Acronyms, Initialisms & Abbreviations Dictionary

Acronyms, Initialisms
& Abbreviations
Dictionary
was named an
***"Outstanding
Reference Source,"***
*the highest honor
given by the
American Library
Association Reference
and User Services
Association.*

ISSN 0270-4404

Acronyms, Initialisms & Abbreviations Dictionary

*A Guide to Acronyms, Abbreviations,
Contractions, Alphabetic Symbols, and Similar Condensed Appellations*

Covering: Aerospace, Associations, Banking, Biochemistry, Business, Data Processing,
Domestic and International Affairs, Economics, Education, Electronics, Genetics,
Government, Information Technology, Internet, Investment, Labor, Language, Law, Medicine, Military
Affairs, Pharmacy, Physiology, Politics, Religion, Science, Societies, Sports, Technical
Drawings and Specifications, Telecommunications, Trade, Transportation, and Other Fields

30th Edition

Volume 1

Part 3

J-P

Mary Rose Bonk,
Editor

GALE GROUP
THOMSON LEARNING

*Detroit • New York • San Diego • San Francisco
Boston • New Haven, Conn. • Waterville, Maine
London • Munich*

Athens Regional Library
2025 Baxter Street
Athens, GA 30606

Editor: Mary Rose Bonk
Associate Editor: Pamela A. Dear
Assistant Editor: Phyllis Spinelli

Data Capture Manager: Ronald D. Montgomery
Project Administrator: Gwendolyn S. Tucker
Data Capture Associate: Nikkita Bankston

Manufacturing Manager: Dorothy Maki
Buyer: NeKita McKee

Graphic Services Manager: Barbara J. Yarrow
Graphic Artist: Mike Logusz
Editorial Training Specialist: Susan Lamb

Director, Technical Support Services: Theresa A. Rocklin
Oracle Applications Specialist: Xiaoyun Lewis

TRADEMARKS AND PROPRIETARY RIGHTS

Acronyms, Initialisms, and Abbreviations Dictionary, its supplement, *Acronyms, Initialisms, and Abbreviations Dictionary Supplement*, and its companion volume, *Reverse Acronyms, Initialisms, and Abbreviations Dictionary*, are not, and are not intended to be in any way, sources of legal authority. The inclusion of an acronym, initialism, or abbreviation (acronym) does not represent an expression of the publisher's opinion as to any legal rights, trademark or otherwise, in such acronym, nor should it be relied upon as having any bearing on the validity or ownership of any trademark. The failure to indicate that an acronym is a trademark is not intended as a representation by the publisher that no trademark right exists in the acronym and does not affect any legal rights in such acronym. A reference to an owner of an acronym or to an acronym as a trademark likewise should not be relied on for legal authority.

While every effort has been made to ensure the reliability of the information presented in this publication, Gale Group does not guarantee the accuracy of the data contained herein. Gale accepts no payment for listing; and inclusion in the publication of any organization, agency, institution, publication service, or individual does not imply endorsement of the editors or publisher.

Errors brought to the attention of the publisher and verified to the satisfaction of the publisher will be corrected in future editions.

This publication is a creative work fully protected by all applicable copyright laws, as well as by misappropriation, trade secret, unfair competition, and other applicable laws. The authors and editors of this work have added value to the underlying factual material herein through one or more of the following: unique and original selection, coordination, expression, arrangement, and classification of the information.

Gale Group and design is a trademark used herein under license. All rights to this publication will be vigorously defended.

Copyright © 2002 by Gale Group, Inc.
27500 Drake Rd.
Farmington Hills, MI 48331-3535

Library of Congress Catalog Card Number 84-643188
ISBN 0-7876-4097-2 (Volume 1 Complete)
ISBN 0-7876-4098-0 (Part 1: A-C only)
ISBN 0-7876-4099-9 (Part 2: D-I only)
ISBN 0-7876-4100-6 (Part 3: J-P only)
ISBN 0-7876-5802-2 (Part 4: Q-Z only)
ISSN 0270-4404

Printed in the United States of America

Athens Regional Library
2025 Baxter Street
Athens, GA 30606

User's Guide

The following examples illustrate possible elements of entries in *AIAD*:

```
        ①            ②                ③              ④        ⑤
    FATAC...Force Aeirienne Tactique [Tactical Air Force] [French] (NATG)

                                      ⑥                    ⑦
    MMT...Multiple-Mirror Telescope [Mount Hopkins, AZ ] [Jointly operated by
    Smithsonian Institiution and the University of Arizona] [Astronomy]
                                                        ⑧
```

① Acronym, Initialism, or Abbreviation

② Meaning or Phrase

③ English Translation

④ Language (for non-English entries)

⑤ Source code (Allows you to verify entries or find additional information. Decoded in the List of Selected Sources)

⑥ Location or Country of origin (Provides geographic identifiers for airports, colleges and universities, libraries, military bases, political parties, radio and television stations, and others)

⑦ Sponsoring organization

⑧ Subject category (Clarifies entries by providing appropriate context)

The completeness of a listing is dependent upon both the nature of the term and the amount of information provided by the source. If additional information becomes available during future research, an entry is revised.

Arrangement of Entries

Acronyms, initialisms, and abbreviations are arranged alphabetically in letter-by-letter sequence. Spacing, punctuation, and capitalization are not considered. If the same term has more than one meaning, the various meanings are subarranged in word-by-word sequence.

Should you wish to eliminate the guesswork from acronym formation and usage, a companion volume could help. *Reverse Acronyms, Initialisms and Abbreviations Dictionary* contains essentially the same entries as *AIAD*, but arranges them alphabetically by meaning, rather than by acronym or initialism.

List of Selected Sources

Each of the sources included in the following list contributed at least 50 terms. It would be impossible to cite a source for every entry because the majority of terms are sent by outside contributors, are uncovered through independent research by the editorial staff, or surface as miscellaneous broadcast or print media references.

For sources used on an ongoing basis, only the latest edition is listed. For most of the remaining sources, the edition that was used is cited. The editors will provide further information about these sources upon request.

(AABC)   *Catalog of Abbreviations and Brevity Codes*. Washington, DC: U.S. Department of the Army, 1981. [Use of source began in 1969]

(ABAC)   "Abbreviations, Acronyms, and Initialisms." <http://www.pnl.gov/ag/usage/acroel.html> (27 January 2000)

(AAEL)   "Common Abbreviations and Acronyms in Electronics." By Gunham Kaytaz. <http://www.seas.smu.edu/~kaytaz/menu.html> (27 April 1999)

(AAG)   *Aerospace Abbreviations Glossary*. Report Number AG60-0014. Prepared by General Dynamics/Astronautics. San Diego, CA: 1962.

(AAGC)   *Acronyms and Abbreviations in Government Contracting*. 2d ed. By Patricia A. Tobin and Joan Nelson Phillips. Washington, DC: George Washington University, 1997.

(AAMN)   *Abbreviations and Acronyms in Medicine and Nursing*. By Solomon Garb, Eleanor Krakauer, and Carson Justice. New York, NY: Springer Publishing Co., 1976.

(ABBR)   *Abbreviations: The Comprehensive Dictionary of Abbreviations and Letter Symbols*. Vol. 1 C. By Edward Wall. Ann Arbor, MI: The Pierian Press, 1984.

(AC)   *Associations Canada 1995/96*. Edited by Ward McBurney. Toronto: Canadian Almanac & Directory Publishing Co. Ltd., 1995.

(ACAE)   *Aerospace and Defense Acronyms*. 2d ed. Compiled by Fernando B. Morinigo. Washington, DC: American Institute of Aeronautics and Astronautics, 1992

(ACII)   "Acronym and Initials Index." 7 February 1996. <http://www.ioi.ie/~readout/cl.html> (7 November 1996)

(AD)   *Abbreviations Dictionary*. 8th ed. By Ralph De Sola. Boca Raton, FL: CRC Press, 1992.

(ADA)   *The Australian Dictionary of Acronyms and Abbreviations*. 2d ed. Compiled by David J. Jones. Leura, NSW, Australia: Second Back Row Press Pty. Ltd., 1981.

(ADDR)   *Army Dictionary and Desk Reference*. By Tim Zurick. Harrisburg, PA: Stackpole Books, 1992.

(ADWA)   *Abbreviations Dictionary; A Practical Compilation of Today's Acronyms and Abbreviations*. By Robert S. Wachal. Boston: Houghton Mifflin Co., 1999.

(AEBE) *Acronyms in Electronics Business and Engineering.* By Ken Westover. Boulder, CO: Cliff Canyon Publishing Co., 1998.

(AEBS) *Acronyms in Education and the Behavioral Sciences.* By Toyo S. Kawakami. Chicago, IL: American Library Association, 1971.

(AEE) *American Educators' Encyclopedia.* By Edward L. Dejnozka and David E. Kapel. Westport, CT: Greenwood Press, 1991.

(AEPA) *U.S. Environmental Protection Agency.* ACCESS EPA. 1995/96 ed. Washington, DC: Office of Information Resources Management, 1996.

(AF) *Reference Aid: Abbreviations in the African Press.* Arlington, VA: Joint Publications Research Service, 1979.

(AFIT) *Compendium of Authenticated Systems and Logistics.* Washington, DC: Air Force Institute of Technology, 1984.

(AFM) *Air Force Manual of Abbreviations.* Washington, DC: U.S. Department of the Air Force, 1975. [Use of source began in 1969]

(AIA) *Aviation Insurance Abbreviations, Organisations and Institutions.* By M.J. Spurway. London, England: Witherby & Co. Ltd., 1983.

(AIE) *Acronyms and Initialisms in Education.* 6th ed. Compiled by John Hutchins. Norwich, England: Librarians of Institutes and Schools of Education, 1995.

(AL) "Acronyms & Abbreviations." American Library Association. <http://www.ala.org/> (2 December 1997)

(ALHF) "Alaska Housing Finance Corporation Glossary." <http://www.ahfc.state.ak.us.index.htm> (18 October 1999)

(ANA) "Abbreviations" - U.S. Navy Dictionary. 3rd revision. Washington, DC: DCP, 1989.

(ANEX) *American Novel Explication 1969-1980.* Compiled by Catherine Glitsch. New Haven, CT: Archon Books, 2000.

(AGLO) *Abbreviations, Acronyms, Glossary for American Readers.* 13th ed. San Jose, CA: American Readers Publishing Co., 2001.

(AMHC) *Glossary of Managed Care Medical Terms, Abbreviations and Acronyms.* By Margaret D. Bischel, M.D. Santa Barbara, CA: Apollo Managed Care Consultants, 1998.

(APTA) *Australian Periodical Title Abbreviations.* Compiled by David J. Jones. Leura, NSW, Australia: Second Back Row Press Pty. Ltd., 1985.

(ARC) *Agricultural Research Centres: A World Directory of Organizations and Programmes.* 2 vols. Edited by Nigel Harvey. Harlow, Essex, England: Longman Group, 1983.

(ARCH) *Dictionary of Architecture and Construction.* Edited by Cyril M. Harris. New York, NY: McGraw-Hill, Inc., 1975.

(ARMP) "Global Change Acronyms and Abbreviations." <http://www.arm.gov/docs/index/html> (8 February 2000)

(ASC) *Associations Canada 1995/96*. Edited by Ward McBurney. Toronto: Canadian Almanac & Directory Publishing Co Ltd., 1995.

(ASF) *Guide to Names and Acronyms of Organizations, Activities, and Projects*. By Food and Agriculture Organization of the United Nations. Fishery Information, Data, and Statistics Service and U.S. National Oceanic and Atmospheric Administration. Aquatic Sciences and Fisheries Information System Reference Series, Number 10, 1982. n.p.

(AUEG) "Acronyms Used by Environmental Groups and Agencies." <http://www.etd.ameslab.gov/etd/library/acronyms/acronym.html> (2000)

(AVGL) "Aircraft Owners and Pilots Association Aviation Glossary." <http://www.aopa.ch/xgloss.htm> (20 October 1999)

(BABM) *Bailliere's Abbreviations in Medicine*. 5th ed. By Edwin B. Steen. London, England: Bailliere Tindall, 1984.

(BARN) *The Barnhart Abbreviations Dictionary*. Edited by Robert K. Barnhart. New York, NY: John Wiley & Sons, Inc., 1995.

(BCP) "BCP Guidebook." <http://www.dtic.dla.mil/environdod/> (Fall 1995)

(BEE) "The Beeline." http://www.bton.com/tb17/abbr/a.html (17 November 1999)

(BI) *British Initials and Abbreviations*. 3rd ed. By Ian H. Wilkes. London, England: Leonard Hill Books, 1971.

(BIB) *Bibliotech*. Ottawa: National Library of Canada, 1988-89.

(BJA) *Biblical and Judaic Acronyms*. By Lawrence Marwick. New York, NY: Ktav Publishing House, Inc., 1979.

(BRI) *Book Review Index*. 1997 Cumulation. Edited by Beverly Baer. Detroit, MI: Gale Research, 1998.

(BROA) *Broadcasting and Cable Yearbook 2000*. Donald V. West, Group Editor in Chief. New Providence, NJ: R.R. Bowker, 2000.

(BTTJ) *Breaking Through Technical Jargon: A Dictionary of Computer and Automation Acronyms*. By Mark S. Merkow. New York, NY: Van Nostrand Reinhold, 1990.

(BUAC) *Buttress's World Guide to Abbreviations of Organizations*. 11th ed. Revised by L.M. Pitman. London, England: Blackie Academic and Professional, 1997.

(BUR) *Computer Acronyms and Abbreviations Handbook*. Tokyo, Japan: Burroughs Co. Ltd., 1978.

(BYTE) *Byte: The Small Systems Journal*. Peterborough, NH: McGraw-Hill Information Systems, Inc., 1987-89.

(CAAL) *CAAL COMOPTEVFOR Acronym and Abbreviation List*. Norfolk, VA: (CAAL-U) Operational Test and Evaluation Force, 1981.

(CARB) "Carbon Dioxide Information Analysis Center—Acronyms and Abbreviations."
        <http://www.cdiac.esd.oorni.gov/cdiac/pns/acronyms.html> (18 July 1996)

(CB)   *Centres & Bureaux: A Directory of Concentrations of Effort, Information and Expertise.* Edited by
        Lindsay Sellar. Beckenham, Kent, England: CBD Research Ltd., 1987.

(CCCA) *ABC Pocket Guide for the Field on C3 Acronyms; An Anthology of Command, Control, and
        Communications Acronyms and Abbreviations.* 2d. ed. Edited by Charles R. Wolfson.
        Geneva, IL: ABC TeleTraining, Inc., 1986.

(CDAI) *Concise Dictionary of Acronyms and Initialisms.* By Stuart W. Miller. New York, NY: Facts on File
        Publications, 1988.

(CDE)   *The Computer Desktop Encyclopedia.* By Alan Freedman. New York, NY: AMACOM, 1996.

(CDI)   *The Cancer Dictionary.* By Roberta Altman and Michael Sarg, M.D. New York, NY: Facts
        on File, 1992.

(CED)   *Current European Directories.* 2d ed. Edited by G.P. Henderson. Beckenham, Kent, England: CBD
        Research, 1981.

(CET)   *Communications-Electronics Terminology.* AFM 11-1. Vol. 3. U.S. Department of the Air Force, 1973.

(CGWS) *The Comprehensive Guide to Wireless Resources; Definitions and Acronyms, and National
        Trade Shows, Association and Publication Listings.* By Lawrence Harte and Steven Kellogg.
        Fuquay-Varina, NC: APDG Publishing, 1998.

(CINC) *A CINCPAC Glossary of Commonly Used Abbreviations and Short Titles.* By Ltc. J.R. Johnson. Wash-
        ington, DC: 1968.

(CIST) *Computer & Information Science & Technology Abbreviations & Acronyms Dictionary.* Edited by David
        W. South. Boca Raton, FL: CRC Press, Inc., 1994.

(CMD) *Complete Multilingual Dictionary of Computer Terminology.* Compiled by Georges Nania. Chicago, IL:
        National Textbook Co., 1984.

(CNC)   *American National Standard Codes for the Representation of Names of Countries, Dependencies, and
        Areas of Special Sovereignty for Information Interchange.* U.S. National Bureau of Standards. Washing-
        ton, DC: Government Printing Office, 1986. [Use of source began in 1977]

(COBU) "Common Business and Professional Abbreviations and Acronyms."
        <http://www.instantaccess.co.uk/infozone/abbraviations.html> (27 January 2000)

(COE)   *Cooper's Comprehensive Environmental Desk Reference.* Edited by Andre R. Cooper.
        New York, NY: John Wiley & Sons, 1990.

(CPGU) *Canadian Parliamentary Guide, Parlementaire Canadien, 1998-1999.* Edited by Kathryn
        O'Handley. Farmington Hills, MI: Gale Group, Inc., 1999.

(CPH)   *The Charles Press Handbook of Current Medical Abbreviations.* 3rd ed. Philadelphia, PA: The
        Charles Press Publishers, Inc., 1991.

(CRD)   *Computer-Readable Databases: A Directory and Data Sourcebook*. 6th ed. Edited by Kathleen Young Marcaccio. Detroit, MI: Gale Research, 1990.

(CROSS)   *Cross-Border Links: A Directory of Organizations in Canada, Mexico, and the United States*. Edited by Ricardo Hernandez and Edith Sanchez. Albuquerque, NM: Inter-Hemispheric Education Resource Center, 1992.

(CSR)   *Computer Science Resources: A Guide to Professional Literature*. Edited by Darlene Myers. White Plains, NY: Knowledge Industry Publications, Inc., 1981.

(CTAS)   "CTAS Acronym Dictionary." <http://www.ctas.arc.nase.gov/acronyms> (10 October 2000)

(CTT)   *Corporate TrendTrac*. Edited by A. Dale Timpe. Detroit, MI: Gale Research, 1988-89.

(CWA)   "Civil War Acronyms."<http://www.antiqueresources.com/articles/cwacronyms.html>(1998)

(DA)   *Dictionary of Aviation*. By R. J. Hall and R. D. Campbell. Chicago, IL: St. James Press, 1991.

(DAS)   *Dictionary of Abbreviations and Symbols*. By Edward Frank Allen. London, England: Cassell and Co. Ltd., 1949.

(DAVI)   *Medical Abbreviations; 14,000 Conveniences at the Expense of Communications and Safety*. 9th ed. By Neil M. Davis. Huntingdon Valley, PA: Neil M. Davis Associates, 1999.

(DB)   *Dictionary of Biomedical Acronyms and Abbreviations*. 2d ed. By Jacques Dupayrat. New York, NY: John Wiley & Sons, 1990.

(DBA)   *Directory of British Associations*. Edited by G.P. Henderson and S.P.A. Henderson. Beckenham, Kent, England: CBD Research, Ltd., 1990.

(DBQ)   *A Dictionary of British Qualifications*. London, England: Kogan Page Ltd., 1985.

(DCDG)   *The Dictionary of Computing & Digital Media; Terms & Acronyms*. Edited by Brad Hansen. Wilsonville, OR: Franklin, Beedle & Associates, Inc., 1999.

(DCTA)   *Dictionary of Commercial Terms and Abbreviations*. By Alan E. Branch. London, England: Witherby & Co. Ltd., 1984.

(DD)   *The Financial Post Directory of Directors 1997*. Toronto, Canada: The Financial Post, 1996.

(DDC)   *The International Dictionary of Data Communications*. By Robert A. Saigh. Chicago, IL: The Glenlake Publishing Company, Ltd., 1998.

(DDSO)   *D & D Standard Oil Abbreviator*. 4th ed. Compiled by the Association of Desk and Derrick Clubs. Tulsa, OK: PennWell Books, 1994.

(DEMM)   "Department of Emergency Management Master List of Acronyms." <http://bcem.co.bay.fl.us/dem/htm> (27 January 2000)

(DEN)   *Dictionary of Electronics and Nucleonics*. By L.E.C. Hughes, R.W.B. Stephens, and L. D. Brown. New York, NY: Barnes & Noble, 1969.

(DET)   *Dictionary of Educational Terms*. Edited by David Blake and Vincent Hanley. Brookfield, VT: Ashgate Publishing Co., 1995.

(DFIT)   *Dictionary of Finance and Investment Terms*. 4th ed. Edited by John Downes and Jordan Elliot Goodman. Hauppauge, NY: Barron's Educational Series, 1995.

(DGA)   *Dictionary of Graphic Arts Abbreviations*. By L. W. Wallis. Rockport, MA: Rockport Publishers, Inc., 1986.

(DHP)   *Dictionary of Abbreviations and Acronyms in Helping Professions*. By John W. Hollis. Muncie,   IN: Accelerated Development, Inc., 1987.

(DHSM)   *Dictionary of Health Services Management*. 2d ed. By Thomas C. Timmreck. Owings Mills, MD: Rynd Communications, 1987.

(DI)   *The Dictionary of Initials—What They Mean*. Compiled and edited by Harriette Lewis. Kingswood, Surrey, England: Paper Fronts Elliot Right Way Books, 1983.

(DIAR)   *The Dictionary of Art*. Edited by Jane Turner. London, England: MacMillan Publishers Limited, 1996.

(DICI)   *The Dictionary of Initials*. By Betsy M. Parks. Secaucus, NJ: Citadel Press, 1981.

(DIPS)   *The Dictionary of Psychology*. By Raymond J. Corsini. Philadelphia: Taylor and Francis, 1999.

(DIT)   *Dictionary of Informatics Terms in Russian and English*. By G.S. Zhdanov, E.S. Kolobrodov, V.A. Polushkin, and A.I. Cherny. Moscow: Nauka, 1971.

(DLA)   *Bieber's Dictionary of Legal Abbreviations*. 3rd ed. By Mary Miles Prince. Buffalo, NY: William S. Hein & Co., 1988.

(DMA)   *Dictionary of Military Abbreviations: British, Empire, Commonwealth*. By B.K.C. Scott. Hastings, East Sussex, England: Tamarisk Books, 1982.

(DMAA)   *Dictionary of Medical Acronyms and Abbreviations*. 3rd ed. Edited by Stanley Jablonski. Philadelphia, PA: Hanley & Belfus, Inc., 1998.

(DMC)   *Webster's New World Dictionary of Media and Communications*. Revised ed. By Richard Weiner. New York, NY: Macmillan, 1996.

(DNAB)   *Dictionary of Naval Abbreviations*. 3rd ed. Compiled and edited by Bill Wedertz. Annapolis, MD: Naval Institute Press, 1984.

(DOAD)   *The Dictionary of Advertising*. Edited by Laurence Urdang. Lincolnwood, IL: NTC Business Books, 1986.

(DOG)   *A Dictionary of Genetics*. 5th ed. By Robert C. King and William D. Stansfield. New York, NY: Oxford University Press, 1997.

(DOGT)   "List of Acronyms." <http://www.em.doe.gov/rtc1994/loa.html> (5 March 1997)

(DOM)   *The Dictionary of Multimedia: Terms & Acronyms*. By Brad Hansen. Wilsonvillee, OR: Franklin, Beedle & Associates, 1997.

(DOMA)   *Dictionary of Military Abbreviations.* By Norman Polmar, Mark Warren, and Eric Wertheim. Annapolis, MD: Naval Institute Press, 1994.

(DS)   *Dictionary of Shipping International Trade Terms and Abbreviations*. 3rd ed. By Alan E. Branch. London, England: Witherby & Co. Ltd., 1986.

(DSA)   *Dictionary of Sigla and Abbreviations to and in Law Books before 1607*. By William Hamilton Bryson. Charlottesville: University Press of Virginia, 1975.

(DSUE)   *A Dictionary of Slang and Unconventional English*. 8th ed. By Eric Partridge. New York, NY: Macmillan Publishing Co., 1984.

(DUND)   *Directory of United Nations Databases and Information Services*. 4th ed. Compiled by the Advisory Committee for the Coordination of Information Systems. New York, NY: United Nations, 1990.

(DWSG)   *Defense Weapon Systems Glossary.* By David Trotz. Piscataway, NJ: Target Marketing, 1992.

(EA)   *Encyclopedia of Associations*. 34th ed. Vol. 1, National Oranizations of the U.S. Edited by Christine Maurer and Tara E. Sheets. Farmington Hills, MI: Gale Group, 1999.
           [Use of source began in 1960]

(EAAP)   *Encyclopedia of Associations: Association Periodicals*. 3 vols. Edited by Denise M. Allard and Robert C. Thomas. Detroit, MI: Gale Research, 1987.

(EAIO)   *Encyclopedia of Associations: International Organizations*. 29th ed. Edited by Linda Irvin. Detroit, MI: Gale Research, 1995. [Use of source began in 1985]

(EBF)   *Encyclopedia of Banking and Finance*. 10th ed. Edited by Charles J. Woelfel. Chicago, IL: Probus
           Publishing Co., 1994.

(ECED)   *The European Communities Encyclopedia and Directory 1992*. London, England: Europa Publications Ltd., 1991; distributed in U.S. by Gale Research, Detroit, MI.

(ECII)   *Electronics, Computers and Industrial Instrumentation Abbreviations and Acronyms.* Edited by Sergio Sobredo. Miami, FL: Sergio Sobredo Technical Services, 1986.

(ECON)   *The Economist. London, England: The Economist Newspaper Ltd., 2001.* [Use of source began in 1988]

(EDAC)   *Dictionary of Educational Acronyms, Abbreviations, and Initialisms.* 2d ed. Edited by James C. Palmer and Anita Y. Colby. Phoenix, AZ: Oryx Press, 1985.

(EDCT)   *Encyclopedic Dictionary of Chemical Technology.* By Dorit Noether and Herman Noether. New York, NY: VCH Publishers, Inc., 1993.

(EE)   *Eastern Europe and the Commonwealth of Independent States 1992*. London, England: Europa Publications Ltd., 1992; distributed in U.S. by Gale Research, Detroit, MI.

(EECA)   *Dictionary of Electrical, Electronics, and Computer Abbreviations*. By Phil Brown. London, England: Buttersworth, 1985.

(EES)   *A Dictionary of Ecology, Evolution and Systematics*. 2d ed. Edited by Roger Lincoln, Geoff Boxshall and Paul Clark. New York, NY: Cambridge University Press, 1998.

(EEVL)   *Environmental Engineering Dictionary*. 3rd ed. Edited by C.C. Lee. Rockville, MD: Government Institutes, 1998.

(EFIS)   *Corporate Acronym Resource Guide, 1800s-1995*. Seattle, WA: Environmental Financial Information Services, Inc. (EFIS), 1996.

(EG)   *Environmental Glossary*. 4th ed. Edited by G. William Frick and Thomas F.P. Sullivan. Rockville, MD: Government Institutes, Inc., 1986.

(EGAO)   *Encyclopedia of Governmental Advisory Organizations*. 9th ed. Edited by Donna Batten. Detroit, MI: Gale Research, 1994-95 (and supplement, 1995). [Use of source began in 1975]

(EMRF)   *The St. James Encyclopedia of Mortgage & Real Estate Finance*. By James Newell, Albert Santi, and Chip Mitchell. Chicago, IL: St. James Press, 1991.

(ELAL)   *Computer Acronyms & Abbreviations; Over 4,000 Entries and What They Stand For*. Compiled by Elie Albala. Quebec, Canada: Alpel Publishing, 1992.

(EOSA)   "Earth Observing System (EOS) Acronyms and Abbreviations." http://eospso.gsfc.nasa/eos_homepage/misc (5 October 1999)

(EPA)   *Glossary of EPA Acronyms*. Washington, DC: Environmental Protection Agency, 1987.

(EPAT)   "Terms of Environment." http://www.epa.gov/OCEPAterms/aaad.html (3 November 1999)

(ERG)   *Environmental Regulatory Glossary*. 5th ed. Edited by G. William Frick and Thomas F.P. Sullivan. Rockville, MD: Government Institutes, Inc., 1990.

(EY)   *The Europa World Year Book 1992*. London: Europa Publications Ltd., 1992. distributed in U.S. by Gale Research, Detroit, MI.

(FAAC)   *Contractions Handbook*. Changes. U.S. Department of Transportation. Federal Aviation Administration, 1993. [Use of source began in 1969]

(FAAL)   *Location Identifiers*. U.S. Department of Transportation. Federal Aviation Administration. Air Traffic Service, 1982.

(FEA)   *The Far East and Australasia 1987*. 18th ed. London, England: Europa Publications Ltd., 1986; distributed in U.S. by Gale Research, Detroit, MI.

(FFDE)   *The Facts on File Dictionary of Environmental Science*. By L. Harold Stevenson and Bruce Wyman. New York, NY: Facts on File, 1991.

(FUCW)   "Frequently Used Contractions in National Weather Service Products." <http://www.awc-kc.noaa.gov/info/domestic_contractions.html>

(GAAI)   "Glossary of Abbreviations, Acronyms, and Initialisms." <http://www.em.doe.gov/idb97/acropdf.html> (17 February 1998)

(GAVI)   "Glossary of Aviation Acronyms and Abbreviations." <http://olias.arc.nasa.gov/AFO_Acronyms_.html> (5 March 1997)

(GEA)   *Government Economic Agencies of the World: An International Directory of Governmental Organisations Concerned with Economic Development and Planning.* A Keesing's Reference Publication. Edited by Alan J. Day. Harlow, Essex, England: Longman Group Ltd., 1985.

(GEAB)   "Genealogy Abbreviations." http://www.genweb.net/~samcasey/abbre.html (17 November 1999)

(GEOI)   "Dictionary of Abbreviations and Acronyms in Geographic Information Systems, Cartography, and Remote Sensing." By Philip Hoehn and Mary Lynette Larsgaard. http://www.lib.berkeley.edu/EART/abbrev.html (June 1999)

(GFGA)   *Guide to Federal Government Acronyms.* Edited by William R. Evinger. Phoenix, AZ: The Oryx Press, 1989.

(GOBB)   *The Gobbledygook Book; Dictionary of Acronyms, Abbreviations, Initializations & Esoteric Terminology.* Compiled by Franklin W. Fox, III. Troy, MI: Momentum Books, Ltd., 1996.

(GNE)   *The Green Encyclopedia.* By Irene Franck and David Brownstone. New York, NY: Prentice Hall General Reference, 1992.

(GPO)   *Style Manual.* Washington, DC: Government Printing Office, 1984. [Terms are included in Chapter 24, Foreign Languages]

(GRD)   *Government Research Directory.* 8th ed. Edited by Joseph M. Palmisano. Detroit, MI: Gale Research, 1994. (and supplement, 1994).

(GROV)   "Abbreviation List." <http://www.grovemusic.com/grovemusic/az/general00.html> (16 January 2001)

(GRST)   "Glossary of Remote Sensing Terms." <http://ceo1409.ceo.sai.jrc.it:8080...2/tutorials/glossary> (5 October 1999)

(GVA)   "Glossary of Veterinary Acronyms." http://www/spvs.org.uk/glossary.htm (October 1999)

(HAWK)   "Hawkman's Automotive Abbreviations." http://www3.sympatico.ca/dhaughey/index2.htm (19 October 2000)

(HCT)   *Health Care Terms.* 2d ed. By Vergil N. Slee and Debora A. Slee. St. Paul, MN: Tringa Press, 1991.

(HEAS)   "Acronyms and Abbreviations Used in Health and Safety Executive Information Services." <http://www.healthandsafety.co.uk/acronyms.html> (26 September 2000)

(HGAA)   *The Handy Guide to Abbreviations and Acronyms for the Automated Office.* By Mark W. Greenia. Seattle, WA: Self-Counsel Press, Inc., 1986.

(HGEN)   "Human Genome Acronym List." <http://www.ornl.gov/hgmis/acronym.html> (2 December 1998)

(HLLA) "Honeywell Abbreviation and Acronym Dictionary."
        <http://www.cas.honeywell.com/ats/acronym.html> (27 January 2000)

(HRG)   *The Human Resources Glossary: The Complete Desk Reference for HR Executives, Managers, and Practitioners.* 2d ed. By William R. Tracey. Boca Raton, FL: St. Lucie Press, 1998.

(IAA)   *Index of Acronyms and Abbreviations in Electrical and Electronic Engineering.* Compiled by Buro Scientia. New York, NY: VCH Publishers, 1989.

(IAS)   "International Arctic Science Committee." <http://www.iasc.no/acronyms.htm> (20 October 1999)

(IBMDP) *IBM Data Processing Glossary.* 6th ed. White Plains, NY: IBM Corp., 1977.

(ICAO) *Aircraft Type Designators.* 13th ed. International Civil Aviation Organization, August, 1981.

(ICDA) *Designators for Aircraft Operating Agencies, Aeronautical Authorities and Services.* 49th ed. International Civil Aviation Organization, June, 1982.

(ICLI) *Location Indicators.* 51st ed. International Civil Aviation Organization, February, 1987.

(IDAI) *The International Dictionary of Artificial Intelligence.* By William Raynor. Chicago: Glenlake Publishing Co., Ltd., 1999.

(IDOE) T*he Illustrated Dictionary of Electronics.* 6th ed. By Stan Gibilisco. New York, NY: TAB Books, 1994.

(IEEE) *IEEE Standard Dictionary of Electrical and Electronics Terms.* Edited by Frank Jay. New York, NY: The Institute of Electrical and Electronics Engineers, Inc., 1977, 1984.

(IGQR) *The Internet Glossary & Quick Reference Guide.* By Alan Freedman, Alfred Glossbrenner and Emily Glossbrenner. New York, NY: AMACOM, 1998.

(IGSL) *International Reference Guide to Space Launch Systems.* 3rd ed. Edited by Steven J. Isakowitz, Joseph P. Hopkins, Jr., Joshua B. Hopkins. Reston, VA: American Institute of Aeronautics and Astronautics, 1999.

(IIA)   *Index of Initials and Acronyms.* Compiled by Richard Kleiner. New York, NY: Auerbach Publishers, 1971.

(IID)   *Information Industry Directory.* 15th ed. Edited by Annette Novallo. Detroit, MI: Gale Research, 1995. (and supplement, 1995).

(ILCA) *Index to Legal Citations and Abbreviations.* By Donald Raistrick. Abingdon, Oxfordshire, England: Professional Books Ltd., 1981.

(IMH)   *International Marketing Handbook.* 2d ed. Edited by Frank Bair. Detroit, MI: Gale Research, 1985.

(INF)   *Infantry.* Fort Benning, GA: U.S. Army Infantry Training School, 1996. [Use of source began in 1983]

(IOWA) "Iowa Department of Natural Resources Quick Facts." <http://www.state.ia.us/government/dnr/part1.htm> (19 October 1999)

(IRC)   *International Research Centers Directory 1992-93.* 6th ed. Edited by Annette Piccirelli. Detroit, MI: Gale Research, 1991.

(IRUK)   *Industrial Research in the United Kingdom*. 12th ed. Harlow, Essex, England: Longman Group UK Ltd., 1987.

(IT)   *Information Today: The Newspaper for Users and Producers of Electronic Information Services*. Medford, NJ: Learned Information, Inc., 1988-89.

(ITCA)   *Internet Terms and Computer Acronyms, A Useful Guide*. By Mary Brookhart. Charlotte, NC: Southeast Consulting, Inc., 1998.

(ITD)   *International Tradeshow Directory*. 5th ed. Frankfurt, Germany: M + A Publishers for Fairs, Exhibitions and Conventions Ltd., 1989.

(IUSS)   "IUSS Acronyms." http://206.239.241.41/Acronym/1.html (12 October 1999)

(IYR)   *The 1989-92 International Yacht Racing Rules*. London, England: International Yacht Racing Union, 1989.

(JAGO)   *Export Terms and Acronyms: Glossary of the Export Sales and Marketing Manual*. By. John R. Jagoe. Minneapolis, MN: Export Institute, 2000.

(KSC)   *A Selective List of Acronyms and Abbreviations*. Compiled by the Documents Department, Kennedy Space Center Library, 1971, 1973.

(LAIN)   *Latest Intelligence: An International Directory of Codes Used by Government, Law Enforcement, Military, and Surveillance Agencies*. By James E. Tunnell. Blue Ridge Summit, PA: TAB BOOKS, 1990.

(LCCP)   *MARC Formats for Bibliographic Data*. Appendix II. Washington, DC: Library of Congress, 1982.

(LCLS)   *Symbols of American Libraries*. 14th ed. Edited by the Enhanced Cataloging Division. Washington, DC: Library of Congress, 1992. [Use of source began in 1980]

(LWAP)   *Legal Words and Phrases: Speed Abbreviations*. By Joel Larus. Boston, MA: Aurico Publishing, 1965.

(MAE)   *Medical Abbreviations and Eponyms*. By Sheila B. Sloane. Philadelphia, PA: W.B. Saunders Co., 1985.

(MARI)   "Glossary of Marine Abbreviations." <http://www.royalsunalliance.ca/rsa.arine/glossabbrevdisp.html> (26 September 2000)

(MAH)   *Medical Abbreviations Handbook.* 2d ed. Oradell, NJ: Medical Economics Co., Inc., 1983.

(MCD)   *Acronyms, Abbreviations, and Initialisms*. Compiled by Carl Lauer. St. Louis, MO: McDonnell Douglas Corp., 1989. [Use of source began in 1969]

(MDG)   *Microcomputer Dictionary and Guide*. By Charles J. Sippl. Champaign, IL: Matrix Publishers, Inc., 1975.

(ME)   *The Marine Encyclopaedic Dictionary*. 5th ed. By Eric Sullivan. London, England: LLP Ltd., 1996.

(MEC)   *Macmillan Encyclopedia of Chemistry*. Vol. 1. Edited by Joseph J. Lagowski. New York, NY: Macmillan Reference USA, 1997.

(MED)   *McGraw-Hill Electronic Dictionary*. 5th ed. Edited by John Markus and Neil Sclater. New York,   NY: McGraw-Hill, Inc., 1994.

(MEDA)   *Medical Acronyms.* 2d ed. By Marilyn Fuller Delong. Oradell, NJ: Medical Economic Books, 1989.

(MELL)   *Melloni's Illustrated Dictionary of Medical Abbreviations*. By John Melloni and Ida G. Dox. Pearl River, NY: Parthenon Publishing Group, Inc., 1998.

(MENA)   *The Middle East and North Africa 1987*. 33rd ed. London, England: Europa Publications Ltd., 1986; distributed in U.S. by Gale Research, Detroit, MI.

(MGMA)   "Medical Group Management Associations Book of Acronyms for Medical Practice Executives." <http://www.mgma.com/library/acronyms.html> (19 October 1999)

(MHDB)   *McGraw-Hill Dictionary of Business Acronyms, Initials, and Abbreviations*. By Jerry M. Rosenberg. New York, NY: McGraw-Hill, Inc., 1992.

(MHDI)   *McGraw-Hill Dictionary of Information Technology and Computer Acronyms, Initials, and Abbreviations*. By Jerry M. Rosenberg. New York, NY: McGraw-Hill, Inc., 1992.

(MHDW)   *McGraw-Hill Dictionary of Wall Street Acronyms, Initials, and Abbreviations*. By Jerry M. Rosenberg. New York, NY: McGraw-Hill, Inc., 1992.

(MILB)   *The Military Balance 1998/99*. London: Oxford University Press for the International Institute for Strategic Studies, 1998.

(MLOA)   "Marconi—List of Acronyms." <http://www.fore.com/atm-edu/acronyms.html> (1999)

(MSA)   *Military Standard Abbreviations for Use on Drawings, and in Specifications, Standards, and Technical Documents*. MIL-STD-12D. U.S. Department of Defense, 1981. [Use of source began in 1975]

(MSC)   *Annotated Acronyms and Abbreviations of Marine Science Related Activities*. 3rd ed. Revised by Charlotte M. Ashby and Alan R. Flesh. Washington, DC: U.S. Department of Commerce. National Oceanographic and Atmospheric Administration. Environmental Data Service. National Oceanographic Data Center, 1976, 1981.

(MUGU)   *The Mugu Book of Acronyms and Abbreviations*. Missile Range, CA: Management Engineering Office, 1963, 1964.

(MUSM)   *Dictionary of Modern United States Military*. By S.F. Tomajczyk. Jefferson, NC: McFarland and   Co., Inc., 1996.

(NADA)   *The New American Dictionary of Abbreviations*. By Mary A. De Vries. New York, NY: Signet, 1991.

(NAKS)   "NASA/KSC Aronym List." <http://www.ksc.nasa.gov/facts/acronyms.html> (27 May 1999)

(NASA)   *Space Transportation System and Associated Payloads: Glossary, Acronyms, and Abbreviations*. Washington, DC: U.S. National Aeronautics and Space Administration, 1985.

(NATG)   *Glossary of Abbreviations Used in NATO Documents*. AAP 15(B), n.p., 1979. [Use of source began in 1976]

(NAU)   "The Nautical Institute: Acronyms & Abbreviations." <http://www.nautinst.org/Acronyms.htm> (20 October 1999)

(NAV)   "Navoceano Acronym List." <http://www.navo.hpc.mil> (12 November 1993)

(NCC)   *NCC The National Centre for Information Technology. Guide to Computer Aided Engineering, Manufacturing and Construction Software*. Manchester, England: NCC Publications, The National Computing Centre Ltd., 1985.

(NDBD)   *The New Dickson Baseball Dictionary*. By Paul Dickson. San Diego, CA: Harcourt, Brace, and Co., 1999.

(NFD)   *The NSFRE Fund-Raising Dictionary*. Edited by Barbara R. Levy. New York, NY: John Wiley & Sons, Inc., 1996.

(NFLA)   "National Football League Abbreviations and Team Histories." http://maxwell.uhh.hawaii.edu/football/archive/nflAbbreviations.html (1998)

(NFPA)   *Standard for Fire Safety Symbols/NFPA170*. Quincy, MA: National Fire Protection Association, 1994.

(NG)   *NAVAIR Glossary of Unclassified Common-Use Abbreviated Titles and Phrases*. NAVAIRNOTE 5216 AIR-6031, n.p., July, 1969.

(NGC)   *Catalogue of the National Gallery of Canada*. Compiled by National Gallery of Canada. Ottawa, Canada: National Gallery of Canada, 1998.

(NHD)   *The New Hacker's Dictionary*. Edited by Eric Raymond. Cambridge, MA: MIT Press, 1991.

(NITA)   *Dictionary of New Information Technology Acronyms*. 2d ed. By Michael Gordon, Alan Singleton, and Clarence Rickards. London, England: Kogan Page, Ltd., 1986.

(NLC)   *Symbols of Canadian Libraries*. 12th ed. National Library of Canada. Minister of Supply and Services Canada, 1987.

(NOAA)   *NOAA Directives Manual*. 66-13 Acronyms. 1977.

(NQ)   *NASDAQ Company Directory*. New York, NY: National Association of Securities Dealers, Inc., 1990. [Use of source began in 1983]

(NRCH)   *A Handbook of Acronyms and Initialisms*. Washington, DC: U.S. Nuclear Regulatory Commission. Division of Technical Information and Document Control, 1985.

(NRGU)   *NORD Resource Guide*. 4th ed. New Fairfield, CT: National Organization for Rare Disorders, Inc., 2000.

(NTCM)   *NTC's Mass Media Dictionary*. R. Terry Ellmore. Lincolnwood, IL: National Textbook Co., 1991.

(NTIO)   *NTC's Dictionary of Acronyms and Abbreviations*. Compiled by Steven R. Kleinedler. Edited by Richard A. Spears. Lincolnwood, IL: NTC Publishing Group, 1996.

(NTPA)   *NTPA '97: National Trade and Professional Associations of the United States*. 32d ed. Edited by John J. Russell. Washington, DC: Columbia Books, Inc., 1997.

(NUCP) *A Dictionary of Nuclear Power and Waste Management with Abbreviations and Acronyms.* Foo-Sun Lau. Letchworth, England: Research Studies Press Ltd., 1987.

(NUJO) "Initials, Credentials, Abbreviations Found on Medical Resumes." <http://www.nursesearch.net/initials.html> (1 February 2000)

(NUMA) "The Numa Dictionary of Derivatives Acronyms." <http://www.numa.com/ref/acronym.html> (24 February 1999)

(NVT) *Naval Terminology.* NWP3. Rev. B. U.S. Department of the Navy. Office of the Chief of Naval Operations, 1980. [Use of source began in 1974]

(OA) *Ocran's Acronyms: A Dictionary of Abbreviations and Acronyms Used in Scientific and Technical Writing.* By Emanuel Benjamin Ocran. London, England: Routledge & Kegan Paul Ltd., 1978.

(OAG) *Official Airline Guide Worldwide Edition.* Oak Brook, IL: Official Airlines Guide, Inc., 1984. [Use of source began in 1975]

(OCD) *Oxford Classical Dictionary.* 2d ed. Edited by N.G. Hammond and H.H. Scullard. London, England: Oxford University Press, 1970.

(OCLC) *OCLC Participating Institutions Arranged by OCLC Symbol.* Dublin, OH: OCLC, 1981.

(ODBW) *The Oxford Dictionary for the Business World.* New York, NY: Oxford University Press, Inc., 1993.

(ODCC) *The Oxford Dictionary of the Christian Church.* Edited by F.L. Cross and E.A. Livingstone. New York, NY: Oxford University Press, 1997.

(OICC) *Abbreviations and Acronyms.* Des Moines: Iowa State Occupational Information Coordinating Committee, 1986.

(OLDSS) *Online Database Search Services Directory.* 2d ed. Edited by Doris Morris Maxfield. Detroit, MI: Gale Research, 1988.

(OPSA) "Official Postal Service Abbreviations." <http://www.usps.gov/ncsc/lookups/abbr_suffix.txt> (17 December 1996)

(OSI) *OSI Standards and Acronyms.* 3rd ed. Compiled by Adrian V. Stokes. United Kingdom: Stokes, 1991.

(OTD) *Official Telecommunications Dictionary.* Edited by Thomas F.P. Sullivan. Rockille, MD: Government Institutes, Inc., 1997.

(PA) "Planning Acronyms." <http://www.planning.org/info/acronyms/html> (24 February 1999)

(PAZ) *Parenting A to Z.* By Irene M. Franck and David M. Brownstone. New York, NY: HarperCollins Publishers, Inc., 1996.

(PCM) *PC Magazine.* New York, NY: Ziff-Davis Publishing Co., 1997. [Use of source began in 1987]

(PD) *Political Dissent: An International Guide to Dissident, Extra-Parliamentary, Guerrilla and Illegal Political Movements. A Keesing's Reference Publication.* Compiled by Henry W. Degenhardt. Edited by Alan J. Day. Harlow, Essex, England: Longman Group, 1983.

(PDAA) *Pugh's Dictionary of Acronyms and Abbreviations: Abbreviations in Management, Technology and Information Science*. 5th ed. By Eric Pugh. Chicago, IL: American Library Association, 1987.

(PGP) *Peterson's Graduate Programs in the Humanities, Arts & Social Sciences*. 31st ed. Princeton, NJ: Peterson's 1997.

(PHSD) *1998/1999 Public Human Services Directory*. Vol 59. Washington, DC: American Public Human Services Association, 1998.

(PIAV) "Pilot's Magazine's A to Z Aviation Jargon." Compiled by James Allan and Mike Jerran. <http://web1.hiway.co.uk/avaition/pterms.html> (10 October 2000)

(PIPO) *Pilot's Pocket Handbook*. 4th ed. N.p.: Flight Time Publishing, 1999.

(PPE) *Political Parties of Europe*. 2 vols. Edited by Vincent E. McHale. The Greenwood Historical Encyclopedia of the World's Political Parties. Westport, CT: Greenwood Press, 1983.

(PPW) *Political Parties of the World*. 2d ed. A Keesing's Reference Publication. Compiled and edited by Alan J. Day and Henry W. Degenhardt. Harlow, Essex, England: Longman Group, 1980, 1984.

(PROS) *Prospector's Choice*. User's Guide. Detroit: The Taft Group, 1997.

(PS) *Popular Science*. New York, NY: Times-Mirror Magazines, Inc., 2001. [Use of source began in 1992]

(PSS) *Peterson's Sports Scholarships & College Athletic Programs*. 3rd ed. Edited by Ron Walker. Princeton, NJ: Peterson's, 1998.

(QUAC) "Dictionary of Quaternary Acronyms." http://www.ualberta.ca/abeaudoi/cap/diction/atoc.html (12 October 1999)

(RALS) *Encyclopedia of Computer Science*. 4th ed. Edited by Anthony Ralston, Edwin E. Reilly, and David Hemmendinger. London: Nature Publishing Group, 2000.

(RCD) *Research Centers Directory*. 19th ed. Edited by Thomas J. Cichonski. Detroit, MI: Gale Research,1994. [Use of source began in 1986]

(RDA) *Army RD and A Magazine*. Alexandria, VA: Development, Engineering, and Acquisition Directorate, Army Materiel Command, 1997. [Use of source began in 1979]

(REAL) "Abbreviations." <http://www.reboc.on.ca/abbreviations.html> (24 February 1999)

(RIMS) "Rimship AS Forkortelser." <http://www.rimship.no/sider/liste.html> (26 September 2000)

(RION) *Religion Index One: Periodicals; a Subject Index to Periodical Literature including an Author/Editor Index and a Scripture Index*. Semiannual edition 1999. Edited by Carolyn K. Coates. Evanston, IL: American Theological Library Association, 1999.

(ROAS) "Acronym and Abbreviation Server Results." <http://www.ucc.ie/cgi-bin/acronym> (20 September 1999)

(ROG) *Dictionary of Abbreviations*. By Walter T. Rogers. London, England: George Allen & Co. Ltd., 1913; reprinted by Gale Research, 1969.

(SAA) *Space-Age Acronyms, Abbreviations and Designations*. 2d ed. By Reta C. Moser. New York, NY: IFI/ Plenum, 1969.

(SAG)   *Stock Abbreviation Guide*. New York, NY: Associated Press. [Database]

(SARE)   "Safety and Related Acronyms." <http://www.labsafety.org/acro.htm> (1999)

(SAUO)   *International Encyclopedia of Abbreviations and Acronyms of Organizations*. 3rd ed. Compiled by Paul Spillner and Peter Wennrich. 6 vol. set. Munich, Germany: K. G. Saur, 1990.

(SAUS)   *International Encyclopedia of Abbreviations and Acronyms in Science and Technology*. Compiled by Michael Peschke. 8 vol. set. Munich, Germany: K.G. Saur, 1996.

(SDI)   *Report to the Congress on the Strategic Defense Initiative*. U.S. Department of Defense. Strategic Defense Initiative Organization, April, 1987.

(SEIS)   *Seismograph Station Codes and Characteristics*. Geological Survey. Circular 791. By Barbara B. Poppe, Debbi A. Naab, and John S. Derr. Washington, DC: U.S. Department of the Interior, 1978.

(SEWL)   "Space and Electronic Warfare Lexicon." <http://www.sew-lexicon.com> (10 October 2000)

(SG)   *Standard & Poor's Stock Guide*. New York, NY: Standard & Poor's, 2001.

(SHCU)   *Short Cuts; The Dictionary of Useful Abbreviations*. Edited by Steven Kleinedler. Lincolnwood, IL: NTC Publishing Group, 1997.

(SLS)   *World Guide to Scientific Associations and Learned Societies/Internationales Verzeichnis Wissenschaftlicher Verbande und Gesellschaften*. 4th ed. Edited by Barbara Verrel. New York, NY: K.G. Saur, 1984.

(SPSG)   *Security Owner's Stock Guide*. New York, NY: Standard & Poor's Corp., 1994. [Use of source began in 1988]

(SPST)   "Space Station Acronyms." <http://www.spacefllight.nasa.gov/cgi-bi> (1999)

(SRA)   *State and Regional Associations of the United States*. 9th ed. Edited by Tracey E. Chirico, Buck J. Downs and John J. Russell. Washington, DC: Columbia Books, Inc., 1997.

(SSD)   *Space Station Directory and Program Guide*. Edited and compiled by Melinda Gipson, Jane Glass, and Mary Linden. Arlington, VA: Pasha Publications, Inc., 1988.

(STED)   *Stedman's Abbreviations, Acronyms and Symbols*. Edited by William R. Hensyl. Baltimore, MD: Williams & Wilkins, 1992.

(TAD)   *The AIDS Dictionary*. By Sarah Barbara Watstein and Karen Chandler. New York, NY: Facts on File, Inc., 1998.

(TAG)   *Transportation Acronym Guide 1996*. U.S. Department of Transportation. Washington, DC: Bureau of Transportation Statistics, 1996.

(TBD)   *Thomson Bank Directory*. Skokie, IL: Thomson Financial Publishing, 1991.

(TDOB)   *The Dictionary of Banking*. By Charles J. Woelfel. Chicago, IL: Probus Publishing Company, 1994.

(TEL)   *Telephony's Dictionary*. 2d ed. By Graham Langley. Chicago, IL: Telephony Publishing Corp., 1986.

(TELE)   "List of Libraries Abbreviations Encountered in the Context of EU R&D." <http://www2.echo.lu/libraries/
          en/acronym.html> (24 February 1999)

(TES)   *Tests: A Comprehensive Reference for Assessments in Psychology, Education, and Business*. 3rd ed.
          Austin, TX: PRO-ED, Inc., 1991.

(TIMI)   "Texas Instruments Military Acronym List."
          <http://www.ti.com/sc/docs/military/millprdov/acroindx.htm> (28 September 2000)

(TMMY)   *The Thirteenth Mental Measurements Yearbook*. Edited by James C. Impara and Barbara S. Plake.
          Lincoln: NE: The Buros Institute of Mental Measurements of the University of Nebraska-Lincoln, 1998.

(TNIG)   *Telecommunications, Networking and Internet Glossary*. By George S. Machovec. Chicago, IL:
          American Library Association, 1993.

(TOCD)   *The Official Catholic Directory 1997*. New Providence, NJ: P.J. Kennedy & Sons, 1997.

(TRID)   "Travel Industry Dictionary." <http://www.hometravelagency.com/dictionary/itra/html>
          (15 August 2000)

(TSPED)   *Trade Shows and Professional Exhibits Directory*. 2d ed. Edited by Robert J. Elster. Detroit, MI: Gale
          Research, 1987. [Use of source began in 1986]

(TSSD)   *Telecommunications Systems and Services Directory*. 4th ed. (and supplement). Edited by John Krol.
          Detroit, MI: Gale Research, 1989. [Use of source began in 1985]

(TVEL)   *The Travel Dictionary.* By Claudine Dervaes. Tampa, FL: Solitaire Publishing, 1998.

(USCA)   "U.S. Census Bureau Abbreviations and Acronyms."
          <http://www.census.gov/cgi-bin/main/allacro.pl> (20 October 1999)

(USDC)   "Glossary of Acronyms." U.S. Department of Commerce. <http://www.pmel.noaa.gov/pubs/
          acronym.html> (5 March 1997)

(USGC)   "U.S. Government Commonly Used Abbreviations and Acronyms." <http://www.fed.gov/hptext/infohwy/
          gov_acro.html> (5 March 1997)

(USMO)   *The Military Online: A Directory for Internet Access to the Development of Defense*. Edited by
          William M. Arkin. Washington, DC: Brassey's, 1997.

(VERA)   "VERA-Virtual Entity of Relevant Acronyms." <http://www/thphy.uni~duesseldorf. de/~gnu/info/VERA/
          vera_2.html#SEC3> (1 December 1998)

(VLIE)   *Dictionary of Acronyms and Technical Abbreviations: For Information and Communication
          Technologies and Related Areas.* 2d ed. By Jakob Vliestra. London, England: Springer, 2001.

(VNW)   *Words of the Vietnam War*. By Gregory R. Clark. Jefferson, NC: McFarland and Co., Inc., 1990.

(VRA)   *VRA Special Bulletin*. No. 2, 1987: Standard Abbreviations for Image Descriptions for Use in Fine Arts
          Visual Resources Collections. Compiled by Nancy S. Schuller. Austin, TX: Visual Resources Associa-
          tion, 1987.

(WA)   *Whitakers Almanack 1998.* London: The Stationery Office, Ltd., 1997.

(WDAA)   *Webster's New World Dictionary of Acronyms and Abbreviations*. By Auriel Douglas and Michael Strumpf. New York, NY: Webster's New World, 1989.

(WDMC)   *Webster's New World Dictionary of Media and Communications*. Revised and updated ed. By Richard Weiner. New York, NY: Webster's New World, 1996.

(WEAT)   "Weather Abbreviations." <http://www.ukweather.freeserve.co.uk/abbrev.html> (16 November 1999)

(WGA)   *Webster's Guide to Abbreviations*. Springfield, MA: Merriam-Webster, Inc., 1985.

(WORL)   *World Guide to Libraries*. Edited by Willemina van der Meer. 14th ed. Munich, Germany: Saur, 1999.

(WPI)   "Selected Acronyms and Abbreviations for Wood Products, Forest Industry and Governmental Affairs." <http://www.ari.net/awpi/acronyms.html> (3 March 1999)

(WYGK)   *HR Words You Gotta Know!* By William R. Tracey. New York, NY: AMACOM, 1994.

J
By Acronym

J .... Action Variable [*Physics*] (BARN)
J .... Air Force Training Category [*Officer training program*]
J .... Angular Momentum [*Physics*] (BARN)
J .... Australian Journalist [*A publication*]
J .... Business Class [*Also, C*] [*Airline fare code*]
J .... Cable Jointing [*Section of the British Royal Navy*]
J .... Chain [*Symbol*] [*A part of the immunoglobulin molecular structure*] (DAVI)
J .... Clubs [*Public-performance tariff class*] [*British*]
j .... Dissenting Opinion Citation in Dissenting Opinion [*Used in Shepard's Citations*] [*Legal term*] (DLA)
J .... Durham (SAUS)
J .... Dynamic Movement of Inertia (STED)
J .... Electric Current Density [*Symbol*] [*IUPAC*] (DEN)
J .... Electromechanical [*JETDS nomenclature*]
J .... Field Testing Division (SAUO)
J .... Flux [*Symbol*] [*IUPAC*]
J .... Institutes of Justinian [*Roman law*] [*A publication*] (DLA)
J .... Irradiation Correction
J .... Jack [*In card game*]
J .... Jack [*Technical drawings*]
J .... Jackpot Enterprises [*NYSE symbol*] (TTSB)
J .... Jackpot Enterprises, Inc. [*NYSE symbol*] (CTT)
J .... Jacobeian Determinant (ROG)
J .... Jacobus de Porta Ravennate [*Deceased, 1178*] [*Authority cited in pre-1607 legal work*] (DSA)
J .... Jaeger point (SAUS)
J .... Jammer (CCCA)
J .... Jamming (ACAE)
J .... January
J .... Japan [*IYRU nationality code*]
J .... Japonica (SAUO)
J .... Jargon [*Used in correcting manuscripts, etc.*]
j .... Jaundice [*Medicine*] (DMAA)
J .... Jenkins Fine Arts Center (SAUS)
J .... Jerusalem Talmud (BJA)
J .... Jesus (ROG)
J .... Jet [*Aircraft*]
J .... Jet Fuel
J .... Jet Route [*Followed by identification*]
J .... Jewels Horology (BARN)
J .... Jewish
J .... Jewish Chaplain [*Territorial Force*] [*Military*] [*British*] (ROG)
J .... Jewish School [*British*]
J .... Jig [*Phonetic alphabet*] [*World War II*] (DSUE)
J .... Job (IEEE)
J .... Jobber [*Merchant middleman*]
J .... Johannes Galensis [*Flourished, 13th century*] [*Authority cited in pre-1607 legal work*] (DSA)
J .... Johnnie [*Phonetic alphabet*] [*Royal Navy*] [*World War I*] (DSUE)
J .... Johnny [*Phonetic alphabet*] [*Pre-World War II*] (DSUE)
J .... Johnson's New York Reports [*A publication*] (DLA)
J .... Join
J .... Joinable Containers [*Shipping*] (DCTA)
J .... Joiner [*Machinery*]
J .... Joining [*Also, JNG*] [*Genetics*]
J .... Joint
J .... Joint Matriculation Board [*British*]
J .... Joist [*Technical drawings*]
J .... Jonckheere Test [*Fisheries*]
J .... Joshua [*Old Testament book*] [*Freemasonry*]
J .... Joule [*Symbol*] [*SI unit of energy*] (GPO)
j .... Jour [*Day*] [*French*]
j .... Journal (RION)
J .... Journal
J .... Journalism
J .... Judaeo-Persian
J .... Judean or Yahwistic [*Used in biblical criticism to designate Yahwistic material*]
J .... Judex [*Judge*] [*Latin*]
J .... Judge
J .... Judgment
J .... Judiciary (journ.) (SAUS)
J .... Juice
J .... Juliett [*Phonetic alphabet*] [*International*] (DSUE)
J .... July

J .... Jump (PIPO)
J .... Junction
J .... Junction Devices [*JETDS nomenclature*] [*Military*] (CET)
J .... Junction Services (SAUS)
J .... June
J .... Jungle
J .... Junior
J .... Jupiter
J .... Juris [*Of Law*] [*Latin*] (ADA)
J .... Jus [*Law*] [*Latin*]
J .... Justice [*i.e., a judge; plural is JJ*]
J .... Justiciary Cases [*Scotland*] [*A publication*] (DLA)
J .... Justification (WDMC)
J .... Juta's South African Reports [*A publication*] (DLA)
J .... Jute-Asphalted [*Nonmetallic armor*] (AAG)
J .... Juvenile
J .... Juvenile (Amaurotic Idiocy) [*Medicine*] (DAVI)
J .... Kansas City [*Branch in the Federal Reserve regional banking system*] (BARN)
J .... Lower Canada Jurist, Quebec [*1848-91*] [*A publication*] (DLA)
J .... Magnetic Poparization [*Physics*] (BARN)
J .... Massieu Function [*Symbol*] [*IUPAC*]
J .... Mechanical Equivalent of Heat [*Symbol*]
J .... Polypeptide Chain in Polymeric Immunoglobulins (STED)
J .... Radiant Intensity [*Symbol*]
J .... Scottish Jurist [*1829-73*] [*A publication*] (DLA)
J .... Sound Intensity (STED)
J .... Special Test, Temporary [*Aircraft classification letter*]
j .... Total Angular Momentum Quantum Number of a Single Particle [*Symbol*] [*Spectroscopy*]
J .... Total Angular Momentum Quantum Number of a System [*Symbol*] [*Spectroscopy*]
J .... VEB Fahlberg-List [*East Germany*] [*Research code symbol*]
J .... Yahwist Source [*Biblical scholarship*]
j .... Yellow [*Symbol*] (DAVI)
J-1 .... Jaeger Test Type One [*Ophthalmology*]
J-1 .... Personnel Section [*of a joint military staff; also, the officer in charge of this section*]
J2 .... Djibouti [*Aircraft nationality and registration mark*] (FAAC)
J-2 .... Intelligence Section [*of a joint military staff; also, the officer in charge of this section*]
J2 .... JTwo Communications [*Associated Press*] (SAG)
J2 Com ...... JTwo Communications [*Associated Press*] (SAG)
J2EE.......... Java 2 Enterprise Edition (SAUS)
J2ME .... Java 2 Micro Edition (SAUS)
J2SE .... Java 2 Standard Edition (SAUS)
J3 .... Grenada [*Aircraft nationality and registration mark*] (FAAC)
J-3 .... Operations and Training Section [*of a joint military staff; also, the officer in charge of this section*]
J-4 .... fuel jet-engine fuel (SAUS)
J-4 .... Logistics Section [*of a joint military staff; also, the officer in charge of this section*]
J-4/JCS .... Medical Readiness Division, Office of the Joint Chiefs of Staff (SAUO)
J-5 .... General Administration Section [*of a joint military staff; also the officer in charge of this section*]
J5 .... Guinea-Bissau [*International civil aircraft marking*] (ODBW)
J-6 .... Command, Control and Communications Systems Directorate (SAUO)
J-6 .... Communications-Electronics Section [*of a joint military staff; also, the officer in charge of this section*]
J6 .... Director for Command, Control, Communications and Computer Systems, Joint Staff (SAUO)
J6 .... St. Lucia [*Aircraft nationality and registration mark*] (FAAC)
J7 .... Dominica [*Aircraft nationality and registration mark*] (FAAC)
J-7 .... Joint Interoperability (SAUO)
J8 .... St. Vincent and the Grenadines [*Aircraft nationality and registration mark*] (FAAC)
J-14/CA .... Jet 14 Class Association (EA)
J17............ Just Seventeen (journ.) (SAUS)
J31............ British Aerospace Jetstream 31 [*Airplane code*]
J-54 .... MAC Aeromedical Evacuation System (SAUO)
JA .... Bankair [*ICAO designator*] (AD)
JA .... FRY Armed Forces (SAUO)
JA .... Jack Adapter

Ja	Jacobus Balduini [*Deceased, 1235*] [*Authority cited in pre-1607 legal work*] (DSA)
Ja	Jacobus de Albenga [*Flourished, 13th century*] [*Authority cited in pre-1607 legal work*] (DSA)
Ja	Jacobus de Ravanis [*Deceased, 1296*] [*Authority cited in pre-1607 legal work*] (DSA)
ja	Jade (VRA)
JA	Jama'at Ahmadiyyah [*Ahmadiyya Muslim Association*] (EAIO)
Ja	Jamaica (MILB)
JA	Jamaica
JA	January
ja	Japan [*ry (Ryukyu Islands, Southern) used in records cataloged before January 1978*] [*MARC country of publication code*] [*Library of Congress*] (LCCP)
JA	Japan Academy (SAUS)
JA	Japan Architect (journ.) (SAUS)
JA	Japan Association (SAUO)
JA	Jetevator Assembly
JA	Jewelers of America (EA)
JA	Jewish Advocate (journ.) (SAUS)
JA	Jewish Agency
JA	Jewish Agency for Palestine (SAUO)
JA	Jewish Art, An Illustrated History [*A publication*] (BJA)
JA	Job Accounting (SAUS)
JA	Job Aid
JA	Job Analysis
JA	Job Authorization (TIMI)
JA	Jockey's Association [*Defunct*] (EA)
JA	John Adams [*US president, 1735-1826*]
JA	John Alden Financial [*NYSE symbol*] (SPSG)
J/A	Joint Account (SHCU)
JA	Joint Account
JA	Joint Agency (SAUO)
JA	Joint Agent
JA	Joint Air Defense Operation Center (SAUS)
JA	Journal Announcement [*Dialog*] [*Searchable field*] [*Information service or system*] (NITA)
JA	Journal A Presses Academiques Europeenes (journ.) (SAUS)
JA	Journal Article (SAUS)
JA	Journal of Aesthetics (SAUO)
JA	Journal of Andrology (journ.) (SAUS)
JA	Journal of Apocrypha (journ.) (SAUS)
JA	Judge Advocate
JA	Judge of Appeal
JA	Judicature Act (ROG)
JA	Judicial Authority [*British*]
JA	Jump Address
JA	Jump If Above [*Computer science*] (PCM)
JA	Jump of Above (SAUS)
JA	Junior Achievement [*Stamford, CT*] (EA)
JA	Junior Ambassadors [*Defunct*] (EA)
JA	Justice of Appeal [*Legal term*] (DLA)
JA	Juvenile Arthritis (MELL)
JA	Juvenile Atrophy [*Medicine*] (DAVI)
JA	Juxta-Articular [*Orthopedics*] (DAVI)
JAA	American Dental Association, Chicago, IL [*OCLC symbol*] (OCLC)
JAA	Jamiat Adduwal Alarabia [*League of Arab States - LAS*] (EAIO)
JAA	Japan Asia Airways
JAA	Japan Asia Airways Co. Ltd. [*ICAO designator*] (FAAC)
JAA	Japanese Archaeologists Association (SAUO)
JAA	Japanese Association of Anatomists (SAUO)
JAA	Jewish Athletic Association (SAUO)
JAA	Joint Airways Association (SAUO)
JAA	Joint Airworthiness Authorities (or Authority) (SAUO)
JAA	Joint Airworthiness Authority [*Aviation*]
JAA	Joint Aviation Authorities (BUAC)
JAA	Journal. British Archaeological Association (journ.) (SAUS)
JAA	Journal of Accounting Auditing and Finance (journ.) (SAUS)
JAA	Journal of African Administration (journ.) (SAUS)
JAA	Journal of Anthropological Archaeology (journ.) (SAUS)
JAA	Journal of Astrophysics and Astronomy (journ.) (SAUS)
JAA	Judge Advocates Association (EA)
JAAA	Jabara Award for Airmanship [*Military decoration*]
JAAA	Japan Amateur Athletic Association (SAUO)
JAAA	Journal of the American Academy of Audiology (journ.) (SAUS)
JAAB	Joint Airlift Allocations Board
JAAC	Joint Airlift Allocations Committee
JAAC	Journal of Aesthetics and Art Criticism [*A publication*] (BRI)
JAACP	Journal. American Chamber of Commerce of the Philippines (journ.) (SAUS)
JAACS	John A. Andrew Clinical Society (EA)
JA(ACT)	Jobless Action (Australian Capital Territory) [*An association*]
JAAD	Journal of the American Academy of Dermatology (SAUO)
JAAD	Justification, Approval and Acquisition Documentation (SAUO)
JAADDB	Journal. American Academy of Dermatology (journ.) (SAUS)
JAAF	Japanese Army Air Force
JAAF	Joint Action Armed Forces
JAAF	Joint Army-Air Force
JAAFAR	Joint Army-Air Force Adjustment Regulations
JAAFCTB	Joint Army-Air Force Commercial Traffic Bulletin
JAAFPC	Joint Army-Air Force Procurement Circular
JAAFU	Joint Anglo-American Foul Up [*World War II slang*] [*Bowdlerized version*]
JAAG	Judge Advocate General Legal Service Office (ACAE)
JAAGL	Journal of the American Association of Gynecologic Laparoscopists (SAUO)
JAAGL	Journal of the American Association of Gynecologic Laparoscopists (journ.) (SAUS)
JAAHA	Journal of the American Animal Hospital Association (SAUO)
JAAHBL	Journal. American Animal Hospital Association (journ.) (SAUS)
JAAL	Jewish Anti-Abortion League (EA)
JAAL	Journal of Adolescent & Adult Literacy [*A publication*] (BRI)
JAAL	Junior Auxiliary of the American Legion (SAUO)
JAALD	Japanese Association of Agricultural Librarians and Documentalists (SAUS)
JAAM	Japanese Association for Acute Medicine (SAUO)
JAAMI J Assoc Adv Med Instrum...	JAAMI Journal. Association for the Advancement of Medical Instrumentation (journ.) (SAUS)
JAAML	Journal. American Academy of Matrimonial Lawyers [*A publication*] (DLA)
JAAMRS	Joint Air-to-Air Missile Requirement (SAUS)
JAAMRS	Joint Air-to-Air Missile Requirement Study (MCD)
JA & FC	Jonrnal of Agricultural and Food Chemistry (journ.) (SAUS)
Ja Ann Int Law...	Japanese Annual of International Law (journ.) (SAUS)
J AANNT	Journal. American Association of Nephrology Nurses and Technicians (journ.) (SAUS)
JAAOC	Joint Antiaircraft Operation Center [*NATO*] (NATG)
JAAOS	Journal of the American Academy of Orthopaedic Surgeons (SAUO)
JAAOS	Journal of the American Academy of Orthopaedic Surgeons (journ.) (SAUS)
JAAP	Joint Airborne Advance Party [*Military*] (AFM)
JAAP	Joliet Army Ammunition Plant (AABC)
JAAP	Journal of the Amecian Academy of Psychoanalysis (journ.) (SAUS)
JAAPA	Journal of the American Academy of Physician Assistants (SAUO)
JAAPA	Journal of the American Academy of Physician Assistants (journ.) (SAUS)
JAAR	Job Area Acceptance Range (AAGC)
JAAR	Journal. American Academy of Religion (journ.) (SAUS)
JAAR	Journal of the American Academy of Religion [*A publication*] (BRI)
Jaarb Inst Biol Scheih Onden Landb Gewss...	Jaarboek. Instituut voor Biologisch en Scheikundig Ondenoek van Landbouwgewassen (journ.) (SAUS)
Ja Are	Jacobus de Arena [*Deceased, 1297*] [*Authority cited in pre-1607 legal work*] (DSA)
JAARS	Joint After-Action Reporting System (COE)
JAARS	Jungle Aviation & Radio Service, Inc. [*Mission plane service*]
JAART	Joint Attack of Artillery (SAUS)
JAAR Thematic St...	Journal. American Academy of Religion. Thematic Studies (journ.) (SAUS)
JAAS	Jewish Academy of Arts and Sciences (EA)
JAAS	Journal. Aberystwyth Agriculture Society (journ.) (SAUS)
JAAS	Journal of Analytical Atomic Spectrometry [*Formerly, ARAAS*] [*A publication*]
JAASAJ	Journal. Alabama Academy of Science (journ.) (SAUS)
JAASD	Journal. American Audiology Society (journ.) (SAUS)
JAASPO	Joint Army-Air Force Special Project Office (ACAE)
JAAT	Joint Air Attack Team [*Military*] (INF)
JAATT	Joint Air Attack Team Tactics (MCD)
JA/ATT	Joint Airborne/Air Transportability Training
JAAW	Juvenile Arthritis Awareness Week [*Arthritis Foundation*]
JAAWSC	Joint Anti-Air Warfare Shore Co-ordination Network (SAUO)
JAB	American Library Association, Booklist, Chicago, IL [*OCLC symbol*] (OCLC)
JAB	Jackson Air Base (SAUS)
JAB	January Assumption Budget [*Budget based on economic forecasts available as of January*]
JAB	Japan Accreditation Board for Conformity Assessment (SAUO)
JAB	Jet Business Airlines [*Belgium*] [*ICAO designator*] (FAAC)
JAB	Job Analysis and Billing (SAUS)
JAB	Join Amphibious Board (SAUS)
JAB	Joint Activity Briefing [*Military*] (AFM)
JAB	Joint Amphibious Board [*Military*]
JAB	Joint Audit Board (SAUO)
JAB	Journal of Applied Biomechanics (journ.) (SAUS)
JAB	Junior Advisory Board
JAB	Juvenile Aid Bureau (SAUO)
JABA	Jefferson Area Board for Aging (SAUO)
JABA	Journal of Applied Behavior Analysis (journ.) (SAUS)
JABAA4	Journal of Applied Bacteriology (journ.) (SAUS)
JABC	Japan Audit Bureau of Circulations (SAUO)
JABCAA	Journal of Abnormal Child Psychology (journ.) (SAUS)
J Abdom Surg...	Journal of Abdominal Surgery (journ.)
JABE	John A. Blume and Associates, Engineers (SAUO)
JABES	Just Another Break-Even Situation [*Slang*]
JABGDP	Journal. Adelaide Botanic Gardens (journ.) (SAUS)
Jabil	Jabil Circuit, Inc. [*Associated Press*] (SAG)
J Abnorm Child Psychol...	Journal of Abnormal Child Psychology (journ.) (SAUS)
J Abnorm Psychol Monogr...	Journal of Abnormal Psychology. Monographs (journ.)
J Abnorm S Psychol...	Journal of Abnormal and Social Psychology (journ.) (SAUS)
JABOWA	Janak-Botkin-Wallis [*Data processing program regarding forest growth; named for three men involved in program*]
JabP	Journal of Abnormal Psychology (journ.)
JABPAF	Journal of Abnormal Psychology. Monographs (journ.) (SAUS)
JABPPC	Joint Animal By Products Parliamentary and Advisory Committee [*British*] (DBA)
JABQC	Job Assembly Breakdown and Quality Control Section [*Social Security Administration*]
JABREG	Journal of Animal Breeding and Genetics (journ.) (SAUS)

JABRO .... James Broadwell [Custom-built racing car]

JABS .... Justice, Awareness & Basic Support (WDAA)

JABSBP .... Journal of Abdominal Surgery (journ.) (SAUS)

J Abstr Br Ship ... Journal of Abstracts. British Ship Research Association (journ.) (SAUS)

J Abstr Int Educ ... Journal of Abstracts in International Education (journ.) (SAUS)

JABUP .... Joint Air Base Utilization Plan (MCD)

Jac .... Book of Jacob (SAUS)

JAC .... CEGEP [College d'Enseignement General et Professionnel] John Abbott College Library [UTLAS symbol]

JAC .... Jackson [Wyoming] [Airport symbol] (OAG)

JAC .... Jacksonville [Florida] [Seismograph station code, US Geological Survey] [Closed] (SEIS)

Jac .... Jacksonville Jaguars [National Football League] [1995-present] (NFLA)

JAC .... Jackson, WY [Location identifier] [FAA] (FAAL)

JAC .... Jacobean (WDAA)

Jac .... Jacob's English Chancery Reports [1821-22] [A publication] (DLA)

Jac .... Jacob's Law Dictionary [A publication] (DLA)

Jac .... Jacobus [James] [King of England] (DLA)

Jac .... Jacobus Balduini [Deceased, 1235] [Authority cited in pre-1607 legal work] (DSA)

JAC .... Japan Advisory Committee (SAUO)

JAC .... Japan Air Commuter Co. Ltd. [ICAO designator] (FAAC)

JAC .... Jet Age Conference

JAC .... Jet Aircraft Coating

JAC .... Jeunesse Anarchiste Communiste [French student group]

JAC .... Jewellery Advisory Centre (BUAC)

JAC .... Job Assistance Center (DOMA)

JAC .... Johnstown American Co. (MHDW)

JAC .... Joint Action Co. [Marine Corps]

JAC .... Joint Advisory Airworthiness Committee (SAUS)

JAC .... Joint Advisory Committee [Military]

JAC .... Joint Aircraft Committee [World War II]

JAC .... Joint Airworthiness Committee (SAUO)

JAC .... Joint Analysis Center (SAUO)

JAC .... Joint Apprenticeship Committee

JAC .... Joint Apprenticeship Council (SAUO)

JAC .... Joint Arms Control

JAC .... Joint Automatic Control (SAUS)

JAC .... Journal of Ancient Civilizations (journ.) (SAUS)

JAC .... Journal of Applied Chemistry [A publication]

JAC .... Junior American Citizens [An association] (EA)

JAC .... Junior Association of Commerce (BARN)

JAC .... Juvenile Advisory Council (SAUO)

JACA .... Journal of the American Chiropractic Association (SAUO)

JACA .... Journal of the American Chiropractic Association (journ.) (SAUS)

J Acad Gen Dent ... Journal. Academy of General Dentistry (journ.) (SAUS)

J Acad Libr ... Journal of Academic Librarianship (journ.) (SAUS)

J Acad Nat Sci Phila ... Journal. Academy of Natural Sciences of Philadelhia (journ.) (SAUS)

JACADS .... Johnston Atoll Chemical Agent Disposal System (SAUO)

JACADS .... Johnston Atoll Chemical Agents Disposal System

Jac & W ...... Jacob and Walker's English Chancery Reports [37 English Reprint] [A publication] (DLA)

Jac & Walk ... Jacob and Walker's English Chancery Reports [37 English Reprint] [A publication] (DLA)

Jac & Walk ... Jacob and Walkers English Chancery Reports (journ.) (SAUS)

Jac & W (Eng) ... Jacob and Walker's English Chancery Reports [37 English Reprint] [A publication] (DLA)

JACAPHO ..... Joint Commission on Allied Health in Ophthalmology (ADWA)

JACARI .... Joint Action Committee Against Racial Interference (BUAC)

JACBB .... Journal of Applied Chemistry and Biotechnology (journ.) (SAUS)

JACB-E .... Joint Acquisition Coordinating Board-Europe (AAGC)

Jacbn .... Jacobean (VRA)

Jacbsn .... Jacobson Stores, Inc. [Associated Press] (SAG)

JACC .... Jayhawk Acceptance [NASDAQ symbol] (TTSB)

JACC .... Jayhawk Acceptance Corp. [NASDAQ symbol] (SAG)

JACC .... Joint Admissions Centre for Colleges (SAUO)

JACC .... Joint Airborne Command Center (SAUO)

JACC .... Joint Airborne Communications Center (MCD)

JACC .... Joint Air Command Center [Army] (DOMA)

JACC .... Joint Alternate Command Center [Military] (CINC)

JACC .... Joint Area Collection Center (SAUS)

JACC .... Joint Area Collection Centre (SAUO)

JACC .... Joint Automatic Control Conference [IEEE]

JACC .... Journalism Association of Community Colleges (EA)

JACC .... Journal of the American College of Cardiology [A publication] (ROAS)

JACCC .... Japanese-American Cultural and Community Center (SAUO)

JACCC .... Joint Air Control and Coordination Center [Air Force] (AFM)

JACC/CP ...... Joint Airborne Command Center/Command Post (SAUO)

JACC/CP ...... Joint Airborne Communications Center/Command Post (AFM)

JACCDI .... Journal. American College of Cardiology (journ.) (SAUS)

J Accel Sci Technol ... Journal of Accelerator Science and Technology (journ.) (SAUS)

JACCI .... Joint Allocation Committee Civil Intelligence [of US and Great Britain] [World War II]

J Accid Emerg Med ... Journal of Accident and Emergency Medicine (journ.) (SAUS)

J Account ...... Journal of Accountancy [A publication] (BRI)

J Account Audit Finance ... Journal of Accounting Auditing and Finance (journ.) (SAUS)

J Account EDP ... Journal of Accounting and EDP (journ.) (SAUS)

JACCP .... Joint Airborne Communication and Command Post (IAA)

JACCS .... Japanese Cloud and Climate Study (SAUO)

J Acct .... Journal of Accountancy [A publication] (DLA)

J Acct Res ... Journal of Accounting Research (journ.) (SAUS)

J Accy .... Journal of Accountancy (journ.) (SAUS)

JACD .... Joint Architectural Control Document (SAUS)

JACD .... Journal of the American College of Dentists (SAUO)

JACDA .... Journal. American College of Dentists (journ.) (SAUS)

Jac Dict ...... Jacob's Law Dictionary [A publication] (DLA)

JACE .... Joint Allied Communications Element (AFM)

JACE .... Joint Alternate Command Element

JACE .... Judge Advocate Civil Law, Environmental (SAUO)

JACE .... Just Another Confused Elephant

JACEB .... JACEP Journal of the American College of Emergency Physicians (journ.) (SAUS)

JACEE .... Japanese-American Cooperative Emulsion Experiment (SAUO)

JACEP .... Journal. American College of Emergency Physicians and the University Association for Emergency Medical Services (journ.) (SAUS)

JACERS .... Japan Research Committee of Environmental Remote Sensing (SAUO)

JACES .... Joint Advisory Committee for Engineering Services (BUAC)

Jac Fish Dig ... Jacob's American Edition of Fisher's English Digest [A publication] (DLA)

JACFU .... Joint American-Chinese Foul Up [World War II slang] [Bowdlerized version]

JACG .... Joint Aeronautical Commanders Group (ACAE)

JACGUAR .... Johns and Call Girls United Against Repression (EA)

J A Che J ...... Journal. Agricultural Chemical Society of Japan (journ.) (SAUS)

Ja Christ Q ... Japan Christian Quarterly (journ.) (SAUS)

JACHS .... Australian Catholic Historical Society. Journal (journ.) (SAUS)

JACIBY .... Journal of Allergy and Clinical Immunology (journ.) (SAUS)

Jac Int .... Jacob's Introduction to the Common, Civil, and Canon Law [A publication] (DLA)

JACK .... Golden Bear Golf, Inc. [NASDAQ symbol] (SAG)

JACK .... Jackpot Enterprises Inc. (SAUO)

JACK .... Junior American Coin Klub (EA)

JACK .... Junior Assistant Cook [British military] (DMA)

Jack & G Landl & Ten ... Jackson and Gross' Treatise on the Law of Landlord and Tenant in Pennsylvania [A publication] (DLA)

Jack & G Landl & Ten ... Jackson and Gross Treatise on the Law of Landlord and Tenant in Pennsylvania (journ.) (SAUS)

Jack & L ...... Jackson and Lumpkin's Reports [59-64 Georgia] [A publication] (DLA)

Jack Geo Ind ... Jackson's Index to the Georgia Reports [A publication] (DLA)

JackHwt .... Jackson Hewitt [Associated Press] (SAG)

Jack Journal ... Jackson Journal of Business (journ.) (SAUS)

JACKPHY .... Japanese, Arabic, Chinese, Korean, Persian, Hebrew, Yiddish [Nonroman languages] [Library of Congress]

Jack Pl .... Jackson on Pleadings [1933] [A publication] (DLA)

Jack Pl .... Jackson on Pleadings (journ.) (SAUS)

Jackpot .... Jackpot Enterprises, Inc. [Associated Press] (SAG)

JACKPOT .... Joint Airborne Communications Center and Command Post

Jackpt .... Jackpot Enterprises [Associated Press] (SAG)

Jackson ...... Jackson's Reports [46-58 Georgia] [A publication] (DLA)

Jackson ...... Jackson's Reports [1-29 Texas Court of Appeals] [A publication] (DLA)

Jackson & Lumpkin ... Jackson and Lumpkin's Reports [59-64 Georgia] [A publication] (DLA)

Jackson St U ... Jackson State University (GAGS)

Jacksonville St U ... Jacksonville State University (GAGS)

Jacksonville U ... Jacksonville University (GAGS)

Jack Tex App ... Jackson's Reports [A publication] (DLA)

JACL .... Japanese American Citizens League (EA)

JACLAP .... Joint Advisory Committee on Local Authority Purchasing (SAUO)

Jac Law Dict ... Jacob's Law Dictionary [A publication] (DLA)

Jac Law Dict ... Jacobs Law Dictionary (journ.) (SAUS)

Jac LD .... Jacob's Law Dictionary [A publication] (DLA)

Jac L Dict ... Jacob's Law Dictionary [A publication] (DLA)

Jac Lex Mer ... Jacob's Lex Mercatoria [A publication] (DLA)

Jac LG .... Jacob's Law Grammar [A publication] (DLA)

Jaclyn .... Jaclyn, Inc. [Associated Press] (SAG)

JACM .... Journal. Association for Computing Machinery (journ.) (SAUS)

JACM .... Journal of Alternative and Complementary Medicine (journ.) (SAUS)

JACM .... Journal of the Association for Computing Machinery [A publication]

JACMAS ...... Joint Approach Central Meteorological Advisory Service (SAUO)

JACNE .... Joint Advisory Committee on Nutrition Education [British]

JACO .... Jaco Electronics [NASDAQ symbol] (TTSB)

JACO .... Jaco Electronics, Inc. [NASDAQ symbol] (NQ)

JACO .... Joint Actions Control Office (AABC)

Jacob .... Jacob's English Chancery Reports [1821-22] [A publication] (DLA)

Jacob .... Jacob's Law Dictionary [A publication] (DLA)

JACOB .... Junior Achievement Corporation of Business (SAUO)

Jacob Ardiz ... Jacobus de Ardizone [Flourished, 1213-50] [Authority cited in pre-1607 legal work] (DSA)

Jacobs .... Jacobs Engineering Group, Inc. [Associated Press] (SAG)

JACODEC ..... Japan Agricultural Chemicals Overseas Development Commission (SAUO)

JACODK .... Journal of Altered States of Consciousness (journ.) (SAUS)

JacoEl .... Jaco Electronics, Inc. [Associated Press] (SAG)

JacoElec ...... Jaco Electronics, Inc. [Associated Press] (SAG)

JACOLA .... Joint Airports Committee of Local Authorities (SAUS)

JACOPIS ...... Joint Advisory Committee on Pets in Society [British] (DI)

JACOPIS ..... Joint Advisory Committee on Poets in Society (SAUO)

JacorC .... Jacor Communications, Inc. [Associated Press] (SAG)

JacorCm ...... Jacor Communications, Inc. [Associated Press] (SAG)

J Acoust Soc Am Spl... Journal. Acoustical Society of America. Supplement (journ.) (SAUS)
J Acoust Soc India... Journal. Acoustical Society of India (journ.) (SAUS)
J Acoust Soc India... Journal of the Acoustical Society of India (journ.) (SAUS)
J Acoust Soc Jpn... Journal. Acoustical Society of Japan (journ.) (SAUS)
J Acoust Soc Jpn... Journal of the Acoustical Society of Japan (journ.) (SAUS)
JACP Japanese American Curriculum Project (EA)
JACPA Journal. American Academy of Child Psychiatry (journ.) (SAUS)
J Acquir Immune Defic Syndr Hum Retrovirol... Journal of Acquired Immune Deficiency Syndromes and Human Retrovirology (journ.) (SAUS)
JACR Joint Advisory Committee Report (HEAS)
JACRAQ Journal of Apicultural Research (journ.) (SAUS)
JacrCm Jacor Communications, Inc. [Associated Press] (SAG)
JACRD Joint Committee for Agricultural Research and Development (BUAC)
JACS Japan-American Cultural Society (EAIO)
JACS Jet Attitude Control System (KSC)
JACS Jewish Alcoholics, Chemically Dependent Persons, and Significant Others
JACS Joint Action in Community Service (EA)
JACS Journal of American Chemical Society (SAUO)
JACS Journal of Applied Communication Series (journ.) (SAUS)
JACS Journal of the Acoustical Society of America (journ.) (SAUS)
JACS Journal of the American Ceramic Society (journ.) (SAUS)
JACS Journal of the American Chemical Society (journ.) (SAUS)
Jac Sea laws... Jacobsens Law of the Sea (journ.) (SAUS)
Jac Sea Laws... Jacobsen's Law of the Sea [A publication] (DLA)
JACSPAC Joint Air Communications of the Pacific
JACT [The] Joint Association of Classical Teachers [British]
JACTA Journal. American Ceramic Society (journ.) (SAUS)
JACTA Journal. Australasian Commercial Teachers Association (journ.) (SAUS)
JACTRU Joint Air Traffic Control RADAR Unit (IAA)
JACult Journal of American Culture [A publication] (ANEX)
JACWA Joint Allied Command Western Approaches [NATO] (LAIN)
JAD Jamaican Dollar (SAUS)
JAD Joint Analyses Directorate (SAUO)
JAD Joint Analysis and Design (ABAC)
JAD Joint Analysis Directorate (ACAE)
JAD Joint Application Design [Computer science]
JAD Joint Application Development [Computer science] (CIST)
JAD Joint Application Point (SAUS)
JAD Joint Assembly Demonstration (SAUS)
JAD Joint Resource Assessment Database
JAD Julian Astronomical Day (SAUS)
JAD Wheaton Public Library, Wheaton, IL [OCLC symbol] (OCLC)
JADA Japan Automobile Dealers Association (SAUO)
JADA Joint Agency Data Agreement (SAUO)
JADA Journal of American Dental Association [A publication] (DHP)
JADA Journal of the American Dental Association (journ.) (SAUS)
JADARA Journal for Professionals Networking for Excellence in Service Delivery with Individuals who are Deaf and Hard of Hearing (SAUO)
Jadav J Comp Lit... Jadavpur Journal of Comparative Literature (journ.) (SAUS)
JADB Joint Air Defense Board
JADC Joint Administrative Committee [Military]
JADC Joint Air Defence Centre (SAUO)
JADD Joint Air Defense Division (SAA)
J Addict Dis... Journal of Addictive Diseases (journ.) (SAUS)
J Addict Res Found... Journal. Addiction Research Foundation (journ.) (SAUS)
JADDIN Joint Air Defence Digital Information System (SAUO)
JADE Japan Area Defense Environment
JADE Japan Asian Dance Event
JADE Japanese Air Defence (or Defense) Environment (SAUS)
JADE Japanese Air Defense Environment
JADE Jasmine Application Development Environment (SAUS)
JADE Joint Allied Defense Experiment (ACAE)
JADE Journal Abstracts Delivered Electronically (SAUO)
JADE Journal of Alcohol and Drug Education (journ.) (SAUS)
JADE Junior Administrator Development Examination (AFM)
J Adelaide Bot Gard... Journal. Adelaide Botanic Gardens (journ.) (SAUS)
JADF Japan Air Defense Force
JADF Joint Air Defense Force (AAG)
JADF Jordan Airports Duty Free
J Adhes Sci Technol... Journal of Adhesion Science and Technology (journ.) (SAUS)
J Adhes Sealant Counc... Journal. Adhesive and Sealant Council (journ.) (SAUS)
J Adhes Soc Jpn... Journal. Adhesion Society of Japan (journ.) (SAUS)
JADI Japan Association of Defence Industries (SAUO)
JADID7 Journal of Affective Disorders (journ.) (SAUS)
JADIS Joint Air Defense Interoperability Study
JADITBHKNYC... Just a Drop in the Basket Helps Keep New York Clean [Antilitter campaign]
JADITBHKYCC... Just a Drop in the Basket Helps Keep Your City Clean (SAUS)
JADMAG Joint Aeronautics Depot Maintenance Action Group (ACAE)
JADO Joint Air Defense Operations [Marine Corps] (DOMA)
JADO Journal of Administration Overseas (journ.) (SAUS)
JADOC Joint Air Defense Operation Center
J Adolesc Health... Journal of Adolescent Health (journ.) (SAUS)
J Adolesc Health Care... Journal of Adolescent Health Care (journ.) (SAUS)
JADOR Joint Advertising Directors of Recruiting [Navy] (NVT)
JADPDS Journal of Applied Developmental Psychology (journ.) (SAUS)
JADPU Joint Automatic Data Processing Unit
JAD/RAD Joint Application Design/Rapid Application Design [Computer science]
JADREP Joint Resource Assessment Damage Report (SAUO)

JADREP Joint Resource Assessment Data Base Report [Military] (AABC)
JADS Joint Advanced Distributed Simulation [Military]
JADS Journal Article Delivery Service [Carnegie Mellon University]
jadt Jadeite (VRA)
J Adult Ed... Journal of Adult Education (journ.) (SAUS)
J Adv Judge Advocate [Legal term] (DLA)
J Adv Ed Journal of Advanced Education [A publication]
J ADV GEN... Judge Advocate General [Military] (WDAA)
J Adv Nurs... Journal of Advanced Nursing (journ.) (SAUS)
J Adv Z Journal of Advanced Zoology (journ.) (SAUS)
JADW Joint Air Defense Wing (SAA)
JAE Illinois Agricultural Association & Affiliated Co., Bloomington, IL [OCLC symbol] (OCLC)
JAE Jacksonville [Illinois] [Airport symbol] (AD)
JAE Jaeger Machine Company (SAUO)
JAE Japan Aviation Electronics Industry Ltd.
JAE Java Application Environment (SAUS)
JAE Joint Atomic Exercise [NATO] (NATG)
JAE Journal of Accounting and Economics (journ.) (SAUS)
JAE Journal of Advanced Education [A publication] (ADA)
JAE Journal of Agricultural Economics [A publication]
JAE Jump If Above or Equal [Computer science] (PCM)
JAEC Japan Atomic Energy Commission
JAEC Joint Atomic Energy Commission
JAEC Joint Atomic Energy Committee (SAUO)
JAED Journal of Agricultural Economics and Development (SAUO)
JAEG Jaegdtiger [Tank-destroyer] [German military - World War II]
Jaeger Labor Law... Jaeger's Cases and Statutes on Labor Law [A publication] (DLA)
Jaeger Labor Law... Jaegers Cases and Statutes on Labor Law (journ.) (SAUS)
JAEH Journal of Aquatic Ecosystem Health [A publication]
JAEIA Japan Atomic Energy Industrial Association (SAUO)
JAEIC Joint Atomic Energy Intelligence Center [Military]
JAEIC Joint Atomic Energy Intelligence Committee (KSC)
JAEIP Japan Atomic Energy Insurance Pool
JAEL JSC Avionics Engineering Laboratory (SAUO)
JAEMA Journal. Albert Einstein Medical Center (journ.) (SAUS)
JAENFS Journal of Agricultural Entomology (journ.) (SAUS)
JAERES Journal of Agricultural Engineering Research (journ.) (SAUS)
JAERI Japan Atomic Energy Research Institute [Tokyo]
JAERI Japanese Atomic Energy Research Institute (SAUS)
J Aeronaut Mater... Journal of Aeronautical Materials (journ.) (SAUS)
J Aeronaut Soc India... Journal of the Aeronautical Society of India (journ.) (SAUS)
J Aeronaut Soc S Afr... Journal. Aeronautical Society of South Africa (journ.) (SAUS)
J Aero Sci ... Journal of the Aeronautical Sciences (journ.) (SAUS)
J Aerosol Sci... Journal of Aerosol Science (journ.) (SAUS)
J Aero/Space Sci... Journal of the Aero/Space Sciences (journ.) (SAUS)
J Aerosp Trans Div Am Soc Civ Eng... Journal. Aerospace Transpon Division. American Society of Civil Engineering (journ.) (SAUS)
JAERT Journal. Association for Education by Radio-Television (journ.) (SAUS)
JAERT Journal of the Association for Education by Radio-Television (SAUO)
JAERT Journal of the Association for Education by Radio-Television (journ.) (SAUS)
JAES Japan Atomic Energy Society (BUAC)
JAES Journal of African Earth Sciences (journ.) (SAUS)
J Aes Art Crit... Journal of Aesthetic and Art Criticism (journ.) (SAUS)
J Aes Ed Journal of Aesthetic Education [A publication] (BRI)
J Aesthetics Art Criticism... Journal of Aesthetics and Art Criticism. American Society of Aesthetics. Johns Hopkins University. Baltimore (SAUO)
JAEU Journal of Asia Electronics Union (SAUO)
JAEU Journal of Asia Electronics Union (journ.) (SAUS)
JAEW Japanese Airborne Early Warning
JAF Corn Belt Library System, Normal, IL [OCLC symbol] (OCLC)
JAF Jaffna [Ceylon] [Airport symbol] (AD)
JAF James A. Fitzpatrick [Nuclear power plant] (NRCH)
JAF Jamestown Area Furniture Haulers Association, Inc., Buffalo NY [STAC]
JAF Jamestown Area Furniture Haulets Association, Inc (SAUS)
JAF Japan-Australia Foundation
JAF Japan Automobile Federation
JAF Job Accounting Facility
JAF John Augustus Foundation (EA)
JAF Joint Armed Forces (SAUO)
JAF Joint Attack Fighter [Air Force] [Navy] [DoD] (DOMA)
JAF Jordanian Air Force
JAF Journal of American Folklore [A publication] (BRI)
JAF Judge Advocate of the Fleet
JAF Judge-Advocate of the Fleet (SAUO)
JAFA Japan Auto-Focus Association (SAUO)
JAFA Japanese Art Festival Association (SAUO)
JAFAE Japan Auto-Focus Association in Europe (SAUO)
JAFB Johnson Air Force Base (SAUS)
JAFC James Allen Fan Club (EA)
JAFC Jammie Ann Fan Club (EA)
JAFC Japan Atomic Fuel Corp.
JAFC Japan Atomic Fuel Corporation (SAUO)
JAFC Japanese Atomic Fuel Corp. (SAUS)
JAFC John Anderson Fan Club [Defunct] (EA)
JAFC Junior Acting Field Captain [Military] [British] (ROG)
JAFE Joint Advanced Fighter Engine
JAFE Joint Advance Fighter Engine (SAUS)
JAFF Electronic and Chaff Jamming (IEEE)

JAFHRO ...... Joint Armed Forces Housing Referral Office (MCD)
JAFNA......... Joint Air Force (SAUS)
JAFNA......... Joint Air Force NASA Facility (SAUS)
JAFNC......... Joint Air Force-Navy Committee
JAFO......... Junior Acting Field Officer [Military] [British] (ROG)
JAFP......... Jewish Agency for Palestine
JAFPUB....... Joint Armed Forces Publication
JAFPUB....... Joint Army-Air Force Publication (SAUO)
JAFRC......... Joint Anti-Fascists Refugee Committee (SAUO)
J Afr Earth Sci... Journal of African Earth Sciences (journ.) (SAUS)
J Afr Earth Sci Middle East... Journal of African Earth Sciences and the Middle
          East (journ.) (SAUS)
J African L... Journal of African Law [A publication] (DLA)
JAfrS......... Journal of the African Society (SAUO)
JAfrS......... Journal of the African Society (journ.) (SAUS)
J Afr Soc... Journal. African Society (journ.) (SAUS)
JAFS .... Japan Asian Association and Asian Friendship Society (BUAC)
JAFS .... Journal. Audio Engineering Society (journ.) (SAUS)
JAFSA......... Japan Foundation For Shipbuilding Advancement (SAUS)
JaG............. Book of Jarom (SAUS)
JAG............. Indian Trails Public Library District, Wheeling, IL [OCLC symbol]
          (OCLC)
JAG............. Jaguar [Automobile]
JAG............. James Abram Garfield [US president, 1831-1881]
jag............. jargonish (SAUS)
JAG............. Jetag AB [Switzerland] [ICAO designator] (FAAC)
JAG............. Jobs for America's Graduates [An association] (EA)
JAG............. Joint Action Group (SAUO)
JAG............. Joint Analyses Group (SAUO)
JAG............. Journal. Alaska Geological Society (journ.) (SAUS)
JAG............. Judge Advocate General [Air Force, Army, Navy]
JAG-A......... Judge Advocate General-Army (SAUO)
JAGA........... Judge Advocate General, United States Army (SAUS)
JAGA........... Military Affairs Division, Office of Judge Advocate General, United
          States Army (DLA)
JAGAR .... Judge Advocate General Area Representatives (SAUO)
JAGAR .... Judge Advocate General's Area Representatives
JAGB........... Jockeys' Association [British] (DBA)
JAGB........... Jockeys Association of Great Britain (BUAC)
JAG Bull ...... Judge Advocate General Bulletin [Air Force] [A publication] (DLA)
JAGC........... Judge Advocate General's Corps
JAG CMR (AF)... Judge Advocate General Court-Martial Reports [Air Force]
          [A publication] (DLA)
JAG Comp CMO (Navy)... Judge Advocate General Compilation of Court-Martial
          Orders [Navy] [A publication] (DLA)
JAGD .... Judge Advocate General's Department [Air Force, Army]
JAG Dig Op... Judge Advocate General Digest of Opinions [A publication] (DLA)
JAGDR......... Judge Advocate General's Department Reserve
JAGET......... Judge Advocates General Network
Jagg Torts ... Jaggard on Torts [A publication] (DLA)
JAGINST ...... Office of the Judge Advocate General Instructions [Navy]
JAGIS.......... Journalism and GIS Interest Group (SAUO)
JAGIT.......... Joint Air-Ground Instruction (SAUS)
JAGIT.......... Joint Air-Ground Instruction Team
JAG Journal... Judge Advocate General of the Navy. Journal (journ.) (SAUS)
JAG L Rev ... Judge Advocate General. Law Review (journ.) (SAUS)
JAG L Rev ... United States. Air Force Judge Advocate General. Law Review
          [A publication] (DLA)
JAG Man...... Judge Advocate General Manual (journ.) (SAUS)
JAG Man...... Judge Advocate General Manual (Navy) [A publication] (DLA)
JAG-N......... Judge Advocate General-Navy (SAUS)
JAGN .... Judge Advocate General of the Navy
J Ag New Zlnd... New Zealand Journal of Agriculture (SAUS)
JAGO .... Judge Advocate General's Office
JAGOS .... Joint Air-Ground Operations System [Military]
JAGOS .... Joint Air-Ground Operations Systems (SAUO)
JAGRA .... Journal of Agricultural Research (journ.) (SAUS)
J Agr Eng Soc Jap... Journal. Agricultural Engineering Society of Japan (journ.)
          (SAUS)
J Agric......... Journal of Agriculture (journ.) (SAUS)
J Agric Chem Soc Jpn... Journal. Agricultural Chemical Society of Japan (journ.)
          (SAUS)
J Agric Eng... Journal of Agricultural Engineering (journ.) (SAUS)
J Agric Entomol... Journal of Agricultural Entomology (journ.) (SAUS)
J Agric Food Chem... Journal of Agriculturul and Food Chemistry (journ.) (SAUS)
J Agric For... Journal of Agriculture and Forestry (journ.) (SAUS)
J Agric Res China... Journal of Agricultural Research of China (journ.) (SAUS)
J Agric Res Icel... Journal of Agricultural Research in Iceland (journ.) (SAUS)
J Agric Sci Finl... Journal of Agricultural Science in Finland (journ.) (SAUS)
J Agric Sci Res... Journal of Agricultural and Scientific Research (journ.) (SAUS)
J Agric Soc Jpn... Journal. Agricultural Society of Japan (journ.) (SAUS)
J Agric Soc Trin & Tobago... Journal. Agricultural Society of Trinidad and Tobago
          (journ.) (SAUS)
J Agric Soc Univ Coll Wales... Journal. Agricultural Society. University College of
          Wales (journ.) (SAUS)
J Agric Vict Dep Agric... Journal of Agriculture. Victoria Department of Agriculture
          (journ.) (SAUS)
J Agric Water Resour Res... Journal of Agriculture and Water Resources Research
          (journ.) (SAUS)
J Agric W Aust... Journal of Agriculture of Western Australia [A publication]
J Agr Ind SA... Journal of Agricultural Industry, South Australia [A publication]
J Agr Ind SA... Journal of Agricultural Industry, South Australia (journ.) (SAUS)
J Agron Crop Sci... Journal of Agronomy and Crop Science (journ.) (SAUS)
J Agr Res Tokai-Kinki Reg... Journal of the Agricultural Research in the Tokai-Kinki
          Region (journ.) (SAUS)

J Agr Soc Wales... Journal. Agricultural Society. University College of Wales
          (journ.) (SAUS)
J Agr Tax'n & L... Journal of Agricultural Taxation and Law [A publication] (DLA)
J Agr Taxn & L... Journal of Agricultural Taxation and Law (journ.) (SAUS)
JAGRY .... Jaguar PLC (MHDW)
JAGS............ Joint Army-Air Force Air-Ground Study
JAGS............ Journal of the American Geriatrics Society (journ.) (SAUS)
JAGS............ Judge Advocate General's School (DLA)
JAGSA .... Journal. American Geriatrics Society (journ.) (SAUS)
JAGSAF........ Journal. American Geriatrics Society (journ.) (SAUS)
JAGT........... Judge Advocate General, United States Army (SAUS)
JAGT........... Procurement Division, Judge Advocate General, United States
          Army (DLA)
J Ag T and L... Journal of Agricultural Taxation and Law (journ.) (SAUS)
Ja Guara..... Jacobus Guaraguilia [Authority cited in pre-1607 legal work] (DSA)
JAGUAR-V ... Jamming Guarded Radio - VHF [Very High Frequency] (PDAA)
JAGUAR-V ... Jamming Guarded Radio. VHF frequency hopping radio system
          (SAUS)
JAH............. Glencoe Public Library, Glencoe, IL [OCLC symbol] (OCLC)
JAH............. John Adams House (SAUO)
JAH............. Journal of African History [A publication]
JAH............. Journal of American History [A publication] (BRI)
JAHCD9 .... Journal of Adolescent Health Care (journ.) (SAUS)
JAHEDF........ Journal of Allied Health (journ.) (SAUS)
JAHI........... Jordan Amer Hldgs [NASDAQ symbol] (TTSB)
JAHI........... Jordan American Holdings, Inc. [NASDAQ symbol] (SAG)
JAHIW .... Jordan Amer Hldgs Wrrt [NASDAQ symbol] (TTSB)
Jahrb f Cl Phil Suppl... Jahrbucher fuer Classische Philologie. Supplementband
          [A publication] (OCD)
Jahresb....... Jahresberichte ueber die Fortschritte der Altertumswissenschaft
          [1873-] [A publication] (OCD)
JAHRS......... Journal. Andhra Historical Research Society (journ.) (SAUS)
JAHWGS ..... Joint Ad Hoc Working Group on Shipping [ASEAN]
JAI............. JAI Press [Division of Johnson Associates, Inc.]
JAI............. Jaipur [India] [Airport symbol] (OAG)
JAI............. Jaipur [India] [Geomagnetic observatory code]
JAI............. Jami'at Al Islan [Defunct] (EA)
JAI............. Japan-America Institute [Defunct] (EA)
JAI............. Jewish Agency for Israel [United Israel Appeal] [Absorbed by] (EA)
JAI............. Job Accounting Interface
JAI............. Johnson Associates Inc. (GAAI)
Jai............. Johnson Associates Incorporated (SAUO)
Jai............. Johnson Associates, Incorporated, Greenwich, CT [Library symbol]
          [Library of Congress] (LCLS)
JAI............. Joint Administrative Instruction
JAI............. Joint Airdrop Inspection (SAUO)
JAI............. Joint Staff Administrative Instruction [Military]
JAI............. Journal of American Insurance (journ.) (SAUS)
JAI............. Journal of Anthropological Institute of Great Britain (SAUO)
JAI............. Journal of Artificial Intelligence [A publication]
JAIS........... Journal of the Anthropological Institute (journ.) (SAUS)
JAI............. Journal of the Anthropological Institute of America (SAUO)
JAI............. Journal of the Royal Anthropological Institute (SAUO)
JAI............. Journal. Royal Archaeological Institute (journ.) (SAUS)
JAI............. Juvenile Amaurotic Idiocy [Medicine]
JAI............. Lake Forest Library, Lake Forest, IL [OCLC symbol] (OCLC)
JAI............. M/S Jet Airways Ltd. [India] [FAA designator] (FAAC)
JAIA........... Japan Automobile Importers Association
JAIA........... Journal. Archaeological Institute of America (journ.) (SAUS)
JAIA........... Journal. Australian Indonesian Association [A publication]
JAIA........... Journal. Australian Indonesian Association (journ.) (SAUS)
JAIA........... Journal of the Archaeological Institute of America (journ.) (SAUS)
JAIAS......... Journal. Australian Institute of Agricultural Science (journ.) (SAUS)
JAIB........... Journal of the Royal Anthropological Institute (SAUO)
JAIC........... Joint Air Intelligence Center (DOMA)
J Aic Ass China New Ser... Journal. Agricultural Association of China. New Series
          (journ.) (SAUS)
JAICC.......... Joint Arab-Irish Chamber of Commerce (BUAC)
J Aichi Med Univ Assoc... Journal. Aichi Medical University Association (journ.)
          (SAUS)
JAICI........... Japanese Association for International Chemical Information [Tokyo]
JAIEA.......... Joint Atomic Information Exchange Agency (SAA)
JAIEE.......... Journal American Institute Electrical Engineer (SAUO)
JAIEG.......... Joint Atomic Information Exchange Group [DoD]
JAIF........... Japan Atomic Industrial Forum
JAIH........... Journal of Ancient Indian History (journ.) (SAUS)
JAII........... Johnstown America Indus [NASDAQ symbol] (TTSB)
JAII........... Johnstown America Industries, Inc. [NASDAQ symbol] (SAG)
JAIL........... Adtec, Inc. (SAUO)
JAIL........... Japanese Annual of International Law (journ.) (SAUS)
JAIL........... Justice Against Identification Laws (SAUS)
JAIM........... Job Analysis and Interest Measurement
JAIMS......... Japan-American Institute of Management Science
JAIMS......... Jobber Automatic Inventory Management System (TIMI)
JAIN........... Japan Academic Inter-University Network
JAINAA .... Journal. Anatomical Society of India (journ.) (SAUS)
Jaina Antiq... Jaina Antiquary (journ.) (SAUS)
Jain J......... Jain Journal (journ.) (SAUS)
Ja Interp..... Japan Interpreter (journ.) (SAUS)
JAIO........... Joint Assessment and Initiatives Office [Military]
Jaipur LJ ..... Jaipur Law Journal [India] [A publication] (DLA)
J Air Pollut Contr A... Air Pollution Control Association. Journal (journ.) (SAUS)
J Air Pollut Control Assoc... Journal of the Air Pollution Control Association
          (journ.) (SAUS)

J Air Transp Div Am Soc Civ Eng... Journal. Air Transport Division. American Society of Civil Engineers (journ.) (SAUS)
J Air Waste Manag Assoc... Journal of the Air and Waste Management Association (SAUO)
JAIS Japan Aircraft Industry Society (BUAC)
JAIS Japan Air Intelligence System (SAUO)
JAISDS Journal. All India Institute of Medical Sciences (journ.) (SAUS)
JAISPAC Joint Area Information System Pacific (SAUO)
JAJ J. A. Jones Construction Services Co. (SAUO)
JAJ Judge Advocate Journal (journ.) (SAUS)
JAJ Waubonsee Community College, Sugar Grove, IL [OCLC symbol] (OCLC)
JAJC Journalism Association of Junior Colleges [Later, JACC]
JAJO January, April, July, and October [Denotes quarterly payments of interest or dividends in these months] [Business term]
Ja J Rel Stud... Japanese Journal of Religious Studies (journ.) (SAUS)
Jak Jakowlew (SAUS)
Jakarta Jakarta Growth Fund [Associated Press] (SAG)
JAKE Jakes Pizza International [NASDAQ symbol] (SAG)
JAKE Jakes Pizza Intl [NASDAQ symbol] (TTSB)
JakePza Jakes Pizza International [Associated Press] (SAG)
JAKFORCE... Jammu and Kashmir Force [British military] (DMA)
JAKIS Japanese Keyword Indexing Simulation (or Simulator) (SAUS)
JAKIS Japanese Keyword Indexing Simulator
JAKIS System... Japanese Keyword Indexing Simulation (or Simulator) System (SAUS)
JAKK JAKKS Pacific [NASDAQ symbol] (TTSB)
JAKK Jakks Pacific, Inc. [NASDAQ symbol] (SAG)
JAL Japan Air Lines
JAL Japan Air Lines Co. Ltd. (SAUO)
JAL Japan Air Lines Ltd. [ICAO designator] (FAAC)
JAL Jet Approach and Landing (SAUS)
JAL Jet Approach Landing Charts (FAAC)
JAL Jewish Apocryphal Literature [A publication] (BJA)
JAL Job Account Log (SAUS)
JAL Journal of Academic Librarianship [A publication] (BRI)
JAL Journal of African Law (journ.) (SAUS)
JAL Judge Advocate Library, Department of the Navy, Alexandria, VA [OCLC symbol] (OCLC)
J Ala Acad Sci... Journal. Alabama Academy of Science (journ.) (SAUS)
J Alab Acd Sci... Journal. Alabama Academy of Science (journ.) (SAUS)
Ja Labor B... Japan Labor Bulletin (journ.) (SAUS)
JALAM Japanese Association for Laboratory Animal Medicine (GVA)
JALAP Jalapae [Jalap] [Pharmacology] (ROG)
Jalate Jalate, Inc. [Associated Press] (SAG)
JALB Joint Administration and Logistics Board (SAUO)
JALB Journal. American Physical Therapy Association (journ.) (SAUS)
J Alberta Soc Pet Geol... Journal. Alberta Society of Petroleum Geologists (journ.) (SAUS)
J Albert Einstein Med Cent... Journal. Albert Einstein Medical Center (journ.) (SAUS)
JAlbert Einstein MedCent... Journal of the Albert Einstein Medical Center (SAUO)
J Albert Einstein Med Cent... Journal of the Albert Einstein Medical Center (journ.) (SAUS)
JALC Japan American Lumber Conference (BUAC)
JALC Jet Approach and Landing Chart (AFM)
JALC John Adams Life Corporation (SAUO)
JALC Journal of Air Law and Commerce (journ.) (SAUS)
JALCBR Journal of Alcoholism (journ.) (SAUS)
J Alc Drug... Journal of Alcohol and Drug Education (journ.) (SAUS)
J Alcohol... Journal of Alcoholism (journ.) (SAUS)
J Alcohol & Drug Educ... Journal of Alcohol and Drug Education (journ.) (SAUS)
JAlden Alden [John] Financial Corp. [Associated Press] (SAG)
J Al Dent Assoc... Journal. Alabama Dental Association (journ.) (SAUS)
J Algebra... Journal of Algebra (journ.) (SAUS)
J Algorithms... Journal of Algorithms (journ.) (SAUS)
JALL Journal of African Languages and Linguistics (journ.) (SAUS)
J Allied Dent Soc... Journal. Allied Dental Societies (journ.) (SAUS)
J Allied Health... Journal of Allied Health (journ.) (SAUS)
J All India Dent Assoc... Journal. All India Dental Association (journ.) (SAUS)
J All India Inst Med Sci... Journal. All India Institute of Medical Sciences (journ.) (SAUS)
J All India Inst Ment Health... Journal. All India Institute of Mental Health (journ.) (SAUS)
J All India Ophthalmol S... Journal. All-India Ophthalmological Society (journ.) (SAUS)
J All Ind Ophth Soc... Journal. All-India Ophthalmological Society (journ.) (SAUS)
J Alloy Phase Diagrams... Journal of Alloy Phase Diagrams (journ.) (SAUS)
JALMA Japan Leprosy Mission for Asia (BUAC)
JALP Japan Annual of Law and Politics (journ.) (SAUS)
JALPAS Japan Airlines Passenger Autoprocessing System (SAUS)
JALPG Joint Automatic Language Processing Group
J ALS Journal. American Liszt Society (journ.) (SAUS)
JALT Japan Association for/of Language Teachers (SAUO)
JALT Journal. Association of Law Teachers [A publication] (DLA)
J Altered States Conscious... Journal of Altered States of Consciousness (SAUS)
JALTOS Japan Air Lines Computerized Air Cargo Terminal System (SAUS)
JAM Jail Accounting Microcomputer System
JAM Jamaica [ANSI three-letter standard code] (CNC)
Jam Jamaica (SHCU)
JAM Jamaica Exports. Complimentary Guide to Trade and Investment Opportunities (journ.) (SAUS)
Jam Jamaican (DIAR)
JAM James [New Testament Book] (WDAA)

JaM J A Micropublishing, Inc., Eastchester, NY [Library symbol] [Library of Congress] (LCLS)
JAM Jamieson Scotch Dictionary [A publication] (ROG)
Jam Jamieson Scotch Dictionary (journ.) (SAUS)
JAM Jammed (SAUS)
JAM Jamming [Military] (NVT)
JAM Jet Age Malfunction (IAA)
JAM Job Analysis Memorandum
JAM Job Assignment Memo (SAUS)
JAM Job Assignment Memorandum
JAM Joint Action for Mission (SAUO)
JAM Joint Analysed Make-up [Computer-controlled attachment] (PDAA)
JAM Joslyn Art Museum (SAUO)
JAM Journal of American Musicology (journ.) (SAUS)
JAM Journal of Applied Mechanics (journ.). (SAUS)
JAM Journal of Audiological Medicine (journ.) (SAUS)
JAM JUMPS [Joint Uniform Military Pay System] Action Memorandum (NVT)
JAM Junction Adhesion Molecule
JAM Just a Minute [Computer hacker terminology] (NHD)
JAM Just a Moment (SAUS)
JAM Justified Ancients of Mummus (SAUO)
JAM Jyacc Application Manager (SAUO)
JAM Moraine Valley Community College, Palos Hills, IL [OCLC symbol] (OCLC)
Jama Jamaica (VRA)
JAMA Japan Air Materiel Area (SAUO)
JAMA Japan Automobile Manufacturers Association (SAUO)
JAMA Japan Automobile Manufacturers Association, Washington Office (EA)
JAMA Journal of the American Medical Association [A publication]
JAMA Moslem People's Revolutionary Movement [Iran] [Political party] (PPW)
JAMAC Job Analysis Memorandum Activity Chart
JAMAC Joint Aeronautical Materials Activity [Military] (AABC)
JAMAC Joint Aeronautical Materials Agency (SAUO)
J Am Acad Appl Nutr... Journal. American Academy of Applied Nutrititin (journ.) (SAUS)
J Am Acad Audiol... Journal of the American Academy of Audiology (SAUO)
J Am Acad Audiol... Journal of the American Academy of Audiology (journ.) (SAUS)
J Am Acad Cbild Psychiatry... Journal. American Academy of Child Psychiatry (journ.) (SAUS)
J Am Acad Child Adolesc Psychiatry... Journal. American Academy of Child and Adolescent Psychiatry (journ.) (SAUS)
J Am Acad Child Adolesc Psychiatry... Journal of the American Academy of Child and Adolescent Psychiatry (SAUO)
J Am Acad Child Adolesc Psychiatry... Journal of the American Academy of Child and Adolescent Psychiatry (journ.) (SAUS)
J Am Acad Child Psych... Journal. American Academy of Child Psychiatry (journ.) (SAUS)
J Am Acad Dermatol... Journal. American Academy of Dermatology (journ.) (SAUS)
J Am Acad Dermatol... Journal of the American Academy of Dermatology (SAUO)
J Am Acad Dermatol... Journal of the American Academy of Dermatology (journ.) (SAUS)
J Am Acad Gnathol Orthop... Journal. American Academy of Gnathologic Orthopedics (journ.) (SAUS)
J Am Acad Gold Foil Oper... Journal. American Academy of Gold Foil Operators (journ.) (SAUS)
J Am Acad Psychoanal... Journal of the American Academy of Psychoanalysis (SAUO)
J Am Acad Psychoanal... Journal of the American Academy of Psychoanalysis (journ.) (SAUS)
J Am Ac Chil... Journal. American Academy of Child Psychiatry (journ.) (SAUS)
JAMAET Journal. American Mosquito Control Association (journ.) (SAUS)
JAMAG Joint American Military Advisory Group
Jamaica English-speaking West Indian island nation (SAUS)
Jamaica Agr Soc J... Jamaica Agricultural Society. Journal (journ.) (SAUS)
Jamaica Archt... Jamaica Architect (journ.) (SAUS)
Jamaica Geol Survey Dept Ann Rept... Jamaica. Geological Survey Department. Annual Report (journ.) (SAUS)
Jamaica Geol Survey Dept Bull... Jamaica. Geological Survey Department. Bulletin (journ.) (SAUS)
Jamaica Geol Survey Dept Occ Pap... Jamaica. Geological Survey Department. Occasional Paper (journ.) (SAUS)
Jamaica Geol Survey Dept Short Pap... Jamaica. Geological Survey Department. Short Paper (journ.) (SAUS)
JAMAL Jamaican Movement for the Advancement of Literacy (BUAC)
J Am Analg Soc... Journal. American Analgesia Society (journ.) (SAUS)
J Am Anim Hosp Assoc... Journal. American Animal Hospital Association (journ.) (SAUS)
J Am Anim Hosp Assoc... Journal of the American Animal Hospital Association (SAUO)
J Am Anim Hosp Assoc... Journal of the American Animal Hospital Association (journ.) (SAUS)
JAMASS Japanese Medical Abstract Scanning System [International Medical Information Center] [Japan] (NITA)
J Am Ass Med Rec Libr... Journal. American Association of Medical Record Librarians (journ.) (SAUS)
J Am Assoc... Journal. American Association for Hygiene and Baths (journ.) (SAUS)
J Am Assoc Cereal Chem... Journal American Association of Cereal Chemists (journ.) (SAUS)

J Am Assoc Nephrol Nurses Tech... Journal. American Association of Nephrology Nurses and Technicians (journ.) (SAUS)
J Am Assoc Nurse Anesth... Journal. American Association of Nurse Anesthetists (journ.) (SAUS)
J Am Assoc Promot Hyg Public Baths... Journal. American Association for Promoting Hygiene and Public Baths (journ.) (SAUS)
J Am Assoc Var Star Obs... Journal of the American Association of Variable Star Observers (journ.) (SAUS)
J Am Ass Teach Educ Agric... Journal. American Association of Teacher Educators in Agriculture (journ.). (SAUS)
J Am Audiol Soc... Journal. American Audiology Society (journ.) (SAUS)
J Am Aud Soc... Journal. American Auditory Society (journ.) (SAUS)
JAMB .... Joint Air Movements Board [*Military*]
JAMBA .... Japan-Australia Migratory Birds Agreement (SAUO)
J Am Bankers' Assn... Journal. American Bankers Association [*A publication*] (DLA)
J Am Bankers Assoc... Journal. American Bankers Association (journ.) (SAUS)
J Am Board Fam Pract... Journal of the American Board of Family Practice (SAUO)
J Am Board Fam Pract... Journal of the American Board of Family Practice (journ.) (SAUS)
JAMC .... Japan Aircraft Manufacturers Corporation (SAUO)
JAMC .... Japan Aircraft Manufacturing Corporation (SAUO)
JAMC .... Joint Amphibious Mines Countermeasures [*Military*]
Jamcaia Geol Survey Pub... Jamaica. Geological Survey Department. Publication (journ.) (SAUS)
JAMCAT ...... Jammer Communications Attachment (SAUS)
J Am Ceram... Journal. American Ceramic Society (journ.) (SAUS)
J Am Ceram Soc... Journal of American Ceramic Society (journ.) (SAUS)
J Am Ceram Soc... Journal of the American Ceramic Society (SAUO)
J Am Chem Soc... Journal of American Chemical Society (MEC)
J Am Chem Soc... Journal of the American Chemical Society (SAUO)
JAMCO .... Japan Aircraft Maintenance Company Ltd. (SAUO)
JAMColl .... Journal of the American Medical College (SAUO)
J Am Coll Cardiol... Journal. American College of Cardiology (journ.) (SAUS)
J Am Coll Cardiol... Journal of the American College of Cardiology (SAUO)
J Am Coll Cardiol... Journal of the American College of Cardiology (journ.) (SAUS)
J Am Coll Dent... Journal of the American College of Dentists (SAUO)
J Am Coll Dent... Journal of the American College of Dentists (journ.) (SAUS)
J Am Coll H... Journal. American College Health Association (journ.) (SAUS)
J Am Coll Health... Journal of American College Health (journ.) (SAUS)
J Am Coll Health... Journal of the American College of Health (journ.) (SAUS)
J Am Coll Nutr... Journal. American College of Nutrition (journ.) (SAUS)
J Am Coll Nutr... Journal of the American College of Nutrition (SAUO)
J Am Coll Nutr... Journal of the American College of Nutrition (journ.) (SAUS)
J Am Coll Surg... Journal of the American College of Surgeons (SAUO)
J Am Coll Surg... Journal of the American College of Surgeons (journ.) (SAUS)
J Am Coll Toxicol... Journal. American College of Toxicology (journ.) (SAUS)
J Am Coll Toxicol... Journal of the American College of Toxicology (journ.) (SAUS)
J Am Concr Inst... Journal. American Concrete Institute (journ.) (SAUS)
Jam Cre... Jamaican Creole (SAUS)
J Am Cult .... Journal of American Culture [*A publication*] (BRI)
J Am Cult .... Journal of American Culture (journ.) (SAUS)
JAMDA .... Journal of the American Medical Directors Association (SAUO)
JAMDAY ...... Journal. American Medical Technologists (journ.) (SAUS)
J Am Dent Assoc... Journal of the American Dental Association (SAUO)
J Am Dent Assoc... Journal of the American Dental Association (journ.) (SAUS)
J Am Dent Assoc Dent Cosmos... Journal. American Dental Association and the Dental Cosmos (journ.) (SAUS)
J Am Dent Hyg Assoc... Journal. American Dental Hygienists Association (journ.) (SAUS)
J Am Dent Soc Anesthesiol... Journal. American Dental Society of Anesthesiology (journ.) (SAUS)
J Am Diet Assoc... Journal of the American Dietetic Association (SAUO)
JAME .... Jamesbury Corp. (SAUO)
Jam Eng ...... Jamaican English (SAUS)
J Amer Ceram Soc... Journal of the American Ceramic Society (SAUO)
J Amer Chem Soc... Journal of the American Chemical Society (SAUO)
J Amer Dent Assoc... Journal of the American Dental Association (SAUO)
J Amer Diet Assoc... Journal of the American Dietetic Association (SAUO)
J Amer Geriat Soc... Journal of the American Geriatrics Society (SAUO)
J Amer Geriat Soc... Journal of the American Geriatrics Society (journ.) (SAUS)
J Amer Inst Planners... Journal of the American Institute of Planners (SAUO)
J Amer Inst Planners... Journal of the American Institute of Planners (journ.) (SAUS)
J Amer Med Assoc... Journal of the American Medical Association (journ.) (SAUS)
J Amer Oil Chem Soc... Journal of the American Oil Chemists Society (SAUO)
J Amer Osteopath Assoc... Journal of the American Osteopathic Association (SAUO)
J Amer Pharm Assoc... Journal of the American Pharmaceutical Association (SAUO)
J Amer Pharm Assoc... Journal of the American Pharmaceutical Association (journ.) (SAUS)
J Amer Podiatry Assoc... Journal of the American Podiatry Association (SAUO)
J Amer Podiatry Assoc... Journal of the American Podiatry Association (journ.) (SAUS)
J Amer S Farm Manage Rural Appraisers... Journal. American Society of Farm Managers and Rural Appraisers (journ.) (SAUS)
J Amer Soc Hort Sci... Journal of the American Society for Horticultural Science (SAUO)
J Amer Soc Safety Eng... Journal of the American Society of Safety Engineers (SAUO)
J Amer Soc Safety Eng... Journal of the American Society of Safety Engineers (journ.) (SAUS)
J Amer Soc Sugar Beet Techn... Journal of the American Society of Sugar Beet Technologists (journ.) (SAUS)

J Amer Statist Assoc... Journal of the American Statistical Association (SAUO)
J Amer Statist Assoc... Journal of the American Statistical Association (journ.) (SAUS)
J Amer Stud... Journal of American Studies (journ.) (SAUS)
J Amer Vet Med Assoc... Journal of the American Veterinary Medical Association (SAUO)
J Amer Vet Radiol Soc... Journal of the American Veterinary Radiology Society (SAUO)
JAmerWater Works Assoc... Journal of the American Water Works Association (SAUO)
J Amer Water Works Assoc... Journal of the American Water Works Association (journ.) (SAUS)
James .... James' Reports [*2 Nova Scotia*] [*A publication*] (DLA)
JAMES .... Java Architecture for Mobile Extended Service [*Computer science*]
JAMES .... Joint Automated Message Editing Software (SAUO)
James & Mont... Jameson and Montagu's English Bankruptcy Reports [*Vol. 2 of Glyn and Jameson*] [*1821-28*] [*A publication*] (DLA)
James Arthur Lect Evol Hum Brain... James Arthur Lecture on the Evolution of the Human Brain (journ.) (SAUS)
James Bk L... James Bankrupt Law (journ.) (SAUS)
James Bk L... James' Bankrupt Law PB (DLA)
James Const Con... Jameson's Constitutional Convention [*A publication*] (DLA)
James Ct Mar... James on Courts-Martial [*A publication*] (DLA)
James Fr Soc... James' Guide to Friendly Societies [*A publication*] (DLA)
James JS... James' Law of Joint Stock Companies [*A publication*] (DLA)
James JS... James Law of Joint Stock Companies (journ.) (SAUS)
James Madison U... James Madison University (GAGS)
JamesnIn... Jameson Inns, Inc. [*Associated Press*] (SAG)
James (N Sc)... James' Reports [*2 Nova Scotia*] [*A publication*] (DLA)
James Op .... James' Opinions, Charges, Etc. [*A publication*] (DLA)
James Salv... James on Salvage [*1867*] [*A publication*] (DLA)
James Sel Cas... James' Select Cases [*1835-55*] [*Nova Scotia*] [*A publication*] (DLA)
James Sel Cases... James' Select Cases [*1835-55*] [*Nova Scotia*] [*A publication*] (DLA)
James Sh .... James' Merchant Shipping [*1866*] [*A publication*] (DLA)
James Sprunt Hist Publ... James Sprunt Historical Publications (journ.) (SAUS)
James Sprunt Hist Stud... James Sprunt Historical Studies (journ.) (SAUS)
JAMEX .... Jamming Exercise [*Military*] (NVT)
J Am Folk .... Journal of American Folklore. American Folklore Society. Washington (SAUO)
JAMG .... Jamming
JAMG .... Juvenile Autoimmune Myasthenia Gravis [*Medicine*] (DAVI)
Jam Geol Surv Dep Econ Geol Rep... Jamaica. Geological Survey Department. Economic Geology Report (journ.) (SAUS)
JAMGIS .... Jamaica GIS (SAUO)
J Am Health Care As... Journal. American Health Care Association (journ.) (SAUS)
J Am Helicopter Soc... Journal. American Helicopter Society (journ.) (SAUS)
J Am Helicopter Soc... Journal of the American Helicopter Society (journ.) (SAUS)
JAMHEP ...... Joint Aircraft Hurricane Plan
J Am Hist .... Journal of the American History (journ.) (SAUS)
Jam Hist Rev... Jamaican Historical Review (journ.) (SAUS)
Jam Hist Soc... Jamaican Historical Society Bulletin. Jamaican Historical Society. Kingston (SAUO)
Jam Hist Soc... Jamaican Historical Society Bulletin. Jamaican Historical Society. Kingston (journ.) (SAUS)
JAMI .... Japan Association for Medical Informatics (SAUO)
JAMIA .... Journal of the American Medical Informatics Association [*A publication*] (DMAA)
JAMIE .... Joint Analogue Microelectronics Initiative of Europe (SAUS)
J Am Ind Hyg Assoc... Journal. American Industrial Hygiene Association (journ.) (SAUS)
J Am Indian Ed... Journal of American Indian Education (journ.) (SAUS)
J Am Inst Archit... Journal of the American Institute of Architects. Washington (journ.) (SAUS)
J Am Inst Electr Eng... Journal. American Institute of Electrical Engineers (journ.) (SAUS)
J Am Inst Electr Eng... Journal of the American Institute of Electrical Engineers (journ.) (SAUS)
JAMINTEL .... Jamaica International Telecommunications Ltd. [*Kingston*] [*Telecommunications service*]
J Am Intraocul Implant Soc... Journal. American Intraocular Implant Society (journ.) (SAUS)
JAMIP .... Journal of the Alliance of Medical Internet Professionals (SAUO)
Ja Mission B... Japan Missionary Bulletin (journ.) (SAUS)
JAMIT .... Japanese Society of Medical Imaging Technology (SAUO)
Jam J .... Jamaica Journal. Institute of Jamaica. Kingston (journ.) (SAUS)
J Am Jud Soc... Journal. American Judicature Society (journ.) (SAUS)
JamKI-L .... Institute of Jamaica, National Library of Jamaica, Kingston, Jamaica [*Library symbol*] [*Library of Congress*] (LCLS)
JamKLS .... Jamaica Library Service, Kingston, Jamaica [*Library symbol*] [*Library of Congress*] (LCLS)
JamKU .... University of the West Indies, Mona, Kingston, Jamaica [*Library symbol*] [*Library of Congress*] (LCLS)
JAML .... Journal of Arts Management, Law & Society [*A publication*] (BRI)
J Am Leather Chem Assoc... Journal of the American Leather Chemists Association (journ.) (SAUS)
Jam LJ .... Jamaica Law Journal [*A publication*] (DLA)
Jam Lt .... Jamaica Law Journal (journ.) (SAUS)
JAMLW .... Journal of Applied Metalworking (journ.) (SAUS)
JAMM .... Journal for Australian Music and Musicians (journ.) (SAUS)
JAMMAT ...... Joint American Military Mission for Aid to Turkey (MUGU)
JAMMAT ...... Joint Military Mission for Aid to Turkey (SAUS)
J Am Math Soc... Journal of the American Mathematical Society (journ.) (SAUS)

JAMMD........ Journal. Australian Mathematical Society. Series B. Applied Mathematics (journ.)
J Am Med Inform Assoc... Journal of the American Medical Informatics Association (SAUO)
J Am Med Inform Assoc... Journal of the American Medical Informatics Association (journ.) (SAUS)
J Am Med Rec Assoc... Journal. American Medical Record Association (journ.) (SAUS)
Jam Med Rev... Jamaica Medical Review (journ.) (SAUS)
J Am Med Technol... Journal. American Medical Technologists (journ.) (SAUS)
J Am Med Wom Assoc... Journal of the American Medical Womens Association (SAUO)
J Am Med Wom Assoc... Journal of the American Medical Womens Association (journ.) (SAUS)
Jam Mines Geol Div Spec Publ... Jamaica. Mines and Geology Division. Special Publication (journ.) (SAUS)
Jam Minist Agric Bull... Jamaica. Ministry of Agriculture. Bulletin (journ.) (SAUS)
Jam Minist Agric Fish Bull... Jamaica. Ministry of Agriculture and Fisheries. Bulletin (journ.) (SAUS)
Jam Minist Agric Lands Annu Rep... Jamaica. Ministry of Agriculture and Lands. Annual Report (journ.) (SAUS)
Jam Minist Agric Lands Bull... Jamaica. Ministry of Agriculture and Lands. Bulletin (journ.) (SAUS)
J Am Mosq Control Assoc... Journal. American Mosquito Control Association (journ.) (SAUS)
J Am Mosq Control Assoc... Journal of the American Mosquito Control Association (SAUO)
J Am Mosq Control Assoc... Journal of the American Mosquito Control Association (journ.) (SAUS)
J Am Mosq Control Assoc Suppl... Journal of the American Mosquito Control Association. Supplement (journ.) (SAUS)
J Am Mus In... Journal. American Musical Instrument Society (journ.) (SAUS)
J Am Optom Assoc... Journal. American Optometric Association (journ.) (SAUS)
J Am Optom Assoc... Journal of the American Optometric Association (SAUO)
J Am Optom Assoc... Journal of the American Optometric Association (journ.) (SAUS)
J Am Or Soc... Journal of the American Oriental Society (SAUO)
J Am Osteopath Assoc... Journal of the American Osteopathic Association (SAUO)
JAMOT........ Julie/Jesebel Airborne Maintenance Operator Training (SAUS)
JAMOT........ Julie/Jezebel [Sonobuoy Systems] Airborne Maintenance Operator Trainee [Navy] (MCD)
JAMP.......... JINTACCS [Joint Interoperability of Tactical Command and Control System] Army Management Plan (MCD)
JAMP.......... Joint Automated Mapping Project (SAUO)
JAMPA2....... Journal of Animal Morphology and Physiology (journ.) (SAUS)
JAMPAC....... Jamming Package [Air Force]
JAMPACK .... Jamming Package [Air Force] (MCD)
J Am Paraplegia Soc... Journal of the American Paraplegia Society (journ.) (SAUS)
J Am Paraplegics Soc... Journal. American Paraplegics Society (journ.) (SAUS)
J Am Peat S... Journal. American Peat Society (journ.) (SAUS)
J Am Penut Res Educ Ass... Journal. American Peanut Research and Education Association (journ.) (SAUS)
JAMPO........ Joint Allied Military Petroleum Office [NATO]
J Am Podiatr Med Assoc... Journal. American Podiatric Medical Association (journ.) (SAUS)
J Am Podiatr Med Assoc... Journal of the American Podiatric Medical Association (SAUO)
J Am Podiatr Med Assoc... Journal of the American Podiatric Medical Association (SAUS)
J Am Podiatry Assoc... Journal. American Podiatry Association (journ.) (SAUS)
JAMPRE....... Journal. American Peanut Research and Education Association (journ.) (SAUS)
JAMPRESS... Jamaican Government News Agency (BUAC)
JAMPS........ Japan Medical Programming System (SAUS)
JAMPS........ JINTACCS Automated Message Preparation System (SAUO)
J Am Psychoanal Assoc... Journal of the American Psychoanalytic Association (SAUO)
J Am Psychoanal Assoc... Journal of the American Psychoanalytic Association (journ.) (SAUS)
J Am Real Estate Urban Econ Assoc... Journal. American Real Estate and Urban Economics Association (journ.) (SAUS)
JAMREP....... Jamming Report
J Am Rocket S... Journal. American Rocket Society (journ.) (SAUS)
JAMS.......... Jameson Inns [NASDAQ symbol] (TTSB)
JAMS.......... Jameson Inns, Inc. [NASDAQ symbol] (SAG)
JAMS.......... Jamming Analysis Measurement System
JAMS.......... Japan Association for Mathematical Sciences (SAUO)
JAMS.......... Job Activities Management System (SAUS)
JAMS.......... Joint Agency for Municipal Securities Dealers
JAMS.......... Journal. Academy of Marketing Science [A publication]
JAMS.......... Journal. Academy of Marketing Science (journ.) (SAUS)
JAmS.......... Journal of American Studies [A publication] (ANEX)
JAmS.......... Journal of American Studies (journ.) (SAUS)
JAMS.......... Journal of the American Musicological Society [A publication] (WDAA)
JAMS.......... Judicial Arbitration and Mediation Services (SAUS)
JAMSA........ Journal. Arkansas Medical Society (journ.) (SAUS)
JAMSAT...... Japanese Satellite for Amateur Radio (SAUS)
Jamsat........ Japan radio Amateur Satellite (SAUS)
JAMSAT....... Japan Radio Amateur Satellite Corp. (BUAC)
J Am Soc Brew Chem... Journal. American Society of Brewing Chemists (journ.) (SAUS)
J Am Soc Brew Chem... Journal of the American Society of Brewing Chemists (journ.) (SAUS)

J Am Soc Echocardiogr... Journal of the American Society of Echocardiography
J Am Soc Echocardiogr... Journal of the American Society of Echocardiography (journ.) (SAUS)
J Am Soc Geriatr Dent... Journal. American Society for Geriatric Dentistry (journ.)
J Am Soc Heat Vent Eng... Journal. American Society of Heating and Ventilating Engineers (journ.) (SAUS)
J Am Soc Inf Sci... Journal of the American Society for Information Science (journ.) (SAUS)
J Am Soc Inf Sci... Journal of the American Society of Information Science (SAUO)
J Am Soc Inf Sci... Journal of the American Society of Information Science (journ.) (SAUS)
J Am Soc Mech Eng... Journal. American Society of Mechanical Engineers (journ.) (SAUS)
J Am Soc Nav Eng... Journal. American Society of Naval Engineers (journ.) (SAUS)
J Am Soc Nephrol... Journal of the American Society of Nephrology (SAUO)
J Am Soc Nephrol... Journal of the American Society of Nephrology (journ.) (SAUS)
J Am Soc Prev Dent... Journal. American Society for Preventive Dentistry (journ.) (SAUS)
J Am Soc Study Orthod... Journal. American Society for the Study of Orthodontics (journ.) (SAUS)
JAMSS........ Japan Manned Space Systems Corporation (SAUO)
Jam St........ Jamaica Statutes [A publication] (DLA)
J Am St .... Journal of American Studies [A publication] (BRI)
J Am Stat Assoc... Journal of the American Statistical Association (SAUO)
JAMSTEC.... Japanese Marine Science and Technology Center (SAUS)
JAMSTEC.... Japan Marine Science and Technology Center (or Centre) (SAUS)
JAMTD........ Journal. Canadian Association for Music Therapy (journ.) (SAUS)
JAMTO........ Joint Airlines Military Traffic Office
JAMTRAC ... Jammers Tracked by Azimuth Crossings [RADAR]
JAMTS........ Japan Association of Motor Trade and Service (BUAC)
J Am Vener Dis Assoc... Journal. American Venereal Disease Association (journ.) (SAUS)
J Am Vet Med Assoc... Journal of the American Veterinary Medical Association (SAUO)
JAMWA........ Journal of the American Medical Womens Association (journ.) (SAUS)
J Am Water Works Assoc... Journal of the American Water Works Association (journ.) (SAUS)
Jamwich ...... Jam Sandwich (SAUS)
J Am Zinc Inst... Journal. American Zinc Institute (journ.) (SAUS)
JAN............. Emerald Airways Ltd. [British] [FAA designator] (FAAC)
JAN............. Jackson [Mississippi] [Airport symbol] (OAG)
JAN............. Jackson, MS [Location identifier] [FAA] (FAAL)
JAN............. Janes Aviation 748 Ltd. [British] [ICAO designator] (FAAC)
JAN............. Janina [Greece] [Seismograph station code, US Geological Survey] (SEIS)
JAN............. Janitor
JAN............. Jantar Resources Corp. [Vancouver Stock Exchange symbol]
Jan.............. January (ASC)
JAN............. January (EY)
jan .... Janvier [January] [French] (ASC)
JAN............. Japanese Accepted Name (DMAA)
JAN............. Japanese Animation Network (EA)
JAN............. Japan. The Economic and Trade Picture (journ.) (SAUS)
JAN............. Jet Aircraft Noise
JAN............. Job Accommodation Network [President's Committee on Employment of the Handicapped] [Information service or system] (IID)
JAN............. Job Action Network
JAN............. Joint Army and Navy
JAN............. Judgment Analysis [Psychology]
JAN............. Justification for Authority to Negotiate [Military]
JAN............. Lincoln Christian College, Lincoln, IL [OCLC symbol] (OCLC)
JANA........... Jamahiriyah News Agency [Libya]
JANAC .... Joint Army-Navy Assessment Committee [World War II]
JANAC .... Journal of the Association of Nurses in AIDS Care (journ.) (SAUS)
JANAF........ Joint Army-Navy-Air Force
JANAFPAC ... Joint Army-Navy-Air Force, Pacific General Message [Serially numbered] (CINC)
JANAF Panel... Joint Army-Navy-Air Force Panel (SAUO)
JANAIA .... Joint Army-Navy Aircraft Instrument Action (MCD)
JANAIC .... Joint Army-Navy Air Intentions-of-the-Enemy Council (SAUO)
JANAIR .... Joint Army-Navy Aircraft Instrumentation (ACAE)
JANAIR .... Joint Army-Navy Aircraft Instrument Research
J Anal Appl Pyrolysis... Journal of Analytical and Applied Pyrolysis (journ.) (SAUS)
J Anal Chem USSR... Journal of the Analytical Chemistry of the USSR (journ.) (SAUS)
JANALP....... Joint Army-Navy-Air Force Logistics Policy
JANALP....... Joint Army-Navy-Air Force Logistics Publication
J Anal Toxicol... Journal of Analytical Toxicology (journ.) (SAUS)
Jan Angl...... Jani Anglorum Facies Nova [1680] [A publication] (DLA)
JANAP .... Joint Army-Navy Acceptance Procedures (SAUS)
JANAP .... Joint Army-Navy-Air Force Procedure [NATO] (NATG)
JANAP .... Joint Army, Navy, Air Force Publication
JANAP .... Joint Army-Navy-Air Force Publication
JANAP .... United States Joint Services Side Word GPO Index (SAUS)
JANARS ...... Joint Army-Navy-Air Force Radiotelephone System (IAA)
JANAST...... Joint Army-Navy-Air Force Sea Transport (SAUO)
JANAST...... Joint Army-Navy-Air Force Sea Transportation Message
JANAST Message... Joint Army-Navy-Air-Force Sea Transportation Message (SAUS)
J Anat........ Journal of Anatomy (SAUO)
J Anat......... Journal of Anatomy (journ.) (SAUS)

J Anat Phys... Journal of Anatomy and Physiology (journ.) (SAUS)
JanBell .... Jan Bell Marketing, Inc. [*Associated Press*] (SAG)
JANBEMI..... Jan Bell Marketing, Inc. (SAUO)
JANBMC ..... Joint Army-Navy Ballistic Missile Committee
JANC........ Junior Army and Navy Club [*British*] (DSUE)
J Anc Ind Hist... Journal of Ancient Indian History (journ.) (SAUS)
JANCOM ...... Joint Army-Navy Communications
JANCPEC ..... Japan National Committee for Pacific Economic Cooperation
JANCWR ...... Joint Army and Navy Committee on Welfare and Recreation
J&A............. Justification and Analysis (SAUS)
J & A .... Justification and Approval [*Army*]
J & B .... Justerini and Brooks [*Scotch*]
J & C .... Jones and Cary's Irish Exchequer Reports [*1838-39*] [*A publication*] (DLA)
J & D .... June and December [*Denotes semiannual payments of interest or dividends in these months*] [*Business term*]
J & E .... Jehovistic and Elohistic [*Theology*]
J&F............. Job & Function (SAUS)
J & F .... Job and Function [*Air Force*] (AAG)
J & H .... Johnson and Hemming's English Vice-Chancellors' Reports [*A publication*] (DLA)
J & H Hind L... Johnson and Houghton's Institutes of Hindoo Law [*A publication*] (DLA)
J Andhra Hist Res Soc... Journal. Andhra Historical Research Society (journ.) (SAUS)
J & J .... January and July [*Denotes semiannual payments of interest or dividends in these months*] [*Business term*]
J & J .... Johnson and Johnson [*Commercial firm*] (DAVI)
J & J Sn...... J & J Snack Foods Corp. [*Associated Press*] (SAG)
J & K.......... All India Reporter, Jammu and Kashmir [*A publication*] (DLA)
J&K............. Jammu and Kashmir (SAUO)
J&K............. University of Jamu and Kashmir (SAUO)
J & L .... Jones and La Touche's Irish Chancery Reports [*A publication*] (DLA)
J & La T ..... Jones and La Touche's Irish Chancery Reports [*A publication*] (DLA)
J & L SpSt... J & L Specialty Steel [*Associated Press*] (SAG)
J & P .... Joannou & Paraskevaides [*Construction company*] [*British*]
J & P .... Joists and Planks [*Technical drawings*]
J & P .... Journal and Proceedings [*Australia*] [*A publication*]
J & P .... Justice and Peace [*An association*] [*Scotland*] (EAIO)
J & Proc Aust Chem Inst... Journal and Proceedings. Australian Chemical Institute. [*A publication*]
J & Proc Aust Chem Inst... Journal and Proceedings. Australian Chemical Institute. (journ.) (SAUS)
J & Proc Roy Soc WA... Journal and Proceedings. Royal Society of Western Australia [*A publication*]
J Androl....... Journal of Andrology (journ.) (SAUS)
J & S .... Jebb and Symes' Irish Queen's Bench Reports [*A publication*] (DLA)
J & S .... Jones and Spencer's Superior Court Reports [*33-61 New York*] [*A publication*] (DLA)
J & S .... Judah and Swan's Jamaica Reports [*1839*] [*A publication*] (DLA)
J & S Jam... Judah and Swan's Jamaica Reports [*1839*] [*A publication*] (DLA)
J & V .... Jones and Varick's Laws of New York [*A publication*] (DLA)
J&V............. Jones and Varicks Laws of New York (journ.) (SAUS)
J & W .... Jacob and Walker's English Chancery Reports [*A publication*] (DLA)
J&W............. Jacob and Walkers English Chancery Reports (journ.) (SAUS)
J & WO....... Jettison and Washing Overboard
JANE........... Joint Air Force-Navy Experiment (MUGU)
JANE........... Journalists Against Nuclear Extermination [*British*] (DI)
JANES.......... Journal. Ancient Near Eastern Society. Columbia University (journ.) (SAUS)
J Anesth ...... Journal of Anesthesia (journ.) (SAUS)
JANET........ Computing Joint Academic Network (SAUS)
JANET........ Joint Academic Network [*Proposed supercomputer network*]
JANET........ Joint Army-Navy Experimental and Testing Board
JANET........ Joint Army-Navy Expetimental and Testing Board (SAUS)
JANET........ Just Another Network [*University of Waterloo*] [*Canada*]
Janex........ Janex International, Inc. [*Associated Press*] (SAG)
JANF........... Joint Army-Navy Facility (SAUO)
Jan-Feb ...... January and February
JANFU....... Joint Army-Navy Foul Up [*Military slang*] [*Bowdlerized version*]
J Anglo-Mongol Soc... Journal. Anglo-Mongolian Society (journ.) (SAUS)
JANGO........ Junior Army-Navy Guild Organization [*Organization of teenage daughters of military officers, who helped out in war work*] [*World War II*]
JAN grid ...... Joint Army-Navy Grid
JANGRID..... Joint Army-Navy Grid System [*NATO*]
JANIC........... Japanese NGO Center for International Cooperation (SAUO)
JANIC.......... Joint Army-Navy Information Center
J Anim Breed Genet... Journal of Animal Breeding and Genetics (journ.) (SAUS)
J Anim Physiol Anim Nutr... Journal of Animal Physiology and Animal Nutrition (SAUS)
J Anim Prod Res... Journal of Animal Production Research (journ.) (SAUS)
JANIS........... Joint ANZECC/MCFFA NFPS Implementation Sub-Committee (SAUO)
JANIS........... Joint Army-Navy Intelligence Studies
JANIS........... Joint Army-Navy Intelligence Surveys (SAUS)
JANMA......... Japanese Nuclear Medicine (journ.) (SAUS)
JANMAT....... Joint Army-Navy Machine Tools Committee (AAG)
JANMAT....... Joint Army-Navy Material
JANMB........ Joint Army and Navy Munitions Board [*Terminated, 1947*]
JANNAF ...... Joint-Army-Navy-NASA-Air Force Interagency Propulsion Committee (MCD)
JANNAF-IPC.. Joint Army-Navy-NASA-Air Force Interagency Propulsion Committee (SAUO)
J Annamalai Univ... Journal. Annamalai University (journ.) (SAUS)

J Annamalai Univ... Journal of the Annamalai University (SAUO)
J Annamalai Univ Part B... Journal. Annamalai University. Part B (journ.) (SAUS)
J Annamalai Univ Part B... Journal of the Annamalai University, Part B (journ.)
JANNF .... Jannock Ltd. [*NASDAQ symbol*] (SAG)
Jannock....... Jannock Ltd. [*Associated Press*] (SAG)
JANNVSA..... Joint Army-Navy War Shipping Administration (SAUS)
JANOT .... Joint Army-Navy Ocean Terminal
JANP.......... Joint Army-Navy Procedure
JANP.......... Joint Army-Navy Publication
JANPA7........ Journal of Analytical Psychology (journ.) (SAUS)
JANPPA ...... Joint Army-Navy Petroleum Purchase Agency
JANS.......... Jet Aircraft Noise Survey
JANS.......... Joint Army-Navy Specification (IAA)
JANSA .... Janatorial Supplies Association (BUAC)
Jans Def Wkly... Janes Defence Weekly (journ.) (SAUS)
JANSPEC..... Joint Army-Navy Specification
JANSRP ...... Jet Aircraft Noise Survey Research Program
JANSTD ...... Joint Army-Navy Standard [*NATO*] (NATG)
JANSX .... Janus Fund [*Mutual fund ticker symbol*] (SG)
JANTA......... Journal of the Australian Natural Therapists Association [*A publication*]
JANTAB....... Joint Army and Navy Technical Aeronautical Board
JANTB........ Joint Army-Navy Technical Board (SAUO)
JAnthrI........ Journal. Royal Anthropological Institute of Great Britain and Ireland (journ.) (SAUS)
J Anthrol Soc Oxford... Journal. Anthropological Society of Oxford (journ.) (SAUS)
J Anthropol Archaeol... Journal of Anthropological Archaeology (journ.) (SAUS)
J Anthrop Soc Bomby... Journal. Anthropological Society of Bombay (journ.) (SAUS)
J Antibiot... Journal of Antibiotics (journ.) (SAUS)
J Antimicrob Chemother... Journal of Antimicrobial Chemotherapy (journ.) (SAUS)
J Ant Ire ..... Journal. Royal Society of Antiquaries of Ireland (journ.) (SAUS)
JANTRL....... Janitorial
JANTX........ Joint Army-Navy Tested Extra
JANUS .... Force Model (SAUS)
JANUS .... Joint Academic Network Using Satellite for European Distance Education and Training (SAUO)
JANUS .... Joint Analog Numeric Understanding System
JANUS .... Joint Army-Navy Uniform Simulation (SAUS)
JANV.......... Janvier [*January*] [*French*]
JANWSA....... Joint Army-Navy War Shipping Administration
JANX.......... Janex International, Inc. [*NASDAQ symbol*] (SAG)
JANX.......... Janex Intl. [*NASDAQ symbol*] (TTSB)
JANXW........ Janex Intl. Wrrt [*NASDAQ symbol*] (TTSB)
JANY.......... January (ROG)
JAO............ Joint Area of Operations (DOMA)
JAO............ Prospect Heights Public Library District, Prospect Heights, IL [*OCLC symbol*] (OCLC)
JAOA.......... Journal of the American Osteopathic Association (SAUO)
JAOA.......... Journal of the American Osteopathic Association (journ.) (SAUS)
JAOAC .... Journal. Association of Official Analytical Chemists (journ.) (SAUS)
JAOAC .... Journal of the Association of Official Agricultural Chemists (SAUO)
J AOAC Int... Journal of AOAC International (SAUS)
JAOC.......... Joint Air Operations Center [*Air Force*]
JAOCS........ Journal. American Oil Chemists Society (journ.) (SAUS)
JAOS.......... Journal. American Oriental Society (journ.) (SAUS)
JAOS.......... Journal of American Oriental Society (journ.) (SAUS)
JAOS.......... Journal of the American Oriental Society (journ.) (SAUS)
J Aoyama Gakuin Womans Jr Coll... Journal. Aoyama Gakuin Womans Junior College (journ.) (SAUS)
JAp............. Against Apion [*Josephus*] (BJA)
JAP............. G. D. Searle & Co., Inc., Skokie, IL [*OCLC symbol*] (OCLC)
JAP............. Jamaica American Party [*Political party*] (BUAC)
JAP............. Japan (KSC)
Jap............. Japan (NTIO)
Jap............. Japanese (ODBW)
JAP............. Japanese (ROG)
jap .... Japanned [*Finished with a hard, glossy varnish*] (BARN)
JAP............. Japan Photo [*Norway*] [*FAA designator*] (FAAC)
JAP............. J. A. Prestwick [*British auto and motorcycle engine maker*]
JAP............. Jerusalem Academic Press (BJA)
JAP............. Jewish Agency for Palestine
JAP............. Jewish-American Princess [*Slang*]
JAP............. Joint Acceptance Plan (AAG)
JAP............. Joint Apprenticeship Program [*Department of Labor*]
JAP............. Journal of American Photography (journ.) (SAUS)
JAP............. Journal of Applied Physics (journ.) (SAUS)
JAP............. Journal of Applied Physiology (SAUO)
JAP............. Judicial Appointments Project (EA)
JAP............. Juntas de Accao Patriotica [*Patriotic Action Boards*] [*Portuguese*] [*Political party*] (PPE)
JAP............. Jupiter Atmospheric Probe
JAP............. Juventudes de Accion Popular [*Spanish*] (PPE)
JAP............. O. D. Searle & Co., Inc. (SAUO)
JAP............. Prestwich and Co. (SAUO)
JAPA.......... Jane Addams Peace Association (EA)
JAPA.......... Japan Aircraft Pilots Association (BUAC)
JAPA.......... Japan Area
JAPA.......... Journal. American Planning Association (journ.) (SAUS)
JAPA.......... Journal of the American Pharmaceutical Association (SAUO)
JAPA.......... Journal of the American Psychoanalytic Association (journ.) (SAUS)
JAPAC........ Japan Atomic Power Company (journ.) (SAUS)
JAPAC......... Joint Air Photo Center (SAUO)
Jap Acad Proc... Japan Academy. Proceedings (journ.) (SAUS)

JAPACS........ Japanese Pacific Climate Studies (or Study) (SAUO)
JAPACS........ Japanese Pacific Climate Study [*Marine science*] (OSRA)
JAPACS........ Japanese Pacific Ocean Climate Studies (USDC)
JAPAEA........ Journal. American Podiatric Medical Association (journ.) (SAUS)
Japan Ann L & Pol... Japan Annual of Law and Politics [*A publication*] (DLA)
Japan Annu Int Law... Japanese Annual of International Law (journ.) (SAUS)
Japan A Soc Psychol... Japanese Annals of Social Psychology (journ.) (SAUS)
Japan Chem... Japan Chemical Week (journ.) (SAUS)
Japanese An Internat Law... Japanese Annual of International Law (journ.) (SAUS)
Japanese Fin and Industry... Japanese Finance and Industry (journ.) (SAUS)
Japanese MT... Japanese Military Technology. Procedures for Transfers to the United States (journ.) (SAUS)
Japan Gensuikyo... Japan Council against A and H Bombs (SAUO)
Japan J Math... Japanese Journal of Mathematics (journ.) (SAUS)
Japan J Math NS... Japanese Journal of Mathematics. New Series (journ.) (SAUS)
Japan J Med Sc Pt 4 Pharmacol... Japanese Journal of Medical Sciences. Part 4. Pharmacology (journ.) (SAUS)
Japan Lbr Bul... Japan Labor Bulletin (journ.) (SAUS)
JAPANMEC... Japan International Measuring and Control Industry Show
Japan Med Gaz... Japan Medical Gazette (journ.) (SAUS)
Japan Med World... Japan Medical World (journ.) (SAUS)
Japan Soc B... Japan Society Bulletin (journ.) (SAUS)
Japan Stat... Japan Statistical Yearbook (journ.) (SAUS)
Japan Stud... Japanese Studies (journ.) (SAUS)
Japan TAPPI... Japan Technical Association of the Tulp and Paper Industry (SAUO)
JapARE........ Japanese Antarctic Research Expedition [*1956-*]
Jap Assoc Mineral Petrol Econ Geol J... Japanese Association of Mineralogists Petrologists and Economic Geologists. Journal (journ.) (SAUS)
Jap Assoc Pet Technol J... Japanese Association of Petroleum Technologists. Journal (journ.) (SAUS)
JAPATIC....... Japan Patient Information Center [*Information service or system*] (IID)
JAPC............ Japan Air Proto Center (SAUS)
JAPC............ Joint Air Photo Center [*NATO*] (NATG)
JAPCA.......... Journal. Air Pollution Control Association (journ.) (SAUS)
JAPCA.......... Journal of Air Pollution Control Association [*A publication*] (EPAT)
Jap Chem Week... Japan Chemical Week (journ.) (SAUS)
Jap Circ J... Japanese Circulation Journal (journ.) (SAUS)
JAPCO.......... Jamestown Paint & Varnish Co.
JAPCO.......... Japan Atomic Power Co.
JAPCo.......... Japan Atomic Power Company (BUAC)
JAPCO.......... Japan Power Demonstration Reactor Company (SAUO)
Jap Cur........ Japan Current (SAUS)
JapDic......... Japanese Dictionary (SAUS)
JAPE............ Journal of Australian Political Economy (journ.) (SAUS)
JAPEAI......... Journal of Applied Ecology (journ.) (SAUS)
Jap Econ St... Japanese Economic Studies (journ.) (SAUS)
JAPEX.......... Japan Express (SAUS)
JAPEX.......... Japan Petroleum Exploitation Co. (SAUS)
JAPEX.......... Japan Petroleum Exploration Co. (BUAC)
Jap Geol Surv Bull... Japan Geological Survey. Bulletin (journ.) (SAUS)
Jap Geol Surv Rep... Japan Geological Survey. Report (journ.) (SAUS)
Jap Geotherm Energy Ass J... Japan Geothermal Energy Association. Journal (journ.) (SAUS)
JAPGWC...... Jewish Association for the Protection of Girls, Women and Children (SAUO)
JAPH............ Just Another PERL Hacker (SAUS)
JAPhA.......... Journal of the American Pharmaceutical Association (SAUO)
Jap Heart J... Japanese Heart Journal (journ.) (SAUS)
JAPI............. Journal of the Association of Physicians of India (journ.) (SAUS)
JAPIA.......... Japan Auto Parts Industries Association
JAPIB.......... Joint Air Photographic Intelligence Board (SAUO)
JAPIC.......... Japanese Project Industry Council (SAUO)
JAPIC.......... Japan Pharmaceutical Information Center [*Tokyo*] [*Information service or system*] (IID)
JAPIC.......... Joint Air Photographic Intelligence Center (SAUS)
JAPIC.......... Joint Air Photographic Intelligence Centre (SAUO)
JAPIC.......... Joint Air Photo Interpretation Center (SAUO)
Jap Inst Nav J... Japan. Institute of Navigation. Journal (journ.) (SAUS)
JAPIO.......... Japan Patent Information Organization [*Database producer*]
JAPIsA......... Japan Auto Parts Industries Association (SAUO)
JAPIT........... Japanese Association for the Promotion of International Trade (EY)
JAPIU.......... Joint Air Photo Interpretation Unit (SAUO)
Jap J Allergy... Japanese Journal of Allergy (journ.) (SAUS)
Jap J A Phy... Japanese Journal of Applied Physics (journ.) (SAUS)
Jap J Appl Phys... Japanese Journal of Applied Physics (journ.) (SAUS)
Jap J Appl Phys Suppl... Japanese Journal of Applied Physics. Supplement (journ.) (SAUS)
Jap J Appl Zool... Japanese Journal of Applied Zoology (journ.) (SAUS)
Jap J Astr... Japanese Journal of Astronomy (journ.) (SAUS)
Jap J Astr Geophys... Japanese Journal of Astronomy and Geophysics (journ.) (SAUS)
Jap J Breed... Japanese Journal of Breeding (journ.) (SAUS)
Jap J Canc Res... Japanese Journal of Cancer Research (journ.) (SAUS)
Jap J Child... Japanese Journal of Child Psychiatry (journ.) (SAUS)
Jap J Clin Med... Japanese Journal of Clinical Medicine (journ.) (SAUS)
Jap J Clin Path... Japanese Journal of Clinical Pathology (journ.) (SAUS)
Jap J Ecol... Japanese Journal of Ecology (journ.) (SAUS)
Jap J Edu P... Japanese Journal of Educational Psychology (journ.) (SAUS)
Jap J Geophys... Japanese Journal of Geophysics (journ.) (SAUS)
Jap J Limnol... Japanese Journal of Limnology (journ.) (SAUS)
Jap J Med... Japanese Journal of Medicine (journ.) (SAUS)
Jap J Nurs... Japanese Journal of Nursing (journ.) (SAUS)
Jap J Nurs Educ... Japan Journal of Nurses Education (journ.) (SAUS)

Jap J Nurs Res... Japanese Journal of Nursing Research (journ.) (SAUS)
Jap J Nutr... Japanese Journal of Nutrition (journ.) (SAUS)
Jap J Ophthal... Japanese Journal of Ophthalmology (journ.) (SAUS)
Jap J Palynol... Japanese Journal of Palynology (journ.) (SAUS)
Jap J Parasit... Japanese Journal of Parasitology (journ.) (SAUS)
Jap J Pharmacogn... Japanese Journal of Pharmacognosy (journ.) (SAUS)
Jap J Sanit Zool... Japanese Journal of Sanitary Zoology (journ.) (SAUS)
Jap J Trop Agr... Sapanese Journal of Tropical Agriculture (SAUS)
Jap J Zool... Japanese Journal of Zoology (journ.) (SAUS)
Jap J Zootech Sci... Japanese Journal of Zootechnical Science (journ.) (SAUS)
JAPLA.......... Journal. Atlantic Provinces Linguistic Association/Revue. Association de Linguistique des Provinces Atlantiques (journ.) (SAUS)
JAPLD.......... Japanese Journal of Applied Physics. Part 2. Letters (journ.) (SAUS)
Japlish......... Japanese & English (SAUS)
JAPMAB....... Journal. American Pharmaceutical Association. Scientific Edition (journ.) (SAUS)
Jap Meteorol Agency Volcanol Bull... Japan Meteorological Agency. Volcanological Bulletin (journ.) (SAUS)
JAPN........... Japan Air Lines Co. Ltd. [*NASDAQ symbol*] (NQ)
JapnAr......... Japan Airlines [*Associated Press*] (SAG)
JapnAr......... Japan Airlines Co. Ltd. [*Associated Press*] (SAG)
Jap Nat Ry Ry Tech Res... Japanese National Railways. Railway Technical Research (journ.) (SAUS)
JAPND......... Japanese Journal of Applied Physics. Part 1. Regular Papers and Short Notes (journ.) (SAUS)
JAPNEF........ Journal of Animal Physiology and Animal Nutrition (journ.) (SAUS)
JapnEq......... [*The*] Japan Equity Fund, Inc. [*Associated Press*] (SAG)
JAPNMS...... JTIDS Air Platform Network Management System (SAUS)
J Ap Nutrition... Journal of Applied Nutrition (journ.) (SAUS)
JAPNY......... Japan Airlines Co. Ltd ADR [*NASDAQ symbol*] (TTSB)
JAPO........... Joint Area Petroleum Office
JAPOS......... JAPOS Study Group [*Defunct*] (EA)
JAPOS......... Journalists, Authors and Poets on Stamps Study Group (SAUO)
JAPOS......... Journalists, Authors and Poets on Stamps Study Unit (EA)
JAPP........... Japanese Patent (IAA)
Jap P........... [*The*] Pharmacopoeia of Japan [*A publication*]
Jap Per Ind... Japanese Periodicals Index.(journ.) (SAUS)
J Appl Biochem... Journal of Applied Biochemistry (journ.) (SAUS)
J Appl Biol... Journal of Applied Biology (journ.) (SAUS)
J Appl Biomater... Journal of Applied Biomaterials (journ.) (SAUS)
J Appl Botany... Journal of Applied Botany (journ.) (SAUS)
J Appl Chem... Journal of Applied Chemistry (journ.) (SAUS)
J Appl Chem Abstr... Journal of Applied Chemistry. Abstracts (journ.) (SAUS)
J Appl Chem Biotechnol Abstr... Journal of Applied Chemistry and Biotechnology. Abstracts (journ.) (SAUS)
J Appl Cosmetol... Journal of Applied Cosmetology (journ.) (SAUS)
J Appl Dev Psychol... Journal of Applied Developmental Psychology (journ.) (SAUS)
J Appl Entomol... Journal of Applied Entomology (journ.) (SAUS)
J Appl Gerontol... Journal of Applied Gerontology (journ.) (SAUS)
J Appl Ichthyol... Journal of Applied Ichthyology (journ.) (SAUS)
J Appl Manage... Journal of Applied Management (journ.) (SAUS)
J Appl Med... Journal of Applied Medicine (journ.) (SAUS)
J Appl Metalwork... Journal of Applied Metalworking (journ.) (SAUS)
J Appl Microbiol Biotech... Journal of Applied Microbiology and Biotechnology (journ.) (SAUS)
J Appl Ntr.... Journal of Applied Nutrition (journ.) (SAUS)
J Appl Pneum... Journal of Applied Pneumatics (journ.) (SAUS)
J Appl Polym Sci Appl Polym Symp... Journal of Applied Polymer Science. Applied Polymer Symposium (journ.) (SAUS)
J Appl Spectrosc... Journal of Applied Spectroscopy (journ.) (SAUS)
J Appl Toxicol... Journal of Applied Toxicology (journ.) (SAUS)
J App Nutr... Journal of Applied Nutrition (journ.) (SAUS)
Jap Prog Climatol... Japanese Progress on Climatology (journ.) (SAUS)
Jap Psy Res... Japanese Psychological Research (journ.) (SAUS)
JAPRCP....... Journal of Anthropological Research (journ.) (SAUS)
JAPRDQ....... Journal of Animal Production Research (journ.) (SAUS)
JAPRRCC..... Japan Authors' and Publishers' Reprographic Rights Clearance Centre (BUAC)
JAPRW........ Japanese Association of Photosynthesis Research Workers (BUAC)
JAPS........... Japanese American Philatelic Society [*Later, JASP*]
JAP S........... Japan Sea (SAUS)
JAPS........... Joint Administration Planning Staff (SAUO)
JAPS........... Joint Administrative Planning Section [*Joint Planning Staff*] [*World War II*]
JAPS........... Joint Administrative Planning Staff (SAUO)
JAPsAs........ Journal of the American Psychoanalytic Association (SAUO)
Jap Semicond Tech N... Japanese Semiconductor Technology News (journ.) (SAUS)
Jap Shipbldg Mar Eng... Japan Shipbuilding and Marine Engineering (journ.) (SAUS)
Jap Shipbuild & Mar Engng... Japan Shipbuilding and Marine Engineering (journ.) (SAUS)
Jap Soc....... Japan Society (SAUO)
J Ap Sociol... Journal of Applied Sociology (journ.) (SAUS)
Jap Soc Promot Sci Sub-Comm Phys Chem Stlmaking Spec Rep... Japan Society for the Promotion of Science. Sub-Committee for Physical Chemistry of Steelmaking. Special Report (journ.) (SAUS)
JAPSS.......... Joint Automated Planning Support System [*of JOPS*] [*Military*]
JAPT........... Journal for Approximation Theory (journ.) (SAUS)
JAPT........... Journal of Approximation Theory (journ.) (SAUS)
Jap Telecom... Japan Telecommunications Review (journ.) (SAUS)
Jap Weld Soc Trans... Japan Welding Society. Transactions (journ.) (SAUS)
JAQ............. Jacquinot Bay [*Papua New Guinea*] [*Airport symbol*] (OAG)
JAQ............. Job Activities Questionnaire

JAQ............ Journal of Buyouts and Acquisitions (journ.) (SAUS)
JAQ............. Passionist Academic Institute, Chicago, IL [OCLC symbol] (OCLC)
J Aqiaric & Aquat Sci... Journal of Aquaculture and Aquatic Sciences (journ.) (SAUS)
J Aquaric..... Journal of Aquaculture (journ.) (SAUS)
JA Quart J Automat Control... Journal. A Quarterly Journal of Automatic Control (journ.) (SAUS)
J Aquat Anim Health... Journal of Aquatic Animal Health (journ.) (SAUS)
JAR............ Airlink Luftverkehrsgesellschaft GmbH [Austria] [ICAO designator] (FAAC)
JAR............ Jamming Avoidance Response
JAR............ Jargon (WDAA)
JAR............ J. Arthur Rank [Motion picture company in England]
JAR............ Java Archive [Computer science] (IGQR)
JAR............ Java Archive File (SAUS)
JAR............ JavaSoft Java Archive [Computer science]
JAr............ Jewish Aramaic (BJA)
JAR............ Jewish Autonomous Region [Eastern Siberia]
JAR............ Jews for Animal Rights (EA)
JAR............ Job Appraisal Review (PDAA)
JAR............ Joint Airworthiness Requirements (MCD)
JAR............ Joint Aviation Requirement [FAA] (TAG)
JAR............ Journal of Accounting Research (journ.) (SAUS)
JAR............ Journal of Advertising Research [Advertising Research Foundation] [A publication]
JAR............ Journal of Anthropological Research (journ.) (SAUS)
JAR............ Jump Address Register
JAR............ Junior Admitting Resident [Medicine] (DAVI)
JAR............ Justice Acquisition Regulation [A publication] (AAGC)
JAR............ Zion-Benton Library District, Zion, IL [OCLC symbol] (OCLC)
JAR-145...... Joint Aviation Requirement on Approved Maintenance Organisations (SAUO)
JARA........... Japan Antibiotics Research Association (BUAC)
J Ar Aad Sci... Journal. Arizona Academy of Science (journ.) (SAUS)
J Arab Affairs... Journal of Arab Affairs (journ.) (SAUS)
J Arachnol... Journal of Arachnology (journ.) (SAUS)
Jar & By Conv... Jannan and Bythewoods Conveyancing (journ.) (SAUS)
Jar & By Conv... Jarman and Bythewood's Conveyancing [A publication] (DLA)
JARB........... Joint Acquisition Review Board [Army]
J Arboric...... Journal of Arboriculture (journ.) (SAUS)
J Arb Vet Med As... Journal. Arab Veterinary Medical Association (journ.) (SAUS)
JARC........... Jewish Association for Retarded Citizens (EA)
JARC........... Joint Air Reconnaissance Center [NATO] (NATG)
JARC........... Joint Air Reconnaissance Centre (SAUO)
JARC........... Joint Avionics Research Committee (SAUS)
JARCA .... Journal of Aesthetic and Art Criticism (journ.) (SAUS)
JARCC .... Joint Air Reconnaissance Coordination Center [Military] (MCD)
JARCE......... Journal. American Research Center in Egypt (journ.) (SAUS)
JARCE......... Journal of the American Research Center in Egypt (SAUO)
JARCE......... Journal of the American Research Center in Egypt (journ.) (SAUS)
J Archaeol Chem... Journal of Archaeological Chemistry (journ.) (SAUS)
J Archaeol Res... Journal of Archaeological Research (journ.) (SAUS)
Jar Chancery Pr... Jarmans Chancery Practics (journ.) (SAUS)
J Archit Plan Res... Journal of Architectural and Planning Research (journ.) (SAUS)
Jar Chy Pr... Jarman's Chancery Practice [A publication] (DLA)
Jar Cr Tr... Jardine's Criminal Trials [A publication] (DLA)
Jar Cr Tr...... Jardines Criminal Trials (journ.) (SAUS)
JARD .... Jardines
JARDB......... Joint Advisory Rehabilitation and Disability Board (SAUS)
JardFlCh...... Jardine Fleming China Region [Associated Press] (SAG)
Jard Ind....... Jardine's Index to Howell's State Trials [A publication] (DLA)
JARE.......... Japanese Antarctic Research Expedition [1956-]
JAREB......... Japanese Railway Engineering (journ.) (SAUS)
JARECT....... Japan Annual Reviews in Electronics, Computers and Telecommunications (journ.) (SAUS)
JARE Scientific Reports... Japanese Antarctic Research Expedition Scientific Reports (journ.) (SAUS)
JARF........... Journal. Addiction Research Foundation (journ.) (SAUS)
JAR-FCL ...... JAR on Flight Crew Licensing (SAUS)
jarg............. jargonese (SAUS)
jarg............. jargonize (SAUS)
Jarg Soc...... Jargon Society (SAUO)
J Ar Hist...... Journal of Arizona History (journ.) (SAUS)
JARI........... Japan Association of Railway Industries (SAUO)
JARI........... Japan Automobile Research Institute
JARI........... Japan Automotive Research Institute
JARI........... Japanese Association of Railway Industries (BUAC)
JARI........... Journal of Agricultural Research in Iceland (journ.) (SAUS)
JARI........... Journal of Applied Radiation and Isotopes (journ.) (SAUS)
JARI........... Jute Agricultural Research Institute [India] (BUAC)
JARIB.......... Joint Air Reconnaissance Intelligence Board [Australia]
JARIC......... Joint Aerial Reconnaissance Interpretation Center (MCD)
JARIC......... Joint Air Reconnaissance Centre (SAUO)
JARIC......... Joint Air Reconnaissance Intelligence Center (or Centre) (SAUS)
JARIC......... Joint Air Reconnaissance Intelligence Centre [British]
J Arid Environ... Journal of Arid Environments (journ.) (SAUS)
JARIV......... Joint Air Reconnaissance Intelligence Centre (SAUO)
J Ariz Ner Ad Sci... Journal. Arizona-Nevada Academy of Science(journ.) (SAUS)
J Arkan Med Soc... Journal. Arkansas Medical Society (journ.) (SAUS)
JARL.......... Japan Amateur Radio League (BUAC)
JARM.......... Jammer, Artillery, Radar Missile (ACAE)
JAR-MED..... JAR on Medical (SAUS)
J Arms Armour Soc... Journal. Arms and Armour Society (journ.) (SAUS)
J Arn Arbor... Journal. Arnold Arboretum (journ.) (SAUS)
J Arnold Arbor... Journal. Arnold Arboretum. Harvard University (journ.) (SAUS)

JARO .... Johore Area Rehabilitation Organization (SAUO)
JAR-OPS..... JAR on Flight Operations (SAUS)
JAROS .... Japanese Resources Observation System Organization (SAUS)
JARPA .... Jam-Resistant Phased Array (ACAE)
Jar Pow Dev... Jarman's Edition of Powell on Devises [A publication] (DLA)
Jar Pow Dev... Jarmans Edition of Powell on Devises (journ.) (SAUS)
JARQ Jap Agric Res Q... JARQ Japan Agricultural Research Quarterly (journ.) (SAUS)
JARQ Jpn Agric Res Q... JARQ Japan Agricultural Research Quarterly (journ.) (SAUS)
JARR .... Journal of Architectural Research (journ.) (SAUS)
JARRP .... Japan Association for Radiation Research on Polymers
JARS........... Alltrista Corp. [NASDAQ symbol] (SAG)
JARS........... Jamming Aircraft and Radar Simulation (ACAE)
JARS........... Java Applet Rating Service (SAUO)
JARS........... Job Accounting Report System (MHDI)
JARS........... Joliet Amateur Radio Society (SAUO)
JARS........... Journal. Assam Research Society (journ.) (SAUS)
JARS........... Journalization and Recovery System (PDAA)
JARS........... Journalization and Recovery System (journ.) (SAUS)
J Arthroplasty... Journal of Arthroplasty (journ.) (SAUS)
J Art Mgmt L... Journal of Arts Management and Law (journ.) (SAUS)
JARTRAN ..... James A. Ryder Transportation [Acronym is trade name of truck-rental firm]
JARTS......... Japan Railway Technical Service (BUAC)
JARTS......... Japan Railway Technical Services (SAUO)
J Arts Mgt and L... Journal of Arts Management and Law (journ.) (SAUS)
JAR-TSO..... Joint Aviation Requirement on Technical Standard Orders (SAUO)
Jar Wills...... Jarman on Wills [8 eds.] [1841-51] [A publication] (DLA)
JAS .... Jamaica Agricultural Society (BUAC)
JAS .... Jamaica Air Service (SAUO)
Jas............. James [New Testament book]
JAS .... Jamestown [California] [Seismograph station code, US Geological Survey] (SEIS)
JAS .... Jane Austen Society [Basingstoke, Hampshire, England] (EAIO)
JAS .... Japan Air System
JAS .... Japan Air System Co. Ltd. [ICAO designator] (FAAC)
JAS .... Japan Association of Shipbuilders (BUAC)
JAS .... Japan Astronautical Society (SAUO)
J-A S .... Japan-Australia Society (SAUO)
JAS .... Jasper, TX [Location identifier] [FAA] (FAAL)
JAS .... Jazz Arts Society (EA)
JAS .... Jenkins Activity Survey [Personality development test] [Psychology]
JAS .... Jewish Agricultural Society (EA)
JAS .... Job Accounting System
JAS .... Job Activity Survey
JAS .... Job Analysis Schedule [Department of Labor]
JAS .... Job Analysis System [Computer program]
JAS .... Job Attitude Scale [Employment test]
JAS .... Johnny Alfalfa Sprout [Defunct] (EA)
JAS .... Joint Administration Services
JAS .... Joint Airmiss Section [Aviation] (DA)
JAS .... Joint Anti-Submarine School (SAUO)
JAS .... Joint Association Survey [American Petroleum Institute, Independent Petroleum Association of America, and Mid-Continent Oil and Gas Association]
JAS .... Joint Automated Planning Support System (SAUS)
JAS .... Jordanian Agricultural Society (SAUO)
JAS .... Journal Abbreviation Sources (SAUS)
JAS .... Journal Access Service [Center for Research Libraries]
JAS .... Journal. Acoustical Society of America (journ.) (SAUS)
JAS .... Journal. Asiatic Society of Great Britain and Ireland (journ.) (SAUS)
JAS .... Journal of Aerospace Science [A publication] (NAKS)
JAS .... Journal of Aerospace Science (journ.) (SAUS)
JAS .... Journal of Archaeological Science (journ.) (SAUS)
JAS .... Journal of Asian Studies [A publication] (BRI)
JAS .... Journal of Asiatic Society (journ.) (SAUS)
JAS .... Journal of Atmospheric Sciences [A publication] (SSD)
JAS .... Journal of Australian Studies (journ.) (SAUS)
JAS .... Journal of Austronesian Studies (journ.) (SAUS)
JAS .... Journal of the Acoustical Society (journ.) (SAUS)
JAS .... Journals Access Service [Center for Research Libraries]
J As .... Judicial Assessor [Ghana] [A publication] (DLA)
J As .... Judicial Assessor (journ.) (SAUS)
JAS .... Junior Astronomical Society (EAIO)
JAS .... Just a Second (SAUS)
JAS .... Juvenile Ankylosing Spondylitis [Medicine] (DMAA)
JAS .... Lake Villa District Library, Lake Villa, IL [OCLC symbol] (OCLC)
JAS-1......... Japan Amateur Satellite-1
JASA.......... Japan Amateur Sports Association (SAUO)
JASA.......... Jewish Association for Services for the Aged (EA)
JASA.......... Jewish Association for the Services of the Aged, New York (SAUO)
JASA.......... Jo-Ann Stores "A" [Formerly, Fabri-Centers Amer. "B"] [NYSE symbol]
JASA.......... Joint Airworthiness Steering Committee (SAUS)
JASA.......... Joint Antisubmarine Action
JASA.......... Journal. Acoustical Safety of America (journ.) (SAUS)
JASA.......... Journal. American Scientific Affiliation (journ.) (SAUS)
JASA.......... Journal. American Statistical Association (journ.) (SAUS)
JASA.......... Journal of the Acoustical Society of America (journ.) (SAUS)
JASA.......... Journal of the American Society of Acoustics (journ.) (SAUS)
JASA.......... Journal of the American Statistical Association (SAUO)
JASA.......... Journal of the American Statistical Association (journ.) (SAUS)
JASA.......... Junior Assistant Stores Accountant [British military] (DMA)
J As Aff........ Journal of Asian Affairs (journ.) (SAUS)

JASAP .... Julie [*Sonobuoy System*] Automatic Search and Attack Plotter [*Navy*] (MCD)

JASAR .... Jittered and Swept Active RADAR

JASASA .... Joint Air-Surface Antisubmarine Action

JASAT .... Journal. American Studies Association of Texas (journ.) (SAUS)

JASB .... Jo-Ann Stores "B" [*Formerly, Fabri-Centers Amer. "A"*] [*NYSE symbol*]

JASB .... Joint Advisory Survey Board [*British*]

JASB .... Journal. Asiatic Society of Bengal (journ.) (SAUS)

JAS B .... Journal. Asiatic Society of Bombay (journ.) (SAUS)

JASB .... Journal of the Anthropological Society of Bombay (journ.) (SAUS)

JASB .... Journal of the Asiatic Society of Bengal (SAUO)

JASB .... Journal of the Asiatic Society of Bombay (journ.) (SAUS)

JASC .... Japan Academic Societies Center (SAUS)

JASC .... Japan-America Society of Southern California (SAUO)

JASC .... Japan-America Student Conference (EA)

JASC .... Japan Asia Sea Cable

JASC .... Japan-Asia Sea Cable (SAUS)

JASC .... Japan Sea Cable (SAUS)

JASC .... Joint Actions Steering Committee (SAUO)

JASC .... Journal. Asiatic Society of Calcutta (journ.) (SAUS)

JASC .... JPL [*Jet Propulsion Laboratory*] Astronautical Star Catalog (KSC)

JAS Calcutta ... Journal. Asiatic Society of Calcutta (journ.) (SAUS)

JASCEV .... Journal of Agronomy and Crop Science (journ.) (SAUS)

J A Science ... Journal of Archaeological Science (journ.) (SAUS)

JASCO .... Joint American Study Commission (SAUO)

JASCO .... Joint Assault Signal Co. [*Small unit in Pacific amphibious warfare*] [*World War II*]

JASCO Appl Notes ... Japan Spectroscopic Company. Application Notes (journ.) (SAUS)

J As Cult ...... Journal of Asian Culture (journ.) (SAUS)

JASDA .... Julie [*Sonobuoy System*] Automatic Sonic Data Analyzer [*Navy*]

JASDF .... Japan Air Self-Defense Force (SAUS)

JASDF .... Japanese Air Self-Defense Force

JASE .... Just Another System Error (SAUS)

JASFA .... Japan Sea-Farming Association (SAUO)

JASFE6 .... Journal of Agricultural Science in Finland (journ.) (SAUS)

JASG .... Joint Advanced Study Group

JASGP .... Joint Advanced Study Group

JASH .... Jason, Inc. (SAUO)

J As Ht .... Journal of Asian History (journ.) (SAUS)

JASI .... Joint Asian Surgical Industries (SAUS)

J Asian & Afric Stud ... Journal of Asian and African Studies (journ.) (SAUS)

J Asian Stud ... Journal of Asian Studies (journ.) (SAUS)

J Asiat Soc Bangla ... Journal. Asiatic Society of Bangladesh (journ.) (SAUS)

J Asiat Soc Bangladesh Sci ... Journal. Asiatic Society of Bangladesh. Science (journ.) (SAUS)

J Asiat Soc Bengal Lett ... Journal. Asiatic Society of Bengal. Letters (journ.) (SAUS)

J Asiat Soc Bengal Sci ... Journal. Asiatic Society of Bengal. Science (journ.) (SAUS)

J Asiat Soc Bombay ... Journal. Asiatic Society of Bombay (journ.) (SAUS)

J Asiat Soc Sci ... Journal Asiatic Society. Science (journ.) (SAUS)

J Asiat Stud ... Journal of Asiatic Studies (journ.) (SAUS)

JASIN .... Joint Air Sea Interaction [*National Science Foundation/United Kingdom*]

JASIN .... Joint Air-Sea Interaction Experiment (SAUO)

JASIN .... Joint Air-Sea Interaction Program [*Global Atmospheric Research Program*] (USDC)

JASIN .... Joint Air-Sea Interaction Project (SAUO)

JASIS .... Journal of the American Society for Information Science (SAUO)

JASIS .... Journal of the American Society for Information Science (journ.) (SAUS)

J Asist Soc ... Journal. Asiatic Society (journ.) (SAUS)

JASL .... Joint Archive for Sea Level (SAUO)

JASL .... Journal. Asiatic Society. Letters (journ.) (SAUS)

JASL .... Journal of the Asiatic Society, Letters (SAUO)

JASL .... Journal of the Asiatic Society, Letters (journ.) (SAUS)

JASLS .... Japanese American Society for Legal Studies (EA)

JASMMM ..... Joint Aviation Supply and Maintenance Material Management (DNAB)

JASMU .... Journal pour l'Avancement des Soins Medicaux d'Urgence [*A publication*]

JASN .... Jason, Inc. [*NASDAQ symbol*] (NQ)

JASN .... Journal of the American Society of Nephrology (SAUO)

JASNA .... Jane Austen Society of North America (EA)

JASO .... Japan Standards Organization (SAUS)

Ja Soc Lond B ... Japan Society of London. Bulletin (journ.) (SAUS)

JASON .... Group of physicists at Stanford that study various projects and are funded by government defense money (SAUO)

Jason .... Jason, Inc. [*Associated Press*] (SAG)

JASON .... Journal Articles Sent On Demand (SAUO)

JASON .... Scientific panel MITRE Corporation (SAUO)

JASORS ...... Joint Advanced Special Operations Radio System [*Military*] (RDA)

JASP .... Japanese American Society for Philately (EA)

JASP .... Journal. Asiatic Society of Pakistan (journ.) (SAUS)

JASp .... Journal of Applied Social Psychology (journ.) (SAUS)

JASPA .... Jesuit Association of Student Personnel Administrators (EA)

JASPA .... Jobs and Skills Programme for Africa (BUAC)

J As Pac World ... Journal of Asian-Pacific and World Perspectives (journ.) (SAUS)

JASPER .... Joint Academic Services Providers to Education and Research (AIE)

JASPR .... Jasper [*Gem*] (ROG)

JASPR .... Journal. American Society for Psychical Research Technologists (journ.) (SAUS)

JASR .... JTPA [*Job Training and Partnership Act*] Annual Status Report (OICC)

JASRAC ...... Japanese Society of Rights of Authors and Composers (SAUO)

JASRES .... Journal of Agricultural and Scientific Research (journ.) (SAUS)

JASS .... Javascript-Accessible Style Sheets (SAUS)

JASS .... Joint Antisatellite Study

JASS .... Joint Anti-Submarine School [*British military*] (DMA)

JASS .... JUMPS [*Joint Uniform Military Pay System*] Automated Support System [*or Supplemental*] [*Military*]

JASSA .... JASSA. Journal of the Australian Society of Security Analysts (journ.) (SAUS)

JASSA .... Journal of Applied Science in Southern Africa (SAUO)

JASS-AC ...... JUMPS [*Joint Uniform Military Pay System*] Automated Supplemental System-Active Component [*Military*]

J Assa Hosp Med Educ ... Journal. Association for Hospital Medical Education (journ.) (SAUS)

J Assam Res Soc ... Journal. Assam Research Society (journ.) (SAUS)

J Assam Sci Soc ... Journal. Assam Science Society (journ.) (SAUS)

JASSC .... Japan-America Society of Southern California

JASSCC .... Japan Academic Society System for Copyright Clearance (BUAC)

J Ass Comput Mach ... Journal of the Association of Computing Machinery (SAUO)

J Ass Comput Mach ... Journal of the Association of Computing Machinery (journ.) (SAUS)

JASSM .... Joint Acoustic Surveillance System Model [*Military*] (CAAL)

JASSM .... Joint Air-to-Surface Standoff Missile [*Military*]

J Assn Law Teachers ... Journal. Association of Law Teachers (journ.) (SAUS)

J Ass'n L Teachers ... Journal. Association of Law Teachers [*A publication*] (DLA)

J Assoc Acad Minor Phys ... Journal of the Association for Academic Minority Physicians (SAUO)

J Assoc Acad Minor Phys ... Journal of the Association for Academic Minority Physicians (journ.) (SAUS)

J Assoc Am Med Coll ... Journal. Association of American Medical Colleges (journ.) (SAUS)

J Assoc Care Child Health ... Journal. Association for the Care of Childrens Health (journ.) (SAUS)

J Assoc Care Child Hos ... Journal. Association for the Care of Children in Hospitals (journ.) (SAUS)

J Assoc Comput Mach ... Journal of the Association for Computing Machinery (journ.) (SAUS)

J Assoc Eng Archit Isr ... Journal. Association of Engineers and Architects in Israel (journ.) (SAUS)

J Assoc Eng Archit Palest ... Journal. Association of Engineers and Architects in Palestine (journ.) (SAUS)

J Assoc Eng Soc ... Journal. Association of Engineering Societies (journ.) (SAUS)

J Assoc Law Teachers ... Journal. Association of Law Teachers (journ.) (SAUS)

J Assoc L Teachers ... Journal. Association of Law Teachers [*A publication*] (DLA)

J Assoc Lunar and Planet Obs Strolling Astron ... Journal. Association of Lunar and Planetary Observers. Strolling Astronomer (journ.) (SAUS)

J Assoc Lunar Planet Obs Strolling Astron ... Journal of the Association of Lunar and Planetary Observers, Strolling Astronomer (journ.) (SAUS)

J Assoc Med Illus ... Journal. Association of Medical Illus- trators (journ.) (SAUS)

J Assoc Nurses AIDS Care ... Journal of the Association of Nurses in Aids Care (SAUO)

J Assoc Nurses AIDS Care ... Journal of the Association of Nurses in AIDS Care (journ.) (SAUS)

J Assoc Off Anal Chem ... Journal of the Association of Official Analytical Chemists (SAUO)

J Assoc Off Anal Chem ... Journal of the Association of Official Analytical Chemists (journ.) (SAUS)

J Assoc Pediatr Oncol Nurses ... Journal. Association of Pediatric Oncology Nurses (journ.) (SAUS)

J Assoc Physicians India ... Journal of the Association of Physicians of India (SAUO)

J Assoc Physicians India ... Journal of the Association of Physicians of India (journ.) (SAUS)

J Assoc Phys Ment Rehabil ... Journal. Association for Physical and Mental Rehabilitation (journ.) (SAUS)

J Ass Off Agric Chem ... Journal. Asciation of Official Agricultural Chemists (journ.) (SAUS)

J Asso Teach Ja ... Journal. Association of Teachers of Japanese (journ.) (SAUS)

J Assot Pers Comput Chem ... Journal. Association of Personal Computers for Chemists (journ.) (SAUS)

J Ass Physicians India ... Journal. Association of Physicians of India (journ.) (SAUS)

JASS-RC ...... JUMPS [*Joint Uniform Military Pay System*] Automated Support System - Reserve Corps

JAST .... Jamaican Association of Sugar Technologists (BUAC)

JAST .... Japan Association of Sugar Technologists (SAUO)

JAST .... Jazz Action Society of Tasmania

JAST .... Joint Advanced Strike Technology [*Program*] [*Air Force*] [*Navy*] (DOMA)

JAST .... Joint Air Support Tactics [*Military*]

JASTAA .... Journal. Agricultural Society of Trinidad and Tobago (journ.) (SAUS)

JASTD .... Junior Assistant Steward [*British military*] (DMA)

JASTIS .... Japan Science and Technology Information System (SAUS)

JASTOP .... Jet-Assisted Stop (SAUS)

JASTOP .... Jet Assist Stop

JASTP .... Joint Advanced Srike Technology Program (SAUS)

J Astronomical Soc Vic ... Journal. Astronomical Society of Victoria (journ.) (SAUS)

J Astron Soc Egypt ... Journal of the Astronomical Society of Egypt (journ.) (SAUS)

JAStud .... Journal of American Studies (journ.) (SAUS)

JASU .... Jet Aircraft Starting Unit (AFM)

JASW .... Japan-America Society of Washington (EA)

JASWG .... Joint Safety Assurance Working Group [*NASA*] (SPST)

JAT .... Jabat [*Marshall Islands*] [*Airport symbol*] (OAG)

JAT .... Jam Angle Tracking

JAT .... Job Accounting Table

JAT	Joint Agency Training
JAT	Journal of Accounting and Public Policy (journ.) (SAUS)
JAT	Journal of Analytical Toxicology (SAUO)
JAT	Journal of Applied Toxicology (journ.) (SAUS)
JAT	Jugoslovenski Aerotransport [*Yugoslav Air Transport*] [*ICAO designator*]
JAT	Junior Aptitude Tests [*Educational test*]
JAT	Mennonite Hospital, Health Sciences Library, Bloomington, IL [*OCLC symbol*] (OCLC)
JAT	Yugoslav Airlines (SAUS)
JATAAQ	Journal. Animal Technicians Association (journ.) (SAUS)
JATAN	Japan Tropical Rainforest Action Network
JATC	Japan Association for Tissue Culture (BUAC)
JATC	Joint Apprenticeship and Training Committee [*Bureau of Apprenticeship and Training*] [*Department of Labor*]
JATC	Joint Apprenticeship Training Committee (SAUS)
JATC	Journal of Air Traffic Control (journ.) (SAUS)
JATCA	Joinery and Timber Construction Association (SAUO)
JATCC	Joint Air Traffic Control Center [*Military*]
JATCC	Joint Aviation Telecommunications Co- ordination Committee (SAUS)
JATCC	Joint Aviation Telecommunications Coordination Committee (BUAC)
JATCCCP	Joint Advanced Tactical Command, Control, and Communications Program [*Military*]
JATCCCS	Joint Advanced Tactical Command, Control, and Communications System [*Military*] (MCD)
JATCCS	Joint Advanced Tactical Command and Control System [*Military*] (SAA)
JATCO	Japan Automatic Transmission Co.
JATCRU	Joint Air Traffic Control Radar Unit (SAUO)
JATE	Japan Techno-Economics Society
JATE	Joint Air Transport Establishment [*Military*] [*British*]
JATEC	Japan Technical Committee to Aid US Anti-War Deserter (BUAC)
J At Energy Soc Jpn	Journal. Atomic Energy Society of Japan (journ.) (SAUS)
J At Energy Soc Jpn	Journal of the Atomic Energy Society of Japan (journ.) (SAUS)
JATES	Japan Techno-Economics Society (EA)
JATF	Joint Amphibious Task Force (NVT)
JATFC	JATF Commander (SAUO)
JATFOR	Joint Amphibious Task Force (SAUO)
JATFS	Japan Technno-Economics Society (SAUO)
JATI	Journal. Association of Teachers of Italian (journ.) (SAUS)
JATIS	Japan Technical Information Service (SAUS)
JATJ	Journal-Newsletter. Association of Teachers of Japanese (journ.) (SAUS)
JATLA	Journal. American Trial Lawyers Association [*A publication*] (DLA)
JATM	Joint Antitactical Missile System (Provisional) [*Army*] (RDA)
JATMA	Japan Automobile Tire Manufacturers Association
J Atmos Chem	Journal of Atmospheric Chemistry (journ.) (SAUS)
J Atmos Sci	Journal of Atmospheric Science (MEC)
J Atmos Sci	Journal of Atmospheric Sciences (journ.) (SAUS)
JATO	Jet-Assisted Take-Off. More correct: Rocket-Assisted Take-Off (SAUO)
JATOD3	Journal of Analytical Toxicology (journ.) (SAUS)
JATOP	Army Topographic Service (SAUO)
JATO unit	Jet-Assisted Takeoff Unit
JATP	Jazz at the Philharmonic
JATP	Joint Air Training Plan
JATP	Joint Air Transportation Plan (AABC)
JATR	Japan Advanced Thermal Reactor (SAUS)
JATS	Jamming Analysis & Transmission Selection (SAUS)
JATS	Job Application Tracking System (SAUO)
JATS	Joint Air Transportation Service
JATT	Joint Air Attack Team (SAUO)
JAU	American Hospital Supply Corp., Evanston, IL [*OCLC symbol*] (OCLC)
JAU	Jacksboro, TN [*Location identifier*] [*FAA*] (FAAL)
JAUA	Jiangxi Agricultural University (SAUO)
JAUA	Just Another Useless Answer (SAUS)
JAUCB	Journal of Autism and Childhood Schizophrenia (journ.) (SAUS)
J Audio Eng Soc	Journal of the Audio Engineering Society (SAUO)
J Audio Eng Soc	Journal of the Audio Engineering Society (journ.) (SAUS)
J Audiov Media Med	Journal of Audiovisual Media in Medicine (journ.) (SAUS)
J Aud Res	Journal of Auditory Research (journ.) (SAUS)
JAUEA	Journal of Automotive Engineering (journ.) (SAUS)
JAUMA	Journal. Australasian Universities Modern Language Association (journ.) (SAUS)
JAUMLA	Journal of the Australasian Universities Modern Language Association (SAUO)
JAUMLA	Journal of the Australasian Universities Modern Language Association (journ.) (SAUS)
JAUMS	Journal. Australian Mathematical Society (journ.) (SAUS)
JAUN	Jaundice [*Medicine*]
JAUND	Jaundice [*Medicine*]
JAUNT	Jefferson Area United Transportation (SAUO)
JAURA	Journal of Auditory Research (journ.) (SAUS)
J Aus Mat B	Journal. Australian Mathematical Society. Series B. Applied Mathematics (journ.) (SAUS)
J Aus Math A	Journal. Australian Mathematical Society. Series A. Pure Mathematics and Statistics (journ.) (SAUS)
J Aust Cath Hist S	Journal. Australian Catholic Historical Society (journ.) (SAUS)
J Aust Ceram Soc	Journal of the Australian Ceramic Society (SAUO)
J Aust Ceram Soc	Journal of the Australian Ceramics Society (journ.) (SAUS)
J Aust Coll Speech Ther	Journal. Australian College of Speech Therapists (journ.) (SAUS)
J Aust Entomol Soc	Journal of the Australian Entomological Society (SAUO)

J Aust Entomol Soc	Journal of the Australian Entomological Society (journ.) (SAUS)
J Aust Inst Agric Sci	Journal of the Australian Institute of Agricultural Science (SAUO)
J Aust Inst Agric Sci	Journal of the Australian Institute of Agricultural Science (journ.) (SAUS)
J Aust Inst Metals	Journal of the Australian Institute of Metals (SAUO)
J Aust Inst Metals	Journal of the Australian Institute of Metals (journ.) (SAUS)
J Aust Inst Surg Dent Tech	Journal. Australian Institute of Surgical and Dental Technicians (journ.) (SAUS)
J Aust Math Soc	Journal. Australian Mathematical Society (journ.) (SAUS)
J Aust Planning Inst	Journal. Australian Planning Institute (journ.) (SAUS)
J Aust Polit Econ	Journal of Australian Political Economy (journ.) (SAUS)
J Austral Math Soc Ser A	Journal. Australian Mathematical Society. Series A. Pure Mathematics and Statistics (journ.) (SAUS)
J Austral Math Soc Ser B	Journal. Australian Mathematical Society. Series B. Applied Mathematics (journ.) (SAUS)
J Austronesian Stud	Journal of Austronesian Studies (journ.) (SAUS)
J Aust Stud	Journal of Australian Studies [*A publication*]
J Aust Stud	Journal of Australian Studies (journ.) (SAUS)
J Aus War M	Journal. Australian War Memorial [*A publication*]
J Aus War M	Journal. Australian War Memorial (journ.) (SAUS)
J Autoimmun	Journal of Autoimmunity (journ.) (SAUS)
J Autom Chem	Journal of Automatic Chemistry (journ.) (SAUS)
J Automot Eng	Journal of Automotive Engineering (journ.) (SAUS)
J Autom Reasoning	Journal of Automated Reasoning (journ.) (SAUS)
J Auton Nerv Syst	Journal of the Autonomic Nervous System (journ.) (SAUS)
J Auton Pharmacol	Journal of Autonomic Pharmacology (journ.) (SAUS)
JAUW	Japanese Association of Unversity Women (BUAC)
JAV	Chicago, IL [*Location identifier*] [*FAA*] (FAAL)
JAV	Dr. William M. Scholl College of Podiatric Medicine, Chicago, IL [*OCLC symbol*] (OCLC)
JAV	Janes Aviation Ltd. [*British*] [*ICAO designator*] (FAAC)
JAV	Java
Jav	Javanese (DIAR)
jav	Javanese [*MARC language code*] [*Library of Congress*] (LCCP)
Jav	Javolenus Priscus [*Flourished, 60-120*] [*Authority cited in pre-1607 legal work*] (DSA)
JAV	Job Analysis Vocabulary (OICC)
JAVA	Jamaica Association of Villas and Apartments [*Later, JRJ*]
JAVA	Jamming Amplitude Versus Azimuth (NVT)
JAVA	Jandel Video Analysis System
JAV/A	Journal. South African Veterinary Association (journ.) (SAUS)
JAVAC	Java Compiler (VLIE)
JavaCt	Java Centrale, Inc. [*Associated Press*] (SAG)
JavaCtrl	Java Centrale, Inc. [*Associated Press*] (SAG)
JAVADS	Journal. American Venereal Disease Association (journ.) (SAUS)
JAVAOS	Java Operating System (SAUS)
JAVC	Java Centrale [*NASDAQ symbol*] (TTSB)
JAVC	Java Centrale, Inc. [*NASDAQ symbol*] (SAG)
JAVCF	Japan Australia Venture Capital Fund
JAVEA	Japan Audio-Visual Education Association (SAUO)
Javelin	Javelin Systems, Inc. [*Associated Press*] (SAG)
JAVHS	Jane Addams Vocational High School (SAUO)
JAVI	Javelin International Ltd. (SAUO)
J Avian Biol	Journal of Avian Biology (SAUO)
J Aviat Hist S Aust	Aviation Historical Society of Australia, Journal (journ.) (SAUS)
J Aviation Med	Journal of Aviation Medicine (journ.) (SAUS)
JAVIC	Japan Audio-Visual Information Centre (BUAC)
JAVLX	Janus Twenty Fund [*Mutual fund ticker symbol*] (SG)
JAVMA	Journal of American Veterinary Medical Association [*A publication*] (GVA)
Javole	Javolenus Priscus [*Flourished, 60-120*] [*Authority cited in pre-1607 legal work*] (DSA)
JAVR	Jewish Audio-Visual Review (journ.) (SAUS)
JAVRAJ	Journal. American Veterinary Radiology Society (journ.) (SAUS)
JAVS	Josephson Array Voltage Standards (VLIE)
JAVS	JOVIAL Automated Verification System (MCD)
JAVTX	Janus Venture Fund [*Mutual fund ticker symbol*] (SG)
JAW	Jamahiriya Airways [*Libya*] [*ICAO designator*] (FAAC)
JAW	Standard Oil Co. (Indiana), Central Research Library, Naperville, IL [*OCLC symbol*] (OCLC)
JAWA	Janes All the World Aircraft (SAUS)
JAWAA7	Journal of Agriculture of Western Australia (journ.) (SAUS)
JAWC	Joint Animal Welfare Council (BUAC)
JAWF	Jet Augmented Wing Flap
JAWF	Joint Agriculture Weather Facility [*Marine science*] (OSRA)
JAWG	Joint Airmiss Working Group (BUAC)
JAWG	Joint Atomic Demolition Munitions Working Group (SAUO)
JAWOP	Joint Automated Weather Observation Program (ACAE)
JAWOP	Joint Automated Weather Observing (or Observation) Program (SAUO)
JAWPB	Joint Atomic Weapons Publications Board (AABC)
JAWPM	Joint Atomic Weapons Planning Manual (AFM)
JAWPS	Joint Atomic Weapons Publication System
JAWRFS	Journal of Agriculture and Water Resources Research (journ.) (SAUS)
JAWS	Jamming and Warning System (MCD)
JAWS	Japan Animal Welfare Society [*London, England*]
JAWS	Jet Advance Warning System (PDAA)
JAWS	Joint AAR Warfighting System
JAWS	Joint Action for Water Services (BUAC)
JAWS	Joint Air Force Systems Command War Game System (SAUO)

JAWS........... Joint Airport Weather Studies [*National Center for Atmospheric Research*]
JAWS........... Joint All Weather Seeker (ACAE)
JAWS........... Joint Arctic Weather Stations [*Canada-US*]
JAWS........... Joint Attack Weapon System [*Military*] (MCD)
JAWS........... Josephson AttoWeber Switch [*Data processor circuitry*]
JAWS........... Junk Acronyms When Speaking [*Program*]
JAWS........... Just Another Windows Shell (SAUS)
JAWS........... Just Another Work Station [*Jargon*] (NITA)
JAWSAT...... Joint Air Force-Weber State College Satellite (SAUO)
JAWTR........ Junior Assistant Writer [*British military*] (DMA)
JAWWA....... Journal. American Water Works Association (journ.) (SAUS)
JAWWAS...... American Water Works Association (SAUO)
JAWYS........ Join Airways (FAAC)
JAX............. Chicago School of Professional Psychology, Chicago, IL [*OCLC symbol*] (OCLC)
JAX............. Jacksonville [*Florida*] [*Airport symbol*] (OAG)
JAX............. J. Alexander's Corp. [*NYSE symbol*] (SG)
JAX............. JanAir, Inc. [*ICAO designator*] (FAAC)
JAX............. Mister Jax Fashions, Inc. [*Toronto Stock Exchange symbol*]
JAY............. J & J Air Charters Ltd. [*British*] [*ICAO designator*] (FAAC)
JAY............. Jayapura [*Indonesia*] [*Seismograph station code, US Geological Survey*] (SEIS)
JAY............. Journal of Applied Psychology (journ.) (SAUS)
JAy.............. Travenol Laboratories, Monon Grove (SAUS)
JAY............. Travenol Laboratories, Morton Grove, IL [*OCLC symbol*] (OCLC)
JAYA........... Jayark Corp. [*NASDAQ symbol*] (NQ)
Jayark........ Jayark Corp. [*Associated Press*] (SAG)
JAYCEES..... Junior Chamber of Commerce (ADWA)
JAYF........... Jersey Association of Youth and Friendship (SAUO)
Jayhwk........ Jayhawk Acceptance Corp. [*Associated Press*] (SAG)
JAYJ........... Jay Jacobs [*NASDAQ symbol*] (TTSB)
JAYJ........... Jay Jacobs, Inc. [*NASDAQ symbol*] (NQ)
JAYT........... Jacobs [*Jay*], Inc. (MHDW)
JAZ............. Japan Air Charter Co. Ltd. [*ICAO designator*] (FAAC)
JAZ............. JCC Holding 'A' [*AMEX symbol*] (SG)
JAZODX....... Journal of Advanced Zoology (journ.) (SAUS)
JB............... Bachelor of Laws (SAUS)
JB............... British Caledonian Airways Ltd. (SAUO)
J-B.............. Fr. Jean-Baptiste (SAUS)
JB............... IML Air Services Ltd. [*British*] [*ICAO designator*] (ICDA)
Jb............... Jaarboek [*Yearbook*] [*Netherlands*] (BJA)
JB............... Jahrbuch [*Yearbook*] [*German*]
JB............... James Boswell [*Initials used as pseudonym*]
JB............... James Buchanan [*US president, 1791-1868*]
JB............... Jerusalem Bible
JB............... Jervis Bay (SAUS)
J-B.............. Jet Barrier
JB............... Jet Black [*Derogatory nickname for a black person*]
JB............... Jet Bomb
JB............... Jet powered Bomb (SAUS)
JB............... Jiffy Bag
JB............... Job (MCD)
Jb............... Job [*Old Testament book*]
JB............... Job Bank (OICC)
JB............... Job Blank (SAUS)
JB............... Job Book
JB............... Jodrell Bank (SAUS)
JB............... Joggle Blocks (MCD)
JB............... Johannes Baptista [*John the Baptist*] [*Authority cited in pre-1607 legal work*] (DSA)
JB............... John Bull [*The typical Englishman*]
JB............... Johore Bahru [*Refers to Europeans named after Malaysian towns*] (DSUE)
JB............... Joint Army-Navy Board
JB............... Joint Bond
JB............... Journal of Bacteriology (SAUO)
JB............... Journal of Biochemistry (SAUO)
JB............... Juggle Box
JB............... Jukeboxes [*Public-performance tariff class*] [*British*]
JB............... Jump If Below [*Computer science*] (PCM)
JB............... Jump of Below (SAUS)
JB............... Junction Box [*Technical drawings*]
JB............... Junior Beadle [*Ancient Order of Foresters*]
JB............... Junior Birdman [*Slang*]
JB............... Junior Bookshelf [*A publication*] (BRI)
JB............... Juris Baccalaureus [*Bachelor of Laws*]
JB............... Lakeside Laboratories, Inc. [*Research code symbol*]
JB............... Pioneer Airways [*ICAO designator*] (AD)
JB............... Stetson Hat [*After John Batterson Stetson, 19th-century American hat manufacturer*] [*Slang*]
JBA............. Helijet Airways [*Canada*] [*ICAO designator*] (FAAC)
JBA............. Japan Bankers Association (BUAC)
JBA............. Japan Binoculars Association (SAUO)
JBA............. Japanese Bioindustry Association (BUAC)
JBA............. Jewel Bearing Assembly
JBA............. Jewish Book Annnal (journ.) (SAUS)
JBA............. Job Buffer A (SAUS)
JBA............. John Burroughs Association (EA)
JBA............. Journal. Board of Agriculture (journ.) (SAUS)
JBA............. Journal of Belizean Affairs. Belize City (journ.) (SAUS)
JBA............. Journal of Business Administration (journ.) (SAUS)
JBA............. Junction Box Assembly
JBA............. Junior Bluejackets of America (EA)
JBAA........... Journal. British Archaeological Association (journ.) (SAUS)

JBAA........... Journal of the British Archaeological Association [*A publication*] (WDAA)
JBAA........... Journal of the British Astronomical Association (SAUO)
J BAC......... Journal. International Union of Bricklayers and Allied Craftsmen (journ.) (SAUS)
J Bacteriol... Journal of Bacteriology (SAUO)
JBADC........ Journal of the Bar Association of the District of Columbia (SAUO)
JBAFC........ Jan Berry and the Alohas Fan Club (EA)
JBAK.......... Baker [*J.*], Inc. [*NASDAQ symbol*] (NQ)
JBAKC........ John Brown Anti-Klan Committee (EA)
J Ballist....... Journal of Ballistics (journ.) (SAUS)
J Baltimore Coll Dent Surg... Journal. Baltimore College of Dental Surgery
JBANC........ Joint Baltic American National Committee (EA)
JB&C.......... John Brown and Company (SAUO)
JB&Co........ John Brown and Company (SAUO)
J Band Res... Journal of Band Research (journ.) (SAUS)
J Bangladesh Ad Sci... Journal. Bangladesh Academy of Sciences (journ.) (SAUS)
J Bangladesh Acad Sci... Journal of the Bangladesh Academy of Sciences (journ.) (SAUS)
J Bank Financ... Journal of Banking and Finance (journ.) (SAUS)
J-Bar........... Jet Runway Barrier [*Aviation*] (FAAC)
J Barbados Mus Hist Soc... Journal of the Barbados Museum and Historical Society. Bridgetown (SAUO)
J Barbados Mus Hist Soc... Journal of the Barbados Museum and Historical Society (journ.) (SAUS)
JBAS........... Jussi Bjorling Appreciation Society [*British*] (DBA)
J Basic Clin Physiol Pharmacol... Journal of Basic and Clinical Physiology and Pharmacology (journ.) (SAUS)
J Basic Microbiol... Journal of Basic Microbiology (journ.) (SAUS)
J Basic Sci Hanyng Inst Basic Sci... Journal of Basic Sciences. Hanyang Institute of Basic Science (journ.) (SAUS)
J Bas S........ Journal of Basque Studies (journ.) (SAUS)
JBB............. John Birch Society (SAUO)
JBBF.......... Judo Black Belt Federation [*Later, USJE*]
JBBFC......... James Bond British Fan Club (EAIO)
JBBL.......... Jamming of Beacons and Blind Landing [*Aviation*] (IAA)
JBBMD........ Journal of Biochemical and Biophysical Methods (journ.) (SAUS)
JBC............. Jamaica Broadcasting Corp.
JBC............. Jamaica Broadcasting Corporation (SAUO)
JBC............. Japan Broadcasting Corp. (SAUS)
JBC............. Japan Broadcasting Corporation (SAUO)
JBC............. Japanese Broadcasting Corporation (BUAC)
JBC............. [*The*] Jerome Biblical Commentary [*Englewood Cliffs, NJ*] [*A publication*] (BJA)
JBC............. Jesness Behavior Checklist [*Psychology*] (DAVI)
JBC............. Jewelers' Book Club (EA)
JBC............. Jewish Book Council [*of the National Jewish Welfare Board*] [*Later, JWBJBC*] (EA)
JBC............. Johnson Bible College [*Tennessee*]
JBC............. Joint Blood Council [*Defunct*] (EA)
JBC............. Joint Budget Committee (OICC)
JBC............. Journal of Biological Chemistry (journ.) (SAUS)
JBC............. Journal of Business Communication (journ.) (SAUS)
JBC............. Journal. State Bar of California [*A publication*] (DLA)
JBCA........... Jewish Book Council of America (SAUO)
JBck & L...... Jackson and Lumpkins Reports (journ.) (SAUS)
JBc L Dict.... Jacobs Law Dictionary (journ.) (SAUS)
JBc Lex Mer... Jacobs Lex Mercatoria (journ.) (SAUS)
JBCNS........ Joint Board of Clinical Nursing Studies (SAUS)
JBCNTRL ..... Job Control (SAUS)
JBCOUNT..... Job Account (SAUS)
JBCPS......... Journeyman Bakers' and Confectioners Pension Society [*British*] (BI)
JBCS.......... James Branch Cabell Society (EA)
JBCSA......... Joint British Committee for Stress Analysis (BUAC)
JBCSA......... Journal. British Ceramic Society (journ.) (SAUS)
JBD............. Becton, Dickinson & Co., Paramus, NJ [*OCLC symbol*] (OCLC)
JBD............. James Brake [*Aviation*] (DA)
JBD............. James Brake Decelerometer (SAUS)
JBD............. Jet Blast Deflector
JBD............. Jet Blast Detector (SAUS)
JBD............. Jewish Board of Deputies [*Australia*]
JBD............. Joint Battlefield Digitization (SAUS)
JBDAAFES ... Joint Board of Directors, Army-Air Force Exchange Service (AABC)
JBDFC......... James Bond 007 Fan Club [*Defunct*] (EA)
JBE............. Japanese B Encephalitis [*Medicine*]
JBE............. Journal of Behavioral Economics (journ.) (SAUS)
JBE............. Journal of Business Education (journ.) (SAUS)
JBE............. Jump If Below or Equal [*Computer science*] (PCM)
J Behav Sci... Journal of Behavioral Science (journ.) (SAUS)
J Behav Ther Exp Psychiatry... Journal of Behavior Therapy and Experimental Psychiatry (journ.) (SAUS)
J Beijing Univ Iron Steel Technol... Journal of Beijing University of Iron and Steel Technology (journ.) (SAUS)
Jber............ annual report (SAUS)
Jber............ Jahresbericht [*Journal, Annual Report*] [*German*] (BJA)
J Bergen Cty Dent S... Journal. Betgen County Dental Safety (journ.) (SAUS)
JBES........... Jodrell Bank Experimental Station [*British*]
J Bethune Univ Med Sci... Journal. Bethune Umversity of Medical Sciences (journ.) (SAUS)
JBF............. James Beard Foundation (EA)
JBF............. James Buchanan Foundation (EA)
JBF............. Japan Booksellers' Federation (BUAC)
JBF............. Jeune Ballet de France
JBFC.......... James Bond 007 Fan Club [*British*] (EAIO)

JBFC .... Jennifer Bassey Fan Club (EA)
JBFC .... Jennifer Burnett Fan Club (EA)
JBFC .... Johnny Bernard Fan Club (EA)
JBFCI .... Jon Beryl Fan Club International (EA)
JBFL&P .... Journal of Banking and Finance Law and Practice [A publication]
JBFLP .... Journal of Banking and Finance Law and Practice [A publication]
JBFSAW .... Joint Board on Future Storage of Atomic Weapons
JBG .... Jewish Board of Guardians (EA)
JBG .... Jewish Brigade Group (SAUO)
JBG .... Johannesburg, South Africa Scientology organization (SAUO)
JBHCPIUA .... Journeymen Barbers, Hairdressers, Cosmetologists and Proprietors' International Union of America (EA)
JBHS .... John Bartram High School (SAUO)
JBHS&R ...... Journal of Behavioral Health Services & Research (SAUO)
JBHT .... Hunt(JB)Transport [NASDAQ symbol] (TTSB)
JBHT .... Hunt [J. B.] Transport Services, Inc. [NASDAQ symbol] (NQ)
JBI .... Jacob Blaustein Institute for the Ad- vancement of Human Rights (SAUS)
JBI .... Jacob Blaustein Institute for the Advancement of Human Rights (EA)
JBI .... Jamaica Bauxite Institute (BUAC)
JBI .... James Brake Index (SAUS)
JBI .... Jewish Braille Institute of America (EA)
JBIA .... Jewish Braille Institute of America (EA)
JBIC .... Journal of Biological Inorganic Chemistry [A publication]
JBIG .... Joint Bi-level Group (SAUO)
JBIG .... Joint Bi-Level Image Experts Group (RALS)
JBIG .... Joint Bi-Level Imaging Group (VLIE)
JBIG .... Joint Binary Image Group (VLIE)
J Bihar Agric Coll... Journal. Bihar Agricultural College (journ.) (SAUS)
J Bihar RS... Journal. Bihar Research Society (journ.) (SAUS)
JBIL .... Bildner & Sons Inc. (SAUO)
JBIL .... Jabil Circuit [NASDAQ symbol] (TTSB)
JBIL .... Jabil Circuit, Inc. [NASDAQ symbol] (SAG)
Jb Int R ...... Jahrbuch fuer Internationales und Auslaendisches Oeffentliches Recht [1948-] [A publication] [German] (ILCA)
J Biochem Toxicol... Journal of Biochemical Toxicology (journ.) (SAUS)
J Biocommun... Journal of Biocommunication (journ.) (SAUS)
J Bioelectr... Journal of Bioelectricity (journ.) (SAUS)
J Bioenerg... Journal of Bioenergetics (journ.) (SAUS)
J Bioenerg Biomembr... Journal of Bioenergetics and Biomembranes (journ.) (SAUS)
J Bioeth .... Journal of Bioethics (journ.) (SAUS)
J Biol Board Cn... Journal. Biological Board of Canada (journ.) (SAUS)
J Biol Inorg Chem Soc... Journal of the Biological Inorganic Chemistry Society (SAUO)
J Biol Inorg Chem Soc... Journal of the Biological Inorganic Chemistry Society (journ.) (SAUS)
J Biologicl Ed... Journal of Biological Education (journ.) (SAUS)
J Biol Osaka City Univ... Journal of Biology. Osaka City University (journ.) (SAUS)
J Biol Photogr... Journal of Biological Photography (journ.) (SAUS)
J Biol Photogr Assoc... Journal of the Biological Photographic Association (SAUO)
J Biol Photogr Assoc... Journal of the Biological Photographic Association (journ.) (SAUS)
J Biol Phys... Journal of Biological Physics (journ.) (SAUS)
J Biol Psychol... Journal of Biological Psychology (journ.) (SAUS)
J Biol Regul Homeost Agents... Journal of Biological Regulators and Homeostatic Agents (journ.) (SAUS)
J Biol Sci..... Journal of Biological Sciences (journ.) (SAUS)
J Biol Sci Res Publ... Journal of Biological Sciences Research Publication (journ.) (SAUS)
J Biolumin Chemilumin... Journal of Bioluminescence and Chemiluminescence (journ.) (SAUS)
J Biomater Appl... Journal of Biomaterials Applications (journ.) (SAUS)
J Biomater Sci Polym Ed... Journal of Biomaterials Science, Polymer Edition (journ.) (SAUS)
J Biomech Eng... Journal of Biomechanical Engineering (journ.) (SAUS)
J Biomed Eng... Journal of Biomedical Engineering (journ.) (SAUS)
J Biomed Mater Res... Journal of Biomedical Materials Research (SAUO)
J Biomed Mater Res Biomed Mater Symp... Journal of Biomedical Materials Research. Biomedical Materials Symposium (journ.) (SAUS)
J Biomed Syst... Journal of Biomedical Systems (journ.) (SAUS)
J Biomol NMR... Journal of Biomolecular NMR (journ.) (SAUS)
J Biopharm Stat... Journal of Biopharmaceutical Statistics (journ.) (SAUS)
J Biophys Biochem Cytol... Journal of Biophysical and Biochemical Cytology. (journ.) (SAUS)
J Biophys S Jpn... Journal. Biophysical Society of Japan (journ.) (SAUS)
J Biosoc Sci... Journal of Biosocial Science (journ.) (SAUS)
J Biosoc Sci Suppl... Journal of Biosocial Science. Supplement (journ.) (SAUS)
J Birla Inst Technol Sci... Journal of the Birla Institute of Technology and Science (journ.) (SAUS)
J Birmingham Metall Soc... Journal. Birmingham Metallurgical Society (journ.) (SAUS)
JBIS .... Journal. British Interplanetary Society (journ.) (SAUS)
JBIS .... Journal of Baltic Studies (journ.) (SAUS)
JBIS .... Journal of the British Interplanetary Society (SAUO)
JBIS .... Journal of the British Interplanetary Society (journ.) (SAUS)
JBITD4 .... Journal of Biotechnology (journ.) (SAUS)
JBJ .... Bellum Judaicum [Josephus] [Classical studies] (BJA)
JBJ .... James Bond Journalism [Term coined by leader Sinnathamby Bajaratman of Singapore and referring to Western journalism]
JBJS .... Journal of Bone and Joint Surgery (SAUO)
JBJS .... Journal of Bone and Joint Surgery (journ.) (SAUS)
JBK .... Berkeley, CA [Location identifier] [FAA] (FAAL)
JBK .... Journal of Banking and Finance (journ.) (SAUS)
JBL .... Jabil Circuit [NYSE symbol] (SG)

JBL .... James B. Lansing Sound, Inc.
JBL .... Jonesboro, LA [Location identifier] [FAA] (FAAL)
JBL .... Journal of Biblical Literature [A publication] (BRI)
JBL .... Journal of Business Law [A publication]
JBL .... Jubilee
JBL .... Junior Bird League [British] (BI)
JB Lit Today... Japanese Literature Today (journ.) (SAUS)
J/BLK .... Junction Block [Automotive engineering]
JBLMS .... Journal of Biblical Literature. Monog- raph Series (journ.) (SAUS)
J Bl St .... Journal of Black Studies [A publication] (BRI)
JBM .... Jan Bell Marketing [AMEX symbol] (TTSB)
JBM .... Jan Bell Marketing, Inc. [AMEX symbol] (SPSG)
JBMA .... John Burroughs Memorial Association (EA)
JBMBB .... Journal of Biochemistry, Molecular Biology and Biophysics (SAUO)
JBMBB .... Journal of Biochemistry, Molecular Biology and Biophysics (journ.) (SAUS)
JBMI .... Journalist Biographies Master Index [A publication]
JBMMA .... Japan Business Machine Makers Association (SAUS)
JBMMA .... Japanese Business Machine Makers Association (SAUS)
JB MoU....... Joint Ballistic MoU (SAUS)
JBMTO .... Joint Bus Military Traffic Office (AABC)
JBN .... Judaica Book News (journ.) (SAUS)
JBNC .... Jefferson Bancorp (FL) [NASDAQ symbol] (TTSB)
JBNC .... Jefferson Bancorp, Inc. [NASDAQ symbol] (NQ)
JBNK .... Jefferson Bankshares, Inc. [NASDAQ symbol] (NQ)
JBNQA .... James Bay and Northern Quebec Agreement (SAUS)
JBNSA .... Journal. British Nuclear Energy Society (journ.) (SAUS)
JBO .... Journal of Behavioral Optometry (SAUO)
JBO .... Journal of Economic Behavior and Organization (journ.) (SAUS)
jbo .... Jumbo
J Board Dir Am S Civ Eng... Journal. Board of Direction. American Society of Civil Engineers (journ.) (SAUS)
J Board Greenkeeping Res... Journal. Board of Greenkeeping Research (journ.) (SAUS)
JBOD .... Just a Bunch of Disks [Computer science]
JBOH .... Oxford [J. B.] Oxford Holdings [NASDAQ symbol] (SAG)
J-bolt .... Capital-J-shaped bolt
J Bombay Nat Hist Soc... Journal. Bombay Natural History Society (journ.) (SAUS)
J Bone-Am V... Journal of Bone and Joint Surgery. American Volume (journ.) (SAUS)
J Bone-Br V... Journal of Bone and Joint Surgery. British Volume (journ.) (SAUS)
J Bone Joint Surg... Journal of Bone and Joint Surgery (journ.) (SAUS)
J Bone Miner Res... Journal of Bone and Mineral Research (journ.) (SAUS)
JBOR .... Job Bank Operations Review [Employment and Training Administration] [Department of Labor]
J Borderl Stud... Journal of Borderlands Studies (journ.) (SAUS)
JBORS .... Journal. Bihar and Orissa Research Society (journ.) (SAUS)
JBORS .... Journal of the Bihar and Orissa Research Society (SAUO)
JBORS .... Journal of the Bihar and Orissa Research Society (journ.) (SAUS)
JBOS........... Job Banks Opening Summary [Department of Labor]
J Boston S Civ Eng Sect ASCE... Journal. Boston Society of Civil Engineers Section. American Society of Civil Engineers (journ.) (SAUS)
J Boston Soc Civ Eng... Journal. Boston Society of Civil Engineers (journ.) (SAUS)
J Bot Br Foreign... Journal of Botany. British and Foreign (journ.) (SAUS)
J Bot Soc S Afr... Journal. Botanical Society of South Africa (journ.) (SAUS)
J Bot UAR.... Journal of Botany. United Arab Republic (journ.) (SAUS)
J Bowman Grsy Scb Med Wake For Coll... Journal. Bowman Gray School of Medicine. Wake Forest College (journ.) (SAUS)
J-box .... J-shaped bleaching box (SAUS)
JB Oxfrd ...... JB Oxford Holdings [Associated Press] (SAG)
JBP .... Jettison Booster Package [NASA]
JBP .... Jewel Bearing Program (SAUS)
JBP .... John B. Piera Foundation Laboratory (SAUO)
JBP .... John B. Pierce Foundation Laboratory [New Haven, CT]
JBP .... Joint Blood Program (COE)
JBP .... Junior Bowhunter Program (EA)
JBPA .... Japan Book Publishers (SAUS)
JBPA .... Japan Book Publishers Association (BUAC)
JBPAA .... Journal. Biological Photographic Association (journ.) (SAUS)
JBPI .... Japanese Bicycle Promotion Institute (SAUO)
JBPI .... Journal of Biological Physics (journ.) (SAUS)
JBPO .... Joint Blood Program Office (DOMA)
JBPS .... Jamaica Banana Producers Steamship (SAUO)
JBPVE .... Joint Board for Pre-Vocational Education (BUAC)
JBR .... Job Air Ltd. [Czechoslovakia] [FAA designator] (FAAC)
JBR .... Jonesboro [Arkansas] [Airport symbol] (OAG)
JBR .... Jonesboro, AR [Location identifier] [FAA] (FAAL)
JBR .... Journal of Bible and Religion (journ.) (SAUS)
JBR .... Journal of Biological Rhythms (SAUS)
J BRANNAM... Just Brand Names [Division of F. W. Woolworth Co.]
JBRAS .... Journal of Bombay Branch of the Royal Asiatic Society (journ.) (SAUS)
J Br Astron Assoc... Journal. British Astronomical Association (journ.) (SAUS)
J Br Astron Assoc... Journal of the British Astronomical Association (journ.) (SAUS)
J Br Boot Shoe Instn... Journal. British Boot and Shoe Institution (journ.) (SAUS)
J Br Dent Assoc... Journal. British Dental Association (journ.) (SAUS)
J Br Endod Soc... Journal. British Endodontic Society (journ.) (SAUS)
J Brew Soc Jpn... Journal. Brewing Society of Japan (journ.) (SAUS)
J Br Fire Serv Ass... Journal. British Fire Services Association (journ.) (SAUS)
J Br Grassl Soc... Journal of the British Grassland Society (SAUO)
J Br Inst Radio Eng... Journal. British Institution of Radio Engineers (journ.) (SAUS)
J Brit Archaeol Ass 3 Ser... Journal. British Archaeological Association. Series 3 (journ.) (SAUS)
J Brit Ceram Soc... Journal. British Ceramic Society (journ.) (SAUS)
J Brit Interplanet S... Journal. British Interplanetary Society (journ.) (SAUS)

JBrit IRE...... Journal of the British Institute of Radio Engineers (SAUO)
J Brit Ship Res Ass... Journal. British Ship Research Association (journ.) (SAUS)
J Brit Soc Phenomenol... Journal. British Society for Phenomenology (journ.)
    (SAUS)
JBRM.......... Journal of Biological Response Modifiers (journ.) (SAUS)
J Br Nucl Energy Soc... Journal of the British Nuclear Energy Society (SAUO)
J Br Nucl Energy Soc... Journal of the British Nuclear Energy Society (journ.)
    (SAUS)
J Broadcst... Journal of Broadcasting and Electronic Media [A publication] (BRI)
J Bromeliad Soc... Journal. Bromeliad Society (journ.) (SAUS)
JBRS.......... Journal. Burma Research Society (journ.) (SAUS)
JBRS.......... Journal of the Burma Research Society (SAUO)
JBRS.......... Journal of the Burma Research Society (journ.) (SAUS)
J Br S Ph..... Journal. British Society for Phenomenology (journ.) (SAUS)
J Br Waterworks As... Journal. British Waterworks Association (journ.) (SAUS)
J Br Waterworks Assoc... Journal of the British Waterworks Association (SAUO)
J Br Wood Preserv Ass... Journal. British Wood Preserving Association (journ.)
    (SAUS)
J Bryol......... Journal of Bryology (journ.) (SAUS)
JBS.............. Jagdbomberfliegerstaffel (SAUO)
JBS.............. Jamaican Bureau of Standards (SAUS)
JBS.............. Jane Badler Society (EA)
JBS.............. Japan British Society (SAUO)
JBS.............. Japan Broadcasting System (SAUO)
JBS.............. Japanese Biochemical Society (BUAC)
JBS.............. Japanese Broadcast Satellite (SAUS)
JBS.............. Jewish Burial Society [Australia]
JBS.............. Job Search [Job Training and Partnership Act] (OICC)
JBS.............. John Birch Society (EA)
JBS.............. Joly Black Screen
JBS.............. Josephine Butler Society (EAIO)
JBS.............. Journal of Biopharmaceutical Statistics (SAUO)
JBS.............. Journal of Black Studies [A publication] (ANEX)
JBS.............. Journal of British Studies (journ.) (SAUS)
JBS.............. Journal of Business Research (journ.) (SAUS)
JBS.............. Journal of Byelorussian Studies (journ.) (SAUS)
JBSDD6....... Journal of Biomolecular Structure and Dynamics (journ.) (SAUS)
JBSRES....... Journal of Biological Sciences Research (journ.) (SAUS)
JBSS.......... Sanfilippo [John B.] & Son [NASDAQ symbol] (SPSG)
JBSTD......... Journal of Biological Standardization (journ.) (SAUS)
JB St Univ ... John B. Stetson University (SAUO)
JBSW.......... Joseph Bulova School of Watchmaking (SAUO)
JBT............. Bethel, AK [Location identifier] [FAA] (FAAL)
JBT............. Jewelers Board of Trade (EA)
JBTS.......... Journal of the Buddhist Text Society (SAUO)
JBTS.......... Journal of the Buddhist Text Society (journ.) (SAUS)
JBU............. John Brown University [Siloam Springs, AR]
JBUA.......... Journal. Bombay University. Arts (journ.) (SAUS)
JB Univ ...... John Brown University (SAUO)
J Bus.......... Journal of Business. University of Chicago (SAUO)
J Busan Med Coll... Journal. Busan Medical College (journ.) (SAUS)
JBUSDC...... Joint Brazil-United States Defense Commission [Terminated, 1977]
J Bus Ethics... Journal of Business Ethics (journ.) (SAUS)
JBUSMC...... Joint Brazil-United States Military Commission
JBUSMC...... Joint Brazil-US Military Commission (SAUS)
J Bus Strategy... Journal of Business Strategy (journ.) (SAUS)
JBV............. Jolt Beverage Co. Ltd. [Vancouver Stock Exchange symbol]
JBYC.......... Jamaica Bay Yacht Club (SAUO)
JC .... All Seasons Aviation Ltd. (SAUO)
JC .... Community Colleges [Educational Resources Information Center
    (ERIC) Clearinghouse] [University of California at Los Angeles
    (UCLA)] (PAZ)
JC .... Jack Connection [Electronics] (IAA)
JC .... Jack Cover
JC .... Jacket Crown (MELL)
JC .... Jackson College (SAUO)
JC .... Jacksonville College (SAUO)
JC .... Jakob-Creutzfeldt [Disease or syndrome] [Neurology] (DAVI)
JC .... Jam Contact (SAUS)
JC .... Jamestown College (SAUO)
JC .... Janitor Closet (MSA)
JC .... Jayhawk Conference (PSS)
JC .... J. C. Smith Marketing Corp. [Vancouver Stock Exchange symbol]
JC .... Jeanswear Communication (EA)
JC .... Jefferson City [Diocesan abbreviation] [Missouri] (TOCD)
JC .... Jefferson College (SAUS)
JC .... Jenny Craig [NYSE symbol] (SPSG)
JC .... Jersey Central Railroad
JC .... Jersey City (SAUO)
JC .... Jesus Christ
JC .... Jesus College [Oxford or Cambridge] [England] (DAS)
JC .... Jet Club (SAUO)
JC .... Jewelcor, Inc. (SAUO)
JC .... Jewish Care [British] (EAIO)
JC .... [The] Jewish Community: Its History and Structure to the American
    Revolution [A publication] (BJA)
JC .... Jimmy Carter [James Earl Carter, Jr.] [US president, 1924-]
JC .... Job Card
JC .... Job Center
JC .... Job Club
JC .... Job Control (VLIE)
JC .... Job Corps [Department of Labor]
JC .... Jockey Club [Later, TJC] (EA)
JC .... Johannesburg Consolidated (SAUS)
JC .... Johnson Controls, Inc. (SAUO)

JC.............. Johnson Counter (SAUS)
JC.............. Johnson's New York Cases [or Reports] [A publication] (DLA)
JC.............. Johnstown College (SAUO)
JC.............. Joint Commission (SAUS)
JC.............. Joint Committee (SAUO)
JC.............. Joint Communications (ELAL)
JC.............. Joint Compound [Plumbing]
JC.............. Joint Conference (SAUS)
JC.............. Joint Contracture [Medicine] (MELL)
JC.............. Joist Chair (SAUS)
JC.............. Joliet College (SAUO)
JC.............. Joule Cycle [Physics]
J/C............. Joule per Coulomb [Physics] (DAVI)
JC.............. Journal Citation (NITA)
JC.............. Journal Code [Online database field identifier]
JC.............. Journal Coden [Searchable fields] (NITA)
JC.............. Journalists' Club [Australia]
JC.............. Journal of Chromatography [A publication]
JC.............. Journal of Communication [A publication] (BRI)
JC.............. JOVIAL Compiler [Computer science]
JC.............. Judicial Council (SAUO)
JC.............. Judson College (SAUO)
Jc.............. Juglans cinerea [Butternut tree]
JC.............. Juice
jc.............. Juice
JC.............. Julius Caesar [Shakespearean work]
JC.............. Jump Command (SAUS)
JC.............. Jump Condition (VLIE)
JC.............. Jump if Carry set (SAUO)
JC.............. Jump on Carry (SAUS)
JC.............. Jump on Condition [Computer science] (BUR)
JC.............. Jump-to-Contact [Physics]
JC.............. Junction (ADA)
JC.............. Junction Center [Civil engineering] (IAA)
JC.............. Juniata College (SAUO)
JC.............. Junior Chamber (SAUO)
JC.............. Junior Chamber of Commerce (WDAA)
JC.............. Junior Clinicians [Medical students] (DAVI)
JC.............. Junior College
JC.............. Jurisconsult
JC.............. Just Compensation [Business term] (MHDB)
JC.............. Justice Clerk
JC.............. Justiciary Case (SAUS)
JC.............. Justiciary Cases [Scotland] [A publication] (DLA)
JC.............. Juvenile Cataract (MELL)
JC.............. Juvenile Corps (SAUO)
JC.............. Juvenile Coupled Radioactivity (SAUS)
JC.............. Juvenile Court
JC.............. Rocky Mountain Airways [ICAO designator] (AD)
JC2WC....... Joint Command and Control Warfare Center (SAUS)
JC3CM....... Joint Command, Control and Communications Countermeasures
    (SAUO)
JC3SOC...... Joint C3 Staff And Operations Course (SAUO)
JCA............. Jamming Control Authority (NATG)
JCA............. Japan Container Association (BUAC)
JCA............. Javelin Class Association (EA)
JCA............. Jetcom SA [Switzerland] [ICAO designator] (FAAC)
JCA............. Jewelry Crafts Association [Later, JMA]
JCA............. Jewish Ceremonial Art [A publication] (BJA)
JCA............. Jewish Colonization Association [British]
JCA............. Job Communication Area (TIMI)
JCA............. Job Control Administrator (SAUS)
JCA............. Job Control Area (TIMI)
JCA............. Johnston(e) Clan in America (EA)
JCA............. Johore Consumers Association (SAUO)
JCA............. Joint Church Aid [Biafra relief program in late 1960's] [Defunct]
JCA............. Joint Commission on Accreditation (SAUS)
JCA............. Joint Commission on Accreditation of Universities [Military]
JCA............. Joint Communication Activity
JCA............. Joint Communications Agency [Military]
JCA............. Joint Construction Agency
JCA............. Joint Cooperative Agreement (SAUO)
JCA............. Joint Countermine Application [Military]
JCA............. Joint Cultural Appeal (EA)
JCA............. Joint Custody Association (EA)
JCA............. Journal of Clinical Anesthesia (SAUO)
JCA............. Journal of Color and Appearance (journ.) (SAUS)
JCA............. Junior Catering Accountant [British military] (DMA)
JCA............. Junior College of Albany (SAUO)
JCA............. Juvenile Chronic Arthritis [Medicine] (DAVI)
JCAA.......... Japanese Civil Aviation Authority (SAUO)
JCAAD........ Joint Counter Air/Air Defense (SAUO)
JCAAI......... Joint Council of Allergy, Asthma, and Immunology (NTPA)
JCAB.......... Japan Civil Aviation Bureau (MCD)
JCAB.......... Japanese Civil Aviation Bureau (SAUS)
JCAC.......... Joint Civil Affairs Committee
JCACC........ Joint Combat Airspace Command and Control Course (DOMA)
JCACDM..... Journal of Carbohydrate Chemistry (journ.) (SAUS)
JCAD.......... Joint Committee on Agricultural Research and Development (SAUO)
JCADIS ...... Joint Continental Aerospace Defense Integration Staff [Military]
    (AABC)
JCADM....... Joint Committee on Antarctic Data Management (SAUO)
JCADR........ Japan Centre for Area Development (BUAC)
JCAE.......... Joint Committee on Atomic Energy [of the US Congress]
    [Terminated]

JCAEC......... Joint Congressional Atomic Energy Commission (MUGU)
JCAEC......... Joint Congressional Atomic Energy Committee (SAUO)
JCAESSL...... Joint Council of the Associated Engineering Societies of St. Louis (SAUO)
JCAFB......... James Connally Air Force Base (SAUO)
JCAH......... Joint Commission for/on Accreditation of Hospitals (SAUO)
JCAH......... Joint Commission on Accreditation of Hospitals [*Later, JCAHO*] (EA)
JCAH......... Joint Committee on Accreditation of Hospitals (SAUS)
JCAHCA...... Joint Commission on Accreditation of Health Care Organizations
JCAHO......... Joint Commission on Accreditation of Healthcare Organizations [*An association*]
JCAHPO...... Joint Commission on Allied Health in Ophthalmology (SAUS)
JCAHPO...... Joint Commission on Allied Health Personnel in Ophthalmology (EA)
JCAHPO...... Joint Committee on Allied Health Personnel in Ophthalmology (SAUO)
JCAI......... Joint Council of Allergy and Immunology (EA)
J Calif Dent Assoc... Journal. California Dental Association (journ.) (SAUS)
J Calif Hortic Soc... Journal. California Horticultural Society (journ.) (SAUS)
J CalifState Dent Ass... Journal. California State Dental Association (journ.) (SAUS)
J Calif State Dent Assoc... Journal of the California State Dental Association (SAUO)
J Calif State Dent Assoc... Journal of the California State Dental Association (journ.) (SAUS)
JCALM......... Joint Committee on Aboriginal Lands and Mining [*Australia*]
JCALS......... Joint Computer-Aided Acquisition and Logistic Support [*DoD*]
JCALS......... Joint Computer Aided Acquisition and Logistic Support System (SAUO)
JCALS......... Joint Computer-Aided Acquisition Logistics System [*Army*] (RDA)
JCALS......... Joint Computer-Aided Logistics System (SAUS)
JCAM......... Joint Commission on Atomic Masses
J Camborne Sch Mines... Journal. Camborne School of Mines (journ.) (SAUS)
JCAN........... Jewish Children's Adoption Network (EA)
J Can Art Hist... Journal of Canadian Art History (journ.) (SAUS)
J Can Assoc Radiol... Journal. Canadian Association of Radiologists (journ.) (SAUS)
J Can Ath Ther Assoc... Journal. Canadian Athletic Therapists Association (journ.) (SAUS)
J Can B........ Juris Canna Baccalaureus [*Bachelor of Canon Law*]
J Can Ceram Soc... Journal. Canadian Ceramic Society (journ.) (SAUS)
J Can Ceram Soc... Journal of the Canadian Ceramic Society (SAUO)
J Can Ceram Soc... Journal of the Canadian Ceramic Society (journ.) (SAUS)
J Cancer Educ... Journal of Cancer Education (journ.) (SAUS)
J Cancer Res... Journal of Cancer Research (journ.) (SAUS)
J Cancer Res Clin Oncol... Journal of Cancer Research and Clinical Oncology (journ.) (SAUS)
J Cancer Res Comm... Journal. Cancer Research Committee. University of Sydney [*A publication*]
J Can Ch H... Journal Canadian Church Historical Society (journ.) (SAUS)
J Can Chiro Ass... Journal. Canadian Chiropractic Associa- tion (journ.) (SAUS)
J Can D....... Juris Canna Doctor [*Doctor of Canon Law*]
JC & ED....... Journal of Chemical and Engineering Data (journ.) (SAUS)
J Can Dent Assoc... Journal of the Canadian Dental Association (SAUO)
J Can Dent Assoc... Journal of the Canadian Dental Association (journ.) (SAUS)
J Can Inst Food Sci Technol... Journal. Canadian Institute of Food Science and Technology (journ.) (SAUS)
J Can M....... Juris Canna Magister [*Master of Canon Law*]
J Can Min Inst... Journal. Canadian Mining Institute (journ.) (SAUS)
J Can S Forensic Sci... Journal. Canadian Society of Forensic Science (journ.) (SAUS)
J Cant Bot Soc... Journal. Canterbury Botanical Society (journ.) (SAUS)
JCAP........... Joint Committee on Aviation Pathology (BUAC)
JCAP........... Joint Conventional Ammunition Panel (SAUO)
JCAP........... Joint Conventional Ammunition Program [*Army*]
JCAP........... Joint Coordinated Ammunition Production (MCD)
JCAP........... Journal of Child and Adolescent Psychopharmacology (SAUO)
JCAP........... Journal of Child and Adolescent Psychotherapy (SAUO)
JCAP-CG...... Joint Conventional Ammunition Program Coordinating Group [*Army*]
J Cap Inst Med... Journal Capital Institute of Medicine (journ.) (SAUS)
J Cap Mgmt... Journal of Capacity Management (journ.) (SAUS)
JCAPN........ Journal of Child and Adolescent Psychiatric Nursing (SAUO)
JCAPN........ Journal of Child and Adolescent Psychiatric Nursing (journ.) (SAUS)
JCAR........... Joint Commission on Applied Radioactivity
JCARA........ Journal. Canadian Association of Radiologists (journ.) (SAUS)
J card......... Jacket Card [*A printed card inside the box holding a cassette tape or compact disc*] (WDMC)
JCARD......... Joint Committee on Agricultural Research and Development [*Agency for International Development*]
J Cardciogr... Journal of Cardiography (journ.) (SAUS)
J Cardiol...... Journal of Cardiology (journ.) (SAUS)
J Cardiol Suppl... Journal of Cardiology. Supplement (journ.) (SAUS)
J Cardiothorac Vasc Anesth... Journal of Cardiothoracic and Vascular Anesthesics (journ.) (SAUS)
J Cardiovasc Electrophysiol... Journal of Cardiovascular Electrophysiology (journ.) (SAUS)
J Cardiovasc Med... Journal of Cardiovascular Medicine (journ.) (SAUS)
J Cardiovasc Nurs... Journal of Cardiovascular Nursing (journ.) (SAUS)
J Cardiovasc Pharmacol... Journal of Cardiovascular Pharmacology (journ.) (SAUS)
J Cardiovasc Risk... Journal of Cardiovascular Risk (journ.) (SAUS)
J Cardiovasc Ultrason... Journal of Cardiovascular Ultrasonography (journ.) (SAUS)
J Cardpulm Rehabil... Journal of Cardiopulmonary Rehabilitation (journ.) (SAUS)
J Card Surg... Journal of Cardiac Surgery (journ.) (SAUS)
J Car Ed...... Journal of Career Education (journ.) (SAUS)
J Caribb Hist... Journal of Caribbean History. St. Lawrence (journ.) (SAUS)
J Caribb Stud... Journal of Caribbean Studies (journ.) (SAUS)
JCarlFut...... Jack Carl/312 Futures, Inc. [*Associated Press*] (SAG)

J Car P & E... Journal of Career Planning and Employment [*A publication*] (BRI)
J Cars......... Designation for certain General Motors frontwheel-drive cars (SAUS)
JCASR......... Joint Committee on Avionic Systems Research (SAUS)
JCAT........... Joint Crisis Action Team [*Environmental science*] (COE)
JCAT........... Journal of Computer Assisted Tomography (SAUO)
J Catal........ Journal of Catalysis (MEC)
J Cat & Class... Journal of Cataloging and Classification (journ.) (SAUS)
J Cataract Refract Surg... Journal of Cataract and Refractive Surgery (journ.) (SAUS)
J-CATCH...... Joint Countering Attack Helicopter Exercises (RDA)
JCATD......... Journal of Computer Assisted Tomography (journ.) (SAUS)
J Cathol Med Coll... Journal. Catholic Medical College (journ.) (SAUS)
J Cathol Nurses Guild Engl Wales... Journal. Catholic Nurses Guild of England and Wales (journ.) (SAUS)
JCATS......... Journal of the Centre of Advanced Television Studies (journ.) (SAUS)
JCAUDB...... Journal of Cardiovascular Ultrasonography (journ.) (SAUS)
JCA-USA...... Joint Church Aid - United States of America [*See also JCA*] [*Defunct*] (EA)
JCB........... Bachelor of Canon Law (SAUS)
JCB........... Bachelor of Civil Law (SAUS)
JCB........... Japan California Bank (SAUO)
JCB........... Japan Convention Bureau (EA)
JCB........... Japan Credit Bank (SAUO)
JCB........... J. C. Bamford Excavators [*British*]
JCB........... Joacaba [*Brazil*] [*Airport symbol*] (AD)
JCB........... Job Control Block [*Computer science*] (BUR)
JCB........... Joint Coal Board (BUAC)
JCB........... Joint Communications Board
JCB........... Joint Computer Bureau [*Office of Population Census and Surveys*] [*British*]
JCB........... Joint Consultative Board [*NATO*] (NATG)
JCB........... Joint Coordinating Board (SAUO)
JCB........... Joseph Cyril Bamford (WDAA)
JCB........... Journal of Cell Biology (journ.) (SAUS)
JCB........... Journal of Cellular Biochemistry (journ.) (SAUS)
JCB........... Journal of Creative Behavior (journ.) (SAUS)
JCB........... Junior College of Business (ACAE)
JCB........... Juris Canonici Baccalaureus [*Bachelor of Canon Law*]
JCB........... Juris Civilis Baccalaureus [*Bachelor of Civil Law*]
JCB........... Justification Control Bit (SAUS)
JCBA........... Jewish Conciliation Board of America (EA)
JCBADL........ Biomedical Applications (journ.) (SAUS)
J Cbangchun Univ Earth Sci... Journal. Changchun University of Earth Science (journ.) (SAUS)
JCBAS......... Journal of the Ceylon Branch of the Royal Asiatic Society (SAUO)
JCBC........... Joint Committee on Building Codes [*Later, Model Code Standardization Council*] (EA)
JCBC........... Junior College of Broward County (SAUO)
JCBC........... Jute Carpet Backing Council (EA)
J Cbem Soc Jpn... Journal of the Chemical Society of Japan (journ.) (SAUS)
JCBF........... Journal of Cerebral Blood Flow and Metabolism (journ.) (SAUS)
JCBL........... John Carter Brown Library (SAUO)
JCBMDN...... Journal of Cerebral Blood Flow and Metabolism (journ.) (SAUS)
JCBMI......... Joint Committee for the British Memorial Industry (DBA)
JCBMI......... Joint Committee for the British Monumental Industry (SAUO)
JCBS........... Jacobson Stores, Inc. [*NASDAQ symbol*] (NQ)
JCBSD7....... Journal of Cellular Biochemistry. Supplement (journ.) (SAUS)
JCBSF......... Joint Commission for Black Sea Fisheries
JCBSSA....... Jersey Cattle Breeders Society of South Africa (BUAC)
JCC........... Jamestown Community College [*New York*]
JCC........... Janney Cylinder Co.
JCC........... Japan Cotton Center (SAUO)
JCC........... Japanese Chamber of Commerce of New York [*Later, JCCINY*] (EA)
JCC........... Jarvis Christian College [*Hawkins, TX*]
JCC........... Jarvis Christian College, Hawkins, TX [*OCLC symbol*] (OCLC)
JCC........... Java Competence Center (SAUO)
JCC........... Jefferson Community College (SAUO)
JCC........... Jesus College, Cambridge [*England*] (ROG)
JCC........... Jet Circulation Control
JCC........... Jewish Chaplains Council (EA)
JCC........... Jewish Community Center
JCC........... Jharkhand Coordination Committee [*Jharkhand Samanvaya Samiti*] [*India*] [*Political party*]
JCC........... Jilin Chemical Inc ADS [*NYSE symbol*] (TTSB)
JCC........... Jilin Chemical Industrial Co. Ltd. [*NYSE symbol*] (SAG)
JCC........... Job Control Card [*Computer science*] (ELAL)
JCC........... Job Control Command (SAUS)
JCC........... Job Corps Camp [*Department of Labor*]
JCC........... Job Corps Center (SAUO)
JCC........... Joint Committee on Contraception (DMAA)
JCC........... Joint Communications Center (MCD)
JCC........... Joint Communications Committee (SAUO)
JCC........... Joint Computer Committee (SAUO)
JCC........... Joint Computer Conference
JCC........... Joint Conciliation Committee (SAUO)
JCC........... Joint Conference Committee (SAUS)
JCC........... Joint Consultative Committee [*of the National Joint Advisory Council*] [*British*] [*World War II*]
JCC........... Joint Consultative Council of the Fresh Fruit and Vegetable Industry (BUAC)
JCC........... Joint Contracting Center
JCC........... Joint Control Center (MCD)
JCC........... Joint Coordinating Committee (SAUO)
JCC........... Joint Coordination Center (NVT)
JCC........... Joint Cryptographic Centre (SAUO)

JCC .... JORN Co-ordination Centre (SAUO)
JCC .... Journal of Carbohydrate Chemistry (journ.) (SAUS)
JCC .... Journal of Clinical Chiropratic (SAUO)
JCC .... Journal of Computational Chemistry (journ.) (SAUS)
JCC .... Jowett Car Club (EA)
JCC .... Junior Carlton Club (SAUO)
JCC .... Junior Chamber of Commerce
JCC .... Junior Command Course [British military] (DMA)
JCC .... San Francisco [California] China Bas [Airport symbol] (OAG)
JCC(1) .... Joint Consultants Committee (SAUO)
JCC(2) .... Joint Consultative Committee (SAUO)
JCCA .... Japanese Canadian Citizens' Association
JCCA .... Japanese Chin Club of America (EA)
JCCA .... Jewish Community Centers Association of North America (NTPA)
JCCA .... Joint CONEX [Container Express] Control Agency
JCCA .... Journal of Canadian Chiropractic Association (SAUO)
JCCAE .... Joint Congressional Committee on Atomic Energy (SAUO)
JCCANA ...... Jewish Community Centers Association of North America (EA)
JCCB .... Joint Configuration Control Board [DoD]
JCCBD .... Journal of Clinical Chemistry and Clinical Biochemistry (journ.) (SAUS)
JCCBI .... Joint Committee for the Conservation of British Insects (BUAC)
JCCBI .... Joint Committee for the Conservation of British Invertebrates (BUAC)
JCCC .... Japanese Canadian Citizens' Council
JCCC .... Joint Committee on Contemporary China (EA)
JCCC .... Joint Communications Control Center (COE)
JCCC .... Joint COMSEC Coordination Center (MCD)
JCCC .... Joint Configuration Control Committee [DoD]
JCCD .... Japanese Canadian Committee for Democracy
JCCD .... Journal of Childhood Communications Disorders (journ.) (SAUS)
JCCDG .... Joint Command and Control Development Group [DoD]
JCCDS .... Joint Committee on Cartographic Data Standardization (SAUO)
JCCE .... Joint Committee on Communications and Electronics (SAUS)
JCCEA .... Joint Committee of Customs and Excise Associations (SAUO)
JCCEM .... Joint Committee of Cultural and Education Ministers [Australia]
JCCEM .... Joint Coordinating Committee for Environmental Restoration and Waste Management (SAUO)
JCCEP .... Joint Crisis Communications Exercise Program (MCD)
JCCF .... Jamaica Combined Cadet Force (BUAC)
JCCFC .... June Carter Cash Fan Club (EA)
JCCFE .... Joint Coordination Center, Far East [Military] (CINC)
JCCFEP .... Joint Commission on Cooperation in the Field of Environmental Protection [US-USSR] [Marine science] (OSRA)
JCC-FPM ..... Joint Coordinating Committee on Fundamental Properties of Matter [US Department of Energy and USSR State Committee on Peaceful Uses of Atomic Energy]
JCCG .... Joint/Combined Coordinating Group (SAUO)
JCCI .... Japan Chamber of Commerce and Industry (BUAC)
JCCINY .... Japanese Chamber of Commerce and Industry of New York (EA)
JCCIS .... Japan Chamber of Commerce and Industry, Sydney [Australia]
JCCIUK .... Japanese Chamber of Commerce and Industry in the United Kingdom (DS)
JCCL .... Japanese Canadian Citizens' League
JCCLE .... Joint Committee on Continuing Legal Education [Later, ALI-ABA Committee on Con tinuing Professional Education] (EA)
JCCMB .... Journal of Coordination Chemistry (journ.) (SAUS)
JCCMI .... Joint Committee for the Church Music in Ireland (BUAC)
JCCN .... Journal of Critical Care Nutrition (SAUO)
JCCN .... Journal of Critical Care Nutrition (journ.) (SAUS)
JCCO .... Joint Container Control Office (MCD)
JCCom .... Japan Computers and Communication
JCCOMNET... Joint Coordination Center Communications Network
JCCP .... Joint Casualty Collection Point [Environmental science] (COE)
JCCP .... Journal of Cross-Cultural Psychology (journ.) (SAUS)
JCCR .... Joint Command and Control Requirements [Military] (GFGA)
JCCR .... Joint Committee on Cellular Roaming (SAUO)
JCCRG .... Joint Command and Control Requirements Group [Joint Chiefs of Staff] [DoD]
JCCRS .... Joint Contingency Construction Requirements System (SAUO)
JCCS .... Jewish Cultural Clubs and Societies (EA)
JCCSA .... Joint Communication Contingency Station Assets (SAUO)
JCCSA .... Joint Communications Contingency Station Activity (MCD)
JCCSC .... Joint Command and Control Standards Committee (AFM)
JCCSMAS .... Joint Commission on Competitive Safeguards and the Medical Aspects of Sports [Later, JCSMS] (EA)
JCCSO .... Jewish Community Center Symphony Orchestra (SAUO)
JCCSO .... Jewish Community Center Symphony Orchestra America (SAUS)
JCCSWO ...... Joint Committee on Cooperation in Studies of the World Ocean [US-USSR] [Marine science] (OSRA)
JCCSWO ...... Joint Committee on Cooperation on Studies of the World Ocean [US-USSR] (USDC)
JCCTC .... Joint Customs Consultative Technical Committee [British] (DCTA)
JCD .... Doctor of Canon Law (SAUS)
JCD .... Doctor of Civil Law (SAUS)
JCD .... John Chard Decoration [British military] (DMA)
JCD .... Journal of Community Development [A publication]
JCD .... Journal of Counseling and Development [A publication] (DHP)
JCD .... Journal of Crime and Delinquency (SAUS)
JCD .... Junior College District
JCD .... Juris Canonici Doctor [Doctor of Canon Law] [Latin]
JCD .... Juris Civilis Doctor [Doctor of Civil Law] [Latin]
JCDA .... Journal of the Canadian Dental Association (SAUO)
JCDA .... Junior Catholic Daughters of America (SAUO)
JCDA .... Junior Catholic Daughters of the Americas [Defunct] (EA)
JCDAA .... Journal. Canadian Dental Association (journ.) (SAUS)

JCDalT .... Journal. Chemical Society. Dalton Transactions (journ.) (SAUS)
JCDEA .... Journal. California State Dental Association (journ.) (SAUS)
JCDIA .... Journal of Communication Disorders (journ.) (SAUS)
JCDSC .... Joint Communication Decision Support Center
JCDSG .... Joint Civil Defense Support Group
JCDSI .... Joint Continental Defense Systems Integration (ACAE)
JCDSIPS ...... Joint Continental Defense Systems Integration Planning Staff [Air Force]
JCDT .... Jamaica Conservation and Development Trust (BUAC)
JCDTA .... Joint Commission on Dance and Theatre Accreditation (EA)
JCDVA .... Journal of Child Development (journ.) (SAUS)
JCE .... Java Cryptographic Extension (SAUS)
JCE .... Jet Control Electronics (ACAE)
JCE .... Jockey Club of Egypt, Alexandria (SAUO)
JCE .... Joint Cadet Executive [British military] (DMA)
JCE .... Joint Committee on Education (SAUO)
JCE .... Journal of Chemical Education [A publication] (WDAA)
JCE .... Journal of Christian Education (journ.) (SAUS)
JCE .... Journal of Clinical Epidemiology (SAUS)
JCE .... Junior Certificate Examination (SAUO)
JCEA .... Jesuit Conference of East Asia (BUAC)
JCEA .... Joint Committee for European Affairs [Defunct] (EA)
JCEADF .... Joint Central Air Defense Force (SAA)
JCEAG .... Joint Civilian Employee Advisory Group [Military] (CINC)
JCEB .... Joint Council on Educational Broadcasting [Later, JCET] (EA)
JCEBD .... Journal of Cellular Biochemistry (journ.) (SAUS)
JCEC .... Joint Chapters - Educational Council
JCEC .... Joint Chiefs Electronic Committee (ACAE)
JCEC .... Joint Communications-Electronics Committee [Military]
JCECPAC..... Joint Communications-Electronics Committee, Pacific [Military] (CINC)
JCED .... Japan Committee for Economic Development (SAUO)
JCEE .... Joint Council on Economic Education (EA)
JCEG .... Joint Communications-Electronics Group [Military]
JCEG .... Joint Concepts and Evaluation Group [Military] (CINC)
JCEGP .... Joint Communications-Electronics Group [Military]
JCEHP .... Journal of Continuing Education in the Health Professions (SAUO)
JCEHP .... Journal of Continuing Education in the Health Professions (journ.) (SAUS)
JCEI .... Joint Council of Engineering Institutions (SAUO)
J Cell Biochem... Journal of Cellular Biochemistry (journ.) (SAUS)
J Cell Biochem Suppl... Journal of Cellular Biochemistry. Supplement (journ.) (SAUS)
J Cell Biol ... Journal of Cell Biology (journ.) (SAUS)
J Cell Comp Physiol... Journal of Cellular and Comparative Physiology (journ.) (SAUS)
J Cell Physiol Suppl... Journal of Cellular Physiology. Supplement (journ.) (SAUS)
J Cell Sci..... Journal of Cell Science (journ.) (SAUS)
J Cell Sci Suppl... Journal of Cell Science. Supplement (journ.) (SAUS)
JCEM .... Joint Center for Energy Management [Research center] (RCD)
JCEM .... Journal of Clinical Endocrinology and Metabolism (journ.) (SAUS)
JCEM .... Junior Control Electrical Mechanic [British military] (DMA)
JCEN .... Journal of Continuing Education in Nursing (journ.) (SAUS)
JCEND .... Journal of Clinical Engineering (journ.) (SAUS)
JCENS......... Joint Communications-Electronics Nomenclature System [Military]
J Cent Bur Anim Husb Dairy India... Journal. Central Bureau for Animal Husbandry and Dairying in India (journ.) (SAUS)
J Cent China Norm Univ Nat Sci... Journal. Central China Normal University. Natural Sciences (journ.) (SAUS)
J Cent Eur Aff... Journal of Central European Affairs (journ.) (SAUS)
J Cent S Inst Min Metall... Journal of Central-South Institute of Mining and Metallurgy (journ.) (SAUS)
JCEOI........... Joint Communications-Electronics Operating Instructions [Military] (CET)
JCEPC.......... Joint United States/Canada Civil Emergency Planning Committee
JCEPF......... Federation of Junior Economic Chambers in Francophone Countries (SAUO)
JCER .... Japan Center for Economic Research (SAUS)
J Ceram Assoc Jpn... Journal. Ceramic Association of Japan (journ.) (SAUS)
J Ceram Soc Jpn... Journal. Ceramic Society of Japan (journ.) (SAUS)
J Ceram Soc Jpn... Journal of the Ceramic Society of Japan (journ.) (SAUS)
J Cereb Blood Flow Metab... Journal of Cerebral Blood Flow and Metabolism (journ.) (SAUS)
J Cerebral Sci... Journal of Cerebral Science (journ.) (SAUS)
J Cer Soc Jap... Journal. Ceramic Society of Japan (journ.) (SAUS)
JCESR......... Job Control Engineering Service Request (SAUO)
JCESS......... Joint Centre for Earth System Science (SAUO)
JCET .... Joint Committee on Educational Telecommunications (SAUS)
JCET .... Joint Committee on Educational Television (SAUO)
JCET .... Joint Council on Educational Telecommunications [Defunct] (EA)
JCET .... Joint Council on Educational Television (SAUO)
JCEW .... Joint Communications Electronic Warfare Simulation
JCEWG......... Joint Communications and Electronics Working Group [NATO] (NATG)
JCEWS......... Joint Command, Control, and Electronic Warfare School
JCEWS......... Joint Commanders Electronic Warfare Staff (SAUO)
JCEWS......... Joint Force Commander's Electronic Warfare Staff [Military]
J Ceylon Br Brit Med Ass... Journal. Ceylon Branch. British Medical Association (journ.) (SAUS)
J Ceylon Law... Journal of Ceylon Law [A publication] (ILCA)
JCF .... Jamaican Constabulary Force (BUAC)
JCF .... Jaycees Community Foundation [Australia]
JCF .... JESSI Common Framework (SAUS)
JCF .... Jet Center Flight Training SA [Spain] [ICAO designator] (FAAC)
JCF .... Job Control File (SAUS)

JCF .... Joint Communications Facility (SAUO)
JCF .... Joint Coordinating Forum (SAUS)
JCF .... Journal of Canadian Fiction (journ.) (SAUS)
JCF .... Juvenile Calcaneal Fracture [*Medicine*] (DMAA)
JCFA .... Japan Chemical Fibres Association (BUAC)
JCFAS .... Joint Council on Food and Agricultural Sciences (SAUO)
JCF AWE ...... Joint Contingency Force Advanced Warfighting Experiment [*Army*]
JCFBC .... Joint Committee on Fire Brigade Communications (WDAA)
JCFBO .... Joint Committee on Fire Brigade Operations (WDAA)
JCFBS .... Joint Commission on the Fisheries in the Black Sea (BUAC)
JCFC .... Jesse Couch Fan Club (EA)
JCFC .... John Conlee Fan Club (EA)
JCFC .... Judaica Captioned Film Center (EA)
JCFI .... Job Control File Internal (IAA)
JCFR .... Junior College of Flat River [*Missouri*]
JCFRB .... Journal of Coffee Research (journ.) (SAUS)
JCFS .... Job Control File Source (IAA)
JCFS .... Journal of Comparative Family Studies (journ.) (SAUS)
JCFSBFC ..... Jerry Campbell and Five Star Band Fan Club (EA)
JCFSO .... Joint Council of Fire Service Organizations [*Defunct*] (EA)
JCG .... Jacobi Conjugate Gradient (SAUS)
JCG .... Joint Commanders Group (ACAE)
JCG .... Joint Conservation Group
JCG .... Joint Consultative Group (SAUO)
JCG .... Joint Coordinating Group [*Military*] (AFIT)
JCG .... Joint Coordination Group (SAUO)
JCG .... Journal of Crystal Growth (journ.) (SAUS)
JCGP .... Joint Consultative Group on Policy (SAUO)
JCGRO .... Joint Central Graves Registration Office [*Military*] (CINC)
JCGS .... Joint Center for Graduate Study [*Research center*] (RCD)
J Ch .... Johnson's New York Chancery Reports [*A publication*] (DLA)
JCHA .... Joint Commission on Hospital Accreditation
J Changcbun Coll Geol... Journal. Changchun College of Geology (journ.) (SAUS)
J Changchun Geol Inst... Journal. Changchun Geological Institute (journ.) (SAUS)
JCHARS .... Joint Commission of High Altitude Research Stations (SAUS)
J Chart Inst Transp... Journal. Chartered Institute of Transport (journ.) (SAUS)
JCHAS .... Journal. Cork Historical and Archaeological Society (journ.) (SAUS)
JCHC .... Journal of Compliance in Health Care (SAUO)
JCHC .... Journal of Compliance in Health Care (journ.) (SAUS)
JCHC .... Journal of Correctional Health Care (SAUO)
JCHC .... Journal of Correctional Health Care (journ.) (SAUS)
JCHE .... Joint Center for Higher Education (SAUO)
J Chekiang Univ... Journal. Chekiang University (journ.) (SAUS)
J Chem An... Japan Chemical Annual (journ.) (SAUS)
J Chem Ecol... Journal of Chemical Ecology (journ.) (SAUS)
J Chem Ed... Journal of Chemical Education [*A publication*] (BRI)
J Chem Ed... Journal of Chemical Education. American Chemical Society. Division of Chemical Education. Easton (SAUO)
J Chem Educ Softwe... Journal of Chemical Education. Software (journ.) (SAUS)
J Chem Eng Educ... Journal of Chemical Engineering Education (journ.) (SAUS)
J Chem Eng Jap... Journal of Chemical Engineering of Japan (journ.) (SAUS)
J Chem Eng Jpn... Journal of Chemical Engineering of Japan (journ.) (SAUS)
J Chem Metall Min Soc S Afr... Journal. Chemical, Metallurgical and Mining Society of South Africa. (journ.) (SAUS)
J Chem Neuroanat... Journal of Chemical Neuroanatomy (journ.) (SAUS)
J Chemom... Journal of Chemometrics (journ.) (SAUS)
J Chemother... Journal of Chemotherapy (journ.) (SAUS)
J Chemother Adv Ther... Journal of Chemotherapy and Advanced Therapeutics (journ.) (SAUS)
J Chem Phys... Journal of Chemical Physics (journ.) (SAUS)
J Chem Phys... Journal of Physical Chemistry (MEC)
J Chem Res... Journal of Chemical Research (journ.) (SAUS)
J Chem Res M... Journal of Chemical Research. Part M (journ.) (SAUS)
J Chem Res Miniprint... Journal of Chemical Research. Miniprint (journ.) (SAUS)
J Chem Res S... Journal of Chemical Research. Part S (journ.) (SAUS)
J Chem Res Synop... Journal of Chemical Research. Synopses (journ.) (SAUS)
J Chem Rev... Japan Chemical Review. Japan Chemical Week Supplement (journ.) (SAUS)
J Chem S..... Japan Chemical Week. Supplement (journ.) (SAUS)
J Chem S Dalton Trans... Journal. Chemical Society. Dalton Trans- actions (SAUS)
J Chem S Dalton Trans... Journal. Chemical Society. Dalton Transactions (SAUO)
J Chem S D Chem Commun... Journal. Chemical Society. D. Chemical Communications (journ.) (SAUS)
J Chem SF I... Journal. Chemical Society. Faraday Transactions I (journ.) (SAUS)
J Chem SF II... Journal. Chemical Society. Faraday Transactions. II (journ.) (SAUS)
J Chem Soc... Journal of the Chemical Society (MEC)
J Chem Soc A... Journal. Chemical Society. A. Inorganic, Physical, Theoretical (journ.) (SAUS)
J Chem Soc A... Journal of the Chemical Society, A. Inorganic Physical Theoretical (SAUS)
J Chem Soc A... Journal of the Chemical Society A (journ.) (SAUS)
J Chem Soc Abstr... Journal. Chemical Society. Abstracts (journ.) (SAUS)
J Chem Soc B... Journal. Chemical Society. B. Physical, Organic (journ.) (SAUS)
J Chem Soc B... Journal of the Chemical Society, B. Physical Organic (SAUS)
J Chem Soc C... Journal of the Chemical Society, C. Organic (SAUS)
J Chem Soc Chem Commum... Journal of the Chemical Society, Chemical Communications (journ.) (SAUS)
J Chem Soc Da... Journal. Chemical Society. Dalton Transactions (journ.) (SAUS)
J Chem Soc Jap Ind Chem Sect... Journal. Chemical Society of Japan. Industrial Chemistry Section (journ.) (SAUS)
J Chem Soc Jpn Chem Ind Chem... Journal. Chemical Society of Japan. Chemistry and Industrial Chemistry (journ.) (SAUS)
J Chem Soc Jpn Pure Chem Sect... Journal. Chemical Society of Japan. Pure Chemistry Section (journ.) (SAUS)

J Chem Tech and Biotech... Journal of Chemical Technology and Biotechnology (MEC)
J Chem Technol Biotechnol A Chem Technol... Journal of Chemical Technology and Biotechnology. A. Chemical Technology (journ.) (SAUS)
J Chem Technol Biotechnol B Biotechnology... Journal of Chemical Technology and Biotechnology. B. Biotechnology (journ.) (SAUS)
J Chem UAR... Journal of Chemistry. United Arab Republic (journ.) (SAUS)
J Cheng Kung Univ Sci Eng... Journal. Cheng Kung University. Science and Engineering (journ.) (SAUS)
J Chiba Med S... Journal. Chiba Medical Society (journ.) (SAUS)
J Child Contemp Soc... Journal of Children in Contemporary Society (journ.)
J Child Neurol... Journal of Child Neurology (journ.) (SAUS)
J Child Psychol Psychtry Book Suppl... Journal of Child Psychology and Psychiatry. Book Supplement (journ.) (SAUS)
J Child Psychotherapy... Journal of Child Psychotherapy (journ.) (SAUS)
J Chin Agri Chem Soc... Journal. Chinese Agricultural Chemical Society (journ.) (SAUS)
J China Pharm Univ... Journal. China Pharmaceutical University (journ.) (SAUS)
J China Soc Chem Ind... Journal. China Society of Chemical Industry (journ.) (SAUS)
J Chin Assoc Refrig... Journal. Chinese Association of Refrigeration (journ.) (SAUS)
J China Univ Sci Technol... Journal. China University of Science and Technology (journ.) (SAUS)
J Chin Biothem Soc... Journal Chinese Biochemical Society (journ.) (SAUS)
J Chin Ceram Soc... Journal. Chinese Ceramic Society (journ.) (SAUS)
J Chin Ceram Soc... Journal of the Chinese Ceramic Society (journ.) (SAUS)
J Chin Chem Soc... Journal of the Chinese Chemical Society (journ.) (SAUS)
J Chin Colloid Interface Soc... Journal. Chinese Colloid and Interface Society (journ.) (SAUS)
J Chin Electron Microsc Soc... Journal of Chinese Electron Microscopy Society (journ.) (SAUS)
J Chinese Inst Chem Engrs... Journal. Chinese Institute of Chemical Engineers (journ.) (SAUS)
J Chin Foundmens Assoc... Journal of Chinese Foundrymens Association (journ.) (SAUS)
J Ching Hua Univ... Journal. Ching Hua University (journ.) (SAUS)
J Chin Inst Chem Eng... Journal of the Chinese Institute of Chemical Engineers (journ.) (SAUS)
J Chin Inst Eng... Journal of Chinese Institute of Engineers (journ.) (SAUS)
J Chin Lang Teach Asso... Journal. Chinese Language Teachers Association (journ.) (SAUS)
J Chin Rare Earth Soc... Journal. Chinese Rare Earth Society (journ.) (SAUS)
J Chin Rare Earth Soc... Journal of the Chinese Rare Earth Society (journ.) (SAUS)
J Chin Silic Soc... Journal of the Chinese Silicate Society (journ.) (SAUS)
J Chins Inst Commun... Journal of the China Institute of Communications (journ.) (SAUS)
J Chin Soc Mech Eng... Journal of the Chinese Society of Mechanical Engineers (journ.) (SAUS)
J Chin Soc Vet Sci... Journal. Chinese Society of Veterinary Science (journ.) (SAUS)
J Chiro......... Journal of Chiropractic (journ.) (SAUS)
J Ch L.......... Journal of Child Language (journ.) (SAUS)
JCHMT......... Joint Committee for Higher Medical Training (CMD)
JCHO........... Joint Commission on Healthcare Organizations (SAUS)
JCHOD......... Journal of Clinical Hematology and Oncology (journ.) (SAUS)
J Chongqing Unir... Journal. Chongqing University (journ.) (SAUS)
J Chosen Med Assoc... Journal. Chosen Medical Association (journ.) (SAUS)
JCHPME....... Joint Commission on Higher Professional Medical Education (SAUS)
JCHPME....... Joint Committee on the Higher Professional Medical Education [*Nigeria*] (BUAC)
JCHPME....... WAPMC-WACP/WACS Joint Committee on Higher Professional Medical Education (SAUO)
JCHQA......... Japan Chemical Quarterly (journ.) (SAUS)
JChr............ Jewish Chronicle (SAUO)
J Christ Med Assoc India... Journal. Christian Medical Association of India (journ.) (SAUS)
J Chromat Chromat Rev... Journal of Chromatography. Chromatographic Reviews (journ.) (SAUS)
J Chromatogr B Biomed Appl... Journal of Chromatography. B, Biomedical Applications (SAUS)
J Chromatogr Libr... Journal of Chromatography Library (journ.) (SAUS)
J Chr Philos... Journal of Christian Philosophy (journ.) (SAUS)
JCHST.......... Joint Committee for Higher Surgical Training (SAUO)
JCHST.......... Joint Committe on Higher Surgical Training [*Royal College of Surgeons*] (PDAA)
J Ch St .... Journal of Church and State [*A publication*] (BRI)
J Church S... Journal of Church and State [*A publication*] (DLA)
JCI .... Jaycees International (EA)
JCI .... Job Characteristics Inventory
JCI .... Job Control Information (VLIE)
JCI .... Johnson Controls [*NYSE symbol*] (TTSB)
JCI .... Johnson Controls, Inc. [*NYSE symbol*] (SPSG)
JCI .... Joint Communications Instruction
JCI .... Journal of Clinical Investigation (SAUO)
JCI .... Junior Chamber International (EAIO)
JCI .... Jute Corp. of India
JCI .... Olathe [*Kansas*] [*Airport symbol*] (OAG)
JCIA .... Japan Camera Industry Association (SAUO)
JCIA .... Japan Communication Industrial Association (SAUO)
JCIAMR....... Joint Commission on the International Aspects of Mental Retardation (BUAC)
JCIC .... Japan Center for Intercultural Communications (SAUS)
JCIC .... Japan Consumer Information Center (SAUO)

JCIC	Jewish Community Information Center [Australia]
JCIC	Johannesburg Consolidated Investment Co.
JCIC	Johannesburg Consolidated Investment Company (SAUO)
JCIC	Joint Committee for Intersociety Coordination (SAUO)
JCIC	Joint Committee on Intersociety Coordination [Defunct] (EA)
JCIC	Joint Compliance & Inspection Commission (SAUO)
JCIC	Joint Compliance & Inspection Committee (SAUO)
JCICS	Journal of Chemical Information and Computer Sciences (journ.) (SAUS)
JCIDO	Joint Combat Identification Office [Military]
JCIE	Joint Center for International Exchange (SAUS)
JCIEABJ	Joint Commission for the Investigation of the Effects of the Atomic Bomb in Japan (SAUO)
JCIE/USA	Japan Center for International Exchange (EA)
JCIF	Japan Center for International Finance (SAUO)
JCIFC	Johnny Comfort International Fan Club [Defunct] (EA)
JCIHCA	Joint Council to Improve Health Care of the Aged [Defunct] (EA)
JCII	Japan Camera and Optical Instruments Inspection and Testing Institute (BUAC)
JCII	Japan Camera Inspection Institute (SAUO)
JCIM	Joint Council of Immunohistochemical Manufacturers
JCIMD	Journal of Clinical Immunology (journ.) (SAUS)
J Cin BA	Journal. Cincinnati Bar Association [A publication] (DLA)
JCIOC	Joint Counterintelligence Operations Center (SAUO)
JCIOMATIC	Job Control Language Automatic Generator (SAUS)
JCIPP	Jewish Committee for Israeli-Palestinian Peace (EA)
J Cir Eng Des	Journal of Civil Engineering Design (journ.) (SAUS)
JCIS	Joint Command Information Systems (SAUO)
JCIS	Joint Counterintelligence Section (SAUO)
JCIT	Jerusalem Conference on Information Technology (ELAL)
JCIT	Joint Combat Information Terminal [Military]
J City Plan Dir Am Soc Civ Eng	Journal. City Planning Division. American Society of Civil Engineers (journ.) (SAUS)
J Civ D	Journal of Civil Defense (journ.) (SAUS)
JCIWG	Joint Cutover Integrated Working Group [Military] (RDA)
JCJ	Journalist Committee of Japan (BUAC)
JCJC	Jasper County Junior College (SAUO)
JCJC	Jefferson City Junior College [Discontinued operation, 1958] [Missouri]
JCJC	Jefferson County Junior College (SAUO)
JCJC	Jones County Junior College [Ellisville, MS]
JCJCCIFC	Johnny Cash and June Carter Cash International Fan Club (EA)
JCJDMU	Jewel Case & Jewellery Display Makers' Union (WDAA)
JCK	Jackson Air Services Ltd. [Canada] [ICAO designator] (FAAC)
JCK	Joint Commission on Korea
JCK	Julia Creek [Australia] [Airport symbol] (OAG)
JCL	Jackson County Library System, Medford, OR [OCLC symbol] (OCLC)
JCL	Jet Cargo-Liberia [ICAO designator] (FAAC)
JCL	Job Command Language (NITA)
JCL	Job Control Language [High-level programming language] [1979] [Computer science]
JCL	John Crerar Library [National Translation Center]
JCL	Johnny Come Lately [Slang]
JCL	Joint Logistics Commanders (SAUO)
JCL	Journal of Commonwealth Literature [A publication] (ANEX)
JCL	Journal of Commonwealth Literature (journ.) (SAUS)
JCL	Journal of Contract Law [Australia] [A publication]
JCL	Journal of Corporation Law (journ.) (SAUS)
JCL	Junior Classical League (EA)
JCL	Juris Canonici Lector [Reader in Canon Law]
JCL	Juris Canonici Licentiatus [Licentiate in Canon Law]
JCL	Juris Civilis Licentiatus [Licentiate of Civil Law]
JCLA	Joint Council of Language Associations [British]
JCLa	Journal. Canadian Linguistic Association (journ.) (SAUS)
JCLa	Journal of Child Language (journ.) (SAUS)
JCLA	Journal of Comparative Literature and Aesthetics (journ.) (SAUS)
JCLA	Journal of the Canadian Language Association (SAUO)
JCLA	Journal of the Canadian Linguistic Association (SAUO)
J Classif	Journal of Classification (journ.) (SAUS)
J Clay Prod Inst Am	Journal. Clay Products Institute of America (journ.) (SAUS)
J Clay Res Group Jpn	Journal. Clay Research Group of Japan (journ.) (SAUS)
J Clay Sci Soc Jpn	Journal. Clay Science Society of Japan (journ.) (SAUS)
JCIC	Joint Committee on Intersociety Coordination (SAUO)
JCLC	Joint Committee [of Congress] on the Library of Congress
JCLE	Joint Committee on Library Education
JCIE/USA	Japan Center for Intertiational Exchange (SAUS)
J Cleveland Eng Soc	Journal. Cleveland Engineering Society (journ.) (SAUS)
JCLGEN	Job Control Language Generation [Computer science] (MHDB)
JCLI	Joint Council for Landscape Industries (BUAC)
JCLIC	Joint Center for Low-Intensity Conflict (SAUO)
JCLIL	Journal of Comparative Legislation and International Law [A publication]
J Climatol	Journal of Climatology (journ.) (SAUS)
J Clin Anesth	Journal of Clinical Anesthesia (journ.) (SAUS)
J Clin Apheresis	Journal of Clinical Apheresis (journ.) (SAUS)
J Clin Biochem Nu	Journal of Clinical Biochemistry and Nutrition (journ.) (SAUS)
J Clin Chem Clin Biochem	Journal of Clinical Chemistry and Clinical Biochemistry (journ.) (SAUS)
J Clin Child	Journal of Clinical Child Psychology (journ.) (SAUS)
J Clin Comput	Journal of Clinical Computing (journ.) (SAUS)
J Clin Dent	Journal of Clinical Dentistry (journ.) (SAUS)
J Clin Dermatol	Journal of Clinical Dermatology (journ.) (SAUS)
J Clin Dysmorphol	Journal of Clinical Dysmorphology (journ.) (SAUS)
J Clin Elecn Microsc	Journal of Clinical Electron Microscopy (journ.) (SAUS)
J Clin Electron Mic Soc Jpn	Journal. Clinical Electron Microscopy Society of Japan (journ.) (SAUS)
J Clin Endocrinol Metab	Journal of Clinical Endocrinology and Metabolism (journ.) (SAUS)
J Clin Eng	Journal of Clinical Engineering (journ.) (SAUS)
J Clin Ethics	Journal of Clinical Ethics (journ.) (SAUS)
J Clin Exp Gerontol	Journal of Clinical and Experimental Gerontology (journ.) (SAUS)
J Clin Exp Hypn	Journal of Clinical and Experimental Hypnosis (journ.) (SAUS)
J Clin Exp Neuropsychol	Journal of Clinical and Experimental Neuropsychology (journ.) (SAUS)
J Clin Exp Psychopathol	Journal of Clinical and Experimental Psychopathology (journ.) (SAUS)
J Clin Exp Psychopathol Q Rev Psychiahy Neurol	Journal of Clinical and Experimental Psychopathology and Quarterly Review of Psychiatry and Neurology (journ.) (SAUS)
J Clin Gastroenterol	Journal of Clinical Gastroenterology (journ.) (SAUS)
J Clin Hematol Oncol	Journal of Clinical Hematology and Oncology (journ.) (SAUS)
J Clin Hosp Pharm	Journal of Clinical and Hospital Pharmacy (journ.) (SAUS)
J Clin Immunoassay	Journal of Clinical Immunoassay (journ.) (SAUS)
J Clin Immunol	Journal of Clinical Immunology (journ.) (SAUS)
J Clin Lab Anal	Journal of Clinical Laboratory Analysis (journ.) (SAUS)
J Clin Lab Autom	Journal of Clinical Laboratory Automatiton (journ.) (SAUS)
J Clin Lab Immunol	Journal of Clinical and Laboratory Immunology (journ.) (SAUS)
J Clin Med	Journal of Clinical Medicine (journ.) (SAUS)
J Clin Monit	Journal of Clinical Monitoring (journ.) (SAUS)
J Clin Neuro-Ophthalmol	Journal of Clinical Neuro-Ophthalmology (journ.) (SAUS)
J Clin Neurophysiol	Journal of Clinical Neurophysiology (journ.) (SAUS)
J Clin Neuropsychol	Journal of Clinical Neuropsychology (journ.) (SAUS)
J Clin Nurs	Journal of Clinical Nursing (journ.) (SAUS)
J Clin Oncol	Journal of Clinical Oncology (journ.) (SAUS)
J Clin Orthod	Journal of Clinical Orthodontics (journ.) (SAUS)
J Clin Pathol	Journal of Clinical Pathology (journ.) (SAUS)
J Clin Periodontol	Journal of Clinical Periodontology (journ.) (SAUS)
J Clin Pharm	Journal of Clinical Pharmacy (journ.) (SAUS)
J Clin Pharmacol J New Drugs	Journal of Clinical Pharmacology and the Journal of New Drugs (journ.) (SAUS)
J Clin Pharmacol New Drugs	Journal of Clinical Pharmacology and New Drugs (journ.) (SAUS)
J Clin Pharm Ther	Journal of Clinical Pharmacy and Therapeutics (journ.) (SAUS)
J ClinPsyc	Journal of Clinical Psychiatry [A publication] (BRI)
J Clin Psychiatry	Journal of Clinical Psychiatry (journ.) (SAUS)
J Clin Psychopharmacol	Journal of Clinical Psychopharmacology (journ.) (SAUS)
J Clin Stomatol Conf	Journal of Clinical Stomatology Conferences (journ.) (SAUS)
J Clin Surg	Journal of Clinical Surgery (journ.) (SAUS)
J Clin Ultrasound	Journal of Clinical Ultrasound (journ.) (SAUS)
J Clin Virol	Journal of Clinical Virology (journ.) (SAUS)
JCLL	Joint Center for Lessons Learned (DOMA)
JCLMS	Journal of Clinical Laser Medicine and Surgery (SAUO)
JCLMS	Journal of Clinical Laser Medicine and Surgery (journ.) (SAUS)
JCL-OMATIC	Job Control Language Automatic Generator [Computer science]
JCLOT	Joint Closed Loop Operations Test (SAA)
JCLPB	Journal of Consulting and Clinical Psychology (journ.) (SAUS)
JCLPREP	Job Control Language Preprocessor [Computer science] (MHDB)
JCLS	Junior College Libraries Section [Association of College and Research Libraries]
JCLTA	Journal. Chinese Language Teachers Association (journ.) (SAUS)
J Cluster Sci	Journal of Cluster Science (journ.) (SAUS)
JCLWC	Joint Committee on Library Work as a Career (SAUO)
JCM	Jacobina [Brazil] [Airport symbol] (OAG)
JCM	Jettison Control Module
JCM	Jeunesse Canada Monde (AC)
JCM	Jeunesse Chretienne Malgache [Malagasy Christian Youth]
JCM	Job Cylinder Map [Computer science] (IBMDP)
JCM	Joint Committee on Microcards (SAUO)
JCM	Joint Conflict Model [Military]
JCM	Joint Countermeasures [Military]
JCM	Joule Ceramic Melter (PDAA)
JCM	Journal of Clinical Microbiology (SAUO)
JCM	Juris Civilis Magister [Master of Civil Law]
JCM	Malagasy Christian Youth (SAUO)
JCM	Standing Conference of Jews, Christians and Muslims in Europe (SAUO)
JCMA	Junior Clergy Missionary Association [British]
JCMB	Joint Committee on Medicine and Biology (SAUS)
JCMBS	Journeymen Curriers' Mutual Benefit Society [A union] [British]
JCMC	Joint Conference on Medical Conventions (BUAC)
JCMC	Joint Crisis Management Capability [DoD]
JCMC	Junta Civico-Militar Cubana [An association] (EA)
JCMD	Joint Committee on Mobility for the Disabled [British]
JCMEB	Joint Civil-Military Engineering Board (COE)
JCMEC	Joint Captured Materiel Exploitation Center (SAUO)
JCMEDK	Journal of Cardiovascular Medicine (SAUO)
JCMHC	Joint Commission on Mental Health of Children
JCMIH	Joint Commission on Mental Illness and Health [Defunct] (EA)
JCMJC	Joint Committee of Master and Journeyman Cloggers (SAUO)
JCML	Juvenile Chronic Myelogenous [or Myelocytic] Leukemia [Medicine] (DMAA)
JCMOS	Joint Complementary Metal Oxide Semiconductor (SAUS)
JCMP	Joint Cruise Missile Project (ACAE)

JCMPO......... Joint Cruise Missile Program (SAUS)
JCMPO......... Joint Cruise Missile Program [*or Project*] Office (MCD)
JCMPO......... Joint Cruise Missile Project Office (SAUO)
JCMR.......... Japan Congress on Materials Research (SAUS)
JCMRFA...... Joseph Cox and Mary Rue Family Association (EA)
JCMS.......... Jackson Country Medical Society (SAUO)
JCMS.......... Journal of Crystal and Molecular Structure (journ.) (SAUS)
JCMSPO....... Joint Cruise Missile System Program Office (ACAE)
JCMST........ Journal of Computers in Math and Science Teaching (NITA)
JCMT .... James Clerk Maxwell Telescope [*Mauna Kea, HI*] [*Operated by the Royal Observatory in Edinburgh, Scotland*]
JCMT .... Joint Collection Management Tools [*Army*] (RDA)
JCMT .... Journal of Cranio-Maxillofacial Trauma (SAUO)
JCMVASA .... Journal of the Central Mississippi Valley American Studies Association (SAUO)
JCMVASA .... Journal of the Central Mississippi Valley American Studies Association (journ.) (SAUS)
JCMWA .... Joint Christian Ministry in West Africa (BUAC)
JCN............ Jewish Communication Network (SAUS)
JCN............ Job Change Notice [*Form*] (AAG)
JCN............ Job Control Number
JCN............ Joint Communications Network (COE)
JCN............ Joint Control Number
JCN............ Journal of Cardiovascular Nursing (SAUO)
JCN............ Journal of Child Neurology (SAUO)
JCN............ Journal of Christian Nursing (SAUO)
JCN............ Jump Conditionally (SAUS)
JCN............ Jump on Condition [*Computer science*]
JCN............ Junction (NITA)
JCNA.......... Jaguar Clubs of North America (EA)
JCNAFF....... Joint Canadian Navy-Army-Air Force (SAUO)
JCNEA........ Journal of Comparative Neurology (journ.) (SAUS)
JCNFC........ Jimmy C. Newman Fan CLub (EA)
JCNM.......... Jewel Cave National Monument (SAUO)
JCNMT........ Joint Committee of Nordic Marine Technology [*See also NSTM*] (EAIO)
JCNMT........ Joint Committee of Nordic Master Tailors (EA)
JCNNM........ Johnson Controls Northern New Mexico (SAUO)
JCNNSRC..... Joint Committee of the Nordic Natural Science Research Councils (EA)
JCNOD........ Journal of Clinical Neuro-Ophthalmology (journ.) (SAUS)
JCNP......... Joint Committee on Nuclear Power (SAUS)
JCNPS .... Joint Committee on Nuclear Power Standards (SAUS)
JCNRD........ Journal of Cyclic Nucleotide Research (journ.) (SAUS)
JCNSW .... Judicial Commission of New South Wales [*Australia*]
JCO............ Jesus College, Oxford [*England*] (ROG)
JCO............ Joint Consultative Organization for Research and Development in Agriculture and Food (SAUO)
JCO............ Joint Contracting Offices [*Army*]
JCO............ Jordan Cooperative Organization (SAUO)
JCO............ Journal of Clinical Oncology (journ.) (SAUS)
JCO............ Journal of Clinical Orthodontics (journ.) (SAUS)
JCO............ Justification for Conditional Operation (SAUO)
JCO............ Justification for Continued Operation [*Nuclear energy*] (NRCH)
JCOA.......... Japanese Clinical Orthopaedic Association (SAUO)
JCOA.......... Jazz Composers Orchestra Association (EA)
J Coal Min Eng Assoc Kyushu... Journal. Coal Mining Engineers Association of Kyushu (journ.) (SAUS)
J-COARE...... Japanese COARE [*Coupled Ocean-Atmosphere Response Experiment*] (USDC)
JCOARE .... Japanese Coupled Ocean-Atmosphere Response Experiment [*Marine science*] (OSRA)
J Coastal Res... Journal of Coastal Research (journ.) (SAUS)
J Coast Res... Journal of Coastal Research (SAUO)
J Coated Fibrous Mater... Journal of Coated Fibrous Materials (journ.) (SAUS)
JCOC........... Joint Civilian Orientation Conference [*DoD*]
JCOC........... Joint Combat Operations Center [*Navy*] (NVT)
JCOC........... Joint Combined Operations Center (SAUO)
JCOC........... Joint Command Operations Center [*NATO*] (NATG)
JCOCG........ Joinl Cadre Operation Control Group (SAUS)
JCOCG........ Joint Cadre Operation Control Group [*Military*]
J Coconut Ind... Journal of Coconut Industries (journ.) (SAUS)
J-CODE....... Justification Code (LAIN)
J codes........ Joint Staff Positions (SAUS)
JC of C .... Junior Chamber of Commerce
J Cogn Rehab... Journal of Cognitive Rehabilitation (SAUS)
JCOI............ Journal. Cama Oriental Institute (journ.) (SAUS)
J Co Kildare Archaeol Soc... Journal. County Kildare Archaeological Society (journ.) (SAUS)
J Colfee Res... Journal of Coffee Research (journ.) (SAUS)
J Coll Agric Hokkaido Imp Univ... Journal. College of Agriculture. Hokkaido Imperial University (journ.) (SAUS)
J Coll Agric Tokyo... Journal. College of Agriculture. Tokyo Imperial University (journ.) (SAUS)
J Coll & Univ L... Journal of College and University Law (journ.) (SAUS)
J Coll & Univ Personnel Assn... Journal. College and University Personnel Association (journ.) (SAUS)
J Coll Arts Sci Chiba Unir... Journal College of Arts and Sciences. Chiba University (journ.) (SAUS)
J Coll Ceram Technol Univ Calcutta... Journal College of Ceramic Technology. University of Calcutta (journ.) (SAUS)
J Collect Negotiations Public Sect... Journal of Collective Negotiations in the Public Sector (journ.) (SAUS)
J College Place... Journal of College Placement (journ.) (SAUS)

J Coll Eng Technol Jadrapur Univ... Journal. College of Engineering and Technology Jadrapur University (journ.) (SAUS)
J Coll Eng Tokyo Imp Univ... Journal. College of Engineering. Tokyo Imperial University (journ.) (SAUS)
J Coll Gen Pract... Journal. College of General Practitioners (journ.) (SAUS)
J Coll Ind Technol Nihon Univ... Journal. College of Industnal Technology. Nihon University (journ.) (SAUS)
J Coll Ind Technol Nihon Univ A... Journal. College of Industrial Technology. Nihon University. Series A (journ.) (SAUS)
J Coll Ind Technol Nihon Univ B... Journal. College of Industrial Technology. Nihon University. Series B (journ.) (SAUS)
J Coll I Sc... Journal of Colloid and Interface Science (journ.) (SAUS)
J Coll Msr Sci Technol Tokai Univ... Journal. College of Marine Science and Technology. Tokai University (journ.) (SAUS)
J Coll Radiol Aust... Journal. College of Radiologists of Australia (journ.) (SAUS)
J Coll Sci Eng Natl Chung Hsing Univ... Journal. College of Science and Engineering. National Chung Hsing University (journ.) (SAUS)
J Coll Sci Imp Univ Tokyo... Journal. College of Science. Imperial University of Tokyo (journ.) (SAUS)
J Coll Sci King Saud Univ... Journal. College of Science. King Saud University (journ.) (SAUS)
J Coll Sci Teach... Journal of College Science Teaching (journ.) (SAUS)
J Coll Univ... Journal. College and University Personnel Association (journ.) (SAUS)
J Colo Dent Assoc... Journal. Colorado Dental Association (journ.) (SAUS)
J Colo-Wyo Acad Sci... Journal. Colorado-Wyoming Academy of Science (journ.) (SAUS)
JCOM........... Journal of Clinical Outcomes Management (SAUO)
JCOM........... Journal of Clinical Outcomes Management (journ.) (SAUS)
J Comb Theory... Journal of Combinatorial Theory (journ.) (SAUS)
JCOMCEN .... Joint Communications Center
JCOME........ Jewish Committee on the Middle East (EA)
JCOMM........ Joint Commission for Ocean and Marine Measurements (SAUO)
J Com Mkt S... Journal of Common Market Studies (journ.) (SAUS)
J Comm Mt Stud... Journal of Common Market Studies [*A publication*] (DLA)
J Common Market Stud... Journal of Common Market Studies (journ.) (SAUS)
J Commun Dis... Journal of Communicable Diseases (journ.) (SAUS)
J Communist Stud... Journal of Communist Studies. London (journ.) (SAUS)
J Community Health Nurs... Journal of Community Health Nursing (journ.) (SAUS)
J Community Psychol... Journal of Community Psychology (journ.) (SAUS)
J Commun Res Lab... Journal of the Communications Research Laboratory (journ.) (SAUS)
J Comp Corp L... Journal of Comparative Corporate Law and Securities Regulation [*A publication*] (ILCA)
J Comp Ethol... Journal of Comparative Ethology (journ.) (SAUS)
J Com Physl... Journal of Comparative and Physiological Psychology (journ.) (SAUS)
J Comp Leg... Journal of the Society of Comparative Legislation (SAUO)
J Comp Leg... Journal. Society of Comparative Legislation [*A publication*] (DLA)
J Complex ... Journal of Complexity (journ.) (SAUS)
J Comp Lg... Journal. Society of Comparative Legislation (journ.) (SAUS)
J Compliance Health Care... Journal of Compliance in Health Care (journ.) (SAUS)
J Comp Med and Vet Arch... Journal of Comparative Medicine and Veterinary Archives (journ.) (SAUS)
J Compos Technol Res... Journal of Composites Technology and Research (journ.) (SAUS)
J Comp Pathol Ther... Journal of Comparative Pathology and Therapeutics (journ.) (SAUS)
J Comp Physiol A... Journal of Comparative Physiology. A. Sensory, Neural and Behavioral Physiology (journ.) (SAUS)
J Comp Physiol B... Journal of Comparative Physiology. B. Biochemical, Systemic and Environmental Physiology (journ.) (SAUS)
J Comp Physiol B Metab Transp Funct... Journal of Comparative Physiology. B. Metabolic and Transport Functions (journ.) (SAUS)
J Comp Psychol... Journal of Comparative Psychology (journ.) (SAUS)
J Comput Aided Mol Des... Journal of Computer-Aided Molecular Design (journ.) (SAUS)
J Comput Appl Math... Journal of Computational and Applied Mathematics (journ.) (SAUS)
J Comput Assist Microsc... Journal of ComputerAssisted Microscopy (journ.) (SAUS)
J Comput Based Instr... Journal of Computer-Based Instruction (journ.) (SAUS)
J Comput Biol... Journal of Computational Biology (journ.) (SAUS)
J Comput Chem... Journal of Computational Chemistry (journ.) (SAUS)
J Comput Graph Stat... Journal of Computational and Graphical Statistics (SAUS)
J Comput Math... Journal of Computational Mathematics (journ.) (SAUS)
J Comput Math and Sci Teach... Journal of Computers in Mathematics and Science Teaching (journ.) (SAUS)
J Comput Neurosci... Journal of Computational Neuroscience (journ.) (SAUS)
J Comput Soc India... Journal. Computer Society of India (journ.) (SAUS)
J Comput Syst Sci... Journal of Computer System Sciences (journ.) (SAUS)
J Comput Tomogr... Journal of Computed Tomography (journ.) (SAUS)
J Con A........ Journal of Consumer Affairs [*A publication*] (BRI)
J Conat Law... Journal of Conational Law [*A publication*] (DLA)
J Conchol .... Journal of Conchology (journ.) (SAUS)
J Cond Monit... Journal of Condition Monitoring (journ.) (SAUS)
J Conf Chem Inst Can Am Chem Soc Abstr Pap... Joint Conference. Chemical Institute of Canada/American Chemical Society. Abstracts of Papers (journ.) (SAUS)
J Conn State Dent Assoc... Journal. Connecticul State Dental Association (journ.) (SAUS)
J Conn State Med Soc... Journal. Connecticut State Medical Society (journ.) (SAUS)
J Cons ASCE... Journal. Construction Division. Proceedings of the American Society of Civil Engineers (journ.) (SAUS)

J Constr Steel Res... Journal of Constructional Steel Research (journ.) (SAUS)
J Consumer Res... Journal of Consumer Research (journ.) (SAUS)
J Consumer Studies and Home Econ... Journal of Consumer Studies and Home Economics (journ.) (SAUS)
J Contam Hydrol... Journal of Contaminant Hydrology (SAUS)
J Cont Bus... Journal of Contemporary Business (journ.) (SAUS)
J Contemp Afr Stud... Journal of Contemporary African Studies (journ.) (SAUS)
J Contemp Health Law Policy... Journal of Contemporary Health Law and Policy (journ.) (SAUS)
J Contemp Hist... Journal of Contemorary History (journ.) (SAUS)
J Contemp RDL... Journal of Contemporary Roman-Dutch Law [A publication] (DLA)
J Contin Educ Obstet Gynecol... Journal of Continuing Education in Obstetrics and Gynecology (journ.) (SAUS)
J Cont Psychoth... Journal of Contempotary Psychotherapy (journ.) (SAUS)
J Contracept... Journal of Contraception (journ.) (SAUS)
J Cooling Tower Inst... Journal. Cooling Tower Institute (journ.) (SAUS)
J Coop Educ... Journal of Cooperative Education (journ.) (SAUS)
JCOP... JCS Concept and Objectives Paper
J Copr Soc'y... Journal. Copyright Society of the USA [A publication] (DLA)
J Copyright Ent & Sports L... Journal of Copyright, Entertainment, and Sports Law [A publication] (DLA)
J Copyright Entertainment Sports L... Journal of Copyright, Entertainment, and Sports Law [A publication] (DLA)
JCOR ... Jacor Communications [NASDAQ symbol] (TTSB)
JCOR ... Jacor Communications, Inc. [NASDAQ symbol] (NQ)
J Cork Hist Archaeol Soc... Journal. Cork Historical and Archaeological Society (journ.) (SAUS)
J Corp Tax'n... Journal of Corporate Taxation [A publication] (DLA)
J Corros Sci Soc Korea... Journal. Corrosion Science Society of Korea (journ.) (SAUS)
JCORW ... Jacor Communications Wrrt [NASDAQ symbol] (TTSB)
JCOS... Job Corps Opportunity Specialist [Department of Labor]
JCOS... Joint Chiefs of Staff [Military]
JCOS... Joint Countermine Operational Simulation [Military]
J Cost Manage Manuf Ind... Journal of Cost Management for the Manufacturing Industry (journ.) (SAUS)
JCOT... Joint Committee on College Teaching
J Coun Psyc... Journal of Counseling Psychology (journ.) (SAUS)
J Counsel & Devt... Journal of Counseling and Development (journ.) (SAUS)
JCP... Jamaican Communist Party [Political party] (BUAC)
JCP... Janna Contact Personal [Janna Systems] [Computer interface] (PCM)
JCP... Japan Communist Party [Nikon Kyosanto] [Political party] (PPW)
JCP... J. C. Penney Co. Inc. (SAUO)
JCP... J.C.Penney Company (SAUO)
JCP... Jetcopter [Denmark] [ICAO designator] (FAAC)
JCP... Jettison Control Panel
JCP... Jewish Communist Party [Political party] (BJA)
JCP... Job Content Protection [UAW]
JCP... Job Control Parameter (SAUS)
JCP... Job Control Processor (SAUS)
JCP... Job Control Program (CMD)
JCP... Job Creation Programme [Manpower Services Commission] (AIE)
JCP... John Crowe Productions, Inc. [Houston, TX] [Telecommunications] (TSSD)
JCP... Joint Chiefs of Staff Publications [Military]
JCP... Joint Committee for Palestine (BUAC)
JCP... Joint [Congressional] Committee on Printing
JCP... Joint Contact Point Division [Desert Test Center] [Fort Douglas, UT]
JCP... Joint Power Conditions [NASA] (LAIN)
JCP... Jordanian Communist Party [Political party] (PD)
JCP... Journal of Clinical Pathology (SAUS)
JCP... Journal of Clinical Pathology (journ.) (SAUS)
JCP... Journal of Clinical Psychiatry (journ.) (SAUS)
JCP... Journal of Communication Pathology (journ.) (SAUS)
JCP... Journal of Comparative Psychology (journ.) (SAUS)
JCP... Journal of Counseling Psychology (journ.) (SAUS)
JCP... JOVIAL [Joule's Own Version of the International Algorithmic Language] Control Program [Computer science]
JCP... Junction Call Processing (SAUS)
JCP... Jungle Canopy Penetration
JCP... Junior Collegiate Players [Later, Associate Collegiate Players] (EA)
JCP... Justice of the Common Pleas [Legal term] (DLA)
JCP... Juvenile Chronic Polyarthritis [Medicine] (DB)
JCP... Penney [J. C.] Co., Inc. [NYSE symbol] (SPSG)
JCP... Penney (J.C.) [NYSE symbol] (TTSB)
JCPC... J. C. Penney Communications, Inc. [J. C. Penney Co., Inc.] [Telecommunications service] (TSSD)
JCPC... Judicial Committee of the Privy Council (SAUO)
JCPCap... JCP & L Capital LP [Associated Press] (SAG)
JCPCI... Junior College of Packer Collegiate Institute (SAUO)
JCPCUS... Joint Committee on Printing of the Congress of the United States (SAUO)
JCPDS... Joint Committee on Powder Diffraction Standards (MCD)
JCPDS... Joint Committee on Powder Diffraction Studies (SAUS)
JCPDS... Joint Committee on Power Diffraction Standards (BUAC)
JCPDS-ICDD... Joint Committee on Powder Diffraction Standards-International Center for Diffraction Data (SAUS)
JCPE... Jersey City Port of Embarkation
JCPES... Joint Center for Political and Economic Studies (EA)
JCPES... Joint Contingency Planning and Execution Support (SAUO)
JCPHA... Journal of Consulting and Clinical Psychology (journ.) (SAUS)
JCPI... Japan Cotton Promotion Institute (BUAC)

JCPN... Journal of Child and Adolescent Psychiatric and Mental Health Nursing (SAUO)
JCPOA... Joint Council of Post Office Associations [South Africa]
JCP/PO... Joint Climate Program/Projects Office (SAUO)
JCPPRFNA... Joint Commission on Political Prisoners and Refugees in French North Africa [World War II]
JCPS... Joint Center for Political Studies [Later, JCPES] (EA)
JCPS... Journal of Constitutional and Parliamentary Studies (journ.) (SAUS)
JCPS... Junction Call Processing Subsystem (SAUS)
JCPSB... Journal of Cellular Physiology. Supplement (journ.) (SAUS)
JCPSD... Journal of Community Psychology (journ.) (SAUS)
JCPT... Journal of Canadian Petroleum Technology (journ.) (SAUS)
JCPT... Journal of Comparative Pathology and Therapeutics (journ.) (SAUS)
JCPTGP... Joint Committee on Postgraduate Training for General Practice (SAUO)
JCPT J Can Pet Technol... JCPT. Journal of Canadian Petroleum Technology (journ.) (SAUS)
JCPWG... Joint Certification Procedures Working Group (SAUO)
JCPX... Joint Command Post Exercise [Military] (AABC)
JCPYA... Journal of Clinical Psychology (journ.) (SAUS)
JCQ... Jacqueline Gold [Vancouver Stock Exchange symbol]
JCQ... Jefferson City, MO [Location identifier] [FAA] (FAAL)
JCQD... Jersey City Quartermaster Depot
JCQE... Joint Council on Quantum Electronics (MCD)
JCR... Jack Criswell Resources [Vancouver Stock Exchange symbol]
JCR... Jesus Cares Refuge Incorporated [Australia] [An association]
JCR... Johnson's New York Chancery Reports [A publication] (DLA)
JCR... Johnsoris New York Chancery Reports (journ.) (SAUS)
JCR... Joint Casualty Resolution (SAUS)
JCR... Joint Council for Repatriation (EA)
JCR... Journal Citation Reports [A publication]
JCR... Journal of Cardiopulmonary Rehabilitation (journ.) (SAUS)
JCR... Journal of Christian Reconstruction (journ.) (SAUS)
JCR... Journal of Clinical Rheumatology (journ.) (SAUS)
JCR... Journal of Coastal Research (journ.) (SAUS)
JCR... Journal of Conflict Resolution (journ.) (SAUS)
JCR... Journal of Consumer Research (journ.) (SAUS)
JCR... Journal of Court Reporting [A publication]
JCR... Judicial Council Reports [A publication] (DLA)
JCR... Junction Current Recovery [in silicon devices]
JCR... Junior Common Room [in British colleges and public schools]
JCR... Junta for Revolutionary Coordination [Argentina] [Political party] (BUAC)
JCRA... Jewish Committee for Relief Abroad
J Craniofac Genet Dev Biol Suppl... Journal of Craniofacial Genetics and Developmental Biology Supplement (journ.) (SAUS)
J Craniomandibular Pract... Journal of Cranio-Mandibular Practice (journ.) (SAUS)
J Craniomaxillofac Surg... Journal of Cranio-Maxillo-Facial Surgery (journ.) (SAUS)
JCRAS... Journal. Ceylon Branch. Royal Asiatic Society (journ.) (SAUS)
JCRAS... Journal of the Ceylon Branch of the Royal Asiatic Society (SAUO)
JCRAS... Journal of the Ceylon Branch of the Royal Asiatic Society (journ.) (SAUS)
JCRC... Jewish Community Relations Council (BARN)
JCRC... Joint Casualty Resolution Center (MCD)
JCRC... Joint Concept Review Committee (AAGC)
JCRDD... Journal of Clinical Research and Drug Development (SAUO)
JCRDD... Journal of Clinical Research and Drug Development (journ.) (SAUS)
JCRe... Judentum im Christlichen Religionsunterricht (BJA)
JC Rettie... Rettie, Crawford, and Melville's Session Cases, Fourth Series [1873-98] [Scotland] [A publication] (DLA)
JCRF... Joint Climate Research Fund (SAUO)
JCRFC... Jeannie C. Riley Fan Club (EA)
JCRFD... Joint Commission for Regulation of Fishing on the Danube (SAUO)
J Criminal Law and Criminology... Journal of Criminal Law and Criminology (journ.) (SAUS)
J Crim L & Crim... Journal of Criminal Law and Criminology [A publication] (DLA)
J Crim Sci... Journal of Criminal Science [A publication] (DLA)
J Crit Anal... Journal of Critical Analysis (journ.) (SAUS)
J Crit Care... Journal of Critical Care (journ.) (SAUS)
JCRLCMP... Joint Computer Resource Life Cycle Management Program (SAUO)
JCRMOD... Joint Center for Research in the Management of Ocean Data (SAUO)
JCRNFE... Joint Committee on Reduction of Nonessential Federal Expenditures (SAUO)
J Croatian Studies... Journal of Croatian Studies (journ.) (SAUS)
JCRPCC... Joint Council on Research in Pastoral Care and Counseling [Later, COMISS] (EA)
JCRS... Joint Casualty Resolution Center [Established in 1973 to coordinate U.S. military activities regarding American MIA/POWs] (VNW)
JCRT... Joint Center for Radiation Therapy (SAUS)
JCRWD... Jersey Committee of Resistance Workers and Deportees (EAIO)
J Cryptol... Journal of Cryptology (journ.) (SAUS)
J Crysllogr Soc Jap... Journal. Crystalioaphic Society of Japan (journ.) (SAUS)
J Crystallogr Soc Jpn... Journal of Crystallographic Society of Japan (journ.) (SAUS)
J Cryurg... Journal of Cryosurgery (journ.) (SAUS)
JCS... Jaicos [Brazil] [Airport symbol] (AD)
JCS... James Connolly Society (BUAC)
JCS... JANET Connection Service (SAUO)
JCS... Japan Club of Sydney [Australia]
JCS... Jazz Centre Society [British]
JCS... Jersey Cattle Society [British] (DBA)
JCS... Jersey Cattle Society of the United Kingdom (BUAC)
JCS... Jewish Chautauqua Society (EA)
JCS... Jewish Community Center (SAUO)
JCS... Job Control Statement [Computer science]

JCS .... Job Control System (IAA)
JCs .... Job Corpsmen (SAUS)
JCS .... Job Cost Sheet (DGA)
JCS .... Job Creation Scheme [Department of Employment] [British]
JCS .... Job Creation Subsidy (SAUS)
JCS .... Joint Chiefs of Staff [United States] [Military]
JCS .... Joint Commission for Spectroscopy (SAUO)
JCS .... Joint Commonwealth Societies (BUAC)
JCS .... Joint Coordinate System (SAUS)
JCS .... Journal. Chemical Society (journ.) (SAUS)
JCS .... Journal of Cardiac Surgery (journ.) (SAUS)
JCS .... Journal of Cell Science (journ.) (SAUS)
JCS .... Journal of Chromatographic Science [A publication]
JCS .... Journal of Croatian Studies (journ.) (SAUS)
JCS .... Journal of Curriculum Studies (journ.) (SAUS)
JCS .... Journal of Management Consulting (journ.) (SAUS)
JCS .... Journal of the Chemical Society (SAUO)
JCS .... JTWG Joint Test Working Group
JCS .... Justices' Clerks' Society [British] (DBA)
JCSA .... Jewish Communal Service Association of North America (EA)
JCSA .... Joint Committee for Soviet Aid (SAUO)
JCSA .... Joseph Conrad Society of America (EA)
JCSA .... Journal. Chemical Society. Abstracts (journ.) (SAUS)
JCS-ACA ..... JCS Automatic Conference Arranger (SAUS)
JCS-ACA ..... Joint Chiefs of Staff Automatic Conference Arranger [Military] (CET)
JCSAN .... Joint Chiefs of Staff Alerting Network [Military]
JCSAS .... Joint Chiefs of Staff Alerting System (MCD)
JCSat .... Japan Communications Satellite (SAUS)
JCSC .... Joint Communications Satellite Center (COE)
JCSCA .... Journal of Colloid and Interface Science (journ.) (SAUS)
JC/SCAMEP... Joint Commonwealth/States Committee on the Adult Migration
                    Education Program [Australia]
JCSCCF .... Joint Commission of the Socialist Countries on Cooperation in the
                    Field of Fisheries (PDAA)
JCS Chem Comm... Journal. Chemical Society. Chemical Communications
                    (journ.) (SAUS)
JCS Chem Commun... Journal of the Chemical Society, Chemical Communications
                    (journ.) (SAUS)
JCS Dalton... Journal. Chemical Society. Dalton Transactions. Inorganic Chemistry
                    (journ.) (SAUS)
JCS Dalton... Journal of the Chemical Society, Dalton Transactions (journ.) (SAUS)
JCSE .... Joint Communications Support Element [DoD]
JCSE .... Joint Communications Systems Elements (MCD)
JCSEA .... JCS Emergency Actions (SAUS)
JCSEA .... Joint Chiefs of Staff Emergency Actions (SAUO)
JCS Faraday I... Journal. Chemical Society. Faraday Transactions. I Physical
                    Chemistry (journ.) (SAUS)
JCS Faraday I... Journal of the Chemical Society, Faraday Transactions I (journ.)
                    (SAUS)
JCS Faraday II... Journal. Chemical Society. Faraday Transactions. II Chemical
                    Physics (journ.) (SAUS)
JCS Faraday II... Journal of the Chemical Society, Faraday Transactions II
                    (journ.) (SAUS)
JCSI .... Joint Combat Systems Integrating
JCSI .... Joint Command Systems Initiative (SAUO)
JCSIDBAD.... Joint Chiefs of Staff Identification Badge [Military decoration] (GFGA)
JCSIdentBad... Joint Chiefs of Staff Identification Badge [Military decoration]
                    (AABC)
JCSIDTN ...... Joint Chiefs of Staff Interim Data Transmission Network [Military]
                    (CET)
JCS-IDTN ..... Joint Chiefs of Staff-Interim Data Transmission Network (SAUO)
JCSLHG .... Joint Center for the Study of Law and Human Genetics
JCSM .... JCS Memorandum (SAUS)
JCSM .... Joint Chiefs of Staff Memorandum [Military]
J/CSM .... Junior Company Sergeant-Major [British military] (DMA)
JCSMC .... JCS Message Center (SAUS)
JCSMC .... Joint Chiefs of Staff Message Center (SAUO)
JCSMR .... John Cultin School of Medical Research (SAUS)
JCSMS .... Joint Commission on Sports Medicine and Science (EA)
JCS NICA ..... Joint Chiefs of Staff NICA Support (SAUO)
JCSNMCC ... Joint Chiefs of Staff National Military Command Center (DNAB)
JCSO .... Joint Chiefs of Staff Organization [Military] (MCD)
JCSOS .... Joint and Combined Staff Officer School
JCSP .... Joint Chiefs of Staff Plans
JCSP .... Joint Chiefs of Staff Publication (SAUO)
JCSP .... Journal of College Student Personnel [A publication] (DHP)
JCS Perkin I... Journal. Chemical Society. Perkin Trans- actions. I Organic and
                    Bioorganic Chemistry (journ.) (SAUS)
JCS Perkin II... Journal. Chemical Society. Perkin Transactions. II Physical Oiganic
                    Chemistry (journ.) (SAUS)
JCSPUB .... Joint Chiefs of Staff Publications [Military]
JCSR .... Journal of Crystallographic and Spectroscopic Research (journ.)
                    (SAUS)
JCSRE .... Joint Chiefs of Staff Representative, Europe [NATO] (NATG)
JCSRG .... Joint Chiefs of Staff Requirements Group (SAUO)
JCSS .... Jaffee Center for Strategic Studies [Israel] (BUAC)
JCSS .... Japan Calibration Service System (SAUO)
JCSS .... Jesuit Center for Social Studies [Defunct] (EA)
JCSS .... Jesus Christ Superstar [Rock opera]
JCSS .... Joint Committee on Slavic Studies (SAUO)
JCSS .... Joint Communications Support Squadron
JCSS .... Journal of Computer and System Sciences (journ.) (SAUS)
JCSSA .... Journal of the Cactus and Succulent Society of America (SAUO)
JCSSAB........ Joint Committee of the States to Study Alcoholic Beverage Laws
                    (EA)

JCS(SASM)... Joint Chiefs of Staff (Special Assistant for Strategic Mobility) (DNAB)
JCST .... Joint Combined System Test (KSC)
JC St.......... Journal of Caribbean Studies (journ.) (SAUS)
JCST .... Journal of Chemical Society Transactions (journ.) (SAUS)
JCSTC .... Joint Council for Scientific and Technical Communication [British]
JCSTD .... Journal of Contemporary Studies (journ.) (SAUS)
JCSTELECON... Joint Chiefs of Staff Teletypwriter Conference Network [Military]
                    (MCD)
JCSTI .... Joint Council for Scientific and Technical Information (SAUO)
JCSTR .... Joint Commission on Solar and Terrestrial Relationships (BUAC)
JCSUCR ...... Joint Commission on Standards, Units and Constants of
                    Radioactivity (SAUO)
JCSUK .... Jersey Cattle Society of the United Kingdom (SAUO)
JCT .... Jacket (ROG)
JCT .... James Cook University of North Queensland Herbarium (SAUO)
JCT .... James Cook University of North Queensland Herbarium International
                    Acronym (SAUS)
JCT .... Jerusalem College of Technology (SAUS)
JCT .... Jewett-Cameron [Vancouver Stock Exchange symbol]
JCT .... Jewish Cemetery Trust [Australia]
JCT .... Job Control Table (CMD)
JCT .... Job-Control-Tecknique (SAUS)
JCT .... Johnstown/Consolidated Realty Trust (MHDW)
JCT .... Joint Central Team (SAUS)
JCT .... Joint Committee on Taxation [US Congress]
JCT .... Joint Contracts Tribunal for the Standard Form of Building Contract
                    (BUAC)
JCT .... Joint Tribunal on the Standard Form of Building Contract (SAUS)
JCT .... Jordan Cosmological Theory
JCT .... Journal Control Table (IAA)
JCT .... Journal of Corporate Taxation (journ.) (SAUS)
JCT .... Junction [Texas] [Seismograph station code, US Geological
                    Survey] (SEIS)
jct .... Junction (SHCU)
Jct.......... Junction (TBD)
JCT .... Junction, TX [Location identifier] [FAA] (FAAL)
JCT .... Jurisconsult (ROG)
JCT & M .... Jordan, Case, Taylor & McGrath [Advertising agency]
JCTC .... Japanese Cultural and Trade Center (or Centre) (SAUS)
JCTC .... Jewett-Cameron Trading Co. Ltd. [NASDAQ symbol] (SAG)
JCTC .... Juneau County Teachers College (SAUO)
JCTCF .... Jewett-Cameron Trading [NASDAQ symbol] (TTSB)
JCTFI .... Joint Committee for Training in Foundry Industry (SAUO)
JCTFI .... Joint Committee for Training in the Foundry Industry (SAUS)
JCTG .... Joint Contingency Task Group [Military] (VNW)
JCTI .... James Crowe Traders International [Commercial firm] [British]
JCTI .... Jurisconsulti [Counselors at Law] [Latin] (ROG)
JCTION .... Junction [Commonly used] (OPSA)
JCTN .... Joint Composite Tracking Net [Military]
JCTN .... Junction [Commonly used] (OPSA)
JCTNS .... Junctions [Commonly used] (OPSA)
JCTOD .... Journal of Combustion Toxicology (journ.) (SAUS)
JCTPT .... Junction Point (IAA)
JCTS .... Junctions [Postal Service standard] (OPSA)
JCTUS .... Jurisconsultus [Counselor at Law] [Latin] (ROG)
JCTV .... Japan Cable Television Company Ltd. (SAUO)
JCTV .... Joint Committee on Tactical Vehicles (SAUO)
JCU .... John Carroll University [University Heights, OH]
JCU .... John Carroll University, Grasselli Library, University Heights, OH
                    [OCLC symbol] (OCLC)
JCU .... Joist Chair Upper (SAUS)
JCU .... Journal of Clinical Ultrasound (journ.) (SAUS)
JCUDI .... Japan Computer Usage Development Institute (BUAC)
JCUF .... Joint Communications Unit, Falkland Islands (SAUO)
JCUIS .... Joint Committee on the Union List of Serials (SAUO)
JCU J Clin Ultrasound... JCU, Journal of Clinical Ultrasound (journ.) (SAUS)
JCULS .... Joint Committee on the Union List of Serials
J Cult Geogr... Journal of Cultural Geography (SAUS)
JC Univ:...... John Carroll University (SAUS)
JCUNQ .... James Cook University of North Queensland (BUAC)
J Curric St ... Journal of Curriculum Studies (journ.) (SAUS)
J Curr Laser Abstr... Journal of Current Laser Abstracls (journ.) (SAUS)
J Curr Stud... Journal of Curriculum Studies (journ.) (SAUS)
JCUS .... Joint Center for Urban Studies of MIT [Massachusetts Institute of
                    Technology] and Harvard University [Research center] (RCD)
JCUS .... Judicial Conference of the United States (SAUO)
JCUSD .... Joint Committee on Urban Storm Drainage (BUAC)
JCV .... Jamestown Canyon Virus [Medicine] (DMAA)
JCV .... JC Virus (SAUS)
JCV .... Jentech Ventures Corp. [Vancouver Stock Exchange symbol]
JCV .... Joule-Clausius Velocity [Physics]
JCVI .... Joint Committee on Vaccination and Immunisation (BUAC)
JCVS .... JOVIAL Compiler Validation System [Computer science]
JCW .... Japan Chemical Week (journ.) (SAUS)
JCW .... Jim Creek [Washington] [Seismograph station code, US Geological
                    Survey] (SEIS)
JCW .... Journal of Comparative Business and Capital Market Law (journ.)
                    (SAUS)
JCWA .... Japan Child Welfare Association (SAUO)
JCWA .... Japan Clock and Watch Association (BUAC)
JCWE .... Joint Contingency Warfighting Experiment [Military]
JCWG .... Joint Checklist Working Group [Military] (AFIT)
JCWG .... Joint Configuration Working Group (SAUO)
JCWI .... Joint Council for the Welfare of Immigrants [British] (DI)
JCWP .... Joint Conservation Working Party [Australia] [Political party]

JCWTS......... Journal. Civil War Token Society (journ.) (SAUS)
JCY............. Johnson City, TX [Location identifier] [FAA] (FAAL)
J Cycle Res... Journal of Cycle Research (journ.) (SAUS)
J Cyclic Nucleotide Protein Phosphor Res... Journal of Cyclic Nucleotide and Protein Phosphorylation Research (journ.) (SAUS)
J Cytol Genet... Journal of Cytology and Genetics (journ.) (SAUS)
JD............. Diploma in Journalism (ADA)
JD............. Doctor of Jurisprudence (DD)
JD............. Doctor of Jurisprudence Laws (SAUS)
JD............. Doctor of Laws or Jurisprudence (SAUS)
JD............. Jack Daniels [A brand name of whiskey]
JD............. Jaundice [Medicine] (MELL)
JD............. J-Band Detector
JD............. Jejunal Diverticulitis [Gastroenterology] (DAVI)
JD............. Jet Driver (KSC)
JD............. Jewish Division [New York Public Library] (BJA)
JD............. Job Description [Department of Labor]
JD............. Job Development (OICC)
JD............. Joggle Die (MCD)
JD............. Joined (AABC)
JD............. Joint Dependency (SAUS)
JD............. Joint Determination (AFM)
JD............. Joint Dictionary [Dictionary of US Military Terms for Joint Usage] [A publication] (AFM)
JD............. Jordan Dinar (SAUS)
JD............. Jordanian Dinar [Monetary unit] (BJA)
Jd............. Jude [New Testament book] (BJA)
JD............. Jugulodigastric [Node] [Gastroenterology] (DAVI)
JD............. Julian Date [or Day]
JD............. Julian Day (SAUO)
JD............. Junction Diode (SAUS)
JD............. Junior Deacon [Freemasonry]
JD............. Junior Dean
jd............. Junior Debutante (SAUS)
JD............. Junior Division [British military] (DMA)
JD............. Junta Democratica [Democratic Junta] [Spain] [Political party] (PPE)
JD............. Jurisdiction [Legal shorthand] (LWAP)
JD............. Juris Doctor [Doctor of Jurisprudence] [Latin]
JD............. Jurum Doctor [Doctor of Laws] [Latin]
JD............. Jury Duty (WGA)
JD............. Justice Department
JD............. Juvenile Delinquency [or Delinquent]
JD............. Juvenile Delinquent (NTIO)
JD............. Juvenile Diabetes [Medicine] (DAVI)
JD............. Toa Domestic Airlines [ICAO designator] (AD)
JDA............. Japan Defence (or Defense) Agency (SAUS)
JDA............. Japan Defense Agency-Japan Domestic Airline (SAUS)
JDA............. Japan Domestic Airlines (PDAA)
JDA............. Japanese Defense Agency (MCD)
JDA............. Jefferson Davis Association (EA)
JDA............. Jewelery Distributors Association [British] (DBA)
JDA............. Jewellery Distributors Association of the United Kingdom (BUAC)
JDA............. Jewish Direct Action (SAUS)
JDA............. Joint Defense Appeal [Defunct] (EA)
JDA............. Joint Deployment Agency [DoD]
JDA............. Joint Development Agency [DoD]
JDA............. Joint Development Agreement [Business term] (PCM)
JDA............. Joint Duty Assignment (DOMA)
JDA............. Journal of Developing Areas (journ.) (SAUS)
JDA............. Juvenile Delinquency Act
J Dairy Res... Journal of Dairy Research (journ.) (SAUS)
J Dairy Sci... Journal of Dairy Science (journ.) (SAUS)
JDAL............. Joint Duty Assignment List (DOMA)
JDAL............. Jurisdictional [Legal shorthand] (LWAP)
J Dalian Eng Inst... Journal. Dalian Engineering Institute (journ.) (SAUS)
J Dalian Inst Technol... Journal. Dalian Institute of Technology (journ.) (SAUS)
J Dalian Univ Technol... Journal of Dalian University of Technology (journ.) (SAUS)
JDAM............. Joint Direct Attack Munition (DOMA)
JDAM............. Joint Direct Attack Munition programme (SAUS)
JDAM............. Joint Direct Attack Munitions [DoD]
JDAMIS....... Joint Duty Assignment Management Information System (DOMA)
JDAP............. Joint Direct Attack Program [Air Force] (DOMA)
JDAS............. JDA Software Group [NASDAQ symbol] (TTSB)
JDAS............. JDA Software Group, Inc. [NASDAQ symbol] (SAG)
JDASoft....... JDA Software Group, Inc. [Associated Press] (SAG)
J Data Ed... Journal of Data Education (journ.) (SAUS)
J Data Manage... Journal of Data Management (journ.) (SAUS)
J Data Mgt... Journal of Data Management (journ.) (SAUS)
J-day........... Judas Day (SAUS)
JDB............. Japan Development Bank (PDAA)
JDB............. Java Debugger (SAUS)
JDBC............. Java Database Connect [Computer science]
JDBC............. Java Database Connection (SAUS)
JDBC............. Java Data Base Connectivity [Computer science] (IGQR)
JDBP............. Journal of Developmental and Behavioral Pediatrics (journ.) (SAUS)
JDC............. American Jewish Joint Distribution Committee (EA)
JDC............. Deere & Co. [ICAO designator] (FAAC)
JDC............. Jackson Development Corporation
JDC............. Japan Airlines Development Co.
JDC............. Japan Digital Cellular (SAUO)
JDC............. Japan Documentation Center [Columbia University]
JDC............. Jet Deflection Control (AAG)
JDC............. Jet Detection Control (SAUS)
JDC............. Jeunesse Democratique Camerounaise [Cameroonian Democratic Youth]

JDC............. Jewish Documentation Centre [See also BJVN] (EAIO)
JDC............. Job Description Card
JDC............. Joint Deployment Community [Military] (INF)
JDC............. Joint Development Community [DoD]
JDC............. Joint Doctrine Center (COE)
JDC............. Joslin Diabetes Center (EA)
JDC............. Junction Diode Circuit
JDC............. Junior Doctors Committee (SAUO)
JDC............. Just Discriminable Change (IAA)
JDC............. Juvenile Delinquency Control (SAUS)
JDC............. Juvenile Detention Center
JDCA............. Japan Designer and Craftsman Association (BUAC)
JDCC............. Juneau-Douglas Community College (SAUO)
J DC DentS... Journal. District of Columbia Dental Society (journ.) (SAUS)
JDCE............. Jeunes Democrates Chretiens Europeens [European Young Christian Democrats - EYCD] (EA)
JDCHA........ Journal of Dentistry for Children (journ.) (SAUS)
JDCMC........ Joint Department of Defense Configuration Management Committee (MCD)
JDCS............. Joint Deputy Chiefs of Staff [Military]
JDCU............. Jamming Detection Control Unit (SAUS)
JDD............. Joint Doctrine Division (COE)
JDDD............. Judicial Discipline and Disability Digest [American Judicature Society] [Information service or system] (CRD)
JDE............. Air Med Jetoperations [Austria] [ICAO designator] (FAAC)
JDE............. Journal of Dental Education (SAUO)
JDE............. Journal of Development Economics (journ.) (SAUS)
J De Agric Un S Afr... Journal. Department of Agriculture. Union of South Africa (journ.) (SAUS)
JDEC............. J D Edwards [NYSE symbol] (SG)
JDEC............. Joint Documents Exploitation Center (SAUO)
J Decor Propag Arts... Journal of Decorative and Propaganda Arts. Wolfson Foundation of Decorative and Propaganda Arts. Miami (SAUO)
JDECU........ Journal. Department of English. Calcutta University (journ.) (SAUS)
J/deg........... Joule per degree (SAUS)
JDEG............. Joules per Degree [Physics] (IAA)
J Dendrol..... Journal of Dendrology (journ.) (SAUS)
JDENL......... Joined by Enlistment [Military]
J Denning LS... Journal. Denning Law Society [Tanzania] [A publication] (DLA)
J Denning L Soc'y... Journal. Denning Law Society [Tanzania] [A publication] (DLA)
J Dent.......... Journal of Dentistry (journ.) (SAUS)
J Dent Assoc S Afr... Journal. Dental Association of South Africa (journ.) (SAUS)
J Dent Assoc Thai... Journal. Dental Association of Thailand (journ.) (SAUS)
JDent Aux.... Journal of the Dental Auxiliaries (journ.) (SAUS)
J Dent Educ... Journal of Dental Education (journ.) (SAUS)
J Dent Eng... Journal of Dental Engineering (journ.) (SAUS)
J Dent Guid Counc Handicap... Journal. Dental Guidance Council on the Handicapped (journ.) (SAUS)
JDent Handicap... Journal of Dentistry for the Handicapped (journ.) (SAUS)
J Dent Med... Journal of Dental Medicine (journ.) (SAUS)
J Dent Sch NU Univ Iran... Journal of the Dental School. National University of Iran (journ.) (SAUS)
J Dent Tech... Journal of Dental Technics (journ.) (SAUS)
JDEP............. Juvenile Delinquency Evaluation Project
J Dep Agric Fish Irl... Journal. Department of Agriculture and Fisheries. Republic of Ireland (journ.) (SAUS)
J Dep Agric Kyushu Imp Univ... Journal. Department of Agriculture. Kyushu Imperial University (journ.) (SAUS)
J Dep Geogr Natl Univ Malaysia... Journal. Department of Geography. National University of Malaysia (journ.) (SAUS)
J Dept Ag Ireland... Journal. Irish Free State Department of Agriculture (journ.) (SAUS)
J Dept Ag S Africa... Journal. Department of Agriculture. South Africa (journ.) (SAUS)
J Dermatol Sci... Journal of Dermatological Science (journ.) (SAUS)
J Dermatol Surg... Journal of Dermatologic Surgery (journ.) (SAUS)
J Dermatol Surg Oncol... Journal of Dermatologic Surgery and Oncology (journ.) (SAUS)
JDES............. Joint Density of Electronic State [Semiconductor technology] (OA)
J Des Autom Fault Tolerant Comput... Journal of Design Automation and Fault Tolerant Computing (journ.) (SAUS)
J Deterg Collect Chem... Journal of Detergents and Collective Chemistry (journ.) (SAUS)
J Dev Behav Pediatr... Journal of Developmental and Behavioral Pediatrics (journ.) (SAUS)
J Develop Read... Journal of Development Reading (journ.) (SAUS)
J Devon Trust Nat Conserv... Journal. Devon Trust for Nature Conservation (journ.) (SAUS)
J Dev Studies... Journal of Development Studies (journ.) (SAUS)
JDEWN........ John Denver Early Warning Network (EA)
JDF............. Jamaican Defense Forces
JDF............. Jamming Direction Finder [Military] (CAAL)
JDF............. Job Description Form (SAUO)
JDF............. Juiz De Fora [Brazil] [Airport symbol] (OAG)
JDF............. Juvenile Diabetes Foundation [Later, JDFI] (EA)
JDF............. Juvenile Diabetes Foundation International (SAUO)
JDFA............. Juvenile Diabetes Foundation Australia (NRGU)
JDFAA........ Japanese Defense Facilities Administration Agency (SAUO)
JDFC............. James Darren Fan Club [Defunct] (EA)
JDFC............. Jimmie Dale Fan Club (EA)
JDFC............. Joanie Dale Fan Club (EA)
JDFC........ Joint Danube Fishery Commission [See also ZKRVD] [Zilina, Czechoslovakia] (EAIO)
JDFCG........ Jamaica Defence Force Coast Guard (SAUO)

JDFI............ Joslin Diabetes Foundation, Inc. [*Later, JDC*] (EA)
JDFI............ Juvenile Diabetes Foundation International (EA)
JDF International... Juvenile Diabetes Foundation International (SAUO)
JDFR............ Joined From [*Military*]
JdFR............ Juan de Fuca Ridge [*Marine science*] (OSRA)
JDFR............ Juan de Fuca Ridge (USDC)
JDG............ Judge
JDH............ Jodhpur [*India*] [*Airport symbol*] (OAG)
JDH............ Journal of Dental Hygiene (SAUO)
JDHE............ Joint Directory of Higher Education [*A publication*]
JDHHFC............ John Denver Heart to Heart Fan Club (EA)
JDHQ-SV-W... Joint Defense Headquarters Services Washington (ACAE)
JDHS............ Jefferson Davis High School (SAUO)
JDHTC .... Jaguar-Daimler Heritage Trust Collection
JDI............ JDS Investments Ltd. [*Toronto Stock Exchange symbol*]
JDI............ Job Description Index
JDI............ Joint Declaration of Interest (DS)
JDI............ Juvenile Delinquency Index (SAUS)
J Diabetes Complications...   Journal of Diabetes and Its Complica- tions (journ.) (SAUS)
J Diabetic Assoc India... Journal. Diabetic Association of India (journ.) (SAUS)
JDIAD .... Journal of Dialysis (journ.) (SAUS)
J Diarrhoeal Dis Res... Journal of Diarrhoeal Diseases Research (journ.) (SAUS)
JDIC............ Justice Data Interface Controller (SAUS)
J Digit Imaging... Journal of Digital Imaging (journ.) (SAUS)
JDIMP.......... Joint Data and Information Management Panel (SAUO)
JDIND .... Joined by Induction [*Military*]
JDIND .... Joint by Induction (SAUS)
JDipMA....... Joint Diploma in Management Accounting Services [*British*]
JDIS............ Joint Defense/Deployable Intelligence Support (SAUS)
J Dispersion Sci Technol... Journal of Dispersion Science and Technology (journ.) (SAUS)
JDISS.......... Joint Deployable Intelligence Support System (SAUO)
J Distrib ...... Journal of Distribution (journ.) (SAUS)
JDK............ Java Developer's Kit (PCM)
JDK............ Joodsch-Democratische Kiespartij [*Political party*] (BJA)
JDL............ Japan Digital Laboratory (SAUS)
JDL............ Jewish Defense League (EA)
JDL............ Job Description Language [*Computer science*]
JDL............ Job Description Library
JDL............ Job Descriptor Language (NITA)
JDL............ Job Drawing List (MCD)
JDL............ Joint Directors of Laboratories [*Military*]
JDL............ Juneau, AK [*Location identifier*] [*FAA*] (FAAL)
JDL............ Junior Drama League (SAUO)
JDL............ Lynn-01, AK [*Location identifier*] [*FAA*] (FAAL)
JDM............ Jarso Democratic Movement (SAUO)
JDM............ Jersey Democratic Movement (SAUO)
JDM............ Journal of Data Management (journ.) (SAUS)
JDM............ Juvenile Diabetes Mellitus [*Medicine*]
JDMA.......... Japan Diet Marketing Association (BUAC)
JDMAG .... Joint Depot Maintenance Analysis Group [*Military*]
JDMC.......... James Dean Memory Club (EA)
JDMC.......... Joint Depot Maintenance Command (SAUO)
JDMC.......... JOPES Development Management Center (SAUO)
JDMP......... Joint Deployment Master Plan [*Military*] (MUSM)
JDMS......... Journal of Diagnostic Medical Sonography (SAUO)
JDMS......... Juvenile Dermatomyositis [*Medicine*] (DAVI)
JDN............ JDN Realty [*NYSE symbol*] (TTSB)
JDN............ JDN Realty Corp. [*NYSE symbol*] (SAG)
JDN............ Joint Data Network [*Army*]
JDN............ Jordan (SAUS)
JDN............ Jordan, MT [*Location identifier*] [*FAA*] (FAAL)
JDN............ Jordan Petroleum Ltd. [*Toronto Stock Exchange symbol*]
JDN............ Julian Day Number
JDNB .... Jewish Telegraphic Agency. Daily News Bulletin (journ.) (SAUS)
JDO............ Jewish Defense Organization (EA)
JDO............ Job Delivery Orders (MCD)
JDO............ Junior Duty Officer (MCD)
J Doc Reprod... Journal of Documentary Reproduction (journ.) (SAUS)
JDOP.......... Joint Development Objectives Plan (SAA)
JDOP .... Joint Doppler Operational Project [*For tornado warning*] [*Meteorology*]
JDOYM .... Jewish Defense Organization Youth Movement (EA)
JDP............ Covington/Cincinnati, OH [*Location identifier*] [*FAA*] (FAAL)
JDP............ Job Development Program
JDP............ Joint Declaration of Principles
JDP............ Joint Development Program
JDP............ Joint Development Project (SAUS)
JDP............ Paris-Moulineaux [*France*] [*Airport symbol*] (OAG)
JDPA.......... Japan Dairy Products Association (SAUO)
JDPA.......... Japan Directory of Professional Associations [*Japan Publications Guide Service*] [*Information service or system*] (CRD)
JDPA.......... Journal of Dental Practice Administration (SAUO)
JDPA.......... Juvenile Justice Planning Agency (OICC)
JDPC.......... Joint Defense Production Committee [*Later, Joint War Production Committee*] [*World War II*]
JDPC.......... Junior Daughters of Peter Claver (EA)
JDR............ Japanese Depository Receipts (SAUS)
JDR............ Job Distribution Register (SAUS)
JDR............ Journal of Dairy Research (journ.) (SAUS)
JDR............ Journal of Defense Research (journ.) (SAUS)
JDR............ Journal of Dental Research (SAUO)
JDR............ Junior Dispatch Riders (SAUS)

JDR............ Juta's Daily Reporter, Cape Provincial Division [*South Africa*] [*A publication*] (DLA)
JDR3.......... John D. Rockefeller III [*American philanthropist, 1906-1978*]
JDREENL .... Joined by Reenlistment [*Military*]
JDREMC ...... Joint Departmental Radio and Electronics Measurements Committee (BUAC)
JDRMA .... Japanese Digital Road Mapping Association
JDRP .... Joint Dissemination Review Panels
J Drug Dev... Journal of Drug Development (journ.) (SAUS)
J Drug Educ... Journal of Drug Education (journ.) (SAUS)
J Drugther Res... Journal for Drugtherapy and Research (journ.) (SAUS)
JDS............ Doctor of Juridical Science
JDS............ Jaguar Diagnostic System [*Automotive engineering*]
JDS............ JDS Capital Ltd. [*Toronto Stock Exchange symbol*]
JDS............ Job Data Sheet (IEEE)
JDS............ Job Diagnosis Survey (PDAA)
JDS............ John Dewey Society (EA)
JDS............ Joint Defense Staff [*NATO*] (NATG)
JDS............ Joint Deployment System
JDS............ Joint Disciplinary Scheme [*British*]
JDS............ Journal of Development Studies (journ.) (SAUS)
JDS............ Judaean Desert Studies (SAUS)
JDS............ Jugoslovenska Demokratska Stranka [*Yugoslav Democratic Party*] [*Political party*] (PPE)
JDS............ Julian Day of Spring
JDS............ Justice Data System (SAUS)
JDSC.......... Junior Division Staff College (SAUO)
JDSCS .... Joint Defense Space Communications Station
JDSFA......... Japan Self-Defense Forces Academy (SAUO)
JDSIP......... JDS Interface Processor (SAUS)
JDSIR .... JDS Incident Reporting (SAUO)
JDSQP .... JDS Query Processor (SAUS)
JDSSC .... Joint Data Systems Support Center [*Military*]
JDSU......... JDS Uniphase Corp. [*NASDAQ symbol*] (SG)
JDSUP .... JDS Update Processor (SAUS)
JDT............ Joint Design Team [*Military*]
JDT............ Joint Development Team (MCD)
JDT............ Joint Development Testing
JDT............ Journal of Dental Technology (SAUO)
Jdt .... Judith [*Old Testament book*] [*Roman Catholic canon*]
JDT............ Judson Dance Theater
JDU............ Journal. Durham University (journ.) (SAUS)
J Durham Sch Agr... Journal. Durham School of Agriculture (journ.) (SAUS)
JDW........... Jacket Decladding Waste (PDAA)
JDW........... Jacket Declatting Waste (SAUS)
JDWC......... Jazz Dance World Congress
JDW Solution... Jacket Declatting Waste Solution (SAUS)
JDY............ Downey (SAUS)
JDY............ Downey, CA [*Location identifier*] [*FAA*] (FAAL)
JDYD .... Juvenile Delinquency and Youth Development Office [*Federal government*]
JDZ............ Jingdezhen [*China*] [*Airport symbol*] (OAG)
JE............ Eurojet SA (SAUS)
JE............ Jacksonian Epilepsy [*Medicine*] (MELL)
JE............ Jamin Effect [*Electronics*]
JE............ Jamming Effect (SAUS)
JE............ Jamming Equipment
JE............ Japanese Encephalitis [*Medicine*]
J/E............ Japan/Europe (SAUS)
Je............ Jeremiah [*Old Testament book*] (BJA)
JE............ Jerseyville & Eastern [*AAR code*]
JE............ Jet Engine
JE............ Jet Exhaust
JE............ Jewish Encyclopaedia [*A publication*] (BJA)
JE............ Job Enlargement (MHDB)
JE............ Job Enrichment (MHDB)
JE............ Job Entry (SAUS)
JE............ Job Estimate (AAG)
JE............ Johnson Engineering Corp. (SAUO)
JE............ Joint Engineers [*Army*] (RDA)
JE............ Joint Enterprise
JE............ Joshi Effect [*Physics*]
JE............ Joule Effect [*Physics*]
JE............ Journal Entry (TIMI)
JE............ Journal of Education [*A publication*] (BRI)
JE............ Jump If Equal [*Computer science*] (PCM)
JE............ Junctional Escape [*Cardiology*] (DAVI)
JE............ Junction Exchange [*Telecommunications*] (OA)
Je............ June (RION)
JE............ June
JE............ Manx Airlines [*Airline flight code*] (ODBW)
JE............ Yosemite Airlines [*ICAO designator*] (AD)
JEA .... Jamaica Exporters Association (BUAC)
JEA .... Japan Electric Association (BUAC)
JEA .... Japan Environmental Agency (QUAC)
JEA .... Japan Export Association (SAUO)
JEA .... Jersey European Airways [*British*] [*ICAO designator*] (FAAC)
JEA .... Jesuit Educational Association [*Later split into AJCU and JSEA*] (EA)
JEA .... Jewish Education Association
JEA .... Jewish Educators Assembly (EA)
JEA .... Joint Endeavor Agreement
JEA .... Joint Engineering Agency
JEA .... Joint Export Agent
JEA .... Joint Export Association [*Department of Commerce*]
JEA .... Jordan Engineers Association (SAUO)

JEA .... Journalism Education Association (EA)
JEAB .... Journal of the Experimental Analysis of Behavior (journ.) (SAUS)
JEAC .... Journal of Electroanalytical Chemistry [A publication]
JEADF .... Joint Eastern Air Defense Force (MUGU)
JEADV .... Journal of the European Academy of Dermatology and Venereology (SAUO)
JEADV .... Journal of the European Academy of Dermatology and Venereology (journ.) (SAUS)
Jeaf .... Jeaffreson's Book about Lawyers [A publication] (DLA)
JEAH .... Jewish Endowment for the Arts and Humanities
JEAL .... Junction Emitting Avalanche Light
JEAN .... Jean Philippe Fragrances [NASDAQ symbol] (TTSB)
JEAN .... Jean Philippe Fragrances, Inc. [NASDAQ symbol] (NQ)
JEAN .... JOSS-Based Expression Analyser for the Nineteen Hundred (NITA)
Jean Charcot... French research vessel (SAUS)
JeanPhl .... Jean Philippe Fragrances, Inc. [Associated Press] (SAG)
JEARD .... Journal of Eastern African Research and Development [A publication]
J Earth Sci... Journal of Earth Sciences (journ.) (SAUS)
J Earth Sci Nagoya Unir... Journal of Earth Sciences. Nagoya University (journ.) (SAUS)
JEAS .... Journal of East Asiatic Studies (journ.) (SAUS)
JEASC .... Journal. East African Swahili Committee [A publication]
J East Afr Nat Hist Soc Natl Mus... Journal. East Africa Natural History Society and National Museum (journ.) (SAUS)
J East Afr Res Develop... Journal of Eastern African Research and Development (journ.) (SAUS)
J East Chin Inst Text Sci Technol... Journal. East China Institute of Textile Science Technology (journ.) (SAUS)
J East Chin Petrol Inst... Journal. East China Petroleum Institute (journ.) (SAUS)
J East West Stud... Journal of East and West Studies (journ.) (SAUS)
JEAT .... Joint Emergency Airlift Traffic (SAUS)
JEAT .... Joint Emergency Airlift Traffic Management Plan [DoD]
JEB .... James Ewell Brown Stuart [American Confederate general known as Jeb Stuart, 1833-1864]
JEB .... Jansen Engineering Building (SAUS)
JEB .... Japan Evangelical Board (SAUO)
JEB .... Jewish Education Bureau [British] (CB)
JEB .... Joint Economy Board [Abolished, 1947] [Army-Navy]
JEB .... Joint Electronics Board
JEB .... Joint Emergency Board (SAUO)
JEB .... Journal of Economic Behavior (journ.) (SAUS)
JEB .... Journal of Economics and Business (journ.) (SAUS)
JEB .... Journal of Experimental Biology (journ.) (SAUS)
JEB .... Journal of Experimental Botany (journ.) (SAUS)
JEB .... Junctional Epidermolysis Bullosa [Medicine]
JEB .... Junctional Escape Beat [Medicine] (MELL)
Jebb............ Jebb's Irish Crown Cases [1822-40] [A publication] (DLA)
Jebb............ Jebbs Irish Crown Cases (journ.) (SAUS)
Jebb & B ..... Jebb and Bourke's Irish Queen's Bench Reports [1841-42] [A publication] (DLA)
Jebb & B ..... Jebb and Bourkes Irish Queens Bench Reports (journ.) (SAUS)
Jebb & B (Ir)... Jebb and Bourke's Irish Queen's Bench Reports [1841-42] [A publication] (DLA)
Jebb & S ..... Jebb and Symes' Irish Queen's Bench Reports [A publication] (DLA)
Jebb & S (Ir)... Jebb and Symes' Irish Queen's Bench Reports [A publication] (DLA)
Jebb & Sym... Jebb and Symes' Irish Queen's Bench Reports [A publication] (DLA)
Jebb CC....... Jebb's Irish Crown Cases [1822-40] [A publication] (DLA)
Jebb CC (Ir)... Jebb's Irish Crown Cases [1822-40] [A publication] (DLA)
Jebb Cr & Pr Cas... Jebb's Irish Crown and Presentment Cases [A publication] (DLA)
JEBC .... Jefferson Bancorp, Inc. (Los Angeles) [NASDAQ symbol] (SAG)
JEBC .... Jefferson Bancorp(LA) [NASDAQ symbol] (TTSB)
JEBD .... Journal of Emotional and Behavioral Disorders (SAUO)
JEBG .... Japan Electronics Buyers Guide (journ.) (SAUS)
JEBH .... Journal of Economic and Business History (journ.) (SAUS)
JEBM .... Jet Engine Base Maintenance
JEBM-RR ..... Jet Engine Base Maintenance - Return Rate (PDAA)
JEC .... Jacobs Engineering Group, Inc. [NYSE symbol] (SPSG)
JEC .... Jacobs Engr Group [NYSE symbol] (TTSB)
JEC .... Japanese Electrotechnical Committee
JEC .... Jardine Engineering Corp. (SAUS)
JEC .... Jeisey Electric Co. (SAUS)
JEC .... Jersey Electric Co. [British]
JEC .... Jeunesse Etudiante Catholique Internationale [International Young Catholic Students] (EAIO)
JEC .... John E. Chance & Associates (SAUO)
JEC .... Joint Economic Committee (COE)
JEC .... Joint Economic Committee of Congress
JEC .... Joint Economic Congress (SAUO)
JEC .... Joint Economics Committee (ACAE)
JEC .... Joint Emergency Committee (SAUO)
JEC .... Joint European Committee of Paper Experts (SAUO)
JEC .... Joint European Committee of Paper Exporters (BUAC)
JEC .... Joint Evaluation Committee [NSF-UCAR]
JEC .... Joint Exchanges Committee [British] (NUMA)
JEC .... Journal Editorial Committee (ACII)
JECA .... Japan Electrical Construction Association (SAUS)
JECA .... Japan Electrical Construction Association, Inc. (SAUO)
JECA .... Jewel Cave National Monument
JECA .... John E. Chance & Associates (SAUO)
JECA .... Joint Engineers Council of Alabama (SAUO)
JECAB .... Journal of Electrocardiology (journ.) (SAUS)

JECB .... Jet Engine Control Bearing
JECC .... Japan Electric Computer Corporation [Japan] (NITA)
JECC .... Japan Electronic Computer Center (SAUO)
JECC .... Japan Electronic Computer Company, Ltd. (SAUO)
JECC .... Japan Electronic Computer Corporation (SAUO)
JECC .... Japanese Electronic Computer Co.
JECC .... Joint Economic Committee of Congress (MCD)
JECC .... Joint Egyptian Cotton Committee (BUAC)
JECC .... Joint Electronic Components Conference (SAUS)
JECC .... Joint Exercise Control Center (MCD)
JECCS .... Joint Enhanced Core Communications System [Military]
JECEJA .... Joint Emergency Committee for European Jewish Affairs (SAUO)
JECEWSI....... Joint Electronic Combat Electronic Warfare Simulator (SAUS)
JECFA .... Joint Expert Committee of/on Food Additives (SAUS)
JECFA .... Joint Expert Committee on Food Additives [FDA/WHO]
JECFA .... Joint FAO/WHO Expert Committee of/on Food Additives (SAUO)
JECFI .... Joint Expert Committee on Food Irradiation (BUAC)
JECG .... Joint Exercise Control Group (SAUO)
JECH .... Journal of Epidemiology & Community Health (SAUO)
JECH .... Journal of Epidemiology and Community Health (journ.) (SAUS)
J E China Inst Chem Technol... Journal of the East China Institute of Chemical Technology (journ.) (SAUS)
JECI .... Jeunesse Etudiante Catholique Internationale [International Young Catholic Students]
Je Ci .... Jewish Civilisation (journ.) (SAUS)
JECL .... JEC Lasers Inc. (SAUO)
JECL .... Job Entry Control Language
JECMA .... Japan Export Clothing Makers Association (BUAC)
JECMA .... Journal of Electronic Materials (journ.) (SAUS)
JECMB .... Joint Executive Committee on Medicine and Biology
JECMB .... Joint Experimental Committee on Medicine and Biology (SAUS)
JECMOS........ Joint Electronic Countermeasures Operation Section [NATO] (NATG)
JECNS.......... Joint Electronic Communications Nomenclature System [Military] (IAA)
J Ecol .... Journal of Ecology (journ.) (SAUS)
J Ecom Dynamics Control... Journal of Economic Dynamics and Control (journ.) (SAUS)
J Econ Aff.... Journal of Economic Affairs (journ.) (SAUS)
J Econ Biol... Journal of Economic Biology (journ.) (SAUS)
J Econ Bs .... Journal of Economics and Business (journ.) (SAUS)
J Econ Bus Hist... Journal of Economic and Business History (journ.) (SAUS)
J Econ Dev... Journal of Economic Development. Chung-Ang Univ., Economic Research Institute. Seoul (journ.) (SAUS)
J Econ Dyn and Control... Journal of Economic Dynamics and Control (journ.) (SAUS)
J Econ Ed .... Journal of Economic Education (journ.) (SAUS)
J Econ S Hist Or... Journal of the Economic and Social History of the Orient (journ.) (SAUS)
J Econ Soc Meas... Journal of Economic and Social Measurement (journ.) (SAUS)
J Econ Studies... Journal of Economic Studies (journ.) (SAUS)
J Econ Taxon Bot... Journal of Economic and Taxonomic Botany (journ.) (SAUS)
JECOR .... U.S.-Saudi Arabian Joint Commission of Economic Cooperation (SAUO)
JECPA.......... Journal of Experimental Child Psychology (journ.) (SAUS)
JECRA.......... Jewish Committee for Relief Abroad (SAUO)
JECS .... Job Entry Central Services (MCD)
JECSS.......... Japan and East China Seas Study [Marine science] (OSRA)
JED .... Japan Economic Daily [Database] [Kyodo News International, Inc.] [Information service or system] (CRD)
JED .... Japan Engineering Development (SAUO)
JED .... Jeddah [Saudi Arabia] [Airport symbol] (OAG)
Jed............. Jedediah (BJA)
JED .... Jet East, Inc. [ICAO designator] (FAAC)
JED .... Jet Engine Duct
J Ed .... Jewish Education (journ.) (SAUS)
JED .... Job Entry Definition (SAUS)
JED .... Joint Educational Development (EA)
JED .... Joint Exercise Division (SAUO)
JED .... Journal of Economic Dynamics and Control (journ.) (SAUS)
JED .... Journal of Electronic Defense (SAUO)
JED .... Journal of Esthetic Dentistry (SAUO)
JED .... Julian Ephemeris Data (MCD)
JEDA........... Joint Environmental Data Analysis Center [Army] [Marine science] (OSRA)
J Ed Admin... Journal of Educational Administration (journ.) (SAUS)
J Ed Data Process... Journal of Educational Data Processing (journ.) (SAUS)
JEDDS .... Joint Electronic Document Delivery Software (SAUS)
JEDEC.......... Joint Electron Device Engineering Council (EA)
JEDI........... Jobs for Employable Dependent Individuals Program [Federal government]
JEDI........... Joint Electronic Data Interchange [International trade]
JEDMICS...... Joint Engineering and Data Management Information and Control System [Military]
JEDPE......... Joint Emergency Defense Plan Europe [NATO] (NATG)
JEDS........... Japanese Expeditions to the Deep Sea
JEDS........... Jedburgh Teams [Allied intelligence-gathering units in Europe] [World War II]
J Ed Soc ..... Journal of Educational Sociology. Payne Educational Sociology Foundation. New York (SAUO)
JEDTC .... Joint Electron Device Tube Council (SAUO)
J Educ Adm... Journal of Educational Administration (journ.) (SAUS)
J Educ Adm Hist... Journal of Educational Administration and History (journ.) (SAUS)
J Educ Comput Res... Journal of Educational Computing Research (journ.) (SAUS)
J Educ Data Proc... Journal of Educational Data Processing (journ.) (SAUS)

J Educ Dept Nugata Univ... Journal Education Department. Nugata University (journ.) (SAUS)
J Educ DP.... Journal of Educational Data Processing (journ.) (SAUS)
J Educ for Teach... Journal of Education for Teaching (journ.) (SAUS)
J Educ Media Science... Journal of Educational Media Science (journ.) (SAUS)
J Educ Method... Journal of Educational Method (journ.) (SAUS)
J Educ Modules Mater Sci Eng... Journal of Educational Modules for Materials Science and Engineering (journ.) (SAUS)
J Educ Soc... Journal of Education for Social Work (journ.) (SAUS)
J EducTh...... Journal of Educational Thought (journ.) (SAUS)
JEE.............. Japan Electronic Engineering (journ.) (SAUS)
JEE.............. Japan Environment Agency (SAUO)
JEE.............. Japanese Equine Encephalitis [Medicine]
JEE.............. Jet Engine Exhaust
JEE.............. Journal of Electronic Engineering (journ.) (SAUS)
JEE.............. Journal of Engineering Education (journ.) (SAUS)
JEE.............. Journal of Experimental Education (journ.) (SAUS)
JEEC .... Joint ETSI/ECMA Committee (SAUO)
JEEC .... Kenneth E. Johnson Environmental and Energy Center [University of Alabama in Huntsville] [Research center] (RCD)
JEED .... Journal. Environmental Engineering Division. Proceedings of the American Society of Civil Engineers (journ.) (SAUS)
JEEGA .... Journal. Environmental Engineering Division. American Society of Civil Engineers (journ.) (SAUS)
JEEJ Electron Eng... JEE. Journal of Electronic Engineering (journ.) (SAUS)
JEEM .... Journal of Embryology and Experimental Morphology (SAUO)
JEEM .... Journal of Embryology and Experimental Morphology (journ.) (SAUS)
JEEP .... General Purpose Military Utility Vehicle (SAUS)
JEEP .... General-Purpose Quarter-Ton Military Utility Vehicle
Jeep........... Graduated Payment Mortgage (DFIT)
JEEP .... Joint Effort Evaluation Program [Military] (AFM)
JEEP .... Joint Emergency Evacuation Plan [Military] (AABC)
JEEP .... Joint Environmental Effects Program [Military] (AFM)
JEEP .... Joint Establishment Experimental Pile [Nuclear reactor] [Norway]
JEEP .... Joint Ethics Enforcement Plan (SAUO)
JEEP .... Joint Export Establishment Promotion [Trade exhibition] [Department of Commerce]
JEEPS .... GNMA Graduated Payment Mortgage Securities (EBF)
JEF.............. Jacobi Elliptic Function [Mathematics]
JEF.............. Jefferies Group [NYSE symbol] (TTSB)
JEF.............. Jefferson City [Missouri] [Airport symbol] (OAG)
JEF.............. Jefferson City, MO [Location identifier] [FAA] (FAAL)
JEF.............. Jefferson Educational Foundation (EA)
JEF.............. Jefjen Capital [Vancouver Stock Exchange symbol]
JEF.............. JEM Exposure Facility (SAUS)
JEF.............. Jet Engine Fuel
JEF.............. Jetflite OY [Finland] [ICAO designator] (FAAC)
JEF.............. Jeunesses Europeennes Federalistes
JEF.............. Jewish Expeditionary Force
JEF.............. Jugoslavia Esperanto-Federacio (SAUO)
JEFAD .... Joint ECA/FAO Agriculture Division (SAUO)
JefBsh .... Jefferson Bankshares, Inc. [Associated Press] (SAG)
JEFDSS....... Journal of the English Folk Dance and Song Society (SAUO)
JEFDSS....... Journal of the English Folk Dance and Song Society (journ.) (SAUS)
JEFF........... JeffBanks, Inc. [NASDAQ symbol] (SAG)
JEFF........... Jefferson National Corp. (SAUO)
JEFF........... Jefferson National Expansion Memorial National Historic Site
Jeff............ Jefferson's Virginia General Court Reports [A publication] (DLA)
JEFF........... Judiciously Efficient Fixed Frame [Computer science] (MCD)
JeffBanks.... JeffBanks, Inc. [Associated Press] (SAG)
JeffBcLA..... Jefferson Bancorp, Inc. [Los Angles] [Associated Press] (SAG)
JeffBcp .... Jefferson Bancorp, Inc. [Associated Press] (SAG)
Jeff Man...... Jefferson's Manual of Parliamentary Law [A publication] (DLA)
JeffPilot...... Jefferson-Pilot Corp. [Associated Press] (SAG)
JeffPlt......... Jefferson Pilot [Associated Press] (SAG)
JeffPOO ...... Jefferson Pilot [Associated Press] (SAG)
JeffrGp........ Jefferies Group, Inc. [Associated Press] (SAG)
JeffSvg .... Jefferson Savings Bancorp [Associated Press] (SAG)
Jeff (VA)...... Jefferson's Virginia General Court Reports [A publication] (DLA)
JEFG .... Jefferies Group, Inc. [NASDAQ symbol] (NQ)
JEFM .... Jet Engine Field Maintenance
JefSmrf....... Jefferson Smurfit Corp. [Associated Press] (SAG)
JEG .... Joint Evaluation Group (SAUO)
JEG .... Joint Exploratory Group [NATO] (NATG)
J Eg Or Soc... Journal Egyptian and Oriental Society (journ.) (SAUS)
JEGP........... Journal of English and Germanic Philology [A publication] (BRI)
JEGPA......... Journal. Egyptan Public Health Association (journ.) (SAUS)
JEGR........... Jegeroil Corp. (SAUO)
J Egypt Med Soc... Journal Egyptian Medical Society (journ.) (SAUS)
J Egypt Pharm... Journal of Egyptian Pharmacy (journ.) (SAUS)
J Egypt Public Health Assoc... Journal. Egyptian Public Health Association (journ.) (SAUS)
J Egypt Public Health Assoc... Journal of the Egyptian Public Health Association (SAUO)
J Egypt Public Health Assoc... Journal of the Egyptian Public Health Association (journ.) (SAUS)
J Egypt Soc Parasitol... Journal. Egyptian Society of Parasitology (journ.) (SAUS)
J Egypt Soc Parasitol... Journal of the Egyptian Society of Parasitology (journ.) (SAUS)
J Egypt Vet Med Ass... Journal. Egyptian Veterinary Medical Association (journ.) (SAUS)
JEH .... Journal of Ecclesiastical History [A publication] (ODCC)
JEH .... Journal of Economic History [A publication] (BRI)
JEHFC......... Jon-Erik Hexum Fan Club (EA)
JEHO........... Jehosaphat [Biblical] (ROG)

JEHU........... Joint Experimental Helicopter Unit [British military] (DMA)
JEI .... Japana Esperanto-Instituto (SAUO)
JEI .... Japan Economic Institute of America (EA)
JEI .... Japan Electronics Industry (journ.) (SAUS)
JEI .... Jones Environmental, Inc. (EFIS)
JEI .... Journal. English Institute (journ.) (SAUS)
JEI .... Journal of Economic Issues (journ.) (SAUS)
JEI .... Journal of Electronic Imaging (SAUS)
JEIA .... Japanese Electronic Industries Association
JEIA .... Joint Electronics Information Agency
JEIA .... Joint Export-Import Agency [Munich] [Allied German Occupation Forces]
J El Ass J .... Journal. Electrochemical Association of Japan (journ.) (SAUS)
JEIB .... Joint Export Import Board (SAUO)
JEIDA......... Japanese Electronic Industry Development Association (CDE)
JEIM .... Jet Engine Intermediate Maintenance
JEIND......... Journal of Endocrinological Investigation (journ.) (SAUS)
JEIOG......... Joint Emissions Inventory Oversight Group (SAUO)
JEIPAC........ Japan Electronic Information Processing Automatic Computer (SAUS)
JEIPAC........ JICST [Japan Information Center of Science and Technology] Electronic Information Processing Automatic Computer (NITA)
JEISSO........ Joint Expeditions in the Indian Ocean Sector of the Southern Ocean (SAUO)
JEIT .... Joint Equipment Identification Team [Military] (CINC)
JEJ............. Japan Economic Journal (journ.) (SAUS)
JEJ............. Jejunum [Medicine]
JEJ............. Jets Ejecutivos SA [Mexico] [ICAO designator] (FAAC)
JEJUN .... Jejunectomy (ABBR)
JEJUN .... Jejunitis (ABBR)
JEL............. Aerojelk, SA de CV [Mexico] [FAA designator] (FAAC)
JEL............. Jackson Estuarine Laboratory [University of New Hampshire] [Research center] (RCD)
JEL............. Jeunesses Europeennes Liberales [Liberal European Youth]
JEL............. Johnson Elastic Limit (SAUS)
JEL............. Joint Electronic Library [Military]
JEL............. Journal of Economic Literature [A publication] (BRI)
JEL............. Young European Liberals (SAUS)
J Elastomers Plast... Journal of Elastomers and Plastics (journ.) (SAUS)
J Elastoplast... Journal of Elastoplastics (journ.) (SAUS)
JELC .... Joint Effort Against Lefthanded Complications
J Elec .... Journal of Electricity (journ.) (SAUS)
J Elechochem Soc... Journal. Electrochemical Society (journ.) (SAUS)
J Electr Eng... Journal of Electrical Engineering (journ.) (SAUS)
J Electroanal Chem... Journal of Electroanalytical Chemistry (journ.) (SAUS)
J Electroanal Chem Abstract... Journal of Electroanalytical Chemistry. Abstract Section (journ.) (SAUS)
J Electroanal Chem Interfacial Elechochem... Journal of Electroanalytical Chemistry and Interfacial Electrochemistry (journ.) (SAUS)
J Electrocardiol... Journal of Electrocardiology (journ.) (SAUS)
J Electrochem Soc... Journal of the Electrochemical Society (MEC)
J Electrochem Soc India... Journal. Electrochemical Society of India (journ.) (SAUS)
J Electrochem Soc India... Journal of Electrochemical Society of India (journ.) (SAUS)
J Electrochem Soc Japan... Journal. Electrochemical Society of Japan (journ.) (SAUS)
J Electrodepositors Tech S... Journal. Electrodepositors Technical Society (journ.) (SAUS)
J Electromagn Waves Appl... Journal of Electromagnetic Waves and Applications (journ.) (SAUS)
J Electromyography Kinesiol... Journal of Electromyography and Kinesiology (SAUS)
J Electron .... Journal of Electronics (journ.) (SAUS)
J Electron Comput Res... Journal of Electronics and Computers Research (journ.) (SAUS)
J Electron Control... Journal of Electronics and Control (journ.) (SAUS)
J Electron Microsc Tech... Journal of Electron Microscopy Technique (journ.) (SAUS)
J Electron Micry... Journal of Electron Microscopy (journ.) (SAUS)
J Electron Spectrosc... Journal of Electron Spectroscopy (journ.) (SAUS)
J Electro Th... Journal of Electrophysiological Techniques (journ.) (SAUS)
J Electr West Ind... Journal of Electririty and Western Indus- try (journ.) (SAUS)
J Elisha Mitchell Scient Soc... Journal. Elisha Mitchell Scientific Society (journ.) (SAUS)
JEI J Electron Ind... JEL Journal of the Electronics Industry (journ.) (SAUS)
JELM .... Japanese Experiment Logistics Module (SAUO)
JELOS......... Jealous (ABBR)
JELOSY........ Jealousy (ABBR)
JEM .... Japanese Experiment Module
JEM .... Japan Experiment Module (SAUS)
JEM .... Jerusalem and the East Mission
JEM .... Jet Engine Modulation (MCD)
JEM .... Jewelmasters, Inc. (SAUS)
JEM .... Joint Endeavor Manager
JEM .... Joint Environmental Monitoring (SAUS)
JEM .... Joint Exercise Manual (MCD)
JEM .... Joint Experts Meeting (SAUO)
JEM .... Jordon Electronic Manufacturing Co. (SAUO)
JEM .... Journal of Enterprise Management (journ.) (SAUS)
JEM .... Journal of Environmental Economics and Management (journ.) (SAUS)
JEM .... Journal of Experimental Medicine (SAUO)
JEM .... Journey's End Motel Corp. [Toronto Stock Exchange symbol]
JEMA .... Japan Electronic Messaging Association (DDC)
JEM(A)........ Junior Electrical Mechanic (Air) [British military] (DMA)

JEMAA......... Journal. Egyptian Medical Association (journ.) (SAUS)
JEM(AW)..... Junior Electrical Mechanic (Air Weapon) [British military] (DMA)
JEMC........... Joint Engineering Management Conference
J Emerg Med... Journal of Emergency Medicine (journ.) (SAUS)
J Emerg Med Serv... Journal of Emergency Medical Services (journ.) (SAUS)
JEMI............. Joint Electromagnetic Interference [Military]
JEMI............. Joint Equipment Manufacturers Initiative (SAUS)
JEMIC........... Japan Electric Meters Inspection Corp. (BUAC)
JEMIMA....... [The] Japan Electrical Measurements Manufacturers' Association (ACII)
JEMP........... Joint Engineers Management Panel [Army] (RDA)
J Empl Coun... Journal of Employment Counseling (journ.) (SAUS)
JEMR........... Jem Records Inc. (SAUS)
JEMR........... Jem Reeords Inc. (SAUO)
JEMRB......... Joint European Medical Research Board (BUAC)
JEMS........... Journal of Emergency Medical Services (SAUO)
JEMS........... Journal of Emergency Medical Services (journ.) (SAUS)
JEMSA........ Journal. Elisha Mitchell Scientific Society (journ.) (SAUS)
JEN............. Japan Economic Newswire [Kyodo News International, Inc.] [Information service or system] (CRD)
JEN............. Jena [German Democratic Republic] [Seismograph station code, US Geological Survey] [Closed] (SEIS)
JEN............. Jenair Ltd. [Cyprus] [ICAO designator] (FAAC)
JEN............. Journal of Emergency Nursing (journ.) (SAUS)
J En........... Journal of English (journ.) (SAUS)
JEN............. Junta de Energia Nuclear [Spanish nuclear agency]
JEN............. Junularo Esperantista de Nord-Ameriko (SAUO)
JEN............. Nuclear Energy Authority (SAUS)
JENAKAT...... Jeunesse Nationale Katangaise [Katangan National Youth]
Jena Rev..... Jena Review (journ.) (SAUS)
Jena Rev Suppl... Jena Review. Supplement (journ.) (SAUS)
JENC........... Joint Emergency National Committee for the Building Industry (SAUO)
Jenck Bills... Jencken's Bills of Exchange [1880] [A publication] (DLA)
Jenck Neg S... Jencken's Negotiable Securities [1880] [A publication] (DLA)
JenCrg........ Jenny Craig [Associated Press] (SAG)
JENDD......... Journal of Energy and Development (journ.) (SAUS)
J Endocrinol Invest... Journal of Endocrinological Investigation (journ.) (SAUS)
J Endourol... Journal of Endourology (journ.) (SAUS)
JENDRPC..... Joint Euratom Nuclear Data and Reactor Physics Committee (BUAC)
JENER......... Joint Establishment for Nuclear Energy Research
J Energy..... Journal of Energy (journ.) (SAUS)
J Energy & Devel... Journal of Energy and Development [A publication] (DLA)
J Energy Eng... Journal of Energy Engineering (journ.) (SAUS)
J Energy LP... Journal of Energy Law and Policy (journ.) (SAUS)
J Energy Resour Technol Trans ASME... Journal of Energy Resources Technology. Transactions of the American Society of Mechanical Engineers (journ.) (SAUS)
JENER Report... Joint Establishment for Nuclear Energy Research Report (journ.) (SAUS)
JENEX.......... Japanese El Nino Experiment [Marine science] (OSRA)
JenfCv........ Jennifer Convertibles, Inc. [Associated Press] (SAG)
J Eng and Germ Philol... Journal of English and Germanic Philology (journ.) (SAUS)
J Eng Ind..... Journal of Engineering for Industry (SAUS)
J.Engl Agric Soc... Journal. English Agricultural Society (journ.) (SAUS)
J Eng Mat & Tech... Journal of Engineering Materials and Technology (journ.) (SAUS)
J Eng Mater Technol Trans ASME... Journal of Engineering Materials and Technology. Transactions of the American Society of Mechanical Engineers (journ.) (SAUS)
J Eng Mech... Journal of Engineering Mechanics (journ.) (SAUS)
J Eng Mech Div Amer Soc... Journal of the Engineering Mechanics Division, Proceedings of the American Society (journ.) (SAUS)
Jengo.......... Junior Engineering Officer (SAUO)
J Eng Power... Journal of Engineering for Power (SAUS)
J Eng Power... Journal of Engineering for Power (journ.) (SAUS)
J Eng Psychol... Journal of Engineering Psychology (journ.) (SAUS)
J Engrg Math... Journal of Engineering Mathematics (journ.) (SAUS)
J Engrg Phys... Journal of Engineering Physics (journ.) (SAUS)
J Eng Sci King Saud Univ... Journal of Engineering King Saud University (journ.) (SAUS)
J Eng Technol Manage... Journal of Engineering and Technology Management (journ.) (SAUS)
Jenk........... Jenkins' Eight Centuries of Reports, English Exchequer [145 English Reprint] [1220-1623] [A publication] (DLA)
Jenk & Formoy... Jenkinson and Formoy's Select Cases in the Exchequer of Pleas [Selden Society Publication, Vol. 48] [A publication] (DLA)
Jenk Cent .... Jenkins' Eight Centuries of Reports, English Exchequer [145 English Reprint] [1220-1623] [A publication] (DLA)
Jenk Cent .... Jenkins Eight Centuries of Reports, Eng- lish Exchequer (journ.) (SAUS)
Jenkins (Eng)... Jenkins' Eight Centuries of Reports, English Exchequer [145 English Reprint] [1220-1623] [A publication] (DLA)
Jenks.......... Jenks' Reports [58 New Hampshire] [A publication] (DLA)
JENN........... Jennifer Convertibles, Inc. (SAUO)
Jenn........... Jennison's Reports [14-18 Michigan] [A publication] (DLA)
Jenn Sug A... Jennett's Sugden Acts [A publication] (DLA)
J Enriron Econ Manage... Journal of Environmental Economics and Management (journ.) (SAUS)
Jen-Soc J.... Jen-Soc Journal (journ.) (SAUS)
J Ent .... Journal of Entomology (journ.) (SAUS)
JENTAC........ Jentaculum [Breakfast] [Pharmacy]
J Enterostom Ther... Journal of Enterostomal Therapy (journ.) (SAUS)

J Entomol A... Journal of Entomology. Series A. General Entomology (journ.) (SAUS)
J Entomol B... Journal of Entomology. Series B. Taxonomy (journ.) (SAUS)
J Entomol Sci... Journal of Entomological Science (journ.) (SAUS)
J Entomol Ser A Physiol Behav... Journal of Entomology. Series A. Physiology and Behaviour (journ.) (SAUS)
J Entomol Ser B Taxon Syst... Journal of Entomology. Series B. Taxonomy and Systematics (journ.) (SAUS)
J Entomol Soc BC... Journal. Entomological Society of British Columbia (journ.) (SAUS)
J Entomol Zool... Journal of Entomology and Zoology (journ.) (SAUS)
J Ent Soc Qd... Journal. Entomological Society of Queensland (journ.) (SAUS)
JENV........... Joint Environmental Department (SAUO)
JENV COLL LOND... Jewish College, London (SAUS)
J Envir Eng... Journal. Environmental Engineering Division. American Society of Civil Engineers (journ.) (SAUS)
J Envir Mgm... Journal of Environmental Management (journ.) (SAUS)
J Environ Biol... Journal of Environmental Biology (journ.) (SAUS)
J Environ Eng... Journal of Environmental Engineering (journ.) (SAUS)
J Environ Engng Dir Proc ASCE... Journal. Environmental Engineering Division. Proceedings of the American Society of Civil Engineering (journ.) (SAUS)
J Environ Health... Journal of Environmental Health (journ.) (SAUS)
J Environ Manage... Journal of Environmental Management (SAUO)
J Environ Pathol Toxicol... Journal of Environmental Pathology and Toxicology (journ.) (SAUS)
J Environ Pathol Toxicol Oncol... Journal of Environmental Pathology, Toxicology and Oncology (journ.) (SAUS)
J Environ Plan Pollut Control... Journal of Environmental Planning and Pollution Control (journ.) (SAUS)
J Environ Polym Degrad... Journal of Environmental Polymer Degradation (journ.) (SAUS)
J Environ Radioact... Journal of Environmental Radioactivity (journ.) (SAUS)
J Envir Sci Hlth... Journal of Environmental Science and Health (journ.) (SAUS)
J Enzym Inhib... Journal of Enzyme Inhibition (journ.) (SAUS)
JEOCN .... Joint European Operations Communications Network
JEOF........... Joint Exercise Observation File (SAUO)
JEOL........... Japan Electron Optics Co., Limited (SAUO)
JEOL........... Japan Electron Optics Laboratory Co. (BUAC)
JEOL........... Japan Electro-Optics Laboratories (or Laboratory) (SAUS)
JEOLCO........ Japan Electron Optics Laboratory Co. (SAUS)
JEOLCO........ Japan Electron Optics Laboratory Company (SAUO)
JEOP........... Jeopardy (ABBR)
JEOPZ......... Jeopardize (ABBR)
JEOPZD........ Jeopardized (ABBR)
JEOPZG........ Jeopardizing (ABBR)
JEOS........... Janus Earth Observation Satellite (SAUS)
JEOS........... Japanese Earth Observation System (SAUS)
JEOS........... Japanese Earth Observing Satellite (EOSA)
JEOS........... Japanese Earth Observing System (CARB)
Jep............. Jeopardy (BARN)
JEP............. Jepson Corp. (SAUO)
JEP............. Jet Engine Processor
JEP............. Jewish Elite Person
JEP............. Joint Experiments Program (ACAE)
JEP............. Journal of Economic Psychology (journ.) (SAUS)
JEP............. Journal of Educational Psychology (journ.) (SAUS)
JEP............. Jupiter Entry Probe
JEPA........... Job Evaluation Policy Act (SAUS)
JEPA........... Job Evaluation Policy Act of 1970
JEPABP........ Journal of Experimental Psychology: Animal Behavior Processes (journ.) (SAUS)
JEPAP......... Joint Emergency Personnel Augmentation Plan [Military] (CINC)
JEPCE......... Joint Exercise Planning Committee (SAUO)
JEPDS......... Jet Exhaust Powered Decontamination System (ACAE)
JEPES .... Joint Engineering Planning Execution System (VLIE)
JEPES .... Joint Engineer Planning and Execution System [Environmental science] (COE)
JEPG........... Joint Exercise Planning Group [Military]
JEPI........... Joint Electronic Payment Intitiative [Proposed] [Computer science]
JEPI........... Joint Electronic Payments Initiative
JEPI........... Junior Eysenck Personality Inventory [Psychology]
JEPIA......... Japan Electronic Parts Industry Association
J Epidemiol Community Health... Journal of Epidemiology and Community Health (journ.) (SAUS)
J Epilepsy.... Journal of Epilepsy (journ.) (SAUS)
JEPLA .... Journal of Elastomers and Plastics (journ.) (SAUS)
JEPO........... Jet Engine Project Office (SAUO)
JEPO........... Joint Engine Project Office (MCD)
JEPOSS....... Javelin Experimental and Theoretical Physics Protection Oil Sands System (SAUS)
JEPOSS....... Javelin Experimental Protection Oil Sands System (SAUS)
JEPP........... Japan English Publications in Print [Japan Publications Guide Service] [Japan] [Information service or system] (CRD)
JEPP........... Japanese Earthquake Prediction Plan
JEPP........... Joint Emergency Planning Program (SAUS)
JEPS .... Job Effectiveness Prediction System [Test for insurance company employees]
JEPS .... Job Entry Peripheral Services [IBM Corp.] (MCD)
JEPS .... Joint Exercise Planning Staff [NATO] (NATG)
JEPSBL........ European Journal of Steroids (SAUS)
JEPTO......... Journal of Environmental Pathology, Toxicology and Oncology (journ.) (SAUS)
JEQ............. Japan Equity Fund [NYSE symbol] (SPSG)
JEQ............. Jequie [Brazil] [Airport symbol] (OAG)

JEQ.............. Jump Equal (SAUS)
J Equine Med Surg... Journal of Equine Medicine and Surgery (journ.) (SAUS)
JER.............. Japan Economic Review [A publication] (WDAA)
JER.............. Japanese Erection Ring [Medicine] (BABM)
Jer.............. Jeremiah [Old Testament book]
Jer.............. Jeremiah, The Book of the Prophet (SAUS)
Jer.............. Jeremias (BJA)
Jer.............. Jericho (BJA)
JER.............. Jersey [Channel Islands] [Airport symbol] (OAG)
JER.............. Jerusalem [Israel] [Seismograph station code, US Geological Survey] (SEIS)
Jer.............. Jerusalem Talmud (BJA)
Jer.............. Jerushalmi (BJA)
JER.............. Journal of Educational Research (journ.) (SAUS)
JER.............. Junctional Escape Rhythm (STED)
JERA.............. James E. Rush Associates, Inc. [Also, an information service or system] (IID)
JERAC.............. Jerramungup Extension and Research Advisory Committee (SAUO)
JERC.............. Japan Economic Research Centre (BUAC)
JERC.............. Japan-Europe Economic Research Center (SAUS)
JerC.............. Jersey Central Power & Light [Associated Press] (SAG)
JERC.............. Joint Electsonic Research Committee (SAUS)
Jerc.............. Junior Executive Research Consultant [Fictitious position in Commerce Bank of Beverly Hills created for Jethro Bodine on the television show "The Beverly Hillbillies"]
Jer Car ...... Jeremy on Carriers [A publication] (DLA)
Jer Dig .... Jeremy's Digest [1817-49] [A publication] (DLA)
Jeremy Eq ... Jeremy's Equity Jurisdiction [A publication] (DLA)
Jeremy Eq Jur... Jeremy's Equity Jurisdiction [A publication] (DLA)
Jer Eq Jur ... Jeremy's Equity Jurisdiction [A publication] (DLA)
JERI.............. Japan Economics Research Institute (BUAC)
JERI.............. Joint Economic Research Institute (SAUO)
JERK.............. Journalists Easy Road to Knowledge (journ.) (SAUS)
JerM.............. Jersey Microfilming, Clifton, NJ [Library symbol] [Library of Congress] (LCLS)
JEROB.............. Jeroboam (WDAA)
jeroboam..... Five-liter resealable container for ethanol-water solutions (SAUS)
JerPes.......... Jerusalem Talmud. Pesahim (BJA)
Jerr Copyr ... Jerrold on Copyright [A publication] (DLA)
JERS.............. Japan Earth Remote Sensing Satellite
JERS.............. Japan Ergonomics Research Society (BUAC)
JERS.............. Japanese Earth Resource Remote-Sensing Satellite (SAUS)
JERS.............. Japanese Earth Resources Satellite
JERS.............. Japanese Ergonomics Research Society (SAUO)
JERS.............. Joint Emergency Relocation Site
JERS-1.......... Japanese Earth Remote-Sensing Satellite-1 (EOSA)
Jersey City St C... Jersey City State College (GAGS)
JERS-I .... Japan Earth Resources Satellite [Marine science] (OSRA)
JERS-OPS... Japanese Earth Resources Satellite-OPS Sensor (SAUO)
JERTD.......... Journal of Energy Resources Technology (journ.) (SAUS)
JERU.............. Joint Environmental Research Unit (MCD)
Jerus .... Jerusalem (BJA)
Jerus Symp Quantum Chem Biochem... Jerusalem Symposia on Quantum Chemistry and Biochemistry (journ.) (SAUS)
Jerv Cor...... Jervis. Coroners [9th ed.] [1957] [A publication] (DLA)
Jerv NR .... Jervis' New Rules [A publication] (DLA)
JerW.............. Jerusalemer Warte (BJA)
JerYeb.......... Jerusalem Talmud. Yebamoth (BJA)
Jes.............. Analysis and Digest of the Decisions of Sir George Jessel, by A. P Peter [England] [A publication] (DLA)
JES .... James Ewing Society (SAUO)
JES .... Japan/East Sea (SAUS)
JES .... Japan Electronics Show
JES .... Japan Engineering Standards (SAUS)
JES .... Japan Environmental Systems
JES .... Japanese Economic Studies. A Journal of Translations (journ.) (SAUS)
JES .... Japanese Electroplating Society (BUAC)
JES .... Japanese Export Standard
JES .... Jes Air [Bulgaria] [ICAO designator] (FAAC)
JES .... Jesuit (DSUE)
JES .... Jesup, GA [Location identifier] [FAA] (FAAL)
JES .... Jesus
Jes.............. Jesus College, Cambridge (SAUO)
JES.............. Jet Ejector System
JES .... Job Entry Subsystem (SAUS)
JES .... Job Entry System [or Subsystem] [IBM Corp.] [Computer science]
JES .... John Ericsson Society (EA)
JES .... Joint Efficiency Study (AIE)
JES .... Joint Environmental Service (SAUS)
JES .... Joint Environmental Simulator (SAUS)
JES .... Joint Environment Simulator (SAUS)
JES .... Journal of Economics and Siology (journ.) (SAUS)
JES .... Journal of Economic Studies (journ.) (SAUS)
JES .... Journal of Ecumenical Studies (journ.) (SAUS)
JES .... Journal of European Studies (journ.) (SAUS)
JESA.............. Japanese Engineering Standards Association (BUAC)
JESAC.......... Joint Engineering Student Activity Committee (SAUS)
JESAP.......... Jet Engine Smoke Abatement Program
JESAUG ...... Journal of the Environmental Satellite Amateur Users Group (journ.) (SAUS)
JESC.............. Japanese Engineering Standards Committee (BUAC)
JESC.............. Joint Electronics Standardisation Committee (BUAC)
JESC.............. Joint Equipment Standardization Committee (SAUO)
JES COLL..... Jesus College [Oxford or Cambridge] [England] (ROG)

Jes Coll....... Jesus College, Cambridge (SAUS)
JESCOM...... Jesuits in Communication in the US (EA)
JESHO .... Journal of Economic and Social History of the Orient (journ.) (SAUS)
JESHO .... Journal of the Economic and Social History of the Orient (journ.) (SAUS)
JESIA........ Journal. Electrochemical Society of India (journ.) (SAUS)
JESNA........ Jewish Education Service of North America (EA)
JES/NJE ...... Job Entry System/Network Job Entry
JESOA........ Journal. Electrochemical Society (journ.) (SAUS)
JES/RES....... Job Entry System/Remote Entry Subsystem (SAUS)
JESS .... Joint Exercise Simulation System [DoD]
JESS .... Joint Exercise Support System [Military]
J Essent Oil Res... Journal of Essential Oil Research (journ.) (SAUS)
JESSI........ Joint European Semiconductor Consortium (SAUO)
JESSI........ Joint European Semiconductor Silicon Initiative
JESSI........ Joint European Submicron Silicon [Project]
JESSI........ Joint European Submicron Silicon Initiative (BUAC)
JESSI........ Junior Engineers' and Scientists' Summer Institute
JESS-TACSIM... Joint Exercise Simulation System (SAUS)
JESS-TACSIM... Joint Exercise Simulation System-Tactical Simulation (SAUO)
JEST .... Journal of Extraneous Scientific Topics (journ.) (SAUS)
JEST .... Jungle Environmental Survival Training [Military]
JEST .... Jungle Environmental Survival Training School (SAUO)
JEST School... Jungle Environmental Survival Training School (SAUS)
Jesus .... Jesus College Oxford (SAUS)
JESUS........ Job Entry System of the University of Saskatuan (SAUO)
JET.............. European Jet Ltd. [British] [ICAO designator] (FAAC)
JET.............. Frankfort (SAUS)
JET.............. Frankfort, KY [Location identifier] [FAA] (FAAL)
JET.............. Jam Exceeds Threshold
JET.............. Japanese Exchange and Teaching Programme (SAUO)
JET.............. Japan-Europa-Trade Co., Ltd. (SAUO)
JET.............. Java Enabled Type (SAUS)
JET.............. JDS Evaluation Team (SAUO)
JET.............. Jetronic Industries, Inc. [AMEX symbol] (SPSG)
JET.............. Jetsam (ABBR)
JET.............. Jettison
JET.............. Jitter Equivalent Target (CCCA)
JET.............. Job Element Text (AFM)
JET.............. Job English Training
JET.............. Job Express Transportation (SAUS)
JET.............. Jobs Evaluation and Training
JET.............. Joint Economic Team
JET.............. Joint Effort for Talent [Navy] (NG)
JET.............. Joint Engine Technology (SAUS)
JET.............. Joint Enroute Terminal (SAUS)
JET.............. Joint European TOKAMAK [Toroidal Kamera Magnetic] [or Torus] [Nuclear reactor]
JET.............. Joint European Transport (SAUS)
JET.............. Jointly Endorsed Training [Union-management]
JET.............. Journal Entries Transfer [Computer science] (MHDI)
JET.............. Journal of Economic Theory (journ.) (SAUS)
JET.............. Journal of Real Estate Taxation (journ.) (SAUS)
JET.............. Judicial Education Teleseminar System [Defunct] (TSSD)
JET.............. Junior Enlisted Travel [Entitlement] (MCD)
JET.............. Junior Executives Training (SAUO)
JETA.......... Jet America Inc. (SAUO)
JET-A1 .... Jet Fuel type A1 (SAUS)
JETAA.......... Journal. Faculty of Engineering. University of Tokyo. Series A. Annual Report (journ.) (SAUS)
JETAI .... Journal of Experimental and Theoretical Artificial Intelligence (journ.) (SAUS)
JETAM .... Jet Engine Thrust Augmentation Mix (SAA)
JETAV .... Jet Aviation (SAA)
JETBA.......... Journal. Faculty of Engineering. University of Tokyo. Series B (journ.) (SAUS)
JETCA .... Journal of Ethnic Studies (journ.) (SAUS)
JETCO........ Jamaican Export Trading Co. (SAUS)
JETCO........ Jamaican Export Trading Company (SAUO)
JETCO........ Japan Export Trading Co. (SAUS)
JETCO........ Japan Export Trading Company (SAUO)
JETD.......... Jetted (ABBR)
JETD.......... Joint Electronics Type Designator [Military] (AABC)
JETDLAG...... Joint European Development of Tunable Diode Laser Absoprtion Spectometry for the Measurement of Atmospheric Gases (SAUO)
JETDS........ Joint Electronics Type Data System (ACAE)
JETDS........ Joint Electronics Type Designation System [Military] (AFM)
JETEC .... Joint Electron Tube Engineering Council [Later, JEDEC] (MCD)
JETEC........ Joint Expendable Turbine Engine Concept (SAUS)
JET FAG...... Jet Flight Fatigue (SAUS)
JetForm ...... Jet Form Corp. [Associated Press] (SAG)
JETG .... Jetting (ABBR)
J Eth L .... Journal of Ethiopian Law [A publication] (DLA)
J Eth L .... Journal of Ethiopian Law (journ.) (SAUS)
J Ethnopharmacol... Journal of Ethnopharmacology (journ.) (SAUS)
JEthS.......... Journal of Ethiopian Studies (journ.) (SAUS)
JETI.......... JETI. Japan Energy and Technology Intelligence (journ.) (SAUS)
JETLNR........ Jetliner (ABBR)
JETMA .... Jet Mechanic (SAUS)
JETN.......... Jettison
JETOAS........ European Journal of Toxicology (journ.) (SAUS)
JETOC........ Japan Chemical Industry Ecology-Toxicology & Information Center (SAUO)
JETP .... Jet-Propelled
JETP .... Journal of Experimental and Theoretical Physics (journ.) (SAUS)

JETP .... Journal of Experimental Purpose (journ.) (SAUS)
JETP .... Journal of Experimental Theoretical Physics (journ.) (SAUS)
JETPA .... Jet Propulsion (journ.) (SAUS)
Jet Propul... Jet Propulsion (journ.) (SAUS)
Jet Propul Lab Publ... Jet Propulsion Laboratory. Publication (journ.) (SAUS)
Jet Propul Lab Tech Memo... Jet Propulsion Laboratory. Technical Memorandum
    (journ.) (SAUS)
JETR .... Japan Engineering Test Reactor
JETR .... Jetevator
JETRO......... Japanese External Trade Recovery Organization (SAUO)
JETRO......... Japan Export and Trade Research Organization (SAUO)
JETRO......... Japan Exterior Trade Research Organization (SAUO)
JETRO......... Japan External Trade Organization [New York, NY] (EA)
JETRON ...... Jetronic Industries, Inc. (SAUO)
Jetronic .... Jetronic Industries, Inc. [Associated Press] (SAG)
JETS .... Jammer Technique Simulation (ACAE)
JETS .... Jetbome International, Inc. (SAUO)
JETS .... Jet Express Ticketing System
JETS .... Job Executive and Transport Satellite [NCR Corp.]
JETS .... Joint Electronics Type [Designation] System [Military] (NASA)
JETS .... Joint Enroute Terminal System [Canada] (MCD)
JETS .... Journal. Evangelical Theological Society (journ.) (SAUS)
JETS .... Junior Engineering Technical Society
JETS .... Junior Engineers Technical Society (SAUO)
JETS .... Junior Engineers, Technicians, Scientists Organization of Zambia
    (SAUO)
JETSB .... Joint European Torus Supervisory Board (BUAC)
JET Scheme... Jobs, Education & Training Scheme [Australia] (WDAA)
JETT............ Jettison (KSC)
JET-X .... Joint European Telescope for X-rays on Spectrum-X-Gamma (SAUO)
JETXA .... Journal of Existentialism (journ.) (SAUS)
JEU .... Journal of European Industrial Training (journ.) (SAUS)
J Eukaryot Microbiol... Journal of Eukaryotic Microbiology (journ.) (SAUS)
J Eur Ceram S... Journal. European Ceramic Society (journ.) (SAUS)
J Eur Ceram Soc... Journal of the European Ceramic Society (journ.) (SAUS)
J Eur Econ Hist... Journal of European Economic History (journ.) (SAUS)
J Eur Stud ... Journal of European Studies (journ.) (SAUS)
JEV .... Japanese Encephalitis Virus [Medicine]
JEV .... Jesuit European Volunteers [An association] (BUAC)
JEVA .... Jammer Evaluation Versus Amplitude (ACAE)
JEVA .... Japan Electric Vehicle Association (SAUO)
JEVA .... Japan Electric Vehicle Birthday Association (SAUO)
J Eval Clin Pract... Journal of Evaluation in Clinical Practice (journ.) (SAUS)
J Evang Th S... Journal. Evangelical Theological Society (journ.) (SAUS)
Jev Cr Law... Jevons on Criminal Law [A publication] (DLA)
Jev Cr Lw... Jevons on Criminal Law (journ.) (SAUS)
JEVED......... Journal of Environmental Education (journ.) (SAUS)
JEVQA........ Journal of Environmental Quality (journ.) (SAUS)
JEVSB......... Journal of Environmental Systems (journ.) (SAUS)
JEW .... Jewellery [British] (ROG)
Jew............ Jewelry (SAUS)
Jew............ Jewish (DIAR)
JEW .... Jewish
JEWC.......... Joint Electronic Warfare Center (MCD)
JEW COLL LOND... Jewish College, London [England] (ROG)
Jewel.......... Jewellery (DIAR)
JEWEL .... Joint Endeavor for Welfare, Education, and Liberation [Part of
    Grenadian political party, the New JEWEL Movement]
JewettC....... Jewett-Cameron Trading Co. Ltd. [Associated Press] (SAG)
Jew Hist Soc Engl Trans... Jewish Historical Society of England. Transactions
    (journ.) (SAUS)
Jewish Soc Stud... Jewish Social Studies (journ.) (SAUS)
JEWLF........ IWI Holding Ltd. [NASDAQ symbol] (SAG)
JEWOC........ Joint Electronic Warfare Orientation Course (SAUO)
JEWSOC ..... Joint Electronic Warfare Staff Officer Course (DOMA)
JewSocSt..... Jewish Social Studies (journ.) (SAUS)
Jew Soc Stud... Jewish Social Studies. Conference on Jewish Social Studies. New
    York (SAUS)
JEWT .... Jungle Exercise without Trees [British military] (DMA)
Jew YB Int'l L... Jewish Yearbook of International Law [A publication] (DLA)
Jew YB Intl L... Jewish Yearbook of International Law (journ.) (SAUS)
JEX .... Jenks, OK [Location identifier] [FAA] (FAAL)
JEX .... Jet Express, Inc. [ICAO designator] (FAAC)
JEX .... Joint Exercise (NVT)
JEXAM .... Japanese Experiment on Asia Monsoon (SAUO)
J Ex An Beh... Journal of the Experimental Analysis of Behavior (journ.) (SAUS)
J Excep Child... Journal of Exceptional Children (journ.) (SAUS)
J Existent..... Journal of Existentialism (journ.) (SAUS)
JExP........... Journal of Experimental Psychology (journ.) (SAUS)
J Exp Anal Behav... Journal of Experimental Analysis of Behavior (SAUS)
J Exp Anim Sci... Journal of Experimental Animal Science (journ.) (SAUS)
J Exp Biol Med... Journal of Experimental Biology and Medicine (journ.) (SAUS)
J Exp Clin Cancer Res... Journal of Experimental and Clinical Cancer Research
    (journ.) (SAUS)
J Ex PHP ..... Journal of Experimental Psychology Human Perception and
    Performance (journ.) (SAUS)
JEx PL .... Journal of Experimental Psychology Human Learning and Memory
    (journ.) (SAUS)
J Expl Eng ... Journal of Explosives Engineering (journ.) (SAUS)
J Exp Mar Biol Ecol... Journal of Experimental Marine Biology and Ecology
    (journ.) (SAUS)
J Exp Marine Biol... Journal of Experimental Marine Biology (journ.) (SAUS)
J Exp Med Sci... Journal of Experimental Medical Sciences (journ.) (SAUS)
J Expo Anal Environ Epidemiol... Journal of Exposure Analysis and Environmental
    Epidemiology (journ.) (SAUS)

J Exp Pathol... Journal of Experimental Pathology (journ.) (SAUS)
J Exp Psychol... Journal of Experimental Psychology (journ.) (SAUS)
J Exp Psychol Hum Learn Mem... Journal of Experimental Psychology Human
    Learning and Memory (journ.) (SAUS)
J Exp Psychol Monogr... Journal of Experimental Psychology Monograph (journ.)
    (SAUS)
J Exp Psy H... Journal of Experimental Psychology Human Learning and Memory
    (journ.) (SAUS)
J Exp Psy P... Journal of Experimental Psychology Human Perception and
    Performance (journ.) (SAUS)
J Exp Res Pers... Journal of Experimental Research in Personality (journ.) (SAUS)
J Exp Ther... Journal of Experimental Therapeutics (journ.) (SAUS)
J Exp Zool ... Journal of Experimental Zoology (journ.) (SAUS)
J Exp Zool Suppl... Journal of Experimental Zoology. Supplement (journ.) (SAUS)
J Ext .... Journal of Extension (journ.) (SAUS)
J Extra Corporeal Technol... Journal of Extra-Corporeal Technology (journ.) (SAUS)
JEY .... Journal of Employment Counseling (journ.) (SAUS)
J Eye .... Journal of the Eye (journ.) (SAUS)
JEZ .... Joint Engagement Zone [Marine Corps] (DOMA)
JEZEX .... Jezebel [Sonobuoy] Exercise [Navy] (NVT)
JF .... Crest Aviation (SAUS)
jf................ distant fog (SAUS)
JF .... Jack Field
JF .... Jackstone Froster Ltd. [Commercial firm] [British]
JF .... Jamestown Foundation (EA)
JF .... Japan Foundation [Also, Kokusai Koryu] (EA)
JF .... Japan Fund (SAUS)
JF .... Jefferson Foundation (EA)
JF .... Jet Fighter (SAUS)
JF .... Jet Flap
JF .... Jewish Federation (SAUO)
J/F .... Jigs and Fixtures (SAUS)
JF .... John Flanagan [Designer's mark, when appearing on US coins]
JF .... Joint Filler [Technical drawings]
JF .... Joint Fluid [Orthopedics] (DAVI)
JF .... Joint Force [Military]
JF .... Jordan Foundation (SAUO)
JF .... Journal Folio (ROG)
JF .... Jugular Forainen [Anatomy] (DAVI)
JF .... Jugular Foramen (STED)
JF .... Jump Function (SAUS)
JF .... Junctional Fold [Anatomy] (DAVI)
JF .... Junction Frequency [Telecommunications] (TEL)
JF .... Junctor Frame [Telecommunications] (TEL)
JF .... Jundt Growth Fund [NYSE symbol] (SPSG)
JF .... Junior Fiction [Library science] (TELE)
JF .... Justice Fellowship (EA)
JF .... LAB Flying Service [ICAO designator] (AD)
JF .... Trehaven Aviation Ltd. [British] [ICAO designator] (ICDA)
JFA .... Aviones Ejecutivos, JFA [Mexico] [FAA designator] (FAAC)
JFA .... Jaffa [Israel] [Airport symbol] (AD)
JFA .... Japanese Food Agency (SAUO)
JFA .... Japan Fisheries Agency (SAUO)
JFA .... Japan Fishery Agency (BUAC)
JFA .... Journal of Field Archaeology (journ.) (SAUS)
JFA .... Judkins Family Association (EA)
JFAAD......... Joint Forward-Area Air Defense (MCD)
JFAADS....... Joint Forward-Area Air Defense System
JFAC .... Joint Flight Acceptance Composite Test [Gemini] [NASA] (IAA)
J Fac Agric Hokkaido Univ... Journal. Faculty of Agriculture. Hokkaido University
    (journ.) (SAUS)
J Fac Agric Hokkaido Univ Ser Entomol... Journal. Faculty of Agriculture. Hokkaido
    University. Series Entomology (journ.) (SAUS)
J Fac Agric Iwate Univ... Journal. Faculty of Agriculture. Iwate University (journ.)
    (SAUS)
J Fac Agric Kyushu Univ... Journal. Faculty of Agriculture. Kyushu University
    (journ.) (SAUS)
J Fac Agric Shinshu Univ... Journal. Faculty of Agriculture. Shinshu University
    (journ.) (SAUS)
J Fac Agric Tottori Univ... Journal. Faculty of Agriculture. Tottori University
    (journ.) (SAUS)
J Fac Appl Biol Sci Hirosbima Univ... Journal. Faculty of Applied Biological
    Science. Hiroshima University (journ.) (SAUS)
JFACC.......... Joint Force Air Component Commander (DOMA)
J Fac Ed Saga Univ... Journal. Faculty of Education. Saga University (journ.)
    (SAUS)
J Fac Ed Saga Univ Part 1... Journal. Faculty of Education. Saga University. Part 1
    (journ.) (SAUS)
J Fac Educ Nat Sci Tottori Univ... Journal. Faculty of Education. Natural Sciences.
    Tottori University (journ.) (SAUS)
J Fac Engng Univ Tokyo... Journal. Faculty of Engineering. University of Tokyo
    (journ.) (SAUS)
J Fac Eng Shinshu Univ... Journal. Faculty of Engineering. Shinshu University
    (journ.) (SAUS)
J Fac Eng Univ Tokyo Ser A... Journal. Faculty of Engineering. University of Tokyo.
    Series A. Annual Report (journ.) (SAUS)
J Fac Fish Anim Husb Hiroshima Univ... Journal. Faculty of Fisheries and Animal
    Husbandry. Hiroshima University. (journ.) (SAUS)
J Fac Fish Prefect Univ Mie... Journal. Faculty of Fisheries. Prefectural University
    of Mie (journ.) (SAUS)
J Fac Lib Arts Shinshu Univ Part II Nat Sci... Journal. Faculty of Liberal Arts.
    Shinshu University. Part II Natural Sciences (journ.) (SAUS)
J Fac Liberal Arts Yamaguchi Univ... Journal. Faculty of Liberal Arts. Yamaguchi
    University (journ.) (SAUS)

J Fac Mar Sci King Abdulalaz Univ... Journal. Faculty of Marine Science. King Abdulaziz University (journ.) (SAUS)
J Fac Mar Sci Technol Tokai Univ... Journal. Faculty of Marine Science and Technology. Tokai University (journ.) (SAUS)
J Fac Med Shin Univ... Journal. Faculty of Medicine. Shinshu University (journ.) (SAUS)
J Fac Med Univ Ankara... Journal. Faculty of Medicine. University of Ankara (journ.) (SAUS)
J Fac Med Univ Ankara Suppl... Journal. Faculty of Medicine. University of Ankara. Supplement (journ.) (SAUS)
J Fac Oceanogr Tokai Univ... Journal. Faculty of Oceanography. Tokai University (journ.) (SAUS)
J Fac Pharm Istanbul Univ... Journal. Faculty of Pharmacy. Istanbul University (journ.) (SAUS)
J Fac Polit Sci Econ Tokai Univ... Journal. Faculty of Political Science and Economics. Tokai University (journ.) (SAUS)
J Fac Sci Ege Univ Ser A... Journal. Faculty of Science. Ege University. Series A (journ.) (SAUS)
J Fac Sci Hokkaido Imp Univ Ser 4... Journal. Faculty of Science. Hokkaido Imperial University. Series 4. Geology and Mineralogy (journ.) (SAUS)
J Fac Sci Hokkaido Imp Univ Ser 5... Journal. Faculty of Science. Hokkaido Imperial University. Series 5. Botany (journ.) (SAUS)
J Fac Sci Hokkaido Univ Ser I... Journal. Faculty of Science. Hokkaido University Series I Mathematics (journ.) (SAUS)
J Fac Sci Hokkaido Univ Ser IV... Journal. Faculty of Science. Hokkaido University. Series IV. Geology and Mineralogy (journ.) (SAUS)
J Fac Sci Hokkaido Univ Ser V Bot... Journal. Faculty of Science. Hokkaido University. Series V. Botany (journ.) (SAUS)
J Fac Sci Hokkaido Univ Ser VI... Journal. Faculty of Science. Hokkaido University. Series VI Zoology (journ.) (SAUS)
J Fac Sci Hokkaido Univ Ser VII... Journal. Faculty of Science. Hokkaido University. Series VII Geophysics (journ.) (SAUS)
J Fac Sci Hokkaido Univ Ser VIII Zool... Journal. Faculty of Science. Hokkaido University. Series VIII Zoology (journ.) (SAUS)
J Fac Sci Imp Univ Tokyo Sect II... Journal. Faculty of Science. Imperial University of Tokyo. Section II Geology, Mineralogy, Geography, Seismology (journ.) (SAUS)
J Fac Sci Ser A Ege Univ... Journal. Faculty of Science. Series A. Ege University (journ.) (SAUS)
J Fac Sci Ser B Ege Univ... Journal. Faculty of Science. Series B. Ege University (journ.) (SAUS)
J Fac Sci Shinshu Univ... Journal. Faculty of Science. Shinshu University (journ.) (SAUS)
J Fac Sci Tokyo Univ... Journal. Faculty of Science. Tokyo University (journ.) (SAUS)
J Fac Sci Univ Tokyo Sect IA... Journal. Faculty of Science. University of Tokyo. Section IA. Mathematics (journ.) (SAUS)
J Fac Sci Univ Tokyo Sect II General Mineral Geogr Geophys... Journal. Faculty of Science. University of Tokyo. Section II Geology, Mineral- ogy, Geography, Geophysics (journ.) (SAUS)
J Fac Sci Univ Tokyo Sect III Bot... Journal. Faculty of Science. University of Tokyo. Section III. Botany (journ.) (SAUS)
J Fac Sci Univ Tokyo Sect IV... Journal. Faculty of Science. University of Tokyo. Section IV. Zoology (journ.) (SAUS)
J Fac Sci Univ Tokyo Sect V... Journal. Faculty of Science. University of Tokyo. Section V. Anthropology (journ.) (SAUS)
JFACSU....... Joint Forward Air Controllers Training and Standards Unit (SAUS)
J-FACT......... Joint Flight Acceptance Composite Test [*Gemini*] [*NASA*]
J-FACT......... Joint Flight Acceptance Test (ACAE)
J Fac Text Sci Technol Sbinshu Univ Ser F... Journal. Faculty of Textile Science and Technology. Shinshu University. Series F. Physics and Mathematics (journ.) (SAUS)
J Fac Text Sci Technol Shinshu Univ Ser A... Journal. Faculty of Textile Science and Technology. Shinshu University. Se- ries A. Biology (journ.) (SAUS)
J Fac Text Sci Technol Shinshu Univ Ser B... Journal. Faculty of Textile Science and Technology. Shinshu University. Series B. Textile Engineering (journ.) (SAUS)
J Fac Text Sci Technol Shinshu Univ Ser C... Journal. Faculty of Textile Science and Technology. Shinshu University. Se- ries C. Chemistry (journ.) (SAUS)
J Fac Text Sci Technol Shinshu Univ Ser D... Journal. Faculty of Textile Science and Technology. Shinshu University. Series D. Arts (journ.) (SAUS)
J Fac Tok I... Journal. Faculty of Science. University of Tokyo. Section I. Mathematics, Astronomy, Physics, Chemistry (journ.) (SAUS)
JFACTSU...... Joint Forward Air Controllers Training and Standards Unit [*British*]
J Faculty Arts Roy Univ Malta... Journal. Faculty of Arts. Royal University of Malta (journ.) (SAUS)
J Fac Vet Med Univ Tokyo... Journal. Faculty of Veterinary Medicine. University of Anka (journ.) (SAUS)
JFAI .... Joint Formal Acceptance Inspection [*NATO*] (NATG)
JFAKA......... Journal. Faculty of Agriculture. Kyushu University (journ.) (SAUS)
J Fam Hist... Journal of Family History (journ.) (SAUS)
J Family L... Journal of Family Law (journ.) (SAUS)
JFAP......... Joint Frequency Allocation Panel
J Farnham Mus Soc... Journal. Farnham Museum Society (journ.) (SAUS)
JFAST......... Joint Flow and Analysis System for Transportation [*Model USA*]
JFAST .... Joint Flow and Analysis System Test [*Environmental science*] (COE)
JFAX............ JFAX.COM, Inc. [*NASDAQ symbol*] (SG)
JFB .... Jet Flying Belt (PDAA)
JFB .... John Freeman Building (SAUS)
JFC .... Japan Film Center (SAUO)
JFC .... Japan Food Co. (SAUS)

JFC .... Jardine Fleming China Reg Fd [*NYSE symbol*] (TTSB)
JFC .... Jardine Fleming China Regular Fund [*NYSE symbol*] (SPSG)
JFC .... Java Foundation Classes [*Sun Microsystems, Inc.*] (IGQR)
JFC .... Jewish Folk Center [*Australia*]
JFC .... John Forsyth Co., Inc. [*Toronto Stock Exchange symbol*]
JFC .... Joint Force Commander [*DoD*]
JFC .... Joint Formulary Committee (SAUO)
JFC .... Journal of Business Forecasting (journ.) (SAUS)
JFC .... Jupiter-family Comets [*Astronomy*]
JFC .... LTV Jet Fleet Corp. [*ICAO designator*] (FAAC)
JFCA .... Japan Fine Ceramics Association (SAUO)
JFCB .... Job File Control Block [*Computer science*] (BUR)
JFCC .... Japanese Federation of Culture Collections of Microorganisms (BUAC)
JFCC .... Japan Federation of Culture Collections (SAUS)
JFCC .... Joint Force Fires Coordinator
JFCC .... Joint Frequency Coordination Committee (SAUO)
JFCL .... Jump if Flag Set and Then Clear the Flag [*Computer science*] (NHD)
JFCS .... Jewish Family and Child Services (SAUO)
JFD .... Joint Frequency Distribution (SAUO)
JFDA .... Jewish Funeral Directors of America (EA)
J Fd Hyg Soc Jp... Journal. Food Hygienic Society of Japan (journ.) (SAUS)
JFDP .... Joint Force Development Process [*or Program*] [*Army*]
JFDP .... Junior Faculty Development Program
JFE............. Joint Fighter Engine (DWSG)
JFE............. Journal of Farm Economics (journ.) (SAUS)
JFE............. Journal of Financial Economics (journ.) (SAUS)
JFE............. Journal of Fluids Engineering (journ.) (SAUS)
JFE............. Justified Field Entry (SAUS)
JFEA .... Japan Federation of Employers Association
JFEA .... Joint Foreign Exchange Agency [*Berlin*] [*Post-World War II, Germany*]
JFEB .... Japan Fast Experimental Breeder (SAUS)
JFED .... Junction Field-Effect Device
J Feng Chi Univ... Journal. Feng Chia University (journ.) (SAUS)
JFEO .... Japanese Federation of Economic Organizations
JFER .... Junction Field-Effect Resistor (SAUS)
J Ferment Ass Jpn... Journal. Fermentation Association of Japan (journ.) (SAUS)
J Ferment Ind... Journal of Fermentation Industries (journ.) (SAUS)
J Ferment Techn... Journal of Fermentation Technology (journ.) (SAUS)
J Ferment Technol (1944-1976)... Journal of Fermentation Technology (1944-1976) [*Japan*] [*A publication*]
J Fert Issues... Journal of Fertilizer Issues (journ.) (SAUS)
JFES .... Japan Federation of Engineering Societies (SAUO)
JFET .... Junction Field-Effect Transistor
JFETT .... Junction Field-Effect Transistor Tetrode (SAUS)
JFEW .... Jewish Foundation for Education of Women (EA)
JFF.............. Aguadilla, PR [*Location identifier*] [*FAA*] (FAAL)
JFF.............. Jobs for the Future [*An association*]
JFF.............. Junior Fashion Fair International [*British*] (ITD)
JFf .... Junior Firefighter (WDAA)
JFF.............. Just for Fun (SAUS)
JFFC .... Jewish Fighting Force Committee [*British*]
JFFC .... John Fricke Fan Club [*Defunct*] (EA)
JFFC .... Judy Fields Fan Club (EA)
JFFSC .... Joint Force Fire Support Coordinator (SAUO)
JFG .... Jumbogroup Frequency Generator [*Bell System*]
JFH .... Jam Frequency Hopper
JFH .... Joint Force Harrier (SAUO)
JFHQ .... Joint Force Headquarters [*Military*]
JFHS .... Journal. Flintshire Historical Society (journ.) (SAUS)
JFI .... James Franck Institute [*University of Chicago*] [*Research center*] (RCD)
JFI .... Japanese Fermentation Institute
JFI .... Jardine Fleming India Fund [*NYSE symbol*] (SAG)
JFI .... Jet Flight Information (AFM)
JFI .... John La Farge Institute (EA)
JFI .... Journal of the Franklin Institute (SAUO)
JFI .... New Orleans, LA [*Location identifier*] [*FAA*] (FAAL)
JFIAP .... Joint Foreign Intelligence Assistance Program (AFM)
JFIC .... Juneau Family Investment Center (SAUO)
JFIDS........... J-5 Force Structure Information Display System (SAUO)
JFIF .... JPEG [*Joint Photographic Experts Group*] File Interchange Format [*Computer science*] (CDE)
J Film & Vid... Journal of Film & Video [*A publication*] (BRI)
J Financ Quant Anal... Journal of Financial and Quantitative Analysis (journ.) (SAUS)
JFIndia .... Jardine Fleming India Fund [*Associated Press*] (SAG)
J Fin Planning... Journal of Financial Planning (journ.) (SAUS)
JFINT .... Joint Field Interrogation Team (SAUO)
J Fire Flamm... Journal of Fire and Flammability (journ.) (SAUS)
J Fire Retardant Chem... Journal of Fire Retardant Chemistry (journ.) (SAUS)
J Fire Sci..... Journal of Fire Sciences (journ.) (SAUS)
J Fish Biol... Journal of Fish Biology (journ.) (SAUS)
J Fisheries Res Board Can... Journal. Fisheries Research Board of Canada (journ.) (SAUS)
J Fish Res Board Can... Journal of the Fisheries Research Board of Canada (SAUO)
J Fish Res Board Can... Journal of the Fisheries Research Board of Canada (journ.) (SAUS)
JFIT .... Joint Framework for Information Technology [*British*]
JFJ............... Jewish Fund for Justice (EA)
JFJ............... Jews for Jesus (EA)
JFK .... John Fitzgerald Kennedy [*US president, 1917-1963*]
JFK .... John F. Kennedy International Airport (NTIO)

JFK .... Kennedy International Airport [*New York*] [*Airport symbol*]
JFKC .... John Fitzgerald Kennedy Center for the Performing Arts
JFKC .... John F. Kennedy Center (SAUS)
JFKC .... John F. Kennedy Center for the Performing Arts (SAUO)
JFKCAS ...... John F. Kennedy College of Arts and Sciences (SAUO)
JFKCPA ...... John F. Kennedy Center for the Performing Arts (SAUO)
JFKCTRMA... John F. Kennedy Center for Military Assistance (MCD)
JFK FDC SU... John F. Kennedy First Day Cover Study Unit (EA)
JFK Fdn ...... John F. Kennedy Foundation (EA)
JFKI .... John F. Kennedy Library (SAUS)
JFKL .... John F. Kennedy Library
JFKLF .... John F. Kennedy Library Foundation (EA)
JFKMF .... John F. Kennedy Memorial Forest (SAUO)
JFKMH........ John F. Kennedy Memorial Highway (SAUO)
JFKML .... John F. Kennedy Memorial Library (SAUO)
JFKMR .... John F. Kennedy Memorial Highway (SAUS)
JFKPS .... John F. Kennedy Philatelic Society (EA)
JFKSC.......... John Fitzgerald Kennedy Spaceflight Center [*Also known as KSC*] [*NASA*]
JFKSC.......... John F. Kennedy Spaceflight Center (SAUO)
JFKYCC........ John F. Kennedy Youth Correctional Center (SAUO)
JFL.............. Joint Frequency List
JFL.............. Judy Farquharson Ltd. [*British*]
JFLA .... Jewish Free Loan Association (EA)
J Fla Acad Gen Pract... Journal. Florida Academy of General Practice (journ.) (SAUS)
J Fla Med Ass... Journal. Florida Medical Association (journ.) (SAUS)
J Fla Med Assoc... Journal of the Florida Medical Association (SAUO)
J Fla Med Assoc... Journal of the Florida Medical Association (journ.) (SAUS)
J Fla State Dent Soc... Journal. Florida State Dental Society (journ.) (SAUS)
JFLC .... Joint Forces Land Component (DOMA)
JFLCC.......... Joint Forces Land Component Commander (DOMA)
J Florida MA... Journal. Florida Medical Association (journ.) (SAUS)
JFLU .... Japan Federation of Labour Unions (SAUO)
J Fluid Control... Journal of Fluid Control (journ.) (SAUS)
J Fluid Eng Trans ASME... Journal of Fluids Engineering. Transactions of the American Society of Mechanical Engineers (journ.) (SAUS)
J Fluids Eng... Journal of Fluids Engineering (journ.) (SAUS)
J Fluids Struct... Journal of Fluids and Structures (journ.) (SAUS)
J Fluorescence... Journal of Fluorescence (journ.) (SAUS)
J Fluoresc Miner S... Journal. Fluorescent Mineral Society (journ.) (SAUS)
JFM .... Jet Flap Model
JFM .... Jews for Morality (EA)
JFM .... Job Function Manual (AAG)
JFM .... Joint Force Memorandum [*Military*]
JFM .... Journal of Fluid Mechanics (journ.) (SAUS)
JFM .... Journal of Forms Management (journ.) (SAUS)
JFM .... Journal of Futures Markets (journ.) (SAUS)
JFM .... June Fourth Movement (SAUO)
JFM .... Jupiter Flyby Mission [*Aerospace*]
JFMA .... Journal. Florida Medical Association (journ.) (SAUS)
JFMAMJJASOND... January, February, March, April, May, June, July, August, September, October, November, December (SAUS)
JFMCC .... Joint Force Maritime Component Commander (SAUO)
JFMCC .... Joint Forces Maritime Component Commander (SAUO)
JFMIP .... Joint Financial Management Improvement Program
JFMO .... Joint Financial Management Office (ACAE)
JFMO .... Joint Frequency Management Office (MCD)
JFMSES ...... Joint Frequency Management and Spectrum Engineering System (SAUO)
JFMU .... Joint Force Meteorological and Oceanographic Forecast Unit (COE)
JFN .... Jefferson, OH [*Location identifier*] [*FAA*] (FAAL)
JFN .... Job File Number
JFNF .... Jewish Family Name File [*Association for the Study of Jewish Languages*] [*Information service or system*] (CRD)
JFNP .... John Forest National Park (SAUS)
JFNP .... Joseph M. Farley Nuclear Plant (NRCH)
JFNPP.......... James A. FitzPatrick Nuclear Power Plant (NRCH)
JFO .... Just for Openers [*An association*] (EA)
J Foetal Med... Journal of Foetal Medicine (journ.) (SAUS)
JF of L......... Japan National Federation of Labor (SAUO)
J Folk Res... Journal of Folklore Research (journ.) (SAUS)
J Food Biochem... Journal of Food Biochemistry (journ.) (SAUS)
J Food Compos Anal... Journal of Food Composition and Analysis (journ.) (SAUS)
J Food Eng... Journal of Food Engineering (journ.) (SAUS)
J Food Hygienic Soc Jap... Journal. Food Hygienic Society of Japan (journ.) (SAUS)
J Food Process Eng... Journal of Food Process Engineering (journ.) (SAUS)
J Food Process Eng... Journal of Food Processing Engineering (journ.) (SAUS)
J Food Process Preserv... Journal of Food Processing and Preservation (journ.) (SAUS)
J Food Qual... Journal of Food Quality (journ.) (SAUS)
J Food Resour Dev... Journal of Food Resources Development (journ.) (SAUS)
J Food Saf... Journal of Food Safety (journ.) (SAUS)
J Food Serv Syst... Journal of Food Service Systems (journ.) (SAUS)
J Foot Ankle Surg... Journal of Foot and Ankle Surgery (journ.) (SAUS)
J Foot Surg... Journal of Foot Surgery (journ.) (SAUS)
J For Comm... Journal. Forestry Commission (journ.) (SAUS)
J Forecasting... Journal of Forecasting (journ.) (SAUS)
J Forensic Odontostomatol... Journal of Forensic Odonto-Stomatology (journ.) (SAUS)
J Forensic Sci Soc... Journal-Forensic Science Society (SAUO)
J For Hist .... Journal of Forest History (journ.) (SAUS)
J Formosan Med Ass... Journal. Formosan Medical Association (journ.) (SAUS)
J Formos Med Assoc... Journal of the Formosan Medical Association (SAUO)

J Formos Med Assoc... Journal of the Formosan Medical Association (journ.) (SAUS)
J For Prod Res Soc... Journal. Forest Products Research Society (journ.) (SAUS)
J For Sci Soc... Journal. Forensic Science Society [*A publication*] (DLA)
J Forth Appl Res... Journal of Forth Application and Research (journ.) (SAUS)
JFP .... Jewish Family Purity (BJA)
JFP .... Jobs For Progress (SAUS)
JFP .... Joint Frequency Panel
JFP .... Journal of Family Practice (SAUO)
JFP .... Journal of Financial Planning Today (journ.) (SAUS)
JFPA .... Jamaica Family Planning Association (BUAC)
JFPC .... Joint Fire Prevention Committee (WDAA)
JFPCC .... Joint Fusion Power Coordination Committee (SAUS)
JFPH .... JUMPS [*Joint Uniform Military Pay System*] Field Procedures Handbook (NVT)
JFPRD .... Journal of Food Protection (journ.) (SAUS)
JFPS .... Japan Fire Prevention Service (SAUS)
JFPS .... Japan Fire Prevention Society (BUAC)
JFR .... Jamie Frontier Resources, Inc. [*Toronto Stock Exchange symbol*]
JFR .... Jet Flap Rotor
JFR .... Jet Flog Rotor (SAUS)
JFR .... Joint Fiction Reserve
JFR .... Journal of Financial Research (journ.) (SAUS)
JFR .... Journal of Folklore Research (journ.) (SAUS)
J Franklin Inst Mono... Journal. Franklin Institute. Monograph (journ.) (SAUS)
JFRC .... James Forrestal Research Center [*Princeton University*] (MCD)
JFRCA .... Japanese Fisheries Resources Conservation Association (BUAC)
JFRCD .... Journal of Fire Retardant Chemistry (journ.) (SAUS)
JFRDD .... Journal of Food Resources Development (journ.) (SAUS)
J Freshwater... Journal of Freshwater (journ.) (SAUS)
JFRF .... Japan Frame Relay Forum (DDC)
JFRO........... Joint Fire Research Organisation (HEAS)
JFRO........... Joint Fire Research Organization (SAUO)
JFRO........... Joint Fisheries Research Organisation [*Malawi, Zambia*] (BUAC)
JFRY .... Jeffrey Manin, Inc. (SAUO)
JFS .... Jamaica Freight and Shipping Co. Ltd. (EY)
JFS .... Java File System (SAUS)
JFS .... Jet Fuel Starter
JFS .... Jewish Family Service (EA)
JFS .... Jewish Friends Society (EA)
JFS .... Job Findcar System
JFS .... Job Finder System
JFS .... Johnston & Frye [*Vancouver Stock Exchange symbol*]
JFS .... Joint Foundation Support (EA)
JFS .... Journaled File System (SAUO)
JFS .... Journalized File System (VLIE)
JFS .... Journal of Food Science (journ.) (SAUS)
JFS .... Juanda Flying School [*Indonesia*] [*ICAO designator*] (FAAC)
JFS .... Jugular Foramen Syndrome [*or Vernet's syndrome*] [*Medicine*] (DAVI)
JFS .... Jumbogroup Frequency Supply [*Bell System*]
JFS .... Justice for Scotland (SAUO)
JFSC .... Joint Forces Staff College (SAUO)
JFSE .... Japan Federation of Small Enterprises (SAUO)
JFSEO .... Japan Federation of Smaller Enterprises (BUAC)
JFSG .... Joint Feasibility Study Group [*Air Force*] (MCD)
JFSNY......... Jewish Folk Schools of New York (EA)
JFSOC......... Junior Foreign Service Officers Club (SAUO)
JFSOCC....... Joint Force Special Operations Component Commander (SAUS)
JFSP .... Joint Forecast System Project [*Marine science*] (OSRA)
JFSR .... Jewish Fund for Soviet Russia (SAUO)
JFSS .... Joint Force Signals Staff [*Military*]
JFSSG .... Joint Food Safety and Standards Group [*British*] (GVA)
JFSUR .... Journal of Foot Surgery (journ.) (SAUS)
JFT............. Jet Fret [*France*] [*ICAO designator*] (FAAC)
JFT............. Job File Table (PCM)
JFT............. Joint Field Trial (NATG)
JFTC .... Japan Foreign Trade Council (BUAC)
JFTC .... Joint for Trade Committee (SAUS)
JFTC .... Joint Fur Trade Committee (BUAC)
JFTCG......... Joint Flight Test Control Group (AAG)
JFTEC .... Journal of Fermentation Technology (journ.) (SAUS)
JFTG .... Joint Fuze Task Group [*Army*]
JFTOT......... Jet Fuel Thermal Oxidation Test [*or Tester*] [*Analytical chemistry*] [*Air Force*]
JFTR .... Joint Federal Travel Regulations (DOMA)
JFTS .... Jet Fuel Thermal Stability
JFTU .... Jordan Federation of Trade Unions
JFTX .... Joint Field Training Exercise [*Military*]
JFU .... Jersey Farmers' Union [*British*] (DBA)
JFUB .... Joint Facilities Utilization Board [*Military*]
J Fudan Univ Nat Sci... Journal. Fudan University. Natural Science (journ.) (SAUS)
J Fuel Heat Technol... Journal of Fuel and Heating Technology (SAUS)
J Fuel Heat Technol... Journal of Fuel and Heat Technology (journ.) (SAUS)
J Fuel Soc Jap... Journal. Fuel Society of Japan (journ.) (SAUS)
J Fuel Soc Jpn... Journal of the Fuel Society of Japan (journ.) (SAUS)
J Fujian Agric Coll... Journal. Fujian Agricultural College (journ.) (SAUS)
J Fujian Teach Univ Nat Sci Ed... Journal. Fujian Teachers University. Natural Science Edition (journ.) (SAUS)
J Fur Higher Educ... Journal of Further and Higher Education (journ.) (SAUS)
JFUS........... Journal of Forestry (SAUS)
J Fusion Energy... Journal of Fusion Energy (journ.) (SAUS)
J Futures Markets... Journal of Futures Markets (journ.) (SAUS)
JFuU .... Fukui University, Fukui-shi, Japan [*Library symbol*] [*Library of Congress*] (LCLS)

JFV .... Jersey Farmers Union (SAUS)
JFV .... Jobs for Veterans (SAUO)
JFV .... Jobs for Veterans National Committee [Defunct] (EA)
JFV .... Jupiter Flyby Vehicle [Aerospace]
JFW .... Jamaica Federation of Women (BUAC)
JFW .... Justice for Women (EA)
JFY .... Foster Yeoman Ltd. [British] [ICAO designator] (FAAC)
JFY .... Japanese Fiscal Year (CINC)
JFY .... Jiffy (ABBR)
JFYI .... Just For Your Information (SAUS)
JG .... Bumthills Aviation Ltd. (SAUO)
JG .... Jahrgang [Year of Publication/Volume] [German]
JG .... Jerusalem und Seine Gelaende [A publication] (BJA)
JG .... Jockeys' Guild (EA)
J/g .... Joule per gram (SAUS)
JG .... Joules Gram (SAUS)
JG .... Joules per Gram [Physics] (IAA)
JG .... Journal of Geography (journ.) (SAUS)
Jg .... Judges [Old Testament book] (BJA)
JG .... Judgment [Legal shorthand] (LWAP)
JG .... Juedisches Gemeindeblatt fuer die Britische Zone [A publication] (BJA)
JG .... Jumbogroup (SAUO)
JG .... Jump if Greater (VLIE)
JG .... Junction Grammar [Machine translation term] (NITA)
JG .... Junction Grammar [Computer science]
JG .... June Grass [Test] [Medicine] (DAVI)
JG .... Junior Girls [School department] [British] (DI)
JG .... Junior Grade
jg .... Juxtaglomerular (STED)
jg .... Juxtaglomerular [Histology]
JG .... Swedair [ICAO designator] (AD)
JGA .... Jamnagar [India] [Airport symbol] (OAG)
JGA .... Japan Gas Association (BUAC)
JGA .... Japan Golf Association (BUAC)
JGA .... Jojoba Growers Association (EA)
JGA .... Joseph Guzman & Associates, Inc. [Palatine, IL] [Telecommunications] [Defunct] (TSSD)
JGA .... Jute Goods Association (SAUO)
JGA .... Juxtaglomerular Apparatus [Histology]
JGAB .... Joint Government Agencies Board (SSD)
J GA Dent Assoc... Journal. Georgia Dental Association (journ.) (SAUS)
J Gakugei Tokushima Univ Nat Sci... Journal. Gakugei Tokushima University. Natural Science (journ.) (SAUS)
J Galway Archaeol Hist S... Journal. Galway Archaeological and Historical Society (journ.) (SAUS)
JGAM .... Junior Gas Association of Manchester (SAUO)
JG & C .... Joint Guidance and Control (KSC)
JG-APP .... Joint Group on Acquisition Pollution Prevention (BCP)
J Gas Chromatogr... Journal of Gas Chromatography (journ.) (SAUS)
J Gas Light Water Supply Sanit Improv... Journal of Gas Lighting, Water Supply and Sanitary Improvement (journ.) (SAUS)
J Gastroenterol... Journal of Gastroenterology (journ.) (SAUS)
J Gastroenterol Hepatol... Journal of Gastroenterology and Hepatology (journ.) (SAUS)
JGB .... Japanese Government Bond (ECON)
JGB .... Jewish Guild for the Blind (EA)
JGC .... Grand Canyon [Arizona] [Airport symbol] (OAG)
JGC .... Jacob Gold Corp. [Vancouver Stock Exchange symbol]
JGC .... Japan Gas Chemical (SAUO)
JGC .... Japan Gasoline Co. (SAUS)
JGC .... JGC Corp. [Formerly, Japan Gasoline Co. Ltd.]
JGC .... Journal of General Chemistry (journ.) (SAUS)
JGC .... Juxtaglomerular Cells [Histology]
JGCC .... Juxtaglomerular Cell Count [Endocrinology]
JGCEA .... Journal of Geochemical Exploration (journ.) (SAUS)
JGCRA .... Journal of Gas Chromatography (journ.) (SAUS)
JGCT .... Juxtaglomerular Cell Tumor [Histology] (DAVI)
JGD .... JOPES Global Dictionary (SAUO)
JG/D .... Judgement for the Defendant [Legal shorthand] (LWAP)
JGD .... Junior Grand Deacon [Freemasonry]
JGDI .... Joggle Die (SAUS)
J/Gdsmn ...... Junior Guardsman [British military] (DMA)
JGE .... Jaguar Equity, Inc. [Vancouver Stock Exchange symbol]
JGE .... Joint Group of Experts [Marine science] (MSC)
JGE .... Journal of General Education (journ.) (SAUS)
JGE .... Jump if Greater or Equal (VLIE)
J Gemmol... Journal of Gemmology (journ.) (SAUS)
J Gen Chem... Journal of General Chemistry (journ.) (SAUS)
J Gen Chem USSR... Journal of General Chemistry of the USSR (journ.) (SAUS)
J Genet... Journal of Genetics (journ.) (SAUS)
J Genet & Breed... Journal of Genetics and Breeding (journ.) (SAUS)
J Gen Intern Med... Journal of General Internal Medicine (journ.) (SAUS)
J Gen Manag... Journal of General Management (journ.) (SAUS)
J Gen Virol... Journal of General Virology (journ.) (SAUS)
J Geobot... Journal of Geobotany (journ.) (SAUS)
J Geochem Soc India... Journal. Geochemical Society of India (journ.) (SAUS)
JGEOD .... Journal of Geophysics (journ.) (SAUS)
J Geodyn... Journal of Geodynamics (journ.) (SAUS)
J Geog... Journal of Geography (journ.) (SAUS)
J Geo Higher Educ... Journal of Geography in Higher Education (journ.) (SAUS)
J Geolectr... Journal of Geoelectricity (journ.) (SAUS)
J Geol Educ... Journal of Geological Education (journ.) (SAUS)
J Geol Sci Appl Geophys... Journal of Geological Sciences. Applied Geophysics (journ.) (SAUS)

J Geol Sci Palaeontol... Journal of Geological Sciences. Palaeontology (journ.) (SAUS)
J Geol Soc... Journal of Geological Society (journ.) (SAUS)
J Geol Soc Aust... Journal of the Geological Society of Australia (SAUO)
J Geol Soc Aust... Journal of the Geological Society of Australia (journ.) (SAUO)
J Geol Soc In... Journal. Geological Society of India (journ.) (SAUS)
J Geol Soc India... Journal of the Geological Society of India (SAUO)
J Geol Soc India... Journal of the Geological Society of India (journ.) (SAUS)
J Geol Soc Iraq... Journal. Geological Society of Iraq (journ.) (SAUS)
J Geol Soc Jam... Journal. Geological Society of Jamaica (journ.) (SAUS)
J Geol Soc Jam... Journal of the Geological Society of Jamaica (journ.) (SAUS)
J Geol Soc Jpn... Journal. Geological Society of Japan (journ.) (SAUS)
J Geol Soc london... Journal. Geological Society of London (journ.) (SAUS)
J Geol Soc Philipp... Journal. Geological Society of the Philippines (journ.) (SAUS)
J Geol Soc Thailand... Journal. Geological Society of Thailand (journ.) (SAUS)
J Geol Soc Tokyo... Journal. Geological Society of Tokyo (journ.) (SAUS)
J Geol UAR... Journal of Geology. United Arab Republic (journ.) (SAUS)
J Geol Ukr Aad Sci Inst Geol... Journal of Geology. Ukrainian Academy of Sciences. Institute of Geology (journ.) (SAUS)
J Geom Phys... Journal of Geometry and Physics (journ.) (SAUS)
J Geophys ... Journal of Geophysics (journ.) (SAUS)
J Geophys Prospect... Journal of Geophysical Prospecting (journ.) (SAUS)
J Geophys Res D Atm... Journal of Geophysical Research. Series D. Atmospheres (journ.) (SAUS)
J Geo R-SP... Journal of Geophysical Research. Space Physics (journ.) (SAUS)
J Geosci Osska City Univ... Journal of Geosciences. Osaka City University (journ.) (SAUS)
J Geotech Eng... Journal of Geotechnical Engineering (journ.) (SAUS)
J Geotech Eng Div Amer Soc Civil Eng Proc... Journal. Geotechnical Engineering Division. Proceedings of the American Society of Civil Engineers (journ.) (SAUS)
J Geotech Engng Div ASCE... Journal Geotechnical Engineering Division. American Society of Civil Engineers (journ.) (SAUS)
J Geotech Engng Div Proc ASCE... Journal. Geotechnical Engineering Division. Proceedings of the American Society of Civil Engineers (journ.) (SAUS)
J Geotherm Energy Res Dev Co Ltd... Journal. Geothermal Energy Research and Development Company, Limited (journ.) (SAUS)
J Geriatr Psychiatry Neurol... Journal of Geriatric Psychiatry and Neurology (journ.) (SAUS)
J Gerontol A Biol Sci Med Sci... Journals of Gerontology. Series A, Biological Sciences and Medical Sciences (journ.) (SAUS)
J Gerontol B Psychol Sci Soc Sci... Journals of Gerontology. Series B, Psychological Sciences and Social Sciences (journ.) (SAUS)
J Gerontol Nurs... Journal of Gerontological Nursing (journ.) (SAUS)
J Gerontol Soc Work... Journal of Gerontological Social Work (journ.) (SAUS)
JGF .... Jakarta Growth Fund [NYSE symbol] (SPSG)
JGF .... Junctor Grouping Frame [Telecommunications] (TEL)
JGFC .... Joe Gallison Fan Club (EA)
JGFC .... John Gilbert Fan Club (EA)
JGFC .... John Gill Fan Club (EA)
JGFET .... Junction Gate Field-Effect Transistor [Electronics] (IAA)
JGGAS .... Journal. Hongkong University. Geographical, Geological and Archaeological Society (journ.) (SAUS)
JGH .... Jig Grinder Head
JGI .... Jejunogastric Intussusception [Gastroenterology] (DAVI)
JGI .... Joint Genome Institute (HGEN)
JGI .... Juxtaglomerular Granulation Index [Endocrinology]
JGI .... Juxtaglomerular Index [Endocrinology]
JGIFC .... John Gary International Fan Club (EA)
JGIM .... Journal of General Internal Medicine (SAUO)
JGIM .... Journal of General Internal Medicine (journ.) (SAUS)
JGIN .... JG Industries [NASDAQ symbol] (TTSB)
JGIN .... JG Industries, Inc. [NASDAQ symbol] (NQ)
JG Ind .... JG Industries, Inc. [Associated Press] (SAG)
JGL .... Java Generic Library (VLIE)
J Glass Stud... Journal of Glass Studies (journ.) (SAUS)
JGLC .... Joint Government Liaison Committee [Composed of Association of Brass and Bronze Ingot Manufacturers and Brass and Bronze Ingot Institute] (EA)
JGLMA .... Journal of the Gay and Lesbian Medical Association (SAUO)
JGLMA .... Journal of the Gay and Lesbian Medical Association (journ.) (SAUS)
JGLRD .... Journal of Great Lakes Research (journ.) (SAUS)
JGLS .... Journal of the Gypsy Lore Society (SAUO)
JGM .... Jig Grinding Machine
JGM .... Job Guide Manual (PDAA)
JGM .... Journal of General Microbiology (journ.) (SAUS)
JGMC .... Judy Garland Memorial Club (EA)
J GMS OSU... Journal. Graduate Music Students. Ohio State University (journ.) (SAUS)
JGN .... Junction Gate Number
J Gnathol..... Journal of Gnathology (journ.) (SAUS)
Jgn J Aerosp Med Psychol... Japanese Journal of Aerospace Medicine and Psychology (journ.) (SAUS)
JGNP .... Japanese Gross National Product (SAUS)
JGOFS .... Joint Global Ocean Flux Study [International experiment]
JGOFS .... Joint Global Ocean Flux Study Program of the IGBP (SAUO)
JGOFS GS... JGOFS Global Synthesis (SAUO)
JGOFS GS... Joint Global Ocean Flux Study Global Synthesis (SAUO)
JGOFS PM... JGOFS Photosynthetic Measurements (SAUS)
JGOFS-SSC... JGOFS Scientific Steering Committee (SAUS)
JGOFS-SSC... Joint Global Ocean Flux Study Scientific Steering Committee (SAUO)
J-GOOS........ Joint Global Ocean Flux Study Scientific and Technical Committee (SAUO)
J-GOOS........ Joint GOOS Scientific and Technical Committee (SAUS)

J-GOOS....... Joint Scientific and Technical Committee for GOOS (SAUS)
JGOS .... Journal of the German Oriental Society (SAUO)
JGOS .... Journal of the German Oriental Society (journ.) (SAUS)
JGO-US....... Job Guarantee Office of the United States (OICC)
J Gov Info.... Journal of Government Information [*A publication*] (BRI)
JGP............. Houston [*Texas*] Greenway [*Airport symbol*] (OAG)
JGP............. Jem Group Products [*Vancouver Stock Exchange symbol*]
JGP............. Journal of General Physiology (journ.) (SAUS)
JG/P............ Judgement for the Plaintiff [*Legal shorthand*] (LWAP)
JGP............. Juvenile General Paralysis [*Medicine*] (DAVI)
JGP............. Juvenile General Paresis [*Medicine*] (DMAA)
JGPA............ Jobbing Grinders' Provident Association [*A union*] [*British*]
JGPN .... Journal of Geriatric Psychiatry and Neurology (journ.) (SAUS)
JGQ............. Houston [*Texas*] Guest Quarters [*Airport symbol*] (OAG)
JGR............. Belize Trans Air [*ICAO designator*] (FAAC)
JGR............. Jaldapara Game Reserve (SAUO)
JGR............. Journal of Geophysical Research
J Grad Res Cent... Journal. Graduate Research Center (journ.) (SAUS)
J Grad Res Cent South Metbodist Univ... Journal. Graduate Research Center. Southern Methodist University (journ.) (SAUS)
J Graph Theory... Journal of Graph Theory (journ.) (SAUS)
J Grey Syst... Journal of Grey Systems (journ.) (SAUS)
JGRIP .... Japanese Government and Public Research in Progress [*International database*]
J Group Experts Sci Aspects Mr Pollut... Joint Group of Experts on the Scientific Aspects of Marine Pollution (SAUO)
J Group Experts Sci Aspects Mr Pollut... Joint Group of Experts on the Scientific Aspects of Marine Pollution (journ.) (SAUS)
J Growth...... Journal of Growth (journ.) (SAUS)
JGRP .... Jesup Group, Inc. (SAUO)
JGS............. James Griffiths & Sons [*AAR code*]
JGS............. Jewish Genealogical Society (EA)
JGS............. Joint General Staff [*Military*] (NATG)
JGS............. Journal of Glass Studies (journ.) (SAUS)
Jgs............. Judges [*Old Testament book*]
JGSA........... John G. Shedd Aquarium (SAUO)
JGSDF .... Japanese Ground Self-Defense Forces (AABC)
JGSLA......... Journal. Geological Society of London (journ.) (SAUS)
JGSTD .... Journal. Gyeongsang National University. Science and Technology (journ.) (SAUS)
JGSW......... Jigsaw (ABBR)
JGSW......... Journal of Gerontological Social Work (journ.) (SAUS)
JGT............. Judgment [*Legal term*] (ROG)
JGT............. Junction Growth Technique
JGTC........... Junior Girls' Training Corps [*British*] [*World War II*]
JG-TE.......... Jumbogroup-Translation Equipment (SAUO)
JGTL........... Job Grading System for Trades and Labor Occupations
JGTOI.......... [*The*] Judge GTO International (EA)
JGU............. Japanese Geomorphological Union (SAUO)
JGUAG .... Joint Government/UNICEF Advisory Group (SAUO)
J Guid Control and Dyn... Journal of Guidance, Control and Dynamics (journ.) (SAUS)
JGW............. Junior Grand Warden [*Freemasonry*]
JGWTC........ Jungle and Guerrilla Warfare Training Center [*Army*]
J Gyeongsang Ntl Univ Nat Sci... Journal. Gyeongsang National University. Natural Sciences (journ.) (SAUS)
J Gyeongsang Ntl Univ Sci Technol... Journal. Gyeongsang National University. Science and Technology (journ.) (SAUS)
J Gynecol Pract... Journal of Gynecological Practice (journ.) (SAUS)
JH................. Echovirus 28 [*Virology*] (DAVI)
JH................. Harland [*John H.*] Co. [*NYSE symbol*] (SPSG)
JH................. Harland (John H.) [*NYSE symbol*] (TTSB)
JH................. Jacob's Horse [*British military*] (DMA)
JH................. Jogger's Heel (MELL)
JH/P............. Journal of History (journ.) (SAUS)
J H.............. Journal of Hygiene (journ.) (SAUS)
JH................. Journal of the House of Representatives [*United States*] [*A publication*] (DLA)
JH................. Juvenile Hormone [*Entomology*]
JH................. Nordeste-Lineas Aereas Regionais [*ICAO designator*] (AD)
JHA............. Japan Hour Association [*Later, JHB*] (EA)
JHA............. Job Hazard Analysis (PDAA)
JHA............. John Howard Association (EA)
JHA............. Justice and Home Affairs (SAUO)
JHA............. Juvenile Hormone Analog [*Entomology*]
JHAH .... John Howard Association of Hawaii (SAUO)
JHAI........... John Herron Art Institute (SAUO)
J Hand Surg... Journal of Hand Surgery (journ.) (SAUS)
J Hand Ther... Journal of Hand Therapy (journ.) (SAUS)
JHAR .... Johns Hopkins Autopsy Resource (SAUO)
J Harbin Ind Coll... Journal. Harbin Industrial College (journ.) (SAUS)
J Harbin Inst Tecbnol... Journal. Harbin Institute of Technology (journ.) (SAUS)
J Harbin Inst Technol... Journal of the Harbin Institute of Technology (journ.) (SAUS)
JHAS........... John Herron Art School (SAUO)
JHAT........... Japan Helicopter Air Transport Company (SAUO)
J Hattori Bot Lab... Journal. Hattori Botanical Laboratory (journ.) (SAUS)
J Hattori Bot Lab... Journal of the Hattori Botanical Laboratory (SAUO)
J Hawaii Dent Ass... Journal. Hawaii Dental Association (journ.) (SAUS)
J Hawaii State Dent Assoc... Journal. Hawaii State Dental Association (journ.) (SAUS)
J Hazard Mater... Journal of Hazardous Materials (journ.) (SAUS)
J Hazard Waste Hazard Mater... Journal of Hazardous Waste and Hazardous Materials (journ.) (SAUS)
JHB............. Japan Hour Broadcasting (EA)

JHB............. Job Hazard Breakdown (SAUS)
JHB............. Johannesburg [*South Africa*] (ABBR)
JHB............. Johore Bahru [*Malaysia*] [*Airport symbol*] (OAG)
JHBLEN....... Journal of Human Behavior and Learning (journ.) (SAUS)
JHBP........... Juvenile Hormone Binding Protein [*Entomology*]
JHBSA .... Journal of the History of the Behavioral Sciences (journ.) (SAUS)
JHC............. Garden City [*New York*] [*Airport symbol*] (OAG)
JHC............. John Hancock Center (SAUO)
JHC............. Johnson Canyon [*California*] [*Seismograph station code, US Geological Survey*] (SEIS)
JHC............. Joint Helicopter Control (SAUS)
JHC............. Joint High Command (DNAB)
JHC............. Joint Hulls Committee (MARI)
JHCM .... Journal of Health Care Marketing (journ.) (SAUS)
JHCNHS....... John Henry Cardinal Newman Honorary Society [*Defunct*] (EA)
JHD............. Jehuda [*On Hebrew coins of the fourth century*]
JHD............. Joint Hypocenter Determination [*Earthquake study*]
JHD............. Journal of the Hellenic Diaspra (journ.) (SAUS)
JHDA........... Journal. Hawaii Dental Association (journ.) (SAUS)
JHDA........... Junior Hospital Doctors Association [*British*]
Jhdf............ Japanese haakon-dahl feet (SAUS)
JHe............. Jewish Heritage [*A publication*] (BJA)
JHE............. Johns Hopkins University, Baltimore, MD [*OCLC symbol*] (OCLC)
JHE............. Journal of Higher Education (journ.) (SAUS)
JHE............. Juvenile Hormone Esterase [*An enzyme*]
J Health Adm Educ... Journal of Health Administration Education (journ.) (SAUS)
J Health Care Finance... Journal of Health Care Finance (journ.) (SAUS)
J Health Care Poor Underserved... Journal of Health Care for the Poor and Underserved (journ.) (SAUS)
J Health Care Technol... Journal of Health Care Technology (journ.) (SAUS)
J Healthc Mater Manage... Journal of Healthcare Material Management (journ.) (SAUS)
J Healthc Prot Manage... Journal of Healthcare Protection Management (journ.) (SAUS)
J Health Econ... Journal of Health Economics (journ.) (SAUS)
J Health Hum Behav... Journal of Health and Human Behavior (journ.) (SAUS)
J Health Phys Radiat Prot... Journal of Health Physics and Radiation Protection (journ.) (SAUS)
J Heart Lung Transplant... Journal of Heart and Lung Transplantation (journ.) (SAUS)
J Heart Valve Dis... Journal of Heart Valve Disease (journ.) (SAUS)
J Heat Recovery Syst... Journal of Heat Recovery Systems (journ.) (SAUS)
J Heat Transfer... Journal of Heat Transfer (SAUS)
J Heat Treat... Journal of Heat Treating (journ.) (SAUS)
J Hebei Univ Nat Sci Ed... Journal. Hebei University. Natural Science Edition (journ.) (SAUS)
J Hebr St..... Journal of Hebraic Studies (journ.) (SAUS)
JHEL........... Journal of Hellenic Studies (journ.) (SAUS)
JHellSt........ Journal of Hellenic Studies (journ.) (SAUS)
J Helth Phys Ed Rec... Journal of Health, Physical Education, Recreation (journ.) (SAUS)
J Hematother... Journal of Hematotherapy (journ.) (SAUS)
J Hepatol..... Journal of Hepatology (journ.) (SAUS)
J Herpetol ... Journal of Herpetology (journ.) (SAUS)
J Herpetol Assoc Afr... Journal. Herpetological Association of Africa (journ.) (SAUS)
JHF............. Jackson, MS [*Location identifier*] [*FAA*] (FAAL)
JHF............. John Hancock Fin'l Svcs. [*NYSE symbol*] (SG)
JHFC........... Jan Howard Friends Club (EA)
JHFC........... Jeff Healey Fan Club (EA)
JHG............. Joule Heat Gradient (IEEE)
JHGA .... Jewish Historical General Archives [*Jerusalem*] (BJA)
JHGSOWA..... Joint Household Goods Shipping Office
JHGSOWA..... Joint Household Goods Shipping Office, Washington Area [*Military*] (AABC)
JHGSW .... Journal. Heraldic and Genealogical Society of Wales (journ.) (SAUS)
JHH............. John Hopkins Hospital
JHH............. Johns Hopkins Hospital (SAUO)
JHH............. Journal of Health and Human Resources Administration (journ.) (SAUS)
JHHGSO....... Joint Household Goods Shipping Office [*Military*]
JHI............. Hancock, John, Investors Trust [*NYSE symbol*] (SAG)
JHI............. Jacob Hiatt Institute (SAUO)
JHI............. Jeffreys Henry International (BUAC)
JHI............. Jesuit Historical Society (SAUO)
JHI............. Jewish Historical Society (SAUO)
JHI............. John Hancock Investors, Incorporated (SAUO)
JHI............. John Hancock Investors Trust [*NYSE symbol*] (SPSG)
JHI............. John Hancock Inv Tr [*NYSE symbol*] (TTSB)
JHI............. Journal of Hospital Infection (SAUO)
JHI............. Journal of the History of Ideas [*A publication*] (BRI)
J Hi E .... Journal of Higher Education [*A publication*] (BRI)
J High Resolut Chromatogr Chromatogr Commun... Journal of High Resolution Chromato-graphy and Chromatography Communications (journ.) (SAUS)
J High Temp Soc... Journal. High Temperature Society (journ.) (SAUS)
J High Temp Soc Jpn... Journal of High Temperature Society of Japan (journ.) (SAUS)
J Highw Dir Am Soc Civ Eng... Journal. Highway Division. American Society of Civil Engineers (journ.) (SAUS)
J Hillside Hosp... Journal. Hillside Hospital (journ.) (SAUS)
JHINDS........ Journal of Hospital Infection (SAUS)
J Hiroshim Univ Dent Soc... Journal. Hiroshima University. Dental Society (journ.) (SAUS)
J Hist Arabic Sci... Journal for the History of Arabic Science (journ.) (SAUS)
J Hist Astron... Journal of the History of Astronomy (journ.) (SAUS)

J Hist Biol ...   Journal of the History of Biology (journ.) (SAUS)
J Hist G ......   Journal of Historical Geography [*A publication*] (BRI)
J Hist Med Allied Sci...   Journal of the History of Medicine and Allied Sciences, Department of the History of Medicine. Yale University. New Haven (SAUO)
J Histochem Biochem...   Journal of Histochemistry and Biochemistry (journ.) (SAUS)
J Histotechnol...   Journal of Histotechnology (journ.) (SAUS)
J Hist Res ...   Journal of Historical Research (journ.) (SAUS)
J Hist Soc Church Wales...   Journal. Historical Society of the Church in Wales (journ.) (SAUS)
J Hist Sociol...   Journal of the History of Sociology (journ.) (SAUS)
J Hist Soc Nigeria...   Journal. Historical Society of Nigeria (journ.) (SAUS)
J Hist Soc QD...   Historical Society of Queensland. Journal (journ.) (SAUS)
J Hist Soc SA...   Journal. Historical Society of South Australia [*A publication*]
J Hist Stud...   Journal of Historical Studies (journ.) (SAUS)
JHjelm.........   Hjelms [*Jim*] Private Collection [*Associated Press*] (SAG)
JHjelm.........   Jim Hjelms Private Collection [*Associated Press*] (SAG)
JHL.............   Jet Heritage Ltd. [*British*] [*ICAO designator*] (FAAC)
JHL.............   John Harvard Library (SAUO)
JHLB...........   Journal of the Federal Home Loan Bank Board (SAUO)
JHM............   Dr. J. Howard Mueller
JHM............   Journal of the History of Medicine (journ.) (SAUS)
JHM............   Juvenile Hormone Mimic [*Entomology*]
JHMA..........   Japan Heat Management Association (SAUO)
JHMCO ....   J. H. Morgan Consultants [*Morristown, NJ*] [*Information service or system*] [*Telecommunications*] (TSSD)
JHMCS........   Joint Helmet-Mounted Cueing System [*Military*]
JHMEDL......   Journal of Holistic Medicine (journ.) (SAUS)
JHMET........   Joint Health-Care Management Engineering Team (ACAE)
JHMI ....   Johns Hopkins Medical Institutions (SAUO)
JHMO ....   Junior Hospital Medical Officer
JHMSDT .....   Journal of Human Movement Studies (journ.) (SAUS)
JHM Virus ...   Dr. J. Howard Mueller Virus (SAUS)
JHN............   Japanese Helicopter Network (SAUS)
JHN............   John Henry Newman [*Initials used as pseudonym*]
JHN............   Johnson Air, Inc. [*ICAO designator*] (FAAC)
JHN............   Johnson, KS [*Location identifier*] [*FAA*] (FAAL)
JHNBX ....   Hancock(J) Bond Cl.A [*Mutual fund ticker symbol*] (SG)
JHNPD ....   Johnson Products Co., Inc. (SAUO)
JHO............   Jam Handy Organization (SAUO)
JHO............   Japan Hydrographic Office (SAUO)
JHO............   Junior House Officer [*Military*]
JHOGB ....   Jewish Health Organization of Great Britain (SAUO)
J Hokkaido Dent Assc...   Journal. Hokkaido Dental Association (journ.) (SAUS)
J Hokkaido Fish Sci Inst...   Journal. Hokkaido Fisheries Scientific Institution (journ.) (SAUS)
J Hokkaido Forest Prod Res Inst...   Journal Hokkaido Forest Products Research Institute (journ.) (SAUS)
J Hokkaido Gakugei Univ...   Journal. Hokkaido Gakugei University (journ.) (SAUS)
J Hokkaido Gakugei Univ Sect B...   Journal. Hokkaido Gakugei University. Section B (journ.) (SAUS)
J Hokkaido Gynecol Obstet Soc...   Journal. Hokkaido Gynecology and Obstetrical Society (journ.) (SAUS)
J Hokkaido Univ Ed Sect II-A...   Journal. Hokkaido University of Education. Section II-A (journ.) (SAUS)
J Hokkaido Univ Educ...   Journal. Hokkaido University of Education (journ.) (SAUS)
J Hokkaido Univ Educ II-B...   Journal. Hokkaido University of Education. Section II-B (journ.) (SAUS)
J Hokkaido Univ Educ Sect II-C...   Journal. Hokkaido University of Education. Section II-C (journ.) (SAUS)
J Holistic Med...   Journal of Holistic Medicine (journ.) (SAUS)
J Holistic Nurs...   Journal of Holistic Nursing (journ.) (SAUS)
J Homosex...   Journal of Homosexuality [*A publication*] (BRI)
J Hopeh Univ Nat Sci...   Journal. Hopeh University. Natural Science (journ.) (SAUS)
J Horol Inst Jpn...   Journal. Horological Institute of Japan (journ.) (SAUS)
J Horol Inst Jpn...   Journal of the Horological Institute of Japan (journ.) (SAUS)
J Hortic Assoc London...   Journal. Horticulture Association of London (journ.) (SAUS)
JHOS ....   John Hopkins Oceanographic Studies (SAUS)
JHOS ....   Johns Hopkins Oceanographic Studies (SAUO)
JHOS ....   Johns Hopkins Oceanographic Studies (journ.) (SAUS)
J Hosp Dent Pract...   Journal of Hospital Dental Practice (journ.) (SAUS)
J Hosp Infect...   Journal of Hospital Infection (journ.) (SAUS)
J Hospitality Educ...   Journal of Hospitality Education (journ.) (SAUS)
J Hosp Supply Process Distrib...   Journal of Hospital Supply, Processing and Distribution (journ.) (SAUS)
JHP.............   Jacketed Hollow-Point [*Ammunition*]
JHP.............   Jackson Hole Preserve (EA)
JHP.............   Johns Hopkins Press (SAUO)
JHP.............   Journal of Hispanic Philology (journ.) (SAUS)
JHP.............   Peabody Institute of Johns Hopkins University, Conservatory Library Baltimore (SAUO)
JHP.............   Peabody Institute of Johns Hopkins University, Conservatory Library, Baltimore, MD [*OCLC symbol*] (OCLC)
JHPC...........   Jim Hielms Private Coll'n [*NASDAQ symbol*] (TTSB)
JHPC...........   Jim Hjelms Private Collection [*NASDAQ symbol*] (SPSG)
JHPC...........   JLM Couture [*NYSE symbol*] (SG)
JHPN ....   Journal of Hospice and Palliative Nursing (SAUO)
JHPPL.........   Journal of Health Politics, Policy and Law (SAUO)
JHPS ....   Japan Hydraulics and Pneumatics Society (SAUO)
JHPS...........   Judaica Historical Philatelic Society (EA)
JHQ............   Job Hazards Questionnaire (SAUS)
JHQ............   Joint Headquarters [*British military*] (DMA)
JHQ............   Shute Harbour [*Australia*] [*Airport symbol*]

JHR............   Jarisch-Herxheimer Reaction [*Immunology*] (DAVI)
JHR............   Journal Holdings Report (AEPA)
JHR............   Journal of Human Resources (journ.) (SAUS)
JHRP ....   Joint Highway Research Project [*Purdue University*] [*Research center*] (RCD)
JHS............   Hancock, John, Income Securities Trust [*NYSE symbol*] (SAG)
JHS............   Jesus Hominum Salvator [*Jesus, Savior of Men*] (ROG)
JHS............   Jewish History Series (journ.) (SAUS)
JHS............   Job Hunter's Sourcebook [*A publication*]
JHS............   John Hampden Society (BUAC)
JHS............   John Hancock Income Securities Trust [*NYSE symbol*] (SPSG)
JHS............   John Hancock Inc. Sec [*NYSE symbol*] (TTSB)
JHS............   John Howard Society (SAUO)
JHS............   Judaic Heritage Society (SAUO)
JHS............   Junior High School
JHS............   School of Advanced International Studies Johns Hopkins University (SAUO)
JHS............   School of Advanced International Studies, Johns Hopkins University, Washington, DC [*OCLC symbol*] (OCLC)
JHS-AR ....   Journal of Hellenic Studies. Archaeological Reports (journ.) (SAUS)
JHSCW ....   Journal Historical Society of the Church in Wales (journ.) (SAUS)
JHSE..........   JCI Health, Safety & Environmental Department (SAUO)
JHSE..........   Jewish Historical Society of England
JHSEM........   Jewish Historical Society of England. Miscellanies (journ.) (SAUS)
JHSET........   Jewish Historical Society of England. Transactions (journ.) (SAUS)
JHSF..........   Japan Health Sciences Foundation (BUAC)
JHSN..........   Johnson Electronics, Inc. (SAUO)
JHSN..........   Journal. Historical Society of Nigeria [*A publication*]
JHSPCW .....   Journal. Historical Society of the Presbyterian Church of Wales (journ.) (SAUS)
JHSRLL.......   Johns Hopkins Studies in Romans Language and Literature (journ.) (SAUS)
JHSS ....   Journal of History for Senior Students (journ.) (SAUS)
JHSSA ....   Journal. Historical Society of South Australia (journ.) (SAUS)
JHSU ....   Joint Helicopter Support Unit (SAUO)
JHSUR ....   Journal of Hand Surgery (journ.) (SAUS)
JHTR..........   Japan High Tech Review [*Database*] [*Kyodo News International, Inc.*] [*Information service or system*] (CRD)
JHU...........   Johns Hopkins University [*Maryland*]
JHU/AJE......   American Journal of Epidemiology. Johns Hopkins University, School of Hygiene. Baltimore (SAUS)
JHU/APL .....   John Hopkins University/Applied Physics Laboratory (SAUS)
JHU/APL .....   Johns Hopkins University Applied Physics Laboratory [*Laurel, MD*]
J Huazhong Inst Tech...   Journal. Huazhong Institute of Technology. English Edition (journ.) (SAUS)
J Huazhong Inst Technol...   Journal. Huazhong Institute of Technology (journ.) (SAUS)
J Huazhong Univ Sci Tech...   Journal. Huazhong University of Science and Technology. English Edition (journ.) (SAUS)
JHUC ....   Journal. Hebrew Union College (journ.) (SAUS)
JHUCCP ......   Johns Hopkins University Center for Communications Programs (SAUO)
JHU-CRSC ...   Johns Hopkins University - Center for Research in Scientific Communication (PDAA)
JHU-CRSC ...   Johns Hopkins University-Center for Research in Scientific Communication (SAUO)
JHU-DDB .....   Johns Hopkins University - Dyslexia and Dysgraphia Batteries
JHU-DDB .....   Johns Hopkins University-Dyslexica and Dysgraphica Batteries (SAUO)
JHUL...........   Johns Hopkins University Library (SAUO)
J Hum Behav Lrn...   Journal of Human Behavior and Learning (journ.) (SAUS)
J Hum Evol...   Journal of Human Evolution (journ.) (SAUS)
J Hum Hypertens...   Journal of Human Hypertension (journ.) (SAUS)
J Hum Nut...   Journal of Human Nutrition (journ.) (SAUS)
J Hum Relat...   Journal of Human Relations (journ.) (SAUS)
J Hum Sci Technol Univ...   Journal. Human Science and Technology University (journ.) (SAUS)
J Hunan Sci Technol Univ...   Journal of Hunan Science and Technology University (journ.) (SAUS)
J Hunan Univ...   Journal. Hunan University (journ.) (SAUS)
J Hung Vet Surg...   Journal. Hungarian Veterinary Surgeons (journ.) (SAUS)
J Hunter Valley Research Foundrtion...   Journal. Hunter Valley Research Foundation (journ.) (SAUS)
JHUP ....   Johns Hopkins University Press
JHUSM ....   Johns Hopkins University School of Medicine (SAUO)
JHU Studies...   Johns Hopkins University. Studies in Historical and Political Science (journ.) (SAUS)
JHVA..........   Jehovah (ROG)
JHVH ....   Jehovah (ABBR)
JHW...........   Jamestown [*New York*] [*Airport symbol*] (OAG)
JHW...........   Jamestown, NY [*Location identifier*] [*FAA*] (FAAL)
JHW...........   Johns Hopkins University, Welch Medical Library, Baltimore, MD [*OCLC symbol*] (OCLC)
JHWC.........   Joint Hurricane Warning Center (CINC)
JHWH ....   Jehovah (ADWA)
JHWRP ....   Joint Hawaii Warm Rain Project (SAUO)
J Hyderabad Geol Surv...   Journal. Hyderabad Geological Survey (journ.) (SAUS)
J Hydraul Div Amer Soc Civil Eng Proc...   Journal. Hydraulics Division. Proceedings of the American Society of Civil Engineers (journ.) (SAUS)
J Hydraul Div Am Soc Civ Eng...   Journal. Hydraulics Division. American Society of Civil Engineers (journ.) (SAUS)
J Hydraul Div Pr ASCE...   Journal. Hydraulics Division. Proceedings of the American Society of Civil Engineers (journ.) (SAUS)
J Hydr-E ......   Journal Hydraulics Division. American Society of Civil Engineers (journ.) (SAUS)

J Hydrogeol... Journal of Hydrogeology (journ.) (SAUS)
J Hydrol Sci... Journal of Hydrological Sciences (journ.) (SAUS)
J Hydronaut... Journal of Hydronautics (journ.) (SAUS)
J Hydrosci Hydraul Eng... Journal of Hydroscience and Hydraulic Engineering (journ.) (SAUS)
J Hyg Chem... Journal of Hygiene Chemistry (journ.) (SAUS)
J Hyg Chem... Journal of Hygienic Chemistry (journ.) (SAUS)
J Hyg Chem Soc Jpn... Journal. Hygienic Chemical Society of Japan (journ.) (SAUS)
J Hyogo Coll Med... Journal. Hyogo College of Medicine (journ.) (SAUS)
J Hypertens... Journal of Hypertension (journ.) (SAUS)
J Hypertens Suppl... Journal of Hypertension. Supplement (journ.) (SAUS)
JI .... Air Balear [ICAO designator] (ICDA)
JI .... Gull Air [ICAO designator] (AD)
JI .... Jamaat-i-Islami [Pakistan] [Political party] (FEA)
JI .... Japan Institute [Defunct] (EA)
JI .... Japan Interpreter (journ.) (SAUS)
JI .... Jazz Interactions (EA)
JI .... Jazz International
JI .... Jejunal Intestinal [Medicine] (DB)
JI .... Jejunoileitis [Gastroenterology] (DAVI)
JI .... Jejunoileostomy [Gastroenterology] (DAVI)
JI .... Jersey Institute
JI .... Jesness Inventory [Psychology]
JI .... Jet Express [ICAO designator] (AD)
JI .... Jet Interaction (RDA)
JI .... Jigging Information
JI .... Job Information (SAUS)
JI .... Job Instruction
JI .... Job Insurance [Job Service] (OICC)
ji .... Johnston Atoll [MARC country of publication code] [Library of Congress] (LCCP)
JI .... Joint Identification (DNAB)
JI .... Joint Implementation
JI .... Josephson Interferometer [Optics] (IAA)
JI .... Journal. American Musical Instrument Society (journ.) (SAUS)
JI .... Journal of Immunology (journ.) (SAUS)
JI .... Jump Instruction (SAUS)
JI .... Junction Isolation [Electronics]
JI .... Jupiter Inlet [NASA] (KSC)
JI .... Justice, Inc. (SAUS)
JIA .... Japanese Interchange Association (SAUO)
JIA .... Jetstream International Airlines [ICAO designator] (FAAC)
JIA .... Joint Interest Audiovisual Requirements (MCD)
JIA .... Jordan International Airline
JIA .... Journal of Industrial Archaeology (journ.) (SAUS)
JIA .... Journal of International Affairs (journ.) (SAUS)
JIA .... Jute Importers' Association [British] (DBA)
JIAA .... Joint Institute for Aeronautics and Acoustics [Stanford University] (PDAA)
JIAD .... Joint Integrated Avionics Directorate (DOMA)
JIAFS .... Joint Institute for Acoustics and Flight Sciences (MCD)
JIAFS .... Joint Institute for Advancement of Flight Science [Research center] (RCD)
Jiangsu Med J... Jiangsu Medical Journal (journ.) (SAUS)
JIAP .... Journal. Indian Academy of Philosophy (journ.) (SAUS)
JIAS .... Japan International Artists Society (SAUO)
JIAS .... Jewish Immigrant Aid Society (SAUO)
JIAS .... Jewish Immigration Aid Society (SAUO)
JIAS .... Journal. Indian Anthropological Society (journ.) (SAUS)
JIAS .... Journal of Inter-American Studies (SAUO)
JIAS .... Journal of Interamerican Studies and World Affairs (journ.) (SAUS)
JIASRA .... Journal. International Arthur Schnitzler Research Association (journ.) (SAUS)
JIAWG .... Joint Integrated Avionics Working Group [DoD]
JIB .... Djibouti [Airport symbol] (OAG)
JIB .... Foodmaker Inc. (SAUO)
JIB .... Jack-in-the-Box Dummy [CIA]
JIB .... Japan International Bank (SAUO)
JIB .... Jejunoileal Bypass [Gastroenterology] (DAVI)
JIB .... Jewish Information Bureau [Defunct] (EA)
JIB .... Job Information Block [Computer science] (BUR)
JIB .... Jobs Impact Bulletin [National Committee for Full Employment] [A publication]
JIB .... Joint Industry Board for the Electrical Contracting Industry (HEAS)
JIB .... Joint Information Bureau [Military] (MCD)
JIB .... Joint Intelligence Bureau [British] (MCD)
JIB .... Jordan Information Bureau (EA)
JIB .... Journal of International Business Studies [A publication] (BRI)
JIBA .... Japanese Institute of Business Administration (BUAC)
JIBA .... Japan Institute of Business Administration (SAUO)
JIBC .... Japan International Biological Program (SAUS)
JIBECI .... Joint Industry Board for the Electrical Contracting Industry (BUAC)
JIBEI .... Joint Industry Board of the Electrical Industry (EA)
JIBF .... Jerusalem International Book Fair (SAUO)
JIBG .... Jibing (ABBR)
JIBICO .... Japan International Bank and Investment (BUAC)
JIBICO .... Japan International Bank and Investment Co. (SAUS)
JIBP .... Japan International Biological Programme (SAUO)
JI Brewing... Journal. Institute of Brewing (journ.) (SAUS)
JIBS .... Journal of Indian and Buddhist Studies (journ.) (SAUS)
Jibuti .... Djibouti (SAUS)
JIC .... Japan Information Center (SAUS)
JIC .... Japan International Cooperation (SAUS)
JIC .... Jet Induced Circulation (SAUS)

JIC .... Jet-Induced Circulation [Combustor]
JIC .... Jet Induced Combustion (SAUS)
JIC .... Jet Interaction Control (MCD)
JIC .... Jewelry Industry Council (EA)
JIC .... Jewelry Information Center (NTPA)
JIC .... Job Information Card (SAUS)
JIC .... Job Information Centre [Canada]
JIC .... Job Instruction and Communication (PDAA)
JIC .... Joint Ice Center [US Navy] [Marine science] (OSRA)
JIC .... Joint Imperial Committee (SAUO)
JIC .... Joint Implementation Committee [Military] (SAA)
JIC .... Joint Industrial Company (SAUO)
JIC .... Joint Industrial Council [Defunct] (EA)
JIC .... Joint Industry Committee (SAUO)
JIC .... Joint Industry Conference (SAUS)
JIC .... Joint Industry Council (EAIO)
JIC .... Joint Information Center (SAUO)
JIC .... Joint Insurance Committee [under the Trading with the Enemy Act] [World War II]
JIC .... Joint Intelligence Center
JIC .... Joint Intelligence Committee
JIC .... Joint Intelligence Curriculum (SAUO)
JIC .... Joint Interrogation Center (MCD)
JIC .... Joint Iron Council (SAUO)
JIC .... Junior International Club (EA)
JIC .... Just in Case (WDMC)
JIC .... Juventudes Inconformes de Colombia [Political party] (EY)
JIC .... Morgan Stanley Group, Inc. [AMEX symbol] (SAG)
JICA .... Japan International Cooperation Agency
JICA .... Jiangsu Provincial Institute of Culture and Art [China] (BUAC)
JICA .... Joint Intelligence Center, Africa
JICA .... Joint Intelligence Collecting Agency
JICACBI .... Joint Intelligence Collecting Agency, China, Burma, India [World War II]
JICAME .... Joint Intelligence Collecting Agency, Middle East [World War II]
JICANA .... Joint Intelligence Collecting Agency, North Africa [World War II]
JICARC .... Joint Intelligence Collecting Agency, Reception Committee [Navy]
JICC .... Japanese ICC (SAUO)
JICC .... Japan Information and Cultural Centre (BUAC)
JICC .... Job Item Cost Code (MCD)
JICC .... Joint Interservice Coordinating Committee (SAUO)
JICCAR .... Joint Industry Committee for Cable Audience Research [Television] [British]
JICG .... Joint International Coordination Group (MSC)
JICGI .... Joint Industrial Council for the Gas Industry (SAUO)
JICHS .... Joint Industrial Conference on Hydraulic Standards
J Ichthyol... Journal of Ichthyology (journ.) (SAUS)
JICI .... Jeunesse Independante Chretienne Internationale [International Independent Christian Youth - IICY] (EA)
JICJ .... Journal. International Commission of Jurists [A publication] (DLA)
Jick Est... Jickling. Legal and Equitable Estates [1829] [A publication] (DLA)
JICMARS .... Joint Industry Committee of Medical Advertisers for Readership Surveys (BUAC)
JICMB .... Joint Interface Configuration Management Board (SAUO)
JICNARS .... Joint Industry Committee for National Readership Surveys [British]
JICOA .... Japan Information and Communication Association [Information service or system] (IID)
JICPAC .... Joint Intelligence Center Pacific (DOMA)
JICPAR .... Joint Industry Committee for Postal Audience Research (BUAC)
JICPAS .... Joint Industry Committee for Poster Audience Surveys [British]
JICPOA .... Joint Intelligence Center, Pacific Ocean Areas
JICP/PO .... Joint International Climate Projects/Planning Office (SAUO)
JICRAR .... Joint Industry Committee for Radio Audience Research (BUAC)
JICRAR .... Joint Industry Committee for Radio Audience Research [British]
JICS .... Joint Intelligence Coordination Staff [Central Intelligence Agency] (AABC)
JICS .... Joint Interpreting and Conference Service (BUAC)
JICST .... Japan Information Center for Science and Technology
JICST .... Japan Information Center of Science and Technology [Tokyo] (IID)
JICST .... Japan International Center of Science and Technology (USGC)
JICT .... Japan Information Center of Science and Technology (SAUO)
JICTAR .... Joint Industry Committee for Television Advertising Research [Database producer]
JICUF .... Japan International Christian University Foundation (EA)
JID .... Air Condal SA [Spain] [ICAO designator] (FAAC)
JID .... Journal of Infectious Diseases (journ.) (SAUS)
JID .... Journal of Investigative Dermatology (journ.) (SAUS)
JIDA .... Japan Industrial Designers Association (BUAC)
JIDA .... Jewelry Industry Distributors Association (EA)
J Idaho Acad Sci... Journal. Idaho Academy of Science (journ.) (SAUS)
JIDC .... Jamaica Industrial Development Corp. (BUAC)
JIdeD .... Inter-American Defense Board (SAUO)
JIDS .... Job Information Delivery System [US Employment Service] [Department of Labor]
JIDSDP .... Journal. Idaho Academy of Science (journ.) (SAUS)
JIDXA .... Journal. Indiana State Medical Association (journ.) (SAUS)
JIE .... Japan Information Exchange [Comtex Scientific Corp.] [Information service or system] [Defunct] (CRD)
JIE .... Jobs in Energy (EA)
JIE .... Journal of Industrial Economics (journ.) (SAUS)
JIE .... Journal of International Economics (journ.) (SAUS)
JIE .... Junior Institute of Engineers
JIEA .... Japan Industrial Explosives Association (BUAC)
JI/EC .... Joint Interrogation/Exploitation Center (SAUS)
JIECh .... Journal of Industrial and Engineering Chemistry (journ.) (SAUS)

JIEE .... Japanese Institute of Electrical Engineers
JIEE .... Japanese Institution of Electrical Engineers (SAUS)
JIEE .... Journal of the Institution of Electrical Engineers (SAUO)
J IEE .... Journal of the Institution of Electrical Engineers (journ.) (SAUS)
JIEEJ............ Journal of the Institute of Electrical Engineers of Japan (SAUO)
JIEEJ............ Journal of the Institute of Electrical Engineers of Japan (journ.) (SAUS)
JIEO .... Joint Interoperability and Engineering Organization [DoD]
JIEO .... Joint Interoperability Engineering Organization (SAUS)
JIEP .... Joint Intelligence Estimate for Planning (AFM)
JIES .... Joint Interoperability Evaluation System (SAUO)
JIES .... Journal of Indo-European Studies (journ.) (SAUS)
JIF .... French Lick, IN [Location identifier] [FAA] (FAAL)
JIF .... Janus Information Facility [Later, J2CP Information Services] (EA)
JIF .... Jet Interaction Fuel
JIF .... Job Information Form (SAUS)
JIF .... Joint Integrated Firepower [Task force] (MCD)
JIF .... Joint Interrogation Facility (DOMA)
JIF .... Journal of Information Systems Management (journ.) (SAUS)
JIF .... JPEG Interchange Format (SAUS)
JIFA .... Japanese Institute for Foreign Affairs (BUAC)
JIFA .... Japan Institute of Foreign Affairs (SAUS)
JIFC .... Janis Ian Fan Club (EA)
JIFC .... Julio Iglesias Fan Club [Defunct] (EA)
JIFDATS...... Joint In-Flight Data Acquisition and Transmission System (SAUS)
JIFDATS...... Joint In-Flight Data Transmission System [Army] (MCD)
JIFE .... Junta Internacional de Fiscalizacion de Estupefacientes [International Narcotics Control Board]
JIFFQ .... Jiffy Foods Corp. (SAUO)
JIFS .... Jerusalem Institute for Federal Studies (BUAC)
JIFSA .... Journal. Indian Academy of Forensic Sciences (journ.) (SAUS)
JIFSAN........ Joint Institute of Food Safety and Applied Nutrition
JIFTS .... Joint In-Flight Transmission System [Army] (IEEE)
JIFUA .... Journal. Institute of Fuel (journ.) (SAUS)
JIFY .... Jiffy Industries (SAUS)
JIG .... Jigging (SAUS)
JIG .... Jinotega [Nicaragua] [Seismograph station code, US Geological Survey] (SEIS)
JIG .... Joint Implementation Committee (SAUO)
JIG .... Joint Industry Group [An association] (EA)
JIG .... Joint Intelligence Group [Military]
JIG .... Joule Impulse Generator [Physics]
JIG .... Journal of Irish Genealogy (journ.) (SAUS)
JIGFET .... Junction and Insulated Gate Field Effect Transistor (MCD)
JIGG............ Jet Interaction Gas Generator
JIGI .... Java Interface for Geospatial Information (SAUO)
JIGL .... Jiggle (ABBR)
JIGLD.......... Jiggled (ABBR)
JIGLG.......... Jiggling (ABBR)
JIGLY .... Jiggly (ABBR)
JIGR............ Jigger (ABBR)
JIGS............ Joule Impulse Generator System [Physics]
JIGTSC........ Joint Industry-Government Tall Structures Committee
JIH .... Joint Interval Histogram [Histology] (DAVI)
JIH .... Journal of Indian History (journ.) (SAUS)
JIH .... Journal of Interdisciplinary History [A publication] (BRI)
JIHI .... John Innes Horticultural Institution (SAUO)
JIHIR .... Joint Institute for Heavy Ion Research (SAUO)
JIHTA .... Journal of Industrial Hygiene and Toxicology (journ.) (SAUS)
JIHVE.......... Journal. Institution of Heating and Ventilating Engineers (journ.) (SAUS)
JII .... John Innes Institute [British] (ARC)
JII .... Johnston Industries [NYSE symbol] (TTSB)
JII .... Johnston Industries, Inc. [NYSE symbol] (SPSG)
JIIA............ Japan Institute of International Affairs (BUAC)
JIIB............ Jewish Immigrants Information Bureau (BJA)
JIIG-CAL ...... Job Ideas and Information Generator - Computer Assisted Learning (AIE)
JIII .... Japan Institute of Invention and Innovation (BUAC)
JIIKS........... Joint Imagery Interpretation Key Structure (MCD)
JIIM .... Journal of Information and Image Management (journ.) (SAUS)
JIIP .... Joint Interface Implementation Program [Army] (MCD)
JIISC.......... Joing Industrial Investment Service Center (SAUS)
JIIST .... Japan Institute for International Studies and Training
Jikeitai Med J... Jikeikai Medical Journal (journ.) (SAUS)
JIL .... George Washington Journal of International Law and Economics (journ.) (SAUS)
JIL .... Jet-Induced Lift
JIL .... Journal of Irish Literature (journ.) (SAUS)
JIL .... Joy Industries Ltd. [Vancouver Stock Exchange symbol]
JILA............ Japanese Institute of Landscape Architects (BUAC)
JILA............ Joint Institute for Laboratory Astrophysics [University of Colorado, National Bureau of Standards] (EA)
JILA-IC........ Joint Institute for Laboratory Astrophysics-Information Center [University of Colorado] (PDAA)
JILA IniCent Rep... Joint Institute for Laboratory Astrophysics. Informatinn Center. Report (journ.) (SAUS)
JILE .... Joint Intelligence Liaison Element (MCD)
JILEA .... Journal. Institution of Locomotive Engineers (journ.) (SAUS)
JILI .... Journal. Indian Law Institute (journ.) (SAUS)
JilinCh .... Jilin Chemical Industrial Co. Ltd. [Associated Press] (SAG)
JILL .... Jobs Illustrated [CD-ROM]
JillEnt .... Jillians Entertainment Corp. [Associated Press] (SAG)
J Illum Eng Inst Jap... Journal. Illuminating Engineering Institute of Japan (journ.) (SAUS)

J Illum Eng Inst Jpn... Journal of the Illuminating Engineering Institute of Japan (journ.) (SAUS)
J Illum Eng Soc... Journal of the Illuminating Engineering Society (journ.) (SAUS)
JILM .... Japan Institute of Light Metals (SAUS)
JILO .... Joint Information Liaison Office [Military]
JILSMT .... Joint Integrated Logistics Support Management Team (ACAE)
JILSP .... Joint Integrated Logistic Support Plan (ACAE)
JILTA .... Journal. Indian Law Teachers Association [A publication] (DLA)
JIM .... Jakarta Informal Meetings (SAUS)
JIM .... Japan Institute of Metals (SAUO)
JIM .... Jevreiski Istoriski Muzej (BJA)
JIM .... Jimma [Ethiopia] [Airport symbol] (OAG)
JIM .... Job Information Memorandum (SAUS)
JIM .... Job Instruction Manual
JIM .... Journal of Information Management (journ.) (SAUS)
JIM .... Journal of Investigative Medicine (SAUO)
JIM .... Junctor Isolated Monolithic (SAUS)
JIM .... Junior Index of Motivation (SAUS)
JIM .... Memphis, TN [Location identifier] [FAA] (FAAL)
JIM .... Sark International Airways Ltd. [British] [ICAO designator] (FAAC)
JIMA .... Japan Industrial Management Association (BUAC)
JIMA .... JDS Interface Method of Access (SAUS)
JIMA .... John Innes Manufacturers Association (DBA)
J IMA .... Journal. Islamic Medical Association of the United States and Canada (journ.) (SAUS)
JIMA .... Journal of the Indian Medical Associations (journ.) (SAUS)
JIMA .... Journal of the Israel Medical Association (journ.) (SAUS)
J Imaging Sci... Journal of Imaging Science (journ.) (SAUS)
J Imaging Technol... Journal of Imaging Technology (journ.) (SAUS)
JIMAR........ Joint Institute for Marine and Atmospheric Research [Honolulu, HI] [National Oceanic and Atmospheric Administration] (GRD)
JIMC .... Japan Immuno-Monitoring Centre (BUAC)
JIMEA .... Journal. Institute of Metals (journ.) (SAUS)
JIMGA .... Journal of Immunogenetics (journ.) (SAUS)
J Img Guided Surg... Journal of Image Guided Surgery (journ.) (SAUS)
JIMI .... Jimi Hendrix Information Management Institute (EA)
JIMIS .... Japan Institute of Metals International Symposium (SAUS)
J Immunoassay... Journal of Immunoassay (journ.) (SAUS)
J Immunopharmacol... Journal of Immunopharmacology (journ.) (SAUS)
J Immunother... Journal of Immunotherapy (journ.) (SAUS)
J Immunother Emphasis Tumor Immunol... Journal of Immunotherapy with Emphasis on Tumor Immunology (journ.) (SAUS)
JIMP .... Center for the Study of Japanese Industry and Management of Technology (SAUO)
JIMPACS...... Joint Improved Multimission Payload Aerial Surveillance Combat Survivable (ACAE)
J Imp Coll Chem Eng S... Journal. Imperial College. Chemical Engineering Society (journ.) (SAUS)
J Imp Coll Chem Soc... Journal. Imperial College. Chemical Society (journ.) (SAUS)
JIMPP .... Joint Industrial Mobilization Planning Process [Environmental science] (COE)
JIMR .... Journal of International Medical Research (SAUO)
JIMS .... Job Information Matrix System
JIMS .... Joint Industrial Measurement Programme (ACII)
JIMS .... Journal. Indian Mathematical Society (journ.) (SAUS)
JIMS .... Journal of Indian Mathematical Society (journ.) (SAUS)
JIMS .... Jukebox Interface Management System (ACAE)
JIMSA .... Journal. Irish Medical Association (journ.) (SAUS)
JIMSDZ....... Journal of Interdisciplinary Modeling and Simulation (journ.) (SAUS)
JIMTOF....... Japan International Machine Tool Fair (SAUS)
JIN .... Japanese Institution of Navigation (BUAC)
JIN .... Japan Institute of Navigation (SAUS)
JIN .... Jindabyne [Australia] [Seismograph station code, US Geological Survey] [Closed] (SEIS)
JIN .... Jinja [Uganda] [Airport symbol] (AD)
JIN .... Joint Implementation Network (CARB)
JIN .... Jump Indirectly [Computer science]
JIN .... Justice Institute of British Columbia, Instructional Service [UTLAS symbol]
JINBA......... Journal. Institute of Brewing (journ.) (SAUS)
J Inc Aust Insurance Inst... Journal. Incorporated Australian Insurance Institute (journ.) (SAUS)
J Inc Brew Guild... Journal. Incorporated Brewers Guild (journ.) (SAUS)
J Inc Clerks Works Ass GB... Journal. Incorporated Clerks of Works Association of Great Britain (SAUO)
J Inc Clerks Works Ass GB... Journal. Incorporated Clerks of Works Association of Great Britain (journ.) (SAUS)
J Inclusion Phenom Mol Recognit Chem... Journal of Inclusion Phenomena and Molecular Recognition in Chemistry (journ.) (SAUS)
J Ind Arts Ed... Journal of Industrial Arts Education (journ.) (SAUS)
J Ind Ch S ... Journal. Indian Chemical Society (journ.) (SAUS)
J Ind Econ ... Journal of Industrial Economics (journ.) (SAUS)
J Ind Eng.... Journal of Industrial Engineering (journ.) (SAUS)
J Ind Hyg... Journal of Industrial Hygiene (journ.) (SAUS)
J Indian Acad Dent... Journal. Indian Academy of Dentistry (journ.) (SAUS)
J Indian Acad Geosci... Journal. Indian Academy of Geoscience (journ.) (SAUS)
J Indian Acad Sci... Journal. Indian Academy of Sciences (journ.) (SAUS)
J Indian Acad Wood Sci... Journal. Indian Academy of Wood Science (journ.) (SAUS)
J Indian Acad Wood Sci... Journal of the Indian Academy of Wood Science (SAUS)
J Indian Acad Wood Sci... Journal of the Indian Academy of Wood Science (journ.) (SAUS)
J Indiana Dent Assoc... Journal. Indiana Dental Association (journ.) (SAUS)

J Indiana MA... Journal. Indiana State Medical Association (journ.) (SAUS)

J Indianap Dist Dent S... Journal. Indianapolis District Dental Society (journ.) (SAUS)

J Indian Assoc Commun Dis... Journal. Indian Association for Communicable Diseases (journ.) (SAUS)

JIndiana State MedAssoc... Journal of Indiana State Medical Association (SAUO)

J Indiana State Med Assoc... Journal of Indiana State Medical (journ.) (SAUS)

J Indian Bot Soc... Journal of the Indian Botanical Society (SAUO)

J Indian Bot Soc... Journal of the Indian Botanical Society (journ.) (SAUS)

J Indian Ceram Soc... Journal. Indian Ceramic Society (journ.) (SAUS)

J Indian Chem Soc... Journal. Indian Chemical Society (journ.) (SAUS)

J Indian Chem Soc... Journal of the Indian Chemical Society (SAUO)

J Indian Chem Soc... Journal of the Indian Chemical Society (journ.) (SAUS)

J Indian Chem Soc Ind News Ed... Journal. Indian Chemical Society. Industrial and News Edition (journ.) (SAUS)

J Indian Dent Assoc... Journal. Indian Dental Association (journ.) (SAUS)

JIndian Dent Assoc... Journal of the Indian Dental Association (SAUO)

J Indian Dent Assoc... Journal of the Indian Dental Association (journ.) (SAUS)

J Indian Geophys Union... Journal. Indian Geophysical Union (journ.) (SAUS)

J Indian Gesci Assoc... Journal. Indian Geoscience Association (journ.) (SAUS)

J Indian Ind Labour... Journal of Indian Industries and Labour (journ.) (SAUS)

J Indian Inst Sci... Journal of the Indian Institute of Science (journ.) (SAUS)

J Indian Inst Sci A... Journal of the Indian Institute of Science A (journ.) (SAUS)

J Indian Inst Sci B... Journal of the Indian Institute of Science B (journ.) (SAUS)

J Indian Inst Sci C... Journal of the Indian Institute of Science C (journ.) (SAUS)

J Indian Inst Sci Sect A... Journal. Indian Institute of Science. Section A (journ.) (SAUS)

J Indian Inst Sci Sect B... Journal. Indian Institute of Science. Section B (journ.) (SAUS)

J Indian Leather Technol Assoc... Journal. Indian Leather Technologists Association (journ.) (SAUS)

J Indian Math Soc... Journal. Indian Mathematical Society (journ.) (SAUS)

J Indian Med Assoc... Journal of the Indian Medical Association (SAUO)

J Indian Med Assoc... Journal of the Indian Medical Associations (journ.) (SAUS)

J Indian Med Prof... Journal of the Indian Medical Profession (journ.) (SAUS)

J Indian Nat Soc Soil Mech Found Eng... Journal. Indian National Society of Soil Mechanics and Foundation Engineering (journ.) (SAUS)

J Indian Pediatr Soc... Journal. Indian Pediatric Society (journ.) (SAUS)

J Indian Plywood Ind Res Inst... Journal. Indian Plywood Industries Research Institute (journ.) (SAUS)

J Indian Potato Assoc... Journal. Indian Potato Association (journ.) (SAUS)

J Indian Refract Makers Asc... Journal of Indian Refractory Makers Association (journ.) (SAUS)

J Indian Refract Makers Ass... Journal. Indian Refractory Makers Association (journ.) (SAUS)

J Indian Roads Congr... Journal. Indian Roads Congress (journ.) (SAUS)

J Indian Soc Pedod Prev Dent... Journal. Indian Society of Pedodontics and Preventive Dentistry (journ.) (SAUS)

J Indian Soc Soil Sci... Journal. Indian Society of Soil Science (journ.) (SAUS)

J Indian Soc Statist Oper Res... Journal. Indian Society of Statistics and Operations Research (journ.) (SAUS)

J Indian State Med Assoc... Journal. Indiana State Medical Association (journ.) (SAUS)

J Indian Statist Assoc... Journal. Indian Statistical Association (journ.) (SAUS)

J Indian Waterworks Assoc... Journal of the Indian Waterworks Association (journ.) (SAUS)

J India Soc Eng... Journal. India Society of Engineers (journ.) (SAUS)

J Indina State Dent Assoc... Journal. Indiana State Dental Association (journ.) (SAUS)

J Ind Irradiat Technol... Journal of Industrial Irradiation Technology (journ.) (SAUS)

J Ind L Inst... Journal. Indian Law Institute [A publication] (DLA)

J Indn Acad Math... Journal Indian Academy of Mathematics (SAUS)

J Indn St A... Journal. Indian Statistical Association (journ.) (SAUS)

J Ind Philo... Journal of Indian Philosophy (journ.) (SAUS)

J Ind Pollut Control... Journal of Industrial Pollution Control (journ.) (SAUS)

J Ind R... Journal of Industrial Relations [A publication]

J Ind Technol... Journal of Industrial Technology (journ.) (SAUS)

J Ind Trade... Journal of Industry and Trade (journ.) (SAUS)

J Indush Econ... Journal of Industrial Economics (journ.) (SAUS)

J Indust Hyg... Journal of Industrial Hygiene (journ.) (SAUS)

J Indust Rel... Journal of Industrial Relations [A publication]

JINEA... Journal. Indian Chemical Society. Industrial and News Edition (journ.) (SAUS)

J Infect... Journal of Infection (journ.) (SAUS)

J Infect Dis... Journal of Infectious Diseases (journ.) (SAUS)

J Inferential Deductive Biol... Journal of Inferential and Deductive Biology (journ.) (SAUS)

J InfImage Manage... Journal of Information and Image Management (journ.) (SAUS)

J Inflamm.... Journal of Inflammation (journ.) (SAUS)

J Inf Process Cybern... Journal of Information Processing and Cybernetics (journ.) (SAUS)

J Inf Process Soc Jap... Journal. Information Processing Society of Japan (journ.) (SAUS)

J Inf Sci... Journal of Information Science (journ.) (SAUS)

J Inf Sci Princ Pract... Journal of Information Science, Principles and Practice (journ.) (SAUS)

J Inf Syst Manage... Journal of Information Systems Management (journ.) (SAUS)

J Inf Technol... Journal of Information Technology (journ.) (SAUS)

J Infus Chemother... Journal of Infusional Chemotherapy (journ.) (SAUS)

JINGLD... Jingled (ABBR)

JINGLG... Jingling (ABBR)

J Inherit Metab Dis... Journal of Inherited Metabolic Disease (journ.) (SAUS)

J Inl Fish Soc India... Journal. Inland Fisheries Society of India (journ.) (SAUS)

J Inorg Mat... Journal of Inorganic Materials (journ.) (SAUS)

J Inorg Organomet Polym... Journal of Inorganic and Organometallic Polymers (journ.) (SAUS)

J INOR NUCL CHEM... Journal of Inorganic and Nuclear Chemistry [A publication] (WDAA)

JINR... Joint Institute of Nuclear Research [Dubna, USSR]

JINS... Japan Institute of Nuclear Safety (SAUO)

J Ins... Journal of Insurance (journ.) (SAUS)

JINS... Journal of the International Neuropsychological Society (SAUO)

JINS... Juveniles in Need of Supervision [Classification for delinquent children]

JINSA... Jewish Institute for National Security Affairs (EA)

Jinsen Med J... Jinsen Medical Journal (journ.) (SAUS)

J Inst Agric Resour Utiliz Chinju Agric Coll... Journal. Institute for Agricultural Resources Utilization. Chinju Agricultural College (journ.) (SAUS)

J Inst Anim Tech... Journal. Institute of Animal Technicians (journ.) (SAUS)

J Inst Brew... Journal. Institute of Brewing (journ.) (SAUS)

J Inst Brew Suppl... Journal. Institute of Brewing. Supplement (journ.) (SAUS)

J Inst Chem Irel... Journal. Institute of Chemistry of Ireland (journ.) (SAUS)

J Inst Civ Eng... Journal. Institution of Civil Engineers (journ.) (SAUS)

J Inst Comput Sci... Journal. Institution of Computer Sciences (journ.) (SAUS)

J Inst Def Stud Anal... Journal. Institute for Defence Studies and Analyses (journ.) (SAUS)

JINSTE... Junior Institution of Engineers [British]

J Inst Elec Eng Jpn... Journal. Institution of Electrical Engineers of Japan (journ.) (SAUS)

J Inst Elec Eng Part 1... Journal. Institution of Electrical Engineers. Part 1. General (journ.) (SAUS)

J Inst Electr Commun Eng Jap... Journal. Institute of Electrical Communication Engineers of Japan (journ.) (SAUS)

J Inst Electr Eng... Journal. Institute of Electrical Engineers (journ.) (SAUS)

J Inst Electr Eng... Journal. Institution of Electrical Engineers (journ.) (SAUS)

J Inst Electr Eng (1949-63)... Journal. Institution of Electrical Engineers (1949-63) [A publication]

J Inst Electr Eng (1889-1940)... Journal. Institution of Electrical Engineers (1889-1940) [A publication]

J Inst Electr Eng Part 2... Journal. Institution of Electrical Engineers. Part 2. Power Engineering (journ.) (SAUS)

J Inst Electr Eng Part 3... Journal. Institution of Electrical Engi- neers. Part 3. Radio and Communica- tion Engineering (journ.) (SAUS)

J Inst Electron Commun EngJap... Journal. Institute of Electronics and Communication Engineers of Japan (journ.) (SAUS)

J Inst Electron Inf Commun Eng... Journal of the Institute of Electronics, Information and Communication Engineers (journ.) (SAUS)

J Inst Electron Radio Eng... Journal of the Institution of Electronic and Radio Engineers (journ.) (SAUS)

J Inst Electron Telecommun... Journal of the Institution of Electronics and Telecommunication Engineers (journ.) (SAUS)

J Inst Electron Telecommun Eng... Journal Institution of Electronics and Telecommunication Engineers (journ.) (SAUS)

J Inst Energy... Journal. Institute of Energy (journ.) (SAUS)

J Inst Energy... Journal of the Institute of Energy (journ.) (SAUS)

J Inst Eng Aust... Journal of the Institution of Engineers, Australia (SAUS)

J Inst Fuel... Journal of the Institute of Fuel (SAUO)

J Inst Fuel... Journal of the Institute of Fuel (journ.) (SAUS)

J Inst Fuel Suppl... Journal. Institute of Fuel. Supplement (journ.) (SAUS)

J Inst Gas Eng... Journal. Institution of Gas Engineers (journ.) (SAUS)

J Inst Gas Engrs... Journal. Institution of Gas Engineers (journ.) (SAUS)

J Inst Geol Vikram Univ... Journal. Institute of Geology. Vikram University (journ.) (SAUS)

J Inst Highw Eng... Journal. Institute of Highway Engineers (journ.) (SAUS)

J Inst Math Appl... Journal of the Institute of Mathematics and its Applications (journ.) (SAUS)

J Inst Met.... Journal of the Institute of Metals with Bulletin and Metallurgical Abstracts (SAUO)

J Inst Met.... Journal of the Institute of Metals with Bulletin and Metallurgical Abstracts (journ.) (SAUS)

J Inst Meth Appl... Journal of the Institute of Mathematics and its Applications (SAUO)

J Inst Met Suppl... Journal. Institute of Metals. Supplement (journ.) (SAUS)

J Inst Nav.... Journal of the Institute of Navigation (journ.) (SAUS)

J Inst Navig... Journal. Institute of Navigation (journ.) (SAUS)

J Instn Eng Aust... Journal. Institution of Engineers of Australia. [A publication]

J Instn Heat Vent Engrs... Journal. Institution of Heating and Ventilating Engineers (journ.) (SAUS)

J Instn Highw Engrs... Journal. Institution of Highway Engineers (journ.) (SAUS)

J Instn Loc Engrs... Journal. Institution of Locomotive Engineers (journ.) (SAUS)

J Inst Nucl Eng... Journal of the Institution of Nuclear Engineers (SAUO)

J Inst Nucl Eng... Journal of the Institution of Nuclear Engineers (journ.) (SAUS)

J Inst Nucl Mater Manage... Journal. Institute of Nuclear Materials Management (journ.) (SAUS)

J Inst Pet... Journal. Institute of Petroleum (journ.) (SAUS)

J Inst Pet Absh... Journal. Institute of Petroleum. Abstracts (journ.) (SAUS)

J Inst Pet Technol... Journal. Institution of Petroleum Technologists (journ.) (SAUS)

J Inst Polytech Osaka City Univ... Journal. Institute of Polytechnics. Osaka City University (journ.) (SAUS)

J Inst Polytech Osaka City Univ Ser C... Journal. Institute of Polytechnics. Osaka City University. Series C. Chemistry (journ.) (SAUS)

J Inst Polytech Osaka City Univ Ser D... Journal. Institute of Polytechnics. Osaka City University. Series D. Biology (journ.) (SAUS)

J Inst Polytech Osaka City Univ Ser E... Journal. Institute of Polytechnics. Osaka City University. Series E. Engineering (journ.) (SAUS)

J Inst Polytech Osaka City Univ Ser G... Journal. Institute of Polytechnics. Osaka City University. Series G. Geoscience (journ.) (SAUS)

J Inst Prod Eng... Journal. Institution of Production Engineers (journ.) (SAUS)

J Inst Public Health Eng... Journal. Institution of Public Health Engineers (journ.) (SAUS)

J Inst Refract Eng... Journal of the Institute of Refractories Engineers (journ.) (SAUS)

J Instr Psychol... Journal of Instructional Psychology (journ.) (SAUS)

J Instrum Soc Am... Journal. Instrument Society of America (journ.) (SAUS)

J Instrum Soc India... Journal. Instrument Society of India (journ.) (SAUS)

J Inst Saf High Pressure Gas Eng... Journal. Institute of Safety of High Pressure Gas Engineering (journ.) (SAUS)

J Inst Sanit Eng... Journal. Institution of Sanitary Engineers (journ.) (SAUS)

J Inst Sci Tech Inf Czech Acad Agric... Journal. Institute for Scientific and Technical Information. Czechoslovak Academy of Agriculture (journ.) (SAUS)

J Inst Sci Technol... Journal. Institute of Science Technology (journ.) (SAUS)

J Inst Sewgae Purif... Journal. Institute of Sewage Purification (journ.) (SAUS)

J Inst Socioecon Stud... Journal. Institute for Socioeconomic Studies (journ.) (SAUS)

J Inst Telecommun Eng... Journal. Institution of Telecommunication Engineers (journ.) (SAUS)

J Inst Telecommun Eng... Journal of the Institution of Telecommunication Engineers (SAUO)

J Inst Telecommun Eng... Journal of the Institution of Telecommunication Engineers (journ.) (SAUS)

J Inst Telev Eng Jpn... Journal. Institute of Television Engineers of Japan (journ.) (SAUS)

J Inst Telev Eng Jpn... Journal of the Institute of Television Engineers of Japan (journ.) (SAUS)

J Inst Water Eng Environ Manage... Journal of the Institution of Water Engineers and Environmental Management (journ.) (SAUS)

J Inst Wood Sci... Journal of the Institute of Wood Science (journ.) (SAUS)

JINTACCS .... Joint Interoperability Command and Control System (SAUS)

JINTACCS .... Joint Interoperability of Tactical Command and Control Systems (MCD)

J Int Ad Pre Med... Journal. International Academy of Preventive Medicine (journ.) (SAUS)

J Int Ass Dent Child... Journal International Association of Dentistry for Children (journ.) (SAUS)

J Int Ass Math Geol... Journal International Association for Mathematical Geology (journ.) (SAUS)

J Int Biomed Inf Data... Journal of International Biomedical Information and Data (journ.) (SAUS)

JINTCCS ...... Joint Interoperability of Tactical Command and Control Systems (DOMA)

JINTD.......... Journal of Industrial Technology. Myong-Ji University (journ.) (SAUS)

J Integral Equations... Journal of Integral Equations (journ.) (SAUS)

J Intell Syst... Journal of Intelligent Systems (journ.) (SAUS)

J Intensiv Care Med... Journal of Intensive Care Medicine (journ.) (SAUS)

J Interam Stud World Aff... Journal of Interamerican Studies and World Affairs (journ.) (SAUS)

J Interferon Res... Journal of Interferon Research (journ.) (SAUS)

J Internat Affairs... Journal of International Affairs (journ.) (SAUS)

J Intern Med... Journal of Internal Medicine (journ.) (SAUS)

J Int Fed Gynael Obstet... Journal. International Federation of Gynaecology and Obstetrics (journ.) (SAUS)

J Int Inst Aerial Surv Earth Sci... Journal. International Institute for Aerial Survey and Earth Sciences (journ.) (SAUS)

J Int Inst Sugar Beet Res... Journal. International Institute for Sugar Beet Research (journ.) (SAUS)

J Int'l & Comp L... Journal of International and Comparative Law [*A publication*] (DLA)

J Int'l Comm Jur... Journal. International Commission of Jurists [*A publication*] (DLA)

J Int'l L & Dipl... Journal of International Law and Diplomacy [*A publication*] (DLA)

J Int'l L & Pol... Journal of International Law and Politics [*A publication*] (DLA)

J Intl L & Pol... Journal of International Law and Politics (journ.) (SAUS)

J Int Market Market Res... Journal of International Marketing and Marketing Research (journ.) (SAUS)

J Int Money Financ... Journal of International Money and Finance. Guildford (journ.) (SAUS)

J Int Phonetic As... Journal. International Phonetic Association (journ.) (SAUS)

J Int Relations... Journal of International Relations (journ.) (SAUS)

J Int Res Commun... Journal of International Research Communications (journ.) (SAUS)

J Int Soc Leather Trades Chem... Journal. International Society of Leather Trades Chemists (journ.) (SAUS)

J Investig Allergol Clin Immunol... Journal of Investigational Allergology and Clinical Immunology (journ.) (SAUS)

J Investig Med... Journal of Investigative Medicine (journ.) (SAUS)

J Invest Surg... Journal of Investigative Surgery (journ.) (SAUS)

J In Vitro Fert Embryo Transf... Journal of In Vitro Fertilization and Embryo Transfer (journ.) (SAUS)

JIO .... Joint Information Office [*Military*]

JIO .... Joint Integration Office [*Department of Energy*] [*Albuquerque, NM*] (GAAI)

JIO .... Joint Intelligence Organization (BUAC)

JIO .... Ontario, CA [*Location identifier*] [*FAA*] (FAAL)

JIOA.......... Joint Intelligence Objectives Agency (MCD)

JIOC.......... Jensen Interceptor Owners Club (EA)

JIOP.......... Joint Interface Operational Procedures (COE)

JIOS.......... Journal of Information and Optimization Sciences (journ.) (SAUS)

J Iowa Acad Sci... Journal of the Iowa Academy of Sciences (journ.) (SAUS)

J Iow Acad Sci... Journal. Iowa Academy of Science (journ.) (SAUS)

J Iowa Med S... Journal. Iowa Medical Society (journ.) (SAUS)

J Iowa State Med Soc... Journal. Iowa State Medical Society (journ.) (SAUS)

JIP .... Jipijapa [*Ecuador*] [*Airport symbol*] (AD)

JIP .... Job Improvement Plan

JIP .... Job the Impatient (BJA)

JIP .... Join in Progress [*Broadcasting*] (WDMC)

JIP .... Joint Identifier Program (SAUO)

JIP .... Joint Impact Protection

JIP .... Joint Implementation Plan [*Military*]

JIP .... Joint Input

JIP .... Joint Input Processing (IEEE)

JIP .... Joint Installation Plan (AAG)

JIP .... Joint Interface Plan (ACAE)

JIP .... Joint Interface Program (SAUS)

JIP .... Joint Investment Plan (SAUO)

JIP .... Journal of Indian Philosophy (journ.) (SAUS)

JIPA .... Journal. Indian Potato Association (journ.) (SAUS)

JIPA .... Journal. International Phonetic Association (journ.) (SAUS)

JIPA .... Journal of International Phonetic Association, London (SAUO)

JIP/AMD ...... JIP/Areal Marketing Database [*Toyo Keizai Shinposha Co. Ltd.*] [*Japan*] [*Information service or system*] (CRD)

JIPC .... Joint Imagery Processing Complex (SAUS)

JIPC .... Joint Imagery Production Complex (DOMA)

JIPC .... Jordan Is Palestine Committee (EA)

JIPD .... JINTACCS Interoperability Planning Document (SAUO)

JIPDC .... Japan Iraq Petroleum Development Corporation (SAUO)

Jipdec .... Japanese Informations Processing Development Center (SAUO)

JIPDEC ...... Japan Information Processing Development Center (NITA)

JIPEA .... Journal. Institute of Petroleum (journ.) (SAUS)

JIPEX .... Johannesburg International Philatelic Exhibition (SAUO)

JIPG .... Joint Interoperability Planners Group (SAUO)

JIPHA .... Journal of Insect Physiology (journ.) (SAUS)

JIPID .... Japanese International Protein Information Database

JIPID .... Japanese International Protein Sequence Database (SAUO)

JIPMER....... Jawahrlal Institute of Postgraduate Medical Education and Research [*India*]

JIPNET........ Japan Information Processing Network (SAUS)

JIPO .... Jordan Investment Promotion Office (SAUO)

JIPS .... JANET Internet Protocol Service (SAUS)

JIPS .... JANET IP Service (SAUS)

JIPS .... Japanese Information Processing Service (SAUO)

JIPS .... Joint Internet Protocol Service (SAUS)

JIR .... Jewish Institute of Religion

JIR .... Jiri [*Nepal*] [*Airport symbol*] (OAG)

JIR .... Job Improvement Request

JIR .... Joint Intelligence Room (SAUS)

JIR .... JOPES Information Requirements (SAUO)

JIR .... Journal of Industrial Relations (journ.) (SAUS)

JIR .... Journal of Irreproducible Results (journ.) (SAUS)

JIRA .... Japanese Industrial Robot Association (CIST)

JIRA .... Japan Industrial Robot Association (BUAC)

J Iraqi Chem Soc... Journal. Iraqi Chemical Society (journ.) (SAUS)

JIRC .... Journal of Information Research Communications [*British*] (NITA)

JIRCAS .... Japan International Research Center for Agricultural Sciences (SAUO)

J Ir Coll Physicians Surg... Journal. Irish Colleges of Physicians and Surgeons (journ.) (SAUS)

JIRCSM........ Joint Industry Research Committee for Standardization of Miniature Precision Coaxial Connectors

J Ir Dent Ass... Journal. Irish Dental Association (journ.) (SAUS)

JIREDJ......... Journal of Interferon Research (journ.) (SAUS)

JIRI .... Johnson Informal Reading Inventory (EDAC)

J Irish CP... Journal. Irish Colleges of Physicians and Surgeons (journ.) (SAUS)

J Irish Lit... Journal of Irish Literature (journ.) (SAUS)

J Irish MA ... Journal. Irish Medical Association (journ.) (SAUS)

J Ir Med Assoc... Journal. Irish Medical Association (journ.) (SAUS)

J Iron & Steel Eng... Journal of Iron and Steel Engineering (journ.) (SAUS)

J Iron Steel Assoc... Journal. Iron and Steel Association (journ.) (SAUS)

J Iron Steel Inst Jpn... Journal. Iron and Steel Institute of Japan (journ.) (SAUS)

J Iron Steel Inst Jpn... Journal of the Iron and Steel Institute of Japan (journ.) (SAUS)

J Iron Steel Inst West Scotl... Journal. Iron and Steel Institute of West Scotland (journ.) (SAUS)

JIRP .... Juneau Icefield Research Project [*University of Idaho*] [*Research center*]

J Irrig Drain Div; Amer Soc... Journal of the Irrigation and Drainage Division, Proceedings of the American Society (journ.) (SAUS)

J Irrig Drain Div Am Soc Civ Eng... Journal. Irrigation and Drainage Division. Proceedings of the American Society of Civil Engineers (journ.) (SAUS)

JIRS .... Jewish Information and Referral Service Directory [*A publication*] (EAAP)

JIRS .... Joint Information and Retrieval System [*DoD*] (MCD)

JIRV .... Jet Interaction Reentry Vehicle (SAUS)

JIS .... Jail Inspection Service (SAUO)

JIS .... Jamaica Information Service (BUAC)

JIS .... Japanese Industrial Standards

JIS .... Japanese Institute for Standards (SAUS)

JIS .... Japanese Institute of Standards (SAUS)

JIS .... Japan Investment Service [*Reuters Holdings Ltd.*] [*British*] [*Information service or system*] (CRD)

JIS .... Jet Inlet System

JIS .... Jet Interaction Steering

JIS .... Jewish Information Society (SAUS)

JIS .... Jewish Information Society of America (EA)

JIS .... Job Information Service [*Department of Labor*]

JIS .... Job Information Station [*Department of Labor*] (IAA)

JIS .... Job Information System (NITA)

JIS	Job Input Station (SAUS)
JIS	Job Input Stream (SAUS)
JIS	Job Input System (NITA)
JIS	Joint Information System (SAUO)
JIS	Joint Integrated Simulation (NASA)
JIS	Joint Intelligence Staff
JIS	Joint Interoperability System (SAUO)
JIS	Joint Operations Interim Software (MCD)
JIS	JOPS Interim System
JIS	Journal of Information Science [*A publication*] (NITA)
JIS	Just-In-Sequence [*Manufacturing operations*]
JIS	Juvenile Idiopathic Scoliosis [*Medicine*] (DMAA)
JISA	Japan Industrial Safety Association (SAUO)
JISA	Japan Information Service Association (SAUO)
JISAO	Joint Institute for Study of the Atmosphere and Ocean [*Seattle, WA*] [*University of Washington, NOAA*] (GRD)
JISAO	Joint Institute for the Study of the Atmosphere and Ocean (SAUO)
JISC	Japanese Industrial Standards Committee [*Agency of Industrial Science and Technology, Ministry of International Trade and Industry*]
JISC	Joint Implementation Steering Committee (SAUO)
JISC	Joint Information Services Committee (BUAC)
JISC	Joint Information Systems Committee [*British*] (TELE)
JISCII	Japanese Industrial Standard Code for Information Interchange (SAUS)
JISCR	Judicial Information System Committee Rules (SAUO)
JISEA	Japan Iron and Steel Exporters Association (BUAC)
JISETA	Joint Investigation of the Southeastern Tropical Atlantic [*Angola, US*] (MSC)
JISF	Japan Iron and Steel Federation (BUAC)
JISHA	Japan Industrial Safety and Health Association (BUAC)
JISHS	Journal of the Illinois State Historical Society (SAUO)
JISHS	Journal of the Illinois State Historical Society (journ.) (SAUS)
JI/SI	Jet Interaction / Secondary Injection
JISI	Journal of Iron and Steel Industry (journ.) (SAUS)
J Islam & Comp L	Journal of Islamic and Comparative Law [*Nigeria*] [*A publication*] (DLA)
JIS-Link	Judicial Information System (SAUO)
JISM	Jordan Institution for Standards and Metrology (SAUO)
JISO	Japanese International Satellite Organization [*Cable-television system*]
JISP	Jack Island State Park (SAUO)
JISPB	Joint Intelligence Studies Publishing Board
JISR	Joint Information Search and Retrieval (SAUO)
JISR	Joint Information Search Unit Retrieval System (MCD)
J Isr Med Assoc	Journal. Israel Medical Association (journ.) (SAUS)
JISS	Japan Intelligence Support System (SAUO)
JISS	Jet Impurity Survey Spectrometer [*Nuclear energy*] (NUCP)
JISS	Journal. Indian Sociological Society (journ.) (SAUS)
JISTA	Journal of the Indian Scientific Translators Association (SAUO)
JISTEC	Japan International Science and Technology Exchange Center
JIS Technique	Junction Insulated Schottky Technique (SAUS)
JISTIC	Japan Iron and Steel Technical Information Center (SAUS)
JIT	Frozen Food Express Industries, Inc. (SAUO)
JIT	Jamiat-i-Talaba [*Pakistan*] [*Political party*] (PD)
JIT	Job Information Table (TIMI)
JIT	Job Information Test [*Military*] (AFM)
JIT	Job Instruction Training
JIT	Joint Interest Test [*Navy*] (NG)
JIT	Just in Time
jit	Just-In-Time [*Industry*] (ODBW)
JIT	Just-in-Time Inventory (TDOB)
JITA	Japanese Industrial Technology Association
JITA	Jet Interaction Test Apparatus (MCD)
J Ital Dairy Sci Assoc	Journal. Italian Dairy Science Association (journ.) (SAUS)
JITC	Jewelry Industry Tax Committee [*Defunct*] (EA)
JITC	Joint Interoperability Technology Center (SAUO)
JITC	Joint Interoperability Test Center [*Military*]
JIT compiler	Just-in-Time Compiler [*Computer science*] (IGQR)
JITE	Journal. Institution of Telecommunication Engineers (journ.) (SAUS)
JITE	Journal of Institutional and Theoretical Economics (SAUO)
JITF	Japan International Trade Fair (SAUO)
JITF	Joint Interface Test Facility [*Army*] (RDA)
JITF	Joint Interface Test Force [*Military*] (RDA)
JITF	Joint Interservice Task Force (MCD)
JITH	Journal of Indian Textile History (journ.) (SAUS)
JITHA	Journal of Ichthyology (journ.) (SAUS)
JITOL	Just in Time Open Learning (SAUO)
JITPA	Japanese International Trade Promotion Association (BUAC)
JITR	Jitter (ABBR)
JITRBG	Jitterbug (ABBR)
JITRY	Jittery (ABBR)
JITS	Joint Interface Test System (SAUO)
JITT	Just-In Time Training (AGLO)
JIT/TQC	Just-In-Time/Total Quality Control (SAUS)
JITUD	Journal of Industrial Technology. Daegu University (journ.) (SAUS)
JIU	Joint Inspection Unit [*United Nations*]
JIU	Jones International University
JIVA	Joint Intelligence Virtual Architecture [*Military*]
JIVE	Joint Institute for VLBI in Europe (SAUS)
JIVPAZ	Journal of Invertebrate Pathology (journ.) (SAUS)
JIW	J. Inglis Wright [*Advertising agency*] [*New Zealand*]
JIW	Jiwani [*Pakistan*] [*Airport symbol*] (OAG)
J Iwate Med Assoc	Journal. Iwate Medical Association (journ.) (SAUS)
JIWC	Joint Industrial Whitley Council (SAUO)
JIWE	Journal of Indian Writing in English (journ.) (SAUS)
JIWP	Joint Interim Working Party
JIWSA	Journal. Institute of Wood Science (journ.) (SAUS)
JJ	Coddair Air East [*ICAO designator*] (AD)
JJ	Jaw Jerk [*Medicine*]
JJ	Jeep Junior [*Automobile model designation*]
JJ	Jejunojejunostomy [*Gastroenterology*] (DAVI)
JJ	Jennifer Jo [*In TV series "The Governor and JJ"*]
JJ	Jews for Jews [*Defunct*] (EA)
JJ	Josephson Junction [*Cryogenics*] (IAA)
JJ	Judges [*Old Testament book*]
JJ	Judges, Justices (SAUS)
JJ	Jungle Jeep (SAUS)
JJ	Junior Judge [*Legal term*] (DLA)
JJ	Justices
JJ	Just Joking (SAUS)
JJA	Jack and Jill of America (EA)
JJA	Judges of Appeal [*Legal term*]
JJA	June-July-August [*Marine science*] (OSRA)
JJA	Justices of Appeal [*Legal term*] (DLA)
JJAF	Jack and Jill of America Foundation (EA)
JJAMD	Jaw Joints and Allied Musculo-Skeletal Disorders Foundation (EA)
J Jan Acad Surg Metab Nutr	Journal. Japan Academy of Surgical Metabolism and Nutrition (journ.) (SAUS)
JJAP	Japanese Journal of Applied Physics (journ.) (SAUS)
JJAP	Japan Society of Applied Physics (SAUO)
J Japanese Trade and Industry	Journal of Japanese Trade and Industry (journ.) (SAUS)
J Jap Ass Philos Sci	Journal. Japan Association for Philosophy of Science (journ.) (SAUS)
J Jap Biochem S	Journal. Japanese Biochemical Society (journ.) (SAUS)
J Jap Chem	Journal of Japanese Chemistry (journ.) (SAUS)
J Jap Soc Air Pol	Journal. Japan Society of Air Pollution (journ.) (SAUS)
J Jap Soc Food Nutr	Journal. Japanese Society of Food and Nutrition (journ.) (SAUS)
J Jap Soc Grassland Sci	Journal. Japanese Society of Grassland Science (journ.) (SAUS)
J Jap Soc Technol Plast	Journal. Japan Society for Technology of Plasticity (journ.) (SAUS)
J Jap S Powder Met	Journal. Japan Society of Powder and Powder Metallurgy (journ.) (SAUS)
J Jap Stud	Journal of Japanese Studies (journ.) (SAUS)
JJATS	Journal of the Japanese Association for Thoracic Surgery (SAUS)
JJC	Jackson Junior College [*Florida; Michigan*]
JJC	James Jones Company (SAUO)
JJC	Japanese Joint Committee (SAUS)
JJC	Jiffy Junction Connector
JJC	Joliet Junior College [*Illinois*]
JJC	Juvenile Justice Center (SAUO)
JJC	Juvenile Justice Clearinghouse (SAUS)
JJCCJ	John Jay College of Criminal Justice (SAUO)
JJCL	Jadavpur Journal of Comparative Literature (journ.) (SAUS)
JJCRA	Japanese Journal of Clinical Radiology (journ.) (SAUS)
JJDP	Juvenile Justice and Delinquency Prevention
JJDPA	Juvenile Justice and Delinquency Prevention Act
JJE	Japanese Journal of Ethnology (journ.) (SAUS)
J Jew Lore Ph	Journal of Jewish Lore and Philosophy (journ.) (SAUS)
JJ FAD	Just Jammin' Fresh and Def [*Rap recording group*]
JJFC	Jana Jae Fan Club (EA)
JJFC	Jim and Jesse Fan Club (EA)
JJFC	Joan Jett Fan Club (EA)
JJFC	Johnny and Jack Fan Club (EA)
J Jgn Pap Pulp Assoc	Journal. Japan Paper and Pulp Association (journ.) (SAUS)
JJHL	John Jay Hopkins Laboratory (SAUS)
JJHL	John Jay Hopkins Laboratory for Pure and Applied Science (SAUO)
JJHS	John Jay High School (SAUO)
JJHS	John Jay Hopkins School (SAUS)
JJI	Juanjui [*Peru*] [*Airport symbol*] (OAG)
J Jinsen Med Sci	Journal of Jinsen Medical Sciences (journ.) (SAUS)
JJITC	Jayco Jafari International Travel Club (EA)
JJL	Josephson Junction Logic (ELAL)
JJM	John Judkyn Memorial (EA)
JJ Marsh (KY)	Marshall's Reports [*Kentucky*] [*A publication*] (DLA)
JJMAS	Jack Jones Music Appreciation Society [*Defunct*] (EAIO)
JJN	Jinjiang [*China*] [*Airport symbol*] (OAG)
JJN	J.J.Newberry Company (SAUO)
JJO	Mountain City, TN [*Location identifier*] [*FAA*] (FAAL)
J Johannesburg Hist Found	Journal. Johannesburg Historical Foundation (journ.) (SAUS)
JJOPA7	Japanese Journal of Ophthalmology (journ.) (SAUS)
JJP	Jatiya Janata Party [*National People's Party*] [*Bangladesh*] [*Political party*] (PPW)
JJP	Journal of Juristic Papyrology (journ.) (SAUS)
JJPHDP	Japanese Journal of Phycology (journ.) (SAUS)
J Jpn Air Clean Asc	Journal of the Japan Air Cleaning Association (journ.) (SAUS)
J Jpn Assoc Infect Dis	Journal. Japanese Association for Infectious Diseases (journ.) (SAUS)
J Jpn Assoc Phys Med Bineol Climatol	Journal. Japanese Association of Physical Medicine, Balneology and Climatology (journ.) (SAUS)
J Jpn Assoc Thorac Surg	Journal. Japanese Association for Thoracic Surgery (journ.) (SAUS)
J Jpn Boiler Assoc	Journal. Japan Boiler Association (journ.) (SAUS)
J Jpn Bot	Journal of Japanese Botany (SAUO)

J Jpn Bot..... Journal of Japanese Botany (journ.) (SAUS)
J Jpn Chem... Journal of Japanese Chemistry (journ.) (SAUS)
J Jpn Chem Suppl... Journal of Japanese Chemistry. Supplement (journ.) (SAUS)
J Jpn Compos Mater... Journal of Japan Composite Materials (journ.) (SAUS)
J Jpn Dent Assoc... Journal. Japan Dental Association (journ.) (SAUS)
J Jpn Diabetes Soc... Journal. Japan Diabetes Society (journ.) (SAUS)
J Jpn Electr Assoc... Journal. Japan Electric Association (journ.) (SAUS)
J Jpn Health Phys Soc... Journal. Japan Health Physics Society (journ.) (SAUS)
J Jpn Hydraul Pneum Soc... Journal of the Japan Hydraulics and Pneumatics Society (journ.) (SAUS)
J Jpn Inst Light Met... Journal of the Japan Institute of Light Metals (journ.) (SAUS)
J Jpn Inst Met... Journal of the Japan Institute of Metals (journ.) (SAUS)
J Jpn Inst Nevig... Journal of the Japan Institute of Navigation (journ.) (SAUS)
J Jpn Obstet Gynecol... Journal. Japanese Obstetrics and Gynecology (journ.) (SAUS)
J Jpn Psychosom S... Journal. Japanese Psychosomatic Society (journ.) (SAUS)
J Jpn Sewage Works Assoc... Journal of the Japan Sewage Works Association (journ.) (SAUS)
J Jpn Soc Aeronaut Space Sci... Journal of the Japan Society for Aeronautical and Space Sciences (journ.) (SAUS)
J Jpn Soc Air Pollut... Journal of the Japan Society of Air Pollution (journ.) (SAUS)
J Jpn Soc Artf Intell... Journal of the Japanese Society for Artificial Intelligence (journ.) (SAUS)
J Jpn Soc Civ Eng... Journal of the Japan Society of Civil Engineers (journ.) (SAUS)
J Jpn Soc Colour Mater... Journal of the Japan Society of Colour Material (journ.) (SAUS)
J Jpn Soc Compos Mater... Journal of the Japan Society for Composite Materials (journ.) (SAUS)
J Jpn Soc Heat Treat... Journal of the Japan Society of Heat Treatment (journ.) (SAUS)
J Jpn Soc Lubr Eng... Journal of the Japan Society of Lubrication Engineers (journ.) (SAUS)
J Jpn Soc Mech Eng... Journal. Japan Society of Mechanical Engineers (journ.) (SAUS)
J Jpn Soc Powder Powder Metall... Journal of the Japan Society of Powder and Powder Metallurgy (journ.) (SAUS)
J Jpn Soc Precis Eng... Journal of the Japan Society of Precision Engineering (journ.) (SAUS)
J Jpn Soc Simul Technol... Journal of the Japan Society for Simulation Technology (journ.) (SAUS)
J Jpn Soc Strength Fract Mater... Journal of the Japanese Society for Strength and Fracture of Materials (journ.) (SAUS)
J Jpn Soc Technol Plast... Journal of the Japan Society for Technology of Plasticity (journ.) (SAUS)
J Jpn Soc Tribol... Journal Japanese Society of Tribologists (journ.) (SAUS)
J Jpn Soc Tribol... Journal of the Japanese Society of Tribologists (journ.) (SAUS)
J Jpn Stud... Journal of Japanese Studies (journ.) (SAUS)
J Jpn Sur Soc... Journal. Japanese Surgical Society (journ.) (SAUS)
J Jpn Vet Med Asc... Journal. Japan Veterinary Medical Association (journ.) (SAUS)
J Jpn Water Works Asc... Journal of the Japan Water Works Association (journ.) (SAUS)
J Jpn Weld Soc... Journal of the Japan Welding Society (journ.) (SAUS)
J Jpn Wood Res Soc... Journal of the Japan Wood Research Society (journ.) (SAUS)
JJPTP .... Joint Jet-Pilot Training Programme (SAUS)
JJS.............. James Joyce Society (EA)
JJS.............. Journal of Japanese Studies (journ.) (SAUS)
JJS.............. Jumping-JacksShoes, Inc. (SAUS)
JJSAAG....... Japanese Journal of Studies on Alcohol (journ.) (SAUS)
JJSC .... Jefferson Smurfit [NASDAQ symbol] (TTSB)
JJSC .... Jefferson Smurfit Corp. [NASDAQ symbol] (SAG)
JJSC .... Justices of the Supreme Court [Legal term] (DLA)
JJSC .... Juvenile Justice Standards Committee (SAUO)
JJSF............ J&J Snack Foods [NASDAQ symbol] (TTSB)
JJSF............ J & J Snack Foods Corp. [NASDAQ symbol] (NQ)
J-J S-S .... Jean-Jacques Servan-Schreiber [French publisher]
JJSSPA....... Jewish Social Service Professionals Association (NTPA)
JJSWC .... Jiffy Junction Single Wire Connector
JJT.............. Josephson Junction Transistor [Electronics] (AAEL)
JJT.............. Jumbo Jet Transport
JJTCAR........ Japanese Journal of Tuberculosis and Chest Diseases (journ.) (SAUS)
JJU .... Julienhaab [Greenland] [Airport symbol] (AD)
J Jur........... Journal of Jurisprudence [A publication] (DLA)
J Jur Papyrol... Journal of Juristic Papyrology [A publication] (DLA)
J Juvenile Res... Journal of Juvenile Research (journ.) (SAUS)
J Juv L .... Journal of Juvenile Law (journ.) (SAUS)
JJW .... Sternair, Inc. [FAA designator] (FAAC)
JJWC .... Jiffy Junction Wire Connector
JJWFC .... Jerry Jeff Walker Fan Club (EA)
JJZOAP........ Japanese Journal of Zoology (journ.) (SAUS)
JK .... Central Caribbean Air Ltd. (SAUO)
JK .... Flip-Flop Circuit [Computer science]
JK .... Jack (MSA)
JK .... J and K input (SAUS)
JK .... Jishu Kanri [Voluntary Management] [Japanese method for increasing productivity of industrial workers by involving them in planning]
J/K .... Joule per Kelvin [Physics]
J/K .... Joules per Kelvin (SAUS)
JK .... Jumper's Knee (MELL)
JK .... Junk [Ship's rigging] (ROG)

JK .... Just Kidding [Online dialog]
JK .... Sun World [ICAO designator] (AD)
JK .... Trabajos Aereos y Enlaces SA [Spain] [ICAO designator] (ICDA)
JKA .... Jakarta [Indonesia] (ABBR)
Jk^a .... Kidd A [Blood group] (DAVI)
JKAA........... Japan Karate Association of Australia
J Kagawa Nutr Coll... Journal. Kagawa Nutrition College (journ.) (SAUS)
JKAHS......... Journal. Kerry Archaeological and Historical Society (journ.) (SAUS)
J Kanagawa Odontol S... Journal. Kanagawa Odontological Society (journ.) (SAUS)
J Kanagawa Prefect J Coll Nutr... Journal. Kanagawa Prefectural Junior College of Nutrition (journ.) (SAUS)
J Kanazawa Med Univ... Journal. Kanazawa Medical University (journ.) (SAUS)
J Kan B Ass'n... Journal. Kansas Bar Association [A publication] (DLA)
JK & A......... John Krucek & Associates [Telecommunications service] (TSSD)
J Kansai Med Univ... Journal. Kansai Medical University (journ.) (SAUS)
J Kansas Geol Surv... Journal. Kansas Geological Survey (journ.) (SAUS)
J Kans Dent Assoc... Journal. Kansas Dental Association (journ.) (SAUS)
J Kans Med Soc... Journal of the Kansas Medical Society (SAUO)
J Kans Med Soc... Journal of the Kansas Medical Society (journ.) (SAUS)
J Kans State Dent Assoc... Journal. Kansas State Dental Association (journ.) (SAUS)
J Kanto-Tosan Agr Exp Sta... Journal. Kanto-Tosan Agricultural Experiment Station (journ.) (SAUS)
J Karnatak Univ... Journal. Karnatak University (journ.) (SAUS)
J Karnatak Univ Hum... Journal. Karnatak University. Humanities (journ.) (SAUS)
J Karnatak Univ Sci... Journal. Karnatak University. Science (journ.) (SAUS)
J Karntak Univ Soc Sci... Journal. Karnatak University. Social Sciences (journ.) (SAUS)
J Karyopathol Esp Tumor Tumorvirus... Journal of Karyopathology Especially Tumor and Tumorvirus (journ.) (SAUS)
JKAS .... Jackass (ABBR)
JKAS .... Jack Knight Airmail Society (EA)
JKAUA .... Journal. Karnatak University (journ.) (SAUS)
JKB .... Justice of the King's Bench (ROG)
Jk^b .... Kidd B [Blood group] (DAVI)
JKBIR .... Justice of the King's Bench, Ireland (ROG)
JKBT .... Jackboot (ABBR)
JKBX .... Jukebox (ABBR)
JKC .... Japan Kennel Club (SAUO)
JKC .... Jidosha Kiki Co. Ltd.
JKC .... Shreveport, LA [Location identifier] [FAA] (FAAL)
JKCL .... Jockey Club, Inc. [NASDAQ symbol] (SAG)
JKD .... Jacked (ABBR)
JKE .... Journal of Post Keynesian Economics (journ.) (SAUS)
J Kerala Ad Biol... Journal. Kerala Academy of Biology (journ.) (SAUS)
J Kerry Archaeol Hist Soc... Journal. Kerry Archaeological and Historical Society (journ.) (SAUS)
JKET .... Jacket (ABBR)
JKETD .... Jacketted (ABBR)
JKFC .... Japan-Republic of Korea Joint Fisheries Commission [Marine science] (OSRA)
JKFCFC........ Jimmy Kish "The Flying Cowboy" Fan Club (EA)
JKFF .... JK Flip-Flop (SAUS)
JKFSD .... Journal. Korean Forestry Society (journ.) (SAUS)
JKG .... Jacking (ABBR)
JKG .... Jonkoping [Sweden] [Airport symbol] (OAG)
J/kg .... Joule per Kilogram [Physics]
Jkg .... Joules per kilogram (SAUS)
J/(KG K)...... Joules per Kilogram Kelvin
JKH .... Chios [Greece] [Airport symbol] (OAG)
JKHHA .... Journal. Korea Institute of Electronics Engineers (journ.) (SAUS)
JKHY........... Henry (Jack) & Assoc [NASDAQ symbol] (TTSB)
JKHY........... Henry, Jack Associates [NASDAQ symbol] (SAG)
JKHY........... Jack Henry & Associates, Inc. (SAUO)
JKIEA .... Journal. Korean Institute of Electrical Engineers (journ.) (SAUS)
J Kirin Univ Nt Sci... Journal. Kirin University. Natural Science (journ.) (SAUS)
JKKB .... Jeunesse du Kwilu-Kwango-Bateke [Kwilu-Kwango-Bateke Youth]
JkksPac .... Jakks Pacific, Inc. [Associated Press] (SAG)
JKL .... Jackal (ABBR)
JKL .... Jackson, KY [Location identifier] [FAA] (FAAL)
JKLF .... Jammu and Kashmir Liberation Front [India] [Political party] (ECON)
JKMAD......... Journal. Korea Military Academy (journ.) (SAUS)
JKMR........... Jackhammer (ABBR)
JKMS........... Jack Knight Air Mail Society (EA)
JKMS........... Joint Key Management System (SAUO)
JKMSA......... Journal. Kansas Medical Society (journ.) (SAUS)
JKMSD......... Journal. Korean Mathematical Society (journ.) (SAUS)
JKNC........... Jammu and Kashmir National Conference [India] [Political party] (PPW)
JKNC........... Jammu and Kashmir National Congress (BUAC)
JKNCD .... Journal. Kongju National Teachers College (journ.) (SAUS)
JKNIF .... Jackknife (ABBR)
J Kongju Natl Teach Coll... Journal. Kongju National Teachers College (journ.) (SAUS)
J Korea Electr Assoc... Journal. Korea Electric Association (journ.) (SAUS)
J Korea Inf Sci Soc... Journal of the Korea Information Science Society (journ.) (SAUS)
J Korea Inst Electron Eng... Journal. Korea Institute of Electronics Engineers (journ.) (SAUS)
J Korea Inst Electron Eng... Journal of the Korea Institute of Electronics Engineers (journ.) (SAUS)
J Korea Merch Mar Coll Nat Sci Ser... Journal. Korea Merchant Marine College. Natural Sciences Series (journ.) (SAUS)
J Korea Mil Acad... Journal. Korea Military Academy (journ.) (SAUS)

J Korean Acad Maxillofac Radiol... Journal. Korean Academy of Maxillofacial Radiology (journ.) (SAUS)
J Korean Acad Periodontol... Journal. Korean Academy of Periodontology (journ.)
J Korean Agric Chem Soc... Journal. Korean Agricultural Chemical Society (journ.) (SAUS)
J Korean Ass Radit Prot... Journal. Korean Association for Radiation Protection (journ.) (SAUS)
J Korean Astron Soc... Journal. Korean Astronomical Society (journ.) (SAUS)
J Korean Cancer Res Ass... Journal. Korean Cancer Research Association (journ.) (SAUS)
J Korean Ceram Soc... Journal. Korean Ceramic Society (journ.) (SAUS)
J Korean Ceram Soc... Journal of the Korean Ceramic Society (journ.) (SAUS)
J Korean Chem Soc... Journal. Korean Chemical Society (journ.) (SAUS)
J Korean Dent Assoc... Journal. Korean Dental Association (journ.) (SAUS)
J Korean Inst Chem Eng... Journal. Korean Institute of Chemical Engineers (journ.) (SAUS)
J Korean Inst Chem Eng... Journal of the Korean Institute of Chemieal Engineers (journ.) (SAUS)
J Korean Inst Electr Eng... Journal. Korean Institute of Electrical Engineers (journ.) (SAUS)
J Korean Inst Electron Eng... Journal. Korean Institute of Electronics Engineers (journ.) (SAUS)
J Korean Inst Met... Journal. Korean Institute of Metals (journ.) (SAUS)
J Korean Inst Met... Journal of the Korean Institute of Metals (journ.) (SAUS)
J Korean Inst Min... Journal. Korean Institute of Mining (journ.) (SAUS)
J Korean Inst Miner Min Eng... Journal of the Korean Institute of Mineral and Mining Engineers (journ.) (SAUS)
J Korean Inst Miner Mining Eng... Journal. Korean Institute of Mineral and Mining Engineers (journ.) (SAUS)
J Korean Inst Min Geol... Journal. Korean Institute of Mining Geology (journ.) (SAUS)
J Korean Inst Rubber Ind... Journal. Korean Institute of Rubber Industry (journ.) (SAUS)
J Korean Inst Telemet Electron... Journal of the Korean Institute of Telematics and Electronics (journ.) (SAUS)
J Korean Math Soc... Journal. Korean Mathematical Society (journ.) (SAUS)
J Korean Med Assoc... Journal. Korean Medical Association (journ.) (SAUS)
J Korean Med Sci... Journal of Korean Medical Science (journ.) (SAUS)
J Korean Meteorol Soc... Journal. Korean Meteorological Society (journ.) (SAUS)
J Korean Nucl Soc... Journal. Korean Nuclear Society (journ.) (SAUS)
J Korean Nucl Soc... Journal of the Korean Nuclear Society (journ.) (SAUS)
J Korean Ophthalmol Soc... Journal. Korean Ophthalmological Society (journ.) (SAUS)
J Korean Orient Med Soc... Journal. Korean Oriental Medical Society (journ.) (SAUS)
J Korean Pharm Sci... Journal of Korean Pharmaceutical Sciences (journ.) (SAUS)
J Korean Phys Soc... Journal. Korean Physical Society (journ.) (SAUS)
J Korean Phys Soc... Journal of the Korean Physical Society (journ.) (SAUS)
J Korean Radiol Soc... Journal. Korean Radiological Society (journ.) (SAUS)
J Korean Res Inst Better Living... Journal. Korean Research Institute for Better Living (journ.) (SAUS)
J Korean Res Soc Dent Hypn... Journal. Korean Research Society for Dental Hypnosis (journ.) (SAUS)
J Korean Res Soc Radiol Technol... Journal. Korean Research Society of Radiolocal Technology (journ.) (SAUS)
J Korean Soc Agric Eng... Journal. Korean Society of Agricultural Engineers (journ.) (SAUS)
J Korean Soc Agric Mach... Journal. Korean Society of Agricultural Machinery (journ.) (SAUS)
J Korean Soc Civ Eng... Journal. Korean Society of Civil Engineers (journ.) (SAUS)
J Korean Soc Crop Sci... Journal. Korean Society of Crop Science (journ.) (SAUS)
J Korean Soc Mech Eng... Journal. Korean Society of Mechanical Engineers (journ.) (SAUS)
J Korean Soc Microbiol... Journal. Korean Society for Microbiology (journ.) (SAUS)
J Korean Soc Soil Sci Fert... Journal. Korean Society of Soil Science and Fertilizer (journ.) (SAUS)
J Korean Soc Text Eng Chem... Journal. Korean Society of Textile Engineers and Chemists (journ.) (SAUS)
J Korean Statist Soc... Journal. Korean Statistical Society (journ.) (SAUS)
J Korean Surg Soc... Journal. Korean Surgical Society (journ.) (SAUS)
J Koren For Soc... Journal. Korean Forestry Society (journ.) (SAUS)
J Kores Inf Sci Soc... Journal. Korean Infomation Science Society (journ.) (SAUS)
JKORS .... Journal. Korean Operations Research Society (journ.) (SAUS)
J Koyasan Univ... Journal. Koyasan University (journ.) (SAUS)
JKP .... James Knox Polk [US president, 1795-1849]
JKPC .... Junior Knights of Peter Claver (EA)
JKPMA .... James K. Polk Memorial Association (EA)
JKPT .... Jackpot (ABBR)
JKPT .... Jackpot Enterprises [NASDAQ symbol] (SAG)
JKPTW .... Jackpot Enterprises Wrrt [NASDAQ symbol] (TTSB)
JKR .... Janakpur [Nepal] [Airport symbol] (OAG)
JKS .... Jacks (ABBR)
JKS .... Jacks Creek, TN [Location identifier] [FAA] (FAAL)
JKS .... Jackson [Diocesan abbreviation] [Mississippi] (TOCD)
JKSCR .... Jackscrew [Mechanical engineering]
Jksnvll .... Jacksonville Bancorp, Inc. [Associated Press] (SAG)
JksnvlSL ...... Jacksonville Savings & Loan Association [Texas] [Associated Press] (SAG)
JksnvSB ...... Jacksonville Savings Bank (Illinois) [Associated Press] (SAG)
JKST .... Johnson-Kenney Screening Test [Psychology] (DAVI)
JKT .... Djakarta [Java, Indonesia] [Airport symbol] (AD)
JKT .... Jacket (KSC)
jkt .... Jacket
JKT .... Jakarta [Indonesia] [Airport symbol] (OAG)

JKT .... Job Knowledge Test [Military] (AFM)
JKTD .... Jacketed (ABBR)
JKTG .... Jacketing (ABBR)
JKU .... Kyoto University, Kyoto, Japan [Library symbol] [Library of Congress] (LCLS)
J Kumamoto Med Soc... Journal. Kumamoto Medical Society (journ.) (SAUS)
J Kumamoto Womens Univ... Journal. Kumamoto Womens University (journ.) (SAUS)
J Kumasi Univ Sci Technol... Journal. Kumasi University of Science and Technology (journ.) (SAUS)
JKUR .... Jammu and Kashmir University Review (journ.) (SAUS)
J Kurume Med Assoc... Journal. Kurume Medical Association (journ.) (SAUS)
J Kuwait Med Ass... Journal. Kuwait Medical Association (journ.) (SAUS)
JKW .... Juvonen, K. W., Winnipeg, Manitoba CDA [STAC]
J KY Med Assoc... Journal. Kentucky Medical Association (journ.) (SAUS)
J Ky Med Assoc... Journal of the Kentucky Medical Association (SAUO)
J Ky Med Assoc... Journal of the Kentucky Medical Association (journ.) (SAUS)
JKYND .... Journal. Materials Science Research Institute. Dongguk University (journ.) (SAUS)
J Kyorin Med Soc... Journal. Kyorin Medical Society (journ.) (SAUS)
J Kyoto Med Assoc... Journal. Kyoto Medical Association (journ.) (SAUS)
J Kyoto Prefect Med Univ... Journal. Kyoto Prefectural Medical University (journ.) (SAUS)
J Kyoto Prefect Univ Med... Journal. Kyoto Prefectural University of Medicine (journ.) (SAUS)
J Ky State Med Assoc... Journal. Kentucky State Medical Association (journ.) (SAUS)
J Kyungpook Eng... Journal. Kyungpook Engineering (journ.) (SAUS)
J Kyungpook Eng Kyungpook Natl Univ... Journal. Kyungpook Engineering. Kyungpook National University (journ.) (SAUS)
J Kyushu Coal Min Tech Assoc... Journal. Kyushu Coal Mining Technicians Association (journ.) (SAUS)
J Kyushu Dent Soc... Journal. Kyushu Dental Society (journ.) (SAUS)
J Kyushu Hematol Soc... Journal. Kyushu Hematological Society (journ.) (SAUS)
JL .... Jadassohn-Lewandowsky [Syndrome] [Thickening of the nails] [Medicine] (DAVI)
JL .... Jaffe-Lichtenstein [Syndrome] [or Fibrous dysplasia] [Orthopedics] (DAVI)
JL .... Jaksch-Luzet [Disease] [Medicine] (DB)
JL .... Jamming Locator (SAUS)
JL .... J & L Specialty Steel [NYSE symbol] (SPSG)
JL .... Japan Air Lines [ICAO designator] (OAG)
JL .... Japan Line (SAUS)
JL .... Javan LASER
JL .... Jazz-Lift [Provides jazz records to persons in Iron Curtain countries] [Defunct] (EA)
JL .... Jefferson Lyons [Commercial firm] [British]
JI .... Jejunoileal [Medicine] (MEDA)
JL .... Job Library [Computer science] (ELAL)
JI .... Joel [Old Testament book]
JL .... Johnny Lightnings [Topper Toys]
JL .... Johnson Line (SAUS)
JI .... Joliotium [Chemistry] (MEC)
JL .... Joule's Law [Physics]
JL .... Journal [Online database field identifier]
JL .... Journal. American Liszt Society (journ.) (SAUS)
JL .... Journal of Linguistics (journ.) (SAUS)
JI .... July (ADWA)
JL .... July
JL .... Jump if Less (VLIE)
JL .... Jump Last (SAUS)
JL .... Junior Leaders Regiment [British military] (DMA)
JL .... Jurin Law [Electronics]
JL .... JustLife [Defunct] (EA)
JL .... Just Looking [A browser] [Retail slang]
JL .... Lab. Jacques Logeais [France] [Research code symbol]
JLA .... Cooper Landing, AK [Location identifier] [FAA] (FAAL)
JLA .... Jack L. Ahr [Designer's mark on US bicentennial quarter]
JLA .... Jalna Resources [Vancouver Stock Exchange symbol]
JLA .... Jamaica Library Association* (SAUO)
JLA .... Japanese Library Association (BUAC)
JLA .... Jet Lift Aircraft
JLA .... Jewish Law Association (BUAC)
JLA .... Jewish Librarians Association [Later, AJL] (EA)
JLA .... Jordan Library Association (BUAC)
J Label Compound Radiopharm... Journal of Labelled Compounds and Radiopharmaceuticals (journ.) (SAUS)
J Labor Research... Journal of Labor Research (journ.) (SAUS)
J Labour Hyg Iron Steel Ind... Journal of Labour Hygiene in Iron and Steel Industry (journ.) (SAUS)
J LA Dent Assoc... Journal. Louisiana Dental Association (journ.) (SAUS)
JLAEA .... Journal. Language Association of Eastern Africa (journ.) (SAUS)
JI Aesthet... Journal of Aesthetic and Art Criticism (journ.) (SAUS)
JLAF .... Joint Lithuanian-American Fund (BUAC)
J Lanchow Univ Nat Sci... Journal. Lanchow University. Natural Sciences (journ.) (SAUS)
J L and Com... Journal of Law and Commerce (journ.) (SAUS)
JL & Com S... Journal. Law and Commerce Society (journ.) (SAUS)
JL & Com Soc... Journal. Law and Commerce Society [Hong Kong] [A publication] (DLA)
JL & Information Science... Journal of Law and Information Science [A publication]
J L & Information Science... Journal of Law and Information Science (journ.) (SAUS)
JL & Pol... Journal of Law and Politics [A publication] (DLA)
JL & Pol... Journal of Law and Politics (journ.) (SAUS)

JL & Religion... Journal of Law and Religion [*A publication*] (DLA)
JL & Religion... Journal of Law and Religion (journ.) (SAUS)
J Lang Teach... Journal for Language Teaching (journ.) (SAUS)
JLA:NWO.... Justice League of America: New World Order (SAUS)
J Laparoendosc Surg... Journal of Laparoendoscopic Surgery (journ.) (SAUS)
J Laryngol Otol Suppl... Journal of Laryngology and Otology. Supplement (journ.) (SAUS)
J Laryng Otol... Journal of Laryngology and Otology (MEC)
JLAS........... Jordanian Laboratories Accreditation System (SAUO)
JLAS........... Journal. Linguistic Association of the Southwest (journ.) (SAUS)
JLAS........... Journal of Latin American Studies (journ.) (SAUS)
JLAS........... JUMPS [*Joint Uniform Military Pay System*] Leave Accounting System (DNAB)
J La State Med Soc... Journal of the Louisiana State Medical Society (SAUO)
J La State Med Soc... Journal of the Louisiana State Medical Society (journ.) (SAUS)
J Lat Am Stud... Journal of Latin American Studies (journ.) (SAUS)
J Law & Ed... Journal of Law and Education [*A publication*] (DLA)
J Law Reform... Journal of Law Reform [*A publication*] (DLA)
J Law Soc ... Journal of Law and Society (journ.) (SAUS)
J Law Soc'y Scotland... Law Society of Scotland. Journal [*A publication*] (DLA)
JLB .... Jewish Labor Bund (EA)
JLB .... Jewish Lads' Brigade [*British*] (DI)
JLB .... Journal of Labor Economics (journ.) (SAUS)
JLBD........... Jailbird (ABBR)
JLBRK........ Jailbreak (ABBR)
J Lbr Res.... Journal of Labor Research (journ.) (SAUS)
JLB Smith Inst Ichthyol Spec Publ... J. L. B. Smith Institute of Ichthyology. Special Publication (journ.) (SAUS)
JLBTS......... Japanese Land-Based Test Site (MCD)
Jl Bus Fin... Journal of Business Finance and Accounting (journ.) (SAUS)
Jl Bus Strat... Journal of Business Strategy (journ.) (SAUS)
JLC .... Houston [*Texas*] Allen Center [*Airport symbol*] (OAG)
JLC .... Jaeger LeCoultre
JLC .... Japanese Linear Collider [*High energy physics*]
JLC .... Japan Logistical Command (SAUO)
JLC .... Jewish Labor Committee (EA)
JLC .... Joint Logistic Commander (ACAE)
JLC .... Joint Logistics Command (SAUO)
JLC .... Joint Logistics Commanders [*Military*]
JLC .... Joint Logistics Committee [*Military*]
JLC .... Junction Latching Circulator
JLC & E... Justification for Limited Competition (COE)
JLC & E.... Jonesboro, Lake City & Eastern Railroad
JLCAT......... Joint Logistics Commanders' Action Team [*Military*]
JLCC .... Joint Logistics Co-ordination Centre (SAUS)
JLCD......... Joint Liaison Committee on Documents [*Used in the international carriage of goods*] (BUAC)
J L-C Met .... Journal of the Less-Common Metals (journ.) (SAUS)
Jl Commun... Journal of Communication (journ.) (SAUS)
Jl Consmr R... Journal of Consumer Research (journ.) (SAUS)
JLCPA......... Journal of Counseling Psychology (journ.) (SAUS)
J/L/Cpl....... Junior Lance-Corporal [*British military*] (DMA)
JLCRD .... Journal of Labelled Compounds and Radiopharmaceuticals (journ.) (SAUS)
JLCST .... Joint Legislative Committee on Science and Technology (SAUO)
JLCU .... Johnson Line Container Unit (SAUS)
JLD .... Jammer Locator Detector (CCCA)
J/Ldr......... Junior Leader [*British military*] (DMA)
JLDS.......... Journal. Lancashire Dialect Society (journ.) (SAUS)
JLE............ Japanese Language Enveronment (SAUS)
JLE............ Jet Lift Engine
JLE............ Journal of Law and Economics (journ.) (SAUS)
JLE............ Jump if Less than or Equal To (VLIE)
Jl E Asiat Stud... Journal of East Asiatic Studies (journ.) (SAUS)
J Leather Ind Res Inst S Afr... Journal. Leather Industries Research Institute of South Africa (journ.) (SAUS)
J Leather Res... Journal of Leather Research (journ.) (SAUS)
J Leeds Univ Text Stud Assa... Journal. Leeds University Textile Students. Association (journ.) (SAUS)
J Legal Prof... Journal of the Legal Profession (journ.) (SAUS)
J Leg Hist.... Journal of Legal History (journ.) (SAUS)
Jl Electrochem Soc... Journal of the Electrochemical Society (SAUO)
JLEM.......... Jerusalem (ABBR)
JLEMA .... Journal of Engineering Mathematics (journ.) (SAUS)
JLEN .... Julienne (ABBR)
JLEP .... Julep (ABBR)
J Lepid Soc... Journal. Lepidopterists Society (journ.) (SAUS)
JLER .... Journal of Leisure Research (journ.) (SAUS)
J Less-Common Met... Journal of Less-Common Metals (journ.) (SAUS)
J Leukoc Biol Suppl... Journal of Leukocyte Biology. Supplement (journ.) (SAUS)
JLF............ Joint Landing Force
JLF............ Joint Live Fire [*Military*]
JLF............ Joint Live-Fire programme (SAUS)
JLFB.......... Joint Landing Force Board
JLFC.......... Joan Lunden Fan Club [*Defunct*] (EA)
JLFC.......... Johnny Len Fan Club (EA)
JLG........... Jewish Lawyers Guild (EA)
JLG........... JLG Industries, Inc. [*Associated Press*] (SAG)
JLG........... Joint Liaison Group (ECON)
JLGA.......... James L. Grant and Associates (EFIS)
JLGI.......... JLG Indus [*NASDAQ symbol*] (TTSB)
JLGI.......... JLG Industries Inc. (SAUO)
JLH........... Arlington Heights, IL [*Location identifier*] [*FAA*] (FAAL)
JLH........... Journal of Legal History [*A publication*]

JLH........... Journal of Library History (journ.) (SAUS)
JLH........... Journal of Library History, Philosophy and Comparative Librarianship (journ.) (SAUS)
JLHC.......... Just Like Home [*NASDAQ symbol*] (TTSB)
JLHC.......... Just Like Home, Inc. [*NASDAQ symbol*] (SAG)
JLI .... Jiffy Lube International, Inc. (EFIS)
JLI .... Julian, CA [*Location identifier*] [*FAA*] (FAAL)
JLIA.......... Japan Lumber Importers Association (BUAC)
J Lib Admin... Journal of Library Administration (journ.) (SAUS)
J Lib Arts Nat Sci Sapporo Med Coll... Journal of Liberal Arts and Natural Sciences. Sapporo Medical College (journ.) (SAUS)
J Lib Arts Sci Kitasato Unir... Journal of Liberal Arts and Sciences. Kitasato University (journ.) (SAUS)
J Lib Arts Sci Sapporo Med Coll... Journal of Liberal Arts and Sciences. Sapporo Medical College (journ.) (SAUS)
J Lib Automation... Journal of Library Automation (journ.) (SAUS)
JLIEA .... Journal of Industrial Engineering (journ.) (SAUS)
J Life Sci R Dublin Soc... Journal of Life Sciences. Royal Dublin Society (journ.) (SAUS)
J Light Met Weld Constr... Journal of Light Metal Welding and Construction (journ.) (SAUS)
J Light Vis Environ... Journal of Light and Visual Environment (journ.) (SAUS)
J Lightwave Technol... Journal of Lightwave Technology (journ.) (SAUS)
J Limnol Soc South Afr... Journal. Limnological Society of South Africa (journ.) (SAUS)
J Linguist Anthropol... Journal of Linguistic Anthropology (journ.) (SAUS)
J Linn Soc Lond Bot... Journal. Linnean Society of London. Botany (journ.) (SAUS)
J Linn Soc Lond Zool... Journal. Linnean Society of London. Zoology (journ.) (SAUS)
JLIOOF......... Junior Lodge, Independent Order of Odd Fellows (EA)
JLIP.......... Joint Level Interface Protocol (SAUS)
J Lipid Mediat Cell Signal... Journal of Lipid Mediators and Cell Signalling (journ.) (SAUS)
J Lipid Mediators... Journal of Lipid Mediators (journ.) (SAUS)
J Lipos Res... Journal of Liposome Research (journ.) (SAUS)
JLIRI.......... Jinan Light Industry Research Institute (BUAC)
JLIS .... Journal of Law and Inforrnation Science (journ.) (SAUS)
J-List .... Journalist (ADWA)
J Lit Sem..... Journal of Literary Semantics (journ.) (SAUS)
JLK .... JLK Direct Distribution'A' [*NYSE symbol*] (SG)
JLL .... Jones Lang LaSalle [*NYSE symbol*] (SG)
JLM .... Journal of Law and Medicine (SAUS)
JLM .... Journal of Lipid Mediators (journ.) (SAUS)
JLM .... Junior Legacy Melbourne [*Australia*] [*An association*]
JLMA.......... Japan Light Metal Association (SAUO)
JLMC.......... Joint Labor Management Committee of the Retail Food Industry (EA)
JLMIC......... Japan Light Machinery Information Center (EA)
JLMPA......... Journal of Microwave Power (journ.) (SAUS)
JLMS .... Journal. London Mathematical Society (journ.) (SAUS)
JLMS .... Journal of the London Mathematical Society (journ.) (SAUS)
JLMSA......... Jewish Liturgical Music Society of America (EA)
Jl Musicology... Journal of Musicology (journ.) (SAUS)
JLN .... Jaclyn, Inc. [*AMEX symbol*] (SPSG)
JLN .... Joplin [*Missouri*] [*Airport symbol*] (OAG)
JLN .... Joplin, MO [*Location identifier*] [*FAA*] (FAAL)
Jl NY Ent S... Journal. New York Entomological Society (journ.) (SAUS)
JLO .... Jesolo [*Italy*] [*Airport symbol*] (AD)
JLO .... Joint Liaison Organization (SAUO)
JLO .... Junction Light Output
Jl of Research... Journal of Research in Music Education (journ.) (SAUS)
J Log Program... Journal of Logic Programming (journ.) (SAUS)
JLOIC......... Joint Logistics, Operations, Intelligence Center [*NATO*] (NATG)
JLOIC......... Joint Logistics, Operations, Intelligence Centre (SAUO)
J London School Trop Med... Journal. London School of Tropical Medicine (journ.) (SAUS)
JLOTA......... Journal of Laryngology and Otology (journ.) (SAUS)
JLOTS......... Joint Logistics Over-the-Shore [*Military*] (RDA)
J Louis St Med Soc... Journal. Louisiana State Medical Society (journ.) (SAUS)
J Low Freq Noise Vib... Journal of Low Frequency Noise and Vibration (journ.) (SAUS)
JLP .... Jamaica Labour Party [*Political party*] (PPW)
JLP .... Jazz for Life Project [*Defunct*] (EA)
JLP .... Jig Leg Plate (SAUS)
JLP .... John Lewis Partnership [*British*] (ECON)
JLP .... Juan-les-Pins [*France*] [*Airport symbol*] (AD)
JLP .... Juvenile Laryngeal Papilloma [*Medicine*] (DAVI)
JLPB .... Joint Logistics Planning Board
JLPC .... Joint Logistics Planning Committee (SAUO)
JLPC .... Joint Logistics Plans Committee [*Military*]
JLPG .... Joint Logistics Plans Group [*Military*]
JLPPG......... Joint Logistics and Personnel Policy Guidance [*Military*] (AFM)
JLR .... Jabalpur [*India*] [*Airport symbol*] (OAG)
JLR .... Jailer (ABBR)
JLR .... Jamaica Law Reports [*1953-55*] [*A publication*] (DLA)
JLR .... Jeweler (ABBR)
JLR .... Jewish Language Review (journ.) (SAUS)
JLR .... Johore Law Reports [*India*] [*A publication*] (DLA)
JLR .... Journal of Labor Research (journ.) (SAUS)
JLR .... Journal of Linguistic Research (journ.) (SAUS)
JLR .... Junction Loudness Rating (SAUS)
JLR .... Junior Leaders Regiment [*British military*] (DMA)
Jl R Agric S... Journal. Royal Agricultural Society of England (journ.) (SAUS)
Jl R Anthrop Inst... Journal. Royal Anthropological Institute of Great Britain and Ireland (journ.) (SAUS)
Jl R Aust Hist S... Royal Australian Historical Society (SAUO)

JLRB .... Joint Labor Relations Board
JLRB .... Joint Logistics Review Board [*Military*]
JLRC .... Jack London Research Center (EA)
JLREID .... Joint Long-Range Estimative Intelligence Document [*Military*]
Jl R Hist Soc Qd... Journal. Royal Historical Society of Queensland (journ.) (SAUS)
Jl R Hort Soc... Journal. Royal Horticulture Society (journ.) (SAUS)
JLRPG .... Joint Long-Range Proving Ground (KSC)
JLRRT.......... Jordan Left-Right Reversal Test [*Educational test*]
JLRSA.......... Joint Long-Range Strategic Appraisal [*Military*]
JLRSA.......... Joint Long-Range Strategic Assessment (SAUO)
Jl RS Arts .... Journal. Royal Society of Arts (journ.) (SAUS)
JLRSE.......... Joint Long-Range Strategic Estimates [*Military*]
JLRSS.......... Joint Long-Range Strategic Study [*Military*] (AFM)
jlry .... Jewelry (VRA)
JLS .... Jail Library Service (SAUO)
JLS .... Jet Alsace [*France*] [*ICAO designator*] (FAAC)
JLS .... Jet Lag Syndrome (MELL)
JLS .... Jet Lift System
JLS .... Jewels (ADA)
JLS .... Joint Least Squares [*Statistics*]
JLS .... Journal of Law and Society [*A publication*]
JLS .... Journal of Literary Semantics (journ.) (SAUS)
JLS .... Junior Literary Society (SAUO)
JLSC .... Joint Electronics Standardization Committee (SAUO)
JLSC .... Joint Logistics System Center (SAUO)
JLSC .... Joint Logistics System Command (DOMA)
Jl S-East Agric Coll... Journal. South-Eastern Agricultural College (journ.) (SAUS)
JLSGI.......... Japanese Local Self Government Institute (SAUO)
J/L/Sgt ...... Junior Lance-Sergeant [*British military*] (DMA)
JLSMA......... Journal. Louisiana State Medical Society (journ.) (SAUS)
Jl Small Bus... American Journal of Small Business (journ.) (SAUS)
JL Soc .... Journal. Law Society of Scotland [*A publication*] (DLA)
Jl Sol State Cir... Journal of Solid State Circuits (SAUS)
JLSP .... Joint Logistics Support Plan
JLSPAO....... Joint United States Public Affairs Office (SAUS)
JLST .... Joint Laser Safety Team (SAUO)
J L Studies... Journal of Legal Studies (journ.) (SAUS)
JLT............. Jalate, Inc. [*AMEX symbol*] (SAG)
JLT............. Jalate Ltd [*AMEX symbol*] (TTSB)
JLT............. Junior Leader Training [*Boy Scouts of America*]
JLT............. Junior Lord of the Treasury
Jl Test Eval... Journal of Testing and Evaluation (journ.) (SAUS)
JLTF.......... Jewish Librarians Caucus (SAUO)
JLTF.......... Jewish Librarians Task Force (EA)
JLTPB .... Joint Logistics Techniques and Procedures Board [*Military*]
JLTR .... Jilter (ABBR)
JLU .... Jilin University (BUAC)
JLUAC .... Joint Land Use Advisory Committee
JLUS .... Jealous (ABBR)
JLUSLY....... Jealously (ABBR)
JLUSNS ...... Jealousness (ABBR)
JLUSY .... Jealousy (ABBR)
J LUU Chem Soc... Journal. Leeds University Union Chemical Society (journ.) (SAUS)
JLW .... Jahrbuch fuer Liturgiewissenschaft [*A publication*] (ODCC)
JLW-155 ...... Joint Lightweight 155mm Howitzer (RDA)
JLY .... Jelly (ABBR)
JLY .... Jena, LA [*Location identifier*] [*FAA*] (FAAL)
JLYBN.......... Jellybean (ABBR)
JLYD .... Jellied (ABBR)
JLYFSH....... Jellyfish (ABBR)
JLYLK .... Jellylike (ABBR)
J Lymphol ... Journal of Lymphology (journ.) (SAUS)
JM .... Air Jamaica Ltd. [*ICAO designator*] (OAG)
JM .... Jactitation of Marriage [*Legal*] [*British*] (ROG)
JM .... Jakarta Mandate on Coastal and Marine Biodiversity (SAUS)
JM .... Jakarta Mandate on Marine and Coastal Biodiversity (or Biological Diversity) (SAUO)
JM .... Jamaica [*ANSI two-letter standard code*] (CNC)
jm .... Jamaica [*MARC country of publication code*] [*Library of Congress*] (LCCP)
Jm .... James [*New Testament book*] (BJA)
JM .... James Madison [*US president, 1751-1836*]
JM .... James Monroe [*US president, 1758-1831*]
JM .... Japan Mail (SAUS)
JM .... Jesuit Missions (EA)
JM .... Jet Mixing (SAUS)
J/M .... Jettison Motor (KSC)
JM .... Jewish Male [*Classified advertising*]
JM .... Jewish Museum (SAUS)
JM .... Jiyu-Minshuto [*Liberal-Democratic Party*] [*Japan*] [*Political party*]
JM .... Job Management (SAUS)
JM .... Job Memory [*Computer science*] (ELAL)
JM .... John Mercanti [*Designer's mark, when appearing on US coins*]
JM .... Johns Manville Corp. (MCD)
JM .... Joint Mission (SAUO)
JM .... Journal of Marketing [*A publication*] (BRI)
JM .... Journal of Micrographics (NITA)
JM .... Jugomaxillary [*Dentistry*] (DAVI)
JM .... Julia MacRae [*Publisher*] [*British*]
JM .... Julian Messner [*Publisher's imprint*]
JM .... Jump on Minus (SAUS)
JM .... Junction Module [*Deep Space Instrumentation Facility, NASA*]
JM .... Juris Magister [*Master of Laws*]
JM .... Juris Master (SAUS)

JM .... Justizminister [*Minister of Justice*] [*German*] (ILCA)
JM .... Justizministerium [*Ministry of Justice*] [*German*] (ILCA)
JM .... Juxtamembrane Domain
jM .... Mass Transfer Factor [*Physics*] (DAVI)
J/M² .... Joules per Square Meter
J/m3 .... Joule per Cubic Metre (SAUS)
J/M³ .... Joules per Cubic Meter [*Physics*]
JMA .... Houston [*Texas*] Astrodome [*Airport symbol*] (OAG)
JMA .... Jamaica Manufacturers Association (BUAC)
JMA .... Jamara Memorial Association (BUAC)
JMA .... James Martin Associates [*Database consulting group*] [*British*]
JMA .... Jamming Modulation Analysis
JMA .... Japanese Meteorological Agency (SAUO)
JMA .... Japanese Military Administration
JMA .... Japan Management Association (BUAC)
JMA .... Japan Medical Association (SAUO)
JMA .... Japan Meteorological Agency
JMA .... Japan Meteorological Association (SAUO)
JMA .... Japan Microfilm Association (SAUO)
JMA .... Japan Microphotography Association
JMA .... Jewelry Manufacturers Association (EA)
JMA .... Jewish Music Alliance (EA)
JMA .... John More Association (EA)
JMA .... Joinery Managers' Association [*British*] (BI)
JMA .... Joint Mission Analysis
JMA .... Joint Mission Application (SAUO)
JMA .... Joint Mobilization Augmentation (SAUO)
JMA .... Journal of Macronomics (journ.) (SAUS)
JMA .... Julia Morgan Association [*Defunct*] (EA)
JMA .... Junior Management Assistant
JMA .... Junior Medical Assistant [*British military*] (DMA)
JMA .... Junior Military Aviator
JMA .... Juvenile Missionary Association [*British*] (BI)
JMAAD........ Joint Military Assistance Affairs Division (CINC)
JMAC .... Joint Munitions Allocation Committee
J Macomb Dent Soc... Journal. Macomb Dental Society (journ.) (SAUS)
J Macromol Chem... Journal of Macromolecular Chemistry (journ.) (SAUS)
J Macromol Sci... Journal of Macromolecular Science (SAUS)
J Macromol Sci A... Journal of Macromolecular Science. Part A (journ.) (SAUS)
J Macromol Sci C... Journal of Macromolecular Science. Part C (journ.) (SAUS)
J Macromol Sci Chem... Journal of Macromolecular Science. Chemistry (journ.) (SAUS)
J Macromol Sci Chem A... Journal of Macromolecular Science. Part A. Chemistry (journ.) (SAUS)
J Macromol Sci Part A... Journal of Macromolecular Science. Part A. Chemistry (journ.) (SAUS)
J Macromol Sci Part C... Journal of Macromolecular Science. Part C. Reviews in Macromolecular Chemistry (journ.) (SAUS)
J Macromol Sci Part D... Journal of Macromolecular Science. Part D. Reviews in Polymer Technology (journ.) (SAUS)
J Macromol Sci Phys... Journal of Macromolecular Science. Part B. Physics (journ.) (SAUS)
J Macromol Sci Phys... Journal of Macromolecular Science-Physics (journ.) (SAUS)
J Macromol Sci Rev Macromol Chem... Journal of Macromolecular Science. Part C. Reviews in Macromolecular Chemistry (journ.) (SAUS)
J Macromol Sci Rev Macromol Chem Phys... Journal of Macromolecular Science. Reviews in Macromolecular Chemistry and Physics (journ.) (SAUS)
J Macromol Sci Rev Polym Technol... Journal of Macromolecular Science. Part D. Reviews in Polymer Technology (journ.) (SAUS)
J Macr S Ch... Journal of Macromolecular Science. Part A. Chemistry (journ.) (SAUS)
J Macr S Ph... Journal of Macromolecular Science. Part B. Physics (journ.) (SAUS)
J Madras Agric Stud Union... Journal. Madras Agricultural Students. Union (journ.) (SAUS)
J Madras Inst Technol... Journal. Madras Institute of Technology (journ.) (SAUS)
J Madras Univ... Journal. Madras University (journ.) (SAUS)
JMADSN....... James Madison Ltd. (SAUO)
J Madurai Kamaraj Univ... Journal. Madurai Kamaraj University (journ.) (SAUS)
J Madurai Univ... Journal Madurai University (journ.) (SAUS)
JMAG .... Journal of Molecular and Applied Genetics (journ.) (SAUS)
J Magn Reson B... Journal of Magnetic Resonance. Series B (journ.) (SAUS)
J Magn Reson Imaging... Journal of Magnetic Resonance Imaging (journ.) (SAUS)
J Maharaja Sayayira Univ Baroda... Journal. Maharaja Sayayira University of Baroda (journ.) (SAUS)
J Maharasbtra Agric Univ... Journal. Maharasbtra Agricultural Universities (journ.) (SAUS)
JMAHEP....... Joint Military Aircraft Hurricane Evacuation Plan (AFM)
J Maine Dent Assoc... Journal. Maine Dental Association (journ.) (SAUS)
J Maine Med Assoc... Journal. Maine Medical Association (journ.) (SAUS)
J Malac Soc Aust... Journal. Malacological Society of Australia (journ.) (SAUS)
J Mal & Comp L... Journal of Malaysian and Comparative Law (journ.) (SAUS)
J Malar Inst India... Journal. Malaria Institute of India (journ.) (SAUS)
J Malaya Branch Br Med Assoc... Journal. Malaya Branch. British Medical Association (journ.) (SAUS)
J Malaya Branch Br Med Assoc... Journal. Malayan Branch. British Medical Association (journ.) (SAUS)
J Malay Branch Roy Asiatic Soc... Journal. Malaysian Branch. Royal Asiatic Society (journ.) (SAUS)
J Mal Br Brit Med Ass... Journal. Malayan Branch. British Medical Association (journ.) (SAUS)
J Mal Vasc... Journal des Maladies Vasculaires (journ.) (SAUS)
JMAM .... Journal of Mammalogy (journ.) (SAUS)
J Mammal... Journal of Mammalogy (journ.) (SAUS)

J Mammal Soc Jpn... Journal. Mammalogical Society of Japan (journ.) (SAUS)
J Manage .... Journal of Management (journ.) (SAUS)
J Manage Inf Syst... Journal of Management Information Systems (journ.) (SAUS)
J Manage Stud... Journal of Management Studies (journ.) (SAUS)
J Manch Geogr Soc... Journal. Manchester Geographical Society (journ.) (SAUS)
J Manch Geol Ass... Journal. Manchester Geological Association (journ.) (SAUS)
J MAN GS.... Journal of the Manchester Geographical Society [A publication] (ROG)
J MAN GS.... Journal of the Manchester Geographical Society (journ.) (SAUS)
J Manuf Oper Manage... Journal of Manufacturing and Operations Management (journ.) (SAUS)
J Manuf Syst... Journal of Manufacturing Systems (journ.) (SAUS)
JMAP........... Joint Mutual Aid Program (SAUO)
JMAPI.......... Java Management Application Program Interface [Computer science] (IGQR)
JMAR.......... JMAR Industries [NASDAQ symbol] (SPSG)
JMAR.......... JMAR Technologies [NASDAQ symbol] [Formerly, JMAR Industries]
J Mar Eng Soc Jpn... Journal. Marine Engineering Society in Japan (journ.) (SAUS)
J Mar J Prac & Proc... John Marshall Journal of Practice and Procedure (journ.) (SAUS)
J Mark........ Journal ot Marketing (journ.) (SAUS)
J Market Research Society Vic... Journal. Market Research Society of Victoria (journ.) (SAUS)
J Market Res Soc... Journal. Market Research Society (journ.) (SAUS)
J Market Res Soc... Journal of the Market Research Society (SAUO)
J Market Res Soc... Journal of the Market Research Society (journ.) (SAUS)
J Mark Prof... Journal of Marketing for Professions (journ.) (SAUS)
J Mar L Rev... John Marshall Law Review (journ.) (SAUS)
J Mar Sci... Journal of Marine Science (journ.) (SAUS)
JMARW........ JMAR Inds Wrrt [NASDAQ symbol] (TTSB)
JMAS........... Joint Manpower Automation System (COE)
JMAS........... Joint Mission Application Software (SAUO)
JMAS........... Journal of Modern African Studies (journ.) (SAUS)
J-Mass........ Joint-Modeling and Simulation System
J Mass Dent Soc... Journal Massachusetts Dental Society (journ.) (SAUS)
JMAT........... Joint Medium-calibre Automatic cannon Technology (SAUS)
J Mater........ Journal of Materials (journ.) (SAUS)
J Mater Energy Syst... Journal of Materials for Energy Systems (journ.) (SAUS)
J Mater Eng... Journal of Materials Engineering (journ.) (SAUS)
J Mater Process Technol... Journal of Materials Processing Technology (journ.) (SAUS)
J Mater Res... Journal of Materials Research (journ.) (SAUS)
J Mater Sci Res Inst Dongguk Univ... Journal. Malerials Science Research Institute. Dongguk University (journ.) (SAUS)
J Mater Sci Soc Jpn... Journal. Materials Science Society of Japan (journ.) (SAUS)
J Mater Sci Soc Jpn... Journal of the Materials Science Society of Japan (journ.) (SAUS)
J Mater Shaping Technol... Journal of Materials Shaping Technology (journ.) (SAUS)
J Mater Technol... Journal of Materials Technology (journ.) (SAUS)
J Math Biol... Journal of Mathematical Biology (journ.) (SAUS)
J Math Chem... Journal of Mathematical Chemistry (journ.) (SAUS)
J Math Econom... Journal of Mathematical Economics (journ.) (SAUS)
J Math Kyoto Univ... Journal of Mathematics. Kyoto University (journ.) (SAUS)
J Math Mech... Journal of Mathematics and Mechanics (journ.) (SAUS)
J Math Modelling Teach... Journal of Mathematical Modelling for Teachers (journ.) (SAUS)
J Math NS ... Journal of Mathematics. New Series (journ.) (SAUS)
J Math Physics... Journal of Mathematical Physics (MEC)
J Math Res Exposition... Journal of Mathematical Research and Exposition (journ.) (SAUS)
J Math Soc Jpn... Journal. Mathematical Society of Japan (journ.) (SAUS)
J Math Soc Jpn... Journal of the Mathematical Society of Japan (journ.) (SAUS)
J Math Tokushima Univ... Journal of Mathematics. Tokushima University (journ.) (SAUS)
J Matsumoto Dent Coll Soc... Journal. Matsumoto Dental College Society (journ.) (SAUS)
J Maulana Acad College Tech... Journal. Maulana Acad College of Technology (journ.) (SAUS)
J Maxillofac Orthop... Journal of Maxillofacial Orthopedics (journ.) (SAUS)
J Maxillofac Surg... Journal of Maxillofacial Surgery (journ.) (SAUS)
J Mayan Linguist... Journal of Mayan Linguistics (journ.) (SAUS)
JMB............. Jamb (ABBR)
JMB............. Jewelers Memorandum Bureau (EA)
JMB............. Johnson Matthey Bankers [Commercial firm] [British]
JMB............. Joint Matriculation Board [British] (DCTA)
JMB............. Joint Meteorological Board (AAG)
JMB............. Joint Movements Branch [NATO] (NATG)
JMB............. Journal of Molecular Biology (journ.) (SAUS)
JMBA.......... Journal of the Marine Biological Association (SAUO)
JMBA.......... Journal of the Marine Biological Association (journ.) (SAUS)
JMBL.......... Jumble (ABBR)
JMBLD........ Jumbled (ABBR)
JMBLG........ Jumbling (ABBR)
JMBR.......... JMB Reality Trust (SAUS)
JMBRE........ Jamboree (ABBR)
JMC............ James Mitchell & Co. (EFIS)
JMC............ Japan Map Center (SAUO)
JMC............ Japan Medical Congress (journ.) (SAUS)
JMC............ Japan Metals and Chemicals (SAUO)
JMC............ Japan Monopoly Corp. (BUAC)
JMC............ JASC Media Center
JMC............ Jefferson Medical College (SAUO)
JMC............ Jerden Manufacturing Corporation (SAUO)
JMC............ Jerusalem Music Centre (SAUO)

JMC............ Jewish Marriage Council (BUAC)
JMC............ Jiangxi Medical College [China] (BUAC)
JMC............ Joint Management Centers (SAUS)
JMC............ Joint Management Committee (SAUO)
JMC............ Joint Maritime Commission
JMC............ Joint Maritime Congress [Washington, DC] (EA)
JMC............ Joint Maritime Course (SAUO)
JMC............ Joint Mathematical Council of the United Kingdom (BUAC)
JMC............ Joint Message Center
JMC............ Joint Meteorological Committee
JMC............ Joint Military Commission [US, North Vietnam, South Vietnam, Viet Cong]
JMC............ Joint Monitoring Commission (SAUO)
JMC............ Joint Movement Center (COE)
JMC............ Journal of Medicinal Chemistry (journ.) (SAUS)
JMC............ Justice Mining Corp. [Vancouver Stock Exchange symbol]
JMC............ Justi Mining Corp.
JMC............ Sausalito, CA [Location identifier] [FAA] (FAAL)
Jmca......... Jamaica (SAUS)
JMCA........ Jewish Ministers Cantors Association of America and Canada (EA)
JMCA........ John M. Cockerham and Associates (SAUO)
JMCA........ Joint Movement Coordination Agency
JMCA........ Judges, Marshals, and Constables Association
JMCAA....... Jewish Minister and Cantors Association of America [Later, JMCA] (EA)
JMCAAC..... Jewish Ministers Cantors Association of America and Canada (EA)
JMCAD....... Journal of Molecular Catalysis (journ.) (SAUS)
JMCC........ Joint Manoeuvre Control Command (SAUO)
JMCC........ Joint Maritime Communications Centre (SAUO)
JMCC........ Joint Message Co-ordinating Centre (SAUO)
JMCC........ Joint Message Coordinating Committee (SAUS)
JMCC........ Joint Mobile Command Capability (SAUS)
JMCC........ Joint Mobile Communications Center [NATO] (NATG)
JMCC........ Joint Mobile Communications Centre (SAUO)
JMCC........ Joint Movement Control Center (SAUO)
JMCC........ Joint Movements Coordinating Committee [British]
JM Cenet.... Journal of Medical Genetics (journ.) (SAUS)
JMCG........ JMC Group [NASDAQ symbol] (TTSB)
JMCG........ JMC Group, Inc. [NASDAQ symbol] (SAG)
JMC Gp....... JMC Group, Inc. [Associated Press] (SAG)
JMCHP....... Jubilee. A Magazine of the Church and Her People (journ.) (SAUS)
JMCI......... Journal of Molecular and Cellular Immunology (journ.) (SAUS)
JMCI J Mol Cell Immunol... JMCI. Journal of Molecular and Cellular Immunology (journ.) (SAUS)
JMCIS........ Joint Maritime Command Information System (SAUO)
JMCM........ Journal of Managed Care Medicine (SAUO)
JMCOL....... JUMPS [Joint Uniform Military Payment System] Monthly Compute Output Listing [Military] (AABC)
JMCP......... Jefferson Medical College of Philadelphia
JMCP......... Journal of Managed Care Pharmacy (SAUO)
JMCQ........ Journalism & Mass Communication Quarterly [A publication] (BRI)
JMCS........ Junior Mountaineering Club of Scotland (SAUO)
JMCSSG..... Joint Management Control System Study Group (SAUO)
JMCY........ Joseph Malins Crusade of Youth [British] (BI)
JMD.......... Jamaican Dollar (SAUS)
JMD.......... Japan Medical Depot (SAUO)
JMD.......... Joint Managing Director (DCTA)
JMD.......... Joint Monitor Display
JMD.......... JOPES Management Division (SAUO)
JMD.......... Journal of Management Development (journ.) (SAUS)
JMD.......... Jungle Message Decoder (SAUS)
JMD.......... Justice Management Division [U.S. Department of Justice] (BARN)
JMD.......... Juvenile Macular Degeneration [Medicine] (MEDA)
J MD Acad Sci... Journal. Maryland Academy of Sciences (journ.) (SAUS)
JMDC......... Japan Machinery Design Center (or Centre) (SAUS)
JMDC......... Joint Manual Direction Center [Air Force]
JMDC......... Joint Message Distribution Centre (SAUO)
Jm Dep Agric Bull... Jamaica. Department of Agriculture. Bulletin (journ.) (SAUS)
JMDR........ Journal of Mental Defficiency Research (journ.) (SAUS)
JMDR........ Journal of Missile Defense Research (journ.) (SAUS)
JMDS........ Joint Manpower Data System (SAUS)
J MD State Dent Assoc... Journal. Maryland State Dental Association (journ.) (SAUS)
J Md State Dent Assoc... Journal of the Maryland State Dental Association (SAUO)
J Md State Dent Assoc... Journal of the Maryland State Dental Association (journ.) (SAUS)
JME.......... James Industries [Vancouver Stock Exchange symbol]
JME.......... Joint Maximum Effort
JME.......... Journal of Mathematical Economics (journ.) (SAUS)
JME.......... Journal of Monetary Economics (journ.) (SAUS)
JME.......... Jungle Message Encoder (SAUS)
JME.......... Juvenile Myoclonic Epilepsy [Medicine]
JMEA......... Japan Machinery Exporters Association (BUAC)
JMEA......... Jewish Music Educators Association [Defunct] (EA)
JMEC......... Joint Materiel Exploitation Center (SAUO)
J Mech ...... Journal of Mechanisms (journ.) (SAUS)
J Mech Behav Mater... Journal of the Mechanical Behavior of Materials (journ.) (SAUS)
J Mech Eng Assoc Witwatersrand... Journal. Mechanical Engineers Association of Witwatersrand (journ.) (SAUS)
J Mech Eng Lab... Journal of Mechanical Engineering Laboratory (journ.) (SAUS)
J Mech Lab Jap... Journal. Mechanical Laboratory of Japan (journ.) (SAUS)
JMED......... Jones Medical Indus [NASDAQ symbol] (TTSB)
JMED......... Jones Medical Industries, Inc. [NASDAQ symbol] (NQ)
JMED......... Jones Pharma [NASDAQ symbol] [Formerly, Jones Medical Indus.]

J Med.......... Journal of Medicine (journ.) (SAUS)
JMED.......... Jungle Message Encoder-Decoder (MCD)
JMEDA........ Journal of Medical Education (journ.) (SAUS)
J Med Ass Form... Jonrnal. Medical Association of Formosa (journ.) (SAUS)
J Med Assoc Ga... Journal of the Medical Association of Georgia (SAUO)
J Med Assoc Ga... Journal of the Medical Association of Georgia (journ.) (SAUS)
J Med Assoc Isr... Journal. Medical Assiation of Israel (journ.) (SAUS)
J Med Assoc Iwate Prefect Hosp... Journal. Medical Association of Iwate Prefectural Hospital (journ.) (SAUS)
J Med Assoc Jam... Journal. Medical Assoriation of Jamaica (journ.) (SAUS)
J Med Assoc Thai... Journal of the Medical Association of Thailand (SAUO)
J Med Assoc Thai... Journal of the Medical Association of Thailand (journ.) (SAUS)
J Med Ass Ok... Journal. Medical Association of Okayama (journ.) (SAUS)
J Med Chem... Journal of Medicinal Chemistry (journ.) (SAUS)
J Med Chir... Journal Medico-Chirurgical (journ.) (SAUS)
J Med Coll Keijo... Journal. Medical College in Keijo (journ.) (SAUS)
J Med Dent Assoc Botswana... Journal. Medical and Dental Association of Botswana (journ.) (SAUS)
J Med Enzymol... Journal of Medical Enzymology (journ.) (SAUS)
J Med Exp Clin... Journal of Medicine. Experimental and Clinical (journ.) (SAUS)
J Med Genet... Journal of Medical Genetics (journ.) (SAUS)
J Medicinal Chem... Journal of Medicinal Chemistry (MEC)
J Mediev Hi... Journal of Medieval History (journ.) (SAUS)
J Mediterr Anthropol Archaeol... Journal of Mediterranean Anthropology and Archaeology (journ.) (SAUS)
J Med Lab Technol... Journal of Medical Laboratory Technology (journ.) (SAUS)
J Med Mie Prefect Univ... Journal of Medicine. Mie Prefectural University (journ.) (SAUS)
J Med Pharm Chem... Journal of Medicinal and Pharmaceutical Chemistry (journ.) (SAUS)
J Med Pharm Soc Wkan Yaku... Journal. Medical and Pharmaceutical Society for Wakan-Yaku (journ.) (SAUS)
J Med Prof Ass... Journal. Medical Professions Association (journ.) (SAUS)
J Med Sci... Journal of Medical Sciences (journ.) (SAUS)
J Med Sci Banaras Hindu Univ... Journal of Medical Sciences. Banaras Hindu University (journ.) (SAUS)
J Med Screen... Journal of Medical Screening (journ.) (SAUS)
J Med Soc NJ... Journal of the Medical Society of New Jersey (SAUO)
J Med Soc Toho Univ... Journal. Medical Society of Toho University (journ.) (SAUS)
J Med Syst... Journal of Medical Systems (journ.) (SAUS)
J Med Vet Mycol... Journal of Medical and Veterinary Mycology (journ.) (SAUS)
JMeH.......... Journal of Medieval History (journ.) (SAUS)
J Mell Soc Jpn... Journal. Metallurgical Society of Japan (journ.) (SAUS)
JMEM .... Job Memory [Computer science] (MHDB)
JMEM .... Joint Munitions Effectiveness Manual [Military] (AFM)
JMEM .... Joint Munitions Effects Manual (SAUO)
JMEM .... Junior Marine Engineering Mechanic [British military] (DMA)
JMEM/AS..... Joint Munitions Effectiveness Manuals, Air-to-Surface (SAUS)
J Membrane Sci... Journal of Membrane Science (MEC)
JMEMS .... Joint Munition Effectiveness Manual [Navy] (DOMA)
JMEM-SO .... Joint Munitions Effectiveness Manual-Special Operations (SAUO)
JMEMT .... John Morgan Evans of Merthyr Tydil [An association] (EA)
JMEMTF ...... Joint Munitions Effectiveness Manual Task Force (MCD)
JMENS .... Joint Mission Element Need Statement (MCD)
J Ment Defic Res... Journal of Mental Deficiency Research (journ.) (SAUS)
J Ment Health... Journal of Mental Health (journ.) (SAUS)
J Ment Health Adm... Journal. Mental Health Admin, istlation (journ.) (SAUS)
J Mercer Dent Soc... Journal. Mercer Dental Society (journ.) (SAUS)
JMES .... Journal. Middle East Society (journ.) (SAUS)
J Metab Res... Journal of Metabolic Research (journ.) (SAUS)
J Metall Club R Coll Sci Technol... Journal. Metallurgical Club. Royal College of Science and Technology (journ.) (SAUS)
J Metall Club Univ Strathclyde... Journal. Metallurgical Club. University of Strathclyde (journ.) (SAUS)
J Metamorph Geol... Journal of Metamorphic Geology (journ.) (SAUS)
J Meteorol Res... Journal of Meteorological Research (journ.) (SAUS)
J Meteorol Soc Jpn... Journal. Meteorological Society of Japan (journ.) (SAUS)
J Met Finish Soc Jp... Journal. Metal Finishing Society of Japan (journ.) (SAUS)
J Met Finish Soc Jpn... Journal of the Metal Finishing Society of Japan (journ.) (SAUS)
J Met Finish Soc Korea... Journal. Metal Finishing Society of Korea (journ.) (SAUS)
J Met Finish Soc Korea... Journal of the Metal Finishing Society of Korea (journ.) (SAUS)
JMETL .... Joint Mission Essential Task List (DOMA)
J Met Soc Jap... Journal. Meteorological Society of Japan (journ.) (SAUS)
J Mex Am Hist... Journal of Mexican American History (journ.) (SAUS)
JMF .... James Madison Foundation (EA)
JMF .... Java Media Framework [Computer science]
JMF .... Jet Mixing Flow
JMF .... Jewish Music Forum
JMF .... John Marshall Foundation (EA)
JMF .... Johnston Mutual Fund, Inc. (SAUO)
JMF .... Journal of Marriage and the Family [A publication] (BRI)
JMF .... Juilliard Musical Foundation (SAUO)
JMFC .... Jared Martin Fan Club [Defunct] (EA)
JMFC .... Jayne Mansfield Fan Club (EA)
JMFC .... Jimmy Murphy Fan Club (EA)
JMFT .... Journal of Milk and Food Technology (journ.) (SAUS)
JMFU .... Joint force Meteorological and oceanographic Forecast Unit (SAUO)
JMFU .... Joint METOC Forecast Unit (SAUO)
JMG .... Jewelry Manufacturers Guild (EA)
JMG .... Joint Meteorological Group [DoD]
JMG .... Joint Monitoring Group (SAUO)
JMG .... Journal of Management Consulting (journ.) (SAUS)

JMG .... Journal of Medical Genetics (SAUO)
JMG .... Journal of Molecular Graphics (journ.) (SAUS)
JMGR .... JCI Site Management (SAUO)
JMGS .... Journal of Modern Greek Studies (journ.) (SAUS)
J Mgt .... Journal of Management (journ.) (SAUS)
JMH .... John Milton Hagen [Antibody] [Immunology] (DAVI)
JMH .... Joint Mission Hardware (SAUO)
JMH .... Journal of Mississippi History (journ.) (SAUS)
JMH .... Journal of Modern History [A publication] (BRI)
JMH .... Journal of Modern History (journ.) (SAUS)
JMHC .... Joint Mission Hardware Contractor (SAUO)
JMHO .... Just My Honest Opinion (SAUS)
JMHO .... Just My Humble Opinion (SAUS)
JMHS .... James Madison High School (SAUO)
JMHS .... James Monroe High School (SAUO)
JMHS .... John Muir High School (SAUO)
JMI .... Jackson & Moreland, Inc. (MCD)
JMI .... Jackson & Moreland, Incorporated (SAUO)
JMI .... Jan Mayen Island [Seismograph station code, US Geological Survey] (SEIS)
JMI .... Japan Machinery and Metal Inspection (SAUS)
JMI .... Japan Management Institute (BUAC)
JMI .... Japan Metals Institute (SAUS)
JMI .... John Muir Institute (SAUS)
JMI .... John Muir Institute for Environmental Studies [Defunct] (EA)
JMI .... Jones Medical Industries, Inc. (EFIS)
JmI .... Jorm Microlab, Inc., Cedar Rapids, IA [Library symbol] [Library of Congress] (LCLS)
JMI .... Journal of Medical Imaging (journ.) (SAUS)
JMI .... Justice Management Institute
JMI .... Justice Mortgage Investors (SAUO)
JMIA .... Japan Mining Industry Association (BUAC)
JMIA .... JCI Internal Auditor (SAUO)
JMIC .... Joint Maritime Intelligence Centre (SAUO)
J Mich Dent Assoc... Journal. Michigan Dental Association (journ.) (SAUS)
J Mich State Dent Assoc... Journal. Michigan State Dental Association (journ.)
J Mich State Dent Assoc... Journal of the Michigan State Dental Association (SAUO)
J Mich State Dent Assoc... Journal of the Michigan State Dental Association (journ.) (SAUS)
J Mich State Dent Soc... Journal. Michigan State Dental Society (journ.) (SAUS)
J Micr and Nat Sc... Journal of Microscopy and Natural Science (journ.) (SAUS)
J Microb Biotechnol... Journal of Microbial Biotechnology (journ.) (SAUS)
J Microbiol UAR... Journal of Microbiology of the United Arab Republic (journ.) (SAUS)
J Microcomput Appl... Journal of Microcomputer Applications (journ.) (SAUS)
J Microcomput Syst Manage... Journal of Microcomputer Systems Management (journ.) (SAUS)
J Micronutr Anal... Journal of Micronutrient Analysis (journ.) (SAUS)
J Microorg Ferment... Journal of Microorganisms and Fermentation (journ.) (SAUS)
J Microsurg... Journal of Microsurgery (journ.) (SAUS)
J Microw Power Electromagn Energy... Journal of Microwave Power and Electromagnetic Energy (journ.) (SAUS)
JMIE .... Joint Maritime Information Element [Coast Guard]
JMIE .... Joint Maritime Information Exchange
J Mie Med Coll... Journal. Mie Medical College (journ.) (SAUS)
JMIF .... Japan Motor Industrial Federation (BUAC)
JMIFC .... Jeanette MacDonald International Fan Club (EA)
JMIFC .... Johnny Mathis International Fan Club (EA)
JMiH .... Journal of Mississippi History (journ.) (SAUS)
J Mil H .... Journal of Military History [A publication] (BRI)
J Mil Serv Inst... Journal of the Military Institution (journ.) (SAUS)
J Mil Soc..... Journal of Political and Military Sociology. (journ.) (SAUS)
J Min Coll Akita Univ Ser A... Journal. Mining College. Akita Univer- sity. Series A. Mining Geology (journ.) (SAUS)
J Mineral Petrol Econ Geol... Journal of Mineralogy, Petrology and Economic Geology (journ.) (SAUS)
J Mineral Soc Jpn... Journal. Mineralogical Society of Japan (journ.) (SAUS)
J Mine Vent Soc S Afr... Journal. Mine Ventilation Society of South Africa (journ.) (SAUS)
J Mine Vent Soc S Afr... Journal of the Mine Ventilation Society of South Africa (journ.) (SAUS)
J Min Geol... Journal of Mining and Geology (journ.) (SAUS)
J Minist Health... Journal. Ministry of Health (journ.) (SAUS)
J Min Mater Process Inst Jpn... Journal of the Mining and Materials Processing Institute of Japan (journ.) (SAUS)
J Min Mat Process Inst Jpn... Journal. Mining and Materials Processing Institute of Japan (journ.) (SAUS)
J Min Metall Foundry... Journal of Mining and Metallurgy. Foundry (journ.) (SAUS)
J Min Metall Inst Jpn... Journal of the Mining and Metallurgical Institute of Japan (journ.) (SAUS)
J Min Metall Metall... Journal of Mining and Metallurgy. Metallurgy (journ.) (SAUS)
J Minn Acad Sci... Journal. Minnesota Academy of Science (journ.) (SAUS)
JMIR .... Journal of Medical Internet Research (SAUO)
J Miss Acad Sci... Journal. Mississippi Academy of Sciences (journ.) (SAUS)
J Miss Hist... Journal of Mississippi History. Mississippi Historical Society. Jackson (SAUO)
J Miss State Med Assoc... Journal of the Mississippi State Medical Association (SAUO)
J Miss State Med Assoc... Journal of the Mississippi State Medical Association (journ.) (SAUS)
JMJ .... James J. Johnston [FAA designator] (FAAC)
JMJ .... Jesus, Mary, and Joseph
JMJ .... Johnston Airways (SAUO)

JMK .... Mikonos [Greece] [Airport symbol] (OAG)
J Mktg Res... Journal of Marketing Research (journ.) (SAUS)
JMKU.......... Journal of Mathematics. Kyoto University (journ.) (SAUS)
JMKU.......... Journal of Mathematics of Kyoto University (journ.) (SAUS)
JmKU.......... University of the West Indies (SAUO)
JMKWA2....... Annual Reports. Institute of Population Problems (journ.) (SAUS)
JML .... James Madison Ltd. (EFIS)
JML .... Job Method Learning (PDAA)
JML .... Journal of Modern Literature [A publication] (ANEX)
JML .... Journal of Modern Literature (journ.) (SAUS)
JML .... JW Martin Laboratory (SAUS)
JML .... Taxi Aereo de Jimulco SA de CV [Mexico] [ICAO designator] (FAAC)
JMLC .... JCI Legal Counsel (SAUO)
JmLibS .... Jamaica Library Service (SAUS)
JM Ling .... Journal of Mayan Linguistics (journ.) (SAUS)
JMLR .... John Marshall Law Review (journ.) (SAUS)
JMLS .... John Marshall Law School [Chicago, IL] (DLA)
JMLS .... John Menzies Library Services [Information service or system] (IID)
J MI Vet Med Ass... Journal. Malayan Veterinary Medical Association (journ.)
              (SAUS)
JMM .... Jacobi Matrix Method [Mathematics]
JMM .... Jamaica Merchant Marine (EY)
JMM .... Joint Man Machine (IAA)
JMM .... Journal of Macromarketing (journ.) (SAUS)
JMM .... Journal of Microbiological Methods (journ.) (SAUS)
JMM .... Journal of Molecular Medicine [A publication]
JMMA .... Japan Materials Management Association (BUAC)
JMMA .... Japan Microscope Manufacturers Association (BUAC)
JMMAA .... Journal. Maine Medical Association (journ.) (SAUS)
JMMAT .... Joint Military Mission for Aid to Turkey (SAUO)
JMMC .... James Madison Memorial Commission (SAUO)
JMMC .... Joint Military Medical Command (SAUO)
JMMF .... James Monroe Memorial Foundation (EA)
JMMII .... Japan Machinery and Metals Inspection Institute (BUAC)
JMMMD .... Journal of Magnetism and Magnetic Materials (journ.) (SAUS)
JMMO .... Joint Medical Mobilization Office (SAUO)
JMMSD .... Journal. Korea Merchant Marine College. Natural Sciences Series
              (journ.) (SAUS)
JMM System... Joint Man-Machine System (SAUS)
JMN .... Jeweled-Orifice Misting Nozzle
JMN .... Johan Mangku Negara [Malaysian Honour]
JMN .... Justification for Mission Need (SAUO)
JMNA .... Joint Military Net Assessment [A publication] (RDA)
JMNCL .... Jeunesse du Mouvement National Congolaise - Lumumba [Youth of
              the Lumumba Wing of the Congolese National Movement]
J/Mne .... Junior Marine [British military] (DMA)
JMNR.......... Journal of Military Nursing and Research (SAUO)
JMNR.......... Journal of Military Nursing and Research (journ.) (SAUS)
JMO .... Jesuit Mission Office [Australia]
JMO .... Joint Force Meteorological and Oceanographic Officer (COE)
JMO .... Joint Maritime Operations (COE)
JMO .... Jomsom [Nepal] [Airport symbol] (OAG)
JMO .... Jugoslovenska Muslimanska Organizacija [Yugoslav Moslem
              Organization] [Political party] (PPE)
JMO .... Just My Opinion [Online dialog]
JMOA .... Joint Memorandum of Agreement (ACAE)
JMOB .... Joint Mobile Offshore Base [Military]
JMOC .... Joint METOC Operations Center (SAUO)
J Mo Dent Assoc... Journal. Missouri Dental Association (journ.) (SAUS)
JModH .... Journal of Modern History (SAUS)
J Mod Lit..... Journal of Modern Literature (journ.) (SAUS)
J Mod Opt ... Journal of Modern Optics (journ.) (SAUS)
JMOF .... Joint Meteorological Observing Facility (SAUO)
J/MOL .... Joules per Mole [Physics]
J Molec Struct... Journal of Molecular Structure (MEC)
J Mol Electron... Journal of Molecular Electronics (journ.) (SAUS)
J Mol Endocrinol... Journal of Molecular Endocrinology (journ.) (SAUS)
J Mol Evol ... Journal of Molecular Evolution (journ.) (SAUS)
J Mol Graph.. Journal of Molecular Graphics (journ.) (SAUS)
J/(MOL K)... Joules per Mole Kelvin [Physics]
J Mol Liq..... Journal of Molecular Liquids (journ.) (SAUS)
J Molluscan Stud... Journal of Molluscan Studies (journ.) (SAUS)
J Molluscan Stud Suppl... Journal of Molluscan Studies. Supple- ment (journ.)
              (SAUS)
J Mol Med... Journal of Molecular Medicine (MEC)
J Mol Med... Journal of Molecular Medicine (journ.) (SAUS)
J Mol Recognit... Journal of Molecular Recognition (journ.) (SAUS)
J Mol Sci..... Journal of Molecular Science (journ.) (SAUS)
J Mol Struct... Journal of Molecular Structure (journ.) (SAUS)
J Monetary Econ... Journal of Monetary Economics (journ.) (SAUS)
J Money Credit Bank... Journal of Money, Credit and Banking. Columbus (SAUS)
JMOOC .... Just My Opinion of Course (SAUS)
JMOP.......... Joint Memorandum of Policy [Military]
J Mormon Hist... Journal of Mormon History (journ.) (SAUS)
JMOS.......... Job Management Operations System (PDAA)
JMOTS......... Joint Maritime Operational Training Staffs (SAUO)
J Mo Water Sewerage Conf... Journal. Missouri Water and Sewerage Conference
              (journ.) (SAUS)
JMP .... Jack Morton Productions, Inc. [New York, NY]
              [Telecommunications] (TSSD)
JMP .... Jen Min Piao [or Yuan] [Peoples money of China] (BARN)
JMP .... Job Monitor Protocol (SAUS)
JMP .... John M. Poindexter [National Security Advisor during the Reagan
              Administration]
JMP .... Johnson Matthey Public Ltd. Co. [Toronto Stock Exchange symbol]

JMP .... Joint Manpower Program [Military] (CINC)
JMP .... Joint Mission Processor (SAUO)
JMP .... Joint Monitoring Programme (SAUO)
JMP .... Journal of Public Policy and Marketing (journ.) (SAUS)
JMP .... Jump [Computer science]
JMPA2 .... Joint Military Passenger Equalization Agreement (SAUO)
JMPAB .... Joint Materiel Priorities and Allocation Board [Military] (AABC)
JMPC .... Joint Mapping and Photography Committee (SAUO)
JMPC .... Joint Military Procurements Control [World War II]
JMPC .... Joint Session of the Manpower Committees (SAUO)
JMPD .... Jumped (ABBR)
JMPE .... Joint Mission Processing Environment (SAUO)
JMPE .... Joint Mission Processing Equipment (SAUO)
JMPG .... Jumping (ABBR)
JMPI .... Jumpmaster Personnel Inspection [Army] (ADDR)
J M Plant Res... Journal of Medicinal Plant Research. Planta Medica (journ.)
              (SAUS)
JMPMA........ Journal of Medical Primatology (journ.) (SAUS)
JMPNS........ Jumpiness (ABBR)
JMPO .... Joint MILSTAR Program Office (SAUO)
JMPO .... Journal of Microwave Power (journ.) (SAUS)
JMPOF .... Jumpoff (ABBR)
JMPP .... Joint Munitions Production Panel (MCD)
JMPR.......... Joint FAO/WHO Meeting and/on Pesticide Residues (SAUO)
JMPR.......... Joint Meeting on Pesticide Residues [Environmental Protection
              Agency] (EPAT)
JMPR.......... Jumper (MSA)
JMPSB .... Journal of Mathematical and Physical Sciences (journ.) (SAUS)
JMPT .... Joint Military Potential Test (MCD)
JMPT .... Journal of Manipulative and Physiological Therapeutics (journ.)
              (SAUS)
JMPTC .... Joint Military Packaging Training Center
JMR .... Alexandair, Inc. [Canada] [ICAO designator] (FAAC)
JMR .... Jamair Inc. (SAUO)
JMR .... Job Manager Request (TIMI)
JMR .... Johannesburg Mounted Rifles [British military] (DMA)
JMR .... Journal of Magnetic Resonance (journ.) (SAUS)
JMR .... Journal of Marketing Research (journ.) (SAUS)
JMR .... Journal of Materials Research (journ.) (SAUS)
JMR .... Journal of Molecular Recognition (journ.) (SAUS)
JMRAS......... Journal of the Malayan Branch of the Royal Asiatic Society (SAUO)
JMRAS......... Journal of the Malayan Branch of the Royal Asiatic Society (journ.)
              (SAUS)
JMRC.......... Joint Mobile Relay Center (MCD)
JMRC.......... Joint Mobile Relay Center (or Centre) (SAUO)
JMRCM........ Journal of Muscle Research and Cell Motility (journ.) (SAUS)
JMRE.......... JM Resources, Inc. (SAUO)
JMRI .... Journal of Magnetic Resonance Imaging (journ.) (SAUS)
JMRMA........ John and Mable Ringling Museum of Art (SAUO)
JMRNSC ...... Joint Meteorological Rocket Network Steering Committee (SAUO)
JMRO.......... Joint Medical Regulating Office (AABC)
JMRO.......... Joint Military Regulating Office
JMRP.......... Joint Meteorological Radio Propagation (SAUS)
JMRP.......... Joint Meteorological Radio Propagation Committee [British] (MCD)
JMRP.......... Joint Meteorological Radio Propagation Sub-Committee (BUAC)
JMRP Committee... Joint Meteorological Radio Propagation Committee (SAUS)
JMRPDC ...... Japan Medical Research Foundation. Publication (journ.) (SAUS)
JMRPS........ Joint Meteorological Radio Propagation Subcommittee (SAUS)
JMRS .... Journal of Medieval and Renaissance Studies (journ.) (SAUS)
JMRT .... Junior Members Round Table [American Library Association]
J Mr Technol Soc... Journal. Marine Technology Society (journ.) (SAUS)
JMS .... Jacob More Society (EA)
JMS .... James Madison Society (SAUO)
JMS .... Jamestown [North Dakota] [Airport symbol] (OAG)
JMS .... Jamestown, ND [Location identifier] [FAA] (FAAL)
JMS .... Japan Medical Society (SAUO)
JMS .... Java Message Service (SAUS)
JMS .... Java Messaging Service (VLIE)
JMS .... Jewish Media Service [Defunct] (EA)
JMS .... Job Management System (SAUS)
JMS .... Johannesburg Musical Society (SAUO)
JMS .... John Milton Society for the Blind [Later, JMSB] (EA)
JMS .... Joint Mission Software (SAUO)
JMS .... Joint Movements Staff [British]
J/MS .... Joules per Cubic Meter (SAUS)
J/Ms .... Joules per Square Meter (SAUS)
JMS .... Journal of Maltese Studies (journ.) (SAUS)
JMS .... Journal of Management Studies (journ.) (SAUS)
JMS .... Journal of Manufacturing Systems (journ.) (SAUS)
JMS .... Jump to Subroutine Instruction [Computer science]
JMS .... Junior Medical Student (DAVI)
JMS .... Morgan Stanley Group, Inc. [AMEX symbol] (SAG)
JMSA .... Japanese Maritime Safety Association (SAUS)
JMSA .... Japan Marine Safety Agency [Marine science] (OSRA)
JMSAC .... Joint Meteorological Satellite Advisory Committee
JMSB .... John Milton Society for the Blind (EA)
JMSBA......... Journal of Mental Subnormality (journ.) (SAUS)
JMSC .... Japanese MIDI Standard Committee (SAUS)
JmSC .... Japan Microfilm Service Center Co. Ltd., Tokyo, Japan [Library
              symbol] [Library of Congress] (LCLS)
JMSC .... Japan MIDI Standard Committee (SAUS)
JMSC .... Joint Meteorological Satellite Communication (SAUO)
JMSCA......... Journal of Mental Science (journ.) (SAUS)
JMSDC......... Joint Merchant Shipping Defence Committee [General Council of
              British Shipping] (DS)

JMSDF......... Japanese Maritime Self-Defense Force
JMSDF......... Japan Maritime Self-Defense Force (SAUS)
JMSEP......... Joint Modeling and Simulation Executive Panel [DoD]
JMSJ .... Journal. Mathematical Society of Japan (journ.) (SAUS)
JMSJ .... Journal of the Mathematical Society of Japan (journ.) (SAUS)
JMSLS......... Joliet Three-Minute Speech and Language Screen [Test]
JMSMD....... Journal of Materials for Energy Systems (journ.) (SAUS)
JMSNA....... Journal. Medical Society of New Jersey (journ.) (SAUS)
JMSNS......... Justification for Major System New Start (SAUO)
JMSNS......... Justification of Major System New Start [Military]
JMSO........... Joint Meetings of Seafarers Organization (SAUS)
JMSPO......... Joint Meteorological Satellite Program Office
JMSPO......... Joint Meteorological System Project Office (ACAE)
JMSW......... Joint Mission Software Subsystem (SAUO)
JMSW......... Journal of Multicultural Social Work [A publication] (BRI)
JMSWG........ Joint Message Standard Working Group (SAUO)
JMSWG........ Joint Multi-TADIL Standards Working Group (SAUO)
JMSX........... Job Memory Switch Matrix
JMT .... Job Methods Training
JMT .... Johnson, Mirmiran and Thompson (SAUO)
JMT .... Jointly-Managed Trust (SAUS)
JMT .... Joint Management Team (MCD)
JMT .... Journal of Music Therapy (journ.) (SAUS)
JMT .... Judgment (DCTA)
JMTAA........ Journal. Institute of Mathematics and Its Applications (journ.) (SAUS)
JMTB .... Joint Military Transportation Board
JMTBA......... Japan Machine Tool-Builders Association (BUAC)
JMTC .... Joint Military Transportation Committee
JMTE .... Journal. Michigan Teachers of English (journ.) (SAUS)
J M Technol... Journal of Medical Technology (journ.) (SAUS)
JMTG.......... Joint Military Task Group (MUGU)
JMTG.......... Joint Military Terminology Group (AFM)
JMTG.......... Joint Missile Task Group (SAUO)
JMTK .... Joint Mapping Tool Kit
JMTR .... Japan Materials Testing Reactor (SAUS)
JMTR .... Japan Material Testing Reactor (SAUS)
J Mt Sinai Hosp... Journal Mount Sinai Hospital (journ.) (SAUS)
JMTSS .... Joint Multichannel Trunking and Switching System (MCD)
JMTTA .... Japan Machine Tool Trade Association (SAUO)
JMU .... James Madison University [Virginia]
JMU .... James Millikin University (SAUO)
JMU .... Jamshedpur Mazdoor Union [India]
JMU .... Job Management Unit (SAUS)
JMU .... John Moores University [British]
JMUA .... Joint Meritorious Unit Award [Military decoration] (GFGA)
JMUSA........ Journal. American Musicological Society (journ.) (SAUS)
JMUSDC ..... Joint Mexican-United States Defense Commission
JMUSDC ..... Joint Mexico-United States Defense Commission (SAUO)
J Music Res... Journal of Musicological Research (journ.) (SAUS)
J Music Thr... Journal of Music Theory (journ.) (SAUS)
J/Musn........ Junior Musician [British military] (DMA)
J Mus Therapy... Journal of Music Therapy (journ.) (SAUS)
JMV .... Justice for Murder Victims [An association]
JMVA .... Joint Meritorious Unit Award (SAUO)
JMVB.......... Joint Merchant Vessels Board [World War II]
JMW .... James McNeill Whistler [Nineteenth-century American painter and etcher]
JMWH......... Journal Watch: Womens Health (SAUS)
JMWU......... Johannesburg Municipal Workers Union (SAUO)
JMX .... Jumbogroup Multiplex [Bell System]
JMY .... Jamesway Corp. (SAUO)
JMY .... Jimmy (ABBR)
J/my........... Joule per meter squared (SAUS)
JMYG.......... Jimmying (ABBR)
J Mysore Agr Exp Union... Journal. Mysore Agricultural and Experimental Union (journ.) (SAUS)
J Mysore Med Assoc... Journal. Mysore Medical Association (journ.) (SAUS)
J Mysore U Arts... Journal. Mysore University. Section A. Arts (journ.) (SAUS)
JMYUAP ...... Journal. Mysore University. Section B. Science (journ.) (SAUS)
JN................ Jam Nut (SAUS)
jn .... Jan Mayen [MARC country of publication code] [Library of Congress] (LCCP)
JN................ Jannock Ltd. [Toronto Stock Exchange symbol]
jn .... January (RION)
J-N............... Jet Navigation (AAG)
JN................ Jet Navigation Chart
JN ;.............. Jim's Neighbors (EA)
JN................ Job Number
Jn................ John [New Testament book]
JN................ Johnson Noise [Thermal noise, that made by a resistor at a temperature above absolute zero]
JN................ Join (MSA)
JN................ Journal Name [Online database field identifier]
JN................ Journal of Neurophysiology (SAUS)
JN................ Journal of Nutrition (SAUS)
Jn................ Juglans nigra [Eastern black walnut]
JN................ Junction
JN................ Junctional Nevus [Medicine] (MELL)
JN................ June (ROG)
JN................ Junior (ROG)
JN................ Justice Now [An association]
Jn................ King John [Shakespearean work]
JNA............. Januaria [Brazil] [Airport symbol] (AD)
JNA............. Jena Nomina Anatomica [Also, INA] [Anatomy]
JNA............. Jewish News Agency (BJA)

JNA............. John Nurminen, OY [Finland] [FAA designator] (FAAC)
JNA............. Joint Navy (IAA)
JNA............. Jordanian News Agency
JNA............. Jordan News Agency (SAUS)
JNA............. Journal of Nursing Administration (SAUO)
JNA............. Jump If Not Above [Computer science] (PCM)
JNA............. Junior Naval Airman [British military] (DMA)
JNA............. Northern Illinois University, De Kalb, IL [OCLC symbol] (OCLC)
JNA............. Yugoslav People's Army
JNABD......... Journal of Nuclear Agriculture and Biology (journ.) (SAUS)
JNAC........... Japan-North American Commission on Cooperative Mission (EA)
JNACC......... Joint Nuclear Accident Coordinating Center
JNADPI .... Japan National Assembly of Disabled Peoples' International (EAIO)
JNAE........... Jump If Not Above or Equal [Computer science] (PCM)
JNAF........... Japanese Navy Air Force
JNAF........... Joint Navy-Air Force
J Nagasaki Earth Sci Ass... Journal. Nagasaki Earth Science Associa- tion (journ.) (SAUS)
J Nagasaki Public Health Soc... Journal. Nagasaki Public Health Society (journ.) (SAUS)
J Nagoya Med Assoc... Journal. Nagoya Medical Association (journ.) (SAUS)
J Nagoy City Univ Med Ass... Journal. Nagoya City University Medical Association (journ.) (SAUS)
J Nakanihon Automot Jr Coll... Journal. Nakanihon Automotive Junior College (journ.) (SAUS)
JNALA......... Journal of the New African Literature and the Arts (journ.) (SAUS)
JNAM.......... Junior Naval Air Mechanic [British military] (DMA)
J Nanjing Agric Coll... Journal. Nanjing Agricultural College (journ.) (SAUS)
J Nanjing Coll Pharm... Journal. Nanjing College of Pharmacy (journ.) (SAUS)
J Nanjing Inst For... Journal. Nanjing Institute of Forestry (journ.) (SAUS)
J Nanjing Inst Technol... Journal. Nanjing Institute of Technology (journ.) (SAUS)
J Nanjing Technol Coll For Prod... Journal. Nanjing Technological College of Forest Produds (journ.) (SAUS)
J Nanjing Univ Nat Sci Ed... Journal. Nanjing University. Natural Science Edition (journ.) (SAUS)
J Nara Gakugei Univ... Journal. Nara Gakugei University (journ.) (SAUS)
J Nara Gakugei Univ Nat Sci... Journal. Nara Gakugei University. Natural Science (journ.) (SAUS)
JNA Referees Bank... Journal. National Association of Referees in Bankruptcy [A publication] (DLA)
J Narr Tech... Journal of Narrative Technique (journ.) (SAUS)
J Natal Zulu Hist... Journal of Natal and Zulu History (journ.) (SAUS)
J Nat Chiao Tung Univ... National Chiao Tung University (SAUO)
J Nating Inst Technol... Journal of Nating Institute of Technology (journ.) (SAUS)
J Nat Inst Hospitl Adm... Journal. National Institute of Hospital Administration (journ.) (SAUS)
J Nat Inst Soc Sci... Journal. National Institute of Social Sciences (journ.) (SAUS)
J Natl Acad Sci... Journal. National Academy of Sciences (journ.) (SAUS)
J Natl Analg Soc... Journal. National Analgesia Society (journ.) (SAUS)
J Natl Assoc Hosp Dev... Journal. National Association for Hospital Development (journ.) (SAUS)
J Natl Assoc Priv Psychiatr Hosp... Journal. National Association of Private Psychiatric Hospitals (journ.) (SAUS)
J Natl Cancer Inst... Journal of the National Cancer Institute (SAUO)
J Natl Cancer Inst... Journal of the National Cancer Institute (journ.) (SAUS)
J Natl Chem Lab Ind... Journal of the National Chemical Laboratory for Industry (journ.) (SAUS)
J Natl Chiao Tung Univ... Journal. National Chiao Tung University (journ.) (SAUS)
J Natl Def Med Coll... Journal. National Defense Medical College (journ.) (SAUS)
J Natl Inst Agric Bot... Journal. Nabonal Institute of Agricultural Botany (journ.) (SAUS)
J Natl Inst Pers Res S Afr CSIR... Journal. National Institute for Personnel Research. South African Council for Scientific and Industrial Research (journ.) (SAUS)
J Natl Med Ass... Journal. National Medical Association (journ.) (SAUS)
J Natl Med Assoc... Journal of the National Medical Association (SAUO)
J Natl Med Assoc... Journal of the National Medical Association (journ.) (SAUS)
J Natl Res Counc Thail... Journal of the National Research Council of Thailand (journ.) (SAUS)
J Natl Tech Assoc... Journal of the National Technical Asso- ciation (journ.) (SAUS)
J Natn Cancer Inst... Journal. National Cancer Institute (journ.) (SAUS)
J Natn Inst Agric Bot... Journal. National Institute of Agricultural Botany (journ.) (SAUS)
J Nat Prod... Journal of Natural Products (journ.) (SAUS)
J Nat Rubber Res... Journal of Natural Rubber Research (journ.) (SAUS)
J Nat Sci ..... Jeju University Journal. Natural Sciences (journ.) (SAUS)
J Nat Sci and Math... Journal of National Science and Mathematics (journ.) (SAUS)
J Nat Sci Coll Gen Stud Seoul Natl Univ... Journal of Natural Sciences. College of General Studies. Seoul National University (journ.) (SAUS)
J Nat Sci Res Inst Yonsei Univ... Journal. Natural Science Research Institute. Yonsei University (journ.) (SAUS)
J Nat Sci Soc Ichimura Gakuen J Coll... Journal. Natural Scientific Society. Ichimura Gakuen Junior College (journ.) (SAUS)
J Nat Sci Yeungnam Univ... Journal of Natural Sciences. Yeungnam University (journ.) (SAUS)
JNAU .... Jawaharlal Nehru Agricultural University [India] (BUAC)
J Naut Soc Jpn... Journal. Nautical Society of Japan (journ.) (SAUS)
J Navig .... Journal of Navigation (journ.) (SAUS)
JNB............. Johannesburg [South Africa] [Airport symbol] (OAG)
JNB............. Joinable (ABBR)
JNB............. Jump If Not Below [Computer science] (PCM)
JNBE........... Jump If Not Below or Equal [Computer science] (PCM)
JNBIA.......... Journal. Newark Beth Israel Hospital (journ.) (SAUS)
JNBK........... Jefferson National Bank (SAUO)
JNBMDW ..... Journal. New Brunswick Museum (journ.) (SAUS)

JNBNA........ Journal of National Black Nurses Association (SAUO)
JNBNA........ Journal of National Black Nurses Association (journ.) (SAUS)
JNC............. Jet Navigation Chart
JNC............. John Nuveen 'A' [NYSE symbol] (TTSB)
JNC............. Joint National Council (AIE)
JNC............. Joint Negotiating Committee (SAUO)
JNC............. Joint Negotiating Council [British] (DCTA)
JNC............. Journal. National Cancer Institute (SAUS)
JNC............. Journal of the National Cancer Institute (SAUO)
JNC............. Jump If No Carry [Computer science] (PCM)
JNC............. Jump on No Carry (SAUS)
JNC............. Junction (ADA)
JNC............. Nuveen [John] & Co. [NYSE symbol] (SPSG)
JNCA.......... Junior Naval Cadets of America (SAUO)
JNCC.......... Joint National Conciliation Committee (SAUO)
JNCC.......... Joint Nature Conservation Committee (BUAC)
JNCC.......... Joint Nuclear Control Commission (SAUO)
JNCC.......... Junior Naval Command Course
J NC Dent Soc... Journal. North Carolina Dental Society (journ.) (SAUS)
JNCG.......... Japan Nuclear Codes Group
JNChBAS ..... Journal of the North China Branch of the Royal Asiatic Society (SAUO)
Jn Chem Q... Japan Chemical Quarterly (journ.) (SAUS)
J N Ch RAS... Journal. North China Branch. Royal Asiatic Society (journ.) (SAUS)
JNCI............. Jounal of the National Cancer Institute (SAUO)
JNCIMC....... Japanese National Committee of the International Music Council (EAIO)
JNCL........... Joint National Committee for Languages (EA)
JNCLA......... Journal. National Chemical Laboratory for Industry (journ.) (SAUS)
JNCN .... Journal of Neuropsychiatry and Clinical Neurosciences (journ.) (SAUS)
JNCN .... Junction (ABBR)
JNCO........... Junior Non-Commissioned Officer [British military] (DMA)
JNCP........... Justification for Non-Competitive Procurement (GFGA)
JNCQ .... Journal of Nursing Care Quality (journ.) (SAUS)
JNC Referees Bank... Journal. National Conference of Referees in Bankruptcy [A publication] (DLA)
J NC Sect Am Water Works Assoc NC Water PollutConhol Assoc... Journal. North Carolina Section of the American Water Works Association and North Carolina Water Pollution Control Association (journ.) (SAUS)
JNCUD......... Journal of Natural Science. Chonnam Natianal University (journ.) (SAUS)
JNCUR........ Juncture (ABBR)
JNCYA........ Journal of Neurocytology (journ.) (SAUS)
JND............. Air East Africa Ltd. [Kenya] [FAA designator] (FAAC)
JND............. Joined (ABBR)
JND............. Just Noticeable Difference [Psychology]
jnd............. Just-Noticeable Difference (DIPS)
JND............. Just-Noticeable Distortion (DIPS)
JNDC........... Juvenile Narcotics Division (SAUO)
JNDC........... Jamaica National Dance Company (SAUO)
JNDI........... Java Naming and Directory Interface (VLIE)
J NDI .... Journal of Nondestructive Inspection (journ.) (SAUS)
JNDR........... Joinder (ABBR)
JNDRA......... Journal of New Drugs (journ.) (SAUS)
JNDSPI........ Java Naming and Directory Service Provider Interface (SAUS)
JNE............. Ja Niin Edespain [And So On] [Finnish]
JNE............. Journal of Negro Education [A publication] (BRI)
JNE............. Journal of Nursing Education (journ.) (SAUS)
JNE............. Jump Not Equal [Computer science] (OA)
JNE............. June (ABBR)
J Nebr Dent Assoc... Journal. Nebraska Dental Association (journ.) (SAUS)
JNEC........... Jamaica National Export Corp. (BUAC)
JNEC........... Jamaican National Export Corp. (SAUS)
J Ne Exp Ne... Journal of Neuropathology and Experimental Neurology (journ.) (SAUS)
JNELDA....... Journal of Nutrition for the Elderly (journ.) (SAUS)
JNEMA........ Jefferson National Expansion Memorial Association (SAUO)
J Nematol... Journal of Nematology (journ.) (SAUS)
J Ne Ne Psy... Journal of Neurology, Neurosurgery and Psychiatry (journ.) (SAUS)
J N Engl Water Pollut Control Assoc... Journal. New England Water Pollution Control Association (journ.) (SAUS)
J Nepal Chem Soc... Journal. Nepal Chemical Society (journ.) (SAUS)
J Nephrol Nurs... Journal of Nephrology Nursing (journ.) (SAUS)
J Nerv Ment Disord... Journal of Nervous and Mental Disorder (journ.) (SAUS)
JNES........... Journal of Near Eastern Studies (journ.) (SAUS)
JNET........... Japanese Network (SAUO)
J Neumpsychiatr Suppl... Journal of Neuropsychiatry. Supplement (journ.) (SAUS)
J Neural Transm Gen Sect... Journal of Neural Transmission. General Section (journ.) (SAUS)
J Neural Transm Park Dis Dement Sect... Journal of Neural Transmission. Parkinsons Disease and Dementia Section (journ.) (SAUS)
J Neural Transm Suppl... Journal of Neural Transmission. Supplementum (journ.) (SAUS)
J Neural Transplant Plast... Journal of Neural Transplantation and Plasticity (journ.) (SAUS)
J Neurobiol... Journal of Neurobiology (journ.) (SAUS)
J Neurochem... Journal of Neurochemistry (journ.) (SAUS)
J Neuroendocrinol... Journal of Neuroendocrinology (journ.) (SAUS)
J Neuroimaging... Journal of Neuroimaging (journ.) (SAUS)
J Neurol Soc Indi... Journal. Neurological Society of India (journ.) (SAUS)
J Neuro-Oncol... Journal of Neuro-Oncology (journ.) (SAUS)
J Neuroophthalmol... Journal of Neuro-Ophthalmology (journ.) (SAUS)

J Neuropsychiatry Clin Neurosci... Journal of Neuropsychiatry and Clinical Neurosciences (journ.) (SAUS)
J Neuroradiol... Journal of Neuroradiology (journ.) (SAUS)
J Neurosci Methods... Journal of Neuroscience Methods (journ.) (SAUS)
J Neurosci Nurs... Journal of Neuroscience Nursing (journ.) (SAUS)
J Neurosci Res... Journal of Neuroscience Research (journ.) (SAUS)
J Neurosurg... Journal of Neurosurgery (journ.) (SAUS)
J Neurosurg Anesthesiol... Journal of Neurosurgical Anesthesiology (journ.) (SAUS)
J Neurosurg Nurs... Journal of Neurosurgical Nursing (journ.) (SAUS)
J Neurotrauma... Journal of Neurotrauma (journ.) (SAUS)
J Neurovirol... Journal of Neurovirology (journ.) (SAUS)
J Newark Beth Isr Med Cent... Journal. Newark Beth Israel Medical Center (journ.) (SAUS)
J Newcastle Sch Arts... Newcastle School of Arts (SAUS)
J New Drugs... Journal of New Drugs (journ.) (SAUS)
J New Gener Comput Syst... Journal of New Generation Computer Systems (journ.) (SAUS)
J New Rem Clin... Journal of New Remedies and Clinics (journ.) (SAUS)
J New World Archaeol... Journal of New World Archaeology (journ.) (SAUS)
JNF............. Japan Nuclear Fuel Co. (BUAC)
JNF............. Jewish National Fund (EA)
JNF............. Junior Non-Fiction [Library science] (TELE)
JNFA............ Jewish National Fund of Australia
JNFA............ Journal of Numismatic Fine Arts (journ.) (SAUS)
JNFC............ Joint National Frequency Committee (SAUO)
JNFC............ Juice Newton Fan Club (EA)
JNFI............ Japan's Nuclear Fuel Industries (BUAC)
JNG............. [The] Jews in NAZI Germany; A Handbook of Facts Regarding Their Present Situation [A publication] (BJA)
JNG............. Joining [Also, J]
JNG............. Jump if Not Greater (VLIE)
JNGE............ Jump if Not Greater or Equal (VLIE)
JNGL............ Jonquil (ABBR)
JNGL............ Jungle (ABBR)
JNH............. Journal of Negro History [A publication] (GEAB)
JNHAC .... Jewish National Home for Asthmatic Children
J NH Dent Soc... Journal. New Hampshire Dental Society (journ.) (SAUS)
JNI............. Java Native Interface [Computer science] (IGQR)
JNI............. Journal of the Nautical Institute (journ.) (SAUS)
JNIB........... Jamaica National Investment Bank (BUAC)
JNICT........... National Board of Scientific and Technical Research Portugal (SAUO)
J Nigeria Assoc Dent Stud... Journal. Nigeria Association of Dental Students (journ.) (SAUS)
J Nigerian Inst Oil Palm Res... Journal. Nigerian Institute for Oil Palm Research (journ.) (SAUS)
J Nihon Univ Med Ass... Journal. Nihon University Medical Association (journ.) (SAUS)
J Nihon Univ Sch Dent... Journal. Nihon University School of Dentistry (journ.) (SAUS)
J Nihon Univ Sch Dent... Journal of Nihon University School of Dentistry (SAUO)
J Nihon Univ Sch Dent... Journal of Nihon University School of Dentistry (journ.) (SAUS)
J Niigata Agric Exp Shi... Journal. Niigata Agricultural Experiment Station (journ.) (SAUS)
JNIP............ Jamaica National Investment Promotions (BUAC)
JNIP............ Jamaican National Investment Promotion (SAUS)
J Nippon Dent Coll... Journal. Nippon Dental College (journ.) (SAUS)
J Nippon UnivSch Dent... Journal. Nippon University School of Dentistry (journ.) (SAUS)
JNIPRMSI.... Japan. National Institute of Polar Research. Memoirs. Special Issue (journ.) (SAUS)
J Nissei Hosp... Journal. Nissei Hospital (journ.) (SAUS)
JNJ............. Johnson & Johnson [NYSE symbol] (SPSG)
JNJ............. Journal of Nursing Jocularity (journ.) (SAUS)
J NJ Dent Assoc... Journal. New Jersey Dental Association (journ.) (SAUS)
J NJ Dent Hyg Assoc... Journal. New Jersey Dental Hygienists Association (journ.) (SAUS)
J NJ State Dent Soc... Journal. New Jersey State Dental Society (journ.) (SAUS)
J NJ State Dent Soc... Journal of the New Jersey State Dental Society (SAUO)
J N J State Dent Soc... Journal of the New Jersey State Dental Society (journ.) (SAUS)
JNKD .... Junked (ABBR)
JNKG .... Junking (ABBR)
JNKI........... Junkie (ABBR)
JNKMA........ Junkman (ABBR)
JNKT........... Junket (ABBR)
JNKTD .... Junketed (ABBR)
JNKTG .... Junketing (ABBR)
JNKTR .... Junketer (ABBR)
JNL............. Atchison, KS [Location identifier] [FAA] (FAAL)
JNL............. Japanese National Laboratory
JNL............. Jefferson National Life Insurance Co. (EFIS)
JNL............. Jenolan [Australia] [Seismograph station code, US Geological Survey] (SEIS)
JNL............. Journal
JNL............. Jump Not Last (SAUS)
JNLA........... Japan National Laboratory Accreditation System (SAUO)
Jnl Asn Stud... Journal of Asian Studies (journ.) (SAUS)
Jnl Basque Stud... Journal of Basque Studies (journ.) (SAUS)
Jnl Constr Div Am Soc Civ Eng... Journal. Construction Division. American Society of Civil Engineers (journ.) (SAUS)
Jnl Consuel Psych... Journal of Counseling Psychology (journ.) (SAUS)
Jnl Diet Home Ec... Journal of Dietetics and Home Economics (journ.) (SAUS)
JNLE........... Jump if Not Less or Equal (SAUO)
Jnl Engl Ger Philol... Journal of English and Germanic Philology (journ.) (SAUS)

Jnl Gen Ed... Journal of General Education (journ.) (SAUS)
Jnl Heptol.... Journal of Hepatology (journ.) (SAUS)
Jnl Higher Ed... Journal of Higher Education (journ.) (SAUS)
Jnl Ital Ling... Journal of Italian Linguistics (journ.) (SAUS)
Jnl Lib Hist... Journal of Library History (journ.) (SAUS)
Jnl Marketing... Journal of Marketing (journ.) (SAUS)
Jnl Mol Appl Genet... Journal of Molecular and Applied Genetics (journ.) (SAUS)
Jnl Negro Ed... Journal of Negro Education (journ.) (SAUS)
Jnl Negro Hist... Journal of Negro History (journ.) (SAUS)
JNLNO .... Journal Number (SAUS)
Jnl Ocular Ther Surg... Journal of Ocular Therapy and Surgery (journ.) (SAUS)
Jnl of Archtl Education... Journal of Architectural Education (journ.) (SAUS)
Jnl of Archtl Research... Journal of Architectural Research (journ.) (SAUS)
Jnl of Canadian Art History... Journal of Canadian Art History (journ.) (SAUS)
Jnl of Environmental Psychology... Journal of Environmental Psychology (journ.) (SAUS)
Jnl Orthomol Psych... Journal of Orthomolecular Psychiatry (journ.) (SAUS)
Jnl Polit Econ... Journal of Political Economy (journ.) (SAUS)
Jnl Politics... Journal of Politics (journ.) (SAUS)
JNLS .... Journals (ADA)
JNLST .... Journalist
JNM .... JNM. Journal of Nuclear Medicine (journ.) (SAUS)
JNM .... Journal of Nuclear Medicine (journ.) (SAUS)
JNMA.......... Journal of the National Medical Association (SAUO)
JNMA.......... Journal of the National Medical Association (journ.) (SAUS)
JNMA.......... Journal of the Nepal Medical Association (journ.) (SAUS)
JNMED........ Journal of Neuroscience Methods (journ.) (SAUS)
JNMM .... Journal of Nuclear Materials Management (journ.) (SAUS)
JNMM .... Journal of the Institute of Nuclear Materials Management (journ.) (SAUS)
JNMR.......... Joint National Media Research [Database producer]
JNMS .... Journal of the Neuromusculoskeletal System (SAUO)
JNMS .... Journal of the Neuromusculoskeletal System (journ.) (SAUS)
JNMSD ...... Journal of Nuclear Medicine and Allied Sciences (journ.) (SAUS)
JNMT .... Journal of Nuclear Medicine Technology (SAUO)
JNMT .... Journal of Nuclear Medicine Technology (journ.) (SAUS)
JNMTA........ Journal of Nonmetals (journ.) (SAUS)
JNN .... Japan News Network (SAUO)
JNN .... Journal of Neonatal Nursing (journ.) (SAUS)
JNND .... Just Not Noticeable Difference (MSA)
JNNP .... Journal of Neurology, Neurosurgery, & Psychiatry (SAUS)
JNNPA........ Journal of Neurology, Neurosurgery and Psychiatry (journ.) (SAUS)
JNNS .... Japanese Neural Network Society (BUAC)
JNO............ Journal of Neuro-Oncology (journ.) (SAUS)
JNO............ Jump if No Overflow (VLIE)
JNOC .... Japan National Oil Corp. (BUAC)
JNODC .... Japanese National Oceanographic Data Center (SAUO)
JNODC .... Japanese National Oceanographic Data Center (or Centre) (SAUS)
J Non-Desh Insp... Journal of Non-Destructive Inpesction (journ.) (SAUS)
J Nondestr Eval... Journal of Nondestructive Evaluation (journ.) (SAUS)
J Non-Equilib Thermodyn... Journal of Non-Equilibrium Thermodynamics (journ.) (SAUS)
J Nonlinear Sci... Journal of Nonlinear Science (journ.) (SAUS)
J Nonmet..... Journal of Nonmetals (journ.) (SAUS)
J Non-Newtonian Fluid Mech... Journal of Non-Newtonian Fluid Mechanics (journ.) (SAUS)
J Nonverbal Behav... Journal of Nonverbal Behavior (journ.) (SAUS)
J Northampton Mus... Journal. Northampton Museum and Art Gallery (journ.) (SAUS)
J Northamptonshire Natur Hist Soc Field Club... Journal. Northamptonshire Natural History Society and Field Club (journ.) (SAUS)
J Northeast Asian Studies... Journal of Northeast Asian Studies (journ.) (SAUS)
J Northeast Univ Technol... Journal of Northeast University of Technology (journ.) (SAUS)
J Northwest Atl Fish Sci... Journal of Northwest Atlantic Fishery Science (journ.) (SAUS)
J Northwest Univ Nt Sci Ed... Journal. Northwest University. Natural Science Edition (journ.) (SAUS)
J Norw Med Ass... Journal. Norwegian Medical Association (journ.) (SAUS)
JNOV .... Judgment Not Withstanding Verdict (HGAA)
JNP............. Jasper National Park [Alberta] [Airport symbol] (AD)
JNP............. Joint Nuclear Plot (CINC)
JNP............. Jump if No Parity (SAUO)
JNP............. Newport Beach, CA [Location identifier] [FAA] (FAAL)
J NPA .... Journal. Nepal Pharmautical Association (journ.) (SAUS)
JNPC........... Joint Nuclear Power Committee (SAUO)
JNPE........... Joint Nuclear Planning Element (MCD)
JNPGC .... Japan Nuclear Power Generation Corp. (SAUS)
JNPGC .... Japan Nuclear Power Generation Corporation (SAUO)
JNPI........... Jetevator Null Position Indicator
JNPR .... Juniper (ABBR)
JNPR .... Juniper Networks [NASDAQ symbol] (SG)
JNPRD .... Journal of Natural Products (journ.) (SAUS)
JNPT .... Johnson Noise Power Thermometer (SAUS)
JNR............. Hamilton Aeroservices (SAUS)
JNR............. Jammer-to-Noise Ratio (CCCA)
JNR............. Japanesae National Railways (BARN)
JNR............. Japan National Railways (SAUO)
JNR............. Joiner (ABBR)
JNR............. June Resources, Inc. [Vancouver Stock Exchange symbol]
JNR............. Junior (EY)
JNR............. Unalakleet, AK [Location identifier] [FAA] (FAAL)
JNRC .... Joint Nuclear Research Center [EURATOM]
JNRI........... Joint Nuclear Research Institute [Former USSR]

JNRM.......... Journal of Natural Resources Management and Interdisciplinary Studies (journ.) (SAUS)
JNRM.......... Journal of Nursing Risk Management (SAUO)
JNROTC ..... Junior Naval Reserve Officer Training Corps
JNRREQ ...... Journal of Natural Rubber Research (journ.) (SAUS)
Jnr Tech ..... Junior Technician (SAUS)
JNS............ Chic by HIS, Inc. [NYSE symbol] (SPSG)
JNS............ International Graduate School, St. Louis, MO [OCLC symbol] (OCLC)
JNS............ Jet Noise Survey
JNS............ Jugoslovenska Nacionalna Stranka [Yugoslav National Party] [Political party] (PPE)
JNS............ Jump if No Sign (VLIE)
JNS............ Justification for New Start (SAUS)
JNS............ Just Noticeable Shift (PDAA)
JNS............ Minneapolis, MN [Location identifier] [FAA] (FAAL)
JNSC.......... Japanese Nuclear Ship Corp. (SAUS)
JNSC.......... Japan Nuclear Safety Commission (BUAC)
JNSC.......... Joint Navigation Satellite Committee
JNSCA .... Journal of the Neurological Sciences (journ.) (SAUS)
JNSD .... Journal of Nurses in Staff Development (SAUO)
JNSD .... Journal of Nursing Staff Development (journ.) (SAUS)
JNSI.......... Journal. Numismatic Society of India (journ.) (SAUS)
JNSMP .... Journal Numismatic Society of Madhya Pradesh (journ.) (SAUS)
JNSNA .... Journal of Neurosurgical Nursing (journ.) (SAUS)
JNSP.......... Joint WHO/UNICEF Nutrition Support Programme (SAUO)
Jn Spectros Co Appl Notes... Japan Spectroscopic Company. Application Notes (SAUO)
Jn Spectros Co Appl Notes... Japan Spectroscopic Company. Application Notes (journ.) (SAUS)
JNSRDA...... Japan Nuclear Ship Research and Development Agency (BUAC)
JNSSB .... Journal of Neurosurgical Sciences (journ.) (SAUS)
JNSV.......... Jones &. Vining, Inc. (SAUO)
J NSW Council for Mentally Handicapped... Journal. New Soulh Wales Council for the Mentally Handicapped (journ.) (SAUS)
JNT .... Jaunt (ABBR)
JNT .... Java Network Technology (SAUS)
JNT .... Joint
JNT .... Joint Network Scheme [British]
JNT .... Joint Network Team [British] (NITA)
JNT .... Jonathan [Italy] [FAA designator] (FAAC)
JNT .... Journal of Narrative Technique [A publication] (ANEX)
JNT .... Journal of Narrative Technique (journ.) (SAUS)
JNT .... Junction (ABBR)
JNT .... Juncture (ABBR)
JNT .... New York, NY [Location identifier] [FAA] (FAAL)
JNTA.......... Japan National Tourist Association (BUAC)
JNTAD .... Journal. National Technical Association (journ.) (SAUS)
JNTD.......... Jointed (ABBR)
JNTINS ...... Jauntiness (ABBR)
JNTIR......... Jauntier (ABBR)
JNTLY........ Jauntily (ABBR)
JNTLY........ Jointly (ABBR)
JNTO.......... Japan National Tourist Office (SAUO)
JNTO.......... Japan National Tourist Organization (EA)
JNTR.......... Janitor (ABBR)
JNTR.......... Jointer (ABBR)
JNTST........ Jauntiest (ABBR)
JNT STK CO... Joint Stock Co. (DLA)
JNT STK CO... Joint Stock Company (SAUO)
JNTUR........ Jointure (ABBR)
JNTURD....... Jointured (ABBR)
JNTURG....... Jointuring (ABBR)
JNT VEN ..... Joint Venture [Legal term] (DLA)
JNTY.......... Jaunty (ABBR)
JNTY.......... Jointly (ABBR)
JNU............ Jiangnan University [China] (BUAC)
JNU............ Jiangxi Normal University [China] (BUAC)
JNU............ Juneau [Alaska] [Airport symbol] (OAG)
JNU............ Juneau, AK [Location identifier] [FAA] (FAAL)
JNU............ Universal Jet Navigation Charts [Air Force]
JNU............ Universal Set Navigation Charts (SAUS)
JNUCA .... Journal of Nuclear Energy (journ.) (SAUS)
J Nucl Agric Biol... Journal of Nuclear Agriculture and Biology (journ.) (SAUS)
J Nucl Energy Part A... Journal of Nuclear Energy. Part A. Reactor Science (journ.) (SAUS)
J Nucl Energy Part B... Journal of Nuclear Energy. Part B. Reactor Technology (journ.) (SAUS)
J Nucl Energy Part C... Journal of Nuclear Energy. Part C. Plasma Physics, Acceleralors, Thermonuclear Research (journ.) (SAUS)
J Nucl Energy Parts A/B... Journal of Nuclear Energy. Parts A/B. Reactor Science and Technology (journ.) (SAUS)
J Nucl Mater Manage... Journal of Nuclear Materials Management (journ.) (SAUS)
J Nucl Med Allied Sci... Journal of Nuclear Medicine and Allied Sciences (journ.) (SAUS)
J Nucl Med Pam... Journal of Nuclear Medicine. Pamphlet (journ.) (SAUS)
J Nucl Med Suppl... Journal of Nuclear Medicine. Supplement (journ.) (SAUS)
J Nucl Med Technol... Journal of Nuclear Medicine Technology (journ.) (SAUS)
JNUL.......... Jewish National and University Library
J Number Theory... Journal of Number Theory (journ.) (SAUS)
J Nurs Care... Journal of Nursing Care (journ.) (SAUS)
J Nurs Care Qual... Journal of Nursing Care Quality (journ.) (SAUS)
J Nurs Ed..... Journal of Nursery Education (journ.) (SAUS)
J Nurse Midwifery... Journal of Nurse-Midwifery (journ.) (SAUS)
J Nurs Ethics... Journal of Nursing Ethics (journ.) (SAUS)
J Nurs Hist... Journal of Nursing History (journ.) (SAUS)

J Nurs Manag...   Journal of Nursing Management (journ.)   (SAUS)
J Nurs Meas...   Journal of Nursing Measurement (journ.)   (SAUS)
J Nurs Staff Dev...   Journal of Nursing Staff Development (journ.)   (SAUS)
J Nutr ....   Journal of Nutrition (journ.)   (SAUS)
J Nutr Ass ...   Journal of Nutritional Assessment (journ.)   (SAUS)
J Nutr Biochem...   Journal of Nutritional Biochemistry (journ.)   (SAUS)
J Nutr Diet..   Journal of Nutrition and Dietetics (journ.)   (SAUS)
J Nutr Educ...   Journal of Nutrition Education (journ.)   (SAUS)
J Nutr Elderly...   Journal of Nutrition for the Elderly (journ.)   (SAUS)
J Nutr Growth Cancer...   Journal of Nutrition, Growth and Cancer (journ.)   (SAUS)
J Nutr Sci...   Journal of Nutritional Sciences (journ.)   (SAUS)
J Nutr Supl...   Journal of Nutrition. Supplement (journ.)   (SAUS)
JNuveen ......   Nuveen [John] Co. [Associated Press]   (SAG)
JNVBDV ....   Journal of Nonverbal Behavior (journ.)   (SAUS)
JNVOA ....   Jewish Nazi Victims Organization of America   (EA)
JNW.............   Joint Committee on New Weapons and Equipment
JNW.............   Joint Nuclear Research Institute   (SAUS)
JNW.............   Newport, OR [Location identifier] [FAA]   (FAAL)
JNWEB.........   Joint New Weapons and Equipment Board   (ACAE)
JNWOC ....   Joint Warfare Operations Center
JNWP.........   Joint Numerical Weather Prediction   (SAUS)
JNWP.........   Joint Numerical Weather Prediction Unit   (IAA)
JNWPS ....   Joint Nuclear Weapons Publication Systems   (MCD)
JNWPU ....   Joint Numerical Weather Prediction Unit
JNW Semi ...   Journal of the Northwest Semitic Languages (journ.)   (SAUS)
J Nw SL......   Journal of the Northwest Semitic Languages (journ.)   (SAUS)
JNX.............   Jackson [Michigan] [Airport symbol]   (AD)
JNY.............   January   (ABBR)
JNY.............   Jenney Beechcraft, Inc. [ICAO designator]   (FAAC)
JNY.............   Jones Apparel Group [NYSE symbol]   (SPSG)
JNY State Nurses Ass...   Journal. New York State Nurses Association (journ.)   (SAUS)
JNY State Sch Nurse Teach Assoc...   Journal. New York State School Nurse Teachers Association (journ.)   (SAUS)
JNZ.............   Jennings, LA [Location identifier] [FAA]   (FAAL)
JNZ.............   Jewelers of New Zealand   (SAUO)
JNZ.............   Jump if Not Zero   (VLIE)
JNZ.............   Jump on Not Zero [Computer science]   (PCM)
JNZ Ass Bacteriol...   Journal. New Zealand Association of Bacteriologists (journ.)   (SAUS)
JNZ Fed Hist S...   Journal. New Zealand Federation of Historical Societies (journ.)   (SAUS)
JNZ Inst Chem...   Journal. New Zealand Institute of Chemistry (journ.)   (SAUS)
JNZ Inst Med Lab Technol...   Journal. New Zealand Institute of Medical Laboratory Technology (journ.)   (SAUS)
JNZ Soc Periodontol...   Journal. New Zealand Society of Periodontology (journ.)   (SAUS)
JO.............   Holiday Airlines [ICAO designator]   (AD)
JO.............   Jewish Orphanage   (SAUO)
JO.............   Job Order
Jo.............   Joel [Old Testament book]   (BJA)
JO.............   Jogging Operation   (SAUS)
Jo.............   Johannes Faventius [Deceased circa 1187] [Authority cited in pre-1607 legal work]   (DSA)
JO.............   Joint Organization
JO.............   Joint Ownership [Business term]
Jo.............   Jones' Irish Exchequer Reports [A publication]   (DLA)
JO.............   Jordan [ANSI two-letter standard code]   (CNC)
jo.............   Jordan [MARC country of publication code] [Library of Congress]   (LCCP)
Jo.............   Joseph   (BJA)
JO.............   Journalist [Navy rating]
JO.............   Journal Officiel des Communautes Europeennes [Official Journal of the European Communities] [A publication]   (ILCA)
JO.............   Judicial Officer [Department of Agriculture]   (GFGA)
JO.............   Jump Order   (SAUS)
JO.............   Junction Office [Telecommunications]   (OA)
JO.............   Junior Officer
JO.............   Jupiter Orbiter [NASA]
JO.............   Juvenile Offenders
JO.............   Senior Chief Journalist   (SAUS)
JO1.............   Journalist, First Class [Navy rating]
JO2.............   Journalist, Second Class [Navy rating]
JO3.............   Journalist, Third Class [Navy rating]
JOA.............   Joint Objective Agreement   (SAUS)
JOA.............   Joint Objective Area   (NVT)
JOA.............   Joint Oceanographic Assembly [Marine science]   (MSC)
JOA.............   Joint Operating Agency   (SAUO)
JOA.............   Joint Operating Agreement
JOA .....   Joint Operations Area   (COE)
JOABAW .....   Journal of Applied Behavior Analysis (journ.)   (SAUS)
Joa Bologne...   Johannes Bolognetus [Deceased, 1575] [Authority cited in pre-1607 legal work]   (DSA)
JOAC.............   Joachim Bancorp [NASDAQ symbol]   (TTSB)
JOAC.............   Joachim Bancorp, Inc. [NASDAQ symbol]   (SAG)
JOAC.............   Junior Officers Advisory Council   (SAUO)
Joachim.......   Joachim Bancorp, Inc. [Associated Press]   (SAG)
JOAD ....   Journal. American Dietetic Association (journ.)   (SAUS)
JOAD ....   Junior Olympic Archery Development
JOADEB ......   Journal of Adolescence (journ.)   (SAUS)
JOAEEB.......   Journal of Applied Entomology (journ.)   (SAUS)
JOAG ....   Juvenile Open Angle Glaucoma [Ophthalmology]
JO AI ....   Jahreshefte des Oesterreichischen Archaeologischen Instituts in Wien [A publication]   (OCD)

Joa Imo ......   Johannes de Imola [Deceased, 1436] [Authority cited in pre-1607 legal work]   (DSA)
JOALAS........   Journal of Allergy (journ.)   (SAUS)
JOAN ....   Journal of Applied Nutrition (journ.)   (SAUS)
Joan Andr....   Johannes Andreae [Deceased, 1348] [Authority cited in pre-1607 legal work]   (DSA)
JOANAY ......   Journal of Anatomy (journ.)   (SAUS)
Joan Bapt Villalob...   Johannes Baptista Villalobos [Authority cited in pre-1607 legal work]   (DSA)
Joan Bologne...   Johannes Bolognetus [Deceased, 1575] [Authority cited in pre-1607 legal work]   (DSA)
Joan Borcholt...   Johannes Borcholten [Deceased, 1593] [Authority cited in pre-1607 legal work]   (DSA)
Jo & Car......   Jones and Cary's Irish Exchequer Reports [1838-39] [A publication]   (DLA)
Joan de Ces...   Johannes de Cesena [Flourished, 13th century] [Authority cited in pre-1607 legal work]   (DSA)
Joan de Lign...   Johannes de Lignano [Deceased, 1383] [Authority cited in pre-1607 legal work]   (DSA)
Jo & La T...   Jones and La Touche's Irish Chancery Reports [A publication]   (DLA)
JOANDR.......   Journal of Andrology (journ.)   (SAUS)
Joan Fan ...   Johannes Faventius [Deceased circa 1187] [Authority cited in pre-1607 legal work]   (DSA)
Joan Mon ....   Johannes Monachus [Deceased, 1313] [Authority cited in pre-1607 legal work]   (DSA)
Joann.........   Johannes Teutonicus [Deceased circa 1246] [Authority cited in pre-1607 legal work]   (DSA)
Joannes........   Johannes Franciscus Pavinus [Flourished, 1448-82] [Authority cited in pre-1607 legal work]   (DSA)
Joann Teut...   Johannes Teutonicus [Deceased, 1246] [Authority cited in pre-1607 legal work]   (DSA)
Joan Vaud ...   Johannes Vaudus [Flourished, 16th century] [Authority cited in pre-1607 legal work]   (DSA)
JOAP............   Joint Oil Analysis Program [Military]   (NVT)
JOAP............   Journal of Applied Psychology (journ.)   (SAUS)
JOAP-CG......   Joint Oil Analysis Program Coordinating Group   (MCD)
JOAP-TSC......   Joint Oil Analysis Program Technical Support Center   (MCD)
JOAT............   Jack Of All Trades   (SAUS)
JOB.............   Aerojobeni SA de CV [Mexico] [ICAO designator]   (FAAC)
JOB.............   General Employment Enterprises, Inc. [AMEX symbol]   (SPSG)
JOB.............   Genl Employ Enterpr [AMEX symbol]   (TTSB)
JOB.............   Jobber
Jo B ....   Johannes Bassianus [Flourished, 12th century] [Authority cited in pre-1607 legal work]   (DSA)
JOB.............   Journal of Business Administration (journ.)   (SAUS)
JOB.............   Journal of Occupational Behaviour (journ.)   (SAUS)
JOB.............   Judicial Officers Bulletin [A publication]
JOB.............   Just One Break   (EA)
JOBAPT........   John the Baptist
JOBCAT.......   Job Catalog   (HGAA)
JOBD............   Jobbed   (ABBR)
JOBDOC.......   Job Documentation   (SAUS)
J Obes Weight Regul...   Journal of Obesity and Weight Regulation (journ.)   (SAUS)
JOBG............   Jobbing   (ABBR)
JOBHLDR....   Jobholder   (ABBR)
JOBLIB.........   Job Library [Computer science]
JOBM............   Journal of Behavioral Medicine (journ.)   (SAUS)
JOBMAN ......   Job Management   (SAUS)
JOBNO .....   Job Number   (SAUS)
Jobns Hopkins Ser in Math Sci...   Johns Hopkins Series in the Mathematical Sciences (journ.)   (SAUS)
Jobns Hopkins Univ Stud...   Johns Hopkins University. Studies in Historical and Political Science (journ.)   (SAUS)
Jobns HU Stud...   Johns Hopkins University. Studies in Historical and Political Science (journ.)   (SAUS)
JOBOL ....   Job Organization Language   (SAUS)
Job Outlk.....   Job Outlook for College Graduates through 1990 (journ.)   (SAUS)
JOBR ....   Jobber   (ABBR)
JOBRESA .....   Joint Board of Remote Sensing Activities   (SAUS)
JOBS............   Job Opportunities for Better Skills   (SAUS)
JOBS............   Job Opportunities in the Business Sector   (WDAA)
JOBS............   Job Oriented Basic Skills [Program] [Military]
JOBS............   Josephson Broadband Spectrometer   (SAUS)
Job Safe & H...   Job Safety and Health (journ.)   (SAUS)
Jobsons Min Yearb...   Jobsons Mining Yearbook (journ.)   (SAUS)
J Obstet Gynaecol Br Commonw...   Journal of Obstetrics and Gynaecology of the British Commonwealth   (SAUO)
J Obstet Gynaecol Br Emp...   Journal of Obstetrics and Gynaecology of the British Empire (journ.)   (SAUS)
J Obstet Gynecol Neonatal Nurs...   Journal of Obstetric, Gynecologic and Neonatal Nursing (journ.)   (SAUS)
JOBTAP........   Job Training Assessment Program [Vocational guidance test]
JOBTICS ......   Job and Time Control System   (SAUS)
JOC.............   Cambria County Library System, Johnstown, PA [OCLC symbol]   (OCLC)
JOC.............   Chief Journalist [Navy rating]
JOC.............   Japan Olympic Committee   (SAUO)
JOC.............   Jewett Owners Club   (EA)
JOC.............   Jewish Occupational Council [Later, NAJVS]   (EA)
JOC.............   Job Order Contract   (SAUO)
JOC.............   Job Order Contracting
JOC.............   Job Order Costing   (MHDI)
JOC.............   Job Ordering Contract
JOC.............   Jocose [or Jocular]
JOC.............   Jocular   (ABBR)

JOC.............. John Coutts Library Services [ACCORD] [UTLAS symbol]
JOC.............. Joint Operational Community (SAUO)
JOC.............. Joint Operation Center (SAUS)
JOC.............. Joint Operations Center
JOC.............. Joint Operations Committee (SAUO)
JOC.............. Joint Opposition Council (SAUO)
JOC.............. Joint Organizing Committee [Global Atmospheric Research Program]
JOC.............. Journal of Communication Management (journ.) (SAUS)
JOC.............. Journal of Organic Chemistry [A publication]
JOC.............. Junior Officer Council [Army]
JOC.............. Junior Optimist Clubs (EA)
JOC.............. New York, NY [Location identifier] [FAA] (FAAL)
JOCAR......... Joint Communications Allocation Requirement (SAUO)
JOCARG....... Joint Wideband Circuit Allocation and Requirement Group (SAUO)
JOCARG....... Joint Wideband Circuit Allocation and Requirement Group, Thailand [Military] (CINC)
JOCAS .... Job Order Cost Accounting System (MCD)
JOCC........... Jeunesse Ouvriere Catholique Canadienne [Young Canadian Catholic Workers] [Established 1930]
JOCC........... Joint Operations Command Centre (SAUO)
JOCC........... Joint Operations Control Center
J OCCA........ Journal of the Oil and Colour Chemists Association (journ.) (SAUS)
J OCCA........ Journal Oil and Colour Chemists Association (journ.) (SAUS)
J Occ Health Safety Aust... Journal of Occupational Health and Safety in Australia [A publication]
J Occup Accid... Journal of Occupational Accidents (journ.) (SAUS)
J Occup Behav... Journal of Occupational Behaviour (journ.) (SAUS)
J Occup Environ Med... Journal of Occupational and Environmental Medicine (journ.) (SAUS)
J Occup Health Safety... Journal of Occupational Health and Safety-Australia and New Zealand (journ.) (SAUS)
J Occup Med... Journal of Occupational Medicine (journ.) (SAUS)
J Oceanogr Soc Jpn... Journal. Oceanographic Society of Japan (journ.) (SAUS)
J Oceanol Soc Kor... Journal. Oceanological Society of Korea (journ.) (SAUS)
J Ocean Technol... Journal of Ocean Technology (journ.) (SAUS)
JOCF........... Joint Operations Capability File (SAUO)
JOCG .... Joint Ordnance Commanders Group
Jo Ch .... Johnson's New York Chancery Reports [A publication] (DLA)
JOCH .... Journal of Community Health (journ.) (SAUS)
JOCI .... Jeunesse Ouvriere Chretienne Internationale [International Young Christian Workers - IYCW] (EAIO)
JOCK........... Jockey (ABBR)
JOCK........... Jockstrap (ABBR)
JockeyC....... Jockey Club, Inc. [Associated Press] (SAG)
JOCM.......... Master Chief Journalist [Navy rating]
JOCMA........ Journal of Occupational Medicine (journ.) (SAUS)
JOCNEE....... Journal of Child Neurology (journ.) (SAUS)
JOCO .... Jointly-Owned Contractor-Operated Facility (MCD)
JOCOMEX .... Joint Communication Exercise (SAUS)
Jo Comm Eur... Journal Officiel des Communautes Europeennes [Official Journal of the European Communities] [A publication] (ILCA)
JOCOTAS ..... Joint Committee on Tactical Shelters (MCD)
JOCR .... Joint Observation for Cometary Research (MCD)
Jo Cre .... Johannes Bassianus de Cremona [Flourished, 12th century] [Authority cited in pre-1607 legal work] (DSA)
JOCS........... Japan Overseas Christian Medical Cooperative Service (SAUO)
JOCS........... Joint Operational Climatological Support (SAUO)
JOCS........... Joint Operations Command System [Military]
JOCS........... Senior Chief Journalist [Navy rating]
JOCSG .... Joint Ordnance Commanders Supply Group [DoD]
J-OCT.......... Joint Operational Compatibility Tests
JOCT........... Junior Officers Common Training
J Ocul Pharmacol... Journal of Ocular Pharmacology (journ.) (SAUS)
J Ocul Pharmacol Ther... Journal of Ocular Pharmacology and Therapeutics (journ.) (SAUS)
JOCV........... Japan Overseas Cooperation Volunteers (SAUO)
JOD............. Joint Occupancy Data (NAKS)
JOD............. Joint Occupancy Date (MCD)
JOD............. Joint Operations Division (SAUO)
JOD............. Jordanian Dinar (SAUS)
JOD............. Journal of Development (ELAL)
JOD............. Journal of Development (journ.) (SAUS)
JOD............. Juvenile Onset Diabetes [Medicine]
JODC .... Japanese Oceanographic Data Center (or Centre) (SAUS)
JODC .... Japanese Oceanographic Data Centre (SAUO)
JODC .... Japan Ocean Data Center (SAUO)
JODC .... Japan Oceanographic Data Center [Information service or system] (IID)
JODC .... Japan Overseas Development Corp. (SAUS)
JODC .... Journal of Dentistry for Children (journ.) (SAUS)
JODC .... Juvenile Osteochondritis Dissecans [Medicine]
JODCO .... Japan Oil Development Co. (BUAC)
JODE........... Journal of Drug Education (journ.) (SAUS)
Jo de Ana.... Johannes de Anania [Deceased, 1457] [Authority cited in pre-1607 legal work] (DSA)
Jo de Anna... Johannes de Anania [Deceased, 1457] [Authority cited in pre-1607 legal work] (DSA)
Jo de Bor.... Johannes de Borbonio [Flourished, 1317-30] [Authority cited in pre-1607 legal work] (DSA)
Jo de Cre..... Johannes Bassianus de Cremona [Flourished, 12th century] [Authority cited in pre-1607 legal work] (DSA)
Jo de F........ Johannes de Fintona [Flourished, 13th century] [Authority cited in pre-1607 legal work] (DSA)
Jo de Fi....... Johannes de Fintona [Flourished, 13th century] [Authority cited in pre-1607 legal work] (DSA)

Jo de Imol... Johannes de Imola [Deceased, 1436] [Authority cited in pre-1607 legal work] (DSA)
Jo de Mo..... Johannes de Monciaco [Flourished, 1263-66] [Authority cited in pre-1607 legal work] (DSA)
JODI............ Journal of Drug Issues (journ.) (SAUS)
JODIN .... Iodinium [Iodine] [Symbol is I] [Chemical element] [Pharmacy] (ROG)
JODIV .... John the Divine
JODM.......... Juvenile Onset Diabetes Mellitus [Medicine]
JODS........... Jasmine Object Database Server (SAUS)
JODV .... Journal of Divorce (journ.) (SAUS)
joe .... Java Objects Everywhere [Computer science] (IGQR)
Joe............. Java Objects Everywhere [Computer science]
JOE............. Joensuu [Finland] [Airport symbol] (OAG)
JOE............. Joensuu [Finland] [Seismograph station code, US Geological Survey] [Closed] (SEIS)
JOE............. Journal of Endodontics (journ.) (SAUS)
JOE............. Juvenile Opportunities Endeavor
JOE............. Juvenile Opportunities Extension (SAUO)
JOEEA......... Journal of Emotional Education (journ.) (SAUS)
JOEG.......... Joint Operations Evaluation Group (AABC)
JOEG-V .... Joint Operations Evaluation Group, Vietnam [Air Force] (MCD)
JOEM.......... Journal of Occupational and Environmental Medicine (SAUO)
JOEM.......... Junior Ordnance Electrical Mechanic [British military] (DMA)
JOENA......... Journal of Endocrinology (journ.) (SAUS)
JOERA......... Japan Optical Engineering Research Association (BUAC)
JOERA......... Journal of Educational Research (journ.) (SAUS)
JOERS......... Joint Opto-Electronics Research Scheme [British]
JOET........... Journal of Education for Teaching (journ.) (SAUS)
JOEVANG..... John the Evangelist
Jo Ex Ir ...... Jones' Irish Exchequer Reports [A publication] (DLA)
Jo Ex Pro W... Jones' Exchequer Proceedings Concerning Wales [1939] [A publication] (DLA)
JOF............. Japan OTC Equity Fund [NYSE symbol] (TTSB)
JOF............. Japan OTC Equity Fund, Inc. [NYSE symbol] (SPSG)
Jo F .... Johannes de Fintona [Flourished, 13th century] [Authority cited in pre-1607 legal work] (DSA)
JOF............. Journal of Forecasting (journ.) (SAUS)
Jo Fa .... Johannes Faventius [Deceased circa 1187] [Authority cited in pre-1607 legal work] (DSA)
J of Air L & Commerce... Journal of Air Law and Commerce (journ.) (SAUS)
Jo Fav .... Johannes Faventinus [Deceased circa 1187] [Authority cited in pre-1607 legal work] (DSA)
J of Ceylon L... Journal of Ceylon Law [Colombo, Ceylon] [A publication] (DLA)
J of E......... Journal of Education [A publication] (ROG)
J of EL........ Journal of Electric Lighting [A publication] (ROG)
J of Ethiop L... Journal of Ethiopian Law [Addis Ababa, Ethiopia] [A publication] (DLA)
J of Home Econ Ed... Journal of Home Economics Education (journ.) (SAUS)
J of Human Rel... Journal of Human Relations (journ.) (SAUS)
J of Ins of Arbitrators... Journal. Institute of Arbitrators [A publication] (DLA)
J of Internat L and Econ... Journal of International Law and Economics (journ.) (SAUS)
JOFL .... Johnstown Flood National Memorial
JOFOC .... Justification for Other Than Full and Open Competition (SAUO)
J of Pract APP... Journal of Practical Approaches to Developmental Handicapped (journ.) (SAUS)
J of Relig Thought... Journal of Religious Thought (journ.) (SAUS)
JOFRO .... Joined Fisheries Research Organization of Northern Rhodesia and Nyassaland (SAUO)
J of the Assoc of Anal Chem... Journal of the Association of Analytical Chemists (SAUO)
J of the Assoc of Anal Chem... Journal of the Association of Analytical Chemists (journ.) (SAUS)
JOG............. Joggle [Engineering]
JOG............. Jogyakarta [Indonesia] [Airport symbol] (OAG)
JOG............. Joint Operating Group [SLA/ASIS]
JOG............. Joint Operations Graphics [Military]
JOG............. Joint Operations Group [DoD]
JOG............. Junior Ocean Group (SAUO)
JOG............. Junior Offshore Group [Racing] [British]
JOG-A......... Joint Operations Graphics - Air [Military] (PDAA)
JOGD .... Jogged (ABBR)
JOGEA .... Journal of Gerontology (journ.) (SAUS)
JOGG .... Jogging (ABBR)
JOG-G .... Joint Operations Graphics - Ground (PDAA)
JOGG A .... Journal of Geography (journ.) (SAUS)
JOGL .... Joggle (ABBR)
JOGLD .... Joggled (ABBR)
JOGLG .... Joggling (ABBR)
JOGNN .... Journal of Obstetric, Gynecologic and Neonatal Nursing (journ.) (SAUS)
JOGR .... Jogger (ABBR)
JOG-R .... Joint Operations Graphic-Radar (SAUS)
JOGS .... Joint Operation Graphics System (COE)
JOH............ Johannesburg [South Africa] [Seismograph station code, US Geological Survey] [Closed] (SEIS)
Joh............. Johannine (BJA)
Joh............. John [New Testament book] (BJA)
JOH............. Johnstone Point, AK [Location identifier] [FAA] (FAAL)
JOH............. Journal of Housing (journ.) (SAUS)
JOH............. St. John's College [Cambridge, England] (DAS)
Joh Ch Rep... Johnson's New York Chancery Reports [A publication] (DLA)
JOHE........... Journal of Health Economics (journ.) (SAUS)
JOHEA .... Journal of Heredity (journ.). (SAUS)

JOHH........... Journal of Holistic Health (journ.) (SAUS)
J Ohio Herpetol Soc... Journal. Ohio Herpetological Society (journ.) (SAUS)
John............ Chase's United States Circuit Court Decisions, Edited by Johnson [*A publication*] (DLA)
John............ Johnson's English Vice-Chancellors' Reports [*A publication*] (DLA)
John............ Johnson's Maryland Chancery Reports [*A publication*] (DLA)
John............ Johnson's New York Reports [*A publication*] (DLA)
John............ Johnson's New York Supreme Court Reports [*A publication*] (DLA)
John Alexander Monogr Ser Var Phases Thorac Surg... John Alexander Monograph Series on Various Phases of Thoracic Surgery (journ.) (SAUS)
John Am Not... John's American Notaries [*A publication*] (DLA)
John & H..... Johnson and Hemming's English Chancery Reports [*70 English Reprint*] [*A publication*] (DLA)
John Carroll U... John Carroll University (GAGS)
John Cas..... Johnson's New York Cases [*A publication*] (DLA)
John Chan... Johnson's New York Chancery Reports [*A publication*] (DLA)
John Ch Rep... Johnson's New York Chancery Reports [*A publication*] (DLA)
JohnCn........ Johnson Controls, Inc. [*Associated Press*] (SAG)
John Dewey Soc Yrbk... John Dewey Society. Yearbook (journ.) (SAUS)
John Dict...... Johnson's English Dictionary [*A publication*] (DLA)
John Did...... Johnsons English Dictionary (journ.) (SAUS)
John Eng Ch... Johnson's English Vice-Chancellors' Reports [*A publication*] (DLA)
John Herron Art Inst Bul... John Herron Art Institute. Bulletin (journ.) (SAUS)
John Innes Horhc Inst Annu Rep... John Innes Horticultural Institution. Annual Report (journ.) (SAUS)
John Innes Sym... John Innes Symposium (journ.) (SAUS)
John Jay C (CUNY)... John Jay College of Criminal Justice of The City University of New York (GAGS)
JohnJn........ Johnson & Johnson [*Associated Press*] (SAG)
John Lawrence Interdiscip Symp Phys Biomed Sci... John Lawrence Interdisciplinary Symposium on the Physical and Biomedical Sciences (journ.) (SAUS)
John Marshall Law Sch... John Marshall Law School (GAGS)
John Marshall LQ... John Marshall Law Quarterly [*A publication*] (DLA)
John Marsh LJ... John Marshall Law Journal [*A publication*] (DLA)
John Marsh LQ... John Marshall Law Quarterly [*A publication*] (DLA)
JOHNNIAC... John Neumann Integrator and Automatic Computer (SAUS)
JOHNNIAC... John's [*Von Neumann*] Integrator and Automatic Computer [*An early computer*]
John Oxley J... John Oxley Journal [*A publication*]
John Rylands Lib Bul... John Rylands Library. Bulletin (journ.) (SAUS)
Johns.......... Chase's United States Circuit Court Decisions, Edited by Johnson [*A publication*] (DLA)
Johns.......... Johnson's English Vice-Chancellors' Reports [*A publication*] (DLA)
Johns.......... Johnson's Maryland Chancery Reports [*A publication*] (DLA)
Johns.......... Johnson's New York Supreme Court Reports [*A publication*] (DLA)
Johns & H... Johnson and Hemming's English Chancery Reports [*70 English Reprint*] [*A publication*] (DLA)
Johns & Hem... Johnson and Hemming's English Chancery Reports [*70 English Reprint*] [*A publication*] (DLA)
Johns & H (Eng)... Johnson and Hemming's English Chancery Reports [*70 English Reprint*] [*A publication*] (DLA)
Johns Bills... Johnson's Bills of Exchange [*2nd ed.*] [*1839*] [*A publication*] (DLA)
Johns C....... Johnson's New York Cases [*A publication*] (DLA)
Johns Cas.... Johnson's New York Cases [*A publication*] (DLA)
Johns Cases... Johnson's New York Cases [*A publication*] (DLA)
Johns Cas (NY)... Johnson's New York Cases [*A publication*] (DLA)
Johns Ch..... Johnson's English Vice-Chancellors' Reports [*A publication*] (DLA)
Johns Ch..... Johnson's Maryland Chancery Decisions [*A publication*] (DLA)
Johns Ch..... Johnson's New York Chancery Reports [*A publication*] (DLA)
Johns Ch Cas... Johnson's New York Chancery Reports [*A publication*] (DLA)
Johns Ch (NY)... Johnson's New York Chancery Reports [*A publication*] (DLA)
Johns Civ L Sp... Johnson's Civil Law of Spain [*A publication*] (DLA)
Johns Civ L Sp... Johnsons Civil Law of Spain (journ.) (SAUS)
Johns Ct Err... Johnson's New York Court of Errors Reports [*A publication*] (DLA)
Johns Dec... Johnson's Maryland Chancery Decisions [*A publication*] (DLA)
Johns Eccl L... Johnson's Ecclesiastical Law [*A publication*] (DLA)
Johns Eccl L... Johnsons Ecclesiastical Law (journ.) (SAUS)
Johns Eng Ch... Johnson's English Chancery Reports [*A publication*] (DLA)
Johns H....... Johns Hopkins University (SAUO)
Johns Hopkins Hp Bull... Johns Hopkins Hospital. Bulletin (journ.) (SAUS)
Johns Hopkins Mag... Johns Hopkins Magazine. Johns Hopkins University. Baltimore (SAUO)
Johns Hopkins Med J Suppl... Johns Hopkins Medical Journal. Supplement (journ.) (SAUS)
Johns Hopkins Oceanogr Stud... Johns Hopkins Oceanographic Studies (journ.) (SAUS)
Johns Hopkins U... [*The*] Johns Hopkins University (GAGS)
Johns Hopkins Univ Appl Phys Lab Spec Rep... Johns Hopkins University. Applied Physics Laboratory. Sperial Report (journ.) (SAUS)
Johns Hopkins Univ Appl Phys Lab Tech Dig... Johns Hopkins University. Applied Physics Laboratory. Technical Digest (journ.) (SAUS)
Johns Hopkins Univ Chesapeake Bay Inst Tech Rept... Johns Hopkins University. Chesapeake Bay Institute. Technical Report (journ.) (SAUS)
Johns Hopkins Univ Cir... Johns Hopkins University. Circular (journ.) (SAUS)
Johns Hopkins Univ McCollum Pratt Inst Contrib... Johns Hopkins University. McCollum Pratt Institute. Contribution (journ.) (SAUS)
Johns Hopkins Univ Studies in Geology... Johns Hopkins University. Studies in Geology (journ.) (SAUS)
Johns HRV... Johnson's English Chancery Reports [*A publication*] (DLA)
Johns Mar R... Johnson on Maritime Rights [*A publication*] (DLA)
Johns (NY)... Johnson's New York Reports [*A publication*] (DLA)
Johns NZ..... Johnson's New Zealand Reports [*A publication*] (DLA)
Johnson....... Johnson's English Vice-Chancellors' Reports [*A publication*] (DLA)
Johnson....... Johnson's Maryland Chancery Decisions [*A publication*] (DLA)
Johnson....... Johnson's New York Reports [*A publication*] (DLA)
Johnson NYR... Johnson's New York Reports [*A publication*] (DLA)
Johnson R... Johnson's New York Reports [*A publication*] (DLA)
Johnson's Quarto Dict... Johnson's Quarto Dictionary [*A publication*] (DLA)
Johnson's Rep... Johnson's New York Reports [*A publication*] (DLA)
Johns Pat Man... Johnson's Patent Manual [*A publication*] (DLA)
Johns Pat Man... Johnsons Patent Manual (journ.) (SAUS)
Johns R....... Johnson's New York Reports [*A publication*] (DLA)
Johns Rep... Johnson's New York Supreme Court Reports [*A publication*] (DLA)
Johnst Inst... Johnston's Institutes of the Laws of Spain [*A publication*] (DLA)
Johnst Inst... Johnstons Institutes of the Laws of Spain (journ.) (SAUS)
JohnstnA...... Johnstown America Industries, Inc. [*Associated Press*] (SAG)
Johnst (NZ)... Johnston's New Zealand Reports [*A publication*] (DLA)
Johnston...... Johnston Industries, Inc. [*Associated Press*] (SAG)
Johns Tr...... Johnson's Impeachment Trial [*A publication*] (DLA)
Johns US..... Johnson's Reports of Chase's United States Circuit Court Decisions [*A publication*] (DLA)
Johns VC..... Johnson's English Vice-Chancellors' Reports [*A publication*] (DLA)
Johns VC (Eng)... Johnson's English Vice-Chancellors' Reports [*A publication*] (DLA)
JOHPER....... Journal of Health, Physical Education, Recreation (journ.) (SAUS)
Johs............ Johannes Galensis [*Flourished, 13th century*] [*Authority cited in pre-1607 legal work*] (DSA)
Joh Teut...... Johannes Teutonicus [*Deceased circa 1246*] [*Authority cited in pre-1607 legal work*] (DSA)
JOHX.......... Johnson Flying Service [*Air carrier designation symbol*]
JOHX.......... Journal of Homosexuality (journ.) (SAUS)
JOI............. Jewish Outreach Institute (SAUS)
JOI............. Joint Oceanographic Institution (USDC)
JOI............. Joint Oceanographic Institutions, Inc. [*Research center*] (RCD)
JOI............. Joinville [*Brazil*] [*Airport symbol*] (OAG)
JOIA........... Japan Ocean Industries Association (BUAC)
JOI-BOG....... JOI Board of Governors (SAUS)
JOICA.......... Journal. Institution of Chemists (journ.) (SAUS)
JOICFP......... Japanese Organisation for International Cooperation in Family Planning (BUAC)
JOIDES........ JODC [*Japan Oceanographic Data Center*] On-Line Information and Data Exchange Service [*Marine science*] (OSRA)
JOIDES........ Joint Oceanographic Institutes for Deep Earth Sampling (SAUO)
JOIDES........ Joint Oceanographic Institutions for Deep Earth Sampling
JOIDESP...... Joint Oceanographic Institutions Deep Earth Sampling Program (SAUO)
J Oil Colour Chem Assoc... Journal of the Oil and Colour Chemists Association (journ.) (SAUS)
J Oilseeds Res... Journal of Oilseeds Research (journ.) (SAUS)
JOIN............ Job Opportunities in Neighbourhoods (SAUO)
JOIN............ Job Orientation in Neighborhoods (AEBS)
JOIN............ Job Orientation in the Neighbourhoods (SAUO)
JOIN............ Jobs or Income Now [*Students for a Democratic Society*] [*Defunct*]
JOIN............ Joinery (ADA)
JOIN............ Joint Optical Information Network [*Army*]
JOIN............ Jones Intercable [*NASDAQ symbol*] (TTSB)
JOIN............ Jones Intercable, Inc. [*NASDAQ symbol*] (NQ)
JOINA.......... Jones Intercable CI'A' [*NASDAQ symbol*] (TTSB)
Joining Mater... Joining and Materials (journ.) (SAUS)
JOINREP...... Joining Report (MCD)
Joint Automat Contr Conf PreprTech Pap... Joint Automatic Control Conference. Preprints of Technical Papers (journ.) (SAUS)
JOINTCINCEASTLANT... Commander-in-Chief Eastern Atlantic Area, Air Commander-in-Chief Eastern Atlantic Area (SAUO)
Joint Four.... Joint Executive Committee of Associations of Head Masters, Head Mistresses, Assistant Masters and Assistant Mistresses (SAUO)
JOIP............ Joint Operations Interface Procedure (NASA)
JOIS............ Japan Online Information System [*Database*]
JOISTS......... Joint Operational Interface Simulation Training System (SAUO)
JOJA........... July, October, January, and April [*Denotes quarterly payments of interest or dividends in these months*] [*Business term*]
JOJAA.......... Journal of Otolaryngology of Japan (journ.) (SAUS)
Jo Je S........ Journal of Jewish Studies (journ.) (SAUS)
JOJO........... Jojoba Horizons, Inc. (SAUO)
Jo Jur.......... Journal of Jurisprudence [*A publication*] (DLA)
JOK............. Airtaxi Bedarfsluftverkehrsges GmbH [*Austria*] [*ICAO designator*] (FAAC)
J Okayama Dent Soc... Journal. Okayama Dental Society (journ.) (SAUS)
J Okayama Med Soc... Journal. Okayama Medical Society (journ.) (SAUS)
J Okayama Med Soc Suppl... Journal. Okayama Medical Society. Supplement (journ.) (SAUS)
JOKG........... Joking (ABBR)
JOKGLY....... Jokingly (ABBR)
JOKGY......... Jokingly (ABBR)
JOKI............ John Fitzgerald Kennedy National Historical Site
JOKING........ Joint Kinematics and Geometry (PDAA)
J Okla Dent Assoc... Journal. Oklahoma Dental Association (journ.) (SAUS)
J Okla State Dent Ass... Journal. Oklahoma State Dental Association (journ.) (SAUS)
J Okla State Med Assoc... Journal of the Oklahoma State Medical Association (journ.) (SAUS)
J Okla State Med Assoc... Journal-Oklahoma State Medical Association (SAUO)
JOKP........... Junior Order, Knights of Pythias (EA)
JOKSTR....... Jokester (ABBR)
JOL............. Job Organization Language [*1979*] [*Computer science*] (CSR)
JOL............. Job Orientation Language (SAUS)
JOL............. Joilet in Illinois [*Diocesan abbreviation*] [*Illinois*] (TOCD)
JOL............. Jolo [*Philippines*] [*Airport symbol*] (OAG)

JOL............. Jolon [California] [Seismograph station code, US Geological Survey] (SEIS)
JOL............. Joule, Inc. [AMEX symbol] (SPSG)
JOL............. Journal of Online Law (SAUO)
JOL............. Journal of Oriental Literature (journ.) (SAUS)
JOL............. Judgements of Learning (SAUS)
JOLA........... Journal of Library Automation (journ.) (SAUS)
JOLD........... Jollied (ABBR)
Jo Le.......... Johannis Lectura [A publication] (DSA)
JOLIS.......... Joint Library and Information System (SAUS)
JOLT........... Java Online Transactions (SAUS)
JOLT........... Java Open Language Toolkit [Computer science] (DCDG)
JOLT........... Juvenile Offenders Learn the Truth [Program]
JOLTGLY..... Joltingly (ABBR)
JOM............ Jeunesse Ouvriere Marocaine [Moroccan Working Youth]
JOM............ Job Operation Manual (AAG)
JOM............ Job-Oriented Manual (AAG)
JOM............ Johnson-O'Malley Act [1934]
JOM............ Joining of Materials (SAUS)
JOM............ Journal of Management (journ.) (SAUS)
JOM............ Journal of Metals (journ.) (SAUS)
JOM............ Journal of Orthomolecular Medicine (SAUS)
JOM............ Njombe [Tanzania] [Airport symbol] (AD)
JOMA.......... Japan Oriental Music Association (BUAC)
JOMA.......... Journal of Military Assistance (journ.) (SAUS)
JOMAC........ Judgement, Orientation, Memory, Abstraction, and Calculation [Medicine] (DAVI)
JOMACI....... Judgment, Orientation, Memory, Abstraction, and Calculation Intact [Medicine] (DAVI)
JOMAR........ John and Margaret Seidel [Children of US importer after whom British sports car was named]
JOMAR........ Joint Office for Mapping and Research (SAUO)
JOMI........... International Journal of Oral & Maxillofacial Implants (SAUO)
JOM J Occup Med... JOM. Journal of Occupational Medicine (journ.) (SAUS)
JOML.......... Journal of Organometallic Chemistry (journ.) (SAUS)
JOMMA....... Journal of Mathematics and Mechanics (journ.) (SAUS)
JOMN......... Jeweled-Orifice Misting Nozzle
JOMO......... Job Mix Optimization [Computer science] (MHDB)
JOMO......... Junta of Militant Organizations (SAUO)
Jo Mon .... Johannes Monachus [Deceased, 1313] [Authority cited in pre-1607 legal work] (DSA)
JOMU.......... John Muir National Historic Site
JON............ Jeweled-Orifice Nozzle
JON............ Job Order Number (MCD)
JON............ Johnston Island [Airport symbol] (OAG)
Jon............. Jonah [Old Testament book]
JON............ Jonas [Old Testament book] [Douay version]
JON............ Jones' Irish Exchequer Reports [A publication] (DLA)
JON............ Jonpol Explorations Ltd. [Toronto Stock Exchange symbol]
JONA.......... Journal of Nursing Administration (SAUO)
JONAH........ Jews Organised for a Nuclear Arms Halt [An association] (BUAC)
Jon & Car.... Jones and Cary's Irish Exchequer Reports [1838-39] [A publication] (DLA)
Jon & L ...... Jones and La Touche's Irish Chancery Reports [A publication] (DLA)
Jon & La T... Jones and La Touche's Irish Chancery Reports [A publication] (DLA)
JONEA .... Journal of Neurophysiology (journ.) (SAUS)
Jonel .... Jones Intercable, Inc. [Associated Press] (SAG)
JoneInt .... Jones Intercable Investors Ltd. [Associated Press] (SAG)
J Onenl Tianjin Med J Suppl... Journal of Oncology. Tianjin Medical Journal. Supplement (journ.) (SAUS)
Jones.......... Jones' Irish Exchequer Reports [A publication] (DLA)
Jones.......... Jones' North Carolina Equity Reports [54-59] [1853-63] [A publication] (DLA)
Jones.......... Jones' North Carolina Law Reports [A publication] (DLA)
Jones.......... Jones' Reports [43-48, 52-57, 61, 62 Alabama] [A publication] (DLA)
Jones.......... Jones' Reports [22-30 Missouri] [A publication] (DLA)
Jones.......... Jones' Reports [11, 12 Pennsylvania] [A publication] (DLA)
Jones.......... Jones' Upper Canada Common Pleas Reports [A publication] (DLA)
Jones & C .. Jones and Cary's Irish Exchequer Reports [1838-39] [A publication] (DLA)
Jones & H Hind Law... Jones and Haughton's Hindoo Law [A publication] (DLA)
Jones & H Hind law... Jones and Hauglitons Hindoo Law (journ.) (SAUS)
Jones & L.... Jones and La Touche's Irish Chancery Reports [A publication] (DLA)
Jones & La T... Jones and La Touche's Irish Chancery Reports [A publication] (DLA)
Jones & L (Ir)... Jones and La Touche's Irish Chancery Reports [A publication] (DLA)
Jones & McM... Jones and McMurtrie's Pennsylvania Supreme Court Reports [A publication] (DLA)
Jones & McM (PA)... Jones and McMurtrie's Pennsylvania Supreme Court Reports [A publication] (DLA)
Jones & S ... Jones and Spencer's Superior Court Reports [33-61 New York] [A publication] (DLA)
Jones & Sp... Jones and Spencer's Superior Court Reports [33-61 New York] [A publication] (DLA)
Jones & Spen... Jones and Spencer's Superior Court Reports [33-61 New York] [A publication] (DLA)
Jones & V Laws... Jones and Varick's Laws of New York [A publication] (DLA)
JonesAp....... Jones Apparel Group, Inc. [Associated Press] (SAG)
Jones B .... Jones' Law of Bailments [A publication] (DLA)
Jones Bailm... Jones' Law of Bailments [A publication] (DLA)
Jones B & W (MO)... Jones, Barclay, and Whittelsey's Reports [31 Missouri] [A publication] (DLA)
Jones Barclay & Whittelsey... Jones, Barclay, and Whittelsey's Reports [31 Missouri] [A publication] (DLA)

Jones Ch Mort... Jones on Chattel Mortgages [A publication] (DLA)
Jones curities... Jones on Railroad Securities (journ.) (SAUS)
Jones Easem... Jones' Treatise on Easements [A publication] (DLA)
Jones Eq...... Jones' North Carolina Equity Reports [54-59] [1853-63] [A publication] (DLA)
Jones Eq (NC)... Jones' North Carolina Equity Reports [54-59] [1853-63] [A publication] (DLA)
Jones Exch... Jones' Irish Exchequer Reports [A publication] (DLA)
Jones Fr Bar... Jones' History of the French Bar [A publication] (DLA)
Jones French Bar... Jones' History of the French Bar [A publication] (DLA)
Jones Inst.... Jones' Institutes of Hindoo Law [A publication] (DLA)
Jones Intr.... Jones' Introduction to Legal Science [A publication] (DLA)
Jones Intr.... Jones Introduction to the Science (journ.) (SAUS)
Jones Ir.... Jones' Irish Exchequer Reports [A publication] (DLA)
Jones L....... Jones' Law Reports [A publication] (DLA)
Jones L....... Jones Law Reports (journ.) (SAUS)
Jones Law... Jones' North Carolina Law Reports [A publication] (DLA)
Jones Lib.... Jones on Libel [1812] [A publication] (DLA)
Jones L Of T... Jones on Land and Office Titles [A publication] (DLA)
JonesM....... Jones Medical Industries, Inc. [Associated Press] (SAG)
Jones Mort... Jones on Mortgages [A publication] (DLA)
Jones NC.... Jones' North Carolina Law Reports [A publication] (DLA)
Jones NC.... Jones North Carolina Law Reports (journ.) (SAUS)
Jones PA.... Jones' Reports [11, 12 Pennsylvania] [A publication] (DLA)
JonesPl....... Jones Plumbing Systems, Inc. [Associated Press] (SAG)
Jones Pledges... Jones on Pledges and Collateral Securities [A publication] (DLA)
Jones Ry Sec... Jones on Railway Securities [A publication] (DLA)
Jones Salv... Jones' Law of Salvage [A publication] (DLA)
Jones Securities... Jones on Railroad Securities [A publication] (DLA)
JonesSp....... Jones Spacelink Ltd. [Associated Press] (SAG)
Jones UC.... Jones' Upper Canada Common Pleas Reports [A publication] (DLA)
Jones Uses... Jones' Law of Uses [A publication] (DLA)
Jones Uses... Jones Law of Uses (journ.) (SAUS)
Jon Ex ...... Jones' Irish Exchequer Reports [A publication] (DLA)
Jon Exch... Jones' Irish Exchequer Reports [A publication] (DLA)
JONFSPL ..... Jones Plumbing Systems, Inc. (SAUO)
JonIcbl........ Jones Intercable, Inc. [Associated Press] (SAG)
Jon Ir Exch... Jones' Irish Exchequer Reports [A publication] (DLA)
JONR .... Joiner (ABBR)
JONS .... Journal of Northern Studies (journ.) (SAUS)
JONS .... Juntas de Ofensiva Nacional Sindicalista [Syndicalist Juntas of the National Offensive] [Spain] [Political party] (PPE)
JONSDAP..... Joint North Sea Data Acquisition Project [An informal group of Belgian, German, British, Dutch, and Swedish scientific institutes] (PDAA)
JONSIS .... Joint North Sea Information Systems (PDAA)
JONSWAP.... Joint North Sea Wave Analysis Project (SAUS)
JONSWAP.... Joint North Sea Wave Atmosphere Program [Global Atmospheric Research Program] (USDC)
JONSWAP.... Joint North Sea Wave Project [An informal group of Belgian, German, British, Dutch, and Swedish scientific institutes] (PDAA)
JONT.......... Journal of Ophthalmic Nursing and Technology (SAUO)
JONT.......... Journal of Ophthalmic Nursing and Technology (journ.) (SAUS)
J Ont Dent Assoc... Journal. Ontario Dental Association (journ.) (SAUS)
JONUDL...... Journal. American College of Nutrition (journ.) (SAUS)
JONUS .... Joint Nutrient Studies (SAUO)
JOO............ Jonesboro, GA [Location identifier] [FAA] (FAAL)
JOOD .... Junior Officer of the Day [or Deck] [Navy]
JOOD .... Junior Officer of the Deck (SAUO)
JOOI.......... Junior Optimist Octagon International [An association] (EA)
JOOM......... Junior Observers of Meteorology (SAUO)
JOOMS .... Junior Observers of Meteorology [Trainees for government service to replace Weather Bureau men who had gone to war] [World War II]
JOOP .... Journal of Object Orientated Programming (SAUS)
JOOS .... Job-Oriented Organizational Structure (AAG)
JOOW .... Junior Officer of the Watch [Navy]
JOP............ Job Opportunity Program (OICC)
JOP............ Jobs Optional Program [Combination job opportunities in the business sector and on the job training] (OICC)
JOP............ Joint Observing Program [NASA]
JOP............ Joint Operating Plan
JOP............ Joint Operating Procedure (SAUO)
JOP............ Joint Operation Procedure (AAG)
JOP............ Joint Optoelectronics Project [Japan] [Agreement for conducting cooperative global research]
JOP............ Journal of Occupational Psychology (journ.) (SAUS)
JOP............ Junior Officer Pilot (SAUO)
JOp............ Jupiter Orbiter Probe [Later, Project Galileo] [NASA]
JOP............ Jupiter Orbiter with Probe (SAUS)
JOPA.......... Junior Officers and Professional Association
JOPA.......... Juventud Organizada del Pueblo en Armas [Armed People's Organized Youth] [Guatemala] (PD)
JOPC.......... Junior Olympic Pistol Championship [National Rifle Association]
JOPCN .... Job Order Program Control Number
JO/PCN...... Job Order/Program Control Number [Army]
JOPD .... Journal of Psychoactive Drugs (journ.) (SAUS)
JOPD .... Junior Officer Professional Development Program [Army] (RDA)
JOPDA .... Journal of Pediatrics (journ.) (SAUS)
J Open Educ Ass Qld... Journal. Open Education Association of Queensland (journ.) (SAUS)
J Operational Psychiatr... Journal of Operational Psychiatry (journ.) (SAUS)
J Operator Theory... Journal of Operator Theory (journ.) (SAUS)
J Oper Manage... Journal of Operations Management (journ.) (SAUS)
J Oper Res Soc... Journal of the Operational Research Society (SAUO)

J Oper Res Soc... Journal of the Operation and Research Society (journ.) (SAUS)
J Oper Res Soc Am... Journal. Operation Research Society of America (journ.) (SAUS)
JOPES......... Joint Operating Planning and Execution System (SAUS)
JOPES......... Joint Operation Planning and Execution System [DoD]
JOPES......... Joint Operations Planning and Execution System [Military]
JOPES ROLSTK... JOPES-Rolling Stock Summary Report (SAUO)
JOPh............ Journal of Physiology (journ.) (SAUS)
JOPHA .... Journal de Physiologie (journ.) (SAUS)
J Ophthalmic Nurs Technol... Journal of Ophthalmic Nursing and Technology (journ.) (SAUS)
JOPID .... Journal of Pipelines (journ.) (SAUS)
JOPL............ Journal of Paleolimnology (journ.) (SAUS)
JOPM.......... Joint Occupancy Plan Memorandum (AAG)
JOPM.......... Joint Operation Procedure Memorandum (AAG)
JOPP........... Joint Operational Policies and Procedures (MCD)
JOPP........... Journal of Primary Prevention (journ.) (SAUS)
JOPR........... Joint Operation Procedure Report (AAG)
JOPREP ...... Joint Operational Report [Military] (AFM)
JOPREP ...... Joint Operational Reporting System (SAUO)
JOPS .... Joint Operating Study (SAUS)
JOPS .... Joint Operational Planning System [Military]
JOPS .... Joint Operations Planning System (SAUS)
JOPS .... Journal of the Patent Office Society (journ.) (SAUS)
JOPSA .... Journal of Psychology (journ.) (SAUS)
JOPS III .... Joint Operations Planning Software Support System (SAUO)
JOPSREP .... Joint Operations Planning System Reporting System (SAUO)
JOPSREP ..... JOPS Reporting System (SAUS)
JOPS ROLSTK... Joint Operations Planning System Rolling Stock Summary Report (SAUO)
JOPS ROLSTK... JOPS Rolling Stock Summary Report (SAUS)
JOPSRSS..... Joint Operations Planning System Rolling Stock Sum System (SAUO)
JOPSRSS..... JOPS Rolling Stock Sum System (SAUS)
J Opt Commun... Journal of Optical Communications (journ.) (SAUS)
J Opt Soc Am A... Journal of the Optical Society of America A. Optics and Image Science (SAUO)
J Opt Soc Am A... Journal. Optical Society of America. A. Optics and Image Science (journ.) (SAUS)
J Opt Soc Am B Opt Phys... Journal. Optical Society of America. B. Optical Physics (journ.) (SAUS)
J Opt Soc Am Rev Sci Instrum... Journal. Optical Society of America and Review of Scientific Instruments (journ.) (SAUS)
J Opt Soc Cum Ind... Journal. Optical Society of America. Cumulative Index (journ.) (SAUS)
JOQ.............. Job Order Quantity [Military] (AFIT)
JOR.............. Jet Operations Requirements
JOR.............. Job Operations Report
JOR.............. Job Order Request (AAG)
JOR.............. Joint Occupancy Rate (ACAE)
JOR.............. Joint Operational Requirement (SAUO)
JOR.............. Joint Operations Requirements [Military] (AFM)
JOR.............. Jordan [ANSI three-letter standard code] (CNC)
Jor.............. Jordan (VRA)
JOR.............. Journal of Oriental Research (journ.) (SAUS)
JOR.............. Yorkshire European Airways Ltd. [British] [ICAO designator] (FAAC)
JORAC .... Joint Operations Radar Airspace Control (SAUO)
Jo Radio Law... Journal of Radio Law [A publication] (DLA)
J Oral Implantol... Journal of Oral Implantology (journ.) (SAUS)
J Oral Implant Transplant Surg... Journal of Oral Implant and Transplant Surgery (journ.) (SAUS)
J Oral Maxillofac Surg... Journal of Oral and Maxillofacial Surgery (journ.) (SAUS)
J Oral Med... Journal of Oral Medicine (journ.) (SAUS)
J Oral Pathol... Journal of Oral Pathology (journ.) (SAUS)
J Oral Pathol Med... Journal of Oral Pathology and Medicine (journ.) (SAUS)
J Oral Rehabil... Journal of Oral Rehabilitation (journ.) (SAUS)
J Oral Surg... Journal of Oral Surgery (journ.) (SAUS)
J Oral Surg Anesth Hp Dent Serv... Journal of Oral Surgery Anesthesia and Hospital Dental Service (journ.) (SAUS)
J Oral Therp Pharmacol... Journal of Oral Therapeutics and Pharmacology (journ.) (SAUS)
JORC .... Jeddah Oil Refinery Co. [Saudi Arabia] (BUAC)
JORC .... Junior Olympic Rifle Championship [National Rifle Association]
JORD .... Jordan (ABBR)
Jord .... Jordanian (DIAR)
Jordan .... Jordan American Holdings, Inc. [Associated Press] (SAG)
Jordan Dent J... Jordan Dental Journal (journ.) (SAUS)
Jordan Med J... Jordan Medical Journal (journ.) (SAUS)
Jord Jt St Comp... Jordan on Joint Stock Companies [A publication] (DLA)
Jord PJ....... Jordan's Parliamentary Journal [A publication] (DLA)
JOREA .... Journal of Rehabilitation (journ.) (SAUS)
JOREDR ...... Journal of Orthopaedic Research (journ.) (SAUS)
JOREES....... Journal of Oilseeds Research (journ.) (SAUS)
J Oreg Dent Assoc... Journal Oregon Dental Association (journ.) (SAUS)
JORG .... Joint Oceanographic Research Group
J Organomet Chem Libr... Journal. Organometallic Chemistry Library (journ.) (SAUS)
J Org Chem... Journal of Organic Chemistry (MEC)
J Org Chem USSR... Journal of Organic Chemistry of the USSR (journ.) (SAUS)
J Orgl Behav Mgt... Journal of Organizational Behavior Management (journ.) (SAUS)
J Orgl Com... Journal of Organizational Communica- tion (journ.) (SAUS)
J Or Inst ...... Journal. Oriental Institute (journ.) (SAUS)
J Orissa Bot Soc... Journal Orissa Botanical Society (journ.) (SAUS)
J Orissa Math Soc... Journal. Orissa Mathematical Society (journ.) (SAUS)
JORITDS....... Joint Optical Range Instrumentation Type Designation System

JORN .... Jindalee Perational/OTH Radar Network (SAUS)
Jor of Indian Art and Ind... Journal of Indian Art and Industry (journ.) (SAUS)
JORP .... Jet Operations Requirements Panel (SAUS)
JORRI .... Journal. Operating Room Research Institute (journ.) (SAUS)
JORS .... Journal. Operational Research Society (journ.) (SAUS)
JORSJ .... Journal of the Operations Research Society of Japan (SAUO)
JORSJ .... Journal of the Operations Research Society of Japan (journ.) (SAUS)
JORSJ .... Journal. Operations Research Society of Japan (journ.) (SAUS)
J Or Stud..... Journal of Oriental Studies (journ.) (SAUS)
J Orthomol Psychiatry... Journal of Orthomolecular Psychiatry (journ.) (SAUS)
J Orthop Sports Phys Ther... Journal of Orthopaedic and Sports Physical Therapy (journ.) (SAUS)
J Orthop Tech... Journal of Orthopaedic Techniques (journ.) (SAUS)
J Orthop Trauma... Journal of Orthopaedic Trauma (journ.) (SAUS)
JOS............ Java-based Operating System (SAUS)
JOS............ Jeunesse Ouvriere du Senegal [Senegalese Working Youth]
JOS............ Job Opportunity System (TIMI)
JOS............ Job Order Sheet (SAUS)
JOS............ Job Order Supplement (MCD)
JOS............ Joint Oil Staff (SAUO)
JOS............ Joint Operations Staff [Military]
JOS............ Jos [Nigeria] [Airport symbol] (OAG)
Jos............ Joseph (BJA)
Jos............ Joseph's Reports [21 Nevada] [A publication] (DLA)
Jos............ Josephus (BJA)
Jos............ Joshua [Old Testament book]
Jos............ Josiah (BJA)
JOS............ Joss Energy Ltd. [Toronto Stock Exchange symbol]
JOS............ Jostens, Inc. [NYSE symbol] (SPSG)
JOS............ Josvafo [Hungary] [Seismograph station code, US Geological Survey] (SEIS)
JOS............ Journal of Oriental Studies (journ.) (SAUS)
JOS............ Journal of Quaternary Science [A publication] (QUAC)
JOS............ Junior Ordinary Seaman (SAUO)
JOSA.......... Journal of the Optical Society of America (SAUO)
JOSA.......... Seaman Apprentice, Journalist, Striker [Navy rating]
JOSAF......... Joint Operations Support Activity Frankfurt [National Security Agency]
J Osaka City Med Cent... Journal. Osaka City Medical Center (journ.) (SAUS)
J Osaka Dent Univ... Journal. Osaka Dental University (journ.) (SAUS)
J Osaka Ind Univ Nat Sci... Journal. Osaka Industrial University. Natural Sciences (journ.) (SAUS)
J Osaka Odontol Soc... Journal. Osaka Odontological Society (journ.) (SAUS)
J Osaka Univ Dent Soc... Journal. Osaka University Dental Society (journ.) (SAUS)
J Osakg Univ Dent Sch... Journal. Osaka University Dental School (journ.) (SAUS)
J Osak Inst Sci Technol Part 1... Journal. Osaka Institute of Science and Technology Part 1 (journ.) (SAUS)
J Osak Med Coll... Journal. Osaka Medical College (journ.) (SAUS)
Jos & Bev.... Joseph and Beven's Digest of Decisions [Ceylon] [A publication] (DLA)
JosAnt .... Jewish Antiquities [Josephus] (BJA)
JosApion... Against Apion [Josephus] (BJA)
JOSB.......... Bank [Joseph A.] Clothiers, Inc. [NASDAQ symbol] (SAG)
JOSB.......... Jos.A. Bank Clothiers [NASDAQ symbol] (TTSB)
JOSB.......... Joseph A Bank Clothiers [NASDAQ symbol] (SAG)
JosBank...... Bank [Joseph A.] Clothiers, Inc. [Associated Press] (SAG)
JosBank...... Joseph A. Bank Clothiers [Associated Press] (SAG)
JOSCO .... Joint Overseas Shipping Control Office
JOSDEPS .... Joint Strategic Defense Concept Plan (SAUO)
JOSE........... Joint Optics Structures Experiment (ACAE)
Joseph .... Josephus [First century AD] [Classical studies] (OCD)
JOSH .... Job Safety and Health [Bureau of National Affairs] [Information service or system] (CRD)
Josh............. Joshua [Old Testament book]
JOSH .... Journal of School Halth (journ.) (SAUS)
JOSHUA...... Joint Sticking Hemoglobin Universal Assay [Sickle cell anemia test]
JOSIC.......... Joint Ocean Surveillance Information Centre (SAUO)
JOSL........... Joslyn Corp. (SAUO)
JO/SL.......... Jupiter Orbiter Satellite Lander [NASA]
JosLife........ Life of Josephus (BJA)
J Oslo City Hosp... Journal Oslo City Hospital (journ.) (SAUS)
JOSM.......... Jesuit Office of Social Ministry [Later, NOJSM] (EA)
J Osmania Univ... Journal. Osmania University (journ.) (SAUS)
JOSN .... Seaman, Journalist, Striker [Navy rating]
JOSO .... Joint Organization for Solar Observations
JOSP........... Junior Olympic Shooting Program [National Rifle Association]
JOSPRO...... Joint Ocean [or Overseas] Shipping Procedure
JOSPT......... Journal of Orthopaedic and Sports Physical Therapy (journ.) (SAUS)
JOSS........... Job Sharing System (SAUS)
JOSS........... JOHNNIAC [John's Integrator and Automatic Computer] Open Shop System [Time-sharing language] [Rand Corp.] [1962] [Computer science]
JOSS........... Joint Object Services Submission (SAUO)
JOSS........... Joint Ocean Surface Study
JOSS........... Joint Office for Science Support (SAUO)
JOSS........... Joint Overseas Switchboard (SAUS)
JOSS........... Joint Overseas Switchboard Switch (SAUO)
JOSS........... Joint Overseas Switching System [Military] (AABC)
Jostens........ Jostens, Inc. [Associated Press] (SAG)
JosWars ...... Wars [Josephus] (BJA)
JOT............. Jam on Target
JOT............. Job-Oriented Terminal
Jo T............ John of Tynemouth [Deceased, 1221] [Authority cited in pre-1607 legal work] (DSA)
JOT............. Joint Observer Team (SAUO)
JOT............. Joint Operational Test

JOT .... Joliet, IL [*Location identifier*] [*FAA*] (FAAL)
JOT .... Journal of Orthopaedic Trauma (journ.) (SAUS)
JOT .... Journal of Taxation (journ.) (SAUS)
JOT .... Jump-Oriented Terminal (SAUS)
JOT .... Junction Optimization Technique (SAUS)
JOT .... Junior Officer Trainee (GOBB)
JOTA .... Jamboree on the Air [*Boy Scouts of America*]
JOT & E ...... Joint Operational Test and Evaluation (MCD)
JOT&E .... Joint Operational Test and Evaluation (SAUS)
JOTB .... Jungle Operations Training Battalion [*Military*]
JOTC .... Joint Oil Targets Committee [*World War II*]
JOTC .... Jungle Operations Training Center [*Army*] (INF)
JOTD .... Jotted (ABBR)
Jo Te .... Johannes Teutonicus [*Deceased circa 1246*] [*Authority cited in pre-1607 legal work*] (DSA)
JOTFOC .... Justification for Other than Full and Open Competition (AAGC)
JOTG .... Jotting (ABBR)
J Otolaryngol... Journal of Otolaryngology (journ.) (SAUS)
J Otolaryngol Soc Aust... Journal. Oto-laryngological Society of Australia (journ.) (SAUS)
J Otolaryngol Suppl... Journal of Otolaryngology. Supplement (journ.) (SAUS)
J Oto-Rhino-Laryngol Soc Jpn... Journal. Oto-Rhino-Laryngological Society of Japan (journ.) (SAUS)
JOTPA .... Journal of Oral Therapeutics and Pharmacology (journ.) (SAUS)
JOTR .... Joint Operational and Technical Reviews [*Military*] (AFIT)
JOTR .... Joshua Tree National Monument
JOTS .... Job-Oriented Training Standards (AFM)
JOTS .... Joint Operational Tactical System [*Navy*] (DOMA)
JOTS .... Joint Operational Telephone System (SAUO)
JOTS II .... Joint Operational Tactical System Version II (SAUS)
JOTT .... Junior Officer Tactics Team (SAUO)
JOU .... Osaka University, Kita-ku (SAUO)
JOU .... Osaka University, Kita-ku, Osaka, Japan [*Library symbol*] [*Library of Congress*] (LCLS)
JOU .... Sioux Falls, SD [*Location identifier*] [*FAA*] (FAAL)
JOUAM .... Junior Order of United American Mechanics (SAUO)
JOULE .... Joint Opportunities for Unconventional or Long-Term Energy Supply (SAUO)
Joule .... Joules, Inc. [*Associated Press*] (SAG)
JOU-N .... Osaka University, Nakanishima Library (SAUO)
JOU-N .... Osaka University, Nakanishima Library, Osaka, Japan [*Library symbol*] [*Library of Congress*] (LCLS)
JOUR .... Journal (ABBR)
Jour .... Journal (EBF)
jour............. Journal (SHCU)
JOUR .... Journalist (GOBB)
JOUR .... Journey (WGA)
JOUR .... Journeyman
Jour Acoust Soc... Journal. Acoustical Society of America (journ.) (SAUS)
Jour Acoust Soc... Journal of the Acoustical Society of America (SAUO)
Jour Aesthetics and Art Crit... Journal of Aesthetic and Art Criticism (journ.) (SAUS)
Jour Amer Inst Arch... Journal of the American Institute of Architects. Washington (journ.) (SAUS)
Jour Am Inst Archit... Journal. American Institute of Architecture (journ.) (SAUS)
Jour Brit Hond agri soc... Journal of the British Honduras Agricultural Society. Belize (SAUO)
Jour Brit Hond Agri Soc... Journal of the British Honduras Agricultural Society (journ.) (SAUS)
Jour Brit Studies... Journal of British Studies (journ.) (SAUS)
Jour bus ...... Journal of Business of the University of Chicago. Chicago (SAUO)
Jour Chem Physics... Journal of Chemical Physics (journ.) (SAUS)
Jour Church and State... Journal of Church and State (journ.) (SAUS)
Jour Comp Leg... Journal. Society of Comparative Legislation [*A publication*] (DLA)
Jour Conat Law... Journal of Conational Law [*A publication*] (DLA)
Jour Contemp Hist... Journal of Contemporary History (journ.) (SAUS)
Jour Crim L... Journal of Criminal Law and Criminology (journ.) (SAUS)
Jour D C bar assoc... Journal of the District of Columbia bar association. District of Columbia (SAUS)
Jour Devel Ares... Journal of Developmental Areas (journ.) (SAUS)
Jour Eccl Hist... Journal of Ecclesiastical History (journ.) (SAUS)
Jour ecol ..... Journal of Ecology. British Ecological Society. London (SAUO)
Jour Econ and Bus Hist... Journal of Economic and Business History (journ.) (SAUS)
Jour Econ Hist... Journal of Economic History (journ.) (SAUS)
Jour educ soc... Journal of Educational Sociology. Payne Educational Sociology Foundation, Inc. New York (SAUO)
Jour Farm Econ... Journal of Farm Economics (journ.) (SAUS)
Jour Farm Hist... Journal of Farm History (journ.) (SAUS)
Jour forestry... Journal of Forestry. Official Organ of the Society of American Foresters. Washington (SAUO)
Jour Geol Eductihon... Journal of Geological Education (journ.) (SAUS)
Jour Hist Ideas... Journal of the History of Ideas (journ.) (SAUS)
Jour Hist Med... Journal of the History of Medicine (journ.) (SAUS)
Jour Hist Phil... Journal of the History of Philosophy (journ.) (SAUS)
Jour Human Rel... Journal of Human Relations (journ.) (SAUS)
Jour Inst Petrol... Journal of the Institute of Petroleum (journ.) (SAUS)
Jour Interam Studies... Journal of Interamerican Studies and World Affairs (journ.) (SAUS)
Jour Jamaica agric soc... Journal of the Jamaica Agricultural Society. Kingston (SAUO)
Jour Jur....... Journal of Jurisprudence [*A publication*] (DLA)
Jour Juris .... Hall's Journal of Jurisprudence [*A publication*] (DLA)
Jour Jur Sc... Journal of Jurisprudence and Scottish Law Magazine [*A publication*] (DLA)

Jour Land Public Uhlity Econ... Journal of Land and Public Utility Economics (journ.) (SAUS)
Jour land publ util econ... Journal of Land & Public Utility Economics. University of Wisconsin. Madison (SAUO)
Jour Law ..... Journal of Law [*A publication*] (DLA)
Jour Law and Econ... Journal of Law and Economic Development (journ.) (SAUS)
Jour Legal Ed... Journal of Legal Education (journ.) (SAUS)
Jour Lib Hist... Journal of Library History (journ.) (SAUS)
Jour meteorology... Journal of Meteorology. American Meteorological Society. Lancaster (SAUO)
Jour Miss Hist... Journal of Mississippi History (journ.) (SAUS)
Jour Mod Hist... Journal of Modern History (journ.) (SAUS)
JOURN .... Journal
Journ .... Journalism (DD)
JOURN .... Journey (ABBR)
Journal Geomorph... Journal of Geomorphology (journ.) (SAUS)
Journal Greater India Soc... Journal. Greater India Society (journ.) (SAUS)
Journalism Educ... Journalism Educator (journ.) (SAUS)
Journal-Net... International Journalist Network (SAUS)
Journal of RPS... Journal. Royal Photographic Society (journ.) (SAUS)
Journal Q... Journalism Quarterly. Association for Education in Journalism; American Association of Schools and Departments of Journalism; Kappa Tau Alpha Society; University of Minnesota (SAUO)
Journal Q... Journalism Quarterly (journ.) (SAUS)
Journ Atm Terr Phys... Journal of Atmospheric and Terrestrial Physics (journ.) (SAUS)
Journ Bib Lit... Journal of Biblical Literature [*A publication*] (OCD)
Journ Bib Lit... Journal of Biblical Literature (journ.) (SAUS)
Journ Biophys Biochem Cytol... Journal of Biohysical and Biochemical Cytology (journ.) (SAUS)
Journ Bot Brit For... Journal of Botany. British and Foreign (journ.) (SAUS)
Journ Br Astr Ass... Journal. British Astronomical Association (journ.) (SAUS)
Journ Ceyl Obstet Gyn Ass... Journal. Ceylon Obstetric and Gynaecological Association (journ.) (SAUS)
Journ Chem Phys... Journal of Chemical Physics (journ.) (SAUS)
Journ Chim Phys Chim... Journal de Chimie Physique et de Physico-Chimie Biologique (journ.) (SAUS)
Journ Clin Ophthal... Journal of Clinical Ophthalmology (journ.) (SAUS)
Journ Clin Path... Journal of Clinical Pathology (journ.) (SAUS)
Journ Clin Psychol... Journal of Clinical Psychology (journ.) (SAUS)
Jour negro hist... Journal of Negro History. Association for the Study of Negro Life and History, Inc. (SAUO)
Jour New York Bot Garden... Journal of the New York Botanical Garden. New York (journ.) (SAUS)
Journ Hist Behavioral Sci... Journal of the History of the Behavioral Sciences (journ.) (SAUS)
Journ Jur..... Journal of Jurisprudence [*A publication*] (DLA)
Journl Cork Hist S... Journal. Cork Historical and Archaeological Society (journ.) (SAUS)
Journ Phil.... Journal of Philology [*A publication*] (OCD)
Journ Phil.... Journal of Philology (journ.) (SAUS)
Journ Sav ... Journal des Savants [*A publication*] (OCD)
Jour of ecology... Journal of ecology, British Ecological Society (SAUO)
Jour of Int Affairs... Journal of International Affairs (journ.) (SAUS)
Jour of Relig... Journal of Religion (journ.) (SAUS)
Jour of Soc Issues... Journal of Social Issues (journ.) (SAUS)
Jour Pac Hist... Journal of Pacifc History (journ.) (SAUS)
Jour Pol Econ... Journal of Political Economy (journ.) (SAUS)
Jour Polit... Journal of Politics (journ.) (SAUS)
Jour Presby Hist... Journal of Presbyterian History (journ.) (SAUS)
Jour Ps Med... Journal of Psychological Medicine and Medical Jurisprudence [*A publication*] (DLA)
Jour Ps Med... Journal of Psychological Medicine and Medical Jurisprudence (journ.) (SAUS)
Jour Relig Hist... Journal of Religious History (journ.) (SAUS)
Jour soc arch hist... Journal of the Society of Architectural Historians. Urbana (SAUO)
Jour Soc Civ... Journal des Societes Civiles et Commerciales [*A publication*] (DLA)
Jour Society Archit Historians... Journal. Society of Architecture and Historians (journ.) (SAUS)
Jour Speech Disorders... Journal of Speech Disorders (journ.) (SAUS)
Jour Trib Com... Journal des Tribunaux de Commerce [*A publication*] (DLA)
Jour Warburg Courtauld Inst... Journal of the Warburg and Courtauld Institutes (journ.) (SAUS)
JOUSD .... Journal of Science. Busan National University (journ.) (SAUS)
Jov.............. Hymnus in Jovem [*of Callimachus*] [*Classical studies*] (OCD)
JOV............. Japanese Overseas Volunteers (SAUS)
JOV............. Joint Venture (SAUO)
JOVE........... Job Placement on the Job Training Vocational Education Educational Assistance (SAUS)
JOVE........... Joint Operations Visualization Environment [*Military*]
JOVE........... Jonathans Own Version of Emacs (SAUS)
JOVE........... Jupiter Orbiting Vehicle for Exploration (MCD)
JOVIAL........ Joule's Own Version of the International Algebraic [*or Algorithmic*] Language [*1958*] [*Computer science*]
JOVIAL........ Joules Own Version of the International Algorithmic Language (SAUS)
JOVIAL........ Jules Own Version of the International Algebraic Language (SAUO)
Jow Dict ..... Jowitt's Dictionary of English Law [*2nd ed.*] [*1977*] [*A publication*] (DLA)
JOWIP .... Joint Ocean Wave Investigation Project [*US and Canadian venture*]
JOWOG .... Joint Working Group
JOWRDN...... Journal of Obesity and Weight Regulation (journ.) (SAUS)
JOY............. Job Opportunity for Youth [*NASA employment program*]
JOY............. Joy [*Poland*] [*ICAO designator*] (FAAC)

JOY.............	Joy Technologies Inc. (SAUO)
JOYA...........	Journal of Youth and Adolescence (journ.) (SAUS)
Joy Acc........	Joy's Evidence of Accomplices [1836] [A publication] (DLA)
Joyce Ins......	Joyce on Insurance [A publication] (DLA)
Joyce Ins.....	Joyce on Insurance (journ.) (SAUS)
Joyce Lim....	Joyce on Limitations [A publication] (DLA)
Joyce Prac Inj...	Joyce's Law and Practice of Injunctions [1872] [A publication] (DLA)
Joyce Prac Inj...	Joyces Law and Practice of Injunctions (journ.) (SAUS)
Joyce Prin Inj...	Joyce's Doctrines and Principles of Injunctions [1877] [A publication] (DLA)
Joy Chal	Joy's Peremptory Challenge of Jurors [1844] [A publication] (DLA)
Joy Conf	Joy. Admissibility of Confessions [1842] [A publication] (DLA)
Joy Ev.........	Joy's Evidence of Accomplices [1836] [A publication] (DLA)
Joy Leg Ed....	Joy on Legal Education [A publication] (DLA)
Joyn Lim	Joynes on Limitations [A publication] (DLA)
JOYO...........	Japanese Breeder Reactor (SAUS)
JOY Program...	Job Opportunity for Youth Program (SAUS)
JOYS...........	Journal of Youth Services in Libraries [American Library Association]
JOZ.............	Jozini [South Africa] [Seismograph station code, US Geological Survey] (SEIS)
JP	Adria Airways [Airline flight code] (ODBW)
JP	Die Juedische Presse [The Jewish Press] [German] (BJA)
JP	Fighter [Russian aircraft symbol]
JP	Indo-Pacific International [ICAO designator] (AD)
JP	Jack Panel
JP	Jackson-Pratt [Drain] [Surgery] (DAVI)
JP	Jacobi Polynomial [Mathematics]
JP	Jacobi Polynominal (SAUS)
JP	James M. Peed [Designer's mark when appearing on US coins]
JP	Janata Party [India] [Political party] (PPW)
JP	Japan [ANSI two-letter standard code] (CNC)
Jp	Japanese (SAUS)
JP	Japan Paper
JP	Japan Press (SAUO)
JP	Jarrow Press, Inc.
JP	Jatiya Party [Bangladesh] [Political party]
JP	Jean Pierre Cosmetiques, Inc. [Vancouver Stock Exchange symbol]
JP	Jefferson Pilot [NYSE symbol] (SAG)
JP	Jefferson-Pilot Corp. [NYSE symbol] (SPSG)
JP	Jet Penetration
JP	Jet Petroleum (AFM)
JP	Jet Pilot
JP	Jet Pipe
JP	Jet Power
jp	Jet Propellant (NAKS)
JP	Jet Propellant [or Propulsion]
JP	Jet-Propelled (SAUS)
jp	Jet Propulsion (NAKS)
JP	Jet Propulsion Fuel
JP	Jet Publications [DoD]
JP	Jet Pump [Bioinstrumentation]
JP	Jewish Press [Brooklyn, NY] [A publication] (BJA)
JP	Jig Pin (SAUS)
JP	Jiji Press, Ltd. (SAUO)
JP	Jobbing Printer [A publication] (DGA)
JP	Job Placement [Job Service] (OICC)
JP	Job Processing (SAUS)
JP	Job Processor
JP	Jobst Pump [Medicine]
JP	Job the Patient (BJA)
JP	Joining Peptide [Medicine] (DMAA)
JP	Joint Pacific [Military] (CINC)
JP	Joint Protection (STED)
JP	Joint Publication [Military]
JP	Jones Party [Malta] [Political party] (PPE)
JP	Jones Plug [Electricity] (IAA)
JP	Joseph Pennell [Specification-made paper]
JP	Journal of Paleontology (journ.) (SAUS)
JP	Journal of Parapsychology [A publication] (BRI)
JP	Judge of Probate [British] (ROG)
JP	Juice Packed (SAUS)
JP	Jumper (IAA)
JP	Jump on Positive (SAUS)
JP	Junction Panel [or Point] [Electronics]
JP	Junction Point (SAUS)
JP	Junge Pioniero
JP	Jungle Penetrator [A helicopter rescue device] [Military] (VNW)
JP	Junior Partner [i.e., a husband] [Slang]
JP	Junior Principal [Freemasonry] (ROG)
JP	Junior Probationer [British] (ROG)
JP	Justice of the Peace
JP	Justice of the Peace and Local Government Review [A publication] (DLA)
JP	Justice of the Peace. Weekly Notes of Cases [England] [A publication] (DLA)
JP	Justice Party [Turkey] [Political party]
JP	Jute-Protected (SAUS)
JP	Jute Protection [Telecommunications] (TEL)
JP	Juvenile Periodontist [Dentistry] (DAVI)
JP	Juventud Peronista [Peronist Youth] [Argentina]
JP	Kim Jong Pil [South Korean politician]
JPA	Jack Panel Assembly
JPA	Jamaica Press Association (BUAC)
JPA	Japan Petroleum Association (BUAC)

JPA.............	Japan Procurement Agency
JPA.............	Jesuit Philosophical Association of the United States and Canada (EA)
JPA.............	Jet Pioneers Association of the United States of America (EA)
JPA.............	Jewish Palestinian Aramaic (BJA)
JPA.............	Joao Pessoa [Brazil] [Airport symbol] (OAG)
JPA.............	Job Application Aid (SAUS)
JPA.............	Job Pack Area [Computer science] (IBMDP)
JPA.............	Job Performance Aid
JPA.............	Job Performance Assistance (SPST)
JPA.............	Joint Palestine Appeal (SAUO)
JPA.............	Joint Passover Association (SAUS)
JPA.............	Joint Passover Association of the City of New York (EA)
JPA.............	Joint Permitting Agency (SAUO)
JPA.............	Joint Permitting Agreement (COE)
JPA.............	Joint Planning Activity [DoD]
JPA.............	Joint Powers Agreement (SAUO)
JPA.............	Junior Philatelists of America (EA)
JPA.............	Justices of the Peace Association [Australia]
JPA.............	Juvenile Pilocytic Astrocytoma [Medicine] (DMAA)
JPA.............	Juvenile Psoriatic Arthritis [Medicine] (MELL)
JPA.............	La Porte, TX [Location identifier] [FAA] (FAAL)
J PA Acad Sci...	Journal. Pennsylvania Academy of Science (journ.) (SAUS)
J-PAAS	Jubilation - Paul Anka Admiration Society [Defunct] (EA)
JPAC...........	Joint Planning Advisory Committee (SAUO)
JPAC...........	Joint Public Advisory Committee (SAUO)
J Pac H.......	Journal of Pacific History [A publication]
J Packag Technol...	Journal of Packaging Technology (journ.) (SAUS)
JPACO.........	Job Pack Area Control Queue (VLIE)
JPACQ.........	Job Pack Area Control Queue
J Paediatr Child Health...	Journal of Paediatrics and Child Health (journ.) (SAUS)
J Paediatr Dent...	Journal of Paediatric Dentistry (journ.) (SAUS)
J Pain Symptom Manage...	Journal of Pain and Symptom Management (journ.) (SAUS)
J Paint Tec...	Journal of Paint Technology (journ.) (SAUS)
J Pak Hist Soc...	Journal. Pakistan Historical Society (journ.) (SAUS)
J Pal Ada Modul-2...	Journal of Pascal, Ada and Modula 2 (journ.) (SAUS)
J Palaegr Soc...	Journal. Palaeographical Society (journ.) (SAUS)
J Palest Arab Med Ass...	Journal. Palestine Arab Medical Association (journ.) (SAUS)
J Palliat Care...	Journal of Palliative Care (journ.) (SAUS)
J Palynol Palynol Soc India...	Journal of Palynology. Palynological Society of India (journ.) (SAUS)
JPAM..........	Joint Program Assessment Memorandum (MCD)
JPANDA.......	Journal of Psychoanalytic Anthropology (journ.) (SAUS)
J Pang Med S...	Journal. Pangasinan Medical Society (journ.) (SAUS)
J Pang Med Soc...	Journal. Pangasinan Medical Society (journ.) (SAUS)
JPAO..........	Joint Public Affairs Office (DOMA)
J Pa Or Soc...	Journal. Palestine Oriental Society (journ.) (SAUS)
JPAP..........	Jet Penetration Approach
JPAPS.........	Job Performance Aids Production System (SAUO)
J Papua NG Society...	Journal. Papua and New Guinea Society (journ.) (SAUS)
J Parametrics...	Journal of Parametrics (journ.) (SAUS)
J Parenter Drug Ass...	Journal. Parenteral Drug Association (journ.) (SAUS)
J Parenter Sci Technol...	Journal of Parenteral Science and Technology (journ.) (SAUS)
J Park Rec Adm...	Journal of Park and Recreation Administration (journ.) (SAUS)
J Parlia Info...	Journal of Parliamentary Information (journ.) (SAUS)
JPAT..........	Joint Process Action Team
J Pathol.......	Journal of Pathology (journ.) (SAUS)
J Patient Acc Manage...	Journal of Patient Account Management (journ.) (SAUS)
JPATS.........	Joint Primary Aircraft Trainer System (SAUS)
JPATS.........	Joint Primary Aircraft Training System [Air Force] [Navy] (DOMA)
JPAV...........	Joint Personnel Asset Visibility [Military]
J PA Water Works Oper Assoc...	Journal. Pennsylvania Water Works Operators Assiation (journ.) (SAUS)
JPB.............	Joint Planning Board
JPB.............	Joint Procurement Board [Military] (AABC)
JPB.............	Joint Production Board [US and Great Britain]
JPB.............	Joint Purchasing Board
JPB.............	Junctional Premature Beat [Cardiology]
JPBAEB........	Journal of Psychopathology and Behavioral Assessment (journ.) (SAUS)
JPBHS	Judah P. Benjamin High School (SAUO)
JPBPB.........	Journal of Pharmacokinetics and Biopharmaceutics (journ.) (SAUS)
JPBS...........	Jettison Pushbutton Switch
JPC.............	Jack Patch Cord
JpC	Japanese Columbia [Record label]
JPC.............	Japan Productivity Center (SAUO)
JPC.............	Japan Productivity Centre (BUAC)
JPC.............	Jet Propulsion Center (SAUO)
JPC.............	Jeunesse pour Christ [Youth for Christ International - YFCI] (EA)
JPC.............	Jeunesse Progressiste Casamancaise [Casamance Progressive Youth] [Senegal]
JPC.............	Johnson Products (EFIS)
JPC.............	Johnson Products Company, Inc. (SAUO)
JPC.............	Joint Partnering Contracting
JPC.............	Joint Pensions Committee (WDAA)
JPC.............	Joint Planning Center
JPC.............	Joint Planning Committee
JPC.............	Joint Planning Conference (SAUO)
JPC.............	Joint Planning Council (SAUO)
JPC.............	Joint Power Condition [Aerospace] (NAKS)
JPC.............	Joint Power Conditioner
JPC.............	Joint Practice Committee (SAUO)

JPC .... Joint Production Committee [*British*] (DCTA)
JPC .... Joint Production Council (SAUO)
JPC .... Joint Project Committee (SAUO)
JPC .... Joint Publishers Committee (SAUO)
JPC .... Journal of Pharmaceutical Care (journ.) (SAUS)
JPC .... Journal of Planar Chromatography (journ.) (SAUS)
JPC .... Journal of Popular Culture [*A publication*] (BRI)
JPC .... Judgement Purchase Corp.
JPC .... Judge of the Prize Court (DLA)
JPC .... Judicial Planning Council (OICC)
JPC .... Junctional Premature Contraction [*Cardiology*]
JPC .... Justice of the Peace Clerk [*British*] (ROG)
JPC .... Just Prior Condition [*Computer science*]
JPC .... Polar Air Co. [*Russian Federation*] [*ICAO designator*] (FAAC)
JPCA .... Japan Petrochemical Industry Association (BUAC)
JPCA .... Jewish Penicillin Connoisseurs Association (EA)
JPCAAC .... Journal. Air Pollution Control Association (journ.) (SAUS)
JP Cable ..... Jute-Protected Cable (SAUS)
JPCC .... Joint Pacific Command Control Network (MCD)
JPCC .... Joint Petroleum Coordination Center (SAUO)
JPCC .... Joint Petroleum Coordination Center/Committee [*NATO*] (NATG)
JPCC .... Joint Petroleum Coordination Committee (SAUO)
JPCCA .... Journal of Physical and Colloid Chemistry (journ.) (SAUS)
JPCD .... Just Perceptible Color Difference [*Telecommunications*] (TEL)
J Pce Sci .... Journal of Peace Science (journ.) (SAUS)
JPCG .... Joint Policy Coordinated Group (SAUO)
JPCG-CRM ... Joint Policy Coordinating Group on Computer Resources Management (MCD)
JPCG/DIMM... Joint Policy Coordinating Group on Defense Integrated Materiel Management (AFIT)
JPCG/DIMM... Joint Policy Coordinating Group on Defense Integrated Materiel Management (SAUS)
JPCG-DMI .... Joint Policy Coordinating Group on Depot Maintenance Interservicing
J PCI .... Journal of the Prestressed Concrete Institute (journ.) (SAUS)
JPCMA .... Journal of Photochemistry (journ.) (SAUS)
JP COMNET... Joint Pacific Command Teletype Network (SAUO)
JPCRM .... Joint Policy Coordinating Group on Computer Resources (SAUO)
JPCRSP .... John Pennekamp Coral Reef State Park (SAUO)
JPCS .... Journal of Physics and Chemistry of Solids. Supplement (journ.) (SAUS)
JP Ct .... Justice of the Peace's Court [*Legal term*] (DLA)
JPD .... Japan Publishers Directory [*Japan Publications Guide Service*] [*Japan*] [*Information service or system*] (CRD)
JPD .... Joint Planning Document (COE)
JPD .... Joint Potential Designator [*DoD*]
JPD .... Just Perceptible Difference (SAUS)
JPD .... Juvenile Plantar Dermatosis [*Medicine*] (DAVI)
JPDAAH ...... Journal. American Podiatry Association (journ.) (SAUS)
JPDADK ...... Journal. Parenteral Drug Association (journ.) (SAUS)
JPDC .... Japan Petroleum Development Co.
JPDC .... Japan Petroleum Development Corporation (SAUO)
JPDEN .... Journal of Prosthetic Dentistry (journ.) (SAUS)
JPDF .... Joint Probability Density Function (SAUS)
JPDMB .... American Society of Psychosomatic Dentistry and Medicine. Journal (journ.) (SAUS)
JPDPA .... Journal of Periodontology-Periodontics (journ.) (SAUS)
JPDR .... Japan Power Demonstration Reactor
JPDRD .... Joint Program Definition and Requirements Document (SAUS)
JPDS .... Joint Petroleum Data System (SAUO)
JPE .... Job Performance Evaluation (PDAA)
J PE .... Journal of Physical Education and Program (journ.) (SAUS)
JPE .... Journal of Political Economy [*A publication*] (BRI)
JPE .... JPE, Inc. [*Associated Press*] (SAG)
JPE .... Jump if Parity Even (VLIE)
JPE .... Jump in Parity Even (SAUS)
JPE .... Jump on Parity Even (SAUS)
J Peas Stud... Journal of Peadant Studies (journ.) (SAUS)
JPEC .... Joint Planning and Execution Community (DOMA)
JPEC .... Joint Planning and Execution Course (SAUO)
JPEC .... JOPES Planning and Execution Community (SAUO)
JP ECON ...... Journal of Political Economy [*A publication*] (ROG)
J PED .... Journal of Pedagogy [*New York*] [*A publication*] (ROG)
JPEDB .... Joint Planning and Execution Data Base (SAUO)
JPEDD .... Journal of Physics Education (journ.) (SAUS)
J Pediat ...... Journal of Pediatrics (SAUS)
J Pediatr Endocrinol Metab... Journal of Pediatric Endocrinology and Metabolism (journ.) (SAUS)
J Pediatr Hematol Oncol... Journal of Pediatric Hematology/Oncology (journ.) (SAUS)
J Pediatr Nurs... Journal of Pediatric Nursing (journ.) (SAUS)
J Pediatr Nurs... Journal of Pediatric Nursing, Nursing Care of Children and Families (journ.) (SAUS)
J Pediatr Oncol Nurs... Journal of Pediatric Oncology Nursing (journ.) (SAUS)
J Pediatr Ophtbalmol... Journal of Pediatric Ophthalmology (journ.) (SAUS)
J Pediatr Ophthalmol Strabismus... Journal of Pediatric Ophthalmology and Strabismus (journ.) (SAUS)
J Pedi Endocr... Journal of Pediatric Endocrinology (journ.) (SAUS)
J Pedod ...... Journal of Pedodontics (journ.) (SAUS)
JPEG .... Joint Photographic Experts Group [*International video standard*] (PCM)
jpeg .... Joint Photographic Experts Group [*Computer science*]
JPEG .... Joint Picture Experts Group (SAUO)
JPEG .... Joint Planning and Execution Graphics (SAUO)
JPEI .... JPE, Inc. [*NASDAQ symbol*] (SAG)
JPEL .... Journal of Planning and Environment Law (journ.) (SAUS)

JPEN .... Journal of Parenteral & Enteral Nutrition (SAUO)
JPEN .... Journal of Parenteral and Enteral Nutrition (journ.) (SAUS)
JPEN J Parenter Enteral Nutr... JPEN. Journal of Parenteral and Enteral Nutrition (journ.)
J Penn Way Instn... Permanent Way Institution. Journal (SAUS)
J Perinat Med... Journal of Perinatal Medicine (journ.) (SAUS)
J Periodontal Res Suppl... Journal of Periodontal Research. Supplement (journ.) (SAUS)
J Periodontol-Periodontics... Journal of Periodontology-Periodontics (journ.) (SAUS)
J Pers Assess... Journal of Personality Assessment (journ.) (SAUS)
JPERSTAT.... Joint Personnel Status and Casualty Report (COE)
J Perth Hosp... Journal. Perth Hospital (journ.) (SAUS)
JPESC .... Joint Planning and Execution Steering Committee (SAUO)
JPESJ .... Jewish Palestine Exploration Society. Journal [*A publication*] (BJA)
J Pestic Sci... Journal of Pesticide Science (journ.) (SAUS)
JPET .... Job Placement and Employment Training
JPET .... Journal of Pharmacology and Experimental Therapeutics (SAUO)
J Petrol....... Journal of Petrology (journ.) (SAUS)
J Petrol Geol... Journal of Petrology and Geology (journ.) (SAUS)
J Petrol Techn... Journal of Petroleum Technology (journ.) (SAUS)
JPF .... Jewish Peace Fellowship (EA)
JPF .... Jewish Philanthropic Fund (SAUO)
JPF .... Jewish Philanthropic Fund of 1933 (EA)
JPF .... Job Planning Form
JPF .... Justice of the Peace Fiscal [*British*] (ROG)
JPFAEV ...... Journal of Psychotherapy and the Family (journ.) (SAUS)
JPFC .... Jane Powell Fan Club (EA)
JPFC .... Jeanne Pruett Fan Club (EA)
JPFC .... Judas Priest Fan Club (EA)
JPFFI .... Jiangsu Provincial Freshwater Fisheries Institute [*China*] (BUAC)
JPFI .... Joslin Diabetes Foundation I (SAUO)
JPFMP .... Journal of Physics. F Metal Physics (journ.) (SAUS)
JPFO .... Jews for the Preservation of Firearms Ownership (EA)
JP Food .... JP Foodservice, Inc. [*Associated Press*] (SAG)
JPFR .... Japan Prototype Fast Reactor (SAUO)
JPFS .... JP Foodservice [*NASDAQ symbol*] (TTSB)
JPFS .... JP Foodservice, Inc. [*NASDAQ symbol*] (SAG)
JPFT .... Joiner Pilaster Fumetight [*Technical drawings*]
J-P Fuel....... Jet-Propulsion Fuel (SAUS)
JPG .... Jefferson Proving Ground [*Madison, IN*] [*Army*] (AABC)
JPG .... Job Performance [*or Proficiency*] Guide (AFM)
JPG .... Job Proficiency Guide (SAUS)
JPG .... Joint Photographic experts Group (SAUO)
JPG .... Joint Planning Group [*NATO*] (NATG)
JPG .... Joint Presidents Group (SAUO)
JPG .... JOPES Project Group (SAUO)
JPG .... JPEG/JFIF compliant image format (SAUS)
JPG .... Jumping (SAUS)
JPGA .... Japan Professional Golf Association (SAUO)
JPGC .... Joint Power Generation Conference
JPGEN .... Journal of Experimental Psychology: General (SAUS)
JPGM .... Joint Planning Graphics Module (SAUO)
JPGM .... J Paul Getty Museum (SAUO)
JPGR .... Journal of Plant Growth Regulation (journ.) (SAUS)
JPGS .... Japan Publications Guide Service [*Information service or system*] (IID)
JPH .... Jones, Paul H., Romulus MI [*STAC*]
JPH .... Journal of Pacifc History (journ.) (SAUS)
JPH .... Journal of Policy History (SAUO)
JPH .... Journal of Presbyterian History (journ.) (SAUS)
JPHA .... John Pelham Historical Association (EA)
JPHAA .... Journal. American Pharmaceutical Association (journ.) (SAUS)
JPHAC .... Journal of Physics. A Mathematical and General (journ.) (SAUS)
J Phann Market Manage... Journal of Pharmaceutical Marketing and Management (journ.) (SAUS)
J Pharmacobiodyn... Journal of Pharmacobio-Dynamics (journ.) (SAUS)
J Pharmacol Methods... Journal of Pharmacological Methods (journ.) (SAUS)
J Pharmacol Toxicol Methods... Journal of Pharmacological Toxicol Methods (journ.) (SAUS)
J Pharmac Sci... Journal of the Pharmaceutical Sciences (journ.) (SAUS)
J Pharm Assoc Thailand... Journal. Pharmaceutical Association of Thailand (journ.) (SAUS)
J Pharm Med... Journal of Pharmaceutical Medicine (journ.) (SAUS)
J Pharm Pharmacol Suppl... Journal of Pharmacy and Pharmacology. Supplement (journ.) (SAUS)
J Pharm Sci... Journal of Pharmaceutical Science (MEC)
J Pharm Sci UAR... Journal of Pharmaceutical Sciences of the United Arab Republic (journ.) (SAUS)
J Pharm Soc Jap... Journal. Pharmaceutical Society of Japan (journ.) (SAUS)
J Pharm Soc Jpn... Journal of the Pharmaceutical Society of Japan (journ.) (SAUS)
J Pharm Soc Jpn... Journal. Pharmaceutical Society of Japan (journ.) (SAUS)
J Pharm Soc Korea... Journal. Pharmaceutical Society of Korea (journ.) (SAUS)
J Pharm Technol... Journal of Pharmacy Technology (journ.) (SAUS)
J Pharm Univ Karachi... Journal of Pharmacy. University of Karachi (journ.) (SAUS)
J Ph Ch Ref Data... Journal of Physical and Chemical Reference Data (journ.) (SAUS)
JPHD .... Journal of Public Health Dentistry (journ.) (SAUS)
J Phenomen... Journal of Phenomenological Psychology (journ.) (SAUS)
JPHGB .... Journal of Physics. G Nuclear Physics (journ.) (SAUS)
J Phil .... Journal of Philosophy [*A publication*] (BRI)
J Phila Ass Psychoanal... Journal. Philadelphia Association for Psychoanalysis (journ.) (SAUS)
J Phila County Dent Soc... Journal. Philadelphia County Dental Society (journ.) (SAUS)

J Philadelphia Gen Hosp... Journal. Philadelphia General Hospital (journ.) (SAUS)

J Phildelphia Coll Pharm... Journal. Philadelphia College of Pharmacy (journ.) (SAUS)

J Phil Educ... Journal of Philosophy of Education (journ.) (SAUS)

J Philipp Dent Assoc... Journal. Philippine Dental Association (journ.) (SAUS)

J Philipp Fed Priv Med Pract... Journal. Philippine Federation of Private Medical Practitioners (journ.) (SAUS)

J Philippine MA... Journal. Philippine Medical Association (journ.) (SAUS)

J Philipp Isl Med Assoc... Journal. Philippine Islands Medical Association (journ.) (SAUS)

J Philipp Med Assoc... Journal. Philippine Medical Association (journ.) (SAUS)

J Philipp Pharm Assoc... Journal. Philippine Pharmaceutical Association (journ.) (SAUS)

J Philipp Vet Med Assoc... Journal. Philippine Veterinary Medical Association (journ.) (SAUS)

J Phil Stat... Journal of Philippine Statistics (journ.) (SAUS)

J Phil Stud... Journal of Philosophical Studies (journ.) (SAUS)

JPHMD Journal of Experimental Psychology Human Learning and Memory (journ.) (SAUS)

JPhon Journal of Phonetics (journ.) (SAUS)

J Photoacoust... Journal of Photoacoustics (journ.) (SAUS)

J Photochem... Journal of Photochemistry (journ.) (SAUS)

J Photochem Etching... Journal of Photochemical Etching (journ.) (SAUS)

J Photochem Photobiol B... Journal of Photochemistry and Photobiology. B, Biology (journ.) (SAUS)

J Photogr Soc Am... Journal. Photographic Society of America (journ.) (SAUS)

J Photomicrogr Soc... Journal. Photomicroaphic Society (journ.) (SAUS)

J Phot Soc Amer... Journal. Photographic Society of America (journ.) (SAUS)

JPHP Journal of Public Health Policy (journ.) (SAUS)

JPHPD Journal of Experimental Psychology Human Perception and Performance (journ.) (SAUS)

JPHS Journal of the Presbyterian Historical Society (SAUO)

JPHS Journal of the Presbyterian Historical Society (journ.) (SAUS)

JPHS Journal. Presbyterian Historical Society (journ.) (SAUS)

JPHS Pakistan Historical Society (SAUO)

JPHYA Journal of Physiology (journ.) (SAUS)

J Phys Journal of Physics (journ.) (SAUS)

J Phys A Gen Phys... Journal of Physics. A General Physics (journ.) (SAUS)

J Phys A Math Nucl Gen... Journal of Physics. A Mathematical, Nuclear and General (journ.) (SAUS)

J Phys B At Mol Opt Phys... Journal of Physics B, Atomic, Molecular and Optical Physics (journ.) (SAUS)

J Phys Chem... Journal of Physical Chemistry (MEC)

J Phys Chem Ref Data Suppl... Journal of Physical and Chemical Reference Data. Supplement (journ.) (SAUS)

J Phys Chem Solids Suppl... Journal of Physics and Chemistry of Solids. Supplement (journ.) (SAUS)

J Phys D Appl Phys... Journal of Physics. D Applied Physics (journ.) (SAUS)

J Phys Earth... Journal of Physics of the Earth (journ.) (SAUS)

J Phys Educ Rec & Dance... Journal of Physical Education, Recreation and Dance (journ.) (SAUS)

J Phys Educ Recr... Journal of Physical Educalion and Recreation (journ.) (SAUS)

J Physiol Soc Jpn... Journal. Physiological Society of Japan (journ.) (SAUS)

J Phys Jap... Journal. Physical Society of Japan (journ.) (SAUS)

J Phys Org Chem... Journal of Physical Organic Chemistry (journ.) (SAUS)

J Phys Soc... Journal of the Physical Society (journ.) (SAUS)

J Phys Soc Jp... Journal. Physical Society of Japan (journ.) (SAUS)

J Phys Soc Jpn... Journal of Physical Society of Japan (journ.) (SAUS)

J Phys Soc Jpn... Journal of the Physical Society of Japan (SAUO)

J Phys Soc Jpn... Journal of the Physical Society of Japan (SAUS)

J Phys Soc Jpn Suppl... Journal. Physical Society of Japan. Supplement (journ.) (SAUS)

JPI Jackson Personality Inventory [Personality development test] [Psychology]

JPI Japan Packaging Institute (BUAC)

JPI Jianghan Petroleum Institute [China] (BUAC)

JPI Job Performance Illustrations (MCD)

JPI Joint Packaging Instruction

JPI Joint Precision Interdiction [NATO] (DOMA)

JPI JP Industries, Inc. (SAUO)

JPI Jupiter Industries, Inc. (SAUO)

JPI Jupiter National, Inc. (SPSG)

JPI Sitka, AK [Location identifier] [FAA] (FAAL)

JPIA Japan Plastics Industry Association (BUAC)

JPIC Joint Program Integration Committee [NASA] (NASA)

JPIC Joint Public Information Center (COE)

JPIFA1 Japan Pesticide Information (journ.) (SAUS)

JPIM Journal of Product Innovation Management [Product Development and Management Association] [A publication]

J Pineal Res... Journal of Pineal Rearch (journ.) (SAUS)

J Pipeline Div Am Soc Civ Eng... Journal. Pipeline Division. American Society of Civil Engineers (journ.) (SAUS)

J Pipelines... Journal of Pipelines (journ.) (SAUS)

JPJ Justice of the Peace and Local Government Review [A publication] (DLA)

JPJ Justice of the Peace Journal [A publication]

JPJ Justice of the Peace. Weekly Notes of Cases [England] [A publication] (DLA)

JPJ Paterson, NJ [Location identifier] [FAA] (FAAL)

JPJo Justice of the Peace. Weekly Notes of Cases [England] [A publication] (DLA)

JPJu Journal of Psychology and Judaism (journ.) (SAUS)

J Pkg Technol... Journal of Packaging Technology (journ.) (SAUS)

J PL Jack Plug (SAUS)

JPL Jacksonville Public Library System, Jacksonville, FL [OCLC symbol] (OCLC)

JPL JAM Programming Language (SAUS)

JPL Japan Planetarium Laboratory

JPL Java Pacific Line (SAUO)

JPL Java Perl Lingo (SAUS)

JPL Jet Propulsion Laboratory [Renamed H. Allen Smith Jet Propulsion Laboratory, 1973, after a retiring congressman. However, JPL is used officially] [California Institute of Technology] [Pasadena, CA] [NASA] [Research center]

JPL Jet Propulsion Laboratory of Caltech (SAUS)

JPL Jewish Peace Lobby (EA)

JPL Job Parts List (AAG)

JPL Job Plans List (SAUS)

JPL Joint Propulsion Laboratory (SAUO)

JPL Journal of Philosophical Logic (journ.) (SAUS)

JPL Journal of Products Liabilily (journ.) (SAUS)

JPL Jyacc Procedural Language (SAUS)

J Plankton Res... Journal of Plankton Research (journ.) (SAUS)

J Plan Property Law... Journal of Planning and Property Law (journ.) (SAUS)

J Plant Breed... Journal of Plant Breeding (journ.) (SAUS)

J Plant Dis Prot... Journal of Plant Diseases and Protection (journ.) (SAUS)

J Plant Growth Regul... Journal of Plant Growth Regulation (journ.) (SAUS)

J Plant Growth Regul... Journal of Plant Orowth Regulation (journ.) (SAUS)

J Plant Nutr Soil Sci... Journal of Plant Nutrition and Soil Science (journ.) (SAUS)

J Plant Physiol... Journal of Plant Physiology (journ.) (SAUS)

J Plant Prot... Journal of Plant Protection (journ.) (SAUS)

J Plast An... Japan Plastics Industry Annual (journ.) (SAUS)

J Plast Film Sheet... Journal of Plastic Film and Sheeting (journ.) (SAUS)

J Plast Reconstr Surg Nurs... Journal of Plastic and Reconstructive Surgical Nursing (journ.) (SAUS)

JPLDIS Jet Propulsion Laboratory Display Information System (SAUO)

JPLE Journal of Professional Legal Education [Australia] [A publication]

JPL/ETR Jet Propuision Laboratory Field Station, Air Force Eastern Test Range (SAUS)

JPL/ETR Jet Propulsion Laboratory Field Station, Air Force Eastern Test Range

J Pln & Prop L... Journal of Planning and Property Law (journ.) (SAUS)

JPL/PODS Jet Propulsion Laboratory/Pilot Ocean Data System (MCD)

JPL Publ 78... Jet Propulsion Laboratory. Publication 78 (journ.) (SAUS)

JPLRC Joint Port Labor Relations Committee (SAUO)

JPLSA Journal. Polarographic Society (journ.) (SAUS)

JPL Space Programs Summ... Jet Propulsion Laboratory. Space Programs Summary (journ.) (SAUS)

JPL-STAR Jet Propulsion Laboratory Self Testing and Repairing Computer [California Institute of Technology] (PDAA)

JPL/STAR Computer... Jet Propulsion Laboratory/Self-Testing and Repair Computer (SAUS)

JPM Jet-Piercing Machine

JPM Job Performance Manual (MCD)

JPM Job Performance Measure

JPM Joint Program Manager (ACAE)

JPM Joint Project Manager

JPM Journal of Property Management (journ.) (SAUS)

JPM Journal of Purchasing and Materials Management (journ.) (SAUS)

JPM J. P. Morgan & Co., Inc. (SAUO)

JPM Morgan [J. P.] & Co., Inc. [NYSE symbol] (SPSG)

JPM Morgan (J.P.) [NYSE symbol] (TTSB)

JPMA Japan Plywood Manufactures Association (BUAC)

JPMA Japan Powder Metallurgy Association (SAUO)

JPMA Juvenile Products Manufacturers Association (EA)

JPMA J Pak Med Assoc... JPMA. Journal of the Pakistan Medical Association (SAUO)

JPMA J Pak Med Assoc... JPMA. Journal of the Pakistan Medical Association (journ.) (SAUS)

JPMC JPM Co. [NASDAQ symbol] (TTSB)

JPMCo JPM Co. (The) [Associated Press] (SAG)

JPMEA Journal. Philippine Medical Association (journ.) (SAUS)

JPMI JPM Industries, Inc. (SAUO)

JPMO Jersey Potato Marketing Organisation (BUAC)

JPMO Joint Program Management Office (MCD)

JPMPrA Morgan(JP) Adj Rt A Pfd [NYSE symbol] (TTSB)

JPMPrH Morgan(JP)6.625% Dep'H'Pfd [NYSE symbol] (TTSB)

JPMR Joint Program Management Review (ACAE)

JPMR Joint Projected Manpower Requirements [Military] (AABC)

JPMS J. P. Morgan Securities

JPMSA Journal of Pharmaceutical Sciences (journ.) (SAUS)

JPMT Joint Patient Movement Team (SAUO)

JPMX JPM Co. (The) [NASDAQ symbol] (SAG)

JPN Japan [ANSI three-letter standard code] (CNC)

Jpn Japan (SHCU)

jpn Japanese [MARC language code] [Library of Congress] (LCCP)

JPN Japan Fund, Inc. (SAUO)

JPN Memrykord Ltd. [British] [ICAO designator] (FAAC)

JPN Washington, DC [Location identifier] [FAA] (FAAL)

Jpn Agric Res Q... Japan Agricultural Research Quarterly (journ.) (SAUS)

Jpn Alum News... Japan Aluminum News (journ.) (SAUS)

Jpn Analyst... Japan Analyst (journ.) (SAUS)

Jpn Annu Rev Electron Comput Telecommun... Japan Annual Reviews in Electronics, Computers and Telecommunications (journ.) (SAUS)

Jpn Arch Histol... Japanese Archives of Histology (journ.) (SAUS)

Jpn Arch Intern Med... Japanese Archives of Internal Medicine (journ.) (SAUS)

Jpn Archit... Japan Architect (journ.) (SAUS)

Jpn At Energy Res Inst Annu Rep Acc... Japan. Atomic Energy Research Institute. Annual Report and Account (journ.) (SAUS)

Jpn At Energy Res Inst Rep Res Rep...   Japan. Atomic Energy Research Institute. Report. Research Report (journ.) (SAUS)
Jpn Chem Ind...   Japan Chemical Industry (journ.) (SAUS)
Jpn Chem Rev...   Japan Chemical Review (journ.) (SAUS)
Jpn Chem Week...   Japan Chemical Week (journ.) (SAUS)
Jpn Circ J....   Japanese Circulation Journal (journ.) (SAUS)
Jpn Dent J...   Japanese Dental Journal (journ.) (SAUS)
Jpn EA........   Japan Economic Almanac (SAUS)
Jpn Elec I....   Japan Electronics Industry (journ.) (SAUS)
Jpn Electron Eng...   Japan Electronic Engineering (journ.) (SAUS)
Jpn Energy Technol Intell...   Japan Energy and Technology Intelligence (journ.) (SAUS)
Jpn Export...   Export Statistical Schedule (journ.) (SAUS)
Jpn Gas Assoc J...   Japan Gas Association. Journal (journ.) (SAUS)
Jpn-Ger Med Rep...   Japan-Germany Medical Reports (journ.) (SAUS)
Jpn Heart J...   Japanese Heart Journal (journ.) (SAUS)
Jpn Hosp .....   Japan Hospitals (journ.) (SAUS)
Jpn Import...   Import Statistical Schedule (journ.) (SAUS)
Jpn Ind Technol Bull...   Japan Industrial and Technological Bulletin (journ.) (SAUS)
Jpn J Alcohol Stud & Drug Degend...   Japanese Journal of Alcohol Studies and Drug Dependence (journ.) (SAUS)
Jpn J Allergy...   Japanese Journal of Allergy (journ.) (SAUS)
Jpn J Anim Reprod...   Japanese Journal of Animal Reproduction (journ.) (SAUS)
Jpn J Antibiot...   Japanese Journal of Antibiotics (journ.) (SAUS)
Jpn J Appl Entomol Zool...   Japanese Journal of Applied Entomology and Zoology (journ.) (SAUS)
Jpn J Appl Phys...   Japanese Journal of Applied Physics (journ.) (SAUS)
Jpn J Appl Phys...   Japan Journal of Applied Physics (journ.) (SAUS)
Jpn J Appl Phys 2 Lett...   Japanese Journal of Applied Physics. Part 2. Letters (journ.) (SAUS)
Jpn J Appl Phys Part 2...   Japanese Journal of Applied Physics. Part 2. Letters (journ.) (SAUS)
Jpn J Appl Phys Suppl...   Japanese Journal of Applied Physics. Supplement (journ.) (SAUS)
Jpn J Astron...   Japanese Journal of Astronomy (journ.) (SAUS)
Jpn J Astron Geophys...   Japanese Journal of Astronomy and Geophysics (journ.) (SAUS)
Jpn J Bacteriol...   Japanese Journal of Bacteriology (journ.) (SAUS)
Jpn J Breed...   Japanese Journal of Breeding (journ.) (SAUS)
Jpn J Cancer Clin...   Japanese Journal of Cancer Clinics (journ.) (SAUS)
Jpn J Cancer Res...   Japanese Journal of Cancer Research (journ.) (SAUS)
Jpn J Chem...   Japanese Journal of Chemistry (journ.) (SAUS)
Jpn J Chest Dis...   Japanese Journal of Chest Diseases (journ.) (SAUS)
Jpn J Child Adoles Psychiatry...   Japanese Journal of Child and Adolescent Psychiatry (journ.) (SAUS)
Jpn J Clin Electron Microsc...   Japanese Journal of Clinical Electron Microscopy (journ.) (SAUS)
Jpn J Clin Exp Med...   Japanese Journal of Clinical and Experimental Medicine (journ.) (SAUS)
Jpn J Clin Hematol...   Japanese Journal of Clinical Hematology (journ.) (SAUS)
Jpn J Clin Med...   Japanese Journal of Clinical Medicine (journ.) (SAUS)
Jpn J Clin Oncol...   Japanese Journal of Clinical Oncology (journ.) (SAUS)
Jpn J Clin Ophthalmol...   Japanese Journal of Clinical Ophthalmology (journ.) (SAUS)
Jpn J Clin Pathol...   Japanese Journal of Clinical Pathology (journ.) (SAUS)
Jpn J Clin Pathol Suppl...   Japanese Journal of Clinical Pathology. Supplement (journ.) (SAUS)
Jpn J Clin Pharmacol...   Japanese Journal of Clinical Pharmacology (journ.) (SAUS)
Jpn J Clin Radiol...   Japanese Journal of Clinical Radiology (journ.) (SAUS)
Jpn J Clin Urol...   Japanese Journal of Clinical Urology (journ.) (SAUS)
Jpn J Const Med...   Japanese Journal of Constitutional Medi- cine (journ.) (SAUS)
Jpn J Crop Sci...   Japanese Journal of Crop Science (journ.) (SAUS)
Jpn J Dairy Food Sci...   Japanese Journal of Dairy and Food Science (journ.) (SAUS)
Jpn J Dairy Sci...   Japanese Journal of Dairy Science (journ.) (SAUS)
Jpn J Dermatol...   Japanese Journal of Dermatology (journ.) (SAUS)
Jpn J Ecol ...   Japanese Journal of Ecology (journ.) (SAUS)
Jpn J Eng Abstr...   Japanese Journal of Engineering. Abstracts (journ.) (SAUS)
Jpn J Ethnol...   Japanese Journal of Ethnology (journ.) (SAUS)
Jpn J Exp Med...   Japanese Journal of Experimental Medicine (journ.) (SAUS)
Jpn J Exp Morphol...   Japanese Journal of Experimenlal Morphology (journ.) (SAUS)
Jpn J Fertil Steril...   Japanese Journal of Fertility and Sterility (journ.) (SAUS)
Jpn J Freezing Dying...   Japanese Journal of Freezing and Dying (journ.) (SAUS)
Jpn J Gastroenterol...   Japanese Journal of Gastroenterology (journ.) (SAUS)
Jpn J Genet...   Japanese Journal of Genetics (journ.) (SAUS)
Jpn J Genet Suppl...   Japanese Journal of Genetics. Supple- ment (journ.) (SAUS)
Jpn J Geol Geogr...   Japanese Journal of Geology and Geography (journ.) (SAUS)
Jpn J Geriatr...   Japanese Journal of Geriatrics (journ.) (SAUS)
Jpn J Herpetol...   Japanese Journal of Herpetology (journ.) (SAUS)
Jpn J Hum Genet...   Japanese Journal of Human Genetics (journ.) (SAUS)
Jpn J Hyg ....   Japanese Journal of Hygiene (journ.) (SAUS)
Jpn J Ind Health...   Japanese Journal of Industrial Health (journ.) (SAUS)
Jpn J Lepr ...   Japanese Journal of Leprosy (journ.) (SAUS)
Jpn J Limnol...   Japanese Journal of Limnology (journ.) (SAUS)
Jpn J Malacol...   Japanese Journal of Malacology (journ.) (SAUS)
Jpn J Med ...   Japanese Journal of Medicine (journ.) (SAUS)
Jpn J Med Sci 1...   Japanese Journal of Medical Sciences. Part 1 (journ.) (SAUS)
Jpn J Med Sci 2...   Japanese Journal of Medical Sciences. Part 2. Biochemistry (journ.) (SAUS)
Jpn J Med Sci 3...   Japanese Journal of Medical Sciences. Part 3. Biophysics (journ.) (SAUS)
Jpn J Med Sci 5...   Japanese Journal of Medical Sciences. Part 5. Pathology (journ.) (SAUS)

Jpn J Med Sci 6...   Japanese Journal of Medical Sciences. Part 6. Bacteriology and Parasitology (journ.) (SAUS)
Jpn J Med Sci 7...   Japanese Journal of Medical Sciences. Part 7. Social Medicine and Hygiene (journ.) (SAUS)
Jpn J Med Sci 8...   Japanese Journal of Medical Sciences. Part 8. Internal Medicine, Pediatry and Psychiatry (journ.) (SAUS)
Jpn J Med Sci 9...   Japanese Journal of Medical Sciences. Part 9. Surgery, Onhopedy and Odontology (journ.) (SAUS)
Jpn J Med Sci 10...   Japanese Journal of Medical Sciences. Part 10. Ophthalmology (journ.) (SAUS)
Jpn J Med Sci 11...   Japanese Journal of Medical Sciences. Part 11 (journ.) (SAUS)
Jpn J Med Sci 12...   Japanese Journal of Medical Sciences. Part 12. Oto-Rhino-Laryngology (journ.) (SAUS)
Jpn J Med Sci 13...   Japanese Journal of Medical Sciences. Part 13. Dermatology and Urology (journ.) (SAUS)
Jpn J Med Sci Biol...   Japanese Journal of Medical Science and Biology (journ.) (SAUS)
Jpn J Michurin Biol...   Japanese Journal of Michurin Biology (journ.) (SAUS)
Jpn J Microbiol...   Japanese Journal of Microbiology (journ.) (SAUS)
Jpn J Nephrol...   Japanese Journal of Nephrology (journ.) (SAUS)
Jpn J Neurol Psychiatry...   Japanese Journal of Neurology and Psychiatry (journ.) (SAUS)
Jpn J Nucl Med...   Japanese Journal of Nuclear Medicine (journ.) (SAUS)
Jpn J Nurs...   Japanese Journal of Nursing (journ.) (SAUS)
Jpn J Nutr ...   Japanese Journal of Nutrition (journ.) (SAUS)
Jpn J Obstet Gynecol...   Japanese Journal of Obstetrics and Gynecology (journ.) (SAUS)
Jpn J Ophthalmol...   Japanese Journal of Ophthalmology (journ.) (SAUS)
Jpn J Oral Biol...   Japanese Journal of Oral Biology (journ.) (SAUS)
Jpn J Palynol...   Japanese Journal of Palynology (journ.) (SAUS)
Jpn J Parasitol...   Japanese Journal of Parasitology (journ.) (SAUS)
Jpn J Pediat...   Japanese Journal of Pediatrics (journ.) (SAUS)
Jpn J Pediat Surg Med...   Japanese Journal of Pedatric Surgery and Medicine (journ.) (SAUS)
Jpn J Pharmacol...   Japanese Journal of Pharmacology (journ.) (SAUS)
Jpn J Pharm Chem...   Japanese Journal of Pharmacy and Chemistry (journ.) (SAUS)
Jpn J Phys...   Japanese Journal of Physics (journ.) (SAUS)
Jpn J Phys Educ...   Japanese Journal of Physical Education (journ.) (SAUS)
Jpn J Phys Fitess Sports Med...   Japanese Journal of Physical Fitness and Sports Medicine (journ.) (SAUS)
Jpn J Physiol...   Japanese Journal of Physiology (journ.) (SAUS)
Jpn J Plast Reconstr Surg...   Japanese Journal of Plastic and Reconstructive Surgery (journ.) (SAUS)
Jpn J Psychiatry Neurol...   Japanese Journal of Psychiatry and Neurology (journ.) (SAUS)
Jpn J Psychol...   Japanese Journal of Psychology (journ.) (SAUS)
Jpn J Psychopharmacol...   Japanese Journal of Psychopharmacology (journ.) (SAUS)
Jpn J Psychosom Med...   Japanese Journal of Psychosomatic Medicine (journ.) (SAUS)
Jpn J Radiol Technol...   Japanese Journal of Radiological Technology (journ.) (SAUS)
Jpn J Relig...   Japanese Journal of Religious Studies (journ.) (SAUS)
Jpn J Sanit Zool...   Japanese Journal of Sanitary Zoology (journ.) (SAUS)
Jpn J Smooth Muscle Res...   Japanese Journal of Smooth Muscle Research (journ.) (SAUS)
Jpn J Stud Alcohol...   Japanese Journal of Studies on Alcohol (journ.) (SAUS)
Jpn J Surg...   Japanese Journal of Surgery (journ.) (SAUS)
Jpn J Tborac Dis...   Japanese Journal of Thoracic Diseases (journ.) (SAUS)
Jpn J Trop Agric...   Japanese Journal of Tropical Agriculture (journ.) (SAUS)
Jpn J Trop Med Hyg...   Japanese Journal of Tropical Medicine and Hygiene (journ.) (SAUS)
Jpn J Tuberc Chest Dis...   Japanese Journal of Tuberculosis and Chest Diseases (journ.) (SAUS)
Jpn J Urol ...   Japanese Journal of Urology (journ.) (SAUS)
Jpn J Vet Sci...   Japanese Journal of Veterinary Science (journ.) (SAUS)
Jpn J Water Pollut Res...   Japanese Journal of Water Pollution Research (journ.) (SAUS)
Jpn J Water Res...   Japan Journal of Water Research (journ.) (SAUS)
Jpn J Zool ...   Japanese Journal of Zoology (journ.) (SAUS)
Jpn J Zootech Sci...   Japanese Journal of Zootechnical Science (journ.) (SAUS)
JPNL...........   Judged Perceived Noise Level (OA)
Jpn Light Met Weld...   Japan Light Metal Welding (journ.) (SAUS)
Jpn Math .....   Japanese Journal of Mathematics (journ.) (SAUS)
Jpn Med J...   Japanese Medical Journal (journ.) (SAUS)
Jpn Med Res Found Publ...   Japan Medical Research Foundation. Publication (journ.) (SAUS)
Jpn Met Bull...   Japan Metal Bulletin (journ.) (SAUS)
Jpn Msrket...   Dentsu Japan Marketing/Advertising Yearbook (journ.) (SAUS)
JPNNB ....   Journal of Psychiatric Nursing and Mental Health Services (journ.) (SAUS)
Jpn Nucl Med...   Japanese Nuclear Medicine (journ.) (SAUS)
Jpn P Comp...   Japanese Invasion of Americas Personal Computer Market (journ.) (SAUS)
Jpn Pestic Inf...   Japan Pesticide Information (journ.) (SAUS)
Jpn Petrol...   Japan Petroleum and Energy Weekly (journ.) (SAUS)
Jpn P Indx...   Japan Price Indexes Annual (journ.) (SAUS)
Jpn Plast .....   Japan Plastics (journ.) (SAUS)
Jpn Plast Age...   Japan Plastics Age (journ.) (SAUS)
Jpn Plast Ind Ann...   Japan Plastics Industry Annual (journ.) (SAUS)
Jpn Poult Sci...   Japanese Poultry Science (journ.) (SAUS)
Jpn Printer...   Japan Printer (journ.) (SAUS)
Jpn Psychol Res...   Japanese Psychological Research (journ.) (SAUS)

Jpn Pulp Paper... Japan Pulp and Paper (journ.) (SAUS)

Jpn Railw Eng... Journal of Railway Engineering (journ.) (SAUS)

Jpn Rev Clin Ophthalmol... Japanese Review of Clinical Ophthalmology (journ.) (SAUS)

Jpn Rilw Eng... Japanese Railway Engineering (journ.) (SAUS)

JPNS........... Journal of the Peripheral Nervous System (journ.) (SAUS)

Jpn S Aeronaut Space Sci Trans... Japan Society for Aeronautical and Space Sciences. Transactions (journ.) (SAUS)

Jpn Sci Mon... Japanese Scientific Monthly (journ.) (SAUS)

Jpn Sci Rer Med Sci... Japan Science Review. Medical Sciences (journ.) (SAUS)

Jpn Sci Rev Min Metall... Japanese Science Review. Mining and Metallurgy (journ.) (SAUS)

Jpn Soc Tuberc Annu Rep... Japanese Society for Tuberculosis. Annual Report (journ.) (SAUS)

Jpn Steel Bull... Japan Steel Bulletin (journ.) (SAUS)

Jpn Steel Tube Tb Rev... Japan Steel and Tube Technical Review (journ.) (SAUS)

Jpn Steel Works... Japan Steel Works (journ.) (SAUS)

Jpn Steel Works Tech News... Japan Steel Works. Technical News (journ.) (SAUS)

Jpn Stud Hist Sci... Japanese Studies in the History of Science (journ.) (SAUS)

JPNT........... Joiner Pilaster Nontight [*Technical drawings*]

Jpn Telecomun Rev... Japan Telecommunications Review (journ.) (SAUS)

JPO............. Japanese Patent Office (TELE)

JPO............. Japan Patent Office (SAUS)

JPO............. Joint Personal Property Shipping Office (SAUS)

JPO............. Joint Petroleum Office

JPO............. Joint Planning Office (SAUO)

JPO............. Joint Program Office [*Military*] (SDI)

JPO............. Joint Project Office [*or Officer*]

JPO............. Journal of Portfolio Management (journ.) (SAUS)

JPO............. Journal of Prosthetics and Orthotics (journ.) (SAUS)

JPO............. Jump if Parity Odd (VLIE)

JPO............. Jump on Parity Odd (SAUS)

JPO............. Junior Police Officer (SAUO)

JPO............. Junior Professional Officer [*United Nations*]

JPO............. Juvenile Probation Officer (OICC)

JPO............. Pomona [*California*] [*Airport symbol*] (AD)

JPOAA .... Junior Panel Outdoor Advertising Association [*Later, ESOAA*]

JPO-BD .... Joint Program Office for Biological Defense [*Army*] (RDA)

JPOC........... Johnson Space Center Payload Operations Center (SAUO)

JPOC........... Joint Planning Orientation Course (SAUO)

JPOC........... JSC [*Johnson Space Center*] Payload Operations Center (MCD)

J Poditr Med Educ... Journal of Podiatric Medical Education (journ.) (SAUS)

JPOG .... Journal of Psychosomatic Obstetrics and Gynecology (SAUO)

JPOGDP....... Journal of Psychosomatic Obstetrics and Gynaecology (journ.) (SAUS)

J-Point........ Junction Point (SAUS)

JPO J Prc Ortbod... JPO Journal of Practical Orthodontics (journ.) (SAUS)

J Pol........... Journal of Politics [*A publication*] (BRI)

J Polar Soc... Journal. Polarographic Society (journ.) (SAUS)

J Pol Econ... Journal of Political Economy. University of Chicago. Department of Political Economy. Chicago (SAUO)

J Policy Anal Mnage... Journal of Policy Analysis and Management (journ.) (SAUS)

J Policy Analysis and Mgt... Journal of Policy Analysis and Management (journ.) (SAUS)

J Policy Model... Journal of Policy Modeling (journ.) (SAUS)

J Pol S .... Journal. Polynesian Society (journ.) (SAUS)

J Pol Sci & Admin... Journal of Police Science and Administration [*A publication*] (DLA)

J Pol Sc PC... Journal of Polymer Science. Polymer Chemistry Edition (journ.) (SAUS)

J Pol Sc PL... Journal of Polymer Science. Polymer Letters Edition (journ.) (SAUS)

J Pol Sc PP... Journal of Polymer Science. Polymer Physics Edition (journ.) (SAUS)

J Polym Eng... Journal of Polymer Engineering (journ.) (SAUS)

J Polym Mater... Journal of Polymer Materials (journ.) (SAUS)

J Polym Sci Lett... Journal of Polymer Science Letters (journ.) (SAUS)

J Polym Sci Macromol Rev... Journal of Polymer Science. Macromolecular Reviews (journ.) (SAUS)

J Polym Sci Polym Chem... Journal of Polymer Science. Polymer Chemistry Edition (journ.) (SAUS)

J Polym Sci Polym Chem Ed... Journal of Polymer Science. Polymer Chemistry Edition (journ.) (SAUS)

J Polym Sci Polym Lett... Journal of Polymer Science. Polymer Letters Edition (journ.) (SAUS)

J Polym Sci Polym Phys... Journal of Polymer Science. Polymer Physics Edition (journ.) (SAUS)

J Polym Sci Polym Phys Ed... Journal of Polymer Science. Polymer Physics Edition (journ.) (SAUS)

J Polym Sci Polym Symp... Journal of Polymer Science. Polymer Symposia Edition (journ.) (SAUS)

J Pomology... Journal of Pomology and Horticultural Science (journ.) (SAUS)

JPONED....... Journal of Psychosonal Oncology (journ.) (SAUS)

JPOP.......... Japanese Polar Orbiting Platform (EOSA)

J Pop F&TV... Journal of Popular Film and Television [*A publication*] (BRI)

J Pop Res... Journal of Population Research (journ.) (SAUS)

J Popul........ Journal of Population (journ.) (SAUS)

J Popul Behar Soc Environ Issues... Journal of Population. Behavioral, Social and Environmental Issues (journ.) (SAUS)

JPOS........... Journal of Pediatric Ophthalmology and Strabismus (journ.) (SAUS)

JPOS........... Journal of the Palestine Oriental Society (SAUO)

JPOS........... Journal of the Patent Office Society (SAUO)

JPOS........... Journal of the Patent Office Society (journ.) (SAUS)

JPOS........... Journal. Palestine Oriental Society (journ.) (SAUS)

J POS .... Journal. Patent Office Society (journ.) (SAUS)

J Post Anesth Nurs... Journal of Post Anesthesia Nursing (journ.) (SAUS)

J Post Grd Sch Indian Agr Res Inst... Journal. Post Graduate School. Indian Agricultural Research Institute (journ.) (SAUS)

J Post Keynes Econ... Journal of Post Keynesian Economics (journ.) (SAUS)

JpOTC......... Japan OTC Equity Fund, Inc. [*Associated Press*] (SAG)

JPOTS......... Joint Panel on Oceanographic Tables and Standards [*Marine science*] [*United Nations*] (OSRA)

JPO-TT........ Joint Program Offrice-Transition Team [*DoD*]

J Power Div; Amer Soc Civi... Journal of the Power Division; Proceedings of the American Society of Civil Engineering (journ.) (SAUS)

J Power Div Am S Civ Eng... Journal. Power Division. American Society of Civil Engineers (journ.) (SAUS)

J Power Sources... Journal of Power Sources (journ.) (SAUS)

JPP .... Jalkeen Puolenpaiuan [*Afternoon*] [*Finland*]

JPP .... Japan Paper Proofs

JPP .... Joint Planning Process [*Military*] (NVT)

jpp .... Joint Program Plan (NAKS)

JPP .... Joint Program Plan (NASA)

JPP .... Journal of Pastoral Practice (journ.) (SAUS)

JPPDA .... Journal of Child Psychology and Psychiatry and Allied Disciplines (journ.) (SAUS)

JPPL .... JAR-FCL Private Pilots License (SAUS)

JPPL .... Joint Personnel Priority List

JPPL .... Journal of Planning and Property Law (journ.) (SAUS)

JpPol .... Japanese Polydor-Deutsche Grammophon [*Record label*]

JPPP .... Jewish People, Past and Present [*Jewish Encyclopedic Handbooks*] [*A publication*] (BJA)

JPPR .... Journal of Psychotherapy Practice and Research (journ.) (SAUS)

JPPRI........... Jewish Planning Policy and Research Institute (BUAC)

JPPRI........... , Jewish Policy Planning and Research Institute [*Synagogue Council of America*]

JPPS........... Jack Point Preservation Society (EA)

JPPS........... Japan Pearl Promoting Society (SAUO)

JPPS........... Joint Petroleum Products Subcommittee (SAUS)

JPPS........... Journal of Pharmacy and Pharmaceutical Sciences (journ.) (SAUS)

JPPSA........ Journal of Pharmacy and Pharmacology. Supplement (journ.) (SAUS)

JPPSO........ Joint Personal Property Shipping Office [*Military*] (DNAB)

JPPSOWA ... Joint Personal Property Shipping Office, Washington, DC [*Military*] (AABC)

JPPSST........ Joseph Preschool and Primary Self-Concept Screening Test [*Child development test*] [*Psychology*]

JpPV .... Japanese Polydor Variable Microgroove [*Record label*]

JPQ............. Jung Personality Questionnaire [*Personality development test*] [*Psychology*]

JPR............. Air International (Holdings) PLC [*British*] [*ICAO designator*] (FAAC)

JPR............. Inversiones Ayacucho, SA, "Jet Privado" [*Peru*] [*FAA designator*] (FAAC)

JPR............. Joint Procurement Regulations [*of Army and Air Force*]

JPR............. Journal of Peace Research [*A publication*] (BRI)

JPR............. Journal of Purchasing and Materials Management [*A publication*] (AAGC)

JPR............. JP Realty [*NYSE symbol*] (SPSG)

jpr............... Judaeo-Persian [*MARC language code*] [*Library of Congress*] (LCCP)

JPR............. Justice of the Peace and Local Government Review Reports [*A publication*] (DLA)

JPR............. Justice Procurement Regulation [*A publication*] (AAGC)

JPRA........... Japanese Phonograph Record Association [*An association*] (NITA)

JPRA........... Japan Phonographic Record Association (SAUS)

JPRA........... Joint Personnel Recovery Agency [*Military*]

J Pract Nurs... Journal of Practical Nursing (journ.) (SAUS)

J Prag.......... Journal of Pragmatics (journ.) (SAUS)

JPRC........... Joint Personnel Recovery Center [*Military*]

J PR CT....... Judge Prerogative Court, Canterbury [*British*] (ROG)

JPRDY .... Jeopardy (ABBR)

JPRDZ .... Jeopardize (ABBR)

JPRDZG ...... Jeopardizing (ABBR)

J Presby H... Journal of Presbyterian History (journ.) (SAUS)

J Presby Hist Soc... Journal. Presbyterian Historical Society (journ.) (SAUS)

J Pressure Vessel Technol... Journal of Pressure Vessel Technology (journ.)

J Prestressed Concrete Inst... Journal of the Prestressed Concrete Institute (journ.) (SAUS)

J Prestressed Concr Iost... Journal. Prestressed Concrete Institute (journ.) (SAUS)

J Prev Dent... Journal of Preventive Dentistry (journ.) (SAUS)

J Prev Psychiatry... Journal of Preventive Psychiatry (journ.) (SAUS)

JPRH .... Journal of Prison Health (journ.) (SAUS)

J Print Hist S... Journal Printing Historical Society (journ.) (SAUS)

JP Rlty......... JP Realty [*Associated Press*] (SAG)

JPRO .... Joint Photographic Reconnaissance Organization [*World War II*]

JPROB......... Judge of Probate [*British*] (ROG)

J Proc Am Hort S... Journal of Proceedings. American Horticultural Society (journ.) (SAUS)

J Proc Asiat Soc Bengal... Journal and Proceedings. Asiatic Society of Bengal (journ.) (SAUS)

J Proc Boken Hill Hist S... Broken Hill Historical Society. Journal and Proceedings (journ.) (SAUS)

J Proc Inst Rd Transp Engrs... Journal and Proceedings. Institute of Road Transport Engineers (journ.) (SAUS)

J Proc Inst Sewage Purif... Journal and Proceedings. Institute of Sewage Purification (journ.) (SAUS)

J Proc Newcastle Hunter Dist Hist Soc... Journal and Proceedings. Newcastle and Hunter District Historical Society (journ.) (SAUS)

J Proc Oil Technol Ass... Journal and Proceedings. Oil Technologists Association (journ.) (SAUS)

J Proc Parramatta Dist Hist S... Journal and Proceedings. Parramatta and District Historical Society (journ.) (SAUS)
J Proc R Aust Hist Soc... Journal and Proceedings. Royal Australian Historical Society (journ.) (SAUS)
J Proc Roy Soc NSW... Journal and Proceedings. Royal Society of New South Wales (journ.) (SAUS)
J Proc Roy Soc NWW... Journal and Proceedings of the Royal Society of New South Wales (SAUO)
J Proc Sydney Tech Coll Chem S... Journal and Proceedings. Sydney Technical College. Chemical Society (journ.) (SAUS)
J Proc W Aust Hist Soc... Journal and Proceedings. Western Australian Historical Society (journ.) (SAUS)
J Prod Agric... Journal of Production Agriculture (journ.) (SAUS)
J Prod Innov Manage... Journal of Product Innovation Management (journ.) (SAUS)
J Prod L...... Journal of Products Law (DLA)
J Prod L...... Journal of Products Law (journ.) (SAUS)
J Prod Liab... Journal of Products Liabilily (journ.) (SAUS)
J Prof Legal Ed... Journal of Professional Legal Education (journ.) (SAUS)
J Prof Nurs... Journal of Professional Nursing (journ.) (SAUS)
J Proj Tech... Journal of Projective Techniques. Society for Projective Techniques and Rorschach Institute. Glendale (SAUO)
J Prop Power... Journal of Propulsion and Power (journ.) (SAUS)
J Propul P... Journal of Propulsion and Power (journ.) (SAUS)
J Prot Coatings Linings... Journal of Protective Coatings and Linings (journ.) (SAUS)
J Protein Chem... Journal of Protein Chemistry (journ.) (SAUS)
J Protozool... Journal of Protozoology (journ.) (SAUS)
JPRRI.......... Japan Public Relations Research Institute (SAUS)
JPRS.......... Joint Publications Research Service [*Department of Commerce*]
JPRSA.......... Journal and Proceedings. Royal Society of New South Wales (journ.) (SAUS)
J Prsbyt Hist... Journal of Presbyterian History (journ.) (SAUS)
JPRS-GUO... Joint Publications Research Service Translations - Government Use Only [*Department of Commerce*]
JPRST-GUO... Joint Publications Research Service Translations-Government Use Only (SAUO)
JPS.......... Japan Physical Society (SAUO)
JPS.......... Japan Press Service
JPS.......... Javad Positioning Systems, Inc. (SAUO)
JPS.......... Jean Piaget Society [*Later, JPSSSKD*] (EA)
JPs.......... Jesuit Priests (SAUS)
JPS.......... Jet Plume Simulation
JPS.......... Jeunesse Populaire Senegalaise [*Senegalese People's Youth*]
JPS.......... Jewish Publication Society (EA)
JPS.......... JICST Photoduplication Service (SAUS)
JPS.......... Johannesburg Philharmonic Society (SAUO)
JPS.......... John Player Special [*Sponsor of British Lotus Formula I racing car*]
JPS.......... Joint Parliamentary Secretary (SAUS)
JPS.......... Joint Planning Staff [*US and Great Britain*] [*World War II*]
JPS.......... Joint Position Sense [*Medicine*]
JPS.......... Jones Plumbing Systems, Inc. [*AMEX symbol*] (SPSG)
JPS.......... Journal of Peadant Studies (journ.) (SAUS)
JPS.......... Journal of Plant Studies (journ.) (SAUS)
JPS.......... Journal of Polymer Science (journ.) (SAUS)
JPS.......... Journal. Polynesian Society (journ.) (SAUS)
JPS.......... Junior Philatelic Society [*British*] (BI)
JPS.......... Juvenile Polyposis Syndrome [*Medicine*]
JPS.......... Juvenile Probation Services (SAUO)
JPSA.......... Jacob's Prevocational Skills Assessment
JPSA.......... Japanese Plating Supplier's Association [*Environmetal science*]
JPSA.......... Jewish Pharmaceutical Society of America (EA)
JPSA.......... Jewish Publication Society of America (DGA)
JPSA.......... Joint Program for the Study of Abortion
JPSA.......... Journal of Police Science and Administation (journ.) (SAUS)
JPSA.......... Journal. Photographic Society of America (journ.) (SAUS)
JPSA.......... Junior Philatelic Society of America [*Later, JPA*] (EA)
JPSBA.......... Journal of Psychology of the Blind (journ.) (SAUS)
JPSC.......... Joint Production Survey Committee
JPSCD.......... Journal of Polymer Science. Part C Polymer Symposia (journ.) (SAUS)
JPSDTF.......... Joint Precision Strike Demonstration Task Force (SAUO)
JPSG.......... Joint Planning and Scheduling Group
JPSJ.......... Journal of the Physical Society of Japan (SAUO)
JPSO.......... Jamaica Philharmonic Symphony Orchestra (SAUO)
JPSO.......... Journal of Psychosocial Oncology (journ.) (SAUS)
JPSP.......... Journal of Personality and Social Psychology [*A publication*] (DHP)
JPSRB.......... Journal of Psychological Researches (journ.) (SAUS)
JPSS.......... Journal of Personality and Social Systems (journ.) (SAUS)
JPSS.......... Just, Participatory, and Sustainable Society [*World Council of Churches*]
JPSSSKD..... Jean Piaget Society: Society for the Study of Knowledge and Development (EA)
JPST.......... Journal of Parenteral Science and Technology [*A publication*] (EAAP)
JPSTH.......... Joint Peristimulus Time Histograms [*For study of physiology*]
J Psychiatr Law... Journal of Psychiatry and Law (journ.) (SAUS)
J Psychiatr Mental Health Nurs... Journal of Psychiatric & Mental Health Nursing (journ.) (SAUS)
J Psychiatr Nurs... Journal of Psychiatric Nursing and Mental Health Services (journ.) (SAUS)
J Psychiatr Treat Eval... Journal of Psychiatric Treatment and Evaluation (journ.) (SAUS)
J Psychiatry Neurosci... Journal of Psychiatry and Neuroscience (journ.) (SAUS)
J Psychoanal Anthropol... Journal of Psychoanalytic Anthropology (journ.) (SAUS)
J Psycho Drugs... Journal of Psychoactive Drugs (MEC)
J Psychohist... Journal of Psychohistory (journ.) (SAUS)
J Psychol..... Journal of Psychology (journ.) (SAUS)
J Psychological Medicine... Journal of Psychological Medicine and Medical Jurisprudence [*A publication*] (DLA)
J Psychologic Medicine... Journal of Psychological Medicine and Medical Jurisprudence (journ.) (SAUS)
J Psychol Res... Journal of Psychological Researches (journ.) (SAUS)
J Psychol T... Journal of Psychology and Theology (journ.) (SAUS)
J Psychopathol Behav Assess... Journal of Psychopathology and Behavioral Assessment (journ.) (SAUS)
J Psychosom Obstet Gynaecol... Journal of Psychosomatic Obstetrics and Gynaecology (journ.) (SAUS)
J Psychos Oncol... Journal of Psychosocial Oncology (journ.) (SAUS)
J Psychother & Fm... Journal of Psychotherapy and the Family (journ.) (SAUS)
J Psych Th... Journal of Psychology and Theology (journ.) (SAUS)
JPsyR.......... Journal of Psycholinguistic Research (journ.) (SAUS)
JPT.......... Houston [*Texas*] Park-Ten [*Airport symbol*] (OAG)
JPT.......... Japanese Proficiency Test [*Educational test*]
JPT.......... Jet Pipe Temperature
JPT.......... Job Process Ticket (SAUS)
JPT.......... Job Progress Ticket
JPT.......... Joint Planning Team (COE)
JPT.......... Joint Project Team (SAUO)
JPT.......... Journal of Paint Technology (journ.) (SAUS)
JPT.......... Journal of Psychology and Theology (journ.) (SAUS)
JPT.......... Jupiter Resources Ltd. (SAUO)
JPT.......... Jupitor Resources Ltd. [*Vancouver Stock Exchange symbol*]
JPTDS.......... Joint Photographic Type Designation System [*Military*]
JPTDS.......... Junior Participating Tactical Data System [*Also known as "Jeep"*] (MCD)
JPTEA.......... Journal of Projective Techniques (journ.) (SAUS)
JPTF.......... Joint Parachute Test Facility [*DoD*]
JPTL.......... Jet Pipe Temperature Limiter (MCD)
JPTM.......... Joint Procedures Training Manual (SAUO)
JPTO.......... Jet-Propelled Takeoff
JPTS.......... Jet Petroleum, Thermally Stable (DOMA)
JPTUN.......... Japanese Journal of Tuberculosis (journ.) (SAUS)
JPU.......... Job Processing Unit
JPU.......... Journal of Public Economics (journ.) (SAUS)
JPU.......... Journal. Poona University (journ.) (SAUS)
JPU.......... Just Publishable Unit
J Public and Internat Affairs... Journal of Public and International Affairs (journ.) (SAUS)
J Public Health... Journal of Public Health (journ.) (SAUS)
J Public Health Dent... Journal of Public Health Dentistry (journ.) (SAUS)
J Public Health Med... Journal of Public Health Medicine (journ.) (SAUS)
J Public Health Med Technol Korea Univ... Journal of Public Health and Medical Technology. Korea University (journ.) (SAUS)
J Public Health Policy... Journal of Public Health Policy (journ.) (SAUS)
J Public Health Pract... Journal of Public Health Practice (journ.) (SAUS)
J Public Policy... Journal of Public Policy (journ.) (SAUS)
J Pul and Pap Sci... Journal of Pulp and Paper Science (journ.) (SAUS)
J-Punkt....... EKG: Junction Point (am Ende des QRS-Komplex, Beginn der ST Strecke) (SAUS)
J Purch Mater Manage... Journal of Purchasing and Materials Management (journ.) (SAUS)
J Pure Appl Algebra... Journal of Pure and Applied Algebra (journ.) (SAUS)
J Pure Appl Ultrason... Journal of Pure and Applied Ultrasonics (journ.) (SAUS)
J Pusan Med Coll... Journal. Pusan Medical College (journ.) (SAUS)
JpV.......... Japanese Victor [*Record label*]
JPV.......... Japan Peace Volunteers (SAUO)
JPV.......... Joint Pacific Voice [*Military*] (CINC)
JPVDA.......... Journal of Preventive Dentistry (journ.) (SAUS)
JP VOICE..... Joint Pacific Command Control Voice Network (SAUO)
JPVTA.......... Journal of Pressure Vessel Technology (journ.) (SAUS)
JPW.......... Job Processing Word
JPW.......... Just Plain Weird (SAUS)
JPWC.......... Joint Postwar Committee
JPWC.......... Joint Psychological Warfare Committee (LAIN)
JPWG.......... Joint Projects Working Group (SAUO)
JP-X.......... Jet-Propellant rocket fuel (SAUS)
JPYBA.......... Journal of Polymer Science. Polymer Letters Edition (journ.) (SAUS)
JPz4-5.......... German tank-destroyer (SAUS)
JQ.......... Job Questionnaire
JQ.......... Job Queue (SAUS)
JQ.......... Journalism Quarterly [*A publication*] (BRI)
JQ.......... J-Q Resources, Inc. [*Toronto Stock Exchange symbol*]
JQ.......... Trans-Jamaican Airlines [*ICAO designator*] (AD)
JQ.......... Trans Jamaican Airlines Ltd. (SAUO)
JQA.......... Japan Quality Assurance Organization (SAUO)
JQA.......... John Quincy Adams [*US president, 1767-1848*]
JQA.......... Trans Jamaican Airlines Ltd. [*ICAO designator*] (FAAC)
JQAH.......... John Quincy Adams House (SAUO)
JQAP.......... Joint Quality Assurance Department (SAUO)
JQB.......... Justice of the Queen's Bench [*Legal term*] (DLA)
JQC.......... Dayton, OH [*Location identifier*] [*FAA*] (FAAL)
JQD.......... Jeffersonville Quartermaster Depot (SAUO)
JQE.......... Jaque [*Panama*] [*Airport symbol*] (OAG)
JQG.......... Joint Question Group (SAUO)
JQH.......... Hammons [*John Q.*] Hotels, Inc. [*NYSE symbol*] (SAG)
JQHamm...... Hammons [*John Q.*] Hotel, Inc. [*Associated Press*] (SAG)
J Qing Hua Univ... Journal Qing Hua University (journ.) (SAUS)
JQP.......... Josephson Quasi Particle (AAEL)
JQR.......... Hammons(John Q)Hotels'A' [*NYSE symbol*] (TTSB)
JQR.......... Jewish Quarterly Review [*A publication*] (ODCC)
JQS.......... Job Qualification Standard (SAUO)

JQS............. Journal of Quaternary Science (journ.) (SAUS)
JQSRT .... Journal of Quantitative Spectroscopy and Radiative Transfer (journ.) (SAUS)
JQT............. Journal of Quality Technology (journ.) (SAUS)
J Quant Trait Loci... Journal of Quantitative Trait Loci (journ.) (SAUS)
J Quat Sci ... Journal of Quaternary Science (SAUS)
J Quekett Microsc Club... Journal. Quekett Microscopical Club (journ.) (SAUS)
JR................ Air Yugoslavia (SAUS)
JR................ Jacobus Rex [King James]
JR................ James River Corp. [NYSE symbol] (TTSB)
JR................ James River Corp. of Virginia [NYSE symbol] (SPSG)
JR................ Jam Resistant
JR................ Japan Railways (SAUS)
JR................ Jar (MCD)
jr................. Jarosite (SAUS)
Jr................. Jeremiah [Old Testament book] (BJA)
JR................ [The] Jewish Right (EA)
JR................ Jigger [Ship's rigging] (ROG)
jr................. jinx ratio (SAUS)
JR................ Job Request (SAUS)
JR................ Job Rotation [Computer science] (MHDB)
JR................ Job Routed [Military] (AFIT)
JR................ John Ross Ewing, Jr. [Character in TV series "Dallas"]
JR................ Johnson's New York Reports [A publication] (DLA)
JR................ Joint Research
JR................ Joint Resolution [Usually, of the US Senate and House of Representatives]
JR................ Joint Return (MHDB)
JR................ Joint Review
JR................ Jolly Reaction (STED)
JR................ Jolly's Reaction [Neurology] (DAVI)
JR................ Jordan Register (EA)
JR................ Jour [Day] [French]
JR................ Journal (ADA)
JR................ Journal of Religion [A publication] (BRI)
JR................ Judge's Remand (WDAA)
JR................ Judges' Rules [A publication] (DLA)
Jr................. Juglans regia [Persian walnut]
JR................ Junctional Rhythm [Cardiology]
JR................ Junction Rack (KSC)
Jr................. Junior (ASC)
jr................. Junior (SHCU)
JR................ Junior
JR................ Juridical Review (journ.) (SAUS)
JR................ Jurist Reports [1873-78] [New Zealand] [A publication] (DLA)
JR................ Juror
JR................ Juvenile Rheumatoid Arthritis [Also, JRA] [Medicine] (DAVI)
JRA............. Jam Resistant Aerial (or Antenna) (SAUS)
JRA............. Jam-Resistant Antenna
JRA............. Japanese Racing Association
JRA............. Japanese Red Army (SAUO)
JRA............. Japan Racing Association (ECON)
JRA............. Japan Ryokan Association (SAUO)
JRA............. Jewish Royalty Association (EA)
JRA............. Job Release Analysis
JRA............. Joint Rear Area (SAUO)
Jr A............. Journal of Arizona History (journ.) (SAUS)
JRA............. Journal of Radiation Research (journ.) (SAUS)
JRA............. Journal of Roman Archaeology (journ.) (SAUS)
JRA............. Journal. Royal African Society (journ.) (SAUS)
JRA............. Journal. Society of Research Administrators (journ.) (SAUS)
JRA............. Junior Rheumatoid Arthritis
JRA............. Juvenile Rheumatoid Arthritis [Medicine]
JRA............. New York, NY [Location identifier] [FAA] (FAAL)
J Race Dev... Journal of Race Development (journ.) (SAUS)
J Racial AFF... Journal of Racial Affairs (journ.) (SAUS)
JRAD .... Joint Resource Assessment Data
JRAD .... Judicial Recommendation against Deportation
JRADA .... Journal of Radiology (journ.) (SAUS)
J Radiat Res... Journal of Radiation Research (journ.) (SAUS)
J Radioanal Nucl Chem... Journal of Radioanalytical and Nuclear Chemistry (journ.) (SAUS)
J Radio L..... Journal of Radio Law [A publication] (DLA)
J Radiol Phys Ther Univ Kanzawa... Journal of Radiology and Physical Therapy. University of Kanazawa (journ.) (SAUS)
J Radiol Prot... Journal of Radiological Protection (journ.) (SAUS)
J Radio Res Lab... Journal of the Radio Research Laboratories (journ.) (SAUS)
J Radit Curing... Journal of Radiation Curing (journ.) (SAUS)
J Radit Res Radiat Process... Journal of Radiation Research and Radiation Processing (journ.) (SAUS)
JRADS .... Joint Resource Assessment Data Base System (SAUO)
J R Afr Soc... Journal. Royal African Society (journ.) (SAUS)
J R Agric Soc Engl... Journal. Royal Agricultural Society of England (journ.) (SAUS)
JRAGSOC.... Journal. Royal Agricultural Society of England (journ.) (SAUS)
JRAHS .... Journal. Royal Australian Historical Society (journ.) (SAUS)
JRAI .... Journal. Royal Anthropological Institute of Great Britain and Ireland (journ.) (SAUS)
J R Aic Soc... Journal. Royal Agricultural Society (journ.) (SAUS)
J Rakuno Gakuen Univ Nt Sci... Journal. Rakuno Gakuen University. Natural Science (journ.) (SAUS)
JRAMA......... Journal. Royal Army Medical Corps (journ.) (SAUS)
J Raman Spectrosc... Journal of Raman Spectroscopy (journ.) (SAUS)
JRAN.......... Junior Resident Admission Note (STED)
J Range Manage... Journal of Range Management (journ.) (SAUS)

J R Anthropol Inst GB Irel... Journal. Royal Anthropological Institute of Great Britain and Ireland (journ.) (SAUS)
J R Army Med Corps... Journal of the Royal Army Medical Corps (SAUO)
J R Army Med Corps... Journal. Royal Army Medical Corps (journ.) (SAUS)
J R Army Vet Corps... Journal. Royal Army Veterinary Corps (journ.) (SAUS)
JRAS........... Journal of the Royal Agricultural Society [A publication] (ROG)
JRAS........... Journal. Royal Asiatic Society of Great Britain and Ireland (journ.) (SAUS)
JRASA .... Journal. Royal Astronomical Society of Canada (journ.) (SAUS)
JRAS Bengl... Journal. Royal Asiatic Society of Bengal (journ.) (SAUS)
JRASCB ...... Journal. Royal Asiatic Society. Ceylon Branch (journ.) (SAUS)
JRASHKB.... Journal. Royal Asiatic Society. Hong Kong Branch (journ.) (SAUS)
JR Asiat Soc GB Irel... Journal. Royal Asiatic Society of Great Britain and Ireland (journ.) (SAUS)
J R Astron Soc Can... Journal of the Royal Astronomical Society of Canada (journ.) (SAUS)
JRATA......... Joint Research and Test Activities (or Activity) (SAUS)
JRATA......... Joint Research and Test Activity (MCD)
JRATA......... Joint Research and Test Agency [Terminated, 1966] [Military]
J R Aust Hist Soc... Journal. Royal Australian Historical Society (journ.) (SAUS)
JRB............. Jig Rest Button (SAUS)
JRB............. Joint Radio Board
JRB............. Joint Reconnaissance Board [Military] (AABC)
JRB............. Joint Rennaissance Board (SAUS)
JRB............. Joint Review Board (MCD)
jrb............. Judaeo-Arabic [MARC language code] [Library of Congress] (LCCP)
JRB............. New York, NY [Location identifier] [FAA] (FAAL)
JRBA-A .... Journal. Royal Institute of British Architects (journ.) (SAUS)
JRBEDZ....... Journal of Reproductive Biology and Comparative Endocrinology (journ.) (SAUS)
Jr BF.......... Junior Baby Food (STED)
JRBK.......... James River Bankshares [NASDAQ symbol] (TTSB)
JRBK.......... James River Bankshares, Inc. [NASDAQ symbol] (SAG)
JRBM.......... Journal of Renaissance and Baroque Music (journ.) (SAUS)
Jr Br AssocTeach Deaf... Journal. British Association of Teachers of the Deaf (journ.) (SAUS)
JRBSDA ...... British Columbia Forest Service-Canadian Forestry Service (SAUS)
JRC............. Jamaica Railway Corp. (SAUS)
JRC............. Japan Red Cross (SAUO)
JRC............. Japan Research Center (SAUS)
JRC............. Japan Research Council (SAUO)
JRC............. Jet Reaction Control
JRC............. Jewish Refugees Committee (EAIO)
JRC............. Johnson Reprint Corp. (SAUS)
JrC............. Johnson Reprint Corporation, New York, NY [Library symbol] [Library of Congress] (LCLS)
JRC............. Joint Railroad Conference
JRC............. Joint Reconnaissance Center [Military] (AFM)
JRC............. Joint Recovery Center (MCD)
JRC............. Joint Replacement Center [Medicine] (STED)
JRC............. Joint Reporting Center (SAUO)
JRC............. Joint Representation Committee [British] (DCTA)
JRC............. Joint Research Center [Commission of the European Communities]
JRC............. Joint Research Centre (HEAS)
JRC............. Joint Rivers Commission (SAUO)
JRC............. Journal Register [NYSE symbol] (SG)
JRC............. Junior Red Cross
JRCA.......... Junior Ruritan Clubs of America (SAUO)
JRCAS........ Journal. Royal Central Asian Society (journ.) (SAUS)
JRCAT........ Joint Research Center for Atom Technology [Japan]
JRCC.......... Joint Radiation Control Center (SAUO)
JRCC.......... Joint Radiological Control Center (SAUO)
JRCC.......... Joint Reconnaissance Control Center (MCD)
JRCC.......... Joint Regional Continuing Committee [Later, RCEAC] [Civil Defense]
JRCC.......... Joint Rescue Coordination Center [Military] (AFM)
JRCC.......... Joint Roland Control Committee (ACAE)
JRC-CVT ..... Joint Review Committee on Education in Cardiovascular Technology (DAVI)
JRCD.......... Journal of Research in Crime and Delinquency (journ.) (SAUS)
JRCDMS ..... Joint Review Committee on Education in Diagnostic Medical Sonography (EA)
JRCE-A .... Journal. Irrigation and Drainage Division. Proceedings of the American Society of Civil Engineers (journ.) (SAUS)
JRC-EEG ..... Joint Review Committee on Education in Electroencephalographic [Technology] (DAVI)
JRCEPPA .... Joint Review Committee on Educational Programs for Physician Assistants (EA)
JRCERT....... Joint Review Committee on Education in Radiologic Technology (EA)
JRCEST....... Joint Review Committee on Education for the Surgical Technologist (EA)
JRCEST....... Joint Review Committee on Education for the Surgical Technology (SAUS)
JRCI........... Jamming RADAR Coverage Indicator (MSA)
JRCI........... Journal of the Royal Colonial Institute (ROG)
JRCI........... Journal. Regional Cultural Institute (journ.) (SAUS)
JRC-ISPRA... Joint Research Center at Ispra (SAUS)
JRCN.......... Japan Committee for Research Networks (SAUS)
JRC-NMT .... Joint Review Committee on Educational Programs in Nuclear Medicine Technology (DAVI)
J R Coll Gen Pract... Journal. Royal College of General Practitioners (journ.) (SAUS)
J R Coll Gen Pract Ocs Pp... Journal. Royal College of General Prac- titioners. Occasional Paper (journ.) (SAUS)
J R Coll Physicians Lond... Journal of the Royal College of Physicians of London (SAUO)

J R Coll Physicians Lond... Journal of the Royal College of Physicians of London (journ.) (SAUS)

J R Coll Physicians Lond... Journal. Royal College of Physicians of London (journ.) (SAUS)

J R Coll Surg Edinb... Journal of the Royal College of Surgeons of Edinburgh (SAUO)

J R Coll Surg Edinb... Journal of the Royal College of Surgeons of Edinburgh (journ.) (SAUS)

J R Coll Surg Irel... Journal. Royal College of Surgeons in Ireland (journ.) (SAUS)

JRCOMA ...... Joint Review Committee for the Ophthalmic Medical Assistant (EA)

JRCOMP ...... Joint Review Committee for Ophthalmic Medical Personnel (EA)

JRCP .... Joint Reinforced Concrete Pavement

JRC-PA .... Joint Review Committee on Educational Programs for Physician Assistants (EA)

JRCPE .... Joint Review Committee for Perfusion Education (DAVI)

JRC Rev ...... JRC Review (journ.) (SAUS)

JRCRTE .... Joint Review Committee for Respiratory Therapy Education (EA)

JRCS .... Jet Reaction Control System

JRCS .... John Reich Collectors Society (EA)

JRCSA .... Journal. Royal College of Surgeons of Edinburgh (journ.) (SAUS)

JRC-ST .... Joint Review Committee on Education for the Surgical Technologist (DAVI)

JRD .... Japan Reconfiguration and Digitization (SAUO)

JRD .... Jarred (ABBR)

JRD .... Joint Research and Development (SAUS)

JRD .... Jumbo Random Driver (SAUS)

JRD .... Justification Review Document (AAGC)

JRD .... Riverside, CA [*Location identifier*] [*FAA*] (FAAL)

JRD-3 .... Japan Reconfiguration & Digitisation Program Phase III (SAUS)

JRDA .... Jeunesse du Rassemblement Democratique Africain [*Youth of the African Democratic Rally*]

JRDACI .... Jeunesse du Rassemblement Democratique Africain de Cote d'Ivoire [*Youth of the African Democratic Rally of the Ivory Coast*]

JRDB .... Joint Research and Development Board [*1946-1947*]

JRDC .... Japan Research and Development Corp. (SAUS)

JRDCA .... Journal of Radiation Curing (journ.) (SAUS)

JRDF .... Joint Rapid Deployment Force (SAUO)

JRDF .... Joint Rapid Development Force [*Military*] (WDAA)

JRDL .... Jam Resistant Data Link (ACAE)

JRDOD .... Joint Research and Development Objectives Document [*Military*] (AABC)

JRE .... Java Runtime Environment (SAUS)

JRE .... Joint Readiness Exercise (SAUS)

JRE .... Journal of Real Estate Taxation (journ.) (SAUS)

JRE .... Journal of Religious Ethics (journ.) (SAUS)

JRE .... JR Energy Ltd. [*Vancouver Stock Exchange symbol*]

JRE .... New York [*New York*] E. 60th Street [*Airport symbol*] (OAG)

JREA .... James Robison Evangelistic Association (EA)

JREA .... Japanese Railway Engineering Association (SAUS)

JREA .... Japan Railway Engineering Association (SAUS)

J Read .... Journal of Reading (journ.) (SAUS)

J Read Writ Learn Dissabil Int... Journal of Reading, Writing and Learning Disabilities International (journ.) (SAUS)

J Real Est Tax... Journal of Real Estate Taxation (journ.) (SAUS)

JREB .... Jewish Religion Education Board (SAUO)

J receptor.... Juxtapulmonary-Capillary Receptor [*Medicine*] (STED)

J Recept Res... Journal of Receptor Research (journ.) (SAUS)

J Recept Signal Transduct Res... Journal of Receptor and Signal Transduction Research (journ.) (SAUS)

J Reconstr Microsurg... Journal of Reconstructive Microsurgery (journ.) (SAUS)

J Recreational Math... Journal of Recreational Mathematics (journ.) (SAUS)

J Refrig .... Journal of Refrigeration (journ.) (SAUS)

J-Reg .... Junction Register (SAUS)

J Rehabil Asia... Journal of Rehabilitalion in Asia (journ.) (SAUS)

J Rehabil D... Journal of Rehabilitation of the Deaf (journ.) (SAUS)

J Rehabil Res Dev... Journal of Rehabilitation Research and Development (journ.) (SAUS)

J Rehabil Res Dev Clin Suppl... Journal of Rehabilitation Research and Development Clinical Supplement (journ.) (SAUS)

J Rehab RD... Journal of Rehabilitation Research and Development [*A publication*] (BRI)

JRE/JRX... Joint Readiness Exercise (SAUO)

J Rel Africa... Journal of Religion in Africa (journ.) (SAUS)

J R Electric Mech Eng... Journal of the Royal Electrical and Mechanical Engineers (journ.) (SAUS)

J Rel Eth ..... Journal of Religious Ethics (journ.) (SAUS)

J Rel Hth ..... Journal of Religion and Health (journ.) (SAUS)

J Relig Afr... Journal of Religion in Africa (journ.) (SAUS)

J Relig Educ... Journal of Religious Education (journ.) (SAUS)

J Rel Psych Res... Journal of Religion and Psychical Research (journ.) (SAUS)

JREM .... Junior Radio Electrical Mechanic [*British military*] (DMA)

J Remote Smsing... Journal of Remote Sensing (journ.) (SAUS)

J Remount Vet Cors... Journal of the Remount and Veterinary Corps (journ.) (SAUS)

J Ren & Bar Mus... Journal of Renaissance and Baroque Music (journ.) (SAUS)

J Rep .... Johnson's Maryland Chancery Reports [*A publication*] (DLA)

J Rep .... Johnson's New York Reports [*A publication*] (DLA)

J Rep .... Johnson's Reports of Chase's United States Circuit Court Decisions [*A publication*] (DLA)

J Reprints Antitrust L & Econ... Journal of Reprints for Antitrust Law and Economics [*A publication*] (DLA)

J Reprints Antitrust L & Econ... Journal of Reprints for Antitrust Law and Economics (journ.) (SAUS)

J Reprod Biol Comp Endocrinol... Journal of Reproductive Biology and Comparative Endocrinology (journ.) (SAUS)

J Reprod Fertil... Journal of Reproduction and Fertility (journ.) (SAUS)

J Reprod Fertil Abstr Ser... Journal of Reproduction and Fertility. Abstract Series (journ.) (SAUS)

J Reprod Fertil Suppl... Journal of Reproduction and Fertility. Supplement (journ.) (SAUS)

J Reprod Immunol... Journal of Reproductive Immunology (journ.) (SAUS)

J Reprod Med... Journal of Reproductive Medicine (journ.) (SAUS)

J Reprod Med Lying-In... Journal of Reproductive Medicine. Lying-In (journ.) (SAUS)

JRERDM ...... Journal of Receptor Research (journ.) (SAUS)

JRES-A .... Journal of Regional Science (journ.) (SAUS)

JRes Assam Agric Univ... Journal of Research. Assam Agricultural University (journ.) (SAUS)

J Res Comput Educ... Journal of Research on Computing in Education (journ.) (SAUS)

J Res Dev Lab Portland Cem Ass... Journal. Research and Development Laboratories. Portland Cement Association (journ.) (SAUS)

J Research M Eduation... Journal of Reascarch in Music Education (journ.) (SAUS)

J Res Haryana Agric Univ... Journal of Reascarch Haryana Agricultural University (journ.) (SAUS)

J Res Indian Med... Journal of Research in Indian Medicine (journ.) (SAUS)

J Res Indian Med Yog Homoeopathy... Journal of Research in Indian Medicine, Yoga and Homoeopathy (journ.) (SAUS)

JRes Inst Med Sci Kor... Journal. Research Institute of Medical Science of Korea (journ.) (SAUS)

J Res Lepid... Journal of Research on the Lepidoptera (journ.) (SAUS)

J Res M & T... Journal of Resource Management and Technology (journ.) (SAUS)

J Res Math Educ... Journal for Research in Mathematics Education (journ.) (SAUS)

J Res Nat Bur Stand St A Phys Chem... Journal of Research. National Bureau of Standards. Section A. Physics and Chemistry (journ.) (SAUS)

J Res Nat Bur Stand St B Math Sci... Journal of Research. National Bureau of Standards. Section B. Mathematical Sciences (journ.) (SAUS)

J Res Nat Bur Stand St D Radio Sci... Journal of Research. National Bureau of Standards. Section D. Radio Science (journ.) (SAUS)

J Res Natl Bur Stand A... Journal of Research. National Bureau of Standards. Section A. Physics and Chemistry (journ.) (SAUS)

J Res Natl Bur Stand B... Journal of Research. National Bureau of Standards. Section B. Mathematics and Mathematical Physics (journ.) (SAUS)

J Res Natl Bur Stand C... Journal of Research. National Bureau of Standards. Section C. Engineering and Instrumentation (journ.) (SAUS)

J Res Natl Inst Stand Technol... Journal of Research of the National Institute of Standards and Technology (journ.) (SAUS)

J Res NBS... Journal of Research. National Bureau of Standards (journ.) (SAUS)

J Res NBS A... Journal of Research. National Bureau of Standards. Section A. Physics and Chemistry (journ.) (SAUS)

J Res NBS B... Journal of Research. National Bureau of Standards. Section B. Mathematical Sciences (journ.) (SAUS)

J Res NIST... Journal of Research of the National Institute of Standards and Technology (journ.) (SAUS)

J Res Pers... Journal of Research in Personality (journ.) (SAUS)

J Res Read... Journal of Research in Reading (journ.) (SAUS)

J Res Sci Agra Univ... Journal of Research in Science. Agra University (journ.) (SAUS)

J Res Sci Teach... Journal of Research in Science Teaching (journ.) (SAUS)

J Res Soc Pak... Journal. Research Society of Pakistan (journ.) (SAUS)

J Res US GS... Journal of Research. United States Geological Survey (journ.) (SAUS)

JRF .... Jackie Robinson Foundation (EA)

JRF .... Jewish Reconstructionist Foundation (EA)

JRF .... Job Request Form (SAUS)

JRF .... Jog Request Form (SAUS)

JRF .... John-Roger Foundation (EA)

JRF .... Journal of Reproduction and Fertility (SAUO)

JRF .... Judicial Research Foundation [*Defunct*]

JRF .... Julius Rosenwald Fund (SAUO)

JRF .... Junior Road Fellowship (SAUO)

JRFC .... Jerry Reed Fan Club [*Defunct*] (EA)

JRFC .... Johnny Rodriguez Fan Club (EA)

JRFL .... Jarful (ABBR)

JRFS .... Janssen Research Foundation Series (journ.) (SAUS)

JRFTNG .... Jet Refresher Training [*Navy*] (NVT)

JRG .... Jarring (ABBR)

JRG .... Joint Rapporteurs Group (SAUO)

JRG .... Journal of Regional Science (journ.) (SAUS)

JRG .... Junction Register (IAA)

JRGN .... Jargon (ABBR)

Jr Gr .... Junior Grade (SAUS)

JRGS .... Journal of the Royal Geographical Society (SAUO)

JRGS .... Journal of the Royal Geographical Society (journ.) (SAUS)

JRH .... Jorhat [*India*] [*Airport symbol*] (OAG)

JRH .... Journal of Religious History (journ.) (SAUS)

JRH .... Journal of Rural Health (journ.) (SAUS)

JRH .... Journal. Royal Historical Society of Queensland (journ.) (SAUS)

J Rheumatol... Journal of Rheumatology (journ.) (SAUS)

J Rheumatol Suppl... Journal of Rheumatology Supplement (journ.) (SAUS)

JRHS .... Julia Richman High School (SAUO)

JR HS .... Junior High School (WDAA)

JRHSQ .... Journal. Royal Historical Society of Queensland [*A publication*]

JRI .... Jail Release Information

JRI .... Japan Research Institute (SAUS)

JRI .... Jewel Resources [*Vancouver Stock Exchange symbol*]

JRI .... Journal of Risk and Insurance (journ.) (SAUS)

JRI .... Jules Richard Instruments (SAUS)

JRIA .... Japan Radio-Isotope Association (SAUO)

JRID............ Job Run Identification (SAUS)
JRIM............ Joint Requirements Integration Manager (SAUO)
JRIMD .... Journal of Reproductive Immunology (journ.) (SAUS)
JRINA .... Journal. Research Institute for Catalysis. Hokkaido University (journ.) (SAUS)
J R Inst Br Archit... Journal. Royal Institute of British Architects (journ.) (SAUS)
J R Inst Chem... Journal. Royal Institute of Chemistry (journ.) (SAUS)
J R Inst Hist Res... Journal. Rajasthan Institute of Historical Research (journ.) (SAUS)
J R Inst Public Health... Journal. Royal Institute of Public Health (journ.) (SAUS)
J R Inst Public Health Hyg... Journal. Royal Institute of Public Health and Hygiene (journ.) (SAUS)
J Rio Grande Val Hortic Soc... Journal. Rio Grande Valley Horticulture Society (journ.) (SAUS)
JRISDON...... Jurisdiction (ROG)
J RI State Dent Soc... Journal. Rhode Island State Dental Society (journ.) (SAUS)
JRivBsh .... James River Bankshares, Inc. [*Associated Press*] (SAG)
JRiver.......... James River Corp. of Virginia [*Associated Press*] (SAG)
JRJ .... Jamaica Association of Villas and Apartments (EA)
JRJ .... JAVA [*Jamaica Association of Villas and Apartments*] Reservations Jamaica (EA)
JRJ .... Journal of Reform Judaism (journ.) (SAUS)
JRKD .... Jerked (ABBR)
JRKG .... Jerking (ABBR)
JRKIR .... Jerkier (ABBR)
JRKLY.......... Jerkily (ABBR)
JRKN .... Jerkin (ABBR)
JRKNS .... Jerkiness (ABBR)
JRKR .... Jerker (ABBR)
JRKST.......... Jerkiest (ABBR)
JRL............. Cincinnati G&E8.28%JrSubDebs [*NYSE symbol*] (TTSB)
JRL............. Cincinnati Gas & Electric [*NYSE symbol*] (SAG)
JRL............. Jarvis Resources [*Vancouver Stock Exchange symbol*]
JRL............. Jet Research Laboratory (MCD)
JRL............. John Rylands Library (SAUO)
jrl.............. Journal (DAVI)
JRL............. Journal of Retailing (journ.) (SAUS)
Jrl Audit ..... Journal of Accounting Auditing and Finance (journ.) (SAUS)
JRL/B.......... Bulletin of the John Rylands Library. Manchester (journ.) (SAUS)
JRLB........... John Rylands Library. Bulletin (journ.) (SAUS)
Jrl Bldg S... Journal. Chartered Institution of Building Services (journ.) (SAUS)
Jrl Bus........ Journal of Business (journ.) (SAUS)
Jrl Comm..... Journal of Commerce (journ.) (SAUS)
Jrl Def& D... Journal of Defense and Diplomacy (journ.) (SAUS)
Jrl Elec I..... Journal of the Electronics Industry (journ.) (SAUS)
Jrl Eng Pwr... Journal of Engineering for Power (journ.) (SAUS)
JRLI............ Life Outreach International (EA)
Jr Lib .... Junior Libraries (journ.) (SAUS)
Jrl Int B ...... Journal of International Business Studies (journ.) (SAUS)
Jrl Irrep ...... Journal of Irreproducible Results (journ.) (SAUS)
Jrl Market.... Journal of Marketing (journ.) (SAUS)
Jrl Metals.... Journal of Metals (journ.) (SAUS)
Jrl Mkt R ... Journal of Marketing Research (journ.) (SAUS)
Jrl P.......... Journal. Patent Office Society (journ.) (SAUS)
Jrl Petro ..... Journal of Petroleum Technology (journ.) (SAUS)
Jrl Retail ..... Journal of Retailing (journ.) (SAUS)
Jrl RE Tax ... Journal of Real Estate Taxation (journ.) (SAUS)
Jr LS.......... Junior Life Saving [*Red Cross*]
Jrl Solar ..... Journal of Solar Energy Engineering (journ.) (SAUS)
Jrl Sol Engr... Journal of Solar Energy Engineering (journ.) (SAUS)
J Rly Div Inst Mech Engrs... Institution of Mechanical Engineers. Railway Division. Journal (journ.) (SAUS)
J Rly Div Inst Mech Engrs... Journal. Institution of Mechanical Engineers. Railway Division (journ.) (SAUS)
JRM............. Jettison Release Mechanism
JRM............. Joule-Rowland Method [*Physics*]
JRM............. Journal of Reproductive Medicine (SAUO)
JRM............. McDermott [*J. Ray*] SA [*NYSE symbol*] (SAG)
JRMA .... Japan Hubber Manufacturers Association (SAUO)
JRMB .... Joint Requirements and Management Board [*Later, JROC*] [*Military*]
JRMB .... Joint Resources Management Board [*Military*]
JRMET .... Joint Reliability and Maintainability Evaluation Team (ACAE)
JRMF .... Joseph R. McCarthy Foundation (EA)
JRMIEZ .... Journal of Reconstructive Microsurgery (journ.) (SAUS)
JRMMRA ..... Journal. Rocky Mountain Medieval and Renaissance Association (journ.) (SAUS)
JRMO.......... Junior Resident Medical Office (SAUS)
JRMO.......... Junior Resident Medical Officer (SAUO)
JRMPO .... Joint Regional Medical Planning Office (SAUO)
JRMS.......... Journal. Royal Meteorological Society (journ.) (SAUS)
JRMTO........ Joint Rail Military Traffic Office (AABC)
JRMX .... JRM Holdings, Inc. (SAUO)
JRN............. Japan Radio Network (SAUO)
JRN............. Jet Rent SA [*Mexico*] [*ICAO designator*] (FAAC)
JRN............. Junior Resident Note [*Medical records*] (DAVI)
JrNAD......... Junior National Association for the Deaf [*Defunct*] (EA)
J R Nav Med Serv... Journal of the Royal Naval Medical Service (SAUO)
J R Nav Med Serv... Journal of the Royal Naval Medical Service (journ.) (SAUS)
J R Nav Med Serv... Journal. Royal Naval Medical Service (journ.) (SAUS)
JRNBA .... Journal of Research (journ.) (SAUS)
JRNBA .... Journal of Research. National Bureau of Standards (journ.) (SAUS)
JRNCDM...... Journal of Radioanalytical and Nuclear Chemistry (journ.) (SAUS)
JRNDEX....... Journal Index
JRNIST .... Journalist
JRNL........... Journal

JRNLM........ Journalism (ABBR)
JRNLSM....... Journalism (ABBR)
JRNLST....... Journalist (ABBR)
JRNLSTC ...: Journalistic (ABBR)
JRNLT......... Journalist (ABBR)
JRNLTC .... Journalistic (ABBR)
JRNLTCY ...... Journalistically (ABBR)
JRNLZ......... Journalize (ABBR)
JRNLZD .... Journalized (ABBR)
JRNLZG ...... Journalizing (ABBR)
JRNLZR ...... Journalizer (ABBR)
JRNMA .... Journal. Royal Naval Medical Service (journ.) (SAUS)
JRNS .... Journal of the Russian Numismatic Society (SAUO)
JRNSCA .... Jurist Reports, New Series, Court of Appeal [*New Zealand*] [*A publication*] (DLA)
JRNSML ..... Jurist Reports, New Series, Cases in Mining Law [*New Zealand*] [*A publication*] (DLA)
JRNSSC .... Jurist Reports, New Series, Supreme Court [*New Zealand*] [*A publication*] (DLA)
JRNY .... Journey (ABBR)
JRNYD .... Journeyed (ABBR)
JRNYG .... Journeying (ABBR)
JRNYMAN .... Journeyman (ABBR)
JRO............. Jicamarca Radar Observatory [*Peru*]
JRO............. J. Robert Oppenheimer
JRO............. J. Robert Oppenheimer Fellowship (SAUO)
JRO............. Junior Radio Operator [*British military*] (DMA)
JRO............. Kilimanjaro [*Tanzania*] [*Airport symbol*] (OAG)
J Robot Syst... Journal of Robotic Systems (journ.) (SAUS)
JROC .... Joint Requirements Oversight Council [*Military*]
JROFC .... James "Rebel" O'Leary Fan Club (EA)
JROJATC...... James "Rebel" O'Leary and Jammie Ann Tape Club [*Defunct*] (EA)
J Root Crops... Journal of Root Crops (journ.) (SAUS)
JROSC .... J. Robert Oppenheimer Study Center (SAUO)
JROt........... Joint Requirements Oversight Council (SAUO)
JROTC .... Junior Reserve Officers' Training Corps (AABC)
J Roy Agr Soc... Journal. Royal Agricultural Society of England (journ.) (SAUS)
J Royal Aust Hist Soc... Journal. Royal Australian Historical Society (journ.) (SAUS)
J Royal Military College Aust... Journal. Royal Military College of Australia (journ.) (SAUS)
J Royal Soc New Zeal... Journal. Royal Society of New Zealand (journ.) (SAUS)
J Roy Artil... Journal of the Royal Artillery (journ.) (SAUS)
J Roy ASC ... Journal of the Royal Astronomical Society of Canada (SAUO)
JRoyASC...... Journal of the Royal Astronomical Society of Canada (journ.) (SAUS)
J Roy Astron Soc Can... Journal of the Royal Astronomical Society of Canada (SAUO)
J Roy At ...... Journal. Royal Australian Historical Society (journ.) (SAUS)
J Roy Col P... Journal. Royal College of Physicians of London (journ.) (SAUS)
J Roy Inst Cornwall N Ser... Journal. Royal Institution of Cornwall. New Series (journ.) (SAUS)
J Roy Satist Soc Ser B... Journal. Royal Statistical Society. Series B. Methodological (journ.) (SAUS)
J Roy Soc Ant Ir... Journal. Royal Society of Antiquaries of Ireland (journ.) (SAUS)
J Roy Soc NSW... Journal. Royal Society of New South Wales (journ.) (SAUS)
J Roy Soc West Aust... Journal of the Royal Society of Western Australia (SAUO)
J Roy Soc West Aust... Journal of the Royal Society of Western Australia (journ.) (SAUS)
J Roy Sta A... Journal. Royal Statistical Society. Series A. General (journ.) (SAUS)
J Roy Statis Soc... Journal of the Royal Statistical Society (SAUO)
J Roy Statis Soc... Journal of the Royal Statistical Society (journ.) (SAUS)
J Roy Statist Soc Ser A... Journal. Royal Statistical Society. Series A. General (journ.) (SAUS)
J Roy Stats... Journal. Royal Statistical Society (journ.) (SAUS)
J Roy Stat Soc A J Verb Learn Verb Beh... Journal. Royal Statistical Society. A Journal of Verbal Learning and Verbal Behavior (journ.) (SAUS)
J Roy St B ... Journal. Royal Statistical Society. Series B. Methodological (journ.) (SAUS)
J Roy St C ... Journal. Royal Statistical Society. Series C. Applied Statistics (journ.) (SAUS)
JRP............. Job Readiness Posture (OICC)
JRP............. Joint Requirements Planning (CDE)
JRP............. Jute Reinforced Plastics (SAUS)
JRPB............ Joint Radio Propagation Bureau (SAUO)
JRPB............ Joint Radio Propogation Bureau (SAUO)
JRPE............ Job-Relevant Professional Experience (SAUS)
JRPG .... Joint RADAR Planning Group [*Military*] (CET)
JRPM........... Joint Registered Publications Memorandum
JRPO .... Joint Research Projects Office [*Army and NASA joint operation*] (RDA)
JRPrK......... James River$3.375Cv Ex K Pfd [*NYSE symbol*] (TTSB)
JRPrL......... James River Dep Cv Ex Pfd [*NYSE symbol*] (TTSB)
JRPrO........ James River 8.25% Dep Pfd [*NYSE symbol*] (TTSB)
JRPrP........ James River 9% 'DECS' [*NYSE symbol*] (TTSB)
JRPS........... Japan Reinforced Plastics Society (SAUO)
JRPUA .... Journal of Research. Punjab Agricultural University (journ.) (SAUS)
JRR............. Japanese Research Reactor
JRR............. Joint Radio Reporting (SAUS)
JRR............. Juror (ABBR)
JRRC .... Japanese Reprographic Rights Center (SAUO)
JRRC .... Joint Regional Reconnaissance Center [*NATO*] (NATG)
JRRI .... Journal of Rubber Research Institute of Malaya (journ.) (SAUS)
JRRI .... Juvenile Risk Reduction Initiative
JRRIAN........ Journal. Rubber Research Institute of Malaysia (journ.) (SAUS)
J RRI Malaysia... Journal. Rubber Research Institute of Malaysia (journ.) (SAUS)
J RRI Sri Lanka... Journal. Rubber Research Institute of Sri Lanka (journ.) (SAUS)

JRRLA	Journal. Radio Research Laboratories (journ.) (SAUS)
JRRS	Japan Hadiation Research Society (SAUO)
JRRT	John Ronald Renel Tolkien [*British author, 1892-1973*]
JRS	Japanese Rocket Society
JRS	Jersey [*Channel Islands*] [*Seismograph station code, US Geological Survey*] [*Closed*] (SEIS)
JRS	Jerusalem [*Israel*] [*Airport symbol*] (OAG)
JRS	Jet Repair Service
JRS	Job Rehearsal Scheme (AIE)
JRS	Job Release Scheme (PDAA)
JRS	John R. Sinnock [*Designer's mark, when appearing on US coins*]
JRS	Joint Reconnaissance Structure (CCCA)
JRS	Joint Reporting Structure [*Military*] (AFM)
JRS	Journal of Refractive Surgery (SAUS)
JRS	Journal of Regional Science (journ.) (SAUS)
JRS	Journal of Roman Studies (journ.) (SAUS)
JRS	Journal. Roentgen Society [*A publication*] (ROG)
JRS	Judges and Judicial Retirement System (SAUO)
JRS	Junction Relay Set (IAA)
JRSA	Japan Raw Silk Association (SAUO)
JRSA	Justice Research and Statistics Association (NTPA)
JRSAA	Journal. Royal Society of Arts (journ.) (SAUS)
JRSAI	Journal. Royal Society of Antiquaries of Ireland (journ.) (SAUS)
JRSAnH	Journal. Royal Society of Antiquaries of Ireland (journ.) (SAUS)
JRSC	Jam-Resistant Secure Communications
JRSC	Joint Rescue Sub-Center (COE)
JRSC	Joint Resistant Secure Communications [*DoD*]
Jr Schol	Junior Scholastic (journ.) (SAUS)
JRSDCNL	Jurisdictional (ABBR)
JRSH	Journal. Royal Society of Health (journ.) (SAUS)
JRSI	Journal of the Royal Sanitary Institute (journ.) (SAUS)
JR Sigls Inst	Journal. Royal Signals Institution (journ.) (SAUS)
J R Signals Inst	Journal of the Royal Signals Institution (journ.) (SAUS)
JRSM	Journal of the Royal Society of Medicine (SAUO)
J/RSM	Junior Regimental Sergeant-Major [*British military*] (DMA)
J RSNZ	Journal. Royal Society of New Zealand (journ.) (SAUS)
JRSO	Jewish Restitution Successor Organization (EA)
J R Soc Encour Art Manuf Commer	Journal. Royal Society for the Encouragement of Arts, Manufactures and Commerce (journ.) (SAUS)
J R Soc Health	Journal of the Royal Society of Health (SAUO)
J R Soc Health	Journal of the Royal Society of Health (journ.) (SAUS)
J R Soc Health	Journal. Royal Society of Health (journ.) (SAUS)
J R Soc Med	Journal of the Royal Society of Medicine (MEC)
J R Soc Med	Journal of the Royal Society of Medicine (journ.) (SAUS)
J R Soc Med	Journal. Royal Society of Medicine (journ.) (SAUS)
J R Soc NZ	Journal. Royal Society of New Zealand (journ.) (SAUS)
JRSOD	Journal. Reticuloendothelial Society (journ.) (SAUS)
JRSPDN	Jurisprudent (ABBR)
JRSPDNC	Jurisprudence (ABBR)
JRSPDTL	Jurisprudential (ABBR)
JRSS	Journal of the Royal Statistical Society (SAUO)
JRSS	Journal of the Royal Statistical Society (journ.) (SAUS)
JRSS	Journal. Royal Statistical Society (journ.) (SAUS)
JRST	Jurist (ABBR)
J R Stat Soc	Journal of the Royal Statistical Society (SAUO)
J R Stat Soc	Journal. Royal Statistical Society (journ.) (SAUS)
JRSTE	Junior Suite [*Travel industry*] (TRID)
JRS/USA	Jesuit Refugee Service/USA (EA)
JRSVC	Jam-Resistant Secure Voice Communications (MCD)
JRSWG	Joint Reentry System Working Group
JRSY	Jersey (ABBR)
JRT	Jaguar-Rover-Triumph
JRT	Jaguar Rover Triumph Inc. (SAUO)
JRT	Job Relations Training
JRT	Joint Rapporteur Team (SAUO)
JRT	Journal of Retailing (journ.) (SAUS)
JRT	Jugoslovenska Radiotelevizija [*Association of Yugoslav Radio and Television Organizations*] (EY)
JRT	Junctional Recovery Time [*Medicine*] (DMAA)
JRT	Tampa, FL [*Location identifier*] [*FAA*] (FAAL)
JRTC	Joint Readiness Training Center [*Fort Chaffee, AR*] (INF)
JRTCA	Jack Russell Terrier Club of America (EA)
JRTC-IS	Joint Readiness Training Center Instrumentation System [*DoD*]
JRTC-OIS	Joint Readiness Training Objective Instrumentation System (SAUS)
J R Telev Soc	Journal. Royal Television Society (journ.) (SAUS)
JRTIG	Joint Radiophone Technical Interfaces Group (SAUO)
JRTOC	Joint Rear Tactical Operations Center (SAUO)
JRTP	Jub Readiness Training Program (SAUS)
J Rubber Res Inst Malays	Journal. Rubber Research Institute of Malaysia (journ.) (SAUS)
J Rubber Res Inst Sri Lanka	Journal. Rubber Research Institute of Sri Lanka (journ.) (SAUS)
JRUL	Journal. Rutgers University Library (journ.) (SAUS)
J R United Serv Inst	Journal. Royal United Service Institution (journ.) (SAUS)
J Rurai Coop Int Res Cent Rural Coop Communities	Journal of Rural Cooperation. Inter- national Research Center on Rural Cooperative Communities (journ.) (SAUS)
J Rural Dev	Journal of Rural Development (journ.) (SAUS)
J Rural Econ and Derebpment	Journal of Rural Economics and Development (journ.) (SAUS)
J Rural Educ	Journal of Rural Education (journ.) (SAUS)
J Rural Eng Dev	Journal of Rural Engineering and Development (journ.) (SAUS)
J Rur Coop	Journal of Rural Cooperation (journ.) (SAUS)
JRUSI	Journal of the Royal United Service Institution [*A publication*] (ROG)
J Russell Soc	Journal of the Russell Society (SAUO)
J Russell Soc	Journal. Russell Society (journ.) (SAUS)
J Rutgers Univ Libr	Journal. Rutgers University Library (journ.) (SAUS)
JRV	Javelin Rocket Vehicle
JRvr	James River Corp. of Virginia [*Associated Press*] (SAG)
JRVSB	Jena Review. Supplement (journ.) (SAUS)
JRWG	Job Redesign Working Group
JRX	Joint Readiness Exercise (MCD)
JRY	Jury (ABBR)
JRYBLD	Jerrybuild (ABBR)
JRYBLDG	Jerrybuilding (ABBR)
JRYBLDR	Jerrybuilder (ABBR)
JRYBLT	Jerrybuilt (ABBR)
JryDeli	Jerrys Famous Deli, Inc. [*Associated Press*] (SAG)
JRYMA	Juryman (ABBR)
JRZ	Jugoslovenska Radikalna Zajednica [*Yugoslav Radical Union*] [*Political party*] (PPE)
JS	Jack Screw
JS	Jamestowne Society (EA)
JS	Jamestown Society (SAUO)
J/S	Jammer-to-Signal Ratio (SAUO)
J/S	Jamming to Signal
JS	Jam Strobe (IEEE)
J/S	Jam to Signal Ratio
JS	Janus. Supplements (journ.) (SAUS)
JS	Japan Society (EA)
JS	Japan Society for the Study of Economic Policy (SAUO)
JS	Jargon Society (EA)
JS	JCS [*Joint Chiefs of Staff*] Support (MCD)
JS	Jefferson Smurfit Group PLC [*NYSE symbol*] (SAG)
JS	Jefferson Smurfit Grp ADS [*NYSE symbol*] (TTSB)
JS	Jejunal Segment [*Gastroenterology*] (DAVI)
JS	Jetevator Sensor
JS	Jet Stabilization
JS	Jet Stream
JS	Jet Study (AAG)
JS	Jettison Signal
J S	Jewish Studies (journ.) (SAUS)
JS	Job Scheduler (SAUS)
JS	Job Search [*Job Training and Partnership Act*] (OICC)
JS	Job Service (ELAL)
JS	Job Set (ELAL)
JS	Job Specification [*Department of Labor*]
JS	Job Statement (ELAL)
JS	Job Stream [*Computer science*]
JS	John R. Sinnock [*Designer's mark, when appearing on US coins*]
JS	Johnson Society (EA)
JS	Joint Services [*British military*] (DMA)
JS	Joint Spacing [*Mining technology*]
JS	Joint Sparing (SAUS)
JS	Joint Staff [*Military*] (CINC)
JS	Joint Station (SAUS)
JS	Joint Support [*Military*] (AFM)
JS	Jones and Spencer's Superior Court Reports [*33-61 New York*] [*A publication*] (DLA)
JS	Joshua [*Old Testament book*]
J/s	Joules per Second (IDOE)
JS	Jourdain Society [*British*]
JS	Journal. Arnold Schoenberg Institute (journ.) (SAUS)
JS	Judaic Studies (journ.) (SAUS)
JS	Judaisme Sepharadi (BJA)
JS	Judean Society (EA)
JS	Judgment Summons [*British*] (ROG)
JS	Judicial Separation [*British*] (ROG)
JS	Jump if Sign (SAUO)
JS	Junctional Slowing [*Cardiology*] (DAVI)
JS	Junior Sailor (SAUS)
JS	Junior Scholastic (journ.) (SAUS)
JS	Junior Seaman [*British military*] (DMA)
JS	Junkman-Shoeller Unit (MAE)
JS	Jury Sittings (Faculty Cases) [*Scotland*] [*A publication*] (DLA)
J/S	Justified
JS	Justifying Space [*Typography*] (DGA)
JS	Just Scale
JS	Korean Airways [*ICAO designator*] (AD)
JS	Sea of Japan
JSA	Jammer System Analysis
JSA	Japanese Standards Association (NTCM)
JSA	Japan Silk Association (EA)
JSA	Jesuit Seismological Association (EA)
JSA	Jet Show Assembly
JSA	Jewelers Security Alliance (SAUS)
JSA	Jewelers Security Alliance of the United States (SAUO)
JSA	Jewelers Shipping Association (EA)
JSA	Jewish Society of America
JSA	Job Safety Analysis
JSA	Job Search Allowance
JSA	Job Seekers' Allowance (WDAA)
JSA	Joint Security Area (MCD)
JSA	Joint Steering Assembly (SAUO)
JSA	Joint Supportability Assessment [*Army*]
JSA	Journal of Substance Abuse (SAUO)
JSA	Journeymen Stonecutters Association (SAUO)
JSA	Journeymen Stone Cutters Association of North America [*Defunct*]
JSA	Junior State of America (SAUS)

JSA.............. Junior Statesmen of America (EA)
Js[a].............. Sutter Antigen [Of Kell system blood group] [Hematology] (DAVI)
JSAAE......... Japanese Society for Alternatives to Animal Experiments
JSAC.......... Jet Strategic Airlift Capability [of Military Air Command] (AAG)
JSAC.......... Joint Strategy and Action Committee [Defunct] (EA)
JSACA......... Journal. South African Chemical Institute (journ.) (SAUS)
J SA Chem I... Journal. South African Chemical Institute (journ.) (SAUS)
JSACT......... Jetstream Anti-Countermeasure Trainer (SAUS)
JSACT........ Joint Strategic Air Control Team (SAUO)
JSAE.......... Japan Society of Automotive Engineers (SAUO)
JSAE.......... Journal of the Society of Automotive Engineers (SAUO)
JSAE.......... Journal of the Society of Automotive Engineers (journ.) (SAUS)
JSAE.......... Journal Society of Automotive Engineers of Japan (journ.) (SAUS)
JSAED......... Journal of Strain Analysis for Engineering Design (journ.) (SAUS)
JSAFA4....... Journal. South African Forestry Association (journ.) (SAUS)
JSAFE....... Journal of South-East Asia and the Far Fast (journ.) (SAUS)
J S Afr Biol S... Journal. South African Biological Society (journ.) (SAUS)
J S Afr Bot Suppl Vol... Journal of South African Botany. Supplementary Volume (journ.) (SAUS)
J S Afr Inst Eng... Journal. South African Institution of Engineers (journ.) (SAUS)
J S Afr Speech Hear Assoc... Journal. South African Speech and Hearing Association (journ.) (SAUS)
J S Afr Vet Assoc... Journal of the South African Veterinary Association (SAUO)
J S Afr Vet Assoc... Journal of the South African Veterinary Association (journ.) (SAUS)
J S Afr Vet Med Assoc... Journal. South African Veterinary Medical Association (journ.) (SAUS)
JSAG........... Joint Service Advisory Group
JSAH........... Journal of Southeast Asian History (journ.) (SAUS)
JSAH........... Journal. Society of Architectural Historians (journ.) (SAUS)
JSAI........... Japanese Society for Artificial Intelligence (SAUS)
JSAI........... Japan Society fot Artificial Intelligence (SAUS)
J Sailama Univ Fac Ed Math Natur Sci... Journal. Sailama University. Faculty of Education. Mathematics and Natural Science (journ.) (SAUS)
J Sailama Univ Nt Sci... Journal. Sailama University. Natural Science (journ.) (SAUS)
J SA I Min... Journal. South African Institute of Mining and Metallurgy (journ.) (SAUS)
J Sains Nukl... Jernal Sains Nuklear (journ.) (SAUS)
J S Air-Cond Refrig Eng Korea... Journal Society of Air-Conditioning and Refrigerating Engineers of Korea (journ.) (SAUS)
JSAIS.......... Junior South African Individual Scales [Intelligence test]
J-SAK.......... Joint Attack of the Second Echelon (MCD)
JSAL.......... Journal of South African Law [A publication] (ILCA)
JSAL.......... Journal of South Asian Languages (journ.) (SAUS)
JSALO......... Journal of Studies on Alcohol (journ.) (SAUS)
JSAM........ Joint Security Assistance Memorandum [Military]
JSAM........ Joint Service Achievement Medal [Military decoration]
JSAMA........ Journal. South African Institute of Mining and Metallurgy (journ.) (SAUS)
JSAMSA....... Joint Security Assistance Memorandum Supporting Analysis (MCD)
JSAN........ Joint Staff Automation of the Nineties (SAUS)
J San Antonio Dent Soc... Journal. San Antonio District Dental Society (journ.) (SAUS)
JS&CS......... Jewish Family and Child Services (SAUO)
JS&TIC........ Joint Scientific and Technical Intelligence Committee (SAUO)
J Sanit Eng Div; Amer Soc... Journal of the Sanitary Engineering Division; Proceedings of American Society of Sanitary Engineering (SAUO)
J Sanit Eng Div Proc Am S Civ Eng... Journal. Sanitary Enneering Division. Proceedings. American Society of Civil Engineers (journ.) (SAUS)
JSAP........... Joint Security Assistance Planning (SAUO)
JSAP........... Joint Statement of Agreed Principles [US-USSR]
JSAP........... Journal of Small Animal Practice [A publication] (GVA)
JSAP........... Junior School of Applied Photography (SAUO)
J Sapporo Munic Gen Hp... Journal. Sapporo Municipal General Hospital (journ.) (SAUS)
JSAR........... Joint Search and Rescue [Military] (DNAB)
JSAR........... Joint Service Agreement Report [Defense Supply Agency]
JSARC......... Joint Search and Rescue Center [Military] (AABC)
J S Archit .... Journal. Society of Architectural Historians (journ.) (SAUS)
JSAS........... Jammer System Analysis Simulator
JSAS........... Journal of Southeast Asian Studies (journ.) (SAUS)
JSAS........... Journal Supplement Abstract Service [American Psychological Association]
J S Asia L ... Journal of South Asian Literature (journ.) (SAUS)
JSASS......... Japan Society for Aeronautical and Space Sciences (SAUO)
JSASWE....... Joint Services Anti-Submarine Warfare Establishment (SAUO)
JSAT.......... Japan Satellite Systems [Commercial firm]
JSAT.......... Joint System Acceptance Test (MCD)
JSAT.......... Junior Scholastic Aptitude Test [Education] (AEBS)
JSATC......... Joint Service Air Trooping Centre (SAUO)
JSATG......... Joint Services Actions Task Group (MCD)
JSATP........ Joint Services Automatic Testing Panel (AAGC)
JSA-US........ Jewelers' Security Alliance of the United States (NTPA)
JSAVLA....... Joint Services Advanced Vertical Lift Aircraft (ACAE)
JSAWC......... Joint Services Amphibious Warfare Centre (SAUS)
JSB.......... Bachelor of Judicial Science
JSB.......... Japanese Society in Brisbane [Australia]
JSB.......... Jaswant Singh and Bhattacharji [Staining method for blood cells, named for its discoverers] [Medicine]
JSB.............. Jewish Society for the Blind (EA)
JSB.......... Jewish Statistical Bureau (EA)
JSB[a].......... Job Status Block (TIMI)
JSB.......... Joint Signal Board (SAUO)
JSB.............. Joint-Stock Bank [Banking]

JSB............. JSB Financial [NYSE symbol] (SG)
JSB............. Judicial Science Bachelor (SAUS)
JSBA........... Jefferson Savings Bancorp [NASDAQ symbol] (SAG)
JSBCD3....... Journal. American Society of Brewing Chemists (journ.) (SAUS)
JSBF........... JSB Financial [NASDAQ symbol] (TTSB)
JSBF........... JSB Financial, Inc. [NASDAQ symbol] (SPSG)
JSB Fn........ JSB Financial, Inc. [Associated Press] (SAG)
JSBK.......... Johnstown Savings Bank (SAUO)
JSBS.......... Joint Strategic Bomber Study
JSC.......... ICSU/WMO Joint Scientific Committee for WCRP (SAUS)
JSC.......... Jackson State College [Later, Jackson State University] [Mississippi]
JSC.......... Janiaica Schools Certificate (SAUS)
JSC.......... Japanese Studies Center [Monash University] [Australia]
JSC.......... Jascan Resources, Inc. [Toronto Stock Exchange symbol]
JSC.......... Jenkinsville [South Carolina] [Seismograph station code, US Geological Survey] (SEIS)
JS-C.......... Jesus College-Cambridge (SAUO)
JSC.......... Job-Site Component
JSC.......... Johnson Space Center (USDC)
JSC.......... Johnstown & Stony Creek Rail Road Co. [AAR code]
JSC.......... Joint Scientific Committee [WMO/ICSU]
JSC.......... Joint Scientific Committee, World Climate Research Program (SAUS)
JSC.......... Joint Sectoral Committee (SAUO)
JSC.......... Joint Security Control
JSC.......... Joint Selection Committee
JSC.......... Joint Service Committee [Military]
JSC.......... Joint Setup Cost
JSC.......... Joint Signal Committee (SAUO)
JSC.......... Joint Staff Council [Japanese] [Military] (CINC)
JSC.......... Joint Standing Committee (ADA)
JSC.......... Joint Steering Committee (SAUS)
JSC.......... Joint Steering Committee for Revision of Anglo-American Cataloging Rules (AL)
JSC.......... Joint Stock Co. (SAUS)
JSC.......... Joint Stock Company (SAUO)
JSC.......... Joint-Stock Company
JSC.......... Joint Strategic Capabilities [Military]
JSC.......... Joint Strategic Committee [Military]
JSC.......... Joint Support Command [Navy]
JSC.......... Joly Steam Calorimeter
J-SC.......... Journal of Solid State Circuits (SAUS)
JSC.......... Journal of Structural Chemistry (journ.) (SAUS)
JSC.......... Judgments of the Supreme Court of Cyprus [A publication] (ILCA)
JSC.......... Junior Staff Course [British]
JSC.......... Justice of the Supreme Court
JSC.......... Justice of the Supreme Court (journ.) (SAUS)
JSC.......... Justice Statistics Clearinghouse (SAUS)
JSCA........... Japanese Spaniel Club of America [Later, JCCA] (EA)
JSCA........... Journeymen Stone Cutters Association of North America [Defunct] (EA)
JSCAACR ..... Joint Steering Committee for Revision of AACR [Anglo-American Cataloging Rules]
JSCAEN....... Joint Schools Committee for Academic Excellence Now (EA)
J S Calif State Dent Assoc... Journal of the Southern California State Dental Association (journ.) (SAUS)
JSCAMPS .... Joint Service Common Airframe Multiple Purpose System [Military] (MCD)
JSCAS......... Japan Society for Computer Aided Surgery (SAUO)
JSCAS......... Johnson Space Center Astronomical Society
JSCAT......... Joint Staff Crisis Action Team [Environmental science] (COE)
JSCB.......... Job Step Control Block [Computer science] (BUR)
JSCC.......... Japan Securities Clearing Corp.
JSCC.......... Japan Society for Composite Materials (SAUO)
JSCC.......... Joint Service Coordination Committee [Military] (DOMA)
JSCC.......... Joint Staff Consultative Committee [British] (DI)
JSCC.......... Joint Synod of the Convocation of Canterbury (SAUO)
JSCC.......... Scott Cable Communications Inc. (SAUO)
JSCCB......... Joint Services Configuration Control Board [Military] (AFIT)
JSCCMP...... Joint Services Committee of Conservative Members of Parliament (SAUO)
J Sc D ...... Doctor of Juridical Science
JScD .... Doctor of Juristic Science (SAUO)
JScD .... Doctor of Iuristic Science (SAUS)
JScE........... Eimac [Division of Varian Associates] Technical Library, San Carlos, CA [Library symbol] [Library of Congress] (LCLS)
JSCE .... Japanese Society of Civil Engineers (SAUS)
JSCE .... Japan Society of Civil Engineers (SAUS)
JSCE .... Japan Society of Corrosion Engineers (SAUO)
JSCE .... Joint Services Communications Element (CCCA)
JSCERDCG... Joint Service Civil Engineering Research and Development Coordination Group [Military] (RDA)
JSCFA.......... Japan Steel Castings and Forgings Association (SAUO)
J Sc Food Agriculture... Journal of the Science of Food and Agriculture (journ.) (SAUS)
J Sch Health... Journal of School Halth (journ.) (SAUS)
J school...... Journalism School (WDMC)
J-School....... Journalism School (journ.) (SAUS)
J School Libr Ass Qd... Journal. School Library Association of Queensland [A publication]
J Sch Pharm Univ Tehran... Journal. School of Pharmacy. University of Tehran (journ.) (SAUS)
J Sci .... Journal of Science (journ.) (SAUS)
JSCI........... Journal of the Society of Chemical Industry (SAUO)
JSCI........... Journal of the Society of Chemical Industry (journ.) (SAUS)

J Sci Assoc Maharajahs Coll...   Journal. Science Association. Maharajahs College (SAUS)

J Sci Busan Natl Univ...   Journal of Science. Busan National University (journ.) (SAUS)

JSCIC...........   Joint Space Command Intelligence Center [*Air Force*]

J Sci Club....   Journal of the Science Club (journ.) (SAUS)

J Sci Coll Gen Educ Unir Tokushima...   Journal of Science. College of General Education. University of Tokushima (journ.) (SAUS)

J Sci Comput...   Journal of Scientific Computing (journ.) (SAUS)

J Sci Edc Chungbuk Natl Univ...   Journal of Science Education. Chungbuk National University (journ.) (SAUS)

J Sci Educ Chonnam Natl Univ...   Journal of Science Education. Chonnam National University (journ.) (SAUS)

J Sci Educ Sci Educ Res Inst Teach Coll Kyungpook Univ...   Journal of Science Education. Science Education Research Institute Teachers College. Kyungpook University (journ.) (SAUS)

J Sci Educ Technol...   Journal of Science Education and Technology (journ.) (SAUS)

J Scient Ind Res...   Journal of Scientific and Industrial Research (journ.) (SAUS)

J Sci Food Agric Abstr...   Journal of the Science of Food and Agriculture. Abstracts (journ.) (SAUS)

J Sci Hiroshima Univ Ser A Math Phys Chem...   Journal of Science. Hiroshima University. Series A. Mathematics, Physics, Chemistry (journ.) (SAUS)

J Sci Hiroshima Univ...   Journal of Hiroshima University (journ.) (SAUS)

J Sci Hiroshima Univ...   Journal of Science. Hiroshima University (journ.) (SAUS)

J Sci Hiroshima Univ A...   Journal of Hiroshima University, Series A (journ.) (SAUS)

J Sci Hiroshima Univ B...   Journal of Hiroshima University, Series B (journ.) (SAUS)

J Sci Hiroshima Univ Ser A-II...   Journal of Science. Hiroshima University. Series A-II (journ.) (SAUS)

J Sci Hiroshima Univ Ser B Div 2 Bot...   Journal of Science. Hiroshima University. Series B. Division 2. Botany (journ.) (SAUS)

J Sci Ind Res Sect A...   Journal of Scientific and Industrial Research. Section A. General (journ.) (SAUS)

J Sci Ind Res Sect B...   Journal of Scientific and Industrial Research. Section B (journ.) (SAUS)

J Sci Ind Res Sect D...   Journal of Scientific and Industrial Research. Section D Technolgy (journ.) (SAUS)

J Sci Instrum Phys Ind...   Journal of Scientific Instruments and Physics in Industry (journ.) (SAUS)

J Sci Instrum Suppl...   Journal of Scientific Instruments. Supplement (journ.) (SAUS)

J Sci Labor...   Journal of Science of Labor (journ.) (SAUS)

J Sci Labour Prt 2...   Journal of Science of Labour. Part 2 (journ.) (SAUS)

J Sci Res...   Journal of Scientific Research (journ.) (SAUS)

J Sci Res Banaras Hindu Univ...   Journal of Scientific Research. Banaras Hindu University (journ.) (SAUS)

J Sci Res Banaras Hindu Univ...   Journal of Scientific Research of the Banaras Hindu University (journ.) (SAUS)

J Sci Res Counc Jam...   Journal. Scientific Research Council of Jamaica (journ.) (SAUS)

J Sci Res Plants & Med...   Journal of Scientific Research in Plants and Medicines (journ.) (SAUS)

J Sci Soc Thail...   Journal of the Science Society of Thai- land (journ.) (SAUS)

J Sci Soc Thiland...   Journal. Science Society of Thailand (journ.) (SAUS)

JSCLC...........   Joint Standing Committee on Library Cooperation [*British*] (NITA)

JSCM...........   Japanese Society for Contemporary Music (SAUO)

JSCM...........   Japan Society for Composite Materials (SAUO)

JSCM...........   Joint Service Commendation Medal [*Military decoration*] (AFM)

JSCM...........   JSC [*Johnson Space Center*] Manual [*NASA*] (NASA)

JSCMA...........   Journal. South Carolina Medical Association (journ.) (SAUS)

J S C Med Assoc...   Journal of the South Carolina Medical Association (journ.) (SAUS)

J S C Med Assoc...   Journal-South Carolina Medical Association (SAUO)

J SC Med Assoc...   Journal. South Carolina Medical Association (journ.) (SAUS)

JSCMPO......   Joint Service Cruise Missile Program Office (MCD)

JSCNOET.....   Joint Standing Committee on Nuclear and Other Energy Technologies (SAUO)

JSCO...........   Joint Staff Communications Office [*Military*] (AABC)

JSCO...........   Journal Status Central Operations Table (SAA)

JSCOM...........   Joint Services Commendation Medal (RDA)

JS Com Ind L...   Journal. Society of Commercial and Industrial Law [*A publication*] (ILCA)

J S Com Ind L...   Journal. Society of Commercial and Industrial Law (journ.) (SAUS)

J S Cosm Ch...   Journal. Society of Cosmetic Chemists (journ.) (SAUS)

J Scott.........   Reporter, English Common Bench Reports [*A publication*] (DLA)

J Scott As Geogr Teach...   Journal. Scottish Association of Geography Teachers (journ.) (SAUS)

JSCP...........   Joint Strategic Capabilities Plan [*Military*]

JSCR...........   Job Schedule Change Request

JSCR...........   Joint Standing Committee Report (HEAS)

Jscript.........   Java Script [*Microsoft Corp.*]

JSCS...........   Job Shop Control System (MHDI)

JSCS...........   Joint Strategic Connectivity Committee [*Joint Chiefs of Staff*]

JSCS...........   Joint Strategic Connectivity Staff

JSCS...........   Junior Slovak Catholic Sokol (EA)

JSCSA...........   Journal of Statistical Computation and Simulation (journ.) (SAUS)

JSCSC...........   Joint Service Command and Staff College (SAUO)

JSCU...........   Joint Supply Council for Union of South Africa [*World War II*]

JSCUD.........   Journal of Science Education. Chungbuk National University (journ.) (SAUS)

J Scunthorpe Mus Soc...   Journal. Scunthorpe Museum Society (journ.) (SAUS)

JSC-WCRP...   Joint Scientific Committee for the WCRP (SAUS)

JSC/WCRP...   Joint Steering Committee of the World Climate Reseach Programme (SAUS)

JSD...........   Doctor of Judicial [*or Juridical*] Science [*or Doctor of the Science of Law*]

JSD...........   Doctor of Juristic Science (SAUS)

JSD...........   Doctor of the Science of Law (SAUS)

JSD...........   Jackson Structured Design (COE)

JSD...........   Jackson System Development [*Systems development methodology*] (NITA)

JSD...........   Jalousie Storm Door (SAUS)

JSD...........   Jatiya Samajtantrik Dal [*National Socialist Party*] [*Bangladesh*] [*Political party*] (PPW)

JSD...........   Jeunesse Social Democrate [*Social Democratic Youth*] [*Malagasy*]

JSD...........   Jewish Society for the Deaf [*Later, New York Society for the Deaf*] (EA)

JSD...........   JiJi Securities Data Service [*JiJi Press Ltd.*] [*Japan*] [*Information service or system*] (CRD)

JSD...........   Joint Standards Documents (SAUO)

JSD...........   Joint System Development (SAUS)

JSD...........   Judicial Science Doctor (SAUS)

JSD...........   Justification Service Digit [*Telecommunications*] (TEL)

JSD...........   Stratford, CT [*Location identifier*] [*FAA*] (FAAL)

JSDA...........   Japanese Securities Dealers Association (ECON)

JSDA...........   Japanese Self-Defense Agency

JSDA...........   Japan Self-Defense Agency (SAUS)

JSDC...........   Joint Service Defence College (SAUO)

JSDC...........   Joint System Development Corporated (SAUS)

JSDF...........   Japanese Self-Defense Forces (SAUS)

JSDF...........   Japan Self-Defense Force (CINC)

JSDF...........   Jin Shin Do Foundation for Bodymind Acupressure (EA)

JSDFA...........   Japan Self Defence Force Agency (SAUO)

JSDFA...........   Japan Self-Defense Forces Academy (SAUO)

JSDFs...........   Japan Self-Defense Forces (SAUO)

JSDIC...........   Joint Services Detailed Interrogation Center (SAUO)

JSDK...........   Java Servlet Development Kit (SAUS)

JSDM...........   June, September, December, and March [*Denotes quarterly payments of interest or dividends in these months*] [*Business term*]

JSDOP.........   Joint Strategic Defense Operations Plan (SAUO)

JSDP...........   Jewish Social Democratic Party [*Political party*] (BJA)

JSDTI...........   John S. Donaldson Technical Institute (SAUO)

JSDTI...........   Sohn S Donaldson Technical Institute (SAUS)

JSE.............   Jakarta Stock Exchange (SAUO)

JSE.............   Jam Strobe Extractor

JSE.............   JOPES Support Element (SAUO)

JSEA...........   Jesuit Secondary Education Association (EA)

JSEAC...........   Joint Societies Employment Advisory Committee

J-SEAD.......   Joint Suppression of Enemy Air Defenses [*Military*] (INF)

J SE Asian Hist...   Journal of Southeast Asian History (journ.) (SAUS)

J Seattle King Cty Dent Soc...   Journal. Seattle-King County Dental Society (journ.) (SAUS)

JSEC...........   Joint Services Electrical and Electronics Committee (SAUS)

J Sec Ed......   Journal of Secondary Education (journ.) (SAUS)

JSEDM...........   Japan Society of Electrical-Discharge Machining (SAUO)

JSEE...........   Japanese Society for Engineering Education (SAUO)

JSEE...........   Japan Society for Engineering Education (SAUS)

JSEI...........   Joint Second Echelon Interdiction

J Seismol Soc Jpn...   Journal of the Seismological Society of Japan (journ.) (SAUS)

JSE/J...........   Japanese Journal of Ethnology. Japanese Society of Ethnology. Tokyo (SAUO)

JSE/J...........   Japanese Journal of Ethnology. Japanese Society of Ethnology. Tokyo (journ.) (SAUS)

J Semant.....   Journal of Semantics (journ.) (SAUS)

J Senticust ICs...   Journal of Semicustom ICs (journ.) (SAUS)

JSEOD...........   Joint Service Explosive Ordnance Disposal (SAUS)

JSEODOC.....   Joint Service Explosive Ordnance Disposal Operations Centre (SAUO)

J Seoul Womans Coll...   Journal. Seoul Womans College (journ.) (SAUS)

JSEP...........   Job Skills Education Program [*Military*]

JSEP...........   Joint Services Electronics Program [*Military*]

J Serb Chem Soc...   Journal of the Serbian Chemical Society (journ.) (SAUS)

J Serb Chem Soc...   Journal. Serbian Chemical Society (journ.) (SAUS)

J Seric Sci Jpn...   Journal of Sericultural Science of Japan (journ.) (SAUS)

JSESP...........   Joint Surface Effect Ships Program (SAUS)

JSESPO.......   Joint [*Maritime Administration - Navy*] Surface-Effects Ship Program Office

JSET...........   Journal of Sex Education and Therapy (journ.) (SAUS)

JSeTU.........   Tohoku University, Sendai, Japan [*Library symbol*] [*Library of Congress*] (LCLS)

J Severance Union Med Coll...   Journal. Severance Union Medical College (journ.) (SAUS)

J Sex Marital Ther...   Journal of Sex and Marital Therapy (journ.) (SAUS)

JSEXP...........   Joint Services Explosives Program (MCD)

J Sex Res...   Journal of Sex Research (journ.) (SAUS)

JSEY...........   Jersey [*One of the Channel Islands*] (ROG)

JSF...........   Japan Scholarship Foundation (EA)

JSF...........   Jesse Stuart Foundation (EA)

JSF...........   Jewish Student Federation (SAUO)

JSF...........   Job Services File

JSF...........   Joint Security Force [*Army*] (INF)

JSF...........   Joint Stipulated Facts and Figures (AAGC)

JSF...........   Joint Strike Fighter

JSF...........   Junctor Switch Frame [*Telecommunications*] (TEL)

JSF...........   Junior Statesman Foundation (SAUO)

JSF...........   Junior Statesmen Foundation (EA)

JSFA...........   Journal of Science of Food and Agriculture (SAUS)

JSFA...........   Journal of the Science of Food and Agriculture (journ.) (SAUS)

JSFC .... Jack Scalia Fan Club (EA)
JSFC .... Japanese-Soviet Fisheries Commission (SAUS)
JSFC .... Japanese-Soviet Fisheries Commission for the Northwest Pacific
JSFC .... Joe Stampley Fan Club [Defunct] (EA)
JSFM .... Japan Society for Strength and Fracture of Materials (SAUO)
JSFP .... Joint Service Fuze Plan [Army]
JSFT .... Health and Safety Department (SAUO)
JSFU .... Joint Services Flail Unit (SAUS)
JSG .... Jamaica (BWI) Study Group [Defunct] (EA)
JSG .... Jamaica Study Group (SAUO)
JSG .... Job Seekers Guide to Private and Public Companies [A publication]
JSG .... Jugoslavia Study Group (EA)
JSGCC .... Joint Service Guidance and Control Committee
JSGLL .... Japanese Studies in German Language and Literature (journ.)
                 (SAUS)
JSGMF .... John Simon Guggenheim Memorial Foundation (SAUO)
JSGMRAM ... Joint Study Group for Material Resource Allocation Methodology
                 (SAUO)
JSGMRAM ... Joint Study Group on Military Resources Allocation Methodology
                 (SAUO)
JSGOMRAM... Joint Study Group on Military Resources Allocation Methodology
                 (MCD)
JSGPM .... Joint Service General Purpose Mask [Army]
J S Gr .... Greens Law Reports (journ.) (SAUS)
JSGRP .... Jewish Symbols in the Greco-Roman Period [A publication] (BJA)
JSG/TCCS .... Joint Standardization Group for Tactical Communications and Control
                 Systems (SAUO)
JSH .... Jetstream Ltd. [Hungary] [ICAO designator] (FAAC)
JSH .... Journal of Social History (journ.) (SAUS)
JSH .... Journal of Southern History [A publication] (BRI)
JSHA .... Johannes Schwalm Historical Association (EA)
JSHABP .... Journal. South African Speech and Hearing Association (journ.)
J Shangbi Coll Text Technol... Journal. Shanghai College of Textile Technology
                 (journ.) (SAUS)
J Shanghai Jiaotong Univ... Journal of the Shanghai Jiaotong University (journ.)
                 (SAUS)
J Shanghai Sci Inst Sect 1... Journal. Shanghai Science Institute. Section 1.
                 Experimental Biology and Medicine (journ.) (SAUS)
J Shanghai Sci Inst Sect 1... Journal. Shanghai Science Institute. Section 1.
                 Mathematics, Astronomy, Physics, Geophysics, Chemistry and
                 Allied Sciences (journ.) (SAUS)
J Shanghai Sci Inst Sect 2... Journal. Shanghai Science Institute. Section 2.
                 Geology Palaeontology, Mineralogy and Petrology (journ.)
                 (SAUS)
J Shanghai Sci Inst Sect 3... Journal. Shanghai Science Institute. Section 3.
                 Systematic and Morphological Biology (journ.) (SAUS)
J Shanghai Sci Inst Sect 5... Journal. Shanghai Science Institute. Section 5.
                 General (journ.) (SAUS)
J Shanxi Univ Nat Sci Ed... Journal. Shanxi University. Natural Science Edition
                 (journ.) (SAUS)
J SHASE ...... Journal. Society of Heating, Air conditioning and Sanitary Engineers
                 of Japan (SAUO)
J SHASE ...... Journal. Society of Heating, Air conditioning and Sanitary Engineers
                 of Japan (journ.) (SAUS)
J Shaw .... John Shaw's Justiciary Reports [1848-52] [Scotland] [A publication]
                 (DLA)
J Shaw Just... John Shaw's Justiciary Reports [1848-52] [Scotland]
                 [A publication] (DLA)
JSHDFC .... Jean S. Harris Defense Fund Committee (EA)
JSHEA .... Journal of School Halth (journ.) (SAUS)
J Sheffield Univ Metall Soc... Journal of the Sheffield University Metallurgical
                 Society (journ.) (SAUS)
J Sheffield Univ Met Soc... Journal. Sheffield University Metallurgical Society
                 (journ.) (SAUS)
J Shellfish Res... Journal of Shellfish Research (journ.) (SAUS)
JSHG .... Hokkai Gakuen University, Sapporo, Japan [Library symbol] [Library
                 of Congress] (LCLS)
JSHG/J .... Japanese Journal of Human Genetics. Japan Society of Human
                 Genetics. Tokyo (SAUO)
JSHG/J .... Japanese Journal of Human Genetics. Japan Society of Human
                 Genetics. Tokyo (journ.) (SAUS)
J Shimane Med Assoc... Journal. Shimane Medical Association (journ.) (SAUS)
J Shimonoseki Coll Fish... Journal. Shimonoseki College of Fisheries (journ.)
                 (SAUS)
J Shimonoseki Univ Fish... Journal. Shimonoseki University of Fisheries (journ.)
                 (SAUS)
J Ship Prod... Journal of Ship Production (journ.) (SAUS)
J Ship Res... Journal of Ship Research (journ.) (SAUS)
J Shivaji Univ... Journal. Shivaji University (journ.) (SAUS)
J Shnw Jt... John Shaws Justiciary Reports (journ.) (SAUS)
J Shoreline Manage... Journal of Shoreline Management (journ.) (SAUS)
J Shoulder Elbow Surg... Journal of Shoulder and Elbow Surgery (journ.) (SAUS)
JSHQ .... Job Safety & Health Quarterly (SAUO)
JSHR .... Journal of Speech and Hearing Research (journ.) (SAUS)
JSHS .... Jewish Society for Human Service [British]
JSHS .... Junior Science and Humanities Symposia [Terminated, 1977]
JSHS .... Junior Science and Humanities Symposium (SAUO)
J-S H Sch Clearing House... Junior-Senior High School Clearing House (journ.)
                 (SAUS)
JSHT .... Japan Society of Heat Treatment (SAUO)
J S Ht .... Journal of Southern History (journ.) (SAUS)
JSI .... Jacobi Semi-Iterative (SAUS)
JSI .... Jansky Screening Index [Psychology] (DAVI)
JSI .... Japanese Studies Institute (SAUS)

JSI .... Java Script Index (SAUS)
JSI .... Job Satisfaction Inventory [Guidance]
JSI .... Job Schedule Items (MCD)
JSI .... Job Search Information
JSI .... Job Search Inventory [Test] (TMMY)
JSI .... Job Sensitivity Inventory [Interpersonal skills and attitudes test]
JSI .... Job Step Index [Computer science] (IAA)
JSI .... Job Style Indicator [Test] (TMMY)
JSI .... John Snow Inc. (SAUO)
JSI .... Joint Support Item (DNAB)
JSI .... Journal. American Society for Information Science (journ.) (SAUS)
JSI .... Journal of Social Issues (journ.) (SAUS)
JSI .... JumboSports, Inc. [NYSE symbol] (SG)
JSI .... Skiathos [Greece] [Airport symbol] (OAG)
JSIA .... Japan Software Industry Association (CIST)
JSIA .... Joint Service Induction Area
JSIA .... Justice System Improvement Act [1979]
JSIAM .... Japan Society of Industrial and Applied Mathematics (SAUO)
J Siam Soc... Journal. Siam Society (journ.) (SAUS)
JSIC .... Joint Securities Industry Committee (SAUS)
JSIC .... Joint Space Command Intelligence Center (SAUO)
JSIC .... Joint Space Intelligence Center
J-SIDS .... Joint Service Intrusion Detection System [Military] (INF)
JSIF .... Japan Shipbuilding Industry Foundation (SAUO)
JSIF .... Japan Spinners Inspecting Officer Foundation (SAUS)
JSIID .... Joint Service Interior Intrusion Detection Devices [Military] (MCD)
JSIIDS .... Joint Service Interior Intrusion Detection System [Military]
JSIIDS .... Joint-Services Interior Intruder Detection System (SAUS)
JSIM .... Joint Service Intelligence Manual
JSIMS .... Joint Simulation System [DoD]
JSIN .... Journal. Society for International Numismatics (journ.) (SAUS)
J Singap Natl Acad Sci... Journal of the Singapore National Academy of Science
                 (journ.) (SAUS)
J Singapore Paediatr Soc... Journal of the Singapore Paediatric Society (SAUO)
J Singapore Paediatr Soc... Journal of the Singapore Paediatric Society (journ.)
                 (SAUS)
J Singapore Pediatr Soc... Journal. Singapore Paediatric Society (journ.) (SAUS)
JSIP .... Job Service Improvement Program [Department of Labor]
JSIPS .... Joint Service Image Processing System (SAUS)
JSIPS .... Joint Services Imagery Processing System [Military]
JSIPS .... Joint Strategic Integrated Planning Staff (CCCA)
JSIPS .... Joint Strategic Integration Planning Staff (SAUO)
JSIPS .... Joint Systems Integration Planning Staff [Air Force]
JSIPS-N ...... Joint Service Imagery Processing System-Navy (SAUS)
JSIS .... Japan Society of Iron and Steel (SAUO)
JSISD .... Journal of Current Social Issues (journ.) (SAUS)
JSIT .... JDS Information Trace (SAUO)
JSJ .... Journal for the Study of Judaism (journ.) (SAUS)
JSJHS .... Journal of the Southern Jewish Historical Society (SAUO)
JSJHS .... Journal of the Southern Jewish Historical Society (journ.) (SAUS)
JSK .... St. Cloud, MN [Location identifier] [FAA] (FAAL)
J Skt .... Jack Socket (SAUS)
JSL .... Japanese Studies in German Language and Literature (journ.)
                 (SAUS)
JSL .... Jet Select Logic (MCD)
JSL .... Job Shop Labor (ACAE)
JSL .... Job Specification Language
JSL .... Johnson Society of London (EA)
JSL .... Joint Stock List [Military] (AFIT)
JSL .... Joint Support List [Military]
JSL .... Journal of Surgical Research (journ.) (SAUS)
JSL .... Journal of Symbolic Logic (journ.) (SAUS)
JSL .... Journal. School of Languages (journ.) (SAUS)
JSL .... Jurong Shipyard Limited (SAUO)
JSLAE .... Japanese Society for Laboratory Animal and Environment (GVA)
JSLB .... Japan Society of London. Bulletin (journ.) (SAUS)
JSLB .... Joint Services Liaison Staff (SAUS)
JSLB .... Joint Stock Land Banks [New Deal]
JSLC .... Jiuquan Satellite Launch Center (IGSL)
JSLE .... Japan Society of Lubrication Engineers (SAUO)
J Sleep Res... Journal of Sleep Research (journ.) (SAUS)
JSLGWCM ... Joint Services LASER-Guided Weapons Countermeasures (MCD)
JSLHR .... Journal of Speech, Language, and Hearing Research (SAUS)
JSLI .... Johnson-Sea-Link I [A submersible for deep sea studies]
JSLO .... Joint Services Liaison Organization (SAUO)
JSLPA .... Journal of Speech-Language Pathology and Audiology (SAUS)
JSLPC .... Joint Service Local Planning Committee
JSLQ .... Journal of Symbolic Logic Quarterly (journ.) (SAUS)
JSLRMDO ... Joint Service Large Rocket Motor Disposal Office [Army]
JSLS .... Japan Society of Library Science (NITA)
JSLS .... Joint Services Liaison Staff [British]
JSLWG .... Joint Spacelab Working Group [NASA] (NASA)
JSM .... Jesus Salvator Mundi [Jesus the Savior of the World] [Latin] (ROG)
JSM .... Job Stream Manager [Computer science] (IAA)
JSM .... Joint Staff Memorandum (MCD)
JSM .... Joint Staff Mission [British] [World War II]
JSM .... Jose de San Martin [Argentina] [Airport symbol] (OAG)
JSM .... Journal of Synagogue Music (journ.) (SAUS)
JSM .... Journal of Systems Management (journ.) (SAUS)
JSM .... Judicial Science Master (SAUS)
JSM .... Juilliard School of Music (SAUO)
JSM .... Master of Judicial Science
JSMA .... Joint Sealer Manufacturers Association
J Smal Bus Mgt... Journal of Small Business Management (journ.) (SAUS)
JSMB .... Japan Society of Mechanical Engineers (SAUO)

JSMB.......... Joint Sealift Movements Board [*Military*] (AFM)
JSMC.......... Joint Staff Message Control (SAUS)
JSMDA........ Japan Ship Machinery Development Association (SAUO)
JSME .... Japan Society of Mechanical Engineers
JSME .... Joint Soil Moisture Experiment
JSMEBE .... Japan Society of Medical Electronics and Biological Engineering (SAUO)
JSMIN.......... Jasmine (ABBR)
JSMMART.... Journal. Society for Mass Media and Resource Technology (journ.) (SAUS)
J Smooth Muscle Res... Journal of Smooth Muscle Research (journ.) (SAUS)
JSMP .... JSIMS [*Joint Simulation (System)*] Master Plan [*DoD*]
JSMPE .... Journal of the Society of Motion Picture Engineers (SAUO)
JSMPE .... Journal of the Society of Motion Picture Engineers (journ.) (SAUS)
JSmrfG .... Jefferson Smurfit Group PLC [*Associated Press*] (SAG)
JSMRU .... Joint Service Medical Rehabilitation Unit
JSMS .... Japan Society of Materials Science (SAUO)
JSMS .... Job Service Matching Systems [*US Employment Service*] [*Department of Labor*]
JSMSM .... Joint Service Meritorious Service Medal [*Military decoration*]
JSMTC .... Joint Service Mountain Training Centre (SAUO)
JSMUG-K.... Joint US Military Affairs Group, Korea (SAUO)
JSN............. Job Sequence Number
JSN............. Joint Space Narrowing [*Medicine*]
JSN............. Junction Switch Number (SAUS)
JSNA........... Jaspers Society of North America (EA)
JSNM........... Japan Society of New Metals (AAEL)
JSNOOFC..... Judson Scott Is Number 1 Official Fan Club (EA)
JSNP........... Japan Satellite News Pool (SAUO)
JSNPE.......... Joint Staff Nuclear Planning Element (MCD)
JSNPE.......... Joint Strategic Nuclear Planning Element (SAUO)
JSNT........... Johnson Tower (SAUS)
JSNT........... Journal for the Study of the New Testament (journ.) (SAUS)
JSO............. Jackson Symphony Orchestra (SAUO)
JSO............. Jacksonville Symphony Orchestra (SAUO)
JSO............. Jacksonville, TX [*Location identifier*] [*FAA*] (FAAL)
JSO............. Job-Specific Orientation (SAUS)
JSO............. Joint Service Office
JSO............. Joint Services Organization (SAUO)
JSO............. Joint Specialty Officer (DOMA)
JSOA........... Joint Special Operations Agency (SAUO)
JSOA........... Joint Special Operations Area [*Military*] (INF)
JSOACC ...... Joint Special Operations Air Component Commander (SAUO)
J So AL........ Journal of South Asian Literature (journ.) (SAUS)
JSOC........... Joint Ship Operations Center
JSOC........... Joint Ship Operations Committee
JSOC........... Joint Special Operations Center (MCD)
JSOC........... Joint Special Operations Command [*Military*]
JSOC........... Joint Strategic Operations Command (MCD)
J Soc Arch... Journal. Society of Archivists (journ.) (SAUS)
J Soc Archit Hist... Journal of the Society of Architectural Historians (SAUO)
J Soc Archit Hist... Journal of the Society of Architectural Historians (journ.) (SAUS)
J Soc Army Hist Res... Journal. Society for Army Historical Research (journ.) (SAUS)
J Soc Arts... Journal of the Society of Arts (journ.) (SAUS)
J Soc Arts... Journal. Society of Arts (journ.) (SAUS)
J Soc Automot Eng... Journal. Society of Automotive Engineers (journ.) (SAUS)
J Soc Automot Eng Jpn Inc... Journal. Society of Automotive Engineers of Japan, Inc. (journ.) (SAUS)
J Soc Automot Engrs Australas... Journal. Society of Automotive Engineers of Australasia (SAUO)
J Soc Bibliogr Nat Hist... Journal. Society for the Bibliography of Natural History (journ.) (SAUS)
J Soc Chem Ind Vic... Journal. Society of Chemical Industry of Victoria (journ.) (SAUS)
J Soc Comp Leg... Journal. Society of Comparative Legislation (journ.) (SAUS)
J Soc Cosmet Chem... Journal of the Society of Cosmetic Chemists (SAUO)
J Soc Cosmet Chem... Journal of the Society of Cosmetic Chemists (journ.) (SAUS)
J Soc Cosmet Chem... Journal. Society of Cosmetic Chemists (journ.) (SAUS)
J Soc Dairy Technol... Journal. Society of Dairy Technology (journ.) (SAUS)
J Soc Dyers Color... Journal of the Society of Dyers and Colorists (journ.) (SAUS)
J Soc Eng Miner Springs... Journal. Society of Engineers for Mineral Springs (journ.) (SAUS)
J Soc Environ Eng... Journal of the Society of Environmental Engineers (journ.) (SAUS)
J Soc Exp Agric... Journal. Society of Experimental Agriculturists (journ.) (SAUS)
J Soc Glass Technol... Journal. Society of Glass Technology (journ.) (SAUS)
J Soc H........ Journal of Social History [*A publication*] (BRI)
J Soc Health Syst... Journal of the Society for Health Systems (SAUO)
J Soc Health Syst... Journal of the Society for Health Systems (journ.) (SAUS)
J Social and Econ Studies... Journal of Social and Economic Studies (journ.) (SAUS)
J Social and Pol Studies... Journal of Social and Political Studies (journ.) (SAUS)
J Social Casework... Journal of Social Casework (journ.) (SAUS)
J Social Forces... Journal of Social Forces (journ.) (SAUS)
J Social Pol and Econ Studies... Journal of Social, Political and Economic Studies (journ.) (SAUS)
J Soc Instrum and Control... Journal. Society of Instrument and Control Engineers (journ.) (SAUS)
J Soc Instrum Control Eng... Journal of the Society of Instrument and Control Engineers (journ.) (SAUS)
J Soc Int Dev... Journal of the Society for International Development (journ.) (SAUS)

J Soc Int Dev... Journal of the Society for International Development. Society for International Development. Rome (SAUO)
J Soc Leath Technol Chem... Journal. Society of Leather Technologists and Chemists (journ.) (SAUS)
J Soc Leath Trades Chem... Journal. Society of Leather Trades Chemists (journ.) (SAUS)
J Soc Mater Sci Jpn... Journal of the Society of Materials Science, Japan (journ.) (SAUS)
J Soc Nav Archit Jpn... Journal. Society of Naval Architects of Japan (journ.) (SAUS)
J Soc Nav Arch Japan... Journal. Society of Naval Architects of Japan (journ.) (SAUS)
J Soc Non-Destr Test... Journal. Society for Non-Destructive Testing (journ.) (SAUS)
J Soc Occup Med... Journal of the Society of Occupational Medicine (journ.) (SAUS)
J Soc Pet Eng... Journal. Society of Petroleum Engineers (journ.) (SAUS)
J Soc Photogr Sci and Technol Jpn... Journal. Society of Photographic Science and Technology of Japan (journ.) (SAUS)
J Soc Photo Opt Instrum Eng... Journal. Society of Photo-Optical Instrumentation Engineers (journ.) (SAUS)
J Soc Photo Sci Technol Jpn... Journal of the Society of Photographic Science and Technology of Japan (journ.) (SAUS)
J Soc Psych Res... Journal. Society for Psychical Research (journ.) (SAUS)
J Soc Pub Teach Law N S... Journal. Society of Public Teachers of Law. New Series (journ.) (SAUS)
J Soc Radiol Prot... Journal. Society for Radiological Protection (journ.) (SAUS)
J Soc Res.... Journal of Social Research (journ.) (SAUS)
J Soc Res Adm... Journal of the Society of Research Administrators (journ.) (SAUS)
J Soc Rheol... Journal of the Society of Rheology (journ.) (SAUS)
J Soc Rheol Jpn... Journal of the Society of Rheology of Japan (journ.) (SAUS)
J Soc Rubber Ind... Journal of the Society of Rubber Industry (journ.) (SAUS)
J Soc Sci Hum... Journal of Social Sciences and Humanities (journ.) (SAUS)
J Soc Sci PhotogrJpn... Journal. Society of Scientific Photography of Japan (journ.) (SAUS)
J Soc Ther... Journal of Social Therapy (journ.) (SAUS)
J Soc Underwater Technol... Journal. Society for Undetwater Technology (journ.) (SAUS)
J Soc Welfare L... Journal of Social Welfare Law (journ.) (SAUS)
J Soc Work & Hum Sex... Journal of Social Work and Human Sexuality (journ.) (SAUS)
J Soc'y Comp Leg... Journal. Society of Comparative Legislation [*A publication*] (DLA)
J Soe Archit Hist... Journal of the Society of Architectural Historians. Louisville (SAUO)
JSOF............ Joint Special Operations Force (SAUO)
JSOFI........... Joint Special Operations Force Institute [*DoD*]
J Soil Biol & Etnl... Journal of Soil Biology and Ecology (journ.) (SAUS)
J Soil Mech Found Div; Ame... Journal of the Soil Mechanics and Foundations Division; Proceedings of the America (SAUO)
J Soil Mech Found Div Am Soc Civ Eng... Journal. Soil Mechanics and Foundations Division. American Society of Civil Engineers (journ.) (SAUS)
J Soil Sci..... Journal of Soil Science (journ.) (SAUS)
J Soil Sci Soc Am... Journal. Soil Science Society of America (journ.) (SAUS)
J Soil Water Conserv India... Journal of Soil and Water Conservation in India (journ.) (SAUS)
J Sol Energy Eng... Journal of Solar Energy Engineering (journ.) (SAUS)
J Sol Energy Res... Journal of Solar Energy Research (journ.) (SAUS)
J Sol Energy S Korea... Journal. Solar Energy Society of Korea (journ.) (SAUS)
J Solid Lubr... Journal of Solid Lubrication (journ.) (SAUS)
J Solid-Phase Biochem... Journal of Solid-Phase Biochemistry (journ.) (SAUS)
J Solid State Chem... Journal of Solid State Chemistry (journ.) (SAUS)
J Solid Wastes... Journal of Solid Wastes (journ.) (SAUS)
J Solid Wastes Manage... Journal of Solid Wastes Management (journ.) (SAUS)
J Sol Sci Soc Philipp... Journal. Soil Science Society of the Philippines (journ.) (SAUS)
J Somerset Mines Res Group... Journal. Somerset Mines Research Group (journ.) (SAUS)
JSON .... Joint Services Operational Notice
JSON .... Josephson International Inc. (SAUO)
JSONOM ...... Joint Specialty Officer Nominee (DOMA)
J Soonchunhyang Coll... Journal. Soonchunhyang College (journ.) (SAUS)
JSOP........... Dominican Oblates of Jesus (Spain) (TOCD)
JSOP........... Joint School of Photography (SAUO)
JSOP........... Joint Strategic Objectives Plan [*Military*]
JSOR........... Joint Services Operational Requirement [*Military*]
JSOR........... Joint Services Organizational Requirements (ACAE)
JSOR........... Joint Statements of Requirements (DOMA)
JSOR........... Joint Systems Operational Requirements (SAUO)
JSOR .... Journal. Society of Oriental Research (journ.) (SAUS)
JSORD........ Joint System Operational Requirements [*Document*] (DOMA)
JSORD........ Joint Systems Operational Requirements Document (SAUO)
JSORS........ Joint Service Operational Requirement Statement (MCD)
JSOSE......... Joint Special Operations Support Element [*DoD*]
JSOTF......... Joint Special Operations Task Force [*DoD*]
J South Afr Chem Inst... Journal. South African Chemical Institute (journ.) (SAUS)
J South Afr Stud... Journal of Southern African Studies (journ.) (SAUS)
J South Afr Wildl Manage Ass... Journal. Southern African Wildlife Management Association (journ.) (SAUS)
J South Am Earth Sci... Journal of South American Earth Sciences (SAUS)
J South Calif Dent Assistants Assoc... Journal. Southern California Dental Assistants Association (journ.) (SAUS)

J South Calif Dent Assoc... Journal. Southern California Dental Association (journ.) (SAUS)
J South California Dent Ass... Journal. Southern California Dental Association (SAUS)
J South Calif State Dent Assoc... Journal. Southern California State Dental Association (journ.) (SAUS)
J Southeast Asian Stud... Journal of Southeast Asian Studies (journ.) (SAUS)
J Southeast Sect Am Water Works Ass... Journal. Southeastern Section. American Water Works Association (journ.) (SAUS)
J South Orthop Assoc... Journal of the Southern Orthopaedic Association (SAUO)
J South Orthop Assoc... Journal of the Southern Orthopaedic Association (journ.) (SAUS)
J South Res... Journal of Southern Research (journ.) (SAUS)
J Southwest... Journal of the Southwest (journ.) (SAUS)
J South West Afr Sc Soc... Journal. South West African Scientific Society (journ.) (SAUS)
J Sov Cardiovasc Res... Journal of Soviet Cardiovascular Research (journ.) (SAUS)
J Soviet Math... Journal of Soviet Mathematics (journ.) (SAUS)
J Sov Laser Res... Journal of Soviet Laser Research (journ.) (SAUS)
J Sov Oncol... Journal of Soviet Oncology (journ.) (SAUS)
JSOW........... Joint Service Stand-Off Weapon (SAUS)
JSOW........... Joint Standoff Weapons Program
JSOW........... Joint Statement of Work (ABAC)
JSP............. Jacketed Soft-Point [Ammunition]
JSP............. Jackson Structured Programming [Program design tool] (NITA)
JSP............. Japanese Society of Periodontology (SAUO)
JSP............. Japan Socialist Party [Nikon Shakaito] [Political party] (PPW)
jsp............. Jasper (VRA)
JSP............. Job Support Program
JSP............. Joint Services Development Program
JSP............. Joint Services Publication
JSP............. Joint Staff Planners [Joint Chiefs of Staff]
JSP............. Joint Strategic Planning (SAUO)
JSP............. Joint Support Plan (SAUO)
JSP............. Journal of Sedimentary Petrology (journ.) (SAUS)
JSP............. Journal of Statistical Planning and Inference (journ.) (SAUS)
JSP............. Judicial Selection Project (EA)
JSP............. Jupiter, Saturn, and Pluto Mission (MCD)
JSP............. Jurisdictional Separation Process
JSPA........... Japan Screen Printing Association (SAUO)
J Space Astron Res... Journal of Space and Astronomy Research (journ.) (SAUS)
J Space L... Journal of Space Law (AAGC)
J Spac Rock... Journal of Spacecraft and Rockets (journ.) (SAUS)
J Span Stud... Journal of Spanish Studies (journ.) (SAUS)
J Span Stud... Journal of Spanish Studies. Twentieth Century (journ.) (SAUS)
JSPB........... Joint Staff Pension Board [United Nations]
JSPC........... Japan Sports Prototype Championship [Auto racing]
JSPC........... Joint Service Parachute Centre (SAUO)
JSPC........... Joint Sobe Processing Center [Okinawa] [Military]
JSPC........... Joint Strategic Plans Committee [Military]
JSPC........... Joint Strobe Processing Center
JSPD........... Joint Strategic Planning Document (MCD)
JSPD........... Joint Subsidiary Plans Division [Military] (MUGU)
JSPDSA...... Joint Strategic Planning Document Supporting Analysis [Military] (AABC)
JSPE........... Japan Society of Precision Engineering (SAUO)
JSPEB......... Journal of Social Education (journ.) (SAUS)
J Spec Philos... Journal of Speculative Philosophy (journ.) (SAUS)
J Spec Philos... Journal of the Speculative Philosophy (journ.) (SAUS)
J Spectrosc Soc Jpn... Journal of the Spectroscopical Society of Japan (journ.)
J Spectros Soc Jpn... Journal. Spectroscopical Society of Japan (journ.) (SAUS)
J Sp Educators... Journal for Special Educators (journ.) (SAUS)
J Speech D... Journal of Speech and Hearing Disorders (journ.) (SAUS)
JSPF........... Joint Staff Pension Fund [United Nations]
JSPFL......... Jointly Sponsored Program for Foreign Libraries [Defunct]
JSPG........... Joint Strategic Plans Group [Military]
JSPI........... Joint School of Photographic Interpretation (SAUO)
JSPIJ......... Journal of Social and Political Ideas in Japan (journ.) (SAUS)
J Spinal Disord... Journal of Spinal Disorders (journ.) (SAUS)
JSPMA......... Journal of Supramolecular Structure (journ.) (SAUS)
JSPMRC...... Joint Service Program Management Review Committee [Military]
JSPN........... Journal of the Society of Pediatric Nurses (SAUO)
JSPN........... Journal of the Society of Pediatric Nurses (journ.) (SAUS)
JSPO........... Joint System Program Office (ACAE)
JSPOG......... Joint Strategic Plans and Operations Group
J Sport Beh... Journal of Sport Behavior (journ.) (SAUS)
J Sport Hist... Journal of Sport History (journ.) (SAUS)
J Sport Med... Journal of Sports Medicine and Physical Fitness (journ.) (SAUS)
J Sports Med... Journal of Sports Medicine (journ.) (SAUS)
JSPP........... Japan Society of Plant Physiologists (SAUO)
JSPP........... Joint Service Program Plan [Military] (RDA)
JSPPM......... Japan Society of Powder and Powder Metallurgy (SAUO)
JSPR........... Journal. Society for Psychical Research (journ.) (SAUS)
JSPRS......... Japan Society of Photogrammetry and Remote Sensing (SAUO)
JSPS........... Japan Society for the Promotion of Science
JSPS........... Japan Sword Preservation Society (SAUO)
JSPS........... Jewish Student Press Service (EA)
JSPS........... Joint Strategic Planning System [Military]
JSPSE......... Journal. Society of Photographic Scientists and Engineers (journ.) (SAUS)
JSPTL......... Journal. Society of Public Teachers of Law (journ.) (SAUS)
JSQ............. Jewish Studies Quarterly (journ.) (SAUS)
JSQC........... Japan Society for/of Quality Control (SAUO)
JSQC........... Japan Society of Quality Control (SAUS)

JSQL........... Java SQL (SAUS)
JSR............. Jackson Resources Ltd. [Vancouver Stock Exchange symbol]
JSR............. Jammer Saturation Range (SAUS)
JSR............. Jam to Signal Ratio (MCD)
JSR............. Japanese Sociological Review (journ.) (SAUS)
JSR............. Japan Science Review [A publication]
JSR............. Japan Synthetic Rubber Co. Ltd.
JSR............. Jessore [Bangladesh] [Airport symbol] (OAG)
JSR............. Jewish Student Review (journ.) (SAUS)
JSR............. Joint Staffing Review
JSR............. Joint Status Review (ACAE)
JSR............. Joint Strategic Review (DOMA)
JSR............. Journal of Sex Research (SAUS)
JSR............. Journal of Ship Research [A publication] (DNAB)
JSR............. Journal of Social Research (journ.) (SAUS)
JSR............. Journal of Spacecraft and Rockets [A publication] (AAGC)
JSR............. Jump to Subroutine [Computer science] (BUR)
JSRA........... Job Search and Relocation Assistance Projects (OICC)
JSRA........... Joint Sponsored Research Agreement (GAVI)
JSRAAM...... Joint Short Range Air to Air Missile (ACAE)
J/S Ratio...... Jamming to Signal Ratio (SAUS)
JSRBA......... Journal of Scientific Research. Banaras Hindu University (journ.) (SAUS)
JSRC........... Joint Services Review Committee
JSRC........... Joint Ship Repair Committee
JSRCC......... Joint Search and Rescue Coordination Center (MCD)
JSRCSC...... Joint Services Radio Component Standardization Committee (SAUS)
JSRHS......... Japan Science Review. Humanistic Studies (journ.) (SAUS)
JSRJ........... Joint Services Recognition Journal (SAUS)
JSRK........... Jeunesse Socialiste Royale Khmere [Royal Cambodian Socialist Youth] [Political party]
JSRLPH....... Japan Science Review. Literature, Philosophy and History (journ.) (SAUS)
JSRP........... Joint Services Reading Panel [Military] [British]
JSRR........... Jamming To Signal Ratio Required (SAUS)
JSRR........... Jam/Signal Ratio Required (SAUS)
JSRS........... Jewish Social Research Series (journ.) (SAUS)
JSRS........... Jury System Reform Society [British]
JSRT........... Joint Short-Range Technology (MCD)
JSRU........... Joint Speech Research Unit [British] (NITA)
JSRWG........ JSIMS [Joint Simulation (System)] Requirements Working Group [Military]
JSS............. Jacob Sheep Society [British] (DBA)
JSS............. Japanese Society of Sydney [Australia]
JSS............. Java-Script Style Sheet (SAUS)
JSS............. Jet Steering System
JSS............. Jet String System (SAUS)
JSS............. Jet Strip System (PDAA)
JSS............. Jewish Social Studies [A publication] (BRI).
JSS............. Jim Smith Society (EA)
JSS............. Job Schedule Status (SAA)
JSS............. Job Segment Schedule (TIMI)
JSS............. Job Shop Simulation (SAUS)
JSS............. Job Shop Simulator
JSS............. Johnson Scan Star (SAUO)
JSS............. Joint Services Seeker (ACAE)
JSS............. Joint Services Standard (SAUS)
JSS............. Joint Signal Staff
JSS............. Joint Surveillance System [FAA] [Air Force]
JSS............. Joshua Slocum Society (EA)
JSS............. Journal of Social Sciences (journ.) (SAUS)
JSS............. Journal of Sports Sciences (journ.) (SAUS)
JSS............. Journal of Systems and Software (journ.) (SAUS)
JSS............. Journal of the Siam Society (SAUO)
JSS............. Junior Secondary School
JSSA........... Japan Science Student Awards (SAUS)
JSSA........... Japan Society for System Audits (SAUO)
JSSA........... John Steinbeck Society of America (EA)
JSSA........... Joint Services Survival, evasion, resistance & escape Agency (SAUO)
JSSA........... Joint Stealth Strike Aircraft [DoD] (DOMA)
JSSADC...... Joint Service Subaqua Diving Centre (SAUO)
JSSAM......... Joint Service Small Arms Management Committee (MCD)
JSSAP......... Joint Service Small Arms Panel (MCD)
JSSAP......... Joint Service Small Arms Program (RDA)
JSSAP......... Joint Service Small Arms Program Office [Dover, NJ] [Military]
JSSC........... Joint Services Staff College [or Course] [Obsolete] [British]
JSSC........... Joint Services Staff Course (SAUS)
JSSC........... Joint Services Standardization Committee (SAUS)
JSSC........... Joint Shop Stewards Committee [British]
JSSC........... Joint Space Surveillance Center (ACAE)
JSSC........... Joint Strategic Service Committee (SAUO)
JSSC........... Joint Strategic Survey Committee [or Council] [DoD]
JSSC........... Joint Strategic Survey Council (SAUO)
JSSC........... Journal of Solid State Circuits (SAUS)
JSSE........... Japanese Software Support Environment
JSSEA......... Journal. American Society of Safety Engineers (journ.) (SAUS)
JSSEE......... Joint Service Software Engineering Environment (SAUO)
JSSF........... Japanese Society of Scientific Fisheries (SAUO)
JSSFM......... Japan Society for Strength and Fracture of Materials (SAUO)
JSSG........... Jamming Signal Source Generator (ACAE)
JSSG........... Joint Signal Support Group (SAUO)
JSSI........... Japan Society of Snow and Ice (SAUO)
JSSIS......... Joint Staff Support Information System [Military] (GFGA)
JSSL........... Joint Services School of Linguists (SAUO)

JSSM........... Joint Services Staff Manual [Military] [British]
JSSMFE....... Japanese Society of Soil Mechanics and Foundation Engineering (SAUO)
JSSPA......... Jewish Social Services Professional Association (EA)
JSSPG .... Job Shop Simulation Program Generator (KSC)
JSSQ........... Jewish Social Service Quarterly (journ.) (SAUS)
JSSR........... Journal of Social Services Research (journ.) (SAUS)
JSSRel........ Journal for the Scientifc Study of Religion (journ.) (SAUS)
JSSS .... Job Seeking Skills Survey [Test] [Donald S. Tackley] (TES)
JSSST......... Japan Society for Software Science and Technology (SAUO)
JSST .... Job Seeking Skills Training (OICC)
JSSTD......... Joint SSTD (SAUS)
JSSU........... Joint Services Signals Unit (SAUS)
JSSUP........ Japanese Space Shuttle Utilization Program (MCD)
JSS/US .... Japanese Sword Society of the United States (EA)
JST .... Jamming Station (IAA)
JST .... Japanese Society of Translators (SAUO)
JST .... Japanese Standard Time
JST .... Japan Society of Tribologists (SAUO)
JST .... Japan Standard Time (SAUO)
JST .... Japan Universal System Transport Co. Ltd. [ICAO designator] (FAAC)
JST .... Javanese Standard Time (SAUS)
JST .... Jet STOL [Short Takeoff and Landing] Transport [Aircraft]
JST .... Jet Stream Turbulence (SAUS)
JST .... Jinpan Intl. [AMEX symbol] (SG)
JST .... Job Safety Training (SAUS)
JST .... Job Skills Training
JST .... Job Step Task (SAUS)
JST .... Johnstown [Pennsylvania] [Airport symbol] (OAG)
JST .... Johnstown, PA [Location identifier] [FAA] (FAAL)
JST .... Joint Systems Test (KSC)
JST .... Journal of Business Strategy (journ.) (SAUS)
JST .... Journal of Science and Technology (journ.) (SAUS)
JSTA.......... Justice System Training Association [Defunct] (EA)
JSTAA......... Journal. Royal Statistical Society. Series A. General (journ.) (SAUS)
J Starch Sweet Technol Res Soc Japan... Journal. Starch Sweetener Technological Research Society of Japan (journ.) (SAUS)
J Starch Technol Res Soc Jpn... Journal of Starch Technology. Research Society of Japan (journ.) (SAUS)
JSTARS....... Joint Strategic Airborne Reconnaissance System (MILB)
JSTARS....... Joint Surveillance and Target Attack RADAR System
JSTARS....... Joint Surveillance Target Acquisition and Reconnaissance System (ACAE)
JSTARS....... Joint Surveillance Target Attack Radar System
JSTARS-GSM... Joint Surveillance/Target Attack RADAR System Ground Station Module (RDA)
JSTASM....... Joint Surveillance/Target Attack Radar System Ground Station Module (SAUS)
J Stat Comput Simul... Journal of Statistical Computation and Simulation (SAUS)
J Statis Soc... Journal of the Statistical Society (SAUO)
J Statis Soc... Journal of the Statistical Society (journ.) (SAUS)
J Statis Soc... Journal. Statistical Society (journ.) (SAUS)
J Statist Res... Journal of Statistical Research (journ.) (SAUS)
J Stat Rsr.... Journal of Statistical Research (journ.) (SAUS)
JSTB .... Jesuit School of Theology at Berkeley (SAUS)
J St Bar Calif... Journal. State Bar of California [A publication] (DLA)
J St Barnabas Med Cent... Journal. Saint Barnabas Medical Center (journ.) (SAUS)
JSTC.......... Japan-Singapore Training Center (SAUO)
JSTC.......... Job Skills Training Course
JSTC.......... Joint Scientific and Technical Committee (SAUO)
JSTC.......... Joint Services Test Command (ACAE)
JSTC.......... Justice
JSTCB........ Job Step Task Control Block (SAUS)
JSTE .... Joint System Training Exercise [Military]
J Sterile Serv Manage... Journal of Sterile Services Management (journ.) (SAUS)
J Steroid Biochem Mol Biol... Journal of Steroid Biochemistry and Molecular Biology (journ.) (SAUS)
J Steward Anthropol Soc... Journal. Steward Anthropological Society (journ.) (SAUS)
JSTF .... Japan Science and Technology Foundation (SAUO)
JstFeet........ Just For Feet, Inc. [Associated Press] (SAG)
JSTG .... Jahressteuergesetz
JSTI .... Jamaican Sugar Technologists Institution (SAUS)
J St Ju........ Journal for the Study of Judaism in the Persian, Hellenistic and Roman Periods (journ.) (SAUS)
J St Jud...... Journal for the Study of Judaism (journ.) (SAUS)
J St Med...... Journal of State Medicine (journ.) (SAUS)
JSTN.......... Justin Indus [NASDAQ symbol] (TTSB)
JSTN.......... Justin Industries, Inc. [NASDAQ symbol] (NQ)
J Stoch Process Appl... Journal of Stochastic Processes and their Applications (journ.) (SAUS)
JSTOR .... Journal Storage (journ.) (SAUS)
JSTOR .... Journal Storage Project
JSTP .... Japan Society for Technology of Plasticity (SAUO)
JSTP .... Job Search Training Program
JSTP .... Joint Services Test Plan (CCCA)
JSTP .... Joint Strike Technology Program (SAUS)
JSTP .... Joint System Test Plan [Initial Defense Communications Satellite Program] (DNAB)
JSTP .... Joint System Test Program (SAUO)
JSTPA......... Joint Strategic Target Planning Agency (NATG)
JSTPPC....... Joint Services Technical Publication Policy Committee [Ministry of Defence] (PDAA)
JSTPS.......... Joint Strategic Target Planning Staff [DoD]

JSTR........... Job-Specific Training Required (SAUS)
JSTR........... Joint Systematic Troop Review [Military]
J Strain Mal.... Journal of Strain Malysis (journ.) (SAUS)
JSTRC......... Joint Services Telecommunications Requirements Contract (SAUO)
J Struct Biol... Journal of Structural Biology (journ.) (SAUS)
J Struct Chem... Journal of Structural Chemistry (MEC)
J Struct Div; Amer Soc Ci... Journal of the Structural Division; Proceedings of the American Society of Civil Engineering (SAUO)
J Struct Div Proc ASCE... Journal. Structural Division. Proceedings of the American Society of Civil Engineers (journ.) (SAUS)
J Struct Eng... Journal of Structural Engineering (journ.) (SAUS)
J Struct Geol... Journal of Structural Geology (journ.) (SAUS)
JSTSSB........ Journal. Royal Statistical Society. Series B. Methodological (journ.) (SAUS)
J St Tax'n.... Journal of State Taxation [A publication] (DLA)
J St Taxn..... Journal of State Taxation (journ.) (SAUS)
JSTU .... Joint Services Trials Unit (SAUO)
JSTU .... Tohoku University, Sendai, Japan [Library symbol] [Library of Congress] (LCLS)
J Stud Alcohol Suppl... Journal of Studies on Alcohol. Supplement (journ.) (SAUS)
J Stud Amer Med Ass... Journal. Student American Medical Association (journ.) (SAUS)
JSTX .... Joro Spider Toxin [Biochemistry]
JSU .... Hokkaido University, Sapporo, Japan [Library symbol] [Library of Congress] (LCLS)
JSU .... Jacksonville State University [Jacksonville, AL]
JSU .... Jewish Student Union (SAUO)
JSU .... Junta Socialista Unida [United Socialist Party] [Spain]
JSU .... Sukkertoppen [Greenland] [Airport symbol] (AD)
J Submicrosc Cytol Pathol... Journal of Submicroscopic Cytology and Pathology (journ.) (SAUS)
J Subst Abuse... Journal of Substance Abuse (journ.) (SAUS)
J Subst Abuse Treat... Journal of Substance Abuse Treatment (journ.) (SAUS)
J Suffolk Acad L... Journal. Suffolk Academy of Law (journ.) (SAUS)
JSUM.......... Japan Society of Ultrasonics in Medicine (SAUO)
JSUN.......... Jupiter, Saturn, Uranus, and Neptune (PDAA)
JS Unit .... Junkmann-Schoeller Unit (SAUS)
J Supercomput... Journal of Supercomputing (journ.) (SAUS)
J Supercond... Journal of Superconductivity (journ.) (SAUS)
J Supramol Struct Cell Biochem... Journal of Supramolecular Structure and Cellular Biochemistry (journ.) (SAUS)
J Supra St ... Journal of Supramolecular Structure (journ.) (SAUS)
J Surf Sci Soc Jpn... Journal of the Surface Science Society of Japan (journ.) (SAUS)
J Surg Oncol... Journal of Surgical Oncology (journ.) (SAUS)
J Surg Oncol Suppl... Journal. of Surgical Oncology. Supplement (journ.) (SAUS)
J Surg Res... Journal of Surgical Research (journ.) (SAUS)
JSV............ Jerry-Slough Virus [Medicine] (DMAA)
JSVA........... Jewish Socialist Verband of America [Defunct] (EA)
JSVIA.......... Journal of Sound and Vibration (journ.) (SAUS)
JSVS .... Japanese Society of Veterinary Science (GVA)
JSW............ Junctor Switch (VLIE)
JSWA.......... Japan Sewage Works Association (SAUO)
JSWAP........ Job Swapping (SAUS)
JSWAP........ Job Swapping Memory [Computer science] (MHDB)
J SWA Sci S... Journal. South West African Scientific Society (journ.) (SAUS)
JSWC.......... Journal of Soil and Water Conservation (journ.) (SAUS)
JSWDL........ Joint Services Weapon Data Link (MCD)
JSWG.......... Joint Science Working Group (ACAE)
JSWL.......... Journal of Social Welfare Law (journ.) (SAUS)
JSWPB........ Joint Special Weapons Publications Board
JSWPR........ Japan Society on Water Pollution Research (SAUO)
JSWS.......... Journal of Social Work and Human Sexuality (journ.) (SAUS)
JSY............ Jersey Airlines (SAUS)
JSY............ New Jersey Airways Inc. (SAUO)
JSYB.......... Jewish Socialist Youth Bund [Later, MJSG] (EA)
J Syd Univ Eng Soc... Journal. Sydney University Engineering Society. [A publication]
J Syd Univ Eng Soc... Journal. Sydney Univetsity Engineering Society (journ.) (SAUS)
J Symb Anthropol... Journal of Symbolic Anthropology (journ.) (SAUS)
J Symb Comput... Journal of Symbolic Computation (journ.) (SAUS)
J Synth Lubr... Journal of Synthetic Lubrication (journ.) (SAUS)
J Systems Software... Journal of Systems and Software (journ.) (SAUS)
JSZ............ Yugoslav Welding Association (SAUO)
JSZT .... Japan Society of Zoological Science (SAUO)
JT .... Air Oregon (SAUS)
JT .... Iowa Airways [ICAO designator] (AD)
JT .... Jahn-Teller (AAEL)
JT .... Jamaica Air Service (SAUS)
JT .... James Taylor [Singer]
JT .... Japanese Tokamak (SAUS)
JT .... Japan Times [A publication] (BARN)
JT .... Japan Tobacco, Inc.
JT .... Jarno Taper (VLIE)
JT .... Java Time (SAUO)
JT .... Jejunostomy Tube [Medicine] (DMAA)
JT .... Jerusalem Talmud (BJA)
JT .... Jig Template (MSA)
JT .... Job Table [Computer science] (IAA)
JT .... Job Ticket (SAUS)
JT .... Job Time (SAUS)
JT .... Job Timing (SAUS)
JT .... John Tyler [US president, 1790-1862]
Jt .... Joint (EBF)

jt................	Joint (RION)
JT	Joint
JT	Joint Tenancy (MHDW)
J-T	Joule-Thompson (SAUS)
J-T	Joule-Thomson [*Physics*]
JT	Journal Tape (SAUS)
JT	Journal. Thailand Research Society (journ.) (SAUS)
JT	Junction Transistor [*Electronics*] (IAA)
JT	Juridisk Tidsskrift [*A publication*] (ILCA)
Jt	Justiciary (SAUS)
JT	Juvenile Templar [*Freemasonry*]
JT-60	Japanese Torus (SAUS)
JTA	Azia Keizai Kenkyujo [*Institute for Developing Economies*], Tokyo, Japan [*Library symbol*] [*Library of Congress*] (LCLS)
JTA	Japanese Technical Abstracts [*A publication*]
JTA	Japan Tourist Association (SAUO)
JTA	Japan Transocean Air Co. Ltd. [*ICAO designator*] (FAAC)
JTA	Jewish Telegraphic Agency (EA)
JTA	Job Table Area (SAUS)
JTA	Job Task Analysis
JTA	Joint Table of Allowance
JTA	Joint Tactical Air (SAUO)
JTA	Joint Tariff Agreement (SAUS)
JTA	Joint Technical Architecture [*Office of the Secretary of Defense*]
JTA	Joint Tenancy Agreement [*Military*]
JTA	Joint Test Assembly (SAUO)
JTA	Journal of Thermal Analysis (journ.) (SAUS)
JTA-Army....	Joint Technical Architecture-Army
JTAC	Joint Technical Advisory Committee [*Electronics*]
JTAC	Joint Technical Advisory Council (SAUO)
JTAC	Joint Telecommunications Advisory Committee (SAUS)
JTACC	Joint Tactical Air Control Center
JTACM........	Joint Tactical Missile (SAUS)
JTACMA......	Joint Tactical Missile System-Army (SAUS)
JTACMIS-A..	Joint Tactical Missile System - Army
JTACMS......	Joint Tactical Cruise Missile System (ACAE)
JTACMS......	Joint Tactical Missile System
JTACMS-A ..	Joint Tactical Missile System - Army
JTACS	Japanese TACS System (SAUO)
JTACS	Joint Tactical Area Communications System [*Army*] (RDA)
JTAD...........	Joint Tactical Aids Detachment [*Military*]
JTAG	Japan Trade Advisory Group [*British Overseas Trade Board*] (DS)
JTAG	Joint Test Action Group [*European automotive industry*]
JTAGG	Joint Turbine Advanced Gas Generator [*DoD*]
JTAGS	Joint Tactical Ground Station [*Army*] (RDA)
JTAGS	Joint Tactical Ground System (SAUS)
JTAGS	Joint Target Acquistion Ground Station [*Military*]
JT AGT........	Joint Agent (WDAA)
J Taiwan Mus...	Journal. Taiwan Museum (journ.) (SAUS)
JTA-M	Jewish Teachers Association - Morim (EA)
JTAMD........	Joint Theater Air and Missile Defense [*Army*]
JT & E	Joint Test and Evaluation [*DoD*]
JT & SEV	Joint and Several [*Legal shorthand*] (LWAP)
JTAO...........	Joint Tactical Air Operations (SAUO)
JTAP	JISC Technology Applications Programme (SAUS)
JTAP	JTC1 TAG Application Portability Study Group (SAUO)
JTAPI..........	JAVA Telephony API (SAUO)
JTAPI..........	Java Telephony Application Program Interface (VLIE)
JTAPI..........	Java Telephony Application Programming Interface (SAUS)
J TAPPIK	Journal of the Technical Association of Pulp and Paper Industry of Korea (journ.) (SAUS)
JTARS.........	Joint Tactical Aerial Reconnaissance/Surveillance [*Military*] (DNAB)
JTARS MISREP...	Joint Tactical Aerial Reconnaissance/Surveillance Mission Report [*Military*] (DNAB)
JTASA.........	Journal. Tennessee Academy of Science (journ.) (SAUS)
JTASB.........	Joint Tactical Air Support Board
JTASC........	Joint Training and Analysis Simulation Center (SAUO)
jt asp	Joint Aspiration [*Orthopedics*] (DAVI)
jt auth........	Joint Author
JTAV	Joint Total Asset Visibility [*Military*]
JTAW	Joint Tactical Autonomous Weapons (ACAE)
JTAWG	Joint Targeting and Weapon Guidance (MCD)
JTAX	Jackson Hewitt [*NASDAQ symbol*] (SAG)
JTB	Japanese Tourist Board
JTB	Joint Bar
JTB	Joint Targeting Board (SAUO)
JTB	Joint Training Board (SAUS)
JTB	Joint Transportation Board [*Military*]
JTB	Journal of Theoretical Biology (journ.) (SAUS)
JTB	Jump Trace Buffer (SAUS)
JTBBD7........	Journal of Chemical Technology and Biotechnology. B. Biotechnology (journ.) (SAUS)
JTBI	Japan Travel Bureau International (TVEL)
JTBSMHS ...	Jacques Timothe Boucher Sieur de Montbrun Heritage Society (EA)
JTC	Houston [*Texas*] Town/Country [*Airport symbol*] (OAG)
JTC	Japan Tobacco Corporation (SAUS)
JTC	Jets Corporativos SA de CV [*Mexico*] [*ICAO designator*] (FAAC)
JTC	Jewish Thought and Civilization (BJA)
JTC	Jewish Trust Corporation for Germany (SAUO)
JTC	JIRI Technical School (SAUS)
JTC	Joint Targeting Coordination (SAUO)
JTC	Joint Technical Committee (CDE)
JTC	Joint Technical Coordinating (SAUS)
JTC	Joint Technology Center (ACAE)
JTC	Joint Telecommunications Committee [*Military*] (AFM)
JTC	Joint Training Committee (WDAA)
JTC	Joint Transfer Correlation (SAUS)
JTC	Joint Transform Correlator [*Instrumentation*]
JTC	Joke to Come (WDMC)
JTC	Jordan Telecommunications Company (SAUO)
JTC	Joule-Thompson Coefficient (SAUS)
JTC	Joule-Thompson Cooler (SAUS)
JTC	Joule-Thomson Coefficient [*Physics*]
JTC	Joule-Thomson Cooler (SAUS)
JTC	Junior Training Corps [*British*]
JTC	Jurong Town Corp. [*Singapore*]
JTC1	ISO standards Committee on IT (SAUO)
JTC1	Joint Technical Committee 1 (SAUO)
JTC2	Joint Tactical Command and Control (SAUO)
JTC3A	Joint Tactical Command, Control, and Communications Agency (USGC)
JTC3-CDBS...	Joint Tactical Command, Control and Communications-Central Data Base System (SAUO)
JTC³S	Joint Tactical Command and Control and Communications System [*Military*] (RDA)
JTCA	Japanese Technical Communication Association (SAUO)
JTCB	Joint Targeting Coordination Board (SAUO)
JTCC	Joint Test Coordinating Committee (MCD)
JTCCCA........	Joint Tactical Command, Control, and Communications Agency (ACAE)
JTCCCS........	Joint Tactical Command, Control, and Communications System [*Military*] (MCD)
JTCCG.........	Joint Technical Configuration Control Group [*Military*] (AABC)
JTCCS.........	Joint Tactical Command and Control and Communications System (SAUS)
JTCE	Journal of Transportation Engineering. Proceedings. American Society of Civil Engineers (journ.) (SAUS)
JTCG..........	Joint Technical Coordinating Group [*Military*] (MCD)
JTCG/ALNNO...	Joint Technical Coordinating Group for Air Launched Non-Nuclear Ordnance [*Military*] (AFM)
JTCG/AS	Joint Technical Coordinating Group for Aircraft Survivability [*Military*]
JTCG-DLA	Joint Technical Coordinating Group for Data Link Acquisitions (MCD)
JTCG-DMI	Joint Technical Coordinating Group for Depot Maintenance Interservicing [*Military*] (AFIT)
JTCG-EER	Joint Technical Coordinating Group for Electronic Equipment Reliability (MCD)
JTCG-ESR	Joint Technical Coordinating Group for Electronics Systems Reliability (MCD)
JTCG-ESR	Joint Technical Coordinating Group for Electronic Systems Reliability (SAUS)
JTCG/EW......	Joint Technical Coordinating Group For Electronic Warfare (SAUO)
JTCGFSR	Joint Technical Coordinating Group for Electronics Systems Reliability (SAUO)
JTCG/MD	Joint Technical Coordinating Group for Munitions Development [*Military*]
JTCG/ME	Joint Technical Coordinating Group for Munitions Effectiveness [*Military*] (AFM)
JTCG/MS......	Joint Technical Coordinating Group on Munitions Survivability [*Military*] (RDA)
JTCGP.........	Joint Technical Coordinating Group [*Military*]
JTCGPaME...	Joint Technical Coordinating Group for Munitions Effectiveness (SAUO)
JTCGP/ME ...	Joint Technical Coordinating Group for Munitions Effectiveness [*Military*]
JTCGP-TACS...	Joint Technical Coordinating Group for Tactical Air Control System [*Military*]
JTCG-STD	Joint Technical Coordinating Group on Simulators and Training Devices (MCD)
JTCGSTD	Joint Technical Coordinating Group on Simulators and Training Devices (SAUS)
JTC I...........	Joint Technical Committee I (SAUO)
JTCIEDI........	Joint Technical Committee for EDI (SAUO)
JTCMD........	Journal of Tissue Culture Methods (journ.) (SAUS)
JTCMEC.......	Journal of Traditional Chinese Medicine (journ.) (SAUS)
JTCMF........	Joint Technical Commission of the Marine Front (SAUO)
JTCMF........	Joint Technical Committee on Marine Front (SAUS)
JTCO..........	Jacksonville Terminal Co. [*AAR code*]
JTCO..........	Joint Tactical Communications Office (SAUO)
JTCO...........	Junior Tactical Communications Operator (SAUS)
Jt Comm J Qual Improv...	Joint Commission Journal on Quality Improvement (journ.) (SAUS)
JT COMP	Joint Compiler (SAUS)
JTCP	JOVIAL [*Joule's Own Version of the International Algorithmic Language*] Test Control Program [*Computer science*] (SAA)
JTCTS	Joint Tactical Combat Training System [*Military*]
JTCY-P........	Jig Transit Central Y-Plane
JTD	Jahn-Teller Distortion (SAUS)
JTD	Jet Turbo Diesel [*Automotive engineering*]
JTD	Joint Table of Distribution [*Military*] (AFM)
JTD	Joint Technology Demonstration (SAUS)
JTD	Joint Test Director (SAUS)
JTD	Joint Test Directorate [*Military*] (CAAL)
JTDA...........	Joint Track Data Storage
JTDAA.........	Journal. Tennessee Dental Association (journ.) (SAUS)
JTDARMVAL...	Joint Test Directorate Advanced Antiarmor Vehicle Evaluation [*Military*] (DNAB)
JTDE...........	Joint Technology Demonstration Engine (SAUS)
JTDE...........	Joint Technology Demonstrator Engine [*Air Force*] (MCD)
JTDP...........	Joint Technical Development Plan
JTDS	Joint Track Data Storage

JTE.............. Jahn-Teller Effect (SAUS)
JTE.............. Jamming Tactics Evaluation
JTE.............. Javelin Thrower's Elbow (MELL)
JTE.............. Joint Technical Evaluation (MCD)
JTE.............. Joint Test Element
JTE.............. Joule-Thompson Effect
JTE.............. Joule-Thomson Effect [*Physics*]
JTE.............. Journal of Teacher Education (journ.) (SAUS)
JTE.............. Junction Tandem Exchange [*Electronics*] (IAA)
JTE.............. Junction Termination Extension (PDAA)
J Teach Ed.. Journal of Teacher Education [*A publication*] (BRI)
J-teacher..... Journalism teacher (SAUO)
J-teacher..... Journalism teacher (journ.) (SAUS)
J Teach Learn... Journal of Teaching and Learning (journ.) (SAUS)
JTEC .... Japanese Technology Evaluation Center (SAUS)
JTEC .... Japan Telecommunications Engineering and Consultancy
JTEC .... Jeep-Truck Engine Controller
JTEC .... Joint Training Enhancement Committee [*Military*]
JTEC .... Joint Transmission-Engine Controller [*Automotive engineering*]
JTECH......... Japanese Technology Evaluation Database (SAUO)
J Tech Ass Fur Ind... Journal. Technical Association of the Fur Industry (journ.) (SAUS)
J Tech Bengal Engrg College... Journal of Technology. Bengal Engineering College (journ.) (SAUS)
J Tech Councils ASCE Proc ASCE... Journal. Technical Councils of ASCE. Proceedings of the American Society of Civil Engineers (journ.) (SAUS)
J Teching PE... Journal of Teaching in Physical Education (journ.) (SAUS)
J Techn Meth... Journal of Technical Methods and Bulletin (journ.) (SAUS)
J Technol Eng... Journal of Technology and Engineering (journ.) (SAUS)
J Tech Phys... Journal of Technical Physics (journ.) (SAUS)
J Tech Voct Educ S Afr... Journal for Technical and Vocational Education South Africa (journ.) (SAUS)
J Tech Writ Commun... Journal of Technical Writing and Communication (journ.) (SAUS)
JT ED .... Joint Editor
J Teflon....... Journal of Teflon (journ.) (SAUS)
J Tenn Acad Sci... Journal of the Tennessee Academy of Science (journ.) (SAUS)
J Tenn Acad Sci... Journal. Tennessee Academy of Science (journ.) (SAUS)
J Tenn Dent Assoc... Journal. Tennessee Dental Association (journ.) (SAUS)
J Tenn Med Assoc... Journal of the Tennessee Medical Association (SAUO)
J Tenn Med Assoc... Journal of the Tennessee Medical Association (journ.) (SAUS)
J Tenn State Dent Assoc... Journal. Tennessee State Dental Association (journ.) (SAUS)
J-TENS........ Joint Tactical Exploitation of National Systems [*Army*] (ADDR)
J Terramech... Journal of Terramechanics (SAUO)
J Terramech... Journal of Terramechanics (journ.) (SAUS)
J Tert Ed Admin... Journal of Tertiary Educational Administration [*A publication*]
JTES .... Japan Techno-Economics Society (SAUO)
JTETF.......... Joint Test and Evaluation Task Force [*Air Force*]
JTEV .... Joint Tactical Electric Vehicle [*Military*]
JTEVA .... Journal of Testing and Evaluation (journ.) (SAUS)
JTEX .... Jaytex Oil & Gas (SAUS)
JTEX .... Jemez Tomography Experiment (SAUO)
J Texas Dent Hyg Assoc... Journal. Texas Dental Hygienists Association (journ.) (SAUS)
J Text Inst... Journal of the Textile Institute (journ.) (SAUS)
J Text Inst Abstr... Journal. Textile Institute. Abstracts (journ.) (SAUS)
J Text Inst Proc... Journal. Textile Institute. Proceedings (journ.) (SAUS)
J Text Inst Proc Abstr... Journal. Textile Institute. Proceedings and Abstracts (journ.) (SAUS)
J Text Inst Trans... Journal. Textile Institute. Transactions (journ.) (SAUS)
J Text Mach Soc Jap... Journal. Textile Machinery Society of Japan (journ.) (SAUS)
JTF............. Japan Textile Federation
JTF............. Jet Tear-Down Facility (MCD)
JTF............. Joint Tactical Fusion [*Army*] (RDA)
JTF............. Joint Task Force [*Military*]
JTF............. Joint Test Force [*Military*]
JTF............. Joule-Thompson Flow (SAUS)
JTF............. Joule-Thomson Flow [*Physics*]
JTF............. Junior Tennis Foundation (EA)
JTF2........... Joint Task Force Two [*Sandia Base, NM*]
JTF-7......... Joint Task Force 7 Automation Support (SAUO)
JTF-A.......... Joint Task Force-Alaska (SAUS)
JTFA .... Joint Time-Frequency Analysis [*Electronics*]
JTFA .... Joint Time-Frequency Analysis [*Military*]
JTFAK .... Joint Task Force Alaska [*Military*]
JTF-AL........ Joint Task Force-Aleutians (SAUO)
JTF/ASAS.... Joint Tactical Fusion/All Source Analysis System (AAGC)
JTFEX .... Joint Task Force Exercise (SAUO)
JTF-FA .... Joint Task Force-Full Accounting [*DoD*]
JTFHQ......... Joint Task Force Headquarters [*Military*] (MCD)
JTF/LOCE.... Joint Tactical Division/Limited Operational Capability Europe (SAUO)
JTF-LOCE.... Joint Task Force-Limited Operational Capability, Europe (SAUS)
JTFME .... Joint Task Force Middle East (DOMA)
JTFOA .... Joint Task Force Operating Area [*Military*] (NVT)
JTFP .... Joint Tactical Fusion Program [*Military*] (RDA)
JTFPMO....... Joint Tactical Fusion Program Management Office [*Army*] (RDA)
JTFREP........ Joint Task Force Report [*Military*]
JTFS .... Joint Tactical Fusion System [*Military*] (LAIN)
JTFS .... JTF [*Joint Task Force*] Simulation [*Model*] [*DoD*]
JTG .... Joint Task Group [*Military*]
JTG .... Joint Test Group [*Nuclear energy*] (NRCH)
JTG .... Joint Training Group [*NASA*] (NASA)
JTG .... Jordan Technology Group (ACAE)

JTGCD .... Joint Task Group Coordination Draft (SAUO)
JTGED......... Joint Task Group Evaluation Draft (SAUO)
JTGGAA .... Journal of Tropical Geography (journ.) (SAUS)
Jth .... Judith [*Old Testament book*] [*Roman Catholic canon*] (BJA)
J Thanatol ... Journal of Thanatology (journ.) (SAUS)
J Theol St... Journal of Theological Studies (journ.) (SAUS)
J Theol Sthn Afr... Journal of Theology for Southern Africa (journ.) (SAUS)
J Theor N... Journal of Theoretical Neurobiology (journ.) (SAUS)
J Thermal Biol... Journal of Themal Biology (SAUS)
J Thermophys Heat Transf... Journal of Thermophysics and Heat Transfer (journ.) (SAUS)
J Therm Spray Technol... Journal of Thermal Spray Technology (journ.) (SAUS)
J Therm Stresses... Journal of Thermal Stresses (journ.) (SAUS)
J Thought ... Journal of Thought (journ.) (SAUS)
JTHP .... Joule-Thompson High Pressure (SAUS)
JTHP .... Joule-Thomson High Pressure [*Physics*]
J Th So Africa... Journal of Theology for Southern Africa (journ.) (SAUS)
JTI .... Jatai [*Brazil*] [*Airport symbol*] (AD)
JTI .... Journal of Taxation of Investments (journ.) (SAUS)
JTI .... Jydsk Teknologisk Institut [*Technological Institute of Jutland*] [*Denmark*]
JTIAP .... Joint Foreign Intelligence Assistance Program (SAUS)
JTIC .... Japan Trade Information Center (SAUO)
JTIC .... Joint Transportation Intelligence Center (COE)
JTIDS.......... Joint Tactical Information Distribution System [*DoD*]
JTIDS.......... Joint Tactical Integrated Display System (SAUO)
JTIDS.......... Joint Tactical Interoperable Data System (ACAE)
J-TIES .... Japan Technology Information and Evaluation Service (IID)
JTIG .... Joint Target Intelligence Group [*Military*] (CINC)
JTII .... Japan Telescopes Inspection Institute (SAUO)
J Timber Dev Assoc India... Journal. Timber Development Association of India (journ.) (SAUS)
J Time Ser Anal... Journal of Time Series Analysis (journ.) (SAUS)
Jt Inst Lab Astrophy Rep... Joint Institute for Laboratory Astrophysics. Report (journ.) (SAUS)
JTIP .... Joint Technology Insertion Program (ACAE)
JTIR .... Justice Court Traffic Infraction Rules (SAUO)
JTIRS......... Japanese Technical Information Research Service (SAUO)
JTIS .... Japanese Technical Information Service [*University Microfilms International*] [*Information service or system*] (IID)
JTIS .... Japan Technical Information Service (SAUO)
J Tissue Cut Meth... Journal of Tissue Culture Methods (journ.) (SAUS)
JTJ............. Japan Information Center of Science and Technology, Tokyo, Japan [*Library symbol*] [*Library of Congress*] (LCLS)
JTJ............. Japan Information Center (or Centre) for/of Science and Technology (SAUS)
JTKU .... Keio University, Tokyo, Japan [*Library symbol*] [*Library of Congress*] (LCLS)
JTL............. Jetall Holdings, Corp. [*Canada*] [*ICAO designator*] (FAAC)
JTL............. Joint Target List (SAUO)
JTL............. Josephson Transmission Line [*Physics*]
JTL............. Josephson Tunneling Logic (SAUS)
JTL............. Joutel Resources Ltd. [*Toronto Stock Exchange symbol*]
Jtl............. Joutel ResourcesLtd. (SAUO)
JTLAS .... Jet Transport Landing Approach Simulator
JTLC .... Joint Technical Language Service, London (SAUO)
J-TIES......... Japan Technology Information and Evaluation Service (SAUS)
JTLS .... Joint Theater Level Simulation [*Model*] [*DoD*]
JTLS .... Joint Theater Level Simulator (SAUO)
JTLY .... Jointly
JTM .... Job Transfer and Management (ACRL)
JTM .... Job Transfer and Manipulation [*Telecommunications*] (OSI)
JTM .... Josephson Tunneling Memory
JTM .... Josephson Tunnelling Memory (VLIE)
JTMA .... Joint Traffic Management Agency (MCD)
JTMAE .... Job Transfer and Manipulation Application Entity (SAUS)
JTM & H ...... Journal of Tropical Medicine and Hygiene [*A publication*] (WDAA)
JTM&H .... Journal of Tropical Medicine and Hygiene (journ.) (SAUS)
JTMB .... Joint Transportation Movements Board [*Military*] (CINC)
JTMD .... Joint Table of Mobilization Distribution (COE)
JTMD .... Joint Theater Missile Defense [*DoD*]
JTML .... Junior Town Meeting League (EA)
JTMLS .... Joint Tactical Microwave Landing System (MCD)
JTMMA .... Journal. Tennesse Medical Assiation (journ.) (SAUS)
JTMMR .... Joint Tactical Multi-Mode Radio (SAUS)
JTMP .... Job Transfer and Manipulation Protocol (NITA)
JTMPO........ Joint Tactical Missile Project Office (ACAE)
JTMS .... Jamb Template Machine Screw (SAUS)
JTMS .... Joint Tactical Missiles Signature Program [*Military*]
JTMS .... Justification based Truth Maintenance System (SAUS)
JTMSS .... Joint Tactical Multichannel Switch System (MCD)
JTMTDE .... Journal of Trace and Microprobe Techniques (journ.) (SAUS)
JTN .... Jewish Television Network
JTN .... Joint Targeting Network (SAUO)
JTNDL......... Kokuritsu Kokkai Toshokan [*National Diet Library*], Tokyo, Japan [*Library symbol*] [*Library of Congress*] (LCLS)
JTNM .... Joshua Tree National Monument (SAUO)
JTNS .... Nihon Shinbun Kyokai [*Japanese Newspaper Association*], Tokyo, Japan [*Library symbol*] [*Library of Congress*] (LCLS)
JTO .... Jeunesse Travailleuse Oubanguienne [*Ubangi Working Youth*]
JTO .... Jewish Territorial Organization (SAUO)
JTO .... Joint Technical Operations (AAG)
JTO .... Joint Test Organization [*Joint Tactical Communications Office*] [*Fort Huachuca, AZ*]

JTO .... JOPES [*Joint Operations, Planning, and Execution System*] Training Organization (DOMA)
JTO .... Jordan Tourist Office (SAUO)
JTO .... Jump Takeoff (WDAA)
JTO .... Junction Temperature, Operating
JTOC .... Joint Tactical Operations Center
J Tohoku Dent Univ... Journal. Tohoku Dental University (journ.) (SAUS)
J Tohoku Min Sa... Journal. Tohoku Mining Society (journ.) (SAUS)
J Tokyo Coll Fish... Journal. Tokyo College of Fisheries (journ.) (SAUS)
J Tokyo Dent Coll Soc... Journal. Tokyo Dental College Society (journ.) (SAUS)
J Tokyo Med Assoc... Journal. Tokyo Medical Association (journ.) (SAUS)
J Tokyo Med Coll... Journal. Tokyo Medical College (journ.) (SAUS)
J Tokyo Univ Fish... Journal. Tokyo University of Fishenes (journ.) (SAUS)
J Tokyo Womens Med Coll... Journal. Tokyo Womens Medical College (journ.)
J Tonghi Univ... Journal of Tonghi University (journ.) (SAUS)
J Tongi Med Univ... Journal. Tongi Medical University (journ.) (SAUS)
J Tongji Med Univ... Journal of Tongji Medical University (SAUO)
JTOR........... Joint Terms of Reference (MCD)
J Tottori Daigaku Nogaku... Journal. Tottori Daigaku Nogaku-Buo (journ.) (SAUS)
J Town Pl I... Journal of Town Planning Institute (journ.) (SAUS)
J Town Reg Plann... Journal for Town and Regional Planning (journ.) (SAUS)
J Toxicol Clin Toxicol... Journal of Toxicology. Clinical Toxicol- ogy (journ.) (SAUS)
J Toxicol Cutaneous Ocul Toxicol... Journal of Toxicology. Cutaneous and Ocular Toxicology (journ.) (SAUS)
J Toxicol Environ Chem... Journal of Toxicological and Environmental Chemistry (journ.) (SAUS)
J Toxicol Sci... Journal of Toxicological Sciences (journ.) (SAUS)
J Toxicol Toxin Rev... Journal of Toxicology. Toxin Reviews (journ.) (SAUS)
JTP .... Job Ticket Processor (RALS)
JTP .... Job Training Package
JTP .... Job Training Program (OICC)
JTP .... Joint Technical Panel [*Aerospace*]
JTP .... Joint Technology Program (CCCA)
JTP .... Joint Training Package
JTP .... Journeyman Training Program
JTP .... Juventud Trabajadora Peronista [*Working Peronist Youth*] [*Argentina*]
JTPA .... Job Training Partnership Act [*Formerly, CETA*] [*1982*]
JTPA .... Job Training Partnership Administration
JTPS .... Job and Tape Planning System
JTPS .... Juvenile Tropical Pancreatitis Syndrome [*Medicine*] (DMAA)
JTPT .... Job Task Performance Test
JTQ .... Wrightstown, NJ [*Location identifier*] [*FAA*] (FAAL)
JTR .... Jet-Air Bedarfsflugunternehmen [*Austria*] [*ICAO designator*] (FAAC)
JTR .... Joint Rate (SAUS)
JTR .... Joint Tactical Radio [*Army*]
JTR .... Joint Termination Regulation
JTR .... Joint Travel Regulations
JTR .... Jordan Travel Research (SAUS)
JTR .... Journal of European Industrial Training (journ.) (SAUS)
JTR .... Journal of Travel Research (journ.) (SAUS)
JTR .... Journal of Typographic Research (journ.) (SAUS)
JTR .... Journal Tape Reader (SAUS)
JTR .... Santorini [*Thira Islands*] [*Airport symbol*] (OAG)
JTR .... Thira [*Greece*] [*Airport symbol*] (AD)
JTRA .... Job Task Requirements Analysis (PDAA)
JTRAC .... JPL [*Jet Propulsion Laboratory*] Transient Radiation Analysis by Computer Program [*NASA*]
J Trace Elem Exp Med... Journal of Trace Elements in Experimental Medicine (journ.) (SAUS)
J Trace Elem Med Biol... Journal of Trace Elements in Medicine and Biology (journ.) (SAUS)
J Trace Microprobe Tech... Journal of Trace and Microprobe Techniques (journ.) (SAUS)
J Tradit Chin Med... Journal of Traditional Chinese Medicine (journ.) (SAUS)
J Transp Eng Dir Amer Soc Civil Eng Proc... Journal. Transportation Engineering Division. American Society of Civil Engineers. Proceedings (journ.) (SAUS)
J Transp Hist... Journal of Transport History (journ.) (SAUS)
J Transp Med... Journal of Transportation Medicine (journ.) (SAUS)
J Transp Res Forum... Journal of the Transportation Research Forum (journ.) (SAUS)
J Trauma..... Journal of Trauma (journ.) (SAUS)
J Trauma Stress... Journal of Traumatic Stress (journ.) (SAUS)
J Travis County Med Soc... Journal. Travis County Medical Society (journ.) (SAUS)
JTRB .... Joint Telecommunications Resource Board [*Office of Science and Technology Policy*] [*Washington, DC*] (EGAO)
JTRC .... Joint Theater Reconnaissance Committee (SAUS)
JTRC .... Joint Theatre Reconnaissance Committee [*NATO*] (NATG)
JTRCP .... Joint Travel Regulations, Department of Defense Civilian Personnel
JTRE .... JIMAP [*Joint Institute for Marine and Atmospheric Research*] Tsunami Research Effort [*Marine science*] (OSRA)
JTRE .... JIMAR [*Joint Institute for Marine and Atmospheric Research*] Tsunami Research Effort (USDC)
JTRE .... Joint Tsunami Research Effort
JTRL .... Janitorial (ABBR)
J Trog Vet Sc... Journal of Tropical Veterinary Science (journ.) (SAUS)
J Trop For ... Journal of Tropical Forestry (journ.) (SAUS)
J Trop Pediatr Afr Child Health... Journal of Tropical Pediatrics and African Child Health (journ.) (SAUS)
J Trop Pediatr Environ Child Health... Journal of Tropical Pediatrics and Environmental Child Health (journ.) (SAUS)
J Trop Pediatr Environ Child Health Monogr... Journal of Tropical Pediatrics and En- vironmental Child Health. Monograph (journ.) (SAUS)
JTRS .... Joint Tactical Radio System [*Army*]

JTRS .... Joint Tenant with Right of Survivorship [*Legal term*] (DLA)
JTRU .... Joint-Services Tropical Research Unit (SAUO)
JTRU .... Joint Tropical Research Unit [*Australia*]
JTRUS .... Joint Travel Regulations
JTS .... Arrendamiento de Aviones Jets, SA [*Mexico*] [*FAA designator*] (FAAC)
JTS .... Jahn-Teller Stripes [*Solid state physics*]
JTS .... Japan Troposcatter Systems
JTS .... Java Transaction Service (SAUO)
JTS .... Jewish Theological Seminary (SAUO)
JTS .... JICST Translation Service (SAUS)
JTS .... Job Tracking System (SAUS)
JTS .... Job Trainer Standard (SAUS)
JTS .... Job Training Scheme [*Government initiative*] [*British*]
JTS .... Job Training Standard
JTS .... Joint Test Subassembly (SAUO)
JTS .... Joint Training Scheme (AIE)
JTS .... Joint Training Squadron (SAUO)
JTS .... Joint Training Standards [*Military*] (KSC)
JTS .... Journal of Theological Studies [*A publication*] (ODCC)
JTS .... JTS Corp. [*AMEX symbol*] [*Formerly, Atari Corp.*] (SG)
JTS .... Justice Telecommunications Service [*Department of Justice*] (TSSD)
JTSA .... Jewish Theological Seminary of America
JTSA .... Joint Tactical Support Activity
JTSA .... Joint Technical Support Activity
JTSB .... Joint Target Selection Board (SAUO)
JTSC .... Joint Technical Steering Committee (ACAE)
JTSCC .... Joint Telecommunications Standards Coordinating (SAUS)
JTSCC .... Joint Telecommunications Standards Coordinating Committee [*American National Standards Institute*] [*Telecommunications*]
JTS Corp...... JTS Corp. [*Associated Press*] (SAG)
JTSG .... Joint Targeting Steering Group (SAUO)
JTSG .... Joint Trials Subgroup [*NATO*] (NATG)
JTSH .... Joint Threat Simulator Handbook (SAUO)
JTSIN .... Joint Transmission Services Information Network
J Tsinghua Univ... Journal of Tsinghua University (journ.) (SAUS)
J Tsing Hua Univ... Journal. Tsing Hua University (journ.) (SAUS)
JTSMA .... Jennifer Trust for Spinal Muscular Atrophy [*Established in 1985*] (NRGU)
JTSN .... Jettison (MSA)
JTSSG .... Joint Telecommunications Standards Steering Group (SAUO)
JTST .... Jet Stream
JTSTR .... Jet Stream
J Tsuda College... Journal. Tsuda College (journ.) (SAUS)
JTT.............. Executive Aircraft Leasing, Inc. (SAUO)
JTT/CIBSM... Joint Tactical Terminal/Common Integrated Broadcast System Module [*Military*] (RDA)
JTTCW .... Jesus to the Communist World [*Later, CMCW*] (EA)
JT TEN......... Joint Tenancy (SAUS)
JT TEN......... Joint Tenant (SAUS)
JTTP .... Joint Tactics, Techniques, and Procedures (DOMA)
JTTPRG....... Joint Tactics, Techniques, and Procedures Review Group
JTTRD9........ Journal of Toxicology. Toxin Reviews (journ.) (SAUS)
JTTU .... Jet Transitional Training Unit [*Navy*]
JTU .... Jackson Turbidity Unit [*Water pollution*]
JTU .... Jet Training Unit
JTUAC .... Joint Trade Union Advisory Committee
JT-UAV .... Joint Tactical Unmanned Aerial Vehicle [*DoD*]
JTUAV .... Joint Tactical Unmanned Aerial Vehicle
J Tuberc Lepr... Journal of Tuberculosis and Leprosy (journ.) (SAUS)
JTUFA .... Journal. Tokyo University of Fishenes (journ.) (SAUS)
J Tung-Chi Univ... Journal. Tung-Chi University (journ.) (SAUS)
J Turk Phytopathol... Journal of Turkish Phytopathology (journ.) (SAUS)
JTV .... Jet Test Vehicle
JTV .... Jones Intercable Inv CI'A' [*AMEX symbol*] (TTSB)
JTV .... Jones Intercable Investors Ltd. [*AMEX symbol*] (SPSG)
JTV .... Jones Intercable Investors Ltd. Class A (SAUO)
JT VENT...... Joint Venture (SAUS)
JTVI .... Journal of Transactions. Victoria Institute (journ.) (SAUS)
J-T-W .... Journey to Work [*FHWA*] (TAG)
JTWC .... Joint Typhoon Warning Center
JTWO .... J2 Communications [*NASDAQ symbol*] (TTSB)
JTWO .... JTwo Communications [*NASDAQ symbol*] (SAG)
JTWOW .... J2 Communications Wrrt'A' [*NASDAQ symbol*] (TTSB)
JTWROS ..... Joint Tenants with Right of Survivorship [*Legal term*]
JTWS .... Journal of Third World Studies [*A publication*]
JTX .... Jet Aspen Air Lines, Inc. [*FAA designator*] (FAAC)
JTX .... Joint Test Exercises
JTX .... Joint Training Exercise [*Military*]
JTX .... Journal of Taxation (journ.) (SAUS)
J-type .... Jungian judging type (SAUS)
J Typogr Res... Journal of Typographic Research (journ.) (SAUS)
JTYWTK...... Just Thought You Wanted To Know (SAUS)
JTZ............. Oklahoma City, OK [*Location identifier*] [*FAA*] (FAAL)
JTZ............. Zantop Airways, Inc. (SAUO)
JU.............. Jacksonville University (SAUO)
JU.............. Jack-Up (SAUS)
JU.............. Jadavpore University (SAUO)
JU.............. Jeunesse Universelle
JU.............. Joint Use [*Military*] (AFIT)
JU.............. Joint User [*Telecommunications*] (TEL)
JU.............. Joygerms Unlimited (EA)
Ju.............. Judges [*Old Testament book*] (BJA)
JU.............. Juilliard Review. Annual (journ.) (SAUS)
JU.............. Julep (ROG)

JU .... Jump Unit
JU .... June
JU .... Junker [German aircraft type] [World War II]
Ju .... Junkers (SAUS)
JU .... Jure Uxoris [In Right of His Wife] [Latin] (ROG)
JU .... Yugoslav Airlines [ICAO designator] (AD)
JU-52 .... German Junkers transport (SAUS)
JUA .... Joint Underwriting Association [Generic term] (DHSM)
JUA .... Joint Underwriting Authority [Insurance]
JUA .... Joint Usage Agreement (SAUO)
JUARA .... Journal of Chemistry. United Arab Republic (journ.) (SAUS)
JUB .... Job Unit Block [Computer science] (IAA)
JUB .... Journal. Bombay University (journ.) (SAUS)
JUB .... Juba [Sudan] [Airport symbol] (OAG)
Jub .... Jubilate (GROV)
JUB .... Jubilate
Jub .... Jubilees [Pseudepigrapha] (BJA)
JUB .... Justice of the Upper Bench [Legal term] (DLA)
JUBU .... Journalistutbildningsutredningen [Sweden]
JUCG .... Joint Utilization Coordination Group [DoD]
JUCO .... Junior College (OICC)
JuCR .... Juvenile Court Rules (SAUO)
JUCSPA ..... Joint University Council for Social and Public Administration (SAUO)
JUCUND ..... Jucunde [Pleasantly] [Latin]
JUD .... Doctor of Canon and Civil Law (SAUS)
JuD .... Doctor of Law (SAUS)
JUD .... Duluth, MN [Location identifier] [FAA] (FAAL)
JUD .... Jam Until Destroyed (SAUS)
JUD .... Jeunesse d'Union Dahomeene [Dahomean Youth Union]
JUD .... Judah (WDAA)
Jud .... Judaic (BJA)
JUD .... Judea (WDAA)
Jud .... Judean (BJA)
JUD .... Judge (WDAA)
JUD .... Judges [Old Testament book] (ROG)
JUD .... Judgment
JUD .... Judicial
Jud .... Judith [Old Testament book] [Roman Catholic canon]
jud .... juditial (SAUS)
jud .... judo (SAUS)
JUD .... Jurisdiction (SAUS)
JUD .... Juris Utriusque Doctor [Doctor of Both Laws; i.e., Canon and Civil Law]
JUD .... US Department of Justice [ICAO designator] (FAAC)
Jud-Alg ...... Judeo-Algerian (SAUS)
Jud-Amer .... Judeo-American (SAUS)
Jud & Sw.... Judah and Swan's Jamaica Reports [1839] [A publication] (DLA)
Jud-Arg ...... Judeo-Argentinian (SAUS)
Jud-Ash ..... Judeo-Ashkenazic (SAUS)
Jud-Aus ..... Judeo-Austrian (SAUS)
Jud-Aust ..... Judeo-Australian (SAUS)
Jud-Bel ...... Judeo-Belgian (SAUS)
Jud-Bol ...... Judeo-Bolivian (SAUS)
Jud-Bra ...... Judeo-Brazilian (SAUS)
Jud-Bul ...... Judeo-Bulgarian (SAUS)
Jud-Can ..... Judeo-Canadian (SAUS)
Jud-Chi ...... Judeo-Chilean (SAUS)
Jud-Chr ...... Judeo-Christian (SAUS)
Jud Chr ...... Judicial Chronicle [A publication] (DLA)
Jud Chr ...... Judicial Chronicle (journ.) (SAUS)
Jud-Col ...... Judeo-Colombian (SAUS)
Jud Com PC... Judicial Committee of the Privy Council [A publication] (DLA)
Jud Com PC... Judicial Committee of the Privy Council (journ.) (SAUS)
Jud Conduct Rep... Judicial Conduct Reporter [A publication] (DLA)
Jud Conduct Rep... Judicial Conduct Reporter (journ.) (SAUS)
Jud Coun (NY)... Judicial Council (New York). Annual Reports [A publication] (DLA)
Jud-CR .... Judeo-Costa Rican (SAUS)
Jud-Cub ..... Judeo-Cuban (SAUS)
Jud-Czech.... Judeo-Czechoslovakian (SAUS)
Judd .... Judd's Reports [4 Hawaii] [A publication] (DLA)
Jud-Dan ..... Judeo-Danish (SAUS)
Jud-Dut ...... Judeo-Dutch (SAUS)
JUDE .... Committee on Juvenile Delinquency (SAUO)
Jude .... General Epistle of Jude (SAUS)
JUDE .... Judicature (ROG)
Jud-Ecu ..... Judeo-Ecuadorean (SAUS)
Jud-Egy ...... Judeo-Egyptian (SAUS)
Jud-Eng ..... Judeo-English (SAUS)
Jud-Eth ...... Judeo-Ethiopian (SAUS)
Jud-Fin ...... Judeo-Finnish (SAUS)
Jud-Fre ...... Judeo-French (SAUS)
JUDG .... Judge
Judg .... Judges [Old Testament book]
JUDG .... Judicate, Inc. [NASDAQ symbol] (NQ)
Jud GCC ..... Judgments, Gold Coast Colony [A publication] (DLA)
Jud GCC ..... Judgments, Gold Coast Colony (journ.) (SAUS)
JUDGE .... Judged Utility Decision Generator
Judge Adv Gen... Judge Advocate General (SAUS)
Judge Advo J... Judge Advocate Journal (journ.) (SAUS)
Jud-Ger ...... Judeo-German (SAUS)
Jud-Gib ...... Judeo-Gibraltarian (SAUS)
Jud-Gre ...... Judeo-Grecian (SAUS)
JUDGT .... Judgment
Jud-Guat ..... Judeo-Guatemalan (SAUS)

Judg UB ..... Judgments of Upper Bench [England] [A publication] (DLA)
Jud-His .... Judeo-Hispanic (SAUS)
Jud-HK .... Judeo-Hong Kongese (SAUS)
Jud-Hung ..... Judeo-Hungarian (SAUS)
Judic .... Judicature (journ.) (SAUS)
judic .... Judicial (GEAB)
JUDIC .... Judicial
Judicate ...... Judicate, Inc. [Associated Press] (SAG)
Jud-Ind .... Judeo-Indian (SAUS)
Jud-Ire .... Judeo-Irish (SAUS)
Jud-Irn .... Judeo-Iranian (SAUS)
Jud-Isr .... Judeo-Israeli (SAUS)
Jud-Itl .... Judeo-Italian (SAUS)
Juditure ...... Journal. American Judicature Society (journ.) (SAUS)
Jud-Jam ...... Judeo-Jamaican (SAUS)
Jud-Jap ...... Judeo-Japanese (SAUS)
Jud-Jor ...... Judeo-Jordanian (SAUS)
JUDL .... Judicial (ROG)
Jud-Lad ...... Judeo-Ladino (SAUS)
Jud-Leb ...... Judeo-Lebanese (SAUS)
Jud-Mex ..... Judeo-Mexican (SAUS)
Jud-Mor ..... Judeo-Moresque (SAUS)
Jud-Mor ..... Judeo-Moroccan (SAUS)
Jud-Nor ...... Judeo-Norwegian (SAUS)
Jud-NZ .... Judeo-New Zealand (SAUS)
JUDO .... Judicial Officer Case Tracking System (SAUO)
Jud-Pan ...... Judeo-Panamanian (SAUS)
Jud Pan Mult Lit... Rulings of the Judicial Panel on Multidistrict Litigation [A publication] (DLA)
Jud-Par ...... Judeo-Paraguayan (SAUS)
Jud-Per ...... Judeo-Peruvian (SAUS)
Jud-Pol ...... Judeo-Polish (SAUS)
Jud-Port ...... Judeo-Portuguese (SAUS)
Jud QR .... Judicature Quarterly Review [1896] [A publication] (DLA)
JUDr .... Juris Utriusque Doctor [Doctor of Both Laws; i.e., Canon and Civil Law]
JUDRE .... Judicature
Jud Rep ...... New York Judicial Repository [A publication] (DLA)
Jud Repos ... Judicial Repository [New York] [A publication] (DLA)
Jud-Rho ...... Judeo-Rhodesian (SAUS)
Jud-Rom ..... Judeo-Romanian (SAUS)
Jud-Rus ...... Judeo-Russian (SAUS)
Jud-SAf ...... Judeo-South African (SAUS)
Jud-Scot ..... Judeo-Scottish (SAUS)
Jud-Sep ...... Judeo-Sephardic (SAUS)
Jud-Sin ...... Judeo-Singaporan (SAUS)
Jud-Slav ..... Judeo-Slavic (SAUS)
Jud-Span ..... Judeo-Spanish (SAUS)
Jud-Sur ...... Judeo-Surinamer (SAUS)
Jud-Swe ..... Judeo-Swedish (SAUS)
Jud-Swiss ... Judeo-Swiss (SAUS)
Jud-Syr ...... Judeo-Syrian (SAUS)
Jud-Tun ...... Judeo-Tunisian (SAUS)
Jud-Tur ...... Judeo-Turkish (SAUS)
Jud-Uru ...... Judeo-Uruguayan (SAUS)
Jud-Ven ...... Judeo-Venezuelan (SAUS)
JUDY .... Just a Useful Device for You (PDAA)
Jud-Yem ..... Judeo-Yemenite (SAUS)
Jud-Yug ...... Judeo-Yugoslavian (SAUS)
JUE .... Journal of Urban Economics (journ.) (SAUS)
JUE .... Julich [Federal Republic of Germany] [Seismograph station code, US Geological Survey] (SEIS)
JUF .... Joint Users File (SAUO)
J U Film As... Journal. University Film Association (journ.) (SAUS)
JUG .... Java User Group (SAUO)
JUG .... Jet Upgrading (SAUS)
JUG .... Joint Users Group [Computer science]
JUG .... JOPES Users Group (SAUO)
JUG .... Jugenheim [Federal Republic of Germany] [Seismograph station code, US Geological Survey] [Closed] (SEIS)
JUG .... Jugoslav (DSUE)
Jug .... Jugoslavia (SAUS)
Jug .... Jugoton [Former Yugoslavia] [Record label]
jug .... Jugular [Anatomy] (DAVI)
JUG .... Jugulo [To the Throat] [Pharmacy]
JUG .... Junction Gate (IAA)
jug comp ..... Jugular Compression [Test] [Neurology] (DAVI)
JUGD .... Java User Group Deutschland (SAUO)
JUGFET ...... Junction Gate Field-Effect Transistor (TEL)
Jughead ...... Jonzy's Universal Gopher Hierarchy Excavation and Display [Internet]
JUGHEAD.... Jonzys Universal Gopher Hierarchy Excavation and Display (SAUS)
JUGL .... JANET User Group for Libraries (SAUO)
JUH-MTF ..... Joint User Handbook for Message Text Formats (SAUO)
JUI .... Jamiatul Ulama-i-Islam [Pakistan] [Political party] (FEA)
JUI .... Juist [Germany] [Airport symbol] [Obsolete] (OAG)
Juilliard R .... Juilliard Review (journ.) (SAUS)
Juilliard ...... [The] Juilliard School (GAGS)
JUJ .... Jujuy [Argentina] [Airport symbol] (OAG)
JUJ .... Jujuy [Argentina] [Seismograph station code, US Geological Survey] (SEIS)
JUJAMCYN... Jujamcyn Theaters [Established by William McKnight, and named for his three grandchildren, Judy, James, and Cynthia]
JUKE .... Video Jukebox Network [NASDAQ symbol] (SAG)
JUKE .... Video Jukebox Network, Inc. (SAUO)
JUKGS .... Journal of Ukrainian Graduate Studies (journ.) (SAUS)

J Ukr Stud ...	Journal of Ukrainian Studies (journ.) (SAUS)
JUL	Joint University Libraries
JUL	Journal of Urban Law (journ.) (SAUS)
JUL	Julepus [*Julep*] [*Pharmacy*] (ROG)
JUL	Juliaca [*Peru*] [*Airport symbol*] (OAG)
JUL	Julian [*Calendar*]
JUL	Julianehab [*Denmark*] [*Later, NAQ*] [*Geomagnetic observatory code*]
JUL	July (AFM)
Jul	July (ODBW)
JUL	Juris Utriusque Licentiatus [*Licentiate in Both Laws; i.e., Canon and Civil Law*]
Jul Caes	Julius Caesar [*Shakespearean work*] (BARN)
Jul Frontin...	Julius Frontinus [*Roman soldier and author, 40-103*] (DLA)
Julian	Julianus Imperator [*332-363AD*] [*Classical studies*] (OCD)
Julians	Julian Alps (SAUS)
JULIE	Joint Utility Locating Information for Excavators [*Telecommunications*] (TEL)
JULIE	Joint Utilization of Laser Integrated Experiments (SAUS)
JULIEX........	Julie [*Sonobuoy System*] Exercise [*Navy*] (NVT)
JULIEX........	Julie Exercise (SAUS)
JULLS	Joint Universal Lessons Learned System (DOMA)
JUL Res......	Journal of Ultrastructure Research (journ.) (SAUS)
J Ultrasound Med...	Journal of Ultrasound in Medicine (journ.) (SAUS)
J Ultrastr Res...	Journal of Ultrastructural Research (journ.) (SAUS)
J Ultrastruct Mol Struct Res...	Journal of the Ultrastructure and Molecular Structure Research (journ.) (SAUS)
J Ultrastruct Mol Struct Res...	Journal of Ultrastructure and Molecular Structure Research (journ.) (SAUS)
J Ultrastruct Res...	Journal of Ultrastructure Research (journ.) (SAUS)
J Ultrastruct Res Suppl...	Journal of Ultrastructure Research. Supplement (journ.) (SAUS)
Julust...........	July and August (SAUS)
JUM	Judaism (journ.) (SAUS)
JUM	Jumla [*Nepal*] [*Airport symbol*] (OAG)
JUMAC.......	Joint Union Management Advisory Committee (SAUO)
JUMBO	Java Universal Molecular Browser for Objects (SAUS)
JUMIP	Juror Utilization and Management Incentive Program (SAUS)
JUMO..........	Junkers-Motor [*Junkers aircraft engine*] [*German military - World War II*]
JUMP..........	Joint UHF Modernization Project (MCD)
JUMP..........	Joint Urban Program (SAUS)
JUMPER	Joint Unit for Minorities Policy & Research (WDAA)
JUMPS........	Joint Uniform Military Pay Service [*or System*]
JUMPS........	Joint Uniform Military Pay System (SAUO)
JUMPS/MMS...	Joint Uniform Military Pay System/Manpower Management System (DNAB)
JUMPS-RC...	Joint Uniform Military Pay System - Reserve Components (MCD)
JUN...	Jump Unconditionally [*Computer science*]
JUN...	Jundah [*Queensland*] [*Airport symbol*] (AD)
JUN.............	June (AFM)
Jun..............	June (ODBW)
JUN.............	Juneau [*Diocesan abbreviation*] [*Alaska*] (TOCD)
Jun..............	Junior (EBF)
jun	Junior (NTIO)
JUN.............	Junior
JUN.............	Junius (ROG)
JUN.............	Jupiter, Uranus and Neptune (SAUS)
JUNAC	Grupo Andino - Junta del Acuerdo de Cartagena [*Andean Group - Cartagena Agreement Board - ANCOM*] (EAIO)
JUNC	Jeunesse d'Union Nationale Congolaise [*Congolese National Youth Union*]
Junc............	Junction (ADWA)
junc	Junction (NTIO)
JUNC	Junction
Jun Col J	Junior College Journal (journ.) (SAUS)
JUNCT	Junction
JUNCTION...	Junction [*Commonly used*] (OPSA)
JUNCTIONS...	Junctions [*Commonly used*] (OPSA)
JUNCTN......	Junction [*Commonly used*] (OPSA)
JUNCTON.....	Junction [*Commonly used*] (OPSA)
J Undergrad Res Phys...	Journal of Undergraduate Research in Physics (journ.) (SAUS)
Jundt	Jundt Growth Fund [*Associated Press*] (SAG)
JUNE...........	Joint Utility Notification for Excavators (IEEE)
JUNET........	Japanese University Network (ACRL)
JUNET........	Japanese UNIX Network (SAUS)
JUNET........	Japan UNIX Network [*Japan*] [*Computer science*] (TNIG)
JunF...........	Juniper Features Ltd. [*Associated Press*] (SAG)
JUNI	Juniper Features Ltd. [*NASDAQ symbol*] (SAG)
JUNIC	Joint United Nations Information Committee (SAUO)
Junior Coll J...	Junior College Journal (journ.) (SAUS)
JUNIP	Juniperus [*Juniper*] [*Pharmacy*] (ROG)
JuniprF........	Juniper Features Ltd. [*Associated Press*] (SAG)
J United Serv Inst India...	Journal. United Service Institution of India (journ.) (SAUS)
J Univ Bombay NS...	Journal. University of Bombay. New Series (journ.) (SAUS)
J Univ Bomby...	Journal. University of Bombay (journ.) (SAUS)
J Univ Durban-Westville...	Journal. University of Durban-Westville (journ.) (SAUS)
J Univ F Ass...	Journal. University Film Association (journ.) (SAUS)
J Univ Gauhati...	Journal. University of Gauhati (journ.) (SAUS)
J Univ Kuwait...	Journal of the University of Kuwait (journ.) (SAUS)
J Univ Poona...	Journal. Univetsity of Poona (journ.) (SAUS)
J Univ Poona Sci Technol...	Journal. University of Poona. Science and Technology (journ.) (SAUS)
J Univ Saugar...	Journal. University of Saugar (journ.) (SAUS)

J Univ Saugr Part 2 St A...	Journal. University of Saugar. Part 2. Section A. Physical Sciences (journ.) (SAUS)
J Univ Sci Technol Bejing...	Journal of the University of Science and Technology Bejing (journ.) (SAUS)
J Univ Sheffield Geol Soc...	Journal. University of Sheffield. Geological Society (journ.) (SAUS)
J Univ S Med S...	Journal. University of Sydney. Medical Society (journ.) (SAUS)
J Univ Stud...	Journal of University Studies (journ.) (SAUS)
JUNIW	Juniper Features Wrr'A' [*NASDAQ symbol*] (TTSB)
JUNIZ..........	Juniper Features Wrrt'B' [*NASDAQ symbol*] (TTSB)
JUNO	Juno Lighting [*NASDAQ symbol*] (TTSB)
JUNO	Juno Lighting, Inc. [*NASDAQ symbol*] (NQ)
JunoLt	Juno Lighting, Inc. [*Associated Press*] (SAG)
Jun Part......	Junior Partner (SAUS)
junr.............	Junior (GEAB)
JUNR	Junior
JUNS	Journal of Undergraduate Nursing Scholarship (SAUO)
JUNT...........	Juntae (ROG)
Junta del Acuer...	Grupo Andino - Junta del Acuerdo de Cartagena [*Andean Group - Cartagena Agreement Board - ANCOM*] (EA)
Jununly.........	June and July (SAUS)
J Unv Peshawar...	Journal. University of Peshawar (journ.) (SAUS)
JUO..............	Junior Under-Officer [*British military*] (DMA)
JUP..............	Jamiatul Ulama-i-Pakistan [*Political party*] (FEA)
JUP..............	Journal. University of Poona. Humanities Section (journ.) (SAUS)
JUP..............	Jupiter (KSC)
JUP..............	Juventud Universitaria Peronista [*University Peronist Youth*] [*Argentina*]
JUP..............	Juventud Uruguaya de Pie [*Upstanding Uruguayan Youth*] (PD)
JUP..............	Upland, CA [*Location identifier*] [*FAA*] (FAAL)
JUPD-A........	Journal. Urban Planning and Development Procedings. American Society of Civil Engineers (journ.) (SAUS)
JUPIND........	Jupiter Industries Inc. (SAUO)
JUPITER	Judicial Precedent Information Trace by Electronic Retrieval [*Database*] [*Toyo Information Systems Co.*] [*Information service or system*] (CRD)
JUPITER	JUGL Project for Information Transfer, Education and Research (SAUS)
JUPITER	Juvenescent Pioneering Technology for Robots (SAUS)
JupNatl........	Jupiter National, Inc. [*Associated Press*] (SAG)
JUPOA	Journal of Undergraduate Psychological Research (journ.) (SAUS)
JUPOA	Journal. University of Poona. Science and Technology (journ.) (SAUS)
JUPPIE	Japanese Urban Professional [*Lifestyle classification*]
JUPSA	Journal. Physical Society of Japan (journ.) (SAUS)
JUR..............	Julia Resources [*Vancouver Stock Exchange symbol*]
JUR..............	Jurassic [*Period, era, or system*] [*Geology*]
JUR..............	Juridical (ROG)
JUR..............	Jurisprudence (ROG)
Jur	[*The*] Jurist [*Washington, DC*] [*A publication*] (DLA)
Jur	Jurist. Quarterly Journal of Jurisprudence (journ.) (SAUS)
Jur	Jurist Reports [*18 vols.*] [*England*] [*A publication*] (DLA)
Jur	London Jurist [*1854*] [*A publication*] (DLA)
JURA	JPEG Utilities Registration Authority (SAUO)
J Urban H....	Journal of Urban History [*A publication*] (BRI)
Jur Com Brux...	Jurisprudence Commerciale de Bruxelles (journ.) (SAUS)
JUR D	Juris Doctor [*Doctor of Law*] [*Latin*] (ADA)
JUR DIG	Jure Dignitatis [*By Right of Rank*] [*Latin*] (ROG)
JURE...........	Junta Revolucionaria Cubana [*Exile action group*]
Jur Ex	Hargrave's Francis-Jurisconsult Exercitations [*A publication*] (DLA)
Jur Ex	Hargraves Francis-Jurisconsult Exercitations (journ.) (SAUS)
JURG	Joint Users Requirements Group (NASA)
JURG	Jurgensetis (SAUS)
Jurid Soc'y Pap...	Juridical Society Papers [*England*] [*A publication*] (DLA)
JURIS	Jurisdiction (AABC)
Juris	Jurisdiction (DIAR)
JURIS	Jurisprudence (ADA)
JURIS	Juristisches Informationssystem [*Judicial Information System*] [*Federal Ministry of Justice*] [*Legal database*] [*Germany*] (IID)
JURIS	Justice Retrieval and Inquiry System [*Department of Justice*] [*Legal databank*] [*Information service or system*] (IID)
JURIS	Juvenile Referral Information System (SAUS)
JURISD........	Jurisdiction
JURISDN	Jurisdiction (ROG)
JURISDON ...	Jurisdiction (ROG)
JURISP	Jurisprudence
Jurispr	Jurisprudence (DLA)
Jur M..........	Master of Jurisprudence
Jur Mar........	Molloy's De Jure Maritimo [*A publication*] (DLA)
J Urn Affairs...	Journal of Urban Affairs (journ.) (SAUS)
Jur NY........	Jurist, or Law and Equity Reporter [*New York*] [*A publication*] (DLA)
Jur Ouv........	Jurisprudence de Louage d Ouvrage (journ.) (SAUS)
Jur Ros........	Roscoe's Jurist [*London*] [*A publication*] (DLA)
Jur (Sc).......	[*The*] Scottish Jurist [*Edinburgh*] [*A publication*] (DLA)
Jur Sc D	Doctor of Judicial Science [*or Doctor of the Science of Jurisprudence*]
Jur Sc D	Doctor of the Science of Jurisprudence (SAUS)
JurScD........	Jurisprudence Science Doctor (SAUS)
Jur Soc P.....	Juridical Society Papers [*1858-74*] [*Scotland*] [*A publication*] (DLA)
Jur St..........	Juridical Styles [*Scotland*] [*A publication*] (DLA)
JURUE........	Joint Unit for Research on the Urban Environment [*British*]
J Urusvati Himalayan Res Inst Roerich Mus...	Journal. Urusvati Himalayan Research Institute of Roerich Museum (journ.) (SAUS)
Jur Utr Dr	Juris Utriusque Doctor [*Doctor of Both Laws; i.e., Canon and Civil Law*]

JUS.............. Active Aero Charter [*FAA designator*] (FAAC)
JUS.............. Department of Justice (SAUO)
JUS.............. Department of Justice Library [*UTLAS symbol*]
Jus.............. Jacobus de Porta Ravennate [*Deceased, 1178*] [*Authority cited in pre-1607 legal work*] (DSA)
JUS.............. Japan-U.S. Cable Network (SAUO)
JUS.............. Justice
JUS.............. Nenana, AK [*Location identifier*] [*FAA*] (FAAL)
J US Artillery... Journal. United States Artillery (journ.) (SAUS)
JUS AVEN.... Jusculum Avenaceum [*Gruel*] [*Pharmacy*] (ROG)
JUSC.......... Jusculum [*Broth*] [*Pharmacy*] (ROG)
JUSCADS..... Joint United States Canadian Air Defense Study (CCCA)
JUSCADS..... Joint US-Canada Air Defense Study (SAUS)
JUSCANZ.... Japan, United States, Canada, Australia and New Zealand, Norway and Switzerland (SAUS)
JUSCANZ..... Japan, United States of America, Canada, Australia and New Zealand (SAUO)
JUSCIMPC... Joint United States/Canada Industrial Mobilization Planning Committee [*NATO*] (NATG)
JUS/CIV .... Department of Justice, Civil Division
Jus Code ..... Code of Justinian [*A publication*] (DLA)
Jus Code ..... Code of Justinian (journ.) (SAUS)
Jus Code ..... Justices' Code [*Oregon*] [*A publication*] (DLA)
Juscul.......... Jusculum [*Broth*] [*Pharmacy*]
JUSE.......... Japanese Union of Scientists and Engineers [*Databank originator*] (NITA)
JUSE.......... Japan Union of Scientists and Engineers (BARN)
JUSE-AESOPP... Japanese Union of Scientists and Engineers-An Estimator of Physical Properties (SAUO)
JUSE-AESOPP... JUSE [*Japanese Union of Scientists and Engineers*] an Estimator of Physical Properties (NITA)
Jus Ecl........ Jus Eclesiasticum (journ.) (SAUS)
J-US FC........ Japan-United States Friendship Commission (SAUO)
JUSII.......... Journal. United Service Institution of India (journ.) (SAUS)
Jus Inst....... Institutes of Justinian [*Roman law*] [*A publication*] (DLA)
Jus Inst....... Institutes of Justinian (journ.) (SAUS)
JUSMAAG.... Joint United States Military Assistance Advisory Group
JUSMAG..... Joint United States Military Advisory Group
JUSMAG...... Joint United States Military Aid Group to Greece (SAUO)
JUSMAG...... Joint U.S. Military Assistance Group
JUSMAGG.... Joint United States Military Aid Group, Greece
JUSMAG-K.. Joint United States Military Advisor Group-Korea (DOMA)
JUSMAGPHIL... Joint United States Military Advisory Group to the Republic of the Philippines [*World War II*]
JUSMAGPHL... Joint United States Military Advisory Group to the Republic of the Philippines (SAUS)
JUSMAGTHAI... Joint United States Military Assistance Group, Thailand
JUSMAGTHAI... Joint United States Military Assistance Group Thailand (SAUS)
JUSMAP...... Joint United States Military Advisory and Planning Group
JUSMAT...... Joint United States Military Assistance, Turkey (SAUO)
JUSMG....... Joint United States Military Group
JUSMGP ...... Joint United States Military Group
JUSMMAT.... Joint United States Military Mission for Aid to Turkey
JUSMMAT.... Joint U.S. Military Mission Aid Training (ACAE)
Jus Nav Rhod... Jus Navale Rhodiorum [*A publication*] (DLA)
Jus Nav Rhod... Jus Navale Rhodiorum (journ.) (SAUS)
JUSNC........ Journal of the United States National Committee (journ.) (SAUS)
JUSNC........ Journal. United States National Committee (journ.) (SAUS)
JUSO.......... Jungsozialist [*Young Socialist*] [*Germany*]
JUSPAO .... Joint United States Public Affairs Office [*Vietnam*]
JUSS.......... Jussien (ROG)
JUSS.......... Jussive
JUSSC........ Joint United States Strategic Committee
JUSSIM....... Justice System Interactive Model (PDAA)
JUST.......... Joint Users of Siemens Telecommunications (SAUO)
JUST.......... Justice (ROG)
JUST.......... Justice Sector Support (SAUO)
Just.......... Justices' Law Reporter [*Pennsylvania*] [*A publication*] (DLA)
Just.......... Justiciary [*Legal term*] (DLA)
JUST.......... Justification (AABC)
Just.......... Justin (BJA)
JUST.......... Justinian (ROG)
Just.......... Justis Law Reporter (journ.) (SAUS)
JUST.......... Just Toys [*NASDAQ symbol*] (TTSB)
JUST.......... Just Toys, Inc. [*NASDAQ symbol*] (SAG)
JUST ANGL... Justiciarius Anglie [*Chief Justiciary of England*] [*Latin*] (ROG)
JUST CP ...... Justice of the Common Pleas (ROG)
Just Dig...... Digest of Justinian [*A publication*] (DLA)
Just Econ.... Just Economics (journ.) (SAUS)
Justice........ Department of Justice (SAUS)
JUSTICE....... Journeymen Under Specific Training in Construction Employment (PDAA)
Justices' LR (PA)... Justices' Law Reporter [*Pennsylvania*] [*A publication*] (DLA)
JUSTIFON .... Justification (ROG)
Justin........ Justinian [*483-565, Byzantine emperor*] [*Authority cited in pre-1607 legal work*] (DSA)
Justin........ Justin Industries, Inc. [*Associated Press*] (SAG)
Just Inst ...... Justinian's Institutes [*A publication*] (DLA)
JUSTINTAC... Joint User Supplier TIA ICEA NEMA Technical Advisory Committee (SAUO)
JUSTIS........ Japan-United States of America Textile Information (SAUS)
JUSTIS........ Japan-United States Textile Information Service (SAUO)
JUSTIS........ Judicial State Information System (OICC)
JUST ITIN .... Justice Itinerant [*Legal term*] (DLA)
JUST KB ...... Justice of the King's Bench [*British*] (ROG)

JUST KB ...... Justice of the Kings Bench (journ.) (SAUS)
JustLHo ...... Just Like Home, Inc. [*Associated Press*] (SAG)
Just LR........ Justices' Law Reporter [*Pennsylvania*] [*A publication*] (DLA)
Justn.......... Justinian [*Australia*] [*A publication*]
JUSTOS ...... Japan-U.S. Tropical Ocean Study (SAUS)
Just P .... Justice of the Peace and Local Government Review [*A publication*] (DLA)
Just Peace.... Justice of the Peace and Local Government Review [*A publication*] (DLA)
Just SL .... Justice's Sea Law [*A publication*] (DLA)
JustToys ...... Just Toys, Inc. [*Associated Press*] (SAG)
JUT............ Jamaica Union of Teachers (SAUO)
JUT............ Jet Utility Transport
JUT............ Jeunesse de l'Unite Togolaise [*Togolese Unity Youth*]
Juta .... Juta's Daily Reporter [*South Africa*] [*A publication*] (DLA)
Juta .... Juta's Prize Cases [*South Africa*] [*A publication*] (DLA)
Juta .... Juta's Supreme Court Reports [*1880-1910*] [*Cape Of Good Hope, South Africa*] [*A publication*] (DLA)
JUTCPS....... Joint Uniform Telephone Communications Precedence System (DNAB)
Jute Bull...... Jute Bulletin (journ.) (SAUS)
Jute Jute Fabr Bangladesh Newsl... Jute and Jute Fabrics. Bangladesh Newsletter (journ.) (SAUS)
JUTEM .... Japan Ultrahigh Temperature Materials Research Center (SAUS)
Jutendo Med... Jutendo Medicine (journ.) (SAUS)
J Utiliz Agr Prod... Journal of Utilzation of Agricultural Products (journ.) (SAUS)
JUV............ Juvenal [*Roman poet, 60-140AD*] [*Classical studies*] (ROG)
Juv............ Juvenile (AL)
juv............ Juvenile (SHCU)
JUV............ Juvenile
JUV............ Juvenis [*Young*] [*Latin*]
Juv & Dom Rel Ct... Juvenile and Domestic Relations Court [*Legal term*] (DLA)
Juv Ct J ...... Juvenile Court Journal [*A publication*] (DLA)
JUVE.......... Juvenile
Juve Delinq... Juvenile Delinquent (SAUS)
juven .... juvenilization (SAUS)
juven .... juvenilized (SAUS)
juven .... juvenilizing (SAUS)
juvenile SMA... Spinal Muscular Atrophy [*Kugelberg-Welander disease*] (PAZ)
juvie.......... Juvenile (ADWA)
JUV JUST .... Juvenile Justice [*Legal term*] (DLA)
JUVOS .... Joint Unemployment, Vacancy, and Operating Statistics [*Department of Employment*] [*British*]
JUWAT........ Joint Unconventional Warfare Assessment Team [*Military*]
JUWC.......... Joint Unconventional Warfare Command (MCD)
JUWTF........ Joint Unconventional Warfare Task Force
JUWTFA...... Joint Unconventional Warfare Task Force, Atlantic
jux............ juxtapose (SAUS)
JUX........... Juxtaposition (WDAA)
JUXT.......... Juxta [*Near*] [*Pharmacy*]
JUY........... Andalusia, AL [*Location identifier*] [*FAA*] (FAAL)
JV............. Air Charters [*Senegal*] [*ICAO designator*] (ICDA)
JV............. Bearskin Lake [*ICAO designator*] (AD)
JV............. Jagdverband [*German aircraft fighter unit*] [*World War II*]
JV............. Jamahiriva Airways (SAUO)
JV............. Janesbury Valve [*Aerospace*] (KSC)
JV............. Japanese Vellum
Jv............. Java (SAUO)
JV............. Jersey European Airways [*ICAO designator*] (AD)
JV............. Jet Ventilation [*Medicine*]
JV............. Jewish Vegetarians of North America (EA)
JV............. Job Variable (SAUS)
JV............. Joint Venture [*Legal term*] [*Business term*]
JV............. Journal. Violin Society of America (journ.) (SAUS)
JV............. Journal Voucher [*Accounting*]
JV............. Jugular Vein [*Anatomy*]
JV............. Jugular Venous [*Pressure and pulse*] [*Cardiology*] (DAVI)
JV............. Jugulovenous (SAUS)
JV............. Junin Virus [*Medicine*] (DMAA)
JV............. Junior Varsity
JVA........... Ankavandra [*Madagascar*] [*Airport symbol*] (OAG)
JVA........... Genavia SRL [*Italy*] [*ICAO designator*] (FAAC)
JVA........... Jet Vane Actuators
JVA........... Jewish Vacation Association [*Superseded by Association of Jewish Sponsored Camps*] (EA)
JVA........... Joint Voluntary Agency (SAUS)
JVA........... Jordan Valley Authority (SAUO)
JVA........... Journal of Volunteer Administration (journ.) (SAUS)
JVA........... Junior Victory Army [*World War II*]
JVAA.......... Jewish Visual Artists Association [*Defunct*] (EA)
J Vac Soc Jpn... Journal of the Vacuum Society of Japan (journ.) (SAUS)
J Vac Soc Jpn... Journal. Vacuum Society of Japan (journ.) (SAUS)
J Value Eng... Journal of Value Engineering (journ.) (SAUS)
J Value Inq... Journal of Value Inquiry (journ.) (SAUS)
JVAN.......... Journal of Vascular Access Nursing (SAUO)
Jv & Dom Rel Ct... Juvenile and Domestic Relations Court (SAUS)
JVAP.......... Joint Vaccine Acquisition Program
JVAR.......... Jordan Valley Applied Radiation Ltd. (SAUO)
JVAS.......... Jandel Video Analysis System
J Vasc Interv Radiol... Journal of Vascular and Interventional Radiology (journ.) (SAUS)
J Vasc Res... Journal of Vascular Research (journ.) (SAUS)
J Vasc Surg... Journal of Vascular Surgery (journ.) (SAUS)
JVB........... James V. Brown Library of Williamsport and Lycoming County, Williamsport, PA [*OCLC symbol*] (OCLC)

JVB	Joint Vulnerability Board
JVC	Japan Victor Co.
JVC	Japan Volunteer Center (SAUS)
JVC	Jesuit Volunteer Corps (SAUO)
JVC	Jesuit Volunteer Corps: Northwest (EA)
JVC	Jet Vane Control (MCD)
JVC	Jewelers Vigilance Committee (EA)
JVC	Jewelry Valuers' Council [Australia]
JVC	Joint Verification Committee (SAUS)
JVC	Jugular Venous Catheter [Medicine] (DMAA)
JVC	Jules Verne Circle (EA)
JVC	Junior Vice Commander
JVC	Victory Company of Japan (SAUO)
JVCC	Joint Vocabulary Coordination Committee (SAUO)
JVD	Jet Vapor Deposition [Coating technology]
JVD	Jugular Venous Distention [Medicine]
JVD	Junction Varactor Doubler (SAUS)
JVD	Juris Utriusque Doctor [Doctor of Both Laws; i.e., Canon and Civil Law]
JVDHS	Jahresverzeichnis der Deutschen Hochschulschriften [A bibliographic publication] [Germany]
JVE	Jeans Viscosity Equation [Physics]
JVE	Joint Verification (SAUS)
JVE	Joint Verification Experiment (SAUO)
J Veg Sci	Journal of Vegetation Science
J Vener Dis Inf	Journal of Venereal Disease Information (journ.) (SAUS)
JVER	Journal of Vocational Education Research [A publication] (EAAP)
J Vertebr Paleontol	Journal of Vertebrate Paleontology (journ.) (SAUS)
J Vet Diagn Invest	Journal of Veterinary Diagnostic Investigation (journ.) (SAUS)
J Vet Fac Univ Tehran	Journal. Veterinary Faculty. University of Tehran (journ.) (SAUS)
J Vet Intern Med	Journal of Veterinary Internal Medicine (journ.) (SAUS)
J Vet Med Educ	Journal of Veterinary Medical Education (journ.) (SAUS)
J Vet Med Sci	Journal of Veterinary Medical Science (journ.) (SAUS)
J Vet Pharmacol TherJVPTD9	Journal of Veterinary Pharmacology and Therapeutics (SAUS)
J Vet Sci UAR	Journal of Veterinaiy Science of the United Arab Republic (journ.) (SAUS)
JVH	Bangor, ME [Location identifier] [FAA] (FAAL)
JVI	Journal of Virology (journ.) (SAUS)
JVI	Jugular Venous Pulse Tracing (SAUS)
JVIB	Journal of Visual Impairment & Blindness [A publication]
JVIBDM	Journal of Visual Impairment and Blindness (journ.) (SAUS)
J Vic Teachers Union	Journal of the Victorian Teachers Union (journ.) (SAUS)
JVIDS	Joint Visually Integrated Display System (DOMA)
J Vinyl Technol	Journal of Vinyl Technology (journ.) (SAUS)
J Viola da Gamba Soc Amer	Journal. Viola da Gamba Society of America (journ.) (SAUS)
JVIR	Journal of Vascular and Interventional Radiology (journ.) (SAUS)
J Virol Methods	Journal of Virological Methods (journ.) (SAUS)
JVIS	Jackson Vocational Interest Survey [Vocational guidance test]
JVIS	Joint Visual Information Services [DoD] (DOMA)
J Visual Impairment & Blind	Journal of Visual Impairment and Blindness (journ.) (SAUS)
JVita	Life of Josephus (BJA)
J Vitaminol	Journal of Vitaminology (journ.) (SAUS)
JVL	Beloit/Janesville [Wisconsin] [Airport symbol] (OAG)
JVL	Janesville, WI [Location identifier] [FAA] (FAAL)
JVLN	Javelin Systems, Inc. [NASDAQ symbol] (SAG)
JVLVB	Journal of Verbal Learning and Verbal Behavior (journ.) (SAUS)
JVM	Java Virtual Machine [Computer science]
JVME	Journal of Veterinary Medical Education (SAUO)
JVMED	Journal of Virological Methods (journ.) (SAUS)
JVMF	Joint Variable Message Format
JVNC	John von Neumann Center (SAUO)
JVNC	John Von Neumann National Supercomputer Center [Princeton, NJ] (GRD)
JvNCnet	John von Neumann Center Network
JvNCnet	John Von Neumann Computer Center Network (ACRL)
JVNL	Juvenile
JVNTSC	John Volpe National Transportation Systems Center (SAUO)
J Voet Com ad Pand	Jan Voet's Commentarius ad Pandectas [A publication] (DLA)
J Voice	Journal of Voice (journ.) (SAUS)
J Volanol Geotherm Res	Journal of Volcanology and Geothermal Research (journ.) (SAUS)
J Volun Act	Journal of Voluntary Action Research (journ.) (SAUS)
J Volunteer Adm	Journal of Volunteer Administration (journ.) (SAUS)
JVP	Janatha Vimukhti Peramuna [People's Liberation Front] [Sri Lanka] [Political party] (PPW)
JVP	Janet-Viscount-Public libraries project (SAUS)
JVP	Japanese Vellum Proofs
JVP	Joint Venture Partners
JVP	Juedische Volkspartei (BJA)
JVP	Jugular Vein Pressure (WDAA)
JVP	Jugular Vein [or Venous] Pulse [Medicine]
JVP	Jugular Venous Pressure [Cardiology] (DAVI)
JVP	Jugular Venous Pulse
JVP	Junior Vice-President [Freemasonry] (ROG)
JVPT	Jugular Venous Pulse Tracing [Medicine]
JVR	Jury Verdict Research, Inc. [Information service or system] (IID)
JVS	Jamaican Vomiting Sickness (MELL)
JVS	Jewish Vegetarian Society - America [Later, JVSNA] (EA)
JVS	Jewish Vocational Services
JVS	Joint Venture Scheme
JVS	Joint Vocational School
JVSNA	Jewish Vegetarian Society-North America (EA)
JVSPLNMQNSC	Je Vous Salue par les Noms Maconniques que Nous Seul Connoissons [I Salute You by the Masonic Names, Which We Only Know] [Freemasonry] [French]
JVSR	Journal of Vertebral Subluxation Research (SAUO)
JVSR	Journal of Vertebral Subluxation Research (journ.) (SAUS)
JVST	Journal of Vacuum Science and Technology (journ.) (SAUS)
JVSUES	Journal of Vascular Surgery (journ.) (SAUS)
JVT	Current-density Voltage Temperature (SAUS)
JVVVA	Justice for Veteran Victims of the Veterans Administration (EA)
JVX	Joint Service Vertical-Lift Aircraft, Experimental [Military] (RDA)
JVX	Joint Vertical Lift Airlift (SAUS)
JVY	Jeffersonville, IN [Location identifier] [FAA] (FAAL)
JW	Arrow Airways, Inc. (SAUO)
JW	Jacket Water
JW	Jamming War (SAUS)
JW	Jehovah's Witnesses (ADA)
JW	[The] Jewish War [A publication] (BJA)
JW	John Wiley [& Sons] [Publisher]
JW	Joint Warfare
JW	Jordan Watch [Database] [Jordan & Sons Ltd.] [Information service or system] (CRD)
jw	jugwell (SAUS)
JW	Jump Walker [Rehabilitation] (DAVI)
JW	Junction Wide [Telecommunications] (OA)
JW	Junior Warden [Freemasonry]
JW	Junior Wolf [A young philanderer] [Slang]
JW	Junior Woodward [Ancient Order of Foresters]
JW	Juvenile Water (SAUS)
JW	Polar Avia [ICAO designator] (AD)
JW	Royal American [ICAO designator] (AD)
JW	Wiley [John] & Sons [NYSE symbol] (SAG)
JWA	Japan Whaling Association (SAUO)
JWA	Japati Whaling Association (SAUO)
JWA	Jetworld Airways Ltd. [Antigua and Barbuda] [ICAO designator] (FAAC)
JWA	Johnson Worldwide Associates, Inc. [Associated Press] (SAG)
JWA	Journal of World Anthroplogy (journ.) (SAUS)
JWA	Jwalamukhi [India] [Seismograph station code, US Geological Survey] [Closed] (SEIS)
JWABAQ	Journal for Water and Wastewater Research (journ.) (SAUS)
JWAC	Jacket Water After Cooled (SAUS)
JWADF	Joint Western Air Defense Force (MUGU)
JWAI	Johnson Worldwide Associates, Inc. [NASDAQ symbol] (NQ)
JWAIA	Johnson Worldwide'A' [NASDAQ symbol] (TTSB)
J Wakayama Med Soc	Journal Wakayama Medical Society (journ.) (SAUS)
J Walter Roth Mus	Journal of the Walter Roth Museum of Archaeology and Anthropology (journ.) (SAUS)
JW & NW	Jamestown, Westfield & Northwestern Railroad (IIA)
J WA Nurses	Journal. Western Australian Nurses Association (journ.) (SAUS)
JWAR	Jehovah's Witnesses for Animal Rights [An association] (EA)
JWARS	Joint Warfare System (SAUS)
J Wash Ac Sci	Journal of the Washington Academy of Sciences (journ.) (SAUS)
J Washington Acad Sci	Journal. Washington Academy of Sciences (journ.)
JWAT	Jamaica Water Properties (SAUS)
J Water PC	Journal. Water Pollution Control Federation (journ.) (SAUS)
J Water Resour	Journal of Water Resources (journ.) (SAUS)
J Water Resour Plann Manage Div Am Soc Civ Eng	Journal. Water Resources Planning and Management Division. Proceedings of the American Society of Civil Engineers (journ.) (SAUS)
J Water Waste	Journal of Water and Waste (journ.) (SAUS)
J Water Wastewater Res	Journal for Water and Wastewater Research (journ.) (SAUS)
J Waterway	Journal. Waterways, Harbors and Coastal Engineering Division. American Society of Civil Engineers (journ.) (SAUS)
J Waterway Port Coastal & Ocean Div Proc ASCE	Journal. Waterways, Ports, Coastal and Ocean Division. American Society of Civil Engineers. Proceedings (journ.) (SAUS)
J Waterway Port Coastal Ocean Div Amer S Civil Eng Proc	Journal. Waterways, Ports, Coastal and Ocean Division. American Society of Civil Engineers. Proceedings (journ.) (SAUS)
J Waterw Harbors Div Am Soc Civ Eng	Journal. Waterways and Harbors Division. American Society of Civil Engineers (journ.) (SAUS)
J Water Works Assoc	Journal. Water Works Association (journ.) (SAUS)
J Waterw Port Coastal Ocean Div ASCE	Journal. Waterways, Ports, Coastal and Ocean Division. American Society of Civil Engineers (journ.) (SAUS)
JWB	Jewish Welfare Board (SAUO)
JWB	Joint Wages Board (DAS)
JWB	Joint Welfare Board (SAUO)
JWB	National Jewish Welfare Board [Later, JCCANA] (EA)
JWBC	Joint Whole Blood Center [Military]
JWBCA	Joint Whole Blood Control Agency (MCD)
JWBJBC	JWB [Jewish Welfare Board] Jewish Book Council (EA)
JWBJCC	JWB Jewish Chaplains Council (NTPA)
JWBS	Journal. Welsh Bibliographic Society (journ.) (SAUS)
JWC	Jayhawk Western Conference (PSS)
JWC	Joint Warfare Center [DoD]
JWC	Joint Warfare Committee (SAUO)
JWC	Joint Working Committee (SAUO)
JWC	Junction Wire Connector
JWC	Jungle Warfare Course [Military] (MCD)
JWCA	Joint Warfighter Capability Assessment (SAUS)

JWD............	Journal of Workforce Diversity [*A publication*]
JWDSC........	JOPES/WIS Data Standardization Committee (SAUO)
JWE............	Joint Warfare Establishment [*British*]
J Weather Modif...	Journal of Weather Modification (journ.) (SAUS)
JWEB..........	Juno Online Svcs. [*NASDAQ symbol*] (SG)
JWEC..........	Jefferson-Williams Energy Corp. (SAUS)
JWEC..........	Jefferson-Williams Energy Corporation (SAUO)
JWEF..........	Joinery and Woodwork Employers' Federation [*British*] (BI)
J West Afr Inst Oil Palm Res...	Journal. West African Institute for Oil Palm Research (journ.) (SAUS)
J West Aust Nurses...	Journal. West Australian Nurses (journ.) (SAUS)
J West Scot Iron Steel Inst...	Journal. West of Scotland Iron and Steel Institute (journ.) (SAUS)
J West Soc Eng...	Journal. Western Society of Engineers (journ.) (SAUS)
JWF............	Job Work Folder (AABC)
JWFC..........	Jacky Ward Fan Club [*Defunct*] (EA)
JWFC..........	Jimmy Wakely Fan Club [*Defunct*] (EA)
JWFC..........	Joe Waters Fan Club (EA)
JWFC..........	Joint Warfighting Center [*DoD*]
JWG............	GCOS/GOOS Joint Working Group (SAUS)
JWG............	Joint Working Group [*Military*]
JWG............	Jugendwohlfahrtsgesetz [*Youth Welfare Law*] [*German*] (ILCA)
JWG............	JWGenesis Financial [*AMEX symbol*] [*Formerly, Charles Financial Services*]
JWGA..........	Joint War Games Agency [*JCS*] [*DoD*]
JWGA..........	Joint Working Group ATMOS (SAUO)
JWGCG........	Joint War Games Control Group [*Military*] (CINC)
JWGFC........	John Wilson Gill Fan Club (EA)
JWGM..........	Joint Working Group Meeting [*NASA*] (KSC)
JWH............	Journal of World History (journ.) (SAUS)
JWI............	Jack Winter (SAUS)
JWI............	Jehovahs Witnesses Information (SAUS)
JWI............	Jewish Women International (EA)
JWI............	Joint Worldwide Intelligence (SAUO)
JWICS........	Joint Worldwide Intelligence Communications System (COE)
JWID..........	Joint Warrior Interoperability Demonstration (SAUS)
JWIDA........	Journal of Wildlife Diseases (journ.) (SAUS)
JWIDS........	Joint Worldwide Interoperability Demonstration System (SAUO)
J Wildl Dis...	Journal of Wildlife Diseases (journ.) (SAUS)
J Wildlife Mgt...	Journal of Wildlife Management (journ.) (SAUS)
J Wildl Manage...	Journal of Wildlife Management (SAUO)
JWIM..........	Journal of Wildlife Management (journ.) (SAUS)
J Wind Eng and Ind...	Journal of Wind Engineering and Industrial Aerodynamics (journ.) (SAUS)
J Wind Engng & Ind Aerodyn...	Journal of Wind Engineering and Industrial Aerodynamics (journ.) (SAUS)
J Wind Engng Ind Aerodyn...	Journal of Wind Engineering and Industrial Aerodynamics (journ.) (SAUS)
JWIS..........	Joint WWMCCS Information System (SAUO)
J Wis Dent Ass...	Journal. Wisconsin Dental Association (journ.) (SAUS)
J Wis State Dent Soc...	Journal. Wisconsin State Dental Society (journ.) (SAUS)
JWJL..........	JW Jagger Library (SAUO)
JWKB..........	Jordan-Wentzel-Kramers-Brillouin [*Physics*]
JWL............	Johnston Warren Lines (SAUS)
JWL............	Whitehall Jewellers [*NYSE symbol*] (SG)
JWLMST......	Jewelmasters, Inc. (SAUO)
JWLO..........	Joint Warfare Liaison Officer (SAUO)
jwlr............	Jeweler (ADWA)
JWLR..........	Jeweler
JWLR..........	Jeweller [*British*] (ADA)
JWLRY........	Jewelry (WDAA)
JWMO..........	Japan Waste Management Office (SAUO)
JWMPO........	Japan Waste Management Program Office (SAUO)
JWNS..........	Jewish News Service (BJA)
JWO............	Jardine Waugh Organization (SAUO)
jwo............	Jettisoning and Washing Overboard [*Inventor*] (ODBW)
JWO............	Job Work Order
JWOC..........	Joint Warrant Officer Course (SAUO)
JWOCN........	Journal of Wound, Ostomy and Continence Nursing (SAUO)
JWOCN........	Journal of Wound, Ostomy and Continence Nursing (journ.) (SAUS)
JWOD.........	Javits-Wagner-O'Day Act
J Womens Hist...	Journal of Womens History (journ.) (SAUS)
J Won Kwang Public Health JrColl...	Journal. Won Kwang Public Health Junior College (journ.) (SAUS)
J Wood Chem Technol...	Journal of Wood Chemistry and Technology (journ.) (SAUS)
J World Hist...	Journal of World History (journ.) (SAUS)
J World Prehist...	Journal of World Prehistory (journ.) (SAUS)
JWP............	Jamaican Workers' Party [*Political party*] (PPW)
JWP............	Jamaica Water Properties (EFIS)
JWP............	Joint Working Paper
JWP............	Joint Working Party (ADA)
JWPAC........	Joint Waste Paper Advisory Council (SAUO)
JWPC..........	Joint War Plans Committee
JWPC..........	Joint War Production Committee
JWPCF........	Journal of the Water Pollution Control Federation (SAUO)
JWPNN........	Jobs with Peace National Network [*Later, NJWPC*] (EA)
JWPS..........	Joint War Production Staff
JWPT..........	Jersey Wildlife Preservation Trust (EAIO)
JWR............	Janes World Railways (SAUS)
JWR............	Joint War Room [*Military*]
JWRA..........	Joint War Room Annex [*Military*] (CINC)
JWRC..........	Jewish Women's Resource Center (EA)
JWRC..........	Joint Warfighter Range Complex [*Army*]
JWREEG	Journal of Water Resources (journ.) (SAUS)
JWRI..........	Japan Welding Research Institute (SAUS)
JWRS..........	Japan Wood Research Society (SAUO)
JWRV..........	Jewish War Relief Volunteers (SAUO)
JWS............	James W. Sewall Company, Inc. (SAUO)
JWS............	Japanese Weekend School
JWS............	Japan Welding Society (SAUO)
JWS............	Java Web Server (SAUS)
JWS............	Java Workshop (SAUO)
JWS............	Jazz World Society (EA)
JWS............	Jewish Welfare Society [*Australia*]
JwS............	John Wiley & Sons, New York, NY [*Library symbol*] [*Library of Congress*] (LCLS)
JWS............	Joint Warfare Staff [*British*]
JWS............	Joint Work Statement (SAUO)
JWS............	Journal of Western Speech (journ.) (SAUS)
JWS............	Judson Welliver Society (EA)
JWSL..........	Journal of Womens Studies in Literature (journ.) (SAUS)
JWSOL........	Joint Warfare Simulation Object Library [*DoD*]
JWSS..........	James Willard Schultz Society (EA)
JWSS..........	Joint Work Study School (SAUO)
JWST..........	Jewish Studies (journ.) (SAUS)
JWS/TD.......	Jungle Warfare School Trial and Development Wing [*Johore Bahru, Malaysia*]
JWSTP........	Joint Warfighting Science and Technology Plan [*Defense Technical Information Center*]
JWT............	J. Walter Thompson (WDAA)
JWTC..........	Jungle Warfare Training Center [*Army*]
JWTDC........	Joint Warfare Tactical Doctrine Committee (SAUO)
JWU............	International Jewelry Workers Union [*Later, Service Employees International Union*]
JWU............	Jewelry Workers Union (SAUO)
JWU............	Sumter, SC [*Location identifier*] [*FAA*] (FAAL)
JWV............	Jewish War Veterans (WDAA)
JWV............	Jewish War Veterans of the USA (EA)
JWVA..........	Jewish War Veterans of the USA - National Ladies Auxiliary (EA)
JW Vir Phil Soc...	Journal. West Virginia Philosophical Society (journ.) (SAUS)
JWV-NMI.....	National Museum of American Jewish Military History (EA)
JWVUSANM...	Jewish War Veterans USA National Memorial (EA)
JWWJA........	Journal. Japan Water Works Association (journ.) (SAUS)
JWY............	Jet Way, Inc. [*ICAO designator*] (FAAC)
JWYCC........	Jamestown-Williamsburg-Yorktown Celebration Committee
JX	Bougainville Air Service (SAUS)
JX	Bougair [*ICAO designator*] (AD)
JX	International Jet Air Ltd. (SAUO)
JX	Jesus Christ (SAUS)
JX	Jesus Christus [*Jesus Christ*] [*Latin*] (ROG)
JX	Jorex Ltd. [*Toronto Stock Exchange symbol*]
JXCG..........	Joint Exercise Control Group [*Military*] (AABC)
JXG............	Juvenile Xanthogranuloma [*Ophthalmology*]
J Xian Inst Metall Constr Eng...	Journal of Xian Institute of Metallurgy and Construction Engineering (journ.) (SAUS)
JXN............	Jackson [*Michigan*] [*Airport symbol*] (OAG)
Jxpan J Nurs Art...	Japanese Journal of Nursing Art (journ.) (SAUS)
JXSB..........	Jacksonville Savings Bank (Illinois) [*NASDAQ symbol*] (SAG)
JXT............	Morristown, TN [*Location identifier*] [*FAA*] (FAAL)
JXVL..........	Jacksonville Bancorp, Inc. [*NASDAQ symbol*] (SAG)
JXVL..........	Jacksonville Savings & Loan Association [*Texas*] [*NASDAQ symbol*] (SAG)
J XXII........	Extravagantes Johannes XXII [*A publication*] (DSA)
JY	British United Channel Islands Airways (SAUS)
JY	European Airways (SAUS)
Jy	Jansky [*A unit of electromagnetic flux density*]
JY	Japanese Yen [*Monetary unit*]
JY	Jersey European [*ICAO designator*] (AD)
Jy	July (ADWA)
JY	July
JY	Jury [*Ship's rigging*] (ROG)
JYA............	Junior Year Abroad [*Collegiate term*]
JYADA6.......	Journal of Youth and Adolescence (journ.) (SAUS)
J Yamashina Inst Ornithol...	Journal. Yamashina Institute for Ornithology (journ.) (SAUS)
J Yamgata Agric For S...	Journal. Yamagata Agriculture and Forestry Society (journ.) (SAUS)
JYC............	Interstate Helicopters, Inc. (SAUO)
JYC............	Jacques-Yves Cousteau [*French marine explorer*] [*Initialism pronounced "Jheek" when used as nickname*]
JYC............	Judicial Youth Corps (SAUS)
JYCE-A........	Journal. Hydraulics Division. Proceedings of the American Society of Civil Engineers (journ.) (SAUS)
JYL............	Jugolinja-Yugoslav Line (SAUO)
J Yokohama Munic Univ...	Journal. Yokohama Municipal University (journ.) (SAUS)
J Yonago Med Assoc...	Journal. Yonago Medical Association (journ.) (SAUS)
JYP............	JCP & L Capital LP [*NYSE symbol*] (SAG)
JYP............	Jersey Central Power & Light Co. [*NYSE symbol*] (SAG)
JYPPr.........	Jersey Cent P&L 4%cmPfd [*NYSE symbol*] (TTSB)
JYPPrE........	Jersey Cent P&L7.88% Pfd [*NYSE symbol*] (TTSB)
JYPPrZ........	JCP&L Cap L.P.8.56%'MIPS' [*NYSE symbol*] (TTSB)
JYV............	Houston, TX [*Location identifier*] [*FAA*] (FAAL)
JYV............	Jyvaskyla [*Finland*] [*Airport symbol*] (OAG)
JZ	Alamo Commuter Airlines [*ICAO designator*] (AD)
JZ	Jazz [*A radio station format*] (WDMC)
JZ	Juedische Zeremonialkunst [*A publication*] (BJA)
JZ	Jump if Zero (VLIE)
JZ	Jump on Zero [*Computer science*] (PCM)
JZ	Zaire Aero Services (SAUS)

JZF.............. Jannasch-Zafirion-Farrington [*Marine sediment trap*]

JZG .... Juedische Zeitschrift fuer Wissenschaft und Leben (A. Geiger) [*A publication*] (BJA)

J Zhejiang Med Univ... Journal. Zhejiang Medical University (journ.) (SAUS)

J Zhejiang Univ... Journal of Zhejiang University (journ.) (SAUS)

JZI .... Charleston, SC [*Location identifier*] [*FAA*] (FAAL)

JZM .... Jazzman Resources, Inc. [*Vancouver Stock Exchange symbol*]

J Zoo Anim Med... Journal of Zoo Animal Medicine (journ.) (SAUS)

J Zool Res... Journal of Zoological Research (journ.) (SAUS)

J Zool Ser A... Journal of Zoology. Series A (journ.) (SAUS)

J Zool Ser B... Journal of Zoology. Series B (journ.) (SAUS)

J Zool Soc Indi... Journal. Zoological Society of India (journ.) (SAUS)

J Zool Sys Evol Res... Journal of Zoological Systematics and Evolutionary Research (journ.) (SAUS)

JZP .... Jersey Zoological Park (SAUO)

JZQ .... Norfolk, VA [*Location identifier*] [*FAA*] (FAAL)

JZS .... Jersey Zoological Society (SAUO)

JZS .... Speleological Association of Slovenia (SAUO)

JZSAEU........ Journal of Zoology. Series A (journ.) (SAUS)

JZSBEX........ Journal of Zoology. Series B (journ.) (SAUS)

K
By Acronym

K................ Absolute Zero [*Temperature*] (MAE)
K................ Absorption Index (SAUS)
K................ Amphibious [*JETDS*]
K................ Black (WDMC)
K................ Boltzmann Constant [*Symbol*] [*IUPAC*]
k................ Bulk Modulus of Elasticity [*Symbol*] (DEN)
K................ Calcium in the Solar Spectrum [*Astronomy*] (BARN)
K................ Calix [*Anatomy*] (MAE)
K................ Capacity (AAG)
K................ Capital [*Factor of production*]
K................ Capsular Antigen [*Immunology*] (MAE)
K................ Cara [*Dear One*] [*Latin*]
K................ Carat [*Unit of measure for precious stones or gold*]
K................ Care
K................ Carissimus [*Dearest*] [*Latin*]
K................ Carlo Erba [*Italy*] [*Research code symbol*]
K................ Carrying Capacity [*Genetics*] (DAVI)
K................ Carus
K................ Cathode [*Electron device*] (MSA)
K................ Cellophane (AAG)
K................ Certified Kosher [*Food labeling*]
K................ Chritiania Bank og Kreditkasse [*Bank*] [*Norway*]
K................ Circuses [*Public-performance tariff class*] [*British*]
k................ Coefficient of Alienation [*Psychology*]
K................ Coefficient of Scleral Rigidity [*Ophthalmology*] (DAVI)
k................ Cold Air Mass [*Meteorology*] (BARN)
K................ Computer [*JETDS nomenclature*]
K................ Consonantal [*Linguistics*]
K................ Constant
K................ Contract [*Legal shorthand*] (LWAP)
K................ Cornea (SAUS)
K................ Cretaceous [*Period, era, or system*] [*Geology*]
K................ Cumulus [*Cloud*] [*Meteorology*]
K................ Dallas [*Branch in the Federal Reserve regional banking system*] (BARN)
K................ Danish National Museum (SAUO)
K................ Declared or Paid This Year on a Cumulative Issue with Dividends in Arrears [*Investment term*] (DFIT)
K................ Degrees Kelvin
K................ Dielectric Constant
K................ Electrostatic Capacity [*Symbol*] (AAMN)
K................ Equilibrium Constant [*Symbol*] [*Chemistry*]
K................ Ionization Constant [*Symbol*] [*Chemistry*]
K................ Kadenz [*Cadence*] [*Music*]
K................ Kaempferol [*Biochemistry*]
K................ Kainic Acid [*Biochemistry*]
K................ Kaiser [*In radio call signs west of the Mississippi River*] (ROG)
K................ Kaken Chemical Co. [*Japan*] [*Research code symbol*]
K................ Kalendas [*Calends*]
K................ Kalium [*Potassium*] [*Chemical element*]
K................ Kallikrein [*or Kininogenin*] Inhibiting Unit [*Hematology*]
K................ Kanamycin [*Antibacterial compound*]
K................ Kanone [*Gun*] [*German military - World War II*]
K................ Kansas State Library, Topeka, KS [*Library symbol*] [*Library of Congress*] (LCLS)
K................ Kappa [*Tenth letter of the Greek alaphabet*] (DAVI)
k................ Karat (SHCU)
K................ Karat [*A twenty-fourth part; unit of value for gold*]
K................ Karolus de Tocco [*Flourished, 13th century*] [*Authority cited in pre-1607 legal work*] (DSA)
K................ Karyotype [*Clinical chemistry*]
K................ Kathode [*Cathode*]
K................ Kayak
K................ Kayser
K................ K Capture [*A type of radioactive decay*]
K................ Keel
K................ Keg
K................ Kell [*Blood group*]
K................ Kell Factor (DMAA)
K................ Kellogg Co. [*NYSE symbol*] (SPSG)
K................ Keloid (MELL)
K................ Kelp [*Quality of the Bottom*] [*Nautical charts*]
K................ Kelvin [*Symbol*] [*SI unit of thermodynamic temperature*]
K................ Kennedy Space Center [*NASA*]
K................ Kensal Press [*Publisher*] [*British*]
K................ Kentish

K................ Kenyon's English King's Bench Reports [*A publication*] (DLA)
K................ Keratometry (MELL)
K................ Kerma (DMAA)
K................ Kern Wave [*Earthquakes*]
K................ Kerosene (AAG)
K................ Kerr Constant [*Optics*]
K................ Ketamine [*An anesthetic*]
K................ Ketch (ROG)
K................ Ketib (BJA)
K................ Ketotifen [*Pharmacology*]
K................ Key
k................ Keyboard
K................ Keyes' New York Court of Appeals Reports [*A publication*] (DLA)
K................ KGB [*Komitet Gossudarstvennoi Bezopasnosti*] Agent
K................ Kicker [*Football*]
K................ Kidney [*Anatomy*] (MAE)
K................ Kill [*Military*] (ACAE)
K................ Killed
K................ Killer [*Cells*] [*Cytology*] (DAVI)
K................ Kilo [*Phonetic alphabet*] [*International*] (DSUE)
k................ Kilo [*A prefix meaning multiplied by 10³*] [*SI symbol*]
K................ Kilobyte [*10³ bytes*] [*Computer science*]
K................ Kilocalorie (MELL)
K................ Kilocycle
K................ Kilodalton (MELL)
K................ Kilogram (SHCU)
K................ Kilogram [*Also, kg*] [*Symbol*] [*SI unit for mass*]
k................ Kilohm
K................ Kilometer (WDAA)
K................ Kilowatt (WDMC)
K................ Kindergarten
K................ Kinesthetic (AAG)
K................ Kinetic Energy [*Symbol*] [*IUPAC*]
K................ King [*Phonetic alphabet*] [*Royal Navy*] (DSUE)
K................ King [*Monetary unit*][*Papua, New Guinea*] (BARN)
K................ King [*Chess, card games*]
k................ King (GEAB)
K................ Kingdom (ROG)
K................ Kings [*Old Testament book*] (BJA)
K................ Kip [*1000 lbs.*]
K................ Kip [*Monetary unit*] [*Laos*]
K................ Kirk (ROG)
K................ Kirschner [*Wire*] [*Orthopedics*] (DAVI)
K................ Kitchen
K................ Klebsiella [*Genus of microorganisms*] (DAVI)
K................ Klinge [*Germany*] [*Research code symbol*]
K................ Klystron
K................ Knee [*Anatomy*] (DAVI)
K................ Knight [*Chess, card games*]
K................ Knighthood
K................ Knit
K................ Knock [*Cardiology*]
K................ Knots [*Also, KT*] [*Nautical speed unit*]
K................ Knudsen Number
K................ Koechel [*Catalogue of Mozart's works*] (ODBW)
K................ Koechel Numeration [*Of Mozart's Works*] [*Music*] (WA)
K................ Kollaborateur [*Nickname given Alain Robbe-Grillet*] [*World War II*]
K................ Kontra [*Contra*] [*Music*]
K................ Kopeck [*Monetary unit*] [*Former USSR*]
K................ K-Orbital (MEC)
K................ Koruna [*Monetary unit*] [*Former Czechoslovakia*]
K................ Kosher
K................ Kosmos [*Publisher*] [*Holland*]
K................ Kotze's Transvaal High Court Reports [*South Africa*] [*A publication*] (DLA)
K................ Kouyunjik [*or Kuyounjik*] [*Collection of cuneiform tablets from Kuyounjik in the British Museum, London*] (BJA)
K................ Kraft [*Paper*] (DGA)
K................ Kraftfahrwesen [*Motor transport*] [*German military - World War II*]
K................ Kraftrad [*Motorcycle*] [*German military - World War II*]
K................ Krazy Kat [*Cartoon character by George Herriman*]
K................ Krona [*Monetary unit*] [*Iceland, Sweden*]
K................ Krone [*Crown*] [*Monetary unit*] [*Denmark, Norway*]
K................ Kroon [*Monetary unit*] [*Estonia*]
K................ Krupp Gun
K................ Kurus [*Monetary unit*] [*Turkey*]

K	Kwacha [*Monetary unit*] [*Malawi, Zambia*]
K	Kyat [*Monetary unit*] [*Myanmar*]
K	Luminous Efficiency [*Physics*] (BARN)
K	Lysine [*One-letter symbol; see Lys*]
k	Magnetic Susceptibility (STED)
k	Mass Transfer Coefficient [*Symbol*] [*IUPAC*]
K	Motor Coordination [*Neurology and orthopedics*] (DAVI)
K	Multiplication Factor [*or Constant*]
K	NCO Logistics Program [*Army skill qualification identifier*] (INF)
K	Okay (SAUS)
K	One Thousand (NASA)
K	Phylloquinone [*Vitamin K*] [*Also, PMQ*] [*Biochemistry*]
K	Potassium [*Chemical element*]
K	Promotional Fare [*Also, L, Q, V*] [*Airline fare code*]
K	Radius of Curvature of Flattest Meridian of Apical Cornea [*Ophthalmology*] (DAVI)
k	Rate (DAVI)
k	Rate Constant [*Symbol*] [*Chemistry*]
k	Reaction Rate Constant [*Chemistry*] (DAVI)
K	Reactor Development Division (SAUO)
K	Red Star of Maximum Intensity of Metal [*Astronomy*] (BARN)
K	Relay (CET)
K	Required Rate of Return [*Finance*]
K	Smoke [*Weather charts*]
K	Solar Absorption Index (CET)
K	Strikeout [*Baseball symbol*]
K	symbol for planetary wave number (SAUS)
K	Tanker [*Designation for all US military aircraft*]
K	Telemetering [*JETDS*]
K	Thermal Conductivity [*Symbol*] [*IUPAC*]
K	Thousand (ADA)
k	Torsion Constant [*Physics*] (BARN)
K	United Kingdom [*IYRU nationality code*] (IYR)
k	Velocity [*Physics*] (DAVI)
K	Wetboek van Koophandel [*Commercial Code*] [*Dutch*] (ILCA)
K1	Kayak, Single Person (ADA)
K2	Coefficient of Nondetermination (DIPS)
K2	Kayak, Two Person (ADA)
K2	Mount Godwin-Austen [*Initialism denotes that mountain is second highest (to Everest) in the Karakoram range in the Himalayas*] [*Initialism also used as brand name of skiing equipment*]
K-2	Taegu Air Base (SAUO)
K2Desgn	K2 Design, Inc. [*Associated Press*] (SAG)
K2Dsgn	K2 Design, Inc. [*Associated Press*] (SAG)
K-3	Krasnogorsk-3 [*A 16mm film camera*] (WDMC)
K-3	Kummer, Kneser, and Kodaira [*Surfaces*] [*Mathematics*]
K_3	Menadione [*Vitamin K3*] (DAVI)
K4	Kayak, Four Person (ADA)
K_4	Menadiol Sodium Diphosphate [*Vitamin K4*] (DAVI)
K-5	Kindergarten-Fifth Grade (SAUO)
K9	Canine [*K9 Corps - Army Dogs*] [*World War II*]
K-10	Gastric Tube [*Medicine*] (STED)
K-12	Kindergarten through 12th Grade (WDAA)
K-12	Kindergarten-Twelfth Grade (WDAA)
K24H	Potassium, Urine 24 Hour [*Biochemistry*] (DAVI)
K-25	Oak Ridge Gaseous Diffusion Plant (SAUS)
K-25	Oak Ridge K-25 Site [*Department of Energy*] [*Oak Ridge, TN*] (GAAI)
K25	Oak Ridge Uranium Separation Plant [*Code designation*] (DEN)
K-25 Site	Oak Ridge K-25 Site (SAUO)
K_a	Acid Ionization Constant [*Physics*] (DAVI)
KA	Alkair [*Denmark*] [*ICAO designator*] (ICDA)
KA	Alkaline Phosphatase [*An enzyme*] (DAVI)
Ka	Auroral Absorption Index (CET)
KA	Australia [*IYRU nationality code*] (IYR)
Ka	Cathode [*Electron device*] (AAMN)
KA	Coastal Plains Commuter [*ICAO designator*] (AD)
KA	Concrete Arch [*Bridges*]
KA	Dragon Air Hong Kong (SAUS)
KA	Eha-Kibbuts ha-Artsi (BJA)
KA	HMS King Alfred [*British military*] (DMA)
KA	Kainic Acid [*Biochemistry*]
KA	Kaiser Engineering (SAUO)
Ka	Kallikrein (MEDA)
KA	Kamov [*Former USSR*] [*ICAO aircraft manufacturer identifier*] (ICAO)
Ka	Kaolinite [*A mineral*]
Ka	Karolus de Tocco [*Flourished, 13th century*] [*Authority cited in pre-1607 legal work*] (DSA)
KA	Kathode [*Cathode*] (AAG)
KA	Keratoacanthoma [*Dermatology*] (DAVI)
KA	Keren Ami (BJA)
KA	Keto Acid (DMAA)
KA	Ketoacidosis [*Medicine*]
KA	Ketoaciduria (MELL)
K/A	Ketogenic to Anti-Ketogenic [*Ratio*] [*In diets*]
KA	Keyed Address (IAA)
KA	Keyed Alike [*Locks*] (ADA)
KA	Kill Assessment [*Military*] (ACAE)
ka	Killed in Action
KA	Kilmarnock [*Postcode*] (ODBW)
kA	Kiloampere
KA	King-Armstrong Unit [*Clinical chemistry*]
KA	King of Arms
KA	King Pin Angle [*Automotive engineering*]
KA	Knight of St. Andrew [*Russia*] [*Obsolete*]
KA	Knight of the Order of Australia (WDAA)
K/A	Knights of the Altar (EA)
KA	Knolls Atomic Power Laboratory (SAUO)
K-A	Kuhlmann-Anderson Intelligence Tests [*Education*]
KA	Kuwait Airways Corp.
KA	Kynurenic Acid [*Biochemistry*] (OA)
KA	Kypriakes Aerogrammes [*Cyprus Airlines*]
KA	Thousands of Amperes
ka	thousands of year ago (SAUO)
ka	thousands of years (SAUO)
KAA	Asia Aero Survey & Consulting Engineers, Inc. [*Korea*] [*ICAO designator*] (FAAC)
Ka A	Kansas Appeals Reports [*A publication*] (DLA)
kaa	Karakalpak [*MARC language code*] [*Library of Congress*] (LCCP)
KAA	Karratha [*Australia*] [*Seismograph station code, US Geological Survey*] [*Closed*] (SEIS)
KAA	Kasama [*Zambia*] [*Airport symbol*] (OAG)
KAA	Keep-Alive Anode
KAAA	Kingman, AZ [*AM radio station call letters*]
KAAB	Batesville, AR [*AM radio station call letters*]
KAAC	Korean Association of Automatic Control (SAUO)
KAAD	Kerosene, Alcohol, Acetic Acid, and Dioxane (DMAA)
KAAH	Honolulu, HI [*Television station call letters*] (BROA)
KAAK	Great Falls, MT [*FM radio station call letters*]
KAAL	Austin, MN [*Television station call letters*]
KAAM	Huntsville, MO [*FM radio station call letters*]
KAAM	Plano, TX [*AM radio station call letters*] (RBYB)
KAAN	Bethany, MO [*AM radio station call letters*]
KAAN-FM	Bethany, MO [*FM radio station call letters*]
KAAO	Kabul [*Afghanistan*] [*Seismograph station code, US Geological Survey*] (SEIS)
KAAO	Korean Air Area of Operations (SAUO)
KAAP	Kansas Army Ammunition Plant (AABC)
KAAQ	Alliance, NE [*FM radio station call letters*]
KAAR	Butte, MT [*FM radio station call letters*]
KAAS	Keele Assessment of Auditory Style (DMAA)
KAAS	Salina, KS [*Television station call letters*]
KAAT	Oakhurst, CA [*FM radio station call letters*]
KAAX	Avenal, CA [*FM radio station call letters*]
KAAY	Little Rock, AR [*AM radio station call letters*]
KAb	Abilene Free Public Library, Abilene, KS [*Library symbol*] [*Library of Congress*] (LCLS)
KAB	Kabansk [*Former USSR*] [*Seismograph station code, US Geological Survey*] (SEIS)
Kab	Kabul (SAUO)
KAB	Kaneb Services [*NYSE symbol*] (TTSB)
KAB	Kaneb Services, Inc. [*NYSE symbol*] (SPSG)
KAB	Kariba Dam [*Zimbabwe*] [*Airport symbol*] (OAG)
KAB	Katholieke Arbeidersbeweging [*Netherlands*]
KAB	Keep America Beautiful (EA)
KAB	Knowledge, Attitudes, and Behavior Survey [*Department of Health and Human Services*] (GFGA)
KAB	Korean Accreditation Board (SAUO)
ka-band	0.8 cm wavelength radar (SAUS)
KABB	San Antonio, TX [*Television station call letters*]
K-ABC	Kaufman Assessment Battery for Children [*Diagnostic assessment test*] (PAZ)
KABC	Los Angeles, CA [*AM radio station call letters*]
KABCC	Korea Australia Business Cooperation Council
KABC-DT	Los Angeles, CA [*Television station call letters*] (BROA)
KABC-TV	Los Angeles, CA [*Television station call letters*]
KAbE	Dwight D. Eisenhower Library, Abilene, KS [*Library symbol*] [*Library of Congress*] (LCLS)
KABF	Little Rock, AR [*FM radio station call letters*]
KABG-FM	Los Alamos, NM [*FM radio station call letters*] (BROA)
KABH	Shawnee, OK [*FM radio station call letters*]
KABI	Abilene, KS [*AM radio station call letters*]
KABI	Abilene/Municipal [*Texas*] [*ICAO location identifier*] (ICLI)
KABINS	Knowledge, Attitude, Behavior, and Improvement in Nutritional Status (STED)
KABIR	Kapitalist Birokrat [*Capitalist Bureaucrat*] [*Term for foreigner*] [*Indonesia*]
KABK	Augusta, AR [*FM radio station call letters*]
KABL	Oakland, CA [*AM radio station call letters*]
KABLE	Kennedy Space Center Atmospheric Boundary Layer Experiment (ACAE)
KABN	Long Island, AK [*AM radio station call letters*]
KABO	Lewiston, MT [*Television station call letters*] (BROA)
KABPrA	Kaneb Svc Adj Rt A Pfd [*NYSE symbol*] (TTSB)
KABQ	Albuquerque/International [*New Mexico*] [*ICAO location identifier*] (ICLI)
KABQ	Albuquerque, NM [*AM radio station call letters*]
KABR	Alamo Community, NM [*AM radio station call letters*]
KABS	Great Falls, MT [*AM radio station call letters*]
KABU-FM	Fort Totten, ND [*FM radio station call letters*] (RBYB)
KABX	Merced, CA [*FM radio station call letters*]
KABY	Aberdeen, SD [*Television station call letters*]
kac	Kachin [*MARC language code*] [*Library of Congress*] (LCCP)
KAC	Kaman Aircraft Corporation (SAUO)
KAC	Kamishli [*Syria*] [*Airport symbol*] (AD)
KAC	Kanian Aircraft Corporation (SAUO)
KAC	Key Access Code (SAUO)
KAC	Kinetics and Catalysis
KAC	Knight Armament Co. (SAUO)
KAC	Komatsu America Corporation (SAUO)
KAC	Korean American Coalition (EA)

KAC .... Kuwait Airways Corp. [*ICAO designator*] (FAAC)
KACB .... San Angelo, TX [*Television station call letters*]
KACC .... Alvin, TX [*FM radio station call letters*]
KACC .... Kaiser Aluminum & Chemical Corporation (SAUO)
KACC .... Kansas Association of Community Colleges (SAUO)
KACC .... Korean-American Chamber of Commerce [*Later, AAACC*]
KACD .... Kansas Association of Soil Conservation Districts (SRA)
KACD .... Santa Monica, CA [*FM radio station call letters*]
KACE .... Inglewood, CA [*FM radio station call letters*]
KACEEE .... Kansas Advisory Council on Environmental Education (EDAC)
KACF .... Korean-American Cultural Foundation (EA)
KACH .... Preston, ID [*AM radio station call letters*]
KACHA .... Kentuckiana Automated Clearing House (TBD)
KACHAPAG.. Karlsruhe Charged Particle Group (NITA)
KACI .... The Dalles, OR [*AM radio station call letters*]
KACIA .... Korea-American Commerce and Industry Association [*Later, KS*]
KACI-FM ...... The Dalles, OR [*FM radio station call letters*]
KACK .... Nantucket [*Massachusetts*] [*ICAO location identifier*] (ICLI)
KACL-FM ..... Bismarck, ND [*FM radio station call letters*] (RBYB)
KACO-FM .... Ardmore, OK [*FM radio station call letters*] (RBYB)
KACP .... Custer, SD [*FM radio station call letters*]
KACP .... Kansas Association of Chiefs of Police (SRA)
KACQ .... Lometa, TX [*FM radio station call letters*] (RBYB)
KACS .... Chehalis, WA [*FM radio station call letters*]
KACT .... Andrews, TX [*AM radio station call letters*]
KACT .... Waco/Waco Municipal [*Texas*] [*ICAO location identifier*] (ICLI)
KACT-FM ..... Andrews, TX [*FM radio station call letters*]
KACTUS ...... Modelling Knowledge About Complex Technical Systems for Multiple Use (SAUO)
KACU .... Abilene, TX [*FM radio station call letters*]
KACV .... Amarillo, TX [*FM radio station call letters*]
KACV-TV ..... Amarillo, TX [*Television station call letters*]
KACW .... North Bend, OR [*FM radio station call letters*]
KACY .... Atlantic City/Atlantic City [*New Jersey*] [*ICAO location identifier*] (ICLI)
KACY .... Lafayette, LA [*AM radio station call letters*]
KAD .... Kadena Air Base, Ryuku Islands (NASA)
KAD .... Kadrey Energy [*Vancouver Stock Exchange symbol*]
KAD .... Kaduna [*Nigeria*] [*Airport symbol*] (OAG)
KAD .... Karad [*India*] [*Seismograph station code, US Geological Survey*] (SEIS)
KAD .... Kathmandu Association of Deaf (SAUO)
KAD .... Keyboard and Display [*Computer science*]
KADA .... Ada, OK [*AM radio station call letters*]
KADA .... Kemubu Agricultural Development Authority (SAUO)
KADA .... Kemuta Agricultural Development Authority (SAUO)
KADA-FM ..... Ada, OK [*FM radio station call letters*]
KADD .... Laughlin, NV [*FM radio station call letters*]
KADE .... San Luis Obispo, CA [*Television station call letters*]
KaDeWe ...... Kaufhaus des Westens [*Department Store of the West*] [*Germany*]
KADF .... Kuwait Air Defense Force (MCD)
KADI .... Republic, MO [*FM radio station call letters*]
KADM .... Ardmore [*Oklahoma*] [*ICAO location identifier*] (ICLI)
KADM .... Odessa, TX [*FM radio station call letters*]
KADN .... Lafayette, LA [*Television station call letters*]
KADOS .... Knowledge-Based Automated Design of Silencers [*Automotive engineering*]
KADP .... Kaduna State Agricultural Development Project [*Nigeria*] (ECON)
KADQ .... Rexburg, ID [*FM radio station call letters*]
KADR .... Elkader, IA [*AM radio station call letters*]
KADS .... Elk City, OK [*AM radio station call letters*]
KADS .... Kabul Amateur Dramatic Society (SAUO)
KADS .... Knowledge Acquisition and Documentation System (VLIE)
KADS .... Knowledge Acquisition Data System (SAUS)
KADS .... Korea Air Defense System (CINC)
KADSE .... Korean Air Defense Sector (SAUO)
KADSE .... Knowledge Assisted Decision Support Environment
KADU .... Hibbing, MN [*FM radio station call letters*]
KADU .... Kenya African Democratic Union [*Political party*] (PPW)
KADV .... Modesto, CA [*FM radio station call letters*]
KADW .... Camp Springs/Andrews Air Force Base [*Maryland*] [*ICAO location identifier*] (ICLI)
KADX .... Houston, AK [*FM radio station call letters*]
KADY .... Oxnard, CA [*Television station call letters*]
KAE .... Kaena [*Hawaii*] [*Seismograph station code, US Geological Survey*] (SEIS)
KAE .... Kake [*Alaska*] [*Airport symbol*] (OAG)
KAE .... Keighley Association of Engineers (SAUO)
KAE .... Kinesthetic Aftereffect (DIPS)
KAE .... Knitting Arts Expo (TSPED)
KAEA .... Korean Association of Electronics and Automation (SAUO)
KAEC .... Kentucky Association of Electric Cooperatives (SRA)
KAECT .... Kansas Association for Educational Communications & Technology
KAEDS .... Keystone Association for Educational Data Systems (HGAA)
KAEF .... Arcata, CA [*Television station call letters*]
KAEH .... Beaumont, CA [*FM radio station call letters*]
KAEH .... King Air Equivalent Hours (SAUS)
KAEP .... Spokane, WA [*FM radio station call letters*] (RBYB)
KAERI .... Korean Atomic Energy Research Institute (SAUO)
KAESP .... Kansas Association of Elementary School Principals (SAUO)
KAET .... Phoenix, AZ [*Television station call letters*]
KAEX .... Alexandria/England Air Force Base [*Louisiana*] [*ICAO location identifier*] (ICLI)
KAEZ .... Amarillo, TX [*FM radio station call letters*]
KAF .... Conglutinogen Activating Factor [*Medicine*] (MELL)

KAF .... Kafue International Air Services Ltd. [*Zambia*] [*FAA designator*] (FAAC)
KAF .... Karato [*Papua New Guinea*] [*Airport symbol*] (OAG)
KAF .... Kazakhstan Air Force (SAUO)
KAF .... Kenya Air Force
KAF .... Khmer [*Cambodia*] Air Force (VNW)
KAF .... Killer-Assistng Factor (DAVI)
KAF .... Kinase-Activating Factor [*Organic chemistry*] (DAVI)
KAF .... Kuwaiti Air Force (DOMA)
KAFAD .... Kuwait Air Force & Air Defence (SAUO)
KAFB .... Keesler Air Force Base [*Mississippi*]
KAFB .... Kirtland Air Force Base [*New Mexico*]
KAFC .... Kenny Antcliff Fan Club (EA)
KAFC-FM ..... Anchorage, AK [*FM radio station call letters*] (BROA)
KAFE .... Bellingham, WA [*FM radio station call letters*]
KAFF .... Flagstaff, AZ [*AM radio station call letters*]
KAFF-FM ..... Flagstaff, AZ [*FM radio station call letters*]
KAFFR .... Kaffaria [*South Africa*] (ROG)
Kaff R .... Kaffrarian Rifles (SAUO)
KAFH .... Ku-Band Antenna Feed Horn
KAFN-FM ..... Gould, AR [*FM radio station call letters*] (BROA)
KAFO .... Knee-Ankle-Foot Orthosis [*Medicine*]
KAFP .... Kansas Academy of Family Physicians (SRA)
KAFP .... Kentucky Academy of Family Physicians (SRA)
KAFR .... Angel Fire, NM [*FM radio station call letters*]
KAFT .... Fayetteville, AR [*Television station call letters*]
KAFU .... Enid, OK [*Television station call letters*]
KAFW .... Wilson, AR [*FM radio station call letters*] (RBYB)
KAFX-FM ..... Diboll, TX [*FM radio station call letters*]
KAFY .... Bakersfield, CA [*AM radio station call letters*]
KAG .... Cryptographic Aid, General Publication (CET)
KAG .... Kagoshima [*Japan*] [*Seismograph station code, US Geological Survey*] (SEIS)
KAG .... Kagoshima Space Center [*Japan*]
KAG .... Kelvin Astatic Galvanometer [*Electronics*]
KAGA .... Santa Ynez, CA [*FM radio station call letters*]
KAGC .... Bryan, TX [*AM radio station call letters*]
KAGE .... Winona, MN [*AM radio station call letters*]
KAGE-FM ..... Winona, MN [*FM radio station call letters*]
KAGG .... Madisonville, TX [*FM radio station call letters*]
KAGH .... Crossett, AR [*AM radio station call letters*]
KAGH-FM..... Crossett, AR [*FM radio station call letters*]
KAGI .... Grants Pass, OR [*AM radio station call letters*]
KAGI .... Kesatuan Aksi Guru Indonesia [*Action Front of Indonesian Teachers*]
KAGJ .... Ephraim, UT [*FM radio station call letters*]
KAGL .... El Dorado, AR [*FM radio station call letters*] (RBYB)
KAGM .... Strasburg, CO [*FM radio station call letters*]
KAGO .... Klamath Falls, OR [*AM radio station call letters*]
KAGO-FM..... Klamath Falls, OR [*FM radio station call letters*]
KAGP .... Grants, NM [*FM radio station call letters*]
KAGR .... Bemidji, MN [*Television station call letters*] (BROA)
KAGR .... Morro Bay, CA [*FM radio station call letters*] (RBYB)
KAGU .... Spokane, WA [*FM radio station call letters*]
KAGY .... Port Sulphur, LA [*AM radio station call letters*]
KAH .... Keilschrifttexte aus Assur Historischen Inhalts [*A publication*] (BJA)
KAH .... Kent Aviation Ltd. [*Canada*] [*ICAO designator*] (FAAC)
KAH .... Kiloampere Hour (IAA)
KAHF-FM ..... Ortonville, MN [*FM radio station call letters*] (RBYB)
KAHI .... Auburn, CA [*AM radio station call letters*]
KAHI .... Keilschrifttexte aus Assur Historischen Inhalts [*A publication*] (BJA)
KAHK-FM ..... Georgetown, TX [*FM radio station call letters*] (BROA)
Kahler .... Kahler Corp. [*Associated Press*] (SAG)
KAHM .... Prescott, AZ [*FM radio station call letters*]
KAHO .... Junction, TX [*FM radio station call letters*]
KAHP .... Kentucky Allied Health Project (EDAC)
KAHR .... Poplar Bluff, MO [*FM radio station call letters*]
KAHRP........ Knob-Associated Histidine-Rich Protein [*Cytology*]
KAHS .... Thousand Oaks, CA [*AM radio station call letters*] (RBYB)
KAHSLC ...... Knoxville Area Health Science Consortium [*Library network*]
KAHTAFU .... Kenya African National Traders and Farmers Union (SAUO)
KAHU .... Hilo, HI [*AM radio station call letters*]
KAHX-FM ..... Ingleside, TX [*FM radio station call letters*] (RBYB)
KAHY .... Myrtle Point, OR [*FM radio station call letters*]
KAHZ .... Fort Worth, TX [*AM radio station call letters*]
KAI .... Kaieteur [*Guyana*] [*Airport symbol*] (OAG)
KAI .... Kaimata [*New Zealand*] [*Seismograph station code, US Geological Survey*] (SEIS)
KAI .... Kanaanaeische und Aramaeische Inschriften [*A publication*] (BJA)
KAI .... Kazan Aviation Institute
KAI .... Keep America Independent [*Defunct*] (EA)
KAI .... Korean Affairs Institute (EA)
KAI .... Kurzweil Applied Intelligence [*Computer science*]
KAIC .... Komatsu America Industries Corporation (SAUO)
KAICA .... Korea Auto Industries Cooperation Association (SAUO)
KAID .... Boise, ID [*Television station call letters*]
KAIE .... Honolulu, HI [*Television station call letters*] (BROA)
KAIG .... Kearfott Acceleration Integrating Gyroscope
KAIGBZ ...... Japanese Journal of Nuclear Medicine (journ.) (SAUS)
KAIH .... Jacksboro, TX [*FM radio station call letters*] (RBYB)
KAII .... Kiddie Academy International, Inc. [*NASDAQ symbol*] (SAG)
KAII .... Kiddie Academy Intl [*NASDAQ symbol*] (TTSB)
KAII .... Wailuku, HI [*Television station call letters*]
KAIIW .... Kiddie Academy Intl Wrrt [*NASDAQ symbol*] (TTSB)
KAIL .... Fresno, CA [*Television station call letters*]
KAIM .... Honolulu, HI [*AM radio station call letters*]

KAIM-FM	Honolulu, HI [*FM radio station call letters*]
KAIMH	Kansas Association for Infant Mental Health (SAUO)
KAIN	Vidalia, LA [*AM radio station call letters*]
KAIO	Rio Grande City, TX [*Television station call letters*] (BROA)
KAIR-AM	Atchison, KS [*AM radio station call letters*] (RBYB)
KAIRE	Ecumenical Group of Women (SAUO)
KAIR-FM	Horton, KS [*FM radio station call letters*] (RBYB)
KAIS	Korean Air Intelligence System (MCD)
KaisA	Kaiser Aluminum & Chemical Corp. [*Associated Press*] (SAG)
KaisAl	Kaiser Aluminum & Chemical Corp. [*Associated Press*] (SAG)
KAIST	Korea Advanced Institute of Science and Technology [*Seoul*] [*Information service or system*] (IID)
KaisVent	Kaiser Ventures, Inc. [*Associated Press*] (SAG)
KAIT	Jonesboro, AR [*Television station call letters*]
KAIT	Katzman Automatic Imaging Telescope [*University of California*]
KAIT	Kaufman Adolescent and Adult Intelligence Test (DIPS)
KAIU-FM	Grants, NM [*FM radio station call letters*] (BROA)
KAJ	Kajaani [*Finland*] [*Airport symbol*] (OAG)
KAJ	Kashiwara [*Japan*] [*Seismograph station code, US Geological Survey*] (SEIS)
KAJ	Keilschrifttexte aus Assur Juridischen Inhalts [*A publication*] (BJA)
KAJA	San Antonio, TX [*FM radio station call letters*]
KAJB	Calipatria, CA [*Television station call letters*] (BROA)
KAJF	Kids Against Junk Food [*An association*] (EA)
KAJI	Keilschrifttexte aus Assur Juridischen Inhalts [*A publication*] (BJA)
KAJI	Point Comfort, TX [*FM radio station call letters*] (RBYB)
KAJK	Fortuna, CA [*AM radio station call letters*]
KAJK-FM	Ferndale, CA [*FM radio station call letters*]
KAJL	Winters, TX [*FM radio station call letters*] (RBYB)
KAJN	Crowley, LA [*FM radio station call letters*]
KAJO	Grants Pass, OR [*AM radio station call letters*]
KAJP	Firebaugh, CA [*FM radio station call letters*] (RBYB)
KAJQ	Sibley, IA [*FM radio station call letters*] (RBYB)
KAJW	Tolleson, AZ [*Television station call letters*] (RBYB)
KAJX	Aspen, CO [*FM radio station call letters*]
KAJZ-FM	Killeen, TX [*FM radio station call letters*] (RBYB)
KAK	Kakioka [*Japan*] [*Seismograph station code, US Geological Survey*] (SEIS)
KAK	Key-Auto-Key [*Computer science*]
KAK	Kungliga Automobil Klubben
KAKA-FM	Salina, KS [*FM radio station call letters*] (BROA)
KAKC	Tulsa, OK [*AM radio station call letters*]
KAKD	Eureka, CA [*FM radio station call letters*] (RBYB)
KAKE	Wichita, KS [*Television station call letters*]
KAKJ	Marianna, AR [*FM radio station call letters*]
KAKM	Anchorage, AK [*Television station call letters*]
kakm	Kakemono (VRA)
KAKN	Naknek, AK [*FM radio station call letters*]
KAKO	Gooding, ID [*FM radio station call letters*] (RBYB)
KAKP	Bagdad, AZ [*FM radio station call letters*] (RBYB)
KAKP-FM	Chino Valley, AZ [*FM radio station call letters*] (BROA)
KAKQ	Fairbanks, AK [*FM radio station call letters*]
KAKQ-FM	Fairbanks, AK [*FM radio station call letters*]
KAKR	Akron [*Ohio*] [*ICAO location identifier*] (ICLI)
KAKR-FM	Sterling City, TX [*FM radio station call letters*] (RBYB)
KAKT-FM	Phoenix, OR [*FM radio station call letters*] (RBYB)
KAKU-FM	Springfield, MO [*FM radio station call letters*] (RBYB)
KAKV-FM	Lompoc, CA [*FM radio station call letters*] (RBYB)
KAKW	Kileen, TX [*TV station call letters*] (RBYB)
KAKX	Mendocino, CA [*FM radio station call letters*] (RBYB)
KAKZ	Juneau, AK [*FM radio station call letters*] (RBYB)
KAL	Caltech Data Ltd. [*Vancouver Stock Exchange symbol*]
KAL	Kalamazoo [*Diocesan abbreviation*] [*Michigan*] (TOCD)
KAL	Kalamein [*Trademark*]
KAL	Kalendae [*The Kalends*] [*First day of the ancient Roman month*]
Kal	Kalium [*Potassium*] (STED)
KAL	Kalium [*Potassium*] [*Pharmacy*]
Kal	Kallah (BJA)
KAL	Kallmann [*Syndrome*] [*Medicine*] (DMAA)
KAL	Kalocsa [*Hungary*] [*Seismograph station code, US Geological Survey*] [*Closed*] (SEIS)
KAL	Kaltag [*Alaska*] [*Airport symbol*] (OAG)
KAL	Kappa Application Language [*Artificial intelligence system*] [*IntelliCorp*] (PCM)
KAL	Key Assets List (COE)
KAL	Keywords and Learning (AIE)
KAL	Korean Air Lines Co. Ltd. [*ICAO designator*] (FAAC)
KAL	Korean Air Lines, Inc.
KALA	Davenport, IA [*FM radio station call letters*]
KALB	Albany/Albany [*New York*] [*ICAO location identifier*] (ICLI)
KALB-TV	Alexandria, LA [*Television station call letters*]
KALC	Denver, CO [*FM radio station call letters*]
KALC	Krypton Absorption in Liquid Carbon Dioxide [*Nuclear energy*] (NRCH)
KALCC	Korean Airlift Control Center (SAUO)
KALD	Kalamein [*Trademark*] Door
KALDAS	Kidsgrove ALGOL [*Algorithmic Language*] Digital Analogue Simulation [*Computer science*] [*British*]
KALE	Richland, WA [*AM radio station call letters*]
KALF	Red Bluff, CA [*FM radio station call letters*]
KALG	Chadron, NE [*FM radio station call letters*] (RBYB)
KALI	Alice/International [*Texas*] [*ICAO location identifier*] (ICLI)
KALI	San Gabriel, CA [*AM radio station call letters*]
KALI-FM	Santa Ana, CA [*FM radio station call letters*] (RBYB)
KALK	Winfield, TX [*FM radio station call letters*]

KALL	Salt Lake City, UT [*AM radio station call letters*]
KALM	Thayer, MO [*AM radio station call letters*]
KALN	Iola, KS [*AM radio station call letters*]
KALO	Port Arthur, TX [*AM radio station call letters*]
KALP	Alpine, TX [*FM radio station call letters*]
KAL PPT	Kali Praeparatum [*Prepared Kali*] [*Carbonate of potash*] [*Pharmacy*] (ROG)
KALQ	Alamosa, CO [*FM radio station call letters*]
KALR	Hot Springs, AR [*FM radio station call letters*]
KalR	Kallah Rabbati (BJA)
KALS	Kalispell, MT [*FM radio station call letters*]
KALT	Atlanta, TX [*AM radio station call letters*]
KALT-FM	Alturas, CA [*FM radio station call letters*] (BROA)
KALU	Langston, OK [*FM radio station call letters*]
KALV	Alva, OK [*AM radio station call letters*]
KALW	San Francisco, CA [*FM radio station call letters*]
KALX	Berkeley, CA [*FM radio station call letters*]
KALY	Los Ranchos de Albuquerque, NM [*AM radio station call letters*]
KALZ-FM	Fresno, CA [*FM radio station call letters*] (BROA)
KAM	Benedictine College, South Campus, Atchison, KS [*Library symbol*] [*Library of Congress*] (LCLS)
KAM	Kamaran Island [*South Arabia (Yemen)*] [*Airport symbol*] (AD)
kam	Kamba [*MARC language code*] [*Library of Congress*] (LCCP)
Kam	Kames' Dictionary of Decisions, Scotch Court of Session [*A publication*] (DLA)
Kam	Kames' Remarkable Decisions, Scotch Court of Session [*2 vols.*] [*1716-52*] [*A publication*] (DLA)
KAM	Kameyama [*Japan*] [*Seismograph station code, US Geological Survey*] (SEIS)
KAM	Kansas Association of Mappers (SAUO)
KAM	Kaupapa Atawhai Manager (SAUO)
KAM	Keep-Alive Memory [*Computer science*]
KAM	Kehillath Anshe Mayriv (BJA)
KAM	Kenya African Movement
KAM	Keyboard Attach Machine [*Computer science*] (TIMI)
KAM	Kinematic Analysis Method
KAM	Knudsen Absolute Manometer [*Physics*]
KAM	Kolmogorov-Arnold-Moser [*Statistical mechanics*]
KAMA	Amarillo/Amarillo Air Terminal [*Texas*] [*ICAO location identifier*] (ICLI)
KAMA	El Paso, TX [*AM radio station call letters*]
KAMA	Korean-American Medical Association (EA)
Kaman	Kaman Corp. [*Associated Press*] (SAG)
KAMB	Merced, CA [*FM radio station call letters*]
KAMC	Komatsu America Manufacturing Corp. [*Chattanooga, TN*]
KAMC	Lubbock, TX [*Television station call letters*]
KAMD	Camden, AR [*AM radio station call letters*]
KAMD-FM	Camden, AR [*FM radio station call letters*] (RBYB)
KAME	Reno, NV [*Television station call letters*]
Kam Eluc	Kames' Elucidation of the Laws of Scotland [*A publication*] (DLA)
Kam Eq	Kames' Principles of Equity [*A publication*] (DLA)
Kames	Kames' Dictionary of Decisions, Scotch Court of Session [*A publication*] (DLA)
Kames	Kames' Remarkable Decisions, Scotch Court of Session [*2 vols.*] [*1716-52*] [*A publication*] (DLA)
Kames Dec...	Kames' Dictionary of Decisions, Scotch Court of Session [*A publication*] (DLA)
Kames Dict Dec...	Kames' Dictionary of Decisions, Scotch Court of Session [*A publication*] (DLA)
Kames Elucid...	Kames' Elucidation of the Laws of Scotland [*A publication*] (DLA)
Kames Eq	Kames' Principles of Equity [*A publication*] (DLA)
Kames Rem...	Kames' Remarkable Decisions, Scotch Court of Session [*2 vols.*] [*1716-52*] [*A publication*] (DLA)
Kames Rem Dec...	Kames' Remarkable Decisions [*Scotland*] [*A publication*] (DLA)
Kames Sel Dec...	Kames' Select Decisions [*Scotland*] [*A publication*] (DLA)
KAMFES	Kentucky Association of Milk, Food, and Environmental Sanitarians (SRA)
KAMFR	Kinesthetic Application of Mechanical Force Reflection
KAMFT	Kansas Association of Marriage and Family Therapy (SRA)
KAMFT	Kentucky Association for Marriage and Family Therapy (SRA)
KAMG	Victoria, TX [*AM radio station call letters*]
KAMI	Cozad, NE [*AM radio station call letters*]
KAMI	Kasatuan Aksi Mahasiswa Indonesia [*Political party*] (BARN)
KAMI-FM	Cozad, NE [*FM radio station call letters*]
KAMJ	Gosnell, AR [*FM radio station call letters*] (RBYB)
KAMK	National Council for Quality and Accreditation (SAUO)
KAMK-FM	Forest City, IA [*FM radio station call letters*] (RBYB)
KAML	Gillette, WY [*FM radio station call letters*]
KAML	Kenedy-Karnes City, TX [*AM radio station call letters*]
KamLAND	Kamioka Liquid Scintillator Anti-Neutrino Detector
Kam L Tr	Kames' Historical Law Tracts [*Scotland*] [*A publication*] (DLA)
KAMM	Karlsruhe Atmospheric Mesoscale Model (SAUO)
KAMM	Madison, SD [*FM radio station call letters*] (RBYB)
KAMN	Kaman Corp. [*NASDAQ symbol*] (NQ)
KAMNA	Kaman Corp. Cl'A' [*NASDAQ symbol*] (TTSB)
KAMNZ	Kaman Cp $3.25 Ser 2 Cv Dep Pfd [*NASDAQ symbol*] (TTSB)
KAMO	Korean Airlift Management Office (SAUO)
KAMO	Rogers, AR [*AM radio station call letters*]
KAMO-FM	Rogers, AR [*FM radio station call letters*]
KAMP..........	El Centro, CA [*AM radio station call letters*]
KAMQ	Carlsbad, NM [*AM radio station call letters*]
KAMR	Amarillo, TX [*Television station call letters*]
Kam Rem	Kames' Remarkable Decisions, Scotch Court of Session [*2 vols.*] [*1716-52*] [*A publication*] (DLA)
KAMS	Korea Ammunition Management System (MCD)
KAMS	Mammoth Spring, AR [*FM radio station call letters*]

Kam Sel	Kames' Select Decisions [Scotland] [A publication] (DLA)
Kam Sel Dec	Kames' Select Decisions [Scotland] [A publication] (DLA)
KAMT	Juneau, AK [FM radio station call letters] (RBYB)
KAMT	Keeping Abreast of Medical Transcription (SAUO)
KAMU	College Station, TX [FM radio station call letters]
KAMU-TV	College Station, TX [Television station call letters]
KAMX	Luling, TX [FM radio station call letters] (RBYB)
KAMY	Lubbock, TX [FM radio station call letters]
KAN	Kanazawa [Japan] [Seismograph station code, US Geological Survey] (SEIS)
kan	Kannada [MARC language code] [Library of Congress] (LCCP)
KAN	Kano [Nigeria] [Airport symbol] (OAG)
Kan	Kansas (ODBW)
KAN	Kansas
Kan	Kansas Power & Light Co. (SAUO)
Kan	Kansas Supreme Court Reports [A publication] (DLA)
Kan	Kantorei [Record label] [Germany]
KAN	Kriegsausruestungsnachweisung [Table of Basic Allowances] [German military - World War II]
KANA	Kamut Association of North America (NTPA)
Kan Admin Regs	Kansas Administration Regulations [A publication] (DLA)
Kan Ann	Vernon's Kansas Statutes, Annotated [A publication] (DLA)
Kan App	Kansas Appeals Reports [A publication] (DLA)
Kanb	Kaneb Services, Inc. [Associated Press] (SAG)
Kan City L Rep	Kansas City Law Reporter [A publication] (DLA)
Kan City L Rev	Kansas City Law Review [A publication] (DLA)
Kan Civ Pro Stat Ann	Vernon's Kansas Statutes, Annotated, Code of Civil Procedure [A publication] (DLA)
Kan Civ Pro Stat Ann (Vernon)	Vernon's Kansas Statutes, Annotated, Code of Civil Procedure [A publication] (DLA)
Kan CL & IWC	Kansas Commission of Labor and Industry Workmen's Compensation Department Reports [A publication] (DLA)
Kan CL Rep	Kansas City Law Reporter [A publication] (DLA)
Kan Crim Code & Code of Crim Proc	Criminal Code and Code of Criminal Procedure [Kansas] [A publication] (DLA)
Kan Crim Code & Code of Crim Proc (Vernon)	Vernon's Kansas Statutes, Annotated, Criminal Code and Code of Criminal Procedure [A publication] (DLA)
Kan Ct App	Kansas Appellate Reports [A publication] (DLA)
KAND	Corsicana, TX [AM radio station call letters]
K & B	Kotze and Barber's Transvaal (High Court) Reports [1885-88] [A publication] (DLA)
K & B Dig	Kerford and Box's Victorian Digest [A publication] (DLA)
K & CL	Kensington and Chelsea Law Group [British]
K & D	Kitchen and Dining Room [Real estate terminology]
K & E Conv	Key and Elphinstone's Conveyancing [15th ed.] [1953-54] [A publication] (DLA)
K & F NSW	Knox and Fitzhardinge's New South Wales Reports [A publication] (DLA)
K & G	Keane and Grant's English Registration Appeal Cases [1854-62] [A publication] (DLA)
K & G	Kerbing and Guttering [British] (ADA)
K & Gr	Keane and Grant's English Registration Appeal Cases [1854-62] [A publication] (DLA)
K & GRC	Keane and Grant's English Registration Appeal Cases [1854-62] [A publication] (DLA)
K&H	Memory Time Value (SAUS)
KANDIDATS	Kansas Digital Data System
KANDIDATS	Kansas Digital Image Data System (SAUO)
KANDIDATS	University of Kansas Landsat Software System (SAUO)
Kan Dig	Hatcher's Kansas Digest [A publication] (DLA)
K & J	Kay and Johnson's English Vice-Chancellors' Reports [69, 70 English Reprint] [A publication] (DLA)
K & J	Kenrick & Jefferson (DGA)
K & O	Knapp and Ombler's English Election Cases [A publication] (DLA)
K & R	Kent and Radcliff's Law of New York, Revision of 1801 [A publication] (DLA)
K&R	Kernighan & Ritchie (VLIE)
K&R	Kernighan + Ritchie (SAUO)
K and R	Kidnaping and Ransom [Insurance policy]
K&SEAFA	Korea and South East Asia Forces Association of Australia (SAUO)
K & W	Kames and Woodhouselee's Folio Dictionary, Scotch Court of Session [A publication] (DLA)
K & W Dic	Kames and Woodhouselee's Folio Dictionary, Scotch Court of Session [A publication] (DLA)
K & Z	Kipp and Zonen Recorders
KANE	New Iberia, LA [AM radio station call letters]
Kaneb	Kaneb Services, Inc. [Associated Press] (SAG)
Kanex	Kansai Agricultural Commodities Exchange (NUMA)
KANGA	Kangaroo (DSUE)
KANG-FM	Carrington, ND [FM radio station call letters] (RBYB)
KANG-FM	lake Havasu City, AZ [FM radio station call letters] (BROA)
KANI	Wharton, TX [AM radio station call letters]
KANJ-FM	Giddings, TX [FM radio station call letters] (RBYB)
KankakB	Kankakkee Bancorp, Inc. [Associated Press] (SAG)
KANL	Elko, NV [Television station call letters] (RBYB)
Kan Law	Kansas Lawyer [A publication] (DLA)
Kan LJ	Kansas Law Journal [A publication] (DLA)
KANM	Modesto, CA [AM radio station call letters] (BROA)
KANM	Winnemucca, NV [Television station call letters] (RBYB)
KANN	Kentucky Nurses Association (SAUO)
KANN	Roy, UT [AM radio station call letters]
KANO-FM	Hilo, HI [FM radio station call letters] (BROA)
KANP	St. Charles, MN [FM radio station call letters] (RBYB)
KanPip	Kaneb Pipe Line Partners Ltd. [Associated Press] (SAG)
KanPipSn	Kaneb Pipe Line Partners LP [Associated Press] (SAG)
KANQ	Grand Marais, MN [FM radio station call letters] (RBYB)
KANR	Belle Plaine, KS [FM radio station call letters]
KANr	Kanamycin Resistant [Genetics]
KANS	Kansas (AFM)
Kans	Kansas (ODBW)
Kans	Kansas Reports [A publication] (DLA)
KANS	Larned, KS [AM radio station call letters]
KANS	Osage City, KS [FM radio station call letters] (RBYB)
Kans App	Kansas Appeals Reports [A publication] (DLA)
Kansas LJ	Kansas Law Journal [A publication] (DLA)
Kansas R	Kansas Reports [A publication] (DLA)
Kans BA	Kansas City Bar Journal [A publication] (DLA)
Kan SCC	Kansas State Corporation Commission Reports [A publication] (DLA)
Kansenshogaku Zasshi	Kansenshogaku Zasshi. Journal of the Japanese Association for Infectious Diseases (SAUO)
Kan Sess Laws	Session Laws of Kansas [A publication] (DLA)
Kans R	Kansas Reports [A publication] (DLA)
Kans St U	Kansas State University of Agriculture and Applied Science (GAGS)
Kan Stat	Kansas Statutes [A publication] (DLA)
Kan Stat Ann	Kansas Statutes Annotated [A publication] (AAGC)
Kan St LJ	Kansas State Law Journal [A publication] (DLA)
Kan Subject Ann Vernon's	Vernon's Kansas Statutes, Annotated [A publication] (DLA)
KANT	Roseau, MN [FM radio station call letters] (RBYB)
KANU	Kenya African National Union [Political party] (PPW)
KANU	Lawrence, KS [FM radio station call letters]
Kan UCC Ann (Vernon)	Vernon's Kansas Statutes, Annotated, Uniform Commercial Code [A publication] (DLA)
Kan U Lawy	Kansas University Lawyer [A publication] (DLA)
Kan Univ Lawy	Kansas University Lawyer [A publication] (DLA)
KANW	Albuquerque, NM [FM radio station call letters]
KANX-FM	Pine Bluff, AR [FM radio station call letters] (RBYB)
KANZ	Garden City, KS [FM radio station call letters]
KANZUS	Korea, Australia, New Zealand, and the United States
kao	Kaolin (BARN)
KAO	Kappa Alpha Order
KAO	Kinesthetic Anharmonic Oscillator [Facetious term for a swing]
KAO	Kirtland Area Office [Department of Energy]
KAO	Knee-Ankle Orthosis [Medicine] (DAVI)
KAO	Knights of Aquarius Order (EAIO)
KAO	Kuiper Airborne Observatory [NASA]
KAO	Kuusamo [Finland] [Airport symbol] (OAG)
KAOA EXP STN	New Orleans, LA [Radio expansion station] (RBYB)
KAOB	Devils Lake, ND [FM radio station call letters] (RBYB)
KAOC	Cavalier, ND [FM radio station call letters] (RBYB)
KAOD	Babbitt, MN [FM radio station call letters] (RBYB)
KAOE	Hilo, HI [FM radio station call letters]
KAOG	Jonesboro, AR [FM radio station call letters] (RBYB)
KAOH-FM	Lompoc, CA [FM radio station call letters] (RBYB)
KAOI	Kihei, HI [AM radio station call letters]
KAOI-FM	Wailuku, HI [FM radio station call letters]
KAOK	Lake Charles, LA [AM radio station call letters]
KAOL	Carrollton, MO [AM radio station call letters]
KAOM	Kansas Association of Osteopathic Medicine (SRA)
KAON	Canadian high energy physics project (SAUO)
KAOR	Vermillion, SD [FM radio station call letters]
KAOS	Killer as an Organized Sport [Campus game]
KAOS	Olympia, WA [FM radio station call letters]
KAOW-FM	Fort Smith, AR [FM radio station call letters] (RBYB)
KAOX-FM	Kemmerer, WY [FM radio station call letters] (RBYB)
KAOY	Kealakekua, HI [FM radio station call letters]
KAP	CapMAC Holdings [NYSE symbol] (SAG)
KAP	Hyannis Air Service, Inc. [ICAO designator] (FAAC)
KAP	Kaphearst Resources [Vancouver Stock Exchange symbol]
KAP	Keyboard Automation Program [Computer science] (TIMI)
KAP	Khalistan Armed Police (SAUO)
KAP	Kids Against Pollution
KAP	Kinematical Analysis Program
KAP	Knowledge, Aptitudes, and Practices [Fertility] (STED)
KAP	Knowledge, Attitudes, and Practice [Sociology]
KAP	Kuwait Action Plan [Advisory Committee on Pollution of the Sea]
KAPA	Kaneohe, HI [TV station call letters] (RBYB)
KAPA	Potassium Aminopropylamide [Organic chemistry]
KAPB	Marksville, LA [AM radio station call letters]
KAPB-FM	Marksville, LA [FM radio station call letters]
KAPC-FM	Butte, MT [FM radio station call letters] (RBYB)
KAPCS	Kansas Association of Private Career Schools (SRA)
KAPE	Cape Girardeau, MO [AM radio station call letters]
KAPE	Kansas Association of Public Employees (SRA)
KAPE	Keeping the Army in the Public Eye [British military] (DMA)
KAPES	Knowledge-Aided Process Planning and Estimation (VLIE)
KAPF-FM	Taos, NM [FM radio station call letters] (RBYB)
KAPG	Kluwer Academic Publishers Group (SAUO)
KAPI	Kasatuan Aksi Peladjar Indonesia [Political party] (BARN)
KAPI-FM	Ruston, LA [FM radio station call letters] (RBYB)
KAPK-FM	Grants Pass, OR [FM radio station call letters] (RBYB)
KAPL	Kaplan Industries Inc. (SAUO)
KAPL	Kennedy Approved Parts List [NASA] (KSC)
KAPL	Knolls Atomic Power Laboratory [Schenectady, NY] [Department of Energy]
KAPL	KSC Approved Parts List (SAUS)
KAPL	Phoenix, OR [AM radio station call letters] (RBYB)
K-APM	Kennedy Space Center Automated Payloads Plan/Requirement (NAKS)

K-APM	KSC Automated Payloads Plan/Requirement (SAUS)
KAPM-FM	Alexandria, LA [*FM radio station call letters*] (RBYB)
KAPMO	Kent Apple and Pear Marketing Organization (SAUO)
K-APN	KSC [*Kennedy Space Center*] Automated Payloads Notice [*NASA*] (NASA)
KAPN	Salt Lake City, UT [*AM radio station call letters*]
KAPO	Kameradschaftpolizei (BJA)
KAPP	Key Asset Protection Plan [*National Guard*] (INF)
KAPP	Kimberley Aboriginal Pastoralists Project (SAUO)
KAPP	Knolls Atomic Power Plant
KAPP	Yakima, WA [*Television station call letters*]
KAPPA	Kappa Networks, Inc. (SAUO)
KAPPA	Kappa Site (SAUO)
K-APPS	KSC [*Kennedy Space Center*] Automated Payloads Project Specification [*NASA*] (NASA)
KAPR	Douglas, AZ [*AM radio station call letters*]
KAPS	Kawasaki Automatic Power-Drive System [*Kawasaki Motors Corp.*]
KAPS	Kentucky Association of Land Surveyors (SAUO)
KAPS	Kuopio Atherosclerosis Prevention Study
KAPS	Mount Vernon, WA [*AM radio station call letters*]
KAPSE	Kernel Ada Programming Support Environment (SAUO)
KAPSE	Kernel APSE [*ADA Program Support Environment*] [*Computer science*]
KapsnSn	Kapson Senior Quarters Corp. [*Associated Press*] (SAG)
KAPU-FM	Amarillo, TX [*FM radio station call letters*] (RBYB)
KAPV-FM	Elma, WA [*FM radio station call letters*] (RBYB)
KAPWA	Kite Aerial Photography Worldwide Association (SAUO)
KAPY	Port Angeles, WA [*AM radio station call letters*]
KAPZ	Bald Knob, AR [*AM radio station call letters*]
KAQA-FM	Kilauea, HI [*FM radio station call letters*] (RBYB)
KAQD-FM	Abilene, TX [*FM radio station call letters*] (RBYB)
KAQE-FM	St. Martinville, LA [*FM radio station call letters*] (RBYB)
KAQF-FM	Clovis, NM [*FM radio station call letters*] (RBYB)
KAQQ	Spokane, WA [*AM radio station call letters*]
KAQR-FM	Helena, MT [*FM radio station call letters*] (RBYB)
KAQS	Shawnee, OK [*TV station call letters*] (RBYB)
KAQU	Huntington, TX [*FM radio station call letters*]
KAQX-FM	Bonanza, OR [*FM radio station call letters*] (RBYB)
KAQY	Columbia, LA [*Television station call letters*] (BROA)
Kar	Indian Law Reports, Karachi Series [*A publication*] (DLA)
KAR	Kamarang [*Guyana*] [*Airport symbol*] (OAG)
KAR	Kansas Administrative Regulations [*A publication*]
KAR	Kap Resources [*Vancouver Stock Exchange symbol*]
KAR	Karabiner [*Carbine*] [*German military - World War II*]
KAR	Karachi [*Pakistan*] [*Seismograph station code, US Geological Survey*] (SEIS)
KAR	Kar-Air OY [*Finland*] [*ICAO designator*] (FAAC)
kar	Karen [*MARC language code*] [*Library of Congress*] (LCCP)
Kar	Karolus de Tocco [*Flourished, 13th century*] [*Authority cited in pre-1607 legal work*] (DSA)
KAR	Kars [*Turkey*] [*Airport symbol*] (AD)
KAR	Keilschrifttexte aus Assur Religioesen Inhalts [*A publication*] (BJA)
KAR	Kentucky Administrative Regulations [*A publication*] (AAGC)
KAR	King's African Rifles [*Military unit*] [*British*]
KAR	Knot Area Ratio (PDAA)
KAR	Kodak Automated Registration [*Eastman Kodak Co.*] (CIST)
KAR	Kodak Automated Retrieval [*Kodak*] [*Microfilm office information system*] (NITA)
Kar	Pakistan Law Reports, Karachi Series [*A publication*] (DLA)
K/Ar	Potassium/Argon (SAUS)
KARA	Santa Clara, CA [*FM radio station call letters*]
KARAC	Kustoms and Rodders Association of Canada
Karachi Univ J Sci	Karachi University Journal of Science (SAUO)
KARB	Price, UT [*FM radio station call letters*]
KARD	West Monroe, LA [*Television station call letters*]
KARE	Koala Corp. [*NASDAQ symbol*] (SAG)
KARE	Minneapolis, MN [*Television station call letters*]
KARF	Washington [*District of Columbia*] [*ICAO location identifier*] (ICLI)
KARF-FM	Independence, KS [*Television station call letters*] (BROA)
KARG-FM	Poteau, OK [*Television station call letters*] (BROA)
KARH-FM	Forrest City, AR [*Television station call letters*] (BROA)
KARI	Blaine, WA [*AM radio station call letters*]
KARI	Keilschrifttexte aus Assur Religioesen Inhalts [*A publication*] (BJA)
KARI	Ketol-Acid Reductoisomerase [*An enzyme*]
KARI	Korea Aerospace Research Institute (SAUO)
KARK	Little Rock, AR [*Television station call letters*]
KARL	Karlsruhe Architectural Language [*Computer science*] (CSR)
KARL	Tracy, MN [*FM radio station call letters*]
KARM	Visalia, CA [*FM radio station call letters*]
Karman Inst Fluid Dynam Lecture Ser	Von Karman Institute for Fluid Dynamics Lecture Series (SAUS)
KARMEN	Karlsruhe-Rutherford Medium-Energy Neutrino Experiment
KARN	Humnoke, AR [*FM radio station call letters*] (RBYB)
KARN	Little Rock, AR [*AM radio station call letters*]
KARO	Caldwell, ID [*FM radio station call letters*] (RBYB)
KARP	Glencoe, MN [*FM radio station call letters*]
KARP	Korea Association for Radiation Protection (SAUO)
KARPEN	Karyawan Pegawai Negeri [*Indonesia*]
KARQ	Ashdown, AR [*FM radio station call letters*]
KARR	Karrington Health, Inc. [*NASDAQ symbol*] (SAG)
KARR	Kirkland, WA [*AM radio station call letters*]
KarrHlth	Karrington Health, Inc. [*Associated Press*] (SAG)
KARS	Belen, NM [*AM radio station call letters*]
KARS	Kansas Applied Remote Sensing Program [*University of Kansas*] [*Research center*] (RCD)

KARS	Kennedy Athletic Recreation and Social [*NASA*] (KSC)
KART	Jerome, ID [*AM radio station call letters*]
KART	Watertown/International [*New York*] [*ICAO location identifier*] (ICLI)
KARV	Russellville, AR [*AM radio station call letters*]
KARV-FM	Ola, AR [*FM radio station call letters*] (BROA)
KARW	Longview, TX [*FM radio station call letters*]
KARX	Claude, TX [*FM radio station call letters*]
KARY	Grandview, WA [*FM radio station call letters*]
KARY	Prosser, WA [*AM radio station call letters*]
KARZ	Burney, CA [*FM radio station call letters*]
KARZ-FM	Marshall, MN [*FM radio station call letters*] (BROA)
KAS	Benedictine College, North Campus, Atchison, KS [*Library symbol*] [*Library of Congress*] (LCLS)
KAS	Kansas [*Obsolete*] (ROG)
Kas	Kansas Reports [*A publication*] (DLA)
kas	Kashmiri [*MARC language code*] [*Library of Congress*] (LCCP)
KAS	Kaskada Resources Ltd. [*Vancouver Stock Exchange symbol*]
KAS	Kasler Corp. (SAUO)
KAS	Kasler Holdings [*NYSE symbol*] (SPSG)
KAS	Kastamonu [*Turkey*] [*Seismograph station code, US Geological Survey*] (SEIS)
KAS	Katz Adjustment Scales [*Psychology*]
KAS	Keep-Alive Signal [*Military*]
KAS	Kentucky Academy of Science (SAUO)
KAS	Kenya-Australia Society
KAS	Ketoacyl-ACP Synthase [*An enzyme*]
KAS	Killed on Active Service (SAUS)
KAS	Kingston Air Services [*Canada*] [*ICAO designator*] (FAAC)
KAS	Kiva Administrative Server [*Computer science*]
KAS	Knowledge Access System [*Interface*]
KAS	Knowledge Acquisition System
KAS	Konrad Adenauer Stiftung [*Germany*] [*Political party*]
KAS	Kroeber Anthropological Society (EA)
KAS	Kulanka Afka Somalyed
KASA	Kentucky Association of School Administrators (SRA)
KASA	Phoenix, AZ [*AM radio station call letters*]
KASA	Santa Fe, NM [*Television station call letters*]
KASB	Bellevue, WA [*FM radio station call letters*]
KASB	Kansas Association of School Boards (SRA)
KASC	Knowledge Availability Systems Center [*University of Pittsburgh*]
KASE	Austin, TX [*FM radio station call letters*]
KASF	Alamosa, CO [*FM radio station call letters*]
KASH	Anchorage, AK [*FM radio station call letters*]
Kash	Kashmir (VRA)
KASH	Kash n'Karry Food Stores [*NASDAQ symbol*] (TTSB)
KASH	Kash n Karry Food Stores, Inc. [*NASDAQ symbol*] (SAG)
KASH	Knowledge, Abilities, Skills, and Habits (STED)
KASH	Knowledge, Attitude, Skills, Habits [*Formula*] [*LIMRA*]
Kashmir LJ	Kashmir Law Journal [*India*] [*A publication*] (DLA)
KashrK	Kash n Karry Food Stores, Inc. [*Associated Press*] (SAG)
KASI	Ames, IA [*AM radio station call letters*]
KASI	Kesatuan Aksi Sardjana Indonesia [*Action Front of Indonesian Scholars*]
KASK-FM	Fairfield, CA [*FM radio station call letters*] (BROA)
KASL	Kansas Association of School Librarians (or Libraries) (SAUO)
KASL	Kasler Corp. (SAUO)
KASL	Newcastle, WY [*AM radio station call letters*]
Kasler Holding Co	Kasler Corp. [*Associated Press*] (SAG)
KASM	Albany, MN [*AM radio station call letters*]
KASM-FM	Albany, MN [*FM radio station call letters*]
KASMS	Korean Air Support Management System (SAUO)
KASN	Pine Bluff, AR [*Television station call letters*]
KASO	Minden, LA [*AM radio station call letters*]
KASO-FM	Minden, LA [*FM radio station call letters*]
KASP	Kehr-Activated Sludge Process (PDAA)
KAS/P	Kroeber Anthropological Society Papers. University of California. Berkeley (SAUO)
Kas R	Kansas Reports [*A publication*] (DLA)
KASR	Perry, OK [*AM radio station call letters*]
KASR-FM	Conway, AR [*FM radio station call letters*] (BROA)
KASR-FM	Perry, OK [*FM radio station call letters*] (BROA)
KASRP	Kaiser Steel Corp. Pfd (SAUO)
KASS	Casper, WY [*FM radio station call letters*] (RBYB)
KASS	Kagan Affective Sensitivity Scales [*Psychology*] (DHP)
Kass	Kassinin [*Biochemistry*]
KASS	Kent Automated Serials System [*Kent State University*] [*Automated library system*] (NITA)
KASSP	Kentucky Association of Secondary School Principals (SRA)
KASSR	Kalmyk Autonomous Soviet Socialist Republic (SAUO)
KA SSR	Kazakh Soviet Socialist Republic (SAUO)
KASSR	Komi Autonomous Soviet Socialist Republic (SAUO)
KAST	Astoria, OR [*AM radio station call letters*]
KAST	Kalman Automatic Sequential TMA [*Military*] (CAAL)
KAST	Kindergarten Auditory Screening Test [*Otorhinolaryngology*] (DAVI)
KAST-FM	Astoria, OR [*FM radio station call letters*]
KASU	Jonesboro, AR [*FM radio station call letters*]
KASV-FM	Borger, TX [*FM radio station call letters*] (BROA)
KASW	Phoenix, AZ [*Television station call letters*]
KASX-FM	Pine Bluffs, WY [*FM radio station call letters*] (BROA)
KASY	Albuquerque, NM [*FM radio station call letters*]
KASY-TV	Albuquerque, NM [*Television station call letters*]
KAT	Asbury Theological Seminary, Wilmore, KY [*OCLC symbol*] (OCLC)
KAT	Die Keilinschriften und das Alte Testament [*A publication*] (BJA)
KAT	Kaitaia [*New Zealand*] [*Airport symbol*] (OAG)
KAT	Kanamycin Acetyltransferase [*An enzyme*]

KAT	Kappa Alpha Theta [*Sorority*]
kat	Katal [*Unit of enzyme activity*]
KAT	Kattegat Air, AS [*Denmark*] [*ICAO designator*] (FAAC)
KAT	Kenosha Auto Transport (SAUO)
KAT	Key-to-Address Transformation [*Computer science*] (PDAA)
KAT	Kizyl-Arvat [*Former USSR*] [*Seismograph station code, US Geological Survey*] (SEIS)
KAT	Kommentar zum Alten Testament [*A publication*] (BJA)
KATA	Arcata, CA [*AM radio station call letters*]
KATB	Anchorage, AK [*FM radio station call letters*]
KATC	Katz Digital Technologies [*NASDAQ symbol*] (TTSB)
KATC	Katz Digital Technologies, Inc. [*NASDAQ symbol*] (SAG)
KATC	Korean Army Training Center
KATC	Lafayette, LA [*Television station call letters*]
KATCA	Korean-American Technical Cooperation Association
Katch Pr Law	Katchenovsky's Prize Law [*2nd ed.*] [*1867*] [*A publication*] (DLA)
KATD	Pittsburg, CA [*AM radio station call letters*]
KATE	Albert Lea, MN [*AM radio station call letters*]
KATE	Knowledge Based Automatic Test Equipment (ACAE)
KatechBR	Katechetische Blaetter [*Berlin-Grunewald*] [*A publication*] (BJA)
KATF	Dubuque, IA [*FM radio station call letters*]
KATH	Bozeman, MT [*FM radio station call letters*]
KATH-FM	El Paso, TX [*FM radio station call letters*] (BROA)
KathM	Die Katholischen Missionen (BJA)
KATI	California, MO [*FM radio station call letters*] (RBYB)
KATIE	Killer Alert Threat Identification & Evasion (SAUS)
KATJ	George, CA [*FM radio station call letters*]
KATK	Carlsbad, NM [*AM radio station call letters*]
KATK-FM	Carlsbad, NM [*FM radio station call letters*]
KATL	Atlanta/The William B. Hartsfield Atlanta International [*Georgia*] [*ICAO location identifier*] (ICLI)
KATL	Miles City, MT [*AM radio station call letters*]
KATM	Katmai National Monument
KATM	Modesto, CA [*FM radio station call letters*]
KATN	Fairbanks, AK [*Television station call letters*]
KATO	Safford, AZ [*AM radio station call letters*]
KATP	Amarillo, TX [*FM radio station call letters*]
KATQ	Plentywood, MT [*AM radio station call letters*]
KATQ-FM	Plentywood, MT [*FM radio station call letters*]
KATR	Wray, CO [*FM radio station call letters*]
KATS	Campus Antenna Television System (SAUS)
KATS	Kennedy Avionics Test Set
KATS	Kennedy Space Center Avionics Test Set [*NASA*] (NASA)
KATS	Yakima, WA [*FM radio station call letters*]
KatShing	Katorikku Shingaku [*Catholic Theology*] [*Tokyo*] [*A publication*] (BJA)
KATSI	Kommentar zum Alten Testament [*E. Sellin*] [*A publication*] (BJA)
KATT	Oklahoma City, OK [*FM radio station call letters*]
KATU	Portland, OR [*Television station call letters*]
KATU-DT	Portland, OR [*Television station call letters*] (BROA)
KATUSA	Korean Augmentation to the United States Army
KATUSA	Korean Augmentee to U.S. Army
KATV	Little Rock, AR [*Television station call letters*]
KATW	Lewiston, ID [*FM radio station call letters*]
KATY	Idyllwild, CA [*FM radio station call letters*]
KatyInd	Katy Industries, Inc. [*Formerly, Missour-Kansas-Texas R.R. Co., with Wall Street slang name of "Kathy"*] [*Associated Press*] (SAG)
KATYP	Kallitype (VRA)
KATZ	St. Louis, MO [*AM radio station call letters*]
KatzDig	Katz Digital Technologies, Inc. [*Associated Press*] (SAG)
KATZ-FM	Alton, IL [*FM radio station call letters*] (BROA)
KatzM	Katz Media Group, Inc. [*Associated Press*] (SAG)
kau	Kanuri [*MARC language code*] [*Library of Congress*] (LCCP)
KAU	Kaohsiung [*Takao*] [*Republic of China*] [*Seismograph station code, US Geological Survey*] (SEIS)
KAU	Kauhava [*Finland*] [*Airport symbol*] (AD)
KAU	Kenya African Union [*1944*] [*Political party*] (PPW)
KAU	Kenya Africa Union (SAUO)
KAU	Kerala Agricultural University (SAUO)
KAU	Keystation Adapter Unit [*Computer science*]
KAU	Kilo Accounting Units (NASA)
KAU	King-Armstrong Unit [*Clinical chemistry*]
KAUB-FM	Reedsport, OR [*FM radio station call letters*] (BROA)
KaufBH	Kaufman & Broad Home Corp. [*Associated Press*] (SAG)
KAUF-FM	Kennett, MO [*FM radio station call letters*] (BROA)
KaufHW	Kaufman [*H. W.*] Financial Group [*Associated Press*] (SAG)
Kauf Mack	Kaufmann's Edition of Mackeldey's Civil Law [*A publication*] (DLA)
Kaufm Mackeld Civ Law	Kaufmann's Edition of Mackeldey's Civil Law [*A publication*] (DLA)
KAUFX	Kaufmann Fund [*Mutual fund ticker symbol*] (SG)
KAUG	Augusta [*Maine*] [*ICAO location identifier*] (ICLI)
KAUG-FM	El Dorado, AR [*FM radio station call letters*] (BROA)
KAUI	Kekaha, HI [*FM radio station call letters*]
KAUJ-FM	Walhalla, ND [*FM radio station call letters*] (BROA)
KAUL-FM	Ellington, MO [*FM radio station call letters*] (BROA)
KAUM	Colorado City, TX [*FM radio station call letters*]
KAUN	Sioux Falls, SD [*Television station call letters*] (BROA)
KAUO	Santa Fe, NM [*Television station call letters*] (BROA)
KAUP	Pendleton, OR [*Television station call letters*] (BROA)
KAUQ-FM	Omak, WA [*FM radio station call letters*] (BROA)
KAUR	Sioux Falls, SD [*FM radio station call letters*]
KAUS	Austin, MN [*AM radio station call letters*]
KAUS	Austin/Robert Mueller Municipal [*Texas*] [*ICAO location identifier*] (ICLI)
KAUS-FM	Austin, MN [*FM radio station call letters*]
KAUV-FM	Viola, AR [*FM radio station call letters*] (BROA)

KAUY-FM	LaJunta, CO [*FM radio station call letters*] (BROA)
KAUZ	Wichita Falls, TX [*Television station call letters*]
KAV	Cambourne Resources [*Vancouver Stock Exchange symbol*]
KAV	Kavieng [*New Ireland*] [*Seismograph station code, US Geological Survey*] [*Closed*] (SEIS)
KAV	Keilschrifttexte aus Assur Verschiedenen Inhalts [*A publication*] (BJA)
KAVA	Burney, CA [*AM radio station call letters*]
KAVA	Pueblo, CO [*AM radio station call letters*] (BROA)
KAVAS	Knowledge Acquisition Visualization and Assessment Study (SAUO)
KAVC	Rosamond, CA [*FM radio station call letters*]
KAVD-FM	Limon, CO [*FM radio station call letters*] (BROA)
KAVE	Oakridge, OR [*FM radio station call letters*]
KAVG-FM	Beulah, ND [*FM radio station call letters*] (BROA)
KAVH-FM	Eudora, AR [*FM radio station call letters*] (BROA)
KAVI	Keilschrifttexte aus Assur Verschiedenen Inhalts [*A publication*] (BJA)
KAVJ-FM	Sutherlin, OR [*FM radio station call letters*] (BROA)
KAVK-FM	Many, LA [*FM radio station call letters*] (BROA)
KAVL	Lancaster, CA [*AM radio station call letters*]
KAVO-FM	Borger, TX [*FM radio station call letters*] (BROA)
KAVP-AM	Colona, CO [*AM radio station call letters*] (BROA)
KAVS	Mojave, CA [*FM radio station call letters*]
KAVT-AM	Fresno, CA [*AM radio station call letters*] (BROA)
KAVU	Victoria, TX [*Television station call letters*]
KAVV	Benson, AZ [*FM radio station call letters*]
KAVW-FM	Amarillo, TX [*FM radio station call letters*] (BROA)
KAVX-FM	Lufkin, TX [*FM radio station call letters*] (BROA)
KAW	Kawthaung [*Myanmar*] [*Airport symbol*] (OAG)
KAWA	Floydada, TX [*FM radio station call letters*]
KAWAD	Karnataka Watersheds Development
KAWB	Brainerd, MN [*Television station call letters*]
KAWC	Yuma, AZ [*AM radio station call letters*]
KAWC-FM	Yuma, AZ [*FM radio station call letters*]
KAWD-FM	Tahoka, TX [*FM radio station call letters*] (BROA)
KAWE	Bemidji, MN [*Television station call letters*]
KAWF-FM	Los Molinos, CA [*FM radio station call letters*] (BROA)
KAWJ	Hutchinson, KS [*Television station call letters*] (BROA)
KAWJ	Korrespondenzblatt des Vereins zur Gruendung und Erhaltung der Akademie fuer dieWissenschaft des Judentums [*A publication*] (BJA)
KAWK-FM	Custer, SD [*FM radio station call letters*] (RBYB)
KAWL	York, NE [*AM radio station call letters*]
KAWN	Carswell [*Texas*] [*ICAO location identifier*] (ICLI)
KAWOL	Knowledgeable, Absent Without Leave
KAWOL	Knowledge, Absent Without Leave [*Army*] (ADDR)
KAWQ-FM	Bridgeport, NE [*FM radio station call letters*] (BROA)
KAWS	Hemphill, TX [*AM radio station call letters*]
KAWT-FM	Princeville, HI [*FM radio station call letters*] (BROA)
KAWU-FM	Newberry Springs, CA [*FM radio station call letters*] (BROA)
KAWV-FM	Lihue-Kauai, HI [*FM radio station call letters*] (BROA)
KAWW	Heber Springs, AR [*AM radio station call letters*]
KAWW-FM	Heber Springs, AR [*FM radio station call letters*]
KAWX-FM	Weaverville, CA [*FM radio station call letters*] (BROA)
KAWY-FM	Denver City, TX [*FM radio station call letters*] (BROA)
KAWZ	Twin Falls, ID [*FM radio station call letters*]
KAX	Kalbarri [*Australia*] [*Airport symbol*] (OAG)
KAXA-FM	Pioche, NV [*FM radio station call letters*] (BROA)
KAXB-FM	Tuba City, AZ [*FM radio station call letters*] (BROA)
KAXE	Grand Rapids, MN [*FM radio station call letters*]
KAXF-FM	Huntsville, TX [*FM radio station call letters*] (BROA)
KAXG-FM	Gillette, WY [*FM radio station call letters*] (BROA)
KAXH-FM	Pampa, TX [*FM radio station call letters*] (BROA)
KAXI-FM	Willcox, AZ [*FM radio station call letters*] (BROA)
KAXJ-FM	Sunrise Beach, MO [*FM radio station call letters*] (BROA)
KAXL	Green Acres, CA [*FM radio station call letters*]
KAXM	Agana, Guam [*Television station call letters*] (BROA)
KAXR-FM	Arkansas City, KS [*FM radio station call letters*] (BROA)
KAXT	Hollister, CA [*FM radio station call letters*] (RBYB)
KAXV-FM	Bastrop, LA [*FM radio station call letters*] (BROA)
KAXW-AM	Merced, CA [*AM radio station call letters*] (BROA)
KAXX	Ventura, CA [*FM radio station call letters*]
KAXX-AM	Eagle River, AK [*AM radio station call letters*] (BROA)
KAXY-AM	Waco, TX [*AM radio station call letters*] (BROA)
KAY	Katlanovo [*Yugoslavia*] [*Seismograph station code, US Geological Survey*] (SEIS)
Kay	Kay's English Vice-Chancellors' Reports [*69 English Reprint*] [*A publication*] (DLA)
KAY	Wakaya [*Fiji*] [*Airport symbol*] [*Obsolete*] (OAG)
KAYA-FM	Hubbard, NE [*FM radio station call letters*] (BROA)
Kay & J	Kay and Johnson's English Vice-Chancellors' Reports [*69, 70 English Reprint*] [*A publication*] (DLA)
Kay & J (Eng)	Kay and Johnson's English Vice-Chancellors' Reports [*69, 70 English Reprint*] [*A publication*] (DLA)
Kay & John	Kay and Johnson's English Vice-Chancellors' Reports [*69, 70 English Reprint*] [*A publication*] (DLA)
Kay & Johns	Kay and Johnson's English Vice-Chancellors' Reports [*69, 70 English Reprint*] [*A publication*] (DLA)
KAYB-FM	Sunnyside, WA [*FM radio station call letters*] (BROA)
KAYC-FM	Durant, OK [*FM radio station call letters*] (BROA)
KAYD	Beaumont, TX [*AM radio station call letters*] (RBYB)
KAYD-FM	Beaumont, TX [*FM radio station call letters*] (BROA)
Kaydon	Kaydon Corp. [*Associated Press*] (SAG)
KAYE	Kaye Group [*NASDAQ symbol*] (TTSB)
KAYE	Kaye Group, Inc. [*NASDAQ symbol*] (SAG)
KAYE	Tonkawa, OK [*FM radio station call letters*]
KayeGrp	Kaye Group, Inc. [*Associated Press*] (SAG)

KayeK .... Kaye Kotts Associates, Inc. [Associated Press] (SAG)
Kay (Eng) ..... Kay's English Vice-Chancellors' Reports [69 English Reprint]
     [A publication] (DLA)
KAYF-FM ..... Starbuck, MN [FM radio station call letters] (BROA)
KAYG-FM ..... Camp Wood, TX [FM radio station call letters] (BROA)
KAYH-FM ..... Fayetteville, AR [FM radio station call letters] (BROA)
KAYI-FM ...... Princeville, HI [FM radio station call letters] (BROA)
KAYK-AM ..... Arvada, CO [AM radio station call letters] (BROA)
KAYL .... Storm Lake, IA [AM radio station call letters]
KAYL-FM ..... Storm Lake, IA [FM radio station call letters]
KAYM-FM ..... Weatherford, OK [FM radio station call letters] (BROA)
KAYO-FM ..... Aberdeen, WA [FM radio station call letters]
KAYP-FM ..... Mount Pleasant, IA [FM radio station call letters] (BROA)
KAYQ .... Warsaw, MO [FM radio station call letters]
KAYR .... Van Buren, AR [AM radio station call letters]
KAYS .... Hays, KS [AM radio station call letters]
KAYSEE .... Kansas City [Missouri] [Slang]
Kay Ship ...... Kay. Shipmasters, and Seamen [2nd ed.] [1894] [A publication]
     (DLA)
KAYT-FM ..... Jena, LA [FM radio station call letters] (BROA)
KAYU .... Spokane, WA [Television station call letters]
KAYW-FM ..... Meeker, CO [FM radio station call letters] (BROA)
KAYX .... Richmond, MO [FM radio station call letters]
KAYY-FM ..... Clearwater, KS [FM radio station call letters] (BROA)
KAZ .... Karuizawa [Also, KRZ] [Japan] [Seismograph station code, US
     Geological Survey] (SEIS)
kaz .... Kazakh [MARC language code] [Library of Congress] (LCCP)
KAZ .... Kazakhstan (ADWA)
Kaz............. Kazakstan (MILB)
KAZA .... Gilroy, CA [AM radio station call letters]
KAZAIR .... Kazakhstan Airlines [ICAO designator] (FAAC)
KAZB-FM ..... Coalinga, CA [FM radio station call letters] (BROA)
KAZC-FM ..... Tishomingo, OK [FM radio station call letters] (BROA)
KAZD-FM ..... Montrose, CO [FM radio station call letters] (BROA)
KAZE-FM ..... Coalgate, OK [FM radio station call letters] (BROA)
KAZF-FM...... Hebronville, TX [FM radio station call letters] (BROA)
KAZG .... Ogden, UT [Television station call letters] (BROA)
KAZI .... Austin, TX [FM radio station call letters]
KAZJ .... Seattle, WA [AM radio station call letters] (BROA)
KAZL .... Castle Rock, WA [FM radio station call letters]
KAZM .... Sedona, AZ [AM radio station call letters]
KAZN .... Pasadena, CA [AM radio station call letters]
KAZP-AM ..... Bellevue, NE [AM radio station call letters] (BROA)
KAZQ .... Albuquerque, NM [Television station call letters]
KAZR-FM ..... Pella, IA [FM radio station call letters] (RBYB)
KazSSR .... Kazakh Soviet Socialist Republic
KAZT-AM ..... Redding, CA [AM radio station call letters] (BROA)
KAZU .... Pacific Grove, CA [FM radio station call letters]
KAZW-AM ..... College Station, TX [AM radio station call letters] (BROA)
KAZX-FM ..... Kirtland, NM [FM radio station call letters] (BROA)
KAZY-FM ..... Winfield, KS [FM radio station call letters] (BROA)
KAZZ .... Deer Park, WA [FM radio station call letters]
KB .... Bermuda [IYRU nationality code] (IYR)
KB .... Burnthills [ICAO designator] (AD)
KB .... Construction Bureau (SAUO)
KB .... English Law Reports, King's Bench Division [1901-52]
     [A publication] (DLA)
KB .... Kashin-Bek Disease [Medicine] (DMAA)
KB .... Kaufman & Broad, Inc. (MHDW)
KB .... Kauri-Butanol Value [Measure of relative solvent power]
KB .... Keel Bending (SSD)
KB .... Keilinschriftliche Bibliothek [Berlin] [A publication] (BJA)
KB .... Kelly Bushing [Drilling] (DICI)
KB .... Ketone Bodies [Clinical chemistry]
KB .... Keyboard [Computer science]
KB .... Kickback (MHDB)
kb .... Kilobar
kb .... Kilobase
KB .... Kilobaud (IAA)
kb .... KiloBIT [Binary Digit] [Computer science]
KB .... Kilobit (NAKS)
KB .... Kilo BTU [British Thermal Unit]
kb .... Kilobyte (ELAL)
Kb .... Kilobyte (NFD)
KB .... Kilobyte [10^3 bytes] [Computer science]
KB .... Kimball International Inc. (SAUO)
KB .... Kincheng Banking Corp. [Hong Kong]
KB .... King's Bench [of law courts] [British]
KB .... King's Bishop [Chess]
KB .... Kitchen and Bathroom
KB .... Kitchen Biddy [Female kitchen worker] [Restaurant slang]
KB .... Kite Balloon [Air Force]
K-B .... Kleihauer-Betke [Stain] [Medicine] (MEDA)
KB .... Knee Bearing [Prosthesis]
KB .... Knee Brace [Technical drawings]
KB .... Knight Bachelor [or Knight Companion] of the Order of the Bath
     [British]
Kb .... Knight of the Bath (SAUO)
Kb .... Knit into Back of Stitch [Knitting] (BARN)
KB .... Knockback (WDAA)
KB .... Knowledgeability Brief (MCD)
KB .... Knowledge Base [Computer science] (IAA)
KB .... Knuckle-Bender Splint [Orthopedics] (DAVI)
KB .... Komercni Bank [Czech Republic Bank]
KB .... Komercni Banka AS [Czech Republic] [Banking]

KB .... Kommanditbolaget [Limited Partnership] [German] (ILCA)
KB .... Koninklijk Besluit [Royal Decree] [Dutch] (ILCA)
Kb .... Kontrabass [Double Bass] [German] [Music] (WDAA)
KB .... Kontrabass [Double Bass] [Music]
KB .... Korpus Bezpieczenstwa (BJA)
KB .... Korrespondenz-Blatt des Verbandes der Deutschen Juden
     [A publication] (BJA)
KB .... Kuiper Belt [Planetary science]
KB .... Kulturbund
KB .... Kunstgeschichte in Bildern [A publication] (OCD)
KBA .... Barbados [IYRU nationality code] (IYR)
KBA .... Beni Abbes [Algeria] [Airport symbol] (AD)
KBA .... Kabala [Sierra Leone] [Airport symbol] (OAG)
KBA .... Kansas Bankers Association (SRA)
KBA .... Kansas Bar Association (SRA)
KBA .... Kenn Borek Air Ltd. [Canada] [ICAO designator] (FAAC)
KBA .... Kentucky Bar Association
KBA .... Kentucky Broadcasters Association (SRA)
KBA .... Ketobutyraldehyde Dimethyl Acetal [Biochemistry]
KBA .... Keyboard Assembly (DWSG)
KBA .... Killed by Action [In reference to the enemy] [Vietnam] (VNW)
KBA .... Killed by Air [Military]
KBA .... Killed by Artillery [In reference to the enemy] [Vietnam] (VNW)
KBA .... Kleinwort Benson Aus [NYSE symbol] (TTSB)
KBA .... Kleinwort Benson Australian Income Fund, Inc. [NYSE symbol]
     (SPSG)
KBA .... Knight of St. Benedict of Avis
KBAB .... Marysville/Beale Air Force Base [California] [ICAO location
     identifier] (ICLI)
KBAB-FM ..... Kerrville, TX [FM radio station call letters] (BROA)
KBAC .... Kennedy Booster Assembly Contractor (MCD)
KBAC .... Las Vegas, NM [FM radio station call letters]
KBAD .... Shreveport/Barksdale Air Force Base [Louisiana] [ICAO location
     identifier] (ICLI)
KBAD-AM ..... Las Vegas, NV [AM radio station call letters] (BROA)
KBAE .... Llano, TX [FM radio station call letters] (RBYB)
KBAH-FM ..... Plainview, TX [FM radio station call letters] (BROA)
KBAI .... Morro Bay, CA [AM radio station call letters]
KBAJ-FM ..... Deer River, MN [FM radio station call letters] (BROA)
KBAK .... Bakersfield, CA [Television station call letters]
KBAL .... Kimball International, Inc. [NASDAQ symbol] (NQ)
KBAL .... Kleine Beitraege zum Assyrischen Lexikon [A publication]
KBAL .... San Saba, TX [AM radio station call letters]
KBALB .... Kimball Intl CI'B' [NASDAQ symbol] (TTSB)
KBAL-FM ..... San Saba, TX [FM radio station call letters] (RBYB)
K-BALL .... Cannibalize (MCD)
KBAM .... Longview, WA [AM radio station call letters]
KB&TS .... Kuwait Broadcasting and Television Service (SAUO)
KBAP-FM ..... King City, CA [FM radio station call letters] (BROA)
KBAQ .... Phoenix, AZ [FM radio station call letters]
KBAR .... Burley, ID [AM radio station call letters]
kbar .... Kilobar (ABAC)
KBAR .... Kilobar
KBART .... Kings Bay Army Terminal
KBAS .... Bullhead City, AZ [AM radio station call letters]
KBASSR ...... Kabardino-Balkar Autonomous Soviet Socialist Republic (SAUO)
KBAT .... Midland, TX [FM radio station call letters]
KBAU .... Big Sandy, TX [FM radio station call letters] (RBYB)
KBAust .... Kleinwort Benson Australian Income Fund, Inc. [Associated Press]
     (SAG)
KBAW-FM ..... Zapata, TX [FM radio station call letters] (BROA)
KBAX .... Fallbrook, CA [FM radio station call letters]
KBAY .... San Jose, CA [FM radio station call letters]
KBB .... Baker University, Baldwin City, KS [Library symbol] [Library of
     Congress] (LCLS)
KBB .... Bear Stearns Companies, Inc. [AMEX symbol] (SAG)
KBB .... Bear Stearns Cos.'CUBS''98 [AMEX symbol] (TTSB)
KBB .... King's Bad Bargain [Undesirable serviceman] [Slang] [British]
     (DSUE)
KBB .... Kitchens, Bedrooms, and Bathrooms Equipment Exhibition [British]
     (ITD)
KBBA .... Abilene, TX [AM radio station call letters]
KBBB-FM ..... Billings, MT [FM radio station call letters] (RBYB)
KBBC .... Lake Havasu City, AZ [FM radio station call letters]
KBBE .... McPherson, KS [FM radio station call letters]
KBBF .... Santa Rosa, CA [FM radio station call letters]
KBBG .... Waterloo, IA [FM radio station call letters]
KBBI .... Homer, AK [AM radio station call letters]
KBBJ .... Havre, MT [Television station call letters] (BROA)
KBBK .... Rupert, ID [AM radio station call letters]
KBBL .... Cabot, AR [AM radio station call letters]
KBBL-FM ..... Cabot, AR [FM radio station call letters]
KBBN .... Broken Bow, NE [FM radio station call letters]
KBBO .... Yakima, WA [AM radio station call letters]
KBBQ .... Fort Smith, AR [FM radio station call letters]
KBBR .... North Bend, OR [AM radio station call letters]
KBBS .... Buffalo, WY [AM radio station call letters]
KBBT.......... Portland, OR [AM radio station call letters]
KBBT-FM ..... Banks, OR [FM radio station call letters] (BROA)
KBBV .... Big Bear Lake, CA [AM radio station call letters]
KBBW .... Waco, TX [AM radio station call letters]
KBBX .... Omaha, NE [AM radio station call letters]
KBBY-FM ..... Ventura, CA [FM radio station call letters]
KBBZ .... Kalispell, MT [FM radio station call letters]
KBC .... Bellarmine College, Louisville, KY [OCLC symbol] (OCLC)

KBC............ Birch Creek [*Alaska*] [*Airport symbol*] (OAG)
KBC............ K-Band Circulator
KBC............ King's Bench Court [*British*]
KBC............ Kiowa Business Committee [*An association*]
KBC............ Kyushu Asahi Broadcasting (SAUO)
KBCA............ Elk City, OK [*Television station call letters*] (BROA)
KBCA............ Keystone Bituminous Coal Association
KBCB............ Bellingham, WA [*Television station call letters*]
KBCC............ Helena, MT [*Television station call letters*] (BROA)
KBCD............ Newport Beach, CA [*FM radio station call letters*]
KBCE............ Boyce, LA [*FM radio station call letters*]
KBCH............ Kings Beach, CA [*FM radio station call letters*] (RBYB)
KBCH............ Lincoln City, OR [*AM radio station call letters*]
KBCI............ Boise, ID [*Television station call letters*]
KBCJ............ Vernal, UT [*Television station call letters*] (BROA)
KBCK............ Diamondville, WY [*FM radio station call letters*]
KBCL............ Shreveport, LA [*AM radio station call letters*]
KBCM............ Fort Worth, TX [*AM radio station call letters*] (BROA)
KBCN............ Marshall, AR [*FM radio station call letters*]
KBCO............ Boulder, CO [*AM radio station call letters*]
KBCO-FM..... Boulder, CO [*FM radio station call letters*]
KBCQ............ Roswell, NM [*FM radio station call letters*]
KBCR............ Steamboat Springs, CO [*AM radio station call letters*]
KBCR-FM..... Steamboat Springs, CO [*FM radio station call letters*] (RBYB)
KBCS............ Bellevue, WA [*FM radio station call letters*]
KBCT............ Boca Raton [*Florida*] [*ICAO location identifier*] (ICLI)
KBCT-FM..... Waco, TX [*FM radio station call letters*] (RBYB)
KBCU............ North Newton, KS [*FM radio station call letters*]
KBCV-FM..... Paris, TX [*FM radio station call letters*] (BROA)
KBCW-FM..... McAlester, OK [*FM radio station call letters*] (BROA)
KBCX-FM..... Big Spring, TX [*FM radio station call letters*] (BROA)
KBCY............ Tye, TX [*FM radio station call letters*]
KBCZ............ Holbrook, AZ [*Television station call letters*] (BROA)
KBD............ Kaschin-Beck Disease [*Medicine*]
kbd............ Keyboard (WDAA)
KBD............ Keyboard
KBD............ King's Bench Division [*of law courts*] [*British*] (ROG)
KBD............ Thousand Barrels per Day [*Also, TBD*]
KBDA-FM..... Great Bend, KS [*FM radio station call letters*] (BROA)
KBDC............ King's Bench Divisional Court [*British*]
KBDC-FM..... Mason City, IA (BROA)
KBDD-FM..... Winfield, KS [*FM radio station call letters*] (BROA)
KBDE............ Baudette [*Minnesota*] [*ICAO location identifier*] (ICLI)
KBDE-FM..... Gatesville, TX [*FM radio station call letters*] (BROA)
KBDG............ Turlock, CA [*FM radio station call letters*]
KBDH-FM..... San Ardo, CA [*FM radio station call letters*] (BROA)
KBDI............ Broomfield, CO [*Television station call letters*]
KB Div'l Ct... King's Bench Divisional Court [*England*] (DLA)
KBDJ-FM..... Ruston, LA [*FM radio station call letters*] (BROA)
KBDK............ Hoisington, KS [*Television station call letters*] (BROA)
KBDL............ Windsor Locks/Bradley International [*Connecticut*] [*ICAO location identifier*] (ICLI)
KBDN............ Bandon, OR [*FM radio station call letters*] (RBYB)
KBDO-FM..... Des Arc, AR [*FM radio station call letters*] (BROA)
KBDQ-FM..... Owensville, MO [*FM radio station call letters*] (BROA)
KBDR............ Mirando City, TX [*FM radio station call letters*]
KBDS-FM..... Arvin, CA [*FM radio station call letters*] (BROA)
KBDT-FM..... Oraibi, AZ [*FM radio station call letters*] (BROA)
KBDU-FM..... Hayden, CO [*FM radio station call letters*] (BROA)
KBDZ............ Perryville, MO [*FM radio station call letters*]
KBE............ Bell Island, AK [*Location identifier*] [*FAA*] (FAAL)
KBE............ Berea College, Berea, KY [*OCLC symbol*] (OCLC)
KBE............ Keyboard Encoder [*Computer science*]
KBE............ Keyboard Entry [*Computer science*]
KBE............ Key British Enterprises [*Dun & Bradstreet Ltd.*] [*Information service or system*] (IID)
KBE............ Knight Commander of the [*Order of the*] British Empire
KBE............ Knight of the Black Eagle [*Russia*] [*Obsolete*]
KBE............ Knowledge-Based Engineering [*Expert systems*] [*Computer-aided design*]
KBE............ Knowledge Base Environment
KBEB-FM..... Hamilton, MT [*FM radio station call letters*] (BROA)
KBEC............ Waxahachie, TX [*AM radio station call letters*]
KBED............ Bedford/Laurence G. Hanscom Field [*Massachusetts*] [*ICAO location identifier*] (ICLI)
KBED-FM..... Shreveport, LA [*FM radio station call letters*] (BROA)
KBEE............ Modesto, CA [*AM radio station call letters*]
KBEE............ Salt Lake City, UT [*FM radio station call letters*] (RBYB)
KBEF-FM..... Gibsland, LA [*FM radio station call letters*] (BROA)
KBEG............ Clovis, CA [*AM radio station call letters*] (BROA)
KBEH............ Bellevue, WA [*Television station call letters*]
KBEI............ Durango, CO [*Television station call letters*] (BROA)
KBEJ............ Fredericksburg, TX [*Television station call letters*] (BROA)
KBEK............ Mora, MN [*FM radio station call letters*]
KBEL............ Idabel, OK [*AM radio station call letters*]
KBEL-FM..... Idabel, OK [*FM radio station call letters*]
KBEM............ Minneapolis, MN [*FM radio station call letters*]
KBEN............ Carrizo Springs, TX [*AM radio station call letters*]
KBENC............ Keyboard Encoder (NITA)
KB (Eng)...... English Law Reports, King's Bench Division [*1901-52*] [*A publication*] (DLA)
KBEO............ Jackson, WY [*Television station call letters*] (BROA)
KBEQ............ Blue Springs, MO [*AM radio station call letters*]
KBEQ............ Kansas City, MO [*FM radio station call letters*]
KBER............ Ogden, UT [*FM radio station call letters*]
KBES............ Ceres, CA [*FM radio station call letters*]
KBES............ Knowledge-Based Expert System
KBET............ Canyon Country, CA [*AM radio station call letters*]
KBEV-FM..... Dillon, MT [*FM radio station call letters*] (BROA)
KBEW............ Blue Earth, MN [*AM radio station call letters*]
KBEW-FM.... Blue Earth, MN [*FM radio station call letters*]
KBEX-FM..... Billings, MT [*FM radio station call letters*] (BROA)
KBEZ............ Tulsa, OK [*FM radio station call letters*]
KBF............ K-Band Feed
KBF............ Kyburz Flat [*California*] [*Seismograph station code, US Geological Survey*] (SEIS)
KBFA............ Wolfforth, TX [*Television station call letters*] (BROA)
KBFB-FM..... Dallas, TX [*FM radio station call letters*] (BROA)
KBFC............ Forrest City, AR [*FM radio station call letters*]
KBFC............ Karen Brooks Fan Club (EA)
KBFC............ Kippe Brannon Fan Club [*Defunct*] (EA)
KBFD............ Honolulu, HI [*Television station call letters*]
KBFE-FM..... Grand Junction, CO [*FM radio station call letters*] (BROA)
KBFF-FM..... Gallup, NM [*FM radio station call letters*] (BROA)
KBFG-FM..... Santa Fe, NM [*FM radio station call letters*] (BROA)
KBFH-FM..... Moose Lake, MN [*FM radio station call letters*] (BROA)
KBFI............ Bonners Ferry, ID [*AM radio station call letters*]
KBFI............ Seattle Boeing Field/King Country International [*Washington*] [*ICAO location identifier*] (ICLI)
KBFJ-FM..... Mountain Home, AR [*FM radio station call letters*] (BROA)
KBFL............ Bakersfield/Meadows Field [*California*] [*ICAO location identifier*] (ICLI)
KBFL............ Buffalo, MO [*FM radio station call letters*]
KBFM............ Edinburg, TX [*FM radio station call letters*]
KBFM............ Mobile/Aerospace [*Alabama*] [*ICAO location identifier*] (ICLI)
KBFN-FM..... Big Sky, MT [*FM radio station call letters*] (BROA)
KBFO-FM..... Aberdeen, SD [*FM radio station call letters*] (BROA)
KBFQ............ Enid, OK [*AM radio station call letters*] (BROA)
KBFR-FM..... Bridgeport, TX [*FM radio station call letters*] (BROA)
KBFS............ Belle Fourche, SD [*AM radio station call letters*]
KBFV-FM..... Carlsbad, NM [*FM radio station call letters*] (BROA)
KBFW............ Bellingham-Ferndale, WA [*AM radio station call letters*]
KBFX............ Anchorage, AK [*FM radio station call letters*]
KBFZ-FM..... Kimball, NE [*FM radio station call letters*] (BROA)
KBGA-FM..... Missoula, MT [*FM radio station call letters*] (RBYB)
KBGC............ Pullman, WA [*Television station call letters*] (BROA)
KBGD............ Farwell, TX [*Television station call letters*] (BROA)
KBGE............ Bellevue, WA [*Television station call letters*] (RBYB)
KBGF............ Douglas, AZ [*Television station call letters*] (BROA)
KBGG............ Des Moines, IA [*AM radio station call letters*] (BROA)
KBGG............ San Francisco, CA [*FM radio station call letters*] (RBYB)
KBGH............ Filer, ID [*Television station call letters*]
KBGIS............ Knowledge Based Geographical Information System (SAUO)
KBGJ-FM..... Marble Hill, MO [*FM radio station call letters*] (BROA)
KBGL............ Larned, KS [*FM radio station call letters*] (BROA)
KBGM-FM..... Park Hills, MO [*FM radio station call letters*] (BROA)
KBGN............ Caldwell, ID [*AM radio station call letters*]
KBGO-FM..... Las Vegas, TX [*FM radio station call letters*] (RBYB)
KBGP-FM..... Bellview, MN [*FM radio station call letters*] (BROA)
KBGQ-FM..... Harrisburg, AR [*FM radio station call letters*] (BROA)
KBGR............ Bangor/International [*Maine*] [*ICAO location identifier*] (ICLI)
KBGS............ Big Spring/Webb Air Force Base [*Texas*] [*ICAO location identifier*] (ICLI)
KBGT-FM..... Hastings, NE [*FM radio station call letters*] (BROA)
KBGU-FM..... Ingalls, KS [*FM radio station call letters*] (BROA)
KBGV-FM..... Clear Lake, SD [*FM radio station call letters*] (BROA)
KBGX-FM..... Newport, OR [*FM radio station call letters*] (BROA)
KBGY-FM..... Fairbault, MN [*FM radio station call letters*] (BROA)
KBGZ-FM..... Galena, KS [*FM radio station call letters*] (BROA)
KBH............ Kaufman & Broad Home [*NYSE symbol*] (TTSB)
KBH............ Kaufman & Broad Home Corp. [*NYSE symbol*] (SPSG)
KBH............ Killed by Helicopter [*In reference to the enemy*] [*Vietnam*]
KBHA-FM..... Wake Village, TX [*FM radio station call letters*] (BROA)
KBHB............ Sturgis, SD [*AM radio station call letters*]
KBHC............ Nashville, AR [*AM radio station call letters*]
KBHD-FM..... Gregory, TX [*FM radio station call letters*] (BROA)
KBHE............ Rapid City, SD [*FM radio station call letters*]
KBHE-TV...... Rapid City, SD [*Television station call letters*]
KBHH-FM..... Kerman, CA [*FM radio station call letters*] (BROA)
KBHI-FM..... Miner, MO [*FM radio station call letters*] (BROA)
KBHJ-FM..... Jackson, WY [*FM radio station call letters*] (BROA)
KBHK............ San Francisco, CA [*Television station call letters*]
KBHL............ Osakis, MN [*FM radio station call letters*]
KBHM............ Birmingham [*Alabama*] [*ICAO location identifier*] (ICLI)
KBHM-FM..... Johannesburg, CA [*FM radio station call letters*] (BROA)
KBHN-FM..... Hydesville, CA [*FM radio station call letters*] (BROA)
KBHO-FM..... Boonville, MO [*FM radio station call letters*] (BROA)
KBHP............ Bemidji, MN [*FM radio station call letters*]
KBHQ-FM..... Moapa Valley, NV [*FM radio station call letters*] (BROA)
KBHR............ Big Bear City, CA [*FM radio station call letters*]
KBHS............ Hot Springs, AR [*AM radio station call letters*]
KBHT............ Crockett, TX [*FM radio station call letters*]
KBHU............ Spearfish, SD [*FM radio station call letters*]
KBHV-FM..... Wellton, AZ [*FM radio station call letters*] (BROA)
KBHW............ International Falls, MN [*FM radio station call letters*]
KBHX-FM..... Shingletown, CA [*FM radio station call letters*] (BROA)
KBHY-FM..... Atkins, AR [*FM radio station call letters*] (BROA)
KBHZ-FM..... Willmar, MN [*FM radio station call letters*] (RBYB)
KBI............ Kawecki Berylco Industries (ACAE)
KBI............ Keyboard Immortals [*Recording label*]

KBI............... Key Buying Influence (WDMC)
KBI............... Kill Before Intercept [*Military*] (ACAE)
Kb/i............... Kilobits per Inch (VLIE)
KBI............... Klan Bureau of Investigation (SAUO)
KBI............... Kribi [*Cameroon*] [*Airport symbol*] (OAG)
KBIA............. Columbia, MO [*FM radio station call letters*]
KBIA............. Kent Barlow Information Associates [*British*] (NITA)
KBIB............. Marion, TX [*AM radio station call letters*]
KBIC............. Raymondville, TX [*FM radio station call letters*] (RBYB)
KBID............. Bakersfield, CA [*AM radio station call letters*]
KBIE-FM ...... Ingalls, KS [*FM radio station call letters*] (BROA)
KBIF............. El Paso/Biggs Air Force Base [*Texas*] [*ICAO location identifier*] (ICLI)
KBIF............. Fresno, CA [*AM radio station call letters*]
KBIG............. Los Angeles, CA [*FM radio station call letters*]
KBIH-FM ...... Coeur d'Alene, ID [*FM radio station call letters*] (BROA)
KBII-FM .... Hatfield, AR [*FM radio station call letters*] (BROA)
KBIJ-FM .... Mena, AR [*FM radio station call letters*] (BROA)
KBIL............. Breckenridge, TX [*AM radio station call letters*]
KBIL-FM ...... Grand Isle, LA [*FM radio station call letters*] (BROA)
KBIM............ Keyboard Interface Module (MCD)
KBIM............ Roswell, NM [*AM radio station call letters*]
KBIM-FM ..... Roswell, NM [*FM radio station call letters*]
KBIM-TV ..... Roswell, NM [*Television station call letters*]
KBIN............ Council Bluffs, IA [*Television station call letters*]
KBIO-FM ..... Natchitoches, LA [*FM radio station call letters*] (BROA)
KBIQ............ Fountain, CO [*FM radio station call letters*]
KBIQ-FM ..... Manitou Springs, CO [*FM radio station call letters*] (RBYB)
KBIS............. Kitchen and Bath Industry Show West (ITD)
KBISKK....... Kodak Business Information Services K.K. (EFIS)
Kbit............. Kilobit
KBIT............ Knowledge Based Intelligent Tracking (ACAE)
KBIT/S........ KiloBITS [*Binary Digits*] per Second [*Transmission rate*] [*Computer science*] (TEL)
Kbit/s.......... Kilobits/Second (VLIE)
KBIU............ Lake Charles, LA [*FM radio station call letters*]
KBIV............ El Paso, TX [*AM radio station call letters*] (BROA)
KBIX............ Biloxi/Keesler Air Force Base [*Mississippi*] [*ICAO location identifier*] (ICLI)
KBIX............ Muskogee, OK [*AM radio station call letters*]
KBIY-FM ...... Van Buren, MO [*FM radio station call letters*] (BROA)
KBIZ............ Ottumwa, IA [*AM radio station call letters*]
KBJ............... Kentucky State Bar Journal [*A publication*] (DLA)
KBJA............ Sandy, UT [*AM radio station call letters*] (BROA)
KBJC............ Kansas City, KS [*AM radio station call letters*] (BROA)
KBJD............ Denver, CO [*AM radio station call letters*] (BROA)
KBJE............ Monroe, LA [*AM radio station call letters*] (BROA)
KBJF-FM ..... Shelby, MT [*FM radio station call letters*] (BROA)
KBJG-FM ..... Mesquite, NV [*FM radio station call letters*] (BROA)
KBJJ............ Marshall, MN [*FM radio station call letters*]
KBJL............ Sheridan, WY [*Television station call letters*] (BROA)
KBJM........... Lemmon, SD [*AM radio station call letters*]
KBJN............ Ely, NV [*Television station call letters*] (BROA)
KBJO............ Avalon, CA [*Television station call letters*] (BROA)
KBJQ-FM ..... Bronson, KS [*FM radio station call letters*] (BROA)
KBJR............ Superior, WI [*Television station call letters*]
KBJS............ Jacksonville, TX [*FM radio station call letters*]
KBJT............ Fordyce, AR [*AM radio station call letters*]
KBJU-FM ..... Bagdad, AZ [*FM radio station call letters*] (BROA)
KBK............. KBK Capital [*AMEX symbol*] (TTSB)
KBK............. KBK Capital Corp. [*AMEX symbol*] (SAG)
KBK............. Kirkjubaejar [*Iceland*] [*Airport symbol*] (AD)
KBKB........... Fort Madison, IA [*AM radio station call letters*]
KBKB-FM ..... Fort Madison, IA [*FM radio station call letters*]
KBKC........... KBK Capital Corp. [*NASDAQ symbol*] (SAG)
KBK Cap...... KBK Capital Corp. [*Associated Press*] (SAG)
KBKC-FM ..... Moberly, MO [*FM radio station call letters*] (BROA)
KBKF-FM ..... Snyder, OK [*FM radio station call letters*] (BROA)
KBKG........... Corning, AR [*FM radio station call letters*]
KBKH-FM ..... Ilwaco, WA [*FM radio station call letters*] (BROA)
KBKK........... Spanish Fork, UT [*FM radio station call letters*] (RBYB)
KBKK-FM ..... Pillager, MN [*FM radio station call letters*] (BROA)
KBKL........... Grand Junction, CO [*FM radio station call letters*]
KBKO........... Billings, MT [*FM radio station call letters*] (RBYB)
KBKO-AM..... Santa Barbara, CA [*AM radio station call letters*] (BROA)
KBKR........... Baker City, OR [*AM radio station call letters*]
KBKS-FM ..... Tacoma, WA [*FM radio station call letters*] (RBYB)
KBKW.......... Aberdeen, WA [*AM radio station call letters*] (RBYB)
KBL............. Design, Development and Implementation of a Knowledge-Based Leitstand (SAUO)
KBL............. Hebraeisches und Aramaeisches Lexikon zum Alten Testament [*L. Koehler and W. Baumgarther*] [*A publication*] (BJA)
KBL............. Kabul [*Afghanistan*] [*Airport symbol*] (OAG)
KBL............. Kabul [*Afghanistan*] [*Seismograph station code, US Geological Survey*] (SEIS)
KBL............. Keebler Foods [*NYSE symbol*] (SG)
KBL............. Keyboard Listener [*Computer science*] (MHDI)
KBL............. Kill Before Launch [*Military*] (ACAE)
KBL............. Kilusan ng Bangong Lipunan [*New Society Movement*] [*Philippines*] (PD)
KBL............. Kraft Black Liquor [*Pulping technology*]
KBL............. Kredietbank Luxembourgeoise [*Luxembourg*]
KBL............. Lexicon in Veteris Testamenti Libros. Supplementum [*L. Koehler and W. Baumgartner*] [*A publication*] (BJA)
KBLA............ Santa Monica, CA [*AM radio station call letters*]
KBLD-FM ..... Kennewick, WA [*FM radio station call letters*] (BROA)

KBLE............ Seattle, WA [*AM radio station call letters*]
KBLF............ Red Bluff, CA [*AM radio station call letters*]
KBLG............ Billings, MT [*AM radio station call letters*]
KBLH............ Keel Blade Height [*Botany*]
KBLI............. Bellingham/International [*Washington*] [*ICAO location identifier*] (ICLI)
KBLI............. Blackfoot, ID [*AM radio station call letters*] (BROA)
KBLJ............ La Junta, CO [*FM radio station call letters*]
KBLK........... Burnet, TX [*FM radio station call letters*]
KBLL........... Helena, MT [*AM radio station call letters*]
KBLL........... Keel Blade Length [*Botany*]
KBLL-FM ..... Helena, MT [*FM radio station call letters*]
KBLP........... Lindsay, OK [*FM radio station call letters*]
KBLPS .... Knowledge-Based Logistics Planning Shell
KBLQ........... Logan, UT [*FM radio station call letters*]
KBLR........... Paradise, NV [*Television station call letters*]
KBLS........... North Fort Riley, KS [*FM radio station call letters*]
KBLT-FM ..... Leakey, TX [*FM radio station call letters*] (BROA)
KBLU........... Yuma, AZ [*AM radio station call letters*]
KBLUP .... Kootenay/Boundary Land Use Plan (SAUO)
KBLUPHLP.. Kootenay/Boundary Land Use Plan Higher Level Plan (SAUO)
KBLV........... Bellerville/Scott Air Force Base [*Illinois*] [*ICAO location identifier*] (ICLI)
KBLV........... Bellevue, WA [*AM radio station call letters*]
KBLX........... Berkeley, CA [*FM radio station call letters*] (RBYB)
KBLZ........... Kaneohe, HI [*FM radio station call letters*]
KBM............. Kabwum [*Papua New Guinea*] [*Airport symbol*] (OAG)
KBM............. Karissimo Bene Merenti [*To the Most Dear and Well-Deserving*] [*Correspondence*]
KBM............. Keyboard Monitor [*Computer science*]
KBM............. Knowledge-Based Manufacturing
KBM............. Knowledge Base Machine [*Computer science*]
KBMA........... Bryan, TX [*FM radio station call letters*]
KBMB-FM .... Sacramento, CA [*FM radio station call letters*] (BROA)
KBMC........... Bozeman, MT [*FM radio station call letters*]
KBME........... Bismarck, ND [*Television station call letters*]
KBME........... Houston, TX [*AM radio station call letters*] (BROA)
KBMEDM...... Knowledge Based Model of the Experienced Decision Maker (VLIE)
KBME-DT..... Bismarck, ND [*Television station call letters*] (BROA)
KBMG........... Hamilton, MT [*FM radio station call letters*]
KBMI............ Roma, TX [*FM radio station call letters*]
KBMJ........... Hardin, MT [*FM radio station call letters*]
KBMR........... Bismarck, ND [*AM radio station call letters*]
KBMS........... Knowledge Based Management System
KBMS........... Knowledge Base Management System [*Computer science*]
KBMS........... Vancouver, WA [*AM radio station call letters*]
KBMT.......... Beaumont, TX [*Television station call letters*]
KBMT.......... Knowledge-Based Machine Translation [*Computer science*]
KB-MUSICA-2671... Knowledge-Based Multi-Sensor Systems in CIM Applications (SAUO)
KBMV........... Birch Tree, MO [*AM radio station call letters*]
KBMV-FM ..... Birch Tree, MO [*FM radio station call letters*]
KBMW .... Breckenridge, MN [*AM radio station call letters*]
KBMX........... Eldon, MO [*FM radio station call letters*]
KBMY........... Bismarck, ND [*Television station call letters*]
KBN .... Kill Bad Name [*Marketing*] (WDMC)
KBNA .... El Paso, TX [*AM radio station call letters*]
KBNA .... Nashville/Metropolitan [*Tennessee*] [*ICAO location identifier*] (ICLI)
KBNA-FM .... El Paso, TX [*FM radio station call letters*]
KBNB-AM ..... Gilmer, TX [*AM radio station call letters*] (RBYB)
KBND .... Bend, OR [*AM radio station call letters*]
KBNF-FM ..... Chester, CA [*FM radio station call letters*] (BROA)
KBNJ .... Corpus Christi, TX [*FM radio station call letters*]
KBNL .... Laredo, TX [*FM radio station call letters*]
KBNN-AM ..... Lebanon, MO [*AM radio station call letters*] (BROA)
KBNO .... Denver, CO [*AM radio station call letters*]
KBNP .... Portland, OR [*AM radio station call letters*]
KBNR .... Brownsville, TX [*FM radio station call letters*]
KBNU-FM ..... Uvalde, TX [*FM radio station call letters*] (RBYB)
KBNWR........ Klamath Basin National Wildlife Refuges (SAUO)
KBO .... Kabalo [*Zaire*] [*Airport symbol*] (AD)
KBO .... Keep Buggering On [*Perseverance*] [*Slang*] [*British*] (DSUE)
KBo............. Keilschrifttexte aus Boghazkoi [*A publication*] (BJA)
KBO .... Kite and Balloon Officer [*Navy*]
KBO .... Kommunistischer Bund Oesterreichs [*Communist League of Austria*] [*Political party*] (PPW)
KBO .... Kuiper Belt Objects [*Planetary science*]
KBO .... Organization for the Management and Development of the Kagera River Basin (EA)
KBOA .... Kennett, MO [*AM radio station call letters*]
KBOA .... Piggott, AR [*FM radio station call letters*] (RBYB)
KBOB .... Muscatine, IA [*FM radio station call letters*]
KBOC .... Bridgeport, TX [*AM radio station call letters*]
KBOE .... Oskaloosa, IA [*AM radio station call letters*]
KBOE-FM ..... Oskaloosa, IA [*FM radio station call letters*]
KBOF .... Washington/Bolling Air Force Base [*District of Columbia*] [*ICAO location identifier*] (ICLI)
KBOI .... Boise/Boise Air Terminal [*Idaho*] [*ICAO location identifier*] (ICLI)
KBOI .... Boise, ID [*AM radio station call letters*]
KBOK .... Malvern, AR [*AM radio station call letters*]
KBOK-FM ..... Malvern, AR [*FM radio station call letters*]
KBOM .... Los Alamos, NM [*FM radio station call letters*]
KBON-FM ..... Mamou, LA [*FM radio station call letters*] (BROA)
KBOO .... Portland, OR [*FM radio station call letters*]
KBOP .... Pleasanton, TX [*AM radio station call letters*]
KBOP-FM ..... Jourdanton, TX [*FM radio station call letters*] (BROA)

KBOQ .... Carmel, CA [*FM radio station call letters*] (RBYB)
KBOR .... Brownsville, TX [*AM radio station call letters*]
KBOS .... Boston/Logan International [*Massachusetts*] [*ICAO location identifier*] (ICLI)
KBOS .... Tulare, CA [*FM radio station call letters*]
KBOT .... Kansas City Board of Trade
KBOT .... Pelican Rapids, MN [*FM radio station call letters*]
KBOV .... Bishop, CA [*AM radio station call letters*]
KBOW .... Butte, MT [*AM radio station call letters*]
KBOX .... Lompoc, CA [*FM radio station call letters*]
KBOY .... Medford, OR [*FM radio station call letters*]
KBOZ .... Bozeman, MT [*AM radio station call letters*]
KBP .... Kainate-Binding Protein [*Biochemistry*]
KBP .... Kappa Beta Pi [*Society*]
KBP .... Kent-Barlow Publications Ltd. [*Information service or system*] (IID)
KBP .... Keyboard Process [*Computer science*]
KBP .... Kiev Borispol Airport [*Former USSR*] [*Airport symbol*] (OAG)
kbp .... Kilobase Pairs [*Genetics*]
KBP .... King's Bishop's Pawn [*Chess*] (IIA)
KBP .... Kite Balloon Pilot
KBP .... Koala Bear Park [*Adelaide*] [*Airport symbol*] (AD)
KBPA .... Knowledge-Based Programming Assistant (PDAA)
KBPA-AM .... Palo Alto, CA [*AM radio station call letters*] (BROA)
KBPAP .... Kidney Bean Purple Acid Phosphatase [*An enzyme*]
KBPI .... Denver, CO [*FM radio station call letters*]
KBPK .... Buena Park, CA [*FM radio station call letters*]
KBPL .... Communist League Proletarian Left [*Netherlands*] [*Political party*] (PPW)
KBPR .... Brainerd, MN [*FM radio station call letters*]
KBPRC .... Keyboard and Printer Controller [*Computer science*] (NITA)
KBPS .... Kilobits per Second (NAKS)
Kbps .... Kilobits per Second [*Computer science*]
KBPS .... Kilobytes Per Second (NITA)
KBps .... Kilobytes per Second [*Computer science*] (DOM)
KBPS .... Portland, OR [*AM radio station call letters*]
Kbps .... thousand bits per second (SAUS)
KBPS-FM .... Portland, OR [*FM radio station call letters*]
KBPT .... Beaumont Port-Arthur/Jefferson County [*Texas*] [*ICAO location identifier*] (ICLI)
KBPX .... Flagstaff, AZ [*Television station call letters*] (BROA)
KBQQ .... Minot, ND [*FM radio station call letters*]
KBR .... Kaaba Resources [*Vancouver Stock Exchange symbol*]
KBR .... Kota Bharu [*Malaysia*] [*Airport symbol*] (OAG)
KBr .... Potassium Bromide [*An anticonvulsant and sedative*] (DAVI)
KBRA-FM .... Freer, TX [*FM radio station call letters*] (BROA)
KBRB .... Ainsworth, NE [*AM radio station call letters*]
KBRB-FM .... Ainsworth, NE [*FM radio station call letters*]
KBRC .... Mount Vernon, WA [*AM radio station call letters*]
KBRD .... Lacey, WA [*AM radio station call letters*] (RBYB)
KBRE .... Cedar City, UT [*AM radio station call letters*]
KBRE-FM .... Cedar City, UT [*FM radio station call letters*]
KBRF .... Fergus Falls, MN [*AM radio station call letters*]
KBRG .... Fremont, CA [*FM radio station call letters*]
KBRH .... Baton Rouge, LA [*AM radio station call letters*]
KBRI .... Brinkley, AR [*AM radio station call letters*]
KBRJ .... Anchorage, AK [*AM radio station call letters*]
KBRK .... Brookings, SD [*AM radio station call letters*]
KBRK-FM .... Brookings, SD [*FM radio station call letters*]
KBRL .... McCook, NE [*AM radio station call letters*]
KBRN .... Boerne, TX [*AM radio station call letters*]
KBRO .... Bremerton, WA [*AM radio station call letters*]
KBRO .... Brownsville/International [*Texas*] [*ICAO location identifier*] (ICLI)
KBRQ .... Hillsboro, TX [*FM radio station call letters*]
KBRR .... Thief River Falls, MN [*Television station call letters*]
KBRS .... Springdale, AR [*FM radio station call letters*]
KBRT .... Avalon, CA [*AM radio station call letters*]
KBRU .... Fort Morgan, CO [*FM radio station call letters*]
KBRV .... Soda Springs, ID [*AM radio station call letters*]
KBRW .... Barrow, AK [*AM radio station call letters*]
KBRW-FM .... Barrow, AK [*FM radio station call letters*] (RBYB)
KBRX .... O'Neill, NE [*AM radio station call letters*]
KBRX-FM .... O'Neill, NE [*FM radio station call letters*]
KBRZ .... Freeport, TX [*AM radio station call letters*]
KBS .... Bo [*Sierra Leone*] [*Airport symbol*] [*Obsolete*] (OAG)
KBS .... Gamair Ltd. [*Gambia*] [*ICAO designator*] (FAAC)
KBS .... Kellogg Biological Station [*Michigan State University*]
kbs .... KiloBITS [*Binary Digits*] per Second [*Transmission rate*] [*Computer science*]
Kb/s .... Kilobits per Second (VLIE)
KBS .... Kilobytes per Second [*Computer science*]
KBS .... Kinematic Bombing System
KBS .... Kingsbay [*Spitsbergen*] [*Seismograph station code, US Geological Survey*] (SEIS)
KBS .... Kinki Broadcasting System (SAUO)
KBS .... Kluver-Bucy Syndrome [*Psychiatry*] (DAVI)
KBS .... Knight of the Blessed Sacrament
KBS .... Knowledge-Based System [*Computer model*] [*Computer science*]
KBS .... Korea Base Section (SAUO)
KBS .... Korean Broadcasting System [*South Korea*] (FEA)
KBS .... Korean Bureau of Standards, Seoul (SAUO)
KBS .... Stites, McElwain & Fowler, Bellarmine College Library, Louisville, KY [*OCLC symbol*] (OCLC)
KBSA .... El Dorado, AR [*FM radio station call letters*]
KBSA .... Kassian Benevolent Society in America (EA)
KBSA .... Knowledge-Based Software Assistant [*Computer science*]

KBSB .... Bemidji, MN [*FM radio station call letters*]
KBSC .... Knowledge-Based Systems Centre [*Polytechnic of the South Bank*] [*British*] (CB)
KBSD .... Ensign, KS [*Television station call letters*]
KBSE .... Knowledge-Based Software Engineering (RALS)
KBSEA .... Bulletin. Kyoto Educational University. Series B. Mathematics and Natural Science (journ.) (SAUS)
KBSF .... Springhill, LA [*AM radio station call letters*]
KBSG .... Auburn, WA [*AM radio station call letters*]
KBSG .... Tacoma, WA [*FM radio station call letters*]
KBSH .... Hays, KS [*Television station call letters*]
KBSI .... Cape Girardeau, MO [*Television station call letters*]
KBSL .... Goodland, KS [*Television station call letters*]
KBSL .... Knowledge Base Services Ltd. (SAUO)
KBSM .... Austin/Bergstrom Air Force Base [*Texas*] [*ICAO location identifier*] (ICLI)
KBSM .... McCall, ID [*FM radio station call letters*]
KBSN .... Moses Lake, WA [*AM radio station call letters*]
KBSO .... Corpus Christi, TX [*FM radio station call letters*]
KBSP .... Salem, OR [*Television station call letters*]
KBSR .... Kankakee, Beaverville & Southern Railroad Co. [*AAR code*]
KBSR .... Laurel, MT [*AM radio station call letters*]
KBST .... Big Spring, TX [*AM radio station call letters*]
KBST-FM .... Big Spring, TX [*FM radio station call letters*]
KBSU .... Boise, ID [*AM radio station call letters*]
KBSU-FM .... Boise, ID [*FM radio station call letters*]
KBSV-TV .... Ceres, CA [*TV station call letters*] (RBYB)
KBSW .... Twin Falls, ID [*FM radio station call letters*]
KBSX-FM .... Boise, ID [*FM radio station call letters*] (BROA)
KBSY-FM .... Burley, ID [*FM radio station call letters*] (BROA)
KBSZ .... Wickenburg, AZ [*AM radio station call letters*] (RBYB)
KBT .... Kerry Blue Terrier (ROAS)
KBTA .... Batesville, AR [*AM radio station call letters*]
KBTA-FM .... Batesville, AR [*FM radio station call letters*] (BROA)
KBTC .... Houston, MO [*AM radio station call letters*]
KBTC .... Knoxville Building Trades Council (SAUO)
KBTC .... Tacoma, WA [*FM radio station call letters*]
KBTC-TV .... Tacoma, WA [*Television station call letters*] (BROA)
KBTD .... Knee Board Training Device [*Military*] (MCD)
KBTE-FM .... Rockport, TX [*FM radio station call letters*] (BROA)
KBTG .... Keep Britain Tidy Group (DCTA)
KBTL-FM .... El Dorado, KS [*FM radio station call letters*] (BROA)
KBTM .... Jonesboro, AR [*AM radio station call letters*]
KBTN .... Neosho, MO [*AM radio station call letters*]
KBTN-FM .... Neosho, MO [*FM radio station call letters*] (RBYB)
KBTO .... Bottineau, ND [*FM radio station call letters*]
KBTR .... Baton Rouge/Ryan Field [*Louisiana*] [*ICAO location identifier*] (ICLI)
KBTS .... Big Spring, TX [*FM radio station call letters*]
KBTT .... Bridgeport, TX [*FM radio station call letters*]
KBTU .... Kilo British Thermal Unit (WDAA)
KBTV .... Burlington/International [*Vermont*] [*ICAO location identifier*] (ICLI)
KBTX .... Bryan, TX [*Television station call letters*]
KBU .... Keyboard Unit [*Computer science*] (NASA)
KBU .... Knuckle Buster University [*Facetious term*]
KBU .... Kotabaru [*West Irian, Indonesia*] [*Airport symbol*] (AD)
KBUA-FM .... San Fernando, CA [*FM radio station call letters*] (BROA)
KBUB-FM .... Brownwood, TX [*FM radio station call letters*] (BROA)
KBUC .... Pleasonton, TX [*FM radio station call letters*]
KBUC .... Upper Canada King's Bench Reports [*A publication*] (DLA)
KBUE .... Long Beach, CA [*FM radio station call letters*] (RBYB)
KBUF .... Buffalo/Greater Buffalo International [*New York*] [*ICAO location identifier*] (ICLI)
KBUF .... Holcomb, KS [*AM radio station call letters*]
KBUG .... Osceola, MO [*AM radio station call letters*]
KBUK .... La Grange, TX [*FM radio station call letters*]
KBUL .... Billings, MT [*AM radio station call letters*] (BROA)
KBUL .... Carson City, NV [*FM radio station call letters*]
KBUL-AM .... Modesto, CA [*AM radio station call letters*] (BROA)
KBUL-FM .... Carson City, NV [*FM radio station call letters*] (BROA)
KBUN .... Bemidji, MN [*AM radio station call letters*]
KBUQ-FM .... Paradise Valley, AZ [*FM radio station call letters*] (RBYB)
KBUR .... Burbank/Hollywood-Burbank [*California*] [*ICAO location identifier*] (ICLI)
KBUR .... Burlington, IA [*AM radio station call letters*]
KBUS .... Paris, TX [*FM radio station call letters*]
KBUT .... Crested Butte, CO [*FM radio station call letters*]
KBUW-FM .... Buffalo, WY [*FM radio station call letters*] (BROA)
KBUX .... Quartzsite, AZ [*FM radio station call letters*]
KBUY .... Ruidoso, NM [*AM radio station call letters*]
KBUY-FM .... Amarillo, TX [*FM radio station call letters*]
KBUZ .... Topeka, KS [*FM radio station call letters*]
KBV .... Kobold Resources Ltd. [*Vancouver Stock Exchange symbol*]
KBV .... Kustbevakningen [*Sweden*] [*ICAO designator*] (FAAC)
KBVA .... Bella Vista, AR [*FM radio station call letters*]
KBVC-FM .... Buena Vista, CO [*FM radio station call letters*] (BROA)
KBVI .... Boulder, CO [*AM radio station call letters*] (RBYB)
KBVM .... Portland, OR [*FM radio station call letters*]
KBVR .... Corvallis, OR [*FM radio station call letters*]
KBVU .... Eureka, CA [*Television station call letters*]
KBVU-FM .... Alta, IA [*FM radio station call letters*] (BROA)
KBVV .... Enid, OK [*FM radio station call letters*]
KBW .... Klan Border Watch (SAUO)
KBW .... Kommunistischer Bund Westdeutschland [*Communist League of West Germany*] [*Political party*] (PPW)
KBWB .... San Francisco, CA [*Television station call letters*] (BROA)

KBWC	Marshall, TX [*FM radio station call letters*]
KBWD	Brownwood, TX [*AM radio station call letters*]
KBWI	Baltimore/Baltimore-Washington International [*Maryland*] [*ICAO location identifier*] (ICLI)
KBWS	Sisseton, SD [*FM radio station call letters*]
KBXB-FM	Sikeston, MO [*FM radio station call letters*] (RBYB)
KBXL	Caldwell, ID [*FM radio station call letters*]
KBXR	Ashland, MO [*FM radio station call letters*]
KBXX	Houston, TX [*FM radio station call letters*]
KBXY	Baker, CA [*FM radio station call letters*]
KBY	Streaky Bay [*Australia*] [*Airport symbol*] (OAG)
KBYB	El Dorado, AR [*FM radio station call letters*]
KBYE	Oklahoma City, OK [*AM radio station call letters*]
KBYG	Big Spring, TX [*AM radio station call letters*]
KBYG	Coahoma, TX [*FM radio station call letters*]
KBYH	Blytheville Air Force Base [*Arkansas*] [*ICAO location identifier*] (ICLI)
KBYN	Arnold, CA [*FM radio station call letters*]
KBYO	Tallulah, LA [*AM radio station call letters*]
KBYO-FM	Tallulah, LA [*FM radio station call letters*]
KBYR	Anchorage, AK [*AM radio station call letters*]
kbyte/sec	kilobytes per second (SAUS)
Kbytes/sec	Kilobytes per Second [*Computer science*] (IGQR)
KBYU	Provo, UT [*FM radio station call letters*]
KBYU-TV	Provo, UT [*Television station call letters*]
KBYZ	Bismarck, ND [*FM radio station call letters*]
KBZE	Berwick, LA [*FM radio station call letters*]
KBZG-FM	Payson, AZ [*FM radio station call letters*] (BROA)
KBZK-FM	Morro Bay, CA [*FM radio station call letters*] (BROA)
KBZN	Ogden, UT [*FM radio station call letters*]
KBZO	Lubbock, TX [*AM radio station call letters*] (RBYB)
KBZQ	Lawton, OK [*FM radio station call letters*]
KBZR	Coolidge, AZ [*FM radio station call letters*] (RBYB)
KBZS-AM	Grand Junction, CO [*AM radio station call letters*] (RBYB)
KBZT	San Diego, CA [*FM radio station call letters*]
KBZX-FM	Paso Robles, CA [*FM radio station call letters*] (BROA)
KBZY	Salem, OR [*AM radio station call letters*]
KBZZ	La Junta, CO [*AM radio station call letters*]
KC	Canada [*IYRU nationality code*] (IYR)
KC	Cook Islands International [*ICAO designator*] (AD)
KC	Kalamazoo College (SAUO)
KC	[*The*] Kanawha Central Railway Co. [*AAR code*]
KC	Kangaroo Care [*Medicine*] (MELL)
KC	Kansas Central Railways (SAUO)
KC	Kansas City [*Missouri*] [*Slang*]
KC	Kansas City Area Office (SAUO)
KC	Kansas City Chiefs [*National Football League*] [*1963-present*] (NFLA)
KC	Kansas City Plant (SAUO)
KC	Kansas City-St. Joseph [*Diocesan abbreviation*] [*Missouri*] (TOCD)
KC	Karman Constant [*Physics*]
KC	Kartell Convent Deutscher Studenten Juedischen Glaubens (BJA)
KC	Kathodal Closing [*Medicine*]
KC	Keble College (SAUO)
KC	Kendall College (SAUO)
KC	Kennedy Center (SAUO)
KC	Kennel Club
KC	Kent Chemical Co. Ltd. (SAUO)
KC	Kenyon College (SAUO)
KC	Keratoconjunctivitis [*Ophthalmology*]
KC	Keratoconus [*Ophthalmology*] (DAVI)
KC	Keratoma Climacterium [*Dermatology*] (DAVI)
KC	Kerr Cell [*Optics*]
KC	Keston College (SAUO)
KC	Ketocyclazocine [*Biochemistry*]
KC	Keuka College (SAUO)
KC	Key Company (SAUO)
KC	Keystone Center [*An association*] (EA)
KC	Keystone College (SAUO)
KC	Kilgore College (SAUO)
kc	Kilocalorie
KC	Kilocharacter (BUR)
KC	Kilocurie (IAA)
kc	Kilocurie (IDOE)
KC	Kilocycle (AEBE)
kc	Kilocycle [*Radio*]
kc	Kilograms per Square Centimeter (DS)
KC	King's Colonials [*British military*] (DMA)
KC	Kings Council (SAUO)
KC	King's Counsel [*British*]
KC	Kings County [*Sussex, New Brunswick*] (DAS)
KC	King's Cross [*British*] (ADA)
KC	Kirksville College (SAUO)
KC	Kiting Check [*Investment*] (MHDB)
KC	Knees to Chest [*Position*] [*Medicine*] (DAVI)
KC	Knickerbocker Conference (PSS)
KC	Knight Club (EA)
KC	Knight Commander
KC	Knight of the Crescent [*Turkey*]
KC	Knights of Columbus
KC	Knox College (SAUO)
KC	Knoxville College (SAUO)
KC	Knuckle Cracking [*Orthopedics*] (DAVI)
Kc	Koruna [*Czech Coin*] (BARN)
Kc	Kupffer Cell [*Histology*]
KC	Kyle Classification [*Library science*]
KC	Strikeout, Called [*Baseball term*] (NDBD)
KC-10	Extender (SAUS)
KCA	Kansas Chiropractic Association (SRA)
KCA	Kansas Contractors Association (SRA)
KCA	Keeshond Club of America (EA)
KCA	Keesings Contemporary Archives [*A publication*] [*Also, an information service or system*]
KCA	Kentucky Callers Association (EA)
KCA	Kentucky Cattlemen's Association (SRA)
KCA	Kentucky Coal Association (SRA)
KCA	Kikuyu Central Association (SAUO)
KCA	Kindness Club of Africa (SAUO)
KCA	Kiowa-Comanche-Apache
KCA	Kitchen Cabinet Association (SAUO)
KCA	Komondor Club of America (EA)
KCA	Kuvasz Club of America (EA)
KCAB	Dardanelle, AR [*AM radio station call letters*]
KCAC	Camden, AR [*FM radio station call letters*]
KCAC	Kansas Collegiate Athletic Conference (PSS)
KCAC	Korean Civil Assistance Command (SAUO)
KCAD-FM	Dickinson, ND [*FM radio station call letters*] (RBYB)
KCAG	Korean Civil Action Group (SAUO)
KCAH	Watsonville, CA [*Television station call letters*]
KCAILUC	Kiowa-Commanche-Apache Intertribal Land Use Committee
KCAJ-FM	Roseau, MN [*FM radio station call letters*] (BROA)
Kcal	Kilcalorie (NTIO)
Kcal	Kilocalorie (SHCU)
kcal	Kilocalorie
KCAL	Redlands, CA [*AM radio station call letters*] (RBYB)
KCAL-FM	Redlands, CA [*FM radio station call letters*]
KCAL-TV	Los Angeles, CA [*Television station call letters*]
KCAM	Glennallen, AK [*AM radio station call letters*]
KCAN	Albion, NE [*Television station call letters*]
KC&C	Kembla Coal and Coke (SAUO)
KCAO	Kansas City Area Office [*Energy Research and Development Administration*]
KCAP	Helena, MT [*AM radio station call letters*]
KCAQ	Oxnard, CA [*FM radio station call letters*]
KCAR	Caribou [*Maine*] [*ICAO location identifier*] (ICLI)
KCAR	Clarksville, TX [*AM radio station call letters*]
KCAS	Knots Calibrated Airspeed (MCD)
KCAS-FM	McCook, TX [*FM radio station call letters*] (BROA)
KCAT	Kemptville College of Agricultural Technology [*Canada*] (ARC)
KCAT	Pine Bluff, AR [*AM radio station call letters*]
KCAU	Sioux City, IA [*Television station call letters*]
KCAW	Sitka, AK [*FM radio station call letters*]
KCAY	Russell, KS [*FM radio station call letters*]
KCAZ	Mission, KS [*AM radio station call letters*] (RBYB)
KCB	Kansas City Ballet
KCB	Kartell Convent Blaetter (BJA)
KCB	Kenya Commercial Bank (SAUO)
KCB	Keyboard Change Button [*Computer science*]
KCB	Knight Commander of the [*Order of the*] Bath [*British*] (GPO)
KCBA	King County Bar Association (SAUO)
KCBA	Salinas, CA [*Television station call letters*]
KCBC	Riverbank, CA [*AM radio station call letters*]
KCBD	Lubbock, TX [*Television station call letters*]
KCBF	Fairbanks, AK [*AM radio station call letters*]
KCBI	Dallas, TX [*FM radio station call letters*]
KCBL-AM	Fresno, CA [*AM radio station call letters*] (BROA)
KCBM	Colombus Air Force Base [*Mississippi*] [*ICAO location identifier*] (ICLI)
KCBN	Reno, NV [*AM radio station call letters*]
KCBNAY	Annals. Kurashiki Central Hospital (journ.) (SAUS)
KCBQ	San Diego, CA [*AM radio station call letters*]
KCBQ-FM	San Diego, CA [*FM radio station call letters*]
KCBR	Monument, CO [*AM radio station call letters*]
KCBS	Los Angeles, CA [*FM radio station call letters*]
KCBS	San Francisco, CA [*AM radio station call letters*]
KCBS-TV	Los Angeles, CA [*Television station call letters*]
KCBT	Board of Trade of Kansas City, MO (EA)
KCBX	San Luis Obispo, CA [*FM radio station call letters*]
KCBY	Coos Bay, OR [*Television station call letters*]
KCBZ	Cannon Beach, OR [*FM radio station call letters*] (RBYB)
KCC	Centre College of Kentucky, Danville, KY [*OCLC symbol*] (OCLC)
KCC	Coffman Cove, AK [*Location identifier*] [*FAA*] (FAAL)
KCC	Kansas City Connecting Railroad Co. [*AAR code*]
KCC	Kansas Co-Operative Council (SRA)
KCC	Karamea Consultative Committee (SAUO)
KCC	Kathodal Closure Contraction [*Medicine*]
KCC	Kellogg Community College (SAUO)
KCC	Kenai Community College (SAUO)
KCC	Kennedy Cultural Center (SAUO)
KCC	Kentucky Chamber of Commerce (SRA)
KCC	Keokuk Community College [*Iowa*]
KCC	Kernel Command & Control (SAUS)
KCC	Ketchikan Community College (SAUO)
KCC	Keyboard Common Contact [*Computer science*]
KCC	Key Control Characteristic
KCC	K-III Communications [*NYSE symbol*] (TTSB)
KCC	K-III Communications Corp. [*NYSE symbol*] (SPSG)
KCC	Kingsborough Community College (SAUO)
KCC	Kiwi Conservation Club (SAUO)
KCC	Knapp Communications Corporation (SAUO)
KCC	Knife Collectors Club (EA)
KCC	Knight Commander of the [*Order of the*] Crown [*Belgium*]

KCC............ Kona Coffee Council [*Defunct*] (EA)

KCC............ Koplar Communications Center [*St. Louis, MO*] [*Telecommunications*] (TSSD)

KCC............ Korea Church Coalition for Peace, Justice and Reunification (EA)

KCC............ Korean Chamber of Commerce (SAUO)

KCCA .... Colorado City, AZ [*FM radio station call letters*]

KCCA .... Korean Chamber of Commerce in America (SAUO)

KCCB .... Corning, AR [*AM radio station call letters*]

KCCC .... Carlsbad, NM [*AM radio station call letters*]

KCCC .... Key Chain Collectors Club (EA)

KCCD .... Kentucky Council on Crime and Delinquency (SAUO)

KCCD .... Moorhead, MN [*FM radio station call letters*]

KCCE .... Keystone Center for Continuing Education (SAUO)

KCCF .... Cave Creek, AZ [*AM radio station call letters*]

KCCF .... Ferndale, WA [*AM radio station call letters*] (BROA)

KCCG-FM .... Ingleside, TX [*FM radio station call letters*] (BROA)

KCCH .... Knight Commander of Court of Honor [*British*]

KCCI .... Des Moines, IA [*Television station call letters*]

KCCI .... Kansas Chamber of Commerce and Industry (SRA)

KCCI .... Korean Chamber of Commerce and Industry (SAUO)

KCCK .... Cedar Rapids, IA [*FM radio station call letters*]

KCCM .... Kupffer Cell Conditioned Medium

KCCM .... Moorhead, MN [*FM radio station call letters*]

KCCN .... Honolulu, HI [*AM radio station call letters*]

KCCN .... Monterey, CA [*Television station call letters*]

KCCN-FM ..... Honolulu, HI [*FM radio station call letters*]

KCCO .... Alexandria, MN [*Television station call letters*]

KCCO .... Kansas City Commodity Office (SAUO)

KCCPr .... K-III Commun$2.875SrExPfd [*NYSE symbol*] (TTSB)

KCCQ .... Ames, IA [*FM radio station call letters*]

KCCR .... Pierre, SD [*AM radio station call letters*]

KCCS .... Salem, OR [*AM radio station call letters*]

KCCT .... Corpus Christi, TX [*AM radio station call letters*]

KCCT .... Kaolin Cephalin Clotting Time (PDAA)

KCCU .... Lawton, OK [*FM radio station call letters*]

KCCV .... Overland Park, KS [*AM radio station call letters*]

KCCV-FM ..... Olathe, KS [*FM radio station call letters*]

KCCW .... Walker, MN [*Television station call letters*]

KCCX-FM ..... Lexington, MO [*AM radio station call letters*] (BROA)

KCCY .... Pueblo, CO [*FM radio station call letters*]

KCDA .... Coeur D'Alene, ID [*FM radio station call letters*]

KCDC .... Longmont, CO [*AM radio station call letters*]

KCDD .... Hamlin, TX [*FM radio station call letters*]

KCDI .... Oro Valley, AZ [*FM radio station call letters*]

KCDL .... Cordell, OK [*FM radio station call letters*]

KCDMA .... Kiln, Cooler, and Dryer Manufacturers Association (SAUO)

KCDQ .... Key Centre for Design Quality (SAUO)

KCDQ .... Monahans, TX [*FM radio station call letters*]

KCDR .... Turlock, CA [*AM radio station call letters*] (RBYB)

KCDS .... Angwin, CA [*AM radio station call letters*]

KCDS .... Childress [*Texas*] [*ICAO location identifier*] (ICLI)

KCDT .... Coeur D'Alene, ID [*Television station call letters*]

KCDU-FM ..... Hollister, CA [*FM radio station call letters*] (RBYB)

KCDV-FM ..... Cordova, KS [*FM radio station call letters*] (RBYB)

KCDX .... San Carlos, AZ [*FM radio station call letters*]

KCDY .... Carlsbad, NM [*FM radio station call letters*]

KCDZ .... Twentynine Palms, CA [*FM radio station call letters*]

KCE............ Collinsville [*Australia*] [*Airport symbol*] (OAG)

KCE............ Key Configuration Element (DNAB)

KCEA .... Atherton, CA [*AM radio station call letters*]

KCEC .... Denver, CO [*Television station call letters*]

KCED .... Centralia, WA [*FM radio station call letters*]

KCEE .... Tucson, AZ [*AM radio station call letters*]

KCEF .... Chicopee Falls/Westover Air Force Base [*Massachusetts*] [*ICAO location identifier*] (ICLI)

KCEL-FM ..... California City, CA [*FM radio station call letters*] (BROA)

KCEN .... Temple, TX [*Television station call letters*]

KCEO .... Vista, CA [*AM radio station call letters*]

KCEP .... Las Vegas, NV [*FM radio station call letters*]

KCER .... Kananaskis Centre for Environmental Research [*University of Calgary*] [*Research center*] (RCD)

KCES .... Eufaula, OK [*FM radio station call letters*]

KCET .... Los Angeles, CA [*Television station call letters*]

KCET-DT ..... Los Angeles, CA [*Television station call letters*] (BROA)

KCEW .... Crestview/Bob Sikes [*Florida*] [*ICAO location identifier*] (ICLI)

KCEY .... Huntsville, TX [*FM radio station call letters*]

KCEZ .... Corning, CA [*FM radio station call letters*]

KCF............ Key-Click Filter

KCF............ Key Clinical Finding [*Medicine*] (HCT)

KCF............ Khalistan Commando Force (SAUO)

KCF............ Thousand Cubic Feet

KCFA .... Arnold, CA [*FM radio station call letters*]

KCFB .... King City Federal Savings Bank (SAUO)

KCFB .... St. Cloud, MN [*FM radio station call letters*]

KCFC .... Karen Carpenter Fan Club [*Defunct*] (EA)

KCFD .... Bryan/Coulter Field [*Texas*] [*ICAO location identifier*] (ICLI)

KCFE .... Eden Prairie, MN [*FM radio station call letters*]

KCFF .... Korean Cultural and Freedom Foundation (EA)

KCFG .... Flagstaff, AZ [*Television station call letters*] (BROA)

KCFMC .... Kevin Collins Foundation for Missing Children (EA)

KCFM-FM .... Okmulgee, OK [*FM radio station call letters*] (BROA)

KCFN .... Wichita, KS [*FM radio station call letters*]

KCFO .... Tulsa, OK [*AM radio station call letters*]

KCFP-FM ..... Pueblo, CO [*FM radio station call letters*] (RBYB)

KCFR .... Denver, CO [*FM radio station call letters*]

KCFS .... Sioux Falls, SD [*FM radio station call letters*]

KCFV .... Ferguson, MO [*FM radio station call letters*]

KCFW .... Kalispell, MT [*Television station call letters*]

KCFX .... Harrisonville, MO [*FM radio station call letters*]

KCFY .... Yuma, AZ [*FM radio station call letters*]

KCG............ Chignik, AK [*Location identifier*] [*FAA*] (FAAL)

KCG............ Key Calling [*Telecommunications*] (IAA)

KCG............ Kinetocardiogram [*Cardiology*]

KCGB .... Hood River, OR [*FM radio station call letters*]

KCGL .... Diamondville (SAUS)

KCGL .... Kyocera Graphic Language (SAUS)

KCGM .... Scobey, MT [*FM radio station call letters*]

KCGN .... Sioux Falls, SD [*AM radio station call letters*]

KCGN-FM ..... Ortonville, MN [*FM radio station call letters*]

KCGQ .... Cape Girardeau, MO [*AM radio station call letters*]

KCGQ-FM .... Gordonville, MO [*FM radio station call letters*]

KCGR .... Cottage Grove, OR [*FM radio station call letters*]

KCGS .... Marshall, AR [*AM radio station call letters*]

KCGS .... United States Army, Command and General Staff College Library, Fort Leavenworth (SAUS)

KCGX .... Broken Bow, OK [*FM radio station call letters*] (RBYB)

KCGY .... Laramie, WY [*FM radio station call letters*]

KCH .... Ketch

KCH .... Ketchum & Co. , Inc. (SAUO)

kch .... Kilocharacter (MHDB)

KCH .... King's College Hospital

KCH .... Knight Commander of the Guelphic Order of Hanover [*British*]

KCH .... Kuching [*Malaysia*] [*Airport symbol*] (OAG)

KCHA .... Charles City, IA [*AM radio station call letters*]

KCHA .... Chattanooga/Lovell [*Tennessee*] [*ICAO location identifier*] (ICLI)

KCHA-FM ..... Charles City, IA [*FM radio station call letters*]

KCHC .... Conroe, TX [*AM radio station call letters*] (BROA)

KCHC-FM ..... Conroe, TX [*FM radio station call letters*] (RBYB)

KCHD .... Chandler/Williams Air Force Base [*Arizona*] [*ICAO location identifier*] (ICLI)

KCHE .... Cherokee, IA [*AM radio station call letters*]

KCHE-FM ..... Cherokee, IA [*FM radio station call letters*]

KCHF .... Santa Fe, NM [*Television station call letters*]

KCHG .... Somerset, TX [*AM radio station call letters*]

KCHI .... Chicago/Metropolitan Area [*Illinois*] [*ICAO location identifier*] (ICLI)

KCHI .... Chillicothe, MO [*AM radio station call letters*]

KCHI-FM ..... Chillicothe, MO [*FM radio station call letters*]

KCHJ .... Delano, CA [*AM radio station call letters*]

KCHK .... New Prague, MN [*AM radio station call letters*]

KCHK-FM ..... New Prague, MN [*FM radio station call letters*]

KCHL .... San Antonio, TX [*AM radio station call letters*]

KCHN-AM ..... Liberty, TX [*AM radio station call letters*] (BROA)

KCHO .... Chico, CA [*FM radio station call letters*]

KCHQ .... Altamont, OR [*FM radio station call letters*]

KCHR .... Charleston, MO [*AM radio station call letters*]

kchr .... Kilocharacter (MHDB)

KCHS .... Charleston/Municipal and Air Force Base [*South Carolina*] [*ICAO location identifier*] (ICLI)

KCHS .... Kilo Characters per Second (IAA)

KCHS .... Knight Commander of the Holy Sepulchre

KCHS .... Truth or Consequences, NM [*AM radio station call letters*]

KCHT .... Astoria, OR [*AM radio station call letters*] (BROA)

KCHT .... Kechabta [*Tunisia*] [*Seismograph station code, US Geological Survey*] (SEIS)

KCHT-AM ..... Selah, WA [*AM radio station call letters*] (RBYB)

KCHU .... Valdez, AK [*AM radio station call letters*]

KCHX .... Midland, TX [*FM radio station call letters*]

KCHZ-FM ..... Ottawa, KS [*FM radio station call letters*] (RBYB)

KCI............ Aeromech Commuter Airlines (SAUS)

KCI............ Key Club International (EA)

KCI............ Key Collectors International (EA)

kCi............ Kilocurie (DEN)

KCI............ Kit Collectors International (EA)

KCI............ Potassium Chloride (MELL)

KCIA........... Korean Central Intelligence Agency (SAUO)

KCIA........... Medford, OR [*FM radio station call letters*]

KCIA........... South Korean Central Intelligence Agency [*Later, Agency for National Security Planning*] (PD)

KCIB........... Milan, NM [*AM radio station call letters*] (RBYB)

KCIC........... Grand Junction, CO [*FM radio station call letters*]

KCID........... Caldwell, ID [*AM radio station call letters*]

KCID-FM ..... Caldwell, ID [*FM radio station call letters*]

KCIE........... Dulce, NM [*FM radio station call letters*]

KCIE........... Knight Commander of the [*Order of the*] Indian Empire [*British*]

KCIF-FM ..... Hilo, HI [*FM radio station call letters*] (BROA)

KCII........... Washington, IA [*AM radio station call letters*]

KCII-FM ..... Washington, IA [*FM radio station call letters*]

KCIJ........... North Fort Polk, LA [*FM radio station call letters*]

KCIL........... Houma, LA [*FM radio station call letters*]

KCIM........... Carroll, IA [*AM radio station call letters*]

KCIN........... Tacoma, WA [*AM radio station call letters*] (RBYB)

KCIO........... King's Commissioned Indian Officer [*British military*] (DMA)

KCIR........... Twin Falls, ID [*FM radio station call letters*]

KCIS........... Edmonds, WA [*AM radio station call letters*]

KCIT........... Amarillo, TX [*Television station call letters*]

K-CITEM ...... Kennedy Space Center Cite Plan/Requirement (NAKS)

K-CITEM ...... KSC CITE Plan (or Requirement) (SAUS)

KCIV........... Mount Bullion, CA [*FM radio station call letters*]

KCIX........... Garden City, ID [*FM radio station call letters*]

KCIY........... Liberty, MO [*FM radio station call letters*] (RBYB)

KCJ	Kolel Chibas Jerusalem [An association] (EA)
KCJB	Minot, ND [AM radio station call letters]
KCJC	Dardanelle, AR [FM radio station call letters] (RBYB)
KCJH	Stockton, CA [FM radio station call letters]
KCJJ	Iowa City, IA [AM radio station call letters]
KCJK	Iowa City, IA [AM radio station call letters] (BROA)
KCJZ	Terrell Hills, TX [FM radio station call letters] (RBYB)
KCK	Kansas City, KS [Location identifier] [FAA] (FAAL)
KCKA	Centralia, WA [Television station call letters]
KCKC	San Bernardino, CA [AM radio station call letters]
KCKI	Henryetta, OK [FM radio station call letters]
KCKK-FM	Longmont, CO [FM radio station call letters] (BROA)
KCKL	Malakoff, TX [FM radio station call letters]
KCKN	Roswell, NM [AM radio station call letters]
KCKR	Waco, TX [FM radio station call letters]
KCKS	Concordia, KS [FM radio station call letters]
KCKX	Stayton, OR [AM radio station call letters]
KCKY	Coolidge, AZ [AM radio station call letters]
KCL	Chignik, AK [Location identifier] [FAA] (FAAL)
KCL	Keystation Control Language [Computer science] (MHDI)
KCL	King's College, London
KCL	Kirchhoff's Current Law [Electronics] (IAA)
KCL	Kitchen, Company Level
KCL	Klamath County Library, Klamath Falls, OR [OCLC symbol] (OCLC)
KCL	Knitting Cylinder Lubrication (PDAA)
KCL	Knudsen Cosine Law [Physics]
KCLA	Pine Bluff, AR [AM radio station call letters]
KCLB	Coachella, CA [AM radio station call letters]
KCLB-FM	Coachella, CA [FM radio station call letters]
KCLC	Kinder-Care Learning Centers, Inc. [NASDAQ symbol] (SAG)
KCLC	Kinder-Care Learning Ctrs [NASDAQ symbol] (TTSB)
KCLC	St. Charles, MO [FM radio station call letters]
KCLCW	Kinder-Care Lrng Ctr Wrrt [NASDAQ symbol] (TTSB)
KCLD	St. Cloud, MN [FM radio station call letters]
KCLE	Cleburne, TX [AM radio station call letters]
KCLE	Cleveland/Cleveland-Hopkins International [Ohio] [ICAO location identifier] (ICLI)
KCLE	Continuing Legal Education, University of Kentucky College of Law (DLA)
KCLE	Glen Rose, TX [FM radio station call letters] (RBYB)
KCLH-FM	Yankton, SD [FM radio station call letters] (BROA)
KCLI	Clinton, OK [FM radio station call letters]
KCLI	Kansas City Life Ins [NASDAQ symbol] (TTSB)
KCLI	Kansas City Life Insurance Co. [NASDAQ symbol] (NQ)
KCLI-AM	Clinton, OK [AM radio station call letters] (RBYB)
KCLJ	Knight Commander of the Order of St. Lazarus of Jerusalem (DD)
KCLJ	Knight Commander, Order of St. Lazarus of Jerusalem [British] (WA)
KCLK	Asotin, WA [AM radio station call letters]
KCLK	Clarkston, WA [FM radio station call letters]
KCLL	College Station/Easterwood Field [Texas] [ICAO location identifier] (ICLI)
KCLL	Lompoc, CA [AM radio station call letters]
KCLM	Newport, OR [FM radio station call letters]
KCLN	Clinton, IA [FM radio station call letters]
KCLO	Rapid City, SD [Television station call letters]
KCLQ	Lebanon, MO [FM radio station call letters]
KCLR	Boonville, MO [FM radio station call letters]
KCLR	Ralls, TX [AM radio station call letters]
KCLR-FM	Boonville, MO [FM radio station call letters] (BROA)
KCLS	Flagstaff, AZ [AM radio station call letters]
KCLS	Kern County Library System [Library network]
KCLS	Knight Commander of the Lion and the Sun
KCLS-FM	Ely, NV [FM radio station call letters] (BROA)
KCLT	West Helena, AR [FM radio station call letters]
KCLU	Korean Council of Organization [South Korea]
KCLU	Thousand Oaks, CA [FM radio station call letters]
KCLV	Clovis, NM [AM radio station call letters]
KCLV-FM	Clovis, NM [FM radio station call letters]
KCLW	Hamilton, TX [AM radio station call letters]
KCLX	Colfax, WA [AM radio station call letters]
KCLY	Clay Center, KS [FM radio station call letters]
KCLY	Kent and County of London Yeomanry [Military unit] [British]
KCM	Kam Creed Mines Ltd. [Vancouver Stock Exchange symbol] [Toronto Stock Exchange symbol]
KCM	Kansas City Museum (SAUO)
KCM	Keratinocyte-Conditioned Medium [Biochemistry]
KCM	Key Center for Mines [University of Wollongong] [Australia]
KCM	Kilenge Mission [New Britain] [Seismograph station code, US Geological Survey] (SEIS)
KCM	Kirchhoff Coda Migration [For seismic wave imaging]
KCM	Kupffer Cell Medium
KCMA	Holdenville, OK [FM radio station call letters] (RBYB)
KCMA	Kitchen Cabinet Manufacturers Association (EA)
KCM & B	Kansas City, Memphis & Birmingham Railroad
KCMB	Baker City, OR [FM radio station call letters]
KCMC	Texarkana, TX [AM radio station call letters]
KCME	Kuznetsk Commodity and Raw Materials Exchange [Russian Federation] (EY)
KCME	Manitou Springs, CO [FM radio station call letters]
KCMG	Knight Commander of St. Michael and St. George [Facetiously translated, "Kindly Call Me God"] [British]
KCMG	Mountain Grove, MO [AM radio station call letters]
KCMG-FM	Los Angeles, CA [FM radio station call letters] (BROA)
KCMG-FM	Mountain Grove, MO [FM radio station call letters]
KCMH	Columbus/Port Columbus International [Ohio] [ICAO location identifier] (ICLI)
KCMH	Mountain Home, AR [FM radio station call letters]
KCMI	Terrytown, NE [FM radio station call letters]
KCMJ	Indio, CA [FM radio station call letters]
KCMJ	Palm Springs, CA [AM radio station call letters]
KCML-FM	St. Joseph, MN [FM radio station call letters] (BROA)
KCMLN	Kansas City Metropolitan Library Network Council [Library network]
KCMN	Colorado Springs, CO [AM radio station call letters]
KCMO	Kansas City, Mexico & Orient [AAR code]
KCMO	Kansas City, MO [AM radio station call letters]
KCMO-FM	Kansas City, MO [FM radio station call letters]
KCMQ	Columbia, MO [FM radio station call letters]
KCMR	Mason City, IA [FM radio station call letters]
KCMS	Edmonds, WA [FM radio station call letters]
KCMS	Kodak Color Management System [Eastman Kodak Co.] (PCM)
KCMT	Chester, CA [FM radio station call letters]
KCMT-FM	Billings, MT [FM radio station call letters] (BROA)
KCMU	Seattle, WA [FM radio station call letters]
KCMW	Warrensburg, MO [FM radio station call letters]
KCMX	Ashland, OR [AM radio station call letters]
KCMX	Keyset Central Multiplexer
KCMX-FM	Ashland, OR [FM radio station call letters]
KCMY	Sacramento, CA [Television station call letters]
KCN	Chernofski Harbor, AK [Location identifier] [FAA] (FAAL)
KCN	Intetnational Colin Energy [NYSE symbol] (SAG)
KCN	Intl Colin Energy [NYSE symbol] (TTSB)
KCN	Kids' Clubs Network (AIE)
KCN	Kit Configuration Notice (MCD)
KCN	Kit Control Number [Navy] (NG)
KCN	Potassium Cyanide (SAUS)
KCNA	Cave Junction, OR [FM radio station call letters]
KCNA	Korean Central News Agency [North Korea]
KCNC	Denver, CO [Television station call letters]
KCND	Bismarck, ND [FM radio station call letters]
KCNE	Chadron, NE [FM radio station call letters]
KCNF	Fort Worth [Texas] [ICAO location identifier] (ICLI)
KCNI	Broken Bow, NE [AM radio station call letters]
KCNM	Carlsbad/Cavern City Air Terminal [New Mexico] [ICAO location identifier] (ICLI)
KCNM	San Jose, Philippines [AM radio station call letters]
KCNN	East Grand Forks, MN [AM radio station call letters]
KCNO	Alturas, CA [AM radio station call letters]
KCNO-FM	Alturas, CA [FM radio station call letters] (RBYB)
KCNP	Kings Canyon National Park (SAUO)
KCNP	Ku-ring-gai Chase National Park (SAUO)
KCNQ	Kernville, CA [FM radio station call letters]
KCNR	Salt Lake City, UT [AM radio station call letters]
KCNS	San Francisco, CA [Television station call letters]
KCNT	Hastings, NE [FM radio station call letters]
KCNW	Fairway, KS [AM radio station call letters]
KCNW	Kelly's Creek & Northwestern Railroad Co. [AAR code]
KCNW	Waco/James Connally [Texas] [ICAO location identifier] (ICLI)
KCNZ	Cedar Falls, IA [AM radio station call letters] (RBYB)
KCO	Keep Cost Order [Telecommunications] (TEL)
KCOB	Newton, IA [AM radio station call letters]
KCOBE	Knight Commander-Order of the British Empire (SAUO)
KCOB-FM	Newton, IA [FM radio station call letters]
KCOF	Cocoa/Patrick Air Force Base [Florida] [ICAO location identifier] (ICLI)
KCOG	Centerville, IA [AM radio station call letters]
KCOH	Houston, TX [AM radio station call letters]
KCOIC	Korean Combat Operations Intelligence Center (SAUO)
KCOL	Fort Collins, CO [AM radio station call letters]
KCoIC	Colby Community College, Colby, KS [Library symbol] [Library of Congress] (LCLS)
KCole	Kenneth Cole Productions, Inc. [Associated Press] (SAG)
KColePd	Kenneth Cole Productions, Inc. [Associated Press] (SAG)
KCOM	Comanche, TX [AM radio station call letters]
KCOMZ	Korean Communications Zone [Military]
KCON	Conway, AR [AM radio station call letters]
KCOO-FM	Shafter, CA [FM radio station call letters] (BROA)
KCOP	Kencope Energy Companies (SAUO)
KCOP	Los Angeles, CA [Television station call letters]
KCOP-DT	Los Angeles, CA [Television station call letters] (BROA)
KCOR	San Antonio, TX [AM radio station call letters]
KCOS	Colorado Springs/Peterson Field [Colorado] [ICAO location identifier] (ICLI)
KCOS	El Paso, TX [Television station call letters]
KCOT	Cotulla/Municipal [Texas] [ICAO location identifier] (ICLI)
KCOT	San Augustine, TX [FM radio station call letters]
KCOU	Columbia, MO [FM radio station call letters]
KCOW	Alliance, NE [AM radio station call letters]
KCOY	Santa Maria, CA [Television station call letters]
KCOZ	Point Lookout, MO [FM radio station call letters] (RBYB)
KCP	Kansas City Plant [Department of Energy] [Kansas City, MO] (GAAI)
KCP	Kansas City Public Library, Kansas City, MO [OCLC symbol] (OCLC)
KCP	Keene's Cement Plaster [Technical drawings]
KCP	Kenneth Cole Productions'A' [NYSE symbol] (TTSB)
KCP	Kenneth Cole Productions, Inc. [NYSE symbol] (SAG)
KCP	Keyboard-Controlled Phototypesetter (NITA)
KCP	Key Crude Prices [Database] [Petroleum Intelligence Weekly] [Information service or system] (CRD)
KCP	Kirghiz Communist Party [Political party]
KCP	Knee-Chest Position (MELL)

KCP	Knight Commander of [*the Order of*] Pius IX
KCP	Korean Communist Party [*Political party*] [*North Korea*] (FEA)
KCPA	Kaolin Clay Producers Association (DGA)
KCPA	Kennedy Center for the Performing Arts (SAUO)
KCPA	Kentucky College Placement Association (SAUO)
KCP & G	Kansas City, Pittsburgh & Gulf Railroad
KCPB	Thousand Oaks, CA [*FM radio station call letters*]
KCPC	Keene's Cement Plaster Ceiling [*Technical drawings*]
KCPCA	Kansas Committee for Prevention of Child Abuse (EDAC)
KCPI	Albert Lea, MN [*FM radio station call letters*]
KCPL	Kansas City Power & Light Co. [*Associated Press*] (SAG)
KCPL	Kansas City Public Library (SAUO)
KCPL	Olympia, WA [*AM radio station call letters*]
KCPM	Chico, CA [*Television station call letters*]
KCPO	Kansas City Philharmonic Orchestra (SAUO)
KCPQ	Tacoma, WA [*Television station call letters*]
KCPR	San Luis Obispo, CA [*FM radio station call letters*]
KCPS	Burlington, IA [*AM radio station call letters*]
KCPS	Kansas City Public Service R. R. [*AAR code*]
kcps	Kilocycles per Second
KCPT	Kansas City, MO [*Television station call letters*]
KCPT-DT	Kansas City, MO [*Television station call letters*] (BROA)
KCPW	Salt Lake City, UT [*FM radio station call letters*]
KCPX	Centerville, UT [*FM radio station call letters*]
KCPX-AM	Centerville, UT [*AM radio station call letters*] (RBYB)
KCQL	Aztec, NM [*AM radio station call letters*]
KCQQ	Davenport, IA [*FM radio station call letters*] (RBYB)
KCQV	Arthur, ND [*FM radio station call letters*]
KCR	Colorado Creek, AK [*Location identifier*] [*FAA*] (FAAL)
KCR	Kansas City Law Review [*A publication*] (DLA)
KC r	Kansas City Terminal Railway Co. (SAUO)
KCR	Key Call Receiver [*Telecommunications*] (TEL)
KCR	[*The*] Kowloon Canton Railway [*Hong Kong*] (DCTA)
KCR	Reports Tempore Chancellor King [*A publication*] (DLA)
KCRA	Sacramento, CA [*Television station call letters*]
KCRABB	Annual Report. Cancer Research Institute. Kanazawa University (journ.) (SAUS)
KCRB	Bemidji, MN [*FM radio station call letters*]
KCRC	Enid, OK [*AM radio station call letters*]
KCRC	Kansas City Records Center [*Military*]
KCRC	Kowloon-Canton Railway Corp. [*Commercial firm*] [*Hong Kong*]
KCRCC	Korean Combined Rescue Coordination Center (SAUO)
KCRCHE	Kansas City Regional Council for Higher Education [*Library network*]
KCRE	Crescent City, CA [*FM radio station call letters*]
KCRF	Korean Conflict Research Foundation [*Defunct*]
KCRF	Newport, OR [*FM radio station call letters*] (RBYB)
KCRG	Cedar Rapids, IA [*AM radio station call letters*]
KCRG-TV	Cedar Rapids, IA [*Television station call letters*]
KCRH	Hayward, CA [*FM radio station call letters*]
KCRI-FM	Mojave, CA [*FM radio station call letters*] (BROA)
KCRK	Colville, WA [*FM radio station call letters*]
KCRL	Rayne, LA [*FM radio station call letters*]
KCRL-FM	Sunrise Beach, MO [*FM radio station call letters*] (BROA)
KCRM-FM	Lubbock, TX [*FM radio station call letters*] (BROA)
KCRN	San Angelo, TX [*AM radio station call letters*]
KCRN-FM	San Angelo, TX [*FM radio station call letters*]
KCRO	Omaha, NE [*AM radio station call letters*]
KCRP	Corpus Christi/International [*Texas*] [*ICAO location identifier*] (ICLI)
KCRR	Grundy Center, IA [*FM radio station call letters*] (RBYB)
KCRS	Midland, TX [*AM radio station call letters*]
KCRS-FM	Midland, TX [*FM radio station call letters*]
KCRT	KCR Technology, Inc. (SAUO)
KCRT	Keyboard Cathode Ray Tube (MCD)
KCRT	Trinidad, CO [*AM radio station call letters*]
KCRT-FM	Trinidad, CO [*FM radio station call letters*]
KCRU	Oxnard, CA [*FM radio station call letters*]
KCRV	Caruthersville, MO [*AM radio station call letters*]
KCRW	Santa Monica, CA [*FM radio station call letters*]
KCRX	Roswell, NM [*AM radio station call letters*]
KCRY	Indio, CA [*FM radio station call letters*]
KCRZ	Tucson, AZ [*FM radio station call letters*]
KCRZ-FM	Tipton, CA [*FM radio station call letters*] (BROA)
KCS	Conston Corp. (SAUO)
KCS	[*The*] Kansas City Southern Railway Co. [*AAR code*]
KCS	Kansas City Standard [*Audio tape technology*] (EECA)
KCS	KCS Energy, Inc. [*Formerly, KCS Group, Inc.*] [*NYSE symbol*] (SPSG)
KCS	Keratoconjunctivitis Sicca [*Ophthalmology*]
KCS	Keyboard Configuration Studies (NASA)
KCS	Keyboard Controlled Sequencer [*Computer science*]
KCS	Keyboards, Computers, and Software [*A publication*]
KCS	Key Configuration Studies (NASA)
KCS	Kilocharacters per Second (IAA)
kcs	Kilocycles per Second
KCS	King's College School [*British*]
KCS	Kinki Chemical Society (SAUO)
KCS	Knight of [*the Order of*] Charles III of Spain
KCS	Knight of the Order of Charles XIII of Sweden [*Freemasonry*]
KCS	Knoxville Air Courier Service, Inc. (SAUO)
KCS	Kockums Computer Systems AB (SAUO)
KCS	Korean Chemical Society
KCS	Thousand Characters per Second
KC/SO	Kilocycles per Second (SAUS)
KCSA	Kerr Center for Sustainable Agriculture [*Research center*] (RCD)
KCSB	Santa Barbara, CA [*FM radio station call letters*]
KCSC	Edmond, OK [*FM radio station call letters*]
KCSC	Kansas City Service Center [*IRS*]
KCSC	Kansas Cosmosphere and Space Center [*Hutchinson, KS*]
KCSC	Kidde Computer Services Company (SAUO)
KCSC	Korean Cold Store Corporation (SAUO)
KCSD	Sioux Falls, SD [*FM radio station call letters*]
KCSD-TV	Sioux Falls, SD [*Television station call letters*] (RBYB)
KCSE-FM	Ballinger, TX [*FM radio station call letters*] (RBYB)
KCSF	Stanton Foundation (EA)
KCSG	Cedar City, UT [*Television station call letters*] (BROA)
KCSG	Knight Commander of Saint Gregory the Great (SAUO)
KCSG	Knight Commander of [*the Order of*] St. Gregory [*British*]
KCSH-FM	Ellensburg, WA [*FM radio station call letters*] (BROA)
KCSI	Kansas City Southern Industries, Inc.
KCSI	Knight Commander of the [*Order of the*] Star of India [*British*]
KCSI	Red Oak, IA [*FM radio station call letters*]
KCSJ	Pueblo, CO [*AM radio station call letters*]
KCSM	San Mateo, CA [*FM radio station call letters*]
KCSM-TV	San Mateo, CA [*Television station call letters*]
KCSN	Northridge, CA [*FM radio station call letters*]
KCSo	Kansas City Southern Industries, Inc. [*Associated Press*] (SAG)
KCSO	Kansas City Support Office (SAUO)
KCSO	Kansas City Symphony Orchestra (SAUO)
KCSO	Modesto, CA [*Television station call letters*]
KCSou	Kansas City Southern Industries, Inc. [*Associated Press*] (SAG)
KCSP	Casper, WY [*FM radio station call letters*]
KCSR	Chadron, NE [*AM radio station call letters*]
KCSRy	Kansas City Southern Railway Co.
KCSS	Key Center for Statistical Services [*Deakin University*] [*Australia*]
KCSS	Knight Commander of [*the Order of*] St. Sylvester
KCSS	Korean Combat Support System (SAUO)
KCSS	Turlock, CA [*FM radio station call letters*]
KCS/SO	Keyboard Class Select / Statistics Output [*Computer science*] (MHDI)
KCST	Florence, OR [*AM radio station call letters*]
KCST-FM	Florence, OR [*FM radio station call letters*]
KCStJ & CB	Kansas City, St. Joseph & Council Bluffs Railroad
KCSU	Fort Collins, CO [*FM radio station call letters*]
KCSX-FM	Moberly, MO [*FM radio station call letters*] (BROA)
KCT	Kansas City Terminal Railway Co. [*AAR code*]
KCT	Kaolin Cephalin Time [*Clinical chemistry*]
KCT	Kaolin Clotting Time [*Clinical chemistry*]
KCT	Kathodal Closing Tetanus [*Medicine*]
KCT	Kelvin Circulation Theorem [*Physics*]
KCT	Knight Commander of the Temple [*Freemasonry*] (ROG)
KCT	Knox's Cube Test [*Short-term memory and attention span test*]
KCTA	Corpus Christi, TX [*AM radio station call letters*]
KCTA	Kootenay Christmas Tree Association (SAUO)
KCTAX	Kemper State TF Inc. Ser: Cal. Cl.A [*Mutual fund ticker symbol*] (SG)
KCTB	Cut Bank [*Montana*] [*ICAO location identifier*] (ICLI)
KCTC	Sacramento, CA [*AM radio station call letters*]
KCTD-AM	Los Angeles, CA [*AM radio station call letters*] (BROA)
KCTE	Independence, MO [*AM radio station call letters*]
KCTE	Kathodal Closure Tetanus [*Medicine*]
KCTF	Waco, TX [*Television station call letters*]
KCTG	Ozark, MO [*FM radio station call letters*] (RBYB)
KCTI	Gonzales, TX [*AM radio station call letters*]
KCTI-FM	Gonzales, TX [*FM radio station call letters*] (RBYB)
KCTM	Rio Grande City, TX [*FM radio station call letters*]
KCTMLPCC	Key Chain Tag and Mini License Plate Collectors Club [*Later, LPKCMLPCC*] (EA)
KCTN	Garnavillo, IA [*FM radio station call letters*]
KCTO	Columbia, LA [*AM radio station call letters*]
KCTO-FM	Columbia, LA [*FM radio station call letters*]
KCTR-FM	Billings, MT [*FM radio station call letters*]
KCTS	Knight Commander of the Tower and Sword [*Portugal*] (ROG)
KCTS	Seattle, WA [*Television station call letters*]
KCTT	Yellville, AR [*FM radio station call letters*]
KCTV	Kansas City, MO [*Television station call letters*]
KCTX	Childress, TX [*AM radio station call letters*]
KCTY	Salinas, CA [*AM radio station call letters*]
KCtyPL	Kansas City Power & Light Co. [*Associated Press*] (SAG)
KCTZ	Bozeman, MT [*Television station call letters*]
KCU	Keyboard Control Unit
KCU	Kilocurie (IAA)
KCUA	Coalville, UT [*FM radio station call letters*]
KCUB	Stephenville, TX [*FM radio station call letters*]
KCUB	Tucson, AZ [*AM radio station call letters*]
KCUE	Red Wing, MN [*AM radio station call letters*]
KCUI	Pella, IA [*FM radio station call letters*]
KCUK	Chevak, AK [*FM radio station call letters*]
KCUL-AM	Marshall, TX [*AM radio station call letters*] (BROA)
KCUL-FM	Marshall, TX [*FM radio station call letters*] (BROA)
KCUR	Kansas City, MO [*FM radio station call letters*]
KCUS	Columbus/Municipal [*New Mexico*] [*ICAO location identifier*] (ICLI)
KCUV	Englewood, CO
KCUZ	Clifton, AZ [*AM radio station call letters*]
KCV	Kancana Ventures Ltd. [*Vancouver Stock Exchange symbol*]
KCV	Knight of Gustavus Vasa (SAUO)
KCVG	Cincinnati/Greater Cincinnati [*Ohio*] [*ICAO location identifier*] (ICLI)
KCVI	Blackfoot, ID [*FM radio station call letters*]
KCVL	Colville, WA [*AM radio station call letters*]
KCVL	Kentucky Commonwealth Virtual Library
KCVM-FM	Hudson, IA [*FM radio station call letters*] (BROA)
KCVO	Camdenton, MO [*FM radio station call letters*]
KCVO	Knight Commander of the Royal Victorian Order [*British*]

KCVP .... Konservativ-Christlichsoziale Volkspartei [*Conservative Christian-Social Party*] [*Switzerland*] [*Political party*] (PPE)

KCVQ-FM ..... Knob Noster, MO [*FM radio station call letters*] (BROA)

KCVR .... Lodi, CA [*AM radio station call letters*]

KCVS .... Clovis/Cannon Air Force Base [*New Mexico*] [*ICAO location identifier*] (ICLI)

KCVS .... Salina, KS [*FM radio station call letters*]

KCVT-FM ..... Silver Lake, KS [*FM radio station call letters*] (RBYB)

KCVU .... Paradise, CA [*Television station call letters*]

KCVW-FM ..... Kingman, KS [*FM radio station call letters*] (RBYB)

KCWA .... Arnold, MO [*FM radio station call letters*]

KCWA .... Kern County Water Agency (SAUO)

KCWB .... Kansas City Westport Belt [*AAR code*]

KCWB-TV ..... Kansas City, MO [*TV station call letters*] (RBYB)

KCWC .... Lander, WY [*Television station call letters*]

KCWC .... Riverton, WY [*FM radio station call letters*]

KCWC-TV ..... Lander, WY [*Television station call letters*] (BROA)

KCWD .... Harrison, AR [*FM radio station call letters*]

KCWD .... Kaleidoscope: Current World Data [*ABC-CLIO*] [*Information service or system*] (IID)

KCWE .... Kansas City, MO [*Television station call letters*] (BROA)

KCWM .... Hondo, TX [*AM radio station call letters*] (RBYB)

KCWM-FM ... Hondo, TX [*FM radio station call letters*] (RBYB)

KCWN .... New Sharon, IA [*FM radio station call letters*]

KCWR .... Bakersfield, CA [*AM radio station call letters*]

KCWS .... Merkel, TX [*FM radio station call letters*]

KCWT........... Wenatchee, WA [*Television station call letters*]

KCWU-FM ..... Ellensburg, WA [*FM radio station call letters*] (BROA)

KCWW .... Tempe, AZ [*AM radio station call letters*]

KCWX .... Columbia Falls, MT [*FM radio station call letters*]

KCWY .... Casper, WY [*Television station call letters*] (BROA)

KCXL .... Calexico/International [*California*] [*ICAO location identifier*] (ICLI)

KCXL .... Liberty, MO [*AM radio station call letters*] (RBYB)

KCXX .... Lake Arrowhead, CA [*FM radio station call letters*] (RBYB)

KCXY .... Camden, AR [*FM radio station call letters*]

KCYC .... King's Cheshire Yeomanry Cavalry [*British military*] (DMA)

KCYL .... Lampasas, TX [*AM radio station call letters*]

KCYN-FM ..... Moab, UT [*FM radio station call letters*] (RBYB)

KCYO-FM ..... Ozark, MO [*FM radio station call letters*] (BROA)

KCYQ-FM ..... Richfield, UT [*FM radio station call letters*] (BROA)

KCYS .... Cheyenne [*Wyoming*] [*ICAO location identifier*] (ICLI)

KCYS-FM ..... Seaside, OR [*FM radio station call letters*] (BROA)

KCYT-FM ..... Houston, AK [*FM radio station call letters*] (RBYB)

KCYT-FM ..... Lead, SD [*FM radio station call letters*] (BROA)

KCYY .... San Antonio, TX [*FM radio station call letters*]

KCZ .... Kochi [*Japan*] [*Airport symbol*] (OAG)

KCZE .... New Hampton, IA [*FM radio station call letters*]

KCZN-FM ..... Santa Paula, CA [*FM radio station call letters*] (BROA)

KCZO .... Carrizo Springs, TX [*FM radio station call letters*]

KCZQ .... Cresco, IA [*FM radio station call letters*]

KCZY .... Osage, IA [*FM radio station call letters*]

KCZZ .... British Island Airways Ltd. (SAUO)

KD .... Batch Distribution Coefficient (SAUS)

KD .... Cathodal Duration [*Medicine*] (DMAA)

Kd .... Coefficient of Soil-Water Absorption (GNE)

K$_d$ .... Dissociation Constant [*Physics*] (DAVI)

K$_d$ .... Distribution Coefficient [*Partition coefficient*] [*Physics*] (DAVI)

KD .... Kallidin [*Biochemistry*]

KD .... Kappa Delta (EA)

KD .... Kathodal Duration [*Medicine*]

KD .... Kawasaki Disease [*Also, KS, MLNS*] [*Medicine*]

KD .... Keep It Dark [*Say nothing about it*] [*Slang*]

KD .... Kendell Airlines [*ICAO designator*] (AD)

KD .... Kennnedy Disease [*Medicine*] (DMAA)

KD .... Kentucky Dam [*TVA*]

KD .... Keto-Diastix [*Miles Inc.*] [*Pharmacology*] (DAVI)

KD .... Kettledrum

KD .... Keyboard and Display [*Computer science*] (MHDB)

K/D .... Keyboard/Display (ACRL)

KD .... Key Definition (MHDB)

KD .... Keyed to Differ [*Locks*] (ADA)

KD .... Khaki Drill [*British military*] (DMA)

KD .... Kidderpore Docks (SAUO)

KD .... Kidney Donor (STED)

KD .... Killed (AABC)

KD .... Kiln-Dried [*Lumber*]

kd .... Kilodalton (STED)

kD .... Kilodalton [*Molecular mass measure*]

KD .... Kilter Diagram

KD .... Klinge [*Germany*] [*Research code symbol*]

KD .... Knee Disarticulation [*Medicine*]

KD .... Knitted Dacron (MEDA)

kd .... Knocked Down (EBF)

KD .... Knocked Down [*i.e., disassembled*]

KD .... Known-Distance [*Range*] [*Weaponry*] (INF)

KD .... Kohler Disease (MELL)

KD .... Komitet Domowy. Warsaw Ghetto (BJA)

KD .... Korsakoff's Disease [*Medicine*]

KD .... Kriegs Dekoration [*War Decoration*] [*German*]

KD .... Kuwaiti Dinar [*Monetary unit*] (BJA)

KD .... Pilotless Aerial Target [*Navy*]

KDA .... Kansas Dental Association (SAUO)

KDA .... Kendall Airlines [*Australia*] [*ICAO designator*] (FAAC)

kDa .... Kilodalton [*Physics*] [*Chemistry*] (DOG)

KDA .... Kit Design Approach

KDA .... Known Drug Allergies [*Medicine*] (DMAA)

KDA .... Kolda [*Senegal*] [*Airport symbol*] (AD)

KDA .... Kuranda [*Australia*] [*Seismograph station code, US Geological Survey*] [*Closed*] (SEIS)

KDA .... Potassium Dihydrogen Arsenate (SAUS)

KDAA .... Rolla, MO [*FM radio station call letters*] (RBYB)

KDAB .... Prairie Grove, AR [*FM radio station call letters*]

KDAC .... Fort Bragg, CA [*AM radio station call letters*]

KDAE .... Sinton, TX [*AM radio station call letters*]

KDAF .... Dallas, TX [*Television station call letters*]

KDAG .... Farmington, NM [*FM radio station call letters*]

KDAK .... Carrington, ND [*AM radio station call letters*]

KDAL .... Dallas/Dallas-Love Field [*Texas*] [*ICAO location identifier*] (ICLI)

KDAL .... Duluth, MN [*AM radio station call letters*]

kdal .... Kilodalton (STED)

KDAL-FM ..... Duluth, MN [*FM radio station call letters*]

KDAM .... Monroe City, MO [*FM radio station call letters*]

KDAO .... Marshalltown, IA [*AM radio station call letters*]

KDAO-FM ..... Eldora, IA [*FM radio station call letters*]

KDAP .... Douglas, AZ [*AM radio station call letters*]

KDAP-FM ..... Douglas, AZ [*FM radio station call letters*]

KDAQ .... Shreveport, LA [*FM radio station call letters*]

KDAR .... Oxnard, CA [*FM radio station call letters*]

KDAT .... Cedar Rapids, IA [*FM radio station call letters*] (RBYB)

KDAT .... Kiln-Dried After Treatment [*Lumber*]

KDAV .... Lubbock, TX [*AM radio station call letters*] (BROA)

KDAY .... Dayton/James M. Coxdayton Municipal [*Ohio*] [*ICAO location identifier*] (ICLI)

KDAY .... Independence, CA [*FM radio station call letters*]

KDAZ .... Albuquerque, NM [*AM radio station call letters*]

KDB .... Kambalda [*Australia*] [*Airport symbol*] (OAG)

KDB .... Keller-Dorian, Berthon [*Method*] [*Photography*]

KDB .... Kelvin Double Bridge [*Physics*]

KDB .... Konedobu [*Papua New Guinea*] [*Seismograph station code, US Geological Survey*] (SEIS)

KDB .... Korea Development Bank

KDB .... Santa Barbara, CA [*FM radio station call letters*]

KDBB .... Bonne Terre, MO [*FM radio station call letters*]

KDBC .... El Paso, TX [*Television station call letters*]

KDBH .... Natchitoches, LA [*FM radio station call letters*]

KDBM .... Dillon, MT [*AM radio station call letters*]

KDBM-FM ..... Dillon, MT [*FM radio station call letters*]

KDBR .... Kalispell, MT [*FM radio station call letters*]

KDBS-AM ..... Alexandria, LA [*AM radio station call letters*] (RBYB)

KDBX .... Banks, OR [*FM radio station call letters*]

KDc .... Dodge City Public Library, Dodge City, KS [*Library symbol*] [*Library of Congress*] (LCLS)

KDC .... Kathodal Duration Contraction [*Medicine*]

KDC .... KD Air Corp. [*ICAO designator*] (FAAC)

KDC .... Keil and Delitzsch Commentaries [*A publication*] (BJA)

KDC .... Kerberos key Distribution Center (SAUO)

KDC .... Key Distribution Center (MCD)

KDC .... Keyed Display Console

KDC .... Kidney Disease Treatment Center (DMAA)

KDC .... Kodak Digital Camera [*Image format*] (AAEL)

KDC .... Kodiak [*Alaska*] [*Seismograph station code, US Geological Survey*] (SEIS)

KDC .... Kosher Dining Club (BJA)

KDCA .... Washington/National [*District of Columbia*] [*ICAO location identifier*] (ICLI)

KDCC .... Dodge City, KS [*AM radio station call letters*]

KDCC .... Washington [*District of Columbia*] [*ICAO location identifier*] (ICLI)

KDCD .... San Angelo, TX [*FM radio station call letters*]

KDCE .... Espanola, NM [*AM radio station call letters*]

KDCG .... San Diego Coast Guard Air Base [*California*] [*ICAO location identifier*] (ICLI)

KDCI .... Key Display Call Indicator

KDCK .... Cadec Systems, Inc. (SAUO)

KDCK .... Dodge City, KS [*Television station call letters*] (BROA)

KDCL .... Knocked Down, in Carloads

KDCP .... Kidney Disease Control Program [*Public Health Service*]

KDCQ .... Coos Bay, OR [*FM radio station call letters*] (RBYB)

KDCR .... Sioux Center, IA [*FM radio station call letters*]

KDCV .... Blair, NE [*FM radio station call letters*]

KDD .... Knowledge Discovery in Databases (RALS)

KDD .... Kokusai Denshin Denwa Co. Ltd. [*Telegraph & Telephone Corp.*] [*Tokyo, Japan*] [*Telecommunications*]

KDDA .... Dumas, AR [*AM radio station call letters*]

KDDB .... Paso Robles, CA [*FM radio station call letters*]

KDDD .... Dumas, TX [*AM radio station call letters*]

KDDG-FM .... Albany, MN [*FM radio station call letters*] (BROA)

KDDJ-FM .... Globe, AZ [*FM radio station call letters*] (BROA)

KDDK .... Jacksonville, AR [*FM radio station call letters*]

KDDQ .... Comanche, OK [*FM radio station call letters*]

KDDR .... Oakes, ND [*AM radio station call letters*]

KDDS-AM ..... Duluth, MN [*AM radio station call letters*] (BROA)

KDDX .... Spearfish, SD [*FM radio station call letters*] (RBYB)

KDDZ-AM ..... San Diego, CA [*AM radio station call letters*] (RBYB)

KDE .... 4 Kids Entertainment [*NYSE symbol*]

KDe .... Derby Public Library, Derby, KS [*Library symbol*] [*Library of Congress*] (LCLS)

KDE .... Kappa Delta Epsilon [*An association*] (NTPA)

KDE .... K-Desktop Environment [*Linux*] (RALS)

KDE .... Keyboard Data Entry

KDE........... Kidde, Inc. (SAUO)

KDE............ Kinetic Depth Effect [Cognitive science]
KDE............ Koroba [Papua New Guinea] [Airport symbol] [Obsolete] (OAG)
KDEA......... New Iberia, LA [FM radio station call letters]
KDEB......... Springfield, MO [Television station call letters]
KDEC......... Decorah, IA [AM radio station call letters]
KDEC-FM... Decorah, IA [FM radio station call letters]
KDEDC....... Kaslo and District Economic Development Committee (SAUO)
KDEF......... Albuquerque, NM [AM radio station call letters]
KDEL......... Arkadelphia, AR [FM radio station call letters]
KDEM........ Deming, NM [FM radio station call letters]
KDEM........ Kurzweil Data Entry Machine [for optical character recognition]
KDEN........ Denver/Stapleton International [Colorado] [ICAO location identifier] (ICLI)
KDEN-TV.... Longmont, CO [TV station call letters] (RBYB)
KDEO-FM... Waipahu, HI [FM radio station call letters]
KDEP......... Kentucky Department of Environmental Protection
KDEP......... Smoke Layer Estimated (Feet) Deep [Meteorology] (FAAC)
KDEP-FM.... Depoe Bay, OR [FM radio station call letters] (RBYB)
KDES......... Palm Springs, CA [AM radio station call letters] (RBYB)
KDES-FM.... Palm Springs, CA [FM radio station call letters]
KDET......... Center, TX [AM radio station call letters]
KDET......... Detroit/Detroit City [Michigan] [ICAO location identifier] (ICLI)
KDET-FM.... Center, TX [FM radio station call letters]
KDEW........ De Witt, AR [AM radio station call letters] (RBYB)
KDEW-FM... De Witt, AR [FM radio station call letters] (RBYB)
KDEX......... Dexter, MO [AM radio station call letters]
KDEX-FM.... Dexter, MO [FM radio station call letters]
KDEZ......... Jonesboro, AR [FM radio station call letters]
KDF........... Kalamein [Trademark] Door and Frame
KDF........... Knob Door Fastener
KDF........... Knocked Down Flat
KDF........... Kraft durch Freude [Strength through Joy Movement] [Pre-World War II] [German]
KDFC......... Kenny Dale Fan Club (EA)
KDFC......... Korea Development Finance Corp.
KDFC......... Palo Alto, CA [AM radio station call letters]
KDFC......... San Francisco, CA [FM radio station call letters]
KDFI.......... Dallas, TX [Television station call letters]
KDFM-FM... Falfurrias, TX [FM radio station call letters] (BROA)
KDFN......... Doniphan, MO [AM radio station call letters]
KDFR......... Des Moines, IA [FM radio station call letters]
KDFT......... Ferris, TX [AM radio station call letters]
KDFW........ Dallas-Fort Worth/Regional Airport [Texas] [ICAO location identifier] (ICLI)
KDFW........ Dallas, TX [Television station call letters]
KDFW-DT... Dallas, TX [Television station call letters] (BROA)
KDFX......... Dallas, TX [AM radio station call letters] (RBYB)
KDG.......... Kedougou [Senegal] [Seismograph station code, US Geological Survey] [Closed] (SEIS)
KDG.......... King's Dragoon Guards [Later, QDG] [Military unit] [British]
KDGB........ Dodge City, KS [FM radio station call letters]
KDGE........ Gainesville, TX [FM radio station call letters]
KDGNBX..... Annual Report. Kinki University. Atomic Energy Research Institute (journ.) (SAUS)
KDGO......... Durango, CO [AM radio station call letters]
KDGS......... Andover, KS [FM radio station call letters] (RBYB)
KDH.......... Kandahar [Afghanistan] [Airport symbol] (OAG)
KDH.......... Key Depression per Hour [Computer science] (IAA)
KDH.......... Korean Direct Hire
KDH.......... Kosher Dining Hall (BJA)
KDHE......... Kansas Department of Health and Environment (SAUO)
KDHI......... Twentynine Palms, CA [FM radio station call letters]
KDHL......... Faribault, MN [AM radio station call letters]
KDHN........ Dimmitt, TX [AM radio station call letters]
KDHN........ Dothan [Alabama] [ICAO location identifier] (ICLI)
KDHNM...... Kill Devil Hill National Memorial (SAUO)
KDHT......... Dalhart [Texas] [ICAO location identifier] (ICLI)
KDHX......... St. Louis, MO [FM radio station call letters]
KDI........... Kendari [Indonesia] [Airport symbol] (OAG)
KDI........... Knowledge and Distributed Intelligence
KDI........... Korea Development Institute (ECON)
KDI........... Kuwaiti Dinar [Monetary unit] (DS)
KDIA......... Korea Defense Industry Association (SAUO)
KDIA......... Oakland, CA [AM radio station call letters]
KDIC......... Grinnell, IA [FM radio station call letters]
KDIF......... Riverside, CA [AM radio station call letters]
KDIG......... Orland, CA [FM radio station call letters]
KDII.......... Key Defense Intelligence Issue (MCD)
KDIN......... Des Moines, IA [Television station call letters]
KDIO......... Ortonville, MN [AM radio station call letters]
KDIS-AM.... Los Angeles, CA [AM radio station call letters] (BROA)
KDIU......... Dimmitt, TX [FM radio station call letters]
KDIX......... Dickinson, ND [AM radio station call letters]
KDIZ-AM.... Golden Valley, MN [AM radio station call letters] (RBYB)
KDJ........... Njdole [Gabon] [Airport symbol] (AD)
KDJI.......... Holbrook, AZ [AM radio station call letters]
KDJK......... Oakdale, CA [FM radio station call letters]
KDJR......... De Soto, MO [FM radio station call letters]
KDJS......... Willmar, MN [AM radio station call letters]
KDJS-FM.... Willmar, MN [FM radio station call letters]
KDJW........ Amarillo, TX [AM radio station call letters]
KDK.......... Khodzhikent [Former USSR] [Seismograph station code, US Geological Survey] [Closed] (SEIS)
KDK.......... Knit de Knit Texturing (IAA)
KDK.......... Kodiak Airways Inc. (SAUO)

KDK........... Kodiak [Alaska] Municipal Airport [Airport symbol] [Obsolete] (OAG)
KDKA......... Pittsburgh, PA [First station to broadcast a baseball game, August 5, 1921] [AM radio station call letters]
KDKA-DT... Pittsburgh, PA [Television station call letters] (BROA)
KDKA-TV... Pittsburgh, PA [Television station call letters]
KDKB-FM... Mesa, AZ [FM radio station call letters] (RBYB)
KDKD......... Clinton, MO [AM radio station call letters]
KDKD-FM... Clinton, MO [FM radio station call letters]
KDKF......... Klamath Falls, OR [Television station call letters]
KDKK......... Park Rapids, MN [FM radio station call letters]
KDKO......... Littleton, CO [AM radio station call letters]
KDKR-FM... Decatur, TX [FM radio station call letters] (RBYB)
KDKS-FM... Haughton, LA [FM radio station call letters]
KDL........... Kerrisdale Resources Ltd. [Vancouver Stock Exchange symbol]
KDL........... Kinshasa-Dilolo-Lubumbashi Railway Co. (SAUO)
KDL........... Koronadal [Mindanao, Philippines] [Airport symbol] (AD)
KDL........... Kreisinger Development Laboratory (KSC)
KDLA......... De Ridder, LA [AM radio station call letters]
KDLB......... Henryetta, OK [AM radio station call letters]
KD lcl........ Knocked Down in Less Than Carload Lots (EBF)
KDLCL....... Knocked Down, in Less than Carloads
KDLF......... Del Rio/Laughlin Air Force Base [Texas] [ICAO location identifier] (ICLI)
KDLG......... Dillingham, AK [AM radio station call letters]
KDLH......... Duluth/International [Minnesota] [ICAO location identifier] (ICLI)
KDLH......... Duluth, MN [Television station call letters]
KDLK......... Del Rio, TX [AM radio station call letters] (RBYB)
KDLK-FM... Del Rio, TX [FM radio station call letters]
KDLL......... Kenai, AK [FM radio station call letters] (RBYB)
KDLM......... Detroit Lakes, MN [AM radio station call letters]
KDLO......... Watertown, SD [FM radio station call letters]
KDLO-TV... Florence, SD [Television station call letters]
KDLP......... Bayou Vista, LA [AM radio station call letters]
KDLR......... Devils Lake, ND [AM radio station call letters]
KDLS......... Perry, IA [AM radio station call letters]
KDLS-FM... Perry, IA [FM radio station call letters]
KDLT......... Mitchell, SD [Television station call letters]
kdlth......... Kodalith (VRA)
KDLT-TV... Sioux Falls, SD [Television station call letters] (BROA)
KDLV......... Sioux Falls, SD [Television station call letters] (BROA)
KDLV-TV... Mitchell, SD [Television station call letters] (BROA)
KDLX......... Makawao, HI [FM radio station call letters]
KDLY......... Lander, WY [FM radio station call letters]
KDM.......... K Display Manager (SAUS)
KDM.......... Key Decision Memorandum (ACAE)
KDM.......... Kingdom (WGA)
KDM.......... Kyrgyzstan Democratic Movement [Political party]
KDMA......... Montevideo, MN [AM radio station call letters]
KDMA......... Tucson/Davis Monthan Air Force Base [Arizona] [ICAO location identifier] (ICLI)
KDMD......... Anchorage, AK [Television station call letters]
KDMG......... Burlington, IA [FM radio station call letters]
KDMI......... Des Moines, IA [FM radio station call letters]
KDMI......... Thousands of Delivered Machine Instructions [Computer science]
KDMI-AM... Des Moines, IA [AM radio station call letters] (RBYB)
KDMM......... Herington, KS [FM radio station call letters]
KDMM......... Highland Park, TX [AM radio station call letters]
KDMN......... Buena Vista, CO [AM radio station call letters]
KDMO......... Carthage, MO [AM radio station call letters]
KDMS......... El Dorado, AR [AM radio station call letters]
KDMS......... Kennedy Space Center Data Management System [NASA] (NASA)
KDMS......... Kork Digital Mapping System (SAUO)
KDMX......... Dallas, TX [FM radio station call letters]
KDN.......... Kaydon Corp. [NYSE symbol] (SAG)
K/DN......... Kickdown [Automotive engineering]
KDN.......... Kinetically Designed Nozzle (NASA)
KdN.......... Koninkrijk der Nederlanden [Kingdom of the Netherlands] [Dutch] (BARN)
KDN.......... N'Dende [Gabon] [Airport symbol] (OAG)
K-DNA...... Deoxyribonucleic Acid - Kinetoplast [Biochemistry, genetics]
kDNA........ Kinetoplast DNA[Deoxyribonucleic Acid] [Genetics] (DOG)
KDNA........ Yakima, WA [FM radio station call letters]
KDNE......... Crete, NE [FM radio station call letters]
KDNI......... Duluth, MN [FM radio station call letters]
KDNK......... Carbondale, CO [FM radio station call letters]
KDNL......... St. Louis, MO [Television station call letters]
KDNO......... Delano, CA [FM radio station call letters]
KDNP......... Keresztenydemokrata Neppart [Christian Democratic People's Party] [Hungary] [Political party] (EY)
KDNR......... Los Lunas, NM [FM radio station call letters] (RBYB)
KDNS......... Downs, KS [FM radio station call letters]
KDNW......... Duluth, MN [FM radio station call letters]
KDNY......... Home Intensive Care Inc. (SAUO)
KDNZ......... Cedar Falls, IA [AM radio station call letters] (BROA)
KDO.......... 3-Deoxy-D-Manno-2-Octulosonate-8-Phosphate
KDO.......... Ketodeoxyoctonate [Biochemistry]
KDO.......... Ketodeoxyoctonic Acid (STED)
KDO.......... Key District Office [IRS]
KDOC......... Anaheim, CA [Television station call letters]
K-DODM.... Kennedy Space Center Department of Defense Plan/Requirement (NAKS)
K-DODM.... KSC DOD Plan/Requirement (SAUS)
KDOG......... North Mankato, MN [FM radio station call letters]
KDOK......... Tyler, TX [FM radio station call letters]
KDOL......... Henderson, NV [AM radio station call letters]

KDOM.......... Windom, MN [*AM radio station call letters*]
KDOM-FM.... Windom, MN [*FM radio station call letters*]
KDON.......... Kaydon Corp. (SAUO)
KDON.......... Salinas, CA [*FM radio station call letters*]
KDOR.......... Bartlesville, OK [*Television station call letters*]
KDOS.......... Key Display Operating System
KDOS.......... Key to Disk Operating System
KDOS.......... Laredo, TX [*AM radio station call letters*]
KDOS-FM...... Gainesville, TX [*FM radio station call letters*] (BROA)
KDOT-FM...... Reno, NV [*FM radio station call letters*] (RBYB)
KDOV.......... Dover Air Force Base [*Delaware*] [*ICAO location identifier*] (ICLI)
KDOV.......... Medford, OR [*FM radio station call letters*] (RBYB)
KDOX.......... Henderson, NV [*AM radio station call letters*] (BROA)
KDP............ Deuterated Potassium dideuterium phosphate (SAUS)
KDP............ Kalabagh Dam Project (SAUO)
KDP............ Kandep [*Papua New Guinea*] [*Airport symbol*] [*Obsolete*] (OAG)
KDP............ Kappa Delta Pi [*Honor society*] (AEE)
KDP............ Keyboard, Display, and Printer [*Computer science*]
KDP............ Key Data Points (MCD)
KDP............ Key Decision Point [*USCG*] (TAG)
KDP............ Key Development Plan [*Telecommunications*] (TEL)
KDP............ Known Datum Point
KDP............ Korean Democratic Party [*North Korea*] [*Political party*] (FEA)
KDP............ Kurdish Democratic Party [*Iran*] [*Political party*]
KDP............ Potassium Dideuterium Phosphate
KDP............ Potassium [*Kalium*] Dihydrogen Phosphate [*Inorganic chemistry*]
KDPA.......... Knitgoods Dyers and Processors Association
KDPA.......... West Chicago/Du Page County [*Illinois*] [*ICAO location identifier*] (ICLI)
KDPI.......... Kurdish Democratic Party of Iran [*Political party*] (PPW)
K-DPM........ Kennedy Space Center Department of Defense Payloads Plan/Requirement (NAKS)
K-DPM........ KSC DOD Payloads Plan (or Requirement) (SAUS)
K-DPN......... Kennedy Space Center Department of Defense Payloads Notice (NAKS)
K-DPN......... KSC [*Kennedy Space Center*] DOD Payloads Notice [*Department of Defense*] [*NASA*] (NASA)
KDPP.......... Keyboard/Display/Printer/Punch (ACAE)
K-DPPS....... Kennedy Space Center Department of Defense Payloads Project Specification (NAKS)
K-DPPS....... KSC DOD Payloads Project Specification (SAUS)
K-DPPS....... KSC [*Kennedy Space Center*] DOD Payloads Projects Specification [*Department of Defense*] [*NASA*] (NASA)
KDPR.......... Dickinson, ND [*FM radio station call letters*]
KDPS.......... Des Moines, IA [*FM radio station call letters*]
KDPS.......... Kurdish Democratic Party of Syria [*Political party*]
KDQN.......... De Queen, AR [*AM radio station call letters*]
KDQN-FM .... De Queen, AR [*FM radio station call letters*]
KDR............ Kandrian [*Papua New Guinea*] [*Airport symbol*] (OAG)
KDR............ Kangeld Resources Ltd. [*Vancouver Stock Exchange symbol*]
KDR............ Kappa Delta Rho [*Fraternity*]
KDR............ Keyboard Data Recorder [*Computer science*]
KDR............ Key Descriptor Record (TIMI)
KDR............ Kidderminster [*British depot code*]
KDR............ Kill/Detection Ratio (SAUS)
K/DR.......... Kitchen/Dining Room [*Classified advertising*] (ADA)
KDR............ Knockdown Resistance [*Pesticide technology*]
KDRE.......... North Little Rock, AR [*FM radio station call letters*]
KDRG.......... Deer Lodge, MT [*AM radio station call letters*]
KDRH.......... Glenwood Springs, CO [*FM radio station call letters*]
KDRK.......... Spokane, WA [*FM radio station call letters*]
KDRM.......... Moses Lake, WA [*FM radio station call letters*]
KDRNBK ...... Annual Report. Noto Marine Laboratory (journ.) (SAUS)
KDRO.......... Sedalia, MO [*AM radio station call letters*]
KDRQ.......... Wishek, ND [*AM radio station call letters*]
KDRS.......... Paragould, AR [*AM radio station call letters*]
KDRSM........ Democratic Committee To Support the Malagasy Socialist Revolution (SAUS)
KDRT.......... Del Rio/International [*Texas*] [*ICAO location identifier*] (ICLI)
KDRV.......... Medford, OR [*Television station call letters*]
KDRY.......... Alamo Heights, TX [*AM radio station call letters*]
KDS............ K2 Del Aire SA de CV [*Mexico*] [*ICAO designator*] (FAAC)
KDS............ Kamad Silver Co. Ltd. [*Vancouver Stock Exchange symbol*]
KDS............ Kathode Dark Space
KDS............ Kaufman Developmental Scale [*Child development test*]
KDS............ Kedougou [*Senegal*] [*Seismograph station code, US Geological Survey*] (SEIS)
KDS............ Keel Depth Simulator
KDS............ Keyboard Display Station [*Computer science*] (DA)
KDS............ Key Data Station (NITA)
KDS............ Key Display System [*Computer science*] (MDG)
KDS............ Key to Disc System
KDS............ Khuzistan Development Service (SAUO)
KDS............ Kiting Detection System (HGAA)
KDS............ Knowledge Directory Server
KDS............ Komma Dimokratikou Sosialismou [*Party for Democratic Socialism*] [*Greek*] [*Political party*] (PPE)
KDS............ Kristen Demokratisk Samling [*Christian Democratic Union*] [*Sweden*] [*Political party*] (PPE)
KDSD.......... Aberdeen, SD [*Television station call letters*]
KDSD.......... Pierpont, SD [*FM radio station call letters*]
KDSE.......... Dickinson, ND [*Television station call letters*]
kd/sec........ Kilocycles per Second [*Measurement*] (DAVI)
KDSI.......... Alice, TX [*AM radio station call letters*]
KDSI.......... Knowledge Data System Inc. (SAUO)

KDSI.......... Thousands of Delivered Source Instructions [*Computer science*]
KDSJ.......... Deadwood, SD [*AM radio station call letters*]
KDSL.......... Thousands of Delivered Source Lines of Code [*Computer science*]
KDSM.......... Des Moines [*Iowa*] [*ICAO location identifier*] (ICLI)
KDSM.......... Des Moines, IA [*Television station call letters*]
KDSM.......... Keratinizing Desquamative Squamous Metaplasia [*Medicine*]
KDSN.......... Denison, IA [*AM radio station call letters*]
KDSN-FM ..... Denison, IA [*FM radio station call letters*]
KDSR.......... Williston, ND [*AM radio station call letters*]
KDSRA2....... Annals of Science. Kanazawa University. Part 2. Biology-Geology (journ.) (SAUS)
KDSS.......... Ely, NV [*FM radio station call letters*]
KDSS.......... Key-to-Disk Subsystem [*Computer science*] (MHDB)
KDST.......... Dyersville, IA [*AM radio station call letters*]
KDSU.......... Fargo, ND [*FM radio station call letters*]
KDSX.......... Denison-Sherman, TX [*AM radio station call letters*]
KDT............ Kammer der Technik
KDT............ Kathodal Duration Tetanus [*Medicine*]
KDT............ Keyboard and Display Test (MCD)
KDT............ Keyboard Display Terminal (MCD)
KDT............ Key Data Terminal
KDT............ Key Definition Table [*Computer science*] (PCM)
KDT............ Key-to-Disk-to-Tape (MCD)
KDT............ Knowledge Discovery in Text (IDAI)
KDTA.......... Delta, CO [*AM radio station call letters*]
KDTB.......... Keg and Drum Trade Board (SAUO)
KDTE.......... Kathodal Duration Tetanus [*Medicine*] (ROG)
KDTH.......... Dubuque, IA [*AM radio station call letters*]
KDTK.......... Prescott Valley, AZ [*FM radio station call letters*]
KDTL-FM ..... Lake Village, AR [*FM radio station call letters*] (RBYB)
KDTN.......... Denton, TX [*Television station call letters*]
KDTV.......... San Francisco, CA [*Television station call letters*]
KDTW.......... Detroit/Metropolitan Wayne County [*Michigan*] [*ICAO location identifier*] (ICLI)
KDTX.......... Dallas, TX [*Television station call letters*]
KDU............ Christian Democratic Union [*Czechoslavakia*] [*Political party*] (ECON)
KDU............ Keyboard Display Unit (MCD)
KDU............ Kidney Dialysis Unit (MELL)
KDU............ Skardu [*Pakistan*] [*Airport symbol*] (AD)
KDUC.......... Barstow, CA [*FM radio station call letters*]
KDUG.......... Douglas/Bisbee International [*Arizona*] [*ICAO location identifier*] (ICLI)
KDUH.......... Scottsbluff, NE [*Television station call letters*]
KDUK.......... Eugene, OR [*AM radio station call letters*]
KDUK.......... Florence, OR [*FM radio station call letters*]
KDUN.......... Reedsport, OR [*AM radio station call letters*]
KDUQ.......... Ludlow, CA [*FM radio station call letters*]
KDUR.......... Durango, CO [*FM radio station call letters*]
KDUS.......... Cadus Pharmaceutical Corp. [*NASDAQ symbol*] (SAG)
KDUS-AM ..... Tempe, AZ [*AM radio station call letters*] (BROA)
KDUV.......... Visalia, CA [*FM radio station call letters*]
KDUX.......... Aberdeen, WA [*FM radio station call letters*]
KDUZ.......... Hutchinson, MN [*AM radio station call letters*]
KDV............ Kandavu [*Fiji*] [*Airport symbol*] (OAG)
KdV............ Korteweg-deVries [*Equation*] [*Mathematics*]
kDVC.......... Kilovolts, Direct Current (KSC)
KDVE-FM ..... Denison-Sherman, TX [*FM radio station call letters*] (RBYB)
KDVL.......... Devils Lake, ND [*FM radio station call letters*]
KDVR.......... Denver, CO [*Television station call letters*]
KDVS.......... Davis, CA [*FM radio station call letters*]
KDVV.......... Topeka, KS [*FM radio station call letters*]
KDW........... Keep Digging, Watson (SAUS)
KDWA.......... Hastings, MN [*AM radio station call letters*]
KDWB.......... Richfield, MN [*FM radio station call letters*]
KDWG.......... Billings, MT [*AM radio station call letters*] (RBYB)
KDWN.......... Las Vegas, NV [*AM radio station call letters*]
KDX............ Klondex Mines [*Vancouver Stock Exchange symbol*]
KDX............ Klondex Mines Ltd [*VS, exchange symbol*] (TTSB)
KDX............ Knock Down Export [*Automotive engineering*]
KDX............ Korea Defence Experiment (SAUO)
KDXE.......... Sulphur Springs, TX [*FM radio station call letters*]
KDXL.......... St. Louis Park, MN [*FM radio station call letters*]
KDXU.......... St. George, UT [*AM radio station call letters*]
KDXX.......... Dallas, TX [*AM radio station call letters*] (BROA)
KDXX-FM..... Corsicana, TX [*FM radio station call letters*] (BROA)
KDXY-FM .... Lake City, AR [*FM radio station call letters*] (RBYB)
KDY........... Kennedy Resources [*Vancouver Stock Exchange symbol*]
KDYA.......... Vallejo, CA [*AM radio station call letters*] (BROA)
KDYL.......... Salt Lake City, UT [*AM radio station call letters*]
KDYN.......... Ozark, AR [*AM radio station call letters*]
KDYN-FM.... Ozark, AR [*FM radio station call letters*]
KDYS.......... Abilene/Dyess Air Force Base [*Texas*] [*ICAO location identifier*] (ICLI)
KDYS-AM..... Lafayette, LA [*AM radio station call letters*] (RBYB)
KdyWils...... Kennedy Wilson, Inc. [*Associated Press*] (SAG)
KDZ........... Kurdzhali [*Bulgaria*] [*Seismograph station code, US Geological Survey*] (SEIS)
KDZA.......... Pueblo, CO [*AM radio station call letters*]
KDZA-FM..... Pueblo, CO [*FM radio station call letters*] (RBYB)
KDZN.......... Glendive, MT [*FM radio station call letters*]
KDZY-FM.... McCall, ID [*FM radio station call letters*] (BROA)
KDZZ.......... Albuquerque, NM [*AM radio station call letters*]
K$_e$.......... Exchangeable Body Potassium [*Biochemistry*] (DAVI)
KE............ Kagel Exercise (MELL)
KE............ Kaiser Engineers (NRCH)

Ke	Keen's English Rolls Court Reports [48 English Reprint] [A publication] (DLA)
KE	Kendall's Compound E [Cortisone]
KE	Kenya [ANSI two-letter standard code] (CNC)
ke	Kenya [MARC country of publication code] [Library of Congress] (LCCP)
KE	Kerr Effect [Optics]
KE	Kessering Site Office (SAUO)
KE	Key Equipment [Telecommunications] (TEL)
KE	Kinetic Energy
KE	King Edward (ROG)
KE	Kitchen Exhaust (OA)
KE	Knight of the Eagle
KE	Knight of the Elephant [Denmark]
KE	Knights of Equity (EA)
KE	Knowledge Engineer [Computer science]
KE	Koger Equity [AMEX symbol] (TTSB)
KE	Koger Equity, Inc. [AMEX symbol] (CTT)
KE	Korea Fund [NYSE symbol] (TTSB)
KE	Korean Air [Airline flight code] (ODBW)
KE	Korean Air Lines [ICAO designator] (AD)
KE	Korean AirLines, Inc. (SAUO)
KE	Kroger Equity [NYSE symbol] (SG)
KEA	Carcino Embryonales Antigen (SAUS)
KEA	Kanada Esperanto-Asocio [Canadian Esperanto Association]
KEA	Kealakomo [Hawaii] [Seismograph station code, US Geological Survey] [Closed] (SEIS)
KEA	Keane, Inc. [AMEX symbol] (SPSG)
KEA	Kent Executive Aviation Ltd. [British] [ICAO designator] (FAAC)
KEA	Kentucky Education Association (SAUO)
KEA	Kiwifruit Exporters Association (SAUO)
KEA	Knitwear Employers Association (EA)
KEA	Kuba Esperanto-Asocio (SAUO)
KEAG	Anchorage, AK [FM radio station call letters]
KEAH	Kill Everyone After Hours (SAUS)
KEAL-FM	Douglas, AZ [FM radio station call letters] (RBYB)
KEAN	Abilene, TX [AM radio station call letters]
Kean C NJ	Kean College of New Jersey (GAGS)
Keane	Keane, Inc. [Associated Press] (SAG)
Keane & Gr	Keane and Grant's English Registration Appeal Cases [1854-62] [A publication] (DLA)
Keane & GRC	Keane and Grant's English Registration Appeal Cases [1854-62] [A publication] (DLA)
KEAN-FM	Abilene, TX [FM radio station call letters]
KEAR	San Francisco, CA [FM radio station call letters]
KEAS	Eastland, TX [AM radio station call letters]
KEAS	Knots Equivalent Airspeed (MCD)
KEASAT	Kinetic Energy Anti-Satellite
KEAS-FM	Eastland, TX [FM radio station call letters]
Keat Fam Sett	Keatinge's Family Settlements [1810] [A publication] (DLA)
KEAZ	De Ridder, LA [FM radio station call letters]
KEB	English Bay, AK [Location identifier] [FAA] (FAAL)
KEB	Keban [Turkey] [Seismograph station code, US Geological Survey] (SEIS)
Keb	Keble's English King's Bench Reports [83, 84 English Reprint] [A publication] (DLA)
KEB	Korea Exchange Bank (IMH)
KEBC	Oklahoma City, OK [FM radio station call letters]
KEB COLL	Keble College [Oxford University] (ROG)
KEBE	Jacksonville, TX [AM radio station call letters]
KEBI	Kentucky Enterprise Bancorp [NASDAQ symbol] (SAG)
Keb J	Keble's Justice of the Peace [A publication] (DLA)
KEBK	Korea Exchange Bank (SAUO)
Kebl	Keble's English King's Bench Reports [83, 84 English Reprint] [A publication] (DLA)
Keble	Keble College (SAUO)
Keble	Keble's English King's Bench Reports [83, 84 English Reprint] [A publication] (DLA)
Keble (Eng)	Keble's English King's Bench Reports [83, 84 English Reprint] [A publication] (DLA)
KEBN	Salem, OR [Television station call letters]
KEBR	North Highlands, CA [FM radio station call letters]
KEBR	Rocklin, CA [AM radio station call letters]
Keb Stat	Keble's Statutes [A publication] (DLA)
KEC	KDD Engineering and Consulting Inc. (NITA)
KEC	Kecskemet [Hungary] [Seismograph station code, US Geological Survey] (SEIS)
KEC	Klebsiella, Enterobacter, Citrobacter [Bacteriae] [Microbiology] (DAVI)
KEC	Korea Explosives Co. Ltd. (SAUO)
KECC	Keystone Empire Collegiate Conference (PSS)
KECC	Miles City, MT [FM radio station call letters]
KECG	El Cerrito, CA [FM radio station call letters]
KECG	Elizabeth City Coast Guard Air Base (SAUS)
KECG	Elizabeth City Coast Guard Air Base/Municipal [North Carolina] [ICAO location identifier] (ICLI)
KECH	Sun Valley, ID [FM radio station call letters]
KECI	Korean Existing Chemicals Inventory (SAUO)
KECI	Missoula, MT [Television station call letters]
KECME	Kuzbass Commodity and Raw Materials Exchange [Russian Federation] (EY)
KECN-AM	Blackfoot, ID [AM radio station call letters] (RBYB)
KECO	Elk City, OK [FM radio station call letters]
KECO	Kent Electronics Corporation (SAUO)
KECO	Korea Electric Company (SAUO)
KECP	Kit Engineering Change Proposal (KSC)
KECR	El Cajon, CA [AM radio station call letters]
KECS	Gainesville, TX [FM radio station call letters] (RBYB)
KECY	El Centro, CA [Television station call letters] (RBYB)
KED	Kaedi [Mauritania] [Airport symbol] (OAG)
KED	Kedougou [Senegal] [Seismograph station code, US Geological Survey] [Closed] (SEIS)
KED	Kendrick Extrication Device (SAUS)
KED	Kill Enhancement Device [Military] (ACAE)
KED	Known Enemy Dead [Military]
KEDA	San Antonio, TX [AM radio station call letters]
KEDD-FM	Johannesburg, CA [FM radio station call letters] (BROA)
KEDDS	Kansas Education Dissemination/Diffusion System (EDAC)
KEDG	Las Vegas, NV [FM radio station call letters]
KEDG-FM	Alexandria, LA [FM radio station call letters] (BROA)
KEDI	Korean Education Development Institute (BUAC)
KEDJ	Sun City, AZ [FM radio station call letters]
KEDM	Monroe, LA [FM radio station call letters]
KEDO	Korea Energy Development Organisation [A consortium formed by the US, North Korea, and South Korea to finance and build reactors] (ECON)
KEDO	Longview, WA [AM radio station call letters]
KEDP	Las Vegas, NM [FM radio station call letters]
KEDR	Sacramento, CA [FM radio station call letters]
KEDS	Knowledge Express Data Systems
KEDT	Corpus Christi, TX [FM radio station call letters]
KEDT-TV	Corpus Christi, TX [Television station call letters]
KEDW	Edwards Air Force Base [California] [ICAO location identifier] (ICLI)
KEE	Emporia State University, School of Library Science, Emporia, KS [OCLC symbol] (OCLC)
KEE	Kelle [Congo] [Airport symbol] (OAG)
KEE	Kerr Electro-Optical Effect [Optics]
KEE	Keychart Educational Equipment [for use with an electronic typewriter]
KEE	Keystone Air Services Ltd. [Canada] [ICAO designator] (FAAC)
KEE	Knowledge Engineering Environment [An artificial intelligence system]
KEED	Eugene, OR [AM radio station call letters] (RBYB)
KEEE	Nacogdoches, TX [AM radio station call letters]
KEEF	Los Angeles, CA [Television station call letters]
KEEH	Spokane, WA [FM radio station call letters]
KEEI	Key Energy Enterprises, Incorporated (SAUO)
KEEL	Kent European Enterprises Ltd. [British]
KEEL	Shreveport, LA [AM radio station call letters]
Keen	Keen's English Rolls Court Reports [48 English Reprint] [A publication] (DLA)
KEEN	Palmer, AK [FM radio station call letters] (RBYB)
Keen Ch	Keen's English Rolls Court Reports [48 English Reprint] [A publication] (DLA)
Keen (Eng)	Keen's English Rolls Court Reports [48 English Reprint] [A publication] (DLA)
Keener Quasi Contr	Keener's Cases on Quasi Contracts [A publication] (DLA)
Keene St C	Keene State College (GAGS)
KEEP	Bandera, TX [FM radio station call letters]
KEEP	Kamehameha Early Education Program [Hawaii] (EDAC)
KEEP	Kentucky Environmental Education Program (EDAC)
KEEP	Kuroshio Edge Exchange Processes (SAUO)
KEEP	Kyosato Education Experiment Project [Self-help program for Japanese farmers established by Americans in 1948]
KEEPS	Kodak Ektaprint Electronic Publishing System [Hardware and software components] [Eastman Kodak Co.]
KEES	Gladewater, TX [AM radio station call letters]
KEET	Eureka, CA [Television station call letters]
Keet	Parakeet [Bird]
KEEX	Kee Exploration, Inc. (SAUO)
KEEY	St. Paul, MN [FM radio station call letters]
KEEZ	Mankato, MN [FM radio station call letters]
KEF	Keflavik [Iceland] [Airport symbol] (AD)
KEF	Korea Equity Fund [NYSE symbol] (SPSG)
KEF	Reykjavik [Iceland] Keflavik Airport [Airport symbol] (OAG)
KEFD	Houston/Ellington Air Force Base [Texas] [ICAO location identifier] (ICLI)
KEFE	Los Alamos, NM [FM radio station call letters]
KEFH-FM	Clarendon, TX [FM radio station call letters] (BROA)
KEFM	Omaha, NE [FM radio station call letters]
KEFR	Le Grand, CA [FM radio station call letters]
KEFX-FM	Twin Falls, ID [FM radio station call letters] (BROA)
KEG	Keg Restaurants Ltd. [Toronto Stock Exchange symbol] [Vancouver Stock Exchange symbol]
KEG	Key Energy Group [AMEX symbol] (SPSG)
KEG	Key Gap [Computer science] (MHDI)
KEGE	Richfield, MN [AM radio station call letters]
KEGEAC	Japanese Journal of Plastic and Reconstructive Surgery (journ.) (SAUS)
KEGE-FM	Minneapolis, MN [FM radio station call letters]
KEGG	Daingerfield, TX [AM radio station call letters]
KEGG	Kyoto Encyclopedia of Genes and Genomes [Computer network]
KEGL	Fort Worth, TX [FM radio station call letters]
KEGP	Eagle Pass/Municipal [Texas] [ICAO location identifier] (ICLI)
KEGR	Red Bluff, CA [FM radio station call letters] (RBYB)
KEGS	Kenworth Engine Governing System [Automotive engineering]
KEGS	King Edward VI Grammar School (SAUO)
KEGT	Lake Village, AR [FM radio station call letters]
KEGX	Richland, WA [FM radio station call letters]
KEH	Kaiser Engineers Hanford (SAUO)
KEH	King Edward's Horse Regiment [Military unit] [British]

KEH	Kurzgefasstes Exegetisches Handbuch zum Alten Testament [Leipzig] [A publication] (BJA)
KEHK-FM	Brownsville, OR [FM radio station call letters] (RBYB)
KEI	Keithley Instruments [NYSE symbol] (TTSB)
KEI	Keithley Instruments, Inc. [AMEX symbol] (SPSG)
KEI	Kepi [Indonesia] [Airport symbol] (OAG)
KEI	Kresge Eye Institute
KEIA	Korea Economic Institute of America (EA)
KEIA	Korea Electronics Industries Association (SAUO)
KEIDANREN	Federation of Economic Organizations, Japan (SAUO)
Keil	Keilway's English King's Bench Reports [72 English Reprint] [A publication] (DLA)
KEIL	Key Essential Item List [Defense Supply Agency]
Keilw	Keilway's English King's Bench Reports [72 English Reprint] [A publication] (DLA)
Keilway	Keilway's English King's Bench Reports [72 English Reprint] [A publication] (DLA)
Keilw (Eng)	Keilway's English King's Bench Reports [72 English Reprint] [A publication] (DLA)
KEIN	Great Falls, MT [AM radio station call letters]
KEIN-FM	Conrad, MT [FM radio station call letters] (BROA)
KEIS	Kentucky Economic Information System [University of Kentucky] [Lexington] [Database producer] [Information service or system]
Keith Ch PA	Registrar's Book, Keith's Court of Chancery [Pennsylvania] [A publication] (DLA)
Keithly	Keithley Instruments, Inc. [Associated Press] (SAG)
KEJC	Modesto, CA [FM radio station call letters] (RBYB)
KEJJ-FM	Gunnison, CO [FM radio station call letters] (BROA)
KEJO	Corvallis, OR [FM radio station call letters]
KEJO	Kelly-Johnston Enterprises (SAUO)
KEJS	Lubbock, TX [FM radio station call letters]
KEK	Ekwok [Alaska] [Airport symbol] (OAG)
KEK	Kappa Eta Kappa [Fraternity]
KEK	Kinetic Energy Kill (SAUS)
KEK	Konferenz Europaeischer Kirchen [Conference of European Churches - CEC] (EA)
KEK	Koo Energy Ken
KEK	Kypriakon Ethnikon Komma [Cypriot National Party (1944-1960)] [Greek Cypriot] [Political party] (PPE)
KEKA	Eureka, CA [FM radio station call letters]
KEKB	Fruita, CO [FM radio station call letters]
Ke/Kg	Exchangeable Potassium per Kilogram of Body Weight [Biochemistry] (DAVI)
KEKO-FM	Hebronville, TX [FM radio station call letters] (BROA)
KEL	Karntner Einheitsliste [Carinthian Unity List] [Austria] [Political party] (PPE)
KEL	Keles [Later, TKT] [Former USSR] [Geomagnetic observatory code]
Kel	Kelim (BJA)
KEL	Kelsey-Hayes Canada Ltd. [Toronto Stock Exchange symbol]
KEL	Kelud [Java] [Seismograph station code, US Geological Survey] [Closed] (SEIS)
KEL	Known Enemy Location [Military]
KEL	Koroska Enotna Lista [Carinthian Unity List] [Austria] [Political party] (PPE)
KEL	Kroatia Esperanto-Ligo (SAUO)
KELA	Centralia-Chehalis, WA [AM radio station call letters]
Kel An	Kelly's Life Annuities [1835] [A publication] (DLA)
Kel Cont	Kelly on Contracts of Married Women [A publication] (DLA)
KELD	El Dorado, AR [AM radio station call letters]
KELD	El Dorado/Goodwin Field [Arkansas] [ICAO location identifier] (ICLI)
Kel Draft	Kelly's Draftsman [14th ed.] [1978] [A publication] (DLA)
KELE-AM	Mountain Grove, MO [AM radio station call letters] (RBYB)
KELE-FM	Mountain Grove, MO [FM radio station call letters] (BROA)
Kel-f	Polymonochlorotrifluoroethylene (IDOE)
KELG	Elgin, TX [AM radio station call letters]
Kel GA	Kelly's Reports [1-3 Georgia] [A publication] (DLA)
Kelh	Kelham's Norman French Law Dictionary [A publication] (DLA)
Kelham	Kelham's Norman French Law Dictionary [A publication] (DLA)
Kelh Dict	Kelham's Norman French Law Dictionary [A publication] (DLA)
KELI	Kristana Esperantista Ligo Internacia [International Christian Esperanto Association] (EAIO)
KELI	San Angelo, TX [FM radio station call letters]
K-ELISA	Kinetic Measurement of Enzyme-Linked Immunosorbant Assay
KELK	Elko, NV [AM radio station call letters]
Kelk Jud Acts	Kelke's Judicature Acts [A publication] (DLA)
KELL	Kellstrom Industries [NASDAQ symbol] (TTSB)
KELL	Kellstrom Industries, Inc. [NASDAQ symbol] (SAG)
Kellen	Kellen's Reports [146-55 Massachusetts] [A publication] (DLA)
Kel Life Ann	Kelly on Life Annuities [A publication] (DLA)
KellOG	Kelley Oil and Gas Corp. [Associated Press] (SAG)
Kellogg	Kellogg Co. [Associated Press] (SAG)
KELLOGG	W.K. Kellogg Foundation Institute (SAUO)
KELLW	Kellstrom Inds Wrrt [NASDAQ symbol] (TTSB)
Kellwood	Kellwood Co. [Associated Press] (SAG)
Kelly	Kelly's Reports [1-3 Georgia] [A publication] (DLA)
Kelly & C	Kelly and Cobb's Reports [4, 5 Georgia] [A publication] (DLA)
Kelly & Cobb	Kelly and Cobb's Reports [4, 5 Georgia] [A publication] (DLA)
KellyRus	Kelly Russell Studios, Inc. [Associated Press] (SAG)
KellyS	Kelly Services, Inc. [Associated Press] (SAG)
KELN	Kell Negative [Hematology] (DAVI)
KELN	North Platte, NE [FM radio station call letters]
KELO	Sioux Falls, SD [AM radio station call letters]
KELO-FM	Sioux Falls, SD [FM radio station call letters]
KELO-TV	Sioux Falls, SD [Television station call letters]
KELP	Coronal Emission Line Polarimeter (SAUS)

KELP	El Paso/International [Texas] [ICAO location identifier] (ICLI)
KELP	El Paso, TX [AM radio station call letters]
KELP	Kindergarten Evaluation for Learning Potential [McGraw Hill]
KELR	Chariton, IA [FM radio station call letters]
KELS	Kohlman Evaluation of Living Skills [Occupational therapy]
Kel Sc Fac	Kelly's Scire Facias [2nd ed.] [1849] [A publication] (DLA)
Kelstr	Kellstrom Industries, Inc. [Associated Press] (SAG)
Kelstrm	Kellstrom Industries, Inc. [Associated Press] (SAG)
KELT-FM	Riverside, CA [FM radio station call letters] (BROA)
KELU	Kuching Employees and Labourers' Union [Sarawak]
Kel Us	Kelly on Usury [1835] [A publication] (DLA)
KELY	Ely, NV [AM radio station call letters]
KELY	Kelly Services, Inc. [NASDAQ symbol] (NQ)
KELYA	Kelly Services 'A' [NASDAQ symbol] (TTSB)
KELYB	Kelly Services 'B' [NASDAQ symbol] (TTSB)
KELY-FM	Ely, NV [FM radio station call letters]
KELYOG	Kelley Oil & Gas Partnership Ltd. (SAUO)
KEm	Emporia Public Library, Emporia, KS [Library symbol] [Library of Congress] (LCLS)
KEM	Kemi [Finland] [Airport symbol] (OAG)
KEM	Kemper Corp. [NYSE symbol] (SPSG)
KEM	Kinetic Energy Missile (INF)
KEMA	Kitchen Equipment Manufacturers Association (SAUO)
KEMAR	Knowles Electronics Manikin for Acoustic Research
KEMB	Emmetsburg, IA [FM radio station call letters]
Kemble Sax	Kemble's The Saxons in England [A publication] (DLA)
KEMC	Billings, MT [FM radio station call letters]
KEmC	College of Emporia, Emporia, KS [Library symbol] [Library of Congress] (LCLS)
KEMC	Kaiserslautern Equipment Maintenance Center (SAUO)
KEMC	Kemper Corp. (MHDW)
KEMEDB	Infection, Inflammation and Immunity (journ.) (SAUS)
Kemet	Kemet Corp. [Associated Press] (SAG)
KEMM	Commerce, TX [FM radio station call letters]
KEMM	Kennesaw Mountain National Battlefield Park
Kemo Tx	Chemical Therapy [or Chemotherapy] [Pharmacology] (DAVI)
Kemper	Kemper Corp. [Associated Press] (SAG)
KEMRI	Kenya Medical Research Institute (BUAC)
KEMRI	Kenyan Medical Research Institute (SAUO)
KEMS	Kaiser Engineers Management System (SAUO)
KEmT	Kansas State Teachers College, Emporia, KS [Library symbol] [Library of Congress] [Obsolete] (LCLS)
KEmU	Emporia State University, Emporia, KS [Library symbol] [Library of Congress] (LCLS)
KEM-V	Kinetic Energy Missile Vehicle [Army]
KEMV	Mountain View, AR [Television station call letters]
KEMX	Locust Grove, OK [FM radio station call letters]
Ken	Kendall [Record label]
KEN	Kenema [Sierra Leone] [Airport symbol] (OAG)
KEN	Kenridge Mineral [Vancouver Stock Exchange symbol]
KEN	Kentucky (ODBW)
KEN	Kentucky
KEN	Kenya [ANSI three-letter standard code] (CNC)
Ken	Kenya (VRA)
KEN	Kenyon College, Gambier, OH [OCLC symbol] (OCLC)
Ken	Kenyon's English King's Bench Reports [A publication] (DLA)
KEN	National Mental Health Services Knowledge Exchange Network (SAUO)
KENA	Kenai Corp. (SAUO)
KENA	Mena, AR [AM radio station call letters]
KENA-FM	Mena, AR [FM radio station call letters]
Kenan	Kenan's Reports [76-91 North Carolina] [A publication] (DLA)
Kenan	Kenan Transportation Co. [Associated Press] (SAG)
KENATCO	Kenya National Transport Co. (BUAC)
KENC	Kentucky Central Life Insurance Co. (SAUO)
KENCLIP	Kentucky Cooperative Library and Information Project [Library network]
KENCO	Kendrick & Co. [Telecommunications service] (TSSD)
KEND	Enid/Vance Air Force Base [Oklahoma] [ICAO location identifier] (ICLI)
KEND	Roswell, NM [FM radio station call letters]
KENDA	Kenya National Democratic Alliance Party (SAUO)
Ken Dec	Kentucky Decisions (Sneed) [2 Kentucky] [A publication] (DLA)
KENE	Toppenish, WA [AM radio station call letters]
Kenetech	Kenetech Corp. [Associated Press] (SAG)
KENGO	Kenya Energy and Environment Organisations (BUAC)
KENI	Anchorage, AK [AM radio station call letters]
Kenkyu Hokoku Sci Pap Cent Res Inst Jap Tob Salt Public Corp	Kenkyu Hokoku. Scientific Papers. Central Research Institute. Japan Tobacco and Salt Public Corporation (SAUO)
Ken LR	Kentucky Law Reporter [A publication] (DLA)
Ken L Re	Kentucky Law Reporter [A publication] (DLA)
KENN	Farmington, NM [AM radio station call letters]
KENN	Kennecott Co. Railroad [AAR code]
KENN	Kennewick School District (SAUO)
KENN	Kennington Ltd. (SAUO)
Kenn Ch	Kennedy's Chancery Practice [2nd ed.] [1852-53] [A publication] (DLA)
Kenn C Mar	Kennedy on Courts-Martial [A publication] (DLA)
Kennett	Kennett's Glossary [A publication] (DLA)
Kennett	Kennett upon Impropriations [A publication] (DLA)
Kennett Gloss	Kennett's Glossary [A publication] (DLA)
Kennett Par Ant	Kennett's Parochial Antiquities [A publication] (DLA)
Kenn Gloss	Kennett's Glossary [A publication] (DLA)
Kenn Imp	Kennett upon Impropriations [A publication] (DLA)

Kenn Jur......	Kennedy on Juries [*A publication*] (DLA)
Kennmtl......	Kennametal, Inc. [*Associated Press*] (SAG)
Kenn Par Antiq...	Kennett's Parochial Antiquities [*A publication*] (DLA)
Kenn Pr	Kennedy's Chancery Practice [*2nd ed.*] [*1852-53*] [*A publication*] (DLA)
KENO	Las Vegas, NV [*AM radio station call letters*]
Ken Opin	Kentucky Opinions [*A publication*] (DLA)
Kenora.........	Keewatin, Norman, and Rat Portage [*Communities that merged to form town in Ontario, Canada*]
KENPRO........	Kenyan Committee on Trade Procedures (BUAC)
KENR	Hudson, TX [*AM radio station call letters*]
Ken R	Kenyon Review [*A publication*] (BRI)
KENS	Kenilwurth Systems Corp. (SAUO)
KENS	Kensington [*West London*] (ROG)
KENS	San Antonio, TX [*AM radio station call letters*]
KenseyN	Kensey Nash Corp. [*Associated Press*] (SAG)
KENS-TV	San Antonio, TX [*Television station call letters*]
KENT..........	Kent Financial Services [*NASDAQ symbol*] (SPSG)
KENT..........	Kent Financial Svcs [*NASDAQ symbol*] (TTSB)
Kent..........	Kent's Commentaries on American Law [*A publication*] (DLA)
KENT..........	Odessa, TX [*AM radio station call letters*]
Kent & R St...	Kent and Radcliff's Law of New York, Revision of 1801 [*A publication*] (DLA)
Kentch	Kenetech Corp. [*Associated Press*] (SAG)
Kent Com.....	Kent's Commentaries on American Law [*A publication*] (DLA)
Kent Comm...	Kent's Commentaries on American Law [*A publication*] (DLA)
Kentekl	Kentek Information Systems, Inc. [*Associated Press*] (SAG)
KentEl........	Kent Electronics [*Associated Press*] (SAG)
KentEnt.......	Kentucky Enterprise Bancorp [*Associated Press*] (SAG)
KENT-FM	Odessa, TX [*FM radio station call letters*]
KentFn........	Kent Financial Services, Inc. [*Associated Press*] (SAG)
KENTING.....	Kenting Earth Sciences (SAUS)
Kent's Commen...	Kent's Commentaries on American Law [*A publication*] (DLA)
Kent St U.....	Kent State University (GAGS)
KENU	Enumclaw, WA [*AM radio station call letters*]
KENV	Wendover Auxiliary Air Base (SAUS)
KENV	Wendover/Wendover Auxiliary Air Base [*Utah*] [*ICAO location identifier*] (ICLI)
KENV-TV	Elko, NV [*TV station call letters*] (RBYB)
KENW	Portales, NM [*FM radio station call letters*]
KENWIN......	Kenwin Shops, Inc. (SAUO)
KENW-TV	Portales, NM [*Television station call letters*]
Ke:nx	Connects [*Macintosh*] [*Computer science*]
Keny	Kenyon's English King's Bench Reports [*A publication*] (DLA)
Kenya LR......	Kenya Law Reports [*A publication*] (DLA)
Keny Ch.......	Chancery Cases [*2 Notes of King's Bench Cases*] [*England*] [*A publication*] (DLA)
KENZ-FM	Orem, UT [*FM radio station call letters*] (RBYB)
KEO...........	Keld'Or Resources, Inc. [*Vancouver Stock Exchange symbol*]
KEO...........	King Edward's Own [*British military*] (DMA)
KEO...........	Odienne [*Ivory Coast*] [*Airport symbol*] (OAG)
KEOC.........	King Edward's Own Cavalry [*British military*] (DMA)
KEOG.........	King Edward VII Own Gurkhas (SAUO)
KEOJ.........	Caney, KS [*FM radio station call letters*]
KEOK	Tahlequah, OK [*FM radio station call letters*]
KEOL.........	King Edward's Own Lancers [*British military*] (DMA)
KEOL.........	La Grande, OR [*FM radio station call letters*]
KEOM.........	Mesquite, TX [*FM radio station call letters*]
KEOR.........	Atoka, OK [*AM radio station call letters*]
KEOS	College Station, TX [*FM radio station call letters*] (RBYB)
KEOT-FM	St. George, UT [*FM radio station call letters*] (BROA)
KEP..........	Kaneb Energy Partners Ltd. (MHDW)
KEP..........	Kellner Eye Piece
KEP..........	Key Entry Processing
KEP..........	King Edward Point [*South Georgia Island*] [*Seismograph station code, US Geological Survey*] (SEIS)
KEP..........	Knight of the Eagle and Pelican [*Freemasonry*]
KEP..........	Korea Electric Power ADS [*NYSE symbol*] (TTSB)
KEP..........	Korea Electric Power Corp. [*NYSE symbol*] (SAG)
KEP..........	Nepalganj [*Nepal*] [*Airport symbol*] (OAG)
KEPB.........	Eugene, OR [*Television station call letters*]
KE/PB........	Kaiser Engineers, Inc./Parsons Brinckerhoff Quade & Douglas, Inc. (SAUO)
KEPC........	Colorado Springs, CO [*FM radio station call letters*]
KEPCO........	Korea Electric Power Corp.
KEPCO........	Kyushu Electric Power Company (SAUO)
KEPD	Kinetic Energy Penetrator Destructor (SAUS)
KEPE.........	Kentron Programmatismou kai Oikonomikon Ereunon [*Centre of Planning and Economic Research*] [*Greece*]
KEPG	Victoria, TX [*FM radio station call letters*]
KEPI.........	Eagle Pass, TX [*FM radio station call letters*] (RBYB)
KEPOA	Keep This Office Advised
KEPR.........	Pasco, WA [*Television station call letters*]
KEPROM......	Keyed-Access, Erasable, Programmable Read-Only Memory [*Computer science*]
KEPS.........	Eagle Pass, TX [*AM radio station call letters*]
KEPX.........	Eagle Pass, TX [*FM radio station call letters*]
KEPZ.........	Kaohsiung Export Processing Zone [*Reexport manufacturing complex*] [*Taiwan*]
KEQ..........	Kebar [*Indonesia*] [*Airport symbol*] (OAG)
KEQU	Kewaunee Scientific [*NASDAQ symbol*] (TTSB)
KEQU	Kewaunee Scientific Corp. [*Formerly, Kewaunee Science Equipment*] [*NASDAQ symbol*] (NQ)
Ker...........	Indian Law Reports, Kerala Series [*A publication*] (DLA)
Ker...........	Kerithoth (BJA)

KER...........	Kerman [*Iran*] [*Airport symbol*] (OAG)
KER...........	Kermanshah [*Iran*] [*Seismograph station code, US Geological Survey*] (SEIS)
KER...........	Kerr-Addison Mines [*TS, exchange symbol*] (TTSB)
KER...........	Kerr Addison Mines Ltd. [*Toronto Stock Exchange symbol*]
KER...........	Kerry [*County in Ireland*] (ROG)
KER...........	Kinetic Energy Release
KERA.........	Dallas, TX [*FM radio station call letters*]
KERA.........	Kentucky Education Reform Act
Kera..........	Keratitis [*Ophthalmology*] (DAVI)
KERA.........	KeraVision, Inc. [*NASDAQ symbol*] (SAG)
Kerala........	All Indian Law Reports, Kerala Series [*A publication*] (DLA)
Kerala LJ.....	Kerala Law Journal [*A publication*] (DLA)
KERA-TV......	Dallas, TX [*Television station call letters*]
KeraVis......	KeraVision, Inc. [*Associated Press*] (SAG)
KeraVs........	KeraVision, Inc. [*Associated Press*] (SAG)
KERB.........	Kermit, TX [*AM radio station call letters*]
KERB-FM	Kermit, TX [*FM radio station call letters*]
KERC	Marked Tree, AR [*FM radio station call letters*]
KERD	Kinetic Energy Release Distribution [*Of ions for spectral studies*]
KERE.........	Atchison, KS [*AM radio station call letters*]
KERE.........	Kuroshio Extension Regional Experiment (SAUO)
KERE-FM	Horton, KS [*FM radio station call letters*]
KEREN-OR ...	Jerusalem Institutions for the Blind (EA)
KERI..........	Kia Economic Research Institute
KERI..........	Wasco, CA [*AM radio station call letters*]
KERIS	Kiel Ecosystem Research Information System (SAUO)
KERKHFF......	Kerkhoff Industries Inc. (SAUO)
KERM.........	Torrington, WY [*FM radio station call letters*]
KERMA	Kinetic Energy Released in Materials (ACAE)
KERMA	Kinetic Energy Released per Unit Mass (DEN)
KERN.........	Bakersfield, CA [*AM radio station call letters*]
Kern..........	Kernan's Reports [*11-14 New York*] [*A publication*] (DLA)
Kern..........	Kern's Reports [*100-116 Indiana*] [*A publication*] (DLA)
KERN-FM	Bakersfield, CA [*FM radio station call letters*]
KERO.........	Bakersfield, CA [*Television station call letters*]
KERO.........	Kerosine [*British*]
KERO.........	Kuwait Emergency Recovery Office (SAUO)
KERP.........	Kuwait Emergency Recovery Programme (SAUS)
KERP.........	Pueblo, CO [*FM radio station call letters*]
Kerr	Kerr Group [*Associated Press*] (SAG)
KERR	Kerrier [*England*]
Kerr	Kerr's New Brunswick Reports [*A publication*] (DLA)
Kerr	Kerr's Reports [*18-22 Indiana*] [*A publication*] (DLA)
Kerr	Kerr's Reports [*27-29 New York Civil Procedure*] [*A publication*] (DLA)
KERR	Kinetic Energy Recovery Rope (SAUS)
KERR	Polson, MT [*AM radio station call letters*]
Kerr Act	Kerr's Actions at Law [*3rd ed.*] [*1861*] [*A publication*] (DLA)
Kerr Anc L ...	Kerr on Ancient Lights [*A publication*] (DLA)
Kerr Black.....	Kerr's Blackstone [*12th ed.*] [*1895*] [*A publication*] (DLA)
Kerr Disc	Kerr's Discovery [*1870*] [*A publication*] (DLA)
Kerr Ext	Kerr on Inter-State Extradition [*A publication*] (DLA)
Kerr F & M...	Kerr's Fraud and Mistake [*7th ed.*] [*1952*] [*A publication*] (DLA)
Kerr Fr	Kerr's Fraud and Mistake [*7th ed.*] [*1952*] [*A publication*] (DLA)
KerrGp	Kerr Group [*Associated Press*] (SAG)
Kerr Inj	Kerr on Injunctions [*A publication*] (DLA)
KerrMc	Kerr McGee Corp. [*Associated Press*] (SAG)
Kerr (NB)....	Kerr's New Brunswick Reports [*A publication*] (DLA)
Kerr Rec	Kerr on Receivers [*A publication*] (DLA)
Kerr Stu Black...	Kerr's Student's Blackstone [*A publication*] (DLA)
Kerr W & M Cas...	Kerr's Water and Mineral Cases [*A publication*] (DLA)
Kerse	Kerse's Manuscript Decisions, Scotch Court of Session [*A publication*] (DLA)
KERUK-NASI...	Kerukunan Nasional [*Campaign for National Harmony*] [*Indonesia*]
KERV	Kentucky Equine Respiratory Virus [*Veterinary science*] (DMAA)
KERV	Kerrville, TX [*AM radio station call letters*]
Kerwin	Kerwin Shops, Inc. [*Associated Press*] (SAG)
KERX	Paris, AR [*FM radio station call letters*]
KES...........	Karg-Elert Society (BUAC)
KES...........	Key Element Search (MCD)
KES...........	Keystone Consolidated Industries, Inc. [*NYSE symbol*] (SPSG)
KES...........	Keystone Consol Ind [*NYSE symbol*] (TTSB)
KES...........	Knigovedenie: Entsiklopedicheskil Slovar [*A publication*]
KES...........	Knowledge Engineering System [*Software Architecture and Engineering Inc.*] (NITA)
KES...........	Ksar Es Souk [*Seismograph station code, US Geological Survey*] [*Closed*] (SEIS)
KES...........	Kvakera Esperantista Societo [*Quaker Esperanto Society - QES*] (EAIO)
KESAB	Keep South Australia Beautiful (SAUO)
KESC.........	Karachi Electric Supply Corporation (SAUO)
KESCO........	Kowloon Electricity Supply Company (SAUO)
KESD	Brookings, SD [*FM radio station call letters*]
KESD-TV	Brookings, SD [*Television station call letters*]
KESE.........	Bentonville-Bella Vista, AR [*AM radio station call letters*] (RBYB)
KESF.........	Alexandria/Esler Field [*Louisiana*] [*ICAO location identifier*] (ICLI)
KESFF........	Kinetic Energy Self Forging Fragments (ACAE)
KESH.........	State Electricity Cooperative of Albania (BUAC)
KESI..........	Kentucky Electric Steel [*NASDAQ symbol*] (TTSB)
KESI..........	Kentucky Electric Steel Co. [*NASDAQ symbol*] (SAG)
KESI..........	Kurzweil Educational Systems, Inc.
KESM.........	El Dorado Springs, MO [*AM radio station call letters*]
KESM-FM	El Dorado Springs, MO [*FM radio station call letters*]
KESO-FM	South Padre Island, TX [*FM radio station call letters*] (BROA)

KESP-FM	Payson, AZ [FM radio station call letters] (BROA)
KESQ	Indio, CA [AM radio station call letters] (BROA)
KESQ	Palm Springs, CA [Television station call letters]
KESS	Fort Worth, TX [AM radio station call letters]
KESS	Kesselring Site [Knolls Atomic Power Laboratory] (GAAI)
KESS	Kinetic Energy Storage System
KEST	Kestrel Energy [NASDAQ symbol] (TTSB)
KEST	Kestrel Energy, Inc. [NASDAQ symbol] (SAG)
KEST	San Francisco, CA [AM radio station call letters]
Kestrel	Kestrel Energy, Inc. [Associated Press] (SAG)
KESY	Omaha, NE [FM radio station call letters]
KESZ	Phoenix, AZ [FM radio station call letters]
KET	Cat Kargo Hava Tasima, AS [Turkey] [FAA designator] (FAAC)
KET	Kengtung [Myanmar] [Airport symbol] (OAG)
KET	Keravat [New Britain] [Seismograph station code, US Geological Survey] [Closed] (SEIS)
KET	Ketamine [An anesthetic]
Ket	Kethuboth (BJA)
KET	Kiel Electron Telescope
KET	Krypton Exposure Technique (MCD)
KETA	Kenya External Trade Authority (BUAC)
KETA	Oklahoma City, OK [Television station call letters]
KETAL	Kalamazoo Area Library Consortium [Library network]
KET BD	Ketone Bodies [Endocrinology] (DAVI)
KETC	St. Louis, MO [Television station call letters]
KETG	Arkadelphia, AR [Television station call letters]
KETH	Houston, TX [Television station call letters]
Keth	Kethuboth (BJA)
KETK	Jacksonville, TX [Television station call letters]
keto	Ketosteroid [Endocrinology]
KETO-AM	Rupert, ID [AM radio station call letters] (BROA)
KE-TP	Kinetic Energy-Training Projectile (MCD)
KETR	Commerce, TX [FM radio station call letters]
KETRI	Kenya Trypanosomiasis Research Institute
KETS	Little Rock, AR [Television station call letters]
K'ETTE	Kitchenette [Classified advertising] (ADA)
KETV	Omaha, NE [Television station call letters]
KETX	Livingston, TX [AM radio station call letters]
KETX-FM	Livingston, TX [FM radio station call letters]
KEU	Eastern Kentucky University, Richmond, KY [OCLC symbol] (OCLC)
KEUG-FM	Cottage Grove, OR [FM radio station call letters] (BROA)
KEUL-FM	Girdwood, AK [FM radio station call letters] (BROA)
KEUN	Eunice, LA [AM radio station call letters]
KEV	Kevo [Finland] [Seismograph station code, US Geological Survey] (SEIS)
keV	Kiloelectron Unit (ADWA)
keV	Kilo Electron Volt (AAEL)
keV	Kiloelectron Volt (ABAC)
KEV	Kinetic Energy Vehicle (ACAE)
KEV	King's Empire Veterans [British military] (DMA)
KEV	Komisarstvo za Evreiskiie Vuprosi [Bulgaria] (BJA)
KEVA	Evanston, WY [AM radio station call letters]
KEVAS	Key Educational Vocational Assessment System (TES)
KEVEVAPI	Kenyan Veterinary Vaccines Production Institute (SAUO)
KEVII	King Edward VII [British]
KEVIII	King Edward VIII [British]
Kevlin	Kevlin Corp. [Associated Press] (SAG)
KEVN	Kimmins Environmental Service Corp. (SAUO)
KEVN	Rapid City, SD [Television station call letters]
KEVT	Cortaro, AZ [AM radio station call letters]
KEVU	Eugene, OR [Television station call letters]
KEVX	Kevex Corp. (SAUO)
KEW	Kew [England] [Seismograph station code, US Geological Survey] [Closed] (SEIS)
KEW	Kewatin
keW	Kiloelectron Watt
KEW	Kinetic Energy Weapons [Military] (RDA)
KEWB	Anderson, CA [FM radio station call letters]
KEWB	Kinetic Experiment on Water Boiler [Nuclear reactor]
Kew Bull	Kew Bulletin (SAUO)
KEWC	Kinetic Energy Weapon, Chemically Propelled (ACAE)
KEWE	Kinetic Energy Weapon, Electromagnetically Propelled (ACAE)
KEWE	Oroville, CA [FM radio station call letters]
KEWG	Kinetic Energy Weapon, Ground (ACAE)
KEWI	Benton, AR [AM radio station call letters]
KEWL	New Boston, TX [FM radio station call letters] (RBYB)
KEWN	New Bern/Simmons-Nott [North Carolina] [ICAO location identifier] (ICLI)
KewnSc	Kewaunee Scientific Corp. [Associated Press] (SAG)
KEWO	Kinetic Energy Weapon, Orbital (ACAE)
KEWR	Newark/International [New Jersey] [ICAO location identifier] (ICLI)
KEWS	Koger Equity Wrrt [AMEX symbol] (TTSB)
KEWS-AM	Portland, OR [AM radio station call letters] (BROA)
KEWS-FM	Arlington, TX [FM radio station call letters] (RBYB)
KEWU	Cheney, WA [FM radio station call letters]
KEX	Kanabea [Papua New Guinea] [Airport symbol] (OAG)
KEX	Kirby Corp. [AMEX symbol] (SPSG)
KEX	Portland, OR [AM radio station call letters]
KEXD	Kirby Exploration Co. , Inc. (SAUO)
KEXL	Norfolk, NE [FM radio station call letters]
KEXO	Grand Junction, CO [AM radio station call letters]
KEXS	Excelsior Springs, MO [AM radio station call letters]
KEXT	Bosque Farms, NM [FM radio station call letters] (RBYB)
KEY	Key [Commonly used] (OPSA)
KEY	Key Anacon Mines Ltd. [Toronto Stock Exchange symbol]

KEY	KeyCorp [NYSE symbol] (SPSG)
Key	Keyes' New York Court of Appeals Reports [A publication] (DLA)
KEYA	Belcourt, ND [FM radio station call letters]
Key & Elph Conv	Key and Elphinstone's Conveyancing [15th ed.] [1953-54] [A publication] (DLA)
KEYB	Altus, OK [FM radio station call letters]
KEYBBE	foreign language KEYBoard program-BElgium (SAUS)
KEYBBR	Foreign language KEYBoard program - Brazil (SAUS)
KEYBCF	foreign language KEYBoard program-Canadian-French (SAUS)
KEYBCZ	Foreign language KEYBoard program - Czechoslovakia (Czech) (SAUS)
KEYBD	Keyboard [Computer science]
KEYBDF	foreign language KEYBoard program-Denmark (SAUS)
KEYBDK	Foreign language KEYBoard program-Denmark (SAUS)
KEYBFR	foreign language KEYBoard program-FRance (SAUS)
KEYBGR	Foreign language KEYBoard program - Germany (SAUS)
KEYBHU	foreign language KEYBoard program-HUngary (SAUS)
KEYBIT	Foreign language KEYBoard program - Italy (SAUS)
KEYBLA	foreign language KEYBoard program-Latin America (SAUS)
KEYBNL	Foreign language KEYBoard program - Netherlands (SAUS)
KEYBNO	foreign language KEYBoard program - NOrway (SAUS)
KEYBPL	Foreign language KEYBoard program - Poland (SAUS)
KEYBPO	foreign language KEYBoard program-Portugal (SAUS)
KEYBSF	Foreign language KEYBoard program - Swiss-French (SAUS)
KEYBSG	foreign language KEYBoard program-Swiss-German (SAUS)
KEYBSL	Foreign language KEYBoard program - Czechoslovakia (Slovak) (SAUS)
KEYBSP	foreign language KEYBoard program-SPain (SAUS)
KEYBSU	Foreign language KEYBoard program - Finland (SAUS)
KEYBSV	foreign language KEYBoard program - Sweden (SAUS)
KEYBUK	Foreign language KEYBoard program - United Kingdom (SAUS)
KEYBUS	foreign language KEYBoard program-United States (SAUS)
KEYBYU	Foreign language KEYBoard program - Yugoslavia (SAUS)
KEYC	Key Centurion Bancshares (EFIS)
KEYC	Key Centurion Bancshares, Inc. (SAUO)
KEYC	Mankato, MN [Television station call letters]
KEYCA	Keystone Camera Products Corp. (SAUO)
Key Ch	Keyes on Future Interest in Chattels [A publication] (DLA)
KeyCon	Keystone Consolidated Industries [Associated Press] (SAG)
Keycorp	Keycorp [Associated Press] (SAG)
Keycp	Keycorp [Associated Press] (SAG)
KEYE	Perryton, TX [AM radio station call letters]
KEYE-FM	Perryton, TX [FM radio station call letters]
KeyEng	Key Energy Group [Associated Press] (SAG)
Keyes	Keyes' New York Court of Appeals Reports [A publication] (DLA)
KEYE-TV	Austin, TX [Television station call letters] (RBYB)
KEYF	Cheney, WA [FM radio station call letters]
KEYF	Dishman, WA [AM radio station call letters]
KeyFn	Keyston Financial, Inc. [Associated Press] (SAG)
KEYG	Grand Coulee, WA [AM radio station call letters]
KEYG-FM	Grand Coulee, WA [FM radio station call letters]
KEYH	Houston, TX [AM radio station call letters]
KEYI	San Marcos, TX [FM radio station call letters]
KeyInt	Keystone International [Associated Press] (SAG)
KEYJ	Abilene, TX [FM radio station call letters]
Keyl	Keylway's [or Keilway's] English King's Bench Reports [A publication] (DLA)
KEYL	Long Prairie, MN [AM radio station call letters]
Key Lands	Keyes on Future Interest in Lands [A publication] (DLA)
Keylway	Keylway's [or Keilway's] English King's Bench Reports [A publication] (DLA)
KEYMAT	Keying Material [Computer science] (NVT)
KEYN	Wichita, KS [FM radio station call letters]
keypal	Internet Penpal (ADWA)
KEYPER	Keywords Permuted (DIT)
KEYPrA	KeyCorp 10% cm Dep Pfd [NYSE symbol] (TTSB)
KeyPrd	Key Production Co., Inc. [Associated Press] (SAG)
KEYQ	Fresno, CA [AM radio station call letters]
KEYR	Marlin, TX [FM radio station call letters]
Key Rem	Keyes on Remainders [A publication] (DLA)
KEYS	Corpus Christi, TX [AM radio station call letters]
KEYS	FFTF access control keycard system (SAUS)
KEYS	Keys [Commonly used] (OPSA)
KEYS	Keystone Automotive Industries, Inc. [NASDAQ symbol] (SAG)
KeysAut	Keystone Automotive Industries, Inc. [Associated Press] (SAG)
KeysHer	Keystone Heritage Group, Inc. [Associated Press] (SAG)
Keys St Ex	Keyser's Stock Exchange [1850] [A publication] (DLA)
KeystFn	Keystone Financial [Associated Press] (SAG)
KEYSTN	Keystone
KEYT	Santa Barbara, CA [Television station call letters]
KeyTech	Key Technology, Inc. [Associated Press] (SAG)
KEYTECT	Keyword Detection (NITA)
Key Trn	Key Tronics Corp. [Associated Press] (SAG)
KEYV	Las Vegas, NV [FM radio station call letters]
KEYW	Key West/Key West International [Florida] [ICAO location identifier] (ICLI)
KEYW	Pasco, WA [FM radio station call letters]
KEYY	Provo, UT [AM radio station call letters]
KEYZ	Williston, ND [AM radio station call letters]
KEZA	Fayetteville, AR [FM radio station call letters]
KEZB	Hempstead, TX [FM radio station call letters]
KEZC	Yuma, AZ [AM radio station call letters]
KEZD	Windsor, CA [AM radio station call letters]
KEZE-FM	Spokane, WA [FM radio station call letters] (RBYB)
KEZF	Tigard, OR [AM radio station call letters]

KEZF-FM..... Albuquerque, NM [*FM radio station call letters*] (BROA)
KEZG........... Lincoln, NE [*FM radio station call letters*]
KEZH........... Hastings, NE [*FM radio station call letters*]
KEZI............ Eugene, OR [*Television station call letters*]
KEZJ........... Twin Falls, ID [*AM radio station call letters*]
KEZJ-FM...... Twin Falls, ID [*FM radio station call letters*]
KEZK........... St. Louis, MO [*FM radio station call letters*]
KEZL........... Fowler, CA [*FM radio station call letters*]
KEZM........... Sulphur, LA [*AM radio station call letters*]
KEZN........... Palm Desert, CA [*FM radio station call letters*]
KEZO........... Omaha, NE [*AM radio station call letters*]
KEZO-FM..... Omaha, NE [*FM radio station call letters*]
KEZP........... Bunkie, LA [*FM radio station call letters*]
KEZQ........... Little Rock, AR [*AM radio station call letters*] (RBYB)
KEZQ........... Sheridan, AR [*FM radio station call letters*]
KEZQ-FM ..... Island Park, ID [*FM radio station call letters*] (BROA)
KEZR........... San Jose, CA [*FM radio station call letters*]
KEZS........... Cape Girardeau, MO [*FM radio station call letters*]
KEZT........... Ames, IA [*FM radio station call letters*]
KEZU........... Booneville, AR [*FM radio station call letters*]
KEZW........... Aurora, CO [*AM radio station call letters*]
KEZX........... Seattle, WA [*AM radio station call letters*]
KEZY........... Anaheim, CA [*FM radio station call letters*]
KEZZ........... Aitkin, MN [*FM radio station call letters*]
KEZZ........... Estes Park, CO [*AM radio station call letters*] (BROA)
KF.............. Catskill Airways [*ICAO designator*] (AD)
KF.............. Family Key (SAUS)
KF.............. Fiji [*IYRU nationality code*] (IYR)
kf.............. Flocculation Speed in Antigen-Antibody Reactions [*Immunology*] (DAVI)
KF.............. Gold Coast Judgments and the Masai Cases, by King-Farlow [*1915-17*] [*Ghana*] [*A publication*] (DLA)
KF.............. Karl Fischer [*Reagent*] [*Analytical chemistry*]
KF.............. Kellogg Foundation (SAUO)
KF.............. Kenner-Fecal Medium [*Organic chemistry*] (DAVI)
KF.............. Kent Foundation (SAUO)
KF.............. Keramos Fraternity [*An association*] (NTPA)
KF.............. Kerr-Fourier [*Imaging*]
KF.............. Key Field
KF.............. Key File [*Computer science*] (ELAL)
KF.............. Kidney Foundation (SAUO)
KF.............. Kidney Function [*Nephrology*] (DAVI)
KF.............. KIDS Fund (EA)
KF.............. Kleine Flote [*Piccolo*] [*German*]
KF.............. Klenow Fragment [*Genetics*]
KF.............. Klippel-Feil [*Syndrome*] [*Neurology*] (DAVI)
KF.............. Knight of Ferdinand [*Spain*]
KF.............. Knudsen Flow [*Physics*]
KF.............. Koff [*Type of ship*] (DS)
KF.............. Koinonia Foundation (EA)
KF.............. Konservative Folkeparti [*Conservative People's Party (Commonly called the Conservative Party)*] [*Denmark*] [*Political party*] (PPE)
KF.............. Kontrafagott [*Double Bassoon*] [*Organ stop*] [*Music*]
KF.............. Korea Fund, Inc. [*NYSE symbol*] (SPSG)
KF.............. Kosciuszko Foundation (EA)
KF.............. Kossuth Foundation (EA)
K+F............. Kummerly + Frey AG (SAUS)
KF.............. Potassium Fluoride (SAUS)
KF.............. Rhine Air AG [*Sweden*] [*ICAO designator*] (ICDA)
KFA............. Keep Fit Association [*British*]
KFA............. Kelowna Flightcraft Air Charter Ltd. [*Canada*] [*ICAO designator*] (FAAC)
KFA............. Kenya Farmers Association (BUAC)
KFA............. Kernforschungsanlage [*Julich, Germany*]
KFA............. Kiffa [*Mauritania*] [*Airport symbol*] (OAG)
KFA............. Kinesthetic Figural Aftereffects [*Also, KFAE*] [*Psychometrics*]
KFA............. Krishnamurti Foundation of America (EA)
KFAA........... Rogers, AR [*Television station call letters*]
KFAB........... Kidney-Fixing Antibody [*Immunology*]
KFAB........... Omaha, NE [*AM radio station call letters*]
KFAC........... Santa Barbara, CA [*FM radio station call letters*]
KFAD........... Alexandria, LA [*FM radio station call letters*]
KFAE........... Kinesthetic Figural Aftereffects [*Also, KFA*] [*Psychometrics*]
KFAE........... Richland, WA [*FM radio station call letters*]
KFAED........ Kuwait Fund for Arab Economic Development
KFAI........... Minneapolis, MN [*FM radio station call letters*]
KFAL........... Fulton, MO [*AM radio station call letters*]
KFAM........... Keyed File Access Method [*Computer science*] (PDAA)
KFAM........... North Salt Lake City, UT [*AM radio station call letters*]
KFAN........... Johnson City, TX [*FM radio station call letters*]
KFAN........... Minneapolis, MN [*AM radio station call letters*]
KF&R........... Knight, Frank & Rutley (WDAA)
KFAO........... Knee-Foot-Ankel Orthosis [*Orthopedics*] (DAVI)
KFAR........... Fairbanks, AK [*AM radio station call letters*]
KFAS........... Casa Grande, AZ [*AM radio station call letters*]
KFAS........... Keyed File Access System
KFAS........... Kuwait Foundation for the Advancement of Sciences (SAUO)
KFAS........... Kuwait Foundation for the Advancement of Science (BUAC)
KFASSR........ Karelo-Finnish Autonomous Soviet Socialist Republic (SAUO)
K-FAST........ Kaufman Functional Academic Skills Test (TMMY)
KFAT........... Corvallis, OR [*FM radio station call letters*]
KFAT........... Fresno/Fresno Air Terminal [*California*] [*ICAO location identifier*] (ICLI)
KFAT-FM...... Anchorage, AK [*FM radio station call letters*] (BROA)
KFAV........... Warrenton, MO [*FM radio station call letters*]

KFAX........... San Francisco, CA [*AM radio station call letters*]
KFAY........... Bentonville, AR [*FM radio station call letters*] (RBYB)
KFAY........... Farmington, AR [*AM radio station call letters*]
KFB............. Air Botnia OY, AB, Finland [*FAA designator*] (FAAC)
KFB............. Bethany College, Lindsborg, KS [*OCLC symbol*] (OCLC)
KFB............. Kuwait French Bank
KFBB........... Great Falls, MT [*Television station call letters*]
KFBC........... Cheyenne, WY [*AM radio station call letters*]
KFBD........... Waynesville, MO [*FM radio station call letters*]
KFBG........... Fort Bragg/Simons Auxiliary Air Base [*North Carolina*] [*ICAO location identifier*] (ICLI)
KfBH........... Kaufman & Broad Home Corp. [*Associated Press*] (SAG)
KFBI........... Klamath First Bancorp [*NASDAQ symbol*] (TTSB)
KFBI........... Klamath First Bancorp, Inc. [*NASDAQ symbol*] (SAG)
KFBI........... Pahrump, NV [*FM radio station call letters*]
KFBK........... Sacramento, CA [*AM radio station call letters*]
KFBN........... Lincoln, NE [*FM radio station call letters*]
KFBN-FM..... Fargo, ND [*FM radio station call letters*] (BROA)
KFBQ........... Cheyenne, WY [*FM radio station call letters*]
KFBT........... Las Vegas, NV [*Television station call letters*]
KFC............. Kajagoogoo Fan Club [*Defunct*] (EA)
KFC............. Katholieke Film-Centrale [*Netherlands*]
KFC............. Kentfield [*California*] [*Seismograph station code, US Geological Survey*] (SEIS)
KFC............. Kentucky Fried Chicken Corp. [*Later, KFC Corp.*] (ADA)
KFC............. Korea Friendship Committee [*British*] (EAIO)
KFC............. Kropp Forge Company (SAUO)
KFCA........... Conway, AR [*AM radio station call letters*]
KFCB........... Concord, CA [*Television station call letters*]
KFCC........... Bay City, TX [*AM radio station call letters*] (RBYB)
KFCF........... Fresno, CA [*FM radio station call letters*]
KFCI........... Knife and Fork Club International (EA)
KFCM........... Cherokee Village, AR [*FM radio station call letters*]
KFCR........... Custer, SD [*AM radio station call letters*]
KFCT........... Fort Collins, CO [*FM radio station call letters*]
KFD............. Key Financial Data (ADA)
KFD............. Kinetic Family Drawing [*Psychology*]
KFD............. Kyasanur Forest Disease
KFDA........... Amarillo, TX [*Television station call letters*]
KFDC .... Washington/National Flight Data Center [*District of Columbia*] [*ICAO location identifier*] (ICLI)
KFDF........... Van Buren, AR [*AM radio station call letters*]
KFDI........... Wichita, KS [*AM radio station call letters*]
KFDI-FM...... Wichita, KS [*FM radio station call letters*]
KFDM........... Beaumont, TX [*Television station call letters*]
KfdO........... Komitee fuer den Osten (BJA)
KFDT........... Kinetic Family Drawing Test [*Psychology*] (DAVI)
KFDX........... Wichita Falls, TX [*Television station call letters*]
KFE............. Kathode Flicker Effect
KFEA........... Korean Federation of Education Associations
KFEB-FM..... Campbell, MO [*FM radio station call letters*] (BROA)
KFEL........... Pueblo, CO [*AM radio station call letters*]
KFEQ........... St. Joseph, MO [*AM radio station call letters*]
KFER........... Santa Cruz, CA [*FM radio station call letters*]
KFEZ........... Kansas City, MO [*AM radio station call letters*]
KFF............. Kvinnenes Frie Folkevalgte [*Women's Freely Elected Representatives*] [*Norway*] [*Political party*] (PPE)
KFFA........... Helena, AR [*AM radio station call letters*]
KFFA-FM...... Helena, AR [*FM radio station call letters*] (RBYB)
KFFB........... Fairfield Bay, AR [*FM radio station call letters*]
KFFG........... Los Altos, CA [*FM radio station call letters*] (RBYB)
KFFLBA........ Konglomerati Florida Foundation for Literature and the Book Arts (EA)
KFFM........... Yakima, WA [*FM radio station call letters*]
KFFN-AM..... Tucson, AZ [*AM radio station call letters*] (RBYB)
KFFO........... Dayton/Wright-Patterson Air Force Base [*Ohio*] [*ICAO location identifier*] (ICLI)
KFFR........... Eagle River, AK [*AM radio station call letters*]
KFFX........... Emporia, KS [*FM radio station call letters*]
KFGA-FM ..... Clayton, LA [*FM radio station call letters*] (BROA)
KFGE........... Lincoln, NE [*FM radio station call letters*]
KFGG........... Corpus Christi, TX [*FM radio station call letters*]
KFGI-FM ..... Brainerd, MN [*FM radio station call letters*] (RBYB)
KFGO .... Fargo, ND [*AM radio station call letters*]
KFGO-FM..... Fargo, ND [*FM radio station call letters*]
KFGQ........... Boone, IA [*AM radio station call letters*]
KFGQ-FM..... Boone, IA [*FM radio station call letters*]
KFGX-FM..... Detroit Lakes, MN [*FM radio station call letters*] (RBYB)
KFGY-FM..... Healdsburg, CA [*FM radio station call letters*] (RBYB)
KFGH........... Fort Hays State University, Hays, KS [*OCLC symbol*] (OCLC)
KFH............. Kaiser Foundation Hospital (SAUO)
KFH............. Ku-Band Feed Horn
KFH............. Kuwait Finance House (BUAC)
KFH............. Wichita, KS [*AM radio station call letters*]
KFI............. Kinetic Fluid Induction
KFI............. Krause's Furniture [*AMEX symbol*] (SG)
KFI............. Los Angeles, CA [*AM radio station call letters*]
KFIA........... Carmichael, CA [*AM radio station call letters*]
KFIA........... King Fahd International Airport [*Saudi Arabia*]
KFIE........... Merced, CA [*FM radio station call letters*]
KFIG........... Fresno, CA [*AM radio station call letters*]
KFIL........... Preston, MN [*AM radio station call letters*]
KFIL-FM...... Preston, MN [*FM radio station call letters*]
KFIN........... Jonesboro, AR [*FM radio station call letters*]
KFIR........... Sweet Home, OR [*AM radio station call letters*]

KFIS............. Soda Springs, ID [FM radio station call letters]
KFIT............. Lockhart, TX [AM radio station call letters]
KFIT EXP STN... San Antonio, TX [Radio expansion station]
KFIV............. Modesto, CA [AM radio station call letters]
KFIX-FM ..... Plainville, KS [FM radio station call letters] (RBYB)
KFIZ............. Fond Du Lac, WI [AM radio station call letters]
KFIZ-FM ..... Fond du Lac, WI [FM radio station call letters] (RBYB)
KFJB............. Marshalltown, IA [AM radio station call letters]
KFJC............. Los Altos, CA [FM radio station call letters]
KFJM............. Grand Forks, ND [AM radio station call letters]
KFJM-FM..... Grand Forks, ND [FM radio station call letters]
KFJO-FM...... Walnut Creek, CA [FM radio station call letters] (BROA)
KFJY............. Grand Forks, ND [AM radio station call letters] (RBYB)
KFJZ............. Fort Worth, TX [AM radio station call letters]
KFKA............. Greeley, CO [AM radio station call letters]
KFKF............. Kansas City, KS [FM radio station call letters]
KFKQ............. New Holstein, WI [AM radio station call letters]
KFKX-FM..... Hastings, NE [FM radio station call letters] (RBYB)
KFL............. Kenya Federation of Labour
KFL............. Kenya Flamingo Airways Ltd. [ICAO designator] (FAAC)
KFL............. Key Facilities List [AEC]
KFL............. Lifestream Technologies [AMEX symbol]
KFL............. University of Kansas, Law Library, Lawrence, KS [OCLC symbol] (OCLC)
KFLA............. Scott City, KS [AM radio station call letters]
KFIAH .... United States Army Hospital, Fort Leavenworth, KS [Library symbol] [Library of Congress] (LCLS)
KFLD............. Pasco, WA [AM radio station call letters] (RBYB)
KFLG............. Bullhead City, AZ [AM radio station call letters]
KFLG-FM ..... Bullhead City, AZ [FM radio station call letters]
KFIGS .... United States Army, Command and General Staff College Library, Fort Leavenworth, KS [Library symbol] [Library of Congress] (LCLS)
KFLL............. Floydada, TX [FM radio station call letters]
KFLL............. Fort Lauderdale/Fort Lauderdale-Hollywood International [Florida] [ICAO location identifier] (ICLI)
KFLN............. Baker, MT [AM radio station call letters]
KFLO............. Florence/Municipal [South Carolina] [ICAO location identifier] (ICLI)
KFLO............. Shreveport, LA [AM radio station call letters]
KFLOPS......... Kilo Floating Point Operations per Second [Computer science] (CIST)
KFLP-AM ..... Floydada, TX [AM radio station call letters] (RBYB)
KFLQ............. Albuquerque, NM [FM radio station call letters]
KFLR............. Phoenix, AZ [FM radio station call letters]
KFLS............. Klamath Falls, OR [AM radio station call letters]
KFLS............. Tulelake, CA [FM radio station call letters]
KFLT............. Tucson, AZ [AM radio station call letters]
KFLV-FM..... Wilber, NE [FM radio station call letters] (BROA)
KFLW............. St. Robert, MO [FM radio station call letters] (RBYB)
KFLX............. Kachina Village, AZ [AM radio station call letters]
KFLX-FM...... Kachina Village, AZ [FM radio station call letters] (BROA)
KFLY............. Corvallis, OR [FM radio station call letters]
KFLZ............. Bishop, TX [FM radio station call letters]
KFM............. K File Manager (SAUS)
KFM............. Klystron Frequency Multiplier
KFM............. Knight of St. Ferdinand and Merit [Italy]
KFMA-FM .... Green Valley, AZ [FM radio station call letters] (RBYB)
KFMB............. San Diego, CA [AM radio station call letters]
KFMB-DT ..... Sand Diego, CA [Television station call letters] (BROA)
KFMB-FM .... San Diego, CA [FM radio station call letters]
KFMB-TV .... San Diego, CA [Television station call letters]
KFMC............. Fairmont, MN [FM radio station call letters]
KFMD............. Delta, UT [FM radio station call letters]
KFME............. Fargo, ND [Television station call letters]
KFMF............. Chico, CA [FM radio station call letters]
KFMG............. Pella, IA [FM radio station call letters]
KFMH............. Falmouth/Otis Air Force Base [Massachusetts] [ICAO location identifier] (ICLI)
KFMI............. Eureka, CA [FM radio station call letters]
KFMJ-FM..... Ketchikan, AK [FM radio station call letters] (RBYB)
KFMK............. Winton, CA [FM radio station call letters]
KFMK-FM..... Round Rock, TX [FM radio station call letters] (BROA)
KFML............. Kommunistiska Foerbundet Marxist-Leninisterna [Communist League of Marxist-Leninists] [Sweden] [Political party] (PPE)
KFML............. Little Falls, MN [FM radio station call letters]
KFMM............. Thatcher, AZ [FM radio station call letters]
KFMN............. Farmington [New Mexico] [ICAO location identifier] (ICLI)
KFMN............. Lihue, HI [FM radio station call letters]
KFMO............. Park Hills, MO [AM radio station call letters]
KFMQ-FM .... Gallup, NM [FM radio station call letters] (RBYB)
KFMR-FM .... Winslow, AZ [FM radio station call letters] (RBYB)
KFMS-FM .... Las Vegas, NV [FM radio station call letters]
KFMT............. Fremont, NE [FM radio station call letters]
KFMU............. Oak Creek, CO [FM radio station call letters]
KFMV............. Franklin, LA [FM radio station call letters]
KFMW............. Waterloo, IA [FM radio station call letters]
KFMX............. Lubbock, TX [FM radio station call letters]
KFMY............. Fort Myers/Page Field [Florida] [ICAO location identifier] (ICLI)
KFMY-FM .... South Bend, WA [FM radio station call letters] (RBYB)
KFMZ............. Columbia, MO [FM radio station call letters]
KFNA............. El Paso, TX [AM radio station call letters]
KFNB............. Casper, WY [Television station call letters]
KFNE............. Riverton, WY [Television station call letters]
KFNF............. Oberlin, KS [AM radio station call letters]
KFNN............. Mesa, AZ [AM radio station call letters]
KFNO............. Fresno, CA [FM radio station call letters]

KFNP .... Kaieteur Falls National Park (SAUO)
KFNR .... Rawlins, WY [Television station call letters]
KFNS .... Wood River, IL [AM radio station call letters]
KFNV .... Ferriday, LA [AM radio station call letters]
KFNV-FM ..... Ferriday, LA [FM radio station call letters]
KFNW .... West Fargo, ND [AM radio station call letters]
KFNW-FM ..... Fargo, ND [FM radio station call letters]
KFNX .... Cave Creek, AZ [AM radio station call letters] (BROA)
KFNZ-AM ..... Salt Lake, UT [AM radio station call letters] (RBYB)
KFO .... Killing Federal Officer
KFO .... King Solomon Resources [Vancouver Stock Exchange symbol]
KFO .... Klamath Falls [Oregon] [Seismograph station code, US Geological Survey] (SEIS)
KFOC .... Kaiser-Frazer Owners Clubs of America [Later, KFOCI] (EA)
KFOCI .... Kaiser-Frazer Owners Club International (EA)
KFOE .... Topeka/Forbes Air Force Base [Kansas] [ICAO location identifier] (ICLI)
KFOG .... San Francisco, CA [FM radio station call letters]
KFOK .... West Hampton Beach/Suffolk County [New York] [ICAO location identifier] (ICLI)
KFON .... Austin, TX [AM radio station call letters]
KFOR .... Lincoln, NE [AM radio station call letters]
KFOR-TV ..... Oklahoma City, OK [Television station call letters]
KFOS .... Korean Fragmentary Order System (SAUO)
KFOX .... Redondo Beach, CA [FM radio station call letters]
KFOX-TV ..... El Paso, TX [Television station call letters]
KFP .... False Pass [Alaska] [Airport symbol] (OAG)
KFP .... Kenya Freedom Party (SAUO)
KFP .... Konstitutionella Folkpartiet [Constitutional People's Party] [Finland] [Political party] (PPE)
KFP .... Korean Fighter Program
KFP .... Pittsburg State University, Pittsburg, KS [OCLC symbol] (OCLC)
KFPC .... Kansas Foundation for Private Colleges (SAUO)
KFPR .... Redding, CA [FM radio station call letters]
KFPW .... Fort Smith, AR [AM radio station call letters]
KFPX .... Newton, IA [Television station call letters] (BROA)
KFQC .... Davenport, IA [AM radio station call letters]
KFQD .... Anchorage, AK [AM radio station call letters]
KFQX-FM ..... Merkel, TX [FM radio station call letters'] (BROA)
KFQX-TV ..... Grand Junction, CO [TV station call letters] (RBYB)
KFR .... Kayser-Fleischer Ring [Medicine] (DMAA)
KFR .... Keefer Resources, Inc. [Vancouver Stock Exchange symbol]
KFRA .... Franklin, LA [AM radio station call letters]
KFRB-FM ..... Bakersfield, CA [FM radio station call letters] (RBYB)
KFRC .... San Francisco, CA [AM radio station call letters]
KFRC-FM ..... San Francisco, CA [FM radio station call letters]
KFRD .... Bellville, TX [AM radio station call letters]
KFRE .... Fresno, CA [AM radio station call letters]
KFRG .... San Bernardino, CA [FM radio station call letters]
KFRL .... Kansas Flight Research Laboratory
KFRM .... Salina, KS [AM radio station call letters]
KFRN .... Long Beach, CA [AM radio station call letters]
KFRO .... Gilmer, TX [FM radio station call letters]
KFRO .... Longview, TX [AM radio station call letters]
KFRQ .... Harlingen, TX [FM radio station call letters]
KFRQ-FM ..... Harlingen, TX [FM radio station call letters]
KFRR .... Woodlake, CA [FM radio station call letters]
KFRST .... Killing Frost [NWS] (FAAC)
KFRU .... Columbia, MO [AM radio station call letters]
KFRX .... Lincoln, NE [FM radio station call letters]
KFRY-FM ..... Manteca, CA [FM radio station call letters] (BROA)
KFRZ-FM ..... Green River, WY [FM radio station call letters] (BROA)
KFS .... Kalitta Flying Service, Inc. [FAA designator] (FAAC)
KFS .... Kalman Filtering System
KFS .... Keyed File System [Computer science]
KFS .... Klippel-Feil Syndrome [Medicine]
KFS .... Kohles, F. S., Montebello CA [STAC]
KFS .... University of Kansas, Spencer Library, Lawrence, KS [OCLC symbol] (OCLC)
KFSA .... Fort Smith, AR [AM radio station call letters]
KFSA .... Keep Fit South Australia
KFSB .... Joplin, MO [AM radio station call letters]
KFSB .... Korean Federation of Small Businesses (BUAC)
KFSD .... Keratosis Follicularis Spinulosa Decalvans [Medicine] (DMAA)
KFSD .... San Diego, CA [FM radio station call letters]
KFSG .... Los Angeles, CA [FM radio station call letters]
KFSH-AM ..... Seward, AK [AM radio station call letters] (BROA)
KFSH & RC... King Faisal Specialist Hospital and Research Center [Saudi Arabia]
KFSI .... Rochester, MN [FM radio station call letters]
KFSK .... Petersburg, AK [FM radio station call letters]
KFSM .... Fort Smith, AR [Television station call letters]
KFSM .... Fort Smith/Municipal [Arkansas] [ICAO location identifier] (ICLI)
KFSN .... Fresno, CA [Television station call letters]
KFSO .... Visalia, CA [FM radio station call letters]
KFSR .... Fresno, CA [FM radio station call letters]
KFSR .... Karakul Fur Sheep Registry [Later, AKFSR] (EA)
KFST .... Fort Stockton, TX [AM radio station call letters]
KFST-FM ..... Fort Stockton, TX [FM radio station call letters]
KFT .... Kalman Filter Theory
KFT .... Kidney Function Test [Medicine] (MELL)
KFTCIC........ Kuwait Foreign Trade (or Trading) Contracting and Investment Company (SAUO)
KFTCIC........ Kuwait Foreign Trading, Contracting & Investment Co.
KFTE .... Breaux Bridge, LA [FM radio station call letters]
KFTG........... Pasadena, TX [FM radio station call letters] (RBYB)

KFTH........... Marion, AR [*FM radio station call letters*]
KFTL........... Keptel, Inc. (SAUO)
KFTL........... Stockton, CA [*Television station call letters*]
KFTM........... Fort Morgan, CO [*AM radio station call letters*]
KFTS........... Klamath Falls, OR [*Television station call letters*]
KFTU........... Korean Federation of Trade Unions [*North Korea*]
KFTV........... Hanford, CA [*Television station call letters*]
KFTW........... Fort Worth/Meacham [*Texas*] [*ICAO location identifier*] (ICLI)
KFTW........... Fredericktown, MO [*AM radio station call letters*]
KFTX........... Kingsville, TX [*FM radio station call letters*] (RBYB)
KFTY........... Santa Rosa, CA [*Television station call letters*]
KFTZ........... Idaho Falls, ID [*FM radio station call letters*]
KFU........... Friends University, Wichita, KS [*OCLC symbol*] (OCLC)
KFU........... King Fahd University (SAUO)
KFU........... King Faisal University [*Saudi Arabia*] (BUAC)
KFUK........... Kristelig Forening for Unge Kvinder [*Young Women's Christian Associations - YWCA*] [*Denmark*]
KFUM........... Kristelig Forening for Unge Maend [*Young Men's Christian Associations - YMCA*] [*Denmark*]
KFUN........... Las Vegas, NM [*AM radio station call letters*]
KFUO........... Clayton, MO [*AM radio station call letters*]
KFUO-FM........... Clayton, MO [*FM radio station call letters*]
KFV........... Quest for Value Dual Fd [*NYSE symbol*] (TTSB)
KFV........... Quest for Value Fund [*NYSE symbol*] (SAG)
KFVE........... Honolulu, HI [*Television station call letters*]
KFVPr........... Quest For Value Income Shrs [*NYSE symbol*] (TTSB)
KFVR........... Crescent City, CA [*AM radio station call letters*]
KFVS........... Cape Girardeau, MO [*Television station call letters*]
KfW........... Kreditanstalt fur Wiederaufbau [*Finance*] [*Germany*]
KFW........... Wichita Public Library, Wichita, KS [*OCLC symbol*] (OCLC)
KFWB........... Los Angeles, CA [*AM radio station call letters*]
KFWD........... Fort Worth, TX [*Television station call letters*]
KFWH........... Fort Worth/Carswell Air Force Base [*Texas*] [*ICAO location identifier*] (ICLI)
KFWJ........... Lake Havasu City, AZ [*AM radio station call letters*]
KFWU........... Fort Bragg, CA [*Television station call letters*]
KFX........... KFX Inc. [*AMEX symbol*] (TTSB)
KFX........... Korean Foreign Exchange (IMH)
KFXA........... Cedar Rapids, IA [*Television station call letters*] (RBYB)
KFXB........... Dubuque, IA [*Television station call letters*] (RBYB)
KFXD........... Nampa, ID [*AM radio station call letters*]
KFXD-FM........... Nampa, ID [*FM radio station call letters*]
KFXE........... Cuba, MO [*AM radio station call letters*]
KFXE........... Fort Lauderdale/Executive [*Florida*] [*ICAO location identifier*] (ICLI)
KFXE-FM........... Cuba, MO [*FM radio station call letters*] (BROA)
KFXF........... Fairbanks, AK [*Television station call letters*] (RBYB)
KFXI........... KFx, Inc. [*NASDAQ symbol*] (SAG)
KFXI........... Marlow, OK [*FM radio station call letters*]
KFX Inc........... KFx, Inc. [*Associated Press*] (SAG)
KFXJ........... Abilene, TX [*FM radio station call letters*]
KFXJ-FM........... Nampa, ID [*FM radio station call letters*] (BROA)
KFXK........... Longview, TX [*Television station call letters*]
KFXP........... Pocatello, ID [*Television station call letters*] (BROA)
KFXR........... Chinle, AZ [*FM radio station call letters*] (RBYB)
KFXS........... Rapid City, SD [*FM radio station call letters*] (RBYB)
KFXT........... Sulphur, OK [*FM radio station call letters*]
KFXX........... Hugoton, KS [*FM radio station call letters*]
KFXX........... Oregon City, OR [*AM radio station call letters*]
KFXX........... Vancouver, WA [*AM radio station call letters*] (BROA)
KFXY........... Morgan City, LA [*FM radio station call letters*]
KFXZ........... Maurice, LA [*FM radio station call letters*]
KFY........... KISS [*Knights in the Service of Satan*] - Flaming Youth [*Defunct*] (EA)
KFY........... Korn/Ferry Intl. [*NYSE symbol*] (SG)
KFYI........... Phoenix, AZ [*AM radio station call letters*]
KFYN........... Bonham, TX [*AM radio station call letters*]
KFYO........... Lubbock, TX [*AM radio station call letters*]
KFYR........... Bismarck, ND [*AM radio station call letters*]
KFYR-TV........... Bismarck, ND [*Television station call letters*]
KFYV........... Fayetteville/Drake Field [*Arkansas*] [*ICAO location identifier*] (ICLI)
KFYZ........... Bonham, TX [*FM radio station call letters*]
KG........... Catalina Airlines [*ICAO designator*] (AD)
KG........... Center of Gravity above Keel (MCD)
KG........... Kammergericht [*District Court, Berlin*] [*German*] (DLA)
KG........... Kampfgeschwader [*Bombardment wing*] [*German military - World War II*]
KG........... Karmann-Ghia [*Volkswagen model designation*]
KG........... Keg
KG........... Keratoglobus [*Medicine*] (MELL)
KG........... Ketoglutarate (DMAA)
KG........... Ketoglutaric [*Biochemistry*]
KG........... Key Generator (MCD)
kG........... Kilogauss
KG........... Kilogram (GAVI)
kg........... Kilogram [*Also, k*] [*Symbol*] [*SI unit for mass*]
KG........... Kindergarten
KG........... Kinder, Gentler [*America*] [*In a George Bush speech during the 1989 Republican Convention*]
KG........... King
KG........... King Pharmaceuticals [*NYSE symbol*]
KG........... Kininogen [*Biochemistry*]
KG........... Knifemakers Guild (EA)
KG........... Knight of [*the Order of*] the Garter [*British*]
KG........... Known Gambler [*Police slang*]
KG........... Kommanditgesellschaft [*Limited Partnership*] [*German*]
KG........... Kultusgemeinde (BJA)
KG........... Kumagai Gumi Co. (EFIS)
KG........... Kyrgyzstan [*Internet country code*]
KG........... Orion Airways Ltd. (SAUO)
KG-1........... Koeffler Golde-1 [*Cell line*] [*Cytology*] (DAVI)
KG5........... HMS King George V [*British military*] (DMA)
KGA........... Kananga [*Zaire*] [*Airport symbol*] (OAG)
KGA........... Ketoglutaric Acid (MELL)
KGA........... King's German Artillery [*British military*] (DMA)
KGA........... Kitchen Guild of America
KGA........... Kyrghyzstan Airlines [*ICAO designator*] (FAAC)
KGA........... Spokane, WA [*AM radio station call letters*]
KGAB-AM........... Orchard Valley, WY [*AM radio station call letters*] (BROA)
KGAC........... Kentucky Guild of Artists and Craftsmen (SRA)
KGAC........... St. Peter, MN [*FM radio station call letters*]
KGAF........... Gainesville, TX [*AM radio station call letters*]
KGAG........... Gage [*Oklahoma*] [*ICAO location identifier*] (ICLI)
KgAG........... Kurzgefasste Assyrische Grammatik [*A publication*] (BJA)
KGAK........... Gallup, NM [*AM radio station call letters*]
KGAL........... Lebanon, OR [*AM radio station call letters*] (RBYB)
KGAL/MIN........... Kilogallons per Minute (MCD)
kgal/min........... Kilogallons per Minute (NAKS)
KGAM-AM........... Palm Springs, CA [*AM radio station call letters*] (BROA)
KGAN........... Cedar Rapids, IA [*Television station call letters*]
KGAP........... Clarksville, TX [*FM radio station call letters*]
KGAR-FM........... Garden City, MO [*FM radio station call letters*] (BROA)
KGAS........... Carthage, TX [*AM radio station call letters*]
KGAS-FM........... Carthage, TX [*FM radio station call letters*]
KGB........... Committee for State Security (SAUS)
KGB........... Kewaunee, Green Bay & Western R. R. [*AAR code*]
KGB........... Kindly Gunn Bunch [*Refers to the Metropolitan Transit Authority of New York City; Gunn is the MTA chairman*]
KGB........... Known Good Board (AAEL)
KGB........... Komitet Gosudarstvennoi Bezopasnosti [*Committee of State Security*] [*Russian Secret Police*] [*Also satirically interpreted as Kontora Grubykh Banditov, or "Office of Crude Bandits"*]
KGB........... Konge [*Papua New Guinea*] [*Airport symbol*] (OAG)
KGB........... San Diego, CA [*FM radio station call letters*]
KGBA........... Holtville, CA [*FM radio station call letters*]
KGbB........... Barton County Community College, Great Bend, KS [*Library symbol*] [*Library of Congress*] (LCLS)
KGBC........... Galveston, TX [*AM radio station call letters*]
KGBI........... Omaha, NE [*FM radio station call letters*]
KGbLS........... Central Kansas Library System, Great Bend, KS [*Library symbol*] [*Library of Congress*] (LCLS)
KGbMC........... Central Kansas Medical Center, Great Bend, KS [*Library symbol*] [*Library of Congress*] (LCLS)
KGBR........... Gold Beach, OR [*FM radio station call letters*]
KGBS........... Krypton Gas Bottling Station [*Nuclear energy*] (NRCH)
KGBT........... Harlingen, TX [*AM radio station call letters*]
KGBT-TV........... Harlingen, TX [*Television station call letters*]
KGBW........... Kewaunee, Green Bay and Western (SAUO)
KGBX........... Nixa, MO [*FM radio station call letters*]
KGBY........... Sacramento, CA [*FM radio station call letters*]
KGC........... Keflin, Gentamicin, and Carbenicellin [*Antibiotics*] (DAVI)
kgc........... Kilogram-Calorie (IDOE)
KGC........... Kingscote [*Australia*] [*Airport symbol*] (OAG)
KGC........... Kinross Gold [*NYSE symbol*] (TTSB)
KGC........... Kinross Gold Corp. [*NYSE symbol*] (SAG)
KGC........... Kiwi Growers of California (EA)
KGC........... Knight Grand Commander
KGC........... Knight of the Golden Circle
KGC........... Knight of the Grand Cross
KGC........... Knights of the Golden Circle (SAUO)
KGC........... W. M. Krogman Center for Research in Child Growth and Development [*University of Pennsylvania*] [*Research center*] (RCD)
kgcal........... Kilogram-Calorie
KGCB........... Knight Grand Cross of the [*Order of the*] Bath [*British*]
KGCB........... Prescott, AZ [*FM radio station call letters*]
KGCF........... Kahlil Gibran Centennial Foundation (EA)
KGCHS........... Knight Grand Cross of the Equestrian Order of the Holy Sepulchre of Jerusalem
KGCK........... Garden City [*Kansas*] [*ICAO location identifier*] (ICLI)
KGCR........... Goodland, KS [*FM radio station call letters*]
KGCSG........... Knight Grand Cross of the Order of Saint Gregory the Great (SAUO)
KGCSG........... Knight Grand Cross of the Order of St. Gregory the Great [*British*] (ADA)
kg/cum........... Kilograms per Cubic Meter
KGD........... Karaganda [*Former USSR*] [*Geomagnetic observatory code*]
KGD........... Known Good Die (AAEL)
KGDC........... Walla Walla, WA [*AM radio station call letters*] (RBYB)
KGDD........... Paris, TX [*AM radio station call letters*]
KGDE........... Lincoln, NE [*FM radio station call letters*] (RBYB)
KGDN........... Pasco, WA [*FM radio station call letters*]
KGDP........... Orcutt, CA [*AM radio station call letters*]
KGDP-FM........... Orcutt, CA [*FM radio station call letters*] (BROA)
KGE........... Kansas Gas and Electric Co. (SAUO)
KGE........... King-Errington Resources Ltd. [*Vancouver Stock Exchange symbol*]
KGE........... Klein-Gordon Equation [*Physics*]
KGE........... Knights of the Golden Eagle (EA)
KGEE........... Monahans, TX [*FM radio station call letters*]
KGEG........... Spokane/International [*Washington*] [*ICAO location identifier*] (ICLI)
KGEM........... Boise, ID [*AM radio station call letters*]
KGEN........... Hanford, CA [*FM radio station call letters*] (RBYB)

KGEN .... Tulare, CA [*AM radio station call letters*]
KGEO .... Bakersfield, CA [*AM radio station call letters*]
KGER .... Long Beach, CA [*AM radio station call letters*]
KGER-AM...... Yakima, WA [*AM radio station call letters*] (BROA)
KGER-FM ..... Quincy, WA [*FM radio station call letters*] (BROA)
KGET .... Bakersfield, CA [*Television station call letters*]
KGEZ........... Kalispell, MT [*AM radio station call letters*]
KGF .... Keilinschriften und Geschichtsforschung [*A publication*] (BJA)
KGF .... Keratinocyte Growth Factor [*Biochemistry*]
kg-f .... Kilogram-Foot
kgf .... Kilogram-Force [*Unit of force*]
KGF .... Knight of the Golden Fleece [*Spain and Austria*]
KGF .... Kriegsgefangener [*Prisoner of War*] [*German*]
KGFA .... Great Falls/Malmstrom Air Force Base [*Montana*] [*ICAO location identifier*] (ICLI)
KGFC-FM ..... Great Falls, MT [*FM radio station call letters*] (RBYB)
KGF/CM² ..... Kilogram Force per Square Centimeter
KGFE........... Grand Forks, ND [*Television station call letters*]
KGFF .... Shawnee, OK [*AM radio station call letters*]
KGFJ........... Los Angeles, CA [*AM radio station call letters*]
KGFJ-FM...... Markham, TX [*FM radio station call letters*] (BROA)
KGFK .... Grand Forks/International [*North Dakota*] [*ICAO location identifier*] (ICLI)
KGFL........... Clinton, AR [*AM radio station call letters*]
KGFM........... Bakersfield, CA [*FM radio station call letters*]
KGF/M .... Kilogram Force per Meter
KGF/M² .... Kilogram Force per Square Meter
KGFR .... Keratinocyte Growth Factor Receptor [*Biochemistry*]
KGFS .... King George's Fund for Sailors [*British*]
KGFST .... Korean General Federation of Science and Technology (SAUO)
KGFT........... Pueblo, CO [*FM radio station call letters*]
KGFW .... Kearney, NE [*AM radio station call letters*]
KGFX .... Pierre, SD [*AM radio station call letters*]
KGFX-FM ..... Pierre, SD [*FM radio station call letters*]
KGFY .... Stillwater, OK [*FM radio station call letters*]
KGG .... Consolidated Goldwest [*Vancouver Stock Exchange symbol*]
KGG .... Kedougou [*Senegal*] [*Airport symbol*] (OAG)
KGG .... Knight of the Guelphic Order of Hanover (SAUO)
KgGBAS ...... Kurzgefasste Grammatik der Biblisch Aramaeischen Sprache [*A publication*] (BJA)
KGGF .... Coffeyville, KS [*AM radio station call letters*]
KGGF-FM ..... Fredonia, KS [*FM radio station call letters*] (BROA)
KGGG........... Longview/Gregg County [*Texas*] [*ICAO location identifier*] (ICLI)
KGGG........... Sterling, KS [*FM radio station call letters*] (RBYB)
KGGI........... Riverside, CA [*FM radio station call letters*]
KGGK-FM..... Winner, SD [*FM radio station call letters*] (RBYB)
KGGL........... Missoula, MT [*FM radio station call letters*] (RBYB)
KGGM........... Delhi, LA [*FM radio station call letters*] (RBYB)
KGGN........... Gladstone, MO [*AM radio station call letters*]
KGGO........... Des Moines, IA [*FM radio station call letters*]
KGGR........... Dallas, TX [*AM radio station call letters*]
KGGY........... Dubuque, IA [*FM radio station call letters*]
KGH .... Kidney Goldblatt Hypertension Scale
KGH .... Knight of the Guelphic Order of Hanover [*British*]
KGHF .... Pueblo, CO [*AM radio station call letters*]
KGHL .... Billings, MT [*AM radio station call letters*]
KGHO-AM ..... Olympia, WA [*AM radio station call letters*] (RBYB)
KGHO-FM ..... Hoquiam, WA [*FM radio station call letters*]
KGHP .... Gig Harbor, WA [*FM radio station call letters*]
KG/HR......... Kilograms per Hour (WDAA)
KGHR.......... Tuba City, AZ [*FM radio station call letters*]
KGHS .... International Falls, MN [*AM radio station call letters*]
KGHT .... Kidney Goldblatt Hypertension [*Medicine*] (DAVI)
KGHT .... Sheridan, AR [*AM radio station call letters*]
KGI............. Cryderman Gold, Inc. [*Vancouver Stock Exchange symbol*]
KGI............. Kalgoorlie [*Australia*] [*Airport symbol*] (OAG)
KGI............. Kellogg [*Idaho*] [*Seismograph station code, US Geological Survey*] (SEIS)
KGII .... King George II [*British*]
KGIL-AM ...... Beverly Hills, CA [*AM radio station call letters*] (BROA)
KGIM .... Aberdeen, SD [*AM radio station call letters*]
KGIM-FM...... Redfield, SD [*FM radio station call letters*] (BROA)
KGIN .... Grand Island, NE [*Television station call letters*]
KGIR-AM...... Cape Giradeau, MO [*AM radio station call letters*] (RBYB)
KGIW .... Alamosa, CO [*AM radio station call letters*]
KGJ .... Karonga [*Malawi*] [*Airport symbol*] (OAG)
KG/J .... Kilograms per Joule
KGJ .... King Jack Resources [*Vancouver Stock Exchange symbol*]
KGK .... Kabushiki Goshi Kaisha [*Partnership*] [*Japan*]
KGK .... Koliganek [*Alaska*] [*Airport symbol*] (OAG)
KGKL .... San Angelo, TX [*AM radio station call letters*]
KGKL-FM...... San Angelo, TX [*FM radio station call letters*]
KGKS-FM..... Scott City, MO [*FM radio station call letters*] (BROA)
KGL .... Kaufel Group Ltd. [*Toronto Stock Exchange symbol*]
KGL .... Key Geographic Location (SAUS)
KGL .... Kigali [*Rwanda*] [*Airport symbol*] (OAG)
kg/L .... Kilogram Per Liter (STED)
KGL .... King's German Legion [*British military*] (DMA)
KGL .... Koeniglich [*Royal*] [*German*]
KGL .... Port-Aux-Francais [*Formerly, Kerguelen*] [*France*] [*Geomagnetic observatory code*]
KGLA .... Gretna, LA [*AM radio station call letters*]
KGLB .... Okmulgee, OK [*Television station call letters*]
KGLC .... Miami, OK [*AM radio station call letters*]
KGLD .... Tyler, TX [*AM radio station call letters*]

KGLE........... Glendive, MT [*AM radio station call letters*]
KGLE........... South Lake Tahoe, CA [*FM radio station call letters*]
KGLF........... Robstown, TX [*AM radio station call letters*]
KGLI........... Sioux City, IA [*FM radio station call letters*]
KGLL........... Greeley, CO [*FM radio station call letters*]
KGLM........... Anaconda, MT [*FM radio station call letters*]
KGLN........... Glenwood Springs, CO [*AM radio station call letters*]
KGLO........... Mason City, IA [*AM radio station call letters*]
KGLP........... Gallup, NM [*FM radio station call letters*]
KGLQ-FM....... Phoenix, AZ [*FM radio station call letters*] (BROA)
KGLS........... Galveston/Scholes Field [*Texas*] [*ICAO location identifier*] (ICLI)
KGLS........... Pratt, KS [*FM radio station call letters*]
KGLT........... Bozeman, MT [*FM radio station call letters*]
KGLW........... San Luis Obispo, CA [*AM radio station call letters*]
KGLX........... Gallup, NM [*AM radio station call letters*]
KGLY........... Tyler, TX [*FM radio station call letters*]
KGM .... Keratinocyte Growth Medium [*Cell culture*]
KGM .... Kerr Glass Manufacturing Corp. (SAUO)
KGM .... Kerr Glass Mfg. (EFIS)
KGM .... Kerr Group [*NYSE symbol*] (SPSG)
KGM .... Key Generator Module
KGM .... Kiena Gold Mines Ltd. [*Toronto Stock Exchange symbol*]
kgm .... Kilogram [*Also, k, kg*] [*SI unit for mass*] (DAVI)
kg-m .... Kilogram-Meter (ADWA)
kgm .... Kilogram-Meter (IDOE)
KGM .... Kluang [*Malaysia*] [*Seismograph station code, US Geological Survey*] (SEIS)
KG/M² .... Kilograms per Square Meter
kg/m³ .... Kilograms per Cubic Meter (IDOE)
KG/M³ .... Kilograms per Cubic Meter
KGMB .... Honolulu, HI [*Television station call letters*]
KGMC .... Clovis, CA [*Television station call letters*]
KGMD .... Hilo, HI [*Television station call letters*]
KGME .... Glendale, AZ [*AM radio station call letters*]
KGMens....... K & G Mens Center, Inc. [*Associated Press*] (SAG)
KGMI .... Bellingham, WA [*AM radio station call letters*]
KGMM .... Abilene, TX [*AM radio station call letters*] (BROA)
KGMN .... Kingman, AZ [*FM radio station call letters*]
KGMO .... Cape Girardeau, MO [*FM radio station call letters*]
KGMS .... Green Valley, AZ [*FM radio station call letters*]
KGMT .... Fairbury, NE [*AM radio station call letters*]
KGMV .... Wailuku, HI [*Television station call letters*]
KGMX .... Lancaster, CA [*FM radio station call letters*]
KGMY .... Aurora, MO [*FM radio station call letters*]
KGMY .... Springfield, MO [*AM radio station call letters*]
KGMZ........... Aiea, HI [*FM radio station call letters*]
Kgn .... Kingsman (SAUS)
KGNB .... New Braunfels, TX [*AM radio station call letters*]
KGNC .... Amarillo, TX [*AM radio station call letters*]
KGNC-FM..... Amarillo, TX [*FM radio station call letters*]
KGND .... Ketchum, OK [*FM radio station call letters*]
KGNM .... St. Joseph, MO [*AM radio station call letters*]
KGNN .... Cuba, MO [*AM radio station call letters*]
KGNN-FM .... Cuba, MO [*FM radio station call letters*] (RBYB)
KGNO .... Dodge City, KS [*AM radio station call letters*]
KGNP .... Kalahari Gemsbok National Park (SAUO)
KGNP .... Katherine Gorge National Park (SAUO)
KGNS .... Laredo, TX [*Television station call letters*]
KGNT .... Grants/Grants-Milan [*New Mexico*] [*ICAO location identifier*] (ICLI)
KGNT-FM ..... Smithfield, UT [*FM radio station call letters*] (BROA)
KGNU .... Boulder, CO [*FM radio station call letters*]
KGNV .... Gainesville [*Florida*] [*ICAO location identifier*] (ICLI)
KGNV .... Washington, MO [*FM radio station call letters*]
KGNW .... Burien-Seattle, WA [*AM radio station call letters*]
KGNZ .... Abilene, TX [*FM radio station call letters*]
KGO .... Kasongo [*Zaire*] [*Airport symbol*] (AD)
KGO .... King's Gurkha Officer [*British military*] (DMA)
KGO .... San Francisco, CA [*AM radio station call letters*]
KGO-DT........ San Francisco, CA [*Television station call letters*] (BROA)
KGOE .... Eureka, CA [*AM radio station call letters*]
KGOK .... Pauls Valley, OK [*FM radio station call letters*]
KGOL .... Humble, TX [*AM radio station call letters*]
KGON .... Portland, OR [*FM radio station call letters*]
KGOR .... Omaha, NE [*FM radio station call letters*]
KGOS .... Torrington, WY [*AM radio station call letters*]
KGOT .... Anchorage, AK [*FM radio station call letters*]
KGO-TV .... San Francisco, CA [*Television station call letters*]
KGOU .... Norman, OK [*FM radio station call letters*]
KGOZ .... Gallatin, MO [*FM radio station call letters*]
KGP .... Komma Georgiou Papandreou [*Party of George Papandreou*] [*Greek*] [*Political party*] (PPE)
KG/(PA S M²)... Kilograms per Pascal Second Square Meter
KGPL .... Dermott, AR [*AM radio station call letters*]
KGPQ-FM..... Monticello, AR [*FM radio station call letters*] (RBYB)
KGPR .... Great Falls, MT [*FM radio station call letters*]
KGPS .... Kilograms per Second (GOBB)
kgps........... Kilograms per Second
KGPS .... Kinematic GPS (SAUS)
KGPX .... Spokane, WA [*Television station call letters*] (BROA)
KGPZ .... Coleraine, MN [*FM radio station call letters*]
KGR .... Kanonengranate [*Shell for a gun*] [*German military - World War II*]
KGR .... Kengate Resources [*Vancouver Stock Exchange symbol*]
KGR .... Key Generator Receiver (MCD)
kgr .... Kilograin (BARN)

kgr	Kirghiz Soviet Socialist Republic [*MARC country of publication code*] [*Library of Congress*] (LCCP)
KGR	Klydonograph Type Gradient Recorder (IAA)
KGRA	Jefferson, IA [*FM radio station call letters*]
KGRA	Known Geothermal Resource Area [*Department of the Interior*]
KGRAX	Kemper Growth Cl.A [*Mutual fund ticker symbol*] (SG)
KGRB	Greenbay/Austin Straubel [*Wisconsin*] [*ICAO location identifier*] (ICLI)
KGRB	West Covina, CA [*AM radio station call letters*]
KGRBX	Kemper Growth Cl.B [*Mutual fund ticker symbol*] (SG)
KGRC	Hannibal, MO [*FM radio station call letters*]
KGRD	Orchard, NE [*FM radio station call letters*]
KGRE	Greeley, CO [*AM radio station call letters*]
KGRG	Auburn, WA [*FM radio station call letters*]
KGRI	Henderson, TX [*FM radio station call letters*]
KGRK	Killeen/Robert Gray Army Air Field [*Texas*] [*ICAO location identifier*] (ICLI)
KGRM	Grambling, LA [*FM radio station call letters*]
KGRN	Grinnell, IA [*AM radio station call letters*]
KGRO	Pampa, TX [*AM radio station call letters*]
KGRP-FM	Calistoga, CA [*FM radio station call letters*] (BROA)
KGRR	Epworth, IA [*FM radio station call letters*]
KGRR	Grand Rapids/Kent County Cascade [*Michigan*] [*ICAO location identifier*] (ICLI)
KGRS	Burlington, IA [*FM radio station call letters*]
KGRT	Las Cruces, NM [*AM radio station call letters*]
KGRT-FM	Las Cruces, NM [*FM radio station call letters*]
KGRV	Winston, OR [*AM radio station call letters*]
KGRW	Friona, TX [*FM radio station call letters*]
KGRZ	Missoula, MT [*AM radio station call letters*]
KGS	Kansas Geological Society (SAUO)
KGS	Kansas Geological Survey (SAUO)
KGS	Kate Greenaway Society (EA)
KGS	Kentucky Geological Survey (SAUO)
KGS	Ketogenic Steroid [*Endocrinology*]
KGS	Kigezi Gorilla Sanctuary (SAUO)
kg/s	Kilograms per Second
Kgs	Kings [*Old Testament book*]
KGS	Kos [*Greece*] [*Airport symbol*] (OAG)
KGSB	Goldsboro/Seymour-Johnson Air Force Base [*North Carolina*] [*ICAO location identifier*] (ICLI)
KGSG-FM	Pasco, WA [*FM radio station call letters*] (BROA)
KGSP	Parkville, MO [*FM radio station call letters*]
KGSR	Bastrop, TX [*FM radio station call letters*]
KGST	Fresno, CA [*AM radio station call letters*]
kgst	Kilograms Static Thrust (DOMA)
KGStJ	Knight of Grace of the Order of Saint John of Jerusalem (SAUO)
KGStJ	Knight of Grace, Order of St. John of Jerusalem
KGT	Kemper Intermediate Government Trust [*NYSE symbol*] (SPSG)
KGT	Kemper Interm Gvt Tr [*NYSE symbol*] (TTSB)
KGTF	Agana, GU [*Television station call letters*]
KGTF	Great Falls/International [*Montana*] [*ICAO location identifier*] (ICLI)
KGTL	Homer, AK [*AM radio station call letters*]
KGTM	Rexburg, ID [*FM radio station call letters*]
KGTO	Tulsa, OK [*AM radio station call letters*]
KGTR	Larned, KS [*FM radio station call letters*] (RBYB)
KGTS	College Place, WA [*FM radio station call letters*]
KGTV	San Diego, CA [*Television station call letters*]
KGTV-DT	San Diego, CA [*Television station call letters*] (BROA)
KGTW	Ketchikan, AK [*FM radio station call letters*]
KGU	Honolulu, HI [*AM radio station call letters*]
KGU	Keningau [*Malaysia*] [*Airport symbol*] (OAG)
KGU	Kobe Gakuin University [*UTLAS symbol*]
KGUL	Port Lavaca, TX [*AM radio station call letters*]
KGUL-FM	Edna, TX [*FM radio station call letters*] (BROA)
KGUM	Agana, GU [*AM radio station call letters*]
KGUM-FM	Dededo, GU [*FM radio station call letters*] (BROA)
KGUN	Tucson, AZ [*Television station call letters*]
KGUS	Peru/Grisson Air Force Base [*Indiana*] [*ICAO location identifier*] (ICLI)
KGV	King George V [*British*]
KGV	Knight of Gustavus Vasa [*Sweden*]
KGVA	Fort Belknap Agency, MT [*FM radio station call letters*] (RBYB)
KGVE	Grove, OK [*FM radio station call letters*]
KGVL	Greenville, TX [*AM radio station call letters*]
KGVM	Gardnerville-Minden, NV [*FM radio station call letters*]
KGVO	King George the Fifth's Own [*British military*] (DMA)
KGVO	Missoula, MT [*AM radio station call letters*]
KGVT	Greenville/Majors Field [*Texas*] [*ICAO location identifier*] (ICLI)
KGVW	Belgrade, MT [*AM radio station call letters*]
KGVW	Grandview/Richards-Gebaur Air Force Base [*Missouri*] [*ICAO location identifier*] (ICLI)
KGVY	Green Valley, AZ [*AM radio station call letters*]
KGW	Kagi [*Papua New Guinea*] [*Airport symbol*] (OAG)
KGW	Kreeger, George W., Atlanta GA [*STAC*]
KGW	Portland, OR [*Television station call letters*]
KGWA	Enid, OK [*AM radio station call letters*]
KGWB	Wahpeton, ND [*FM radio station call letters*]
KGWC	Casper, WY [*Television station call letters*]
KGWC	Offutt Air Force Base, Omaha [*Nebraska*] [*ICAO location identifier*] (ICLI)
KGW-DT	Portland, OR [*Television station call letters*] (BROA)
KGWL	Lander, WY [*Television station call letters*]
KGWN	Cheyenne, WY [*Television station call letters*]
KGWO	Greenwood-Leflore [*Mississippi*] [*ICAO location identifier*] (ICLI)
KGWR	Rock Springs, WY [*Television station call letters*]

KGWS	Keoladeo Ghana Wildlife Sanctuary (SAUO)
KGWT	Kilogram Weight (IAA)
KGWY	Gillette, WY [*FM radio station call letters*]
KGX	Grayling [*Alaska*] [*Airport symbol*] (OAG)
KGXL-AM	Costa Mesa, CA [*AM radio station call letters*] (BROA)
KGXY	Lenwood, CA [*FM radio station call letters*]
kGy	Kilo Gray [*Absorbed dose*] [*Radiology*]
KGY	Kingaroy [*Australia*] [*Airport symbol*] (OAG)
KGY	Olympia, WA [*AM radio station call letters*]
KGY-FM	McCleary, WA [*FM radio station call letters*]
KGYN	Guymon, OK [*AM radio station call letters*]
kg/yr	Kilograms per Year (COE)
KGZ	Glacier Creek, AK [*Location identifier*] [*FAA*] (FAAL)
KGZ	Kyrgyzstan (ADWA)
Kgz	Kyrgyzstan (MILB)
KGZC	Folsom, LA [*FM radio station call letters*]
KGZF	Emporia, KS [*FM radio station call letters*]
KGZH	Nyssa, OR [*FM radio station call letters*]
KGZO-FM	Shafter, CA [*FM radio station call letters*] (RBYB)
KH	Cambodia [*ANSI two-letter standard code*] (CNC)
KH	Cook Islandair [*ICAO designator*] (AD)
KH	Cook Island Airways Ltd. (SAUO)
KH	Hong Kong [*IYRU nationality code*] (IYR)
KH	Hungary [*License plate code assigned to foreign diplomats in the US*]
KH	Kadosh [*Freemasonry*] (ROG)
KH	Kawasaki Heavy Industries Ltd. [*Japan*] [*ICAO aircraft manufacturer identifier*] (ICAO)
KH	Kelvin-Helmholtz [*Waves*] [*Meteorology*]
KH	Kelvin Hughes A/S (SAUO)
KH	Keren Hayesod (BJA)
KH	Kersten Hurik Group [*Commercial firm*] [*British*]
KH	Key Hole [*Reconnaissance satellite series*] (DOMA)
KH	Keyhole Series [*Optical reconnaissance satellites*]
Kh	Khirbet (BJA)
KH	Kilohenry
kH	Kilohertz
kh	Kilohour (ELAL)
Kh	Kilohour (VLIE)
KH	King's Hussars [*Military unit*] [*British*]
KH	Kneller Hall [*British military*] (DMA)
KH	Knight of Honor
KH	Knight of the Guelphic Order of Hanover [*British*]
KH	Kramers-Henneberger [*Coordinate frame for electron movement*] [*Physics*]
KH	Krebs-Henseleit [*Cycle*] [*or Ornithine cycle*] [*Analytical biochemistry*] (DAVI)
KH	Krebs-Henseleit Buffer [*Analytical biochemistry*] (DMAA)
KH	Kupat Holim (BJA)
KHA	Kansas Hospital Association (SRA)
KHA	Khancoban [*Australia*] [*Seismograph station code, US Geological Survey*] (SEIS)
kha	Khasi [*MARC language code*] [*Library of Congress*] (LCCP)
KHA	Killed by Hostile Action [*Military*]
KHA	Kitty Hawk Airways, Inc. [*ICAO designator*] (FAAC)
KHAC	Tse Bonito, NM [*AM radio station call letters*]
KHAD	De Soto, MO [*AM radio station call letters*]
KHAI	Kharkov Aviation Institute (SAUO)
KHAK-FM	Cedar Rapids, IA [*FM radio station call letters*]
KHalH	Hertzler Research Foundation, Halstead, KS [*Library symbol*] [*Library of Congress*] (LCLS)
KHAM-FM	Saint Ansgar, IA [*FM radio station call letters*] (BROA)
KHAP	Chico, CA [*FM radio station call letters*]
KHAR	Anchorage, AK [*AM radio station call letters*]
KHAR	Harrisburg/Capital City [*Pennsylvania*] [*ICAO location identifier*] (ICLI)
KHAS	Hastings, NE [*AM radio station call letters*]
KHAS-TV	Hastings, NE [*Television station call letters*]
KHAT	Kurzer Handkommentar zum Alten Testament [*Tuebingen*] [*A publication*] (BJA)
KHAT	Lincoln, NE [*AM radio station call letters*]
KHAW	Hilo, HI [*Television station call letters*]
KHAY	Ventura, CA [*FM radio station call letters*]
KHayF	Fort Hays State University, Hays, KS [*Library symbol*] [*Library of Congress*] (LCLS)
KHayv	Haysville Community Library, Haysville, KS [*Library symbol*] [*Library of Congress*] (LCLS)
KHAZ	Hays, KS [*FM radio station call letters*]
KHB	Khabarovsk [*Former USSR*] [*Geomagnetic observatory code*]
KHB	King's Hard Bargain [*British military slang for undesirable sailor or soldier*]
KHB	Korea Housing Bank (IMH)
KHB	Krebs-Henseleit Bicarbonate [*A buffer*] [*Analytical biochemistry*]
KHB	KSC [*Kennedy Space Center*] Handbook [*NASA*] (KSC)
KHb	Kurzgefasstes Exegetisches Handbuch zum Alten Testament [*Leipzig*] [*A publication*] (BJA)
KHb	Potassium Hemoglobinate (AAMN)
KHBC	Hilo, HI [*Television station call letters*]
KHBG	Healdsburg, CA [*FM radio station call letters*] (RBYB)
KHBM	Monticello, AR [*AM radio station call letters*]
KHBM-FM	Monticello, AR [*FM radio station call letters*]
KHBR	Hillsboro, TX [*AM radio station call letters*]
KHBR	Hobart [*Oklahoma*] [*ICAO location identifier*] (ICLI)
KHBS	Fort Smith, AR [*Television station call letters*]
KHBT	Humboldt, IA [*FM radio station call letters*]
KHBX-FM	El Dorado, AR [*FM radio station call letters*] (BROA)

KHByF	Fort Hays State University (SAUO)
KHC	135 Airways [FAA designator] (FAAC)
KHC	Karen Horney Clinic (EA)
KHC	Karen Horney Psychoanalytic Clinic (SAUO)
KHC	Kasperske Hory [Czechoslovakia] [Seismograph station code, US Geological Survey] (SEIS)
KHC	Kinesin Heavy Chain [Physiology]
KHC	Kinetic Hemolysis Curve [Biochemistry] (DAVI)
KHCA	King's Honorary Chaplain [British]
KHCA	Wamego, KS [FM radio station call letters]
KHCB	Galveston, TX [AM radio station call letters]
KHCB	Houston, TX [FM radio station call letters]
KHCC	Hutchinson, KS [FM radio station call letters]
KHCD	Kenya High Court Digest [A publication] (DLA)
KHCD	Salina, KS [FM radio station call letters]
KHCE	Khabarovsk Commodity Exchange [Russian Federation] (EY)
KHCE	San Antonio, TX [Television station call letters]
KHCH	Huntsville, TX [AM radio station call letters] (BROA)
KHCK	Denton, TX [FM radio station call letters] (RBYB)
KHCME	Kharkov Commodity and Raw Materials Exchange [Ukraine] (EY)
KHCR	Potosi, MO [FM radio station call letters]
KHCS	Palm Desert, CA [FM radio station call letters]
KHCT	Great Bend, KS [FM radio station call letters]
KHCV	Seattle, WA [Television station call letters]
KHD	Kinky Hair Disease [Medicine] (DMAA)
KHDC	Chualar, CA [FM radio station call letters]
KHDN	Hardin, MT [AM radio station call letters] (RBYB)
KHDR-FM	Victorville, CA [FM radio station call letters'] (BROA)
KHDS	Honorary Dental Surgeon to the King (SAUS)
KHDS	King's Honorary Dental Surgeon [British]
KHDT	Caldwell, ID [Television station call letters]
KHDX	Conway, AR [FM radio station call letters]
KHDY-FM	Plainview, TX [FM radio station call letters] (RBYB)
KHE	Kanfey-Ha'Emek Aviation [Israel] [FAA designator] (FAAC)
KHE	Kheis [Former USSR] [Seismograph station code, US Geological Survey] (SEIS)
KHE	Kherson [USSR] [Airport symbol] (AD)
KHEP	Phoenix, AZ [AM radio station call letters]
KHER	Crystal City, TX [FM radio station call letters]
KHET	Honolulu, HI [Television station call letters]
KHEY	El Paso, TX [AM radio station call letters]
KHEY-FM	El Paso, TX [FM radio station call letters]
KHF	Know How Fund [European economic development fund]
KHF	Korean Hemorrhagic Fever [Medicine]
KHFD	Hartford/Brainard Field [Connecticut] [ICAO location identifier] (ICLI)
KHFD-FM	Hereford, TX [FM radio station call letters] (BROA)
KHFI	Georgetown, TX [FM radio station call letters]
KHFM	Albuquerque, NM [FM radio station call letters]
KHFN	Los Ranchos de Albuquerque, NM [AM radio station call letters] (RBYB)
KHFS-AM	Fort Smith, AR [AM radio station call letters] (BROA)
KHFT	Hobbs, NM [Television station call letters]
KHFX-FM	Ball, LA [FM radio station call letters] (BROA)
KHG	Kashi [China] [Airport symbol] (OAG)
KHG	Keystone Heritage Group [AMEX symbol] (TTSB)
KHG	Keystone Heritage Group, Inc. [AMEX symbol] (SAG)
K hgb	Potassium Hemoglobinate [Organic chemistry] (DAVI)
KHGI	Kearney, NE [Television station call letters]
KHGI	Keystone Heritage Group, Incorporated (SAUO)
KHGN-FM	Kirksville, MO [FM radio station call letters] (BROA)
KHH	Kaohsiung [Taiwan] [Airport symbol] (OAG)
KHH	Kirchoff, H. H., St. Paul MN [STAC]
KHHK-FM	Naches, WA [FM radio station call letters] (RBYB)
KHHO-AM	Tacoma, WA [AM radio station call letters] (RBYB)
KHHT	Killeen, TX [FM radio station call letters]
KHI	Kakhk [Iran] [Seismograph station code, US Geological Survey] (SEIS)
KHi	Kansas State Historical Society, Topeka, KS [Library symbol] [Library of Congress] (LCLS)
KHI	Karachi [Pakistan] [Airport symbol] (OAG)
KHI	Kawasaki Heavy Industries (ACAE)
KHI	Kawasaki Heavy Industries Ltd (SAUS)
KHI	Kelvin-Helmholtz Instability (PDAA)
KHI	Kemper High Income [NYSE symbol] (SPSG)
KHIB	Durant, OK [FM radio station call letters]
KHIB	Hibbing/Chisholm-Hibbing [Minnesota] [ICAO location identifier] (ICLI)
KHID	McAllen, TX [FM radio station call letters]
KHIF	Keeping House of Ill Fame
KHIF	Ogden/Hill Air Force Base [Utah] [ICAO location identifier] (ICLI)
KHIH-FM	Denver, CO [FM radio station call letters] (RBYB)
KHII	Security, CO [FM radio station call letters]
KHIL	Willcox, AZ [AM radio station call letters]
KHILS	Kill-vehicle In-the-Loop Simulator (SAUS)
KHIIT	Tabor College, Hillsboro, KS [Library symbol] [Library of Congress] (LCLS)
KHIM-FM	Mangum, OK [FM radio station call letters] (BROA)
KHIM-TV	Conroe, TX [TV station call letters] (RBYB)
KHIN	Red Oak, IA [Television station call letters]
KHIP	Felton, CA [FM radio station call letters]
KHIS	Bakersfield, CA [AM radio station call letters]
KHIS-FM	Bakersfield, CA [FM radio station call letters]
KHIT	Reno, NV [FM radio station call letters]
KHIT-AM	Reno, NV [AM radio station call letters] (RBYB)
KHIX-FM	Ely, NV [FM radio station call letters] (BROA)
KHIZ	Barstow, CA [Television station call letters]
KHJJ	Lancaster, CA [AM radio station call letters]
KHJM	Taft, OK [FM radio station call letters]
KHJP-FM	Leone, AS [FM radio station call letters] (BROA)
KHJQ-FM	Susanville, CA [FM radio station call letters] (BROA)
KHJS-FM	Pago Pago, AS (BROA)
KHK	Khark [Iran] [Airport symbol] [Obsolete] (OAG)
KHK	Kurzer Handkommentar zum Alten Testament [A publication] (BJA)
KHKC	Atoka, OK [FM radio station call letters]
KHKE	Cedar Falls, IA [FM radio station call letters]
KHKI	Des Moines, IA [FM radio station call letters]
KHKK-FM	Modesto, CA [FM radio station call letters] (RBYB)
KHKR	East Helena, MT [AM radio station call letters]
KHKR-FM	East Helena, MT [FM radio station call letters]
KHKS	Denton, TX [FM radio station call letters]
KHKY	Hickory/Municipal [North Carolina] [ICAO location identifier] (ICLI)
KHL	Kennedy-Heaviside Layer [Electronics]
KHL	Keren Hajesod Ljisroel (BJA)
KHL	Khulna [Bangladesh] [Airport symbol] (AD)
KHL	Kupat Holim Le-'Ovdim Le'umiyim [A publication] (BJA)
KHLA	Lake Charles, LA [FM radio station call letters]
KHLB	Burnet, TX [AM radio station call letters]
KHLB-FM	Burnet, TX [FM radio station call letters]
KHLL	Richwood, LA [FM radio station call letters]
KHLO	Hilo, HI [AM radio station call letters]
KHLOS	Kilo High Level Language Operations per Second (CCCA)
KHLR	Cameron, TX [FM radio station call letters]
KHLR	Kahler Corp. [NASDAQ symbol] (NQ)
KHLR	KahlerRealty [NASDAQ symbol] (TTSB)
KHLS	Blytheville, AR [FM radio station call letters]
KHLT	Hallettsville, TX [AM radio station call letters] (RBYB)
KHM	Cambodia [ANSI three-letter standard code] (CNC)
KHM	Khamtis [Myanmar] [Airport symbol] (OAG)
KHM-M	King's Harbour Master [Obsolete] [British]
KH-M	Yad V'Kidush Hashem, House of Martyrs (EA)
KHMA	Kentucky Hotel and Motel Association (SRA)
KHMB	Hamburg, AR [FM radio station call letters]
KHMC	Goliad, TX [FM radio station call letters]
KHME	Winona, MN [FM radio station call letters]
KHMG	Barrigada, GU [FM radio station call letters] (RBYB)
KHMN	Alamogordo/Holloman Air Force Base [New Mexico] [ICAO location identifier] (ICLI)
KHMO	Hannibal, MO [AM radio station call letters]
KHMS	Victorville, CA [FM radio station call letters]
KHMT	Hardin, MT [Television station call letters] (RBYB)
KHMX	Houston, TX [FM radio station call letters]
KHN	Knoop Hardness Number
KHN	Nanchang [China] [Airport symbol] (OAG)
KHN	Northern Kentucky University, Highland Heights, KY [OCLC symbol] (OCLC)
KHNC	Johnstown, CO [AM radio station call letters]
KHND	Harvey, ND [AM radio station call letters]
KHNE	Hastings, NE [FM radio station call letters]
KHNE-TV	Hastings, NE [Television station call letters]
KHNL	Honolulu, HI [Television station call letters]
KHNR	Honolulu, HI [AM radio station call letters]
KHNS	Haines, AK [FM radio station call letters]
KHNS	Honorary Nursing Sister to the King (SAUS)
KHNS	King's Honorary Nursing Sister [British]
KHO	Khorog [Former USSR] [Seismograph station code, US Geological Survey] (SEIS)
KHO	Khors Aircompany [Ukraine] [FAA designator] (FAAC)
kho	Khotanese [MARC language code] [Library of Congress] (LCCP)
KHOB	Hobbs/Les County [New Mexico] [ICAO location identifier] (ICLI)
KHOB	Hobbs, NM [AM radio station call letters]
KHOC-FM	Casper, WY [FM radio station call letters] (BROA)
KHOE	Fairfield, IA [FM radio station call letters]
KHOG	Fayetteville, AR [Television station call letters]
KHOK	Hoisington, KS [FM radio station call letters]
KHOL	Beulah, ND [AM radio station call letters]
KHOM	Houma, LA [FM radio station call letters]
KHON	Honolulu, HI [Television station call letters]
KHOP	Hopkinsville/Campbell Army Air Field [Kentucky] [ICAO location identifier] (ICLI)
KHOP	Modesto, CA [FM radio station call letters]
KHOS	Sonora, TX [AM radio station call letters]
KHOS-FM	Sonora, TX [FM radio station call letters]
KHOT	Globe, AZ [FM radio station call letters] (RBYB)
KHOT	Madera, CA [AM radio station call letters]
KHOU	Houston, TX [Television station call letters]
KHOU	Houston/William P. Hobby [Texas] [ICAO location identifier] (ICLI)
KHOU-DT	Houston, TX [Television station call letters] (BROA)
KHOW	Denver, CO [AM radio station call letters]
KHOX	Hoxie, AR [FM radio station call letters]
KHOY	Laredo, TX [FM radio station call letters]
KHOZ	Harrison, AR [AM radio station call letters]
KHOZ-FM	Harrison, AR [FM radio station call letters]
KHP	Honorary Physician to the King [British]
KHP	Koppers Hydrate Process
KHP	Potassium Hydrogen Phthalate (SAUS)
KHPA	Hope, AR [FM radio station call letters]
KHPC	Karen Horney Psychoanalytic Clinic (SAUO)
KHPE	Albany, OR [FM radio station call letters]
KHPN	Loveland, CO [AM radio station call letters] (BROA)
KHPN	White Plains/Westchester [New York] [ICAO location identifier] (ICLI)

KHPQ .... Clinton, AR [FM radio station call letters]
KHPR .... Honolulu, HI [FM radio station call letters]
KHPS .... Kilo Hops per Second (CCCA)
KHPU-FM ..... Brownwood, TX [FM radio station call letters] (BROA)
KHPY .... Moreno Valley, CA [AM radio station call letters]
KHQ .... Spokane, WA [Television station call letters]
KHQA .... Hannibal, MO [Television station call letters]
KHQN .... Spanish Fork, UT [AM radio station call letters]
KHR .... Khazar [Turkmenistan] [ICAO designator] (FAAC)
KHR .... Khorongon [Former USSR] [Seismograph station code, US
                  Geological Survey] [Closed] (SEIS)
KHRI .... Kresge Hearing Research Institute [University of Michigan] [Research
                  center]
KHRL .... Harlingen/Industrial Airpack [Texas] [ICAO location identifier] (ICLI)
KHRN .... Hearne, TX [FM radio station call letters] (RBYB)
KHRO .... Harrison/Boone County [Arkansas] [ICAO location identifier] (ICLI)
KHRP .... Kurdish Human Rights Project (BUAC)
KHRR .... Tucson, AZ [Television station call letters]
KHRT .... Mary Esther/Eglin Air Field Auxiliary [Florida] [ICAO location
                  identifier] (ICLI)
KHRT .... Minot, ND [AM radio station call letters]
KHS .... Honorary Surgeon to the King [British]
KHS .... Kennedy High School (SAUO)
KHS .... Kinky Hair Syndrome [Medicine] (DMAA)
KHS .... Knight of the Holy Sepulchre
KHS .... Knight of the Holy Sepulchre of Jerusalem (DD)
KHS .... Krebs-Henseleit Solution (DB)
KHS .... Kushtia [Bangladesh] [Airport symbol] (AD)
KHSA .... Kentucky Human Services Association (SRA)
KHSC .... Ontario, CA [Television station call letters]
KHSD .... Lead, SD [Television station call letters]
KHSH .... Alvin, TX [Television station call letters]
KHSL .... Paradise, CA [FM radio station call letters]
KHSL-TV ...... Chico, CA [Television station call letters]
KHSN .... Coos Bay, OR [AM radio station call letters]
KHSP .... Ashdown, AR [FM radio station call letters]
KHSP .... Texarkana, TX [AM radio station call letters]
KHSR-FM ..... Crescent City, CA [FM radio station call letters] (BROA)
KHSS .... Walla Walla, WA [FM radio station call letters]
KHST .... Homestead/Homestead Air Force Base [Florida] [ICAO location
                  identifier] (ICLI)
KHST .... Lamar, MO [FM radio station call letters]
KHSU .... Arcata, CA [FM radio station call letters]
KHSX .... Irving, TX [Television station call letters]
KHT .... Kathode Heating Time
KHT .... Khost [Afghanistan] [Airport symbol] [Obsolete] (OAG)
KHTC .... Phoenix, AZ [FM radio station call letters] (RBYB)
KHTE-FM ...... Lonoke, AR [FM radio station call letters] (BROA)
KHTH .... Dillon, CO [AM radio station call letters]
KHTK .... Sacramento, CA [AM radio station call letters]
KHTL .... Albuquerque, NM [AM radio station call letters] (RBYB)
KHTL .... Houghton Lake/Roscommon [Michigan] [ICAO location identifier]
                  (ICLI)
KHTN .... Los Banos, CA [FM radio station call letters]
KHTO .... Mount Vernon, MO [FM radio station call letters]
KHTQ .... Hayden, ID [FM radio station call letters] (RBYB)
KHTR .... Pullman, WA [FM radio station call letters]
KHTS .... El Cajon, CA [FM radio station call letters] (RBYB)
KHTT .... Muskogee, OK [FM radio station call letters]
KHTTA .... Kanata High Technology Training Association [Canada] (EDAC)
KHTV .... Houston, TX [Television station call letters]
KHTW-FM ..... Caledonia, MN [FM radio station call letters] (BROA)
KHTX .... Salinas, CA [AM radio station call letters] (RBYB)
KHTY .... Santa Barbara, CA [FM radio station call letters]
KHTZ .... Albuquerque, NM [AM radio station call letters] (BROA)
KHu .... Hutchinson Public Library, Hutchinson, KS [Library symbol] [Library
                  of Congress] (LCLS)
KHU .... Kahuku [Hawaii] [Seismograph station code, US Geological
                  Survey] (SEIS)
KHUB .... Fremont, NE [AM radio station call letters]
KHuC .... Hutchinson Community Junior College, Hutchinson, KS [Library
                  symbol] [Library of Congress] (LCLS)
KHUG .... Rocky Ford, CO [FM radio station call letters]
KHUG-FM .... England, AR [FM radio station call letters] (BROA)
KHUL .... Houlton/International [Maine] [ICAO location identifier] (ICLI)
KHUL-FM ..... Waipahu, HI [FM radio station call letters] (BROA)
KHUM .... Garberville, CA [FM radio station call letters] (RBYB)
KHUT .... Hutchinson, KS [FM radio station call letters]
KHV .... Khabarovsk [Former USSR] [Airport symbol] (OAG)
KhV .... Khranit' Vechno [To be Kept in Perpetuity] [KGB file status]
KhV .... Khristianski Vostok (BJA)
KHVH .... Honolulu, HI [AM radio station call letters]
KHVN .... Fort Worth, TX [AM radio station call letters]
KHVO .... Hilo, HI [Television station call letters]
KHVO-DT ..... Hilo, HI [Television station call letters] (BROA)
KHVR .... Havre [Montana] [ICAO location identifier] (ICLI)
KHWG-FM ..... Kings Beach, CA [FM radio station call letters] (RBYB)
KHWI .... Hilo, HI [FM radio station call letters]
KHWK .... Tonopah, NV [FM radio station call letters]
KHWO .... Hollywood/North Perry [Florida] [ICAO location identifier] (ICLI)
KHWS-FM ..... North Pole, AK [FM radio station call letters] (BROA)
KHWY .... Essex, CA [FM radio station call letters]
KHWZ-FM ..... Ludlow, CA [FM radio station call letters] (RBYB)
KHX .... Hugo Rizzuto [ICAO designator] (FAAC)
KHXR-FM ..... Sun Valley, NV [FM radio station call letters] (BROA)

KHXS .... Abilene, TX [FM radio station call letters]
KHYAX .... Kemper High Yield Cl.A [Mutual fund ticker symbol] (SG)
KHYB .... Kupat Holim Year Book [A publication] (BJA)
KHYBX .... Kemper High Yield Cl.B [Mutual fund ticker symbol] (SG)
KHYF .... Know How You Feel (ADWA)
KHYF-FM ...... Taos, NM [FM radio station call letters] (BROA)
KHYI .... Howe, TX [FM radio station call letters]
KHYL .... Auburn, CA [FM radio station call letters]
KHYM .... Gilmer, TX [AM radio station call letters]
KHYM-FM ..... Copeland, KS [FM radio station call letters] (BROA)
KHYS .... Port Arthur, TX [FM radio station call letters]
KHYT-FM ...... Tucson, AZ [FM radio station call letters] (RBYB)
KHYZ .... Mountain Pass, CA [FM radio station call letters]
KHZ .... Kilohertz [FAA] (TAG)
KHz .... Kilohertz (VLIE)
kHz .... Kilohertz [Electronics]
KHZL .... Shingletown, CA [FM radio station call letters] (RBYB)
KI .... Absorption index for the daylight end of a day-night electromagnetic
                  transmission path (SAUS)
KI .... Kach International (EA)
KI .... Kanaanaeische Inschriften [A publication] (BJA)
KI .... Kangaroo Island (SAUO)
KI .... Karyopyknotic Index [Cytology] (MAE)
KI .... Karyotype Instability [Genetics]
KI .... Kennarasamband Islands [Iceland] (BUAC)
KI .... Keyette International (EA)
KI .... Key Industry [Business term]
KI .... Khmer Insurgents [Cambodian rebel force]
KI .... Kilo (WDAA)
KI .... Kinase Insert
Ki .... Kings [Old Testament book]
KI .... Kiribati [Internet country code]
KI .... Kirtland Area Office (SAUO)
KI .... Kitchen (AABC)
KI .... Kiwanis International (EA)
KI .... Knesset Israel (BJA)
KI .... Know, Incorporated (SAUO)
KI .... Knowledge Integrity [Electronic information] (IT)
KI .... Kovats [Retention] Index
KI .... Kroenig's Isthmus [Of resonance] [Medicine]
KI .... Potassium Iodide (AAMN)
Ki .... Secret Identity Key (CGWS)
KiA .... Die Keilinschriften der Achaemeniden [A publication] (BJA)
KIA .... Kachin Independence Army [Myanmar] [Political party] (EY)
KIA .... Kaiapit [New Guinea] [Airport symbol] (AD)
KIA .... Kansai International Airport [Japan]
KIA .... Kent International Airport [British]
KIA .... Kenya Institute of Administration (BUAC)
KIA .... Kibbutz Industries Association [Israel] (BUAC)
KIA .... Killed in Action [Military]
KIA .... KIWI International Air Lines, Inc. [ICAO designator] (FAAC)
KIA .... Kligler Iron Agar [Medium]
KIA .... Korean Inferior Automobile (SAUO)
KIA .... Kotoka International Airport [Ghana]
KIAA .... Kangaroo Industries Association of Australia
KIAA .... Korea Industrial Advancement Administration (SAUO)
KIAB .... Wichita/McConnell Air Force Base [Kansas] [ICAO location
                  identifier] (ICLI)
KIA - BNR ..... Killed in Action - Body Not Recovered (MCD)
KIAC .... Kansai International Airport Co. [Japan]
KIAC .... Kansai International Airport Company (SAUO)
KIAC .... Kerr Industrial Applications Center [Southeastern Oklahoma State
                  University] [Durant] [Information service or system] (IID)
KIAD .... Washington/Dulles International [District of Columbia] [ICAO location
                  identifier] (ICLI)
KIAG .... Niagara Falls/International [New York] [ICAO location identifier]
                  (ICLI)
KIAH .... Houston/Intercontinental [Texas] [ICAO location identifier] (ICLI)
KIAI .... Mason City, IA [FM radio station call letters]
KIAK .... Fairbanks, AK [AM radio station call letters]
KIAK-FM ...... Fairbanks, AK [FM radio station call letters]
KIAL .... Unalaska, AK [AM radio station call letters]
KIAM .... Nenana, AK [AM radio station call letters]
KIAQ .... Clarion, IA [FM radio station call letters]
KIAR .... Kiwanis International Accredited Representative
KIAR .... Kuzell Institute for Arthritis Research [Medical Research Institute at
                  Pacific Medical Center] [Research center] (RCD)
KIAS .... Knots Indicated Airspeed (MCD)
KIAS .... Korea Advanced Institute of Science
KIB .... Ivanof Bay, AK [Location identifier] [FAA] (FAAL)
KIB .... Kansas Inspection Bureau (SAUO)
KIB .... Keilinschriftliche Bibliothek [A publication] (BJA)
KIB .... Kentucky Inspection Bureau (SAUO)
kib .... Kilopounds (NAKS)
KIBB-FM ...... Los Angeles, CA [FM radio station call letters] (RBYB)
KIBC .... Burney, CA [FM radio station call letters]
KIBG-FM ...... Merced, CA [FM radio station call letters] (RBYB)
KIBIC .... Karolinska Institutets Bibliotek och Informationscentral [Karolinska
                  Institute Library and Information Center] [Sweden] [Information
                  service or system] (IID)
KIBL .... Beeville, TX [AM radio station call letters]
KIBN .... Wichita, KS [FM radio station call letters]
KIBO .... Knowledge In, Bullshit Out (SAUO)
KIBR-FM ...... Sandpoint, ID [FM radio station call letters] (BROA)
KIBS .... Bishop, CA [FM radio station call letters]

KIBZ	Lincoln, NE [*FM radio station call letters*]
KIC	Kansas Information Circuit [*Library network*]
KIC	Karlsruhe Isochronous Cyclotron
KIC	Kart Industry Council
KIC	Kellogg International Corporation (SAUO)
KIC	Kenya Indian Congress (SAUO)
KIC	Kernal Input Controller [*Computer science*] (CIST)
KIC	Ketoisocaproate [*Biochemistry*]
KIC	Keto Isocaproic Acid (DMAA)
KIC	King City, CA [*Location identifier*] [*FAA*] (FAAL)
KIC	Knight of the Iron Crown [*British*] (ROG)
KIC	Kollsman Instrument Corporation (SAUO)
KIC	Kosan Boka [*Ivory Coast*] [*Seismograph station code, US Geological Survey*] (SEIS)
KIC	Kurdistan Information Centre (BUAC)
KIC	Kuwait Insurance Co. (BUAC)
KICA	Clovis, NM [*AM radio station call letters*]
KICA	Farwell, TX [*FM radio station call letters*]
KICAX	Kemper Inc. Cap. Pres. Cl.A [*Mutual fund ticker symbol*] (SG)
KICB	Fort Dodge, IA [*FM radio station call letters*]
KICB	Killed Intracellular Bacteria [*Microbiology*] (DAVI)
KICD	Spencer, IA [*AM radio station call letters*]
KICD-FM	Spencer, IA [*FM radio station call letters*]
KICE	Bend, OR [*FM radio station call letters*]
KICF	Kentucky Independent College Foundation (SAUO)
KICI	Corsicana, TX [*FM radio station call letters*] (RBYB)
KICI	Denton, TX [*AM radio station call letters*] (RBYB)
KICK	Master Glaziers Karate Intl. [*NASDAQ symbol*] (SAG)
KICK	Palmyra, MO [*FM radio station call letters*]
KICKW	Master Glaziers Karate Wrrt'A' [*NASDAQ symbol*] (TTSB)
KICKZ	Master Glaziers Karate Wrrt'B' [*NASDAQ symbol*] (TTSB)
KICM	Healdton, OK [*FM radio station call letters*]
KICN	Idaho Falls, ID [*AM radio station call letters*]
KICO	Calexico, CA [*AM radio station call letters*]
KICR	Oakdale, LA [*AM radio station call letters*]
KICR-FM	Oakdale, LA [*FM radio station call letters*]
KICS	Hastings, NE [*AM radio station call letters*]
KICS	Kansas Individualized Curriculum Sequencing (EDAC)
KICT	Wichita, KS [*FM radio station call letters*]
KICT	Wichita/Mid-Continent [*Kansas*] [*ICAO location identifier*] (ICLI)
KICU	Keyboard Interface Control Unit [*Computer science*]
KICU	San Jose, CA [*Television station call letters*]
KICX	McCook, NE [*FM radio station call letters*]
KICY	Nome, AK [*AM radio station call letters*]
KICY-FM	Nome, AK [*FM radio station call letters*]
KID	Idaho Falls, ID [*AM radio station call letters*]
KID	Kent Infant Development Scale (EDAC)
KID	Keratitis, Ichthyosis, and Deafness Syndrome [*Medicine*] (DMAA)
KID	Keyboard Input Device (MCD)
KID	Key Industry [*Business term*] (DS)
KID	Khmer Institute of Democracy [*Phnom Penh, Cambodia*]
KID	Kiddie
KID	Kidd Resources Ltd. [*Vancouver Stock Exchange symbol*]
Kid	Kiddushin (BJA)
KID	Kidnaping [*FBI standardized term*]
KID	Kidney [*Anatomy*] (DAVI)
KID	Kildare [*County in Ireland*] (ROG)
KID	Kinase-Inducible Domain [*Biochemistry*]
KID	Kristianstad [*Sweden*] [*Airport symbol*] (OAG)
KIDA	Ida Grove, IA [*FM radio station call letters*]
KIDA	Korea Institute for Defence Analyses (SAUO)
KIDA	Korean International Development Agency (BUAC)
KidAInt	Kiddie Academy International, Inc. [*Associated Press*] (SAG)
KIDC	Kentucky Industrial Development Council (SRA)
KIDC	Kiowa Industrial Development Commission
KIDD	First Yars Inc. (The) [*NASDAQ symbol*] (SAG)
KIDD	First Years [*NASDAQ symbol*] (TTSB)
KIDD	Kiddie Products, Inc. [*NASDAQ symbol*] (NQ)
KIDD	Monterey, CA [*AM radio station call letters*]
KiddAcInt	Kiddie Academy International, Inc. [*Associated Press*] (SAG)
KIDDCOS	Kitchens Design Drawing and Costing [*Kitchens International DMS Electronics Ltd.*] [*Software package*] (NCC)
KIDE	4 Kids Entertainment [*NASDAQ symbol*] (TTSB)
KIDE	For Kids Entertainment, Inc. [*NASDAQ symbol*] (SAG)
KIDE	Hoopa, CA [*FM radio station call letters*]
Kideo	Kideo Productions [*Associated Press*] (SAG)
KID-FM	Idaho Falls, ID [*FM radio station call letters*]
KIDH	Eagle, ID [*AM radio station call letters*]
KIDI	Guadalupe, CA [*FM radio station call letters*]
KIDK	Idaho Falls, ID [*Television station call letters*]
KIDN	Hayden, CO [*FM radio station call letters*]
KIDO	Boise, ID [*AM radio station call letters*]
KIDO	Kideo Productions [*NASDAQ symbol*] (SAG)
KIDQ	New Horizon Kids Quest [*NASDAQ symbol*] (TTSB)
KIDQ	New Horizon Kids Quest, Inc. [*NASDAQ symbol*] (SAG)
KIDR	Phoenix, AZ [*AM radio station call letters*]
KIDS	Children's Comprehensive Services [*NASDAQ symbol*] (SAG)
KIDS	Children's Comp Svcs [*NASDAQ symbol*] (TTSB)
KIDS	Kent Infant Development Scale [*Neonatology*] (DAVI)
KIDS	Kestrel Interactive Development System [*Computer science*]
KIDS	Kids in Integrated Day Care Settings (MELL)
KIDS	Kindergarten Inventory of Developmental Skills [*Child development test*]
KIDS	Knowledge-Based Integrated Design System (DOMA)
KIDS	Magic Years Child Care & Learning Centers, Inc. (SAUO)
KIDS	Springfield, MO [*AM radio station call letters*]
Kidult	Kid-Adult [*Television viewer aged 12-34*]
KIDWE	Direct Connect Intl Wrrt [*NASDAQ symbol*] (TTSB)
KIDX	Billings, MT [*FM radio station call letters*]
KIDY	San Angelo, TX [*Television station call letters*]
KIDZ	Direct Connection International, Inc. (SAUO)
KIE	Kenia Industrial Estates Limited (SAUO)
KIE	Kennedy Institute of Ethics, Washington, DC [*OCLC symbol*] (OCLC)
KIE	Kieta [*Papua New Guinea*] [*Airport symbol*] (OAG)
KIE	Kinetic Isotope Effect [*Physical chemistry*]
KIE	Kirklees Information Exchange [*Formerly, Huddersfield and District Information*] (NITA)
KIE	Kodak Image Enhancement
KIEE	Knoxville International Energy Exposition [*1982*]
KIEE	Korean Institute of Electrical Engineers
KI-EF	Kiwanis International - European Federation [*An association*]
KIEI	Kundu Introversion-Extraversion Inventory [*Personality development test*] [*Psychology*]
KIEM	Eureka, CA [*Television station call letters*]
KIEMP	Kenya Industrial Energy Management Program (BUAC)
KIER	Korea Institute of Energy and Resources (BUAC)
KIESEC	Korea International Exchange Society for Education and Culture (SAUO)
KIET	Korea Institute for Economics and Technology (BUAC)
KIET	Korea Institute for Industrial Economics and Technology (SAUO)
KIET	Korea Institute for Industrial Economics and Trade (ECON)
KIEV	Glendale, CA [*AM radio station call letters*]
KIEZ	Carmel Valley, CA [*AM radio station call letters*]
KIF	Key Index File [*Computer science*] (VLIE)
KIF	Kiwanis International Foundation [*An association*]
KIF	Knitting Industries Federation (BUAC)
KIF	Knitting Industries Foundation [*British*] (DBA)
KIF	Knowledge Interchange Format [*Computer science*]
KIF	Kodak Industrial Film
KIF	Korean Investment Fund [*NYSE symbol*] (SAG)
KIF	Name and Address Key Index File [*IRS*]
Kif Aus	Kiffa Australis [*Constellation*] (WDAA)
Kif Bor	Kiffa Borealis [*Constellation*] (WDAA)
KIFG	Iowa Falls, IA [*AM radio station call letters*]
KIFG-FM	Iowa Falls, IA [*FM radio station call letters*]
KIFI	Idaho Falls, ID [*Television station call letters*]
KIFIS	Kollsman Integrated Flight Instrumentation System [*Aviation*]
KIFM	San Diego, CA [*FM radio station call letters*]
KIFO	Pearl City, HI [*AM radio station call letters*]
KIFP	Korean Institute for Family Planning (BUAC)
KIFTSG	Kiftsgate [*England*]
KIFV	Korean Infantry Fighting Vehicle (SAUS)
KIFW	Sitka, AK [*AM radio station call letters*]
KIFX	Roosevelt, UT [*FM radio station call letters*]
KIG	Koingnaas [*South Africa*] [*Airport symbol*] (OAG)
KIGAM	Korean Institute of Geology, Mining and Minerals (SAUO)
KIGC	Oskaloosa, IA [*FM radio station call letters*]
KIGL	Spencer, IA [*FM radio station call letters*]
KIGN-FM	Cheyenne, WY [*FM radio station call letters*] (RBYB)
KIGO	St. Anthony, ID [*AM radio station call letters*]
KIGS	Hanford, CA [*AM radio station call letters*]
KIH	Coast Independent Hi-Tech [*Vancouver Stock Exchange symbol*]
KIH	Kaisar-I-Hind [*Indian medal*]
KIH	Kilometres in the Hour [*Rate of march*] [*Military*] [*British*]
KIH	Kish Island [*Iran*] [*Airport symbol*] (OAG)
KIHA	Kodiak Island Housing Authority (SAUO)
KIHASA	Korea Institute for Health and Social Affairs (BUAC)
KIHK-FM	Rock Valley, IA [*FM radio station call letters*] (BROA)
KIHM-AM	Sun Valley, NV [*AM radio station call letters*] (BROA)
KIHN	Hugo, OK [*AM radio station call letters*]
KIHR	Hood River, OR [*AM radio station call letters*]
KIHR	Korean Institute for Human Rights (EA)
KIHT	St. Louis, MO [*FM radio station call letters*]
K-II	Karyovirus-II (ECON)
KII	Keystone International, Inc. [*NYSE symbol*] (SPSG)
KII	Kuder Interest Inventory [*Occupational information*] (OICC)
KIIC	Kuwait International Investment Company (SAUO)
KIIC-FM	Lamoni, IA [*FM radio station call letters*] (BROA)
KIII	Corpus Christi, TX [*Television station call letters*]
K-III	K-III Communications Corp. [*Associated Press*] (SAG)
KIIK	Fairfield, IA [*FM radio station call letters*]
KIIM	Tucson, AZ [*FM radio station call letters*]
KIIN	Iowa City, IA [*Television station call letters*]
KIIS	Keller Industries Ltd. (SAUO)
KIIS	Korean Institute of International Studies
KIIS	Los Angeles, CA [*AM radio station call letters*]
KIIS-FM	Los Angeles, CA [*FM radio station call letters*]
KIIX	Wellington, CO [*AM radio station call letters*]
KIIZ	Killeen, TX [*FM radio station call letters*]
KIJ	Independence Community Junior College, Independence, KS [*Library symbol*] [*Library of Congress*] (LCLS)
KIJ	Kawah Idjen [*Java*] [*Seismograph station code, US Geological Survey*] [*Closed*] (SEIS)
KIJ	Niigata [*Japan*] [*Airport symbol*] (OAG)
KIJK	Prineville, OR [*FM radio station call letters*]
KIJN	Farwell, TX [*AM radio station call letters*]
KIJN-FM	Farwell, TX [*FM radio station call letters*]
KIJV	Huron, SD [*AM radio station call letters*]
KIK	Kentucky's Individualized Kindergartens (EDAC)
kik	Kikuyu [*MARC language code*] [*Library of Congress*] (LCCP)

KIK............. Kirkuk [Iraq] [Airport symbol] (AD)
KIK............. Kozawa, Iwatsuru, and Kawaguchi [Factor involving injection of cancerous gastric juices into rabbits, named for its discoverers] [Medicine]
KIK............. Kuwait Intertiational Investment Co. (SAUO)
KIKC........... Forsyth, MT [AM radio station call letters]
KIKC-FM...... Forsyth, MT [FM radio station call letters]
KIKD-FM...... Lake City, IA [FM radio station call letters] (BROA)
KIKF........... Garden Grove, CA [FM radio station call letters]
KIKI............ Honolulu, HI [AM radio station call letters]
KIKI-FM....... Honolulu, HI [FM radio station call letters]
KIKK........... Pasadena, TX [AM radio station call letters]
KIKK-FM...... Houston, TX [FM radio station call letters]
KIKM........... Sherman, TX [FM radio station call letters]
KIKN........... Port Angeles, WA [AM radio station call letters] (BROA)
KIKN........... Salem, SD [FM radio station call letters]
KIKO........... Claypool, AZ [FM radio station call letters]
KIKO........... Miami, AZ [AM radio station call letters]
KIKR........... Asbury, IA [FM radio station call letters]
KIKS........... Iola, KS [FM radio station call letters]
KIKT........... Greenville, TX [FM radio station call letters]
KIKU........... Honolulu, HI [Television station call letters]
KIKV........... Alexandria, MN [FM radio station call letters]
KIKX........... Manitou Springs, CO [FM radio station call letters]
KIKX-FM...... Ketchum, ID [FM radio station call letters] (BROA)
KIKY........... Hutto, TX [FM radio station call letters] (RBYB)
KIKY-FM...... Hutto, TX [FM radio station call letters] (RBYB)
KIKZ........... Seminole, TX [AM radio station call letters]
KIL............. Keyed Input Language
KIL............. Keystone Intl [NYSE symbol] (TTSB)
Kil............. Kil'aim (BJA)
KIL............. Kilderkin [Unit of measurement] [British] (ROG)
KIL............. Kilembe Resources Ltd. [Vancouver Stock Exchange symbol]
KIL............. Kilogram
KIL............. Kilometer
KIL............. Krypton Ion LASER
KILA........... Las Vegas, NV [FM radio station call letters]
Kilamco...... Kilwa Ammonia Co. [Tanzania] (BUAC)
Kilb........... Kilburn's English Magistrates' Cases [A publication] (DLA)
KILD........... Kildare [County in Ireland] (ROG)
KILD........... Kilderkin [Unit of measurement] [British]
KILE........... Bellaire, TX [AM radio station call letters] (BROA)
KILE........... Kile Technology Corp. (SAUO)
KILE-AM...... Port Lavaca, TX [FM radio station call letters] (RBYB)
Kilern....... Killearn Properties, Inc. [Associated Press] (SAG)
KILG........... Wilmington/Greater Wilmington [Delaware] [ICAO location identifier] (ICLI)
KILJ........... Mount Pleasant, IA [AM radio station call letters]
KILJ-FM...... Mount Pleasant, IA [FM radio station call letters]
KILK........... Kilkenny [County in Ireland]
Kilk.......... Kilkerran's Scotch Court of Session Decisions [A publication] (DLA)
Kilkerran...... Kilkerran's Scotch Court of Session Decisions [A publication] (DLA)
kill........... Kilowatt (NAKS)
KILLS......... Ka-Inertial Launch and Leave System
KILM........... Wilmington/New Hannover County [North Carolina] [ICAO location identifier] (ICLI)
KILN........... Kirlin Holding [NASDAQ symbol] (TTSB)
KILN........... Kirlin Holding Corp. [NASDAQ symbol] (SAG)
KILO........... Colorado Springs, CO [FM radio station call letters]
kilo.......... Kilogram (ADWA)
KILO........... Kilogram
KILO........... Kilometer
KILOBAUD ... One Thousand Bits per Second (AGLO)
KILOL......... Kiloliter
KILOM......... Kilometer
KILOPAC...... Thousand Packages (SAUS)
KILOPACS... Thousand Package Switchings (SAUS)
kilovar...... Kilovolt-Ampere Reactive Hour (BARN)
KILR........... Estherville, IA [AM radio station call letters]
KILR-FM...... Estherville, IA [FM radio station call letters]
KILS........... Minneapolis, KS [FM radio station call letters]
KILT........... Houston, TX [AM radio station call letters]
KILT-FM...... Houston, TX [FM radio station call letters]
KILU........... Paauilo, HI [FM radio station call letters] (RBYB)
KIM............. Joint Struggle Committee (SAUS)
KIM............. Kenya Independence Movement (SAUO)
KIM............. Kenya Institute of Management (BUAC)
KIM............. Keyboard Input Matrix [Computer science]
KIM............. Kimberley [South Africa] [Airport symbol] (OAG)
KIM............. Kimberley [South Africa] [Seismograph station code, US Geological Survey] (SEIS)
KIM............. Kimco Realty [NYSE symbol] (SPSG)
KIM............. Kinetic Impact Munition (ACAE)
KIM............. Knowledge-Based Integrated Machine [Computer science]
KIMA........... Yakima, WA [Television station call letters]
KIMB........... Kimball, NE [AM radio station call letters]
KIMB........... Kimbark Oil & Gas Co. (SAUO)
Kimbal....... Kimball International, Inc. [Associated Press] (SAG)
KimbClk...... Kimberly Clark [Associated Press] (SAG)
KIMC........... Kimco Energy Corp. (SAUO)
Kimc.......... Kimco Realty Corp. [Associated Press] (SAG)
Kimco........ Kimco Realty Corp. [Associated Press] (SAG)
KIMCODE..... Kimble Method for Controlled Devacuation
KimEnv...... Kimmins Environmental Services [Associated Press] (SAG)
KIMG........... Key Image Systems Inc. (SAUO)

KIML........... Gillette, WY [AM radio station call letters]
KIMM........... Rapid City, SD [AM radio station call letters]
KIMMA........ Kongres Indian Muslim Malaysia [Malaysia Indian Moslem Congress] [Political party] (PPW)
KIMN .... Fort Collins, CO [FM radio station call letters]
KIMO........... Anchorage, AK [Television station call letters]
KIMO........... Kings Mountain National Military Park
KIMP........... Mount Pleasant, TX [AM radio station call letters]
KIMPrA .... Kimco Rlty 7.75% Sr'A'Dep Pfd [NYSE symbol] (TTSB)
KIMPrB .... Kimco Rlty 8.50% Sr'B'Dep Pfd [NYSE symbol] (TTSB)
KIMPrC .... Kimco Rlty 8.375% Sr'C'Dep [NYSE symbol] (TTSB)
KIMS........... Kennedy Inventory Management System [NASA] (SSD)
KIMS........... Kodak Image Management System (HGAA)
KIMSA .... Kirsten Murine Sarcoma [Virus] [Oncology] (DAVI)
KiMSV .... Kirsten Murine Sarcoma Virus
KIMT........... Mason City, IA [Television station call letters]
KI MUSV...... Kirsten Murine Sarcoma Virus
KIMX........... Laramie, WY [FM radio station call letters]
KIMY........... Watonga, OK [FM radio station call letters]
KIN............. Association of Kinsmen Clubs (EA)
KIN............. Keyboard Input [Computer science] (VLIE)
KIN............. Kinark Corp. [AMEX symbol] (SPSG)
KIN............. Kinescope
kin............. Kinetic (VRA)
Kin............. Kinetics (SAUS)
KIN............. Kingston [Jamaica] [Airport symbol] (OAG)
KIN............. Kingston [Jamaica] [Seismograph station code, US Geological Survey] (SEIS)
Kin............. Kinnim (BJA)
KIN............. Kinross-Shire [Former county in Scotland] (WGA)
kin............. Kinyarwanda [MARC language code] [Library of Congress] (LCCP)
KIN............. K Mart Information Network (EFIS)
KINA........... Salina, KS [AM radio station call letters]
Kinark........ Kinark Corp. [Associated Press] (SAG)
KINC........... Las Vegas, NV [Television station call letters] (RBYB)
KIND........... Independence, KS [AM radio station call letters]
KIND........... Indianapolis/International [Indiana] [ICAO location identifier] (ICLI)
KIND........... Kinder-Care Learning Centers, Inc. (SAUO)
KIND........... Kindergarten (WDAA)
KIND........... Kindness in Nature's Defense [Elementary school course]
KINDERGTN.... Kindergarten
KIND-FM..... Independence, KS [FM radio station call letters]
KINE........... Honolulu, HI [FM radio station call letters]
KINE........... Kinescope
KINE........... Kingsville, TX [AM radio station call letters] (RBYB)
Kinetic....... Kinetic Concepts, Inc. [Associated Press] (SAG)
KINF-AM...... Denton, TX [AM radio station call letters] (RBYB)
KING........... Kinetic Intense Neutron Generator
King............ King's Reports [5, 6 Louisiana] [A publication] (DLA)
King............ Select Cases in Chancery Tempore King, Edited by Macnaghten [1724-33] [England] [A publication] (DLA)
King Cas...... Cases in King's Colorado Civil Practice [A publication] (DLA)
King Cas Temp... Select Cases in Chancery Tempore King [1724-33] [England] [A publication] (DLA)
KINGD......... Kingdom
King Dig ...... King's Tennessee Digest [A publication] (DLA)
KING-DT ..... Seattle, WA [Television station call letters] (BROA)
King-Farlow... Gold Coast Judgments and the Masai Cases, by King-Farlow [1915-17] [Ghana] [A publication] (DLA)
KING-FM...... Seattle, WA [FM radio station call letters]
KINGMAP..... King's Music Analysis Package [King's College] [University of London] [British] (NITA)
Kings .... Kingsway [Record label]
KINGSBR ..... Kingsbridge [England]
King's Con Cs... King's Conflicting Cases [Texas] [A publication] (DLA)
King's Conf Ca... King's Conflicting Cases [Texas] [A publication] (DLA)
KINGTEL ...... Kingston upon Thames Viewdata Service (SAUO)
KING-TV...... Seattle, WA [Television station call letters]
KingWd........ King World Productions [Associated Press] (SAG)
KINI .... Crookston, NE [FM radio station call letters]
KINIT .... Korea Institute of Industry & Technology Information [South Korea] (DDC)
KINK .... Portland, OR [FM radio station call letters]
KINK .... Wink/Winkler County [Texas] [ICAO location identifier] (ICLI)
KINL .... Eagle Pass, TX [FM radio station call letters]
KINL .... International Falls [Minnesota] [ICAO location identifier] (ICLI)
KINN .... Alamogordo, NM [AM radio station call letters]
KINN .... Kinnard Investments [NASDAQ symbol] (TTSB)
KINN .... Kinnard Investments, Inc. [NASDAQ symbol] (NQ)
Kinnard........ Kinnard Investments, Inc. [Associated Press] (SAG)
Kinney Law Dict & Glos... Kinney's Law Dictionary and Glossary [A publication] (DLA)
KINO .... Winslow, AZ [AM radio station call letters]
Kinross........ Kinross Gold Corp. [Associated Press] (SAG)
KINS .... Eureka, CA [AM radio station call letters]
KINS .... Indian Springs/Indian Springs Army Air Field [Nevada] [ICAO location identifier] (ICLI)
KINSA .... Kodak International Newspaper Snapshot Awards
KINSYM ...... Kinematic Synthesis (PDAA)
KINT .... El Paso, TX [Television station call letters]
KINT .... Koninklijk Instituut voor het duurzame beheer van de Natuurlijke rijkdommen en de bevordering van schone Technologie (SAUO)
KINT .... Winston Salem/Smith-Reynolds [North Carolina] [ICAO location identifier] (ICLI)
KINTB .... Kintbury [England]

KINT-FM	El Paso, TX [*FM radio station call letters*]
KINV	Kentucky Investors Inc. (SAUO)
KINY	Juneau, AK [*AM radio station call letters*]
KINY	Kinney System Inc. (SAUO)
KINZ-FM	Humboldt, KS [*FM radio station call letters*] (BROA)
KINZ-TV	Arlington, TX [*TV station call letters*] (RBYB)
KIo	Iola Free Public Library, Iola, KS [*Library symbol*] [*Library of Congress*] (LCLS)
KIO	Kachin Independence Organization [*Myanmar*] [*Political party*] (EY)
KIO	Kenya Information Office (BUAC)
KIO	Kick It Off [*Slang*] (DOMA)
KIO	Kili [*Marshall Islands*] [*Airport symbol*] (OAG)
KIO	Kraiaero [*Russian Federation*] [*ICAO designator*] (FAAC)
KIO	Kuwait Investment Office (BUAC)
KIOA	Des Moines, IA [*AM radio station call letters*]
KIOA-FM	Des Moines, IA [*FM radio station call letters*]
KIOC	Orange, TX [*FM radio station call letters*]
KIOD-FM	McCook, NE [*FM radio station call letters*] (BROA)
KIOI	San Francisco, CA [*FM radio station call letters*]
KIOK	Richland, WA [*FM radio station call letters*]
KIOL	Lamesa, TX [*FM radio station call letters*]
KION	Monterey, CA [*Television station call letters*] (BROA)
KIOO	Porterville, CA [*FM radio station call letters*]
KIOPI	Kienzle Input/Output Peripheral Interface
KIOPI	Kienzle Input/Output Processor Interface (NITA)
KIOQ	Folsom, CA [*AM radio station call letters*]
KIOS	Omaha, NE [*FM radio station call letters*]
KIoS	Southeast Kansas Library System, Iola, KS [*Library symbol*] [*Library of Congress*] (LCLS)
KIOT	Los Lunas [*FM radio station call letters*]
KIOU	Shreveport, LA [*AM radio station call letters*]
KIOV	Payette, ID [*AM radio station call letters*]
KIOW	Forest City, IA [*FM radio station call letters*]
KIOX	El Campo, TX [*FM radio station call letters*]
KIOZ	Oceanside, CA [*FM radio station call letters*]
KIP	Keep Alone if Possible [*Travel industry*] (TRID)
KIP	Keyboard Input Processor [*Computer science*] (NASA)
KIP	Key Indigenous Personnel (MCD)
KIP	Key Intelligence Position (AFM)
KIP	Key Intermediary Proteins (DAVI)
KIP	Kilopound (IAA)
KIP	Kipapa [*Hawaii*] [*Seismograph station code, US Geological Survey*] (SEIS)
KIP	Kit, Individual Protection [*British army*] (INF)
KIP	Knowledge Industry Publications, Inc. [*Telecommunications*]
KIP	Knowledge Information Processing [*Computer science*]
KIP	Korean Industry Participation (SAUS)
KIP	Thousand Pounds
KIPA	Hilo, HI [*AM radio station call letters*]
KIP-FT	Thousand Foot-Pounds
KIPI	Knowledge Industry Publications, Inc. [*White Plains, NY*] [*Telecommunications*] [*Information service or system*]
KIPIC	Kuwait International Petroleum Investment Co. (BUAC)
KIPL	Imperial/Imperial County [*California*] [*ICAO location identifier*] (ICLI)
Kiplinger	Kiplinger's Personal Finance Magazine [*A publication*] (BRI)
KIPO	Honolulu, HI [*FM radio station call letters*]
KIPO	Keyboard Input Printout [*Computer science*] (IEEE)
KIPR	Pine Bluff, AR [*FM radio station call letters*]
KIPS	10³ (K) of Instructions Per Second [*Unit of computer processing speed*] (NITA)
KIPS	Kaufman Infant and Preschool Scale [*Child development test*] [*Psychology*]
KIPS	Key Indicators, Probes, and a Scoring Method [*Health care*] (HCT)
KIPS	Kilo-Instructions per Second
KIPS	Kilowatt Isotope Power System (IEEE)
KIPS	Knowledge Information Processing Systems [*Computer science*]
KIPT	Kharkov Institute for Science and Technology (SAUO)
KIPT	Twin Falls, ID [*Television station call letters*]
KIQ	Key Intelligence Question [*CIA*]
KIQ	Key Intelligence Requirement [*Military*] (MUSM)
KIQ	Kira [*Papua New Guinea*] [*Airport symbol*] (OAG)
KIQI	San Francisco, CA [*AM radio station call letters*]
KIQK	Rapid City, SD [*FM radio station call letters*]
KIQN	Tooele, UT [*AM radio station call letters*] (BROA)
KIQO	Atascadero, CA [*FM radio station call letters*]
KIQQ	Barstow, CA [*AM radio station call letters*]
KIQS	Willows, CA [*AM radio station call letters*]
KIQX	Durango, CO [*FM radio station call letters*]
KIQZ	Rawlins, WY [*FM radio station call letters*]
KIR	Key Intelligence Requirement (MCD)
KIR	Killer-Cell Inhibitory Receptor [*Immunology*]
Kir	Kirby's Connecticut Reports and Supplement [*1785-89*] [*A publication*] (DLA)
kir	Kirghiz [*MARC language code*] [*Library of Congress*] (LCCP)
KIR	Kiruna [*Sweden*] [*Seismograph station code, US Geological Survey*] (SEIS)
KIR	Knight's Industrial Reports [*A publication*] (DLA)
KIR	Kyocera Image Refinement (SAUS)
Kirb	Kirby's Connecticut Reports and Supplement [*1785-89*] [*A publication*] (DLA)
KIRBS	Korean Institute for Research in the Behavioral Sciences
Kirby	Kirby Exploration Co., Inc. [*Associated Press*] (SAG)
Kirby	Kirby's Connecticut Reports and Supplement [*1785-89*] [*A publication*] (DLA)
Kirby's Conn R	Kirby's Connecticut Reports [*A publication*] (DLA)

Kirby's R	Kirby's Connecticut Reports [*A publication*] (DLA)
Kirby's Rep	Kirby's Connecticut Reports [*A publication*] (DLA)
KIRC	Seminole, OK [*FM radio station call letters*]
KIRDI	Kenya Industrial Research and Development Institute (BUAC)
KirinBr	Kirin Brewery Co. Ltd. [*Associated Press*] (SAG)
KIRIS	Kentucky Instructional Results Information System
KIRK	Kirkcaldy [*Seaport in Scotland*]
KIRK	Lebanon, MO [*FM radio station call letters*]
KIRK-AM	Bethany, MO [*AM radio station call letters*] (BROA)
KIRKCUDB	Kirkcudbrightshire [*County in Scotland*]
KIRL	St. Charles, MO [*AM radio station call letters*]
Kirlin	Kirlin Holding Corp. [*Associated Press*] (SAG)
KIRO	Seattle, WA [*AM radio station call letters*]
KIRO-DT	Seattle, WA [*Television station call letters*] (BROA)
KIRO-FM	Seattle, WA [*FM radio station call letters*]
KIRO-TV	Seattle, WA [*Television station call letters*]
KIRP	Kodak Infrared Phosphor
KIRQ	Lawton, OK [*FM radio station call letters*] (RBYB)
KIRS	Kodak Infrared Scope
KIRS	Sun Valley, NV [*AM radio station call letters*] (RBYB)
KirSeph	Kirjath Sepher [*Jerusalem*] (BJA)
KirSSR	Kirghiz Soviet Socialist Republic
KIRT	Mission, TX [*AM radio station call letters*] (BUAC)
KIRTAK	Kirghiz Telegraph Agency, Frunze (BUAC)
Kirt Sur Pr	Kirtland on Practice in Surrogates' Courts [*A publication*] (DLA)
KIRV	Fresno, CA [*AM radio station call letters*]
KIRX	Kirksville, MO [*AM radio station call letters*]
KIS	Contactair Flugdienst & Co. [*Germany*] [*ICAO designator*] (FAAC)
KIS	Keep it Short (ELAL)
KIS	Keep It Simple (ADA)
KIS	Kenny Information Systems [*Database producer*] (IID)
KIS	Kenya Independent Squadron [*British military*] (DMA)
KIS	Kenya Inspection Service (BUAC)
KIS	Keyboard Input Simulation [*Computer science*]
KIS	Kishinev [*Former USSR*] [*Seismograph station code, US Geological Survey*] (SEIS)
KIS	Kisumu [*Kenya*] [*Airport symbol*] (OAG)
KIS	Kitting Instruction Sheet [*NASA*] (NASA)
KIS	Knowbot Information Service (VLIE)
KIS	Kodak Infrared Scope
KIS	Krankenhaus Information System (DAVI)
KISA	Honolulu, HI [*AM radio station call letters*]
KISA	Karaoke International Sing-Along Association (EA)
KISA	Korean International Steel Associates (BUAC)
KISA	Korean International Steel Association (SAUO)
KISA	Voluntary International Service Assignments [*of the Society of Friends*]
Kisb Ir Land L	Kisbey on the Irish Land Law [*A publication*] (DLA)
KISC	Kimmins Corporation (SAUO)
KISC	Knowledge Industry Systems Concept [*Publishing and education*] [*Pronounced "kiss"*]
KISC	Knowledge Information Skills and Curriculum [*Project*] (AIE)
KISC	Spokane, WA [*FM radio station call letters*]
KISD	Pipestone, MN [*FM radio station call letters*]
KISE-FM	Seaside, CA [*FM radio station call letters*] (RBYB)
KISEH	Kent Incorporated Society for Experiments in Horticulture (SAUO)
KISF	Lexington, MO [*FM radio station call letters*]
KISF-FM	Las Vegas, NV [*FM radio station call letters*] (BROA)
KISI	Malvern, AR [*FM radio station call letters*]
KISK-FM	Shasta Lake City, CA [*FM radio station call letters*] (BROA)
KISL	Avalon, CA [*FM radio station call letters*]
KISM-FM	Bellingham, WA [*FM radio station call letters*] (RBYB)
KISMIF	Keep It Simple, Make It Fun
KISN	Salt Lake City, UT [*AM radio station call letters*]
KISN	Williston/International [*North Dakota*] [*ICAO location identifier*] (ICLI)
KISN-FM	Salt Lake City, UT [*FM radio station call letters*]
KISNOPI	Keyboard Input Stimulation Noise Problem Input (IAA)
KISO	Kol Israel Symphony Orchestra (SAUO)
KISO	Phoenix, AZ [*AM radio station call letters*]
KISP	Blair, NE [*FM radio station call letters*]
KISP	Islip/MacArthur Field [*New York*] [*ICAO location identifier*] (ICLI)
KISQ-FM	San Francisco, CA [*FM radio station call letters*] (BROA)
KISR	Fort Smith, AR [*FM radio station call letters*]
KISR	Kuwait Institute for Science Research (SAUO)
KISR	Kuwait Institute for Scientific Research (BUAC)
KISS	Kanton Island Sounding System (SAUS)
KISS	Keep It Safe and Simple (VLIE)
KISS	Keep It Short and Simple (MCD)
KISS	Keep It Short and Sweet [*Radio messages*]
KISS	Keep It Simple, Sir (SAA)
KISS	Keep It Simple, Stupid [*Bridge bidding term*]
KISS	Keep It Straight and Simple [*Computer science*]
KISS	Keyed Indexed Sequential Search
KISS	Key Integrative Social Systems
KISS	Knights in the Service of Satan [*Rock music group*]
KISS	Knowledge-Based Interactive Signal Monitoring System (SAUO)
KISS	Knowledge Integrating Simulation System
KISS	Korean Information Science Society (SAUO)
KISS	Korean Intelligence Support System (DOMA)
KISS	San Antonio, TX [*FM radio station call letters*]
KISS	Saturated Solution of Potassium Iodide [*Pharmacology*] (DAVI)
KI SSR	Kirgiz Soviet Socialist Republic (SAUO)
KIST	Keyword Index to Serial Titles [*A publication*]
KIST	Korean Institute for Science and Technology
KIST	Santa Barbara, CA [*AM radio station call letters*]

KIST-FM ...... Santa Barbara, CA [*FM radio station call letters*] (BROA)
KISU .... Pocatello, ID [*Television station call letters*]
KISU-FM ...... Pocatello, ID [*FM radio station call letters*] (BROA)
KiSV .... Kirsten Sarcoma Virus
KISV-FM ...... Bakersfield, CA [*FM radio station call letters*] (BROA)
KISW .... Seattle, WA [*FM radio station call letters*]
KISX .... Whitehouse, TX [*FM radio station call letters*]
KISZ .... Cortez, CO [*FM radio station call letters*]
KISZ .... Kommunista Ifjusagi Szovetseg [*Communist Youth Organization*] [*Hungary*]
KISZAR .... Japanese Journal of Parasitology (journ.) (SAUS)
KIT .... Kahn Intelligence Test (DMAA)
KIT .... KAPSE Interface Team (SAUO)
KIT .... Kaufman Ion Thrustor
KIT .... Keep in Touch [*Slang*] (DNAB)
KIT .... Kent Information Technology Conference (NITA)
KIT .... Kentucky & Indiana Terminal Railroad Co. [*AAR code*]
KIT .... Kermit [*Texas*] [*Seismograph station code, US Geological Survey*] (SEIS)
KIT .... Key Intelligence Topic (AAEL)
KIT .... Key Issue Tracking [*Database*]
KIT .... Kitchen (ADA)
kit .... Kitchen (ADWA)
Kit .... Kitchin's Retourna Brevium [*4 eds.*] [*1581-92*] [*A publication*] (DLA)
KIT .... Kithira [*Greece*] [*Airport symbol*] (OAG)
KIT .... Kit Manufacturing Co. [*AMEX symbol*] (SPSG)
KIT .... Kit Mfg [*AMEX symbol*] (TTSB)
KIT .... Kittrell Junior College, Kittrell, NC [*Inactive*] [*OCLC symbol*] (OCLC)
KIT .... Knowledge-based Information Tutorial (SAUO)
KIT .... Korean International Telecommunications (SAUO)
KIT .... KWIC Interactive Tagger [*University of Minnesota*] [*Text editing system*] (NITA)
KIT .... Yakima, WA [*AM radio station call letters*]
KITA .... Kesatuan Insaf Tanah Air [*National Consciousness Party*] [*Malaysia*] [*Political party*] (PPW)
KITA .... Kick in the Afterdeck [*Bowdlerized version*]
KITA .... Little Rock, AR [*AM radio station call letters*]
KITC .... Kentucky-Indiana-Tennessee Conference (PSS)
kitch .... Kitchen (BARN)
Kitch .... Kitchin on Jurisdictions of Courts-Leet, Courts-Baron, Etc. [*A publication*] (DLA)
Kitch Courts... Kitchin on Jurisdictions of Courts-Leet, Courts-Baron, Etc. [*A publication*] (DLA)
Kitch Cts ...... Kitchin on Courts [*A publication*] (DLA)
Kitchen .... Griqualand West Reports [*Cape Colony, South Africa*] [*A publication*] (DLA)
KITCO .... Kenala Industry and Technical Consultancy Organisation [*India*] (BUAC)
KITCO .... Kerala Industry and Technical Consultancy Organization (SAUO)
Kit Ct .... Kitchin on Jurisdictions of Courts-Leet, Courts-Baron, Etc. [*A publication*] (DLA)
KITE .... Kerrville, TX [*FM radio station call letters*]
KITE .... Kinetic energy kill vehicle Integrated Technology Experiments (SAUS)
KITE .... Kinetic Energy Weapon Integrated Test Experiment (MCD)
KITE .... Kinetic Isolation Tether Experiment (SAUS)
KITE .... Kuiper Infrared Technology Experiment (ACAE)
KITES .... Kinescope Image Test and Evaluation System (MCD)
KITG .... Kiting (ABBR)
KITI .... Centralia-Chehalis, WA [*AM radio station call letters*]
KITI .... Winlock, WA [*FM radio station call letters*] (RBYB)
KITIA .... KAPSE Interface Team for Industry and Academia (SAUO)
Kit Jur .... Kitchin on Jurisdictions of Courts-Leet, Courts-Baron, Etc. [*A publication*] (DLA)
KITK .... Kit Karson Corp. (SAUO)
KITL .... King International Corp. (SAUO)
KITLV .... Royal Institute of Linguistics and Anthropology (SAUO)
Kit Mfg .... Kit Manufacturing Co. [*Associated Press*] (SAG)
KITN .... Kitten (ABBR)
KITN .... Worthington, MN [*FM radio station call letters*] (RBYB)
KITO .... Vinita, OK [*AM radio station call letters*]
KITO-FM ...... Vinita, OK [*FM radio station call letters*]
KITR .... Creston, IA [*FM radio station call letters*]
Kit Rd Trans... Kitchin's Road Transport Law [*19th ed.*] [*1978*] [*A publication*] (DLA)
KITS .... Campus Instructional Television System (SAUS)
KITS .... Meridian Diagnostics [*NASDAQ symbol*] (TTSB)
KITS .... Meridian Diagnostics, Inc. (SAUO)
KITS .... San Francisco, CA [*FM radio station call letters*]
KITT .... Kinetic Tree Theory (PDAA)
KITT .... Knight Industries Two Thousand [*Acronym is name of computerized car in TV series "Knight Rider"*]
KITT .... Korean International Telephone & Telegraph
KITT .... Shreveport, LA [*FM radio station call letters*]
KITTY .... Kentucky-Illinois-Tennessee League [*Old baseball league*]
KittyHk .... Kitty Hawk, Inc. [*Associated Press*] (SAG)
KITU .... Beaumont, TX [*Television station call letters*]
KITV .... Honolulu, HI [*Television station call letters*]
KITV-DT ...... Honolulu, HI [*Television station call letters*] (BROA)
KITX .... Hugo, OK [*FM radio station call letters*]
KITZ .... Silverdale, WA [*AM radio station call letters*]
KIU .... Kainantu [*New Guinea*] [*Airport symbol*] (AD)
KIU .... Kallikrein Inactivator Unit [*Analytical biochemistry*]
KIU .... Kallikrein-Inhibiting Unit [*Analytical biochemistry*] (DAVI)
KIU .... Krein Inactivator Unit (DB)
KIUL .... Garden City, KS [*AM radio station call letters*]
KIUN .... Pecos, TX [*AM radio station call letters*]
KIUP .... Durango, CO [*AM radio station call letters*]
K-IUSM .... KSC IUS Plan (or Requirement) (SAUS)
K-IUSN .... KSC IUS Notice (SAUS)
K-IUSPS ...... KSC IUS Project Specification (SAUS)
KIV .... Air Kiev [*Ukraine*] [*FAA designator*] (FAAC)
KIV .... Kali Venture Corp. [*Vancouver Stock Exchange symbol*]
KIV .... Keep in View
KIV .... Ketoisovalerate [*Biochemistry*]
KIV .... Kiev [*Former USSR*] [*Geomagnetic observatory code*]
KIV .... Kishinev [*Former USSR*] [*Airport symbol*] (OAG)
KIVA .... Corrales, NM [*AM radio station call letters*]
Kiva .... Kiva. University of Arizona. Arizona Archaeological and Historical Society. Arizona State Museum. Tucson (SAUO)
KIVA .... Workgroup for Indians of North America [*Acronym is based on foreign phrase*] [*Netherlands*]
KIVI .... Koninklijk Instituut van Inginieurs [*Netherlands*] (ACII)
KIVI .... Nampa, ID [*Television station call letters*]
KIvI .... Royal Institution of Engineers in the Netherlands (SAUO)
KIVV .... Lead, SD [*Television station call letters*]
KIVY .... Crockett, TX [*AM radio station call letters*]
KIVY-FM ...... Crockett, TX [*FM radio station call letters*]
KIW .... Kitwe [*Zambia*] [*Airport symbol*] (OAG)
KIW .... Royal New Zealand Air Force [*FAA designator*] (FAAC)
KIWA .... Keuringsinstituut voor Waterleidingartikelen
KIWA .... Sheldon, IA [*AM radio station call letters*]
KIWA-FM ..... Sheldon, IA [*FM radio station call letters*]
KIWI .... Bakersfield, CA [*FM radio station call letters*]
KIWI-A .... Nuclear Rocket Propulsion Experiments (SAUO)
KIWR .... Council Bluffs, IA [*FM radio station call letters*]
KIWW .... Harlingen, TX [*FM radio station call letters*]
KIX .... Kerkhoff Industries, Inc. (SAUO)
KIXA .... Lucerne Valley, CA [*FM radio station call letters*]
KIXB .... El Dorado, AR [*FM radio station call letters*]
KIXC .... Quanah, TX [*FM radio station call letters*]
KIXD-FM ...... Oracle, AZ [*FM radio station call letters*] (BROA)
KIXE .... Redding, CA [*Television station call letters*]
KIXF .... Baker, CA [*FM radio station call letters*]
KIXF .... Kodak Industrial X-Ray Film
KIXI .... Mercer Island-Seattle, WA [*AM radio station call letters*]
KIXK .... Canton, SD [*FM radio station call letters*] (RBYB)
KIXK-FM ...... Linden, TX [*FM radio station call letters*] (BROA)
KIXL .... Del Valle, TX [*AM radio station call letters*]
KIXN .... Hobbs, NM [*FM radio station call letters*] (RBYB)
KIXO-FM ...... Sulphur, OK [*FM radio station call letters*] (BROA)
KIXQ .... Webb City, MO [*FM radio station call letters*]
KIXR .... Ponca City, OK [*FM radio station call letters*]
KIXS .... Victoria, TX [*FM radio station call letters*]
KIXT-FM ...... Grover City, CA [*FM radio station call letters*]
KIXV .... Brady, TX [*FM radio station call letters*]
KIXW .... Apple Valley, CA [*AM radio station call letters*] (RBYB)
KIXW .... Lenwood, CA [*FM radio station call letters*]
KIXX .... Watertown, SD [*FM radio station call letters*]
KIXY .... San Angelo, TX [*FM radio station call letters*]
KIXZ .... Amarillo, TX [*AM radio station call letters*]
KIY .... Kilwa [*Tanzania*] [*Airport symbol*] (OAG)
KIY .... Kiyosumi [*Japan*] [*Seismograph station code, US Geological Survey*] [*Closed*] (SEIS)
KIYS .... Jonesboro, AR [*FM radio station call letters*]
KIYU .... Galena, AK [*AM radio station call letters*]
KIYX-FM ...... Sageville, IA [*FM radio station call letters*] (RBYB)
KIZ .... Kanaf-Arkia Airlines Ltd. [*Israel*] [*ICAO designator*] (FAAC)
KIZ .... Kunming Institute of Zoology (BUAC)
KIZN .... Boise, ID [*FM radio station call letters*]
KIZZ .... Minot, ND [*FM radio station call letters*]
KJ .... Air Guyane [*ICAO designator*] (AD)
KJ .... Crescent Air Transport (SAUS)
KJ .... Jamaica [*IYRU nationality code*] (IYR)
KJ .... Karaoke Jockey
kJ .... Kilojoule
KJ .... King James [*Version of the Bible*] (WDAA)
KJ .... Kirchenmusikalisches Jahrbuch [*A publication*]
KJ .... Knee Jerk [*Medicine*]
KJ .... Knight of St. Joachim
KJ .... Knights of Jurisprudence
KJA .... Avistar (Cyprus) Ltd. [*ICAO designator*] (FAAC)
KJAA .... Globe, AZ [*AM radio station call letters*]
KJAB .... Mexico, MO [*FM radio station call letters*]
KJAC .... Port Arthur, TX [*Television station call letters*]
KJAE .... Leesville, LA [*FM radio station call letters*]
KJAK .... Slaton, TX [*FM radio station call letters*]
KJAM .... Madison, SD [*AM radio station call letters*]
KJAM-FM ..... Madison, SD [*FM radio station call letters*]
KJAN .... Atlantic, IA [*AM radio station call letters*]
KJAN .... Jackson/Allen C. Thompson Field [*Mississippi*] [*ICAO location identifier*] (ICLI)
KJAS-FM ...... Jasper, TX [*FM radio station call letters*] (RBYB)
KJAV .... Alamo, TX [*FM radio station call letters*]
KJAX .... Jacksonville/International [*Florida*] [*ICAO location identifier*] (ICLI)
KJAX .... Stockton, CA [*AM radio station call letters*]
KJAY .... Sacramento, CA [*AM radio station call letters*]
KJAZ .... McFarland, CA [*AM radio station call letters*]
KJB .... Kinder- und Jugendlichenberatung (SAUO)
KJB .... Korea-Japan Board (SAUO)
KJBC .... Midland, TX [*AM radio station call letters*]

KJBN — Little Rock, AR [*AM radio station call letters*]
KJBR-FM — Marked Tree, AR [*FM radio station call letters*] (RBYB)
KJBX-FM — Trumann, AR [*FM radio station call letters*] (BROA)
KJBZ — Laredo, TX [*FM radio station call letters*]
KJc — fracture toughness calculated from the J-integral Jc at the point of cleavage (SAUS)
KJC — Jefferson Community College, Louisville, KY [*OCLC symbol*] (OCLC)
KJC — Kaiser Jeep Corporation (SAUO)
KJC — Keystone Junior College [*Pennsylvania*]
KJCB — Lafayette, LA [*AM radio station call letters*]
KJCC — Lake Havasu City, AZ [*FM radio station call letters*]
KJCCC — Kansas Jayhawk Community College Conference (PSS)
KJCE — Rollingwood, TX [*AM radio station call letters*]
KJCF — Festus, MO [*AM radio station call letters*]
KJCK — Junction City, KS [*AM radio station call letters*]
KJCK-FM — Junction City, KS [*FM radio station call letters*]
KJCPL — Koninklijke Java-China-Paketvaart Lijnen
KJCR — Keene, TX [*FM radio station call letters*]
KJCS — Nacogdoches, TX [*FM radio station call letters*]
KJCT — Grand Junction, CO [*Television station call letters*]
KJDJ — San Luis Obispo, CA [*AM radio station call letters*]
KJDX — Susanville, CA [*FM radio station call letters*]
KJDY — John Day, OR [*AM radio station call letters*]
KJDY-FM — Canyon City, OR [*FM radio station call letters*] (RBYB)
KJEE — Montecito, CA [*FM radio station call letters*]
KJEF — Jennings, LA [*AM radio station call letters*]
KJEF-FM — Jennings, LA [*FM radio station call letters*]
KJEL — Lebanon, MO [*AM radio station call letters*]
KJEM — Seligman, MO [*FM radio station call letters*] (RBYB)
KJEO — Fresno, CA [*Television station call letters*]
KJET — Hoquiam, WA [*AM radio station call letters*] (RBYB)
KJEZ — Poplar Bluff, MO [*FM radio station call letters*]
KJF — Kajaani [*Finland*] [*Seismograph station code, US Geological Survey*] (SEIS)
KJF — Karl-Jaspers Foundation (EA)
KJF — Kutta-Joukowski Force
KJFA — Grass Valley, CA [*FM radio station call letters*]
KJFF-AM — Festus, MO [*AM radio station call letters*] (RBYB)
KJFK — New York/John F. Kennedy International [*New York*] [*ICAO location identifier*] (ICLI)
KJFK-FM — Lampasas, TX [*FM radio station call letters*] (BROA)
KJFM — Louisiana, MO [*FM radio station call letters*]
KJFX — Fresno, CA [*FM radio station call letters*]
KJGM — Fredonia, KS [*FM radio station call letters*] (RBYB)
KJHA-FM — Houston, AK [*FM radio station call letters*] (BROA)
KJHK — Lawrence, KS [*FM radio station call letters*]
KJHY — Emmett, ID [*FM radio station call letters*]
KJI — Kay Jewelels Inc. (SAUO)
KJI — Kay Jewelers, Incorporated (SAUO)
KJIB — South Padre Island, TX [*FM radio station call letters*]
KJIL — Copeland, KS [*FM radio station call letters*]
KJIM — Sherman, TX [*AM radio station call letters*]
KJIN — Houma, LA [*AM radio station call letters*]
KJIW — West Helena, AR [*AM radio station call letters*]
KJIW-FM — West Helena, AR [*FM radio station call letters*]
KJJ — Kuhner, J. J., Cleveland OH [*STAC*]
KJJB — Eunice, LA [*FM radio station call letters*]
KJJC — Osceola, IA [*FM radio station call letters*]
KJJJ-FM — Seligman, AZ [*FM radio station call letters*] (RBYB)
KJJK — Fergus Falls, MN [*AM radio station call letters*]
KJJK-FM — Fergus Falls, MN [*FM radio station call letters*]
KJJL-AM — Cheyenne, WY [*AM radio station call letters*] (RBYB)
KJJM-FM — Baker, MT [*FM radio station call letters*] (BROA)
KJJO — St. Louis Park, MN [*AM radio station call letters*]
KJJQ — Volga, SD [*AM radio station call letters*]
KJJR — Whitefish, MT [*AM radio station call letters*]
KJJY — Ankeny, IA [*FM radio station call letters*]
KJJZ — Kodiak, AK [*FM radio station call letters*]
KJJZ-FM — Indio, CA [*FM radio station call letters*] (BROA)
KJKB-FM — Jacksboro, TX [*FM radio station call letters*] (RBYB)
KJKJ — Grand Forks, ND [*FM radio station call letters*]
KJKS — Cameron, TX [*FM radio station call letters*]
KJKT — Joplin, MO [*FM radio station call letters*]
KJL — Kenneth J. Lane [*Jewelry designer*]
KJLA — Ventura, CA [*Television station call letters*] (BROA)
KJLF — El Paso, TX [*Television station call letters*]
KJLH — Compton, CA [*FM radio station call letters*]
KJLO — Monroe, LA [*FM radio station call letters*]
KJLS — Hays, KS [*FM radio station call letters*]
KJLT — North Platte, NE [*AM radio station call letters*]
KJLT-FM — North Platte, NE [*FM radio station call letters*]
KJLU — Jefferson City, MO [*FM radio station call letters*]
KJLY — Blue Earth, MN [*FM radio station call letters*]
KJMB — Blythe, CA [*FM radio station call letters*]
KJME — Denver, CO [*AM radio station call letters*]
KJMH — Burlington, IA [*Television station call letters*]
KJMK-FM — Webb City, MO [*FM radio station call letters*] (BROA)
KJML-FM — Columbus, KS [*FM radio station call letters*] (BROA)
KJMM — Bixby, OK [*FM radio station call letters*]
KJMN-FM — Castle Rock, CO [*FM radio station call letters*] (RBYB)
KJMO — Jefferson City, MO [*FM radio station call letters*]
kJ mol — Kilojoule Mole [*Chemistry*] (MEC)
KJMS — Memphis, TN [*AM radio station call letters*]
KJMX — Tulia, TX [*FM radio station call letters*]
KJMY — Seaside, CA [*FM radio station call letters*] (RBYB)

KJMZ — Henderson, NV [*FM radio station call letters*] (RBYB)
KJMZ-FM — Lawton, OK [*FM radio station call letters*] (RBYB)
KJN — Kajaani [*Finland*] [*Seismograph station code, US Geological Survey*] [*Closed*] (SEIS)
KJNA — Jena, LA [*AM radio station call letters*]
KJNA-FM — Jena, LA [*FM radio station call letters*]
KJNO — Juneau, AK [*AM radio station call letters*]
KJNP — North Pole, AK [*AM radio station call letters*]
KJNP-FM — North Pole, AK [*FM radio station call letters*]
KJNP-TV — North Pole, AK [*Television station call letters*]
KJNT — Hempsted [*New York*] [*ICAO location identifier*] (ICLI)
KJO — Kommunistische Jugend Oesterreich [*Communist Youth of Austria*]
KJOC — Davenport, IA [*AM radio station call letters*]
KJOE — Slayton, MN [*FM radio station call letters*] (RBYB)
KJOI — Dinuba, CA [*FM radio station call letters*]
KJOJ — Conroe, TX [*AM radio station call letters*]
KJOJ-FM — Freeport, TX [*FM radio station call letters*]
KJOK — Yuma, AZ [*FM radio station call letters*]
KJOL — Grand Junction, CO [*FM radio station call letters*]
KJON-AM — Anadarko, OK [*AM radio station call letters*] (BROA)
KJOP — Lemoore, CA [*AM radio station call letters*]
KJOT — Boise, ID [*FM radio station call letters*]
KJOV-FM — Woodward, OK [*FM radio station call letters*] (RBYB)
KJOX-AM — Yakima, WA [*AM radio station call letters*] (RBYB)
KJOY — Stockton, CA [*FM radio station call letters*]
KJPN — Waipahu, HI [*AM radio station call letters*]
KJPW — Waynesville, MO [*AM radio station call letters*]
KJPW-FM — Waynesville, MO [*FM radio station call letters*]
KJQN-FM — Stockton, CA [*FM radio station call letters*] (BROA)
KJQY — San Diego, CA [*FM radio station call letters*]
KJR — Seattle, WA [*AM radio station call letters*]
KJRB — Spokane, WA [*AM radio station call letters*]
KJRE — Ellendale, ND [*Television station call letters*]
KJR-FM — Seattle, WA [*FM radio station call letters*]
KJRG — Newton, KS [*AM radio station call letters*]
KJRH — Tulsa, OK [*Television station call letters*]
KJRR — Jamestown, ND [*Television station call letters*]
KJRT — Amarillo, TX [*FM radio station call letters*]
KJS — Kansas Journal of Sociology
KJS — Karl-Jaspers Stiftung [*Karl-Jaspers Foundation - KJF*] (EA)
KJS — Kiva Java Server [*Computer science*]
KJS — Kodak Job Sheet
KJS — V-Groove on One Side [*Lumber*]
KJSA — Mineral Wells, TX [*AM radio station call letters*]
KJSK — Columbus, NE [*AM radio station call letters*]
KJSL — St. Louis, MO [*AM radio station call letters*]
KJSN — Modesto, CA [*FM radio station call letters*]
KJSR — Tulsa, OK [*FM radio station call letters*] (RBYB)
KJStJ — Knight of Justice, Order of St. John of Jerusalem
KJTA — Flagstaff, AZ [*FM radio station call letters*]
KJTL — Wichita Falls, TX [*Television station call letters*]
KJTT — Oak Harbor, WA [*AM radio station call letters*]
KJTV — Lubbock, TX [*Television station call letters*]
KJTX — Jefferson, TX [*FM radio station call letters*]
KJTY — Topeka, KS [*FM radio station call letters*]
KJU — Kamiraba [*Papua New Guinea*] [*Airport symbol*] [*Obsolete*] (OAG)
KJUD — Juneau, AK [*Television station call letters*]
KJUG — Tulare, CA [*AM radio station call letters*]
KJUG-FM — Tulare, CA [*FM radio station call letters*]
KJUL — North Las Vegas, NV [*FM radio station call letters*]
KJUN — Eatonville, WA [*FM radio station call letters*]
KJUN — Puyallup, WA [*AM radio station call letters*]
KJUN-FM — Tillamook, OR [*FM radio station call letters*] (BROA)
KJUS — Beaumont, TX [*AM radio station call letters*] (RBYB)
KJV — King James Version [*or Authorized Version of the Bible, 1611*]
KJVC — Mansfield, LA [*FM radio station call letters*]
KJVD — Kommunistischer Jugendverband Deutschlands [*Communist Youth Club of Germany*]
KJVH — Longview, WA [*FM radio station call letters*]
KJVI — Jackson, WY [*Television station call letters*]
KJWA — Grand Junction, CO [*Television station call letters*]
KJWL — Fresno, CA [*FM radio station call letters*]
KJWY-TV — Jackson, WY [*TV station call letters*] (RBYB)
KJYE — Grand Junction, CO [*FM radio station call letters*]
KJYL — Eagle Grove, IA [*FM radio station call letters*]
KJYO — Oklahoma City, OK [*FM radio station call letters*]
KJZY — Sebastopol, CA [*FM radio station call letters*] (RBYB)
KJZZ — Phoenix, AZ [*FM radio station call letters*]
KJZZ-TV — Salt Lake City, UT [*Television station call letters*]
KK — Arab International Aviation Co. (SAUO)
KK — Confirmed [*Travel industry*] (TVEL)
KK — Die Welt der Bibel. Kleinkommentare zur Heiligen Schrift [*Duesseldorf*] [*A publication*] (BJA)
KK — Kabushiki Kaishi [*Joint stock company*] [*Japan*]
KK — Kahal Kadosh. Holy Congregation (BJA)
KK — Kallikrein (DB)
KK — Kaluza-Klein [*Theories*] [*Physics*]
KK — Kar-Kraft [*Automotive industry supplier*]
KK — Kenya [*IYRU nationality code*] (IYR)
KK — Key-Encrypting Key [*Computer science*] (VLIE)
kK — Kilokayser
KK — Kilokelvin
KK — Kings
KK — Kingston Korner (EA)

K-K	Kirov-Kiev [*Former USSR*]
KK	Kleinkaliber [*Small Caliber*] [*German military*]
KK	Knee Kick [*Neurology*]
KK	Knock-for-Knock (MARI)
KK	Know That You Know (VLIE)
KK	Kokusai Koryu [*Japan Foundation*] (EAIO)
KK	Komisja Koordynacyjna. Zydowskie Instytucje Opiekuncze (BJA)
KK	Kosher Kitchen (BJA)
KK	Kremlin Kommandant
KK	Kulutusosuuskuntien Keskusliitto [*Co-Operative Union*] [*Finland*] (EY)
KK	Kurtis-Kraft [*US racecar maker*]
KK	Kurzgefasster Kommentar zu den Heiligen Schriften Alten und Neuen Testaments [*Munich*] [*A publication*] (BJA)
KKA	Benedictine College, Atchison, KS [*OCLC symbol*] (OCLC)
KKA	Kelsey Kindred of America (EA)
KKA	Kitchen Klutzs of America [*Inactive*] (EA)
KKA	Knights of King Arthur (EA)
KKA	Koyukuk [*Alaska*] [*Airport symbol*] (OAG)
KKAA	Aberdeen, SD [*AM radio station call letters*]
KKAG	Porterville, CA [*Television station call letters*]
KKAJ-FM	Ardmore, OK [*FM radio station call letters*]
KKAL	Arroyo Grande, CA [*AM radio station call letters*]
KKAM	Lubbock, TX [*AM radio station call letters*]
KKAN	Phillipsburg, KS [*AM radio station call letters*]
KKAP	Little Rock, AR [*Television station call letters*] (BROA)
KKAQ	Thief River Falls, MN [*AM radio station call letters*]
KKAR	Omaha, NE [*AM radio station call letters*]
KKAS	Silsbee, TX [*AM radio station call letters*]
KKASSR	Kara-Kalpak Autonomous Soviet Socialist Republic (SAUO)
KKAT	Ogden, UT [*FM radio station call letters*]
KKAW-FM	Albin, WY [*FM radio station call letters*] (BROA)
KKAY	Donaldsonville, LA [*FM radio station call letters*]
KKAY	White Castle, LA [*AM radio station call letters*]
KKAZ	Cheyenne, WY [*FM radio station call letters*]
KKB	Baker University, Baldwin City, KS [*OCLC symbol*] (OCLC)
KKB	Kitoi [*Alaska*] [*Airport symbol*] (OAG)
KKBA	Kingsville, TX [*FM radio station call letters*] (RBYB)
KKBB	Bakersfield, CA [*FM radio station call letters*]
KKBC	Baker City, OR [*FM radio station call letters*]
KKBC	Korea Kuwait Banking Corp.
KKBE-FM	Ojai, CA [*FM radio station call letters*] (BROA)
KKBG	Hilo, HI [*FM radio station call letters*]
KKBH	San Diego, CA [*FM radio station call letters*] (RBYB)
KKBI	Broken Bow, OK [*FM radio station call letters*]
KKBJ	Bemidji, MN [*AM radio station call letters*]
KKBJ-FM	Bemidji, MN [*FM radio station call letters*]
KKBL	Monett, MO [*FM radio station call letters*]
KKBN	Twain Harte, CA [*FM radio station call letters*]
KKBQ	Houston, TX [*AM radio station call letters*]
KKBQ	Pasadena, TX [*FM radio station call letters*]
KKBR	Billings, MT [*FM radio station call letters*]
KKBS	Guymon, OK [*FM radio station call letters*]
KKBT	Los Angeles, CA [*FM radio station call letters*]
KKBY-AM	Puyallup, WA [*AM radio station call letters*] (RBYB)
KKBY-FM	Eatonville, WA [*FM radio station call letters*] (RBYB)
KKBZ	Clarinda, IA [*FM radio station call letters*]
KKc	Kansas City Public Library, Kansas City, KS [*Library symbol*] [*Library of Congress*] (LCLS)
KKC	Kansas City Public Library, Kansas City, KS [*OCLC symbol*] (OCLC)
KKC	Khon Kaen [*Thailand*] [*Airport symbol*] (OAG)
KKC	Knox College Library, University of Toronto [*UTLAS symbol*]
KKCA	Fulton, MO [*FM radio station call letters*]
KKcB	Central Baptist Theological Seminary, Kansas City, KS [*Library symbol*] [*Library of Congress*] (LCLS)
KKCB-FM	Duluth, MN [*FM radio station call letters*] (RBYB)
KKcBM	Bethany Medical Center, Kansas City, KS [*Library symbol*] [*Library of Congress*] (LCLS)
KKcD	Donnelly College, Kansas City, KS [*Library symbol*] [*Library of Congress*] (LCLS)
KKCD	Omaha, NE [*FM radio station call letters*]
KKCH-FM	Glenwood Springs, CO [*FM radio station call letters*] (BROA)
KKCI	Goodland, KS [*FM radio station call letters*]
KKcJS	Jensen-Salsbery Laboratories, Kansas City, KS [*Library symbol*] [*Library of Congress*] (LCLS)
KKCK	Marshall, MN [*FM radio station call letters*]
KKCL	Lorenzo, TX [*FM radio station call letters*]
KKCM	Shakopee, MN [*AM radio station call letters*]
KKCN	Trumann, AR [*FM radio station call letters*] (RBYB)
KKCN-FM	Sterling City, TX [*FM radio station call letters*] (BROA)
KKCO-TV	Grand Junction, CO [*TV station call letters*] (RBYB)
kKCP	Koala Conservation Program (SAUO)
KKcP	Providence - Saint Margaret Health Center, Kansas City, KS [*Library symbol*] [*Library of Congress*] (LCLS)
KKcPS	Kansas City Kansas Public Schools, Kansas City, KS [*Library symbol*] [*Library of Congress*] (LCLS)
KKCQ	Fosston, MN [*AM radio station call letters*]
KKCQ-FM	Fosston, MN [*FM radio station call letters*]
KKCR-FM	Hanalei, HI [*FM radio station call letters*] (RBYB)
KKCS	Colorado Springs, CO [*AM radio station call letters*]
KKCS-FM	Colorado Springs, CO [*FM radio station call letters*]
KKCT	Bismarck, ND [*FM radio station call letters*]
KKCV	Cedar Falls, IA [*FM radio station call letters*]
KKCW	Beaverton, OR [*FM radio station call letters*]
KKCY	Colusa, CA [*FM radio station call letters*]
KKD	Kokoda [*Papua New Guinea*] [*Airport symbol*] (OAG)

KKD	Korintji-Kaba-Dempo [*Sumatra*] [*Seismograph station code, US Geological Survey*] [*Closed*] (SEIS)
KKDA	Dallas, TX [*FM radio station call letters*]
KKDA	Grand Prairie, TX [*AM radio station call letters*]
KKDD	Katalog Kandidatskikh i Doktorskikh Dissertatsii [*A bibliographic publication*]
KKDD	North Las Vegas, NV [*AM radio station call letters*] (RBYB)
KKDD	San Bernardino, CA [*AM radio station call letters*] (BROA)
K K-D-H	Knight Kadosch [*Freemasonry*]
KKDJ	Fresno, CA [*FM radio station call letters*]
KKDKA	Bulletin. Kyushu Institute of Technology (journ.) (SAUS)
KKDL	Detroit Lakes, MN [*FM radio station call letters*]
KKDM	Des Moines, IA [*FM radio station call letters*]
KKDQ	Thief River Falls, MN [*FM radio station call letters*]
KKDS	South Salt Lake, UT [*AM radio station call letters*]
KKDY	West Plains, MO [*FM radio station call letters*]
KKDZ	Seattle, WA [*AM radio station call letters*]
KKE	Kerikeri [*New Zealand*] [*Airport symbol*] (OAG)
KKE	Kleena Kleene Gold Mines [*Vancouver Stock Exchange symbol*]
KKE	Kommunistiko Komma Ellados [*Communist Party of Greece*] [*Political party*] (PPW)
KKED-FM	Fairbanks, AK [*FM radio station call letters*] (BROA)
KKEE	Long Beach, WA [*FM radio station call letters*]
KKEes	Kommunistiko Komma Ellados - Esoterikou [*Communist Party of Greece - Interior*] [*Political party*] (PPE)
KKEex	Kommunistiko Komma Ellados - Exoterikou [*Communist Party of Greece - Exterior*] [*Political party*] (PPE)
KKEG	Fayetteville, AR [*FM radio station call letters*]
KKEL	Hobbs, NM [*AM radio station call letters*]
KKEN	Duncan, OK [*AM radio station call letters*] (BROA)
KKEN-FM	Duncan, OK [*FM radio station call letters*] (BROA)
KKEQ-FM	Fosston, MN [*FM radio station call letters*] (RBYB)
KKER-FM	Kerrville, TX [*FM radio station call letters*] (BROA)
KKES	Kommunistiko Komma Ellados - Esoterikou [*Communist Party of Greece - Interior*] [*Political party*] (PPW)
KKEX	Preston, ID [*FM radio station call letters*]
KKEY	Portland, OR [*AM radio station call letters*]
KKEZ	Fort Dodge, IA [*FM radio station call letters*]
KKFC	KISS [*Knights in the Service of Satan*] Konnection Fan Club (EA)
KKFG	Bloomfield, NM [*FM radio station call letters*]
KKFI	Kansas City, MO [*FM radio station call letters*]
KKFJ-AM	Alturas, CA [*AM radio station call letters*] (RBYB)
KKFM	Colorado Springs, CO [*FM radio station call letters*]
KKFN	Denver, CO [*AM radio station call letters*]
KKFO	Coalinga, CA [*AM radio station call letters*]
KKFR	Glendale, AZ [*FM radio station call letters*]
KKG	Kappa Kappa Gamma [*Sorority*]
KKG	Konawaruk [*Guyana*] [*Airport symbol*] [*Obsolete*] (OAG)
KKG	Kootenay King Resources [*Vancouver Stock Exchange symbol*]
KKG	Thousand Kilograms (EG)
KKGB	Sulphur, LA [*FM radio station call letters*]
KKGJ	Grand Junction, CO [*AM radio station call letters*] (BROA)
KKGL-FM	Nampa, ID [*FM radio station call letters*] (BROA)
KKGM	Grand Junction, CO [*FM radio station call letters*] (RBYB)
KKGO	Frazier Park, CA [*AM radio station call letters*]
KKGO-FM	Los Angeles, CA [*FM radio station call letters*]
KKGR-AM	East Helena, MT [*AM radio station call letters*] (BROA)
KKGT	Portland, OR [*AM radio station call letters*] (BROA)
KKH	Kailua-Kona [*Hawaii*] [*Seismograph station code, US Geological Survey*] (SEIS)
KKH	Karakoram Highway [*Asia*]
KKH	Kongiganak [*Alaska*] [*Airport symbol*] (OAG)
KKHB-FM	Eureka, CA [*FM radio station call letters*] (RBYB)
KKHG	Tucson, AZ [*FM radio station call letters*]
KKHI	San Rafael, CA [*AM radio station call letters*]
KKHI-FM	San Rafael, CA [*FM radio station call letters*]
KKHJ	Los Angeles, CA [*AM radio station call letters*]
KKHK-FM	Denver, CO [*FM radio station call letters*] (RBYB)
KKHL	Klung Kidney-Heart-Lung [*Machine*]
KKHN-FM	Naipahu, HI [*FM radio station call letters*] (BROA)
KKHQ	Odem, TX [*FM radio station call letters*]
KKHR	Anson, TX [*AM radio station call letters*]
KKHT	Conroe, TX [*FM radio station call letters*] (RBYB)
KKI	Akiachak [*Alaska*] [*Airport symbol*] (OAG)
KKI	Karkar Island [*Papua New Guinea*] [*Seismograph station code, US Geological Survey*] (SEIS)
KKI	Kenpo Karate International (EA)
KKIC	Boise, ID [*AM radio station call letters*]
KKID	Sallisaw, OK [*AM radio station call letters*]
KKIFC	Kris Kristofferson International Fan Club (EA)
KKIH	King Khalid International Hospital [*Saudi Arabia*] (WDAA)
KKIK	Temple, TX [*FM radio station call letters*] (RBYB)
KKIK-FM	La Junta, CO [*FM radio station call letters*] (BROA)
KKIM	Albuquerque, NM [*AM radio station call letters*]
KKIN	Aitkin, MN [*AM radio station call letters*]
KKIN-FM	Aitkin, MN [*FM radio station call letters*] (RBYB)
KKIQ	Livermore, CA [*FM radio station call letters*]
KKIS	Concord, CA [*AM radio station call letters*]
KKIS	Soldotna, AK [*FM radio station call letters*]
KKIT	Taos, NM [*AM radio station call letters*]
KKIX	Fayetteville, AR [*FM radio station call letters*]
KKJ	Kita Kyushu [*Japan*] [*Airport symbol*] [*Obsolete*] (OAG)
KKJG	San Luis Obispo, CA [*FM radio station call letters*]
KKJI	Gallup, NM [*FM radio station call letters*]
KKJJ-FM	Ashland, OR [*FM radio station call letters*] (RBYB)

KKJL.......... San Luis Obispo, CA [*AM radio station call letters*] (RBYB)
KKJM.......... St Joseph, MN [*FM radio station call letters*]
KKJO.......... St. Joseph, MO [*FM radio station call letters*]
KKJQ.......... Garden City, KS [*FM radio station call letters*]
KKJR.......... Hutchison, MN [*FM radio station call letters*]
KKJT.......... Joshua Tree, CA [*FM radio station call letters*]
KKJW-FM.... Stanton, TX [*FM radio station call letters*] (BROA)
KKJY-AM.... Lake Oswego, OR [*AM radio station call letters*] (BROA)
KKJZ.......... Lake Oswego, OR [*FM radio station call letters*]
KKK.......... Invisible Empire Knights of the Ku Klux Klan (EA)
KKK.......... Kissel Kar Klub (EA)
KKK.......... Knight of the Ku Klux Klan (EA)
KKK.......... Kolmer, Kline, Kahn [*Test for syphilis*] [*Medicine*] (DAVI)
KKK.......... Kuehnle, Kopp, & Kausch [*Auto industry supplier*]
KKKIS.......... K.K. Kodak Information Systems (EFIS)
KKKK.......... Knights of the Ku Klux Klan (BUAC)
KKKK.......... Odessa, TX [*FM radio station call letters*]
KKKK.......... White Knights of the Ku-Klux-Klan (SAUO)
KKKUK.......... Ku-Klux-Klan in the United Kingdom (SAUO)
KKL.......... Kam-Kotia Mines Ltd. [*Toronto Stock Exchange symbol*]
KKL.......... Karluk Lake, AK [*Location identifier*] [*FAA*] (FAAL)
KKL.......... Keren Kayemeth Leisrael (BJA)
KKL.......... Kol-Kol Airlines Ltd. [*Nigeria*] [*FAA designator*] (FAAC)
KKLA.......... Los Angeles, CA [*FM radio station call letters*]
KKLA.......... San Bernardino, CA [*AM radio station call letters*] (RBYB)
KKLB.......... Elgin, TX [*FM radio station call letters*]
KKLD-FM.... Prescott Valley, az [*FM radio station call letters*] (RBYB)
KKLE.......... Winfield, KS [*AM radio station call letters*]
KKLF.......... Denison-Sherman, TX [*AM radio station call letters*] (BROA)
KKLH-FM.... Marshfield, MO [*FM radio station call letters*] (RBYB)
KKLI.......... Widefield, CO [*FM radio station call letters*]
KKLK-FM.... Daingerfield, TX [*FM radio station call letters*] (BROA)
KKLL.......... Webb City, MO [*AM radio station call letters*]
KKLL-FM.... Webb City, MO [*FM radio station call letters*]
KKLO.......... Leavenworth, KS [*AM radio station call letters*]
KKLQ.......... Oceanside, CA [*AM radio station call letters*] (RBYB)
KKLQ-FM.... San Diego, CA [*FM radio station call letters*]
KKLQ-FM.... Vancouver, WA [*FM radio station call letters*] (BROA)
KKLR.......... Poplar Bluff, MO [*FM radio station call letters*]
KKLS.......... Rapid City, SD [*AM radio station call letters*]
KKLS-FM.... Sioux Falls, SD [*FM radio station call letters*]
KKLT.......... Phoenix, AZ [*FM radio station call letters*]
KKLV.......... Honolulu, HI [*FM radio station call letters*]
KKLX.......... Worland, WY [*FM radio station call letters*]
KKLY-FM.... Pecos, TX [*FM radio station call letters*] (RBYB)
KKLZ.......... Las Vegas, NV [*FM radio station call letters*]
KKM.......... Kota Kinabalu [*Malaysia*] [*Seismograph station code, US Geological Survey*] (SEIS)
KKM.......... North Central Kansas Library, Manhattan, KS [*OCLC symbol*] (OCLC)
KKMA.......... Le Mars, IA [*FM radio station call letters*]
KKMC.......... Gonzales, CA [*AM radio station call letters*]
KKMC.......... King Khalid Military City [*Saudi Arabia*] (DOMA)
KKMG.......... Pueblo, CO [*FM radio station call letters*]
KKMI.......... Burlington, IA [*FM radio station call letters*]
KKMJ.......... Austin, TX [*FM radio station call letters*]
KKMK.......... Rapid City, SD [*FM radio station call letters*]
KKMO.......... Tacoma, WA [*AM radio station call letters*]
KKMS-AM.... Richfield, MN [*AM radio station call letters*] (BROA)
KKMT-FM.... Columbia Falls, MT [*FM radio station call letters*] (BROA)
KKMV.......... Rupert, ID [*FM radio station call letters*]
KKMX.......... Tri City, OR [*FM radio station call letters*]
KKMY.......... Orange, TX [*FM radio station call letters*]
KKN.......... Kansas Newman College, Wichita, KS [*OCLC symbol*] (OCLC)
KKN.......... Kirkenes [*Norway*] [*Airport symbol*] (OAG)
KKNB.......... Crete, NE [*FM radio station call letters*]
KKND.......... Tucson, AZ [*AM radio station call letters*] (RBYB)
KKND-FM.... Port Sulphur, LA [*FM radio station call letters*] (RBYB)
KKNG.......... Laramie, WY [*FM radio station call letters*]
KKNN.......... Delta, CO [*FM radio station call letters*] (RBYB)
KKNO.......... Gretna, LA [*AM radio station call letters*]
KKNU.......... Springfield-Eugene, OR [*FM radio station call letters*]
KKNW-AM.... Port Angeles, WA [*AM radio station call letters*] (BROA)
KKNX-AM.... Eugene, OR [*AM radio station call letters*] (RBYB)
KKO.......... Kaikohe [*New Zealand*] [*Airport symbol*] [*Obsolete*] (OAG)
KKO.......... National Citizens' Committee [*Poland*] [*Political party*]
KKO.......... Ottawa University, Ottawa, KS [*OCLC symbol*] (OCLC)
KKOA.......... Kustom Kemps of America (EA)
KKOA.......... Volcano, HI [*FM radio station call letters*]
KKOB.......... Albuquerque, NM [*AM radio station call letters*]
KKOB Exp Stn... Santa Fe, NM [*Radio expansion station*] (RBYB)
KKOB-FM.... Albuquerque, NM [*FM radio station call letters*]
KKOH.......... Reno, NV [*AM radio station call letters*] (RBYB)
KKOJ.......... Jackson, MN [*AM radio station call letters*]
KKOK.......... Morris, MN [*FM radio station call letters*]
KKOL.......... Hampton, AR [*FM radio station call letters*]
KKOL-AM.... Seattle, WA [*AM radio station call letters*] (BROA)
KKON.......... Kealakekua, HI [*AM radio station call letters*]
KKOR.......... Gallup, NM [*FM radio station call letters*]
KKOS-FM.... Palacios, TX [*FM radio station call letters*] (RBYB)
KKOT.......... Columbus, NE [*FM radio station call letters*]
KKOW.......... Pittsburg, KS [*AM radio station call letters*]
KKOW-FM.... Pittsburg, KS [*FM radio station call letters*]
KKOY.......... Chanute, KS [*AM radio station call letters*]
KKOY-FM.... Chanute, KS [*FM radio station call letters*]
KKOZ.......... Ava, MO [*AM radio station call letters*]
KKOZ-FM.... Ava, MO [*FM radio station call letters*]
KKP.......... Canadian Communist Party [*Political party*]
KKP.......... Chinese Communist Party [*Political party*]
KKP.......... Cuban Communist Party [*Political party*]
KKP.......... Cypriot Communist Party [*Political party*]
KKP.......... Kappa Kappa Psi [*Society*]
KKP.......... Kina Kommunista Partja [*Communist Party of China*] [*Political party*]
KKP.......... King's Knight's Pawn [*Chess*] (IIA)
KKP.......... Komisja Kontroli Partyjnej (SAUO)
KKp.......... University of Kansas Medical Library (SAUO)
KKP.......... University of Kansas, Medical Library, Kansas City, KS [*OCLC symbol*] (OCLC)
KKPC.......... Pueblo, CO [*FM radio station call letters*]
KKPC-AM.... Pueblo, CO [*AM radio station call letters*] (RBYB)
KKPL.......... Opportunity, WA [*AM radio station call letters*]
KKPN-FM.... Houston, TX [*FM radio station call letters*] (BROA)
KKPR.......... Kearney, NE [*AM radio station call letters*]
KKPR-FM.... Kearney, NE [*FM radio station call letters*]
KKPS.......... Brownsville, TX [*FM radio station call letters*]
KKPT.......... Little Rock, AR [*FM radio station call letters*]
KKPX.......... San Jose, CA [*Television station call letters*] (BROA)
KKPZ.......... Portland, OR [*AM radio station call letters*] (RBYB)
KKQ.......... Sterling College, Sterling, KS [*OCLC symbol*] (OCLC)
KKQQ.......... Volga, SD [*FM radio station call letters*]
KKQY-FM.... HillCity, KS [*FM radio station call letters*] (RBYB)
KKR.......... Emporia State University, Emporia, KS [*OCLC symbol*] (OCLC)
KKR.......... Kaukura [*French Polynesia*] [*Airport symbol*] (OAG)
KKR.......... Kohlberg Kravis Roberts (BUAC)
KKR.......... Kohlberg Kravis Roberts & Co.
KKR.......... Kokanee Resources Ltd. [*Vancouver Stock Exchange symbol*]
KKR.......... Kurtis-Kraft Register [*Defunct*] (EA)
KKR.......... Kurukshetra [*India*] [*Seismograph station code, US Geological Survey*] (SEIS)
KKRB.......... Klamath Falls, OR [*FM radio station call letters*]
KKRC.......... Granite Falls, MN [*FM radio station call letters*]
KKRD.......... Wichita, KS [*FM radio station call letters*]
KKRF.......... Stuart, IA [*FM radio station call letters*]
KKRH.......... Salem, OR [*FM radio station call letters*] (RBYB)
KKrJS.......... Jensen-Salsbery Laboratories, Kansas City (SAUS)
KKRK.......... Douglas, AZ [*FM radio station call letters*]
KKRL.......... Carroll, IA [*FM radio station call letters*]
KKRN-FM.... Cabot, AR [*FM radio station call letters*] (RBYB)
KKRO.......... Anchorage, AK [*FM radio station call letters*]
KKRO.......... Koo Koo Roo [*NASDAQ symbol*] (TTSB)
KKRO.......... Koo Koo Roo, Inc. [*NASDAQ symbol*] (SAG)
KKRQ.......... Iowa City, IA [*FM radio station call letters*]
KKRR-FM.... Casper, WY [*FM radio station call letters*] (BROA)
KKRS-FM.... Davenport, WA [*FM radio station call letters*] (BROA)
KKRT.......... Wenatchee, WA [*AM radio station call letters*]
KKRV-FM.... Wenatchee, WA [*FM radio station call letters*]
KKRW.......... Houston, TX [*FM radio station call letters*]
KKRX.......... Lawton, OK [*AM radio station call letters*]
KKRX-FM.... Lawton, OK [*FM radio station call letters*]
KKRY-FM.... Miles City, MT [*FM radio station call letters*] (BROA)
KKRZ.......... Portland, OR [*FM radio station call letters*]
KKS.......... Kansas State University, Farrell Library, Manhattan, KS [*OCLC symbol*] (OCLC)
KKS.......... Konstanta Kongresa Sekretario (SAUO)
KKSA.......... Keith Keating Society for the Arts [*Defunct*] (EA)
KKSA.......... San Angelo, TX [*AM radio station call letters*] (RBYB)
KKSB-FM.... Goleta, CA [*FM radio station call letters*] (BROA)
KKSC.......... Brawley, CA [*AM radio station call letters*] (BROA)
KKSD-FM.... Milbank, SD [*FM radio station call letters*] (BROA)
KKSF.......... San Francisco, CA [*FM radio station call letters*]
KKSI.......... Eddyville, IA [*FM radio station call letters*]
KKSJ.......... San Jose, CA [*AM radio station call letters*]
KKSL.......... Lake Oswego, OR [*AM radio station call letters*] (RBYB)
KKSM-AM.... Oceanside, CA [*AM radio station call letters*] (RBYB)
KKSN.......... Oregon City, OR [*AM radio station call letters*] (BROA)
KKSN.......... Portland, OR [*FM radio station call letters*]
KKSN.......... Vancouver, WA [*AM radio station call letters*]
KKSO.......... Des Moines, IA [*AM radio station call letters*]
KKSR.......... Sartell, MN [*FM radio station call letters*]
KKSS.......... Santa Fe, NM [*FM radio station call letters*]
KKST-FM.... Oakdale, LA [*FM radio station call letters*] (BROA)
KKSU.......... Manhattan, KS [*AM radio station call letters*]
KKSY.......... Bald Knob, AR [*FM radio station call letters*]
KKt.......... King's Knight (ADWA)
KKT.......... King's Knight [*Chess*]
KKTK-AM.... Waco, TX [*AM radio station call letters*] (RBYB)
KKTL-FM.... Cleveland, TX [*FM radio station call letters*] (BROA)
KKTO-FM.... Tahoe City, CA [*FM radio station call letters*] (RBYB)
KKTP.......... King's Knight's Pawn [*Chess*] (IIA)
KKTR.......... Fresno, CA [*AM radio station call letters*]
KKTT-FM.... Eugene, OR [*FM radio station call letters*] (BROA)
KKTU.......... Cheyenne, WY [*Television station call letters*]
KKTV.......... Colorado Springs, CO [*Television station call letters*]
KKTX.......... Kilgore, TX [*AM radio station call letters*]
KKTX-FM.... Kilgore, TX [*FM radio station call letters*]
KKTY.......... Douglas, WY [*AM radio station call letters*]
KKTY-FM.... Douglas, WY [*FM radio station call letters*]
KKTZ.......... Mountain Home, AR [*FM radio station call letters*]
KKU.......... Ekuk [*Alaska*] [*Airport symbol*] (OAG)

KKU .... Keanakolu [Hawaii] [Seismograph station code, US Geological Survey] (SEIS)
KKU .... Khon Kaen University (SAUO)
KKU .... University of Kansas, Lawrence, KS [OCLC symbol] (OCLC)
KKUA .... Wailuku, HI [FM radio station call letters]
KKUB .... Brownfield, TX [AM radio station call letters]
KKUH .... King Khalid University Hospital [Saudi Arabia]
KKUL .... King Kullen Grocery Co. Inc. (SAUO)
KKUL-FM ..... Lincoln, NE [FM radio station call letters] (RBYB)
KKUP .... Cupertino, CA [FM radio station call letters]
KKUS .... Tyler, TX [FM radio station call letters]
KKUU-FM ..... Indio, CA [FM radio station call letters] (BROA)
KKUZ .... Sallisaw, OK [FM radio station call letters]
KKUZ-AM ..... Sallisaw, OK [AM radio station call letters] (RBYB)
KKV .... Central Kansas Library System, Book Processing Center, Great Bend, KS [OCLC symbol] (OCLC)
KKV .... Kinetic-Kill Vehicle [Military] (SDI)
KKVI .... Twin Falls, ID [Television station call letters]
KKVO .... Altus, OK [FM radio station call letters]
KKVV .... Las Vegas, NV [AM radio station call letters]
KKW .... Kainokawa [Japan] [Seismograph station code, US Geological Survey] (SEIS)
KKW .... Kikwit [Zaire] [Airport symbol] (OAG)
KKW .... Kinetic Kill Weapon (SAUS)
KKW .... Washburn University of Topeka, Topeka, KS [OCLC symbol] (OCLC)
KKWB .... El Paso, TX [Television station call letters] (BROA)
KKWM .... Winfield, KS [FM radio station call letters]
KKWQ .... Warroad, MN [FM radio station call letters]
KKWS .... Wadena, MN [FM radio station call letters]
KKWY .... Fox Farm, WY [AM radio station call letters] (BROA)
KKWZ .... Richfield, UT [FM radio station call letters]
KKX .... Kikaiga Shima [Japan] [Airport symbol] (OAG)
KKX .... Southwestern College, Winfield, KS [OCLC symbol] (OCLC)
KKXK .... Montrose, CO [FM radio station call letters]
KKXL .... Grand Forks, ND [AM radio station call letters]
KKXL-FM ..... Grand Forks, ND [FM radio station call letters]
KKXO .... Eugene, OR [AM radio station call letters]
KKXX .... Delano, CA [FM radio station call letters]
KKXX .... Paradise, CA [AM radio station call letters]
KKYA .... Yankton, SD [FM radio station call letters]
KKYC .... Muleshoe, TX [FM radio station call letters]
KKYC-FM ..... Clovis, NM [FM radio station call letters] (BROA)
KKYD .... Denver, CO [AM radio station call letters]
KKYK-TV ..... El Dorado, AR [Television station call letters] (BROA)
KKYN .... Plainview, TX [AM radio station call letters]
KKYN-FM ..... Plainview, TX [FM radio station call letters]
KKYR .... Texarkana, AR [AM radio station call letters]
KKYR-FM ..... Texarkana, TX [FM radio station call letters]
KKYS .... Bryan, TX [FM radio station call letters]
KKYT .... McCook, NE [FM radio station call letters]
KKYX .... San Antonio, TX [AM radio station call letters]
KKYY .... Gunnison, CO [FM radio station call letters]
KKYZ .... Sierra Vista, AZ [FM radio station call letters]
KKZIS.......... Komisja Koordynacyjna Zydowskich Instytucji Spolecznych (BJA)
KKZN-FM ..... Haltom City, TX [FM radio station call letters] (BROA)
KKZQ .... Lowell, AR [FM radio station call letters]
KKZQ-FM ..... Tehachapi, CA [FM radio station call letters] (BROA)
KKZX .... Spokane, WA [FM radio station call letters]
KKZY-FM ..... Bemidji, MN [FM radio station call letters] (BROA)
KKZZ .... Santa Paula, CA [AM radio station call letters]
KL .... Air Atlantique [ICAO designator] (AD)
KL .... Confirmed Waitlist [Travel industry] (TVEL)
KL .... Kahunen-Loeve [Mathematics] (CCCA)
KL .... Kaliszer Leben (BJA)
KL .... Kansalaisvallen Liitto [League of Civil Power] [Finland] [Political party] (PPW)
K-L .... Kansas State Library, Law Department, Topeka, KS [Library symbol] [Library of Congress] (LCLS)
KL .... Karl Lagerfeld [Fashion designer]
K-L .... Karl-Lorimar Home Video, Inc.
KL .... Keel (ROG)
KL .... Keller's Language [1977] [Computer science] (CSR)
KL .... Kelly [Tire casing code]
KL .... Kelvin Law [Physics]
KL .... Kerley Lines [Radiology]
KL .... Key Length [Computer science] (BUR)
KL .... Key Lever (IAA)
KL .... Key Locker
KL .... Kidney Lobe
kL .... Kilolambert
kl .... Kiloliter (ADWA)
kL .... Kiloliter
KL .... Klaeger [Plaintiff] [German] (ILCA)
kl .... Klang [Musical Overtone] [German]
KI .... Klarinette [Clarinet] [German] [Music] (WDAA)
KL .... Klebs-Loeffler [Bacteriology]
KL .... Kleine-Levin [Syndrome] [Medicine] (DAVI)
KL .... Kleinmann-Low [Astronomy]
KL .... Klemm Flugzeugbau GmbH & Apparatebau Nabern [Germany] [ICAO aircraft manufacturer identifier] (ICAO)
KL .... KLM [Koninklijke Luchtvaart Maatschappij] Royal Dutch Airlines [ICAO designator] (OAG)
KL .... Knight of Leopold [Austria, Belgium] (ROG)
KL .... Knight of [the Order of] Leopold of Austria
KL .... Knights of Lithuania

KL .... Konzentrationslager [Concentration Camp] [German] (BJA)
KL .... Kuala Lumpur [Malaysia]
KL .... Kullback-Leibler [Mathematics]
KLA .... Air Lietuva [Lithuania] [ICAO designator] (FAAC)
KLA .... Ka-Ahari Resources [Vancouver Stock Exchange symbol]
KLA .... Kampala [Uganda] [Airport symbol] (AD)
KLA .... Kansas Library Association
KLA .... Karachi Library Association [Pakistan] (BUAC)
KLA .... Kentucky Library Association (SAUO)
KLA .... Kenya Library Association (BUAC)
KLA .... Key Learning Area [Education]
KLA .... Kingdom of Libya Airways, Bengasi (SAUO)
KLA .... KLA Instruments Corp. [Associated Press] (SAG)
KLA .... Klystron Amplifier
KLA .... Knight of [the Order of] Leopold of Austria
KLA .... Korean Library Association (BUAC)
KLA .... Kosovo Liberation Army [Yugoslavia]
KLAA .... Tioga, LA [FM radio station call letters]
KLAC .... KLA Instruments [NASDAQ symbol] (TTSB)
KLAC .... KLA Instruments Corp. [NASDAQ symbol] (NQ)
KLAC .... KLA-Tencor Corp. [NASDAQ symbol] (NQ)
KLAC .... Los Angeles, CA [AM radio station call letters]
KLAD .... Klamath Falls, OR [AM radio station call letters]
KLAD-FM ..... Klamath Falls, OR [FM radio station call letters]
KLAK .... Durant, OK [FM radio station call letters]
KLAL-FM..... Wrightsville, AR [FM radio station call letters] (BROA)
KLAM .... Cordova, AK [AM radio station call letters]
Klamath ...... Klamath First Bancorp, Inc. [Associated Press] (SAG)
KLAN .... Glasgow, MT [FM radio station call letters]
KLAN .... Lansing/Capital Region [Michigan] [ICAO location identifier] (ICLI)
KLANSS ...... Keep That Local Area Network Simple, Stupid [Telecommunications]
KLAQ .... El Paso, TX [FM radio station call letters]
KLAR .... Laredo, TX [AM radio station call letters]
KLAS............ Las Vegas/McCarran International [Nevada] [ICAO location identifier] (ICLI)
KLAS............ Las Vegas, NV [Television station call letters]
KLaSH .... Larned State Hospital, Larned, KS [Library symbol] [Library of Congress] (LCLS)
Klass Phil Stud... Klassische Philologische Studien [A publication] (OCD)
KLAT........... Houston, TX [AM radio station call letters]
KLAV........... Las Vegas, NV [AM radio station call letters]
KLaw .... Lawrence Free Public Library, Lawrence, KS [Library symbol] [Library of Congress] (LCLS)
KLAW .... Lawton, OK [FM radio station call letters]
K Law Rep... Kentucky Law Reporter [A publication] (DLA)
KLAX........... Long Beach, CA [FM radio station call letters]
KLAX........... Los Angeles/International [California] [ICAO location identifier] (ICLI)
KLAX-TV ..... Alexandria, LA [Television station call letters]
KLAY .... Lakewood, WA [AM radio station call letters]
KLAZ .... Hot Springs, AR [FM radio station call letters]
KLB .... Audio Book Club (SG)
KLB .... Kalabo [Zambia] [Airport symbol] (OAG)
KLB .... Kilopound (MCD)
KLB .... Knight of [the Order of] Leopold [Belgium]
KLB .... Korea Longterm Credit Bank (BUAC)
KLBA .... Albia, IA [AM radio station call letters]
KL Bac........ Klebs-Loeffler Bacillus (AAMN)
KLBA-FM ..... Albia, IA [FM radio station call letters]
KLBB........... Lubbock/Regional [Texas] [ICAO location identifier] (ICLI)
KLBB........... St. Paul, MN [AM radio station call letters]
KLBC .... Durant, OK [FM radio station call letters]
KLBF .... Kilopound-Force (WDAA)
KLBG .... Alexandria, LA [AM radio station call letters] (RBYB)
KLBJ .... Austin, TX [AM radio station call letters]
KLBJ-FM ..... Austin, TX [FM radio station call letters]
KLBK........... Lubbock, TX [Television station call letters]
KLBM .... La Grande, OR [AM radio station call letters]
KLBN .... Auberry, CA [FM radio station call letters] (RBYB)
KLBO .... Monahans, TX [AM radio station call letters]
KLBQ .... El Dorado, AR [FM radio station call letters]
KLBS........... Los Banos, CA [AM radio station call letters]
KLBY .... Colby, KS [Television station call letters]
KLC .... Kaingaroa Logging Company (SAUO)
KLC .... Kaolack [Senegal] [Airport symbol] (AD)
KLC .... Kern County Library System, Bakersfield, CA [OCLC symbol] (OCLC)
KLC .... Kinesin Light Chain [Cytology]
KLC .... Kirkland Lake [Ontario] [Seismograph station code, US Geological Survey] [Closed] (SEIS)
KLC .... KLM Cityhopper BV [Netherlands] [ICAO designator] (FAAC)
KLC .... Kodiak Launch Complex (IGSL)
KLCA-FM ..... Tahoe City, CA [FM radio station call letters] (BROA)
KLCB........... Libby, MT [AM radio station call letters]
KLCC .... Eugene, OR [FM radio station call letters]
KLCC .... Kuala Lumpur City Center [Malaysia] (ECON)
KLCCL .... Kilocycle (ABBR)
KLCD .... Decorah, IA [FM radio station call letters]
KLCE .... Blackfoot, ID [FM radio station call letters]
KLCE .... Kuala Lumpur Commodity Exchange [Malayia] (NUMA)
KLCH .... Lake Charles/Lake Charles [Louisiana] [ICAO location identifier] (ICLI)
KLCI............ Nampa, ID [FM radio station call letters]
KLCI-FM ..... Princeton, MN [FM radio station call letters] (BROA)
KLCK........... Goldendale, WA [AM radio station call letters]
KLCK........... Rickenbacker Air Force Base [Ohio] [ICAO location identifier] (ICLI)
KLCL........... Lake Charles, LA [AM radio station call letters]

KLCM Lewistown, MT [*FM radio station call letters*]

KLCN Blytheville, AR [*AM radio station call letters*]

KLCO Newport, OR [*FM radio station call letters*]

KLCQ Healdsburg, CA [*FM radio station call letters*]

KLCR-FM Lakeview, OR [*FM radio station call letters*] (BROA)

KLCS Los Angeles, CA [*Television station call letters*]

KLCU-FM Ardmore, OK [*FM radio station call letters*] (BROA)

KLCV-FM Lincoln, NE [*FM radio station call letters*] (RBYB)

KLCX Indio, CA [*FM radio station call letters*] (RBYB)

KLCX-FM St. Charles, MN [*FM radio station call letters*] (BROA)

KLCY East Missoula, MT [*AM radio station call letters*]

KLCY-FM Vernal, UT [*FM radio station call letters*]

KLCZ Corcoran, CA [*FM radio station call letters*]

KLD Kelly, Douglas & Co. Ltd. [*Toronto Stock Exchange symbol*]

KLD King's Light Dragoons [*British military*] (DMA)

KLD Kongres Liberalno-Demokratyczny [*Liberal Democratic Congress*] [*Poland*] [*Political party*] (EY)

KLDC Commerce City, CO [*AM radio station call letters*] (RBYB)

KLDC-AM Brighton, CO [*AM radio station call letters*] (RBYB)

KLDE Houston, TX [*FM radio station call letters*]

KLDG Liberal, KS [*FM radio station call letters*]

KLDI Laramie, WY [*AM radio station call letters*]

KLDJ-FM Duluth, MN [*FM radio station call letters*] (RBYB)

KLDN Lufkin, TX [*FM radio station call letters*]

KLDO Laredo, TX [*Television station call letters*]

KLDR Harbeck-Fruitdale, OR [*FM radio station call letters*]

KLDR Killdeer (ABBR)

KLDS-AM Falfurrias, TX [*AM radio station call letters*] (BROA)

KLDSOP Kaleidoscope (ABBR)

KLDSOPC Kaleidoscopic (ABBR)

KLDT Lake Dallas, TX [*Television station call letters*]

KLDY-AM Lacey, WA [*AM radio station call letters*] (BROA)

KLDZ Lincoln, NE [*FM radio station call letters*]

KLDZ-FM Fremont, CA [*FM radio station call letters*] (BROA)

KLE Kaele [*Cameroon*] [*Airport symbol*] (AD)

KLE Kala Explorations [*Vancouver Stock Exchange symbol*]

KLe Leavenworth Public Library, Leavenworth, KS [*Library symbol*] [*Library of Congress*] (LCLS)

KLEA Lovington, NM [*AM radio station call letters*]

KLEA-FM Lovington, NM [*FM radio station call letters*]

KLEB Golden Meadow, LA [*AM radio station call letters*]

Kleb Klebsiella [*Genus of microorganisms*] (MAH)

KleBl Klerusblatt [*Munich*] [*A publication*] (BJA)

Klebs Klebsiella [*A genus of bacteria*]

KLEE Ottumwa, IA [*AM radio station call letters*]

KleerVu Kleer-Vu Industries, Inc. [*Associated Press*] (SAG)

KLEF Anchorage, AK [*FM radio station call letters*]

KLEH Anamosa, IA [*AM radio station call letters*]

KLEI Kailua-Kona, HI [*AM radio station call letters*]

Kleinrt Kleinert's, Inc. [*Associated Press*] (SAG)

KLEL San Jose, CA [*FM radio station call letters*]

KLEM Le Mars, IA [*AM radio station call letters*]

KLEN Cheyenne, WY [*FM radio station call letters*]

KLEO Kahaluu, HI [*FM radio station call letters*]

KLEP Newark, AR [*Television station call letters*]

KLEPTO Kleptomania (ABBR)

KLER Orofino, ID [*AM radio station call letters*]

KLER-FM Orofino, ID [*FM radio station call letters*]

KLERW Kleer-Vu Industries, Inc. (SAUO)

KLeS Saint Mary College, Leavenworth, KS [*Library symbol*] [*Library of Congress*] (LCLS)

KLES-FM Mabton, WA [*FM radio station call letters*] (BROA)

KLeVA United States Veterans Administration Center, Leavenworth, KS [*Library symbol*] [*Library of Congress*] (LCLS)

KLEW Lewiston, ID [*Television station call letters*]

KLEX Lexington, MO [*AM radio station call letters*]

KLEY Wellington, KS [*AM radio station call letters*]

KLEY-FM Floresville, TX [*FM radio station call letters*] (BROA)

KLF Kopyright Liberation Front (SAUO)

KLFA King City, CA [*FM radio station call letters*]

KLFB Lubbock, TX [*AM radio station call letters*]

KLFC Branson, MO [*FM radio station call letters*]

KLFD Litchfield, MN [*AM radio station call letters*]

KLFE Seattle, WA [*AM radio station call letters*] (RBYB)

KLFF San Luis Obispo, CA [*FM radio station call letters*] (RBYB)

KLFI Hampton/Langley Air Force Base [*Virginia*] [*ICAO location identifier*] (ICLI)

KLFJ Springfield, MO [*AM radio station call letters*]

KLFK Lufkin/Angelina County [*Texas*] [*ICAO location identifier*] (ICLI)

KLFM Great Falls, MT [*FM radio station call letters*]

KLFO Florence, OR [*FM radio station call letters*] (BROA)

KLFT Lafayette/Regional [*Louisiana*] [*ICAO location identifier*] (ICLI)

KLFX Nolanville, TX [*FM radio station call letters*] (RBYB)

KLFY Lafayette, LA [*Television station call letters*]

KLG Kalgoorlie [*Australia*] [*Seismograph station code, US Geological Survey*] (SEIS)

KLG Kalskag [*Alaska*] [*Airport symbol*] (OAG)

KLG Kenelm Lee Guinness (SAUO)

KLG Keto-Laevo-Gulonic Acid [*Organic chemistry*]

KLG Keto-L-glutonic (Acid) [*Biochemistry*]

KLG Killing (ABBR)

KLG Knudsen Leaf Gauge [*Physics*]

KLG University of Louisville, Louisville, KY [*OCLC symbol*] (OCLC)

KLGA Algona, IA [*AM radio station call letters*]

KLGA New York/La Guardia [*New York*] [*ICAO location identifier*] (ICLI)

KLGA-FM Algona, IA [*FM radio station call letters*]

KLGB Long Beach [*California*] [*ICAO location identifier*] (ICLI)

KLGM Kilogram (ABBR)

KLGN Logan, UT [*AM radio station call letters*]

KLGR Knight's Local Government Reports [*A publication*] (DLA)

KLGR Redwood Falls, MN [*AM radio station call letters*]

KLGR-FM Redwood Falls, MN [*FM radio station call letters*]

KLGT Buffalo, WY [*FM radio station call letters*]

KLGT-TV Minneapolis, MN [*Television station call letters*]

KLH Kapapala Ranch [*Hawaii*] [*Seismograph station code, US Geological Survey*] (SEIS)

KLH Keyhole Limpet Hemocyanin [*Immunology*]

KLH Kingdom of Lesotho Handicrafts (BUAC)

KLH KLH Computers, Inc. (SAUO)

KLH KLM Helicopters NV [*Netherlands*] [*ICAO designator*] (FAAC)

KLH Kloss, Low, and Hofmann [*Initialism is name of electronics company and brand name of its products*]

KLH Knight of the Legion of Honor [*France*]

KLH Knight of the Legion of Honour (DD)

KLH Long Akha [*Malaysia*] [*Airport symbol*] (AD)

KLH Minister of State for Population and Research Environment, Indonesia (SAUO)

KLHB-FM Odem, TX [*FM radio station call letters*] (RBYB)

KLHI Lahaina, HI [*FM radio station call letters*]

KLHS Lewiston, ID [*FM radio station call letters*]

KLHT Honolulu, HI [*AM radio station call letters*]

KLI Kaliber Resources Ltd. [*Vancouver Stock Exchange symbol*]

KLI King's Light Infantry [*Military unit*] [*British*]

KLI Klingon Language Institute

KLI Kolyma-Avia [*Former USSR*] [*FAA designator*] (FAAC)

Kliatt Kliatt Young Adult Paperback Book Guide [*A publication*] (BRI)

KLIAU Korea Land Improvement Association Union (BUAC)

KLIC Keyletter-in-Context [*Computer science*]

KLIC Kulicke & Soffa Ind [*NASDAQ symbol*] (TTSB)

KLIC Kulicke & Soffa Industries, Inc. [*NASDAQ symbol*] (NQ)

KLIC Kulicke & Soffia Industries, Inc. (SAUO)

KLIC Monroe, LA [*AM radio station call letters*]

KLID Poplar Bluff, MO [*AM radio station call letters*]

KLIF Dallas, TX [*AM radio station call letters*]

KLIH-AM Little Rock, AR [*AM radio station call letters*] (BROA)

KLIK Jefferson City, MO [*AM radio station call letters*]

KLIL Moreauville, LA [*FM radio station call letters*]

KLIM Limon, CO [*AM radio station call letters*] (RBYB)

KLiMN Alamogordo/Holloman Air Force Base (SAUS)

KLIN Lincoln, NE [*AM radio station call letters*]

KLINA K, Li, and Na [*For the chemical elements potassium, lithium, and sodium*] [*Beckman flame system*] [*Trademark*]

KLindB Bethany College, Lindsborg, KS [*Library symbol*] [*Library of Congress*] (LCLS)

KLIP Monroe, LA [*FM radio station call letters*]

KLIPS Kilo Logical Inferences Per Second (SAUS)

KLIPS Thousands of Logical Inferences Per Second (SAUS)

KLIR Columbus, NE [*FM radio station call letters*]

KLIS Palestine, TX [*FM radio station call letters*]

KLIT Little Rock/Adams Field [*Arkansas*] [*ICAO location identifier*] (ICLI)

KLIT-FM Avalon, CA [*FM radio station call letters*] (BROA)

KLIV San Jose, CA [*AM radio station call letters*]

KLIX Twin Falls, ID [*AM radio station call letters*]

KLIX-FM Twin Falls, ID [*FM radio station call letters*]

KLIZ Brainerd, MN [*AM radio station call letters*]

KLIZ Korea Limited Identification Zone

KLIZ Limestone/Loring Air Force Base [*Maine*] [*ICAO location identifier*] (ICLI)

KLIZ-FM Brainerd, MN [*FM radio station call letters*]

KLJ Jewish Hospital, Louisville, KY [*OCLC symbol*] (OCLC)

KLJ Knight of [*the Order of*] St. Lazarus of Jerusalem [*British*]

KLJ Knight of the Military and Hospitalier Order of St. Lazarus (DD)

KLJB Davenport, IA [*Television station call letters*]

KLJC Kansas City, MO [*FM radio station call letters*]

KLJT-FM Jacksonville, TX [*FM radio station call letters*] (BROA)

KLJY Killjoy (ABBR)

KLJZ Port Sulphur, LA [*FM radio station call letters*] (RBYB)

KLJZ-FM Yuma, AZ [*FM radio station call letters*] (BROA)

KLK Kealakekua [*Hawaii*] [*Seismograph station code, US Geological Survey*] [*Closed*] (SEIS)

KLK Killick Gold Co. [*Vancouver Stock Exchange symbol*]

KLKC Parsons, KS [*AM radio station call letters*]

KLKC-FM Parsons, KS [*FM radio station call letters*]

KLKE Albion, NE [*Television station call letters*] (RBYB)

KLKI Anacortes, WA [*AM radio station call letters*]

KLKK Clear Lake, IA [*FM radio station call letters*]

KLKL Benton, LA [*FM radio station call letters*]

KLKN-TV Lincoln, NE [*TV station call letters*] (RBYB)

KLKO Elko, NV [*FM radio station call letters*]

KLKS Breezy Point, MN [*FM radio station call letters*]

KLKX Rosamond, CA [*FM radio station call letters*]

KLKY Milton-Freewater, OR [*AM radio station call letters*]

KLKY-FM Milton-Freewater, OR [*FM radio station call letters*] (RBYB)

KLL Kalltalsperre [*Federal Republic of Germany*] [*Seismograph station code, US Geological Survey*] (SEIS)

KLL Levelock [*Alaska*] [*Airport symbol*] (OAG)

KLLA Leesville, LA [*AM radio station call letters*]

KLLB West Jordan, UT [*AM radio station call letters*]

KLLC-FM San Francisco, CA [*FM radio station call letters*] (RBYB)

KLLF Wichita Falls, TX [*AM radio station call letters*]

KLLI............ Hooks, TX [*FM radio station call letters*]
KLLK............ Fort Bragg, CA [*FM radio station call letters*]
KLLK............ Willits, CA [*AM radio station call letters*]
KLLL............ Lubbock, TX [*AM radio station call letters*]
KLLL-FM...... Lubbock, TX [*FM radio station call letters*]
KLLM........... Forks, WA [*FM radio station call letters*]
KLLM........... KLLM Transport Services, Inc. [*NASDAQ symbol*] (NQ)
KLLM........... KLLM Transport Sv [*NASDAQ symbol*] (TTSB)
KLLN........... Newark, AR [*AM radio station call letters*]
KLLR........... Amarillo, TX [*FM radio station call letters*] (RBYB)
KLLS........... Augusta, KS [*FM radio station call letters*]
KLLT............ Vinton, IA [*FM radio station call letters*]
KLLU-AM .... Reedsport, OR [*AM radio station call letters*] (BROA)
KLLV........... Breen, CO [*AM radio station call letters*]
KLLY........... Oildale, CA [*FM radio station call letters*]
KLLZ........... Walker, MN [*AM radio station call letters*]
KLLZ-FM ..... Walker, MN [*FM radio station call letters*]
KL/M........... Kiloliters per Minute
KLM........... Kilometer
KLM........... KLM Royal Dutch Air [*NYSE symbol*] (TTSB)
KLM........... KLM [*Koninklijke Luchtvaart Maatschappij*] Royal Dutch Airlines
              [*NYSE symbol*] (SPSG)
KLM........... KLM Royal Dutch Airlines [*Netherlands*] [*ICAO designator*] (FAAC)
KLM........... Koninklijke Luchtvaart Maatschappij [*Royal Dutch Airlines*]
KLM........... Kuala Lumpur [*Malaysia*] [*Seismograph station code, US Geological
              Survey*] (SEIS)
KLM........... University of Louisville, School of Music Library, Louisville, KY [*OCLC
              symbol*] (OCLC)
KLMA.......... Hobbs, NM [*FM radio station call letters*]
KLMB-FM ..... Bastrop, LA [*FM radio station call letters*] (RBYB)
KLMC.......... Knights of Life Motorcycle Club (EA)
KLME.......... Kuala Lumpur Metal Exchange (BUAC)
KLMJ........... Hampton, IA [*FM radio station call letters*]
KLMN.......... Amarillo, TX [*FM radio station call letters*]
KLMO.......... Longmont, CO [*AM radio station call letters*]
KLMP.......... Rapid City, SD [*FM radio station call letters*]
KLMR.......... Lamar, CO [*AM radio station call letters*]
KLMS-AM ... Lincoln, NE [*AM radio station call letters*] (BROA)
KLMTR......... Kilometer (ABBR)
KLMX-AM .... Clayton, NM [*AM radio station call letters*] (RBYB)
KLMY........... Seaside, CA [*FM radio station call letters*]
KLN............ Kelan Resources [*Vancouver Stock Exchange symbol*]
KLN............ Larsen Bay [*Alaska*] [*Airport symbol*] (OAG)
KLN............ Norton-Children's Hospital Medical Library, Louisville, KY [*OCLC
              symbol*] (OCLC)
KLNA .... West Palm Beach/Palm Beach County Park [*Florida*] [*ICAO location
              identifier*] (ICLI)
KLNA-FM ..... Dunnigan, CA [*FM radio station call letters*] (RBYB)
KLNC-FM ..... Killeen, TX [*FM radio station call letters*] (BROA)
KLND.......... Little Eagle, SD [*FM radio station call letters*] (RBYB)
KLNE.......... Lexington, NE [*FM radio station call letters*]
KLNE-TV ..... Lexington, NE [*Television station call letters*]
KLNG.......... Council Bluffs, IA [*AM radio station call letters*]
KLNI........... Decorah, IA [*FM radio station call letters*]
KLNITE........ Knitting, Lace, and Net Industry Training Board (BUAC)
KLNK.......... Lincoln/Municipal [*Nebraska*] [*ICAO location identifier*] (ICLI)
KLNQ-FM ..... Des Moines, IA [*FM radio station call letters*] (BROA)
KLNR.......... Panaca, NV [*FM radio station call letters*]
KLNT........... Clinton, IA [*AM radio station call letters*]
KLNT........... Laredo, TX [*AM radio station call letters*] (BROA)
KLNV-FM ..... San Diego, CA [*FM radio station call letters*] (BROA)
KLO............ Kalibo [*Philippines*] [*Airport symbol*] (OAG)
KLO............ Klystron Oscillator
KLO............ Ogden, UT [*AM radio station call letters*]
KLOA .... Ridgecrest, CA [*AM radio station call letters*]
KLOA-FM ..... Ridgecrest, CA [*FM radio station call letters*]
KLOB .... Thousand Palms, CA [*FM radio station call letters*]
KLOC .... Ceres, CA [*AM radio station call letters*]
KLOC .... Kilo Lines of Code [*Computer science*] (IGQR)
KLOC .... Kush Locke [*NASDAQ symbol*] (SAG)
KLOC .... Kushner-Locke [*NASDAQ symbol*] (TTSB)
KLOC .... [*The*] Kushner-Locke Co. [*NASDAQ symbol*] (NQ)
KLOC .... Kushner-Locke Company (SAUO)
KLOC .... Thousand Lines of Code (SAUS)
KLOC .... Thousands of Lines of Code (SAUS)
KLOCW .... Kushner-Locke Wrrt [*NASDAQ symbol*] (TTSB)
KLOD .... Shafter, CA [*FM radio station call letters*]
KLOE .... Goodland, KS [*AM radio station call letters*]
KLOF .... Kloof Gold Mining Co. Ltd. [*NASDAQ symbol*] (NQ)
KLOFFE........ Kuala Lumpur Options and Financial Futures Exchange [*Maylaysia*]
              (NUMA)
KLOFY .... Kloof Gold Mining ADR [*NASDAQ symbol*] (TTSB)
KLOG .... Kelso, WA [*AM radio station call letters*]
KLOH .... Pipestone, MN [*AM radio station call letters*]
KLOK .... San Jose, CA [*AM radio station call letters*]
KLOK-FM ..... Greenfield, CA [*FM radio station call letters*] (RBYB)
KLOL .... Houston, TX [*FM radio station call letters*]
KLOM .... Lompoc, CA [*AM radio station call letters*]
KLON .... Long Beach, CA [*FM radio station call letters*]
KLOO .... Corvallis, OR [*AM radio station call letters*]
KloofG .... Kloof Gold Mining Co. Ltd. [*Associated Press*] (SAG)
KLOO-FM ..... Corvallis, OR [*FM radio station call letters*] (BROA)
KLOQ .... Merced, CA [*AM radio station call letters*]
KLOQ-FM ..... Winton, CA [*FM radio station call letters*] (RBYB)
KLOR .... Ponca City, OK [*FM radio station call letters*]

KLOS .... Kloss Video Corp. (SAUO)
KLOS .... Los Angeles, CA [*FM radio station call letters*]
KloS .... Southeast Kansas Library System, Iola (SAUS)
KLOU .... Louisville/Bowman [*Kentucky*] [*ICAO location identifier*] (ICLI)
KLOU .... St. Louis, MO [*FM radio station call letters*]
KLOV .... Loveland, CO [*AM radio station call letters*]
KLOV-FM ..... Winchester, OR [*FM radio station call letters*] (BROA)
KLOW ..... Caruthersville, MO [*FM radio station call letters*]
KLOZ ..... Eldon, MO [*FM radio station call letters*]
KLP ..... Korean Labor Party [*Political party*]
KLP ..... Louisville Free Public Library, Louisville, KY [*OCLC symbol*] (OCLC)
KLP ..... Redding Aero Enterprises, Inc. [*FAA designator*] (FAAC)
KLPA ..... Alexandria, LA [*Television station call letters*]
KLPA ..... Khan-Lewis Phonological Analysis [*Speech evaluation test*]
KLPA ..... Knuckeys Lagoon Protected Area (SAUO)
KI Pauly ..... Der Kleine Pauly [*A publication*] (OCD)
KLPB ..... Lafayette, LA [*Television station call letters*]
KLPC ..... Krypton Laser Photocoagulation [*Medicine*] (MELL)
KLPI ..... Ruston, LA [*FM radio station call letters*]
KLPL ..... Lake Providence, LA [*AM radio station call letters*]
KLPL-FM ..... Lake Providence, LA [*FM radio station call letters*]
KLPQ ..... Sherweeod, AR [*FM radio station call letters*]
KLPQ-FM ..... Arkansas City, KS [*FM radio station call letters*] (BROA)
KLPR-FM ..... Keamey, NE [*FM radio station call letters*] (RBYB)
KLPTMN ..... Kleptomania (ABBR)
KLPTMNC ..... Kleptomaniac (ABBR)
KLPW ..... Union, MO [*AM radio station call letters*]
KLPW-FM ..... Union, MO [*FM radio station call letters*]
KLPX ..... Tucson, AZ [*FM radio station call letters*]
KLPZ ..... Parker, AZ [*AM radio station call letters*]
KLQB ..... Oracle, AZ [*FM radio station call letters*]
KLQL ..... Luverne, MN [*FM radio station call letters*]
KLQP ..... Madison, MN [*FM radio station call letters*]
KLQV-FM ..... San Diego, CA [*FM radio station call letters*] (BROA)
KLQZ ..... Paragould, AR [*FM radio station call letters*]
KLR ..... Columbus Air Transport, Inc. [*ICAO designator*] (FAAC)
KLR ..... Kalmar [*Sweden*] [*Airport symbol*] (OAG)
KLR ..... Kathiawar Law Reports [*India*] [*A publication*] (DLA)
KLR ..... Kentucky Law Reporter [*A publication*] (DLA)
KLRA ..... England, AR [*AM radio station call letters*]
KLRA-FM ..... England, AR [*FM radio station call letters*]
KLRB ..... Aurora, NE [*FM radio station call letters*]
KLRC ..... Siloam Springs, AR [*FM radio station call letters*]
KLRD ..... Laredo/International [*Texas*] [*ICAO location identifier*] (ICLI)
KLRD ..... Yucaipa, CA [*FM radio station call letters*]
KLRE ..... Little Rock, AR [*FM radio station call letters*]
KLRF ..... Brownsville, OR [*FM radio station call letters*]
KLRF ..... Jacksonville/Little Rock Air Force Base [*Arkansas*] [*ICAO location
              identifier*] (ICLI)
KLRG ..... North Little Rock, AR [*AM radio station call letters*]
KLRK ..... Vandalia, MO [*FM radio station call letters*]
KLRN ..... San Antonio, TX [*Television station call letters*]
KLRO-FM ..... Nile, WA [*FM radio station call letters*] (BROA)
KLRQ ..... Clinton, MO [*FM radio station call letters*]
KLRR ..... Redmond, OR [*FM radio station call letters*]
KLRS ..... Chico, CA [*FM radio station call letters*]
KLRT ..... Kleinert's, Inc. [*NASDAQ symbol*] (NQ)
KLRT ..... Little Rock, AR [*Television station call letters*]
KLRU ..... Austin, TX [*Television station call letters*]
KLRU-DT ..... Austin, TX [*Television station call letters*] (BROA)
KLRX-FM ..... Madrid, IA [*FM radio station call letters*] (BROA)
KLRZ ..... Larose, LA [*FM radio station call letters*]
KLS ..... Faculty of Library and Information Science, University of Toronto
              [*UTLAS symbol*]
KLS ..... Karlskrona [*Sweden*] [*Seismograph station code, US Geological
              Survey*] [*Closed*] (SEIS)
KLS ..... Kaskaskia Library System [*Library network*]
KLS ..... Kelso Resources [*Vancouver Stock Exchange symbol*]
KLS ..... Kelso, WA [*Location identifier*] [*FAA*] (FAAL)
KLS ..... Key Lock Switch
KLS ..... Kidney, Liver, Spleen [*Medicine*]
KLS ..... Kleine-Levin Syndrome [*Medicine*] (MELL)
Kls ..... Kloster (SAUO)
KLS ..... Knight of the Lion and Sun [*Persia*] (ROG)
KLS ..... Knotted List Structure (BUR)
KLS ..... Kreuzbein Lipomatous Syndrome [*Medicine*] (DMAA)
KLS ..... Kreuzbein's Lipomatous Syndrome [*Medicine*] (DB)
KLS ..... Krypton LASER System
KLSA ..... Alexandria, LA [*FM radio station call letters*]
KLSB ..... Nacogdoches, TX [*Television station call letters*]
KLSC ..... Korean Logistic Service Corps (CINC)
KLSC-FM ..... Fayette, MO [*FM radio station call letters*] (RBYB)
KI Schr ..... Kleine Schriften [*of various authors*] [*Classical studies*] (OCD)
KLSD ..... Kiribati Land and Survey Division (SAUO)
KLSE ..... Kuala Lumpur Stock Exchange
KLSE ..... Rochester, MN [*FM radio station call letters*]
KLSIFC ..... Kathy Lynn Sacra International Fan Club (EA)
KLSI-FM ..... Hutchinson, KS [*FM radio station call letters*] (BROA)
KLSK ..... Santa Fe, NM [*FM radio station call letters*]
KLSN ..... New London, MO [*FM radio station call letters*] (RBYB)
KLSN-FM ..... Santa Cruz, CA [*FM radio station call letters*] (BROA)
KLSP ..... Angola, LA [*FM radio station call letters*]
KLSQ ..... Laughlin, NV [*AM radio station call letters*] (RBYB)
KLSQ EXP STN... East Las Vegas, NV [*Radio expansion station*] (RBYB)
KLSR ..... Memphis, TX [*AM radio station call letters*]

KLSR-FM ..... Memphis, TX [*FM radio station call letters*]
KLSR-TV ...... Eugene, OR [*Television station call letters*] (BROA)
KLSS............ Korean Library Science Society (BUAC)
KLSS-FM ..... Mason City, IA [*FM radio station call letters*]
KLST .... Kindergarten Language Screening Test
KLST .... San Angelo, TX [*Television station call letters*]
KLSU .... Baton Rouge, LA [*FM radio station call letters*]
KLSV .... Las Vegas/Nellis Air Force Base [*Nevada*] [*ICAO location identifier*] (ICLI)
KLSX............ Los Angeles, CA [*FM radio station call letters*]
KLSY .... Bellevue, WA [*FM radio station call letters*]
KLSZ .... Van Buren, AR [*FM radio station call letters*]
KLT .... Kansas City Power & Light Co. [*NYSE symbol*] (SPSG)
KLT .... Kansas City Pwr & Lt [*NYSE symbol*] (TTSB)
KLT .... Karhunen-Loeve Transform [*Mathematics*]
KLT .... Kiloton [*Nuclear equivalent of 1000 tons of high explosives*] (AAG)
KIT .... Kleine Texte fuer Theologische und Philosophische Vorlesungen [*A publication*] (BJA)
KLT .... Klystron Life Test
KLTA............ Breckenridge, MN [*FM radio station call letters*]
KLTB............ Boise, ID [*FM radio station call letters*]
KLTC............ Dickinson, ND [*AM radio station call letters*]
KLTCB.......... Korean Long Term Credit Bank
KLTD............ Temple, TX [*FM radio station call letters*]
KLTE............ Kirksville, MO [*FM radio station call letters*]
KLTF............ Little Falls, MN [*AM radio station call letters*]
KLTG............ Corpus Christi, TX [*FM radio station call letters*]
KLTH............ Kansas City, MO [*FM radio station call letters*]
KLTI............ Macon, MO [*AM radio station call letters*]
KLTI-FM ...... Ames, IA [*FM radio station call letters*] (BROA)
KLTJ .... Galveston, TX [*Television station call letters*]
KLTK............ South West City, MO [*AM radio station call letters*]
KLTL............ Lake Charles, LA [*Television station call letters*]
KLTM............ Monroe, LA [*Television station call letters*]
KLTN............ Kiloton (ABBR)
KLTN............ Port Arthur, TX [*FM radio station call letters*]
KLTO............ Knurling Tool
KLTO............ Rosenberg, TX [*FM radio station call letters*] (RBYB)
KLTP-FM ..... Galveston, TX [*AM radio station call letters*] (RBYB)
KLTPrA........ Kansas City P&L 3.80% Pfd [*NYSE symbol*] (TTSB)
KLTPrD........ Kansas City P&L 4.35% Pfd [*NYSE symbol*] (TTSB)
KLTPrE........ Kansas City P&L 4.50% Pfd [*NYSE symbol*] (TTSB)
KLTQ........... Sparta, MO [*FM radio station call letters*]
KLTR............ Franklin, TX [*FM radio station call letters*] (RBYB)
KLTR............ Kilter (ABBR)
KLTS............ Altus Air Force Base [*Oklahoma*] [*ICAO location identifier*] (ICLI)
KLTS............ Shreveport, LA [*Television station call letters*]
KLTT............ Brighton, CO [*AM radio station call letters*]
KLTV............ Tyler, TX [*Television station call letters*]
KLTW-AM ..... Sierra Vista, AZ [*AM radio station call letters*] (RBYB)
KLTW-FM .... Rayne, LA [*FM radio station call letters*] (BROA)
KLTX............ Harker Heights, TX [*FM radio station call letters*]
KLTX............ Long Beach, CA [*AM radio station call letters*] (BROA)
KLTY............ Fort Worth, TX [*FM radio station call letters*]
KLTZ............ Glasgow, MT [*AM radio station call letters*]
KLU .... Kaiser Aluminum [*NYSE symbol*] (TTSB)
KLU .... Kaiser Aluminum & Chemical Corp. [*NYSE symbol*] (SPSG)
KLU .... Key and Lamp Units [*Telecommunications*]
KLU .... Klagenfurt [*Austria*] [*Airport symbol*] (OAG)
KLU .... Klutina [*Alaska*] [*Seismograph station code, US Geological Survey*] (SEIS)
KLUA .... Kailua-Kona, HI [*FM radio station call letters*]
KLUB .... Bloomington, TX [*FM radio station call letters*]
KLUC-FM ..... Las Vegas, NV [*FM radio station call letters*]
KLUE............ Knowledge Legacy of the Unavailable Expert [*Computer science*] (BTTJ)
KLUE............ Soledad, CA [*FM radio station call letters*]
KLUF............ Phoenix/Luke Air Force Base [*Arizona*] [*ICAO location identifier*] (ICLI)
KLUH .... Poplar Bluff, MO [*FM radio station call letters*]
KLUJ............ Harlingen, TX [*Television station call letters*]
KLUK............ Cincinnati/Municipal-Lunken Field [*Ohio*] [*ICAO location identifier*] (ICLI)
KLUK .... Laughlin, NV [*FM radio station call letters*] (RBYB)
KLUP .... Terrell Hills, TX [*AM radio station call letters*]
KLUPrD........ Kaiser Alum 8.255% 'PRIDES' [*NYSE symbol*] (TTSB)
KLUR............ Wichita Falls, TX [*FM radio station call letters*]
KLUV .... Dallas, TX [*FM radio station call letters*]
KLUX .... Robstown, TX [*FM radio station call letters*]
KLUZ............ Albuquerque, NM [*Television station call letters*]
KLV .... Karlovy Vary [*Former Czechoslovakia*] [*Airport symbol*] (OAG)
KLVA............ Casa Grande, AZ [*FM radio station call letters*] (RBYB)
KLVB-AM ..... Medford, OR [*AM radio station call letters*] (BROA)
KLVC............ Magalia, CA [*FM radio station call letters*]
KLVE............ Los Angeles, CA [*FM radio station call letters*]
KLVF............ Las Vegas, NM [*FM radio station call letters*]
KLVG............ Garberville, CA [*FM radio station call letters*] (RBYB)
KLVH-FM ..... Leavenworth, WA [*FM radio station call letters*] (BROA)
KLVI............ Beaumont, TX [*AM radio station call letters*]
KLVJ............ Mountain Home, ID [*AM radio station call letters*]
KLVJ-FM ...... Julian, CA [*FM radio station call letters*] (BROA)
KLVJ-FM ...... Mountain Home, ID [*FM radio station call letters*]
KLVK............ Dimmitt, TX [*FM radio station call letters*] (RBYB)
KLVK-FM ..... Kingsburg, CA [*FM radio station call letters*] (BROA)
KLVL............ Pasadena, TX [*AM radio station call letters*]

KLVM............ Prunedale, CA [*FM radio station call letters*]
KLVN .... Chowchilla, CA [*FM radio station call letters*] (RBYB)
KLVO .... Belen, NM [*FM radio station call letters*] (RBYB)
KLVP .... Tigard, OR [*AM radio station call letters*] (BROA)
KLVP-FM ..... Cherryville, OR [*FM radio station call letters*] (BROA)
KLVQ .... Athens, TX [*AM radio station call letters*]
KLVR............ Santa Rosa, CA [*FM radio station call letters*]
KLVS............ Las Vegas [*New Mexico*] [*ICAO location identifier*] (ICLI)
KLVS-FM ..... Kingsburg, CA [*FM radio station call letters*] (RBYB)
KLVT .... Levelland, TX [*AM radio station call letters*]
KLVT-FM ..... Levelland, TX [*FM radio station call letters*]
KLVU .... Haynesville, LA [*AM radio station call letters*]
KLVU-FM ..... Sweet Home, OR [*FM radio station call letters*] (BROA)
KLVV .... Ponca City, OK [*FM radio station call letters*]
KLVW .... Julian, CA [*FM radio station call letters*] (RBYB)
KLVW-FM ..... Odessa, TX [*FM radio station call letters*] (BROA)
KLVX .... Las Vegas, NV [*Television station call letters*]
KLVY-FM ..... Fairmead, CA [*FM radio station call letters*] (BROA)
KLW .... Claw Resources Ltd. [*Vancouver Stock Exchange symbol*]
KLW .... Faculty of Law Library, University of Toronto [*UTLAS symbol*]
KLW .... Klawock [*Alaska*] [*Airport symbol*] (OAG)
KLWD-FM ..... Gillette, WY [*FM radio station call letters*] (BROA)
KLWJ............ Umatilla, OR [*AM radio station call letters*]
KLWN .... Lawrence, KS [*AM radio station call letters*]
KLWS-FM ..... Moses Lake, WA [*FM radio station call letters*] (BROA)
KLWT .... Kilowatt (ABBR)
KLWT .... Kirsch Laser Welding Technique [*Medicine*] (MELL)
KLWT .... Lebanon, MO [*AM radio station call letters*]
KLWY .... Cheyenne, WY [*Television station call letters*]
KLX .... Kalamata [*Greece*] [*Airport symbol*] (OAG)
KLX .... Kalix Air [*Nigeria*] [*FAA designator*] (FAAC)
KLX .... Kidney and Lung Extract
KLXK............ Duluth, MN [*FM radio station call letters*]
KLXK-FM ..... Breckenridge, TX [*FM radio station call letters*] (BROA)
KLXM-FM ..... Salinas, CA [*FM radio station call letters*] (BROA)
KLXO .... El Centro, CA [*Television station call letters*]
KLXQ .... Hot Springs, AR [*FM radio station call letters*]
KLXQ-FM ..... Hot Springs, AR [*FM radio station call letters*] (BROA)
KLXR............ Redding, CA [*AM radio station call letters*]
KLXS............ Pierre, SD [*FM radio station call letters*]
KLXV .... San Jose, CA [*Television station call letters*]
KLXX .... Bismarck-Mandan, ND [*AM radio station call letters*]
KLY .... Kalima [*Zaire*] [*Airport symbol*] (AD)
KLY .... Klyuchi [*Former USSR*] [*Seismograph station code, US Geological Survey*] (SEIS)
KLYC............ McMinnville, OR [*AM radio station call letters*]
KLYD .... Shafter, CA [*FM radio station call letters*] (RBYB)
KLYF............ Des Moines, IA [*FM radio station call letters*]
KLYF............ Thousand Oaks, CA [*AM radio station call letters*] (BROA)
KLYK............ Longview, WA [*FM radio station call letters*]
KLYN............ Lynden, WA [*FM radio station call letters*]
KLYQ .... Hamilton, MT [*AM radio station call letters*]
KLYR............ Clarksville, AR [*AM radio station call letters*]
KLYR............ Smoke Layer Aloft [*Meteorology*] (FAAC)
KLYR-FM ..... Clarksville, AR [*FM radio station call letters*]
KLYT............ Albuquerque, NM [*FM radio station call letters*]
KLYV............ Dubuque, IA [*FM radio station call letters*]
KLYY-FM ..... Arcadia, CA [*FM radio station call letters*] (RBYB)
KLZ .... Denver, CO [*AM radio station call letters*]
KLZ .... Kleinzee [*South Africa*] [*Airport symbol*] (OAG)
KLZA-FM ..... Falls City, NE [*FM radio station call letters*] (BROA)
KLZE............ Owensville, MO [*FM radio station call letters*]
KLZK............ Brownfield, TX [*FM radio station call letters*]
KLZR............ Lawrence, KS [*FM radio station call letters*]
KLZX-FM ..... Brigham City, UT [*FM radio station call letters*] (RBYB)
KLZY............ Powell, WY [*FM radio station call letters*]
KLZZ............ Waite Park, MN [*FM radio station call letters*]
KM .... Air Malta [*ICAO designator*] (AD)
KM .... Comoros [*ANSI two-letter standard code*] (CNC)
KM .... Draepelin-Morel [*Disease*] [*Psychiatry*] (DAVI)
KM .... Ha-Kibbuts ha-Me'uhad (BJA)
KM .... Kabataang Makabayan [*Nationalist Youth*] [*Philippines*]
KM .... Kaffrarian Museum (SAUO)
KM .... Kanamycin [*Antibacterial compound*]
KM .... [*The*] Kansas & Missouri Railway & Terminal Co. [*Formerly, KMRT*] [*AAR code*]
KM .... Kansas Mapper (SAUO)
kM .... Kilomega
Km .... Kilometer (TBD)
km .... Kilometer
KM .... K-Immunoglobulin Light Chains [*Immunology*] (DAVI)
KM .... Kinetic Momentum
KM .... King and Martyr [*Church calendars*]
KM .... Kingdom
KM .... King's Medal [*or Medallist*] [*British*]
KM .... King's Messenger [*British*] (ROG)
KM .... Kirchoff Method [*Telecommunications*] (OA)
KM .... Kirk-Mayer, Inc. (SAUO)
KM .... Kitchen Mechanic [*Restaurant slang*]
KM .... Klystron Mount
KM .... Kmart [*NYSE symbol*] (TTSB)
KM .... K Mart Corp. [*NYSE symbol*] (SPSG)
KM .... K mart Financing Trust I [*NYSE symbol*] (SAG)
KM .... Kneading Massage (MELL)
KM .... Knight of Malta

KM	Knight of the Sovereign and Military Order of Malta (DD)
KM	Knowledge Management
KM	Knowledge Manager
KM	Kraepelin-Morel [Disease] [Psychiatry] (DAVI)
KM	Kubelka-Munk [Optics]
KM	Kurram Militia [British military] (DMA)
KM	Manhattan Public Library, Manhattan, KS [Library symbol] [Library of Congress] (LCLS)
Km	Michaelis Constant [In enzyme assays] (STED)
Km	Michaelis-Menten Dissociation Constnat (DAVI)
KM2	Kermit [Texas] [Seismograph station code, US Geological Survey] (SEIS)
km2	Square Kilometer
K M²/W	Kelvin Square Meters per Watt
KM³	Cubic Kilometer
KM5	Kermit [Texas] [Seismograph station code, US Geological Survey] (SEIS)
KM6	Kermit [Texas] [Seismograph station code, US Geological Survey] (SEIS)
KM9	Kermit [Texas] [Seismograph station code, US Geological Survey] (SEIS)
KMA	Kerema [Papua New Guinea] [Airport symbol] (OAG)
KMA	Kinematograph Manufacturers Association, Inc. (SAUO)
KMA	Korea Military Academy
KMA	Ku-Band Multiple Access (MCD)
KMA	Royal Military Academy for Army & Air Force (SAUO)
KMA	Shenandoah, IA [AM radio station call letters]
KMAA	Kart Marketing Association of America (EA)
KMAC	Gainesville, MO [FM radio station call letters]
KMAC	Kushi Macrobiotic Corp. [NASDAQ symbol] (SAG)
KMAC	Kushi Macrobiotics [NASDAQ symbol] (TTSB)
KMACW	Kushi Macrobiotics Wrrt [NASDAQ symbol] (TTSB)
KMAD	Madill, OK [AM radio station call letters]
KMAD-FM	Madill, OK [FM radio station call letters]
KMAF	Midland/Regional Air Terminal [Texas] [ICAO location identifier] (ICLI)
KMAG	Fort Smith, AR [FM radio station call letters]
KMAG	Komag, Inc. [NASDAQ symbol] (NQ)
KMAG	Korea Military Advisory Group [United States]
KMAGV	Korean Military Assistance Group, Vietnam (VNW)
KMAJ	Topeka, KS [AM radio station call letters]
KMAJ-FM	Topeka, KS [FM radio station call letters]
KMAK	Orange Cove, CA [FM radio station call letters]
KMAL	Malden, MO [FM radio station call letters]
KMAM	Butler, MO [AM radio station call letters]
KMAN	Manhattan, KS [AM radio station call letters]
KMAP-FM	Castana, IA [FM radio station call letters] (BROA)
KMAQ	Marquoketa, IA [AM radio station call letters]
KMAQ-FM	Maquoketa, IA [FM radio station call letters]
KMAR	Winnsboro, LA [AM radio station call letters]
KMAR-FM	Winnsboro, LA [FM radio station call letters]
K mart	K Mart Corp. [Associated Press] (SAG)
KmartF	K mart Financing Trust I [Associated Press] (SAG)
KMAS	Korean Medical Association of America (EA)
KMAS	Shelton, WA [AM radio station call letters]
KMAT-FM	Seadrift, TX [FM radio station call letters] (BROA)
KMAU	Wailuku, HI [Television station call letters]
KMAU-DT	Wailuku, HI [Television station call letters] (BROA)
KMAV	Mayville, ND [AM radio station call letters]
KMAV-FM	Mayville, ND [FM radio station call letters]
KMAX	Arcadia, CA [FM radio station call letters]
KMAX-AM	Opportunity, WA [AM radio station call letters] (RBYB)
KMAX-TV	Sacramento, CA [Television station call letters] (BROA)
KMAY	Billings, MT [AM radio station call letters]
KMAZ	Las Cruces, NM [Television station call letters] (BROA)
KMB	Kimbe [New Britain] [Seismograph station code, US Geological Survey] [Closed] (SEIS)
KMB	Kimberly-Clark [NYSE symbol] (TTSB)
KMB2	Kimberly-Clark Corp. [NYSE symbol] (SPSG)
KMB	Koinambe [Papua New Guinea] [Airport symbol] (OAG)
KMBAX	Kemper Municipal Bond Cl.A [Mutual fund ticker symbol] (SG)
KMBC	Kansas City, MO [Television station call letters]
KMBD	Tillamook, OR [AM radio.station call letters]
KMBH	Harlingen, TX [Television station call letters]
KMBH-FM	Harlingen, TX [FM radio station call letters]
KMBI	Spokane, WA [AM radio station call letters]
KMBI-FM	Spokane, WA [FM radio station call letters]
KMBL	Junction, TX [AM radio station call letters]
KMBO	Keith Martin Ballet Oregon
KMBQ	Wasilla, AK [FM radio station call letters]
KMBR-FM	Butte, MT [FM radio station call letters] (BROA)
KMBS	West Monroe, LA [AM radio station call letters]
KMBV	Navasota, TX [FM radio station call letters]
KMBY	Capitola, CA [AM radio station call letters] (RBYB)
KMBY-FM	Gonzales, CA [FM radio station call letters] (RBYB)
KMBZ	Kansas City, MO [AM radio station call letters]
KMC	Kamloops CableNet [Vancouver Stock Exchange symbol]
KMC	Kane-Miller Corp. (EFIS)
KMC	Kenya Meat Commission (BUAC)
KMC	Kernel Migration Coefficient (PDAA)
kMc	Kilomegacycle
KMC	Kinetic Monte Carlo [Simulation]
KMC	Knowledge Management Consortium (SAUO)
KMC	Knowledge Management Network (SAUO)
KMC	Korean Marine Corps [North Korea]

KMC	Manhattan Christian College, Manhattan, KS [Library symbol] [Library of Congress] (LCLS)
KMCA-AM	Burney, CA [AM radio station call letters] (BROA)
KMCC	Lake Havasu City, AZ [Television station call letters] (BROA)
KMCC	Sacremento/McClellan Air Force Base [California] [ICAO location identifier] (ICLI)
KMCD	Fairfield, IA [AM radio station call letters]
KMCF	Tampa/MacDill Air Force Base [Florida] [ICAO location identifier] (ICLI)
KMCG	Casper, WY [AM radio station call letters] (BROA)
KMCG-FM	Carlsbad, CA [FM radio station call letters] (BROA)
KMCH	Manchester, IA [FM radio station call letters]
KMCI	Kansas City/International [Missouri] [ICAO location identifier] (ICLI)
KMCI	Lawrence, KS [Television station call letters]
KMCK	Siloam Springs, AR [FM radio station call letters]
KMCL	McCall, ID [AM radio station call letters]
KMCL-FM	McCall, ID [FM radio station call letters]
KMCM	Miles City, MT [FM radio station call letters]
K-MCM	Potassium-Containing Minimal Capacitation Medium [Medicine] (BABM)
KMCM-FM	Odessa, TX [FM radio station call letters] (BROA)
KMCO	McAlester, OK [FM radio station call letters]
KMCO	Orlando/McCoy Air Force Base [Florida] [ICAO location identifier] (ICLI)
KMCP	Kodak Metal Clad Plate (IAA)
KMcpC	McPherson College, McPherson, KS [Library symbol] [Library of Congress] (LCLS)
kMcps	Kilomegacycle per Second (STED)
kMcps	Kilomegacycles per Sound [Measurement] (DAVI)
KMCQ	The Dalles, OR [FM radio station call letters]
KMCR	Montgomery City, MO [FM radio station call letters]
kMcs	Kilomegacycles per Second (AABC)
KMCT	West Monroe, LA [Television station call letters]
KMCX	Ogallala, NE [FM radio station call letters]
KMCY	Minot, ND [Television station call letters]
KMD	Kamlode Resources, Inc. [Vancouver Stock Exchange symbol]
KMD	Kentucky Manpower Development (SAUO)
KMDAT	KeyMath Diagnostic Arithmetic Test
KMDC	Kirschner Medical Corporation (SAUO)
KMDL	Kaplan, LA [FM radio station call letters]
KMDO	Fort Scott, KS [AM radio station call letters]
KMDT	Middletown/Harrisburg International-Olmsted Field [Pennsylvania] [ICAO location identifier] (ICLI)
KMDW	Chicago/Chicago Midway [Illinois] [ICAO location identifier] (ICLI)
KMDX-FM	San Angelo, TX [FM radio station call letters] (BROA)
KMDY-FM	Keokuk, IA [FM radio station call letters] (BROA)
KME	Kappa Mu Epsilon [Society]
KME	Kermit [Texas] [Seismograph station code, US Geological Survey] [Closed] (SEIS)
KME	Kerr Magneto-Optical Effect [Optics]
KME	Kraft Mill Effluent [Pulp and paper processing]
KME	Media Center, Audio Visual Library, University of Toronto [UTLAS symbol]
KMEA	Kansas Music Educators Association (SAUO)
KMEA	Kentucky Music Educators Association (SAUO)
KMEB	Wailuku, HI [Television station call letters]
KMEC	Keystone Medical Corporation (SAUO)
KMED	K MED Centers, Inc. (SAUO)
KMED	Medford, OR [AM radio station call letters]
KMEF	Keratin, Myosin, Epidermin, Fibrin [Biochemistry]
KMEG	Sioux City, IA [Television station call letters]
KMEIA	Kodaly Music Education Institute of Australia
KMEL	San Francisco, CA [FM radio station call letters]
KMEM	Lincoln, NE [AM radio station call letters]
KMEM	Memphis/International [Tennessee] [ICAO location identifier] (ICLI)
KMEM	Memphis, MO [FM radio station call letters]
KMEN	San Bernardino, CA [AM radio station call letters]
KMER	Kemmerer, WY [AM radio station call letters]
KMER	Kodak Metal Etch Resist
KMER	Merced/Castle Air Force Base [California] [ICAO location identifier] (ICLI)
KMET	Banning, CA [AM radio station call letters]
KMET	Kemet Corp. [NASDAQ symbol] (SAG)
KMEX	Los Angeles, CA [Television station call letters]
KMEZ	Belle Chasse, LA [FM radio station call letters]
KMF	Kamina [Papua New Guinea] [Airport symbol] (OAG)
KMF	Koussevitzky Music Foundation (EA)
KMFA	Austin, TX [FM radio station call letters]
KMFB	Mendocino, CA [FM radio station call letters]
KMFC	Centralia, MO [FM radio station call letters]
KMFC	Kimberly McCullough Fan Club (EA)
KMFE	McAllen/Miller International [Texas] [ICAO location identifier] (ICLI)
KMFG-FM	Nashwauk, MN [FM radio station call letters] (BROA)
KMFM	Premont, TX [FM radio station call letters]
KMFX	Lake City, MN [FM radio station call letters]
KMFX	Wabasha, MN [AM radio station call letters]
KMFY	Grand Rapids, MN [FM radio station call letters]
KMG	Kerr-McGee [NYSE symbol] (TTSB)
KMG	Kerr-McGee Corp. [NYSE symbol] [Toronto Stock Exchange symbol] (SPSG)
KMG	Kumagaya [Japan] [Seismograph station code, US Geological Survey] (SEIS)
KMG	Kunming [China] [Airport symbol] (OAG)
KMGA	Albuquerque, NM [FM radio station call letters]
KMGC	Camden, AR [FM radio station call letters] (RBYB)

KMGE........... Eugene, OR [*FM radio station call letters*]

KMGE........... Marietta/Dobbins Air Force Base [*Georgia*] [*ICAO location identifier*] (ICLI)

KMGG .... Monte Rio, CA [*FM radio station call letters*]

KMGH .... Denver, CO [*Television station call letters*]

KMGI .... Pocatello, ID [*FM radio station call letters*]

KMGK .... Glenwood, MN [*FM radio station call letters*]

KMGL .... Oklahoma City, OK [*FM radio station call letters*]

KMGM .... Montevideo, MN [*FM radio station call letters*]

KMGN .... Flagstaff, AZ [*FM radio station call letters*]

KMGO .... Centerville, IA [*FM radio station call letters*]

KMGPrD...... Kerr Group $1.70 Cv Pfd [*NYSE symbol*] (TTSB)

KMGQ .... Goleta, CA [*FM radio station call letters*]

KMGR .... Murray, UT [*AM radio station call letters*]

KMGW .... Casper, WY [*FM radio station call letters*]

KMGX .... Rio Dell, CA [*FM radio station call letters*] (RBYB)

KMGZ .... Lawton, OK [*FM radio station call letters*] (RBYB)

kmh .... Kilometers per Hour

KMH............. Kleinhans Music Hall (SAUO)

KMH............. Knight of Merit of Holstein

KMHA .... Four Bears, ND [*FM radio station call letters*]

KMHD .... Gresham, OR [*FM radio station call letters*]

KMHI-AM ..... Mountain Home, ID [*AM radio station call letters*] (BROA)

KMHK-FM ..... Hardin, MT [*FM radio station call letters*] (RBYB)

KMHL......... Marshall, MN [*AM radio station call letters*]

KMHM-FM ..... Lutesvile, MO [*FM radio station call letters*] (RBYB)

KM/HR .... Kilometers per Hour

KMHR .... Sacramento/Mather Air Force Base [*California*] [*ICAO location identifier*] (ICLI)

KMHS-AM .... Coos Bay, OR [*AM radio station call letters*] (BROA)

KMHT.......... Marshall, TX [*AM radio station call letters*]

KMHX-FM ..... Windsor, CA [*FM radio station call letters*] (BROA)

kMHZ .... Kilomega Hertz (MCD)

KMI .... Keilschrifttexte Medizinischen Inhalts [*A publication*] (BJA)

KMI .... Kentucky Military Institute (SAUO)

KMI .... Kessler Marketing Intelligence [*Information service or system*] (IID)

KMI .... Kirk-Mayer, Inc. (SAUO)

KMI .... KSC [*Kennedy Space Center*] Management Instruction [*NASA*] (KSC)

KMI .... Miyazaki [*Japan*] [*Airport symbol*] (OAG)

KMIA........... Jasper, TX [*FM radio station call letters*]

KMIA........... Miami/International [*Florida*] [*ICAO location identifier*] (ICLI)

KMIB........... Minot/Minot Air Force Base [*North Dakota*] [*ICAO location identifier*] (ICLI)

KMID .... Midland, TX [*Television station call letters*]

KMIDC .... Korean Marine Industry Development Corporation (SAUO)

KMIH .... Mercer Island, WA [*FM radio station call letters*]

KMiJ .... Johnson County Mental Health Center, Mission, KS [*Library symbol*] [*Library of Congress*] (LCLS)

KMIL .... Cameron, TX [*AM radio station call letters*]

KMIN .... Grants, NM [*AM radio station call letters*]

KMIP .... Key Management Interface Processor (ACAE)

KMIPS .... Kaist Map and Image Processing Station (SAUO)

KMIQ .... Robstown, TX [*FM radio station call letters*]

KMIR .... Palm Springs, CA [*Television station call letters*]

KMIS .... New Madrid, MO [*FM radio station call letters*]

KMIS .... Portageville, MO [*AM radio station call letters*]

KMIT .... Mitchell, SD [*FM radio station call letters*]

KMIV .... Millville/Millville [*New Jersey*] [*ICAO location identifier*] (ICLI)

KMIX .... Tracy, CA [*FM radio station call letters*] (RBYB)

KMIZ .... Columbia, MO [*Television station call letters*]

KMJ .... Fresno, CA [*AM radio station call letters*]

KMJ .... Knight of Maximilian Joseph [*Bavaria*]

KMJ .... Kumamoto [*Japan*] [*Airport symbol*] (OAG)

KMJ .... Kume Jima [*Ryukyu Islands*] [*Seismograph station code, US Geological Survey*] (SEIS)

KMJC .... Mount Shasta, CA [*AM radio station call letters*] (RBYB)

KMJC-FM..... Mount Shasta, CA [*FM radio station call letters*] (RBYB)

KMJE-FM..... Gridley, CA [*FM radio station call letters*] (RBYB)

KMJI .... Sacramento, CA [*AM radio station call letters*] (RBYB)

KMJJ .... Shreveport, LA [*FM radio station call letters*]

KMJK .... Buckeye, AZ [*FM radio station call letters*]

KMJM .... St. Louis, MO [*FM radio station call letters*]

KMJM-FM..... Columbia, IL [*FM radio station call letters*] (BROA)

KMJQ .... Houston, TX [*FM radio station call letters*]

KMJX .... Conway, AR [*FM radio station call letters*]

KMJY .... Newport, WA [*AM radio station call letters*]

KMJY-FM..... Newport, WA [*FM radio station call letters*]

KMJZ-FM..... St. Louis Park, MN [*FM radio station call letters*] (RBYB)

KMK............. Kamakura [*Japan*] [*Seismograph station code, US Geological Survey*] [*Closed*] (SEIS)

KMK............. Kansas State University, Manhattan, KS [*Library symbol*] [*Library of Congress*] (LCLS)

KMK............. Keren Mif'alim Konstruktiviyim [*Constructive Enterprises Fund*] (BJA)

KMK............. Konyvtartudomanyi es Modszertani Kozpont [*Center for Library Science and Methodology*] [*Hungary*] [*Information service or system*] (IID)

KMK............. Makabana [*Congo*] [*Airport symbol*] (AD)

KMK............. Perhaps...Kids Meeting Kids Can Make A Difference [*An association*] (EA)

KMKC.......... Kansas City/Kansas City [*Missouri*] [*ICAO location identifier*] (ICLI)

KMKE.......... Grand Junction, CO [*FM radio station call letters*]

KMKE.......... Milwaukee/General Mitchell Field [*Wisconsin*] [*ICAO location identifier*] (ICLI)

KMKF.......... Manhattan, KS [*FM radio station call letters*]

KMKM .... Kansas City [*Missouri*] [*ICAO location identifier*] (ICLI)

KMKO .... Muskogee/Davis [*Oklahoma*] [*ICAO location identifier*] (ICLI)

KMKP-FM..... Honolulu, HI [*FM radio station call letters*] (BROA)

KMKRY........ Kvutzat Mesahake Kadur Regel Yehudit (BJA)

KMKS.......... Bay City, TX [*FM radio station call letters*]

KMKT-FM ..... Bells, TX [*FM radio station call letters*] (BROA)

KMK-V .... Kansas State University, Veterinary Medicine Library, Manhattan, KS [*Library symbol*] [*Library of Congress*] (LCLS)

KMKX.......... San Diego, CA [*FM radio station call letters*] (RBYB)

KMKX-FM ..... Rock Springs, WY [*FM radio station call letters*] (BROA)

KMKY.......... Oakland, CA [*AM radio station call letters*] (BROA)

KMKZ.......... Lahoma, OK [*FM radio station call letters*]

KML .... Carmel Container Sys [*AMEX symbol*] (TTSB)

KML .... Carmel Container Systems Ltd. [*AMEX symbol*] (SPSG)

KML .... Kamileroi [*Australia*] [*Airport symbol*] [*Obsolete*] (OAG)

KML .... Kamuela [*Hawaii*] [*Seismograph station code, US Geological Survey*] [*Closed*] (SEIS)

KMLA-FM ..... El Rio, CA [*FM radio station call letters*] (RBYB)

KMLB.......... Melbourne/Cape Kennedy Regional [*Florida*] [*ICAO location identifier*] (ICLI)

KMLB.......... Monroe, LA [*AM radio station call letters*]

KMLC.......... McAlester/Municipal [*Oklahoma*] [*ICAO location identifier*] (ICLI)

KMLD-FM ..... Casper, WY [*FM radio station call letters*] (BROA)

KMLE.......... Chandler, AZ [*FM radio station call letters*]

KMLM .... Odessa, TX [*Television station call letters*]

KMLO-FM ..... Lowry, SD [*FM radio station call letters*] (RBYB)

KMLT.......... Millinocket/Millinocke [*Maine*] [*ICAO location identifier*] (ICLI)

KMLT-FM...... Thousand Oaks, CA [*FM radio station call letters*] (BROA)

KMLU.......... Monroe/Monroe Municipal [*Louisiana*] [*ICAO location identifier*] (ICLI)

KMLW.......... Moses Lake, WA [*FM radio station call letters*] (RBYB)

KMM............ Kamigamo [*Japan*] [*Seismograph station code, US Geological Survey*] [*Closed*] (SEIS)

KMM............ Kemper Multi-Market Income [*NYSE symbol*] (SPSG)

KMM............ Kimam [*Indonesia*] [*Airport symbol*] (OAG)

KMM............ Knight of the Order of Military Merit [*Prussia*] (ROG)

KMM............ Morehead State University, Morehead, KY [*OCLC symbol*] (OCLC)

KMMA......... Knitting Machine Manufacturers Association [*Defunct*] (EA)

KMMA......... Korean Merchant Marine Academy (SAUO)

KMMC......... Kangaroo Marketing and Management Committee [*Australia*]

KMMC......... Kerala Minerals and Metals Corp. [*India*] (BUAC)

KMMC......... Salem, MO [*FM radio station call letters*]

KMMG-FM ... Santa Fe, NM [*FM radio station call letters*] (BROA)

KMMJ .... Grand Island, NE [*AM radio station call letters*]

KMML .... Amarillo, TX [*FM radio station call letters*]

KMMM........ Madera, CA [*FM radio station call letters*]

KMMO......... Marshall, MO [*AM radio station call letters*]

KMMO-FM .... Marshall, MO [*FM radio station call letters*]

KMMPI........ Khatena-Morse Multitalent Perception Inventory [*Test*] (TMMY)

KMMR .... Malta, MT [*FM radio station call letters*]

KMMS .... Bozeman, MT [*AM radio station call letters*]

K-MMSEM ... KSC MMSE Plan (or Requirement) (SAUS)

K-MMSEN ... KSC [*Kennedy Space Center*] MMSE Notice [*Multiuse Mission Support Equipment*] [*NASA*] (NASA)

K-MMSEPS... KSC [*Kennedy Space Center*] MMSE Project Specification [*Multiuse Mission Support Equipment*] [*NASA*] (NASA)

KMMS-FM ... Bozeman, MT [*FM radio station call letters*]

KMMT......... Mammoth Lakes, CA [*FM radio station call letters*]

KMMX......... Lamesa, TX [*FM radio station call letters*]

KMMY......... Muskogee, OK [*FM radio station call letters*]

KMN .... Kamina [*Zaire*] [*Airport symbol*] (OAG)

KMN .... Kumano [*Japan*] [*Seismograph station code, US Geological Survey*] (SEIS)

KMNC .... North Central Kansas Libraries, Manhattan, KS [*Library symbol*] [*Library of Congress*] (LCLS)

KMND......... Midland, TX [*AM radio station call letters*]

KMNE......... Bassett, NE [*FM radio station call letters*]

KMNE-TV ..... Bassett, NE [*Television station call letters*]

KMNL .... Kinetic Minerals, Inc. (SAUO)

KMNO .... Kimono (ABBR)

KMnO......... Potassium Permanganate [*Pharmacology*] (DAVI)

KMNR .... Rolla, MO [*FM radio station call letters*]

KMNS .... Sioux City, IA [*AM radio station call letters*]

KMNT .... Centralia, WA [*FM radio station call letters*]

KMNY .... Pomona, CA [*AM radio station call letters*]

KMNZ .... Oklahoma City, OK [*Television station call letters*]

KMO........... Kobe Marine Observatory (BARN)

KMO........... Manokotak [*Alaska*] [*Airport symbol*] (OAG)

KMOB .... Mobile/Bates Field [*Alabama*] [*ICAO location identifier*] (ICLI)

KMOC......... Wichita Falls, TX [*FM radio station call letters*]

KMOD......... Kuwait Ministry of Defence (SAUO)

KMOD .... Tulsa, OK [*FM radio station call letters*]

KMOE......... Butler, MO [*FM radio station call letters*]

KMOG......... Payson, AZ [*AM radio station call letters*]

KMOH......... Kingman, AZ [*Television station call letters*]

KMOJ......... Minneapolis, MN [*FM radio station call letters*]

KMOK......... Lewiston, ID [*FM radio station call letters*]

KMOL......... San Antonio, TX [*Television station call letters*]

KMOM......... Monticello, MN [*AM radio station call letters*]

KMON......... Great Falls, MT [*AM radio station call letters*]

KMON......... Keyboard Monitor [*Digital Equipment Corp.*]

KMON-FM..... Great Falls, MT [*FM radio station call letters*]

KMOO-FM..... Mineola, TX [*FM radio station call letters*]

KMOQ......... Baxter Springs, KS [*FM radio station call letters*]

KMOR......... Scottsbluff, NE [*FM radio station call letters*]

KMOS......... Sedalia, MO [*Television station call letters*]

KMOT	Minot/International [North Dakota] [ICAO location identifier] (ICLI)
KMOT	Minot, ND [Television station call letters]
KMOU	Roswell, NM [FM radio station call letters]
KMOV	St. Louis, MO [Television station call letters]
KMOV-DT	St. Louis, MO [Television station call letters] (BROA)
KMOX	St. Louis, MO [AM radio station call letters]
KMOZ	Rolla, MO [AM radio station call letters]
KMP	Kaiser Metal Products (SAUO)
KMP	Kangaroo Management Program [Australia]
KMP	Keetmanshoop [South-West Africa] [Airport symbol] (OAG)
KMP	Kent Mathematics Project [British] (AIE)
KMP	Kilusang Mabubukid ng Pilipinas [Philippine Peasant Federation] [Political party]
KMP	Kommunistak Magyarorszagi Partja [Communist Party of Hungary] [Political party] (PPE)
KMP	Policy and Regulations Division, Information Resources Management Service (AAGC)
KMPA	Korean Maritime and Port Administration (SAUO)
KMPC	Abilene, TX [AM radio station call letters] (BROA)
KMPC	Los Angeles, CA [AM radio station call letters]
KMPD	Kingston Military Products Division (SAA)
KMPG	Hollister, CA [AM radio station call letters]
KMPH	Hanford, CA [FM radio station call letters]
kmph	Kilometers per Hour (AABC)
KMPH	Visalia, CA [Television station call letters]
KmpHi	Kemper High Income Trust [Associated Press] (SAG)
KmpIGv	Kemper Intermediate Government Trust [Associated Press] (SAG)
KMPL	Sikeston, MO [AM radio station call letters]
KmpMI	Kemper Multi-Market Income Trust [Associated Press] (SAG)
KmpMu	Kemper Municipal Income Fund [Associated Press] (SAG)
KMPO	Modesto, CA [FM radio station call letters]
KMPP	Kisan Mazdoor Praja Party [India] [Political party]
KMPQ	Rosenberg-Richmond, TX [AM radio station call letters]
KMPQ-FM	Woodward, OK [FM radio station call letters] (BROA)
KMPR	Minot, ND [FM radio station call letters]
KMPS	Kernel Multiple Processing System [Computer science]
KMPS	Kilometers per Second (GOBB)
kmps	Kilometers per Second
KMPS	Seattle, WA [AM radio station call letters]
KMPS-FM	Seattle, WA [FM radio station call letters]
KmpSInc	Kemper Strategic Income Fund [Associated Press] (SAG)
KmpStr	Kemper Strategic Municipal Income Trust [Associated Press] (SAG)
KMP-TUCP	Katipunang Manggagawang Pilipino [Trade Union Congress of the Philippines] (EY)
KMPV	Montpelier/Edward F. Knapp [Vermont] [ICAO location identifier] (ICLI)
KMPX	Decatur, TX [Television station call letters]
KMQ	Komatsu [Japan] [Airport symbol] (OAG)
KMQA	West Covina, CA [FM radio station call letters]
KMQT	Marquette/Marquette County [Michigan] [ICAO location identifier] (ICLI)
KMQUT	Kumquat (ABBR)
KMQX	Springtown, TX [FM radio station call letters] (RBYB)
KMR	Cambria Resources Ltd. [Vancouver Stock Exchange symbol]
KMR	Kafrarian Mounted Rifles [British military] (DMA)
KMR	Karimui [Papua New Guinea] [Airport symbol] (OAG)
KMR	Kremsmuenster [Austria] [Seismograph station code, US Geological Survey] (SEIS)
KMR	Kwajalein Missile Range (AABC)
KMR	Western Pacific Airlines, Inc. [FAA designator] (FAAC)
KMRA	Knitwear Mill Representatives Association [Defunct] (EA)
KMRC	Morgan City, LA [AM radio station call letters]
KMRE	Dumas, TX [FM radio station call letters]
KMRF	Keyswitch Magic Relay Finder (IAA)
KMRF	Marshfield, MO [AM radio station call letters]
KMRI-AM	West Valley City, UT [AM radio station call letters] (BROA)
KMrJ	Johnson County Library, Merriam, KS [Library symbol] [Library of Congress] (LCLS)
KMRJ-FM	Rancho Mirage, CA [FM radio station call letters] (RBYB)
KMRK	Odessa, TX [FM radio station call letters]
KMRL	Buras, LA [FM radio station call letters] (RBYB)
KMRN	Cameron, MO [AM radio station call letters]
KMRO	Camarillo, CA [FM radio station call letters]
KMRR	South Tucson, AZ [AM radio station call letters]
KMRS	Morris, MN [AM radio station call letters]
KMrS	Shawnee Mission Medical Center, Merriam, KS [Library symbol] [Library of Congress] (LCLS)
KMRT	Dallas, TX [AM radio station call letters]
KMRT	[The] Kansas & Missouri Railway & Terminal Co. [Later, KM] [AAR code]
KMRT-FM	Granbury, TX [FM radio station call letters] (RBYB)
KMRV-FM	Blair, NE [FM radio station call letters] (RBYB)
KMRX-FM	Collinsville, OK [FM radio station call letters] (BROA)
KMRY	Cedar Rapids, IA [AM radio station call letters]
KMRZ-AM	San Bernardino, CA [AM radio station call letters] (BROA)
KMS	Camas Resources Ltd. [Vancouver Stock Exchange symbol]
KMS	Kabuki Make-Up Syndrome [Medicine] (DMAA)
KMS	Kansas Medical Society (SAUO)
KMS	Karitane Mothercraft Society [Australia]
KMS	Keysort Multiple Selector
km/s	Kilometers per Second
KMS	King's Magnetic Ore Separator (ROG)
KMS	Knowledge Management System [Computer science]
KMS	Komatsu Mining Systems [Japan]
KMS	Kumasi [Ghana] [Airport symbol] (OAG)
KMS	Kwashiorkormarasmus Syndrome [Medicine] (DMAA)
KMS	K-Words Times Millions of Seconds [Unit of measure] (GFGA)
KMS	Murray State University, Murray, KY [OCLC symbol] (OCLC)
KMSA	Grand Junction, CO [FM radio station call letters]
KMSB	Committee for Public Opinion Information (SAUS)
KMSB	Tucson, AZ [Television station call letters]
KMSC	Sioux City, IA [FM radio station call letters]
KMSD	Milbank, SD [AM radio station call letters]
KMSE-FM	Rochester, MN [FM radio station call letters] (BROA)
KMSG	Sanger, CA [Television station call letters]
KMSI	KMS Industries, Inc. (SAUO)
KMSI	Moore, OK [FM radio station call letters]
KMSK	Austin, MN [FM radio station call letters]
KMSL	Great Falls, MT [AM radio station call letters]
KMSL	Ontario, CA [AM radio station call letters] (BROA)
KMSM	Butte, MT [FM radio station call letters]
KMSN	Madison/Truax Field [Wisconsin] [ICAO location identifier] (ICLI)
KMSO	Missoula, MT [FM radio station call letters]
KMSP	Minneapolis/Minneapolis-St. Paul International [Minnesota] [ICAO location identifier] (ICLI)
KMSP	Minneapolis, MN [Television station call letters]
KMSR	Sauk Centre, MN [FM radio station call letters]
KMSS	Massena/Richards Field [New York] [ICAO location identifier] (ICLI)
KMSS	Shreveport, LA [Television station call letters]
KMSU	Mankato, MN [FM radio station call letters]
KMSV	Kirsten Murine Sarcoma Virus [Medicine] (DB)
KMSX-FM	Carlsbad, CA [FM radio station call letters] (BROA)
KMSY	New Orleans/International [Louisiana] [ICAO location identifier] (ICLI)
KMT	Kennametal, Inc. [NYSE symbol] (SPSG)
KMT	Kinomoto [Japan] [Seismograph station code, US Geological Survey] [Closed] (SEIS)
KMT	Knight of St. Maria Theresa [Austria] (ROG)
KMT	Kuomintang [Nationalist Party of Taiwan] [Political party] (PD)
KMTA	Miles City, MT [AM radio station call letters]
KMTB	Kibris Milli Turk Birligi [Cypriot National Turkish Union] (PPE)
KMTB	Murfreesboro, AR [AM radio station call letters]
KMTC	Korea Marine Transport Company (SAUO)
KMTC	Mount Clemens/Selfridge Air Force Base [Michigan] [ICAO location identifier] (ICLI)
KMTC	Russellville, AR [FM radio station call letters]
KMTF	Helena, MT [Television station call letters] (BROA)
KMTH	Maljamar, NM [FM radio station call letters]
KMTI	Manti, UT [AM radio station call letters]
KMTL	Sherwood, AR [AM radio station call letters]
KMTN	Jackson, WY [FM radio station call letters]
KMTNC	King Mahendra Trust for Nature Conservation [Nepal] (BUAC)
KMTP	San Francisco, CA [Television station call letters]
KMTPS	Key Makers' Trade Protection Society [A union] [British]
KMTR	Eugene, OR [Television station call letters]
KMTS	Glenwood Springs, CO [FM radio station call letters]
KMTT	Tacoma, WA [AM radio station call letters]
KMTT-FM	Tacoma, WA [FM radio station call letters]
KMTV	Omaha, NE [Television station call letters]
KMTX	Helena, MT [AM radio station call letters]
KMTX-FM	Helena, MT [FM radio station call letters]
KMTX-TV	Roseburg, OR [Television station call letters]
KMTY-FM	Holdrege, NE [FM radio station call letters] (RBYB)
KMTZ	Coos Bay, OR [Television station call letters]
KMU	Kamikineusu Station [Japan] [Seismograph station code, US Geological Survey] (SEIS)
KMU	Karl Marx University (SAUO)
KMU	Kilusang Mayo Uno [May First Movement] [Philippines] [Political party]
KMU	Kismayu [Somalia] [Airport symbol] (OAG)
KMU	Kit Munition Unit [Air Force] (MCD)
KMUD	Garberville, CA [FM radio station call letters]
KMUE-FM	Eureka, CA [FM radio station call letters] (RBYB)
KMUFA	Central Technological Development Fund (SAUS)
KMUL	Muleshoe, TX [FM radio station call letters]
KMUN	Astoria, OR [FM radio station call letters]
KMUO	Mountain Home/Mountain Home Air Force Base [Idaho] [ICAO location identifier] (ICLI)
KMUS	Burns, WY [FM radio station call letters]
KMUS-AM	Muskogee, OK [AM radio station call letters] (RBYB)
KMUW	Wichita, KS [FM radio station call letters]
KMUZ	Gresham, OR [AM radio station call letters] (RBYB)
KMV	Kalemyo [Myanmar] [Airport symbol] (OAG)
KMV	Keen Mountain [Virginia] [Seismograph station code, US Geological Survey] [Closed] (SEIS)
KMV	Killed Measles-Virus Vaccine
KMVC	Marshall, MO [FM radio station call letters]
KMVI	Wailuku, HI [AM radio station call letters]
KMVI-FM	Pukalani, HI [FM radio station call letters]
KMVK	Benton, AR [FM radio station call letters]
KMVL	Madisonville, TX [AM radio station call letters]
KMVL-FM	Madisonville, TX [FM radio station call letters] (RBYB)
KMVP-AM	Phoenix, AZ [AM radio station call letters] (BROA)
KMVR	Mesilla Park, NM [FM radio station call letters]
KMVT	Twin Falls, ID [Television station call letters]
KMVU	Medford, OR [Television station call letters]
KMVX	Jerome, ID [FM radio station call letters]
kmw	Kilomegawatt (WGA)
KMW	KMW Systems Corp. (SAUO)
kmwh	Kilomegawatt-Hour (WGA)
KMWL	Mineral Wells [Texas] [ICAO location identifier] (ICLI)

KMWX .... Yakima, WA [*AM radio station call letters*]
KMX............. Circuit City Strs-CarMx Grp [*NYSE symbol*] (SG)
KMXA-AM .... Aurora, CO [*AM radio station call letters*] (RBYB)
KMXA-FM .... Minot, ND [*FM radio station call letters*]
KMXB.......... Orem, UT [*FM radio station call letters*]
KMXB-FM .... Henderson, NV [*FM radio station call letters*] (BROA)
KMXC.......... Sioux Falls, SD [*FM radio station call letters*]
KMXD.......... Ankeny, IA [*FM radio station call letters*]
KMXE.......... Red Lodge, MT [*FM radio station call letters*]
KMXF........... Montgomery/Maxwell Air Force Base [*Alabama*] [*ICAO location identifier*] (ICLI)
KMXF-FM .... Lowell, AR [*FM radio station call letters*] (BROA)
KMXG .... Clinton, IA [*FM radio station call letters*]
KMXI........... Chico, CA [*FM radio station call letters*] (RBYB)
KMXJ-FM .... Sallisaw, OK [*FM radio station call letters*] (RBYB)
KMXK.......... Cold Spring, MN [*FM radio station call letters*]
KMXL.......... Carthage, MO [*FM radio station call letters*]
KMXM-FM ... Gooding, ID [*FM radio station call letters*] (RBYB)
KMXN.......... Santa Rosa, CA [*AM radio station call letters*]
KMXO .... Merkel, TX [*AM radio station call letters*]
KMXP-FM .... Phoenix, AZ [*FM radio station call letters*] (BROA)
KMXQ.......... Socorro, NM [*FM radio station call letters*]
KMXR.......... Corpus Christi, TX [*FM radio station call letters*]
KMXS.......... Anchorage, AK [*FM radio station call letters*] (RBYB)
KMXT.......... Kodiak, AK [*FM radio station call letters*]
KMXU.......... Manti, UT [*FM radio station call letters*]
KMXV.......... Kansas City, MO [*FM radio station call letters*]
KMXX.......... Imperial, CA [*FM radio station call letters*]
KMXY-FM .... Grand Junction, CO [*FM radio station call letters*] (RBYB)
KMXZ-FM .... Tucson, AZ [*FM radio station call letters*] (RBYB)
KMY............. Moser Bay [*Alaska*] [*Airport symbol*] (OAG)
kmy............. square kilometer (or kilometre) (SAUS)
KMYC.......... Marysville, CA [*AM radio station call letters*]
KMYF.......... Kiss Me You Fool (SAUS)
KMYI........... Kirtland, NM [*FM radio station call letters*]
KMYL-AM .... Tolleson, AZ [*AM radio station call letters*] (BROA)
KMYL-FM .... Wickenburg, AZ [*FM radio station call letters*] (BROA)
KMYR .... Myrtle Beach/Myrtle Beach Air Force Base [*South Carolina*] [*ICAO location identifier*] (ICLI)
KMYR .... Wichita, KS [*AM radio station call letters*] (BROA)
KMYX.......... Taft, CA [*AM radio station call letters*]
KMYX-FM .... Taft, CA [*FM radio station call letters*]
KMYY.......... Monroe, LA [*FM radio station call letters*]
KMYZ.......... Pryor, OK [*AM radio station call letters*]
KMYZ-FM .... Pryor, OK [*FM radio station call letters*]
KMZ............. Kangaroo Management Zone
KMZA.......... Seneca, KS [*FM radio station call letters*]
KMZE.......... Woodward, OK [*FM radio station call letters*]
KMZK-AM .... Billings, MT [*AM radio station call letters*] (BROA)
KMZL-FM .... Missoula, MT [*FM radio station call letters*] (BROA)
KMZN.......... Farwell, TX [*Television station call letters*]
KMZQ.......... Henderson, NV [*FM radio station call letters*]
KMZU.......... Carrollton, MO [*FM radio station call letters*]
KMZX.......... Lonoke, AR [*FM radio station call letters*]
KN.............. Air Kentucky [*ICAO designator*] (AD)
KN.............. GKN Group Services Ltd. [*British*] [*ICAO designator*] (ICDA)
KN.............. Kennecott Copper Corporation (SAUO)
KN.............. Kenya Navy
KN.............. Khan (ABBR)
kN.............. Kilonewton
KN.............. Kinetics of Neutralization [*Chemistry*]
KN.............. King's Knight [*Chess*] (GOBB)
KN.............. Kings Norton Mint [*British*]
KN.............. Kitting Notice [*NASA*] (NASA)
KN.............. Klamath Northern Railway Co. [*Later, KNOR*] [*AAR code*]
Kn.............. Knapp's Privy Council Appeal Cases [*1829-36*] [*England*] [*A publication*] (DLA)
kn.............. Knee
KN.............. Knight (ABBR)
KN.............. Knot
kn.............. Knot
kn.............. Known (VRA)
KN.............. Known
KN.............. Know-Nothing [*American political party, 1855-60*]
Kn.............. Knudsen Number [*IUPAC*]
KN.............. Kol Nidre (BJA)
kn.............. Korea, North [*MARC country of publication code*] [*Library of Congress*] (LCCP)
KN.............. Krone (ABBR)
KN.............. Kronen (ABBR)
KN.............. KSC [*Kennedy Space Center*] Notice [*NASA*] (NASA)
KN.............. St. Christopher-Nevis [*ANSI two-letter standard code*] (CNC)
KN.............. Temsco Airlines [*ICAO designator*] (AD)
KNA............ Katholische Nachrichten-Agentur [*Catholic Press Agency*] [*Germany*]
KNA............ Kenar Resources [*Vancouver Stock Exchange symbol*]
KNA............ Kentucky Nurses Association (SAUO)
KNA............ Kenya News Agency
KNA............ Kex National Association (EA)
KNA............ Killed; Not Enemy Action [*Military*]
KNA............ Knight Air Ltd. [*Canada*] [*ICAO designator*] (FAAC)
KNA............ Knogo North America [*AMEX symbol*] (TTSB)
KNA............ Knogo North America, Inc. [*AMEX symbol*] (SAG)
KNA............ Korean National Airlines
KNA............ Korean National Association (EA)
KNA............ Kuki National Assembly [*India*] [*Political party*] (PPW)

KNA............ Kununurra [*Australia*] [*Seismograph station code, US Geological Survey*] (SEIS)
KNA............ St. Christopher-Nevis [*ANSI three-letter standard code*] (CNC)
KNAA-FM..... Show Low, AZ [*FM radio station call letters*] (BROA)
KNAB.......... Albany/Albany Naval Air Station [*Georgia*] [*ICAO location identifier*] (ICLI)
KNAB.......... Burlington, CO [*AM radio station call letters*]
KNAB-FM..... Burlington, CO [*FM radio station call letters*]
KNAC.......... Earlimart, CA [*FM radio station call letters*] (RBYB)
Kn AC .... Knapp's Privy Council Appeal Cases [*1829-36*] [*England*] [*A publication*] (DLA)
KNAD-FM..... Page, AZ [*FM radio station call letters*] (BROA)
KNAF.......... Fredricksburg, TX [*AM radio station call letters*]
KNAI........... Phoenix, AZ [*FM radio station call letters*]
KNAIR......... Kuehne & Nagel Air Cargo Ltd. [*British*]
KNAK.......... Delta, UT [*AM radio station call letters*]
KNAL........... Victoria, TX [*AM radio station call letters*]
Kn & O .... Knapp and Ombler's English Election Cases [*A publication*] (DLA)
Kn & Omb ... Knapp and Ombler's English Election Cases [*A publication*] (DLA)
KNAP.......... Knape & Vogt Manufacturing Co. [*NASDAQ symbol*] (NQ)
KNAP.......... Knape & Vogt Mfg [*NASDAQ symbol*] (TTSB)
KNAP.......... Knapwell [*England*]
KnapeV....... Knape & Vogt Manufacturing Co. [*Associated Press*] (SAG)
Knapp........ Knapp's Privy Council Reports [*England*] [*A publication*] (DLA)
Knapp & O... Knapp and Ombler's English Election Cases [*A publication*] (DLA)
KNAQ.......... Flagstaff, AZ [*FM radio station call letters*] (RBYB)
KNAS.......... Kenya National Academy of Arts and Sciences (BUAC)
KNAS.......... Nashville, AR [*FM radio station call letters*]
KNAT........... Albuquerque, NM [*Television station call letters*]
KNAU.......... Flagstaff, AZ [*FM radio station call letters*]
KNAX.......... Fresno, CA [*FM radio station call letters*]
KNAZ.......... Flagstaff, AZ [*Television station call letters*]
KNB............ Kanab [*Utah*] [*Airport symbol*] (OAG)
KNB............ Kanab [*Utah*] [*Seismograph station code, US Geological Survey*] (SEIS)
KNB............ Kanab, UT [*Location identifier*] [*FAA*] (FAAL)
KNB............ Kansas-Nebraska Natural Gas Company, Inc. (SAUO)
KNB............ Kita-Nihon Broadcasting (SAUO)
KNBA-FM..... Anchorage, AK [*FM radio station call letters*] (RBYB)
KNBC.......... Beaufort/Beaufort Marine Corps Air Station [*South Carolina*] [*ICAO location identifier*] (ICLI)
KNBC.......... Los Angeles, CA [*Television station call letters*]
KNBC-DT..... Los Angeles, CA [*Television station call letters*] (BROA)
KNBE.......... Dallas/Hensley Field Naval Air Station [*Texas*] [*ICAO location identifier*] (ICLI)
KNBG.......... New Orleans/Alvin Callender Naval Air Station [*Louisiana*] [*ICAO location identifier*] (ICLI)
KNBJ........... Bemidji, MN [*FM radio station call letters*]
KNBL........... Knife Blade
KNBO.......... New Boston, TX [*AM radio station call letters*]
KNBR.......... Knobbier (ABBR)
KNBR.......... San Francisco, CA [*AM radio station call letters*]
KNBR-FM..... Haltom City, TX [*FM radio station call letters*] (RBYB)
KNBST........ Knobbiest (ABBR)
KNBT.......... New Braunfels, TX [*FM radio station call letters*]
KNBU.......... Baldwin City, KS [*FM radio station call letters*]
KNBW......... Kirin Brewery Co. Ltd. [*NASDAQ symbol*] (NQ)
KNBWY....... Kirin Brewery ADS [*NASDAQ symbol*] (TTSB)
KNBY......... Knobby (ABBR)
KNBY......... Newport, AR [*AM radio station call letters*]
KNBZ-FM .... Redfield, SD [*FM radio station call letters*] (BROA)
KNC........... Canadian Crew Energy [*Vancouver Stock Exchange symbol*]
KNC........... Kalamazoo Nature Center (SAUO)
KNC........... Kamerun National Congress
KNC........... Kansas Newman College [*Formerly, Sacred Heart College*] [*Wichita*]
KNC........... Karenni National Council [*Burma*] (BUAC)
KNC........... Kingcome Navigation [*AAR code*]
KNCA......... Burney, CA [*FM radio station call letters*]
KNCA......... Jacksonville/New River Marine Corps Air Station [*North Carolina*] [*ICAO location identifier*] (ICLI)
KNCB......... Vivian, LA [*AM radio station call letters*]
KNCB-FM.... Vivian, LA [*FM radio station call letters*]
KNCC......... Elko, NV [*FM radio station call letters*]
KNCCI........ Kenya National Chamber of Commerce and Industry (BUAC)
KNCD......... Kincaid Furniture Co., Inc. (SAUO)
KNCI.......... Kinetic Concepts [*NASDAQ symbol*] (TTSB)
KNCI.......... Kinetic Concepts, Inc. [*NASDAQ symbol*] (NQ)
KNCI.......... Sacramento, CA [*FM radio station call letters*]
KNCIAWPRC... Korean National Committee of the International Association on Water Pollution Research and Control (EAIO)
KNCIAWPRC... Kuwaiti National Committee of the International Association on Water Pollution Research and Control (EAIO)
Kn Civ Proc... Knox on Civil Procedure in India [*A publication*] (DLA)
KNCK......... Concordia, KS [*AM radio station call letters*]
KNCK-AM..... Concordia, KS [*AM radio station call letters*] (BROA)
KNCKBT...... Knockabout (ABBR)
KNCKDN..... Knockdown (ABBR)
KNCKKN..... Knock-knee (ABBR)
KNCKOT..... Knockout (ABBR)
KNCKR....... Knocker (ABBR)
KNCM-FM.... Appleton, MN [*FM radio station call letters*] (RBYB)
KNCN......... Sinton, TX [*FM radio station call letters*]
KNCO......... Grass Valley, CA [*AM radio station call letters*]
KNCO......... Quonset Point/Quonset Point Naval Air Station [*Rhode Island*] [*ICAO location identifier*] (ICLI)

KNCO-FM.... Grass Valley, CA [FM radio station call letters]
KNCQ......... Redding, CA [FM radio station call letters]
KNCR......... Paso Robles, CA [FM radio station call letters] (RBYB)
Kn Cr Law ... Knox on Bengal Criminal Law [A publication] (DLA)
KNCT......... Belton, TX [Television station call letters]
KNCT......... Killeen, TX [FM radio station call letters]
KnCtyL....... Kansas City Life Insurance [Associated Press] (SAG)
KNCU......... Kilimanjaro Native Cooperation Union (SAUO)
KNCW-FM.... Omak, WA [FM radio station call letters] (BROA)
KNCY......... Nebraska City, NE [AM radio station call letters]
KNCY-FM.... Auburn, NE [FM radio station call letters] (RBYB)
KND.......... Kindu [Zaire] [Airport symbol] (OAG)
KNDA......... Alice, TX [FM radio station call letters] (RBYB)
KNDC......... Hettinger, ND [AM radio station call letters]
KNDC......... KwaNdebele National Development Corporation (SAUO)
KNDD......... Seattle, WA [AM radio station call letters]
KNDGTN..... Kindergarten (ABBR)
KNDHTD..... Kindhearted (ABBR)
KNDHTDNS... Kindheartedness (ABBR)
KNDI......... Honolulu, HI [AM radio station call letters]
KNDK......... Langdon, ND [AM radio station call letters]
KNDK-FM.... Langdon, ND [FM radio station call letters]
KNDL......... Kindle (ABBR)
KNDLD....... Kindled (ABBR)
KNDLES...... Kindless (ABBR)
KNDL-FM..... Angwin, CA [FM radio station call letters] (BROA)
KNDLG....... Kindling (ABBR)
KNDLIR...... Kindlier (ABBR)
KNDLNS..... Kindliness (ABBR)
KNDLST..... Kindliest (ABBR)
KNDLY....... Kindly (ABBR)
KNDN........ Farmington, NM [AM radio station call letters]
KNDN-FM.... Sacramento, CA [FM radio station call letters] (BROA)
KNDNS...... Kindness (ABBR)
KNDO........ Karen National Defense Organization [Burma]
KNDO........ Yakima, WA [Television station call letters]
KNDP........ Kamerun National Democratic Party [Later, UNC]
KNDR........ Kinder (ABBR)
KNDR........ Kinder-Care Learning Centers, Inc. (SAUO)
KNDR........ Mandan, ND [FM radio station call letters]
KNDRD...... Kindred (ABBR)
KNDRG...... Kindergarten (ABBR)
KNDRGR..... Kindergartener (ABBR)
KndrL........ Kinder-Care Learning Centers, Inc. [Associated Press] (SAG)
KndrLr....... Kinder-Care Learning Centers, Inc. [Associated Press] (SAG)
KNDST...... Kindest (ABBR)
KNDU........ Richland, WA [Television station call letters]
KNDX........ Bismarck, ND [Television station call letters] (BROA)
KNDY........ Kindly (ABBR)
KNDY........ Marysville, KS [AM radio station call letters]
KNDY-FM.... Marysville, KS [FM radio station call letters]
KNE.......... KN Energy [NYSE symbol] (TTSB)
KNE.......... KN Energy, Inc. [NYSE symbol] (SPSG)
KNE.......... Knie Resources, Inc. [Vancouver Stock Exchange symbol]
KNEA......... Brunswick/Glynco Naval Air Station [Georgia] [ICAO location identifier] (ICLI)
KNEA......... Jonesboro, AR [AM radio station call letters]
K-NEA........ Kansas-National Education Association (SAUO)
KNEA......... Kentucky Negro Education Association (SAUO)
KNEB......... Scottsbluff, NE [AM radio station call letters]
KNEB-FM.... Scottsbluff, NE [FM radio station call letters]
KNEB-TV..... Ketchikan, AK [Television station call letters] (RBYB)
KNEC-FM.... Yuma, CO [FM radio station call letters] (BROA)
KNECP....... Kneecap (ABBR)
KNED........ Knife Edge
KNED........ McAlester, OK [AM radio station call letters]
KNEDP....... Kneedeep (ABBR)
KNEI......... Waukon, IA [AM radio station call letters]
KNEI-FM..... Waukon, IA [FM radio station call letters]
KNEK........ Washington, LA [AM radio station call letters]
KNEK-FM.... Washington, LA [FM radio station call letters]
KNEL........ Brady, TX [AM radio station call letters]
KNEL........ Lakehurst/Lakehurst Naval Air Station [New Jersey] [ICAO location identifier] (ICLI)
KNEL-FM..... Brady, TX [FM radio station call letters] (RBYB)
KNELG....... Kneeling (ABBR)
KNELR....... Kneller (ABBR)
KNEM........ Nevada, MO [AM radio station call letters]
KNEN........ Norfolk, NE [FM radio station call letters]
KN Engy...... KN Energy, Inc. [Associated Press] (SAG)
KNEO........ Neosho, MO [FM radio station call letters]
KNeo......... W. A. Rankin Memorial Library, Neodesha, KS [Library symbol] [Library of Congress] (LCLS)
KNES........ Fairfield, TX [FM radio station call letters]
KNET........ Palestine, TX [AM radio station call letters]
KNET-FM..... Lincoln, NE [FM radio station call letters] (RBYB)
KNEU........ Roosevelt, UT [AM radio station call letters]
KNEV........ Reno, NV [FM radio station call letters]
KNEW........ New Orleans [Louisiana] [ICAO location identifier] (ICLI)
KNEW........ Oakland, CA [AM radio station call letters]
KNEX-FM.... Laredo, TX [FM radio station call letters] (BROA)
KNEZ-AM.... Creedmoor, TX [AM radio station call letters] (BROA)
KNF.......... Klein-Nishina Formula [Physics]
KNF.......... Knife (ABBR)
KNF.......... Konjunktive Normalform (SAUO)

KNFC......... Kenya National Federation of Cooperatives (BUAC)
KNFD........ Knifed (ABBR)
KNFG........ Knifing (ABBR)
KNFL......... Tremonton, UT [AM radio station call letters]
KNFL-FM..... Tremonton, UT [FM radio station call letters]
KNFLK....... Kinfolk (ABBR)
KNFLK....... Knifelike (ABBR)
KNFM........ Midland, TX [FM radio station call letters]
KNFO........ Basalt, CO [FM radio station call letters] (RBYB)
KNFP........ Kellogg National Fellowship Program
KNFR........ Opportunity, WA [FM radio station call letters]
KNFT........ Bayard, NM [AM radio station call letters]
KNFT-FM..... Bayard, NM [FM radio station call letters]
KNFX........ Austin, MN [AM radio station call letters]
KNFX-FM.... Spring Valley, MN [FM radio station call letters]
KNG.......... Kaimana [Indonesia] [Airport symbol] (OAG)
KNG.......... Kaliningrad [Former USSR] [Geomagnetic observatory code]
KNG.......... King Aviation [British] [ICAO designator] (FAAC)
KNG.......... Kininogen (DMAA)
KNG.......... Konigsberg [Kaliningrad] [Former USSR] [Seismograph station code, US Geological Survey] [Closed] (SEIS)
KNGA........ St. Peter, MN [FM radio station call letters]
KNGDM...... Kingdom (ABBR)
KNGDM...... Kinhdom
KNGFSH..... Kingfish (ABBR)
KNGFSHR... Kingfisher (ABBR)
KNGHT....... Knight
KnghtR....... Knight Ridder, Inc. [Associated Press] (SAG)
KNGL........ McPherson, KS [AM radio station call letters]
KNGLNS..... Kingliness (ABBR)
KNGLR...... Kinglier (ABBR)
KNGLST..... Kingliest (ABBR)
KNGLY...... Kingly (ABBR)
KNGM........ Emporia, KS [FM radio station call letters]
KNGN........ McCook, NE [AM radio station call letters]
KNGP........ Corpus Christi/Corpus Christi Naval Air Station [Texas] [ICAO location identifier] (ICLI)
KNGPN...... Kingpin (ABBR)
KNGR........ Kangaroo (ABBR)
KNGR........ Kruger National Game Reserve (SAUO)
KNGS........ Coalinga, CA [FM radio station call letters]
KngsRd...... Kings Road Entertainment, Inc. [Associated Press] (SAG)
KNGSZ...... Kingsize (ABBR)
KNGT........ Jackson, CA [FM radio station call letters]
KNGT........ Knight (ABBR)
KNGT........ Knight Transportation [NASDAQ symbol] (SAG)
KNGTHD..... Knighthood (ABBR)
KNGTLY..... Knightly (ABBR)
KNGT-RNT... Knight-Errant (ABBR)
KNGU........ Norfolk/Norfolk Naval Air Station [Virginia] [ICAO location identifier] (ICLI)
KNGY........ Kingly (ABBR)
KNGZ........ Alameda/Alameda Naval Air Station [California] [ICAO location identifier] (ICLI)
KNH.......... Kipuka Nene [Hawaii] [Seismograph station code, US Geological Survey] (SEIS)
KNHC........ Seattle, WA [FM radio station call letters]
KNHD-AM.... Camden, AR [AM radio station call letters] (BROA)
KNHK........ Patuxent River/Patuxent River Naval Air Station [Maryland] [ICAO location identifier] (ICLI)
KNHK-FM.... Reno, NV [FM radio station call letters] (BROA)
KNHN........ Kansas City, KS [AM radio station call letters]
KNHT........ Knight (ABBR)
KNHZ........ Brunswick/Brunswick Naval Air Station [Maryland] [ICAO location identifier] (ICLI)
KNI.......... Centaur Resources Ltd. (SAUO)
KNI.......... Kalallit Niuerfiat [Greenland Trade] (EY)
KNI.......... Kantorberita Nasional Indonesia [News service] [Indonesia] (EY)
KNI.......... Katmai New Instructions [Computer science]
KNI.......... Knight-Ridder Newspapers Incorporated (SAUO)
KNI.......... Koyna Nagar [India] [Seismograph station code, US Geological Survey] [Closed] (SEIS)
KNI.......... Kyodo News International, Inc. [Information service or system] (IID)
KNIA......... Knoxville, IA [AM radio station call letters]
KNIC......... [The] Knickerbocker [L.L.] Company, Inc. [NASDAQ symbol] (SAG)
Knick........ [The] Knickerbocker [L. L.] Co., Inc. [Associated Press] (SAG)
KnickL....... [The] Knickerbocker [L. L.] Company, Inc. [Associated Press] (SAG)
KNID......... Enid, OK [FM radio station call letters]
Knight Mech Dict... Knight's American Mechanical Dictionary [A publication] (DLA)
Knight's Ind... Knight's Industrial Reports [A publication] (DLA)
KnightTr....... Knight Transportation [Associated Press] (SAG)
KNIK......... Anchorage, AK [FM radio station call letters]
KNIL......... Koninklijk Nederlandsch-Indisch Leger [Royal Dutch Indies Army]
KNIM........ Maryville, MO [AM radio station call letters]
KNIM-FM.... Maryville, MO [FM radio station call letters]
KNIN-FM..... Wichita Falls, TX [FM radio station call letters]
KNIN-TV..... Caldwell, ID [TV station call letters] (RBYB)
KNIP......... Jacksonville/Jacksonville Naval Air Station [Florida] [ICAO location identifier] (ICLI)
KNIR......... Beeville/Chase Field Naval Air Station [Texas] [ICAO location identifier] (ICLI)
KNIS......... New Iberia, LA [AM radio station call letters]
KNIS......... Carson City, NV [FM radio station call letters]
KNIT......... Techknits, Inc. [NASDAQ symbol] (SAG)
KNITG....... Knitting (ABBR)

KNITR .... Knitter (ABBR)
KNIX .... Phoenix, AZ [*FM radio station call letters*]
KNJ............. Kindamba [*Congo*] [*Airport symbol*] (OAG)
KNJK........... El Centro Naval Air Station [*California*] [*ICAO location identifier*] (ICLI)
KNJO .... Thousand Oaks, CA [*FM radio station call letters*]
KNJP........... Sargent, NE [*FM radio station call letters*]
KNJU .... Raton, NM [*FM radio station call letters*]
KNJY .... Spokane, WA [*FM radio station call letters*]
KNJZ .... Alton, IL [*FM radio station call letters*]
KNK .... Compact Sodium-Cooled Nuclear Reactor Plant, Karlsruhe (SAUS)
KNK .... Kakhonak [*Alaska*] [*Airport symbol*] (OAG)
KNK .... Kankakee Bancorp [*AMEX symbol*] (TTSB)
KNK .... Kankakee Bancorp, Inc. [*AMEX symbol*] (SAG)
KNK .... Klondike Air, Inc. (SAUO)
KNK .... Knik Glacier [*Alaska*] [*Seismograph station code, US Geological Survey*] (SEIS)
KNKA .... Kansas City [*Missouri*] [*ICAO location identifier*] (ICLI)
KNKE .... Jasper, TX [*FM radio station call letters*]
KNKI-FM ...... Sherman, TX [*FM radio station call letters*] (BROA)
KNKK-FM..... Needles, CA [*FM radio station call letters*] (BROA)
KNKL .... Knuckle (ABBR)
KNKLD .... Knuckled (ABBR)
KNKLG .... Knuckling (ABBR)
KNKN .... Pueblo, CO [*FM radio station call letters*]
KNKR .... Kinkier (ABBR)
KNKRS........ Knickers (ABBR)
KNKST .... Kinkiest (ABBR)
KNKT .... Armijo, NM [*FM radio station call letters*] (RBYB)
KNKT .... Cherry Point Marine Corps Air Station [*North Carolina*] [*ICAO location identifier*] (ICLI)
KNKX .... Miramar Naval Air Station [*California*] [*ICAO location identifier*] (ICLI)
KNL............. Centaur Resources Ltd. [*Vancouver Stock Exchange symbol*]
KNL............. Darrow's Solution [*For antidiarrhea potassium therapy*] (DAVI)
KNL............. Keller, N. L., Washington DC [*STAC*]
KNL............. Kennel (ABBR)
KNL............. Knight of the Netherlands Lion
KNL............. Knoll (ABBR)
KNLA .... Karen National Liberation Army [*Myanmar*] [*Political party*]
KNLA .... White Rock, NM [*FM radio station call letters*]
KNLB .... Lake Havasu City, AZ [*FM radio station call letters*]
KNLC .... Hanford/Lemorre Naval Air Station [*California*] [*ICAO location identifier*] (ICLI)
KNLC .... St. Louis, MO [*Television station call letters*]
KNLD .... Duluth, MN [*Television station call letters*]
KNLD .... Kenneled (ABBR)
KNLE........... Round Rock, TX [*FM radio station call letters*]
KNLF........... Karen National Liberation Front [*Myanmar*] [*Political party*] (PD)
KNLF........... Quincy, CA [*FM radio station call letters*]
KNLG .... Kenneling (ABBR)
KNLG-FM..... New Bloomfield, MO [*FM radio station call letters*] (BROA)
Kn LGR .... Knight's Local Government Reports [*A publication*] (DLA)
KNLH-FM..... Cedar Hill, MO [*FM radio station call letters*] (BROA)
KNLJ .... Jefferson City, MO [*Television station call letters*]
KNLM-FM..... Marshfield, MO [*FM radio station call letters*] (BROA)
KNLP-FM..... Potosi, MO [*FM radio station call letters*] (BROA)
KNLR .... Bend, OR [*FM radio station call letters*]
KNLS .... Kenya National Library Service (BUAC)
KNLS .... Knolls (MCD)
KNLT........... Walla Walla, WA [*FM radio station call letters*]
KNLU .... Monroe, LA [*FM radio station call letters*]
KNLV .... Ord, NE [*AM radio station call letters*]
KNLV-FM ..... Ord, NE [*FM radio station call letters*]
KNM........... Katmai National Monument (SAUO)
KNM........... Keene State College, Keene, NH [*OCLC symbol*] (OCLC)
KNM........... Kenya National Museum
KNM........... Mennonite Historical Society, Newton, KS [*Library symbol*] [*Library of Congress*] (LCLS)
KNMA-FM .... Reserve, NM [*FM radio station call letters*] (BROA)
KNMC .... Havre, MT [*FM radio station call letters*]
KNMC .... Knutson Mortgage Corporation (SAUO)
KNME.......... Albuquerque, NM [*Television station call letters*]
KNMH .... Coast Guard Station, Washington [*District of Columbia*] [*ICAO location identifier*] (ICLI)
KNMI .... Farmington, NM [*FM radio station call letters*]
KNML-AM .... Los Ranchos de Albuquerque, NM [*AM radio station call letters*] (RBYB)
KNMO.......... Nevada, MO [*FM radio station call letters*]
KNMR .... Kenai National Moose Range (SAUO)
KNMT.......... Portland, OR [*Television station call letters*]
KNMTCS ..... Kinematics
KNMvD .... Royal Netherlands Veterinary Association (GVA)
KNMX .... Las Vegas, NM [*FM radio station call letters*]
KNMZ-FM .... Alamogordo, NM [*FM radio station call letters*] (RBYB)
KNN .... Kankan [*Guinea*] [*Airport symbol*] (AD)
KNN .... Kenton Natural Resources Corp. [*Vancouver Stock Exchange symbol*]
KNN .... K-Nearest-Neighbor [*Algorithm*]
KNnB .... Bethel College, North Newton, KS [*Library symbol*] [*Library of Congress*] (LCLS)
KNNB .... Whiteriver, AZ [*FM radio station call letters*]
KNNC .... Georgetown, TX [*FM radio station call letters*]
KNND .... Cottage Grove, OR [*AM radio station call letters*]
KNNG .... Sterling, CO [*FM radio station call letters*]
KNNK-FM..... Dimmitt, TX [*FM radio station call letters*] (RBYB)

KNNN.......... Central Valley, CA [*FM radio station call letters*]
KNNS .... Beverly Hills, CA [*AM radio station call letters*] (RBYB)
KNNS .... Larned, KS [*AM radio station call letters*] (BROA)
Kn NSW .... Knox's New South Wales Reports [*A publication*] (DLA)
KNNT .... Farmington, NM [*AM radio station call letters*] (BROA)
KNNZ .... Costa Mesa, CA [*FM radio station call letters*] (RBYB)
KNO .... Beginn der Knospenbildung (SAUS)
KNO .... Kano, Nigeria [*Remote site*] [*NASA*] (NASA)
KNO .... Keep Needle Open [*Reference to intravenous fluid lines*] (DAVI)
KNO .... Kennedy Space Center Notice (NAKS)
KNO .... Knogo Corp. (SAUO)
KNO .... Knox Ranch [*California*] [*Seismograph station code, US Geological Survey*] [*Closed*] (SEIS)
KNO .... Koch, Neff, Oetlinger [*Germany*] (NITA)
KNO .... Korrespondenzblatt der Nachrichtenstelle fuer den Orient [*A publication*] (BJA)
KNOB .... San Rafael, CA [*AM radio station call letters*] (RBYB)
KNOBA......... Knowledge-Based Real-Time Systems for Fault Diagnosis of Flexible Manufacturing Systems (SAUO)
KNOBS......... Knowledge-Based System
KNOC .... Natchitoches, LA [*AM radio station call letters*] (RBYB)
KNOD .... Harlan, IA [*FM radio station call letters*]
KNOE .... Monroe, LA [*AM radio station call letters*]
KNOE-FM ..... Monroe, LA [*FM radio station call letters*]
KNOE-TV ..... Monroe, LA [*Television station call letters*]
KNOF .... St. Paul, MN [*FM radio station call letters*]
KNOG-FM ..... Nogales, AZ [*FM radio station call letters*] (RBYB)
KnogNA....... Knogo North America, Inc. [*Associated Press*] (SAG)
KNOL .... Knoll [*Commonly used*] (OPSA)
KNOLL .... Knoll [*Commonly used*] (OPSA)
KNOLLS....... Knolls [*Commonly used*] (OPSA)
KNOM .... Nome, AK [*FM radio station call letters*]
KNOM-FM.... Nome, AK [*FM radio station call letters*]
KNON .... Dallas, TX [*FM radio station call letters*]
KNOOM .... Knowledge Orientated Office Model (SAUO)
KNOP .... North Platte, NE [*Television station call letters*]
KNOR .... Klamath Northern Railway Co. [*AAR code*]
KNOR .... Norman, OK [*AM radio station call letters*]
knork .... Knife and Fork [*Pharmacology*] (DAVI)
KNOS .... Albuquerque, NM [*AM radio station call letters*] (RBYB)
KNOS-FM..... Omaha, NE [*FM radio station call letters*] (RBYB)
KNoSH .... Norton State Hospital, Norton, KS [*Library symbol*] [*Library of Congress*] (LCLS)
KNOT .... Prescott, AZ [*AM radio station call letters*]
KNOT-FM ..... Prescott, AZ [*FM radio station call letters*]
Know .... Knowledge [*Record label*]
KNOW .... Knowledge Ware Inc. (SAUO)
KNOW .... Port Angeles Coast Guard Air Station [*Washington*] [*ICAO location identifier*] (ICLI)
KNOW-FM.... Minneapolis-St. Paul, MN [*FM radio station call letters*]
Knowl .... Knowledge (DIAR)
Knowles....... Knowles' Reports [*3 Rhode Island*] [*A publication*] (DLA)
KNOWLT...... Knowlton [*England*]
KNOW-NET.... Knowledge Network of Washington (EDAC)
KNOX .... Grand Forks, ND [*AM radio station call letters*]
Knox .... Knox's New South Wales Reports [*A publication*] (DLA)
Knox & F...... Knox and Fitzhardinge's New South Wales Reports [*A publication*] (DLA)
KNOX-FM..... Grand Forks, ND [*FM radio station call letters*]
KNOZ .... Cameron, MO [*FM radio station call letters*]
KNP .... Kafue National Park (SAUO)
KNP .... Kakadu National Park (SAUO)
KNP .... Kalahari National Park (SAUO)
KNP .... Kalbarri National Park (SAUO)
KNP .... Kanha National Park (SAUO)
KNP .... Katholieke Nationale Partij [*Catholic National Party*] [*Netherlands*] [*Political party*] (PPE)
KNP .... Katholisk Nederlands Persbureau [*Catholic Netherlands Press Agency*] [*Netherlands*]
KNP .... Kejimkujik National Park (SAUO)
KNP .... Kenya National Party (SAUO)
KNP .... Kinabalu National Park (SAUO)
KNP .... Kinchega National Park (SAUO)
KNP .... Kinetics of Nonhomogeneous Processes
KNP .... King's Knight's Pawn [*Chess*] (BARN)
KNP .... Kootenay National Park (SAUO)
KNP .... Korea National Party [*South Korea*] [*Political party*] (PPW)
KNP .... Korean National Police (SAUO)
KNP .... Kosciuszko National Park (SAUO)
KNP .... Koshkonong Nuclear Plant (NRCH)
KNP .... Kruger National Park (SAUO)
KNPA .... Pensacola/Pensacola Naval Air Station [*Florida*] [*ICAO location identifier*] (ICLI)
KNPB .... Reno, NV [*Television station call letters*]
Kn PC .... Knapp's Privy Council Appeal Cases [*1829-36*] [*England*] [*A publication*] (DLA)
KNPC .... Korea National Party [*Political party*] (BUAC)
KNPC .... Kuwait National Petroleum Co.
KNPI .... Kundu's Neurotic Personality Inventory [*Psychology*]
KNPP .... Karenni National Progressive Party [*Myanmar*] [*Political party*] (EY)
KNPP .... Kewaunee Nuclear Power Plant (NRCH)
KNPP .... Kola Nuclear Power Plant (SAUO)
KNPR .... Las Vegas, NV [*FM radio station call letters*]
KNPSK .... Knapsack (ABBR)
KNPT .... Newport, OR [*AM radio station call letters*]

KNQ .... Kone [*New Caledonia*] [*Airport symbol*] [*Obsolete*] (OAG)
KNQI .... Kingsville Naval Air Station [*Texas*] [*ICAO location identifier*] (ICLI)
KNQX .... Key West/Key West Naval Air Station [*Florida*] [*ICAO location identifier*] (ICLI)
KNR .... Kalaallit Nunaata Radioa [*Greenland*] (EY)
KNR .... Kidnap and Ransom [*Insurance terminology*]
KNR .... King's National Roll
KNR .... Kinki Nippon Railway (SAUO)
KNR .... Klamath Northern Railway (MHDW)
KNR .... Korean National Railroad (DCTA)
KNRB .... Mayport/Mayport Naval Station [*Florida*] [*ICAO location identifier*] (ICLI)
KNRC .... Reno, NV [*AM radio station call letters*] (RBYB)
KNRIS .... Kentucky Natural Resources Information System (SAUO)
KNRK .... Camas, WA [*FM radio station call letters*] (RBYB)
KNRK .... Kirsten Sarcoma Virus in Normal Rat Kidney [*Medicine*] (DMAA)
KNRL .... Kernel (ABBR)
KNRL .... Knurl [*Engineering*]
KNRO .... Redding, CA [*AM radio station call letters*]
KNRQ .... Springfield, OR [*AM radio station call letters*] (RBYB)
KNRQ-FM .... Creswell, OR [*FM radio station call letters*] (RBYB)
KNRR .... Pembina, ND [*Television station call letters*]
KNRS .... Salt Lake City, UT [*AM radio station call letters*] (BROA)
KNRV-FM .... Harker Heights, TX [*FM radio station call letters*] (RBYB)
KNRX .... Castle Rock, CO [*FM radio station call letters*] (RBYB)
KNRX-FM .... Oklahoma City, OK [*FM radio station call letters*] (RBYB)
KNRY .... Monterey, CA [*AM radio station call letters*]
KNS .... Kazan [*Formerly, Kazanskaya*] [*Former USSR*] [*Geomagnetic observatory code*]
KNS .... Kenuz Airlines Ltd. [*Nigeria*] [*ICAO designator*] (FAAC)
KNS .... King Island [*Tasmania*] [*Airport symbol*] (OAG)
KNS .... Kinney Services, Inc. (SAUO)
KNS .... Knight of [*the Order of*] the Royal Northern Star [*Sweden*]
KNS .... Korean Nuclear Society (SAUO)
KNSA .... Unalakleet, AK [*AM radio station call letters*]
KNSCP .... Kinescope (ABBR)
KNSD .... San Diego, CA [*Television station call letters*]
KNSD-DT ..... San Diego, CA [*Television station call letters*] (BROA)
KNSE .... Ontario, CA [*AM radio station call letters*]
KNSF .... Washington Naval Air Facility [*District of Columbia*] [*ICAO location identifier*] (ICLI)
KNSG .... Springfield, MN [*FM radio station call letters*] (RBYB)
KNSHP .... Kinship (ABBR)
KNSI .... San Nicolas Auxiliary Air Base (SAUS)
KNSI .... San Nicolas Island/San Nicolas Auxiliary Air Base [*California*] [*ICAO location identifier*] (ICLI)
KNSI .... St. Cloud, MN [*AM radio station call letters*]
KNSJA .... Journal. Korean Nuclear Society (journ.) (SAUS)
KNSMN .... Kinsman (ABBR)
KNSN .... Chico, CA [*AM radio station call letters*] (RBYB)
KNSO .... Merced, CA [*Television station call letters*]
KNSP .... Staples, MN [*AM radio station call letters*]
KNSP-FM ..... Staples, MN [*FM radio station call letters*]
KNSQ .... Mount Shasta, CA [*FM radio station call letters*]
KNSR .... Collegeville, MN [*FM radio station call letters*]
KNSS .... Wichita, KS [*AM radio station call letters*]
KNST .... Tucson, AZ [*AM radio station call letters*]
KNSU .... Thibodaux, LA [*FM radio station call letters*]
KNSW .... Knife Switch
KNSWMN ..... Kinswoman (ABBR)
KNSX-FM ..... Steelville, MO [*FM radio station call letters*] (BROA)
KNSY .... Kensey Nash [*NASDAQ symbol*] (TTSB)
KNSY .... Kensey Nash Corp. [*NASDAQ symbol*] (SAG)
KNSY-FM ..... Amarillo, TX [*FM radio station call letters*] (BROA)
KNT .... Kent Electronics [*NYSE symbol*] (TTSB)
KNT .... Kent Electronics Corp. [*NYSE symbol*] (SPSG)
knt .... Knight (GEAB)
KNT .... Knight [*British title*]
KNT .... Knight-Knott Hotels Corp. (SAUO)
KNT .... Knightway Air Charter Ltd. [*British*] [*ICAO designator*] (FAAC)
KNT .... Knitting
KNT .... Sanandaj [*Iran*] [*Airport symbol*] (AD)
KNT .... Short-Cycle Gas Nitriding (SAUS)
KNTA .... Santa Clara, CA [*AM radio station call letters*]
KNTA .... Lakewood, WA [*AM radio station call letters*] (BROA)
KNTB .... Los Alamitos/Los Alamitos Naval Air Station [*California*] [*ICAO location identifier*] (ICLI)
KNTB-FM ..... Lakewood, WA [*FM radio station call letters*] (RBYB)
KNTC .... Kenya National Trading Company (SAUO)
KNTC .... Kenya National Trading Corp. (BUAC)
KNTC .... Kinetic (ABBR)
KNTC .... Korea National Tourism Corp. (BUAC)
KNTC .... Korean National Tourism Corporation (SAUO)
KntckyEl ...... Kentucky Electric Steel Co. [*Associated Press*] (SAG)
KNTD .... Knotted (ABBR)
KNTD .... Point Mugu Naval Air Station [*California*] [*ICAO location identifier*] (ICLI)
KNTE .... Lakewood, WA [*AM radio station call letters*]
KNTG .... Knotting (ABBR)
KNTHL .... Knothole (ABBR)
KNTI .... Lakeport, CA [*FM radio station call letters*]
KNTK .... Kentek Information Sys [*NASDAQ symbol*] (TTSB)
KNTK .... Kentek Information Systems, Inc. [*NASDAQ symbol*] (SAG)
KNTL .... Bethany, OK [*FM radio station call letters*]
KNtl .... Kinetic Concepts, Inc. (SAUO)

KNTLK .... Knotlike (ABBR)
KNTLS .... Knotless (ABBR)
KNTN .... Thief River Falls, MN [*FM radio station call letters*]
KNTO .... Livingston, CA [*FM radio station call letters*]
KNTR .... Ferndale, WA [*AM radio station call letters*]
KNTS .... Abilene, TX [*AM radio station call letters*]
KNTTD .... Knitted
KNTU .... Denton, TX [*FM radio station call letters*]
KNTU .... Virginia Beach/Oceana Naval Air Station [*Virginia*] [*ICAO location identifier*] (ICLI)
KNTV .... San Jose, CA [*Television station call letters*]
KNTWR .... Knitwear
KNTY .... Knotty (ABBR)
KNU .... Kanpur [*India*] [*Airport symbol*] (OAG)
KNU .... Karen National Union [*Myanmar*] (PD)
KnU .... Knowledge Utility (SAUS)
KNU .... Knuckle [*Automotive engineering*]
KNU .... Kyungpook National University (SAUO)
KNUC .... Smithfield, UT [*FM radio station call letters*]
KNUDO .... Kore Nationality Union Democratic Organization (SAUO)
KNUE .... Tyler, TX [*FM radio station call letters*]
KNUFNS ...... Kampuchean National United Front for National Salvation (PD)
KNUI .... Kahului, HI [*AM radio station call letters*]
KNUI-FM ..... Kahului, HI [*FM radio station call letters*]
KNUJ .... New Ulm, MN [*AM radio station call letters*]
KNUJ .... Sleepy Eye, MN [*FM radio station call letters*]
KNUP .... Karen National Unity Party [*Burma*]
KNUQ .... Mountain View/Moffett Naval Air Station [*California*] [*ICAO location identifier*] (ICLI)
KNUQ-FM .... Paauilo, HI [*FM radio station call letters*] (RBYB)
KNUS .... Denver, CO [*AM radio station call letters*]
KNUU .... Paradise, NV [*AM radio station call letters*]
KNUW .... Whidbey Island/Whidbey Island Naval Air Station [*Washington*] [*ICAO location identifier*] (ICLI)
KNUW-FM .... Central, NM [*FM radio station call letters*] (RBYB)
KNUZ .... Houston, TX [*AM radio station call letters*]
KNUZ Exp Stn... Houston, TX [*Radio expansion station*]
KNV .... Knave (ABBR)
KNVA .... Austin, TX [*Television station call letters*]
KNVC .... Consolidated Nevada Goldfields Corp. [*NASDAQ symbol*] (SAG)
KNVCF .... Consolidated Nev Goldfields [*NASDAQ symbol*] (TTSB)
KNVH .... Knavish (ABBR)
KNVHLY ...... Knavishly (ABBR)
KNVN .... Chico, CA [*Television station call letters*] (BROA)
KNVO .... McAllen, TX [*Television station call letters*]
KNVRY .... Knavery (ABBR)
KNW .... Konawaena [*Hawaii*] [*Seismograph station code, US Geological Survey*] [*Closed*] (SEIS)
KNW .... New Stuyahok [*Alaska*] [*Airport symbol*] (OAG)
KNWA .... Bellefonte, AR [*AM radio station call letters*]
KNWB .... Hilo, HI [*FM radio station call letters*] (RBYB)
KNWB .... Knowable (ABBR)
KNWC .... Sioux Falls, SD [*AM radio station call letters*]
KNWC-FM .... Sioux Falls, SD [*FM radio station call letters*]
KNWD .... Natchitoches, LA [*FM radio station call letters*]
KNWDV .... Knickerbocker L L Wrrt [*NASDAQ symbol*] (TTSB)
KNWG .... Knowing (ABBR)
KNWGNS ..... Knowingness (ABBR)
KNWGY .... Knowingly (ABBR)
KNWHW .... Know-How (ABBR)
KNWL .... Knowledge (ABBR)
KNWLB .... Knowledgeable (ABBR)
KNWLDG ..... Knowledge (ABBR)
KNWLDGB ... Knowledgeable (ABBR)
KNWNTHG ... Know-Nothing (ABBR)
KNWO .... Cottonwood, ID [*FM radio station call letters*]
KNWP-FM .... Port Angeles, WA [*FM radio station call letters*] (BROA)
KNWR .... Ellensburg, WA [*FM radio station call letters*] (RBYB)
KNWR .... Kirwin National Wildlife Refuge (SAUO)
KNWR .... Knower (ABBR)
KNWS .... Kwame Nkrumah Welfare Society (SAUO)
KNWS .... Waterloo, IA [*AM radio station call letters*]
KNWS-FM .... Waterloo, IA [*FM radio station call letters*]
KNWS-TV .... Katy, TX [*Television station call letters*]
KNWV-FM .... Clarkston, WA [*FM radio station call letters*] (RBYB)
KNWX .... Seattle, WA [*AM radio station call letters*] (RBYB)
KNWY .... Yakima, WA [*FM radio station call letters*]
KNWZ .... Thousand Palms, CA [*AM radio station call letters*]
KNWZ-FM .... Yucca Valley, CA [*FM radio station call letters*]
KNX .... Knighthawk Air Express Ltd. [*Canada*] [*ICAO designator*] (FAAC)
KNX .... Knoxville [*Diocesan abbreviation*] [*Tennessee*] (TOCD)
KNX .... Kununurra [*Australia*] [*Airport symbol*] (OAG)
KNX .... Los Angeles, CA [*AM radio station call letters*]
KNXN .... Sierra Vista, AZ [*AM radio station call letters*]
KNXR .... Rochester, MN [*FM radio station call letters*]
KNXT .... Visalia, CA [*Television station call letters*]
KNXV .... Knoxville [*Tennessee*] (ABBR)
KNXV .... Phoenix, AZ [*Television station call letters*]
KNXV-DT ..... Phoenix, AZ [*Television station call letters*] (BROA)
KNXX .... Willow Grove/Willow Grove Naval Air Station [*Pennsylvania*] [*ICAO location identifier*] (ICLI)
KNY .... Kanoya [*Japan*] [*Geomagnetic observatory code*]
KNY .... Kearney National, Inc. (SAUO)
KNY .... Kenergy Resource Corp. [*Vancouver Stock Exchange symbol*]
KNYC .... New York (City) [*New York*] [*ICAO location identifier*] (ICLI)

KNYD .... Broken Arrow, OK [*FM radio station call letters*]
KNYL .... Yuma/Vincent Marine Corps Air Station [*Arizona*] [*ICAO location identifier*] (ICLI)
KNYN .... Santa Fe, NM [*FM radio station call letters*]
KNYN-FM..... Fort Bridger, WY [*FM radio station call letters*] (BROA)
KNZ .... Kanozan [*Japan*] [*Geomagnetic observatory code*]
KNZ .... Kenieba [*Mali*] [*Airport symbol*] (OAG)
KNZA .... Hiawatha, KS [*FM radio station call letters*]
KNZJ .... El Toro Marine Corps Air Station [*California*] [*ICAO location identifier*] (ICLI)
KNZR .... Bakersfield, CA [*AM radio station call letters*]
KNZS .... Montecito, CA [*AM radio station call letters*]
KNZW .... South Weymouth/South Weymouth Naval Air Station [*Massachusetts*] [*ICAO location identifier*] (ICLI)
KNZY .... San Diego/North Island Naval Air Station [*California*] [*ICAO location identifier*] (ICLI)
KNZZ .... Grand Junction, CO [*AM radio station call letters*]
Ko .... C. H. Boehringer Sohn, Ingelheim [*Germany*] [*Research code symbol*]
KO .... [*The*] Coca-Cola Co. [*NYSE symbol*] (SPSG)
KO .... Commanding Officer [*Military slang*]
KO .... Contracting Officer [*Also, CO, CONTRO*]
KO .... Kashrut Observance (BJA)
KO .... Kattoo [*Ship's rigging*] (ROG)
KO .... Keep Off [*i.e., avoid assuming the risk on an application, pending further investigation*] [*Insurance*]
KO .... Keep On [*Continue*] [*Medicine*] (DAVI)
KO .... Keep Open (AMHC)
K/O .... Keep Open [*Medicine*]
KO .... Key Output (SAUS)
KO .... Kickoff (MSA)
KO .... Killarney Oscillation [*Climatology*]
KO .... Killed Organism [*Medicine*] (DMAA)
KO .... Kilogram (ROG)
KO .... Kilohm (ABBR)
KO .... King's Own [*Military unit*] [*British*]
KO .... Klystron Oscillator
KO .... Knee Orthosis [*Medicine*]
K/O .... Knocked Out [*To write or produce something quickly*] [*Also called knock off*] (WDMC)
ko .... Knock Out [*Boxing*] (WA)
KO .... Knockout [*Partly cut out or loosened area which can be easily removed, as in a junction box*] [*Technical drawings*]
KO .... Knockout [*Boxing*]
KO .... Kodiak-Western Alaska Airlines, Inc. [*CAB official abbreviation*]
Ko .... Korea (SAUO)
ko .... Korea, South [*MARC country of publication code*] [*Library of Congress*] (LCCP)
KO .... Kraus-Thomson Organization [*Publisher*]
KOA .... Communications on Alternatives in Education [*Defunct*] (EA)
KOA .... Denver, CO [*AM radio station call letters*]
KOA .... Kailua-Kona, HI [*Location identifier*] [*FAA*] (FAAL)
KOA .... Kampground Owners Association [*Phoenix, AZ*] (EA)
KOA .... Kampgrounds of America
KOA .... Kentucky Opera Association (SAUO)
KOA .... Kentucky Optometric Association (SRA)
KOA .... Knocked-on-Atom
KOA .... Koala Technologies Corp. (SAUO)
KOA .... Kobuan [*Solomon Islands*] [*Seismograph station code, US Geological Survey*] [*Closed*] (SEIS)
KOA .... Kona [*Hawaii*] [*Airport symbol*] (OAG)
KOA .... Kone Air Ltd. [*Finland*] [*ICAO designator*] (FAAC)
KOA .... Korean Operation Area (SAUO)
KOAA .... Pueblo, CO [*Television station call letters*]
KOAB .... Bend, OR [*FM radio station call letters*]
KOAB-TV ..... Bend, OR [*Television station call letters*]
KOAC .... Corvallis, OR [*AM radio station call letters*]
KOAC-TV ..... Corvallis, OR [*Television station call letters*]
KOAI .... Fort Worth, TX [*FM radio station call letters*]
KOAI A .... Koala Technologies Corp. (SAUO)
KOAK .... Oakland/Metropolitan Oakland International [*California*] [*ICAO location identifier*] (ICLI)
KOAK .... Red Oak, IA [*AM radio station call letters*]
KOAL .... Price, UT [*AM radio station call letters*]
KOALA .... Keyfile Open Access Layer [*Workflow automation software*] (PCM)
Koala .... Koala Corp. [*Associated Press*] (SAG)
KOALAS .... Knowledgeable Observation Analysis Advisory System (SAUO)
KOAM .... Korean-American Oil Co.
KOAM .... Pittsburg, KS [*Television station call letters*]
KO & G .... Kansas, Oklahoma & Gulf Railway Co.
KO&G .... Kansas, Oklahoma & Gulf Railway Company (SAUO)
KOAQ .... Terrytown, NE [*AM radio station call letters*]
KOAS .... Broken Arrow, OK [*FM radio station call letters*] (RBYB)
KOAT .... Albuquerque, NM [*Television station call letters*]
KOAZ-FM ..... Glendale, AZ [*FM radio station call letters*] (RBYB)
KOB .... Albuquerque, NM [*Television station call letters*]
KOB .... King's Own Borderers [*British military*] (DMA)
KOB .... Kob Air Ltd. [*Uganda*] [*ICAO designator*] (FAAC)
KOB .... Kobe [*Japan*] [*Seismograph station code, US Geological Survey*] (SEIS)
KoB .... Koehler and Baumgartner Lexikon in Veteris Testamenti Libros [*Leiden*] [*A publication*] (BJA)
KOB .... Koutaba [*Cameroon*] [*Airport symbol*] (OAG)
KOB .... Kriegsoffizier-Bewerber [*Applicant for Wartime Commission*] [*German military - World War II*]

KOBB .... Bozeman, MT [*AM radio station call letters*]
KOBC .... Joplin, MO [*FM radio station call letters*]
KOBE .... Las Cruces, NM [*AM radio station call letters*]
Kobe UL Rev... Kobe University. Law Review [*A publication*] (DLA)
KOBF .... Farmington, NM [*Television station call letters*]
KOBI .... Medford, OR [*Television station call letters*]
KOBN .... Honolulu, HI [*Television station call letters*]
KOBO .... Yuba City, CA [*AM radio station call letters*]
KOBOL .... Keystation On-Line Business-Oriented Language [*Computer science*]
KOBR .... Roswell, NM [*Television station call letters*]
Koc .... Coefficient of Organic Carbon Partition (GNE)
KOC .... Kathodal Opening Contraction [*Medicine*]
KOC .... Key Operational Capability [*Military*] (RDA)
KOC .... Knight of the [*Order of the*] Oak Crown
KOC .... Kochi [*Japan*] [*Seismograph station code, US Geological Survey*] (SEIS)
KOC .... Kollmorgen Optical Corporation (SAUO)
KOC .... Koumac [*New Caledonia*] [*Airport symbol*] (OAG)
KOC .... Kuwait Oil Co.
Koc .... Measure of Soil Absorption (GNE)
KOC .... Occupational and Environmental Health Unit, University of Toronto [*UTLAS symbol*]
KOC .... TCC Beverages Ltd. [*Toronto Stock Exchange symbol*]
KOCB .... Oklahoma City, OK [*Television station call letters*]
KOCC .... Oklahoma City, OK [*FM radio station call letters*]
KOCCCG .... Kenya Operations Control Center Coordination Group (SAUO)
KOCCCG .... Kunia Operations Control Center Coordination Group (CINC)
KOCD .... Columbus, KS [*FM radio station call letters*]
KOCE .... Huntington Beach, CA [*Television station call letters*]
KOCE .... Komi Commodity Exchange [*Russian Federation*] (EY)
Koch .... Koch's Supreme Court Decisions [*Ceylon*] [*A publication*] (DLA)
KOCL-FM .... Arthur, ND [*FM radio station call letters*] (BROA)
KOCN .... Pacific Grove, CA [*FM radio station call letters*]
KOCO .... Korea Oil Corporation (SAUO)
KOCO .... Oklahoma City, OK [*Television station call letters*]
KOCP .... Camarillo, CA [*FM radio station call letters*] (RBYB)
KOCR-AM .... Joplin, MO [*AM radio station call letters*] (BROA)
KOCT .... Carlsbad, NM [*Television station call letters*]
KOCV .... Odessa, TX [*FM radio station call letters*]
KOCV-TV .... Odessa, TX [*Television station call letters*]
KOCY-FM .... Hoxie, AR [*FM radio station call letters*] (RBYB)
KO'd .... Knocked Out [*Boxing*] (DAVI)
KOD .... Kodaikanal [*India*] [*Seismograph station code, US Geological Survey*] (SEIS)
KOD .... Kodaikanal [*India*] [*Geomagnetic observatory code*]
KODA .... Houston, TX [*FM radio station call letters*]
KODC .... Korea Oceanographic Data Center [*Marine science*] (OSRA)
KODCH .... Kodachrome (VRA)
KODCO .... Korean Overseas Development Co. [*Korean government agency*]
KODE .... Joplin, MO [*Television station call letters*]
KODI .... Cody, WY [*AM radio station call letters*]
KODJ .... Salt Lake City, UT [*FM radio station call letters*]
KODL .... The Dalles, OR [*AM radio station call letters*]
KODM .... Odessa, TX [*FM radio station call letters*]
KODR .... King's Overseas Dominions Regiment [*British military*] (DMA)
KODS .... Carnelian Bay, CA [*FM radio station call letters*]
KODY .... North Platte, NE [*AM radio station call letters*]
KODZ .... Eugene, OR [*FM radio station call letters*]
KOE .... Kilograms Oil Equivalent [*Petroleum industry*]
kOe .... Kilooersted
KOE .... Koppel [*Federal Republic of Germany*] [*Seismograph station code, US Geological Survey*] (SEIS)
KOE .... Kupang [*Indonesia*] [*Airport symbol*] (OAG)
KOE .... MER Leasing [*FAA designator*] (FAAC)
KOE .... Northland Aviation, Inc. [*ICAO designator*] (FAAC)
KOEA .... Doniphan, MO [*FM radio station call letters*]
KOEBES .... Koelner Bibliothekserschliessungssystem [*Automated library system*] (NITA)
KOED .... Tulsa, OK [*Television station call letters*]
KOEL .... Oelwein, IA [*AM radio station call letters*]
KOEL-FM .... Oelwein, IA [*FM radio station call letters*]
KOEN .... Koenig, Inc. (SAUO)
KOEO .... Key-On Engine-Off [*Automotive engineering*]
KOER .... Key-On Engine-Running [*Automotive engineering*]
KOES-FM .... Stamford, TX [*FM radio station call letters*] (BROA)
KOET .... Eufaula, OK [*Television station call letters*]
KOEX .... Korea Exhibition Center (SAUO)
KOEX .... Oklahoma City [*Oklahoma*] [*ICAO location identifier*] (ICLI)
KOEZ .... Newton, KS [*FM radio station call letters*]
KOF .... Coca-Cola FEMSA [*NYSE symbol*] (SPSG)
KOF .... Coca-Cola FEMSA ADS [*NYSE symbol*] (TTSB)
KOF .... Knitted Outerwear Foundation (EA)
KOF .... Kofu [*Japan*] [*Seismograph station code, US Geological Survey*] (SEIS)
KOFC .... Fayetteville, AR [*AM radio station call letters*]
K of C .... Knights of Columbus (EA)
K of E .... Knights of Equity (SAUO)
KOFE .... St. Maries, ID [*AM radio station call letters*]
KOFF .... Offutt Air Force Base, Omaha [*Nebraska*] [*ICAO location identifier*] (ICLI)
K of H .... Knight of Hanover
KOFH-FM .... Nogales, AZ [*FM radio station call letters*] (BROA)
KOFI .... Kalispell, MT [*AM radio station call letters*]
KOFI-FM .... Kalispell, MT [*FM radio station call letters*]
K of L .... Knights of Labor

K of L	Knights of Lithuania (EA)
KOFM	Enid, OK [FM radio station call letters]
KOFO	Ottawa, KS [AM radio station call letters]
K of P	Knights of Pythias
KOFR-FM	Post, TX [FM radio station call letters] (BROA)
KOFS	Key Officers of Foreign Service Posts [A publication]
KOFSE	Kuwait Oil-Fire Smoke Experiment (SAUO)
KOFST	Korean Federation of Science and Technology
KOFT	Farmington, NM [Television station call letters] (BROA)
KOFT	Gallup, NM [Television station call letters]
KOFX	El Paso, TX [FM radio station call letters]
KOFY	San Francisco, CA [Television station call letters]
KOFY	San Mateo, CA [AM radio station call letters]
KOG	Kansas, Oklahoma & Gulf Railway Co. [AAR code]
KOG	Kindly Old Gentleman [Slang]
KOG	Koger Properties Inc. (SAUO)
KOGA	Ogallala, NE [AM radio station call letters]
KOGA-FM	Ogallala, NE [FM radio station call letters]
KOGC	Kelley Oil and Gas Corp. [NASDAQ symbol] (SAG)
KOGCC	Kelley Oil & Gas [NASDAQ symbol] (SG)
KogEq	Koger Equity, Inc. [Associated Press] (SAG)
KOGG	Wailuku, HI [Television station call letters]
KOGM	Opelousas, LA [FM radio station call letters]
KOGO	San Diego, CA [AM radio station call letters]
KogrEq	Koger Equity, Inc. [Associated Press] (SAG)
KOGS	Ogdensburg [New York] [ICAO location identifier] (ICLI)
KOGT	Orange, TX [AM radio station call letters]
KOH	King's Own Hussars [British military] (DMA)
KOH	Kohala [Hawaii] [Seismograph station code, US Geological Survey] (SEIS)
Koh	Koheleth (BJA)
KOH	Koolatah [Australia] [Airport symbol] [Obsolete] (OAG)
KOH	Potassium Hydroxide [Organic chemistry]
KOHEMA	Korean Heavy Machinery Industries (SAUO)
KOHEPFC	King of Our Hearts Elvis Presley Fan Club (EA)
KOHI	St. Helens, OR [AM radio station call letters]
KOHL	Fremont, CA [FM radio station call letters]
Kohls	Kohls Corp. [Associated Press] (SAG)
KOHM	Kilohm (MCD)
KOHM	Lubbock, TX [FM radio station call letters]
KOHO	Honolulu, HI [AM radio station call letters]
KohR	Kohelet Rabbah (BJA)
KOHS	Orem, UT [FM radio station call letters]
KOHT	Marana, AZ [FM radio station call letters]
KOHU	Hermiston, OR [AM radio station call letters]
KOHYNO	Nordic Coordinating Committee of Hydrology (SAUO)
KOI	Kennedy Operating Instructions [NASA] (KSC)
K-OI	Keren-OR, Inc. [An association] (EA)
KOI	Kirkwall [Orkney Islands] [Airport symbol] (OAG)
KOI	KSC [Kennedy Space Center] Operation Instruction [NASA] (NASA)
KOI	Olathe Public Library (SAUS)
KOI	Ontario Institute for Studies in Education Library [UTLAS symbol]
KOICA	Korea International Cooperation Agency (BUAC)
KOIL	Bellevue, NE [AM radio station call letters]
KOIL	Kelley Oil Corp. (SAUO)
KOIN	Portland, OR [Television station call letters]
KOIN-DT	Portland, OR [Television station call letters] (BROA)
KOIR	Edinburg, TX [FM radio station call letters]
KOIS	Kuder Occupational Interest Survey [Aptitude and skills test]
KOIT	San Francisco, CA [AM radio station call letters]
KOIT-FM	San Francisco, CA [FM radio station call letters]
KOJ	Kagoshima [Japan] [Airport symbol] (OAG)
KOJ	Keen on the Job (ADA)
KOJJ	East Porterville, CA [FM radio station call letters]
KOJM	Havre, MT [AM radio station call letters]
KOJO	Lake Charles, LA [FM radio station call letters]
KOK	Horizon Cargo Transport, Inc. [ICAO designator] (FAAC)
KOK	Kansallinen Kokoomus [National Coalition Party] [Finland] [Political party] (EAIO)
KOK	Kokkola [Finland] [Airport symbol] (OAG)
kok	Konkani [MARC language code] [Library of Congress] (LCCP)
KOKA	Shreveport, LA [AM radio station call letters]
KOKB	Blackwell, OK [AM radio station call letters]
KOKC	Guthrie, OK [AM radio station call letters]
KOKC	Oklahoma City/Will Rogers World [Oklahoma] [ICAO location identifier] (ICLI)
KOKE	Giddings, TX [FM radio station call letters]
KOKE	Pflugerville, TX [AM radio station call letters] (BROA)
KOKF	Edmond, OK [FM radio station call letters]
KOKH	Oklahoma City, OK [Television station call letters]
KOKI	Tulsa, OK [Television station call letters]
KOKK	Huron, SD [AM radio station call letters]
KOKL	Okmulgee, OK [AM radio station call letters]
KO-KO	Kommerzielle Koordination [Former East German political party]
KOKO	Warrensburg, MO [AM radio station call letters]
KOKP	Perry, OK [AM radio station call letters] (BROA)
KOKR	Newport, AR [FM radio station call letters]
KOKS	Poplar Bluff, MO [FM radio station call letters]
KOKU	Agana, GU [FM radio station call letters]
KOKX	Keokuk, IA [AM radio station call letters]
KOKX-FM	Keokuk, IA [FM radio station call letters]
KOKX-FM	Sherwood, AR [FM radio station call letters] (BROA)
KOKZ	Waterloo, IA [FM radio station call letters]
KOL	King's College, Wilkes-Barre, PA [OCLC symbol] (OCLC)
KOL	Knights of Lithuania (EA)
KOL	Kollmorgen Corp. [NYSE symbol] (SPSG)
KOI-FM	Olathe Public Library, Olathe, KS [Library symbol] [Library of Congress] (LCLS)
KOLA	Keep Old Los Angeles (SAUO)
KOLA	San Bernardino, CA [FM radio station call letters]
KOLAS	Korean Laboratory Accreditation Scheme (SAUO)
KOLD	Tucson, AZ [Television station call letters]
KOLE	Port Arthur, TX [AM radio station call letters]
KOLF	Kolff Medical, Inc. (SAUO)
KOLH	Olathe Commumity Hospital (SAUS)
KOIH	Olathe Commumity Hospital, Olathe, KS [Library symbol] [Library of Congress] (LCLS)
KOLI	King's Own Light Infantry [Military unit] [British]
KOLI-FM	Electra, TX [FM radio station call letters] (BROA)
KOLIN	Consortium of East Slovakian Libraries (SAUO)
KOLJL	Johnson County Law Library Olathe (SAUS)
KOIJL	Johnson County Law Library, Olathe, KS [Library symbol] [Library of Congress] (LCLS)
KOLK-FM	Onawa, IA [FM radio station call letters] (RBYB)
KOLL	Maumelle, AR [FM radio station call letters]
KollRE	Koll Real Estate Group [Associated Press] (SAG)
KollRI	Koll Real Estate Group [Associated Press] (SAG)
KOLM	Rochester, MN [AM radio station call letters]
KOIMN	Mid-America Nazarene College, Olathe, KS [Library symbol] [Library of Congress] (LCLS)
Kolmor	Kollmorgen Corp. [Associated Press] (SAG)
KOLN	Lincoln, NE [Television station call letters]
KOLO	Reno, NV [Television station call letters]
KOLR	Springfield, MO [Television station call letters]
KOLS	Dodge City, KS [FM radio station call letters]
KOLS	Nogales/International [Arizona] [ICAO location identifier] (ICLI)
KOLT	Scottsbluff, NE [AM radio station call letters]
KOLT-FM	Gering, NE [FM radio station call letters] (BROA)
KOLT-FM	Santa Fe, NM [FM radio station call letters]
KOLU	Pasco, WA [FM radio station call letters]
KOLV	Olivia, MN [FM radio station call letters]
KOLX	Barling, AR [FM radio station call letters]
KOLY	Mobridge, SD [AM radio station call letters]
KOLY-FM	Mobridge, SD [FM radio station call letters]
Kolze	Transvaal Reports, by Kolze [A publication] (DLA)
KOLZ-FM	Cheyenne, WY [FM radio station call letters] (BROA)
KOM	Kansas-Oklahoma-Missouri League [Old baseball league]
KOM	Kennedy Space Center Operation instruction (SAUO)
KOM	Kennedy Space Center Organizational Manual (SAUO)
KOM	Kentucky, Ohio, Michigan [Medical library network]
KOM	Kilometric Wavelength [Radio astronomy]
KOM	Knight of the Order of Malta (WDAA)
KOM	Komaba [Japan] [Seismograph station code, US Geological Survey] [Closed] (SEIS)
KOM	Komitet Opiekunczy Miejski (BJA)
KOM	Komo-Manda [Papua New Guinea] [Airport symbol] [Obsolete] (OAG)
KoM	Korea Microforms, Seoul, Korea [Library symbol] [Library of Congress] (LCLS)
KOM	KSC [Kennedy Space Center] Organizational Manual [NASA] (NASA)
KOMA	Oklahoma City, OK [AM radio station call letters]
KOMA	Omaha/Eppley Air Field [Nebraska] [ICAO location identifier] (ICLI)
KOMA-FM	Oklahoma City, OK [FM radio station call letters]
Komag	Komag, Inc. [Associated Press] (SAG)
KOMB	Fort Scott, KS [FM radio station call letters]
KomBeiANT	Kommentare und Beitraege zum Alten und Neuen Testament [Duesseldorf] [A publication] (BJA)
KOMC	Branson, MO [AM radio station call letters]
KOMC-FM	Kimberling City, MO [FM radio station call letters] (BROA)
KOME	San Jose, CA [FM radio station call letters]
KOMH-AM	Pawhuska, OK [AM radio station call letters] (RBYB)
KOMO	Seattle, WA [AM radio station call letters]
KOMO-DT	Seattle, WA [Television station call letters] (BROA)
KOMO-TV	Seattle, WA [Television station call letters]
KOMP	Las Vegas, NV [FM radio station call letters]
KOMRML	Kentucky, Ohio, Michigan Regional Medical Library (SAUO)
KOMRMLN	Kentucky-Ohio-Michigan Regional Medical Library [Library network]
KOMS	Poteau, OK [FM radio station call letters]
KOMSAT	Korean Multi-Purpose Satellite System (SAUO)
KOMSOMOL	Communist Youth League [From the Russian]
KOMU	Columbia, MO [Television station call letters]
KOMW	Omak, WA [AM radio station call letters]
KOMW-FM	Omak, WA [FM radio station call letters]
KOMX	Pampa, TX [FM radio station call letters]
KOMY-AM	Watsonville, CA [AM radio station call letters] (BROA)
KON	Kongcha [Publisher]
kon	Kongo [MARC language code] [Library of Congress] (LCCP)
KON	Kongsberg [Norway] [Seismograph station code, US Geological Survey] (SEIS)
KON	Kontum [South Vietnam] [Airport symbol] (AD)
KONA	Kennewick, WA [AM radio station call letters]
KONA-FM	Kennewick, WA [FM radio station call letters]
KOND-FM	Cleveland, TX [FM radio station call letters] (RBYB)
KONE	Lubbock, TX [FM radio station call letters]
KONG	Everett, WA [Television station call letters]
KONI	Lanai City, HI [FM radio station call letters]
KONO	San Antonio, TX [AM radio station call letters]
KONO-FM	Fredricksburg, TX [FM radio station call letters]
KONP	Port Angeles, WA [AM radio station call letters]
KONQ	Dodge City, KS [FM radio station call letters]

Konst & W Rat App... Konstam and Ward's Rating Appeals [*1909-12*] [*A publication*] (DLA)

Konst Rat App... Konstam's Rating Appeals [*1904-08*] [*A publication*] (DLA)

KONT Ontario/International [*California*] [*ICAO location identifier*] (ICLI)

KONX Elkonix Corp. (SAUO)

KONY Washington, UT [*AM radio station call letters*]

KONY-FM Kanab, UT [*FM radio station call letters*]

KONZ Arizona City, AZ [*FM radio station call letters*]

KOO Kongolo [*Zaire*] [*Airport symbol*] (OAG)

KOOC Belton, TX [*FM radio station call letters*]

KOOD Hays, KS [*Television station call letters*]

KOOG Ogden, UT [*Television station call letters*]

KOOI Jacksonville, TX [*FM radio station call letters*]

KOOJ Riverside, CA [*FM radio station call letters*]

KOOK-FM Junction, TX [*FM radio station call letters*] (BROA)

KOOKR Kookier (ABBR)

KooKR Koo Koo Roo, Inc. [*Associated Press*] (SAG)

KOOKST Kookiest (ABBR)

KOOL Insta Cool Inc. of North America (SAUO)

KOOL Phoenix, AZ [*AM radio station call letters*]

KOOL Thermagenesis Corp. [*NASDAQ symbol*] (SAG)

KOOL Thermogenesis Corp. [*NASDAQ symbol*] (SAG)

KOOL-FM Phoenix, AZ [*FM radio station call letters*]

KOOO-AM Dallas, TX [*AM radio station call letters*] (BROA)

KOOP drkoop.com, Inc. [*NASDAQ symbol*] (SG)

KOOP Hornsby, TX [*FM radio station call letters*]

KOOQ North Platte, NE [*AM radio station call letters*]

KOOR Clovis, CA [*AM radio station call letters*] (BROA)

Koor Koor Industries Ltd. [*Associated Press*] (SAG)

KOOS North Bend, OR [*FM radio station call letters*]

KOOU Hardy, AR [*FM radio station call letters*]

KOOV Copperas Cove, TX [*FM radio station call letters*]

KOOZ Great Falls, MT [*FM radio station call letters*]

KOP Kansallis-Osake-Pankki [*National Capital Stock Bank*] [*Finland*]

KOP Kickoff Point [*Diamond drilling*]

KOP Klippfontain Organic Product Corporation (SAUO)

KOP Kopeck [*Monetary unit in Russia*]

KOP Koppers Co., Inc. (SAUO)

KOP Nakhon Phanom [*Thailand*] [*Airport symbol*] [*Obsolete*] (OAG)

KOPA Scottsdale, AZ [*AM radio station call letters*]

KOPB Portland, OR [*FM radio station call letters*]

KOPB-TV Portland, OR [*Television station call letters*]

KOPCC Kunzang Odsal Palyul Changchub Choling [*An association*] (EA)

KOPE Medford, OR [*FM radio station call letters*]

KOPEC Korea National Committee for Pacific Economic Cooperation

KOPF Miami/Opa Locka [*Florida*] [*ICAO location identifier*] (ICLI)

Kopin Kopin Corp. [*Associated Press*] (SAG)

KOPN Columbia, MO [*FM radio station call letters*]

KOPN Kopin Corp. [*NASDAQ symbol*] (SAG)

KOPR Butte, MT [*FM radio station call letters*]

KOPS K (10³) Operations Per Second (NITA)

KOPS Keep Off Pounds Sensibly [*Club*]

KOPS Thousands of Operations per Second (NASA)

KOPX Oklahoma City, OK [*Television station call letters*] (BROA)

KOPY-AM Alice, TX [*AM radio station call letters*] (RBYB)

KOPY-FM Alice, TX [*FM radio station call letters*] (RBYB)

KOQI Soquel, CA [*AM radio station call letters*]

KOQL Columbia, MO [*FM radio station call letters*]

KOQO Clovis, CA [*AM radio station call letters*]

KOQO Fresno, CA [*FM radio station call letters*]

KOR Air Koryo [*North Korea*] [*ICAO designator*] (FAAC)

KOR Contracting Officer

KOR King's Own Royal [*Military unit*] [*British*]

KOR Klein Offset Rotation [*Typography*] (DGA)

KOR Knowledge of Results [*Visual monitoring*]

KOR Koala Resources Ltd. [*Vancouver Stock Exchange symbol*]

KOR Kodak Ortho Resist

KOR Kokoro [*Papua New Guinea*] [*Airport symbol*] (OAG)

KOR Koor Indus Ltd ADS [*NYSE symbol*] (TTSB)

KOR Koor Industries Ltd. [*NYSE symbol*] (SAG)

KOR Koracorp Industries, Inc. (SAUO)

KOR Koran (ROG)

Kor Korea (VRA)

Kor Korean (DIAR)

kor Korean [*MARC language code*] [*Library of Congress*] (LCCP)

KOR Koror [*Palau Islands*] [*Seismograph station code, US Geological Survey*] [*Closed*] (SEIS)

KOR Republic of Korea [*ANSI three-letter standard code*] (CNC)

KOR Seaplane [*Russian symbol*]

KOR Social Self-Defense Committee [*Also, SSDC*] [*Poland*] (PD)

KORA Bryan, TX [*FM radio station call letters*]

KORB Bettendorf, IA [*FM radio station call letters*] (RBYB)

KORC Waldport, OR [*AM radio station call letters*]

KORD Chicago/O'Hare [*Illinois*] [*ICAO location identifier*] (ICLI)

KORD-FM Richland, WA [*FM radio station call letters*]

KORDI Korea Ocean Research and Development Institute (USDC)

KORE Kinetic Analysis Using Over-Relaxation [*FORTRAN computer program*] [*Physical chemistry*]

KORE Springfield-Eugene, OR [*AM radio station call letters*]

Korea Korea Fund, Inc. [*Associated Press*] (SAG)

KoreaElc Korea Electric Power Corp. [*Associated Press*] (SAG)

Korea Inf Sci Soc Rev... Korea Information Science Society Review (SAUO)

KoreaInv Korean Investment Fund [*Associated Press*] (SAG)

Korea LR Korea Law Review [*A publication*] (DLA)

KoreaM Korea Mobile Telecommunications [*Associated Press*] (SAG)

Korean J Comp L... Korean Journal of Comparative Law [*A publication*] (DLA)

Korean J Int'l L... Korean Journal of International Law [*A publication*] (DLA)

Korean J of Internat L... Korean Journal of International Law [*A publication*] (DLA)

Korean L Korean Law [*A publication*] (DLA)

KorEIN Korea Electric Power Corp. [*Associated Press*] (SAG)

KORF Norfolk/Norfolk Regional Airport [*Virginia*] [*ICAO location identifier*] (ICLI)

KORG Anaheim, CA [*AM radio station call letters*]

KORI Mansfield, LA [*FM radio station call letters*]

KORK Las Vegas, NV [*AM radio station call letters*]

KORL Honolulu, HI [*AM radio station call letters*]

KORL Orlando [*Florida*] [*ICAO location identifier*] (ICLI)

KORL-FM Honolulu, HI [*FM radio station call letters*] (RBYB)

KORMEX Korea Monsoon Experiment (SAUO)

KORN Mitchell, SD [*AM radio station call letters*]

KORO Corpus Christi, TX [*Television station call letters*]

KOROC Keep Out of Reach of Children (DI)

KORP Charles, [*J. W.*] Financial Services [*NASDAQ symbol*] (SAG)

KORP Charles (JW) Finl Svcs [*NASDAQ symbol*] (TTSB)

KORP Corporate Management Group, Inc. (SAUO)

KORQ-FM Abilene, TX [*FM radio station call letters*]

KORR American Falls, ID [*FM radio station call letters*] (RBYB)

KORR King's Own Royal Regiment [*Military unit*] [*British*]

KORSTIC Korea Scientific and Technical Information Centre (NITA)

KORSTIC Korea Scientific and Technological Information Center [*INSPEC operator*]

KORT Grangeville, ID [*AM radio station call letters*]

KORT-FM Grangeville, ID [*FM radio station call letters*]

KORV Oroville, CA [*AM radio station call letters*]

KOS Kent University On-Line System [*Computer science*] (PDAA)

KO's Knockout Drops [*A drug producing unconsciousness*] [*Slang*]

KOS Kosmodemyansk [*Former USSR*] [*Seismograph station code, US Geological Survey*] [*Closed*] (SEIS)

KOS Kosovaair [*Yugoslavia*] [*ICAO designator*] (FAAC)

KOSA Odessa, TX [*Television station call letters*]

KOSAA Korea Shipping Agencies Association (SAUO)

KOSAMI Korea Society for the Advancement of Machine Industry (SAUO)

KOSAMP Kuwait Oil-Fire Smoke Atmospheric Measurements Program (SAUO)

KOSB King's Own Scottish Borderers [*Military unit*] [*British*]

KOSB-FM Perry, OK [*FM radio station call letters*] (BROA)

KOSC Oscoda/Wurtsmith Air Force Base [*Michigan*] [*ICAO location identifier*] (ICLI)

KOSCO Korea Oil Storage Company (SAUO)

KOSCOT Cosmetics for the Community of Tomorrow [*Acronym used as brand name*]

KOSE Osceola, AR [*AM radio station call letters*]

KOSEF Korea Science and Engineering Foundation (SAUO)

KOSE-FM Osceola, AR [*FM radio station call letters*]

KOSG Camden, AR [*AM radio station call letters*]

KOSH Osawatomie State Hospital, Osawatomie, KS [*Library symbol*] [*Library of Congress*] (LCLS)

KOSI Denver, CO [*FM radio station call letters*]

KOSI Kaiser Optical Systems Inc. (SAUO)

KOSJ Nebraska City, NE [*FM radio station call letters*] (RBYB)

KOSM Cascade International Inc. (SAUO)

KOSN Kosan Biosciences [*NASDAQ symbol*]

KoSNU Seoul National University, Seoul, Korea [*Library symbol*] [*Library of Congress*] (LCLS)

KOSO Patterson, CA [*FM radio station call letters*]

KOSP Kos Pharmaceuticals

KOSP Willard, MO [*FM radio station call letters*]

KOSR-AM Omaha, NE [*AM radio station call letters*] (RBYB)

KOSS Koss Corp. [*NASDAQ symbol*] (SAG)

KOSS-FM Rosamond, CA [*FM radio station call letters*] (BROA)

KOST Los Angeles, CA [*FM radio station call letters*]

KOSU Stillwater, OK [*FM radio station call letters*]

KOSY-FM Spanish Fork, UT [*FM radio station call letters*] (BROA)

KoSYU Yonsei University, Seoul, Korea [*Library symbol*] [*Library of Congress*] (LCLS)

KOSZ Vermillion, SD [*AM radio station call letters*]

KOSZ-FM Idaho Falls, ID [*FM radio station call letters*]

KOT Knowledge of Occupations Test [*Psychology*] (DAVI)

KOT Kotlik [*Alaska*] [*Airport symbol*] (OAG)

KOTA Rapid City, SD [*AM radio station call letters*]

KOTAR Korean Tactical Range (SAUO)

KOTA-TV Rapid City, SD [*Television station call letters*]

KOTB Evanston, WY [*FM radio station call letters*]

KOTC Kennett, MO [*AM radio station call letters*] (RBYB)

KOTC Kuwait Oil Tanker Co. (BUAC)

KOTD Plattsmouth, NE [*AM radio station call letters*]

KOTD-FM Plattsmouth, NE [*FM radio station call letters*]

KOTE Eureka, KS [*FM radio station call letters*]

KOTI Klamath Falls, OR [*Television station call letters*]

KOTK Portland, OR [*AM radio station call letters*] (RBYB)

KOTL Kiss on The Lips (SAUS)

KOTM Ottumwa, IA [*FM radio station call letters*]

KOTN Keep on Truckin' News [*A publication*] (EAAP)

KOTN Pine Bluff, AR [*AM radio station call letters*]

KOTO Telluride, CO [*FM radio station call letters*]

KOTR Cambria, CA [*FM radio station call letters*]

KOTRA Korea Trade Promotion Center (EA)

KOTRA Korea Trade Promotion Co. (BUAC)

KOTS Deming, NM [*AM radio station call letters*]

KOTT Otterville, MO [*FM radio station call letters*]

KOtU .... Ottawa University, Ottawa, KS [*Library symbol*] [*Library of Congress*] (LCLS)
KOTV .... Tulsa, OK [*Television station call letters*]
KOTZ............ Kotzebue, AK [*AM radio station call letters*]
Kotze .... Kotze's Transvaal High Court Reports [*South Africa*] [*A publication*] (DLA)
Kotze & B .... Supreme Court Reports, Transvaal [*1885-88*] [*South Africa*] [*A publication*] (DLA)
Kotze & Barb... Supreme Court Reports, Transvaal [*1885-88*] [*South Africa*] [*A publication*] (DLA)
Kotze & Barber... Transvaal Court Reports [*A publication*] (DLA)
KOU .... Koula Moutou [*Gabon*] [*Airport symbol*] (OAG)
KOU .... Koumac [*New Caledonia*] [*Seismograph station code, US Geological Survey*] (SEIS)
KOUL .... Sinton, TX [*FM radio station call letters*]
KOURIR ...... Association for Parents of Children with Juvenile Chronic Arthritis (SAUO)
KOUT .... Rapid City, SD [*FM radio station call letters*]
KOUU .... American Falls, ID [*FM radio station call letters*]
KOUU .... Pocatello, ID [*AM radio station call letters*] (BROA)
KOUZ .... Alexandria, LA [*FM radio station call letters*] (RBYB)
KOV .... Key Operated Valve
KOV .... Knock Out Vessel (EEVL)
Kov .... N. A. Kovach, Los Angeles, CA [*Library symbol*] [*Library of Congress*] (LCLS)
KOVA-FM..... Rosenberg, TX [*FM radio station call letters*] (BROA)
KOVC .... Valley City, ND [*AM radio station call letters*]
KOVC-FM..... Valley City, ND [*FM radio station call letters*]
KOVE .... Lander, WY [*AM radio station call letters*]
KOVE-FM .... Port Arthur, TX [*FM radio station call letters*] (BROA)
KOVO .... Provo, UT [*AM radio station call letters*]
KOvpJ .... Johnson County Community College, Overland Park, KS [*Library symbol*] [*Library of Congress*] (LCLS)
KovpST .... St. Thomas High School, Overland Park, KS [*Library symbol*] [*Library of Congress*] (LCLS)
KOVR .... Stockton, CA [*Television station call letters*]
KOVT .... Silver City, NM [*Television station call letters*]
Kow .... Coefficient of Octanolwater Partition (GNE)
KOW .... Ghanzhou [*China*] [*Airport symbol*] (OAG)
KOW .... Keen on Waller [*A coterie of women admirers of British stage actor, Lewis Waller (1860-1915)*] (ROG)
KOW .... Knock-Off Wheels [*Automotive accessory*]
KOW .... Kowkash Gold [*Vancouver Stock Exchange symbol*]
KOWACO...... Korea Water Resources Development Corporation (SAUO)
KOWB .... Laramie, WY [*AM radio station call letters*]
KOWF .... Escondido, CA [*FM radio station call letters*]
KOWL .... South Lake Tahoe, CA [*AM radio station call letters*]
KOWO .... Waseca, MN [*AM radio station call letters*]
KOWS .... Texarkana, TX [*AM radio station call letters*] (BROA)
KOWS-FM .... Ashdown, AR [*FM radio station call letters*] (BROA)
KOWW-AM.... Blue Springs, MO [*AM radio station call letters*] (RBYB)
KOWZ-FM .... Blooming Prairie, MN [*FM radio station call letters*] (RBYB)
KOX .... Keyboard Operated Transmission [*Computer science*] (VLIE)
KoX .... Knights of Xenu (SAUO)
KOX .... Kokonao [*West Irian, Indonesia*] [*Airport symbol*] (AD)
KOXE .... Brownwood, TX [*FM radio station call letters*]
KOXR .... Oxnard, CA [*AM radio station call letters*]
KOXZ-FM .... Comanche, TX [*FM radio station call letters*] (BROA)
KOY .... Koyama [*Japan*] [*Seismograph station code, US Geological Survey*] [*Closed*] (SEIS)
KOY .... Olga Bay [*Alaska*] [*Airport symbol*] (OAG)
KOY .... Phoenix, AZ [*AM radio station call letters*]
KOYE .... Laredo, TX [*FM radio station call letters*]
KOYLI .... King's Own Yorkshire Light Infantry [*Military unit*] [*British*]
KOYN .... Paris, TX [*FM radio station call letters*]
KOZ .... Kozyrevsk [*Former USSR*] [*Seismograph station code, US Geological Survey*] (SEIS)
KOZ .... Ouzinkie, AK [*Location identifier*] [*FAA*] (FAAL)
KOZA .... Odessa, TX [*AM radio station call letters*]
KOZE .... Lewiston, ID [*AM radio station call letters*]
KOZE-FM .... Lewiston, ID [*FM radio station call letters*]
KOZI .... Chelan, WA [*AM radio station call letters*]
KOZI-FM ..... Chelan, WA [*FM radio station call letters*]
KOZJ .... Joplin, MO [*Television station call letters*]
KOZK .... Springfield, MO [*Television station call letters*]
KOZL-FM ..... New Boston, TX [*FM radio station call letters*] (BROA)
KOZN-FM.... Kansas City, MO [*FM radio station call letters*] (BROA)
KOZO-FM.... Branson, MO [*FM radio station call letters*] (RBYB)
KOZQ .... Waynesville, MO [*AM radio station call letters*]
KOZT.......... Fort Bragg, CA [*FM radio station call letters*]
KOZX .... Cabool, MO [*FM radio station call letters*]
KOZY .... Grand Rapids, MN [*AM radio station call letters*]
KOZZ .... Reno, NV [*AM radio station call letters*]
KOZZ-FM .... Reno, NV [*FM radio station call letters*]
KP................ Commission Percentage [*Travel industry*] (TVEL)
KP................ Democratic People's Republic of Korea [*ANSI two-letter standard code*] (CNC)
kp................ geomagnetic planetary index (SAUS)
K-P............. Kaiser-Permanente [*Diet*]
kp................ Kaliophilite [*CIPW classification*] [*Geology*]
KP................ Kaufmann-Peterson Base [*Medicine*] (DMAA)
KP................ Kensington Palace [*British*]
KP................ Keogh Plan [*Business term*]
KP................ Keratic Precipitate (SAUS)
KP................ Keratitic Precipitate [*Ophthalmology*]

KP................ Keratitis Punctata [*Ophthalmology*]
KP................ Keskustapuolue [*Center Party of Finland*] [*Political party*] (PPW)
KP................ Keyboard Perforator
KP................ Key Personnel
KP................ Key Production Co. [*NYSE symbol*] (SAG)
KP................ Key Pulsing
KP................ Keypunch [*Computer science*]
KP................ Kickpipe [*Building construction*]
KP................ Kick Plate
KP................ Kidder, Peabody & Co. (EFIS)
KP................ Kidney Pore
KP................ Kidney Protein [*Nephrology*] (DAVI)
KP................ Kidney Punch [*Medicine*] (DAVI)
KP................ Kids of Preachers
KP................ Killed Parenteral [*Vaccine*] [*Immunology*] (DAVI)
KP................ Kill Probability (MCD)
KP................ Kilometer Post
KP................ Kilopond
kp................ Kilopulse
KP................ Kinetic Percolation
KP................ Kinetic Potential
KP................ King Post
KP................ King's Parade [*British*] (DSUE)
KP................ King's Pawn [*Chess*] (ADA)
KP................ King's Pleasure [*British*]
KP................ King's Proctor [*British*]
KP................ Kitchen Police [*Kitchen helpers*] [*Military*]
KP................ Kitchen Punishment (SAUO)
KP................ Klebsiella Pneumoniae [*Genus of microorganism*] (DAVI)
KP................ Klein Paradox [*Physics*]
KP................ Knight of Pius IX
KP................ Knight of St. Patrick [*British*]
KP................ Knights of Pythias (EA)
KP................ Knotty Pine
KP................ Kodak Process Resist [*Photography*] (DICI)
KP................ Komma Proodeftikon [*Progressive Party*] [*Greek*] [*Political party*] (PPE)
KP................ Kommunistesch Partei [*Communist Party*] [*Luxembourg*] [*Political party*] (PPE)
KP................ Kommunistische Partei [*Communist Party*] [*German*] [*Political party*]
KP................ Kurdish Heritage Foundation of America
KP................ Kurdish Program (EA)
KP................ Kurie Plot [*Physics*]
kp................ low magnetic activity (SAUS)
KP................ North Korea [*Internet country code*]
KP................ Papua New Guinea [*IYRU nationality code*] (IYR)
KP................ Safair [*ICAO designator*] (AD)
KPA............. Innkeepers USA Trust [*NYSE symbol*] (SAG)
KPA............. Kalenjin Political Alliance (SAUO)
KPA............. Kansas Pharmaceutical Association (SAUO)
KPA............. Kentucky Pharmaceutical Association (SAUO)
KPA............. Key Personnel Analysis (TIMI)
KPA............. Key-Process Area (AAEL)
KPA............. Key Pulse Adapter [*Telecommunications*] (TEL)
KPA............. Kidney Plasminogen Activator [*Anticlotting agent*]
kPa............. Kilopascal
KPA............. Klystron Power Amplifier
KPA............. Kopiago [*Papua New Guinea*] [*Airport symbol*] (OAG)
KPA............. Korean People's Army [*Democratic People's Republic of Korea*] (BUAC)
KPA............. Korea Procurement Agency
KPA............. Kraft Paper Association [*Later, API*] (EA)
KPAC .... San Antonio, TX [*FM radio station call letters*]
KPAE .... Erwinville, LA [*FM radio station call letters*]
KPAE .... Everett/Snohomish County-Paine Field [*Washington*] [*ICAO location identifier*] (ICLI)
KPAG .... Pagosa Springs, CO [*AM radio station call letters*]
KPAL-AM .... North Little Rock, AR [*AM radio station call letters*] (RBYB)
KPAM .... Panama City/Tyndall Air Force Base [*Florida*] [*ICAO location identifier*] (ICLI)
KPAM .... Troutdale, OR [*AM radio station call letters*] (BROA)
KPAN .... Hereford, TX [*AM radio station call letters*]
KP & D .... Kick Plate and Drip (AAG)
KPAN-FM.... Hereford, TX [*FM radio station call letters*]
KPAR .... Granbury, TX [*AM radio station call letters*]
KParSH ...... Parsons State Hospital, Parsons, KS [*Library symbol*] [*Library of Congress*] (LCLS)
KPAS .... Fabens, TX [*FM radio station call letters*]
KPAT-FM .... San Luis Obispo, CA [*FM radio station call letters*] (BROA)
KPAW .... Fort Collins, CO [*FM radio station call letters*] (RBYB)
KPAWU ...... Kenya Plantation and Agricultural Workers Union (BUAC)
KPAX .... Missoula, MT [*Television station call letters*]
KPAY .... Chico, CA [*AM radio station call letters*]
KPAZ.......... Phoenix, AZ [*Television station call letters*]
KPB............. Kalium [*Potassium*] Phosphate Buffer [*Biochemistry*] (DAVI)
KPB............. Kenai Peninsula Borough [*Alaska*]
KPB............. Kenya Pyrethrum Board (BUAC)
KPB............. Ketophenylbutazone [*or Kebuzone*] [*An antirheumatic*] (DAVI)
KPB............. Kommunistische Partij van Belgie [*Communist Party of Belgium*] [*See also PCB*] [*Political party*] (PPE)
KPB............. Point Baker, AK [*Location identifier*] [*FAA*] (FAAL)
KPBA .... Pine Bluff, AR [*AM radio station call letters*]
KPBC .... Garland, TX [*AM radio station call letters*]
KPBE-FM .... Brownwood, TX [*FM radio station call letters*] (BROA)
KPBF........... Pine Bluff/Grider Field [*Arkansas*] [*ICAO location identifier*] (ICLI)

KPBG .... Plattsburg/Plattsburg Air Force Base [*New York*] [*ICAO location identifier*] (ICLI)
KPBI .... Greenwood, AR [*AM radio station call letters*]
KPBI .... West Palm Beach/Palm Beach International [*Florida*] [*ICAO location identifier*] (ICLI)
KPBL-AM ..... Hemphill, TX [*AM radio station call letters*] (BROA)
KPBM-FM ..... McCamey, TX [*FM radio station call letters*] (BROA)
KPBQ .... Pine Bluff, AR [*FM radio station call letters*]
KPBRS .... Korean Peace Bioreserves System
KPBS .... San Diego, CA [*Television station call letters*]
KPBS-FM ..... San Diego, CA [*FM radio station call letters*]
KPBX .... Spokane, WA [*FM radio station call letters*]
KPC .... Kappa Resources [*Vancouver Stock Exchange symbol*]
KPC .... Kembata People's Congress [*Ethiopia*]
KPC .... Kentucky Power Co. [*NYSE symbol*] (SAG)
KPC .... Kentucky Pwr 8.72% Sr'A'Debs [*NYSE symbol*] (TTSB)
KPC .... Keratinocyte Precursor Cell
KPC .... Keratoconus Posticus Circumscriptus [*Medicine*] (DMAA)
KPC .... Keyboard/Printer Control [*Computer science*]
KPC .... Keyboard Priority Controller [*Computer science*] (HGAA)
KPC .... Key Personnel Course (MCD)
KPC .... Key Product Characteristic
KPC .... Keypunch Cabinet [*Computer science*]
KPC .... Khapcheranga [*Former USSR*] [*Seismograph station code, US Geological Survey*] (SEIS)
kpc .... Kiloparsec [*Astronomy*]
KPC .... Kilo Parsecs [*Astronomy*] (GOBB)
KPC .... Kinetic Process Control
KPC .... Klystron Phase Control
KPC .... Knights of Peter Claver (EA)
KPC .... Koblenz Procurement Center [*Federal Republic of Germany*] [*Military*] (NATG)
KPC .... Kodak Photofabrication Center
KPC .... Kohn Problem Checklist (TES)
KPC .... Korean Productivity Center (SAUO)
KPC .... Korean Productivity Council (SAUO)
KPC .... Korea Productivity Centre (BUAC)
KPC .... Kuwait Petroleum Corporation (SAUO)
KPC .... Paducah Junior College, Paducah, KY [*OCLC symbol*] (OCLC)
KPC .... Port Clarence [*Alaska*] [*Airport symbol*] (OAG)
KPC .... Port Clarence, AK [*Location identifier*] [*FAA*] (FAAL)
KPCB-TV ...... Snyder, TX [*TV station call letters*] (RBYB)
KPCC .... Pasadena, CA [*FM radio station call letters*]
KPCH .... Dubach, LA [*FM radio station call letters*]
KPCI........... Key Production [*NASDAQ symbol*] (TTSB)
KPCI........... Key Production Co., Inc. [*NASDAQ symbol*] (NQ)
KPCK .... Kopeck (ABBR)
KPC/KSC ..... Kohn Problem Checklist/Kohn Social Competence Scale [*Test*] (TMMY)
KPCL .... Farmington, NM [*FM radio station call letters*]
KPCMS .... Kodak Precision Color Management System (SAUS)
KPCO .... Quincy, CA [*AM radio station call letters*]
KPCR .... Bowling Green, MO [*AM radio station call letters*]
KPCR-FM ..... Bowling Green, MO [*FM radio station call letters*]
KPCU .... Kenyan Planters Co-Operative Union (BUAC)
KPCW .... Park City, UT [*FM radio station call letters*]
KPD .... Kennedy Program Directive [*NASA*] (NASA)
KPD .... Knowledge-Based Producibility Decision-Maker [*Productivity technology*] (RDA)
KPD .... Kommunistische Partei Deutschlands [*Communist Party of Germany*] [*Political party*] (PPW)
KPDES .... Kentucky Pollutant Discharge Elimination System (SAUO)
KPDL .... Kyocera Page Description Language (SAUS)
KPDL .... Kyocera Printer Description Language [*Computer science*] (VLIE)
KPD-ML .... Kommunistische Partei Deutschlands/Marxisten-Leninisten [*Communist Party of Germany/Marxists-Leninists*] [*Political party*] (PPW)
KPDQ .... Portland, OR [*AM radio station call letters*]
KPDQ-FM ..... Portland, OR [*FM radio station call letters*]
KPDR .... Korean People's Democratic Republic (BUAC)
KPDR .... Wheeler, TX [*FM radio station call letters*]
KPDU .... Kaffa People's Democratic Union [*Ethiopia*] [*Political party*] (EY)
KPDX .... Portland/International [*Oregon*] [*ICAO location identifier*] (ICLI)
KPDX .... Vancouver, WA [*Television station call letters*]
KPE .... Kelman Phakoemulsification [*Ophthalmology*] (DAVI)
KPE .... Key Point Error [*Computer science*] (IAA)
KPE .... Kilman Phacoemulsification [*Medicine*] (MEDA)
kpe .... Kpelle [*MARC language code*] [*Library of Congress*] (LCCP)
KPEJ .... Odessa, TX [*Television station call letters*]
KPEK-FM ..... Albuquerque, NM [*FM radio station call letters*] (RBYB)
KPEL .... Lafayette, LA [*AM radio station call letters*]
KPEL-FM...... Erath, LA [*FM radio station call letters*]
KPENC .... Korean Centre of International PEN (EAIO)
KPEN-FM ..... Soldotna, AK [*FM radio station call letters*]
KPER .... Hobbs, NM [*FM radio station call letters*]
KPET .... Lamesa, TX [*AM radio station call letters*]
KPEZ .... Austin, TX [*FM radio station call letters*]
KPF .... Kangaroo Protection Foundation (EA)
KPF .... Katadyn Pocket Filter
KPF .... Kenya Patriotic Front [*Political party*] (BUAC)
KPF .... Key Pulse on Front Cord [*Telecommunications*] (TEL)
KPFA .... Berkeley, CA [*FM radio station call letters*]
KPFA .... Knackery and Pet Food Association [*Australia*]
KPFB .... Berkeley, CA [*FM radio station call letters*]
KPFC.......... Kuwait Pacific Finance Company (SAUO)

KPFC-FM ..... Callisburg, TX [*FM radio station call letters*] (BROA)
KPFK.......... Los Angeles, CA [*FM radio station call letters*]
KPFM.......... Mountain Home, AR [*FM radio station call letters*]
KPFN-FM ..... Seward, AK [*FM radio station call letters*] (BROA)
KPFSM........ King's Police and Fire Services Medal for Distinguished Service [*British*]
KPFSM........ King's Police & Fire Services Medal for Gallantry [*British*] (WDAA)
KPFT .... Houston, TX [*FM radio station call letters*]
KPFX .... Fargo, ND [*FM radio station call letters*]
KPG .... Keeping
KPG .... King Power Intl. [*AMEX symbol*] (SG)
KPG .... Kurupung [*Guyana*] [*Airport symbol*] (OAG)
KPGA .... Kansas Personnel and Guidance Association (SAUO)
KPGA .... Kentucky Personnel and Guidance Association (SAUO)
KPGE .... Page, AZ [*AM radio station call letters*]
KPGR .... Pleasant Grove, UT [*FM radio station call letters*]
KPH .... Kaena Point [*Hawaii*] [*Seismograph station code, US Geological Survey*] [*Closed*] (SEIS)
KPH .... Keystrokes Per Hour (NITA)
kph .... Kilometers per Hour
KPH .... Know Problems of Hydrocephalus (EA)
KPH .... Komunisticka Partija Hrvatske [*Communist Party of Croatia*] [*Political party*]
KPH .... Ktav Publishing House, Inc. [*New York*] (BJA)
KPH .... Pauloff Harbor/Sanak Island, AK [*Location identifier*] [*FAA*] (FAAL)
KPhA .... Kansas Pharmacists Association (SRA)
KPHA .... Kansas Public Health Association (SAUO)
KPhA .... Kentucky Pharmacists Association (SRA)
KPHF .... Newport News/Patrick Henry [*Virginia*] [*ICAO location identifier*] (ICLI)
KPHF .... Phoenix, AZ [*FM radio station call letters*]
KPHL .... Philadelphia/International [*Pennsylvania*] [*ICAO location identifier*] (ICLI)
KPHN .... Kansas City, MO [*AM radio station call letters*] (BROA)
KPHN .... Pittsburg, KS [*AM radio station call letters*]
KPHN .... Port Huron [*Michigan*] [*ICAO location identifier*] (ICLI)
KPHO .... Phoenix, AZ [*Television station call letters*]
KPHO-DT ..... Phoenix, AZ [*Television station call letters*] (BROA)
KPHR .... Milbank, SD [*FM radio station call letters*]
KPHR-FM ..... Ortonville, MN [*FM radio station call letters*] (BROA)
KPHS-FM ..... Plains, TX [*FM radio station call letters*] (RBYB)
KPHT .... Kindred, ND [*FM radio station call letters*] (RBYB)
KPHX .... Phoenix, AZ [*AM radio station call letters*]
KPHX .... Phoenix/Sky Harbor International [*Arizona*] [*ICAO location identifier*] (ICLI)
KPI............. Kapit [*Malaysia*] [*Airport symbol*] (OAG)
KPI............. Karyopyknotic Index [*Cytology*]
KPI............. Kernel Programming Interface [*Computer science*]
KPI............. Key Performance Indicator (EBF)
KPI............. Killearn Properties, Inc. [*AMEX symbol*] (SPSG)
KPI............. King Pin Inclination [*Automotive engineering*]
kpi............. Kips [*Thousands of Pounds*] per Square Inch
KPI............. Kontron Personal Instrumentation [*Kontron Electronics*] (NITA)
KPI............. Kunitz Protease Inhibitor [*Medicine*]
KPI............. Kuwait Petroleum International (BUAC)
KPI............. KWIK Products International Corp. [*Vancouver Stock Exchange symbol*]
KPIB........... Key Points Intelligence Branch (SAUO)
KPIC........... Key Phrase in Context
KPIC........... Roseburg, OR [*Television station call letters*]
KPICO .... Kuwait Pharmaceutical Industries Co. (BUAC)
KPIE .... St. Petersburg/Clearwater International [*Florida*] [*ICAO location identifier*] (ICLI)
KPIG .... Freedom, CA [*FM radio station call letters*]
KPIK .... Beebe, AR [*FM radio station call letters*]
KPIN-FM ..... Pinedale, WY [*FM radio station call letters*] (RBYB)
KPIT .... Pittsburgh/Greater Pittsburgh [*Pennsylvania*] [*ICAO location identifier*] (ICLI)
KPIX .... San Francisco, CA [*AM radio station call letters*] (RBYB)
KPIX-DT ...... San Francisco, CA [*Television station call letters*] (BROA)
KPIX-FM ..... San Francisco, CA [*FM radio station call letters*] (RBYB)
KPIX-TV ...... San Francisco, CA [*Television station call letters*]
KPJ .... Komunisticka Partija Jugoslavije [*Communist Party of Yugoslavia*] [*Political party*] (PPE)
KPK .... Communist Party of Kazakhstan [*Political party*] (BUAC)
KPK .... Kanaka Peak [*California*] [*Seismograph station code, US Geological Survey*] (SEIS)
KPK .... Kapok (ABBR)
KPK .... Kappa Phi Kappa [*Fraternity*]
KPK .... Parks [*Alaska*] [*Airport symbol*] (OAG)
KPK .... Parks, AK [*Location identifier*] [*FAA*] (FAAL)
KPKE-AM ..... Gunnison, CO [*AM radio station call letters*] (RBYB)
KPKX .... Livingston, MT [*FM radio station call letters*] (RBYB)
KPKY .... Pocatello, ID [*FM radio station call letters*]
KPL .... Copeland Resources [*Vancouver Stock Exchange symbol*]
KPL .... Key Personnel Locator (SAUO)
KPL .... Khao San Pathet Lao [*News agency*] [*Laos*] (FEA)
KPL .... Kick Plate [*Building construction*]
KPL .... Killearn Properties [*AMEX symbol*] (TTSB)
KPL .... Knoxville Public Library (SAUO)
KPL .... Kommunistisch Partei vu Leetzebuerg [*Communist Party of Luxembourg*] [*Political party*] (PPW)
KPI............. Kuwait Petroleum Corporation (SAUO)
K-PL.......... Potassium-Plasma [*Biochemistry*] (DAVI)
KPLA.......... Columbia, MO [*FM radio station call letters*] (RBYB)

KPLC............ Lake Charles, LA [*Television station call letters*]
KPLG-FM .... Plains, MT [*FM radio station call letters*]   (BROA)
KPLM .... Palm Springs, CA [*FM radio station call letters*]
KPLN-FM .... Plains, TX [*FM radio station call letters*]
KPLN-FM .... San Diego, CA [*FM radio station call letters*]   (BROA)
KPLO .... Reliance, SD [*AM radio station call letters*]
KPLO-TV ..... Reliance, SD [*Television station call letters*]
KPLR .... St. Louis, MO [*Television station call letters*]
KPLS............ Key Pulsing   (MSA)
KPLS............ Orange, CA [*AM radio station call letters*]
KPLT............ Paris, TX [*AM radio station call letters*]
KPLT-FM ..... Paris, TX [*FM radio station call letters*]
KPLU .... Tacoma, WA [*FM radio station call letters*]
KPLV .... Port Lavaca, TX [*FM radio station call letters*]
KPLW-FM .... Wenatchee, WA [*FM radio station call letters*]   (RBYB)
KPLX .... Fort Worth, TX [*FM radio station call letters*]
KPLY .... Sparks, NV [*AM radio station call letters*]
KPLZ .... Seattle, WA [*FM radio station call letters*]
KPM .... Kahler Process Model [*Computer science*]
KPM .... Kathode Pulse Modulation
KPM .... Kensington Palace Gardens [*British interrogation center*]
Kpm .... Kilopondmeter
KPM .... Kilo/Pound/Meters   (STED)
KPM .... King's Police Medal
KPM .... King's Police Medal for Distinguished Service [*British*]
KPM .... King's Police Medal for Gallantry [*British*]
KPM .... Kronig-Penny Model
KPMB........... Pembina [*North Dakota*] [*ICAO location identifier*]   (ICLI)
KPMD .... Palmdale/Air Force Plant No. 42 [*California*] [*ICAO location identifier*]   (ICLI)
KPMG .... Klynveld Peat Marwick Goerdeler [*Commercial firm*] [*British*]
KPMG .... KPMG Peat Marwick   (SAUO)
KPMI .... Kraner Preschool Math Inventory [*Educational test*]
KPMO .... Mendocino, CA [*AM radio station call letters*]
KPMR .... Santa Barbara, CA [*Television station call letters*]   (BROA)
KPMW .... Hallimaile, HI [*FM radio station call letters*]
KPMX........... Sterling, CO [*FM radio station call letters*]
KPN .... Confederation for an Independent Poland   (PD)
KPN .... Kipnuk [*Alaska*] [*Airport symbol*]   (OAG)
KPN .... Kipnuk, AK [*Location identifier*] [*FAA*]   (FAAL)
KPN .... Koninklijke PTT Nederland [*Post and telecommunications company*]   (ECON)
KPN .... KPN [*NYSE symbol*]   (SAG)
KPN .... Kupiano [*Papua New Guinea*] [*Seismograph station code, US Geological Survey*]   (SEIS)
KPN .... Royal PTT Nederland ADS [*NYSE symbol*]   (TTSB)
KPNC .... Ponca City [*Oklahoma*] [*ICAO location identifier*]   (ICLI)
KPNC .... Ponca City, OK [*FM radio station call letters*]
KPND .... Sandpoint, ID [*FM radio station call letters*]
KPNE .... North Platte, NE [*Television station call letters*]
KPNE .... Philadelphia/North Philadelphia [*Pennsylvania*] [*ICAO location identifier*]   (ICLI)
KPNE-FM .... North Platte, NE [*FM radio station call letters*]
KPNLF .... Khmer People's National Liberation Front [*Cambodia*] [*Political party*]   (PD)
KPNO .... Kitt Peak National Observatory [*Tucson, AZ*] [*National Science Foundation*]
KPNO .... Norfolk, NE [*FM radio station call letters*]
KPNOB......... Kitt Peak National Observatory [*Tucson, AZ*]
KPNS .... Pensacola/Regional [*Florida*] [*ICAO location identifier*]   (ICLI)
KPNT-FM ..... Ste. Genevieve, MO [*FM radio station call letters*]   (RBYB)
KPNW .... Eugene, OR [*AM radio station call letters*]
KPNWR .... Kern-Pixley National Wildlife Refuge   (SAUO)
KPNX-DT ..... Mesa, AZ [*Television station call letters*]   (BROA)
KPNX-TV ..... Mesa, AZ [*Television station call letters*]
KPNY .... Alliance, NE [*FM radio station call letters*]
KPO .... Key Performance Objectives   (VLIE)
KPO .... Keypunch Operator [*Computer science*]
KPO .... King Pin Offset [*Automotive engineering*]
KPO .... Kitt Peak National Observatory, Tucson, AZ [*OCLC symbol*]   (OCLC)
KPO .... Kommunistische Partei Oesterreichs [*Communist Party of Austria*] [*Political party*]   (PPW)
KPO .... Korean Post Office   (SAUO)
KPOA .... Lahaina, HI [*FM radio station call letters*]
KPOB .... Fayetteville/Pope Air Force Base [*North Carolina*] [*ICAO location identifier*]   (ICLI)
KPOB .... Poplar Bluff, MO [*Television station call letters*]
KPOC .... Key Prep on Campus [*Slang*]
KPOC .... Pocahontas, AR [*AM radio station call letters*]
KPOC-FM .... Pocahontas, AR [*FM radio station call letters*]
KPOD .... Crescent City, CA [*AM radio station call letters*]
KPOD-FM .... Crescent North, CA [*FM radio station call letters*]
KPOF .... Denver, CO [*AM radio station call letters*]
KPOI .... Honolulu, HI [*FM radio station call letters*]
KPOK .... Bowman, ND [*AM radio station call letters*]
KPOM .... Fort Smith, AR [*Television station call letters*]
KPOO .... San Francisco, CA [*FM radio station call letters*]
KPOP .... Kerberized Post Office Protocol   (SAUS)
KPOP .... San Diego, CA [*AM radio station call letters*]
KPOS .... Post, TX [*AM radio station call letters*]
KPOS-FM .... Post, TX [*FM radio station call letters*]
KPOW .... Powell, WY [*AM radio station call letters*]
KPOW-FM .... La Monte, MO [*FM radio station call letters*]   (BROA)
KPOWU .... Kenya Petroleum and Oil Workers' Union
KPOZ-AM .... San Antonio, TX [*AM radio station call letters*]   (BROA)

KPP .... Kaneb Pipeline Partnership LP [*NYSE symbol*]   (SPSG)
KPP .... Kaneb Pipe Line PtnrsL.P. [*NYSE symbol*]   (TTSB)
KPP .... Keeper of the Privy Purse [*British*]
KPP .... Komunistyczna Partia Polski [*Communist Party of Poland (1925-1938)*] [*Political party*]   (PPE)
KPP .... Korean Pacific Press   (SAUO)
KPP .... K-Profile Parameterization scheme   (SAUS)
KPPA .... Kosovo Patriotic and Political Association   (BUAC)
KPPC .... Pasadena, CA [*AM radio station call letters*]
KPPL .... Colusa, CA [*FM radio station call letters*]
KPPR .... Williston, ND [*FM radio station call letters*]
KPPS .... Kilopackets per Second [*Telecommunications*]
KPPS .... Kilopulses per Second   (NAKS)
kpps............ Kilopulses per Second
KPPT-AM .... Toledo, OR [*AM radio station call letters*]   (BROA)
KPPT-FM ..... Toledo, OR [*FM radio station call letters*]   (BROA)
KPPV .... Prescott Valley, AZ [*FM radio station call letters*]
KPPX .... Tolleson, AZ [*Television station call letters*]   (BROA)
KPQ .... Wenatchee, WA [*AM radio station call letters*]
KPQ-FM ...... Wenatchee, WA [*FM radio station call letters*]
KPQI .... Presque Isle/Presque Isle [*Maine*] [*ICAO location identifier*]   (ICLI)
KPQX .... Havre, MT [*FM radio station call letters*]
KPQZ-FM ..... Amarillo, TX [*FM radio station call letters*]   (BROA)
KPR .... Keeper   (ABBR)
KPR .... Kenya Police Reserve
KPR .... Key Pulse Rate [*Cardiology*]   (DAVI)
KPR .... Keypunch Replacement [*Computer science*]   (MHDI)
KPR .... Knight of Polonia Restituta [*British*]
KPR .... Knots per Revolution
KPR .... Kodak Photo Resist
KPR .... Krasnaya Polyana [*Former USSR*] [*Seismograph station code, US Geological Survey*] [*Closed*]   (SEIS)
KPR .... Kuder Preference Record [*Psychology*]   (DAVI)
KPR .... Port Williams [*Alaska*] [*Airport symbol*]   (OAG)
KPR .... Port Williams, AK [*Location identifier*] [*FAA*]   (FAAL)
KPRA .... Ukiah, CA [*FM radio station call letters*]
KPRB-FM .... Brush, CO [*FM radio station call letters*]   (BROA)
KPRC .... Houston, TX [*AM radio station call letters*]
KPRC-DT ..... Houston, TX [*Television station call letters*]   (BROA)
KPRC-TV ..... Houston, TX [*Television station call letters*]
KPRD .... Hays, KS [*FM radio station call letters*]   (RBYB)
KPRD .... KSC [*Kennedy Space Center*] Program Requirements Document [*NASA*]   (NASA)
KPRE .... Vail, CO [*FM radio station call letters*]   (RBYB)
KPRG .... Agana, GU [*FM radio station call letters*]   (RBYB)
KPRH-FM .... Montrose, CO [*FM radio station call letters*]   (BROA)
KPRI .... Fagaitua, AS [*FM radio station call letters*]   (RBYB)
KPRI .... Kinshasa Peace Research Institute   (SAUO)
KPRJ .... Jamestown, ND [*FM radio station call letters*]
KPRK .... Livingston, MT [*AM radio station call letters*]
KPRL .... Paso Robles, CA [*AM radio station call letters*]
KPRM .... Park Rapids, MN [*AM radio station call letters*]
KPRN .... Grand Junction, CO [*FM radio station call letters*]
KPRNA .... Konza Prairie Research Natural Area   (SAUO)
KPRO .... Riverside, CA [*AM radio station call letters*]
KPRP .... Kampuchean [*or Khmer*] People's Revolutionary Party [*Political party*]   (PD)
KPR-P .... Kuder Preference Record - Personal [*Psychology*]
KPRQ .... Price, UT [*FM radio station call letters*]
KPRR .... El Paso, TX [*FM radio station call letters*]
KPRS .... Kansas City, MO [*FM radio station call letters*]
KPRT .... Kansas City, MO [*AM radio station call letters*]
KPRU-FM .... Delta, CO [*FM radio station call letters*]   (BROA)
KPRV .... Heavener, OK [*FM radio station call letters*]
KPR-V .... Kuder Preference Record - Vocational [*Psychology*]   (DAVI)
KPRV .... Poteau, OK [*AM radio station call letters*]
KPRV-FM .... Heavener, OK [*FM radio station call letters*]   (BROA)
KPRW-FM .... Perham, MN [*FM radio station call letters*]   (RBYB)
KPRX .... Bakersfield, CA [*FM radio station call letters*]
KPRY .... Pierre, SD [*Television station call letters*]
KPRZ .... San Marcos, CA [*AM radio station call letters*]
KPRZ-FM ..... Fountain, CO [*FM radio station call letters*]   (RBYB)
KPS .... Keeper of the Privy Seal   (SAUO)
KPS .... Kempsey [*Australia*] [*Airport symbol*]   (OAG)
KPS .... Keypunch Performance System [*Computer science*]   (PDAA)
KPS .... Kilometers per Second   (NASA)
KPS .... Kirbati Philatelic Society   (EA)
KPS .... Klystron Power Supply
KPS .... Knight of the (Order of the) Polar Star [*Sweden*]   (ROG)
KPS .... Knowledge Processing System [*Expert system shell*]   (NITA)
KPS .... Kommunistische Partei der Schweiz [*Communist Party of Switzerland*] [*Political party*]   (PPE)
KPS .... Kommunistische Partij Suriname [*Communist Party of Surinam*] [*Political party*]   (PPW)
KPS .... Korean Physical Society   (SAUO)
KPS .... One Thousand Pulses per Second   (KSC)
KPSA .... Alamogordo, NM [*AM radio station call letters*]
KPSA .... La Luz, NM [*FM radio station call letters*]
KPSC .... Palm Springs, CA [*FM radio station call letters*]
KPSD .... Faith, SD [*FM radio station call letters*]
KPSD-TV ..... Eagle Butte, SD [*Television station call letters*]
KPSG .... Oklahoma City, OK [*Television station call letters*]   (BROA)
KPSH .... Kepco Power Supply Handbook
KPSI .... Kip [*Thousands of Pounds*] per Square Inch
KPSI .... Palm Springs, CA [*AM radio station call letters*]

KPSI-FM ...... Palm Springs, CA [*FM radio station call letters*]
KPSK .... Keepsake (ABBR)
KPSL .... Thousand Palms, CA [*AM radio station call letters*]
KPSM .... Brownwood, TX [*FM radio station call letters*]
KPSM .... Klystron Power Supply Modulator
KPSM .... Portsmouth/Pease Air Force Base [*New Hampshire*] [*ICAO location identifier*] (ICLI)
KPSNSW ...... Koala Preservation Society of New South Wales [*Australia*]
KPSO .... Falfurrias, TX [*AM radio station call letters*]
KPSO-FM ..... Falfurrias, TX [*FM radio station call letters*]
KPSQ .... Kapson Senior Quarters Corp. [*NASDAQ symbol*] (SAG)
KPSS .... Kommunisticheskaya Partiya Sovietskogo Soyuza [*Communist Party of the Soviet Union*] [*Political party*]
KPST .... Vallejo, CA [*Television station call letters*]
KPSU .... Goodwell, OK [*FM radio station call letters*]
KPSX .... Palacios [*Texas*] [*ICAO location identifier*] (ICLI)
KPT .... Kaena Point Station [*Hawaii*] [*Military*]
KPT .... Kai's Power Tools for Windows [*HSC Software*] (PCM)
KPT .... Karpatair [*Hungary*] [*ICAO designator*] (FAAC)
KPT .... Keeprite, Inc. [*Toronto Stock Exchange symbol*]
KPT .... Kenner Parker Toys, Inc. (SAUO)
KPT .... Kidney Punch Test [*or Murphy's test*] (DAVI)
KPT .... Konover Property [*Formerly, FAC Realty Trust*] [*NYSE symbol*]
KPT .... Kuder Performance Test [*Psychology*] (DAVI)
KPT .... Pittsburgh State University (SAUS)
KPT .... Pittsburg State University, Pittsburg, KS [*Library symbol*] [*Library of Congress*] (LCLS)
KPT3 .... Kai's Power Tools [*Computer science*]
KPTB .... Lubbock, TX [*Television station call letters*] (RBYB)
KPTC .... Kuwait Public Transport Co. (BUAC)
KPTE-FM ..... Durango, CO [*FM radio station call letters*] (BROA)
KPTH .... Sioux City, IA [*Television station call letters*] (BROA)
KPTI .... Kunitz Pancreatic Trypsin Inhibitor [*Medicine*] (MAE)
KPTL .... Carson City, NV [*AM radio station call letters*]
KPTM .... Omaha, NE [*Television station call letters*]
KPTS .... Hutchinson, KS [*Television station call letters*]
KPTT .... Kaolin Partial Thromboplastin Time [*Clinical chemistry*] (MAE)
KPTT .... Reno, NV [*AM radio station call letters*] (BROA)
KPTV .... Portland, OR [*Television station call letters*]
KPTX .... Pecos, TX [*FM radio station call letters*]
KPTY-FM ..... Gilbert, AZ [*FM radio station call letters*] (BROA)
KPU .... Kaneb Pipe Line Partners LP [*NYSE symbol*] (SAG)
KPU .... Kaneb Pipe Ln Ptnrs LP Pref Ut [*NYSE symbol*] (TTSB)
KPU .... Kaszubian Pomeranian Union [*Poland*] [*Political party*] (BUAC)
KPU .... Ketchikan Public Utilities (SAUO)
KPU .... Keyboard Printer Unit (SAUS)
KPU .... Khapalu [*Pakistan*] [*Airport symbol*] (AD)
KPU .... Kommunisticheskaia Partiia Ukrainy [*Communist Party of the Ukraine*] [*Political party*]
KPUA .... Hilo, HI [*AM radio station call letters*]
KPUB .... Pueblo Memorial [*Colorado*] [*ICAO location identifier*] (ICLI)
KPUB-FM ..... Prescott, AZ [*FM radio station call letters*] (BROA)
KPUC .... Korean Presidential Unit Citation [*Military award*]
KPUG .... Bellingham, WA [*AM radio station call letters*]
KPUP .... Key Personnel Upgrade Program [*National Guard*]
KPUR .... Amarillo, TX [*AM radio station call letters*]
KPUR-FM ..... Canyon, TX [*FM radio station call letters*]
KPUZ .... Kommunisticheskaia Partiia Uzbekistana [*Communist Party of Uzbekistan*] [*Political party*]
KPV .... Keypunch Verifier (VLIE)
KPV .... Kid-Powered Vehicle
KPV .... Killed Parenteral Vaccine [*Immunology*] (DAVI)
KPV .... Killed Polio Vaccine [*Medicine*] (STED)
KPVD .... Providence/Theodore Francis Greene State [*Rhode Island*] [*ICAO location identifier*] (ICLI)
KPV HMG..... Krupnokalibernyi Pulemyoy Vladimirova Heavy Machine Gun [*Soviet-made weaponry used extensively by the People's Army of North Vietnam*] (VNW)
KPVI........... Pocatello, ID [*Television station call letters*]
KPVS .... Hilo, HI [*FM radio station call letters*]
KPVU .... Prairie View, TX [*FM radio station call letters*]
KPVY .... Amarillo, TX [*FM radio station call letters*]
KPW .... North Korean Won (SAUS)
KPWA .... Korean Patriotic Women's Association in America [*Defunct*] (EA)
KPWB .... Piedmont, MO [*AM radio station call letters*]
KPWB-FM ..... Piedmont, MO [*FM radio station call letters*]
KPWB-TV ..... Ames, IA [*Television station call letters*] (BROA)
KPWB-TV ..... Sacramento, CA [*Television station call letters*] (RBYB)
KPWM .... Portland/International Jetport [*Maine*] [*ICAO location identifier*] (ICLI)
KPWR .... Los Angeles, CA [*FM radio station call letters*]
KPWS .... Crowley, LA [*AM radio station call letters*]
KPWU .... Korean Port Worker's Union (BUAC)
KPWW-FM... Hooks, TX [*FM radio station call letters*] (BROA)
KPXA .... Sisters, OR [*FM radio station call letters*]
KPXB .... Conroe, TX [*Television station call letters*] (BROA)
KPXC .... Indian Springs, NV [*FM radio station call letters*]
KPXC-TV ..... Denver, CO [*Television station call letters*] (BROA)
KPXD .... Arlington, TX [*Television station call letters*] (BROA)
KPXE .... Kansas City, MO [*Television station call letters*] (BROA)
KPXE .... Liberty, TX [*FM radio station call letters*]
KPXF .... Lacombe, LA [*FM radio station call letters*]
KPXF........... Porterville, CA [*Television station call letters*] (BROA)
KPXG .... Salem, OR [*Television station call letters*]
KPXH .... Garapan-Saipan, MP [*FM radio station call letters*]
KPXI........... Mount Pleasant, TX [*FM radio station call letters*]

KPXK .... Odessa, TX [*Television station call letters*] (BROA)
KPXL .... Uvalde, TX [*Television station call letters*] (BROA)
KPXM .... St. Cloud, MN [*Television station call letters*] (BROA)
KPXN .... San Bernardino, CA [*Television station call letters*] (BROA)
KPXO .... Kaneohe, HI [*Television station call letters*] (BROA)
KPXP .... Garapan-Saipan, MP [*FM radio station call letters*]
KPXQ-AM ..... Phoenix, AZ [*AM radio station call letters*] (RBYB)
KPXR .... Cedar Rapids, IA [*Television station call letters*] (BROA)
KPY .... Port Bailey [*Alaska*] [*Airport symbol*] (OAG)
KPY .... Port Bailey, AK [*Location identifier*] [*FAA*] (FAAL)
KPYK .... Terrell, TX [*AM radio station call letters*]
KPYN .... Atlanta, TX [*FM radio station call letters*]
KPZA .... Espanola, NM [*FM radio station call letters*] (RBYB)
KQ .... Air South, Inc. [*Airline code*]
KQ .... Kenya Airways [*ICAO designator*] (AD)
KQ .... Kenya Airways [*Airline flight code*] (ODBW)
KQ .... Kenya Airways Ltd. (SAUO)
KQ .... Line Squall [*Meteorology*] (WDAA)
KQA .... Akutan [*Alaska*] [*Airport symbol*] (OAG)
KQA .... Akutan, AK [*Location identifier*] [*FAA*] (FAAL)
KQA .... Kenya Airways Ltd. [*ICAO designator*] (FAAC)
KQAA .... Aberdeen, SD [*FM radio station call letters*]
KQAB-AM ..... Lake Isabella, CA [*AM radio station call letters*] (BROA)
KQAC .... Amarillo, TX [*FM radio station call letters*]
KQAD .... Luverne, MN [*AM radio station call letters*]
KQAK .... Bend, OR [*FM radio station call letters*]
KQAL .... Winona, MN [*FM radio station call letters*]
KQAM .... Wichita, KS [*AM radio station call letters*]
KQAR-FM ..... Jacksonville, AR [*FM radio station call letters*] (BROA)
KQAY .... Tucumcari, NM [*FM radio station call letters*]
KQAZ .... Springerville-Eager, AZ [*FM radio station call letters*]
KQBE .... Ellensburg, WA [*FM radio station call letters*]
KQBR .... Davis, CA [*FM radio station call letters*]
KQBT-FM ..... Taylor, TX [*FM radio station call letters*] (BROA)
KQC .... King's College London [*British*] (IRUK)
KQCA .... Stockton, CA [*Television station call letters*] (RBYB)
KQCD .... Dickinson, ND [*Television station call letters*]
KQCL .... Faribault, MN [*FM radio station call letters*]
KQCP .... King's and Queen's College of Physicians [*Ireland*]
KQCT .... Davenport, IA [*Television station call letters*]
KQCV .... Oklahoma City, OK [*AM radio station call letters*]
KQDI .... Great Falls, MT [*AM radio station call letters*] (BROA)
KQDI-FM ..... Great Falls, MT [*FM radio station call letters*]
KQDJ .... Jamestown, ND [*AM radio station call letters*]
KQDJ-FM ..... Valley City, ND [*FM radio station call letters*] (RBYB)
KQDS .... Duluth, MN [*AM radio station call letters*]
KQDS-FM ..... Duluth, MN [*FM radio station call letters*]
KQDY .... Bismarck, ND [*FM radio station call letters*]
KQED .... San Francisco, CA [*FM radio station call letters*]
KQED-DT ..... San Francisco, CA [*Television station call letters*] (BROA)
KQED-TV ..... San Francisco, CA [*Television station call letters*]
KQEG .... La Crescent, MN [*FM radio station call letters*]
KQEN .... Roseburg, OR [*AM radio station call letters*]
KQEO-FM ..... Grants, NM [*FM radio station call letters*] (BROA)
KQEP .... Rock Valley, IA [*FM radio station call letters*]
KQEQ .... Fowler, CA [*AM radio station call letters*] (RBYB)
KQEW .... Fordyce, AR [*FM radio station call letters*]
KQEX .... Fortuna, CA [*FM radio station call letters*]
KQEZ-FM ..... Houston, AK [*FM radio station call letters*] (BROA)
KQF .... Krupp Quick-Firing Gun
KQFC .... Boise, ID [*FM radio station call letters*]
KQFE .... Springfield, OR [*FM radio station call letters*]
KQFM .... Hermiston, OR [*FM radio station call letters*]
KQFN .... Fargo, ND [*AM radio station call letters*] (RBYB)
KQFX .... Borger, TX [*FM radio station call letters*]
KQHC-FM ..... Burns, OR [*FM radio station call letters*] (RBYB)
KQHN .... Nederland, TX [*AM radio station call letters*]
KQHT .... Crookston, MN [*FM radio station call letters*]
KQIB-FM ..... Idabel, OK [*FM radio station call letters*] (BROA)
KQIC .... Willmar, MN [*FM radio station call letters*]
KQID .... Alexandria, LA [*FM radio station call letters*]
KQIK .... Lakeview, OR [*AM radio station call letters*]
KQIK-FM ..... Lakeview, OR [*FM radio station call letters*]
KQIL .... Grand Junction, CO [*AM radio station call letters*]
KQIP .... Odessa, TX [*FM radio station call letters*]
KQIS-FM ..... Basile, LA [*FM radio station call letters*] (BROA)
KQIX .... Grand Junction, CO [*FM radio station call letters*]
KQIZ .... Amarillo, TX [*FM radio station call letters*]
KQJD .... West Fargo, ND [*AM radio station call letters*] (BROA)
KQJM .... King, Queen, Jack Meld [*Canasta*]
KQJZ-FM ..... Grover City, CA [*FM radio station call letters*] (BROA)
KQKD .... Redfield, SD [*AM radio station call letters*]
KQKD-FM ..... Redfield, SD [*FM radio station call letters*]
KQKI .... Bayou Vista, LA [*FM radio station call letters*]
KQKK-FM ..... Walker, MN [*FM radio station call letters*] (BROA)
KQKQ .... Council Bluffs, IA [*FM radio station call letters*]
KQKS .... Longmont, CO [*FM radio station call letters*]
KQKY .... Kearney, NE [*FM radio station call letters*]
KQL .... Kol [*Papua New Guinea*] [*Airport symbol*] (OAG)
KQLA .... Ogden, KS [*FM radio station call letters*]
KQLB .... Los Banos, CA [*FM radio station call letters*]
KQLI-FM ..... Geneseo, IL [*FM radio station call letters*] (BROA)
KQLL .... Owasso, OK [*FM radio station call letters*]
KQLL .... Tulsa, OK [*AM radio station call letters*]
KQLM-FM ..... Odessa, TX [*FM radio station call letters*] (RBYB)

KQLO	Reno, NV [*AM radio station call letters*]
KQLS	Colby, KS [*FM radio station call letters*]
KQLT	Casper, WY [*FM radio station call letters*]
KQLV-FM	Grants, NM [*FM radio station call letters*] (BROA)
KQLX	Lisbon, ND [*AM radio station call letters*]
KQLX-FM	Lisbon, ND [*FM radio station call letters*]
KQM	Kolson Quick Modality Test [*Education*]
KQMA	Phillipsburg, KS [*FM radio station call letters*]
KQMB-FM	Midvale, UT [*FM radio station call letters*] (RBYB)
KQMC	Brinkley, AR [*FM radio station call letters*]
KQMG	Independence, IA [*AM radio station call letters*]
KQMG-FM	Independence, IA [*FM radio station call letters*]
KQML	Knowledge Query and Manipulation Language [*Computer science*]
KQMN	Thief River Falls, MN [*FM radio station call letters*]
KQMO-FM	Ash Grove, MO [*FM radio station call letters*] (RBYB)
KQMQ	Honolulu, HI [*AM radio station call letters*]
KQMQ-FM	Honolulu, HI [*FM radio station call letters*]
KQMS	Redding, CA [*AM radio station call letters*]
KQMX-FM	Clinton, OK [*FM radio station call letters*] (RBYB)
KQNA	Prescott Valley, AZ [*AM radio station call letters*]
KQNC	Quincy, CA [*FM radio station call letters*]
KQNG	Lihue, HI [*AM radio station call letters*]
KQNG-FM	Lihue, HI [*FM radio station call letters*]
KQNK	Norton, KS [*AM radio station call letters*]
KQNK-FM	Norton, KS [*FM radio station call letters*]
KQNN	Alice, TX [*FM radio station call letters*]
KQNS	Lindsborg, KS [*FM radio station call letters*]
KQNV	Sparks, NV [*FM radio station call letters*] (RBYB)
KQOD	Stockton, CA [*FM radio station call letters*]
KQOL	Boulder City, NV [*FM radio station call letters*] (RBYB)
KQPM	Ukiah, CA [*FM radio station call letters*]
KQPR	Albert Lea, MN [*FM radio station call letters*]
KQPT	Sacramento, CA [*FM radio station call letters*]
KQQA	Creedmoor, TX [*AM radio station call letters*] (BROA)
KQQK	Galveston, TX [*FM radio station call letters*]
KQQL	Anoka, MN [*FM radio station call letters*]
KQQQ	Pullman, WA [*AM radio station call letters*]
KQQQ-FM	Hutto, TX [*FM radio station call letters*] (BROA)
KQR	Cobequid Resources Ltd. [*Vancouver Stock Exchange symbol*]
KQR	Kit Quotation Request (MCD)
KQRC-FM	Leavenworth, KS [*FM radio station call letters*]
KQRK	Ronan, MT [*FM radio station call letters*]
KQRN	Mitchell, SD [*FM radio station call letters*]
KQRS	Golden Valley, MN [*AM radio station call letters*]
KQRS-FM	Golden Valley, MN [*FM radio station call letters*]
KQRV-FM	Deer Lodge, MT [*FM radio station call letters*] (BROA)
KQRX	Midland, TX [*FM radio station call letters*]
KQSB	Santa Barbara, CA [*AM radio station call letters*]
KQSC	Willows, CA [*FM radio station call letters*]
KQSD	Lowry, SD [*Television station call letters*]
KQSK	Chadron, NE [*FM radio station call letters*]
KQSN-FM	Toppenish, WA [*FM radio station call letters*] (BROA)
KQSR-FM	Oklahoma City, OK [*FM radio station call letters*] (BROA)
KQSS	Miami, AZ [*FM radio station call letters*]
KQST	Sedona, AZ [*FM radio station call letters*]
KQSW	Rock Springs, WY [*FM radio station call letters*]
KQSY	Nowata, OK [*FM radio station call letters*] (RBYB)
KQT	Konkordanz zu den Qumrantexten [*A publication*] (BJA)
KQTL	Sahuarita, AZ [*AM radio station call letters*]
KQTN-FM	Lordsburg, NM [*FM radio station call letters*] (BROA)
KQTP	St. Marys, KS [*FM radio station call letters*]
KQTV	St. Joseph, MO [*Television station call letters*]
KQTY	Borger, TX [*AM radio station call letters*]
KQTZ	Hobart, OK [*FM radio station call letters*]
KQUA	Lutesville, MO [*FM radio station call letters*]
KQUE	Houston, TX [*FM radio station call letters*]
KQUL	Lake Ozark, MO [*FM radio station call letters*]
KQUS	Hot Springs, AR [*FM radio station call letters*]
KQUY	Butte, MT [*FM radio station call letters*]
KQV	Pittsburgh, PA [*AM radio station call letters*]
KQVO	Calexico, CA [*FM radio station call letters*]
KQWB	Fargo, ND [*AM radio station call letters*] (BROA)
KQWB	Moorhead, MN [*FM radio station call letters*]
KQWC	Webster City, IA [*AM radio station call letters*]
KQWC-FM	Webster City, IA [*FM radio station call letters*]
KQWK-FM	Wallace, ID [*FM radio station call letters*] (BROA)
KQWS-FM	Omak, WA [*FM radio station call letters*] (BROA)
KQXC	Wichita Falls, TX [*FM radio station call letters*]
KQXI	Aruada, CO [*AM radio station call letters*]
KQXL	New Roads, LA [*FM radio station call letters*]
KQXR	Payette, ID [*FM radio station call letters*] (RBYB)
KQXT	San Antonio, TX [*FM radio station call letters*]
KQXX	McAllen, TX [*FM radio station call letters*]
KQXY	Beaumont, TX [*FM radio station call letters*]
KQYB	Spring Grove, MN [*FM radio station call letters*]
KQYN	Twentynine Palms, CA [*FM radio station call letters*]
KQYX	Joplin, MO [*AM radio station call letters*]
KQZE	St. Johns, AZ [*FM radio station call letters*]
KQZZ-FM	Devils Lake, ND [*FM radio station call letters*] (RBYB)
KR	Contractor [*Navy*]
KR	Kallah Rabbati (BJA)
KR	Kar-Air [*ICAO designator*] (AD)
KR	Karat (ABBR)
KR	Keesom Relationship
KR	Kennedy Round
K-R	Kent-Rosanoff Free Association Test [*Psychology*]
KR	Kenya Railways
KR	Kenya Regiment (SAUO)
KR	Ketoaldonate Reductase [*An enzyme*]
KR	Ketoreductase [*An enzyme*]
KR	Keying Relay
KR	Key Records [*Record label*]
KR	Key Register
KR	Khmer Rouge (BARN)
kR	Kilorayleigh
kR	Kiloroentgen
KR	Kimberley Regiment (SAUO)
KR	Kinetic Reaction
KR	King's Regiment [*Military unit*] [*British*]
KR	King's Regulations for the Army and the Army Reserves [*British*]
KR	King's Remembrancer [*British*]
KR	King's Rook [*Chess*]
KR	Kipp Relay
KR	Kirkus Review [*A publication*] (BRI)
KR	Knight of the [*Order of the*] Redeemer [*Greece*]
KR	Knight-Ridder
KR	Knowledge of Results
KR	Knowledge Representation [*Computer science*]
KR	Koloniale Rundschau (BJA)
KR	Kopper Reppart [*Medium*] [*Biochemistry*] (DAVI)
KR	Korean Register of Shipping (SAUO)
KR	Kreuzer [*Monetary unit*] [*German*]
KR	Kroger Co. [*NYSE symbol*] (TTSB)
KR	Krona [*Crown*] [*Monetary unit*] [*Iceland, Sweden*] (EY)
KR	Krone [*Crown*] [*Monetary unit*] [*Denmark, Norway*] (EY)
K-R	Krueger-Ringier [*Book manufacturer*]
Kr	Krypton [*Chemical element*]
K-R	Kuder-Richardson Formula [*Education*] (AEE)
KR	Republic of Korea [*ANSI two-letter standard code*] (CNC)
KR20	Kuder-Richardson Formula 20
KR21	Kuder-Richardson Formula 21
KRA	Contractor Responsible Action (MCD)
KRA	Karenni Revolutionary Army [*Myanmar*] [*Political party*] (EY)
KRA	Kerang [*Victoria, Australia*] [*Airport symbol*] (AD)
KRA	Key Recovery Alliance (VLIE)
KRA	Key Result Area
KRA	Kickback Racket Act
KRA	Klinefelter-Reifenstein-Albright [*Syndrome*] [*Medicine*] (DAVI)
KRA	Kraftco Corp. (SAUO)
KRA	Krakow [*Poland*] [*Seismograph station code, US Geological Survey*] (SEIS)
KRA	Waft, Inc. (SAUO)
KRAB	Greenacres, CA [*FM radio station call letters*]
KRAC	Kaiserslautern Community Relations Advisory Committee (SAUO)
KRAD	Kilorad (WDAA)
KRAD	Portland, TX [*FM radio station call letters*]
KRAE	Cheyenne, WY [*AM radio station call letters*]
KRAF	Holdenville, OK [*AM radio station call letters*]
KRAG-JORG	Krag-Jorgensen Rifle
KRAI	Craig, CO [*AM radio station call letters*]
KRAI-FM	Craig, CO [*FM radio station call letters*]
KR Air	King's Regulations and Orders for the Royal Canadian Air Force
KRAJ	Johannesburg, CA [*FM radio station call letters*]
KRAK-FM	Sacramento, CA [*FM radio station call letters*]
KRAL	Rawlins, WY [*AM radio station call letters*]
KRAM	St. Louis, MO [*AM radio station call letters*] (RBYB)
KRAM	West Klamath, OR [*AM radio station call letters*] (BROA)
KRAN	Krantor Corp. [*NASDAQ symbol*] (SAG)
KR & ACI	King's Regulations and Air Council Instructions [*British military*] (DMA)
KR & AI	King's Regulations and Admiralty Instructions [*Navy*] [*British*]
KR & O (Can)	King's Regulations and Orders for the Royal Canadian Army
Krantor	Krantor Corp. [*Associated Press*] (SAG)
Krantr	Krantor Corp. [*Associated Press*] (SAG)
KRANW	Krantor Corp.Wrrt'A' [*NASDAQ symbol*] (TTSB)
Kranzc	Kranzco Realty Trust [*Associated Press*] (SAG)
KRAO	Colfax, WA [*FM radio station call letters*]
KRAQ	Jackson, MN [*FM radio station call letters*]
KRAR-FM	Brigham City, UT [*FM radio station call letters*] (BROA)
KRAS	Keyworded References to Archaeological Science [*Department of Archaeology*] [*University of Leicester British*] [*Database*] (NITA)
KRAT-FM	Altamont, OR [*FM radio station call letters*] (BROA)
KRAU	Kellogg Rural Adjustment Center, University of New England (SAUO)
Krause	Krauses Furniture, Inc. [*Associated Press*] (SAG)
KrauseF	Krauses Furniture, Inc. [*Associated Press*] (SAG)
KRAV	Tulsa, OK [*FM radio station call letters*]
KRAW-FM	Lake Arthur, LA [*FM radio station call letters*] (BROA)
KRAY	Salinas, CA [*FM radio station call letters*]
KRAZ	Sutter Creek, CA [*FM radio station call letters*]
KRB	Kansas River Basin
KRB	Kariba [*Zimbabwe*] [*Seismograph station code, US Geological Survey*] [*Closed*] (SEIS)
KRB	Karumba [*Australia*] [*Airport symbol*] (OAG)
KRB	Krebs-Ringer-Bicarbonate [*Buffer solution*]
KRB	Krebs-Ringer Bicarbonate Buffer [*Biochemistry*] (DAVI)
KRB	MBNA Corp. [*NYSE symbol*] (SPSG)
KRBA	Lufkin, TX [*AM radio station call letters*]
KRBB	Krebs-Ringer Bicarbonate Buffer [*Biochemistry*] (DAVI)
KRBB	Wichita, KS [*FM radio station call letters*]
KRBC	Abilene, TX [*Television station call letters*]

KRBD .... Ketchikan, AK [*FM radio station call letters*]
KRBE .... Houston, TX [*FM radio station call letters*]
KRBF .... Bonners Ferry, ID [*FM radio station call letters*]
KRBFC .... Kenny Roberts and Bettyanne Fan Club [*Defunct*] (EA)
KRBG .... Canadian, TX [*FM radio station call letters*]
KRBG .... Krebs-Ringer Bicarbonate Buffer [*Containing*] Glucose (DAVI)
KRBG .... Krebs-Ringer Bicarbonate Buffer with Glucose [*Medicine*] (DMAA)
KRB-GA .... Krebs-Ringer-Bicarbonate Glucose-Albumin [*Buffer solution*]
KRBH-FM ..... Hondo, TX [*FM radio station call letters*] (RBYB)
KRBI .... St. Peter, MN [*AM radio station call letters*]
KRBI-FM ...... St. Peter, MN [*FM radio station call letters*]
KRBL .... Idalou, TX [*FM radio station call letters*] (RBYB)
KRBM .... Pendleton, OR [*FM radio station call letters*]
KRBN .... Boston [*Massachusetts*] [*ICAO location identifier*] (ICLI)
KRBO .... Las Vegas, NV [*FM radio station call letters*]
KRBPrA .... MBNA Corp.7.50% Sr'A'Pfd [*NYSE symbol*] (TTSB)
KRBR-FM ..... Superior, WI [*FM radio station call letters*] (RBYB)
KRBS .... Krebs-Ringer Bicarbonate Solution
KRBSG .... Krebs-Ringer Bicarbonate Solution with Glucose
KRBT .... Eveleth, MN [*AM radio station call letters*] (BROA)
KRBT .... Fresno, CA [*FM radio station call letters*]
KRBV .... Dallas, TX [*FM radio station call letters*] (RBYB)
KRBW-FM ..... Ottawa, KS [*FM radio station call letters*] (BROA)
KRBZ .... Reedsport, OR [*FM radio station call letters*]
KRC .... Keweenaw Research Center [*Houghton, MI*] [*Army*] [*Research center*] (GRD)
KRC .... Kilroy Realty [*NYSE symbol*] (SG)
KRC .... King Ranch [*California*] [*Seismograph station code, US Geological Survey*] [*Closed*] (SEIS)
KRC .... Knight of the Red Cross [*Freemasonry*]
KRC .... Knowledge Resource Center [*Computer-based information delivery system in libraries*] [*Generic term*]
KRC .... Knowledge, Responsibility, Control (SAUO)
KRC .... Kodak Reflex Camera
KRC .... Regis College Library, University of Toronto [*UTLAS symbol*]
KRCA .... Rapid City/Ellsworth Air Force Base [*South Dakota*] [*ICAO location identifier*] (ICLI)
KRCA .... Riverside, CA [*Television station call letters*]
KRCB .... Santa Rosa, CA [*FM radio station call letters*]
KRCB-TV ...... Cotati, CA [*Television station call letters*]
KRCC .... Colorado Springs, CO [*FM radio station call letters*]
KRCC .... Kingston Regional Cancer Center [*Canada*] (PDAA)
KRCD .... Chubbuck, ID [*AM radio station call letters*]
KRCG .... Jefferson City, MO [*Television station call letters*]
KRCH .... Rochester, MN [*FM radio station call letters*]
KRCHF .... Kerchief (ABBR)
KRCI .... Avalon, CA [*FM radio station call letters*]
KRCK .... Burbank, CA [*AM radio station call letters*]
KRCL .... Salt Lake City, UT [*FM radio station call letters*]
KRCM .... Beaumont, TX [*AM radio station call letters*] (BROA)
KRCN .... King's Regulations and Orders for the Royal Canadian Navy
KRCO .... Prineville, OR [*AM radio station call letters*]
KRCQ .... Detroit Lakes, MN [*FM radio station call letters*] (RBYB)
KRCR .... Redding, CA [*Television station call letters*]
KRCRA .... Known Recoverable Coal Resource Area (PDAA)
KRCS .... Sturgis, SD [*FM radio station call letters*]
KRCU .... Cape Girardeau, MO [*FM radio station call letters*]
KRCW .... Royal City, WA [*FM radio station call letters*]
KRCX .... Roseville, CA [*AM radio station call letters*]
KRCY .... Kingman, AZ [*FM radio station call letters*]
KRD .... Kourday [*Former USSR*] [*Seismograph station code, US Geological Survey*] [*Closed*] (SEIS)
KRD .... Krieger Data International Corp. [*Vancouver Stock Exchange symbol*]
KRDC .... St. George, UT [*FM radio station call letters*]
KRDD .... Roswell, NM [*AM radio station call letters*]
KRDE .... Denver [*Colorado*] [*ICAO location identifier*] (ICLI)
KRDF .... Spearman, TX [*FM radio station call letters*]
KRDG .... Redding, CA [*AM radio station call letters*]
KRDG-FM ..... Shingletown, CA [*FM radio station call letters*] (BROA)
KRDO .... Colorado Springs, CO [*AM radio station call letters*]
KRDO-FM ..... Colorado Springs, CO [*FM radio station call letters*]
KRDO-TV ..... Colorado Springs, CO [*Television station call letters*]
KRDR .... Red River/Grand Forks Air Force Base [*North Dakota*] [*ICAO location identifier*] (ICLI)
KRDR-FM ..... Red River, NM [*FM radio station call letters*] (BROA)
KRDS .... Tolleson, AZ [*AM radio station call letters*]
KRDS .... Wickenburg, AZ [*FM radio station call letters*]
KRDU .... Dinuba, CA [*AM radio station call letters*]
KRDU .... Raleigh/Raleigh-Durham [*North Carolina*] [*ICAO location identifier*] (ICLI)
KRDZ .... Wray, CO [*AM radio station call letters*]
KRE .... Aerosucre, SA [*Colombia*] [*FAA designator*] (FAAC)
KRE .... Capital Re [*NYSE symbol*] (TTSB)
KRE .... Capital Real Estate [*NYSE symbol*] (SPSG)
KRE .... Capital Re Corporation1 [*NYSE symbol*] (SAG)
KRE .... Consolidated Regal Resources Ltd. [*Vancouver Stock Exchange symbol*]
KRE .... Knight of the Red Eagle [*Prussia*]
KRE .... Kobe Rubber Exchange (NUMA)
KRE .... Kure [*Japan*] [*Seismograph station code, US Geological Survey*] [*Closed*] (SEIS)
KREA .... Ontario, CA [*FM radio station call letters*]
KREB .... Huntsville, AR [*FM radio station call letters*]
KREC .... Brian Head, UT [*FM radio station call letters*]
KRED-FM ..... Eureka, CA [*FM radio station call letters*]

KREE .... Lubbock/Reese Air Force Base [*Texas*] [*ICAO location identifier*] (ICLI)
KREEP .... Potassium and Rare-Earth Elements and Phosphorus (SAUS)
KREEP .... Potassium [*Chemical symbol: K*], Rare-Earth Elements, and Phosphorus [*Acronym used to describe crust material brought from the moon by astronauts*]
KREEP .... Potassium, Rare Earth Elements, Phosphorus (SAUS)
KREG .... Glenwood Springs, CO [*Television station call letters*]
KREG .... Koll Real Estate Group [*NASDAQ symbol*] (SAG)
KREG .... Koll Real Estate Grp [*NASDAQ symbol*] (TTSB)
KREGP .... Koll Real Estate Cv'A'Pfd [*NASDAQ symbol*] (TTSB)
KREH .... Oakdale, LA [*AM radio station call letters*]
KREI .... Farmington, MO [*AM radio station call letters*]
KREIC .... Kuwait Real Estate Investment Consortium (BUAC)
Kreislr .... Kreisler Manufacturing Co. [*Associated Press*] (SAG)
KREJ .... Medicine Lodge, KS [*FM radio station call letters*]
KREK .... Bristow, OK [*FM radio station call letters*]
KREL .... California, MO [*AM radio station call letters*] (RBYB)
KREM .... Krispy Kreme Doughnuts [*NASDAQ symbol*] (SG)
KREM .... Spokane, WA [*Television station call letters*]
KREMS .... Kiernan Reentry Measurement Site
KREMU .... Kenya Department of Resources Surveys and Remote Sensing (BUAC)
KREMU .... Kenya Rangeland Ecological Monitoring Unit
KREN .... Kings Road Entertainment, Inc. [*NASDAQ symbol*] (NQ)
KREN .... Kings Road Entmt [*NASDAQ symbol*] (TTSB)
KREN .... Reno, NV [*Television station call letters*]
KREO-FM ..... Superior, MT [*FM radio station call letters*] (BROA)
KREP .... Belleville, KS [*FM radio station call letters*]
KREPrL .... Capital Re LLC'MIPS' [*NYSE symbol*] (TTSB)
KRES .... Moberly, MO [*FM radio station call letters*]
KRESS .... Kinetic Ring Energy Storage System
Kress .... Kress' Reports [*2-12 Pennsylvania Superior Court*] [*166-194 Pennsylvania*] [*A publication*] (DLA)
Krestintern... International Farmer and Peasant Council (SAUO)
KREU-FM ..... Roland, OK [*FM radio station call letters*] (RBYB)
KREUZ .... Kreuzer [*Monetary unit*] [*German*] (ROG)
KREV .... Lakeville, MN [*FM radio station call letters*]
KREW .... Sunnyside, WA [*AM radio station call letters*]
KREW-FM ..... Sunnyside, WA [*FM radio station call letters*]
KREX .... Grand Junction, CO [*Television station call letters*]
KREX .... Keel Blade Tip Reflex [*Botany*]
KREY .... Montrose, CO [*Television station call letters*]
KREZ .... Durango, CO [*Television station call letters*]
KRF .... Kathode Ray Furnace
KRF .... Kentucky Research Foundation (SAUO)
KRF .... Kerf Petroleums [*Vancouver Stock Exchange symbol*]
KRF .... Knowledge of Results Feedback
KRF .... Kramfors [*Sweden*] [*Airport symbol*] (OAG)
KrF .... Kristelig Folkpartiet [*Christian People's Party*] [*Norway*] [*Political party*] (PPE)
KrF .... Kristeligt Folkeparti [*Christian People's Party*] [*Denmark*] [*Political party*] (PPE)
KRF .... No. 32 (The Royal) Squadron [*British*] [*FAA designator*] (FAAC)
KRFA .... Moscow, ID [*FM radio station call letters*]
KRFC .... KISS [*Knights in the Service of Satan*] Rocks Fan Club (EA)
KRFE .... Lubbock, TX [*AM radio station call letters*] (RBYB)
KRFM .... Show Low, AZ [*FM radio station call letters*]
KRFN .... Knight-Ridder Financial News [*Database*] (IT)
KRFO .... Owatonna, MN [*AM radio station call letters*]
KRFO-FM ..... Owatonna, MN [*FM radio station call letters*]
KRFS .... Superior, NE [*AM radio station call letters*]
KRFS-FM ..... Superior, NE [*FM radio station call letters*]
KRFT .... Knowledge of Results Feedback Task (SAA)
KRFW .... Fort Worth [*Texas*] [*ICAO location identifier*] (ICLI)
KRFX .... Denver, CO [*FM radio station call letters*]
KRG .... Kakapo Recovery Group (SAUO)
KRG .... Karasabai [*Guyana*] [*Airport symbol*] (OAG)
KRG .... Kerema [*Papua New Guinea*] [*Seismograph station code, US Geological Survey*] [*Closed*] (SEIS)
KRG .... Kiwi Recovery Group (SAUO)
KRG .... Knight of the Redeemer of Greece (ROG)
KRG .... Kokako Recovery Group (SAUO)
KRG .... Krebs-Ringer-Glucose [*Buffer solution and growth medium*]
KRG .... KRG Management, Inc. [*Toronto Stock Exchange symbol*]
KrG .... Kriegsgericht [*War Tribunal*] [*German*]
KRG .... Krug International Corp. [*AMEX symbol*] (SAG)
KRG .... Quantum Restaurant Group, Inc. [*NYSE symbol*] (SPSG)
KRGC .... Chicago [*Illinois*] [*ICAO location identifier*] (ICLI)
KRGD-FM ..... Burlington, CO [*FM radio station call letters*] (BROA)
KRGE .... Weslaco, TX [*AM radio station call letters*]
KRGI .... Grand Island, NE [*AM radio station call letters*]
KRGI-FM ...... Grand Island, NE [*FM radio station call letters*]
KRGN .... Amarillo, TX [*FM radio station call letters*]
KRGO .... Fowler, CA [*AM radio station call letters*]
KRGQ .... West Valley City, UT [*AM radio station call letters*]
KRGQ-FM ..... Roy, UT [*FM radio station call letters*]
KRGS .... Rifle, CO [*AM radio station call letters*]
K Rgt .... Kenya Regiment (SAUO)
KRGV .... Weslaco, TX [*Television station call letters*]
Krh .... Karachi (SAUO)
KRH .... Redhill [*England*] [*Airport symbol*]
KRHCF .... Rich Coast Res Ltd [*NASDAQ symbol*] (TTSB)
KRHCF .... Rich Coast Resouces [*NASDAQ symbol*] (SAG)
KRHD .... Duncan, OK [*AM radio station call letters*]

KRHD-FM .... Duncan, OK [*FM radio station call letters*]
KRHS .... Overland, MO [*FM radio station call letters*]
KRHT-AM .... Concord, CA [*AM radio station call letters*] (RBYB)
KRHV .... Big Pine, CA [*FM radio station call letters*] (RBYB)
KRHW-AM .... Sikeston, MO [*AM radio station call letters*] (BROA)
KRI .... Karin Lake Explorations [*Vancouver Stock Exchange symbol*]
KRI .... Kikori [*Papua New Guinea*] [*Airport symbol*] (OAG)
KRI .... King Research, Inc. [*Computer consultant*] [*Information service or system*] (IID)
KRI .... King's Royal Irish [*Military unit*] [*British*]
KRI .... Knight-Ridder, Inc. [*NYSE symbol*] (SPSG)
KRI .... Krilo [*Former USSR*] [*FAA designator*] (FAAC)
KRIB .... Mason City, IA [*AM radio station call letters*]
KRIC .... Korean Reinsurance Company (SAUO)
KRIC .... Rexburg, ID [*FM radio station call letters*]
KRIC .... Richmond/Richard Evelyn Byrd International [*Virginia*] [*ICAO location identifier*] (ICLI)
KRIG .... Nowata, OK [*FM radio station call letters*]
KRIG .... Pawhuska, OK [*AM radio station call letters*] (RBYB)
KRIH .... King's Royal Irish Hussars [*British military*] (DMA)
KRII .... Knight-Ridder Information Inc.
KRIL .... Odessa, TX [*AM radio station call letters*]
KRIM .... Payson, AZ [*FM radio station call letters*]
KRIN .... Waterloo, IA [*Television station call letters*]
KRIO .... Floresville, TX [*FM radio station call letters*]
KRIO .... McAllen, TX [*AM radio station call letters*]
KRIPA .... Korean Research Institute of Public Administration (BUAC)
KRIPES .... K-Resolved Inverse Photoelectron Spectroscopy
KRIPES .... K-Resolved Inverse Photoemission Spectroscopy (SAUS)
KRIPO .... Kriminalpolizei [*Ordinary Criminal Police*] [*German*]
KRIS .... Corpus Christi, TX [*Television station call letters*]
KRIS .... Kentucky Resources Information System (SAUO)
KRISO .... Korea Research Institute of Ship and Ocean (BUAC)
KRISP .... Kenya Rift International Seismic Project
KRISS .... Korean Research Institute of Standards and Science (SAUO)
KRISS .... Korea Research Institute of Standards and Science (SAUO)
KRITIC .... Knowledge Representation and Inference Techniques in Industrial Control (SAUO)
KRITIC .... Knowlege based Review and Intervention to Impose Constraints (SAUO)
KRIV .... Houston, TX [*Television station call letters*]
KRIV .... Riverside/March Air Force Base [*California*] [*ICAO location identifier*] (ICLI)
KRIV-DT...... Houston, TX [*Television station call letters*] (BROA)
KRIZ .... Renton, WA [*AM radio station call letters*]
KRJ .... Kamimuroga [*Japan*] [*Seismograph station code, US Geological Survey*] (SEIS)
KRJB.......... Ada, MN [*FM radio station call letters*]
KRJC.......... Elko, NV [*FM radio station call letters*]
KRJT.......... Bowie, TX [*AM radio station call letters*]
KRJT-FM...... Bowie, TX [*FM radio station call letters*]
KRK .... Kirkenes [*Norway*] [*Seismograph station code, US Geological Survey*] [*Closed*] (SEIS)
KRK .... Krakow [*Poland*] [*Airport symbol*] (OAG)
KRKC.......... Kansas City [*Missouri*] [*ICAO location identifier*] (ICLI)
KRKC.......... King City, CA [*AM radio station call letters*]
KRKC-FM..... King City, CA [*FM radio station call letters*]
KRKE .... Aspen, CO [*AM radio station call letters*]
KRKH-FM..... Harwood, ND [*FM radio station call letters*] (BROA)
KRKI .... Estes Park, CO [*AM radio station call letters*]
KRKK .... Rock Springs, WY [*AM radio station call letters*]
KRKL .... Yountville, CA [*AM radio station call letters*]
KRKM .... Kremmling, CO [*FM radio station call letters*]
KRKN .... Eldon, IA (RBYB)
KRKN .... Kraken (ABBR)
KRKO .... Everett, WA [*AM radio station call letters*]
KRKQ-FM..... Boone, IA [*FM radio station call letters*] (RBYB)
KRKR-FM..... Lincoln, NE [*FM radio station call letters*] (BROA)
KRKR-FM..... Roy, UT [*FM radio station call letters*] (RBYB)
KRKS .... Boulder, CO [*FM radio station call letters*]
KRKS .... Denver, CO [*AM radio station call letters*]
KRKT.......... Albany, OR [*AM radio station call letters*]
KRKT-FM ..... Albany, OR [*FM radio station call letters*]
KRKX .... Billings, MT [*AM radio station call letters*]
KRKY .... Granby, CO [*AM radio station call letters*]
KRKZ .... Altus, OK [*FM radio station call letters*]
KRL............. Karlsruhe [*Federal Republic of Germany*] [*Seismograph station code, US Geological Survey*] (SEIS)
KRL............. Kathode Ray Lamp
KRL............. Kingdom Resources Ltd. [*Vancouver Stock Exchange symbol*]
KRL............. Kirchhoff Radiation Law [*Physics*]
KRL............. Knowledge Representation Language
KRL............. Korla [*China*] [*Airport symbol*] (OAG)
KRL............. Kryla [*Ukraine*] [*FAA designator*] (FAAC)
KRLA .... Los Angeles [*California*] [*ICAO location identifier*] (ICLI)
KRLA .... Pasadena, CA [*AM radio station call letters*]
KRLB .... Lubbock, TX [*FM radio station call letters*]
KRLC .... Lewiston, ID [*AM radio station call letters*]
KRLD .... Dallas, TX [*AM radio station call letters*]
KRLF .... Pullman, WA [*FM radio station call letters*]
KRLI .... Malta Bend, MO [*FM radio station call letters*]
KRLK .... Cassville, MO [*FM radio station call letters*]
KRLN .... Canon City, CO [*AM radio station call letters*]
KRLN-FM ..... Canon City, CO [*FM radio station call letters*]
KRLR .... Las Vegas, NV [*Television station call letters*]

KRLS .... Keweenaw Rocket Launch Site [*University of Michigan*]
KRLS .... Knoxville, IA [*FM radio station call letters*]
KRLT .... South Lake Tahoe, CA [*FM radio station call letters*]
KRLV .... Las Vegas, NV [*AM radio station call letters*] (RBYB)
KRLW .... Walnut Ridge, AR [*AM radio station call letters*]
KRLW-FM .... Walnut Ridge, AR [*FM radio station call letters*]
KRLX .... Northfield, MN [*FM radio station call letters*]
KRLz .... Krelitz Industries, Inc. (SAUO)
KRM........... Karma (ABBR)
KRM........... Klein-Rydberg Method [*Physics*]
KRM........... Kurmenty [*Former USSR*] [*Seismograph station code, US Geological Survey*] (SEIS)
KRM........... Kurzweil Reading Machine
KRM........... Royal Ontario Museum Library [*UTLAS symbol*]
KRMA .... Denver, CO [*Television station call letters*]
KRMB-FM .... Bisbee, AZ [*FM radio station call letters*] (RBYB)
KRMC .... Douglas, AZ [*FM radio station call letters*] (RBYB)
KRMC .... Karmic (ABBR)
KRMD .... Shreveport, LA [*AM radio station call letters*]
KRMD-FM..... Shreveport, LA [*FM radio station call letters*]
KRME........... Rome/Griffiss Air Force Base [*New York*] [*ICAO location identifier*] (ICLI)
KRME-FM .... Shafter, CA [*FM radio station call letters*] (RBYB)
KRMG .... Tulsa, OK [*AM radio station call letters*]
KRMH-FM .... Red Mesa, AZ [*FM radio station call letters*] (BROA)
KRMJ.......... Grand Junction, CO [*Television station call letters*] (BROA)
KRMJ-FM .... Grand Junction, CO [*FM radio station call letters*] (RBYB)
KRML.......... Carmel, CA [*AM radio station call letters*]
KRMN-FM .... Shamrock, TX [*FM radio station call letters*] (BROA)
KRMO .... Monett, MO [*AM radio station call letters*]
KRMP-FM..... Portland, TX [*FM radio station call letters*] (BROA)
KRMS .... Osage Beach, MO [*AM radio station call letters*]
KRMS-FM..... Osage Beach, MO [*FM radio station call letters*] (BROA)
KRMT.......... Denver, CO [*Television station call letters*] (RBYB)
KRMX .... Pueblo, CO [*AM radio station call letters*]
KRMY .... Kileen, TX [*AM radio station call letters*]
KRN .... Food Magazine (journ.) (SAUS)
KRN .... Kiruna [*Sweden*] [*Airport symbol*] (OAG)
KRN .... Knight Ridder Newspapers [*Viewdata Corp.*] [*Videotex producer*] (NITA)
KRNA .... Iowa City, IA [*FM radio station call letters*]
KRNB .... Decatur, TX [*FM radio station call letters*] (RBYB)
KRNC-FM ..... Fresno, CA [*FM radio station call letters*] (BROA)
KRND .... San Antonio/Randolf Air Force Base [*Texas*] [*ICAO location identifier*] (ICLI)
KRNE .... Merriman, NE [*FM radio station call letters*]
KRNE-TV..... Merriman, NE [*Television station call letters*]
KRNG .... Fallon, NV [*FM radio station call letters*] (RBYB)
KRNH .... Comfort, TX [*FM radio station call letters*]
KRNI .... Mason City, IA [*AM radio station call letters*]
KRNL .... Kernel (ABBR)
KRNL .... Mount Vernon, IA [*FM radio station call letters*]
KRNM-FM..... Saipan, MP [*FM radio station call letters*] (BROA)
KRNN-AM ..... North Little Rock, AR [*AM radio station call letters*] (RBYB)
KRNO .... Reno/International [*Nevada*] [*ICAO location identifier*] (ICLI)
KRNO .... Reno, NV [*FM radio station call letters*]
KRNQ-FM ..... Keokuk, IA [*FM radio station call letters*] (RBYB)
KRNR .... Roseburg, OR [*AM radio station call letters*]
KRNT .... Des Moines, IA [*AM radio station call letters*]
KRNU .... Lincoln, NE [*FM radio station call letters*]
KRNV .... Reno, NV [*Television station call letters*]
KRNV-FM ..... Reno, NV [*FM radio station call letters*] (RBYB)
KRNW .... Chillicothe, MO [*FM radio station call letters*]
KRNY .... Kearney, NE [*FM radio station call letters*]
KRNY .... New York [*New York*] [*ICAO location identifier*] (ICLI)
KRO .... Aliblu Airways SpA [*Italy*] [*ICAO designator*] (FAAC)
KRO .... Kathode Ray Oscilloscope
KRO .... Katholieke Radio Omroep [*Catholic Broadcasting Association*] [*Netherlands*]
KRO .... Kreis Resident Officer (SAUO)
kro .... Kru [*MARC language code*] [*Library of Congress*] (LCCP)
KROA .... Grand Island, NE [*FM radio station call letters*]
KROAG........ Committee for the Revolution in Oman and the Arabian Gulf [*Denmark*]
KROC .... Rochester, MN [*AM radio station call letters*]
KROC .... Rochester/Rochester-Monroe County [*New York*] [*ICAO location identifier*] (ICLI)
KROC-FM..... Rochester, MN [*FM radio station call letters*]
KROD .... El Paso, TX [*AM radio station call letters*]
KROE .... Sheridan, WY [*AM radio station call letters*]
Kroeber Anthr Soc Pap... Kroeber Anthropological Society Papers. Berkeley (SAUO)
KROE-FM .... Sheridan, WY [*FM radio station call letters*]
KROF .... Abbeville, LA [*AM radio station call letters*]
KROF-FM ..... Abbeville, LA [*FM radio station call letters*]
KROG .... Kroll-O'Gara [*Stock market symbol*]
KROG .... Phoenix, OR [*FM radio station call letters*]
Kroger .... [*The*] Kroger Co. [*Associated Press*] (SAG)
KROK .... De Ridder, LA [*FM radio station call letters*]
KROL .... Las Cruces, NM [*FM radio edition call letters*]
KROM .... San Antonio, TX [*FM radio station call letters*]
KRON .... Kronos, Inc. [*NASDAQ symbol*] (SAG)
KRON .... San Francisco, CA [*Television station call letters*]
KRON-DT..... San Francisco, CA [*Television station call letters*] (BROA)
Kronos .... Kronos, Inc. [*Associated Press*] (SAG)

KROO .... Breckenridge, TX [*FM radio station call letters*]
KROP .... Brawley, CA [*AM radio station call letters*]
KROQ .... Pasadena, CA [*FM radio station call letters*]
KROR-FM .... Hastings, NE [*FM radio station call letters*] (BROA)
KROS .... Clinton, IA [*AM radio station call letters*]
KROTOS...... Test facility at Joint Research Center Ispra for studying steam explosions (SAUO)
KROU .... Spencer, OK [*FM radio station call letters*]
KROW .... Mariposa, CA [*FM radio station call letters*]
KROW .... Roswell/Industrial Air Center [*New Mexico*] [*ICAO location identifier*] (ICLI)
KROW-FM.... Huntsville, MO [*FM radio station call letters*] (BROA)
KROX .... Crookston, MN [*AM radio station call letters*]
KROX-FM..... Giddings, TX [*FM radio station call letters*] (RBYB)
KROY .... Kroy Inc. (SAUO)
KROY .... Victorville, CA [*AM radio station call letters*] (RBYB)
KROZ .... Roseburg, OR [*Television station call letters*]
KRP .... Karapiro [*New Zealand*] [*Seismograph station code, US Geological Survey*] (SEIS)
KRP .... Karup [*Denmark*] [*Airport symbol*] (OAG)
KRP .... Key Resource People [*US Chamber of Commerce*]
KRP .... Kinesin-Related Polypeptide [*Biochemistry*]
KRP .... King's Rook's Pawn [*Chess*]
KRP .... Known Reference Point
KRP .... Kodak Relief Plate
KRP .... Kolmer [*Test with*] Reiter Protein [*Serology*]
KRP .... Krebs-Ringer-Phosphate [*Buffer solution*]
KRP .... Kurdistan Revolutionary Party [*Iraq*] [*Political party*] (PPW)
KRPA .... Rancho Palos Verdes, CA [*Television station call letters*]
KRPB .... Krebs-Ringer-Phosphate Buffer [*Solution*]
KRPH-FM..... Dodge City, KS [*FM radio station call letters*] (BROA)
KRPI .... Kinshasa Peace Research Institute (SAUO)
KRPL .... Moscow, ID [*AM radio station call letters*]
KRPM .... Tacoma, WA [*FM radio station call letters*]
KRPM-AM..... Seattle, WA [*AM radio station call letters*] (RBYB)
KRPQ .... Rohnert Park, CA [*FM radio station call letters*]
KRPR .... Rochester, MN [*FM radio station call letters*]
KRPS .... Krebs-Ringer-Phosphate Buffer Solution (MAE)
KRPS .... Pittsburg, KS [*FM radio station call letters*]
KRPT .... Anadarko, OK [*AM radio station call letters*]
KRPT-FM ..... Anadarko, OK [*FM radio station call letters*]
KRPV .... Roswell, NM [*Television station call letters*]
KRPX .... Price, UT [*AM radio station call letters*]
KRQ .... Crimsonstar Resources [*Vancouver Stock Exchange symbol*]
KRQC .... Marina, CA [*FM radio station call letters*]
KRQE .... Albuquerque, NM [*Television station call letters*]
KRQK .... Lompoc, CA [*FM radio station call letters*]
KRQQ .... Tucson, AZ [*FM radio station call letters*]
KRQR .... San Francisco, CA [*FM radio station call letters*]
KRQS .... Pagosa Springs, CO [*FM radio station call letters*]
KRQT-FM..... Castle Rock, WA [*FM radio station call letters*] (RBYB)
KRQU .... Laramie, WY [*FM radio station call letters*]
KRQX .... Mexia, TX [*AM radio station call letters*]
KRQZ-FM..... Wagoner, OK [*FM radio station call letters*] (RBYB)
KRR .... Kansai Research Reactor [*Japan*]
KRR .... Karoi [*Zimbabwe*] [*Seismograph station code, US Geological Survey*] (SEIS)
KRR .... Kettle River Resources Ltd. [*Vancouver Stock Exchange symbol*]
KRR .... King's Royal Rifles [*Military unit*] [*British*]
KRR .... Krasnodar [*Former USSR*] [*Airport symbol*] (OAG)
KRRA-AM..... West Covina, CA [*AM radio station call letters*] (BROA)
KRRB .... Dickinson, ND [*FM radio station call letters*]
KRRC .... King's Royal Rifle Corps [*Military unit*] [*British*]
KRRC .... Portland, OR [*FM radio station call letters*]
KRRD .... Dickinson, ND [*FM radio station call letters*]
KRRE-FM..... Shingle Springs, CA [*FM radio station call letters*] (BROA)
KRRF-AM..... Denver, CO [*AM radio station call letters*] (RBYB)
KRRG .... Laredo, TX [*FM radio station call letters*]
KRRK .... Bennington, NE [*FM radio station call letters*]
KRRK-FM..... Lake Havasu City, AZ [*FM radio station call letters*] (BROA)
KRRM .... Rogue River, OR [*FM radio station call letters*]
KRRNY .... King's Royal Regiment of New York (GEAB)
KRRO .... Sioux Falls, SD [*FM radio station call letters*]
KRRP .... Coushatta, LA [*AM radio station call letters*]
KRRQ .... Lafayette, LA [*FM radio station call letters*]
KRRR-FM .... Cheyenne, WY [*FM radio station call letters*] (RBYB)
KRRS .... Kinetic Resonance Raman Spectroscopy (DAVI)
KRRS .... Santa Rosa, CA [*AM radio station call letters*]
KRRT .... Kerrville, TX [*Television station call letters*]
KRRU .... Pueblo, CO [*AM radio station call letters*]
KRRV .... Alexandria, LA [*AM radio station call letters*]
KRRV-FM..... Alexandria, LA [*FM radio station call letters*]
KRRW .... Dallas, TX [*FM radio station call letters*]
KRRW-FM.... St. James, MN [*FM radio station call letters*] (BROA)
KRRX-FM..... Burney, CA [*FM radio station call letters*] (BROA)
KRRY .... Canton, MO [*FM radio station call letters*] (RBYB)
KRRZ .... Minot, ND [*AM radio station call letters*]
KRS .... Kearney State College, Kearney, NE [*OCLC symbol*] (OCLC)
KRS .... Kentucky Revised Statutes [*A publication*]
KRS .... Kerato-Refractive Society (EA)
KRS .... Kernighan + Ritchie Standard (SAUO)
KRS .... Kinematograph Renter's Society
KRS .... Knowledge-based Replanning System (SAUO)
KRS .... Knowledge Retrieval System [*KnowledgeSet Corp.*]
KRS .... Korsar [*Russian Federation*] [*ICAO designator*] (FAAC)

KRS .... Krasnogorka [*Former USSR*] [*Seismograph station code, US Geological Survey*] [*Closed*] (SEIS)
KRS .... Kristiansand [*Norway*] [*Airport symbol*] (OAG)
KRSA .... Petersburg, AK [*AM radio station call letters*]
KRSB .... Roseburg, OR [*FM radio station call letters*]
KRSC .... Claremore, OK [*Television station call letters*]
KRSC .... Kaiser Resources, Inc. [*NASDAQ symbol*] (SAG)
KRSC .... Kaiser Ventures [*NASDAQ symbol*] (TTSB)
KRSC .... Kaiser Ventures, Inc. [*NASDAQ symbol*] (SAG)
KRSC .... Othello, WA [*AM radio station call letters*]
KRSC-FM ..... Claremore, OK [*FM radio station call letters*] (RBYB)
KRSD .... Sioux Falls, SD [*FM radio station call letters*]
KRSE .... Seattle [*Washington*] [*ICAO location identifier*] (ICLI)
KRSE .... Yakima, WA [*FM radio station call letters*]
KRSEN .... Kerosene (ABBR)
KRSH .... Middletown, CA [*FM radio station call letters*]
KRSHB .... Annals of Science. Kanazawa University (journ.) (SAUS)
KRSI .... Garapan-Saipan, MP [*FM radio station call letters*]
KRSI .... Kelly Russell Studios, Inc. [*NASDAQ symbol*] (SAG)
KRSI .... Kreisler Mfg [*NASDAQ symbol*] (TTSB)
KRSJ .... Durango, CO [*FM radio station call letters*]
KRSK-FM ..... Salem, OR [*FM radio station call letters*] (BROA)
KRSL .... Kreisler Manufacturing Co. [*NASDAQ symbol*] (NQ)
KRSL .... Russell, KS [*AM radio station call letters*]
KRSM .... Dallas, TX [*FM radio station call letters*]
KRSN .... Kerosene (MSA)
KRSN .... Los Alamos, NM [*AM radio station call letters*]
KRS-ONE ..... Knowledge Reigns Supreme Over Nearly Everyone [*Rap recording artist*]
KRSP .... Salt Lake City, UT [*FM radio station call letters*]
KRSQ .... Laurel, MT [*FM radio station call letters*]
KRSR .... Coos Bay, OR [*AM radio station call letters*]
KRSR-FM..... Santa Rosa, NM [*FM radio station call letters*] (BROA)
KRSS .... Chubbuck, ID [*FM radio station call letters*]
KRST .... Albuquerque, NM [*FM radio station call letters*]
KRSTL .... Knowledge Representation Systems Trials Laboratory [*Pronounced "crystal"*] [*Artificial intelligence*]
KRSU .... Appleton, MN [*FM radio station call letters*]
KRSV .... Afton, WY [*AM radio station call letters*]
KRSV-FM..... Afton, WY [*FM radio station call letters*]
KRSW .... Worthington-Marshall, MN [*FM radio station call letters*]
KRSY .... Roswell, NM [*AM radio station call letters*]
KRT .... Cretan Airlines SA [*Greece*] [*ICAO designator*] (FAAC)
KRT .... Karate
KRT .... Kathode Ray Tube (AAG)
KRT .... Keratin (DMAA)
KRT .... Keravat [*New Britain*] [*Seismograph station code, US Geological Survey*] [*Closed*] (SEIS)
KRT .... Khartoum [*Sudan*] [*Airport symbol*] (OAG)
KRT .... Kranzco Realty Trust [*NYSE symbol*] (SPSG)
KRTA .... Medford, OR [*AM radio station call letters*] (RBYB)
KRTE .... Karate (ABBR)
KRTH .... Los Angeles, CA [*FM radio station call letters*]
KRTI .... Grinnell, IA [*FM radio station call letters*]
KRTK .... Chubbuck, ID [*AM radio station call letters*] (BROA)
KRTL .... Atlanta [*Georgia*] [*ICAO location identifier*] (ICLI)
KRTM .... Temecula, CA [*FM radio station call letters*]
KRTN .... Karatin (ABBR)
KRTN .... Raton, NM [*AM radio station call letters*]
KRTN-FM..... Raton, NM [*FM radio station call letters*]
KRTO .... Kathode Ray Tube Oscillograph
KRTO-FM..... West Covina, CA [*FM radio station call letters*] (RBYB)
KRTR .... Kailua, HI [*FM radio station call letters*]
KRTS .... Kathode Ray Tube Shield
KRTS .... Seabrook, TX [*FM radio station call letters*]
KRTT .... Kathode Ray Tube Tester
KRTU .... San Antonio, TX [*FM radio station call letters*]
KRTV .... Great Falls, MT [*Television station call letters*]
KRTX .... Galveston, TX [*FM radio station call letters*]
KRTY .... Los Gatos, CA [*FM radio station call letters*]
KRTZ .... Cortez, CO [*FM radio station call letters*]
KRU .... Karasu [*Former USSR*] [*Seismograph station code, US Geological Survey*] (SEIS)
KRU .... Krueger Brewing Company (SAUO)
kru .... Kurukh [*MARC language code*] [*Library of Congress*] (LCCP)
KRUA .... Anchorage, AK [*FM radio station call letters*]
KRUC-FM..... Las Cruces, NM [*FM radio station call letters*] (BROA)
KRUE .... Waseca, MN [*FM radio station call letters*]
KRUF-FM..... Shreveport, LA [*FM radio station call letters*] (RBYB)
KRUG .... KRUG International [*NASDAQ symbol*] (TTSB)
KRUG .... KRUG International Corp. [*NASDAQ symbol*] (NQ)
KRUGW .... KRUG Intl Wrrt [*NASDAQ symbol*] (TTSB)
KRUI .... Iowa City, IA [*FM radio station call letters*]
KRUI .... Ruidoso Downs, NM [*AM radio station call letters*]
Krummeck ... Decisions of the Water Courts [*1913-36*] [*South Africa*] [*A publication*] (DLA)
KRUN .... Ballinger, TX [*AM radio station call letters*]
KRUN-FM .... Ballinger, TX [*FM radio station call letters*]
KRUP .... Dillingham, AK [*FM radio station call letters*] (RBYB)
KRUS .... Ruston, LA [*AM radio station call letters*]
KRUU .... Boone, IA [*FM radio station call letters*]
KRUX .... Las Cruces, NM [*FM radio station call letters*]
KRUZ .... Europa Cruises [*NASDAQ symbol*] (TTSB)
KRUZ .... Europa Cruises Corp. [*NASDAQ symbol*] (SAG)
KRUZ .... Santa Barbara, CA [*FM radio station call letters*]

KRV	Kilham Rat Virus [Medicine]
KRV	Kirovabad [Former USSR] [Seismograph station code, US Geological Survey] (SEIS)
KRVA	Cockrell Hill, TX [AM radio station call letters]
KRVA	McKinney, TX [FM radio station call letters]
KRVC	Medford, OR [AM radio station call letters]
KRVE	Brusly, LA [FM radio station call letters]
KRVH	Rio Vista, CA [FM radio station call letters]
KRVK-FM....	Midwest, WY [FM radio station call letters] (BROA)
KRVL	Kerrville, TX [FM radio station call letters]
KRVM	Eugene, OR [FM radio station call letters]
KRVN	Lexington, NE [AM radio station call letters]
KRVN-FM....	Lexington, NE [FM radio station call letters]
KRVQ-FM....	Blanchard, LA [FM radio station call letters] (BROA)
KRVR	Copperopolis, CA [FM radio station call letters] (RBYB)
KRVS	Lafayette, LA [FM radio station call letters]
KRVV	Bastrop, LA [FM radio station call letters]
KRVZ	Springerville-Eager, AZ [AM radio station call letters]
KRW	Karlsruhe - West [Federal Republic of Germany] [Seismograph station code, US Geological Survey] (SEIS)
KRWA	Waldron, AR [FM radio station call letters]
KRWA	Washington [District of Columbia] [ICAO location identifier] (ICLI)
KRWB	Roseau, MN [AM radio station call letters]
KRWB-FM....	Roseau, MN [FM radio station call letters] (RBYB)
KRWC	Buffalo, MN [AM radio station call letters]
KRWF	Redwood Falls, MN [Television station call letters]
KRWG	Las Cruces, NM [FM radio station call letters]
KRWG-TV	Las Cruces, NM [Television station call letters]
KRWM	Bremerton, WA [FM radio station call letters]
KRWN	Farmington, NM [FM radio station call letters]
KRWQ	Gold Hill, OR [FM radio station call letters]
KRWV-FM....	Emporia, KS [FM radio station call letters] (BROA)
KRX	Christina Exploration [Vancouver Stock Exchange symbol]
KRX	Kar Kar [Papua New Guinea] [Airport symbol] (OAG)
KRXI	Reno, NV [Television station call letters]
KRXK	Rexburg, ID [AM radio station call letters]
KRXL	Kirksville, MO [FM radio station call letters]
KRXO	Oklahoma City, OK [FM radio station call letters]
KRXQ	Roseville, CA [FM radio station call letters]
KRXR	Gooding, ID [AM radio station call letters]
KRXS	Globe, AZ [FM radio station call letters]
KRXT	Rockdale, TX [FM radio station call letters]
KRXV	Yermo, CA [FM radio station call letters]
KRXX-FM	Kodiak, AK [FM radio station call letters] (RBYB)
KRXY	Shelton, WA [FM radio station call letters] (BROA)
KRXZ	Ardmore, OK [FM radio station call letters] (RBYB)
KRXZ-FM	Erath, LA [FM radio station call letters] (BROA)
KRY	Crystallex Intl. [AMEX symbol] (SG)
KRY	Karamay [China] [Airport symbol] (OAG)
KRYD	Telluride, CO [FM radio station call letters]
KRYK	Chinook, MT [FM radio station call letters]
KRYL	Gatesville, TX [FM radio station call letters]
KRYPN	Krypton (ABBR)
KRYS	Corpus Christi, TX [AM radio station call letters]
KRYS	Krystal Co. [NASDAQ symbol] (SAG)
KRYS-FM	Corpus Christi, TX [FM radio station call letters]
KRYSQ	Krystal Company [NASDAQ symbol] (TTSB)
Krystal	Krystal Co. [Associated Press] (SAG)
KRZ	Karuizawa [Japan] [Also, KAZ] [Seismograph station code, US Geological Survey] (SEIS)
KRZ	Kiri [Zaire] [Airport symbol] (OAG)
KRZA	Alamosa, CO [FM radio station call letters]
KRZB-FM	Olney, TX [FM radio station call letters] (BROA)
KRZE	Farmington, NM [AM radio station call letters]
KRZI	Waco, TX [AM radio station call letters]
KRZK	Branson, MO [FM radio station call letters]
KRZN	Albuquerque, NM [FM radio station call letters]
KRZQ	Tahoe City, CA [FM radio station call letters]
KRZR	Hanford, CA [FM radio station call letters]
KRZY	Albuquerque, NM [AM radio station call letters]
KRZY-FM	Santa Fe, NM [FM radio station call letters] (RBYB)
KRZZ	Derby, KS [FM radio station call letters]
KS	Directorate of Mission Support (SAUO)
KS	Kafus Environmental Industries [AMEX symbol] [Formerly, Kafus Capital] (SG)
KS	Kallmann's Syndrome [Medicine] (MELL)
KS	Kansas [Postal code]
KS	Kansas Reports [A publication] (DLA)
KS	Kaposi's Sarcoma [Medicine]
KS	Kartagener's Syndrome [Medicine] (DAVI)
KS	Katoptric System [Optics]
KS	Kawasaki Syndrome [Also, KD, MLNS]
KS	Keep Type Standing [Printing]
KS	Kehr's Sign [Medicine] (MELL)
KS	Kelly-Springfield Tire Co.
KS	Keltic Society (SAUO)
KS	Keltic Society and the College of Druidism (EA)
KS	Kentucky State College (SAUO)
KS	Kernig's Sign [Medicine] (MELL)
KS	Ketosteroid [Medicine] (MELL)
KS	Key Seated [Freight]
KS	Keyset [Navy] (NVT)
KS	Key Stage [Of National Curriculum] [British] (AIE)
KS	Keystone (IAA)
K/S	Kick Stage [NASA] (NASA)
KS	Kidney Sac
KS	Kilostere
KS	King Solomon [Freemasonry] (ROG)
KS	King's Scholar [British]
KS	King's Serjeant [British] (ROG)
KS	King's Speech [British]
KS	Kipling Society of North America - USA and Canada (EA)
KS	Kirjath Sepher [Jerusalem] (BJA)
KS	Kiting Stock [Investment term]
KS	Klinefelter's Syndrome [Medicine]
KS	Knee Society (SAUO)
KS	Knife Switch
KS	Knight of the Sword [of Sweden]
KS	Knock Sensor [Automotive engineering]
KS	Knowledge Source (IAA)
KS	Kodak Standard [Photography]
KS	Kokoxili Suture [Paleogeography]
KS	Kolmogorov-Smirnoff Tests (DIPS)
KS	Kolmogorov - Smirnov Test [Statistics]
KS	Konungariket Sverige [Kingdom of Sweden] (BARN)
KS	Koplik's Spots [Medicine] (MELL)
KS	Korean Bureau of Standards (SAUO)
KS	Korea Shipping (SAUO)
KS	Korea Society (EA)
KS	Korsakoff Syndrome [Medicine] [Medicine] (DMAA)
KS	Krackow Suture [Medicine] (MELL)
KS	Kraemer System
KS	Kugel-Stoloff [Syndrome] [Medicine] (DAVI)
KS	Kurze Sicht [Short Sight] [German]
Ks	Kush (BJA)
KS	Kveim-Seltzback (Test) [Medicine]
KS	Peninsula Airways [ICAO designator] (AD)
ks	Potassium Metasilicate [CIPW classification] [Geology]
KS	Session Key (SAUS)
KS	Singapore [IYRU nationality code] (IYR)
KS	Storm of Drifting Snow [Meteorology] (WDAA)
KS	Strikeout, Swinging [Baseball term] (NDBD)
KSA	Kafka Society of America (EA)
KSA	Kaiserslautern Support Activity (SAUO)
KSA	Kalman Saffran Associates (SAUO)
KSA	Kansas Motor Carriers Association, Topeka KS [STAC]
KSA	Kansas Statutes, Annotated [A publication]
K-SA	Keats-Shelley Association of America (SAUO)
KSA	Kindle, Stone & Associates, Inc. (EFIS)
KSA	Kitchen Specialists Association [British] (DBA)
KSA	Kite-Supported Antenna
KSA	Klinefelter's Syndrome Association (BUAC)
KSA	Klinefelter Syndrome and Associates (EA)
KSA	Knight of St. Anne [Russia] [Obsolete]
KSA	Knowledge, Skills, and Abilities [Psychology] (DAVI)
KSA	Ksara [Lebanon] [Seismograph station code, US Geological Survey] (SEIS)
KSA	Ku-Band Single Access (MCD)
KSA	Kwajalein Standard Atmosphere
KSA	St. Augustine's Seminary Library, University of Toronto [UTLAS symbol]
KSAA	Keats-Shelley Association of America (EA)
KSAB	Robstown, TX [FM radio station call letters]
KSAC	Kingston and Saint Andrew Corp. [Jamaica] (BUAC)
KSAC	Sacramento/Executive [California] [ICAO location identifier] (ICLI)
KSAC	Sutter Creek, CA [FM radio station call letters] (RBYB)
KSAE	Kansas Society of Association Executives (SRA)
KSAE	Kentucky Society of Association Executives (SRA)
KSAF	K-Band, Single Access Forward (SSD)
KSAF	Santa Fe [New Mexico] [ICAO location identifier] (ICLI)
KSAH	Universal City, TX [AM radio station call letters]
KSAI	Saipan, MP [AM radio station call letters]
KSAJ	Abilene, KS [FM radio station call letters]
KSAK	Royal Aero Club of Sweden (SAUO)
KSAK	Walnut, CA [FM radio station call letters]
KSAL	Salina, KS [AM radio station call letters]
KSAL	Salina Public Library (SAUS)
KSal	Salina Public Library, Salina, KS [Library symbol] [Library of Congress] (LCLS)
KSalM	Marymount College, Salina, KS [Library symbol] [Library of Congress] (LCLS)
KSalW	Kansas Wesleyan University, Salina, KS [Library symbol] [Library of Congress] (LCLS)
KSAM	Huntsville, TX [AM radio station call letters]
KSAM	Keyed Sequential Access Method [Computer science] (CMD)
KSAM	Key Field Sequential Access Method (NITA)
KSAM-FM	Huntsville, TX [FM radio station call letters]
KSAMI	Korea Society for the Advancement of Machine Industry (SAUO)
KSAN	San Diego/International-Lindbergh Field [California] [ICAO location identifier] (ICLI)
KSAN	San Francisco, CA [FM radio station call letters]
KSANG	Kansas Air National Guard (MUSM)
KSAR	K-Band, Single Access Return (SSD)
KSAR	Salem, AR [FM radio station call letters]
KSAS	Wichita, KS [Television station call letters]
KSAT	San Antonio/International [Texas] [ICAO location identifier] (ICLI)
KSAT	San Antonio, TX [Television station call letters]
KSAU	Nacogdoches, TX [FM radio station call letters]
KSAV	KS Bancorp [NASDAQ symbol] (TTSB)
KSAV	KS Bancorp, Inc. [NASDAQ symbol] (SAG)

KSAV	Savannah/Municipal [*Georgia*] [*ICAO location identifier*] (ICLI)
KSAW	Gwinn/K. I. Sawyer Air Force Base [*Michigan*] [*ICAO location identifier*] (ICLI)
KSAX	Alexandria, MN [*Television station call letters*]
KSAY	Fort Bragg, CA [*FM radio station call letters*]
KSAZ	Tucson, AZ [*AM radio station call letters*]
KSAZ-TV	Phoenix, AZ [*Television station call letters*]
KSB	Keyboard Status Block [*Computer science*] (TIMI)
KSB	Kradschuetzen-Bataillon [*Motorcycle Battalion*] [*German military - World War II*]
KSBA	Coos Bay, OR [*FM radio station call letters*]
KSBA	Kentucky School Boards Association (SAUO)
KSB Bc	KSB Bancorp [*Associated Press*] (SAG)
KSBC	Hot Springs, AR [*FM radio station call letters*]
KS Bcp	KS Bancorp, Inc. [*Associated Press*] (SAG)
KSBD	San Bernardino/Norton Air Force Base [*California*] [*ICAO location identifier*] (ICLI)
KSBH	Coushatta, LA [*FM radio station call letters*]
KSBI	Oklahoma City, OK [*Television station call letters*]
KSBJ	Humble, TX [*FM radio station call letters*]
KSBK	KSB Bancorp [*NASDAQ symbol*] (SAG)
KSBL	Carpinteria, CA [*FM radio station call letters*]
KSBN	Spokane, WA [*AM radio station call letters*]
KSBN	Springdale, AR [*Television station call letters*]
KSBQ	Santa Maria, CA [*AM radio station call letters*]
KSBR	Mission Viejo, CA [*FM radio station call letters*]
KSBS	Pago Pago, AS [*FM radio station call letters*]
KSBS	Steamboat Springs, CO [*Television station call letters*]
KSBT	Steamboat Springs, CO [*FM radio station call letters*]
KSBW	Salinas, CA [*Television station call letters*]
KSBY	Salisbury/Wicomico County [*Maryland*] [*ICAO location identifier*] (ICLI)
KSBY	San Luis Obispo, CA [*Television station call letters*]
KSBZ	Sitka, AK [*FM radio station call letters*]
KSC	Council of State Governments, Lexington, KY [*OCLC symbol*] (OCLC)
KSC	Kagoshima Space Center [*Japan*]
KSC	Kansas State College of Applied Sciences (SAUO)
KSC	Kathodal Closing Contraction [*Medicine*] (DAVI)
KSC	Kennedy Space Center [*NASA*]
KSC	Kentucky State College (SAUO)
KSC	King's School, Canterbury (ROG)
KSC	Knight of St. Columba
KSC	Knights of St Columbanus (BUAC)
KSC	Kohn Social Competence Scale [*Psychology*] (DHP)
KSC	Komunisticka Strana Ceskoslovenska [*Communist Party of Czechoslovakia*] [*Political party*] (PPW)
KSC	Korean Service Corps
KSC	Kosice [*Former Czechoslovakia*] [*Airport symbol*] (OAG)
KSC	KSC, Inc. (SAUO)
KSC	Kutztown State College (SAUO)
KSCA	Glendale, CA [*FM radio station call letters*]
KSCAP	Kennedy Space Center Area Permit [*NASA*] (MCD)
KSCAX	Kemper Small Cap. Equity Cl.A [*Mutual fund ticker symbol*] (SG)
KSCB	Khe Sanh Combat Base [*Vietnam*] [*Marine Corps*] (VNW)
KSCB	Liberal, KS [*AM radio station call letters*]
KSCB-FM	Liberal, KS [*FM radio station call letters*]
KSCC	Hutchinson, KS [*Television station call letters*] (BROA)
KSCE	El Paso, TX [*Television station call letters*]
KSCF	Thousand Standard Cubic Feet
KSch (Alt)	Kleine Schriften zur Geschichte de Volkes Israel [*A. Alt*] [*A publication*] (BJA)
KSCI	Long Beach, CA [*Television station call letters*] (BROA)
KSCI	San Bernardino, CA [*Television station call letters*]
KSCI	San Clemente Naval Auxiliary Air Base [*California*] [*ICAO location identifier*] (ICLI)
KSCJ	Sioux City, IA [*AM radio station call letters*]
KSCK	Stockton/Stockton Metropolitan [*California*] [*ICAO location identifier*] (ICLI)
KSCL	Shreveport, LA [*FM radio station call letters*]
KSCN	Potassium Thiocyanate [*Broth*] [*A reagent*] [*Pharmacology*] (DAVI)
KSCO	Santa Cruz, CA [*AM radio station call letters*]
KSCQ	Silver City, NM [*FM radio station call letters*]
KSCR	Benson, MN [*AM radio station call letters*]
KSCR-FM	Benson, MN [*FM radio station call letters*]
KSCS	Fort Worth, TX [*FM radio station call letters*]
KSCU	Santa Clara, CA [*FM radio station call letters*]
KSC/ULO	Kennedy Space Center/Unmanned Launch Operations [*NASA*]
KSCV	Kearney, NE [*FM radio station call letters*]
KSC-WTROD	Kennedy Space Center - Western Test Range Operations Division [*NASA*]
KSCY	Belgrade, MT [*FM radio station call letters*]
KSD	C. H. Boehringer Sohn, Ingelheim [*Germany*] [*Research code symbol*]
KSD	Karlstad [*Sweden*] [*Airport symbol*] (OAG)
KSD	St Louis, MO [*AM radio station call letters*]
KSDA	Agat, GU [*FM radio station call letters*]
KSDA	Korean Securities Dealers' Association (ECON)
KSDB	Kommunal Statistisk DataBank [*Danmarks Statistik*] [*Denmark*] [*Information service or system*] (CRD)
KSDB	Manhattan, KS [*FM radio station call letters*]
KSD-FM	St. Louis, MO [*FM radio station call letters*]
KSDIC	Kerala State Industrial Development Corp. [*India*] (BUAC)
KSDJ	Brookings, SD [*FM radio station call letters*]
KSDK	St. Louis, MO [*Television station call letters*]
KSDL	Sedalia, MO [*FM radio station call letters*]
KSDM	International Falls, MN [*FM radio station call letters*]
KSDN	Aberdeen, SD [*AM radio station call letters*]
KSDN	Kennedy Switched Data Network (SAUO)
KSDN-FM	Aberdeen, SD [*FM radio station call letters*]
KSDO	San Diego, CA [*AM radio station call letters*]
KSDP	Sand Point, AK [*AM radio station call letters*]
KSDR	Watertown, SD [*AM radio station call letters*]
KSDR-FM	Watertown, SD [*FM radio station call letters*]
KSDS	Key Sequenced Data Set (CMD)
KSDS	San Diego, CA [*FM radio station call letters*]
KSDT	Hemet, CA [*AM radio station call letters*] (RBYB)
KSDZ	Gordon, NE [*FM radio station call letters*]
KSE	Karachi Stock Exchange [*Pakistan*]
KSE	Kasese [*Uganda*] [*Airport symbol*] (OAG)
KSE	Kewdale Structural Engineers (SAUS)
KSE	Keyspan Energy [*NYSE symbol*] [*Formerly, Brooklyn Union Gas*]
KSE	Kids for Saving Earth [*An association*] (EA)
KSE	Kisbee Air Ltd. [*New Zealand*] [*ICAO designator*] (FAAC)
KSE	Knight of Saint-Esprit [*France*]
KSE	Knight of the Star of the East (ROG)
KSE	Korea Stock Exchange (ECON)
KSEA	Greenfield, CA [*FM radio station call letters*]
KSEA	Korean Scientists and Engineers Association in America (EA)
KSEA	Seattle/Seattle-Tacoma International [*Washington*] [*ICAO location identifier*] (ICLI)
KSEAFA	Korea and South-East Asia Forces Association (SAUO)
KSEC	Korea Shipbuilding and Engineering Corporation (SAUO)
KSEC	Lamar, CO [*FM radio station call letters*]
KSED	Sedona, AZ [*FM radio station call letters*]
KSEE	Fresno, CA [*Television station call letters*]
KSEG	Sacramento, CA [*FM radio station call letters*]
KSEI	Pocatello, ID [*AM radio station call letters*]
KSEK	Girard, KS [*FM radio station call letters*]
KSEL	Portales, NM [*AM radio station call letters*]
KSEL-FM	Portales, NM [*FM radio station call letters*]
KSEM	Selma/Craig Air Force Base [*Alabama*] [*ICAO location identifier*] (ICLI)
KSEM	Seminole, TX [*FM radio station call letters*]
KSEN	Shelby, MT [*AM radio station call letters*]
KSEO	Durant, OK [*AM radio station call letters*]
KSEQ	Visalia, CA [*Television station call letters*]
KSER	Everett, WA [*FM radio station call letters*]
KSES	Selma/Selfield [*Alabama*] [*ICAO location identifier*] (ICLI)
KSES-FM	Yucca Valley, CA [*FM radio station call letters*] (RBYB)
KSET	El Paso, TX [*AM radio station call letters*]
KSEV	Tomball, TX [*AM radio station call letters*]
KSEY	Seymour, TX [*AM radio station call letters*]
KSEY-FM	Seymour, TX [*FM radio station call letters*]
KSEZ	Sioux City, IA [*FM radio station call letters*]
KSF	Karen Silkwood Fund (EA)
KSF	Kashmiri Students Federation (BUAC)
KSF	Kassel [*Germany*] [*Airport symbol*] (OAG)
KSF	K-Band Shuttle Forward (SSD)
KSF	Keel Shock Factor (NATG)
KSF	Key Success Factor (VLIE)
ksf	Kips [*Thousands of Pounds*] per Square Foot
KSF	Knight of San Fernando [*Spain*]
KSF	Knight of St. Ferdinand [*Sicily*] (ROG)
KSF	Kulkyne State Forest (SAUO)
KSF	Quaker State Corp. [*NYSE symbol*] (SPSG)
KSFA	Nacogdoches, TX [*AM radio station call letters*]
KSFC	Karnataka State Financial Corp. [*India*] (BUAC)
KSFC	Keith Sewell Fan Club (EA)
KSFC	Spokane, WA [*FM radio station call letters*]
KSFF	Spokane/Felts [*Washington*] [*ICAO location identifier*] (ICLI)
KSFF-FM	Caledonia, MN [*FM radio station call letters*] (BROA)
KSFH	Mountain View, CA [*FM radio station call letters*]
KSFI	Salt Lake City, UT [*FM radio station call letters*]
KSFM	Knight of St. Ferdinand and Merit [*Italy*]
KSFM	Woodland, CA [*FM radio station call letters*]
KSFN-AM	North Las Vegas, NV [*AM radio station call letters*] (BROA)
KSFO	San Francisco, CA [*AM radio station call letters*]
KSFO	San Francisco/International [*California*] [*ICAO location identifier*] (ICLI)
KSFQ-FM	White Rock, NM [*FM radio station call letters*] (BROA)
KSFR	Santa Fe, NM [*FM radio station call letters*]
KSFS	San Francisco Coast Guard Air Station [*California*] [*ICAO location identifier*] (ICLI)
KSFS	Sioux Falls, SD [*AM radio station call letters*] (BROA)
KSFT	St. Joseph, MO [*AM radio station call letters*]
KSFT-FM	South Sioux City, NE [*FM radio station call letters*] (RBYB)
KSFUS	Korean Student Federation of the United States (EA)
KSFX	Roswell, NM [*FM radio station call letters*]
KSFY	Sioux Falls, SD [*Television station call letters*]
KSG	Harvard University, Kennedy School for Government, Cambridge, MA [*OCLC symbol*] (OCLC)
KSG	Kniest Syndrome Group (NRGU)
KSG	Knight of St. George [*Russia*] [*Obsolete*]
KSG	Knight of St. Gregory
KSGB	Kite Society of Great Britain (BUAC)
KSGC	Tusayan, AZ [*FM radio station call letters*]
KSGI	Cedar City, UT [*Television station call letters*]
KSGI	St. George, UT [*AM radio station call letters*]

KSGI-FM	St George, UT [*FM radio station call letters*]
KSGL	Wichita, KS [*AM radio station call letters*]
KSGM	Chester, IL [*AM radio station call letters*]
KSGN	Riverside, CA [*FM radio station call letters*]
KSGS-AM	St. Louis Park, MN [*AM radio station call letters*] (RBYB)
KSGT	Jackson, WY [*AM radio station call letters*]
KSGW	Sheridan, WY [*Television station call letters*]
KSH	K-Band Shuttle (SSD)
KSH	Kenya Shilling [*Monetary unit*] (IMH)
KSh	Kenya Shilling [*Monetary unit*] (ODBW)
KSH	Kermanshah [*Iran*] [*Airport symbol*] (AD)
ksh	Key Strokes per Hour (VLIE)
KSH	Key Strokes per Hour
KSH	Knight of St. Hubert [*Bavaria*]
KSH	Kolel Shomre Hachomos [*An association*] (EA)
ksh	Korn Shell [*Written by David Korn of Bell Labs, a standard Unix shell*] (DCDG)
KSH	Kuh Shi [*Republic of China*] [*Seismograph station code, US Geological Survey*] (SEIS)
KSHA	Redding, CA [*FM radio station call letters*]
KSHB	Kansas City, MO [*Television station call letters*]
KSHE	Crestwood, MO [*FM radio station call letters*]
KSHI	Zuni, NM [*FM radio station call letters*]
KSHL	Gleneden Beach, OR [*FM radio station call letters*]
KshLc	Kush Locke [*Associated Press*] (SAG)
KShm	Johnson County Public Library, Shawnee Mission, KS [*Library symbol*] [*Library of Congress*] (LCLS)
KSHN	Liberty, TX [*FM radio station call letters*]
KSHO	Lebanon, OR [*AM radio station call letters*]
KSHP-AM	North Las Vegas, Nv [*AM radio station call letters*] (RBYB)
KSHR	Coquille, OR [*FM radio station call letters*]
KSHR	Kosher (ABBR)
KSH/RMBH	Kolel Shomre Hachomos/Reb Meir Baal Haness (EA)
KSHS	Kansas State Historical Society (BUAC)
KSHS	Kansas State Horticultural Society (SAUO)
KSHSR	Kentucky State Historical Society Register (SAUO)
KSHU	Huntsville, TX [*FM radio station call letters*]
KSHV	Kaposi's Sarcoma Associated Herpesvirus [*Medicine*]
KSHV	Shreveport, LA [*Television station call letters*] (RBYB)
KSHV	Shreveport/Regional Airport [*Louisiana*] [*ICAO location identifier*] (ICLI)
KSHY	Cheyenne, WY [*AM radio station call letters*]
KSI	Karsanskaya [*Later, TFS*] [*Former USSR*] [*Geomagnetic observatory code*]
KSI	Kemgas Sydney, Inc. [*Vancouver Stock Exchange symbol*]
KSI	Kilopounds per Square Inch (SAA)
KSI	Kips [*Thousands of Pounds*] per Square Inch (MCD)
KSI	Kissidougou [*Guinea*] [*Airport symbol*] (AD)
KSI	Kleine Schriften zur Geschichte des Volkes Israel [*A. Alt*] [*A publication*] (BJA)
KSI	Knight of [*the Order of*] the Star of India [*British*]
KSIB	Creston, IA [*AM radio station call letters*]
KSIB-FM	Creston, IA [*FM radio station call letters*] (BROA)
K sicca	Keratoconjunctivitis sicca (SAUS)
KSID	Sidney, NE [*AM radio station call letters*]
KSIDC	Kerala State Industrial Development Corporation (SAUO)
KSID-FM	Sidney, NE [*FM radio station call letters*]
KSIG	Basile, LA [*FM radio station call letters*]
KSIG	Crowley, LA [*AM radio station call letters*]
KSII	El Paso, TX [*FM radio station call letters*] (RBYB)
KSIIMK	Kratkie Soobshcheniia o Dokladakh i Polevykh Issledovaniiakh Instituta Istorii Materialnoi Kulturi [*A publication*] (BJA)
KSIL-FM	Wallace, ID [*FM radio station call letters*] (BROA)
K-SIM	K-Band Simulation (SSD)
KSIM	Sikeston, MO [*AM radio station call letters*]
KSIN	Sioux City, IA [*Television station call letters*]
KSIP	Kent Scientific & Industrial Projects Ltd. [*University of Kent*] [*Research center*] [*British*] (IRUK)
KSIQ	Brawley, CA [*FM radio station call letters*]
KSIR	Brush, CO [*AM radio station call letters*]
KSIR-FM	Brush, CO [*FM radio station call letters*]
KSIS	Sedalia, MO [*AM radio station call letters*]
KSIT	Rock Springs, WY [*FM radio station call letters*]
KSIV	Clayton, MO [*AM radio station call letters*]
KSIV-FM	St. Louis, MO [*FM radio station call letters*] (RBYB)
KSIW	Woodward, OK [*AM radio station call letters*]
KSIX	Corpus Christi, TX [*AM radio station call letters*]
KSIZ	Jacksonville, TX [*FM radio station call letters*]
KSIZ-FM	Maumelle, AR [*FM radio station call letters*] (BROA)
KSJ	Kashima [*Japan*] [*Seismograph station code, US Geological Survey*] (SEIS)
KSJ	Kasos Island [*Greece*] [*Airport symbol*] (OAG)
KSJ	Knight of St. Januarius [*Naples*]
KSJ	Knights of St. John (EA)
KSJB	Jamestown, ND [*AM radio station call letters*]
KSJC	Stockton, CA [*AM radio station call letters*]
KSJD	Cortez, CO [*FM radio station call letters*]
KSJE	Farmington, NM [*FM radio station call letters*]
KSJJ	Redmond, OR [*FM radio station call letters*]
KSJK	Talent, OR [*AM radio station call letters*]
KSJL	San Antonio, TX [*FM radio station call letters*]
KSJM-FM	Oro Valley, AZ [*FM radio station call letters*] (RBYB)
KSJN	Minneapolis, MN [*FM radio station call letters*]
KSJO	San Jose, CA [*FM radio station call letters*]
KSJQ	Savannah, MO [*FM radio station call letters*]
KSJR	Collegeville, MN [*FM radio station call letters*]
KSJS	San Jose, CA [*FM radio station call letters*]
KSJSC	Knights of St. John Supreme Commandery (EA)
KSJT	San Angelo/Mathis Field [*Texas*] [*ICAO location identifier*] (ICLI)
KSJT	San Angelo, TX [*FM radio station call letters*]
KSJV	Fresno, CA [*FM radio station call letters*]
KSJX	San Jose, CA [*AM radio station call letters*]
KSJY	Lafayette, LA [*FM radio station call letters*]
KSJZ	Jamestown, ND [*FM radio station call letters*]
KSK	Alcohol-free variety of ethyl iodoacetate (SAUS)
KSK	Kappa Sigma Kappa [*Later, Theta Xi*] [*Fraternity*]
KSK	Karlskoga [*Sweden*] [*Airport symbol*] (OAG)
KSK	Kathodenschliessungs-Kontaktion [*or kathodal closing contraction*] [*Medicine*] (DAVI)
KSK	Kiosk (ABBR)
KSKA	Anchorage, AK [*FM radio station call letters*]
KSKA	Spokane/Fairchild Air Force Base [*Washington*] [*ICAO location identifier*] (ICLI)
KSKB	Brooklyn, IA [*FM radio station call letters*]
KSKD	Sweet Home, OR [*FM radio station call letters*]
KSKD-FM	Chowchilla, CA [*FM radio station call letters*] (BROA)
KSKE	Vail, CO [*AM radio station call letters*]
KSKE-FM	Vail, CO [*FM radio station call letters*]
KSKF	Klamath Falls, OR [*FM radio station call letters*]
KSKF	San Antonio/Kelly Air Force Base [*Texas*] [*ICAO location identifier*] (ICLI)
KSKG	Salina, KS [*FM radio station call letters*]
KSKI	Sun Valley, ID [*FM radio station call letters*]
KSKJ	American Slovenian Catholic Union of the USA (EA)
KSKK	Staples, MN [*FM radio station call letters*]
KSKL	Scott City, KS [*FM radio station call letters*]
KSKN	Spokane, WA [*Television station call letters*]
KSKO	McGrath, AK [*AM radio station call letters*]
KSKS	Fresno, CA [*FM radio station call letters*]
KSKU	Lyons, KS [*FM radio station call letters*]
KSKX-FM	Security, CO [*FM radio station call letters*] (RBYB)
KSKY	Balch Springs, TX [*AM radio station call letters*]
KSKY	Sandusky/Griffing [*Ohio*] [*ICAO location identifier*] (ICLI)
KSKZ	Leoti, KS [*FM radio station call letters*] (RBYB)
KSL	Kanadska Slovenska Liga [*Canadian Slovak League - CSL*]
KSL	Kassala [*Sudan*] [*Airport symbol*] (OAG)
KSL	Keio University [*EDUCATSS*] [*UTLAS symbol*]
KSL	Kentucky Department of Libraries, Library Extension Division, Frankfort, KY [*OCLC symbol*] (OCLC)
KSL	Keyboard Simulated Lateral Telling [*Computer science*]
KSL	Kinsel Drug Company (SAUO)
KSL	Knight of the Sun and Lion [*Persia*]
KSL	Salt Lake City, UT [*AM radio station call letters*]
KSLA	Shreveport, LA [*Television station call letters*]
KSLC	McMinnville, OR [*FM radio station call letters*]
KSLC	Salt Lake City/International [*Utah*] [*ICAO location identifier*] (ICLI)
KSLD	Soldotna, AK [*AM radio station call letters*]
KSLI	King's Shropshire Light Infantry [*Military unit*] [*British*]
KSLJ	Knight of [*the Order of*] St. Lazarus of Jerusalem [*British*]
KSLK	Visalia, CA [*FM radio station call letters*]
K-SLM	Kennedy Space Center Spacelab Plan/Requirement (NAKS)
K-SLM	KSC Spacelab Plan (or Requirement) (SAUS)
KSLM	Salem, OR [*AM radio station call letters*]
K-SLN	KSC [*Kennedy Space Center*] Spacelab Notice [*NASA*] (NASA)
KSLNRC	Knowledge Systems Laboratory of the National Research Council (SAUO)
KSLO	Opelousas, LA [*AM radio station call letters*]
KSLOC	Thousands of Source Lines of Code (SAUS)
K-SLPS	KSC [*Kennedy Space Center*] Spacelab Project Specification [*NASA*] (NASA)
KSLQ	Washington, MO [*AM radio station call letters*]
KSLQ-FM	Washington, MO [*FM radio station call letters*]
KSLR	San Antonio, TX [*AM radio station call letters*]
KSLS	Liberal, KS [*FM radio station call letters*]
KSLT	Spearfish, SD [*FM radio station call letters*]
KSL-TV	Salt Lake City, UT [*Television station call letters*]
KSLU	Hammond, LA [*FM radio station call letters*]
KSLV	Monte Vista, CO [*AM radio station call letters*]
KSLV-FM	Monte Vista, CO [*FM radio station call letters*]
KSLX	Scottsdale, AZ [*FM radio station call letters*]
KSLY	San Luis Obispo, CA [*FM radio station call letters*]
KSLZ-FM	St. Louis, MO [*FM radio station call letters*] (BROA)
KSM	Kane Security Monitor [*Computer security device*]
KSM	Katubsanan sa Mamumio [*Philippine United Labor Congress*]
KSM	Kemper Strategic Municipal Trust [*NYSE symbol*] (SPSG)
KSM	Kemper Strategic Muni Tr [*NYSE symbol*] (TTSB)
KSM	Kooperative Serbaguna Malaysia [*Bank*]
KSM	Korean Service Medal [*Military decoration*]
K-SM	KSC [*Kennedy Space Center*] Shuttle Management [*Document*] [*NASA*] (NASA)
KSM	Saint Mary's [*Alaska*] [*Airport symbol*] (OAG)
KSM	Saint Mary's, AK [*Location identifier*] [*FAA*] (FAAL)
KSM	Shawnee Medical Center Medical Library, Shawnee Mission, KS [*OCLC symbol*] (OCLC)
KSM	St. Michael's College Library, University of Toronto [*UTLAS symbol*]
Ksm	thousand square meters (SAUS)
KSMA	Keats-Shelley Memorial Association (BUAC)
K-SMA	Keats-Shelley Memorial Association [*British*] (DBA)
KSMA	Kentucky School Media Association
KSMA	Kentucky State Medical Association (SAUO)

KSMA.......... Santa Maria, CA [*AM radio station call letters*]
KSM & SG... Knight of Saint Michael and Saint George [*Ionian Islands*]
KSMB.......... Lafayette, LA [*FM radio station call letters*]
KSMC.......... Moraga, CA [*FM radio station call letters*]
KSMF.......... Ashland, OR [*FM radio station call letters*]
KSMF.......... Sacramento/Sacramento Metropolitan [*California*] [*ICAO location identifier*] (ICLI)
KSMG.......... Seguin, TX [*FM radio station call letters*]
KSMH.......... Auburn, CA [*AM radio station call letters*] (BROA)
KSMJ-FM..... Bakersfield, CA [*FM radio station call letters*] (BROA)
KSML.......... Diboll, TX [*AM radio station call letters*] (RBYB)
KSML.......... Kosher Meal [*Airline notation*]
KSMM.......... Shakopee, MN [*AM radio station call letters*] (BROA)
KSMMP........ Kind Seeking Missing Military Personnel (SAUO)
KSMMP........ Kin Seeking Missing Military Personnel [*Organization of parents with sons missing in action with purpose of supplementing US government search for missing personnel*] [*Post-World War II*]
KSMN.......... Worthington, MN [*Television station call letters*] (RBYB)
KSMO.......... Kansas City, MO [*Television station call letters*]
KSMO.......... Salem, MO [*AM radio station call letters*]
KSMQ.......... Austin, MN [*Television station call letters*]
KSMR.......... Winona, MN [*FM radio station call letters*]
KSMS.......... Point Lookout, MO [*FM radio station call letters*]
KSMS-TV..... Monterey, CA [*Television station call letters*]
KSMT.......... Breckenridge, CO [*FM radio station call letters*]
KSMT.......... Kismet (ABBR)
KSMU.......... Komunistycha Spilka Molodi Ukrainy
KSMU.......... Springfield, MO [*FM radio station call letters*]
KSMX.......... Clovis, NM [*FM radio station call letters*] (RBYB)
KSN............ Kassan Resources [*Vancouver Stock Exchange symbol*]
KSN............ Kit Serial Number (SAUO)
KSN............ Kit Shortage Notice
KSN............ Sam Neua [*Laos*] [*Airport symbol*] (AD)
KSNA.......... Kansas State Nurses Association (SAUO)
KSNA-FM..... Laramie, WY [*FM radio station call letters*] (BROA)
K-SNAP....... Kaufman Short Neuropsychological Assessment Procedure [*Test*] (TMMY)
KSNB.......... Superior, NE [*Television station call letters*]
KSNC.......... Great Bend, KS [*Television station call letters*]
KSND.......... Lincoln City, OR [*FM radio station call letters*]
KSNE-FM..... Las Vegas, NV [*FM radio station call letters*] (RBYB)
KSNF.......... Joplin, MO [*Television station call letters*]
KSNG.......... Garden City, KS [*Television station call letters*]
KSNI.......... Santa Maria, CA [*FM radio station call letters*]
KSNK.......... McCook, NE [*Television station call letters*]
KSNM.......... Thousands of square nautical miles (SAUS)
KSNM.......... Truth or Consequences, NM [*FM radio station call letters*]
KSNN.......... Arlington, TX [*FM radio station call letters*]
KSNN-FM..... St. George, UT [*FM radio station call letters*] (BROA)
KSNO.......... Snowmass Village, CO [*FM radio station call letters*]
KSNOPI....... Keyboard Input Simulation-Noise-Problem Input [*Computer science*] (SAA)
KSNP.......... Burlington, KS [*FM radio station call letters*]
KSNP.......... Khao Salob National Park (SAUO)
KSNR.......... Thief River Falls, MN [*FM radio station call letters*]
KSNS-FM..... Medicine Lodge, KS [*FM radio station call letters*] (BROA)
KSNT.......... Topeka, KS [*Television station call letters*]
KSNU-FM..... Roy, UT [*FM radio station call letters*] (BROA)
KSNW.......... Wichita, KS [*Television station call letters*]
KSNX-FM..... Show Low, AZ [*FM radio station call letters*] (BROA)
KSNY.......... Snyder, TX [*AM radio station call letters*]
KSNY-FM..... Snyder, TX [*FM radio station call letters*]
KSO............ Kalamazoo Symphony Orchestra (SAUO)
KSO............ Kansas City Support Office (SAUO)
KSO............ Kastoria [*Greece*] [*Airport symbol*] (OAG)
KSO............ Knoxville Symphony Orchestra (SAUO)
KSOB-FM..... Dell Rapids, SD [*FM radio station call letters*] (BROA)
KSoc.......... Kamashastra Society (SAUO)
KSOC.......... Key Symbol Out of Context [*Computer science*] (DIT)
KSOF.......... Caledonia, MN [*FM radio station call letters*]
KSOF-FM..... Dinuba, CA [*FM radio station call letters*] (BROA)
KSOH.......... Wapato, WA [*FM radio station call letters*]
KS/OI......... Kaposi's Sarcoma and Opportunistic Infection [*Infectious disease*] (DAVI)
KSOK.......... Arkansas City, KS [*AM radio station call letters*]
KSOK-FM..... Winfield, KS [*FM radio station call letters*] (RBYB)
KSOL.......... San Francisco, CA [*FM radio station call letters*]
KSOM.......... Audubon, IA [*FM radio station call letters*] (RBYB)
KSON.......... San Diego, CA [*AM radio station call letters*]
KSON-FM..... San Diego, CA [*FM radio station call letters*]
KSOO.......... Sioux Falls, SD [*AM radio station call letters*]
KSOP.......... Salt Lake City, UT [*FM radio station call letters*]
KSOP.......... South Salt Lake, UT [*AM radio station call letters*]
KSOR.......... Ashland, OR [*FM radio station call letters*]
KSOS.......... Brigham City, UT [*AM radio station call letters*]
KSOS.......... Kernelized Secure Operating System (CCCA)
KSOS-FM..... Brigham City, UT [*FM radio station call letters*]
KSOU-AM..... Sioux Center, IA [*AM radio station call letters*] (RBYB)
KSOU-FM..... Sioux Center, IA [*FM radio station call letters*] (RBYB)
KSOX.......... Raymondville, TX [*AM radio station call letters*]
KSOX-FM..... Raymondville, TX [*FM radio station call letters*]
KSP............ Karolinska Scales of Personality [*Medicine*] (DMAA)
KSP............ Kentucky Department of Libraries, Processing Center, Frankfort, KY [*OCLC symbol*] (OCLC)
KSP............ Kerala Socialist Party (SAUO)
KSP............ Keyset Panel
KSP............ Kidney-Specific Protein [*Medicine*] (DAVI)
KSP............ Knight of Saint Patrick (SAUO)
KSP............ Knight of Saint Stanislaus of Poland (SAUO)
KSP............ Knight of St. Stanislaus of Poland
KSP............ Kodak Special Plate
KSP............ Ksiaz [*Poland*] [*Seismograph station code, US Geological Survey*] (SEIS)
Ksp............ Potassium Solubility Product [*Biochemistry*] (DAVI)
KSP............ Servicios Aereos Especializados en Transportes Petroleros [*Colombia*] [*ICAO designator*] (FAAC)
KSPA.......... Escondido, CA [*AM radio station call letters*]
KSPB.......... Pebble Beach, CA [*FM radio station call letters*]
KSPC.......... Claremont, CA [*FM radio station call letters*]
KSPC.......... Kuwait Spanish Petroleum Co. (BUAC)
KSPD.......... Boise, ID [*AM radio station call letters*]
KSPE.......... Kentucky Society of Professional Engineers (SAUO)
KSPE.......... Santa Barbara, CA [*AM radio station call letters*]
KSPE-FM..... Ellwood, CA [*FM radio station call letters*] (RBYB)
KSPG.......... Clearwater, KS [*FM radio station call letters*]
KSPG.......... St. Petersburg/Albert Whitted [*Florida*] [*ICAO location identifier*] (ICLI)
KSPI.......... Stillwater, OK [*AM radio station call letters*]
KSPI-FM..... Stillwater, OK [*FM radio station call letters*]
KSPK.......... Walsenburg, CO [*FM radio station call letters*]
KSPL-FM..... Kalispell, MT [*FM radio station call letters*] (RBYB)
KSPM.......... Keystrokes Per Minute (SAUS)
KSPN.......... Aspen, CO [*FM radio station call letters*]
K-SPN......... KSC [*Kennedy Space Center*] Shuttle Project Notice [*NASA*] (NASA)
KSPO.......... Spokane, WA [*FM radio station call letters*]
KSPQ.......... West Plains, MO [*FM radio station call letters*]
KSPR.......... Springfield, MO [*Television station call letters*]
KSPS.......... Kilo Symbols per Second (MCD)
K-SPS......... KSC [*Kennedy Space Center*] Shuttle Project Specification [*NASA*] (NASA)
KSPS.......... Spokane, WA [*Television station call letters*]
KSPS.......... Wichita Falls/Sheppard Air Force Base and Municipal [*Texas*] [*ICAO location identifier*] (ICLI)
K-SPT......... Potassium-Urine [*Spot*] [*Biochemistry*] (DAVI)
KSPT.......... Sandpoint, ID [*AM radio station call letters*]
KSPT-FM..... Sandpoint, ID [*FM radio station call letters*] (RBYB)
KSPX.......... Sacramento, CA [*Television station call letters*] (BROA)
KSPY.......... Quincy, CA [*FM radio station call letters*]
KSPZ.......... Colorado Springs, CO [*FM radio station call letters*]
KSQA.......... Wallace, ID [*FM radio station call letters*]
KSQB-FM..... Flandreau, SD [*FM radio station call letters*] (BROA)
KSQD.......... Lowry, SD [*FM radio station call letters*]
KSQQ.......... Morgan Hill, CA [*FM radio station call letters*]
KSQR.......... Sacramento, CA [*AM radio station call letters*] (RBYB)
KSQY.......... Deadwood, SD [*FM radio station call letters*]
KSR............ Kaiser (ABBR)
KSR............ K-Band Shuttle Return (SSD)
KSR............ Keyboard Send and Receive [*Computer science*]
KSR............ Knowledge of Stock Remaining [*Machine tools*]
KSR............ Koster [*South Africa*] [*Seismograph station code, US Geological Survey*] (SEIS)
KSR............ Sandy River, AK [*Location identifier*] [*FAA*] (FAAL)
KSRA.......... Salmon, ID [*AM radio station call letters*]
KSRA-FM..... Salmon, ID [*FM radio station call letters*]
KSRC.......... Kuwait Shipbuilding & Repairyard Company (SAUO)
KSRE.......... Minot, ND [*Television station call letters*]
KSRF.......... Poipu, HI [*FM radio station call letters*]
KSRG.......... Ashland, OR [*FM radio station call letters*] (RBYB)
KSRH.......... San Rafael, CA [*FM radio station call letters*]
KSRI.......... Korea Standards Research Institute, Seoul (SAUO)
KSRM.......... Soldotna, AK [*AM radio station call letters*]
KSRN.......... Sparks, NV [*FM radio station call letters*]
KSRO.......... Santa Rosa, CA [*AM radio station call letters*]
KSRQ.......... Thief River Falls, MN [*FM radio station call letters*]
KSRR.......... Provo, UT [*AM radio station call letters*]
KSRS.......... Roseburg, OR [*FM radio station call letters*]
KSR/T......... Keyboard Send/Receive Terminal [*Computer science*] (MHDI)
KSRTC........ Karnataka State Road Transport Corp. [*India*] (BUAC)
KSR terminal... Keyboard Send Receive Terminal [*Computer science*]
KSRV.......... Ontario, OR [*AM radio station call letters*]
KSRV-FM..... Ontario, OR [*FM radio station call letters*]
KSRW.......... Childress, TX [*FM radio station call letters*]
KSRX.......... El Dorado, KS [*AM radio station call letters*]
KSRZ-FM..... Omaha, NE [*FM radio station call letters*] (BROA)
KSS............ Kearns-Sayre Syndrome [*Ophthalmology*]
KSS............ Keep Sunday Special [*Campaign*] (BUAC)
KSS............ Kellogg Switchboard and Supply
KSS............ Kent State University, School of Library Science, Kent, OH [*OCLC symbol*] (OCLC)
KSS............ Keying Switching Station
KSS............ Knee Signature System [*Orthopedics*]
KSS............ Knight of St. Sylvester
KSS............ Knight of the Southern Star [*Brazil*]
KSS............ Knight of the Sword of Sweden
KSS............ Knock Sensor System [*Automotive engineering*]
KSS............ Kohl's Corp. [*NYSE symbol*] (SPSG)
KSS............ Komunisticka Strane Slovenska [*Communist Party of Slovakia*] [*Former Czechoslovakia*] [*Political party*] (PPW)
KSS............ Korea Stamp Society (EA)
KSSB.......... Calipatria, CA [*FM radio station call letters*]

KSSB .... Kissable (ABBR)

KSSC .... KSC [Kennedy Space Center] Security Steering Committee [NASA] (SSD)

KSSC .... Sumter/Shaw Air Force Base [South Carolina] [ICAO location identifier] (ICLI)

KSSD .... Cedar City, UT [FM radio station call letters]

KSSE .... Kurdish Students' Society in Europe (BUAC)

KSSE-FM ..... Riverside, CA [FM radio station call letters] (BROA)

KSSI .... China Lake, CA [FM radio station call letters]

KSSJ .... Shingle Springs, CA [FM radio station call letters]

KSSK .... Honolulu, HI [AM radio station call letters]

KSSK .... Waipahu, HI [FM radio station call letters]

KSSM .... Sault Ste. Marie/Sault Ste. Marie Municipal [Michigan] [ICAO location identifier] (ICLI)

KSSN .... Little Rock, AR [FM radio station call letters]

KSSQ .... Conroe, TX [AM radio station call letters]

KSSR .... Kazakh Soviet Socialist Republic (SAUO)

KSSR .... Kirghizian Soviet Socialist Republic (SAUO)

KSSR .... Kisser (ABBR)

KSSR .... Santa Rosa, NM [AM radio station call letters]

KSSS .... Bismarck, ND [FM radio station call letters]

KSSS .... Kennedy Space Center Station Set Specification (SAUO)

K-SSS .... KSC [Kennedy Space Center] Shuttle Project Station Set Specification [NASA] (NASA)

KSST .... Sulphur Springs, TX [AM radio station call letters]

KSSU .... Kiev T.G. Shevchenko State University (SAUO)

KSSU-FM ..... Durant, OK [FM radio station call letters] (RBYB)

KST .... Kallistatin (DMAA)

KST .... Kathodenschilessungs-Tetanus [or Kathodal closing tetanus] [Medicine] (DAVI)

KST .... Keilinschriftliche Studien [A publication] (BJA)

KST .... Kemper Strategic Income [AMEX symbol] (TTSB)

KST .... Kemper Strategic Income Fund [NYSE symbol] (SAG)

KST .... Keyboard Skills Test (TES)

KST .... Keyseat (KSC)

KST .... Key Station Terminal [Computer science]

KST .... King-Seeley Thermos Company (SAUO)

KST .... King Solomon's Temple [Freemasonry]

KST .... Known Segment Table [Computer science] (IAA)

KST .... Kolcsonos Segito Takarekpenztarak [Mutual Savings Banks] [Hungarian]

KST .... Korean Society of Translators, Seoul (SAUO)

KST .... Kosti [Sudan] [Airport symbol] (AD)

KSTA .... Coleman, TX [AM radio station call letters]

KSTA-FM ..... Coleman, TX [FM radio station call letters]

K-State .... Kansas State University (SAUO)

KSTB-FM ..... Crystal Beach, TX [FM radio station call letters] (RBYB)

KSTC .... Sterling, CO [AM radio station call letters]

KSTE .... Rancho Cordova, CA [AM radio station call letters]

KSteC .... Sterling College, Sterling, KS [Library symbol] [Library of Congress] (LCLS)

KSTF .... Scottsbluff, NE [Television station call letters]

KSTG .... Sikeston, MO [FM radio station call letters]

KStJ .... Knight Commander of [the Order of] St. John of Jerusalem [British]

KStJ .... Knight of the Order of St. John of Jerusalem (DD)

KStJ .... Knight Venerable, Order of St. John of Jerusalem [Decoration] (CMD)

KSTJ-FM ..... Boulder City, NV [FM radio station call letters] (BROA)

K ST J of J... Knight of St. John of Jerusalem [Freemasonry] (ROG)

KSTK .... Wrangell, AK [FM radio station call letters]

KSTKBO .... Clean Air. Special Edition (journ.) (SAUS)

KSTL .... St. Louis/Lambert-St. Louis International [Missouri] [ICAO location identifier] (ICLI)

KSTL .... St. Louis, MO [AM radio station call letters]

KSTM .... Indianola, IA [FM radio station call letters]

KSTN .... Keystone Financial [NASDAQ symbol] (TTSB)

KSTN .... Keystone Financial, Inc. [NASDAQ symbol] (NQ)

KSTN .... Kriegsstaerke-Nachweisung [Table of Organization] [German military - World War II]

KSTN .... Stockton, CA [AM radio station call letters]

KSTN-FM ..... Stockton, CA [FM radio station call letters]

KSTO .... Agana, GU [AM radio station call letters]

K stoff .... Chloromethyl Chloroformate [Organic chemistry] (DAVI)

KSTP .... St. Paul, MN [AM radio station call letters]

KSTP-FM ..... St. Paul, MN [FM radio station call letters]

KSTP-TV ..... St. Paul, MN [Television station call letters]

KSTQ .... Alexandria, MN [FM radio station call letters]

KSTR .... Montrose, CO [FM radio station call letters]

KSTRL .... Kestrel (ABBR)

KSTS .... San Jose, CA [Television station call letters]

K-STSM .... KSC [Kennedy Space Center] Space Transportation System Management [Document] [NASA] (NASA)

K-STSN .... KSC [Kennedy Space Center] Shuttle Test Station Notice [NASA] (GFGA)

K-STSPS ..... KSC [Kennedy Space Center] Shuttle Test Station Project Specification [NASA] (GFGA)

KSTT .... Los Osos-Baywood Park, CA [FM radio station call letters]

KSTU .... Salt Lake City, UT [Television station call letters]

KSTV .... Stephenville, TX [AM radio station call letters]

KSTV .... Ventura, CA [Television station call letters]

KSTV-FM ..... Dublin, TX [FM radio station call letters] (BROA)

KSTW .... Tacoma, WA [Television station call letters]

KSTX .... San Antonio, TX [AM radio station call letters]

KSTY .... Canon City, CO [FM radio station call letters]

KSTZ .... Des Moines, IA [FM radio station call letters]

KSU .... C-14 dates produced by Kyoto Sangyo University (SAUS)

ksu .... Kansas [MARC country of publication code] [Library of Congress] (LCCP)

KSU .... Kansas City So. Ind. [NYSE symbol] (TTSB)

KSU .... Kansas City Southern Industries, Inc. [NYSE symbol] (SPSG)

KSU .... Kansas State University

KSU .... Kent State University, Kent, OH [OCLC symbol] (OCLC)

KSU .... Key Service Unit (IEEE)

KSU .... Key System Control Unit [Telecommunications]

KSU .... Kharkov State University (SAUO)

KSU .... Kousour [Djibouti] [Seismograph station code, US Geological Survey] (SEIS)

KSU .... Kristiansund [Norway] [Airport symbol] (OAG)

KSU .... Kyoto Sangyo University [UTLAS symbol]

KSUA .... College, AK [FM radio station call letters]

KSUAAS .... Kansas State University of Agriculture and Applied Science (SAUO)

KSUB .... Cedar City, UT [AM radio station call letters]

KSUD .... West Memphis, AR [AM radio station call letters]

KSUE .... Susanville, CA [AM radio station call letters]

KSUH .... Puyallup, WA [AM radio station call letters] (BROA)

KSUI .... Iowa City, IA [FM radio station call letters]

KSUM .... Fairmont, MN [AM radio station call letters]

KSUN .... Phoenix, AZ [AM radio station call letters]

KSUP .... Juneau, AK [FM radio station call letters]

KSUPr .... Kansas City So. Ind 4% Pfd [NYSE symbol] (TTSB)

KSUT .... Ignacio, CO [AM radio station call letters]

KSUU .... Cedar City, UT [FM radio station call letters]

KSUU .... Fairfield/Travis Air Force Base [California] [ICAO location identifier] (ICLI)

KSUV-FM ..... McFarland, CA [FM radio station call letters]

KSUW-FM ..... Sheridan, WY [FM radio station call letters] (BROA)

KSUX .... Sioux City [Iowa] [ICAO location identifier] (ICLI)

KSUX .... Winnebago, NE [FM radio station call letters]

KSV .... Knight of Saint Vladimir (SAUO)

KSVA .... Corrales, NM [FM radio station call letters]

KSVC .... Richfield, UT [AM radio station call letters]

KSVE .... El Paso, TX [AM radio station call letters]

KSVI .... Billings, MT [Television station call letters]

KSVN .... Ogden, UT [AM radio station call letters]

KSVP .... Artesia, NM [AM radio station call letters]

KSVR .... Mount Vernon, WA [FM radio station call letters]

KSVY .... Opportunity, WA [AM radio station call letters]

KSW .... C. H. Boehringer Sohn, Ingelheim [Germany] [Research code symbol]

KSW .... Keeping Scientology Working (SAUO)

KSW .... Knight of Saint Wladimir (SAUO)

KSW .... Wichita State University, Wichita, KS [OCLC symbol] (OCLC)

KSWA .... Graham, TX [AM radio station call letters]

KSWA .... Swan Islands [ICAO location identifier] (ICLI)

KSWB .... Seaside, OR [AM radio station call letters] (RBYB)

KSWB-TV ..... San Diego, CA [TV station call letters] (RBYB)

KSWC .... Winfield, KS [FM radio station call letters]

KSWD .... Seward, AK [AM radio station call letters]

KSWF .... Newburgh/Stewart [New York] [ICAO location identifier] (ICLI)

KSWG-FM ..... Wickenburg, AZ [FM radio station call letters] (RBYB)

KSWH .... Arkadelphia, AR [FM radio station call letters]

K Swiss .... K Swiss, Inc. [Associated Press] (SAG)

KSWK .... Lakin, KS [Television station call letters]

KSWM .... Aurora, MO [AM radio station call letters]

KSWN-FM ..... McCook, NE [FM radio station call letters] (BROA)

KSWO .... Lawton, OK [AM radio station call letters]

KSWO-TV ..... Lawton, OK [Television station call letters]

KSWP .... Lufkin, TX [FM radio station call letters]

KSWR .... Clinton, OK [FM radio station call letters]

KSWS .... K Swiss, Inc. [NASDAQ symbol] (SAG)

KSWS .... K Swiss Inc. 'A' [NASDAQ symbol] (TTSB)

KSWS .... Sisseton, SD [FM radio station call letters]

KSWT .... Yuma, AZ [Television station call letters]

KSWV .... Santa Fe, NM [AM radio station call letters]

KSWW .... Raymond, WA [FM radio station call letters]

KSXX .... Marysville, CA [FM radio station call letters]

KSYC .... Yreka, CA [AM radio station call letters]

KSYC-FM ..... Yreka, CA [FM radio station call letters] (RBYB)

KSYD .... Reedsport, OR [FM radio station call letters]

KSYE .... Frederick, OK [FM radio station call letters]

KSYG .... Little Rock, AR [FM radio station call letters] (RBYB)

KSYG-FM ..... Little Rock, AR [FM radio station call letters] (RBYB)

KSYL .... Alexandria, LA [AM radio station call letters]

KSYM .... San Antonio, TX [FM radio station call letters]

KSYM .... Smyrna/Sewart Air Force Base [Tennessee] [ICAO location identifier] (ICLI)

KSYN .... Joplin, MO [FM radio station call letters]

KSYR .... Syracuse/Hancock International [New York] [ICAO location identifier] (ICLI)

KSYR-FM ..... Minden, LA [FM radio station call letters] (BROA)

KSYS .... Medford, OR [Television station call letters]

KSYV .... Solvang, CA [FM radio station call letters]

KSYY-FM ..... Fallbrook, CA [FM radio station call letters] (RBYB)

KSYZ .... Grand Island, NE [FM radio station call letters]

KSZL .... Barstow, CA [AM radio station call letters]

KSZL .... Knobnoster/Whiteman Air Force Base [Missouri] [ICAO location identifier] (ICLI)

KSZZ .... San Bernardino, CA [AM radio station call letters] (RBYB)

KT .... British Airtours Ltd. [British] [ICAO designator] (ICDA)

KT .... Canadian-Tech Industries, Inc. [Vancouver Stock Exchange symbol]

kt	Cassiterite (SAUS)
KT	Contract [*Navy*]
K-T	Cretaceous-Tertiary
KT	Cretaceous-Tertiary [*Geology*]
K/T	Cretaceous/Tertiary boundary (SAUO)
KT	Kangmar Thrust [*Geophysics*]
kt	Karat (NTIO)
KT	Karat [*Also, CT*]
KT	Karuna Trust [*Multinational association based in England*] (EAIO)
KT	Katy Indus [*NYSE symbol*] (TTSB)
KT	Katy Industries, Inc. [*Formerly, Missouri-Kansas-Texas R. R. Co., with Wall Street slang name of "Kathy"*] [*NYSE symbol*] (SPSG)
KT	Keel Torsion (SSD)
KT	Kelling's Test [*Medicine*] (MELL)
KT	Kentucky & Tennessee Railway [*AAR code*]
KT	Kenya Times [*A publication*]
KT	Kermit [*Texas*] [*Seismograph station code, US Geological Survey*] (SEIS)
KT	Kerner's Test [*Medicine*] (MELL)
KT	Ketamine [*An anesthetic*]
KT	Keying Time [*Computer order entry*]
KT	Key Tape (ELAL)
KT	Khaksar Tehrik [*Pakistan*] [*Political party*] (FEA)
KT	Khotanese Texts (BJA)
KT	Kidney Transplant [*Medicine*] (DMAA)
KT	Killian's Test [*Medicine*] (MELL)
KT	Kiloton (MILB)
kt	Kiloton [*Nuclear equivalent of 1000 tons of high explosives*]
KT	Kinberg's Test [*Medicine*] (MELL)
KT	Kinetic Theory
KT	Kinetin [*Plant growth regulator*]
KT	Kingston-upon-Thames [*Postcode*] (ODBW)
KT	Kit
KT	Klimow's Test [*Medicine*] (MELL)
KT	Klippel-Trenaunay [*Syndrome*] [*Medicine*] (DAVI)
KT	Knapp's Test [*Medicine*] (MELL)
Kt	Knight [*British title*] (WA)
KT	Knight [*British title*]
KT	Knight [*Chess*]
Kt	Knight Bachelor (SAUO)
KT	Knighted
KT	Knight of Tabor [*Freemasonry*] (ROG)
KT	Knight of the Thistle [*British*]
KT	Knights Templar
kt	Knot (COE)
KT	Knots [*Also, K*] [*Nautical speed unit*]
KT	Kober Test [*Medicine*] (MELL)
KT	Koopman's Theorem
K-T	Kosterlitz-Thouless Theory [*Physics*]
KT	Kuder Test [*Psychology*] (DAVI)
KT	Kungtang [*Labor party*] [*Taiwan*] [*Political party*] (EY)
KT	Potassium Titanate (SAUS)
KT	Topeka Public Library, Topeka, KS [*Library symbol*] [*Library of Congress*] (LCLS)
KT	Trinidad and Tobago [*IYRU nationality code*] (IYR)
KT	Turtle Airways [*ICAO designator*] (AD)
KTA	Journal. Korean Physical Society (journ.) (SAUS)
KTA	Kansas Telecommunications Association (SRA)
KTA	Karratha [*Australia*] [*Airport symbol*] (OAG)
KTA	Kentucky Telephone Association (SRA)
KTA	Kentucky Thoroughbred Association (SRA)
KTA	Keyboard Teachers Association (EA)
KTA	Key Telephone Adapter [*Telecommunications*] (TEL)
KTA	Kindergarten Teachers Association (BARN)
KTA	Kite Trade Association International (EA)
KTA	Knitted Textile Association (EA)
KTA	Knots True Airspeed
KTA	Korean Telecommunication Authority (SAUO)
KTA	Korean Traders Association, Seoul (SAUO)
KTA	Korea Tourist Association (EAIO)
KTA	Kotzebue [*Alaska*] [*Seismograph station code, US Geological Survey*] (SEIS)
KTA	Potassium Turbo-Alternator
KTAA	Kerman, CA [*FM radio station call letters*]
KTAAK	Korea Trading Agents Association (SAUO)
KTAB	Abilene, TX [*Television station call letters*]
KTAC	Ephrata, WA [*FM radio station call letters*] (RBYB)
KTACS	Korean Tactical Air Control System (SAUO)
KTAE	Taylor, TX [*AM radio station call letters*]
KTAG	Cody, WY [*FM radio station call letters*]
KTAG	Korea Trade Advisory Group [*British Overseas Trade Board*] (DS)
KTAI	Keyboard Teachers Association International (NTPA)
KTAI	Kingsville, TX [*FM radio station call letters*]
KTAI	Kite Trade Association International [*Later, KTA*] (EA)
KTAJ	St. Joseph, MO [*Television station call letters*]
KTAK	Riverton, WY [*FM radio station call letters*]
KTAL	Texarkana, TX [*FM radio station call letters*]
KTAL-TV	Texarkana, TX [*Television station call letters*]
KTAM	Bryan, TX [*AM radio station call letters*]
KTAN	Sierra Vista, AZ [*AM radio station call letters*]
KTAO	Taos, NM [*FM radio station call letters*]
KTAP	Santa Maria, CA [*AM radio station call letters*]
KTAQ	Greeneville, TX [*FM radio station call letters*]
KTAR	Phoenix, AZ [*AM radio station call letters*]
KTAS	Knots True Airspeed [*Navy*] (NVT)

KTAS	San Luis Obispo, CA [*Television station call letters*] (BROA)
KTAT	Frederick, OK [*AM radio station call letters*]
KTAX	Kaye Kotts Associates, Inc. [*NASDAQ symbol*] (SAG)
KTAX	Kay Kotts Assoc [*NASDAQ symbol*] (TTSB)
KTAXW	Kaye Kotts Assoc Wrrt [*NASDAQ symbol*] (TTSB)
KTB	German continental deep-drilling project (SAUS)
KTB	Kosterlitz-Thouless-Berezinskii Layers [*Physics*]
KTB	Kriegstagebuch [*War Diary*] [*German military - World War II*]
KTB	Thorne River, AK [*Location identifier*] [*FAA*] (FAAL)
KTBA	Ketothiomethylbutyric Acid [*Organic chemistry*]
KTBA	Tuba City, AZ [*AM radio station call letters*]
Kt Bach	Knight Bachelor
KTBB	Tyler, TX [*AM radio station call letters*]
KTBC	Austin, TX [*Television station call letters*]
KTBI	Ephrata, WA [*AM radio station call letters*]
KTBJ-FM	Festus, MO [*FM radio station call letters*] (RBYB)
KTBK	Denison-Sherman, TX [*AM radio station call letters*] (BROA)
KTBL-FM	Albuquerque, NM [*FM radio station call letters*] (RBYB)
KTBN	Santa Ana, CA [*Television station call letters*]
KTBO	Oklahoma City, OK [*Television station call letters*]
KTBQ	Nacogdoches, TX [*FM radio station call letters*]
KTBR	Roseburg, OR [*AM radio station call letters*]
KTBR-FM	Myrtle Point, OR [*FM radio station call letters*] (BROA)
KTBS	Shreveport, LA [*Television station call letters*]
KTBT-FM	New Iberia, LA [*FM radio station call letters*] (BROA)
KTBU	Conroe, TX [*Television station call letters*] (BROA)
KTBW	Tacoma, WA [*Television station call letters*]
KTBY	Anchorage, AK [*Television station call letters*]
KTBZ	Lake Jackson, TX [*FM radio station call letters*] (RBYB)
KTC	Kellogg Telecommunications Corp. [*Littleton, CO*] [*Telecommunications*] (TSSD)
KTC	Kentucky Tourism Council (SRA)
KTC	Keystone Tankship Corporation (SAUO)
KTC	Kindergarten Teachers College (SAUO)
KTC	Kodiak Tracking Station (SAUO)
KTC	Korea Technologies Corp. (SAUS)
KTC	Korea Telecom ADS [*NYSE symbol*] (SG)
KTC	Kutchino [*Later, MOS*] [*Former USSR*] [*Geomagnetic observatory code*]
KTC	Somerset Community College, Somerset, KY [*OCLC symbol*] (OCLC)
KTC	Trinity College Library, University of Toronto [*UTLAS symbol*]
KTCA	St. Paul, MN [*Television station call letters*]
KTCAX	Kemper Technology Cl.A [*Mutual fund ticker symbol*] (SG)
KTCB	Malden, MO [*AM radio station call letters*]
KTCC	Colby, KS [*FM radio station call letters*]
KTCC	Key Tronic Corp. [*NASDAQ symbol*] (TTSB)
KTCC	Key Tronics Corp. [*NASDAQ symbol*] (NQ)
KTCC	Tucumcari [*New Mexico*] [*ICAO location identifier*] (ICLI)
KTCCA	Kotwali Thana Central Cooperative Association [*Bangladesh*] (BUAC)
KTCE	Payson, UT [*FM radio station call letters*]
KTCF	Crosby, MN [*FM radio station call letters*]
ktch	Kitchen (ADWA)
KTCH	Wayne, NE [*AM radio station call letters*]
KTCH-FM	Wayne, NE [*FM radio station call letters*]
KTCHN	Kitchen
KTCHP	Ketchup (ABBR)
KTCI	St. Paul, MN [*Television station call letters*]
KTCI-DT	St. Paul, MN [*Television station call letters*] (BROA)
KTCJ	Minneapolis, MN [*AM radio station call letters*]
KTCK	Dallas, TX [*AM radio station call letters*]
KTCL	Fort Collins, CO [*FM radio station call letters*]
KTCM	Kingman, KS [*FM radio station call letters*]
KTCM	Tacoma/McChord Air Force Base [*Washington*] [*ICAO location identifier*] (ICLI)
KTCN	Eureka Springs, AR [*FM radio station call letters*]
KTCN	Kitchen (ABBR)
KTCNET	Kitchennette (ABBR)
KTCNWR	Kitchenware (ABBR)
KTCO	Duluth, MN [*FM radio station call letters*]
KTCO	Kenan Transport [*NASDAQ symbol*] (TTSB)
KTCO	Kenan Transportation Co. [*NASDAQ symbol*] (NQ)
KTCO	Kenan Transport Company (SAUO)
KTCOOTN	Keep This Crap Out of This Newsgroup (SAUO)
KTCR	Kennewick, WA [*AM radio station call letters*]
KTCS	Fort Smith, AR [*AM radio station call letters*]
KTCS	Truth Or Consequences/Municipal [*New Mexico*] [*ICAO location identifier*] (ICLI)
KTCS-FM	Fort Smith, AR [*FM radio station call letters*]
KTCT-AM	San Mateo, CA [*AM radio station call letters*] (BROA)
KTCU	Fort Worth, TX [*FM radio station call letters*]
KTCV	Kennewick, WA [*FM radio station call letters*]
KTCWAO	Kenya Thirsty Child and Women Aid Organisation (BUAC)
KTCX-FM	Beaumont, TX [*FM radio station call letters*] (RBYB)
KTCY	Denison, TX [*FM radio station call letters*]
KTCZ	Minneapolis, MN [*FM radio station call letters*]
KTD	Killed Target Detector [*Military*] (PDAA)
KTD	Kita-Daito [*Japan*] [*Airport symbol*] (OAG)
KTDA	Kenya Tea Development Authority (BUAC)
KT/DA	Kidney Transplant/Dialysis Association (SAUO)
KTDB	Ramah, NM [*FM radio station call letters*]
KTDC	Kenya Tourist Development Corp. (BUAC)
KTDO	Columbia, CA [*FM radio station call letters*] (RBYB)
KTDR	Del Rio, TX [*FM radio station call letters*]
KTDS	Key to Disk Software
KTDX	Mountain Pine, AR [*FM radio station call letters*] (RBYB)

KTDY .... Lafayette, LA [*FM radio station call letters*]
KTE .... Kennedy-Thorndike Experiment
KTE .... Kermit [*Texas*] [*Seismograph station code, US Geological Survey*] (SEIS)
K-TEA .... Scientific Society for Transport (SAUO)
K-TEA .... Kaufman Test of Educational Achievement
KTEB .... Teterboro [*New Jersey*] [*ICAO location identifier*] (ICLI)
KTEC .... Key Technologies, Inc. [*NASDAQ symbol*] (SAG)
KTEC .... Key Technology [*NASDAQ symbol*] (TTSB)
KTEC .... Klamath Falls, OR [*FM radio station call letters*]
KTEF .... Knights Templar Educational Foundation (SAUO)
KTEG .... Albuquerque, NM [*FM radio station call letters*] (RBYB)
KTEH .... San Jose, CA [*Television station call letters*]
KTEJ .... Jonesboro, AR [*Television station call letters*]
KTEK .... Alvin, TX [*AM radio station call letters*]
K-TEL .... Kives-Television [*In company name K-Tel International. Derived from name of company president and fact that it markets its products on television*]
KTEL .... K-Tel International [*NASDAQ symbol*] (TTSB)
K-Tel .... K-tel International, Inc. [*Associated Press*] (SAG)
KTEL .... K-tel International, Inc. [*NASDAQ symbol*] (SAG)
KTEL .... Walla Walla, WA [*AM radio station call letters*]
KTEL-FM .... Walla Walla, WA [*FM radio station call letters*]
KTEM .... Temple, TX [*AM radio station call letters*]
KTEN .... Ada, OK [*Television station call letters*]
KTEO .... Wichita Falls, TX [*FM radio station call letters*]
KTEP .... El Paso, TX [*FM radio station call letters*]
KTEQ .... Rapid City, SD [*FM radio station call letters*]
KTEX .... Brownsville, TX [*FM radio station call letters*]
KTF .... Kansas Turfgrass Foundation (EA)
KTF .... Kauai Test Facility [*AEC*]
KTF .... Kemper Municipal Income Fund [*NYSE symbol*] (CTT)
KTF .... Kemper Muni Income [*NYSE symbol*] (TTSB)
KTF .... Kuwaiti [*Civil Affairs*] Task Force (DOMA)
KTFA .... Groves, TX [*FM radio station call letters*]
KTFC .... Sioux City, IA [*FM radio station call letters*]
KTFG .... Sioux Rapids, IA [*FM radio station call letters*]
KTFH .... Conroe, TX [*Television station call letters*]
KTFI .... Twin Falls, ID [*AM radio station call letters*]
KTFJ .... Dakota City, NE [*AM radio station call letters*]
KTFL .... Flagstaff, AZ [*Television station call letters*] (BROA)
KTFM .... San Antonio, TX [*FM radio station call letters*]
KTFN-AM .... Merced, CA [*AM radio station call letters*] (BROA)
KTFO .... Tulsa, OK [*Television station call letters*]
KTFR .... Claremore, OK [*FM radio station call letters*]
KTFR .... Kodak Thin-Film Resist [*Cathode coating*]
KTFS-AM .... Texarkana, TX [*AM radio station call letters*] (RBYB)
KTFW-FM .... Stamford, TX [*FM radio station call letters*] (BROA)
KTFX .... Sand Springs, OK [*FM radio station call letters*] (RBYB)
KTG .... Kap Tobin [*Greenland*] [*Seismograph station code, US Geological Survey*] (SEIS)
KTG .... Ketapang [*Indonesia*] [*Airport symbol*] (OAG)
KTG .... Nuclear Technical Society of the German Atomic Forum, Inc. (SAUO)
KTGA .... Kenya Tea Growers Association (BUAC)
KTGE .... Salinas, CA [*AM radio station call letters*]
KTGF .... Great Falls, MT [*Television station call letters*]
KTGF .... Keratinocyte T-Cell Growth Factor [*Immunology*]
KTGG .... Spring Arbor, MI [*AM radio station call letters*]
KTGIFC .... Karen Taylor-Good International Fan Club [*Defunct*] (EA)
KTGL .... Beatrice, NE [*FM radio station call letters*]
KTGM .... Tamuning, GU [*Television station call letters*]
KTGO .... Tioga, ND [*AM radio station call letters*]
KTGP-FM .... Pawhuska, OK [*FM radio station call letters*] (RBYB)
KTGR .... Columbia, MO [*AM radio station call letters*]
KTGS-FM .... Ada, OK [*FM radio station call letters*] (BROA)
KTH .... Kungliga Tekniska Hoegskolan [*Royal Institute of Technology*] [*Stockholm, Sweden*] (ARC)
KTHB .... Kungliga Tekniska Hogskolans Bibliotek [*Royal Institute of Technology Library*] [*Information service or system*] (IID)
KTHC .... Sidney, MT [*FM radio station call letters*] (RBYB)
KTHE .... Thermopolis, WY [*AM radio station call letters*]
KTHK .... Okmulgee, OK [*FM radio station call letters*]
KTHK-FM .... Milton-Freewater, OR [*FM radio station call letters*] (BROA)
KTHN-FM .... Hooks, TX [*FM radio station call letters*] (BROA)
KTHO .... South Lake Tahoe, CA [*AM radio station call letters*]
KTHQ-FM .... Eagar, AZ [*FM radio station call letters*] (RBYB)
KTHR-FM .... Grants, NM [*FM radio station call letters*] (RBYB)
KTHS .... Berryville, AR [*AM radio station call letters*]
KTHS-FM .... Berryville, AR [*FM radio station call letters*]
KTHT .... Fresno, CA [*FM radio station call letters*]
KTHU-FM .... Los Molinos, CA [*FM radio station call letters*] (BROA)
KTHV .... Little Rock, AR [*Television station call letters*]
KTHX .... Visalia, CA [*AM radio station call letters*]
KTHX-FM .... Carson City, NV [*FM radio station call letters*]
KTI .... Kalingrad Technological Institute (SAUO)
KTI .... Kallikrein-Trypsin Inhibitor (DB)
KTI .... Kano Transport International Ltd. KATI Air [*Nigeria*] [*ICAO designator*] (FAAC)
KTI .... Keyboard Training, Incorporated (SAUO)
KTI .... Kinai Technologies, Inc. [*Formerly, Kinai Resources Corp.*] [*Vancouver Stock Exchange symbol*]
KTI .... Kirsch Technologies, Inc. [*Software manufacturer*] [*St. Clair, MI*]
KTI .... Kitchen Table International [*David D. Busch's vaporware software company*]
KTI .... Kratie [*Cambodia*] [*Airport symbol*] (AD)

KTI .... KTI, Inc. [*Associated Press*] (SAG)
KTI .... Kunitz Trypsin Inhibitor (DB)
KTIB .... Thibodaux, LA [*AM radio station call letters*]
KTIC .... West Point, NE [*AM radio station call letters*] (RBYB)
KTIE .... Bakersfield, CA [*FM radio station call letters*]
KTIE .... KTI, Inc. [*NASDAQ symbol*] (SAG)
KTIG .... Pequot Lakes, MN [*FM radio station call letters*]
KTII .... K-Tron International, Inc. [*NASDAQ symbol*] (NQ)
KTII .... K-Tron Intl [*NASDAQ symbol*] (TTSB)
KTIJ .... Elk City, OK [*FM radio station call letters*]
KTIK .... Nampa, ID [*AM radio station call letters*]
KTIK .... Oklahoma City/Tinker Air Force Base [*Oklahoma*] [*ICAO location identifier*] (ICLI)
KTIL-FM ..... Tillamook, OR [*FM radio station call letters*]
KTIM .... Wickenburg, AZ [*AM radio station call letters*]
KTIN .... Fort Dodge, IA [*Television station call letters*]
KTIP .... Porterville, CA [*AM radio station call letters*]
KTIS .... Minneapolis, MN [*AM radio station call letters*]
KTIS-FM ..... Minneapolis, MN [*FM radio station call letters*]
KTIV .... Sioux City, IA [*Television station call letters*]
KTIX .... Pendleton, OR [*AM radio station call letters*]
KTJC .... Rayville, LA [*FM radio station call letters*]
KTJJ .... Farmington, MO [*FM radio station call letters*]
KTJN .... Mercedes, TX [*FM radio station call letters*]
KTJO .... Ottawa, KS [*FM radio station call letters*]
KTJS .... Hobart, OK [*AM radio station call letters*]
KTJX .... Mission, TX [*FM radio station call letters*]
KTKA .... Topeka, KS [*Television station call letters*]
KTKC .... Springhill, LA [*FM radio station call letters*]
KTKK .... Sandy, UT [*AM radio station call letters*]
KTKN .... Ketchikan, AK [*AM radio station call letters*]
KTKO .... Beeville, TX [*FM radio station call letters*]
KTKR .... San Antonio, TX [*AM radio station call letters*]
KTKS .... Versailles, MO [*FM radio station call letters*]
KTKT .... Tucson, AZ [*AM radio station call letters*]
KTKU .... Juneau, AK [*FM radio station call letters*]
KTKX .... Crystal Beach, TX [*FM radio station call letters*]
KTKY-FM .... Refugio, TX [*FM radio station call letters*] (BROA)
KTKZ .... Sacramento, CA [*AM radio station call letters*] (BROA)
ktl .... Kai ta Loipa [*And the Rest, And So Forth*]
KTL .... Kettle (ABBR)
KTL .... Key-Edit Terminal Language [*Computer science*] (MHDI)
KTL .... Kitale [*Kenya*] [*Airport symbol*] (AD)
KTL .... K-Tel International, Inc. [*Toronto Stock Exchange symbol*] (SPSG)
KTL .... Kuratorium fuer Technik in der Landwirtschaft
KTLA .... Los Angeles, CA [*Television station call letters*]
KTLA-DT .... Los Angeles, CA [*Television station call letters*] (BROA)
KTLB .... Twin Lakes, IA [*FM radio station call letters*]
KTLC .... Oklahoma City, OK [*Television station call letters*]
KTLC-FM .... Canon City, CO [*FM radio station call letters*] (BROA)
KTLD .... Pineville, LA [*AM radio station call letters*]
KTLDR .... Kettledrum (ABBR)
KTLE .... Tooele, UT [*FM radio station call letters*]
KTLF .... Colorado Springs, CO [*FM radio station call letters*]
KTLH .... Tallahassee/Dale Mabry Field [*Florida*] [*ICAO location identifier*] (ICLI)
KTLI .... El Dorado, KS [*FM radio station call letters*]
KTLK .... Thornton, CO [*AM radio station call letters*]
KTLM .... Rio Grande City, TX [*Television station call letters*] (BROA)
KTLN .... Thibodaux, LA [*FM radio station call letters*] (RBYB)
KTLO .... Mountain Home, AR [*AM radio station call letters*]
KTLO-FM .... Mountain Home, AR [*FM radio station call letters*]
KTLQ .... Tahlequah, OK [*AM radio station call letters*]
KTLR .... Terrell, TX [*FM radio station call letters*]
KTLS .... Ada, OK [*FM radio station call letters*]
KTLT .... Wichita Falls, TX [*FM radio station call letters*]
KTLU .... Rusk, TX [*AM radio station call letters*]
KTLV .... Midwest City, OK [*AM radio station call letters*]
KTLW .... Lancaster, CA [*FM radio station call letters*] (RBYB)
KTLX .... Columbus, NE [*FM radio station call letters*]
KTM .... Katmai [*Alaska*] [*Seismograph station code, US Geological Survey*] (SEIS)
KTM .... Katmandu [*Nepal*] [*Airport symbol*] (OAG)
KTM .... Keep to Top of Mast (RIMS)
KTM .... Ketema, Inc. (SAUO)
KTM .... Key Transport Module
KTM .... Menninger Clinic Library, Topeka, KS [*Library symbol*] [*Library of Congress*] (LCLS)
KTM .... Thomas More College, Fort Mitchell, KY [*OCLC symbol*] (OCLC)
KTMA .... Ketema, Inc. (SAUO)
KT MAR SC... Knight Mareschal of Scotland (ROG)
KT MAR SC... Knight Marschal of Scotland (SAUO)
KTMB .... Miami/New Tamiami [*Florida*] [*ICAO location identifier*] (ICLI)
KTMC .... McAlester, OK [*AM radio station call letters*]
KTMC-FM ... McAlester, OK [*FM radio station call letters*]
KTMD .... Galveston, TX [*Television station call letters*]
KTME .... Lompoc, CA [*AM radio station call letters*]
KTMF .... Missoula, MT [*Television station call letters*]
KTMG .... Deer Trail, CO [*AM radio station call letters*]
KTMN .... Los Alamos, NM [*FM radio station call letters*]
KTMO .... Kennett, MO [*FM radio station call letters*]
KTMP .... Heber City, UT [*AM radio station call letters*]
KTMR .... Edna, TX [*AM radio station call letters*]
KTMS .... Knapp Time Metaphor Scale
KTMS .... Knowledge-Based Tank Management System (VLIE)

KTMS.......... Santa Barbara, CA [*AM radio station call letters*]
KTMT.......... Medford, OR [*AM radio station call letters*]
KTMT.......... Phoenix, OR [*AM radio station call letters*]
KTMW.......... Salt Lake City, UT [*Television station call letters*] (BROA)
KTMX.......... York, NE [*FM radio station call letters*]
KTN.......... Keltic, Inc. [*Toronto Stock Exchange symbol*]
KTN.......... Ketchikan [*Alaska*] [*Airport symbol*] (OAG)
KTN.......... Ketchikan, AK [*Location identifier*] [*FAA*] (FAAL)
KTN.......... Kitten (ABBR)
KTN.......... Kuratorium fuer die Tagungen der Nobelpreistrager [*Standing Committee for Nobel Prize Winners' Congresses - SCNPWC*] [*Germany*] (EA)
KTN.......... Potassium Tantalate Niobate (MCD)
KTNA.......... Talkeetna, AK [*FM radio station call letters*]
KTNC.......... Falls City, NE [*AM radio station call letters*]
KTNC-TV...... Concord, CA [*TV station call letters*] (RBYB)
KTND.......... Ojai, CA [*FM radio station call letters*] (RBYB)
KTNE.......... Alliance, NE [*FM radio station call letters*]
KTNE-TV...... Alliance, NE [*Television station call letters*]
KTNF.......... Kodak Timing Negative Film
KTNH.......... Kittenish (ABBR)
KTNI.......... Kansas Neurological Institute, Topeka, KS [*Library symbol*] [*Library of Congress*] (LCLS)
KTNL.......... Sitka, AK [*Television station call letters*]
KTNM.......... Tucumcari, NM [*AM radio station call letters*]
KTNN.......... Window Rock, AZ [*AM radio station call letters*]
KTNO.......... Fort Worth, TX [*AM radio station call letters*]
KTNP-FM...... Bennington, NE [*FM radio station call letters*] (RBYB)
KTNQ.......... Los Angeles, CA [*AM radio station call letters*]
KTNR.......... Kenedy, TX [*FM radio station call letters*]
KTNS.......... Oakhurst, CA [*AM radio station call letters*]
KTNT.......... Edmund, OK [*FM radio station call letters*]
KTNT.......... Miami/Dade-Collier Training and Transition Airport [*Florida*] [*ICAO location identifier*] (ICLI)
KTNV.......... Las Vegas, NV [*Television station call letters*]
KTNV.......... Washbuni University of Topeka (SAUO)
KTNW.......... Richland, WA [*Television station call letters*]
KTNY.......... Libby, MT [*FM radio station call letters*]
KTNZ.......... Amarillo, TX [*AM radio station call letters*] (RBYB)
KTO.......... K2, Inc. [*NYSE symbol*] [*Formerly, Anthony Industries*] (SG)
KTO.......... Kato [*Guyana*] [*Airport symbol*] (OAG)
KTO.......... Kraus-Thomson Organization [*Publishing*]
KtO.......... KTO Microform, Millwood, NY [*Library symbol*] [*Library of Congress*] (LCLS)
KTO.......... Kuwaiti Theatre of Operation [*Operation Desert Storm*]
KTO.......... Kuwait Theater (or Theatre) of Operations (SAUO)
KTO.......... Kuwait Theatre of Operations (SAUS)
KTOB.......... Petaluma, CA [*AM radio station call letters*]
KTOC.......... Jonesboro, LA [*AM radio station call letters*]
KTOC-FM...... Jonesboro, LA [*FM radio station call letters*]
KTOD.......... Conway, AR [*FM radio station call letters*]
KTOE.......... Mankato, MN [*AM radio station call letters*]
KTOF.......... Cedar Rapids, IA [*FM radio station call letters*]
KTOK.......... Oklahoma City, OK [*AM radio station call letters*]
KTOL.......... Lacey, WA [*AM radio station call letters*]
KTOM.......... Salinas, CA [*AM radio station call letters*]
KTOM-FM...... Salinas, CA [*FM radio station call letters*]
KTON.......... Belton, TX [*AM radio station call letters*]
KTON.......... Ketone [*Organic chemistry*] (ABBR)
KTOO.......... Juneau, AK [*FM radio station call letters*]
KTOO-TV...... Juneau, AK [*Television station call letters*]
KTOP.......... Topeka, KS [*AM radio station call letters*]
KTOQ.......... Rapid City, SD [*AM radio station call letters*]
KTOS.......... Kratos, Inc. (SAUO)
KTOW.......... Sand Springs, OK [*AM radio station call letters*]
KTOW-FM...... Sand Springs, OK [*FM radio station call letters*]
KTOX.......... Needles, CA [*AM radio station call letters*]
KTOZ.......... Marshfield, MO [*FM radio station call letters*]
KTOZ.......... Springfield, MO [*AM radio station call letters*]
KTP.......... Kentucky Truck Plant [*Ford Motor Co.*]
KTP.......... Keyboard Typing Perforator (NITA)
KTP.......... Kingstip, Inc. (SAUO)
KTP.......... Kingston-Tinson [*Jamaica*] [*Airport symbol*] (OAG)
KT P.......... Knight's Pawn [*Chess*] (ROG)
KTP.......... Kommunistinen Tyovaenpuolue [*Communist Workers' Party*] [*Finland*] [*Political party*] (EY)
KTP.......... Potassium Titanyl Phosphate (SAUS)
KTPA.......... Prescott, AR [*AM radio station call letters*]
KTPA.......... Tampa/International [*Florida*] [*ICAO location identifier*] (ICLI)
KTPB.......... Kilgore, TX [*FM radio station call letters*]
KTPC.......... Korea Trade Promotion Corporation (SAUO)
KTPH.......... Tonopah, NV [*FM radio station call letters*]
KTPI.......... Kaum-Tani Persatuan Indonesia [*Indonesian Farmers' Party*] [*Surinam*] [*Political party*] (PPW)
KTPI.......... Tehachapi, CA [*FM radio station call letters*]
KTPK.......... Topeka, KS [*FM radio station call letters*]
KTPP.......... Potassium Tripolyphosphate (SAUS)
KTPR.......... Fort Dodge, IA [*FM radio station call letters*]
KTPX.......... Okmulgee, OK [*Television station call letters*] (BROA)
KTPZ-FM...... Mountain Home, ID [*FM radio station call letters*] (BROA)
KTQM.......... Clovis, NM [*FM radio station call letters*]
KTQX.......... Bakersfield, CA [*FM radio station call letters*]
KTR.......... Contractor
KTR.......... Helikoptertransport AB [*Sweden*] [*ICAO designator*] (FAAC)
KTR.......... K-2 Resources, Inc. [*Vancouver Stock Exchange symbol*]

KTR.......... Katherine [*Northern Territory, Australia*] [*Airport symbol*] (AD)
KTR.......... Katuura [*Japan*] [*Later, HTY*] [*Geomagnetic observatory code*]
KTR.......... Kauai Test Range (SAUO)
KTR.......... Keyboard Typing Reperforator [*Computer science*]
KTR.......... Knowledge Template Repository (VLIE)
KTRA.......... Farmington, NM [*FM radio station call letters*]
KTRAX.......... Kemper Total Return Cl.A [*Mutual fund ticker symbol*] (SG)
KTRB.......... Modesto, CA [*AM radio station call letters*]
KTRBX.......... Kemper Total Return Cl.B [*Mutual fund ticker symbol*] (SG)
KTRC.......... Santa Fe, NM [*AM radio station call letters*]
KTRE-TV...... Lufkin, TX [*Television station call letters*]
KTRF.......... Thief River Falls, MN [*AM radio station call letters*]
KTRG.......... Del Rio, TX [*Television station call letters*]
KTRH.......... Houston, TX [*AM radio station call letters*]
KTRI.......... Mansfield, MO [*FM radio station call letters*]
KTRJ-AM...... Frazier Park, CA [*AM radio station call letters*] (RBYB)
KTRK.......... Houston, TX [*Television station call letters*]
KTRK-DT...... Houston, TX [*Television station call letters*] (BROA)
KTRM-FM...... Kirksville, MO [*FM radio station call letters*] (BROA)
KTRN.......... Silverton, CO [*FM radio station call letters*]
KTRN-FM...... White Hall, AR [*FM radio station call letters*] (BROA)
KTRO.......... Port Hueneme, CA [*AM radio station call letters*]
KTron.......... K-Tron International, Inc. [*Associated Press*] (SAG)
KTRQ-FM...... Brinkley, AR [*FM radio station call letters*] (BROA)
KTRQ-FM...... Quincy, WA [*FM radio station call letters*] (RBYB)
KTRR.......... Loveland, CO [*FM radio station call letters*]
KTRS.......... Casper, WY [*FM radio station call letters*]
KTRS.......... St. Louis, MO [*AM radio station call letters*] (BROA)
KTRT.......... Claremore, OK [*AM radio station call letters*]
KTRU.......... Houston, TX [*FM radio station call letters*]
KTRV.......... Nampa, ID [*Television station call letters*]
KTRW.......... Spokane, WA [*AM radio station call letters*]
KTRX.......... Tarkio, MO [*FM radio station call letters*]
KTRY.......... Bastrop, LA [*AM radio station call letters*]
KTRY-FM...... Bastrop, LA [*FM radio station call letters*]
KTRZ.......... Riverton, WY [*FM radio station call letters*]
KTS.......... Brevig Mission [*Alaska*] [*Airport symbol*] (OAG)
KTS.......... Kagoshima Television Station (SAUO)
KTS.......... Kelvin Temperature Scale
KTS.......... Kethoxal Thiosemicarbazone [*An antiviral*] [*Pharmacology*] (DAVI)
KTS.......... Key Telephone System [*Telecommunications*] (AAG)
KTS.......... Kiersley Temperament Sorter [*Psychiatry*] (DAVI)
KTS.......... Klippel-Trenaunay Syndrome [*Medicine*] (DMAA)
KTS.......... Knight of the Tower and Sword [*Portugal*]
KTS.......... Knots (ADA)
KTS.......... Kodiak Tracking Station [*NASA*] (MCD)
KTS.......... Korea National Tourist Service (SAUO)
KTS.......... Kotas Joint Civil Aviation Enterprise [*Former USSR*] [*FAA designator*] (FAAC)
KTS.......... Kumbheshwor Technical School (SAUO)
KTS.......... Kwajalein Test Site (MCD)
KTS.......... Southern Baptist Theological Seminary, Louisville, KY [*OCLC symbol*] (OCLC)
KTS.......... Teller Mission, AK [*Location identifier*] [*FAA*] (FAAL)
KTSA.......... Kahn Test of Symbol Arrangement [*Psychology*]
KTSA.......... San Antonio, TX [*AM radio station call letters*]
KTSB.......... Sioux Center, IA [*FM radio station call letters*]
KTSC.......... Kitsch (ABBR)
KTSC.......... Pueblo, CO [*FM radio station call letters*]
KTSCHOOL.... Karnali Technical School (SAUO)
KTSC-TV...... Pueblo, CO [*Television station call letters*]
KTSD.......... Reliance, SD [*FM radio station call letters*]
KTSD-TV...... Pierre, SD [*Television station call letters*]
KTSF.......... San Francisco, CA [*Television station call letters*]
KTSG.......... Klippel-Trenaunay Support Group (EA)
KTSH.......... Tishomingo, OK [*FM radio station call letters*]
KTSH.......... Topeka State Hospital, Topeka, KS [*Library symbol*] [*Library of Congress*] (LCLS)
KTSJ.......... Pomona, CA [*AM radio station call letters*]
KTSL.......... Medical Lake, WA [*FM radio station call letters*]
KTSM.......... El Paso, TX [*AM radio station call letters*]
KTSM-FM...... El Paso, TX [*FM radio station call letters*]
KTSM-TV...... El Paso, TX [*Television station call letters*]
KTSN-AM...... Elko, NV [*AM radio station call letters*] (RBYB)
KTSP.......... St. George, UT [*AM radio station call letters*] (BROA)
KTSR.......... College Station, TX [*FM radio station call letters*]
KTST.......... Oklahoma City, OK [*FM radio station call letters*] (RBYB)
KTSU.......... Houston, TX [*FM radio station call letters*]
KTSV.......... Stormont-Vail Hospital, Topeka, KS [*Library symbol*] [*Library of Congress*] (LCLS)
KTSW.......... San Marcos, TX [*FM radio station call letters*]
KTSY.......... Caldwell, ID [*FM radio station call letters*]
KTT.......... Kermit [*Texas*] [*Seismograph station code, US Geological Survey*] [*Closed*] (SEIS)
KTT.......... Key to Tape (VLIE)
KTT.......... Kittila [*Finland*] [*Airport symbol*] (OAG)
KTTA-FM...... Esparto, CA [*FM radio station call letters*] (BROA)
KTTC.......... Keesler Technical Training Center
KTTC.......... Kingston-upon-Thames Technical College (SAUO)
KTTC.......... Rochester, MN [*Television station call letters*]
KTTG.......... Mena, AR [*FM radio station call letters*] (RBYB)
KTTL.......... Yuma, AZ [*FM radio station call letters*]
KTTL.......... Alva, OK [*FM radio station call letters*]
KTTL.......... Korea Tactical Target List (MCD)
KTTM.......... Huron, SD [*Television station call letters*]

KTTN	Trenton/Mercer County [*New Jersey*] [*ICAO location identifier*] (ICLI)
KTTN	Trenton, MO [*AM radio station call letters*]
KTTN-FM	Trenton, MO [*FM radio station call letters*]
KTTR	Rolla, MO [*AM radio station call letters*]
KTTR	St. James, MO [*FM radio station call letters*]
KTTS	Springfield, MO [*AM radio station call letters*]
KTTS-FM	Springfield, MO [*FM radio station call letters*]
KTTT	Columbus, NE [*AM radio station call letters*]
KTTU	Tucson, AZ [*Television station call letters*]
KTTV	Los Angeles, CA [*Television station call letters*]
KTTV-DT	Los Angeles, CA [*Television station call letters*] (BROA)
KTTW	Sioux Falls, SD [*Television station call letters*]
KTTX	Brenham, TX [*FM radio station call letters*]
KTTY	Kitty Hawk, Inc. [*NASDAQ symbol*] (SAG)
KTTY	San Diego, CA [*Television station call letters*]
KTTZ	Ajo, AZ [*FM radio station call letters*]
KTU	Key Telephone Unit
KTU	Kidney Transplant Unit [*National Health Service*] [*British*] (DI)
KTU	Kota [*India*] [*Airport symbol*] (OAG)
KTU	Kutaisi [*USSR*] [*Airport symbol*] (AD)
KTU	Kyushu Tokai University (SAUO)
KTU	Transylvania University (SAUO)
KTU	Transylvania University, Lexington, KY [*OCLC symbol*] (OCLC)
KTUB	Farmersville, TX [*AM radio station call letters*] (BROA)
KTUC	Kiribati Trades Union Congress (BUAC)
KTUC	Tucson, AZ [*AM radio station call letters*]
KTUE	Tulia, TX [*AM radio station call letters*]
KTUF	Kirksville, MO [*FM radio station call letters*]
KTUH	Honolulu, HI [*FM radio station call letters*]
KTUI	Sullivan, MO [*AM radio station call letters*]
KTUI-FM	Sullivan, MO [*FM radio station call letters*]
KTUL	Tulsa/International [*Oklahoma*] [*ICAO location identifier*] (ICLI)
KTUL	Tulsa, OK [*Television station call letters*]
KTUN-FM	Eagle, CO [*FM radio station call letters*] (RBYB)
KTUO	Sonora, CA [*FM radio station call letters*]
KTUR	Tooele, UT [*AM radio station call letters*]
KTUS	Tucson/International [*Arizona*] [*ICAO location identifier*] (ICLI)
KTUU-TV	Anchorage, AK [*Television station call letters*]
KTUX	Carthage, TX [*FM radio station call letters*]
KTUZ-FM	Chickasha, OK [*FM radio station call letters*] (BROA)
KTV	Kamarata [*Venezuela*] [*Airport symbol*] (OAG)
KTV	Kuwait Television
KTVA	Anchorage, AK [*Television station call letters*]
KTVA	United States Veterans Administration Hospital, Topeka, KS [*Library symbol*] [*Library of Congress*] (LCLS)
KTVB	Boise, ID [*Television station call letters*]
KTVC	Cedar Rapids, IA [*Television station call letters*]
KTVD	Denver, CO [*Television station call letters*]
KTVE	El Dorado, AR [*Television station call letters*]
KTVF	Fairbanks, AK [*Television station call letters*]
KTVF-DT	Fairbanks, AK [*Television station call letters*] (BROA)
KTVG	Grand Island, NE [*Television station call letters*]
KTVH	Helena, MT [*Television station call letters*]
KTVI	St. Louis, MO [*Television station call letters*]
KTVI-DT	St. Louis, MO [*Television station call letters*] (BROA)
KTVJ	Boulder, CO [*Television station call letters*]
KTVK	Phoenix, AZ [*Television station call letters*]
KTVL	Medford, OR [*Television station call letters*]
KTVM	Butte, MT [*Television station call letters*]
KTVN	Reno, NV [*Television station call letters*]
KTVO	Kirksville, MO [*Television station call letters*]
KTVQ	Billings, MT [*Television station call letters*]
KTVR	La Grande, OR [*Television station call letters*]
KTVS	Keystone Telebinocular Visual Survey (STED)
KTVS	Sterling, CO [*Television station call letters*]
KTVT	Fort Worth, TX [*Television station call letters*]
KTVT-DT	Fort Worth, TX [*Television station call letters*] (BROA)
KTVU	Oakland, CA [*Television station call letters*]
KTVU-DT	Oakland, CA [*Television station call letters*] (BROA)
KTVW	Phoenix, AZ [*Television station call letters*]
KTVX	Salt Lake City, UT [*Television station call letters*]
KTVZ	Bend, OR [*Television station call letters*]
KTW	Katowice [*Poland*] [*Airport symbol*] (OAG)
KTW	Klippel-Trenaunay-Weber Syndrome [*Medicine*] (DMAA)
KTW	Washburn University of Topeka, Topeka, KS [*Library symbol*] [*Library of Congress*] (LCLS)
KTWA	Ottumwa, IA [*FM radio station call letters*]
KTWB	Sioux Falls, SD [*FM radio station call letters*]
KTWC	Glendale, AZ [*FM radio station call letters*]
KTWG	Agana, GU [*AM radio station call letters*]
KTWI	Warm Springs, OR [*FM radio station call letters*]
KTWK	Colorado Springs, CO [*AM radio station call letters*]
KTW-L	Washburn University of Topeka, School of Law, Topeka, KS [*Library symbol*] [*Library of Congress*] (LCLS)
KTWN	Texarkana, TX [*AM radio station call letters*]
KTWN-FM	Texarkana, AR [*FM radio station call letters*]
KTWO	Casper, WY [*AM radio station call letters*]
KTWO	K2 Design, Inc. [*NASDAQ symbol*] (SAG)
KTWO-TV	Casper, WY [*Television station call letters*]
KTWS	Bend, OR [*FM radio station call letters*]
KTWS	Klippel-Trenaunay-Weber Syndrome [*Medicine*] (DMAA)
KTWU	Topeka, KS [*Television station call letters*]
KTWV	Los Angeles, CA [*FM radio station call letters*]
KTWY-FM	Walla Walla, WA [*FM radio station call letters*] (RBYB)
KTX	Keith Railway Equipment Co. [*AAR code*]
KTX	Kermit [*Texas*] [*Seismograph station code, US Geological Survey*] (SEIS)
KTXA	Arlington, TX [*Television station call letters*]
KTXB	Beaumont, TX [*Television station call letters*]
KTXC	Cuero, TX [*AM radio station call letters*] (RBYB)
KTXH	Houston, TX [*Television station call letters*]
KTXI-FM	Ingram, TX [*FM radio station call letters*] (BROA)
KTXJ	Jasper, TX [*AM radio station call letters*]
KTXK	Texarkana/Municipal-Webb Field [*Arkansas*] [*ICAO location identifier*] (ICLI)
KTXK	Texarkana, TX [*FM radio station call letters*]
KTXL	Sacramento, CA [*Television station call letters*]
KTXM-FM	Hallettsville, TX [*FM radio station call letters*] (BROA)
KTXN	Victoria, TX [*Television station call letters*]
KTXQ	Fort Worth, TX [*FM radio station call letters*]
KTXR	Springfield, MO [*FM radio station call letters*]
KTXS	Sweetwater, TX [*Television station call letters*]
KTXT	Lubbock, TX [*FM radio station call letters*]
KTXT-TV	Lubbock, TX [*Television station call letters*]
KTXX	Devine, TX [*FM radio station call letters*]
KTXX	Salinas, CA [*AM radio station call letters*] (BROA)
KTXY	Jefferson City, MO [*FM radio station call letters*]
KTXZ	West Lake Hills, TX [*AM radio station call letters*]
KTY	Kitty (ABBR)
KTY	Terror Bay [*Alaska*] [*Airport symbol*] (OAG)
KTY	Terror Bay, AK [*Location identifier*] [*FAA*] (FAAL)
KTYCR	Kitty-Corner (ABBR)
KTYD	Katydid (ABBR)
KTYD	Santa Barbara, CA [*FM radio station call letters*]
KTYL	Tyler, TX [*FM radio station call letters*]
KTYM	Inglewood, CA [*AM radio station call letters*]
KTYN	Minot, ND [*AM radio station call letters*]
KTYR	Tyler/Pounds Field [*Texas*] [*ICAO location identifier*] (ICLI)
KTYS	Knoxville/McGee Tyson [*Tennessee*] [*ICAO location identifier*] (ICLI)
KTYX-FM	Jonesville, LA [*FM radio station call letters*] (BROA)
KTZ	Katz Media [*AMEX symbol*] (TTSB)
KTZ	Katz Media Group, Inc. [*AMEX symbol*] (SAG)
KTZ	Kutztown [*Pennsylvania*] [*Seismograph station code, US Geological Survey*] (SEIS)
KTZA	Artesia, NM [*FM radio station call letters*]
KTZN	Anchorage, AK [*AM radio station call letters*] (BROA)
KTZR	Tucson, AZ [*AM radio station call letters*]
KTZZ	Seattle, WA [*Television station call letters*]
KU	Kallikrein Unit (DMAA)
KU	Kalmar Union (SAUO)
KU	Kanazawa University (SAUO)
KU	Kansas University (SAUO)
KU	Kapuskasing Uplift [*Geology*] [*Canada*]
KU	Karachi University (SAUO)
KU	Karmen Unit [*Medicine*] (MAE)
KU	Kasetsart University (SAUO)
KU	Keep Up [*Typography*] (DGA)
KU	Keio University (SAUO)
KU	Kentucky University (PDAA)
KU	Kentucky Utilities Co. (EFIS)
KU	Keyboard Unit [*Computer science*] (NASA)
KU	Kilourane (ABBR)
KU	Kimbel Unit (AAMN)
KU	Kimbrel Unit (STED)
KU	Kinski University (SAUO)
KU	Kitvei Ugarit (BJA)
KU	Knightsbridge University [*Denmark*] (ECON)
KU	Knowledge Universe
KU	Kobe University (SAUO)
KU	Kochi University (SAUO)
KU	Kogakuin University (SAUO)
KU	Kogoshima University (SAUO)
KU	Kokushukan University (SAUO)
K-U	Kremers-Urban Co. (DAVI)
KU	KU Energy [*NYSE symbol*] (TTSB)
KU	KU Energy Co. [*NYSE symbol*] (SPSG)
KU	Kumamoto University
KU	Kumho [*Tire casing code*]
Ku	Kurchatovium [*See also Rf*] [*Proposed name for chemical element 104*]
Ku	Kurtosis [*The relative degree of flatness in the region about the mode of a frequency curve*]
ku	Kuwait [*MARC country of publication code*] [*Library of Congress*] (LCCP)
KU	Kuwait Airways [*ICAO designator*] (AD)
KU	Kuwait Airways Corp. (SAUO)
KU	Kyoto University (SAUO)
KU	Kyushu University (SAUO)
KU	Unit Key (SAUS)
KU	University of Kansas, Lawrence, KS [*Library symbol*] [*Library of Congress*] (LCLS)
KUA	Kit Upkeep Allowance [*British*]
KUA	Kuantan [*Malaysia*] [*Airport symbol*] (OAG)
KUAB-FM	Fairbanks, AK [*FM radio station call letters*] (BROA)
KUAC	Fairbanks, AK [*FM radio station call letters*]
KUAC-TV	Fairbanks, AK [*Television station call letters*]
KUAD	Windsor, CO [*FM radio station call letters*]
KUAF	Fayetteville, AR [*FM radio station call letters*]
KUAI	Eleele, HI [*AM radio station call letters*]
KUAM	Agana, GU [*AM radio station call letters*]

KUAM-FM .... Agana, GU [*FM radio station call letters*]
KUAM-TV .... Agana, GU [*Television station call letters*]
KUAP .... Pine Bluff, AR [*FM radio station call letters*]
KUAR .... Little Rock, AR [*FM radio station call letters*]
KUAS .... Tucson, AZ [*Television station call letters*]
KUAT .... Tucson, AZ [*AM radio station call letters*]
KUAT-FM .... Tucson, AZ [*FM radio station call letters*]
KUAT-TV .... Tucson, AZ [*Television station call letters*]
KUAU .... Haiku, HI [*AM radio station call letters*]
KUAV .... Annual Reports. Research Reactor Institute. Kyoto University (journ.) (SAUS)
KUAZ .... Tucson, AZ [*FM radio station call letters*]
KUB .... Keilschrifturkunden aus Boghazkoi [*A publication*] (BJA)
KUB .... Kidney and Upper Bladder
KUB .... Kidney and Urinary Bladder (STED)
KUB .... Kidney Ultrasound Biopsy [*Medicine*] (MELL)
KUB .... Kidney, Ureter, Bladder [*X-ray*]
KUB .... Kubota Corp. ADR [*NYSE symbol*] (SPSG)
KUB .... Kubota Motor (SAUS)
KUBA .... Yuba City, CA [*AM radio station call letters*]
KuBand .... Satellite to Satellite communication frequency (SAUS)
KUBB .... Mariposa, CA [*FM radio station call letters*]
KUBC .... Montrose, CO [*AM radio station call letters*]
KUBD .... Denver, CO [*Television station call letters*]
KUBD .... Ketchikan, AK [*Television station call letters*] (BROA)
KUBE .... Seattle, WA [*FM radio station call letters*]
KUBL .... Salt Lake City, UT [*FM radio station call letters*] (RBYB)
KUBO .... Calexico, CA [*FM radio station call letters*]
Kubota .... Kubota Corp. [*Associated Press*] (SAG)
KUBQ .... La Grande, OR [*FM radio station call letters*]
KUBR .... San Juan, TX [*AM radio station call letters*]
KUBS .... Newport, WA [*FM radio station call letters*]
KUC .... Kucino [*Former USSR*] [*Seismograph station code, US Geological Survey*] [*Closed*] (SEIS)
KUC .... Kuria [*Kiribati*] [*Airport symbol*] (OAG)
KUCA .... Conway, AR [*FM radio station call letters*]
KUCB .... Des Moines, IA [*FM radio station call letters*]
KUCD .... Pearl City, HI [*FM radio station call letters*]
KUCE .... Kiev Universal Commodity Exchange [*Ukraine*] (EY)
KUCI .... Irvine, CA [*FM radio station call letters*]
KUCOG .... Kunia Coordinating Group (SAA)
KUCR .... Riverside, CA [*FM radio station call letters*]
KUCU-AM .... Hobbs, NM [*AM radio station call letters*] (RBYB)
KUCV .... Lincoln, NE [*FM radio station call letters*]
KUD .... Kudat [*Malaysia*] [*Airport symbol*] (OAG)
KUDL .... Kansas City, KS [*FM radio station call letters*]
KUDU-FM .... Tok, AK [*FM radio station call letters*] (RBYB)
KUDY .... Spokane, WA [*AM radio station call letters*]
KUED .... Kodak Unitized Engineering Data
KUED .... Salt Lake City, UT [*Television station call letters*]
KUEL .... Fort Dodge, IA [*FM radio station call letters*]
KU Engy .... KU Energy Corp. [*Associated Press*] (SAG)
KUER .... Salt Lake City, UT [*FM radio station call letters*]
KUES .... Richfield, UT [*Television station call letters*] (BROA)
KUET .... Black Canyon, AZ [*AM radio station call letters*] (RBYB)
KUEZ .... Lufkin, TX [*FM radio station call letters*]
KUF .... Kabul Union of Furriers [*Afghanistan*] (BUAC)
KUF .... Kidney Ultrafiltration Rate [*Nephrology*] (DAVI)
KUFM .... Missoula, MT [*FM radio station call letters*]
KUFM-TV .... Missoula, MT [*Television station call letters*]
KUFNCD .... Kampuchean United Front for National Construction and Defence [*Political party*] (PPW)
KUFN-FM .... Hamilton, MT [*FM radio station call letters*] (RBYB)
KUFNS .... Kampuchean National United Front for National Salvation
KUFO .... Portland, OR [*FM radio station call letters*]
KUFPEC .... Kuwait Foreign Petroleum Exploration Co. (BUAC)
KUFR .... Salt Lake City, UT [*FM radio station call letters*]
KUFX .... Gilroy, CA [*FM radio station call letters*]
KUG .... Kupang [*Timor*] [*Seismograph station code, US Geological Survey*] (SEIS)
KUGB .... Karate Union of Great Britain
KUGBNC .... Karate Union of Great Britain National Championship
KUGN .... Eugene, OR [*AM radio station call letters*]
KUGN-FM .... Eugene, OR [*FM radio station call letters*]
KUGR .... Green River, WY [*AM radio station call letters*]
KUGS .... Bellingham, WA [*FM radio station call letters*]
KUGT .... Jackson, MO [*AM radio station call letters*]
KUH .... Kaapuna [*Hawaii*] [*Seismograph station code, US Geological Survey*] (SEIS)
KUH .... Kuhlman Corp. [*NYSE symbol*] (SPSG)
KUH .... Kushiro [*Japan*] [*Airport symbol*] (OAG)
KUHB .... St. Paul, AK [*AM radio station call letters*] (BROA)
KUHB .... St. Paul Island, AK [*FM radio station call letters*]
KUHCA .... Journal. Korean Institute of Metals (journ.) (SAUS)
KUHD .... Port Neches, TX [*AM radio station call letters*]
KUHF .... Houston, TX [*FM radio station call letters*]
KUHG .... Milford, NE [*FM radio station call letters*]
KUHL .... Santa Maria, CA [*AM radio station call letters*]
Kuhlm .... Kuhlman Corp. [*Associated Press*] (SAG)
KUHM-FM .... Helena, MT [*FM radio station call letters*] (RBYB)
KUHT .... Houston, TX [*Television station call letters*]
KUIC .... Vacaville, CA [*FM radio station call letters*]
KUID .... Moscow, ID [*Television station call letters*]
KUIK .... Hillsboro, OR [*AM radio station call letters*]
KUIP .... Kernel User Interface Package (VLIE)
KUIPNET .... Kyoto University Information Processing Network (SAUO)
KUIS .... Kentucky Union List of Serials (SAUO)
KUISA .... Japanese Journal of Aerospace Medicine and Psychology (journ.) (SAUS)
KUJ .... Walla Walla, WA [*AM radio station call letters*]
KUJ-FM .... Walla Walla, WA [*FM radio station call letters*] (BROA)
KUK .... College of Universal Knowledge (SAUO)
KUK .... Kasigluk [*Alaska*] [*Airport symbol*] (OAG)
KUK .... University of Kentucky, Lexington, KY [*OCLC symbol*] (OCLC)
KUKA .... San Diego, TX [*FM radio station call letters*]
KUKI .... Ukiah, CA [*AM radio station call letters*]
KUKI-FM .... Ukiah, CA [*FM radio station call letters*]
KUKL .... Kalispell, MT [*FM radio station call letters*] (RBYB)
KUKN .... Kelso, WA [*FM radio station call letters*]
KUKQ .... Tempe, AZ [*AM radio station call letters*]
KUKU .... Willow Springs, MO [*AM radio station call letters*]
KUKU-FM .... Willow Springs, MO [*FM radio station call letters*]
KUL .... Kabul University Library (SAUO)
KUL .... Karachi University Library (SAUO)
KUL .... Kinjo Gakuin University Library [*UTLAS symbol*]
KUL .... Kuala Lumpur [*Malaysia*] [*Airport symbol*] (OAG)
KUL .... Kulyab [*Former USSR*] [*Seismograph station code, US Geological Survey*] (SEIS)
KUL .... Kyoto University Library (SAUO)
KUL .... Sterling Central Union List of Serials, Sterling, KS [*OCLC symbol*] (OCLC)
KU-L .... University of Kansas, School of Law, Lawrence (SAUS)
KU-L .... University of Kansas, School of Law, Lawrence, KS [*Library symbol*] [*Library of Congress*] (LCLS)
KULA .... Maunawili, HI [*AM radio station call letters*]
KULC .... Ogden, UT [*Television station call letters*]
Kulcke .... Kulicke & Soffa Industries, Inc. [*Associated Press*] (SAG)
KULE .... Ephrata, WA [*AM radio station call letters*]
KULE-FM .... Ephrata, WA [*FM radio station call letters*]
KULF .... Brenham, TX [*FM radio station call letters*]
KULH-FM .... Wheeling, MO [*FM radio station call letters*] (BROA)
KULL-FM .... Abilene, TX [*FM radio station call letters*] (BROA)
KULM .... Columbus, TX [*FM radio station call letters*]
KULP .... El Campo, TX [*AM radio station call letters*]
Kulp .... Kulp's Luzerne Legal Register Reports [*Pennsylvania*] [*A publication*] (DLA)
KULR .... Billings, MT [*Television station call letters*]
KULS .... Kentucky Union List of Serials [*Library network*]
KULSAA .... Karachi University Library Science Alumni Association (SAUO)
KULY .... Ulysses, KS [*AM radio station call letters*]
KUM .... Cape Kumukahi, Hawaii (SAUS)
KUM .... Kumamoto [*Japan*] [*Seismograph station code, US Geological Survey*] (SEIS)
KU-M .... University of Kansas, School of Medicine, Kansas City, KS [*Library symbol*] [*Library of Congress*] (LCLS)
KUM .... University of Kentucky, Medical Center, Lexington, KY [*OCLC symbol*] (OCLC)
KUM .... Yaku Shima [*Japan*] [*Airport symbol*] (OAG)
KUMA .... Pendleton, OR [*AM radio station call letters*]
KUMA-FM .... Pendleton, OR [*FM radio station call letters*]
KUMBX .... Kemper U.S. Mtge Cl.B [*Mutual fund ticker symbol*] (SG)
KUMD .... Duluth, MN [*FM radio station call letters*]
KUMM .... Morris, MN [*FM radio station call letters*]
KUMMI .... Kobe University Medical Mission to Indonesia
KUMR .... Rolla, MO [*FM radio station call letters*]
KuMSIC .... Kuwait Medical Student International Committee (SAUO)
KUMT .... Centerville, UT [*FM radio station call letters*]
KUMU .... Honolulu, HI [*AM radio station call letters*]
KUMU-FM .... Honolulu, HI [*FM radio station call letters*]
KUMV .... Williston, ND [*Television station call letters*]
KU-MW .... University of Kansas, School of Medicine-Witchita, Witchita, KS [*Library symbol*] [*Library of Congress*] (LCLS)
KUMX-FM .... Houma, LA [*FM radio station call letters*] (BROA)
KUN .... Kunia, Oahu, HI [*Location identifier*] [*FAA*] (FAAL)
KUN .... Kunming [*Republic of China*] [*Seismograph station code, US Geological Survey*] (SEIS)
KUNA .... Indio, CA [*AM radio station call letters*]
KUNA .... Kuwait News Agency (BUAC)
KUNA-FM .... La Quinta, CA [*FM radio station call letters*]
KUNC .... Greeley, CO [*FM radio station call letters*]
KUND-AM .... Grand Forks, ND [*AM radio station call letters*] (BROA)
KUND-FM .... Grand Forks, ND [*FM radio station call letters*] (BROA)
KUNI .... Cedar Falls, IA [*FM radio station call letters*]
KUNM .... Albuquerque, NM [*FM radio station call letters*]
KUNO .... Corpus Christi, TX [*AM radio station call letters*]
KUNQ .... Houston, MO [*FM radio station call letters*]
KUNR .... Reno, NV [*FM radio station call letters*]
KUNV .... Las Vegas, NV [*FM radio station call letters*]
KUNY .... Mason City, IA [*FM radio station call letters*]
KUO .... Kuopio [*Finland*] [*Airport symbol*] (OAG)
KUOA .... Siloam Springs, AR [*AM radio station call letters*]
KUOI .... Moscow, ID [*FM radio station call letters*]
KUOL .... San Marcos, TX [*AM radio station call letters*]
Kuom .... Kuomintang (SAUO)
KUOM .... Minneapolis, MN [*AM radio station call letters*]
KUON .... Lincoln, NE [*Television station call letters*]
KUOO .... Spirit Lake, IA [*FM radio station call letters*]
KUOP .... Stockton, CA [*FM radio station call letters*]
KUOR .... Redlands, CA [*FM radio station call letters*]
KUOW .... Seattle, WA [*FM radio station call letters*]

KUP .... Kupang [Timor] [Seismograph station code, US Geological Survey] [Closed] (SEIS)
KUP .... Kupiano [Papua New Guinea] [Airport symbol] (OAG)
KUP .... Kwacha United Press [Angola] (BUAC)
KUP .... University of Kentucky, Plestonburg Community College (SAUO)
KUP .... University of Kentucky, Prestonburg Community College, Prestonburg, KY [OCLC symbol] (OCLC)
KUPB .... Midland, TX [Television station call letters] (BROA)
KUPC .... Carlsbad, NM [Television station call letters] (BROA)
KUPD .... Tempe, AZ [FM radio station call letters]
KUPH-FM .... Mountain View, MO [FM radio station call letters] (BROA)
KUPI .... Idaho Falls, ID [AM radio station call letters]
KUPI-FM ..... Idaho Falls, ID [FM radio station call letters]
KUPK-TV ..... Garden City, KS [Television station call letters]
KUPL .... Portland, OR [AM radio station call letters] (BROA)
KUPL-FM ..... Portland, OR [FM radio station call letters]
KUPN .... Las Vegas, NV [Television station call letters] (RBYB)
KUPN .... Mission, KS [AM radio station call letters] (BROA)
KUPR .... Carlsbad, CA [FM radio station call letters] (RBYB)
KUPS .... Tacoma, WA [FM radio station call letters]
KUPX .... Provo, UT [Television station call letters] (BROA)
KUQQ-FM .... Milford, IA [FM radio station call letters] (RBYB)
KUR .... Kit Use Ratio [Statistics]
kur .... Kurdish [MARC language code] [Library of Congress] (LCCP)
KUR .... Kurilsk [Former USSR] [Seismograph station code, US Geological Survey] (SEIS)
KUR .... Kyoto University Reactor
KURA .... Ouray, CO [FM radio station call letters]
KURB .... Little Rock, AR [AM radio station call letters]
KURB-FM ..... Little Rock, AR [FM radio station call letters]
KURCHATOV... Kurchatov Institute-Russia (SAUO)
KURE .... KURE Foundation
KURE-FM ..... Ames, IA [FM radio station call letters] (RBYB)
KUREX .... Kursk Experiment (SAUO)
KURL .... Billings, MT [AM radio station call letters]
KURM .... Kurzweil MusicSystems, Inc. (SAUO)
KURM .... Rogers, AR [AM radio station call letters]
KURR-FM .... Bountiful, UT [FM radio station call letters] (RBYB)
KURRI .... Kyoto University Research Reactor Institute [Japan] (BUAC)
KURS .... San Diego, CA [FM radio station call letters]
KURV .... Edinburg, TX [AM radio station call letters]
KURY .... Brookings, OR [AM radio station call letters]
KURY-FM ..... Brookings, OR [FM radio station call letters]
KURZ .... Kurzweil Applied Intelligence, Inc. [NASDAQ symbol] (SAG)
Kurzweil ...... Kurzweil Applied Intelligence, Inc. [Associated Press] (SAG)
KUS .... Kidney, Ureter, and Spleen [Anatomy] (MAH)
KUS .... Kulusuk Island [Greenland] [Airport symbol] (AD)
KUS .... Kursk State Air Enterprise [Former USSR] [FAA designator] (FAAC)
KUS .... Kushiro [Japan] [Seismograph station code, US Geological Survey] (SEIS)
KU-S .... University of Kansas, Kenneth Spencer Research Library, Lawrence, KS [Library symbol] [Library of Congress] (LCLS)
KUS .... University of Kentucky, Southeast Center, Cumberland, KY [OCLC symbol] (OCLC)
KUSA .... Denver, CO [Television station call letters]
KUSAX .... Kemper U.S. Govt. Secs. Cl.A [Mutual fund ticker symbol] (SG)
KUSC .... Los Angeles, CA [FM radio station call letters]
KUSD .... Vermillion, SD [AM radio station call letters]
KUSD-FM ..... Vermillion, SD [FM radio station call letters]
KUSD-TV ..... Vermillion, SD [Television station call letters]
KUSF .... San Francisco, CA [FM radio station call letters]
KUSG .... St. George, UT [Television station call letters]
KUSH .... Cushing, OK [AM radio station call letters]
Kush .... Kushan (VRA)
Kushi .... Kushi Macrobiotic Corp. [Associated Press] (SAG)
KushLc .... Kush Locke [Associated Press] (SAG)
KushLc .... [The] Kushner-Locke Co. [Associated Press] (SAG)
KushLk .... Kush Locke [Associated Press] (SAG)
KushLk .... [The] Kushner-Locke Co. [Associated Press] (SAG)
KUSI .... San Diego, CA [Television station call letters]
KUSK .... Prescott, AZ [Television station call letters]
KUSM .... Bozeman, MT [Television station call letters]
KUSN .... Coffeyville, KS [FM radio station call letters]
KuSNU .... Seoul National University (SAUO)
KUSP .... Ku-Band Signal Processor (MCD)
KUSP .... Ku-Band Single Processor (MCD)
KUSP .... Santa Cruz, CA [FM radio station call letters]
KUSR .... Ames, IA [FM radio station call letters]
KUST .... Kustom Electronics Inc. (SAUO)
KUST-FM ..... Huntsville, TX [FM radio station call letters] (BROA)
KUSU .... Logan, UT [FM radio station call letters]
KUSZ .... Proctor, MN [FM radio station call letters] (RBYB)
KUT .... Austin, TX [FM radio station call letters]
KUT .... Kutahya [Turkey] [Airport symbol] (AD)
kut .... Kutenai [MARC language code] [Library of Congress] (LCCP)
KUT .... Kutsu-Ga-Hara [Japan] [Seismograph station code, US Geological Survey] (SEIS)
Kut .... Kuttim (BJA)
KUT .... Lexington Technical Institute, Lexington, KY [OCLC symbol] (OCLC)
KUT .... University of Toronto Union Catalogue Section [UTLAS symbol]
KUTA .... Blanding, UT [AM radio station call letters]
Kutch .... All India Reporter, Kutch [1949-56] [A publication] (DLA)
KUTD .... Keep Up to Date (KSC)
KUTE-FM ..... Ignacio, CO [FM radio station call letters] (BROA)
KUTGW .... Keep Up the Good Work

KUTI .... Selah, WA [AM radio station call letters]
KUTP .... Phoenix, AZ [Television station call letters]
KUTQ .... Bountiful, UT [AM radio station call letters]
KUTT .... Fairbury, NE [FM radio station call letters]
KUTV .... Salt Lake City, UT [Television station call letters]
KUTX .... San Angelo, TX [FM radio station call letters] (RBYB)
KUTY .... Palmdale, CA [AM radio station call letters]
KUTZ .... Lampasas, TX [FM radio station call letters]
Kutztown U... Kutztown University of Pennsylvania (GAGS)
KUU .... Kulu [India] [Airport symbol] (AD)
KUUG .... Karlsruher UNIX User Group (SAUO)
KUUL .... Davenport, IA [FM radio station call letters]
KUUL-FM ..... East Moline, IL [FM radio station call letters] (BROA)
KUUY .... Orchard Valley, WY [AM radio station call letters]
KUUY-FM ..... Glendo, WY [FM radio station call letters] (BROA)
KUUZ .... Lake Village, AR [FM radio station call letters]
KUVA .... Uvalde, TX [FM radio station call letters]
KUVI .... Bakersfield, CA [Television station call letters] (BROA)
KUVN .... Garland, TX [Television station call letters]
KUVO .... Denver, CO [FM radio station call letters]
KUVR .... Holdrege, NE [AM radio station call letters]
KUVR-FM ..... Holdrege, NE [FM radio station call letters]
KUVS .... Modesto, CA [Television station call letters] (BROA)
KUW .... Kuwait (ABBR)
Kuw .... Kuwait (VRA)
KUWA-FM .... Afton, WY [FM radio station call letters] (BROA)
KUWB .... Ogden, UT [Television station call letters] (BROA)
KUWC-FM .... Casper, WY [FM radio station call letters] (BROA)
KUWG-FM .... Gillette, WY [FM radio station call letters] (BROA)
KUWJ .... Jackson, WY [FM radio station call letters]
KUWL .... Fairbanks, AK [FM radio station call letters]
KUWN-FM .... Newcastle, WY [FM radio station call letters] (BROA)
KUWR .... Laramie, WY [FM radio station call letters]
KUWS .... Superior, WI [FM radio station call letters]
KUWZ .... Rock Springs, WY [FM radio station call letters]
KUX .... Kumix Resources Corp. [Vancouver Stock Exchange symbol]
KUY .... Kuyper [Indonesia] [Later, TNG] [Geomagnetic observatory code]
KUY .... Uyak [Alaska] [Airport symbol] (OAG)
KUY .... Uyak, AK [Location identifier] [FAA] (FAAL)
KUYI-FM ...... Holevilla, AZ [FM radio station call letters] (BROA)
KUYO .... Evansville, WY [AM radio station call letters]
KUZZ .... Bakersfield, CA [FM radio station call letters]
KUZZ-TV ..... Bakersfield, CA [Television station call letters]
KV .... British Virgin Island [IYRU nationality code] (IYR)
KV .... Kanamycin-Vancomycin [An antibiotic] (DAVI)
KV .... Karnaugh Veitch (SAUO)
KV .... Kerr Vector [Optics]
KV .... Key Verifier [Computer science]
KV .... Kidney Valve
KV .... Killed Vaccine [Immunology] (MAE)
KV .... Killed Virus [Pharmacology] (DAVI)
KV .... Kill Vehicle
KV .... Kilovolt (AAEL)
kV .... Kilovolt
KV .... Kinematic Viscosity
KV .... Knights of Vartan (EA)
KV .... Kochel-Verzeichnis [List of Mozart's works] (IIA)
KV .... Kriegsverwendungsfaehig [Fit for Active Service] [German military - World War II]
KV .... K-V Pharmaceutical Co. [AMEX symbol] (SPSG)
KV .... Transkei Airways [ICAO designator] (AD)
KV1 .... Kalanchoe Virus 1 [Plant pathology]
KVA .... Karavia [Zaire] [Geomagnetic observatory code]
KVA .... Kavala [Greece] [Airport symbol] (OAG)
KVA .... Kill Vehicle Assembly [Military] (ACAE)
kVA .... Kilovolt Ampere
KVA .... Kilovolt-Ampere (VLIE)
KVA .... Korean Veterans Association (SAUO)
KVA .... Royal Academy of Science (SAUS)
KVAB-FM ..... Clarkston, WA [FM radio station call letters] (RBYB)
KVAC .... Forks, WA [AM radio station call letters]
KVAC .... Kilovolt Alternating Current (IAA)
KVAD .... Valdosta/Moody Air Force Base [Georgia] [ICAO location identifier] (ICLI)
KVAG-FM ..... Rugby, ND [FM radio station call letters] (RBYB)
kVAH .... Kilovolt-Ampere Hour
kVAhm .... Kilovolt-Ampere Hour Meter (MSA)
KVAK .... Valdez, AK [AM radio station call letters]
KVAK-FM ..... Valdez, AK [FM radio station call letters] (BROA)
KVAL .... Eugene, OR [Television station call letters]
kVAM .... Kilovolt-Ampere Meter
KVAN .... Korean Voice Alerting Network (SAUO)
KVAN .... Vancouver, WA [AM radio station call letters]
kvar .... Kilovar
kVAr .... Kilovolt-Ampere Reactive
KVAR .... Riverside, CA [FM radio station call letters]
kvarh .... Kilovar-Hour
kVARh .... [Reactive] Kilovolt-Ampere-Hour (IDOE)
KVAS .... Astoria, OR [AM radio station call letters]
KVAW .... Eagle Pass, TX [Television station call letters]
KVAY .... Lamar, CO [FM radio station call letters]
KVAZ .... Henryetta, OK [FM radio station call letters]
KVBA .... Kanamycin-Vancomycin Blood Agar [Microbiology]
KVBC .... Las Vegas, NV [Television station call letters]
KVBC-FM ..... Las Vegas, NV [FM radio station call letters] (RBYB)

KVBG .... Lompoc/Vandenberg Air Force Base [*California*] [*ICAO location identifier*] (ICLI)
KVBM .... Minneapolis, MN [*Television station call letters*]
KVBR .... Brainerd, MN [*AM radio station call letters*]
KVBR-FM ..... Brainerd, MN [*FM radio station call letters*]
KVC .... King Cove [*Alaska*] [*Airport symbol*] (OAG)
KVC .... King Cove, AK [*Location identifier*] [*FAA*] (FAAL)
KVCA-AM ..... Simi Valley, CA [*AM radio station call letters*] (BROA)
KVCE .... Fallon, NV [*FM radio station call letters*]
KVCI .... Mineola, TX [*AM radio station call letters*]
KVCK .... Wolf Point, MT [*AM radio station call letters*]
KVCK-FM ..... Wolf Point, MT [*FM radio station call letters*]
KVCL .... Winnfield, LA [*AM radio station call letters*]
KVCL-FM ..... Winnfield, LA [*FM radio station call letters*]
KVCM .... Helena, MT [*FM radio station call letters*]
KVCO .... Concordia, KS [*FM radio station call letters*]
kVcp .... Kilovolt Constant Potential (STED)
kVCP .... Kilovolt Constant Potential
KVCQ .... Cuero, TX [*FM radio station call letters*] (RBYB)
KVCR .... San Bernardino, CA [*FM radio station call letters*]
KVCR-TV ..... San Bernardino, CA [*Television station call letters*]
KVCS .... KXE6S Verein Chess Society (EA)
KVCS-AM ..... Perry, OK [*AM radio station call letters*] (RBYB)
KVCS-FM ..... Perry, OK [*FM radio station call letters*] (RBYB)
KVCT .... Victoria, TX [*Television station call letters*]
KVCU .... Boulder, CO [*AM radio station call letters*] (BROA)
KVCV .... Victorville/George Air Force Base [*California*] [*ICAO location identifier*] (ICLI)
KVCX .... Gregory, SD [*FM radio station call letters*]
KVCY .... Fort Scott, KS [*FM radio station call letters*]
KVDA .... San Antonio, TX [*Television station call letters*]
KVDB .... Sioux Center, IA [*AM radio station call letters*]
kVdc .... Kilovolt Direct Current (IEEE)
KVDL .... Quanah, TX [*AM radio station call letters*]
KVDP .... Dry Prong, LA [*FM radio station call letters*]
KVDT .... Keyboard Visual Display Terminal (MCD)
KVE .... Kaposi's Varicelliform Eruption [*Medicine*] [*Medicine*] (DMAA)
KVEA .... Corona, CA [*Television station call letters*]
KVEC .... San Luis Obispo, CA [*AM radio station call letters*]
KVEG .... North Las Vegas, NV [*AM radio station call letters*]
KVEL .... Vernal, UT [*AM radio station call letters*]
KVEN .... Ventura, CA [*AM radio station call letters*]
KVEO .... Brownsville, TX [*Television station call letters*]
KVER .... El Paso, TX [*FM radio station call letters*]
KVET .... Austin, TX [*AM radio station call letters*]
KVET-FM ..... Austin, TX [*FM radio station call letters*]
KVEW .... Kennewick, WA [*Television station call letters*]
KVEZ-FM ..... Parker, AZ [*FM radio station call letters*] (RBYB)
KVF .... Kent Volunteer Fencibles [*British military*] (DMA)
KVFC .... Cortez, CO [*AM radio station call letters*]
KVFD .... Fort Dodge, IA [*AM radio station call letters*]
KVFM .... Logan, UT [*FM radio station call letters*]
K-V Funds.... Knutson-Vandenberg Funds (WPI)
KVFX .... Manteca, CA [*FM radio station call letters*]
KVFX-FM ..... Logan, UT [*FM radio station call letters*] (BROA)
KVG .... Kavieng [*New Ireland*] [*Airport symbol*] (AD)
KVG .... Kavieng [*Papua New Guinea*] [*Airport symbol*] (OAG)
KVG .... Kavieng [*Papua New Guinea*] [*Seismograph station code, US Geological Survey*] (SEIS)
KVG .... Keyed Video Generator
KVG .... Key Variable Generator (COE)
KVGB .... Great Bend, KS [*AM radio station call letters*]
KVGB-FM ..... Great Bend, KS [*FM radio station call letters*]
KVGO-FM ..... Spring Valley, MN [*FM radio station call letters*] (RBYB)
KVHI .... KVH Industries [*NASDAQ symbol*] (TTSB)
KVHI .... KVH Industries, Inc. [*NASDAQ symbol*] (SAG)
KVHInd .... KVH Industries, Inc. [*Associated Press*] (SAG)
KVHP .... Lake Charles, LA [*Television station call letters*]
KVHS .... Concord, CA [*FM radio station call letters*]
KVHS .... Kanawha Valley Historical Society (SAUO)
KVHT .... Vermillion, SD [*FM radio station call letters*]
KVI .... Carlsbad Ventures [*Vancouver Stock Exchange symbol*]
KVI .... Known Value Item (VLIE)
KVI .... Korean Veterans International (EA)
KVI .... Seattle, WA [*AM radio station call letters*]
KVIA .... El Paso, TX [*Television station call letters*]
KVIC .... Khadi & Village Industries Commission (SAUO)
KVIC .... Victoria, TX [*FM radio station call letters*]
KVIE .... Sacramento, CA [*Television station call letters*]
KVIH .... Clovis, NM [*Television station call letters*]
KVII .... Amarillo, TX [*Television station call letters*]
KVIK .... Decorah, IA [*FM radio station call letters*] (RBYB)
KVIL-FM ..... Highland Park, TX [*FM radio station call letters*]
KVIN-AM ..... Turlock, CA [*AM radio station call letters*] (BROA)
KVIP .... Redding, CA [*AM radio station call letters*]
KVIP-FM ..... Redding, CA [*FM radio station call letters*]
KVIQ .... Eureka, CA [*Television station call letters*]
KVIS .... Miami, OK [*AM radio station call letters*]
KVIV .... El Paso, TX [*AM radio station call letters*]
KViWM .... Wesley Medical Center, Wichita (SAUS)
KVJM-FM ..... Hearme, TX [*FM radio station call letters*] (BROA)
KVJY .... Pharr, TX [*AM radio station call letters*]
KVK .... Kriegsverdienstkreuz [*War Service Cross*] [*German military decoration - World War II*]
KVKI .... Shreveport, LA [*FM radio station call letters*]

KVL .... Kingsvale Resources [*Vancouver Stock Exchange symbol*]
KVL .... Kirchhoff's Voltage Law (PDAA)
KVL .... Kivalina [*Alaska*] [*Airport symbol*] (OAG)
KVL .... Kivalina, AK [*Location identifier*] [*FAA*] (FAAL)
KVLA .... Vidalia, LA [*AM radio station call letters*]
KVLBA .... Kanamycin-Vancomycin Labeled Blood Agar [*Microbiology*]
KVLC .... Hatch, NM [*FM radio station call letters*] (RBYB)
KVLD .... Valdez, AK [*AM radio station call letters*]
KVLE .... Gunnison, CO [*AM radio station call letters*]
KVLF .... Alpine, TX [*AM radio station call letters*]
KVLG .... La Grange, TX [*AM radio station call letters*]
KVLH .... Pauls Valley, OK [*AM radio station call letters*]
KVLI .... Lake Isabella, CA [*AM radio station call letters*]
KVLI-FM ..... Lake Isabella, CA [*FM radio station call letters*]
KVLL .... Woodville, TX [*AM radio station call letters*]
KVLL-FM ..... Woodville, TX [*FM radio station call letters*]
KVLM .... Kevlin Corp. [*NASDAQ symbol*] (NQ)
KVLO-FM ..... Sheridan, AR [*FM radio station call letters*] (RBYB)
KVLR .... Twisp, WA [*FM radio station call letters*]
KVLT .... Victoria, TX [*FM radio station call letters*]
KVLU .... Beaumont, TX [*FM radio station call letters*]
KVLV .... Fallon, NV [*AM radio station call letters*]
KVLV-FM ..... Fallon, NV [*FM radio station call letters*]
KVLY .... Edinburg, TX [*FM radio station call letters*]
KVLY-TV ..... Fargo, ND [*Television station call letters*] (RBYB)
KVM .... Keyboard-Video-Mouse [*Computer science*]
kVM .... Kilovolt Meter
KVM .... K Virtual Machine (SAUS)
KVM .... Rusaerolizing Airling [*Former USSR*] [*FAA designator*] (FAAC)
KVMA .... Kansas Veterinary Medical Association (GVA)
KVMA .... Kentucky Veterinary Medical Association (GVA)
KVMA .... Magnolia, AR [*AM radio station call letters*]
KVMA-FM .... Magnolia, AR [*FM radio station call letters*]
KVMC........... Colorado City, TX [*AM radio station call letters*]
KVMD-TV ..... Twentynine Palms, CA [*TV station call letters*] (RBYB)
KVML .... Sonora, CA [*AM radio station call letters*]
KV/mm .... Kilovolt per Millimeter (VLIE)
KVMR .... Nevada City, CA [*FM radio station call letters*]
KVMV .... McAllen, TX [*FM radio station call letters*]
KVMX .... Eastland, TX [*FM radio station call letters*]
KVN .... Kaiserville [*Nevada*] [*Seismograph station code, US Geological Survey*] (SEIS)
KVN .... Kimmins Corp. [*NYSE symbol*] (TTSB)
KVN .... Kimmins Environmental Services [*NYSE symbol*] (SPSG)
KVNA .... Flagstaff, AZ [*AM radio station call letters*]
KVNA-FM ..... Flagstaff, AZ [*FM radio station call letters*]
KVNE .... Tyler, TX [*FM radio station call letters*]
KVNF .... Paonia, CO [*FM radio station call letters*]
KVNI .... Coeur D'Alene, ID [*AM radio station call letters*]
KVNO .... Omaha, NE [*FM radio station call letters*]
KVNP .... Kidepo Valley National Park (SAUO)
KVNR .... Santa Ana, CA [*AM radio station call letters*] (BROA)
KVNU .... Logan, UT [*AM radio station call letters*]
KVO .... Keep Vein Open [*Medicine*]
KVO .... Kraftverkehrsordnung fuer den Gueterfernverkehr mit Kraftfahrzeugen [*Regulation for the Carriage of Goods by Motor Vehicles*] [*German*] [*Business term*] (ILCA)
KVOA .... Tucson, AZ [*Television station call letters*]
KVOC .... Casper, WY [*AM radio station call letters*]
KVO C D5W... Keep Vein Open Cum [*with*] Dextrose 5% in Water [*Pharmacology*] (DAVI)
KVOD .... Denver, CO [*FM radio station call letters*]
KVOE .... Emporia, KS [*AM radio station call letters*]
KVOE-FM ..... Emporia, KS [*FM radio station call letters*]
KVOI .... Oro Valley, AZ [*AM radio station call letters*]
KVOK .... Kodiak, AK [*AM radio station call letters*]
KVOL .... Lafayette, LA [*AM radio station call letters*]
KVOL .... Opelousas, LA [*AM radio station call letters*]
KVOM .... Morrilton, AR [*AM radio station call letters*]
KVOM-FM .... Morrilton, AR [*FM radio station call letters*]
KVON .... Napa, CA [*AM radio station call letters*]
KVOO .... Tulsa, OK [*AM radio station call letters*]
KVOO-FM ..... Tulsa, OK [*FM radio station call letters*]
KVOP .... Plainview, TX [*AM radio station call letters*]
KVOP-FM ..... Plainview, TX [*FM radio station call letters*] (BROA)
KVOR .... Colorado Springs, CO [*AM radio station call letters*]
KVOS-TV ..... Bellingham, WA [*Television station call letters*]
KVOU .... Uvalde, TX [*AM radio station call letters*]
KVOW .... Riverton, WY [*AM radio station call letters*]
KVOX .... Moorhead, MN [*AM radio station call letters*]
KVOX-FM ..... Moorhead, MN [*FM radio station call letters*]
KVOY .... Mojave, CA [*AM radio station call letters*]
KVOZ .... Laredo, TX [*AM radio station call letters*]
KVP .... Katholieke Volkspartij [*Catholic People's Party*] [*Netherlands*] [*Political party*] (PPE)
kVP .... Kilovolt Peak
KVP .... Kodak Vacuum Probe
KVP .... Kodak Versamat Processor
KVPA .... Port Isabel, TX [*FM radio station call letters*]
KVPC .... San Joaquin, CA (RBYB)
KVPC-FM ..... San Joaquin, CA [*FM radio station call letters*] (BROA)
KV Ph .... K-V Pharmaceutical Co. [*Associated Press*] (SAG)
KVPI .... Ville Platte, LA [*AM radio station call letters*]
KVPI-FM ..... Ville Platte, LA [*FM radio station call letters*]
KVPR .... Fresno, CA [*FM radio station call letters*]

KVPS .... Valparaiso/Eglin Air Force Base [*Florida*] [*ICAO location identifier*] (ICLI)
KVPT .... Fresno, CA [*Television station call letters*]
KVRB .... Vero Beach/Vero Beach [*Florida*] [*ICAO location identifier*] (ICLI)
KVRC .... Arkadelphia, AR [*AM radio station call letters*]
KVRD .... Cottonwood, AZ [*AM radio station call letters*]
KVRD-FM ..... Cottonwood, AZ [*FM radio station call letters*]
KVRE .... Hot Springs Village, AR [*FM radio station call letters*]
KVRG .... Seaside, CA [*FM radio station call letters*]
KVRG .... Soledad, CA [*AM radio station call letters*] (RBYB)
KVRH .... Salida, CO [*AM radio station call letters*]
KVRH-FM ..... Salida, CO [*FM radio station call letters*]
KVRN-FM ..... Marvell, AR [*FM radio station call letters*] (BROA)
KVRO-FM ..... Stillwater, OK [*FM radio station call letters*] (BROA)
KVRP .... Haskell, TX [*FM radio station call letters*]
KVRP .... Stamford, TX [*AM radio station call letters*]
KVRQ .... Atwater, CA [*FM radio station call letters*]
KVRR .... Fargo, ND [*Television station call letters*]
KVRS .... Lawton, OK [*FM radio station call letters*]
KVRT .... Victoria, TX [*FM radio station call letters*] (RBYB)
KVRW .... Lawton, OK [*FM radio station call letters*]
KVRX .... Austin, TX [*FM radio station call letters*]
KVRY .... Mesa, AZ [*FM radio station call letters*]
KVS .... Kansanvalistusseura [*Society for Culture and Education*] [*Finland*] (EAIO)
KVS .... Kelvin-Varley Slide [*Electronics*]
KVS .... Keyboard/Video Switch [*Computer science*]
KVS .... Kurzweil VoiceSystem [*Voice-recognition computer device*]
KVSA .... McGehee, AR [*AM radio station call letters*]
KVSC .... St. Cloud, MN [*FM radio station call letters*]
KVSF .... Santa Fe, NM [*AM radio station call letters*]
KVSH .... Valentine, NE [*AM radio station call letters*]
KVSI .... Montpelier, ID [*AM radio station call letters*]
KVSL .... Show Low, AZ [*AM radio station call letters*]
KVSN .... Tumwater, WA [*AM radio station call letters*]
KVSO .... Ardmore, OK [*AM radio station call letters*] (RBYB)
KVSP .... Oklahoma City, OK [*AM radio station call letters*]
KVSR-FM ..... Fresno, CA [*FM radio station call letters*] (BROA)
KVST .... Huntsville, TX [*FM radio station call letters*]
KVST .... Keystone Visual Survey Test [*Ophthalmology*]
KVSV .... Beloit, KS [*AM radio station call letters*]
KVSV-FM ..... Beloit, KS [*FM radio station call letters*]
KVT .... Kavak [*Turkey*] [*Seismograph station code, US Geological Survey*] (SEIS)
KVTF .... Williams, AZ [*FM radio station call letters*]
KVTH .... Hot Springs, AR [*Television station call letters*] (RBYB)
KVTI .... Tacoma, WA [*FM radio station call letters*]
KVTJ-TV ...... Jonesboro, AR [*TV station call letters*] (RBYB)
KVTN .... Pine Bluff, AR [*Television station call letters*]
KVTO .... Berkeley, CA [*AM radio station call letters*]
KVTT .... Dallas, TX [*FM radio station call letters*]
KVTV .... Laredo, TX [*Television station call letters*]
KVTY-FM ..... Lewiston, ID [*FM radio station call letters*] (BROA)
KVU .... Kleer-Vu Industries [*AMEX symbol*] (TTSB)
KVU .... Kleer-Vu Industries, Inc. [*AMEX symbol*] (SPSG)
KVU .... Victoria University Library, University of Toronto [*UTLAS symbol*]
KVUE .... Austin, TX [*Television station call letters*]
KVUT .... Little Rock, AR [*Television station call letters*]
KVUU .... Pueblo, CO [*FM radio station call letters*]
KVVA .... Phoenix, AZ [*AM radio station call letters*]
KVVA-FM ..... Apache Junction, AZ [*FM radio station call letters*]
KVVN .... Santa Clara, CA [*AM radio station call letters*] (BROA)
KVVP .... Leesville, LA [*FM radio station call letters*]
KVVQ .... Hesperia, CA [*AM radio station call letters*]
KVVQ .... Victorville, CA [*FM radio station call letters*]
KVVS .... Windsor, CO [*AM radio station call letters*]
KVVU .... Henderson, NV [*Television station call letters*]
KVVV .... Baytoun, TX [*Television station call letters*]
KVW .... Kansas City, Kaw Valley R. R., Inc. [*AAR code*]
KVW .... Kurzweil Voice Writer
KVWB .... Las Vegas, NV [*Television station call letters*] (BROA)
KVWC .... Vernon, TX [*AM radio station call letters*]
KVWC-FM .... Vernon, TX [*FM radio station call letters*]
KVWG .... Pearsall, TX [*AM radio station call letters*]
KVWG-FM ... Pearsall, TX [*FM radio station call letters*]
KVWM .... Show Low, AZ [*AM radio station call letters*]
KVWM-FM ... Show Low, AZ [*FM radio station call letters*]
KVY .... CAI [*Compagnia Aeronautica Italiana SpA*] [*Italy*] [*ICAO designator*] (FAAC)
KVYE-TV ...... El Centro, CA [*TV station call letters*] (RBYB)
KVYF .... Wilson Creek, WA [*FM radio station call letters*]
KVYN .... St. Helena, CA [*FM radio station call letters*]
KVYS .... St. George, UT [*FM radio station call letters*]
KVYY-FM ..... Ventura, CA [*FM radio station call letters*] (RBYB)
KVZK-2 .... Pago Pago, AS [*Television station call letters*]
KVZK-4 .... Pago Pago, AS [*Television station call letters*]
KVZK-5 .... Pago Pago, AS [*Television station call letters*]
Kw .... Afrikan Airlines Ltd. (SAUO)
K$_w$ .... Dissociation Constant of Water [*Physics*] (DAVI)
KW .... Dorado Wings [*Airline code*]
KW .... Kaiser Wilhelm [*King William*] [*Name of two Prussian kings and emperor of Germany*] (ROG)
KW .... Kaliszer Woch (BJA)
KW .... Kampfwagen [*Tank*] [*German military - World War II*]
KW .... Katabatic Wind

KW .... Keith-Wagener [*Ophthalmology*]
KW .... Kenworth Truck Co.
KW .... Key West [*Florida*]
KW .... Key Word [*Online database field identifier*]
KW .... Killer Weed [*Slang for phencyclidine; also called PCP and Sernyl*] (DAVI)
kW .... Kilohm [*Formerly, K*] [*Unit of electrical resistance*] (DAVI)
Kw .... Kilowatt (EBF)
kw .... Kilowatt (ELAL)
kW .... Kilowatt
KW .... Kiloword (BUR)
KW .... Kimmelstiel-Wilson [*Medicine*]
KW .... Kirkwall, Orkney [*Postcode*] (ODBW)
KW .... Knight of William [*Netherlands*]
KW .... Knight of Windsor (ROG)
KW .... Knitwise [*Knitting*]
KW .... Know (ADWA)
KW .... Korean War
KW .... Kraftwagen [*Motor Vehicle*] [*German*]
KW .... Kruskal-Wallis Test [*Fisheries*]
KW .... Kugelberg-Welander Disease (DAVI)
KW .... Kuwait [*ANSI two-letter standard code*] (CNC)
KWA .... Keyword Adapted [*Computer science*]
KWA .... Kodiak Western Alaska Airlines (SAUO)
KWA .... Kwajalein [*Marshall Islands*] [*Airport symbol*] (OAG)
KWA .... Kwantlen College Library [*UTLAS symbol*]
KWA .... Kweiyang [*Republic of China*] [*Seismograph station code, US Geological Survey*] (SEIS)
KWAB .... Big Spring, TX [*Television station call letters*]
KWAC .... Bakersfield, CA [*AM radio station call letters*]
KWAC .... Keyword and Context [*Indexing*] (DIT)
KWAD .... Wadena, MN [*AM radio station call letters*]
KWADE .... Key Word as a Dictionary Entry [*IBM*] [*Indexing system*] (NITA)
K-W AG....... Kitchener-Waterloo Art Gallery (SAUO)
KWAI .... Honolulu, HI [*AM radio station call letters*]
KWAJ .... Kwajalein Atoll (AABC)
KWAK .... Stuttgart, AR [*AM radio station call letters*]
KWAK-FM ... Stuttgart, AR [*FM radio station call letters*]
KWAL .... Wallace, ID [*AM radio station call letters*]
KWAL .... Wallops Island/Wallops Station [*Virginia*] [*ICAO location identifier*] (ICLI)
KWAM .... Memphis, TN [*AM radio station call letters*]
KWAN .... Gualala, CA [*FM radio station call letters*]
Kwansei Gak L Rev... Kwansei Gakuin University. Law Review [*A publication*] (DLA)
Kwansei Gakuin Univ Annual Stud... Kwansei Gakuin University. Annual Studies. Kwansei Gakuin University, Nishinomiya (SAUO)
KWAR .... Waverly, IA [*FM radio station call letters*]
KWAS .... Joplin, MO [*AM radio station call letters*]
KWAT .... Watertown, SD [*AM radio station call letters*]
KWAU .... Korea Women's Associations United (BUAC)
KWAV .... Monterey, CA [*FM radio station call letters*]
KWAX .... Eugene, OR [*FM radio station call letters*]
KWAY .... Waverly, IA [*AM radio station call letters*]
KWAY-FM .... Waverly, IA [*FM radio station call letters*]
KWAZ.......... Needles, CA [*FM radio station call letters*]
KWB............ Keith, Wagener, Barker [*Ophthalmology*]
KWB............ Koch-Weeks Bacillus [*Medicine*] (MELL)
KWBA .... Sierra Vista, AZ [*Television station call letters*] (BROA)
KWBC .... Navasota, TX [*AM radio station call letters*]
KWBC .... Washington [*District of Columbia*] [*ICAO location identifier*] (ICLI)
KWBE.......... Beatrice, NE [*AM radio station call letters*]
KWBF.......... Flagstaff, AZ [*Television station call letters*] (RBYB)
KWBF.......... Katholische Welt-Bibelfoderation [*World Catholic Federation for the Biblical Apostolate - WCFBA*] (EAIO)
KWBG .... Boone, IA [*AM radio station call letters*]
KWBH .... Rexburg, ID [*AM radio station call letters*]
KWBI .... Morrison, CO [*FM radio station call letters*]
KWBK-AM... Beaumont, TX [*AM radio station call letters*] (BROA)
KWBM .... Harrison, AR [*Television station call letters*] (BROA)
KWBN .... Honolulu, HI [*AM radio station call letters*] (BROA)
KWBP .... Salem, OR [*Television station call letters*] (RBYB)
KWBQ .... Santa Fe, NM [*Television station call letters*] (BROA)
KWBR .... Pismo Beach, CA [*FM radio station call letters*]
KWBT .... Muskogee, OK [*Television station call letters*] (BROA)
KWBU .... Waco, TX [*FM radio station call letters*]
KWBW .... Hutchinson, KS [*AM radio station call letters*]
KWBY .... Woodburn, OR [*AM radio station call letters*]
KWC............ K-Band Waveguide Circulator
KWC............ Kentucky Wesleyan College [*Owensboro*]
KWC............ Kierownictwo Walki Cywilnej (BJA)
KWC............ Wycliffe College Library, University of Toronto [*UTLAS symbol*]
KWCB .... Floresville, TX [*FM radio station call letters*]
KWCC .... Kootenay Weed Control Committee (SAUO)
KWCC .... KTACS Warning and Control Center (SAUO)
KWCC-FM ... Muscatine, IA [*FM radio station call letters*] (RBYB)
KWCD .... Bisbee, AZ [*FM radio station call letters*]
KWCH .... Hutchinson, KS [*Television station call letters*]
KWCK .... Searcy, AR [*AM radio station call letters*]
KWCK-FM ... Searcy, AR [*FM radio station call letters*]
KWCL .... Oak Grove, LA [*FM radio station call letters*]
KWCM .... Appleton, MN [*Television station call letters*]
KWCO .... Chickasha, OK [*AM radio station call letters*]
KWCR .... Ogden, UT [*FM radio station call letters*]
KWCV .... Wichita, KS [*Television station call letters*]

KWCW	Walla Walla, WA [FM radio station call letters]
KWCX	Wilcox, AZ [FM radio station call letters]
KWCY-FM	Glendale, AZ [FM radio station call letters] (BROA)
KWD	Consolidated Westrex Development [Vancouver Stock Exchange symbol]
KWD	Draco [Sweden] [Research code symbol]
KWD	Kellwood Co. [NYSE symbol] (SPSG)
KWDA	White Hall, AR [FM radio station call letters]
KWDF	Ball, LA [AM radio station call letters]
KWDK	Tacoma, WA [Television station call letters]
KWDM	West Des Moines, IA [FM radio station call letters]
KWDQ	Woodward, OK [FM radio station call letters]
KWDX	Silsbee, TX [FM radio station call letters]
KWE	Guiyang [China] [Airport symbol] (OAG)
KWE	Keith-Welti-Ernst [Method] [Radiology] (DAVI)
KWE	Kilowatt Electric [DOE] (TAG)
kWe	Kilowatts of Electric Energy
KWE	Knight of the White Eagle [Poland]
KWE	Kweiyang [China] [Airport symbol] (AD)
KWEB	Rochester, MN [AM radio station call letters]
KWED	Seguin, TX [AM radio station call letters]
KWEG-FM	Warm Springs, OR [FM radio station call letters] (BROA)
KWEI	Weiser, ID [AM radio station call letters]
KWEI-FM	Fruitland, ID [FM radio station call letters] (RBYB)
KWEL	Midland, TX [AM radio station call letters]
KWEN	Tulsa, OK [FM radio station call letters]
KWEO	Garberville, CA [FM radio station call letters]
KWES	Ruidoso, NM [FM radio station call letters]
KWES-TV	Odessa, TX [Television station call letters]
KWET	Cheyenne, OK [Television station call letters]
KWEX	San Antonio, TX [Television station call letters]
KWEY	Weatherford, OK [AM radio station call letters]
KWEY-FM	Weatherford, OK [FM radio station call letters]
KWEZ-FM	Santa Margarita, CA [FM radio station call letters] (BROA)
KWF	Kirschner Wire Fixation (MELL)
KWF	Waterfall, AK [Location identifier] [FAA] (FAAL)
KWFC	Kelli Warren Fan Club [Defunct] (EA)
KWFC	Springfield, MO [FM radio station call letters]
KWFH	Parker, AZ [FM radio station call letters]
KWFJ	Roy, WA [FM radio station call letters]
KWFL	Roswell, NM [FM radio station call letters]
KWFM	Kurt Weill Foundation for Music (EA)
KWFM-FM	Tucson, AZ [FM radio station call letters]
KWFR	San Angelo, TX [FM radio station call letters] (RBYB)
KWFS	Wichita Falls, TX [FM radio station call letters]
KWFS-FM	Wichita Falls, TX [FM radio station call letters] (RBYB)
KWFT	Kilowatt Foot (IAA)
KWFT	Wichita Falls, TX [AM radio station call letters]
KWFX	Woodward, OK [FM radio station call letters]
KWG	Kerguelen Working Group (SAUO)
KWG	Stockton, CA [AM radio station call letters]
KWGB-FM	Colby, KS [FM radio station call letters] (BROA)
KWGDF	KWG Resources, Inc. [NASDAQ symbol] (SAG)
KWGN	Denver, CO [Television station call letters]
KWG Rs	KWG Resources, Inc. [Associated Press] (SAG)
KWGS	Tulsa, OK [FM radio station call letters]
Kwh	Kilowatt Hour (EBF)
KWH	Kilowatt Hour [DOE] (TAG)
KWh	Kilowatt-Hour (VLIE)
kWh	Kilowatt-Hour
KWHB	Tulsa, OK [Television station call letters]
KWHD	Castle Rock, CO [Television station call letters]
KWHE	Honolulu, HI [Television station call letters]
kWhe	Kilowatt-Hour Electric
KWHH	Hilo, HI [Television station call letters]
KWHI	Brenham, TX [AM radio station call letters]
KWHL	Anchorage, AK [FM radio station call letters]
KWHM	Kilowatt-Hour Meter
KWHM	Wailuku, HI [Television station call letters]
KWHN	Fort Smith, AR [AM radio station call letters]
KWHN	Haynesville, LA [FM radio station call letters]
KWHO	Weed, CA [FM radio station call letters]
KWHQ	Kenai, AK [FM radio station call letters]
kW-hr	Kilowatt-Hour (ADWA)
kwhr	Kilowatt-Hour (NTIO)
kWhr	Kilowatt-Hour
KWHR	Kilowatthour (ABBR)
KWHT	Pendleton, OR [FM radio station call letters]
KWHW	Altus, OK [AM radio station call letters]
KWHY	Los Angeles, CA [Television station call letters]
KWHY-DT	Los Angeles, CA [Television station call letters] (BROA)
KWI	Kosher Wine Institute (EA)
KWI	Kuwait [Airport symbol] (OAG)
KWi	Wichita Public Library, Wichita, KS [Library symbol] [Library of Congress] (LCLS)
KWiB	Boeing Co., Wichita Division Library (SAUO)
KWiB	[The] Boeing Co., Wichita Division Library, Wichita, KS [Library symbol] [Library of Congress] (LCLS)
KWIC	Kennedy Wilson, Inc. [NASDAQ symbol] (SAG)
KWIC	Kentucky Women's Intercollegiate Conference (PSS)
KWIC	Keyword in Context [Indexing]
KWIC	Topeka, KS [FM radio station call letters]
KWiF	Friends University, Wichita, KS [Library symbol] [Library of Congress] (LCLS)

KWiGS	Church of Jesus Christ of Latter-Day Saints Genealogical Society Library, Wichita Branch (SAUO)
KWiGS	Church of Jesus Christ of Latter-Day Saints, Genealogical Society Library, Wichita Branch, Wichita, KS [Library symbol] [Library of Congress] (LCLS)
KWiIL	Institute of Logopedics, Wichita, KS [Library symbol] [Library of Congress] (LCLS)
KWiK	Kansas Newman College, Wichita, KS [Library symbol] [Library of Congress] (LCLS)
KWIK	KWIK Products International Corp. (SAUO)
KWIK	Pocatello, ID [AM radio station call letters]
KWIL	Albany, OR [AM radio station call letters]
KWiIL	Institute of Logopedics, Wichita (SAUS)
KWIM	Window Rock, AZ [FM radio station call letters]
KWIN	Lodi, CA [FM radio station call letters]
KWIP	Dallas, OR [AM radio station call letters]
KWIP	Keyword Word in Permutation [Indexing] (PDAA)
KWIPS	Kilo Whetstones Per Second (SAUO)
KWIQ	Moses Lake, WA [AM radio station call letters]
KWIQ-FM	Moses Lake, WA [FM radio station call letters]
K-wire	Kirschner wire (SAUS)
KWiSF	Saint Francis Hospital, Wichita, KS [Library symbol] [Library of Congress] (LCLS)
KWiSJ	Saint Joseph Hospital, Wichita, KS [Library symbol] [Library of Congress] (LCLS)
KWIT	Keyword in Title [Indexing]
KWIT	Sioux City, IA [FM radio station call letters]
KWiU	Wichita State University, Wichita, KS [Library symbol] [Library of Congress] (LCLS)
KWiVA	United States Veterans Administration Hospital, Wichita, KS [Library symbol] [Library of Congress] (LCLS)
KWiWC	Wichita Clinic, Wichita, KS [Library symbol] [Library of Congress] (LCLS)
KWiWM	Wesley Medical Center, Wichita, KS [Library symbol] [Library of Congress] (LCLS)
KWIX	Moberly, MO [AM radio station call letters]
KWIZ	Santa Ana, CA [AM radio station call letters]
KWIZ-FM	Santa Ana, CA [FM radio station call letters]
KWJC	Liberty, MO [FM radio station call letters]
KWJG-FM	Kasilof, AK [FM radio station call letters] (BROA)
KWJJ	Portland, OR [AM radio station call letters]
KWJJ-FM	Portland, OR [FM radio station call letters]
KWJM	Farmerville, LA [FM radio station call letters]
KWJZ	Seattle, WA [FM radio station call letters] (RBYB)
KWK	Kampfwagenkanone [Tank Gun] [German military - World War II]
KWK	Kwigillingok [Alaska] [Airport symbol] (OAG)
KWK	Kwigillingok, AK [Location identifier] [FAA] (FAAL)
KWKA	Clovis, NM [AM radio station call letters]
KWKB-TV	Iowa City, IA [TV station call letters] (RBYB)
KWKH	Shreveport, LA [AM radio station call letters]
KWKH-FM	Shreveport, LA [FM radio station call letters]
KWKK	Dardanelle, AR [FM radio station call letters]
KWKM-FM	St. Johns, AZ [FM radio station call letters] (BROA)
KWKQ	Graham, TX [FM radio station call letters]
KWKT	Waco, TX [Television station call letters]
KWKW	Los Angeles, CA [AM radio station call letters]
KWKY	Des Moines, IA [AM radio station call letters]
KWKZ	Charleston, MO [FM radio station call letters]
KWL	Guilin [China] [Airport symbol] (OAG)
KWLA	Many, LA [AM radio station call letters]
KWLC	Decorah, IA [AM radio station call letters]
KWLD	Plainview, TX [FM radio station call letters]
KWLF	Fairbanks, AK [FM radio station call letters]
KWLF	Kodak Wratten Light Filter
KWLL	Casa Grande, AZ [AM radio station call letters]
KWLM	Willmar, MN [AM radio station call letters]
KWLO	Waterloo, IA [AM radio station call letters]
KWLS	Pratt, KS [AM radio station call letters]
KWLT	North Crossett, AR [FM radio station call letters]
KWLV	Many, LA [FM radio station call letters]
KWLW	North Salt Lake City, UT [AM radio station call letters] (BROA)
kWm	Kilowatt Meter
KWM	Korean War Memorial (EA)
KWM	Kowanyama [Australia] [Airport symbol] (OAG)
KWM	K Window Manager (SAUS)
KW/M²	Kilowatts per Square Meter
KWMC	Del Rio, TX [AM radio station call letters]
KWME	Wellington, KS [FM radio station call letters]
KWMJ	Tulsa, OK [Television station call letters]
KWMM-FM	Osage, IA [FM radio station call letters] (BROA)
KWMO	Washington, MO [AM radio station call letters] (BROA)
KWMQ	Southwest City, MO [FM radio station call letters]
KWMR-FM	Point Reyes Station, CA [FM radio station call letters] (BROA)
KWMT	Fort Dodge, IA [AM radio station call letters]
KWMU	St. Louis, MO [FM radio station call letters]
KWMW	Maljamar, NM [FM radio station call letters]
KWMX	Lakewood, CO [FM radio station call letters]
KWMX-FM	Williams, AZ [FM radio station call letters] (BROA)
KWN	Kenwin Shops [AMEX symbol] (TTSB)
KWN	Kenwin Shops, Inc. [AMEX symbol] (SPSG)
KWN	Korean Wideband Network [Communications] [Military] (MCD)
KWN	Quinhagak [Alaska] [Airport symbol] (OAG)
KWN	Quinhagak, AK [Location identifier] [FAA] (FAAL)
KWNA	Winnemucca, NV [AM radio station call letters]
KWNA-FM	Winnemucca, NV [FM radio station call letters]

KWNB .... Hayes Center, NE [*Television station call letters*]
KWNC .... Quincy, WA [*AM radio station call letters*]
KWND .... Kenetech Corp. [*NASDAQ symbol*] (SAG)
KWND .... Springfield, MO [*AM radio station call letters*]
KWNDZ .... KENETECH Cp 8.25% Cv Dep Pfd [*NASDAQ symbol*] (TTSB)
KWNE .... Ukiah, CA [*FM radio station call letters*]
KWNG .... Red Wing, MN [*FM radio station call letters*]
KWNK .... Simi Valley, CA [*AM radio station call letters*]
KWNN .... Turlock, CA [*FM radio station call letters*] (RBYB)
KWNO .... Rushford, MN [*FM radio station call letters*]
KWNO .... Winona, MN [*AM radio station call letters*]
KWNR .... Henderson, NV [*FM radio station call letters*]
KWNS .... Winnsboro, TX [*FM radio station call letters*]
KWNV-TV .... Winnemucca, NV [*TV station call letters*] (RBYB)
KWNWR .... Key West National Wildlife Refuge (SAUO)
KWNX .... Keyword Index Subsystem (SAUO)
KWNZ .... Carson City, NV [*FM radio station call letters*]
KWOA .... Worthington, MN [*AM radio station call letters*]
KWOA-FM .... Worthington, MN [*FM radio station call letters*]
KWOC .... Keyword out of Context [*Indexing*]
KWOC .... Poplar Bluff, MO [*AM radio station call letters*]
KWOCA .... Key Word Online Catalogue Access
KWOD .... Sacramento, CA [*FM radio station call letters*]
KWOF .... Waterloo, IA [*AM radio station call letters*] (RBYB)
KWOK .... Novato, CA [*Television station call letters*] (BROA)
KWOM .... Watertown, MN [*AM radio station call letters*] (RBYB)
KWON .... Bartlesville, OK [*AM radio station call letters*]
KWOR .... Worland, WY [*AM radio station call letters*]
KWOS .... Jefferson City, MO [*AM radio station call letters*]
KWOT .... Keyword out of Title [*Indexing*]
KWOT .... Kilometer-Wave Orbiting Telescope [*NASA*]
KWOW .... Clifton, TX [*FM radio station call letters*]
KWOX .... Woodward, OK [*FM radio station call letters*]
KWOZ .... Mountain View, AR [*FM radio station call letters*]
KWP .... Kierowinctwo Walki Podziemnej (BJA)
KWP .... King World Prod'ns [*NYSE symbol*] (TTSB)
KWP .... King World Productions, Inc. [*NYSE symbol*] (SPSG)
KWP .... Korean Workers' Party [*North Korea*] [*Political party*] (PD)
KWP .... West Point [*Alaska*] [*Airport symbol*] (OAG)
KWP .... West Point, AK [*Location identifier*] [*FAA*] (FAAL)
KWPA-AM .... Pomona, CA [*AM radio station call letters*] (RBYB)
KWPC .... Muscatine, IA [*AM radio station call letters*]
KWPL .... Kitchener-Waterloo Public Library (SAUO)
KWPM .... West Plains, MO [*AM radio station call letters*]
KWPN-FM .... West Point, NE [*FM radio station call letters*]
KWPX .... Bellevue, WA [*Television station call letters*] (BROA)
KWPZ-FM .... Lynden, WA [*FM radio station call letters*] (RBYB)
KWQC .... Davenport, IA [*Television station call letters*]
KWQH-FM ... San Luis Obispo, CA [*FM radio station call letters*] (RBYB)
KWQJ-FM .... Anchorage, AK [*FM radio station call letters*] (RBYB)
KWQL .... Dishman, WA [*AM radio station call letters*]
kWr .... Kilowatts Reactive
KWR .... KW Resources Ltd. [*Vancouver Stock Exchange symbol*]
KWRB .... Bisbee, AZ [*FM radio station call letters*] (RBYB)
KWRB .... Macon/Robins Air Force Base [*Georgia*] [*ICAO location identifier*]
                   (ICLI)
KWRD .... Henderson, TX [*AM radio station call letters*]
KWRD-FM .... Arlington, TX [*FM radio station call letters*] (BROA)
KWRE .... Warrenton, MO [*AM radio station call letters*]
KWRF .... Warren, AR [*AM radio station call letters*]
KWRF-FM .... Warren, AR [*FM radio station call letters*]
KWRI .... Wrightstown/McGuire Air Force Base [*New Jersey*] [*ICAO location identifier*] (ICLI)
KWRK .... Window Rock, AZ [*FM radio station call letters*]
KWRL .... La Grande, OR [*FM radio station call letters*]
KWRM .... Corona, CA [*AM radio station call letters*]
KWRN .... Apple Valley, CA [*AM radio station call letters*] (RBYB)
KWRO .... Coquille, OR [*AM radio station call letters*]
KWRP .... San Jacinto, CA [*FM radio station call letters*]
KWRQ .... Clifton, AZ [*FM radio station call letters*] (RBYB)
KWRR-FM.... Ethete, WY [*FM radio station call letters*] (RBYB)
KWRRI .... Kansas Water Resources Research Institute [*Kansas State University*] [*Department of the Interior*] [*Research center*] (RCD)
KWRRI......... Kentucky Water Resources Research Institute [*University of Kentucky*] [*Lexington, KY*] [*Department of the Interior*] [*Research center*] (RCD)
KWRS .... Spokane, WA [*FM radio station call letters*]
KWRT .... Boonville, MO [*AM radio station call letters*]
KWRV .... Sun Valley, ID [*FM radio station call letters*]
KWRW .... Rusk, TX [*FM radio station call letters*]
KWS............ Kaziranga Wildlife Sanctuary (SAUO)
KWS............ Kenya Wildlife Service
KWS............ Korean Welfare Society [*Australia*]
KWS............ Southwestern College, Winfield, KS [*Library symbol*] [*Library of Congress*] (LCLS)
KWSA .... West Klamath, OR [*AM radio station call letters*]
KWSB .... Gunnison, CO [*FM radio station call letters*]
KWSC .... Wayne, NE [*FM radio station call letters*]
KWSD .... White Sands/Condron Army Air Field [*New Mexico*] [*ICAO location identifier*] (ICLI)
KWSE.......... Williston, ND [*Television station call letters*]
KWSH .... Wewoka, OK [*AM radio station call letters*]
KWSH-FM.... Wewoka, OK [*FM radio station call letters*] (BROA)
KWSJ.......... Saint John's College, Winfield, KS [*Library symbol*] [*Library of Congress*] (LCLS)

KWSJ-FM ... Haysville, KS [*FM radio station call letters*] (RBYB)
KWSK-FM... Daingerfield, TX [*FM radio station call letters*] (RBYB)
KWSL .... Sioux City, IA [*AM radio station call letters*] (RBYB)
KWSM .... Korean War Service Medal (SAUO)
KWSM .... Sherman, TX [*FM radio station call letters*]
KWSN .... Sioux Falls, SD [*AM radio station call letters*]
KWSO .... Warm Springs, OR [*FM radio station call letters*]
KWSP .... Santa Margarita, CA [*FM radio station call letters*]
KWST .... Brawley, CA [*FM radio station call letters*]
KWSU .... Pullman, WA [*AM radio station call letters*]
KWSU-TV ... Pullman, WA [*Television station call letters*]
KWSW .... Eureka, CA [*AM radio station call letters*]
KWSWA ...... Kansas Wine and Spirits Wholesalers Association (SRA)
kWt .... Kilowatt, Thermal
KWT .... Kuwait [*ANSI three-letter standard code*] (CNC)
Kwt .... Kuwait (MILB)
KWT .... Kwethluk [*Alaska*] [*Airport symbol*] (OAG)
KWT .... Kwethluk, AK [*Location identifier*] [*FAA*] (FAAL)
kW(th) .... Kilowatt, Thermal
KWTO .... Springfield, MO [*AM radio station call letters*]
KWTO-FM ... Springfield, MO [*FM radio station call letters*]
KWTR .... Georgetown, TX [*AM radio station call letters*]
KWTR-FM ... Big Lake, TX [*FM radio station call letters*] (BROA)
KWTS.......... Canyon, TX [*FM radio station call letters*]
KWTV .... Oklahoma City, OK [*Television station call letters*]
KWTX .... Waco, TX [*AM radio station call letters*]
KWTX-FM ... Waco, TX [*FM radio station call letters*]
KWTX-TV ... Waco, TX [*Television station call letters*]
KWTY .... Cartago, CA [*FM radio station call letters*]
KWU .... Kansas Wesleyan University [*Salina*]
KWU .... Kawau Island [*New Zealand*] [*Airport symbol*] (AD)
KWU .... Kraftwerksunion [*Germany*]
KWUA .... Clovis, NM [*FM radio station call letters*]
KWUC .... Keyword and Universal Decimal Classification (PDAA)
KWUF-AM ... Pagosa Springs, CO [*AM radio station call letters*] (BROA)
KWUF-FM ... Pagosa Springs, CO [*FM radio station call letters*] (BROA)
KWUN-AM ... Murray, UT [*AM radio station call letters*] (BROA)
KWUR .... Clayton, MO [*FM radio station call letters*]
KWVA .... Eugene, OR [*FM radio station call letters*]
KWVA .... Korean War Veterans Association (EA)
KWVE .... San Clemente, CA [*FM radio station call letters*]
KWVM .... Korean War Veterans Memorial [*Defunct*] (EA)
KWVR .... Enterprise, OR [*AM radio station call letters*]
KWVR-FM ... Enterprise, OR [*FM radio station call letters*]
KWVV .... Homer, AK [*FM radio station call letters*]
KWW .... Asbury College, Wilmore, KY [*OCLC symbol*] (OCLC)
KWWC .... Columbia, MO [*FM radio station call letters*]
KWWD .... Wildwood/Cape May County [*New Jersey*] [*ICAO location identifier*] (ICLI)
KWWF-FM ... West Yellowstone, MT [*FM radio station call letters*] (RBYB)
KWWJ.......... Baytown, TX [*AM radio station call letters*]
KWWK .... Rochester, MN [*FM radio station call letters*]
KWWL .... Waterloo, IA [*Television station call letters*]
KWWR .... Mexico, MO [*FM radio station call letters*]
KWWS-FM ... Walla Walla, WA [*FM radio station call letters*] (RBYB)
KWwUT........ United Telecommunications/U.S. Sprint, Westwood, KS [*Library symbol*] [*Library of Congress*] (LCLS)
KWWV .... Morro Bay, CA [*FM radio station call letters*]
KWWW .... Quincy, WA [*AM radio station call letters*]
KWWX .... Wenatchee, WA [*FM radio station call letters*]
KWX .... Kiwai Island [*Papua New Guinea*] [*Airport symbol*] (OAG)
KWXA .... Durango, CO [*FM radio station call letters*]
KWXD .... Asbury, MO [*FM radio station call letters*]
KWXE .... Glenwood, AR [*FM radio station call letters*]
KWXH .... Sun City, CA [*FM radio station call letters*]
KWXI .... Glenwood, AR [*AM radio station call letters*]
KWXI-AM .... Glenwood, AR [*AM radio station call letters*] (RBYB)
KWXT .... Dardanelle, AR [*AM radio station call letters*]
KWXX .... Hilo, HI [*FM radio station call letters*]
KWXY .... Cathedral City, CA [*AM radio station call letters*]
KWXY-FM ... Cathedral City, CA [*FM radio station call letters*]
KWY .... Key Way
KWYB .... Butte, MT [*Television station call letters*]
KWYD .... Colorado Springs, CO [*AM radio station call letters*]
KWYI .... Kawaihae, HI [*FM radio station call letters*]
KWYK .... Aztec, NM [*FM radio station call letters*]
KWYN .... Wynne, AR [*AM radio station call letters*]
KWYN-FM ... Wynne, AR [*FM radio station call letters*]
KWYO .... Sheridan, WY [*AM radio station call letters*]
KWYO-FM ... Sheridan, WY [*FM radio station call letters*]
KWYR .... Winner, SD [*AM radio station call letters*]
KWYR-FM ... Winner, SD [*FM radio station call letters*]
KWYS .... West Yellowstone, MT [*AM radio station call letters*]
KWYX .... Jasper, TX [*FM radio station call letters*]
KWYY-FM ... Casper, WY [*FM radio station call letters*] (BROA)
KWYZ.......... Everett, WA [*AM radio station call letters*]
KXZ............. Kolwezi [*Zaire*] [*Airport symbol*] (AD)
KX .... Cayman Airways [*ICAO designator*] (AD)
KX .... Cayman Airways [*Airline flight code*] (ODBW)
KX .... Cayman Airways Ltd. (SAUO)
KX .... [*The*] Holy Bible (1955) [*R.A. Knox*] [*A publication*] (BJA)
KXA .... Kasaan, AK [*Location identifier*] [*FAA*] (FAAL)
KXAA .... Rock Island, WA [*FM radio station call letters*]
KXAC .... St. James, MN [*FM radio station call letters*]
KXAL........... Pittsburg, TX [*FM radio station call letters*]

KXAM Mesa, AZ [*AM radio station call letters*]
KXAM-TV Llano, TX [*Television station call letters*]
KXAN Austin, TX [*Television station call letters*]
KXAR Hope, AR [*AM radio station call letters*]
KXAR-FM Hope, AR [*FM radio station call letters*]
KXAS Fort Worth, TX [*Television station call letters*]
KXAS-DT Fort Worth, TX [*Television station call letters*] (BROA)
KXAX St. James, MN [*FM radio station call letters*]
KXAZ Page, AZ [*FM radio station call letters*]
KXBA-FM Nikiski, AK [*FM radio station call letters*] (BROA)
KXBJ Victoria, TX [*FM radio station call letters*]
KXBK Bryan, TX [*FM radio station call letters*] (BROA)
KXBR-AM Minneapolis, MN [*AM radio station call letters*] (BROA)
KXBS Santa Paula, CA [*FM radio station call letters*]
KXBT Vallejo, CA [*AM radio station call letters*]
KXBX Lakeport, CA [*AM radio station call letters*]
KXBX-FM Lakeport, CA [*FM radio station call letters*]
KXBZ-FM Manhattan, KS [*FM radio station call letters*] (RBYB)
KXC Keleket X-Ray Corp.
KXCA Lawton, OK [*AM radio station call letters*] (BROA)
KXCC Rockport, TX [*FM radio station call letters*]
KXCI Tucson, AZ [*FM radio station call letters*]
KXCL Yuba City, CA [*FM radio station call letters*]
KXCR El Paso, TX [*FM radio station call letters*]
KXCV Maryville, MO [*FM radio station call letters*]
KXDA Las Cruces, NM [*FM radio station call letters*] (RBYB)
KXDC Carmel, CA [*FM radio station call letters*] (RBYB)
KXDD Yakima, WA [*FM radio station call letters*]
KXDG Webb City, MO [*FM radio station call letters*] (RBYB)
KXDL Browerville, MN [*FM radio station call letters*]
KXEB Sherman, TX [*AM radio station call letters*]
KXED Los Angeles, CA [*AM radio station call letters*]
KXEG Tolleson, AZ [*AM radio station call letters*]
KXEI Havre, MT [*FM radio station call letters*]
KXEL Waterloo, IA [*AM radio station call letters*]
KXEM Bakersfield, CA [*AM radio station call letters*] (RBYB)
KXEN Festus-St. Louis, MO [*AM radio station call letters*]
KXEO Mexico, MO [*AM radio station call letters*]
KXEQ Reno, NV [*AM radio station call letters*]
KXEW South Tucson, AZ [*AM radio station call letters*]
KXEX Fresno, CA [*AM radio station call letters*]
KXEZ Los Angeles, CA [*FM radio station call letters*]
KXEZ-FM Farmersville, TX [*FM radio station call letters*] (BROA)
KXF Kodak X-Ray Film
KXF Koro [*Fiji*] [*Airport symbol*] (OAG)
KXFE Dumas, AR [*FM radio station call letters*]
KXFG-FM Sun City, CA [*FM radio station call letters*] (RBYB)
KXFM Santa Maria, CA [*FM radio station call letters*]
KXFS Ventura, CA [*AM radio station call letters*] (BROA)
KXFX Santa Rosa, CA [*FM radio station call letters*]
KXGA Glennallen, AK [*FM radio station call letters*] (RBYB)
KXGE-FM Dubuque, IA [*FM radio station call letters*] (BROA)
KXGF Great Falls, MT [*AM radio station call letters*]
KXGJ Bay City, TX [*FM radio station call letters*]
KXGL-FM San Diego, CA [*FM radio station call letters*] (BROA)
KXGM Muenster, TX [*FM radio station call letters*]
KXGN Glendive, MT [*AM radio station call letters*]
KXGN-TV Glendive, MT [*Television station call letters*]
KXGO Arcata, CA [*FM radio station call letters*]
KXGR Green Valley, AZ [*Television station call letters*]
KXGT-FM Jamestown, ND [*FM radio station call letters*] (RBYB)
KXHA Shafter, CA [*FM radio station call letters*]
KXHT-FM Marion, AR [*FM radio station call letters*] (BROA)
KXHV Sacramento, CA [*FM radio station call letters*]
KXIA Marshalltown, IA [*FM radio station call letters*]
KXIC Iowa City, IA [*AM radio station call letters*]
KXII Sherman, TX [*Television station call letters*]
KXIL-FM Sanger, TX [*FM radio station call letters*] (BROA)
KXIO Clarksville, AR [*FM radio station call letters*]
KXIT Dalhart, TX [*AM radio station call letters*]
KXIT-FM Dalhart, TX [*FM radio station call letters*]
KXIX Bend, OR [*FM radio station call letters*]
KXJB Valley City, ND [*Television station call letters*]
KXJK Forrest City, AR [*AM radio station call letters*]
KXJZ Sacramento, CA [*FM radio station call letters*]
KXKB Tahoe City, CA [*FM radio station call letters*]
KXKC New Iberia, LA [*FM radio station call letters*]
KXKK Lordsburg, NM [*FM radio station call letters*]
KXKK-FM Park Rapids, MN [*FM radio station call letters*] (BROA)
KXKL Denver, CO [*AM radio station call letters*]
KXKL-FM Denver, CO [*FM radio station call letters*]
KXKM McCarthy, AK [*FM radio station call letters*] (RBYB)
KXKQ Safford, AZ [*FM radio station call letters*]
KXKS Albuquerque, NM [*AM radio station call letters*]
KXKT Atlantic, IA [*FM radio station call letters*]
KXKX Knob Noster, MO [*FM radio station call letters*]
KXKZ Ruston, LA [*FM radio station call letters*]
KXL Portland, OR [*AM radio station call letters*]
KXLA Rayville, LA [*AM radio station call letters*]
KXLC La Crescent, MN [*FM radio station call letters*]
KXLE Ellensburg, WA [*AM radio station call letters*]
KXLE-FM Ellensburg, WA [*FM radio station call letters*]
KXLF Butte, MT [*Television station call letters*]
KXL-FM Portland, OR [*FM radio station call letters*] (BROA)
KXLI St. Cloud, MN [*Television station call letters*]
KXLK Haysville, KS [*FM radio station call letters*]
KXLM Oxnard, CA [*FM radio station call letters*]
KXLN Rosenburg, TX [*Television station call letters*]
KXLO Lewistown, MT [*AM radio station call letters*]
KXLP New Ulm, MN [*FM radio station call letters*]
KXLQ Indianola, IA [*AM radio station call letters*] (RBYB)
KXLR Fairbanks, AK [*FM radio station call letters*]
KXLS Alva, OK [*FM radio station call letters*]
KXLT Eagle, ID [*FM radio station call letters*]
KXLT-TV Rochester, MN [*Television station call letters*]
KXLU Los Angeles, CA [*FM radio station call letters*]
KXLY Spokane, WA [*AM radio station call letters*]
KXLY-DT Spokane, WA [*Television station call letters*] (BROA)
KXLY-FM Spokane, WA [*FM radio station call letters*]
KXLY-TV Spokane, WA [*Television station call letters*]
KXMA Dickinson, ND [*Television station call letters*]
KXMB Bismarck, ND [*Television station call letters*]
KXMC Minot, ND [*Television station call letters*]
KXMD Williston, ND [*Television station call letters*]
KXME-FM Kaneohe, HI [*FM radio station call letters*] (BROA)
KXMG-AM Los Angeles, CA [*AM radio station call letters*] (RBYB)
KXMR Bismarck, ND [*AM radio station call letters*] (RBYB)
KXMS Joplin, MO [*FM radio station call letters*]
KXMX Cedar Rapids, IA [*FM radio station call letters*] (RBYB)
KXND Minot, ND [*Television station call letters*] (BROA)
KXNE Norfolk, NE [*FM radio station call letters*]
KXNE-TV Norfolk, NE [*Television station call letters*]
KXNO North Las Vegas, NV [*AM radio station call letters*]
KXNP North Platte, NE [*FM radio station call letters*]
KXNT North Las Vegas, NV [*AM radio station call letters*] (BROA)
KXO El Centro, CA [*AM radio station call letters*]
KXOA Sacramento, CA [*AM radio station call letters*]
KXOA-FM Sacramento, CA [*FM radio station call letters*]
KXOF Bloomfield, IA [*FM radio station call letters*]
KXO-FM El Centro, CA [*FM radio station call letters*]
KXOI Crane, TX [*AM radio station call letters*]
KXOJ Sapulpa, OK [*AM radio station call letters*]
KXOJ-FM Sapulpa, OK [*FM radio station call letters*]
KXOK Florissant, MO [*FM radio station call letters*]
KXOL Brigham City, UT [*AM radio station call letters*] (BROA)
KXOL Clinton, OK [*AM radio station call letters*]
KXOO Elk City, OK [*FM radio station call letters*] (RBYB)
KXOQ Kennett, MO [*FM radio station call letters*] (RBYB)
KXOR Thibodaux, LA [*FM radio station call letters*]
KXOW Hot Springs, AR [*AM radio station call letters*]
KXOX Sweetwater, TX [*AM radio station call letters*]
KXOX-FM Sweetwater, TX [*FM radio station call letters*]
KXOZ Mountain View, MO [*FM radio station call letters*]
KXPA-AM Pasadena, CA [*AM radio station call letters*] (RBYB)
KXPC Lebanon, OR [*FM radio station call letters*]
KXPK Evergreen, CO [*FM radio station call letters*]
KXPO Grafton, ND [*AM radio station call letters*]
KXPO-FM Grafton, ND [*FM radio station call letters*]
KXPR Sacramento, CA [*FM radio station call letters*]
KXPS Thousand Palms, CA [*AM radio station call letters*] (BROA)
KXPT Las Vegas, NV [*FM radio station call letters*]
KXPW Belle Plaine, IA [*FM radio station call letters*]
KXPX Stillwater, OK [*FM radio station call letters*] (RBYB)
KXPZ Lytle, TX [*FM radio station call letters*]
KXRA Alexandria, MN [*AM radio station call letters*]
KXRA-FM Alexandria, MN [*FM radio station call letters*]
KXRB Sioux Falls, SD [*AM radio station call letters*]
KXRD Victorville, CA [*FM radio station call letters*]
KXRE Manitou Springs, CO [*AM radio station call letters*]
KXRJ Russellville, AR [*FM radio station call letters*]
KXRK Provo, UT [*FM radio station call letters*]
KXRM Colorado Springs, CO [*Television station call letters*]
KXRO Aberdeen, WA [*AM radio station call letters*]
KXRQ-FM Roosevelt, UT [*FM radio station call letters*] (BROA)
KXRS Hemet, CA [*FM radio station call letters*]
KXRX Walla Walla, WA [*FM radio station call letters*]
KXS Kiva Executive Server [*Computer science*]
KXSA-FM Dermott, AR [*FM radio station call letters*]
KXSB Big Bear Lake, CA [*FM radio station call letters*] (RBYB)
KXSM Saint Mary College, Xavier, KS [*Library symbol*] [*Library of Congress*] (LCLS)
KXSP Ventura, CA [*AM radio station call letters*] (RBYB)
KXSR Groveland, CA [*FM radio station call letters*]
KXSS Waite Park, MN [*AM radio station call letters*]
KXST-FM Oceanside, CA [*FM radio station call letters*] (RBYB)
KXTA Los Angeles, CA [*AM radio station call letters*] (BROA)
KXTC Thoreau, NM [*FM radio station call letters*]
KXTD Wagoner, OK [*AM radio station call letters*]
KXTE-FM Rahrump, NV [*FM radio station call letters*] (RBYB)
KXTF Twin Falls, ID [*Television station call letters*] (BROA)
KXTJ Beaumont, TX [*FM radio station call letters*]
KXTK-AM Des Moines, IA [*AM radio station call letters*] (RBYB)
KXTL Butte, MT [*AM radio station call letters*]
KXTN San Antonio, TX [*AM radio station call letters*]
KXTN-FM San Antonio, TX [*FM radio station call letters*]
KXTO Reno, NV [*AM radio station call letters*]
KXTP Superior, WI [*AM radio station call letters*]
KXTQ Lubbock, TX [*AM radio station call letters*]
KXTQ-FM Lubbock, TX [*FM radio station call letters*]
KXTR Kansas City, MO [*FM radio station call letters*]

KXTV............ Sacramento, CA [*Television station call letters*]
KXTX............ Dallas, TX [*Television station call letters*]
KXTZ-FM...... Pismo Beach, CA [*FM radio station call letters*] (BROA)
KXU............. Kastamonu [*Turkey*] [*Airport symbol*] (AD)
KXU............. Keyword Transformation Unit [*Computer science*] (MHDI)
KXUS............ Springfield, MO [*FM radio station call letters*]
KXUX............ Bend, OR [*AM radio station call letters*]
KXVO............ Omaha, NE [*Television station call letters*] (RBYB)
KXXI............. Gallup, NM [*FM radio station call letters*]
KXXK............ Chickasha, OK [*FM radio station call letters*]
KXXL............ Crane, TX [*FM radio station call letters*]
KXXL-FM...... Sun Valley, NV [*FM radio station call letters*] (BROA)
KXXM-FM..... San Antonio, TX [*FM radio station call letters*] (BROA)
KXXO............ Olympia, WA [*FM radio station call letters*]
KXXR-FM...... Minneapolis, MN [*FM radio station call letters*] (BROA)
KXXS............ Toppenish, WA [*FM radio station call letters*]
KXXT............ Santa Barbara, CA [*AM radio station call letters*] (BROA)
KXXV............ Waco, TX [*Television station call letters*]
KXXX............ Colby, KS [*AM radio station call letters*]
KXXY............ Oklahoma City, OK [*AM radio station call letters*]
KXXY-FM...... Oklahoma City, OK [*FM radio station call letters*]
KXXZ............ Barstow, CA [*FM radio station call letters*]
KXYL............ Brownwood, TX [*AM radio station call letters*]
KXYL-FM...... Brownwood, TX [*FM radio station call letters*]
KXYQ............ Milwaukie, OR [*AM radio station call letters*]
KXYZ............ Houston, TX [*AM radio station call letters*]
KXZN-FM...... Sanger, TX [*FM radio station call letters*] (BROA)
KXZZ............ Lake Charles, LA [*AM radio station call letters*]
KY............... Cayman Islands [*ANSI two-letter standard code*] (CNC)
KY............... Kabaka Yekka [*The King Alone*] [*Uganda*] [*Suspended*] [*Political party*]
KY............... Kabaka Yekka Party (SAUO)
KY............... Kapustin Yar [*Test Facility*] [*US prefix for Soviet-Russian developmental missiles*] (DOMA)
KY............... Kentucky [*Postal code*] (AFM)
Ky............... Kentucky (ODBW)
Ky............... Kentucky Department of Libraries, Frankfort, KY [*Library symbol*] [*Library of Congress*] (LCLS)
Ky............... Kentucky Reports [*A publication*] (AAGC)
KY............... Kentucky Supreme Court Reports [*1879-1951*] [*A publication*] (DLA)
KY............... Kent Yeomanry [*Military unit*] [*British*]
KY............... Key
KY............... Keyhole [*United States reconnaissance satellite*] (DOMA)
KY............... Keying (VLIE)
KY............... Keying Devices [*JETDS nomenclature*] [*Military*] (CET)
KY............... Kol Yisroel [*Israeli Broadcasting Service*]
Ky............... Kyrie (GROV)
KY............... Kyrie [*Liturgical*]
KY............... Sun West [*ICAO designator*] (AD)
KY............... thousand years (SAUS)
KyA............. Ashland Public Library, Ashland, KY [*Library symbol*] [*Library of Congress*] (LCLS)
Kya............. Kenya (MILB)
KYA............. Konya [*Turkey*] [*Airport symbol*] (AD)
KYA............. Kyakhta [*Former USSR*] [*Seismograph station code, US Geological Survey*] [*Closed*] (SEIS)
kya.............. thousands of years ago (SAUO)
KYA............. Yana Air Cargo (Kenya) Ltd. [*ICAO designator*] (FAAC)
KY Admin Reg... Kentucky Administrative Register [*A publication*] (DLA)
KY Admin Regs... Kentucky Administration Regulations Service [*A publication*] (DLA)
Ky Admin Regs... Kentucky Administrative Regulations [*A publication*] (AAGC)
KYAJ............ Merced, CA [*FM radio station call letters*]
KYAK............ Anchorage, AK [*AM radio station call letters*]
Ky-Ar........... Kentucky Department of Libraries and Archives, Kentucky State Archives, Frankfort, KY [*Library symbol*] [*Library of Congress*] (LCLS)
KYAT............ Keokuk, IA [*FM radio station call letters*]
KYAX............ Alturas, CA [*FM radio station call letters*]
KYB............. Kayaba Industry Co. [*Auto industry supplier*]
KYB............. Know Your Body (DAVI)
KYBA............ Stewartville, MN [*FM radio station call letters*]
KyBB............ Berea College, Berea, KY [*Library symbol*] [*Library of Congress*] (LCLS)
KYBB-FM...... Canton, SD [*FM radio station call letters*] (BROA)
KYBC-AM..... Cottonwood, AZ [*AM radio station call letters*] (RBYB)
KYBD............ Copeland, KS [*FM radio station call letters*]
KYBD............ Keyboard (MSA)
KYBE............ Frederick, OK [*FM radio station call letters*]
KYBG............ Aurora, CO [*AM radio station call letters*]
KyBgW......... Western Kentucky University, Bowling Green, KY [*Library symbol*] [*Library of Congress*] (LCLS)
KyBgW-K...... Western Kentucky University, Kentucky Library, Bowling Green, KY [*Library symbol*] [*Library of Congress*] (LCLS)
KYBI-FM...... Huntington, TX [*FM radio station call letters*] (RBYB)
KYBJ............ Lake Jackson, TX [*FM radio station call letters*] (RBYB)
Ky-BPH......... Kentucky Library for the Blind and Physically Handicapped, Frankfort, KY [*Library symbol*] [*Library of Congress*] (LCLS)
KYBRD......... Keyboard
KYBR-FM...... Espanola, NM [*FM radio station call letters*] (RBYB)
KyBrU.......... Union College, Barbourville (SAUO)
KyBvU.......... Union College, Barbourville, KY [*Library symbol*] [*Library of Congress*] (LCLS)
KYC............. HCL Aviation, Inc. [*ICAO designator*] (FAAC)
KYC............. Keystone Camera Products Corp. (SAUO)
KYC............. Klan Youth Corps (SAUO)
KYC............. Knickerbocker Yacht Club (SAUO)
KYC............. Know Your Customer [*Investment term*] (DFIT)
KYCA........... Prescott, AZ [*AM radio station call letters*]
KyCambC..... Campbellsville College, Campbellsville, KY [*Library symbol*] [*Library of Congress*] (LCLS)
KyCarD........ Dow Corning Corp., TIS Library, Carrollton, KY [*Library symbol*] [*Library of Congress*] (LCLS)
KYCC-FM..... Livingston, CA [*FM radio station call letters*] (BROA)
KYCH........... Convent General of the Knights York Cross of Honour (EA)
KYCK........... Crookston, MN [*FM radio station call letters*]
KYCM-FM.... Bastrop, TX [*FM radio station call letters*] (BROA)
KYCN........... Wheatland, WY [*AM radio station call letters*]
KYCN-FM..... Wheatland, WY [*FM radio station call letters*]
KyColW........ Lindsey Wilson College, Columbia, KY [*Library symbol*] [*Library of Congress*] (LCLS)
KY Comment'r... Kentucky Commentator [*A publication*] (DLA)
KyCov.......... Kenton County Public Library, Covington, KY [*Library symbol*] [*Library of Congress*] (LCLS)
KyCovStE..... Saint Elizabeth Medical Center, Covington, KY [*Library symbol*] [*Library of Congress*] (LCLS)
KYCP........... Keystone Camera Products Corporation (SAUO)
KYCR........... Golden Valley, MN [*AM radio station call letters*]
KYCS........... Rock Springs, WY [*FM radio station call letters*]
KYCW........... Seattle, WA [*FM radio station call letters*]
KYCX........... Mexia, TX [*FM radio station call letters*]
KYCY........... San Francisco, CA [*FM radio station call letters*]
KYD............. Kilo Yard
Kyd............. Kyd on Bills of Exchange [*A publication*] (DLA)
Kyd Aw........ Kyd on Awards [*A publication*] (DLA)
Kyd Bills...... Kyd on Bills of Exchange [*A publication*] (DLA)
KyDC........... Centre College of Kentucky, Danville, KY [*Library symbol*] [*Library of Congress*] (LCLS)
Kyd Corp...... Kyd on Corporations [*A publication*] (DLA)
KYDE........... Pine Bluff, AR [*AM radio station call letters*]
KY Dec......... Sneed's Kentucky Decisions [*2 Kentucky*] [*A publication*] (DLA)
KYDKAJ...... Annual Report. Kyoritsu College of Pharmacy (journ.) (SAUS)
KYDS........... Kiloyards (MCD)
KYDS........... Sacramento, CA [*FM radio station call letters*]
KYDT-FM..... Sundance, WY [*FM radio station call letters*] (RBYB)
KYDZ........... Cody, WY [*FM radio station call letters*]
KYEA........... West Monroe, LA [*FM radio station call letters*]
KYEE........... Alamogordo, NM [*FM radio station call letters*]
KYEG-FM..... Canadian, TX [*FM radio station call letters*] (RBYB)
KyeKtts....... Kaye Kotts Associates, Inc. [*Associated Press*] (SAG)
KYERI.......... Know Your Endorsers - Require Identification [*Advice to businessmen and others who cash checks for the public*]
KyErP.......... Seminary of Saint Pius X, Erlanger, KY [*Library symbol*] [*Library of Congress*] (LCLS)
KYES........... Anchorage, AK [*Television station call letters*]
KYET........... Williams, AZ [*AM radio station call letters*]
KYEZ........... Salina, KS [*FM radio station call letters*]
KYF............. Kentucky First Bancorp [*AMEX symbol*] (TTSB)
KYF............. Kentucky First Bancorp, Inc. [*AMEX symbol*] (SAG)
KYF............. Yeelirie [*Australia*] [*Airport symbol*] (OAG)
KYFA........... Amarillo, TX [*FM radio station call letters*]
KYFC........... Kansas City, MO [*Television station call letters*]
KyFc........... United States Army, Fort Campbell Post Library (R. F. Sink Memorial Library), Fort Campbell, KY [*Library symbol*] [*Library of Congress*] (LCLS)
KyFCE.......... Kentucky Council on Higher Education, Frankfort, KY [*Library symbol*] [*Library of Congress*] (LCLS)
KyFkAS........ United States Army Armor School, Fort Knox, KY [*Library symbol*] [*Library of Congress*] (LCLS)
KYFL........... Monroe, LA [*FM radio station call letters*]
KyFLR.......... Legislative Research Commission, Library, Frankfort, KY [*Library symbol*] [*Library of Congress*] (LCLS)
KYFM........... Bartlesville, OK [*FM radio station call letters*]
KyFmTM....... Thomas More College, Fort Mitchell, KY [*Library symbol*] [*Library of Congress*] (LCLS)
KYFO........... Ogden, UT [*AM radio station call letters*]
KYFO-FM..... Ogden, UT [*FM radio station call letters*]
Ky For Lang Q... Kentucky Foreign Language Quarterly. University of Kentucky. Lexington (SAUO)
KYFP-FM..... Palestine, TX [*FM radio station call letters*] (BROA)
KYFR........... Shenandoah, IA [*AM radio station call letters*]
KYFS........... San Antonio, TX [*FM radio station call letters*]
KyFSC.......... Kentucky State University, Frankfort, KY [*Library symbol*] [*Library of Congress*] (LCLS)
KY Fst......... Kentucky First Bancorp, Inc. [*Associated Press*] (SAG)
KY FstB....... Kentucky First Bancorp, Inc. [*Associated Press*] (SAG)
KYFT........... Lubbock, TX [*FM radio station call letters*]
KYFW........... Wichita, KS [*FM radio station call letters*]
KYFX........... Little Rock, AR [*FM radio station call letters*]
Ky-G........... Kentucky Department of Libraries and Archives, Kentucky Guide Project, Frankfort, KY [*Library symbol*] [*Library of Congress*] (LCLS)
KyGeC.......... Georgetown College, Georgetown, KY [*Library symbol*] [*Library of Congress*] (LCLS)
KYGL........... Texarkana, AR [*FM radio station call letters*] (RBYB)
KYGO........... Lakewood, CO [*AM radio station call letters*]
KYGO-FM..... Denver, CO [*FM radio station call letters*]
KyHaHi......... Harrodsburg Historical Society, Harrodsburg, KY [*Library symbol*] [*Library of Congress*] (LCLS)

KyHhN .... Northern Kentucky University, Highland Heights, KY [*Library symbol*] [*Library of Congress*] (LCLS)

KyHhN-L ..... Northern Kentucky University, B. P. Chase College of Law, Covington (SAUS)

KyHhN-L ..... Northern Kentucky University, B. P. Chase College of Law, Covington, KY [*Library symbol*] [*Library of Congress*] (LCLS)

KyHi............ Kentucky Historical Society, Frankfort, KY [*Library symbol*] [*Library of Congress*] (LCLS)

KYHL .... Keyhole (ABBR)

KyHopC........ Hopkinsville Community College, Hopkinsville, KY [*Library symbol*] [*Library of Congress*] (LCLS)

KYHT .... Yermo, CA [*FM radio station call letters*]

KyHzC.......... Hazard Community College, Hazard, KY [*Library symbol*] [*Library of Congress*] (LCLS)

KYI E .... Kyle Technology Corp. (SAUO)

KYIN........... Mason City, IA [*Television station call letters*]

KYIP............ Detroit/Willow Run [*Michigan*] [*ICAO location identifier*] (ICLI)

KYIS............ Oklahoma City, OK [*FM radio station call letters*]

KYIX............ South Oroville, CA [*FM radio station call letters*] (RBYB)

KYIZ............ Renton, WA [*AM radio station call letters*] (BROA)

KYJC-FM...... Grants Pass, OR [*FM radio station call letters*]

KYJT........... Yuma, AZ [*FM radio station call letters*] (RBYB)

KYK............. Karluk [*Alaska*] [*Airport symbol*] (OAG)

KYK............. Karluk, AK [*Location identifier*] [*FAA*] (FAAL)

KYK............. Kayak (ABBR)

KYK............. Kayak Island [*Alaska*] [*Seismograph station code, US Geological Survey*] (SEIS)

KYK............. Kelley-Kerr Energy [*Vancouver Stock Exchange symbol*]

KYKA .... Naches, WA [*FM radio station call letters*]

KYKC .... Byng, OK [*FM radio station call letters*]

KYKD .... Bethel, AK [*FM radio station call letters*]

KYKF........... San Fernando, CA [*FM radio station call letters*]

KYKK .... Hobbs, NM [*AM radio station call letters*]

KYKM.......... Yoakum, TX [*FM radio station call letters*] (RBYB)

KYKN .... Keizer, OR [*AM radio station call letters*]

KYKN .... Nephi, UT [*FM radio station call letters*]

KYKN .... Pkynocytes [*Hematology*] (DAVI)

KYKR .... Beaumont, TX [*FM radio station call letters*]

KYKS .... Lufkin, TX [*FM radio station call letters*]

KYKX .... Longview, TX [*FM radio station call letters*]

KYKY .... St. Louis, MO [*FM radio station call letters*]

KYKZ .... Lake Charles, LA [*FM radio station call letters*]

KY L............ Kentucky Law Reporter [*A publication*] (DLA)

KYL............. Kyle Resources, Inc. [*Vancouver Stock Exchange symbol*]

KYLA-FM...... Homer, LA [*FM radio station call letters*] (BROA)

KY Law Rep... Kentucky Law Reporter [*A publication*] (DLA)

KYLC........... Osage Beach, MO [*FM radio station call letters*]

KYLD .... San Mateo, CA [*FM radio station call letters*]

KYLE .... Bryan, TX [*Television station call letters*]

KYLM.......... Yuma Marine Corps Air Station (SAUS)

KyLo .... Louisville Free Public Library, Louisville, KY [*Library symbol*] [*Library of Congress*] (LCLS)

KyLoB .... Bellarmine College, Louisville, KY [*Library symbol*] [*Library of Congress*] (LCLS)

KyloB-M....... Bellarmine College, Thomas Merton Studies Center (SAUS)

KyLoB-M...... Bellarmine College, Thomas Merton Studies Center, Louisville, KY [*Library symbol*] [*Library of Congress*] (LCLS)

KyLoBW....... Brown & Williamson Tobacco Corp., Research Department Library, Louisville, KY [*Library symbol*] [*Library of Congress*] (LCLS)

KyLoC.......... Courier-Journal & Louisville Times Co., Inc., Louisville, KY [*Library symbol*] [*Library of Congress*] (LCLS)

KyLoF .... Filson Club, Louisville, KY [*Library symbol*] [*Library of Congress*] (LCLS)

KyloJ .... Jefferson Community College, Louisville (SAUS)

KyLoJ.......... Jefferson Community College, Louisville, KY [*Library symbol*] [*Library of Congress*] (LCLS)

KyLoL .... Louisville Presbyterian Seminary, Louisville, KY [*Library symbol*] [*Library of Congress*] (LCLS)

KyLoM......... Louisville Medical Library, Louisville, KY [*Library symbol*] [*Library of Congress*] (LCLS)

KyLoN......... Spalding College, Louisville, KY [*Library symbol*] [*Library of Congress*] (LCLS)

KyLoS .... Southern Baptist Theological Seminary, Louisville, KY [*Library symbol*] [*Library of Congress*] (LCLS)

KyLoU......... University of Louisville, Louisville, KY [*Library symbol*] [*Library of Congress*] (LCLS)

KyLoU-Ar ..... University of Louisville, University Archives and Records Center, Louisville, KY [*Library symbol*] [*Library of Congress*] (LCLS)

KyLoU-HS .... University of Louisville, Health Sciences Library, Louisville, KY [*Library symbol*] [*Library of Congress*] (LCLS)

KyLoU-L....... University of Louisville, Law Library, Louisville, KY [*Library symbol*] [*Library of Congress*] (LCLS)

KyLoU-Mu.... University of Louisville, Dwight Anderson Music Library, Louisville, KY [*Library symbol*] [*Library of Congress*] (LCLS)

KyLoV .... United States Veterans Administration Hospital, Louisville, KY [*Library symbol*] [*Library of Congress*] (LCLS)

KYLR .... Huntsville, TX [*AM radio station call letters*]

KY LR.......... Kentucky Law Reporter [*A publication*] (DLA)

KY L Rep...... Kentucky Law Reporter [*A publication*] (DLA)

KY L Rev ..... Kentucky Law Review [*A publication*] (DLA)

KY L Rptr..... Kentucky Law Reporter [*A publication*] (DLA)

KYLS-AM ..... Fredericktown, MO [*AM radio station call letters*] (BROA)

KYLS-FM ..... Ironton, MO [*FM radio station call letters*] (BROA)

KYLT........... Missoula, MT [*AM radio station call letters*]

KYLV-FM ..... Oklahoma City, OK [*FM radio station call letters*] (BROA)

KyLx............ Lexington Public Library, Lexington, KY [*Library symbol*] [*Library of Congress*] (LCLS)

KyLxCB .... Lexington Theological Seminary, Lexington, KY [*Library symbol*] [*Library of Congress*] (LCLS)

KyLxCS .... Council of State Governments, State Information Center, Lexington, KY [*Library symbol*] [*Library of Congress*] (LCLS)

KyLxI .... IBM Corp., Office Products Division, Lexington, KY [*Library symbol*] [*Library of Congress*] (LCLS)

KyLxIMM ...... Institute for Mining and Minerals Research, Lexington, KY [*Library symbol*] [*Library of Congress*] (LCLS)

KyLxK .... Keeneland Association, Inc., Lexington, KY [*Library symbol*] [*Library of Congress*] (LCLS)

KyLxT.......... Transylvania University, Lexington, KY [*Library symbol*] [*Library of Congress*] (LCLS)

KyLxTI .... Lexington Technical Institute, Lexington, KY [*Library symbol*] [*Library of Congress*] (LCLS)

KyLxV .... United States Veterans Administration Hospital, Lexington, KY [*Library symbol*] [*Library of Congress*] (LCLS)

KYLZ .... Santa Cruz, CA [*FM radio station call letters*]

KYMA.......... Yuma, AZ [*Television station call letters*]

KyMadC .... Madisonville Community College, Media Center, Madisonville, KY [*Library symbol*] [*Library of Congress*] (LCLS)

KyMan .... Clay County Public Library, Manchester, KY [*Library symbol*] [*Library of Congress*] (LCLS)

KYMC .... Ballwin, MO [*FM radio station call letters*]

KYMD .... Kentucky Medical Insurance Co. [*NASDAQ symbol*] (NQ)

KyMdC......... Midway Junior College and Pinkerton High School, Midway, KY [*Library symbol*] [*Library of Congress*] (LCLS)

KyMed .... Kentucky Medical Insurance Co. [*Associated Press*] (SAG)

KYMG .... Anchorage, AK [*FM radio station call letters*]

KYMI .... Los Ybanez, TX [*FM radio station call letters*]

KYMN .... Northfield, MN [*AM radio station call letters*]

KYMO .... East Prairie, MO [*AM radio station call letters*]

KYMO .... Kymograph (ABBR)

KYMO-FM ..... East Prairie, MO [*FM radio station call letters*]

KyMoreU ..... Morehead State University (SAUO)

KyMoreU ..... Morehead State University, Morehead, KY [*Library symbol*] [*Library of Congress*] (LCLS)

KYMS.......... Keep Your Mouth Shut

KYMS.......... Santa Ana, CA [*FM radio station call letters*]

KyMurT........ Murray State University, Murray, KY [*Library symbol*] [*Library of Congress*] (LCLS)

KYMV.......... Kennedya Yellow Mosaic Virus [*Plant pathology*]

KYMX.......... Sacramento, CA [*FM radio station call letters*]

KyMyC .... Maysville Community College, Maysville, KY [*Library symbol*] [*Library of Congress*] (LCLS)

KYN .... Kynurenic Acid (DMAA)

KYN .... Kynurenine [*Biochemistry*]

KYN .... Kyrnair [*France*] [*ICAO designator*] (FAAC)

KyNaM........ Nazareth Mother House Archives, Nazareth, KY [*Library symbol*] [*Library of Congress*] (LCLS)

KYND .... Cypress, TX [*AM radio station call letters*]

KYNE .... Omaha, NE [*Television station call letters*]

KYNG .... Dallas, TX [*FM radio station call letters*]

KYNG .... Youngstown [*Ohio*] [*ICAO location identifier*] (ICLI)

KYNO .... Fresno, CA [*AM radio station call letters*]

KYNP .... Khao Yai National Park (SAUO)

KYNT .... Keynote (ABBR)

KYNT .... Yankton, SD [*AM radio station call letters*]

KYNTG .... Keynoting (ABBR)

KYNU .... Jamestown, ND [*FM radio station call letters*]

KYNZ .... Lone Grove, OK [*FM radio station call letters*]

KYO .... Kyocera Corp. [*NYSE symbol*] (SPSG)

KYO .... Kyocera Corp.ADR [*NYSE symbol*] (TTSB)

KYO .... Kyoeera Corp. (SAUO)

KYO .... Kyoto [*Japan*] [*Seismograph station code, US Geological Survey*] (SEIS)

Kyocer .... Kyocera Corp. [*Associated Press*] (SAG)

KYOD-FM...... Casper, WY [*FM radio station call letters*] (BROA)

KYOK .... Houston, TX [*AM radio station call letters*]

KYOO .... Bolivar, MO [*AM radio station call letters*]

KYOO-FM ..... Halfway, MO [*FM radio station call letters*]

KY Op .... Kentucky Court of Appeals Opinions [*A publication*] (DLA)

KY Opin ...... Kentucky Opinions [*A publication*] (DLA)

KYOR-FM ..... Yucca Valley, CA [*FM radio station call letters*] (BROA)

KYOS .... Merced, CA [*AM radio station call letters*]

KYOT-FM ..... Phoenix, AZ [*FM radio station call letters*]

Kyoto L Rev... Kyoto Law Review [*A publication*] (DLA)

Kyot Univ .... Kyoto University (SAUO)

KYOU .... Wendover, NV [*FM radio station call letters*]

KYOU-TV ..... Ottumwa, IA [*Television station call letters*]

KyOw .... Owensboro-Daviess County Public Library, Owensboro, KY [*Library symbol*] [*Library of Congress*] (LCLS)

KyOwB .... Brescia College, Owensboro, KY [*Library symbol*] [*Library of Congress*] (LCLS)

KyOwC .... Owensboro Community College, Owensboro, KY [*Library symbol*] [*Library of Congress*] (LCLS)

KyOwK .... Kentucky Wesleyan College, Owensboro, KY [*Library symbol*] [*Library of Congress*] (LCLS)

KYP............. Kyaukpyu [*Myanmar*] [*Airport symbol*] (OAG)

KYPA-AM ..... Los Angeles, CA [*AM radio station call letters*] (RBYB)

KyPad .... Paducah Public Library, Paducah, KY [*Library symbol*] [*Library of Congress*] (LCLS)

KyPadC........ Paducah Community College, Paducah, KY [*Library symbol*] [*Library of Congress*] (LCLS)

KyParF......... John Fox, Jr. Memorial Library, Paris, KY [*Library symbol*] [*Library of Congress*] (LCLS)

kyph............. Kyphosis [*Orthopedics*] (DAVI)

KyPikC......... Pikeville College, Pikeville, KY [*Library symbol*] [*Library of Congress*] (LCLS)

KYPL-FM .... Yakima, WA [*FM radio station call letters*] (RBYB)

KyPpA.......... Alice Lloyd College, Pippa Passes, KY [*Library symbol*] [*Library of Congress*] (LCLS)

KyPrbC......... Prestonburg Community College, Prestonsburg, KY [*Library symbol*] [*Library of Congress*] (LCLS)

KyPw25........ Kentucky Power Co. [*Associated Press*] (SAG)

KYPX .... Little Rock, AR [*Television station call letters*] (BROA)

KYQQ .... Arkansas City, KS [*FM radio station call letters*]

KYQX .... Weatherford, TX [*FM radio station call letters*] (RBYB)

KY R .... Kentucky Reports [*A publication*] (DLA)

Kyr............... Kiloyear (SAUS)

KYR .... Kyber Resources [*Vancouver Stock Exchange symbol*]

KyRE............ Eastern Kentucky University, Richmond, KY [*Library symbol*] [*Library of Congress*] (LCLS)

KY Rev Stat... Kentucky Revised Statutes [*A publication*] (DLA)

KY Rev Stat & Rules Serv... Kentucky Revised Statutes and Rules Service (Baldwin) [*A publication*] (DLA)

KY Rev Stat Ann... Baldwin's Kentucky Revised Statutes, Annotated [*A publication*] (DLA)

Kyrgyz.......... Kyrgyzstani (DIAR)

KYRK-FM ..... Eunice, NM [*FM radio station call letters*] (RBYB)

KYRM-FM .... Yuma, AZ [*FM radio station call letters*] (BROA)

KYRO .... Potosi, MO [*AM radio station call letters*]

KYRS .... Atwater, NM [*FM radio station call letters*]

KYRV-FM ..... Concordia, MO [*FM radio station call letters*] (BROA)

KYRX .... Chaffee, MO [*FM radio station call letters*]

KYS.............. Kayes [*Mali*] [*Airport symbol*] (OAG)

KYS.............. Kentucky State University, Frankfort, KY [*OCLC symbol*] (OCLC)

KYS.............. Keycorp Industries [*Vancouver Stock Exchange symbol*]

KYS.............. Keys

KYS.............. Kiyosumi - Telemeter [*Japan*] [*Seismograph station code, US Geological Survey*] (SEIS)

KY SBJ .... Kentucky State Bar Journal [*A publication*] (DLA)

KYSC .... Yakima, WA [*FM radio station call letters*]

KYSG .... Coos Bay, OR [*FM radio station call letters*] (RBYB)

Kyshe........... Kyshe's Reports [1808-90] [*A publication*] (DLA)

KYSL............ Frisco, CO [*FM radio station call letters*]

KYSM........... Mankato, MN [*AM radio station call letters*]

KYSM-FM .... Mankato, MN [*FM radio station call letters*]

KYSN .... East Wenatchee, WA [*FM radio station call letters*]

KySoC.......... Somerset Community College, Somerset, KY [*Library symbol*] [*Library of Congress*] (LCLS)

Kysor .... Kysor Industrial Corp. [*Associated Press*] (SAG)

KYSR .... Los Angeles, CA [*FM radio station call letters*]

KYSS-FM ..... Missoula, MT [*FM radio station call letters*]

kyst.............. Keystone (VRA)

KYST............ Texas City, TX [*AM radio station call letters*]

KY St BJ ...... Kentucky State Bar Journal [*A publication*] (DLA)

KY St Law ... Morehead and Brown. Digest of Kentucky Statute Laws [*A publication*] (DLA)

KYSTN .... Keystone (ABBR)

KYSY-FM ..... Ankeny, IA [*FM radio station call letters*] (BROA)

KYT.............. Corporate High Yield Fd II [*NYSE symbol*] (TTSB)

KYT.............. Corporate High Yield II [*NYSE symbol*] (SAG)

KYT.............. Keystone Explorations [*Vancouver Stock Exchange symbol*]

KYT.............. Kyauktaw [*Myanmar*] [*Airport symbol*] (OAG)

KYTC .... Northwood, IA [*FM radio station call letters*]

KYTE .... Newport, OR [*FM radio station call letters*]

KYTI-FM ..... Sheridan, WY [*FM radio station call letters*] (BROA)

KYTN .... Wrightsville, AR [*FM radio station call letters*]

KYTOON....... Kite Balloon [*Air Force*]

KyTrA........... Abbey of Gethsemani, Trappist, KY [*Library symbol*] [*Library of Congress*] (LCLS)

KYTT............ Coos Bay, OR [*FM radio station call letters*]

KYTV........... Springfield, MO [*Television station call letters*]

KYTX........... Beeville, TX [*FM radio station call letters*]

kyu............... Kentucky [*MARC country of publication code*] [*Library of Congress*] (LCCP)

KYU .... Koyukuk [*Alaska*] [*Airport symbol*] (OAG)

KYU .... Koyukuk, AK [*Location identifier*] [*FAA*] (FAAL)

KyU.............. University of Kentucky (SAUO)

KyU.............. University of Kentucky, Chemistry/Physics Library (SAUO)

KyU.............. University of Kentucky, Lexington, KY [*Library symbol*] [*Library of Congress*] (LCLS)

KyU-A .... University of Kentucky, Ashland Community College, Ashland, KY [*Library symbol*] [*Library of Congress*] (LCLS)

KyU-ASC ...... University of Kentucky, Agricultural Science Center, Lexington, KY [*Library symbol*] [*Library of Congress*] (LCLS)

KYUC .... Roland, OK [*FM radio station call letters*]

KyU-C .... University of Kentucky, Southeast Center, Cumberland, KY [*Library symbol*] [*Library of Congress*] (LCLS)

KyU-E .... University of Kentucky, Elizabethtown Community College, Elizabethtown, KY [*Library symbol*] [*Library of Congress*] (LCLS)

KyU-F .... University of Kentucky, Fort Knox Center, Fort Knox, KY [*Library symbol*] [*Library of Congress*] (LCLS)

KYUF .... Uvalde, TX [*FM radio station call letters*]

KyU-H .... University of Kentucky, Northwest Center, Henderson, KY [*Library symbol*] [*Library of Congress*] (LCLS)

KYUK .... Bethel, AK [*AM radio station call letters*]

KYUK-TV ...... Bethel, AK [*Television station call letters*]

KyU-L .... University of Kentucky, Law Library, Lexington, KY [*Library symbol*] [*Library of Congress*] (LCLS)

KYUL-FM ..... Harker Heights, TX [*FM radio station call letters*] (BROA)

KyU-M .... University of Kentucky, Medical Center, Lexington, KY [*Library symbol*] [*Library of Congress*] (LCLS)

KYUM .... Yuma/Yuma Marine Corps Air Station, Yuma International [*Arizona*] [*ICAO location identifier*] (ICLI)

KyU-N .... University of Kentucky, Northern Center, Covington, KY [*Library symbol*] [*Library of Congress*] (LCLS)

KYUNGHEE... KYUNG Hee Nepal Friendship Medical Center (SAUS)

KyU-P .... University of Kentucky, Prestonburg Community College, Prestonburg, KY [*Library symbol*] [*Library of Congress*] (LCLS)

KYUS .... Miles City, MT [*Television station call letters*]

KYUU .... Liberal, KS [*AM radio station call letters*]

KYV.............. Kibris Turk Hava Yollari Ltd. [*Turkey*] [*FAA designator*] (FAAC)

KYVA .... Gallup, NM [*AM radio station call letters*]

KYVE .... Yakima, WA [*Television station call letters*]

KYVU .... Kentucky Virtual University

KYW .... Philadelphia, PA [*AM radio station call letters*]

KyWA .... Asbury College, Wilmore, KY [*Library symbol*] [*Library of Congress*] (LCLS)

KyWAT........ Asbury Theological Seminary, Wilmore, KY [*Library symbol*] [*Library of Congress*] (LCLS)

KyWAT12..... Asbury Theological Seminary, Wilmore (SAUS)

KyWavH....... Waverly Hills Tuberculosis Sanatorium, Waverly Hills, KY [*Library symbol*] [*Library of Congress*] (LCLS)

KY WC Dec . Kentucky Workmen's Compensation Board Decisions [*A publication*] (DLA)

KYW-DT....... Philadelphia, PA [*Television station call letters*] (BROA)

KyWilC......... Cumberland College, Williamsburg, KY [*Library symbol*] [*Library of Congress*] (LCLS)

KyWn .... Clark County Public Library, Winchester, KY [*Library symbol*] [*Library of Congress*] (LCLS)

KyWnS .... Southeastern Christian College, Winchester, KY [*Library symbol*] [*Library of Congress*] (LCLS)

KYW-TV .... Philadelphia, PA [*Television station call letters*]

KYX............. Yalumet [*Papua New Guinea*] [*Airport symbol*] (OAG)

KYXE........... Selah, WA [*AM radio station call letters*]

KYXK .... Gurdon, AR [*FM radio station call letters*]

KYXS .... Mineral Wells, TX [*FM radio station call letters*]

KYXX .... Ozona, TX [*FM radio station call letters*]

KYXY .... San Diego, CA [*FM radio station call letters*]

KYYA .... Billings, MT [*FM radio station call letters*]

KYYD .... Abilene, TX [*AM radio station call letters*]

KYYI .... Burkburnett, TX [*FM radio station call letters*]

KYYK .... Palestine, TX [*FM radio station call letters*]

KYYS .... Kansas City, MO [*FM radio station call letters*]

KYYT .... Goldendale, WA [*FM radio station call letters*]

KYYX .... Minot, ND [*FM radio station call letters*]

KYYY .... Bismarck, ND [*FM radio station call letters*]

KYYZ .... Williston, ND [*FM radio station call letters*]

KYZ............. Kayseri [*Turkey*] [*Airport symbol*] (AD)

Kyzen.......... Kyzen Corp. [*Associated Press*] (SAG)

KYZN........... Kyzen Corp. [*NASDAQ symbol*] (SAG)

KYZN........... Kyzen Corp.'A' [*NASDAQ symbol*] (TTSB)

KYZNW........ Kyzen Corp.Wrrt'A' [*NASDAQ symbol*] (TTSB)

KYZS-L........ Tyler, TX [*AM radio station call letters*]

KYZX........... Pueblo, CO [*FM radio station call letters*]

KYZZ .... San Angelo, TX [*FM radio station call letters*]

KZ .... Dust/Sand Storm [*Meteorology*] (WDAA)

kZ .... duststorm (SAUS)

KZ .... Kaplan-Zuelzer [*Syndrome*] (DAVI)

KZ .... Kazakhstan [*Internet country code*]

KZ .... Ketoconazole (DMAA)

KZ .... Killing Zone [*Military*] [*British*]

KZ .... Kilohertz [*Preferred form is kHz*] [*Electronics*] (MCD)

KZ .... Konzentrationslager [*Concentration Camp*] [*Initials also used in medicine to indicate a psychiatric syndrome found in surviving victims of the World War II camps*] [*German*]

KZ .... Kuhns Zeitschrift fuer Vergleichende Sprachforschung [*A publication*] (BJA)

Kz .... Kwanza [*Monetary Unit*][*Angola*] (BARN)

KZ .... Kysor Indl [*NYSE symbol*] (TTSB)

KZ .... Kysor Industrial Corp. [*NYSE symbol*] (SPSG)

KZ .... New Zealand [*IYRU nationality code*] (IYR)

KZ .... Oriens & King [*ICAO designator*] (AD)

KZA .... Kazakhstan Airlines [*ICAO designator*] (FAAC)

KZAB........... Albuquerque [*New Mexico*] [*ICAO location identifier*] (ICLI)

KZAC........... Esparto, CA [*FM radio station call letters*] (RBYB)

KZAK........... Incline Village, NV [*FM radio station call letters*]

KZAL........... Desert Center, CA [*FM radio station call letters*]

KZAM-FM .... Ganado, TX [*FM radio station call letters*] (RBYB)

KZAP........... Paradise, CA [*FM radio station call letters*] (RBYB)

KZAR-TV ...... Provo, UT [*Television station call letters*] (RBYB)

KZAT........... Kommentar zum Alten Testament [*A publication*] (BJA)

KZAT-FM .... Belle Plaine, IA [*FM radio station call letters*] (BROA)

KZAU........... Chicago, Aurora [*Illinois*] [*ICAO location identifier*] (ICLI)

KZAZ........... Bellingham, WA [*FM radio station call letters*]

KZB............. Zachar Bay [*Alaska*] [*Airport symbol*] (OAG)

KZB............. Zachar Bay, AK [*Location identifier*] [*FAA*] (FAAL)

KZBA........... Shafter, CA [*FM radio station call letters*]

KZBB........... Poteau, OK [*FM radio station call letters*]

KZBE........... Pleasant Hope, MO [*FM radio station call letters*] (RBYB)

KZBE-FM .... Omak, WA [*FM radio station call letters*] (BROA)

KZBK........... Brookfield, MO [*AM radio station call letters*]

KZBK-FM ..... Brookfield, MO [*FM radio station call letters*]
KZBL .... Natchitoches, LA [*FM radio station call letters*]
KZBN .... Santa Barbara, CA [*AM radio station call letters*] (BROA)
KZBQ-FM ..... Pocatello, ID [*FM radio station call letters*]
KZBR-FM ..... Mountain Pine, AR [*FM radio station call letters*] (RBYB)
KZBW .... Boston, Nashua [*New Hampshire*] [*ICAO location identifier*] (ICLI)
KZBZ .... Salina, KS [*FM radio station call letters*]
KZCD .... Lawton, OK [*FM radio station call letters*]
KZCO-FM ..... Oroville, CA [*FM radio station call letters*] (RBYB)
KZCR .... Fergus Falls, MN [*FM radio station call letters*]
KZCY-FM ..... Cheyenne, WY [*FM radio station call letters*] (BROA)
KZDC .... San Antonio, TX [*AM radio station call letters*] (RBYB)
KZDC .... Washington, Leesburg [*Virginia*] [*ICAO location identifier*] (ICLI)
KZDF-FM ..... McKinney, TX [*FM radio station call letters*] (BROA)
KZDG .... Greeley, CO [*FM radio station call letters*]
KZDL-FM ..... Terrell, TX [*FM radio station call letters*] (BROA)
KZDV .... Denver, Longmont [*Colorado*] [*ICAO location identifier*] (ICLI)
KZDX .... Burley, ID [*FM radio station call letters*]
KZDY-FM ..... Cawker City, KS [*FM radio station call letters*] (BROA)
KZEE .... Weatherford, TX [*AM radio station call letters*]
KZEG-FM ..... Clinton, IA [*FM radio station call letters*] (BROA)
KZEL .... Eugene, OR [*FM radio station call letters*]
KZEN .... Central City, NE [*FM radio station call letters*]
KZEP-FM ..... San Antonio, TX [*FM radio station call letters*]
KZEW-FM ..... Wheatland, WY [*FM radio station call letters*] (BROA)
KZEY .... Tyler, TX [*AM radio station call letters*]
KZEY-FM ..... Marshall, TX [*FM radio station call letters*]
KZEZ .... St. George, UT [*FM radio station call letters*]
KZF .... Kaintiba [*Papua New Guinea*] [*Airport symbol*] (OAG)
KZFM .... Corpus Christi, TX [*FM radio station call letters*]
KZFN .... Moscow, ID [*FM radio station call letters*]
KZFO .... Madera, CA [*FM radio station call letters*]
KZFR .... Chico, CA [*FM radio station call letters*]
KZFT .... Merced, CA [*FM radio station call letters*] (RBYB)
KZFW .... Fort Worth, Euless [*Texas*] [*ICAO location identifier*] (ICLI)
KZFX-FM ..... Lincoln, NE [*FM radio station call letters*] (BROA)
KZGL .... Cottonwood, AZ [*FM radio station call letters*]
KZGO .... Glenwood Springs, CO [*FM radio station call letters*] (RBYB)
KZGT .... Great Falls [*Montana*] [*ICAO location identifier*] (ICLI)
KZGZ .... Agana, GU [*FM radio station call letters*]
KZHE .... Stamps, AR [*FM radio station call letters*]
KZHK-FM ..... St. George, UT [*FM radio station call letters*] (BROA)
KZHR .... Dayton, WA [*FM radio station call letters*]
KZHT .... Provo, UT [*FM radio station call letters*]
KZHU .... Houston, Humble [*Texas*] [*ICAO location identifier*] (ICLI)
KZI .... Kozani [*Greece*] [*Airport symbol*] (OAG)
KZIA .... Las Cruces, NM [*Television station call letters*]
KZIA-FM ..... Cedar Rapids, IA [*FM radio station call letters*] (BROA)
KZID .... Indianapolis [*Indiana*] [*ICAO location identifier*] (ICLI)
KZIG .... Cave City, AR [*FM radio station call letters*]
KZII .... Lubbock, TX [*FM radio station call letters*]
KZIM .... Cape Girardeau, MO [*AM radio station call letters*]
KZIN .... Shelby, MT [*FM radio station call letters*]
KZIO .... Superior, WI [*FM radio station call letters*]
KZIO-FM ..... Two Harbors, MN [*FM radio station call letters*] (BROA)
KZIP .... Amarillo, TX [*AM radio station call letters*]
KZIQ .... Ridgecrest, CA [*AM radio station call letters*]
KZIQ-FM ..... Ridgecrest, CA [*FM radio station call letters*]
KZIZ .... Sumner, WA [*AM radio station call letters*]
KZJC .... Flagstaff, AZ [*Television station call letters*]
KZJG .... Longmont, CO [*Television station call letters*]
KZJH .... Jackson, WY [*FM radio station call letters*]
KZJL .... Houston, TX [*Television station call letters*]
KZJM-FM ..... Rockport, TX [*FM radio station call letters*] (BROA)
KZJX .... Jacksonville Hillard [*Florida*] [*ICAO location identifier*] (ICLI)
KZJZ .... St. Louis, MO [*AM radio station call letters*] (BROA)
KZKC .... Kansas City Olathe [*Kansas*] [*ICAO location identifier*] (ICLI)
KZKE .... Seligman, AZ [*FM radio station call letters*] (RBYB)
KZKI .... San Bernardino, CA [*Television station call letters*]
KZKK .... Huron, SD [*FM radio station call letters*]
KZKL .... Rio Rancho, NM [*FM radio station call letters*]
KZKS .... Rifle, CO [*FM radio station call letters*]
KZKX .... Seward, NE [*FM radio station call letters*]
KZKZ .... Greenwood, AR [*FM radio station call letters*]
KZLA .... Los Angeles, CA [*FM radio station call letters*]
KZLA .... Los Angeles Palmdale [*California*] [*ICAO location identifier*] (ICLI)
KZLC .... Salt Lake City [*Utah*] [*ICAO location identifier*] (ICLI)
KZLE .... Batesville, AR [*FM radio station call letters*]
KZLN .... Othello, WA [*FM radio station call letters*]
KZLO .... Bozeman, MT [*AM radio station call letters*]
KZLO-FM ..... Bozeman, MT [*FM radio station call letters*] (BROA)
KZLS .... Great Bend, KS [*FM radio station call letters*]
KZLT .... East Grand Forks, MN [*FM radio station call letters*]
KZLZ .... Keamy, AZ [*FM radio station call letters*]
KZMA .... Miami [*Florida*] [*ICAO location identifier*] (ICLI)
KZMA .... Poplar Bluff, MO [*FM radio station call letters*]
KZME .... Hudson, IA [*FM radio station call letters*]
KZME .... Memphis [*Tennessee*] [*ICAO location identifier*] (ICLI)
KZMG .... New Plymouth, ID [*FM radio station call letters*]
KZMI .... San Jose, MP [*FM radio station call letters*]
KZMK .... Sierra Vista, AZ [*FM radio station call letters*]
KZMM .... Troy, MO [*FM radio station call letters*]
KZMP .... Fort Worth, TX [*AM radio station call letters*] (BROA)
KZMP .... Minneapolis, Farmington [*Minnesota*] [*ICAO location identifier*] (ICLI)
KZMQ .... Greybull, WY [*AM radio station call letters*]
KZMQ-FM ..... Greybull, WY [*FM radio station call letters*]
KZMS .... Patterson, CA [*FM radio station call letters*]
KZMT .... Helena, MT [*FM radio station call letters*]
KZMU .... Moab, UT [*FM radio station call letters*]
KZMX .... Hot Springs, SD [*AM radio station call letters*]
KZMX-FM ..... Hot Springs, SD [*FM radio station call letters*]
KZMZ .... Alexandria, LA [*FM radio station call letters*]
KZN .... Kazan [*Former USSR*] [*Airport symbol*] (OAG)
KZN .... Kozani [*Greece*] [*Seismograph station code, US Geological Survey*] (SEIS)
KZN .... KwaZulu Natal [*South Africa*]
KZN .... Zaimische [*Later, KNS*] [*Former USSR*] [*Geomagnetic observatory code*]
KZNA .... Hill City, KS [*FM radio station call letters*]
KZNC .... Huron, SD [*FM radio station call letters*]
KZNG .... Hot Springs, AR [*AM radio station call letters*]
KZNM .... Grants, NM [*FM radio station call letters*]
KZNN .... Rolla, MO [*FM radio station call letters*]
KZNO .... Nogales, AZ [*FM radio station call letters*] (RBYB)
KZNR-FM ..... Lakeville, MN [*FM radio station call letters*] (BROA)
KZNT-FM ..... Cambridge, MN [*FM radio station call letters*] (BROA)
KZNX-FM ..... Astoria, OR [*FM radio station call letters*] (BROA)
KZNY .... New York, Ronkonkoma [*New York*] [*ICAO location identifier*] (ICLI)
KZNZ-FM ..... Eden Prairie, MN [*FM radio station call letters*] (BROA)
KZOA .... KZ Owners' Association [*Defunct*] (EA)
KZOA .... Oakland, Freemont [*California*] [*ICAO location identifier*] (ICLI)
KZOB .... Cleveland, Oberlin [*Ohio*] [*ICAO location identifier*] (ICLI)
KZOE .... Longview, WA [*FM radio station call letters*]
KZOK .... Seattle, WA [*FM radio station call letters*]
KZOL-FM ..... Santa Cruz, CA [*FM radio station call letters*] (RBYB)
KZON .... Phoenix, AZ [*FM radio station call letters*]
KZOO .... Honolulu, HI [*AM radio station call letters*]
KZOQ .... Missoula, MT [*FM radio station call letters*]
KZOR .... Hobbs, NM [*FM radio station call letters*]
KZOT .... Marianna, AR [*AM radio station call letters*]
KZOZ .... San Luis Obispo, CA [*FM radio station call letters*]
KZP .... Kwartalnik dla Historji Zydow w Polsce [*A publication*] (BJA)
KZPA .... Fort Yukon, AK [*AM radio station call letters*]
KZPD .... Ash Grove, MO [*FM radio station call letters*]
KZPE .... Ford City, CA [*FM radio station call letters*]
KZPH .... Cashmere, WA [*FM radio station call letters*]
KZPI-FM ..... Deming, NM [*FM radio station call letters*] (RBYB)
KZPK .... Paynesville, MN [*FM radio station call letters*]
KZPM .... Bakersfield, CA [*AM radio station call letters*]
KZPN .... Bayside, CA [*FM radio station call letters*]
KZPO .... Lindsay, CA [*FM radio station call letters*]
KZPR .... Minot, ND [*FM radio station call letters*]
KZPS .... Dallas, TX [*FM radio station call letters*]
KZPT-FM ..... Tucson, AZ [*FM radio station call letters*] (BROA)
KZQD .... Liberal, KS [*FM radio station call letters*]
KZQZ-FM ..... San Francisco, CA [*FM radio station call letters*] (BROA)
kzr .... Kazakh Soviet Socialist Republic [*MARC country of publication code*] [*Library of Congress*] (LCCP)
KZR .... Khuzdar [*Pakistan*] [*Airport symbol*] (AD)
KZRA .... Springdale, AR [*AM radio station call letters*]
KZRB .... New Boston, TX [*FM radio station call letters*]
KZRK .... Canyon, TX [*AM radio station call letters*] (RBYB)
KZRK-FM ..... Canyon, TX [*FM radio station call letters*] (RBYB)
KZRO .... Dunsmuir, CA [*FM radio station call letters*]
KZRQ .... Santa Fe, NM [*FM radio station call letters*]
KZRR .... Albuquerque, NM [*FM radio station call letters*]
KZS .... Kutztown State College, Kutztown, PA [*OCLC symbol*] (OCLC)
KZSA .... Placerville, CA [*FM radio station call letters*]
KZSC .... Santa Cruz, CA [*FM radio station call letters*]
KZSD .... Martin, SD [*FM radio station call letters*]
KZSD-TV ..... Martin, SD [*Television station call letters*]
KZSE .... Rochester, MN [*FM radio station call letters*]
KZSE .... Seattle, Auburn [*Washington*] [*ICAO location identifier*] (ICLI)
KZSF .... Alameda, CA [*FM radio station call letters*] (RBYB)
KZSF .... San Jose, CA [*AM radio station call letters*] (BROA)
KZSJ .... San Martin, CA [*AM radio station call letters*] (RBYB)
KZSN .... Hutchinson, KS [*FM radio station call letters*]
KZSN .... Wichita, KS [*AM radio station call letters*]
KZSP .... South Padre Island, TX [*FM radio station call letters*]
KZSQ .... Sonora, CA [*FM radio station call letters*]
KZSR .... Reno, NV [*FM radio station call letters*]
KZSS .... Albuquerque, NM [*AM radio station call letters*]
KZST .... Santa Rosa, CA [*FM radio station call letters*]
KZSU .... Stanford, CA [*FM radio station call letters*]
KZTA .... Yakima, WA [*AM radio station call letters*]
KZTA-FM ..... Yakima, WA [*FM radio station call letters*]
KZTB-FM ..... Sunnyside, WA [*FM radio station call letters*] (RBYB)
KZTL .... Atlanta, Hampton [*Georgia*] [*ICAO location identifier*] (ICLI)
KZTO .... Ottawa, KS [*FM radio station call letters*]
KZTQ .... Laredo, TX [*FM radio station call letters*]
KZTR-FM ..... Franklin, TX [*FM radio station call letters*] (BROA)
KZTS-AM ..... Tacoma, WA [*AM radio station call letters*] (BROA)
KZTU .... Eugene, OR [*AM radio station call letters*] (RBYB)
KZTU-AM ..... Eugene, OR [*AM radio station call letters*] (RBYB)
KZTV .... Corpus Christi, TX [*Television station call letters*]
KZTW .... Fairview, OR [*AM radio station call letters*] (RBYB)
KZTX .... Refugio, TX [*FM radio station call letters*]
KZTY .... Winchester, NV [*AM radio station call letters*]
KZUA .... Holbrook, AZ [*FM radio station call letters*]
KZUB .... Tahoka, TX [*FM radio station call letters*]

KZUE............ El Reno, OK [*AM radio station call letters*]
KZUL............ Lake Havasu City, AZ [*FM radio station call letters*]
KZUM........... Lincoln, NE [*FM radio station call letters*]
KZUN........... Zuni Pueblo/Blackrock [*New Mexico*] [*ICAO location identifier*] (ICLI)
KZUS.......... Toledo, OR [*AM radio station call letters*]
KZUS-FM..... Toledo, OR [*FM radio station call letters*]
KZUU........... Pullman, WA [*FM radio station call letters*]
KZV............. Kartell Zionistischer Verbindungen (BJA)
KZWA.......... Lake Charles, LA [*FM radio station call letters*]
KZWC........... Walnut Creek, CA [*FM radio station call letters*]
KZWY-FM.... Sheridan, WY [*FM radio station call letters*] (BROA)
KZXA........... Santa Fe, NM [*FM radio station call letters*]
KZXB........... Homer, LA [*FM radio station call letters*]
KZXC........... Anchorage, AK [*Television station call letters*]
KZXR........... Prosser, WA [*FM radio station call letters*]
KZXX........... Kenai, AK [*AM radio station call letters*]
KZXY-FM..... Apple Valley, CA [*FM radio station call letters*]
KZYP........... Pine Bluff, AR [*FM radio station call letters*]
KZYQ-FM..... Lake Village, AR [*FM radio station call letters*] (BROA)
KZYR.......... Avon, CO [*FM radio station call letters*]
KZYX........... Philo, CA [*FM radio station call letters*]

KZYZ............ Willits, CA [*FM radio station call letters*] (RBYB)
KZZB........... Beaumont, TX [*AM radio station call letters*]
KZZC-FM..... Tipton, CA [*FM radio station call letters*] (RBYB)
KZZD-FM..... Wichita, KS [*FM radio station call letters*] (BROA)
KZZE........... Eagle Point, OR [*FM radio station call letters*] (RBYB)
KZZF-FM..... South Lake Tahoe, CA [*FM radio station call letters*] (RBYB)
KZZI............ Belle Fourche, SD [*FM radio station call letters*] (RBYB)
KZZJ........... Rugby, ND [*AM radio station call letters*] (RBYB)
KZZK-FM..... New London, MO [*FM radio station call letters*] (RBYB)
KZZL............ Pullman, WA [*FM radio station call letters*]
KZZM-FM..... Dayton, WA [*FM radio station call letters*] (BROA)
KZZN........... Littlefield, TX [*AM radio station call letters*]
KZZO-FM..... Sacramento, CA [*FM radio station call letters*] (BROA)
KZZP........... Winner, SD [*FM radio station call letters*] (RBYB)
KZZP-FM..... Mesa, AZ [*FM radio station call letters*] (BROA)
KZZQ........... Winterset, IA [*FM radio station call letters*] (RBYB)
KZZR........... Burns, OR [*AM radio station call letters*]
KZZT........... Moberly, MO [*FM radio station call letters*]
KZZU........... Spokane, WA [*FM radio station call letters*]
KZZX........... Alamogordo, NM [*FM radio station call letters*]
KZZY........... Devils Lake, ND [*FM radio station call letters*]
KZZZ............ Kingman, AZ [*FM radio station call letters*]

L

By Acronym

L .... Angle
L .... Angular Momentum [*Symbol*] [*IUPAC*]
I---- .... Atlantic Ocean [*MARC geographic area code*] [*Library of Congress*] (LCCP)
L .... Avogadro Constant [*Symbol*] [*IUPAC*]
I .... Azimuthal Quantum Number [*or Orbital Angular Momentum Quantum Number*] [*Symbol*]
L .... Azimuthal Quantum Number [*or Orbital Angular Momentum Quantum Number*] - Total [*Symbol*]
L .... Cleared to Land (SAUS)
L .... Coefficient of Physics [*Physics*] (DAVI)
L .... Concerts and Recitals of Serious Music (Permits) [*Public-performance tariff class*] [*British*]
L .... Countermeasures [*JETDS nomenclature*]
L .... Days before Launch [*Usually followed by a number*] [*NASA*] (KSC)
L .... Difference of Latitude [*Navigation*]
L .... Drizzle [*Meteorology*]
L .... Electrical [*in British naval officers' ranks*]
L .... Electromagnet Radiance [*Astronomy*] (BARN)
L .... Element
L .... Elevated [*Railway*] [*Also, EL*]
L .... Equipped with Search Light [*Suffix to plane designation*] [*Navy*]
L .... extra insulation (SAUS)
L .... Fifty [*Roman numeral*]
L .... Finland [*IYRU nationality code*] (IYR)
L .... Glider Aircraft [*When first letter in Navy aircraft designation*]
L .... Inductance [*Symbol*] (AAG)
L .... Induction (SAUS)
L .... Inductor (SAUS)
L .... Kinetic Potential [*Symbol*]
L .... Labaz [*Belgium, France*] [*Research code symbol*]
L .... Label (MDG)
L .... Labetalol [*Pharmacology*]
L .... Labor
L .... Laboratory
L .... Laboratory Attendant [*Ranking title*] [*British Royal Navy*]
L .... Lactobacillus
L .... Ladestreifen [*Ammunition Clip*] [*German military - World War II*]
L .... Ladinian [*Geology*]
L .... Lady [*or Ladyship*]
L .... Lagrangian Function
L .... Lake [*Maps and charts*]
L .... Lambda (WDAA)
L .... Lambda Index (DIPS)
L .... Lambert [*Unit of luminance*] [*Preferred unit is lx, Lux*]
L .... Lameness [*Used by immigration officials*] [*Obsolete*]
L .... Laminated
L .... Lamp
L .... Lancashire Flats [*British*] (DCTA)
L .... Lancers
L .... Land
L .... Landing
L .... Landplane
L .... Land Transportation [*FCC*] (NTCM)
L .... Landulfus Acconzaioco [*Flourished, 13th century*] [*Authority cited in pre-1607 legal work*] (DSA)
L .... Lane
L .... Langmuir [*Unit of measure*]
L .... Language
L .... Language Score (DIPS)
L .... Lansing's New York Supreme Court Reports [*A publication*] (DLA)
L .... Lansing's Select Cases in Chancery [*1824, 1826*] [*New York*] [*A publication*] (DLA)
L .... Lanthanum [*Chemical element; symbol is La*]
L .... Larceny [*FBI standardized term*]
I .... Large (WDMC)
L .... Large [*Size designation for clothing, etc.*]
L .... Larva [*Biology*]
L .... Laser
L .... Laser Research and Technology Division (SAUO)
L .... L-Asparaginase [*Also, A, L-ase, L-asnase, L-Asp*] [*An enzyme, an antineoplastic*]
L .... Lat [*Monetary unit*] [*Latvia*]
I .... Latching [*Electronics*]
L .... Late (WDMC)
L .... Late

L .... Latent Heat
L .... Lateral (IAA)
L .... Latex (DMAA)
L .... Latin
L .... Latitude
L .... Laudatur [*Latin*]
L .... Launch [*or Launcher*]
L .... Laurentius Hispanus [*Deceased, 1248*] [*Authority cited in pre-1607 legal work*] (DSA)
L .... Lavender [*Botany*]
L .... Law
L .... Lawson's Notes of Decisions, Registration [*A publication*] (DLA)
L .... Layer [*Officer's rating*] [*British Royal Navy*]
L .... "Lay" Source (BJA)
L .... Leader (ADA)
L .... Leader Sequence (DMAA)
L .... Lead Sheath (AAG)
L .... Leaf [*Bibliography*] [*Botany*]
L .... Leaflet
L .... League
L .... Learner
L .... Learning [*Denotes learning drivers before they receive their automobile driving licenses*] [*British*]
L .... Leasehold (ROG)
L .... Leather
L .... Leave
L .... Leave without pay (SAUO)
L .... Lederle Laboratories [*Research code symbol*]
L .... Leeward
I .... Left (WDMC)
L .... Left [*Politics*]
L .... Left [*Direction*]
L .... Left Eye [*Opthalmology*] (DAVI)
L .... Left Hand [*Music*] (ROG)
L .... Legal Division [*Coast Guard*]
L .... Leges [*Laws*] [*Latin*] (ROG)
L .... Legge [*Law, Act, Statute*] [*Italian*] (ILCA)
L .... Legionella [*A bacteria*] (DAVI)
L .... Legitimate
L .... Lehrregiment (SAUO)
L .... Leishmania [*Microbiology*] (MAE)
L .... Lek [*Monetary unit*] [*Albania*] (BARN)
L .... Lempira [*Monetary unit*] [*Honduras*]
L .... Lenad Subgroup [*Leucite, nephelite, halite, thenardite*] [*CIPW classification*] [*Geology*]
L .... Length [*or Lengthwise*]
I .... Length [*Symbol*] [*IUPAC*]
L .... Lens
L .... Lente Insulin [*Pharmacology*] (DAVI)
L .... Leo (WDAA)
L .... Lepetit [*Italy*] [*Research code symbol*]
L .... Lepidocrocite [*A mineral*]
L .... Leptin (MELL)
L .... Leptospira [*A bacteria*] (DAVI)
L .... Leptotrichia [*A bacteria*] (DAVI)
L .... Lesser (DAVI)
L .... Lethal
L .... Letter
L .... Leu [*Monetary unit*] [*Romania*]
L .... Leucine [*One-letter symbol; see Leu*] [*An amino acid*]
L .... Leuconostoc [*An algae*] [*Biochemistry*] (DAVI)
L .... Leukocyte (MELL)
L .... Lev [*Monetary unit*] [*Bulgaria*]
L .... Level (KSC)
L .... Lever
L .... Levo [*or Laevo*] [*Configuration in chemical structure*]
I .... Levorotary [*or Levorotatory*] [*Chemistry*]
L .... Levorotatory [*Organic chemistry*] (DIPS)
L .... Lewisite [*War gas*] [*Army symbol*]
L .... Lexical Rule [*Linguistics*]
L .... Liaison [*Airplane designation*]
L .... Liber [*Book*] [*Latin*]
L .... Liberal [*Politics*]
L .... Liberty Financial Companies, Inc. [*NYSE symbol*] (SAG)
L .... Liberty Financial Cos. [*NYSE symbol*] (TTSB)
L .... Libra [*Pound*]

L	Library
L	Libration [Space exploration]
L	Licenciatus [Academic Qualification] [Latin]
L	License
L	Licensed to Practice [Medicine]
L	Licentiate
L	Lidocaine [Topical anesthetic]
L	Lidoflazine [A vasodilator]
L	Lies [Read] [German]
L	Lieutenant [Navy] [British]
L	Life [Insurance]
L	Lifestyle [Wire service code]　(NTCM)
L	Lift
L	Ligament [or Ligamentum]
L	Ligand [Chemistry]
L	Light [Chain] [Biochemistry, immunochemistry]
L	Lighting [As part of a code]
L	Lightning [Meteorology]
L	Light Sense
L	Lignite　(WDAA)
L	Lilac
L	Lilangeni [Monetary unit] [Swaziland]　(BARN)
L	Lima [Phonetic alphabet] [International]　(DSUE)
L	Lime
L	Limen or Threshold [Psychology]
L	Limes [Boundary] [Pharmacology]　(DAVI)
L	Limestone [Petrology]
L	Limit
L	Limited　(DLA)
L	Limited security clearance　(SAUO)
L	Lincoln and Welland Regiment　(SAUO)
L	Lincomycin　(STED)
l	Line　(WDMC)
L	Line
L	Line Assembly　(AAG)
L	Line Drive [Baseball term]　(NDBD)
L	Linen [Deltiology]
L	Line (of Print) [Publishing]　(NTCM)
L	Liner [Nautical]
L	Lines Dose [Medicine]
L	Lingual [Dentistry]
L	Link
L	Linnaean
L	Lip
L	Lipoid [Biochemistry]
(l)	Liquid [Chemistry]
(l)	Liquidity [Business term]
L	Liquor　(STED)
L	Lira [Monetary unit] [Italy]
L	List　(MSA)
L	Listed [Stock exchange term]
L	Listening Post [In symbol only]
L	Listeria [A bacteria]　(DAVI)
L	Lit
L	Litas [Monetary unit] [Lithuania]
L	Liter [Also, l] [Metric measure of volume]
l	Liter
L	Literate
L	Lithium [Chemical element]　(ROG)
L	Lithuania　(MILB)
L	Little
L	Live [Wiring code] [British]
L	Liver　(MAE)
L	Liverpool [Postcode]　(ODBW)
L	Living　(DAVI)
L	Living Room　(ROG)
L	Livre [Monetary unit] [Obsolete] [French]
L	Load　(MDG)
L	Loam [Agronomy]
L	Lobe [Of a leaf] [Botany]
L	Loblaw Companies Ltd. [Toronto Stock Exchange symbol] [Vancouver Stock Exchange symbol]
L	Loblaw Cos. [TS, exchange symbol]　(TTSB)
L	Local [Broadcasting program]　(NTCM)
l	Local　(WDMC)
L	Locative (Case) [Linguistics]
L	Locator [Compass]
L	Locator Beacon
L	Loch
L	Lockheed Aircraft Corp. [ICAO aircraft manufacturer identifier]　(ICAO)
L	Locking [Lamp base type]　(NTCM)
L	Locus [Place] [Latin]
L	Lodge
L	Logarithm [Mathematics]
L	Long
L	Longacre [James B.] [Designer's mark, when appearing on US coins]
L	Longitude
L	Longo Catalogue [A. Scarlatti]　(GROV)
L	Long, Rolling Sea [Meteorology]
L	Loop [Fingerprint description]
L	Looper [Computer science]　(MDG)
L	LORAN [Long-Range Navigation]　(IAA)
L	Lorazepam [A tranquilizer]
L	Lord [or Lordship]
L	Lorentz Unit [Electronics]
L	Losing Pitcher [Baseball term]　(NDBD)
L	loss　(WDAA)
L	Lost [RADAR]
L	Lost [Sports statistics]
L	Loti [Monetary unit] [Lesotho]　(BARN)
L	Lough [Maps and charts]
L	Louisiana Reports [A publication]　(DLA)
L	Louisiana State Library, Baton Rouge, LA [Library symbol] [Library of Congress]　(LCLS)
L	Louisville [Diocesan abbreviation] [Kentucky]　(TOCD)
L	Love [Phonetic alphabet] [World War II]　(DSUE)
l	Low　(IDOE)
L	Low [or Lower]
L	Low Altitude　(PIPO)
L	Lower Bow [Music]　(ROG)
L	Lower Limit of a Class Interval [Psychology]
L	Low Season [Airline fare code]
L	Loyalty
L	Lues [or Syphilis] [Medicine]　(DAVI)
L	Luitingh [Holland]
l	Lumbar [Medicine]
l	Lumen　(IDOE)
L	Lumen [Unit of luminous flux]
L	Luminance　(DMAA)
L	Lunch　(CDAI)
L	Lung [Anatomy]　(DAVI)
L	Luteolin [Botany]
L	Luxembourg
L	Luxury [In automobile model name "Cordia L"]
L	Lymph [A fluid] [Biochemistry]　(DAVI)
L	Lymphocyte [Biochemistry]　(DAVI)
L	Lymphogranuloma [Pathology]　(DAVI)
L	Lysosome [Biochemistry]　(DAVI)
l	Lyxose [As substituent on nucleoside] [Biochemistry]
l	Mean Free Path [Symbol] [IUPAC]
L	Merck & Co., Inc. [Research code symbol]
L	Promotional Fare [Also, K, Q, V] [Airline fare code]
L	Quinquaginta [Fifty] [Latin]
L	Radiance [Symbol] [IUPAC]
L	Requires Fuel and Oil [Search and rescue symbol that can be stamped in sand or snow]
L	Sandoz Pharmaceuticals [Research code symbol]
L	San Francisco [Branch in the Federal Reserve regional banking system]　(BARN)
L	Searchlight Control [JETDS nomenclature]
L	Self-Inductance [Symbol] [IUPAC]
L	Shape Descriptor [Dining el, for example. The shape resembles the letter for which it is named]
L	Silo Launched [Missile launch environment symbol]
L	Single Acetate　(AAG)
L	Timber [Lumber] [Vessel load line mark]
L	Time of Launch [NASA]
L0	Raw SAR data　(SAUS)
L1	First language　(SAUS)
L1	First Language　(ADA)
L_1	First Lumbar Nerve [Second lumbar nerve is L_2, etc., through L_5] [Medicine]　(DAVI)
L_1	First Lumbar Vertebra [Second lumbar vertebra is L_2, etc., through L_5] [Medicine]
L1A	Processed SAR data　(SAUS)
L1B	Processed and Geocoded SAR data　(SAUS)
L1TC	Level 1 Trauma Center [Medicine]　(DMAA)
L-2	Launch Minus 2 Days　(SAUS)
L02	Liquid Oxygen　(NAKS)
L2D2	Lightweight Loran Digital Dropsonde　(SAUS)
L2TP	Layer Two Tunneling Protocol [Computer science]　(DCDG)
L/3	Lower Third [Referring to long bones] [Orthopedics]　(DAVI)
L3S	LNG [Liquefied Natural Gas] Seabed Supported System
L4	Automatic Lockup Four Speed [DOE]　(TAG)
L4	Fourth lumbar vertebra　(SAUS)
L5	Fifth of five lumbar vertebra　(SAUS)
L5	Long Quinto [Pt. 10 of Year Books] [A publication]　(DSA)
L-5HTP	L-5-Hydroxytryptophan [Pharmacology]　(DAVI)
L6	Laboratories Low-Level Linked List Language [Bell Systems]　(DIT)
L-10-W	Levulose (10 Percent) in Water
L15	Leibovitz 15　(SAUS)
L123UA	Lotus 1-2-3 Users' Association
LA	Concerts and Recitals of Serious Music (Annual Licence) [Public-performance tariff class] [British]
LA	Fighter [Russian aircraft symbol]
LA	Hoffmann-La Roche, Inc. [Research code symbol]
La	[The] Holy Bible from Ancient Eastern Manuscripts [G. M. Lamsa] [A publication]　(BJA)
La	Lab. Aron [France] [Research code symbol]
La	Labial [Dentistry]
LA	Labor Administration　(SAUO)
LA	Labor Arbitration Reports [A publication]　(DLA)
LA	Labor Area
LA	Laboratory Analytical procedure　(SAUO)
LA	Laboratory of Anthropology　(SAUO)
La	Laches [of Plato] [Classical studies]　(OCD)
LA	Lactalbumin [Biochemistry]
LA	Lactic Acid [Biochemistry]
LA	Lactic Acidosis [Medicine]　(MELL)

LA	Lag Amplifier
LA	Lag Angle (IAA)
LA	LA Gear, Inc. [NYSE symbol] (CTT)
La	Lagulanda (BJA)
La	Laira [Plymouth] [British depot code]
LA	Lake Aircraft [ICAO aircraft manufacturer identifier] (ICAO)
LA	Lama Foundation (EA)
LA	Lambda Alpha
La	Lambert [Unit of luminance] [Preferred unit is lx, Lux] (ADA)
La	Lamellar Phase [Physical chemistry]
La	Lamentations [Old Testament book] (BJA)
LA	LAN Analyzer (SAUS)
LA	Lancaster [Postcode] (ODBW)
LA	Lancastrian [Of the royal house of Lancaster] [British] (ROG)
LA	Lan Chile [Airline flight code] (ODBW)
LA	Land Agent [Ministry of Agriculture, Fisheries, and Food] [British]
L/A	Landing Account [Shipping]
La	Landulfus Acconzaioco [Flourished, 13th century] [Authority cited in pre-1607 legal work] (DSA)
LA	Lane
La	Lane's English Exchequer Reports [1605-12] [A publication] (DLA)
La	Lanfrancus [Deceased, 1089] [Authority cited in pre-1607 legal work] (DSA)
La	Lanfrancus Cremensis [Deceased, 1229] [Authority cited in pre-1607 legal work] (DSA)
LA	Langley Alloys Limited (SAUO)
LA	Language [Online database field identifier]
LA	Language Age [Score]
LA	Language Arts [A publication] (BRI)
LA	Lanthanum (NAKS)
La	Lanthanum [Chemical element]
LA	Laos [or Lao People's Democratic Republic] [ANSI two-letter standard code] (CNC)
La	Lapus de Castiglionchio [Flourished, 1353-81] [Authority cited in pre-1607 legal work] (DSA)
La	Lapus Tatti [Flourished, 14th century] [Authority cited in pre-1607 legal work] (DSA)
LA	Lard Association (BUAC)
LA	Large Amount [Medicine]
LA	Large Aperture [Photography] (ROG)
LA	Laryngeal Atresia [Medicine] (MELL)
LA	LASER Altimeter [NASA]
LA	LASER Angioplasty [Cardiology] (DMAA)
LA	LASER [Gyro] Axis (IEEE)
LA	Last [Wool weight]
la	Late (VRA)
LA	Late Abortion [Medicine] (DMAA)
LA	Late Antigen [Biochemistry] (DAVI)
LA	Latex Agglutination [Test] [Clinical chemistry]
LA	Latex Allergy (MELL)
LA	Lathe [Division in the county of Kent] [British]
LA	Latin America
LA	Launch Abort [NASA] (KSC)
LA	Launch Aft
LA	Launch Analyst [Aerospace] (AAG)
LA	Launch Area [NASA] (KSC)
LA	Launch Azimuth [NASA] (KSC)
LA	Laureate in Arts
La	Laurentius Hispanus [Deceased, 1248] [Authority cited in pre-1607 legal work] (DSA)
LA	Lava [Maps and charts]
LA	Lavatory (DSUE)
LA	Lavochkin [USSR aircraft type] [World War II]
LA	Law Agent
LA	Law Association (SAUO)
LA	Lawyers' Reports, Annotated [A publication] (DLA)
LA	Lead Adapter [Electric equipment]
LA	Lead Agent (COE)
LA	Lead Amplifier
LA	Lead Angle (MSA)
LA	Leading Aircraftsman [RAF] [British]
LA	Leading Article (ROG)
LA	Leaf Abscission [Botany]
LA	Learning Activity (ADA)
LA	Leasehold Area (ADA)
L/A	Leave Address (DNAB)
L/A	Leave Advance [Military]
LA	Lebanese Army (BUAC)
LA	Lebensalter [Chronological Age] [Psychology]
LA	Ledger Account (ROG)
LA	Ledger Asset
LA	Left Angle
LA	Left Angulation [Orthopedics] (DAVI)
LA	Left Arm [Medicine]
LA	Left Ascension
LA	Left Atrial [or Avricular] Appendage [Cardiology] (DAVI)
LA	Left Atrium [Anatomy]
LA	Left Auricle [Anatomy]
LA	Left Axilla (KSC)
LA	Legal Adviser
LA	Legal Advisor (SAUO)
LA	Legal Asset [Business term]
LA	Lege Artis [According to the Art] [Pharmacy]
LA	Legislative Affairs
LA	Legislative Assembly
LA	Legislative Assistant [US Congress]
LA	Legitimate Access [British police term]
LA	Legum Allegoriae [Philo] (BJA)
LA	LeMans America (EA)
LA	Lemko Association [Poland] (BUAC)
LA	Lemko Association of US and Canada (EA)
LA	Lenticular Astigmatism (MELL)
LA	Lesbian Activities (WDAA)
LA	Leschetizky Association (EA)
LA	Lethal Area [Of indirect-fire weapon systems] [Military]
LA	Letter of Activation [Military]
L/A	Letter of Authority (EBF)
LA	Letters Abroad (EA)
L/A	Lettre d'Avis [Letter of Advice] [French]
LA	Leucinamide (MELL)
LA	Leucine Aminopeptidase [Also, LP, LPAP] [An enzyme]
LA	Leukemia Antigen [Immunochemistry] (DAVI)
LA	Leukoagglutinating [Immunochemistry]
LA	Leukogglutination (DMAA)
LA	Leuprolide Acetate (DMAA)
LA	Levator Ani [Anatomy]
LA	Level Absolute (SSD)
LA	Level Alarm [Engineering]
LA	Level Amplifier (IAA)
LA	Levulinic Acid [Organic chemistry]
LA	Liberal Arts
LA	Liberator Atlanta [An association] (EA)
LA	Libertarian Alliance [British] (EAIO)
LA	Library Administrator (SAUO)
LA	Library Association [British] (NITA)
LA	Library Automation
LA	Library of Art [A publication]
LA	License Application (SAUO)
LA	Licensing Act (DLA)
LA	Licensing Assistant (NRCH)
LA	Licensing Authority (DCTA)
LA	Licentiate in Arts
LA	Lichen Amyloidosis [Dermatology] (DAVI)
LA	Lieutenant-at-Arms [British]
LA	Light Ale (ADA)
LA	Light Alloy
LA	Light Armor [Telecommunications] (TEL)
LA	Light Artillery
LA	Lighter Association (EA)
LA	Lighter-than-Air [Aircraft]
LA	Lighter Than Air Airship (PIPO)
LA	Lighting Association (SAUO)
LA	Lightning Arrester
LA	Lightwood-Albright [Syndrome] [Nephrology] (DAVI)
LA	Limited Area
LA	Limited Availability [Tire design]
LA	Linea Aerea Nacional de Chile [Chilean airline] [ICAO designator] (OAG)
LA	Linea Aspera (MELL)
LA	Line Adapter [Computer science] (CMD)
LA	Line Adaptor (NITA)
LA	Linear Arithmetic [Computer science]
LA	Linear Assembly
LA	Line Art (ELAL)
LA	Linguoaxial [Dentistry]
LA	Link Address (IAA)
LA	Link Allotter
LA	Link Analysis
LA	Link Aviation, Inc. (SAUO)
LA	Linnaean Society
LA	Linoleic Acid (AAMN)
LA	Linolenic Acid (MELL)
LA	Liquid Asset [Business term]
LA	Listed Address [Telecommunications] (TEL)
LA	Listing Agent [Classified advertising] (ADA)
la	Listing Agent [Real estate] (REAL)
LA	Literate in Arts
LA	Lithuanian National Accreditation Bureau (SAUO)
LA	Live Action (NTCM)
LA	Liverpool Academy [British]
LA	Living Allowance
L/A	Lloyd's Agent
LA	Load Address (IAA)
LA	Load Adjuster (CET)
LA	Load Allocation [Environmental science] (FFDE)
LA	Loan Amount [Dialog] [Searchable field] [Information service or system] (NITA)
LA	Lobuloalveolar [Medicine] (DAVI)
LA	Local Address
LA	Local Agent
LA	Local Alarm (NRCH)
LA	Local Anesthetic [Medicine]
LA	Local Authority
LA	Location Area (SAUO)
LA	Lock Actuator (MCD)
LA	Locomotor Ataxia [Medicine] (MELL)
LA	Locus Allowed (ROG)
LA	Lodging Allowance [British military] (DMA)
LA	Log Analyzer (SAUO)
LA	Log Analyzer Processor [Computer science]

LA .... Logarithmic Amplifier
LA .... Logical Address
LA .... Logical Area (ELAL)
LA .... Logistics Assistance (SAUO)
LA .... Loners of America [*An association*] (EA)
LA .... Long-Acting [*Pharmacy*]
LA .... Long-Arm [*Cast*] [*Orthopedics*] (DAVI)
LA .... Longitudinal Acoustic [*Spectroscopy*]
LA .... Look Ahead (IAA)
LA .... Look Angle (ACAE)
LA .... Loop Antenna (DEN)
LA .... Lord Advocate of Scotland (DLA)
LA .... Los Alamos Scientific Laboratory [*USAEC*] (MCD)
LA .... Los Angeles [*California*] [*Slang*]
LA .... Louisiana [*Postal code*] (AFM)
La .... Louisiana (BEE)
LA .... Louisiana & Arkansas (SAUO)
LA .... Louisiana & Arkansas Railway Co. [*AAR code*]
LA .... Louisiana Reports [*A publication*] (DLA)
LA .... Louisiana Supreme Court Reports [*A publication*] (DLA)
LA .... Louvain Association (SAUO)
LA .... Low Alcohol [*Trademark of Anheuser-Busch, Inc.*]
LA .... Low Altitude
LA .... Low Angle [*RADAR*] (DEN)
LA .... Low Anxiety (MAE)
LA .... Lower Arm
LA .... Ludwig's Angina [*Medicine*] (DAVI)
LA .... Lunula (MELL)
LA .... Lupus Anticoagulant [*Medicine*] (MELL)
LA .... Luscombe Association (EA)
LA .... Lyme Arthritis (MELL)
LA .... Lymphadenopathy [*Medicine*]
LA .... National Leukemia Association (SAUO)
La 2000 ...... Old Latin Version (BJA)
LA 2000 ...... Los Alamos 2000 Strategic Planning and Allocation (SAUO)
LAA .... Amphibious Assault Ship [*Military*]
LAA .... International Legal Aid Association (SAUO)
LAA .... Jamahiriya Libyan Arab Airlines [*ICAO designator*] (FAAC)
LAA .... Laboratory Animal Allergy (HEAS)
LAA .... Lamar [*Colorado*] [*Airport symbol*] (OAG)
LAA .... Lamar, CO [*Location identifier*] [*FAA*] (FAAL)
LAA .... Laser Association of America [*Later, LEMA*] (EA)
LAA .... LASER Attenuator Assembly
LAA .... Lateral Accelerometer Assembly (MCD)
LAA .... Latex Advisors Association (NTPA)
LAA .... Latin American Association (BUAC)
LAA .... Launch Area Antenna (MCD)
LAA .... Laundrette Association of Australia
LAA .... Lead Agency Attorney (EPAT)
LAA .... League of Advertising Agencies [*New York, NY*] (EA)
LAA .... Leather Apparel Association (EA)
LAA .... Left Atrial Abnormality [*Medicine*] (STED)
LAA .... Left Atrial Appendage [*Medicine*] (STED)
LAA .... Left Auricular Appendage [*Medicine*] (STED)
LAA .... Leukemia-Associated Antigen [*Medicine*] (STED)
LAA .... Leukocyte Ascorbic Acid [*Clinical chemistry*] (AAMN)
LAA .... Library Association of Alberta [*Canada*] (BUAC)
LAA .... Library Association of Australia (BUAC)
LAA .... Libyan Arab Airlines (BUAC)
LAA .... Licentiate of the Central Association of Accountants (SAUO)
LAA .... Lieutenant-at-Arms [*British*] (DMA)
LAA .... Life Insurance Advertisers Association [*Later, LCA*] (EA)
LAA .... Light Antiaircraft [*Guns*]
LAA .... Light Army Aircraft
LAA .... Lighterage Assembly Area
LAA .... Limited Access Authorization [*Military*] (GFGA)
LAA .... Lipizzan Association of America (EA)
LAA .... Lithuanian Agriculture Academy (BUAC)
LAA .... Lithuanian Alliance of America (EA)
LAA .... Little America [*Antarctica*] [*Seismograph station code, US Geological Survey*] [*Closed*] (SEIS)
LAA .... Little Athletics Association [*Australia*]
LAA .... Live Assembly Area (MCD)
LAA .... Liverpool Academy of Arts [*England*]
LAA .... Local Airport Advisory [*Aviation*] (FAAC)
LAA .... Locally Administered Address [*Computer science*] (CIST)
LAA .... Los Angeles Airways, Inc.
LA A .... Louisiana Annual Reports [*A publication*] (DLA)
LA A .... Louisiana Courts of Appeal Reports [*A publication*] (DLA)
LAA .... Low-Altitude Attack
LAA .... Lymphoedema Association of Australia (SAUO)
LAAA .... Latin American Association of Archives [*See also ALA*] (EAIO)
LAAAS ...... Latin American Association for Afro-Asian Studies [*Mexico*] (EAIO)
LAAAS ...... Low-Altitude Airfield Attack System (MCD)
LAAB .... Landscape Architectural Accreditation Board (GAGS)
LAAB .... Light Armored Assault Battalion [*Marine Corps*]
LAABAM ...... Latin American Association of Behavior Analysis and Modification [*Uruguay*] (EAIO)
LAABF .... Ladies' Auxiliary of the American Beekeeping Federation (EA)
LAAC .... Library Association's Annual Conference [*British*]
LAAC .... Lord Chancellor's Legal Aid Advisory Committee [*British*] (DLA)
LAACC .... Light Antiaircraft Control Center (NATG)
LAACG .... Los Alamos Accelerator Code Group (SAUO)
LAACP .... Local Alcohol Abuse Control Program (SAUO)
LAACT .... Legislative Assembly of the Australian Capital Territory

LA Acts .... State of Louisiana: Acts of the Legislature [*A publication*] (DLA)
LAAD .... Latin American Agribusiness Development Corp.
LAAD .... Los Angeles Aircraft Division [*Rockwell International*]
LAAD .... Low Altitude Air Defense (SAUO)
LAADBN .... Low Altitude Air Defense Battalion [*Navy*] (ANA)
LAADIW .... Latin American Association for the Development and Integration of Women [*See also ALADIM*] [*Chile*] (EAIO)
LA Admin Code... Louisiana Administrative Code [*A publication*] (DLA)
LA Admin Reg... Louisiana Administrative Register [*A publication*] (DLA)
LAADS .... Los Angeles Air Defense Sector [*ADC*]
LAADS .... Low Altitude Aircraft Detection System (SAUS)
LAADS .... Low-Altitude Air Defense [*or Delivery*] System
LAADS .... Low-Altitude Air Dropped Stores (MCD)
LAAEMCTS... Latin American Association of Environmental Mutagens, Carcinogens, and Teratogens Societies [*Mexico*] (EAIO)
LAAF .... Lawson Army Airfield [*Fort Benning, GA*] (MCD)
LAAF .... Libby Army Airfield
LAAF .... Libyan Arab Air Force (BUAC)
LAAFS .... Los Angeles Air Force Station
LAAG .... Latin American Anthropology Group (EA)
LAAG .... Light Anti-Aircraft Gun (SAUS)
LAAGOWRNAFE... Local Authority Associations Group of Work Related Non-Advanced Further Education (AIE)
LAAI .... Licentiate of the Institute of Administrative Accountants [*British*] (DBQ)
LAAIB .... Latin American Air Intelligence Brief (MCD)
LAAM .... Large-Animal Anesthesia Machine [*Instrumentation*]
LAAM .... Levo-alpha-Acetylmethadol [*Drug alternative to methadone*]
LAAM .... Light Antiaircraft Missile
LAAMBN .... Light Antiaircraft Missile Battalion (MUGU)
LAAME .... Large Antenna Assembly & Measurement Experiment (SAUO)
LAAMM .... London Association in Aid of Moravian Missions (SAUO)
LAAMS .... Land Armaments Movement Model (SAUO)
LAAMSF .... Latin American Association of Medical Schools and Faculties [*See also ALAFEM*] [*Ecuador*] (EAIO)
La An .... Lawyers' Reports, Annotated [*A publication*] (DLA)
LA & LR ...... Livonia Avon & Lakeville Railroad (MHDB)
LA & M .... Library Administration and Management
LAANG .... Louisiana Air National Guard (MUSM)
LA Ann .... Louisiana Annual Reports [*A publication*] (DLA)
LA Ann Reps... Louisiana Annual Reports [*A publication*] (DLA)
LA An R ...... Louisiana Annual Reports [*A publication*] (DLA)
LA An Rep ... Louisiana Annual Reports [*A publication*] (DLA)
L A Ant ...... Latin America Antiquity [*A publication*]
LA Ant .... Latin American Antiquity [*A publication*] (BRI)
LAAO .... L-Amino Acid Oxidase [*An enzyme*]
LAAO .... Los Alamos Area Office [*Energy Research and Development Administration*]
LAAO-ES&H... Los Alamos Area Office/Environment, Safety & Health Branch (SAUO)
LAAO-FOB.... Los Alamos Area Office/Facilities Operations Branch (SAUO)
LAAO-PMB... Los Alamos Area Office/Project Management Branch (SAUO)
LA A (Orleans)... Louisiana Court of Appeals (Parish of Orleans) (DLA)
LAAP .... Language Arts Assessment Portfolio [*Test*] (TMMY)
LAAP .... Law Association for Asia and the Pacific [*Australia*]
LAAP .... Longhorn Army Ammunition Plant (MCD)
LAAP .... Louisiana Army Ammunition Plant (AABC)
LAAPD .... Los Angeles Air Procurement District
LAAPI .... Latin American Association of Pharmaceutical Industries [*See also ALIFAR*] (EAIO)
LA App .... Louisiana Courts of Appeal Reports [*A publication*] (DLA)
LA App (Orleans)... Louisiana Court of Appeals (Parish of Orleans) (DLA)
LAAPS .... Laptop Automated Aid Positioning System [*Coast Guard*] [*Computer science*] (DOMA)
LAAPS .... Latin American Association of Physiological Sciences (SAUO)
LAAR .... Liquid Air Accumulator Rocket
LAAR .... Low-Altitude Air Refuelling (SAUS)
LAARD .... Long-Acting Antirheumatic Drug [*Medicine*] (STED)
LAA Regt ..... Light Anti-Aircraft Regiment (SAUO)
LAARS .... LASER-Augmented Air-Rescue System (PDAA)
LAAS .... Latin American Association for Afro-Asian Studies (SAUO)
LAAS .... Light Armor Antitank System (MCD)
LAAS .... Lincolnshire Architectural and Archaeological Society (SAUO)
LAAS .... Local Area Augmentation System (HLLA)
LAAS .... London Amateur Aviation Society (SAUO)
LAAS .... Los Angeles Air Service, Inc.
LAAS .... Low Altitude Airfield Attack System (SAUO)
LAAS .... Low-Altitude Alerting System
LAAS .... Low Altitude Alert System [*Aviation*] (PIPO)
LAASCA .... Long-Range Antisubmarine Capability Aircraft
LAASH .... LITEF Analogue Air data System for Helicopters (SAUS)
LAASL .... Latin American Association for the Study of the Liver [*Mexico*] (EAIO)
LAASP .... Latin American Association for Social Psychology [*Formerly, Latin American Social Psychology Committee*] (EA)
LAAT .... Laser Augmented Airborne TOW (SAUS)
LAAT .... LASER-Augmented Airborne TOW Sight [*Army*] (MCD)
LAAT .... LASER-Augmented Airborne Track
LAAT .... Logistics Assessment and Assistance Team (MCD)
LAATC .... Latin American Association of Trading Companies [*Brazil*] (BUAC)
LAAUW .... Los Alamos Area United Way
LAAV .... Light Airborne ASW [*Antisubmarine Warfare*] Vehicle
LA Avgas ..... Los Alamos Aviation Gas Association (SAUO)
LAAW .... Legal Automated Army-Wide
LAAW .... Light Assault Antitank Weapon
LAAW .... Local Antiair Warfare (NVT)

LAAWC	Local Antiair Warfare Commander (NVT)
LAAWC	Local Anti-Air Warfare Co-ordinator (SAUS)
LAAWS	Legal Automation Army-Wide Systems
LAB	CIE color space, Laboratory (SAUS)
Lab	Labatt's California District Court Reports [1857-58] [A publication] (DLA)
LAB	Label [or Labelling] (IAA)
LAB	Lablab [Papua New Guinea] [Airport symbol] (OAG)
LAB	Labmin Resources Ltd. [Toronto Stock Exchange symbol]
LAB	Labor
LAB	Labor Advisory Board [New Deal]
LAB	Laboratories for Applied Biology Ltd. (WDAA)
Lab	Laboratory (AL)
LAB	Laboratory
lab	Laboratory (WDMC)
LAB	Laboratory Animals Bureau (BUAC)
LAB	Laboratory Automation Based (VLIE)
LAB	Laboratory for Applied Biophysics [MIT] (MCD)
LAB	Labor Officer [Foreign service]
LAB	Labour Party [British] [Political party]
Lab	Labrador (NTIO)
LAB	Labrador [Canada]
LAB	Labrador Retriever [Dog breed]
LAB	Labuan [Island in Malaysia] (ROG)
LAB	Lactic Acid Bacteria [Food microbiology]
Lab	Lambertus de Ramponibus [Deceased, 1304] [Authority cited in pre-1607 legal work] (DSA)
LAB	Land Air Battle (ACAE)
LAB	Language Assessment Battery (SAUO)
LAB	Latin America Bureau [British] (EAIO)
LAB	Lead Acid Battery
LAB	Leave Authorization Balance [Air Force] (AFM)
LAB	Legal Advisory Board (TELE)
LAB	Legal Aid Board (BUAC)
LAB	Leisure Activities Blank [Vocational guidance test]
LAB	Level of Aspiration Board [Psychology]
LAB	Liber Antiquitatum Biblicarum. Pseudo-Philo (BJA)
LAB	Library Association of Barbados (BUAC)
LAB	Library of American Biography (SAUO)
LAB	Licentiate of the Associated Board (SAUO)
LAB	Licentiate of the Associated Board of Royal Schools of Music [British]
LAB	Licquor Administration Board (SAUO)
LAB	Light Assault Bridge [Military program] (INF)
LAB	Light Attack Battalion (INF)
LAB	Line Adapter Base (VLIE)
LAB	Linear Alkylbenzene [Organic chemistry]
LAB	Lithosphere-Asthenosphere Boundary [Geology]
LAB	Live Animals Board [IATA] (DS)
LAB	Lloyd Aereo Boliviano SA [Lloyd Bolivian Air Line]
LAB	Local Area Broadcast (NVT)
LAB	Logic Array Block (SAUS)
LAB	Los Angeles Branch [AEC]
LAB	Low-Altitude Bombing [Military]
LABA	Laboratory Animal Breeders Association (EA)
Lab AC	Labour Appeal Cases [India] [A publication] (DLA)
LABAC	Licentiate Member of the Association of Business and Administrative Computing [British] (DBQ)
LABAN	Lakas ng Bayan [Peoples' Power Movement - Fight] [Philippines] [Political party] (PPW)
Lab & Auto Bull...	Labor and Automation Bulletin [A publication] (DLA)
LA Bar	Louisiana Bar. Official Publication of the Louisiana State Bar Association [A publication] (DLA)
Lab Arb	Labor Arbitration Reports [Bureau of National Affairs] [A publication] (DLA)
Lab Arb & Disp Settl...	Labor Arbitration and Dispute Settlements [A publication] (DLA)
Lab Arb Awards...	Labor Arbitration Awards [Commerce Clearing House] [A publication] (DLA)
LaBarg	La Barge, Inc. [Associated Press] (SAG)
LABB	Legal Abbreviations [Database]
LABBS	Ladies Association of British Barbershop Singers (BUAC)
LABC	Local Automatic Brightness Control (ACAE)
LABC	Lymphadenosis Benigna Cutis [Medicine]
LabChile	Laboratorio Chile SA [Associated Press] (SAG)
LABCOM	Laboratory Command [Adelphi, MD] [Army] (RDA)
LABCOM	US Army Laboratory Command (SAUS)
LAB-CO-OP...	Labour and Co-Operative Party [British]
LabCp	Laboratory Corp. of America Holdings [Associated Press] (SAG)
LABE	Lava Beds National Monument
LABE	Louisiana Association of Business Educators (EDAC)
LABECO	Laboratory Equipment Corp. [Auto industry supplier]
LABEL	Law Students Association for Buyers' Education in Labeling [Student legal action organization]
LABELS	Region 3 Mail Labels System (SAUS)
LABEX	International Laboratory Apparatus and Material Exhibition (SAUO)
LABEX	Laboratory Equipment Exhibition (TSPED)
LABF	Latin American Banking Federation [Bogota, Colombia] (EA)
LABH	Lab Holdings [NASDAQ symbol] (SG)
Lab His	Labour History [A publication]
LABIB	LASER Bibliography
LABIL	Light Aircraft Binary Information Link
LABIM	Licentiate, American Board of International Medicine (CMD)
Lab Ind	Labour and Industry [A publication]
LabInd	Labour Independent (SAUO)
LABIS	Laboratory Information Systems (DNAB)
Lab J Aust ...	Laboratory Journal of Australasia [A publication]
LABK	Lafayette American Bank & Trust [NASDAQ symbol] (SAG)
LABK	Lafayette American Bk & Tr [NASDAQ symbol] (TTSB)
LABL	Australian Co. Secretary's Business Law Manual [A publication]
LABL	Multi-Color Corp. [NASDAQ symbol] (NQ)
Lab L Rep ...	Labor Law Reporter [Commerce Clearing House] [A publication] (DLA)
LABMIS	Laboratories Management Information System
LABN	Lake Ariel Bancorp [NASDAQ symbol] (SAG)
LABNET	Los Alamos National Laboratory Network (SAUO)
LABO	Licentiate, American Board of Ophthalmology (CMD)
LabOne	LabOne, Inc. [Associated Press] (SAG)
Labor C	Labor Code [A publication] (DLA)
LABORDOC...	International Labour Documentation [International Labour Office] [Geneva, Switzerland] [Bibliographic database]
LABORINFO...	Labour Information Database [International Labour Office] [Information service or system] (IID)
LABORSTAT...	International Labor Organization, Bureau of Statistics Database (GFGA)
LABP	Latin American Book Programs [Defunct]
LABP	Lethal Aid for Bomber Penetration (MCD)
LABP	Licentiate, American Board of Pediatrics (CMD)
LABPIE	Low-Altitude Bombing Position Indicator Equipment [Military]
LABPR	Local Advisory Board Procedural Regulation (Office of Rent Stabilization) [Economic Stabilization Agency] [A publication] (DLA)
LAB PROC ...	Laboratory Procedure [Medicine] (BABM)
LabProg	Labour Progressive (SAUO)
LABPROP	Laboratory Property Management System (SAUO)
LabPty	Labour Party (SAUO)
LabPU	Labour Party of Ukraine [Political party] (BUAC)
labr	Laborer (GEAB)
LABR	Laborer
LABR	Licentiate, American Board of Radiology (CMD)
L Abr	Lilly's Abridgment [England] [A publication] (DLA)
LABRAPS	Laboratoire de Recherche en Administration et Politique Scolaires [Canada]
Lab Rel Guide (P-H)...	Labor Relations Guide (Prentice-Hall, Inc.) [A publication] (DLA)
LABREV	Laboratoire de Recherche sur l'Emploi, la Repartition, et la Securite du Revenu [University of Quebec at Montreal] [Research center] (RCD)
LABROC	Laboratory Rocket
LABRV	Large Advanced Ballistic Re-entry Vehicle (SAUS)
LABS	LabOne, Inc. [NASDAQ symbol] (SAG)
LABS	Laboratory Admission Baseline Studies
Labs	Laboratory classes (SAUS)
LABS	LASER Active Boresight System (PDAA)
LABS	Learning about Basic Science [Education program]
LABS	Linear Alkylbenzene Sulfonate (EDCT)
LABS	Los Alamos Bright Source (SAUO)
LABS	Low-Altitude Bombing System [Air Force]
LABSAP	Laboratoire des Sciences de l'Activite Physique [Laval University] [Canada] [Research center] (RCD)
LABS I/II	Los Alamos Bright Source Laser Facility (SAUO)
LabSpc	Laboratory Specialists of America, Inc. [Associated Press] (SAG)
LabSpec	Laboratory Specialists of America, Inc. [Associated Press] (SAG)
LABSTAT	Labor Statistics [Database] [Department of Labor]
LABSTAT	United States Bureau of Labor Statistics (SAUO)
LabStatBull...	United States Bureau of Labor Statistics Bulletin (SAUO)
LAB TECH ...	Laboratory Technologies Corp. (PCM)
LABU	Latin American Blind Union [See also ULAC] [Uruguay] (EAIO)
LA Bus	Los Alamos Bus System (SAUO)
LABUT	Labor Utilization (MCD)
LAbV	Vermilion Parish Library, Abbeville, LA [Library symbol] [Library of Congress] (LCLS)
LabVIEW	Laboratory Virtual Instrument Engineering Workbench
LABVT	Left Atrial Ball-Valve Thrombus [Medicine] (STED)
LABZ	Laboratory Specialists Amer [NASDAQ symbol] (TTSB)
LABZ	Laboratory Specialists of America, Inc. [NASDAQ symbol] (SAG)
LABZW	Laboratory Specialists Wrrt [NASDAQ symbol] (TTSB)
LAC	AB Bofors [Sweden] [Research code symbol]
LAC	Fort Lewis, WA [Location identifier] [FAA] (FAAL)
LaC	Labiocervical [Dentistry]
LAC	Laboratory Accreditation Committee (SAUO)
LAC	Laboratory Animals Centre (BUAC)
LAC	Labour Appeal Cases [India] [A publication] (ILCA)
LAC	Labour Arbitration Cases [Canada Law Book, Inc.] [Information service or system] [A publication] [A publication] (CRD)
Lac	Laceration [Medicine] (AMHC)
Lac	Laceration [Medicine]
Lac	Lacerta [Constellation]
LAC	Lac Minerals Ltd. (SAUO)
lac	Lacquer (VRA)
LAC	Lacquer (WDAA)
LAC	La Crosse [A bunyavirus]
LAC	Lactation (WDAA)
LAC	Lactose [Cardiology] (DAVI)
LAC	Lae-City [Papua New Guinea] [Airport symbol] (OAG)
LAC	Landers [California] [Seismograph station code, US Geological Survey] (SEIS)
LAC	Landscape Advisory Committee (BUAC)
LAC	Language Across the Curriculum
LAC	Large Acrocentric Chromosome [Medicine]
LAC	Large Anechoic Chamber (ACAE)

LAC............. Large-Area-Counter [Astronomy] [Instrumentation]
LAC............. Large Area Counter on Ginga (SAUO)
LAC............. Large Area Coverage [Marine science] (OSRA)
LAC............. LASER Amplifier Chain
LAC............. Latin American Center (BUAC)
LAC............. Latvian Academy of Culture (BUAC)
LAC............. Launch Analyst's Console [Aerospace] (AAG)
LAC............. Launcher Assignment Console
LAC............. Law-abiding Citizen (BARN)
LAC............. Lead Angle Compensator (ACAE)
LAC............. Leading Aircraftsman [RAF] [British]
LAC............. League of Arab Countries (SAUO)
LAC............. Learning Assistance Center [Stanford University]
LAC............. Left Atrial Contraction [Cardiology] (DAVI)
LAC............. Legal Advice Centre (SAUO)
LAC............. Legal Advisory Committee [of NYSE]
LAC............. Legislative Action Conference (SAUO)
LAC............. Lemon Administrative Committee (EA)
LAC............. Liberal Academic Complex
LAC............. Liberated Areas Committee [World War II]
LAC............. Liberty Amendment Committee of the USA (EA)
LAC............. Library Advisory Council [Department of Education and Science]
     [British] (NITA)
LAC............. Library Assistants Certificate [City and Guilds Institute] [British]
     (NITA)
LAC............. Library Association of China (BUAC)
LAc............. Licensed Acupuncturist [Medicine]
LAC............. Licentiate of the Apothecaries' Company [British]
LAC............. Lights Advisory Committee [General Council of British Shipping] (DS)
LAC............. Limited Area Coverage [Data]
LAC............. Limiting Admissible Concentration
LAC............. Limits to Acceptable Change [Park tourism management]
LAC............. Lindamood Auditory Conceptualization Test [Psychology] (DAVI)
LAC............. Linear Absorption Coefficient
LAC............. Linear Aeronautical Chart (BARN)
LAC............. Linear Amplitude-Continuous (PDAA)
LAC............. Linguoaxiocervical [Dentistry]
LAC............. Liposome-Antibody-Complement [Immunochemistry]
LAC............. Liquid Affinity Chromatography
LAC............. List of Assessed Contractors [Military] (RDA)
LAC............. Lithuanian American Community (EA)
LAC............. Lithuanian American Council
LAC............. Live Action Camera (WDMC)
LAC............. Livestock Advisory Committee (SAUO)
LAC............. Load Accumulator
LAC............. Local Advisory Council [British labor]
LAC............. Local Agency Check (AFM)
LAC............. Local Area Controller (SAUO)
LAC............. Local Area Coverage [Meteorology]
LAC............. Local Arrangements Committee [National Court Reporters
     Association]
LAC............. Local Authority Circular (HEAS)
LAC............. Lockheed Aircraft Corp. [ICAO designator] (FAAC)
LAC............. Logistics Area Coordinator (MCD)
LAC............. London Assembly Centre (SAUO)
LAC............. Long Arm Cast [Medicine] (MEDA)
LAC............. Longitudinal Aerodynamic Characteristics
LAC............. Long-Run Average Cost Curve [Economics]
LAC............. Loop Assignment Center (VLIE)
LA-C............. Los Alamos Conference (SAUO)
LAC............. Los Alamos County (SAUO)
LAC............. Los Angeles Chargers [National Football League] [1960] (NFLA)
LAC............. Lotus Authorized Consultants (SAUS)
LAC............. Low-Altitude Cruise (MCD)
LAC............. Low Amplitude Contraction [Neurology] (DAVI)
LAC............. Lunar Aeronautical Chart [Air Force]
LAC............. Lunar Atlas Chart [Aerospace] (SAA)
LAC............. Lung Adenocarcinoma Cell [Medicine] (STED)
LAC............. Lupus Anticoagulant [Immunochemistry]
LACA........... Ladies Apparel Contractors Association (EA)
LACA........... Latin America Coffee Agreement (BUAC)
LACA........... Latin American Coffee Agreement (SAUO)
LACA........... Life Agency Cashiers Association of the United States and Canada
     (EA)
LACA........... Local Authority Caterers Association (BUAC)
LACA........... London Association of Certified Accountants (SAUO)
LACA........... Low-Altitude Control Area
LACAC......... Latin American Civil Aviation Commission [See also CLAC] (EAIO)
lac & cont ... Lacerations and Contusions [Medicine] (STED)
LACAP......... Latin American Cooperative Acquisitions Program [or Project]
LACAP......... Los Alamos Civil Air Patrol (SAUO)
LACAS......... LASER Applications in Close Air Support [Air Force]
LACas......... Latin American Casinos, Inc. [Associated Press] (SAG)
LACAS......... Lineas Aereas Costarricenses SA [Costa Rica] [ICAO designator]
     (FAAC)
LACAS......... Local Authority Catering Advisory Service (AIE)
LACAS......... Low Altitude Close Aircraft Support (SAUO)
LACAS......... Low-Altitude Close Air Support [Military]
LACASA...... Latin American and Caribbean Solidarity Association (EA)
LACAT........ Legislative Alliance of Creative Arts Therapies [Defunct] (EA)
LACATA...... Laundry and Cleaners Allied Trades Association [Later, TCATA] (EA)
LACATE...... Low Atmospheric Composition and Temperature Experiment (SAUO)
LACATE...... Lower Atmosphere Composition and Temperature Experiment
     [National Science Foundation]
LACB........... Landing Aids Control Building [NASA] (NASA)

LACB........... Look Angles of Celestial Bodies (KSC)
LACBWR...... LaCrosse Boiling Water Reactor [Also, LCBWR]
LACC........... Latin American and Caribbean Center [Florida International
     University] [Research center] (RCD)
LACC........... Latin-American Council of Churches (BUAC)
LACC........... Lloyd's Aviation Claims Centre (AIA)
LACC........... Local Area Control Center (VLIE)
LACC........... Los Angeles City College [California]
l'ACCAB ...... L'Association Canadienne des Centres d'Action Benevole (AC)
LACCB .... Latin American Confederation of Clinical Biochemistry [Colombia]
     (EAIO)
LACCD .... Los Angeles Community College District (ACAE)
LACCSM ..... Latin American and Caribbean Council for Self-Management (EAIO)
LACD........... Limited-Amplitude, Controlled-Decay (PDAA)
LACDL .... Louisiana Association of Criminal Defense Lawyers (SRA)
LACE........... Alpine Lace Brands [NASDAQ symbol] (SPSG)
LACE........... Landline Air defense Communications Encryption (SAUS)
LACE........... Language for ALGOL [Algorithmic Language] Compiler Extension
     [Computer science] (CSR)
LACE........... LASER Aerospace Communications Experiment
LACE........... Laser Communication Experiment (ACAE)
LACE........... Launch Angle Condition Evaluator
LACE........... Launch Automatic Checkout Equipment
LACE........... Library Advisory Council for England (NITA)
LACE........... [The] Lingerie and Corsetry Exhibition [British] (ITD)
LACE........... Linkage Assistance and Cooperation for the European Border
     Regions (BUAC)
LACE........... Liquid Air Collection Engine
LACE........... Liquid Air Cycle Engine [Aerospace plane engine concept]
LACE........... Local Automatic Circuit Exchange [Telecommunications]
LACE........... Low-Power Atmospheric Compensation Experiment [Strategic
     Defense Initiative]
LACE........... Low-power Atmospheric Compensation Experiment satellite (SAUS)
LACE........... Lunar Atmospheric Composition Experiment [Apollo] [NASA]
LACE........... Luton Analogue Computing Engine [British] (DEN)
LACE........... Lysergic Acid Cryptoethelane (IIA)
LACEF .... Los Alamos Critical Experiments Facility (SAUO)
LACES......... London Airport Cargo Electronic-Data-Processing Scheme
LACES...... Los Angeles Council for Engineering Societies (SAUO)
Lacey Dig .... Lacey's Digest of Railroad Decisions [A publication] (DLA)
LACF........... Low Acid Canned Food
LACFD .... Los Alamos County Fire Department (SAUO)
LACFFP....... Latin-American Commission on Forestry and Forest Products (SAUO)
LACFFP....... Latin-American Commission on Forestry and Forestry Products
     (BUAC)
Lach............ Laches [of Plato] [Classical studies] (OCD)
LACH .... Lightweight Amphibious Container Handler (MCD)
LACHESIS .... Laterally Archiving Containment, Health, Environment & Safety
     System (SAUO)
LACHEX ...... Los Alamos Chess Experiment (SAUO)
LACI .... Land Air Campaign Initiative (SAUO)
LACI .... Latin Amer Casinos [NASDAQ symbol] (TTSB)
LACI .... Latin American Casinos, Inc. [NASDAQ symbol] (SAG)
LACI .... Lipoprotein-Associated Coagulation Inhibitor [Hematology]
LACI .... Lockheed Aeromod Centers Inc. (SAUO)
LACI .... London Association of Conference Interpreters (SAUO)
LACIE......... Large Area Crop Inventory Experiment [NASA]
LACIM......... Latin American and Caribbean International Moving [Panama] (EAIO)
LACIP......... Large Area Crop Inventory Program [NASA] (NASA)
LACIRS .... Latin American Communications Information Retrieval System
     (SAUO)
LA Civ Code Ann (West)... West's Louisiana Code of Civil Procedure, Annotated
     [A publication] (DLA)
LACIW .... Latin Amer Casinos Wrrt [NASDAQ symbol] (TTSB)
LACJ .... Los Angeles County Jail (SAUO)
L'ACJE........ L'Association Canadienne pour les Jeunes Enfants (AC)
Lacka Leg News... Lackawanna Legal News [Pennsylvania] [A publication] (DLA)
Lackawanna B... Lackawanna Bar Reporter [Pennsylvania] [A publication] (DLA)
Lack Bar R... Lackawanna Bar Reporter [Pennsylvania] [A publication] (DLA)
Lack Co (PA)... Lackawanna County Reports [Pennsylvania] [A publication] (DLA)
Lack Leg N... Lackawanna Legal News [Pennsylvania] [A publication] (DLA)
Lack Leg News (PA)... Lackawanna Legal News [Pennsylvania] [A publication]
     (DLA)
Lack Leg R... Lackawanna Legal Record [Pennsylvania] [A publication] (DLA)
Lack Leg Rec... Lackawanna Legal Record [Pennsylvania] [A publication] (DLA)
Lack LN ...... Lackawanna Legal News [Pennsylvania] [A publication] (DLA)
Lack LR ...... Lackawanna Legal Record [Pennsylvania] [A publication] (DLA)
LACL........... Latin American Citizens League (SAUO)
LACLA......... Latin American Constitutional Law Association [Argentina] (EAIO)
LacledeSt .... Laclede Steel Co. [Associated Press] (SAG)
LaclGas...... Laclede Gas Co. [Associated Press] (SAG)
LACM.......... Latin America Common Market [Proposed]
LACM.......... Latin American Common Market (SAUO)
LACM.......... Load Accumulator with Magnitude (HGAA)
LACM.......... Los Angeles County Museum (SAUO)
LACM.......... Los Angeles County Museum of Natural History [California]
LACMA........ Latin American and Caribbean Movers Association (EAIO)
LACMA........ Los Angeles Conservatory of Music and Arts (SAUO)
LACMA........ Los Angeles County Medical Association (SAUO)
LACMA........ Los Angeles County Museum of Art
LACMedA.... Los Angeles County Medical Association (SAUO)
LACMN........ Leading Aircrewman [British military] (DMA)
LACMNH/Q... Quarterly. Los Angeles County Museum of Natural History. Los
     Angeles (SAUS)
lac-mRNA .... Ribonucleic Acid, Messenger - lac operon [Biochemistry, genetics]

Lac-mRNA... Ribonucleic Acid, Messenger-Lac operon (SAUS)
LACN........... Local Area Communications Network (DMAA)
LACNSW..... Legal Aid Commission of New South Wales [Australia]
LACNT........ Legal Aid Commission of the Northern Territory [Australia]
LACO .... Erich Lacher Co.
LACO .... LASER Communication (SSD)
LACO .... Liberty American Corporation (SAUO)
LACO .... Los Angeles Chamber Orchestra (SAUO)
LACO .... Los Angeles College of Optometry [California]
LA Co Art Mus... Los Angeles County Art Museum
LA Code Civ Pro Ann... West's Louisiana Code of Civil Procedure, Annotated
                    [A publication] (DLA)
LA Code Crim Pro Ann... West's Louisiana Code of Criminal Procedure, Annotated
                    [A publication] (DLA)
LAC of AMFC... Library Affairs Committee of the Associated Mid-Florida Colleges
                    [Library network]
LACOM........ Low-Altitude Contour Matching (MCD)
LACONIQ..... Laboratory Computer Online Inquiry
LA Const Art... Louisiana Constitution [A publication] (DLA)
LACOTS ...... Local Authorities' Coordinating Body on Training Standards [British]
LACP........... Large Area Coverage Processor (ACAE)
LACP........... Latin American Co-operative Acquisition Project (SAUO)
LACP........... Lignes Aeriennes Canadiennes Pacifiques
LA-CP......... Los Alamos Controlled Publication (SAUO)
LACPA........ Los Angeles County Purchasing Agent (ACAE)
LACQ .... Lacquer
LACQLD ...... Legal Aid Commission of Queensland [Australia]
Lacr .... Lacerta [Constellation]
lacr .... Lacrimal [Ophthalmology] (DAVI)
LACR .... Lancer Corp. (SAUO)
LACR .... Low-Altitude Coverage RADAR
LACRC........ Locally Assigned Convoy Route Carrier Code
LAC REC ..... Lactis Recentis [New Milk] [Pharmacy] (ROG)
LaCrose...... LaCrosse Footwear, Inc. [Associated Press] (SAG)
Lac RR Dig... Lacey's Digest of Railroad Decisions [A publication] (DLA)
LACS........... Laboratory Automated Calibration System (MCD)
LACS........... Large-Area Chemical Sensor (ABAC)
LACS........... League Against Cruel Sports (EA)
LACS........... Listener Active State (IAA)
LACS........... Lithuanian-American Catholic Services [Defunct] (EA)
LACS........... Los Angeles Catalyst Study [Environmental Protection Agency]
LACS........... Los Angeles Copyright Society (EA)
LACSA .... Lineas Aereas Costarricenses Sociedad Anonima [Airline] [Costa
                    Rica]
LACSAB .... Local Authorities' Conditions of Service Advisory Board [British]
                    (DCTA)
LACSD .... Los Angeles County Sanitation District (SAUO)
L'ACSQ .... Association Canadienne des Cinq Quilles [Formerly, Canadian
                    Bowling Congress] (AC)
lact .... Lactate [or Lactating] (AAMN)
lact .... Lactating [Medicine] (MAE)
LACT........... Lactic Acid [Biochemistry] (DAVI)
LAC T.......... Lactose Tolerance [Gastroenterology] (DAVI)
LACT........... Lease Automatic Custody Transfer
LACT........... Legal Aid Commission of Tasmania [Australia]
LACT........... Library of Anglo-Catholic Theology [A publication] (ODCC)
LACT........... Lindamood Auditory Conceptualization Test [Psychology] (STED)
LACT........... London Association of Classical Teachers (SAUO)
LACT........... Low-Affinity Choline Transport
LACT-ART..... Lactate Arterial (STED)
LACTC......... Los Angeles County Transportation Commission (ACAE)
lact hyd ...... Lactalbumin Hydrolysate (STED)
LACTOZ....... Laboratory Studies of the Chemistry of Atmospheric Ozone (SAUO)
LACUS .... Linguistic Association of Canada and the United States (EA)
LACUSA ...... Liberty Amendment Committee of the USA (EA)
LACUSA ...... Lithuanian-American Community of the USA [Later, LAC] (EA)
LAC/USC ...... Los Angeles County/University of Southern California Medical
                    Center (DAVI)
LACV........... Light Amphibious Cargo Vehicle (MCD)
LACV........... Light Armored Combat Vehicle
LACV........... Lighter, Air-Cushion Vehicle [Usually used in combination with
                    numerals] [Military] (RDA)
LACV-30 ...... Lighter, Air Cushion Vehicle, 30 Tons [Military] (MCD)
LACW......... Leading Aircraft Woman [RAF] [British]
LACWA .... Legal Aid Commission of Western Australia
LACYMCA .... Latin American Confederation of YMCAs [See also CLACJ] (EAIO)
LAD........... Laboratory Astrophysics Division (SAUO)
LAD........... Lactate Dehydrogenase [Also, LD, LDH] [An enzyme]
LAD........... Lactic Acid Dehydrogenase [See also LDH] [An enzyme]
LAD........... Ladder (MSA)
lad .... Ladino [MARC language code] [Library of Congress] (LCCP)
LAD........... Ladron Mountain [New Mexico] [Seismograph station code, US
                    Geological Survey] (SEIS)
LAD........... Landing Assist Device [Aviation] (NG)
LAD........... Language Acquisition Device
LAD........... Large Area Detector [Instrumentation]
LAD........... Large Area Display
LAD........... LASER Acoustic Delay
LAD........... LASER Acquisition and Direction
LAD........... LASER Acquisition Device (MCD)
LAD........... LASER Air Defense
LAD........... Last Appearance Datum [Geology]
LAD........... Last Appearance of Date (or Datum) (SAUO)
LAD........... Lateral Awareness and Directionality Test [Sensorimotor skills test]
LAD........... Latest Arrival Date (AABC)

LAD........... Launch Assist Device (SAUS)
LAD........... Leaf Area Duration [Botany]
LAD........... Least Absolute Deviation (IDAI)
LAD........... Lebanon Airport Development Corp. [ICAO designator] (FAAC)
LAD........... Left Anterior Descending [Artery]
LAD........... Left Anterior Digestive [Gland]
LAD........... Left Axis Deviation [Medicine]
LAD........... Leukocyte Adhesion Deficiency [Medicine]
LAD........... Liberation Army Daily (SAUS)
LAD........... Library Administration Division [American Library Association] [Later,
                    LAMA] (EA)
LAD........... Ligament Augmentation Device [Sports medicine]
LAD........... Light Aid Detachment [Military] [British]
LAD........... Light Area Defense (MCD)
LAD........... Linoleic Acid Depression [Clinical chemistry] (AAMN)
LAD........... Lipoamide Dehydrogenase [An enzyme]
LAD........... Liquid Agent Detector (AABC)
LAD........... Lithia Motors'A' [NYSE symbol] (SG)
LAD........... Lithium Aluminum Deuteride [Inorganic chemistry]
LAD........... Lloyd's Aviation Department (AIA)
LAD........... Load Address (IAA)
LAD........... Local Air Defence (SAUS)
LAD........... Local Area Disk (VLIE)
LAD........... Location Aid Device (MCD)
LAD........... Logical Analysis Device
LAD........... Logical Aptitude Device (BUR)
LAD........... Logic and Adder (IAA)
LAD........... Logistic Approval Data
LAD........... Logistics Anchor Desk [Military]
LAD........... Lookout Assist Device [Navigation] (OA)
LAD........... Low-Accuracy Data/Designation [System]. (MUGU)
LAD........... Low Alcohol Drinking [Rat strain]
LAD........... Low Altitude Dispenser (SAUO)
LAD........... Low-Altitude Dispenser
LAD........... Low-Angle Dolly
LAD........... Luanda [Angola] [Airport symbol] (OAG)
LAD........... Lunar Atmosphere Detector [Aerospace]
LAD........... Lymphocyte-Activating Determinant (DAVI)
LAD........... Lymphocyte-Activating Determinate (STED)
LAD........... Our Lady of Angels College, Aston, PA [OCLC symbol] (OCLC)
LADA........... Laboratory Animal Dander Allergy (DAVI)
LADA........... Left Acromio-Dorso-Anterior [A fetal position] [Obstetrics]
LADA........... Left Anterior Descending Artery [Anatomy] (DAVI)
LADA........... Lesson Analysis Design Approach
LADA........... Light Air Defense Artillery [Army]
LADA........... London Air Defence Area [British military] (DMA)
LADA........... London Alley Dwelling Authority (SAUO)
LADAPT ...... Lookup Dictionary Adaptor Program (IEEE)
LADAR........ LASER Detection and Ranging
LADAR........ LASER Doppler RADAR (MCD)
LADB .... Laboratory Animal Data Bank [Battelle Memorial Institute] [Columbus,
                    OH] [No longer available online] [Information service or
                    system] (IID)
LADB .... Latin American Data Bank [University of Florida] (IID)
LADB .... Latin American Data Base [An association] (EA)
LADB .... Lesotho Agricultural Development Bank (BUAC)
LADC........... LASER Advanced Development Center (IAA)
L'ADC .... L'Association Dentaire Canadienne (AC)
LADC........... Left Anterior Descending Coronary Artery [Anatomy]
LADC........... Los Alamos Document Center (SAUO)
LADCA........ Left Anterior Descending Coronary Artery [Medicine] (STED)
LADCP .... Lowered Acoustic Doppler Current Profiler (SAUS)
Ladd .... Ladd's Reports [59-64 New Hampshire] [A publication] (DLA)
LADD........... Left Anterior Descending Diagonal [Branch of coronary artery]
                    [Anatomy] (DAVI)
LADD........... Lens Antenna Deployment Demonstration (ACAE)
LADD........... Low-Altitude Drogue Delivery (AFM)
LADD........... Lowest Acceptable Daily Dose (EPAT)
LADDER...... Language Access to Distributed Data with Error Recovery
LaddFr........ Ladd Furniture, Inc. [Associated Press] (SAG)
LADDR........ Layered Device Driver Architecture [Microsoft Corp.] [Computer
                    science] (PCM)
LADDS........ Laundry and Decontamination Drycleaning System [Military] (DWSG)
LADE........... Language Definition Environment
LADE........... Lineas Aereas del Estada [Argentine Air Force airline]
La de Castigl... Lapus de Castiglionchio [Flourished, 1353-81] [Authority cited in
                    pre-1607 legal work] (DSA)
LADECO........ Linea Aerea del Cobre SA [Chile] (EY)
La de Rampo... Lambertus de Ramponibus [Deceased, 1304] [Authority cited in
                    pre-1607 legal work] (DSA)
LADF........... Ladd Furniture [NASDAQ symbol] (SAG)
LADF........... Ladd Furniture, Inc. (SAUO)
LADFU......... Large Area Detector Flight Unit (SAUS)
LADGA........ Layered Acrylic Directed Graph with Attributes (VLIE)
LADH........... Lactic Acid Dehydrogenase [An enzyme] (DAVI)
LADH........... Liver Alcohol Dehydrogenase [An enzyme]
LADIES....... Lapan Digital Image Evaluation System (SAUO)
LADIES....... Life after Divorce Is Eventually Sane (EA)
LADIES....... Los Alamos Digital Image Enhancement Software (PDAA)
LADIES....... Los Alamos Digital Image Enhancement System (SAUO)
LADIES....... Low-Altitude Air Defense Identification and Engagement Study
LADIR........ Low-Cost Arrays for Detection of Infrared (PDAA)
LADIZ......... Leaving Air Defense Identification Zone
LADLE......... Librarians Antidefamation League

LAD-LOMS.... Library Administration Division, Library Organization and Management Section [*American Library Association*] (AEBS)
LADM.......... Laboratory Automated Data Management
LADME........ Liberation, Absorption, Distribution, Metabolism, and Excretion [*Medicine*] (STED)
LADME........ Liberation, Absorption, Distribution, Metabolism, Excretion [*Medicine*] (DAVI)
LAD-MIN..... Left Axis Deviation Minimal [*Cardiology*] (DAVI)
LADMIS ...... Low Altitude Air Defense Missile (ACAE)
LADMS .... Lightweight Air Defense Missile System (SAUS)
LADO .... Latin American Defense Organization (SAUO)
LADO .... Latin American Development Organization (SAUO)
LADO .... Los Angeles District Office (SAUO)
LADOG........ Low-Altitude Drive on Ground (IAA)
Ladp .... Ladyship (BARN)
LADP .... Leadership Assessment and Development Program [*Army*] (INF)
LADP .... Left Acromio-Dorso-Posterior [*A fetal position*] [*Obstetrics*]
LADP .... Locally-Acting Drug Product [*Drug evalution*]
LA/DP .... Office of Development Programs, Bureau for Latin America (SAUO)
LADPOP....... Lethal Agent Disposal Process Optimization Program (MCD)
LADR .... Linear Accelerator-Driven Reactor (BARN)
LADRAP...... Lethal Area Data Reduction and Plotting (SAA)
LADS .... LASER Actuator Director System [*DoD*]
LADS .... LASER Airborne Depth Sounder
LADS .... LASER Air Defense System
LADS .... Light Air Defense System (SAUS)
LADS .... Light Area Defense System (MCD)
LADS .... Lightweight Actuator Detector Weapons System (SAUO)
LADS .... Lightweight Air Defense System (MCD)
LADS .... Limited Attack Defense System
LADS .... Linear Analysis and Design of Structure (IAA)
LADS .... Listener Addressed State (IAA)
LADS .... Literary and Debating Society (SAUO)
LADS .... Local Area Data Service [*Telecommunications*] (ACRL)
LADS .... Local Area Data Set
LADS .... Logic Automation Documentation System (VLIE)
LADS .... Low-Altitude Defense System (MCD)
LADS .... Low-Altitude Detection System [*Air Force*]
LADS .... Low-Altitude Dispensing System [*Missiles*]
LADSIRLAC... Liverpool and District Scientific Industrial and Research Library Advisory Council [*Library cooperative scheme*] [*British*] (NITA)
LADSR .... Low Altitude Defense System Radar (ACAE)
LADT .... Local Access Data Transport (SAUO)
LADT.......... Local Area Data Transport [*AT & T*]
LADT.......... Local Area Digital Transmission (WGA)
LADT.......... Low-Altitude Drop Test [*NASA*]
LADTAC ...... Light Area Defense Technical Assistance Control (ACAE)
LADu.......... Lobuloalveolar-Ductal (STED)
L Adv .... Lord Advocate [*British*] (DAS)
L Advertiser... Law Advertiser [*1823-31*] [*A publication*] (DLA)
LADWP .... Los Angeles Department of Water and Power (SAUO)
LADY .... Tennis Lady, Inc. (SAUO)
LadyLuck .... Lady Luck Gaming Corp. [*Associated Press*] (SAG)
LAE.......... Lae [*Papua New Guinea*] [*Airport symbol*] (OAG)
LAE.......... Lae [*Papua New Guinea*] [*Seismograph station code, US Geological Survey*] [*Closed*] (SEIS)
LAE.......... Launcher Adapter Electronics (MCD)
LAE.......... Lead Angle Error
LAE.......... Leadership Ability Evaluation [*Psychology*]
LAE.......... Left Arithmetic Element
LAE.......... Left Atrial Enlargement [*Cardiology*]
LAE.......... Lethal Area Estimate
LAE.......... Linear Alcohol Ethoxylate [*Surfactant*]
LAE.......... Lineas Aereas Colombianas Ltd. [*Colombia*] [*ICAO designator*] (FAAC)
LAE.......... London Association of Engineers [*England*] (BUAC)
LAE.......... Long Above-Elbow [*Cast*] (STED)
LAE.......... "Love Is All" for Enge (EA)
LAE.......... Low Altitude Extraction (SAUS)
LAEADA ...... Alabama. Agricultural Experiment Station. Leaflet (SAUS)
LAEC......... Los Angeles Electric Club (SAUO)
LAEC......... Los Angeles Electronic Club (SAUO)
LAEC......... Lotus Authorized Education Center (SAUO)
LAECC......... Groupe International Laicat et Communaute Chretienne [*International Laity and Christian Community Group - ILCCG*] [*Defunct*] (EA)
LAECG .... Local Aboriginal Education Consultative Group [*Australia*]
LAED.......... Large Area Electronic Display
LAED.......... Low Angle Electron Diffraction (PDAA)
LAEDP .... Large Area Electronic Display Panel
LAEDV .... Left Atrial End-Diastolic Volume [*Medicine*] (STED)
LAEDV .... Left Atrial Volume in End Diastole [*Medicine*] (DMAA)
LAEE.......... Lithuanian Association for Energy Economics (BUAC)
LAEF.......... Luso-American Education Foundation (EA)
LAEI.......... Left Atrial Emptying Index [*Medicine*] (STED)
LAE NOTE.... Licensed Aircraft Engineers' Notice (DNAB)
LAEO.......... Low-Altitude Electro-Optical (SAUS)
LAEP.......... Large Area Electronic Panel
LAEPC......... Local Aboriginal Employment Promotion Committee [*Australia*]
LAER.......... Lowest Achievable Emission Rate [*Environmental Protection Agency*]
LAERF......... Lewisville Aquatic Ecosystem Research Facility [*Texas*]
LAEs........ Aircraft Engineers (SAUS)
LAES........ Latin American Economic System
LAESV........ Left Atrial End-Systolic Volume [*Medicine*] (STED)
LAET.......... Limiting Actual Exposure Time (KSC)

LAETRILE.... Laevo-Mandelonitrile-beta-glucuronic Acid [*Possible anticancer compound*]
LAEU.......... Launching Adapter Electronic Unit (ACAE)
LAEV.......... Laevus [*Left*] [*Pharmacy*]
LAF.......... Lafarge Corp. [*NYSE symbol*] (SPSG)
LAF.......... Lafayette [*Indiana*] [*Airport symbol*] (OAG)
LAF.......... Lafayette [*Rhode Island*] [*Seismograph station code, US Geological Survey*] [*Closed*] (SEIS)
LAF.......... Lafayette [*Diocesan abbreviation*] [*Louisiana*] (TOCD)
LAF.......... Lafayette College, Easton, PA [*OCLC symbol*] (OCLC)
LAF.......... Lafayette, IN [*Location identifier*] [*FAA*] (FAAL)
LAF.......... Lake Acidification and Fisheries (SAUO)
LAF.......... Laminar Airflow (KSC)
LAF.......... Land Acquisition Fund (SAUO)
LAF.......... Landscape Architecture Foundation (EA)
Laf.......... Lanfrancus [*Deceased, 1089*] [*Authority cited in pre-1607 legal work*] (DSA)
Laf.......... Lanfrancus Cremensis [*Deceased, 1229*] [*Authority cited in pre-1607 legal work*] (DSA)
LAF.......... Latin American Female [*Classified advertising*] (DMAA)
LAF.......... Left Anterior Fascicle [*Anatomy*]
LAF.......... Legal Aid Fund (SAUO)
LAF.......... Leukocyte-Activating Factor [*Immunochemistry*]
LAF.......... Light Assault Ferry (SAUS)
LAF.......... Limited Amplifier Filter
LAF.......... Limits and Fits [*System*] [*Precision of tolerance*] [*Automotive engineering*]
LAF.......... Live Aid Foundation (EA)
LAF.......... Living Arts Foundation (EA)
LAF.......... Load Alleviation Function (ACAE)
LAF.......... Logistic Availability Factor (CAAL)
LAF.......... Long Address Form (NITA)
LAF.......... Low Animal Fat (STED)
LAF.......... Low Frequency Active System (SAUS)
LAF.......... Luteal Angiogenic Factor [*Biochemistry*]
LAF.......... Lymphocyte Activating Factor [*Immunology*]
LAF.......... Lyophilized Allantoic Fluid [*Endocrinology*]
Lafarge....... Lafarge Corp. [*Associated Press*] (SAG)
Lafay .... Lafayette Industries, Inc. [*Associated Press*] (SAG)
LafayABk.... Lafayette American Bank & Trust [*Associated Press*] (SAG)
Lafaye .... Lafayette Industries, Inc. [*Associated Press*] (SAG)
LAFB.......... Langley Air Force Base (MCD)
LAFB.......... Left Anterior Fascicular Block [*Cardiology*]
LAFB.......... Libyan Arab Foreign Bank
LAFB.......... Light Assault Floating Bridge [*British military*] (DMA)
LAFB.......... Lincoln Air Force Base (AAG)
LAFB.......... Local Authority Fire Brigade [*British*]
LAFB.......... Lockland Air Force Base (SAUO)
LAFB.......... Lowry Air Force Base (SAA)
LAFB.......... Luke Air Force Base (SAUO)
LAFC.......... Latin-American Forestry Commission
LAFC.......... Loan America Financial Corporation (SAUO)
LAFC.......... Lynn Anderson Fan Club (EA)
LAFD.......... Los Alamos Fire Department (SAUO)
LAFD.......... Los Angeles Fire Department (SAUO)
LAFF.......... Launcher Air Filtration Facility
LAFF.......... Luso-American Fraternal Federation (EA)
LAFFX........ Lord Abbett: Affiliated CI.A [*Mutual fund ticker symbol*] (SG)
LAFI.......... Lafayette Industries, Inc. [*NASDAQ symbol*] (SAG)
Lafico .... Libyan Arab Foreign Investment (BUAC)
LAFIE......... Lafayette Industries [*NASDAQ symbol*] (TTSB)
LAFIS......... Local Authority Financial Information System (PDAA)
LAFIS......... Local Authority Financial Institution System (AIE)
LAFL.......... Latin American Football League [*British*]
LAFM.......... Limited-Area Fine Mesh
LAFM.......... Los Alamos Fuel Model [*Department of Energy*] (GFGA)
LAFO.......... Los Alamos Field Office (SAUO)
LAFO.......... Los Angeles Foundation of Otology (SAUO)
LA FONT..... La Fontaine [*French author, 1621-1695*] (ROG)
LAFR.......... Laminar Air Flow Room (STED)
LaFr.......... Laminar Airflow Room [*Medicine*] (DAVI)
LAFS.......... Los Angeles Funeral Society (SAUO)
LAFTA........ Latin American Association of Freight and Transport Agents [*Paraguay*] (EAIO)
LAFTA........ Latin American Free Trade Association (SAUO)
LAFTA........ Latin-American Free Trade Association [*Later, LAIA*]
LAFTC........ Latin American Federation of Thermalism and Climatism [*See also FLT*] [*Argentina*] (EAIO)
LAFTO........ Latin American Confederation of Tourist Organizations [*Argentina*] (EAIO)
LAFTS........ LASER and FLIR [*Forward-Looking Infrared*] Test Set [*Air Force*]
LAFTS........ Los Alamos Fourier Transform Spectrometer [*Department of Energy*] (GRD)
LAFU.......... Ladies Amateur Fencing Union [*British*] (DBA)
LAFU.......... Laminar Airflow Unit [*Medicine*] (DAVI)
LAFUC........ Los Alamos Fleet Users Committee (SAUO)
LAFUS......... Latvian Association of Foresters in the United States [*Defunct*] (EA)
LAFV.......... Light Armoured Fighting Vehicle [*British military*] (DMA)
LAFWE........ Lafayette Industries Wrrt [*NASDAQ symbol*] (TTSB)
LAFY.......... Lafayette United (SAUO)
LAG.......... Aerovias de Lagos SA de CV [*Mexico*] [*ICAO designator*] (FAAC)
LaG.......... Labiogingival [*Dentistry*]
Lag .... Lagena [*Flask*] [*Latin*]
LAG.......... Lagging [*Engineering*]
LAG.......... Lagoon [*Maps and charts*]

LAG............ La Guaira [Venezuela] [Airport symbol] (AD)
LAG............ LaGuardia Community College Library [UTLAS symbol]
LAG............ Langila [Cape Gloucester] [New Britain] [Seismograph station code, US Geological Survey] (SEIS)
LAG............ LASER Absolute Gravimeter
LAG............ Laser Advisory Group (SAUO)
LAG............ Lastenausgleichsgesetz (BJA)
LAG............ Layton Art Gallery (SAUO)
LAG............ Legal Action Group [British] (DBA)
LAG............ Legislative Advisory Group (SAUO)
LAG............ Librarians Automation Group [Australia] (NITA)
LAG............ Liga Armada Gallega [Armed Galician League] [Spain] (PD)
LAG............ Line of Arrested Growth [Biology]
LAG............ Linguoaxiogingival [Dentistry]
LAG............ Listen Address Group (SAUO)
LAG............ [A] Literary Atlas and Gazetteer of the British Isles [A publication]
LAG............ Livermore Action Group [Defunct] (EA)
LAG............ Load and Go (NITA)
LAG............ Load and Go Assembler (BUR)
LAG............ Local Address Group (VLIE)
LAG............ Logical Address Group (SAUO)
LAG............ Logical Applications Group [Social Security Administration]
LAG............ London Amusement Guide
LAG............ Lympangiosium [Medicine]
LAG............ Lymphangiogram [or Lymphangiography]
LAGAP........ LASER-Guided Artillery Projectile (TIMI)
LAGB.......... Linguistics Association of Great Britain
LAGB.......... Linhas Aereas da Guine-Bissau [Airline] [Guinea-Bissau]
LAGD.......... Louisiana Academy of General Dentistry (SAUO)
LAGE.......... Los Angeles Grain Exchange (EA)
LA Gear...... LA Gear, Inc. [Associated Press] (SAG)
LAGEO........ LASER Geodynamic Satellite [NASA] (PDAA)
LAGEOS...... Laser Geodetic Satellite (SAUO)
LAGEOS...... LASER Geodynamic Satellite [NASA]
LAGER........ Layout Generating Routine (VLIE)
LAGER........ Lesbian and Gay Employment Rights (BUAC)
LAGER........ Liberal Action Group for Electoral Reform [British] (DI)
LAGEX........ Lord Abbett: Global Equity Cl.A [Mutual fund ticker symbol] (SG)
LAGG.......... Fighter [Russian aircraft symbol]
LAGIC........ Life and General Insurance Committee (SAUO)
LAGIC........ Louisiana Geographic Information Center (SAUO)
LaGIN......... Louisiana Government Information Network [Louisiana State Library] [Baton Rouge] [Information service or system] (IID)
LAGIX........ Lord Abbett: Global Income Cl.A [Mutual fund ticker symbol] (SG)
LAGLG........ Library Association Government Libraries Group (PDAA)
LAGMA....... Lawn and Garden Manufacturers Association [Defunct] (EA)
LAGN.......... Lagoon [Board on Geographic Names]
LAGO.......... Light Atomic Gas Oil [Petroleum product]
Lagos HCR... Lagos High Court Reports [A publication] (DLA)
Lagos R....... Judgments in the Supreme Court, Lagos [1884-92] [Nigeria] [A publication] (DLA)
LAGR.......... Los Angeles Gear, Inc. (SAUO)
LaGrange C... LaGrange College (GAGS)
LAGS.......... LASER-Activated Geodetic Satellite [AFCRL]
LAGS.......... Launch Abort Guide Simulation [NASA] (NASA)
LAGS.......... Los Angeles Geographic Society (SAUO)
LAGUMS...... LASER-Guided Missile System (MCD)
LAGVX........ Lord Abbett: U.S. Govt. Secs. Cl.A [Mutual fund ticker symbol]
LAGWX....... Lord Abbett: Developing Growth Cl.A [Mutual fund ticker symbol] (SG)
Lah .... Indian Law Reports, Lahore Series [A publication] (DLA)
Lah .... Indian Rulings, Lahore Series [A publication] (DLA)
LAH............ Labuha [Indonesia] [Airport symbol] (OAG)
LAH............ Lactalbumin Hydrolysate [Biochemistry] (MAE)
LAH............ LA Helicopter, Inc. [ICAO designator] (FAAC)
lah .... Lahnda [MARC language code] [Library of Congress] (LCCP)
LAH............ Lahore [Pakistan] [Seismograph station code, US Geological Survey] [Closed] (SEIS)
LAH............ Latex Agglutination-Inhibition (DB)
LAH............ Launch Axis, Horizontal (MCD)
LAH............ Lebanon, NH [Location identifier] [FAA] (FAAL)
LAH............ Left Anterior Hemiblock [Cardiology]
LAH............ Left Atrial Hypertrophy [Cardiology]
LAH............ Licentiate of Apothecaries (SAUO)
LAH............ Licentiate of the Apothecaries' Hall [Dublin]
LAH............ Light-Armed Helicopter [Military] (PDAA)
LAH............ Lithium Aluminum Hydride [Inorganic chemistry]
LAH............ Logical Analyzer of Hypothesis (IEEE)
LA-H.......... Los Alamos History (SAUO)
LAH............ Low-Altitude Hold [Military] (CAAL)
Lah .... Pakistan Law Reports, Lahore Series [A publication] (DLA)
LAH............ Pakistan Law Repos, Lahore Series (SAUS)
LAHA.......... Linear Array Hybrid Assembly
LAHAWS...... LASER Homing and Warning System [Military] (PDAA)
LAHB.......... Left Anterior Hemiblock [Medicine] (STED)
LAHB.......... Local Authorities Historic Buildings Act [Town planning] [British]
LAHC.......... Los Angeles Harbor College (SAUO)
LAHC.......... Los Angeles Harbor Commission (SAUO)
LAHC.......... Low Affinity-High Capacity [Medicine] (DMAA)
Lah Cas...... Lahore Cases [India] [A publication] (DLA)
LAHCG........ Look Ahead Carry Generator [Computer science] (NITA)
LAHCP........ Los Alamos Health Care Plan (SAUO)
LAHD.......... Los Angeles Harbor Department (SAUO)
LAHF.......... Latin American Hospital Federation [Mexico] (EAIO)
Lahhs.......... Large Hydrofoil Hybrid Ship

LAHIVE .... Low-Altitude/High-Velocity Experiment
Lah LJ .... Lahore Law Journal [India] [A publication] (DLA)
Lah LT .... Lahore Law Times [India] [A publication] (DLA)
LAHM.......... Limited Area HIBU [Hydrological Institute and Belgrade University] (USDC)
Lahore .... All India Reporter, Lahore Series [A publication] (ILCA)
Lahore L Times... Lahore Law Times [India] [A publication] (DLA)
LAHPERD.... Louisiana Association for Health, Physical Education, Recreation, and Dance (SRA)
LAHRC........ Libyan Arab Human Rights Committee (BUAC)
LAHS.......... Leicestershire Archaeological and Historical Society (SAUO)
LAHS.......... Local Authority Health Services [British]
LAHS.......... Los Alamos High School (SAUO)
LAHS.......... Low-Altitude, High-Speed
LAHSO........ Land and Hold Short Operation (SAUO)
LAHV.......... Leukocyte-Associated Herpesvirus [Medicine] (STED)
LAHV.......... Leukocyte-Associates Herpes Virus [Medicine] (DAVI)
LAI............. LaBat-Anderson, Inc. (EFIS)
LAI............. Labioincisal [Dentistry]
LAI............. Laboratory Audit Inspection [Environmental Protection Agency] (EPAT)
LAI............. Lact-Aid International [Commercial firm] (EA)
LAI............. Lamb Associates Incorporated (SAUO)
LAI............. LAN [Linked Access Network] Automatic Inventory [Brightwork Development, Inc.] [Computer science] (PCM)
LAI............. Lannion [France] [Airport symbol] (OAG)
LAI............. Lasir Gold, Inc. [Vancouver Stock Exchange symbol]
LAI............. Latex Agglutination-Inhibition (PDAA)
LAI............. Latin American Institute [University of New Mexico] [Research center] (RCD)
LAI............. Leaf Area Index [Forestry]
LAI............. Lean Aircraft Initiative (SAUS)
LAI............. Left Atrial Involvement [Medicine] (STED)
LAI............. Lesotho Airways Corp. [ICAO designator] (FAAC)
LAI............. Lesson Administrative Instructions [Military]
LAI............. Leukocyte Adherence Inhibition [Immunochemistry]
LAI............. Library Association of Ireland (EAIO)
LAI............. Life Adjustment Inventory [Psychology]
LAI............. Light Armored Infantry [Marine Corps] (DOMA)
L-A-I .... Linkage, Ability, Interest [Fundraising term] (NFD)
LAI............. Load Address Immediate (BUR)
LAI............. Loaded Applicator Impedance
LAI............. Location-Activity Inventory (DB)
LAI............. Love Attitudes Inventory [Premarital relations test] [Psychology]
LAI............. Low-Altitude Indicator
LAIA.......... Latin American Industrialists Association [Uruguay] (EAIO)
LAIA.......... Latin American Integration Association [Formerly, LAFTA] [See also ALADI] [Uruguay] (EAIO)
LAIC.......... Latin America Information Centre (BUAC)
LAIC.......... Lesbian Archive and Information Centre (BUAC)
LAIC.......... Lithuanian-American Information Center [Defunct]
LA-ICP-MS... LASER Ablation-Inductively Coupled Plasma-Mass Spectrometry [Analytical chemistry]
LAICS........ Los Alamos Integrated Communications System (SAUO)
LaidlwA...... Laidlaw, Inc. [Associated Press] (SAG)
LaidlwB...... Laidlaw, Inc. [Associated Press] (SAG)
LAIEC........ Latin American Institute of Educational Communication [Mexico] (EAIO)
LAIF .... Leukocyte Adherence Inhibition Factor (DAVI)
LAIFS......... Los Angeles International Fern Society (EA)
LAIG.......... LA Industrial Group (NITA)
LAIG.......... Library Association Industrial Group (BUAC)
LAII........... Land-Atmosphere-Ice-Interactions (SAUO)
LAIICS .... Latin American Institute for Information and Computer Sciences [Chile] (PDAA)
LAILA........ Latin American Indian Literatures Association (EA)
LAIMP........ Lunar-Anchored Interplanetary Monitoring Platform [Aerospace] (MCD)
LAINS........ Low-Altitude Inertial Navigation System [Air Force]
LAIR.......... Laser & Atomic Research & Development (SAUS)
LAIR.......... Letterman Army Institute of Research [San Francisco, CA]
LAIR.......... Liquid Air (NASA)
LAIRS .... Labor Agreement Information Retrieval System [Office of Management and Budget]
LAIRS .... Land-Air Integrated Reduction System (MUGU)
LAIRS .... Laser Imaging and Ranging System (ACAE)
LAIRS .... Light Aircraft Reconnaissance System (SAUS)
LAIRS .... Lightweight Advanced Inertial Reference Sphere
LAIRTS ...... Large Aperture Infrared Telescope System
LAIS .... Advanced Interventional Systems (SAUS)
LAIS .... Labor Arbitration Information System [LRP Publications] [Information service or system] (CRD)
LAIS .... Labyrinth Air Induction Silencer [Automotive engineering]
LAIS .... Labyrinth Air Induction System [Automotive engineering]
LAIS .... Leiter Adult Intelligence Scale [Intelligence test] [Psychology]
LAIS .... Library Acquisitions Information System
LAIS .... Lithium Aluminium Iron Sulphide (SAUS)
LAIS .... Loan Accounting Information System [Agency for International Development]
LAIS .... Local Automatic Intercept System (VLIE)
LAIS .... Logistics Attrition Information System (SAUO)
LAISDSS..... Latin American Institute of Social Doctrine and Social Studies [Chile] (EAIO)
LAISPS....... Los Angeles Institute and Society for Psychoanalytic Studies (SAUO)
LAIT........... Langdon Adult Intelligence Test (TES)

LAIT............	Latex Agglutination Inhibition Test [*for pregnancy*] [*Medicine*]
LAIT............	Library Association Information Technology Group [*British*] (NITA)
LAIT............	Logistics Assistance and Instruction Team [*Military*] (AABC)
LAITG..........	Library Association Information Technology Group (AIE)
LAITS..........	Latin American Institute for Transnational Studies (EA)
LAIU............	Launch Abort Interface Unit [*NASA*] (MCD)
LAIV............	Loss Adjusters Institute of Victoria (SAUO)
LAIWS	Land-Air White Sands (MUGU)
LAJ.............	British Mediterranean Airways Ltd. [*FAA designator*] (FAAC)
LAJ	Lajes [*Brazil*] [*Airport symbol*] (OAG)
LAJ	London Airtours Ltd. [*British*] [*ICAO designator*] (FAAC)
LAJ	Los Angeles Junction Railway Co. [*AAR code*]
LAJC	Latin American Jewish Congress (BUAC)
LAJC	London Agreement Joint Committee (SAUO)
LaJolIPh	La Jolla Pharmaceutical [*Associated Press*] (SAG)
LaJolP	La Jolla Pharmaceutical [*Associated Press*] (SAG)
LAJPEL	Latin American Journal of Politics, Economics, and Law [*A publication*] (DLA)
LAK............	Aklavik [*Canada*] [*Airport symbol*] (OAG)
LAK............	Laker Resources [*Vancouver Stock Exchange symbol*]
LAK............	Lennox Airways [*Kenya*] [*ICAO designator*] (FAAC)
LAK............	Leukocyte-Activated Killer [*Cells*] [*Oncology*] (DAVI)
LAK............	Lightweight Antenna Kit
LAK............	Lymphokine-Activated Killer [*Cells*] [*Immunotherapy*]
LAKBC	Los Angeles Kings Booster Club (EA)
LAKE..........	Clean Lakes Database (SAUO)
LAKE..........	Lake [*Commonly used*] (OPSA)
LAKE..........	Lakeland Indus [*NASDAQ symbol*] (TTSB)
LAKE..........	Lakeland Industries, Inc. [*NASDAQ symbol*] (SAG)
LakeAriel	Lake Ariel Bancorp [*Associated Press*] (SAG)
LakehdP	Lakehead Pipe Line Partners Ltd. [*Associated Press*] (SAG)
Lake-ICE	Lake-Induced Convection Experiment (SAUO)
LakeInd........	Lakeland Industries, Inc. [*Associated Press*] (SAG)
LAKES	Lakes [*Commonly used*] (OPSA)
LakevwF	Lakeview Financial Corp. [*Associated Press*] (SAG)
LAKFC.........	Los Angeles Kings Fan Club (EA)
LakldFt	Lakeland First Fianancial Group, Inc. [*Associated Press*] (SAG)
LaL	Labiolingual [*Dentistry*]
LAL	Labrador Airways Ltd. [*Canada*] [*ICAO designator*] (FAAC)
LAL	Lakeland [*Florida*] [*Airport symbol*] (AD)
LAL	Lakeland, FL [*Location identifier*] [*FAA*] (FAAL)
LAL	Lana Gold Corp. [*Vancouver Stock Exchange symbol*]
LAL	Landcare Australia Limited (SAUO)
LAL	Langley Aeronautical Laboratory [*NASA*]
LAL	Launch and Leave [*Military*] (MUSM)
LAL	Left Axillary Line [*Medicine*] (DMAA)
LAL	Limulus Amebocyte Lysate [*Medicine*]
LAL	Livonia, Avon & Lakeville Railroad Corp. [*AAR code*]
LAL	Local Adjunct Language (PDAA)
LAL	Los Almos Laboratory (SAUO)
LAL	Loudspeaker Acoustical Labyrinth
LAL	Low Air Loss
LAL	Lower Acceptance Level
LAL	Lysinoalanine [*An amino acid*]
L-Ala...........	L-Alanine [*Biochemistry*] (DAVI)
LALA...........	Large Amplitude Late Arrival [*Seismology*]
LALA...........	Linoletic Acid-Like Activity (PDAA)
LA(L)A	Local Authorities (Land) Act [*Town planning*] [*British*]
LALA...........	Low-Altitude Alert [*Air traffic control*]
LaLand	Louisiana Land & Exploration Co. [*Associated Press*] (SAG)
LALD...........	Low-Angle Low-Drag
L Alem........	Law of the Alemanni [*A publication*] (DLA)
LALF...........	Light Aviation & Land Forces (SAUO)
LALI...........	Labiolingual [*Dentistry*]
LALI...........	Latin American-Caribbean Labor Institute (EA)
LALI...........	Lymphocyte Antibody-Lymphocytolytic Interaction [*Medicine*] (DMAA)
La Ligue......	Ligue nationale contre le cancer (SAUO)
LALIS.........	Luso-American Life Insurance Society
LA LJ	Louisiana Law Journal [*New Orleans*] [*A publication*] (DLA)
LALL	Longest Allowed Lobe Length (SAUO)
LALLL	Low-Altitude Low-Light Level
LALLS.........	Low-Angle LASER Light Scattering
LALM	Limulus Amebocyte Lysate Method
LALO..........	Low-Altitude Observation
LALOC	Laser Locator (ACAE)
Lalor..........	Lalor's Supplement to Hill and Denio's New York Reports [*A publication*] (DLA)
Lalor Pol Econ...	Lalor's Cyclopaedia of Political Science, Political Economy, Etc. [*A publication*] (DLA)
Lalor's Supp...	Lalor's Supplement to Hill and Denio's New York Reports [*A publication*] (DLA)
Lalor's Supp (Hill and Denio)...	Lalor's Supplement to Hill and Denio's New York Reports [*A publication*] (DLA)
Lalor Supp...	Lalor's Supplement to Hill and Denio's New York Reports [*A publication*] (DLA)
LALP..........	Longest Activity from Longest Project
LALP..........	Los Alamos Laboratory Publication (SAUO)
LALR..........	Latin American Literary Review. Carnegie-Mellon University, Department of Modern Languages. Pittsburgh (SAUO)
LALR..........	Lookahead Left to Right [*Computer science*]
LALR..........	Rapides Parish Library, Alexandria (SAUS)
LAIR...........	Rapides Parish Library, Alexandria, LA [*Library symbol*] [*Library of Congress*] (LCLS)
Lal RP	Lalor's Law of Real Property [*A publication*] (DLA)

LALS...........	LaGuardia Automated Library System [*LaGuardia Community College*] [*Information service or system*] (IID)
LALS...........	LASER Alarm Locator System
LALS...........	Linkless Ammunition Loading System (MCD)
LALSD.........	Language for Automated Logic and System Design [*Computer science*] (CSR)
LALUC	Local Authority Land Use Classification (PDAA)
LALV	Lucerne Australian Latent Virus [*Plant pathology*]
L'AM	L'Alliance Monarchiste (EA)
Lam	Lamarck [*Biology*] (BARN)
lam	Lamba [*MARC language code*] [*Library of Congress*] (LCCP)
Lam	Lambert [*Unit of luminance*] [*Preferred unit is lx, Lux*]
Lam	Lambertus de Ramponibus [*Deceased, 1304*] [*Authority cited in pre-1607 legal work*] (DSA)
Lam	Lamentations [*Old Testament book*]
LAM	Lamina [*Medicine*] (DAVI)
Lam	Lamina (STED)
LAM	Laminate (MSA)
lam	Laminated (WDMC)
Lam	Laminectomy [*Medicine*] (AMHC)
LAM	Laminectomy [*Medicine*]
lam	Laminogram (MAE)
LAM	Land Attack Mode [*Navy*] (CAAL)
LAM	Laramide Resources Ltd. [*Vancouver Stock Exchange symbol*]
LAM	LASER [*Light Amplification by Stimulated Emission of Radiation*] Aiming Module
LAM	L-Asparaginase and Methotrexate [*Antineoplastic drug regimen*] (DAVI)
LAM	Late Ambulatory Monitoring [*Medicine*]
LAM	Latin America Inv Fd [*NYSE symbol*] (TTSB)
LAM	Latin America Mission (EA)
LAM	Latin American Investment Fund [*NYSE symbol*] (SPSG)
LAM	Latin American Male (DAVI)
LAM	Latin American Mission [*Air Force*]
LAM	Leading Air Mechanic [*British military*] (DMA)
LAM	Learner-Approved Motorcycle
LAM	Left Anterior Measurement [*Medicine*] (STED)
LAM	Left Artial Myxoma [*Cardiology*] (DAVI)
LAM	Left Atrial Myxoma [*Medicine*] (STED)
LAM	Levator Ani Muscle (MELL)
LAM	Liberal Alliance of Montenegro (BUAC)
LAM	Liberalium Artium Magister [*Master of the Liberal Arts*]
LAM	Library Association of Malaysia (BUAC)
LAM	Life Action Ministries (EA)
LAM	Light-Absorbing Molecules
LAM	Lightweight Analog Motor (MCD)
LAM	Limited Area Model [*Marine science*] (OSRA)
LAM	Limpet Assembly Modular [*Navy*] (CAAL)
LAM	Linhas Aereas de Mocambique [*Mozambique*] [*ICAO designator*] (FAAC)
LAM	Lipoarabinomannan [*Biochemistry*]
LAM	Liquid Apogee Motor (ACAE)
LAM	Lithuanian Academy of Music (BUAC)
LAM	Load Acceptance Module
LAM	Load Accumulator with Magnitude
LAM	Lobe Attachment Module [*Computer science*]
LAM	Lobe Attachment Unit [*Computer science*] (ACRL)
LAM	Local Area Missile (ACAE)
LAM	Logical Acknowledgement Message [*Aviation*] (DA)
LAM	London Academy of Music
LAM	Long Aerial Mine [*Military*]
LAM	Longitudinal Acoustic [*or Acoustical*] Mode [*Spectroscopy*]
LAM	Look at Me (IAA)
LAM	Loop Access Module (TIMI)
LAM	Loop Adder and Multiplier (NITA)
LAM	Loop Addition and Modification [*Computer science*]
LAM	Los Alamos [*New Mexico*] [*Airport symbol*] (OAG)
LAM	Los Alamos Airport (SAUO)
LA-M	Los Alamos Manual (SAUO)
LAM	Los Alamos, NM [*Location identifier*] [*FAA*] (FAAL)
LAM	Louisiana Motor Freight Bureau [*STAC*]
LAM	Lousiana Maneuvers [*Military*]
LAM	Low-Altitude Missile (MCD)
LAM	Low-Attack Mode (MCD)
LAM	Lunar Excursion Module (ACAE)
LAM	Lymphangioleiomyomatosis [*Medicine*]
LAM	Master of Liberal Arts
LAMA	Laboratory Animal Management Association (EA)
LAMA	Laminin A (DMAA)
LAMA	Large Array for Millimeter Astronomy
LAMA	Laser-Assisted Microanastomosis [*Medicine*] (MELL)
LAMA	Latin American Manufacturers Association [*Washington, DC*] (EA)
LAMA	Lead Air Materiel Area [*Air Force*]
LAMA	Legal Assistant Management Association (EA)
LAMA	Library Administration and Management Association (EA)
LAMA	Light Aircraft Manufacturers' Association (EA)
LAMA	Livestock Auction Markets Association
LAMA	Local Authority Members Association [*Ireland*] (BUAC)
LAMA	Local Automatic Message Accounting [*Telecommunications*] (TEL)
LAMA	Locomotive and Allied Manufacturers' Association [*British*] (BI)
LAMA	Los Angeles Maintainability Association (SAUO)
LAMA BES ...	LAMA [*Library Administration and Management Association*] Buildings and Equipment Section
LAMACHA	Louisiana-Alabama-Mississippi Automated Clearing House Association

LAMA FRFDS... LAMA [*Library Administration and Management Association*] Fund Raising and Financial Development Section
LAMAHRS.... Human Resources Section
LAMA LOMS... LAMA [*Library Administration and Management Association*] Library Organization and Management Section
LaMan .... LaMan Corp. [*Associated Press*] (SAG)
lam & fus.... Laminectomy and Fusion [*Medicine*] (DAVI)
LAMA PAS ... LAMA [*Library Administration and Management Association*] Personnel Administration Section
LAMA PRS ... LAMA [*Library Administration and Management Association*] Public Relations Section
Lamar........... Lamar's Reports [*25-40 Florida*] [*A publication*] (DLA)
LAMAR .... Large Amplitude Modular Array (SAUS)
LAMAR .... Large Area Modular Array of Reflectors [*Astronomy*]
LAMAR .... Linear-Elastic Matrix Analysis Routine
LAMARS ..... Large Amplitude Multimode Aerospace Research Simulator
Lamar U ...... Lamar University (GAGS)
LAMAS .... Location and Movement Analysis System (MCD)
LAMAS........ London and Middlesex Archaeological Society [*England*] (BUAC)
LAMA SASS... LAMA [*Library Administration and Management Association*] Systems and Services Section
LAMA SS .... LAMA [*Library Administration and Management Association*] Statistics Section
LAMA SSS ... LAMA [*Library Administration and Management Association*] Systems and Services Section
LA-MAX ...... Maximal Left Atrial [*Dimension*] [*Medicine*] (STED)
Lamb .... Lambard's Archaionomia [*A publication*] (DLA)
Lamb .... Lambard's Archeion [*1635*] [*A publication*] (DLA)
Lamb .... Lambard's Eirenarcha [*A publication*] (DLA)
Lamb .... Lambard's Explication [*A publication*] (DLA)
LAMB.......... Lambeth [*Degrees granted by Archbishop of Canterbury*] [*British*] (ROG)
LAMB.......... Lambourne [*England*]
Lamb .... Lamb's Reports [*103-105 Wisconsin*] [*A publication*] (DLA)
LAMB.......... Light Armoured Motor Brigade [*British military*] (DMA)
LAMB.......... Lively Arts Market Builder (ACAE)
LAMB.......... Local Area Multiuser Board [*American Micronics*] [*Computer science*]
LAMB.......... Los Alamos Water Boiler (NRCH)
LAMB.......... Low-Altitude Multiburst Code (MCD)
LAMBADA.... Amazon Basin Experiment (SAUO)
Lamb Arch... Lambard's Archaionomia [*A publication*] (DLA)
Lamb Arch... Lambard's Archeion [*1635*] [*A publication*] (ILCA)
Lamb Archaion... Lambard's Archaionomia [*A publication*] (DLA)
LAMBC........ Los Angeles Motor Boat Club (SAUO)
Lamb Const.. Lambard's Duties of Constables, Etc. [*A publication*] (DLA)
LAMBDA...... Language for Manufacturing Business and Distribution Activity (IAA)
Lamb de Ramp... Lambertus de Ramponibus [*Deceased, 1304*] [*Authority cited in pre-1607 legal work*] (DSA)
Lamb Dow.... Lambert's Law of Dower [*A publication*] (DLA)
Lamb Eir..... Lambard's Eirenarcha [*A publication*] (DLA)
Lamb Eiren... Lambard's Eirenarcha [*A publication*] (DLA)
Lamber de Sal... Lambertus de Salinis [*Flourished, 14th century*] [*Authority cited in pre-1607 legal work*] (DSA)
Lamb Explic... Lambard's Explication [*A publication*] (DLA)
Lam Bk Rpt... Lambda Book Report [*A publication*] (BRI)
LAMBR .... Laminin B Receptor (DMAA)
LAMBS......... Laboratory Animal Management and Business Systems [*Computer science*]
LAMC.......... Laminin C (DMAA)
LAMC.......... Language and Mode Converter [*Computer science*] (TEL)
LAMC.......... Last Maneuver Calculation [*Orbit identification*]
LAMC.......... Letterman Army Medical Center (AABC)
LAMC.......... Lima Army Modification Center (RDA)
LAMC.......... Livestock Auctioneers' Market Committee [*British*] (DBA)
LAMC.......... Livestock Auctioneers Market Committee for England and Wales (BUAC)
LAMC.......... Los Alamos Medical Center (SAUO)
LAMC.......... Los Angeles Metropolitan College (SAUO)
LAMC.......... Los Angeles Music Center (SAUO)
LAMCIS........ Los Angeles Multiple Corridor Identification System (SAA)
LAMCO .... Liberian American-Swedish Minerals Co.
LAMCS........ Latin American-American Communications Systems (PDAA)
LAMCS........ Latin American Military Communications System
LAMD......... London Association of Master Decorators (SAUO)
LAMDA .... [*The*] London Academy of Music and Dramatic Art
LAME.......... Lake Mead National Recreation Area
LAME.......... Licensed Aircraft Maintenance Engineer (ADA)
LAMEF......... Los Alamos Medium Energy Facility
La Mennais Brothers... Brothers of Christian Instruction of Ploermel (SAUO)
LAMG.......... Laban Art of Movement Guild [*Later, LG*] (EA)
LAMI........... Laminectomy [*Medicine*] (MELL)
lami........... Laminotomy [*Medicine*] (STED)
LAMIDA .... Lancashire and Merseyside Industrial Development Association (SAUO)
Lamin......... Laminating Technologies, Inc. [*Associated Press*] (SAG)
LAMINAR..... Low Altitude, Mapping, Interception, Navigation (ACAE)
Laminat....... Laminating Technologies, Inc. [*Associated Press*] (SAG)
LAMIS......... Local Authority Management Information System (SAUO)
LAMIS......... Los Angeles Municipal Information System (SAUO)
LAMIT......... Local Authorities' Mutual Investment Trust [*British*]
LAMM .... Land Armament Manpower and Material Data Base (SAUO)
LAMM .... Los Angeles Master Morticians (SAUO)
LAMM .... Lutheran-American Melancthon Movement (SAUO)
LAMMA......... LASER Microprobe Mass Analyzer [*Spectrometry*]
LAMMP........ Lower Acceptable Mean Maximum Pressure (SAA)

LAMMR........ Large Antenna Multichannel Microwave Radiometer (SAUS)
LAMMR........ Large Antenna Multifrequency Microwave Radiometer (MCD)
LAMMS........ LASER Microprobe Mass Spectrometry [*or Spectroscopy*]
LAMN.......... La Man Corp. [*NASDAQ symbol*] (TTSB)
LAMOPH....... Ladies Auxiliary, Military Order of the Purple Heart (SAUO)
LAMOPH....... Ladies Auxiliary, Military Order of the Purple Heart, United States of America (EA)
LAMOST ...... Large Area Multi Object Fiber Spectroscopic Telescope [*Proposed, China*]
LAMOST ...... Large Sky Area Multi-Objects Fiber Spectoscopic Telescope [*China*]
LAMP.......... Center for the Study of Legal Authority and Mental Patient Status (EA)
LAMP.......... Center for the Study of the Authority and Mental Patient Status (SAUS)
LAMP.......... Lake Acidification Mitigation Project [*Environmental Protection Agency*] (GFGA)
LAMP.......... Lakewide Management Plan [*Great Lakes*] [*Environmental Protection Agency*]
LAMP.......... Lanier Academic Motivational Program [*Military*]
LAMP.......... Laos Ammunition Procedures (CINC)
LAMP.......... Large Advanced Mirror Program [*Military*] (SDI)
LAMP.......... LASER and MASER Patents
LAMP.......... LASER and Mixing Program
LAMP.......... Laser Microbeam Program [*Research center*] (RCD)
LAMP.......... Laser Modulation Program (ACAE)
LAMP.......... Latin America Mass Media Project (BUAC)
LAMP.......... Latin American Maize Project (SAUO)
LAMP.......... Latin American Market Planning Centre (BUAC)
LAMP.......... Leap and Stamp [*Dance terminology*]
LAMP.......... Library Addition and Maintenance Program
LAMP.......... Life Agency Management Program [*GAMC*]
LAMP.......... Light Airborne Multipurpose System [*Navy*] (MCD)
LAMP.......... Lighthouse Automation and Modernization Project [*US Coast Guard*] (PDAA)
LAMP.......... Linux, Apache, MySQL, PHP (SAUS)
LAMP.......... Lockheed Adaptive Modular Payload (SAUS)
LAMP.......... Logic Analysis for Maintenance Planning (MHDB)
LAMP.......... Logistics Automation Master PLan [*Military*]
LAMP.......... Louis Armstrong Memorial Project
LAMP.......... Low-Altitude Manned Penetrator
LAMP.......... Low Altitude Mapping Photogrammetry (SAUO)
LAMP.......... Lunar Analysis and Mapping Program [*NASA*] (IAA)
LAMP.......... Lysosome-Associated Membrane Protein [*Biochemistry*]
LAMP.......... SOI Industries, Inc. (SAUO)
LAMPEX ...... Large Area Marine Productivity-Pollution Experiments (SAUO)
LAMPF........ Los Alamos Meson Physics Facility [*Later, Clinton P. Anderson Meson Physics Facility at Los Alamos*] [*Department of Energy*]
LAMP-H ...... Lighter, Amphibian Heavy Lift
LAMPP........ Los Alamos Molten Plutonium Program
LAMPRE ..... Los Alamos Molten Plutonium Reactor Experiment
LAMPS........ Large Amplitude SLOSH [*Sea, Lake, Overland Surge from Hurricanes*] [*NASA*]
LAMPS........ Light Airborne Multiple Package System
LAMPS........ Light Airborne Multipurpose System [*Navy*]
LAMPS........ Limited Area Mesoscale Prediction System (MCD)
LAMPS........ Logistics Assessment of Modifications Program (SAUO)
LAMPS........ London Area Mobile Physiotherapy Service (SAUO)
LAMPSOP...... Light Airborne Multipurpose System Standard Operating Procedures Manual [*Navy*] (DNAB)
LA/MPSS ...... Large Area/Mobile Projected Smoke System [*Military*] (RDA)
LAMR.......... Lamar Advertising 'A' [*NASDAQ symbol*] (SG)
LamR.......... Lamentations Rabbah (BJA)
LAMR.......... Large Aperture Microwave Radiometer (SSD)
LAMRDT....... Large Aperture Microwave Radiometer Development Test (SAUO)
LAMRL........ Logistic Area Material Readiness List [*Military*] (AFIT)
LamRsch ..... Lam Research Corp. [*Associated Press*] (SAG)
LAMRTPI ..... Legal Associate Member of the Royal Town Planning Institute [*British*] (DBQ)
LAMS.......... Lake Analysis Management System (SAUO)
LAMS.......... Land Acoustical Monitoring System [*NASA*]
LAMS.......... Land Acquisition and Management Schemes [*British*]
LAMS.......... Large Atypical Mole Syndrome [*Medicine*]
LAMS.......... Light Aircraft Maintenance Schedule (PIAV)
LAMS.......... Lightweight Artillery Meteorological System (SAUO)
LAMS.......... Limited Area Models (SAUO)
LAMS.......... Load Alleviation and Mode Stabilization
LAMS.......... Local Area Missile System (SAUO)
LAMS.......... Local Asset Management System (ACAE)
LAMS.......... London Aero Motor Services
LA-MS .... Los Alamos Manuscript (SAUO)
LAMS.......... Los Alamos Scientific Laboratory [*USAEC*] (MCD)
LAMSA........ Lineas Aereas Mexicana, Sociedad Anonima
LAMSAC ...... Local Authorities' Management Services and Computer Committee [*British*]
LAMSAC Committee... Local Authorities Management Services and Computer Committee (SAUO)
LAMSAS ...... Linguistic Atlas of the Middle and South Atlantic States
LamSes .... [*The*] Lamson & Sessions Co. [*Associated Press*] (SAG)
LAMSIM .... Launcher and Missile Simulator
L Am Soc.... Law in American Society [*A publication*] (DLA)
L Am Soc'y... Law in American Society [*A publication*] (DLA)
LAMSS........ Laser Air Motion Sensing System (SAUO)
LAMT.......... Laminating Technologies, Inc. [*NASDAQ symbol*] (SAG)
LAmT.......... Tangihoa Parish Library, Amite (SAUS)

LAmT .... Tangipahoa Parish Library, Amite, LA [*Library symbol*] [*Library of Congress*] (LCLS)

LAMTD .... Laminated

LAMTPI .... Legal Associate Member of the Town Planning Institute (SAUO)

LAMTS .... Launcher Adapter Missile Test Set

LAN .... Inland [*Aviation code*]

LAN .... Laboratory Automation News (SAUO)

LAN .... Lanarkshire [*County in Scotland*]

LAN .... Lancer Corp. [*AMEX symbol*] (SPSG)

LAN .... Lanchow [*Republic of China*] [*Seismograph station code, US Geological Survey*] [*Closed*] (SEIS)

LAN .... Landau [*Automotive classified advertising*]

LAN .... Landing Aid [*Navigation*] (IAA)

Lan .... Landulfus Acconzaioco [*Flourished, 13th century*] [*Authority cited in pre-1607 legal work*] (DSA)

Lan .... Lanfrancus [*Deceased, 1089*] [*Authority cited in pre-1607 legal work*] (DSA)

Lan .... Lanfrancus Cremensis [*Deceased, 1229*] [*Authority cited in pre-1607 legal work*] (DSA)

LAN .... Langley [*Unit of sun's heat*] (IAA)

lan .... Langue d'Oc [*MARC language code*] [*Library of Congress*] (LCCP)

LAN .... Lansing [*Michigan*] [*Airport symbol*] (OAG)

LAN .... Lansing, MI [*Location identifier*] [*FAA*] (FAAL)

Lan .... Lanthionine (DB)

LAN .... Lateral Access Network (NITA)

LAN .... Latin American Newsletters [*British*] [*Information service or system*] (IID)

LAN .... Latin American Newsletters Ltd. (SAUO)

LAN .... Library Advocacy Now [*American Library Association*]

LAN .... Library Automation and Networks

LAN .... Lime-Ammonium-Nitrate [*Fertilizer*]

LAN .... Linea Aerea Nacional [*National Airline*] [*Chile*]

LAN .... Linea Aerea Nacional de Chile [*ICAO designator*] (FAAC)

LAN .... Linked Access Network

LAN .... Local Apparent Noon [*Navigation*]

LAN .... Local Area Networks [*Information Gatekeepers, Inc.*] [*No longer available online*] [*Information service or system*] (CRD)

LAN .... Long-Acting Neuroleptic [*Pharmacology*] (DAVI)

LAN .... Longitude of the Ascending Node

LAN .... Los Alamos National Laboratory (SAUO)

LAN .... Lymphadenopathy (STED)

LAN .... Mesa Public Library, Los Alamos, NM [*OCLC symbol*] (OCLC)

LAN .... Panorama Air Tour, Inc. (SAUO)

LANA .... Language Analog [*Project*]

LANA .... Lipizzan Association of North America (NTPA)

LANA .... Liquid Air Corp. (SAUO)

LANA .... Lithuanian American National Alliance (EA)

LANA .... Llama Association of North America (EA)

LANA .... Local Area Network Accelerator [*Computer science*] (CIST)

LANA .... Low-Altitude Night Attack (DOMA)

LANABS ...... Light Attack Navigation and Bombing System (MCD)

LANAC .... Laminar Air Navigation and Anticollision [*Air Force*]

LANAC .... Lawyers Alliance for Nuclear Arms Control [*Later, LAWS*] (EA)

Lan Acon ..... Landulfus Acconzaioco [*Flourished, 13th century*] [*Authority cited in pre-1607 legal work*] (DSA)

LANAP .... Latin American Natural Areas Program (BUAC)

Lanarks. ...... Lanarkshire (GROV)

LANBY .... Large Automatic Navigational Buoy [*Shipping*] (DS)

LANC .... Lancaster [*England*] (ROG)

LANC .... Lancaster Colony [*NASDAQ symbol*] (SAG)

Lanc. .... Lancellottus [*Authority cited in pre-1607 legal work*] (DSA)

LANC .... Lancer [*Military*] [*British*] (ROG)

LANC .... Liga Apararii Nationale Crestine [*League of National Christian Defense*] [*Romania*] [*Political party*] (PPE)

LANC .... Local Application Control Bus System (SAUS)

LANC .... Local Application Numerical Control [*Sony Corp.*] (DOM)

LANC .... Long-Arm Navicular Cast [*Orthopedics*] (DAVI)

Lancastr ...... Lancaster Colony [*Associated Press*] (SAG)

LANCC .... Local Area Network Communications Controller (SAUO)

LANCC .... Local Area Network Control Center (SAUO)

LANCC/SM .. Local Area Network Control Center and Security Monitor (SAUO)

LANCE .... Ballistic Missile with Self Contained Guidance (SAUO)

Lance. .... Lance, Inc. [*Associated Press*] (SAG)

LANCE .... Local Area Network Controller for Ethernet [*Mostek*] (NITA)

Lance Cpl ... Lance Corporal (SAUO)

Lance FDS ... Lance Fire Direction System (SAUO)

Lancell Galiaul... Lancellottus Galiaula [*Flourished, 16th century*] [*Authority cited in pre-1607 legal work*] (DSA)

Lancer .... Lancer Corp. [*Associated Press*] (SAG)

LANCET .... Library Association National Council for Educational Technology (NITA)

LanChile ...... Linea Aerea Nacional de Chile

Lancit .... Lancit Media Productions Ltd. [*Associated Press*] (SAG)

Lanc Law Rev... Lancaster Law Review [*A publication*] (DLA)

Lanc L Rev... Lancaster Law Review [*A publication*] (DLA)

LANCO .... Landscape Nursery Council (EA)

LANCRA .... Landing Craft

LANCRAB ..... Landing Craft and Bases [*Military*]

LANCRABEU... Landing Craft and Bases, Europe [*Navy*]

LANCRABNAW... Landing Craft and Bases, Northwest African Waters [*World War II*] [*Navy*]

Lan Cre .... Lanfrancus Cremensis [*Deceased, 1229*] [*Authority cited in pre-1607 legal work*] (DSA)

Lanc Rev ..... Lancaster Review [*Pennsylvania*] [*A publication*] (DLA)

Lancs .... Lancashire (ADWA)

LANCS .... Lancashire [*County in England*]

LAND .... Land [*Postal Service standard*] (OPSA)

LAND .... Landair Services [*NASDAQ symbol*] (SAG)

LAND .... League Against Nuclear Dangers [*Defunct*] (EA)

LAND .... Local Access Network Directory [*Frye Computer Systems*] [*Telecommunications*] (PCM)

LANDA .... Ladies Auxiliary to the National Dental Association [*Later, ANDA*] (EA)

LANDA .... LAN [*Local Area Network*] Dealers Association (CDE)

L & A .... Landing and Ascent [*NASA*]

L & A .... Leembruggen and Asirvatham's Appeal Court Reports [*Ceylon*] [*A publication*] (DLA)

L & A .... Light and Accommodation [*Ophthalmology*] (DAVI)

L & A .... Living and Active (DAVI)

L & A .... Louisiana & Arkansas Railway Co.

LANDAC ...... Land Development Accounting System (MHDB)

Landair .... Landair Services [*Associated Press*] (SAG)

LANDASSESS... CSIRO Program to assess land degradation (SAUS)

LANDATA ..... Land Division Data Base [*Australia*] (BUAC)

Landaur .... Landauer, Inc. [*Associated Press*] (SAG)

L & B .... Leadam and Baldwin's Select Cases before the King's Council [*England*] [*A publication*] (DLA)

L & B .... Left and Below [*Medicine*]

L & B .... Lothians and Border Horse [*British military*] (DMA)

L & Bank .... Lawyer and Banker [*A publication*] (DLA)

L & B, Bull ... Daily Law and Bank Bulletin [*Ohio*] [*A publication*] (DLA)

L & B Fin .... L & B Financial, Inc. [*Associated Press*] (SAG)

L & B Ins Dig... Littleton and Blatchley's Insurance Digest [*A publication*] (DLA)

LandBnc ...... Landmark Bancshares [*Associated Press*] (SAG)

L & B Prec.. Leake and Bullen's Precedents of Pleading [*A publication*] (DLA)

L & BR .... London & Blackwall Railway [*British*] (ROG)

L&C .... Laboratory and Checkout (NAKS)

L & C .... Laboratory and Checkout (NASA)

L & C .... Laxatives and Cathartics (MELL)

L & C .... Lefroy and Cassel's Practice Cases [*1881-83*] [*Ontario*] [*A publication*] (ILCA)

L & C .... Leigh and Cave's English Crown Cases Reserved [*1861-65*] [*A publication*] (DLA)

LANDCARE... CSIRO Program on management improvement to prevent degradation (SAUS)

L&CC .... Lewis and Clark College (SAUO)

L & CCC ...... Leigh and Cave's English Crown Cases Reserved [*1861-65*] [*A publication*] (DLA)

LANDCENT... Allied Land Forces Central Europe [*NATO*]

L & CM .... Lime and Cement Mortar (DAC)

L&CMPS ...... London and Counties Medical Protection Society (SAUO)

L & Comm... Law and Communication [*A publication*] (DLA)

Land Comp Rep... Land Reports, by Roche, Dillon, and Kehoe [*1881-82*] [*Ireland*] [*A publication*] (DLA)

L & Computer Tech... Law and Computer Technology [*A publication*] (DLA)

Land Com Rep... Land Reports, by Roche, Dillon, and Kehoe [*1881-82*] [*Ireland*] [*A publication*] (DLA)

L & CONTEM PROB... Law and Contemporary Problems [*A publication*] (LWAP)

LANDCRA ..... Landing Craft and Bases [*Military*] (AFIT)

LANDCRAB... Landing Craft and Bases [*Military*] (AABC)

L & D .... Labor and Delivery [*Area of a hospital*]

L & D .... Landing and Deceleration [*NASA*] (NASA)

l&d .... Loans and Discounts (EBF)

L & D .... Loans and Discounts [*Banking*]

l&d .... Loss and Damage (EBF)

L & D .... Loss and Damage

L & D Conv... Leigh and Dalzell. Conversion of Property [*1825*] [*A publication*] (DLA)

Land Dec ..... Land Decisions, United States [*A publication*] (DLA)

L & E .... English Law and Equity Reports [*American Reprint*] [*A publication*] (DLA)

LANDENMARK... Allied Land Forces Denmark [*NATO*]

L & Eq Rep... Law and Equity Reporter [*United States*] [*A publication*] (DLA)

L & E Rep ... English Law and Equity Reports [*American Reprint*] [*A publication*] (DLA)

Land Est C... Landed Estates Court [*England*] (DLA)

LANDEX .... Landing Exercise [*Navy*] (CAAL)

LANDFAE ..... Large Area Nozzle Delivery of Fuel Air Explosive (RDA)

LANDFOR .... Landing Force [*Military*]

LANDFORASCU... Landing Force Air Support Control Unit [*Navy*]

L & G Temp Plunk... Lloyd and Goold's Irish Chancery Reports Tempore Plunkett [*A publication*] (DLA)

L & G Temp Sugd... Lloyd and Goold's Irish Chancery Reports Tempore Sugden [*1835*] [*A publication*] (DLA)

L & GTP ...... Lloyd and Goold's Irish Chancery Reports Tempore Plunkett [*A publication*] (DLA)

L & GT Plunk... Lloyd and Goold's Irish Chancery Reports Tempore Plunkett [*A publication*] (DLA)

L & GTS ...... Lloyd and Goold's Irish Chancery Reports Tempore Sugden [*1835*] [*A publication*] (DLA)

L & GT Sug... Lloyd and Goold's Irish Chancery Reports Tempore Sugden [*1835*] [*A publication*] (DLA)

L & H .... Lamport & Holt Line [*Steamship*] (MHDB)

L & H .... Laurel and Hardy [*The film comedy team of Stan Laurel and Oliver Hardy*]

L&H .... Lernout & Hauspie [*A speech products manufacturer*] (PCM)

L&H .... Lungs and Heart (SAUS)

L & HR .... [*The*] Lehigh & Hudson River Railway Co. [*Absorbed into Consolidated Rail Corp.*]

L & HTC ...... Line and Halftone Combined [*Illustration*] (DGA)

L & I	Launch and Impact (AFM)
L&I	Liver and Iron (DMAA)
L & ID	London and India Docks [Shipping] [British] (ROG)
LANDING	Landing [Commonly used] (OPSA)
LANDIS	Low-Approach Navigation Director System [Aircraft landing aid] [Air Force]
L & J Tr Mar	Ludlow and Jenkyns on the Law of Trade-Marks [A publication] (DLA)
LANDJUT	Allied Land Forces Schleswig-Holstein and Jutland [NATO] (NATG)
L & K	Love and Kisses [Correspondence]
L & L	Latch and Lock (DAC)
L&L	Launch and Landing [Aerospace] (NAKS)
L & L	Leave and Liberty (WDAA)
L & L	Legislative and Liaison [Military]
L&L	Lerner and Loewe [Composers]
L & L	Lewd and Lascivious
L & L	Love and Liquor (IIA)
L&L	Lyrics and Lyricists [Long running New York show]
L & LC	Leeds and Liverpool Canal [Shipping] [British] (ROG)
L & LC	Lift and Lift Cruise (MCD)
LANDLD	Landlord (ROG)
L & Leg GDR	Law and Legislation in the German Democratic Republic [A publication] (DLA)
L & Legis in GDR	Law and Legislation in the German Democratic Republic [A publication] (DLA)
L & LeM	Leigh and Le Marchant. Elections [4th ed.] [1885] [A publication] (DLA)
L & Lib	Law and Liberty [A publication] (DLA)
L&LS	Londonderry and Lough Swilly (SAUO)
L & M	Labor and Material Bond
L&M	L&M Drafting Service (SAUO)
L & M	Layout and Manuscript [Advertising] (WDMC)
L&M	Layout and Manuscript [Publishing] (WDMC)
L & M	Legal and Magnanimous Side [Sarcastic reference to the government of Vietnam and its allies] (VNW)
L & M	[The] Librarian and the Machine [A publication]
L&M	Linotype and Machinery (SAUO)
L & M	Lowndes and Maxwell's English Practice Cases [1852-54] [A publication] (DLA)
LANDMARC	International Land Management Research Centre (SAUO)
L&MM	Logistics and Materiel Management (SAUO)
L&N	Leeds & Northrup (SAUO)
L&N	Lomas & Nettleton Financial Corp. (EFIS)
L & N	Louisville & Nashville Railroad Co.
L & NE	Lehigh & New England Railway Co. [Absorbed into Consolidated Rail Corp.]
LANDNON	Allied Land Forces North Norway [NATO] (NATG)
LANDNON	Land Forces North Norway (SAUO)
LANDNOR	Allied Land Forces, North Norway (SAUO)
LANDNORTH	Allied Land Forces Northern Europe [NATO] (NATG)
LANDNORTH	Land Forces Northern Europe (SAUO)
LANDNORWAY	Allied Land Forces Norway [NATO]
L & NRR	Louisville & Nashville Railroad Co.
L&NWRy	London and North-Western Railway (SAUO)
L&OD	Leadership & Organization Development (SAUO)
L & OD	Lester & Orpen Dennys [Canadian publisher]
L&OG	Logistics and Operations Group (SAUO)
L & Order	Law and Order [A publication] (DLA)
L & P	Latch and Plaster (DAC)
L & P	Lighting and Power
L&P	Literature and Psychology [A publication] (ANEX)
L & PA	Lodging and Pay Allowance [British military] (DMA)
L & PP	Lunar and Planetary Program
L & Psychology Rev	Law and Psychology Review [A publication] (DLA)
L & Psych Rev	Law and Psychology Review [A publication] (DLA)
L & R	Lake and Rail
L & R	Landing and Recovery (KSC)
L & R	Larceny and Receiving
L & R	Left and Right
L & R	Loring and Russell's Election Cases in Massachusetts [A publication] (DLA)
L & R Election Cases	Loring and Russell's Election Cases in Massachusetts [A publication] (DLA)
LANDREST	CSIRO Program on cost effective restoration technologies (SAUS)
L&RScRgt	Lanark and Renfrew Scottish Regiment (SAUO)
Landrys	Landrys Seafood Restaurants, Inc. [Associated Press] (SAG)
L&S	College of Letters and Science (SAUS)
L&S	Language and Speech (SAUO)
L & S	Launch and Servicing (AAG)
L & S	Laurinburg & Southern Railroad Co. (IIA)
L & S	Laverne and Shirley [Television program]
L&S	Liver and Spleen (SAUS)
L & S	Logistics and Support (NASA)
L&SA	Law and Society Association (SAUO)
Landsat	Land Remote Sensing Satellite (EOSA)
LANDSAT	Land Remote Sensing Satellite System (GFGA)
LANDSAT	Land Satellite [Marine science] (OSRA)
LANDSC	Landscape
Landsc Ecol	Landscape Ecology (SAUO)
Landsc J	Landscape Journal (SAUO)
LANDSCPG	Landscaping
Landsc Urban Plan	Landscape and Urban Planning (SAUO)
LandsE	Land's End, Inc. [Associated Press] (SAG)
LANDSONOR	Allied Land Forces South Norway [NATO] (NATG)
LANDSOUTH	Allied Land Forces Southern Europe [NATO]

LANDSOUTHEAST	Allied Land Forces Southeastern Europe [NATO]
LANDSS	Lightweight Advanced Night/Day Surveillance System (SAUO)
Landstr	Landstar Systems, Inc. [Associated Press] (SAG)
L & SWR	London & South-Western Railway (ROG)
L & T	Laboratories and Test (NASA)
L&T	Laboratory and Test (SAUO)
L & T	Landlord and Tenant [A publication] (DLA)
L & T	Line and Terminal [Telecommunications] (TEL)
L & T	Longfield and Townsend's Irish Exchequer Reports [1841-42] [A publication] (DLA)
L&T Camp	Leave and Transit Camp (SAUO)
L & TH	Lethality and Target Hardening [Military] (SDI)
L & U	Loading and Unloading
L & U	Lower and Upper [Anatomy]
LANDUP	Alberta Land Use Planning Data Bank [Alberta Municipal Affairs] [Information service or system] [Defunct] (IID)
Land U Pl Rep	Land Use Planning Reports [A publication] (DLA)
Land Use & Env't L Rev	Land Use and Environment Law Review [A publication] (DLA)
L & W	Living and Well
L & W	Lloyd and Welsby's English Commercial and Mercantile Cases [1829-30] [A publication] (DLA)
L & Welsb	Lloyd and Welsby's English Commercial and Mercantile Cases [1829-30] [A publication] (DLA)
L&WV	Lackawanna and Wyoming Valley Railroad Co. (SAUO)
L&YR	Lancashire and Yorkshire Railway (SAUO)
LANDZEALAND	Allied Land Forces Zealand [NATO] (NATG)
LANE	Lane [Commonly used] (OPSA)
Lane	Lane's English Exchequer Reports [1605-12] [A publication] (DLA)
LANE	Local Area Network Emulation [Telecommunications] (ACRL)
LANES	Lane [Commonly used] (OPSA)
LANES	League for the Advancement of New England Storytelling
LANFLTMATCONOFF	Atlantic Fleet Material Control Office (SAUS)
LANFORTRACOMLANT	Landing Force Training Command, Atlantic [Navy]
LANFORTRAU	Landing Force Training Unit [Marine Corps] (DNAB)
LANFOX	Local Area Network Fiber Optic Transceiver (ACAE)
LANFZT	Latin American Nuclear Free Zone Treaty (SAUO)
LANG	Langley [England]
LANG	Language (AFM)
Lang	Language (AL)
lang	Language (WDAA)
Lang Ca Cont	Langdell's Cases on Contracts [A publication] (DLA)
Lang Ca Sales	Langdell's Cases on the Law of Sales [A publication] (DLA)
Lang Cont	Langdell's Cases on Contracts [A publication] (DLA)
Lang Cont	Langdell's Summary of the Law of Contracts [A publication] (DLA)
Langd Cont	Langdell's Cases on Contracts [A publication] (DLA)
Langd Cont	Langdell's Summary of the Law of Contracts [A publication] (DLA)
Lang Eq Pl	Langdell's Cases in Equity Pleading [A publication] (DLA)
Lang Eq Pl	Langdell's Summary of Equity Pleading [A publication] (DLA)
Langer	[The] Langer Biomechanics Group, Inc. [Associated Press] (SAG)
Lang Sales	Langdell's Cases on the Law of Sales [A publication] (DLA)
Lang Soc	Language in Society [A publication] (BRI)
Lang Sum Cont	Langdell's Summary of the Law of Contracts [A publication] (DLA)
Lang Tr	Langley's Trustees' Act [A publication] (DLA)
Language	Language. Journal of the Linguistic Society of America. Baltimore (SAUO)
LANH	Launch (MSA)
LANIC	LAN [Local Area Network] Interface Card (PCM)
LANIC	Latin American Network Information Center [Internet resource]
LANICA	Lineas Aereas de Nicaragua, SA [Nicaraguan airline]
LANL	Los Alamos National Laboratory [Los Alamos, NM] [Department of Energy]
LANMAS	Local Area Network Material Accounting System (SAUO)
L Ann	Louisiana Annual Reports [A publication] (DLA)
Lannet	Lannet Data Communictions Ltd. [Associated Press] (SAG)
LANNET	Large Artificial Nerve [or Neuron] Network
Lanoptic	Lanoptics Ltd. [Associated Press] (SAG)
LANP	Leucine-Rich Acidic Nuclear Protein [Biochemistry]
LAnP	Louisiana State Penitentiary, Angola, LA [Library symbol] [Library of Congress] (LCLS)
LANP	Plaintree Systems Inc. [NASDAQ symbol] (SAG)
LAN/PDL	Local Area Network / Program Design Language (LAIN)
LANPF	Plaintree Systems [NASDAQ symbol] (TTSB)
LANRAC	Land Army Reunion Association Committee (SAUO)
Lan Reg	Lancashire Regiment (SAUO)
LANRES	Linked Access Network Resource Extension and Service
LANRES	Local Network Resource Extension [Computer science] (CIST)
LAN/RM	Local Area Network Reference Model
Lans	Lansing's New York Supreme Court Reports [A publication] (DLA)
LANS	Large Atypical Nevus Syndrome [Medicine]
LANS	Latin America News Service (BUAC)
LANS	Lightweight Airborne Navigation System (MCD)
LANS	Local Area Network Services (SAUO)
LANS	Local Area Network System [Telecommunications]
LANS	LORAN Airborne Navigation System (IEEE)
LANSA	Latin American Paper Money Society (EA)
LANSA	Lineas Aereas Nacionales Consolidadas Sociedad Anonima
LANSCE	Los Alamos Neutron Scattering Center
LANSCE	Los Alamos Neutron Science Center (SAUO)
Lans Ch	Lansing's Select Cases in Chancery [1824, 1826] [New York] [A publication] (DLA)
Lansg	New York Supreme Court Reports (Lansing) [A publication] (DLA)
LANSHIPRON	Landing Ship Squadron (CINC)
Lansing	New York Supreme Court Reports (Lansing) [A publication] (DLA)

LANSL .... Los Alamos National Scientific Laboratories [*New Mexico*]
Lans Sel Cas... Lansing's Select Cases in Chancery [*1824, 1826*] [*New York*] [*A publication*] (DLA)
LANSW .... Laryngectomee Association of New South Wales [*Australia*]
LANSW .... Legislative Assembly of New South Wales [*Australia*]
LANSW .... Lupus Association of New South Wales [*Australia*]
LANSX .... Lord Abbett: Tax Free Inc.: National Cl.A [*Mutual fund ticker symbol*] (SG)
LANt. .... Atlanten (SAUS)
LANT .... Atlantic
LANT .... Atlantic Area (SAUO)
LANT .... Lannet Data Communications Ltd. [*NASDAQ symbol*] (SAG)
L ANT .... Left Anterior (STED)
LANT .... Legislative Assembly of the Northern Territory [*Australia*]
LANTCOM ...... Atlantic Command [*Navy*]
LANTCOMINSGEN... Atlantic Command Inspector General (DNAB)
LANTCOMMBPO... Atlantic Command Military Blood Program Office (DNAB)
LANTCOMOPCONCEN... Atlantic [*Fleet*] Commander Operational Control Center [*Navy*]
LANTCOMOPSUPPFAC... Atlantic Command Operations Support Facility (DNAB)
LANTDAC ..... Atlantic Command Defense Analysis Center (SAUO)
LANTDIS ...... Atlantic Command Deployable Intelligence System (SAUS)
LANTDIS ...... US Atlantic Command Deployable Intelligence System (SAUO)
LANTFAP ..... Allied Command Atlantic Frequency Allocation Panel [*Obsolete*] [*NATO*] (NATG)
LANTFAST ... Atlantic Forward Area Support Team [*Military*] (DNAB)
LANTFLEASWTACSCOL... Atlantic Fleet Antisubmarine Warfare Tactical School [*Navy*]
LANTFLEASWTASCOL... Atlantic Fleet Antisubmarine Warfare Tactical School (SAUS)
LANTFLT ...... Atlantic Fleet
LANTFLTHEDSUPPACT... Atlantic Fleet Headquarters Support Activity [*Navy*] (DNAB)
LANTFLTMATCONOFF... Atlantic Fleet Material Control Office [*Navy*] (DNAB)
LANTFLTPEB... Atlantic Fleet Propulsion Examining Board [*Navy*] (DNAB)
LANTFLTRANSUPPFAC... Atlantic Fleet Training Support Facilities
LANTFLTWPNRAN... Atlantic Fleet Weapons Range [*Later, AFRSF*] [*Navy*]
LANTFLTWPNTRAFAC... Atlantic Fleet Weapons Training Facility [*Navy*] (DNAB)
L Anti .... Antilles (VRA)
L Anti .... Lesser Antilles (VRA)
LANTICOMIS... LANTCOM Integrated Command and Control Management Information System (MCD)
LANTINCEN... Atlantic Intelligence Center (SAUS)
LANTINTCEN... Atlantic Intelligence Center [*Navy*]
LANTIRN ...... Low-Altitude Navigation and Targeting Infrared [*System*] for Night [*Aviation*]
LANTMS ...... Linked Access Network Transport Management System [*Telecommunications*]
LANTNAVFACENGCOM... Atlantic Division Naval Facilities Engineering Command
LANTOPS ..... Atlantic Operations Supply Facilities (MCD)
LANTOPSSUPFAC... Atlantic Operations Supply Facilities
LANTREADEX... Atlantic Readiness Exercise (MCD)
LANTREPCNAVRES... Atlantic Fleet Chief of Naval Reserve Representative (DNAB)
LANTREPCOMNAVSURFRES... Atlantic Representative for Commander Naval Surface Reserve Force (DNAB)
LANTRESFLT... Atlantic Reserve Fleet
LANTSAR ..... Atlantic International Air and Surface Search and Rescue Seminar (PDAA)
LANTSOC ..... Atlantic Fleet Signals Security Operations Center [*Navy*] (DNAB)
LANTWWMCCS... Atlantic Fleet Worldwide Military Command Control System [*Navy*] (DNAB)
LANUG .... Los Alamos Next Users Group (SAUO)
LANV .... LanVision Systems [*NASDAQ symbol*] (TTSB)
LANV .... Left Atrial Neovascularization [*Cardiology*] (DAVI)
LANWR .... Laguna Atascosa National Wildlife Refuge (SAUO)
LANWR .... Lake Andes National Wildlife Refuge (SAUO)
LANX .... Local Area Network Exchange
LANY .... Linseed Association of New York (SAUO)
LANYX .... Lord Abbett: Tax Free Inc.: N.Y. Cl.A [*Mutual fund ticker symbol*] (SG)
LANZ .... Lancer Orthodontics [*NASDAQ symbol*] (TTSB)
LANZ .... Lancer Orthodontics, Inc. [*NASDAQ symbol*] (SAG)
LAO .... Laboratory Assessment Office (SAUO)
lao .... Lao [*MARC language code*] [*Library of Congress*] (LCCP)
LAO .... Laoag [*Philippines*] [*Airport symbol*] (OAG)
LAO .... Lao Aviaton [*Laos*] [*ICAO designator*] (FAAC)
LAO .... Laos [*or Lao People's Democratic Republic*] [*ANSI three-letter standard code*] (CNC)
Lao .... Laos (MILB)
LAO .... Large Assembly Order (MCD)
LAO .... Lasa Array [*Montana*] [*Seismograph station code, US Geological Survey*] (SEIS)
LAO .... La Teko Resources Ltd. [*Vancouver Stock Exchange symbol*]
LAO .... Lateral Anterior Oblique (DB)
LAO .... Lead Agency Official (MHDB)
LAO .... Left Anterior Oblique [*Cardiology*]
LAO .... Left Anterior Occipital [*Medicine*] (STED)
LAO .... Left Atrial Overloading [*Cardiology*] (DAVI)
LAO .... Legal Aid Office
LAO .... Legal Assistance Officer
LAO .... Legislative Analyst's Office (AGLO)
LAO .... Licensing Authorities Office
LAO .... Licentiate in Obstetric Science (DAVI)
LAO .... Licentiate of the Art of Obstetrics [*British*]
LAO .... Limited Attack Option (COE)

LAO .... Local Area Office (SAUO)
LAO .... Local Area Operations (SAUO)
LAO .... Location Administrative Officer (SARE)
LAO .... Logistics Area Officer (MCD)
LAO .... Logistics Assistance Office [*or Officer*] [*Army Materiel Command*]
LAOAR .... Latin American Office of Aerospace Research [*Air Force*]
LAOCIF .... Logistic Assistance Office Command Interest Flasher [*Military*] (AABC)
LAOCP .... Limited Amateur Operator's Certificate of Proficiency [*Radio*]
LAOD .... Los Angeles Ordnance District [*Military*] (AAG)
LAOF .... Longitudinal Arch of Foot (MELL)
LAOL .... Los Alamos Opacity Library (SAUO)
LAOOC .... Los Angeles Olympic Organizing Committee (EA)
LAOR .... La Teko Resources Ltd. [*NASDAQ symbol*] (SAG)
LAORF .... La Teko Resources Ltd [*NASDAQ symbol*] (TTSB)
LAOS .... Laymen's Overseas Service [*Acronym is now used as official name of the organization*]
LAOSA .... Librarianship and Archives Old Students' Association (DGA)
LAOSC .... Local Authorities Ordnance Survey Committee [*British*]
LAOT .... Los Angeles Opera Theater (SAUO)
LAP .... Laboratory Accreditation Program [*Department of Commerce*]
LAP .... Laboratory of Advertising Performance [*McGraw-Hill*]
LAP .... Laboratory of Architecture and Planning [*Massachusetts Institute of Technology*] [*Research center*] (RCD)
LAP .... Laboratory of Atmospheric Physics (SAUO)
LAP .... Laboratory of Aviation Psychology (SAUO)
LAP .... Labour Action for Peace [*Political party*] (BUAC)
LAP .... Lakewood Public Library, Lakewood, OH [*OCLC symbol*] (OCLC)
LAP .... Landsat Applications Program (SAUO)
lap .... Laparoscopy [*Medicine*]
Lap .... Laparotomy [*Medicine*] (AMHC)
Lap .... Laparotomy [*Sponges*] (DAVI)
LAP .... La Paz [*Mexico*] [*Airport symbol*] (OAG)
LAP .... La Paz [*Mexico*] [*Seismograph station code, US Geological Survey*] (SEIS)
LAP .... Lapland
lap .... Lapp [*MARC language code*] [*Library of Congress*] (LCCP)
Lap .... Lapus de Castiglionchio [*Flourished, 1353-81*] [*Authority cited in pre-1607 legal work*] (DSA)
LAP .... Large Area Panel
LAP .... Large-Area Processing [*For fabricating multichip modules*]
LAP .... Large Scale Advanced Propeller (ACAE)
LAP .... Last Appearance (SAUO)
LAP .... Latin American Parliament [*See also PLA*] [*Colombia*] (EAIO)
LAP .... Lattice Assessment Program [*Civil Defense*]
LAP .... Launch Analyst Panel [*Aerospace*] (AAG)
LAP .... Launch Assist Platform (IGSL)
LAP .... Launcher Adaptable Platform (ACAE)
LAP .... Launcher Avionics Package (ACAE)
LAP .... Learning Ability Profile [*Margarita Henning*] (TES)
LAP .... Learning Accomplishment Profile [*Psychology*]
LAP .... Learning Activity Package (EDAC)
LAP .... Learning Activity Packet (AEE)
LAP .... Learning Assistance Program
LAP .... Leased Attached Pallet (SSD)
LAP .... Left Arterial Pressure [*Cardiology*] (DAVI)
LAP .... Left Atrial Pressure [*Cardiology*]
LAP .... Lesson Assembly Program (IEEE)
LAP .... Lethality Assessment Program
LAP .... Leucine Aminopeptidase [*Also, LA, LP*] [*An enzyme*]
LAP .... Leukocyte Adhesion Stimulator [*Medicine*] (MELL)
LAP .... Leukocyte Alkaline Phosphatase [*An enzyme*]
LAP .... Liberation Action Party [*Trinidad and Tobago*] [*Political party*] (PPW)
LAP .... Liberian Action Party [*Political party*] (BUAC)
LAP .... Library Access Program
LAP .... Library Awareness Program [*FBI*]
LAP .... Line Access Point [*Telecommunications*] (TEL)
LAP .... Linear Arithmetic Processor (IAA)
LAP .... Lineas Aereas Paraguayas [*Paraguay*] [*ICAO designator*] (FAAC)
LAP .... Lingual Antimicrobial Peptide [*Biochemistry*]
LAP .... Link Access Procedure [*Telecommunications*] (TEL)
LAP .... Link Access Protocol [*Telecommunications*] (TEL)
LAP .... Link Asynchronous Protocol [*Telecommunications*]
LAP .... Linux Application Platform (VLIE)
LAP .... List Assembly Programming [*Computer science*]
LAP .... Load, Assemble, Pack [*Army*] (AABC)
LAP .... Loading Assembling and Packing
LAP .... Local Access Port [*Telecommunications*] (ACRL)
LAP .... Local Air Picture (SAUS)
LAP .... Local Analysis and Prediction [*Marine science*] (OSRA)
LAP .... Local Area Power [*Computer science*] (CIST)
LAP .... Location Audit Program [*Navy*] (NG)
LAP .... Logistics Assistance Program
LAP .... Loide Aereo Nacional, SA [*Brazilian airline*]
LAP .... London Airport
LAP .... London Artid Plastics Ltd. (SAUO)
LAP .... Lord's Acre Plan (EA)
LA-P .... Los Alamos Proposal (SAUO)
LAP .... Loudspeaker Acoustical Phase-Inverter
L Ap .... Louisiana Courts of Appeal Reports [*A publication*] (DLA)
LAP .... Low Achievers Project [*Education*] (AIE)
LAP .... Low-Altitude Penetration
LAP .... Low-Altitude Performance
LAP .... Low Altitude Program (ACAE)
LAP .... Low Atmospheric Pressure (DAVI)

LAP	Lyophilized Anterior Pituitary [*Endocrinology*]
LAPA	Latin America Parents Association (EA)
LAPA	Leukocyte Alkaline Phosphatase Activity [*Biochemistry*]
LAPA	Lightweight Aggregate Producers Association (EA)
LAPA	Los Angeles Procurement Agency [*Army*]
LAPAC	Life Amendment Political Action Committee [*Defunct*] (EA)
LaPac	Louisiana-Pacific Corp. [*Associated Press*] (SAG)
LAPADA	London and Provincial Antique Dealers Association [*England*] (BUAC)
LAPADS	Lightweight Acoustic Processing and Display System [*British military*] (DMA)
LAPAM	Low-Altitude Penetrating Attack Missile [*Proposed*]
LAPAN	Institute of Aeronautics and Space (SAUS)
LAPAN	National Aeronautics and Space Agency (SAUS)
LAPAR	Large Phased-Array RADAR
LAPB	Laboratories' Applied Physiology Branch [*Army*]
LAPB	Link Access Procedure [*or Protocol*] Balanced [*Telecommunications*]
LAPB	Link Access Procedure for Balanced Mode (SAUO)
LAP-B	Link Access Protocol-Balanced (MLOA)
LAPB	Link Access Protocol, B Channel [*Telecommunications*]
LAPB	Local Analysis and Prediction Branch (SAUO)
LAPC	Land and Agriculture Policy Centre [*South Africa*]
LAPC	Landmarks of American Popular Culture [*A publication*]
LAPC	Large Area Proportional Counter Array (SAUO)
LAPC	Los Angeles Pacific College [*California*]
LAPC	Los Angeles Pierce College (SAUO)
LAPCO	Lavan Petroleum Co. [*Iran*] (BUAC)
LAPD	Latin American Pollen Database (QUAC)
LAPD	Limited Axial Power Distribution (IEEE)
LAPD	Link Access Procedure-D [*Telecommunications*] (DOM)
LAPD	Link Access Procedure Direct (SAUO)
LAPD	Link Access Procedure for the D Channel (SAUO)
LAPD	Link Access Protocol, D Channel [*Telecommunications*]
LAPD	Los Alamos Police Department (SAUO)
LAPD	Los Angeles Air Procurement District
LAPD	Los Angeles Police Department (WDAA)
LAPD	Los Angeles Police District (SAUO)
LAPD	Los Angeles Procurement District (SAUO)
Lap Dec	Laperriere's Speaker's Decisions [*Canada*] [*A publication*] (DLA)
LAPDis	Los Angeles Procurement District (SAUO)
LAPDOG	Low-Altitude Pursuit Dive on Ground (MCD)
LAPDRY	Lapidary
LAPE	Lineas Aereas Postales Espanoles [*Airline*] [*Spain*]
LAPE	Low Altitude Parachute Extraction System (SAUO)
LAPERS	Labor and Production Effectiveness Reporting System [*DoD*]
LAPES	Low-Altitude Parachute Extraction System [*Military*]
LAPF	Link Access Procedure to Frame Mode Bearer Services [*Telecommunications*] (ACRL)
LAPF	Low-Affinity Platelet Factor (STED)
LAPFA	Laminated Plastics Fabricators Association (SAUO)
LAPF-Core	Core Aspects of the Link Access Procedure to Frame Mode Bearer Services (SAUS)
LAPFO	Los Angeles Procurement Field Office
LAPH	Lithium Aluminum Pentahydride (MCD)
LAPIC	Local Advanced Programmable Interrupt Controller (SAUS)
lapid	Lapideum [*Stony*] [*Latin*] (MAE)
LAPIS	LASER Photoionization Spectroscopy
LAPIS	Legislative Authorization Program Information System [*General Accounting Office*] [*Defunct*] (IID)
LAPIS	Local Automated Personnel Information System (DNAB)
LAPIS	Locality and Practice Information (SAUO)
LAPL	Lead Allowance Parts List
LAPL	Library Association Publishing Ltd. [*British*]
LAPL	Los Angeles Public Library
LaPL	Louisiana Power & Light Co. [*Associated Press*] (SAG)
LAPLS	Lead Allowance Parts List System (DNAB)
LAPM	Last Premidcourse Orbit
LAPM	Link Access Procedure for MODEMs [*Communications protocol*] [*Computer science*] (PCM)
LAPMS	Latin American Paper Money Society (EA)
LAPMS	Long Arm Posterior Molded Splint [*Medicine*] (MEDA)
LAPO	Los Angeles Philharmonic Orchestra (SAUO)
LAPOCA	L-Asparaginase, Prednisone, Oncovin [*Vincristine*], Cytarabine, Adriamycin [*Antineoplastic drug regimen*]
La Pol Inst	Louisiana Polytechnical Institute (SAUO)
LAPP	Land Arctic Physical Processes (SAUO)
LAPP	Lappish [*Language, etc.*] (ROG)
LAPP	Lower Achieving Pupils Project [*British*]
LAPPES	Large Power Plant Effluent Study (NRCH)
Lappie	Live-Alone Person [*Lifestyle classification*]
LAPR	Life Assurance Premium Relief [*Business term*]
LAPR	Los Alamos Power Reactor
LA-PR	Los Alamos Progress Report (SAUO)
LAPRE	Los Alamos Power Reactor Experiment
LAPS	LASER Profile System
LAPS	Latin American Philatelic Society (EA)
LAPS	Latin American, Portuguese, and Spanish [*Division*] [*Library of Congress*]
LAPS	Launcher Avionics Packages (MCD)
LAPS	Left Aft Propulsion System [*or Subsystem*] (NASA)
LAPS	Light-Addressable Potentiometric Sensor [*Semiconductor*]
LAPS	Literary, Artistic, Political, or Scientific [*Value*] [*In obscenity law, a criterion established by the 1973 case of Miller Versus California*]
LAPS	Loan Application Processing System
LAPS	Local Analysis and Prediction System [*Marine science*] (OSRA)
LAPS	Louis-Allen Power Supply
LAPS	Lovelace Aerosol Particle Separator [*Lovelace Foundation for Medical Education and Research*] (PDAA)
LAPS	Low-Altitude Proximity Sensor (MCD)
LAPS	Low Attaining Pupils in Secondary Schools (AIE)
LAPSA	Lineas Aereas Paraguayas Sociedad Anonima [*Airline*] [*Paraguay*]
LAPSE	Longterm Ambulatory Physiological Surveillance Equipment (PDAA)
LAPSS	Large Area Pulsed Solar Simulator (ACAE)
LAPSS	LASER Airborne Photographic Scanning System [*Navy*]
LAPSS	Low-Angle Polycrystalline Silicon Sheet [*Photovoltaic energy systems*]
LAPT	Library Acquisitions: Practice and Theory [*A publication*]
LAPT	Local Apparent Time (MSA)
LAPT	London Association for the Protection of Trade (SAUO)
LAPT	Los Angeles Union Passenger Terminal [*AAR code*]
LAPTA	Local Authorities Passenger Transport Association (SAUO)
LAPTC	Lucas Aerospace Power Transmission Corp. (SAUO)
LAPUT	Light-Activated Programmable Unijunction Transistor
LAPW	Left Atrial Posterior Wall [*Cardiology*] (DAVI)
LAPW	Linear Augmented Plane-Wave [*Physics*]
LAPW	Linearized Augmented Plane Wave [*Physical chemistry*]
LAPX	Link Access Procedure Half-Duplex [*Telecommunications*] (ACRL)
LAQ	Al Bayda [*Libya*] [*Airport symbol*] (AD)
LAQ	Beida [*Libya*] [*Airport symbol*] (OAG)
LAQ	Lacquer (KSC)
LAQ	Latin America Equity Fd [*NYSE symbol*] (TTSB)
LAQ	Latin America Equity Fund [*NYSE symbol*] (SPSG)
LAQ	Leathercrafters' Association of Queensland [*Australia*]
LAQ	Lebanese Air Transport [*ICAO designator*] (FAAC)
LAQ	Legislative Assembly of Queensland [*Australia*]
L'AQORCD	L'Association Quebecoise des Organismes Regionaux de Concertation et de Developpement (AC)
LAQ STNS	Laquer Stains
LAQT	Low-Altitude Qualification Test [*Balloon*]
LaQuinta	La Quinta Motor Inns Ltd. [*Associated Press*] (SAG)
LAR	Division of Labor Relations (SAUO)
LAR	Labor Arbitration Reports [*Bureau of National Affairs*] [*A publication*] (DLA)
LAR	Laboratory Animal Resources
LAR	Land Registry [*British*]
LAR	Laramie [*Wyoming*] [*Airport symbol*] (OAG)
LAR	Laramie [*Wyoming*] [*Seismograph station code, US Geological Survey*] (SEIS)
LAR	Laramie, WY [*Location identifier*] [*FAA*] (FAAL)
LAR	Larceny [*Legal shorthand*] (LWAP)
LAR	Lariat Oil & Gas Ltd. [*Toronto Stock Exchange symbol*]
LAR	Laryngology
lar	Larynx [*Anatomy*] (DAVI)
LAR	LASER-Aided Rocket (MCD)
LAR	Last Address Register (TIMI)
LAR	Late Asthmatic Response [*Medicine*] (DAVI)
LAR	Late Reaction [*Medicine*] (DMAA)
LAR	Launch Acceptability Region (MCD)
LAR	Launch Alert Receiver (DNAB)
LAR	Launcher Adapter Rail (MCD)
LAR	Lawrence Aviation, Inc. [*ICAO designator*] (FAAC)
LAR	Leaf Area Ratio [*Botany*]
LAR	Leaflet Artillery Round [*PSYOP*] (RDA)
LAR	Left Arm Reclining [*or Recumbent*] [*Medicine*]
LAR	Leukocyte Adhesion Receptor [*Immunology*]
LAR	Leukocyte Antigen-Related [*Medicine*] (DMAA)
LAR	Library Association of Rhodesia (SAUO)
LAR	Library Association Record [*A publication*] (BRI)
LAR	Libyan Arab Republic (BUAC)
LAR	Life Assurance Relief [*British*]
LAR	Light Artillery Rocket (MCD)
LAR	Light Attendant Station [*Coast Guard*]
LAR	Light Automatic Rifle (SAUS)
LAR	Limit Address Register [*Computer science*]
LAR	Limited Access Required (ACAE)
LAR	Linhas Aereas Regionais SA [*Portugal*] [*ICAO designator*] (FAAC)
LAR	Liquid Air Rocket
LAR	Load Access Rights (VLIE)
LAR	Local Acquisition RADAR (CET)
LAR	Locus Activation Region [*Genetics*]
LAR	Logistic Assessment Review (ACAE)
LAR	Logistics Assessment Review (SAUO)
LAR	Logistics Assistance Representative [*Army*] (DOMA)
LAR	Loita Armada Revolucionaria [*Armed Revolutionary Struggle*] [*Spain*] (PD)
LAR	Long-Range Aircraft Rocket (NG)
LAR	Long-Range Assessments and Research [*Program*] [*Department of State*] [*Washington, DC*]
LAR	Los Angeles Raiders [*National Football League*] [*1982-94*] (NFLA)
LAR	Lot Age Report (AAEL)
L-Ar	Louisiana Department of State, State Archives and Records, Baton Rouge, LA [*Library symbol*] [*Library of Congress*] (LCLS)
LA R	Louisiana Reports [*A publication*] (DLA)
LAR	Low-Altitude Release
LAR	Low-Angle Reentry [*Aerospace*] (MCD)
LAR	Low-Aspect Ratio
LARA	Land Access Rights Association (BUAC)
LARA	Latin American Railways Association (EA)
LARA	League of Americans Residing Abroad (SAUO)
LARA	Licensed Agencies for Relief in Asia (SAUO)

LARA	Light Armed Reconnaissance Aircraft [Air Force]
LARA	Local Acquisition Radar (ACAE)
LARA	Low-Altitude RADAR Altimeter [Air Force]
LARAC	Local Authority Recycling Advisory Council (BUAC)
LARAM	Line Addressable Random Access Memory [Computer science] (MDG)
LArB	Bienville Parish Library, Arcadia, LA [Library symbol] [Library of Congress] (LCLS)
LArbG	Landesarbeitsgericht [Provincial Labor Court of Appeal] [German] (ILCA)
LARC	Association for Library Automation Research Communications (EA)
LARC	Lambda Amateur Radio Club (EA)
LaRC	Langley Research Center [Hampton, VA] (NAKS)
LARC	Langley Research Center [NASA]
LARC	Larceny [FBI standardized term]
LARC	Large Automatic Research Computer [or Calculator]
LARC	LASER-Activated Recession Compensator (MCD)
LARC	LASER Applications Research Center (RCD)
LARC	Legal Aid Review Committee
LARC	Leukocyte Automatic Recognition Computer [Blood counting]
LARC	Library Automation Research and Consulting Association (NITA)
LARC	Library Automation Research and Consulting Services (IAA)
LARC	Libyan-American Reconstruction Commission
LARC	Light Amphibious Resupply Craft
LARC	Lighter, Amphibious, Resupply, Cargo [Vessel]
LARC	Lindheimer Astronomical Research Center [Northwestern University]
LARC	Livermore Atomic Research Computer
LARC	Livermore Automatic Research Calculator (VLIE)
LARC	Livermore Automatic Research Computer (RALS)
LARC	Local Alcoholism Reception Center
LARC	Locally Assigned Reporting Code [Munitions reports] (AFM)
LARC	Loose Actors Revolving Company [for producing plays; members include actors George C. Scott and Rod Steiger]
LARC	Low-Altitude Ride Control [Shock-absorbing system] [Aviation] (MCD)
LaRC	NASA Langley Research Center (SAUO)
LARC	Regional Conference for Latin America [UN Food and Agriculture Organization]
LARCCH	Latin America Resource Center and Clearinghouse [Defunct] (EA)
LARCEF	Latin American Council for Cosmic Radiation & Physical (SAUO)
LARCF	Lithuanian American Roman Catholic Federation (EA)
LARC Services	Library Automation Research and Consulting Services (SAUO)
LARCT	Last Radio Contact [Aviation]
LARC-V	Lighter, Amphibious, Resupply, Cargo-Five Ton [Vessel] (DNAB)
LARD	Load Adjuster Reference Datum (IAA)
LarDav	Larson-Davis [Associated Press] (SAG)
LARDS	Low-Accuracy RADAR Data Transmission System
LARE	Local Asymptotic Relative Efficiency [Statistics]
LAREHS	Laboratory of Research in Human and Social Ecology [University of Quebec at Montreal] [Canada] [Research center] (RCD)
LA Rep	Louisiana Reports [A publication] (DLA)
LA Rev Stat Ann (West)	West's Louisiana Revised Statutes, Annotated [A publication] (DLA)
LARF	Latin American Reserve Fund (BUAC)
LARF	Lebanese Armed Revolutionary Faction
LARF	Low-Altitude RADAR Fuzing (CET)
LARG	Largamente [Easily] [Music]
LARG	Largo [Very Slow] [Music] (ROG)
LARG	Library-Anthropology Resource Group
LARGE	Laboratory of Regional Geodynamics (SAUO)
LARGE	Moscow Laboratory of Regional Geodynamics (SAUS)
LARGO	Larghetto [Slow] [Music] (ROG)
LARGOS	LASER-Activated Reflecting Geodetic Optical Satellite
LARIA	Local Authorities Research and Intelligence Association [British]
LARIAT	LASER RADAR Intelligence Acquisition Technology
LARIAT	Long-Range Area RADAR for Intrusion Detection and Tracking
LARIS	Louisiana Areal Resource Information System (SAUO)
LARIS	Low-Altitude RADAR Interface System (MCD)
Larizz	Larizza Industries, Inc. [Associated Press] (SAG)
LARK	Landmark Bancshares [NASDAQ symbol] (TTSB)
LARL	Laurel Cap Group [NASDAQ symbol] (TTSB)
LARL	Laurel Capital Group [NASDAQ symbol] (SAG)
LARM	Logistics Assets Requirements Model (PDAA)
LARM	Low-Angle Re-Entry Maneuvering Re-Entry Vehicle (PDAA)
LARMC	Landstuhl Army Regional Medical Center [Germany]
LARO	Latin American Regional Office [United Nations Food and Agricultural Organization] (BARN)
LAROO	Lackland Aircraft Reactors Operations Office (SAA)
LARP	Launch and Recovery Platform (DNAB)
LARP	Line Automatic Reperforator (CET)
LARP	Live-Action Role Playing (ADWA)
LARP	Local and Remote Printing [Computer science]
LARP	Local Approvals Review Program
LARPS	Large Aircraft Robotic Paint-Stripping System (SAUS)
LARPS	Local and Remote Printing Station [Computer science]
LARR	Large Area Record Reader (IAA)
LARR	Latin American Research Review. University of North Carolina Press for the Latin American Studies Association. Chapel Hill (SAUO)
LARR	Linear Accelerator Regenerator Reactor (BARN)
LARRIE	Local Authorities Race Relations Information Exchange (BUAC)
LARRL	Fort Keogh Livestock and Range Research Laboratory [Miles City, MT] [Department of Agriculture] (GRD)
LARRS	Livestock and Range Research Station [Department of Agriculture] (GRD)
LARRS	Low-Altitude Retro Rocket System (DWSG)
LARS	Laboratory for Agricultural Remote Sensing
LARS	Laboratory for Applications of Remote Sensing [Purdue University] [Research center] (RCD)
LARS	Laminar Angular Rate Sensor [Navy]
LARS	Language-Structured Auditory Retention Span Test
LARS	Larscom Inc. [NASDAQ symbol] (SAG)
LARS	LASER-Aided Rocket System [Military] (CAAL)
LARS	LASER Angular Rate Sensor [or Scanner]
LARS	LASER-Articulated Robotic System
LARS	Launch and Recovery System [NASA]
LARS	Learning and Recognition System [GTE]
LARS	Left Add, Right Subtract [Army field artillery technique] (INF)
LARS	Leucyl-Transfer Ribonucleic Acid [Biochemistry] (DAVI)
LARS	Light Artillery Rocket System (NATG)
LARS	Living Aquatic Resources Sector [Aquaculture]
LARS	Low-Altitude RADAR System (NATG)
LARS	Lower Airspace RADAR Advisory Service [British] (DA)
LARS	Lower Atmosphere Research Satellite (SSD)
LARSA	Latin American Rural Sociological Association (EAIO)
Larscom	Larscom Inc. [Associated Press] (SAG)
LARSFRIS	Laboratory for Applications of Remote Sensing Forest (SAUO)
LARSI	Laboratoire de Recherche en Sciences Immobilieres [University of Quebec at Montreal] [Research center] (RCD)
LA RSIS	LA Reference, Special and Information Section [British] (NITA)
LARSIS	Library Association Reference and Special Information Section (PDAA)
LARSP	Language Assessment Remediation and Screening Procedure [for the language impaired]
LARSSYAA	Laboratory for Applications of Remote Sensing System for Aircraft Analysis [NASA] (GFGA)
LARSYS	Laboratory of Applications of Remote Sensing Image Data Processing System (SAUO)
LARSYSAA	Laboratory for Applications of Remote Sensing System for Aircraft Analysis (SAUO)
LART	Lateral Acceleration Response Time
LART	Los Angeles Rapid Transit (SAUO)
LART	Luser Attitude Re-adjustment Tool (SAUS)
LARTS	LOGAIR Real-Time Terminal System (SAUO)
LARU	Latin American Research Unit (SAUO)
LARV	Light Armoured Reconnaissance Vehicle (SAUS)
LARV	Low-Altitude Research Vehicle (IAA)
LARVA	Low-Altitude Research Vehicular Advancements
LARWS	Lightweight Airborne Radar Warning System (SAUO)
laryn	Laryngeal [Medicine] (STED)
laryn	Laryngitis [Otorhinolaryngology] (DAVI)
laryn	Laryngoscopy [Otorhinolaryngology] (DAVI)
Laryng	Laryngology
LARYNGLGST	Laryngologist
LARYNGLGY	Laryngology
Laryngol	Laryngologist (DAVI)
LARYNGOL	Laryngology
LAS	Almiral [Spain] [Research code symbol]
LAS	Label as Such [Pharmacology] (CDAI)
las	Label as Such [Medicine] (WDAA)
LAS	Labor Area Summary [Employment and Training Administration] [Department of Labor]
LAS	Laboratories of Applied Sciences [University of Chicago] (MCD)
LAS	Laboratory Analytical Services (SAUO)
LAS	Laboratory Animal Sciences
LAS	Laboratory Automation System
LAS	Laboratory of Atmospheric Sciences [National Science Foundation]
LAS	LAGEOS Apogee Stage (SAUS)
LAS	Land Agents' Society [British] (DI)
LAS	Land Analysis Software (ACAE)
LAS	Land Analysis System (ACAE)
LAS	Landing Approach Simulator
LAS	Landsat Assessment System (ACAE)
LAS	LANDSAT [Land Remote Sensing Satellite System] Sensor [NASA] (SSD)
LAS	Language Assessment Scales [Test]
LAS	Lapidus Airfloat System (DAVI)
LAS	Large Amplitude Simulator
LAS	Large Astronomical Satellite [ESRO]
LAS	Large-Probe Atmospheric Structure [NASA]
LAS	La Salle College, Philadelphia, PA [OCLC symbol] (OCLC)
LAS	LASER Absorption Spectrometer
LAS	LASER Antiflash System
LAS	LASER Attack System
LAS	Laser Indus Ltd, Ord [AMEX symbol] (TTSB)
LAS	Laser Industries Ltd. [AMEX symbol] (SPSG)
LAS	Las Vegas [Nevada] [Airport symbol] (OAG)
LAS	Las Vegas, NV [Location identifier] [FAA] (FAAL)
LAS	Lateral Amyotrophic Sclerosis [Medicine] (STED)
LAS	Launch Area Supervisor (AFM)
LAS	Launch Auxiliary System
las	Laxative [Medicine] (DAVI)
LAS	Laxative Abuse Syndrome [Medicine] (DAVI)
LAS	Leader Authenticity Scale [Psychology] (EDAC)
LAS	Leadership Appraisal Survey [Interpersonal skills and attitudes test]
LAS	League of Arab States [Tunis, Tunisia]
LAS	Lebanese-American Society of Greater New York [Defunct] (EA)
LAS	Left Anterior-Superior [Anatomy] (DAVI)
LAS	Left Arm Sitting [Blood pressure and pulse measurement] [Cardiology] (DAVI)
LAS	Legal Aid Service (SAUO)
LAS	Legal Aid Society (WDAA)

LAS............	Leipziger Aegyptologische Studien [*A publication*] (BJA)
LAS............	Leucine Acetylsalicylate [*Biochemistry*] (DAVI)
LAS............	Library Access System (SAUO)
LAS............	Library Association of Singapore (BUAC)
LAS............	Library Automation Services [*Oxford University*]
LAS............	Life Assurance of Scotland [*Commercial firm*]
LAS............	Light-Activated Switch
LAS............	Lignes Aerienne Seychelles [*ICAO designator*] (FAAC)
LAS............	Limited Assignment Status [*Military*]
LAS............	Limited Assortment Store (WDMC)
LAS............	Line Apparatus Shop [*Telecommunications*] (OA)
LAS............	Linear Alkylbenzene Sulfonate [*Surfactant*]
LAS............	Linear Alkyl Sulfonate (STED)
LAS............	Link Active Scheduler (ACII)
LAS............	Litha-Alumina-Silicate [*Inorganic chemistry*]
LAS............	Lithuanian Academy of Sciences (BUAC)
LAS............	Liturgical Arts Society (EA)
LAS............	Liverpool Architectural Society (SAUO)
LAS............	Local Adaptation Syndrome [*Medicine*]
LAS............	Local Address Space
LAS............	Local Alignment System [*Optics*]
LAS............	Local Area Screening
LAS............	Location Addressable Storage [*Computer science*] (VLIE)
LAS............	Lockheed Aircraft Services Co. (SAUO)
LAS............	Locum Appointment Service (SAUO)
LAS............	Logical Address Strobe
LAS............	Logical Compare Accumulator with Storage (SAA)
LAS............	Logic Analysis System [*Rohde and Schwartz*] [*Germany*] (NITA)
LAS............	London Appreciation Society
LAS............	Long-Arm Splint [*Orthopedics*] (DAVI)
LAS............	Longitudinal Air Spring
LAS............	Long-Range Assistance Strategy (CINC)
LAS............	Look-Out Aiming Sight [*Military*] (PDAA)
LAS............	Loop Actuating Signal (SAA)
LAS............	Lord Advocate of Scotland
LAS............	Los Alamos Science (SAUO)
LAS............	Los Angeles Shop (SAUO)
LAS............	Louisiana Academy of Sciences (SAUO)
LAS............	Low Air Speed (MCD)
LAS............	Low-Alloy Steel
LAS............	Low-Altitude Satellite
LAS............	Low Apgar Score [*Medicine*] (MELL)
LAS............	Lower Abdominal Surgery (DAVI)
LAS............	Lower Airspace (WDAA)
LAS............	Lunar Attitude System [*Aerospace*]
LAS............	Lung Alveolar Surfactant (SAUS)
LAS............	Lupus Anticoagulant Syndrome [*Medicine*] (MELL)
LAS............	Lutheran Academy for Scholarship [*Defunct*] (EA)
LAS............	Lymphadenopathy Syndrome [*Medicine*]
LAS............	Lymphangioscintigraphy (STED)
LAS............	Lysine Acetylsalicylate [*Biochemistry*]
LAS............	McCarran International Airport [*FAA*] (TAG)
LAS............	Saskatchewan Libraries Retrospective Conversion [*UTLAS symbol*]
LASA............	Laboratory Animal Science Association [*British*]
LASA............	Large Aperture Seismic Array [*Nuclear detection device*]
LASA............	Large Area Solar Array
LASA............	LASER Anti-Satellite Weapon (LAIN)
LASA............	Latin American Shipowners Association (BUAC)
LASA............	Latin American Student Association (SAUO)
LASA............	Latin American Studies Association (EA)
LA(SA)........	Latvian Association of South Australia
LASA............	LIDAR [*Light Detection and Ranging*] Atmospheric Sounder and Altimeter
LASA............	Linear-Analogue Self Assessment (DMAA)
LASA............	London Advice Services Alliance [*England*] (BUAC)
LASAIL........	Land-Sea-Air Interaction Laboratory (SAUO)
La Salette Missionaries...	Missionaries of Our Lady of La Salette (SAUO)
LaSalle........	La Salle Re Holdings Ltd. [*Associated Press*] (SAG)
LASAM........	Laser Anti Tank Semi Active Missile (ACAE)
LASAM........	LASER Semiactive Missile
LASAN........	Los Alamos Systems Analysis (SAUO)
LASA-P	Linear-Analogue Self-Assessment-Pristman (DMAA)
LASAR	Logic Automated Stimulus and Response (MCD)
LASARS	Low Probability of Intercept Antijam Secure Airborne Radio System (MCD)
LASAS	Latin American Secretariat for Academic Services [*Defunct*]
LASA-S	Linear-Analogue Self-Assessment-Selby (DMAA)
LASAT........	Laser Antisatellite Satellite (ACAE)
LASB............	Lackawaxen & Stourbridge Railroad Corp. [*AAR code*]
LASBO	Louisiana Association of School Business Officials (SAUO)
LASC............	Light Armored Squad Carrier
LASC............	Lockheed Aeronautical Systems Corporation (ACAE)
LASC............	Los Angeles State College (SAUO)
LASCA	Large Area Solar Cell Array
LASCA	Los Angeles State and County Arboretum (SAUO)
LASCAR	Language for Simulation of Computer Architecture (CSR)
Lasc H War...	Lascelles' Horse Warranty [*2nd ed.*] [*1880*] [*A publication*] (DLA)
Lasc Juv Off...	Lascelles on Juvenile Offenders [*A publication*] (DLA)
LASCO	Large Angle and Spectrometric Coronagraph Experiment [*For observation of the sun*]
LASCO	Large-Angle Spectrometric Coronagraph [*Marine science*] (OSRA)
LASCO	Large-Angle Spectroscopic Coronagraph [*Instrumentation*]
LASCo	Larkin Aircraft Supply Company (SAUO)
LASCO	Latin American Science Cooperation Office (SAUO)
LASCO	Latin America Science Cooperation Office (MSC)

LASCODOCS...	Linguistic Analysis of Spanish Colonial Documents
LASCOM	Laser Communication (SAUS)
LASCOT	Large Screen Color Television System (NASA)
LASCR	Light-Activated Silicon-Controlled Rectifier
LASCS	Light-Activated Silicon-Controlled Switch (MCD)
LASD	Labor Agreement Settlement Data [*Cast Metals Association*] [*A publication*]
LASD	Large Area Screen Display (VLIE)
LASD	Latin American Serial Documents
LASE	LAMPS Shipboard Element (MCD)
LASE	Large Aperture Seismic Experiment [*Geophysical survey*]
LASE	Laser Adjustable Synethetic Epikeratoplasty (SAUS)
LASE	Laser Atmospheric Sensing Experiment (ACAE)
LASE	Laser-Scan International, Inc. (SAUO)
LASE	Laser Sight, Inc. [*NASDAQ symbol*] (SAG)
L-Ase	L-Asparaginase [*Also, A, L, L-Asp, L-asnase*] [*An enzyme, an antineoplastic*]
LASE	LIDAR [*Light Detection and Ranging*] Atmosphere Sensing Experiment
LASE	Lidar Atmospheric Sensing Experiment (SAUO)
LASE	Logistics Asset Support Estimate
LASED	Latin Americans for Social and Economic Development (SAUO)
LASEDECO...	Land Settlement and Development Corp. [*Philippines*] (BUAC)
LASEORS....	London and South Eastern Operational Research Society (SAUO)
Laser	Laser Industries Ltd. [*Associated Press*] (SAG)
LASER	League for the Advancement of States' Equal Rights (EA)
LASER	Learning About Science, Engineering, and Research (SAUS)
LASER	Learning Achievement through Saturated Educational Resources
LASER	Light Amplification by Stimulated Emission of Radiation [*Acronym was coined in 1957 by scientist Gordon Gould*]
LASER	London and South East Advisory Council [*England*] (BUAC)
LASER	London and South Eastern Library Region [*Information service or system*] (IID)
LASER	London and South Eastern Library Region cooperative (SAUO)
LASERCOM..	LASER Communications (MCD)
LASERCOM..	Light Amplification by Stimulated Emission of Radiation Computer Output Microfilm (EECA)
Lasergte	Lasergate Systems, Inc. [*Associated Press*] (SAG)
LASERS	Learning about Science Easily and Readily (SAUS)
LaserSt........	Laser Storm, Inc. [*Associated Press*] (SAG)
Lasertech.....	Laser Technics [*Associated Press*] (SAG)
LA Sess Law Serv...	Louisiana Session Law Service [*A publication*] (DLA)
LASFB	Left Anterior-Superior Fascicular Block [*Medicine*] (STED)
LASGAM	Laser Semi-Active Guided Anti Tank Missile (ACAE)
LASH	LASER Antitank Semiactive Homing
LASH	Latin American Society of Hepatology [*See also SLH*] (EAIO)
LASH	Left Anterior-Superior Hemiblock [*Medicine*] (STED)
LASH	Left Anterosuperior Hemiblock [*Cardiology*] (DAVI)
LASH	Legislative Action on Smoking and Health (EA)
LASH	Lighter Aboard Ship [*Barge-carrying ship*]
LASHAR	Laser System Hardware (ACAE)
LASHE	Low Altitude Simultaneous HAWK Engagement (SAUS)
LASHST	Latin American Society for the History of Sciences and Technology (BUAC)
LASHUP	Land-Air Synergic Homogeneous Ultra-Processor (SAA)
LASI............	Landing-Site Indicator [*Aviation*]
LASI............	Laser Industries Ltd. (SAUO)
LASI............	Library of Ancient Semitic Inscriptions (BJA)
LASI............	Licentiate of the Ambulance Service Institute [*British*] (DBQ)
LASI............	Lockheed Aircraft Service, Incorporated (SAUO)
LASIC	Laser Application Specific Integrated Circuit (SAUS)
LASIE	Information Bulletin. Library Automated Systems Information Exchange (journ.) (SAUS)
LASIE	Library Automated Systems Information Exchange [*Australia*] (NITA)
LASIK	Laser Assisted In-Situ Keratomileusis [*Ophthalmology*]
LASIK	Laser In-situ Keratomileusis (SAUS)
LASIL	Land and Sea Interaction Laboratory [*Environmental Science Services Administration*]
LASIM	LASER Aiming Simulation (PDAA)
LASIM	Los Angeles Society of Internal Medicine (BUAC)
LASINT	LASER Intelligence (MCD)
LASJ............	Latin American Society of Japan (SAUO)
LASL............	Los Alamos Scientific Laboratory [*USAEC*]
LASLA..........	Laboratoire d'Analyse Statistique des Langues Anciennes [*Laboratory for the Statistical Analysis of Ancient Languages*] [*University of Liege, Belgium*]
LASLA..........	Laboratory for the Statistical Analysis of Ancient Languages (SAUO)
LASM	Land-Attack Standard Missile
LASM	LASER Semiactive Missile (DNAB)
LASMCO	Liberian American-Swedish Minerals Company (SAUO)
LASMEC......	Local Authorities School Meals Equipment Consortium
Lasmo	Lasmo Ltd. [*Associated Press*] (SAG)
LASMO	London & Scottish Marine Oil [*British*]
L-Asnase	L-Asparaginase [*Also, A, L, L-ase, L-Asp*] [*An enzyme, an antineoplastic*]
LASO	Latin American Solidarity Organization (BUAC)
LASO	Los Angeles Society of Ophthalmology (SAUO)
LASO	Low-Altitude Search Option [*Search mode of the BOMARC guidance system*]
L A social econ trans...	Proceedings of the Conference on Latin America in Social and Economic Transition. Inter-American Short Papers. The University of New Mexico Press. (SAUO)
LA-SOP........	Los Alamos Standard Operating Procedure (SAUO)
LASOR	Laser Airborne Simulated Optical Range Tester (ACAE)
LASOR	LASER Spillover and Reflectivity (MCD)

LASP............	Laboratory for Atmosphere and Space Physics (SAUS)
LASP............	Laboratory for Atmospheric and Space Physics [*University of Colorado*] [*Research center*]
L-Asp............	L-Asparaginase [*Also, A, L, L-ase, L-asnase*] [*An enzyme, an antineoplastic*]
LASP............	Local Attached Support Processor
LASP............	Logistics Analysis Simulation Program (VLIE)
LASP............	Low-Altitude Space Platform (MCD)
LASP............	Low-Altitude Surveillance Platform (MCD)
LASPAC.......	Landing Gear, Avionics Systems Package (MCD)
LASPAU.......	Latin American Scholarship Program of American Universities (EA)
LasPMd.......	Laser Pacific Media Corp. [*Associated Press*] (SAG)
LASPOL.......	Leningrad Association of Soviet Polar Explorers (SAUO)
LASR	Laboratories for Astrophysics and Space Research [*University of Chicago*] [*Research center*]
LASR	Laser Precision Corp. (SAUO)
LASR	Letter Writing with Automatic Send-Receive (IAA)
LASR	Library Access, Search and Retrieval (SAUO)
LA-SR	Los Alamos Status Report (SAUO)
LASR	Low-Altitude Surveillance RADAR
LASR-2	Litton Airborne Search RADAR Mark Two [*Canada*] (PDAA)
LASRA	Leather and Shoe Research Association [*New Zealand*] (BUAC)
LASRAM	Low-Altitude Short-Range Missile
LasrCp	Laser Corp. [*Associated Press*] (SAG)
LASRE	Lightweight Advanced Super-Responsive Engine [*Automotive engineering*]
LASREF.......	Los Alamos Spallation Radiation Effects Facility (SAUO)
Lasrgt	Lasergate Systems, Inc. [*Associated Press*] (SAG)
LASRM	Low-Altitude Short-Range Missile
LASRM	Low Altitude Supersonic Ramjet Missile (ACAE)
LASRM	Low-Altitude Supersonic Research Missile
LasrmTc	LaserMaster Technologies, Inc. [*Associated Press*] (SAG)
Lasrscp	Laserscope, Inc. [*Associated Press*] (SAG)
Lasrtch	Laser Technics, Inc. [*Associated Press*] (SAG)
LASS...........	Labile Aggregation-Stimulating Substance [*Hematology*]
LASS...........	Land Applications Satellite System (ACAE)
LASS...........	Language and Assembly Language [*Computer science*] (DNAB)
LASS...........	Laptop Avionics Support System (SAUS)
LASS...........	Large Aircraft Start System (DWSG)
LASS...........	Large Amplitude Space Simulator (SAUS)
LASS...........	Large Aperture Solenoid Spectrometer [*Stanford Linear Accelerator Center*]
LASS...........	Large Area Screening Systems (MCD)
LASS...........	Large Area Sky Survey
LASS...........	Large Area Smoke Screening (SAUS)
LASS...........	Large Area Space Simulator (ACAE)
LASS...........	LASER-Activated Semiconductor Switch (IAA)
LASS...........	LASER-Activated Silicon Switch (MCD)
LASS...........	LASER Applications System Study [*Military*]
LASS...........	Laser Scanning System (ACAE)
LASS...........	Lateral Acceleration Sensing System (PDAA)
LASS...........	Latin American Sleep Society (SAUO)
LASS...........	Launch Area Support Ship
LASS...........	Leisure Accident Surveillance System (HEAS)
LASS...........	Liaoning Academy of Social Sciences (BUAC)
LASS...........	Library Access and Sixth-Form Studies [*British*] (AIE)
LASS...........	Library Automated Service System (IAA)
LASS...........	Light-Activated Silicon Switch
LASS...........	Lighter-than-Air Submarine Simulator
LASS...........	Line Amplifier and Super Sync Mixer
LASS...........	Linguistic Analysis of Speech Samples (DAVI)
LASS...........	Linked Administrative Statistical Sample [*Social Security Administration*] (GFGA)
LASS...........	Local Area Sensor System [*Military*] (LAIN)
LASS...........	Local Area Signaling Service [*Bell Laboratories*]
LASS...........	Local Area Signaling Services [*Telecommunications*] (ACRL)
LASS...........	Local Area Sounding System (SAUO)
LASS...........	Local Authority Social Services [*British*]
LASS...........	Lockheed Airline System Simulation (PDAA)
LASS...........	Logistic-Automated Support System (SSD)
LASS...........	Logistics Activities Status System (SAUO)
LASS...........	Logistics Analysis Simulation System
LASS...........	Logistics Automated Supply System
LASS...........	Los Angeles Special Services (SAUO)
LASS...........	Low-Altitude Space Surveillance System [*Military*] (MUSM)
LASS...........	Low Altitude Surveillance System (SAUS)
LASS...........	Low-Angle Silicon Sheet [*Photovoltaic energy systems*]
LASS...........	Lunar Applications of a Spent Stage [*Aerospace*] (MCD)
LASSA	Licensed Animal Slaughter and Salvage Association (SAUO)
LASSA	Licensed Animal Slaughterers and Salvage Association [*British*] (BI)
LASSC	Latin American Social Sciences Council [*Argentina*] [*Database producer*] (EA)
LASSC	Los Alamos Space and Science Committee (SAUO)
LASSCO	Los Angeles Steamship Company (SAUO)
LASSI..........	Latin American Secretariat of the Socialist International (BUAC)
LASSI-HS....	Learning and Study Strategies Inventory-High School Version [*Test*] (TMMY)
LASSII	Low-Altitude Satellite Studies of Ionospheric Irregularities
LASSM........	Line Amplifier and Super Sync Mixer (MSA)
LASSO	Landing and Approach System, Spiral-Oriented
LASSO	LASER Search and Secure Observer (CET)
LASSO	LASER Synchronization from Stationary Orbit (IEEE)
LASSO	Latin American Student Studies Organization (SAUO)
LASSO	Library Acquisition Services System Online [*Suggested name for the Library of Cogress computer system*]
LASSO	Light Air-to-Surface Semiautomatic Optical [*French missile*]
LASSO	Light Anti-Surface Semi-automatic Optical missile (SAUS)
LASSO	Light Aviation Special Support Operations
LASSO	Linguistic Association of the Southwest (SAUO)
LASSO	Lunar Applications of a Spent Stage in Orbit [*Aerospace*] (MCD)
LASSOS	Library Automation Systems and Services Options Study [*Advisory committee*] (NITA)
LASSP	Laboratory for Atomic and Solid State Physics [*Cornell University*] [*Research center*] (RCD)
LASSP	Los Alamos Students in Science Program (SAUO)
LA SSR	Latvian Soviet Socialist Republic (SAUO)
LASST.........	Laboratory for Surface Science and Technology [*University of Maine at Orono*] [*Research center*] (RCD)
LASSV	Land and Approach System for Space Vehicles [*NASA*] (KSC)
LAST...........	Labor and Sample Tracking (SAUO)
LAST...........	Lactic Acidosis Support Trust [*British*] (NRGU)
LAST...........	Language and Systems Together [*Programming language*] [*Baytec*] [*Bay City, MI*]
LAST...........	Large Aperture Scanning Telescope (TEL)
LAST...........	Laser Aided Search and Track (ACAE)
LAST...........	Last Satellite Position [*Navy Navigation Satellite System*] (DNAB)
LAST...........	Left Anterior Small Thoracotomy [*Medicine*] (DMAA)
LAST...........	Leukocyte-Antigen Sensitivity Testing [*Medicine*] (MEDA)
LAST...........	Light Applique System Technique (SAUS)
LAST...........	Local Area Storage Transport (SAUO)
LAST...........	Local Area System Transport [*Computer science*] (CIST)
LAST...........	Logic Analysis and Simulation Technique (VLIE)
LAST...........	London Association of Science Teachers (SAUO)
LAST...........	Low-Altitude Supersonic Target (RDA)
LASTCHP....	Last Paging Channel (CGWS)
LASTE.........	Low-Altitude Safety and Targeting Equipment (DWSG)
LASTport......	Local Area Storage Transport [*Computer science*] (VLIE)
LASU	Large Aircraft Sector Understanding (SAUO)
LASU	Local Air Supply Unit [*British military*] (DMA)
LA SUQ.......	Louisiana State University. Quarterly [*A publication*] (DLA)
LASUSSR.....	Library of the Academy of Science of the USSR (SAUO)
LASV..........	Low-Altitude Supersonic Vehicle [*Formerly, SLAM*] [*Air Force*]
LASV..........	Low-Altitude Surface Vehicle (WDAA)
LasVDsc	Las Vegas Discount Golf & Tennis, Inc. [*Associated Press*] (SAG)
LasVE	Las Vegas Entertainment Network [*Associated Press*] (SAG)
LasVEE	Las Vegas Entertainment Network [*Associated Press*] (SAG)
LASVEM......	Lightly Armored Structure Vulnerability Estimation Methodology (MCD)
LasVEnt	Las Vegas Entertainment Network [*Associated Press*] (SAG)
LasVMaj	Las Vegas Major League Sports [*Associated Press*] (SAG)
LASW..........	Lightweight Anti-Submarine Weapons (SAUS)
LASWMMR..	London Association of Scale and Weighing Machine Manufacturers and Repairers [*England*] (BUAC)
LASX..........	Laser Technics [*NASDAQ symbol*] (SAG)
LASX..........	Lasertechnics Inc. [*NASDAQ symbol*] (TTSB)
LAT............	Aviation Legere de l'Armee de Terre [*France*] [*ICAO designator*] (FAAC)
LAT............	Laboratory Assessment Team (SAUO)
LaT.............	Lactate Threshold [*Biochemistry*]
LAT............	Lae [*Papua New Guinea*] [*Seismograph station code, US Geological Survey*] (SEIS)
LAT............	Language Aptitude Test [*Military*] (AFM)
LAT............	Large Angle Tagger (MCD)
LAT............	Large Angle Torque (MCD)
LAT............	LASER Acquisition and Tracking (OA)
LAT............	Latch (NASA)
Lat.............	Latch's English King's Bench Reports [*1625-28*] [*A publication*] (DLA)
LAT............	Latent
Lat.............	Lateral [*Medicine*] (AMHC)
LAT............	Lateral (KSC)
lat.............	Lateral (VRA)
LAT............	Latex Agglutination Test [*Clinical chemistry*]
LAT............	Lathwell Resources Ltd. [*Vancouver Stock Exchange symbol*]
Lat.............	Latin (BEE)
lat.............	Latin [*MARC language code*] [*Library of Congress*] (LCCP)
LAT............	Latin
lat.............	Latissimus [*Dorsi*] (STED)
Lat.............	Latitude (ELAL)
Lat.............	Latitude (WA)
LAT............	Latitude
LAT............	Latitude of Target
LAT............	Latrine (DSUE)
lat.............	Latus [*Broad*] [*Latin*] (EES)
LAT............	Latus [*Wide*] [*Pharmacy*]
Lat.............	Latvia (MILB)
LAT............	Latvia
LAT............	Learning Ability Test [*Military*] (AFM)
LAT............	Learning by Advanced Telecommunications (SAUO)
LAT............	Left Anterior Thigh [*Medicine*]
LAT............	Less Active Tetragonal (PDAA)
LAT............	Level above Threshold
LAT............	Licensing Appeals Tribunal [*Australia*]
LAT............	Lidocaine, Adrenaline and Tetracaine (SAUS)
LAT............	Light Anti-Tank (SAUS)
LAT............	Light Artillery Tractor [*British military*] (DMA)
LAT............	Linear Accelerator Tube
LAT............	Linseed Association Terms [*Shipping*]
LAT............	Local Access Transport (AGLO)
LAT............	Local Apparent Time
LAT............	Local Area Transport [*Telecommunications*]

LAT	Lockheed Air Terminal, Inc. [Subsidiary of Lockheed Aircraft Corp.]
LAT	Locum Appointment for Training (SAUO)
LAT	Logistics Assistance Team (MCD)
LAT	Long-Acting Theophylline [Pharmacology]
LA-T	Los Alamos Thesis (SAUO)
LAT	Los Angeles Times [A publication]
LAT	Lot Acceptance Test (NASA)
LAT	Low-Altitude Tactics (DOMA)
LAT	Low-Angle Track (CAAL)
LAT	Lowest Astronomical Tide (PDAA)
LAT	Lumbermen's Association of Texas (SRA)
Lat	Valsts Biblioteka [State Library of Latvia], Riga, Latvia [Library symbol] [Library of Congress] (LCLS)
LAT-A	Latrunculin-A [A toxin]
LATA	Local Access and Transport Area
LATA	Local Access Transport Area [Telecommunications]
LATA	Local Area and Transport Area (CCCA)
LATA	Local-Area Telephone Authority [Telecommunications]
LATA	London Amenity and Transport Association
LATA	Los Alamos Technical Associates, Inc. (SAUO)
LatACas	Latin American Casinos, Inc. [Associated Press] (SAG)
LatADis	Latin American Discovery Fund [Associated Press] (SAG)
LatADIr	Latin America Dollar Income Fund [Associated Press] (SAG)
LAT ADMOV...	Lateri Admoveatum [Let It Be Applied to the Side] [Pharmacy]
LatAEqt	Latin America Equity Fund [Associated Press] (SAG)
LATAF	Logistics Activation Task Force [Air Force] (MCD)
LATAG	LASER Air-to-Air Gunnery Simulator [Military] (CAAL)
LATAG	Latin American Trade Advisory Group [British Overseas Trade Board] (DS)
LatAInv	Latin American Investment Fund [Associated Press] (SAG)
LATAK	Latvian National Accreditation Bureau
LatAm	Index to Latin American Periodicals (journ.) (SAUS)
Lat Am Antiq..	Latin American Antiquity. Society for American Archaeology. Washington (SAUO)
Lat Am Stud/NISC...	Latin American Studies. National Information Services Corporation. Baltimore (SAUO)
lat & loc	Lateralizing and Localizing [Medicine] (STED)
LATAR	LASER-Augmented Target Acquisition and Recognition System (MCD)
LATAS	LASER-Augmented Target Acquisition System
LAT-B	Latrunculin-B [A toxin]
LATB	Lithium Aluminum Tri-tert-Butoxyhydride [Organic chemistry]
LATBR	Los Angeles Times Book Review [A publication] (BRI)
LATC	Los Angeles Theater Center [California]
LATCC	London Air-Traffic Control Center
LATCC	London Air Traffic Control Centre (SAUO)
Latch	Latch's English King's Bench Reports [1625-28] [A publication] (DLA)
LATCH	Literature Attached to Charts [Nursing program]
LATCH	Lower Anchors and Tethers for Children [Car seat safety term]
LATCRS	London Air Traffic Control Radar Station (SAUO)
LATD	Large Area Transmission Density (MCD)
LATD	Latitude (ADA)
LATDISP	Lateral Dispersion (MCD)
LAT DOL	Lateri Dolente [To the Painful Side] [Pharmacy]
LATE	Late Assessment of Thrombolytic Efficacy [Cardiology study]
LATE	Legal Assistance for the Elderly
LATE	London Association for the Teaching of English [British] (AIE)
La Tech U...	Louisiana Tech University (GAGS)
LaTeko	La Teko Resources Ltd. [Associated Press] (SAG)
LATER	Ladies' After Thoughts on Equal Rights [Acronym is used as name of association] [Defunct] (EA)
LATER	[The] Life and Times of Eddie Roberts [TV program]
Later Rom Emp...	[The] Later Roman Empire [A publication] (OCD)
Latex	Latex Resources [Associated Press]
LATEX	Louisiana-Texas Experiment [Gulf Marine Minerals Management] [Marine science] (OSRA)
LatexRs	Latex Resources [Associated Press] (SAG)
LATF	Legal Aid Task Force
LATF	Lloyd's American Trust Fund (AIA)
LATF	Low Altitude Tactical Formation (ACAE)
LATG	Laboratory Automation Trials Group (SAUO)
LATH	Laos and Thailand Military Assistance
La Th	La Themis [A publication] (DLA)
Lath	Lathrop's Reports [115-145 Massachusetts] [A publication] (DLA)
LATH	Libraries of Affiliated Teaching Hospitals - School of Medicine [Library network]
LATH	Long-Wavelength Above the Horizon (ACAE)
La Them LC...	La Themis (Lower Canada) [A publication] (DLA)
LATHES	LASER Terminal Homing Engagement Simulator (PDAA)
Lathrop	Lathrop's Reports [115-145 Massachusetts] [A publication] (DLA)
Lath Wind L...	Latham on the Law of Window Lights [A publication] (DLA)
LATI	Linee Aeree Transcontinentali Italiane
Latin	American Confederation of Clinical Biochemistry (SAUO)
LatinAGr	Latin America Growth Fund, Inc. [Associated Press] (SAG)
LATINAH	Latin America Human Settlements Information Network (BUAC)
LATIS	Lightweight Airborne Thermal Imaging System (MCD)
LATIS	Loop Activity Tracking Information System [Telecommunications] (TEL)
LATIX	Lord Abbett: Tax Free Inc: Texas Cl.A [Mutual fund ticker symbol] (SG)
Lat Jus	Latrobe's Justice [A publication] (DLA)
LATK	Local Administrative Tool Kit [AT & T] [Software development and integration tools] (NITA)
LATKWEPSCOLPAC...	Light Attack Weapons School, Pacific (DNAB)
LATL	Lateral (MSA)

LATLI	Latin American Tax Law Institute [Uruguay] (EAIO)
LATM	Local Asynchronous Transfer Mode (SAUO)
lat men	Lateral Meniscectomy [Orthopedics] (DAVI)
LATN	Low-Altitude Tactical Navigation
LATNET	Latvian Academic Network (TELE)
LATNS	Los Angeles Times News Service
LATO	List of Applicable Technical Orders [Military] (AFIT)
LATO	Los Alamos Technical Office (SAUO)
LATO	Los Alamos Technology Office (SAUO)
LATOFF	Lowest Astronomical Tide of the Foreseeable Future (PDAA)
LATOM	Lowest Astronomical Tide of the Month (PDAA)
LATOY	Lowest Astronomical Tide of the Year (PDAA)
LATP	League of American Theatres and Producers (EA)
LATP	Left Atrial Transmural Pressure [Medicine] (DMAA)
LATP	Lima Army Tank Plant [Ohio]
LATPT	Left Atrial Transesophageal Pacing Test [Medicine] (DMAA)
LATR	Lateral (DNAB)
Latr	Locator [Compass] (DA)
LATR	Los Alamos Translation (SAUO)
LA TR	Louisiana Term Reports (Martin) [A publication] (DLA)
LATR	Low Altitude Threat Radar (ACAE)
LATREC	LASER-Acoustic Time Reversal Expansion and Compression (MCD)
lat Rin	Lactated Ringer [Solution] (STED)
LATRL	Lateral
LA TR (NS)	Louisiana Term Reports, New Series (Martin) [1823-30] [A publication] (DLA)
LATRS	Logistic Air Terminal Reporting System (ACAE)
LATS	Latin American Thyroid Society (SAUO)
LATS	Latin-America Thyroid Society (BUAC)
LATS	L.A. T Sportswear [NASDAQ symbol] (TTSB)
LATS	LA T Sportswear, Inc. [NASDAQ symbol] (SAG)
LATS	LDEF [Long-Duration Exposure Facility] Assembly and Transportation System [NASA] (NASA)
LATS	Leather and Associated Trades Show [British] (ITD)
LATS	Light Armored Turret System (MCD)
LATS	Light Attack Turbofan Single Aircraft [Aviation]
LATS	Lightweight Antenna Terminal Seeker
LATS	Long-Acting Thyroid Stimulator [Endocrinology]
LATS	Long-Acting Transmural Stimulator [Medicine] (STED)
LATS	Long Duration Exposure Facility Assembly and Transportation System (SAUO)
LATS-P	Long Acting Thyroid Stimulator-Protector [Endocrinology]
LA T Spt	LA T Sportswear, Inc. [Associated Press] (SAG)
LatSSR	Latvian Soviet Socialist Republic
LATT	LASER Atmospheric Transmission Test
LATT	Library Association of Trinidad and Tobago (BUAC)
LATTC	Los Angeles Trade-Technical College (SAUO)
Lattice	Lattice Semiconductor Corp. [Associated Press] (SAG)
Latt Pr C Pr...	Lattey's Privy Council Practice [1869] [A publication] (DLA)
LATTU	Latin American Table Tennis Union (BUAC)
LATu	Lobuloalveolar Tumor [Medicine] (DB)
LATUF	Latin America Trade Union Federation (NATG)
Latv	Latvia (VRA)
Latv	Latvian
LATWING	Light Attack Wing [Navy] (NVT)
LATWPNS	Los Angeles Times Washington Post News Service (SAUO)
LATX	Latex Res Inc. [NASDAQ symbol] (TTSB)
LATX	Latex Resources, Inc. [NASDAQ symbol] (SAG)
LAU	Lamu [Kenya] [Airport symbol] (OAG)
LAU	Lauder [New Zealand] [Geomagnetic observatory code]
LAU	Laumontite [A zeolite]
LAU	Launcher Aircraft Unit
LAU	Launcher Armament Unit [Navy] (DOMA)
LAU	Laundry (MSA)
LAU	Laurentian University Library [UTLAS symbol]
Lau	Laurentius Hispanus [Deceased, 1248] [Authority cited in pre-1607 legal work] (DSA)
LAU	Lebanese American University (SAUO)
LAU	Line Access Unit (NITA)
LAU	Line Adapter Unit [Computer science]
LAU	Linear Accelerometer Unit (PDAA)
LAU	Lineas Aereas Suramericanas Ltd. [Colombia] [ICAO designator] (FAAC)
LAU	Lithuanian Artists' Union (BUAC)
LAU	Local Authority Unit (HEAS)
lau	Louisiana [MARC country of publication code] [Library of Congress] (LCCP)
LAU	Lower Arithmetic Unit (IAA)
LAUA	Lloyd's Aviation Underwriters Association [British] (DBA)
LAUD	Layered Access User Diversification (SAUS)
LAUD	League of Americans of Ukrainian Descent (EA)
Lau de Pin...	Laurentius de Pinu [Deceased, 1397] [Authority cited in pre-1607 legal work] (DSA)
Lauder	Fountainhall's Session Cases [1678-1712] [Scotland] [A publication] (DLA)
LAUK	Library Association of the United Kingdom
Lau Lib	Laurentian Library (SAUO)
LAUM	Linguistic Atlas of the Upper Midwest
LAUN	Launch Media [NASDAQ symbol] (SG)
Laun	Laundry Room (ADWA)
LAUNC	Launceston [Municipal borough in England]
LAUND	Laundry [Classified advertising]
La Univ	Louisiana State University (SAUO)
LAUNS	Local Area Underwater Navigation System (SAUS)
LAUP	LASER-Assisted Uvulopalatoplasty [Medicine] (DMAA)

LAUR .... Laurel Bancorp, Inc. [NASDAQ symbol] (SAG)
Laur .... Laurentian Library [Classical studies] (OCD)
Laur .... Laurentius Hispanus [Deceased, 1248] [Authority cited in pre-1607 legal work] (DSA)
LA-UR .... Los Alamos Unlimited Release (SAUO)
LA-UR .... Los Alamos-XXXX Report (SAUO)
Laur .... Reports of the High Court of Griqualand [1882-1910] [South Africa] [A publication] (DLA)
LAURA .... Low-Altitude Unmanned Reconnaissance Aircraft (DOMA)
Laur de Palat... Laurentius de Pallatis [Flourished, 16th century] [Authority cited in pre-1607 legal work] (DSA)
LaurelBc .... Laurel Bancorp, Inc. [Associated Press] (SAG)
Lauren .... Laurentius Hispanus [Deceased, 1248] [Authority cited in pre-1607 legal work] (DSA)
Laurence ..... Laurence's Reports of the High Court of Griqualand [1882-1910] [South Africa] [A publication] (DLA)
Lauren de Rodul... Laurentius de Rodulphis [Flourished, 15th century] [Authority cited in pre-1607 legal work] (DSA)
Laur HC Ca... Lauren's High Court Cases [South Africa] [A publication] (DLA)
LAURIN........ Libraries and Archives collecting newpaper clippings Unified for their integration into Networks (SAUO)
LaurlCa .... Laurel Capital Group [Associated Press] (SAG)
Laur Prim .... Laurence's Primogeniture [1878] [A publication] (DLA)
LAUS .... Local Area Unemployment Statistics (OICC)
LAUSC .... Linguistic Atlas of the United States and Canada [1930]
LAUSD .... Los Angeles United School District (SAUO)
Lauss Eq..... Laussat's Equity Practice in Pennsylvania [A publication] (DLA)
LAUTRO....... Life Assurance and Unit Trust Regulatory Authority (SAUS)
LAUTRO....... Life Assurance and Unit Trust Regulatory Organisation [British] (SAUS)
LAUW .... London Associaton of University Women (SAUO)
LAV.............. Las Vegas [Diocesan abbreviation] [Nevada] (TOCD)
lav .... Latvian [MARC language code] [Library of Congress] (LCCP)
LAV.............. Launch Axis, Vertical (MCD)
LAV.............. Lavaliere [Lapel microphone] (NTCM)
Lav.............. Lavatory (ADWA)
LAV.............. Lavatory (KSC)
lav .... Lavender [Philately]
LAV.............. Law Association of Victoria [Australia]
LAV.............. Leafhopper A Virus [Medicine] (DMAA)
LAV.............. Legislative Assembly of Victoria [Australia]
LAV.............. Leisure Activity Vehicle
LAV.............. Lifting Ascent Vehicle
LAV.............. Light Armored Vehicle [Army] (RDA)
LAV.............. Light Assault Vehicle (SAUS)
LAV.............. Linea Aeropostal Venezolana [Venezuela] [ICAO designator] (FAAC)
LAV.............. Load Average (SAUS)
LAV.............. Lymphadenopathy-Associated Virus
LAV.............. Lymphocyte-Associated Virus
LAV.............. Varah [L. A.] Ltd. [Toronto Stock Exchange symbol]
LAVA............ Linear Acoustic Vernier Analyzer (CAAL)
LAVA............ Linear Amplifier for Various Applications (IEEE)
LAVA............ Local Authorities Videotex Association (BUAC)
LAVA............ Local Authority Valuers Association [British] (DBA)
LAVA............ Look Ahead Variable Acceleration [Computer science] (MHDB)
LAVA............ Los Alamos Vulnerability Assessment (SAUO)
LAVA............ Low-Frequency Acoustic Vernier Analyzer (NVT)
LAVA............ Low-profile Adaptive Vehicular Antenna (SAUS)
LAVAC......... LASER Atmospheric Visibility and Contamination (PDAA)
LAV/AD........ Light Armored Vehicle / Air Defense [Army] (DWSG)
LAV-AD........ Light Armoured Vehicle-Air Defence (SAUS)
LAV/ADS...... Light Armored Vehicle/Air Defense System [Army]
LAV-AF .... Light Armored Vehicle, Air Force (LAIN)
LAV-AG .... Light Armored Vehicle-Assault Gun [Marine Corps] (DOMA)
LAV-AG .... Light Armoured Vehicle-Assault Gun (SAUS)
LAVALIN ...... Lavalin Transport
LavalTPh ..... Laval Theologique et Philosophique [Quebec] [A publication] (BJA)
LAV-AT .... Light Armored Vehicle - Antitank [Canada]
LAVB........... Light Armored Vehicle Battalion [Marine Corps] (DOMA)
LAVC........... Local Area VAX Cluster (SAUO)
LAVc........... Local Area Vaxcluster (USDC)
LAVC........... Los Angeles Valley College (SAUO)
LAVE........... Association Vocanologique Europeenne [European Volcanological Association] [Paris, France] (EAIO)
LaVeLe........ Landesverbindungslehrerin (SAUO)
LAVEND ...... Lavendula [Lavender] [Pharmacology] (ROG)
LAVEPA....... Local Administration of Vocational Education and Practical Arts (OICC)
LAVERS .... Lake Vessel Reporting System
LAVFWUS.... Ladies Auxiliary to the Veterans of Foreign Wars of the United States (EA)
LAVH .... Laparoscopically-Assisted Vaginal Hysterectomy [Medicine]
LAVH .... Leparoscopically Assisted Vaginal Hysterectomy [Medicine]
LAVI........... Lymphadenopathy-Associated Virus (PDAA)
LAVIP.......... Landsurface-Atmosphere (or Atmospheric)-Vegetation Interaction Programme (SAUO)
LAVLX......... Lord Abbett Mid-Cap Value Cl.A [Mutual fund ticker symbol] (SG)
LAVM.......... LORAN [Long-Range Navigation] Automatic Vehicle Monitoring (PDAA)
LAVM.......... Los Alamos Voice Messaging (SAUO)
LAVM.......... Low-Altitude Vulnerability Model [Aerospace] (MCD)
LAVMS........ Los Alamos Voice Messaging System (SAUO)
LAVO .... Lassen Volcanic National Park
LAVO .... Lavatory [Slang] (DSUE)
Lav Pall....... Lavacrum Palladis [of Callimachus] [Classical studies] (OCD)
LAVV........... Left Atrioventricular Valve [Medicine] (MELL)

LAW............. Ladies Against Women (EA)
LAW............. Land Authority for Wales
LAW............. LASER Absorption Wave (PDAA)
LAW............. Lawrence [Kansas] [Seismograph station code, US Geological Survey] (SEIS)
LAW............. Lawter International, Inc. [NYSE symbol] (SPSG)
LAW............. Lawter Intl [NYSE symbol] (TTSB)
LAW............. Lawton [Oklahoma] [Airport symbol] (OAG)
LAW............. Lawton, OK [Location identifier] [FAA] (FAAL)
LAW............. Lawyer (ADA)
LAW............. Leading Aircraft Woman [RAF] [British]
LAW............. League of American Wheelmen
LAW............. Left Atrial Wall [Medicine] (STED)
LAW............. Left Attack Wing [Women's lacrosse position]
LAW............. Left-Handers Against the World [Defunct] (EA)
LAW............. Legal Action for Women [An association] (BUAC)
LAW............. Legal Advocates for Women (EA)
LAW............. Legal Aid Warranty [Fund providing legal services in case of arrest]
LAW............. Library, Amphibious Warfare (DNAB)
LAW............. Light Antiarmor Weapon [Military] (RDA)
LAW............. Light Antitank Weapon
LAW............. Light Area Weapon
LAW............. Light Assault Weapon
LAW............. Light Attack Weapon
LAW............. Link Airways of Australia [Australia] [ICAO designator] (FAAC)
LAW............. Local Air Warning
LAW............. Local Air Wing (DNAB)
LAW............. Local Authority Workstation (SAUO)
LAW............. Logistics Action Worksheet
LAW............. Low-Acid Waste [Nuclear energy] (NRCH)
LAW............. Low Active Waste [Nuclear energy]
LAW............. Low-Altitude Warning (MCD)
LAW............. Loyalist Association of Workers [Trade union] [Northern Ireland]
LAW............. Lubricant, Arctic, Weapon [Military] (INF)
LAW............. Quaere Legal Resources Ltd. [UTLAS symbol]
LAW............. United States Supreme Court Library, Washington, DC [OCLC symbol] (OCLC)
LAWA.......... Legislative Assembly of Western Australia
Law Advert... Law Advertiser [1823-31] [A publication] (DLA)
Law Alm....... Law Almanac [New York] [A publication] (DLA)
Law Amdt J... Law Amendment Journal [1855-58] [A publication] (DLA)
Law Am Jour... Law Amendment Journal [1855-58] [A publication] (DLA)
Law & Bank... Lawyer and Banker [New Orleans] [A publication] (DLA)
Law & Bank... Lawyers' and Bankers' Quarterly [A publication] (DLA)
Law & Banker... Lawyer and Banker and Central Law Journal [A publication] (DLA)
Law & Bk Bull... Weekly Law and Bank Bulletin [Ohio] [A publication] (DLA)
Law & Eq Rep... Law and Equity Reporter [New York] [A publication] (DLA)
Law & Hist Rev... Law and History Review [A publication] (DLA)
Law & Legisl in the German Dem Rep... Law and Legislation in the German Democratic Republic [A publication] (DLA)
Law & Lib... Law and Liberty [A publication] (DLA)
Law & Mag... Lawyer and Magistrate Magazine [1898-99] [Dublin] [A publication] (DLA)
Law & Magis Mag... Lawyer's and Magistrate's Magazine [A publication] (DLA)
Law & Mag Mag... Lawyer and Magistrate Magazine [1898-99] [Dublin] [A publication] (DLA)
Law & Psychology Rev... Law and Psychology Review [A publication] (DLA)
Law & Soc... Law and Social Change [A publication] (DLA)
Law & Soc Inquiry... Law & Social Inquiry: Journal of the American Bar Foundation (SAUO)
LAWASIA ..... LAWASIA. Journal of the Law Association for Asia and the Western Pacific [A publication] (DLA)
LAWASIA ..... Law Association for Asia and the Western Pacific (BUAC)
LAWASIA HRB... LAWASIA [Law Association for Asia and the Pacific] Human Rights Bulletin [A publication]
LAWASIA LJ... LAWASIA [Law Association for Asia and the Pacific] Law Journal [A publication] (DLA)
LAWB.......... Los Alamos Water Boiler [Nuclear reactor] (NRCH)
LAW BBS ..... Legal Access in Washington Bulletin Board System (SAUO)
Law Bk Rev Dig... Law Book Review Digest and Current Legal Bibliography [A publication] (DLA)
Law Bul & Br... Law Bulletin and Brief [A publication] (DLA)
Law Bul IA... Law Bulletin. State University of Iowa [A publication] (DLA)
Law Bull...... Law Bulletin [Zambia] [A publication] (DLA)
Law Bull...... Weekly Law Bulletin [Ohio] [A publication] (DLA)
LAW/BUSA... League of American Wheelman/Bicycle USA (EA)
LAWC.......... Land Air Warfare Committee [Military]
Law Cas Wm I... Law Cases, William I to Richard I [England] [A publication] (DLA)
Law Ch Bdg Soc... Law on Church Building Societies [A publication] (DLA)
Law Ch P..... Lawes on Charterparties [1813] [A publication] (DLA)
Law Chr....... Law Chronicle [England] [A publication] (DLA)
Law Chr....... Law Chronicle [South Africa] [A publication] (ILCA)
Law Chr & Auct Rec... Law Chronicle and Auction Record [A publication] (DLA)
Law Chr & Jour Jur... Law Chronicle and Journal of Jurisprudence [A publication] (DLA)
Law Ch Ward... Law on Church Wardens [A publication] (DLA)
Law Cl........ Law Clerk (DLA)
Law Cl Rec... Law Clerk Record [1910-11] [A publication] (DLA)
Law Com ..... Law Commission (DLA)
Law Com ..... Law Commission Report [A publication] (DLA)
Law Committee News... Lawyers' Committee News [A publication] (DLA)
Law Con ...... Lawson on Contracts [A publication] (DLA)
Law cont prob... Law and Contemporary Problems. School of Law. Duke University. Durham (SAUO)

Law Dept Bull... Law Department Bulletin, Union Pacific Railroad Co. [*A publication*] (DLA)

LAWDS........ LORAN-Aided Weapons Delivery System

LAWEB........ Lake Warning [*or Weather*] Bulletin [*National Weather Service*] [*A publication*]

Law Ecc Law... Law's Ecclesiastical Law [*2nd ed.*] [*1844*] [*A publication*] (DLA)

Law Ed .... Lawyer's Edition, United States Supreme Court Reports [*A publication*] (DLA)

Law Ed 2d ... United States Supreme Court Reports, Lawyers' Edition, Second Series [*A publication*] (DLA)

Law Ed Adv Op... United States Supreme Court Reports, Lawyers' Edition, Advance Opinions [*A publication*] (DLA)

Lawes Ch... Lawes on Charterparties [*1813*] [*A publication*] (DLA)

Lawes Pl .... Lawes on Pleading [*A publication*] (DLA)

Law Ex J...... Law Examination Journal [*A publication*] (DLA)

Law Ex Rep... Law Examination Reporter [*A publication*] (DLA)

Law Fr Dict... Law French Dictionary [*A publication*] (DLA)

LAWG ...... Latin American Working Group [*Canada*] (CROSS)

Law Gaz ...... Law Gazette [*A publication*] (DLA)

Law Guild M... Lawyers Guild Monthly [*A publication*] (DLA)

Law in Cont... Law in Context [*A publication*]

Law Int .... Law Intelligencer [*United States*] [*A publication*] (DLA)

Law J.......... Law Journal Reports [*A publication*] (DLA)

Law J Ch .... Law Journal, New Series, Chancery [*A publication*] (DLA)

Law J Exch... Law Journal, New Series, Exchequer [*A publication*] (DLA)

Law Jour ..... Law Journal Reports [*A publication*] (DLA)

Law Jour (M & W)... Morgan and Williams' Law Journal [*London*] [*A publication*] (DLA)

Law JPD ...... Law Journal, Probate Division [*A publication*] (DLA)

Law JPD & A... Law Journal Reports, New Series, Probate, Divorce, and Admiralty [*1875-1946*] [*A publication*] (DLA)

Law JQB ...... Law Journal, New Series, English Queen's Bench [*A publication*] (DLA)

Law Jr QB ... Law Journal, New Series, English Queen's Bench [*A publication*] (DLA)

Law Jur .... Law's Jurisdiction of the Federal Courts [*A publication*] (DLA)

Law Lat Dic... Law Latin Dictionary [*A publication*] (DLA)

Law Lib N.... Law Library News [*A publication*] (DLA)

Law Lib NS... Law Library, New Series [*Philadelphia, PA*] [*A publication*] (DLA)

Law LJ .... Lawrence Law Journal [*A publication*] (DLA)

LAW M .... Law Magazine and Review [*A publication*] (ROG)

LawM.......... Lawrence Microfilming Service, Fuquay-Varina, NC [*Library symbol*] [*Library of Congress*] (LCLS)

LAWM.......... Light All-Weather Missile (MCD)

Law Mag ..... Law Magazine [*A publication*] (DLA)

Law Mag & Law Rev... Law Magazine and Law Review [*A publication*] (DLA)

Law Mag & R... Law Magazine and Review [*A publication*] (DLA)

Law Mag & Rev... Law Magazine and Review [*A publication*] (DLA)

Law Mo .... Western Law Monthly (Reprint) [*Ohio*] [*A publication*] (DLA)

Law N .... Law News [*A publication*] (DLA)

LAWN .... Local Area Wireless Network [*O'Neill Communications, Inc.*] [*Computer science*] (PCM)

Law of Trusts Tiff & Bul... Tiffany and Bullard on Trusts and Trustees [*A publication*] (DLA)

Law Pat....... Law's United States Patent Cases [*A publication*] (DLA)

Law Pat Dig... Law's Digest of United States Patent Cases [*A publication*] (DLA)

Law Pl .... Lawes' Pleading in Assumpsit [*1810*] [*A publication*] (DLA)

Law Pl .... Lawes' Pleading in Civil Actions [*1806*] [*A publication*] (DLA)

Law Pr........ Law's Practice in United States Courts [*A publication*] (DLA)

Law Q Rev... Law Quarterly Review [*A publication*] (BRI)

Lawr .... Lawrence High Court Reports [*Griqualand*] [*A publication*] (DLA)

LAWRC .... Limited Air Weather Reporting Certificate (IAA)

Law Rec ...... Ceylon Law Recorder [*A publication*] (DLA)

Law Rec ...... Ceylon Law Recorder (journ.) (SAUS)

Law Rec ...... Irish Law Recorder [*1827-38*] [*A publication*] (ILCA)

Law Rec ...... Law Recorder [*1827-31*] [*Ireland*] [*A publication*] (DLA)

Law Rec (NS)... Law Recorder, New Series [*Ireland*] [*A publication*] (DLA)

Law Rec (OS)... Law Recorder, First Series [*Ireland*] [*A publication*] (DLA)

Law Ref Com... Law Reform Committee (DLA)

Law Ref Cttee... Law Reform Committee (DLA)

Law Reg ...... American Law Register [*Philadelphia*] [*A publication*] (DLA)

Law Reg ...... Law Register, Chicago [*A publication*] (DLA)

Law Reg Cas... Lawson's Registration Cases [*England*] [*A publication*] (DLA)

LAWREMS ... Land and Water Resources and Economic Models System (SAUO)

Lawrence....... Lawrence's Reports [*20 Ohio*] [*A publication*] (DLA)

Lawrence Comp Dec... Lawrence's First Comptroller's Decisions [*United States*] [*A publication*] (DLA)

Lawrence Compt Dec... Lawrence's First Comptroller's Decisions [*United States*] [*A publication*] (DLA)

Law Rep...... Law Reporter [*England*] [*A publication*] (DLA)

Law Rep...... Law Reporter (Ramsey and Morin) [*Canada*] [*A publication*] (DLA)

Law Rep...... Law Reports [*England*] [*A publication*] (DLA)

Law Rep...... Louisiana Reports [*A publication*] (DLA)

Law Rep...... New Zealand Law Reports [*A publication*] (DLA)

Law Rep...... Ohio Law Reporter [*A publication*] (DLA)

Law Rep A & E... Law Reports, Admiralty and Ecclesiastical Cases [*1865-75*] [*A publication*] (DLA)

Law Rep App Cas... Law Reports, Appeal Cases [*England*] [*A publication*] (DLA)

Law Rep CC... Law Reports, Crown Cases [*A publication*] (DLA)

Law Rep Ch... Law Reports, Chancery Appeal Cases [*England*] [*A publication*] (DLA)

Law Rep Ch App... Law Reports, Chancery Appeal Cases [*England*] [*A publication*] (DLA)

Law Rep Ch D... Law Reports, Chancery Division [*A publication*] (DLA)

Law Rep CP... Law Reports, Common Pleas [*England*] [*A publication*] (DLA)

Law Rep CPD... Law Reports, Common Pleas Division [*England*] [*A publication*] (DLA)

Law Rep Dig... Law Reports Digest [*A publication*] (DLA)

Law Rep Eq... Law Reports, Equity Cases [*A publication*] (DLA)

Law Rep Ex... Law Reports, Exchequer [*A publication*] (DLA)

Law Rep Ex D... Law Reports, Exchequer Division [*England*] [*A publication*] (DLA)

Law Rep HL... Law Reports, House of Lords, English and Irish Appeal Cases [*A publication*] (DLA)

Law Rep HL Sc... Law Reports, Scotch and Divorce Appeal Cases, House of Lords [*A publication*] (DLA)

Law Rep Ind App... Law Reports, Indian Appeals [*A publication*] (DLA)

Law Rep Ir... Law Reports, Irish [*A publication*] (DLA)

Law Rep Misc D... Law Reports, Miscellaneous Division [*A publication*] (DLA)

Law Rep NS... Law Reports, New Series [*New York*] [*A publication*] (DLA)

Law Repos... Carolina Law Repository [*North Carolina*] [*A publication*] (DLA)

Law Rep P... Law Reports, Probate [*A publication*] (DLA)

Law Rep P & D... Law Reports, Probate and Divorce Cases [*A publication*] (DLA)

Law Rep PC... Law Reports, Privy Council, Appeal Cases [*England*] [*A publication*] (DLA)

Law Rep QB... Law Reports, Queen's Bench [*A publication*] (DLA)

Law Rep QBD... Law Reports, Queen's Bench Division [*A publication*] (DLA)

Law Repr...... Law Reporter (Ramsey and Morin) [*Canada*] [*A publication*] (DLA)

Law Rep (Tor)... Law Reporter (Toronto) [*A publication*] (DLA)

Law Rev & Qu J... Law Review and Quarterly Journal [*London*] [*A publication*] (DLA)

Law Rev J... Law Review Journal [*A publication*] (DLA)

Law Rev Qu... Law Review Quarterly [*Albany, NY*] [*A publication*] (DLA)

Law Rev U Det... Law Review. University of Detroit [*A publication*] (DLA)

LawrG......... Lawrence Insurance Group, Inc. [*Associated Press*] (SAG)

LAWRS........ Limited Aviation Weather Reporting Station [*FAA*] (TAG)

LawrSB........ Lawrence Savings Bank [*Associated Press*] (SAG)

Lawr Wh...... Lawrence's Edition of Wheaton on International Law [*A publication*] (DLA)

LAWS.......... Land and Water Systems [*Michigan*]

LAWS.......... Laser Atmospheric Wind Sound (SAUS)

LAWS.......... LASER Atmospheric Wind Sounder [*NASA*]

LAWS.......... Laser Weapon Simulator (ACAE)

LAWS.......... Lawson Products [*NASDAQ symbol*] (SAG)

LAWS.......... Lawson Products, Inc. (SAUO)

LAWS.......... Lawyers Alliance for World Security (EA)

LAWS.......... Leadership and World Society [*Defunct*]

LAWS.......... Lidar Atmospheric Wind Sounder (SAUS)

LAWS.......... Light Antitank Weapon System (LAIN)

LAWS.......... Low-Altitude Warning System (NVT)

Law School Rec... Law School Record [*Chicago*] [*A publication*] (DLA)

Law School Rev... Law School Review. Toronto University [*A publication*] (DLA)

Laws Cont ... Lawson on Contracts [*A publication*] (DLA)

Law Ser MO Bull... University of Missouri. Bulletin. Law Series [*A publication*] (DLA)

Lawsn.......... Lawson Products, Inc. [*Associated Press*] (SAG)

LAWSO .... Lockheed Antisubmarine Warfare Systems Organization

Law Soc ACT NL... Law Society of the Australian Capital Territory. Newsletter [*A publication*]

Law Soc G... Law Society. Gazette [*A publication*]

Law Soc J... Law Society Journal (SAUO)

Law Soc Jo... Law Society of Massachusetts. Journal [*A publication*] (DLA)

Law Soc Tas NL... Law Society of Tasmania. Newsletter [*A publication*]

Law Soc'y Scotl... Law Society of Scotland. Journal [*A publication*] (DLA)

Lawson Exp Ev... Lawson on Expert and Opinion Evidence [*A publication*] (DLA)

Lawson Pres Ev... Lawson on Presumptive Evidence [*A publication*] (DLA)

Lawson Rights Rem & Pr... Lawson on Rights, Remedies, and Practice [*A publication*] (DLA)

Lawson Usages & Cust... Lawson on the Law of Usages and Customs [*A publication*] (DLA)

Laws Reg Cas... Lawson's Registration Cases, Irish [*1885-1914*] [*A publication*] (DLA)

Law Stud ..... Law Student [*A publication*] (ILCA)

Law Stud Mag... Law Students' Magazine [*A publication*] (DLA)

Law Stud Mag NS... Law Students' Magazine. New Series [*A publication*] (DLA)

Law Stu H ... Law Students' Helper [*A publication*] (ILCA)

Law Stu Mag... Law Students' Magazine [*A publication*] (DLA)

Laws Wom... Laws of Women [*A publication*] (DLA)

Law T .... Law Times Reports [*A publication*] (DLA)

Law Tchr ...... Law Teacher [*A publication*] (DLA)

LAWTE........ Laboratory Animal Welfare Training Exchange (GVA)

Law Tenn Rep... Tennessee Reports [*A publication*] (DLA)

Lawter .... Lawter International, Inc. [*Associated Press*] (SAG)

Law Times (NS)... Law Times. New Series [*Pennsylvania*] [*A publication*] (DLA)

Law Times (OS)... Law Times, Old Series [*Luzerne, PA*] [*A publication*] (DLA)

Law T NS..... Law Times. New Series [*Pennsylvania*] [*A publication*] (DLA)

Law T NS..... Law Times Reports, New Series [*England*] [*A publication*] (DLA)

Law Tr .... Law Tracts [*A publication*] (DLA)

Law T Rep NS... Law Times Reports, New Series [*England*] [*A publication*] (DLA)

Law T Rep OS... Law Times Reports, Old Series [*England*] [*A publication*] (DLA)

Law US Cts... Law's Practice in United States Courts [*A publication*] (DLA)

LAWV.......... [*The*] Lorain & West Virginia Railway Co. [*AAR code*]

Law V & S... Lawrence's Visitation and Search [*A publication*] (DLA)

Law W .... Law Weekly [*A publication*] (DLA)

Law Wheat... Lawrence's Edition of Wheaton on International Law [*A publication*] (DLA)

Lawy........... Lawyer (DLA)

Lawyer & Banker... Lawyer and Banker and Central Law Journal [*A publication*] (DLA)

Lawyers Co-Op... Lawyers Co-Operative Publishing Co. (DLA)

Lawyers guild rev... Lawyers Guild Review with which is combined International Juridical Association Bulletin. Washington (SAUO)
Lawyers' Rep Ann... Lawyers' Reports, Annotated [A publication] (DLA)
Lawyers' Rep Annotated... Lawyers' Reports, Annotated [A publication] (DLA)
Lawyers' Rev... Lawyers' Review [A publication] (DLA)
Lawy Mag.... Lawyers' Magazine [A publication] (DLA)
Lawy Rep Ann... Lawyers' Reports, Annotated [A publication] (DLA)
Lawy Rev..... Lawyers' Review [A publication] (DLA)
LAX............. Bahia De Los Angeles [Mexico] [Seismograph station code, US Geological Survey] (SEIS)
LAX............. Lacrosse [British] (ROG)
LAX............. Laurel Explorations Ltd. [Vancouver Stock Exchange symbol]
Lax............. Laxative [Medicine] (AMHC)
lax .... Laxative [Pharmacy]
lax .... Laxity (STED)
LAX............. Limited Area automatic Extraction (SAUS)
LAX............. Los Angeles [California] [Airport symbol] (OAG)
LAXRAY....... Large X-Ray Survey Experiment (PDAA)
LAXS......... Large-Angle X-Ray Scattering
LAXS......... Low-Angle X-Ray Scattering (MCD)
LAXSM....... Large Area X-ray Spectroscopy Mission (SAUS)
LAY............. Ladysmith [South Africa] [Airport symbol] (OAG)
LAY............. Lanyu [Republic of China] [Seismograph station code, US Geological Survey] (SEIS)
Lay............. Lay's English Chancery Reports [A publication] (DLA)
LAY............. Look After Yourself Project Centre (BUAC)
LAYB......... Library Association Year Book [A publication] (DGA)
LAYCAN...... Layday Cancelling Date (RIMS)
LAYDET....... Layer Detection (SAA)
LAYGEN....... Layout Generator [Ergonomics]
LAYN .... Layne Christensen Co. [NASDAQ symbol] (SAG)
LAYN .... Layne, Inc. [NASDAQ symbol] (SAG)
Layne.......... Layne Christensen Co. [Associated Press] (SAG)
Layne.......... Layne, Inc. [Associated Press] (SAG)
Layos.......... Layos, Hollywood [Record label]
LAZ .... Balkan-Bulgarian Airlines [ICAO designator] (FAAC)
LAZ .... Bom Jesus Da Lapa [Brazil] [Airport symbol] (OAG)
LAZ .... La Luz Mines Ltd. [Toronto Stock Exchange symbol]
LAZ .... Los Angeles Zoo (SAUO)
LaZ Boy .... La-Z Boy Chair Co. [Associated Press] (SAG)
LazKap......... Lazare Kaplan International, Inc. [Associated Press] (SAG)
LAZR........... Laser Storm [NASDAQ symbol] (TTSB)
LAZR........... Laser Storm, Inc. [NASDAQ symbol] (SAG)
LAZRU......... Laser Storm Unit [NASDAQ symbol] (TTSB)
LAZRW .... Laser Storm Wrrt [NASDAQ symbol] (TTSB)
LB.............. Baccalaureus Literarum [Bachelor of Literature] [Latin]
LB.............. Farbwerke Hoechst AG [Germany] [Research code symbol]
LB.............. Graduate in Letters
LB.............. LaBarge, Inc. [AMEX symbol] (SPSG)
LB.............. Laboratory (MAE)
LB.............. Laboratory Bulletin
LB.............. Labrador [Postal code] [Canada]
LB.............. Lactose Broth [Microbiology]
LB.............. Ladies of Bethany (TOCD)
LB.............. Lady Boss
LB.............. Lag Bolt [Technical drawings]
LB.............. Lamellar Body [Physiology]
LB.............. Land Based
LB.............. Landing Barge
LB.............. Landing Beach [Navy]
L/B.............. Landing Book [Tea trade] (ROG)
LB.............. Lane Bryant, Inc.
LB.............. Langmuir-Blodgitt Technique [Optics] (EECA)
LB.............. Large Bowel [Anatomy]
LB.............. Lasa B Ring [Montana] [Seismograph station code, US Geological Survey] (SEIS)
LB.............. Last Brochure
LB.............. Late Babylonian (BJA)
LB.............. Late Bronze [Age] (BJA)
LB.............. Lateral Bending (STED)
LB.............. Latin Bibliography
LB.............. Launch Boost (MCD)
LB.............. Launch Bunker (MUGU)
LB.............. Launch Bus (NASA)
LB.............. Laurentian Bank of Canada [Toronto Stock Exchange symbol]
LB.............. Lavatory Basin
LB.............. Lebanon [ANSI two-letter standard code] (CNC)
LB.............. Lectori Benevolo [To the Kind (or Gentle) Reader] [Latin]
LB.............. Lecture Bottle [Shipment of gas products] [Union Carbide Corp.]
LB.............. Lederer-Brill [Syndrome] [Medicine] (DB)
LB.............. Left Back [Football] (WDAA)
LB.............. Left Base [Aviation] (FAAC)
LB.............. Left Border [Genetics]
LB.............. Left Breast [Medicine] (DMAA)
LB.............. Left Bundle [Cardiology] (DMAA)
LB.............. Left Buttock [Medicine]
LB.............. Left Button (SAUO)
LB.............. Left Fullback [Soccer]
LB.............. Left on Base [Baseball]
LB.............. Legal Bond [Investment term]
LB.............. Leg Bye [Cricket]
LB.............. Legum Baccalaureus [Bachelor of Laws]
LB.............. Leiomyoblastoma [Medicine]
L/B.............. Length/Beam Ratio (DNAB)
Lb.............. Leptosphaerulinia briosiana [A fungus]

LB............. Letterbook (SAUO)
LB............. Letter Box
LB............. Levobunolol [Also, LBUN] [Biochemistry]
LB............. Liaison Branch [BUPERS]
lb............. Liberia [MARC country of publication code] [Library of Congress] (LCCP)
Lb............. Liberia (MILB)
lb............. Libra [Pound] [Latin] (AAG)
LB............. Library Bookseller (NITA)
LB............. Library Buckram (SAUO)
LB............. Library Bulletin
LB............. Library Bureau (SAUO)
L-B............. Liebermann-Burchard [Reaction] [Medicine] (MEDA)
LB............. Lifeboat (AAG)
LB............. Lifeboat Station [Coast Guard]
LB............. Ligand Binding Domain [Genetics]
LB............. Light Battalion [British military] (DMA)
LB............. Light Bombardment [Air Force]
LB............. Light Bomber [Air Force]
LB............. Light Bracket (AAG)
LB............. Lighted Buoy [USCG] (TAG)
LB............. Limited Base [Air Force] (AFM)
LB............. Limited Benefits [Unemployment insurance] (OICC)
LB............. Limited Partner in Brokers Firm [London Stock Exchange]
LB............. Linebacker [Football]
LB............. Line Block (SAUO)
LB............. Line Buffer [Computer science]
LB............. Line Busy
LB............. Link Babler [Telecommunications] (ECII)
LB............. Linoleum Base [Technical drawings]
LB............. Lipid Body [Biochemistry] (MAE)
LB............. Lithium Bromide (DNAB)
LB............. Litterarum Baccalaureus [Bachelor of Letters or Literature] [Latin]
LB............. Litter Bearer (AABC)
LB............. Live Birth
LB............. Liver Biopsy [Medicine] (STED)
LB............. Living Bank (EA)
LB............. Lloyd Aereo Boliviano [ICAO designator] (AD)
LB............. Load Bank [Computer science] (KSC)
LB............. Local Batch (IAA)
LB............. Local Battery [Radio]
LB............. Local Board
LB............. Logan Brothers Book Co.
LB............. Log Book
LB............. Logical Block
LB............. London Borough [England]
LB............. London Bridge
Lb............. Long Bill (EBF)
LB............. Long Bill [Business term]
LB............. Long Binh [Vietnam]
LB............. Long-Bout
LB............. Loose Body [Medicine]
LB............. Low Back [Disorder] [Medicine]
LB............. Low Band (AAG)
LB............. Low Battery [Modem status information light] [Computer science] (IGQR)
LB............. Low Bay (KSC)
LB............. Low Breakage (STED)
LB............. Lower Bearing
LB............. Lower Bound [Computer science]
LB............. Lower Brace (MCD)
LB............. Lunch Break
LB............. Lung Biopsy [Medicine] (STED)
LB............. Luria Broth [For cultivation of cells]
LB............. Photographic Laboratory Specialist [Navy]
lb............. Pound [Libra] [Unit of weight]
LBA............ Bus Adapter (SAUS)
LBA............ Lahr/Bader Area [Germany]
LBA............ Lambada-Baterista and Ambiace (SAUS)
LBA............ Large Scale Biological-Atmosphere Experiment Amazonia (SAUS)
LBA............ Large-scale Biosphere-Atmosphere Field Experiment in Amazonia (SAUS)
LBA............ LASER Beam Analyzer (IAA)
LBA............ Latin Business Association (NTPA)
LBA............ Leeds/Bradford [England] [Airport symbol] (OAG)
LBA............ Left Basal Artery [Medicine] (DMAA)
LBA............ Left Brachial Artery [Medicine] (MELL)
LBA............ Lifting-Body Airship (PDAA)
LBA............ Ligand-Binding Assay [Analytical biochemistry]
LBA............ Lima Bean Agar [Microbiology]
LBA............ Limas Bulgarian Airlines [ICAO designator] (FAAC)
LBA............ Limit of Basic Aircraft (MCD)
LBA............ Linear Boom Actuator (ACAE)
LBA............ Linear-Bounded Automaton
LBA............ Little Books on Art [A publication]
LBA............ Load-Bearing Axis
LBA............ Local Battery Apparatus
LBA............ Local Bus Adapter [Computer science]
LBA............ Local Bus Adaptor (NITA)
LBA............ Logical Block Address [Computer science]
LBA............ Logical Block Addressing [Computer science] (VLIE)
LBA............ London Boroughs Association [British] (DCTA)
LBA............ London Building Acts (SAUO)
LBA............ Longbow Apache [Helicoptor] [Army] (RDA)
LBA............ Louisiana Bankers Association (SRA)

LBA	Lutheran Benevolent Association (EA)
LBA	Luxembourg Brotherhood of America (EA)
LBAB	Lima Bean Advisory Board [*Superseded by California Dry Bean Advisory Board*] (EA)
LBAD	Lexington-Blue Grass Army Depot [*Kentucky*] (AABC)
LBAF	Line Width, Black-to-White-Ratio, Area, Fixation Point
LBAK	Lightweight Broadband Antenna Kit
L-BAND	390 to 1,550 MHz (SAUS)
LB&A	Legislative Budget and Audit (SAUO)
LB&A	Lever Brothers & Associates Ltd. (SAUO)
LB&AL	Lever Brothers and Associates Limited (SAUO)
lb ap	Apothecaries' Pound (BARN)
Lb Ap	Pound, Apothecaries (SAUS)
LBAT	Late Babylonian Astronomical and Related Texts (BJA)
LBAT	Leukocyte Bactericidal Assay Test [*Medicine*] (MELL)
LBA-TESS	Longbow Apache-Tactical Engagement Simulation System
LBAU	Laboratory Automation System (SAUO)
lb av	Pound Avoirdupois (BARN)
LBB	Lancaster Bible College, Lancaster, PA [*OCLC symbol*] (OCLC)
LBB	Left Breast Biopsy [*Medicine*] (STED)
LBB	Left Bundle-Branch [*Cardiology*] (DAVI)
Lbb	Leishmania braziliensis braziliensis [*Microbiology*]
LBB	Life Blower Bearing
LBB	Linear Ball Bushing
LBB	[*The*] Little Black Book [*Cygnet Technologies, Inc.*] [*Database software*]
LBB	Logic Building Block (SAUS)
LBB	Low Back Bend (STED)
LBB	Low Back Bending (DMAA)
LBB	Low Band Basic (TIMI)
LBB	Lubbock [*Texas*] [*Airport symbol*] (OAG)
LBB	Lubbock, TX [*Location identifier*] [*FAA*] (FAAL)
LBBA	London Bacon Buyers' Association Ltd. [*British*]
LBBB	Left Bundle Branch Block [*Cardiology*]
LBBG	Burgas [*Bulgaria*] [*ICAO location identifier*] (ICLI)
LBBM	Ludlow Bone Bed Member [*England*] [*Geology*]
LBBP	Laboratory of Blood and Blood Products [*Public Health Service*]
LBBSB	Left Bundle Branch System Block [*Cardiology*]
LBB/W	Locks, Bolts & Bars/Windows (WDAA)
LBBX	Left Breast Biopsy Examination [*Medicine*] (AAMN)
LBBY	Lobby
LBC	Albanian Airline Co. [*ICAO designator*] (FAAC)
LBC	Laboratoires Bruneau & Cie [*France*] [*Research code symbol*]
LBC	Laboratorio Chile ADS [*NYSE symbol*] (TTSB)
LBC	Laboratorio Chile SA [*NYSE symbol*] (SAG)
LBC	Land Bank Commission
LBC	Landmark Bancshares Corporation (SAUO)
LBC	Large Bobbin Core (SAUS)
LBC	Large Bore Cannon (MCD)
LBC	LASER Beam Cutting [*Welding*]
LBC	Launcher Battery Charger (ACAE)
LBC	Law Book Company (SAUO)
LBC	Layman's Bible Commentary [*London*] [*A publication*] (BJA)
LBC	Left Book Club [*Founded in the 1930's by publisher Victor Gollancz*] [*Defunct*] [*British*]
LBC	Left Bounded Context [*Computer science*] (MHDB)
LBC	Letter Book Copy (GEAB)
LBC	Levesque, Beaubien & Co. [*Toronto Stock Exchange symbol*]
LBC	Liberian Broadcasting Corporation (SAUO)
LBC	Liberty Baptist College [*Virginia*]
LBC	Liberty Bell Communications, Inc. [*Detroit, MI*] [*Telecommunications*] (TSSD)
LBC	Lidocaine Blood Concentration [*Medicine*] (STED)
LBC	Lilliputian Bottle Club (EA)
LBC	Line Balance Converter
LBC	Little British Car
LBC	Load Bus Contactor [*Aviation*]
LBC	Local Baggage Committee [*IATA*] (DS)
LBC	Local Bus Controller
LBC	Logistical Base Command [*Korea*]
LBC	London Ballet Circle
LBC	London Bankruptcy Court
LBC	London Bradcasting Company (SAUO)
LBC	London Brick Co. (WDAA)
LBC	London Broadcasting Co.
LBC	Loose Bladder Construction [*Ball*] (DICI)
LBC	Lothian and Berwick Cavalry [*British military*] (DMA)
LBC	Lowband Color [*Broadcasting*] (NTCM)
LBC	Lubudi [*Zaire*] [*Seismograph station code, US Geological Survey*] (SEIS)
LBC	Lummer-Brodhun Cube [*Physics*]
LBC	Lymphadenosis Benigna Cutis [*Medicine*] (DMAA)
LBC-A	LASER Beam Cutting - Air
LB CAL	Pound Calorie (WDAA)
LBCC	Long Beach City College [*California*]
LBC/CML	Lymphoid Blast Crisis of Chronic Myeloid Leukemia [*Oncology*]
LBCD	Left Border Cardiac Dullness [*Cardiology*]
LBC-EV	LASER Beam Cutting - Evaporative
LBCF	Laboratory Branch Complement Fixation [*Clinical chemistry*]
Lb CHU	Pound Centigrade Heat Unit (SAUS)
LBCI	Liberty Bancorp, Inc. [*NASDAQ symbol*] (SAG)
LBC-IG	LASER Beam Cutting - Inert Gas
LBCL	Liberty Baptist College (SAUO)
LBCL	Louisville Behavior Check List [*Psychology*]
LBCL	Lymphoblastoid B-Cell Line [*Genetics*]
LBCM	Licentiate of the Bandsmen's College of Music (WDAA)
LBCM	Locator at Back Course Marker (PDAA)
LBCM	London Board of Congregational Ministers (SAUO)
Lb Co	Labour Company (SAUO)
LBCO	Lanthanum-Barium-Copper-Oxide [*Inorganic chemistry*]
LBC-O	LASER Beam Cutting - Oxygen
LBcS	Belle Chasse State School, Belle Chasse, LA [*Library symbol*] [*Library of Congress*] (LCLS)
LBCS	Land-Based Classification Standard (PA)
Lb/cu ft	Pound per Cubic Foot (SAUS)
Lb/cu in	Pound per Cubic Inch (SAUS)
Lb/cu yd	Pound per Cubic Yard (SAUS)
LBCV	Left Brachiocephalic Vein [*Medicine*] (MELL)
LBD	Lamellar Body Density [*Medicine*] (MELL)
LBD	Large Bile Duct [*Medicine*] (DMAA)
LBD	Laser Beam Detector (ADWA)
LBD	Laser Beam Directors (SAUO)
LBD	Left Border of Dullness [*Cardiology*]
LBD	Licensed Beverage Distributors (SRA)
LBD	Lifting Body Development
LBD	Ligand-Binding Domain [*Biology*]
LBD	Light Beam Deflection
LBD	Little Black Devils [*Nickname given to the 90th Battalion of the Winnipeg Rifles during the Northwest Rebellion in 1885*]
LBD	Little Black Dress [*Women's fashions*]
LBD	Logic Block Diagram (IAA)
LBD	Low Band Difference (TIMI)
LBD	Lower Back Disability [*Medicine*]
LBDA	Lexington Bluegrass Depot Activity [*Kentucky*] [*Army*]
LBDI	Liberian Bank for Development and Investment (BUAC)
LBDQ	Leader Behavior Description Questionnaire [*Psychology*]
L/Bdr	Lance-Bombardier [*British military*] (DMA)
LBDS	Laser Beam Diagnostic Scanner (ACAE)
LBDS	Leiden-Berkeley Deep Survey [*Astronomy*]
LBDT	Low Bay Dolly Tug (NASA)
LBE	Lakewood Board of Education, Lakewood, OH [*Inactive*] [*OCLC symbol*] (OCLC)
LBE	Lambada-Baterista Experiment (SAUS)
LBE	Lance-Bubbling-Equilibrium [*Steelmaking*]
LBE	Land-Bearing Equipment [*Military*] (INF)
LBE	Landing Barge, Emergency Repair
LBE	Language Based Editor (VLIE)
LBE	Latrobe [*Pennsylvania*] [*Airport symbol*] (OAG)
LBE	Latrobe, PA [*Location identifier*] [*FAA*] (FAAL)
LBE	Libra Energy, Inc. [*Vancouver Stock Exchange symbol*]
LBE	Load-Bearing Equipment (INF)
LBE	Local Business Entities (TIMI)
LBE	Location-Based Entertainment
LBE	Long Below-Elbow [*Cast*] (STED)
LBE	Long Bill of Exchange [*Business term*] (MHDW)
LBE	Lower Band Edge (VLIE)
LBEA	Lutheran Braille Evangelism Association (EA)
LBeB	Bossier Parish Library, Benton, LA [*Library symbol*] [*Library of Congress*] (LCLS)
LBEB	Laboratory of Brain Evolution and Behavior [*National Institute of Mental Health*]
LBEF	Land-Based Evaluation Facility [*Military*] (CAAL)
LBEFM	Low Background Epifluorescence Microscopy
LBEI	Licentiate of the Institution of Body Engineers [*British*] (DBQ)
LBEN	Low-Byte Enable
Lber	Literaturbericht (BJA)
LBES	Laboratory of Biomedical and Environmental Sciences [*Research center*] (RCD)
LBES	Lifeboat Enthusiasts Society (BUAC)
LBETV	Les Brown's Encyclopedia of Television [*A publication*]
LB Eur	Lehman Brothers, Inc. [*Associated Press*] (SAG)
LBF	Botanical Society of Lund (SAUO)
LBF	Lactobacillus bulgaricus Factor [*Biochemistry*]
LBF	Landing Barge Flak [*British military*] (DMA)
LBF	Latin America Dollar Inc.Fd [*NYSE symbol*] (TTSB)
LBF	Latin America Dollar, Inc. Fund [*NYSE symbol*] (SPSG)
LBF	Les Buteaux [*France*] [*Seismograph station code, US Geological Survey*] (SEIS)
LBF	Limb Blood Flow (AAMN)
LBF	Lithuanian Basketball Federation (BUAC)
LBF	Liver Blood Flow [*Physiology*]
LBF	Load Bit Field [*Computer science*] (IAA)
LBF	London Book Fair [*England*]
LBF	Louis Braille Foundation for Blind Musicians [*Defunct*] (EA)
LBF	Lyme Borreliosis Foundation (EA)
LBF	North Platte [*Nebraska*] [*Airport symbol*] (OAG)
LBF	North Platte, NE [*Location identifier*] [*FAA*] (FAAL)
lbf	Pound-Force (WPI)
LBF	Pounds, Force (MCD)
LBFA	Landau Fan Association (SAUO)
LBFA	Official Martin Landau-Barbara Bain Fan Association (EA)
LBFC	Landmark Financial Corporation (SAUO)
LBFC	Lane Brody Fan Club (EA)
LBFC	Laura Branigan Fan Club (EA)
LBFC	Lauralee Bell Fan Club (EA)
LBFC	Long Beach Finl'. [*NASDAQ symbol*] (SG)
LBFCR	Longbow Fire Control RADAR (DWSG)
lbf-ft	Pound Force Foot (STED)
LBFI	L & B Financial, Inc. [*NASDAQ symbol*] (SAG)
LBF/IN²	Pound-Force per Square Inch (WDAA)

LBFL	L&B Financial [*NASDAQ symbol*] (TTSB)
LBF-S	Pound-Force per Second
LBF S/FT²	Pound-Force Seconds per Square Foot
Lbf s/fty	Pound-Force Seconds per Square Foot (SAUS)
lb-ft	Pound-Feet (STED)
Lb-Ft	Pound-Foot (SAUS)
Lb/ft	Pound per Foot (SAUS)
LB/FT	Pounds per Foot
LB/FT²	Pounds per Square Foot
Lb/ft3	Pound per Cubic Foot (SAUS)
Lb/ft3	Pounds per Cubic Foot (SAUS)
LB/FT³	Pounds per Cubic Foot
LB/(FT H)	Pounds per Foot-Hour
LB/(FT S)	Pounds per Foot-Second
Lb/fty	Pound per Square Foot (SAUS)
Lb/fty	Pounds per Square Foot (SAUS)
LBG	Le Bourget Airport [*France*]
LBG	Left Buccal Ganglion [*Medicine*]
LBG	Load Balancing Group [*Computer science*] (ELAL)
LBG	Local Battle Group (ACAE)
LBG	Locust Bean Gum (OA)
LBG	Low BTU Gas (MCD)
LBG	Lucky Break Gold [*Vancouver Stock Exchange symbol*]
LB/GAL	Pounds per Gallon
LBGC	Columbia Lesbian, Bisexual and Gay Coalition (EA)
LBGO	Gorna Orechovitsa [*Bulgaria*] [*ICAO location identifier*] (ICLI)
LBH	Laker Airways (Bahamas) Ltd. [*ICAO designator*] (FAAC)
LBH	LB Ltd. [*FAA designator*] (FAAC)
LBH	Leased Bachelor Housing [*Military*] (DNAB)
LBH	Length, Breadth, Height
LBH	Local Board of Health [*British*]
LBH	Lyman-Birge-Hopfield [*System*] [*Physics*] (MUGU)
LB/H	Pounds per Hour
LBH	Sydney [*Australia*] [*Airport symbol*] (OAG)
LBHA	Little Big Horn Associates (EA)
LBHASA	London Business Houses Amateur Sports Association (SAUO)
LBHB	Low-Barrier Hydrogen Bond [*Enzymology*]
LBHD	Long Beach Harbor Department (SAUO)
LB Horse	Lothians and Border Horse (SAUO)
Lb/HP	Pound-Force per Horsepower (SAUS)
LB/(HP H)	Pounds per Horsepower-Hour
Lb/hphr	Pound per Horsepower-Hour (SAUS)
LBHS	Long Beach High School (SAUO)
LBHS	Longbow Hellfire Seeker (DWSG)
LBHS	Luther Burbank High School (SAUO)
LBHY	Lothians and Border Horse Yeomanry (SAUO)
LBI	Albi [*France*] [*Airport symbol*] (OAG)
LBI	Land Based Interceptor (ACAE)
LBI	Last Byte In (ECII)
LBI	Leo Baeck Institute (EA)
LBI	Liberte Investors [*Formerly, Lomas & Nettleton Mortgage Investors*] [*NYSE symbol*] (SPSG)
LBI	Libra Industries, Inc. [*Vancouver Stock Exchange symbol*]
LBI	Library Bibliographies and Indexes [*A publication*]
LBI	Library Binding Institute (EA)
LBI	Licensed Beverage Industries [*Later, DISCUS*] (EA)
LBI	Lima Bean (trypsin) Inhibitor [*Biochemistry*]
LBI	Little Barrier Island (SAUS)
LBI	Lloyds & BOLSA [*Bank of London & South America*] International Bank Ltd. [*British*]
LBI	Lloyds Bank International (ADA)
LBI	Long-Baseline Interferometer [*or Interferometry*] (PDAA)
LBI	Lost by Inventory (DNAB)
LBI	Low Back Injury [*Medicine*] (DMAA)
LBI	Low Serum-Bound Iron (MAE)
LBIA	Archives of the Leo Baeck Institute (SAUO)
LBI-ALA	Library Binding Institute-American Library Association (SAUO)
LBIB	Bulletin des Leo Baeck Instituts (SAUS)
LBIB	Bulletin of the Leo Baeck Instituts (SAUO)
LBibel	Im Lande der Bibel [*Berlin-Dahlem*] [*A publication*] (BJA)
LBIC	Licensed Beverage Information Council (EA)
Lb/imp gall	Pound per Imperial Gallon (SAUS)
LBIMS	Laban/Bartenieff Institute of Movement Studies (EA)
LBIN	Pound-Force per Inch (MSA)
Lb-in	Pound-Inch (SAUS)
Lb/in	Pound per Inch (SAUS)
LB/IN²	Pounds per Square Inch
Lb/in3	Pound per Cubic Inch (SAUS)
Lb/in3	Pounds per Cubic Inch (SAUS)
LB/IN³	Pounds per Cubic Inch
Lb-in/s	Pound-Inch per Second (SAUS)
Lb/iny	Pound per Square Inch (SAUS)
LBIPP	Licentiate of the British Institute of Professional Photography (DBQ)
LBIR	Laser Beam Image Recorder (ACAE)
LBIR	LASER Beam Image Reproducer
LBIR	Low Background Infrared Radiometry
LBIST	Licentiate of the British Institute of Surgical Technologists (DBQ)
LBIY	Yearbook of the Leo Baeck Institute (SAUO)
LBJ	Lady Bird Johnson [*Mrs. Lyndon Baines Johnson*]
LBJ	Little Brown Job [*Unidentified bird, to a bird watcher*]
LBJ	Load Bank and Jump [*Computer science*]
LBJ	Long Binh Jail [*Vietnam*]
LBJ-S	Lower Ball Joint [*Automotive engineering*]
LBJ	Lyndon Baines Johnson [*US president, 1908-1973*]
LBJL	Lyndon B. Johnson Library

LBJSC	Lyndon B. Johnson Space Center (MSC)
LBJSHP	Lyndon B. Johnson State Historic Park (SAUO)
LBJTMC	Lyndon B. Johnson Tropical Medical Center (SAUO)
LBK	Landing Barge, Kitchen
LBK	Left Bank
LBL	Ernest Orlando Lawrence Berkeley National Laboratory
lbl	Label (ELAL)
LBL	Label (MSA)
LBL	Labeled Lymphoblast [*Oncology*] (DMAA)
LBL	Laminar Boundary Layer
LBL	Lawrence Berkeley Laboratories (or Laboratory) (SAUO)
LBL	Lawrence Berkeley Laboratory [*Berkeley, CA*] [*Department of Energy*] (GRD)
LBL	Left Buttock Line (MCD)
LBL	Liberal [*Kansas*] [*Airport symbol*] (OAG)
LBL	Liberal, KS [*Location identifier*] [*FAA*] (FAAL)
LBL	Limited Broadcasting License [*Australia*]
LBL	Line by Line (ARMP)
LBL	Lloyds Bank Limited (SAUO)
LBL	Low Brightness Laser (ACAE)
LBL	Lymphoblastic Lymphoma [*Oncology*]
LBLG	Large Blast Load Generator (PDAA)
LBLS	Laminar Boundary-Layer Separation
LBLTY	Liability
LBM	Deluxe Paint image format (SAUS)
LBM	LASER Beam Machine (IAA)
LBM	Lean Body Mass [*Exercise*]
LBM	Left Buffer Memory (GFGA)
LBM	Liberty-Bell Mines, Inc. [*Vancouver Stock Exchange symbol*]
LBM	Liquid Boost Module (MCD)
LBM	Little Brown Mushroom (LDT)
LBM	Little Butte [*Montana*] [*Seismograph station code, US Geological Survey*] [*Closed*] (SEIS)
LBM	Load Buffer Memory [*Computer science*]
LBM	Local Battle Manager (ACAE)
LBM	Local Board Memoranda
LBM	Locator Back Marker [*Aviation*] (DA)
LBM	Logic Bus Monitor [*Computer science*] (CET)
LBM	Loose Bowel Movement [*Medicine*] (CPH)
LBM	Lowband Monochrome [*Broadcasting*] (NTCM)
LBM	Lunar Breaking Module [*NASA*] (IAA)
LBM	Lung Basement Membrane [*Medicine*] (DMAA)
LBM	Morehouse Parish Library, Bastrop, LA [*Library symbol*] [*Library of Congress*] (LCLS)
LbM	Pound Mass (SAUS)
LBM	Pounds, Mass (MCD)
LB/M	Pounds per Minute (AAG)
LBMA	London Bullion Market Association
LBMC	Liberty Bell Matchcover Club (EA)
LBMCTX	Local Battery Magneto Call Telephone Exchange (IAA)
LBMI	Lease Base Machine Inventory (MHDB)
LB/MIN	Pounds per Minute
LBMM	Lifetime Book of Money Management [*A publication*]
Lb Mol	Pound Molecule (SAUS)
LBMP	Land-Based Marine Pollution
LBMS	Learmonth & Burchett Management Systems [*British*] (NITA)
LBMS	London Boroughs Management Services (SAUO)
LBM/S-IN2	Pounds of Mass per Second per Square Inch
Lbm/s-iny	Pounds of Mass per Second per Square Inch (SAUS)
LBMSU	London Boroughs Management Service Unit (SAUO)
LBMSY	Learmonth & Burchett Management Systems, Inc. [*NASDAQ symbol*] (SAG)
LBMSY	Learmouth & Burchett Mgt ADS [*NASDAQ symbol*] (TTSB)
LbN	Labial Nerve [*Anatomy*]
LBN	Lawrence Berkeley Laboratory (SAUO)
LBN	Lebanon [*ANSI three-letter standard code*] (CNC)
LBN	Letter Box Number [*Viet Cong equivalent to the US APO*]
LBN	Lewis x Brown Norway [*Rat strain*]
LBN	Liberty Broadcasting Network [*Cable-television system*]
LBN	Line Balancing Network [*Telecommunications*] (TEL)
LBN	Logical Bibliographic Network [*Library science*] (TELE)
LBN	Logical Block Numer [*Computer science*] (CIST)
LBN	Logic Bucket Number (NITA)
LBNA	Liberty Bancorp, Inc., Oklahoma [*NASDAQ symbol*] (SAG)
LBNA	Liberty Bancorp(OK) [*NASDAQ symbol*] (TTSB)
LBNDX	Lord Abbett: Bond Debenture Cl.A [*Mutual fund ticker symbol*] (SG)
LBNL	Lawrence Berkeley National Laboratory (HGEN)
LBNP	Lower Body Negative Pressure [*Boots*] [*Space flight equipment*] [*NASA*]
LBNPD	Lower Body Negative Pressure Device [*Space flight equipment*] [*NASA*]
LBNS	Long Beach Naval Shipyard (DNAB)
LBNSY	Long Beach Naval Shipyard (MUGU)
LBO	Landing Barge Oiler [*British military*] (DMA)
LBO	Lanthanum Boron Oxide [*Inorganic chemistry*]
LBO	Large Bowel Obstruction [*Medicine*]
LBO	Lebanon, MO [*Location identifier*] [*FAA*] (FAAL)
LBO	Leveraged Buy-Out
LBO	Liberal Bosnian Organization (BUAC)
LBO	Light Beam Oscillograph
LBO	Line Building Out
LBO	Line Build Out [*Telecommunications*] (MLOA)
LBO	Line Build-Out [*Computer science*] (VLIE)
LBO	Lithium Boron Oxide [*Inorganic chemistry*]
LBocNS	Northwest State School, Bier City (SAUS)

LBocNS........ Northwest State School, Bossier City, LA [*Library symbol*] [*Library of Congress*] (LCLS)
LBOE........... Local Board of Education (SAUO)
LBOM.......... Local Area Network-Based Object Management (SAUO)
L Book Adviser... Law Book Adviser [*A publication*] (DLA)
Lboro.......... Email address for Loughborough University (SAUO)
LBOT.......... Logical Beginning of Tape (VLIE)
LBP............ Land-Based Plant (NRCH)
LBP............ Laser Beam Printer (NITA)
LBP............ Length Between Perpendiculars [*Technical drawings*]
LBP............ Leucine-Binding Protein [*Biochemistry*]
LBP............ Light Beam Pickup
LBP............ Line Binder Post (IAA)
LBP............ Lipopolysaccharide-Binding Protein [*Biochemistry*]
LBP............ Local Batch Processing [*Computer science*] (VLIE)
LBP............ London Borough Polytechnic (SAUO)
LBP............ Low-Back Pain [*Medicine*]
LBP............ Low Band Processor (TIMI)
LBP............ Low Blood Pressure [*Medicine*]
LBP............ Lumbar Back Pain [*Medicine*] (DMAA)
LBP............ Personnel Landing Boat [*Navy symbol*] [*Obsolete*]
LBPA.......... Lysobisphosphatidic Acid [*Biochemistry*]
LBPC......... London Building Productivity Committee (SAUO)
Lb p cu ft.... Pounds per Cubic Foot (SAUS)
LBPD......... Plovdiv [*Bulgaria*] [*ICAO location identifier*] (ICLI)
LBPF.......... Long Bone or Pelvic Fracture [*Medicine*] (DMAA)
Lb p gal...... Pounds per Gallon (SAUS)
LBPH .... Libraries for the Blind and Physically Handicapped [*Automated system*]
LBPH .... Library for the Blind and Physically Handicapped (SAUO)
L-BPH .... Louisiana State Library, Department for the Blind and Physically Handicapped, Baton Rouge, LA [*Library symbol*] [*Library of Congress*] (LCLS)
LBPI.......... LASER Beam Position Indicator
LBPIS......... LASER Beam Position Indicator System
LBPL.......... Long Beach Public Library (SAUO)
LBPO .... Lifting Body Program Office [*NASA*]
LBPQ .... Low Back Pain Questionnaire [*Medicine*] (DMAA)
LBPR .... Lumped Burnable Poison Rod [*Assembly*] [*Nuclear energy*] (NRCH)
LBPS......... Lead-Based Paint Survey [*Environmental science*] (COE)
Lb p yd...... Pounds per Yard (SAUS)
LBQ .... Lambarene [*Gabon*] [*Airport symbol*] (OAG)
LBQS .... Large Bright Quasar Survey [*Astronomy*]
LBr............ East Baton Rouge Parish Public Library, Baton Rouge, LA [*Library symbol*] [*Library of Congress*] (LCLS)
Lbr............. Labor
LBR............ Laborer
LBR............ Labor Room (MELL)
LBR............ Labrea [*Brazil*] [*Airport symbol*] (AD)
LBR............ Large Business Remote [*Computer science*] (CIST)
LBR............ LASER Beam Recorder [*or Recording*]
LBR............ LASER Beam Rider (RDA)
LBR............ L-Band Radiometer (MCD)
LBR............ Liberia [*ANSI three-letter standard code*] (CNC)
LBR............ Librarian (WDAA)
LBR............ Line of Bomb Release (NATG)
LBR............ Little Bear Resources [*Vancouver Stock Exchange symbol*]
LBR............ Little Books on Religion [*A publication*]
LBR............ Living Benefits Rider [*Insurance*] (WYGK)
LBR............ Local Base Rescue [*Air Force*] (AFM)
LBR............ Low Birth Rate
LBR............ Low BIT [*Binary Digit*] Rate [*Computer science*] (MCD)
LBR............ Lower Burma Rulings [*India*] [*A publication*] (DLA)
LBR............ Low Running Rate (KSC)
LBR............ [*The*] Lowville & Beaver River Railroad Co. [*AAR code*]
LBR............ Lumber (KSC)
LBRA.......... Laboratory of Biochemical Risk Analysis (GNE)
LBrAg.......... Louisiana State Department of Agriculture, Research Library, Baton Rouge, LA [*Library symbol*] [*Library of Congress*] (LCLS)
LBRC .... Loft Bomb Release Computer (MCD)
LBrC.......... Louisiana Commerce Department, Research Library, Baton Rouge, LA [*Library symbol*] [*Library of Congress*] (LCLS)
LBrCJIS....... Commission on Law Enforcement and Criminal Justice, Criminal Justice InformationSystem, Baton Rouge, LA [*Library symbol*] [*Library of Congress*] (LCLS)
LBrcTI......... Louisiana Training Institute, Bridge City Library, Bridge City, LA [*Library symbol*] [*Library of Congress*] (LCLS)
LBrE.......... Ethyl Corp., Chemical Development Library, Baton Rouge, LA [*Library symbol*] [*Library of Congress*] (LCLS)
LBrEd.......... Louisiana Education Department, Baton Rouge, LA [*Library symbol*] [*Library of Congress*] (LCLS)
LBRF.......... Louse-Borne Relapsing Fever [*Medicine*] (AAMN)
LBRF.......... Lower Branchial Filament
LBrG .... Gulf South Research Institute, Baton Rouge, LA [*Library symbol*] [*Library of Congress*] (LCLS)
LBRG .... LASER Beam Rider Guidance (MCD)
LBRG .... Laser Beam-Riding Guidance (SAUS)
LBrGS .... Church of Jesus Christ of Latter-Day Saints, Genealogical Society Library, Baton Rouge
LBrGS .... Church of Jesus Christ of Latter-Day Saints, Genealogical Society Library, BatonRouge Branch, Baton Rouge, LA [*Library symbol*] [*Library of Congress*] (LCLS)
LBrHR......... Louisiana Department of Health and Human Resources, Policy Planning and Evaluation Office, Baton Rouge, LA [*Library symbol*] [*Library of Congress*] (LCLS)

LBrHR-Y ...... Louisiana Department of Health and Human Resources, Office of Youth Services, Baton Rouge, LA [*Library symbol*] [*Library of Congress*] (LCLS)
LBRI.......... Lake Biwa Research Institute (BUAC)
LBrIPA .... Louisiana Information Processing Authority, Baton Rouge, LA [*Library symbol*] [*Library of Congress*] (LCLS)
LBrJ.......... Louisiana Justice Department, Huey P. Long Library, Baton Rouge, LA [*Library symbol*] [*Library of Congress*] (LCLS)
LBrJS.......... Jimmy Swaggart Bible College Library, Baton Rouge, LA [*Library symbol*] [*Library of Congress*] (LCLS)
LBrL.......... Labor Department, Research Library, Baton Rouge, LA [*Library symbol*] [*Library of Congress*] (LCLS)
LBrLAS .... Louisiana Arts and Science Center, Baton Rouge, LA [*Library symbol*] [*Library of Congress*] (LCLS)
LBrLC.......... Louisiana Legislative Council, Reference Division, Baton Rouge, LA [*Library symbol*] [*Library of Congress*] (LCLS)
LBrLH .... Earl K. Long Hospital, Medical Library, Baton Rouge, LA [*Library symbol*] [*Library of Congress*] (LCLS)
LBRM......... Large Basin Runoff Model [*Marine science*] (OSRA)
LBRM......... Laser Beam Rider Missile (ACAE)
LBrNR......... Natural Resources Department, Research and Development Library, Baton Rouge, LA [*Library symbol*] [*Library of Congress*] (LCLS)
LBrNR-F....... Natural Resources Department, Office of Forestry, Baton Rouge, LA [*Library symbol*] [*Library of Congress*] (LCLS)
LBrPS......... Public Service Commission, Baton Rouge, LA [*Library symbol*] [*Library of Congress*] (LCLS)
LBrR.......... Louisiana Revenue Department, Research Department, Baton Rouge, LA [*Library symbol*] [*Library of Congress*] (LCLS)
LBRS......... Low Background Reference System
LBRS......... Rousse [*Bulgaria*] [*ICAO location identifier*] (ICLI)
LBrSP......... State Planning Office, Library, Baton Rouge, LA [*Library symbol*] [*Library of Congress*] (LCLS)
Lbr Svc....... Labor Service (SAUO)
LBRT......... Liberate Technologies [*NASDAQ symbol*] (SG)
LBRT......... Liberty
LBrTD-Av ..... Department of Transportation and Development, Aviation (SAUS)
LBrTD-Av ..... Department of Transportation and Development, Aviation Office, Baton Rouge, LA [*Library symbol*] [*Library of Congress*] (LCLS)
LBrTD-H....... Department of Transportation and Development, Office of Highways, Research and Development Library, Baton Rouge, LA [*Library symbol*] [*Library of Congress*] (LCLS)
LBrTD-Pw .... Department of Transportation and Development, Office of Public Works, Baton Rouge, LA [*Library symbol*] [*Library of Congress*] (LCLS)
LBRTY .... Liberty
LBrUC .... Department of Urban and Community Affairs, Office of Planning and Technical Assistance, Baton Rouge, LA [*Library symbol*] [*Library of Congress*] (LCLS)
LBRV .... Lifting Body Research Vehicle
LBRV .... Low BIT [*Binary Digit*] Rate Voice [*Telecommunications*]
LBrWF-S ...... Department of Wildlife and Fisheries, Louisiana Stream Control Commission, BatonRouge, LA [*Library symbol*] [*Library of Congress*] (LCLS)
LBRY .... Library (MSA)
LBS............ Labasa [*Fiji*] [*Airport symbol*] (OAG)
LBS............ Lactobacillus Selector [*Microbiology*] (DAVI)
LBS............ Laminar Boundary-Layer Separation
LBS............ Land-Based Sources [*of Marine Pollution*] [*Marine science*] (OSRA)
LBS............ Land-Based Sources of Marine Pollution (USDC)
LBS............ Landing Boat, Support [*Navy symbol*]
LBS............ Large Blast Simulator
LBS............ Large Bulb Ship
LBS............ LASER Beam Surgery
LBS............ LASER Bombing System
LBS............ Launch Base Support [*Air Force*]
LBS............ Launch Blast Simulator (MUGU)
LBS............ Lead Belly Society (EA)
LBS............ Lecithin Bile State [*Medicine*]
LBS............ Lectori Benevolo Salutem [*To the Kind (or Gentle) Reader, Greeting*] [*Latin*]
LBS............ Liberation Broadcasting Station (CINC)
LBS............ Life Boat Station (SAUO)
LBS............ Lifeboat Stations (SAUO)
LBS............ Light Bomber Strike [*Air Force*] (NATG)
LBS............ Line Buffer System [*Computer science*]
LBS............ Liquid Bipropellant System (ACAE)
LBS............ Lithuanian Boy Scouts (EA)
LBS............ Load Balance System [*Telecommunications*] (TEL)
LBS............ Load-Bearing Surface (MCD)
LBS............ Load Bearing System
LBS............ Local Battery Signaling [*Telecommunications*] (IAA)
LBS............ Local Battery Supply [*Telecommunications*] (IAA)
LBS............ Local Battery Switchboard [*Telecommunications*] (IAA)
LBS............ Local Battery System [*Telecommunications*] (IAA)
LBS............ Loire Base Section [*World War II*]
LBS............ London Boroughs Association (SAUO)
LBS............ London Business Aviation [*British*] [*ICAO designator*] (FAAC)
LBS............ London Business School [*England*]
LBS............ London Graduate School of Business Studies (SAUO)
LBS............ Low Back Strain (DAVI)
LBS............ Low Back Syndrome [*Medicine*] (DMAA)
LBS............ Lumbar Back Strain [*Medicine*] (DMAA)
LBS............ Lysine-Binding Site [*Hematology*]
LB/S.......... Pounds per Second
LBSA........... Libraries Board of South Australia

LBSA............	Lipid-Bound Sialic Acid [Analytical biochemistry]
LBSA............	Long Binh Subarea [Vietnam]
LBSC............	Licentiate of the British Society of Commerce (DBQ)
LBSC............	London, Brighton and South Coast Railway (SAUO)
LBSC............	Long Beach State College (SAUO)
LBSCR	London, Brighton & South Coast Railway [British]
LBSD	Lightweight Battlefield Surveillance Device
LBSF............	Lions Blind Sports Foundation (EA)
LBSF............	Little Brothers of Saint Francis (TOCD)
LBSF............	Sofia [Bulgaria] [ICAO location identifier] (ICLI)
LBSG............	Letter Box Study Group [British] (DBA)
LBSM...........	Licentiate of Birmingham and Midland Institute School of Music (SAUO)
Lb/sq ft.......	Pound per Square Foot (SAUS)
Lb/sq in.......	Pound per Square Inch (SAUS)
Lb/sq yd	Pound per Square Yard (SAUS)
LBSR	Lightweight Battleweight Surveillance Radar (ACAE)
LBSS...........	Lightweight Battlefield Surveillance System (SAUS)
LBSS...........	Local Boards of the Selective Service System
lbst	Pounds [Libra in Latin] Static Thrust (DOMA)
LBSTR.........	Lobster
LBSZ...........	Stara Zagora [Bulgaria] [ICAO location identifier] (ICLI)
LBT	Air Liberte Tunisie [Tunisia] [ICAO designator] (FAAC)
LBT	Chemical Laboratory Technician [or Technology] [Navy]
LBT	Labatt [John] Ltd. [Toronto Stock Exchange symbol] [Vancouver Stock Exchange symbol]
LBT	Labete [Solomon Islands] [Seismograph station code, US Geological Survey] (SEIS)
LBT	Land-Based Tanker [Aircraft] (DOMA)
LBT	Large Binocular Telescope
LBT	Launch Base Test (ACAE)
LBT	L-Band Tetrode
LBT	L-Band Transmitter
LBT	Lean Best Torque [Automotive engineering]
lbt	Librettist [MARC relator code] [Library of Congress] (LCCP)
LBT	Light-Beam Transmissometer (PDAA)
LBT	Linear Beam Tube
LBT	Listen Before Talk (SAUO)
LBT	Local Battery Telephone [Telecommunications] (IAA)
LBT	Local Bus Target (SAUO)
LBT	Long-Baseline Tiltmeter [For earthquake study]
LBT	Low Back Tenderness [Medicine] (DMAA)
LBT	Low Bandpass Transformer
LBT	Low BIT [Binary Digit] Test [Computer science] (IEEE)
LBT	Lumberton, NC [Location identifier] [FAA] (FAAL)
LBT	Lupus Band Test [Medicine]
LBT	Lutheran Bible Translators (EA)
LBT	Pounds Thrust [NASA] (KSC)
LBT	Pound Troy
LBT CBS	Local-Battery Talking, Common-Battery Signaling [Telecommunications] (TEL)
Lb t/cu ft......	Pound Troy per Cubic Foot (SAUS)
Lb t/cu in.....	Pound Troy per Cubic Inch (SAUS)
Lb t/cu yd	Pound Troy per Cubic Yard (SAUS)
LBTF	Land-Based Test Facility (DNAB)
LBTF	Langmuir-Blodgett Trough Facility (SAUS)
LBTF	Long Beach Test Facility [Missiles]
Lb t/ft.........	Pound Troy per Foot (SAUS)
Lb t/ft3.......	Pound Troy per Cubic Foot (SAUS)
Lb t/fty........	Pound Troy per Square Foot (SAUS)
LBTI	Lima Bean Trypsin Inhibitor (DB)
LBTI	Long-Burning Target Indicator [British military] (DMA)
Lb t/in.........	Pound Troy per Inch (SAUS)
Lb t/in3.......	Pound Troy per Cubic Inch (SAUS)
Lb t/iny........	Pound Troy per Square Inch (SAUS)
LBTMA........	Listen Before Transmission Multiple Access (PDAA)
LBTP...........	Launch Base Test Plan (ACAE)
LBTS...........	Land-Based Test Site
LBTS...........	Land-Based Test System
LBTS...........	Local Battery Telephone Set [Telecommunications] (IAA)
LBTS...........	Local Battery Telephone Switchboard [Telecommunications] (IAA)
LBTS...........	London Blood Transfusion Service (SAUO)
Lb t/sq ft.....	Pound Troy per Square Foot (SAUS)
Lb t/sq yd	Pound Troy per Square Yard (SAUS)
Lb t/sy in.....	Pound Troy per Square Inch (SAUS)
LbtTrm.........	Liberty Term Trust [Associated Press] (SAG)
Lb t Weight...	Pound Troy Weight (SAUS)
LBTX...........	Local Battery Telephone Exchange [Telecommunications] (IAA)
LBTY...........	Liberty Petroleum Co. (SAUO)
LBTY...........	Tele-Communications Class A [NASDAQ symbol] (SAG)
LBTYA.........	Tele-Comm Inc. 'A' Liberty Media [NASDAQ symbol] (TTSB)
LbtyASE.......	Liberty All-Star Equity [Associated Press] (SAG)
LbtyASG.......	Liberty All Star Growth [Associated Press] (SAG)
LBTYB.........	Tele-Comm 'B' Liberty Media [NASDAQ symbol] (TTSB)
LbtyBc	Liberty Bancorp, Inc. [Associated Press] (SAG)
Lb t/yd	Pound Troy per Yard (SAUS)
Lb t/yd3	Pound Troy per Cubic Yard (SAUS)
Lb t/ydy	Pound Troy per Square Yard (SAUS)
LbtyH	Liberty Homes, Inc. [Associated Press] (SAG)
LBU.............	Labuan [Malaysia] [Airport symbol] (OAG)
LBU.............	Large Base Unit [Telecommunications]
LBU.............	Launcher Booster Unit
LBUN	Levobunolol [Also, LB] [Biochemistry]
LBuP	Plaquemines Parish Library, Buras, LA [Library symbol] [Library of Congress] (LCLS)
LBUR	Library Bureau, Inc. (SAUO)
LBUTX	Federated Utility Cl.A [Mutual fund ticker symbol] (SG)
LBV.............	La Belle, FL [Location identifier] [FAA] (FAAL)
LBV.............	Landing Boat, Vehicle [Navy symbol] [Obsolete]
LBV.............	Lateral Boundary Value (QUAC)
LBV.............	Left Brachial Vein [Cardiology] (DAVI)
LBV.............	Libreville [Gabon] [Airport symbol] (OAG)
LBV.............	Load-Bearing Vest [Military] (INF)
LBV.............	Local Bus Video
LBV.............	Luminous Blue Variables [Astronomy]
LBW............	Landing Barge Water [British military] (DMA)
LBW............	LASER Beam Welding
LBW............	Lean Body Weight [Medicine] (DMAA)
lbw.............	Leg before Wicket [Cricket] (WA)
lbw.............	Leg before Wicket [Cricket]
LBW............	Long Bawan [Indonesia] [Airport symbol] (OAG)
LBW............	Long Wheelbase [Automotive term] (GOBB)
LBW............	Low Birth Weight [Obstetrics]
LBW............	Low Body Weight
LBW............	Low-Speed Black and White [Photography]
LBW............	Lutheran Braille Workers (EA)
LBWBUZCALTX...	Local Battery with Buzzer Calling Telephone Exchange [Telecommunications] (IAA)
LBWI..........	Low-Birth-Weight Infant [Obstetrics] (MAE)
LBWMABCTX...	Local Battery with Magneto and Buzzer Calling Telephone Exchange [Telecommunications] (IAA)
LBWN	Varna [Bulgaria] [ICAO location identifier] (ICLI)
LBWOC	Level Bombing Wind Offset Computer [Military] (IAA)
LBWR	Lung-Body Weight Ratio [Medicine] (MAE)
Lb Wt..........	Pound-Weight (SAUS)
Lb wt/cu ft...	Pound-Weight per Cubic Foot (SAUS)
Lb wt/cu in...	Pound-Weight per Cubic Inch (SAUS)
Lb wt/cu yd...	Pound-Weight per Cubic Yard (SAUS)
Lb wt/ft........	Pound-Weight per Foot (SAUS)
Lb wt/ft3......	Pound-Weight per Cubic Foot (SAUS)
Lb wt/fty......	Pound-Weight per Square Foot (SAUS)
Lb wt/hp	Pound-Weight per Horsepower (SAUS)
Lb wt/in	Pound-Weight per Inch (SAUS)
Lb wt/in3	Pound-Weight per Cubic Inch (SAUS)
Lb wt/iny	Pound-Weight per Square Inch (SAUS)
Lb wt/sq ft...	Pound-Weight per Square Foot (SAUS)
Lb wt/sq in...	Pound-Weight per Square Inch (SAUS)
Lb wt/sq yd...	Pound-Weight per Square Yard (SAUS)
Lb wt/yd	Pound-Weight per Yard (SAUS)
Lb wt/yd3.....	Pound-Weight per Cubic Yard (SAUS)
Lb wt/ydy.....	Pound-Weight per Square Yard (SAUS)
LBX.............	Lake Jackson, TX [Location identifier] [FAA] (FAAL)
LBX.............	Local Bus Accelerator (VLIE)
LBX.............	Low Band with X (SAUO)
LBY.............	Hattiesburg, MS [Location identifier] [FAA] (FAAL)
LBY.............	La Baule [France] [Airport symbol] (AD)
LBY.............	Libbey, Inc. [NYSE symbol] (SPSG)
LBY.............	Liberty Fabrics of New York (SAUO)
LBY.............	Libya [ANSI three-letter standard code] (CNC)
Lb/yd	Pound per Yard (SAUS)
LB/YD2	Pounds per Square Yard
Lb/yd3.........	Pound per Cubic Yard (SAUS)
LB/YD3	Pounds per Cubic Yard
Lb/ydy.........	Pound per Square Yard (SAUS)
Lb/ydy.........	Pounds per Square Yard (SAUS)
LBYR	Labyrinth [Engineering]
LBYRPK	Labyrinth Pack [Engineering]
LC	Convention on the Prevention of Marine Pollution by Dumping of Wastes and other Matter (SAUS)
LC	Co-ordinating Committee for the Liberation of Africa (SAUO)
LC	Deferred Cable (EBF)
LC	Ewell's Leading Cases on Infancy, Etc. [A publication] (DLA)
L/C	Inductance/Capacitance (AAG)
LC	Inductor Capacitor circuit (SAUS)
LC	Label Clause
LC	Laboratory Counsel (SAUO)
LC	Laboratory Craftsman (ADA)
LC	Labor Cases [A publication] (DLA)
LC	Labor Code (DNAB)
LC	Labour Canada [See also TRAVC]
LC	Labour Corps [British military] (DMA)
LC	Lackawanna College (SAUO)
LC	La Crosse [Diocesan abbreviation] [Wisconsin] (TOCD)
LC	Lactation Consultant [Medicine] (MEDA)
LC	Ladycliff College (SAUO)
LC	Laennec's Cirrhosis [Medicine] (MAE)
LC	Lafayette College (SAUO)
LC	Lagonda Club, US Section (EA)
LC	Lake Central Airlines
LC	Lake Current (COE)
LC	Lakehead College (SAUO)
LC	Lakeland College (SAUO)
LC	Lakey Clinic Medical Center [Burlington, MA]
LC	Lamb Committee (EA)
LC	Lambuth College (SAUO)
LC	Lancaster & Chester Railway Co. [AAR code]
LC	Lance Corporal
LC	Land Commission [British]
LC	Land Court [Legal] [British]
L/C	Land Cover (CARB)

LC	Lander College (SAUO)		LC	Life Care [Medicine] (BABM)
LC	Landing Craft		LC	Light Car [British]
LC	Lane College (SAUO)		LC	Light Case [Military] (NATG)
LC	Langerhans' Cells [Medicine]		LC	Light Chain [Immunoglobulin]
LC	Langmuir Circulation [Geophysics]		LC	Light Company [British military] (DMA)
LC	Language Code [Online database field identifier]		LC	Light Control [Technical drawings]
LC	Lannois-Cleret [Syndrome] [Medicine] (DB)		LC	Light Current (IAA)
LC	Laredo College (SAUO)		LC	Lightly Canceled
LC	Large Case [Indicator] [IRS]		LC	Lightweight Computer (SAUS)
LC	Large Cell [Lymphoma classification]		LC	Limestone College (SAUO)
LC	Large Cleaved Cell (DB)		LC	Limited Coordinating (NG)
LC	Larval Chamber [Botany]		LC	Limp Cloth [Bookbinding] (DGA)
LC	Lasa C Ring [Montana] [Seismograph station code, US Geological Survey] (SEIS)		LC	Lincoln College (SAUO)
			LC	Lindenwood College (SAUO)
LC	Lassen College (SAUO)		LC	Linear Combination
LC	Last Card		LC	Line-Carrying
LC	Late Clamped [Umbilical cord]		LC	Line Circuit [Telecommunications]
LC	Late Commitment [Reason for missed interception] [Military]		LC	Line Collector
LC	Lateral Component		LC	Line Concentrator
LC	Launch Center		LC	Line Connection
L/C	Launch Complex (ACAE)		LC	Line Connector (NITA)
LC	Launch Complex		LC	Line Construction Tools [JETDS nomenclature] [Military] (CET)
LC	Launch Conference [Aerospace] (AAG)		LC	Line Contractor (MCD)
L/C	Launch Control [Aerospace] (AAG)		LC	Line Control
LC	Launch Coordinator [NASA]		LC	Line Crosser [Deserter] [Military]
LC	Launch Corridor [Aerospace] (AAG)		LC	Line Length Ciceros [Typography] (DGA)
LC	Launch Cost [Aerospace]		LC	Line of Communication [Military]
LC	Launch Count [NASA] (KSC)		LC	Line of Contact [Military]
LC	Launch Countdown [NASA] (NASA)		L/C	Line of Credit [Business term]
LC	Launch Critical (MCD)		LC	Linfield College (SAUO)
LC	Launching Control [Military]		LC	Linguocervical [Dentistry]
LC	Laundry Chute (MSA)		LC	Link Circuit
LC	Laureate of Arts		LC	Link Control [Telecommunications] (OSI)
LC	Laureate of Letters		LC	Links and Chargers (NATG)
LC	Law Commission (DLA)		LC	Linux Computer (SAUS)
LC	Law Court (SAUO)		LC	Lions Club (SAUO)
LC	Law Courts		LC	Lipid Cytosome [Biochemistry] (MAE)
LC	Lawrence College (SAUO)		LC	Liquid Capacity
LC	Lead Covered [or Coated]		LC	Liquid Chromatography
LC	Leading Cases (DLA)		LC	Liquid Crystal
LC	League of Communists [Former Yugoslavia]		LC	Literature Criticism from 1400 to 1800 [A publication]
LC	League of Composers (EA)		LC	Lithocholate [Biochemistry]
LC	League of the Cross [Roman Catholic religious order] (ROG)		LC	Lithocolic Acid [Biochemistry] (DB)
LC	Leander Club (SAUO)		LC	Liturgical Conference (EA)
LC	Learning Curve (MSA)		LC	Liver Cirrhosis [Medicine]
LC	Least Count		LC	Livestock Commission (SAUO)
LC	Lecithin Cholesterol Acyltransferase (DB)		LC	Living Children
LC	Lee College (SAUO)		LC	Livingstone College (SAUO)
LC	Leesona Corp. (KSC)		LC	Load Carrier
LC	Leesona Corporation (SAUO)		LC	Load Cell
lc	Left Center (WDAA)		LC	Load Center (MSA)
LC	Left Center [A stage direction]		LC	Load-Compensating (MSA)
LC	Left Chest [Medicine] (KSC)		LC	Load Computer [or Controller] (MCD)
LC	Left Circumflex (Artery) [Anatomy]		LC	Load Contactor
LC	Left Ear, Cold Stimulus [Medicine] (MEDA)		LC	Load Control [Hydraulics]
LC	Legal Committee (MCD)		L/C	Load Crew (SAUO)
LC	Legal Currency (ADA)		LC	Loading Capacity (RIMS)
lc	Legionaries of Christ (TOCD)		LC	Loading Coil [Telecommunications] (TEL)
LC	Legionaries of Christ [Roman Catholic men's religious order]		LC	Loan Capital [Business term]
LC	Legislative Council [British]		LC	Loan Crowd [Investment term]
LC	Legitimate Child		LC	Local Call [Followed by telephone number]
LC	Leisure Counseling [Medicine] (MEDA)		LC	Local Changes (SAUS)
LC	Length of Chord (MSA)		LC	Local Channel (CET)
LC	Lesley College (SAUO)		LC	Localization Code (IAA)
LC	Lethal Concentration		LC	Localized Corrosion (PDAA)
L/C	Lettera di Credito [Letter of Credit] [Italian] [Business term]		LC	Location Counter [Computer science]
LC	Letter Contract		LC	Locked Closed
l/c	Letter of Credit (EBF)		lc	Loco Citato [At the Place Cited] [Latin] (EES)
LC	Letter of Credit		LC	Loco Citato [In the Place Cited] [Latin]
L/C	Letter of Credit (NTIO)		LC	Locomotive and Carriage Institute (BUAC)
LC	Letters and Cards [US Postal Service]		LC	Locus Ceruleus [Brain anatomy]
LC	Lettre de Credit [Letter of Credit] [Business term] [French]		LC	Locus of Control [Psychology]
lc	Leucite [CIPW classification] [Geology]		LC	Loganair [ICAO designator] (AD)
LC	Level Control		LC	Logical Channel (PDAA)
LC	Level Crossing		LC	Logical Choice (ELAL)
LC	Leverage Contract [Business term]		LC	Logical Comparison (ELAL)
LC	Lewis College (SAUO)		LC	Logic Cell (IAA)
LC	Leydig's Cells [Endocrinology]		LC	Logic Circuit (ELAL)
LC	Leyland Cars [Leyland Daf Ltd.]		LC	Logic Corp.
LC	Liaison-Cargo [Air Force]		LC	Logistics Command (IAA)
LC	Liaison Committee of Rector's Conferences of Member States of the European Communities (BUAC)		LC	London Clause [Business term]
			LC	London Club (EA)
LC	Liaison/Communicator (COE)		LC	Long-Chain [Triglyceride] [Biochemistry] (MAE)
LC	Liberal Conservative		LC	Longwood College (SAUO)
LC	Liberalt Centrum [Liberal Center] [Denmark] [Political party] (PPE)		L/C	Loopback Capability (SAUS)
LC	Liberty Corp. [NYSE symbol] (SPSG)		L/C	Loop Check (MUGU)
LC	Library of Congress		LC	Loop Circuit (ELAL)
LC	Library of Congress Card Number (NITA)		LC	Loose Coupler
LC	Library of Congress Classification		LC	Loras College (SAUO)
LC	License Condition (HEAS)		LC	Lord Chamberlain [British]
L/C	License to Cut (SAUO)		LC	Lord Chancellor [British]
LC	Licensing Committee (SAUO)		LC	Los Californianos (EA)
LC	Licensing Country [Dialog] [Searchable field] [Information service or system] (NITA)		LC	Loss of Contact (IAA)
			LC	Lotta Continua [Continuous Struggle] [Italy] [Political party] (PPE)
LC	Lieutenant Commander		LC	Loud and Clear

LC .... Loudness Control (ELAL)
LC .... Louisburg College (SAUO)
LC .... Louisiana College (SAUO)
LC .... [A] Lover's Complaint [Shakespearean work]
LC .... Low Calorie (AAMN)
LC .... Low Carbon [Content, as low-carbon steel]
L/C .... Low Compression [Automotive engineering]
LC .... Low Conditioners [Psychology]
LC .... Low Cost (ELAL)
LC .... Low Cost Color [Computer science] (CDE)
LC .... Lower California
LC .... Lower Canada
lc .... Lowercase (WDMC)
LC .... Lowercase [i.e., small letters] [Typography]
LC .... Lower Character (IAA)
LC .... Lower Control (IAA)
LC .... Lower Court (SAUO)
LC .... Lower Cylinder
LC .... LOX [Liquid Oxygen] Clean
LC .... Loyola College (SAUO)
LC .... Lubrication Chart
LC .... Luminosity Class [Astronomy] (IAA)
LC .... Lutheran Council [British] (DBA)
LC .... Lutheran Council of Great Britain (BUAC)
LC .... Luther College (SAUO)
LC .... Luzon College (SAUO)
LC .... Lycoming College (SAUO)
LC .... Lyman Continuum [Spectroscopy] (OA)
LC .... Lymphocyte-Mediated Cytotoxicity [Also, LMC] [Immunology]
LC .... Lynchburg College (SAUO)
LC .... Lytic Capacity [Clinical chemistry]
LC .... Scottish Land Court Reports [A publication] (DLA)
L/C .... Single Acetate Single Cotton [Wire insulation] (AAG)
LC .... St. Lucia [ANSI two-letter standard code] (CNC)
LC .... United States Public Health Service Hospital, Carville (SAUS)
LC3 .... Logistics Command, Control and Communications (SAUO)
LC-39 .... Launch Complex 39 (SAUS)
LC₅₀ .... Lethal Concentration, Median [Lethal for 50% of test group]
LCA .... Lacana Mining Corp. [Toronto Stock Exchange symbol]
LCA .... Lake Carriers' Association (EA)
LCA .... Lake Central Airlines
LCA .... Lamborghini Club America (EA)
LCA .... Laminate Council of America [Defunct] (EA)
LCA .... Land Compensation Act [Town planning] [British]
LCA .... Landing Craft, Armored [Used in Vietnam by the French to transport their engineer units] (VNW)
LCA .... Landing Craft, Assault [Navy ship symbol]
LCA .... Larnaca [Cyprus] [Airport symbol] (OAG)
LCA .... Last Common Ancestor [Evolution]
LCA .... Latent Class Analysis
LCA .... Launch Control Amplifier [NASA] (NASA)
LCA .... Launch Control Analyst [NASA] (AAG)
LCA .... Launch [or Launcher] Control Area [Missiles]
LCA .... Lead Contractors Association [British] (EAIO)
LCA .... Leadership Councils of America (EA)
LCA .... Leading Cases, Annotated [A publication] (DLA)
LCA .... Leading Catering Accountant [British military] (DMA)
LCA .... Learning Corporation of America (SAUO)
LCA .... Leber's Congenital Amaurosis [Medicine] (DAVI)
LCA .... LeConte Airlines [ICAO designator] (FAAC)
LCA .... Left Carotid Artery [Cardiology] (DAVI)
LCA .... Left Circumflex Artery [Medicine] (DB)
LCA .... Left Coronary Artery [Cardiology]
LCA .... Lesson Content Analysis
LCA .... Leukocyte Common Antigen [Immunochemistry]
LCA .... Leveling Control Amplifier
LCA .... Ley de Comunidad Aut"noma (SAUO)
LCA .... Library Club of America [Defunct] (EA)
LCA .... Library-College Associates [Defunct] (EA)
LCA .... Library of Congress Authority File [Source file] [UTLAS symbol]
LCA .... Licensed Company Auditor [British]
LCA .... Life Communicators Association [Des Moines, IA] (EA)
LCA .... Life Cycle Analysis [or Assessment] [Environmental science]
LCA .... Life Cycle Assessment (ADWA)
LCA .... Light Combat Aircraft [Military]
LCA .... Light Contact Assist (STED)
LCA .... Lighting Control Assembly [NASA] (KSC)
LCA .... Line Clearance Airdrome [Air Force]
LCA .... Line Control Adapter
LCA .... Liquid Crystal Analog
LCA .... Lithocholic Acid [Biochemistry]
LCA .... Lithuanian Catholic Alliance (EA)
LCA .... Liverpool Cotton Association (BUAC)
LCA .... Living Centers of America [NYSE symbol] (SAG)
LCA .... Load-Carrying Ability (IAA)
LCA .... Load Control Assembly (SAUS)
LCA .... Load Controller Assembly (NASA)
LCA .... Local Communications Adapter [IBM Corp.]
LCA .... Local Communications Area (KSC)
LCA .... Local Cooperation Agreement [Army Corps of Engineers]
LCA .... Local Core Alignment [Telecommunications] (NITA)
LCA .... Log Cabin [Alabama] [Seismograph station code, US Geological Survey] (SEIS)
LCA .... Logic Cell Array (IAA)
LCA .... Logistic Control Activity (AABC)

LCA .... Logistics Control Area (IAA)
LCA .... London City Airport [British]
LCA .... Longitudinal Chromatic Aberration
LCA .... Losely Coupled Architecture (SAUO)
LCA .... Lotus Communications Architecture (SAUO)
LCA .... Louisiana Cattlemen's Association (SRA)
LCA .... Louisiana Chemical Association (SRA)
LCA .... Low Cost Aircraft (ACAE)
LCA .... Low-Cost Automation (WDAA)
LCA .... Lowercase Alphabet
lca .... Lowercase-Alphabet Length [Typesetting] (WDMC)
LCA .... Lussazione Congenita dell'Anca [Congenital Hip Dislocation] [Italian] [Medicine]
LCA .... Lutheran Church in America [Later, ELCA]
LCA .... Lutheran Collegiate Association [Defunct] (EA)
LCA .... Lymphocytotoxic Antibody [Medicine] (STED)
LCA .... St. Lucia [ANSI three-letter standard code] (CNC)
LCAA .... Licensed Clubs Association of Australia
LCAACT .... Licensed Clubs Association of the Australian Capital Territory
LCAAJ .... Language and Culture Atlas of Ashkenazic Jewry [A publication] (BJA)
LCAAP .... Lake City Army Ammunition Plant (AABC)
LCABLS Bull... Law Council of Australia. Business Law Section. Bulletin [A publication]
LCaC .... Cameron Parish Library, Cameron, LA [Library symbol] [Library of Congress] (LCLS)
LCAC .... Landing Craft, Air Cushion [Navy symbol]
LCAC .... Landing Craft, Air Cushioned (SAUO)
LCAC .... Library of Congress Classification - Additions and Changes [A publication]
LCAC .... Light Craft, Air Cushion (ACAE)
LCAC .... Listed Company Advisory Committee [of NYSE]
LCAC .... Low-Cost Automation Centre [British]
LCACCC .... Laymen's Commission of the American Council of Christian Churches (EA)
LCACM .... Liaison Committee of Architects of the Common Market (SAUO)
LCACT .... Law Council of the Australian Capital Territory
LCAD .... Logistics Cost Analysis Data (MCD)
LC-ADD .... Library of Congress - American Doctoral Dissertations [A bibliographic publication]
LCAF .... Lutheran Church in America Foundation
LCA(FT) ...... Landing Craft, Assault (Flamethrower) [British military] (DMA)
LCA-GB .... Lightweight Cycle Association of Great Britain (BUAC)
LCA(H) .... Landing Craft, Assault (Hedgerow)
LCAH .... London and Continental Advertising Holdings [British]
LCAJ .... Low-Cost Anti-Jam system (SAUS)
LCAL .... Lower Conformance Altitude (SAA)
LCAM .... Liver Cell Adhesion Molecule [Cytology]
LCAMIMS .... Logistics Capability Assessment Models Information Management System (SAUO)
LCAMOS ...... Loop Cable Maintenance Operation System (VLIE)
LCAN .... Lockheed Canada Inc. (SAUO)
LC & M Gaz... Lower Courts and Municipal Gazette [Canada] [A publication] (DLA)
LC&TPA .... Lighting Column and Transmission Pole Association (BUAC)
LCANSW ...... Landscape Contractors' Association of New South Wales [Australia]
LCANSW ...... Licensed Clubs Association of New South Wales [Australia]
LCAO .... Leadership Council of Aging Organizations (EA)
LCAO .... Limited Configuration Atomic Orbital (MCD)
LCAO .... Linear Combination of Atomic Orbitals [Physical chemistry]
LCA(OC)...... Landing Craft, Assault (Obstacle Clearance) [British military] (DMA)
LCAofGB ...... Lightweight Cycle Association of Great Britian (DBA)
LCAO-MO...... Linear Combination of Atomic Orbital-Molecular Orbital (DB)
LCAO-MO-SCF... Linear Combination of Atomic Orbitals to Form Molecular Orbitals by a Self-Consistent Field [Quantum mechanics]
LCAP .... Linear Control Analysis Program (ACAE)
LCAP .... Local Combat Air Patrol
LCAP .... Loop Carrier Analysis Program [Bell System]
LCAP .... Low Cost Accurate Programmer (ACAE)
LCAR .... Late Cutaneous Anaphylactic Reaction [Immunology]
LCAR .... Launch Complex Assessment Report [NASA] (KSC)
LCAR .... Lotus Cortina of America Register [Defunct] (EA)
LCAR .... Low-Cost Attack RADAR
LCAR .... Low-Coverage Acquisiton RADAR (PDAA)
LCAR .... Luxury Car (TRID)
LCar .... United States Public Health Service Hospital, Carville, LA [Library symbol] [Library of Congress] (LCLS)
LCARC .... Lake County Amateur Radio Club (SAUO)
LCARS .... Library Computer Access Retrieval System (VLIE)
LCAS .... Land Capability Assessment Strategy (SAUO)
LCAS .... Light Close Air Support (SAUS)
LCAS .... Lithuanian Catholic Academy of Sciences (EA)
LCASA .... Licensed Clubs Association of South Australia
LCAT .... Laser Communications Airborne Testbed (ACAE)
LCAT .... Lecithin-Cholesterol Acyltransferase [An enzyme]
LCAT .... Licensed Clubs Association of Tasmania [Australia]
LCAT .... Lifts and Cranes Appeals Tribunal [Australia]
LCATA .... Laundry and Cleaners Allied Trades Association [Later, TCATA]
LCATS .... Large Capacity Automated Telecommunications System (SAUO)
LCATS .... Laser Communications Airborne Test Set (ACAE)
LCAUE .... Liaison Committee of the Architects of United Europe [EC] (ECED)
LCAUS .... Latvian Choir Association of the United States (SAUO)
LCAV .... Landscape Contractors Association of Victoria [Australia]
LCAV .... LCA-Vision [NASDAQ symbol] (TTSB)
L Cav .... Lucy Cavendish Collegiate Society, Cambridge (SAUO)
LCAVAT .... Landing Craft and Amphibious Vehicle Assignment Table

LCAW........... Low-Cost Anti-Submarine Weapon (SAUS)
LCAX........... Landing Craft, Assault, Experimental [Navy ship symbol]
LCB............. Laboratory Coordinating Board (SAUO)
LCB............. Landing Craft, Vehicle [Navy symbol]
LCB............. Language Control Board (TIMI)
LCB............. Launch Control Building [NASA]
LCB............. Least-Common Bigram [Computer science] (BYTE)
LCB............. Least Common BIT [Binary Digit] (MCD)
LCB............. Left Cornerback [Football]
LCB............. Liefdezusters van de H. Carolus Borromeus [Sisters of Charity of St. Charles Borromeo - SCSCB] (EAIO)
LCB............. Limited Capability Buoy
LCB............. Line Control Block [Computer science]
LCB............. Line to Computer Buffer (VLIE)
LCB............. Link Control Block [Computer science] (ELAL)
LCB............. Liquor Control Board [Canada]
LCB............. Living Country Blues [A publication]
LCB............. Logic Control Block
LCB............. London and Continental Bankers (SAUO)
LCB............. London Centre for Biotechnology [British] (IRUK)
LCB............. Long-Chain Branching [Organic chemistry]
LCB............. Longitudinal Centre of Buoyancy (SAUO)
LCB............. Longitudinal Position of Center of Buoyancy
LCB............. Lord Chief Baron [British]
LCB............. Low Cost Bipolar (VLIE)
LCBA........... Loyal Christian Benefit Association [Erie, PA] (EA)
LCBB........... "Life Can Be Beautiful" [Old radio program; nicknamed "Elsie Beebee"]
LCBBC .... Liquor Control Board of British Columbia (SAUO)
LCBC........... Lake Chad Basin Commission [Chad] (BUAC)
LCBF........... Local Cerebral Blood Flow [Medicine]
LCBM.......... Lifecore Biomedical [NASDAQ symbol] (TTSB)
LCBM.......... LifeCore Biomedical, Inc. [NASDAQ symbol] (SAG)
LCBM.......... Liquor Control Board of Manitoba (SAUO)
LCBO........... Linear Combination of [Semi-localized] Band Orbitals [Atomic physics]
LCBO .... Liquor Control Board of Ontario (SAUO)
LC/BPL........ Laboratory Counsel/Business & Patent Law (SAUO)
LCBS........... Liquor Control Board of Saskatchewan (SAUO)
LCBS........... London Classification of Business Studies [Library classification scheme] [British] (NITA)
LCBWR .... LaCrosse Boiling Water Reactor [Also, LACBWR]
LCBX........... Large Computerized [Private] Branch Exchange (MHDI)
LCC............. Amphibious Command Ship [Formerly, AGC] [Navy symbol]
LCC............. Cameron Parish Library (SAUS)
LCC............. Charles A. Lindbergh Collectors Club (EA)
LCC............. Laboratory of Computer Chemistry (VLIE)
LCC............. Labor Case Comments [Cast Metals Association] [A publication]
LCC............. Labor Class Code (DNAB)
LCC............. Labour Coordinating Committee [British]
LCC............. Lactose Coliform Count [Medicine] (BABM)
LCC............. Land Capability Classes [Agriculture]
LCC............. Land Component Commander (MCD)
LCC............. Land Court Cases [New South Wales] [A publication] (DLA)
LCC............. Landing Control Center
LCC............. Landing Craft, Control
LCC............. Lands Conservation Council (SAUO)
LCC............. Langley Complex Coordination [Device] [NASA]
LCC............. Language for Conversational Computing (MDG)
LCC............. Lansing Community College (SAUO)
LCC............. Large Capacity Cassette [Electronic printing] (DGA)
LCC............. Large Cavitation Channel [Pressurized water tunnel to test submarines and ship models] [Navy]
LCC............. Large Compressor Colorimeter (MCD)
LCC............. Last Clear Chance [Legal shorthand] (LWAP)
LCC............. Late Choice Call (NITA)
LCC............. Launch Command and Control
LCC............. Launch Commit Criteria (MCD)
LCC............. Launch Committee Criteria (SAUO)
LCC............. Launch Control Car (SAUS)
LCC............. Launch Control Center [NASA]
LCC............. Launch Control Console
LCC............. Laurie Cox Conference (PSS)
LCC............. Leach's English Crown Cases [1730-1815] [A publication] (DLA)
LCC............. Lead-Coated Copper (OA)
LCC............. Lead Covered Cable [Telecommunications] (TEL)
LCC............. Leaded Chip Carrier [Electronics] (AAEL)
LCC............. Leadless Ceramic Carrier (TIMI)
LCC............. Leadless Chip Carrier [Motorola, Inc.]
LCC............. League of California Cities (SAUO)
LCC............. Le Cercle Concours d'Elegance (EA)
LCC............. Ledger Card Computer (MHDB)
LCC............. Left Circumflex Coronary Artery [Medicine] (DMAA)
LCC............. Left Coronary Cusp [Medicine] (STED)
LCC............. Legacy Coordinating Council [Australia]
LCC............. Legalise Cannabis Campaign [British] (DBA)
LCC............. Legalize Cannabis Campaign (SAUO)
LCC............. Lesser of Costs or Charges [Medicine] (GFGA)
LCC............. Levo-Carnitine Chloride [Biochemistry]
LCC............. Leyland Cars Council
LCC............. Liang-Chow [Republic of China] [Seismograph station code, US Geological Survey] [Closed] (SEIS)
LCC............. Libertarian Council of Churches [Defunct] (EA)
LCC............. Libraries Consultative Committee [Australia]
LCC............. Libraries Copyright Committee [Australia]

LCC............. Library of Congress Classification
LCC............. Libreville Construction Company (SAUO)
LCC............. Life Cycle Center (SAUO)
LCC............. Life Cycle Cost (ADWA)
LCC............. Life-Cycle Costing [or Costs] [DoD]
LCC............. Lignin-Carbohydrate Complex [Organic chemistry]
LCC............. Ligue Canadienne des Compositeurs [Canadian League of Composers - CLC]
LCC............. Limited Capability Configuration [Army] (DOMA)
LCC............. Lincoln Capital Corp. [Toronto Stock Exchange symbol]
LCC............. Linear Cutting Cord [Aircraft escape technology] (PDAA)
LCC............. Linecaster Control (DGA)
LCC............. Link Control Standard Controller [Telecommunications] (ECII)
LCC............. Liquid Column Chromatography (EDCT)
LCC............. Liquid Crystal Cell (IEEE)
LCC............. Liquid-Cushion Electroplating Cell [Steel production]
LCC............. Liquor Control Commission
LCC............. Lithophane Collectors Club (EA)
LCC............. Little Carter Cay [NASA] (KSC)
LCC............. Liver Cell Carcinoma [Medicine] (DB)
LCC............. Load Controlling Crewman [Helicopter] [Navy]
LCC............. Loading Coil Case [Telecommunications] (TEL)
LCC............. Local Command Centre (SAUO)
LCC............. Local Communications Complex
LCC............. Local Communications Console
LCC............. Local Control Center (SAUO)
LCC............. Local Control Console (CAAL)
LCC............. Local Coordinating Committee
LCC............. Lockheed-California Co. [Division of Lockheed Aircraft Corp.]
LCC............. Lockheed California Company (SAUO)
LCC............. Lockheed Corporation of California (SAUO)
LCC............. Logistic Control Code [Military] (AABC)
LCC............. Logistics Control Center [Military] (INF)
LCC............. Logistics Coordination Center [NATO]
LCC............. Logistics Co-ordination Centre (SAUO)
LCC............. London Chamber of Commerce [British] (DAS)
LCC............. London City Council (SAUO)
LCC............. London Communication Committee (SAUO)
LCC............. London Communications Committee [World War II]
LCC............. London County Council [or Councillor] [Later, GLC]
LCC............. London Cycling Campaign [England] (BUAC)
LCC............. Lost Calls Cleared [Telecommunications] (NITA)
LCC............. Lost Chord Clubs (EA)
LCC............. Low-Cement Castable [Ceramics]
LCC............. Low-Cost Classifier (MCD)
LCC............. Lower Columbia College (SAUO)
LCC............. Lundy Collectors Club (EA)
LCCA........... Late Cortical Cerebellar Atrophy [Neurology]
LCCA........... Lawyers Committee on Central America [Defunct] (EA)
LCCA........... Lead Contamination Control Act of 1988 (COE)
LCCA........... Left Circumflex Coronary Artery [Anatomy]
LCCA........... Left Common Carotid Artery [Cardiology] (DAVI)
LCCA........... Leukocytoelastic Angitis [Cardiology] (DAVI)
LCCA........... Life Cycle Cost Analysis (MCD)
LCCA........... Lionel Collectors Club of America (EA)
LCCA........... Lithuanian Chamber of Commerce of America (EA)
LCCA........... Load Current Contacting Aiding
LCCA........... London Church Choir Association
LCCA........... Low-Cost Computer Attachment (IAA)
LCCB........... Local Change Control Board (MCD)
LCCB........... Local Configuration Control Board (AABC)
LCCB........... Low-Cost Controllable Booster (MCD)
LCCC........... Launch Control Centre Computer (SAUO)
LCCC........... Leadless Ceramic Chip Carrier [Electronics]
LCCC........... Library of Congress Catalogue Card (WDAA)
LCCC........... Library of Congress Computer Catalog (NITA)
LCCC........... Life Care Communities Corporation (SAUO)
LCCC........... Lorain County Community College (SAUO)
LCCC........... Low-Cost Chip Carrier (TIMI)
LCCC........... Lower Canada Civil Code [A publication] (DLA)
LCCC........... Lucas County Corrections Center (SAUO)
LCCC........... Luzerne County Community College [Nanticoke, PA] (TSSD)
LCCC........... Nicosia [Cyprus] [ICAO location identifier] (ICLI)
LCCCN......... Library of Congress Catalog Card Number (NITA)
LCCD........... Launch Commit Criteria Document [NASA] (NASA)
LCCD........... Launch Committee Criteria Document (SAUO)
LCCD........... Low Complexity Color Display [Video technology] (EECA)
LCC/DTC ...... Life Cycle Cost / Design to Cost
LCCE........... Lee County Central Electric [AAR code]
LCCE........... Life-Cycle Cost Estimate (AABC)
LCCEB......... London Chamber of Commerce Examinations Board [British] (AIE)
LCCEP......... Logistics Civilian Career Enhancement Program [Military]
LCCEV......... Low Cost Cryogenic Expendable Vehicle (SAUS)
LCCEWG ..... Large-Core Code Evaluation Working Group (SAUO)
LCCFC........ Launch Control Complex Facility Console [NASA] (IAA)
LCCFCO ...... Lake Cowichan Combined Fire Control Organization (SAUO)
LCCH.......... London College of Clinical Hypnosis (SAUO)
LCCH.......... London County Council Hospital (SAUO)
LCCI........... London Chamber of Commerce and Industry [British] (DCTA)
LCCID......... Life Cycle Cost in Design [Computer program released by US Army Construction Engineering Research Laboratory] (RDA)
LCCIEB........ London Chamber of Commerce and Industry Examinations Board
LCCIS......... Local Common Channel Interoffice Signaling (VLIE)
LCCIW........ Life Cycle Cost Impact Worksheet (SPST)
LCCJ........... Louisiana Council on Criminal Justice (SAUO)

LCCL............	Line Card Cable (VLIE)
LCCLN	Line Card Cable Narrative (VLIE)
LCCM..........	LanClient Control Manager [Computer science]
LCCM..........	Late Choice Call Meter [Telecommunications] (NITA)
LCCM..........	Life Cycle Cost Management (SPST)
LCCM..........	Life Cycle Cost Model (ACAE)
LCCMARC	Library of Congress Current MARC [Machine-Readable Catalog] File (NITA)
LCCMS.........	Launch Control Center Measuring Station [NASA] (KSC)
LCCN	Library of Congress Catalog-Card Number
LCCO	Landing Craft Control Officer [Military]
LCCO	Leadership Career Counseling Officer (DNAB)
LCCO	Life Cycle Cost of Ownership (MCD)
LCCOGA.......	Liaison Committee of Cooperating Oil and Gas Associations (EA)
LC Cont.......	Langdell's Cases on Contracts [A publication] (DLA)
LCCP..........	Landing Craft Control Primary [Military]
LCCP..........	LASER Code Control Panel (MCD)
LCCP..........	Launch Captain's Control Panel [Navy] (CAAL)
LCCP..........	Lower Canada Civil Procedure [A publication] (DLA)
LCC-PDR......	League of Communists of Croatia - Party of Democratic Reform [Political party]
LCCPMP	Life Cycle Computer Program Management Plan (VLIE)
LCCPT.........	Low-Cost Cockpit Procedures Trainer (MCD)
LCCR	Laboratory for Computer and Communications Research [Simon Fraser University] [Canada] [Research center] (RCD)
LCCR	Leadership Conference on Civil Rights (EA)
LCCRUL	Lawyers' Committee for Civil Rights under Law (EA)
LCCS..........	Laboratory Customer Communications System (SAUO)
LCCS..........	Land Capability Classification System (COE)
LCCs..........	Land Care Committees (SAUO)
LCCS..........	Landing Craft Control Secondary (SAUS)
LCCS..........	Large Capacity Core Storage [Computer science] (MDG)
LCCS..........	Launch Checkout and Countdown System [Aerospace] (IAA)
LCCS..........	Launch Control and Checkout System [Aerospace] (IAA)
LCCS..........	Launcher Captain Control System [Military] (NVT)
LCCS..........	Library of Congress Classification Schedules [A publication]
LCCS..........	Life Cycle Contractor Support
LCCS..........	Logistics Control Center System
LCCS..........	London County Council Service (SAUO)
LCCS..........	Low Cervical Caesarean Section
LCCS..........	Lucy Cavendish Collegiate Society (SAUO)
LCCTS.........	Life Cycle Cost Tracking System [Social Security Administration]
LCCU	Lightweight Crewman Communication Umbilical (MCD)
LCCV..........	Large-Component Cleaning Vessel [Nuclear energy] (NRCH)
LCCW..........	Low-Cost Composite Weapon (MCD)
LCD............	Land Conservation District (SAUO)
LCD............	Language for Computer Design (CSR)
LCD............	Launch Control Design [NASA] (AAG)
LCD............	Launch Countdown [NASA] (NASA)
LCD............	Least [or Lowest] Common Denominator [or Divisor] [Mathematics]
lcd............	Least Common Denominator (NTIO)
LCD............	Left Crus of Diaphragm [Medicine] (MELL)
LCD............	Letter Carrier Depot (DD)
LCD............	Light-Chain Deposition (MELL)
LCD............	Lightweight Ceramic Dome
LCD............	Line Control Definer (VLIE)
LCD............	Line Current Disconnect (HGAA)
LCD............	Liquid Crystal Device (SAUS)
LCD............	Liquid Crystal Digital [Battery-powered wristwatch]
LCD............	Liquid Crystal Diode
LCD............	Liquid Crystal Display
LCD............	Liquor Carbonis Detergens [Coal tar solution] [Medicine]
LCD............	LISP Code Directory (SAUS)
LCD............	List of Chosen Descriptors (PDAA)
LCD............	Liver Cell Dysplasia [Medicine]
LCD............	LM [Lunar Module] Change Directive [NASA] (KSC)
LCD............	Load Classification Group (SAUO)
LCD............	Lobster-Claw Deformity (MELL)
LCD............	Local Climatological Data [A publication]
LCD............	Localized Collagen Dystrophy [Medicine] (DAVI)
LCD............	Logistics Communications Division [Military]
LCD............	London College of Divinity
LCD............	London Dumping Convention (SAUO)
LCD............	Lord Chancellor's Department [British]
LCD............	Loss of Cell Delineation (MLOA)
LCD............	Loss of Clock Detector
LCD............	Louis Trichardt [South Africa] [Airport symbol] (OAG)
LCD............	Low Calorie Diet (MELL)
LCD............	Low Cost Drifter [Marine science] (OSRA)
LCD............	Lowest Common Denominator (GOBB)
lcd	Lowest Common Denominator
LCD............	Lumped Constant Dispersion
LCD............	Ohio Lower Court Decisions [A publication] (DLA)
LCDB	Land Cover Database (SAUO)
LCDC	Laboratory Centre for Disease Control [Canada]
LCDC	Land Conservation and Development (SAUO)
LCDC	Land Conservation District Committee (SAUO)
LCDC	Licensed Chemical Dependency Counselor (NUJO)
LCDD	Light Chain Deposition Disease [Medicine] (DMAA)
LCDDS	Leased Circuit Digital Data Service [British Telecom] (EECA)
LCDHWIU	Laundry, Cleaning, and Dye House Workers' International Union [Later, Textile Processors, Service Trades, Health Care, Professional, and Technical Employees International Union] (EA)
LCDLVC	Library of Congress Digital Library Visiotrs' Center (WDAA)
LCDM..........	Large Component Development Management (SAUO)

LCDM..........	Life-Cycle Document Management (SAUO)
LCDM..........	Low Collateral-Damage Munitions (SAUS)
LCDN	Last Called Directory Number (ROAS)
LCDOSEM	Local Civil Defense Operating Systems Evaluation Model (PDAA)
LCDP	Local Career Development Panels (HEAS)
LCDR	Lieutenant Commander (AAG)
LCdr...........	Lieutenant-Commander (SAUO)
LCDR	London, Chatham & Dover Railway [British]
LCDS	Lefschetz Center for Dynamical Systems [Brown University] [Research center] (RCD)
LCDS	Liquid-Crystal Displays [Computer science]
LCDS	Low-Cost Development System [National Semiconductor Corp.]
LCDT	London Contemporary Dance Theatre [Defunct]
LCDTL.........	Load-Compensated Diode Transistor Logic [Computer science]
LCDTL.........	Low Current Diode Transistor Logic [Electronics] (IAA)
LCE............	La Ceiba [Honduras] [Airport symbol] (OAG)
LCE............	Lance (WGA)
LCE............	Land-Covered Earth (OA)
LCE............	Landing Craft, Emergency Repair
LCE............	Latest Cost Estimate (NATG)
LCE............	Launch Complex Engineer [NASA] (KSC)
LCE............	Launch Complex Equipment
LCE............	Launch Control Equipment (AAG)
LCE............	Launch Countdown Exercise [NASA] (AFM)
LCE............	Left Center Entrance [Theater] (WDMC)
LCE............	Legal Counsel for the Elderly (EA)
LCE............	Licentiate in Civil Engineering (WDAA)
LCE............	Life Cycle Energy
LCE............	Load-Carrying Equipment (MCD)
LCE............	Load Circuit Efficiency
LCE............	Logistic Capability Estimate (MCD)
LCE............	Logistics Capability Estimator (COE)
LCE............	London Commodity Exchange (NUMA)
LCE............	Lone Star Cement Corp. (SAUO)
LCE............	Lone Star Indus [NYSE symbol] (TTSB)
LCE............	Lone Star Industries, Inc. [Formerly, Lone Star Cement Corp.] [NYSE symbol] (SPSG)
LCE............	Low-Cost Expendable [Refers to payload type] [NASA]
LCE............	Lyapunov Characteristic Exponent [Mathematics]
LCE.WS	Lone Star Indus Wrrt [NYSE symbol] (TTSB)
LCEA..........	Licentiate of the Association of Cost and Executive Accountants [British] (DBQ)
LCEAPL.......	Lawyers Committee for the Enforcement of Animal Protection Law (EA)
LCEB	Launch Control Equipment Building (AFM)
LCEBM........	Liaison Committee of European Bicycle Manufacturers [Belgium] (EAIO)
LCEC	Liquid Chromatographs with Electrochemical Detection
LCED	Low-Cost Encryption Device [Military] (GFGA)
LCEE	Louisiana Council on Economic Education (EDAC)
LCEE	Low Cost Emplacement Excavator (SAUS)
LCEECSTI....	Liaison Committee of the European Economic Community Steel Tube Industry [Defunct] (EAIO)
LCEHV	Low-Cost Expendable Harassment Vehicle [Air Force] (MCD)
LCEM..........	Leading Control Electrical Mechanic [British military] (DMA)
LCEMD........	Low Cost Expendable Mine Destructor (SAUS)
LCEMM........	Liaison Committee of European Motorcycle Manufacturers [Belgium] (EAIO)
LCEOP	Landing Craft, Engine Overhaul Parties
LCEP..........	Lower Critical End Points [Supercritical extraction]
LCEPS.........	Labor Cooperative Educational and Publishing Society [Defunct] (EA)
LC Eq	White and Tudor's Leading Cases in Equity [A publication] (DLA)
LCER..........	Labour Campaign Electoral Reform [British] [An association] (DBA)
LCES..........	Least Cost Estimating and Scheduling (IAA)
LCES..........	Lightweight Communications Equipment Subsystem (ACAE)
LCETB........	Linen and Cotton Embroidery Trade Board (SAUO)
LCEWS........	Low-Cost Electronic Warfare Suite (NVT)
LCF............	Labour Co-operative Farms (SAUO)
LCF............	Landing Craft, Flak
LCF............	Language Central Facility [Computer science] (IEEE)
LCF............	Large Core Fibre (SAUS)
LCF............	Last Chance Filter (MCD)
LCF............	Last Chance Forever (EA)
LCF............	Latent Cancer Fatalities (PDAA)
LCF............	Launch Control Facility
LCF............	Law Centres Federation [British] (DBA)
LCF............	Lawyers Christian Fellowship (EA)
LCF............	Learning Curve Factor
LCF............	Least [or Lowest] Common Factor [Mathematics]
LCF............	Least Cost Feed Formulation System (ADA)
LCF............	Lederberg-Coxeter-Frucht [Notation] [Graph theory, mathematics]
LCF............	Left Circumflex Artery [Anatomy]
LCF............	Left Common Femoral [Artery] [Anatomy] (DAVI)
LCF............	Leonard Cheshire Foundation (WDAA)
LCF............	Level Control Function [Computer science]
LCF............	Librarians' Christian Fellowship [British] (DBA)
LCF............	Library of Congress Films [Source file] [UTLAS symbol]
LCF............	Lime, Cement, and Flyash (PDAA)
LCF............	Lincomycin Cosynthetic Factor [Biochemistry]
LCF............	Liquid, Complex Fertilizer (PDAA)
LCF............	Little City Foundation (EA)
LCF............	Living Church Foundation (EA)
LCF............	Local area network File System (SAUO)
LCF............	Local Control Facility [FAA] (TAG)

LCF	Local Cycle Fatigue (IEEE)
LCF	Log Cabin Federation (EA)
LCF	Logical Channel Fill
LCF	London College of Fashion [England] (WDAA)
LCF	Longitudinal Centre of Flotation (SAUO)
LCF	Longitudinal Position of Center of Flotation
LCF	Low Cab Forward [Truck configuration]
LCF	Low-Carbon Ferrochrome [Metallurgy]
LCF	Low Coefficient of Friction [Aerodynamics]
LCF	Low-Cycle Fatigue [Rocket engine]
LCF	Lymphocyte Chemoattractant Factor [Biochemistry]
LCFA	Lithuanian Catholic Federation Ateitis (EA)
LCFA	Long-Chain Fatty Acids [Organic chemistry]
LCFA	Lower California Fisheries Association (SAUO)
LCFC	Launch Complex Facility Console [NASA] (IAA)
LCFC	Leslie Charleson Fan Club (EA)
LCFC	Linear Combination of Fragment Configuration (DB)
LCFC	Living Colour Fan Club (EA)
LCFC	Lou Christie Official Fan Club (EA)
LCFC	Low-Cycle Fatigue Counter (PDAA)
LCFDU	Laser Countermeasure Frequency Double Unit (ACAE)
LC(FF)	Landing Craft, Infantry (Flotilla Flagship) [Navy symbol]
LCFIX	Lord Abbett: Cal. Tax-Free Inc. Cl.A [Mutual fund ticker symbol] (SG)
LCFLOLS	Laterally Compounded Fresnel Lens Optical Landing System
LCFLOTSPAC	Landing Craft, Flotilla, Pacific Fleet
LCFNM	Lawyers' Campaign to Free Nelson Mandela [Defunct] (EA)
LCFR	Life Cycle Fuel Requirement
LCFS	Last-Come, First-Served
LCFS	Launch Control Facility Simulator [NASA] (IAA)
LCFSPR	Last Come, First Served Preemptive Resume (PDAA)
LCFU	Laboratory Configured Fire Units (MCD)
LCG	Harvard Laboratory for Computer Graphics (SAUS)
LCG	Laboratory for Computer Graphics (SAUO)
LCG	La Coruna [Spain] [Airport symbol] (OAG)
LCG	Landing Craft Gun (MCD)
LCG	Landing Craft, Gunboat
LCG	Langerhans' Cell Granule [Anatomy]
LCG	Langerhans' Cell Granulomatosis [Oncology]
LCG	Lead Computing Gyro (MCD)
LCG	Left Cerebral Ganglion [Medicine]
LCG	Leon Cerro Gordo [Mexico] [Seismograph station code, US Geological Survey] (SEIS)
LCG	Liquid-Cooled Garment [Spacesuit]
LCG	Liquid Cooling Garment (SAUS)
LCG	Load Classification Group (DA)
LCG	Loads Control Group [Prepares supplies to be airlifted] [Military]
LCG	Logistics Control Group [Air Materiel Command] (AAG)
LCG	London Capital Group (SAUO)
LCG	Longitudinal Position of Center of Gravity
LCG	Lookahead Carry Generator [Computer science] (IAA)
LCG	Low Center of Gravity [Tractor engineering]
LCG	Low-Cost Generator
LCG	Lower Courts Gazette [Ontario] [A publication] (DLA)
LCG	Wayne, NE [Location identifier] [FAA] (FAAL)
LCGB	Letzeburger Chreschtliche Gewerkschaftsbond [Confederation of Christian Trade Unions of Luxembourg]
LCGB	Locomotive Club of Great Britain (BI)
LCGF	Longitudinal Ciliated Groove of Filament
LCGI	Local Common Graphics Interface (SAUS)
LCGIL	Libera Confederazione Generale Italiana dei Lavoratori [Free Italian General Confederation of Workers]
LC/GL	Laboratory Counsel/General Law (SAUO)
LCG(L)	Landing Craft, Gun (Large)
LCG(M)	Landing Craft, Gun (Medium)
LCGMD	Library of Congress Geography and Map Division (SAUO)
LCGME	Liaison Committee on Graduate Medical Education
LCGN	Logical Channel Group Number [Telecommunications] (OSI)
LCGO	Linear Combination of Gaussian Orbitals [Atomic physics]
LCGP	Landing Craft, Group
LCG(S)	Landing Craft, Gun (Small) [British military] (DMA)
LCGS	Lead Computing Gun Sight
LCGT	Listening Comprehension Group Test
LCGT/IGS	Low-Cost Graphics Terminal/Interactive Graphics System (PDAA)
LCGU	Lead Computing Gyroscope Unit (MCD)
LCGU	Lesser Curve Gastric Ulcer (MELL)
LCGU	Local Cerebral Glucose Utilization [Biochemistry]
LCGU	Local Rates of Glucose Utilization (DB)
LCH	Lake Charles [Louisiana] [Airport symbol] (OAG)
LCH	Lake Charles, LA [Location identifier] [FAA] (FAAL)
LCH	Landing Craft Headquarters [British military] (DMA)
LCH	Landing Craft (Heavy) (ADA)
LCH	Landing Craft Hospital [British military] (DMA)
LCH	Larch Resources Ltd. [Vancouver Stock Exchange symbol]
LCH	Latch (MSA)
LCH	Launch
LCH	Launching Charging Header
LCh	Licentiate of the Institute of Chiropodists [British]
L Ch	Licentiatus Chirurgiae [Licentiate in Surgery]
LCH	Life Cycle Hypothesis [Economics]
LCH	Load Channel (IAA)
LCH	Local City Hospital (DAVI)
LCH	Logical Channel Queue [Computer science]
LCH	London Clearing House
L CH	Lord Chancellor [British] (ROG)
LCH	Lost Calls Held [Telecommunications] (NITA)

Lch	Lunch
LCH	Lynch Flying Service, Inc. [ICAO designator] (FAAC)
LCHA	Love Canal Homeowners Association (EA)
LChaMC	Louisiana Universities Marine Consortium, Chauvin, LA [Library symbol] [Library of Congress] (LCLS)
LCHC	Life Cycle Hydrocarbons
LCHE	Luton College of Higher Education (AIE)
LCHIP	Late-Cycle High Injection Pressure [Automotive fuel systems]
LCHM	Life Chemistry, Inc. (SAUO)
LCH/M/T/U/VP	Landing Craft, Heavy/Mechanised/Tank/Utility/Vehicles and Personnel (MILB)
LCHP	Local Control Hydraulic Panel
LCHQ	Local Command Headquarters [NATO] (NATG)
LCHR	Launcher (AAG)
L Chr	Law Chronicle [England] [A publication] (DLA)
LCHR	Lawyers Committee for Human Rights (EA)
LChr	Liberte Chretienne [A publication] (BJA)
L Chron	Law Chronicle [England] [A publication] (DLA)
L Chron & L Stud Mag	Law Chronicle and Law Students' Magazine [A publication] (DLA)
L Chron & L Stud Mag (NS)	Law Chronicle and Law Students' Magazine (New Series) [A publication] (DLA)
LCHS	Large Component Handling System [Nuclear energy] (NRCH)
LCHS	Lund Centre for Habitat Studies (SAUO)
LChSt	Saint Bernard Parish Library, Chalmette, LA [Library symbol] [Library of Congress] (LCLS)
LCHTF	Low-Cycle High-Temperature Fatigue [Rocket engine]
LCHU	Low Cost Home User
LCI	Laboratory of Cellular Immunology [University of Arizona] [Research center] (RCD)
LCI	Labor Cost Index
LCI	Laconia [New Hampshire] [Airport symbol] (OAG)
LCI	Laconia, NH [Location identifier] [FAA] (FAAL)
LCI	Lafarge Canada, Inc. [Toronto Stock Exchange symbol]
LCI	Landing Craft, Infantry [Obsolete]
LCI	Launch Complex Instrumentation (IAA)
LCI	Launcher Control Indicator [Missiles] (AABC)
LCI	LCI International [NYSE symbol] (SAG)
LCI	Leadership Competency Inventory [Test] (TMMY)
LCI	Learner-Centered Instruction (PDAA)
LCI	Legally Correct Interpretation [of the ABM treaty]
LCI	Life Cycle Inventory [Environmental engineering]
LCI	Liga Comunista Internacionalista [International Communist League] [Portugal] [Political party] (PPE)
LCI	Lions Clubs International (EA)
LCI	Liquid Crystal Institute [Kent State University] (PDAA)
LCI	Literary Criticism Index [A publication]
LCI	Livestock Conservation, Incorporated (SAUO)
LCI	Livestock Conservation Institute (EA)
LCI	Local Cerebral Ischemia [Medicine] (MELL)
LCI	Locus of Control Interview [Psychology]
LCI	Logical Channel Indentifier (SAUO)
LCI	Low-Cost Inertial
LCI	Lummus Crest, Inc. [Telecommunications service] (TSSD)
LCI	United States Central Intelligence Agency, McLean, VA [OCLC symbol] (OCLC)
LCI(A)	Landing Craft, Infantry (Ammunition)
LCIA	Life Cycle Impact Assessment [Recycling]
LCIA	London Court of International Arbitration
LCIB	Library of Congress. Information Bulletin [A publication]
LCIC	Leisure Concepts [NASDAQ symbol] (SAG)
LCIC	Leisure Concepts, Incorporated (SAUO)
LCICD	Liquid Crystal Induced Circular Dichroism [Spectroscopy]
LCID	Laboratory Corporate Information Directory (SAUO)
LCI(D)	Landing Craft, Infantry (Demolition) [British military] (DMA)
LCIDIV	Landing Craft, Infantry, Division
LCIE	Large Carnivore Initiative Europe (SAUO)
LCIFC	Lou Christie International Fan Club (EA)
LCIFLOT	Landing Craft, Infantry, Flotilla [Obsolete]
LCI(G)	Landing Craft, Infantry, Gunboat [Obsolete]
LCIGB	Locomotive and Carriage Institution of Great Britain and Eire (BI)
LCIGB	Locomotive and Carriage Institution of Great Britain and Ireland (SAUO)
LCIGRP	Landing Craft, Infantry, Group
LCIGS	Low-Cost Inertial Guidance Subsystem (MCD)
LCIHR	Lawyers Committee for International Human Rights (EA)
LCII	Laser Craft Industries, Incorporated (SAUO)
LCII	Laser Master International, Incorporated (SAUO)
LCI Int	LCI International [Associated Press] (SAG)
LCIL	Landing Craft, Infantry, Large [Obsolete]
LCILFLOT	Landing Craft, Infantry, Large, Flotilla [Obsolete]
LCI(M)	Landing Craft, Infantry (Medium) [British military] (DMA)
LCI(M)	Landing Craft, Infantry (Mortar Ship) [Obsolete]
LCINS	Low Cost Inertial Navigation System (SAUS)
LC Intl	LCI International [Associated Press] (SAG)
LCIOB	Licentiate of the Chartered Institute of Building [British] (DI)
LC/IP	Laboratory Counsel/Intellectual Property (SAUO)
LCIPr	LCI Intl 5% Cv Exch Pfd [NYSE symbol] (TTSB)
LCI(R)	Landing Craft, Infantry (Rocket Ship) [Obsolete]
LC/IR	Liquid Chromatography/Infrared
LCIR	London Centre of International Relations [University of Kent at Canterbury] [British]
LCI(S)	Landing Craft, Infantry (Small) [British military] (DMA)
LCIS	Library of Computer and Information Sciences (SAUO)
LCIS	Lighter Collectors' International Society [Defunct] (EA)

LCIS............	Lobular Carcinoma in Situ [Medicine] (AAMN)
LCISA..........	Lockheed Corporation International SA (SAUO)
LCISC..........	Laundry and Cleaning Industry Sports Club (SAUO)
LCJ..............	Lawyers for Civil Justice (EA)
LCJ..............	Lord Chief Justice [British]
LCJ..............	Low Cost Junction [Optical fibre equipment] (NITA)
LCJ..............	Lower Canada Jurist, Montreal [1848-91] [A publication] (DLA)
LCJC............	Lake City Junior College (SAUO)
LCJC............	Lower Columbia Junior College (SAUO)
LC Jur..........	Lower Canada Jurist [A publication] (DLA)
LCK..............	Columbus, OH [Location identifier] [FAA] (FAAL)
LCK..............	Landing Craft, Kitchen
L Ck.............	Leading Cook [British military] (DMA)
LCK..............	Legion of Christ the King [Defunct] (EA)
LCK..............	Library Construction Kit [Microsoft Corp.] [Computer science] (PCM)
LCK..............	Lock [Postal Service standard] (OPSA)
LCKR............	Locker
LCKS............	Locks
LCKY............	Lucky
LCL..............	Labor Congress of Liberia
LCL..............	Labor Congress of Liberia, Inc. (SAUO)
LCL..............	Lambert Cosine Law [Physics]
LCL..............	Landing Craft, Logistic [British military] (DMA)
LCL..............	Laser Centreline Localiser (SAUS)
LCL..............	Lateral Capsular Ligament [Medicine] (MELL)
LCL..............	Lateral Collateral Ligament [Anatomy]
LCL..............	Leading Catholic Layman
LCL..............	Lens Culinaris Lectin
Lcl...............	Less than Carload (EBF)
LCL..............	Less-than-Carload [Under 60,000 pounds]
LCL..............	Less-than-Carload Lot (DFIT)
lcl...............	Less than Carload Lots (WPI)
LCL..............	Less-than-Container Load [Shipping]
LCL..............	Levinthal-Coles-Lillie Bodies [Microbiology]
LCL..............	Liberal and Country League (SAUO)
LCL..............	Liberal Country League [Australia] (BARN)
LCL..............	Library Control Language (OA)
LCL..............	Library of Congress, Interlibrary Loan Department [UTLAS symbol]
LCL..............	Licentiate in Common Law (SAUO)
LCL..............	Licentiate of Canon Law [British]
LCL..............	Licentiate of Civil Law
LCL..............	Lifting Condensation Level [Meteorology]
LCL..............	Light Center Length
LCL..............	Limited Channel Logout
LCL..............	Linkage Control Language [Computer science] (BUR)
LCL..............	Liverpool Central Library (SAUO)
LCL..............	Local (AFM)
LCL..............	Localizer (CET)
LCL..............	Loeb Classical Library. Harvard University Press [A publication] (BJA)
LCL..............	Logical Comparative LOFAR
LCL..............	Loose Container Load [Shipping] (IMH)
LCL..............	Lot-Car Load
LCL..............	Loughborough Consultants Ltd. (SAUO)
LCL..............	Low-Capacity Link [Telecommunications] (OA)
LCL..............	Lower Confidence Limit [Statistics]
LCL..............	Lower Control Limit [QCR]
LCL..............	Lower of Cost or Market (TDOB)
LCL..............	Lumbocostal Ligament [Medicine] (MELL)
LCL..............	Lymphoblastoid Cell Line
LCL..............	Lymphocytic Leukemia (MAE)
LCL..............	Lymphocytic Lymphosarcoma [Oncology]
LCL..............	Lymphoma Cell Line [Oncology]
LCL..............	Mala Services Ltd. [British] [FAA designator] (FAAC)
LCLA............	Lutheran Church Library Association (EA)
LCLAA..........	Labor Council for Latin American Advancement (EA)
LCLC............	Large Cell Lung Carcinoma [Oncology] (DAVI)
LCLC............	Las Cumbres Learning Center (SAUO)
LCL/CI..........	Limited Calendar Life, Controlled Item
LCLD............	Laclede Steel [NASDAQ symbol] (TTSB)
LCLD............	Laclede Steel Co. [NASDAQ symbol] (SAG)
LCIi..............	Audubon Regional Library, Clinton, LA [Library symbol] [Library of Congress] (LCLS)
LCLJ............	Lower Canada Law Journal [A publication] (DLA)
LCL Jo..........	Lower Canada Law Journal [A publication] (DLA)
LCLK............	Larnaca [Cyprus] [ICAO location identifier] (ICLI)
LCLM............	Low-Cost Lightweight Missile (MCD)
LCLo............	Lethal Concentration Low [Environmental science] (COE)
LCLo............	Lethal Concentration Low (ERG)
LCLOC..........	Line Card Location (VLIE)
LCLS............	Lewis and Clark Library System [Library network]
LCLS............	Livestock Commission Levy Scheme (SAUO)
LCLSC..........	Life-Cycle Logistic Support Cost (PDAA)
LCLS-SLT......	Low Cost Low Speed-Solid Logic Technology (VLIE)
LCLU............	Landing Control Logic Unit [Aviation] (OA)
LCLV............	Liberace Club of Las Vegas (EA)
LCLV............	Lilac Chlorotic Leafspot Virus [Plant pathology]
LCLV............	Liquid-Crystal Light Valve (IEEE)
LCLV............	Low-Cost Launch Vehicle [NASA] (KSC)
LCLZR..........	Localizer (IAA)
LCM.............	Laboratory Contract Manager (MCD)
LCM.............	La Cumbre [Argentina] [Airport symbol] (AD)
LCM.............	Lagos Church Missions (SAUO)
LCM.............	Lake Champlain & Moriah Rail Road Co. [AAR code]
LCM.............	Land Combat Missile
LCM.............	Landing Craft, Mechanized [Navy symbol]
LCM.............	Landing Craft, Medium [Navy]
LCM.............	Lane Change-Merge [Automotive safety]
LCM.............	Large-Core Memory [Computer science]
LCM.............	Laser Capture Microdissection [Biochemistry]
LCM.............	LASER Cloud Mapper
LCM.............	LASER Countermeasure
LCM.............	Last Calls Meter [Telecommunications] (NITA)
LCM.............	Late Change Message [Aviation] (DA)
LCM.............	Latent Cardiomyopathy [Medicine] (STED)
LCM.............	Launch Control Monitor (MCD)
LCM.............	Launch Crew Member (AAG)
LCM.............	Lead-Coated Metal [Technical drawings]
lcm.............	Least Common Multiple (SHCU)
LCM.............	Least Common Multiple [Mathematics]
LCM.............	Least Concave Majorant [Statistics]
LCM.............	Left Costal Margin [Medicine]
LCM.............	Legis Comparativae Magister [Master of Comparative Law] [Latin] (WGA)
LCM.............	Leukocyte-Conditioned Medium [Microbiology]
LCM.............	Library of Congress Maps [Source file] [UTLAS symbol]
LCM.............	Life Cycle Management (EEVL)
LCM.............	Life Cycle Manager (MCD)
LCM.............	Lightning Creek Mines Ltd. [Vancouver Stock Exchange symbol]
LCM.............	Line Concentrator Module
LCM.............	Line Control Module [Telecommunications] (TEL)
LCM.............	Liquid Composite Molding [Plastics]
LCM.............	Liquid Crystal Module (SAUS)
LCM.............	Liquid Curing Medium
LCM.............	Little Company of Mary, Nursing Sisters [Roman Catholic religious order]
LCM.............	LOCA [Loss-of-Coolant Accident] Core Melt [Nuclear energy] (NRCH)
LCM.............	Loer, C. M., Reno NV [STAC]
LCM.............	Logical Connection Manager (VLIE)
LCM.............	Logistics Capability Model (SAUO)
LCM.............	London City Mission
LCM.............	London College of Music (ROG)
LCM.............	Longhaul Customer Modem [Telecommunications] (NITA)
LCM.............	Loose Cubic Meter (DAC)
LCM.............	Lost Circulation Material [Oil well drilling]
LCM.............	Low Cost Module (IAA)
LCM.............	Lower Costal Margin [STED]
LCM.............	Lower of Cost or Market
LCM.............	Lowest Common Multiple [Mathematics]
LCM.............	Lymphocyte Conditioned Medium [Hematology]
LCM.............	Lymphocytic Choriomeningitis [Medicine]
LCM(2)..........	Landing Craft, Mechanized, MKII [Navy symbol]
LCM(3)..........	Landing Craft, Mechanized, MKIII [Navy symbol]
LCM6...........	Landing Craft, Mechanized, MKVI [Navy symbol]
LCM8...........	Landing Craft, Mechanized, MKVIII [Navy symbol]
LCMA...........	Lightweight Cycle Manufacturers Association [British] (DBA)
LCMA...........	Longhaul Customer Modem Adapter [Telecommunications] (NITA)
LCMA...........	Lutheran Campus Ministry Association [Defunct] (EA)
LCMA...........	Lutheran Church Men of America
LC MARC......	Library of Congress Machine Readable Catalog [Washington, DC] [Bibliographic database] [Library of Congress]
LC-MARC......	Library of Congress MARC (SAUO)
LCMARC.......	Library of Congress MARC [Machine-Readable Catalog] Files (NITA)
LCMCFC.......	Liaison Committee for Mediterranean Citrus Fruit Culture [See also CLAM] [Madrid, Spain] (EAIO)
LCMCS.........	Liquid Conditioned Microclimate System [Army] (RDA)
LCMD...........	Laser Countermeasures Materials Development (ACAE)
LCMD...........	Low-Cost Motor Demonstration (MCD)
LCME...........	Large Climate-Moderating Envelope [Energy-conserving form of architecture]
LCME...........	Liaison Committee on Medical Education (EA)
LCM(G).........	Landing Craft, Mechanised (Gun) [British military] (DMA)
LCMG...........	Long-Chain Monoglyceride [Biochemistry] (MAE)
LCMH...........	Lake Charles Memorial Hospital [Lake Charles, LA]
LCMI............	Licentiate Cost and Management Institute (SAUO)
LCMI............	Licentiate of Cost and Management Institute [British]
LCML...........	Library of Congress Minimal Level Cataloguing [Source file] [UTLAS symbol]
LCML...........	Low-Capacity Microwave Link
LC(ML)C.......	Ligue Communiste (Marxiste-Leniniste) du Canada [Canadian Communist League (Marxist-Leninist)]
LCMM...........	Life-Cycle Management Model (AABC)
LCMM...........	Life Cycle Material Manager (MCD)
LCMMD........	Laser Countermeasures Material Development (ACAE)
LCMO...........	Lanthanum/Calcium/Manganese/Oxygen [Inorganic chemistry]
LCMP...........	Launcher Control and Monitoring Panel
LCMP...........	Life Cycle Management Planning [Army]
LCMP...........	Local Commandant, Military Police [British military] (DMA)
LCM-PDR.......	League of Communists of Macedonia - Party for Democratic Reform [Political party]
LCM(R).........	Landing Craft, Mechanised (Rocket) [British military] (DMA)
LCMR...........	Local Cerebral Metabolic Rate (DB)
LCMRGlc.......	Local Cerebral Metabolic Rate for Glucose [Brain research]
LCMS...........	Lake County Medical Society (SAUO)
LCMS...........	Laser Cavity Mode Spacing (ACAE)
LCMS...........	LASER Countermeasure System [Military] (INF)
LCMS...........	Launch Control and Monitoring System [NASA] (AAG)
LCMS...........	Library Collection Management System (NITA)
LCMS...........	Life-Cycle Management System

LC/MS..........	Liquid Chromatography/Mass Spectrometry
LCMS...........	Logistics Capability Measurement System (SAUO)
LCMS...........	Logistics Command Management System
LCMS...........	Longshore Case Management System [*Department of Labor*] (GFGA)
LCMS...........	Low-Cost Modular Spacecraft [*NASA*]
LCMS...........	Lutheran Church - Missouri Synod
LCMSO	Landing Craft, Material Supply Officer
LCMT...........	London Centre for Marine Technology [*British*] (IRUK)
LCMU...........	Load Current Monitoring Unit (ACAE)
LCMV...........	Lymphocytic Choriomeningitis Virus
LCMWG	Life Cycle Management Working Group (SAUO)
LC-MY	League of Communists - Movement for Yugoslavia [*Political party*]
LCN.............	Labor Collection Network (ACAE)
LCN.............	La Cosa Nostra [*Our Thing*]
LCN.............	Landing Craft, Navigation [*Obsolete*]
LCN.............	Large Co-Ops Network [*British*]
LCN.............	Lateral Cervical Nucleus (STED)
LCN.............	Left Caudate Nucleus [*Medicine*] (DMAA)
LCN.............	Liaison Change Notice
LCN.............	Library of Congress Number (MCD)
LCN.............	Lineas Aereas Canarias SA [*Spain*] [*ICAO designator*] (FAAC)
LCN.............	Linked Cluster Network [*Chemistry*]
LCN.............	Load Classification Number (AFM)
LCN.............	Local Civil Noon (ADA)
LCN.............	Local Communication Network (ACRL)
LCN.............	Local Communications Network (GAVI)
LCN.............	Local Computer Network (VLIE)
LCN.............	Local Control Network (SAUS)
LCN.............	Local Control Number (MCD)
LCN.............	Logical Channel Number [*Computer science*] (TNIG)
LCN.............	Logistics Change Notice (SAUS)
LCN.............	Logistics Control Number (MCD)
LCN.............	Loosely Coupled Network [*Telecommunications*] (OSI)
LCNA...........	Lacana Mining Corp. (SAUO)
LCNA...........	Lewis Carroll Society of North America (EA)
LC/NA	Lutherans Concerned/North America (EA)
LCNADE	Liquid-Cooled Naturally Aspirated Diesel Engine
LCNC...........	Local Cartage National Conference [*Later, LSHCNC*]
LCNC...........	Nicosia [*Cyprus*] [*ICAO location identifier*] (ICLI)
LC NGO-EC...	Liaison Committee of Development Non-Governmental Organizations to the European Communities [*Belgium*] (EAIO)
LCNI...........	Landmark Communications, Inc. (EFIS)
LCNM	Lehman Caves National Monument (SAUO)
LCNN	Land Commander Northern Norway (SAUO)
LCNN	Land Commander, North Norway [*NATO*] (NATG)
LCNP	Lawyers' Committee on Nuclear Policy (EA)
LCNP	Licentiate of the National Council of Psychotherapists [*British*]
LCNR	Liquid Core Nuclear Rocket
LCNSD	Licensed
LCNSW	Labor Council of New South Wales [*Australia*]
LCNSW	Legislative Council of New South Wales [*Australia*]
LCNT	Link Celestial Navigation Trainer
LCNTR	Location Counter [*Computer science*]
LC/NUC.......	Library of Congress and National Union Catalog Author Lists, 1942-1962 [*A publication*]
LCNVA	Low-Cost Night Vision Aid (MCD)
LCNVG	Low-Cost Night Vision Goggles (MCD)
LCNY	Linguistic Circle of New York (SAUO)
LCNYC	Lincoln Center New York City (SAUO)
LCNY/W Word...	Journal of the Linguistic Circle of New York (journ.) (SAUS)
LCO.............	Land Conservation Officer (SAUO)
LCO.............	Landing Craft Officer [*British*] (ADA)
LCO.............	Latching Contract Operate (VLIE)
LCO.............	Launch Control Officer (SAUO)
LCO.............	Launch Control Operation (MCD)
LCO.............	Launching Control Office [*or Officer*] [*Military*]
LCO.............	Lee Conservancy Office (SAUO)
LCO.............	Light Cycle Oil [*Petrochemical technology*]
LCO.............	Limiting Conditions for Operation [*Nuclear energy*] (NRCH)
LCO.............	Linea Aerea del Cobre Ltda. [*Chile*] [*ICAO designator*] (FAAC)
LCO.............	Lipo-Chitooligosaccharide [*Botany*]
LCO.............	Logistics Control Office [*Military*] (AABC)
LCO.............	London College of Osteopathy (SAUO)
LCO.............	Lord Chancellor's Office [*British*] (DLA)
LCO.............	Low Cardiac Output [*Cardiology*]
LCO.............	Lowest Cost of Ownership
LCO.............	MMC Uniform Central Number (SAUS)
LCOA...........	Logistics Control Office, Atlantic [*Military*]
LCOC	Launch Control Officer's Console (AAG)
LCOC	Lincoln and Continental Owners Club (EA)
LCOC	Lincoln Continental Owners Club (EA)
LCOCC	Atlantic [*Fleet*] Commander Operational Control Center [*Navy*]
LCOCC	Atlantic Command Operational Control Center (SAUO)
LCOCU	Landing Craft, Obstruction Clearance Unit
LCOD	Last Cutoff Date (ACAE)
LC OFC	Linear Crystal Oxygen Free Copper [*Cable component*] (NITA)
L/COH	Lance-Corporal of Horse [*British military*] (DMA)
L/Col	Lieutenant Colonel (SAUO)
LCOL	Lieutenant Colonel
LColC	Caldwell Parish Library, Columbia, LA [*Library symbol*] [*Library of Congress*] (LCLS)
LColfG	Grant Parish Library, Colfax, LA [*Library symbol*] [*Library of Congress*] (LCLS)
LCOLNT	Low Coolant
LCOM...........	Lieutenant Commander (GOBB)

LCOM...........	Local Committee Operations Manual [*A publication*] (EAAP)
LCOM...........	Logic Control Output Module (MCD)
LCOM...........	Logistics Composite Model
LCOMM.......	Library Council of Metropolitan Milwaukee [*Wisconsin*] [*Library network*]
L Comment...	Law Commentary [*A publication*] (DLA)
L Comment'y...	Law Commentary [*A publication*] (DLA)
L COMP RAM...	Licentiate in Composition, Royal Academy of Music [*British*] (ROG)
L/COMPT	Luggage Compartment [*Automotive engineering*]
LCOP	Launch Control Officer's Panel (AAG)
LCOP	Logistics Control Office, Pacific [*Military*] (AABC)
LCOR	Langley Corporation (SAUO)
LCOR	Lincoln Cosmopolitan Owners Registry [*Defunct*] (EA)
LCOR	Load Character with Offset Register (VLIE)
L-CORP	Lance-Corporal [*Military*] [*British*] (ROG)
LCOS	Launch Checkout Stations (ACAE)
LCOS	Lead Computing Optical Sight
LCOS	Limiting Conditions for Operations Specification (SAUO)
LCOS	Liquid Crystal on Silicon (AEBE)
LCOS	Low Cardiac Output Syndrome [*Medicine*] (DMAA)
LCOS	Lycos Inc. [*NASDAQ symbol*] (TTSB)
LCOSE	Launch Complex Operational Support Equipment
LCOSS	Lead Computing Optical Sighting System (MCD)
LCOSS	Lead Computing Optical Sight System (SAUS)
LCOT	Lower Critical Ordering Transition [*Polymer physics*]
LCouRR	Red River Parish Library, Coushata, LA [*Library symbol*] [*Library of Congress*] (LCLS)
LCovD..........	Delta Regional Primate Research Center, Science Information Service, Covington (SAUS)
LCovD..........	Delta Regional Primate Research Center, Science Information Service, Covington, LA [*Library symbol*] [*Library of Congress*] (LCLS)
LCovSt........	Saint Tammany Parish Library, Covington, LA [*Library symbol*] [*Library of Congress*] (LCLS)
LCP.............	Galbraith Lake Camp, AK [*Location identifier*] [*FAA*] (FAAL)
LCP.............	Landing Craft, Personnel
LCP.............	Language Conversion Program [*Computer science*] (BUR)
LCP.............	Large Coil Program [*Physics*]
LCP.............	Large Computer Project (IAA)
LCP.............	Last Card Program Start (IAA)
LCP.............	Last Complete Program (WDAA)
LCP.............	Lateral Choroid Plexus (PDAA)
LCP.............	Launch Control Panel
LCP.............	Launch Control Post (MCD)
LCP.............	Laws for Construction of Programs (MHDB)
LCP.............	Lawyers Co-Operative Publishing Co. [*Rochester, NY*]
LCP.............	Leader, Company Procurement [*Military*] (AFIT)
LCP.............	League of Canadian Poets [*Canada*] (EAIO)
LCP.............	Left Circular Polarization
LCP.............	Left-Handed Circular Polarization (VLIE)
L-C-P..........	Leg-Calve-Perthes Disease [*Medicine*]
LCP.............	Legg-Calve-Perthes [*Disease*] [*Medicine*] (DB)
LCP.............	Legislative Council for Photogrammetry [*Later, MAPPS*] (EA)
LCP.............	Lehndorff Canadian Prop. [*Limited Partnership Units*] [*Toronto Stock Exchange symbol*]
LCP.............	Letter Carrier Presort [*Canadian postal term*] (NFD)
LCP.............	Liberal and Country Party (SAUO)
LCP.............	Liberal Country Party [*Australia*] (BARN)
LCP.............	Library Company of Philadelphia (SAUO)
LCP.............	Licensed Clinical Psychologist
LCP.............	Licentiate of the College of Preceptors [*British*]
LCP.............	Light Compact Performance [*Filtration systems*] [*Automotive engineering*]
LCP.............	Link Control Procedure [*Telecommunications*]
LCP.............	Link Control Protocol [*Telecommunications*] (ACRL)
LCP.............	Liquid-Crystal Polymer [*Organic chemistry*]
LCP.............	Liquid Cyclone Process [*for making high-protein edible cottonseed flour*]
LCP.............	Little Computer Person [*Activision computer game*]
LCP.............	Liverpool Court of Passage (SAUO)
LCP.............	Load Cell Platform
LCP.............	Loading Control Program (IAA)
LCP.............	Local Calibration Procedure
LCP.............	Local Coastal Program (SAUO)
LCP.............	Local Collaborative Projects [*Between business and education*] [*British*]
LCP.............	Local Contigency Plan (SAUO)
LCP.............	Local Control Panel (CAAL)
LCP.............	Local Control Point [*Telecommunications*] (TEL)
LCP.............	Location Characterization Plan (SAUO)
LCP.............	Loews Cineplex Entertain't. [*NYSE symbol*] (SG)
LCP.............	Logistic Capability Plan [*Navy*]
LCP.............	London College of Printing
LCP.............	Long-Chain Polysaturated Fatty Acid [*Biochemistry*] (MAE)
LCP.............	Lost Cause Press, Louisville, KY [*Library symbol*] [*Library of Congress*] (LCLS)
LCP.............	Low-Calcium Pyroxene [*Mineralogy*]
LCP.............	Low-Cost Production (WDAA)
LCP.............	Lower Control Panel [*Automotive engineering*]
LCP.............	Lower Cost Processor (MCD)
LCPA...........	Lymphocyte Cytosol Polypeptide [*Medicine*] (DMAA)
LCPA...........	Lincoln Center for the Performing Arts (EA)
LC-PAD	Liquid Chromatography plus Pulsed Amperometric Detection [*Analytical chemistry*]

LCP & SA .... Licentiate of Physicians and Surgeons of America
LCP&SA........ Licentiate of the College of Physicians and Surgeons of America (SAUO)
LCP&SO....... Licentiate of the College of Physicians and Surgeons of Ontario (SAUO)
LCPC............ Lancashire and Cheshire Provincial Council (SAUO)
LCPC............ Liquid Cyclone Processed Cottonseed Flour
LCPC............ Low-Cost-to-Produce Classifier (MCD)
LCP-FY........ Logistic Capability Plan - Fiscal Year [Navy] (NG)
LCPG........... Logic Clock Pulse Generator [Computer science]
LCPH .... Paphos [Cyprus] [ICAO location identifier] (ICLI)
LCPIS.......... Low-Cost Propulsion Integration Study (MCD)
LCPL............ Lance Corporal
L/Cpl........... Lance-Corporal (WDAA)
LCPL............ Landing Craft, Personnel, Large [Navy symbol]
LCPL............ Left Circularly Polarized Light
LCPL............ Leon-Jefferson Library System [Library network]
LCPLR.......... Landing Craft, Personnel Leader
LCP(M)........ Landing Craft, Personnel (Medium)
LCP(N)......... Landing Craft, Personnel (Nested) [Obsolete]
LCPO........... Leading Chief Petty Officer (DNAB)
LCPP........... Land Capability Planning Program (SAUO)
LCP(P).......... Landing Craft, Personnel (Plastic)
LCPR........... Landing Craft, Personnel, Ramped [Navy symbol]
LCPRC......... Liquid Crystalline Polymer Research Center [University of Connecticut] [Research center] (RCD)
LCP(S)......... Landing Craft, Personnel (Small) [British military] (DMA)
LCPS........... Large Cloud Particle-Size Spectrometer
LCPS........... Licentiate of the College of Physicians and Surgeons [British]
LCPS........... Lithuanian Catholic Press Society (EA)
LCPS........... London Carthorse Parade Society (SAUO)
LCP(SY)....... Landing Craft, Personnel (Survey)
LCPT........... Lightweight Collapsible Pillolo Tank
LCPTT.......... Low-Cost Part Task Trainer (MCD)
LCP(U)......... Landing Craft, Personnel (Utility) [British military] (DMA)
LCPUFA ...... Long-Chain Polyunsaturated Fatty Acids
LCPVC........ Life Cycle Present Value Costs (SAUO)
LCQ............. Launch Crew Quarters (AFM)
LCQ............. Learning Climate Questionnaire [Medicine] (DMAA)
LCQ............. Liquid Crystal Quartz (WGA)
LCQ............. Logical Channel Queue [Computer science] (BUR)
LCR............. Inductance-Capacitance-Resistance (CET)
LCR............. La Lucha [Costa Rica] [Seismograph station code, US Geological Survey] (SEIS)
LCR............. Landcare Research Limited Lease (SAUO)
LCR............. Land Compensation Reports [A publication] (ILCA)
LCR............. Landing Craft, Raiding [British]
LCR............. Landing Craft, Rocket [British military] (DMA)
LCR............. Landing Craft, Rubber
LCR............. Las Cruces, NM [Location identifier] [FAA] (FAAL)
LCR............. Late Cutaneous Reaction [Immunology]
LCR............. Launch Control Rack (ACAE)
LCR............. Launch Control Room (MCD)
LCR............. Least-Cost Routing [Telecommunications]
LCr............. Letter of Credit
L/CR........... Lettre de Credit [Letter of Credit] [French]
LCR............. Leurocristine [Oncovin, Vincristine] [Also, O, V, VC, VCR] [Antineoplastic drug]
LCR............. Level Crossing Rate (IAA)
LCR............. Level Crossing Resonance [Physical chemistry]
LCR............. Libyan Arab Company for Air Cargo [ICAO designator] (FAAC)
LCr............. Lieutenant Commander [Navy] [British]
LCR............. Ligase Chain Reaction [Genetics]
LCR............. Light Chopping Reticle
LCR............. Ligue Communiste Revolutionnaire [Revolutionary Communist League] [France] [Political party] (PPW)
LCR............. Limit Control Register [Navy Navigation Satellite System] (DNAB)
LCR............. Liquid Chromatographic Reactor
LCR............. Liquide Cephalo-Rachidien [Cerebrospinal Fluid] [French]
LCR............. Liquido Cefaloraquideo [Cerebrospinal Fluid] [Spanish]
LCR............. Load Complement Register (IAA)
LCR............. Local Content Requirement (JAGO)
LCR............. Locus Control Region [Genetics]
LCR............. Logarithmic Correlators Ratiometer (PDAA)
LCR............. Log Cabin Republicans (EA)
LCR............. Log Count Rate [Nuclear energy] (NRCH)
LCR............. Logistic Change Report [Military] (AFM)
LCR............. London & Continental Railways Ltd.
LCR............. Low Compression Ratio [Automotive engineering] (IAA)
LCR............. Low Cost Range
LCR............. Low-Cost Reusable [Refers to payload type] [NASA]
LCR............. Low Count Range [Nuclear energy] (NUCP)
LCR............. Low Cross Range
LCR............. Lower Canada Reports [A publication] (DLA)
LCR............. Lower Circulating Reflux [Chemical engineering]
LCR............. Lowest Current Rate (RIMS)
LCR............. Low Pass Coaxial Relay (ACAE)
LCR............. Lucero Resources Corp. [Vancouver Stock Exchange symbol]
LCR............. Lung Configuration Recorder
LCR............. Lutheran Churches of the Reformation
LCrA........... Acadia Parish Library, Crowley, LA [Library symbol] [Library of Congress] (LCLS)
LCRA........... Akrotiri [Cyprus] [ICAO location identifier] (ICLI)
LCRA........... Labour Cost Research Associates Ltd. [British] (ECON)
LCRA........... Lithuanian Catholic Religious Aid (EA)

LCRA .... Lower Colorado River Authority
LCRC .... Lake Champlain Research Consortium [Marine science] (OSRA)
LCRC .... Laotian Cultural and Research Center (EA)
LCRC .... Lenawee County Railroad Co., Inc. [AAR code]
LCRC .... Lenawee County Railroad Company, Inc. (SAUO)
LCRDP .... Laboratory/Campus Research and Development Program (SAUO)
LCRE .... Lithium Cooled Reactor Experiment
LC Rep S Qu... Lower Canada Seignorial Questions Reports [A publication] (DLA)
LCRES .... Letter Carrier Route Evaluation System [Postal Service]
LCRF .... L'Association Canadienne des Ludotheques et des Centres de Ressources pour la Famille [Canadian Association of Toy Libraries and Parent Resource Centers] [See also TLRC] (EAIO)
LCRI........... Library of Congress Rule Interpretations [A publication]
LCRIS .... Loop Cable Record Inventory System (MCD)
LCR(L)......... Landing Craft, Rubber (Large) [Obsolete]
LCRL .... Lewis and Clark Regional Library [Library network]
LCRM.......... Launch Control Room (AAG)
LCRM.......... Linear Count Rate Meter (NRCH)
LCRO.......... Episkopi [Cyprus] [ICAO location identifier] (ICLI)
LCRO.......... Linear Combination of Rydberg Orbitals [Atomic physics]
LCRO.......... Low Cross-Range Orbiter (KSC)
LCRPM .... Large-Capacity Reciprocating Pultrusion Machine [Plastics]
LCR(R)......... Landing Craft, Rubber (Rocket)
LCRR .... Low-Cost Risk Reduction (PDAA)
LCRR .... Nicosia [Cyprus] [ICAO location identifier] (ICLI)
Lcrs .... Lancers (SAUO)
LCR(S)......... Landing Craft, Rubber (Small) [Obsolete]
LCRS .... Leachate Collection and Removal System (SAUO)
LCRS .... Leachate Control and Removal System [Environmental science] (COE)
LCRS .... Low-Cost Readout Station [NASA]
LCRSMEEC... Liaison Committee of the Rice Starch Manufacturers of the EEC [Belgium] (EAIO)
LCRT .... Lincoln Center Repertory Theater (SAUO)
LCRT .... Low-Contrast Resolution Test [Optics]
LCRU .... Landing Craft, Recovery Unit
LCRU .... Lunar Communications Relay Unit [Apollo] [NASA]
LCRV .... Length of Curve (MSA)
LCRY .... LeCroy Corp. [NASDAQ symbol] (SAG)
LCS .... Ann Arbor Laboratory Computer System (SAUS)
LCS .... Laboratory-Certifying Scientist [Analytical chemistry]
LCS .... Laboratory Computer System (SAUO)
LCS .... Laboratory Control Sample (ABAC)
LCS .... Laboratory for Computational Statistics [Stanford University] (PDAA)
LCS .... Laboratory for Computer Science [Massachusetts Institute of Technology] [Research center] (RCD)
LCS .... Labor Collection System (TIMI)
LCS .... Lancaster Resources [Vancouver Stock Exchange symbol]
LCS .... Land Combat System
LCS .... Landing Craft, Support
LCS .... Landsat Customer Services (SAUO)
LCS .... Lane Control Signal
LCS .... Large Capacity [or Core] Storage [Computer science]
LCS .... Large Core Storage [Computer science] (OA)
LCS .... Laser Communications Subsystem (SAUS)
LCS .... LASER Communications System
LCS .... Laser Cross Section (ACAE)
LCS .... LASER Crosswind System (RDA)
LCS .... Last Cast Syndrome [Fictitious fishing malady]
LCS .... Lateral Channel Stop (IAA)
LCS .... Lateral Control System (MUGU)
LCS .... Lathe Control System
LCS .... Launch Complex Set
LCS .... Launch Control Sequence (AAG)
LCS .... Launch Control Shelter (ACAE)
LCS .... Launch Control Simulator
LCS .... Launch Control Station
LCS .... Launch Control System [or Subsystem]
LCS .... Law of Corresponding States [Physics]
LCS .... LCS Industries, Inc. [Associated Press] (SAG)
LCS .... League Championship Series [Baseball]
LCS .... Leakage Collection System [Nuclear energy] (NRCH)
LCS .... Leak Control System [Nuclear energy] (NRCH)
LCS .... Learning Classifier System [Computer science]
LCS .... Leveling Control System
LCS .... Liaison Call Sheet
LCS .... Library Call Society (SAUO)
LCS .... Library Cat Society (EA)
LCS .... Library Circulation System (SAUO)
LCS .... Library Computer System [University of Illinois] [Library network]
LCS .... Library Control System [Ohio State Library] [Columbus] [Information service or system] (IID)
LCS .... Lichen Chronicus Simplex [Dermatology] (DAVI)
LCS .... Life Care Services
LCS .... Life Cycle Support (SAUO)
LCS .... Life-Cycle Survivability (MSA)
LCS .... Light Cruiser Squadron [British military] (DMA)
LCS .... Limiting Control Settings (SAUO)
LCS .... Lincoln Calibration Sphere
LCS .... Linear Collision Sequence (MCD)
LCS .... Line Coding Storage
LCS .... Link Control Station [Telecommunications] (ECII)
LCS .... Linked Cross Sectional (PDAA)
LCS .... Linux Compatibility Standard (SAUS)
LCS .... Liquid Controlled Solid (KSC)

LCS............	Liquid Cooling System
LCS............	Liquid Crystal Shutter [Epson] [Printer technology]
LCS............	List of Command Signals (MCD)
LCS............	Lithuanian Cultural Society [Defunct] (EA)
LCS............	Litton Computer Services [Information service or system] (IID)
LCS............	Lladro Collectors Society (EA)
LCS............	Loadable Control Storage [Computer science] (NITA)
LCS............	Local Communications Services [British]
LCS............	London Controlling Section [British military] (DMA)
LCS............	Loop Control System [Nuclear energy] (NRCH)
LCS............	LOPO [Local Post] Collectors Society (EA)
LCS............	Lottery Collectors Society (EA)
LCS............	Loudness Contour Selector
LCS............	Low Constant [or Continuous] Suction [Surgical procedure] (DAVI)
LCS............	Low-Cost LASER Seeker (MCD)
LCS............	Low Cost Seeker (SAUS)
LCS............	Low-Cost Sonobuoy (DOMA)
LCS............	Lyon Court, Scotland (SAUO)
LCS............	Region 10 Library Circulation System (SAUS)
LCS............	Statewide Library Computer System [University of Illinois] [Information service or system] (IID)
LCSA..........	Legislative Council of South Australia
LCSA..........	Lewis and Clark Society of America (EA)
LCSA..........	Lotteries Commission of South Australia
LC Sales......	Langdell's Cases on the Law of Sales [A publication] (DLA)
LCSB..........	Launch Control Support Building [Missiles]
LCSC..........	Legislative Council Select Committee (SAUO)
LCSC..........	London Child Study Centre (SAUO)
LCSCU........	Launch Coolant System Control Unit (AAG)
LCSD..........	Laminate Chip Signal Diode (SAUS)
LC-SDP.......	League of Communists-Social Democratic Party [Bosnia-Hercegovina] [Political party] (BUAC)
LCSE..........	LASER Communication Satellite Experiment [NASA]
LCSE..........	Life-Cycle Software Engineering [Army] (RDA)
LCSEC........	Life-Cycle Software Engineering Center [Army]
LCSEFE.......	Labor Committee for Safe Energy and Full Employment [Defunct] (EA)
LCSFP........	Low Cerebrospinal Fluid Pressure [Medicine] (MELL)
LCSG..........	London Construction Safety Group (SAUO)
LCSG..........	Lung Cancer Study Group (ADWA)
LC/SG.........	Scientific Group (SAUO)
LCSH..........	Library of Congress National Union Catalogue Subject Headings (TELE)
LCSH..........	Library of Congress Subject Headings [Formerly, SHDC] [A publication]
LCSI..........	Launch Critical Support Items [NASA] (KSC)
LCSI..........	LCS Industries [NASDAQ symbol] (SAG)
LCSI..........	Licentiate of the Construction Surveyors' Institute [British] (DBQ)
LCSI..........	Logistic Control Shipping Instruction (AAG)
LCSIE.........	Liquid-Cooled Spark Ignition Engine
LCS/IS........	Local Communications Services/Information Services (NITA)
LCS(L)........	Landing Craft, Support (Large) [Obsolete]
LCSLT........	Low-Cost Solid Logic Technology (IAA)
LCS(M).......	Landing Craft, Support (Medium)
LCSM.........	Launch Control and Status Monitor
LCSMM.......	Life-Cycle Systems Management Model
LCSN.........	Local Circuit Switched Network
LCSO.........	Launch Complex Safety Officer (IAA)
LCSO.........	Launch Control Safety Officer (MCD)
LCSO.........	Local Communications Service Order
LCSO.........	Low-Cost Systems Office [NASA] (PDAA)
LCSP..........	Logical Channels Switching Program (MHDB)
LCSP..........	London and Counties Society for Psychologists (SAUO)
LCS-PDR.....	League of Communists of Slovenia - Party of Democratic Reform [Political party]
LCSPL........	Launch Critical Spare Parts List [NASA] (KSC)
LCSR.........	Laboratory for Computer Science Research [Rutgers University] [Research center] (RCD)
LCS(R).......	Landing Craft, Support (Rocket)
LCSR.........	Landing Craft, Swimmer Reconnaissance [Navy symbol]
LCSR.........	Large Caliber Soft Recoil [Weaponry] (MCD)
LCSR(L)......	Landing Craft, Swimmer Recovery (Light) [Navy symbol] (NVT)
LCSRM.......	Loop Current Step Response Method (IEEE)
LCSS..........	Land Combat Support Set (NATG)
LCSS..........	Land Combat Support System (DWSG)
LCSS..........	Land Combat System Study (AFIT)
LCS(S)........	Landing Craft, Support (Small), MKI [Navy symbol] [Obsolete]
LCSS..........	Launch Control and Sequencer System
LCSS..........	Launch Control System Simulator [NASA] (IAA)
LCSS..........	Life Cycle Software Support
LCSS..........	Lightweight Camouflage Screen System (MCD)
LCSs..........	Local Conservation Strategies (SAUO)
LCSS..........	London Council of Social Service
LCSS..........	Low Cost Sonobuoy System (SAUS)
LCSSAP......	Low-Cost Silicon Solar Array Project
LCSSC........	Life-Cycle Software Support Center [Army]
LCSSE........	Life-Cycle Software Support Environment [Army]
LCSSP........	Laboratory of Chemical and Solid-State Physics [MIT] (MCD)
LCSSP........	Laboratory of Chemistry and Solid-State Physics (SAUO)
LCST..........	Licentiate of the College of Speech Therapists [British]
LCST..........	Lower Critical-Solution-Temperature
LCSU..........	Lao Civil Servants' Union
LCSU..........	Local Concentrator Switching Unit [Telecommunications] (TEL)
LCSVF........	Logistics Combat Support Vehicle Family (MCD)
LCSW.........	Latch Checking Switch (MSA)
LCSW.........	Licensed Clinical Social Worker [Medicine]
LCT............	Landing Craft, Tank [Navy symbol]
LCT............	Laplace-Carson Transform [Mathematics]
LCT............	Last Card Total (IAA)
LCT............	Last Compliance Time
LCT............	Latest Closing Time
LCT............	Launch Control Trailer
LCT............	Launch Countdown [NASA] (NASA)
L Ct...........	Law Court (DLA)
LCT............	Legislative Council of Tasmania [Australia]
LCT............	Lencourt Ltd. [Toronto Stock Exchange symbol]
LCT............	Less than Truckload Lot [Under 24,000 pounds] (MHDW)
LCT............	Licensing Commission of Tasmania [Australia]
LCT............	Life Component Tester
LCT............	Light Capital Technology (PDAA)
LCT............	Light Crawler Tractor (SAUS)
LCT............	Ligue Communiste des Travailleurs [Communist Workers' League] [Senegal] [Political party] (PPW)
LCT............	Linear Combination Technique [Nuclear science] (OA)
LCT............	Linkage Control Table [Telecommunications] (IAA)
LCT............	Liquid Crystal Thermography
LCT............	Listening Comprehension Test (TES)
LCT............	Liver Cell Tumor [Medicine] (DMAA)
LCT............	Local Civil Time
LCT............	Local Correlation-Tracking [Instrumental technique]
LCT............	Locate (MSA)
LCT............	Location, Command, and Telemetry (IAA)
LCT............	Locust (MSA)
LCT............	Logical Channel Termination
LCT............	Long Calcined Ton [Bauxite, etc.]
LCT............	Long-Chain Triglyceride [Biochemistry]
LCT............	Loughborough College of Technology (SAUO)
LCT............	Louis Comfort Tiffany [Signature on the art glass designed by Tiffany]
LCT............	Low Cervical Transverse [Position] [Obstetrics] (DAVI)
LCT............	Low-Cost Technology (PDAA)
LCT............	Low Cost Terminal [Telecommunications] (LAIN)
LCT............	Luscher Color Test [Psychology] (DAVI)
LCT............	Lymphocytotoxicity [Medicine] (DMAA)
LCT............	Lymphocytotoxicity Test [Hematology]
LCT-1.........	Lunar Cycle Test One [Aerospace]
LCTA..........	Land Condition-Trend Analysis [Army] (RDA)
LCT(A)........	Landing Craft, Tank (Armored)
LCTA..........	London Corn Trade Association
LCTA..........	Lungs Clear to Auscultation (SAUS)
LCTA..........	Lymphocytotoxic Antibodies [Immunochemistry]
LCTB..........	Launch Control Training Building [NASA] (IAA)
LC/TC.........	Livonia Career/Technical Center
LCTCDE......	Liquid-Cooled Turbocharged Diesel Engine
LCTD..........	Located (AFM)
LCTF..........	Large Coil Test Facility (MCD)
LCTF..........	Lloyd's Canadian Trust Fund (AIA)
LCTGM.......	Library of Congress Thesaurus for Graphic Materials (TELE)
LCT(H)........	Landing Craft, Tank (Hospital) [British military] (DMA)
LCTHF........	Lewis and Clark Trail Heritage Foundation (EA)
LCTI..........	Large Components Test Installation [Nuclear energy] (NRCH)
LCTL..........	Large Component Test Loop [Nuclear energy]
LCTLs........	Less Commonly Taught Languages
LCTMP.......	Little Change in Temperature [NWS] (FAAC)
LCTN.........	Location
LCTP..........	Launcher Control Test Panel
LCT(R)........	Landing Craft, Tank (Rocket)
LCTR.........	Locator
LCTS..........	Lagos City Transport Services (SAUO)
LCT(S)........	Landing Craft, Tank (Slow)
LCTS..........	LASER Coherence Techniques Section
LCTSU........	Launch Control Transfer Switching Unit [Aerospace] (AAG)
LCTT..........	Launch Complex Telemetry Trailer
LCTT..........	Low-Cost Tow Target (SAUS)
LCTV..........	Liquid Crystal Television (CIST)
LCU...........	Lac-Coated Urea Fertilizer
LCU...........	Lancashire Congregational Union (SAUO)
LCU...........	LAN CID Utility (SAUS)
LCU...........	Landing Craft, Utility [Navy symbol]
LCU...........	Large Close-Up (ADA)
LCU...........	Laser Coding Unit (ACAE)
LCU...........	LASER Cooling Unit (MCD)
LCU...........	Last Cluster Used (VLIE)
LCU...........	Launch Control Unit (MCD)
LCU...........	Level Converter Unit [Computer science] (CIST)
LCU...........	Library of Congress Music [Source file] [UTLAS symbol]
LCU...........	Life Change Unit [Psychometrics]
LCU...........	Lightweight Computer Unit [Computer science] (CIST)
LCU...........	Line Control Unit [Data communications]
LCU...........	Line Converter Unit (ACAE)
LCU...........	Line Coupling Unit (NASA)
LCU...........	Link Control Unit [Telecommunications] (TEL)
LCU...........	Local Control Unit (IAA)
LCU...........	London Congregational Union (SAUO)
LCU...........	Loop Control Unit [Computer science] (ELAL)
LCU...........	Lower Control Unit (WDAA)
LCU...........	Loyal Citizens of Ulster (SAUO)
LCU...........	Lucin, UT [Location identifier] [FAA] (FAAL)
LCUC.........	Letter Carriers' Union of Canada
LCuC.........	Liver Copper Concentration [Physiology]

LCUG	Liquid-Cooled Undergarment (MCD)
LCUG	Liquid Cooling under Garment (SAUS)
LCUP	Least Cost Utility Planning (SAUO)
LCUSA	Ladies of Charity of the United States of America [*An association*] (EA)
LC/USA	Lutheran Council in the USA [*Defunct*] (EA)
LCUT	Lifetime Hoan [*NASDAQ symbol*] (TTSB)
LCUT	Lifetime Hoan Corp. [*NASDAQ symbol*] (SAG)
LCV	Labor Cost Variance (ACAE)
LCV	La Cueva [*New Mexico*] [*Seismograph station code, US Geological Survey*] (SEIS)
LCV	Landing Craft, Vehicle [*Navy symbol*]
LCV	Large Compound Vesicle [*Biochemistry*]
LCV	LASER Compatible Vidicon
LCV	League of Conservation Voters (EA)
LCV	Legislative Council of Victoria [*Australia*]
LCV	Level Control Valve (MCD)
LCV	Licentiate of the College of Violinists (SAUO)
LCV	Light Commercial Vehicle
LCV	Light Contingency Vehicle (SAUS)
LCV	Line Coding Violation (SAUS)
LCV	Llymphocryptovirus
LCV	Load Control Valve [*Engineering*]
LCV	Local Control Valve [*Nuclear energy*] (NRCH)
LCV	Longer Combination Vehicle [*Trucks hauling multiple trailers*]
LCV	Lorry Command Vehicle [*British military*] (DMA)
LCV	Lorry Company Vehicle (SAUO)
LCV	Low Calorific Value [*of a fuel*]
LCV	Low Cervical Vertical [*Incision*] [*Obstetrics*] (DAVI)
LCV	Low Cost Visual (ACAE)
LCV	Low-Cost Visual (SAUS)
LCV	Lymphocytic Choriomeningitis Virus [*Medicine*] (DB)
LCVA	Light Commercial Vehicle Association (EA)
LCVAO	Linear Combination of Virtual Atomic Orbitals [*Physical chemistry*]
LCVASI	Low-Cost Visual-Approach Slope Indicator (DNAB)
LCVD	Laser-Assisted Chemical Vapor Deposition [*Coating technology*]
LCVD	LASER Chemical Vapor Deposition [*Coating technology*]
LCVD	Least Coincidence Voltage Detection (MDG)
LCVG	Liquid Cooling and Ventilation Garment [*NASA*] (NASA)
LCVIP	Licensee Contractor Vendor Inspection Report Program [*Nuclear energy*] (NRCH)
LCVM	Log Conversion Voltmeter
LCVP	Landing Craft, Vehicle, Personnel [*Navy symbol*] [*NATO*]
LCW	Limited Conventional War [*Description of Vietnam War*] [*DoD*] (VNW)
LCW	Line Control Word
LCW	Lithuanian American Roman Catholic Women's Alliance
LCW	Lithuanian Catholic Women (EA)
LCW	Lutheran Church Women [*Defunct*] (EA)
LCWA	Legislative Council of Western Australia
LCWA	Lotteries Commission of Western Australia
LCWDS	Low-Cost Weapon Delivery System (MCD)
LCWE	Lausanne Committee for World Evangelization (SAUO)
LCWF	Launch Complex Work Flow (IAA)
LCWHN	Latin American and Caribbean Women's Health Network (EAIO)
LCWI	Left Ventricular Cardiac Work Index [*Physiology*]
LCWIO	Liaison Committee of Women's International Organisations [*British*] (DI)
LCWP	Law Commission Working Paper [*A publication*] (DLA)
LCWR	Leadership Conference of Women Religious of the United States of America (SAUO)
LCWS	Land and Water Conservation Fund (SAUO)
LCWSL	Large Caliber Weapon Systems Laboratory [*ARRADCOM*] (RDA)
LCX	Higginsville, MO [*Location identifier*] [*FAA*] (FAAL)
LCX	Launch Complex
LCx	Left Circumflex [*Artery*] [*Medicine*] (DB)
LCX	Left Circumflex Coronary Artery [*Cardiology*] (DAVI)
LCXT	Large Cosmic X-Ray Telescope (PDAA)
LCY	Guthrie, OK [*Location identifier*] [*FAA*] (FAAL)
LCY	League of Communists of Yugoslavia [*Savez Komunista Jugoslavije*] [*Political party*] (PPW)
LCY	Loose Cubic Yard (DAC)
LCYC	Lemon Creek Yacht Club (SAUO)
LCZ	Laws of the Canal Zone [*A publication*] (DLA)
LCZR	Localizer
LD	Decisions Lost [*Boxing*]
LD	Doctor of Letters
LD	Lab. Dausse [*France*] [*Research code symbol*]
LD	Label Definition (IAA)
LD	Labor and Delivery [*Obstetrics*] (DAVI)
L/D	Labor and Delivery (MELL)
LD	Laboratory Data (MAE)
LD	Labor Daily [*A publication*]
LD	Labor Department
LD	Labor Dispute (DLA)
LD	Labyrinthine Defect [*Physiology*] (MAE)
LD	Labyrinthine Dysfunction [*Medicine*] (MELL)
LD	Lactase Deficiency [*Medicine*] (MELL)
LD	Lactate Dehydrogenase [*Also, LAD, LDH*] [*An enzyme*]
LD	Lady Day [*March 25, the Feast of the Annunciation*] [*British*]
LD	Lamina Densa [*Dermatology*]
LD	Lamp Driver
LD	Land
LD	Land Disposal (EPAT)
LCUP	Landing Distance [*Aviation*] (IAA)
LD	Land Office Decisions, United States [*A publication*] (DLA)

LD	Language Disordered
LD	Large Date [*Numismatic term*]
LD	Large Dollar [*Indicator*] [*IRS*]
LD	Lasa D Ring [*Montana*] [*Seismograph station code, US Geological Survey*] (SEIS)
LD	Laser Designator (ACAE)
LD	LASER Desorption [*of ions for analysis*]
LD	LASER Diode
LD	Laser Disc (DCDG)
LD	LASER Discectomy [*Spinal surgery*]
LD	Last Dose (MELL)
LD	Lateral Direction (MCD)
LD	Lateral Dorsal [*Anatomy*]
LD	Lateral Drift
LD	Lateralis Dorsalis [*Neuroanatomy*]
LD	Launch Director [*NASA*] (KSC)
LD	Launching Division [*Missiles*] (MUGU)
LD	Laus Deo [*Praise to God*] [*Latin*]
LD	Law Dictionary [*A publication*] (DLA)
LD	Layer Depth
ld	Lead (WDMC)
LD	Lead [*or Leads*] [*Publishing*]
LD	Leading (MSA)
ld	Leading (WDMC)
LD	Leading Edge Delay [*Aviation*] (IAA)
LD	Leak Detection [*Nuclear energy*] (IAA)
LD	Learning Disabilities/Differences
LD	Learning Disability [*or Learning-Disabled*]
LD	Learning Disabled (NTIO)
LD	Learning Disorder (DB)
LD	Least Depth [*Nautical charts*]
LD	Lectio Divina [*Paris*] [*A publication*] (BJA)
LD	Left Defense
LD	Left Deltoid [*Medicine*]
LD	Left Door [*Theater*]
LD	Legal Deposit (ADA)
LD	Legal Discriminator (MCD)
LD	Legal Division (SAUO)
LD	Legionnaire's Disease
LD	Legion of Decency (SAUO)
LD	Legislative Department [*Generic term*] (ROG)
LD	Leigh's Disease [*Medicine*] (MELL)
LD	Leipzig Declaration (SAUO)
L-D	Leishman-Donovan (Bodies) [*Microbiology*]
LD	Length-Diameter Ratio
LD	Lepide Dictum [*Wittily Said*] [*Latin*] (ADA)
LD	Letdown [*Nuclear energy*] (NRCH)
LD	Lethal Dose
LD	Let's Discuss
LD	Letter Description (PDAA)
L/D	Letter of Deposit [*Banking*]
LD	Leukodystrophy [*Medicine*] (MELL)
LD	Level Detector
LD	Level Discriminator
LD	Levodopa [*Obstetrics*] (DAVI)
LD	Liberal Democrat (WA)
LD	Library of Devotion [*A publication*]
LD	Libyan Dinar [*Monetary unit*] (BJA)
LD	Licentiate in Dentistry [*British*] (ROG)
LD	Licentiate in Divinity (DAS)
LD	Lifeboat Deck
L:D	Lift-Drag [*Ratio*]
L/D	Lift-Drag Ratio [*Aerodynamics*]
L/D	Lift to Drag Ratio (PIPO)
LD	Light-Dark [*Cycles*]
L/D	Light-Dark [*Ratio*] [*Ophthalmology*] (DAVI)
LD	Light Detail (ELAL)
LD	Light Difference [*Difference between amounts of light perceptible to the two eyes*] [*Ophthalmology*]
LD	Light Dragoons [*Military unit*] [*British*]
LD	Light Driver (IAA)
L/D	Light Duty [*Automotive engineering*]
LD	Lighting Designer (NTCM)
LD	Lighting Director (NTCM)
LD	Light on Dark
LD	Limited
LD	Limited Disease [*Medicine*]
LD	Limited Partner in Dual Capacity Firm [*London Stock Exchange*]
LD	Linear Decision
LD	Linear Dichroism [*Spectra*]
LD	Line Delete [*Computer science*] (VLIE)
LD	Line Dolly (MCD)
LD	Line Drawing (MSA)
LD	Line Driver
LD	Line of Departure [*Military*]
LD	Line of Duty [*Military*]
LD	Linguodistal [*Dentistry*]
LD	Linkage Disequlilibrium [*Genetics*]
LD	Linker Directive [*Telecommunications*] (TEL)
LD	Linz and Donawetz [*Furnace*] [*Metallurgy*] [*Named after two plant sites in Austria*]
LD	Lipodystrophy [*Medicine*] (MELL)
LD	Liquid Drop
LD	Lisfranc Dislocation [*Medicine*] (MELL)
LD	List Down

LD .... List of Drawings [*USN*] (MCD)
LD .... Litera Dominicalis [*Sunday Letter*]
LD .... Litterarum Doctor [*Doctor of Letters or Literature*] [*Latin*] (ROG)
LD .... Liver Disease [*Gastroenterology*] (DAVI)
LD .... Living Donor [*Medicine*]
LD .... Load [*or Loader*] (AAG)
Id .... Load (WDAA)
LD .... Load Draught (IAA)
LD .... Loaded Deployability [*Posture*] [*Military*] (DOMA)
LD .... Loaded Deployability Posture (SAUO)
LD .... Loading Dock (MCD)
LD .... Loading Dose
LD .... Local Delivery
LD .... Local Director (DCTA)
LD .... Local Directory (ACRL)
LD .... Loft Dried Paper (DGA)
LD .... Logical Design
LD .... Logical Diagram (ELAL)
LD .... Logic Driver [*Computer science*]
LD .... Logistics Demonstration (MCD)
LD .... Logistics Document (MCD)
LD .... Lombard-Dowell [*Broth medium*] [*Microbiology*]
LD .... London Division (SAUO)
LD .... London Docks
LD .... Long Day [*Botany*]
LD .... Long Delay
LD .... Long Distance
LD .... Long Duration
LD .... Longitudinal Diameter
LD .... Longitudinal Division [*Cytology*]
LD .... Loop Diagram
LD .... Loop-Disconnect [*Telecommunications*] (TEL)
LD .... Lord
LD .... Loss and Damage (IAA)
LD .... Louis Dreyfus Natural Gas [*NYSE symbol*] (TTSB)
LD .... Louis Dreyfus Natural Gas Holdings Corp. [*NYSE symbol*] (SPSG)
LD .... Low Density
LD .... Low Dispersion [*Optics*]
LD .... Low Door (WDAA)
LD .... Low Dose [*Medicine*]
LD .... Low Drag
LD .... Low Dust
LD .... Low Dutch [*Language, etc.*]
LD .... Low Dynamic
LD .... Lower Deck
LD .... Luminance-Defined (SAUS)
LD .... Luminescence Detector (SSD)
LD .... Luminescence Diode (IAA)
LD .... Lunar Day (KSC)
LD .... Lunar Docking [*NASA*] (IAA)
LD .... Lunar Drill [*NASA*] (KSC)
LD .... Lyme Disease [*Medicine*]
LD .... Lymphocyte Defined [*Immunology*]
LD .... Lymphocyte Depleted [*Medicine*]
LD .... Lymphocyte Depletion [*Hematology*]
LD .... Lymphocytical Determined [*Hematology*] (DAVI)
LD .... Vietnam [*License plate code assigned to foreign diplomats in the US*]
LD50 .... Lethal Dose 50
LD$_{50}$ .... Lethal Dose, Median [*Also, MLD*] [*Lethal for 50% of test group*]
LD 50 .... Low Dose, Fifty Percent Fatality [*Environmental science*] (COE)
LDA .... Ascension Parish Library, Donaldsonville, LA [*Library symbol*] [*Library of Congress*] (LCLS)
LDA .... Laboratory Designated Area (AFIT)
LDA .... Labor Developments Abroad [*A publication*]
LDA .... Ladies Darts Association (SAUO)
LDA .... Land Development Aircraft (PDAA)
LDA .... Landing Directional Aid [*FAA*] (TAG)
LDA .... Landing Distance Available [*ICAO*] (FAAC)
LDA .... Laser Disc Association (NTPA)
LDA .... LASER Doppler Anemometry
LDA .... Last Day of Attendance
LDA .... Late-Differentiation Antigen [*Immunology*]
LDA .... Lauda Air [*Austria*] [*ICAO designator*] (FAAC)
LDA .... Lauryl Diethanolamide [*Also, LDE*] [*Organic chemistry*]
LDA .... Lead Development Association [*British*] (EAIO)
LDA .... Leadership Analysis (SAUO)
LDA .... Learning Disabilities Association (SAUO)
LDA .... Learning Disabilities Association of America (EA)
LDA .... Left Dorso-Anterior [*A fetal position*] [*Obstetrics*]
LDA .... Legitimacy Declaration Act [*British*] (ROG)
LDA .... Lesson Design Approach (MCD)
LDA .... Limited Depository Account
LDA .... Limiting Dilution Analyses [*Analytical biochemistry*]
LDA .... Linear Discriminant Analysis
LDA .... Linear Displacement Analysis (DAVI)
LDA .... Linear Dynamic Analyzer (IAA)
LDA .... Line Driving Amplifier
LDA .... Lithium Diisopropylamide [*Organic chemistry*]
LDA .... Local Data Acquisition
LDA .... Local Data Administrator
LDA .... Local-Density (Functional) Approximation [*Physical chemistry*]
LDA .... Local Design Agency (MCD)
LDA .... Local Display Adapter (MHDB)
LDA .... Local Distribution Accesses (ACAE)
LDA .... Localizer Directional Aid [*Aviation*]

LDA .... Localizer Type Directional Aid (PIPO)
LDA .... Locate Drum Address (CET)
LDA .... Logical Device Address [*Computer science*] (IBMDP)
LDA .... Logic Design Automation (AAEL)
LDA .... Lord's Day Alliance of the United States (EA)
LDA .... Louisiana Dental Association (SAUO)
LDA .... Low-Density Amorph [*Materials science*]
LDA .... Lower-Deck Attitude [*British military*] (DMA)
LDA .... Lowest Designated Assembly
LDA .... Lutheran Deaconess Association (EA)
LDA .... Lymphocyte-Dependent Antibody [*Immunology*]
LDAC .... Learning Disabilities Association of Canada (EAIO)
LDAC .... Lunar Surface Data Acquisition Camera [*Aerospace*]
LDAD .... Local Data Acquisition and Dissemination (SAUO)
LDAI .... Low-Dose Oral Alpha Interferon [*Medicine*] (TAD)
LDAK .... Lidak Pharmaceuticals [*NASDAQ symbol*] (SAG)
LDAKA .... LIDAK Pharmaceuticals'A' [*NASDAQ symbol*] (TTSB)
LDAM .... Local Damage Assessment Model (PDAA)
LDAM .... Logical Data Access Method [*Computer science*] (VLIE)
LD & B .... Lyme Disease and Babesiosis [*Medicine*] (MELL)
LDAO .... Lauryldimethylamine Oxide [*Detergent*]
LDAP .... Light Directory Access Protocol [*Computer science*] (VLIE)
LDAP .... Lightweight Directory Access Protocol [*Computer utility tool*] (PCM)
LDAPAPI ...... Lightweight Directory Access Protocol Application Program Interface (SAUS)
LDAPS .... Long-Duration Auxiliary Power System (NG)
LDAQ .... Association Quebecoise pour les Troubles d'Apprentissage (AC)
LDAQ .... Learning Disabilities Association of Quebec (AC)
LDAR .... Latex Direct Agglutination Reaction [*Medicine*] (DMAA)
LDAR .... Leak Detection and Repair [*Chemical engineering*]
LDAR .... Lightning Detection and Ranging System [*Meteorology*]
LDAS .... LASER Detection and Analysis System (MCD)
LDASE .... Large Deployable Antenna Shuttle Experiment [*NASA*] (PDAA)
Ldata .... Life Data (DIPS)
LDAU .... Laboratory Data Adapter Unit (ACAE)
LdB .... Das Land der Bibel (BJA)
LDB .... Genetic Location Database (SAUO)
LDB .... Lamb Dysentery Bacillus [*Medicine*] (DMAA)
LDB .... Launch Data Bus [*Computer science*] (MCD)
LDB .... Leader Dogs for the Blind (EA)
LDB .... Legionnaires Disease Bacillus [*Medicine*] (DMAA)
LDB .... Legionnaire's Disease Bacterium
LDB .... Legislative Data Base [*Department of Energy*] [*Information service or system*] (IID)
LDB .... Leisure Diagnostic Battery [*Psychology*] (EDAC)
LDB .... Lexington Development Branch (SAA)
LDB .... Light Distribution Box (AAG)
LDB .... Limited Data Block (KSC)
LDB .... Liquidity Data Bank (NUMA)
LDB .... Load Determining Bolt
LDB .... Local Data Buffer (IAA)
LDB .... Logical Database
LDB .... Logistics Data Bank (NASA)
LDB .... Londrina [*Brazil*] [*Airport symbol*] (OAG)
LDB .... Low-Drag Bomb
LDBC .... LD Brinkman Corporation (SAUO)
LDBE .... London Diocesan Board of Education
LDBHS .... Louis D. Brandeis High School (SAUO)
Ld Birk .... Lord Birkenhead's Judgments, House of Lords [*England*] [*A publication*] (DLA)
LDBLC .... Low-Drag Boundary Layer Control [*Military*]
LDBOS .... LASER Designation Battlefield Obscuration Simulator (RDA)
Ld Br Sp ...... Lord Brougham's Speeches [*A publication*] (DLA)
LDBS .... Land Data Bank System (SAUO)
LDBS .... Local Data Base System (MHDI)
LDC .... Laboratory Data Control [*Commercial firm*]
LDC .... Labor Data Collection (MCD)
LDC .... Labor Day Committee [*Australia*]
LDC .... Ladeco Cargo, SA [*Chile*] [*FAA designator*] (FAAC)
LDC .... Lancashire Dynamo & Crypto Ltd. (SAUO)
LDC .... Land Defense of CONUS (SAUO)
LDC .... Large Diameter Core (SAA)
LDC .... LASER Discharge Capacitor (IAA)
LDC .... Latitude Data Computer
LDC .... Launch Detection System (SAUS)
LDC .... Laundry and Dry Cleaning International Union
LDC .... Laydown Code Development (ACAE)
LDC .... Learning Disability Center
LDC .... Learning Disordered Children
LDC .... Least Developed Countries (SAUO)
LDC .... Less Developed Countries (or Country) (SAUO)
LDC .... Less Developed Country (JAGO)
LDC .... Leukocyte Differential Count [*Medicine*] (MEDA)
LDC .... Level Decision Circuit
LDC .... Libertarian Defense Caucus [*Defunct*] (EA)
LDC .... Library Development Center [*Columbia University*]
LDC .... Library Development Consultants, Inc. [*Information service or system*] (IID)
LDC .... Light Direction Center [*Military*]
LDC .... Lightweight Deployable Communications System [*Army*]
LDC .... Limiting Dilution Cloning [*Biochemistry*]
LDC .... Lindeman Island [*Australia*] [*Airport symbol*]
LDC .... Linear Detonating Cord (MSA)
LDC .... Line Directional Coupler
LDC .... Line-Drop Compensator (MSA)

LDC............. Linguistic Data Consortium [*Defense Advanced Research Projects Agency*]
LDC............. Linguistics Documentation Center [*University of Ottawa*] [*Database*] [*Canada*] (NITA)
LDC............. Load Drawer Computer (MCD)
LDC............. Local Damping Control [*Automotive engineering*]
LDC............. Local Data Concentrator [*Telecommunications*]
LDC............. Local Defense Center
LDC............. Local Dental Committee (SAUO)
LDC............. Local Departmental Committee [*British labor*]
LDC............. Local Development Company
LDC............. Local Display Controller
LDC............. Local Distribution Center (CCCA)
LDC............. Local Distribution Center Telephone (SAUO)
LDC............. Local Distribution Company
LDC............. Location Dependent Code (VLIE)
LDC............. Logical Device Coordinates (VLIE)
LDC............. Logistics Data Center [*Army*] (AABC)
LDC............. London Diagnostic Centre [*England*] (WDAA)
LDC............. London Diocesan Council (SAUO)
LDC............. London Dumping Convention [*Sets standards for disposal of wastes in oceans*]
LDC............. Long Day Care
LDC............. Long-Distance Call
LDC............. Long Distance Carrier (VLIE)
LDC............. Long-Distance Communications
LDC............. Lotus Development Corporation (SAUO)
LDC............. Low Density Center (VLIE)
LDC............. Lower Dead Center
LDC............. Low-Speed Data Channel
LDC............. Lutheran Deaconess Conference (EA)
LDCA .... Land Development Contractors' Association [*Australia*]
LDCC .... Laboratory Data Communications Center (SAUO)
LDCC .... Large Diameter Component Cask [*Nuclear energy*] (NRCH)
LDCC .... Lectin-Dependent Cell-Mediated Cytotoxicity [*Biochemistry*]
LDCC .... Local Disease Control Centre (SAUO)
LD-CELP ..... Long Delay-Code Excited Linear Prediction
LD-CELP ..... Low-Delay Code Excited Linear Prediction (SAUS)
LDCF .... Lymphocyte Derived Chemotactic Factor [*Biochemistry*]
LDCIU .... Laundry and Dry Cleaning International Union (NTPA)
LDCM.......... LANDesk Client Manager Technology [*Intel*] [*Computer science*]
LDCMMA ..... Laundry and Dry Cleaners Machinery Manufacturers Association (SAUO)
LDCMWW .... London Diocesan Council for Moral Welfare Work (SAUO)
LDCO .... Laundry and Dry Cleaning Operations [*Military*]
LDCO .... Leader Development Corporation (SAUO)
LDCP .... Landing Dynamics Computer Program [*NASA*]
LDCR .... Light-Duty Common Rail [*Automotive fuel systems*]
LDCR .... Lucas Diesel Common Rail [*Automotive engines*]
L(D)CRS ...... Leachate (Detection) Collection and Removal System (GNE)
LDCRS .... Leachate Detection, Collection, and Removal System (EEVL)
LDCS .... Long-Distance Control System (IEEE)
LDC/SG .... Scientific Group on Dumping (SAUO)
LDCT .... Late Distal Cortical Tubule [*Medicine*] (DMAA)
LDCT.......... Linear Discriminant Classification Tree [*Mathematics*]
LDCV .... Large Dense-Core Vesicle [*Neurobiology*]
LDD .... LASER Detector Diode
LDD .... LASER Diode Driver
LDD .... Late Dedifferentiation (DB)
LDD .... Letter of Determination of Dependency
LDD .... Light-Dark Discrimination [*Ophthalmology*]
LDD .... Light-Dependent Diode [*Instrumentation*]
LDD .... Light Duty Diesel (COE)
LDD .... Lightly Doped Drain (MCD)
LDD .... Little Diomede Island, AK [*Location identifier*] [*FAA*] (FAAL)
LDD .... Loaded
LDD .... Local Data Distribution
LDD .... Local Development District
LDD .... Logical Database Designer [*Computer science*]
LDD .... Logic Design Data [*Telecommunications*] (TEL)
LDD .... Long-Distance Dispersal [*Botany*]
LDD .... Low-Density Data (KSC)
LDD .... Luminaire Dirt Depreciation [*Floodlighting*]
LDD .... Lunar Dust Detector [*NASA*]
LDDC .... Least-Developed Developing Country [*Trade status*]
LDDC .... London Docklands Development Corp. [*British*] (ECON)
LDDC .... Long-Distance Dialing Center (IAA)
LDDC .... Long Distance Direct Current [*Telecommunications*] (CIST)
LDDCS .... Laundry and Decontamination Drycleaning System [*Military*] (DWSG)
LDDI .... Less Developed Defence Industrial nation (SAUO)
LDDI .... Local Distributed Data Interface [*Telecommunications*]
LDDL .... Logical Data Definition Language (IAA)
LDDM.......... LASER Doppler Displacement Meter (AAEL)
LDDMWG.... LGSOWG Data Distribution and Marketing Working Group (SAUO)
LDDO .... Long-Distance Diesel Oil (PDAA)
LDDS .... LDDS Communications, Inc. (SAUO)
LDDS .... Light Division Direct Support [*Artillery system*] (MCD)
LDDS .... Limited Distance Data Service [*Telecommunications*]
LDDS .... Limited Distance Data Set [*Modem*] (NITA)
LDDS .... Local Dentist (DAVI)
LDDS .... Local Digital Distribution Subsystem
LDDS .... Local Doctor of Dental Surgery (MAE)
LDDS .... Long-Distance Discount Service [*Telecommunications*]
LDDS .... Long Distance Discount Services Co. (SAUO)
LDDS .... Low-Density Data System

LDDT .... Light-Duty Diesel Truck [*Automotive emissions*]
LDDV .... Light Duty Diesel Vehicle [*VDOT*] (TAG)
LDDVX .... Lindner Dividend [*Mutual fund ticker symbol*] (SG)
LDE............. Lagrange Differential Equation
LDE............. Laminar Defect Examination (IEEE)
LDE............. Lauryl Diethanolamide [*Also, LDA*] [*Organic chemistry*]
LDE............. Les Dames d'Escoffier (EA)
LDE............. Lighting Director Engineer (NTCM)
LDE............. Linear Differential Equation
LDE............. Lineas Aereas del Estado [*Argentina*] [*ICAO designator*] (FAAC)
LDE............. Local Dynamics Experiment [*Marine science*] (MSC)
LDE............. Long-Delayed Echo
LDE............. Long-Duration Exposure
LDE............. Lourdes/Tarbes [*France*] [*Airport symbol*] (OAG)
LDeB.......... Beauard Parish Library, DeRidder (SAUS)
LDeB.......... Beauregard Parish Library, DeRidder, LA [*Library symbol*] [*Library of Congress*] (LCLS)
L Dec.......... Land Office Decisions, United States [*A publication*] (DLA)
LDEC.......... Lunar Docking Events Controller [*NASA*] (MCD)
LDEF.......... Long-Duration Exposure Facility [*NASA*]
LDEG.......... Laus Deo et Gloria [*Praise and Glory Be to God*] [*Latin*]
LDentSc...... Licentiate in Dental Science (SAUO)
L Dent Sci ... Licentiate in Dental Science (SAUO)
L-DEO......... Lamont-Doherty Earth Observatory (SAUO)
LDEO......... Lamont-Doherty Earth Observatory of Columbia University (SAUO)
LDEP......... Lancashire Dynamo Electronic Products (SAUO)
LDEQ......... Louisiana Department of Environmental Quality (SAUO)
LDERRY....... Londonderry [*County in Ireland*] (ROG)
LDET......... Level Detector (MSA)
LDEX.......... Landing Exercise [*Navy*] (NVT)
LD-EYA........ Lombard-Dowell Egg Yolk Agar [*Microbiology*]
LDF.......... Laboratory Directors Funds (ACAE)
LDF.......... Land Disposal Facility
LDF.......... Landed Duty Free
LDF.......... Laser Demonstration Facility (SAUO)
LDF.......... Latin American Discovery Fund [*NYSE symbol*] (SPSG)
LDF.......... Legal Defense and Educational Fund (SAUO)
LDF.......... Legal Defense Fund (SAUO)
LDF.......... Light Digital FACSIMILE [*Machine*]
LDF.......... Light Distillate Feedstock (PDAA)
LDF.......... Lightweight Digital Facsimile (SAUS)
LDF.......... Linear Discriminant Function [*Mathematics*]
LDF.......... Linear Driving Force
LDF.......... Liquid Drop Experiment Facility (SAUS)
LDF.......... Load Division Fault
LDF.......... Load Factor (IAA)
LDF.......... Local Defense Forces
LDF.......... Local-Density Functional Equation (MCD)
LDF.......... Local Density Functional Theory [*Chemistry*]
LDF.......... London Diocesan Fund
LDF.......... Lyme Disease Foundation
LDF.......... NAACP [*National Association for the Advancement of Colored People*] Legal Defense and Educational Fund (EA)
LDFC.......... Lew DeWitt Fan Club [*Defunct*] (EA)
LDFS.......... London District Friendly Society (SAUO)
LDFSTN....... Landing Direction Finding Station [*Aviation*] (IAA)
LDG .... Lactic Dehydrogenase (DMAA)
LDG .... Lading (WDAA)
LDG .... Landing [*Maps and charts*] (AFM)
LDG .... Leading
LDG .... Left Digestive Gland
LDG .... Lexington Design Group (SAA)
LDG .... Libyan Desert Glass [*Archeology*]
LDG .... Linear Displacement Gauge
LDG .... Lingual Developmental Groove (DMAA)
LDG .... Loading
LDG .... Lodge [*or Lodging*] (MCD)
LDG .... Logistics Data Gateway (SAUO)
LDG .... Longs Drug Stores [*NYSE symbol*] (TTSB)
LDG .... Longs Drug Stores Corp. [*NYSE symbol*] (SPSG)
LDG .... Low-Density Gas
Ldg & Dly .. Landing and Delivery [*Shipping*] (DS)
LDGE .... LEM [*Lunar Excursion Module*] Dummy Guidance Equipment [*NASA*] (KSC)
LDGE .... Lodge [*Commonly used*] (OPSA)
LDGLT .... Leading Light [*Navigation signal*]
LDGO.......... Lamont Doherty Geological Observatory [*Marine science*] (OSRA)
L-DGO......... Lamont-Doherty Geological Observatory [*Formerly, LGO*] [*Columbia University*]
LDGP .... Liverpool Division of General Practice (SAUO)
LDGP .... Low-Drag, General Purpose (SAUO)
LDGPS........ Local DGPS [*Differential*][*Global Positioning System*] (GAVI)
LDGSPTBN... Landing Support Battalion (DNAB)
Ld Gt .... Land Grant (MHDB)
LDGT.......... Light-Duty Gasoline Truck (EPAT)
Ldg Tel .... Leading Telegraphist
LDGV.......... Light-Duty Gasoline Vehicle
LDH .... Lactate Dehydrogenase [*Also, LAD, LD*] [*An enzyme*]
LDH .... Lactic Dehydrogenase
L d'H .... Legion d'Honneur [*French decoration*]
LDH .... Ligue des Droits de l'Homme [*France*]
LDH .... Limiting Dome Height [*Automotive metal stamping*]
LDH .... London District Headquarters (SAUO)
LDH .... Lord Howe Island [*Australia*] [*Airport symbol*] (OAG)
LDHA .... Lactic Dehydrogenase A (DB)

LDHB	Lactic Dehydrogenase B (DB)
LDHC	Lactic Dehydrogenase-C (DMAA)
LDHC	Locker Door Hydraulic Cylinder
LDHD	Lymphocyte-Depletion Hodgkin's Disease [*Medicine*]
LDHI	Lactic Dehydrogenase Isoenzymes
LDHILS	Laser Designator Hardware in the Loop Simulation (ACAE)
LDHK	Lactic Dehydrogenase-K (DMAA)
LDHM	London Diocesan Home Mission [*or Missionary*]
LDHRR	League for the Defense of Human Rights in Romania [*Paris, France*] (EAIO)
LDI	Landing Direction Indicator [*ICAO*] (FAAC)
LDI	LASER Desorption Ionization [*Spectroscopy*]
LDI	Lauda Air [*Italy*] [*ICAO designator*] (FAAC)
LDI	Life Detection Instrument
LDI	Lindi [*Tanzania*] [*Airport symbol*] (OAG)
LDI	Linear Displacement Indicator
LDI	Load Indicator
LDI	Lockheed DataPlan, Inc. [*Information service or system*] (IID)
LDI	Loredi Resources Ltd. [*Vancouver Stock Exchange symbol*]
LDI	Lossless Digital Integrator (IAA)
LDI	Low-Density Indication (MCD)
LDIC	LDI Corp. [*NASDAQ symbol*] (SAG)
LDI Cp	LDI Corp. [*Associated Press*] (SAG)
L Dict	Law Dictionary [*A publication*] (DLA)
LDID	Logical Disk Identifier (SAUS)
LDIH	Left Direct Inguinal Hernia [*Medicine*] (DMAA)
LDII	Larson Davis [*NASDAQ symbol*] (TTSB)
LDIM	Luminescence Digital Imaging Microscopy
LDIN	Lead-In Lighting [*or Lights*] [*Aviation*]
LDIN	Lead in Lighting System (PIPO)
LDIN	Lead-in-Light System [*FAA*] (TAG)
L-Dink	Lower Class - Double [*or Dual*] Income, No Kids [*Lifestyle classification*]
LDIP	Laboratory Data Integrity Program [*Environmental Protection Agency*] (GFGA)
LDIR	Low-Dose Ionizing Radiation (MELL)
L-DISC	Late Direct Injection Stratified Charge
LDISCR	Level Discriminator (MSA)
LD Is FFD	Line of Departure Is Friendly Forward Disposition [*Army*] (AABC)
LDISO	Lactic Dehydrogenase Isoenzymes (DAVI)
LD Is PPOS	Line of Departure Is Present Positions [*Military*] (AABC)
LDIU	Launch Data Interface Unit (MCD)
L Div	Law Division (DLA)
L Div	Licentiate in Divinity
LDJ	Linden, NJ [*Location identifier*] [*FAA*] (FAAL)
LDJ	Load D-Bank and Jump [*Computer science*]
LDJU	Lovers of David Jones United (SAUO)
LDJU	Luvers of David Jones United (EA)
LDK	Lower Deck
Ld Ken	Lord Kenyon's English King's Bench Reports [*1753-59*] [*A publication*] (DLA)
Ld Kenyon	Lord Kenyon's English King's Bench Reports [*1753-59*] [*A publication*] (DLA)
Ld Kenyon (Eng)	Lord Kenyon's English King's Bench Reports [*1753-59*] [*A publication*] (DLA)
LDL	Lambda Delta Lambda (EA)
LDL	Landing Direction Light [*Aviation*] (IAA)
LDL	Language Description Language [*Computer science*]
LDL	Learned Doctor of Laws
LDL	Lighting Design Lumen (PDAA)
LDL	Liquid Delay Line
LDL	Logical Data Language [*Computer science*] (IAA)
LDL	Logical Display List (MCD)
LDL	Long Distance Love [*An association*] (EA)
LDL	Loudness Discomfort Level (MAE)
LDL	Low-Density Lipoprotein [*Biochemistry*]
LDL	Lower Detectable Limit [*Chemical analysis*]
LDL	Lower Detection Limit (AAEL)
LDL	Lower Deviation Level (AABC)
LDL	Lydall, Inc. [*NYSE symbol*] (SPSG)
LDL	University of Nebraska, Lincoln, Lincoln, NE [*OCLC symbol*] (OCLC)
LDLA	Limited Distance Line Adapter
LDLA	Low-Density Lipoprotein Apheresis [*Medicine*] (DMAA)
LD/LC	Line of Departure/Line of Contact [*Army*] (ADDR)
LDL-C	Low-Density Lipoprotein-Cholesterol [*Biochemistry*]
LDLE	Light-Duty Lathe Engine
LdLew	Lewisville Public Library, Lewisville, ID [*Library symbol*] [*Library of Congress*] (LCLS)
LD-LISC	Ligand-Driven Light-Induced Spin Changes [*Physics*]
LD LMT	Load Limit (WDAA)
LDLN	Long Distance Learning Network (SAUO)
LDLO	Lethal Dose Low [*Environmental science*] (COE)
LD LO	Lethal Dose Low (EEVL)
LD^{Lo}	Lethal Dose Low (ERG)
LDLP	Low Density Lipoprotein [*Biochemistry*]
LDLR	Land Development Law Reporter [*A publication*] (DLA)
LDLR	Low-Density Lipoprotein Receptor [*Biochemistry*]
LDLS	Lesotho Department of Lands, Surveys and Physical Planning (SAUO)
Ldlw COO	Laidlaw One, Inc. [*Associated Press*] (SAG)
LdlwOOO	Laidlaw One, Inc. [*Associated Press*] (SAG)
LDM	Laidlaw Transportation Ltd. [*Toronto Stock Exchange symbol*]
LDM	LASER Drilling Machine
LDM	Last Day of the Month (AFM)
LDM	Lee, David M., Los Angeles CA [*STAC*]

LDM	Libby Dam [*Montana*] [*Seismograph station code, US Geological Survey*] (SEIS)
LDM	Licentiate of Dental Medicine
LDM	Limited-Distance MODEM [*Computer science*]
LDM	Linear Delta Modulation
LDM	Load Distribution Matrix (IAA)
LDM	Local Data Management (SAUO)
LDM	Local Data Manager
LDM	Logical Data Model (VLIE)
LDM	Long-Delay Monostable [*Circuitry*]
LDM	Long Distance Modem (VLIE)
LDM	Lord Mayor
LDM	Low-Density Microsome [*Cytology*]
LDM	Ludington, MI [*Location identifier*] [*FAA*] (FAAL)
LDm	Median Lethal Time (EES)
LDMA	London Discount Market Association [*British*] (MHDW)
LDME	LASER Distance Measuring Equipment (DNAB)
LDMI	LASER Distance Measuring Instrument
LDMK	Landmark (KSC)
LdmkBc	Landmark Bancorp [*Associated Press*] (SAG)
LdmkGph	Landmark Graphics Corp. [*Associated Press*] (SAG)
LDMM	Leadville Mining & Milling Corp. (SAUO)
LDMOS	Lateral Double-Diffused Metal-Oxide Semiconductor (MCD)
LDMOS	Laterally Diffused Metal-Oxide Semiconductor (AAEL)
LDMOS	Latterally Diffused MOS (SAUS)
LD-MPT	Ligue Democratique - Mouvement pour le Parti des Travailleurs [*Democratic League - Movement for the Workers' Party*] [*Senegal*] [*Political party*] (PPW)
LDMS	Laboratory Data Management System [*IBM Corp.*]
LDMS	LASER Desorption Mass Spectrometry
LDMS	LASER Distance Measuring System
LDMS	Lunar Distance Measuring System [*Aerospace*]
LDMS	Region 2, Lab Data Management System (SAUS)
LDMTS	Long Distance Message Telecommunications Service (VLIE)
LDMWA	Low Drag Multi/Wire Antenna (CCCA)
LDMWR	Limited Depot Maintenance Work Requirements
LDMX	Local Digital Message Exchange (AABC)
LDN	Greater London (SAUS)
LDN	Lamidanda [*Nepal*] [*Airport symbol*] (OAG)
LDN	Lightning Detection Network [*Electric Power Research Institute*]
LDN	Linden, VA [*Location identifier*] [*FAA*] (FAAL)
LDN	Listed Directory Number [*Bell System*]
LDN	Local Data Network (SAUS)
LDN	Locally Defined Neighborhood
LDN	London [*Ontario*] [*Seismograph station code, US Geological Survey*] (SEIS)
LDN	London [*England*]
LDN	London Silver Corp. [*Vancouver Stock Exchange symbol*]
LDNA	Long-Distance Navigation Aid
LD-NEYA	Lombard-Dowell Neomycin Egg Yolk Agar [*Microbiology*]
LDNF	London Foundation (SAUO)
LDNG	Loading
LDNRX	Lindner Growth Fund [*Mutual fund ticker symbol*] (SG)
LDNS	Laser Doppler Navigation System (SAUS)
LDNS	Lightweight Doppler Navigation System (MCD)
LDO	Ladouanie [*Suriname*] [*Airport symbol*] (OAG)
LDO	Laminated Diatom Ooze [*Oceanography*]
LDO	Language Dependent Objects (VLIE)
LDO	Launch Division Officer [*Missiles*] (MUGU)
LDO	Licensed Deck Officer (SAUO)
LDO	Light Diesel Oil (IAA)
LDO	Limited Duties (or Duty) Officer (SAUO)
LDO	Limited Duty Officer [*Navy*]
LDO	Linear Diophantine Object
LDO	Local Dental Officer
LDO	Logical Device Order [*Computer science*] (IBMDP)
LDO	Long-Distance Oil [*Service mark*] [*Amoco Oil Co.*]
LDO	Low-Density Oil [*Petroleum industry*]
LDO	Low-Density Overlay [*Plywood*]
LDO	Low Drop Out
LDO	St. Mary's Dominican College, New Orleans, LA [*OCLC symbol*] (OCLC)
LDOCE	Longman's Dictionary of Contemporary English [*A publication*]
LDOCF	Long Distance Operational Control Facility (SAUS)
LDOE	Longitude Drift/Orbit Eccentricity (ACAE)
LDOM	Lorenz Domination [*Statistics*]
L-DOPA	Levo-Dihydroxyphenylalanine [*Pharmacology*]
L-dopa	Levodopa (WDAA)
LDOS	Leather Dressers' Old Society [*A union*] [*British*]
LDOS	Local Density of Electron States [*Physical chemistry*]
LDOS	Local Density of States [*Solid state physics*]
LDOS	Lord's Day Observance Society [*British*]
LDP	Laban ng Demokratikong Pilipino [*Democratic Filipino's Struggle*] [*Political party*]
LDP	Label Distribution Protocol (VLIE)
LDP	Laboratory Data Processor (IAA)
LDP	Laboratory Data Products (VLIE)
LDP	Laboratory Distribution Panel
LDP	Ladyship [*or Lordship*]
LDP	Landed Duty Paid [*Military*]
LDP	Langmuir Diffusion Pump [*Engineering*]
LDP	Language Data Processing (MSA)
LDP	Large Developmental Plant [*Project*] [*Department of Energy*]
LDP	Laser Designator Pod (SAUS)
LDP	Leadership Development Projects [*National Science Foundation*]

LDP............. Leaflet Dispensing Pod
LDP............. League for Democracy and Peace [Myanmar] [Political party] (EY)
LDP............. Left Dorso-Posterior [A fetal position] [Obstetrics]
LDP............. Lesotho Democratic Party (SAUO)
LDP............. Liberal Democratic Party [Slovenia] [Political party] (EY)
LDP............. Liberal-Democratic Party of Japan [Jiyu-Minshuto] [Political party] (PPW)
LDP............. Liberal Demokratische Partei [Liberal Democratic Party] [Germany] [Political party] (PPW)
LDP............. Lietuviy Demokraty Partija [Lithuanian Democratic Party] [Political party] (PPE)
LDP............. Limited Denial of Participation (SAUO)
LDP............. Linux Documentation Project (SAUO)
LDP............. Lithuanian Democratic Party (SAUO)
L/DP........... Living/Dying Project (EA)
LDP............. Local Data Package (KSC)
LDP............. Local Data Processor (AABC)
LDP............. Local Distribution Point (SAUS)
LDP............. Logistics Data Package
LDP............. Logistics Development Program (DOMA)
LDP............. Lomas Data Products [Marlboro, MA] [Computer manufacturer]
LDP............. London Daily Price [British]
LDP............. Long-Day Plant [Botany]
LDP............. Lordship [British]
LDP............. Lorentz Doppler Profile [Physics]
LDP............. Low Density Plasma (AAEL)
LDP............. Lumbo-Dorsal Pain (SAUS)
LDP............. Lung Damaging Particle
LDPC........... Logistic Data Processing Centre (SAUO)
LDPD........... Liberal-Demokratische Partei Deutschlands [Liberal Democratic Party of Germany] [Political party] (PPW)
LDPE........... Low-Density Polyethylene [Polymer]
LDP Group... Laboratory Data Products Group (SAUO)
LDPHDN ...... Lead Additive Report for Refineries and Importers and for Manufacturing (SAUO)
LDPN .... Low-Density Phenolic Nylon [Polymer]
LDPS .... L-Band Digital Phase Shifter
LDPT........... Load Point (VLIE)
LDQ .... Laboratory and Data Quality (SAUO)
LDQ .... Leaders Equity Corp. [Vancouver Stock Exchange symbol]
LDQ .... Lobe-Dominated Quasar [Astronomy]
LDR .... Aero Lider SA de CV [Mexico] [ICAO designator] (FAAC)
LDR .... County Londonderry (SAUS)
LDR .... Labor, Delivery, Recovery Room [Medicine]
LDR .... Landauer, Inc. [AMEX symbol] (SPSG)
LDR .... Land Disposal Restriction (COE)
LDR .... Land Disposal Restrictions [Environmental Protection Agency]
LDR .... Landmark Resources Ltd. [Vancouver Stock Exchange symbol]
LDR .... Large Deployable Reflector [Astronomy]
LDR .... LASER Designator Range (MCD)
LDR .... Laser Designator Receiver (ACAE)
LDR .... Latest Date of Release (WDAA)
ldr.............. Leader (GEAB)
LDR .... Leader
LDR .... Leading Deep Recess [Rotary automotive engine]
LDR .... Ledger (ADA)
LDR .... Length-Diameter Ratio
LDR .... Level Distribution Recorder
LDR .... Liberal, Democratic, and Reformist Group [European political movement] (ECON)
Ldr .... Lidar (SAUS)
LDR .... Light Dependent Resistor
LDR .... Light Detect Resistor (SAUS)
LDR .... Light-to-Dark Ratio
LDR .... Limited Distribution Reports (SAUO)
LDR .... Limiting Drawing Ratio (MCD)
LDR .... Linear Decision Rule
LDR .... Linear Dynamic Range
LDR .... Line Driver-Receiver [Computer communication] (TEL)
LDR .... Link Loader (VLIE)
LDR .... Liquid Droplet Radiator (MCD)
LDR .... Llandore [Welsh depot code]
LDR .... Loader (MSA)
LDR .... Lodar [South Arabia] [Airport symbol] (AD)
LDR .... Log Dose Response [Biochemical analysis]
LDR .... Lorentz Double Refraction [Physics]
L/DR .... Lounge/Dining Room [Classified advertising] (ADA)
LDR .... Low Data Rate [RADAR]
LDR .... Low Data Register [Computer science]
LDR .... Low-Density, Recorder
LDR .... Low Dose Rate [Medicine]
LDRA .... Low Data Rate Auxiliary [RADAR]
Ld Ray........ Lord Raymond's King's Bench and Common Pleas Reports [1694-1732] [A publication] (DLA)
Ld Raym...... Lord Raymond's King's Bench and Common Pleas Reports [1694-1732] [A publication] (DLA)
LDRC .... Libel Defense Resource Center (EA)
LDRC .... Lumber Dealers Research Council [Defunct] (EA)
LDRD .... Laboratory-Directed Research and Development (SAUO)
LDRDA........ Long Distance Running Directors Association (EA)
LDRER .... Launderer
LDRF .... Long-Distance Range Finder (SSD)
LDRG .... Liberal, Democratic and Reformist Group [See also GLDR] (EAIO)
LDRI .... Learning Disabilities Research Institute [University of Virginia] (EDAC)

LDRI .... Low Data Rate Input [RADAR]
LDRIACS...... Low Data Rate Integrated Acoustic Communications System [Military] (CAAL)
LDRM .... LASER Designator Rangefinding Module (RDA)
LDRP .... Labor, Delivery, Recovery, Post-Partum [Medicine] (MEDA)
LDRP .... Learning Disability Rating Procedure [Educational test]
LDRPS .... Labor-Delivery-Recovery-Postpartum Suite (HCT)
LDRR .... Laboratory of Diagnostic Radiology Research (ADWA)
LDRRDDB .... Land Disposal Restrictions Rule Development (SAUO)
LDRRIM ...... Low-Density Reinforced Reaction Injection Molding [Plastics]
LDRS .... Labor-Delivery-Recovery Suite (HCT)
LDRS .... LASER Discrimination RADAR System
L/DRS .... Level and Density Recorder Switch [Nuclear energy] (NRCH)
LDRSHP....... Leadership
LDRSP......... Leadership (AFM)
LDRT .... [The] Lake Front Dock & Railroad Terminal Co. [Formerly, LDT] [AAR code]
LDRT .... Low Data Rate [RADAR] (IAA)
LDRTF .... Land Disposal Restrictions Task Force [Environmental Protection Agency] (GFGA)
LDRY .... Landry's Seafood Restaurants [NASDAQ symbol] (TTSB)
LDRY .... Landrys Seafood Restaurants, Inc. [NASDAQ symbol] (SAG)
LDRY .... Laundry (AFM)
LDryNG .... Louis Dreyfus Natural Gas [Associated Press] (SAG)
LDS .... Church of Jesus Christ and Latter Day Saints (SAUO)
LDS .... Havre, MT [Location identifier] [FAA] (FAAL)
LDS .... Labor Distribution System (TIMI)
LDS .... Lakeland Dialect Society (SAUO)
LDS .... Lancashire Dialect Society (SAUO)
LDS .... Landing/Deceleration Subsystem [NASA] (NASA)
LDS .... Landing, Deservicing, and Safing [NASA] (KSC)
LDS .... Langmuir Dark Space [Electronics]
LDS .... Language for Description and Functional Specification (VLIE)
LDS .... Large Disk Storage [Computer science] (IEEE)
LDS .... Laser Dazzle Sight (SAUS)
LDS .... LASER Deep Space
LDS .... LASER Designator System [Rangefinder] (MCD)
LDS .... Laser Detecting Set (SAUS)
LDS .... Laser Detection System
LDS .... Laser Docking Sensor (SAUS)
LDS .... LASER Drilling System
LDS .... Last Data Sample (IAA)
LDS .... Latter-Day Saints [Mormons]
LDS .... Launch Data System [NASA] (KSC)
LDS .... Launch Detection Satellite [Former USSR]
LDS .... Laus Deo Semper [Praise to God Always] [Latin]
LDS .... Layered Defense System (MCD)
LDS .... Lead Design Supervisor [Engineering]
LDS .... Leader Development Study [Army]
LDS .... Leads (VLIE)
LDS .... Leak Detection System [Nuclear energy] (NRCH)
LDS .... Lethal Defense System (MCD)
LDS .... Lexington Developmental Scales [Child development test]
LDS .... Licentiate in Dental Surgery
LDS............. Lietuviu Darbininku Susivienijimas [Association of Lithuanian Workers] (EA)
LDS .... Ligating and Dividing Stapler [Used surgical procedures] (DAVI)
LDS .... Light Distillate Spirit (PDAA)
LDS .... Lightweight Decontamination System (INF)
LDS .... Linear Dynamic System
LDS .... Liquid, Diesel-Cycle, Supercharged
LDS .... Loads [Military]
LDS .... Local Dependant Services (SAUO)
LDS .... Local Development Scheme (SAUO)
LDS .... Local Digital Switch [Telecommunications] (TEL)
LDS .... Local Distribution Service [Cable TV network] (NITA)
LDS .... Local Distribution System [or Service] [Cable television] (MDG)
LDS .... Locked Door Seclusion [Medicine] (DMAA)
LDS .... Logistics Data Sheet
LDS .... Logistics Data System (SAUO)
LDS .... Long Distance Savers
LDS .... Long Distance Swimmer
LDS............. Longitudinal Direct Substitution Imputation Procedure [Bureau of the Census] (GFGA)
LDS............. Loral Defense Systems Corp. (SAUO)
LDS............. Lucey-Driscoll Syndrome [Medicine] (MELL)
LDS............. Lunar Drill System [NASA]
LDSA .... Logistics Doctrine and Systems Agency [Army] (MCD)
LDSC .... Layered Defense Systems Countermeasures (ACAE)
LDSc........... Licentiate in Dental Science [British]
ldscp........... Landscape (VRA)
LDSD .... Lookdown/Shootdown (MCD)
LDSD .... Low Dimensional Structures and Devices [British]
LDSFE......... Fuel Economy (SAUO)
LDSG .... Long Distance Signal Group (SAUO)
LDSH .... Ladish Co. [NASDAQ symbol] (SG)
LDSI........... Licentiate in Dental Surgery, Ireland (SAUO)
LDSJ........... Little Daughters of St. Joseph [Roman Catholic religious order]
LDSO .... Logistics Doctrine and Systems Office [Army]
LDSP .... Lietuvos Socialdemokratu Partija [Social Democratic Party of Lithuania] [Political party] (EAIO)
LDSR .... League of Distilled Spirits Rectifiers [Defunct]
LDSRA .... Logistics Doctrine Systems and Readiness Agency [Army] (AABC)
LDSRCPS..... Licentiate in Dental Surgery of the Royal College of Physicians and Surgeons (SAUO)

LDSRCPS Glas... Licentiate in Dental Surgery of the Royal College of Physicians and Surgeons of Glasgow [*British*]
LDSRCS....... Licentiate in Dental Surgery of the Royal College of Surgeons [*British*]
LDSRCSEd... Licentiate in Dental Surgery of the Royal College of Surgeons of Edinburgh (DI)
LDSRCS Edin... Licentiate in Dental Surgery of the Royal College of Surgeons of Edinburgh [*British*]
LDSRCSEng... Licentiate in Dental Surgery of the Royal College of Surgeons in England (SAUO)
LDSRCS Eng... Licentiate in Dental Surgery of the Royal College of Surgeons of England
LDSRCSI...... Licentiate in Dental Surgery of the Royal College of Surgeons in Ireland (SAUO)
LDSRCS Irel... Licentiate in Dental Surgery of the Royal College of Surgeons in Ireland
LD-SRIM...... Low-Density Structural Reaction Injection Molding [*Plastics*]
LDSS .... LASER Designator Search System
LDSS .... Lunar Deep Seismic Sounding [*Aerospace*] (MCD)
LDSSIG .... Learning Disabled Student SIG [*Special Interest Group*] (EA)
LDST........... Letdown Storage Tank [*Nuclear energy*] (NRCH)
LDSU .... Local Distribution Service Unit (IAA)
LDT............. [*The*] Lake Front Dock & Railroad Terminal Co. [*Later, LDRT*] [*AAR code*]
LDT............. Language Dependent Translator
LDT............. Laser Detector Tracker (SAUS)
LDT............. LASER Discharge Tube
LDT............. Lateral Dorsal Tract [*Neuroanatomy*]
LDT............. L-DOPA Test [*Endocrinology*]
LDT............. Left Dorsotransverse [*Medicine*] (DMAA)
LDT............. Level Delay Time
LDT............. Level Detector (KSC)
LDT............. Library Development Team
LDT............. Licensed Deposit-Taking Institution [*British*]
LDT............. Light Displacement Ton [*MARAD*] (TAG)
LDT............. Light-Duty Truck
LDT............. Lightning Data Transport
LDT............. Linear Differential Transformer
LDT............. Linear Displacement Transduced (MCD)
LDT............. Local Daylight Saving Time
LDT............. Local Descriptor Table [*Computer science*]
LDT............. Logical Design Translator (NITA)
LDT............. Logical Device Table (IAA)
LDT............. Logic Design Translator [*Computer science*]
LDT............. Logistic Delay Time (CAAL)
LDT............. London Dipole Theory
LDT............. Long Distance Transmission (BUR)
LDT............. Long Dry Ton
LDT............. Lowest Dose Tested [*Environmental science*] (EPAT)
LDT............. Lubbock, TX [*Location identifier*] [*FAA*] (FAAL)
LDTA.......... Leak Detection Technology Association (EA)
LDTC........... Lawndale Transportation Co. [*AAR code*]
LDTC........... Learning Disabilities Teacher Consultant
LDTD.......... Lousiana Department of Transportation and Development (SAUO)
LD/TE......... Line Driver/Terminal Equipment (MCD)
LDTEL........ Long Distance Telephone [*Telecommunications*] (IAA)
LDTF.......... Large Dynamic Test Facility (SAUO)
LDTF.......... Light of Divine Truth Foundation (EA)
LDTM.......... Lander Dynamic Test Model [*NASA*]
LDTM.......... Light-Duty Tank Target Mechanism (SAUS)
LDTO.......... Long-Distance Telegraph Office (SAUO)
LDTOF .... LASER Desorption Time-of-Flight [*Spectrometry*]
LDTR .... Load Descriptor Table Register (SAUO)
LDTR .... Long Dwell Time RADAR (NATG)
LDTRC .... Local Descriptor Table Register Cache (SAUO)
LDTS .... Laser Designator Targeting System (ACAE)
LDTS .... Laser Designator Tracker System (ACAE)
LDT/SCAM ... Laser Detector & Tracker-Strike Camera (SAUS)
LDTTY......... Landing Line Teletype
LDU .... Lahad Datu [*Malaysia*] [*Airport symbol*] (OAG)
LDU .... Lamp Dimmer Unit (MCD)
LdU........... Landesring der Unabhaengigen [*Independent Party*] [*Switzerland*] [*Political party*] (PPE)
LDU .... Launcher Display Unit (SAUS)
LDU .... Leather Dressers' Union [*British*]
LDU .... Line Driver Unit [*Computer communication*] (MCD)
LDU .... Local Defence Union (SAUO)
LDUA .... Light-Duty Utility Arm (ABAC)
LDUB .... Long Double Upright Brace [*Medicine*]
LDUH .... Low-Dose Unfractionated Heparin [*Medicine*] (DMAA)
LD/USA........ Long Distance/USA, Inc. [*Honolulu, HI*] [*Telecommunications*] (TSSD)
LDV............ Lactic Dehydrogenase Virus
LDV............ Large Dense-Cored Vesicle [*Medicine*] (DMAA)
LDV............ LASER Doppler Velocimeter
LDV............ Laser Doppler Velocimetry [*Medicine*] (MELL)
LDV............ Leadville [*Nevada*] [*Seismograph station code, US Geological Survey*] [*Closed*] (SEIS)
LDV............ League of Disabled Voters (EA)
LDV............ Lectus Developments Ltd. [*Vancouver Stock Exchange symbol*]
LDV............ Light-Duty Vehicle
LDV............ Linear Differential Vector
LDV............ Local Defence Volunteers [*Later called Home Guards*] [*British*] [*World War II*]
LDV............ Low-Dollar Value

LDVA .... Lodi District Vintners Association (EA)
LDVE.......... Linear Differential Vector Equation
LDVS .... Logistics Data Validation System (SAUO)
LDW........... Laidlaw Inc. [*NYSE symbol*] (SAG)
LDW........... Lane Departure Warning [*Automotive electronics*]
LDW........... Left Defense Wing [*Women's lacrosse position*]
LDW........... Liability Damage Waiver [*Insurance*]
LDW........... Licensed Driver's Waiver (BARN)
LDW........... Loss Damage Waiver [*Insurance*] (TVEL)
LDWA......... Long Distance Walkers Association [*British*] (DBA)
LDWSS .... LASER Designator Weapon System Simulation (RDA)
LDX........... Long-Distance Xerography [*Xerox Corp.*] [*Communications facsimile system*]
LDXL.......... Large Diameter Extended Length (IGSL)
LDY........... Lancashire and Derbyshire Yeomanry (SAUO)
LDY........... Laundry
LDY........... Leicestershire and Derbyshire Yeomanry [*Military unit*] [*British*]
LDY........... Londonderry [*Northern Ireland*] [*Airport symbol*] (OAG)
LDZ........... Lodz [*Poland*] [*Airport symbol*] (AD)
LDZ........... St. Louis, MO [*Location identifier*] [*FAA*] (FAAL)
LE .... Antenna Effective Length for Electric-Field Antennas (IEEE)
LE .... Caribbean Council of Legal Education
LE .... Eunice Public Library, Eunice, LA [*Library symbol*] [*Library of Congress*] (LCLS)
LE .... Laboratory Essential (SAUO)
LE .... Laboratory Evaluation (MUGU)
LE .... Laboratory of Electronics [*Rockefeller University*] [*Research center*] (RCD)
LE .... Labor Exchange
LE .... Labour Exchange (SAUO)
LE .... Lactate Extraction [*Medicine*] (DMAA)
LE .... Lafayette Escadrille (ACAE)
LE .... Lands' End [*NYSE symbol*] (SPSG)
LE .... LAN [*Local Area Network*] Emulation [*Computer science*]
LE .... Large End (OA)
LE .... LASER Electronics (MCD)
LE .... Latent Heat (SAUS)
LE .... Lateral Element
LE .... Lateral Epicondyle [*Anatomy*]
LE .... Latest Estimate [*Business term*]
LE .... Launch Eject
LE .... Launch Electronics
L/E .... Launch Encounter [*NASA*] (KSC)
LE .... Launch Escape [*NASA*] (KSC)
LE .... Launching Equipment
LE .... Law Enforcement
LE .... Laws of Eshnunna (BJA)
LE .... Lawyers' Edition, United States Supreme Court Reports [*A publication*] (DLA)
LE .... Lazy Eye (MELL)
LE .... Lead Engineer (AAG)
LE .... Leading Edge [*Aerospace*]
LE .... Lease
LE .... Leave Edge (DGA)
LE .... Lebanese International Airways (SAUO)
le .... Lebanon [*MARC country of publication code*] [*Library of Congress*] (LCCP)
LE .... Lector
Le .... Ledge
LE .... Lee-Enfield [*British military*] (DMA)
LE .... Left Ear (DMAA)
LE .... Left End
LE .... Left Extremity
LE .... Left Eye
LE .... Leg Exercise [*Sports medicine*]
LE .... Length (IAA)
Le .... Leonard [*Unit for cathode rays*]
LE .... Leone [*Monetary unit*] [*Sierra Leone*]
LE .... Less or Equal (SAUO)
LE .... Less than or Equal
LE .... Leucine Enkephalin [*Biochemistry*]
LE .... Leucocyte Elastase [*An enzyme*]
LE .... Leukemia [*Oncology*]
LE .... Leukocyte Esterase (MELL)
LE .... Leukoerythrogenetic (MAE)
LE .... Levy Industries Ltd. [*Toronto Stock Exchange symbol*]
Le .... Lewis [*Blood group*]
Le .... Lewis Number [*IUPAC*]
LE .... Library Edition (ADA)
LE .... Life Expectancy (MELL)
LE .... Lifting Eye
LE .... Light Equipment
LE .... Limited Edition (ADA)
LE .... Limit of Endurance [*Materials testing*]
LE .... Limits of Error
LE .... Linear Expansion [*Physics*]
LE .... Line Equipment [*Telecommunications*] (TEL)
LE .... Linkage Editor (IAA)
LE .... Linkage Equilibrium [*Genetics*]
LE .... Link Encapsulation (MLOA)
L-E .... List/Enumerate (SAUS)
LE .... Local Area Network Emulation [*Computer science*] (DDC)
LE .... Local Exchange [*Telecommunications*] (TEL)
LE .... Locally Engaged
LE .... Locally Excited [*Physical chemistry*]

LE	Logic Element
LE	Logistic Effectiveness (CAAL)
LE	Logistic Evaluation
LE	Long-Evans Rat
LE	Loop Error [Computer science] (ELAL)
LE	Loop Extender [Telecommunications] (TEL)
LE	Louisiana Eastern Railroad [AAR code]
LE	Low Efficiency
LE	Low Energy (CAAL)
LE	Low Entry [Truck cab]
LE	Lower Epidermis [Botany]
LE	Lower Extremity [Medicine]
LE	Low Explosive [Military]
LE	Low Exposure (MELL)
LE	Lugalbanda and Enmerkar (BJA)
LE	Lugalbanda Epos (BJA)
LE	Lunar Ephemeris
LE	Lupus Erythematosus [Hematology]
LE	Luxury Edition [Automobile model designation]
LE	Magnum Airlines [ICAO designator] (AD)
Le	[The] Twenty-Four Books of the Holy Scriptures (1853) [I. Leeser] (BJA)
LE 2d	Lawyer's Edition, United States Supreme Court Reports, Second Series [A publication] (DLA)
LEA	Laborista Esperanto-Asocio (SAUO)
LEA	Labour Education Authority (SAUO)
LEA	Landes-Entschaedigungsamt (BJA)
LEA	Language Experience Approach [Education]
LEA	Latest Epicardial Activation [Cardiology]
LEA	Launch Enable Alarm (MCD)
LEA	Launcher Electronics Assembly (ACAE)
LEA	Launch Escape Assembly [NASA] (KSC)
LEA	Law Enforcement Agencies (DOMA)
LEA	Law Enforcement Agency (SAUO)
LEA	Law Enforcement Assistance (SAUO)
LEA	Law Enforcement Assistance Program (EA)
LEA	Lead [South Dakota] [Seismograph station code, US Geological Survey] [Closed] (SEIS)
LEA	Lead Air Jet Service [France] [ICAO designator] (FAAC)
LEA	Leader Resources, Inc. [Vancouver Stock Exchange symbol]
LEA	Leaf (SAUS)
lea	League (WDAA)
LEA	League [Unit of measurement]
LEA	Lear Corp. [NYSE symbol] [Formerly, Lear Seating] (SG)
LEA	Learmonth [Australia] [Airport symbol] (OAG)
LEA	Learning Experience Approach [Education] (EDAC)
LEA	Lear Seating Co. [NYSE symbol] (SAG)
Lea	Lea's Tennessee Reports [A publication] (DLA)
lea	Leather (VRA)
LEA	Leather
LEA	Leave
LEA	Letter Enjoyers Association (EA)
LEA	Librarians, Editors, Authors. Pan American Union. Washington (SAUO)
LEA	Light-Emitting Array
LEA	Limited Exclusion Area (SAUO)
LEA	Linear Embedding Algorithm (PDAA)
LEA	Line Equalizing Amplifier (AFM)
LEA	Load Effective Address [Computer science]
LEA	Local Education Agency [School district] [HEW] (OICC)
LEA	Local Educational Agency (SAUO)
LEA	Local Education Area (SAUO)
LEA	Local Education Authority [British] (WDAA)
LEA	Local Employment Act [Town planning] [British]
LEA	Local Enforcement Agency (SARE)
LEA	Local Examination Authority (SAUO)
LEA	Locomotive Engineers Association (SAUO)
LEA	Logistic Evaluation Agency [Army]
LEA	Logistics Engineering Analysis (NASA)
LEA	Logistics Evaluation Activity [Army]
LEA	Logistics Evaluation Agency (SAUO)
LEA	Long-Endurance Aircraft
LEA	Longitudinally Excited Atmosphere [LASER technology] (EECA)
LEA	Loop Extension Amplifier
LEA	Loss Executives Association [Parsippany, NJ] (EA)
LEA	Lower Excess Air [Combustion technology]
LEA	Lower Extremity Amputation [Medicine] (DMAA)
LEA	Low-Excess-Air [Combustion technology]
LEA	Lutheran Education Association (EA)
LEAA	Lace and Embroidery Association of America [Later, Lace Importers Association] (EA)
LEAA	Law Enforcement Assistance Act
LEAA	Law Enforcement Assistance Administration [Closed, functions transferred to Office of Justice Assistance, Research, and Statistics] [Department of Justice]
LEAA Legal Op	Law Enforcement Assistance Administration. Legal Opinions [A publication] (DLA)
LEAB	Albacete [Spain] [ICAO location identifier] (ICLI)
LEA/BZ	Vessel Leased to Brazil [Navy]
LEAC	Levelized Energy Adjustment Clause (NRCH)
LEAC	Madrid [Spain] [ICAO location identifier] (ICLI)
Leach	Leach's English Crown Cases [1730-1815] [A publication] (DLA)
LEA/CH	Vessel Leased to China [Navy]
Leach CC	Leach's Crown Cases, King's Bench [England] [A publication] (DLA)
Leach CL	Leach's Cases in Crown Law [A publication] (DLA)

Leach Cl Cas	Leach's Club Cases [London] [A publication] (DLA)
Leach Cr Cas	Leach's English Crown Cases [1730-1815] [A publication] (DLA)
LEA/CR	Vessel Leased to Greece (SAUS)
LEAD	Law Enforcement Activities Division [National Rifle Association]
LEAD	Law Students Exposing Advertising Deceptions [Student legal action organization]
LEAD	Lead Education Abatement Design Group (SAUO)
LEAD	Leader Effectiveness and Adaptability Description [Test]
Lead	Leader Law Reports [Ceylon] [A publication] (DLA)
LEAD	Leadership and Excellence in Alzheimer's Disease Award Program [Department of Health and Human Services] (GFGA)
LEAD	Leadership, Education, and Development [US Army Corps of Engineers]
LEAD	Leadership for Environment and Development Institute [Non-profit organization] (ECON)
LEAD	Leadership in Educational Administration Development
LEAD	Leadville Corp. [NASDAQ symbol] (SAG)
LEAD	Learn, Execute, and Diagnose
LEAD	Lens Electronic Automatic Design (IAA)
LEAD	Letterkenny Army Depot [Pennsylvania] (AABC)
LEAD	Low-Cost Encryption Authentication Devices (SAUO)
Lead-acid battery	Car battery
Leadam	Leadam's Select Cases before King's Council in the Star Chamber [Selden Society Publications, Vols. 16, 25] [A publication] (DLA)
Leadam Req	Select Cases in the Court of Requests, Edited by I. S. Leadam [Selden Society Publications, Vol. 12] [A publication] (DLA)
Lead Cas Am	American Leading Cases, Edited by Hare and Wallace [A publication] (DLA)
Lead Cas Eq	Leading Cases in Equity, by White and Tudor [A publication] (DLA)
Lead Cas in Eq	Leading Cases in Equity, by White and Tudor [A publication] (DLA)
Lead Cas in Eq (Eng)	Leading Cases in Equity, by White and Tudor [England] [A publication] (DLA)
LEADER	Lehigh Automatic Device for Efficient Retrieval [Center for Information Sciences, Lehigh University] [Bethlehem, PA] [Computer science]
LEADER	Logistics Echelons above Division in Europe (MCD)
LEADER	Low-Emissions Advanced Engine Range [Automotive engineering]
LEADERMART	LEADER Mechanical Analysis and Retrieval of Text (NITA)
LEADEX	Arctic Leads Dynamics Experiment (SAUO)
LEADEX	Lead Dynamics Experiment (SAUS)
LEADEX	Lead Experiment [Marine science] (OSRA)
Lead LR	Leader Law Reports [South Africa] [A publication] (DLA)
LEADR	Lawyers Engaged in Alternative Dispute Resolution [Australia] [An association]
LeadrFn	Leader Financial Corp. [Associated Press] (SAG)
LEADS	Law Enforcement Automated Data System (IEEE)
LEADS	Leigh Airborne Data Acquisition System (SAUO)
LEADS	Library Experimental Automated Demonstration System [Computer science]
LEADS	Line Equipment Assignment and Display System [GTE Corp.]
LEAD USA	Leadership Education and Development USA (EA)
Leadvle	Leadville Corp. [Associated Press] (SAG)
LEA/EC	Vessel Leased to Ecuador [Navy]
LEAF	Interleaf, Inc. [Cambridge, MA] [NASDAQ symbol] (NQ)
LEAF	Land Educational Associates Foundation [Defunct] (EA)
LEAF	Law Enforcement Access Field [Telecommunications]
LEAF	Law, Equality and Freedom (SAUO)
LEAF	Legal Education and Action Fund (SAUO)
LEAF	Legal Environmental Assistance Foundation (EA)
LEAF	Liberal Education for Adoptive Families (EA)
LEAF	LISP Extended Algebraic Facility
LEAF	Lotus Extended Applications Facility
LEAF	Women's Legal Education and Action Fund [Canada]
LEAFAC	Local Employment Acts Financial Advisory Committee (SAUO)
LEA/FR	Vessel Leased to France [Navy]
LEAFS	LASER-Excited Atomic Fluorescent Spectrometry
LEAG	Legislative Extended Assistance Group [University of Iowa] [Research center] (RCD)
LEA/GR	Vessel Leased to Greece [Navy]
LEAGUE	Lesbian, Bisexual, and Gay United Employees at AT & T
League of Nations Off J	League of Nations. Official Journal [A publication] (DLA)
League of Nations OJ	League of Nations. Official Journal [A publication] (DLA)
League of Nations OJ Spec Supp	League of Nations. Official Journal. Special Supplement [A publication] (DLA)
LEAH	Lulov, Esrog, Arrovos, Hadassim (BJA)
LEAHS	Lifetime Evaluation and Analysis of Heterogeneous System (PDAA)
LEAJ	Law Enforcement and Administration of Justice (SAUO)
LEAK	Leak-X Environmental [NASDAQ symbol] (TTSB)
LEAK	Leak-X Environmental Corp. [NASDAQ symbol] (SAG)
LEAK	Liposome-Encapsulated Amikacin [Bactericide]
Leake	Leake on Contracts [1861-1931] [A publication] (DLA)
Leake	Leake's Digest of the Law of Property in Land [A publication] (DLA)
Leake Cont	Leake on Contracts [1861-1931] [A publication] (DLA)
Leake Land	Leake's Digest of the Law of Property in Land [A publication] (DLA)
LEAKW	Leak-X Environmental Wrrt [NASDAQ symbol] (TTSB)
LeakX	Leak-X Environmental Corp. [Associated Press] (SAG)
LEAL	Alicante [Spain] [ICAO location identifier] (ICLI)
LEAM	Almeria [Spain] [ICAO location identifier] (ICLI)
LEAM	Lunar Ejecta and Meteorites [Experiment] [NASA]
Leam & Spic	Learning and Spicer's Laws, Grants, Concessions, and Original Constitutions [New Jersey] [A publication] (DLA)
LEAMS	Law Enforcement Automated Management Subsystem (SAUO)
LEA/MX	Vessel Leased to Mexico [Navy]
LEAN	Law Enforcement Agency Network (SAUO)

LEAN............	Low-Fat Eating for America Now
Le & Ca........	Leigh and Cave's English Crown Cases Reserved [*1861-65*] [*A publication*] (DLA)
LE&S	Logistics Engineering and Support (SAUS)
LE&WRR......	Lake Erie and Western Railroad Co. (SAUO)
LEA/NE........	Vessel Leased to Netherlands [*Navy*]
LEA/NO........	Vessel Leased to Norway [*Navy*]
LEANON.......	Lupus Erythematosus Anonymous (EA)
LEANS	Lehigh Analog Simulator (IAA)
LEAO	Almagro [*Spain*] [*ICAO location identifier*] (ICLI)
LEAO	Law Enforcement Aerial Observation (SAUO)
LEAP	Laboratory Education Advancement Program [*Department of Labor*]
LEAP	Laboratory Evaluation and Accreditation Program
LEAP	Laboratory Evening Academic Program (SAA)
LEAP	Labor Education Advancement Program
LEAP	Lambda Efficiency Analysis Program (VLIE)
LEAP	Landcare and Environment Action Plan (SAUO)
LEAP	Landcare and Environment Action Program (SAUO)
LEAP	Language for Expressing Associative Procedures [*Computer science*]
LEAP	Language for the Expression of Associative Procedures (VLIE)
LEAP	Large Einsteinium Activation Program
LEAP	Large Experimental Aquifer Program [*Oregon Graduate Institute of Science and Technology*] [*Research center*] (RCD)
LEAP	Lasers and Electro-Optics Applications Program
LEAP	Leadership and Education for Advancement of Phoenix [*Arizona*]
LEAP	Leadership and Performance
LEAP	Leading Edge Airborne PANAR
LEAP	Leap Group, Inc. (The) [*NASDAQ symbol*] (SAG)
LEAP	Legal and Educational Aid to the Poor [*Center*]
LEAP	Legislative Evaluation and Accountability Program Committee (SAUO)
LEAP	Lewis Expandable Adjustable Prosthesis [*Orthopedics*]
LEAP	Lifetime Element Advancing Program
LEAP	Lift-Off Elevation and Azimuth Programmer
LEAP	Light Exo-Atmospheric Projectile [*Formerly, Lightweight*] (DOMA)
LEAP	Lightweight Exoatmospheric Advanced Projectile [*Military*] (SDI)
LEAP	Limited Education Assistance Program (SAUO)
LEAP	Linear-Elastic Analysis Program [*SIA Computer Services*] [*Software package*] (NCC)
LEAP	Liquid Engine Air-Augmented Package (MCD)
LEAP	Loan and Educational Aid Programme (SAUO)
LEAP	Loaned Executives Assignment Program [*American Association of Advertising Agencies lobbying group*]
LEAP	Local Education Authorities Project for School Management Training (AIE)
LEAP	Lockheed Electronics Assembly Program
LEAP	Logistic Element Action Proposal (MCD)
LEAP	Logistic Element Alternatives Process (MCD)
LEAP	Logistic Event and Assessment Program
LEAP	Logistics Efficiencies to Increase Army Power (MCD)
LEAP	Logistics Event and Assessment Program (SAUO)
LEAP	Long-Term Equity Anticipations [*Business term*]
LEAP	Louisiana Educational Assessment Program
LEAP	Low-Energy All-Purpose (Collimator) [*Radiology*]
LEAP	Lower Eastside Action Project [*New York City*]
LEAP	Lower-Extremity Amputation Protocol [*Orthopedics*]
LEAP	Low-Power Embedded Application Processor (VLIE)
LEAP	Low-Power Enhanced at Portable (VLIE)
LEAP	Lunar Escape Ambulance Pack [*Aerospace*]
LEA/PA........	Vessel Leased to Panama [*Navy*]
LEA/PE........	Vessel Leased to Peru [*Navy*]
LEA/PG........	Vessel Leased to Paraguay [*Navy*]
LeapGrp.......	Leap Group, Inc. (The) [*Associated Press*] (SAG)
Leap Rom Civ L...	Leapingwell on the Roman Civil Law [*A publication*] (DLA)
LEAPS..........	LASER Electro-Optical Alignment Pole for Surveying [*NASA*]
LEAPS..........	LASER Engineering and Application of Prototype System (MCD)
LEAPS..........	Law Enforcement Agencies Processing System (SAUO)
LEAPS..........	Local Exchange Area Planning Simulation [*Bell Laboratories*]
LEAPS..........	Long-Term Equity Anticipation Securities [*Investment term*] (DFIT)
LEAPS..........	Low Electron Attachment Potential Species (SAUO)
LEAR............	Learn [*Database*]
LEAR............	Lear Petroleum Corp. (SAUO)
LEAR............	Logistics Evaluation and Review
LEAR............	Low-Energy Antiproton Ring [*Particle physics*]
LEAR............	Low Erucic Acid Rapeseed [*Plant variety*]
LearBur........	Learmouth & Burchett Management Systems, Inc. [*Associated Press*] (SAG)
LEARN	Laboratory Experience in Atmospheric Research at NCAR (SAUO)
LEARN	Learnng
LEARN	Los Angeles Educational Alliance for Restructuring Now [*Education-reform project*] (ECON)
Learn & L	Learning and the Law [*A publication*] (DLA)
Learn & Law...	Learning and the Law [*A publication*] (DLA)
Learnl..........	LeaRonal, Inc. [*Associated Press*] (SAG)
LEARS	Long [*Term*] Equity Anticipation Securities [*Finance*]
LearSeat......	Lear Seating Co. [*Associated Press*] (SAG)
LEARSYN.....	Logistics Evaluation and Review Synchronization (IAA)
LEA/RU........	Vessel Leased to Russia [*Navy*]
LEAS............	Aviles/Asturias [*Spain*] [*ICAO location identifier*] (ICLI)
LEAS............	Lata Equal Access System (VLIE)
LEAS............	Lease Electronic Accounting System (IEEE)
LEAs............	Local Education Agencies (PAZ)
LEAS............	Local Education Authorities (ECON)
LEAS............	Lower Echelon Automatic Switchboard
LEAS............	Pride Automotive Gp [*NASDAQ symbol*] (TTSB)
LEAS............	Pride Automotive Group, Inc. [*NASDAQ symbol*] (SAG)

LEA SAT	Leased Communications Satellite (SAUO)
LEASAT.......	Leased Satellite (NITA)
LEASAT.......	Leased Satellite Communications (NVT)
LEASAT.......	Leased Satellite Communications System (SAUO)
LEASATCOM...	Leased Satellite Communications (SAUO)
Leasco.........	Leasco Corporation (SAUO)
LEASCO	Leasing Company-Equipment [*Transportation company classification code*]
LEASE.........	Leasing
LeasEd........	Leasing Edge Corp. [*Associated Press*] (SAG)
LEASESAT...	Leased Satellite (SAUS)
LEAS-FACS...	Lease-Financial Accounting Control System (MHDB)
LEASIB........	Local Education Authorities and Schools Item Banking [*Project*] (AIE)
LEAST.........	Learning Systems Standardization (SAUO)
L East Eur....	Law in Eastern Europe [*A publication*] (DLA)
LEASW........	Pride Automotive Gp Wrrt [*NASDAQ symbol*] (TTSB)
LEATGS.......	Local Education Authority Training Grants Scheme (AIE)
LEATH..........	Leather (ROG)
LEATH..........	Leatherhead [*City in England*]
LeathFac......	Leather Factory, Inc. [*Associated Press*] (SAG)
LEA/UK	Vessel Leased to United Kingdom [*Navy*]
LEA/UR	Vessel Leased to Uruguay [*Navy*]
LEAVERATS...	Leave Rations [*Military*]
LEB	East Baton Rouge Parish Public Library, Baton Rouge, LA [*OCLC symbol*] (OCLC)
LEB	Lateral Efferent Bundle [*Neuroanatomy*]
Leb	Lebanese (DIAR)
LEB	Lebanon [*New Hampshire*] [*Airport symbol*] (OAG)
Leb	Lebanon (VRA)
LEB	Lebanon, NH [*Location identifier*] [*FAA*] (FAAL)
LEB	Lebap [*Turkmenistan*] [*ICAO designator*] (FAAC)
LEB	LeBaron [*Automotive classified advertising*]
LEB	Local Ethernet Bridge [*RAD Network Devices, Inc.*]
LEB	London Electricity Board
LEB	Low-Emissions Bus
LEB	Lower Equipment Bay [*Apollo*] [*NASA*]
LEBA............	Cordoba [*Spain*] [*ICAO location identifier*] (ICLI)
LEBA............	Long Endurance Breathing Apparatus (PDAA)
Lebanon	Lebanon County Legal Journal [*Pennsylvania*] [*A publication*] (DLA)
Lebanon Co LJ (PA)...	Lebanon County Legal Journal [*Pennsylvania*] [*A publication*] (DLA)
LeBAU	American University of Beirut, Beirut, Lebanon [*Library symbol*] [*Library of Congress*] (LCLS)
LEBB............	Bilbao [*Spain*] [*ICAO location identifier*] (ICLI)
LEBC............	Letchworth Indep Bancshares [*NASDAQ symbol*] (TTSB)
LEBC............	Letchworth Independent Bancshares Corp. [*NASDAQ symbol*] (SAG)
LEBCW.........	Letchworth Indep Bcshs Wrrt [*NASDAQ symbol*] (TTSB)
LEBG............	Burgos [*Spain*] [*ICAO location identifier*] (ICLI)
LEBL	Barcelona [*Spain*] [*ICAO location identifier*] (ICLI)
LEBNAP........	Lebanese Kidnap [*Victims*] [*American hostages held in Beirut*]
LEBR............	Bardenas Reales [*Spain*] [*ICAO location identifier*] (ICLI)
LEBS............	London Emergency Bed Service (SAUO)
LEBS............	Low Emission Boiler Systems (SAUO)
LebSeels......	Lebendige Seelsorge (BJA)
LEBT............	Betera [*Spain*] [*ICAO location identifier*] (ICLI)
LEBU............	Large Eddy Breakup Device [*Aerodynamics*]
LEBZ............	Badajoz/Talavera La Real [*Spain*] [*ICAO location identifier*] (ICLI)
LEC	Lake Erie College, Painesville, OH [*OCLC symbol*] (OCLC)
LEC	LAMPS [*Light Airborne Multipurpose System*] Element Coordinator [*Navy*] (CAAL)
LEC	Landed Estates Courts Commission [*England*] (DLA)
LEC	Landmarks of Early Cartography (SAUO)
LEC	LAN [*Local Area Network*] Emulation Client [*Telecommunications*] (ACRL)
LEC	LANTCOM ELINT Center (MCD)
LEC	LASER Electronic Computer
LEC	Launceston Environment Centre (SAUO)
LEC	Launch Escape Control [*NASA*] (KSC)
LEC	Law and Economics Center (SAUO)
LEC	Law Enforcement Center (SAUO)
LEC	Lec Refrigeration Ltd. [*British*] [*ICAO designator*] (FAAC)
LEC	Lecture
LEC	Leukoencephalitis [*Medicine*] (DB)
LEC	Levelized Energy Cost
LEC	Library of English Classics [*A publication*]
LEC	Ligand Exchange Chromatography (DB)
LEC	Light-Emitting Chemical Compound [*Marking agent for equipment used in night operations*] [*Military*] (VNW)
LEC	Light-Emitting Electrochemical Cell [*Chemistry*]
LEC	Light Energy Converter [*Telecommunications*] (TEL)
LEC	Limited Editions Club
LEC	Liquid Encapsulated Czochralski [*Crystal growing technique*] (IEEE)
LEC	List Execution Condition (IAA)
LEC	Little East Conference (PSS)
LEC	Livestock Equipment Council [*Defunct*] (EA)
LEC	Local Emergency Coordinator (SARE)
LEC	Local Employment Committee [*Department of Employment*] [*British*]
LEC	Local Engineering Change [*DoD*]
LEC	Local Exchange Carrier [*Telecommunications*] (PCM)
LEC	Local Export Control [*British*] (DS)
LEC	Lockheed Electronics Company (SAUO)
LEC	Lockheed Electronics Corp. [*Subsidiary of Lockheed Aircraft Corp.*]
LEC	Locking Escape Character [*Computer science*] (VLIE)
LEC	London Education Classification [*Library classification system*] (NITA)
LEC	London Executive Council (SAUO)

LEC.............. Low-Echo-Centroid [Geology]
LEC.............. Low Emitter Concentration (PDAA)
LEC.............. Lower East Coast
LEC.............. Lower Epidermal Cell [Botany]
LEC.............. Low Exchange Carriers (SAUS)
LEC.............. Lumped Element Circulator
LEC.............. Lunar Equipment Conveyor [Aerospace]
LECA............ Landed Estate Companies Association [British] (BI)
LECA............ Launch Escape Control Area [NASA] (KSC)
LECA............ Lehman Caves National Monument
LECA............ Light European Combat Aircraft (PDAA)
LECA............ Light-Expanded Clay Aggregate (DAC)
LECA............ Madrid [Spain] [ICAO location identifier] (ICLI)
LECAM.......... Lectin Adhesion Molecule [Biochemistry]
LECAM.......... Lectin-Cellular Adhesion Molecule [Biochemistry]
LECAPSR ..... Llano Estacado Center for Advanced Professional Studies and
　　　　　　　　Research [Eastern New Mexico University] [Research center]
　　　　　　　　(RCD)
LECB............ Barcelona [Spain] [ICAO location identifier] (ICLI)
LECC............ Lake Erie Cleanup Committee [Defunct] (EA)
LECC............ Linear Error Correcting Code (IAA)
LECCAM........ Leukocyte Endothelial Cell-Cell Adhesion Molecule [Cytology]
LECCE.......... Left Extracapsular Cataract Extraction (MELL)
LECE............ Leasing Edge [NASDAQ symbol] (TTSB)
LECE............ Leasing Edge Corp. [NASDAQ symbol] (SAG)
LECEL.......... Leasing Edge Wrrt'B' [NASDAQ symbol] (TTSB)
LECEP.......... Leasing Edge cm Cv'A'Pfd [NASDAQ symbol] (TTSB)
LECEZ.......... Leasing Edge Wrrt'A' [NASDAQ symbol] (TTSB)
LECH............ Calamocha [Spain] [ICAO location identifier] (ICLI)
LECH............ Lechters, Inc. [NASDAQ symbol] (SAG)
Lechters ...... Lechters, Inc. [Associated Press] (SAG)
LECL............ Linkage Editor Control Language [Computer science] (VLIE)
LECL............ Valencia [Spain] [ICAO location identifier] (ICLI)
LECLU.......... Law Enforcement Civil Liberties Unit (SAUO)
LECM............ Madrid [Spain] [ICAO location identifier] (ICLI)
LECNA.......... Lutheran Educational Conference of North America (EA)
LECO............ La Coruna [Spain] [ICAO location identifier] (ICLI)
LECO............ Leeco Diagnostics, Inc. (SAUO)
LECO............ Lincoln Electric [NASDAQ symbol] (TTSB)
LECO............ [The] Lincoln Electric Co. [NASDAQ symbol] (SAG)
LECO............ Lincoln Electric Holdings [NASDAQ symbol] [Formerly, Lincoln
　　　　　　　　Electric]
LECO............ Local Engineering Control Office [Telecommunications] (TEL)
LECO............ London Engineering Congress (SAUO)
LECOA.......... Lincoln Electric 'A' [NASDAQ symbol] (TTSB)
LEconSc....... License Economic Sciences [Canada] (DD)
LECOS.......... Light Electronic Control System (SAUS)
LECOS.......... Lunar-Environment Construction and Operations Simulator [NASA]
　　　　　　　　(IAA)
LECP............ Low-Energy Charged Particle [Atomic physics]
LECP............ Palma [Spain] [ICAO location identifier] (ICLI)
LECR............ Law Enforcement Candidate Record [Test] (TMMY)
LeCroy.......... LeCroy Corp. [Associated Press] (SAG)
LECS............ LAN [Local Area Network] Emulation Configuration Server
　　　　　　　　[Telecommunications] (ACRL)
LECS............ Launching Equipment Checkout Set
LECS............ Local Economic Consequences Study [Military]
LECS............ Local Enterprise Companies [Scotland] (ECON)
LECS............ Sevilla [Spain] [ICAO location identifier] (ICLI)
LECT............ League for the Exchange of Commonwealth Teachers (EA)
LECT............ LecTec Corp. [NASDAQ symbol] (SAG)
LECT............ Lectern (ROG)
Lect .... Lecture (DIAR)
LECT............ Lecture [or Lecturer]
Lect .... Lecturer (AL)
Lectec.......... LecTec Corp. [Associated Press] (SAG)
Lect LSUC ... Special Lectures. Law Society of Upper Canada [A publication]
　　　　　　　　(DLA)
lectn .... Lectionary (VRA)
Lect Notes Earth Sci... Lecture Notes in Earth Sciences (SAUS)
LECTO.......... Lectotype
LECTR.......... Lecturer
Lect y V ...... Lectura y Vida [A publication]
LECV............ Colmenar Viejo [Spain] [ICAO location identifier] (ICLI)
LED.............. Large Electronic Display
LED.............. Law Enforcement Division [National Park Service]
L Ed .... Lawyers' Edition, United States Supreme Court Reports
　　　　　　　　[A publication] (DLA)
LED.............. Leaded
LED.............. League for Ecological Democracy (EA)
Led .... Ledger (EBF)
led .... Ledger (WDAA)
LED.............. Ledger
LED.............. Leningrad [Former USSR] [Airport symbol] (OAG)
LED.............. Library Education Division [American Library Association] [Defunct]
LED.............. License Expiry Date (WDAA)
LED.............. Light-Emitting Diode [Display component]
LED.............. Line Embossing Device [Computer science]
LED.............. Liquid Element Display
LED.............. Logical Error Detection
LED.............. Logistics Engineering Directorate [ARRCOM] (RDA)
LED.............. London Engine Drivers (SAUO)
LED.............. Longitudinal Establishment Data [Bureau of the Census] (GFGA)
LED.............. Low Echo Defense (ACAE)
LED.............. Low Endoatmospheric Defence (SAUS)

LED.............. Low-Energy Detector
LED.............. Low-Energy Diffraction
LED.............. Lower Emissions Dispatch [Environmental Protection Agency]
LED.............. Lowest Effective Dose [Medicine] (DB)
LED.............. Lowest Emitting Dose [Medicine] (DMAA)
LED.............. Lupus Erythematosus Disseminatus [Medicine]
LED.............. North Platte, NE [Location identifier] [FAA] (FAAL)
L Ed 2d........ Lawyers' Edition, United States Supreme Court Reports, Second
　　　　　　　　Series [A publication] (DLA)
LEDA............ LANDSAT Earthnet Data Availability [ESA-Earthnet Programme
　　　　　　　　Office] [Database]
LEDA............ Lee Data Corporation (SAUO)
LEDA............ Library of Efficient Data Types and Algorithms (VLIE)
LEDA............ Local Employment Development Action (SAUO)
LEDA............ Low-Energy Deasphalting [Petroleum refining]
LEDA............ On-line Earthnet Data Access (SAUS)
L Ed (Adv Ops)... United States Supreme Court Reports, Lawyers' Edition,
　　　　　　　　Advance Opinions [A publication] (DLA)
LEDC............ League for Emotionally Disturbed Children
LEDC............ Local Economic Development Corp.
LEDC............ Logistics Executive Development Course [Army]
LEDC............ Low-Energy Detonating Cord (SAA)
LEDD............ Light-Emitting Diode Display
LEDET.......... Law Enforcement Detachment [Coast Guard]
LED FO .... Ledger Folio (ROG)
LEDI............ Local Employment Development Initiative [Australia]
LEDI............ Low Endo-Atmospheric Defense Interceptor (ACAE)
LEDM............ Valladolid [Spain] [ICAO location identifier] (ICLI)
LEDO............ Laboratory Emergency Duty Officer (SAUO)
LEDO............ Long-Term Effects of Dredging Operations [Coastal Engineering
　　　　　　　　Research Center]
LEDP............ Large Electronic Display Panel
LEDR............ Laboratory for Environmental Data Research [National Oceanic and
　　　　　　　　Atmospheric Administration]
LEDR............ Light-Emitting Diode Recorder (MCD)
LEDS............ Law Enforcement Data System
LEDS............ Liquid Effluents Data System [Environmental Protection Agency]
　　　　　　　　(GFGA)
LEDSHP........ Leadership
LEDT............ Limited Entry Decision Table
LEDU .... Local Employment Development Unit (SAUO)
L Ed (US).... Lawyers' Edition, United States Supreme Court Reports
　　　　　　　　[A publication] (DLA)
L Ed US ...... Supreme Court Reports, Lawyer's Edition [A publication] (NTCM)
LEE .... [The] Lake Erie & Eastern Railroad Co. [AAR code]
LEE .... LASER Energy Evaluator (PDAA)
LEE .... Launch Electronics Equipment
LEE .... Leading Edge Environment
LEE .... Leeds [Utah] [Seismograph station code, US Geological Survey]
　　　　　　　　(SEIS)
LEE .... Lee Enterprises [NYSE symbol] (TTSB)
LEE .... Lee Enterprises, Inc. [NYSE symbol] (SPSG)
LEE .... Leesburg, FL [Location identifier] [FAA] (FAAL)
Lee .... Lee's English Ecclesiastical Reports [A publication] (DLA)
Lee .... Lee's Reports [9-12 California] [A publication] (DLA)
LEE .... Life and Earth Environment (SAUO)
LEE .... Logistics Evaluation Exercise
LEE .... London Electrical Engineers (SAUO)
LEEA .... Law Enforcement Education Agency (SAUO)
LEEA .... Lifting Equipment Engineers Association [British] (EAIO)
Lee Abs ...... Lee's Abstracts of Title [1843] [A publication] (DLA)
Lee & H....... Lee's English King's Bench Reports Tempore Hardwicke [1733-38]
　　　　　　　　[A publication] (DLA)
Lee Bank .... Lee's Law and Practice of Bankruptcy [3rd ed.] [1887]
　　　　　　　　[A publication] (DLA)
LEEBI .... Low-Energy Electron Beam Irradiation [Physics]
LEEC .... LASER-to-Electric Energy Conversion (SSD)
LEEC .... London Environmental Economics Centre (SAUO)
LEEC .... Sevilla-El Copero Base [Spain] [ICAO location identifier] (ICLI)
Lee Cap...... Lee on Captures [A publication] (DLA)
LEED .... LASER-Energized Explosive Device
LEED .... Longitudinal Employer-Employee Data File [Social Security
　　　　　　　　Administration]
LEED .... Low-Energy Electron Diffraction [Spectroscopy]
Lee Dict...... Lee's Dictionary of Practice [A publication] (DLA)
LEEDS.......... Low-Energy Electron Diffraction Spectroscopy (DB)
LeedsFdl...... Leeds FSB [Associated Press] (SAG)
LEEE .... Madrid [Spain] [ICAO location identifier] (ICLI)
Lee Eccl ...... Lee's English Ecclesiastical Reports [A publication] (DLA)
LeeEnt .... Lee Enterprises, Inc. [Associated Press] (SAG)
LEEGS.......... Law Enforcement Explorer Girls (SAUO)
Lee I .... Leeward Islands (SAUO)
LE-EIA.......... Leukocyte Esterase Enzyme Immunoassay
LEEIXS .... Low-Energy-Electron-Induced X-Ray Spectrometry
LEEM .... Low-Energy Electron Microscopy
LEEP .... Law Enforcement Education Program [Department of Justice]
LEEP .... Law Enforcement Explorer Post [Boy Scouts]
LEEP .... Left End-Expiratory Pressure [Medicine] (MELL)
LEEP .... Library Education Experimental Project [Syracuse University]
LEEP .... Loop Electrosurgical Excision Procedure [Medicine]
LeePhr........ Lee Pharmaceuticals [Associated Press] (SAG)
LEER .... Low-Energy Electron Reflection (IEEE)
LEERS .... Long-Endurance Experimental Research Submarine (SAA)
LEES .... Laboratory for Electromagnetic and Electronic Systems
　　　　　　　　[Massachusetts Institute of Technology] [Research center] (RCD)

LEES .... Lake Erie Environmental Studies
LEES .... Launch Equipment Evaluation Set (MCD)
Leese........... Leese's Reports [26 Nebraska] [A publication] (DLA)
Lee Ship...... Lee's Laws of Shipping [A publication] (DLA)
LEET .... Limiting Equivalent Exposure Time (MUGU)
Lee T Hard... Lee's English King's Bench Cases Tempore Hardwicke [1733-38] [England] [A publication] (DLA)
Lee T Hardw... Lee's English King's Bench Cases Tempore Hardwicke [1733-38] [England] [A publication] (DLA)
LEE W .... Lee White Tritium [Clotting Time] [Hematology] (DAVI)
LEF .... Lake Erie, Franklin & Clarion Railroad Co. [AAR code]
LEF .... Landpower Education Fund
LEF .... LASER Excited Fluorescence
LEF .... Leading Edge Flap [Aviation]
LEF .... Left-In Telephone [Telecommunications] (TEL)
LEF .... Leukokinesis-Enhancing Factor [Medicine] (DMAA)
LEF .... Library Exchange Format (SAUO)
LEF .... Licentiate in Economics and Finance
LEF .... Life Extension Foundation (EA)
LEF .... Light-Emitting Film (IEEE)
LEF .... Lincoln Educational Foundation [Defunct] (EA)
LEF .... Linear-Energy Spectrophotofluorometry
LEF .... Line Expansion Function
LEF .... Liquid Expanded Film
LEF .... Lobby Europeen des Femmes [European Women's Lobby] [Belgium] (EAIO)
LEF .... Local Education Fund
LEF .... Loss Entry Form [Insurance]
LEF .... Lupus Erythematosus Factor [Medicine] (DMAA)
LEF .... Lymphoid-Enhanced Binding Factor [Medicine] (DMAA)
LEF .... Lymphoid Enhancer Factor [Biochemistry]
Lef & Cas .... Lefroy and Cassel's Practice Cases [1881-83] [Ontario] [A publication] (DLA)
LEFC .... L-Band Electronic Frequency Converter
Lef Cr L .... Lefroy's Irish Criminal Law [A publication] (DLA)
LEFCS......... Leading Edge Flap Control System [Aviation]
Lef Dec........ Lefevre's Parliamentary Decisions, by Bourke [England] [A publication] (DLA)
LEFE .... Linear Electric Field Effect (PDAA)
LEFI .... Local Electrical Field Instrument (EOSA)
LEFM .... Linear-Elastic Fracture Mechanics
LEFO .... Land's End for Order [Shipping]
Lefroy .... Lefroy's Railroad and Canal Cases [England] [A publication] (DLA)
LEFTA .... Labour Economic, Finance and Taxation Association (SAUO)
LEFU .... Light Ends Fractionating Unit [Petroleum technology]
LEFW .... Lake Erie & Fort Wayne Railroad Co. [AAR code]
LEG .... Aleg [Mauritania] [Airport symbol] (AD)
LEG .... Cabinet Legislation Committee (SAUO)
Leg .... De Legibus [of Cicero] [Classical studies] (OCD)
LEG .... Language of Functions and Graphs (AIE)
LEG .... Law Enforcement Group (WDAA)
LEG .... Legal (AFM)
leg .... Legal (SHCU)
LEG .... Legal Committee (SAUO)
LEG .... Legal Department (SAUO)
LEG .... Legal Questions Relating to Scientific Investigations in the Ocean (SAUO)
leg .... Legate (WDAA)
LEG .... Legate
Leg .... Legatio ad Gaium [of Philo Judaeus] [Classical studies] (OCD)
leg .... Legato (NTIO)
LEG .... Legato [Smoothly and Connectedly] [Music]
LEG .... Legend [Numismatics]
Leg .... Leges [Laws] [Latin] (ILCA)
LEG .... Leggett & Platt [NYSE symbol] (TTSB)
LEG .... Leggett & Platt, Inc. [NYSE symbol] (SPSG)
LEG .... Legislation [or Legislature]
Leg .... Legislative (PHSD)
LEG .... Legislative Library of British Columbia [UTLAS symbol]
LEG .... Legislature (GOBB)
Leg .... Legislature (WDAA)
LEG .... Legit [He, or She, Reads] [Latin]
LEG .... Legunt [They Read] [Latin] (ADA)
LEG .... Library Education Group of the Library Association (NITA)
LEG .... Liquefied Energy Gas
LEG .... Logistical Expediting Group
LEG .... Logistic Evaluation Group
LEGA .... Granada/Armilla [Spain] [ICAO location identifier] (ICLI)
Legacy........ Legacy: A Journal of American Women Writers [A publication] (BRI)
Leg Adv....... Legal Adviser [Chicago] [A publication] (DLA)
Leg Agr........ De Lege Agraria [of Cicero] [Classical studies] (OCD)
LEGAL......... League for Equitable General Aviation Legislation (EA)
Legal Adv .... Legal Advertiser [Chicago] [A publication] (DLA)
Legal Adv .... Legal Adviser [Denver] [A publication] (DLA)
Legal Asp Med Prac... Legal Aspects of Medical Practice [A publication] (DLA)
Leg Alfred ... Leges Alfredi [Laws of King Alfred] [Latin] [A publication] (DLA)
Legal Gaz (PA)... Legal Gazette (Pennsylvania) [A publication] (DLA)
Legal Int...... Legal Intelligencer [A publication] (DLA)
Legal Intel.... Legal Intelligencer [A publication] (DLA)
Legal Intell... Legal Intelligencer [A publication] (DLA)
Legal Obser... Legal Observer [London] [A publication] (DLA)
Legal Observer... New York Legal Observer [A publication] (DLA)
LegalR......... Legal Research Center, Inc. [Associated Press] (SAG)
Legal Rep..... Legal Reporter [Australia] [A publication]
Legal Rep.... Legal Reporter, New Series [Tennessee] [A publication] (DLA)

Legal Resp Child Adv Protection... Legal Response; Child Advocacy and Protection [A publication] (DLA)
Leg & Ins R... Legal and Insurance Reporter [Pennsylvania] [A publication] (DLA)
Leg & Ins Rep... Legal and Insurance Reporter [Philadelphia, PA] [A publication] (DLA)
Leg & Ins Rept... Legal and Insurance Reporter [Philadelphia, PA] [A publication] (DLA)
Legat .... De Lagatione ad Caium [Philo] (BJA)
LEGAT......... Legal Attache [FBI agent posted at an American embassy]
Legato .... Legato Systems, Inc. [Associated Press] (SAG)
LEGATT....... Legal Attache [Foreign service]
Leg Bibl...... Legal Bibliography [A publication] (DLA)
Leg Canut.... Leges Canuti [Laws of King Canute or Knut] [Latin] [A publication] (DLA)
Leg Ch Forms... Leggo's Chancery Forms [Ontario] [A publication] (DLA)
Leg Ch Pr.... Leggo's Chancery Practice [Ontario] [A publication] (DLA)
Leg Chron.... Legal Chronicle Reports, Edited by Foster [Pennsylvania] [A publication] (DLA)
Leg Chron Rep... Legal Chronicle Reports [Pottsville, PA] [A publication] (DLA)
Legco.......... Legislative Council [Hong Kong] (ECON)
LEG COM..... Legally Committed (BABM)
legd .... Legend
LEGE........... Gerona/Costa Brava [Spain] [ICAO location identifier] (ICLI)
Leg Edm ...... Leges Edmundi [Laws of King Edmund] [Latin] [A publication] (DLA)
LEGEN .... Liposome-Encapulated Gentamicin [Bactericide]
LEGEND ...... Legal Electronic Network and Database (IID)
Legend .... Legend Properties, Inc. [Associated Press] (SAG)
Leg Ethel .... Leges Ethelredi [Laws of King Ethelred] [Latin] [A publication] (DLA)
Leg Exam .... Legal Examiner [London or New York] [1831-35; 1862-68; 1869-72] [A publication] (DLA)
Leg Exam & LC... Legal Examiner and Law Chronicle [London] [A publication] (DLA)
Leg Exam & Med J... Legal Examiner and Medical Jurist [London] [A publication] (DLA)
Leg Exam NS... Legal Examiner, New Series [England] [A publication] (DLA)
Leg Exam WR... Legal Examiner Weekly Reporter [A publication] (DLA)
Leg Exch...... Legal Exchange [Des Moines, IA] [A publication] (DLA)
LEGG .... Launch Eject Gas Generator
Leg G.......... Legal Guide [A publication] (DLA)
Legg .... Leggett's Reports [India] [A publication] (DLA)
LEGG .... Leggiero [Light and Rapid] [Music]
Leg Gaz ...... Legal Gazette [A publication] (DLA)
Leg Gaz R ... Campbell's Legal Gazette Reports [Pennsylvania] [A publication] (DLA)
Leg Gaz Re... Campbell's Legal Gazette Reports [Pennsylvania] [A publication] (ILCA)
Leg Gaz Rep... Campbell's Legal Gazette Reports [Pennsylvania] [A publication] (DLA)
Legg Bills L... Leggett on Bills of Lading [A publication] (DLA)
LeggMas...... Legg Mason, Inc. [Associated Press] (SAG)
Leggo .... Leggiero [Light and Rapid] [Music]
Legg Out...... Legge on Outlawry [A publication] (DLA)
LEGGS .... Loyal Escorts of the Green Garters (EA)
Leg HI .... Laws of King Henry the First [A publication] (DLA)
Leg Inf Bul... Legal Information Bulletin [A publication] (DLA)
Leg Inq........ Legal Inquirer [London] [A publication] (DLA)
Leg Int......... Legal Intelligencer [A publication] (DLA)
Leg Intel....... Legal Intelligencer [A publication] (DLA)
Leg Intell..... Legal Intelligencer [A publication] (DLA)
Leg Intl........ Legal Intelligencer [A publication] (DLA)
Legis .... Legislative (AL)
LEGIS.......... Legislative [or Legislature]
LEGIS.......... Legislative Information and Status System [for House of Representatives]
LEGISL .... Legislative (ADA)
LEGISLN ...... Legislation
LEGISN .... Legislation [Legal shorthand] (LWAP)
LEGISNET .... National Legislative Network [National Conference of State Legislatures] [Information service or system] (IID)
LEGISOR...... Legislator [Legal shorthand] (LWAP)
Legis Stud Q... Legislative Studies Quarterly [A publication] (DLA)
Leg Issues ... Legal Issues of European Integration [A publication] (ILCA)
LEGISURE.... Legislature [Legal shorthand] (LWAP)
LEGISV .... Legislative [Legal shorthand] (LWAP)
LEGIT .... Legitimate (DSUE)
legit............ Legitimate (SHCU)
LEGIW .... Co. Counsel Inc. Wrrt [NASDAQ symbol] (TTSB)
Leg J .... Pittsburgh Legal Journal [Pennsylvania] [A publication] (DLA)
Leg Jour...... Pittsburgh Legal Journal [Pennsylvania] [A publication] (DLA)
LEGL........... Co-Counsel, Inc. [NASDAQ symbol] (SAG)
LEGM.......... Low-Energy Gamma Monitor
Leg Misc ..... Legal Miscellany [Ceylon] [A publication] (DLA)
Leg Misc & Rev... Legal Miscellany and Review [India] [A publication] (DLA)
Leg News .... Legal News [Canada] [A publication] (DLA)
Leg Notes.... Legal Notes on Local Government [New York] [A publication] (DLA)
LEGO .... Leg Godt [Play Well] [Acronym is brand of child's building toy] [Denmark]
Leg Obs....... Legal Observer [London] [A publication] (DLA)
Leg Obs....... Legal Observer and Solicitor's Journal [London] [A publication] (DLA)
LEGOL .... Legally Oriented Language [Programming language project] [British] (NITA)
Leg Oler...... Laws of Oleron [Maritime law] [A publication] (DLA)
Leg Op........ Legal Opinion [Pennsylvania] [A publication] (DLA)
Leg Ops (PA)... Legal Opinion [Pennsylvania] [A publication] (DLA)
Leg Out....... Legge on Outlawry [A publication] (DLA)

LegPlat........ Leggett & Platt, Inc. [Associated Press] (SAG)
Leg Port....... Leges Portuum [A publication] (DLA)
Leg Pract & Sol J... Legal Practitioner and Solicitor's Journal [1846-47, 1849-51] [A publication] (DLA)
LEGR.......... Granada [Spain] [ICAO location identifier] (ICLI)
Leg R........... Legal Record Reports [Pennsylvania] [A publication] (DLA)
Leg Rec....... Legal Record [Detroit, MI] [A publication] (DLA)
Leg Rec Rep... Legal Record Reports [Pennsylvania] [A publication] (DLA)
Leg Ref....... Legal Reformer [1819-20] [A publication] (DLA)
Leg Rem...... Legal Remembrancer [Calcutta] [A publication] (DLA)
Leg Rep...... Legal Reporter [1840-43] [Ireland] [A publication] (DLA)
Leg Rep (Ir)... Legal Reporter, Irish Courts [A publication] (DLA)
Leg Rep SL... Legal Reporter Special Leave Supplement [A publication]
Leg Rev....... Legal Review [1812-13] [London] [A publication] (DLA)
LEGRI......... Low Energy Gamma-Ray Imager (SAUS)
Leg R (Tenn)... Legal Reporter Parallel to Shannon Cases [Tennessee] [A publication] (DLA)
LEGS.......... Database Program to write reports with leg (SAUS)
LEGS.......... Lateral Electronic Guidance System [Automotive engineering]
LEGS.......... Learning Experience Guides for Nursing Students [Series of films, games, slides, etc.]
LEGS.......... Legacies (ROG)
LEGS.......... Lethality End Game Simulation (MCD)
LEGS.......... Lighter Electronics Guidance System (MCD)
LEGS.......... Lightweight Engine Generator Set (SAUS)
LEGS.......... Logistic Engine Generator Set (DWSG)
LEGT.......... Lycee d'Enseignement General et Technologique [High School for General and Technical Studies] [French] (BARN)
LEGT.......... Madrid/Getafe [Spain] [ICAO location identifier] (ICLI)
Leg T Cas.... Legal Tender Cases [A publication] (DLA)
Legul......... Leguleian [1850-65] [A publication] (DLA)
LEG (UN)..... Department of Legal Affairs of the United Nations
Legve......... Legislative
Leg W......... Legal World [India] [A publication] (DLA)
Leg Wisb..... Laws of Wisby [Maritime law] [A publication] (DLA)
LEG WT....... Legal Weight (WDAA)
LEGY......... Legacy (ROG)
Leg YB....... Legal Year Book [London] [A publication] (DLA)
LEH............ Launch/Entry Helmet (MCD)
LEH............ Leeds Central Helicopters [British] [FAA designator] (FAAC)
LEH............ Le Havre [France] [Airport symbol] (OAG)
Leh............ Lehigh County Law Journal [Pennsylvania] [A publication] (DLA)
LEH............ Lehigh Valley Industries, Inc. (SAUO)
LEH............ Lehman Br Holdngs [NYSE symbol] (TTSB)
LEH............ Lehman Brothers [NYSE symbol] (SAG)
LEH............ Licentiate in Ecclesiastical History (SAUO)
LEH............ Linear Enamel Hypoplasia (SAUO)
LEH............ Linear Enamel Hypoplasias (QUAC)
LEH............ Liposome Encapsulated Hemoglobin [Biochemistry]
LehAMGN.... Lehman Brothers Holdings, Inc. [Associated Press] (SAG)
LehBr35....... Lehman Brothers [Associated Press] (SAG)
LEHC.......... Huesca [Spain] [ICAO location identifier] (ICLI)
Leh Co LJ (PA)... Lehigh County Law Journal [Pennsylvania] [A publication] (DLA)
LehGTel....... Lehman Brothers, Inc. [Associated Press] (SAG)
LEHI.......... Hinojosa Del Duque [Spain] [ICAO location identifier] (ICLI)
LEHI.......... Lehame Herut Israel [Fighters of the Freedom of Israel]
LEHI.......... Lehigh University (SAUO)
Lehigh .... Lehigh Valley Law Reporter [Pennsylvania] [A publication] (DLA)
Lehigh Co LJ... Lehigh County Law Journal [Pennsylvania] [A publication] (DLA)
LehighGp..... Lehigh Group, Inc. [Formerly, LUI Group] [Associated Press] (SAG)
Lehigh LJ..... Lehigh County Law Journal [Pennsylvania] [A publication] (DLA)
Lehigh U...... Lehigh University (GAGS)
Lehigh Val Law Rep... Lehigh Valley Law Reporter [Pennsylvania] [A publication] (DLA)
Lehigh Val LR... Lehigh Valley Law Reporter [Pennsylvania] [A publication] (DLA)
Lehigh Val L Rep... Lehigh Valley Law Reporter [Pennsylvania] [A publication] (DLA)
LeHK.......... Lehman Brothers, Inc. [Associated Press] (SAG)
Leh LJ .... Lehigh County Law Journal [A publication] (DLA)
Lehman C (CUNY)... Herbert H. Lehman College of The City University of New York (GAGS)
LehmBr........ Lehman Brothers [Associated Press] (SAG)
LEHMIC....... Lumped Element Hybrid Microwave Integrated Circuit [Electronics] (LAIN)
LehMU........ Lehman Brothers, Inc. [Associated Press] (SAG)
LehORCL..... Lehman Brothers Holdings, Inc. [Associated Press] (SAG)
LEHPZ......... Lower Esophageal High Pressure Zone [Gastroenterology] (DAVI)
LEHR.......... Laboratory for Energy-Related Health Research [University of California-D avis] [Department of Energy] (GRD)
LehRgBk..... Lehman Brothers, Inc. [Associated Press] (SAG)
LehSTc .... Lehman Brothers [Associated Press] (SAG)
Leh VLR (PA)... Lehigh Valley Law Reporter [Pennsylvania] [A publication] (DLA)
LEI............ Air UK (Leisure) Ltd. [British] [ICAO designator] (FAAC)
LEI............ Almeria [Spain] [Airport symbol] (OAG)
LEI............ Laboratory Engineering Instruction (ACAE)
LEI............ LASER-Enhanced Ionization [Spectrometry]
LEI............ Leading Economic Indicator
LEI............ Lehigh Group [NYSE symbol] (TTSB)
Lei............ Leijona [Record label] [Finland]
LEI............ Leipzig [German Democratic Republic] [Seismograph station code, US Geological Survey] [Closed] (SEIS)
LEI............ Libertarian Education Institute (EA)
LEI............ Library Equipment Institute [American Library Association]
LEI............ Life Events [or Expectancy] Inventory
LEI............ Literacy and Evangelism International (EA)

LEI............ Lloyd's Electronics, Inc. (EFIS)
LEI............ Local Engineering Instruction (DNAB)
LEI............ Locher Evers International Ltd.
LEI............ Raleigh, NC [Location identifier] [FAA] (FAAL)
LEIA.......... Luminescence Enzyme Immunoassay [Clinical chemistry]
LEIAC......... Livestock Export Industry Advisory Committee (SAUO)
LEIB.......... Ibiza [Spain] [ICAO location identifier] (ICLI)
LEIC.......... Leicestershire [County in England] (ROG)
Leics.......... Leicestershire (DIAR)
LEICS......... Leicestershire [County in England]
LEICSC....... Legal Education Institute, United States Civil Service Commission (DLA)
LEID.......... Limit of Error on Inventory Difference
LEID.......... Low-Energy Ion Detector
LEIDS......... Logistics Electronic Information Delivery System
LeIF.......... Leukocyte Interferon [Genetics]
LEIFS......... Lake Erie Information Forecasting System [Marine science] (OSRA)
LEIFX......... Federated Equity Income Cl.A [Mutual fund ticker symbol] (SG)
Leigh .... Leigh's Virginia Supreme Court Reports [1829-42] [A publication] (DLA)
Leigh .... Ley's English King's Bench Reports [1608-29] [A publication] (DLA)
Leigh Abr..... Leigh's Abridgment of the Law of Nisi Prius [1838] [A publication] (DLA)
Leigh & C..... Leigh and Cave's English Crown Cases Reserved [1861-65] [A publication] (DLA)
Leigh & CCC... Leigh and Cave's English Crown Cases Reserved [1861-65] [A publication] (DLA)
Leigh & D Conv... Leigh and Dalzell. Conversion of Property [1825] [A publication] (DLA)
Leigh & LM Elec... Leigh and Le Marchant. Elections [4th ed.] [1885] [A publication] (DLA)
Leigh GA...... Leigh's Game Act [A publication] (DLA)
Leigh NP ..... Leigh's Abridgment of the Law of Nisi Prius [1838] [A publication] (DLA)
Leigh (VA)... Leigh's Virginia Supreme Court Reports [1829-42] [A publication] (DLA)
LEIM .... Law Enforcement Information Management Section [An association] (EA)
LEIN.......... Law Enforcement Information Network
LEINS R....... Leinster Regiment [Military unit] [British] (ROG)
leio........... Leiomyoma [Gynecology] (DAVI)
LEIP.......... Leipzig [City in East Germany] (ROG)
LEIP.......... Link Eleven Improvement Program (DOMA)
Leipz Stud ... Leipziger Studien zur Klassischen Philosophie [A publication] (OCD)
LEIR.......... Low Energy Ion Ring
LEIS.......... Lander Electrical Interface Simulator [NASA]
LEIS.......... LASER-Enhanced Ionization Spectroscopy (MEC)
Le Is........... Leeward Islands (BARN)
LEIS.......... Legislative Environmental Impact Statement (SAUO)
LEIS.......... LEISURE: Australian Leisure Index (SAUO)
LEIS.......... LeisureLine [Footscray Institute of Technology Library] [Database] [Information service or system] (IID)
LEIS.......... Low-Energy Ion Scattering [For study of surfaces]
LEISA......... Low External Input and Sustainable Agriculture (SAUO)
LeisMkt........ Leisureways Marketing [Associated Press] (SAG)
LEISS......... Low-Energy Ion Scattering Spectroscopy
LEIT .... Leitrim [County in Ireland] (ROG)
LEIT .... Light Emission via Inelastic Tunnelling (IAA)
Leith Black... Leith. Blackstone on Real Property [2nd ed.] [1880] [A publication] (DLA)
Leith R Pr.... Leith's Real Property Statutes [Ontario] [A publication] (DLA)
LEITR......... Leitrim [County in Ireland] (ROG)
LEIU.......... Law Enforcement Intelligence Units [An association] (EA)
LEIX.......... Lowrance Electronics [NASDAQ symbol] (SAG)
LEIX.......... Lowrance Electronics, Inc. (SAUO)
LEJ............ Leipzig [Germany] [Airport symbol] (OAG)
LEJ............ Longitudinal Expansion Joint [Technical drawings]
LEJR.......... Jerez [Spain] [ICAO location identifier] (ICLI)
LeJY .... Lehman Brothers, Inc. [Associated Press] (SAG)
LEK............ Labe [Guinea] [Airport symbol] (AD)
LEK............ Laiko Enotiko Komma [Populist Union Party] [Greece] [Political party] (PPE)
LEK............ LASER Experimental Package
LEK............ Lexington [Kentucky] [Seismograph station code, US Geological Survey] (SEIS)
LEK............ Liquid Encapsulated Kyropoulos [Crystal growing technique]
Leknas........ National Institute for Economic and Social Research (SAUO)
LEKOTEK..... Leksaker, Bibliotek [Program providing meaningful toys for mentally disturbed children; operates on the same principle as a lending library.] [Name formed from Swedish words for "playthings" and "library"]
lekyt.......... Lekythos (VRA)
LEL............ Labor Electoral League (SAUO)
LEL............ Lake Evella [Australia] [Airport symbol] (OAG)
LEL............ Lancashire Enterprise Ltd. [British] (ECON)
LEL............ Large Engineering Loop [NASA] (NRCH)
LEL............ Laureate in English Literature
LEL............ League of Empire Loyalists [British]
LEL............ Learning Expectancy Level [Education]
LEL............ Lens-End-Lamp
LEL............ Letitia Elizabeth Landon [English poet and novelist, 1802-1839]
LEL............ Link-Edit Language [Computer science]
LEL............ Low Energy LASER [Light Amplification by Stimulated Emission of Radiation] [Military]
LEL............ Lower Earnings Limit (MHDB)

LEL	Lower Electrical Limit (NRCH)
LEL	Lower Explosive Limit [of fuel vapor]
LEL	Lowest Effect Level [Toxicology]
LELC	Murcia/San Javier [Spain] [ICAO location identifier] (ICLI)
LELL	Sabadell [Spain] [ICAO location identifier] (ICLI)
LELN	Leon [Spain] [ICAO location identifier] (ICLI)
LELO	Logrono [Spain] [ICAO location identifier] (ICLI)
LELS	Low-Energy LASER System
LELS/OR	Odyssey Review. A quarterly of modern Latin American and European literature in English translation. Latin American and European Literary Society (SAUO)
LELTS	Lightweight Electronic Locating and Tracking System
LELU	Launch Enable Logic Unit
LELU	Lugo [Spain] [ICAO location identifier] (ICLI)
Lely & F Elec	Lely and Foulkes' Elections [3rd ed.] [1887] [A publication] (DLA)
Lely & F Jud Acts	Lely and Foulkes' Judicature Acts [4th ed.] [1883] [A publication] (DLA)
Lely & F Lic Acts	Lely and Foulkes' Licensing Acts [3rd ed.] [1887] [A publication] (DLA)
Lely Railw	Lely's Regulation of Railway Acts [1873] [A publication] (DLA)
LEM	Antenna Effective Length for Magnetic-Field Antennas (IEEE)
LEM	Laboratory Environment Model (MCD)
LEM	Laboratory of Electro-Modeling [Former USSR]
LEM	Lake Exploration Module [University of Wisconsin]
LEM	Language Extension Module (SAUO)
LEM	LASER Energy Monitor
LEM	LASER Exhaust Measurement
LEM	Lateral Eye Movement
LEM	Launch Enclosure Maintenance [Aerospace] (IAA)
LEM	Launcher Electronic Module [Military] (RDA)
LEM	Launch Escape Monitor (MCD)
LEM	Launch Escape Motor [NASA]
LEM	Law Enforcement Manual [IRS]
LEM	Leading Electrical Mechanician
LEM	Legacy Encapsulation Methodology
LEM	Lehman Corp. (SAUO)
LEM	Leibovitz-Emory Medium [Microbiology]
LEM	Lembang [Java] [Seismograph station code, US Geological Survey] (SEIS)
LEM	Lemmon, SD [Location identifier] [FAA] (FAAL)
lem	Lemon [Philately]
LEM	Length of Effectiveness for Magnetic-Field Antennae
LEM	Leukocytic Endogenous Mediator [Immunochemistry]
LEM	Leukoencephalomalacia [Veterinary medicine]
LEM	Library Education and Manpower (SAUO)
LEM	Light Effector Mediator System [Plant physiology]
LEM	Light Emission Microscopy (MELL)
LEM	Light Equipment Maintenance (MCD)
LEM	Linear Electric Motor [Magnetic rapid-transit car] (PS)
LEM	Liquid Emulsion Membrane [Separation technology]
LEM	Logical End of Media
LEM	Logic Enhanced Memory
LEM	Logistic Element Manager
LEM	Logistics Element Manager (SAUO)
LEM	Lower Explosive Mixture (SAUS)
LEM	Luminescences Emission Monitor
LEM	Lunar Excursion Module [Later, LM] [NASA]
LEM	Lunar Exploration Module [NASA] (IAA)
LEMA	Laser and Electro-Optics Manufacturers' Association (EA)
LEM(A)	Leading Electrical Mechanic (Air) [British military] (DMA)
LEMA	Lifting Equipment Manufacturers Association [British] (BI)
LEMA	Lighting Equipment Manufacturers' Association (DAC)
LEMA	Long-term Ecological Modelling Activity (SAUO)
LEMAC	Leading Edge Mean Aerodynamic Chord
LEMAG	Laboratory Equipment and Methods Advisory Group (SAUO)
LEMAR	Legalize Marijuana [Acronym is used for name of an organization]
Le Mar	Le Marchant's Gardner Peerage Case [A publication] (DLA)
LEM(AW)	Leading Electrical Mechanic (Air Weapon) [British military] (DMA)
LEMCA	Low-Echelon Maneuver Control Application (SAUS)
LEMCO	Light Equipment Maintenance Co. (MCD)
LEMD	Madrid/Barajas [Spain] [ICAO location identifier] (ICLI)
LEMDA	Lighting-Electrical Materials Distributors Association (EA)
LEMDE	Lunar Excursion Module Descent Engine [NASA] (MCD)
LEMES	Low-Energy Magnetic Electron Spectrum (IAA)
LEMF	Labour Exchange Managers' Federation [A union] [British]
LEMF	Law Enforcement Memorial Foundation (EA)
LEMF	Local Effective Mole Fraction [Chemistry]
LEMG	Lockyer Resource Management Group (SAUO)
LEMG	Malaga [Spain] [ICAO location identifier] (ICLI)
LEMH	Mahon/Menorca [Spain] [ICAO location identifier] (ICLI)
LEML & AIA	Locomotive Engineers Mutual Life and Accident Insurance Association (EA)
LEMM	Madrid [Spain] [ICAO location identifier] (ICLI)
LEMO	Local Emergency Management Officer
LEMO	Lowest Empty Molecular Orbital [Medicine] (DMAA)
LEMO	Sevilla/Moron [Spain] [ICAO location identifier] (ICLI)
LEMP	Lightning Electromagnetic Pulse (SAUO)
LEMP	Logistics Element Manager Plan (SAUO)
LEMPA	Low-Energy Magnetospheric Particle Analyzer [Atomic physics]
LEMRAS	Law Enforcement Manpower Resource Allocation System (SAUO)
LEMRAS	Law Enforcement Manpower Resources Allocation [IBM program product]
LEMRP	Law Enforcement Memorial Research Project (EA)
LEMS	Lambert-Eaton Myasthenic Syndrome [Medicine] (DB)
LEMS	Linear Econometric Modeling System (BUR)
LEMS	Low-Energy Molecular Scattering (MCD)
LEMSCO	Lockheed Engineering and Management Services Company Inc. (SAUO)
LEMSIP	Laboratory for Experimental Medicine and Surgery in Primates [New York University] [Research center]
LEMT	Lunar Excursion Module Track [NASA] (IAA)
LEMUF	Limits of Error on Material Unaccounted For
LEN	[The] Lake Erie & Northern Railway Co. [AAR code]
LEN	Large Extension Node [Telecommunications] (LAIN)
LEN	Large Extension Node. Communications (SAUS)
LEN	Length
LEN	Leninakan [Former USSR] [Seismograph station code, US Geological Survey] (SEIS)
LEN	Lennar Corp. [NYSE symbol] (SPSG)
LEN	Lenora Explorations Ltd. [Toronto Stock Exchange symbol]
LEN	Lentini Aviation, Inc. [ICAO designator] (FAAC)
LEN	Leon [Mexico] [Airport symbol] (OAG)
LEN	Library of Early Novelists [A publication]
LEN	Light-Emitting Numerics
LEN	Ligue Europeenne de Natation [European Swimming Federation] [Sweden] (EAIO)
LEN	Linear Electrical Network
LEN	Line Equipment Number (SAUS)
LEN	Living Economy Network (SAUO)
LEN	Load Equalization Net [Aircraft arresting barrier] [Trademark]
LEN	Local Employment Network (AIE)
LEN	Local Entry Network (NITA)
LEN	Low Entry Networking (MCD)
LENA	Lower Eastside Neighborhoods Association (SAUO)
LEND	Credit Depot [NASDAQ symbol] (TTSB)
LEND	Credit Depot Corp. [NASDAQ symbol] (SAG)
L en D	Licencie en Droit [Licentiate in Law] [French]
LEND	Lockheed Engineers for National Deployment (SAA)
LENGTH	Length
LENGTHD	Lengthened (ROG)
LENIT	Leniter [Gently] [Pharmacy]
Lennar	Lennar Corp. [Associated Press] (SAG)
LENNI	Local area network Emulation Network Node Interface (SAUS)
Lennk	Low Endoatmospheric Non Nuclear Kill [Military] (ACAE)
LENS	Concord Camera Corp. [NASDAQ symbol] (NQ)
LENS	Large Enthalpy National Shock (SAUO)
LENS	Large Extension Node Switch. Communications (SAUS)
LENS	Lockheed Expendable Neutralization System (SAUS)
LENSCE	Limited Enemy Situation Correlation Element (SAUO)
LEntA	London Enterprise Agency
LENTO	Lentando [With Increasing Slowness] [Music] (ROG)
LENWID	Length to Width Ratio [Of a leaf] [Botany]
LENZ	Vision Sciences, Inc. (SAUO)
LEO	Dreyfus Strategic Municipals [NYSE symbol] (SPSG)
LEO	Law Enforcement Officer (MCD)
LEO	Lear Oil & Gas Corp. [Vancouver Stock Exchange symbol]
Leo	Leonard's King's Bench Reports [1540-1615] [England] [A publication] (DLA)
Leo	Leonardus [Authority cited in pre-1607 legal work] (DSA)
LEO	Leoncito [Argentina] [Seismograph station code, US Geological Survey] (SEIS)
LEO	Leopair SA [Switzerland] [ICAO designator] (FAAC)
LEO	Leopoldville (SAUO)
LEO	Liaison Engineering Order
LEO	Library Entrance Online
LEO	Librating Equidistant Observer
LEO	Link Everything Online (SAUO)
LEO	Littoral Environment Observation [Program] [Oceanography]
LEO	Local Elected Official (OICC)
LEO	Low Earth Orbit
LEO	Lunar Exploration Office [NASA]
LEO	Lyons Electronic Office [J. Lyons & Co] [British] (NITA)
Leoc	Against Leocrates [of Lycurgus] [Classical studies] (OCD)
LEOC	Local Emergency Operations Controller
LEOC	Ocana [Spain] [ICAO location identifier] (ICLI)
LEOCOMM	Low Earth Orbit Mobile Data Communications
LEOD	Lens Extraction, Oculus Dexter [Right eye] [Ophthalmology] (DAVI)
LEOMA	LASER and Electro-Optics Manufacturers' Association
LEOMA	LASER/Electro/Optic Measurement Alignment System
Leon	Leonard's King's Bench, Common Pleas, and Exchequer Reports [England] [A publication] (DLA)
Leon LA Dig	Leonard's Louisiana Digest of United States Cases [A publication] (DLA)
Leon Prec	Leonard's Precedents in County Courts [1869] [A publication] (DLA)
LEOP	Launch and Early Operations Phase (ACAE)
LEOPARD	Lentigines, EKG Abnormalities, Ocular Hypertelorism, Pulmonary Stenosis, Abnormalities of Genitalia, Retardation of Growth, and Deafness Syndrome [Medicine]
LEOPCID	Local Elected Officials Project of the Center for Innovative Diplomacy [Defunct] (EA)
LEOS	IEEE [Institute of Electrical and Electronics Engineers] LASERS and Electro-Optics Society (EA)
LEOS	Large Erectable Optical System (ACAE)
LEOS	Lasers and Electro-Optics Society (SAUO)
LEOS	Loral Electro-Optical Systems (SAUS)
LEOS	Loral Electro-Optical Systems Corp.
LEOS	Low Earth Orbit Satellite (MCD)
LEOS	Low Earth Orbit Satellites (ACRL)
LEOSAR	Low Earth Orbit Search and Rescue (SAUO)
LEOT	Left-End-of-Tape

LEOV............	Oviedo [Spain] [ICAO location identifier] (ICLI)
LEP.............	Air West Airlines, Inc. [ICAO designator] (FAAC)
LEP.............	Laboratory Evaluation Program [Environmental Protection Agency] (GFGA)
LEP..........	Large Electronic Panel
LEP..........	Large Electron-Positron [Accelerator] [in Europe]
LEP..........	Laser Eye Protection (ACAE)
LEP..........	Leadership for Performance (ACAE)
LEP..........	Least Energy Principle
Lep............	Lepidoptera [Entomology]
Lep............	Lepus [Constellation]
LEP............	Lethal Effective Phase [Medicine] (DB)
LEP..........	Library of Exact Philosophy
LEP............	Light Emitting Polymer (SAUS)
LEP..........	Light-Emitting Polymer
LEP..........	Light Evaluation Plan (MCD)
LEP............	Light External Pintle (SAUS)
LEP..........	Lightning-Induced Electron Precipitation [Atmospheric physics]
LEP..........	Limited English Proficiency
LEP............	Limited English Proficient (SAUO)
LEP............	Lipoprotein Electrophoresis [Biochemistry]
LEP............	List of Effective Pages (NVT)
LEP..........	Local Enterprise Program
LEP............	Local Field Potential [Neurobiology]
LEP............	Locally Enlisted Personnel [British military] (DMA)
LEP............	Logistics Excellence Program (SAUO)
LEP............	Low Egg Passage [Rabies vaccine]
LEP............	Low Emissions Partnership
LEP............	Low-Energy Photon (ABAC)
LEP............	Lower End Plug (IEEE)
LEP............	Lower Esophageal [Medicine] (DB)
LEP............	Lowest Effective Power
LEP............	Lowest Evaluated Price (ACAE)
LEP............	Low-Frequency Prediction [Marine science] (OSRA)
LEP............	Lupus Erythematosus Preparation [Hematology] (DAVI)
LEP............	Lycee d'Enseignement Professionel [Professional Secondary School for AdvancedStudies] [French] (BARN)
LEPA............	Laboratoire d'Etudes Politiques et Administratives [Universite Laval, Quebec] [Canada]
LEPA............	Law Enforcement Planning Agency (SAUO)
LEPA............	Palma De Mallorca [Spain] [ICAO location identifier] (ICLI)
LEPC............	Law Enforcement Planning Commission
LEPC............	Local Emergency Planning Commission (SAUO)
LEPC............	Local Emergency Planning Committee [Hazardous waste]
LEPC............	Local Energy Planning Committee (SAUO)
LEPC............	Low Emissions Paint Consortium
LEPD............	Legal Enforcement Policy Division [Environmental Protection Agency] (GFGA)
LEPD............	Low-Energy Photon Detector [Environmental Protection Agency]
LEPEDEA......	Low-Energy Proton-Electron Differential Energy Analyzer [NASA]
LEPG............	Lep Group Ltd. [NASDAQ symbol] (SAG)
LE/PH..........	Local Exchange/Packet Handler (ACRL)
LEPI............	Litton Educational Publishing, Inc.
LEPMA..........	Lithographic Engravers and Plate Makers Association (EA)
LEPO............	Low Exercise Price Options (NUMA)
LEPO............	Pollensa [Spain] [ICAO location identifier] (ICLI)
LEPOR..........	Long-Range and Expanded Oceanic Research (SAUO)
LEPOR..........	Long-Term and Expanded Program of Oceanic Exploration and Research
LEPORE........	Long-Term and Expanded Program of Oceanic Research and Exploration (BARN)
LEPP............	Pamplona/Noain-Pamplona [Spain] [ICAO location identifier] (ICLI)
LEPR............	LASER Electron Paramagnetic Resonance
LEPRA.........	British Leprosy Relief Association (IRUK)
LEPRA.........	Leprosy Relief Association [British] (DI)
LE Prep........	Lupus Erythematosus Preparation [Hematology] (CPH)
LEPS............	Launch Escape Propulsion System [NASA]
Leps............	Lepus [Constellation]
LEPS............	London-Eyring-Polanyi-Sato Method [Reaction dynamics]
LEPS............	Low-Energy Photon Spectroscopy (ABAC)
LEPSOC........	Lepidopterists' Society (EA)
Lept............	Against Leptines [of Demosthenes] [Classical studies] (OCD)
LEPT............	Leptocytes [Biochemistry] (DAVI)
Lept............	Leptospira [Genus of bacteria]
LEPT............	Long-Endurance Patrolling Torpedo
LEPT............	Low-Energy Particle Telescope
LEPTOS........	Leptospirosis Agglutinins [Biochemistry] (DAVI)
LEPW............	Longitudinal Electric Pressure Wave
LEQ............	Lehman Br Hldg 8.30%'QUICS' [NYSE symbol] (TTSB)
LEQ............	Lehman Brothers [NYSE symbol] (SAG)
LEQ............	Level Equivalent (SSD)
LEQ............	Life Events Questionnaire [Psychology] (EDAC)
LEQ............	Line Equipped [Telecommunications] (TEL)
LEQ............	Line of Equipment [Telecommunications] (TEL)
Leq............	Loudness Equivalent [Medicine] (DMAA)
LER............	Land Equivalent Ratio [Agriculture]
LER............	LANSCE/Energy Research Programs (SAUO)
LER............	Launcher Equipment Room [Missiles]
LER............	Leading Edge Radius (MSA)
LER............	Lease Expenditure Request (MCD)
LER............	Leinster [Australia] [Airport symbol] (OAG)
LER............	Lerner Stores Corp. (SAUO)
LER............	Lerwick [United Kingdom] [Geomagnetic observatory code]
LER............	Licensee Event Report [Nuclear energy] (NRCH)
LER............	Life Elongation Ratio (DB)

LER............	Life Extension Refit (SAUS)
LER.............	Light Efficiency Radiator [General Motors Corp.] [Automotive engineering]
LER............	Light-Emitting Resistor [Computer hacker terminology] (NHD)
LER............	Lissajous Electron Plasma (AAEL)
LER............	London Eastern Railway (SAUO)
LER............	London Electric Railway
LER............	Long Eye Relief (MCD)
LER............	Loss Exchange Ratio (MCD)
LER............	Lysozomal Enzyme Release (DB)
LERA..........	Limited Employee Retirement Account (IEEE)
LERAM........	Littoral Ecosystem Risk Assessment Model (SAUO)
LERAM........	Littoral Ecosystem Risk Assessment Model for Prediction of Risk of Chemical Stressors Entering the Aquatic Environment [Environmental Protection Agency] (AEPA)
LERB..........	Line Error Recording Block (MCD)
LERC..........	Laboratory Environmental Review Committee (SAUO)
LERC..........	Language for Export Research Center [University of Western Sydney] [Australia]
LERC..........	Laramie Energy Research Center [Department of Energy]
LERC..........	Law Enforcement Resource Center (SAUO)
LERC..........	Lewis Research Center [NASA] (KSC)
LeRC..........	Lewis Research Center [Cleveland, OH] (NAKS)
LERC..........	Local Emergency Response Committee (EPAT)
LERC..........	London Electric Railway Company (SAUO)
LERF..........	Laboratory Experimental Research Facility [Army] (RDA)
LERG..........	Local Electroretinogram (DB)
LERI..........	Murcia/Alcantarilla [Spain] [ICAO location identifier] (ICLI)
LERIS..........	Low-Energy Recoil Ion Spectroscopy
LERK..........	LASER Experimental Research Kit
LERMISTOR...	Learning Materials Information Store (PDAA)
LERN..........	Learning Resources Network (EA)
LERN..........	Learning Technology, Inc. (SAUO)
LERP..........	Labor Education and Research Project (EA)
LERP..........	Linear Interpolation [Computer science] (NHD)
LERS..........	Reus [Spain] [ICAO location identifier] (ICLI)
LERSC..........	Location Evaluation Recognition and Statistical Comparison (PDAA)
LERSO........	Low Erucic Acid Rapeseed Oil (PDAA)
LERT..........	Lockheed Emergency Reset Timer (IAA)
LERT..........	Rota [Spain] [ICAO location identifier] (ICLI)
LERTCON.....	Alert Condition [Military] (AABC)
LERTCON.....	Alert Condition System (SAUO)
LERTS..........	Laboratoire d'Etudes et de Recherches en Teledetection Spatiale [France] (EOSA)
LERX..........	Leading Edge Root Extension [Aviation]
L-ERX..........	Leukoerythroblastic Reaction [Biochemistry] (DAVI)
LERY..........	Leroy Pharmacies, Inc. (SAUO)
LES............	Automotors Salta SACYF [Argentina] [ICAO designator] (FAAC)
LES.............	Laboratory for Environmental Studies [Ohio State University] [Research center] (RCD)
LES............	Lambert-Eaton Myasthenic Syndrome [Medicine]
LES............	Land Earth Station (SAUO)
LES............	LAN [Local Area Network] Emulation Server [Telecommunications] (ACRL)
LES............	Large Eddy Simulation [For modelling fluid flow]
LES............	Laser Engagement System (ACAE)
LES............	LASER Excitation Spectroscopy
LES............	Lateral Epithelial Space [Anatomy] (DAVI)
LES............	Launch Effects Simulator
LES............	Launch Enabling System
LES............	Launch/Entry Suit [NASA]
LES............	Launch Environmental Simulator (MCD)
LES............	Launch Equipment Shop (MCD)
LES............	Launch Escape System [or Subsystem] [NASA]
LES............	Law Enforcement Squadron
LES............	Lawrence Experiment Station [Agar] [Medicine] (BABM)
LES............	Leading Edge Slats (MCD)
LES............	Leave and Earnings Statement [Military] (AABC)
LES............	Lesbian (DSUE)
LES............	Leslie Fay Companies (SAUO)
LES............	Lesobeng [Lesotho] [Airport symbol] (OAG)
LES............	Lesozavodsk [Former USSR] [Seismograph station code, US Geological Survey] [Closed] (SEIS)
LES............	Licensing Executive Society (SAUO)
LES............	Licensing Executives Society (EA)
LES............	Licensing Executives Society International (SAUO)
LES............	Life Experiences Survey [Psychology]
LES............	Life Extension Society (SAUO)
LES............	Light-Emitting Switch [Electronics] (OA)
LES............	Light Experimental Supercruiser (MCD)
LES............	Light Exposure Speed [Photography] (OA)
LES............	Lilliput Edison Screw
LES............	Limited Early Site [Nuclear energy] (NRCH)
LES............	Limited English Speaking (OICC)
LES............	Lincoln Experimental Satellite [Lincoln Laboratory, MIT]
LES............	Lincoln Laboratory Experimental Satellite (SAUO)
LES............	Line Errored Seconds (SAUS)
LES............	Loaded Equipment Section
LES............	Local Engineering Specifications [DoD]
LES............	Local Engineering Standard (IAA)
LES............	Local Excitatory State
LES............	Locally Engaged Staff
LES............	Locke Egg Serum [Medicine] (MAE)
LES............	Loop Error Signal
LES............	Louisiana Engineering Society (SAUO)

LES	Low-Energy Sputter
LES	Lower Esophageal Sphincter [Medicine]
LES	Lunar Escape System [NASA]
LES	Lupus Erythematosus, Systemic [Medicine] (MAE)
LES	Support Landing Boat [Navy symbol] [Obsolete]
LES-9	Lincoln Experimental Satellite-9 (SAUS)
LES 8/9	Lincoln Laboratories Experimental Satellites Number 8 and 9 (SAUO)
LESA	Lake Erie Steam Association [Defunct]
LESA	Land Evaluation and Site Assessment System [Department of Agriculture]
LESA	Lunar Exploration System for Apollo [NASA]
LESA	Salamanca [Spain] [ICAO location identifier] (ICLI)
LESAP	Law Enforcement Security Access Position
LESAR	Linear Elastic Structural Analysis Routine (ACAE)
LESAT	Leased Satellite [Military] (CAAL)
LESAT	Lockheed Environmental Systems and Technologies Co. (SAUO)
LESC	Launch Escape System Control [NASA] (KSC)
LESC	LE [Lupus Erythematosus] Support Club (EA)
LESC	Liberty Equipment and Supply Company (SAUO)
LESC	Life and Environmental Sciences Committee (SAUO)
LESC	Light-Emitting Switch Control [Electronics] (OA)
LESC	Lockheed Electronic Systems Company (SPST)
LESC	Lockheed Engineering & Sciences Co. (SAUS)
LESC	Lunar-Environment Sample Container [Apollo] [NASA]
Lesco	Lesco, Inc. [Associated Press] (SAG)
LESCS	Launch Escape Stabilization and Control System [NASA] (IAA)
LESD	Letterer-Siwe Disease [Medicine] (DMAA)
LESEM	Low Energy Scanning Electron Microscope (ACAE)
LESG	Late Effects Study Group [for Hodgkins disease]
Lesh	Leshonenu [Jerusalem] (BJA)
LESI	Leif Ericson Society International (EA)
LESJ	Son San Juan Air Force Base [Spain] [ICAO location identifier] (ICLI)
LESL	Law Enforcement Standards Laboratory [National Institute of Standards and Technology]
LESL	Leslie's Poolmart [NASDAQ symbol] (TTSB)
L es L	Licencie es Lettres [Licentiate in Letters] [French] (EY)
Lesli	List of Eligible Surplus Line Insurers
LESM	Longman's Elementary Science Manuals [A publication]
LESM	Murcia [Spain] [ICAO location identifier] (ICLI)
Les Miz	Les Miserables [Musical based on Victor Hugo's novel]
LESNW	Lesnwith [England]
LESO	Lifting Engineering Stop Order (ACAE)
LESO	San Sebastian [Spain] [ICAO location identifier] (ICLI)
LESOC	Lincoln Experimental Satellite Operations Center (MCD)
LESOP	Leveraged Employee Stock Ownership Plan [Procter & Gamble Co.]
LESP	Law Enforcement Standards Program [National Institute of Law Enforcement and Criminal Justice]
LESP	Lower Esophageal Sphincter Pressure [Medicine]
LESP	Madrid [Spain] [ICAO location identifier] (ICLI)
LesPol	Leslie's Poolmart, Inc. [Associated Press] (SAG)
L'Esprit	L'Esprit Createur [A publication] (BRI)
LESR	Limited Early Site Review [Nuclear energy] (NRCH)
LESS	La Esperanto-Spiritista Societo (SAUO)
LESS	LASER-Excited Shpol'skii Spectrometry
LESS	Lateral Electrical Spine Stimulation [Orthopedics] (DAVI)
LESS	Launch Escape System Simulator [NASA] (IAA)
LESS	Law Encounter Severity Scale [Personality development test] [Psychology]
LESS	Leading Edge Structure Subsystem [Aviation] (NASA)
LESS	Leading Edge Subsystem (NAKS)
LESS	Least-Cost Estimating and Scheduling System
LesS	Licencie es Sciences [Licentiate in Science] [French] (BARN)
L/ESS	Loads/Environmental Spectra Survey (MCD)
LESS	Lunar Escape System Simulator [NASA]
L es SC	Licencie es Sciences [Licentiate of Sciences] [French]
LesSc	Licencie es Sciences [Licentiate of Sciences] [French] (ASC)
lessy	lesbian [Psychology] (DAVI)
LEST	Large Earth-Based [formerly, European] Solar Telescope
LEST	Large Earth Survey Telescope
LEST	Launch Electronics System Test
LEST	Launch Enable System Turret (IAA)
Lest	Licencie es Lettres [Licentiate in Letters] [French] (BARN)
LEST	Low-Energy Speech Transmission
LEST	Santiago [Spain] [ICAO location identifier] (ICLI)
Lest & But	Lester and Butler's Supplement to Lester's Georgia Reports [A publication] (DLA)
Lester	Lester's Reports [31-33 Georgia] [A publication] (DLA)
Lester & B.	Lester and Butler's Supplement to Lester's Georgia Reports [A publication] (DLA)
Lester Supp	Lester and Butler's Supplement to Lester's Georgia Reports [A publication] (DLA)
Lest PL	Lester's Decisions in Public Land Cases [A publication] (DLA)
LESTR	Leukocyte-Expressed Seven-Transmembrane-Domain Receptor [Biochemistry]
LESU	Law Enforcement Study Unit [of the American Topical Association] (EA)
LESU	Seo De Urgel [Spain] [ICAO location identifier] (ICLI)
LET	Aerolineas Ejecutivas SA [Mexico] [ICAO designator] (FAAC)
LET	Laboratory Electronics Instruction (IAA)
LET	Laboratory of Electromagnetic Theory (SAUO)
LET	Launch & Escape Time (SAUS)
LET	Launch Effects Trainer [Weaponry] (MCD)
LET	Launch Eject Test
LET	Launch Equipment Test
LET	Launch Escape Tower [NASA] (MCD)

LET	Leader Effectiveness Training [A course of study]
LET	Leading Edge Tracker
LET	Learning Efficiency Test [Educational test]
LET	Legacy Encapsulation Technology
LET	Leonard Euler Telescope (SAUO)
LET	Leticia [Colombia] [Airport symbol] (OAG)
LET	Letter
LET	Lettish [Latvian] (ROG)
LET	Lidocaine, Epinephrine and Tetracaine (SAUS)
LET	Lidocaine, Epinephrine, and Tetracaine Solution [Medicine] (DMAA)
LET	Life Environmental Testing (IAA)
LET	Light Equipment Transporter (MCD)
LET	Limited Environmental Test (MCD)
LET	Lincoln Experimental Terminal [NASA]
LET	Linear Energy Transfer [Radiology]
LET	Lithium Excretion Test [Clinical chemistry]
LET	Live Environment Testing
LET	Live Environment Training [Military] (ADDR)
LET	Local Enterprise Trust [British]
LET	Logical Equipment Table
LET	Logistic Escape Trunk (CAAL)
LET	London and Edinburgh Trust [British]
LET	Low-Emissions Truck
LET	Low-End Torque [Automotive engineering]
LET	Low-Energy Telescope [Geophysics]
LET	Lux e Tenebris [Light Out of Darkness] [Freemasonry] [Latin]
LETA	Latvian Telegraph Agency (EY)
LETA	Sevilla/Tablada [Spain] [ICAO location identifier] (ICLI)
LETAC	Law Enforcement Training Advisory Council (SAUO)
LET&D	Liquid Effluent Treatment and Disposal Liability Act (SAUO)
LETATA	Light Edge Tool and Allied Trades Association [British] (BI)
LETB	Local Exchange Test Bed [Telecommunications] (TEL)
LETC	Laramie Energy Technology Center [Department of Energy] (GRD)
Letch	Letchworth Independent Bancshares Corp. [Associated Press] (SAG)
LetchInd	Letchworth Independent Bancshares Corp. [Associated Press] (SAG)
LETCO	Law Engineering Testing Co. (EFIS)
LETCS	Launch Escape Tower Canard System [NASA] (IAA)
Let D	Doctor of Letters
LETD	Lowest Effective Toxic Dose [Medicine] (DMAA)
LE-TE	Leading Edge - Trailing Edge [Aerodynamics]
LETEC	London East Training and Enterprise Council [British] (AIE)
LETF	Launch Equipment Exposure Facility (SAUS)
LETF	Launch Equipment Test Facility [NASA] (NASA)
LETFO	Letter Follows (NOAA)
LETGS	Low Energy Transmission Grating Spectrometer (SAUS)
leth	Lethal [Pharmacology] (DAVI)
LETHR	Leather
LETI	Leningrad Electrotechnical Institute (SAUO)
LETIS	Leicestershire Technical Information Service [British] (NITA)
LETM	Lake Evaporation and Thermodynamics Model [Marine science] (OSRA)
LETN	Law Enforcement Television Network
LETO	Madrid/Torrejon [Spain] [ICAO location identifier] (ICLI)
LETRI	Leihua Electronic Technology Research Institute (SAUO)
LETS	Large, External Transformation Sensitive [Glycoprotein] [Also known as CSP] [Cytochemistry]
LETS	Launch Equipment Test Set (MCD)
LETS	Law Enforcement Teletype [or Teletypewriter] Service [Phoenix, AZ]
LETS	Law Enforcement Teletypewriter System (SAUO)
LETS	Leading Edge Tracker System
LETS	Learning Experience for Technical Students [NASA]
LETS	Linear-Energy Transfer Spectrometer [Radiology] (KSC)
LETS	Linear-Energy Transfer System [Radiology]
LETS	Live Environment Testing with SAGE (MCD)
LETS	Local Exchange Trading Scheme (WDAA)
LETS	Low-Energy Telescope System [Geophysics]
LETS	Lunar Experiment Telemetry System [Aerospace]
LETT	Letters
LETT	Lettish [Latvian] (ROG)
LEU	Emory University, Division of Librarianship, Atlanta, GA [OCLC symbol] (OCLC)
LEU	Laser Electronic Unit (SAUS)
LEU	Launch Enable Unit
LEU	Launcher Electronic Unit (MCD)
leu	Leucine [An amino acid] (DOG)
Leu	Leucine [Also, L] [An amino acid]
LEU	Leucovorin (DMAA)
LEU	Leukocyte Equivalent Unit (DMAA)
LEU	Lewis, IN [Location identifier] [FAA] (FAAL)
LEU	License to Export Uranium (NRCH)
LEU	Lions-Air, AG [Switzerland] [IATA designator] (FAAC)
LEU	Low-Enriched Uranium [Nuclear energy]
LEU	Seo De Urgel [Spain] [Airport symbol] (OAG)
LEUC	Leucotomy [European term for lobotomy] (DSUE)
LeucNtl	Leucadia National Corp. [Associated Press] (SAG)
Leuk	Leukemia [Medicine]
LEUK	Leukocyte [Biochemistry] (DAVI)
LEUKAP	Leukocyte Alkaline Phosphatase [Biochemistry] (DAVI)
leuko	Leukocyte [Hematology]
LEUP	Leuprlide [Antineoplastic drug] (CDI)
LEV	Bureta [Fiji] [Airport symbol] (OAG)
LEV	Grand Isle, LA [Location identifier] [FAA] (FAAL)
LEV	Launch Escape Vehicle [NASA]
LEV	Leibovitz-Emory Medium for Viral Cultures [Microbiology]

LEV .... Leichtverwundet; Leichtverwundeter [Slightly wounded; minor casualty] [German military - World War II]
LEV .... Levamisole [Antineoplastic drug] (CDI)
LEV .... Levant
lev .... Levator [Muscle] [Medicine] (MEDA)
LEV .... Level
LEV .... Lever
LEV .... Leviathan Gas PL Partners Ltd. [NYSE symbol] (SPSG)
LEV .... Leviathan Gas PLPtnrs LP [NYSE symbol] (TTSB)
Lev............ Levinz's King's Bench and Common Pleas Reports [1660-97] [England] [A publication] (DLA)
LEV .... Levis [Light] [Pharmacy]
Lev............. Leviticus [Old Testament book]
LEV .... Levitz Furniture Corp. (SAUO)
lev .... Levorotatory [Optics] [Chemistry] (DOG)
LEV .... Lev Scientific Industries Ltd. [Vancouver Stock Exchange symbol]
LEV .... Levyne [A zeolite]
LEV .... Lifting Entry Vehicle
LEV .... Loader/Editor/Verifier [Telecommunications] (TEL)
LEV .... Local Exhaust Ventilation [Hazardous material control]
LEV .... Logistics Entry Vehicle
LEV .... Lolium Enation Virus [Plant pathology]
LEV .... Low-Emissions Vehicle
LEV .... Loyal Edinburgh Volunteers [British military] (DMA)
LEV .... Lunar Escape Vehicle (IAA)
LEV .... Lunar Excursion Vehicle [Aerospace]
LEVC .... Valencia [Spain] [ICAO location identifier] (ICLI)
LEVCB .... Low-Emission Vehicle Certification Board [Terminated, 1980] [Environmental Protection Agency]
LEVD .... Valladolid [Spain] [ICAO location identifier] (ICLI)
LevelOne ..... Level One Communications, Inc. [Associated Press] (SAG)
Lev Ent ...... Levinz's Entries [England] [A publication] (DLA)
LevGas .... Leviathan Gas Pipeline [Associated Press] (SAG)
LE-VGF .... Liquid Encapsulation-Vertical Gradient Freeze (PDAA)
Levi Com L... Levi's International Commercial Law [2nd ed.] [1863] [A publication] (DLA)
Levi Merc L... Levi's Mercantile Law [1854] [A publication] (DLA)
LEVIT .... Leviter [Lightly] [Pharmacy]
LEVIT .... Leviticus [Old Testament book] (ROG)
Levitz .... Levitz Furniture, Inc. [Associated Press] (SAG)
Lev JP .... Levinge's Irish Justice of the Peace [A publication] (DLA)
LEVL .... Level One Communications [NASDAQ symbol] (TTSB)
LEVL .... Level One Communications, Inc. [NASDAQ symbol] (SAG)
LEVM .... Valencia [Spain] [ICAO location identifier] (ICLI)
LEVMETR..... Levelometer
LEVN .... Levin Computer Corp. (SAUO)
LEVONORG... Levonorgestrel (SAUS)
LevR .... Leviticus Rabbah (BJA)
LEVS .... Leaves
LEVS .... Lev Scientific Industries Ltd. (SAUO)
LEVS .... Madrid/Cuatro Vientos [Spain] [ICAO location identifier] (ICLI)
LEVT .... Left Extremity Venous Tracing [Cardiology] (DAVI)
LEVT .... Levitt Corporation (SAUO)
LEVT .... Lower Extremity Venous Tracing [Cardiology] (DAVI)
LEVT .... Vitoria [Spain] [ICAO location identifier] (ICLI)
LEVTAB........ Level Table (MHDB)
LEVVA.......... Lunar Extravehicular Visor Assembly [NASA] (KSC)
LEVX .... Vigo [Spain] [ICAO location identifier] (ICLI)
Levy WTM ... Woerterbuch ueber die Talmudim und Midraschim [J. Levy] [A publication] (BJA)
LEW .... Auburn-Lewiston [Maine] [Airport symbol] (AD)
LEW .... Auburn/Lewiston, ME [Location identifier] [FAA] (FAAL)
Lew............. Lewin's English Crown Cases Reserved [1822-38] [A publication] (DLA)
LEW .... Lewis [Rat strain]
Lew............. Lewis' Reports [Nevada] [A publication] (DLA)
Lew............. Lewis' Reports [Missouri] [A publication] (DLA)
LEW .... Lewiston [Maine] [Airport symbol] (OAG)
LEW .... Lyttleton Engineering Works (SAUO)
Lew App ..... Lewin's Appportionment [1869] [A publication] (DLA)
Lew B & S... Lewis on Bonds and Securities [A publication] (DLA)
Lew CC........ Lewin's English Crown Cases [A publication] (DLA)
Lew CL........ Lewis' Criminal Law [A publication] (DLA)
Lew Conv..... Lewis' Principles of Conveyancing [A publication] (DLA)
LEWDD .... Lightweight Early Warning Detection Device (SAUS)
LEWDI .... Light Weight Early Warning Detection Device (ACAE)
Lew Dig Cr L... Lewis' Digest of United States Criminal Law [A publication] (DLA)
Lew Elec...... Lewis' Election Manual [A publication] (DLA)
Lew Eq Dr ... Lewis on Equity Drafting [A publication] (DLA)
LEWEX........ Labrador Extreme Waves Experiment (SAUO)
Lewin........... Lewin on Trusts [A publication] (DLA)
Lewin CC.... Lewin's English Crown Cases Reserved [1822-38] [A publication] (DLA)
Lewin CC (Eng)... Lewin's English Crown Cases [A publication] (DLA)
Lewin Cr Cas... Lewin's English Crown Cases Reserved [A publication] (DLA)
Lew Ind Pen... Lewis' East India Penal Code [A publication] (DLA)
Lewis........... Lewis' Appeals Reports [29-35 Missouri] [A publication] (DLA)
Lewis........... Lewis' Kentucky Law Reporter [A publication] (DLA)
Lewis........... Lewis' Reports [Nevada] [A publication] (DLA)
Lewis & Clark C... Lewis and Clark College (GAGS)
Lewis Em Dom... Lewis on Eminent Domain [A publication] (DLA)
Lewis Perp... Lewis' Law of Perpetuities [A publication] (DLA)
Lew L Cas ... Lewis' Leading Cases on Public Land Law [A publication] (DLA)
Lew LT .... Lewis on Land Titles in Philadelphia [A publication] (DLA)
LEWP........... Line Echo Wave Pattern

Lew Perp..... Lewis' Law of Perpetuities [A publication] (DLA)
Lew St........ Lewis on Stocks, Bonds, Etc. [A publication] (DLA)
Lew Tr........ Lewin on Trusts [A publication] (DLA)
LEWU.......... Lanka Estate Workers' Union [Ceylon]
Lew US Cr L... Lewis' Digest of United States Criminal Law [A publication] (DLA)
LEWWG .... Land Electronic Warfare Working Group (SAUO)
LEX .... Cary Memorial Library, Lexington, MA [OCLC symbol] (OCLC)
LEX .... Land Exercise [Marine Corps]
LEX .... Leading Edge Extension [Aviation]
LEX .... Letter Exchange (EA)
Lex............. Lexical (BJA)
LEX .... Lexicographer (ABBR)
Lex............. Lexicon (DIAR)
LEX .... Lexicon
lex .... Lexicon (WDAA)
LEX .... Lexington [Virginia] [Seismograph station code, US Geological Survey] [Closed] (SEIS)
LEX .... Lexington [Diocesan abbreviation] [Kentucky] (TOCD)
LEX .... Lexington/Frankfort [Kentucky] [Airport symbol] (OAG)
LEX .... L'Express, Inc. [ICAO designator] (FAAC)
LEX .... Line Exchange [Telecommunications]
LEX .... Listing Exchange
LEx............. Liver Extract [Protein/lipid substance] [Immunology]
LEXB .... Lexington Savings Bank (SAUO)
LexBLF .... Lexington B & L Financial Corp. [Associated Press] (SAG)
LexCrpP...... Lexington Corporate Properties [Associated Press] (SAG)
Lex Cust ..... Lex Custumaria [Latin] [A publication] (DLA)
LEXD .... Lexden [England]
LEXD .... Lexidata Corp. (SAUO)
LEXG .... Lexicon Genetics [NASDAQ symbol] (SG)
LexGlbl .... Lexington Global Asset Managers, Inc. [Associated Press] (SAG)
LEXI .... Lexical (ABBR)
LEXI .... Lexicon Corp. (SAUO)
LEXICO .... Lexicographer (ABBR)
lexicog......... Lexicography (WDAA)
LEXICOG...... Lexicography
LEXIS.......... Legal Exchange Information Service (SAUO)
LEXIS.......... Legal Research Service [Registered service mark] (IID)
LEXIS.......... Lexicography Information Service [Germany] [Computer science]
LEXJ .... Santander [Spain] [ICAO location identifier] (ICLI)
Lex Man ...... Lex Maneriorum [Latin] [A publication] (DLA)
Lex Mer Am... Lex Mercatoria Americana [Latin] [A publication] (DLA)
Lex Mess..... Lexicon Messanense [Classical studies] (OCD)
Lexmrk........ Lexmark International Group [Associated Press] (SAG)
LEXN........... Lexicon (ABBR)
LEXOG .... Lexicology (ABBR)
LEXOGL ...... Lexicological (ABBR)
LEXOGT ...... Lexicologist (ABBR)
LEXP .... Language Experience
Lex Parl ...... Lex Parliamentaria [Latin] [A publication] (DLA)
LEXPHR ...... Lexicographer (ABBR)
LEXPHY ...... Lexicography (ABBR)
LEXSWG ...... Lunar Exploration Science Working Group [NASA]
LexSyr........ Lexicon Syriacum [A publication] (BJA)
LEXT........... Lexitech International Documentation Network, Inc. (SAUO)
L/EXT.......... Lower Extremity [Medicine]
Ley............. Ley's English Court of Wards Reports [A publication] (DLA)
Ley............. Ley's English King's Bench Reports [1608-29] [A publication] (DLA)
LEY .... Liberal European Youth
LEYD........... Leyden [Netherlands] (ROG)
Ley Wards.... Ley's English Court of Wards Reports [A publication] (DLA)
LEZ .... Lunar Equatorial Zone [Army Map Service]
LEZA .... Zaragoza [Spain] [ICAO location identifier] (ICLI)
LEZG .... Zaragoza [Spain] [ICAO location identifier] (ICLI)
LEZL .... Sevilla [Spain] [ICAO location identifier] (ICLI)
LEZOR .... Liquid Encapsulation Zone-Refining (PDAA)
LF .... Fighter Aircraft Fitted with Engine Rated for Low-Altitude Performance (SAUS)
LF .... Labile Factor (DB)
LF .... Lacrimatory Factor [Food technology]
LF .... Lacrosse Foundation (EA)
LF .... Lactoferrin [Biochemistry]
LF .... La Fosse Platinum Group, Inc. [Toronto Stock Exchange symbol]
LF .... Lakser Foundation (SAUO)
LF .... Lama Foundation (EA)
LF .... Laminar Flow (AAEL)
LF .... [The] Lancashire Fusiliers [Military unit] [British]
LF .... Land Forces [Military] [British]
LF .... Landing Force [Navy] (NVT)
LF .... Largest Frame (ACRL)
LF .... Laryngofissure (MAE)
LF .... Lassa Fever [Medicine] (MELL)
LF .... Latex Fixation [Test] [Medicine]
LF .... Lathe Fixture (MCD)
LF .... Laucks Foundation (EA)
LF .... Launch Facility
LF .... Launch Forward
LF .... Law French (DLA)
LF .... Lawn Faucet (MSA)
L/F .... Leader/Follower (ACAE)
LF .... Lead Fabricators Ltd. (SAUO)
LF Perp....... Lead-Free
LF .... Leaf [Bibliography] (ROG)
LF .... Leaf (VRA)
lf .... Leaf (WGA)

LF	League of Friendship [Defunct] (EA)
LF	Leapfrog Configuration [Circuit theory] (IEEE)
LF	Least Frequent (AEBS)
LF	Lebanese Forces
LF	Lederer Foundation (EA)
LF	Ledger Folio
LF	Left (ECII)
lf	Left Field [Baseball term] (NDBD)
LF	Left Field [or Fielder] [Baseball]
LF	Left Foot
LF	Left Forward [Football]
LF	Left Front
LF	Left Fullback [Soccer]
LF	Legion of Frontiersmen [British military] (DMA)
LF	Lethal Factor (MELL)
LF	Lettering Faded
LF	Leukotactic Factor [Medicine] (MELL)
LF	Liberty Federation (EA)
LF	Library of Fathers [A publication] (ODCC)
LF	Liederkranz Foundation (EA)
LF	Life (ABBR)
LF	Life Float
LF	Lifeline Foundation (EA)
LF	Lifting Fan [Hovercraft]
LF	Ligamenta Flava [Medicine] (MELL)
LF	Lightface [Type]
lf	Lightface Type (WDMC)
LF	Light Fastness Ink (DGA)
LF	Ligue de Foyer [Salvation Army Home League - SAHL] (EAIO)
LF	Limiting Fragmentation [Physics] (OA)
LF	Limit of Flocculation
LF	Lineal Feet
LF	Linear File [Computer file] (NITA)
LF	Linear Filter
LF	Linear Foot
LF	Linear Fracture (SAUS)
LF	Line Feed [Control character] [Computer science]
LF	Line Finder [Teletype]
L/F	Linen-Faced Paper (DGA)
LF	Linjeflyg [ICAO designator] (AD)
LF	Linoleum Floor [Technical drawings]
LF	Lisle Fellowship (EA)
LF	Listener Function (IAA)
LF	Lituanus Foundation (EA)
LF	Live Fire
LF	Live Flying (NATG)
LF	Liver Fluke [Medicine] (MELL)
LF	Load Factor
LF	Loaf
LF	Loan Forgiveness (DICI)
LF	Local Film
LF	Local Force [Viet Cong combat force]
LF	Local Forces (SAUS)
LF	Locally Funded (AFM)
LF	Lock Forward
LF	Logical File [Computer science] (BUR)
LF	Logic Function
LF	Long Form (SAUS)
LF	Loss Factor (ELAL)
LF	Lost on Foul [Boxing]
LF	Lovelace Foundation for Medical Education and Research [Reorganized to form Lovelace Medical Foundation and Lovelace Biomedical and Environmental Research Institute]
Lf	Lower Left (ACAE)
LF	Low Fat [Diet]
LF	Low Fidelity (ACAE)
LF	Low Filter (ELAL)
LF	Low Flange (DICI)
LF	Low-Fluence [Physics]
LF	Low Foliage Forager [Ecology]
LF	Low Food Density [Ecology]
LF	Low Force
LF	Low Forceps [Delivery] [Obstetrics]
lf	Low Frequency (WDMC)
LF	Low Frequency
lf	Low Rate Forward [Ecology]
LF	Lung Fluke [Medicine] (MELL)
LF	Siebelwerke ATG GmbH [Germany] [ICAO aircraft manufacturer identifier] (ICAO)
LFA	Air Alfa Hava Yollari Ve Tec, AS [Turkey] [FAA designator] (FAAC)
LFA	Klamath Falls, OR [Location identifier] [FAA] (FAAL)
LFA	Land Force Adriatic [British Royal Marines] [World War II]
LFA	Land Force, Airmobility [NATO] (NATG)
LFA	Land Freedom Army (SAUO)
LFA	Landing Force Aviation
LFA	Language Foundation of Australia
LFA	Large Families of America [Defunct] (EA)
LFA	Last Field Address (IAA)
LFA	Lavage Fluid Analysis [Medicine] (MELL)
LFA	Lead Federal Agency (COE)
LFA	Leading Field Activity (MCD)
LFA	Left Femoral Artery [Anatomy]
LFA	Left Forearm (SAUS)
LFA	Left Frontal Craniotomy [Medicine] (DMAA)
LFA	Left Frontoanterior [A fetal position] [Obstetrics]

LFA	Less Favored Areas (WDAA)
LFA	Less Favoured Area (SAUO)
LFA	Leukocyte Function-Associated Antigen [Immunology]
LFA	Leukotactic Factor Activity [Medicine] (DMAA)
LFA	Light Freight Agent (ADA)
LFA	Lime Fly Ash [Aggregate] (DICI)
LFA	Link Field Address (SAUS)
LFA	Littlefield, Adams [AMEX symbol] (TTSB)
LFA	Littlefield, Adams & Co. [AMEX symbol] (SPSG)
LFA	Local Feature Analysis (VLIE)
LFA	Local File Access [Computer science] (VLIE)
LFA	Local Flying Area [Aviation] (DA)
LFA	Local Freight Agent
LFA	London Football Association (SAUO)
LFA	Louisiana Forestry Association (WPI)
LFA	Low Flow Alarm (IEEE)
LFA	Low-Flying Area (SAUS)
LFA	Low Frequency Active (DOMA)
LFA	Low Friction Arthroplasty [Orthopedics] (DAVI)
LFA	Low Functioning Autism
LFA	Lupus Foundation of America (EA)
LFA	Lutheran Fraternities of America (EA)
LFA	Luther Family Association
LFA	Lymphocyte Function-Associated Antigen [Immunochemistry]
LFAA	Ambleteuse [France] [ICAO location identifier] (ICLI)
LFAAV	Landing Force Assault Amphibious Vehicle (MCD)
LFAB	Dieppe/Saint-Aubin [France] [ICAO location identifier] (ICLI)
LFAC	Calais/Dunkerque [France] [ICAO location identifier] (ICLI)
LFACS	Light Future Armored Combat System [Tank]
LFACS	Loop Facilities Assignment and Control System (VLIE)
LFAD	Compiegne/Margny [France] [ICAO location identifier] (ICLI)
LFAE	Eu-Mers/Le Treport [France] [ICAO location identifier] (ICLI)
LFAF	Laon/Chambry [France] [ICAO location identifier] (ICLI)
LFAF	Low-Frequency Accelerometer Flutter (MCD)
LFAG	Leafage (ABBR)
LFAG	Peronne/Saint-Quentin [France] [ICAO location identifier] (ICLI)
LFAH	Soissons/Cuffies [France] [ICAO location identifier] (ICLI)
LFAI	Lifting Fair Air Intake [Hovercraft]
LFAI	Nangis/Les Loges [France] [ICAO location identifier] (ICLI)
LFAJ	Argentan [France] [ICAO location identifier] (ICLI)
LFAK	Dunkerque-Ghyvelde [France] [ICAO location identifier] (ICLI)
LFAL	La Fleche/Thoree-Les-Pins [France] [ICAO location identifier] (ICLI)
LFAL	Lutheran Fraternities of America Life
LFAM	Berck-Sur-Mer [France] [ICAO location identifier] (ICLI)
LFAM	Life of America Insurance Corporation of Boston (SAUO)
LFAM	Low-Frequency Accelerometer Modes (MCD)
LFAN	Conde-Sur-Noireau [France] [ICAO location identifier] (ICLI)
LFAO	Bagnole-De-L'Orne [France] [ICAO location identifier] (ICLI)
LFAP	Lightweight Flow Admission Protocol (SAUS)
LFAP	Low-Frequency Accelerometer POGO [Polar Orbiting Geophysical Observatory] [NASA] (NASA)
LFAP	Rethel-Perthes [France] [ICAO location identifier] (ICLI)
LFAQ	Albert/Bray [France] [ICAO location identifier] (ICLI)
LFAR	Last Frame Address Register
LFAR	Libertarians for Animal Rights (EA)
LFAR	Montdidier [France] [ICAO location identifier] (ICLI)
LFAS	Falaise-Monts-D'Eraines [France] [ICAO location identifier] (ICLI)
LFAS	League of Finnish-American Societies (EAIO)
LFAS	Licentiate of Faculty of Architects and Surveyors (SAUO)
LFAS	Low-Frequency Active Sonar (DOMA)
LFASV	Landing Force Amphibious Support Vehicle (SAA)
LFAT	Le Touquet/Paris-Plage [France] [ICAO location identifier] (ICLI)
LFATDS	Light Field Artillery Tactical Data System (GFGA)
LFaU	Union Parish Library, Farmerville, LA [Library symbol] [Library of Congress] (LCLS)
LFAU	Vauville [France] [ICAO location identifier] (ICLI)
LFAV	Valenciennes/Denain [France] [ICAO location identifier] (ICLI)
LFAW	Villerupt [France] [ICAO location identifier] (ICLI)
LFAX	Mortagne-Au-Perche [France] [ICAO location identifier] (ICLI)
LFAY	Amiens/Glisy [France] [ICAO location identifier] (ICLI)
LFB	Lafayette, TN [Location identifier] [FAA] (FAAL)
LFB	Landing Force Bulletin [Marine Corps]
LFB	Lateral Forebrain Bundle
LFB	Left Fullback [Soccer]
LFB	Leverage Fund of Boston (SAUO)
LFB	Licensed Fishing Boat
LFB	Light Field Battery [British military] (DMA)
LFB	Limited Frequency Band
LFB	Linear Frame Buffer [Computer science] (VLIE)
LFB	London Festival Ballet
LFB	London Fire Brigade
LFB	Longview Fibre [NYSE symbol] (TTSB)
LFB	Longview Fibre Co. [NYSE symbol] (CTT)
LFB	Loop Fluidized Bed [Chemical engineering]
LFB	Low-Frequency Beacon
LFB	Luxol Fast Blue [Biological stain]
LFB2	London Festival Ballet's Ensemble Group
LFBA	Agen/La Garenne [France] [ICAO location identifier] (ICLI)
LFBA	Licentiate of the Corporation of Executives and Administrators [British] (DBQ)
LFBB	Bordeaux [France] [ICAO location identifier] (ICLI)
LFBC	Cazaux [France] [ICAO location identifier] (ICLI)
LFBD	Bordeaux/Merignac [France] [ICAO location identifier] (ICLI)
LFBD	Letters of the First Babylonian Dynasty [A publication] (BJA)
LFBD	Lifeblood (ABBR)

LFBE .... Bergerac/Roumaniere [*France*] [*ICAO location identifier*]   (ICLI)
LFBF .... Louisiana Farm Bureau Federation   (SRA)
LFBF .... Toulouse/Francazal [*France*] [*ICAO location identifier*]   (ICLI)
LFBG .... Cognac/Chateau Bernard [*France*] [*ICAO location identifier*]   (ICLI)
LFBH .... La Rochelle/Laleu [*France*] [*ICAO location identifier*]   (ICLI)
LFBI .... Little Falls Bancorp [*NASDAQ symbol*]   (TTSB)
LFBI .... Poitiers/Biard [*France*] [*ICAO location identifier*]   (ICLI)
LFBJ .... Saint-Junien [*France*] [*ICAO location identifier*]   (ICLI)
LFBK .... Lincoln First Banks   (SAUO)
LFBK .... Montlucon-Gueret [*France*] [*ICAO location identifier*]   (ICLI)
LFBL .... Limoges/Bellegarde [*France*] [*ICAO location identifier*]   (ICLI)
LFBM .... Mont-De-Marsan [*France*] [*ICAO location identifier*]   (ICLI)
LFBN .... Niort/Souche [*France*] [*ICAO location identifier*]   (ICLI)
LFBO .... Toulouse/Blagnac [*France*] [*ICAO location identifier*]   (ICLI)
LFBP .... Pau/Pont-Long-Uzein [*France*] [*ICAO location identifier*]   (ICLI)
LFBQ .... Toulouse [*France*] [*ICAO location identifier*]   (ICLI)
LFBR .... LASER Fusion Breeder Reactor
LFBR .... Liquid Fluidized Bed Reactor
LFBR .... Longview Fibre Co.   (SAUO)
LFBR .... Muret/Lherm [*France*] [*ICAO location identifier*]   (ICLI)
LFBR-CX .... Liquid Fluidized Bed Reactor Critical Experiment
LFBS .... Biscarosse/Parentis [*France*] [*ICAO location identifier*]   (ICLI)
LFBT .... Lifeboat   (ABBR)
LFBT .... Tarbes/Ossun-Lourdes [*France*] [*ICAO location identifier*]   (ICLI)
LFBU .... Angouleme/Brie-Champniers [*France*] [*ICAO location identifier*]   (ICLI)
LFBV .... Brive/La Roche [*France*] [*ICAO location identifier*]   (ICLI)
LFBW .... Mont-De-Marsan [*France*] [*ICAO location identifier*]   (ICLI)
LFBX .... Perigeux/Bassillac [*France*] [*ICAO location identifier*]   (ICLI)
LFBY .... Dax/Seyresse [*France*] [*ICAO location identifier*]   (ICLI)
LFBZ .... Biarritz-Bayonne/Anglet [*France*] [*ICAO location identifier*]   (ICLI)
LFC .... Aero Control Air Ltd. [*Canada*] [*ICAO designator*]   (FAAC)
LFC .... Concordia Parish Library, Ferriday, LA [*Library symbol*] [*Library of Congress*]   (LCLS)
LFC .... Lafayette Flying Corps [*World War I*]
LFC .... Lake Forest College [*Illinois*]
LFC .... Lake Fork Canyon [*New Mexico*] [*Seismograph station code, US Geological Survey*]   (SEIS)
LFC .... Laminar Flow Control [*Aerodynamics*]
LFC .... Lands and Forests Commission [*Australia*]
LFC .... Large Format Camera [*Space exploration*]
LFC .... Laser Film Corporation   (SAUO)
LFC .... Lateral Femoral Condyle [*Anatomy*]
LFC .... L-Band Frequency Converter
LFC .... Level of Free Convection [*Meteorology*]
LFC .... Liberty Financial Corp.   (EFIS)
LFC .... Liberty Football Conference   (PSS)
LFC .... Light Fighter Course [*Army*]
LFC .... Line Feed Character [*Computer science*]   (VLIE)
LFC .... Liquids from Coal
LFC .... Live Fire Component   (MCD)
LFC .... Living Female Child [*Medicine*]   (DMAA)
LFC .... Load Frequency Control   (IEEE)
LFC .... Local Files Check
LFC .... Local Forms Control [*Computer science*]   (CMD)
LFC .... Local Function Capabilities   (VLIE)
LFC .... Logic Flow Chart [*Computer science*]
LFC .... Logo Forum on Compuserve [*Defunct*]   (EA)
LFC .... Lomas Financial Corp. [*NYSE symbol*]   (SPSG)
LFC .... Loverboy Fan Club   (EA)
LFC .... Lowest-Feasible Concentration   (ABAC)
LFC .... Low Fat and Cholesterol Diet   (DMAA)
LFC .... Low-Frequency Choke   (DEN)
LFC .... Low-Frequency Correction   (CET)
LFC .... Low-Frequency Current
LFC .... Lunar Facsimile Capsule [*NASA*]   (KSC)
LFC .... Lunar Farside Chart [*Air Force*]
LFC .... Lutheran Free Church   (WDAA)
LFCA .... Chatellerault/Targe [*France*] [*ICAO location identifier*]   (ICLI)
LFCB .... Bagneres De Luchon [*France*] [*ICAO location identifier*]   (ICLI)
LFCB .... Legal Fees and Costs Board [*Australia*]
LFCC .... Cahors/Lalbenque [*France*] [*ICAO location identifier*]   (ICLI)
LFCC .... Linux Federation for Commercial Customers   (SAUO)
LFCD .... Andernos-Les-Bains [*France*] [*ICAO location identifier*]   (ICLI)
LFCDA .... London Fire and Civil Defence Authority   (HEAS)
LFCE .... Gueret/Saint-Laurent [*France*] [*ICAO location identifier*]   (ICLI)
LFCF .... Figeac/Livernon [*France*] [*ICAO location identifier*]   (ICLI)
LFCG .... Saint-Girons/Antichan [*France*] [*ICAO location identifier*]   (ICLI)
LFCH .... Arcachon/La Teste De Buch [*France*] [*ICAO location identifier*]   (ICLI)
LFCI .... Albi/Le Sequestre [*France*] [*ICAO location identifier*]   (ICLI)
LFCI .... Licentiate of the Faculty of Commerce and Industry [*British*]   (DBQ)
LFCJ .... Jonzac/Neulles [*France*] [*ICAO location identifier*]   (ICLI)
LFCK .... Castres/Mazamet [*France*] [*ICAO location identifier*]   (ICLI)
LFCL .... Less Than Full Container Load
LFCL .... Toulouse/Lasbordes [*France*] [*ICAO location identifier*]   (ICLI)
LFCM .... Liquid-Fed Ceramic Melter   (ABAC)
LFCM .... Low-Frequency Cross-Modulation [*Electronics*]   (OA)
LFCM .... Millau/Larzac [*France*] [*ICAO location identifier*]   (ICLI)
LFCN .... Nogaro [*France*] [*ICAO location identifier*]   (ICLI)
LFCO .... Oloron/Herrere [*France*] [*ICAO location identifier*]   (ICLI)
LFCOp .... Leading Fire Control Operator   (WDAA)
LFCP .... Pons/Avy [*France*] [*ICAO location identifier*]   (ICLI)
LFCQ .... Graulhet/Mondragon [*France*] [*ICAO location identifier*]   (ICLI)
LFCR .... Rodez/Marcillac [*France*] [*ICAO location identifier*]   (ICLI)
LFCS .... Bordeaux/Saucats [*France*] [*ICAO location identifier*]   (ICLI)
LFCS .... Land Forces Classification System   (AABC)

LFCS .... LASER Fire Control System
LFCS .... Licentiate of the Faculty of Secretaries [*British*]   (DBQ)
LFCS .... Low-Flow Cooling System [*Automotive engineering*]
LFCT .... Leader Financial [*NASDAQ symbol*]   (TTSB)
LFCT .... Leader Financial Corp. [*NASDAQ symbol*]   (SAG)
LFCT .... Thouars [*France*] [*ICAO location identifier*]   (ICLI)
LFCU .... Ussel/Thalamy [*France*] [*ICAO location identifier*]   (ICLI)
LFCV .... Villefranche-De-Rouergue [*France*] [*ICAO location identifier*]   (ICLI)
LFCW .... Villeneuve-Sur-Lot [*France*] [*ICAO location identifier*]   (ICLI)
LFCX .... Castelsarrasin/Moissac [*France*] [*ICAO location identifier*]   (ICLI)
LFCY .... Royan/Medis [*France*] [*ICAO location identifier*]   (ICLI)
LFCZ .... Mimizan [*France*] [*ICAO location identifier*]   (ICLI)
LFD .... Lactose-Free Diet
LFD .... Lateral Facial Dysplasia [*Medicine*]   (MELL)
LFD .... Latest Finish Date
LFD .... Launch and Flight Division [*Ballistic Research Laboratory*]   (RDA)
LFD .... Least Fatal Dose
LFD .... Line Fault Detector [*Telecommunications*]   (TEL)
LFD .... Line Feed   (VLIE)
LFD .... Litchfield, MI [*Location identifier*] [*FAA*]   (FAAL)
LFD .... Local Frequency Distribution
LFD .... Longford [*County in Ireland*]   (ROG)
LFD .... Low-Fat Diet
LFD .... Low Fiber Diet   (MELL)
LFD .... Low-Forceps Delivery [*Obstetrics*]
LFD .... Low-Frequency Decoy
LFD .... Low-Frequency Disturbance
LFD .... Lutheran Foundation for Religious Drama   (EA)
LFDA .... Aire-Sur-L'Addour [*France*] [*ICAO location identifier*]   (ICLI)
LFDA .... Land and Facilities Development Administration [*HUD*]
LFDB .... Montauban [*France*] [*ICAO location identifier*]   (ICLI)
LFDC .... Montendre/Marcillac [*France*] [*ICAO location identifier*]   (ICLI)
LFDE .... Egletons [*France*] [*ICAO location identifier*]   (ICLI)
LFDF .... Low-Frequency Direction Finder   (MCD)
LFDF .... Sainte-Foy-La-Grande [*France*] [*ICAO location identifier*]   (ICLI)
LFDG .... Gaillac/Lisle Sur Tarn [*France*] [*ICAO location identifier*]   (ICLI)
LFDH .... Auch/Lamothe [*France*] [*ICAO location identifier*]   (ICLI)
LFDI .... Libourne/Artiques De Lussac [*France*] [*ICAO location identifier*]   (ICLI)
LFDJ .... Pamiers/Les Pujols [*France*] [*ICAO location identifier*]   (ICLI)
LFDK .... Soulac-Sur-Mer [*France*] [*ICAO location identifier*]   (ICLI)
LFDL .... Loudun [*France*] [*ICAO location identifier*]   (ICLI)
LFDM .... Low Flyer, Defense Mode
LFDM .... Marmande/Virazeil [*France*] [*ICAO location identifier*]   (ICLI)
LFDN .... Rochefort/Saint-Agnant [*France*] [*ICAO location identifier*]   (ICLI)
LFDO .... Bordeaux/Souge [*France*] [*ICAO location identifier*]   (ICLI)
LFDP .... Saint-Pierre D'Oleron [*France*] [*ICAO location identifier*]   (ICLI)
LFDQ .... Castelnau-Magnoac [*France*] [*ICAO location identifier*]   (ICLI)
LFDR .... La Reole/Floudes [*France*] [*ICAO location identifier*]   (ICLI)
LFDS .... Sarlat/Domme [*France*] [*ICAO location identifier*]   (ICLI)
LFDT .... Tarbes/Laloubere [*France*] [*ICAO location identifier*]   (ICLI)
LFDU .... Lesparre/St. Laurent Du Medoc [*France*] [*ICAO location identifier*]   (ICLI)
LFDV .... Couhe/Verac [*France*] [*ICAO location identifier*]   (ICLI)
LFDW .... Chauvigny [*France*] [*ICAO location identifier*]   (ICLI)
LFDX .... Fumel/Montayral [*France*] [*ICAO location identifier*]   (ICLI)
LFDY .... Bordeaux-Yvrac [*France*] [*ICAO location identifier*]   (ICLI)
LFDZ .... Condat-Sur-Vezere [*France*] [*ICAO location identifier*]   (ICLI)
LFE .... Brotherhood of Locomotive Firemen and Enginemen [*Later, United Transportation Union*] [*AFL-CIO*]
LFE .... Laboratory for Electronics   (DNAB)
LFE .... Laboratory for Electronics, Inc.   (SAUO)
LFE .... Laminar Flow Element [*Engineering*]
LFE .... Large Flight Envelope   (MCD)
LFE .... LFE Corp.   (SAUO)
LFE .... Logarithmic Feedback Element [*Computer science*]
LFE .... London Fixtures Exchange   (SAUO)
LFE .... London Fur Exchange   (SAUO)
LFEA .... Delle-Ile [*France*] [*ICAO location identifier*]   (ICLI)
LFEB .... Dinan/Trelivan [*France*] [*ICAO location identifier*]   (ICLI)
LFEB .... Launch Facility Equipment Building [*Missiles*]
LFEC .... Ouessant [*France*] [*ICAO location identifier*]   (ICLI)
Lfecore .... LifeCore Biomedical, Inc. [*Associated Press*]   (SAG)
LFED .... Leeds Federal Svgs Bk [*NASDAQ symbol*]   (TTSB)
LFED .... Leeds FSB [*NASDAQ symbol*]   (SAG)
LFED .... Pontivy [*France*] [*ICAO location identifier*]   (ICLI)
LFEE .... Reims [*France*] [*ICAO location identifier*]   (ICLI)
LFEF .... Amboise/Dierre [*France*] [*ICAO location identifier*]   (ICLI)
LFEG .... Argenton-Sur-Creuse [*France*] [*ICAO location identifier*]   (ICLI)
LFEH .... Aubigny-Sur-Nere [*France*] [*ICAO location identifier*]   (ICLI)
LFEI .... Briare/Chatillon [*France*] [*ICAO location identifier*]   (ICLI)
LFEJ .... Chateauroux/Villers [*France*] [*ICAO location identifier*]   (ICLI)
LFEK .... Issoudun/Le Fay [*France*] [*ICAO location identifier*]   (ICLI)
LFEL .... Le Blanc [*France*] [*ICAO location identifier*]   (ICLI)
LfelneS .... Lifeline Systems, Inc. [*Associated Press*]   (SAG)
LFEM .... Montargis/Vimory [*France*] [*ICAO location identifier*]   (ICLI)
LfeMd .... Life Medical Sciences [*Associated Press*]   (SAG)
LfeMed .... Life Medical Sciences [*Associated Press*]   (SAG)
LFEN .... Laboratorio de Fisica e Engenharia Nucleores [*Portugal*]
LFEN .... Tours/Sorigny [*France*] [*ICAO location identifier*]   (ICLI)
LFEO .... Saint-Malo/Saint-Servan [*France*] [*ICAO location identifier*]   (ICLI)
LFEP .... Pouilly-Maconge [*France*] [*ICAO location identifier*]   (ICLI)
LFEQ .... Quiberon [*France*] [*ICAO location identifier*]   (ICLI)
LfeQst .... LifeQuest Medical, Inc. [*Associated Press*]   (SAG)
LFER .... Linear Free Energy Relationship
LFER .... Redon/Bains-Sur-Oust [*France*] [*ICAO location identifier*]   (ICLI)

LFES	Guiscriff-Scaer [France] [ICAO location identifier] (ICLI)
LFET	Til-Chatel [France] [ICAO location identifier] (ICLI)
LfeTch	Life Technologies, Inc. [Associated Press] (SAG)
LFETS	Live Fire Evasive Target System [Army] (INF)
LFEU	Bar-Le-Duc [France] [ICAO location identifier] (ICLI)
LfeUSA	Life USA Holding, Inc. [Associated Press] (SAG)
LFEV	Gray-Saint-Adrien [France] [ICAO location identifier] (ICLI)
LFEW	Saulieu-Liernais [France] [ICAO location identifier] (ICLI)
LF-EX	Life Expectancy [Military]
LFEX	Nancy-Azelot [France] [ICAO location identifier] (ICLI)
LFEY	Ile-D'Yeu/Le Grand Phare [France] [ICAO location identifier] (ICLI)
LFEZ	Nancy-Malzeville [France] [ICAO location identifier] (ICLI)
LFF	La Frestal [France] [Seismograph station code, US Geological Survey] (SEIS)
LFF	Large Formation Flyer (SSD)
LFf	Leading Firefighter (WDAA)
LFF	Light Filter Factor
LFF	Limited Fanout-Free (MHDB)
LFF	Logistic Factors File (DOMA)
LFF	London Film Festival
LFF	Low-Frequency Filter (IAA)
LFFA	CORTA (Orly Ouest) [France] [ICAO location identifier] (ICLI)
LFFB	Buno-Bonnevaux [France] [ICAO location identifier] (ICLI)
LFFC	Mantes-Cherence [France] [ICAO location identifier] (ICLI)
LFFD	Saint-Andre-De L'Eure [France] [ICAO location identifier] (ICLI)
LFFE	Enghien-Moisselles [France] [ICAO location identifier] (ICLI)
LFFET	Low-Frequency Field-Effect Transistor [Electronics] (OA)
LFFEZ	Large Force Fighter Employment Zone (SAUS)
LFFF	Paris [France] [ICAO location identifier] (ICLI)
LFFG	La Ferte-Gaucher [France] [ICAO location identifier] (ICLI)
LFFH	Chateau-Thierry-Belleau [France] [ICAO location identifier] (ICLI)
LFFI	Ancenis [France] [ICAO location identifier] (ICLI)
LFFJ	Joinville-Mussey [France] [ICAO location identifier] (ICLI)
LFFK	Fontenay-Le-Conte [France] [ICAO location identifier] (ICLI)
LFFL	Bailleau-Armenonville [France] [ICAO location identifier] (ICLI)
LFFM	La Motte-Beuvron [France] [ICAO location identifier] (ICLI)
LFFN	Brienne-Le-Chateau [France] [ICAO location identifier] (ICLI)
LFFO	Tonnerre-Moulins [France] [ICAO location identifier] (ICLI)
LFFP	LASER Fusion Feasibility Project [Nuclear fusion]
LFFP	Pithiviers [France] [ICAO location identifier] (ICLI)
LFFQ	La Ferte-Alais [France] [ICAO location identifier] (ICLI)
LFFR	Bar-Sur-Seine [France] [ICAO location identifier] (ICLI)
LFFS	Suippes [France] [ICAO location identifier] (ICLI)
LFFT	Left Front Fluid Temperature [Brake system] [Automotive engineering]
LFFT	Neufchateau-Roucaux [France] [ICAO location identifier] (ICLI)
LFFU	Chateauneuf-Sur-Cher [France] [ICAO location identifier] (ICLI)
LFFV	Vierzon-Mereau [France] [ICAO location identifier] (ICLI)
LFFW	Montaigu-Saint-Georges [France] [ICAO location identifier] (ICLI)
LFFX	Tournus-Cuisery [France] [ICAO location identifier] (ICLI)
LFFY	Etrepagny [France] [ICAO location identifier] (ICLI)
LFFZ	Sezanne-Saint-Remy [France] [ICAO location identifier] (ICLI)
LFG	Landamerica Financial Grp. [NYSE symbol] (SG)
LFG	Landfill Gas
LFG	Lead-Free Glass
LFG	Lexical Functional Grammar [Artificial intelligence]
LFG	Liberty Financial Group, Inc. (SAUO)
LFG	Low-Frequency Generator
LFGA	Colmar/Houssen [France] [ICAO location identifier] (ICLI)
LFGB	Mulhouse/Habsheim [France] [ICAO location identifier] (ICLI)
LFGC	Strasbourg/Neuhof [France] [ICAO location identifier] (ICLI)
LFGD	Arbois [France] [ICAO location identifier] (ICLI)
LFGE	Avallon [France] [ICAO location identifier] (ICLI)
LFGF	Beaune/Challanges [France] [ICAO location identifier] (ICLI)
LFGG	Belfort/Chaux [France] [ICAO location identifier] (ICLI)
LFGG	Low-Frequency Gravity Gradiometer
LFGH	Cosne-Sur-Loire [France] [ICAO location identifier] (ICLI)
LFGI	Dijon/Val Suzon [France] [ICAO location identifier] (ICLI)
LFGJ	Dole/Tavaux [France] [ICAO location identifier] (ICLI)
LFGK	Joigny [France] [ICAO location identifier] (ICLI)
LFGL	Lons Le Saunier/Courlaoux [France] [ICAO location identifier] (ICLI)
LFGM	Montceau Les Mines/Pouilloux [France] [ICAO location identifier] (ICLI)
LFGN	Paray Le Monial [France] [ICAO location identifier] (ICLI)
LFGO	Pont-Sur-Yonne [France] [ICAO location identifier] (ICLI)
LFGP	Saint-Florentin/Cheu [France] [ICAO location identifier] (ICLI)
LFGQ	Semur-En-Auxois [France] [ICAO location identifier] (ICLI)
LFGR	Doncourt-Les-Conflans [France] [ICAO location identifier] (ICLI)
LFGRD	Lifeguard (ABBR)
LFGS	Longuyon/Villette [France] [ICAO location identifier] (ICLI)
LFGT	Sarrebourg/Buhl [France] [ICAO location identifier] (ICLI)
LFGU	Sarreguemines/Neunkirch [France] [ICAO location identifier] (ICLI)
LFGV	Thionville/Yutz [France] [ICAO location identifier] (ICLI)
LFGW	Verdun/Rozelier [France] [ICAO location identifier] (ICLI)
LFGX	Champagnole/Crotenay [France] [ICAO location identifier] (ICLI)
LFGY	Saint-Die/Remoneix [France] [ICAO location identifier] (ICLI)
LFGZ	Nuits-Saint-Georges [France] [ICAO location identifier] (ICLI)
LFH	Left Femoral Hernia [Medicine]
LFH	Lower Fascial Height [Medicine]
LFH	Low Fire Hazard (SAUS)
LFH	Lunar Far Horizon (KSC)
LFHA	Issoire/Le Broc [France] [ICAO location identifier] (ICLI)
LFHB	Moulins/Avermes [France] [ICAO location identifier] (ICLI)
LFHC	Perouges/Meximieux [France] [ICAO location identifier] (ICLI)
LFHD	Pierrelatte [France] [ICAO location identifier] (ICLI)
LFHE	Romans/Saint-Paul [France] [ICAO location identifier] (ICLI)
LFHF	Ruoms [France] [ICAO location identifier] (ICLI)
LFHG	Saint-Chamond/L'Horme [France] [ICAO location identifier] (ICLI)
LFHH	Vienne/Reventin [France] [ICAO location identifier] (ICLI)
LFHI	Morestel [France] [ICAO location identifier] (ICLI)
LFHJ	Lyon/Corbas [France] [ICAO location identifier] (ICLI)
LFHK	Camp De Canjuers [France] [ICAO location identifier] (ICLI)
LFHL	Langogne/L'Esperon [France] [ICAO location identifier] (ICLI)
LFHL	Low-Frequency Hearing Loss (DMAA)
LFHM	Megeve [France] [ICAO location identifier] (ICLI)
LFHN	Bellegarde/Vouvray [France] [ICAO location identifier] (ICLI)
LFHO	Aubenas-Vals-Lanas [France] [ICAO location identifier] (ICLI)
LFHP	Le Puy/Loudes [France] [ICAO location identifier] (ICLI)
LFHQ	Saint-Flour/Coltines [France] [ICAO location identifier] (ICLI)
LFHR	Brioude-Beaumont [France] [ICAO location identifier] (ICLI)
LFHS	Bourg/Ceyreziat [France] [ICAO location identifier] (ICLI)
LFHSC	London Foot Hospital School of Chiropody (SAUO)
LFHT	Ambert-Le-Poyet [France] [ICAO location identifier] (ICLI)
LFHU	L'Alpe D'Huez [France] [ICAO location identifier] (ICLI)
LFHV	Villefrance/Tarare [France] [ICAO location identifier] (ICLI)
LFHW	Belleville-Villie-Morgon [France] [ICAO location identifier] (ICLI)
LFHX	Lapalisse-Perigny [France] [ICAO location identifier] (ICLI)
LFHY	Moulins/Montbeugny [France] [ICAO location identifier] (ICLI)
LFHZ	Sallanches-Mont-Blanc [France] [ICAO location identifier] (ICLI)
LFI	Hampton, VA [Location identifier] [FAA] (FAAL)
LFI	Last File Indicator (VLIE)
LFI	Last Frame Indicator
LFI	Left Front Inside-Drive [Tire maintenance]
LFI	Lethal Force Institute (SAUO)
LFI	Let's Face It [Later, AFLFI] [An association] (EA)
LFI	Levitz Furniture [NYSE symbol] (TTSB)
LFI	Levitz Furniture, Inc. [NYSE symbol] (SPSG)
LFI	Licensed Financial Institution
LFI	Licentiate of the Faculty of Insurance (SAUO)
LFI	Lifting Fan Intake [Hovercraft]
LFI	Linear Function Interpolator
L-FI	Live-Free, Inc. [An association] (EA)
LFI	Long Fiber Injection
LFI	Low-Frequency Inductor
LFIA	Luminescence and Fluorescence Immunoassay [Clinical chemistry]
LFIB	Belves-Saint-Pardoux [France] [ICAO location identifier] (ICLI)
LFIC	Cross Corsen [France] [ICAO location identifier] (ICLI)
LFIC	Landing Force Intelligence Center [Navy] (DNAB)
LFICS	Landing Force Integrated Communications System [Marine Corps]
LFID	Condom-Valence-Sur-Baise [France] [ICAO location identifier] (ICLI)
LF-ID	Logical Frame Identifier (VLIE)
LFIE	Cross Etel [France] [ICAO location identifier] (ICLI)
LFIF	Saint-Afrique-Belmont [France] [ICAO location identifier] (ICLI)
LFIG	Cassagnes-Begonhes [France] [ICAO location identifier] (ICLI)
LFIH	Chalais [France] [ICAO location identifier] (ICLI)
LFIINST	Life Fellow Imperial Institute [British] (ROG)
LFIJ	Cross Jobourg [France] [ICAO location identifier] (ICLI)
LFIK	Riberac-Saint-Aulaye [France] [ICAO location identifier] (ICLI)
LFIL	Rion-Des-Landes [France] [ICAO location identifier] (ICLI)
LFILIE	Libera Federazione Italiana Lavoratori Industrie Estrattive [Free Italian Federation of Workers in Mining Industries]
LFIM	Low-Frequency Instruments and Measurement (MCD)
LFIM	Saint Gaudens Montrejeau [France] [ICAO location identifier] (ICLI)
LFIN	Cross Gris-Nez [France] [ICAO location identifier] (ICLI)
LFIN	Local Financial [NASDAQ symbol] (SG)
LFINT	Low-Frequency Intersection
LFIP	Peyresourde-Balestas [France] [ICAO location identifier] (ICLI)
LFIPA	Laminated Fiberglass Insulation Producers Association [Defunct] (EA)
LFIR	Revel-Montgey [France] [ICAO location identifier] (ICLI)
LFIRSS	Louis Finkelstein Institute for Religious and Social Studies (EA)
LFISWB	Loyal, Free, Industrious Society of Wheelwrights and Blacksmiths [A union] [British]
LFIT	Toulouse-Bourg-Saint-Bernard [France] [ICAO location identifier] (ICLI)
LFIV	Vendays-Montalivet [France] [ICAO location identifier] (ICLI)
LFIX	Itxassou [France] [ICAO location identifier] (ICLI)
LFIY	Saint-Jean-D'Angely [France] [ICAO location identifier] (ICLI)
LFJ	Local Feed Junctor [Telecommunications] (NITA)
LFJ	Low-Frequency Jammer
LFJ	Lumbar Facet Joints [Medicine] (MELL)
LFJG	Cross La Garde [France] [ICAO location identifier] (ICLI)
LFJV	Low Frequency Jet Ventilation [Medicine]
LFK	Lufkin/Nacogdoches [Texas] [Airport symbol] (OAG)
LFK	Lufkin, TX [Location identifier] [FAA] (FAAL)
LFKA	Albertville [France] [ICAO location identifier] (ICLI)
LFKB	Bastia/Poretta, Corse [France] [ICAO location identifier] (ICLI)
LFKC	Calvi/Sainte-Catherine, Corse [France] [ICAO location identifier] (ICLI)
LFKD	Sollieres-Sardieres [France] [ICAO location identifier] (ICLI)
LFKE	Saint-Jean-En-Royans [France] [ICAO location identifier] (ICLI)
LFKF	Figari, Sud-Corse [France] [ICAO location identifier] (ICLI)
LFKG	Ghisonaccia-Alzitone [France] [ICAO location identifier] (ICLI)
LFKH	Saint-Jean-D'Avelanne [France] [ICAO location identifier] (ICLI)
LFKJ	Ajaccio/Campo Dell'Oro, Corse [France] [ICAO location identifier] (ICLI)
LFKL	Lyon-Brindas [France] [ICAO location identifier] (ICLI)
LFKM	Saint-Galmier [France] [ICAO location identifier] (ICLI)
LFKO	Propriano [France] [ICAO location identifier] (ICLI)
LFKP	La Tour-Du-Pin-Cessieu [France] [ICAO location identifier] (ICLI)

LFKS .... Solenzara, Corse [France] [ICAO location identifier] (ICLI)
LFKT .... Corte [France] [ICAO location identifier] (ICLI)
LFKY .... Belley-Peyrieu [France] [ICAO location identifier] (ICLI)
LFKZ .... Saint-Claude-Pratz [France] [ICAO location identifier] (ICLI)
LFL .... Lan Chile ADS [NYSE symbol] [Formerly, Linea Aerea Nac'l. Chile ADS]
LFL .... LASER Flash Lamp
LFL .... League for Liberty (EA)
LFL .... Left Frontolateral [Medicine] (DMAA)
LFL .... Length of Flowering Period [Botany]
LFL .... Lesbian Feminist Liberation (EA)
LFL .... Leukocyte Feeder Layer [Medicine] (DMAA)
LFL .... Libertarians for Life (EA)
LFL .... Linear Field Line
LFl .... Long Flashing Light [Navigation signal]
LFL .... Lower Flammability Limit (EEVL)
LFL .... Lower Flammable Limit
LFL .... Lower Flexibility Limit [Environmental science] (COE)
LFL .... Lower Frequency Limit (ACAE)
LFL .... Lutherans for Life (EA)
LFLA .... Auxerre/Moneteau [France] [ICAO location identifier] (ICLI)
LFLA .... Landing Force Logistics Afloat (MCD)
LFlAA .... Laut-und Formenlehre des Aegyptisch-Aramaeisch [A publication] (BJA)
LFLB .... Chambery/Aix-Les-Bains [France] [ICAO location identifier] (ICLI)
LFLC .... Clermont-Ferrand/Aulnat [France] [ICAO location identifier] (ICLI)
LFLD .... Bourges [France] [ICAO location identifier] (ICLI)
LFLE .... Chambery/Challes-Les-Eaux [France] [ICAO location identifier] (ICLI)
LFLEN .... Leaf Length [Botany]
LFLF .... Orleans [France] [ICAO location identifier] (ICLI)
LFLG .... Grenoble/Le Versoud [France] [ICAO location identifier] (ICLI)
LFLGTH ...... Leaf Length [Botany]
LFLH .... Chalon/Champforgeuil [France] [ICAO location identifier] (ICLI)
LFLI .... Annemasse [France] [ICAO location identifier] (ICLI)
LFLID .... Long Focal Length Imaging Demonstration (ACAE)
LFLJ .... Courchevel [France] [ICAO location identifier] (ICLI)
LFLK .... Lifelike (ABBR)
LFLK .... Oyonnax/Arbent [France] [ICAO location identifier] (ICLI)
LFLL .... Lyon/Satolas [France] [ICAO location identifier] (ICLI)
LFLM .... Macon/Charnay [France] [ICAO location identifier] (ICLI)
LFLN .... Lifeline (ABBR)
LFLN .... Saint-Yan [France] [ICAO location identifier] (ICLI)
LFLO .... Roanne/Renaison [France] [ICAO location identifier] (ICLI)
LFLOW .... Linearized High-Resolution Wind-Field Flow [Model] [Marine science] (OSRA)
LFLP .... Annecy/Meythet [France] [ICAO location identifier] (ICLI)
LFLPU .... Libyan Federation of Labor and Professional Unions
LFLQ .... Montelimar/Ancone [France] [ICAO location identifier] (ICLI)
LFLR .... Saint-Rambert-D'Albon [France] [ICAO location identifier] (ICLI)
LFLRASP .... Lifwynn Foundation for Laboratory Research in Analytical and Social Psychiatry (SAUO)
LFLS .... Grenoble/Saint-Geoirs [France] [ICAO location identifier] (ICLI)
LFLS .... Leafless (ABBR)
LFLSY .... Lifelessly (ABBR)
LFLT .... Left Front Lining Temperature [Brake system] [Automotive engineering]
LFLT .... Montlucon/Domerat [France] [ICAO location identifier] (ICLI)
LFLU .... Valence/Chabeuil [France] [ICAO location identifier] (ICLI)
LFLV .... Vichy/Charmeil [France] [ICAO location identifier] (ICLI)
LFLW .... Aurillac [France] [ICAO location identifier] (ICLI)
LFLWP .... Land Forces Logistics Working Party (MCD)
LFLX .... Chateauroux/Deols [France] [ICAO location identifier] (ICLI)
LFLY .... Lyon/Bron [France] [ICAO location identifier] (ICLI)
LFLZ .... Feurs/Chambeon [France] [ICAO location identifier] (ICLI)
LFM .... Franklin and Marshall College, Lancaster, PA [OCLC symbol] (OCLC)
LFM .... Landing Force Manual [Marine Corps, Navy]
LFM .... Large Function Modules (ACAE)
LFM .... LASER Feedback Microscope
LFM .... LASER Force Microscope
LFM .... Lateral Force Microscopy [Morphology]
LFM .... Launch First Motion
LFM .... Lieutenant Field Marshal
LFM .... Limited-Area Fine-Mesh Model [Marine science] (OSRA)
LFM .... Limited Fine Mesh
LFM .... Linear Feet per Minute
LFM .... Linear Frequency Modulation (CAAL)
LFM .... Link Framing Module (VLIE)
LFM .... Live Firing Monitor (SAUS)
LFM .... Local File Manager
LFM .... Longitudinal Field Modulator
LFM .... Loss Frequency Method [Insurance]
LFM .... Lower Figure of Merit
LFM .... Low Fat Milk [Medicine] (AMHC)
LFM .... Low-Field Magnetometer [Instrumentation]
LFM .... Low-Frequency Magnetic [Field]
LFM .... Low-Frequency Modulation
LFM .... Low-Powered Fan Marker (MUGU)
LFM .... Lubrecht Forest [Montana] [Seismograph station code, US Geological Survey] [Closed] (SEIS)
LFMA .... Aix-Les-Milles [France] [ICAO location identifier] (ICLI)
LFMA .... Laminated Foil Manufacturers' Association [Defunct]
LFMB .... Aix-En-Provence [France] [ICAO location identifier] (ICLI)
LFMC .... Le Luc/Le Cannet [France] [ICAO location identifier] (ICLI)
LFMD .... Cannes/Mandelieu [France] [ICAO location identifier] (ICLI)

LfMd .... Life Medical Sciences [Associated Press] (SAG)
LFME .... Nimes/Courbessac [France] [ICAO location identifier] (ICLI)
LFMER .... Lovelace Foundation for Medical Education and Research [Reorganized to form Lovelace Medical Foundation and Lovelace Biomedical and Environmental Research Institute] (MCD)
LFMF .... Fayence [France] [ICAO location identifier] (ICLI)
LF/MF .... Low Frequency, Medium Frequency
LFMG .... La Montagne Noire [France] [ICAO location identifier] (ICLI)
LFMH .... Saint-Etienne/Boutheon [France] [ICAO location identifier] (ICLI)
LFMI .... Istres/Le Tube [France] [ICAO location identifier] (ICLI)
LFMI .... Lasers for Medicine, Incorporated (SAUO)
LFMJ .... Nice/Mont Agel [France] [ICAO location identifier] (ICLI)
LFMK .... Carcassonne/Salvaza [France] [ICAO location identifier] (ICLI)
LFML .... Little Flower Mission League (EA)
LFML .... Marseille/Marignane [France] [ICAO location identifier] (ICLI)
LFMM .... Aix-En-Provence [France] [ICAO location identifier] (ICLI)
LFMM .... Liquid-Fed Minimelter (ABAC)
LFMN .... Nice/Cote D'Azur [France] [ICAO location identifier] (ICLI)
LFMO .... Orange/Caritat [France] [ICAO location identifier] (ICLI)
LFMOP .... Linear Frequency Modulation on Pulse (MCD)
LFMP .... Perpignan/Rivesaltes [France] [ICAO location identifier] (ICLI)
LFM/PD ...... Local Flow Management/Profile Descent
LFMQ .... Le Castellet [France] [ICAO location identifier] (ICLI)
LFMR .... Barcelonnette/Saint-Pons [France] [ICAO location identifier] (ICLI)
LFMR .... Low-Frequency Microwave Radiometer
LFMS .... Ales/Deaux [France] [ICAO location identifier] (ICLI)
LFMS .... Laminated Ferrite Memory System (MCD)
LFMT .... Montpellier/Frejorgues [France] [ICAO location identifier] (ICLI)
LFMU .... Beziers/Vias [France] [ICAO location identifier] (ICLI)
LFMV .... Avignon/Caumont [France] [ICAO location identifier] (ICLI)
LFMW .... Castelnaudary/Villeneuve [France] [ICAO location identifier] (ICLI)
LFMX .... Chateau-Arnoux/Saint-Auban [France] [ICAO location identifier] (ICLI)
LFMY .... Salon [France] [ICAO location identifier] (ICLI)
LFMZ .... Lezignan-Corbieres [France] [ICAO location identifier] (ICLI)
LFN .... Lactoferrin [Biochemistry] (MAE)
LFN .... Libraries for Nursing (SAUO)
LFN .... Logical File Name
LFN .... Logical File Number [Computer science] (MCD)
LFN .... Long Filename (PCM)
LFN .... Louisburg, NC [Location identifier] [FAA] (FAAL)
LFNA .... Gap/Tallard [France] [ICAO location identifier] (ICLI)
LFNB .... Mende/Brenoux [France] [ICAO location identifier] (ICLI)
LFNBK .... Long File Name BackUp (SAUS)
LFNC .... Mont-Dauphin/Saint-Crepin [France] [ICAO location identifier] (ICLI)
LFND .... Pont-Saint-Esprit [France] [ICAO location identifier] (ICLI)
LFNE .... Salon/Eyguieres [France] [ICAO location identifier] (ICLI)
LFNF .... Vinon [France] [ICAO location identifier] (ICLI)
LFNG .... Montpellier/L'Or [France] [ICAO location identifier] (ICLI)
LFNGFT .... Landing Force Naval Gunfire Team
LFNH .... Carpentras [France] [ICAO location identifier] (ICLI)
LFNI .... Conqueyrac [France] [ICAO location identifier] (ICLI)
LFNJ .... Aspres-Sur-Buech [France] [ICAO location identifier] (ICLI)
LFNK .... Vars-Les-Crosses-Et-Les-Tronches [France] [ICAO location identifier] (ICLI)
LFNL .... Saint-Martin-De-Londres [France] [ICAO location identifier] (ICLI)
LFNM .... La Mole [France] [ICAO location identifier] (ICLI)
LFNO .... Florac-Sainte-Enimie [France] [ICAO location identifier] (ICLI)
LFNP .... Pezenas-Nizas [France] [ICAO location identifier] (ICLI)
LFNQ .... Mont-Louis-La-Quillane [France] [ICAO location identifier] (ICLI)
LFNR .... Berre-La-Fare [France] [ICAO location identifier] (ICLI)
LFNS .... Leafiness (ABBR)
LFNS .... Low-Frequency Navigation System (NG)
LFNS .... Sisteron-Theze [France] [ICAO location identifier] (ICLI)
LFNT .... Avignon-Pujaut [France] [ICAO location identifier] (ICLI)
LFNT .... Low Frequency Intersection (FAAC)
LFNU .... Uzes [France] [ICAO location identifier] (ICLI)
LFNV .... Valreas-Visan [France] [ICAO location identifier] (ICLI)
LFNW .... Puivert [France] [ICAO location identifier] (ICLI)
LFNX .... Bedarieux-La-Tour-Sur-Orb [France] [ICAO location identifier] (ICLI)
LFNY .... Saint-Etienne-En-Devoluy [France] [ICAO location identifier] (ICLI)
LFNZ .... Le Mazet-De-Romanin [France] [ICAO location identifier] (ICLI)
LFO .... Large Follow-On
LFO .... LASER/Fiber-Optic (MCD)
LFO .... Left Front Outside-Drive
LFO .... Light Fuel Oil (BARN)
LFO .... Low-Frequency Oscillator
LFOA .... Avord [France] [ICAO location identifier] (ICLI)
LFOA .... Last Frame of Action [Cinematography] (WDMC)
LFOB .... Beauvais/Tille [France] [ICAO location identifier] (ICLI)
LFOC .... Crateaudun [France] [ICAO location identifier] (ICLI)
LFOC .... Landing Force Operation Center [Navy] (CAAL)
LFOC .... Lea-Francis Owners Club [British] (EAIO)
LFOD .... Saumur/Saint-Florent [France] [ICAO location identifier] (ICLI)
LFOE .... Evreux/Fauville [France] [ICAO location identifier] (ICLI)
LFOF .... Alencon/Valframbert [France] [ICAO location identifier] (ICLI)
LFOG .... Flers/Saint-Paul [France] [ICAO location identifier] (ICLI)
LFOH .... Le Havre/Octeville [France] [ICAO location identifier] (ICLI)
LFOI .... Abbeville [France] [ICAO location identifier] (ICLI)
LFOJ .... Orleans/Bricy [France] [ICAO location identifier] (ICLI)
LFOK .... Chalons/Vatry [France] [ICAO location identifier] (ICLI)
LFOL .... L'Aigle/Saint-Michel [France] [ICAO location identifier] (ICLI)
LFOM .... Lessay [France] [ICAO location identifier] (ICLI)
LFOM .... Low-Frequency Outer Marker (MSA)
LFON .... Dreux/Vernouillet [France] [ICAO location identifier] (ICLI)

LFOO	Les Sables D'Olonne/Talmont [*France*] [*ICAO location identifier*] (ICLI)
LFOP	Landing and Ferry Operations Panel [*NASA*] (NASA)
LFOP	Rouen/Boos [*France*] [*ICAO location identifier*] (ICLI)
LFOQ	Blois/Le Breuil [*France*] [*ICAO location identifier*] (ICLI)
LFOR	Chartres/Champhol [*France*] [*ICAO location identifier*] (ICLI)
LFORM	Landing Force Operational Reserve Material [*Navy*] (NVT)
LFOS	Launch and Flight Operations System
LFOS	Saint-Valery/Vittefleur [*France*] [*ICAO location identifier*] (ICLI)
LFOT	Tours/Saint-Symphorien [*France*] [*ICAO location identifier*] (ICLI)
LFOU	Cholet/Le Pontreau [*France*] [*ICAO location identifier*] (ICLI)
LFOV	Large Field of View [*Radiology*] (DAVI)
LFOV	Large Field-Of-View (SAUS)
LFOV	Laval/Entrammes [*France*] [*ICAO location identifier*] (ICLI)
LFOW	Saint-Quentin/Roupy [*France*] [*ICAO location identifier*] (ICLI)
LFOX	Etampes/Mondesir [*France*] [*ICAO location identifier*] (ICLI)
LFOY	Le Havre/Saint-Romain [*France*] [*ICAO location identifier*] (ICLI)
LFOZ	Orleans/Saint-Denis-De-L'Hotel [*France*] [*ICAO location identifier*] (ICLI)
LFP	Labor-Force Participation
LFP	Large Flat Plate
LFP	LASER Flash Photolysis (MEC)
LFP	Late Flight Plan
LFP	Left Frontoposterior [*A fetal position*] [*Obstetrics*]
LFP	LFP Holdings, Inc. [*Toronto Stock Exchange symbol*]
LFP	Liberala Folkpartiet [*Liberal People's Party*] [*Finland*] [*Political party*] (PPE)
LFP	Libraries for Prisons [*An association*] (EA)
LFP	Life Point, Inc. [*AMEX symbol*] (SG)
LFP	Light Floor Pintle (SAUS)
LFP	Lindbergh Field Plant (SAUO)
LFP	Listen for Pleasure [*Audio books*]
LFP	Livestock Feed Program
LFP	Local Facilities Plan (SAUO)
LFP	Local Field Potential [*Electrophysiology*]
LFP	Low-Frequency Prediction (USDC)
LFPA	Persan-Beaumont [*France*] [*ICAO location identifier*] (ICLI)
LFPAG	Live Firing Program Analysis Group [*Military*] (CAAL)
LFPB	Paris/Le Bourget [*France*] [*ICAO location identifier*] (ICLI)
LFPC	Creil [*France*] [*ICAO location identifier*] (ICLI)
LFPC	Louisiana Foundation for Private Colleges (SAUO)
LFPD	Bernay/Saint-Martin [*France*] [*ICAO location identifier*] (ICLI)
LFPE	Meaux/Esbly [*France*] [*ICAO location identifier*] (ICLI)
LFPEF	Low-Frequency Pulsed Electromagnetic Field
LFPER	Leaf Persistence [*Botany*]
LFPF	Beynes/Thiverval [*France*] [*ICAO location identifier*] (ICLI)
LFPG	Paris/Charles-De-Gaulle [*France*] [*ICAO location identifier*] (ICLI)
LFPH	Chelles/Le Pin [*France*] [*ICAO location identifier*] (ICLI)
LFPI	Paris/Issy-Les-Moulineaux [*France*] [*ICAO location identifier*] (ICLI)
LFPJ	Taverny [*France*] [*ICAO location identifier*] (ICLI)
LFPK	Coulommiers/Voisins [*France*] [*ICAO location identifier*] (ICLI)
LFPL	Lewis Flight Propulsion Laboratory [*NASA*]
LFPL	Lognes/Emerainville [*France*] [*ICAO location identifier*] (ICLI)
LFPM	Melun/Villaroche [*France*] [*ICAO location identifier*] (ICLI)
LFPN	Toussus-Le-Noble [*France*] [*ICAO location identifier*] (ICLI)
LFPO	Paris/Orly [*France*] [*ICAO location identifier*] (ICLI)
LFPP	Le Plessis-Belleville [*France*] [*ICAO location identifier*] (ICLI)
LFPPV	Low-Frequency Positive Pressure Ventilation [*Medicine*] (DMAA)
LFPQ	Fontenay-Tresigny [*France*] [*ICAO location identifier*] (ICLI)
LFPR	Guayancourt [*France*] [*ICAO location identifier*] (ICLI)
LFPRI	London Female Preventive and Reformatory Institution (SAUO)
LFPRL	Lewis Flight Propulsion Research Laboratory [*NASA*] (MUGU)
LFPS	Licentiate of the Faculty of Physicians and Surgeons [*British*]
LFPS	Low-Frequency Phase Shifter [*Telecommunications*]
LFPS	Paris [*France*] [*ICAO location identifier*] (ICLI)
LFPSG	Licentiate of the Faculty of Physicians and Surgeons, Glasgow (ROG)
LFPT	Pontoise/Cormeilles-En-Vexin [*France*] [*ICAO location identifier*] (ICLI)
LFPU	Moret/Episy [*France*] [*ICAO location identifier*] (ICLI)
LFPUB	Leaf Pubescence [*Botany*]
LFPV	Villacoublay/Velizy [*France*] [*ICAO location identifier*] (ICLI)
LFPW	Low-Frequency Plasma Wave
LFPW	Paris, Centre Meteorologique [*France*] [*ICAO location identifier*] (ICLI)
LFPX	Chavenay/Villepreux [*France*] [*ICAO location identifier*] (ICLI)
LFPY	Bretigny-Sur-Orge [*France*] [*ICAO location identifier*] (ICLI)
LFPZ	Saint-Cyre-L'Ecole [*France*] [*ICAO location identifier*] (ICLI)
LFQ	Light Foot Quantizer
LFQ	Limited Flying Quality
LFQA	Reims/Prunay [*France*] [*ICAO location identifier*] (ICLI)
LFQB	Troyes/Barberey [*France*] [*ICAO location identifier*] (ICLI)
LFQC	Luneville/Croismare [*France*] [*ICAO location identifier*] (ICLI)
LFQD	Arras/Roclincourt [*France*] [*ICAO location identifier*] (ICLI)
LFQE	Etain/Rouvres [*France*] [*ICAO location identifier*] (ICLI)
LFQF	Autun/Bellevue [*France*] [*ICAO location identifier*] (ICLI)
LFQG	Nevers/Fourchambault [*France*] [*ICAO location identifier*] (ICLI)
LFQH	Chatillon-Sur-Seine [*France*] [*ICAO location identifier*] (ICLI)
LFQI	Cambrai/Epinoy [*France*] [*ICAO location identifier*] (ICLI)
LFQJ	Maubeuge/Elesmes [*France*] [*ICAO location identifier*] (ICLI)
LFQK	Chalons/Ecury-Sur-Coole [*France*] [*ICAO location identifier*] (ICLI)
LFQL	Lens/Benifontaine [*France*] [*ICAO location identifier*] (ICLI)
LFQM	Besancon-La-Veze [*France*] [*ICAO location identifier*] (ICLI)
LFQN	Saint-Omer/Wizernes [*France*] [*ICAO location identifier*] (ICLI)
LFQO	Lille/Marcq-En-Baroeul [*France*] [*ICAO location identifier*] (ICLI)
LFQP	Phalsbourg/Bourscheid [*France*] [*ICAO location identifier*] (ICLI)
LFQQ	Lille/Lesquin [*France*] [*ICAO location identifier*] (ICLI)
LFQR	Romilly-Sur-Seine [*France*] [*ICAO location identifier*] (ICLI)
LFQS	Vitry-En-Artois [*France*] [*ICAO location identifier*] (ICLI)
LFQT	Merville/Calonne [*France*] [*ICAO location identifier*] (ICLI)
LFQU	Sarre-Union [*France*] [*ICAO location identifier*] (ICLI)
LFQV	Charleville/Mezieres [*France*] [*ICAO location identifier*] (ICLI)
LFQW	Vesoul-Frotey [*France*] [*ICAO location identifier*] (ICLI)
LFQY	Saverne-Steinbourg [*France*] [*ICAO location identifier*] (ICLI)
LFQZ	Dieuze-Gueblange [*France*] [*ICAO location identifier*] (ICLI)
L FR	Franc [*Monetary unit*] [*Luxembourg*]
LFR	Inshore Fire Support Ship [*Navy symbol*]
LFR	Laboratory Facilities Request (MCD)
LFR	La Fria [*Venezuela*] [*Airport symbol*] (OAG)
LFR	Laminar-Flow Reactor [*Engineering*]
LFR	LASERgraphics Film Recorder (PCM)
L Fr	Law French (DLA)
LFR	Leafier (ABBR)
LFR	Lifer (ABBR)
LFR	Linear Flow Reactor [*Chemical engineering*]
LFR	Line Frequency Rejection (IAA)
LFR	Logical Forms Recognition [*Computer science*]
LFR	Lowest Fare Routing [*Travel industry*]
LFR	Low-Flux Reactor
LFR	Low Frequency Radio Range (TAG)
LFR	Low-Frequency Range (MCD)
LFR	Low Frequency Receiver (ACAE)
LFR	Lymphoid Follicular Reticulosis [*Medicine*] (DB)
LFr	Saint Mary Parish Library, Franklin, LA [*Library symbol*] [*Library of Congress*] (LCLS)
LFRA	Angers/Avrille [*France*] [*ICAO location identifier*] (ICLI)
LFRA	League of Federal Recreation Associations (EA)
LFRA	Leatherhead Food Research Association [*British*] (ARC)
LFRAP	Long Feeder Route Analysis Program [*Bell System*]
LFRB	Brest/Guipavas [*France*] [*ICAO location identifier*] (ICLI)
LFRC	Cherbourg/Maupertus [*France*] [*ICAO location identifier*] (ICLI)
LFRC	Latex Foam Rubber Council [*Defunct*] (EA)
LFRC	Laurentian Forest Research Center [*Canadian Forestry Service*] [*Research center*] (RCD)
LFRC	Library Fundraising Resource Center [*American Library Association*]
LFRD	Dinard/Pleurtuit-Saint-Malo [*France*] [*ICAO location identifier*] (ICLI)
LFRD	Lot Fraction Reliability Deviation [*Quality control*]
LFRE	La Baule/Escoublac [*France*] [*ICAO location identifier*] (ICLI)
LFRED	Liquid-Fueled Ramjet Engine Demonstration [*Navy*] (MCD)
LFRED	Liquid-Fuelled Ramjet Engine Development (SAUS)
LFRF	Granville [*France*] [*ICAO location identifier*] (ICLI)
LFRG	Deauville/Saint-Gatien [*France*] [*ICAO location identifier*] (ICLI)
LFRH	Lorient/Lann-Bihoue [*France*] [*ICAO location identifier*] (ICLI)
LFRI	La Roche-Sur-Yon/Les Ajoncs [*France*] [*ICAO location identifier*] (ICLI)
LFRJ	Landivisiau [*France*] [*ICAO location identifier*] (ICLI)
LFRJ	Liquid-Fueled Ramjet [*Navy*] (MCD)
LFRK	Caen/Carpiquet [*France*] [*ICAO location identifier*] (ICLI)
LFRL	Lanveoc/Poulmic [*France*] [*ICAO location identifier*] (ICLI)
LFRM	Le Mans/Arnage [*France*] [*ICAO location identifier*] (ICLI)
LFRN	Lavender Families Resource Network [*An association*] (EA)
LFRN	Rennes/Saint-Jacques [*France*] [*ICAO location identifier*] (ICLI)
LFRO	Lannion/Servel [*France*] [*ICAO location identifier*] (ICLI)
LFRP	Ploermel-Loyat [*France*] [*ICAO location identifier*] (ICLI)
LFRQ	Quimper/Pluguffan [*France*] [*ICAO location identifier*] (ICLI)
LFRR	Brest [*France*] [*ICAO location identifier*] (ICLI)
LFRR	Low-Frequency Radio Range (MCD)
LFRS	Nantes/Chateau Bougon [*France*] [*ICAO location identifier*] (ICLI)
LFRSB	Loose Fuel-Rod Shipping Basket (GAAI)
LFRT	Long Film-Reinforced Thermoplastic
LFRT	Saint-Brieuc Armor [*France*] [*ICAO location identifier*] (ICLI)
LFrtW	Washington Parish Library (SAUO)
LFrtW	Washington Parish Library, Franklinton (SAUS)
LFrtW	Washington Parish Library, Franklinton, LA [*Library symbol*] [*Library of Congress*] (LCLS)
LFRU	Morlaix/Ploujean [*France*] [*ICAO location identifier*] (ICLI)
LFRV	Vannes/Meucon [*France*] [*ICAO location identifier*] (ICLI)
LFRW	Avranches/Le Val Saint-Pere [*France*] [*ICAO location identifier*] (ICLI)
LFRX	Brest [*France*] [*ICAO location identifier*] (ICLI)
LFRY	Cherbourg [*France*] [*ICAO location identifier*] (ICLI)
LFRZ	Saint-Nazaire/Montoir [*France*] [*ICAO location identifier*] (ICLI)
LFS	Amphibious Fire Support Ship [*Navy symbol*]
LFS	Labour Force Survey [*Canada*]
LFS	Lancaster Finishing School [*British military*] (DMA)
LFS	LASER Fluorescence Spectroscopy
LFS	Launch Facility Simulator
LFS	League of Filipino Students
LFS	Leather Finishers' Society [*A union*] [*British*]
LFS	Libertarian Futurist Society (EA)
LFr	Licentiate of the Faculty of Architects and Surveyors [*British*] (DBQ)
LFS	Licentiate Surveyor of the Faculty of Architects and Surveyors (SAUO)
LFS	Li-Fraumeni Syndrome [*Oncology*]
LFS	Liquid Filtration System
LFS	Liquid Flow System
LFS	Liver Function Series [*Clinical chemistry*]
LFS	Local Format Storage
LFS	Logical File Structure [*Computer science*] (OA)
LFS	Logical File System (IAA)
LFS	Logic Fault Simulator [*Computer science*]

LFS	Logistics Feasibility System
LFS	Logistics/Ferry Station
LFS	London Financial Studies
LFS	London Fire Service (SAUO)
LFS	Loop Feedback Signal
LFS	Low-Frequency Stimulation [Neurophysiology]
LFS	Low Frequency Synchronization (ACAE)
LFS	Luftfahrzeug Service - Aircraft Service [Austria] [ICAO designator] (FAAC)
LFSA	Besancon/Thise [France] [ICAO location identifier] (ICLI)
LFSA	List of Frequently Seen Acronyms (SAUO)
LFSA	Logistical Force Structure Assessment (MCD)
LFSB	Bale/Mulhouse [France/Switzerland] [ICAO location identifier] (ICLI)
LFSB	LFS Bancorp [NASDAQ symbol] (SAG)
LFS Bcp	LFS Bancorp [Associated Press] (SAG)
LFSC	Colmar/Meyenheim [France] [ICAO location identifier] (ICLI)
LFSC	Life Sciences, Inc. (SAUO)
LFSC	Limited First-Strike Capability
LFSC	London Fire Salvage Corps (SAUO)
LFSC	Louisville Fear Survey for Children [Psychology]
LFSCWW	Live Food Singles Club - World Wide [Defunct] (EA)
LFSD	Dijon/Longvic [France] [ICAO location identifier] (ICLI)
LFSE	Epinal/Dogneville [France] [ICAO location identifier] (ICLI)
LFSF	Metz/Frescaty [France] [ICAO location identifier] (ICLI)
LFSG	Epinal/Mirecourt [France] [ICAO location identifier] (ICLI)
LFSH	Haguenau [France] [ICAO location identifier] (ICLI)
LFSI	Saint-Dizier/Robinson [France] [ICAO location identifier] (ICLI)
LFSID	Local Form Session Identifier (ACRL)
LFSJ	Sedan/Douzy [France] [ICAO location identifier] (ICLI)
LFSK	Vitry-Le-Francois/Vauclerc [France] [ICAO location identifier] (ICLI)
LFSL	Toul/Rosieres [France] [ICAO location identifier] (ICLI)
LFSM	Montbeliard/Courcelles [France] [ICAO location identifier] (ICLI)
LFSMS	Logistics Force Structure Management Support (ACAE)
LFSMT/S	Liquid Fuel Systems Maintenance Technician/Specialist [Aerospace] (AAG)
LFSN	Lipomyelomeningocele Family Support Network [Founded in 1997] (NRGU)
LFSN	Nancy/Essey [France] [ICAO location identifier] (ICLI)
LFSO	Nancy/Ochey [France] [ICAO location identifier] (ICLI)
LFSP	Landing Force Support Party [Navy] (ANA)
LFSP	Pontarlier [France] [ICAO location identifier] (ICLI)
LFSPT	Long Form System Performance Test (ACAE)
LFSQ	Belfort/Fontaine [France] [ICAO location identifier] (ICLI)
LFSR	Linear Feedback Shift Register [Computer science] (CIST)
LFSR	Reims/Champagne [France] [ICAO location identifier] (ICLI)
LFSS	Landing Force Support Ship [Navy]
LFSS	Launch Facility Security System [NASA] (KSC)
LFST	Largest Feasible Steerable Telescope
LFST	Lifestyle (ABBR)
LFST	Strasbourg/Entzheim [France] [ICAO location identifier] (ICLI)
LFSTK	Leafstalk (ABBR)
LFSU	Rolampont [France] [ICAO location identifier] (ICLI)
LFSV	Landing Force Support Vehicle (MCD)
LFSV	Lifesaver (ABBR)
LFSV	Pont-Saint-Vincent [France] [ICAO location identifier] (ICLI)
LFSW	Epernay/Plivot [France] [ICAO location identifier] (ICLI)
LFSW	Landing Force Support Weapon
LFSX	Luxeuil/Saint-Sauveur [France] [ICAO location identifier] (ICLI)
LFSY	Chaumont-La Vendue [France] [ICAO location identifier] (ICLI)
lf sz	Life Size (VRA)
LFSZ	Lifesize (ABBR)
LFSZ	Vittel/Champ De Courses [France] [ICAO location identifier] (ICLI)
LFT	Aerolift Philippines Corp. [ICAO designator] (FAAC)
LFT	Ladd-Franklin Theory [Color vision]
LFT	Lafayette [Louisiana] [Airport symbol] (OAG)
LFT	Lafayette [Diocesan abbreviation] [Indiana] (TOCD)
LFT	Lafayette, LA [Location identifier] [FAA] (FAAL)
LFT	Laminar Flow Torch [For plasma generation]
LFT	LASER Flash Tube
LFT	Late Finish Time
LFT	Latest Finish Time
LFT	Latex Fixation Test [Medicine]
LFT	Latex Flocculation Test [Clinical chemistry]
LFT	Launch Facility Trainer
LFT	Law Foundation of Tasmania [Australia]
LFT	Leafiest (ABBR)
LFT	Leaflet (ADA)
LFT	Leap-Frog Test
LFT	Left (ABBR)
lft	Left (VRA)
LFT	Left Frontotransverse [A fetal position] [Obstetrics]
LFT	Left Half Indicators, Off Test (SAA)
LFT	Lexford Residential TR SBI [NYSE symbol] (SG)
LFT	Lifetime Corporation (SAUO)
LFT	Lifting (MSA)
LFT	Ligand-Field Theory [Physical chemistry]
LFT	Light Fire Team [Military] (CINC)
LFT	Linear Flash Tube
LFT	Linear Foot (ADA)
LFT	Live Fire Test
LFT	Live Fire Testing (SAUS)
LFT	Liver Function Test [Medicine]
LFT	Long-Fiber Thermoplastic
LFT	Low-Frequency Tetanus [Medicine] (DMAA)
LFT	Low-Frequency Transduction

LFT	Low-Frequency Transfer [Sex factor] (DB)
L/FT²	Lumens per Square Foot (WDAA)
LFTA	London Fur Trade Association (SAUO)
LFTA	Low-Frequency Timing Assembly (IAA)
LFT & E	Live Fire Test and Evaluation [Required testing for major weapon system and munition programs] [Military] (RDA)
LFTB	Lace Finishing Trade Board (SAUO)
LFTB	Liquid Fuels Trust Board (SAUO)
LFTC	Landing Force Training Command [Navy] (NVT)
LFTC	Toulon [France] [ICAO location identifier] (ICLI)
LFTCPAC	Landing Force Training Command, Pacific [Navy] (DNAB)
LFTDWP	Land Force Tactical Doctrine Working Party [NASA] (MCD)
LFTEG	Liquid-Fuelled Thermo-Electric Generator (PDAA)
LFTF	Cuers/Pierrefeu [France] [ICAO location identifier] (ICLI)
LFTF	Liftoff (ABBR)
LFTF	London Furniture Trades Federation (SAUO)
LFTH	Hyeres/Le Palyvestre [France] [ICAO location identifier] (ICLI)
LFTHDD	Lefthanded (ABBR)
LFTHDY	Lefthandedly (ABBR)
LFTINS	Loftiness (ABBR)
LFTIR	Loftier (ABBR)
LFTIT	Loftiest (ABBR)
LFTM	Lifetime (ABBR)
LFTM	Lifetime Communities (SAUO)
LFTN	La Grand'Combe [France] [ICAO location identifier] (ICLI)
LFTOV	Leftover (ABBR)
LFtp	Library Program, Cataloging Department, Recreation Service (SAUO)
LFtp	Library Program, Cataloging Department, Recreation Service, Fort Polk, LA [Library symbol] [Library of Congress] (LCLS)
LFTPR	Long Fiber Thermoplastic Resin
LFTR	Toulon/Saint-Mandrier [France] [ICAO location identifier] (ICLI)
LFTS	Low Frequency Test Station (ACAE)
LFTS	Toulon [France] [ICAO location identifier] (ICLI)
LFTT	Leftist (ABBR)
LFTU	Frejus/Saint-Raphael [France] [ICAO location identifier] (ICLI)
LFTU	Landing Force Training Unit [Marine Corps]
LFTW	Nimes/Garons [France] [ICAO location identifier] (ICLI)
LFTWF	Luftwaffe (ABBR)
LFTWG	Leftwing (ABBR)
LFTWR	Leftwinger (ABBR)
LFTY	Lofty (ABBR)
LFU	Laser Firing Unit (ACAE)
LFU	Least Frequency Unit (NITA)
LFU	Least Frequently Used [Computer science]
LFU	Leonhartsberger Flugunternchmen GmbH [Austria] [ICAO designator] (FAAC)
LFU	LFU Leonhartsberger Flugunternehmen Gesellschaft MbH [Austria] [FAA designator] (FAAC)
LFU	Lipid Fluidity Unit (DB)
LFU	Lunar Flying Unit [NASA]
LFU Memory	Least Frequency Used Memory [Computer science] (ITCA)
LFUS	Littelfuse, Inc. [NASDAQ symbol] (SAG)
LFUSS	Landing Force Organizational Systems Study
LFUSW	Littelfuse Inc. Wrrt'A' [NASDAQ symbol] (TTSB)
LFV	Large Field of View [Radiology] (DAVI)
LFV	Lassa-Fever Virus
LFV	Light Forces Vehicle (SAUS)
LFV	Low-Frequency Vibration
LFV	Lunar Flying Vehicle [NASA]
LFV	Northhampton, MA [Location identifier] [FAA] (FAAL)
LFVLF	Low Frequency, Very Low Frequency (IAA)
LFVM	Miquelon [France] [ICAO location identifier] (ICLI)
LFVO	Library Foundation for Voluntary Organizations [Defunct] (EA)
LFVP	Saint-Pierre, Saint-Pierre-Et Miquelon [France] [ICAO location identifier] (ICLI)
LFW	Liberal Federation of Wales (SAUO)
LFW	Linear Friction Welding [Environmental science]
LFW	Lome [Togo] [Airport symbol] (OAG)
LFW	Looking for Work
LFWB	Sccom Sud-Ouest [France] [ICAO location identifier] (ICLI)
LFWD	Location of Four-Wheel Drive [Automotive emissions]
LFWID	Length of Leaf at Widest Portion [Botany]
LFWK	Lifework (ABBR)
LFX	Limited output Full area automatic Extraction (SAUS)
LFX	Live Fire Exercise [Army] (INF)
LFX	Live-Fire Exercises [Army] (INF)
LFXA	Amberieu [France] [ICAO location identifier] (ICLI)
LFXB	Saintes/Thenac [France] [ICAO location identifier] (ICLI)
LFXC	Contrexeville [France] [ICAO location identifier] (ICLI)
LFXD	Doullens/Lucheux [France] [ICAO location identifier] (ICLI)
LFXE	Camp De Mourmelon [France] [ICAO location identifier] (ICLI)
LFXF	Limoges/Romanet [France] [ICAO location identifier] (ICLI)
LFXG	Camp De Bitche [France] [ICAO location identifier] (ICLI)
LFXH	Camp Du Valdahon [France] [ICAO location identifier] (ICLI)
LFXI	Apt/Saint-Christol [France] [ICAO location identifier] (ICLI)
LFXJ	Bordeaux [France] [ICAO location identifier] (ICLI)
LFXK	Camp De Suippes [France] [ICAO location identifier] (ICLI)
LFXL	Mailly-Le-Camp [France] [ICAO location identifier] (ICLI)
LFXM	Mourmelon [France] [ICAO location identifier] (ICLI)
LFXN	Narbonne [France] [ICAO location identifier] (ICLI)
LFXO	Tours/Cinq-Mars La Pile [France] [ICAO location identifier] (ICLI)
LFXP	Camp De Sissonne [France] [ICAO location identifier] (ICLI)
LFXQ	Camp De Coetquidan [France] [ICAO location identifier] (ICLI)
LFXR	Rochefort/Soubise [France] [ICAO location identifier] (ICLI)
LFXS	Camp De La Courtine [France] [ICAO location identifier] (ICLI)

LFXT .... Camp De Caylus [France] [ICAO location identifier] (ICLI)
LFXU .... Les Mureaux [France] [ICAO location identifier] (ICLI)
LFXV .... Lyon/Mont-Verdun [France] [ICAO location identifier] (ICLI)
LFXW .... Camp Du Larzac [France] [ICAO location identifier] (ICLI)
LFY .... Leafy (ABBR)
LFYA .... Drachenbronn [France] [ICAO location identifier] (ICLI)
LFYD .... Damblain [France] [ICAO location identifier] (ICLI)
LFYF .... Centre Meteorologique de Concentration et de Diffusion, French Air Force [France] [ICAO location identifier] (ICLI)
LFYG .... Cambrai/Niergnies [France] [ICAO location identifier] (ICLI)
LFYH .... Broye-Les-Pesmes [France] [ICAO location identifier] (ICLI)
LFYL .... Lure/Malbouhans [France] [ICAO location identifier] (ICLI)
LFYM .... Marigny-Le-Grand [France] [ICAO location identifier] (ICLI)
LFYO .... Villacoublay [France] [ICAO location identifier] (ICLI)
LFYR .... Romorantin/Pruniers [France] [ICAO location identifier] (ICLI)
LFYS .... Sainte-Leocadie [France] [ICAO location identifier] (ICLI)
LFYT .... Saint-Simon/Clastres [France] [ICAO location identifier] (ICLI)
LFYX .... Paris [France] [ICAO location identifier] (ICLI)
LFZ .... Laminar Flow Zone
LG .... Directorate of Logistics Systems (SAUO)
LG .... Guidotti & C. [Italy] [Research code symbol]
LG .... Laban Guild [Formerly, LAMG] (EA)
LG .... Laboratory of Genetics (GNE)
LG .... Laclede Gas [NYSE symbol] (TTSB)
LG .... Laclede Gas Co. [NYSE symbol] (SPSG)
LG .... Lady [of the Order of the] Garter (BARN)
LG .... Lagoon [Maps and charts] (ROG)
LG .... Landed Gentry
LG .... Landgericht [Regional Court] [German] (ILCA)
L/G .... Land Grant (DLA)
LG .... Landing Gear [Aircraft]
LG .... Landing Ground [Navy]
LG .... Landing Group [Navy] (NVT)
LG .... Lane Grader [Slang for an army instructor] (VNW)
LG .... Language [Online database field identifier]
lg .... Large (BEE)
Lg .... Large (DIAR)
LG .... Large
LG .... Large Grain
LG .... Laryngectomy [Medicine] (MAE)
LG .... LASER Gyro (MCD)
LG .... Lateral Gastrocnemius
LG .... Lateral Geniculate [Medicine] (MELL)
LG .... Launcher Group [Army]
LG .... Law Glossary (DLA)
L-G .... Lawson Gould [Publisher]
LG .... Leathercraft Guild (EA)
LG .... Leaving Group
LG .... Left Gluteus [Medicine]
LG .... Left Guard [Football]
LG .... Leg (IAA)
LG .... Leichtgeschuetz [Light gun for airborne operations] [German military - World War II]
LG .... Length (MSA)
LG .... Leucylglycine (DB)
LG .... Level Gauge
LG .... Lewis Gun
LG .... Lieutenant General [British] (ROG)
LG .... Life Guards [Military unit] [British]
LG .... Light Green
LG .... Light Gun
LG .... Linear Gate
LG .... Line Generator [Computer science]
LG .... Line Graph (OA)
LG .... Line-to-Ground (IAA)
LG .... Linguogingival [Dentistry]
LG .... Lining
LG .... Linkage Group [Genetics] (OA)
LG .... Lipoglycopeptide (DB)
LG .... Liquid Gas
LG .... Liquid Gold (WDAA)
LG .... [The] Literary Guild
LG .... Little Guides [A publication]
LG .... Local Government (ADA)
LG .... Local Ground (ACAE)
LG .... Loganiar Ltd. [British]
LG .... Logistics Group [Military]
LG .... London Group (SAUO)
LG .... Long (KSC)
LG .... Longold Resources, Inc. [Vancouver Stock Exchange symbol]
LG .... Longwood Gardens [Kennett Square, PA]
LG .... Loop Gain
LG .... Low German [Language, etc.]
LG .... Low Glucose [Medicine]
LG .... Lumen Gentium [Dogmatic Constitution on the Church] [Vatican II document]
LG .... Lymph Glands [Medicine]
LGA .... Elgaz [Poland] [ICAO designator] (FAAC)
LGA .... Flight Ground Attack Fighter (ACAE)
LGA .... LaGuardia Airport [New York] (CDAI)
LGA .... Large for Gestational Age [Pediatrics]
LGA .... Left Gastric Artery [Medicine] (MELL)
LGA .... LGA: Local Government Administration [A publication]
LGA .... Light-Gun Amplifier
LGA .... Liptako-Gourma Integrated Development Authority (SAUO)

LGA .... Local Government Act (SAUO)
LGA .... Local Government Administration
LGA .... Local Government Agency (SAUO)
LGA .... Local Government Area (ADA)
LGA .... Local Government Association (GVA)
LGA .... Local Government Audit [British]
LGA .... Local Government Authority (SAUO)
LgA .... Lodging Allowance [British military] (DMA)
LGA .... Low-Gain Antenna
LGA .... New York [New York] La Guardia [Airport symbol] (OAG)
LGAA .... Local Government Auditors Association
LGAANSW .... Local Government Auditors' Association of New South Wales [Australia]
LGAB .... Local Government Advisory Board [Tasmania, Australia]
LGAB .... Local Government Auditors' Board [Queensland, Australia]
LGAC .... Athinai [Greece] [ICAO location identifier] (ICLI)
LgacySft ...... Legacy Software, Inc. [Associated Press] (SAG)
LGAD .... Andravida [Greece] [ICAO location identifier] (ICLI)
LGAES .... Lesbian and Gay Associated Engineers and Scientists [Later, NOGLSTP] (EA)
LGAF .... Flight Ground-Attack Fighter (SAUS)
LGAF .... Light Ground-Attack Fighter
LGAG .... Agrinion [Greece] [ICAO location identifier] (ICLI)
LGAG .... Luggage (ABBR)
LGAL .... Alexandroupolis [Greece] [ICAO location identifier] (ICLI)
LGAM .... Amphiali [Greece] [ICAO location identifier] (ICLI)
LGAM .... Lexington Global Asset Managers, Inc. [NASDAQ symbol] (SAG)
LGAM .... Lexington Global Assets Mgrs [NASDAQ symbol] (TTSB)
LG&E .... Louisville Gas and Electric Co. (EFIS)
LGANSW ..... Local Government Association of New South Wales [Australia]
LGANT .... Local Government Association of the Northern Territory [Australia]
LGAR .... Ladies of the Grand Army of the Republic (EA)
LGAS .... Louisville Gas & Electric Co. [NASDAQ symbol] (SAG)
LGAS .... Low-G Accelerometer System [NASA]
LGASA .... Local Government Association of South Australia
LGASP .... Louiseville G&E 5% Pfd [NASDAQ symbol] (TTSB)
LGAT .... Athinai [Greece] [ICAO location identifier] (ICLI)
LGAT .... Local Government Appeals Tribunal (SAUO)
LGAX .... Alexandria [Greece] [ICAO location identifier] (ICLI)
L Gaz .... Law Gazette [A publication] (DLA)
LGB .... Landry-Guillain-Barre (Syndrome) [Medicine]
LGB .... LASER-Guided Bomb
LGB .... Lateral Geniculate Body
LGB .... Legible (ABBR)
LGB .... Local Government Board
LGB .... Long Beach [California] [Airport symbol] (OAG)
LGB .... Long Beach, CA [Location identifier] [FAA] (FAAL)
LGBA .... Lesbian and Gay Bands of America (EA)
LGBC .... Local Government Boundaries Commission [New South Wales, Australia]
LGBC .... Local Government Boundary Commission (SAUO)
LGBCE .... Local Government Boundary Commission for England
LGBL .... Nea Anghialos [Greece] [ICAO location identifier] (ICLI)
LGBO .... Local Government Board Office [British]
LGBPM .... Lesbian, Gay, and Bisexual People in Medicine (EA)
LGBR .... Loganberry (ABBR)
LGBRPCV ..... Lesbian, Gay, and Bisexual Returned Peace Corps Volunteers (EA)
LGBRU .... Lugubrious (ABBR)
LGBRUY .... Lugubriously (ABBR)
LGBS .... Landry-Guillain-Barre Syndrome [Medicine] (DMAA)
LGBT .... Legibility (ABBR)
LGBT .... Lesbian, Gay, Bisexual, and Transgendered [Lifestyle classifications]
LGBTA .... Lesbian Gay Bisexual Transgender Association
LGBY .... Legibly (ABBR)
LGC .... Laboratory of the Government Chemist [Research center] [British] (IRC)
LGC .... La Grange, GA [Location identifier] [FAA] (FAAL)
LGC .... Lakewood Golf Course [California] [Seismograph station code, US Geological Survey] (SEIS)
LGC .... Large Diameter Gravity Corer [Nuclear energy] (NUCP)
LGC .... Large-Probe Gas Chromatograph [NASA]
LGC .... Launch Guidance Computer
LGC .... Laurentian Group Corp. [Toronto Stock Exchange symbol]
LGC .... Leafy Greens Council (EA)
LGC .... Left Giant Cell [Medicine] (STED)
LGC .... Line Group Controller (ACRL)
LGC .... LM [Lunar Module] Guidance Computer [NASA]
LGC .... Local Government Center [Database producer] (EA)
LGC .... Local Government Chronicle [1855] [A publication] (DLA)
LGC .... Local Government Commission [Victoria, Australia]
LGC .... Local Government Contact (SAUO)
LGC .... Local Government Council
L-G C .... Lockheed-Georgia Company (SAUO)
LGC .... Logic (MSA)
LGC .... Longitude Grid Control (ACAE)
LGC .... Lord Great Chamberlain [British] [A publication] (DLA)
LGC .... Lorry with Gas Containers [British]
LGC .... Lunar Gas Chromatograph
LGC .... Lunar Geological Camera [NASA] (KSC)
LGCA .... Land-Grant College of Agriculture
LGCA .... Late Great Chevrolet Association (EA)
LGCA .... Local Government Clerks' Association [Australia]
LGCA .... London Gregorian Choral Association
LGCANSW .... Local Government Clerks' Association of New South Wales [Australia]

LGCB	Local Government Clerks' Board [*Queensland, Australia*]
LGCC	Letchworth Garden City Corporation (SAUO)
LGCC	Local Government Clerks' Certificate
LGCL	Licentiate of the Guild of Cleaners and Launderers [*British*] (DBQ)
LGCL	Logical (ABBR)
LGCLT	Logicality (ABBR)
LGCLY	Logically (ABBR)
LGCM	Lesbian & Gay Christian Movement (WDAA)
LGCN	Logician (ABBR)
LGCOMB	Large Combatant (DNAB)
LGCP	Lexical-Graphical Composer Printer [*Photocomposition*]
LGCPHW	Lesbian and Gay Caucus of Public Health Workers (EA)
LGCS	Limited Generation Certification Scheme (SAUO)
LGCY	Legacy (ABBR)
LGCY	Legacy Software [*NASDAQ symbol*] (TTSB)
LGCY	Legacy Software, Inc. [*NASDAQ symbol*] (SAG)
LGD	Compagnie Aerienne du Languedoc [*France*] [*ICAO designator*] (FAAC)
LGd	Dorsal Lateral Geniculate Nucleus [*Also, dLGN*] [*Anatomy*]
LGD	La Grande, OR [*Location identifier*] [*FAA*] (FAAL)
LGD	Lambda Gamma Delta [*Society*]
LGD	Large Group Display (MCD)
LGD	Leaderless Group Discussion
lgd	Legend (VRA)
LGD	Local Government Development (SAUO)
LGD	Local Government Division (SAUO)
LGD	Local Government Division, Department of Internal Affairs (SAUS)
LGD	Lou Gehrig Disease [*Medicine*] (MELL)
LGD	Low-Grade Dysplasia [*Medicine*]
LGDA	Lawn and Garden Distributors Association (SAUO)
LGDA	National Lawn and Garden Distributors Association (EA)
LGDHC	Ligue Guineenne des Droits de l'Homme [*Guinea*] [*Political party*] (EY)
LGDM	LASER-Guided Dispenser Munition (PDAA)
LGDMN	Legerdemain (ABBR)
LGDR	Labor of Genetic Disease Research [*National Institutes of Health*]
LGDT	Load Global Descriptor Table (SAUO)
LGE	Landing Ground, Emergency [*British military*] (DMA)
LGE	Large (MSA)
lge	Large (REAL)
LGE	Laser Guidance Element (ACAE)
LGE	League (WDAA)
LGE	LEM [*Lunar Excursion Module*] Guidance Equipment [*NASA*] (KSC)
LGE	LG & E Energy [*NYSE symbol*] (SPSG)
LGE	Light Generation Efficiency (AAEL)
LGE	Local Government Engineer
LGE	Logic Gate Expander [*Computer science*]
LGE	Lunar Geological Equipment [*NASA*]
LGEA	Local Government Electricity Association (SAUO)
LGEANSW	Local Government Electricity Association of New South Wales [*Australia*]
LGEANSW	Local Government Engineers' Association of New South Wales [*Australia*]
LGEB	Local Government Examination Board (SAUO)
LGEC	Lunar Geological Exploration Camera (PDAA)
LGEEQC	Local Government Electrical Engineering Qualifications Committee [*Australia*]
LGEIES	Local Government Environmental Information Exchange Scheme (SAUO)
LGEL	Elefsis [*Greece*] [*ICAO location identifier*] (ICLI)
LGEME	Legion of Greeks from Egypt and the Middle East [*Australia*] [*An association*]
LGEMP	Local Government Energy Management Program
LGEN	Lieutenant General (GOBB)
L/Gen	Lieutenant General (SAUO)
LGen	Lieutenant General [*Navy*] [*British*]
LGEQC	Local Government Engineering Qualifications Committee [*Australia*]
LGER	Low German [*Language, etc.*] (ROG)
LGF	Lateral Giant Fiber (DB)
LGF	Light Guiding Film [*Adhesives*]
LGF	Lions Gate Entertainment [*AMEX symbol*] (SG)
LGF	Yuma/Yuma Proving Ground, AZ [*Location identifier*] [*FAA*] (FAAL)
LGFA	Lattice Girder Floor Association [*British*] (DBA)
LGFC	Lesley Gore Fan Club (EA)
LGFS	Local Government Financial System (MHDB)
LGFSTF	Liquified Gaseous Fuels Spill Test Facility [*Department of Energy*]
LGFSTP	Liquefied Gaseous Fuels Spill Test Facility (USDC)
LGG	Least General Generalization (IDAI)
LGG	Legging (ABBR)
LGG	Liege [*Belgium*] [*Airport symbol*] (OAG)
LGG	Light Gas Gun
LGG	Light-Gun Pulse Generator
LGGBFC	Larry Gatlin and the Gatlin Brothers Fan Club (EA)
LGGBIFC	Larry Gatlin and the Gatlin Brothers International Fan Club (EA)
LGGC	Local Government Grants Commission
LGGE	Laboratory of Glaciology and Geophysics of the Environment [*France*]
LGGG	Athinai [*Greece*] [*ICAO location identifier*] (ICLI)
LGGR	Logger (ABBR)
LGGRHD	Loggerhead (ABBR)
LGH	Lactogenic Hormone [*Also, LTH, PR, PRL*] [*Endocrinology*]
LGH	Lansing General Hospital [*Michigan*]
LGH	Laugh (ABBR)
LGH	Launch Grapnel Hook
LGH	Leigh Creek [*Australia*] [*Airport symbol*] (OAG)
LGH	Length
LGH	Letterman General Hospital (SAUO)
LGH	Liberty Godparent Home [*An association*] (EA)
LGH	Little Growth Hormone [*Medicine*] (STED)
LGH	Logarithmic Histogram Scanning [*Mass spectrometry*]
LGHB	Laughable (ABBR)
LGHBY	Laughably (ABBR)
LGHCS	Lutheran General Health Care System (EA)
LGHD	Laughed (ABBR)
LGHET	Larghetto (ABBR)
LGHG	Laughing (ABBR)
LGHGY	Laughingly (ABBR)
LGHI	Khios [*Greece*] [*ICAO location identifier*] (ICLI)
LGHL	Porto Heli [*Greece*] [*ICAO location identifier*] (ICLI)
LGHN	Leghorn (ABBR)
LGHP	Large Group Health Plan [*Department of Health and Human Services*] (GFGA)
LGHR	Laugher (ABBR)
LGHTR	Laughter (ABBR)
LGHTR	Lighter
LGI	Deadman's Cay [*Bahamas*] [*Airport symbol*] (OAG)
LGI	Large Glucagon Immunoreactivity [*Immunochemistry*]
LGI	Laser Glidescope Indicator (SAUS)
LGI	Lateral Giant Interneuron [*Neurobiology*]
LGI	Linear Gate and Integrator (MHDB)
LGI	Locally Generated Income (MCD)
LGI	Lower Gastrointestinal [*Medicine*] (STED)
LGI	Lunar Geology Investigation [*NASA*]
LGI	Lynx Geosystems Incorporated (SAUO)
LGIB	Lower Gastrointestinal Bleeding (SAUS)
LGIEE	Liaison Group for International Educational Exchange (EA)
LGIO	Ioannina [*Greece*] [*ICAO location identifier*] (ICLI)
LGIO	Local Government Information Office (SAUO)
LGIOM	Lieutenant-Governor of the Isle of Man (SAUO)
LGIR	Iraklion [*Greece*] [*ICAO location identifier*] (ICLI)
LGISC	Louisiana Geographic Information Systems Council (SAUO)
LGITIT	Legitimist (ABBR)
LGITIZ	Legitimize (ABBR)
LGITIZD	Legitimized (ABBR)
LGITIZG	Legitimizing (ABBR)
LGITMA	Legitimate (ABBR)
LGITMAD	Legitimated (ABBR)
LGITMAG	Legitimating (ABBR)
LGITMC	Legitmacy (ABBR)
LGITMY	Legitimately (ABBR)
LGIU	LASER Gyro Interface Unit (NASA)
LGIU	Local Government Information Unit [*British*]
LGJ	Local Government Journal [*A publication*] (ROG)
LGK	Langkawi [*Malaysia*] [*Airport symbol*] (OAG)
LGk	Late Greek [*or Low Greek*] [*Language*] (BARN)
LGKA	Kastoria [*Greece*] [*ICAO location identifier*] (ICLI)
LGKC	Kithira [*Greece*] [*ICAO location identifier*] (ICLI)
LGKF	Kefallinia [*Greece*] [*ICAO location identifier*] (ICLI)
LGKJ	Kastelorizo [*Greece*] [*ICAO location identifier*] (ICLI)
LGKL	Kalamata [*Greece*] [*ICAO location identifier*] (ICLI)
LGKM	Kavala/Amigdhaleon [*Greece*] [*ICAO location identifier*] (ICLI)
LGKO	Kos [*Greece*] [*ICAO location identifier*] (ICLI)
LGKP	Karpathos [*Greece*] [*ICAO location identifier*] (ICLI)
LGKR	Kerkira [*Greece*] [*ICAO location identifier*] (ICLI)
LGKS	Kasos [*Greece*] [*ICAO location identifier*] (ICLI)
LGKV	Kavala/Khrisoupolis [*Greece*] [*ICAO location identifier*] (ICLI)
LGKZ	Kozani [*Greece*] [*ICAO location identifier*] (ICLI)
LGL	Labioglossolaryngeal [*Dentistry*] (DAVI)
LGL	La Gloria [*Colombia*] [*Airport symbol*] (AD)
LGL	Large Granular Leukocyte [*Hematology*]
LGL	Large Granular Lymphocyte [*Hematology*]
LGL	Legal (ABBR)
Lgl	Legal (TBD)
LGL	Lobular Glomerulonephritis [*Medicine*] (STED)
LGL	Local Government Library [*A publication*]
LGL	Local Graphics Library [*Cambridge Computer Graphics Ltd.*] [*Software package*] (NCC)
LGL	Long Lellang [*Malaysia*] [*Airport symbol*] (OAG)
LGL	Lown-Ganong-Levine [*Syndrome*] [*Medicine*]
LGL	Luxair-Societe Luxembourgeoise de Navigation Aerienne SA [*Germany*] [*ICAO designator*] (FAAC)
LGL	Lynch Corp. [*AMEX symbol*] (SPSG)
LGLA	Legislate (ABBR)
LGLAD	Legislated (ABBR)
LGLAG	Legislating (ABBR)
LGLAN	Legislation (ABBR)
LGLAR	Legislator (ABBR)
LGLAR	Legislature (ABBR)
LGLAY	Legislative (ABBR)
LGLC	Libertarians for Gay and Lesbian Concerns (EA)
LGLE	Leros [*Greece*] [*ICAO location identifier*] (ICLI)
LGLM	Legalism (ABBR)
LGLPFA	London and Greater London Playing Fields Association (SAUO)
LGLR	Larissa [*Greece*] [*ICAO location identifier*] (ICLI)
LGLST	Legalist (ABBR)
LGLSTC	Legalistic (ABBR)
LGLSTCY	Legalistically (ABBR)
LGLT	Legality (ABBR)
LGLTC	Legalistic (ABBR)
LGLY	Legally (ABBR)

LGLZ............	Legalize (ABBR)
LGLZD.........	Legalized (ABBR)
LGLZG.........	Legalizing (ABBR)
LGLZN.........	Legalization (ABBR)
LGM............	LASER Ground Mapper
LGM............	LASER-Guided Munition
LGM............	Last Glacial Maximum [Climatology]
LGM............	Liberty Godparent Ministry (EA)
LGM............	Little Green Men [British term for space signals]
LGM............	Little Green Mountain [Idaho] [Seismograph station code, US Geological Survey] [Closed] (SEIS)
LGM............	Local Government Management [A publication]
LGM............	Logistic Guidance Memorandum
LGM............	Logistics Module [Simulation games] [Army] (SSD)
LGM............	Loop Ground Multiplexer (MCD)
LGM............	Loop Group Multiplexer. Communications (SAUO)
LGM............	Lymphogranuloma [Medicine] (MELL)
LGM............	Silo-Launched surface attack Guided Missile (SAUS)
LGMA..........	Lesbian and Gay Medical Association [Defunct] (EAIO)
LGMB..........	Lady Godiva Marching Band (SAUO)
LGMB..........	Local Government Management Board (AIE)
LGMD..........	Limb Girdle Muscular Dystrophy [Medicine]
LGMD..........	Lobular Giant Movement Detector (PDAA)
LGMG..........	Lipid and Glycopeptide Modified Derivative (DB)
LGMG..........	Megara [Greece] [ICAO location identifier] (ICLI)
LGMK..........	Mikonos [Greece] [ICAO location identifier] (ICLI)
LGML..........	Milos [Greece] [ICAO location identifier] (ICLI)
LGMN..........	Ligament (ABBR)
LGMR..........	Laser Guided Magnetical Recording (SAUS)
LGMR..........	Marathon [Greece] [ICAO location identifier] (ICLI)
LGMS..........	LASER Ground Mapping System
LGMS..........	Laser Guided Missile System (SAUO)
LGMT..........	Mitilini [Greece] [ICAO location identifier] (ICLI)
LGN............	Lagoon (ADA)
LGN............	Lagunillas [Venezuela] [Seismograph station code, US Geological Survey] (SEIS)
LGN............	Lateral Geniculate Nucleus
LGN............	Left Green Network [An association] (EA)
LGN............	Legion (ABBR)
LGN............	Legion Resources Ltd. [Vancouver Stock Exchange symbol]
LGN............	Line Gate Number [Computer science]
LGN............	Lobular Glomerulonephritis [Medicine] (MAE)
LGN............	Logical Group Node (SAUO)
LGN............	Logical Group Number [Computer science] (IBMDP)
LGN............	Logicon, Inc. [NYSE symbol] (SPSG)
LGNAP.........	Lagniappe (ABBR)
LGNAR.........	Legionaire (ABBR)
LGNBRY.......	Loganberry (ABBR)
LGND..........	Lateral Geniculate Nucleus Dorsal [Neuroanatomy]
LGND..........	Legend (ABBR)
LGND..........	Ligand Pharmaceuticals, Inc. [NASDAQ symbol] (SAG)
LGND..........	Ligand Pharmaceuticals 'B' [NASDAQ symbol] (TTSB)
LGNDY.........	Legendary (ABBR)
LGNMVTE.....	Lignum Vitae [Botany]
LGNS..........	Largeness (ABBR)
LGNS..........	Leggoons Inc. [NASDAQ symbol] (TTSB)
LGNT..........	LEGENT Corp. (SAUO)
LGNY..........	Legionary (ABBR)
LGNZ..........	Local Government New Zealand (SAUO)
LGO............	Lamont Geological Observatory [Later, L-DGO] [Columbia University]
LGO............	Largo (ABBR)
LGO............	Light Gas Oil [Fuel technology]
LGO............	Local Government Office
LGO............	Logo Resources Ltd. [Vancouver Stock Exchange symbol]
LGO............	Low Gravity Orbit
LGOC..........	Lunar Geoscience Observer (MCD)
LGOC..........	London General Omnibus Co. [British] (DCTA)
LGOFC.........	Linda Gray's Official Fan Club (EA)
LGON..........	Lagoon (ABBR)
LGOR..........	Langor (ABBR)
LGORU........	Langorous (ABBR)
LGORU........	Local Government Operational Research Unit [British] (DI)
LGORUY......	Langorously (ABBR)
LGP............	Labioglossopharyngeal [Dentistry] (DAVI)
LGP............	Laboratory Graduate Participation [Oak Ridge National Laboratory]
LGP............	LASER-Guided Projectile (MCD)
LGP............	Legaspi [Philippines] [Airport symbol] (OAG)
LGP............	Legaspi [Philippines] [Seismograph station code, US Geological Survey] (SEIS)
LGP............	Low G Projectile (ACAE)
LGP............	Low Ground Pressure
LGP............	Lummer-Gehreke Plate [Physics]
LGPA..........	Livestock and Grain Producers Association (SAUO)
LGPA..........	Paros [Greece] [ICAO location identifier] (ICLI)
LGPANSW....	Livestock and Grain Producers' Association of New South Wales [Australia]
LGPIM........	Lesbian and Gay People in Medicine [Later, LGBPM] (EA)
LGPL..........	Lesser General Public License (SAUO)
LGPL..........	Library General Public License (SAUO)
LGPN..........	International Leather Goods, Plastic, and Novelty Workers' Union (EA)
LGPO..........	Local Group Policy Object (SAUO)
LGPZ..........	Preveza [Greece] [ICAO location identifier] (ICLI)
LGQ............	Lago Agrio [Ecuador] [Airport symbol] (OAG)
LGQ............	Linear Gaussian Quadratic (AAEL)
LGQB..........	Local Government Qualifications Board [Victoria, Australia]
LGR............	Knight's Local Government Reports [A publication] (DLA)
LGR............	Lager (ABBR)
LGR............	Laird Group, Inc. [Toronto Stock Exchange symbol]
LGR............	Larger (WGA)
lgr.............	Larger
LGR............	Laser Guidance Receiver (SAUS)
LGR............	Leasehold Ground Rent (ROG)
LGR............	Lethal Ground Range (MCD)
LGR............	Letter of General Representation (PDAA)
LGR............	Light-Water-Cooled, Graphite-Moderated Reactor (NRCH)
LGR............	Local Government Reorganization [British]
LGR............	Local Government Reports [England] [A publication] (DLA)
LGR............	Local Governments Reimbursement Program (SAUO)
LGR............	Localized Gain Region (PDAA)
LGR............	Logrono [Spain] [Seismograph station code, US Geological Survey] (SEIS)
LGR............	London Grand Rank [Freemasonry]
LGR............	Longer (WGA)
LGR............	Loop Gap Resonator [Spectrometry]
LGR............	Low Greek [Language, etc.]
LGR............	Low Group Receiving Unit
LGra...........	Grambling State University, Grambling, LA [Library symbol] [Library of Congress] (LCLS)
LGRD..........	Laggard (ABBR)
LGRD..........	Rodos/Maritsa [Greece] [ICAO location identifier] (ICLI)
LGR (Eng)....	Local Government Reports [England] [A publication] (DLA)
LGRF..........	Loan Guaranty Revolving Fund
LGrJ...........	Jefferson Parish Public Library, Gretna, LA [Library symbol] [Library of Congress] (LCLS)
LGR Laser ...	Localized Gain Region Laser (SAUO)
LGRMG.......	Lesbian/Gay Rights Monitoring Group (EA)
LGRP..........	Rodos/Paradisi [Greece] [ICAO location identifier] (ICLI)
LGR Unit.....	Low Group Receiving Unit (SAUO)
LGRX..........	Araxos [Greece] [ICAO location identifier] (ICLI)
LGS............	Grambling State University, Grambling, LA [OCLC symbol] (OCLC)
LGS............	Lagoons [Maps and charts] (ROG)
LGS............	Landing Guidance System [Aerospace]
LGS............	Large Gray Ship [Slang] [Navy]
LGS............	Large Green Soft [Stool] [Gastroenterology] (DAVI)
LGS............	LASER Guidance System (MCD)
LGS............	Last Glacial Stage (QUAC)
LGS............	Late Glacial Stage [Paleontology]
LGS............	Lega dei Giovani Somali [Somali Youth League]
LGS............	Limerick Generation Station [Nuclear energy] (NRCH)
LGS............	Liquid Asset and Government Securities (ADA)
LGS............	Lithogenic Grain Size [An indicator of wind intensity]
LGS............	Litton Graphics Standard (MCD)
LGS............	Louisiana General Services, Inc. (SAUO)
LGS............	Louisiana Geological Survey (SAUO)
LGS............	Lower Group Stop (NRCH)
LGS............	Lunar Geophysical Surface
LGS............	Lunar Gravity Simulator [Aerospace]
LGSA..........	Khania/Souda [Greece] [ICAO location identifier] (ICLI)
LGSA..........	Langer-Giedion Syndrome Association (NRGU)
LGSA..........	Leinster Guild of Shop Assistants (SAUO)
LGSB..........	Local Government Services Bureau [South Australia]
LGSB..........	Local Government Superannuation Board [Queensland, Australia]
LGSC..........	Large Scale (ABBR)
LGSC..........	Linear Glideslope Capture (SAUS)
LGSD..........	Sedes [Greece] [ICAO location identifier] (ICLI)
L/GSE.........	Launch and Ground Support Equipment
LGS/GJ.......	Geological Journal. Liverpool Geological Society and the Manchester Geological Association. Liverpool
LGSIL.........	Low Grade Squamous Intraepithelial Lesions [Medicine] (WDAA)
LGSK..........	Skiathos [Greece] [ICAO location identifier] (ICLI)
LGSL..........	Lugsail (ABBR)
LGSM..........	Licentiate of Guildhall School of Music [British]
LGSM..........	Light Ground Station Module
LGSM..........	Samos [Greece] [ICAO location identifier] (ICLI)
LGSOWG.....	Landsat Ground Station Operations (or Operators) Working Group (SAUO)
LGSOWOG ...	Landsat Ground Station Operations Working Group (SAUO)
LGSP..........	Sparti [Greece] [ICAO location identifier] (ICLI)
LGSR..........	Santorini [Greece] [ICAO location identifier] (ICLI)
LGsSH........	Greenwell Springs State Hospital, Greenwell Springs, LA [Library symbol] [Library of Congress] (LCLS)
LGST..........	Sitia [Greece] [ICAO location identifier] (ICLI)
lgstc..........	Linguistic (ADWA)
LGSTC........	Logistic (ABBR)
LGSTCL.......	Logistical (ABBR)
LGSTCN......	Logistician (ABBR)
Lgstcs........	Linguistics (ADWA)
LGSV..........	Stefanovikion [Greece] [ICAO location identifier] (ICLI)
LGSY..........	Skyros [Greece] [ICAO location identifier] (ICLI)
LGT............	Langat Encephalitis [Medicine]
LGT............	Largest (ABBR)
LGT............	Late Generalized Tuberculosis [Medicine]
LGT............	Legate (ABBR)
LGT............	Liechtenstein Global Trust
LGT............	Light
lgt.............	Light
LGT............	Liquid Gas Tank
LGT............	Local Geomagnetic Time
LGT............	Logistec Corp. [Toronto Stock Exchange symbol]

LGT............. Longitudinal Survey of Work Experience (SAUO)
LGT............. Low Gelling Temperature [Analytical biochemistry]
LGT............. Low Group Transmit (SAUO)
LGT............. Low Group Transmitting Unit
LGTA........... Ligue Generale des Travailleurs Angolais [General League of Angolan Workers in Exile]
LGTB........... Local Government Training Board [British]
LGTD .... Lighted
LGTE........... Legatee (ABBR)
LGTFGR....... Lightfingered (ABBR)
LGTFTD....... Lightfooted (ABBR)
LGTFTY....... Lightfootedly (ABBR)
LGTG .... Lighting (ABBR)
LGTG .... Tanagra [Greece] [ICAO location identifier] (ICLI)
LGTH .... Length (AFM)
lgth .... Length (VRA)
LGTH .... Lexington Group in Transportation History (EA)
LGTH .... Lightning Hole [Electronics]
LGTHCOLM... Length of Column [Military] (GFGA)
LGTHD......... Lightheaded (ABBR)
LGTHDY....... Lightheadedly (ABBR)
LGTHIY........ Lengthily (ABBR)
LGTHN .... Lengthen (ABBR)
LGTHND...... Lengthened (ABBR)
LGTHNG...... Lengthening (ABBR)
LGTHNS...... Lengthiness (ABBR)
LGTHR .... Lengthier (ABBR)
LGTHRTD..... Lighthearted (ABBR)
LGTHRTNS... Lightheartedness (ABBR)
LGTHRTY..... Lightheartedly (ABBR)
LGTHS .... Lighthouse (ABBR)
LGTHT .... Lengthiest (ABBR)
LGTHWS...... Lengthwise (ABBR)
LGTHY .... Lengthy (ABBR)
LGTI............ Lower Genital Tract Infection [Medicine] (DMAA)
LGTIC.......... Logistic (ABBR)
LGTICL......... Logistical (ABBR)
LGTK........... Logitek, Inc. (SAUO)
LGTL........... Kasteli [Greece] [ICAO location identifier] (ICLI)
LGTMDD ...... Lightminded (ABBR)
LGTMDY ...... Lightmindedly (ABBR)
LGTN .... Legation (ABBR)
LGTN .... Lighten (ABBR)
LG TN .... Long Ton [2240 pounds] (WDAA)
LGTNG........ Lightning (ABBR)
LGTO .... Legato (ABBR)
LGTO .... Legato Systems [NASDAQ symbol] (TTSB)
LGTO .... Legato Systems, Inc. [NASDAQ symbol] (SAG)
LGTP........... Tripolis [Greece] [ICAO location identifier] (ICLI)
LGTPB......... Local Government Town Planners' Board [Queensland, Australia]
LG TPR .... Long Taper (WDAA)
LGTR .... Ligature (ABBR)
LGTR .... Lightener (ABBR)
LGTRD......... Ligatured (ABBR)
LGTRG......... Ligaturing (ABBR)
LGTS........... Lights [Postal Service standard] (OPSA)
LGTS........... Thessaloniki [Greece] [ICAO location identifier] (ICLI)
LGTT........... Dekeleia/Tatoi [Greece] [ICAO location identifier] (ICLI)
LGTUD......... Longitude (ABBR)
LGTUDL....... Longitudinal (ABBR)
LGTUDY....... Longitudinally (ABBR)
LGT Unit...... Low Group Transmitting Unit (SAUO)
LGTWT........ Lightweight (ABBR)
LGTY .... Lightly (ABBR)
LGTYR .... Lightyear (ABBR)
LGU .... Ladies Golf Union
LGU .... Land-Grant University
LGU .... League (ABBR)
LGU .... Legume (ABBR)
LGU .... Local Glucose Utilization [Physiology]
LGU .... Local Government Union (SAUO)
LGU .... Local Government Unit (SAUO)
LGU .... Logan [Utah] [Airport symbol] (OAG)
LGU .... Logan, UT [Location identifier] [FAA] (FAAL)
L Guard .... Law Guardian [A publication] (DLA)
LGUD.......... Leagued (ABBR)
LGUG.......... Leaguing (ABBR)
LGUM.......... Legume, Inc. (SAUO)
LGUNU........ Leguminous (ABBR)
LGUs........... Local Government Units (SAUS)
LGV............. Large Goods Vehicle (SAUO)
LGV............. Large Granular Vesicle (OA)
LGV............. Long Goods Vehicle (SAUO)
LGV............. Lymphogranuloma Venereum [Medicine]
LGVC.......... Local Government Valuers' Committee [New South Wales, Australia]
LGVD.......... Large Group View Display (MCD)
LGVHD........ Lethal Graft-Versus-Host Disease [Medicine] (DMAA)
LGVMA .... Lesbian & Gay Veterinary Medical Association (GVA)
LGVO .... Volos [Greece] [ICAO location identifier] (ICLI)
LGW............ Landing Gear Warning
LGW............ Laser-Guided Weapon (DOMA)
LGW............ London-Gatwick [England] [Airport symbol] (OAG)
LGW............ Longines-Wittnauer Watch Company (SAUO)
LGW............ Love Games Won [Tennis]

LGW............ Lufttarhtgesellschaft Walter GmbH [Germany] [ICAO designator] (FAAC)
LGW/CAS..... Laser Guided Weapons in Close Air Support (SAUO)
LGWCM ...... LASER-Guided Weapons Counter-Measure (PDAA)
LGWD.......... Large Group Wall Display (SAUO)
LGWF.......... Libyan General Workers' Federation
LGWS.......... LASER-Guided Weapons Systems (IEEE)
LGWV .... Long Wave (FAAC)
LGWX .... Logic Works [NASDAQ symbol] (TTSB)
LGWX .... Logic Works, Inc. [NASDAQ symbol] (SAG)
LGX............. Lovington, NM [Location identifier] [FAA] (FAAL)
LGY............. Lagunillas [Venezuela] [Airport symbol] (AD)
LGY............. Largely (ABBR)
LGY............. Leggy (ABBR)
LGZA........... Zakinthos [Greece] [ICAO location identifier] (ICLI)
LH.............. Deutsche Lufthansa AG [Germany] [ICAO designator] (OAG)
LH.............. Laboratory Corp. Amer Hldgs Wrrt [NYSE symbol] (TTSB)
LH.............. Laboratory Corp. of America Holdings [NYSE symbol] (SAG)
LH.............. Labor Historians [Defunct] (EA)
LH.............. Labor Hour [In contract work]
LH.............. Laetolil Hominid
LH.............. Lamphole (ABBR)
LH.............. Langmuir-Hinshelwood Mechanism [Chemistry]
LH.............. Lanugo Hair (MELL)
LH.............. Laparoscopic Herniorrhaphy [Medicine] (MELL)
LH.............. Large Heavy Seeds [Botany]
LH.............. Larval Heart
LH.............. Las Hermanas [Later, LH-USA] (EA)
LH.............. Last Half [of month] [Business term] (DS)
LH.............. Last Harvest [An association] (EA)
LH.............. Last Hope [Facetious name for Chrysler's 1993 sedans]
LH.............. Late Helladic (BJA)
LH.............. Latent Heat (IAA)
LH.............. Lateral Hypothalamic [or Hypothalamus]
LH.............. Learning Handicapped
LH.............. Learning How [An association] (EA)
L/H............. Leasehold [Legal term] (DLA)
LH.............. Left Half (WDAA)
LH.............. Left Halfback [Soccer]
LH.............. Left Hand
LH.............. Left Hemisphere (DB)
LH.............. Left Hyperphoria [Ophthalmology]
LH.............. Legal Holiday (MHDW)
LH.............. Legion d'Honneur [French decoration]
LH.............. Lewisite-Mustard Gas Mix [for land mines] [Army symbol]
LH.............. L. Hungerford [Record label] [Great Britain]
LH.............. Liberty House (SAUO)
LH.............. Licentiate of Hygiene (SAUO)
LH.............. Lidocaine Hydrochloride [Medicine] (MELL)
lh.............. Liechtenstein [MARC country of publication code] [Library of Congress] (LCCP)
LH.............. Light-Harvesting (MEC)
LH.............. Lighthawk [An association] (EA)
LH.............. Light Helicopter [Military] (RDA)
LH.............. Light Horse [Cavalry]
LH.............. Lighthouse [Maps and charts]
LH.............. Lightly Hinged [Philately]
LH.............. Limited Hold
LH.............. Linear Hybrid
LH.............. Link Header (ACRL)
LH.............. Link House Books [Publisher] [British]
LH.............. Lipid Hydrocarbon [Biochemistry]
LH.............. Liquid Helium (IAA)
LH.............. Liquid Hydrogen
LH.............. Litter Hook
LH.............. Little House (WDAA)
LH.............. Load-High [Computer science] (PCM)
LH.............. Local Horizontal
LH.............. Locating Head [Engineering] (OA)
LH.............. Loch's Horse [British military] (DMA)
LH.............. Long Haul (ACAE)
LH.............. Loop of Henle (MEC)
LH.............. Lower Half
LH.............. Lower Hemispherical (MCD)
LH.............. Lower Hold [Shipping]
LH.............. Low Head [Nuclear energy] (NRCH)
L/H............. Low-to-High (MDG)
LH.............. Lues Hereditaria [Medicine]
LH.............. Lufthansa (ABBR)
LH.............. Lufthansa German Airlines [ICAO designator] (AD)
LH.............. Luteinizing-Hormone [Also, ICSH, LSH] [Endocrinology]
LH.WS........ Laboratoy Corp. Amer Hldgs Wrrt [NYSE symbol] (TTSB)
LH2............. Liquid Hydrogen (NAKS)
LH$_2$............ Liquid Hydrogen [NASA]
LHA............. Amphibious Assault Carrier [or Ship] (Landing Helicopter Assault Ship) [Navy symbol]
LHA............. Ladies' Hermitage Association (EA)
LHA............. Landing Helicopter Assault
LHA............. Lanham Housing Act (DLA)
LHA............. Lateral Hypothalamic Area
LHA............. Lay Helpers' Association [British]
LHA............. Left Heart Assistance [Cardiology]
LHA............. Left Hepatic Artery [Medicine] (DMAA)
LHA............. Leisure & Hotel Appointments [Recruitment for the hotel, leisure, and travel industries] [British]

LHA............. Lhasa [*Tibet*] [*Seismograph station code, US Geological Survey*] [*Closed*] (SEIS)
LHA............. Libertarian Humanist Association (EA)
LHA............. Licentiate of the Australian Institute of Hospital Administration (SAUO)
LHA............. Licentiate of the Institute of Health Service Administrators [*British*] (DBQ)
LHA............. Light Helicopter, Attack [*Computer test vehicle*]
LHA............. Lincoln Highway Association [*Motoring history organization*]
LHA............. Livestock Husbandry Adviser [*Ministry of Agriculture, Fisheries, and Food*] [*British*]
LHA............. Local Health Authority [*British*]
LHA............. Local Highway Authority (SAUO)
LHA............. Local Hour Angle [*Navigation*]
LHA............. Local Housing Authority
LHA............. Lord High Admiral [*British*]
LHA............. Lower-Half Assembly
LHA............. Lower Hour Angle [*Navigation*]
LHA............. Lutheran Hospital Association of America (EA)
LHA............. McNeese State University, Lake Charles, LA [*OCLC symbol*] (OCLC)
LHAA.......... Budapest [*Hungary*] [*ICAO location identifier*] (ICLI)
LHAAP........ Longhorn Army Ammunition Plant (AABC)
LHAD.......... Left Heart Assist Device (SAUS)
L/Hadr......... Lance Havidar [*Military*] [*British*]
LHAL........... Lethal (ABBR)
LHAMS........ Local Hour Angle of Mean Sun
LH&HS........ Lutheran Hospitals and Homes Society of America (SAUO)
LHAR.......... London-Hamburg-Antwerp-Rotterdam
LHAR.......... London, Havre, Antwerp, Rouen [*Shipping route*] (ROG)
LHAR.......... London, Hull, Antwerp, or Rotterdam [*Shipping route*]
LHAR.......... Lothario (ABBR)
LHarC......... Catahoula Parish Library, Harrisonburg, LA [*Library symbol*] [*Library of Congress*] (LCLS)
LHAS.......... Luteinizing Hormone Antiserum [*Endocrinology*]
LHASA......... Logic and Heuristic Applied to Synthetic Analysis (VLIE)
LHaSC......... Saint Charles Parish Library, Hahnville, LA [*Library symbol*] [*Library of Congress*] (LCLS)
LHAT.......... League of Historic American Theatres (EA)
LHATS......... Local Hour Angle of True Sun
LHAW......... Liquid High Activity Waste [*Nuclear energy*] (NUCP)
LHAWS....... Laser Homing and Warning System (SAUO)
LHB............. Bachelor of Humane Letter (SAUO)
LHB............. Bachelor of Humane Letters [*or Bachelor of Literature or Bachelor of the More Humane Letters*]
LHB............. Bachelor of Literature (SAUO)
LHB............. Bachelor of the More Humane Letters (SAUO)
LHB............. Laboratory Hazards Bulletin [*Royal Society of Chemistry*] [*Information service or system*] (IID)
LHB............. Late Heavy Bombardment [*Planetary history*]
LHb............. Lateral Habenular (Nucleus) [*Neuroanatomy*]
LHB............. Left Halfback [*Soccer*]
LHB............. Left-Handed Batter [*Baseball term*] (NDBD)
LHB............. Line History Block (SAUS)
LHB............. Lost Heartbeat [*An attractive girl*] [*Slang*]
LHBANA....... Log House Builder's Association of North America (EA)
LHBMA........ Let's Have Better Mottoes Association [*A mythical association*] (EA)
LHBP.......... Budapest/Ferihegy [*Hungary*] [*ICAO location identifier*] (ICLI)
LHBV......... Left Heart Blood Volume [*Medicine*] (DB)
LHC............. Arlington, TN [*Location identifier*] [*FAA*] (FAAL)
LHC............. Heavy Salvage Ship [*Navy symbol*] (VNW)
LHC............. Lakehead University [*Thunder Bay*] [*Ontario*] [*Seismograph station code, US Geological Survey*] (SEIS)
LHC............. L & N Housing Corporation (SAUO)
LHC............. Large Hadron Collider [*Nuclear physics*] (ECON)
LHC............. Lease Housing Coordinator (SAUO)
LHC............. Left-Hand Chain (MHDI)
LHC............. Left-Hand Circular [*Polarization*] (IEEE)
LHC............. Left Hypochondrium [*Medicine*]
LHC............. Light Harvesting Complex
LHC............. Light Hydrocarbon [*Organic chemistry*]
LHC............. Lignin-Hemicellulose-Cellulose [*A complex found in plants*]
LHC............. Lined Hollow Charge
LHC............. Liquid Hydrogen Container
LHC............. LNH Real Estate Investment Trust (SPSG)
LHC............. LNH REIT, Inc. [*NYSE symbol*] (SAG)
LHC............. Local Health Councils [*Scotland*] (DAVI)
LHC............. Local Host Computer (VLIE)
LHC............. Log Homes Council (EA)
LHC............. London Housing Consortium (SAUO)
LHC............. Lord High Chancellor [*British*]
LHC............. Loretto Heights College [*Denver, CO*]
LHC............. Louis, Holland, Callaway [*Advertising agency*]
LHC............. Lovers of the Holy Cross Sisters (TOCD)
LHC............. Lutheran Historical Conference (EA)
LHCA.......... Longshoremen's and Harbor Workers' Compensation Act (DLA)
LHCC.......... Budapest [*Hungary*] [*ICAO location identifier*] (ICLI)
LHCCBA...... London and Home Counties Contract Bridge Association (SAUO)
LHCCBCI..... London and Home Counties Conciliation Board of the Cinematograph Industry (SAUO)
LHCGACS.... Lord High Commissioner to the General Assembly of the Church of Scotland (SAUO)
LHCIMA....... Licentiate of the Hotel, Catering, and Institutional Management Association [*British*] (DBQ)
LHCJEA....... London and Home Counties Joint Electricity Authority (SAUO)
LHCN.......... Long Haul Communication Network (SAUO)

LHCP.......... Left-Hand Circularly Polarized [*LASER waves*]
LHCP.......... Light-Harvesting Chlorophyll A/B-Binding Protein (DB)
LHCRC........ Lapheld Computer Requirements Contract (SAUO)
LHCTL........ Left-Hand Control (IAA)
LHD............. Anchorage, AK [*Location identifier*] [*FAA*] (FAAL)
LHD............. Doctor of Humane Letters (DD)
LHD............. Doctor of Humanities (SAUO)
LHD............. Doctor of Letters (SAUO)
LHD............. Doctor of Letters of Humanity (SAUO)
LHD............. Doctor of Literature (DD)
LHD............. Doctor of Polite Literature (SAUO)
LHD............. Doctor of the Humanities (DD)
LHD............. Doctor of the More Humane Letters (SAUO)
LHD............. Lakehead University Library [*UTLAS symbol*]
LHD............. Large Helical Device [*Plasma physics*]
LHD............. Lateral Head Displacement [*Sperm*] [*Medicine*] (DMAA)
LHD............. Left-Hand Drive [*AEC*]
LHD............. Licentiate in Health, Dublin (ROG)
LHD............. Light Heavy-Duty [*Automotive engineering*]
LHD............. Litterarum Humaniorum Doctor [*Doctor of Humane Letters*] [*Latin*]
LHD............. Load, Haul, Dump [*Mining*]
LHD............. Local Health Department (SAUO)
LHD............. Multipurpose Amphibious Assault Ship
LHDA.......... Lesotho Highlands Development Authority (ECON)
LHDC.......... Debrecen [*Hungary*] [*ICAO location identifier*] (ICLI)
LHDC.......... Lateral Homing Depth Charge
LHDDE........ Light Heavy-Duty Diesel Engine [*Motor vehicle specifications*]
LHDDV........ Light Heavy-Duty Diesel Vehicle (EPAT)
LHDLC........ Logical High-Level Data Lead Control (SAUO)
LHDPE........ Linear High-Density Polyethylene (EDCT)
LHDR.......... Left-Hand Drive [*AEC*]
LHDS.......... LASER Hole Drilling System
LHE............. Lagrange-Helmholtz Equation
LHE............. Lahore [*Pakistan*] [*Airport symbol*] (OAG)
LHE............. Lateral Humeral Epicondylalgia [*Medicine*] (MELL)
LHE............. Lateral Humeral Epicondylitis [*Medicine*] (MELL)
LHe............. Liquid Helium (NAKS)
LHE............. Liquid Helium
LHEA.......... Laboratory for High Energy Astrophysics [*Greenbelt, MD*] [*NASA*] (GRD)
LHEAA........ Low-Income Home Energy Assistance Act of 1981 (COE)
LHeb.......... Late Hebrew (ADWA)
L HEB......... Late Hebrew (WDAA)
LHEB.......... Left-Hand Equipment Bay [*NASA*] (KSC)
LHEF.......... Lesbian Herstory Educational Foundation (EA)
LHEG.......... Local Healthcare Executive Group (HCT)
LHeT.......... Liquid Helium Temperature (PDAA)
LHF............. Labor Heritage Foundation (EA)
LHF............. Lamp Heat Flux
LHF............. Left Heart Failure [*Medicine*]
LHF............. Lighthouse, Fixed [*Maps and charts*] (ROG)
LHF............. List Handling Facility
LHFA.......... Lung Hageman Factor Activator [*Medicine*] (DMAA)
LHFC.......... Laura Hendler Fan Club (EA)
LHFCS........ Long Haul Fuel Conservation System
LHFEB........ Left-Hand Forward Equipment Bay [*NASA*] (KSC)
LHFI.......... Lighthouse, Floating [*Maps and charts*] (ROG)
LHFS.......... Ligand Hyperfine Structure
LHFT.......... Light Helicopter Fireteam [*Navy*] (NVT)
LHG............ Left Hand Grip (DMAA)
LHG............ Library History Group (SAUO)
LHG............ Licentiate of the Institute of Heraldic and Genealogical Studies [*British*] (DBQ)
LHG............ Local Hemolysis in Gel (PDAA)
LHGR.......... Linear Heat Generation Rate [*Nuclear energy*] (NRCH)
LHH............ League of Home Help [*Australia*] [*An association*]
LHH............ League of the Helping Hand (SAUO)
LHH............ Left-Hand Head
LHH............ Lower Hybrid Resonance Heating (MCD)
LHHS.......... Lutheran Hospitals and Homes Society of America (EA)
LHHW......... Langmuir-Hinshelwood-Hougen-Watson Rate Equation [*Chemical kinetics*]
LHI............. Fort Lauderdale, FL [*Location identifier*] [*FAA*] (FAAL)
LHI............. Leadership Housing, Incorporated (SAUO)
LHI............. Lefthanders International (EA)
LHI............. Leigh Instruments Ltd. [*Toronto Stock Exchange symbol*]
LHI............. Library of the Hoover Institution (SAUO)
LHI............. Lighthouse, Intermittent [*Maps and charts*] (ROG)
LHI............. Lipid Hydrocarbon Inclusions [*Biochemistry*] (DAVI)
LHi............. Louisiana Historical Society, New Orleans, LA [*Library symbol*] [*Library of Congress*] (LCLS)
LHIA.......... Logistics Horizontal Integration Analysis (SAUO)
LHID.......... Logical Hardware Interface Description [*Computer science*]
LHITA......... Long Haul Information Transfer Architecture (SAUO)
LHL............. Fort Lauderdale (SAUS)
LHL............. Left Hemisphere Lesion [*Neurology*] (DAVI)
LHL............. Left Hepatic Lobe [*Anatomy*]
LHL............. Leigh Instruments Limited (SAUO)
LHL............. Line and Half Line [*Illustration*] (DGA)
LHL............. Long Haul Link (VLIE)
LHLW.......... Liquid High Level Waste [*Nuclear energy*] (NUCP)
LHM............ Lake Helena [*Montana*] [*Seismograph station code, US Geological Survey*] [*Closed*] (SEIS)
LHM............ Laser Hardened Materials (ACAE)
LHM............ Laser-Hardened Materials (SAUS)

LHM	Left-Hand Circularly Polarized Mode (IAA)
LHM	Licensed Hotel Motel
LHM	Lisuride Hydrogen Maleate [Pharmacology]
LHM	Loop Handling Machine [Nuclear energy] (NRCH)
LHM	Master of Humane Letters [or Master of the More Humane Letters]
LHM	Master of the More Humane Letters (SAUO)
LHMC	London Hospital Medical College [British] (DI)
LHME	LASER HELLFIRE Missile Evaluation (MCD)
LHMEL	LASER-Hardened Materials Evaluation Laboratory
LHMM	Laymen's Home Missionary Movement (EA)
LHMO	Local Hazard Mitigation Officer [Department of Emergency Management] (DEMM)
LHMP	Life Health Monitoring Program (BABM)
LHMU	Ladies' Home Mission Union [British] (BI)
LHN	Express One International, Inc. [ICAO designator] (FAAC)
LHN	Lateral Hypothalamic Nucleus (STED)
LHN	Lillehammer [Norway] [Seismograph station code, US Geological Survey] (SEIS)
LHN	Load Half Name (VLIE)
LHN	Localized Hypertrophic Neuropathy [Medicine]
LHN	Long-Haul Network (RDA)
LHNCBC	Lister Hill National Center for Biomedical Communications [National Library of Medicine] [Information service or system] (IID)
LHO	LaSalle Hotel Properties [NYSE symbol] (SG)
LHO	Local Head Office [British] (DCTA)
LHOB	Longworth House Office Building
LHoC	Clairborne Parish Library, Homer, LA [Library symbol] [Library of Congress] (LCLS)
LHOLD	Leasehold (ROG)
LHON	Leber's Hereditary Optic Neuropathy [Ophthalmology]
LHOR	Load Halfword with Offset Register (VLIE)
LHO ratio	Library Holdings Ratio per Inhabitant
LHOTS	Long-Haul Optical Transmission Set [Telecommunications] (EECA)
LHouT	Terrebonne Parish Library, Houma, LA [Library symbol] [Library of Congress] (LCLS)
LHOX	Low- and High-Pressure Oxygen
LHP	Lakehead Pipe Line Partners Ltd. [NYSE symbol] (SPSG)
LHP	Lakehead Pipe Line Ptrs L.P. [NYSE symbol] (TTSB)
LHP	Lamp of Hope Project [An association] (EA)
LHP	Larval Hemolymph Protein [Entomology]
LHP	Late Hyperpolarizing Potential [Neurophysiology]
LHP	Launcher Handling Procedure
LHP	Left Half Plane (IAA)
LHP	Left-Handed Pitcher [Baseball]
LHP	Left-Hand Page (DGA)
lhp	Left-Hand Page (WDMC)
LHP	Left-Hand Panel
LHP	Left Hemiparesis [Medicine] (MEDA)
LHP	Left Hemiplegia (STED)
LHP	Lehu [Papua New Guinea] [Airport symbol] (OAG)
LHPC	Light-Harvesting Chlorophyll Protein Complex [Botany]
LHPG	LASER-Heated Pedestal Growth [Crystal growing technology]
LHPS	Lead Hydrogen Purge System [Nuclear energy] (IEEE)
LHPT	Loculated Hydropneumothorax [Medicine] (MELL)
LHPZ	Lower Esophageal High-Pressure Zone [Medicine] (STED)
LHQ	Allied Land Headquarters [World War II]
LHQ	Lancaster, OH [Location identifier] [FAA] (FAAL)
LHQ	Life History Questionnaire [Psychology] (DAVI)
LHR	Launcher (ACAE)
LHR	Left-Hand Rule
LHR	[The] Lehigh & Hudson River Railway Co. [Absorbed into Consolidated Rail Corp.] [AAR code]
LHR	Leukocyte Histamine Release [Test]
LHR	Life History Recorder (ACAE)
LHR	Lighthouse, Revolving [Maps and charts] (ROG)
LHR	Liquid-Holding Recovery [of bacterial cells]
LHR	Load Halfword Register (VLIE)
LHR	London-Heathrow [England] [Airport symbol] (OAG)
LHR	Long-Term Heart Rate (PDAA)
LHR	Lower Hybrid Resonance
LHR	Low-Heat-Rejection Engine [Mechanical engineering] (RDA)
LHR	Low heat Release [Adiabatic engines] [Automotive engineering]
LHR	Lumen Hour (ADA)
l-hr	Lumen-Hour [Unit quantity of light] (STED)
LHRAA	Lutheran Human Relations Association of America (EA)
LHRBI	Luteinizing Hormone Receptor Binding Inhibitor [Endocrinology]
LHRE	Low Heat Rejection Engine [Mechanical engineering]
LHRF	Luteinizing Hormone-Releasing Factor [Medicine] (STED)
LH-RF	Luteinizing-Hormone Releasing Factor [Also, GnRF, GnRH, LH-RH, LH-RH/FSH-RH, LRF, LRH] [Endocrinology]
LHRF	Luteotropin Hormone-Releasing Factor [Medicine] (STED)
LHRFDS	Large Heterogeneous Reference Fuel Design Study (SAUO)
LHRH	Left Hand, Right Hand (IAA)
LHRH	Luteinizing Hormone-Releasing Hormone [Medicine] (STED)
LH-RH	Luteinizing-Hormone Releasing Hormone [Also, GnRF, GnRH, LH-RF, LH-RH/FSH-RH, LRF, LRH] [Endocrinology]
LH-RH/FSH-RH	Luteinizing-Hormone Releasing Hormone/Follicle-Stimulating Hormone Releasing Hormone [Also, GnRF, GnRH, LH-RF, LH-RH, LRF, LRH] [Endocrinology]
LHRS	Life History Recorder Set [or System] (MCD)
LHRT	Library History Round Table [American Library Association]
LHS	Lafayette High School (SAUO)
LHS	Lake Hughes, CA [Location identifier] [FAA] (FAAL)
LHS	Lawrence Hall of Science
LHS	Layered Half Space

LHS	Left-Hand Side
LHS	Left-Hand Steering [Automotive engineering]
LHS	Left Heart Strain [Medicine]
LHS	Left Heel Strike (STED)
LHS	Liberty Hill [South Carolina] [Seismograph station code, US Geological Survey] (SEIS)
LHS	Library History Seminar
LHS	Lightweight Hydraulic System [Navy aviation]
LHS	Line Haul Steer [Tire design]
LHS	Load Handling System (SAUS)
LHS	Loop Handling System [Nuclear energy] (NRCH)
LHS	Lunar Horizon Sensor [Aerospace]
LHS	Lymphatic and Hematopoietic System (STED)
LHS	Southeastern Louisiana University, Hammond, LA [Library symbol] [Library of Congress] (LCLS)
LHSC	Lateral Horn of Spinal Cord [Medicine] (MELL)
LHSC	Left-Hand Side Console [NASA] (KSC)
LHSC	Liquid Hydrogen System Complex [NASA] (KSC)
LHSC	Lock Haven State College (SAUO)
LHSC	Luther Hospital Sentence Completions [Nursing school test]
LHSI	Low-Head Safety Injection [Nuclear energy] (NRCH)
LHSLG	Lincoln Health Sciences Library Group [Library network]
LHSP	Lernout & Hauspie Speech Products [NASDAQ symbol] (SAG)
LHSPF	Lernout & Hauspie Speech Pds [NASDAQ symbol] (TTSB)
LHSSC	Left-Hand Side Storage Container [NASA] (KSC)
LHSV	Liquid Hourly Space Velocity [Fluid dynamics]
LHT	Left Hypertropia [Ophthalmology]
LHT	Library Hi Tech [Pierian Press, Inc.] [Information service or system] [A publication] (IID)
LHT	Light (ABBR)
LHT	Lighthouse Tender
LHT	Line and Halftone [Illustration] (DGA)
LHT	Line-Haul Tractor (DOMA)
LHT	Long Holding Time (VLIE)
LHT	Lord High Treasurer [British]
LHT	Lunar Hand Tool [NASA]
LHTD	Lighted (ABBR)
LHTEC	Light Helicopter Turbine Engine Co. [US Army contractor]
LHTEN	Lighten (ABBR)
LHTEND	Lightened (ABBR)
LHTENG	Lightening (ABBR)
LHTF	Lincoln Heritage Trail Foundation (EA)
LHTG	Lighting (ABBR)
LHTH	Left-Hand Thread
L-HTL	L-Histidinol [Biochemistry]
LHTL	Luxury Class Hotel (TVEL)
LHTL	Luxury Hotel (TRID)
LHTN	Library Hi Tech News [A publication]
LHTNG	Lightning (ABBR)
LHTR	Lighter (ABBR)
LHTR	Lighthouse Transmitter Receiver (IAA)
LHTST	Lightest (ABBR)
LHTY	Lightly (ABBR)
LHU	Lake Havasu City [Arizona] [Airport symbol] (OAG)
LHUS	Literary History of the United States (SAUO)
LH-USA	Las Hermanas-United States of America (EA)
LHUSA	Likud-Herut USA (EA)
LHV	Light Horse Volunteers [British military] (DMA)
LHV	Liquid Hydrogen Vessel
LHV	Lock Haven [Pennsylvania] [Airport symbol] (AD)
LHV	Lock Haven, PA [Location identifier] [FAA] (FAAL)
LHV	Lower Heating Value (CARB)
LHV	Low Heat [or Heating] Value (MCD)
LHV	Luchtvaart Historische Vereniging [Society of Aeronautical Historians] [Netherlands] Defunct] (EAIO)
LHW	Hinesville, GA [Location identifier] [FAA] (FAAL)
LHW	Lanzhou [China] [Airport symbol] (OAG)
LHW	Laser-Homing Weapon (SAUS)
LHW	League of Hispanic Women (SAUO)
LHW	Lees-Hromas-Webb [Theory]
LHW	Left Half Word
LHW	Left Hand World [British] [An association] (DBA)
LHW	Lehman Brothers, Inc. [AMEX symbol] (SAG)
LHW	Lower High-Water [Tides and currents]
LHWCA	Longshore and Harbor Workers' Compensation Act (AAGC)
LHWI	Lower High-Water Interval [Tides and currents]
LHWP	Lesotho Highlands Water Project (ECON)
LHX	La Junta [Colorado] [Airport symbol] (AD)
LHX	La Junta, CO [Location identifier] [FAA] (FAAL)
LHX	Light Helicopter, Experimental [Army] (RDA)
LHX	Light Helicopters [Army] (RDA)
LHX	Lochiel Exploration Ltd. [Toronto Stock Exchange symbol]
LHY	Lancashire Hussars Yeomanry [British military] (DMA)
LHY	Lohame Herut Yisrael (BJA)
L Hy	Registered Hypnotist
LHY	Wilkes-Barre, PA [Location identifier] [FAA] (FAAL)
LI	Icelandic Medical Association (SAUO)
LI	Labeling Index [Measurement of cell labeling]
L/I	Labindustries [Commercial firm]
LI	Labor Intensive (MHDW)
LI	Lactose Intolerance [Medicine] (MELL)
LI	Land Institute [An association] (EA)
LI	Landscape Institute [British]
LI	Langelier Index (EEVL)
LI	LAN Interface (SAUS)

LI	Large Intestine [Medicine] (DB)
L/I	Laser Imager (ACAE)
LI	LASER Interferometry (AAEL)
LI	Laser Interrogator (SAUS)
LI	Laser Iridotomy [Medicine] (MELL)
LI	Late Iron [Age] (BJA)
LI	Launch Instructions (SAA)
LI	Lawn Institute (EA)
LI	(Laws of) Lipit-Ishtar (BJA)
LI	Leadership Institute (EA)
LI	Lead In (VLIE)
LI	Leakage of Information [British] [World War II]
LI	Learned Information [Database originator and marketer] (NITA)
LI	Leeward Islands (BARN)
LI	Leeward Islands Air Transport Ltd. (SAUO)
LI	Left In (VLIE)
LI	Left in Place [Telecommunications] (TEL)
LI	Legal Intelligencer [A publication] (DLA)
LI	Legislative Instrument [Ghana] [1960-] [A publication] (ILCA)
LI	Leitender Ingenieur [Chief Engineer] [German military - World War II]
LI	Length Indicator [Computer science] (TNIG)
LI	Leptospirosis Icterohemorrhagica [Medicine] (DB)
L/I	Letter of Indemnity (DS)
L/I	Letter of Intent (ACAE)
LI	Letter of Intent
LI	Letter of Introduction (ADA)
LI	Level Indicator
LI	Liability [Insurance]
LI	Liberal International [World Liberal Union] [British] (EAIO)
LI	Liberia (ABBR)
LI	Libertarian International (EA)
LI	License Inquiry [Police]
LI	Licentiate of Instruction [or Licentiate Instructor]
LI	Liechtenstein [ANSI two-letter standard code] (CNC)
LI	Lifegain Institute (EA)
LI	Lifted Index (ARMP)
LI	Lifting Index [Ergonometrics]
LI	Liga International (EA)
LI	Light Infantry
LI	Lightly Included [Colored gemstone grade]
LI	Lignin Institute (NTPA)
LI	Ligue Internationale de la Representation Commerciale [International League of Commercial Travelers and Agents - ILCTA] (EAIO)
LI	Lilac (ROG)
LI	Lilly Industries, Inc. [NYSE symbol] (SAG)
LI	Lilly Industries 'A' [NYSE symbol] (TTSB)
LI	Lincoln's Inn [London] [One of the Inns of Court]
LI	Linear Interpolator (IAA)
LI	Line Item (AABC)
li	Lines per Vertical Inch (WDMC)
Li	Linguoincisal [Dentistry]
Li	Link (ADWA)
Li	Link
LI	Lions International [Later, LCI] (EA)
LI	Liquid Ionization [Spectrometric instrumentation]
LI	List Item (SAUS)
LI	Litchfield Institute (EA)
LI	Liter [Metric measure of volume] (MCD)
Li	Lithium [Chemical element]
Li	Lithograph [or Lithography] (WDAA)
LI	Lithographer [Navy rating]
LI	Liver Infarct [Medicine] (MELL)
LI	Load Index [Tires] [Automotive engineering]
LI	Local Interneuron [Neuroanatomy]
LI	Local Intraconnect (SAUO)
LI	Location Identifier (IAA)
LI	Logistic Index (CAAL)
LI	Logistics Instructions [Military]
LI	Loglan Institute (EA)
LI	Loitering with Intent [British] (DSUE)
LI	London International [Record label] [Great Britain, USA, etc.]
LI	Long Island
LI	[The] Long Island Rail Road Co. [AAR code]
LI	Long Island Rail Road Co. (SAUO)
LI	Longitudinal Interval (ADA)
LI	Loop of Intestine
LI	Lot Indices
LI	Low Impulsiveness (MAE)
LI	Low Intensity
LI	Lubrication Instructions [Marine Corps]
LI	Lubricity Index (IAA)
LI	Lues I [Primary syphilis] [Infectious diseases] (DAVI)
LI	Lukens, Inc. (EFIS)
LI	Luteinization Inhibitor [Endocrinology]
LI	Lymphoid Cellular Infiltration [Oncology]
LI1	Lithographer, First Class [Navy rating]
LI2	Lithographer, Second Class [Navy rating]
LI3	Lithographer, Third Class [Navy rating]
LIA	International Union of Life Insurance Agents
LIA	Label Information Area (CMD)
LIA	Land Improvement Agreement (SAUO)
LIA	Land Information and Analysis [Program] [Department of the Interior]
LIA	Land Information and Analysis office (SAUO)
LIA	Laser Industry (or Industries) Association (SAUO)
LIA	Laser Institute of America (EA)

LIA	Lead Industries Association [New York, NY] (EA)
LIA	Leather Industries of America (EA)
LIA	Lebanese International Airways
LIA	Leeward Islands Air Transport (1974) Ltd. [Antigua and Barbuda] [ICAO designator] (FAAC)
LIA	Leukemia-Associated Inhibiting Activity [Medicine]
LIA	Leukemia Cell-Derived Inhibitory Activity [Hematology] (DAVI)
LIA	Level Indicating Alarm [Engineering]
LIA	Liaison
LIA	Liberian International Airways (SAUO)
LIA	Licensing Industry Association [Later, ILMA] (EA)
LIA	Licentiate in Accountancy (DD)
LIA	Licentiate Institute of the Accountants and Auditors of Province of Quebec (SAUO)
LIA	Life Insurance Act [Australia]
LIA	Life Insurance Association [British] (DBA)
LIA	Lima [Ohio] [Airport symbol] (OAG)
LIA	Limited Intelligent Agent [Virtual reality technology] (PS)
LIA	Limiting Interval Availability
LIA	Linear Induction Accelerator (MCD)
LIA	Liposome Immunoassay [Clinical chemistry]
LIA	Lithographic Institute of Australia
LIA	Little Ice Age [Geoscience]
LIA	Liver Infusion Agar [Germination medium]
LIA	Livestock Improvement Association (SAUO)
LIA	Livestock Industry Act (SAUO)
LIA	Localized Induction Approximation [Mathematics]
LIA	Lock-In Amplifier (MAE)
LIA	Long Island Association (SAUO)
LIA	Loop Interface Address
LIA	Low-Impact Aerobics
LIA	Low Intensity Area (SAUO)
LIA	Luminescence Immunoassay [Clinical chemistry]
LIA	Lymphocyte-Induced Angiogenesis [Immunology]
LIA	Lysine Iron Agar [Microbiology]
LIAA	Library and Information Association of Australia (SAUO)
LIAA	Life Insurance Association of America [Later, ACLI] (EA)
LIAA	Louisiana Independent Administrators Association (SRA)
Liab	Liability (TBD)
LIAB	Liability
LIAB	Life Insurance Adjustment Bureau [Defunct] (EA)
LIABT	Liability (ABBR)
LIAC	Legal Industry Advisory Council (EA)
LIAC	Liberian International American Corporation [New York]
LIAC	Light-Induced Absorbance Change
LIAC	Local Industry Advisory Committee [Civil defense]
LIADA	Liga Ibero-Americana de Astronomia [Ibero-American Astronomy League] (EAIO)
LIADA	Louisiana Independent Automobile Dealers Association (SRA)
LIAFI	Late Infantile Amaurotic Familial Idiocy [Medicine] (MAE)
LIAI	Licensing Industry Association International (SAUO)
LIAI	Love in Action International (EA)
LIALS	Long Island Airport Limousine Service (SAUO)
LIAMA	Life Insurance Agency Management Association [Later, LIMRA]
LIAR	Lexicon of Inconspicuously Ambiguous Recommendations [Term coined by Robert J. Thornton of Lehigh University]
LIAR	Report Labrador Inuit Association (SAUS)
LIAS	Library Information Access System [Pennsylvania State University Libraries] [University Park] [Information service or system] (IID)
LIASAR	LASER Inertial Aided Synthetic Aperture RADAR (MCD)
LIASE	Linking Industry and School Education (AIE)
LIAT	Leeward Islands Air Transport Services Ltd. [Humorous interpretation: Luggage in Another Town] [Airline]
LIB	Air Liberte [France] [ICAO designator] (FAAC)
LIB	Federal Liberal Agency of Canada Library [UTLAS symbol]
LIB	Harlan Hatcher Graduate Library (SAUS)
LIB	Laboratory Information Bulletin (GNE)
LIB	Left Inboard (MCD)
LIB	Left in Bottle (MAE)
LIB	Liber [Book] [Latin]
lib	Liberal (SHCU)
LIB	Liberal
Lib	Liberal Party (SAUO)
lib	Liberation (SHCU)
LIB	Liberation
LIB	Liberator Bomber Aircraft [British] (DSUE)
Lib	Liberia
lib	Liberty (WDAA)
LIB	Liberty [Geographical division] [British]
LIB	Liberty Aviation, Inc. (SAUO)
LIB	Liberty, NC [Location identifier] [FAA] (FAAL)
LIB	Libra [Pound]
Lib	Libra [Constellation]
Lib	Librarian (DLA)
LIB	Library (AFM)
Lib	Library [A publication] (BRI)
lib	Library (GEAB)
lib	Libretto (WDAA)
LIB	Libretto [Music]
LIB	Light Infantry Brigade (SAUO)
LIB	Light Ion Beam (PDAA)
LIB	Line Interface Base [Telecommunications]
LIB	London Infantry Brigade (SAUO)
LIB	Loudspeaker Intercom Box (SAUS)

LIB-2 .... EC 12-part study on new information technologies in libraries 1988 (SAUS)
LIBA .... Amendola [Italy] [ICAO location identifier] (ICLI)
LIBA .... Licentiate of the Institute of Business Administration
LIBA .... Long Island Biological Association
LIBA .... Long Island Biological Association Inc. (SAUO)
LIBACC .... Library Acquisition Program [Computer program]
LIBACT1 ...... Impact CR-ROM project for National Libraries (SAUS)
Lib & Cult ... Libraries & Culture [A publication] (BRI)
LIB & SL ...... Libel and Slander [Legal term] (DLA)
LIBANOR ...... Lebanese Standards Institution (SAUO)
Lib Ass .... Liber Assisarum [Book of Assizes, or pleas of the crown] [Pt. 5 of Year Books] [A publication] (DLA)
LIBB .... Brindisi [Italy] [ICAO location identifier] (ICLI)
LIBBA .... Long Island Beach Buggy Association (SAUO)
Libbey .... Libbey, Inc. [Associated Press] (SAG)
LIBBKS .... Headquarters Book System (SAUO)
LIBC .... Cray C library (SAUO)
LIBC .... Crotone [Italy] [ICAO location identifier] (ICLI)
LIBC .... Latent Iron-Binding Capacity [Clinical chemistry]
LIBC .... Liberty National Bank [NASDAQ symbol] (SAG)
LIBC .... Lloyd's Insurance Brokers Committee (AIA)
LIB CAT .... Library Catalogue (WDAA)
LIBCEPT ...... LIBRIS Intercept [Sweden] (NITA)
LIBCO .... Liberty Investors Benefit Insurance Company (SAUO)
Lib Colon ..... Libri Coloniarum [Classical studies] (OCD)
LIBCON .... Libertarian Conservative
LIBCON .... Library of Congress
LIBCON/E .... Library of Congress/English [Database on English language monographs] (NITA)
LIB CONG .... Library of Congress (WDAA)
Lib Cong Q .. Library of Congress. Quarterly Journal [A publication] (DLA)
LI Bcp .... Long Island Bancorp, Inc. [Associated Press] (SAG)
LIBD .... Bari/Palese Macchie [Italy] [ICAO location identifier] (ICLI)
Lib-Dem ...... Liberal Democrat (WDAA)
LIBE .... Library Editor (MHDI)
LIBE .... Ligo Internacia de Blindaj Esperantistoj [International League of Blind Esperantists - ILBE] (EAIO)
LIBE .... Monte S. Angelo [Italy] [ICAO location identifier] (ICLI)
LIBEC .... Light Behind Camera [Photographic technique]
LIBECON ..... Monitor of Library Economics (SAUO)
LIBEDIT .... Library Editor (MHDI)
Lib Ent .... Old Books of Entries [A publication] (DLA)
Liber .... Liberia (VRA)
LIBER .... Ligue des Bibliotheques Europeennes de Recherche [League of European Research Libraries] (EAIO)
LIBERATION... Libraries: Electronic Remote Access to Information over Networks (SAUO)
LIBERATOR... Libraries in European Regions-Access to Telematics and Other Resources (SAUO)
LIBERD .... Liberated (ABBR)
LIBERG .... Liberating (ABBR)
LIBERN .... Liberation (ABBR)
LIBERR .... Liberator (ABBR)
LIBERTAS .... Automated library system marketed by SLS Ltd (SAUS)
Liberte .... Liberte Investors, Inc. [Associated Press] (SAG)
LIBF .... Foggia [Italy] [ICAO location identifier] (ICLI)
Lib Feud ...... Liber Feudorum [Book of Feuds] [At the end of the Corpus Juris Civilis] [A publication] (DLA)
LibFin .... Liberty Financial Companies, Inc. [Associated Press] (SAG)
LIBG .... Grottaglie [Italy] [ICAO location identifier] (ICLI)
LIBGIS .... Library General Information Survey [of the National Center for Educational Statistics]
LIBH .... Liberty Homes, Inc. [NASDAQ symbol] (SAG)
LIBH .... Marina Di Ginosa [Italy] [ICAO location identifier] (ICLI)
LIBHA .... Liberty Homes Cl'A' [NASDAQ symbol] (TTSB)
LIBHB .... Liberty Homes Cl'B' [NASDAQ symbol] (TTSB)
LIBI .... Vieste [Italy] [ICAO location identifier] (ICLI)
Libid .... London interbank bid or deposit rate (SAUO)
LIBID .... London Interbank Bid Rate [Finance] [British]
LibInt(BG).... Liberal International (British Group) [World Liberal Union] (EAIO)
LIBISAC .... Livres Bibliotheque Saclay Database [Commissariat a l'Energie Atomique] [France] [Information service or system] (CRD)
LIBJ .... Vibo Valentia [Italy] [ICAO location identifier] (ICLI)
LIBK .... Caraffa Di Catanzaro [Italy] [ICAO location identifier] (ICLI)
LIBL .... Liable (ABBR)
LIBL .... Liberal
LIBL .... Palascia [Italy] [ICAO location identifier] (ICLI)
Lib-Lab .... Liberal-Labour (SAUO)
LIB LAB ...... Liberal-Labour Alliance [British] (DSUE)
Lib L & Eq.... Library of Law and Equity [A publication] (DLA)
Liblit .... Library Literature
LIBLZG .... Liberalizing (ABBR)
LIBM .... Grottammare [Italy] [ICAO location identifier] (ICLI)
LIBMAN .... Library Management (MHDB)
LIBMAS .... Library Master File [FORTRAN program]
LIBMISH ...... Liberia Military Mission [US]
LIBMISH ...... United States Military Mission, Liberia (SAUO)
LIBMRG .... Library Merge Program [Computer program]
LIBN .... Lecce [Italy] [ICAO location identifier] (ICLI)
LIBN .... Liberty National Corp. (SAUO)
LIBN .... Librarian (WGA)
LibNat .... Liberal National (SAUO)
LIBNAT .... Library Network Analysis Theory

LibNBk .... Liberty National Bank [Huntington Beach, CA] [Associated Press] (SAG)
LIBO .... Lincoln Boyhood National Memorial
LIBO .... London Interbank Offered [Rate] [Reference point for syndicated bank loans]
LIBO .... Ortanova [Italy] [ICAO location identifier] (ICLI)
LIB/OL .... Librarian/Online [Database] (MHDI)
LIBOL .... Litton Business-Oriented Language (IAA)
LibOp .... Libraries Operator (SAUO)
LIBOR .... London Interbank Offered Rate [Reference point for syndicated bank loans]
LIBORS .... LASER Ionization Based on Resonant Saturation [Physics]
LIBP .... Pescara [Italy] [ICAO location identifier] (ICLI)
Lib Parl .... Library of Parliament (SAUO)
Lib Plac .... Lilly's Assize Reports [1688-93] [A publication] (DLA)
LIBQ .... Monte Scuro [Italy] [ICAO location identifier] (ICLI)
LIBR .... Brindise/Casale [Italy] [ICAO location identifier] (ICLI)
Libr .... Libra [Constellation]
LIBR .... Librarian (EY)
libr .... Library (VRA)
LIBR .... Library
LIBR .... Librium [Pharmacology] (DAVI)
LIBR .... RTP Library (SAUS)
LIBRA .... Living in the Buff Recreational Associates (SAUO)
LIBRARY ...... Tape Library and Workload Management System (SAUO)
LIBRE .... Living in the Buff Residential Enterprises (SAUO)
Lib Reg .... Register Book [A publication] (DLA)
LIBRI .... Literary Information Bases for Research and Instruction [American Philological Association] [An association] (NITA)
LIBRIME ...... Library and Information Management in Europe (TELE)
LIBRIS .... Land Image-Based Resource Information System (SAUO)
LIBRIS .... Library Information Service [or System] [The Royal Library] [Database] [Information service or system] (IID)
LIBRLZ......... Liberalize (ABBR)
LIBRN .... Librarian
Libr quart .... Library Quarterly. University of Chicago (SAUO)
LibrtyTc .... Liberty Technologies, Inc. [Associated Press] (SAG)
LIBRY .... Library (ABBR)
LIBS .... Campobasso [Italy] [ICAO location identifier] (ICLI)
LIBS .... LASER-Induced Breakdown Spectroscopy
LIBS .... Library Internet Browsing Software
LIBSET .... Library Set [Computer program]
LibSIG .... Libertarian SIG [Special Interest Group] (EA)
LIBSM .... Low Inertia Beam Steering Minor (ACAE)
Lib Soc Sci... Library of Social Science (SAUO)
LIBSOFT ...... Library Software Archives [Computer science] (TNIG)
Libsp .... Librarianship (DIAR)
LIBSTAD ...... Working Party on Library and Book Trade Relations [British]
Libs Unl .... Libraries Unlimited (SAUO)
LIBSYS .... Library System [Computer program]
LIBT .... Liability (ABBR)
LIBT .... Liberty (ABBR)
LIBT .... Liberty Technologies [NASDAQ symbol] (TTSB)
LIBT .... Liberty Technologies, Inc. [NASDAQ symbol] (SAG)
LIBT .... Termoli [Italy] [ICAO location identifier] (ICLI)
LibtProp....... Liberty Property Trust [Associated Press] (SAG)
LibtyCp .... Liberty Corp. [Associated Press] (SAG)
LIBU .... Latronico [Italy] [ICAO location identifier] (ICLI)
LIB (UN) ...... Headquarters Library of the United Nations
Lib UN .... Library of the United Nations (SAUO)
LIBV .... Gioia Del Colle [Italy] [ICAO location identifier] (ICLI)
LibVT .... Libri Veteris Testamenti (BJA)
LIBW .... Bonifati [Italy] [ICAO location identifier] (ICLI)
LIBX .... Martina Franca [Italy] [ICAO location identifier] (ICLI)
LIBY .... Santa Maria Di Leuca [Italy] [ICAO location identifier] (ICLI)
LIBZ .... Potenza [Italy] [ICAO location identifier] (ICLI)
LIC .... Chief Lithographer [Navy rating]
LIC .... Lacquer Insulating Compound
LIC .... Lamto [Ivory Coast] [Seismograph station code, US Geological Survey] (SEIS)
LIC .... Lands Improvement Company (SAUO)
LIC .... Language Identity Code [Army] (INF)
LIC .... Large Integrated Circuit [Electronics]
LIC .... LASER Image Converter
LIC .... LASER-Induced Chemistry (RDA)
LIC .... LASER Intercept Capability [Military] (CAAL)
LIC .... Last in Chain (ELAL)
LIC .... Last Instruction Cycle (IAA)
LIC .... Launcher Interchange Circuit (IAA)
LIC .... Law in Context [Australia] [A publication]
LIC .... Lawson, I. C., St. Paul MN [STAC]
LIC .... League International for Creditors (DCTA)
LIC .... Least Incompatible [Laboratory science] (DAVI)
LIC .... Lecturer in Charge (ADA)
LIC .... Left Iliac Crest [Anatomy] (DAVI)
LIC .... Left Internal Carotid [Artery] [Anatomy] (DAVI)
LIC .... Leisure-Interest Class (MEDA)
LIC .... Less Industrialized Country (MHDW)
LIC .... Level Indicator Controller (NRCH)
LIC .... Library and Information Commission [British] (TELE)
LIC .... Library Information Center [Lunar and Planetary Institute] [Information service or system] (IID)
Lic .... Licenciado [Lawyer] [Spanish] (WA)
lic .... License (BEE)
LIC .... License (KSC)

LIC	Licensed Internal Code (SAUO)
LIC	Licentiate
LIC	Life Insurers Conference [*Richmond, VA*] (EA)
LIC	Limiting Isorrheic Concentration [*Medicine*]
LIC	Limon, CO [*Location identifier*] [*FAA*] (FAAL)
LIC	Linear Integrated Circuit
LIC	Lineas Aereas del Caribe [*Colombia*] [*ICAO designator*] (FAAC)
LIC	Line Integrity Check (SAUS)
LIC	Liquor Industry Council (SAUO)
LIC	List of Instruments and Controls (DNAB)
LIC	Lithuanian Information Center [*Defunct*] (EA)
LIC	Load Interface Circuit (MCD)
LIC	Local Import Control [*British*] (DS)
LIC	Local Indigenous Civilian [*Military*]
LIC	Local Intelligence Committee (SAUO)
LIC	Local Interstellar Cloud [*Astronomy*]
LIC	Logical Link Control (SAUO)
LIC	Logistics Indoctrination Course [*Military*] (DNAB)
LIC	London International College [*British*]
LIC	Loop Insertion Cell [*Nuclear energy*] (NRCH)
LIC	Louisiana Insurers' Conference (SRA)
LIC	Low Income Country
LIC	Low Inertia Clutch
LIC	Low Intensity Conflict (SAUO)
LIC	Low-Intensity Conflict [*Military*]
LIC	Lunar Instrument Carrier [*NASA*] (KSC)
LICA	International League Against Racism and Antisemitisme (SAUO)
LICA	Lamezia/Terme [*Italy*] [*ICAO location identifier*] (ICLI)
LICA	Land Improvement Contractors of America (EA)
LICA	Left Internal Carotid Artery [*Anatomy*] (DAVI)
LICA	Licentiate, International College of Anesthetists (CMD)
LICA	Ligue Internationale Contre le Racisme et l'Antisemitisme [*International League Against Racism and Antisemitism*]
LICA	Lithium Isopropylcyclohexylamide [*Organic chemistry*]
LicAc	Licentiate in Acupuncture [*British*]
Lic Agro	Licentiate in Agronomy [*British*]
LICALM	LORAN Inertial Command Air-Launched Missile
LICAP	LASER-Induced Cut and Patch
LICAS	Low Intensity Conflict Aircraft System (SAUS)
LICB	Comiso [*Italy*] [*ICAO location identifier*] (ICLI)
LICB	Licensable (ABBR)
LICC	Catania/Fontanarossa [*Italy*] [*ICAO location identifier*] (ICLI)
LICC	Land Information Co-ordinating Committee (SAUO)
LICC	League for Innovation in the Community College (EA)
LICC	Litton Industries, Inc. (EFIS)
LICC	Local Interagency Coordinating Council
LICC	London Institute for Contemporary Christianity (SAUO)
LICC	Long Island Council of Churches
LiCCA	Languages in Contact and Conflict in Africa (SAUO)
LICCB	Laboratory Information Calibration Control Board (SAUO)
LICCD	Ligue Internationale Contre la Concurrence Deloyale [*International League Against Unfair Competition*] (EAIO)
LICCRE	Laboratory of Ice Core and Cold Regions Environment (SAUO)
LICCS	Laboratory Information Calibration Control System (SAUO)
LICD	Lampedusa [*Italy*] [*ICAO location identifier*] (ICLI)
LICD	Licensed (ROG)
LicD	Licentiate in Theology, Malta (SAUO)
LICE	Enna [*Italy*] [*ICAO location identifier*] (ICLI)
LICE	LASER Interface Control Electronics (MCD)
LICE	License (ROG)
LIC ECON	Licentiate in Economic Sciences (WDAA)
Lic en Der	Licenciado en Derecho [*Licentiate in Law*] [*Spanish*]
Lic en Fil	Licenciado en Filosofia [*Licentiate in Philosophy*] [*Spanish*]
LICeram	Licentiate of the Institute of Ceramics (SAUO)
LICET	Library of Industrial and Commercial Education and Training
LICF	Laser-Induced Chlorophyll Fluorescence [*Analytical biochemistry*]
LICF	Messina [*Italy*] [*ICAO location identifier*] (ICLI)
LICG	Licensing (ABBR)
LICG	Pantelleria [*Italy*] [*ICAO location identifier*] (ICLI)
LICGF	Land Information & Computer Graphics Facility (SAUO)
LICGS	Lightweight Intermediate Caliber Gun System (MCD)
LICH	Capo Spartivento [*Italy*] [*ICAO location identifier*] (ICLI)
LICh	Licentiate of the Institute of Chiropodists (SAUO)
LICH	Lichfield [*City in England*] (ROG)
LICI	Finale [*Italy*] [*ICAO location identifier*] (ICLI)
LICI	Lilly Industrial Coatings, Incorporated (SAUO)
LICIA	Lilly Industries, Incorporated (SAUO)
LICIT	Labor-Industry Coalition for International Trade [*Washington, DC*] (EA)
LICITA	Life Insurance Co. Income Tax Act of 1959
LICJ	Palermo/Punta Raisi [*Italy*] [*ICAO location identifier*] (ICLI)
LICK	Lightweight Communication Kit (MCD)
LICK	Lightweight Communications Kit (SAUO)
LICL	Gela [*Italy*] [*ICAO location identifier*] (ICLI)
LICM	Calopezzati [*Italy*] [*ICAO location identifier*] (ICLI)
LICM	Left Intercostal Margin [*Anatomy*]
LICM	Master Chief Lithographer [*Navy rating*]
Lic Med	Licentiate in Medicine
LICND	Life Insurance Committee for a Nuclear Disarmament (EA)
LICNWF	Life Insurance Committee for a Nuclear Weapons Freeze [*Later, LICND*] (EA)
LICO	Cozzo Spadaro [*Italy*] [*ICAO location identifier*] (ICLI)
LICO	Low Income Cut-Off [*Canada*]
LiCO3	Lithium Carbonate [*Pharmacology*] (DAVI)
LICOF	Land Lines Communications Facilities (FAAC)

LICOR	Lightning Correlation
LICP	Lead Inventory Control Point (NG)
LICP	Palermo/Boccadifalco [*Italy*] [*ICAO location identifier*] (ICLI)
Lic Phil	Licentiate in Philosophy [*British*]
LICR	Lloyd's Information Casualty Report [*A publication*]
LICR	Reggio Calabria [*Italy*] [*ICAO location identifier*] (ICLI)
LICRA	Ligue Internationale Contre le Racisme et l'Antisemitisme [*France*]
LICROSS	League of International Red Cross Societies
LiCrOx	Lithium/Chromium-Oxide [*Type of battery*]
LICS	Left Intercostal Space [*Cardiology*] (MAE)
Lic S	Licentiate in Surgery [*Academic degree*] (WDAA)
LICS	Lotus International Character Set [*Printer technology*] (PCM)
LICS	Sciacca [*Italy*] [*ICAO location identifier*] (ICLI)
LICS	Senior Chief Lithographer [*Navy rating*]
LICSR	Life Insurance Committee for Social Responsibility (EA)
LICT	Laser Imaging Component Technology (ACAE)
LICT	Trapani/Birgi [*Italy*] [*ICAO location identifier*] (ICLI)
LICTA	Life Insurance Co. Tax Act of 1955
Lic Tech	Licentiate in Technology [*British*]
Lic Theol	Licentiate in Theology [*British*]
LICU	League of IBM [*International Business Machines Corp.*] Employee Credit Unions (EA)
LICU	Ustica [*Italy*] [*ICAO location identifier*] (ICLI)
LICVD	LASER-Induced Chemical Vapor Deposition [*Photovoltaic energy systems*]
LICW	Licentiate of the Institute of Clerks of Works of Great Britain, Inc. (DBQ)
LICX	Prizzi [*Italy*] [*ICAO location identifier*] (ICLI)
LICZ	Sigonella [*Italy*] [*ICAO location identifier*] (ICLI)
LID	Alidaunia SRL [*Italy*] [*ICAO designator*] (FAAC)
LID	Doctor of Letters of Journalism (SAUS)
LID	Laboratory of Infectious Diseases [*Later, Laboratory of Viral Diseases*] [*NIAID*]
LID	Labor Information Database [*International Labor Office*] [*Information service or system*] (IID)
LID	Land Information Division (SAUO)
LID	Laser Illuminator Detector (ACAE)
LID	LASER Image Display (MCD)
LID	LASER Injection Diode
LID	LASER Intrusion Detector
LID	LASER Intrusion Device (MCD)
LID	Laser Irradiation Detector (SAUS)
LID	LASER Isotope Dating
LID	Late Immunoglobulin Deficiency [*Medicine*] (DB)
LID	Leadless Inverted Device
LID	League for Industrial Democracy (EA)
LID	Letters in Digit Strings [*Psychology*]
LID	Library Issue Document (NVT)
LID	Lidco Industries, Inc. [*Toronto Stock Exchange symbol*]
LID	Lift Improvement Device (MCD)
LID	Light Infantry Division [*Army*] (INF)
LID	Limited Instrument Departure (MCD)
LID	Linear Imaging Device (MCD)
LID	Line Isolation Device [*Telecommunications*] (NITA)
LID	Line Item Description (MCD)
LID	Liquid Immersion Development [*Reprography*]
LID	Liquid Interface Diffusion
LID	Literaturdienst Medizin und Umwelt [*Literature Service in Medicine and Environment*] [*Austrian National Institute for Public Health*] [*Information service or system*] (IID)
LID	Local Issue Data [*Telecommunications*] (TEL)
LID	Locked-In Device (MSA)
LID	Logical Identification (MCD)
LID	Logistics Identification Document (NASA)
LID	Low-Iodine Diet [*Medicine*]
LID	Lunar Ionosphere Detector (PDAA)
LIDA	Ligue Internationale des Droits de l'Animal [*International League for Animal Rights*] (EAIO)
LIDA	Lodzer Idishe Dramatishe Aktyorn (BJA)
Lidak	Lidak Pharmaceuticals [*Associated Press*] (SAG)
LIDAR	Atmospheric Light Detection and Ranging Facility [*Los Alamos, NM*] [*Los Alamos National Laboratory*] [*Department of Energy*] (GRD)
LIDAR	Laser Induced Differential Absorption Radar (ACAE)
LIDAR	LASER Infrared RADAR (IEEE)
LIDAR	LASER Intensity Direction and Ranging (IEEE)
LIDAR	Light Detection and Range (SAUO)
LIDAR	Light Detection and Ranging
LIDAR	Light Detection and Ranging Instrument (SAUO)
LIDAS	Laboratory Instrument Data Acquisition
LIDASE	Lecturer in Design and Analysis of Scientific Experiments (SAUO)
LIDB	Line Information Database [*Telecommunications*] (ACRL)
LIDB	Logistics Intelligence Data Base (AABC)
LIDC	Lead Industries Development Council [*British*] (DAS)
LIDC	Ligue Internationale du Droit de la Concurrence [*International League for Competition Law*] [*Paris, France*] (EA)
LIDC	Livestock Industry Development Council (SAUO)
LIDC	Low Intensity - Direct Current
LIDD	Laydown Initialization Data Document (SAUS)
LIDE	LED Light-Emittng Diode Indirect Exposure [*Canon*]
LIDEX	Labrador Ice Dynamics Experiment (SAUO)
LIDF	Line Intermediate Distributing Frame
LIDI	Lions-International Diabetes Institute (SAUO)
LIDIA	Learning in Dialog (PDAA)
LIDIA	Liaison Internationale des Industries de l'Alimentation [*International Liaison for the Food Industries*]

LIDO .... Lidocaine (SAUS)
LIDO .... Logic In, Documents Out (PDAA)
LIDO .... Logistics Inventory Disposition Order (AAG)
LIDOC .... Lidocaine [Topical anesthetic] (WDAA)
LIDQA .... Landsat Image Data Quality and Analysis (SAUO)
LIDS .... Laboratory for Information and Decision Systems [Massachusetts Institute of Technology] [Research center] (RCD)
LIDS .... LASER Illumination Detection System
LIDS .... LASER Infrared Countermeasures Demonstration System [Air Force]
LIDS .... Laser Instrumentation Detection System (ACAE)
LIDS .... Listener Idle State (IAA)
LIDS .... Lithium Ion Drift Semiconductor
LIDS .... Local Inmate Database System (WDAA)
LIDS .... Logistics Item Data Systems [DoD]
LIDT .... LASER-Induced Damage Testing
LIDT .... Load Interrupt Descriptor Table (SAUO)
LIDUS .... Liberal-Demokratische Union der Schweiz [Liberal Democratic Union of Switzerland] [Political party] (PPE)
LIE .... Laterally Inclined Engine
LIE .... Left Inboard Elevon [Aviation] (MCD)
LIE .... Lessio Intellectuale Europeo [Research Institute] [Consiglio Nationale delle Richerche] [Italy] (NITA)
LIE .... Libenge [Zaire] [Airport symbol] [Obsolete] (OAG)
LIE .... Liechtenstein [ANSI three-letter standard code] (CNC)
LIE .... Limited Information Estimation
LIE .... Line Islands Experiment [National Science Foundation]
LIE .... Long Island Expressway (BARN)
LIEA .... Alghero [Italy] [ICAO location identifier] (ICLI)
LIEA .... Low Income Energy Assistance [Later, LIHEAP] [Block grant]
LIEB .... Capo Bellavista [Italy] [ICAO location identifier] (ICLI)
LIEB .... Liebert Corporation (SAUO)
Lieber Civ Lib... Lieber on Civil Liberty and Self Government [A publication] (DLA)
Lieb Herm ... Lieber's Hermeneutics [A publication] (DLA)
Liebigs Ann Chem... Liebigs Annalen der Chemie (MEC)
LIEC .... Capo Carbonara [Italy] [ICAO location identifier] (ICLI)
LIECH .... Liechtenstein (ABBR)
Liech .... Liechtenstein (SHCU)
Liecht .... Liechtenstein
LIECU .... League of IBM [International Business Machines Corp.] Employee Credit Unions [Later, LICU] (EA)
LIED .... Decimomannu [Italy] [ICAO location identifier] (ICLI)
LIED .... Large Industrial Engineering Development (SAUO)
LIED .... LASER Initiating Explosive Device
LIED .... Linkage Editor [Computer science]
LIEE .... Cagliari/Elmas [Italy] [ICAO location identifier] (ICLI)
LIEE .... Law in Eastern Europe [A publication] (DLA)
LIEF .... Capo Frasca [Italy] [ICAO location identifier] (ICLI)
LIEF .... Launch Information Exchange Facility [NASA]
LIEFC .... Long Island Early Fliers Club (EA)
LIEG .... Guardiavecchia [Italy] [ICAO location identifier] (ICLI)
LIEH .... Capo Caccia [Italy] [ICAO location identifier] (ICLI)
LIEJA .... Long Island Equal Justice Association (SAUO)
LIEL .... Capo S. Lorenzo [Italy] [ICAO location identifier] (ICLI)
LIEM .... Macomer [Italy] [ICAO location identifier] (ICLI)
LIEMA .... Long Island Electronics Manufacturers Association (SAUO)
LIEMC .... Long Island Electronics Manufacturers Council (SAUO)
LIEN .... Fonni [Italy] [ICAO location identifier] (ICLI)
LIENS .... Ligue Europeenne pour une Nouvelle Societe [European League for a New Society - ELNS] [Paris, France] (EAIO)
LIEO .... Olbia/Costa Smeralda [Italy] [ICAO location identifier] (ICLI)
LIEP .... Large Internet Exchange Packet (VLIE)
LIEP .... LORAN Integrated Engineering Program
LIEP .... Perdasdefogu [Italy] [ICAO location identifier] (ICLI)
LIEPS .... LORAN Integrated Engineering Program, Shed Light
LIES .... LASER-Induced Emission Spectroscopy (MEC)
LIES .... Library Information and Enquiry System
LIESA .... Long Island Episcopal Schools Association (SAUO)
LIESST .... Light-Induced Excited Spin State Trapping [Physics]
Liet .... Lieutenant (SAUS)
LIETS .... Land Integrated Equipment for Tactical Systems (MCD)
LIEUT .... Lieutenant (EY)
lieut .... Lieutenant (GEAB)
Lieut .... Lieutenant (WDAA)
LIEUTC .... Lieutenancy (ABBR)
Lieut Col ..... Lieutenant Colonel (SAUO)
Lieut-Col ..... Lieutenant-Colonel [British military] (DMA)
Lieut Comdr... Lieutenant Commander (SAUO)
LIEUTE .... Lieutenancy (ABBR)
Lieut Gen .... Lieutenant General (SAUO)
Lieut-Gen .... Lieutenant-General [British military] (DMA)
Lieut Gov .... Lieutenant Governor (SAUO)
Lieut Jg ...... Lieutenant Junior Grade [Navy]
LIF .... Large Isothermal Furnace (SAUS)
LIF .... LASER-Induced Fluorescence [Physical chemistry]
LIF .... LASER Interference Filter
LIF .... Layaway of Industrial Facilities (AABC)
LIF .... Left Iliac Fossa [Medicine]
LIF .... Left Index Finger (MELL)
LIF .... Leukemia Inhibitory Factor [Oncology]
LIF .... Leukocyte Inhibition Factor [Hematology]
LIF .... Leukocytosis-Inducing Factor [Hematology] (DAVI)
LIF .... Lief (ABBR)
LIF .... Lifestyle Restaurants, Inc. (SAUO)
LIF .... Lifu [Loyalty Islands] [Airport symbol] (OAG)
LIF .... Lighting Industry Federation [British] (DBA)

LIF .... Line Interface Feature [Computer science] (ELAL)
LIF .... Logical Interchange Format (SAUS)
LIF .... Logistics Intelligence File (AABC)
LIF .... Lone Indian Fellowship [Later, Lone Indian Fellowship and Lone Scout Alumni] (EA)
LIF .... Low Insertion Force (AAEL)
LIF .... Low-Ionization Filament Component [Galactic science]
LIFA .... Licentiate of the International Faculty of Arts [British]
LIFB .... Life Bancorp [NASDAQ symbol] (TTSB)
LIFB .... Life Bancorp, Inc. [NASDAQ symbol] (SAG)
LIFC .... Lifecell Corp. [NASDAQ symbol] (SAG)
LIFD .... Last In First Drop (SAUS)
LIFE .... Laboratory for International Fuzzy Engineering (SAUO)
LIFE .... Laboratory for International Fuzzy Engineering Research [Japan]
LIFE .... Ladies Involved For Education (SAUO)
LIFE .... Language Improvement to Facilitate Education of Hearing-Impaired Children [A project of NEA]
LIFE .... LASER-Induced Fluorescence Emission
LIFE .... Leadership & Investment in Fighting an Epidemic (SAUO)
LIFE .... League for International Food Education [Defunct] (EA)
LIFE .... League of Independent Ferret Enthusiasts (EA)
LIFE .... Lear Integrated Flight Equipment (MCD)
LIFE .... Learning in a Free Environment [Education program]
LIFE .... Less Infant Fatality Everywhere [In association name, Project LIFE]
LIFE .... Let's Improve Future Environment
LIFE .... Liberia International Foundation for Elevation
LIFE .... Life Issues in Formal Education (EA)
LIFE .... Lifeline Systems [NASDAQ symbol] (TTSB)
LIFE .... Lifeline Systems, Inc. (SAUO)
LIFE .... Lifetime [Cable television channel]
LIFE .... Likelihood Function Estimation (ACAE)
LIFE .... Living in Family Environments
LIFE .... Logistics Evaluation and Review Integrated Flight Equipment [Aviation] (IAA)
LIFE .... Logistics Intelligence File Europe
LIFE .... Logistics Interface for a Factory Environment [Computer science] (VLIE)
LIFE .... London International Futures Exchange (SAUO)
LIFE .... Long Instruction Format Engine [Computer science] (CIST)
LIFE .... Longitudinal Interval Follow-Up Evaluation (MEDA)
LIFE .... Love Is Feeding Everyone (EA)
LIFE .... Low Income Family Emancipation Society
LIFE .... Low Income Family Emergency Center
LIFE .... Lung-Imaging Fluorescent Endoscope [Medicine] (ECON)
Life and Acc Ins R... Bigelow's Life and Accident Insurance Reports [A publication] (DLA)
Life Bcp ...... Life Bancorp, Inc. [Associated Press] (SAG)
Life C .... Life (Health and Accident) Cases [Commerce Clearing House] [A publication] (DLA)
Life Cas ...... Life (Health and Accident) Cases [Commerce Clearing House] [A publication] (DLA)
Life Cas 2d... Life (Health and Accident) Cases, Second Series [Commerce Clearing House] [A publication] (DLA)
Lifecell .... Lifecell Corp. [Associated Press] (SAG)
LifeHoan ..... Lifetime Hoan Corp. [Associated Press] (SAG)
LIFEL .... Limited Functional English Literacy
LIFEMAN ..... Live Fire Evaluation Manikin [Perceptronics, Inc.] [Military]
LifePart .... Life Partners [Associated Press] (SAG)
LIFER .... Language Interface Facility with Ellipsis and Recursion [Computer science] (MHDI)
LifeRe .... Life Re Corp. [Associated Press] (SAG)
LifeRte .... LifeRate Systems, Inc. [Associated Press] (SAG)
LIFES .... LASER-Induced Fluorescence and Environmental Sensing [NASA]
LifeSpir .... [The] Life of the Spirit [London] [A publication] (BJA)
LIFESTA ...... Lifeboat Station [Coast Guard]
LIFETECH .... Long-term Funding for the Environment Through Technology (SAUO)
Lifeway .... Lifeway Foods, Inc. [Associated Press] (SAG)
LIFF .... Lifschultz Inds [NASDAQ symbol] (TTSB)
LIFF .... Lifschultz Industries, Inc. [NASDAQ symbol] (SAG)
Liffe .... London and International Financial Futures Exchange (SAUO)
Liffe .... London International Financial Futures & Options Exchange
LIFFE .... London International Financial Futures and Options Exchange (NUMA)
LIFFE .... London International Financial Futures Exchange (EBF)
LIFFE .... London International Financial Futures Exchange Ltd. [London, England]
LIFFOE .... London International Financial Futures and Options Exchange (EBF)
LiFHAS .... Libertarian Foundation for Human Assistance (EAIO)
LIFI .... Life of Indiana Corp. (SAUO)
LIFireE .... Licentiate of the Institute of Fire Engineers (SAUO)
LI Fire Eng... Licentiate of the Institute of Fire Engineers (SAUO)
LIFLSA .... Lone Indian Fellowship and Lone Scout Alumni (EA)
LIFMA .... Leather Importers, Factors and Merchants Association (SAUO)
LIFMOP .... Linearly Frequency-Modulated Pulse
LIFO .... Last In, First Out [Queuing technique] [Accounting]
LIFO .... Life Orientation (Survey)
LIFPL .... Ligue Internationale de Femmes pour la Paix et la Liberte [Women's International League for Peace and Freedom - WILPF] (EAIO)
LIFPL/SF ..... Ligue Internationale de Femmes pour la Paix et la Liberte, Section Francaise (EAIO)
LIFR .... Leukemia Inhibitory Factor Receptor [Biochemistry]
LIFRAM .... Liquid-Fueled Ramjet [Navy] (MCD)
LIFS .... LASER-Induced Fluorescence Spectroscopy
LIFS .... London International Furniture Show [British] (ITD)
LIFS .... Lowell Institution for Savings (SAUO)

LifschIt	Lifschultz Industries, Inc. [Associated Press] (SAG)
LIFSUM........	Airlift Summary (SAUS)
LIFSUM........	Airlift Summary Report [Air Force]
LIFT	Aviation Group, Inc. (SAUO)
LIFT	Bereavement Services & Community Education (AC)
LIFT	Labor Investing for Tomorrow [Department of Labor]
LIFT	Lead-In Fighter Training (SAUS)
LIFT	Lead-In Flight Training [Air Force] (DOMA)
LIFT	Link Intellectual Functions Tester
LIFT	Literacy Involves Families Together [Arizona]
LIFT	Logically Integrated FORTRAN Translator [UNIVAC]
LIFT	Logistics Improvement Facility Technology (SAUO)
LIFT	London International Festival of Theatre [British]
LIFT	London International Freight Terminal (DS)
LIFT	Lower Inventories for Tomorrow (SAUO)
LIFT	Lower Inventory for Tomorrow [A program of the Canadian government to bring heavy stocks of wheat into line with demand by paying farmers not to produce]
LIFT	Low Interfacial Tension [Physical chemistry]
LIFT	Lymphocyte Immunofluorescence Test (STED)
LIFTG	Lifting (ABBR)
LIFU	Liquid Fuel
LIFUM..........	Airlift Summary Report (SAUS)
LIG	Laboratory Implementation Guidance (SAUO)
LIG	Landcare Liaison Group (SAUO)
LIG	LASER Image Generator (MCD)
LIG	LASERS in Graphics (DGA)
LIG	Last Interglacial (SAUO)
LIG	Last Interglacial Period [Climatology]
LIG	Leichte Infanteriegeschuetz [Light Infantry Howitzer] [German military - World War II]
LIG	Liege (ABBR)
LIG	Ligament [Anatomy] (DAVI)
lig	Ligamentum (STED)
LIG	Ligated [or Ligation] [Medicine]
lig	Ligation (STED)
LIG	Ligature (DGA)
LIG	Limoges [France] [Airport symbol] (OAG)
LIG	London Industrial Group [British]
Lig	Pro Ligario [of Cicero] [Classical studies] (OCD)
LIGA	Liquid Granule Applicator [Device used to disperse pesticides]
LIGA	Lithographic Galvanoforming Abformung [Materials science]
Ligand	Ligand Pharmaceuticals, Inc. [Associated Press] (SAG)
LIGCM	Licentiate of the Incorporated Guild of Church Musicians [British] (ROG)
Lig Dig	Ligon's Digest [Alabama] [A publication] (DLA)
LIGG	Lanzhou Institute of Glaciology and Geocryology (SAUO)
ligg	Ligaments (STED)
LIGG	Ligaments [or Ligamenti]
ligg	Ligature [Surgery] (DAVI)
LIGHT	Lifecycle Global HyperText [Computer science] (VLIE)
LIGHT	Light [Commonly used] (OPSA)
LIGHT	Light Industrial Gas Heat Transfer
LIGHT	Lighting (ABBR)
LIGHT	Lightning (ABBR)
LIGHTEX	Searchlight Illumination Exercise [Also, LITEX] [Military] (NVT)
LightP	LightPath Technologies, Inc. [Associated Press] (SAG)
LIGHTPHOTORON...	Light Photographic Squadron
LIGHTS	Lights [Commonly used] (OPSA)
LightSav	Light Savers USA, Inc. [Associated Press] (SAG)
Lign	Lignum [Wood] [Latin]
LIGO	Laser Interferometer Gravitational Wave Observatory (SAUO)
LIGO	LASER Interferometry Gravitational Wave Observatory [Proposed]
LIH	LASER Interferometric Holography
LIH	Left Inguinal Hernia [Medicine]
LIH	Letters and Inscriptions of Hammurabi [A publication] (BJA)
LIH	Leucine-Induced Hypoglycemia [Medicine] (MELL)
LIH	Leukocyte Inhibiting Factor [Medicine] (MELL)
LIH	Licensed Industrial Hygienist (SARE)
LIH	Light Intensity High
LIH	Lihue [Hawaii] [Airport symbol] (OAG)
LIH	Line Interface Handler
LiH	Lithium Hydride
LIHA	Low Impulsiveness, High Anxiety (MAE)
LIHDC	Low Income Housing Development Corp. [North Carolina] (EA)
LIHE	Lutheran Institute of Human Ecology (EA)
LIHEAP	Low Income Home Energy Assistance Program [Formerly, LIEA] [Block grant]
LIHG	Ligue Internationale de Hockey sur Glace [International Ice Hockey Federation]
LihirGld	Lihir Gold Ltd. [Associated Press] (SAG)
LIHIS	Low Income Housing Information Service (EA)
LIHM	Licentiate of the Institute of Housing Managers [British] (DI)
LIHN	Hieronymi Liber Interpretationis Hebraicorum Nominum (BJA)
LIHPRHA......	Low Income Housing Preservation and Resident Homeownership Act of 1990
LIHRY	Lihir Gold ADS [NASDAQ symbol] (TTSB)
LIHRY	Lihir Gold Ltd. [NASDAQ symbol] (SAG)
LIHS	Long Island Horticultural Society (SAUO)
LIHTC	Low Income Housing Tax Credit
LII	Flight Research Institute, M. Gromov [Former USSR] [FAA designator] (FAAC)
LII	Land Information Infrastructure (SAUO)
LII	Larizza Industries (SAUO)
LII	Larizza Industries, Inc. [AMEX symbol] (SPSG)
LII	Leisure Interest Inventory (STED)
LII	Lennox Intl. [NYSE symbol] (SG)
LII	Life Insurance Index [A publication]
LII	Light Image Intensifier (SAUS)
LII	Linux Internationalisation Inititative (SAUO)
LII	Livestock Industry Institute (EA)
LII	London Insurance Institute (SAUO)
LII	Lues II [or Secondary syphilis] [Infectious diseases] (DAVI)
LII	Mulia [Indonesia] [Airport symbol] (OAG)
LI/IA	Ibero Americana. Scandinavian Association for Research on Latin America. Stockholm (SAUO)
LIIA	Italy International NOTAM Office [Italy] [ICAO location identifier] (ICLI)
LIIB	Roma [Italy] [ICAO location identifier] (ICLI)
LIIC	Italy Military International NOTAM Office [Italy] [ICAO location identifier] (ICLI)
LIICC	Land Information and Inventory Co-ordinating Committee (SAUO)
LIIG	Logistics Item Identification Guide [Military] (AFM)
LIII	Lues III [Teritiary syphilis] [Infectious diseases] (DAVI)
LIII	Roma [Italy] [ICAO location identifier] (ICLI)
li-ion	Lithium Ion
LIIP	LASER-Induced Infrared Photochemistry
LIIR	Italian Agency for Air Navigation Services [Italy] [ICAO location identifier] (ICLI)
LIJ	Lawyers for an Independent Judiciary [Defunct] (EA)
LIJ	Left Internal Jugular Vein [Medicine] (DMAA)
LIJJ, ...	Roma [Italy] [ICAO location identifier] (ICLI)
LIK	Leichte Infanteriekolonne [Light Infantry Supply Column] [German military - World War II]
LIK	Likiep [Marshall Islands] [Airport symbol] (OAG)
LIKE	Learning Inventory of Kindergarten Experience [Owigns, Mills, and O'Dell] (TES)
LIKONA	Limburgse Koepel voor Natuurstudie (SAUO)
LIL	Laboratory Interface Language [Programming language]
LIL	Laporte Industries Limited (SAUO)
LIL	Large Immersion Lens
LIL	Large-Ion Lithophile
LIL	Law of the Iterated Logarithm (PDAA)
LIL	Lead-In Light-System [Aviation]
LIL	Light Intensity Low
LIL	Lilac (ROG)
LIL	Lille [France] [Airport symbol] (OAG)
LIL	Lille [France] [Seismograph station code, US Geological Survey] [Closed] (SEIS)
LIL	Lilliputian (ABBR)
Lil	Lilly's English Assize Reports [1688-93] [A publication] (DLA)
LIL	Lily-Tulip Cup Corporation (SAUO)
LIL	Lincoln's Inn Library [A publication] (DLA)
LIL	Linguaphone Institute Limited (SAUO)
LIL	Lithuanian Airlines [ICAO designator] (FAAC)
LIL	Little (ABBR)
LIL	Live-In Lover [Slang] (DSUE)
LIL	Log-Inject-Log [Petroleum technology]
LIL	Long Island Light'g [NYSE symbol] (TTSB)
LIL	Long Island Lighting Co. [Formerly, LLT] [NYSE symbol] (SPSG)
LIL	Low-Input Landscaping
LIL	Lunar International Laboratory
LILA	Life Insurance Logistics Automated (SAUO)
LILA	Ligue Internationale de la Librairie Ancienne [International League of Antiquarian Booksellers - ILAB] (EAIO)
LILA	Low Impulsiveness, Low Anxiety (MAE)
Lil Abr	Lilly's Abridgment [England] [A publication] (DLA)
LILAC	Low-Intensity Large Area [Headlight]
LILACS........	Latin American and Caribbean Health Sciences Literature (IID)
LILAM.........	Licentiate of the Institute of Leisure and Amenity Management [British] (DBQ)
LILC	Annual Long Island Library Conference
LILCo	Long Island Lighting Co. [Associated Press] (SAG)
Lil Conv	Lilly's Conveyancer [A publication] (DLA)
LILE	Large Ion Lithophile Element [Geochemistry]
Lill Ent........	Lilly's Entries [England] [A publication] (DLA)
Lilly	Lilly [Eli] and Co. [Associated Press] (SAG)
Lilly	Lilly's Reports and Pleadings of Cases in Assize [170 English Reprint] [1688-93] [A publication] (DLA)
Lilly Abr	Lilly's Abridgment [England] [A publication] (DLA)
Lilly Assize...	Lilly's Reports and Pleadings of Cases in Assize [170 English Reprint] [1688-93] [A publication] (DLA)
Lilly Assize (Eng)...	Lilly's Reports and Pleadings of Cases in Assize [170 English Reprint] [1688-93] [A publication] (DLA)
LillyE	Lilly [Eli] & Co. [Associated Press] (SAG)
LillyEli	Lilly [Eli] [Associated Press] (SAG)
LillyInd	Lilly Industries, Inc. [Associated Press] (SAG)
LILO	Last-In, Last-Out [Accounting]
LILO	Link Loader (IAA)
LILO	Linux Loader (RALS)
LILOC	Light Lyne Optical Correlation (MCD)
LILPrA	Long Island Ltg 7.95% Pfd [NYSE symbol] (TTSB)
LILPrB	Long Island Ltg 5% B Pfd [NYSE symbol] (TTSB)
LILPrC	Long Island Ltg 7.66% Pfd [NYSE symbol] (TTSB)
LILPrE	Long Island Ltg 4.35% Cv E Pfd [NYSE symbol] (TTSB)
LILPrI	Long Island Ltg, 5.75% Cv I Pfd [NYSE symbol] (TTSB)
LILPrQ	Long Island Ltg 7.05% Pfd [NYSE symbol] (TTSB)
LILRC	Long Island Library Resources Council [Bellport, NY] [Library network]
Lil Reg	Lilly's Practical Register [A publication] (ILCA)

LilVern.........	Lillian Vernon Corp. [*Associated Press*] (SAG)
LIM	BVBA Lucorp [*Belgium*] [*FAA designator*] (FAAC)
LIM	Compass Locator of Inner Marker Site
LIM	Laboratory Institute of Merchandising [*New York, NY*]
LIM	Land Information Management (SAUO)
LIM	Land Inventory and Management Program (SAUO)
LIM	Language Interface Module (NITA)
LIM	Language Interpretation Module
LIM	Latent Image Memory
LIM	Leg-Inducing Membrane [*Entomology*]
LIM	Leningrad Institute of Metals [*Former USSR*] (MCD)
LIM	Licentiate of the Institution of Metallurgists (SAUO)
LIM	Light Intensity Medium
LIM	Lima [*Peru*] [*Airport symbol*] (OAG)
LIM	Lima [*Peru*] [*Seismograph station code, US Geological Survey*] (SEIS)
LIM	Lima Public Library, Lima, OH [*OCLC symbol*] (OCLC)
LIM	Limber (MSA)
LIM	Limerick [*County in Ireland*] (ROG)
lim	Limes [*Limit*] [*Latin*]
lim	Limit (ELAL)
LIM	Limit
lim	Limitation (STED)
LIM	Limiter [*Electronics*] (ECII)
LIM	Limonene [*Organic chemistry*]
LIM	Linear Induction Motor [*Magnetic rapid-transit car*]
LIM	Line Insulation Monitor (PDAA)
LIM	Line Interface Module
LIM	Liquid Injection Molding
LIM	Locator Inner Marker [*Aviation*] (DA)
LIM	Logic Interface Module (TIMI)
LIM	Losing Inventory Manager [*Army*] (AABC)
LIM	Lotus/Intel/Microsoft [*Computer science*]
LIM	Lower Inlet Module [*Nuclear energy*] (NRCH)
LIM	Low-Inclination Mission (SAUS)
LIMA	Langkawi International Maritime & Aerospace Exhibition (SAUO)
LIMA	LASER-Induced Ion-Mass Analyzer [*Instrumentation*]
LIMA	LASER-Induced Mass Analysis (AAEL)
LIMA	Left Internal Mammary Artery [*Anatomy*] (AAMN)
LIMA	Licentiate of the Institute of Mathematics and Its Applications [*British*] (DBQ)
LIMA	Light Induced Modulation of Absorption (VLIE)
LIMA	Logic-in-Memory Array
LIMA	Long Island Museum Association (SAUO)
LIMA	Lotus/Intel/Microsoft/Ast (SAUO)
LIMA	Torino [*Italy*] [*ICAO location identifier*] (ICLI)
LIMAC	Large Integrated Monolithic Array Computer (MCD)
LIMAC	Linden Industrial Mutual Aid Council (SAUO)
LIM ACT	Limitation of Action [*Legal term*] (DLA)
LIMAD	Linear Magnetic Drive (SAUS)
LIMAP	Landsat Imagery Analysis Package (SAUO)
LIMAS	Lightweight Marking System [*British Army*]
LIMB	Library Instruction Materials Bank [*Loughborough University of Technology*] [*Information service or system*] (IID)
LIMB	Limestone Injection/Multistage Burner
LIMB	Liquid Metal Breeder [*Reactor*]
LIMB	Listing of Molecular Biology Databases (SAUO)
LIMB	Look In Mail Box (VLIE)
LIMB	Milano/Bresso [*Italy*] [*ICAO location identifier*] (ICLI)
LIMBT	Large Injection-Molded Body Technology [*Automotive plastics*]
LIMC	Milano/Malpensa [*Italy*] [*ICAO location identifier*] (ICLI)
LIMD	Grigna Settentrionale [*Italy*] [*ICAO location identifier*] (ICLI)
LIMD	Limited (ROG)
LIMDAT	Limiting Date
LIMDIS	Limited Distribution [*Military*] (AFIT)
LIMDOW	Light Intensity Modulation Direct OverWrite [*Computer science*]
LIMDU	Limited Duty (MCD)
LIME	Bergamo/Orio Al Serio [*Italy*] [*ICAO location identifier*] (ICLI)
LIME	Laser Inducted Microwave Emissions (ADWA)
LIME	Low-Iron, Manganese-Enriched [*Meteorite*]
LIMEA	Low-Iron-Content Monoethanolamine
LIMEAN	London Interbank Median Average Rate
LIM-EMS......	Lotus-Intel-Microsoft Expanded Memory Specification [*Computer science*] (BTTJ)
LIMESCO	Line Memory Scan Converter
limest	Limestone [*Petrology*]
LIMEX	Labrador Ice Margin Experiment (SAUO)
LIMF	Land Information Management Framework (SAUO)
LIMF	Licentiate of the Institute of Metal Finishing [*British*] (DBQ)
LIMF	Torino/Caselle [*Italy*] [*ICAO location identifier*] (ICLI)
LIMFAC........	Limiting Factor (MCD)
LIMG	Albenga [*Italy*] [*ICAO location identifier*] (ICLI)
LIMH	Pian Rosa [*Italy*] [*ICAO location identifier*] (ICLI)
LIMI	Colle Del Gigante [*Italy*] [*ICAO location identifier*] (ICLI)
LIMI	Leningrad International Management Institute [*Joint Venture between Bocconi University, Italy and Leningrad University*] (ECON)
LIMIRIS	LASER-Induced Modulation of Infrared in Silicon
LIMIT	Leicester Intravenous Magnesium Intervention Trial [*Cardiology study*]
LIMIT	Lot-Size Inventory Management Interpolation Technique (BUR)
Limitd	[*The*] Limited, Inc. [*Associated Press*] (SAG)
Limit Ed.......	Limited Edition
LIMITS.........	Development and Evaluation of a New Generation of Real Time Software Engineering Design Tools for Handling the Temporal Aspects of Industrial Applications of Information Technology (SAUO)
LIMJ	Genova/Sestri [*Italy*] [*ICAO location identifier*] (ICLI)
LIMK	Torino/Bric Della Croce [*Italy*] [*ICAO location identifier*] (ICLI)
LIML	Limited Information Maximum Likelihood [*Econometrics*]
LIML	Milano/Linate [*Italy*] [*ICAO location identifier*] (ICLI)
LIMM	Milano [*Italy*] [*ICAO location identifier*] (ICLI)
LIMN	Cameri [*Italy*] [*ICAO location identifier*] (ICLI)
LIMNET	London Insurance Market Network (SAUO)
LIMNOL	Limnology
LIMNURP.....	Lippincott Manual of Nursing Practice (SAUO)
LIMO...........	Land Information Management Office
LIMO...........	Least Input for the Most Output [*Business term*]
LIMO...........	Limousine (DSUE)
Limo	Limousine
LIMO...........	Limousine Industry Manufacturers Organization (EA)
LIMO...........	Monte Bisbino [*Italy*] [*ICAO location identifier*] (ICLI)
LIMON	Limonis [*Of Lemon*] [*Pharmacy*] (ROG)
LIMOS	Laser Intensity Modulation System [*Computer science*]
LIMOSO	Limitation of Supplies Order [*World War II*]
LIMP	Laboratory Instrument Maintenance Program (SAUO)
LIMP	Language-Independent Macro Processor (PDAA)
LIMP	Life-Injury-Money-Problems (SAUO)
LIMP	Louis XIV, James II, Mary, Prince of Wales [*Jacobite toast*]
LIMP	Lunar-Anchored Interplanetary Monitoring Platform [*Aerospace*]
LIMP	Lunar Interplanetary Monitoring Probe (IAA)
LIMP	Parma [*Italy*] [*ICAO location identifier*] (ICLI)
LIMPES.......	Logistics Interactive Mobilization/Planning and Execution System (SAUO)
LIMPS.........	Linear Induction Motor Propulsion System
LIMQ	Govone [*Italy*] [*ICAO location identifier*] (ICLI)
LIMR	Limiter
LIMR	Novi Ligure [*Italy*] [*ICAO location identifier*] (ICLI)
LIMRA	Life Insurance Marketing and Research Association [*Hartford, CT*] (EA)
LIMRC	LRU [*Line Replaceable Unit*] Identification and Maintenance Requirements Catalog (NASA)
LIMRF..........	Life Insurance Medical Research Fund [*Defunct*]
LIMRIC	LRU Identification and Maintenance Requirements Catalog (SAUS)
LIMRV	Linear Induction Motor Research Vehicle [*Magnetic rapid-transit car*]
LIMS	Laban Institute of Movement Studies [*Later, LBIMS*] (EA)
LIMS	Laboratory Information Management System
LIMS	LASER-Induced Mass Spectrometry (AAEL)
LIMS	LASERInduced Microgrough Structures [*Surface Technology*]
LIMS	Laser Ionization Mass Spectrometer (ACAE)
LIMS	Lewis Information Management System (SAUO)
LIMS	Library Information Management System [*University of Maryland*]
LIMS	Light Ion Mass Spectrometer (SAUS)
LIMS	Limb Infrared Monitor of the Stratosphere
LIMS	Limb-Motion Sensor [*System*]
LIMS	Limb Sounder (SSD)
LIMS	Liquid Injection Molding Simulation [*Plastics*]
LIMS	Lithium Metal Sulfide
LIMS	Logistic Inventory Management System [*North American Rockwell*]
LIMS	Logistics Information Management System (SAUO)
LIMS	Logistics Inventory Management System (SAUO)
LIMS	Lotus Intel Microsoft Specifications (VLIE)
LIMS	Piacenza/San Damiano [*Italy*] [*ICAO location identifier*] (ICLI)
LIMSS.........	Logistics Information Management Support System [*Military*]
LIMSW........	Limit Switch (NRCH)
LIMT	Passo Della Cisa [*Italy*] [*ICAO location identifier*] (ICLI)
LIMTV.........	Linear Induction Motor Test Vehicle [*Magnetic rapid-transit car*]
LIMU...........	Capo Mele [*Italy*] [*ICAO location identifier*] (ICLI)
LIMU...........	LASER Inertial Measurement Unit (MCD)
LIMV...........	Lilac Mottle Virus [*Plant pathology*]
LIMV...........	Passo Dei Giovi [*Italy*] [*ICAO location identifier*] (ICLI)
LIMW..........	Aosta [*Italy*] [*ICAO location identifier*] (ICLI)
LIMY...........	Monte Malanotte [*Italy*] [*ICAO location identifier*] (ICLI)
LIMZ...........	Levaldigi [*Italy*] [*ICAO location identifier*] (ICLI)
LIN.............	Law Institute News [*Australia*] [*A publication*]
LIN.............	Linair-Hungarian Regional Airlines [*FAA designator*] (FAAC)
LIN.............	Lincoln [*Nebraska*] [*Seismograph station code, US Geological Survey*] [*Closed*] (SEIS)
LIN.............	Lincoln [*Diocesan abbreviation*] [*Nebraska*] (TOCD)
Lin.............	Lincolnshire Regiment (SAUO)
Lin.............	Linden [*Record label*]
LIN.............	Linden, CA [*Location identifier*] [*FAA*] (FAAL)
LIN.............	Line (WDAA)
LIN.............	Lineal (MSA)
LIN.............	Linear (KSC)
lin.............	Linear (STED)
LIN.............	Line Item Number (ACAE)
LIN.............	Linen (ADA)
lin.............	Linen (VRA)
LIN.............	Linens'n Things [*NYSE symbol*] (SG)
lin.............	Liniment (STED)
LIN.............	Liniment
LIN.............	Liquid Nitrogen (AFM)
LIN.............	Local Interconnect Network (SAUO)
LIN.............	Massachusetts Institute of Technology, Lincoln Laboratory, Lexington, MA [*OCLC symbol*] (OCLC)
LIN.............	Milan [*Italy*] Forlanini-Linate [*Airport symbol*] (OAG)
LIN.............	Nitlyn Airways, Inc. (SAUO)

LINA.............	Liberian News Agency (EY)
LINA.............	Literaturnachweise [*Literature Compilations Database*] [*Fraunhofer Society*] (IID)
LINABOL......	Lineas Navieras Bolivianas [*Shipping line*] [*Bolivia*] (EY)
LINAC.........	Linear [*Electron*] Accelerator
LINAS.........	LASER Inertial Navigation Attack System (IAA)
LINAS.........	LASER-Integrated Navigation/Attack System (MCD)
LINB...........	LIN Broadcasting Corp. (SAUO)
LINC...........	Laboratory Instrument Computer [*Medical analyzer*]
LINC...........	Language Information Network Coordination [*Education*] (AIE)
LINC...........	Language in the National Curriculum [*Project*] (WDAA)
LINC...........	Learning Institute of North Carolina
LINC...........	Legislative Information Network Corp. [*Information service or system*] (IID)
LINC...........	Library & Information Consultants Ltd. [*Information service or system*] (IID)
LINC...........	Library and Information Cooperation Council (SAUO)
LINC...........	Lincolnshire [*County in England*]
LINC...........	Lindas Diversified Holdings [*NASDAQ symbol*] (SAG)
LINC...........	Lucas Industries Noise Centre [*Research center*] [*British*] (IRUK)
LINCA.........	Linda's Flame Roasted Chicken [*NASDAQ symbol*] (TTSB)
L'INCA........	L'Institut National Canadien pour les Aveugles (AC)
Lincare........	Lincare Holdings, Inc. [*Associated Press*] (SAG)
LINCE.........	LASER-Improved Naval Combat Equipment (PDAA)
LincEl.........	[*The*] Lincoln Electric Co. [*Associated Press*] (SAG)
LincElA.......	Lincoln Electric Co. (The) [*Associated Press*] (SAG)
LINCLOE......	Lightweight Individual Combat Clothing and Equipment (AABC)
LinCMOS......	Linear CMOS [*Complementary Metal Oxide Semiconductor*] [*Texas Instruments*] (NITA)
LINCMOS......	Linear Complementary Metal-Oxide Semiconductor [*Electronics*] (EECA)
LincN..........	Lincoln National Corp. [*Associated Press*] (SAG)
LincN..........	Lincoln National Corp. Capital I [*Associated Press*] (SAG)
LincN..........	Lincoln National Corp. Capital II [*Associated Press*] (SAG)
LincNatl.......	Lincoln National Corp. [*Associated Press*] (SAG)
LincNIF.......	Lincoln National Income Fund, Inc. [*Associated Press*] (SAG)
LINCO.........	Linear Composition (PDAA)
LINCO.........	Linearly Organized Chemical Code for Use in Computer Systems (DIT)
Lincoln U.....	Lincoln University (GAGS)
LINCOMPEX...	Linked Compressor and Expander (NATG)
LINCOS........	Lingua Cosmica [*Artificial language consisting of radio signals of varying lengths and frequencies*]
LINCOTT......	Liaison, Interface, Coupling, Technology Transfer
LINCS.........	Language Information Network and Clearinghouse System [*Center for Applied Linguistics*] [*Washington, DC*]
LINCS.........	Leased Interfacility Nas Communications System [*FAA*] (TAG)
Lincs..........	Lincolnshire (DIAR)
LINCS.........	Lincolnshire [*County in England*]
LINCS.........	Literacy Information and Communication System
LinCS.........	Local Independents Collaborating with Stations (SAUO)
LincSB........	Lincoln Savings Bank [*Associated Press*] (SAG)
LincSnk.......	Lincoln Snacks Co. [*Associated Press*] (SAG)
LINCT.........	Linctus [*Tincture*] [*Pharmacy*] (ROG)
LincTel.......	Lincoln Telecommunications Co. [*Associated Press*] (SAG)
LINCW.........	Linda's Flame Rstd Ckn Wrrt'A' [*NASDAQ symbol*] (TTSB)
LINCZ.........	Linda's Flame Rstd Ckn Wrrt'B' [*NASDAQ symbol*] (TTSB)
LIND...........	Lindberg Corp. [*NASDAQ symbol*] (SAG)
LIND...........	Lindbergh Corporation (SAUO)
Linda..........	Lindas Flame Roasted Chicken, Inc. [*Associated Press*] (SAG)
Linda..........	Lindasw Diversified Holdings [*Associated Press*] (SAG)
LINDA.........	Line Drawing Analyzer [*Cybernetics*]
LindasCh......	Lindas Flame Roasted Chicken, Inc. [*Associated Press*] (SAG)
LindasDiv.....	Lindas Diversified Holdings [*Associated Press*] (SAG)
Lindbrg.......	Lindberg Corp. [*Associated Press*] (SAG)
LINDI.........	Line-to-Disk [*Computer science*] (MHDI)
Lind Jur......	Lindley's Study of Jurisprudence [*A publication*] (DLA)
Lindl Copartn...	Lindley on Partnership [*A publication*] (DLA)
Lindley.......	Lindley's Law of Companies [*A publication*] (DLA)
Lindley Comp...	Lindley's Law of Companies [*A publication*] (DLA)
Lindley P.....	Lindley on Partnership [*A publication*] (DLA)
Lindley Part..	Lindley on Partnership [*A publication*] (DLA)
LindlH........	Lindal Cedar Homes, Inc. [*Associated Press*] (SAG)
Lindl Partn..	Lindley on Partnership [*A publication*] (DLA)
Lind Part.....	Lindley on Partnership [*A publication*] (DLA)
Lind Pr	Lindewoode's Provinciales [*A publication*] (DLA)
Lind Prob.....	Lindsay on Probates [*A publication*] (DLA)
Lindsy.........	Lindsay Manufacturing Co. [*Associated Press*] (SAG)
lindwd	Lindenwood (VRA)
LINE...........	Lightweight Inertial Northseeking Equipmet (SAA)
LINE...........	Linear Corp. (SAUO)
LINE...........	Line Ministries (SAUO)
LINE...........	Long Interspersed Element Sequence [*Genetics*]
LINE...........	Long Interspersed Nuclear Element [*Genetics*]
LINEAR.......	Lincoln Near-Earth Asteroid Research
LinearT.......	Linear Technology Corp. [*Associated Press*] (SAG)
L in Eastern Eur...	Law in Eastern Europe [*A publication*] (DLA)
LINED........	Line Editor [*Computer science*] (MHDI)
LINEII.........	Logic and Information Network Compiler II [*Computer science*] (HGAA)
LINER........	Low-Ionization Nuclear Emission-Line Region [*Spectroscopy*]
LINES.........	Library Information Network Exchange Services [*Australia*] [*A publication*]
LINEs.........	Long Interspered Nuclcotide Elements [*Genetics*]
LINES.........	Long-Interspersed Repeated Segments [*of DNA*] [*Genetics*] (DAVI)

Linfield C....	Linfield College (GAGS)
linft.............	Linear Foot (WPI)
LINFT.........	Linear Foot
Ling...........	De Lingua Latina [*of Varro*] [*Classical studies*] (OCD)
LING.........	Learning Independence Through Computers, Inc.
Ling..........	Linguistics (BEE)
ling...........	Linguistics (SHCU)
LING.........	Linguistics
LINGO........	Linguistic Operation (VLIE)
LINGUA......	Linguistic Analysis System (ECII)
LINIM.........	Liniment
Lin Ins........	De Lineis Insecabilibus [*of Aristotle*] [*Classical studies*] (OCD)
Linium........	Linium Technology Corp. [*Associated Press*] (SAG)
LINJET........	Liquid Injection Electric Thruster [*NASA*] (NASA)
LINK..........	Data Link (SAUS)
LINK..........	Interlink Electronics [*NASDAQ symbol*] (TTSB)
LINK..........	Interlink Electronics, Inc. [*NASDAQ symbol*] (SAG)
LINK..........	International Leisure Information Network (SAUO)
LINK..........	Lambeth Information Network [*Information service or system*] [*British*] (NITA)
LINK..........	Library and Information Network [*Planned Parenthood Federation of America, Inc.*] [*Information service or system*] (IID)
LINK..........	Literature in Nursing Kardex
LINKW........	Interlink Electrs Wrrt [*NASDAQ symbol*] (TTSB)
LINLOG.......	Linear-Logarithmic (IEEE)
LINMH........	Linear Meters per Hour (IAA)
LINMOS......	Laser Intensity Modulation (SAUO)
LINN..........	Lincoln Foodservice Products, Inc. (SAUO)
LINN..........	Linnaeus
Linn Ind.......	Linn's Index of Pennsylvania Reports [*A publication*] (DLA)
Linn Laws Prov PA...	Linn on the Laws of the Province of Pennsylvania [*A publication*] (DLA)
LINO..........	Liaison Officer [*Military*]
lino...........	Linocut (VRA)
Lino..........	Linoleum (ADWA)
LINO..........	Linoleum
Lino..........	Linotronic [*Computer science*]
LINO..........	Linotype
Linoco........	Libyan National Oil Corporation (SAUO)
LINOL........	Linoleum (MSA)
LINOSCO......	Libraries in North Staffordshire and South Cheshire in Cooperation [*British*] (NITA)
LINOSCO......	Libraries of North Staffordshire in Cooperation (SAUO)
LINPEX......	London International Invention and New Products Exhibition (SAUO)
LINQ..........	Literature in North Queensland [*A publication*]
LINR..........	Linear Instruments Corp. (SAUO)
LINS..........	Labrador Institute of Northern Studies [*Memorial University of Newfoundland*] [*Canada*] [*Research center*] (RCD)
LINS..........	LASER Inertial Navigation System (MCD)
LINS..........	Lightweight Inertial Navigation System [*Air Force*]
LINS..........	LORAN Inertial System
L in Soc'y...	Law in Society [*A publication*] (DLA)
LInstBB......	Licentiate of the Institute of British Bakers (DBQ)
LInstBCA......	Licentiate of the Institute of Burial and Cremation Administration [*British*] (DBQ)
L Inst P......	Licentiate of the Institute of Physics [*British*]
L Inst Phys...	Licentiate of the Institute of Physics (SAUO)
LInstPRA.....	Licentiate of the Institute of Park and Recreation Administration [*British*] (DI)
LINSU........	Liberian National Student Union (SAUO)
LINTAS......	Lever International Advertising Service (SAUO)
LINTEL.......	Lincoln Telecommunications Co. (EFIS)
LinTelev......	Lin Television Corp. [*Associated Press*] (SAG)
L Intell.......	Law Intelligencer [*United States*] [*A publication*] (DLA)
L in Trans J...	Law in Transition Journal [*A publication*] (DLA)
L in Trans Q...	Law in Transition Quarterly [*A publication*] (DLA)
LINUS.........	Local Independently Nucleated Units of Structure (MELL)
LINUS.........	Local Information Network for Universal Service [*Telecommunications service*] (TSSD)
LINUS.........	Logical Inquiry and Update System
LINV.........	Life Investors, Inc. (SAUO)
LINWR.......	Lake Ilo National Wildlife Refuge (SAUO)
LINX..........	Logistics Information Exchange [*Computer science*] (CIST)
LINZ..........	Land Information New Zealand (SAUO)
LINZ..........	Lindsay Manufacturing [*NASDAQ symbol*] (SAG)
LINZ..........	Lindsay Manufacturing Co. (SAUO)
LINZ..........	Lindsay Mfg [*NASDAQ symbol*] (TTSB)
LIO...........	Air Charter Ltd. (Leiguflug Isleifs Ottesen) [*Iceland*] [*FAA designator*] (FAAC)
LIO...........	Laser Indirect Ophthalmoscope [*Medicine*] (MELL)
LIO...........	Left Inferior Oblique [*Anatomy*] (DAVI)
LIO...........	Legislative Information Office (SAUO)
LIO...........	Lesser Included Offense
LIO...........	Liberian Iron Ore Ltd. [*Toronto Stock Exchange symbol*]
LIO...........	Limon [*Costa Rica*] [*Airport symbol*] (OAG)
LIO...........	Lionel Corporation (SAUO)
LIO...........	Lions International Organization (SAUO)
LIO...........	Liottite [*A zeolite*]
LIO...........	Lithium Organic Battery
LIO...........	Livestock Improvement Organization (SAUO)
LIO...........	Local Interconnect Option [*Wang Laboratories, Inc.*] (BYTE)
LIO...........	National Restaurant Association Large Independent Operators [*Defunct*] (EA)
LIOAS........	LASER-Induced Optoacoustic Spectroscopy
LIOB..........	Licentiate of the Institute of Builders (or Building) (SAUO)

LIOB	Licentiate of the Institute of Building (SAUO)
LIOC	Lighted Independent of Computer
LIOCS	Logical Input/Output Control System [Computer science]
LIOD	Lightweight Optronic Detector (SAUS)
LIOD	Lightweight Optronic Director (MCD)
LIODD	LASER In-Flight Obstacle Detection Device
LiOH	Lithium Hydroxide (NASA)
LIOJ	Language Institute of Japan (SAUO)
LIOL	Legal Information On-Line [Ministry of Labour] [Hamilton, ON] [Information service or system] (IID)
LION	Fidelity National [NASDAQ symbol] (TTSB)
LION	Fidelity National Corp. [NASDAQ symbol] (SAG)
LION	Lehman Investment Opportunity Note
LION	Library Information OnLine [International Atomic Energy Agency] [United Nations] (DUND)
LION	Literature Online [Chadwyck-Healey]
LION	Local Input/Output Nozzle [Computer science]
LION	Local Integrated Optical Network (SAUO)
LI/ON	Logicon Input/Output Network
LION	Low Energy Ion and Electron Instrument (ADWA)
LION	Lunar International Observer Network [NASA]
LionBrw	Lion Brewery, Inc. (The) [Associated Press] (SAG)
Lion-Club	Liberty, Intelligence, Our Nations Safety (SAUO)
LIONS	Library Information and On-Line Network Service [New York Public Library] [Information service or system] (IID)
LIOP	Life in One Position [Telecommunications] (TEL)
LIOP	Limited Initial Operating Production (MCD)
LIP	Boston, MA [Location identifier] [FAA] (FAAL)
LIP	Laboratory for Image Processing (SAUO)
LIP	Large Internet Packet [Computer science] (PCM)
LIP	LASER-Induced Plasma [Spectroscopy]
LIP	Latent Information Parameter
LIP	Lateral Intraparietal Area [Anatomy]
LIP	Launch in Process [NASA] (IAA)
LIP	Legal Inverse Path [Physics]
LIP	Letter Input Procesing [Printing] (DGA)
LIP	Library Information Plan (AIE)
LIP	Life Insurance Policy
LIP	Limited Implementation Program [FAA] (TAG)
lip	Lipemic [Cardiology] (DAVI)
LIP	Lipkovo [Yugoslavia] [Seismograph station code, US Geological Survey] (SEIS)
Lip	Lipoate [Also called Lipoic acid] [Biochemistry] (DAVI)
LIP	Lithium-Induced Polydipsia (DB)
LIP	Local Initiatives Program [Canada]
LIP	Local Interested Party (SAUO)
LIP	London International Press, Ltd. (SAUO)
LIP	Loop Initialization Protocol (SAUS)
LIP	Low Internal Phase [Emulsion chemistry]
LIP	Lunar Impact Probe [Aerospace]
LIP	Lymphoid Interstitial Pneumonitis [Medicine]
LIPA	Aviano [Italy] [ICAO location identifier] (ICLI)
LIPA	Labor Institute of Public Affairs (EA)
LIPA	Lauric [or Lauroyl or Lauryl] Isopropanolamide [Also, LPA] [Organic chemistry]
LIPA	Ligue panafricaine contre le tribalisme, le sectarianisme et le racisme (SAUO)
LIPA	List of Interchangeable Parts and Assemblies
LIPA	Liverpool Institute of Performing Arts [England] (WDAA)
LIPA	Louisiana Independent Physicians Association, Inc.
LIPAD	Ligue Patriotique pour le Developpement [Burkina Faso] [Political party] (EY)
LIPAS	LASER-Induced Photoacoustic Spectroscopy
LIPB	Bolzano [Italy] [ICAO location identifier] (ICLI)
LIPB	Lipase B (DMAA)
LIPB	Lloyd's International Private Banking [Finance]
Lip Bib Jur	Lipenius' Bibliotheca Juridica [A publication] (DLA)
LIPC	Cervia [Italy] [ICAO location identifier] (ICLI)
LIPC	Levenson's Internal, Powerful Others, and Chance Scales (EDAC)
LIPC	Livestock Industry Promotion Corporation (SAUO)
LIPC	Livestock Industry Promotion Council [Australia]
LIPD	Lipase D (DMAA)
LIPD	Udine/Campoformido [Italy] [ICAO location identifier] (ICLI)
LIPE	Bologna/Borgo Panigale [Italy] [ICAO location identifier] (ICLI)
LIPE	Lipe-Rollway Corp. (SAUO)
LIPES	LASER-Induced Plasma Emission Spectroscopy (MEC)
LIPF	Ferrara [Italy] [ICAO location identifier] (ICLI)
LIPF	LASER-Induced Photodissociation and Fluorescence [Coal technology]
LIPFS	Laser-Induced Plasma Fluorescence Spectroscopy (MEC)
LIPG	Gorizia [Italy] [ICAO location identifier] (ICLI)
LIPH	Treviso/San Angelo [Italy] [ICAO location identifier] (ICLI)
LIPHE	Life Interpersonal History Enquiry [Test] [Psychology]
LIPI	Indonesian Institute of Sciences [Marine science] (OSRA)
LIPI	Marine Pollution Monitoring Center (SAUO)
LIPI	Rivolto [Italy] [ICAO location identifier] (ICLI)
LIPID	Logical Page Identifier
LIPJ	Bassano Del Grappa [Italy] [ICAO location identifier] (ICLI)
LIPK	Forli [Italy] [ICAO location identifier] (ICLI)
LIPL	Ghedi [Italy] [ICAO location identifier] (ICLI)
LIPL	Linear Information Processing Language [High-order programming language] [Computer science] (IEEE)
LIPLAFCO	Liberia Plastic Footwear Corporation (SAUO)
LIPN	Verona/Boscomantico [Italy] [ICAO location identifier] (ICLI)
LIPO	Liposome Co. [NASDAQ symbol] (SAG)
LIPO	Liposome Co., Inc. (SAUO)
Lipo	Liposuction (ADWA)
LIPO	Montichiari [Italy] [ICAO location identifier] (ICLI)
Liposm	[The] Liposome Co., Inc. [Associated Press] (SAG)
LIPOZ	Liposome $1.9375 Cv Dep'A'Pfd [NASDAQ symbol] (TTSB)
LIPP	LASER-Induced Pressure Pulse [Medicine] (DMAA)
LIP P	Lipid Profile [Cardiology] (DAVI)
LIPP	Padova [Italy] [ICAO location identifier] (ICLI)
Lipp Cr L	Lippitt's Massachusetts Criminal Law [A publication] (DLA)
LIPQ	Ronchi De'Legionari [Italy] [ICAO location identifier] (ICLI)
LIPR	Rimini [Italy] [ICAO location identifier] (ICLI)
LIPS	Laboratory Information Processing System (SAUO)
LIPS	Laboratory Interface Peripheral Subsystem [Computer science]
LIPS	Lanthanide Ion Probe Spectroscopy
LIPS	Laser Image Processing Scanner (ACAE)
LIPS	Laser Intensify Profile System (ACAE)
LIPS	Late-Inning Pressure Situation [Baseball term] (NDBD)
LIPS	Leiter International Performance Scale [Psychology]
LIPS	Library and Information Plans [British]
LIPS	Linear Inferences per Second (ADWA)
LIPS	Litton Industries Privacy System
LIPS	Logical Inferences per Second [Processing power units] [Computer science]
LIPS	Logic Inference per Second (IAA)
Lips	Low Income, Parents Supporting [Lifestyle classification]
LIPS	Treviso/Istrana [Italy] [ICAO location identifier] (ICLI)
Lipsm	[The] Liposome Co., Inc. [Associated Press] (SAG)
LIPT	Leiter International Performance Test [Psychology] (DAVI)
LIPT	Vicenza [Italy] [ICAO location identifier] (ICLI)
LIPU	Padova [Italy] [ICAO location identifier] (ICLI)
LIPV	Venezia/San Nicolo [Italy] [ICAO location identifier] (ICLI)
LIPX	Large Internetwork Packet Exchange (SAUO)
LIPX	Villafranca [Italy] [ICAO location identifier] (ICLI)
LIPY	Ancona/Falconara [Italy] [ICAO location identifier] (ICLI)
LIPZ	Venezia/Tessera [Italy] [ICAO location identifier] (ICLI)
LIQ	Athens, TX [Location identifier] [FAA] (FAAL)
LIQ	Left Inner Quadrant (SAUS)
LIQ	Liquest International Marketing [Vancouver Stock Exchange symbol]
liq	Liqueur [Solution] [Pharmacy]
LIQ	Liquid (AAG)
liq	Liquid (ELAL)
LIQ	Liquidation (MCD)
LIQ	Liquids of all types (SAUS)
liq	Liquor (NTIO)
LIQ	Liquor
LIQ	Lisala [Zaire] [Airport symbol] (OAG)
LIQ	Lower Inner Quadrant [Anatomy]
LIQB	Arezzo [Italy] [ICAO location identifier] (ICLI)
LIQB	Liqui-Box Corp. [NASDAQ symbol] (SAG)
LIQC	Capri [Italy] [ICAO location identifier] (ICLI)
LIQD	Liquid (ECII)
LIQD	Passo Della Porretta [Italy] [ICAO location identifier] (ICLI)
LIQDTE	Liquidate (ROG)
LIQFRKT	Liquid Fuel Rocket (IAA)
LIQI	Gran Sasso [Italy] [ICAO location identifier] (ICLI)
LIQJ	Civitavecchia [Italy] [ICAO location identifier] (ICLI)
LIQK	Capo Palinuro [Italy] [ICAO location identifier] (ICLI)
LIQM	Rifredo Mugello [Italy] [ICAO location identifier] (ICLI)
LIQN	Rieti [Italy] [ICAO location identifier] (ICLI)
LIQO	Monte Argentario [Italy] [ICAO location identifier] (ICLI)
LIQOR	Liquidator (ROG)
LIQP	Palmaria [Italy] [ICAO location identifier] (ICLI)
LIQQ	Monte Cavo [Italy] [ICAO location identifier] (ICLI)
LIQR	Radicofani [Italy] [ICAO location identifier] (ICLI)
LIQS	Siena [Italy] [ICAO location identifier] (ICLI)
LIQSS	Liquid Steady State (PDAA)
LIQT	Circeo [Italy] [ICAO location identifier] (ICLI)
LIQT	Liquid Transient (PDAA)
LiquiBox	Liqui-Box Corp. [Associated Press] (SAG)
LIQUID	Liquidus [Liquid] [Pharmacy] (ROG)
LIQUON	Liquidation
Liquor Cont L Serv (CCH)	Liquor Control Law Service (Commerce Clearing House) [A publication] (DLA)
LIQV	Volterra [Italy] [ICAO location identifier] (ICLI)
LIQW	Sarzana/Luni [Italy] [ICAO location identifier] (ICLI)
LIQZ	Ponza [Italy] [ICAO location identifier] (ICLI)
LIR	Dover, DE [Location identifier] [FAA] (FAAL)
LIR	Laboratory for Insulation Research [MIT] (MCD)
LIR	Laboratory Implementation Requirements (SAUO)
LIR	Laser Intercept Receiver (SAUS)
LIR	Leader Internode Ratio [Botany]
LIR	Left Iliac Region [Medicine] (MAE)
LIR	Left Inferior Rectus [Muscle] [Ophthalmology and surgery] (DAVI)
LIR	Level Indicator Recorder [Electronics] (ECII)
LIR	Liberia [Costa Rica] [Airport symbol] (OAG)
LIR	Library and Information Resources (NITA)
LIR	Library of International Relations (SAUO)
LIR	Licentiate of the Institute of Population Registration [British] (DBQ)
LIR	Limiting Interval Reliability
LIR	Line Integral Refractometer
LIR	Lionair SA [Luxembourg] [ICAO designator] (FAAC)
lir	Lira [Monetary unit] [Italy]
lir	Lithuanian Soviet Socialist Republic [MARC country of publication code] [Library of Congress] (LCCP)
LIR	Load-Indicating Relay (IAA)

LIR	Load-Indicating Resistor (IAA)
LIR	Location Inventory Report (AAEL)
LIR	London Irish Rifles (SAUO)
LIR	Longitude Independent Reset
LIR	Lost Item Replacement (MCD)
LIRA	Lambeg Industrial Research Association [*British*] (IRUK)
LIRA	Liberal Industrial Relations Association [*British*]
LIRA	Linen Industry Research Association [*British*] (BI)
LIRA	Literature Retrieval Agent (SAUO)
LIRA	Lithospheric Investigation in the Ross Sea Area (SAUO)
LIRA	Little Italy Restoration Association
LIRA	Logging Industry Research Association (SAUO)
LIRA	Low Intensity Reconnaissance Aircraft (SAUS)
LIRA	Roma/Ciampino [*Italy*] [*ICAO location identifier*] (ICLI)
LIRAD	Lidar/Radiometer (CARB)
LIRAQ	Livermore Regional Air Quality Model (SAUO)
LIRB	Liability Insurance Research Bureau (NTPA)
LIRB	Vigna Di Valle [*Italy*] [*ICAO location identifier*] (ICLI)
LIRBM	Liver, Iron, Red Bone Marrow
LIRC	Centocelle [*Italy*] [*ICAO location identifier*] (ICLI)
LIRC	Lebanese Information and Research Center (EA)
LIRC	Level Indicator Recorder Controller [*Electronics*] (ECII)
LIRC	Ligue Internationale de la Representation Commerciale [*International League of Commercial Travelers and Agents - ILCTA*] (EAIO)
LIRC	Low Interest Rate Currency (MHDW)
LIRD	Laser & Infra-red Irradiation Detector (SAUS)
LIRDP	Luangwa Integrated Resource Development Project [*China*] (BUAC)
LIRE	Lincoln Institute for Research and Education (EA)
LIRE	Pratica Di Mare [*Italy*] [*ICAO location identifier*] (ICLI)
LIRES	Literature Retrieval System [*Computer science*]
LIRES-MC	Literature Retrieval System - Multiple Searching, Complete Text [*Computer science*]
LIRF	Low-Intensity Reciprocity Failure [*Of photographic emulsions*]
LIRF	Roma/Fiumicino [*Italy*] [*ICAO location identifier*] (ICLI)
LIRG	Guidonia [*Italy*] [*ICAO location identifier*] (ICLI)
LIRG	Landesverband der Israelitischen Religionsgemeinde (BJA)
LIRG	Library and Information Research Group [*Bristol Polytechnic Library*] [*British*] [*Information service or system*] (IID)
LIRH	Frosinone [*Italy*] [*ICAO location identifier*] (ICLI)
LIRI	Leather Industries Research Institute [*South Africa*] (BUAC)
LIRI	Licentiate of the Institution of the Rubber Industry (SAUO)
LIRI	Salerno/Pontecagnano [*Italy*] [*ICAO location identifier*] (ICLI)
LIRIC	Language Instruction for Recent Immigrants through Computer Technology (EDAC)
LIRJ	Marina Di Campo [*Italy*] [*ICAO location identifier*] (ICLI)
LIRK	Monte Terminillo [*Italy*] [*ICAO location identifier*] (ICLI)
LIRL	Latina [*Italy*] [*ICAO location identifier*] (ICLI)
LIRL	Low Intensity Runway Edge Lights [*FAA*] (TAG)
LIRL	Low-Intensity Runway Lighting
LIRLY	Load-Indicating Relay (MSA)
LIRM	Grazzanise [*Italy*] [*ICAO location identifier*] (ICLI)
LIRMA	London Insurance and Reinsurance Market Association (ECON)
LIRN	Library and Information for the Northwest [*Program of the Fred Meyer Charitable Trust*]
LIRN	Library and Information Research News [*A publication*] (NITA)
LIRN	Library Information Enquiry and Referral Network (TELE)
LIRN	Napoli/Capodichino [*Italy*] [*ICAO location identifier*] (ICLI)
LIROC	Last Instruction Readout Cycle (IAA)
LIROD	Lightweight Radar Optronic Director (SAUS)
LIRP	Pisa [*Italy*] [*ICAO location identifier*] (ICLI)
LIRQ	Firenze [*Italy*] [*ICAO location identifier*] (ICLI)
LIRR	[*The*] Long Island Rail Road Co.
LIRR	Luoyang Institute of Refractories Research [*China*] (BUAC)
LIRR	Roma [*Italy*] [*ICAO location identifier*] (ICLI)
LIRRTP	Lao-IRRI Rice Research and Training Project (SAUO)
LIRS	Grosseto [*Italy*] [*ICAO location identifier*] (ICLI)
LIRS	Lance Information Retrieval System
LIRS	Laser Inertial Reference System (SAUS)
LIRS	Legal Information and Reference Services [*General Accounting Office*] (IID)
LIRS	Level Indicator Recording Switch (NRCH)
LIRS	Library Information Retrieval Service [*Oregon State University*] [*Information service or system*]
LIRS	Library Information Retrieval System [*California Institute of Technology*] [*Pasadena, CA*]
LIRS	Low Impact Resistant Supports [*FAA*] (TAG)
LIRS	Lutheran Immigration and Refugee Service (EA)
LIRS	Texto Refundido del Impuesto General sobre la Renta de las Sociedades (SAUO)
LIRSH	List of Items Requiring Special Handling
LIRT	Library Instruction Round Table [*American Library Association*]
LIRT	Low Input Reduced Tillage [*Cropping systems*] (GNE)
LIRT	Trevico [*Italy*] [*ICAO location identifier*] (ICLI)
LIRTS	Large Infrared Telescope
LIRU	Roma/Urbe [*Italy*] [*ICAO location identifier*] (ICLI)
LIRV	Viterbo [*Italy*] [*ICAO location identifier*] (ICLI)
LIRZ	Perugia [*Italy*] [*ICAO location identifier*] (ICLI)
LIS	Airlis SA [*Spain*] [*ICAO designator*] (FAAC)
LIS	Laboratory Information Systems
LIS	Laboratory Integrated System (ACAE)
LIS	Land Information System (ACAE)
LIS	Land Inventory System (SAUO)
LIS	Landsat Information System (SAUO)
LIS	Language Implementation System (IAA)
LIS	Lanthanide-Induced Shift [*Spectroscopy*]
LIS	Lanthanide-Ion Induced Chemical Shift [*Spectroscopy*]
LIS	LARC Instruction Simulator
LIS	Large Interactive Surface [*Automated drafting table that serves as a computer input and output device*]
LIS	Laser Ignition System [*Military*]
LIS	LASER Illuminator System
LIS	LASER-Induced Separation (MCD)
LIS	LASER Interferometer System
LIS	LASER Isotope Separation
LIS	Lateral Intercellular Space (PDAA)
LIS	Launch Instant Selector
LIS	Laurentide Ice Sheet [*Climatology*]
LIS	Left Intercostal Space [*Cardiology*]
LIS	Legislative Information Service [*New Jersey State Legislature*] [*Trenton*] [*Information service or system*] (IID)
LIS	Legislative Information System [*National Conference of State Legislatures*] [*Information service or system*] (IID)
LIS	Lesbian Information Service (BUAC)
LIS	Libertarian Information Service [*An association*] (EA)
LIS	Library and Information Science
LIS	Library and Information Service
LIS	Library and Information Services [*Institution of Mining and Metallurgy*] [*British*] [*Information service or system*] (IID)
LIS	Library and Information Systems (SAUO)
LIS	Library Information System [*Georgetown University*] [*Information service or system*]
lis	licensed (SAUS)
LIS	Licensing Information Service (IID)
LIS	Licensure Information System [*Public Health Service*] [*Georgetown University Medical Center*] (IID)
LIS	Light Industries Services [*Singapore*] (BUAC)
LIS	Light Industry Services (SAUO)
LIS	Lightning Imaging Sensor (CARB)
LIS	Line Information Store [*Telecommunications*] (TEL)
LIS	Line Isolation Switch [*Reactor level switch*] (IEEE)
LIS	Link Information Sciences (BUR)
LIS	Liposome Immunosensor [*Electrochemistry*]
LIS	Lisbon [*Portugal*] [*Airport symbol*] (OAG)
LIS	Lisbon [*Portugal*] [*Seismograph station code, US Geological Survey*] (SEIS)
LIS	List and Index Society [*British*] (NITA)
LIS	Lithium Diodosalicylate [*Organic chemistry*]
LIS	Lithium Ion Storage (SAUS)
LIS	LM [*Lunar Module*] Interface Control Specification [*NASA*] (KSC)
LIS	Load I-Bank and Jump [*Computer science*]
LIS	Lobular in Situ [*Medicine*]
LIS	Local Implementation Strategy (SAUO)
LIS	Local Interface Station (TIMI)
LIS	Locate in Scotland [*Investment group*] (ECON)
LIS	Locked-in Syndrome [*Medicine*] (MELL)
LIS	Lockheed Information Systems (NITA)
LIS	Logistic Information System (VLIE)
LIS	Logistics Information System (SAUO)
LIS	Loop Input Signal
LIS	Loss Information Service [*Insurance*]
LIS	Low-Impact Switch (MCD)
LIS	Low Inductance Stripline (IAA)
LIS	Low-Intensity Sonication [*Chemistry*]
LIS	Low Intermittent Suction [*Medicine*] (MEDA)
LIS	Low Ionic Strength (DB)
LIS	Lutheran Immigration Service [*Later, LIRS*] (EA)
LIS	Luxembourg Income Study [*Economics*]
LISA	Laboratory for Information Science in Agriculture [*Research center*] [*Defunct*] (RCD)
LISA	Land Information System for Agriculture (SAUO)
LISA	LARC Instruction Assembly
LISA	Large Installations Systems Administration (SAUO)
LISA	Large Installation Systems Administration (VLIE)
LISA	LASER Indirect Fire Semiactive
LISA	Laser Interferometer Space Antenna (SAUS)
LISA	Lateral Integrated Silicon Accelerometer
LISA	Lead-in-Steel Analyser (PDAA)
LISA	Leather Industry Suppliers Associates [*British*] (DBA)
LISA	Leather Industry Suppliers Association (BUAC)
LISA	Library & Science Abstracts
LISA	Library Systems Analysis
LISA	Licht Sammler [*Light Collector*] [*Fluorescent plastic used in commercial displays*] [*German*]
LISA	Life Insurance Society of America (EA)
LISA	Linear Systems Analysis
LISA	Linear Systems Analysis Programme (SAUO)
LISA	Line Impedance Stabilization Network
LISA	Linked Indexed Sequential Access
LISA	Linux Installation & System Administration (SAUS)
LISA	Locally Integrated Software Architecture [*Apple microcomputer*] [*Computer science*]
LISA	Logistics Information Systems Analysis (SAUO)
LISA	London and International School of Acting [*British*]
LISA	Long Island Schizophrenia Association (SAUO)
LISA	Low-Input Sustainable Agriculture
LISA	Seaman Apprentice, Lithographer, Striker [*Navy rating*]
LISAN	Librarians on the Information Superhighway Advocacy Network (AL)
LISAN	Libraries on the Information Superhighway Advocacy Network (TELE)
LISARD	Latest Information Selected and Abstracted for Researchers and Decision-Makers [*Database*]

LISARD........ Library and Information Service Automated Retrieval of Data (NITA)
LISARD........ Library Information Search and Retrieval Data System [*US Navy*] (NITA)
LISARDS...... Library Information Search and Retrieval Data System (VLIE)
LISB............ Lithium Ion Storage Battery (PCM)
LISB............ Long Island Bancorp [*NASDAQ symbol*] (TTSB)
LISB............ Long Island Bancorp, Inc. [*NASDAQ symbol*] (SAG)
LISBMS....... Laboratory Integrated Standards Based Management System (SAUO)
Lisbon Union... Union for the Protection of Appellations of Origin and their International Registration (SAUO)
LISC............ Land Information Strategic Council (SAUO)
LISC............ Land Information System Committee (SAUO)
LISC............ Library and Information Services Council [*British*]
LISC............ Lions International Stamp Club (EA)
LISC............ Local Initiatives Support Corp. (EA)
LISC............ London Institute for the Study of Conflict (SAUO)
LIS/CIV........ Logistics Information System/Critical Item Visibility Systems (SAUO)
LISCO.......... Liberian Iron and Steel Corp. (BUAC)
LISD............ Latest Information Selected and Abstracted for Researchers and Decision-Makers [*Database*]
LISD............ Library and Information Services Division [*National Oceanic and Atmospheric Administration*] (NITA)
LISD............ Logistics Information Systems Division (SAUO)
LISDOK........ Literaturinformationssystem [*Literature Information System*] [*North Rhine-Westphalia Institute for Air Pollution Control*] [*Information service or system*] (IID)
LISDP.......... LOAD [*Low-Altitude Defense*] Interceptor Subsystem Development Plan
LISE............ Laser Integrated Space Experiment (ACAE)
LISE............ Librarians of Institutes and Schools of Education [*British*] (DBA)
LISFA.......... Lost in Space Fannish Alliance (EA)
LISFAN........ Lost in Space Fannish Alliance (EA)
LISH............ Last In, Still Here [*Accounting*] (ADA)
LISI............ Library Interface Systems, Inc. [*Information service or system*] (IID)
LISIC.......... Library and Information Service to Industry and Commerce (NITA)
LISK............ Liskeard [*Municipal borough in England*]
LISL............ Amsterdam Studies in the Theory and History of Linguistic Science. Series V. Library and Information Sources in Linguistics (journ.) (SAUS)
LISI............ Library Interface Systems, Incorporated (SAUO)
LISM............ Licentiate, Institute of Sales and Marketing Executives (ADA)
LISM............ Licentiate of Incorporated Society of Musicians (SAUO)
LISM............ Licentiate of the Incorporated Society of Musicians (ROG)
LISM............ Local Interstellar Medium
LISN............ Library Services Network [*Library network*]
LISN............ Line Impedance Stabilization Network
LISN............ Load Impedance Stabilization Network [*Electrical engineering*]
LISN............ Long Island Sports Network [*Cable-television system*]
LISN............ Seaman, Lithographer, Striker [*Navy rating*]
LISNY.......... Life Insurance Society of New York (SRA)
LISP............ LASER Isotope Separation Program
LISP............ Library and Information Software Package (PDAA)
LISP............ Lightweight Individual Special Purpose [*Weaponry*]
LISP............ Liquid Injector Spray Pattern (MCD)
LISP............ List-Oriented Processing [*Computer science*] (VLIE)
LISP............ List Processing [*Programming language*] [*Facetious translation: "Lots of Insane, Stupid Parentheses"*] [*Computer science*]
LISP............ List Processor [*Standard programming language*] [*1958*] [*Computer science*]
LISP............ Local Initiatives Support Project (VLIE)
LISP............ Lots of Irritating Superfluous (SAUO)
LISP............ Lots of Isolated Silly Parentheses (SAUS)
LISPA.......... Long Island Sound Pilots Association (SAUO)
LISPB.......... Lithospheric Seismic Profile in Britain (PDAA)
LISPER........ Limited Speech Recognition (PDAA)
LISR............ Line Information Storage and Retrieval [*Information service or system*] (NITA)
LISRB.......... Life Insurance Sales Research Bureau [*Later, LIMRA*]
LISREL........ Linear Structural Relationships (NITA)
LISRES-A..... Life Stressors and Social Resources Inventory-Adult Form [*Test*] (TMMY)
LISRES-Y..... Life Stressors and Social Resources Inventory Youth-Form [*Test*] (TMMY)
LI SRR........ Lithuanian Soviet Socialist Republic (SAUO)
LISS............ Laser Illuminator Subsystem (ACAE)
LISS............ Lightweight Integrated Shelter System (DWSG)
LISS............ Linear/Imaging Self-Scanner Sensor (MCD)
LISS............ London Institute of Strategic Studies (SAUO)
LISS............ Los-Ionic-Strength Saline Solution [*Medicine*] (MEDA)
LISS............ Low-Ionic-Strength Saline [*Medicine*] (DMAA)
LISSADA...... Library and Information Science Students Attitudes, Demographics, and Aspirations Survey [*American Libraries Association*]
LISST.......... Laser In Situ Scattering and Transmissometery (SAUS)
LISST.......... Library and Information Scholarship Today [*A publication*]
LIST............ Last In, Still There [*Accounting*]
LIST............ Library and Information Science Trends
LIST............ Library & Information Selective Targeting (WDAA)
LIST............ Library and Information Services, Tees-Side (IEEE)
LIST............ Library and Information Services Today [*A publication*]
LIST............ Library Index Search and Transcribe
LIST............ List-Oriented Interactive Language [*Computer science*] (TIMI)
LIST............ Low Isotonic Strength Titrator
LISTAR........ Lincoln Information Storage and Associative Retrieval System [*Lincoln Laboratory*] [*Massachusetts Institute of Technology*] (NITA)

LISTAR .... Lincoln Information Storage and Retrieval [*MIT*]
LISTD.......... Licentiate of the Imperial Society of Teachers of Dancing [*British*]
LISTED........ Library Integrated Systems for Telematics-Based Education (TELE)
LISTEN........ Low-Income-Schools Teacher Education (SAUO)
LISTS.......... Library Information System Time-Sharing
LISTSERV ... Apparently, the term is a registered trademark licensed to L-Soft international, Inc. (SAUO)
LISTSERV ... List Server [*Computer science*] (VLIE)
LISU............ Library and Information Statistics Unit (AIE)
LISV............ Loyal Independent Sheffield Volunteers [*British military*] (DMA)
LISW............ Licensed Independent Social Worker (ADWA)
LISWG .... Land Interface Sub-Working Group [*NATO*] (NATG)
LIT .... Adams Field [*FAA*] (TAG)
LIT .... Air Littoral [*France*] [*ICAO designator*] (FAAC)
LIT .... Language Imitation Test
LIT .... Language Inventory for Teachers [*Child development test*]
LIT .... Lawrence Institute of Technology [*Later, Lawrence Technological University*]
LIT .... Lead-In Training [*Air Force*] (DOMA)
LIT .... Leukocyte Immunization Therapy [*Medicine*]
LIT .... Librarians Inquiry Terminal (IT)
Lit .... Lietuvos TSR Valstybine Respublikine Biblioteka [*National Library of Lithuania*], Vilnius, Lithuania [*Library symbol*] [*Library of Congress*] (LCLS)
LIT .... Life Insurance Trust (DLA)
LIT .... Light Interface Technology [*Signal transmission*]
LIT .... Light Intratheater Transport [*Air Force*]
LIT .... Light Ion Trough
LIT .... Line Insulation Test [*Telecommunications*]
LIT .... Liquid Injection Technique (IEEE)
Lit .... Lire Italiane [*Italian Lire*] [*Monetary unit*]
lit .... Litany (GROV)
LIT .... Liter [*Metric measure of volume*]
LIT .... Literacy
lit .... Literal (ELAL)
LIT .... Literal
lit .... Literally (ELAL)
Lit .... Literary (WA)
LIT .... Literary
Lit .... Literature (AL)
lit .... Literature (WDMC)
LIT .... Literature
lit .... Lithuanian [*MARC language code*] [*Library of Congress*] (LCCP)
LIT .... Lithuanian Apostolate for Lithuanian Catholics [*Diocesan abbreviation*] (TOCD)
Lit .... Littell's Kentucky Reports [*A publication*] (DLA)
LIT .... Litter (WDAA)
LIT .... Litterae [*Letters*] [*Latin*] (ADA)
Lit .... Little
LIT .... Little Rock [*Arkansas*] [*Airport symbol*] (OAG)
Lit .... Littleton's English Common Pleas Reports [*A publication*] (DLA)
Lit .... Littleton's Tenures [*A publication*] (DLA)
LIT .... Litton Indus [*NYSE symbol*] (TTSB)
LIT .... Litton Industries, Inc. [*NYSE symbol*] (SPSG)
LIT .... Liturgy
LIT .... Load Initial Table [*Computer science*] (ELAL)
LIT .... Local Inclusive Tour (DCTA)
LIT .... Local Income Tax (PDAA)
LIT .... Local Information Transfer (SAUO)
LIT .... Location/Identification Transmitter [*NASA*]
LIT .... Logical Interface Tape (VLIE)
LIT .... London Investment Trust [*British*]
LIT .... Low-Impedance Transmission
LITA............ Library and Information Technology Association (EA)
LITA............ LIbrary and Information Technology Associaton of the ALA (NITA)
LITA............ Local Information Transfer Architecture (SAUO)
LITACS........ Lightweight Integrated Tactical Artillery Command & Control System (SAUO)
LITADLIG ..... Library & Information Technology Associaton Distance Learning Interest Group
LITAEPEJIG... Library & Information Technology Association Electronic Publishing/Electronic Journals Interest Group
LITAETIG...... Library & Information Technology Association Emerging Technologies Interest Group
LITAIRIG...... Library & Information Technology Association Internet Resources Interest Group
LITA/ISAS .... Library and Information Technology Association/Information Science and Automation Section (SAUO)
LITAMUIG .... Library & Information Technology Association Microcomputer Users Interest Group
Lit & BI Dig... Littleton and Blatchley's Insurance Digest [*A publication*] (DLA)
LITAOSSIG... Library & Information Technology Association Open Source Systems Interest Group
LITAS.......... Low Intensity Two-Color Approach Slope Indicator [*Aviation*] (DA)
LITASSIG...... Library & Information Technology Association Secure Systems Interest Group
LITASTOR..... Light Tapping Storage (IAA)
LITATIG........ Library & Information Technology Association Telecommunications Interest Group
LITA/VCCS ... Library and Information Technology Association/Video and Cable Communication-Section (SAUO)
Lit B............ Bachelor of Literature (SAUS)
Lit B............ Litterarum Baccalaureus [*Bachelor of Letters or Literature*] [*Latin*]
LITBIEL........ Lithuania & Byelorussia (SAUS)

Lit Brooke....	Brooke's New Cases, English King's Bench [1515-58] [A publication] (DLA)
LITC	Library Information Technology Centre [British] (TELE)
LITCA	International Licensing, Innovation and Technology Consultants Association (SAUO)
LITCA	Licensing Innovation Technology Consultants Association (BUAC)
LitchFin	Litchfield Financial Corp. [Associated Press] (SAG)
LITCO	Lebanese International Trading Company (SAUO)
LITCO	Lockheed Idaho Technologies Company (SAUO)
Lit Crit	Literary Criticism (ADWA)
Lit D	Doctor of Literature (SAUS)
LITD	Laser-Induced Thermal Desorption
Lit D	Litterarum Doctor [Doctor of Letters or Literature] [Latin]
LITDL	Link-16 Interoperable Tactical Data Link (SAUS)
LitDokAB	Literaturdokumentation zur Arbeitsmarkt- und Berufsforschung [Deutsche Bundesanstalt fuer Arbeit] [Germany] [Information service or system] (CRD)
LITE	BMC International Corp. (SAUO)
LITE	Laptop Imagery Transmission System (SAUS)
LITE	LASER Illuminator Targeting Equipment
LITE	Laser Infrared Tracking Experiment (ACAE)
LITE	LASER In-Space Technology Experiment
LITE	Legal Information Through Electronics [Air Force]
LITE	Let's Improve Today's Education [Newsletter]
LITE	Lidar In-Space Technology Experiment (EOSA)
Litelfuse	Littelfuse, Inc. [Associated Press] (SAG)
LITES	Ladies in Technical Electronic Servicing (SAUO)
LITES	LASER Initiated Transfer Energy Subsystem [Detonator, developed by US Navy]
LITES	LASER Intercept and Technical Exploitation System (MCD)
LITEX	Searchlight Illumination Exercise [Also, LIGHTEX] [Military] (NVT)
LITFASS	Lindenberg Inhomogeneous Terrain, Fluxes between Atmosphere and Surface (SAUS)
LitfldAd	Littlefield, [Adams] & Co. [Associated Press] (SAG)
Litfse	Littelfuse, Inc. [Associated Press] (SAG)
LITFUND	Fund for the Relief of Russian Writers and Scientists in Exile (EA)
litg	Liturgy (VRA)
LITH	Lithium [Pharmacy] (DAVI)
LITH	Lithograph [or Lithography] (ROG)
lith	Lithograph (WDMC)
lith	Lithographic (WDMC)
lith	Lithography (WDMC)
LITH	Lithuania (ROG)
Lith	Lithuania (VRA)
LITH	Lithuanian [Language, etc.]
LITH BRO	Lithium Bromide (DNAB)
LITHD	Lithographed (ROG)
LITHO	Lithograph (AABC)
litho	Lithograph (VRA)
litho	Lithographic (WDMC)
litho	Lithography (WDMC)
litho	Lithotripsy [Medicine] (DAVI)
LITHOC	Lithographic
lithog	Lithograph (WDMC)
lithog	Lithographic (WDMC)
LITHOG	Lithographing
lithog	Lithography (WDMC)
LITHOG	Lithography
lithol	Lithology (BARN)
LITHOR	Lithographer
LITHOT	Lithotomy [Medicine]
LITHOY	Lithography
LITHP	Link Type Description Language for Hypertext Processing [Computer science] (VLIE)
LithSSR	Lithuanian Soviet Socialist Republic
LITHUAN	Lithuanian
Lit Hum	Literae Humaniores [Faculty of Classics and Philosophy, Oxford] [British] (WA)
LIT HUM	Litterae Humaniores [Classic literature] [Latin] (ROG)
Litig	Litigation [A publication] (DLA)
LITIGON	Litigation (ROG)
LITINT	Literacy International
LITINT	Literature Intelligence (MCD)
LITIR	Literary Information and Retrieval [Computer science]
LITIR	Literature Information and Retrieval [Database on Victorian studies literature] [University of Alberta] [Canada] (NITA)
LIT-LIT	Committee on World Literacy and Christian Literature [Later, Intermedia] (EA)
LITM	London International Trade Market (SAUO)
Lit M	Master of Literature
LitMo	Liturgie und Moenchtum [A publication] (BJA)
LITP	Ley del Impuesto sobre Transmisiones Patrimoniales y Actos Juridicos Documentados (SAUO)
LITPrB	Litton Indus.,$2 B Pfd [NYSE symbol] (TTSB)
Litprog	Literate Programming [Computer science] (VLIE)
LITR	Low-Cost Indirect-Fire Training Round [Army] (INF)
LITR	Low-Intensity Test Reactor [ORNL]
LITS	Laboratory for Information Transmission Systems (SAUO)
LITS	Light Interface Technology System (SAUO)
LITS	Local Information Transfer System (SAUO)
LITS	Logistics Information Technology Strategy (SAUO)
Lit Sel Ca	Littell's Select Kentucky Cases [A publication] (DLA)
LITSUR	Litigation Survey System (SAUO)
Litt	Littell's Kentucky Supreme Court Reports [1822-24] [A publication] (DLA)
LITT	Litterateur [French] (ROG)
Litt	Littleton's English Common Pleas Reports [A publication] (DLA)
Litt & S St Law	Littell and Swigert's Digest of Statute Law [Kentucky] [A publication] (DLA)
LittB	Bachelor of Letters or Literature (SAUO)
Litt B	Litterarum Baccalaureus [Bachelor of Letters or Literature] [Latin]
Litt Comp Laws	Littell's Statute Law [Kentucky] [A publication] (DLA)
LittD	Doctor of Letters (SAUO)
LittD	Doctor of Literature (SAUO)
Litt D	Litterarum Doctor [Doctor of Letters or Literature] [Latin]
LittD(Econ)	Doctor of Letters in Economic Studies (ADA)
Litteli	Littell's Kentucky Reports [A publication] (DLA)
LittHD	Doctor of Hebrew Letters (BJA)
Litt (KY)	Littell [Kentucky] [A publication] (DLA)
Litt L	Licentiate in Letters
Little Brooke	Brooke's New Cases, English King's Bench [1515-58] [A publication] (DLA)
Littleton	Littleton's English Common Pleas and Exchequer Reports [A publication] (DLA)
Litt M	Master of Letters
Litton	Litton Industries, Inc. [Associated Press] (SAG)
Litt Rep	Littleton's English Common Pleas and Exchequer Reports [A publication] (DLA)
LITTS	Large Inventory Top-Tier Site [Industrial hazard designation] [British]
Litt Sel Cas	Littell's Select Kentucky Cases [A publication] (DLA)
LITTT	Luoyang Institute of Tracking and Telecommunication Technology [China] (BUAC)
Litt Ten	Littleton's Tenures [A publication] (DLA)
LITTY	Libraries of Idaho Teletype Network - Academics [Library network]
Litur Arts	Liturgical Arts. Liturgical Arts Society. Concord, New Hampshire (SAUO)
Liturg	Liturgical (DIAR)
LITURG	Liturgies (ROG)
LITVC	Liquid Injection Thrust Vector Control
LITW	Longitudinally in Homogeneous Traveling Waves (MCD)
LITZ	Litzendraht [Wire] [German]
LIU	LAN Interface Unit (SAUS)
LIU	Launcher Interface Unit (SAUS)
LIU	Library and Information Unit
LIU	Line Interface Unit [Data communications]
LIU	Line Isolation Unit [Electronics]
LIU	Link Interface Unit [Telecommunications] (ECII)
LIU	Littlefield, TX [Location identifier] [FAA] (FAAL)
LIU	Long Island University [Brooklyn, NY]
LIU	Wood, Wire, and Metal Lathers' International Union [Later, UBC]
LIUNA	Laborers' International Union of North America (EA)
LIUP	Long Island University Press (DGA)
Liuski	Liuski International, Inc. [Associated Press] (SAG)
LIV	Law of Initial Value [Joseph Wilder]
LIV	Left Innominate Vein [Medicine] (MAE)
LIV	Legislative Indexing Vocabulary
LIV	Light Infantry Volunteers [Military unit] [British]
LIV	Linear, Invariant (PDAA)
LIV	Line Item Value
LIV	Lived [or Living]
LIV	Livengood, AK [Location identifier] [FAA] (FAAL)
LIV	Liver Battery Test [Gastroenterology] (DAVI)
LIV	Liverpool (ROG)
Liv	Liverpool University (SAUO)
LIV	Living (DAVI)
LIV	Livingstone Energy [Vancouver Stock Exchange symbol]
Liv	Livingston's Mayor's Court Reports [New York] [A publication] (DLA)
LIV	Livorno [Italy] [Seismograph station code, US Geological Survey] [Closed] (SEIS)
LIV	Livraison [Delivery] [French]
LIV	Livre [Book or Pound] [French]
LIV	Livy [Roman historian, c. 10BC] (ROG)
LIV	Low-Input Voltage (KSC)
LIV	Low Investment Vehicle
LIV	Lunar and Interplanetary Vehicle [Aerospace] (AFM)
Liv Ag	Livermore on Principal and Agent [A publication] (DLA)
LIVB	Passo Del Brennero [Italy] [ICAO location identifier] (ICLI)
LIV-BP	Leucine, Isoleucine, and Valine Binding Protein [Biochemistry] (DMAA)
LIVC	Low-Input Voltage Converter
LIVC	Monte Cimone [Italy] [ICAO location identifier] (ICLI)
Liv Cas	Livingston's Cases in Error [New York] [A publication] (DLA)
LIVCR	Low-Input Voltage Conversion and Regulation
LIVD	Dobbiaco [Italy] [ICAO location identifier] (ICLI)
Liv Dis	Livermore's Dissertation on the Contrariety of Laws [A publication] (DLA)
LIVE	Learning through Industry and Voluntary Educators [Community education program]
LIVE	Liquid Inertia Vibration Eliminator (SAUS)
LIVE	Live Entertainment [NASDAQ symbol] (TTSB)
LIVE	Lunar Impact Vehicle [NASA] (KSC)
LIVE	Passo Resia [Italy] [ICAO location identifier] (ICLI)
LiveEn	LIVE Entertainment, Inc. [Associated Press] (SAG)
LiveEnt	LIVE Entertainment, Inc. [Associated Press] (SAG)
Livent	Livent, Inc. [Associated Press] (SAG)
LIVEP	Live Entmt cm Cv'B' Pfd [NASDAQ symbol] (TTSB)
Liverm Ag	Livermore on Principal and Agent [A publication] (DLA)
Livermore Ag	Livermore on Principal and Agent [A publication] (DLA)
LIVEX	Live Exercise [Military exercise in which live forces participate] (NATG)

LIVF............ Frontone [Italy] [ICAO location identifier] (ICLI)
LIVG............ Monte Grappa [Italy] [ICAO location identifier] (ICLI)
LIVID .... Language Identification and Voice Identification (SAUS)
Livingston U... Livingston University (GAGS)
Liv Jud Cas... Livingston's Judicial Opinions [New York] [A publication] (DLA)
Liv Judic Op... Livingston's Judicial Opinions [New York] [A publication] (DLA)
Liv Jud Op... Livingston's Judicial Opinions [New York] [A publication] (DLA)
Liv La Cr Code... Livingston's Louisiana Criminal Code [A publication] (DLA)
Liv Law Mag... Livingston's Law Magazine [New York] [A publication] (DLA)
Liv L Mag.... Livingston's Law Magazine [New York] [A publication] (DLA)
Liv L Reg.... Livingston's Law Register [New York] [A publication] (DLA)
LIVM.......... Marino Di Ravenna [Italy] [ICAO location identifier] (ICLI)
LivngCtr....... Living Centers of America, Inc. [Associated Press] (SAG)
LIVO.......... Tarvisio [Italy] [ICAO location identifier] (ICLI)
LIVP.......... Paganella [Italy] [ICAO location identifier] (ICLI)
LIVR .... Low-Input Voltage Regulation
LIVR.......... Passo Rolle [Italy] [ICAO location identifier] (ICLI)
liv rm.......... Living Room (BARN)
livrm.......... Living Room (REAL)
LIVT............ Trieste [Italy] [ICAO location identifier] (ICLI)
Liv US Pen Co... Livingston's System of United States Penal Codes [A publication] (DLA)
LIVV.......... Monte Venda [Italy] [ICAO location identifier] (ICLI)
LIW.......... Letters in Words [Psychology]
LIW.......... Lightweight Individual Weapon (PDAA)
LIW.......... Loikaw [Myanmar] [Airport symbol] (OAG)
LIW.......... Long Instruction Word [Teraplex] [Computer science]
LIW.......... Loss in Weight
LIW.......... Lyttleton Engineering Works (SAUO)
LIWAP........ Low-Income Weatherization Assistance Program (SAUO)
LIWB.......... Livermore Water Boiler [Nuclear reactor] [Dismantled]
LIWMS........ Laura Ingalls Wilder Memorial Society (EA)
LIX.......... Liquid Crystal (IDOE)
LIXISCOPE... Low-Intensity X-Ray Imaging Scope
LIY.......... Leicestershire Imperial Yeomanry [British military] (DMA)
LIY.......... Limay [Nicaragua] [Seismograph station code, US Geological Survey] (SEIS)
LIYP.......... Legacy International Youth Program [Later, LIYTP] (EA)
LIYTP.......... Legacy International Youth Training Program (EA)
LIYV.......... Lettuce Infectious Yellows Virus
LIYW.......... Aviano [Italy] [ICAO location identifier] (ICLI)
LIZ.......... Limestone, ME [Location identifier] [FAA] (FAAL)
LIZ.......... Lizard (MSA)
LIZ.......... Liz Claiborne [NYSE symbol] (TTSB)
LIZ.......... Liz Claiborne, Inc. [NYSE symbol] (SAG)
LIZARDS..... Library Information Search and Retrieval Data System (IEEE)
Lizars.......... Lizar's Scotch Exchequer Cases [A publication] (DLA)
LIZC.......... Liz Claiborne, Inc. (SAUO)
LizClab.......... Claiborne [Liz], Inc. [Associated Press] (SAG)
LIZ EI.......... London Initiative Zone Educational Incentives (SAUO)
Liz Sc Exch... Lizar's Scotch Exchequer Cases [A publication] (DLA)
LJ.......... British Guiana Limited Jurisdiction (Official Gazette) [1899-1955] [A publication] (DLA)
LJ.......... Hall's American Law Journal [A publication] (DLA)
LJ.......... House of Lords Journals [England] [A publication] (DLA)
LJ.......... Jennings Public Library, Jennings, LA [Library symbol] [Library of Congress] (LCLS)
LJ.......... Joullie [France] [Research code symbol]
LJ.......... Larsen-Johansson [Disease] [Medicine] (DB)
LJ.......... Law Journal Newspaper [1866-1965] [A publication]
LJ.......... Law Judge (DLA)
LJ.......... Lawson & Jones Ltd. [Toronto Stock Exchange symbol]
LJ.......... Left Justified (TIMI)
LJ.......... Lennard-Jones [Physical chemistry]
LJ.......... Library Journal [A publication] (BRI)
LJ.......... Life Jacket
LJ.......... Limited Partner in Jobbers Firm [London Stock Exchange]
LJ.......... Line Judge [Football]
LJ.......... Little Joe [Early developmental spacecraft] [NASA]
LJ.......... Little John [Rocket] [Military] (AABC)
LJ.......... Lockjaw (MELL)
LJ.......... Long Jump
LJ.......... Lord Justice
L-J.......... Lowenstein-Jensen [Growth medium]
L-J.......... Lower Canada Law Journal [A publication] (DLA)
LJ.......... Ohio State Law Journal (SAUS)
LJ.......... Sierra Leone Airways [ICAO designator] (AD)
LJ.......... University of California, San Diego, La Jolla (SAUO)
LJA.......... Lady Jockeys Association [British] (DBA)
LJA.......... Lodja [Zaire] [Airport symbol] (OAG)
LJA.......... London Jute Association [England] (BUAC)
LJA.......... Lord Justice of Appeal
L JaD.......... Dixon Correctional Institute, Jackson (SAUS)
LJaD.......... Dixon Correctional Institute, Jackson, LA [Library symbol] [Library of Congress] (LCLS)
LJ Adm........ Law Journal, New Series, Admiralty [A publication] (DLA)
LJ Adm NS... Law Journal Reports, Admiralty, New Series [1865-75] [A publication] (DLA)
LJ Adm NS (Eng)... Law Journal Reports, New Series, Admiralty [England] [A publication] (DLA)
LJ App......... Law Journal Reports, New Series, Appeals [A publication] (DLA)
LJ Bank ...... Law Journal Reports, Bankruptcy [A publication] (DLA)
LJ Bank NS... Law Journal Reports, New Series, Bankruptcy [A publication] (DLA)
LJ Bankr...... Law Journal Reports, Bankruptcy [A publication] (DLA)

LJ Bankr NS (Eng)... Law Journal Reports, New Series, Bankruptcy [England] [A publication] (DLA)
LJ Bcy .... Law Journal Reports, New Series, Bankruptcy [A publication] (DLA)
LJBF.......... Let's Just Be Friends [Online dialog]
LJ Bk.......... Law Journal Reports, Bankruptcy [A publication] (DLA)
LJC.......... Lackawanna Junior College (SAUO)
LJC.......... La Jolla [California] [Seismograph station code, US Geological Survey] [Closed] (SEIS)
LJC.......... Lamar Junior College (SAUO)
LJC.......... Laredo Junior College [Texas]
LJC.......... Lasell Junior College [Newton, MA]
LJC.......... Law Journal Reports, New Series, Common Pleas [England] [A publication] (DLA)
LJC.......... Lees Junior College [Jackson, KY]
LJC.......... Lincoln Junior College (SAUO)
LJC.......... London Joint Committee on Graduate and Student Engineers (SAUO)
LJC.......... London Juvenile Court (DAS)
LJC.......... Lord Jesus Christ (ROG)
LJC.......... Loretto Junior College [Kentucky]
LJC.......... Louisville, KY [Location identifier] [FAA] (FAAL)
LJCBDP........ Local Joint Control Boards for Dock Pilots (SAUO)
LJCC.......... Law Journal, County Courts Reporter [A publication] (DLA)
LJCC.......... Local Joint Consultative Committee [British] (DCTA)
LJCCA.......... Law Journal Newspaper, County Court Appeals [England] [A publication] (DLA)
LJCCR.......... Law Journal Reports, New Series, Crown Cases Reserved [England] [A publication] (DLA)
LJCCR (NS)... Law Journal Reports, New Series, Crown Cases Reserved [England] [A publication] (DLA)
LJ Ch.......... Law Journal Reports, New Series, Chancery [A publication] (DLA)
LJ Ch (Eng)... Law Journal Reports, New Series, Chancery [England] [A publication] (DLA)
LJ Ch NS (Eng)... Law Journal Reports, New Series, Chancery [England] [A publication] (DLA)
LJ Ch (OS)... Law Journal Reports, Chancery, Old Series [1822-31] [England] [A publication] (DLA)
LJCP.......... Law Journal Reports, Common Pleas Decisions [England] [A publication] (DLA)
LJCPD.......... Law Journal Reports, Common Pleas Decisions [England] [A publication] (DLA)
LJCP (Eng)... Law Journal Reports, Common Pleas Decisions [England] [A publication] (DLA)
LJCP NS ..... Law Journal Reports, Common Pleas Decisions, New Series [1831-75] [A publication] (DLA)
LJCP NS (Eng)... Law Journal Reports, Common Pleas, New Series [England] [A publication] (DLA)
LJCP (OS)... Law Journal Reports, Common Pleas, Old Series [England] [A publication] (DLA)
LJCRF.......... La Jolla Cancer Research Foundation [Research center] (RCD)
LJCS.......... Lord Justice Clerk of Scotland (DAS)
LJD.......... Doctor of Letters of Journalism
LJD & M...... Law Journal Reports, New Series, Divorce and Matrimonial [England] [A publication] (DLA)
LJDFC.......... Lacy J. Dalton Fan Club (EA)
LJE.......... Local Job Entry
LJ Ecc.......... Law Journal Reports, New Series, Ecclesiastical Cases [A publication] (DLA)
LJ Eccl......... Law Journal Reports, New Series, Ecclesiastical Cases [A publication] (DLA)
LJED.......... Large Jet Engine Department [NASA] (KSC)
LJeL.......... LaSalle Parish Library, Jena, LA [Library symbol] [Library of Congress] (LCLS)
LJ Eq.......... Law Journal Reports, Chancery, New Series [1831-1946] [A publication] (DLA)
LJEWU......... Lanka Jatika Estate Workers' Union [Ceylon National Estate Workers' Union]
LJ Ex.......... Law Journal Reports, New Series, Exchequer Division [England] [A publication] (DLA)
LJ Exch........ Law Journal Reports, New Series, Exchequer Division [England] [A publication] (DLA)
LJ Exch (Eng)... Law Journal Reports, New Series, Exchequer Division [England] [A publication] (DLA)
LJ Exch in Eq (Eng)... English Law Journal. Exchequer in Equity [A publication] (DLA)
LJ Exch NS... Law Journal Reports, New Series, Exchequer [1831-75] [A publication] (DLA)
LJ Exch NS (Eng)... Law Journal Reports, New Series, Exchequer Division [England] [A publication] (DLA)
LJ Exch (OS)... Law Journal Reports, Exchequer, Old Series [A publication] (DLA)
LJ Ex D....... Law Journal Reports, New Series, Exchequer Division [England] [A publication] (DLA)
LJ Ex Eq....... Law Journal, Exchequer in Equity [England] [A publication] (DLA)
LJFC.......... Leon Jordan Fan Club (EA)
LJG.......... Leading Jewelers Guild (NTPA)
LJG.......... Levend Joods Geloof (Liberaal Joodse Gemeente) (BJA)
LJG.......... Lord Justice General [British]
LJHL.......... Law Journal Reports, New Series, House of Lords [England] [A publication] (DLA)
LJI.......... Legal Journals Index [Information service or system] (IID)
LJI.......... Library of Jewish Information (BJA)
LJI.......... List of Journals Indexed (DMAA)
LJI.......... List of Journals Indexed in Index Medicus (SAUO)
LJIF.......... Ludmila Jivkova International Foundation (SAUO)
LJIFS.......... Law Journal, Irish Free State [1931-32] [A publication] (DLA)
LJ Ir.......... Law Journal, Irish [1933-34] [A publication] (DLA)

LJJ.............. Jefferson Davis Parish Library, Jennings, LA [*Library symbol*] [*Library of Congress*] (LCLS)
LJJ.............. Long Josephson Junction (ACAE)
LJJ.............. Lords Justices
LJK.............. Ashland, VA [*Location identifier*] [*FAA*] (FAAL)
LJKB............ Law Journal Reports, King's Bench [*A publication*] (DLA)
LJKB (Eng)... Law Journal Reports, King's Bench [*England*] [*A publication*] (DLA)
LJKB NS...... Law Journal Reports, King's Bench, New Series [*A publication*] (DLA)
LJKB NS (Eng)... Law Journal Reports, King's Bench, New Series [*England*] [*A publication*] (DLA)
LJKB OS...... Law Journal, King's Bench, Old Series [*England*] [*A publication*] (DLA)
LJL.............. Lateral Joint Line [*Orthopedics*] (DAVI)
LJL.............. Little John Launcher [*Military*]
LJLC............ Law Journal (Lower Canada) [*A publication*] (DLA)
LJLT............ Law Journal (Law Tracts) [*A publication*] (DLA)
LJLV............ Little Joe Launch Vehicle [*NASA*]
LJM............. Limited Joint Mobility [*Medicine*] (DMAA)
LJM............. Lowenstein-Jensen Growth Medium (MAE)
LJ Mag....... Law Journal, New Series, Common Law, Magistrates Cases (Discontinued) [*A publication*] (DLA)
LJ Mag Cas... Law Journal Reports, Magistrates' Cases [*1822-31*] [*A publication*] (DLA)
LJ Mag Cas (Eng)... Law Journal Reports, Magistrates' Cases [*England*] [*A publication*] (DLA)
LJ Mag Cas NS... Law Journal Reports, Magistrates' Cases, New Series [*1831-96*] [*A publication*] (DLA)
LJ Mag Cas NS (Eng)... Law Journal Reports, Magistrates' Cases, New Series [*England*] [*A publication*] (DLA)
LJM & W..... Morgan and Williams' Law Journal [*London*] [*A publication*] (DLA)
LJ Mat........ Law Journal, Matrimonial [*England*] [*A publication*] (DLA)
LJ Mat Cas.. Law Journal, New Series, Divorce and Matrimonial [*England*] [*A publication*] (DLA)
LJ Mat (Eng)... Law Journal, Matrimonial [*England*] [*A publication*] (DLA)
LJMC........... Law Journal Reports, New Series, Magistrates' Cases [*England*] [*A publication*] (DLA)
LJMCA........ La Jolla Museum of Contemporary Art (SAUO)
LJM Cas...... Law Journal Reports, New Series, Magistrates' Cases [*England*] [*A publication*] (DLA)
LJMCOS...... Law Journal Reports, Old Series, Magistrates' Cases [*England*] [*A publication*] (DLA)
LJMPA........ Law Journal Reports, Matrimonial, Probate, and Admiralty [*England*] [*A publication*] (DLA)
LJN............. Lake Jackson [*Texas*] [*Airport symbol*] (OAG)
LJNC........... Law Journal, Notes of Cases [*A publication*] (DLA)
LJNCCA....... Law Journal Newspaper, County Court Appeals [*England*] [*A publication*] (DLA)
LJNCCR...... Law Journal Newspaper, County Court Reports [*England*] [*A publication*] (DLA)
LJNC (Eng)... Law Journal, Notes of Cases [*England*] [*A publication*] (DLA)
LJ News...... Law Journal Newspaper [*1866-1965*] [*A publication*] (DLA)
LJ News (Eng)... Law Journal Newspaper [*England*] [*A publication*] (DLA)
LJ Newsp..... Law Journal Newspaper [*1866-1965*] [*A publication*] (DLA)
LJ NS.......... Law Journal, New Series [*England*] [*A publication*] (DLA)
LJo.............. Jackson Parish Library, Jonesboro, LA [*Library symbol*] [*Library of Congress*] (LCLS)
L Jo............ Law Journal Newspaper [*England*] [*A publication*] (DLA)
LJ of the Marut Bunnag Internat L Off... Law Journal. Marut Bunnag International Law Office [*A publication*] (DLA)
L Jo NC...... Law Journal, Notes of Cases [*England*] [*A publication*] (DLA)
LJ OS......... Law Journal, Old Series [*1822-31*] [*London*] [*A publication*] (DLA)
LJ OS Ch..... Law Journal, Old Series, Chancery [*1822-23*] [*A publication*] (DLA)
LJ OS CP.... Law Journal, Old Series, Common Pleas [*1822-31*] [*A publication*] (DLA)
LJ OS Ex..... Law Journal, Old Series, Exchequer [*1830-31*] [*A publication*] (DLA)
LJ OS KB.... Law Journal, Old Series, King's Bench [*1822-31*] [*A publication*] (DLA)
LJOSMC...... Law Journal, Old Series, Magistrates' Cases [*1826-31*] [*A publication*] (ILCA)
LJP............. Law Journal Reports, New Series, Privy Council [*England*] [*A publication*] (DLA)
LJP............. Law Journal Reports, Probate, Divorce, and Admiralty [*England*] [*A publication*] (DLA)
LJP............. Liquid Junction Potential
LJP............. Localized Juvenile Periodontitis [*Dentistry*]
LJP............. Local Job Processing (IAA)
LJP & M...... Law Journal, Probate and Matrimonial [*England*] [*A publication*] (DLA)
LJPC........... La Jolla Pharmaceutical [*NASDAQ symbol*] (SAG)
LJPC........... Law Journal Reports, Privy Council [*England*] [*A publication*] (DLA)
LJ PC (Eng).. Law Journal Reports, Privy Council [*England*] [*A publication*] (DLA)
LJ PC NS.... Law Journal Reports, New Series, Privy Council [*England*] [*A publication*] (DLA)
LJPCW........ La Jolla Pharmaceutical Wrrt [*NASDAQ symbol*] (TTSB)
LJPD & A.... Law Journal Reports, New Series, Probate, Divorce, and Admiralty [*1875-1946*] [*A publication*] (DLA)
LJPD & Adm.. Law Journal Reports, New Series, Probate, Divorce, and Admiralty [*England*] [*A publication*] (DLA)
LJPM & A.... Law Journal Reports, New Series, Probate, Matrimonial, and Admiralty [*England*] [*A publication*] (DLA)
LJ Prob........ Law Journal Reports, New Series, Probate and Matrimonial [*1858-59, 1866-75*] [*A publication*] (DLA)
LJ Prob & Mat... Law Journal, Probate and Matrimonial [*England*] [*A publication*] (DLA)

LJ Prob (Eng)... Law Journal, Probate and Matrimonial [*England*] [*A publication*] (DLA)
LJ Prob NS... Law Journal Reports, New Series, Probate and Matrimonial [*1858-59, 1866-75*] [*A publication*] (DLA)
LJ Prob NS (Eng)... Law Journal, Probate and Matrimonial, New Series [*England*] [*A publication*] (DLA)
LJQB........... Law Journal Reports, New Series, Queen's Bench [*England*] [*A publication*] (DLA)
LJQBD......... Law Journal Reports, New Series, Queen's Bench Division [*England*] [*A publication*] (DLA)
LJQBD NS... Law Journal Reports, New Series, Queen's Bench Division [*England*] [*A publication*] (DLA)
LJQB (Eng)... Law Journal Reports, New Series, Queen's Bench [*England*] [*A publication*] (DLA)
LJQB NS...... Law Journal Reports, New Series, Queen's Bench [*1831-1946*] [*A publication*] (DLA)
LJQB NS (Eng)... Law Journal Reports, Queen's Bench, New Series [*England*] [*A publication*] (DLA)
LJR............. Law Journal Reports [*A publication*]
LJR............. Lead Joint Runner
LJR............. Little John Rocket [*Military*]
LJR............. Lone Jack Resources Ltd. [*Vancouver Stock Exchange symbol*]
LJR............. Low Jet Route (ADA)
LJR (Eng).... Law Journal Reports [*England*] [*A publication*] (DLA)
LJ Rep........ Law Journal Reports [*A publication*] (DLA)
LJ Rep NS... Law Journal Reports, New Series [*A publication*] (DLA)
LJRTC......... London Joint Road Transport Council (SAUO)
LJS............. Lap Joint Strength
LJS............. Lithuanian Journalists' Society (BUAC)
LJ Sm.......... Smith's Law Journal [*London*] [*A publication*] (DLA)
LJST........... Library of Japanese Science and Technology [*England*] (BUAC)
LJSU........... Local Junction Switching Unit [*Telecommunications*] (TEL)
LJTSA......... Library of the Jewish Theological Seminary of America (SAUO)
LJU............. La Jolla University (SAUO)
LJU............. Lithuanian Journalists' Union (BUAC)
LJU............. Ljubljana [*Slovenia*] [*Airport symbol*] (OAG)
LJU............. Ljubljana [*Slovenia*] [*Seismograph station code, US Geological Survey*] (SEIS)
LJU............. Oscoda, MI [*Location identifier*] [*FAA*] (FAAL)
LJUC.......... Law Journal of Upper Canada [*A publication*] (DLA)
LJWG.......... Logistic Joint Work Group [*DoD*]
LJZ............. Lajes [*Brazil*] [*Airport symbol*] (AD)
LK............... Arawak Airlines (OAG)
LK............... Laiko Komma [*Populist Party*] [*Greece*] [*Political party*] (PPE)
Lk............... Lake (SHCU)
LK............... Lake
LK............... Lamellar Keratoplasty [*Medicine*] (MELL)
LK............... Landry-Kussmaul [*Syndrome*] [*Medicine*] (DB)
LK............... Leak (KSC)
LK............... Left Kidney [*Medicine*]
LK............... Lek [*Monetary unit*] [*Albania*]
Lk............... Leptosphaeria korrea [*A fungus*]
LK............... Letaba Airways [*ICAO designator*] (AD)
LK............... Lichenoid Keratosis [*Medicine*] (DMAA)
LK............... Liederkranz [*Type of cheese*] (BJA)
L-K............. Linguistic-Kinesic [*Psychiatry*]
LK............... Link (KSC)
LK............... Lock [*Automotive engineering*]
LK............... Lockheed Aircraft Corp. (SAUO)
LK............... Lockheed Corp. (SAUO)
LK............... Loehr-Kindberg [*Syndrome*] [*Medicine*] (DB)
LK............... Looking for Party [*Telecommunications*] (TEL)
LK............... Lord Keeper [*of the Great Seal*] [*British*] (ROG)
LK............... Lowenfeld Kaleidoblocs [*Psychological testing*]
LK............... Low-Priority Key [*Computer science*]
LK............... Lucas Air Societies (SAUO)
Lk............... Luke [*New Testament book*]
LK............... Lymphokine [*Immunochemistry*]
LK............... Sri Lanka [*ANSI two-letter standard code*] (CNC)
LK1............. Ladies' Kayak, Single Person (ADA)
LK2............. Ladies' Kayak, Two Person (ADA)
LK4............. Ladies' Kayak, Four Person (ADA)
LKA............ Alkair Flight Operations APS [*Denmark*] [*ICAO designator*] (FAAC)
LKA............ Amphibious Cargo Ship [*Navy symbol*]
LKA............ Attack Cargo Ship [*Navy symbol*]
LKA............ Ladies Kennel Association [*British*] (BI)
LKA............ Larantuka [*Indonesia*] [*Airport symbol*] (OAG)
LKA............ Last Known Address (LAIN)
LKA............ Lazare-Klerman-Armour [*Personality inventory*] (STED)
LKA............ Lighthouse Keepers Association (EA)
LKA............ Literarische Keilschrifttexte aus Assur [*A publication*] (BJA)
LKA............ Miraloma, CA [*Location identifier*] [*FAA*] (FAAL)
LKA............ Sri Lanka [*ANSI three-letter standard code*] (CNC)
LKAA.......... Ladies Kennel Association of America (EA)
LKAA.......... Praha [*Former Czechoslovakia*] [*ICAO location identifier*] (ICLI)
LKAAAN....... Annual Report. Laboratory of Algology (journ.) (SAUS)
LK & PRR.... Lahaina-Kaanapali & Pacific Railroad [*Hawaii*]
LK&PRR....... Lahaina-Kaanapali & Pacific Railroad Co. (SAUO)
LKA of A...... Ladies Kennel Association of America (EA)
LKartB......... Landeskartellbehoerde [*Provincial Cartel Authority*] [*German*] (DLA)
LKB............ Lakeba [*Fiji*] [*Airport symbol*] (OAG)
LKB............ Lockwood, Kessler & Bartlett Inc. (SAUO)
LKBB.......... Bratislava [*Former Czechoslovakia*] [*ICAO location identifier*] (ICLI)
LKC............ Lake Chabot [*California*] [*Seismograph station code, US Geological Survey*] (SEIS)

LKC	Lake Charles [Diocesan abbreviation] [Louisiana] (TOCD)
LKC	Lancaster County Library, Lancaster, PA [OCLC symbol] (OCLC)
LKC	Lekana [Congo] [Airport symbol] (OAG)
Lkc	Leukocyte (MELL)
LKCL	LASER Kit Combination Lock
LKD	Locked (KSC)
LKDM	Low K Dielectric Material (AAEL)
LKDP	Lietuviu Krikscioniu Demokratu Partija [Lithuanian Christian Democratic Party] [Political party] (PPE)
LKED	Linkage Editor [Computer science] (CIST)
LKESTR	Leukocyte Esterase (STED)
LKF	Linear Kalman Filter
LKG	League of the Kingdom of God [Church of England]
LKG	Leakage (MSA)
LKG	Linking (IAA)
LKG	Locking (KSC)
LKG	Looking (MSA)
LKG	Loop Key Generator (MCD)
LKGABKG	Leakage and Breakage (IAA)
LKG & BKG	Leakage and Breakage (WDAA)
LKGE	Linkage (MSA)
LKGR	Lake Kyle Game Reserve (SAUO)
LKHO	Holesov [Former Czechoslovakia] [ICAO location identifier] (ICLI)
LKI	Duluth, MN [Location identifier] [FAA] (FAAL)
LKI	Lazare Kaplan International, Inc. [AMEX symbol] (SPSG)
LKI	Lazare Kaplan Intl [AMEX symbol] (TTSB)
LKI	Loki Gold Corp. [Vancouver Stock Exchange symbol]
LKIB	Bratislava/Ivanka [Former Czechoslovakia] [ICAO location identifier] (ICLI)
LKID	Left Kidney [Anatomy] (DAVI)
LKJ	Linton Kwesi Johnson [British musician]
LKK	Kulik Lake, AK [Location identifier] [FAA] (FAAL)
LKK	Lake Shore Mines Ltd. [Toronto Stock Exchange symbol]
LKK	Loka Kongresa Komitato (SAUO)
LKKS	Liver, Kidneys, and Spleen (STED)
LKKV	Karlovy Vary [Former Czechoslovakia] [ICAO location identifier] (ICLI)
LKKZ	Kosice [Former Czechoslovakia] [ICAO location identifier] (ICLI)
LKL	Lakeland Aviation [ICAO designator] (FAAC)
LKL	Lakselv [Norway] [Airport symbol] (OAG)
LKLF	Lung Kruppel-Like Factor [Immunology]
LKLY	Likely (FAAC)
LKM	Lafayette, LA [Location identifier] [FAA] (FAAL)
LKM	Liver-Kidney Microsomal [Antibody] [Medicine] (DMAA)
LKM	Locke Rich Minerals [Vancouver Stock Exchange symbol]
LKM	Low-Key Maintenance
LKM	Nekempt [Ethiopia] [Airport symbol] (AD)
LKMT	Ostrava [Former Czechoslovakia] [ICAO location identifier] (ICLI)
LKN	Leknes [Norway] [Airport symbol] (OAG)
LKN	Lock-In
LK-NDV	Newcastle Disease Virus, L-Kansas Strain
LKNPOS	Last Known Position (MCD)
LKNPT	Last Known Port (MCD)
LKNT	Locknut (MSA)
LKO	Billings, MT [Location identifier] [FAA] (FAAL)
LKO	Lucknow [India] [Airport symbol] (OAG)
LKP	Lake Placid, NY [Location identifier] [FAA] (FAAL)
LKP	Lamellar Keratoplasty [Ophthalmology]
LKP	Landelijke Knokplogen [Netherlands Regional Action Groups] [World War II]
LKP	Last Known Position [Aviation] (NVT)
LKP	Liberaalinen Kansanpuolue [Liberal People's Party] [Finland] [Political party] (PPE)
LKP	Lietuvos Komunisty Partija [Communist Party of Lithuania] [Political party] (PPE)
LKP	Local Knowledge Pool (SAUS)
LKPP	Piestany [Former Czechoslovakia] [ICAO location identifier] (ICLI)
LKPR	Praha/Ruzyne [Former Czechoslovakia] [ICAO location identifier] (ICLI)
LKQ	Like Kind and Quality (Metal) [Auto repair]
LKQCPI	Licentiate of the King's and Queen's College of Physicians of Ireland
LKR	Lake Air Helicopters Ltd. [British] [ICAO designator] (FAAC)
LKR	Lancaster, SC [Location identifier] [FAA] (FAAL)
LKR	Left Knee Right [Guitar playing]
LKR	LK Resources Ltd. [Toronto Stock Exchange symbol]
LKR	Locker (KSC)
LKROT	Locked Rotor
LKRT	Loyal Knights of the Round Table (EA)
LKS	Lakes
LKS	Lakeside Aviation Ltd. [British] [ICAO designator] (FAAC)
LKS	Lambda Kappa Sigma (EA)
LKS	Landau-Kleffer Syndrome [Medicine]
LKS	Landau-Kleffler Syndrome
LKS	Liberation Kanake Socialiste [Socialist Kanak Liberation] [New Caledonia] (PD)
LKS	Liver, Kidney, Spleen [Medicine]
LKS	Logan-Keck-Stickney [Method]
LKS	Louisville, KY [Location identifier] [FAA] (FAAL)
LKS	Lucky 7 Exploration [Vancouver Stock Exchange symbol]
LKS	Lucky Stores, Inc. (SAUO)
LKSB	Liver, Kidney, Spleen, Bladder [Medicine] (DMAA)
LKSCR	Lockscrew
LKSL	Sliac [Former Czechoslovakia] [ICAO location identifier] (ICLI)
LKS NP	Liver, Kidneys, and Spleen Not Palpable [On physical examination] (DAVI)
LKT	Locket (ROG)
LKT	Lookout (MSA)
LKT	Salmon, ID [Location identifier] [FAA] (FAAL)
LKTT	Poprad/Tatry [Former Czechoslovakia] [ICAO location identifier] (ICLI)
LKTYP	Like Type (FAAC)
LKU	Literarische Keilschrifttexte aus Uruk [A publication] (BJA)
LKUP	Lockup
LKV	Laked Kanamycin-Vancomycin [Agar] [Microbiology]
LKV	Lake Ventures Ltd. [Vancouver Stock Exchange symbol]
LKV	Lakeview, OR [Location identifier] [FAA] (FAAL)
LKV	Left Knee Vertical [Guitar playing]
LKV	Lengyel-Kerman-Vargar [Rating] [Psychology] (DAVI)
LKVY	Lykens Valley Railroad Co. [AAR code]
LKW	Lake Wisdom [Papua New Guinea] [Seismograph station code, US Geological Survey] (SEIS)
LKW	Lakewood Mining [Vancouver Stock Exchange symbol]
LKW	Larkana [Pakistan] [Airport symbol] (AD)
LK/WA	Lock Washer [Automotive engineering]
LKWASH	Lock Washer [Automotive engineering]
LKX	La Pryor, TX [Location identifier] [FAA] (FAAL)
LKY	Lucky Strike Resources [Vancouver Stock Exchange symbol]
LKZ	Letaba Airways [South Africa] [ICAO designator] (FAAC)
LL	Aero Lloyd Flugreisen GmbH & Co. KG (SAUO)
LL	All Is Well [Search and rescue symbol that can be stamped in sand or snow]
LL	Bell-Air [ICAO designator] (AD)
LL	Double-Loop Magnetic Mine Sweep [Navy] [British]
LL	International Convention on Load Lines (SAUO)
LL	Lab. Lafon [France] [Research code symbol]
LL	Labor Letter [Cast Metals Association] [A publication]
LL	Lamina Lucida [Dermatology]
LL	Land-Line [Telecommunications] (TEL)
LL	Landline [Aviation]
LL	Land Lines (SAUO)
LL	Land Locomotion Division [Army Tank-Automotive Command] [Warren, MI]
LL	Land Locomotion Laboratory [Army]
LL	Landlord [Legal shorthand] (LWAP)
LL	Language Laboratory (SAUO)
ll	Lapis Lazuli (VRA)
LL	Large Letter
LL	Large Light Seeds [Botany]
LL	Large Lymphocyte [Medicine]
LL	Last (ROG)
LL	Late Latin [Language, etc.]
LL	Latent Lethality [Radiation casualty criterion] [Army]
LL	Lateral Lemniscus [Neuroanatomy]
LL	Lateral Line [Invertebrate zoology]
LL	Lateral Lip
L/L	Latitude/Longitude (IEEE)
LL	Laugh Lovers (EA)
LL	Launch and Landing [NASA] (NASA)
LL	Launch Left (MCD)
LL	Laurentian Life Insurance Co., Inc. [Toronto Stock Exchange symbol]
LL	Law Latin
L-L	Law Library of Louisiana, New Orleans, LA [Library symbol] [Library of Congress] (LCLS)
LL	Law List (ILCA)
LL	Laws (ROG)
LL	Laymen's League (EA)
LL	League (ROG)
LL	Lean Line (EA)
LL	Leased Line [Private telephone or Teletype line] [Telecommunications]
LL	Lease or Loan
LL	Leaves [Bibliography]
LL	Lederle Laboratories [Research code symbol]
LL	Left Lateral [Anatomy] (DAVI)
LL	Left Leg (MAE)
LL	Left Lower [Medicine]
LL	Left Lung [Medicine]
LL	Legal Letter (WDAA)
LL	Lega Lombarda [Italy] [Political party] (ECED)
LL	Leges [Laws] [Latin]
LL	Legislative Liaison
LL	Legum [Of Laws] [Latin] (ADA)
L/L	Leigh Light [British military] (DMA)
LL	Lending Library
LL	Lend-Lease [Bill] [World War II]
LL	Lepromatous-Type Leprosy [Animal pathology]
LL	Lessons Learned
LL	Level Lock (SAUS)
LL	Lever Lock (MCD)
LL	Lewandowsky-Lutz [Syndrome] [Medicine] (DB)
LL	Liberty Lobby (EA)
L/L	Library Labels [Antiquarian book trade]
LL	License in Civil Law
LL	Lighterage Limits
LL	Light Line [Military]
LL	Light Load (AAG)
LL	Light Lock
LL	Light Lorry [British]
LL	Limited Liability [Finance]
LL	Limiting Level

LL	Lincoln Laboratories (or Laboratory) (SAUO)
LL	Lincoln Laboratory [*MIT*] (MCD)
LL	Lincoln Libraries (ACAE)
LL	Lincoln Library of Essential Information
L/L	Line for Line [*Typesetting*] (WDMC)
LL	Line Leg [*Telegraph*] [*Telecommunications*] (TEL)
LL	Line Link (IAA)
ll	Lines (WDMC)
LL	Lines
LL	Lines Layout (MCD)
L-L	Line-to-Line (MCD)
LL	Linking Loader (IAA)
LL	Link Level [*Telecommunications*]
LL	Lipoprotein Lipase (DB)
LL	Liquid Level (ECII)
LL	Liquid Limit (IEEE)
L/L	Liquid/Liquid Extraction [*Laboratory procedure*]
LL	Liquor Law
L-L	List/Leave (SAUS)
LL	Literary Lives [*A publication*]
LL	Litre (ROG)
LL	Little League [*Baseball*]
LL	Live Load
LL	Load Line [*Shipping*] (DS)
LL	Load List (MSA)
LL	Local Lesion [*Pathology*]
LL	Local Line [*Telecommunications*]
LL	Local Linearization
LL	Local Loopback (MHDB)
LL	Locator Lists [*Army*]
LL	Loco Laudato [*In the Place Quoted*] [*Latin*]
LL	Lodges [*Freemasonry*] (ROG)
LL	Loft Line (MSA)
LL	London Lyceum (SAUO)
L/L	Long Lead (ACAE)
LL	Long Lead (NASA)
LL	Long Line [*Telecommunications*] (MCD)
LL	Loose Leaf
LL	Lord Lieutenant
LL	Lords
LL	Loudness Level
LL	Lower Laterals [*Botany*]
LL	Lower Left
LL	Lower Leg
LL	Lower Lid [*Ophthalmology*]
LL	Lower Limb [*Lower edge of sun, moon, etc.*] [*Navigation*]
LL	Lower Limen [*Psychology*]
LL	Lower Limit
LL	Lower Lip [*Anatomy*] (DAVI)
LL	Lower Lobe [*Medicine*]
LL	Low Latin [*Language, etc.*]
LL	Low Level
LL	Low Load [*Finance*]
LL	Lumbar Length [*Anatomy*] (DAVI)
LL	Lunar Landing [*NASA*] (KSC)
LL	Luther League [*Defunct*] (EA)
LL	Lutlag [*Limited Company*] [*Norwegian*]
LL	Lymphoblastic Lymphoma [*Oncology*] (DAVI)
LL	Lymphoid Leukemia [*Medicine*] (DB)
L/L	Lymphoma/Leukemia [*Oncology*]
LL	Lysolecithin [*Biochemistry*]
LLA	Lady Licentiate of Arts [*Scotland*]
LLA	Lady Literate in Arts [*British*]
LLA	Lakeland Aviation (SAUO)
LLA	Language and Literary Agency (SAUO)
LLA	Latin Liturgy Association (EA)
LLA	Latitude, Longitude, Altitude (SAUS)
LLA	Laubach Literacy Action (EA)
LLA	Leased Line Adapter [*Telecommunications*]
LLA	Leased Line Adaptor (NITA)
LLA	Lebanese Library Association (BUAC)
LLA	Lend-Lease Administration [*Defunct*]
LLA	Lesotho Liberation Army (PD)
LLA	Limited Locus Allowed [*Legal*] (ROG)
LLA	Limiting Lines of Approach [*Navy*] (NVT)
LLA	Limulus Lysate Assay (DMAA)
LLA	Link Level Access (SAUO)
LLA	Literary Landmarks Association (EA)
LLA	Little Library [*A publication*]
LLA	Llanada [*California*] [*Seismograph station code, US Geological Survey*] (SEIS)
LLA	Local Lighthouse Authority (SAUO)
LLA	Louisiana Library Association (BUAC)
LLA	Lower Left Abdomen [*Injection Site*]
LLA	Low-Level Analog (MCD)
LLA	Low Low Alarm (ECII)
LLA	Lulea [*Sweden*] [*Airport symbol*] (OAG)
LLA	Luther League of America [*Later, LL*]
LLA	Servicio Leo Lopez SA de CV [*Mexico*] [*ICAO designator*] (FAAC)
LLA	White Lake, LA [*Location identifier*] [*FAA*] (FAAL)
LLAA	Israel Airports Authority Headquarters [*Israel*] [*ICAO location identifier*] (ICLI)
LLAAII	Leurs Altesses Imperiales [*Their Imperial Highnesses*] [*French*]
LLAARR	Leurs Altesses Royales [*Their Royal Highnesses*] [*French*]
LLABL	Liberation Academy Bonded Labourers (SAUO)

LLAD	Ben Gurion [*Israel*] [*ICAO location identifier*] (ICLI)
LLAD	Low-Level Air Defence [*Navy*] [*British*]
LLADI	Low Level Air Defense Interface (SAUS)
LLADS	Low Level Air Defence System (SAUS)
LLafL	Lafayette Public Library, Lafayette, LA [*Library symbol*] [*Library of Congress*] (LCLS)
LLafS	University of Southwestern Louisiana, Lafayette, LA [*Library symbol*] [*Library of Congress*] (LCLS)
LL Alfredi	Leges Alfredi [*Laws of King Alfred*] [*Latin*] [*A publication*] (DLA)
Llam	Lumbar Laminectomy [*Medicine*] (DAVI)
LLAMA	Low-Level Acceleration Measurement Apparatus
LLAN	Llandaff (ROG)
LL & B	Latch, Lock, and Bolt (DAC)
Ll & GTP	Lloyd and Goold's Irish Chancery Reports Tempore Plunkett [*A publication*] (DLA)
Ll & GT Pl	Lloyd and Goold's Irish Chancery Reports Tempore Plunkett [*A publication*] (DLA)
Ll & GTS	Lloyd and Goold's Irish Chancery Reports Tempore Sugden [*1835*] [*A publication*] (DLA)
LL & N.	Language, Literacy and Numeracy Skills Taskforce [*Australia*]
Ll & W.	Lloyd and Welsby's English Mercantile Cases [*A publication*] (DLA)
Ll & Wels	Lloyd and Welsby's English Commercial Cases [*A publication*] (DLA)
LLAP	LocalTalk Link Access Protocol [*Computer science*] (ACRL)
LLap	Saint John Parish Library, La Place, LA [*Library symbol*] [*Library of Congress*] (LCLS)
LLAR	Local Loop Access Ring [*Telecommunications*] (ACRL)
LLAT	Law Latin
LLAT	Lawrence Lowery Apperception Test
LLAT	Left Lateral [*Radiology*] (DAVI)
LLAT	Lysolecithin-Lecithin Acyltransferase (ADWA)
LL Athelst	Laws of Athelstan [*A publication*] (DLA)
LLATIS	Low Light and Thermal Imaging System (PDAA)
LLAW	Liquid Low Activity Waste [*Nuclear energy*] (NUCP)
LLB	Bachelor of Laws (DD)
LLB	Computrac, Inc. [*AMEX symbol*] (SPSG)
LLB	Lawyers' Law Books [*1977*] [*A publication*] (ILCA)
LLB	Left Lateral Bending (SAUS)
LLB	Left Lateral Border [*Medicine*] (DMAA)
LLB	Left Linebacker (WGA)
LLB	Legum Baccalaureus [*Bachelor of Laws*] [*Latin*]
LLB	Line Loop Back [*Telecommunications*] (ITD)
LLB	Liquor Licensing Board [*Australian Capital Territory*]
LLB	Little League Baseball (EA)
LLB	Lloyd Aereo Boliviano SA [*Bolivia*] [*ICAO designator*] (FAAC)
LLB	Local Licensing Bench (SAUO)
LLB	Long Leg Brace [*Orthopedics*]
LLB	Lower Leg Brace [*Medicine*]
LLB	Luluabourg [*Zaire*] [*Airport symbol*] (AD)
LLBA	Language and Language Behavior Abstracts [*Sociological Abstracts*] [*Database*] (NITA)
LLBA	Linguistics and Language Behavior Abstracts (ADWA)
LLBAM	Lincoln Laboratory Boolean Algebra Minimizer (IAA)
LLBBMA	Loose Leaf and Blank Book Manufacturers Association [*Later, ABPM*] (EA)
LLBC	Liquid Large-Bore Cannon (MCD)
LLBCD	Left Lower Border of Cardiac Dullness [*Cardiology*]
LLBD	Meteorological Service [*Israel*] [*ICAO location identifier*] (ICLI)
LLBG	Tel Aviv/D. Ben Gurion [*Israel*] [*ICAO location identifier*] (ICLI)
LLBO	Liquor License Board of Ontario (SAUO)
LL brace	Long Leg Brace (AMHC)
LLBS	Beersheba/Teyman [*Israel*] [*ICAO location identifier*] (ICLI)
LLBS	Low-Level Bombsight (NATG)
LL Burgund	Laws of Burgundians [*A publication*] (DLA)
LLC	Laboratory Leadership Council (SAUO)
LLC	Lac Minerals Ltd. (SAUO)
LLc	Lake Charles Public Library, Lake Charles, LA [*Library symbol*] [*Library of Congress*] (LCLS)
LLC	Lakeland Library Cooperative [*Library network*]
LLC	La Lucha Farm [*Costa Rica*] [*Seismograph station code, US Geological Survey*] (SEIS)
LLC	Lankalink Aircargo (Pvp) Ltd. [*Sri Lanka*] [*FAA designator*] (FAAC)
LLC	Laparoscopic Laser Cholecystectomy [*Medicine*] (MELL)
LLC	Law Certificate
LLC	Left Line Contactor (MCD)
LLC	Lessons-Learned Committee (SAUO)
LLC	Lewis Lung Carcinoma [*Medicine*] (DB)
LLC	Libertarian Law Council (SAUO)
LLC	Library Learning Center (AL)
LLC	Light Salvage Ship [*Navy symbol*] (VNW)
LLC	Lightweight Leader Computer [*Army*] (INF)
LLC	Limited Liability Company
LLC	Limited Life Component (MCD)
LLC	Line Land Control (SAUO)
LLC	Liquid Level Control
LLC	Liquid Level Controller (ECII)
LLC	Liquid-Liquid Chromatography
LLC	Live from the Lost Continent (SAUO)
LLC	Living Learning Center (SAUO)
LLC	Local Line Control [*Electronics*]
LLC	Local Liaison Committee (HEAS)
LLC	Logical Link Control [*Telecommunications*]
LLC	Logic Link Control [*Network interfacing*] (NITA)
LLC	Long Leg Cast [*Orthopedics*]
LLC	Long Lines Coordination (NATG)
LLC	Long-Linking Carbon

LLC	Low Level Code (VLIE)
LLC	Low Liquid Cutoff
LLC	Loyola University, Career Information Center, New Orleans, LA [OCLC symbol] (OCLC)
LLC	Luneberg Lens Commutator [Physics]
LLC	Lymphocytic Leukemia, Chronic (MAE)
LLC	Lyotropic Liquid Crystals [Physical chemistry]
LLC2	Logical Link Control Class 2 (SAUO)
LL Canuti R	Laws of King Canute [or Knut] [A publication] (DLA)
LLCB	Long-Link Carbon Tire [Tire engineering]
LLcC	Calcasieu Parish Public Library, Lake Charles, LA [Library symbol] [Library of Congress] (LCLS)
LLCC	Leadless Chip Carrier (AAEL)
LLCC	Long-Leg Cylinder Cast [Medicine] (MELL)
LLCCA	Low Life Cycle Cost Avionics (ACAE)
LLC/CC	Low Level Code/Continuity Check (VLIE)
LI CC Pr	Lloyd's County Courts Practice [A publication] (DLA)
LLCF	Launch and Landing Computational Facilities [NASA] (NASA)
LLCFR	Lobbyists and Lawyers for Campaign Finance Reform (EA)
LLCLINK	Logical Layer Control Link [Computer science] (VLIE)
LLCM	Licentiate of the London College of Music [British] (DBQ)
LLCM	Low Level Control Module [NASA] (SPST)
LLCM	Master of Comparative Law (DLA)
LLcM	McNeese State University, Lake Charles, LA [Library symbol] [Library of Congress] (LCLS)
LLCM(TD)	Licentiate of the London College of Music (Teacher's Diploma) [British]
LLCO	Licentiate of the London College of Osteopathy
LI Comp	Lloyd's Compensation for Lands, Etc. [6th ed.] [1895] [A publication] (DLA)
LL COOL J	Ladies Love Cool James [Rap recording artist, James Todd Smith]
LLCS	Link Level Communications Subsystem [NCR Corp.]
LLCS	Liquid Level Control Switch
LLCS	Logical Link Control Security [Computer science] (VLIE)
LLCS	Low-Level Compaction Station [Nuclear energy] (NRCH)
LLCSC	Lower Level Computer Software Component
LLCT	Last Line Control (VLIE)
LLCUNAE	Law Library of Congress United Association of Employees
LLD	Deep Laterolog (SAUS)
LLD	Doctor of Laws (CMD)
LLD	Lactobacillus Lactis Dorner Factor [Vitamin B₁₂] [Also, APA, APAF, EF]
LLD	Lamp Lumen Depreciation
LLD	Language Learning Disorder
LLD	LASER Light Detector
LLD	Laser Locator Designator (ACAE)
LLD	Late-Life Depression (MELL)
LLD	Launcher Load Dolly
LLD	Law and Legal Information Directory [A publication]
LLD	Left Lateral Decubitus [Medicine] (AAMN)
LLD	Leg Length Discrepancy [Orthopedics] (DAVI)
LLD	Legum Doctor [Doctor of Laws] [Latin]
LLD	Lipid-Lowering Drug (MELL)
LLD	Live Letter-Drop [Espionage]
LLD	Logic Level Driver [Computer science] (MCD)
LLD	Long-Lasting Depolarization [Neurophysiology]
LLD	Lower Level Discriminator (ACAE)
LLD	Lower Limit of Detection [Spectrometry]
LLD	Lowest Lethal Dose [Medicine] (LDT)
LLD	Low-Level Detector (IEEE)
LLD	Low-Level Dose [Nuclear energy] (NRCH)
LLDB	Luc Luong Dac Biet [South Vietnam]
LLDC	Lesser Developed Country (SAUO)
LLDCs	Least Developed Countries (SAUO)
LLDEF	Lambda Legal Defense and Education Fund (EA)
LLDF	Lactobacillus Lactis Dorner Factor [Vitamin B12] (STED)
LLDH	Liver Lactate Dehydrogenase [An enzyme] (DAVI)
LLDL	Low-Level Differential Logic (IAA)
LLDPE	Linear Low-Density Polyethylene [Plastics technology]
LLD/R	Laser Locator Designator/Rangefinder (ACAE)
LLDR	Lightweight LASER [Light Amplification by Stimulated Emission of Radiation] Designator Range Finder [DoD]
LLDS	Low-Level Weapons Delivery System (MCD)
LLDT	Light Light-Duty Truck
LLDT	Load Local Descriptor Table (VLIE)
LLDV	Light Light-Duty Vehicle [Automotive emissions]
LLDV	Luc-Luong Dac-Viet [Vietnamese special forces]
LLE	Laboratory for LASER Energetics [University of Rochester] [Research center]
LLE	Large Local Exchange [Telecommunications] (TEL)
LLE	Lead Lead Engineer (SAUO)
LLE	Left Lower Extremity [Medicine]
LLE	Lessons-Learned Evaluation (SAUO)
LLE	Lightning Loss Exclusion [Insurance]
LLE	Liquid-Liquid Equilibria [Physical chemistry]
LLE	Liquid-Liquid Extraction
LLE	Load List Element (VLIE)
LLE	Long Line Effect
LLE	Long Line Equipment [Telecommunications] (TEL)
LLE	West Bend, WI [Location identifier] [FAA] (FAAL)
LLEA	Local Law Enforcement Agency
LLEC	Long Lake Energy Corporation (SAUO)
LLECR	Lessons-Learned Evaluation Condition Report (SAUO)
LL Edw Conf	Laws of Edward the Confessor [A publication] (DLA)
LLEE	Leurs Eminences [Their Eminences] [French]
LLEE	Leurs Excellences [Their Excellencies] [French]
LLEI	Lincoln Library of Essential Information (SAUO)
LLEIS	Lower Level End Item Subdivision [Army] (AABC)
LLER	Lessons-Learned Evaluation Request (SAUO)
LLE Ry	LL & E Royalty Trust [Associated Press] (SAG)
LLES	Eyn-Shemer [Israel] [ICAO location identifier] (ICLI)
LLeS	Leesville State School, Leesville, LA [Library symbol] [Library of Congress] (LCLS)
LLET	Elat/J. Hozman [Israel] [ICAO location identifier] (ICLI)
L LETT	Licentiate of Letters (WDAA)
LLETZ	Large Loop Excision of the Transformation Zone [Medicine]
LLeV	Vernon Parish Library, Leesville, LA [Library symbol] [Library of Congress] (LCLS)
LLF	Fibrin-Stabilizing Factor [Hematology] (DAVI)
LLF	Lag Line Filter
LLF	Laki-Lorand Factor [Factor XIII] [Also, FSF] [Hematology]
LLF	Land Level Facility [Navy]
LLF	Latin American Growth Fd [NYSE symbol] (TTSB)
LLF	Laubach Literacy Fund [Later, LLI] (EA)
LLF	Left Lateral Femoral [Site of injection] [Medicine]
LLF	Left Lateral Flexion [Medicine] (DMAA)
LLF	Left Little Finger (SAUS)
LLF	Lehman Brothers Latin American Growth Fund [NYSE symbol] (SAG)
LLF	Light Loss Factor [Floodlighting]
LLF	Line Link Frame [Telecommunications] (TEL)
LLF	Little League Foundation (EA)
LLF	Load List File (AFIT)
LLF	London Liberal Federation (SAUO)
LLF	Lower Limb Fracture (MELL)
LLF	Low Level Format (VLIE)
LLFA	Low-Low Frequency Acoustics (DOMA)
LLFC	Laryssa Lauret Fan Club (EA)
LLFC	Loretta Lynn Fan Club (EA)
LLFET	Linear-Load Field Effect Transistor [Electronics] (PDAA)
LLFM	Land Line Frequency Modulation (AAG)
LLFM	Low-Level Flux Monitor [Nuclear energy] (NRCH)
LLFPB	Linear, Lumped, Finite, Passive, Bilateral
LLG	Chillagoe [Australia] [Airport symbol] [Obsolete] (OAG)
LLG	Labour Life Group (BUAC)
LLG	Landcare Liaison Group (BUAC)
LLG	Line-to-Line to Ground (IAA)
LLG	Logical Language Group [An association] (EA)
LLG	Logical Line Group [Computer science] (IBMDP)
LLG	Loose Lug [Tire maintenance]
LLG	Luggage and Leather Goods Salesmen's Association of America (EA)
LLGA	Leadless Land Grid Array [Electronics] (EECA)
LLGAF	Leslie-Lohman Gay Art Foundation (EA)
LLGDS	Landlocked and Geographically Disadvantaged States [Developing countries]
LLGF	Leather, Leather Goods, Fur [Department of Employment] [British]
LLGL	Low-Level Graphical Language (PDAA)
LLGMA	Luggage and Leather Goods Manufacturers of America (EA)
LLGs	Logical Line Groups (SAUO)
LLGSA	Luggage and Leather Goods Salesmen's Association of America (NTPA)
LL-GXT	Low-Level Graded Exercise Test [Cardiology] (DAVI)
LLH	Ladies Left Handed
LLH	Lahore Light Horse [British military] (DMA)
LLH	Library of Literary History [A publication]
LLH	Light Liaison Helicopter (SAUS)
LLH	Light Lift Helicopter (ACAE)
LLH	Linked-List Histogrammers (ACAE)
LLH	Low-Level Heating [Nuclear energy] (OA)
LLHA	Haifa/U. Michaeli [Israel] [ICAO location identifier] (ICLI)
LL Hen I	Laws of Henry I [A publication] (DLA)
LLHZ	Herzlia [Israel] [ICAO location identifier] (ICLI)
LLI	Lalibella [Ethiopia] [Airport symbol] (OAG)
LLI	Language-Based Learning Impairment [Neurology]
LLI	Late Latent Infection [Medicine]
LLI	Latitude and Longitude Indicator
LLI	Laubach Literacy International (EA)
LLI	Life Line International (EA)
LLI	Ligula Length Index
LLI	Limited Life Item (MCD)
LLI	Link Layer Interface [Computer science] (PCM)
LLI	Lipari [Lipari Islands] [Seismograph station code, US Geological Survey] (SEIS)
LLI	Liquid Level Indicator
LLI	Logical Link Identifier (ACRL)
LLI	Longitude and Latitude Indicator
LLI	Long Lead Item (MUGU)
LLI	Lord Lieutenant of Ireland
LLI	Lower Large Intestine (ABAC)
LLI	Lower Layer Information (SAUO)
LLI	Low-Level Interface
LLIAC-IV	Illinois Integrator & Automatic Computer (SAUO)
LLIB	Load Module Librarian (MHDB)
LLIB	Rosh Pina/Mahanaim-I. Ben-Yaakov [Israel] [ICAO location identifier] (ICLI)
LLIBC	Lotus Lantern International Buddhist Center [South Korea] (EAIO)
LLIC	Lamar Life Corporation (SAUO)
LLIL	Long Lead Item List
LLIL	Long Lead Time Items List (NASA)

LLiLi .... Livingston Parish Library, Livingston, LA [*Library symbol*] [*Library of Congress*] (LCLS)
LL Inse .... Laws of Ina [*A publication*] (DLA)
LLIT .... Liquid-Like Intermediate Transistory
LLIU .... Launch and Landing Interface Unit (MCD)
LLIV .... Low-Level Input Voltage
LLJ .... Challis, ID [*Location identifier*] [*FAA*] (FAAL)
LLJ .... Lahore Law Journal [*India*] [*A publication*] (DLA)
LLJ .... Lalmonirhat [*Bangladesh*] [*Airport symbol*] (AD)
LLJ .... LaTrobe Library Journal [*A publication*]
LLJ .... Leaf Library of Judaica (SAUO)
LLJ .... Liberation of the Lingonberry Juice (SAUO)
LLJ .... Low-Level Jet [*Marine science*] (OSRA)
LLJJ .... Lords Justices
LLJM .... Ministry of Transport [*Israel*] [*ICAO location identifier*] (ICLI)
Ll Jud Act .... Lloyd's Supreme Court of Judicature Acts [*1875*] [*A publication*] (DLA)
LLK .... Liberator Lake, AK [*Location identifier*] [*FAA*] (FAAL)
LLK .... Little Lake Resources Ltd. [*Vancouver Stock Exchange symbol*]
LLK .... Louis Leakey - Korongo [*Anthropological skull*]
LLL .... L-3 Communications Hldgs. [*NYSE symbol*] (SG)
LLL .... Labour Left Liaison [*An association*] (BUAC)
LLL .... La Leche League [*Local affiliates of LLLI*] (EA)
LLL .... Land Locomotion Laboratory [*Army*]
LLL .... Last Look Logic (VLIE)
LLL .... Latitude/Longitude Locator (SAUS)
LLL .... Lawrence Livermore Laboratory [*Also, LLNL*] [*University of California*]
LLL .... Lawrence Livermore National Laboratories (SAUO)
LLL .... Lawyers, Layers, and Limos [*Television broadcasting industry*]
LLL .... Left Liver Lobe (STED)
LLL .... Left Lower Eyelid [*Medicine*]
LLL .... Left Lower Leg (STED)
LLL .... Left Lower Lid (MELL)
LLL .... Left Lower Limb [*Anatomy*] (DAVI)
LLL .... Left Lower Lobe [*of lung*] [*Medicine*]
LLL .... Left Lower Lung (STED)
LLL .... Liberal Liberty League (SAUO)
LLL .... Liberte, Liberation, et Liberation Nationale [*French resistance movement*] [*World War II*]
LLL .... Licence en Droit [*Licentiate in Law*] [*French*] (ASC)
LLL .... Licentiate in Laws
LLL .... Light Living Library (EA)
LLL .... Lillooet [*British Columbia*] [*Seismograph station code, US Geological Survey*] [*Closed*] (SEIS)
LLL .... Long Lead List (MCD)
LL/L .... Long Leadtime/Items List
LLL .... Long Line Loiter [*Aircraft*]
LLL .... Loose Leaf Ledger
LLL .... Love's Labour's Lost [*Shakespearean work*]
LLL .... Lower Lip Length [*Medicine*]
LLL .... Low Level Language [*Computer programming*] (NTCM)
LLL .... Low-Level Logic
LLL .... Low Light Level
LLL .... Low Liquid Level [*Engineering*]
LLL .... Loyal Lusitanian League [*British military*] (DMA)
LLL .... Lutheran Laymen's League [*Later, ILLL*] (EA)
LLL .... University of Nebraska, Lincoln College of Law, Lincoln, NE [*OCLC symbol*] (OCLC)
LLLB .... Left Long Leg Brace [*Medicine*]
L LL brace ... Left Long-Leg Brace (STED)
LLLE .... Low-Level Lead Exposure (MELL)
LLLGB .... Low-Level-LASER Guided Bomb
LLLI .... La Leche League International (EA)
Ll List LR .... Lloyd's List Law Reports [*England*] [*A publication*] (DLA)
LLLLL .... Laboratories Low Level Linked List (NITA)
LLLLLL .... Laboratories Low-Level Linked List Language [*Bell Systems*] (MCD)
Ll LLR .... Lloyd's List Law Reports [*England*] [*A publication*] (DLA)
LLLM .... Low Liquid Level Monitor (STED)
LLLNR .... Left Lower Lobe, No Rales [*Medicine*] (STED)
LLLO .... Lend-Lease Liaison Office [*World War II*]
LL Longobard... Laws of the Lombards [*A publication*] (DLA)
Ll L Pr Cas... Lloyd's List Prize Cases Reports [*England*] [*A publication*] (DLA)
Ll LR .... Lloyd's List Law Reports [*England*] [*A publication*] (DLA)
Ll L Rep ...... Lloyd's List Law Reports [*England*] [*A publication*] (DLA)
LLLT .... Low Level Laser Therapy (SAUO)
LLLT .... Low-Light-Level Television [*Night vision device*] [*Military*] (RDA)
LLLTV .... Low-Level LASER Television
LLLTV .... Low-Light-Level Television [*Night vision device*] [*Military*]
LLLW .... Liquid Low Level Waste [*Nuclear energy*] (NUCP)
LLLW .... Low Level Liquid Waste [*Nuclear energy*] (NUCP)
LLLWT .... Low-Level Liquid Waste Tank [*Nuclear energy*] (NRCH)
LLM .... Launcher Loader Module
LLM .... Lawyers Linked by MODEM [*Computer bulletin board system*] [*FIDO*]
LLM .... Layer Laminate Manufacturing (SAUS)
LLM .... Legum Magister [*Master of Laws*] [*Latin*]
LLM .... Life and Liberty Movement (SAUO)
LLM .... Limb Load Monitor
LLM .... Linear Learning Machine [*Data analysis*]
LLM .... Load Line Method
LLM .... Localized Leukocyte Mobilization
LLM .... Local Linear Model (AAEL)
LLM .... Long Lama [*Malaysia*] [*Airport symbol*] (AD)
LLM .... Low-Level Multiplexer
LLM .... Loyola University, New Orleans, LA [*OCLC symbol*] (OCLC)

LLM .... Lunar Landing Mission [*NASA*]
LLM .... Lunar Landing Module [*NASA*] (MCD)
LLM .... Master of Law (GAGS)
LLM .... Master of Laws
LLMA .... Leavers Lace Manufacturers of America [*Defunct*] (EA)
LL Malcom R Scott... Laws of Malcolm, King of Scotland [*A publication*] (DLA)
Li Mar LN .... Lloyd's Maritime Law Newsletter [*A publication*] (DLA)
LLMC .... Convention on Limitation of Liability for Maritime Claims (SAUS)
LLMC .... International Convention on Limitation of Liability for Maritime Claims (SAUO)
LLM (CL) .... Master of Laws in Comparative Law
LLM Com .... Master of Commercial Law
LLMD .... Lifeline Healthcare Group, Ltd. (SAUO)
LLME .... Leuo Leucine Methylester [*Biochemistry*]
LLMFC .... Laura Lee McBride Fan Club (EA)
LLMH .... Loyal Legion of the Medal of Honor (EA)
LLMI .... Local Labour Market Information/Intelligence [*British*] (AIE)
LLM (Int L)... Master of Laws in International Law
LLMM .... Leurs Majestes [*Their Majesties*] [*French*]
LLMPP .... Liquid Level Monitor Port Plug [*Nuclear energy*] (NRCH)
LLMR .... Mitzpe-Ramon [*Israel*] [*ICAO location identifier*] (ICLI)
LLMRCP ...... Licentiate and Licentiate in Midwifery of the Royal College of Physicians (SAUO)
LLMRCS ...... Licentiate and Licentiate in Midwifery of the Royal College of Surgeons (SAUO)
LLMS .... Longitudinal Layer of Muscles of Stomach (MELL)
LLMW .... Low Level Mixed Waste [*Environmental science*] (COE)
LLMZ .... Metzada/I. Bar Yehuda [*Israel*] [*ICAO location identifier*] (ICLI)
LLN .... Language, Literacy and Numeracy
LLN .... League for Less Noise
LLN .... Levelland, TX [*Location identifier*] [*FAA*] (FAAL)
LLN .... Line Link Network [*Bell System*]
LLN .... Local Line Network [*Telecommunications*] (NITA)
LLN .... Lower Limit of Normal [*Medicine*] (MELL)
LLNE .... Law Librarians of New England (BUAC)
LLNL .... Lawrence Livermore National Laboratory [*Also, LLL*] [*Livermore, CA*] [*Department of Energy*] (GRD)
LLNNR .... Loch Leven National Nature Reserve (SAUO)
LLNO .... Low-Level Night Operations [*Aviation*]
LLNQ .... Least Lots Next Queue (AAEL)
LL NS .... Law Library, New Series [*Philadelphia Reprint of English Treatises*] [*A publication*] (DLA)
LLNWR .... Long Lake National Wildlife Refuge (SAUO)
LLO .... Eliadamello SPA [*Italy*] [*ICAO designator*] (FAAC)
LLO .... Lead Laboratory Office (SAUO)
LLO .... Legionella-Like Organisms [*Medicine*]
LLO .... Legislative Liaison Office (AAGC)
LLO .... Lifer Liaison Officer (WDAA)
LLO .... Llano, TX [*Location identifier*] [*FAA*] (FAAL)
LLO .... Local Lockout (IAA)
LLO .... Low Lunar Orbit
LLOC .... Land Line of Communications [*Military*]
LLOC .... Land Lines of Communications (SAUO)
LLOD .... Lowe Limit of Detection [*Also, LLD*] [*Analytical chemistry*]
LLOE .... Louisiana Land & Offshore Explorations (SAUO)
LLOG .... Lincoln Logs Ltd. (SAUO)
LLOPS .... Law Librarians of Puget Sound (SAUO)
LLOS .... Landmark Line of Sight (KSC)
LLOV .... Low-Level Output Voltage
LLOV .... Ovda [*Israel*] [*ICAO location identifier*] (ICLI)
Lloyd & Goold (T Plunkett) (Ir)... Lloyd and Goold's Irish Chancery Reports Tempore Plunkett [*A publication*] (DLA)
Lloyd & Goold (T Sugden) (Ir)... Lloyd and Goold's Irish Chancery Reports Tempore Sugden [*A publication*] (DLA)
Lloyd & W... Lloyd and Welsby's English Mercantile Cases [*A publication*] (DLA)
Lloyd LR...... Lloyd's List Law Reports [*England*] [*A publication*] (DLA)
Lloyd Pr Cas... Lloyd's List Prize Cases Reports [*England*] [*A publication*] (DLA)
Lloyd Pr Cas NS... Lloyd's List Prize Cases Reports, Second Series [*1939-53*] [*A publication*] (DLA)
Lloyd's List LR... Lloyd's List Law Reports [*England*] [*A publication*] (DLA)
Lloyd's Mar LN... Lloyd's Maritime Law Newsletter [*A publication*] (DLA)
Lloyd's Pr Cas... Lloyd's List Prize Cases Reports [*England*] [*A publication*] (DLA)
Lloyd's Prize Cas... Lloyd's List Prize Cases Reports [*London*] [*A publication*] (DLA)
Lloyd's Rep... Lloyd's List Law Reports [*England*] [*A publication*] (DLA)
LLP .... Lambda Limiting Process
LLP .... LASER Light Pump
LLP .... Late Luteal Phase (DB)
LLP .... Launch and Landing Project [*NASA*] (NASA)
LLP .... Law and Liberty Project [*Defunct*] (EA)
LLP .... Leased Long Lines Program (NATG)
LLP .... Liberian Liberal Party [*Political party*] (EY)
LLP .... Lightning Location and Protection (SAUS)
LLP .... Linear Log Potentiometer
LLP .... Line Link Pulsing [*Telecommunications*]
LLP .... Link Layer Protocol (SAUO)
LLP .... Link Level Protocol (SAUS)
LLP .... Literacy and Learning Program
LLP .... Live Load Punch
LLP .... Lloyd's of London Press [*British*]
LLP .... Local Language Program
LLP .... Lollipop Daycare [*Vancouver Stock Exchange symbol*]
LLP .... London Labour Party [*British*] [*Political party*]
LLP .... Long-Lasting Potentiation (DB)
LLP .... Long Lead Part

LLP	Long Line Program (SAUO)
LLP	Lower Layer Protocol (SAUO)
LLP	Lowest Level Processor [Computer science] (CIST)
LLP	Lunar Landing Program [NASA]
LLP	Lyman Laboratory of Physics [Harvard] (MCD)
LLPA	Low Level Waste Policy Act [1980] (NUCP)
LLPDD	Late Luteal Phase Dysphoric Disorder [Gynecology]
LLPE	Labor's League for Political Education [AFL] [Later merged into Committee on Political Education of AFL-CIO]
LLpEC	East Carroll Parish Library, Lake Providence, LA [Library symbol] [Library of Congress] (LCLS)
LLPI	Linen and Lace Paper Institute [Later, SSI] (EA)
LLPL	Low Low Pond Level (IEEE)
LLPMS	Long Leg Posterior Molded Splint [Medicine] (MEDA)
LLPN	Lumped, Linear, Parametric Network
LLPO	Launch and Landing Project Office [NASA] (NASA)
Ll Pr	Lloyd on Prohibition [1849] [A publication] (DLA)
Ll Pr Cas	Lloyd's List Prize Cases Reports [England] [A publication] (DLA)
Ll Pr Cas NS...	Lloyd's List Prize Cases Reports, New Series [1939-53] [A publication] (DLA)
LLPS	Low-Level Pumping Station (ADA)
LL-PTC	Liquid Liquid Phase Transfer Catalysis [Physical chemistry]
LLQ	Left Lower Quadrant [of abdomen] [Medicine]
LLQA	Limiting Lines of Quiet Approach [Navy] (NVT)
LLR	High Court of Lagos Law Reports [Nigeria] [A publication] (ILCA)
LLR	Lancaster Law Review [A publication] (DLA)
LLR	Large Lattice Relaxation (AAEL)
LLR	Large Local Reaction [Medicine] (DMAA)
LLR	Lawyer Legal Research OnLine (SAUO)
LLR	Leader Law Reports [South Africa] [A publication] (DLA)
LLR	Left Lateral Rectus [Eye muscle] (BABM)
LLR	Left Lateral Rotation [Medicine]
LLR	Left Lumbar Region [Medicine] (MAE)
LLR	Lender of Last Resort
LLR	Leukemia-Like Reaction [Hematology]
LLR	Liberian Law Reports [A publication] (ILCA)
LLR	Line Length Remainder [Graphic arts] (DGA)
LLR	Line of Least Resistance
LLR	Load-Limiting Resistor
LLR	LOFT [Loss-of-Fluid Test] Lead Rod (GAAI)
LLR	Log-Likelihood Ratio (PDAA)
LLR	Long Latency Response [Neurology]
LLR	Long Length Record (IAA)
LLR	Low-Level Radiation
LLR	Low-Level Resistance [to disease]
LLR	Lunar LASER Ranging [Aerospace]
LLRA	LapLink Remote Access [Traveling Software, Inc.] [Computer science] (PCM)
LLRC	Luneberg Lens Rapid Commutator [Physics]
LLRDS	Long Life Recording and Data Storage (MCD)
Ll Rep	Lloyd's List Law Reports [England] [A publication] (DLA)
LLRES	Load-Limiting Resistor (MSA)
LLRF	Low-Level Radio Frequency
LLRF	Lunar Landing Research Facility [Aerospace]
LLRF	Lunar LASER Range-Finder [Aerospace]
LLRI	Low-Level-Run-In (MCD)
LLRM	Low-Level Radio Modulator
LLRMW	Low-Level Radioactive Mixed Waste (ABAC)
LLRP	Long Lead Repair Part
Ll R Pr Cas...	Lloyd's List Prize Cases Reports, Second Series [1939-53] [A publication] (DLA)
LLRR	Log-Likelihood Ratio Representation (MHDB)
LLRR	Lowest Level Remove-Replace (SAA)
LLRS	LASER Lightning Rod System (PDAA)
LLRT	Local Leak Rate Test [Nuclear energy] (NRCH)
LLRT	Low-Level Reactor Test (IEEE)
LLRV	Lunar Landing Research Vehicle [Aerospace]
LLRW	Low-Level Radiological Waste [U.S. Army Corps of Engineers]
LLRWPA	Low-Level Radioactive Waste Policy Act (SAUO)
LLRWPA	Low-Level Radioactive Waste Policy Act of 1980 (GAAI)
LLRWPAA....	Low-Level Radioactive Waste Policy Amendments Act (SAUO)
LLRWPAA....	Low-Level Radioactive Waste Policy Amendments Act of 1985 (GAAI)
LLS	Land Laws Service [Australia] [A publication]
LLS	LASER Light Scattering [Physical chemistry]
LLS	LASER Light Source
LLS	LASER Line Scanner
LLS	Later-Life Sexuality (MELL)
LLS	Launch and Landing Site (MCD)
LLS	Lazy Leukocyte Syndrome [Medicine]
LLS	Linear Least Squares [Mathematics]
LLS	Liquid Level Sensor
LLS	Liquid Level Switch (IAA)
LLS	Little League Shoulder (MELL)
LLS	Localized Light Scatterer (AAEL)
LLS	Local Library System [OCLC]
LLS	Longitudinal Leaf Spring [Automotive engineering]
LLS	Long Left Shift (SAA)
LLS	Long Leg Splint [Orthopedics] (DAVI)
LLS	Louisiana State University, Graduate School of Library Science, Baton Rouge, LA [OCLC symbol] (OCLC)
LLS	Low-Level Sensor (KSC)
LLS	Low-Level Service [Computer science]
LLS	Low-Level Solid [Nuclear energy] (NRCH)
LLS	Lunar Landing Simulator [Aerospace] (AAG)
LLS	Lunar Logistics System [NASA]
LLS	Lyman Limit System [Spectroscopy]
LLSA	Land Lines Assembly [Ground Communications Facility, NASA]
LLSA	Latin Languages Speaking Allergists [See also GAILL] (EAIO)
LLSA	Limiting Lines of Surfaced Approach [Navy] (NVT)
LLSAC	LASER Line Scanner Aerial Camera
LLSAGW	Low-Level Surface-to-Air Guided Weapon (IAA)
LLSB	Left Lower Scapular Border [Medicine] (DMAA)
LLSB	Left Lower Sternal Border [Anatomy]
LLSBA	Leicester Longwool Sheep Breeders Association [England] (BUAC)
LLSC	Israel South Control Area Control Center Unit [Israel] [ICAO location identifier] (ICLI)
LLSD	Tel Aviv/Sde Dov [Israel] [ICAO location identifier] (ICLI)
LLSI	Laser Light Scattering Instrument (SAUS)
LLSIL	Lower Living Standard Income Level [CETA] [Department of Labor]
LLSL	Lakeland Savings & Loan Association (SAUO)
LLSNA	Limiting Lines of Snorkel Approach [Navy] (NVT)
LLSP	Law Library Service to Prisoners [Minnesota State Law Library]
LLSPT	Licentiateship of the London School of Polymer Technology [British] (DBQ)
LLSS	LASER Light Scattering Spectroscopy
LLSS	LASER Light Source Station
LLSS	Long Life Space System (IAA)
LLSS	Low-Level Sounding System [for measuring weather conditions]
Ll St.	Lloyd's Statutes of Practical Utility [A publication] (DLA)
LLSU	Low-Level Signaling Unit [Telecommunications] (TEL)
LLSUA	Limiting Lines of Submerged Approach [Navy] (NVT)
Ll Suc	Lloyd on Succession Laws [1877] [A publication] (DLA)
LLSV	Low-Level Storage Vault [Nuclear energy] (NRCH)
LLSV	Lunar Logistics Supply Vehicle [NASA] (IAA)
LLSV	Lunar Logistics System Vehicle [NASA]
LLSWCP	Low-Level Solid Waste Certification Plan (SAUO)
LLSWV	Low-Level Solid Waste Storage Vault [Nuclear energy] (NRCH)
LLT	Lahore Law Times [India] [A publication] (DLA)
LLT	Lander Local Time [NASA]
LLT	Land-Line Teletypewriter [Military] (IAA)
LLT	Left Lateral [Anatomy] (DAVI)
LLT	Left Lateral Thigh [Medicine]
LLT	Library of Living Thought [A publication]
LLT	London Landed Terms [Shipping]
LLT	Long Lead Time
LLT	Low-Level Terminal
LLT	Low-Level Turbulence
LLT	Low-Light Television
LLT	Loyola University, Law Library, New Orleans, LA [OCLC symbol] (OCLC)
LLT	Lysolecithin (DMAA)
LLTA	Tel Aviv [Israel] [ICAO location identifier] (ICLI)
LLTC	Linear Technology Corp. [NASDAQ symbol] (TTSB)
LLTC	Linear Technology Corporation (SAUO)
LLTCS	Low-Limit Temperature Control Systems
LLTD	Lightweight LASER Target Designator
LLTDS	Launch Landing Test Data System (MCD)
LLTI	Long Lead Time Items (AAG)
LLTIL	Long Lead Time Items List [Military] (CAAL)
LLTM	Long Lead Time Material (DNAB)
LLTR	Large Leak Test Rig [Nuclear energy] (NRCH)
LLTR	Low-Level Transit Route (SAUO)
LLTR	Low-Level Transit Time
Ll Tr M	Lloyd on Trade-Marks [A publication] (DLA)
LLTT	Landline Teletypewriter [Military]
LLTTY	Landline Teletypewriter [Military]
LLTV	Low-Light-Level Television [Night vision device] [Military]
LLTV	Low Light Television (ACAE)
LLTV	Lunar Landing Training Vehicle [Aerospace]
LLTWP	Low-Level Tritiated Water Processing Subsystem (MCD)
LLU	Lamar, MO [Location identifier] [FAA] (FAAL)
LLU	Lending Library Unit
LLU	Lithuanian Liberal Union (BUAC)
LLU	Loma Linda University, Loma Linda, CA [OCLC symbol] (OCLC)
LLu	Saint James Parish Library, Lutcher, LA [Library symbol] [Library of Congress] (LCLS)
LLV	Large Launch Vehicle Planning Group (SAUO)
LLV	Lockheed Launch Vehicle (IGSL)
LLV	Long Life Valve
LLV	Long Life Vehicle [Automotive engineering]
LLV	Lonicera Latent Virus [Plant pathology]
LLV	Low Level Vault (ABAC)
LLV	Loyal London Volunteers [British military] (DMA)
LLV	Lunar Landing Vehicle [NASA]
LLV	Lunar Logistics Vehicle [NASA]
LLV	Lymphocytic Leukemia Virus
LLVIR	Long Line Voice Interface Rack (SSD)
LLVP	Left Lateral Ventricular Preexcitation [Medicine] (DMAA)
LLVPG	Large Launch Vehicle Planning Group [NASA]
LLW	Lilongwe [Malawi] [Airport symbol] (OAG)
LLW	Lower Low Water [Tides and currents]
LLW	Low-Level Radioactive Waste
LLW	Low-Level Waste [Nuclear energy] (NRCH)
LLWAS	Low-Level Windshear Alert System (USDC)
LLWC	Long-Leg Walking Cast [Orthopedics] (DAVI)
LLWCP	Low Level Waste Certification Plan (SAUO)
LLWD	Low-Level Weapons Delivery (SAUS)
LLWDDD	Low-Level Waste Disposal Development and Demonstration
LLWDF	Low-Level Waste Disposal Facilities (SAUO)

LLWI............	Lower Low-Water Interval [*Tides and currents*]
LL Wisegotho...	Laws of the Visigoths [*A publication*] (DLA)
LLWM..........	Low-Level Waste Management (SAUO)
LL Wm Conq...	Laws of William the Conqueror [*A publication*] (DLA)
LL Wm Noth...	Laws of William the Bastard [*A publication*] (DLA)
LLWMP.........	Low-Level Waste Management Program (GAAI)
LLWPA.........	Low-Level Waste Policy Act (SAUO)
LLWPAA........	Low-Level Waste Policy Amendment Act (SAUO)
LLWPSS........	Low-level Waste Processing and Shipping System (SAUO)
LLWQAPP....	Low Level Waste Quality Assurance Program Plan (SAUO)
LLWS..........	Low Level Wind Shear [*Aviation*] (FAAC)
LLWSV........	Low-Level Waste Storage Vault [*Nuclear energy*] (NRCH)
LLX............	Left Lower Extremity (SAUS)
LLX............	Louisiana Land & Exploration Co. [*NYSE symbol*] [*Toronto Stock Exchange symbol*]
LLX............	Louisiana Land/Exp [*NYSE symbol*] (TTSB)
LLX............	Lyndonville, VT [*Location identifier*] [*FAA*] (FAAL)
LLY............	Lilly [*Eli*] & Co. [*NYSE symbol*] (SPSG)
LLY............	Lilly (Eli) [*NYSE symbol*] (TTSB)
LLY............	Llanelly [*Welsh depot code*]
LLYP..........	Long Leaf Yellow Pine [*Lumber*]
LLZ............	Left Lower Zone [*Medicine*] (DMAA)
LLZ............	Localizer [*ICAO designator*] (CET)
LM............	Labiomental [*Lip and chin*] [*Dentistry*] (DAVI)
LM............	Laboratory Manager
LM............	Laboratory Microscope
LM............	Laboratory Module (MCD)
LM............	Labour Mobility [*British*]
LM............	Lactic Acid Mineral (DMAA)
LM............	Lactose Malabsorption [*Gastroenterology*]
LM............	Lacus Mortis [*Lunar area*]
Lm............	Lamentations (ADWA)
LM............	Lamentations [*Old Testament book*]
LM............	Landmark (KSC)
LM............	Land Mine [*Military*]
LM............	Land Mobile
LM............	Land Mobility (TIMI)
LM............	Landsdale Microelectronics (SAUO)
LM............	Language Minority (SAUO)
LM............	Laramie Projects Office (SAUO)
LM............	Large Memory [*Computer science*]
LM............	Large Momentum (ACAE)
LM............	Large Mouth Bass [*Pisciculture*]
LM............	Laryngeal Mask [*Medicine*] (DMAA)
Im............	Laryngeal Muscle (BABM)
LM............	LASER Machine (IAA)
LM............	Late Midcourse (ACAE)
LM............	Late Model [*Class of racing cars*]
LM............	Lateral Malleolus [*Anatomy*]
LM............	Lateral Meniscus [*Anatomy*]
LM............	Laufenden Monats [*Of the Current Month*] [*German*]
LM............	Launch Module
LM............	Launch Mount (AFM)
LM............	Leading Mechanician
LM............	Leave Message [*Word processing*]
LM............	Lee-Metford [*British military*] (DMA)
LM............	Left Male (MSA)
LM............	Left Mid (NASA)
LM............	Legal Medicine
LM............	Legg Mason, Inc. [*NYSE symbol*] (SPSG)
LM............	Legion of Merit [*Military decoration*]
LM............	Leg Multiple [*Telegraph*] [*Telecommunications*] (TEL)
LM............	Lemniscus Medialis (IAA)
LM............	Lentigo Maligna [*Oncology*]
LM............	Leprosy Mission [*Australia*] [*An association*]
LM............	Leptomeningeal Metastasis
LM............	Lethal Material
LM............	Level Meter
LM............	Liability Management (EBF)
LM............	Licentiate in Medicine
LM............	Licentiate in Midwifery
LM............	Licentiate in Music (WDAA)
LM............	Light Machine Gun
LM............	Light Maintenance
LM............	Light Metal
LM............	Light Microscope
LM............	Light Microscopy (AAEL)
LM............	Light Minimum [*Medicine*]
Im............	Light-Minute
LM............	Light Music [*Canadian Broadcasting Corp. record series prefix*]
LM............	Lime Mortar (DAC)
LM............	Limit (IAA)
LM............	Limitation [*Dialog*] [*Searchable field*] [*Information service or system*] (NITA)
LM............	Lincoln Memorial (SAUO)
LM............	Lincoln Mercury [*Division of Ford Motor Co.*]
LM............	Linear Meter
LM............	Linear Mile
LM............	Linear Modulation
LM............	Line Mark (IAA)
I/m............	Lines per Minute (IDOE)
L/M............	Lines per Minute [*Computer science*]
LM............	Linguomesial [*Dentistry*]
LM............	Link Manager
LM............	Lipid Mobilizing Hormone [*Endocrinology*]
LM............	Liquidity-Money Supply [*Economics*]
LM............	Liquid Membrane
LM............	Liquid Metal
Lm............	[*Maltese*] Lira [*Monetary Unit*][*Malta*] (BARN)
LM............	Listeria Monocytogenes [*Microorganism*]
LM............	List of Material [*DoD*]
L/M............	List of Materials (AAG)
LM............	Litchfield & Madison [*AAR code*]
L/M............	Liters per Minute
LM............	Liturgie und Moenchtum [*A publication*] (BJA)
LM............	Load Master (SAUO)
LM............	Load Module (MCD)
LM............	Load Multiple [*Computer command*] (PCM)
LM............	Local Manufacture (AAG)
LM............	Local Memory
LM............	Local Militia [*British military*] (DMA)
LM............	Lockheed Martin Corp. (SAUO)
LM............	Locus Monumenti [*Place of the Monument*] [*Latin*]
LM............	Logical Module (NITA)
LM............	Logic Module [*Computer science*] (MCD)
LM............	Logistics Manager (MCD)
LM............	Logistics Module [*Simulation games*] [*Army*] (SSD)
LM............	London Museum (SAUO)
LM............	Longitudinal Muscle [*Anatomy*]
LM............	Long March [*Launch vehicle*]
LM............	Long Measure (ROG)
LM............	Long Meter [*Music*]
LM............	Longmile [*Tire retread brand*]
LM............	Long Module (MCD)
LM............	Loop Multiplexer
LM............	Looser-Milkman [*Syndrome*] [*Medicine*] (DB)
LM............	Lord Mayor
LM............	Loss Margin (IAA)
LM............	Lost Motion
LM............	Louisiana Midland Railway Co. (IIA)
L-M............	Louisiana State Museum, New Orleans, LA [*Library symbol*] [*Library of Congress*] (LCLS)
LM............	Lower Magazine [*Typography*]
LM............	Lower Motor [*Neurology*]
LM............	Low Meaningfulness [*Psychology*]
L/M............	Low/Medium (MCD)
LM............	Low-Melting (OA)
LM............	Low Molecular [*Chemistry*]
LM............	Luftmine [*Aerial mine*] [*German military - World War II*]
Im............	Lumen (IDOE)
LM............	Lumen [*Symbol*] [*SI unit of luminous flux*]
L/M............	Luminosity to Mass [*Ratio*] [*Astronomy*]
LM............	Lunar Mission
LM............	Lunar Module [*Formerly, LEM*] [*NASA*]
LM............	Maestretti [*Italy*] [*Research code symbol*]
LM............	Middle Latitude [*Navigation*]
LM1A............	Late Minoan 1A [*Archaeology*]
LM1B............	Late Minoan 1B [*Archaeology*]
LM2............	Lima [*Magdalena*] [*Peru*] [*Seismograph station code, US Geological Survey*] (SEIS)
LM2............	Liver Microsomal Band 2
L/(M² D)......	Liters per Square Meter Day
LMA............	Labor Market Area
LMA............	Lake Minchumina [*Alaska*] [*Airport symbol*] (OAG)
LMA............	Laminating Materials Association [*Oradell, NJ*] (EA)
LMA............	Land Mammal Ages [*Paleontology*]
LMA............	Large Model Access (MCD)
LMA............	Laryngeal Mask Airway (SAUS)
LMA............	LASER Microspectral Analysis
LMA............	Last Manufacturers Association [*Defunct*] (EA)
LMA............	Latvian Maritime Academy (BUAC)
LMA............	Leading Medical Assistant [*British military*] (DMA)
LMA............	League for Mutual Aid [*Defunct*] (EA)
LMA............	Leased Management Agreement [*Radio*] [*Television*] (WDMC)
LMA............	Leave Me Alone (SAUS)
LMA............	Lebanese Management Association (BUAC)
LMA............	Lebanese Moslem Association [*Australia*]
LMA............	Left Mentoanterior [*A fetal position*] [*Obstetrics*]
LMA............	Liberian Marketing Association (SAUO)
LMA............	Licensed Merchandisers' Association [*Later, ILMA*] (EA)
LMA............	Limbic Midbrain Area (STED)
LMA............	Lingerie Manufacturers Association [*Later, IAMA*] (EA)
LMA............	Linoleum Manufacturers Association (BUAC)
LMA............	Liquor Merchants' Association [*Australia*]
LMA............	Liver Membrane Antibody [*Medicine*] (STED)
LMA............	Liver Membrane Autoantibody [*Immunochemistry*]
LMA............	Livestock and Meat Authority [*Queensland, Australia*]
LMA............	Livestock Marketing Association (EA)
LMA............	Local Marshalling Areas (MCD)
LMA............	Lock Museum of America (EA)
LMA............	Logsplitter Manufacturers Association [*Defunct*] (EA)
LMA............	London Mayors Association [*England*] (BUAC)
LMA............	London Metropolitan Archives (SAUO)
LMA............	London-Midlands Association (SAUO)
LMA............	Low Moisture Activity [*Brake system*] [*Automotive engineering*]
LMA............	Lunar Meteoroid Analyzer [*NASA*]
LMA............	Lunar Module Adapter [*NASA*] (MCD)
LMAA............	Liquor Merchants' Association of Australia
LMAA............	Logistics Management Association of Australia
LMAB............	London Munitions Assignments Board [*World War II*]

LMAC........... Labor-Management Advisory Committee [*Terminated, 1974*] [*Cost of Living Council*] (EGAO)
LMAC........... Labor Market Advisory Council (SAUO)
LMAC........... Labor Market Advisory Councils [*Department of Labor and Department of Health, Education, and Welfare*] [*Terminated, 1982*] (EGAO)
LMAC........... Lockheed Martin Aeronautics Company (SAUO)
LMaD........... DeSoto Parish Library, Mansfield, LA [*Library symbol*] [*Library of Congress*] (LCLS)
LMAD........... Let's Make a Deal [*TV program*]
LMAE........... Lunar Module Ascent Engine [*NASA*]
LMAES......... Lockheed Martin Advanced Environmental Systems (SAUO)
LMAF........... Live Missile Assembly Facility
LMAF........... Live Motor Assembly Facility (SAUO)
LMAFS......... Lookout Mountain Air Force Station
LM-Ag......... Liver Membrane Antigen [*Immunochemistry*]
L Mag & LR... Law Magazine and Law Review [*A publication*] (DLA)
L Mag & Rev... Law Magazine and Review [*A publication*] (DLA)
LMAGB........ Locomotive Manufacturers Association of Great Britain (BUAC)
LMAL.......... Langley Memorial Aeronautical Laboratory [*NASA*] (AAG)
LMAMA....... Louisa May Alcott Memorial Association (EA)
LMAN.......... Lieberman Enterprises, Inc. (SAUO)
LmAN.......... Limited Area Networks (NITA)
LM & LR...... Law Magazine and Law Review [*A publication*] (DLA)
LM & P....... Lowndes, Maxwell, and Pollock's English Bail Court Practice Reports [*1850-51*] [*A publication*] (DLA)
LM & Sc R... London, Midland & Scottish Railway [*British*] (DCTA)
LManyS .... Sabine Parish Library, Many, LA [*Library symbol*] [*Library of Congress*] (LCLS)
LMAQ.......... Liquor Merchants Association of Queensland [*Australia*]
LMAQ.......... Livestock and Meat Authority of Queensland [*Australia*]
LMAR.......... Lorimar-Telepictures Corp. (SAUO)
LMarA......... Avoyelles Parish Library, Marksville, LA [*Library symbol*] [*Library of Congress*] (LCLS)
LMARS .... Library Management and Retrieval System [*Navy*] [*Information service or system*] (IID)
LMAS.......... London and Middlesex Archaeological Society (SAUO)
LM/ATM...... Lunar Module Apollo Telescope Mount [*NASA*] (MCD)
LMAV.......... LASER Maverick (MCD)
LMAV.......... Lumber Manufacturers Association of Virginia (WPI)
LMAW......... Light Multi-purpose Assault Weapon (SAUS)
LMAW......... Liquid Medium Active Waste (NUCP)
LMB .... Laboratory of Molecular Biophysics (GNE)
LMB .... Labor Market Bulletin (OICC)
LMB .... Laurence-Moon-Biedl [*Medicine*]
LMB .... Left Main-Stem Bronchus [*Medicine*] (MEDA)
LMB .... Left Most BIT [*Binary Digit*] [*Computer science*] (MHDB)
LMB .... Left Mouse Button (VLIE)
LMB .... Leiomyblastoma [*Pathology*] (DAVI)
LMB .... Leptomycin B [*A cytotoxin*]
LMB .... Linear Motion Bearing
LMB .... Liquidation and Manpower Board (SAUO)
LMB .... Local Marine Board (SAUO)
LMB .... Local Master Browser (SAUS)
LMB .... Local Message Box (NATG)
LMB .... Low-Maintenance Battery (MCD)
LMBATA...... Lace Machine Builders and Allied Trades Association (SAUO)
LMBB.......... Laurence-Moon-Bardet-Biedl Syndrome [*Medicine*] (DMAA)
LMBBS........ Laurence-Moon-Bardet-Biedl Syndrome [*Medicine*]
LMBBSN ..... Laurence-Moon-Bardet-Biedl Syndrome Network [*An association*] (EA)
LMBC.......... Lady Margaret Boat Club [*of St. John's College, Cambridge*] [*British*]
LMBC.......... Landmark Bancorp [*NASDAQ symbol*] (SAG)
LMBC.......... Liverpool Marine Biological Committee [*British*] (BARN)
LMBC.......... Liverpool Marine Biology Committee (SAUO)
LMBCS........ Lotus Multi-Byte Character Set [*Computer science*] (VLIE)
LMBDA .... Language for Manufacturing Business and Distribution Activities (SAUO)
LMBF.......... Low and Medium Bleeding Frequency [*Medicine*]
LMBI.......... Local Memory Bus Interface [*Computer science*]
LMBnyS ...... Sabine Parish Library, Many (SAUS)
LMBO.......... Leveraged Management Buy-Out
LMBP.......... Lake Manyara Bird Paradise (SAUO)
LMBR.......... Lumber
LMBS.......... Laurence-Moon-Biedl Syndrome [*Medicine*]
LMC........... Cleveland-Marshall College of Law, Cleveland, OH [*OCLC symbol*] (OCLC)
LMC........... Laboratory of Molecular Carcinogensis (GNE)
LMC........... Labor Market Characteristics (OICC)
LMC........... Labour Management Committee (SAUO)
LMC........... Lake Michigan College (SAUO)
LMC........... Lake Michigan Conference (PSS)
LMC........... Lamacarena [*Colombia*] [*Airport symbol*] [*Obsolete*] (OAG)
LMC........... Lamina Monopolar Cell [*Cytology*]
LMC........... Lamocks [*Republic of China*] [*Seismograph station code, US Geological Survey*] (SEIS)
LMC........... Lancia Motor Club [*Ledbury, Herefordshire, England*] (EAIO)
LMC........... Land Management Code (PA)
LMC........... Lanzhou Medical College [*China*] (BUAC)
LMC........... Large Magellanic Cloud [*Astronomy*]
LMC........... Large Monopolar Cell [*Anatomy*]
LMC........... large Motile Cell [*Medicine*] (STED)
LMC........... LASER Mirror Coating
LMC........... Late Mid Course (ACAE)
LMC........... Lateral Motor Column [*of the spinal cord*] [*Neurobiology*]

LMC........... Latex-Modified Concrete (PDAA)
LMC........... Launch Monitor Console [*or Control*] [*NASA*] (IAA)
LMC........... Least Material Condition (MSA)
LMC........... Left Main Coronary [*Artery*] [*Medicine*] (STED)
LMC........... Left Middle Cerebral [*Artery*] [*Medicine*] (STED)
LMC........... Library Media Center
LMC........... Ligue Monarchiste du Canada [*Monarchist League of Canada*] (EAIO)
LMC........... Lime-Magnesium Carbonate
LMC........... Liquid Media Concentrate [*Cell culture*]
LMC........... Liquid Metal Cycle
LMC........... Living Male Child [*Medicine*] (DMAA)
LMC........... Lloyd's Machinery Certificate [*Shipping*]
LMC........... Local Management Committee
LMC........... Local Mate Competition [*Entomology*]
LMC........... Local Medical Committee [*British*]
LMC........... Lockheed Martin Corporation (SAUO)
LMC........... Logistical Maintenance Computer (VLIE)
LMC........... Logistic Movement Center [*Military*] (CAAL)
LMC........... Logistics Management Center [*Army*] (MCD)
LMC........... Lomas Mortgage Corp. (SAUO)
LMC........... London Montessori Centre [*British*] (AIE)
LMC........... Long-Run Marginal Cost Curve [*Economics*]
LMC........... Lon Morris College [*Texas*]
LMC........... Loss of Mesodermal Competence [*Developmental biology*]
LMC........... Louisville Municipal College [*Kentucky*]
LMC........... Low Middling Clause [*Business term*]
LMC........... Low-Pressure Molding Compound (MCD)
LMC........... Lutheran Medical Center (SAUO)
LMC........... Lymphocyte-Mediated Cytolysis [*Medicine*] (STED)
LMC........... Lymphocyte-Mediated Cytotoxicity [*Also, LC*] [*Immunology*]
LMC........... Lymphocyte Microcytotoxicity [*Medicine*] (STED)
LMC........... Lymphomyeloid Complex [*Medicine*]
LMc........... Morgan City Public Library, Morgan City, LA [*Library symbol*] [*Library of Congress*] (LCLS)
LMCA.......... Laboratory Materiel Control Activity (AFIT)
LMCA.......... Land Management Cooperative Agreement (SAUO)
LMCA.......... Left Main Coronary Artery [*Anatomy*]
LMCA.......... Left Middle Cerebral Artery [*Medicine*] (MAE)
LMCA.......... Logistics Management Course for Auditors [*Army*]
LMCA.......... Logistics Material Control Activity [*Military*]
LMCA.......... Long-Term Medical Conditions Alliance (BUAC)
LMCA.......... Lorry-Mounted Crane Association [*British*] (BI)
LMCAD .... Left Main Coronary Artery Disease
LMCC.......... Land Mobile Communications Council (EA)
LMCC.......... Licentiate of Medical Council of Canada
LMCC.......... Licentiate of the Medical College of Canada (DD)
LMCC.......... Logistic Movement Coordination Center [*Navy*] (ANA)
LMCC.......... Low-Mintage Coin Club (EA)
LMCD .... Liquid Metal Cooled Demonstration (IAA)
LMCFP........ Life Member, College of Family Physicians (CMD)
LMCLQ........ Lloyds Maritime and Commercial Law Quarterly [*A publication*] (DLA)
LMCM^2....... Land Mine Countermeasures (ACAE)
LM/CM^2..... Lumens per Square Centimeter
LMCMS........ Licentiate Ministers and Certified Mediums Society (EA)
LMCN.......... Launch Maintenance Conference Network [*Aerospace*] (AAG)
LMCN.......... Launch Missile Control Network (IAA)
LMCNI......... Livestock Marketing Commission for Northern Ireland (BUAC)
LMCO.......... Lockheed Martin Corporation and Ericsson (SAUO)
LMCP.......... Laboratory Module Computer Program
LMCPA........ London Motor Cab Proprietors Association [*England*] (BUAC)
LMCR.......... Liquid Metal Cooled Reactor
LMCS.......... Laboratory Measurement-Control System (SAUO)
LMCS.......... Leeds Medico-Chirurgical Society (SAUO)
LMCSS........ Letter Mail Code Sort System [*Postal Service*]
LMCT.......... Licensed Motor Car Trader (SAUO)
LMCT.......... Ligand-to-Metal Charge Transfer [*Physical chemistry*]
LMCTF........ Land Managers Cooperative Task Force (SAUO)
LMD........... Laboratory Management Division
LMD........... Laboratory Managers Division (SAUO)
LMD........... Laboratory of Meteorological Dynamics (SAUO)
LMD........... Labor Mobility Demonstration
LMD........... Lamda Airlines [*Greece*] [*ICAO designator*] (FAAC)
LMD........... LASER Microwave Division [*Army*]
LMD........... Last Modification Date (SAUS)
LMD........... Lead Military Department (SAUO)
LMD........... Leaf-Mold (ROG)
LMD........... Left Main Disease [*Cardiology*] (DB)
LMD........... Left Medial Deltoid [*Injection Site*]
LMD........... Left Medline Deviation (SAUS)
LMD........... Library Macro-Definition (VLIE)
LMD........... Licensed Motor Dealer
LMD........... Light Mobile Digger (SAUS)
LMD........... Linear Magnetic Drive (CCCA)
LMD........... Lipid-Moiety Modified Derivative (DB)
LMD........... Liquid Metal Detector
L/(M D)...... Liter per Meter Day
LMD........... Local Medical Doctor
LMD........... Logistics Maintenance Data (ACAE)
LMD........... Logistics Management Data [*Military*] (MCD)
LMD........... Long Meter Double [*Music*]
LMD........... Louisiana Midland Railway Co. [*Later, LMT*] [*AAR code*]
LMD........... Low Modulus Direction [*Mechanical testing*]
LMD........... Low-Molecular-Weight Dextran [*Medicine*]
LMD........... Lunar Meteoroid Detector [*NASA*]

LMDA	Lee's Multidifferential Agar [*Brewery bacteria culture medium*]
LMDA	Literary Managers and Dramaturgs of the Americas (NTPA)
LMDA	Lunar Meteoroid Detector-Analyzer [*NASA*]
LMDC	Leadership and Management Development Center [*Maxwell Air Force Base, AL*]
LMDC	Leadership Management Development Course (SAUO)
LMDE	Limpet Mine Disposal Equipment (SAUS)
LMDE	Lunar Module Descent Engine [*NASA*]
LMDH	Mauritanian Human Rights League (BUAC)
LMDL	Longitudinal Mode Delay Line (VLIE)
LMDM	Little Mission for the Deaf-Mute [*See also PMS*] [*Rome, Italy*] (EAIO)
LMDS	Lightweight Module Display System (ACAE)
LMDS	Local Multipoint Distribution Service [*Telecommunications*]
LMDS	Local Multipoint Distribution System [*Telecommunications*] (ACRL)
LMDS	Local Multipoint Distribution Systems [*Broadcasting term*]
LM/DUP	Launch Module / Defense Unit Platform
LMDX	Low-Molecular-Weight Dextran (MAE)
LME	Labor Market Exposure [*Work Incentive Program*]
LME	Lambda Mercantile Corp. [*Toronto Stock Exchange symbol*]
LME	Large Marine Ecosystem
LME	Launch Monitor Equipment [*NASA*] (KSC)
LME	Layer Management Entity [*Telecommunications*]
LME	Left Mediolateral Episiotomy [*Obstetrics*] (MAE)
LME	Light Mitochondrial Extract (OA)
LME	Link Monitor Equipment (MCD)
LME	Liquid Membrane Extraction [*Separation science and technology*]
LME	Liquid Mercury Engine
LME	Liquid Metal Embrittlement (MCD)
LME	Liquid Motion Experiment (SAUS)
LME	Locally Manufactured Equipment
LME	Logistics Management Engineering, Inc. [*Annapolis, MD*] [*Telecommunications*] (TSSD)
LME	London Metal Exchange
LME	Lunar Module Engine [*NASA*]
LME	Lysine Methyl Ester [*Biochemistry*]
LMEA	Louisiana Music Educators Association (SAUO)
LMEC	Labour Middle East Council (BUAC)
LMEC	Lambda Mercantile Corporation (SAUO)
LMEC	Line Map Editing Console
LMEC	Liquid Metal Engineering Center [*Energy Research and Development Administration*]
L Med	Licentiate in Medicine (SAUO)
LMED	Light Military Electronics Department (SAUO)
LMED	Lyphomed, Inc. (SAUO)
LMed & Ch	Licentiate in Medicine and Surgery (DAVI)
LMEE	Left Middle Ear Exploration [*Otorhinolaryngology*] (DAVI)
LMEE	Light Military Electronics Equipment
LMEED	Light Military Electronics Equipment Department (SAUO)
LMEIC	Life Member of Engineering Institute of Canada
LMEP	Language MOS Evaluation Program [*Army*]
LMER	Land Margin Ecosystem Research [*Marine science*] (OSRA)
LMER	Lockheed Martin Energy Research Corp. (SAUO)
LMer	London Mercury (SAUO)
LMES	Laboratory for Meteorology and Earth Sciences [*NASA*]
LMES	Laboratory of Meteorology and Earth Sciences (SAUO)
LMES	Lockheed Martin Energy Systems, Inc. (GAAI)
LMET	Leadership and Management Education and Training [*Navy*]
L-Meter	Induction Meter (SAUS)
LMetJ	Jefferson Parish Library, Metairie, LA [*Library symbol*] [*Library of Congress*] (LCLS)
LMetR	Jefferson Parish Recreation Department, Metairie, LA [*Library symbol*] [*Library of Congress*] (LCLS)
LMF	Laboratory Microfusion Facility (SAUO)
LMF	Lack of Moral Fibre [*British military*] (DMA)
LMF	Lake Michigan Federation (EA)
LMF	Language Media Format (CET)
LMF	Large Melt Facility, Sandia National Laboratories (SAUO)
LMF	Large Myelinated Fiber [*Neuroanatomy*]
LMF	Large-Scale Melt Facility [*Nuclear reactor test unit*]
LMF	Last Meal Furnished
LMF	Last Month's Forecast (MCD)
LMF	Left Middle Finger (DMAA)
LMF	Le Mans [*France*] [*Seismograph station code, US Geological Survey*] [*Closed*] (SEIS)
LMF	Leukeran [*Chlorambucil*], Methotrexate, Fluorouracil [*Antineoplastic drug regimen*]
LMF	Leukocyte Mitogenic Factor [*Medicine*]
LMF	Levitation Microfurnace (SAUS)
LMF	Linear Matched Filter (IEEE)
LMF	Linear Multistep Formula (PDAA)
LMF	Liquid Metal Fuel
LMF	Logical Mainframe (COE)
LMF	London Musical Festival (SAUO)
LMF	Low and Medium Frequency
LMF	Lower Mid Fuselage (NASA)
L/MF	Low/Medium Frequency (PIPO)
LMF	Lymphocyte Mitogenic Factor [*Endocrinology, hematology*]
LMFA	Light Metal Founders Association [*British*] (DBA)
LMFA	Lucky Mee Family Association (EA)
LMFB	Liquid-Metal Fast Breeder (MEC)
LMFBR	Liquid Metal Fast Breeder Reactor
LMFC	Leigh McCloskey Fan Club (EA)
LMFC	Liza Minnelli Fan Club (EA)
LMFC	Louise Mandrell Fan Club (EA)
LMFE	London Meat Futures Exchange [*British*]

LMFR	Liquid Metal Fueled Reactor
LMFRE	Liquid Metal Fueled Reactor Experiment
LMFS	Lockheed Martin Fairchild Systems (SAUO)
LM/FT²	Lumen per Square Foot (WDAA)
lm/ft²	Lumens per Square Foot (IDOE)
LMG	Laboratory of Molecular Genetics (GNE)
LMG	Lactic Esters of Mono/Diglycerides
LMG	Lamington [*Papua New Guinea*] [*Seismograph station code, US Geological Survey*] (SEIS)
LMG	LASER Milling Gauge
LMG	Lauerer Markin Gibbs, Inc. [*Maumee, OH*] [*Telecommunications*] (TSSD)
LMG	Lawson Mardon Group (EFIS)
LMG	Left Main Gear (MCD)
LMG	Light Machine Gun
LMG	Liquid Methane Gas
LMG	London Medical Group (SAUO)
LMG	Louisiana Mining Corp. [*Vancouver Stock Exchange symbol*]
LMGC	Lunar Module Guidance Computer [*NASA*] (KSC)
LMGEN	Load Module Generator (IAA)
LMGR	Liberation Movement of the German Reich [*An association*] (EAIO)
LMGSM	Latin and Mediterranean Group for Sport Medicine (EA)
LMH	Lady Margaret Hall [*Oxford University*]
LMH	Lewis, M. H., Winchester VA [*STAC*]
LMH	Light Metal Hydride
LMH	Light Military Hovercraft (PDAA)
LMH	Lipid Mobilizing Hormone [*Endocrinology*]
LMH	Lumen Hour (IAA)
LMHA	Lay Mission-Helpers Association (EA)
LMHC	Lockheed Martin Hanford Corp. (SAUO)
LMHF	Lauritz Melchior Heldentenor Foundation (EA)
LMHI	Liga Medicorum Homoeopathica Internationalis [*International Homoeopathic Medical League*] (EA)
LMHR	Lumen Hour (IAA)
lm-hr	Lumen-Hour (IDOE)
LMHS	Lancaster Mennonite Historical Society (EA)
LMHX	Liquid Metal Heat Exchanger (NRCH)
LMI	Collaboration Market Interest (SAUS)
LMI	Labor Market Information [*Department of Labor*]
LMI	Laurentian Mutual Insurance (SAUO)
LMI	Lawn Mower Institute [*Later, OPEI*]
LMI	Leo Minor [*Constellation*]
LMI	Leukocyte Migration Inhibition [*Hematology*]
LMI	Lewis Management Instruction (SAUO)
LMI	Life Management Institute [*Life Office Management Association*]
LMI	Linkage Macro Instruction (VLIE)
LMI	Link Management Interface [*Computer science*]
LMI	Liquid Mercury Isolator
LMI	Liquid Metal Ionization [*Spectrometry*]
LMI	Livestock Merchandising Institute [*Later, LII*] (EA)
LMI	Loaded Motional Impedance
LMI	Local Management Interface [*Telecommunications*] (ACRL)
LMI	Local Memory Image
LMI	Logistics Management Information (SAUO)
LMI	Logistics Management Institute [*Bethesda, MD*] [*Research center*] (AFM)
LMI	Lower Middle Income (SAUO)
LMI	Low-Molecular-Weight Inhibitor [*of protease activity*]
LMI	Lumi [*Papua New Guinea*] [*Airport symbol*] (OAG)
LMI	Luthiers Mercantile International [*Healdsburg, CA*] [*Commercial firm*]
LMI	Lymphocyte Migration Index
LMIA	Louisiana Meat Industry Association (SRA)
LMIAA	Licentiate Architect Member of the Incorporated Association of Architects and Surveyors [*British*] (DAS)
LMIAS	Licentiate Surveyor Member of the Incorporated Association of Architects and Surveyors [*British*] (DAS)
LMI-ATS	Labor Market Information - Analytical Table Series [*Department of Labor - Employment and Training Administration*] (OICC)
LMIB	Light Motorized Infantry Battalion (INF)
LMIC	Land Management Information Center (SAUO)
LMIC	Liberty Mutual Insurance Co.
LMIC	Liquid Metal Information Center (SAUO)
LMIC	Liquid Metals Information Center [*AEC*]
LMIC	Lower Middle Income Country
LMIF	Leukocyte Migration Inhibition Factor [*Hematology*] (DMAA)
LMIG	Liquid Metal Ion Gun [*Surface analysis*]
LMIN	Laboratory of Molecular and Integrative Neuroscience (GNE)
LMIN	Lastminute.com plc ADS [*NASDAQ symbol*] (SG)
LMin	Leo Minor [*Constellation*]
L/min	Liters per Minute (ADWA)
L/MIN	Liters per Minute
LMIS	Labor Market Information System [*Department of Labor*]
LMIS	Liquid Metal Ion Source
LMIS	Lloyd's Maritime Information Services Ltd. [*Information service or system*] (IID)
LMIS	Logistics Management Information System [*Marine Corps*] (GFGA)
LMIT	Lockheed Martin Idaho Technologies (GAAI)
LMiW	Webster Parish Library, Minden, LA [*Library symbol*] [*Library of Congress*] (LCLS)
LMJ	Greer, SC [*Location identifier*] [*FAA*] (FAAL)
LMK	Landmark (NASA)
LMK	Landmark Corp. [*Toronto Stock Exchange symbol*]
LMK	Let Me Know (SAUS)
LML	Lae [*Marshall Islands*] [*Airport symbol*] (OAG)
LML	Landmark Land Co., Inc. (SAUO)

LML	Lankard Materials Laboratory (SAUO)
LML	Large and Medium Lymphocytes [Medicine]
LML	Lean Misfire Limb (PDAA)
LML	Lean Misfire Limit [Automotive engine testing]
LML	Leesona Moos Laboratory
LML	Left Mediolateral [Episiotomy] [Obstetrics]
LML	Left Mentolateral [Episiotomy] [Obstetrics]
LML	Left Middle Lobe [of lung] (DAVI)
LML	Lerner Marine Laboratory (SAUO)
LML	Lightweight Multiple Launcher (SAUS)
LML	Line Message Log (SAUS)
LML	Load Module Library [Computer science] (VLIE)
LML	Logical Memory Level
LML	Lookout Mountain Laboratories [California] (SAA)
LML	Lowest Maintenance Level (MCD)
LMLA	Leisureways Marketing [NASDAQ symbol] (SAG)
LMLA	Lizzadro Museum of Lapidary Arts (SAUO)
LMLAF	Leisureways Marketing Ltd [NASDAQ symbol] (TTSB)
LMLC	Low Mobility Load Carrier (SAUS)
LMLE	Left Mediolateral Episiotomy [Medicine] (STED)
LMLE	Local Maximum Likelihood Estimates [Statistics]
LMLE	Long Magazine Lee-Enfield [British military] (DMA)
LMLI	Liberty Mutual Life Insurance (SAUO)
LMLR	Load Memory Lockout Register
LM/LRV	Lunar Module/Lunar Roving Vehicle [NASA]
LMLSA	Language Monography of the Linguistic Society of America (SAUO)
LML scar w/h	Lower Midline Scar with Hernia [Medicine] (STED)
LMLV	Lockheed Martin Launch Vehicle
LMLW	Liquid Medium Level Waste [Nuclear energy] (NUCP)
LMM	Lactobacillus Maintenance Medium [Microbiology]
LMM	Laser Mortgage Mgmt. [NYSE symbol] (SG)
LMM	Lemming Resources, Inc. [Vancouver Stock Exchange symbol]
LMM	Lentigo Maligna Melanoma [Oncology]
LMM	Library Microfilm & Materials Co.
LMM	Light Meromyosin [Biochemistry]
LMM	Lights Monitor Module [Automotive engineering]
LMM	Linear Multi-Step Method (PDAA)
LMM	Lines per Millimeter (AAG)
LMM	Liquid Money Market [Banking]
LMM	Living Masters of Music [A publication]
LMM	Llanelly & Mynydd Mawr Railway [Wales]
LMM	Locator at Middle Marker [Aviation]
LMM	Los Mochis [Mexico] [Airport symbol] (OAG)
LMM	Lourenco Marques [Mozambique] [Seismograph station code, US Geological Survey] (SEIS)
LMM	Lumbar Motion Monitor [Ergonometrics]
LMM	Lutheran Men in Mission [An association] (EA)
LM/M²	Lumen per Square Meter (WDAA)
lm/m²	Lumens per Square Meter (IDOE)
LMMA	LASER Microprobe Mass Analysis (AAEL)
LMMA	Lutheran Medical Mission Association [Defunct] (EA)
LMMCI	Labor Management Maritime Committee, Inc. (EA)
lmmd	Low Molecular Weight Dextran [Medicine] (MELL)
LMMF	Lederer Messianic Ministries (EA)
LMMF	Lisa Madonia Memorial Fund [An association] (EA)
LMMF	Local Maintenance and Management of Facilities [Military] (AABC)
LMMFHR	Letelier-Moffitt Memorial Fund for Human Rights [Later, LMMFHR/IPS] (EA)
LMMFHR/IPS	Letelier-Moffitt Memorial Fund for Human Rights/Institute for Policy Studies (EA)
LMMHD	Liquid Metal Magnetohydrodynamics
LMM IRSTS	Lightweight Mast-Mounted IRST System (SAUS)
LMML	Malta/Luqa [Malta] [ICAO location identifier] (ICLI)
LMMM	Malta [Malta] [ICAO location identifier] (ICLI)
LMMS	LASER Microprobe Mass Spectrometry [or Spectroscopy]
LMMS	Library Materials Management System
LMMS	Lightweight Multipurpose Missile System (MCD)
LMMS	Local Message Metering Service [Telecommunications] (TEL)
LMMS	Logistics Maintenance Management System (SAUO)
LMMSA	Lightweight Modular Multi-purpose Spanning Assembly (SAUS)
LMMU	Latin Mediterranean Medical Union [See also UMML] [Mantua, Italy] (EAIO)
LMMV	Lamium Mild Mosaic Virus [Plant pathology]
LMN	Lamoni, IA [Location identifier] [FAA] (FAAL)
LMN	Lanthanum Magnesium Double Nitrate
LMN	Lateral Mesencephalic Nucleus [Brain anatomy]
LMN	Lateral Motoneuron [Neurobiology]
LMN	Library Management Network, Inc. [Information service or system] (IID)
LMN	Library Micromation News (NITA)
LMN	Limbang [Malaysia] [Airport symbol] (OAG)
LMN	Lineman (AABC)
LMN	Load Matching Network
LMN	Locomotor Neuron [Neurology]
LMN	Lornex Mining Corp. [Vancouver Stock Exchange symbol]
LMN	Lost Music Network [Defunct] (EA)
LMN	Lower Motor Neuron [Anatomy]
LMN	Northeast Louisiana University, Monroe, LA [Library symbol] [Library of Congress] (LCLS)
LMNA	Label Manufacturers National Association [Defunct]
LMNA	Land-Based Multimission Naval Aircraft (MCD)
LMNA	Long-Range Multipurpose Naval Aircraft (HGAA)
LMNDF	Lesbian Mothers National Defense Fund (EA)
LMNE	Luminent, Inc. [NASDAQ symbol]

LMNED	Laboratories for Molecular Neuroendocrinology and Diabetes [Tulane University] [Research center] (RCD)
LMNL	Lower Motor Neuron Lesion [Medicine]
LMNP	Lake Manyara National Park (SAUO)
LMNRA	Lake Mead National Recreation Area (SAUO)
LMNT	Laminate
LMNTNG	Laminating
LMNX	Luminex Corp. [NASDAQ symbol] (SG)
LMO	LASER Master Oscillator
LMO	Lasmo Canada, Inc. [Toronto Stock Exchange symbol]
LMO	Lens-Modulated Oscillator
LMO	Linear Master Oscillator
LMO	Living Modified Organism
LMO	Living Modified Organisms (SAUS)
LMO	Localized Molecular Orbital (DB)
LMO	Logistics Management Office [Army]
LMO	London Meteorological Office (SAUO)
LMO	Lookout Mountain Observatory [California] [Seismograph station code, US Geological Survey] [Closed] (SEIS)
LMO	Ouachita Parish Public Library, Monroe, LA [Library symbol] [Library of Congress] (LCLS)
LMOA	Locomotive Maintenance Officers' Association (EA)
LMOAC	Local Medical Officers Advisory Committee (SAUO)
LMOAC	Local Medical Officers Advisory Committee (SAUS)
LMOF	Local Media Output Format (SAUO)
LMOI	Labor Market and Occupational Information (OICC)
L/mole	Liters per Mole [Chemistry] (MEC)
LMOP	Landfill Methane Outreach Program [Environmental Protection Agency] (EPAT)
LMOS	Lake Michigan Ozone Study (SAUO)
LMOS	Line-Maintenance Operating System [Telecommunications] (ITD)
LMOs	Living Modified Organisms (SAUS)
LMOS	Loop Maintenance Operations System [Formerly, MLR] [Bell System]
LMOTS	Launcher Maintenance & Operational Training System (SAUS)
LMP	Labor Mobility Project [Department of Labor]
LMP	Lamap [New Hebrides] [Seismograph station code, US Geological Survey] (SEIS)
LMP	Laminated Metal Part
LMP	Lampedusa [Italy] [Airport symbol] (OAG)
LMP	Land Management Planning (SAUO)
LMP	LANTCOM Modernization Program (SAUO)
LMP	Large Multifunctional Protease [Medicine] (DMAA)
LMP	Last Menstrual Period [Medicine]
LMP	Late Middle Paleolithic
LMP	Latent Membrane Potential [Medicine] (DMAA)
LMP	Latent Membrane Protein [Genetics]
LMP	Lawson Mardon Group Ltd. [Toronto Stock Exchange symbol]
LMP	Layered Metal Phosphates [Physical chemistry]
LMP	Left Mentoposterior [A fetal position] [Obstetrics]
LMP	Library Material Processed
LMP	Light Marching Pack [Military]
LMP	Light Metal Products
LMP	Linguistic Minorities Project [Education] (AIE)
LMP	Liquid Metal Plasma Valve (IAA)
LMP	Liquid Monopropellant
LMP	Liquid Oxygen Maintenance Panel (AAG)
LMP	List of Measurement Points (NASA)
LMP	Literary Market Place [A publication]
LMP	LM [Lunar Module] Mission Programmer [NASA] (KSC)
LMP	Longitudinal Muscles of Pinnule
LMP	Low Malignant Potential [Medicine] (MELL)
LMP	Low Melting Point
LMP	Low-Molecular-Weight Polypeptide [Biochemistry]
LMP	Lumbar Puncture [Medicine]
LMP	Lunar Module Pilot [Apollo] [NASA]
LMPA	Library and Museum of the Performing Arts (SAUO)
LMPA	Methodist Local Preachers Mutual Aid Association (BUAC)
LMPA	Qualified Member of the Master Photographers Association [British] (DBQ)
LMPB	Labor-Management Public Board (SAUO)
LMPBLK	Lampblack
LMPCR	Ligation-Mediated Polymerase Chain Reaction [Genetics]
LMPG	Light Mobile Protected Gun (INF)
LMPM	Library Material Preservation Manual
LMPRT	Locally Most Powerful Rank Test [Statistics]
LMPS	Lift Manufacturers Product Section - Material Handling Institute (NTPA)
LMPS	Lunar Module Procedures Simulator [NASA]
LMPT	Laboratory Material Property Transfer (SAUO)
LMPT	Logistics and Material Planning Team (NATG)
LMQ	La Malbaie [Quebec] [Seismograph station code, US Geological Survey] (SEIS)
LMQ	Marsa Brega [Libya] [Airport symbol] (AD)
LMR	Labor-Management Relations
LMR	La Maur, Inc. (SAUO)
LMR	La Mourre [France] [Seismograph station code, US Geological Survey] (SEIS)
LMR	Land Mobile Radio (NITA)
LMR	LASER Magnetic Resonance (MCD)
LMR	Launch Mission Rules [NASA] (KSC)
LMR	Launch Monitor Room [NASA] (MCD)
LMR	Left Medial Rectus [Eye muscle] (BABM)
LMR	Library Maintenance Routine (IAA)
LMR	Licensed Motor Repairer
LMR	Light Modulation Recording

LMR	Ligue Marxiste Revolutionnaire [*Revolutionary Marxist League*] [*Switzerland*] [*Political party*] (PPW)
LMR	Linear Multiple Regression (IAA)
LMR	Line Monitor/Recorder (MCD)
LMR	Linguomandibular Reflex (STED)
LMR	Lipman Management Resources Ltd. (NITA)
LMR	Liquid Metal Reactor
LMR	Liquid Molding Resin [*Organic chemistry*]
LMR	Literary Magazine Review [*A publication*] (BRI)
LMR	Liverpool & Manchester Railway (SAUO)
LMR	Living Marine Resource [*Marine science*] (OSRA)
LMR	Localized Magnetic Resonance (DAVI)
LMR	Log Magnitude Ratio (STED)
LMR	Long Message Recovery (SAUO)
LMR	Longmoor Military Railway [*British military*] (DMA)
LMR	Lowest Maximum Range
LMR	Lymphocytic Meningopolyradiculitis [*Medicine*] (DMAA)
LMR	St. Louis, MO [*Location identifier*] [*FAA*] (FAAL)
LMRA	Labor-Management Relations Act [*1947*]
LMRA	Land Mobile Radio Architecture (SAUO)
LMRC	London Medical Research Council (SAUO)
LMRCP	Licenciate in Midwifery of the Royal College of Physicians [*British*]
LMRD	Launch Mission Rules Document [*NASA*] (KSC)
LMRDA	Labor-Management Reporting and Disclosure Act [*1959*]
LMRDA-IM	Labor-Management Reporting and Disclosure Act - Investigative Matter [*FBI standardized term*]
LMRDFS	Lightweight Man-Transportable Radio Direction-Finding System [*Army*]
LMREP	Lower Mississippi River Environmental Program (SAUO)
LMRI	Living Marine Resources, Inc. (SAUO)
LMRK	Landmark Graphics [*NASDAQ symbol*] (SAG)
LMRP	Lunar Module Replaceable Package [*NASA*] (KSC)
LMRPC	Linear-Motor Resonant-Piston Compressor [*Navy*]
LMRR	Lunar Module Rendezvous RADAR [*NASA*]
LMRS	Labor-Management Relations Service
LMRS	Labor-Management Relations Service of the US Conference of Mayors (EA)
LMRS	Labor-Management Relations Staff [*Department of Agriculture*] (GFGA)
LMRS	Land Mobile Radio Service [*Telecommunications*] (CIST)
LMRS	Livestock Market Reporting Service (SAUO)
LMRS	Lockheed Maintenance Recording System
LMRS	London Military Radar Services (SAUO)
LMRS	Lunar Module Rendezvous Simulator [*NASA*] (IAA)
LMRSH	Licentiate Member of the Royal Society for the Promotion of Health (SAUO)
LMRSH	Licentiate Member of the Royal Society of Health [*British*]
LMRT	Logistics Management Responsibility Transfer (SAUS)
LMRTPI	Legal Member of the Royal Town Planning Institute [*British*] (DBQ)
LMS	Laboratory for Mathematics and Statistics [*University of California at San Diego*] [*Research center*] (RCD)
LMS	Laboratory Management System (SAUO)
LMS	Laboratory of Molecular Structure [*Massachusetts Institute of Technology*]
LMS	Lamsn & Sessions [*NYSE symbol*] (TTSB)
LMS	[*The*] Lamson & Sessions Co. [*NYSE symbol*] (SPSG)
LMS	Land Mass Simulator
LMS	Land Mobile Service (DA)
LMS	LASER Bank Management System [*Computer science*]
LMS	LASER Magnetic Stage
LMS	LASER Magnetic Storage International
LMS	LASER Mapping System
LMS	LASER Mass Spectrometer
LMS	LASER Mass Spectroscopy (EDCT)
LMS	Lateral Medullary Syndrome [*Medicine*] (MELL)
LMS	Latin Mass Society (EAIO)
LMS	Laurence-Moon Syndrome [*Medicine*]
LMS	Lawer Mapping System (SAUO)
LMS	Least Mean Square (IEEE)
LMS	Least Median Squares (ARMP)
LMS	Leave Management System (SAUO)
LMS	Leiomyosarcoma [*Oncology*]
LMS	Lelean Memorial School (SAUO)
LMS	LEM [*Lunar Excursion Module*] Mission Simulator [*NASA*]
LMS	Levator Muscle of Scapula [*Medicine*] (MELL)
LMS	Levator Muscle Syndrome [*Medicine*] (MELL)
LMS	Level Measuring Set [*for test signals*] [*Telecommunications*] (TEL)
LMS	Library Maintenance System (PDAA)
LMS	Library Management System
LMS	License Management Service (SAUO)
LMS	Licentiate in Medicine and Surgery [*British*]
LMS	Licentiate in/of Medicine and Surgery (SAUO)
LMS	Lightning Mapper Sensor [*NASA*]
LMS	Lightweight Multi-purpose Shelter (SAUS)
LMS	Limestone [*Technical drawings*]
LMS	Limited Mass Search [*Chromatography*]
LMS	Linear Measuring System
LMS	Liquid Measuring System
LMS	Liquid Metal System
LMS	List Management System
LMS	Literature Management System
LMS	Loadmaster Systems, Inc. [*Vancouver Stock Exchange symbol*]
LMS	Load Matching Switch
LMS	Load Measurement System (NASA)
LMS	Local Management of Schools [*British*]

LMS	Local Measured Service [*Telecommunications*] (TEL)
LMS	Local Missile Selector (IAA)
LMS	Local Monitoring Station (SAUO)
LMS	Location and Monitoring Service [*Telecommunications*] (OTD)
LMS	Lockheed Marine Services (SAUO)
LMS	Lockheed Martin Services (SAUO)
LMS	Lockheed Missile System (MCD)
LMS	Logistics Management Specialist (MCD)
LMS	Logistics Management Systems (ACAE)
LMS	Logistics Master Schedules (MCD)
LMS	Lomas Helicopters Ltd. [*British*] [*ICAO designator*] (FAAC)
Lms	London, Madrigal Society (SAUO)
LMS	London Malacological Society (SAUO)
LMS	London Mathematical Society [*England*] (BUAC)
LMS	London Medical Schools (SAUO)
LMS	London Medical Society (SAUO)
LMS	London Medieval Society [*England*] (BUAC)
LMS	London Mendicity Society (SAUO)
LmS	London Microfilming Services Ltd., London, ON, Canada [*Library symbol*] [*Library of Congress*] (LCLS)
LMS	London, Midland & Scottish Railway [*British*]
LMS	London Missionary Society
LMS	London Municipal Society (SAUO)
LMS	Lookout Mountain Observatory [*California*] [*Seismograph station code, US Geological Survey*] (SEIS)
LMS	Lotto Management Services (SAUO)
LMS	Louisville, MS [*Location identifier*] [*FAA*] (FAAL)
LMS	Low Moisture Silage (SAUO)
LM/S	Lumens per Second (MCD)
LMS	Lunar Mass Spectrometer [*NASA*]
LMS	Lunar Measuring System [*Aerospace*]
LMS	Lunar Module Simulator [*NASA*] (SSD)
LMS	Lutheran Mission Societies (EA)
LMSA	Labor-Management Services Administration [*Department of Labor*]
LMSA	Large Metoscale Area (PDAA)
LMSA	Large Millimeter and Submillimeter Array (SAUS)
LMSA	Large Millimetre and Submillimetre Array
LMSA	Silber-Messing-Lot (SAUS)
LMSC	LAN/MAN Standards Committee (SAUO)
LMSC	Let Me See Correspondence [*Business term*]
LMSC	Liquid Metals Safety Committee [*AEC*] (MCD)
LMSC	Little Missionary Sisters of Charity (TOCD)
LMSC	Lockheed Missiles and Space Company (SAUO)
LMSC	Lockheed Missiles & Space Corp. [*Subsidiary of Lockheed Aircraft Corp.*]
LMSC	Logistics Management Systems Center [*Military*]
LMSD	Lockheed Missile and Space Division (IAA)
LMSD	Lockheed Missile System Division (SAUO)
LMSE	Laboratory Module Simulation Equipment
LMSE	Liquid Metal Slip Ring
LMSEC	Lumen Second (IAA)
LMSEO	Labor-Management Standards Enforcement Service (SAUO)
LMSFX	Federated Municipal Securities Cl.A [*Mutual fund ticker symbol*] (SG)
LMSG	Lockheed Martin Services Group (SAUO)
LMSG	Low Magnetic Saturation Garnet
LMSI	Association of Lithuanian Foresters in Exile [*Defunct*] (EA)
LMSI	Local Mobile Station Identity (SAUO)
LMSI	Lockheed Martin Services, Incorporated (SAUO)
LMSN	Local Message Switched Network
LMSQFT	Lumen per Square Foot (IAA)
LMSR	Large, Medium Speed RO/RO [*Roll On/Roll Off*] [*Navy*]
LMSR	London, Midland & Scottish Railway [*British*]
LMSR	London, Midland & Scottish Railway Co. (SAUO)
LMSS	Land Mobile Satellite Service [*Rockwell International Corp.*]
LMSS	LANTIRN Mobility Shelter Set (SAUS)
LMSS	Lunar Mapping and Survey System [*NASA*] (MCD)
LMSSA	Licentiate in Medicine and Surgery of the Society of Apothecaries [*British*]
LMST	Learning of Middle Size Task [*Psychology*]
lmst	Limestone (VRA)
LMSW	Load Machine Status Word (SAUO)
LMSWA	Land Management Society of Western Australia
LMT	Air Limousin TA [*France*] [*ICAO designator*] (FAAC)
LMT	Klamath Falls [*Oregon*] [*Airport symbol*] (OAG)
LMT	Large Millimeter Telescope [*US-Mexico project*] [*Proposed, 1994*]
LMT	LASER Marksmanship Trainer (MCD)
LMT	Launch Motor Test
LMT	Leadership and Management Training [*Navy*] (NVT)
LMT	Learning Methods Test [*Mills*] [*Education*]
LMT	Left Mentotransverse [*A fetal position*] [*Obstetrics*]
LMT	Lemonthyme [*Tasmania*] [*Seismograph station code, US Geological Survey*] [*Closed*] (SEIS)
LMT	Length, Mass, Time [*Physics*]
LMT	Length of Mean Turn
LMT	Levtech Medical Technologies Ltd. [*Vancouver Stock Exchange symbol*]
LMT	Licensed Massage Therapist [*Medicine*]
LMT	Lifetime Medical Television
LMT	Limit (AFM)
LMT	Local Mean Time (AFM)
LMT	Lockheed Martin [*NYSE symbol*] (TTSB)
LMT	Lockheed Martin Corp. [*NYSE symbol*] (SAG)
LMT	Logical Mapping Table
LMT	Logic Master Tape (IAA)
LMT	Logic Module Tester (ACAE)

LMT	Logistic Management of the Turnaround (MCD)
LMT	Logistics Management Team [*Navy*]
LMT	Log Mean Temperature
LMT	Louisiana Midland Transport [*AAR code*]
LMT	Lowenfeld Mosaic Test [*Psychology*]
LMTA	Language Modalities Test for Aphasia [*Psychology*]
LMTA	Library/Media Technical Assistant
LMTA	Light Microscopy Trace Analysis
LMTA	Louisiana Motor Transport Association (SRA)
LMTAS	Lockheed Martin Tactical Aircraft Systems
LMTBR	Liquid Metal Thorium Breeder Reactor
LMTBS	Lightweight Multifunction Tactical Beacon System (MCD)
LMTC	Launcher Maintenance Trainer Course
lmtd	Limited (AAMN)
LMTD	Logarithmic Mean Temperature Difference
LMTDNS	Launch Environment, Mission, Type, Design Number, and Series [*Missiles*] (AFM)
LMTG	Limiting (MSA)
LMTI	Louisiana Training Institute, Monroe, LA [*Library symbol*] [*Library of Congress*] (LCLS)
LMTLSS	Limitless
LMTN	Labor Market Training Needs
LMTN	Leamington [*British depot code*]
LMTO	Linear Combination of Muffin Tin Orbitals [*Atomic physics*]
LMTPI	Legal Member of the Town Planning Institute [*British*] (DLA)
LMTR	Limiter [*Electronics*]
LMTS	LaserMaster Technologies [*NASDAQ symbol*] (TTSB)
LMTS	LaserMaster Technologies, Inc. [*NASDAQ symbol*] (SAG)
LMTS	Liquid-Mirror Telescopes
LMTV	Light Medium Tactical Vehicle [*Army*] (RDA)
LMTVT	Light Medium Tactical Vehicle Trailer (SAUS)
LMU	Lake Mountain [*Utah*] [*Seismograph station code, US Geological Survey*] (SEIS)
LMU	Land Management Unit (SAUO)
LMU	Latin Monetary Union [*Established in 1865*]
LMU	Lifer Management Unit (WDAA)
LMU	Lincoln Memorial University [*Tennessee*]
LMU	Line Monitor Unit
LMU	Logical Network Management Unit (SAUO)
LMU	Loyola Marymount University [*Los Angeles, CA*]
LMU	University of Missouri, Law School, Columbia, MO [*OCLC symbol*] (OCLC)
LMUA	Lloyd's Motor Underwriters Association [*British*] (DBA)
L Mus	Licentiate in Music (SAUO)
LMUS	Licentiate in Music, University of Saskatchewan (SAUO)
LMus	Licentiate of Music
LMusLCM	Licentiate in Music, London, College of Music (SAUO)
LMusLCM	Licentiate in Music of the London College of Music [*British*] (DBQ)
LMusTCL	Licentiate in Music, Trinity College of Music, London [*British*] (DBQ)
LMV	Larva Migrans Visceralis [*Medicine*] (MELL)
LMV	Lettuce Mosaic Virus
LMV	Long Market Value [*Investment term*]
LMV	Low Mass Vehicle
LMVD	Licensed Motor Vehicle Dealer (SAUO)
LMVD	Lower Mississippi Valley Division [*Army Engineers*]
LMVE	Linear, Minimum Variance Estimation (PDAA)
LMVUS	League of Men Voters of the United States (SAUO)
LMW	Ladd Mountain [*Washington*] [*Seismograph station code, US Geological Survey*] (SEIS)
LMW	LASER Microwelder
LMW	Lower Midwest
LMW	Low-Molecular Weight [*Chemistry*]
lm/W	Lumens per Watt
LMWA	Low-Molecular-Weight Organic Acid (ABAC)
LMWAGS	Local Medical Workforce Advisory Groups (SAUO)
lmwd	Limewood (VRA)
LMWD	Low-Molecular-Weight Dextran [*Medicine*] (AAMN)
LMWH	Low-Molecular-Weight Heparin [*Biochemistry*]
LMWHC	Low-Molecular-Weight Hydrocarbon (MCD)
LMWK	Low Molecular-Weight Kininogen [*Biochemistry*]
LMWP	Labor-Management Welfare-Pension [*Reports*] [*Department of Labor*]
LMWP	Low-Molecular-Weight Proteinuria [*Medicine*]
LMX	Aerolineas Mexicanas JS SA de CV [*Mexico*] [*ICAO designator*] (FAAC)
LM/X	LAN Manager for Unix (SAUO)
LMX	LMX Resources Ltd. [*Vancouver Stock Exchange symbol*]
LMX	London Market Excess of Loss [*British*] (BUAC)
LMX	L-Type Multiplex [*Telecommunications*] (TEL)
LMXB	Low-Mass X-Ray Binary [*Star system*]
LMY	Lake Murray [*Papua New Guinea*] [*Airport symbol*] (OAG)
LN	Background Noise Level (CAAL)
ln	Central and Southern Line Islands [*gb (Gilbert Islands) used in records cataloged after October 1978*] [*MARC country of publication code*] [*Library of Congress*] (LCCP)
LN	Jamahiriya Libyan Arab Airlines (SAUS)
LN	Labionasal [*lip and nose*] [*Otorhinolaryngology*] (DAVI)
ln	Lane (ELAL)
LN	Lane (MCD)
Ln	Lane (PROS)
Ln	Lanthanide [*Chemical element*] (WGA)
LN	Large Node (SAUS)
LN	Large-Probe Nephelometer [*NASA*]
LN	LASER Nephelometry [*Analytical biochemistry*]
LN	Lateen [*Ship's rigging*] (ROG)
LN	Lateral Neuropil [*Neurology*]
LN	Law Notes, American Bar Association Section of General Practice [*A publication*] (DLA)
LN	Law Notes, London [*A publication*] (DLA)
LN	Leading Note [*Music*] (ROG)
L/N	League of Nations (SAUO)
LN	League of Nations [*1919-1946*]
LN	Legal News [*Canada*] [*A publication*] (DLA)
LN	Legal Notice (OICC)
LN	Legal Notification [*Ghana*] [*A publication*] (DLA)
LN	Lepista Nuda [*A fungus*]
L-N	Lesch-Nyhan [*Medicine*]
LN	Lesion Number [*Pathology*]
L/N	Letter-Numerical [*system*] (DAVI)
LN	Liaison (AFM)
LN	Liber Niger [*Black Book*] [*A publication*] (DLA)
Ln	Librarian (AL)
LN	Libyan Arab Airlines [*ICAO designator*] (AD)
LN	Licensed Nurse
Ln	Lien (EBF)
LN	Lien
LN	Line (AAG)
ln	Line (VRA)
LN	Link Number (MHDB)
LN	Lip Nerve
LN	Lipoid Nephrosis (DB)
LN	Liquid Nitrogen
LN	Lira Nuova [*Monetary unit*] [*Italy*] (ROG)
LN	Lithuanian Navigation (BUAC)
LN	Load Number
Ln	Loan (TBD)
LN	Loan
LN	Local National
ln	Logarithm (Natural) [*Mathematics*]
LN	Logical Network (SAUO)
LN	Logistics Needs (SAUO)
LN	Lot Number
LN	Love Notes [*An association*] (EA)
LN	Low Foliage Nester [*Ecology*]
LN	Low Noise (IAA)
LN	Luminometer Number [*Hydrocarbon fuel rating*]
LN	Lupus Network (EA)
LN	Lymph Node [*Medicine*]
LN	New Orleans Public Library, New Orleans, LA [*Library symbol*] [*Library of Congress*] (LCLS)
ln---	North Atlantic Ocean [*MARC geographic area code*] [*Library of Congress*] (LCCP)
LN$_2$	Liquid Nitrogen [*NASA*] (NASA)
LNA	Airlen [*Russian Federation*] [*ICAO designator*] (FAAC)
LNA	Lahu National Army [*Myanmar*] [*Political party*] (EY)
LNA	Launch Numerical Aperture [*Telecommunications*] (TEL)
LNA	Leading National Advertiser
LNA	League for National Advancement [*Papua New Guinea*] [*Political party*] (EY)
LNA	League of the Norden Associations (EA)
LNA	Leucine Nitroanilide [*Biochemistry*]
LNA	Liberation News Agency [*Vietnam*]
LNA	Liberian National Airways (SAUO)
LNA	Libyan National Alliance (BUAC)
LNA	Lithium Nitrate Ammoniate [*Inorganic chemistry*]
LNA	Lithographers National Association
LNA	Lithuanian Numismatic Association (EA)
LNA	Local Navy Authority
LNA	Local Numbering Area [*Telecommunications*] (TEL)
LnA	London Allowance [*British military*] (DMA)
LNA	Love-N-Addiction [*An association*] (EA)
LNA	Low-Noise Amplifier [*Satellite communications*]
LNA	Low-Noise Antenna
LNA	Lunar Resources Ltd. [*Vancouver Stock Exchange symbol*]
LNA	New Orleans City Archives, New Orleans, LA [*Library symbol*] [*Library of Congress*] (LCLS)
LNA	West Palm Beach, FL [*Location identifier*] [*FAA*] (FAAL)
LNAA	Large Neutral Amino Acid [*Biochemistry*] (DB)
LNAA	Licentiate of the National Association of Auctioneers, House Agents, Rating Surveyors and Valuers (SAUO)
LNAC	Amistad Research Center Library, New Orleans, LA [*Library symbol*] [*Library of Congress*] (LCLS)
LNAC	Librarians for Nuclear Arms Control [*Defunct*] (EA)
LNAC	Limited National Agency Check (AFM)
LNAC	Louisville, New Albany & Corydon Railroad Co. [*AAR code*]
LNA/DC	Low Noise Amplifier/Downconverter (ACAE)
LNADW	Lower North Atlantic Deep Water [*Oceanography*]
LNAH	League of Night Adoration in the Home [*Later, NAH*] (EA)
LNAH	Licentiate of National Association of Auctioneers and House Agents (SAUO)
LNaN	Northwestern State University of Louisiana, Natchitoches, LA [*Library symbol*] [*Library of Congress*] (LCLS)
LNaNa	Natchitoches Parish Library, Natchitoches, LA [*Library symbol*] [*Library of Congress*] (LCLS)
LNAP	Low Nonessential Air Pressure (IEEE)
LNapA	Assumption Parish Library, Napoleonville, LA [*Library symbol*] [*Library of Congress*] (LCLS)
LNAPL	Light Non-Aqueous Phase Liquids
LNAV	Lateral Navigation [*Provides computer description of aircraft's planned lateral flight path*] (GAVI)

lnaz-	Azores Islands [*MARC geographic area code*] [*Library of Congress*] (LCCP)
LNB	Lamen Bay [*Vanuata*] [*Airport symbol*] (OAG)
LNB	Large Navigation Buoy [*Marine science*] (MSC)
LNB	Liberty National Bancorp, Inc. (EFIS)
LNB	Lithium Niobate (PDAA)
LNB	Local Name Base [*Computer science*]
LNB	Louisiana National Bank [*Baton Rouge*] (TSSD)
LNB	Low Nitrogen Oxide Burner [*Combustion technology*]
LNB	Low-Noise Block [*Satellite communications*]
LNB	Low Noise Block Converter (SAUO)
LNB	Lumbar Nerve Block [*Medicine*] (MELL)
LNB	Lymph Node Biopsy [*Medicine*] (MELL)
LNB	New Orleans Baptist Theological Seminary, New Orleans, LA [*Library symbol*] [*Library of Congress*] (LCLS)
LNBA	Bell Aerospace Co., New Orleans, LA [*Library symbol*] [*Library of Congress*] (LCLS)
LNBA	Laymen's National Bible Association (EA)
LNBC	Laymen's National Bible Committee [*Formerly, LNC*] [*Later, LNBA*] (EA)
LNBC	Liberty National Bancorp, Inc. (SAUO)
LNBD	Lens Board [*Mechanical engineering*]
LNBF	Low-Noise Block Feed [*Satellite communications*]
LNBK	Lane Financial, Inc. (SAUO)
lnbm-	Bermuda [*MARC geographic area code*] [*Library of Congress*] (LCCP)
LNBpA	Assumption Parish Library, Napoleonville (SAUS)
LNBS	Lesotho National Broadcasting Service [*South Africa*]
LNC	Lancaster, TX [*Location identifier*] [*FAA*] (FAAL)
LNC	Lance
LNC	Lancer Resources [*Vancouver Stock Exchange symbol*]
LNC	Landscape Nursery Council (EA)
LNC	Laymen's National Committee [*Later, LNBC*] (EA)
LNC	League of Nations Covenant (SAUO)
LNC	Legal Nurse Consultant (NUJO)
LNC	Leith Nautical College (SAUO)
LNC	Leonard Nimoy Club (EA)
LNC	Libertarian National Committee (SAUO)
LNC	Lincoln National Corp. [*NYSE symbol*] (SPSG)
LNC	Lincoln National Corp. Capital I [*NYSE symbol*] (SAG)
LNC	Lincoln National Corp. Capital II [*NYSE symbol*] (SAG)
LNC	Lincoln Natl Corp. [*NYSE symbol*] (TTSB)
LNC	Local Naval Commander
LNC	LORAN Navigation Chart [*Air Force*]
LNC	Low-Noise Cable
LNC	Low Noise Converter (SAUO)
LNC	Low-Noise Converter [*Satellite communications*]
LNC	Lunacharskoye [*Former USSR*] [*Seismograph station code, US Geological Survey*] [*Closed*] (SEIS)
LNC	Lymph Node Cell [*Medicine*]
LNC	New Orleans Public Library, New Orleans, LA [*OCLC symbol*] (OCLC)
lnca-	Canary Islands [*MARC geographic area code*] [*Library of Congress*] (LCCP)
LNCE	Lance, Inc. [*NASDAQ symbol*] (SAG)
LNCFS	Low Nitric Oxide [*Combustion technology*]
LNCH	Launch (AAG)
LNCHR	Launcher
LNCM	Licentiate, National College of Music (SAUO)
LncNtC	Lincoln National Convertible Securities Fund, Inc. [*Associated Press*] (SAG)
L-NCP	Liberal-National Country Party [*Australia*] [*Political party*] (PPW)
LNCPr	Lincln Natl $3.00 Cv Pfd [*NYSE symbol*] (TTSB)
LNCR	Lincare Holdings [*NASDAQ symbol*] (TTSB)
LNCR	Lincare Holdings, Inc. [*NASDAQ symbol*] (SAG)
LNCR	Lincoln Resources, Inc. (SAUO)
LncrOrt	Lancer Orthodontics, Inc. [*Associated Press*] (SAG)
LNCRT	Licentiate of the National College of Rubber Technology [*British*] (DI)
LNCT	Lancit Media Productions [*NASDAQ symbol*] (TTSB)
LNCT	Lancit Media Productions Ltd. [*NASDAQ symbol*] (SAG)
LNCU	Large Node Computer Unit (SAUS)
lncv-	Cape Verde [*Islands*] [*MARC geographic area code*] [*Library of Congress*] (LCCP)
LNCY	Lunacy [*FBI standardized term*]
LND	Dillard University, New Orleans, LA [*Library symbol*] [*Library of Congress*] (LCLS)
LND	Lander, WY [*Location identifier*] [*FAA*] (FAAL)
LND	Lawyers for Nuclear Disarmament [*Defunct*] (EAIO)
LND	Limiting Nose Dive [*Aerospace*]
LND	Lincoln National Direct Placement Fund (SAUO)
LND	Lincoln National Income Fund, Inc. [*Formerly, Lincoln National Direct Placement Fund, Inc.*] [*NYSE symbol*] (SPSG)
LND	Lincoln Natl Income Fd [*NYSE symbol*] (TTSB)
LND	Lined
LND	Local Number Dialed [*Telecommunications*] (TEL)
LND	Local Number Dialling [*Telecommunications*] (NITA)
LND	London [*Ontario*] [*Seismograph station code, US Geological Survey*] (SEIS)
LND	Lymph Node Dissection [*Medicine*]
LND	Skargardsflyg, AB, Finland [*FAA designator*] (FAAC)
LNDB	Landmark Bancshares (SAUO)
LNDB	Lesotho National Development Bank (BUAC)
LNDC	Delgado Community College, New Orleans, LA [*Library symbol*] [*Library of Congress*] (LCLS)
LNDC	Landec Corp. [*NASDAQ symbol*] (TTSB)
LNDC	Lesotho National Development Corp.
LNDCF	Locally-Normalized Discrete Correlation Function [*Mathematics*]
LNDF	Linear Natural Density Filter (AAEL)
LNDFLL	Landfill
LNDG	Landing [*Maps and charts*] (KSC)
Lndg	Lending (TBD)
LNDH	Local Nationals, Direct Hire [*Military*] (AABC)
LNDI	Lotus Notes Document Imaging (SAUO)
LN-DI	Lotus Notes-Document Imaging (VLIE)
LNDL	Least Negative Down Level (IAA)
LNDL	Lindal Cedar Homes [*NASDAQ symbol*] (SAG)
LNDMRK	Landmark
LNDNG	Landing [*Commonly used*] (OPSA)
LNDO	Local Neglect of Differential Overlap [*Physical chemistry*]
Lndr	Lender (TBD)
LNDRMT	Laundromat
LNDRY	Laundry
LNDSCP	Landscape
LndsPc	Landsing Pacific Fund [*Associated Press*] (SAG)
LNDSPTPLT	Landing Support Platoon [*Navy*] (DNAB)
LNE	Late Network Entry (SAUS)
LNE	Lehigh & New England Railway Co. [*Absorbed into Consolidated Rail Corp.*] [*AAR code*]
LNE	Liquid Nitrogen Evaporator
LNE	Local Network Emulator
LNE	Lonorore [*Vanuata*] [*Airport symbol*] (OAG)
LNE	Lymph Node Enlargement [*Medicine*] (DMAA)
LNE	Northeast Louisiana University, Monroe, LA [*OCLC symbol*] (OCLC)
LNEP	Low-Noise Emission Product (GFGA)
LNER	Linear Films, Inc. (SAUO)
LNER	London & North Eastern Railway [*British*]
LNERG	London & North Eastern Railway Group [*British*]
LNESC	LULAC [*League of United Latin American Citizens*] National Educational Service Centers (EA)
LneSStk	Lone Star Steakhouse & Saloon, Inc. [*Associated Press*] (SAG)
LNET	LodgeNet Entertainment [*NASDAQ symbol*] (TTSB)
LNET	Lodgenet Entertainment Corp. [*NASDAQ symbol*] (SAG)
LNewr	Pointe Coupee Parish Library, New Roads, LA [*Library symbol*] [*Library of Congress*] (LCLS)
LNF	Latvian National Foundation [*Stockholm, Sweden*] (EAIO)
LNF	Leon's Furniture Ltd. [*Toronto Stock Exchange symbol*]
LNF	Linfen [*Republic of China*] [*Seismograph station code, US Geological Survey*] (SEIS)
LNF	Liposoluble Neutral Fraction (OA)
LNF	Lithuanian National Foundation (EA)
LNF	Little-Known Fan [*of science fiction or fantastic literature*] [*See also BNF*]
LNF	Local National Forces [*SEATO*] (CINC)
LNF	Lomas & Nettleton Financial Corp. (SAUO)
LNF	London Flights (Biggin Hill) Ltd. [*British*] [*ICAO designator*] (FAAC)
LNF	Low-Noise Feed [*Satellite communications*]
LNFC	Leonard Nimoy Fan Club (EA)
LNFCS	Leonard Nimoy Fan Club, Spotlight (EAIO)
LNFM	Louisiana Masonic Grand Lodge, New Orleans, LA [*Library symbol*] [*Library of Congress*] (LCLS)
LNG	Lateral Nasal Gland [*Anatomy*]
LNG	Length (IAA)
LNG	Lese [*Papua New Guinea*] [*Airport symbol*] (OAG)
LNG	Lining (MSA)
LNG	Liquefied Natural Gas
LNG	Liquid Natural Gas [*BTS*] [*DOE*] (TAG)
LNG	Liste de Noms Geographiques [*A publication*] (BJA)
LNG	Long
LNG	Lounge
LNG	Luning [*Nevada*] [*Seismograph station code, US Geological Survey*] [*Closed*] (SEIS)
Lnge	Lounge [*Classified advertising*] (ADA)
LNGR	Lingerie
LngStk	Longhorn Steaks, Inc. [*Associated Press*] (SAG)
LNH	Large Number Hypothesis [*Medicine*] (DMAA)
LNH	Lengeh [*Iran*] [*Airport symbol*] (AD)
LNH	LNH REIT [*Real Estate Investment Trust*], Inc. [*Associated Press*] (SAG)
LNH	Lunar Near Horizon [*NASA*] (KSC)
LNHA	Louisiana Historical Association, Memorial Hall, New Orleans, LA [*Library symbol*] [*Library of Congress*] (LCLS)
LNHiC	[*The*] Historic New Orleans Collection, New Orleans, LA [*Library symbol*] [*Library of Congress*] (LCLS)
LNHS	London Natural History Society (SAUO)
LNI	Inland Library System, Redlands, CA [*OCLC symbol*] (OCLC)
LNI	Log Neutralization Index [*Microbiology*]
LNI	Lonely, AK [*Location identifier*] [*FAA*] (FAAL)
LNIAC	Los Ninos International Adoption Center (EA)
LNIB	Like New in Box [*Watch collecting*]
LNIB	Loch Ness Investigation Bureau [*Inactive*] (EA)
LNiI	Iberia Parish Library, New Iberia (SAUS)
LNiI	Iberia Parish Library, New Iberia, LA [*Library symbol*] [*Library of Congress*] (LCLS)
LNIS	Atlantic Naval Intelligence Summary (MCD)
LNIT	Local Nasal Immunotherapy
lnjn-	Jan Mayen [*MARC geographic area code*] [*Library of Congress*] (LCCP)
LNK	Airlink Airlines (Pty) Ltd. [*South Africa*] [*ICAO designator*] (FAAC)
LNK	Air Link Corp. (SAUO)
LNK	Clublink Corp. [*Toronto Stock Exchange symbol*] (SG)

L/Nk............. Lance-Naik [*British military*] (DMA)
LNK............. Lenkoran [*Former USSR*] [*Seismograph station code, US Geological Survey*] (SEIS)
LNK............. Lincoln [*Nebraska*] [*Airport symbol*] (OAG)
LNK............. Link
LNKEDT....... Linkage Editor [*Computer science*] (IAA)
LNKPSC...... Link Performance Assessment Program (SAUO)
LNL............. Land O'Lakes [*Wisconsin*] [*Airport symbol*] (AD)
LNL............. Land O' Lakes, WI [*Location identifier*] [*FAA*] (FAAL)
LNL............. Law Library of Louisiana, New Orleans, LA [*OCLC symbol*] (OCLC)
LNL............. Let Nicaragua Live [*An association*] [*Defunct*] (EA)
LNL............. Loyal North Lancashire Regiment
LNL............. Loyola University, Law Library, New Orleans (SAUO)
LNL............. Loyola University, New Orleans, LA [*Library symbol*] [*Library of Congress*] (LCLS)
LNL............. Lymph Node Lymphocyte [*Medicine*] (DMAA)
LNLA........... Lithuanian National League of America (EA)
LNLC........... Ladies' Naval Luncheon Club (WDAA)
LNLI............ League for National Life in Israel (EA)
LNL-L......... Loyola University, Law Library, New Orleans, LA [*Library symbol*] [*Library of Congress*] (LCLS)
LNLM.......... Linoleum
LNLM.......... Low-Noise Level Margin
LNLM.......... United States Bureau of Land Management, New Orleans Outer Continental Shelf Office, New Orleans, LA [*Library symbol*] [*Library of Congress*] (LCLS)
LNL-Phar..... Loyola University, Pharmacy Library, New Orleans, LA [*Library symbol*] [*Library of Congress*] (LCLS)
LNM........... Langimar [*Papua New Guinea*] [*Airport symbol*] (OAG)
LNM........... LAN [*Linked Access Network*] Network Manager
LNM........... Lansdowne Minerals [*Vancouver Stock Exchange symbol*]
LNM........... Lebanese National Movement [*Political party*] (PPW)
LNM........... Leon [*Mexico*] [*Seismograph station code, US Geological Survey*] (SEIS)
LNM........... Level of No Motion [*Oceanography*]
LNM........... Library Cooperative of Macomb [*Library network*]
LNM........... Lithium Nuclear Microprobe
LNM........... Local Notice to Mariners
LNM........... Logical Network Machine (MHDB)
LNM........... Lumen Technologies [*NYSE symbol*] [*Formerly, BEC Group*]
LNM........... Lymph Node Metastases [*Oncology*]
LNM........... Margaret C. Hanson Normal School, New Orleans, LA [*Library symbol*] [*Library of Congress*] [*Obsolete*] (LCLS)
Inma-.......... Madeira Islands [*MARC geographic area code*] [*Library of Congress*] (LCCP)
LNMA.......... New Orleans Museum of Art, New Orleans, LA [*Library symbol*] [*Library of Congress*] (LCLS)
LNMC.......... Monaco [*Monaco*] [*ICAO location identifier*] (ICLI)
LNME.......... Mobil Exploration and Producing U.S., Inc., New Orleans, LA [*Library symbol*] [*Library of Congress*] (LCLS)
LNMMS....... McMain Magnet Secondary School, New Orleans, LA [*Library symbol*] [*Library of Congress*] (LCLS)
LNMP.......... Last Normal Menstrual Period [*Medicine*]
LNMRB....... Laboratory of Nuclear Medicine and Radiation Biology
LNMS.......... Large-Probe Neutral Mass Spectrometer [*NASA*]
LNN............. Leningrad [*Former USSR*] [*Seismograph station code, US Geological Survey*] [*Closed*] (SEIS)
LNN............. Leningrad [*Former USSR*] [*Geomagnetic observatory code*]
LNN............. Lincoln Resources, Inc. [*Vancouver Stock Exchange symbol*]
LNN............. Lindsay Mfg. [*NYSE symbol*] (SG)
LNN............. Linear Nearest Neighbor (MHDB)
LNN............. Lower Nephron Nephrosis [*Medicine*] (MELL)
LNN............. Willoughby, OH [*Location identifier*] [*FAA*] (FAAL)
LNNB.......... Luria-Nebraska Neuropsychological Battery
LNND.......... Notre Dame Seminary, New Orleans, LA [*Library symbol*] [*Library of Congress*] (LCLS)
LNNI........... LAN Emulation Network Node Interface (SAUS)
LNNP.......... Lake Nakuru National Park (SAUO)
LNNR.......... Lindisfarne National Nature Reserve (SAUO)
LNO............. Laona & Northern Railway Co. [*AAR code*]
LNO............. Leonora [*Australia*] [*Airport symbol*] (OAG)
LNO............. Liaison Officer [*Military*]
LNO............. Limited Nuclear Option [*Military*] (MCD)
LNO............. Local Network Operations [*Computer science*] (VLIE)
LNOC.......... Libya National Oil Co.
LNOP.......... Lanoptics Ltd. [*NASDAQ symbol*] (SAG)
LNOP.......... Orleans Parish Medical Society, New Orleans, LA [*Library symbol*] [*Library of Congress*] (LCLS)
LNOPF........ LanOptics Ltd [*NASDAQ symbol*] (TTSB)
L Notes...... Law Notes, England [*A publication*] (DLA)
L Notes Gen Pract... Law Notes for the General Practitioner [*A publication*] (DLA)
LNP............. Bibliotheca Parsoniana, New Orleans, LA [*Library symbol*] [*Library of Congress*] [*Obsolete*] (LCLS)
LNP............. Chieftain Aviation PC [*South Africa*] [*ICAO designator*] (FAAC)
LNP............. Lamington National Park (SAUO)
LNP............. Large Neuronal Polypeptide [*Medicine*] (DMAA)
LNP............. Least Newtonian Path (IAA)
LNP............. Leg Negative Pressure (PDAA)
LNP............. Lehn & Fink Products Corporation (SAUO)
LNP............. Liberal/National Party [*Political party*] [*Australia*]
LNP............. Libertarian Party [*Australia*] [*Political party*]
LNP............. Lincoln National Park (SAUO)
LNP............. Liquefied Natural Petroleum
LNP............. Liquid Nitrogen Processing
LNP............. Local Network Protocol (SAUO)

LNP............. London Northern Polytechnic (SAUO)
LNP............. Loss of Normal Power (IEEE)
LNP............. Low Needle Position [*on dial*]
LNP............. Lunar Neutron Probe [*NASA*] (KSC)
LNP............. Lunping [*Taiwan*] [*Geomagnetic observatory code*]
LNP............. Wise, VA [*Location identifier*] [*FAA*] (FAAL)
LNPA........... Low-Noise Pre-Amplifier (SAUS)
LNP & W..... Laramie, North Park & Western Railroad (IIA)
LNPC.......... Liberian National Petroleum Company (SAUO)
LNPF.......... Lebanese National Patriotic Forces [*Political party*]
LNPF.......... Lymph Node Permeability Factor [*Immunology*]
LNPIB......... Loch Ness Phenomena Investigation Bureau [*Later, LNIB*]
LNPo.......... Polyanthos, New Orleans, LA [*Library symbol*] [*Library of Congress*] (LCLS)
LNPP.......... Leningrad Nuclear Power Plant (SAUO)
LNQ........... Longest Queue
LNR .... Lagos Notes and Records [*A publication*]
LNR .... Last Number Redial [*Telecommunications*] (VLIE)
LNR .... Leeds Northern Railway (SAUO)
LNR .... Linamar Machine (SAUO)
LNR .... Linamar Machine Ltd. [*Toronto Stock Exchange symbol*]
LNR .... Line Number (SAUO)
LNR .... Liner
LNR .... Line Ring [*Telecommunications*] (VLIE)
LNR .... Liquid Natural Rubber
LNR .... Liquid Nitrogen Refrigeration
LNR .... LNR Property [*NYSE symbol*] (SG)
LNR .... Local Nature Reserve (PDAA)
LNR .... Lone Rock, WI [*Location identifier*] [*FAA*] (FAAL)
LNR .... Lonorore [*New Hebrides*] [*Seismograph station code, US Geological Survey*] (SEIS)
LNR .... Loteni Nature Reserve (SAUO)
LNR .... Louisiana Numerical Register [*Louisiana State Library*] [*Baton Rouge, LA*] [*Library network*]
LNR .... Low-Noise Receiver
LNR .... Luftnachrichten-Regiment [*Air forces signal regiment*] [*German military - World War II*]
LNR .... Lymph Node Region [*Medicine*] (DAVI)
LNR .... Sky Liners Air Services Ltd. [*Suriname*] [*ICAO designator*] (FAAC)
LNRA.......... Linear Nested Region Analysis (PDAA)
LNRC.......... Little Nash Rambler Club (EA)
LNRD.......... Land and Natural Resources Division (SAUO)
LNRS.......... Limited Night Recovery System (PDAA)
LNS............. Laboratory for Nuclear Science [*MIT*] (MCD)
LNS............. Labour and National Service (SAUO)
LNS............. Lancaster [*Pennsylvania*] [*Airport symbol*] (OAG)
LNS............. Land Nationalization Society (SAUO)
LNS............. Land Navigation System
LNS............. Lansco Resources [*Vancouver Stock Exchange symbol*]
LNS............. Lanslevillard [*France*] [*Seismograph station code, US Geological Survey*] (SEIS)
LNS............. LASER Night Sensor
LNS............. Lateral Nuclear Stratum [*Medicine*] (DMAA)
LNS............. Lesch-Nyhan Syndrome [*Medicine*]
LNS............. Liberation News Service (EA)
LNS............. London and Northern Securities (SAUO)
LNS............. London Normal School
LNS............. Long Normal Superchron [*Geology*]
LNS............. Lutheran News Service [*Lutheran Church in America*] [*Information service or system*] (IID)
LNS............. Lymph Node Seeking [*Medicine*] (DB)
LNS............. Nicholls State University, Ellender Memorial Library (SAUO)
LNS............. Nicholls State University, Ellender Memorial Library, Thibodaux, LA [*OCLC symbol*] (OCLC)
LNSA .... Local Navy Supervising Activity
LNSB .... Lincoln Savings Bank (SAUO)
Insb-.......... Svalbard and Jan Mayen [*MARC geographic area code*] [*Library of Congress*] (LCCP)
Inscp.......... Landscaped (REAL)
Insd .... Linseed Oil (VRA)
LNSF.......... Light Night Striking Force [*British military*] (DMA)
Lnship .... Librarianship (AL)
LNSL.......... Liberia National Shipping Line (EY)
LNSL.......... Southeast Louisiana Library Network Cooperative (SEALLING), New Orleans, LA [*Library symbol*] [*Library of Congress*] (LCLS)
LNSM.......... Saint Mary's Dominican College, New Orleans, LA [*Library symbol*] [*Library of Congress*] (LCLS)
LNSN .... Local Non-Switched Network
LNsN........... Northwestern State University of Louisiana, Natchitoches (SAUO)
LNSO .... Shell Oil Co., New Orleans, LA [*Library symbol*] [*Library of Congress*] (LCLS)
LNSP .... Lens Speed [*Mechanical engineering*]
LNSTAT....... Line Status (VLIE)
LnStr.......... Lone Star Industries [*Associated Press*] (SAG)
LnStrInd...... Lone Star Industries [*Associated Press*] (SAG)
LNSU .... Library Network of SIBIL Users (EAIO)
LNSU .... United States Department of Agriculture, Southern Utilization and Development Division, Agricultural Research Service, New Orleans, LA [*Library symbol*] [*Library of Congress*] (LCLS)
LNT............. Aerolineas Internacionales, SA de CV [*Mexico*] [*FAA designator*] (FAAC)
LNT............. Alliant Energy [*NYSE symbol*] (SG)
LNT............. Launch Network Test
LNT............. Linear No-Threshold [*Risk model*]
LNT............. Liquid Nitrogen Temperature (IAA)

LNT	Low Noise Tape (ELAL)
LNT	Millinocket, ME [*Location identifier*] [*FAA*] (FAAL)
LNT	Tulane University, New Orleans, LA [*Library symbol*] [*Library of Congress*] (LCLS)
LNT-BA	Tulane University, Graduate School of Business Administration, New Orleans, LA [*Library symbol*] [*Library of Congress*] (LCLS)
LNTC	International House, Cunningham Library, New Orleans, LA [*Library symbol*] [*Library of Congress*] (LCLS)
LNTC	Lymph Node T Cells [*Immunology*]
LNTE	Lante Corp. [*NASDAQ symbol*] (SG)
LNTex	Texas, Inc., New Orleans, LA [*Library symbol*] [*Library of Congress*] (LCLS)
LNTF	Lipid Nurse Task Force (NTPA)
LNTL	Lane Telecommunications, Inc. (SAUO)
LNTL	Lintel
LNT-L	Tulane University, Law Library, New Orleans, LA [*Library symbol*] [*Library of Congress*] (LCLS)
LNT-M	Tulane University, Medical Library, New Orleans, LA [*Library symbol*] [*Library of Congress*] (LCLS)
LNT-MC	Greater New Orleans Microform Cooperative, Tulane University, New Orleans, LA [*Library symbol*] [*Library of Congress*] (LCLS)
LNTO	Lento [*Very Slow*] [*Music*] (ROG)
LNTP	New Orleans Times-Picayune, New Orleans, LA [*Library symbol*] [*Library of Congress*] (LCLS)
LNTS	League of Nations Treaty Series [*A publication*] (DLA)
LNTS	Liquid Nitrogen Transfer System
LNTV	Lin Television Corp. [*NASDAQ symbol*] (SAG)
LNTWA	Low-Noise Traveling Wave Amplifier
LNTWTA	Low-Noise Traveling Wave Tube Amplifier (IAA)
LNTY	L90, Inc. [*NASDAQ symbol*] (SG)
LNU	Last Name Unknown
LNU	League of Nations Union
LNU	University of New Orleans, New Orleans, LA [*Library symbol*] [*Library of Congress*] [*OCLC symbol*] (LCLS)
LNUCA	United States Circuit Court of Appeals, Fifth Circuit Law Library, New Orleans, LA [*Library symbol*] [*Library of Congress*] (LCLS)
LNUrs	Ursuline Academy, New Orleans, LA [*Library symbol*] [*Library of Congress*] (LCLS)
LNV	Lanvin-Parfums, Inc. (SAUO)
LNV	Limit of Night Visibility (SAUS)
LNV	Lincln Natl Cv Sec [*NYSE symbol*] (TTSB)
LNV	Lincoln National Convertible Securities Fund, Inc. [*NYSE symbol*] (SPSG)
LNV	Londolovit [*Papua New Guinea*] [*Airport symbol*] [*Obsolete*] (OAG)
LNV	Longovilo [*Chile*] [*Seismograph station code, US Geological Survey*] (SEIS)
LNV	Lonvest Corp. [*Toronto Stock Exchange symbol*] [*Vancouver Stock Exchange symbol*]
LNVA	United States Veterans Administration Hospital, New Orleans, LA [*Library symbol*] [*Library of Congress*] (LCLS)
lNVALY	Union Valley Corp. (SAUO)
LNVT	Launch Network Verification Test (IAA)
LNW	[*The*] Louisiana & North West Railroad Co. [*AAR code*]
LNWR	Lacassine National Wildlife Refuge
LNWR	Lacreek National Wildlife Refuge (SAUO)
LNWR	London & North Western Railway [*British*]
LNWR	London & North Western Railway Co. (SAUO)
LNWR	Lostwood National Wildlife Refuge (SAUO)
LNWR	Loxahatchee National Wildlife Refuge (SAUO)
LNWS	Large Node Work Station (SAUS)
LNX	Lenex [*Poland*] [*ICAO designator*] (FAAC)
LNX	Lenox, Incorporated (SAUO)
LNX	London Executive Aviation Ltd. [*British*] [*FAA designator*] (FAAC)
LNX	Xavier University, New Orleans, LA [*Library symbol*] [*Library of Congress*] [*OCLC symbol*] (LCLS)
LNY	Lanai City [*Hawaii*] [*Airport symbol*] (OAG)
LNY	Lane Bryant, Incorporated (SAUO)
LNY	Laws of New York [*A publication*] (DLA)
LNYD	Lanyard
LNYL	Leksikon fun der Nayer Yidisher Literatur [*New York*] [*A publication*] (BJA)
LNYT	League of New York Theaters (SAUO)
LNYT	League of New York Theatres [*Later, LNYTP*] (EA)
LNYTP	League of New York Theatres and Producers (EA)
LNYV	Lettuce Necrotic Yellows Virus
LNZ	Linz [*Austria*] [*Airport symbol*] (OAG)
LNZ	Litag K.G. [*Austria*] [*FAA designator*] (FAAC)
LO	Laboratory Outfitting (SSD)
LO	Lamp Oil
LO	Landelijke Organistatie [*Netherlands underground organization*] [*World War II*]
LO	Land Office (SAUO)
LO	Landsorganisasjonen i Norge [*Norwegian Federation of Trade Unions*]
LO	Landsorganisationen i Sverige [*Swedish Federation of Trade Unions*]
LO	Larval Operculum
LO	Laser Optical (RALS)
LO	Lateral Oblique [*X-ray view*] (DAVI)
LO	Launch Operations [*or Operator*] [*NASA*]
LO	Launch Operator (SAUO)
LO	Law Observer [*1872*] [*India*] [*A publication*] (DLA)
LO	Law Officer
LO	Law Opinions [*A publication*] (DLA)
LO	Lay Observer (ILCA)
L/O	Layout (GOBB)

LO	Layout [*Graphic arts*]
LO	Learning Objective
LO	Left On [*Baseball term*] (NDBD)
LO	Left Out (TIMI)
LO	Left Outboard (MCD)
LO	Legal Observer [*British*]
LO	Legal Officer
LO	Legal Opinion [*1870-73*] [*A publication*] (DLA)
LO	Lenticular Opacity [*Ophthalmology*] (DAVI)
lo	Lesotho [*MARC country of publication code*] [*Library of Congress*] (LCCP)
L/O	Letter of Offer
LO	Letter Orders
LO	Leucine Oxidation (STED)
LO	Level Off
LO	Leverage Out (VLIE)
LO	Liaison Office [*or Officer*]
LO	Licensed Officer [*US Merchant Marine*]
LO	Lick Observatory (SAUO)
LO	[*The*] Lifestyles Organization (EA)
LO	Lift-Off (AAG)
LO	Limerent Object [*One who is the object of obsessional romantic love*]
LO	Limited Order [*Business term*]
LO	Line Occupancy
LO	Line Office (USDC)
LO	Linguoocclusal [*Dentistry*]
LO	Liquid Oxygen
LO	Listing Office [*Real estate*] (REAL)
LO	Livestock Office (SAUO)
LO	Loam [*Type of soil*] (ROG)
LO	Loan Officer [*Banking*] (TBD)
LO	Local [*Navy*]
LO	Local Office
LO	Local Order
LO	Local Origination [*Television programming*]
LO	Local Oscillator [*Electronics*]
LO	Locator File [*Information retrieval*]
LO	Locked Open [*Technical drawings*]
LO	Locked Oscillator
LO	Lock-On
LO	Lock-Out
LO	Loco [*As Written*] [*Music*]
LO	Loco [*Place*] [*Latin*]
LO	Logical Operation (AAG)
LO	Logistics Offensive
LO	Log Out [*Computer science*] (VLIE)
LO	London Office
Lo	London Regiment (SAUO)
Lo	London Stock Exchange (SG)
LO	Longitude
LO	Longitudinal Optic
LO	Longitudinal Optical (VLIE)
LO	Look-Out [*Navy*] [*British*]
Lo	Lord (WGA)
Lo	Lotarius [*Flourished, 1191-1212*] [*Authority cited in pre-1607 legal work*] (DSA)
LO	Louisville Orchestra [*Record label*]
LO	Louth [*County in Ireland*] (ROG)
LO	Love Object
lo	Low (IDOE)
LO	Low (KSC)
LO	Lowell Observatory (SAUO)
LO	Lowest Offer [*Business term*]
LO	Low Loaders (DCTA)
LO	Low Oblique [*Aerospace*]
LO	Low Observable (DOMA)
LO	Low Order [*Computer science*] (OA)
LO	Low Ordinary (IAA)
LO	Lubricating Oil
LO	Lubrication Order
LO	Lumber Orthosis (STED)
LO	Lunar Observer (ACAE)
LO	Lunar Orbiter [*Aerospace*] (MCD)
LO	Lutte Ouvriere [*Workers' Struggle*] [*France*] [*Political party*] (PPW)
LO	Lysyl Oxidase [*An enzyme*]
LO	Opelousas-Eunice Public Library (SAUS)
LO	Opelousas-Eunice Public Library, Opelousas, LA [*Library symbol*] [*Library of Congress*] (LCLS)
LO	Solicitor's Law Opinion, United States Internal Revenue Bureau [*A publication*] (DLA)
LO$_2$	Liquid Oxygen [*Also, LOX*] [*NASA*] (KSC)
LO2	Pahute Mesa [*Nevada*] [*Seismograph station code, US Geological Survey*] [*Closed*] (SEIS)
LOA	Landing Operations Area [*NASA*] (NASA)
LOA	LASER Opto-Acoustic
LOA	Lateral Osseous Ampulla [*Medicine*] (MELL)
LOA	Launch on Assessment [*Military*]
LOA	Launch on Attack [*Military*]
LOA	Launch Operations Agency [*NASA*] (KSC)
LOA	Launch Operations Area (MCD)
LOA	Lead Operational Authority (COE)
LOA	Leave of Absence
LOA	Leber Optic Atrophy (STED)
LOA	Leber's Optic Atrophy [*Medicine*] (MELL)
LOA	Left Anterior Oblique [*Medicine*] (MELL)

LOA............. Left Occipitoanterior [*A fetal position*] [*Obstetrics*]
LOA............. Length of Output Area (VLIE)
LOA............. Length Over-All [*Technical drawings*]
LOA............. Leona, TX [*Location identifier*] [*FAA*] (FAAL)
LOA............. Letter of Acceptance
LOA............. Letter of Agreement
LOA............. Letter of Authorization
LOA............. Letter Officers Association (SAUO)
LOA............. Letter Offices Association (SAUO)
LOA............. Letter of Offer and Acceptance (MCD)
LOA............. Letters of Authorization (SAUO)
LOA............. Level of Authority [*Military*] (AFIT)
LOA............. Life Offices' Association [*British*] (DCTA)
LOA............. Light Observation Aircraft
LOA............. Limit of Advance [*Army*] (DOMA)
LOA............. Line of Assurance
LOA............. List of Acronyms (or Abbreviations) (SAUS)
LOA............. Lithuanian Organists Alliance (SAUO)
LOA............. Local Ocean Area (SAUO)
LOA............. Local Overseas Allowance [*British military*] (DMA)
LOA............. Log-Out Analysis (NITA)
LOA............. London Orchestral Association (SAUO)
LOA............. London Orphan Asylum (ROG)
LOA............. Loners of America [*An association*] (EA)
LOA............. Looseness of Associations (STED)
LOA............. Lorcan Resources Ltd. [*Vancouver Stock Exchange symbol*]
LOA............. Lorcan Resours Ltd. (SAUO)
LOA............. Lorraine [*Australia*] [*Airport symbol*] [*Obsolete*] (OAG)
LOA............. Los Alamos [*New Mexico*] [*Seismograph station code, US Geological Survey*] (SEIS)
LOA............. Low Oil Agglomeration [*Coal processing*]
LOA............. Low-Speed Output Adapter (MHDB)
LOAA........... Letter of Agreement and Acceptance
LOAC........... Low Accuracy
LOAD........... Laser Optoacoustic Detection (ACAE)
LOAD........... Low-Altitude Defense (MCD)
LOAD........... Low Altitude Defense Program (SAUO)
LOADEO....... Loading of Explosive Ordnance (SAUS)
LOADEX....... Loading Exercise [*Military*] (NVT)
LOADS......... Lifting of Aerodynamic Decelerators (PDAA)
LOADS......... Low-altitude Air Defence System (SAUS)
LOADS......... Low-Altitude Defense System
LOAEL........ Lowest Observed Adverse Effect Level (EG)
LOAF........... Large Open-Area Floor
LOAF........... Lesbians Over the Age of Forty (SAUO)
LOAF........... Loaf [*Commonly used*] (OPSA)
LOAL........... Lock-On after Launch [*Weaponry*] (CAAL)
LOAL........... Lock-One After Launch [*Military*] (MUSM)
LOAM.......... List of Applicable Material (MCD)
LOAMP........ Logarithmic Amplifier (IEEE)
LOAN.......... Horizon Bancorp, Inc. (TX) [*NASDAQ symbol*] (SAG)
LOAN.......... Horizon Bancorp(TX) [*NASDAQ symbol*] (TTSB)
LOAN.......... Local Officials' Administration Network [*An association*]
LOAN/A....... Vessels Loaned to Army [*Navy*]
LOAN/C....... Vessels Loaned to Coast Guard [*Navy*]
LO & DS...... London Operatic and Dramatic Society (ROG)
LOAN/M....... Vessels Loaned to Miscellaneous Activities [*US Maritime Academy, etc.*] [*Navy*]
LOAN/S....... Vessels Loaned to States [*Navy*]
LOAN/W...... Vessels Loaned to War Shipping Administration [*Terminated, 1946*] [*Navy*]
LOANZ........ Life Offices Association of New Zealand (SAUO)
LOAP.......... Length of Adjacency Process (MHDB)
LOAP.......... List of Applicable Publications [*Air Force*]
LOAPS........ Large Order Assembly Planning System (MCD)
LOAS.......... Lift-Off Acquisition System
LOAS.......... List of Assessed Spares (MCD)
LOAS.......... Loyal Order of Ancient Shepherds [*British*] (BI)
LOAT.......... Trausdorf [*Austria*] [*ICAO location identifier*] (ICLI)
LOAV.......... Lift Owners' Association of Victoria [*Australia*]
LOAV.......... Voslau [*Austria*] [*ICAO location identifier*] (ICLI)
LOAVF........ Lorcan Resources Ltd. (SAUO)
LOAX.......... Log On America
LOB............. Laboratory Office Building
LOB............. [*The*] Land of the Bible: A Historical Geography [*A publication*] (BJA)
LOB............. Launch Operations Branch [*NASA*]
LOB............. Launch Operations Building [*NASA*]
LOB............. Left of Baseline
LOB............. Left on Base [*Baseball*]
LOB............. Left Outboard (MCD)
LOB............. Left Out of Battle [*British*]
LOB............. Legends of Batman
LOB............. Limited Operating Base (AFM)
LOB............. Line of Balance
LOB............. Line of Bearing [*Navy*] (NVT)
LOB............. Line of Business [*Used in corporate reports to Federal Trade Commission*]
LOB............. Lobito [*Angola*] [*Airport symbol*] (AD)
LOB............. Location of Offices Bureau [*British*]
LOB............. Logistics Operating Base
LOB............. Logistics-over-the-Beach Base [*Military*] (VNW)
LOB............. Loyal Order of the Boar (EA)
LObA........... Allen Parish Library, Oberlin, LA [*Library symbol*] [*Library of Congress*] (LCLS)
LOBA.......... Last Offer Binding Arbitration [*Labor negotiations*]

LOBAR........ Long Baseline RADAR
LOBI........... Library Orientation/Bibliographic Instruction [*Florida Library Association caucus*]
LOBI........... Loop Blowdown Investigation (SAUO)
Lobin.......... Lobingier's Extra-Territorial Cases [*United States Court for China*] [*A publication*] (DLA)
LOBL.......... Lock-On Before Launch [*Missile*] (DOMA)
LOBSTER.... Long-Term Ocean Bottom Settlement Test for Engineering Research [*Navy project*]
LOBTP........ League of Off-Broadway Theatres and Producers [*Later, OBL*] (EA)
LOBUND...... Laboratories of Bacteriology, University of Notre Dame (SAUO)
LoC............. Book 6 of the WOT series Lord of Chaos (SAUS)
LOC............. Landing Operations Center (MCD)
LOC............. Landsat Oversight Committee (SAUO)
LOC............. LAN Operations Center (SAUO)
LOC............. Large Optical Cavity [*LASER design*]
LOC............. Launch Operations Center [*NASA*]
LOC............. Launch Operations Complex
LOC............. Launch Operations Control
LOC............. Launch Operator's Console [*Aerospace*] (AAG)
LOC............. Laverda Owner's Club (EA)
LOC............. Laxative of Choice [*Medicine*]
LOC............. Le Groupe Opus Communications, Inc. [*Vancouver Stock Exchange symbol*]
LOC............. LeMoyne-Owen College, Memphis, TN [*OCLC symbol*] (OCLC)
LOC............. Letter of Comment
LOC............. Letter of Compliance [*Program*] [*Coast Guard*]
LOC............. Letter of Consent
LOC............. Letter of Credit (SAUO)
LOC............. Letterpress to Offset Conversion (DGA)
LOC............. Letters of Comment (SAUO)
LOC............. Letters of Credit
LOC............. Level of Care [*Medicine*] (GFGA)
LOC............. Level of Concern [*Environmental Protection Agency*] (ERG)
LOC............. Level of Consciousness [*Medicine*]
LOC............. Liaison Officer Coordinator [*Air Force*] (AFM)
LOC............. Libraries and Our Civilizations [*A publication*]
LOC............. Library of Congress
LoC............. Library of Congress Classification (TELE)
LOC............. Light-Off Catalyst [*Exhaust emissions*] [*Automotive engineering*]
LOC............. Limitation of Cost (AAGC)
LOC............. Limited Operational Capability (CET)
LOC............. Limiting Oxygen Concentration [*For ignition*]
LOC............. Lincoln Owners Club (EA)
LOC............. Lincoln School [*California*] [*Seismograph station code, US Geological Survey*] (SEIS)
LOC............. Line of Code
LOC............. Line of Communication [*Military*]
LOC............. Line of Contact (MCD)
LOC............. Line of Correction
LOC............. Line Office Contact (SAUO)
LOC............. Lines of Code (SAUO)
LOC............. Linked Object Code (TEL)
LOC............. Linked Operational Capability (DOMA)
LOC............. Liquid Organic Compound
LOC............. Load Overcurrent
loc.............. Local (ELAL)
LOC............. Local
loc/............. Localized (STED)
LOC............. Localizer (MSA)
LOC............. Localizer Line of Sight
LOC............. Locally (SAUS)
LOC............. Local Operating Company (SAUO)
LOC............. Local Operations Console (SAUS)
LOC............. Local Original Channel [*Cable television broadcasting*]
LOC............. Locate (MSA)
loc.............. Located (REAL)
LOC............. Location (AFM)
loc.............. Location (VRA)
LOC............. Location Counter [*Computer science*]
LOC............. Locative (Case) [*Linguistics*]
LOC............. Locator (PIPO)
LOC............. Locavia 49 [*France*] [*ICAO designator*] (FAAC)
LOC............. Lock-On Completed (MCD)
LOC............. Loco [*Place*] [*Latin*] (WGA)
LOC............. Loctite Corp. [*NYSE symbol*] (SPSG)
LOC............. Loctite Corporation
LOC............. Locus of Control (STED)
LOC............. Logistical Operations Center (SAUO)
LOC............. Logistic Operation Center [*Military*]
LOC............. Logistics Operations Center (SAUO)
LOC............. Logistics Operations Centre (SAUO)
LOC............. Loop On-line Control (SAUO)
LOC............. Lord of Creation
LOC............. Loss of Consciousness [*Medicine*]
LOC............. Loss of Coolant (GAAI)
LOC............. Louisiana Office of Conservation (SAUO)
LOC............. Low Compression [*Automotive engineering*]
LOC............. Lunar Observer Camera (ACAE)
LOC............. Lyric Opera of Chicago (SAUO)
LOCA.......... Late Onset Cerebellar Ataxia [*Medicine*]
LOCA.......... Loss-of-Coolant Accident [*Nuclear energy*]
LoCa.......... Low Calcium (STED)
LOCA.......... Low-Cost Computer Attachment (IAA)
LOCA.......... Low Osmolar Contrast Agent [*Medicine*]

LOCAAS........	Low-Cost Anti-Armor Submunition programme (SAUS)
LOCAAS........	Low-Cost Anti-Armor Submunitions [Military]
LOC ACC	Location Accuracy [Environmental science] (COE)
LOCAE..........	List of Classified and Authorised Explosives (HEAS)
LOCAL	Laboratory Program for Computer-Assisted Learning (IAA)
LOCAL	Load On-Call [Computer science]
lo cal	Low Calorie (MAE)
Local 464	Local 464, Utility Workers Union of America, AFL-CIO and Utility Workers Union of America, AFL-CIO (SAUO)
lo calc	Low Calcium [Diet] (DAVI)
Local Ct & Mun Gaz...	Local Courts and Municipal Gazette [Toronto, ON] [A publication] (DLA)
Local Gov	Local Government and Magisterial Reports [England] [A publication] (DLA)
Local Gov R Aust...	Local Government Reports of Australia [A publication] (DLA)
Local Gov't...	Local Government and Magisterial Reports [England] [A publication] (DLA)
Local Govt Jl WA...	Local Government Journal of Western Australia [A publication] (DLA)
LOCALS	Low-Cost Alternate LASER Seeker (MCD)
LOCAM	Logistics Cost Analysis Model (MCD)
LOCAN	Location of Canisters [Automotive emissions]
LOCAP	Low Capacitance [Cable] [Bell System]
LOCAP	Low [Altitude] Combat Air Patrol (NVT)
Locarno Union...	Union for the International Classification for/of Industrial Designs (SAUO)
LOCART	Local Cartage Company [Transportation company classification code]
LOCAS	Local Cataloguing Service (NITA)
LOCAT	Location (DAVI)
LOCAT	Low-Altitude Clear-Air Turbulence (MCD)
LOCAT	Low-Cost Aerial Trainer (SAUS)
LOCAT	Low-Cost Air Target (MCD)
LOCAT	Low Cost Artillery Trainer (SAUS)
LOCATE........	Library of Congress Automation Techniques Exchange
LOCATE........	List of Common Abbreviations in Training and Education (AIE)
LOCATE........	Local Area Telecommunications, Inc. [Digital microwave carrier] [New York, NY] (TSSD)
LOCATE........	LORAN/OMEGA Course and Tracking Equipment (MCD)
LOCATM	Low-Cost Advanced Technology Missile (SAUS)
LOCATS	Lockheed Optical Communications and Tracking System
LOCB	London Orchestral Concert Board (SAUO)
LOCC	Launcher Order and Capture Computer (MCD)
LOCC	Launch Operations Control Center
LOCC	Limitation of Cost Clause (AAGC)
Locc............	Loccenius. De Jure Maritimo [A publication] (DLA)
LOCC	Logistical Operations Control Center [Army]
LOCCAP	Transportation Plans LOCs Capacities and Capabilities (SAUO)
LOCCB	Lead on Chip with Center Bond (TIMI)
loc cit	In the Place Cited [Loco citato] [Latin] (WDMC)
LOC CIT	Loco Citato [In the Place Cited] [Latin]
LOCCOZO......	Line of Communication Combat Zone [Military]
LOCCS	Letter of Credit Control System [Department of Housing and Urban Development] (GFGA)
Loc Ct Gaz...	Local Courts and Municipal Gazette [Toronto, ON] [A publication] (DLA)
LOCD	Lines of Communication Designators (MCD)
LOCD	Local Disease
LOC DOL	Loco Dolenti [To the Painful Spot] [Pharmacy]
LOCE	Large Optical Communications Experiment (SAUS)
LOCE	Last Observation Carried Forward
LOCE	Limited Operational Capability Europe (SAUO)
LOCE	Limited Operational Capability for Europe [DoD]
LOCE	Limited Operational Capacity for Europe (SAUO)
LOCE	Linked Operations/intelligence Centers Europe (SAUO)
LOCE	Loss-of-Coolant Experiment [Nuclear energy]
LOCF	Location File (MCD)
LOCF	Loss-of-Coolant Flow [Nuclear energy] (NRCH)
Loc Gov Chron...	Local Government Chronicle [London, England] [A publication] (DLA)
Loc Govt Chr & Mag Rep...	Local Government Chronicle and Magisterial Reporter [London] [A publication] (DLA)
LOCH	Loch Exploration, Inc. (SAUO)
LOCH	London Options Clearing House (NUMA)
LOCI............	Ligue des Originaires de Cote d'Ivoire [League of Ivory Coast Natives]
LOCI............	List of Cancelled Items
LOCI............	Local Course Improvement [National Science Foundation] (EDAC)
LOCI............	Logarithmic Computing Instrument
LOCI............	Low-Cost Interceptor (MCD)
LOCID	Location Identifier [FAA] (TAG)
LOCIG	Limited-Overs Cricket Information Group [British] (DBA)
LOCIS	Library of Congress Information System [Library of Congress] [Information service or system] (IID)
LOCIST	Low Cost Improved Sensors Technology (ACAE)
LO CIT	Loco Citato [In the Place Cited] [Latin]
LOCK	Lock [Commonly used] (OPSA)
LOCK	Logistical Operational Control Key [Army] (AABC)
Lock GL	Locke's Game Laws [5th ed.] [1866] [A publication] (DLA)
LockhM........	Lockheed Martin Corp. [Associated Press] (SAG)
Lock Rev Ca...	Lockwood's Reversed Cases [New York] [A publication] (DLA)
Lock Rev Cas...	Lockwood's Reversed Cases [New York] [A publication] (DLA)
LOCKS	Locks [Commonly used] (OPSA)
LOCKSS........	Lots of Copies Keeps Stuff Safe
LOCL	Local Federal Savings & Loan Association (SAUO)
LOCL	Loyal Order of Catfish Lovers (EA)
LOCLAD	Low-Cost Low Altitude Dispenser (SAUS)

LOC LAUD ...	Loco Laudato [In the Place Quoted] [Latin]
LOCLED	Low-Operating Current Light-Emitting Diode
LOC LF	Local Line Feed [Telecommunications] (DNAB)
LOCM..........	Low Osmolar Contrast Medium (DB)
LOCMOS......	Locally-Oxidized Complementary Metal-Oxide Semiconductor (PDAA)
LOCN	Location
LOCO	Local Copy (VLIE)
LOCO	Locomotion (WDAA)
LOCO	Locomotive (AABC)
LOCO	Long Core [Drilling program]
LOCO	Love Oil Company (SAUO)
Loco...........	On the Spot (EBF)
LOCOM	Local Community (ADA)
LOCOM	Locomotive
LOCOMOTIVE...	Logistics Chain Multidimensional Design Toolbox with Environmental Assessment (SAUO)
LOCOR........	Local Coordinator (FAAC)
LOCOS........	Local Oxidation of Silicon [Transistor technology]
LOCOSS.......	Logic of Computers Operating System (MCD)
LOCO TAC ...	Low-Cost Tactical RADAR (DNAB)
LOCP	Launcher Operation Control Panel
LOCP	Local Operator's Control Panel (ACAE)
LOCP	Logistics Control Office, Pacific (SAUO)
LOCP	Loss-of-Coolant Protection [Nuclear energy] (NRCH)
LOCPOD.......	Low-Cost Powered Dispenser
LOCPOD.......	Low Cost Powered Off-boresight Dispenser (SAUS)
LOCPORT.....	Lines of Communications Ports (AABC)
Loc Primo Cit...	Loco Primo Citato [In the Place First Cited] [Latin] (ILCA)
LOC PRIUS CIT...	Loco Prius Citato [In the Place First Cited] [Latin] (ADA)
LOCPURO....	Local Purchase Order
LOCREP.......	Location Report (SAUO)
LOCRIS	Low-Cost Robot by means of Integrated Servo Control (SAUO)
LOCRV........	Local Review Program (SAUO)
LOCS	Land Ocean Climate Satellite (SAUO)
LOCS	Land-Ocean-Climate Satellite [Marine science] (OSRA)
LOCS	Land Operations Command Systems programme (SAUO)
LOCS	Librascope Operations Control System
LOCS	Local Optical Clean-Up System (ACAE)
LOCS	Local Optical Correction System (ACAE)
LOCS	Logic and Control Simulation (NITA)
LOCS	Logic and Control Simulator [Computer science] (BUR)
LOCT	Layered Open Crypto Toolkit (SAUS)
LOCT	Lockheed Command and Tracking (IAA)
LOC-TFCS	Letter-of-Credit-Treasury Financial Communications System (SAUO)
Loctite	Loctite Corp. [Associated Press] (SAG)
LOCTRACS...	Lockheed Tracking and Control System
LOCUS	Laser Obstacle Cable Unmasking System (SAUS)
LOCUSP.......	Low Cost Uncooled Sensor Prototype [Army]
Locus Standi...	Locus Standi Reports [England] [A publication] (DLA)
LOCV	Loss of Condenser Vacuum [Environmental science] (COE)
LOD	Large Organic Debris [Pisciculture]
LOD	Last Occurrence of Date (QUAC)
LOD	Launch on Demand (SAUS)
LOD	Launch Operations Directive [or Director] [NASA]
LOD	Launch Operations Directorate (SAUO)
LOD	Launch Operations Division [NASA] (KSC)
LOD	Law Officers' Department [British]
LOD	Leading Ones Detector [Computer science]
LoD	Legion of Doom (SAUS)
LOD	Length of Day
LOD	Letter of Declination (ACAE)
LOD	Letter of Direction (ACAE)
LOD	Level of Detail (MCD)
LOD	Light-Off Detector [Military] (CAAL)
LOD	Limit of Detection
LOD	Limits of Disturbance (PA)
LOD	Line of Dance
LOD	Line of Departure [Military] (AFM)
LOD	Line of Direction
LOD	Line of Duty [Military]
LOD	List of Drawings
LOD	Little Oxford Dictionary [A publication]
LOD	Locally One-Dimensional [Engineering] (OA)
LOD	Location Dependent
LOD	Lodgian, Inc. [NYSE symbol] (SG)
LOD	Lodi Metals, Inc. [Vancouver Stock Exchange symbol]
lod	Logarithm of the Odds [Favoring linkage] [Genetics] (DOG)
LOD	Logarithm of the Odds
LOD	Longana [Vanuata] [Airport symbol] (OAG)
LOD	Low Density (IAA)
LOD2	Lightweight Omega Digital Dropwindsonde (SAUO)
LODAC	Low Dispersion Automatic Cannon (TIMI)
LODACS.......	Longitudinal Fame Developing and Conducting System (PDAA)
LODACS.......	Low-Dispersion Automatic Cannon System
LODC	Local Defense District Craft
LODCS	Lunar Orbiter Data Conversion System [Aerospace]
LODE	Comstock Bank [NASDAQ symbol] (SAG)
LODE	Cornstock Bk Carson City Nev [NASDAQ symbol] (TTSB)
LODE	Large Optics Demonstration Experiment [DoD]
LODED	Long Duration Expendable Decoy (SAUS)
LODEM	Loading Dock Equipment Manufacturers Association (EA)
LODESMP.....	Logistics Data Element Standardization and Management Process (IEEE)
LODESTAR...	Logically Organized Data Entry, Storage, and Recording
LODG	Lodge [Commonly used] (OPSA)

LODG .... Sholodge, Inc. [*NASDAQ symbol*] (SAG)
LODGE .... Lodge [*Commonly used*] (OPSA)
LodgEnt ...... Lodgenet Entertainment Corp. [*Associated Press*] (SAG)
LODI .... List of Deleted Items (NG)
LODIF .... Long Distance Infrared Flash Camera (PDAA)
LODISNAV .. Long Distance Navigation (FAAC)
LODOR .... Loaded, Waiting Orders or Assignment [*Navy*]
LODP .... Lunar Orbiter Data Printer [*Aerospace*]
LODR .... Loader
LODSB .... Load String Byte [*Computer science*] (VLIE)
LODSC .... Logistics Operations Decision Support Center (SAUO)
LODTM .... Large Optics Diamond Turning Machine (ACAE)
LODUS .... Low Data Rate UHF [*Ultra-High Frequency*] Satellite [*RADAR*] (MCD)
LODYC .... Laboratoire d'Oceanographie Dynamique et de Climatologie [*France*] [*Marine science*] (OSRA)
LOE .... Late Old English (ADWA)
LOE .... Left Otitis Externa [*Medicine*] (AMHC)
LOE .... Left Outboard Elevon [*Aviation*] (MCD)
LOE .... Letter of Evaluation
LOE .... Letter of Execution (MCD)
LOE .... Level of Effort (KSC)
LOE .... Light-Off Examination [*Navy*] (NVT)
LOE .... Limit of Exploitation (SAUS)
LOE .... Line of Effort (MCD)
LOE .... Line Oriented Evaluation (GAVI)
LOE .... Loei [*Thailand*] [*Airport symbol*] [*Obsolete*] (OAG)
LOE .... Loeser, Luftfahrtgesellschaft GmbH [*Germany*] [*ICAO designator*] (FAAC)
LOE .... Louisiana Eastern Railroad (SAUO)
LOEAT .... Lowest Temperature Equaled for All Time [*NWS*] (FAAC)
LOEC .... List of Effective Cards (NVT)
LOEC .... Lowest Observed Effect Concentration [*Environmental Technology*]
LOEE .... Loyal Order of Overtime Experts (SAUO)
LOEFM .... Lowest Temperature Equaled for the Month [*NWS*] (FAAC)
LOEH .... Loehmann's Inc. [*NASDAQ symbol*] (TTSB)
LOEL .... Lowest-Observed-Effect Level [*Environmental science*] (FFDE)
LOEM(A) ...... Leading Ordnance Electrical Mechanic (Air) [*British military*] (DMA)
LOEP .... List of Effective Pages (NVT)
LOEP .... Loss of Electric Power
LOERO .... Large Orbiting Earth Resources Observatory (IEEE)
LOESE .... Lowest Temperature Equaled So Early [*NWS*] (FAAC)
LOESL .... Lowest Temperature Equaled So Late [*NWS*] (FAAC)
Loewen .... Loewen Group, Inc. [*Associated Press*] (SAG)
LoewenG ..... Loewen Group Capital LP [*Associated Press*] (SAG)
Loews .... Loew's Corp. [*Formerly, Loew's Theatres, Inc.*] [*Associated Press*] (SAG)
LOEX .... Laboratory of Experimental Tissue Engineering (SAUO)
LOEX .... Library Orientation/Instruction Exchange [*Library network*]
LOF .... Lack of Fusion
LOF .... Lecherous Old Fool [*Slang*]
LOF .... Letter of Finding (GFGA)
LOF .... Libbey-Owens-Ford Glass Co. [*Auto industry supplier*]
LOF .... Lift-Off (SAUS)
LOF .... Limitation of Funds (AAGC)
LOF .... Line of Fire
LOF .... Line-of-Flight (MCD)
LOF .... Line of Force
LOF .... List Overflow (VLIE)
LOF .... Lloyd's Open Form (RIMS)
LOF .... Local Oscillator Filter [*Electronics*]
LOF .... Local Oscillator Frequency [*Electronics*]
LOF .... Lock Off-Line [*Computer science*] (VLIE)
LOF .... Lofexidine (DMAA)
LOF .... London and Overseas Freighter
LOF .... Longest Operation First
LOF .... Look Ahead on Fault [*Computer science*] (MHDB)
LOF .... Loss of Feedwater [*Nuclear energy*] (NRCH)
LOF .... Loss of Flow [*Nuclear energy*] (NRCH)
LOF .... Loss of Fluid (BARN)
LOF .... Loss of Frame (MLOA)
LOF .... Lowest Operating Frequency (IEEE)
LOF .... Low Outlet Forceps [*Delivery*] [*Obstetrics*] (DAVI)
LOF .... Lube and Oil Filter
LOF .... Lube, Oil, and Filter [*Automobile servicing*]
LOF .... Trans States Airlines, Inc. [*ICAO designator*] (FAAC)
LOFA .... Leisure and Outdoor Furniture Association [*British*] (DBA)
LOFA .... Loss of Flow Accident [*Nuclear energy*] (NRCH)
LOFAAD .... Low-Altitude Forward Area Air Defense (AABC)
LOFAADS ..... Low-Altitude Forward Area Anti-Aircraft Defense System [*Army*]
LOFAADS ..... Low Level Forward Area Air Defense System (SAUO)
LOFADS .... Low-Altitude Forward Air Defense System (PDAA)
LOFAR .... Low-Frequency Acquisition and Ranging
LOFAR .... Low-Frequency Analysis and Recording [*Sonobuoys*] [*Navy*]
LOFAR .... Low Frequency Omnidirectional Acoustic Frequency Analysis & Recording (SAUS)
LOFARGRAM... Low Frequency Recording & Analysis Gram (SAUS)
LOFAT .... Low-Flying Aerial Target [*Military*] (CAAL)
L of C .... Library of Congress
L of C .... Lines of Communication (SAUO)
LOFC .... Loss of Forced Circulation [*Nuclear energy*] (NRCH)
LOFES .... Load Factor Error Sensor (MCD)
LOFEZ .... Low Fighter Engagement Zone (PDAA)
LOFF .... Leakoff [*Mechanical engineering*]
L Off Econ & Mgt... Law Office Economics and Management [*A publication*] (DLA)

LOFFIRS ...... Low Cost Fire/Forget Infrared Seeker (ACAE)
Lofft .... Lofft's English King's Bench Reports [*1772-74*] [*A publication*] (DLA)
Lofft Append. .... Lofft's Maxims, Appended to Lofft's Reports [*A publication*] (DLA)
Lofft Lib .... Lofft on the Law of Libels [*A publication*] (DLA)
Lofft Max .... Maxims Appended to Lofft's Reports [*A publication*] (DLA)
Lofft's Rep. .. Lofft's English King's Bench Reports [*1772-74*] [*A publication*] (DLA)
Lofft Un L .... Lofft's Elements of Universal Law [*A publication*] (DLA)
L of N .... League of Nations [*1919-1946*]
LOFO .... Low-Frequency Oscillation (MCD)
L of P .... Lodge of Perfection [*Freemasonry*] (DAS)
LOFRECO ...... Low Front End Cost [*Engineering*]
LOFS .... Launch Operations Flow Subgroup (SAUO)
Lofs .... London and Overseas Freighters Society (SAUO)
LOFS .... London & Overseas Freightliners [*NASDAQ symbol*] (SAG)
LOFSY .... London & Overseas Freight ADS [*NASDAQ symbol*] (TTSB)
LOFT .... Line Oriented Flight Training (MCD)
Loft .... Lofft's English King's Bench Reports [*1772-74*] [*A publication*] (DLA)
LOFT .... Loss of Flow [*or Fluid*] Test Facility [*Nuclear energy*]
LOFT .... Loss-of-Fluid Test (GAAI)
LOFT .... Low-Frequency Telescope [*NASA*]
LOFTI .... Low-Frequency Transionospheric Satellite
LOFTPS .... Lube Oil Fill, Transfer, and Purification System (DNAB)
LOFW .... Loss of Feedwater [*Nuclear energy*] (NRCH)
LOG .... Labor Old Guard [*Australia*] [*An association*]
LOG .... Lambda Omicron Gamma Medical Society (NTPA)
LOG .... Lawn-O-Gram [*A publication*] (EAAP)
LOG .... Legion of Guardsmen (EA)
LOG .... Logan [*Utah*] [*Seismograph station code, US Geological Survey*] [*Closed*] (SEIS)
LOG .... Loganair Ltd. [*British*] [*ICAO designator*] (FAAC)
LOG .... Logan Mines Ltd. [*Vancouver Stock Exchange symbol*]
log .... Logarithm (IDOE)
LOG .... Logarithm [*Mathematics*]
log .... log book (SAUS)
log .... Loggia (VRA)
LOG .... Logging
LOG .... Logic
log .... Logistic (MILB)
LOG .... Logistician
LOG .... Logistics (KSC)
log .... Logogram (BJA)
log .... Logographic (BJA)
LOG .... Pago Pago, AQ [*Location identifier*] [*FAA*] (FAAL)
LOG .... Rayonier Timberlands (SAUO)
LOG .... Rayonier Timberlands Cl'A' [*NYSE symbol*] (TTSB)
LOG .... Rayonier Timberlands LP [*NYSE symbol*] (SPSG)
LOGACS .... Low-G Accelerometer Calibration System [*NASA*]
LOGAI .... Logical Addressing and Interoperability (SAUO)
LOGAIR .... Logistics Airlift [*Military*]
LOGAIR .... Logistics Air Network (SAUO)
Logair .... United States Air Force Logistics Command (SAUO)
LOGAIRNET... Logistics Air Network [*Air Force*]
LOGAIS .... Logistics Automated Information System [*Marine Corps*] (DOMA)
LOGAL .... Logical Algorithmic Language [*Computer science*] (CSR)
LogalEd .... Logal Educational Software & Systems Ltd. [*Associated Press*] (SAG)
LOGALGOL... Logical Algorithmic Language [*Computer science*]
LOGAM .... Logistics Analysis Model [*Army*] (RDA)
LOGAMP .... Logarithmic Amplifier (IAA)
LOGAMP ...... Logistics and Acquisition Management Program [*Army*] (RDA)
LOGANDS .... Logical Commands
Logans .... Logan's Roadhouse, Inc. [*Associated Press*] (SAG)
LOGATAK ...... Logistics Attack Model [*BDM Corp.*] (MCD)
LOGBALNET... Logistics Ballistic Missile Network [*Air Force*]
LOGC .... Logic Devices [*NASDAQ symbol*] (TTSB)
LOGC .... Logic Devices, Inc. [*NASDAQ symbol*] (SAG)
LOGC .... Logistics Center [*Army*]
LOG-C3 .... Logistics Command, Control and Communications (SAUO)
LOG-C3I .... Logistics Command, Control, Communications and Intelligence (SAUO)
LOGCAB .... Logistics Center Advisory Board (MCD)
LOGC-AMIP... Logistics Center Involvement in Army Model Improvement Program
LOGCAP .... Logistic and Command Assessment of Projects [*Army*]
LOGCAP .... Logistics Capability
LOGCAP .... Logistics Civil Augmentation Program [*Army*]
LOGCCIS ...... Logistics Command & Control Information System (SAUO)
LOGCCIS ...... Logistics Command Central Information System [*British*]
LOGCEN .... Logistics Center (MCD)
LOGCMD ...... Logistical Command
Log Com ...... Logistical Command (SAUO)
LOGCOM ...... Logistic Communications (CET)
LOGCOM ...... Logistics Command (MCD)
LOGCOMD ... Logistical Command
LOGCOMNET... AFLC Teletypewriter Communications System (SAUO)
Log Comp ..... Logan's Compendium of Ancient Law [*A publication*] (DLA)
LOGCON .... Logic Connection (VLIE)
LOGCON ...... Logistics Readiness Condition System [*DARCOM*] (MCD)
LOGCON ...... Medical Logistics and Contingency Planning system (SAUO)
LOGCOR .... Logistics Coordination (NVT)
LOGCOST ..... Logistics Cost Model (PDAA)
LOG CTR ...... Logistic Center [*Army*]
LOGDB .... Logistics Database
LOGDEC .... Logarithmic Decrement (IAA)
LOGDESMAP... Logistics Data Element Dictionary (SAUO)

LOGDESMAP... Logistics Data Element Standardization and Management Program [*DoD*] (AABC)

LOGDESMO... Logistics Data Element Standardization and Management Office [*DoD*] (AABC)

LOGDET....... Logistics Detachment (SAUO)

LOGDET....... Logistics Detail (SAUO)

LOGDIS .... Logistics Data Integration System (SAUO)

LOGDIV....... Logistics Division [*Supreme Headquarters, Allied Powers Europe*] (NATG)

log$_e$............. Logarithm to the Base e [*Mathematics*] (DAVI)

LOGE .... Logetronics, Inc. (SAUO)

LOGEL .... Logic Generating Language [*Computer science*]

LOGEN .... Aircraft Load Generator (SAUO)

LOGEST .... Annual Logistic Estimate (NATG)

LOGEX .... Logistical Exercise [*Army*] (AABC)

LOGEX .... Logistic Exercise (SAUS)

LOGFAC ...... Logistics Feasibility Analysis Capability (SAUO)

LOGFACREP.. Logistics Factors Report (SAUO)

LOGFED .... Log File Editor (NITA)

LOGFED .... Log File Editor Processor [*Computer science*]

LOGFOR....... Logistics Force [*Military*]

LOGFTC .... Logarithmic Fast Time Constant

LOGHELO..... Logistics Helicopter (NVT)

LOGHOLDAIR... Air Logistics Message (SAUS)

LOGI .... Logarithmic Computing Instrument (HGAA)

LOGI .... Logimetrics, Incorporated (SAUO)

LOGIC .... LASER Optical Guidance Integration Concept [*Missile guidance*]

LOGIC .... Level of Greatest Item Control [*DoD*]

LOGIC .... Local Government Information Center

Logic .... Logic Works, Inc. [*Associated Press*] (SAG)

LOGIC .... Loveland Geographic Information/ Cartographic System (SAUO)

LogicD .... Logic Devices, Inc. [*Associated Press*] (SAG)

LOGICOM..... Logical Communications, Inc. [*East Norwalk, CT*] [*Telecommunications*] (TSSD)

Logicon....... Logicon Corp. [*Associated Press*] (SAG)

LOGICON ..... Logicon, Inc. (ACAE)

LOGIFAMP ... Logarithmic Intermediate Frequency Amplifier (IAA)

LOGIK .... Logical Organizing and Gathering of Information Knowledge (MHDI)

LOGIMP .... Logistic Improvement Program [*Military*]

LOGIN......... Local Government Information Network [*Information service or system*]

LOGIPAC..... Logical Processor and Computer

LOGISTC ..... Logistic

LOGIT .... Logical Inference Tester [*NASA*]

LOGK .... Kapfenberg [*Austria*] [*ICAO location identifier*] (ICLI)

LOGL .... Logal Educational Software & Systems Ltd. [*NASDAQ symbol*] (SAG)

LOGLAN....... Logical Language

LOGLAND ..... Logistics Transport by Land [*Military*]

LOGLF .... Logal Educational Softwr&Sys [*NASDAQ symbol*] (TTSB)

LOGLISP...... Prolog and List Processing

LOGMAN...... Logistics & Manpower Division (SAUO)

LOGMAP..... Logistic Master Plan (SAUO)

LOGMAP..... Logistics System Master Plan [*Army*]

LOGMAPS.... Logistics Master Planning System

LOGMARS.... Logistic Applications of Automated Marking and Reading Symbols [*DoD*]

LOGMDS..... Logistics Management Data System (SAUO)

LOGMET ...... Logistics Management Engineering Team [*Military*]

Log Mgt Cen.. Logistical Management Center (SAUO)

LOGMIS ...... Logistics Management Information System [*USACC*]

LOGMOD..... Logic Model [*Fault isolation device*] [*Army*] (MCD)

LOGMOD..... Logistics Module [*Simulation games*] [*Army*] (INF)

LOGMOD-B... Logistics Module-Base Level (SAUO)

LOGMOD-M.. Logistics Module-Major Command Level (SAUO)

LOGMSG..... Log Message [*Computer science*] (VLIE)

LOGMTD...... Logarithmic Mean Temperature Difference (IAA)

LOGN .... Logansort Financial [*NASDAQ symbol*] (TTSB)

LOGN .... Logansport Financial Corp. [*NASDAQ symbol*] (SAG)

LOGNET...... Logistics Data Network (SAUO)

LOGNET...... Logistics Network (MCD)

LOGNEW...... Logistics Network (SAUO)

Lognspt....... Logansport Financial Corp. [*Associated Press*] (SAG)

LOGO .... Limitation of Government Obligation (MCD)

LOGO .... Limit of Government Obligation (NAKS)

LOGO .... Logotype [*Advertising*] (DSUE)

LOGOIS........ Logistics Operating Information System (AABC)

LOGOS .... Language of Generalized Operational Simulation (VLIE)

LOGP .... Logistics Plans

LOGPAC...... Logistics Package [*Army*] (INF)

LOGPARS .... Logistics Planning & Requirements Simplification (SAUO)

LOGPARS .... Logistics Planning and Requirements Simplification System [*Army*] (RDA)

LOGPLAN..... Logistics Planning Module (SAUO)

LOGPLAN..... Logistics Plans Generation Subsystem (SAUO)

LOG PLAN ... Logistics System Plan [*Navy*] [*DoD*]

LOGR .... Logistical Ratio [*Army*]

LOGRAM...... Logical Program

LOGRAM...... Logistics Readiness Assessment Model (SAUO)

LOGREADI ... Logistics Production/ Maintenance/Readiness (SAUO)

LOGREC....... Log Recording [*Computer science*]

LOGREDI...... Logistics Readiness (SAUO)

LOGREP....... Logistics Replenishment (NVT)

LOGREP....... Logistics Report (SAUO)

LOGREP....... Logistics Representative [*Navy*] (NVT)

LOGREQ...... Logistics Requirements (NVT)

LOGS .... Labor's Old Guard Socialists [*Australia*] [*An association*]

LOGS .... Logistics Supportability (AABC)

LOGS .... Logos Scientific, Inc. (SAUO)

LOGSA .... Logistics Support Activity [*Army*]

LOGSACS ..... Logistics Structure and Composition System (AABC)

LOGSAFE ..... Logistics Sustainability Analysis Feasibility Estimator (DOMA)

LOGSAFE ..... Logistics Sustainment Analysis and Feasibility Estimator (SAUO)

LOGSAM...... Logistics Support Alternative [*or Analysis*] Model (MCD)

LOGSAR...... Logistics Storage and Retrieval System (SAUO)

LOGSARC ... Logistics System Acquisition Review Council (ACAE)

LOGSAT ...... Logistics Special Assistance Team (MCD)

LOGSAT ...... Logistics Support Assistance Team (SAUO)

LOGSEA ...... Logistics Transport by Sea [*Military*]

LOGSHORE... Logistics Short Report message (SAUS)

LOGSIM...... Logic Simulator Program (ACAE)

LOGSIM...... Logistic Simulation (ACAE)

LOGSS .... Logistics Support Squadron [*Military*]

LOGSTAR..... Logistics Status Report (SAUO)

LOGSTAT .... Logistical Status Report [*Military*] (INF)

LOGSTAT .... Logistics State (SAUO)

LOGSTCN... Logistician

LOGSUM..... Logistics Summary (NVT)

LOGSUM..... Logistics Summary Data (SAUO)

LOGSUP..... Logistics Support

LOGSUPREP... Logistics Support Report message (SAUS)

LOGSVC...... Logistics Service [*Military*] (NVT)

LOGTAB...... Logic Tables (IEEE)

LOGTANBG... Logarithm Tangent Bearing (IAA)

LOGTECH..... Logistics Technology (SAUO)

LOGTIES ...... Logistic Technology Initiatives for Existing Systems (ACAE)

LOGWARS ... Logistic Wartime Automated Readiness System (SAUO)

LOgWC .... West Carroll Parish Library, Oak Grove, LA [*Library symbol*] [*Library of Congress*] (LCLS)

LOH .... "Lady of the House" [*Advertising*] (DOAD)

loh............. Lady of the House [*Telephone marketing*] (WDMC)

LOH .... League of Housewives [*Also known as HOW*]

LOH .... Length of Hospitalization

L o H .... Library of Hawaii (SAUO)

LOH .... Light Observation Helicopter

LOH .... Line Overhead (ACRL)

LOH .... Local Osteolytic Hypercalcemia [*Endocrinology*]

LOH .... Loja [*Ecuador*] [*Airport symbol*] (OAG)

LOH .... Loop of Henle [*Medicine*] (DMAA)

LOH .... Loss of Heterozygosity [*Genetics*]

LOHAC........ Loading and Handling Corrective Action Program

LOHAP .... Light Observation Helicopter Avionics Package (MCD)

LOHET .... Linear Output Hall Effect Transducer

LOHF .... Late-Onset Hepatic Failure [*Medicine*] (MELL)

LOHO .... Longhorn Steaks [*NASDAQ symbol*] (TTSB)

LOHO .... Longhorn Steaks, Inc. [*NASDAQ symbol*] (SAG)

Lo Ho .... Lower Hold (RIMS)

LOHP .... Labor Occupational Health Program (SAUO)

LOHS .... Loss of Heat Sink [*Nuclear energy*] (NRCH)

LOHTADS..... Light Observation Helicopter Target Acquisition Designation System (MCD)

LOI............. Laboratory Operating Instructions (MCD)

LOI............. Laredo [*Texas*] [*Airport symbol*] (AD)

LOI............. Laredo, TX [*Location identifier*] [*FAA*] (FAAL)

LOI............. Launch-on-Impact [*Military*] (MUSM)

LOI............. Letter of Indemnity (RIMS)

LOI............. Letter of Instruction

LOI............. Letter of Intent (ACAE)

LOI............. Letter of Interest (NG)

LOI............. Letter of Introduction

LOI............. Level of Incompetence (DMAA)

LOI............. Level of Injury [*Neurology*] (DAVI)

LOI............. Limiting Oxygen Index

LOI............. Limit of Impurities

LOI............. Line of Induction

LOI............. List of Items (AABC)

LOI............. Lock-On Initiated (MCD)

LOI............. Lodge of Instruction [*Freemasonry*]

LOI............. Loss of Imprinting [*Genetics*]

LOI............. Loss-of-Input (COE)

LOI............. Loss on Ignition [*Analytical chemistry*]

LOI............. Loss-on-Ignition (SAUO)

LOI............. Lunar Orbit Insertion [*NASA*]

LOIA............ Liaison Officer for Internal Affairs (SAUO)

LOICZ........... Land-Ocean Interaction in the Coastal Zone [*International Geosphere Biosphere Programme*]

LOICZ-SSC... LOICZ Scientific Steering Committee (SAUO)

LOID .... Location Identifiers [*A publication*] [*FAA*]

LOIH .... Hohenems-Dornbirn [*Austria*] [*ICAO location identifier*] (ICLI)

LOIH .... Left Oblique Inguinal Hernia [*Medicine*] (DMAA)

LOIJ .... St. Johann, Tirol [*Austria*] [*ICAO location identifier*] (ICLI)

LOINC.......... Logical Observation Identifier Names and Codes (RALS)

LOIRA .... Land-Ocean Interactions in the Russian Arctic (SAUO)

LOIS........... Land-Ocean Interaction Study

LOIS........... Langsam Library Online Information Services [*University of Cincinnati*] (OLDSS)

LOIS........... Law Office Information Systems (VLIE)

LOIS........... Legal Office Information System

LOIS........... Lesbians Organising in Solidarity [*An association*]

LOIS............. Library Online Information Services [*Morehead State University*] (OLDSS)
LOIS............. Library Order Information System [*Computer system*] [*Library of Congress*] [*Obsolete*]
LOIS............. Loss of Interim Status [*Environmental Protection Agency*]
Lois Batim... Lois des Batiments [*A publication*] (DLA)
Lois Rec...... Lois Recentes du Canada [*A publication*] (DLA)
LOIT............. Loitering [*FBI standardized term*]
LOIUSA........ Loyal Orange Institution of United States of America (EA)
LOIV............ Loyal Orange Institution of Victoria [*Australia*]
LoJack........ Lo-Jack Corp. [*Associated Press*] (SAG)
LOJN........... LoJack Corp. [*NASDAQ symbol*] (SAG)
LOK............. Lockwood Petroleum, Inc. [*Vancouver Stock Exchange symbol*]
LOKSMTH... Locksmith
LOKTAL....... Locked Octal (IAA)
LOL............. Laughing Out Loud
LOL............. Laugh Out Loud [*Internet language*] [*Computer science*]
LOL............. League of Lefthanders [*Defunct*] (EA)
LOL............. Left Occipitolateral [*A fetal position*] [*Obstetrics*]
LOL............. Length of Lead [*Actual*] [*Technical drawings*]
LOL............. Limited Operating Life
LOL............. Limit of Liability (MCD)
LOL............. Line of Launch [*Navy*] (CAAL)
LOL............. List of Lists (SAUS)
LOL............. Little Old Lady [*Slang*]
LOL............. Lobitos Oilfields Limited (SAUO)
lol.............. Lolo (Bantu) [*MARC language code*] [*Library of Congress*] (LCCP)
LOL............. London-Oiseau-Lyre [*Record label*] [*Great Britain, USA, etc.*]
LOL............. Longitude of Launch
LOL............. Loss of Learning (SAUO)
LOL............. Loss of Life (SAUS)
LOL............. Lovelock [*Nevada*] [*Airport symbol*] [*Obsolete*] (OAG)
LOL............. Low Order Language (ACAE)
LOL............. Loyal Orange Lodge
LOLA........... Layman-Oriented Language (IAA)
LOLA........... Library On-Line Acquisitions [*Washington State University*] [*Data processing system*]
LOLA........... Light Observation Light-Armored Aircraft
LOLA........... London Online Local Authorities (NITA)
LOLA........... Long Line Azimuth [*Survey*]
LOLA........... Lower Leg Artery [*Anatomy*]
LOLA........... Low-Level Oil Alarm (IAA)
LOLA........... Lunar Orbit and Landing Approach [*Simulator*] [*NASA*]
LOLAD........ Low-Altitude LASER Air Defense System
LOLADS...... Low Altitude Laser Air Defense System (ACAE)
LOLAS........ Location of Launching Site [*Army*]
LOLEX........ Low-Level Extraction [*Military aviation*]
LOLI........... Limited Operational-Life Items [*NASA*] (NASA)
LOLI........... Loyal Orange Ladies Institution (EA)
LOLITA...... Language for the On-Line Investigation and Transformation of Abstractions [*Computer science*]
LOLITA....... Library On-Line Information and Text Access [*Oregon State University*] [*Corvallis, OR*] [*Data processing system*]
LOLITS....... Little Old Ladies in Tennis Shoes [*Facetious reference to minor league baseball*]
LO/LO......... Lift-On/Lift-Off
LOLP.......... Loss of Load Probability [*Nuclear energy*] (IEEE)
LOLSD........ Liquid Crystal Large Screen Display (ACAE)
LOLV.......... Lower Leg Vein [*Anatomy*]
LOLVE........ Lower Leg Venule [*Anatomy*]
LOLW......... Laid Off, Lack of Work [*Unemployment insurance and the Bureau of Labor Statistics*] (OICC)
LOLW......... Wels [*Austria*] [*ICAO location identifier*] (ICLI)
LOM............ Laminated Object Manufacturing [*Desktop manufacturing*]
LOM............ Laminated Object Modeling [*Prototyping*]
LOM............ LASER Optical Modulator
LOM............ Launch Operations Manager [*NASA*]
LOM............ League of Mercy [*Salvation Army*]
LOM............ League of Mothers (SAUO)
LOM............ Left Otitis Media [*Medicine*] (CPH)
LOM............ Legion of Merit [*Military award*]
LOM............ Level of Maintenance (MCD)
LOM............ Light-Optic Microscope (MSA)
LOM............ Limitation of Motion [*Neurology*] (DAVI)
LOM............ Limitation of Movement
LOM............ List of Material (SAUO)
LOM............ List of Materials (CET)
LOM............ List of Modifications (AFM)
LOM............ Little Old Man [*Slang*] (DAVI)
LOM............ Living Operating Module (ACAE)
LOM............ Locator at Outer Marker [*Aviation*]
LOM............ Loewen, Ondaatje, McCutcheon, Inc. [*Toronto Stock Exchange symbol*] [*Vancouver Stock Exchange symbol*]
LOM............ Lomas & Nettleton Mortgage Investors (SAUO)
LOM............ Lome [*Togo*] [*Seismograph station code, US Geological Survey*] (SEIS)
LOM............ Loss of Motion [*Medicine*]
LOM............ Loss of Movement (SAUO)
LOM............ Low-Frequency Outer Marker
LOM............ Low-Order Memory (CET)
LOM............ Loyal Order of Moose (EA)
LOM............ Lunar Orbital Map [*Air Force*]
LOM............ Lunar Orbital Mission [*NASA*] (KSC)
LOM............ SERTEL [*Servicios Telereservacios SA de CV*] [*ICAO designator*] (FAAC)

LOMA......... Lange Order Matrix Arithmetic (ACAE)
LOMA......... Life Office Management Association [*Atlanta, GA*] (EA)
LOMA......... Literature on Modern Art
LOMA......... Lutheran Outdoors Ministry Association [*Later, NLOMA*] (EA)
LOMAC...... Logical Machine Corporation (SAUO)
LOMAC...... Logistic Management Advisory Committee
Lomaco....... Lonrho-Mozambique Agroindustrial Company (SAUO)
LOMAD...... Low-to-Medium-Altitude Air Defense (AABC)
LOMADS..... Low Altitude Missile Air Defence System (SAUS)
LOMAH...... Location of Miss and Hit [*Marksmanship training*] [*Army*] (INF)
Lomak........ Lomak Petroleum, Inc. [*Associated Press*] (SAG)
Loma Linda U... Loma Linda University (GAGS)
LOMAR....... Local Manual Attempt Recording (TEL)
LOMAR....... Logistics, Maintenance, and Repair (IAA)
LOMAS....... Law Office Managemnt and Accounting System (HGAA)
Lomax Ex'rs... Lomax on Executors [*A publication*] (DLA)
LOMB......... Lockheed Missile Beacon (IAA)
LOMC......... Logistics Management Committee (AAGC)
Lom CH Rep... Lomas's City Hall Reporter [*New York*] [*A publication*] (DLA)
Lom Dig...... Lomax's Digest of Real Property [*A publication*] (DLA)
Lome III...... Third ACP-EEC convention (SAUO)
Lom Ex....... Lomax on Executors [*A publication*] (DLA)
LOMEZ....... Low-altitude Missile Engagement Zone (SAUO)
LOMF......... Loss of Main Feedwater [*Nuclear energy*] (NRCH)
LOMI......... Letter of Moral Intent [*Business term*]
LOMI......... Low Oxidation State Metallic Ion [*Nuclear energy*] (NUCP)
LOMIS........ Locator Map in Source (IAA)
LOMK........ Lomak Petroleum [*NASDAQ symbol*] (TTSB)
LOMK........ Lomak Petroleum, Inc. [*NASDAQ symbol*] (SAG)
LOMMCA .... Logistics Operations Manpower and Materiel Cost Analysis (SAUO)
LOMMIS ...... Land Ordnance Maintenance Management Information System (PDAA)
LOMO .... London Overseas Mail Office
LOMOR....... Long-Distance Medium Frequency Omni Range (IAA)
LOMP........ Local Office Microcomputer Project (NITA)
LOMS......... Library Organization and Management Section [*Library Administration Division of ALA*]
LOMSA ...... Left Otitis Media Suppurative Acute [*Medicine*]
LOMSACh ... Left Otitis Media Suppurative, Chronic [*Medicine*] (MEDA)
LOMSCH..... Left Otitis Media Suppurative Chronic [*Medicine*]
LOMUSS..... Lockheed Multiprocessor Simulation System (IEEE)
LOMV......... Lolium Mottle Virus [*Plant pathology*]
LON .... Avilond, TAC [*Ukraine*] [*FAA designator*] (FAAC)
LON .... League of Nations (SAUO)
LON .... Letter of Notification
LON .... Line of Nodes
LON .... Local Operating Network [*Computer science*] (AGLO)
LON .... London [*England*] [*Airport symbol*] (OAG)
Lon .... London [*Record label*] [*Export issues of English Decca - mainly USA, Canada, etc.*]
LON .... London European Airways PLC [*British*] [*ICAO designator*] (FAAC)
LON .... Longitude (KSC)
LON .... Longmire [*Washington*] [*Seismograph station code, US Geological Survey*] (SEIS)
LON .... Tupelo, MS [*Location identifier*] [*FAA*] (FAAL)
LON .... University College, London, England [*OCLC symbol*] (OCLC)
LoNa........... Low Sodium [*Dietetics*] (DAVI)
LONAL .... Local Off-Net Access Line [*Telecommunications*] (TEL)
LOND.......... London
Lond........... London Encyclopedia [*A publication*] (DLA)
LOND.......... London International Group Ltd. [*NASDAQ symbol*] (SAG)
LondInt .... London International Group PLC [*Associated Press*] (SAG)
Lond Jur ...... London Jurist Reports [*England*] [*A publication*] (DLA)
Lond Jur NS... London Jurist, New Series [*A publication*] (DLA)
Lond LM ...... London Law Magazine [*A publication*] (DLA)
LondM .... London Magazine (SAUO)
LondMedSt... London Medical Studies (SAUO)
LondonP ...... London Pacific Group Ltd. [*Associated Press*] (SAG)
LONDON SE... London Stock Exchange [*England*]
LondOvr...... London & Overseas Freightliners [*Associated Press*] (SAG)
LondQR...... London Quarterly Review (SAUO)
LondTopogRec... London Topographical Record (SAUO)
LONDY........ London Intl Group plc ADS [*NASDAQ symbol*] (TTSB)
LONEOS...... Lowell Observatory Near-Earth Object Search (SAUO)
LONESHS..... Limited- or Non-English Speaking Handicapped Student
LoneStar...... Lone Star Technologies [*Associated Press*] (SAG)
LoneStr...... Lone Star Technologies, Inc. [*Associated Press*] (SAG)
LONEX .... Laboratory Office Network Experiment [*DoD*]
LONF .... London Financial [*NASDAQ symbol*] (TTSB)
Long .... Longford [*County in Ireland*] (WGA)
LONG .... Longitude (AFM)
long .... Longitude (ELAL)
Long .... Longtitude (WA)
LONG .... Longus [*Long*] [*Pharmacy*]
Long & R..... Long and Russell's Election Cases [*Massachusetts*] [*A publication*] (DLA)
Long & T .... Longfield and Townsend's Irish Exchequer Reports [*1841-42*] [*A publication*] (DLA)
Long Beach B Bull... Long Beach Bar Bulletin [*A publication*] (DLA)
LongDr........ Longs Drug Stores Corp. [*Associated Press*] (SAG)
LongDrg...... Longs Drug Stores [*Associated Press*] (SAG)
LONGF .... Longford [*County in Ireland*] (ROG)
Longf & T .... Longfield and Townsend's Irish Exchequer Reports [*1841-42*] [*A publication*] (DLA)
LONGFD....... Longford [*County in Ireland*]

Longf Dist....	Longfield on Distress and Replevin [*A publication*] (DLA)
LONGFOG ...	Long-Range, Fiber-Optic Guided [*Missiles*]
LONGFOG ...	Long-range FOG (SAUS)
Long Irr	Long on Irrigation [*A publication*] (DLA)
longit...........	Longitudinal (VRA)
LONG LINES...	Long Hydrographic Sections Program (SAUO)
LONGLINES...	Long Hydrographic Sections Programme (SAUO)
LONGN........	Longeron [*Aerospace engineering*]
Long Q........	Long Quinto [*Pt. 10 of Year Books*] [*A publication*] (DLA)
Long Quinto ..	Year Books, Part X [*5 Edw. 4, 1465*] [*A publication*] (DLA)
LONGRAM ...	Long-Range Artillery Missile (SAUS)
Long S........	Long on Sales of Personal Property [*A publication*] (DLA)
LONGT	Longtree [*England*]
LONGV	Longevity (AFM)
LongvF........	Longview Fibre Co. [*Associated Press*] (SAG)
Longwood C...	Longwood College (GAGS)
LONGZ........	Long-Term Terrain Model (SAUO)
LONI	Library of Neuropsychological Information (SAUO)
LonMag	London Magazine (SAUO)
LONO	Letter of No Objection [*FDA*]
LONO	Low Noise
Lon R Bks....	London Review of Books [*A publication*] (BRI)
LONRHO	London and Rhodesian Mining and Land Company (SAUO)
Lonrho	London-Rhodesia Company (SAUO)
LONS	Laboratory Office Network System [*DoD*]
LONS	Light of the Night Sky [*Galaxy*]
LONS	Local Online Network System
LONS	Logistic Office Network System (ACAE)
Lons Cr L....	Lonsdale's Statute Criminal Law [*A publication*] (DLA)
LOO	Laghouat [*Algeria*] [*Airport symbol*] (AD)
LOO	Leave One Out at a Time [*Data analysis*]
LOO	Letter of Offer (ACAE)
LOO	Loumic Resources Ltd. [*Vancouver Stock Exchange symbol*]
LOOM	Light Opera of Manhattan
LOOM	Loyal Order of Moose (EA)
LOOP	Long-Range Open Ocean Patrol [*Navy*] (NVT)
LOOP	Loop [*Postal Service standard*] (OPSA)
LOOP	Loss of Offsite Power [*Nuclear energy*] (NRCH)
LOOP	Louisiana Offshore Oil Port [*Group of major oil companies*]
LOOPE	Loop while Equal (VLIE)
LOOPNE.......	Loop while Not Equal (VLIE)
LOOPNZ.......	Loop while Not Zero (VLIE)
LOOPs	Locally Organized and Operated Partnerships (SAUO)
LOOPS	Local Office Online Payment System [*Unemployment insurance*]
LOOPS........	Loop [*Commonly used*] (OPSA)
LOOPZ	LOOP while Zero (SAUO)
LOOS	League of Older Students (SAUO)
LOOW	Lake Ontario Ordnance Works
LOP............	Laboratory Operating Procedures (SAUO)
LOP............	Lactosuria of Pregnancy (MELL)
LOP............	Lake Ontario Cement Ltd. [*Toronto Stock Exchange symbol*]
LOP............	Last Operation Completed [*Computer science*]
LOP............	Launch Operations [*or Operator's*] Panel [*NASA*]
LOP............	Learning Opportunity [*Education*]
LOP............	Least Objectionable Program [*Television*]
LOP............	Leave on Pass
LOP............	Left Occipitoposterior [*A fetal position*] [*Obstetrics*]
LOP............	Left Outside Position [*Dancing*]
LOP............	Letter of Promulgation [*Navy*] (NVT)
LOP............	Letter of Proposal [*Military*] (AFM)
LOP............	Level of Pain (MELL)
LOP............	Level of Performance (ACAE)
LOP............	Levels-of-Processing [*Psychology*]
LOp............	Lex Operator Gene
LOP............	Life of Program
LOP............	Line of Position [*Electronics*]
LOP............	Line of Power (WDAA)
LOP............	Line-Oriented Protocol
LOP............	Linton-on-Ouse FTU [*British*] [*ICAO designator*] (FAAC)
LOP............	Loanda [*Brazil*] [*Airport symbol*] (AD)
LOP............	Locally-Originated Program [*Broadcasting*] (NTCM)
LOP............	Local Office Project [*Department of Health and Social Security*] [*British*]
LOP............	Local Operating Procedures (AFM)
LOP............	Local Operational Plot
LOP............	Local Operations Plot (SAUS)
LOP............	Logic Processor (IAA)
LOP............	Logistics Officer Program [*Army*]
LOP............	Lookout Post (IAA)
LOP............	Loss of Offsite Power [*Nuclear energy*] (NRCH)
LOP............	Loss of Pointer
LOP............	Loss of Privileges (WDAA)
LOP............	Low Oil Pressure (SAUS)
LOP............	Low-Order Position [*Military*] (AFIT)
LOP............	Lubricating Oil Pump (MSA)
LOP............	Lunar Orbit Plane [*NASA*] (IAA)
LOPA	Layout of Passenger Accommodation (MCD)
LOPA	Local Payment of Airline (MCD)
LOPAC	Load Optimization and Passenger Acceptance Control [*Airport computer*]
LOPACC	Late Quaternary Ocean Palaeocirculation and Climate Change (SAUO)
LOPAD........	Logarithmic Outline [*or Online*] Processing System for Analog Data (IEEE)
LOPAIR........	Long Path Infrared

LOP & G	Live Oak, Perry & Gulf Railroad (IIA)
LOPAR	Long Baseline Position and Rates [*Guidance and tracking system*] [*Air Force*]
LOPAR	Low-Power Acquisition RADAR
LOPBS	List of Organic Persistant and Bioaccumulative Substances (SAUO)
LOPC	Lunar Orbital Photocraft [*NASA*] (IAA)
LOPC	Lunar Orbit Plane Change [*NASA*]
LOPE	Live on Planet Earth (WDAA)
LOPG	Launch Operations Planning Group
LOPG	Live Oak, Perry & Gulf Railroad (SAUO)
LOP-GAP......	Liquid Oxygen Petrol, Guided Aircraft Projectile
LOPI	Loss of Pipe Integrity [*Nuclear energy*] (NRCH)
LOPKGS......	Loose or in Packages [*Freight*]
LOPM	Liaison Office for Personnel Management (SAUO)
LOPO	Local Post (EA)
LOPO	Low-Power Boiler [*US reactor*]
LOPOS	Local Oxidation of Polysilicon over Silicon [*Transistor technology*]
LOPP	Lunar Orbiter Photographic Project [*Aerospace*]
LOPPLAR	LASER Doppler RADAR (IAA)
LOPRA	Low-Power Reactor Assembly [*University of Illinois*] (NRCH)
lopro	low probe (SAUS)
LO-PRO	Low-Profile
LOPRPr........	Santander Overseas Bk'A' Pfd [*NYSE symbol*] (TTSB)
LOPS	Length of Patient Stay [*Medicine*] (AABC)
LOPS	Lunar Orbiting Photographic System [*Aerospace*]
LOPT	Line Output Transformer (IAA)
LOPT..........	Lynx Helicopter Observer Procedure Trainer (SAUS)
LOPU	Logistics Organization Planning Unit
LOQ	Leadership Opinion Questionnaire [*Test*]
LOQ	Left Lower Quadrant (SAUS)
LOQ	Left Outer Quadrant (SAUS)
LOQ	Level of Quantification (SAUO)
LOQ	Level of Quantitation (EEVL)
LOQ	Limit of Quantitation [*Analytical chemistry*]
LOQ	Lobatsi [*Botswana*] [*Airport symbol*] (AD)
LOQ	Loquitur [*He, or She, Speaks*] [*Latin*]
LOQ	Lower Outer Quadrant [*Anatomy*]
LOQ	Lowest Obtainable Quantification (ABAC)
LO-QG	Locked Oscillator-Quadrature Grid [*Computer science*]
LOR	Ladies of Retreads (EA)
LOR	Large Optical Reflector
LOR	League of Remembrance (SAUO)
LOR	Lender's Offered Rate [*Banking*]
LOR	Letter of Readiness (SAUS)
LOR	Letter of Request (AFIT)
LOR	Letters of Response (SAUO)
LOR	Level of Repair
LOR	Licence of Right (DB)
LOr.............	Licentiate in Orientation (SAUO)
LOR	Light Output Ratio (WDAA)
LOR	Likely Operational Range [*Navy*] (ANA)
LOR	Lockout Relay (MCD)
LOR	Long Open Reading [*Frame*] [*Genetics*]
LOR	Loral Corp. [*NYSE symbol*] (SPSG)
LOR	Loral Space Communications [*NYS*] (TTSB)
LOR	Lorazepam [*A tranquilizer*]
LOR	Lorcainide (STED)
LOR	Lorcha [*Ship's rigging*] (ROG)
LOR	Loricrin (DMAA)
LOR	Lormes [*Somee*] [*France*] [*Seismograph station code, US Geological Survey*] (SEIS)
LOR	Loss of Righting Reflex [*Medicine*] (DMAA)
LOR	Lower Operator Rate [*Telecommunications*] [*British*]
LOR	Low-Frequency Omnidirectional Radio Range
LOR	Lunar Orbit [*or Orbital*] Rendezvous [*NASA*]
LOR	Ozark, Fort Rucker, AL [*Location identifier*] [*FAA*] (FAAL)
LOR-1	Level of Rehabilitation Scale 1 (STED)
LORA	Lecturer-Oriented Response Analysis (PDAA)
LOR/A	Letter of Repair/Analysis (AAGC)
LORA	Level of Repair Analysis (MCD)
LORA	Long-Range Adaption (MCD)
LORA	Long-Range Addition (NVT)
LORA	Low Out of Range Alarm (ECII)
LORAAS.......	Long-Range Airborne ASW [*Antisubmarine Warfare*] System (MCD)
LORAC	Long-Range Accuracy [*RADAR*]
LORACON	Local Radioactivity Control (SAUO)
LORAD........	Long-Range Active Detection
LORAD........	Long-Range Air Defense (AABC)
LORADAC	Long-Range Active Detection and Communications System
LORADS.......	LASER Optical Ranging and Designation System
LORADS.......	Long Range Radar & Display System (SAUS)
LORAE	Long-Range Attitude and Event [*Instrumentation system*]
LORAH	Long-Range Area Homing
LORA-HOJ ...	Long-Range - Home on Jam
LORAINE......	Long-Range Interceptor Experiment (SAUS)
Loral	Loral Corp. [*Associated Press*] (SAG)
LORAM	Level of Repair for Aeronautical Material (PDAA)
LORAMS.......	Long-Range Automatic Measuring Station [*Meteorology*]
LORAN	Long-Range Aid to Navigation [*Military*] (DOMA)
LORAN	Long-Range Area Navigation System (SAUO)
loran	Long-Range Navigation (IDOE)
LORAN	Long-Range Navigation
LORAN	Long-Range Radio Navigation (ACRL)
LORAN D	Long-Range Navigation Doppler Inertial (DNAB)
LORAN DM...	Long-Range Navigation Double Master

Lor & Russ...	Loring and Russell's Election Cases in Massachusetts [*A publication*] (DLA)
LORAN DS...	Long-Range Navigation Double Slave
LORAN M...	Long-Range Navigation Master
LORAN S.....	Long-Range Navigation Slave
LORAP......	Level of Repair Analysis Program
LORAPH.....	Long-Range Passive Homing System
LORAPL.....	Long-Range Planning Task Group [*Oversaw military strategy in Vietnam*] (VNW)
LORAS.........	Linear Omnidirectional Airspeed System (PDAA)
LORAS.........	Long-Range Airborne Surveillance (SAUS)
LORAS.........	Low-Range Airspeed System (MCD)
Loras C.......	Loras College (GAGS)
LORBAS.......	Large Off-Line Retrieval Text Base Access System
LORBI.........	Locked-On RADAR Bearing Indicator
LORC..........	Lockheed Radio Command (MUGU)
LORCS........	League of Red Cross and Red Crescent Societies
LORCS........	League of Red Cross Societies
LORD........	Licensing Online Retrieval Data (NRCH)
LORD........	List of Required Documents (NVT)
LORD..........	Long-Range and Detection RADAR (NATG)
lord.........	Lordosis (STED)
LORD..........	Lordosis [*Medicine*]
LORDF........	Loredi Resources Ltd. (SAUO)
LORDS........	Licensing On-Line Retrieval Data System (NRCH)
Lords Jour...	Journals of the House of Lords [*England*] [*A publication*] (DLA)
LORE	Land Ordnance Engineering Branch [*Canada*] [*Military*] (PDAA)
LORE	Line Oriented Editor (VLIE)
LOREC........	Long-Range Earth Current Communications
LORELCO.....	Lower Elevated Serum Cholesterol [*Acronym is trade name of Dow Chemical*]
LORELEI	Long-Range Echo Level Indicator
LORENDAS...	Long-Range Energy Development and Supply (PDAA)
Lorenz	Lorenz's Ceylon Reports [*A publication*] (DLA)
Lorenz App R...	Lorenz's Appeal Reports [*Ceylon*] [*A publication*] (DLA)
Lorenz Rep...	Lorenz's Ceylon Reports [*A publication*] (ILCA)
LOREOR......	Long Range Electro Optical Reconnaissance (ACAE)
LOREORS	Long-Range, Electro-Optical Reconnaissance System
LORES	Long-Range Environmental Studies (SAUO)
LORES	Long-Route Engineering Study [*Bell System*]
LO-RES	Low Resolution [*Computer science*]
Loreto..........	Institute of the Blessed Virgin Mary, Irish Branch (SAUO)
LOREX	Lomonosov Ridge Experiment (SAUO)
LORI	Limited Operational Readiness Inspection (MCD)
LORI	Logistics Operation Readiness Inspection (SAUO)
LoriCp.........	Lori Corp. [*Associated Press*] (SAG)
LORINE........	Limited Range Imagery Networks Elements (SAUO)
Loring & Russel El Cases...	Loring and Russell's Election Cases in Massachusetts [*A publication*] (DLA)
Loring & Russell...	Loring and Russell's Election Cases in Massachusetts [*A publication*] (DLA)
Lor Inst........	Lorimer. Institutes of Law [*A publication*] (ILCA)
LORIS	Long-Range Infra-red System (SAUS)
LORL	Large Orbital Research Laboratory [*NASA*]
LORMODS ...	Long-Range Metal Object Detection System (MCD)
LORMONSTA...	LORAN Monitor Station
LORO	Lobe-On Receive Only [*Electronic counter-countermeasures*]
LOROC........	Long-Range Offboard Chaff (SAUS)
LOROC........	Long-Range Optical Camera (SAUS)
Loronix	Loronix Information Systems, Inc. [*Associated Press*] (SAG)
LOROP........	Long-Range Oblique Photography
LORPGAC ...	Long-Range Proving Ground Automatic Computer (IEEE)
L or RC.......	Leather or Rubber Covered [*Freight*]
LORRE	Laboratory of Renewable Resources Engineering [*Purdue University*]
LORROS	Long-Range Reconnaissance & Observation System (SAUS)
LORS	Labor Organization Reporting System [*Department of Labor*] (GFGA)
LORS	LM [*Lunar Module*] Optical Rendezvous System [*NASA*]
LORS	Long-Range SONAR
LORS	Lunar Orbiting Reconnaissance System [*Aerospace*]
LORSA	Long-Range Steerable Antenna (MCD)
LORSAC......	Long-Range Submarine Communications (AAG)
Lor Sc L	Lorimer's Handbook of Scotch Law [*A publication*] (DLA)
LORS-I........	Level of Rehabilitation Scale-I [*Medicine*] (DAVI)
LORSTA	LORAN Transmitting Station
LORSU........	Long-Range Special Unit [*Military*]
LORT	League of Resident Theaters (EA)
LORTAN.......	Long-Range and Tactical Navigation System
LORTID........	Long Range Target Identification (ACAE)
LORTRAP.....	Long-Range Training and Rotation Plan
LORV	Low-Observability Reentry Vehicle
LORW..........	Light Output Ratio Working (PDAA)
LORX	Loronix Information Systems, Inc. [*NASDAQ symbol*] (SAG)
LORX	Loronix Info Systems [*NASDAQ symbol*] (TTSB)
LOS.............	Laboratory Operating System [*NASA*]
LOS.............	Lagos [*Nigeria*] [*Airport symbol*] (OAG)
LOS.............	Land Observation Satellite (PDAA)
LOS.............	Land Ownership Survey
LOS.............	Latin Old Style (ADA)
LOS.............	Launcher Operation Station (MCD)
LOS.............	Launch on Search [*Navy*] (CAAL)
LOS.............	Launch Operations System [*NASA*] (KSC)
LOS.............	Launch Optional Selector (IAA)
LOS.............	Law of the Sea [*United Nations*] (ASF)
LOS.............	Length of Service
LOS.............	Length of Stay
LOS.............	Level of Service [*BTS*] (TAG)
LOS.............	Level of Support (VLIE)
LOS.............	Liaison Office Support
LOS.............	Licentiate in Obstetrical Science
LOS.............	Lift-Off Simulator [*NASA*] (NASA)
LOS.............	Limited Operational Strategy
LOS.............	Limit Order Switching (PDAA)
LOS.............	Line-Off Simulator (SAUS)
LOS.............	Line of Scrimmage [*Football*]
LOS.............	Line of Sight
LOS.............	Line of Site (SAUS)
LOS.............	Line of Supply
LOS.............	Line-Oriented Simulation (GAVI)
LOS.............	Line Out of Service [*Telecommunications*] (TEL)
LOS.............	Little Orchestra Society (SAUO)
LOS.............	Live Oak Society (EA)
LOS.............	Local Office System (SAUO)
LOS.............	Local Operating Station (DNAB)
LOS.............	Local Operating System (IAA)
LOS.............	Logistic Operation - Streamline [*Military*] (AABC)
LOS.............	Logistic Oriented Schools [*Army*]
LOS.............	London Orphan School (SAUO)
LOS.............	Loop Output Signal (CET)
Los.............	Los Angeles Rams [*National Football League*] [*1946-94*] (NFLA)
LOS.............	Lossiemouth FTU [*British*] [*ICAO designator*] (FAAC)
LOS.............	Loss of Selectivity (AAEL)
LOS.............	Loss of Sight
LOS.............	Loss of Signal
LOS.............	Loss of Site (STED)
LOS.............	Loss of Sync [*Aerospace*] (NAKS)
LOS.............	Loss of Synchronization
LOS.............	Lost in Space [*Television Program*]
LOS.............	Lower (O)Esophageal Sphincter (STED)
LOS.............	Low Output Syndrome (MAE)
LOS.............	Lunar Orbiting Satellite [*or Spacecraft*] [*Aerospace*] (MCD)
LOS.............	Midwestern Baptist Theological Seminary, Kansas City, MO [*OCLC symbol*] (OCLC)
LOS.............	United Nations Convention on the Law of the Sea (SAUO)
LOSACA	Liaison Officer to Supreme Allied Commander (ACAE)
LOSACA	Liaison Officer to the Supreme Allied Commander, Atlantic (SAUO)
LOS-AD.......	Line-of-Sight - Air Defense [*DoD*]
LOSAM	Low-Altitude Surface-to-Air Missiles (NATG)
Los Angeles BAB...	Los Angeles Bar Association. Bulletin [*A publication*] (DLA)
Los Angeles L Rev...	Los Angeles Law Review [*A publication*] (DLA)
LOSARP......	Line-of-Sight - Repeater Placement Program (IAA)
LOSAT	Language-Oriented System Analysis Table (IAA)
LOS-AT.......	Line-of-Sight - Antitank [*DoD*]
LOSC	Laboratory Operations Support Center [*NASA*] (SSD)
LOSC	Law of the Sea Conference [*United Nations*] (MSC)
LOSC	Law of the Sea Convention [*Australia*]
LOSC	Local On-Scene Commander [*Military*] (DNAB)
LOSD	League of St. Dymphna (EA)
LOSE..........	Let Others Share Equally [*Slogan opposing President Gerald R. Ford's anti-inflation WIN campaign*]
LOSE..........	Let's Omit Superfluous Expenses [*Slogan opposing President Gerald R. Ford's anti-inflation WIN campaign*]
LOSE..........	Line of Sight Equipment (ACAE)
LOSE..........	Line-of-Sight Expendables (DNAB)
LOS-F	Line-of-Sight - Forward [*DoD*]
LOS-FH.......	Line-of-Sight - Forward Heavy [*DoD*]
LOS-FL	Line of Sight-Forward Light [*DoD*]
LOSH	Labor Occupational Safety & Health program (SAUO)
LOSI...........	Ad hoc Task Team to Study the Implications, for the Commission, of the United Nations Convention on the Law of the Sea and the New Ocean Regime (SAUS)
LOSI...........	Line-Of-Sight Indicator (SAUS)
LOSIS	Law of the Sea Information System (GNE)
LOSL...........	Saint Landry Parish Library, Opelousas, LA [*Library symbol*] [*Library of Congress*] (LCLS)
LOSM..........	Launch Operations Simulation Model
LOSM..........	Launch Operations Support Manager (SAUO)
LOSM..........	Lunar Orbital Survey Missions (ACAE)
LOSMAD......	Line of Sight Missile for Air Defense (ACAE)
LOS of NA ...	Ladies Oriental Shrine of North America (EA)
LOSOS	Local Oxidation of Silicon on Sapphire [*Transistor technology*] (IAA)
LOSP	Loss of Offsite Power [*Nuclear energy*] (NRCH)
LOSP	Loss of System Pressure [*Nuclear energy*] (NRCH)
LOSP	Lower (O)Esophageal Sphincter Pressure (STED)
LOS(P)........	Lower O-Esophageal Sphincter Pressure [*Medicine*] (DMAA)
LOSP	Low Speed channel connector (SAUS)
LOS PrepCom...	United Nations Preparatory Commission on the International Sea-Bed Authority and for the international Tribunal for the Law of the Sea (SAUO)
LOSR	Limit of Stack Register
LOSR	Line of Sight Range (ACAE)
LOSR	Line-of-Sight Rate (MCD)
LOS-R.........	Line-of-Sight - Rear [*DoD*]
LOSREP	Loss Report [*Aircrew/aircraft*]
LOSS	Landing Observer Signal System (MSA)
LOSS	LAPS Observing System Simulation (USDC)
LOSS	LAPS [*Local Analysis and Prediction System*] Observing System Stimulation [*Marine science*] (OSRA)
LOSS	Large Object Salvage System [*Navy*]
LOSS	Launch Operations Support Services (ACAE)
LOSS	Lunar Orbital Survey System [*NASA*] (KSC)

LOSS	Lunar Orbit Space Station [*NASA*]
Loss & Dam Rev...	Loss and Damage Review [*A publication*] (DLA)
Loss Sec Reg...	Loss' Security Regulations [*A publication*] (DLA)
LOSSYS	Landing Observer Signal System
LOST	Law of the Sea Treaty (MCD)
LOST	Linear One-Step Transition [*Mathematical model for social grouping*]
LOST	Lommel and Steinkopf [*German name for mustard gas, taken from two of the chemists who helped develop it as a chemical warfare agent*]
LOST	Lube Oil Storage Tank (NRCH)
LOST/A	Vessels Lost by Accident, Collision, or Similar Methods [*Navy*]
LOST/E	Vessels Lost through Enemy Action [*Navy*]
LOSTF	Line-of-Sight Test Fixture
LOSTFC	Line-of-Sight Task Force Communications [*Military*] (CAAL)
LOSTFCS	Line-of-Sight Task Force Communications System [*Military*]
LOST/P	Vessels Lost Due to Weather, Perils of the Sea, or Similar Reasons [*Navy*]
LOSTPED	Load, Orientation, Speed, Travel, Precision, Environment, and Duty Cycle (VLIE)
LOSTW	Lostwithiel [*Municipal borough in England*]
LOT	Laminated Overlay Transistor [*Electronics*] (IAA)
LOT	Lapped Orthogonal Transform [*Telecommunications*]
LOT	Large Orbiting Telescope (MCD)
LOT	Lateral Olfactory Tract
LOT	Leak-Off Test
LOT	Left Occipitotransverse [*A fetal position*] [*Obstetrics*]
LOT	Left Outer Thigh [*Injection site*]
LOT	Lengthened Off Time (STED)
LOT	Letter of Transmittal (MCD)
LOT	Life of Type (AFIT)
LOT	Lift-Off Time [*Aerospace*] (MCD)
LOT	Light-Off Temperature [*For steady-state combustion*]
LOT	Light-Off Time [*Exhaust emissions*] [*Automotive engineering*]
LOT	Light Operated Typewriter
LOT	Limited Operational Test
LOT	Linear Optical Trajectory [*Vision*]
LOT	List on Tape (IAA)
LOT	Load on Top [*Oil tankers*]
LOT	Lock on Track
LOT	Lodestar Energy, Inc. [*Vancouver Stock Exchange symbol*]
LOT	Logic Optimization with Testability (VLIE)
Lot	Lotarius Rosario de Cremona [*Deceased, 1227*] [*Authority cited in pre-1607 legal work*] (DSA)
LOT	Lotio [*Lotion*] [*Pharmacy*]
lot	Lotion (STED)
LOT	Lotru [*Romania*] [*Seismograph station code, US Geological Survey*] (SEIS)
LOT	Lower Outer Tube
LOT	Low-Observables Technology (SAUO)
LOT	Low-Observable Technology (MCD)
LOT	Lumisis Operations Team (ACAE)
LOT	Polskie Linie Lotnicze [*Poland*] [*ICAO designator*] (FAAC)
LOT	Romeoville, IL [*Location identifier*] [*FAA*] (FAAL)
LOTA	Loss of Target Accident [*Environmental science*] (COE)
LOTADS	Long Term Air Defense Study (SAUO)
LOTADS	Long-Term Worldwide Air Defense Study [*Army*] (AABC)
LOTAS	Large Optical Tracker - Aerospace
LOTAWS	LASER Obstacle Terrain Avoidance Warning System
LOTC	London Over-the-Counter Market [*Information service or system*] (IID)
LOTCA	Loewenstein Occupational Therapy Cognitive Assessment [*Test*] (TMMY)
LOTCIP	Long-Term Communications Improvement Plan (NATG)
LOTE	Languages Other than English
LOTE	Lesser of Two Evils [*Politics*]
LOTEX	Life-of-Type Extension (SAUO)
LOTH R	Lotharian Regiment [*Military*] [*British*] (ROG)
LOTIS	Logical Structure: The Timing and the Sequencing of Synchronous/Asynchronous Machines [*Computer science*] (CSR)
LOTIS	Logical Timing Sequencing (NITA)
LOTIS	Logic, Timing, and Sequencing (VLIE)
LOTMP	Lowest Temperature [*NWS*] (FAAC)
LO-TO	Longitudinal-Optic-Transverse-Optic [*Spectral characteristic*]
LOTO	Lottery Enterprises [*NASDAQ symbol*] (TTSB)
LOTON	Long Tons Discharged or Loaded
LOTOS	Language of Temporal Ordering of Specifications [*Computer science*]
LOTP	Logical Operation Time Projection (VLIE)
LOTR	[*The*] Lord of the Rings [*A trilogy*]
LOTREX	Land-Ocean Interactions in the Coastal Zone (SAUO)
LOTREX	Land-Surface Traverse Experiment (SAUO)
LOTREX	Working LORAN (SAUS)
LOTS	Large Overland Transporter System (MCD)
LOTS	Launch Operations Television System
LOTS	Launch Optical Trajectory System [*NASA*] (IAA)
LOTS	LEM [*Lunar Excursion Module*] Optical Tracking System [*NASA*] (KSC)
LOTS	Lighter, Over-the-Shore [*Missions*] [*For air-cushion vehicles*] (RDA)
LOTS	Load over the Side
LOTS	Logistics over the Shore [*Military*]
LOTS	LORAN Operational Training School
LOTS	Lotus Development Corp. (SAUO)
LOTS	Low Overhead Time-Sharing System (CIST)
LOTSS	Libraries of the Social Sciences [*Australia*] [*An association*]
LotteryE	Lottery Enterprises, Inc. [*Associated Press*] (SAG)
LottoW	Lotto World, Inc. [*Associated Press*] (SAG)
LOTUS	Ladies Organized to Unfetter Sexuality (SAUO)
LOTUS	Long-Term Upper Ocean Study
LOTV	Launch Operations and Test Vehicle [*NASA*] (KSC)
LOTW	Loaded on Trailers or Wagons [*Freight*]
LOU	Letter of Understanding [*Nuclear energy*] (NRCH)
LOU	Letters of Undertaking [*RSPA*] (TAG)
LOU	Limited Official Use
LOU	Line Output Unit [*Printing*] (DGA)
LOU	Linomatic Operating Unit [*Printing*] (DGA)
LOU	Louisiana
LOU	Louisville Gas & Electric Co. (SAUO)
LOU	Louisville, KY [*Location identifier*] [*FAA*] (FAAL)
Lou	Louth [*County in Ireland*] (WGA)
LOUD	Loudeye Tech [*NASDAQ symbol*] (SG)
LouG	Louisville Gas & Electric Co. [*Associated Press*] (SAG)
LouG 5	Louisville Gas & Electric Co. [*Associated Press*] (SAG)
Lough	Loughborough University of Technology (SAUO)
LOUH	Light Observation Utility Helicopter (NATG)
LOUIS	Logical On-Line User Inquiry System (SAUO)
LOUISA	Lunar Optical-UVIR [*Ultraviolet Infrared*] Synthesis Array [*NASA*]
Louisiana Ann...	Louisiana Annual Reports [*A publication*] (DLA)
Louisiana Ann Rep...	Louisiana Annual Reports [*A publication*] (DLA)
Louisiana Rep...	Louisiana Reports [*A publication*] (DLA)
Louis Rep...	Louisiana Reports [*A publication*] (DLA)
Lou Leg N...	Louisiana Legal News [*A publication*] (DLA)
Lou LJ...	Louisiana Law Journal [*New Orleans*] [*A publication*] (DLA)
Lou L Jour...	Louisiana Law Journal [*A publication*] (DLA)
LOUO	Limited Official Use Only [*Military*]
Lou R...	Louisiana Reports [*A publication*] (DLA)
Lou Rep NS...	Martin's Louisiana Reports, New Series [*A publication*] (DLA)
Lou Reps...	Louisiana Reports [*A publication*] (DLA)
LOV	Large Opaque Vesicle [*Medicine*] (DMAA)
LOV	Limit of Visibility
LOV	London Flight Centre (Stansted) Ltd. [*British*] [*ICAO designator*] (FAAC)
LOV	Loss of Vehicle (KSC)
LOV	Loss of Visibility (NASA)
LOV	Loss of Vision (DAVI)
LOV	Loveland Area Office (SAUO)
LOV	Lovo [*Sweden*] [*Geomagnetic observatory code*]
LOV	Low-Observable Vehicle [*Military*] (MUSM)
LOV	Monclova [*Mexico*] [*Airport symbol*] (AD)
LOV	Societe Miniere Louvem, Inc. [*Toronto Stock Exchange symbol*]
LOVA	Low Vulnerability Ammunition [*Military*] (RDA)
LOVAG	Low Voltage Agreement Group (SAUO)
Lov Arb	Lovesy on Arbitration [*1867*] [*A publication*] (DLA)
LOVE	Language Organization Voicing Esperanto
LOVE	League of Victims and Emphathizers (SAUO)
LOVE	Limited Only to Vans in Europe (SAUO)
LOVE	Linguistics of Visual English [*Sign language system for the hearing impaired*]
Love Bank	Lovesy's Bankruptcy Act [*1869, 1870*] [*A publication*] (DLA)
LOVER	Lunar Orbiting Vehicle for Emergency Rescue (PDAA)
LOVISIM	Low-Visibility Landing Simulation [*Program*] [*Air Force*]
LOVL	Laugh Out Very Loud [*Internet language*] [*Computer science*]
LOVV	Wien [*Austria*] [*ICAO location identifier*] (ICLI)
LOW	Last Open Water (RIMS)
LOW	Launch on Warning [*Missiles*]
LOW	Laws of War (MCD)
LOW	League of Welldoers (SAUO)
LOW	Link Order Wire
LOW	Link Orderwire Project
LOW	Loners on Wheels (EA)
LOW	Low Core Threshold (NITA)
Low	Lowell's District Court Reports [*United States, Massachusetts District*] [*A publication*] (DLA)
low	Lower (VRA)
LOW	Lowe's Companies, Inc. [*NYSE symbol*] (SPSG)
LOW	Lowe's Cos. [*NYSE symbol*] (TTSB)
LOW	West Yellowstone, MT [*Location identifier*] [*FAA*] (FAAL)
LOWAT	Low-Observable Weapon Airframe Technology (SAUS)
LOWBI	Low-Birth-Weight Infant [*Obstetrics*]
Low Can	Lower Canada Reports [*A publication*] (DLA)
Low Can Jur...	Lower Canada Jurist [*A publication*] (DLA)
Low Can Jurist...	Lower Canada Jurist [*A publication*] (DLA)
Low Can LJ...	Lower Canada Law Journal [*A publication*] (DLA)
Low Can R...	Lower Canada Reports [*A publication*] (DLA)
Low Can Rep...	Lower Canada Reports [*A publication*] (DLA)
Low Can Rep SQ...	Lower Canada Seignorial Questions Reports [*A publication*] (DLA)
LOWCAT	Low Cost Air Target (SAUS)
LOW-COST CONTROL...	Adaptable Low-Cost Shop-Floor Control Systems (SAUO)
Low C Seign...	Lower Canada Seignorial Questions Reports [*A publication*] (DLA)
Low Dec (F)...	Lowell's Decisions [*A publication*] (DLA)
Low Dis	Lowell's District Court Reports [*United States, Massachusetts District*] [*A publication*] (DLA)
Low-E	Low-Elevation (CAAL)
LOW-E	Low-Emissivity [*Glass*]
Lowell	Lowell's District Court Reports [*United States, Massachusetts District*] [*A publication*] (DLA)
Lower Can Jur...	Lower Canada Jurist [*A publication*] (DLA)
Lower Can SQ...	Lower Canada Seignorial Questions Reports [*A publication*] (DLA)
Lower Ct Dec...	Ohio Lower Court Decisions [*A publication*] (DLA)
Lowes	Lowe's Companies, Inc. [*Associated Press*] (SAG)
LOWESS	Locally-Weighted Scatterplot Smoother [*Medicine*]

LOWFAR	Low-Frequency Analysis and Recording (MCD)
LOWFER	Low Frequency Experimental Radio (SAUO)
LOWG	Graz [*Austria*] [*ICAO location identifier*] (ICLI)
LOWG	Landing Operations Working Group [*NASA*] (NASA)
LOWG	Launch Operations Working Group (ACAE)
LOWI	Innsbruck [*Austria*] [*ICAO location identifier*] (ICLI)
LOWK	Klagenfurt [*Austria*] [*ICAO location identifier*] (ICLI)
LOWL	Linz [*Austria*] [*ICAO location identifier*] (ICLI)
LOWL	Low Degree Oscillations Experiment (SAUO)
LOWL	Low-Level Language [*Computer programming*]
LOWM	Wien [*Austria*] [*ICAO location identifier*] (ICLI)
Lown & M	Lowndes and Maxwell's English Bail Court Reports [*1852-54*] [*A publication*] (DLA)
Lownd & M	Lowndes and Maxwell's English Bail Court Reports [*1852-54*] [*A publication*] (DLA)
Lownd Av	Lowndes' General Average [*10th ed.*] [*1975*] [*A publication*] (DLA)
Lownd Col	Lowndes on Collisions at Sea [*A publication*] (DLA)
Lownd Cop	Lowndes on Copyright [*A publication*] (DLA)
Lowndes & M	Lowndes and Maxwell's English Bail Court Reports [*1852-54*] [*A publication*] (DLA)
Lowndes & M (Eng)	Lowndes and Maxwell's English Bail Court Reports [*1852-54*] [*A publication*] (DLA)
Lowndes M & P	Lowndes, Maxwell, and Pollock's English Bail Court Reports [*1850-51*] [*A publication*] (DLA)
Lownd Ins	Lowndes on Insurance [*A publication*] (DLA)
Lownd Leg	Lowndes on Legacies [*A publication*] (DLA)
Lownd M & P	Lowndes, Maxwell, and Pollock's English Bail Court Reports [*1850-51*] [*A publication*] (DLA)
LownInST	P. W. Lown Institute. Brandeis University. Studies and Texts (BJA)
Lown Leg	Lowndes on Legacies [*A publication*] (DLA)
Lown M & P	Lowndes, Maxwell, and Pollock's English Bail Court Reports [*1850-51*] [*A publication*] (DLA)
Low Pr Code	Lower Provinces Code [*India*] [*A publication*] (DLA)
LOWR	Lower
Lowranc	Lowrance Electronics, Inc. [*Associated Press*] (SAG)
LOWS	Salzburg [*Austria*] [*ICAO location identifier*] (ICLI)
LOWTRAN	Low Resolution Transmission (ACAE)
LOWW	Wien/Schwechat [*Austria*] [*ICAO location identifier*] (ICLI)
LOWZ	Zell Am See [*Austria*] [*ICAO location identifier*] (ICLI)
LOX	Lipoxygenase [*An enzyme*]
lox	Liquid Oxygen (STED)
LOX	Liquid Oxygen [*Also, LO₂*]
LOX	Liquid Oxygen Expert System (NITA)
LO-X	Low Thermal Expansion [*Synthetic ceramic*]
LOXA	Aigen/Ennstal [*Austria*] [*ICAO location identifier*] (ICLI)
LOXAT	Lowest Temperature Exceeded for All Time [*NWS*] (FAAC)
LOXFM	Lowest Temperature Exceeded for the Month [*NWS*] (FAAC)
LOXG	Graz [*Austria*] [*ICAO location identifier*] (ICLI)
LOXK	Klagenfurt [*Austria*] [*ICAO location identifier*] (ICLI)
LOXL	Horsching [*Austria*] [*ICAO location identifier*] (ICLI)
LOX/LH	Liquid Oxygen and Liquid Hydrogen
LOXN	Wiener Neustadt [*Austria*] [*ICAO location identifier*] (ICLI)
Lox-PLD	Loxoseles reclusus - Phospholipase D [*An enzyme*]
LOXS	Schwaz, Tirol [*Austria*] [*ICAO location identifier*] (ICLI)
LOXSE	Lowest Temperature Exceeded So Early [*NWS*] (FAAC)
LOXSL	lowest Temperature Exceeded So Late [*NWS*] (FAAC)
LOXT	Langenlebarn [*Austria*] [*ICAO location identifier*] (ICLI)
LOXT	Large Orbital X-Ray Telescope [*NASA*]
LOXZ	Zeltweg [*Austria*] [*ICAO location identifier*] (ICLI)
LOY	Loyalty (AABC)
LOY	Loyola - Notre Dame Library, Inc. (SAUO)
LOY	Loyola - Notre Dame Library, Inc., Baltimore, MD [*OCLC symbol*] (OCLC)
LOYA	League of Young Adventurers (SAUO)
LOYC	Loyola Capital [*NASDAQ symbol*] (SAG)
LOYC	Loyola Capital Corp. (SAUO)
Loy Con Prot J	Loyola Consumer Protection Journal [*Los Angeles*] [*A publication*] (DLA)
Loy Dig	Loyola Digest [*A publication*] (DLA)
Loy LA Ent LJ	Loyola of Los Angeles Entertainment Law Journal (SAUO)
Loy LA L Rev	Loyola of Los Angeles Law Review (SAUO)
Loy Law	Loyola Lawyer [*A publication*] (DLA)
Loy LJ	Loyola Law Journal [*New Orleans*] [*1920-32*] [*A publication*] (DLA)
Loy L Rev	Loyola Law Review (SAUO)
Loyola	Loyola Capital Corp. [*Associated Press*] (SAG)
Loyola C (Md)	Loyola College (Maryland) (GAGS)
Loyola Dig	Loyola Digest [*A publication*] (DLA)
Loyola LJ	Loyola Law Journal [*A publication*] (DLA)
Loyola Marymount U	Loyola Marymount University (Los Angeles) (GAGS)
Loyola U Chicago	Loyola University of Chicago (GAGS)
Loyola U (La)	Loyola University (Louisiana) (GAGS)
Loyola ULJ (Chicago)	Loyola University. Law Review (Chicago) [*A publication*] (DLA)
Loyola Univ L Rev	Loyola University. Law Review [*Chicago*] [*A publication*] (DLA)
Loy Pov LJ	Loyola Poverty Law Journal (SAUO)
Loy U Chi LJ	Loyola University Chicago Law Journal (SAUO)
LOZ	Liquid Ozone
LOZ	London [*Kentucky*] [*Airport symbol*] (OAG)
LOZ	Lovozero [*Former USSR*] [*Geomagnetic observatory code*]
LOZ	Lozenge [*Pharmacy*] (DAVI)
LP	Air Alpes [*ICAO designator*] (AD)
LP	Labile Peptide (DB)
LP	Labile Protein (DB)
LP	Laboratory Port [*NASA*] (SPST)
LP	Laboratory Procedure
LP	Labor Pain (MELL)
LP	Labour Party (SAUO)
LP	Labour Party of South Africa [*Political party*] (PPW)
L/P	Lactate/Pyruvate [*Ratio*]
LP	Lactic Peroxidase [*Medicine*] (MELL)
LP	Lactoperoxidase (DB)
LP	Ladyship [*or Lordship*]
LP	Laminated Polyethylene Film
LP	Lamp [*Automotive engineering*]
LP	Landing Point [*British military*] (DMA)
LP	Land Plane
LP	Large-Paper Edition [*of a book*]
LP	Large Particle
LP	Large Post
LP	Laryngeal Pharyngeal [*Medicine*]
LP	Last Paid [*Military*]
LP	Last Performance
LP	Last Post (WDAA)
LP	Latch Pick (VLIE)
LP	Latent Period [*Physiology*]
LP	Lateral Pyloric [*Neuron*]
LP	Launching Platoon [*Army*]
LP	Launch Pad (KSC)
LP	Launch Panel
LP	Launch Platform
LP	Laureate of Philosophy
LP	Law Pamphlet (ROG)
LP	Lay Preacher
LP	Leadership Project [*Defunct*] (EA)
LP	Lead Poisoning (MELL)
LP	Lead Programmer [*Computer science*] (VLIE)
LP	Leaf Protein [*Food industry*]
LP	Learning Prototype (SAUO)
LP	Leathery Pocket [*of pineapple*]
LP	Lecturer Practitioner (WDAA)
LP	Left Pectoral Fin [*Fish anatomy*]
LP	Left Traffic Pattern [*Aviation*] (FAAC)
LP	Legal Process [*British*]
LP	Legal Procurator (WDAA)
LP	Legislative Proposal (GFGA)
LP	Lempira [*Monetary unit*] [*Honduras*]
LP	Lesson Plan
LP	Lettering Piece (ROG)
L/P	Letterpress (ADA)
LP	Letters Patent (ROG)
LP	Leucine Aminopeptidase [*Also, LA, LAP*] [*An enzyme*]
LP	Leucocyte Pyrogen [*Immunology*]
LP	Leukocyte-Poor [*Hematology*]
LP	Liability Policy [*Information service or system*] (DOAD)
LP	Liberal Party [*Canada*] (PPW)
LP	Liberator Party [*Guyana*] [*Political party*] (PPW)
LP	Libertarian Party (EA)
LP	Library of Parliament [*Canada*]
LP	Library of Philosophy [*A publication*]
LP	Lichen Planus (MELL)
L/P	Life Policy [*Insurance*]
LP	Lighting Panel (IAA)
LP	Light Pen
LP	Light Perception [*Ophthalmology*]
LP	Lightproof [*Technical drawings*]
LP	Light Pulse [*Embryology*]
LP	Limited Partnership
LP	Limited Planning (MCD)
LP	Limited Procurement
LP	Limited Production (AABC)
LP	Limited Proprietorship [*Business term*]
LP	Limit of Proportionality [*Mechanics*] (IAA)
LP	Limp [*Binding*] [*Publishing*]
LP	Linear Phase
LP	Linear Polarization
LP	Linear Prediction [*Computer science*]
LP	Linear Programming [*Computer science*]
LP	Linear Programming Language (NITA)
LP	Linen Press (ADA)
lp	Line Pair [*Philately*]
LP	Line Pressure
LP	Line Printer [*Computer science*]
LP	Linguistic Problems
LP	Linguopulpal [*Dentistry*]
LP	Linker Polypeptide [*Biochemistry*]
LP	Linkport [*Electronics*] (ECII)
LP	Link Printer (ACRL)
LP	Lipid Pneumonia (MELL)
Lp	Lipoprotein [*Biochemistry*]
LP	Liquefied Petroleum [*Gas*]
LP	Liquidity Preference [*Economics*]
LP	Liquid Petroleum (SAUS)
LP	Liquid Phase [*Chemistry*]
LP	Liquid Propane (ACAE)
LP	Liquid Propellant
LP	Listening Post
LP	List of Publications [*National Institute of Standards and Technology*]
LP	List Price (BARN)

LP	List Processor [*Standard programming language*] [*1958*] [*Computer science*] (BUR)
LP	Lists of Parts (NATG)
LP	Litter Patient
LP	Little Person
LP	Livens Projector [*Military*]
LP	Live Preview (ELAL)
LP	Liverpool Prison (SAUO)
LP	Liver Protein [*Medicine*]
LP	Liver to Plasma Concentration Ratio (MAE)
LP	Load Point (BUR)
LP	Local-Pair [*Superconductivity*]
LP	Local Pastors [*British*]
LP	Local Primary (OTD)
LP	Local Procurement [*Military*]
LP	Local Purchase (AFM)
LP	Locating Point [*Optical tooling*]
LP	Lodge-Pole Pine [*Utility pole*] [*Telecommunications*] (TEL)
LP	Loewenthal Papers [*Shanghai/Washington, DC*] [*A publication*] (BJA)
LP	Logical Partition (SAUO)
LP	Logic Probe
LP	Logic Programming (SAUS)
LP	Log Periodic [*Antenna*] (NATG)
LP	Lollipop Power [*An association*] (EA)
LP	London Particular [*Marsala*]
LP	London Police (SAUO)
LP	Longest Path
LP	Longest Perpendicular [*IOR*] [*Yacht racing*]
LP	Longitudinal Parity [*Telecommunications*] (TEL)
LP	Long-Pass [*Absorption cell*]
LP	Long Period
LP	Long Persistence
LP	Long Picot
LP	Long Play [*VHS recorder mode*] (NTCM)
LP	Long Playing [*Phonograph record*]
LP	Long Position [*Investment term*]
LP	Long Primer
LP	Long Provost
LP	Loop [*Knitting*]
LP	Lord President of the Court of Session, Scotland (DLA)
LP	Lord Provost [*British*]
LP	Lorentz-Polarization [*Optics*]
LP	Losing Pitcher [*Baseball*]
LP	Loss of Pay [*Court-martial sentence*] [*Marine Corps*]
LP	Lost Planes [*An association*] (EA)
LP	Love Project (EA)
LP	Lower Panel (IAA)
LP	Lower Peninsula [*Michigan*]
LP	Low Pass [*Electronics*]
LP	Low Performance
LP	Low Point
LP	Low Potency (DB)
LP	Low Power [*Microscopy*]
LP	Low Pressure
LP	Low-Pressure Cylinder [*Especially, a locomotive cylinder*]
LP	Low Primary (IAA)
LP	Low-Profile [*Tire design*]
LP	Low Protein [*Nutrition*]
LP	Lumbar-Peritoneal [*Shunt*] (DAVI)
LP	Lumbar Puncture [*Medicine*]
LP	Lumboperitoneal (DB)
LP	Lunar and Planetary [*Aerospace*] (IAA)
LP	Lunar Prospector [*NASA*]
LP	Luster Paper [*Photography*] (DGA)
LP	Lymphocyte Predominant [*Medicine*]
L/P	Lymphocyte to Polymorph Ratio [*Hematology*]
LP	Lymphoid Plasma [*Hematology*] (MAE)
LP	Lymphoid Predominance [*Medicine*] (AAMN)
L/P	Lymph-Plasma [*Ratio*] [*Laboratory science*] (DAVI)
LP	Lymph-Plasma Ratio [*Hematology*] (MAE)
LP	Lythway Press [*British*]
LP	Popular Concerts [*Public-performance tariff class*] [*British*]
LP-28	Ligas Populares de 28 de Febrero [*February 28 Popular Leagues*] [*El Salvador*] (PD)
LPA	Amphibious Transport [*Navy ship symbol*]
LPA	Collaboration Partners Acquired (SAUS)
LPA	Laboratory Products Association (NTPA)
LPA	Labor Party Association (SAUO)
LPA	Labor Policy Association (EA)
LPA	Labor Press Association (SAUO)
LPA	La Plata [*Argentina*] [*Seismograph station code, US Geological Survey*] (SEIS)
LPA	LASER Printer Adapter
LPA	Las Palmas [*Canary Islands*] [*Airport symbol*] (OAG)
LPA	Latex Particle Agglutination [*Immunochemistry*] (DAVI)
LPA	Latvian Privatization Agency
LPA	Launcher Plant Assembly (IAA)
LPA	Launch Phase Analyst
LPA	Lauric [*or Lauroyl or Lauryl*] Isopropanolamide [*Also, LIPA*] [*Organic chemistry*]
LPA	Leaky Pipe Antenna
LPA	Leather Producers' Association for England, Scotland, and Wales (BI)
LPA	Left Pulmonary Artery [*Anatomy*]
LPA	Lightning Position Analyser (QUAC)

LPA	Light Pulser Array
LPA	Limited Period Appointment [*Short-term employment*] [*British*]
LPA	Limited Purpose Agency (OICC)
LPA	Linear Power Amplifier
LPA	Link Pack Area [*Computer science*] (MCD)
LpA	Lipoprotein A [*Biochemistry*]
LPA	Liquid Propellant Analysis
LPA	Literature Primers [*A publication*]
LPA	Lithium Perchlorate Ammoniate [*Inorganic chemistry*]
LPA	Little People of America (EA)
LPA	Load Planning Advisor (SAUS)
LPA	Loan Production Office (EBF)
LPA	Local Pay Authority (AIE)
LPA	Local Planning Assistance (OICC)
LPA	Local Planning Authority [*British*] (DCTA)
LPA	Local Processing Agency [*Department of Housing and Urban Development*] (GFGA)
LPA	Local Public Agency
LPA	Logarithmic Periodic Antenna (MCD)
LPA	Logistics Pipeline Analysis [*Military*] (MCD)
LPA	Log Periodic Antenna
LPA	London Academy of Performing Arts [*England*] (WDAA)
LPA	Louisiana Pharmacists Association (SRA)
LPA	Louisiana Press Association (SRA)
LPA	Louisiana Psychological Association (SRA)
LPA	Low-Power Amplifier (CET)
LPA	Low-Pressure Alarm (IEEE)
LPA	Lysophosphatidic Acid [*Biochemistry*]
LPA	PAL Aerolineas SA de CV [*Mexico*] [*ICAO designator*] (FAAC)
LPAA	League of Pace Amendment Advocates (EA)
LPAA	Log Periodic Array Antenna
LPAA	London Poster Advertising Association (SAUO)
LPAAT	Lysophosphatidic Acid Acyltransferase [*An enzyme*]
LPAB	Legal Practitioners' Admission Board [*Australia*]
LPAC	Labor Policy Advisory Committee for Multilateral Trade Negotiations [*Terminated, 1980*] (EGAO)
LPAC	Lancer Pacific, Inc. (SAUO)
LPAC.	Laser Pacific Media Corp. [*NASDAQ symbol*] (SAG)
LPAC.	Laser-pac Media [*NASDAQ symbol*] (TTSB)
LPAC	Libertarian Party Abolitionist Caucus (EA)
LPAI	La Petite Academy, Incorporated (SAUO)
LPAI	Ligue Populaire Africaine pour l'Independance [*African People's League for Independence*] [*Djibouti*]
LPAM	Lisboa [*Portugal*] [*ICAO location identifier*] (ICLI)
L-PAM	L-Phenylalanine Mustard [*Melphalan*] [*Also, A, M, MPH, MPL*] [*Antineoplastic drug*]
L-PAM	L-Phenylalanin, Procarbazine, Adriamycin, Methotrexate [*Antineoplastic drug regimen*] (DAVI)
LP & KTF	London Printing and Kindred Trades Federation (DGA)
LP&L	Louisiana Power and Light (SAUO)
LP&LC	Louisiana Power & Light Company (SAUO)
LP & M	Liverpool Post and Mercury [*A publication*] (ROG)
LP & P	Logistics Policy and Procedures for Contingency Operations [*DARCOM*] (CINC)
LPAR	Alverca [*Portugal*] [*ICAO location identifier*] (ICLI)
LPAR	Large Phased-Array RADAR
LPAR	Logical Partition [*Computer science*] (CIST)
LPARL	Lockheed Palo Alto Research Laboratory (SAUO)
LPARM	Liquid Propellant Applied Research Motor
LPAS	Luciano Pavarotti Appreciation Society [*British*] (DBA)
LPASA	Linear Pulse-Height Analyzer Spectrum Analysis (PDAA)
L/PAT	Legislative/Political Action Team
L/PAT	Letters Patent (ROG)
LPAT	Lopat Industries, Inc. (SAUO)
LPATS	Lightning Position and Tracing System (MCD)
LPAV	Aveiro [*Portugal*] [*ICAO location identifier*] (ICLI)
LPA-VS	London and Provincial Anti-Vivisection Society (SAUO)
LPAZ	Santa Maria, Santa Maria Island [*Portugal*] [*ICAO location identifier*] (ICLI)
LPB	La Paz [*Bolivia*] [*Airport symbol*] (OAG)
LPB	La Paz [*Bolivia*] [*Seismograph station code, US Geological Survey*] (SEIS)
LPB	Launch Pad Building (ACAE)
LPB	Lighted Pushbutton (ECII)
LpB	Lipoprotein B [*Biochemistry*]
LPB	Lithium Polymer Battery
LPB	Load Program Block [*Computer science*] (ELAL)
LPB	Loan Policy Board [*of SBA*] [*Abolished, 1965*]
LPB	Lollipop Power Books (EA)
LPB	[*The*] Louisiana & Pine Bluff Railway Co. [*AAR code*]
LPB	Low-Level Penetration Bomb
LPB	Low-Probability Behavior
LPB	Lunar and Planetary Bibliography [*Lunar and Planetary Institute*] [*Information service or system*] (IID)
LPB	Paper Book of Laurence, J., in Lincoln's Inn Library [*A publication*] (DLA)
LPBA	Lawyer-Pilots Bar Association (EA)
LPBBA	Log Periodic Broadband Antenna
LPBE	Beja [*Portugal*] [*ICAO location identifier*] (ICLI)
LPBE	Linear Poisson-Boltzmann Equation [*Physical chemistry*]
LPBG	Braganca [*Portugal*] [*ICAO location identifier*] (ICLI)
LPBJ	Beja [*Portugal*] [*ICAO location identifier*] (ICLI)
LPBP	Latino Public Broadcasting Project (SAUO)
LPBP	Low-Profile Bioprosthesis [*Medicine*] (DMAA)
LPBR	Braga [*Portugal*] [*ICAO location identifier*] (ICLI)

LPBT............	Ladies Professional Bowlers Tour (EA)
LPC............	Acyl Lyso-glycerophosphocholine (SAUS)
LPC............	Laboratory Precision Connector (IAA)
LPC............	Laboratory Pulse Compression
LPC............	Labour Party Conference (SAUO)
LPC............	La Cumbre Peak [California] [Seismograph station code, US Geological Survey] (SEIS)
LPC............	Lamina Precursor Cell [Neurology]
LPC............	Landmarks Preservation Commission [New York City]
LPC............	Land Protection Council [Victoria, Australia]
LPC............	Large Particle Count (SAUS)
LPC............	LASER Particle Counter (AAEL)
LPC............	Laser Photocoagulation [Ophthalmology] (DAVI)
LPC............	Late Positive Component (MAE)
LPC............	Launch Pod Container [General Support Rocket System] (MCD)
LPC............	Laurylpyridinium Chloride [Also, DPC] [Organic chemistry]
LPC............	Leader Preparation Course
LPC............	Leaf Protein Concentrate [Food industry]
LPC............	League of Professional Craftsmen [British] (DBA)
LPC............	Least-Preferred Co-Worker [Management term]
LPC............	Leather Personnel Carriers [i.e., boots] [Slang] [Army]
LPC............	Less Prosperous Country
LPC............	Leukocyte Particle Counter [Instrumentation]
LPC............	Licensed Professional Counselor
LPC............	Lieberman Plasma Cell (DB)
LPC............	Light Patrol Car [British]
LPC............	Limiting Permissible Concentration (EEVL)
LPC............	Linear Power Controller
LPC............	Linear Prediction Code
LPC............	Linear Predictive Coding [Digital coding technique] [Telecommunications]
LPC............	Linkport Controller [Electronics] (ECII)
LPC............	Link Priority Change [NASA] (KSC)
LPC............	Lipocortin (DMAA)
LpC............	Lipoprotein C [Biochemistry]
LPC............	Livermore Projects Committee (SAUO)
LPC............	Livestock and Pastoral Company (SAUO)
LPC............	Livestock Publications Council (EA)
LPC............	Local Procedure Call (VLIE)
LPC............	Local Productivity Committee (SAUO)
LPC............	Lockheed Propulsion Co. [Division of Lockheed Aircraft Corp.] (KSC)
LPC............	Logical Processing Capabilities (ACAE)
LPC............	Lompoc, CA [Location identifier] [FAA] (FAAL)
LPC............	London Parochial Charities (SAUO)
LPC............	London Processing Centre (SAUO)
LPC............	London Publicity Club (SAUO)
LPC............	Longitudinal Parity Check [Telecommunications] (IAA)
LPC............	Longitudinal Primary Care [Medicine] (DMAA)
LPC............	Loop-Control [Relay] (IEEE)
LPC............	Loop Preparation Cask [Nuclear energy] (NRCH)
LPC............	Lord President's Committee [British]
LPC............	Lords of the Privy Council Lower Provinces Code [India] [A publication] (DLA)
LPC............	Loss and Prevention Council (HEAS)
LPC............	Lottery Promotion Co. [British] (ECON)
LPC............	Lower Pump Cubicle (IEEE)
LPC............	Low Particle Concentration
LPC............	Low-Power Channel (IAA)
LPC............	Low-Power Counter
LPC............	Low-Pressure Chamber Technician [Navy]
LPC............	Low-Pressure Composite
LPC............	Low Pressure Compressor (SAUS)
LPC............	Low-Pressure Compressor
LPC............	Low Price Center (SAUO)
LPC............	Lumped-Parameter Calorimeter [Heat measure]
LPC............	Lysophosphatidylcholine [Also, Lyso-PC] [Biochemistry]
LPCA............	Louisiana Pest Control Association (SRA)
LPCA............	Louisiana Primary Care Association (SRA)
LPCA............	Lunar Pyrotechnic Control Assembly [Aerospace]
LPCAT............	Laboratory for Pest Control Application Technology [Ohio State University] [Research center] (RCD)
LPCC............	Lamb Promotion Coordination Committee (SAUO)
LPCC............	Legal Practitioners Complaints Committee [South Australia]
LPCC............	London Propaganda Coordinating Committee (SAUO)
LPCC............	Low-Pressure Combustion Chamber
LPCDF.........	Low Profile Combined Distributing Frame (ROAS)
LPCG	LASER Planning and Coordination Group [Energy Research and Development Administration]
LPCH	Chaves [Portugal] [ICAO location identifier] (ICLI)
LPCH	Local Process Control Host (IAA)
LPCI............	Low Pressure Coolant Injection (SAUS)
LPCI............	Low-Pressure Coolant Injection [Nuclear energy] (NRCH)
LPCIS.........	Low-Pressure Coolant Injection System [Nuclear energy] (NRCH)
LPCL............	Laboratory Pulse Compression Loop
LPCL............	Linear Programming Control Language [Computer science] (VLIE)
LPCM............	Linear Phase Code Modulation
LPCM............	Linear Pulse-Code Modulation [Computer science]
LPCM............	London Police Court Mission (SAUO)
LPCM............	Low Placed Conus Medullaris [Medicine] (DMAA)
LPCO............	Coimbra [Portugal] [ICAO location identifier] (ICLI)
LPCO	Laboratory Policy Coordination Office (SAUO)
LPCO	Low-Pressure Cut-Off [Air conditioning system] [Automotive engineering]
LPCOMP......	Logical Physical Comparator (VLIE)
LPCP............	Launcher Preparation Control Panel

LPCR	Low-Pressure Cooling Recirculation Phase [Environmental science] (COE)
LPCRS.........	Low-Pressure Coolant Recirculation System [Nuclear energy] (IEEE)
LPCS............	Cascais [Portugal] [ICAO location identifier] (ICLI)
LPCS............	Laterally to the Pedunculus Cerebellaris Superior [Medicine]
LPCS............	League for the Prohibition of Cruel Sports (SAUO)
LPCS............	Local Post Collectors Society (EA)
LPCS............	Low-Pressure Core Spray [Environmental science] (COE)
LPCS............	Low-Pressure Core Spray System [Nuclear energy] (NRCH)
LPCT............	Late Proximal Cortical Tubule (DB)
LPCV............	Covilha [Portugal] [ICAO location identifier] (ICLI)
LPCVD	Liquid Phase Chemical Vapor Deposition [Photovoltaic energy systems]
LPCVD	Liquid Phase Chemical Vapour Deposition (AAEL)
LPCVD	Low-Pressure Chemical Vapor Deposition [Semiconductor technology]
LP-CW	Long Pulse - Continuous Wave (NG)
LPD............	Amphibious Transport Dock [Landing Platform, Dock] [Navy ship symbol]
LPD............	Labelled Plan Display (PDAA)
LPD............	Labelled Position Display (SAUS)
LPD............	Label Plan Display (SAUS)
LPD............	Labour Party of Dominica [Political party] (EY)
LPD............	Landing Platform, Dock
LPD............	Landing Point Designator [Apollo] [NASA]
LPD............	Language Processing and Debugging [Computer science] (BUR)
LPD............	La Pedrera [Colombia] [Airport symbol] (OAG)
LPD............	Laredo Petroleums [Vancouver Stock Exchange symbol]
LPD............	Large Parallel Databases (SAUO)
LPD............	LASER Polarization Detector
LPD............	LASER Projection Display (AAEL)
LPD............	Lateral Photoelectric Detector (PDAA)
LPD............	Launch Platform Detected [Navy] (CAAL)
LPD............	Launch Point Determination
LPD............	Launch Procedure Document [NASA] (KSC)
LPD............	Least Perceptible Difference [Psychology]
lpd............	Least-Perceptible Difference (DIPS)
LPD............	Legendary Pink Dots (VLIE)
LPD............	Legg-Perthes Disease [Medicine] (MELL)
LPD............	Liberal Publications Department (SAUO)
LPD............	Lighting-Power Density
LPD............	Light Pipe Device [Communications]
LPD............	Light Point Defect (AAEL)
LPD............	Linear Phasing Device [Telecommunications] (OA)
LPD............	Line Printer Daemon (PCM)
LpD............	Lipoprotein D [Biochemistry]
LPD............	Liquid-Protein Diet
LPD............	Liters per Day (KSC)
LPD............	Local Power Density (NRCH)
LPD............	Local Procurement Direct [Military]
LPD............	Logical Physical Design (VLIE)
LPD............	Log Periodic Dipole
LPD............	Low-Performance Drone
LPD............	Low Period Dipole
LPD............	Low-Power Difference (IEEE)
LPD............	Low-Pressure Difference (IEEE)
LPD............	Low Probability of Detection (ADWA)
LPD............	Low Protein Diet
LPD............	Luteal Phase Defect [Gynecology] (DAVI)
LPD............	Lymphoproliferative Disease [Oncology]
LPD............	Lymphoproliferative Disorder [Medicine] (MELL)
LPDA	Linear Photodiode Array [Instrumentation]
LPDA	Link Problem Determination Aid (VLIE)
LPDA	Log Periodic Dipole Antenna [Military] (CAAL)
LPDA	Log Periodic Dipole Array
LPDC	Language Programmes Development Centre (SAUO)
LPDC	LASER Plasmadynamic Converter
LPDC	Least Positive Down Count (VLIE)
LPDC	Leonard Peltier Defense Committee (EA)
LPDC	London Parcels Delivery Co.
LPDC	London Parcels Delivery Company (SAUO)
LPDE............	Leeds Product Data Editor (VLIE)
LPDF............	Lipoprotein-Deficient Fraction [Medicine] (DMAA)
LPD/H	Landing Platform, Dock/Helicopter (MILB)
LpDH............	Lysopine Dehydrogenase [An enzyme]
LPDM............	List of Physical Dimensions (NASA)
LPDR............	Lao People's Democratic Republic
LPDR............	Local Public Document Room (GFGA)
LPDS............	Lipoprotein Deficient Human Serum
LPDT............	Legal Practitioners Disciplinary Tribunal [South Australia]
LPDT............	Low Power Distress Transmitter [Aviation] (DA)
LPDTL.........	Low-Power Diode Transistor Logic [Electronics] (IAA)
LPDU	Link Layer Protocol Data Unit [Telecommunications] (OSI)
LPDU	Link Protocol Data Unit (SAUS)
LPE............	Labour Party Executive (SAUO)
LPE............	Lamda Point Experiment (SAUS)
LPE............	Launch Preparation Equipment (AABC)
LPE............	Layer Primitive Equation (MHDI)
LPE............	Lead Piping Engineer
LPE............	Limited Paperback Editions
LPE............	Linear Parameter Estimation [Physical chemistry]
LPE............	Linear Polyethylene [Organic chemistry]
LPE............	Linkport Extension [Electronics] (ECII)
LpE............	Lipoprotein E [Biochemistry]
LPE............	Lipoprotein Electrophoresis [Biochemistry]

LPE	Liquid Phase Epitaxy [*Magnetic film*]
LPE	Local Peripheral Equipment (VLIE)
LPE	London Petroleum Exchange (SAUO)
LPE	London Press Exchange
LPE	London Provision Exchange (SAUO)
LPE	Loop Preparation Equipment [*Nuclear energy*] (NRCH)
LPE	Low Probability of Exploitation (PDAA)
LPE	Lunar and Planetary Ephemerides Assembly [*Space Flight Operations Facility, NASA*]
LPE	Lysophosphatidylethanolamine [*Biochemistry*]
LPEA	Luis Palau Evangelistic Association (EA)
LPEC	Labour Party Education Committee (SAUO)
LPEC	Launch Preparation Equipment Compartment (AABC)
LPed	Licentiate in Pedagogy (CPGU)
LPEM	Launch Preparation Equipment Monitor (MCD)
LPEO	Local Public Employment Office
LPEP	Le Peep Restaurants, Inc. (SAUO)
LPER	Institute for Regional Economic Research (SAUO)
LPerc	Light Perception [*Ophthalmology*]
LPERE	Linear Phase with Equal Ripple Error (IAA)
LPES	Lamda Point Experiment System (SAUS)
LPES	Launch Preparation Equipment Set (AABC)
LPEV	Evora [*Portugal*] [*ICAO location identifier*] (ICLI)
LPEV	Launch Preparation Equipment Vault (MCD)
LPF	Landsing Pacific Fund [*AMEX symbol*] (CTT)
LPF	Large Payload Fairing (IGSL)
LPF	Latvian Popular Front [*Political party Defunct*] (EAIO)
LPF	Leach-Precipitate Float (BARN)
LPF	Lead Pipe Fracture (MELL)
LPF	League for Programming Freedom (EA)
LPF	Left Posterior Fascicle [*Anatomy*]
LPF	Le Pertre [*France*] [*Seismograph station code, US Geological Survey*] (SEIS)
LPF	Leukocytosis-Promoting Factor [*Hematology*]
LPF	Leukopenia Factor (STED)
LPF	Life Probability Function
LPF	Light Patrol Frigate (ADA)
LPF	Lipopolysaccharide Factor (STED)
LPF	Liquid Pressure Filter
LPF	Liver Plasma Flow [*Medicine*] (STED)
LPF	Localized Plaque Formation [*Dentistry*] (MAE)
LPF	Logically Passive Function
LPF	Lowest Possible Airfare
LPF	Low-Pass Filter [*Electronics*]
lpf	Low-Power Field (STED)
LPF	Low-Power Field [*Microscopy*]
LPF	Low-Profile Flange
LPF	Lutheran Peace Fellowship (EA)
LPF	Lymphocytosis-Promoting Factor [*Hematology*] (DAVI)
LPF	Pop Festivals [*Public-performance tariff class*] [*British*]
LPFA	Laminated Plastics Fabricators Association [*British*] (BI)
LPFA	London Potato Futures Association [*London Stock Exchange*]
LPFB	Left Posterior Fascicular Block [*Cardiology*]
LPFGEN	Linear Programming File Generator [*Computer science*] (IAA)
LPFL	Flores, Flores Island [*Portugal*] [*ICAO location identifier*] (ICLI)
LPFL	Lowpass Filter (MSA)
LPFM	Low-Powered Fan Marker (MSA)
LPFN	Low-Pass-Filtered Noise (STED)
LPFO	London Procurement Field Office
LPFP	Low-Pressure Fuel Pump (KSC)
LPFR	Faro [*Portugal*] [*ICAO location identifier*] (ICLI)
LPFR	Liquid Phase Flow Reactor (KSC)
LPFRS	Low-Profile Frequency Reference Standard
LPFRT	Limited Preliminary Flight Rating Test
LPFS	London Public Fur Sales (SAUO)
LPFS	Low-Pass-Filtered Signal (STED)
LPFSSB	Lone Parents' Family Support Service - Birthright [*Australia*]
LPFT	LOPW Pressure Fuel Turboprop (SAUS)
LPFT	Low-Pressure Fuel Turbopump
LPFTP	Low-Pressure Fuel Turbopump (NASA)
LPFU	Funchal, Madeira Island [*Portugal*] [*ICAO location identifier*] (ICLI)
LPG	Collaboration Programme (SAUS)
LPG	Lake Ponask Gold Corp. [*Toronto Stock Exchange symbol*]
LPG	Langage de Programmation et de Gestion [*French computer language*]
LPG	La Plata [*Argentina*] [*Airport symbol*] (OAG)
LPG	Lapping [*Electricity*]
LPG	Last Page Generator (NASA)
LPG	Launch Preparations Group [*NASA*]
LPG	Le Parti de la Guadeloupe [*Political party*] (EY)
LPG	Library Planning Group (SAUO)
LPG	Licentiate of the Physicians Guild [*British*]
LPG	Life Partners Group [*NYSE symbol*] (TTSB)
LPG	Life Partners Group, Inc. [*NYSE symbol*] (SPSG)
LPG	Linear Predictive Coder (SAUO)
LPG	Lipophosphoglycan [*Biochemistry*]
LPG	Liquefied Petroleum Gas
LPG	Liquid Propane Gas
LPG	Liquid Propane-Gas Shutoff [*NFPA pre-fire planning symbol*] (NFPA)
LPG	Liquid Propellant Gun (NASA)
LPG	List Program Generator (IAA)
LPG	Loan Portfolio Guarantee (SAUO)
LPG	Long Path Gas [*Spectroscopy*]
LPG	Lousy Paying Guest [*Hotel slang*]
LPG	Low-Pressure Gas (NRCH)
LPG	Petrolane Partners (SAUO)
LPGA	Ladies Professional Golf Association (EA)
LPGA	Liquefied Petroleum Gas Association (HEAS)
LPGA	Living Plant Growers Association (EA)
LPGA	Louisiana Pecan Growers' Association (EA)
LPGA	Louisiana Personnel and Guidance Association (SAUO)
LP Gas	Liquefied Petroleum Gas (SAUO)
LPGE	LEM [*Lunar Excursion Module*] Partial Guidance Equipment [*NASA*] (KSC)
LPGG	Liquid Propellant Gas Generator
LPGITA	Liquefied Petroleum Gas Industry Technical Association [*British*]
LPGITA	Liquid Petroleum Gas Industry Technical Association (SAUO)
LPGITC	Liquified Petroleum Gas Industry Technical Committee
LPGL	London Pacific Group Ltd. [*NASDAQ symbol*] (SAG)
LPGLY	London Pacific Grp ADS [*NASDAQ symbol*] (TTSB)
LPGM	Last Pinedale Glacial Maximum [*Climatology*]
LPGR	Graciosa, Graciosa Island [*Portugal*] [*ICAO location identifier*] (ICLI)
LPGS	Liquid Pathway Generic Study [*Nuclear energy*] (NRCH)
LPGS	Liquified Petroleum Gas Report [*American Petroleum Institute*] [*Database*]
LPGTC	Liquified Petroleum Gas Industry Technical Committee (MCD)
LPH	Amphibious assault ship, helicopter (SAUS)
LPH	Amphibious Assault Ship (Landing Platform, Helicopter) [*Navy symbol*]
LPH	Assault Hospital Ship [*Navy symbol*] (VNW)
LPH	Laboratory of Physiological Hygiene [*University of Minnesota*] [*Research center*] (RCD)
LPH	Landing Personnel Helicopter [*British*] (NATG)
LPH	Landing Platform Helicopter (CCCA)
LPh	Late Phoenician (BJA)
LPH	Lee Pharmaceuticals [*AMEX symbol*] (SPSG)
LPH	Left Posterior Hemiblock [*Cardiology*]
LPH	Legrest Pin Handle
LPh	Licentiate of Philosophy
LPH	Light Pintle Head (SAUS)
LPH	Lines per Hour [*Printing*]
LPH	Lipotropic Hormone (ADWA)
LPH	Lipotropic Pituitary Hormone [*Lipotropin*] [*Medicine*] (STED)
LPH	Lipotropin Hormone [*Endocrinology*]
LPH	Liters per Hour (KSC)
LPH	Lochgilphead [*Scotland*] [*Airport symbol*] (OAG)
LPHB	Left Posterior Hemiblock [*Medicine*] (STED)
LPHB	Low-Pressure Heating Boiler
LPHL	Leisureplanet Holdings [*NASDAQ symbol*] (SG)
LPHLDR	Lampholder
LPHR	Horta, Faial Island [*Portugal*] [*ICAO location identifier*] (ICLI)
LPHS	Lunar and Planetary Horizon Scanner [*Aerospace*]
LPhSoc	London, Royal Philharmonic Society (SAUO)
LPHSW	Last Pass Heat Sink Welding [*Nuclear energy*] (NUCP)
LPI	Collaboration Programme Interest (SAUS)
LPI	Colorado Springs, CO [*Location identifier*] [*FAA*] (FAAL)
LPI	Laser Peripheral Iridectomy [*Medicine*] (MELL)
LPI	LASER Peripheral Iridectomy (STED)
LPI	Latent Photographic Image
LPI	Launching Position Indicator
LPI	Leadership Practices Inventory [*Test*] (TMMY)
LPI	Leaf Plastochron Index [*Botany*]
LPI	Learning Preference Inventory
LPI	Lease Plan International (SAUO)
LPI	Left Posterior-Inferior [*Medicine*] (DMAA)
LPI	Lightning Protection Institute (EA)
LPI	Linear Partial Information (PDAA)
Lpi	Lines per Inch (ADWA)
LPI	Lines per Inch [*Printing*]
LPI	Linkoeping [*Sweden*] [*Airport symbol*] (OAG)
LPI	Linus Pauling Institute of Science and Medicine [*Research center*] (RCD)
LPI	Linux Professional Institute (SAUO)
LPI	List per Inch (IAA)
LPI	Logistics Performance Indicator (PDAA)
LPI	Lomond Publications, Inc. [*Telecommunications service*] (TSSD)
LPI	Longitudinally Applied Paper Insulation [*Telecommunications*] (TEL)
LPI	Long Process of Incus [*Medicine*] (MELL)
LPI	Louisiana Polytechnical Institute
LPI	Low-Power Illuminator (NATG)
LPI	Low-Power Injection [*Nuclear energy*] (NRCH)
LPI	Low-Power Interrupt (MCD)
LPI	Low-Pressure Index
LPI	Low-Pressure Injection [*Nuclear energy*] (NRCH)
LPI	Low-Pressure Isolation (AAEL)
LPI	Low Probability of Intercept (NVT)
LPI	Low Probability of Interest
LPI	Lunar and Planetary Institute [*University Space Research Association*] [*Research center*] (RCD)
LPI	Lysinuric Protein Intolerance [*Medicine*] (DMAA)
LPIA	Label Printing Industries of America (EA)
LPIA	Launch Pad Interface Assembly
LPIA	Liquid Propellant Information Agency [*Johns Hopkins Univeristy*]
LPIB	Law and Policy in International Business [*ABA*] [*A publication*] (AAGC)
LPIBSS	Lunar and Planetary Institute Bibliographic Search Service [*University Space Research Association*] [*Information service or system*] (IID)
LPiC	Central Louisiana State Hospital, Medical Library, Pineville, LA [*Library symbol*] [*Library of Congress*] (LCLS)

LPICBM........	Liquid Propellant Intercontinental Ballistic Missile [*Military*] (IAA)
LPID............	Logical Page Identifier (BUR)
LPI/D...........	Low Probability of Intercept/Detection [*Environmental science*] (COE)
LPiL.............	Louisiana College, Pineville, LA [*Library symbol*] [*Library of Congress*] (LCLS)
LPI/LPE.......	Low Probability of Interception & Exploitation (SAUS)
LPIN............	Espinho [*Portugal*] [*ICAO location identifier*] (ICLI)
LPIR............	Limited Partnership Investment Review [*Information service or system*] (IID)
LPIR............	Low-Probability Intercept RADAR
LPIR............	LPI Radar (SAUS)
LPIRB..........	Low Probability of Intercept Radio Brassboard (SAUS)
LPIS............	Land Protection Incentives Scheme (SAUO)
LPIS............	Low-Pressure Injection System [*Nuclear energy*] (NRCH)
LPISM..........	Liquid Photo-Imageable Solder Mask [*Electronics*] (AAEL)
LPISS..........	Low-Power Illuminator Signal Source (MCD)
LPIU............	Lithographers and Photoengravers International Union [*Later, Graphic Arts International Union*]
LPIW..........	Lumber, Production, and Industrial Workers (WPI)
LPJF	Leiria [*Portugal*] [*ICAO location identifier*] (ICLI)
LPJO............	Alijo [*Portugal*] [*ICAO location identifier*] (ICLI)
LPK.............	Lao Pen Kang [*Laotian Neutralist Party*] (CINC)
LPK.............	Liver Pyruvate Kinase [*Medicine*] (DMAA)
LPKCMLPCC...	License Plate, Key Chain, and Mini License Plate Collectors Club (EA)
LPKRR	Logic Programming in Knowledge Representation and Reasoning (SAUO)
LPKS............	Lone Pine Koala Sanctuary (SAUO)
LPL.............	Entergy Louisiana, Inc. [*NYSE symbol*] (SAG)
LPL.............	Entergy Louisiana, Inc. Capital I [*NYSE symbol*] (SAG)
LPL.............	Laborers Political League (EA)
LPL.............	Labour Protection League [*A union*] [*British*]
LPL.............	Lambeth Palace Library (SAUO)
LPL.............	Lamina Propria Lymphocyte [*Hematology*]
LPL.............	Lamp-Pumped LASER (MCD)
LPL.............	Large Project Leader
LPL.............	LASER-Pumped-LASER
LPL.............	Lawton Public Library, Lawton, OK [*OCLC symbol*] (OCLC)
LPL.............	Lawyers Professional Liability [*Insurance*]
LPL.............	Lease-A-Plane International [*ICAO designator*] (FAAC)
LPL.............	Lethbridge Public Library [*UTLAS symbol*]
LPL.............	Lichen Planus-Like Lesion [*Medicine*] (DMAA)
LPL.............	Lightproof Louver [*Technical drawings*]
LPL.............	Linear Polarised Laser (SAUS)
LPL.............	Linear Programming Language [*Intertechnique*] [*French*] [*Computer science*]
LPL.............	Lipoprotein Lipase [*An enzyme*]
LPL.............	Liquid Plastics Limited (SAUO)
LPL.............	List Processing Language [*Computer science*] (IEEE)
LPL.............	Liverpool [*England*] [*Airport symbol*] (OAG)
LPL.............	Liverpool Public Libraries (SAUO)
LPL.............	LM [*Lunar Module*] Plan [*NASA*] (KSC)
LPL.............	Local Processor Link
LPL.............	London Public Library (SAUO)
LPL.............	Long Pulse LASER
LPL.............	Lotus Programming Language (SAUO)
LPL.............	Louisiana Power and Light (SAUO)
LPL.............	Louisiana Power & Light Co. [*NYSE symbol*] (SPSG)
LPL.............	Louisville Public Library (SAUO)
LPL.............	Low Polar Latitude [*Geophysics*]
LPL.............	Low Power Laser (ACAE)
LPL.............	Low-Power Logic
LPL.............	Lunar and Planetary Laboratory [*University of Arizona*] [*Research center*] (MCD)
LPL.............	Lunar Projects Laboratory
LPL.............	Lysophospholipase [*An enzyme*]
LPLA............	Lajes, Terceira Island [*Portugal*] [*ICAO location identifier*] (ICLI)
LPLA............	Lao Peoples Liberation Army (CINC)
LPLA............	Lipoprotein Lipase Activity [*Medicine*] (DMAA)
LPLA............	Log-Periodic Loop Antenna (PDAA)
LPlaI............	Iberville Parish Library, Plaquemine, LA [*Library symbol*] [*Library of Congress*] (LCLS)
LPLC............	Lift-Plus-Lift/Cruise (SAUS)
LPLDF.........	Ley de Protecci"n Jurisdiccional de las Libertades P#blicas y Derechos Fundamentales (SAUO)
LPLE	Leukocyte Pepsin-Like Enzyme (DB)
LPLG............	Lagos [*Portugal*] [*ICAO location identifier*] (ICLI)
LPLG............	Left Pleural Ganglion [*Medicine*]
LPLI.............	LPL Investment Group, Inc. (SAUO)
LPLIS...........	Lipoprotein Lipase Inactivation System [*Biochemistry*] (DAVI)
LPLM...........	Lowest Planned Level of Maintenance (SAA)
LPLNG	Low-Pressure Liquefied Natural Gases (NRCH)
LPLP...........	Language Problems & Language Planning, The University of Texas Press (SAUO)
LPLPr..........	Entergy Louisiana 12.64% cmPfd [*NYSE symbol*] (TTSB)
LPLPrA	Entergy Louisiana 9.68% cm Pfd [*NYSE symbol*] (TTSB)
LPLR...........	Lock Pillar (AAG)
LPL?TMC.....	Low-Pressure Low-Temperature Molding Compound
LPLV...........	Large Payload Life Vehicle (ACAE)
LPLWS........	Launch Pad Lightning Warning System [*NASA*] (KSC)
LPM............	Labour Party of Malaya (SAUO)
LPM............	Lamap [*Vanuatu*] [*Airport symbol*] (OAG)
LPM............	Landing Party Manual (SAUO)
LPM............	Lane Photograph Method
LPM............	LASER Particle Monitor (PDAA)
LPM............	LASER Phase Macroscope
LPM............	Laser Pointing Mirror (ACAE)
LPM............	LASER Precision Microfabrication (IAA)
LPM............	Lateral Pterygoid Muscle (DMAA)
LPM............	Leading Patrolman [*Navy*] [*British*] (DI)
lpm.............	Letters Per Minute (WDMC)
LPM............	Licensing Project Manager [*Nuclear energy*] (NRCH)
LPM............	Light Pulser Matrix
LPM............	Linearly Polarized Mode [*Telecommunications*] (TEL)
LPM............	Linear Power Module [*Computer science*] (CIST)
LPM............	Lines per Millimeter (WDAA)
lpm.............	Lines per Minute (IDOE)
LPM............	Lines per Minute [*Computer science*]
LPM............	Liquid Phase Methanation [*Fuel chemistry*]
LPM............	Liquid Propulsion Module (ACAE)
lpm.............	Liter per Minute (COE)
Lpm............	Liter per Minute (EEVL)
LPM............	Liters per Minute (MCD)
LPM............	Liver Plasma Membrane
LPM............	Local Processor Memory (IAA)
LPM............	Long Particular [*or Peculiar*] Metre [*Music*]
LPM............	Los Pinos Mountain [*New Mexico*] [*Seismograph station code, US Geological Survey*] (SEIS)
LPM............	Low-Pressure Molding [*Plastics*]
LPM............	Lunar Payload Module [*Aerospace*] (MCD)
LPM............	Lunar Portable Magnetometer [*Apollo*] [*NASA*]
LPMA...........	Lead Pencil Manufacturers Association [*Later, Pencil Makers Association*] (EA)
LPMA...........	Loose-Parts-Monitor Assembly [*Nuclear energy*] (NRCH)
LPMAD	Living Personnel Management Authorization Document [*DoD*]
LPMATGEN...	Linear Programming Matrix Generation (IAA)
LPMC...........	Low-Pressure Molding Compound
LPMES.........	Logistics Performance Measurement and Evaluation System (AABC)
LPMF...........	Monfortinho [*Portugal*] [*ICAO location identifier*] (ICLI)
LPMG...........	Liquid Phase Miscibility Gap (SAUS)
LPMG...........	Lisboa [*Portugal*] [*ICAO location identifier*] (ICLI)
LPMI...........	Mirandela [*Portugal*] [*ICAO location identifier*] (ICLI)
LPMO...........	Livestock Promotional Marketing Organisation (SAUO)
LPMOSS.......	Linear Programming Mathematical Optimization Subroutine System (IAA)
LPMP...........	Low-Pressure Molding Process [*Plastics*]
LPMR...........	Monte Real [*Portugal*] [*ICAO location identifier*] (ICLI)
LPM/S..........	Liquid Phase Methanation/Shift Reaction [*Fuel chemistry*]
LPMS...........	Lock Performance Monitoring System [*DOD*] [*COE*] (TAG)
LPMS...........	Logistics Program Management System [*Air Force*] (AFIT)
LPMS...........	Loose-Parts Monitoring System [*Nuclear energy*] (NRCH)
LPMT...........	Montijo [*Portugal*] [*ICAO location identifier*] (ICLI)
LPN.............	Alpenair GmbH & Co. KG [*Austria*] [*ICAO designator*] (FAAC)
LPN.............	Language Planning Newsletter (SAUO)
LPN.............	Licensed Practical Nurse
LPN.............	Logical Page Number (BUR)
LPN.............	Long Part Number
LPN.............	Longview, Portland & Northern Railway Co. [*AAR code*]
LPN.............	Low-Pass Network [*Electronics*]
LPN.............	Lumped Parameter Network (ACAE)
LPN.............	National Federation of Licensed Practical Nurses
LPNA...........	Licensed Practical Nurses Association (SAUO)
LPNA...........	Lithographers and Printers National Association [*Later, PIA*] (EA)
LPNAF..........	Licensed Practical Nurses Association of Florida (SRA)
LPNGP.........	Low-Pressure Noble Gas Processing (NRCH)
LPNI...........	Labour Party of Northern Ireland (SAUO)
LPNI...........	Langley Porter Neuropsychiatric Institute (SAUO)
LPO.............	La Palma Observatory
LPO.............	La Porte [*Indiana*] [*Airport symbol*] (OAG)
LPO.............	Laramie Project Office [*Laramie, WY*] [*Department of Energy*] (GRD)
LPO.............	Late Pleistocene Origins [*Ecology*]
LPO.............	Lateral Preoptic [*Brain anatomy*]
LPO.............	Lattice-Preferred Orientation [*Geophysics*]
LPO.............	Lauroyl Peroxide [*Organic chemistry*]
LPO.............	Leading Petty Officer (SAUO)
LPO.............	Left Posterio Occipital [*A fetal position*] (DAVI)
LPO.............	Left Posterior Oblique [*Cardiology*] (MAE)
LPO.............	Le Pouchou [*France*] [*Seismograph station code, US Geological Survey*] (SEIS)
LPO.............	Liberale Partei Oesterreichs [*Liberal Party of Austria*] [*Political party*] (PPE)
LPO.............	Liberal Party Organization [*British*]
LPO.............	Light Perception Only [*Ophthalmology*]
LPO.............	Likely Preferred Options (ABAC)
LPO.............	Limited Production Option [*Automotive engineering*]
LPO.............	Liquid Phase Oxidation [*Chemical processing*]
LPO.............	Loan Production Office [*Banking*]
LPO.............	Lobus Parolfactorius (PDAA)
LPO.............	Local Purchase Order
LPO.............	Logical Post Office (SAUO)
LPO.............	London Philharmonic Orchestra
LPO.............	London Post Office (SAUO)
LPO.............	Low Power Output (MSA)
LPO.............	Low-Pressure Oxygen
LPO.............	Lunar Parking Orbit [*Apollo*] [*NASA*]
LPO.............	Lunar Polar Orbiter [*NASA*]
LPO.............	Lunar Program Office [*NASA*] (IAA)
LPOC...........	Labile Particulate Organic Carbon [*Environmental science*]
LPOF...........	Low-Pressure Oil-Filled [*Cable*] (DICI)
LpOH	Lysopine Dehydrogenase (BABM)

L/POL........... Life Policy [Insurance] (DCTA)
L Pon Co ..... Light Pontoon Company (SAUO)
LPOOC......... Lake Placid Olympic Organizing Committee (SAUO)
L'POOL......... Liverpool (ROG)
LPOP .... Low-Pressure Oxidizer Turbopump (NASA)
L POST .... Left Posterior [Medicine] (MEDA)
LPOT........... Low-Pressure Oxidizer Turbopump (MCD)
LPOT........... Ota [Portugal] [ICAO location identifier] (ICLI)
LPOTP......... Low-Pressure Oxidizer Turbopump (NASA)
LPOX .... Low-Pressure Oxygen (AFM)
LPP............. Laboratory of Pulmonary Pathobiology (GNE)
LPP............. Labor Protection Plan
LPP............. Labour Progressive Party [Canadian communist party]
LPP............. Lanka Prajatantrawadi Party [Ceylon]
LPP............. Lappeenranta [Finland] [Airport symbol] (OAG)
LPP............. Large Paper Proofs
LPP............. LASER-Produced Plasma
LPP............. Lateral Pterygoid Plate [Medicine] (DMAA)
LPP............. Launcher Preparation Control Panel
LPP............. Leader Preparation Program
LPP............. Leader Preparations Program (SAUO)
LPP............. Learning Prototype Phase (SAUO)
LPP............. Lear Petroleum Partners (SAUO)
LPP............. Lebowa People's Party [South Africa] [Political party] (PPW)
LPP............. Length of Perpendiculars
LPP............. Liberian People's Party [Political party] (EY)
LPP............. Liberia Peoples Party (SAUO)
LPP............. Licensed Program Product (SAUO)
LPP............. Lightweight Presentation Protocol [Telecommunications] (ACRL)
LPP............. Linear Photopolymerization [Organic chemistry]
LPP............. Lines per Page
LPP............. Link Peripheral Processor (ACRL)
LPP............. Lipoprotein Lipase [An enzyme] (DAVI)
LPP............. Liquid Phase Processing [Chemistry]
LPP............. Local Patching Panel
LPP............. Location of Peak Pressure [Automotive engines]
LPP............. Long Periodic Perturbation
LPP............. Long-Period Pulses [Volcanology]
LPP............. Long Plenum Plugs (COE)
LPP............. Low-Power Physics (IEEE)
LPP............. Low-Pressure-Pipe System [Waste water treatment]
LPP............. Lunar Precepts Positioner [Aerospace]
LPPA........... Licensed Pearl Producers' Association [Australia]
LPPC........... Labour Progressive Party of Canada (SAUO)
LPPC........... Lisboa [Portugal] [ICAO location identifier] (ICLI)
LPPC........... Load Point Photocell
LPPC........... Long-Staying Psychiatric Patient Classes (SAUS)
LPPD .... Ponta Delgada, Sao Miguel Island [Portugal] [ICAO location identifier] (ICLI)
LPPH .... Late Postpartum Hemorrhage [Medicine] (DMAA)
LPPH .... Leningrad Prison Psychiatric Hospital [Later, LSPH]
LPPI........... Litton Precision Products International, Incorporated (SAUO)
LPPI........... Pico, Pico Island [Portugal] [ICAO location identifier] (ICLI)
LPPM.......... Low Pressure Permanent Mould (PDAA)
LPPM.......... Portimao [Portugal] [ICAO location identifier] (ICLI)
LPPMUL ...... Lawyers Protecting People from Malicious and Unjustified Lawsuits (EA)
LPPO .... Santa Maria [Portugal] [ICAO location identifier] (ICLI)
LPPP........... Low-Pressure Pump Pad (COE)
LPPR........... Porto [Portugal] [ICAO location identifier] (ICLI)
LPPS........... Low-Pressure Plasma Sprayed [Thermal barrier coating]
LPPS........... Porto Santo, Porto Santo Island [Portugal] [ICAO location identifier] (ICLI)
LPPT........... Lisboa [Portugal] [ICAO location identifier] (ICLI)
LPPT........... Low Pressurization Pressure Test Transmitter (IEEE)
LPPTS......... [The] Library of the Palestine Pilgrims' Text Society (BJA)
LPPV........... Praia Verde [Portugal] [ICAO location identifier] (ICLI)
LPQ........... Learning Process Questionnaire [J. Biggs] (TES)
LPQ........... Luang Prabang [Laos] [Airport symbol] (AD)
LPR............. Amphibious Transport (Small) [Navy ship symbol]
LPR............. Laboratory Property Removal Form (SAUO)
LPR............. Lactate-Pyruvate Ratio (MAE)
LPR............. Lanpar Technologies, Inc. [Toronto Stock Exchange symbol]
LPR............. La Peregrina [Puerto Rico] [Seismograph station code, US Geological Survey] (SEIS)
LPR............. Late Phase Reaction [or Response] [Medicine]
LPR............. Late Position Report [Report of a flight which is off flight plan]
LPR............. Late Procurement Request [Air Force] (AFM)
LPR............. Lawful Permanent Resident [Department of Justice]
LPR............. Leadership Potential Rating [Army] (AABC)
LPR............. Licensed Preacher
LPR............. License Plate Reader
LPR............. Lilly's Practical Register [A publication] (DLA)
LPR............. Linea Aerea Privadas Argentina [ICAO designator] (FAAC)
LPR............. Linear Polarization Resistance (MCD)
LPR............. Line Printer [Computer science] (NASA)
LPR............. Line Printer Redirector (AGLO)
LPR............. Line Printer Remote (PCM)
LPR............. Liquid Propellant Rocket [Air Force]
LPR............. Local Payment Receipt (AABC)
LPR............. London Property Register [London Research Centre] [British] [Information service or system] (IID)
LPR............. Long-Playing Record (IAA)
LPR............. Long-Playing Rocket [Aerospace]
LPR............. Looper Position Regulator

LPR............. Low-cost Packet Radio (SAUS)
LPR............. Low Power Radio
LPR............. Low Priority Request (SAUS)
LPR............. Lymphocyte Proliferative Response [Immunology]
LPR............. Lynchburg Pool Reactor
LPR-5 .... Lease Production Revenue System - 5 File [Petroleum Information Corp.] [Information service or system] (CRD)
LPR-10 .... Lease Production Revenue System - 10 File [Petroleum Information Corp.] [Information service or system] (CRD)
LPRA .... Laws of Puerto Rico Annotated [A publication]
LPRA .... Lost Parts Replacement Authorization (MCD)
LPRB .... Loaded Program Request Block [Computer science] (BUR)
LPRC .... Laboratory Process Review Committee (SAUO)
LPRC .... Launch Pitch Rate Control
LPRC .... Library Public Relations Council (EA)
LPRCO .... Logistics Planning and Reporting Code [Military]
LPRD .... Launch Program Requirement Document [NASA] (IAA)
LPRE........... Launch Prediction (ACAE)
LPRE........... Liquid Propellant Rocket Engine [Air Force]
LPRF........... Low-Power Radio Frequency (MCD)
LPRF........... Low Pulse Recurrence Frequency (MCD)
LPRI........... Licentiate of the Plastics and Rubber Institute [British] (DBQ)
LPRINT .... Lookup Dictionary Print Program (IEEE)
LPRINT .... Lookup Dictionary Print Programme (SAUO)
LPRL........... Laboratory Property Removal/Loan form (SAUO)
LPRL........... Lentz Peace Research Laboratory (EA)
LPRM.......... Local Power Range Monitor (NRCH)
LPRM.......... Low-Power Range Monitor [Nuclear energy] (NRCH)
LPRO .... Legend Properties, Inc. [NASDAQ symbol] (SAG)
LProj........... Light Projection [Ophthalmology]
LPRP .... Lao People's Revolutionary Party [Phak Pasason Pativat Lao] [Political party] (PPW)
LPRPrB .... Santander Overseas Bk 'B'Pfd [NYSE symbol] (TTSB)
LPRR .... Low-Power Research Reactor
LPRRAG....... Labour Party Race Relations Action Group (SAUO)
LPRS .... Local Primary Reference Source
LPRS .... Low Power Radio Service (SAUO)
LPRS .... Low-Pressure Recirculation System (NRCH)
LPRSVR....... Life Preserver
LPRSX .... Low-Pressure Recirculation System Heat Exchanger [Environmental science] (COE)
LPRT........... Laboratory Project Review Team (SAUO)
LPRT........... Low Power Relay Transmitter
LPS............. Laboratory for Planetary Studies (SAUO)
LPS............. Laboratory of Plasma Studies (SAUO)
LPS............. Laboratory Peripheral System
LPS............. Laboratory Program Summary (MCD)
LPS............. Labor Performance System (TIMI)
LPS............. Labour Press Service (SAUO)
LPS............. Landing Performance Score (MCD)
LPS............. Language for Programming-in-the-Small [Computer science] (MHDI)
LPS............. Lanterman-Petris-Short Act [Psychology] (DAVI)
LPS............. La Palma [El Salvador] [Seismograph station code, US Geological Survey] (SEIS)
LPS............. Large Pointing System (MCD)
LPS............. Large Processing Stations (SAUO)
LPS............. LASER Particulate Spectrometer [NASA]
LPS............. LASER Power Supply
LPS............. Laser Printing System (NITA)
LPS............. Last Papanicolaou Smear [Gynecology] (DAVI)
LPS............. Last Period Satisfied [IRS]
LPS............. Laterality Preference Schedule [Psychology]
LPS............. Lateral Premotor System (DMAA)
LPS............. Launch Phase Simulator [NASA]
LPS............. Launch Processing System [NASA] (KSC)
LPS............. Launch Processor System (SAUS)
LPS............. Launch Protection System (ACAE)
LPS............. Layered Protocol Structure [Computer science] (VLIE)
LPS............. L-Band Phase Shifter
LPS............. Learning Preference Scales [Test] (TMMY)
LPS............. Le Play Society (SAUO)
LPS............. Levator Palpebrae Superioris [Muscle] [Anatomy] (AAMN)
LPS............. Liberale Partei der Schweiz [Liberal Party of Switzerland] [Political party] (PPE)
LPS............. Liberal Party of Switzerland (SAUO)
LPS............. Liberian Philatelic Society [Defunct] (EA)
LPS............. Library Processes System [Educomp] [Information service or system] (IID)
LPS............. Library Programs Service (SAUO)
LPS............. Licensed Program Support (VLIE)
LPs............. Licentiate in Psychiatry (CMD)
LPS............. Life-Cycle Productivity System
LPS............. Lightning Protection System [Boating]
LPS............. Light Photo Squadron (SAUO)
LPS............. Lightproof Shade [Technical drawings]
LPS............. Linear Profile Scan [Medicine] (DMAA)
LPS............. Linear Programming System [Computer science]
LPS............. Linear Pulse Sector (OA)
LPS............. Line Procedure Specifications (CMD)
LPS............. Line Program Selector (IAA)
lps............. Lines per Second (VLIE)
LPS............. Lines per Second [Computer science]
LPS............. Lipase (MAE)
LPS............. Lipopolysaccharide [Biochemistry]
LPS............. Liquid-Phase Sintering (MCD)

LPS............. Liquid Propulsion System (ACAE)
LPS............. Liters per Second (KSC)
LPS............. Loan Production System [Department of Veterans Affairs]
LPS............. Local Process Specification (NG)
LPS............. Location Programming Standard [Computer science] (VLIE)
LPS............. Logicon Products [Vancouver Stock Exchange symbol]
LPS............. Logistic Policy Statement [Navy]
LPS............. Logistics Planning Study (MCD)
LPS............. Logistics Planning Support (SAUO)
LPS............. London & Port Stanley Railway Co. [AAR code]
LPS............. London Parcels Section (SAUO)
LPS............. London Press Service
Lps............. London, Royal Philharmonic Society (SAUO)
LPS............. Longfellow Poetry Society (EA)
Lps............. Loops [Military decoration] (AABC)
LPS............. Lopez Island [Washington] [Airport symbol] (OAG)
LPS............. Lord Privy Seal [British]
LPS............. Low-Power Schottky [Electronics]
LPS............. Low-Pressure Sand [Casting] [Automotive engineering]
LPS............. Low-Pressure Scram [Nuclear energy] (IEEE)
LPS............. Low-Pressure Separator [Chemical engineering]
LPS............. Low-Pressure Sodium
LPS............. Low Primary Sequence (VLIE)
LPS............. Lunar Penetrometer System [Aerospace]
LPS............. Lunar Pilotage System [Aerospace]
LPS............. Lyceum Performing Society (SAUO)
LPS............. Lypopolysaccharide [Medicine] (TAD)
LPSA............ Liberal Party of South Africa (SAUO)
LPSA............ Licensed Program Support Agreement [Computer science] (CIST)
LPSA............ Lithographic Preparatory Services Association [Later, GPA] (EA)
LPSA............ Log Periodic Scattering Array
LPSC............ Local Program Support Charges (VLIE)
LPSC............ Lunar and Planetary Science Conference
LPSC............ Luxembourg Philatelic Study Club [Defunct] (EA)
LPSC............ Santa Cruz [Portugal] [ICAO location identifier] (ICLI)
LPS/CDS .... Launch Processing System / Central Data Subsystem [Military]
LPS/CDS .... LPS/Central Data Subsystem (SAUS)
LPSCU .... Ladies Pennsylvania Slovak Catholic Union (EA)
LPSD .... Logically Passive Self-Dual
LPSF........... Lens-Pinhole Spatial Filter (PDAA)
LPSG .... Live Oak, Perry & South Georgia Railway Co. [AAR code]
LPSI........... Low-Pressure Safety Injection [Nuclear energy] (NRCH)
LPSI........... Sines [Portugal] [ICAO location identifier] (ICLI)
LPSIP.......... Low-Pressure Safety Injection Pump [Nuclear energy] (NRCH)
LPSJ........... Sao Jorge, Sao Jorge Island [Portugal] [ICAO location identifier] (ICLI)
LPSM........... Levenson Phase Shift Mask (AAEL)
LPSN........... Local Packet Switched Network
LPSNY .... Lithuanian Philatelic Society of New York (EA)
LPSO .... Laboratory Procurement Supply Office
LPSO .... Lloyd's Policy Signing Office [Lloyd's of London]
LPSOL .... Linear Programming Solution (IAA)
LPS/PIA .... Lothographic Platemakers Section of Printing Industries of America (SAUO)
LPSR........... Lipopolysaccharide Receptor (DB)
LPSS........... Amphibious Transport Submarine [Landing Platform, Submarine] [Navy ship symbol]
LPSS........... Law and Political Science Section [Association of College and Research Libraries]
LPSS........... Line Protection Switching System [Bell System]
LPSS........... Local Population Studies Society [British]
LPSSNJ........ Low-Power Self-Screening Noise Jammer [Military] (CAAL)
LPSSR .... Low-Power Spread Spectrum RADAR (PDAA)
LPST........... Latest Possible Start Time (SAUO)
LPST........... Sintra [Portugal] [ICAO location identifier] (ICLI)
LPSTTL........ Low-Power Schottky Transistor-Transistor Logic [Electronics] (IAA)
LPSU........... Launcher Power Supply Unit (SAUS)
LPSV........... Low-Pressure Solenoid Valve
LPSVD .... Linear Prediction with Singular Value Decomposition [Computer science]
LPSW.......... Load Program Status Word (IAA)
LPSW.......... Low-Pressure Service Water [Nuclear energy] (NRCH)
LPT .... Laboratory Point and Tracking (ACAE)
LPT .... Lampang [Thailand] [Airport symbol] (OAG)
LPT .... Lampang [Thailand] [Seismograph station code, US Geological Survey] (SEIS)
LPT .... Language Proficiency Test [Military] (AFM)
LPT .... Largest Processing Time First [Computer science] (MHDB)
LPT .... LASER Propulsion Test (SSD)
LPT .... LASER Pyrolysis Technique [Inorganic synthesis]
LPT .... Latest Recommended Posting Times [Business term] (DCTA)
LPT .... Leading Physical Trainer [British military] (DMA)
LPT .... Lear Petroleum Corp. (SAUO)
LPT .... Lehigh Portland Cement Company (SAUO)
LPT .... Licensed Physical Therapist
LPT .... Licensed Psychiatric Technician (NUJO)
LPT .... Light Pen Tracking (MCD)
LPT .... Limited Procurement Test
LP-T........... Limited Production - Test (AABC)
LPT .... Line Printer [Computer science]
LPT .... Line Printer Port [Computer science] (DCDG)
LPT .... Line Printer Terminal (RALS)
LPT .... Lipotropin (DMAA)
LPT .... Liquid Penetrant Testing [or Examination] [Nuclear energy] (NRCH)
LPT .... Listed Property Trust

LPT............. Local Point (VLIE)
LPT............. Local Printer Terminal (SAUS)
LPT............. Local Public Transportation
LPT............. Lock Pointer Table
LPT............. Longest Processing Time [Computer science] (VLIE)
LPT............. Long-Period Tremor [Volcanology]
LPT............. Low Point [Technical drawings]
LPT............. Low-Power Test
LPT............. Low-Pressure Test
LPT............. Low-Pressure Transducer
LPT............. Low Pressure Turbine (SAUS)
LPT............. Low-Pressure Turbine [Nuclear energy] (NRCH)
LPT............. Low Pressure Turbocharger
LPT............. Low Profile Turret (SAUS)
LPT............. Luminescent Pigment Tattooing
LPT............. Lymphocyte Transfer (DB)
LPT1............ First Parallel Printer Port (SAUS)
LPT3............ Third Parallel Printer Port (SAUS)
LPTA............ Louisiana Parent-Teacher Association (SAUO)
LPtaW.......... West Baton Rouge Parish Library, Port Allen, LA [Library symbol] [Library of Congress] (LCLS)
LPTB............ London Passenger Transport Board
LPTB............ Low-Pressure Turbine [on a ship] (DS)
LPTC............ Liquid Propellant Travelling Charge (SAUS)
LPTD............ Linear Programmed Thermal Degradation [Instrumentation]
LPTD............ Long Play Talkdown
LPTD-MS ..... Linear Programmed Thermal Degradation - Mass Spectroscopy [Instrumentation]
LPTF............ Low-Power Test Facility [Nuclear energy]
LPTH............ LightPath Technologies, Inc. [NASDAQ symbol] (SAG)
LPTHA .... LightPath Technologes'A' [NASDAQ symbol] (TTSB)
LPTHU .... LightPath Technologies Unit [NASDAQ symbol] (TTSB)
LPTHW .... LightPath Technol Wrrt 'A' [NASDAQ symbol] (TTSB)
LPTHZ .... LightPath Technol Wrrt 'B' [NASDAQ symbol] (TTSB)
LPTIS.......... Laguna Peak Tracking and Injection Station
LPTN........... Tancos [Portugal] [ICAO location identifier] (ICLI)
LPTR........... Line Printer [Computer science] (MSA)
LPTR........... Livermore Pool Type Reactor
LPTS........... Lightweight Protected Turret System (SAUS)
LPTS........... Louisiana Presbyterian Theological Seminary
LPTTL......... Low-Power Transistor-Transistor Logic
LPTTP......... League of Professional Theatre Training Programs [Defunct] (EA)
LPTV........... Large Payload Test Vehicle [Air Force]
LPTV........... Low-Power Television (GOBB)
LPTW.......... Lake Providence, Texarkana & Western R. R. [AAR code]
LPu............ Language Processor Unit
LPu............ Late Punic (BJA)
LPU............ League of Prayer for Unity [Defunct] (EA)
LPU............ Least Publishable Unit [of research data]
LPU............ Legal Practices Update [A publication]
LPU............ Life Preserver Unit
LPU............ Limited Procurement, Urgent (MCD)
LP-U........... Limited Production - Urgent (AABC)
LPU............ Line Printer Unit (COE)
LPU............ Line Processing Unit
LPU............ Lions Philatelic Unit (EA)
LPU............ Liquid Processing Unit
LPU............ Local Programming Unit (SAUS)
LPU............ Low Pay Unit [British]
LPU............ Low-Power Unit (CAAL)
LPUG.......... Lasers in Publishing Users Group (EA)
LPUL.......... Least Positive Uplevel (IAA)
LPUU .... Linear Programming under Uncertainty [Computer science]
LPV............ Houston, TX [Location identifier] [FAA] (FAAL)
LPV............ Landing Platform Vehicle [Navy] [British]
LPV............ Landing Pontoon Vehicle [Military]
LPV............ Laser-Protective Visor (DOMA)
LPV............ Launching Point Vertical (NATG)
LPV............ Launch Preparation Van (IGSL)
LPV............ Left Pulmonary Vein [Anatomy]
LPV............ Light Pen Value (IAA)
LPV............ Lightproof Vent [Technical drawings]
LPV............ Limiting Pressure Velocity (PDAA)
LPV............ Log Periodic V [Antenna]
LPV............ Long Period Variable (ADWA)
LPV............ Low-Pressure Vent (AAEL)
LPV............ Lymphopathia Venereum (MAE)
LPVP........... Lymphotropic Papovavirus [Medicine] (DB)
LPVP........... Left Posterior Ventricular Preexcitation [Medicine] (DMAA)
LPVR........... Vila Real [Portugal] [ICAO location identifier] (ICLI)
LPVS........... Link Packetized Voice Subsystem [Telecommunications] (ACRL)
LPVT........... Large Print Video Terminal
LPVZ........... Viseu [Portugal] [ICAO location identifier] (ICLI)
LPW............ Lateral Pharyngeal Wall [Medicine] (DMAA)
LPW............ Liberal Party of Wales [Political party]
LPW............ Linear Polarized Wave
LPW............ Local Point Warning [Military]
LPW............ Longitudinal Pressure Wave
lp/W........... Lumens per Watt (CET)
LPW............ Lumens per Watt (NAKS)
LPWA.......... Local Public Works Act (OICC)
LPWG .... Logistics Planning Working Group (SAUO)
LPWG .... Lunar and Planetary Working Group [Aerospace] (IAA)
LP w/o proj... LP without projection (SAUS)
LP w/ proj ... LP with projection (SAUS)

LPWS..........	Low-Pressure Warning Switch
Lp-X.............	Lipoprotein-X [*Biochemistry*] (MAE)
LPX..............	Liquid Plume imaging Experiment (SAUS)
LPX..............	Louisiana Pacific [*NYSE symbol*] (TTSB)
LPX..............	Louisiana-Pacific Corp. [*NYSE symbol*] (SPSG)
LPX..............	Low Profile Extended (SAUS)
LPYS............	Labour Party Young Socialists [*British*] [*Political party*]
LPZ..............	La Paz [*San Calixto*] [*Bolivia*] [*Seismograph station code, US Geological Survey*] (SEIS)
LPZ..............	Leipzig [*City and district in East Germany*] (ROG)
LPZ..............	Low Population Zone (NRCH)
LPZ..............	Ruston, LA [*Location identifier*] [*FAA*] (FAAL)
LPZG............	Lincoln Park Zoological Gardens (SAUO)
LQ...............	Inland Empire Airlines [*ICAO designator*] (AD)
LQ...............	Laboratory Quality (SAUO)
LQ...............	Last Quarter [*Moon phase*]
LQ...............	Laterality Quotient [*Neuropsychology*]
LQ...............	Laurentian Capital Corp. (SAUO)
LQ...............	Learning Quotient
LQ...............	Lege Quaeso [*Please Read*] [*Latin*]
LQ...............	Lens Quality [*Optics*]
LQ...............	Letter Quality (PCM)
LQ...............	Library Quarterly [*A publication*] (BRI)
LQ...............	Limited Quantity (SAUO)
LQ...............	Limiting Quality (IAA)
LQ...............	Linear Quadratic [*Mathematics*]
lq...............	Liquid
LQ...............	Living Quarters (SAUO)
LQ...............	Longevity Quotient [*Demography*]
LQ...............	Lordosis Quotients [*Medicine*]
Lq...............	Love Wave [*Earthquakes*]
LQ...............	Lower Quadrant [*Medicine*] (MELL)
LQ...............	Lowest Quadrant
LQ...............	Lowest Quadrille
LQA..............	La Quiaca [*Argentina*] [*Seismograph station code, US Geological Survey*] [*Closed*] (SEIS)
LQA..............	La Quiaca [*Argentina*] [*Geomagnetic observatory code*]
LQA..............	Link Quality Analysis (PDAA)
LQA..............	Link Quality Assessment (SAUS)
LQA..............	Living Quarters Allowance [*Air Force*] (AFM)
LQD	Liquid
LQD	Lowest Quantity Determinable [*Analytical chemistry*]
LQDR	Liquidator
LQER	Lesser Quantity Emission Rates (EPAT)
LQFD	Liquefied
LQG	Large Quantity Generator (AUEG)
LQG	Linear Quadratic Gaussian (MCD)
LQG	Lorain, OH [*Location identifier*] [*FAA*] (FAAL)
LQGLS	Liquid in Glass
LQI	La Quinta Inns [*NYSE symbol*] (SAG)
LQID	Liquid Audio [*NASDAQ symbol*] (SG)
LQIV	Linear, Quasi Invariant (PDAA)
LQK	Pickens, SC [*Location identifier*] [*FAA*] (FAAL)
LQL	Willoughby, OH [*Location identifier*] [*FAA*] (FAAL)
LQM	La Quinta Motor Inns (EFIS)
LQM	La Quinta Motor Inns, Inc. (SAUO)
LQM	Link Quality Monitoring (SAUO)
LQM	Puerto Leguizamo [*Colombia*] [*Airport symbol*] (OAG)
LQMD	LifeQuest Medical [*NASDAQ symbol*] (TTSB)
LQMD	LifeQuest Medical, Inc. [*NASDAQ symbol*] (SAG)
LQMETR	Liquidometer
LQN	Boston, MA [*Location identifier*] [*FAA*] (FAAL)
LQN	Qala-Nau [*Afghanistan*] [*Airport symbol*] [*Obsolete*] (OAG)
LQP	Fort Collins, CO [*Location identifier*] [*FAA*] (FAAL)
LQP	Letter Quality Printer [*Computer science*]
LQP	Linear Quadratic Problem [*Mathematics*]
LQPO	Laboratory Quality & Planning Office (SAUO)
LQQ	Chicago, IL [*Location identifier*] [*FAA*] (FAAL)
LQR	Larned, KS [*Location identifier*] [*FAA*] (FAAL)
LQR	Liquor
LQR	Local Qualitative Radio [*Ratings*] (NTCM)
LQRev..........	Law Quarterly Review (SAUO)
LQRR	Laser Qualitative Research Requirements (SAUO)
LQRR	Low-Quality Recruiting Report (DNAB)
LQS.............	Les Quatre Saisons [*Record label*] [*France*]
LQS.............	Lock Haven State College, Lock Haven, PA [*OCLC symbol*] (OCLC)
LQST	Leadership Q-Sort Test [*Psychology*]
LQT	Linear Quantizer (IAA)
LQT	Liverpool Quay Terms (DS)
LQT	Los Queltehues [*Chile*] [*Seismograph station code, US Geological Survey*] (SEIS)
lqtx.............	Liquitex (VRA)
LQU	Link Quality Analysis (SAUO)
LQU	Quilmes Ind(Quinsa)ADS [*NYSE symbol*] (TTSB)
LQUT	Queensland Unit and Group Titles Law and Practice [*Australia*] [*A publication*]
LQV.............	Leiurus Quinquestriatus Venom (DB)
LQV.............	Pennington Gap, VA [*Location identifier*] [*FAA*] (FAAL)
LQX.............	Lehighton, PA [*Location identifier*] [*FAA*] (FAAL)
LQY.............	Springfield, IL [*Location identifier*] [*FAA*] (FAAL)
LR...............	Dealer
LR...............	Division of Licensing and Regulation (SAUO)
Lr-X.............	King Lear [*Shakespearean work*]
LR...............	Labeled Release [*Mars life detection experiment*]
LR...............	Laboratory Reactor
LR...............	Laboratory Reagent
LR...............	Laboratory Reference (MAE)
LR...............	Laboratory Report
LR...............	Labor Reports (OICC)
LR...............	Labor Review [*A publication*]
LR...............	Labor Room [*Obstetrics*]
LR...............	Lacrimation Reflex [*Medicine*] (MELL)
LR...............	Lactated Ringer [*Medicine*]
LR...............	Ladder Rung (AAG)
LR...............	Lady's Realm [*A publication*] (ROG)
Lr...............	Lancer [*Military*] [*British*] (DMA)
LR...............	Landing RADAR
LR...............	Landing Report (WDAA)
LR...............	Land Registry (DLA)
LR...............	Lapse Ratio [*Insurance*]
LR...............	Large Range (RIMS)
LR...............	Large Ring
LR...............	LASER-RADAR (MCD)
LR...............	Laser Rangefinder (ACAE)
LR...............	Laser Retroreflector (EOSA)
LR...............	Last Record (IAA)
LR...............	Last Renewal
LR...............	Last Resort (SAUS)
LR...............	Latency Reaction [*Medicine*] (DB)
LR...............	Latency Relaxation
LR...............	Lateral Rectus [*Muscle*] [*Anatomy*]
LR...............	Lateral Reversal [*Typography*] (DGA)
LR...............	Lateral Root [*Botany*]
L/R..............	Late Run
lR...............	Laufend Rechnung [*Current Account*] [*German*] [*Business term*]
L/R..............	Launch/Reentry (MCD)
LR...............	Launch Reliability (MCD)
LR...............	Launch Right (MCD)
LR...............	Lawesson Reagent [*Organic chemistry*]
LR...............	Law Record [*1911-12*] [*India*] [*A publication*] (DLA)
LR...............	Law Recorder [*1827-38*] [*Ireland*] [*A publication*] (DLA)
LR...............	Law Register [*1880-1909*] [*A publication*] (DLA)
Lr...............	Lawrencium [*Original symbol, Lw, changed in 1963*] [*Chemical element*]
LR...............	Law Reporter [*1821-22*] [*A publication*] (DLA)
LR...............	Layer Rating [*British military*] (DMA)
LR...............	Lay Reader (ROG)
LR...............	Leaching Rate [*Nuclear energy*] (NUCP)
LR...............	Leaders of Religion [*A publication*]
LR...............	Lead Radial (PIPO)
LR...............	Leaf Rust [*Plant Pathology*]
LR...............	Lear [*ICAO aircraft manufacturer identifier*] (ICAO)
L/R..............	Learning Resources (SAUO)
LR...............	Leave Rations [*Military*]
LR...............	Leave to Appeal Refused [*Legal term*] (ADA)
LR...............	Ledger (ROG)
LR...............	Lee Rubber & Tire Corp. (SAUO)
L - R...........	Left minus Right [*Stereo signals*] (NTCM)
L + R...........	Left plus Right [*Stereo signals*] (NTCM)
LR...............	Left Rear
LR...............	Left Rudder (MCD)
LR...............	Left to Right (MAE)
L/R..............	Left to Right [*Ratio*] (DAVI)
LR...............	Legal Reserve (MHDW)
LR...............	Leicestershire Regiment [*Military unit*] [*British*]
LR...............	Lending Rate [*Banking*] (MHDW)
LR...............	Lent Reading (ROG)
LR...............	Lesion Expansion Rate [*Pathology*]
LR...............	Lethal Radius (ACAE)
LR...............	Letter [*Online database field identifier*]
LR...............	Letter of Requirements (SAUO)
LR...............	Letter Report
LR...............	Letter Requirement
LR...............	Level Recorder
LR...............	Level Regulator (NRCH)
LR...............	Leviticus Rabbah (BJA)
LR...............	Liaison Regiment (SAUO)
LR...............	Liaison Report (AAG)
LR...............	Liaison Request (AAG)
LR...............	Liberia [*ANSI two-letter standard code*] (CNC)
LR...............	Library Review [*A publication*] (BRI)
LR...............	Licensing Registration [*British*]
L/R..............	Life/Revisit [*NASA*] (KSC)
LR...............	Lifespan Resources [*An association*] (EA)
LR...............	Light Reaction (MAE)
LR...............	Light Reflex [*Medicine*] (AAMN)
LR...............	Likelihood Ratio [*Statistics*]
Lr...............	Limes Reacting Dose of Diphtheria Toxin [*Medicine*] (DMAA)
LR...............	Limited Recoverable (IEEE)
LR...............	Limit Register
LR...............	Limit Response (ELAL)
LR...............	Lincoln Red [*Livestock terminology*]
LR...............	Lindblad Resonance [*Planetary science*]
LR...............	Linear Regression [*Mathematics*]
LR...............	Lineas Aereas Costarricenses, Sociedad Anonima (LACSA) [*Costa Rica*] [*ICAO designator*] (ICDA)
LR...............	Line Receiver
LR...............	Line Relay
LR...............	Link Resources, Inc. [*Vancouver Stock Exchange symbol*]
LR...............	Lion Rock Trading Co. (SAUO)

LR	Liquid Rocket
LR	Listing Representative (REAL)
lr	Listing Representative [*Real estate*] (REAL)
LR	Listing Requirement [*Investment term*]
LR	Literary Review [*A publication*] (ANEX)
LR	Little Rock [*Diocesan abbreviation*] [*Arkansas*] (TOCD)
lr	Living Room (SHCU)
LR	Living Room
LR	Lloyd's Register of Shipping
LR	Loaded Radius [*Tires*]
LR	Loading Ramp
LR	Load Ratio
LR	Load Rejection (NRCH)
LR	Load-Resistor Relay (MSA)
LR	Loan Rate [*Banking*]
L/R	Local/Remote [*Telecommunications*] (TEL)
LR	Local Review (SAUO)
LR	Location Register (SAUS)
LR	Lock Rail
LR	Lock Range (IAA)
L/R	Locus of Radius
LR	Logical Record
LR	Logistical Reassignment [*Military*] (AFIT)
LR	Logistical Requirement
LR	Logistic Regression [*Medicine*]
LR	Log Run [*Lumber*]
LR	London Rank [*Freemasonry*]
LR	London Regiment (SAUO)
LR	Long Range
LR	Long Rifle
LR	Long Run [*Economics*]
LR	Louisiana Register [*A publication*] (AAGC)
LR	Louisiana Reports [*A publication*] (DLA)
LR	Lower (ADA)
LR	Lower Rail [*Typography*]
LR	Lower Right
LR	Lower Rule
LR	Low Rate (ACAE)
lr	Low Rate Reverse [*Ecology*]
LR	Low Reduction (NITA)
LR	Low Register (IAA)
LR	Low Renin [*Medicine*] (MELL)
LR	Low Resistance (IAA)
LR	Low Resolution (QUAC)
LR	Low Risk
LR	Loyal Regiment [*Military*] [*British*]
LR	Lugger [*Ship's rigging*] (ROG)
LR	Lunar Rover (ACAE)
LR	New Zealand Law Reports [*A publication*] (DLA)
LR	Ohio Law Reporter [*A publication*] (DLA)
LR	Radiolocation Land Station [*ITU designation*]
Lr	Rayleigh Wave [*Earthquakes*]
LR3	LASER Ranging Retroreflection [*Also, LRRR*] [*Initialism pronounced "LR-cubed"*] [*Apollo 11 experiment*] [*NASA*]
LR³	Logistics Readiness Rating Report [*DoD*]
LRA	Labor Research Associates (SAUO)
LRA	Labor Research Association (EA)
LRA	Lace Research Association [*British*]
LRA	Lagged Reserve Accounting [*Banking*]
LRA	Landing Rights Airport [*US Customs*]
LRA	Larissa [*Greece*] [*Airport symbol*] (OAG)
LRA	LASER [*Gyro*] Reference Axis (IEEE)
LRA	Laser Retroreflector Array (EOSA)
LRA	Last Return Amount [*IRS*]
LRA	Latching Rocker Arm [*Automotive engines*]
LRA	Launcher Relay Assembly [*Navy*] (CAAL)
LRA	Lawyers' Reports, Annotated [*A publication*] (DLA)
LRA	Lease Rental Agreement (MHDB)
LRA	Least Restrictive Alternative [*For the education of the handicapped*]
LRA	left Renal Artery [*Anatomy*] (DAVI)
LRA	Libertarian Republican Alliance (EA)
LRA	Library of Romance [*A publication*]
LRA	Light Replaceable Assemblies
LRA	Lincoln Road Association (SAUO)
LRA	Line Receiving Amplifier (MSA)
LRA	Lithuanian Regeneration Association (EA)
LRA	Little Red Air Service [*Canada*] [*ICAO designator*] (FAAC)
LRA	Little Rock [*Arkansas*] [*Seismograph station code, US Geological Survey*] [*Closed*] (SEIS)
LRA	Load Real Address (HGAA)
LRA	Load Reference Axis
LRA	Local Radio Association (SAUO)
LRA	Local Redevelopment Authority (BCP)
LRA	Locked-Rotor Amperes (MSA)
LRA	Logical Record Access [*Computer science*] (MHDB)
LRA	Logical Record Address (NITA)
LRA	Long-Range Aircraft (SAUO)
LRA	Long-Range Aviation [*Army*] (AABC)
LRA	Lord Ruthven Assembly [*An association*] (EA)
LRA	Louisiana Realtors Association (SRA)
LRA	Louisiana Restaurant Association (SRA)
LRA	Louisiana Retailers Association (SRA)
LRA	Lower Right Abdomen [*Injection site*]
LRA	Low Right Atrium [*Anatomy*]

LRA	North Carolina Union List of Serials for Community Colleges [*Library network*]
LRAA	Long-Range Air Army [*Former USSR*] (MCD)
LRAACA	Long-Range Air Anti-submarine Capability Aircraft (SAUS)
LRAACA	Long-Range Air Antisubmarine Warfare Capable Aircraft (MCD)
LRAAM	Long Range Air-to-Air Missile [*Air Force*]
LRA & E	English Law Reports, Admiralty and Ecclesiastical [*A publication*] (DLA)
LRAAS	Long Range Airborne Air to Surface Systems (ACAE)
LRAC	English Law Reports, Appeal Cases [*A publication*] (DLA)
LRAC	Long-Run Average Costs [*Marketing*]
LRAD	Laboratory for Research on Animal Diseases (SAUO)
LRAD	Licentiate of the Royal Academy of Dancing [*British*]
LRADM	Long-Range Air Defense Missile (MCD)
LR Adm & Ecc	Law Reports, Admiralty and Ecclesiastical Cases [*1865-75*] [*A publication*] (DLA)
LR Adm & Eccl	Law Reports, Admiralty and Ecclesiastical Cases [*1865-75*] [*A publication*] (DLA)
LR Adm & Eccl (Eng)	Law Reports, Admiralty and Ecclesiastical Cases [*England*] [*A publication*] (DLA)
LRADP	Long-Range Active Duty Program [*Army*]
LRAF	Long-Range Air Force
LRAF	Long-Range Aviation Forces (SAUO)
LRAFB	Little Rock Air Force Base (SAUO)
LRALS	Long-Range Approach and Landing System (PDAA)
LRAM	Licentiate of the Royal Academy of Music [*British*] (EY)
LRAMRP	Long-Range Army Materiel Requirements Plan (SAUS)
LRAN	Local Regional Access Node (MCD)
LR Ann	Lawyers' Reports, Annotated [*A publication*] (DLA)
LRA NS	Lawyers' Reports, Annotated, New Series [*A publication*] (DLA)
LRAO	Logistics Review and Analysis Office [*US Army Defense Ammunition Center and School*]
LRAOP	Long-Range Aerospace Observation Platform
LRAP	Leucine-Rich Amelogenin Polypeptide [*Biochemistry of dental enamel*]
LRAP	Long-Range Acoustic Propagation
LRAP	Long Route Analysis Program (VLIE)
LRAPIS	Long Range Advanced Piloted Interceptor System (ACAE)
LR App	English Law Reports, Appeal Cases, House of Lords [*A publication*] (DLA)
LRAPP	Long-Range Acoustic Propagation Project
LR App Cas	English Law Reports, Appeal Cases, House of Lords [*A publication*] (DLA)
LR App Cas (Eng)	English Law Reports, Appeal Cases, House of Lords [*A publication*] (DLA)
LRAR	Arad [*Romania*] [*ICAO location identifier*] (ICLI)
LRaR	Richland Parish Library, Rayville, LA [*Library symbol*] [*Library of Congress*] (LCLS)
LRARFS	Long-Range Airlift Requirements Forecast System (SAUO)
LRAS	Logistics Requirements Allocation Sheet (SSD)
LRAS	Long-Range Autonomous Submersible
LRAS	Lunar Module Replaceable Assembly [*NASA*] (IAA)
LRAS3	Long-Range Advanced Scout Surveillance System (SAUS)
LRASM	Long-Range Air-to-Surface Missile (MCD)
LRASV	Long-Range Air-to-Surface Vessel (IAA)
LRAT	Large Radar Array Technology (ACAE)
LRAT	Lecithin-Retinol Acyltransferase [*An enzyme*]
LRAT	Long-Range Antitank [*Army*] (INF)
LRATC	Long-Run Average Total Costs [*Economics*]
LRATGW	Long-Range Antitank Guided Weapon [*British military*] (DMA)
LRB	Laboratory of Radiation Biology (SAUO)
LRB	Labor Research Bureau (SAUO)
LRB	Labour Relations Board [*Canada*]
LRB	Legislative Reference Bureau (SAUO)
LRB	Level Reference Base
LRB	Liquid Rocket Booster (IGSL)
LRB	Lissamine Rhodamine B [*Fluorescent dye*]
LRB	Load Request Block (IAA)
LRB	Local Reference Beam [*Holography*]
LRB	London Rifle Brigade [*Military unit*] [*British*]
LRB	Loyalty Review Board [*Abolished, 1953*] [*Civil Service Commission*]
LRBB	Bucuresti [*Romania*] [*ICAO location identifier*] (ICLI)
LRBB	Long-Range, Base Bleed (SAUS)
LRBC	Bacau [*Romania*] [*ICAO location identifier*] (ICLI)
LRBC	Left-Right Bounded Context (VLIE)
LRBC	Lift-Right Bounded-Context [*Computer science*] (MHDI)
LRBC	Lloyd's Registry Building Certificate
LRBF	Longitudinal Ridge of Basal Fold
LRBFM	National Labor Relations Board Field Manual
LRBG	Law Reports, British Guiana [*1890-1955*] [*A publication*] (DLA)
LRBM	Baia Mare/Tauti Magherusi [*Romania*] [*ICAO location identifier*] (ICLI)
LRBM	Long-Range Ballistic Missile
LRBR	Long-Range Ballistic Rocket
LRBR	Long-Range Bombardment Round
LRB/RANGERS	London Rifle Brigade/Rangers (SAUO)
LRBS	Bucuresti/Baneasa [*Romania*] [*ICAO location identifier*] (ICLI)
LRBS	LASER Ranging Bombing System
LR Burm	Law Reports, British Burma [*A publication*] (DLA)
LR Burma	Law Reports, British Burma [*A publication*] (DLA)
LRC	Labour Relations Committee (SAUO)
LRC	Labour Representation Committee [*Northern Ireland*] (PPW)
LRC	Labrador Retriever Club (EA)
LRC	Ladies Recreation Club (SAUO)
LRC	Land Reserve Commission (SAUO)

LRC	Langley Research Center [*NASA*]
LRC	Launch/Recovery Visual Landing Aid Change (MCD)
LRC	Law Reform Commission [*Canada*]
LRC	Law Reform Committee (DLA)
LRC	Leadership Reaction Course (SAUO)
LRC	Leaders Reaction Course [*Military training*] (INF)
LRC	Lead Resistance Compensator
LRC	Leander Rowing Club (SAUO)
LRC	Learning Resource Center
LRC	Learning Resources Center
LRC	Lenoir Rhyne College [*Hickory, NC*]
LRC	Lesbian Resource Center (EA)
LRC	Lesser Regional Conflict (SAUO)
LRC	Lesser Regional Contingencies (SAUS)
LRC	Level Recording Controller
LRC	Lewis Research Center [*NASA*]
LRC	Liberia Refining Co.
LRC	Library Research Center [*University of Illinois*] (IID)
LRC	Library Resource Center (SAUO)
LRC	Light Rapid Comfortable [*Train system*]
LRC	Light Reflective Capacitor [*Electronics*] (DA)
LRC	Light Repair Car [*British*]
LRC	Limnological Research Center [*University of Minnesota*] [*Research center*] (RCD)
LRC	Linear Responsibility Charting (PDAA)
LRC	Lineas Aereas Costarricenses SA [*Costa Rica*] [*ICAO designator*] (FAAC)
LRC	Line Rectifier Circuit
LRC	Line Replaceable Components (ACAE)
LRC	Linguistics Research Center [*University of Texas at Austin*] [*Research center*] (RCD)
LRC	Lionel Railroader Club (EA)
LRC	Lipid Research Center [*Washington University*] [*Research center*] (RCD)
LRC	Lipid Research Clinic (SAUO)
LRC	Lipid Research Clinics
LRC	Load Ratio Control (MSA)
LRC	Local Register Cache (VLIE)
LRC	Local Review Committee (WDAA)
LRC	Locomotor Respiratory Coupling [*Physiology*]
LRC	Lode Resources Corp. [*Vancouver Stock Exchange symbol*]
LRC	Logistics Research Center (SAUO)
LRC	Logistics to Relay Converter (MCD)
LRC	London Rowing Club
LRC	London Rubber Company (SAUO)
LRC	Lone Oak Road [*California*] [*Seismograph station code, US Geological Survey*] (SEIS)
LRC	Longitude Rotation Convention (ADWA)
LRC	Longitudinal Redundancy Check [*Computer science*]
LRC	Long-Range Climb (MCD)
LRC	Long Range Communications (NTCM)
LRC	Long-Range Cruise [*Aircraft speed*]
LRC	Lori Corp. [*AMEX symbol*] (SPSG)
LRC	Lower Rib Cage [*Anatomy*]
LRC	Lunar Receiving Center (SAUO)
LRC	Lunar Resources Company (SAUO)
LRC	Luneberg Rapid Commutator [*Physics*]
LRC	Lung Rate Counter
LRC	Lutheran Resources Commission (EA)
LRCA	Law Reports, Court of Appeals of New Zealand [*A publication*] (DLA)
LRCA	Lithuanian Roman Catholic Alliance of America [*Later, LCA*] (EA)
LRCA	Long-Range Combat Aircraft
LRCA	Lop Rabbit Club of America (EA)
LRCA-STS	Long Range Combat Aircraft System Test Station (ACAE)
LRCC	English Law Reports, Crown Cases Reserved [*2 vols.*] [*1865-75*] [*A publication*] (DLA)
LRCC	Library Resources Coordinating Committee of the University of London (NITA)
LRCC	Longitudinal Redundancy Check Character [*Telecommunications*] (TEL)
LRCC (Eng)	English Law Reports, Crown Cases Reserved [*2 vols.*] [*1865-75*] [*A publication*] (DLA)
LRCCM	Long-Range Conventional Cruise Missile (MCD)
LRCCPPT	Lipid Research Clinics Coronary Primary Prevention Trial [*Cardiology*]
LRCCR	Law Reports, Crown Cases Reserved [*England*] [*A publication*] (DLA)
LRCD	Linear Rule of Cumulative Damage (PDAA)
LRCD	Lunar Rock Coring Device (ACAE)
LRCE	LASER Relay Communication Equipment
LRCE	Little Rock Cotton Exchange [*Defunct*]
LRCFA	Lithuanian Roman Catholic Federation of America (EA)
LR Ch	Law Reports, Chancery Appeal Cases [*England*] [*A publication*] (DLA)
LR Ch App	Chancery Appeal Cases [*1865-75*] [*A publication*] (DLA)
LR Ch D	English Law Reports, Chancery Division [*A publication*] (DLA)
LR Ch D (Eng)	Law Reports, Chancery Division, English Supreme Court of Judicature [*A publication*] (DLA)
LR Ch Div (Eng)	Law Reports, Chancery Division, English Supreme Court of Judicature [*A publication*] (DLA)
LR Ch (Eng)	Law Reports, Chancery Appeal Cases [*England*] [*A publication*] (DLA)
LRCI	Legal Research Center [*NASDAQ symbol*] (TTSB)
LRCI	Legal Research Center, Inc. [*NASDAQ symbol*] (SAG)
LRCK	Constanta/M. Kogalniceau [*Romania*] [*ICAO location identifier*] (ICLI)
LRCL	Cluj-Napoca/Someseni [*Romania*] [*ICAO location identifier*] (ICLI)
LRCL	Long-Range Chemical LASER (MCD)
LRCM	Licentiate of the Royal College of Music [*British*]
LRCM	Long-Range Cruise Missile [*Navy*]
LRCNSW	Law Reform Commission of New South Wales [*Australia*]
LRCO	Lead Range Control Officer (SAUO)
LRCO	Limited Remote Communications Outlet (SAUO)
LRCO	Limited Remote [*or Radio*] Communication Outlet
LRCO	Long-Range Capability Objective [*Air Force*]
LRCP	Laboratory Research Cooperative Program [*Scientific Services Program*] [*Army*] (RDA)
LRCP	Law Reports, Common Pleas [*1865-75*] [*England*] [*A publication*] (DLA)
LRCP	Licensed Respiratory Care Practitioner (NUJO)
LRCP	Licentiate of the Royal College of Physicians [*British*]
LRCP	Licentiate, Royal College of Physicians [*British*] (CMD)
LRCP	Long-Range Construction Program [*Military*]
LRCP & S	Licentiate of the Royal College of Physicians and the College of Surgeons of Edinburgh, and of the Faculty of Physicians and Surgeons of Glasgow (ROG)
LRCP & SI	Licentiate of the Royal College of Physicians and Surgeons of Ireland (AAMN)
LRCPD	English Law Reports, Common Pleas Division [*A publication*] (DLA)
LRCP Div	Law Reports, Common Pleas Division [*England*] [*A publication*] (DLA)
LRCP Div (Eng)	English Law Reports, Common Pleas Division [*A publication*] (DLA)
LRCPE	Licentiate of the Royal College of Physicians (Edinburgh)
LRCPEd	Licentiate of the Royal College of Physicians Edinburgh (SAUO)
LRCP (Eng)	Law Reports, Common Pleas [*England*] [*A publication*] (DLA)
LRCPI	Licentiate of the Royal College of Physicians of Ireland
LRCP Irel	Licentiate of the Royal College of Physicians of Ireland
LRCPLA	Lithuanian Roman Catholic Priests' League of America (EA)
LRCPSGlasg	Licentiate of the Royal College of Physicians and Surgeons of Glasgow (DI)
LRCR	Longitudinal Redundancy Check Register [*Telecommunications*] (IAA)
LRCR	Long-Range Chaff Rocket (SAUS)
LR Cr Cas Res	Law Reports, Crown Cases Reserved [*England*] [*A publication*] (DLA)
LRCS	Caransebes/Caransebes [*Romania*] [*ICAO location identifier*] (ICLI)
LRCS	LASER RADAR Cross Section
LRCS	League of Red Cross and Red Crescent Societies [*Switzerland*] (EA)
LRCS	League of Red Cross Societies
LRCS	Licentiate of the Royal College of Surgeons [*British*]
LRCS	Lincoln Red Cattle Society [*British*] (DBA)
LRCS	Load Relief Control System
LRCS	Long-Range Communications System (SAUO)
LRCS	Low Radar Cross-Section (SAUS)
LRCSA	Lincoln Red Cattle Society of Australia
LRCSE	Licentiate of the Royal College of Surgeons (Edinburgh)
LRCS (Edin)	Licentiate of the Royal College of Surgeons (Edinburgh) (DI)
LRCSG	Licentiate of the Royal College of Surgeons, Glasgow (SAUO)
LRCSI	Licentiate of the Royal College of Surgeons in Ireland
LRCS Irel	Licentiate of the Royal College of Surgeons in Ireland
LRCSOW	Long-Range Conventional Standoff Weapon [*Military*]
LRCSS	Logistics Resource Control and Support System (SAUO)
LRCSW	Long-Range Conventional Standoff Weapon (MCD)
LRCT	Licensed Respiratory Care Technician (NUJO)
LRCT	Licentiate of the Royal Conservatory of Toronto [*Canada*]
LRC-TCC	Logistics Readiness Center-Transportation Control Center (SAUO)
LRCU	Landing Rollout Control Unit (SAUS)
L/RCU	Local/Remote Control Unit
LRCU	Logic Refresh Control Unit
LRCV	Craiova [*Romania*] [*ICAO location identifier*] (ICLI)
LRCVS	Licentiate of the Royal College of Veterinary Surgeons [*British*]
LRC-W	Lutheran Resources Commission - Washington [*Later, LRC*] (EA)
LRC-W	Lutheran Resources Commission-Washington (SAUO)
LRCX	Lam Research [*NASDAQ symbol*] (TTSB)
LRCX	Lam Research Corp. [*NASDAQ symbol*] (SAG)
LRD	Labelled RADAR Display (PDAA)
LRD	Labour Research Department [*Trade union*] [*British*]
LRD	Landing and Recovery Division [*NASA*]
LRD	Land Resources Division (SAUO)
LRD	Laredo [*Texas*] [*Airport symbol*] (OAG)
LRD	Laredo Air, Inc. [*ICAO designator*] (FAAC)
LRD	Laser Rangefinder/Designator (SAUS)
LRD	LASER Ranger and Designator (MCD)
LRD	Launch Readiness Demonstration [*NASA*] (KSC)
LRD	Lightning and Radio-Emission Detector [*Instrumentation*]
LRD	Liquid Rocket Division Rocket Propulsion Laboratory (SAUO)
LRD	Living Related Donor [*Medicine*]
LRD	Living Renal Donor [*Nephrology*] (DAVI)
LRD	Logistics Requirements Determination (MCD)
LRD	London Recruiting Depot (SAUO)
LRD	Long-Range Data [*RADAR*]
LRD	Long Range Designator (ACAE)
LRD	Long-Reach Detonator [*Explosive*]
LRD	Lord River Gold [*Vancouver Stock Exchange symbol*]
LRD	Low Rate Demodulator (ACAE)
LRD	Low-Residue Diet (MELL)
LRD	Lysinated Rhodamine Dextran [*Cytology*]
LRDC	Land Resources Development Centre [*British*] (ARC)
LRDC	Learning Research and Development Center [*University of Pittsburgh*] [*Research center*]

LRDCT......... Linear Rotary Differential Capacitance Transducer [*Instrumentation*]
LRDD.......... Limited Rights to Delivered Data
LRDE .... Laboratory for Research and Development of Electronics (SAUO)
LRDE .... Long-Run Deal Effect [*Marketing*]
LRDG .... Learning Resources Development Group [*British*] (DBA)
LRDG .... Long Range Desert Group [*British Army*] [*World War II*]
LR Dig .... Law Reports Digest [*A publication*] (DLA)
LRDL .... Longitudinal Ridge of Dorsal Lip
LRDMM .... Long-Range Dual-Mission Missile (MCD)
LRDP .... Long-Range Development Program (IAA)
LRDR .... Last Revision Date Routine
LRDS .... LASER Ranging and Designation System [*Military*] (CAAL)
LRDSB .... Left Minus Right Double Sideband (IAA)
LRDT .... Laboratory of Reproductive and Developmental Toxicology (GNE)
LRDT .... Living Related Donor Transplant [*Medicine*] (DMAA)
LRD/T .... Long Range Designator/Transceiver (ACAE)
LRDU .... Long-Range Development Unit
LRE............ Lafayette Radio Electronics (SAUO)
LRE............ Lafayette Radio Electronics Corp.
LRE............ Laser Ranger Experiment (SAUO)
LRE............ Latest Revised Estimate (MCD)
LRE............ Law-Related Education (AEE)
LRE............ Least Restrictive Environment [*For the education of the handicapped*]
LRE............ Leukemic Reticuloendotheliosis [*Medicine*] (AAMN)
LRE............ Library Resources Exhibition [*British*]
LRE............ Licentiate in Religious Education
LRE............ Life Re [*NYSE symbol*] (TTSB)
LRE............ Life Real Estate [*NYSE symbol*] (SPSG)
LRE............ Light Responsive Element [*Chemistry*]
LRE............ Limited Regular Expression (SAUO)
LRE............ Liquid Rocket Engine
LRE............ Local Resource Enhancement [*Biology*]
LRE............ Logistics Readiness Elements (MCD)
LRE............ Longreach [*Australia*] [*Airport symbol*] (OAG)
LRE............ Lossless Reciprocal Embedding (IAA)
LRE............ Low Rate Encoding [*Telecommunications*] (LAIN)
LRE............ Low Risk Enhancement (SAUS)
LRE............ Lunar Retrograde Engine [*NASA*] (KSC)
LRE............ Lymphoreticuloendothelial (DB)
LREA......... Law Reports, East Africa [*A publication*] (DLA)
LREA......... Licensed Real Estate Agent (SAUO)
LRE & I App... Law Reports, House of Lords, English and Irish Appeals [*1866-75*] [*A publication*] (DLA)
LREB......... London Regional Examining Board [*British*] (AIE)
L Rec......... Law Recorder [*Dublin, Ireland*] [*A publication*] (DLA)
LREC......... Liaison Residency Endorsement Committee [*RRCEM* [*Superseded by*] (EA)
LREC......... Local Research Ethics Committee (SAUO)
LRECL........ Logical Record Length (VLIE)
LRECL........ Logical Records of Fixed Length (MCD)
L Rec NS..... Law Recorder, New Series [*Ireland*] [*A publication*] (DLA)
L Record..... Law Recorder [*Dublin, Ireland*] [*A publication*] (DLA)
L Rec OS..... Law Recorder, First Series [*Ireland*] [*A publication*] (DLA)
LREDA........ Liberal Religious Education Directors Association (SAUO)
LREDA........ Liberal Religious Educators Association (EA)
LREE.......... Light Rare Earth Elements [*Chemistry*]
LREG .... Leading Regulator [*British*]
LREH .... Laboratory of Radiobiology and Environmental Health (SAUO)
LREH .... Low-Renin Essential Hypertension [*Medicine*]
LREI.......... Life Role Expectations Inventory (EDAC)
LREIS........ Laboratory for Resource and Environmental Information Systems (SAUO)
LREM(A)...... Leading Radio Electrical Mechanic (Air) [*British military*] (DMA)
LR Eng & Ir App... Law Reports, English and Irish Appeals [*1866-75*] [*A publication*] (DLA)
L Rep......... Carolina Law Repository (Reprint) [*North Carolina*] [*A publication*] (DLA)
LREP.......... Left-Bracketed Representation [*Computer science*] (VLIE)
LREP.......... Light Replica Decay (ACAE)
L Rep Mont... Law Reporter, Montreal [*A publication*] (DLA)
L Repos....... Law Repository [*A publication*] (DLA)
LR Eq......... English Law Reports, Equity [*1866-75*] [*A publication*] (DLA)
LR Eq (Eng)... English Law Reports, Equity [*1866-75*] [*A publication*] (DLA)
L-RERP....... Long-Range Effects Research Program (USDC)
LRES.......... Land Resources Corp. (SAUO)
LRES.......... Letters
LRES.......... Linear Rocket Engine System (PDAA)
LRES.......... Long-Range Earth Sensor
LRES.......... Low Rigid Frame (PDAA)
L Rev & Quart J... Law Review and Quarterly Journal [*London*] [*A publication*] (DLA)
L Rev Dig.... Law Review Digest [*A publication*] (DLA)
L Rev U Detroit... Law Review. University of Detroit [*A publication*] (DLA)
LREW......... Long-Range Early Warning (NATG)
LREWP .... Long-Range Electronic Warfare Plan [*Military*] (CAAL)
LREWS .... Long-Range Early Warning System (NATG)
LR Ex......... English Law Reports, Exchequer [*1866-75*] [*A publication*] (DLA)
LR Ex Cas... English Law Reports, Exchequer [*1866-75*] [*A publication*] (DLA)
LR Exch...... English Law Reports, Exchequer [*1866-75*] [*A publication*] (DLA)
LR Exch D... English Law Reports, Exchequer Division [*A publication*] (DLA)
LR Exch Div... Law Reports, Exchequer Division [*England*] [*A publication*] (DLA)
LR Exch Div (Eng)... English Law Reports, Exchequer Division [*A publication*] (DLA)
LR Exch (Eng)... English Law Reports, Exchequer [*1866-75*] [*A publication*] (DLA)
LR Ex D .... Law Reports, Exchequer Division [*England*] [*A publication*] (DLA)

LR Ex Div .... English Law Reports, Exchequer Division [*A publication*] (DLA)
LRF............ Jacksonville, AR [*Location identifier*] [*FAA*] (FAAL)
LRF............ Ladle Refining Furnace [*Nuclear energy*] (NUCP)
LRF............ LASER RADAR Fuze
LRF............ LASER Range-Finder
LRF............ Laser Resonance Fluorescence (ACAE)
LRF............ Last Return Filed [*IRS*]
LRF............ Late Renal Failure [*Medicine*]
LRF............ Latex and Resorcinol Formaldehyde
LRF............ Launch Rate Factor
LRF............ Lepidoptera Research Foundation (EA)
LRF............ Lesson Reference File (ACAE)
LRF............ Leukaemia Research Fund [*British*]
LRF............ Leukemia Research Foundation (SAUO)
LRF............ Lincoln Realty Fund (SAUO)
LRF............ Lincoln Resign Formulation
LRF............ Liquid Rocket Fuel (MCD)
LRF............ Little Rubber Feet (MLOA)
LRF............ Liver Residue Factor [*Molybdenum*] [*Medicine*]
LRF............ London Regional Federation [*League of Nations Union*]
LRF............ Long-Range Facility [*Telecommunications*] (TEL)
LRF............ Long-Range Fighter (SAUS)
LRF............ Long-Range Flight
LRF............ Low Recoil Force (SAUS)
LRF............ Low Refraction Layer
LRF............ Lumber Recovery Factor
LRF............ Luteinizing-Hormone Releasing Factor [*Also, GnRF, GnRH, LH-RF, LH-RH, LH-RH/FSH-RH, LRH*] [*Endocrinology*]
LRFA......... Lymphoma Research Foundation of America (EA)
LRFAX .... Low-Resolution Facsimile [*Telecommunications*] (TEL)
LRFC......... LASER Range-Finder Controller (MCD)
LRFC......... Lymphoma Research Foundation Canada (NRGU)
LRF/D........ LASER Range-Finder/Designator (MCD)
LRFD......... Load and Resistance Factor Design (WPI)
LRFD......... Low Resolution Fault Dictionary (ACAE)
LRFG......... Low-Range Force Gauge
LRFI.......... League for Religious Freedom in Israel [*Later, American Friends of Religious Freedom in Israel*] (EA)
LRF/MTR .... LASER Range-Finder and Marked Target Receiver (MCD)
LRFPB....... Louisiana Rating and Fire Prevention Bureau (SAUO)
LRFPS .... Licentiate of the Royal Faculty of Physicians and Surgeons [*British*]
LRFPS(G) .... Licentiate of the Royal Faculty of Physicians and Surgeons, Glasgow
LRFPWG ..... Long Range Fiscal Planning Working Group (SAUO)
LRFS......... Long-Range Forecasting System (TEL)
LRF/SSC ..... LASER Ranger Finder/Solid State Computer (MCD)
LRFT .... Left Rear Fluid Temperature [*Brake system*] [*Automotive engineering*]
LRG.......... Laboratory Retirees Group (SAUO)
LRG.......... Land Resources Group
LRG.......... Landscape Research Group [*Lutterworth, Leicestershire, England*] (EAIO)
LRG.......... Large [*Classified advertising*]
LRG.......... Leucine-Rich Glycoprotein
LRG.......... License Review Group [*Nuclear energy*] (NRCH)
LRG.......... Lincoln, ME [*Location identifier*] [*FAA*] (FAAL)
LRG.......... Line Relay Group (SAUO)
LRG.......... Liquefied Refinery Gas
LRG.......... Logistic Review Group [*Military*] (CAAL)
LRG.......... Long Range
LRG.......... Long-Range Guidance (MCD)
LRG.......... Lorgues [*France*] [*Seismograph station code, US Geological Survey*] (SEIS)
LRG.......... Lubricant Recommended Guideline
LRGB........ Long-Range Guided Bomb (MCD)
LRGM........ Long Range Guided Missile (CCCA)
LRGPP....... Long-Range Generation Planning Problem [*Energy*]
LRGS .... Local Readout Ground Stations (SAUO)
LRH.......... La Rochelle [*France*] [*Airport symbol*] (OAG)
LRh.......... Liquid Rheostat
LRH.......... Luteinizing-Hormone Releasing Hormone [*Also, GnRF, GnRH, LH-RF, LH-RH, LH-RH/FSH-RH, LRF*] [*Endocrinology*]
LRHB........ Long-Range, Hollow Base (SAUS)
LRHL .... Law Reports, English and Irish Appeals and Peerage Claims, House of Lords [*England*] [*A publication*] (DLA)
LRHL (Eng)... Law Reports, English and Irish Appeals and Peerage Claims, House of Lords [*England*] [*A publication*] (DLA)
LRHL Sc ...... English Law Reports, House of Lords, Scotch and Divorce Appeal Cases [*1866-75*] [*A publication*] (DLA)
LRHL Sc App Cas... Law Reports, House of Lords, Scotch and Divorce Appeal Cases [*1866-75*] [*A publication*] (DLA)
LRHL Sc App Cas (Eng)... English Law Reports, House of Lords, Scotch and Divorce Appeal Cases [*1866-75*] [*A publication*] (DLA)
LRHS .... Large Radioisotope Heat Source [*NASA*] (IAA)
LRHS .... Longitudinal Retirement History Survey [*Social Security Administration*] (GFGA)
LRHSC ...... Large Radioisotope Heat Source Capsule [*NASA*] (KSC)
LRI............ Big Lost River [*Idaho*] [*Seismograph station code, US Geological Survey*] [*Closed*] (SEIS)
LRI............ Collaboration Research Interest (SAUS)
LRI............ Labour Research Institute (SAUO)
LRI............ Lawndale Railway & Industrial Co. [*Terminated*] [*AAR code*]
LRI............ Learning Resources Institute (EA)
LRI............ LeaRonal, Inc. [*NYSE symbol*] (SPSG)
LRI............ Least Recently Loaded (SAUO)
LRI............ Left Rear Inside-Drive [*Tire maintenance*]

LRI............. Left-Right Indicator
LRI............. Legal Resource Index [*Information Access Corp.*] [*Bibliographic database*] [*Information service or system*] (IID)
LRI............. Library Resources, Inc. [*Subsidiary of Encyclopaedia Britannica*]
Lrl............. Library Resources, Incorporated, Chicago, IL [*Library symbol*] [*Library of Congress*] (LCLS)
LRI............. Life Roles Inventory [*Test*] (TMMY)
LRI............. Lighting Research Institute (EA)
LRI............. Limited Range Intercept [*Telecommunications*] [*Navy*] (ANA)
LRI............. Limited Remedial Investigation (SAUO)
LRI............. Line Replaceable Item (CTAS)
LRI............. Literature and Religion of Israel [*A publication*]
LRI............. Load Register Immediate (VLIE)
LRI............. Longboat Resources, Inc. [*Vancouver Stock Exchange symbol*]
LRI............. Long-Range Indicator
LRI............. Long-Range Input (CET)
LRI............. Long-Range Inspector
LRI............. Long-Range Interceptor
LRI............. Long-Range International (DOMA)
LRI............. Long-Range RADAR Input
LRI............. Lorica [*Colombia*] [*Airport symbol*] (AD)
LRI............. Lower Respiratory Infection [*Medicine*]
LRI............. Low Resolution Imager (SAUS)
LRI............. Lymphocyte Reactivity Index (DB)
LRIA........... English Law Reports, Indian Appeals [*A publication*] (DLA)
LRIA........... Iasi [*Romania*] [*ICAO location identifier*] (ICLI)
LRIA........... Level Removable Instrument Assembly [*Nuclear energy*] (IEEE)
LRIBA .... Licentiate of the Royal Institute of British Architects
LRIBA .... Licentiate of the Royal Institute of British Architecture (SAUO)
LRIC........... Licentiate of the Royal Institute of Chemistry [*British*]
LRIC........... Long-Run Incremental Cost [*Business term*] (ADA)
LRIDP......... Land Resources Inventory Demonstration Project (SAUO)
LRIFC......... Lauren Robbins International Fan Club (EA)
LRIICC .... Land and Resource Inventory and Information Co-ordinating Committee (SAUO)
LRIM........... Liquid Reaction Injection Molding (EDCT)
LRIM........... Long-Range Input Monitor [*RADAR*]
LR Ind App... English Law Reports, Indian Appeals [*A publication*] (DLA)
LR Ind App Supp... English Law Reports, Indian Appeals, Supplement [*A publication*] (DLA)
LR Indian App... English Law Reports, Indian Appeals [*A publication*] (DLA)
LR Indian App (Eng)... English Law Reports, Indian Appeals [*A publication*] (DLA)
LRINF .... Longer-Range Intermediate-Range Nuclear Forces
LRIP........... Language Research in Progress (DIT)
LRIP........... Liberia Research and Information Project (EA)
LRIP........... Long-Range Impact Point (MUGU)
LRIP........... Low Rate Industrial Production (ACAE)
LRIP........... Low-Rate Initial Production (RDA)
L Ripuar ...... Law of the Ripuarians [*A publication*] (DLA)
LRIr........... Law Reports, Ireland [*1878-1893*] [*A publication*]
LR Ir .... Law Reports, Irish [*A publication*] (DLA)
LRIR .... Limb Radiance Infrared (SAUS)
LRIR .... Limb Radiance Inversion Radiometer
LRIR .... Low-Resolution Infrared Radiometer
LRIRR .... Low-Resolution Infrared Radiometer (MSA)
LRIS .... Land Registration and Information Service (SAUO)
LRIS .... Low Resolution Imaging Spectrograph [*Instrumentation*]
LR-IST .... Long-Range Infra-Red Search & Track (SAUS)
LRITF.......... Land Resources Inventory Task Force (SAUO)
LRJ............. Lemars, IA [*Location identifier*] [*FAA*] (FAAL)
LRJC.......... Lake Region Junior College (SAUO)
LRK........... Kenya Law Reports [*A publication*] (DLA)
LRK........... LASER Research Kit
LRKB .... English Law Reports, King's Bench Division [*1901-52*] [*A publication*] (DLA)
LRKB .... Quebec Official Reports, King's Bench [*A publication*] (ILCA)
LRL............. Collaboration Research Level (SAUS)
LRL............. Laser Relay Link (ACAE)
LRL............. Lawrence Radiation Laboratory [*Livermore*] [*Later, Lawrence Livermore Laboratory*] [*University of California*]
LRL............. Leakage Resistance Limit
LRL............. Least Recently Loaded (VLIE)
LRL............. Light Railway Loads [*British*]
LRL............. Lightweight Rocket Launcher (SAUS)
LRL............. Limited Raman LASER
LRL............. Lincoln Research Laboratory
LRL............. Linguistics Research Laboratory [*Gallaudet College*] [*Research center*] (RCD)
LRL............. Linking Relocating Loader
LRL............. Livermore Research Laboratory [*University of California*] (KSC)
LRL............. Location Records List [*Computer science*] (VLIE)
LRL............. Logical Record Length
LRL............. Logical Record Location
LRL............. Lunar Receiving Laboratory [*NASA*]
LRL............. Lunar Research Laboratory [*NASA*] (DAVI)
LRL............. Tulane University, Law Library, New Orleans, LA [*OCLC symbol*] (OCLC)
LRLA .... La Raza Legal Alliance (SAUO)
LRLB.......... Lawrence Radiation Laboratory-Berkeley (SAUO)
LRLCX .... Lord Abbett Research: Large Cap [*Mutual fund ticker symbol*] (SG)
LR/LD......... Line Receiver/Line Driver (MCD)
LRLEI......... League for Religious Labor in Eretz Israel (EA)
LRLF.......... Local Radio Luminosity Function [*Cosmology*]
LRLG .... Long-Range Logistics Guidance [*Air Force*]

LRL-L......... Lawrence Radiation Laboratory, Livermore [*Later, Lawrence Livermore Laboratory*] [*University of California*]
LRLL .... Longitudinal Ridge of Lateral Lip
LRLM .... Lower Reject Limit Median (SAA)
LRLS.......... London Regional Library System (SAUO)
LRLSA .... La Raza Law Students Association (SAUO)
LRLT.......... Left Rear Lining Temperature [*Brake system*] [*Automotive engineering*]
LRLTRAN..... Lawrence Radiation Laboratory FORTRAN [*Programming language*] [*1961*] (CSR)
LRLTRAN.... Lawrence Radiation Laboratory Translator (IEEE)
LRM........... Labor Reimbursable Material (ACAE)
LRM........... Labor Relations Reference Manual [*A publication*] (DLA)
LRM........... Land Resources Management (MCD)
LRM........... Language Reference Manual (VLIE)
LRM........... La Rassegna Musicale [*A publication*]
LRM........... La Romana [*Dominican Republic*] [*Airport symbol*] (OAG)
LRM........... Latching Relay Matrix
LRM........... Lead Reactor Manufacturer (NRCH)
LRM........... Leaflet Rolling Machine [*PSYOP*] (RDA)
LRM........... Least Recently Used Master [*Computer science*]
LRM........... Left Radical Mastectomy [*Medicine*] (MAE)
LRM........... Lightweight Ramjet Missile (MCD)
LRM........... Limited Register Machine
LRM........... Linear Radiating Module (ACAE)
LRM........... Line Replacement Module
LRM........... Liquid Reaction Molding
LRM........... Liquid Rocket Motor (KSC)
LRM........... Logarithmic Radiation Monitor (NRCH)
LRM........... Logarithmic Ratio Module
LRM........... Long-Range Missile Launcher
LRM........... Long Reach Manipulator (ABAC)
LRM........... Lower Reject Limit Median
LRM........... Low Rate Multiplexer (SAUS)
LRM........... Lunar Reconnaissance [*or Rendezvous*] Mission [*Aerospace*]
LRM........... Lunar Reconnaissance Module [*Aerospace*]
LR Mad ...... Indian Law Reports, Madras Series [*A publication*] (DLA)
LRMC......... Lloyd's Refrigerating Machinery Certificate
LRMC......... Long-Run Marginal Costs
LRMCO .... Long Run, Mill Cuts Out [*Forest industry*] (WPI)
LRMG .... Hughes Lockless Rifle/Machine Gun (MCD)
LR Misc D ... Law Reports, Miscellaneous Division [*A publication*] (DLA)
LRML .... Long-Range Missile Launcher [*Military*] (IAA)
LRMP......... Land and Resource Management Plan (SAUO)
LRMP......... Last Regular Menstrual Period [*Gynecology*] (DMAA)
LRMP......... Legacy Resource Management Program (DOMA)
LRMP......... Long-Range Maritime Patrol [*Aircraft*] (NATG)
LRMPA .... Long Range Maritime Patrol Aircraft (ACAE)
LRMS.......... Library Routine Management System
LRMS.......... Low Resolution Mass Spectroscopy (COE)
LRMTS .... LASER Range-Finder and Marked Target Seeker (MCD)
LRMV.......... Lilac Ring Mottle Virus [*Plant pathology*]
LRN .... Learning Resource Interchange
LRN .... Long-Range Navigation
LRN .... Long Reference Number
LRN .... LORAN [*Long-Range Aid to Navigation*]
LRN .... Low Recoil Noricum (SAUS)
LRNA .... Laws Relating to the Navy Annotated [*Military law*]
LRNAV .... Long Range Navigation [*FAA*] (TAG)
LRNBA .... La Raza National Bar Association (EA)
LRNC.......... Long Reference Number Code
LRND......... Left Radical Neck Dissection [*Surgical procedure*] (DAVI)
LRNF.......... Longer-Range Nuclear Forces (WDAA)
LRNG .... Learning
LRNG .... Learning Co. [*NASDAQ symbol*] (SAG)
LrngCo........ Learning Co. [*Associated Press*] (SAG)
LrnHaus....... Lernout & Hauspie Speech Products [*Associated Press*] (SAG)
LRNOD........ Long-Range Night Observation Device [*Army*] (AABC)
LRNR .... Low-Resolution Non-Scanning Radiometer (MCD)
LRNRM........ Landowners for Responsible Natural Resource Management [*An association*] (WPI)
LRNS .... Long-Range Navigation System [*Aviation*]
LRNS .... Nova Scotia Law Reports [*A publication*] (DLA)
LRNSW .... Law Reports, New South Wales Supreme Court [*A publication*] (DLA)
LRNTF .... Long Range Intermediate Nuclear Forces (ACAE)
LrnTree....... Learning Tree International, Inc. [*Associated Press*] (SAG)
LRNZ .... Law Reports, New Zealand [*A publication*] (DLA)
LRO .... Laboratory Review Office [*Army*] (RDA)
LRO .... Labor Relations Officer (COE)
LRO .... Large Radio Observatory (KSC)
LRO .... Lathrop, CA [*Location identifier*] [*FAA*] (FAAL)
LRO .... Leading Radio Operator [*British military*] (DMA)
LRO .... Left Rear Outside-Drive [*Tire maintenance*]
LRO .... Loan Review Officer [*Banking*] (TBD)
LRO .... Logistics Readiness Officer [*Military*] (AABC)
LRO .... Long-Range Objectives [*Navy*]
LRO .... Long-Range Order
LRO .... Low-Resistance Ohmmeter
LROA .... Land Rover Owners Association (EA)
LROA USA ... Land Rover Owners Association, USA (EA)
LROC......... Libertarian Republican Organizing Committee [*Defunct*] (EA)
LROD......... Long-Range Overwater Diffusion [*Experiment*] [*Marine science*] (OSRA)
LROD......... Oradea [*Romania*] [*ICAO location identifier*] (ICLI)
LRO(G)....... Leading Radio Operator (General) [*British military*] (DMA)

LROG	Long-Range Objectives Group [*Navy*] (MCD)	
LROI	Legal Rate of Interest [*Business term*] (MHDB)	
LROL	Laboratoire de Recherches en Optique et Laser [*Laval University*] [*Canada*] [*Research center*] (RCD)	
LROP	Bucuresti/Otopeni [*Romania*] [*ICAO location identifier*] (ICLI)	
LROP	Long-Range Optical Pod (SAUS)	
LROP	Lower Radicular Obstetrical Paralysis [*Medicine*] (DMAA)	
LROR	Low-Resolution Omnidirectional Radiometer (MCD)	
LROS	Long Range Optical System (ACAE)	
LRO(W)	Leading Radio Operator (Warfare) [*British military*] (DMA)	
LROY	Leroy Properties & Development Corp.	
LRP	English Law Reports, Probate Division [*A publication*] (DLA)	
LRP	Lancaster, PA [*Location identifier*] [*FAA*] (FAAL)	
LRP	Landscape Research Project (SAUO)	
LRP	Lang Recovery Package (ACAE)	
LRP	Large Repairs to Hull	
LRP	Large Rotating Plug [*Nuclear energy*] (NRCH)	
LRP	LASER Retinal Photocoagulator	
LRP	Lateralized Readiness Potential [*Neurophysiology*]	
LRP	Late Receptor Potential [*Photoreceptor*] [*Physiology*]	
LRP	Latest Reporting Period [*Business term*]	
LRP	Launching Reference Point	
LRP	LDI [*Low Density Lipoprotein*] Receptor-Related Protein [*Biochemistry*]	
LRP	League for the Revolutionary Party (EA)	
LRP	Lebanese Revolutionary Party [*Political party*] (PD)	
LRP	Lesbian Rights Project [*Later, NCLR*] (EA)	
LRP	Lichen Ruber Planus (DMAA)	
LRP	Limited Rate Production	
LRP	Limited Reaction Processing [*Semiconductor technology*]	
LRP	Liporotein Receptor-Related Protein [*Biochemistry*]	
LRP	Live Role Playing (ADWA)	
LRP	LM [*Lunar Module*] Replaceable Package [*NASA*]	
LRP	Loan Repayment Program [*Department of Health and Human Services*] (GFGA)	
LRP	Logical Record Processor (IAA)	
LRP	Logical Request Package [*Computer science*] (CIST)	
LRP	Logistics Recovery Program (SAUO)	
LRP	Logistics Release Point [*Army*] (INF)	
LRP	Longe Range Interceptor (ACAE)	
LRP	Long-Range Path (IEEE)	
LRP	Long-Range Patrol [*Pronounced "lurp"*] [*Formerly, LRRP*] [*Army*] (AABC)	
LRP	Long-Range Penetration	
LRP	Long-Range Plans (NVT)	
LRP	Low Rate Production (RDA)	
LRP	Low Rigging Penalty [*IOR*] [*Yacht racing*]	
LRP	Society for Long Range Planning (SAUO)	
LRPA	Laser Radar Power Amplifier (ACAE)	
LRPA	Little Rock Port Railroad [*AAR code*]	
LRPA	Long-Range Patrol Aircraft (MCD)	
LRP & D	Probate and Divorce Cases [*1865-75*] [*England*] [*A publication*] (DLA)	
LRP & M	Law Reports, Probate and Matrimonial [*1866-75*] [*A publication*] (DLA)	
LRPC	English Law Reports, Privy Council, Appeal Cases [*1866-75*] [*A publication*] (DLA)	
LRPC	Laboratory Review Process Committee (SAUO)	
LRPC	Liberia Rubber Processing Corporation (SAUO)	
LRPC	Lightweight Remote Procedure Call [*Computer science*]	
LRPC	London Regional Passengers Committee [*British*] (ECON)	
LRPC (Eng)	English Law Reports, Privy Council, Appeal Cases [*1866-75*] [*A publication*] (DLA)	
LRPD	Law Reports, Probate Division [*A publication*] (DLA)	
LRP Div	English Law Reports, Probate, Divorce, and Admiralty Division [*A publication*] (DLA)	
LRPDS	Long-Range Position-Determining System [*Army*] (RDA)	
LRPE	Long-Range Procurement Estimate (PDAA)	
LRPE	Long-Run Price Effect [*Marketing*]	
LRPF	Liberal Religious Peace Fellowship (EA)	
LRPG	Long-Range Penetration Group [*Military*] [*World War II*]	
LRPG	Long-Range Proving Ground [*Air Force*]	
LRPGD	Long-Range Proving Ground Division [*Air Force*]	
LRPGR	Long-Range Planning Ground Rules (AAG)	
LRP/GWU	Logistics Research Project, George Washington University	
LRPL	Liquid Rocket Propulsion Laboratory [*Army*] (IEEE)	
LRPL	Little Rock Public Library (SAUO)	
LRPLS	Long-Range Passive Location System (PDAA)	
LRPO	Location Radiation Protection Officer (SARE)	
LRPP	Long-Range Propulsion Plan (MCD)	
LRPPD	Long-Range Planning Purpose Document	
LR Prob & M (Eng)	English Law Reports, Probate, Divorce, and Admiralty Division [*A publication*] (DLA)	
LR Prob Div	English Law Reports, Probate, Divorce, and Admiralty Division [*A publication*] (DLA)	
LR Prob Div (Eng)	English Law Reports, Probate, Divorce, and Admiralty Division [*A publication*] (DLA)	
LRPS	Laser Reliability Prediction Study (ACAE)	
LRPS	Licentiate of the Royal Photographic Society [*British*] (DBQ)	
LRPS	London Railway Preservation Society (SAUO)	
LRPS	Long-Range Planning Service [*Stanford Research Institute*] [*Assists businesses in investment activities*] (IID)	
LRPS	Long-Range Planning System (SAUO)	
LRPS	Long-Range Positioning System	

LRPSI	Long-Range Planning for School Improvement [*Pennsylvania*] (EDAC)	
LRPT	Large Repair Parts Transporter (MCD)	
LRPT	Longest Remaining Processing Time (PDAA)	
LRPT	Low-Resolution Picture Transmission (EOSA)	
LRQ	Lower Right Quadrant (MAE)	
LRQB	English Law Reports, Queen's Bench Division [*1865-75*] [*A publication*] (DLA)	
LRQB	Quebec Queen's Bench Reports [*Canada*] [*A publication*] (DLA)	
LRQBD	English Law Reports, Queen's Bench Division [*1865-75*] [*A publication*] (DLA)	
LRQB Div	English Law Reports, Queen's Bench Division [*1865-75*] [*A publication*] (DLA)	
LRQB Div (Eng)	English Law Reports, Queen's Bench Division [*1865-75*] [*A publication*] (DLA)	
LRQB (Eng)	English Law Reports, Queen's Bench Division [*1865-75*] [*A publication*] (DLA)	
LR-QR	Letter Requirement - Quick Reaction [*Army*]	
LRR	Labyrinthine Righting Reflex [*Physiology*]	
LRR	Lagged Reserve Requirement [*Finance*]	
LRR	Land-Rover Register 1947-1951 [*Petersfield, Hampshire, England*] (EAIO)	
LRR	LASER Radiation Receiver	
LRR	Launch Readiness Report [*or Review*] [*NASA*] (KSC)	
LRR	Launch Readiness Review [*Aerospace*] (NAKS)	
LRR	Leucine-Rich Repeat [*Biochemistry*]	
LRR	Leucine-Rich Repeats [*Genetics*]	
LRR	Logistic Readiness Review [*Navy*]	
LRR	Long-Range RADAR	
LRR	Long-Range Reconnaissance (MCD)	
LRR	Long-Range Requirements [*Navy*]	
LRR	Long-Range Rocket (MUGU)	
LRR	Longreach Resources Ltd. [*Vancouver Stock Exchange symbol*]	
LRR	Long Reduced Rate [*Taxation*] (WDAA)	
LRR	Long Regulatory Region [*Genetics*]	
LRR	Loop Regenerative Repeater	
LRR	Loss of Righting Reflex [*Medicine*]	
LRR	Lot Rejection Rate [*Quality measurement*]	
LRR	Lot Rejection Report	
LRR	Lower Receiving Room (SAUS)	
LRR & MF	Long-Range Resource and Management Forecast	
LRRC	Labor Relations and Research Center [*University of Massachusetts*]	
LRRC	Land Resource Research Centre [*Canada*] (IRC)	
LRRC	Lionel Railroaders Club (EA)	
LRRC	London Regional Reconstruction Committee (SAUO)	
LRRD	Long-Range Reconnaissance Detachment	
LRRDA	Long Range Research, Development, and Acquisition (ACAE)	
LRRDAP	Long-Range Research, Development, and Acquisition Plan (RDA)	
LRRI	Land Resources Research Institute [*Agriculture Canada*] [*Formerly, Soil Research Institute*] [*Research center*] (RCD)	
LRRI	Long-Range Reference Retroreflectance Instrument [*Bicycle test*] [*National Institute of Standards and Technology*]	
LRRM	Labor Relations Reference Manual [*Bureau of National Affairs*] [*A publication*] (DLA)	
LRRM	Loss Ratio Reserve Method [*Insurance*]	
lrRNA	Ribonucleic Acid, Light Ribosomal [*Biochemistry, genetics*]	
LRRO	Land Revenue Record Office (SAUO)	
LRRO	Land Revenue Records and Enrollments Office [*British*]	
LRRP	Law Reports, Restrictive Practices Cases [*1958-72*] [*A publication*] (DLA)	
LRRP	Long-Range Reconnaissance Patrol [*Pronounced "lurp"*] [*Later, LRP*] [*Army*] (AABC)	
LRRP	Lowest Required Radiated Power	
LRRPC	Restrictive Practices Cases [*1958-72*] [*England*] [*A publication*] (DLA)	
LRRR	LASER Ranging Retroreflection [*Also, LR3*] [*Pronounced "LR-cubed"*] [*Apollo 11 experiment*] [*NASA*]	
LRRRC	Liberia Refugee, Repatriation and Resettlement Commission (SAUO)	
LRRS	Library Reports & Research Service, Inc. [*Information service or system*] (IID)	
LRRS	Limited Remaining Radiation Service [*Unit*] [*Military*]	
LRRS	Long-Range RADAR Site (OA)	
LRRS	Long-Range Radar Station (SAUO)	
LRRSA	Light Railway Research Society of Australia	
LRRT	Library Research Round Table [*American Library Association*]	
LRRT	Light Rail Rapid Transit [*TRB*] (TAG)	
LR/RT	Long-Range Radiotelephone (DNAB)	
LRS	Laboratory Recoil Simulator (MCD)	
LRS	Laboratory Release System (MCD)	
LRS	Labor Relations Specialist (AAGC)	
LRS	Lactated Ringer's Solution [*Intravenous solution*]	
LRS	Lake Reporting Service	
LRS	Lamb-Retherford Shift [*Physics*]	
LRS	Lander Radio Subsystem [*NASA*]	
LRS	Language ReSource (SAUO)	
LRS	Lanyard Release Switch	
LRS	Larder Resources, Inc. [*Toronto Stock Exchange symbol*]	
LRS	Lares [*Puerto Rico*] [*Seismograph station code, US Geological Survey*] (SEIS)	
LRS	Large Ring Sparger [*Engineering*]	
LRS	Laser Radiometer System (ACAE)	
LRS	LASER Raman Scattering	
LRS	LASER Raman Spectroscopy	
LRS	Laser Rangefinder Set (ACAE)	
LRS	LASER Ranging System	

LRS	LASER Raster Scanner
LRS	LASER Reflectance Spectrometer (SSD)
LRS	Launch and Recovery Site (COE)
LRS	Launch Recoil Simulator
LRS	Laurinburg & Southern Railroad Co. [AAR code]
LRS	Lawyer Referral Service
LRS	League of Religious Settlements (EA)
LRS	Legislative Reference Service [Later, Congressional Research Service] [Library of Congress]
LRS	Level Recording Switch (NRCH)
LRS	Library Reproduction Service, Microfilm Co. of California, Los Angeles, CA [Library symbol] [Library of Congress] (LCLS)
L/R/S	Library Rubber Stamps [Antiquarian book trade]
LRS	Lifetime Reproductive Success [Demographics]
LRS	Light Radiation Sensor
LRS	Light Repair Section [British military] (DMA)
LRS	Light's Retention Scale [Test]
LRS	Lightweight RADAR Set
LRS	Limited Resources Specialty (AFM)
LRS	Lincoln Record Society (SAUO)
LRS	Linear Referencing System [FHWA] (TAG)
LRS	Linguistics Research System
LRS	Liquid RADWASTE System (NRCH)
LRS	Lloyd's Register of Shipping
LRS	Logistics Requirements System [Navy]
LRS	London Record Society [British] (ILCA)
LRS	London Research Station [British Gas] (WDAA)
LRS	Long-Range Schedule (SAA)
LRS	Long-Range Search
LRS	Long-Range Study
LRS	Long-Range Surveillance [Military] (INF)
LRS	Long Ranging Subsystem (ACAE)
LRS	Long Reversed Superchron [Geology]
LRS	Long Right Shift
LRS	Low-Rate Station
LRS	Low Resolution Spectrometer (SAUS)
LRS	Low Response System (SAUS)
LRSA	Laboratoire de Recherche en Sciences de l'Administration [Laval University] [Canada] [Research center] (RCD)
LRSA	Lamprey River Study Act of 1991 (COE)
LRSA	Long Range Strategic Aircraft (ACAE)
LRSAGW	Long-Range Surface-to-Air Guided Weapon (IAA)
LRSAM	Long-Range Surface-to-Air Missile (NATG)
LRS & D App	Law Reports, Scotch and Divorce Appeals [1866-75] [A publication] (DLA)
LRS & TP	Long-Range Science and Technology Plan [Army]
LRSB	Low Right Sternal Border [Medicine] (MELL)
LRSB	Sibiu/Turnisor [Romania] [ICAO location identifier] (ICLI)
LRSC	Law Reports, New Zealand Supreme Court [A publication] (DLA)
LRSC	Licentiate of the Royal Society of Chemistry [British] (DBQ)
LRSC	Long-Range Surveillance Co. [Military] (INF)
LRSCA	Land Remote Sensing Commercialization Act [1984]
LRSCA	Large Retractable Solar Cell Array
LR Sc & D	English Law Reports, House of Lords, Scotch and Divorce Appeal Cases [1866-75] [A publication] (DLA)
LR Sc & D App	Scottish and Divorce Appeals [1866-75] [A publication] (DLA)
LR Sc & D App	Scottish and Divorce Cases before the House of Lords [A publication] (DLA)
LR Sc & Div	Scotch and Divorce Appeals [1866-75] [A publication] (DLA)
LR Sc App	Law Reports, Scotch Appeals [A publication] (DLA)
LR Sc Div App	Law Reports, Scotch Appeals [A publication] (DLA)
LRSCX	Lord Abbett Research: Small Cap [Mutual fund ticker symbol] (SG)
LRSD	Long-Range Surveillance Detachment [Military] (INF)
LRSDC	Lakes Region Sled Dog Club (EA)
LR Sess Cas	English Law Reports, Sessions Cases [A publication] (DLA)
LRSF	Lactating Rat Serum Factor [Immunology]
LRSF	Liver Regenerating Serum Factor [Medicine] (DMAA)
LRSF	Long-Range Systems Forecast
LRSI	LifeRate Systems [NQS] (TTSB)
LRSI	LifeRate Systems, Inc. [NASDAQ symbol] (SAG)
LRSI	Long-Range SOF [Special Operation Force] Insertion (DOMA)
LRSI	Low-Temperature Reusable Surface Insulation (NASA)
LRSIFC	Lori Robin Smith International Fan Club (EA)
LRSK	Long-Range Station Keeping (NG)
LRSL	Law Reports, Sierra Leone Series [A publication] (DLA)
LRSL	Long-Range Surveillance Leader [Military] (INF)
LRSLA	Long-Range Service Life Analysis (MCD)
LRSLBM	Long Range Sea Launched Ballistic Missile (ACAE)
LRSLC	Long Range Surveillance Leaders Course [Army]
LRSLP	Lietuvos Revoliuciniu Socialistu Liaudininkai Partija [Revolutionary Socialist Populists Party of Lithuania] [Political party] (PPE)
LRSM	Laboratory for Research on the Structure of Matter [University of Pennsylvania]
LRSM	Licentiate of the Royal School of Music, London [British]
LRSM	Long-Range Seismograph Measurements (MCD)
LRSM	Long-Range Standoff Missile [Military] (MUSM)
LRSM	Satu Mare [Romania] [ICAO location identifier] (ICLI)
LRSO	Long-Range Surveillance Outpost (MCD)
LRSOM	Long-Range Stand-Off Missile
LRSOW	Long-Range Conventional Standoff Weapon
LRSP	Long-Range Strategic Planning (PDAA)
LRSP	Long-Range Systems Plan (TIMI)
LRSR	Liquid Redox Sulfur Recovery [Processes for removing hydrogen sulfide from gases]
LRSR	Long-Range Sniper Rifle (PDAA)
LRSR	Long-Range Storage Requirements (SAUO)
LRSS	Logistics Readiness Simulation System (SAUO)
LRSS	Long-Range Scientific Studies (SAUO)
LRSS	Long-Range Strategic Studies [Military] (AFIT)
LRSS	Long-Range Surveillance System (SAUS)
LRSS	Long-Range Survey System [Military]
LR Stat	English Law Reports, Statutes [A publication] (DLA)
LRSTPP	Long-Range Scientific Technical Planning Program (NG)
LRSU	Long Range Sensor Unit (SAUO)
LRSU	Long-Range Surveillance Unit [Military] (INF)
LRSUBRS	Long-Range Surveillance Unit Base Radio Station [Military] (INF)
LRSV	Lychnis Ringspot Virus [Plant pathology]
LRSV	Suceava/Salcea [Romania] [ICAO location identifier] (ICLI)
LRT	LASER Range-Finder Theodolite
LRT	Last Resort Target [Military]
LRT	Launch Readiness Test (ACAE)
LRT	Launch, Recovery, and Transport [Vehicle]
LRT	Lawrenceburg, TN [Location identifier] [FAA] (FAAL)
LRT	Light Rail Transit
LRT	Light Rail Transport (SAUO)
LRT	Light Repair Truck [British]
LRT	Likelihood Ratio Test [Statistics]
LRT	Linear Response Theory [Physics]
LRT	Link Readiness Test (ACAE)
LRT	Little Round Top (SAUO)
LRT	LL&E Royalty Tr UBI [NYSE symbol] (TTSB)
LRT	LL & E Royalty Trust UBI [NYSE symbol] (SPSG)
LRT	Load Ratio Transformer (IAA)
LRT	Local Leak Rate Test [Nuclear energy] (IEEE)
LRT	Local Radiotherapy
LRT	Loki Ranging Transponder
LRT	London Reading Test [Educational test]
LRT	London Regional Transport
LRT	Long-Range Radiotelephone
LRT	Long-Range Transport [Navy] [British]
LRT	Long-Range Typhon [Navy] (NG)
LRT	Long Ring Timer
LRT	Lorentz Reciprocal Theorem
LRT	Lorient [France] [Airport symbol] (OAG)
LRT	Lower Respiratory Tract [Medicine]
LRT	Low Rate Type (SAUS)
LRT	Lymphoreticular Tissue [Medicine] (MELL)
LRTA	Lath Renders' Trade Association [A union] [British]
LRTA	Leisure, Recreation, and Tourism Abstracts [Database] [Commonwealth Agricultural Bureaux International] [Information service or system] (CRD)
LRTA	Light Rail Transit Association [Milton, Keynes, England] (EAIO)
LRTAP	Long Range Transportation of Air Pollution (EEVL)
LRTAP	Long-Range Transport of Atmospheric Pollutants
LRTAP	Long-Range Transport of Atmospheric Pollution (SAUO)
LRTC	Law Reform Commission of Tasmania [Australia]
LRTC	Local Road Transport Co-ordinator (SAUO)
LRTC	Tulcea/Cataloi [Romania] [ICAO location identifier] (ICLI)
LRTD	Living Relative Transplant Donor (MELL)
LRTF	Linear Radial Transmission Filter [Photography]
LRTF	Long-Range Technical Forecast (IEEE)
LRTG	Logistics Reassignment Task Group [DoD] (MCD)
LRTGT	Last Resort Target [Military]
LRThD	Lateral Reach-Through Device (PDAA)
LRTI	Lower Respiratory Tract Illness (DAVI)
LRTI	Lower Respiratory Tract Infection [Medicine] (ADA)
LRTIA	Long-Range Scientific and Technical Intelligence Assessment (SAUO)
LRTL	Light Railway Transport League [British] (DCTA)
LRTM	Long-Range Training Mission [Military]
LRTM	Tirgu Mures/Vidrasau [Romania] [ICAO location identifier] (ICLI)
LRTNF	Long-Range Theater Nuclear Force [Military]
LRTNW	Long-Range Theater Nuclear Weapons [Military]
LRTP	Long-Range Technical Plan (PDAA)
LRTP	Long-Running Thermal Precipitation (DICI)
LRTPP	Long-Range Scientific Technical Planning Program (SAUO)
LRTR	Timisoara/Giarmata [Romania] [ICAO location identifier] (ICLI)
LRTRO	Loaded Radial Tire Run-Out [Automotive engineering]
LRTS	LASER Ranging and Tracking System (RDA)
LRTS	Library Resources & Technical Services [Association for Library Collections and Technical Services] [American Library Association]
LRTx	Living Related Renal Transplantation [Medicine]
LRU	Landowner Relations Unit (SAUO)
LRU	Landscape Response Unit (QUAC)
LRU	Las Cruces [New Mexico] [Airport symbol] (OAG)
LRU	Las Cruces, NM [Location identifier] [FAA] (FAAL)
LRU	Laser Rangefinder Unit (ACAE)
LRU	Laser Recording Unit (SAUS)
LRU	Least Recently Used [Replacement algorithm] [Computer science]
LRU	Least Repairable Unit
LRU	Least Replaceable Unit (IAA)
LRU	Less than Release Unit [Army] (AABC)
LRU	Line Removable Unit
LRU	Line Replaceable Unit (AFM)
LRU	Link Retraction Unit (KSC)
LRU	Little Rock University [Merged with University of Arkansas]
LRU	Lone Replaceable Unit (MCD)
LRU	Lowest Repairable Unit (MCD)
LRU	Lowest Replaceable Unit (SAUO)

LRU	Lowest Replacement Unit (MCD)
LRU	Tulane University, New Orleans, LA [OCLC symbol] (OCLC)
LRuL	Louisiana Technical University, Ruston, LA [Library symbol] [Library of Congress] (LCLS)
LRuLP	Lincoln Parish Library, Ruston, LA [Library symbol] [Library of Congress] (LCLS)
LRUP	La Raza Unida Party (EA)
LRUP	Local Resource Use Plan (SAUO)
LRUPS	Line Replaceable Unit Power Supply (MCD)
LRV	Labor Rate Variance (TIMI)
LRV	Lanarkshire Rifle Volunteers [British military] (DMA)
LRV	Lancashire Rifle Volunteers [British military] (DMA)
LRV	Last Received Value (ACAE)
LRV	Launch & Recovery Vehicle (SAUS)
LRV	Launch Readiness Verification [NASA] (NASA)
LRV	Left Renal Vein [Anatomy] (DAVI)
LRV	Leirvogur [Iceland] [Geomagnetic observatory code]
LRV	Lifting Reentry Vehicle (MCD)
LRV	Light Rail Vehicle
LRV	Light Reconnaissance Vehicle [Military]
LRV	Light Recreational Vehicle [Mitsubishi minivan]
LRV	Liquid Radioactive Waste (SAUO)
LRV	Little Rabbit Valley [California] [Seismograph station code, US Geological Survey] (SEIS)
LRV	Local Radio Workshop (SAUO)
LRV	London Radio Workshop (SAUO)
LRV	Long-Range Vehicle
LRV	Long-Range Video (MCD)
LRV	Low Resolution Visible (SAUO)
LRV	Lunar Rover [or Roving] Vehicle [NASA]
LRVEP	League of Rural Voters Education Project (EA)
LRW	Labor Ready [NYSE symbol] (SG)
LRW	Labor Relations Week [Bureau of National Affairs] [Information service or system] (CRD)
LRW	Liquid Radioactive Waste (SAUS)
LRW	London Radio Workshop [Independent Local Radio] [British]
LRWC	Licensed Residental Wages Council (SAUO)
LRWRO	Loaded Radial Wheel Run-Out [Automotive engineering]
LRY	Lady Robyn Resources, Inc. [Vancouver Stock Exchange symbol]
LRY	Latching Relay (IAA)
LRY	Liberal Religious Youth
LRY	Liberty Property Trust [NYSE symbol] (SAG)
LS	Labologists Society [Farnborough, Hampshire, England] (EAIO)
LS	Laboratory System
LS	Labor Service [Military]
L/S	Lactose/Sucrose [Ratio]
LS	Lacus Somniorum [Lunar area]
LS	Lamb Society (SAUO)
LS	Lamellar Strip [Botany]
LS	Landesschuetzeneinheit [Regional defense force] [German military - World War II]
LS	Landing Ship
LS	Landing Side [Air Force]
LS	Landing Site (KSC)
LS	Landing System (ACAE)
L/S	Landsat (SAUO)
LS	Land Service
LS	Land Surveying Program [Association of Independent Colleges and Schools specialization code]
LS	Land Surveyor
LS	Lange Sicht [Long Sight] [German]
LS	Language Specification (IEEE)
LS	LAN Server (SAUS)
LS	Lantern Slide [Photography]
ls	Laos [MARC country of publication code] [Library of Congress] (LCCP)
LS	Lapped Seam (DNAB)
LS	Larcher's Sign [Medicine] (MELL)
LS	Lasallian Sisters (Vietnam) (TOCD)
LS	Laser Surgery (MELL)
LS	LASER System
LS	Lastensegler; Lastensegelflugzeug [Cargo transport glider] [German military - World War II]
LS	Latch Side
LS	Latent Syphilis (MELL)
LS	Lateral Septum
LS	Lateral Subsylvian Cortex [Neuroanatomy]
LS	Lateral Suspensor [Ligament] [Anatomy] (DAVI)
LS	Late Scramble [Reason for missed interception] [Military]
LS	Late Shock [Medicine]
LS	Late Start (SAUO)
LS	Launching System
LS	Launch Sequence (MCD)
LS	Launch Service
LS	Launch Set
LS	Launch Simulator (MUGU)
LS	Launch Site [NASA] (MCD)
LS	Launch Station (MCD)
LS	Law Society (WDAA)
LS	Law Student (DLA)
LS	Leaders of Science [A publication]
LS	Leading Seaman [Navy] [British]
LS	Leading Stoker
LS	Lead Service (ACAE)
LS	Lead Sheet [Military]
LS	Lead Survey [Environmental science] (COE)
LS	Leaf Spring [Automotive engineering]
L-S	Leap-Second
LS	Learning Step
LS	Lease
LS	Least Significant (IEEE)
LS	Least Squares [Mathematical statistics]
L/S	Lecithin/Sphingomyelin [Ratio] [Clinical chemistry]
LS	Lecithin Supplement (MELL)
LS	Lectori Salutem [Latin]
LS	Left Sacrum [Medicine] (KSC)
LS	Left Safety [Football] (DICI)
LS	Left Shift
LS	Left Side
LS	Left Sign (IAA)
LS	Left Socialists (SAUO)
LS	Legally Separated (MAE)
LS	Legal Scroll
LS	Le Gros Scouts [British military] (DMA)
LS	Leichtenstern's Sign [Medicine] (MELL)
LS	Leiomyosarcoma [Medicine]
LS	Length of Stroke
LS	Lepidopterists' Society
LS	Lesotho [ANSI two-letter standard code] (CNC)
Ls	Lesotho (MILB)
LS	Less
LS	Lessing Society (EA)
LS	Letterer-Siwe [Disease] [Medicine] (DB)
LS	Letter Service
LS	Letter Signed (ACAE)
LS	Letter Signed [Manuscript descriptions]
ls	Letter Signed [Handwritten signature] (WDMC)
LS	Letter Stock
LS	Leukemia Society (SAUO)
LS	Leukemia Society of America
LS	Level Setter
LS	Level Switch
LS	Liaison Squadron (SAUO)
LS	Libman-Sacks [Disease] [Medicine] (DB)
LS	Library Science
LS	Library Search
LS	Library Services
LS	Licensed Surveyor [British] (ADA)
LS	Licentiate in Science
LS	Licentiate in Surgery
LS	Lichen Sclerosis [Medicine] (MELL)
LS	Lichen Simplex [Medicine] (MELL)
LS	Lifesaving Service [Coast Guard]
LS	Life Science (NASA)
LS	Life Sciences (SAUO)
LS	Life Sciences Division (SAUO)
LS	Life Support (AAG)
LS	Life System (MCD)
LS	Lighthouse Service [Coast Guard]
LS	Lighting Supervisor [Television]
LS	Lighting System
LS	Lightning Sensor [Aviation]
ls	Light-Second
LS	Light Shield (SPST)
LS	Light Ship
LS	Light Source
LS	Light Sussex [Poultry]
LS	Light Switch
LS	Lignosulfonate [Pulp and paper processing]
LS	Like-Sexed
LS	Limbic System [Brain anatomy]
LS	Limestone [Petrology] (AAG)
LS	Liminal [or Least] Sensation [Psychology]
LS	Liminal Sensitivity (DIPS)
LS	Limit Switch [Electronics]
LS	Line Scan (DEN)
LS	Line-Sequential (IAA)
LS	Line Speed
L/S	Lines per Second (WDAA)
LS	Line Stretcher
LS	Line Switch [Telecommunications] (TEL)
LS	Linker Scanning [Mutants] [Genetics]
LS	Linksozialisten [Left Socialists] [Austria] [Political party] (PPE)
LS	Link State (ACRL)
LS	Link Status (AGLO)
LS	Linnean Society [Australia]
LS	Liquid Scintillation [Chemical analysis]
LS	Liquid Sensor (AAG)
LS	Listed Securities
LS	Listing Salesperson [Real estate] (REAL)
ls	Listing Salesperson [Real estate] (REAL)
LS	List of Specifications (NATG)
LS	List Total [Banking]
LS	Literature Search
l/s	Liters per Second [SI symbol]
LS	Little Stock (MHDW)
LS	Liver and Spleen [Medicine]
LS	Liver Scan [Medicine] (MELL)
LS	Livestock (DCTA)
LS	Lladro Society (EA)

LS	Loading Splice [Telecommunications] (TEL)
L/S	Load System (MCD)
LS	Lobe Switching (IAA)
LS	Local Store
LS	Local Sunset
LS	Local Sunset Time (WDMC)
LS	Loca Sancta [A publication] (BJA)
LS	Locked Shut (NRCH)
LS	Lockheed Standards
LS	Locus Sepulchri [Place of the Sepulchre] [Latin]
LS	Locus Sigilli [Place of the Seal] [Legal term] [Latin]
LS	Logical Sum [Computer science]
LS	Logic Synthesis (VLIE)
LS	Logistical Support [Army]
LS	Logistics Squadron [Military]
LS	Logistics Summary (SAUO)
LS	Log-Skidder [Tires] (DICI)
LS	London Scottish [Army regiment]
LS	London Scottish Regiment (SAUO)
LS	[The] London Sinfonietta
LS	London Society (SAUO)
Ls	Longear Sunfish [Ichthyology]
LS	Longitudinal Section
LS	Longitudinal Staggering (IAA)
LS	Long Service (ADA)
LS	Long Shot [A photograph or motion picture sequence taken from a distance]
LS	Long Sight (WDAA)
LS	Long Sleeves [Dressmaking]
LS	Long Stub (VLIE)
LS	Loose Shot
LS	Lost Seska [Defunct] (EA)
LS	Loudspeaker
LS	Loudspeaker System [Automotive engineering]
LS	Lovat Scouts [British military] (DMA)
LS	Lower Sprocket (ECII)
LS	Lower Structure
LS	Low-Power Schottky [Electronics]
LS	Low Salt [Dietetics]
LS	Low Secondary (IAA)
LS	Low Similarity [Psychology]
LS	Low-Sodium Diet (DMAA)
LS	Low-Speed
LS	Low Spin (EDCT)
LS	Lumbar Spine [Medicine] (DMAA)
L-S	Lumbosacral [Medicine] (AMHC)
LS	Lumbosacral [Medicine]
LS	Lump Sum
LS	Lunar Surface (KSC)
LS	Lung Sounds [Medicine]
LS	Luteinization Stimulator [Endocrinology]
LS	Lute Society [Harrow, England] (EAIO)
LS	Luxury Sport [In automobile model name "Cordia LS"]
LS	Lymphosarcoma [Medicine]
LS	Marco Island Airways [ICAO designator] (AD)
LS	Sandia Laboratories (SAUO)
ls---	South Atlantic Ocean [MARC geographic area code] [Library of Congress] (LCCP)
LS	Sudanese Pound (IMH)
LS	Summer [Vessel load line mark]
LS2	Lesser Sulphur-Crested Cockatoo [Bird]
LS3	Life Saving, Life Sustaining, Life Supporting (SAUS)
LS3	London Specialist Software Systems (NITA)
LSA	Labor Services Agency (AABC)
LSA	Labor Surplus Area
LSA	Labour Services Association (SAUO)
LSA	Labour Staff Association [National Coal Board] [British]
LSA	Lamesa, TX [Location identifier] [FAA] (FAAL)
LSA	Landing Ship, Assault [Navy] [British]
LSA	Landing Supply Activity
LSA	Landmark Savings Association (EFIS)
LSA	Land Service Assistant [Ministry of Agriculture, Fisheries, and Food] [British]
LSA	Land Settlement Association [British]
LSA	Language Sampling and Analysis [Educational test]
LSA	Large Science Aperture [Spectrometer]
LSA	Large Southern Array (SAUS)
LSA	Large Space Antenna (SSD)
LSA	Large Spherical Array
LSA	Large Submillimeter Array
LSA	Laser Seeker Assembly (ACAE)
LSA	LASER-Supported Absorption (PDAA)
LSA	Lateral Spherical Aberration
LSA	Later Stone Age (SAUO)
LSA	Late Stone Age
LSA	Launcher Structure Assembly (ACAE)
LSA	Launch Services Agreement (MCD)
LSA	Law and Society Association (EA)
LSA	Law Services Association [British] (DBA)
LSA	Layton School of Art [Wisconsin]
LSA	Leading Stores Accountant [British military] (DMA)
LSA	Leading Supply Assistant (WDAA)
L/S	Lead Spring Assembly
LSA	League for Socialist Action [Canada]
LSA	Leaving Scene of an Accident [Traffic offense charge]
LSA	Left Sacroanterior [A fetal position, the breech position] [Obstetrics]
LSA	Left Subclavian Artery [Anatomy] (AAMN)
LSA	Leisure Studies Association [British]
LSA	Leukemia Society of America (EA)
LSA	Leukocyte Specific Activity (DB)
LSA	Level Shift Amplifier
LSA	Lhasa [Tibet] [Seismograph station code, US Geological Survey] (SEIS)
LSA	Library Science Abstracts [A publication]
LSA	Library Service Association (SAUO)
LSA	Library Services Act [1956]
LSA	Licentiate in Agricultural Science
LSA	Licentiate of Science in Agriculture (SAUO)
LSA	Licentiate of the Society of Apothecaries [British]
LSA	Lichen Sclerosis et Atrophicus [Dermatology]
LSA	Life Saving Appliance [or Apparatus] (DS)
LSA	Life Style Analysis [Psychology]
LSA	Lighthouse Society of America (SAUO)
LSA	Light Source Assembly (ACAE)
LSA	Light Strike Aircraft [Military] (PDAA)
LSA	Limbless Soldiers Association (SAUO)
LSA	Limited Space-Charge Accumulation [Electronics]
LSA	Linea Aerea Nacional (Lansa) [Dominican Republic] [ICAO designator] (FAAC)
LSA	Linear Servo Actuator
LSA	Line Sensing Amplifier (IAA)
LSA	Line Sharing Adapter (SAUO)
LSA	Line-Sharing Adapter
LSA	Line Sharing Adaptor (NITA)
LSA	Linguistic Society of America (EA)
LSA	Link State Algorithm (SAUO)
LSA	Lipid-Bound Sialic Acid [Biochemistry] (DAVI)
LSA	Liquid Scintillation Analyzer [Chemistry]
LSA	Liquor Stores Association (SAUO)
LSA	List of Sections Affected (AAGC)
LSA	Lithuanian Scouts Association (EA)
LSA	Lithuanian Society of America (SAUO)
LSA	Lithuanian Students Association (EA)
LSA	Little Sisters of the Assumption [See also PSA] [France] (EAIO)
LSA	Livestock Agent
LSA	Lobor Surplus Area (SAUO)
LSA	Local Security Authority (VLIE)
LSA	Local Supervising Authority
LSA	Locksmith Security Association (EA)
LSA	Logarithmic Sense Amplifier (VLIE)
LSA	Logic Sequential Access [Computer science] (VLIE)
LSA	Logic State Analyzer (IAA)
LSA	Logistics Supply Area
LSA	Logistics Supportability Analysis (SAUO)
LSA	Logistics Support Analysis
LSA	Logistics Systems Applications (SAUO)
LSA	Logistic Support Agreement [Military] (CAAL)
LSA	Logistic Support Aircraft (MCD)
LSA	Logistic Support Analysis
LSA	Logistic Support Area (NVT)
LSA	Logistic Sustainability Analysis [Environmental science] (COE)
LSA	Logistic System Analysis [Navy]
LSA	London Salvage Association (SAUO)
LSA	London School of Accountancy (SAUO)
LSA	Longitudinal Spherical Aberration
LSA	Loss of Situation Awareness (SAUS)
LSA	Losuia [Papua New Guinea] [Airport symbol] (OAG)
LSA	Lotus Solution Architecture (SAUS)
LSA	Loudspeaker Amplifier (DWSG)
LSA	Louisiana Statutes, Annotated [A publication] (DLA)
LSA	Low-Cost Solar Array (IEEE)
LSA	Lowe's Syndrome Association (EA)
LSA	Low Sidelobe Antenna (ACAE)
LSA	Low Specific Activity [Radioisotope]
LSA	Low-Speed Adapter (IAA)
LSA	Lubricant, Small Arms [Weaponry] [Military] (VNW)
LSA	Lumbosacral Agenesis [Medicine] (MELL)
LSA	Lute Society of America (EA)
LSa	Lymphosarcoma [Medicine]
LSA	University of Arizona, Graduate Library School, Tucson, AZ [OCLC symbol] (OCLC)
LSAA	Library Services Authority Act (NITA)
LSAA	Linen Supply Association of America [Later, TRSA] (EA)
LSAA	Low Sidelobe Antenna Array (ACAE)
LSAAP	Lone Star Army Ammunition Plant (AABC)
LSAB	Learning Systems and Access Branch [Education] (AIE)
LSAB	London Society of Air Britain (SAUO)
LSAC	Laboratory Studies in Atmospheric Chemistry
LSAC	Labor Sector Advisory Committee [Terminated, 1980] (EGAO)
LSAC	Law School Admission Council (EDAC)
LSAC	London Sessions Appeal Committee (SAUO)
LSAC	London Small Arms Co. [Military]
LSAC	London Small Arms Company (SAUO)
LSAC	Low-Pressure Suction Air Conveyor (PDAA)
LSAC	Low-Speed Access to a Computer (PDAA)
LSACECC	Lutheran South-East Asia Christian Education Curriculum Committee (SAUO)
LSAC/LSAS	Law School Admission Council/Law School Admission Services (EA)
LSACN	Logistic Support Analysis Control Number (MCD)
LSAD	Launch Safe-and-Arm Device

LSAG	Geneve [*Switzerland*] [*ICAO location identifier*] (ICLI)
LSAH	Launch Site Accommodations Handbook [*NASA*] (NASA)
lsai-	Ascension Island [*MARC geographic area code*] [*Library of Congress*] (LCCP)
LSA/L	Language. Journal of the Linguistic Society of America. Baltimore (SAUO)
LSAL	Left Salivary [*Gland*]
L Salic	Salic Law [*A publication*] (DLA)
LSA/LSAR	Logistic Support Analysis/Logistic Support Analysis Record [*Army*] (RDA)
LSALT	Lowest Safe Altitude [*Aviation*] (DA)
LSAM	Launcher System Angles Matched [*Navy*] (CAAL)
LSAM	Logistics Support Alternative [*or Analysis*] Model (MCD)
LSAM	Lumped Shell Analysis Method
LSA mode	Limited Space Charge Accumulation Mode [*Telecommunications*] (NITA)
LSANA	Leukocyte-Specific Antinuclear Antibody [*Hematology*] (DMAA)
LS & GCM	Long Service and Good Conduct Medal [*Military decoration*] [*British*]
LS&I	Lake Superior & Ishpeming Railroad Co. (SAUO)
LS & MS	Lake Shore & Michigan Southern Railway
LS and MS	Less Sleep and More Speed [*Hobo slang*]
LSANSW	Limbless Soldiers' Association of New South Wales [*Australia*]
LSANSW	Liquor Stores Association of New South Wales [*Australia*]
LSAO	Line Station Assembly Order (MCD)
LSAO	Logistics Systems Analysis Office (ACAE)
LSAP	Laboratory Space Allocation Plan (MCD)
LSAP	Launch Sequence Applications Program (MCD)
LSAP	Letzeburger Sozialistesch Arbechter Partei [*Socialist Workers' Party of Luxembourg*] [*Political party*] (PPE)
LSAP	Life Space Analysis Profile [*Test*] (TMMY)
LSAP	Linear Systems Analysis Program [*Statistics*]
LSAP	Link Layer Service Access Point
LSAP	Local Service Access Point [*Telecommunications*] (OSI)
LSAP	Logistics Support Analysis Plan (SAUO)
LSAP	Logistic Support Analysis Plan [*or Program*] [*Army*]
LSAP	Logistic Support Analysis Process [*Navy*]
LSAPT	Long Service Access Point [*Computer science*] (VLIE)
LSAPT	Lunar Sample Analysis Planning Team [*NASA*]
LSAQ	Limbless Soldiers' Association of Queensland [*Australia*]
LSAR	Local Storage Address Register (IAA)
LSAR	Logistics Support Analysis Report (SAUO)
LSAR	Logistic Support Analysis Record (RDA)
LSAR	Lymphosarcoma Cell [*Oncology*] (DAVI)
LSA/RCS	Lymphosarcoma - Reticulum Cell Sarcoma [*Oncology*] (MAE)
LSARS	West's Louisiana Revised Statutes [*A publication*] (DLA)
LSAS	Law School Admission Services (EDAC)
LSAS	Longitudinal Stability Augmentation System [*Aviation*] (DA)
LSASA	Limbless Soldiers' Association of South Australia
LSAT	Large Scale Applications Test (ACAE)
LSAT	Law School Admission Test
LSAT	Law School Aptitude Test (GAGS)
LSAT	Legal Scholastic Aptitude Test (HGAA)
LSAT	Leveling/Sharpening Aggressions Test [*Psychology*] (EDAC)
LSAT	Logistic Shelter Air Transportable
LSAV	Limbless Soldiers' Association of Victoria [*Australia*]
LSAV	Liquor Stores' Association of Victoria [*Aerospace*]
LSAW	LASER-Supported Absorption-Wave (PDAA)
LSAWA	Liquor Stores' Association of Western Australia
LSAY	Longitudinal Study of American Youth [*Northern Illinois University*] [*Education*]
LSAZ	Zurich [*Switzerland*] [*ICAO location identifier*] (ICLI)
LSB	Bachelor of Life Science
LSB	Labour Supply Board [*British*]
LSB	Landing Ship, Bombardment
LSB	Large-Scale Bypass [*Telecommunications*] (CIST)
LSB	La Sacra Bibbia (BJA)
LSB	Launcher Support Building
LSB	Launch Service Building
LSB	Learned Society Board (ACII)
LSB	Leased Spacecraft Bus (SSD)
LSB	Least Significant BIT [*or Byte*] [*Data compaction*]
LSB	Left Sternal Border
LSB	Lensivavia [*Former USSR*] [*FAA designator*] (FAAC)
LSB	Library of Standard Biographies [*A publication*]
LSB	Life Safety Box
LSB	Lifestyle Beverage Corp. [*Vancouver Stock Exchange symbol*]
LSB	Line Segment Block [*Computer science*]
LSB	Linux Standard Base (SAUS)
LSB	List of Successful Bidders [*DoD*]
LSB	Lithuanian Boy Scouts [*An association*] (EA)
LSB	Logistics Sustaining Base [*Military*] (RDA)
LSB	Logistic Support Base (NVT)
LSB	London School Board
LSB	Longitudinal Studies Branch [*Department of Education*] (GFGA)
LSB	Long Span Bridge (SAUS)
LSB	Lordsburg, NM [*Location identifier*] [*FAA*] (FAAL)
LSB	Louisiana School Board (SAUO)
LSB	Lower Sideband [*Data transmission*]
LSB	Low Silhouette Blade [*Aircraft*]
LSB	Low-Speed Breaker Relay (IEEE)
LSB	Low-Speed Buffer (CET)
LSB	Low-Surface-Brightness [*Galaxies - astronomy*]
LSB	LSB Industries [*NYSE symbol*] (TTSB)
LSB	LSB Industries, Inc. [*NYSE symbol*] (SAG)
LSB	Lucas-Sumitomo Brakes [*Auto industry supplier*]
LSB	Lunar Surface Base [*NASA*] (KSC)
LSB	Southern University, Library, Baton Rouge, LA [*OCLC symbol*] (OCLC)
LSBA	LaSalle and Bureau County Railroad Company (SAUO)
LSBA	Leading Sick Bay Attendant [*Navy*] [*British*]
LSBA	Louisiana School Boards Association (SAUO)
LSBC	[*The*] La Salle & Bureau County Railroad Co. [*AAR code*]
LSB Fn	LSB Financial Corp. [*Associated Press*] (SAG)
LSB Fncl	LSB Financial Corp. [*Associated Press*] (SAG)
LSBGA	Last Sortie Before Ground Alert (SAUO)
LSBI	LSB Financial [*NASDAQ symbol*] (TTSB)
LSBI	LSB Financial Corp. [*NASDAQ symbol*] (SAG)
LSB Ind	LSB Industries, Inc. [*Associated Press*] (SAG)
LSB NC	LSB Bancshares, Inc. of North Carolina [*Associated Press*] (SAG)
LSBPHF	Library Service to the Blind and Physically Handicapped Forum [*Association of Specialized and Cooperative Library Agencies*]
LSBPrC	LSB Ind $3.25 Cv Exch Pfd [*NYSE symbol*] (TTSB)
LS BPS	Laparoscopic Bilateral Partial Salpingectomies [*Gynecology*] (DAVI)
LSBR	Large Seed-Blanket Reactor
LSBR	Liquid Strand Burning Rate (MCD)
LSBRT	Library Service to the Blind Round Table
lsbv-	Bouvet Island [*MARC geographic area code*] [*Library of Congress*] (LCCP)
LSBX	Lawrence Savings Bank [*NASDAQ symbol*] (SAG)
LSBY	Least Significant Byte [*Data compaction*] [*Computer science*]
LSC	Laboratory Support Center (SAUO)
LSC	Labor Service Center (SAUO)
LSC	Labor Socialist Committee [*Australia*]
LSC	Labor Studies Center [*AFL-CIO*]
LSC	Labor Supervision Company (SAUO)
LSC	Lake Survey Center [*National Oceanic and Atmospheric Administration*]
LSC	Landing Ship Carrier [*British military*] (DMA)
LSC	Language and Society Centre [*Monash University*] [*Australia*]
LSC	Languages Services Centre [*South Australia*]
LSC	Large-Scale Computer
LSC	Large Single Copy Region [*Of a chromosome*] [*Genetics*]
LSC	Large Sized Combatant (ACAE)
LSC	Large Solar Concentrator (SSD)
LSC	Large Submetacentric Chromosome [*Medicine*]
LSC	Las Cruces [*Diocesan abbreviation*] [*New Mexico*] (TOCD)
LSC	La Serena [*Chile*] [*Airport symbol*] (AD)
LSC	LASER Spectral Control
LSC	LASER-Supported Combustion (MCD)
LSC	Laser Systems Center (SAUO)
LSC	Last Significant Character (ECII)
LSC	Late Systolic Click [*Cardiology*] (DAVI)
LSC	Latrobe Steel Company (SAUO)
LSC	Launch Sequence Control
L/SC	Launch/Storage Container
L Sc	Laureate of Science
LSC	Law of the Sea Conference [*United Nations*]
LSC	Learning Skills Center Reading and Study Skills Program [*Cornell University*] [*Research center*] (RCD)
LSC	Learning Station.com
LSC	Least Significant Character (IEEE)
LSC	Least Square Center (IAA)
LSC	Least Squares Circle [*Manufacturing term*]
LSC	Least-Squares Collocation [*Mathematics*]
LSC	Left-Sided Colon Cancer [*Oncology*]
LSC	Left Stage Center [*A stage direction*]
LSC	Legal Services Corp. [*Government agency*]
LSC	Legal Services for Children (EA)
LSC	Legislative Service Center [*Washington State Legislature*] [*Information service or system*] (IID)
LSC	Lens Sign Convention
LSC	Liberian Shipowners Council (EA)
LSC	Library Service Center (SAUO)
LSC	Library Services Center, Midwestern Regional Library System [*UTLAS symbol*]
LSC	Library Services Center of Missouri [*Library network*]
LSc	Licentiate in Science (DD)
LSC	Lichen Simplex Chronicus (DB)
LSC	Lid, Sclera, and Conjunctiva [*Opthalmology*] (DAVI)
LSC	Life Safety Code
LSC	Life Sciences Center (SAUO)
LSC	Life Support Cost (SAUO)
LSC	Limit Signaling Comparator
LSC	Lincoln Sesquicentennial Committee [*Terminated, 1960*] [*Government agency*]
LSC	Linear Sequential Circuit
LSC	Linear-Shaped Charge
LSC	Linear Slope Controlled (PDAA)
LSC	Liquid Scintillation Cocktail [*Analytical chemistry*]
LSC	Liquid Scintillation Counter [*or Counting*]
LSC	Liquid Smoke Condensate
LSC	Liquid Solid Chromatography
LSC	Liquids Solids Contact
LSC	Little Sisters of Carmel
LSC	Littleton System Center (ACAE)
LSC	LOAD [*Low Altitude Defense*] Simulation Center
LSC	Load Standardization Crew (MCD)
LSC	Lobbyist Systems Corp. [*Information service or system*] (IID)
LSC	Local Supercluster [*Cosmology*]
LSC	Local Switching Centre [*Telecommunications*] (NITA)

LSC	Loco Sub Citato [*In the Place Cited Below*] [*Latin*] (ROG)
LSC	Loco Supra Citato [*In the Place Cited Above*] [*Latin*]
LSC	Logistical Support Center [*Army*]
LSC	Logistics Support Costs (SAUO)
LSC	Logistic Support Cadre (MCD)
LSC	Logistic Support Command (SAUO)
LSC	Logistic Support Cost (ACAE)
LSC	London Salvage Corps
Lsc	London, Sion College (SAUO)
LSC	London Survey Committee (SAUO)
LSC	Lone Star Conference (PSS)
LSC	Loop Station Connector (MHDB)
LSC	Low-Speed Concentrator
LSC	LSI Logic Corp. of Canada, Inc. [*Toronto Stock Exchange symbol*]
LSC	Luminescent Solar Concentrator
LSC	Luminescent Stamp Club [*Defunct*] (EA)
LSC	Lump-Sum Contract
LSC	Luxury Sport Coupe
LSC	Shopco Laurel Centre (SAUO)
LSC	Shopco Laurel Centre L.P. [*AMEX symbol*] (TTSB)
LSC	Shopco Laurel Centre Ltd. [*AMEX symbol*] (SPSG)
LSC	Southern University, Law Library, Baton Rouge, LA [*OCLC symbol*] (OCLC)
LScA	Left Scapuloanterior [*A fetal position*] [*Obstetrics*]
LSCA	Left Subclavian Artery [*Anatomy*] (DAVI)
LSCA	Library Services and Construction Act [*1963*]
LSCA	Logistics Support Cost Analysis (NASA)
LScAct	Licentiate of Actuarial Science (SAUO)
LScAdmin	Licence in Administration [*Canada*] (DD)
LSCC	Lattice Semiconductor [*NASDAQ symbol*] (TTSB)
LSCC	Lattice Semiconductor Corp. [*NASDAQ symbol*] (SAG)
LSCC	Liberty Seated Collectors Club (EA)
LSCC	Library of the Supreme Court of Canada (SAUO)
LScC	Licentiate in Commercial Science (DD)
LSCC	Line-Sequential Color Composite (IEEE)
LSCC	Local Servicing Control Center [*Telecommunications*] (TEL)
LSCC	London Scottish Cadet Corps [*British military*] (DMA)
LScCom	Licentiate in Commercial Science
LScComm	Licentiate in Commercial Science (DD)
LScCompt	Licencie en Sciences Comptables [*Licentiate of Accounting*] (DD)
L Sc D	Doctor of the Science of Law
LSCD	Large Screen Color Display (ACAE)
LSCD	Leading Seaman Clearance Diver
LSCE	Launch Sequence and Control Equipment
LSCE	Least Square Complex Exponential [*Mathematics*]
LScEco	Licence in Economics [*Canada*] (DD)
LSc(Econ)	Licence in Science (Economics) [*British*] (DI)
LSCG	Law School Computer Group [*Defunct*] (EA)
LSCI	Large-Scale Compound Integration
LSCI	Lymphosarcoma Cell Leukemia [*Medicine*] (DMAA)
LSCL	Limit Switch Closed [*Electronics*] (IAA)
LSCL	Lower Surface Center Line
LSCM	LASER-Scan Confocal Microscope
LSCM	LASER Scanning Confocal Microscopy
LSCM	Logistic Support Coordination Meeting [*Military*] (MCD)
LSCo	Labor Service Company (SAUO)
LSCO	Lanthanum Strontium Copper Oxide [*Inorganic chemistry*]
LSCO	Lesco, Inc. [*NASDAQ symbol*] (SAG)
LScO	Licence in the Science of Optometry [*Canada*] (DD)
LScO	Licentiate of Optometry (SAUO)
LSCP	Laserscope [*NASDAQ symbol*] (SAG)
LSCP	Launching System Control Panel (SAUS)
LScP	Left Scapuloposterior [*A fetal position*] [*Obstetrics*]
LSCP	Logistic Support Control Point [*Military*] (AFM)
LSCP	Low-Speed Card Punch [*Computer science*] (AABC)
LSCP(Assoc)	Associate of the London and Counties Society of Physiologists [*British*] (DBQ)
LScPol	Licence en Science Politique [*French*] (CPGU)
LSCPS	Logistics Support Concept of Pre-Operational Support (ACAE)
LSCRA	Lower Saint Croix River Act of 1972 (COE)
LSCRC	Lapheld Small Computer Requirements Contract (SAUO)
LScRel	Licentiate in Religion (DD)
LSCRRC	Law Students Civil Rights Research Council (EA)
LSCRS	Law School Candidate Referral Service (SAUO)
LSCS	Lower Segment Caesarean Section [*Medicine*]
LScS	Southern University, Scotlandville, Baton Rouge, LA [*Library symbol*] [*Library of Congress*] (LCLS)
LScS-N	Southern University at New Orleans, New Orleans, LA [*Library symbol*] [*Library of Congress*] (LCLS)
LScSoc	Licence in Social Science [*British*]
LSCSS	Limited Scale Command and Control System (ACAE)
LSCT	Lamar State College of Technology (SAUO)
LSCT	LASER Spectral Control Technique
LSCT	Loevinger Sentence Completion Test (EDAC)
LSCT	Low-Speed Compound Terminal (CET)
LSCU	Local Servicing Control Unit [*Telecommunications*] (TEL)
LSCV	Left Subclavian Vein [*Anatomy*] (DAVI)
LSD	Amphibious Ship, Dock
LSD	d-Lysergic acid Diethylamine (SAUS)
LSD	Dock Landing Ship (SAUO)
LSD	Doctor of Library Science
LSD	Doctor of Life Science
LSD	Laboratory Services Division (SAUO)
LSD	Landing Ship Deck
LSD	Landing Ship, Dock [*Navy symbol*]

LSD	Landing-Site Determination [*NASA*] (KSC)
LSD	Landing, Storage, Delivery [*Business term*]
LSD	Land Surface Datum (SAUO)
LSD	Language for Systems Development
LSD	Large Scale Display (ACAE)
LSD	Large-Scale Dynamics (SAUS)
LSD	Large Screen Display
LSD	Large Shallow-Draught [*Bulk carrier*] (PDAA)
LSD	Large Steel Desk [*Position given to ex-astronauts*]
LSD	Laryngeal Sound Discrimination [*Medicine*] (DMAA)
LSD	LASER-Selective Demagnetization [*Analytical technique*]
LSD	LASER Signal Device
LSD	LASER-Supported Detonation Waves (MCD)
LSD	Lashed Secured Dunnage (RIMS)
LSD	Last Safe Date [*Marine insurance*] (DS)
LSD	Latching Semiconductor Diode
LSD	Latest Start Date
LSD	Launch Support Division [*NASA*] (KSC)
LSD	Launch Systems Data
LSD	Law Student Division [*American Bar Association*] (BARN)
LSD	Leadless Sealed Device (PDAA)
LSD	Lead Sulfide Detection
LSD	League for Spiritual Discovery (WDAA)
LSD	League of Safe Drivers [*British*] (BI)
LSD	Leased (WGA)
LSD	Least Separation Distance (MUSM)
LSD	Least Significant Decade (IAA)
LSD	Least Significant Difference [*Statistics*]
LSD	Least Significant Digit [*Data compaction*] (MUGU)
LSD	Legal Sub-division (SAUO)
LSD	Lesson Specification Document (MCD)
LSD	Level Sensor Demonstration
LSD	Lexington, KY [*Location identifier*] [*FAA*] (FAAL)
Lsd	Librae, Solidi, Denari [*Shillings and Pence*] [*British*] (WA)
LSD	Library Service to the Disadvantaged Committee
LSD	Life, Sport, and Drama [*A publication*] [*British*]
LSD	Life-Sustaining Device (MELL)
LSD	Lightermen, Stevedores, and Dockers
LSD	Light-Sensing Device (IAA)
LSD	Lime Juice, Scotch, Drambuie [*A cocktail*] (IIA)
LSD	Limited Saturation Device (PDAA)
LSD	Limited-Slip Differential [*Automotive engineering*]
LSD	Limited Space-Charge Drift [*Electronics*] (IAA)
LSD	Limitswitch Down [*Electronics*] (IAA)
LSD	Line-Sharing Device
LSD	Line Signal Detector
LSD	Linkage System Diagnostic (IAA)
LSD	Lipid Storage Disease (MELL)
LSD	Local Spin Density [*Physics*]
LSD	Logarithmic Series Distribution [*Statistics*]
LSD	Logistics Systems Division [*Air Force*]
LSD	Log-Slope Difference [*Statistics*]
LSD	Lomir Shoyn Davenen (BJA)
LSD	Long Side
LSD	Long, Slow Distance [*Training method for runners*]
LSD	Lowest Significant Dose [*Toxicology*]
LSD	Low Salt Diet (MELL)
LSD	Low-Sodium Diet (DMAA)
LSD	Low-Speed Data
LSD	Low-Sulfur Diesel Fuel [*Petroleum marketing*]
LSD	Lump-Sum Distribution [*Banking*]
LSD	Lunar Surface Drill [*Aerospace*]
LSD	Lysergic Acid Diethylamide [*or Lysergsaeure Diethylamid*] [*Hallucinogenic drug*]
LSD	Lysergide (LDT)
LSD-25	Lysergic Acid Diethylamide (STED)
LSDA	Licentiate of the Speech and Drama Association (ADA)
LSDA	Louisiana Soft Drink Association (SRA)
LSDAS	Law School Data Assembly Service (GAGS)
LSDDP	Library Service to Developmentally Disabled Persons [*ASCLA*] (AL)
LSDF	Large Sodium Disposal Facility [*Nuclear energy*] (NRCH)
LSDF	Library Service to the Deaf Forum [*Association of Specialized and Cooperative Library Agencies*]
LSDG	Latitudinal Species-Diversity Gradient [*Biodiversity*]
LSDH	Ligue Suisse des Droits de l'Homme [*Switzerland*]
LSD/H/M/T	Landing Ship, Dock/Heavy/Medium/Tank (MILB)
LSDIS	Light & Special Division Interim Sensor (SAUS)
LSDM	Lagrangian Stochastic Dispersion Model [*Marine science*] (OSRA)
LSDM	Logical Systems Design Methodology (NITA)
LSDP	Landsat Signature Development Program (SAUO)
LSDP	Lietuvos Socialdemokratu Partija [*Lithuanian Social Democratic Party*] [*Political party*] (PPE)
LSDP	Lithuanian Social Democratic Party (SAUO)
LSDP	Lump-Sum Death Payment
LSDR	Local Store Data Register
LSDRM	Logistic Support Data Responsibility Matrix (MCD)
LSDS	Large-Scale Dynamical System (PDAA)
LSDS	Large Screen Display System
LSDS	Low-Speed Data Service [*RCA Global Communications, Inc.*] [*Piscataway, NJ*] [*Telecommunications*] (TSSD)
LSDS	Low-Speed Digital System
LSDSP	Latvijas Socialdemokratiska Stradnieku Partija [*Latvian Social Democratic Workers' Party*] [*Political party*] (EAIO)
LSDT	Local Sidereal Time (MSA)
LSDU	Link Layer Service Data Unit

LSDV .... Link Segment Delay Value (SAUS)
LS/DW .... Life Safety/Disaster Warning [*Environmental science*] (COE)
LSE .... Laboratory Support Equipment (SSD)
LSE .... La Crosse [*Wisconsin*]/Winona [*Minnesota*] [*Airport symbol*] (OAG)
LSE .... Landing Ship, Emergency Repair
LSE .... Landing Signal Enlisted [*Military*]
LSE .... Land Surface Experiment (SAUO)
LSE .... Language-Sensitive Editor [*Computer science*] (CIST)
LSE .... Large-Scale Equipment (MCD)
LSE .... Laser Systems & Electronics, Inc. (SAUO)
LSE .... Latex Sphere Equivalent (AAEL)
LSE .... Lattice Screen Editor [*Program editor*]
LSE .... Launcher Servo Electronics (ACAE)
LSE .... Launch Sequencer Equipment [*NASA*]
LSE .... Launch Station Equipment
LSE .... Launch Support Equipment [*NASA*] (AAG)
LSE .... Laurence, Scott & Electromotors Ltd. (SAUO)
LSE .... Lease (ROG)
Lse. .... Lease (TBD)
LSE .... Least Squares Estimator [*Statistics*]
LSE .... Left Second Entrance [*Theater*]
LSE .... Left Sternal Edge [*Cardiology*]
LSE .... Legal Services for the Elderly (EA)
lse .... Licensee [*MARC relator code*] [*Library of Congress*] (LCCP)
LSE .... Life Science Experiment (MUGU)
LSE .... Life Support Equipment (KSC)
LSE .... Life Support Evaluator (SAA)
LSE .... Limited Signed Edition (ADA)
LSE .... Lincoln Space Experiment (CCCA)
LSE .... Linkage Stack Entry [*Computer science*] (CIST)
LSE .... Liquid-Solid Extraction [*Chemistry*]
LSE .... Live Sheep Export (SAUO)
LSE .... Living Skin Equivalent [*Synthetic organ*]
LSE .... Local Security Environment (SAUS)
LSE .... Local Services Environment (SAUO)
LSE .... Local Side Effects [*Pharmacology*] (DAVI)
LSE .... Local Subscriber Environment (SAUS)
LSE .... Logistics Support Element
LSE .... Logistics Support Equipment [*Military*] (MCD)
LSE .... London School of Economics
LSE .... London School of English (SAUO)
LSE .... London Stock Exchange
LSE .... Longitudinal-Section Electric (IEEE)
LSE .... Loose
lse .... Loose
LSE .... Louisiana Sugar Exchange (EA)
LSE .... Lower Sternal Edge [*Cardiology*]
LSE .... Low-Set Ear (MELL)
LSE .... Low-Speed Encoder (IAA)
LSE .... Low-Styrene Emission
LSE .... Low Surface Energy [*Adhesives*]
LSE .... Lunar Support Equipment [*Aerospace*] (IAA)
LSE .... Lunar Surface Experiment [*NASA*]
LSE .... Luxembourg Stock Exchange
LSE .... Luxury Sport Euro [*Automobile model designation*] [*General Motors Corp. - Cadillac*]
LSE .... Queen's Bench Library [*Alberta*] [*UTLAS symbol*]
LSEAD .... Lethal Sead (ACAE)
LSE&PS ...... London School of Economics and Political Science (SAUO)
LSE/BJS ...... British Journal of Sociology. Published quarterly for the London School of Economics and Political Sience. London (SAUS)
LSEC .... Australian Company Secretary's Practice Manual [*A publication*]
LSEC .... Life-Cycle Software Engineering Center [*Army*]
l/sec. .... Liters per Second [*Respiration*] [*Medicine*] (DAVI)
LSECS .... Life Support and Environmental Control System (IEEE)
LsEd. .... Leasing Edge Corp. [*Associated Press*] (SAG)
LSEED .... Launch Support Equipment - Engineering Division [*NASA*] (KSC)
LSEG .... Livestock Export Group (SAUO)
LSEG .... Low Styrene Emission Gelcoat
LSEGR .... Linear Solenoid Exhaust Gas Recirculation [*Automotive emissions*]
LSEIF .... Lodestar Energy, Incorporated (SAUO)
LSEL .... Link Selector (VLIE)
LSEL .... London School of Economics Library (SAUO)
LSELR .... Low-Styrene-Emission Laminating Resin
LSEOS .... Lightweight Shipboard Electro-Optical Sensor (TIMI)
LSEP .... Left Somatosensory Evoked Potential (STED)
LSEP .... Legal Service for the Elderly Poor (SAUO)
LSEP .... Legal Services for the Elderly Poor [*Later, LSE*] (EA)
LSEP .... Lifetime Sports Education Project [*of Lifetime Sports Foundation*]
LSEP .... Limited System Evaluation Program (ACAE)
LSEP .... Lunar Surface Experiment Package [*NASA*]
LSE/PS .... Population Studies. A journal of demography. London School of Economics, The Population Investigation Committee. London (SAUS)
LSEQ .... Launch Sequencer [*Navy*] (CAAL)
LSER .... Laser Corp. [*NASDAQ symbol*] (SAG)
LSER .... Linear Solvation Energy Relationship [*Physical chemistry*]
LSER .... Raron [*Switzerland*] [*ICAO location identifier*] (ICLI)
LSERA .... ERL-Duluth Financial Management Package (SAUS)
LSERB .... ERL-Duluth Personnel and Payroll (SAUS)
LSES .... Large Surface Effect Ship (PDAA)
LSES .... Life Support and Environmental System (IAA)
LSE SKDS .... Loose or on Skids [*Freight*]
LSET .... Logistics Supportability Evaluation Team [*Military*] (AFIT)
LSEU .... La Salle Extension University (SAUO)

LSEV .... Lunar Surface Exploration Vehicle [*Aerospace*]
LSEW .... Law Society of England and Wales (SAUO)
LSEZ .... Zermatt [*Switzerland*] [*ICAO location identifier*] (ICLI)
LSF .... Fort Benning (Columbus), GA [*Location identifier*] [*FAA*] (FAAL)
LSF .... Laboratory Simulation Facility (MCD)
LSF .... Lande Splitting Factor
LSF .... Landing Ship, Fighter Direction [*British military*] (DMA)
LSF .... Language System FORTRAN [*Computer science*]
LSF .... La Souterraine [*France*] [*Seismograph station code, US Geological Survey*] (SEIS)
LSF .... Last Spring Frost (QUAC)
LSF .... Launch Support Facility [*NASA*] (KSC)
LSF .... Least Square Fit
LSF .... Lesser Sciatic Foramen [*Medicine*] (MELL)
LSF .... Lightship Screen File [*Computer science*]
LSF .... Lightweight Strike Fighter [*NATO Air Forces*]
LSF .... Limit Switch Forward [*Electronics*] (IAA)
LSF .... Line Spread Function (MCD)
LSF .... Line Switch Frame [*Telecommunications*] (TEL)
LSF .... Liquid-State Submerged Fermentation [*Biochemistry*]
LSF .... Literary Society Foundation (EA)
LSF .... Lloyd Shaw Foundation (EA)
LSF .... Load Sheet Fuel [*Aviation*] (DA)
LSF .... Local Security Force (SAUO)
LSF .... Local Selling Fare [*Travel industry*] (TRID)
LSF .... Lock Security Force (SAUO)
LSF .... Logistic Support Force [*Military*]
LSF .... Loss Factor [*Electronics*] (IAA)
LSF .... Lower Side Frequency [*Electronics*] (ECII)
LSF .... Low Saturated Fat [*Diet*] (DAVI)
LSF .... Lumped Selection Filter [*Telecommunications*] (OA)
LSF .... Lunar Scientific Facility [*NASA*] (KSC)
LSF .... Lymphocyte-Stimulating Factor [*Biochemistry*]
LSFA .... Logistic System Feasibility Analysis (AABC)
LSFAE .... Low-Speed Fuel Air Explosive
LSFC .... Langley Space Flight Center (SAUO)
LSFC .... Lennon Sisters Fan Club (EA)
LSFE .... Life Sciences Flight Experiment [*NASA*] (NASA)
LSFF .... Landing Ship, Flotilla Flagship [*Navy symbol*] [*Obsolete*]
LSFFAR .... Low-Speed Folding-Fin Aircraft Rocket (SAUS)
LSFFAR .... Low-Spin Folding Fin Aircraft Rocket (IEEE)
LSFIAB .... Like Shooting Fish In A Barrel (SAUS)
lsfk- .... Falkland Islands [*MARC geographic area code*] [*Library of Congress*] (LCCP)
LSFN .... List of Selected File Numbers (AABC)
LSFO .... Logistics Support Field Office [*Federal disaster planning*]
LSFO .... Low-Sulfur Fuel Oil
LSFR .... Large-Probe Solar Net Flux Radiometer [*NASA*]
LSFR .... Launch Side Flow Review (SAUS)
LSFR .... Local Storage Function Register
LSFS .... Lateral Separation Focus Sensor (PDAA)
LSFS .... Light Sequence Flasher System (DWSG)
LSFT .... London School of Foreign Trade (SAUO)
LSFT .... Low Steamline Flow Test (IEEE)
LSG .... labial Salivary Gland [*Medicine*] (STED)
LSG .... Laminated Safety Glass [*Automotive engineering*]
LSG .... Landing Ship, Gantry
LSG .... Landing Ship, Gun [*British military*] (DMA)
LSG .... Language Structure Group [*CODASYL*]
LSG .... Large-Scale Geostrophic [*Marine science*] (OSRA)
LSG .... Lateral Superior Geniculate Artery [*Anatomy*]
LSG .... Legal Services Group
LSG .... Legislative Strategy Group [*Reagan administration*]
LSG .... Level Sensor Gradiometer
LSG .... Ligo Samseksamaj Geesperantistoj [*Richmond, Surrey, England*] (EAIO)
LSG .... Limited Subgroup (NATG)
LSG .... Little Sisters of the Gospel (France) (TOCD)
LSG .... Logistics Support Group (AAG)
LSG .... Logistic Support Group (SAUS)
LSG .... Loh's Sinfully Good Ice Cream & Cookies, Inc. [*Vancouver Stock Exchange symbol*]
LSG .... Lone Star Gas Co. (SAUO)
LSG .... Low-Stress Grinding (DICI)
LSG .... Lunar Surface Gravimeter [*Apollo*] [*NASA*]
LSGA .... Laminators Safety Glass Association (EA)
LSGA .... Los Angeles Securities Group (SAUO)
LSGC .... Les Eplatures [*Switzerland*] [*ICAO location identifier*] (ICLI)
LSGC .... London and Surrey Gliding Club (SAUO)
LSGC .... Long Service and Good Conduct (ADA)
LSGD .... Lymphocyte Specific Gravity Distribution [*Medicine*]
LSGE .... Ecuvillens [*Switzerland*] [*ICAO location identifier*] (ICLI)
LSGG .... Geneve/Cointrin [*Switzerland*] [*ICAO location identifier*] (ICLI)
LSGK .... Saanen [*Switzerland*] [*ICAO location identifier*] (ICLI)
LSGL .... Lausanne/Blecherette [*Switzerland*] [*ICAO location identifier*] (ICLI)
LSG/LSU ...... Landing Support Group/Logistics Support Unit (DNAB)
LSGN .... Neuchatel [*Switzerland*] [*ICAO location identifier*] (ICLI)
LSGP .... La Cote [*Switzerland*] [*ICAO location identifier*] (ICLI)
LSGP .... Large-Scale General Purpose
LSGP .... Lateral Simulated Ground Plane [*Aerodynamics*]
LSGR .... Loose Granular Snow [*Skiing condition*]
LSGS .... Left Stellate Ganglion Stimulation [*Physiology*]
LSGS .... Sion [*Switzerland*] [*ICAO location identifier*] (ICLI)
LsgSolu .... Leasing Solutions, Inc. [*Associated Press*] (SAG)
LSGT .... Gruyeres [*Switzerland*] [*ICAO location identifier*] (ICLI)

L Sgt	Lance Sergeant (SAUO)
L/Sgt	Lance Sergeant [British military] (DMA)
LSGT	Lasergate Systems [NASDAQ symbol] (TTSB)
LSGT	Lasergate Systems, Inc. [NASDAQ symbol] (SAG)
LSGTW	Lasergate Sys Wrrt [NASDAQ symbol] (TTSB)
LSGU	Local Spinal Glucose Utilization [Medicine]
LSH	Landing Ship, Headquarters
LSH	Landing Ship, Heavy
LSH	LaSalle Re Holdings [NYSE symbol] (SG)
LSH	Lashio [Myanmar] [Airport symbol] (OAG)
LSH	Latter-day Saints Hospital (SAUO)
LSH	Library Services to the Handicapped (SAUO)
LSH	Library Services to the Handicapped, Alberta Culture [UTLAS symbol]
LSH	Light Ship (IAA)
LSH	London School of Hygiene
LSH	Lowland-Southern Hybrid [Hemoglobin phenotype of Rana pipiens]
LSH	Low Section Height [Automotive engineering]
LSH	Loyal Suffolk Hussars [British military] (DMA)
LSH	Lutein-Stimulating Hormone [Also, ICSH, LH] [Endocrinology]
LSH	Lymphocytosis-Stimulating Hormone [Endocrinology]
LSh	Shreve Memorial and Caddo Parish Extension Library, Shreveport, LA [Library symbol] [Library of Congress] (LCLS)
LSH	Southeastern Louisiana University, Hammond, LA [OCLC symbol] (OCLC)
LSHA	Gstaad-Inn Grund [Switzerland] [ICAO location identifier] (ICLI)
LSHA	Louisiana State Horticultural Association (SAUO)
LShC	Centenary College of Louisiana, Shreveport, LA [Library symbol] [Library of Congress] (LCLS)
LSHC	Light-Saturated Hydrocarbon [Organic chemistry]
LShCa	Caddo Parish Library, Shreveport, LA [Library symbol] [Library of Congress] (LCLS)
LSHCNC	Local and Short Haul Carriers National Conference (EA)
LSHER	Load Sheet Reference (VLIE)
LSHG	Gampel [Switzerland] [ICAO location identifier] (ICLI)
LSHG	Lashing [Engineering]
LSHI	Large-Scale Hybrid Integration
LSHIP	Leadership
LSH(L)	Landing Ship, Headquarters (Large)
Lshld	Leasehold (EBF)
LSHLD	Leasehold
LSH/LSF	Landing Ship, Helicopter/Landing Ship, Fighter Direction (DNAB)
LShN	R. W. Norton Art Foundation, Shreveport, LA [Library symbol] [Library of Congress] (LCLS)
LSHQ	Landing Ship, Headquarters [British military] (DMA)
LSH(S)	Landing Ship, Headquarters (Small)
LSHS	Low Sulphur Heavy Stock (PDAA)
LSHS	Sezegnin [Switzerland] [ICAO location identifier] (ICLI)
LSHSS	Language, Speech, and Hearing Services in Schools (SAUO)
LShTE	Texas Eastern Transmission Corp., Shreveport, LA [Library symbol] [Library of Congress] (LCLS)
LSHTM	London School of Hygiene and Tropical Medicine (DAVI)
LShUG	United Gas Corp., Shreveport, LA [Library symbol] [Library of Congress] (LCLS)
LsHUP	Pennzoil United, Inc., Shreveport, LA [Library symbol] [Library of Congress] (LCLS)
LSHV	Laminated Synthetic High Voltage
LSI	Alis [Former USSR] [FAA designator] (FAAC)
LSI	Labour and Socialist International (SAUO)
LSI	Labour Supply Inspector [British]
LSI	Lake Superior & Ishpeming Railroad Co. [AAR code]
LSI	Landing Ship, Infantry [Navy symbol]
LSI	Large-Scale Integration [of circuits] [Electronics]
LSI	Largest Single Item (AFM)
LSI	LASER Surface Interaction
LSI	Lateral Shear Interferometer (PDAA)
LSI	Launch Success Indicator
LSI	Law of the Sea Institute (EA)
LSI	Law-Science Institute (SAUO)
LSI	Law Society of Ireland (SAUO)
LSI	Laws of the State of Israel (BJA)
LSI	Leadership Skills Inventory [Test] (TMMY)
LSI	Lead Systems Integration
LSI	Learning Style Inventory [Occupational therapy]
LSI	Learning Systems Institute [Florida State University] [Research center] (RCD)
LSI	Lear Siegler Inc. (NITA)
LSI	Legal Support Inspection [Clean Water Act] [Environmental Protection Agency] (EPA)
LSI	Leisure Search Inventory [Test] (TMMY)
LSI	Lerwick [Scotland] [Airport symbol] (OAG)
LSI	Leukemia Society, Incorporated (SAUO)
LSI	Life Satisfaction Index [Medicine] (DMAA)
LSI	Life Space Interviewing [Teaching technique]
LSI	Life Support International Inc. (SAUO)
LSI	Light Scatter Index
LSI	Light Scattering Index (STED)
LSI	Listing Site Inspection [Environmental science] (FFDE)
LSI	List of Serials Indexed for Online Users (SAUO)
LSI	Literacy Support Initiative (SAUO)
LSI	Little Sitkin Island [Alaska] [Seismograph station code, US Geological Survey] [Closed] (SEIS)
LSI	Logistic Supportability Index
LSI	Logistic Support Impact
LSI	LSI Logic [NYSE symbol] (TTSB)
LSI	LSI Logic Corp. [NYSE symbol] (SPSG)
LSI	Lumbar Spine Index [Medicine] (DMAA)
LSI	Lunar Science Institute [Houston]
LSI	Lunar Surface Instrument [Aerospace]
LSIA	Lamp and Shade Institute of America [Defunct] (EA)
LSIA	Licentiate of the Society of Industrial Artists [British]
LSIB	London Stage Information Bank [Lawrence University] [Information service or system] (IID)
LSIC	Large-Scale Integrated Circuit [Electronics] (KSC)
LSIC	Large-Scale Integration Computer
LSIC	Little Servant Sisters of the Immaculate Conception (TOCD)
LSIC	Lockheed System Integration Contractor (ACAE)
LSICA	Liquid and Solid Industrial Control Association (EA)
LSID	Large Scale Integration Development
LSID	Launch Sequence and Interlock Document [NASA] (NASA)
LSID	Local Session Identification [Computer science] (IBMDP)
LSID	Local Session Identifier (SAUO)
LSidFW	United States Fish and Wildlife Service, Sidell, LA [Library symbol] [Library of Congress] (LCLS)
LSIEF	Library Service to the Impaired Elderly Forum [Association of Specialized and Cooperative Library Agencies]
LSI(G)	Landing Craft, Infantry (Gunboat) [Navy symbol] [Obsolete]
LSIG	Least Significant (IAA)
LSIG	Line Scan Image Generator (OA)
LSI(H)	Landing Ship, Infantry (Hand-Hoisted Boats) [British]
LSI Ind	LSI Industries, Inc. [Associated Press] (SAG)
LSI Inds	LSI Industries, Inc. [Associated Press] (SAG)
LSIL	Land and Sea Interaction Laboratory [Environmental Science Services Administration] (NOAA)
LSI(L)	Landing Ship, Infantry (Large) [Obsolete]
LSIL	Low-Grade Squamous Intraepithelial Lesion [Medicine]
LSI Log	LSI Logic Corp. [Associated Press] (SAG)
LSI(M)	Landing Craft, Infantry (Mortar) [Navy symbol] [Obsolete]
LSI(M)	Landing Ship, Infantry (Medium) [British]
LSI-M-CAPS	Large Scale Integrated-Mobile CAPS (SAUO)
LSIMS	Liquid Secondary Ion Mass Spectrometry
LSIO	Lumbosacroiliac Orthosis [Medicine]
LSI-P	Learning Styles Inventory-Primary Version [Occupational therapy] (EDAC)
LSI(R)	Landing Craft, Infantry (Rocket) [Navy symbol] [Obsolete]
LSIR	Limb-Scanning Infrared Radiometer
LSIR	Low-Ship Impact Ranging [Navy] (CAAL)
LSI(S)	Landing Ship, Infantry (Small)
LSIS	Large-Scale Information System (SAUO)
LSIS	LASER Scan Inspection System (PDAA)
LSIS	LASER Shutterable Image Sensor
LSIS	League of Shut-In Sodalists (EA)
LSIS	Learning Style Identification Scale [Educational test]
LSIT	Land Securities Investment Trust (SAUO)
LSIT	Large-Scale Integration Technology (IAA)
LSIT	Linear Strip Ion Thruster
LSITT	Let's Stick It to Them [Acronym used as book title]
LSITV	Liquid Secondary Injection Thrust Vector Control (PDAA)
LSJ	La Societe Jersiaise (EAIO)
LSJ	Liddell and Scott [Greek-English Lexicon, 9th ed., revised by H. Stuart Jones] [A publication] (OCD)
LSJ	Little Sisters of Jesus [See also PSJ] [Italy] (EAIO)
LSJ	London School of Journalism (SAUO)
LSJM	Laus Sit Jesu et Mariae [Praise Be to Jesus and Mary] [Latin]
LSJM	Little Sisters of Jesus and Mary (TOCD)
LSK	Law Society of Kenya (SAUO)
LSK	Leucosulfakinin [Biochemistry]
LSK	Liquid Sample Kit
LSK	Liuski International [NASDAQ symbol] (TTSB)
LSK	Liver, Spleen, Kidney [Medicine]
LSK	Lusk, WY [Location identifier] [FAA] (FAAL)
LSKI	Liuski International, Inc. [NASDAQ symbol] (SAG)
LSKM	Liver-Spleen-Kidney Megaly [Medicine]
LSL	Ladder Static Logic
LSL	Landing Ship, Logistic [British]
LSL	Language Studies Limited London (SAUO)
LSL	Lateral Superlattice [Physics]
LSL	Left Sacrolateral [A fetal position] [Obstetrics]
LSL	Left Short Leg (MELL)
LSL	Life Sciences Laboratory (AAG)
LSL	Link and Selector Language
LSL	Link Support Layer
LSL	Linnaean Society of London
LSL	Litton Systems Ltd. (MCD)
LSL	Load Segment Limit (VLIE)
LSL	Location Systems List (VLIE)
LSL	Logical Shift Left [Computer science]
LSL	Logistics Spares List (KSC)
LSL	Logistics Systems Laboratory
LSL	Long Service Leave (ADA)
LSL	Los Chiles [Costa Rica] [Airport symbol] (OAG)
LSL	Louisiana State Library, Baton Rouge, LA [OCLC symbol] (OCLC)
LSL	Lower Specification Limit (SAUO)
LSL	Lower Specified Limit
LSL	Low Sight Lobe
LSL	Low-Speed Logic (IAA)
LSL	Lucy Stone League (SAUO)
LSL	Lump Sum Leave (COE)
LSL	Lump-Sum Leave Payment [Military] (DNAB)
LSL	Lymphosarcoma Leukemia [Medicine] (MELL)

LSL A............	Chemical Storage and Transfer Facility (SAUS)
LSLA............	Lincoln Savings & Loan Association (SAUO)
LSLA............	Low Speed Line Adaptor (NITA)
LSLAB..........	Life Sciences Laboratory (SAUO)
LSLB............	Land Surveyors' Licensing Board [Western Australia]
LSLB............	Left Short Leg Brace [Medicine]
LSLBP..........	Lump-Sum Leave Payment, Basic Pay [Military] (DNAB)
LSLC............	Loop Side Lobe Canceler (ACAE)
LSLDP	Lietuvos Socialistu Liaudininkai Demokratu Partija [Socialist Populists Democratic Party of Lithuania] [Political party] (PPE)
LSLE............	Life Sciences Laboratory Experiment (SAUO)
LSLI............	Large-Scale Linear Integration (IAA)
LSLM..........	Low Speed Line Manager [Computer science] (VLIE)
LSLP...........	Lietuvos Socialistu Liaudininkai Partija [Socialist Populists Party of Lithuania] [Political party] (PPE)
LSLP...........	Lump-Sum Leave Payment [Air Force] (AFM)
LSL PMA	Lump-Sum Leave Payment, Personal Money Allowance [Military] (DNAB)
LSL QTRS....	Lump-Sum Leave Payment, Quarters [Military] (DNAB)
LSL SUBS....	Lump-Sum Leave Payment, Subsistence [Military] (DNAB)
LSLT............	League to Save Lake Tahoe (EA)
LSM............	Laboratory for the Structure of Matter [Navy] (PDAA)
LSM............	Lakeside & Marblehead R. R. [AAR code]
LSM............	Lancastrian School of Management (SAUO)
LSM............	Landing Ship Mechanized (CCCA)
LSM............	Landing Ship, Medium [Navy symbol]
LSM............	Large Solid Motor [Aerospace]
LSM............	LASER Scanning Microscope
LSM............	LASER Slicing Machine
LSM............	Late Systolic Murmur (MAE)
LSM............	Launcher Status Multiplexer (MSA)
LSM............	Launching System Module
LSM............	Launch Site Maintenance [NASA] (IAA)
LSM............	LAWS Simulation Model (SAUO)
LSM............	Layered Synthetic Microstructure [For optical instruments]
LSM............	Learning Subspace Method (IDAI)
LSM............	Learning Systems Model (EDAC)
LSM............	Least Square Mean [Mathematical statistics]
LSM............	Legal Services Manager (SAUO)
LSM............	Letter Sorting Machine [US Postal Service]
LSM............	Liberation Support Movement Information Center (EA)
LSM............	Life Science Module [NASA] (NASA)
LSM............	Linear Select Memory
LSM............	Linear Sequential Machine
LSM............	Linear Shock Machine
LSM............	Linear Synchronous Motor (IAA)
LSM............	Line-Scanning Mode [Microscopy]
LSM............	Line Selection Module [Telecommunications] (TEL)
LSM............	Line Select Module (NITA)
LSM............	Line Switch Module [Computer science] (CIST)
LSM............	Litera Scripta Manet [The Written Word Remains] [Latin] (ADA)
LSM............	Little Skull Mountain [Nevada] [Seismograph station code, US Geological Survey] (SEIS)
LSM............	Local Service for Mobiles [Computer science]
LSM............	Logical Storage Manager (SAUS)
LSM............	Logic Selection Module (VLIE)
LSM............	Logistics Support Manager (SAUO)
LSM............	Logistic Support Manager
LSM............	Longitudinal Section Magnetic [Electronics] (OA)
LSM............	Long Semado [Malaysia] [Airport symbol] (OAG)
LSM............	Loop Sampling Module
LSM............	Louisiana State Library, Processing Center, Baton Rouge, LA [OCLC symbol] (OCLC)
LSM............	Low-Speed MODEM (IAA)
LSM............	Low-Sulfate Medium [Microbiology]
LSM............	Lunar Surface Magnetometer [NASA]
LSM............	Lymphocyte Separation Medium [Medicine]
LSM............	Lysergic Acid Morpholide
LSM............	Master of Life Science
LSMA..........	Low-Speed Multiplexer Arrangement
LSMC..........	Launching System Module Console [Navy] (CAAL)
LSMC..........	Logistics Specialty Management Committee (SAUO)
LSMD..........	Dubendorf [Switzerland] [ICAO location identifier] (ICLI)
LSMDC........	Labor Service Medical Depot Company (SAUO)
LSME..........	Emmen [Switzerland] [ICAO location identifier] (ICLI)
LSME..........	Logistic Support Maintenance Equipment (MCD)
LSME..........	London Society of Music Engravers [British] (DGA)
LS/MFT........	Lucky Strike Means Fine Tobacco [Advertising slogan]
LSMHT........	List of Standard/Modified Hand Tools (MCD)
LSMI...........	Lake Superior Mining Institute (SAUO)
LSMI...........	Loadmaster Systems, Incorporated (SAUO)
LSMI...........	Logistics Support Management Information [NASA] (NASA)
LSMIS.........	Logistics Support Management Information System (SAUO)
LSMITH.......	Locksmith
LSMLC........	Low-Speed Multiline Controller (MHDB)
L/Smn.........	Leading Seaman [Navy] [British] (DMA)
LSMO..........	Local Sample Management Office (SAUO)
LSMP..........	Logistics Support and Mobilization Plan (SAUO)
LSMP..........	Logistics Systems Modernization Program (SAUO)
LSMP..........	Logistic Support and Mobilization Plan [Military] (NVT)
LSMP..........	Payerne [Switzerland] [ICAO location identifier] (ICLI)
LSM(R)........	Landing Ship, Medium (Rocket) [Later, LFR] [Navy symbol]
LSMR..........	Rocket Ship [Navy symbol]
LSMS..........	Living Standards Management Study [International Monetary Fund]
LSMS..........	Louisiana State Medical Society (SRA)
LSMSC........	Lake Superior Mines Safety Council (SAUO)
LSMSO	Landing Ship, Material Supply Officer
LSMT..........	Landing Ship Marshalling Team (SAUO)
LSMT..........	Land Site Marshalling Team [Military]
LSMTP........	ListServ Simple Mail Transport Protocol [L-Soft International, Inc.] [Computer science]
LSMU..........	LASERcom Space Measurement Unit (IEEE)
LSM-USA.....	Lutheran Student Movement - USA (EA)
LSMV..........	Lettuce Speckles Mottle Virus [Plant pathology]
LSMW..........	London School of Medicine for Women (ROG)
LSN............	Large Scale Networking Committee (SAUO)
LSN............	Leasing Solutions [NYSE symbol] (SG)
LSN............	Left Substantia Nigra (DB)
LSN............	Lesser Sciatic Notch [Medicine] (MELL)
LSN............	Life Services Network of Illinois (SRA)
LSN............	Linear Sequential Network (MUGU)
LSN............	Line Stabilization Network
LSN............	Listen [Amateur radio shorthand] (WDAA)
LSN............	Load Sharing Network
LSN............	Local Stock Number
LSN............	Logical Session Number (VLIE)
LSN............	Los Banos, CA [Location identifier] [FAA] (FAAL)
LSNA	Louisiana State Nurses Association (SAUO)
LSNB	Lake Shore Bancorp (EFIS)
LSND	Liquid Scintillator Neutrino Detector [Physics]
LSNLIS	Lunar Science Natural Language Information System (PDAA)
LSNR	League of Struggle for Negro Rights (SAUO)
LSNSR	Line of Bearing Sensor
LSNSW	Law Society of New South Wales [Australia]
LSNT..........	Law Society of the Northern Territory [Australia]
LSNY	Linnaean Society of New York (EA)
LSNY	Linnean Society of New York (SAUO)
LSO............	Aerolineas del Sol, SA de CV [Mexico] [FAA designator] (FAAC)
LSO............	Kelso, WA [Location identifier] [FAA] (FAAL)
LSO............	Labour Supply Organization (SAUO)
LSO............	Landing Safety Officer (MCD)
LSO............	Landing Signal Officer
LSO............	Landing Support Officer [Navy]
LSO............	Land Surveyors Online (SAUO)
LSO............	Large Solar Observatory [NASA]
LSO............	LASER Safety Officer (COE)
LSO............	LASMO pic ADS [NYSE symbol] (TTSB)
LSO............	Lasmo PLC [NYSE symbol] (SAG)
LSO............	Last Standing Order
LSO............	Lateral Superior Olive [Brain anatomy]
LSO............	Launch/Safety Officer [NASA]
LSO............	Law Schools On-Line (AAGC)
LSO............	Left Salpingo-Oophorectomy [Gynecology] (CPH)
LSO............	Leningrad Symphony Orchestra (SAUO)
LSO............	Lesotho [ANSI three-letter standard code] (CNC)
LSO............	Licensed Science Officer (SAUO)
lso	Licensor [MARC relator code] [Library of Congress] (LCCP)
LSO............	Life Systems Officer [NASA] (KSC)
LSO............	Limited Strategic Option (SAUO)
LSO............	Line Stabilized Oscillator
LSO............	Linseed Oil (PDAA)
LSO............	Linux Standards Organization (SAUO)
LSO............	Local Central Office [Telecommunications] (ITD)
LSO............	Local Service Office (SAUO)
LSO............	Logistics Studies Office [Army] (RDA)
LSO............	London String Orchestra (SAUO)
LSO............	London Symphony Orchestra
LSO............	Lost Lake Resources Ltd. [Vancouver Stock Exchange symbol]
LSO............	Louisiana Southern Railway Co. [AAR code]
LSO............	Lumbosacral Orthosis [Medicine]
LSO............	Lutetium, Silicon, and Oxygen [Inorganic chemistry]
LSOA	Longitudinal Study of Aging (SAUO)
LSOA	Longitudinal Study of the Aging [Department of Health and Human Services] (GFGA)
LSOAD........	Life Sciences Organizations and Agencies Directory [A publication]
LSOC	Launch Support Operations Contractor (SSD)
LSOC	Lockheed Space Operations Co.
LSOC	Logistical Support Operations Center [Army]
LSOCE	Linear Stochastic Optimal Control and Estimation [Computer program]
LSOMT........	Large-Scale Operations Management Test (RDA)
LSON	Lason, Inc. [NASDAQ symbol] (SG)
LSOP	Limit Switch Open [Electronics] (IAA)
LSOP	L-Serine-O-Phosphate [Biochemistry]
LSOP	Lunar Surface Operations Planning [NASA] (KSC)
LSOPrA........	LASMO plc Sr'A'Pref ADS [NYSE symbol] (TTSB)
LSOT..........	Landing Signal Officer Trainer [Navy]
LSOV	Linguistic Survey of the Ottawa Valley [Carleton University] [Canada] [Research center] (RCD)
LSP............	Laboratory Standards Project (SAUO)
LSP............	Laboratory Suggestion Program (SAUO)
LSP............	Laminar Soot Processes (SAUS)
LSP............	Landing Ship Personnel [British military] (DMA)
LSP............	Land Surface Parameterization (SAUO)
LSP............	Land Surface Parmeterization [Environmental science]
LSP............	Las Mesas [Puerto Rico] [Seismograph station code, US Geological Survey] (SEIS)
LSP............	Las Piedras [Venezuela] [Airport symbol] (OAG)
LSP............	Launcher Status Panel (MCD)
LSP............	Launch Sequence Plan [NASA] (IAA)

LSP	Learning Skills Profile [*Test*] (TMMY)
LSP	Least Significant Portion (MCD)
LSP	Least Significant Position (CMD)
LSP	Left Sacroposterior [*Medicine*] (MELL)
LSp	Left Span (MAE)
LSP	Less Sensitive Person (SAUS)
LSP	Level Set Point (NRCH)
LSP	Levitated Spherator (PDAA)
LSP	Liberale Staatspartij [*Liberal State Party*] [*Netherlands*] [*Political party*] (PPE)
LSP	Liberal Socialist Party [*Egypt*] [*Political party*] (PPW)
LSp	Liberal State Party (SAUO)
LSP	Library Software Package (ADA)
LSp	Life Span
LSP	Life Support Package [*Diving apparatus*]
LSP	Light Scattering Photometer
LSP	Lincoln Society of Philately [*Defunct*] (EA)
LSP	Linear Selenium Photocell
LSP	Line Spectrum Pair (IAA)
LSP	Line Synchronizing Pulse
LSP	Linked Systems Project [*of the Library of Congress*]
LSP	Linked Systems Protocol [*Computer science*] (TNIG)
LSP	Link State Packet [*Telecommunications*]
lsp	Liters per Second per Person (ECON)
LSP	Little Sisters of the Poor [*Roman Catholic religious order*]
LSP	Liver-Specific [*Membrane*] Lipoprotein (DAVI)
LSP	Liver-Specific Protein
LSP	LM [*Lunar Module*] Specification [*NASA*] (KSC)
LSP	Loan Service Personnel (SAUS)
LSP	Local Service Provider (SAUO)
LSP	Local Store Pointer
LSP	Logical Signal Processor (IAA)
LSP	Logistics Support Plan
LSP	Logistics Support Priorities (SAUO)
LSP	Loop Splice Plate (ELAL)
LSP	Lot Sensitive Plan (PDAA)
LSP	Lower Sequential Permissive (NRCH)
LSP	Lower Solution Point
LSP	Low-Salinity Plume [*Oceanography*]
LSP	Low-Speed Printer
LSP	Low Support Program (OICC)
LSP	Lucas-Sargent Proposition [*Economics*]
LSP	Lumbar Spine [*Medicine*] (DHSM)
LSP	Lumbosacral Plexus [*Medicine*] (MELL)
LSP	Lunar Spectral Photometrics [*Aerospace*]
LSP	Lunar Surface Probe [*Aerospace*]
LSP	Lunar Survey Probe [*NASA*] (IAA)
LSPA	Amlikon [*Switzerland*] [*ICAO location identifier*] (ICLI)
LSPA	Learning System Pilot Aiding programme (SAUS)
LSPA	Lithuanian State Privatisation Agency
LSPAFRO	Lump-Sum Payment to Air Force Reserve Officers
LSPBP	Large-Solid Propellant Booster Program [*Aerospace*] (IAA)
LSPBV	Load-Sensing Proportioning and Bypass Valve
LSPC	Legal Services for Prisoners with Children (EA)
LSPC	Lewis Space Flight Center (MCD)
LSPC	Linear Selenium Photocell
LSPC	Living Stream Prayer Circle (EA)
LSPC	Logistics Systems Policy Committee [*Navy*]
LSPC	Louisiana Sweet Potato Commission
LSPCC	Logistics Support Planning and Control Center (ACAE)
LSPCJ	London Society for Promoting Christianity amongst the Jews (SAUO)
LSPD	Dittingen [*Switzerland*] [*ICAO location identifier*] (ICLI)
LSPD	Large Screen Plasma Display (SAUS)
LSPD	Low Speed (VLIE)
LSPDF	Life Science Payloads Development Facility (MCD)
LSPDS	Lunar Survey Probe Delivery System [*NASA*] (SAA)
LSPE	Lunar Seismic Profiling Experiment [*NASA*]
LSPES	Logistics System Planning and Execution System (SAUO)
LSPET	Lunar Sample Preliminary Examination Team [*NASA*]
LSPF	Least Square Polynomial Fit (IAA)
LSPF	Library Service to Prisoners Forum [*Association of Specialized and Cooperative Library Agencies*]
LSPF	Schaffhausen [*Switzerland*] [*ICAO location identifier*] (ICLI)
LSPG	Linnean Society Palynology Specialist Group (SAUO)
LSPGA	London School of Printing and Graphic Arts (SAUO)
LSPH	Leningrad Special Psychiatric Hospital [*Formerly, LPPH*]
LSPH	Winterthur [*Switzerland*] [*ICAO location identifier*] (ICLI)
LSPI	Laboratory Service Process Instructors (ACAE)
L-spine	Lumbar Spine [*Medicine*] (AMHC)
LSPK	Hasenstrick [*Switzerland*] [*ICAO location identifier*] (ICLI)
LSPK	Loudspeaker (TEL)
LSPL	Langenthal [*Switzerland*] [*ICAO location identifier*] (ICLI)
LSPN	Lightspan Partnership [*NASDAQ symbol*] (SG)
LSPN	Triengen [*Switzerland*] [*ICAO location identifier*] (ICLI)
LSPO	Lunar Surface Project Office [*NASA*] (KSC)
LSPOJC	La Salle-Peru-Oglesby Junior College (SAUO)
LSPP	Step-by-Step Precedents and Procedures. Companies, Trusts, Superannuation Funds [*Australia*] [*A publication*]
LSPPO	Lead Screw Position Pick-Off
LSPPS	Logistic Support Plan for Preoperational Support (MCD)
LSPR	Library Society of Puerto Rico (SAUO)
LSPR	Logistics Support Property Representative (ACAE)
LSPR	Low-Speed Pulse Restorer (MCD)
LSPS	Limited Serial Project Slip
LSPS	Local Service Planning System [*Telecommunications*] (TEL)
LSPS	Logistic Support Plan Summary
LSPS	Louisiana Society of Professional Surveyors (SAUO)
LSPSD	Low-Speed Packet Switched Data [*Computer science*] (ACRL)
LSPT	Launch Site Performance Test (ACAE)
LSPT	Limited Scope Performance Test [*Environmental science*] (COE)
LSPT	Logistics Support Planning Team (ACAE)
LSPT	London School of Polymer Technology [*British*] (AIE)
LSPTP	Low-Speed Paper Tape Punch [*Telecommunications*] (AABC)
LSPTR	Low-Speed Paper Tape Reader [*Telecommunications*] (TEL)
LSPUD	Lietuvos Socialdemokratu Partijos Uzsienio Delegatura [*Lithuanian Social Democratic Party*] (EAIO)
LSPV	Wangen-Lachen [*Switzerland*] [*ICAO location identifier*] (ICLI)
LSPVPD	Library Service to People with Visual or Physical Disabilities Forum [*Association of Specialized and Cooperative Library Agencies*] [*American Library Association*]
LSPVPDF	Library Service to People with Visual or Physical Disabilities Forum [*ASCLA*] (AL)
LSPZ	Luzern-Beromunster [*Switzerland*] [*ICAO location identifier*] (ICLI)
LSQ	Line Squall [*ICAO*] (FAAC)
LSQ	L'Octogone, Bibliotheque Municipale de LaSalle, Quebec [*UTLAS symbol*]
LSQ	Newark, NJ [*Location identifier*] [*FAA*] (FAAL)
LSQA	Local System Queue Area [*Computer science*] (BUR)
LSQCP	Logistic System Quality Control Program [*Military*] (AFIT)
LSR	Alsair Societe [*France*] [*ICAO designator*] (FAAC)
LSR	Laboratory for Space Research [*Netherlands*]
LSR	Laboratory Standards and Reference (SAUO)
LSR	Landing Ship, Rocket (NATG)
LSR	Land Sea Rescue (NASA)
LSR	Land Speed Record [*Auto racing*]
LSR	Lanthanide Shift Reagent [*Spectroscopy*]
LSR	Large Ship Reactor
lsr	Laser (VRA)
LSR	Laser
LSR	Laser Technology [*AMEX symbol*] (TTSB)
LSR	Laser Technology, Inc. [*AMEX symbol*] (SPSG)
LSR	Last Speed Rating [*of a horse*]
LSR	Launch Signal Responder (AAG)
LSR	Launch Site Recovery [*NASA*] (KSC)
LSR	Launch Support Requirement [*NASA*] (KSC)
LSR	Launch Support Room (SAUS)
LSR	League for Socialist Reconstruction [*Later, IUP*] (EA)
LSR	Lecithin/Sphingomyelin Ratio [*Medicine*] (DMAA)
LSR	Left Superior Rectus [*Muscle*] [*Medicine*] (DMAA)
LSR	Life Science Research Ltd. [*British*] (IRUK)
LSR	Lighthouse Resources, Inc. [*Vancouver Stock Exchange symbol*]
LSR	Light-Scattering Response [*Biology*]
LSR	Light-Sensitive Relay
LSR	Light-Sensitive Resistor
LSR	Light Stopping Reticle
LSR	Light, Straight Run [*Petroleum technology*]
LSR	Limited Style Run
LSR	Limited to Searches (MCD)
LSR	Limit Switch Reverse [*Electronics*] (IAA)
LSR	LINAC Stretcher Ring [*Design for an electron accelerator*]
LSR	Linear Seal Ring
LSR	Linear Sedimentation Rate [*Geology*]
LSR	Line Source Range (IAA)
LSR	Lingual Skills Required [*Civil service*]
LSR	Liquid Slip Ring
LSR	Liver/Spleen Ratio [*Medicine*] (DMAA)
LSR	Load Shifting Resistor (MSA)
LSR	Load Storage Register
LSR	Local Shared Resources [*Computer science*] (IBMDP)
LSR	Local Standard of Rest [*Galactic science*]
LSR	Local Storage Register (NITA)
LSR	Local Sunrise
LSR	Location Stack Register
LSR	Locus Standi Reports [*A publication*] (DLA)
LSR	Logical Shift Right [*Computer science*]
LSR	Logistics Service Representatives (ACAE)
LSR	Logistics Support Requirements (NG)
LSR	Logistic Status Review
LSR	Loop Shorting Relay (MCD)
LSR	Loose Snow on Runway [*NWS*] (FAAC)
LSR	Lost River, AK [*Location identifier*] [*FAA*] (FAAL)
LSR	Lovers of the Stinking Rose (EA)
LSR	Low-Speed Reader
LSR	Low Stocking Rate [*Agriculture*] (OA)
LSR	Luftschutzraum [*Air-Raid Shelter*] [*German military - World War II*]
LSR	Lunar Surface Rendezvous [*NASA*] (KSC)
LSR	Lynchburg Source Reactor
LSR.WS	Laser Technology Wrrt [*AMEX symbol*] (TTSB)
LSRA	Logistic Support Requirement Analysis (MCD)
L/S ratio	Lecithin/Sphingomyelin Ratio (ADWA)
LSRB	Linear Sound Ranging Base (PDAA)
LSRC	Land Settlement Research Centre (SAUO)
LSRC	Launch Site Recovery Commander [*NASA*] (KSC)
LSRC	Logistics Systems Review Committee [*DARCOM*] (MCD)
LSRC	Lunar Surface Return Container [*NASA*] (KSC)
LSRD	Launch Site Requirements Document (ACAE)
LSRD	Logistic Support Readiness Date
LSRE	Leisure
LSREF	LaSalle Re Holdings Ltd. [*NASDAQ symbol*] (SAG)
LSREF	LaSall Re Holdings [*NASDAQ symbol*] (TTSB)

LSRF	LASER Submarine Range-Finder
LSRF	Life Sciences Research Facility (SAUO)
LSRF	Logistic Support Resource Funds [Army]
LSRgt	Lake Superior Regiment (SAUO)
LSRI	Large Screen RADAR Indicator
LSRI	Lumbosacral Root Injury (MELL)
LSRL	Ley de Sociedades de Responsabilidad Limitada (SAUO)
LSRM	Life Science Research Module (MCD)
LSRO	Life Sciences Research Office [NASA] (KSC)
LSRP	Local Switching Replacement Planning [Telecommunications] (TEL)
LSR-P	Loose Snow on Runway-Patchy [Aviation] (DNAB)
LSRRTI	Leningrad Scientific Research Radio Technical Institute (SAUO)
LSRS	LOAD [Low Altitude Defense] System Requirements Simulation
LsrSght	Laser Sight, Inc. [Associated Press] (SAG)
LsrTc	Laser Technology, Inc. [Associated Press] (SAG)
LsrTech	Laser Technology, Inc. [Associated Press] (SAG)
LsrV	Laser Video Network, Inc. [Associated Press] (SAG)
LSRV	London and Scottish Rifle Volunteers [Military] [British] (ROG)
LSRV	Lunar Surface Roving Vehicle [Aerospace]
LsrVd	Laser Video Network, Inc. [Associated Press] (SAG)
LsrVide	Laser Video Network, Inc. [Associated Press] (SAG)
LsrVis	Laser Vision Centers, Inc. [Associated Press] (SAG)
LsrVs	Laser Vision Centers, Inc. [Associated Press] (SAG)
LSS	Exec Express II, Inc. [ICAO designator] (FAAC)
LSS	Laboratory for Surface Studies [University of Wisconsin, Milwaukee] [Research center] (RCD)
LSS	Laboratory Support Service
LSS	Ladies Shoemakers' Society [A union] [British]
LSS	Landing, Separation Simulator (MCD)
LSS	Landing Ship Sternchute [British military] (DMA)
LSS	Landing Ship, Support (NATG)
LSS	Landing-Site Supervisor
LSS	Lane Sensing System [Automotive engineering]
LSS	Language for Symbolic Simulation
LSS	Language Support System (IAA)
LSS	Laparoscopic Surgery (MELL)
LSS	Large-Scale Standard (IAA)
LSS	Large-Scale Structure [Cosmology]
LSS	Large Space Structure (IEEE)
LSS	Large Space Structures (SAUS)
LSS	Large Space System (IEEE)
LSS	Laser Sizing Study (ACAE)
LSS	Lateral Series Servo (MCD)
LSS	Lateral Spinal Stenosis [Medicine] (MELL)
LSS	Launcher Support Structure [Navy] (CAAL)
LSS	Launch Sequence Simulator
LSS	Launch Signature Simulator (MCD)
LSS	Launch Status Summarizer
LSS	Launch Support Section [NASA]
LSS	Launch Support Services (SAUS)
LSS	Launch Support System [NASA] (KSC)
LSS	Law Society of Scotland
LSS	Leipziger Semitische Studien [A publication] (BJA)
LSS	Leopold Stokowski Society (EA)
LSS	Les Saintes [Guadeloupe] [Airport symbol] (OAG)
LSS	Licensing Support System [Department of Energy] (EGAO)
LSS	Licentiate of Sacred Scripture (SAUO)
LSS	Life Saving Service (WDAA)
LSS	Life-Saving Service (SAUO)
LSS	Lifesaving Station [Nautical charts]
LSS	Life Services System [For the disabled]
LSS	Life-Span Study [Environmental science] (FFDE)
LSS	Life Support Subsystem (SAUS)
LSS	Life Support System [or Subsystem]
LSS	Lightning Sensor System (ACAE)
LSS	Lightning Surge Simulator
LSS	Light Spot Scanner
LSS	Limb-Salvage Surgery (MELL)
LSS	Limited Storage Site (AABC)
LSS	Line Scanner System
LSS	Linking Segment Subprogram
LSS	Liquid Scintillation Spectrometer
LSS	Literature Search System (SAUO)
LSS	Liver-Spleen Scan [Medicine] (MEDA)
LSS	Living Situations Survey (SAUO)
LSS	Load Sensing Signal [Hydraulics]
LSS	Load Sensing System (SAUS)
LSS	Local School System (SAUO)
LSS	Local Subscriber Switch (CCCA)
LSS	Local Synchronization Subsystem [Telecommunications] (TEL)
LSS	Lockheed Space Systems (SAUO)
LSS	Logistics Support Station (SAUO)
LSS	Logistic Support Squadron (AAG)
LSS	Logistic Support System (AABC)
LSS	Longitudinal Static Stability
LSS	Loop Surge Suppresser (ELAL)
LSS	Loop Switching System [Telecommunications]
LSS	LOT [Limited Operational Test] Support Services [Military] (DWSG)
LSS	Lumbar Spinal Stenosis [Medicine] (MELL)
LSS	Lumbosacral Spine [Medicine] (MEDA)
LSS	Lunar Soil Stimulant [NASA] (KSC)
LSS	Lunar Surveying System [Aerospace]
LSS	Lunar Survey Sensor [NASA] (KSC)
LSS	Lung Serum Simulant (PDAA)
LSS	Lutheran Social Service System [An association]
LSSA	Law Society of South Australia
LSSA	Leopold Stokowski Society of America (EA)
LSSA	Limnological Society of Southern Africa (SAUO)
LSSA	Lipid Soluble Secondary Antioxidants [Biochemistry]
LSSA	Lithuanian Student Scout Association [Later, Lithuanian Scouts Association College Division] (EA)
LSSA	Logistic System Support Activity [Army]
LSSA	Logistic System Support Agency
LSSA	London Subterranean Survey Association (SAUO)
LSSAS	Longitudinal Static Stability Augmentation System (MCD)
LSSB	Bern Radio [Switzerland] [ICAO location identifier] (ICLI)
LSSB	Lake Sunapee Savings Bank (SAUO)
LSSB	Legal Support Services Branch [General Accounting Office] [Information service or system] (IID)
LSSB	Light SEAL [Sea, Air, and Land] Support Boat [Navy] (DNAB)
LSSC	Lake Superior State College [Sault Ste. Marie, MI]
LSSC	Launch Support Services Contracts (SAUO)
LSSc	Licentiate in Sacred Scriptures
LSSC	Licentiate in Sanitary Science [British] (ROG)
LSSC	Light SEAL [Sea, Air, and Land] Support Craft [Navy symbol]
LSSC	Logistic Support System Characteristics (AAG)
LSSC	Logistic System Support Center [Army]
LSSC	Lower-Sideband Suppressed Carrier (IDOE)
LSSCV	Large Scale Structure Control Verification (SAUS)
LSSD	Level Sensitive Scan Design (MCD)
LSSD	Level-Sensitive Scan Detector (CIST)
LSSD	Lower-Speed Service-Deriving [Telecommunications] (TSSD)
LSSD	Lunar Surface Sampling Device [Aerospace]
LSSDDPMAG	Library Service to Developmentally Disabled Persons Membership Activity Group [Association of Specialized and Cooperative Library Agencies] [American Library Association]
LSSDPF	Library Service to the Developmentally Disabled Persons Forum [Association of Specialized and Cooperative Library Agencies] [American Library Association]
LSSE	Launch Site Support Engineer (SAUO)
LSSE	Licentiate in Social, Economic, & Political Sciences (DD)
LSSF	Land Special Security Force [Army] (AABC)
LSSF	Life Sciences Support Facility [NASA] (NASA)
LSSF	Limited Service Storage Facility
LSSG	Logistics Studies Steering Group (AABC)
LSSG	Logistics Studies Support Group (SAUO)
LSSGR	Local Switching System General Requirement [Telecommunications]
LSSI	Leasing Solutions [NASDAQ symbol] (TTSB)
LSSI	Leasing Solutions, Inc. [NASDAQ symbol] (SAG)
LSSI	Library Systems and Services, Inc. [Information service or system] (IID)
LSSI	Lockheed Support Systems Inc. (SAUS)
LSSL	Landing Ship Support, Large [Military] (VNW)
LSSL	Life Sciences Space Laboratory [NASA]
LSSL	Support Landing Ship (Large) MK III
LSSM	Launch Site Support Manager [NASA] (NASA)
LSSM	Local Scientific Survey Module [NASA]
LSSM	Lunar Surface Scientific Module [NASA]
LSSO	Bern. Office Federal de l'Air [Switzerland] [ICAO location identifier] (ICLI)
LSSO	Launch Site System Operations (ACAE)
LSSO	Library Science Student Organization
LSSP	Lanka Sama Samaja Party [Sri Lanka Equal Society Party] [Political party] (PPW)
LSSP	Latest Scram Set Point (NRCH)
LSSP	Launch Site Support Plan (MCD)
LSSP	Lunar Surveying System Program [Aerospace]
LSSPO	Life Support Systems Project Office [NASA] (MCD)
LSSPS	Libraries Serving Special Populations Section [Association of Specialized and Cooperative Library Agencies]
LSSPSC	Life Sciences Strategic Planning Study Committee [NASA]
LSSR	Amphibious Coastal Reconnaissance Ship [Navy symbol]
LSSR	Berne/Radio Suisse SA [Switzerland] [ICAO location identifier] (ICLI)
LSSR	Lessor
LSSRC	Life Sciences Shuttle Research Centrifuge [NASA] (NASA)
LSSS	Geneve [Switzerland] [ICAO location identifier] (ICLI)
LSSS	LASER Source Signature Simulator
LSSS	Lightweight SHF SATCOM System (SAUO)
LSSS	Lightweight Ship SATCOM Set [Navy] (CAAL)
LSSS	Lime-Sulphur-Synthetic-Solution [Hydrometallurgy]
LSSS	Limiting Safety System Setting [Nuclear energy] (NRCH)
LSSS	London School of Slavonic Studies (SAUO)
LSST	Laser Spot Seeker/Tracker (SAUS)
LSST	Launch Site Support Team (MCD)
lsst	Lead-Sheathed Steel-Taped
LS/ST	Light Shield/Star Tracker (NASA)
LSST	List of Specifications and Standards (MSA)
LSST	Lone Star Technologies [NASDAQ symbol] (SAG)
LSST	Lone Star Technologies, Inc. (SAUO)
LSSTA	Low Supersonic Transport (PDAA)
LSSTA	Lunar Space Tug (PDAA)
LSSU	Lake Superior State University [Michigan]
LSSW	Zurich [Switzerland] [ICAO location identifier] (ICLI)
LST	Amphibious Ship, Tank
LST	Lakewood Forest Products Ltd. [Vancouver Stock Exchange symbol]
LST	Laminated SONAR Transistor
LST	Landing Ship, Tank [Navy symbol]
LST	Landing Ship Transport (MCD)
LST	Land Surface Temperature (SAUO)
LST	Laplace-Stieltjes Transform

LST	Large Scale Telescope (ACAE)
LST	Large Scale Test (SAUS)
LST	Large Simple Trial [Statistics]
LST	Large Space Telescope [Later, Space Telescope] [NASA]
LST	Large Stellar Telescope (KSC)
LST	Large Subsonic Tunnel [NASA]
LST	LASER Spot Tracker (MCD)
LST	Last (BUR)
LST	Lateral Sinus Thrombophlebitis [Medicine] (MEDA)
LST	Lateral Spinothalamic Tract [Neurology] (DAVI)
LST	Late Start Time
LST	Launceston [Tasmania] [Airport symbol] (OAG)
LST	Launch Support Team [NASA] (KSC)
LST	Lauryl Sulfate Tryptose [Growth medium]
LST	Law Society of Tasmania [Australia]
LST	Least Squares Tracking (ACAE)
LST	Left Sacrotransverse [A fetal position] [Obstetrics]
LST	Left Store (SAA)
LST	Licentiate in Sacred Theology [British]
LST	Life-Sustaining Treatment [Medicine] (DMAA)
LST	Light-Sensitive Tube
LST	Lightweight Satellite Terminal (SAUO)
LST	Line Scan Tube
LST	Linux Support Team (SAUO)
LST	Liquid Oxygen Start Tank (AAG)
LST	Liquid Storage Tank (AAG)
LST	Listing of a Program in a File [Computer science]
LST	Living Structures Tank (WDAA)
LST	Local Sidereal Time
LST	Local Solar Time
LST	Local Standard Time
LST	Local Summer Time [Astronomy] (IAA)
LST	Logic Service Terminal [Computer science] (VLIE)
LST	Lone Star [Missouri] [Seismograph station code, US Geological Survey] (SEIS)
LST	Lone Star, TX [Location identifier] [FAA] (FAAL)
LST	Long-Term Stability Test [Chemistry]
LST	Lost (GOBB)
LST	Loud Speaking Telephone (NITA)
LST	Low-Solvent Technology (GNE)
LST	Lunar Surface Telescope [NASA]
LST	Lunar Surface Transponder [Aerospace]
LST	Tank Landing Ship (SAUO)
LSTA	Library Services and Technology Act (SAUO)
LSTAR	Limited Scientific and Technical Aerospace Reports [NASA] (MCD)
LSTAT	Life Support for Trauma And Transport [Northrop Grumman] (PS)
LSTB	Bellechasse [Switzerland] [ICAO location identifier] (ICLI)
LSTB	Long Shoot Terminal Bud [Botany]
LStBA	Saint Joseph's Abbey, St. Benedict, LA [Library symbol] [Library of Congress] (LCLS)
LSTC	London Society of Tie Cutters (SAUO)
LST/CAM	LASER Spot Tracker/Strike Camera (MCD)
LSTD	Leading Steward [British military] (DMA)
LSTD	Lunar Satellite Tracking Data [NASA] (KSC)
lstd-	Tristan da Cunha Island [MARC geographic area code] [Library of Congress] (LCCP)
LSTDM	Low Speed Time Division Multiplexer (ACAE)
LSTE	Large Structure Technology Experiment (SSD)
LSTE	Launch Site Transportation Equipment [NASA] (NASA)
LSTF	Large Scale Test Facility (SAUO)
LSTF	Lead Sulfide Thin Film
LST-G	Large Steam Turbine-Generator
LStgH	Hunt Correctional Center (Louisiana Correctional Institute for Women), St. Gabriel, LA [Library symbol] [Library of Congress] (LCLS)
LST(H)	Landing Ship, Tank (Casualty Evacuation) [Navy symbol] [Obsolete]
LST(H)	Landing Ship, Tank (Hospital) [British military] (DMA)
LSTIS	Laboratory Scientific and Technical Information System (SAUO)
LStjT	Tensas Parish Library, St. Joseph, LA [Library symbol] [Library of Congress] (LCLS)
LSTL	Laparoscopic Tubal Ligation [Gynecology] (DAVI)
LSTM	Lander Static Test Model [NASA]
LSTM	Large-Sample Scanning Tunneling Mode [Microscopy]
LSTM	Liverpool School of Tropical Medicine (SAUO)
LSTM	London School of Tropical Medicine (SAUO)
LSTM	Low Steam
LStmSM	St. Martin Parish Library, St. Martinville, LA [Library symbol] [Library of Congress] (LCLS)
LSTN	Light Station [Coast Guard] (IAA)
LSTNG	Lasting
LSTO	Motiers [Switzerland] [ICAO location identifier] (ICLI)
LSTP	Logistic Systems Training Program (ACAE)
LSTP	Low Speed Tape Processor (ACAE)
LSTR	Landstar System [NASDAQ symbol] (TTSB)
LSTR	Landstar System, Inc. [NASDAQ symbol] (SAG)
LSTR	Launch System Test Rack (ACAE)
LSTR	Montricher [Switzerland] [ICAO location identifier] (ICLI)
LSTS	Landing Ship (Utility) [Navy symbol]
LSTS	Launch Station Test Set (MCD)
LSTS	Low-Pressure Side Temperature Sensor [Air conditioning system] [Automotive engineering]
LSTS	Lunar Surface Thermal Simulator [NASA] (KSC)
LST/SCAM	LASER Spot Tracker / Strike Camera
LSTSRFA	Launch Station Test Set Radio Frequency Adapter (MCD)
LSTT	Labor Service Transportation Truck (SAUO)

LSTT	Lake Superior Terminal & Transfer Railway Co. [AAR code]
LSTTL	Low-Power Schottky Transistor-Transistor Logic [Electronics]
L Stud H	Law Students' Helper [A publication] (DLA)
L Stud Helper	Law Students' Helper [A publication] (DLA)
L Stud J	Law Students' Journal [A publication] (DLA)
L Stu Mag	Law Students' Magazine [A publication] (DLA)
L Stu Mag NS	Law Students' Magazine. New Series [A publication] (ILCA)
L Stu Mag OS	Law Students' Magazine. Old Series [A publication] (ILCA)
lstwx	Lost Wax (VRA)
LSTX	Bex [Switzerland] [ICAO location identifier] (ICLI)
LSTY	Yverdon [Switzerland] [ICAO location identifier] (ICLI)
LSU	Institute of Continuing Legal Education, Louisiana State University Law Center (DLA)
LSU	Labor Service Unit [Military]
LSU	Labour Service Unit (SAUO)
LSU	Lactose Saccharose Urea [Cell growth medium]
LSU	Lamentation over the Destruction of Sumer and Ur (BJA)
LSU	Landing Ship, Utility [Navy symbol] [Obsolete]
LSU	Languages, Sorts, Utilities [Computer science] (VLIE)
LSU	LAN Service Unit (SAUS)
LSU	LASER Scanning Unit [Computer science] (CIST)
LSU	Launcher Selector Unit
LSU	Launcher Switching Unit [Navy] (CAAL)
LSU	Law Society of Upper Canada [UTLAS symbol]
LSU	Leading Signal Unit [Telecommunications] (TEL)
LSU	Liberalsoziale Union [Liberal Social Union] [Germany] [Political party] (PPW)
LSU	Library Storage Unit
LSU	Life Support Umbilical [NASA]
LSU	Life Support Unit [NASA] (KSC)
LSU	Lighthouse Study Unit (EA)
LSU	Limit Switch Up [Electronics] (IAA)
LSU	Line Selection Unit [Telecommunications] (IAA)
LSU	Line-Sharing Unit
LSU	Line Signalling Unit (SAUS)
LSU	Livestock Unit
LSU	Load Storage Unit [Computer science]
LSU	Local Storage Unit [Computer science]
LSU	Local Store Unit (ELAL)
LSU	Local Switching Unit [Telecommunications] (TEL)
LSU	Local Synchronization Utility [Telecommunications] (TEL)
LSU	Logistics Support Unit [Military] (NVT)
LSU	Lone Signalling Unit (NITA)
LSU	Lone Signal Unit [Telecommunications] (TEL)
LSU	Long Sukang [Malaysia] [Airport symbol] (OAG)
LSU	Loughborough Students Union (SAUO)
LSU	Louisiana State University
LSU	Louisiana State University and Agricultural and Mechanical College (GAGS)
LSU	Southern University at New Orleans, New Orleans, LA [OCLC symbol] (OCLC)
LSU-IES	Louisiana State University Institute of Environmental Studies (SAUO)
LSU Med Cent	Louisiana State University Medicine Center (GAGS)
LSUN	Labor Service Unit Navy (SAUO)
LSUNO	Louisiana State University in New Orleans [Later, University of New Orleans]
L Sup	Lake Superior (BARN)
LSUP	Loader Storage Unit Support Program [Computer science] (MHDI)
LSUP	Louisiana State University Press (SAUO)
L Sup H & D	Lalor's Supplement to Hill and Denio's New York Reports [A publication] (DLA)
LSUR	Leisure
LSU Shreveport	Louisiana State University Shreveport (GAGS)
LSUV	Lunar Surface Ultraviolet [Camera] [NASA]
LSUV	Luxury Sport Utility Vehicle
LSV	Alak [Former USSR] [ICAO designator] (FAAC)
LSV	Landing Ship, Vehicle [Navy symbol]
LSV	Large Scale Vehicle (ACAE)
LSV	Las Vegas, NV [Location identifier] [FAA] (FAAL)
LSV	Lateral Sacral Vein [Medicine] (MELL)
LSV	Left Sinus of Valsalva [Medicine] (MELL)
LSV	Left Subclavian Vein [Anatomy]
LSV	Light Strike Vehicle (SAUS)
LSV	Lily Symptomless Virus [Plant pathology]
LSV	Linear Shift-Varying (PDAA)
LSV	Linear Sweep Voltammograms [Electrochemistry]
LSV	Line Status Verifier [Telecommunications] (TEL)
LSV	Logistics Support Vessel [Military]
LSV	Logistic Support Vehicle (SAUS)
LSV	Low-Signature Vehicle [Hazardous materials control]
LSV	Lunar Shuttle Vehicle (AAG)
LSV	Lunar Surface Vehicle [Aerospace]
LSV	Lunar Survey Viewfinder [Aerospace]
LSVC	Left Superior Vena Cava [Medicine] (STED)
LSVC	Lunar Surface Vehicle Communications [Aerospace]
LSvCo	Labor Service Company (SAUO)
LSvCtr	Labor Service Center (SAUO)
LSVG	Lifesaving (MSA)
LSVI	Large Size Visual Interface [Computer science] (VLIE)
LSVI	Little Switzerland [NASDAQ symbol] (TTSB)
LSVI	Little Switzerland, Inc. [NASDAQ symbol] (SAG)
LSVP	Landing Ship, Vehicle and Personnel [Navy symbol]
LSvRwyMPCo	Labor Service Railway Military Police Company (SAUO)
LSVW	Logistic Support Vehicle, Wheeled (SAUS)
LSW	Detroit, MI [Location identifier] [FAA] (FAAL)

LSW	Labrador Sea Water [Oceanography]
LSW	Landslide [Washington] [Seismograph station code, US Geological Survey] [Closed] (SEIS)
LSW	Large Scale Walleye (ACAE)
LSW	LASER Spot Welder
LSW	Least Significant Word (MCD)
LSW	Left-Sided Weakness [Medicine] (STED)
LSW	Licensed Shorthand Writer
LSW	Lifshitz-Slyozov-Wagner Theory of Mineral Recrystallization
LSW	Light Support Weapon (MCD)
LSW	Limit Switch [Electronics]
LSW	Line Switch [Telecommunications] (IAA)
LSWA	Large-Amplitude, Slow Wave Activity [Encephalography]
LSWA	Law Society of Western Australia
LSWMA	Lutheran Society for Worship, Music, and the Arts [Later, Liturgical Conference]
LSWP	Lump-Sum Wage Payments (MCD)
LSWR	London & South-Western Railway (ROG)
LSWS	London Society for Women's Service [British] (WDAA)
LSWT	Low-Speed Wind Tunnel (MCD)
LSWY	League of Socialist Working Youth (SAUO)
LSX	Landing Ship, Experimental
LSX	Land-surface Transfer Scheme (SAUO)
LSXB	Balzers/FL [Switzerland] [ICAO location identifier] (ICLI)
LSXD	Domat-Ems [Switzerland] [ICAO location identifier] (ICLI)
LSXE	Erstfeld [Switzerland] [ICAO location identifier] (ICLI)
LSXH	Holziken [Switzerland] [ICAO location identifier] (ICLI)
lsxj-	St. Helena [MARC geographic area code] [Library of Congress] (LCCP)
LSXL	Lauterbrunnen [Switzerland] [ICAO location identifier] (ICLI)
LSXM	St. Moritz [Switzerland] [ICAO location identifier] (ICLI)
LSXO	Gossau SG [Switzerland] [ICAO location identifier] (ICLI)
LSXS	Schindellegi [Switzerland] [ICAO location identifier] (ICLI)
LSXT	Trogen [Switzerland] [ICAO location identifier] (ICLI)
LSXU	Untervaz [Switzerland] [ICAO location identifier] (ICLI)
LSXV	San Vittore [Switzerland] [ICAO location identifier] (ICLI)
LSXW	Wurenlingen [Switzerland] [ICAO location identifier] (ICLI)
LSY	Lindsay Aviation, Inc. [ICAO designator] (FAAC)
LSY	Lismore [Australia] [Airport symbol] (OAG)
LSYC	League of Socialist Youth of Croatia [Political party]
LSZA	Lugano [Switzerland] [ICAO location identifier] (ICLI)
LSZB	Bern/Belp [Switzerland] [ICAO location identifier] (ICLI)
LSZC	Bad Ragaz [Switzerland] [ICAO location identifier] (ICLI)
LSZD	Ascona [Switzerland] [ICAO location identifier] (ICLI)
LSZE	Bad Ragaz [Switzerland] [ICAO location identifier] (ICLI)
LSZF	Birrfeld [Switzerland] [ICAO location identifier] (ICLI)
LSZG	Grenchen [Switzerland] [ICAO location identifier] (ICLI)
LSZH	Zurich [Switzerland] [ICAO location identifier] (ICLI)
LSZI	Fricktal-Schupfart [Switzerland] [ICAO location identifier] (ICLI)
LSZJ	Courtelary [Switzerland] [ICAO location identifier] (ICLI)
LSZK	Speck-Fehraltorf [Switzerland] [ICAO location identifier] (ICLI)
LSZL	Locarno [Switzerland] [ICAO location identifier] (ICLI)
LSZM	Bale [Switzerland] [ICAO location identifier] (ICLI)
LSZN	Hausen Am Albis [Switzerland] [ICAO location identifier] (ICLI)
LSZP	Biel/Kappelen [Switzerland] [ICAO location identifier] (ICLI)
LSZR	Altenrhein [Switzerland] [ICAO location identifier] (ICLI)
LSZS	Samedan [Switzerland] [ICAO location identifier] (ICLI)
LSZT	Lommis [Switzerland] [ICAO location identifier] (ICLI)
LSZU	Buttwil [Switzerland] [ICAO location identifier] (ICLI)
LSZV	Sitterdorf [Switzerland] [ICAO location identifier] (ICLI)
LSZW	Thun [Switzerland] [ICAO location identifier] (ICLI)
LSZX	Schanis [Switzerland] [ICAO location identifier] (ICLI)
LSZY	Porrentruy [Switzerland] [ICAO location identifier] (ICLI)
LSZZ	Collective address for NOTAM and SNOWTAM [Switzerland] [ICAO location identifier] (ICLI)
LT	Fixed Light [USCG] (TAG)
LT	Great Sierra [ICAO designator] (AD)
LT	Heat-labile Enterotoxin [Biochemistry] (DAVI)
LT	Heat-Labile Toxin (STED)
LT	Labile Toxin (DB)
LT	Laboratory Technology (SAUO)
LT	Laboratory Test (IAA)
LT	[The] Lake Terminal Railroad Co. [AAR code]
LT	Lamaze Technique [Medicine] (MELL)
LT	Laminar Tomography (STED)
LT	Laminated TEFLON
LT	Landed Terms
LT	Landing Team
LT	Landing Time (SAUO)
L/T	Landlord/Tenant (SAUO)
LT	Lands Tribunal [Legal] [British]
LT	Language Translation [Computer science]
LT	Laplace Transform [Mathematics]
LT	Lapped Transform [Telecommunications]
LT	Laptop [Computer] (BARN)
LT	Large Tug [Army]
LT	Larsen and Toubro Ltd. [India] [Commercial firm]
LT	Laser Transmitter (SAUS)
LT	LASER Trimming (PDAA)
LT	Last (ROG)
LT	Last Telecast (NTCM)
LT	Lateral Tooth
LT	Lateral Triceps Brachii [Medicine]
LT	Latest Time [Business term]
LT	Laughter Therapy (EA)

LT	Launch Test [NASA] (IAA)
LT	Laundry Tray
LT	Lawn Tennis
LT	Law Times Journal [A publication] (DLA)
LT	Law Times Newspaper [A publication] (DLA)
LT	Law Times Reports [British]
LT	Layout Template (MCD)
L/T	Leading Telegraphist
LT	Leading Torpedoman [Navy] [British]
LT	Lead Time (NG)
LT	League of Tarcisians (EA)
LT	Lease Time (SAUS)
LT	Left
LT	Left Tackle [Football]
LT	Left Thigh
LT	Left Triceps [Anatomy] (DAVI)
LT	Left Turn (SAUS)
LT	Legal Tender [Currency]
LT	Legal Title [Business term]
lt	Legal Training [Navy] [British]
Lt	Leptosphaerulina Trifolii [A fungus]
LT	Less Than (IBMDP)
LT	Lethal Time (STED)
LT	Letter
LT	Letter of Transmittal (MCD)
LT	Letter Telegram
LT	Leukotriene [Clinical pharmacology]
LT	Level Transmitter (NRCH)
LT	Level Trigger
LT	Levin Tube [Medicine]
LT	Levothyroxine [Pharmacy]
LT	Library Talk [A publication] (BRI)
LT	Licentiate in Teaching [British]
LT	Licentiate in Theology
LT	Lid Tank
LT	Lieutenant (EY)
Lt	Lieutenant (WA)
LT	Light (AAG)
lt	Light (VRA)
LT	Light Tank
LT	Light Terminal (PDAA)
LT	Light Test (IAA)
LT	Light Transportable (SAUS)
LT	Light Trap
LT	Light Truck [British]
LT	Limit (DEN)
LT	Limited Term Employee (OICC)
L/T	Line Telecommunications
LT	Line Telegraphy
LT	Line Terminator
LT	Line Traffic Coordinator (SAUO)
LT	Linked Term [Online database field identifier]
LT	Link Terminal [Telecommunications] (TEL)
LT	Link Testing (NITA)
LT	Link Trailer (SAUO)
LT	Link Trainer Instructor
LT	Liquid Toned [Copier] [Reprography]
LT	Lira Toscana [Tuscany Pound] [Monetary unit] [Italian] (ROG)
LT	Lira Turca [Turkish Pound] [Monetary unit] [Italian] (ROG)
LT	Liter (ECII)
LT	Lithuania [Internet country code]
LT	Loader Trainer (MCD)
LT	Loader-Transporter [British military] (DMA)
L/T	Load Test (MCD)
LT	Local Time
LT	Locum Tenens [In the Place Of] [Latin]
LT	Logical Terminal (SAUS)
LT	Logic Theorist [or Theory] [Computer science]
LT	Logic Tree
LT	Logistics Technology
LT	London-Ducretet-Thomson [Record label] [Great Britain, USA, etc.]
LT	London Transport
LT	Long Term
LT	Long-Term Stay [in hospital] [British]
LT	Long Throw [Speaker system]
LT	Long Ton [2240 pounds]
LT	Long Tour [Military] (GFGA)
LT	Long Treble [Crocheting] (ROG)
LT	Lookthrough (LAIN)
L/T	Loop Test [Aerospace] (AAG)
LT	Lorimar-Telepictures Corp. (SAUO)
LT	Los Alamos Technical Associates (SAUO)
LT	Lot
LT	Lo Ta'aseh (BJA)
LT	Lot Time (SAA)
LT	Lower Torso
LT	Low Temperature
LT	Low Tension
LT	Low Torque
LT	Low Transverse [incision] [Obstetrics] (DAVI)
LT	Lucis Trust (EA)
LT	Lues Test (STED)
LT	Lug Terminal
LT	Lumbar Traction [Orthopedics] (DAVI)
LT	Luxury Tax (MHDB)

LT	Lymphocyte Transformation [Hematology]	LTB	La Trobe University Herbarium (SAUO)
LT	Lymphocyte Transitional [Medicine] (STED)	LTB	Laundry Trade Board (SAUO)
LT	Lymphocytic Thyroiditis [Medicine] (STED)	LTB	Lawrence Traffic Bureau Inc., Kansas City MO [STAC]
LT	Lymphocytotoxin [Medicine] (STED)	LTB	Law Times Bankruptcy Reports [United States] [A publication] (DLA)
LT	Lymphoid Tissue [Biology]	LTB	Lead-Time Bias (MELL)
LT	Lymphotoxin [Immunochemistry]	LTB	Length-Time Bias (MELL)
LT	Turn Left after Takeoff [Aviation] (FAAC)	LTB	Lepers Trust Board (SAUO)
LTA	Land Trust Alliance (EA)	LTB	Leucotriene B [Clinical pharmacology]
LTA	Large Transport Airplane	LTB	Light Bay [Horse racing]
LTA	Laser Training Aid (SAUS)	LTB	Limited Test Ban [Nuclear testing]
LTA	Launch Test Area	LTB	Line Term Buffer [Computer science] (AABC)
LTA	Launch Tube Assembly	LTB	Local Token-Ring Bridge (CIST)
LTA	Lawn Tennis Association (EAIO)	LTB	London Tourist Board [British] (DCTA)
LTA	Lead Tetraacetate [Organic chemistry]	LTB	London Transport Board [British]
LTA	Lead Trial Attorney (SAUO)	LT(B)	Low-Tension (Battery) (DEN)
LTA	Leave Travel Allowance	LTBA	Die Lexikalischen Tafelserien der Babylonier und Assyrer in den Berliner Museen [A publication] (BJA)
LTA	Legionarios del Trabajo in America (EA)		
LTA	Leisure Time Activity	LTBA	Istanbul/Yesilkoy [Turkey] [ICAO location identifier] (ICLI)
LTA	LEM Test Article (MCD)	LTBA	Louisiana Thoroughbred Breeders Association (SRA)
LTA	Less than Adequate (COE)	LTBB	Istanbul [Turkey] [ICAO location identifier] (ICLI)
LTA	Lettera di Transporto Aereo [Air Waybill] [Italian] [Business term]	LTBC	Alasehir [Turkey] [ICAO location identifier] (ICLI)
LTA	Lettre de Transport Aerien [Air Waybill] [French] [Business term]	LTBC	Lawn Tennis Ball Convention [British] (BI)
LTA	Leucotriene A [Clinical pharmacology]	LTBD	Aydin [Turkey] [ICAO location identifier] (ICLI)
LTA	Leveling Torquer Amplifier	LTBE	Bursa [Turkey] [ICAO location identifier] (ICLI)
LTA	Library Technical Assistant	LTBF	Balikesir [Turkey] [ICAO location identifier] (ICLI)
LTA	Lighter-than-Air [Aircraft]	LTBF	Learn To Be Funny (SAUS)
LTA	Light Transport Aircraft (SAUS)	LTBG	Bandirma [Turkey] [ICAO location identifier] (ICLI)
LTA	Linea Aerea Tama [Chile] [ICAO designator] (FAAC)	LTBG	Lightbridge, Inc. [NASDAQ symbol] (SG)
LTA	Linear Triaxial Accelerometer (SAUS)	LTBH	Canakkale [Turkey] [ICAO location identifier] (ICLI)
LTA	Linen Trade Association (EA)	LTBI	Eskisehir [Turkey] [ICAO location identifier] (ICLI)
LTA	Lipoate Transacetylase [An enzyme]	LTBJ	Izmir/Cumaovasi [Turkey] [ICAO location identifier] (ICLI)
LTA	Lipoteichoic Acid [Biochemistry]	LTBK	Izmir/Gaziemir [Turkey] [ICAO location identifier] (ICLI)
LTA	Living Together Arrangement	LTBL	Izmir/Cigli [Turkey] [ICAO location identifier] (ICLI)
LTA	LM [Lunar Module] Test Article [NASA]	LtBI	Light Blend [Horticulture]
LTA	Local Training Area (MCD)	LTBM	Isparta [Turkey] [ICAO location identifier] (ICLI)
LTA	Logical Transient Area	LTBMC	Long-Term Bone Marrow Culture [Cell culture]
LTA	Logic Time Analyzer (IAA)	LTBN	Kutahya [Turkey] [ICAO location identifier] (ICLI)
LTA	Logic Tree Analysis (EA)	LTBO	Linear Time Base Oscillator
LTA	London Traffic Act (SAUO)	LTBO	Usak [Turkey] [ICAO location identifier] (ICLI)
LTA	Long-Term Arrangement (SAUO)	LTBP	London Tanker Broker Panel
LTA	Long-Term Arrangements [Department of State]	LTBP	Yalova [Turkey] [ICAO location identifier] (ICLI)
LTA	Long-Term Average (CAAL)	LTBQ	Topel [Turkey] [ICAO location identifier] (ICLI)
LTA	Lower Torso Assembly [Aerospace] (MCD)	LTBR	Yenisehir [Turkey] [ICAO location identifier] (ICLI)
LTA	Low Temperature Aftercooled [Automotive engineering]	LTBS	Dalaman [Turkey] [ICAO location identifier] (ICLI)
LTA	Low-Temperature Ashing [Analytical chemistry]	LTBT	Akhisar [Turkey] [ICAO location identifier] (ICLI)
LTA	South Lake Tahoe, CA [Location identifier] [FAA] (FAAL)	LTBT	Limited Test Ban Treaty [Signed in 1963; prohibits testing of nuclear devices in certain environments]
LTA	Tzaneen [South Africa] [Airport symbol] (OAG)		
LTAA	Ankara [Turkey] [ICAO location identifier] (ICLI)	LTC	Laboratory Training Center (SAUO)
LTAB	Guvercinlik [Turkey] [ICAO location identifier] (ICLI)	LTC	Lafferty Transportation [AAR code]
LTAB	League to Abolish Billionaires [Fictitious organization mentioned in Donald Duck comic by Carl Barks]	LTC	Lafferty Transportation Company (SAUO)
		LTC	Lai [Chad] [Airport symbol] (AD)
LTAC	Ankara/Esenboga [Turkey] [ICAO location identifier] (ICLI)	LTC	Land Tenure Center [University of Wisconsin] [Research center]
LTAC	Literary Translators Association of Canada (EAIO)	LTC	Land Tenure Centre, Madison, Wisc. (SAUS)
LTACFIRE	Light Tactical Fire (SAUS)	LTC	Land Transfer Committee (SAUO)
LTACFIRE	Lightweight Tactical Fire Direction System [Artillery] [Army] (INF)	LTC	Land Transport Corps [British military] (DMA)
LTAD	Ankara/Etimesgut [Turkey] [ICAO location identifier] (ICLI)	LTC	Land Trust Commission (BARN)
LTADL	Launcher Tube Azimuth Datum Line	LTC	Language and Time-sharing Center (SAUO)
LTAE	Ankara/Murted [Turkey] [ICAO location identifier] (ICLI)	LTC	Language Testing Center [University of Melbourne] [Australia]
LTAE	Long-Term Agroecosystem Experiment	LTC	Language Tuition Centre (SAUO)
LTAF	Adana/Sakirpasa [Turkey] [ICAO location identifier] (ICLI)	LTC	Large Transformed Cell [Medicine] (DMAA)
LTAG	Adana/Incirlik [Turkey] [ICAO location identifier] (ICLI)	LTC	Last Telecast (WDMC)
LTAG	Liaison Training and Advisory Group (SAUO)	LTC	Latcharter [Latvia] [FAA designator] (FAAC)
LTAH	Afyon [Turkey] [ICAO location identifier] (ICLI)	LTC	Lattice (MSA)
LTAI	Antalya [Turkey] [ICAO location identifier] (ICLI)	LTC	Launceston Technical College [Australia]
LTAJ	Gaziantep [Turkey] [ICAO location identifier] (ICLI)	LTC	Launch Vehicle Test Conductor [NASA] (KSC)
LTAK	Iskenderun [Turkey] [ICAO location identifier] (ICLI)	LTC	Lawn Tennis Club [British]
LTAL	Kastamonu [Turkey] [ICAO location identifier] (ICLI)	LTC	Lead Telluride Crystal [Photoconductor]
LTAL	Lower Transition Altitude (SAA)	LTC	Lead to Come [Publishing] (WDMC)
LTALT	Light Alternating (IAA)	LTC	Leaseway Transportation Corp. (WDAA)
LTAM	Kayseri [Turkey] [ICAO location identifier] (ICLI)	LTC	Leave and Transit Camp (SAUO)
LTaM	Madison Parish Library, Tallulah, LA [Library symbol] [Library of Congress] (LCLS)	LTC	Left to Count (DAVI)
		LTC	Legislative Transportation Committee (SAUO)
LTAN	Konya [Turkey] [ICAO location identifier] (ICLI)	LTC	Lesotho Telecommunications Corp. [Ministry of Transport and Communications] [Lesotho] (TSSD)
LT & D	Love, Togetherness, and Devotion [Rock music group]		
LT & S	London, Tilbury & Southend Railway [British]	LTC	Less than Truckload Cargo (MCD)
LT & SR	London, Tilbury & Southend Railway [British] (ROG)	LTC	Letdown Terrain Clearance (DNAB)
LTAO	Malatya/Erhac [Turkey] [ICAO location identifier] (ICLI)	LTC	Le Tourneau College (SAUO)
LTAP	Merzifon [Turkey] [ICAO location identifier] (ICLI)	LTC	Leukotriene C [Clinical pharmacology]
LTAQ	Samsun [Turkey] [ICAO location identifier] (ICLI)	LTC	Level and Timing Controller (ACAE)
LTAR	Sivas [Turkey] [ICAO location identifier] (ICLI)	LTC	Liberia Telecommunications Corp. (IMH)
LTAS	Lead Tetraacetate-Schiff (Reaction) [Clinical chemistry]	LTC	Liberty to the Captives [Later, ACAT] (EA)
LTAS	Lighter than Air Society [An association] (PDAA)	LTC	Library of Trinity College (SAUO)
LTAS	Zonguldak [Turkey] [ICAO location identifier] (ICLI)	LTC	Library Technical Centre [Polytechnic of Central London] (NITA)
LTAT	Malatya/Erhac [Turkey] [ICAO location identifier] (ICLI)	LTC	Licentiate of Trinity College (SAUO)
LTAU	Kayseri/Erkilet [Turkey] [ICAO location identifier] (ICLI)	LTC	Lidocaine Tissue Concentration [Medicine] (DMAA)
LTAV	Sivrihisar [Turkey] [ICAO location identifier] (ICLI)	LTC	Lieutenance Colonel (SAUO)
LTAVD	Low-Temperature Arc Vapor Deposition [Coating technology]	LTC	Lieutenant Colonel (AABC)
LTB	Acute Laryngotracheobronchitis [Commonly known as croup] (PAZ)	Ltc	Lieutenant Colonel
		LTC	Lieutenant Commander (GFGA)
Lt B	Bachelor of Literature	LTC	Lightly Treated Coated [Papermaking]
LTB	Department of Genetics and Human Variation La Trobe University, Melbourne (SAUS)	LTC	Light Terminal Complexes
		LTC	Linear Transformation Converter (IAA)
LTB	Laboratory Test Bed (SAUS)	LTC	Linear Transmission Channel
LTB	Laparoscopic Tubal Banding [Ligation] (DAVI)	LTC	Line Terminal Control (IAA)
LTB	Laryngo-Tracheal Bronchitis	LTC	Line Termination Coordinator (SAUS)
LTB	Last Trunk Busy [Telecommunications] (TEL)		

LTC	Line Time Clock
LTC	Line Traffic Coordinator (CET)
LTC	Lithographic Test Chip (AAEL)
LTC	Living Tree Center (EA)
LTC	Livros Tecnicos e Cientificos Editora Ltda. [Brazil]
LTC	Load Tap Changing
LTC	Local Telephone Circuit [Telecommunications] (TEL)
LTC	Local Terminal Controller
LTC	Local Time Clock
LTC	Location Traction Control Switch [Automotive emissions]
LTC	Lockwood Torday & Carlisle Ltd. [British]
LTC	London Trades Council (SAUO)
LTC	Longitudinal Time Code (NTCM)
LTC	Longitudinal Time Constant
LTC	Long-Term Care [Medicine]
LTC	Long-Term Complication (MELL)
LTC	Long-Term Consequence (MELL)
LTC	Long Term Contract (SAUS)
LTC	Long-Term Contract (ADA)
LTC	Long Term Costing [Military] (RDA)
LTC	Long Time Constant (IEEE)
LTC	Loop Test Conference [Aerospace] (AAG)
LTC	Lotus Cosmetics International (SAUO)
LTC	Lotus Cosmetics International Ltd. [Vancouver Stock Exchange symbol]
LTC	Low-Tar Content [of cigarettes]
LTC	Low-Temperature Carbonization
LTC	Low-Temperature Catalyst
LTC	Low-Temperature Coefficient
LTC	Low-Temperature Cooling
LTC	Low-Tension Current (IAA)
LTC	Low Transverse Cervical [Medicine] (MELL)
LTC	LTC Properties [NYSE symbol] (TTSB)
LTC	LTC Properties, Inc. [NYSE symbol] (SPSG)
LTC	Lunar Terrain [or Topographic] Camera [NASA]
LTC	Lynchburg Technology Center (GAAI)
L(TC)	Tax Cases Leaflets [Legal] [British]
LTCA	Elazig [Turkey] [ICAO location identifier] (ICLI)
LTCAX	Thornburg Ltd. Term Muni-Cal. Cl.A [Mutual fund ticker symbol] (SG)
LTCB	Agri [Turkey] [ICAO location identifier] (ICLI)
LTCB	Long Term Credit Bank [Japan] (ECON)
LTCB	Long-Term Credit Bank of Japan, Ltd. (ECON)
LTCC	Diyarbakir [Turkey] [ICAO location identifier] (ICLI)
LTCC	Language Testing and Curriculum Center [Griffith University] [Australia]
LTCC	Long-Term Care Campaign (EA)
LTCC	Low Temperature Co-Fired Ceramic (AAEL)
LTCCE	Long-term Continuous Cropping Experiment (SAUO)
LTCCM	Loading Training Captive Carry Missile (MCD)
LTCD	Erzincan [Turkey] [ICAO location identifier] (ICLI)
LTCDA	Low Temperature Coal Distillers Association [British] (DBA)
Lt Cdr	Lieutenant Commander (WDAA)
LTCDR	Lieutenant Commander
LTCE	Erzurum [Turkey] [ICAO location identifier] (ICLI)
LTCF	Kars [Turkey] [ICAO location identifier] (ICLI)
LTCF	Long-Term Care Facility [Medicine]
LTCG	Long-Term Capital Gain
LTCG	Trabzon [Turkey] [ICAO location identifier] (ICLI)
LTCH	Litchfield Financial [NASDAQ symbol] (TTSB)
LTCH	Litchfield Financial Corp. [NASDAQ symbol] (SAG)
LTCH	Urfa [Turkey] [ICAO location identifier] (ICLI)
LTCI	Van [Turkey] [ICAO location identifier] (ICLI)
LTCJ	Batman [Turkey] [ICAO location identifier] (ICLI)
LTCL	Licentiate of Trinity College of Music, London [British]
LTCL	Long-Term Capital Loss
LTCM	Licentiate of the Toronto Conservatory of Music [Canada]
LTCM	Long-Term Capital Management
Lt Cmdr	Lieutenant Commander (SAUO)
LTCMDS	Long-Term Care Minimum Data Set [Department of Health and Human Services] (GFGA)
LTCML	Licentiate of Trinity College of Music, London (SAUO)
LtCol	Lieutenant Colonel (ASC)
LTCOL	Lieutenant Colonel
LTCOM	Lieutenant Commander (DNAB)
LT COMDR	Lieutenant Commander (DNAB)
Lt-Comm	Lieutenant-Commander [British military] (DMA)
LT/COR/WR	Light Corner Wear [Deltiology]
LTC Prp	LTC Properties, Inc. [Associated Press] (SAG)
LT/CR	Light Crease [Deltiology]
LTCS	Long-Term Contracting Strategy (COE)
LTCS	Low Transverse Cesarean Section [Medicine] (MEDA)
LTCSB	Long-Term Care Statistics Branch [Department of Health and Human Services] (GFGA)
LTCT	Lower Thermal Comfort Threshold [Environmental heating]
LTCVD	Low-Temperature Chemical Vapor Deposition (AAEL)
LTD	Collaboration Type Details (SAUS)
LTD	Ghadames [Libya] [Airport symbol] (OAG)
LTD	Land Titles Division [South Australia]
LTD	Land Treatment Demonstration [Environmental science] (COE)
LTD	Language Training Detachment [Defense Language Institute] (DNAB)
LTD	Largest Tumor Diameter (SAUS)
LTD	Laron-Type Dwarfism [Medicine]
LTD	LASER Target Designator
LTD	Launch Test Directive [NASA] (KSC)
LTD	Letdown [Nuclear energy] (NRCH)

LTD	Leukotriene D [Clinical pharmacology]
LTD	Lift-Drag [Ratio] (MCD)
LTD	Lift-to-Drag [Aerospace] (NAKS)
LTD	Light Displacement Tonnage (SAUS)
LTD	Lightweight Target Designator
ltd	Limited (DAVI)
Ltd	Limited (DIAR)
LTD	Limited
ltd	limited (SAUO)
LTD	Limited Company (SAUO)
LTD	[The] Limited, Inc. [NYSE symbol] (SPSG)
Ltd	Limited Liability (SAUO)
Ltd	Limited Liability Co. (SAUO)
LTD	Limit to Topographic Development [Of hillsides] [Geology]
LTD	Linear Transport Drive
LTD	Linear Tumor Diameter [Oncology]
LTD	Line Transfer Device
LTD	Litchfield, IL [Location identifier] [FAA] (FAAL)
LTD	Live Test Demonstration
LTD	Local Data Terminal (ACAE)
LTD	Local Test Desk [Telecommunications] (KSC)
LTD	Logistic Technical Data [Navy]
LTD	Long Tank Delta
LTD	Long Term Debt (SAUO)
LTD	Long-Term Depression [Neurophysiology]
LTD	Long-Term Disability
LTD	Lost During Transhipment (SAUO)
LTD	Low-Temperature Drying
LTD	Lumber Transfer and Distribution
LTDA	Licensed Taxi Drivers' Association [British] (DBA)
LTD ED	Limited Edition [Publishing]
LTDI	Learning Technology Dissemination Initiative (AIE)
LTDL	Life Test Data Logger (CAAL)
LTDM	Light Transmittance Difference Meter
LTDP	Long Term Defense Plan (SAUS)
LTDP	Long-Term Defense Program [NATO] (MCD)
LTDQ	Limited Quantity [Refers to a test performed on a scanty specimen] [Biochemistry] (DAVI)
LTDR	Laser Target Designator Rangefinder (ACAE)
LTD/R	LASER Target Designator/Ranger (DWSG)
LTDR	LASER Target Designator Receiver
LTDS	Laser Target Designator Set (ACAE)
LTDS	LASER Target Designator System (MCD)
LTDS	Laser Tracking and Discrimination Study (ACAE)
LTDS	Launch Tracking [or Trajectory] Data System
LTDSS	LASER Target Designator Scoring System (MCD)
LTDSTD	Limited Standard (IAA)
LTDT	Langley Transonic Dynamics Tunnel [NASA] (KSC)
LTD(U)	Land Treatment Demonstration [or Unit] (GNE)
LTE	Land Trust Exchange [Later, LTA] (EA)
LTE	Laplace Transformation Estimator
LTE	Large Table Electroplotter [Computer science]
LTE	Large Terminal Repeats [Genetics] (DAVI)
LTE	Large Thrust per Element
LTE	Launch to Eject
LTE	Letter to the Editor
LTE	Leucotriene E [Clinical pharmacology]
LTE	Levitator Technology Experiment (SAUS)
LT(E)	Lieutenant (Engineer)
LTE	Limited Technical Evaluation (MCD)
LTE	Limited Test Equipment
LTE	Linear Threshold Element [Computer science]
LTE	Line Termination Equipment [Telecommunications] (TEL)
LTE	Local Telephone Exchange (NITA)
LTE	Local Thermal Equilibrium [Physical chemistry]
LTE	Local Thermodynamic Equilibrium [or Equivalent] [Astronautics, astrophysics]
LTE	Local Truncation Error (VLIE)
LTE	Long-Term Effect
LTE	Long-Term Enhancement [Neurophysiology]
LTE	Long-Term Equilibration [Analytical chemistry]
LTE	Low-Thrust Engine
LTE	LTE International Airways SA [Spain] [FAA designator] (FAAC)
LTE	Luxury Touring Edition [Automobile model designation]
LTEA	Leaf Tobacco Exporters Association (EA)
LTEC	Lincoln Telecmmun [NASDAQ symbol] (TTSB)
LTEC	Lincoln Telecommunications Company (SAUO)
LTED	Long-Term Economic Deterioration [Department of Commerce]
LT/ED/WR	Light Edge Wear [Deltiology]
Ltee	Limitee [Limited] [French]
LTEEC	Lake Tahoe Environmental Education Consortium (SAUO)
LTEK	Life Technologies [NASDAQ symbol] (TTSB)
LTEK	Life Technologies, Inc. (SAUO)
LTEL	Lincoln Telecommunications Co. (SAUO)
LTEL	Lorain Telecommunications Corp. (SAUO)
LTEMP	Low Temperature
L T (Eng)	Law Times Journal (England) [A publication] (DLA)
LTEP	Long-Term Equipment Plan [Military] (RDA)
LTEP	Low-Temperature Engine Performance
LTER	Long Term Ecological Research [National Science Foundation]
LTER	Long-Term Ecological Research Project (SAUO)
LTERM	Logical Terminal (TIMI)
LTERM	Long-Term Ecosystem Research and Monitoring (SAUO)
LTERR	Lunar Terrestrial Age
LTEU	Liquor Trades Employees Union (SAUO)

LTF .... Landline Telephony [*Aviation*] (DA)
LTF .... LASER Terrain Follower
LTF .... Latvijas Tautas Fronte [*Popular Front of Latvia*] [*Political party*] (EY)
LTF .... Layman Tithing Foundation (EA)
LTF .... Leucotriene F [*Clinical pharmacology*]
LTF .... Ligand-Responsive Transcription Factor [*Genetics*]
LTF .... Light-Float [*Navigation*]
LTF .... Lightning Training Flight [*British military*] (DMA)
LTF .... Lipotropic Factor [*Choline*] [*Biochemistry*]
LTF .... Liquid Thermal Flowmeter
LTF .... Lithographic Technical Foundation [*Later, GATF*] (MSA)
LTF .... Lithographic Technical Foundation, Inc. (SAUO)
LTF .... Local Training Flight
LTF .... Logical Twin Forward Pointer (MHDI)
LTF .... Logistic Task Force (SAUO)
LTF .... Lymphocyte Transforming Factor [*Immunology*]
LTF .... Nicholls State University, Thibodaux, LA [*Library symbol*] [*Library of Congress*] (LCLS)
LTFC .... Landing Traffic [*Aviation*] (FAAC)
LTFC .... Low-Temperature Fuel Cell [*Energy source*]
LTFCS .... LASER Tank Fire Control System
LTFD .... Logic and Test Function Drawer [*Computer science*] (MCD)
LT/FM .... Long-Term/Frequency Modulation
LTFP .... Long Term Force Programmes (SAUS)
LTFRD .... Lot Tolerance Fraction Reliability Deviation [*Quality control*]
LTFS .... LASER Terrain Following System
LTFS .... London Tax Free Shopping Co. (SAUO)
LTFT .... Long-Term Fuel Trim [*Automotive engineering, fuel systems*]
LTFT .... Long Term Full Time Training (ACAE)
LTFT .... Low-Temperature Filter Test
LTFT .... Low-Temperature Flow Test [*Lubricant technology*]
LTFV .... Less Than Fair Value [*Business term*]
LTG .... Catalina Lighting [*NYSE symbol*] (SAG)
LTG .... Laboratory Test Group (SAUO)
LTG .... Legal Technology Group [*Information service or system*] (IID)
LTG .... Lettering (ADA)
LTG .... Lieutenant General (AABC)
LTG .... Lightening
LTG .... Lighting
LTG .... Lightning [*Meteorology*]
LTG .... Lightning Minerals [*Vancouver Stock Exchange symbol*]
LTG .... Linear Tangent Guidance (MCD)
LTG .... Line Termination Group (SAUO)
LTG .... Line Trunk Group [*Telecommunications*]
ltg .... Lithographer [*MARC relator code*] [*Library of Congress*] (LCCP)
LTG .... Little Theatre Guild [*British*] (DBA)
LTG .... Local Tactical Grid [*Military*] (NVT)
LTG .... Long-Term Goals (DAVI)
LTG .... Low Tension Glaucoma (SAUS)
LTG .... Lunar Traverse Gravimeter [*Experiment*] [*NASA*]
LTGA .... Left [*or Levo*] Transposition of the Great Arteries [*Also called corrected transposition*] [*Cardiology*] (DAVI)
LTGC .... Lieutenant Grand Commander [*Freemasonry*]
LTGCA .... Lightning Cloud-to-Air [*NWS*] (FAAC)
LTGCC .... Lightning Cloud-to-Cloud [*NWS*] (FAAC)
LTGCCCG .... Lightning Cloud-to-Cloud, Cloud-to-Ground [*NWS*] (FAAC)
LTGCG .... Lightning Cloud-to-Ground [*NWS*] (FAAC)
LTGCW .... Lightning Cloud-to-Water [*NWS*] (FAAC)
LTGE .... Lighterage
Lt Gen .... Lieutenant General (WDAA)
LTGEN .... Lieutenant General
LTGF Newl... Lawyers' Title Guaranty Funds Newsletter [*A publication*] (DLA)
LTGH .... Lightening Hole [*Engineering*]
LTGHE .... Low-Temperature Gradient Heating Furnace (SAUS)
LTGIC .... Lightning in Clouds [*NWS*] (FAAC)
LTGL .... Lee-Tse-Goldberg-Lowe [*Theory*]
Lt Gov .... Lieutenant Governor (SHCU)
LT Gov .... Lieutenant Governor (WGA)
Lt grp fl ...... Light, group-flashing (SAUO)
Lt grp occ ... Light, group occulting (SAUO)
LTH .... Enterprise Thesaurus [*Database*]
LTH .... Laboratory Test Handbook
LTH .... Lactogenic Hormone [*Also, LGH, PR, PRL*] [*Endocrinology*]
L Th .... La Themis [*Lower Canada*] [*A publication*] (DLA)
LTH .... Leather [*Automotive advertising*]
LtH .... Left-Handed (ADWA)
LTH .... Less than Honorable Discharge [*Military*] (VNW)
LTH .... Lethality (ACAE)
LTH .... Lethality & Target Hardening (SAUS)
L Th .... Licentiate in Theology
LTH .... Light Towed Howitzer (SAUS)
LTH .... Light Training Helicopter (WDAA)
LTH .... Local Tumor Hyperthermia [*Medicine*] (DB)
LTH .... Logical Track Header
LTH .... London Teaching Hospitals [*National Health Service*] [*British*] (DI)
LTH .... Long-Term Holiday (MHDB)
LTH .... Low-Temperature Herschel (OA)
LTH .... Low-Temperature Holding
LTH .... Low Turret Half
LTH .... Luteotrophic Hormone [*Also, PR, PRL*] [*Endocrinology*]
Lth .... Martin Luther's German Version of the Bible [*A publication*] (BJA)
LTHA .... Long-Term Heat Aging
LTHE .... Low Temperature Heat Exchanger (EEVL)
L Theol .... Licentiate in Theology [*British*] (WA)
LTHG .... Lathing

L Th K .... Lexikon fuer Theologie und Kirche [*A publication*] (ODCC)
LTHO .... Lighthouse
LTHR .... Leather (KSC)
LTHV .... Lucke Tumor Herpesvirus
LTI .... Aerotaxis Latinoamericanos SA de CV [*Mexico*] [*ICAO designator*] (FAAC)
LTI .... Ladder Towers Incorporated (SAUO)
LTI .... Land Training Installations (NATG)
LTI .... Laser Technology Inc. (SAUS)
LTI .... Lawyers Tile [*NYSE symbol*] (TTSB)
LTI .... Lawyers Title Corp. [*NYSE symbol*] (SAG)
LTI .... Licentiate of the Textile Institute [*British*] (DBQ)
LTI .... Life Technologies, Inc. (HGEN)
LTI .... Light Tip-In [*Automotive testing*]
LTI .... Light Transmission Index
LTI .... Limited to Interrogations (MCD)
LTI .... Linear Technology, Inc. [*Toronto Stock Exchange symbol*]
LTI .... Linear Time Invariant (IAA)
LTI .... Lingua Tertii Imperii [*A study of the abuse of language under Nazism by Viktor Klemperer*]
LTI .... Logistic Technical Information (SAUO)
LTI .... Long-Term Inmate (WDAA)
LTI .... Long-Term Integration (CAAL)
LTI .... Lost Time Injuries (SAUO)
LTI .... Lost Time Injury [*Industrial plant safety*]
LTI .... Louisiana Training Institute (SAUO)
LTI .... Lowell Technological Institute [*Massachusetts*]
LTI .... Lowell Textile Institute (SAUO)
LTI .... Low-Temperature Isomerization [*Organic chemistry*]
LTI .... Low-Temperature Isotope
LTI .... Lupus-Type Inclusions [*Medicine*] (DMAA)
LTIB .... Lead Technical Information Bureau [*British*] (BI)
LTIC .... Language Teaching Information Centre [*British*] (CB)
LTID .... LASER Target Interface Device (RDA)
LTID .... Light-Intensity Detector (MSA)
LTID .... Logical Terminal Identifier (SAUS)
Lt Inf .... Light Infantry [*British military*] (DMA)
LTIOV .... Latest Time Information of Value [*Military*] (AFM)
LTIP .... Long-Term Incentive Plan
LTIRF .... Lowell Technological Institute Research Foundation (MCD)
LTIS .... LASER Target Interface System
LTIV .... Lunar Trajectory Injection Vehicle [*NASA*] (KSC)
LTJ .... Law Times Journal [*A publication*] (DLA)
LTJ .... Lutheran Theological Journal [*A publication*] (APTA)
LTJC .... Lyons Township Junior College [*Illinois*]
LTJG .... Lieutenant Junior Grade [*Navy*]
LTjg .... Lieutenant, Junior Grade [*Navy*] (GOBB)
LT Jo (Eng)... Law Times Journal (England) [*A publication*] (DLA)
LTK .... Laser Thermal Keratoplasty (SAUS)
LTK .... Latakia [*Syria*] [*Airport symbol*] (OAG)
LTK .... Lead To Come [*Copyediting*] (WDMC)
LTK1 .... Leukocyte Tyrosine Kinase [*An enzyme*]
LTK1 .... Ladies' Touring Kayak, Single Person (ADA)
L Tk Co ...... Light Tank Company (SAUO)
LTL .... Aerie Airlines (SAUO)
LTL .... Lafourche Parish Library, Thibodaux, LA [*Library symbol*] [*Library of Congress*] (LCLS)
LTL .... Laparoscopic Tubal Ligation [*Gynecology*] (DAVI)
LTL .... Lastourville [*Gabon*] [*Airport symbol*] (OAG)
LTL .... Latvian Airlines [*ICAO designator*] (FAAC)
LTL .... Learning Through Listening [*Recording for the blind*]
LTL .... Learning to Look
LTL .... Less than Lethal (INF)
LTL .... Less than Truckload [*Under 24,000 pounds*]
LTL .... Linear Temporal Logic (RALS)
LTL .... Line-to-Line
LTL .... Lintel [*Technical drawings*]
LTL .... Listing-Time Limit (MSA)
LTL .... Little
LTL .... Lot-to-Lot (AAEL)
LTL .... Lot-Truck Load
LTL .... Low Temperature Loop (SPST)
LTL .... Lytton Minerals (SAUO)
LTL .... Lytton Minerals Ltd. [*Toronto Stock Exchange symbol*] [*Vancouver Stock Exchange symbol*]
LTLA .... Launcher Tube Longitudinal Axis
LTLA .... Louisiana Trial Lawyers Association (SRA)
lt lat .... Left Lateral [*Medicine*] (MAE)
LTLCG .... Little Change (FAAC)
LTLOG .... Landsat Technical Working Group (SAUO)
LTLP .... Low Temperature, Low Pressure [*Plastics*]
LTLS .... Lincoln Trail Libraries System [*Library network*]
LTLS .... Long-Term Lapse Survey [*LIMRA*]
LTLT .... Long Time Low Temperature [*Food processing*]
LTM .... Laici per il Terzo Mondo [*Italy*]
LTM .... LASER Target Marker (RDA)
LTM .... LASER Transfer Module [*Telecommunications*] (LAIN)
LTM .... Leading Torpedoman [*Navy*] [*British*]
LTM .... Lead Time Matrix
LTM .... Learning to Manage Health information (SAUO)
LTM .... Leave Trapping Mode (SAA)
LTM K .... Lethem [*Guyana*] [*Airport symbol*] (OAG)
LTM .... Leverage Transaction Merchant (MHDI)
LTM .... Licentiate in/of Tropical Medicine (SAUO)
LTM .... Licentiate in Tropical Medicine [*British*]

LTM .... Lient Trief Mixed [*Cement*]
LTM .... Life Test Model
LTM .... Limits-to-Throughput Model [*Environmental science*]
LTM .... Line Termination Module (SAUS)
LTM .... Line Transition Monitoring (NITA)
LTM .... Line Type Modulation [*Radio*]
LTM .... Little Maria Mountains [*California*] [*Seismograph station code, US Geological Survey*] (SEIS)
LTM .... Little Theatre Movement (SAUO)
LTM .... Live Traffic Model [*Telecommunications*] (TEL)
LTM .... Load Ton Mile (IAA)
LTM .... Logic Theory Machine (SAA)
LTM .... London Terminal Market (SAUO)
LTM .... Long-Term Memory
LTM .... Long-Term Monitoring [*Environmental science*] (BCP)
LTM .... Low Thermal Mass (PDAA)
LTM .... Low-Trajectory Missiles (NRCH)
LTM1 .... Lunar Tele-Operations Model 1 [*Mooncolony modeling*]
LTMA .... Lithium Trimethoxyaluminium (MEC)
LTMAC .... Lauryltrimethylammonium Chloride [*Organic chemistry*]
LTMC .... Lymphoid Tissue Mononuclear Cell [*Physiology*]
LTMED .... Low-Temperature Multieffect Distillation [*Chemical engineering*]
LTMFM .... Low-Temperature Magnetic Force Microscope
LTMFX .... Thornburg Ltd. Term Munic: Natl. Cl.A [*Mutual fund ticker symbol*] (SG)
LTMO .... Laser Target Marking Operator (SAUS)
LTMR .... Laser Target Marker & Receiver (SAUS)
LTMR .... LASER Target Marker Ranger [*Aviation*] (OA)
LTMR .... Long-Term Multilineage Reconstituting [*Cytology*]
LTMRSC ...... Long-Term Multilineage Reconstituting Stem Cell [*Cytology*]
LTMS .... Lubricant Test Monitoring System [*Automotive engineering*]
LTMS .... Lunar Terrain Measuring System [*Aerospace*]
LTMSH .... Laughing 'Til My Sides Hurt (ADWA)
LTN .... Aerolineas Latinas CA [*Venezuela*] [*ICAO designator*] (FAAC)
LTN .... Alaska Legislative Teleconference Network [*Alaska State Legislative Affairs Agency*] [*Juneau, AK*] [*Telecommunications service*] (TSSD)
LTN .... Liberty Tree Network [*An association*] (EA)
LTN .... Lightning (ADA)
LTN .... Linear Time-Varying Network
LTN .... Listen (IAA)
LTN .... Long-Term Nephelometer [*Instrumentation*]
Ltn .... Long Ton (EBF)
LTN .... Luton [*England*] [*Airport symbol*] (OAG)
LTNG .... Lightning [*Meteorology*]
LTNGARR ..... Lightning Arrester (IAA)
LTNGP .... Low-Temperature Noble Gas Process [*Nuclear energy*] (NRCH)
LTNIF .... Low-Temperature Neutron Irradiation Facility [*Oak Ridge, TN*] [*Oak Ridge National Laboratory*] [*Department of Energy*] (GRD)
LTNP .... Long-Term Nonprogressor [*Of the human immune deficiency virus*]
LT NS .... Law Times. New Series [*Pennsylvania*] [*A publication*] (DLA)
LT NS .... Law Times Reports, New Series [*England*] [*A publication*] (DLA)
LTNS .... Long Time, No See [*Computer science*] (DOM)
LT NS (Eng)... Law Times. New Series [*England*] [*A publication*] (DLA)
LTNYX .... Rochester Limited Term N.Y. Municipal [*Mutual fund ticker symbol*] (SG)
LTO .... Laboratory Training Office (SAUO)
LTO .... Landing and Takeoff
LTO .... Land Transfer Office (SAUO)
LTO .... Leading Torpedoman [*Navy*] [*British*] (DMA)
LTO .... Leading Torpedo Operator (SAUO)
LTO .... Lead-Tin Overlay [*Automotive engineering*]
LTO .... Linear Tape Open [*Computer science*] (DCDG)
LTO .... Local Tax Office [*British*]
LTO .... Loreto [*Mexico*] [*Airport symbol*] (OAG)
LTO .... Lot Time Order
LTO .... Low-Temperature Orthorhombic [*Crystallography*]
LTO .... Low Temperature Oxidation [*Physical chemistry*]
LTO .... Low Temperature Oxide (AAEL)
LTOC .... Landing-Takeoff Cycle (COE)
LTOC .... Lockheed Technical Operations Co. (SAUO)
LTOC .... Lowest Total Overall Cost (MHDI)
LTOE .... Living Table of Organization and Equipment [*Army*] (INF)
LTOF .... Low-Temperature Optical Facility
LTOM .... London's Traded Options Market [*British*] (ECON)
LTOM .... London Traded Options Market (SAUO)
LTON .... Long Ton [*2240 pounds*]
LTOOR .... Light Truck On-Off Road
LTOP .... Lease to Ownership Plan
LTOP .... Lease to Purchase (COE)
LTOS .... Law Times, Old Series [*British*]
LT OS .... Law Times Reports, Old Series [*England*] [*A publication*] (DLA)
LTOS .... Long to Short [*Computer utility tool*] (PCM)
LTOT .... Latest Time over Target (AFM)
LTP .... Laboratory Test Profile [*Medicine*] (DB)
LT-P .... Large Transmitter Coated with Paraffin
LTP .... Laser Trabeculoplasty (SAUS)
LTP .... Latpass [*Latvia*] [*FAA designator*] (FAAC)
LTP .... Leader Training Program [*Army*]
LTP .... Lead, Test, Probe (DWSG)
LTP .... LEM [*Lunar Excursion Module*] Test Procedure [*NASA*] (KSC)
LTP .... Let's Tax Plutocrats [*Humorous interpretation of LTP - Limit on Tax Preferences*]
LTP .... Letterpress
LTP .... Leukocyte Thromboplastin (STED)

LTP .... Library Technology Program [*Formerly, Library Technology Project*] [*ALA*] [*Defunct*]
LTP .... Lient Trief Pure [*Cement*]
LTP .... Life Test Procedure (ACAE)
LTP .... Limit on Tax Preferences
LTP .... Linear Time Plot (MUGU)
LTP .... Line-Throwing Projectile (NG)
LTP .... Line Type Processor [*Radio*] (IAA)
LTP .... Lipid Transfer Protein [*Biochemistry*]
LTP .... Living Together Partner [*Lifestyle classification*]
LTP .... Local Tourism Plan
LTP .... Local Training Plan [*Job Training and Partnership Act*] (OICC)
LTP .... Long-Tailed Pair [*Electronics*] (OA)
LTP .... Long-Term Potentiation [*Neurophysiology*]
LTP .... Long Term Projections [*Townsend-Greenspan & Co., Inc.*] [*Database*]
LTP .... Lower Trip Point
LTP .... Low-Temperature Passivation (PDAA)
LTP .... Low-Temperature Phase (PDAA)
LTP .... Low-Temperature Phosphorimetry [*Analytical chemistry*]
LTP .... Low-Temperature Physics
LTP .... Low-Temperature Polymer (IAA)
LTP .... L-Tryptophan (STED)
LTP .... Lunar Tidal Perturbation
LTP .... Lunar Transient Phenomenon
LTPA .... Leisure-Time Physical Activity (MELL)
LTPA .... Louisiana Travel Promotion Association (SRA)
LTPB .... Lactone Terminated Polybutadiene [*Organic chemistry*] (MCD)
LTPD .... Lot Tolerance Percent Defective [*Quality control*] (MSA)
LTPE .... Long-Term Public Expenditure [*British*]
LTPHOTORON... Light Photographic Squadron
LTPL .... Long-Term Procedural Language
LTPN .... Long-Term Parenteral Nutrition (PDAA)
LTPO .... LASER Technology Program Office [*Navy*]
LTPP .... Lipothiamide-Pyrophosphate
LTPP .... Long-Term Pavement Performance [*FHWA*] (TAG)
LTPP .... Long Term Planning Project (ACAE)
LTPR .... Lightproof [*Technical drawings*] (IAA)
LTPR .... Long Taper
LTPR .... Long-Term Prime Rate [*Finance*]
LTPS .... Lateral Transitional Phase Shift [*Optics*]
LTPS .... Lincoln Tube Process Specification (SAA)
LTPS .... Low Temperature Polysilicon (SAUS)
LTPSTFT ...... Low Temperature Polysilicon Thin Film Transistor (SAUS)
LTPT .... Low-Turbulence Pressure Tunnel [*NASA*]
LTPWG .... LOAD [*Low Altitude Defense*] Test Planning Working Group
LTPWS .... Low Tire-Pressure Warning System [*Automotive engineering*]
LTQ .... Le Touquet [*France*] [*Airport symbol*] (OAG)
LTQ .... Local Track Quality (NVT)
LTQ .... Low Torque
LTQC .... Long-Term Quality-Control [*Analytical chemistry*]
LTR .... Archives of Lithuanian Folklore of the Institute of Lithuanian Literature and Folklore (SAUS)
LTR .... AS Lufttransport [*Norway*] [*ICAO designator*] (FAAC)
LTR .... Lander Trajectory Reconstruction [*Program*] [*NASA*]
LTR .... Lands Tribunal Rules [*Town planning*] [*British*]
LTR .... LASER Tank Range-Finder
LTR .... LASER Target Recognition [*Military*] (CAAL)
LTR .... Lattice Test Reactor
LTR .... Law Times Reports, New Series [*England*] [*A publication*] (DLA)
LTR .... Lead Technical Representative (EEVL)
LTR .... [*The*] Learning Tree [*UTLAS symbol*]
LTR .... Left Test Register (IAA)
LTR .... Left to Right (SAUO)
LTR .... Letter (AFM)
Ltr .... Letter (EBF)
ltr .... Letter (ELAL)
LTR .... Library Technology Reports [*American Library Association*]
L-TR .... Licensing Technical Review [*Nuclear energy*] (NRCH)
LTR .... Lighter
LTR .... Light Tactical Raft
LTR .... Liquid Test Rig [*Apollo*] [*NASA*]
LTR .... List Test Resister (PDAA)
LTR .... Living Together Relationship
LTR .... Load Task Register [*Computer science*] (PCM)
LTR .... Location Transactivating Region [*Medicine*] (DMAA)
LTR .... Lockheed Training Reactor
LTR .... Loew's Corp. [*Formerly, Loew's Theatres, Inc.*] [*NYSE symbol*] (SPSG)
LTR .... London Telecommunications Region (SAUO)
LTR .... Lone Tree Road [*California*] [*Seismograph station code, US Geological Survey*] (SEIS)
LTR .... Longitudinal Triangular Ripples [*Oceanography*]
LTR .... Long Terminal Repeat [*or Redundancy*] [*Genetics*]
LTR .... Long-Term Research (SAUO)
LTR .... Long-Term Reserve [*British military*] (DMA)
LTR .... Long-Term Residential
LTR .... Long-Term Revitalization (OA)
LTR .... Long Treble [*Knitting*]
LTR .... Long-Tube Recirculation [*Evaporator*]
LTR .... Loop Transfer Recovery (SAUS)
LTR .... Lord Treasurer's Remembrancer [*British*]
LTR .... Low-Temperature Reactor [*Chemical engineering*]
LTR .... Low Thermal Regime (ACAE)
LTR .... Lymphocyte Transfer Reaction (STED)

LTRA............ Lands Tribunal Rating Appeals [Legal] [British]
LTRA............ Leukotriene Receptor Antagonist [Biochemistry]
LTRA............ Long Term Remedial Action (SAUO)
L-TRAN........ Lesson Translator (NVT)
L Trans Q .... Law in Transition Quarterly [A publication] (DLA)
LTRB............ Long Term Review Board (WDAA)
LTRC............ Louisiana Transportation Research Center [Louisiana State University] [Research center] (RCD)
LTRCA .... Lawn Tennis Registered Coaches Association [British] (BI)
LTRD............ Lettered
LTRE............ Learning Tree Intl. [NASDAQ symbol] (TTSB)
LTREB........... Long-Term Research in Environmental Biology (SAUO)
LTren........... Left Trendelenburg [Position] [Surgery] (DAVI)
LT Rep......... Law Times Reports, New Series [England] [A publication] (DLA)
LT Rep NS... Law Times Reports, New Series [England] [A publication] (DLA)
LTRF............ LASER Tank Range-Finder
LTRF............ Low Temperature Research Facility [NASA]
LTRI............ Lightning and Transient Research Institute (SAUO)
LTRI............ Lightning and Transients Research Institute [St. Paul, MN] (MCD)
LTRMP.......... Long-Term Resource Monitoring Program (SAUO)
LTRN............ Lantern (MSA)
LTRN .... Lantern Slide (VRA)
Lt RN .... Lieutenant-Royal Navy (SAUO)
LTR NS........ Law Times Reports, New Series [England] [A publication] (DLA)
LTRO............ Lateral Tire Run-Out [Automotive engineering]
LTROM .... Linear Transformer Read Only Memory [Computer science] (IAA)
LTRP............ Long-Term Requirement Plan (NATG)
LTRPRS .... Letterpress
LTRR .... Laboratory for/of Tree Ring Research. Based at the University of Arizona (SAUO)
LTRRS .... Long-Term Regional Research Site (SAUO)
LTRS............ LASER Target Recognition System
LTRS............ Letters Shift [Teleprinters]
LTRS............ Low Temperature Research Station [British]
LT Rulings... Land Tax Rulings [Australia] [A publication]
LTS.............. Altus, OK [Location identifier] [FAA] (FAAL)
LTS.............. Laboratory Test Set
LTS.............. Labor Turnover Statistics (OICC)
LTS.............. Landfall Technique School [Navy]
LTS.............. Language Teaching System
LTS.............. Language Translation System
LTS.............. Laparoscopic Tubal Sterilization [Medicine] (STED)
LTS.............. LASER Target Simulator (MCD)
LTS.............. LASER Test Set (MCD)
LTS.............. LASER Time Sharing (PDAA)
LTS.............. Laser Tracking System (ACAE)
LTS.............. Laser Training System (SAUS)
LTS.............. LASER-Triggered Switch (MCD)
LTS.............. Lateral Test Simulator (IAA)
LTS.............. Launch Telemetry Station
LTS.............. Launch Telemetry Stations (SAUO)
LTS.............. Launch Telemetry System
LTS.............. Launch Test Set
LTS.............. Launch Tracking Station
LTS.............. Launch Tracking Stations (SAUO)
LTS.............. Launch Tracking System
LTS.............. Leadership Training School (SAUO)
LTS.............. Lethality Test System (ACAE)
LTS.............. Levothyroxine Sodium (ACAE)
LTS.............. Library Technical Services [Library network]
LTS.............. Libyan Television Service (SAUO)
LTS.............. Lifetrends Behavioral Systems, Inc. [Vancouver Stock Exchange symbol]
LTS.............. Lift-Off Transmission Subsystem (IAA)
LTS.............. Lighting Test Set (KSC)
LTS.............. Lights
LTS.............. Light Tactile Stimulation [Neurology] (DAVI)
LTS.............. Light Traffic Station (ACAE)
LTS.............. Light Truck Structure [Automotive engineering]
LTS.............. Linearity Test Set
LTS.............. Line Transient Suppression
LTS.............. Link Terminal Simulator
LTS.............. Link Translator System (SAUS)
LTS.............. Linomatic Tape System [Typography] (DGA)
LTS.............. Llantrisant [Welsh depot code]
LTS.............. Load Transfer Switch
LTS.............. Logistics Test Squadron [Military]
LTS.............. Log Tape System (TIMI)
LTS.............. London Transport System (SAUO)
LTS .... London Typographical Society (SAUO)
LTS.............. Long-Term Stability
LTS.............. Long-Term Standard [Lamp for spectrometry]
LTS.............. Long-Term Storage [Memory] [Computer science]
LTS.............. Long-Term Survival [Medicine] (DMAA)
LTS.............. Long-Term Surviving (STED)
LTS.............. Long Tract Sign [Neurology] (STED)
LTS.............. Love Token Society (EA)
LTS.............. Low frequency Transmit Subsystem (SAUS)
LTS.............. Low-Frequency Transmit System (DWSG)
LTS.............. Low-Temperature Separation
LTS.............. Low-Temperature Smoking (PDAA)
LTS.............. Low Temperature Superconductor (ACAE)
LTS.............. Low Threshold Spike [Neurochemistry]
LTS.............. LTU [Lufttransport Unternehmen Sud] GmbH [Germany] [ICAO designator] (FAAC)

LTS.............. Lufttransport-Sud [Airline] [Germany]
LTS.............. Lunar Touchdown System [NASA] (IAA)
LTS.............. Luxury Touring Sedan
LTS.............. Trinity Lutheran Seminary, Columbus, OH [OCLC symbol] (OCLC)
LTSB............ London Trustee Savings Bank (SAUO)
LTSC............ Licentiate in the Technology of Surface Coatings [British] (DBQ)
LTSC............ Licentiate of the Tonic Sol-fa College (WDAA)
LTSC............ Low-Temperature Semiconductor [Electronics]
LTSCP.......... Long Term Ship Communication Plan (SAUO)
LTSDE.......... Low-Temperature Superconducting Device Electronics (DOMA)
LTSEM......... Low-Temperature Scanning Electron Microscopy
LTSF........... Lid Tank Shielding Facility [Nuclear energy] (NRCH)
LTSG........... LASER-Triggered Spark Gap
LTSH........... League of Tarcisians of the Sacred Heart [Later, LT] (EA)
LTSM.......... Long-Range Tactical Strike Missile (MCD)
LT(Sp)......... Lieutenant (Special)
LTSPC.......... L'Union Territoriale des Syndicats Professionelles Caledoniens [Territorial Federation of New Caledonian Unions of Private Employees]
LT-SR .... Large Transmitter Coated with Silicon Rubber
LTSR........... Line Trunk Scanner Register [Computer science] (IAA)
LTSS........... Lawrence Timesharing System (CIST)
LTSS........... Livermore Time-Sharing System (SAUO)
LTSS........... Long-Term Scientific Study [NATO Defense Research Group] (MCD)
LTSS........... Loral Thermal Sight System (SAUS)
LTSS........... Lotus Translation Services for Sametime
LTSTA......... Light Station [Coast Guard]
LTSV........... Light Savers USA [NASDAQ symbol] (TTSB)
LTSV........... Light Savers USA, Inc. [NASDAQ symbol] (SAG)
LTSV........... Lucerne Transient Streak Virus [Plant pathology]
LTSW........... Light Switch
LtSwtz......... Little Switzerland, Inc. [Associated Press] (SAG)
LTT............. Lactose Tolerance Test [Medicine] (STED)
LTT............. Landline Teletypewriter [Military]
LTT............. Land Title Trust (DLA)
LTT............. LASER Target Tracker
LTT............. Laser Thermal Tagger (ACAE)
LTT............. Latakia Type Tobacco [Shipping]
LTT............. Less than Truckload [Under 24,000 pounds] (WGA)
LTT............. Leucine Tolerance Test [Clinical chemistry] (AAMN)
LTT............. Liberty Term Trust-1999 [NYSE symbol] (SPSG)
LT T............ Lieutenant of Treasury [British]
LTT............. Light Tactical Transport (MCD)
LTT............. Light Tracked Tractor (SAUS)
LTT............. Light-Travel-Time [Astronomy]
LTT............. Limited Treadmill Test [Medicine] (DMAA)
LTT............. Liquid Toner Transfer [Typography] (DGA)
LTT............. Lithium Thallium Tartrate [Inorganic chemistry]
LTT............. Long-Term Training (MCD)
LTT............. Long-Term Trend [Finance] (MHDI)
LTT............. Long Term Trends (SAUO)
LTT............. Louis Trichardt [South Africa] [Seismograph station code, US Geological Survey] (SEIS)
LTT............. Low Temperature Teatment [Materials science]
LTT............. Low-Temperature Test
LTT............. Low-Temperature Tetragonal [Crystallography]
LTT............. Lunar Test Table [Aerospace]
LTT............. Lymphoblastic Transformation Test [Biochemistry] (DAVI)
LTT............. Lymphocyte Transformation Test [Medicine]
LTTA........... Logic Tree Trouble-Shooting Aid (PDAA)
LTTA........... Long Tank Thrust-Augmented (PDAA)
LTTAD......... Long Tank Thrust-Augmented Delta (PDAA)
LTTAID........ Long Tank Thrust Augmented Improved Thor (ACAE)
LTTAS......... Light Tactical Transport Aircraft System [Helicopter] [Military] (RDA)
LTTAT......... Long Tank Thrust-Augmented Thor
LTTB........... Listen to the Band (EA)
LTTBT......... Low-Threshold Test Ban Treaty [Proposed]
LTTC........... Lawn-Tennis-Tournier-Club (SAUO)
LTTC........... Lowry Technical Training Center [Air Force] (AFM)
LTTD........... Letter-Type Technical Directive [Navy] (NG)
LTTE........... Liberation Tigers of Tamil Eelam [Sri Lanka]
LTTE........... Link Terminal Terminating Equipment (SAUO)
LTTL........... Low-Power Transistor-Transistor Logic (IEEE)
LTTM........... Longterm Terrain Model (SAUO)
LTTMT .... Low-Temperature Thermomechanical Treatment
LTTO........... Lotto World [NASDAQ symbol] (TTSB)
LTTO........... Lotto World, Inc. [NASDAQ symbol] (SAG)
LTTP........... Long-Term Treatment Plan [Environmental science] (COE)
LTTPBA....... Late Third Trimester Partial Birth Abortion (MELL)
LTTR........... Latter
LTTR........... Long-Term Tape Recorder
LTTV........... Launch Transient Test Vehicle (SAUS)
LTU............. Laboratory Test Unit (SAUO)
LTU............. Land Treatment Unit [Waste disposal]
LTU............. Laser Tracking Unit (ACAE)
LTU............. Laser Transceiver Unit (SAUS)
LTU............. Lawrence Technological University
LTU............. Less Than
LTU............. Lift-Off Time and Update
LTU............. Line Terminating Unit (CET)
LTU............. Line Termination Unit (NITA)
LTU............. Little Mountain [Utah] [Seismograph station code, US Geological Survey] (SEIS)
LTU............. Long-Term Unemployed
LTU............. Long Ton Unit

LTU.............	Loughborough University of Technology (SAUO)
LTU.............	Lufttransport Unternehmen GmbH [Germany] [ICAO designator] (FAAC)
LTU.............	Spencer, IA [Location identifier] [FAA] (FAAL)
LTUAE.........	Life, The Universe, and Everything (SAUS)
LTUI............	Low Transverse Uterine Incision [Medicine] (STED)
LTUM...........	Line Terminating Unit Module (SAUO)
LTUS............	Garden Fresh Restaurant [NASDAQ symbol] (TTSB)
LTUS............	Garden Fresh Restaurant Corp. [NASDAQ symbol] (SAG)
LTUSA	La Trobe University Staff Association [Australia]
LTV.............	Land Transport Vehicle (NVT)
LTV.............	Large Test Vessel [Nuclear energy] (NRCH)
LTV.............	Launch Test Vehicles
LTV.............	Life Test Vehicle
LTV.............	Light Trucks and Vans
LTV.............	Light-Vessel [Navigation]
LTV.............	Linear Velocity Transducer (ACAE)
LTV.............	Ling-Temco-Vaught (WDAA)
LTV.............	Ling-Temco-Vaught Inc. (SAUO)
LTV.............	Ling-Temco-Vought Co.
LTV.............	Load Threshold Value (DA)
LTV.............	Loan-to-Value Ratio [Finance]
LTV.............	Local Thickness Variation (AAEL)
LTV.............	Long-Term Vibration
LTV.............	Long Tube Vertical
LTV.............	LTV Corp. [Formerly, Ling-Temco-Vought, Inc.] [NYSE symbol] (SPSG)
LTV.............	Lucke Tumor Virus [Medicine] (STED)
LTV.............	Lunar Excursion Module Test Vehicle [NASA] (IAA)
LTV.............	Lung Thermal Volume [Medicine] (STED)
LTVC............	Launcher Tube Vertical Centerline
LTVC............	Long-Term Venous Catheter [Medicine] (MELL)
LTVSM.........	Long-Term Visiting Staff Member (SAUO)
LTW.............	League of Tasmanian Wheelmen [Australia]
LTW.............	Leydig-Cell Tumor in Wistar Rat [Medicine] (DMAA)
LTW.............	Long-Term Waviness [Metal surface finish]
LTW.............	Los Trancos Woods [California] [Seismograph station code, US Geological Survey] (SEIS)
LTW.............	Low-Tension Winding
LTW.............	NV Luchtvaartmaatschappij Twente [Netherlands] [ICAO designator] (FAAC)
LTWA...........	Lawn Tennis Writers' Association of America [Later, USTWA] (EA)
LTWA...........	Log Tape Write Ahead [Computer science] (ELAL)
LTWA...........	Long Trailing Wire Antenna (MCD)
LTWG...........	Landsat Technical Working Group (SAUO)
LTWG...........	Launch Test Working Group
LTWO...........	Learn2.com, Inc. [NYSE symbol] (SG)
LTWT...........	Lightweight
LTX.............	Lap-Top Expansion [Computer science]
ltx.............	Latex (VRA)
LTX.............	Leo Taxi Aereo SA de CV [Mexico] [ICAO designator] (FAAC)
LTX.............	Lintronics International Ltd. [Vancouver Stock Exchange symbol]
LTX.............	LTX Corp. [Associated Press] (SAG)
LTXRD	Low-Temperature X-Ray Diffraction [Instrumentation]
LTXW..........	Latex Resources Wrrt [NASDAQ symbol] (TTSB)
LTXX...........	LTX Corp. [NASDAQ symbol] (SAG)
LTY.............	Collaboration Type (SAUS)
LTYR...........	Light Year
Lu...............	H. Lundbeck [Denmark] [Research code symbol]
LU...............	Labor Union (OICC)
LU...............	Lamentations over the Destruction of Ur (BJA)
LU...............	Langston University (SAUO)
LU...............	Laurentian University (SAUO)
LU...............	Laval University (SAUO)
LU...............	Laws of Ur Nammu (BJA)
LU...............	Left Unity Group [European political movement] (ECON)
LU...............	Left Upper [Medicine]
LU...............	Lehigh University (SAUO)
LU-.............	Leningrad University (SAUS)
LU...............	Lethbridge University (SAUO)
LU...............	Liberal Unionist (SAUO)
LU...............	Liberal-Unionist [British] (ROG)
LU...............	Libraries Unlimited [Library network]
LU...............	Library Utility [Computer science]
LU...............	Lighting Unit (WDAA)
LU...............	Ligue Universelle [Esperantiste]
LU...............	Lincoln University (SAUO)
LU...............	Line Unit (IAA)
LU...............	Line-Up
LU...............	List Up
LU...............	Liverpool University (SAUO)
LU...............	Load Unit
LU...............	Lock Up (ADA)
LU...............	Logical Unit [Computer science]
LU...............	Logistical Unit (NATG)
LU...............	London University (SAUO)
LU...............	Looking Up [An association] (EA)
LU...............	Loudness Unit
LU...............	Louisiana State University, Baton Rouge, LA [Library symbol] [Library of Congress] (LCLS)
LU...............	Loyola University (SAUO)
LU...............	Lucent Technologies [NYSE symbol] (TTSB)
LU...............	Lucent Technologies, Inc. [NYSE symbol] (SAG)
LU...............	Lues [Syphilis] [Latin] (WDAA)
Lu...............	Lumbar [Anatomy] (DAVI)
Lu...............	Lumen [Anatomy]
LU...............	Lund University (SAUO)
lu...............	Lute
Lu...............	Lutetium [Chemical element]
Lu...............	Lutheran [Blood group]
LU...............	Luxembourg [ANSI two-letter standard code] (CNC)
lu...............	Luxembourg [MARC country of publication code] [Library of Congress] (LCCP)
LU...............	Lytic Unit (DB)
LU...............	St. Luke's Gospel [New Testament book] (ROG)
LU...............	Theron Airways [ICAO designator] (AD)
LU...............	Upper Limen [Psychology]
LUA.............	Launch under Attack [Nuclear warfare option]
LUA.............	Left Upper Arm [Medicine]
LUA.............	Lens Users Association (SAUO)
LUA.............	Library Users of America (EA)
LUA.............	Life Underwriters Association (SAUO)
LUA.............	Liverpool Underwriters Association (DS)
LUA.............	Lloyd's Underwriters' Association [British] (DBA)
LUA.............	Local Unit of Administration (SAUO)
LUA.............	London Underwriters Association (SAUO)
LU-A	Louisiana State University in Alexandria, Alexandria, LA [Library symbol] [Library of Congress] (LCLS)
LUA.............	Luanda [Angola] [Seismograph station code, US Geological Survey] [Closed] (SEIS)
LUA.............	Luanda Belas [Angola] [Geomagnetic observatory code]
LUA.............	Lukla [Nepal] [Airport symbol] (OAG)
LUA.............	Luray, VA [Location identifier] [FAA] (FAAL)
LUAA............	Life Underwriters Association of Australia (SAUO)
LUAC	Land Use Advisory Council (SAUO)
LUAC	Life Underwriters Association of Canada
LUAM...........	Land Use Allocation Model
LUAMC	Leading Underwriters' Agreement for Marine Cargo Business (DS)
LUAMH	Leading Underwriters' Agreement for Marine Hull Business (DS)
LUANZ	Life Underwriters Association of New Zealand (SAUO)
LUAP	Land Use Adjustment Program
LUAR	Liga de Uniao e Acao Revolucionaria [Portugal]
LU-Ar	Louisiana State University, Department of Archives and Manuscripts, Baton Rouge, LA [Library symbol] [Library of Congress] (LCLS)
LUB.............	Least [or Lowest] Upper Bound
LUB.............	Left Upper Lobe Bronchus [Anatomy]
LUB.............	Logical Unit Block [Computer science]
lub.............	Luba [MARC language code] [Library of Congress] (LCCP)
LUB.............	Lubbock [Texas] [Seismograph station code, US Geological Survey] (SEIS)
LUB.............	Lubricant (WDAA)
LUB.............	Lubricate [or Lubrication] (AAG)
LUB.............	Luby's Cafeterias [NYSE symbol] (TTSB)
LUB.............	Luby's Cafeterias, Inc. [NYSE symbol] (SPSG)
LUB.............	Lusiana [Czechoslovakia] [ICAO designator] (FAAC)
LUBA	Limited Underwater Breathing Apparatus (NG)
LUBC	Liberty United Bancorp (SAUO)
LUBE...........	AutoSpa Corp. (SAUO)
LUBE...........	Lubricate (ADA)
LUBEE.........	Lubrication
Lube Eq	Lube on Equity Pleading [A publication] (DLA)
Lube PL	Lube on Equity Pleading [A publication] (DLA)
LUBIX.........	Lutheran Bro. Income [Mutual fund ticker symbol] (SG)
LUBO	Lubricating Oil
LUBR	Lubricant
LUBR	Lubricate (ADA)
Lubrizol	[The] Lubrizol Corp. [Associated Press] (SAG)
LUBS	Large Undisturbed-Bottom Sampler (PDAA)
LUBS	Loughborough University Business School (SAUO)
LUBT	Lubricant (MSA)
Lubys..........	Luby's Cafeterias, Inc. [Associated Press] (SAG)
LUC.............	Land Use Commission (SAUO)
LUC.............	Land Use Committee (SAUO)
LUC.............	Land Use Concurrence [Acquisition of real estate for the use of US forces on a rent-free basis] [Vietnam]
LUC.............	Large Unstained Cells [Cytology]
LUC.............	Laucala Island [Fiji] [Airport symbol] (OAG)
LUC.............	League of Ukrainian Catholics of America (EA)
LUC.............	Limburg University Centre (SAUO)
LUC.............	Living under Canvas [British military] (DMA)
LUC.............	London Union Catalogue (SAUO)
LU-C	Louisiana State University, Chemistry Library, Baton Rouge, LA [Library symbol] [Library of Congress] (LCLS)
LUC.............	Louisiana Union Catalog [Library network]
LUC.............	Louisiana University Center (SAUO)
Luc.............	Lucan [39-65AD] [Classical studies] (OCD)
Luc.............	Lucas: an Evangelical History Review [A publication] (APTA)
Luc.............	Lucas' Reports [Modern Reports, Part X] [A publication] (DLA)
LUC.............	Lucifer (WDAA)
LUC.............	Luciferase [An enzyme]
Luc.............	Lucullus [of Plutarch] [Classical studies] (OCD)
Luc.............	Lucullus or Academica Posteriora [of Cicero] [Classical studies] (OCD)
LUC.............	Lukens, Inc. [NYSE symbol] (SPSG)
LUC.............	Lukens Steel Company (SAUO)
Luc.............	[The] Rape of Lucrece [Shakespearean work]
LUCALOX....	Translucent Aluminum Oxide [Ceramic]
LUCAS	Line Utilization Cable Assignment System (MCD)
Lucas..........	Lucas' Reports [Modern Reports, Part X] [A publication] (DLA)
LucasV........	Lucasvarity PLC [Associated Press] (SAG)

LUCB .... Library of the University of California at Berkeley (SAUO)
LUCC .... Land Use and Climate Change (SAUO)
LUCC .... Land Use and Cover Change [*Environmental studies*] (ECON)
LUCC .... Lehigh University Computing Center [*Pennsylvania*] [*Research center*] (RCD)
LUCCAS ...... Land Use and Cover Change Analysis System (SAUO)
LUCC-CPPC... LUCC Core Project Planning Committee (SAUO)
LUCCO .... Land Utilization Coordination Committee (SAUO)
LUCE .... Low Urinary Calcium Excretion [*Medicine*] (MELL)
Lucent .... Lucent Technologies, Inc. [*Associated Press*] (SAG)
LUCF .... Load, Unload, Cool, Fracture (PDAA)
LUCHIP .... Lutheran Church and Indian People [*An association*] [*Defunct*] (EA)
LUCID .... Language for Utility Checkout and Instrumentation Development
LUCID .... Language Used to Communicate Information System Design
LUCID .... Loughborough University Computerized Information and Drawings Project [*British*]
LUCIE .... Study of circulation north and west of Australia (SAUO)
LUCIFS .... Land Use and Climate Impacts on Fluvial Systems during the Period of Agriculture (SAUO)
Lucil .... Lucilius [*Second century BC*] [*Classical studies*] (OCD)
Lucile .... Lucille Farms, Inc. [*Associated Press*] (SAG)
LucileFr ...... Lucille Farms, Inc. [*Associated Press*] (SAG)
LUCIS .... London University Central Information Services (SAUO)
Luck .... Indian Law Reports, Lucknow Series [*A publication*] (DLA)
LUCK .... Lady Luck Gaming'A' [*NASDAQ symbol*] (TTSB)
LUCK .... Lady Luck Gaming Corp. [*NASDAQ symbol*] (SAG)
LUCK .... Logical Unit and Checker (NITA)
Luck .... Lucknow University (SAUO)
LUCKN .... Lucknow [*City in India*] (ROG)
Luck Ser ..... Indian Law Reports, Lucknow Series [*A publication*] (DLA)
LUCO .... Land-Use Coordination Office (SAUO)
LUCO .... Lloyd's Underwriters Claims Office (AIA)
LUCOLA ...... Lutheran Coalition on Latin America (EA)
LUCOLED .... Luminescence Conversion LED (SAUS)
LUCOLED .... Luminescence Conversion Light-Emitting Diode (AAEL)
LUCOM .... Lunar Communication [*System*] [*Aerospace*]
Lucor .... Lucor, Inc. [*Associated Press*] (SAG)
LUCP .... League to Uphold Congregational Principles [*Defunct*] (EA)
LUC PRIM ... Luce Primo [*At Daybreak*] [*Pharmacy*]
LUCR .... Lucor, Inc. [*NASDAQ symbol*] (SAG)
LUCR .... Lucor Inc.'A' [*NASDAQ symbol*] (TTSB)
Lucr .... [*The Rape of*] Lucrece [*Shakespearean Work*] (BARN)
LUCR .... Lucretius [*Roman poet, 96-55BC*] [*Classical studies*] (ROG)
LUCRE .... Lower Unit Costs and Related Earnings (MHDB)
LUCS .... Land Use Cost Studies (SAUO)
LUCS .... London University Computer Services (IAA)
LUCS .... London University Computing Services (SAUO)
LUCY .... Lucille Farms [*NASDAQ symbol*] (TTSB)
LUCY .... Lucille Farms, Inc. [*NASDAQ symbol*] (SAG)
LUCYW .... Luclle Farm Wrrt [*NASDAQ symbol*] (TTSB)
LUD .... Land Use Designation [*US Forest Service*]
LUD .... Lift-Up Door [*Technical drawings*]
LUD .... Luderitz [*South-West Africa*] [*Airport symbol*] (OAG)
LUD .... Ludlow Corporation (SAUO)
LUD .... Lundin Explorations [*Vancouver Stock Exchange symbol*]
LUDA .... Land Use Data
LUDA .... Land Use Development Assistance (SAUO)
LUDA .... USGS Land Use Data Analysis (SAUS)
Lud & J Tr M... Ludlow and Jenkyns on Trade-Marks [*A publication*] (DLA)
Lud Bolog.... Ludovicus Bologninus [*Deceased, 1508*] [*Authority cited in pre-1607 legal work*] (DSA)
Ludd .... Ludden's Reports [*43, 44 Maine*] [*A publication*] (DLA)
Ludden .... Ludden's Reports [*43, 44 Maine*] [*A publication*] (DLA)
Lud de Ro ... Ludovicus Pontanus de Roma [*Deceased, 1439*] [*Authority cited in pre-1607 legal work*] (DSA)
Lud EC .... Luder's Election Cases [*England*] [*A publication*] (DLA)
Lud El Cas... Luder's Election Cases [*England*] [*A publication*] (DLA)
Luder Elec Cas... Luder's Election Cases [*England*] [*A publication*] (DLA)
Luders Elec Cas (Eng)... Luder's Election Cases [*England*] [*A publication*] (DLA)
ludes .... Quaaludes [*Methaqualone*] [*Pharmacology*] (DAVI)
Lud Gozad ... Ludovicus Gozzadini [*Deceased, 1536*] [*Authority cited in pre-1607 legal work*] (DSA)
Ludo .... Ludovicus Pontanus de Roma [*Deceased, 1439*] [*Authority cited in pre-1607 legal work*] (DSA)
Ludo Bolog... Ludovicus Bologninus [*Deceased, 1508*] [*Authority cited in pre-1607 legal work*] (DSA)
Ludo Ro .... Ludovicus Pontanus de Roma [*Deceased, 1439*] [*Authority cited in pre-1607 legal work*] (DSA)
LUE .... Dallas, TX [*Location identifier*] [*FAA*] (FAAL)
LUE .... Left Upper Entrance [*Theater*]
LUE .... Left Upper Extremity [*Anatomy*] (DMAA)
LUE .... Life, the Universe and Everything (SAUO)
LUE .... Linear Unbiased Estimator [*Statistics*]
LUE .... Link Utilization Efficiency
LUE .... Local Unit Establishment (SAUO)
LU-E .... Louisiana State University in Eunice, Eunice, LA [*Library symbol*] [*Library of Congress*] (LCLS)
LU-ECT .... Louisiana State at Baton Rouge, Eighteenth Century Short Title Catalogue, Baton Rouge, LA [*Library symbol*] [*Library of Congress*] (LCLS)
LUEMA......... Land Use and Environmental Management Authority (SAUO)
LUEV .... Lucerne Enation Virus [*Plant pathology*]
LUF .... Glendale, AZ [*Location identifier*] [*FAA*] (FAAL)
LUF .... Labour Unity Front (SAUO)
LUF .... Lift Unit Frame [*Shipping*] (DS)

LUF .... Limiting System Utilization Factor (MHDB)
LUF .... Local Utah Freight Bureau, Omaha NE [*STAC*]
LUF .... Lowest Usable [*or Useful*] Frequency [*Radio*]
LUF .... Luteinized Unruptured Follicle [*Medicine*] (DMAA)
LUFK .... Lufkin Industries [*NASDAQ symbol*] (TTSB)
LUFK .... Lufkin Industries, Inc. [*NASDAQ symbol*] (SAG)
Lufkin .... Lufkin Industries, Inc. [*Associated Press*] (SAG)
LUFO .... Last Used, First Out (VLIE)
LUFO .... Least Used, First Out [*Computer science*]
LUFO .... Longest Unused, First Out (VLIE)
LUFORO....... London Unidentified Flying Objects Research Organization (SAUO)
LUFS .... Land Use and Forest Resource Survey of Taiwan (SAUO)
LUFS .... Luteinized Unruptured Follicle Syndrome [*Medicine*] (DMAA)
LUFT .... Leaking Underground Fuel Tank (SARE)
LUG .... Lesbian Until Graduation
LUG .... Lewisburg, TN [*Location identifier*] [*FAA*] (FAAL)
LUG .... Light Utility Glider
LUG .... Linux User Group (SAUO)
LUG .... LOCAS Users Group (NITA)
LUG .... Lock-Up Garage
lug .... Luganda [*MARC language code*] [*Library of Congress*] (LCCP)
LUG .... Lugano [*Switzerland*] [*Airport symbol*] (OAG)
LUG .... Lugano Resources Ltd. [*Vancouver Stock Exchange symbol*]
LUG .... Luganville [*New Hebrides*] [*Seismograph station code, US Geological Survey*] (SEIS)
LUG .... Luggage
LUG .... Lugger [*Boat*]
LUG BAT ..... Lugdunum Batavorum [*Leyden*] [*Imprint*] (ROG)
LUGD .... Lugdunum [*Lyons*] [*Imprint*] (ROG)
LUGG .... Luggage
LUGL .... Lumen and Glare Calculations [*Facet Ltd.*] [*Software package*] (NCC)
LUGS .... Land Use Game Simulation
LUH .... Light Utility Helicopter (SAUS)
LUH .... Lumen Hour
LUHF .... Lowest Usable [*or Useful*] High-Frequency [*Radio*]
LUHGLSD ... Lock-Up Helical Gear Limited-Slip Differential [*Automotive engineering*]
LUI .... Land Use Intensity (PA)
LUI .... La Union [*Honduras*] [*Airport symbol*] [*Obsolete*] (OAG)
LUI .... Load Upper Immediate [*Computer science*]
LUI .... Logical Unit of Information (IAA)
LUI .... London United Investments [*British*]
lui .... Luiseno [*MARC language code*] [*Library of Congress*] (LCCP)
LUIE .... Leeds University Institute of Education [*British*] (AIE)
LUIP .... London University Institute of Psychiatry (SAUO)
LUIS .... Label Use Information System [*Environmental Protection Agency*] (EPAT)
LUIS .... Library User Information Service (SAUO)
LUIS .... Library User Information System [*Detroit, MI*] [*Library network*]
LUIS .... Low-Dose Urea in Invert Sugar (AAMN)
LUISA .... Leicester University Interactive Structural Analysis Project (SAUO)
LUISA Project... Leicester University Interactive Structural Analysis Project (SAUO)
LUJ .... Big Lake, TX [*Location identifier*] [*FAA*] (FAAL)
LUJ .... Lesotho Union of Journalists (EAIO)
LUJB .... Left Umbilical Junction Box [*Aerospace*] (AAG)
LUJBM .... London Union of Journeymen Basket Makers (SAUO)
LUK .... Cincinnati, OH [*Location identifier*] [*FAA*] (FAAL)
LUK .... Leucadia National [*NYSE symbol*] (TTSB)
LUK .... Leucadia National Corp. [*NYSE symbol*] (SPSG)
Lukens .... Lukens, Inc. [*Associated Press*] (SAG)
LukMed .... Lukens Medical Corp. [*Associated Press*] (SAG)
LUKN .... Lukens Med [*NASDAQ symbol*] (TTSB)
LUKN .... Lukens Medical Corp. [*NASDAQ symbol*] (SAG)
LUKY .... Lucky Chance Mining (SAUO)
LUL .... Language, Unseamanlike [*Slang*] [*Military*] (DNAB)
LUL .... Laurel, MS [*Location identifier*] [*FAA*] (FAAL)
LUL .... Left Upper Eyelid [*Medicine*]
LUL .... Left Upper Lid (SAUS)
LUL .... Left Upper Limb [*Medicine*]
LUL .... Left Upper Lobe [*of lung*] [*Medicine*]
LUL .... London Underground Ltd. [*British*] (ECON)
LUL .... London University Library (SAUO)
LU-L .... Louisiana State University, Law Library, Baton Rouge, LA [*Library symbol*] [*Library of Congress*] (LCLS)
LULA .... Loyola University of Los Angeles [*Later, Loyola Marymount University*]
LULAC .... League of United Latin American Citizens (EA)
LULL .... Loyola University, Law Library (SAUO)
LULOP .... London Union List of Periodicals
LULS .... Lunar Logistics System [*NASA*]
LULU .... Locally Unwanted Land Use [*i.e. garbage incinerators, prisons, roads, etc.*]
LULU .... Logical Unit to Logical Unit
LUM .... Bellingham, WA [*Location identifier*] [*FAA*] (FAAL)
LUM .... Launch Utility Mode
LUM .... Living Utility Module [*NASA*] (KSC)
LUM .... Local Urgent Mail [*British*]
LU-M .... Louisiana State University, Medical Center, New Orleans, LA [*Library symbol*] [*Library of Congress*] (LCLS)
LUM .... Lumbago (WDAA)
LUM .... Lumbar [*Medicine*] (WDAA)
LUM .... Lumber (WDAA)
Lum .... Lumen [*Record label*] [*France*]
LUM .... Lumex, Inc. [*AMEX symbol*] (SPSG)

LUM............ Luminairs Components (SAUS)
LUM............ Luminous (MSA)
LUM............ Lumonics, Inc. [*Toronto Stock Exchange symbol*]
LUM............ Maputo [*Mozambique*] [*Airport symbol*]
LUM............ University of Maryland, School of Law, Baltimore, MD [*OCLC symbol*] (OCLC)
Lum Ann..... Lumley on the Law of Annuities [*A publication*] (DLA)
LUMAS .... Lunar Mapping System [*Aerospace*]
lumb .... Lumbar [*Medicine*] (MAE)
Lum Bast..... Lumley on Bastardy [*A publication*] (DLA)
Lum BL....... Lumley on Bye-Laws [*A publication*] (DLA)
LUMC.......... Laval University Medical Center (SAUO)
LUMCON...... Louisiana Universities Marine Consortium
LUMD.......... Lowest Usual Maintenance Dose [*Medicine*] (MELL)
LUME.......... Light Utilization More Efficient (MCD)
LUMEN .... Loyola University Medical Education Network
Lumen Vitae... International Center for Studies in Religious Education (SAUO)
Lumex......... Lumex, Inc. [*Associated Press*] (SAG)
LUMF.......... Lockheed Underwater Missile Facilities (SAUO)
LUMF.......... Lockheed Underwater Missile Facility (AAG)
LUMI........... Lumisys, Inc. [*NASDAQ symbol*] (SAG)
LUMIS .... Land Use Management Information System [*NASA*]
Lumisys...... Lumisys, Inc. [*Associated Press*] (SAG)
Lumley PLC... Lumley's Poor Law Cases [*1834-42*] [*A publication*] (DLA)
LUMO.......... Lowest Unoccupied Molecular Orbit (SAUS)
LUMO .... Lowest Unoccupied Molecular Orbital [*Atomic physics*]
LUMP......... Last Unattached Male Person
Lum Parl Pr... Lumley's Parliamentary Practice [*A publication*] (DLA)
Lumpkin..... Lumpkin's Reports [*59-77 Georgia*] [*A publication*] (DLA)
Lum PLC..... Lumley's Poor Law Cases [*1834-42*] [*A publication*] (DLA)
Lum PL Cas... Lumley's Poor Law Cases [*1834-42*] [*A publication*] (DLA)
Lumps .... Life-Giving Unselfish Middle-Class Parent Survivors [*Facetious term coine d by columnist Erma Bombeck to describe the Yuppies' progenitors*] [*Lifestyle classification*]
Lum Pub H... Lumley's Public Health Acts [*12th ed.*] [*1950-55 and supplements*] [*A publication*] (DLA)
LUMS.......... Land Use Management System (SAUO)
Lum Sett..... Lumley on the Law of Settlements [*A publication*] (DLA)
LUN .... League of United Nations (SAUO)
LUN .... Logical Unit Number
LUN .... Ludington & Northern Railway [*AAR code*]
LUN .... Lunar (KSC)
LUN .... Lund [*Sweden*] [*Seismograph station code, US Geological Survey*] [*Closed*] (SEIS)
lun .... Lunette (VRA)
LUN .... Lunette
LUN .... Lusaka [*Zambia*] [*Airport symbol*] (OAG)
LUNA.......... Language for Users' Needs and Aims (NITA)
Lunar......... Lunar Corp. [*Associated Press*] (SAG)
LUNARG ..... Lunar Gravity Simulator [*Aerospace*] (MCD)
LUNCO....... Lloyd's Underwriters Non-Marine Claims Office (AIA)
LUND.......... Lund International [*NASDAQ symbol*] (TTSB)
LUND.......... Lund International Holdings, Inc. [*NASDAQ symbol*] (SAG)
LundInt....... Lund International Holdings, Inc. [*Associated Press*] (SAG)
Lund Pat..... Lund on Patents [*A publication*] (DLA)
Lundqua Rep... Lundqua Report (SAUO)
Lung Cancer... Lung Cancer (SAUS)
LUNHA .... Land Use History of North America (SAUO)
LUNK .... Line/Trunk (MCD)
LUNN .... Lunn Industries [*NASDAQ symbol*] (SAG)
LUNN .... Lunn Industries, Inc. (SAUO)
Lunnl......... Lunn Industries, Inc. [*Associated Press*] (SAG)
LUNO........ Logical Unit Number (TIMI)
LUNOS........ Lightweight Universal Night Observation System (SAUS)
LUNR .... Land Use and Natural Resource Information System (SAUO)
LUNR .... Lunar Corp. [*NASDAQ symbol*] (SAG)
LUO .... Laboratory Unit Operation
LUO .... Left Ureteral Orifice [*Medicine*]
LUO .... Luena [*Angola*] [*Airport symbol*] (OAG)
LUOQ .... Luogo [*As Written*] [*Music*]
LUOQ .... Left Upper Outer Quadrant [*of abdomen*] [*Medicine*]
LUOTC .... London University Officers Training Corps [*British military*] (DMA)
LUP........... Kalaupapa [*Hawaii*] [*Airport symbol*] (OAG)
LUP........... Land Use and Planning [*British*]
LUP........... Laying-Up Position [*British military*] (DMA)
LUP........... Liberia Unification Party [*Political party*]
LUP........... Liverpool University Press (SAUO)
LUP........... Loyola University Press (SAUO)
LUP........... Lupenga Air Charters [*Zambia*] [*ICAO designator*] (FAAC)
Lup........... Lupus [*Constellation*]
LUPAC .... Life Underwriters Political Action Committee
LUPF......... Linear Utility Prediction Function [*Mathematics*]
LUPI.......... Laser Unequal Path Interferometer (ACAE)
Lupi.......... Lupus [*Constellation*]
LUPIN .... Land Use Planning Information Network (SAUO)
LUPIS .... Land Use Planning Information System (SAUO)
LUPS .... Logistics Unit Productivity Study [*or System*] [*Army*]
LUPUL .... Lupulus [*Hops*] [*Pharmacy*] (ROG)
LUPWT .... Langley Unitary Plan Wind Tunnel [*NASA*] (KSC)
LUQ .... Laval University, Quebec (SAUO)
LUQ .... Left Upper Quadrant [*of abdomen*] [*Medicine*]
LUQ .... San Luis [*Argentina*] [*Airport symbol*] (OAG)
LUR .... Cape Lisburne [*Alaska*] [*Airport symbol*] (OAG)
LUR .... Land Use Ratio (PA)
LUR .... Laurasia Resources Ltd. [*Toronto Stock Exchange symbol*]

LUR .... Laureate [*Numismatics*]
LUR .... Lineas Aereas Latur SA de CV [*Mexico*] [*ICAO designator*] (FAAC)
LUR .... London Underground Railway
LUR .... Luria [*L.*] & Sons, Inc. [*NYSE symbol*] (SAG)
LUR .... Luria (L)& Son [*NYSE symbol*] (TTSB)
LURE .... Lunar Ranging Experiment [*Aerospace*]
Luria .... Luria [*L.*] & Sons, Inc. [*Associated Press*] (SAG)
LURS .... Land Use and Requirements Study (MCD)
LURS .... Logistic Unit Productivity System [*Army*]
LURTx......... Living Unrelated Renal Transplantation [*Medicine*]
LUS .... Land Utilization Survey (WDAA)
LUS .... Laparoscopic Ultrasonography [*Medicine*]
LUS .... Large Ultimate Size [*Telecommunications*] (TEL)
LUS .... Latch Up Screen
LUS .... Laws of the United States [*A publication*] (DLA)
LUS .... Library of Useful Stories [*A publication*]
LUS .... Liquid Upper Stage (NASA)
LUS .... Load, Update, Subset
LUS .... Local Use Study (SAUO)
LUS .... Lock-Up Solenoid [*Automotive engineering*]
LUS .... London Union of Sailmakers (SAUO)
LUS .... Louisiana State University in Shreveport, Library, Shreveport, LA [*OCLC symbol*] (OCLC)
LU-S .... Louisiana State University in Shreveport, Shreveport, LA [*Library symbol*] [*Library of Congress*] (LCLS)
LUS .... Lusaka [*Zambia*] [*Seismograph station code, US Geological Survey*] (SEIS)
LUS .... Lusitanair-Transportes Aereos Comercials SA [*Portugal*] [*ICAO designator*] (FAAC)
lus .... Lustre (VRA)
LUSA .... Life USA Holding, Inc. [*NASDAQ symbol*] (SAG)
LUSA .... Life USA Holdings [*NASDAQ symbol*] (TTSB)
LUSB .... Left Upper Sternal Border [*Anatomy*] (DAVI)
LUSCC .... Latymer Upper School Cadet Corps [*British military*] (DMA)
LUSCS .... Lower Uterine Segment Caesarian Section [*Medicine*] (WDAA)
LUSER .... Loser USER (SAUS)
LUSEX .... Lunar Surface Explorer Simulation Program [*Aerospace*] (MCD)
Lush........... Lushington's English Admiralty Reports [*1859-62*] [*A publication*] (DLA)
Lush Adm .... Lushington's English Admiralty Reports [*1859-62*] [*A publication*] (DLA)
Lush Pr...... Lush's Common Law Practice [*A publication*] (DLA)
Lush Pr L.... Lushington on Prize Law [*A publication*] (DLA)
LUSI.......... Lunar Surface Inspection [*Aerospace*]
LUSING........ Lusingando [*Coaxingly*] [*Music*]
LUSL.......... Loyola University School of Law (DLA)
LU-SM .... Louisiana State University in Shreveport, Medical Center Library, Shreveport, LA [*Library symbol*] [*Library of Congress*] (LCLS)
LUSO.......... Luso-American Fraternal Federation
LUSOLT ...... Lakehead University School of Library Technology [*Canada*]
LUST.......... Latrine Urinal Shower Toilet [*A unit of mobility equipment*] [*Military*]
LUST.......... Leaking Underground Storage Tank [*Environmental chemistry*]
LUST.......... List Updated Sort and Total (PDAA)
LUST.......... Lustrous (WDAA)
LUST.......... Wanderlust Interactive [*NASDAQ symbol*] (TTSB)
LUST.......... Wanderlust Interactive, Inc. [*NASDAQ symbol*] (SAG)
LUSTER ...... Lunar Dust and Earth Return [*NASA*] (IAA)
LUSTW .... Wanderlust Interactive Wrrt [*NASDAQ symbol*] (TTSB)
LUSURF....... Lunar Surface (PDAA)
LUSVC .... Logical Unit Services Manager (MHDB)
LUT........... Former abbreviation for Loughborough University of Technology (SAUS)
LUT............ Launcher-Umbilical Tower [*Aerospace*] (NAKS)
LUT............ Launch Umbilical Tower [*NASA*]
LUT............ Laura Station [*Australia*] [*Airport symbol*] [*Obsolete*] (OAG)
LUT............ Limited User Test [*Military*] (RDA)
LUT............ Limited User Testing
LUT............ Line Unit [*Computer science*] (BUR)
LUT............ Lining Up Table (DGA)
LUT............ Local User Terminal
LUT............ Lookup Table [*Computer science*] (BYTE)
LUT............ Loughborough University of Technology [*British*] (IRUK)
LUT............ Luteum [*Yellow*] [*Latin*]
LUT............ Miri [*Malaysia*] [*Airport symbol*] (AD)
LUTA.......... Library of the University of Texas at Austin (SAUO)
LUTC.......... Life Underwriter Training Council [*Washington, DC*] (EA)
LUTC.......... Life Underwriter Training Course
LUTCAM...... Language Used to Conceal Actual Meaning
LUTE.......... Language Understander Translator and Editor (NITA)
LUTEA........ Land Use in Temperate East Asia (SAUS)
Lut Elec Cas... Lutwyche's English Election Cases [*A publication*] (DLA)
Lut Ent....... Lutwyche's Entries [*1704; 1718*] [*A publication*] (DLA)
LUTET........ Lutetia Parisiorum [*Paris*] [*Imprint*] (ROG)
LUTFCSUSTC... Librarians United to Fight Costly, Silly, Unnecessary Serial Title Changes [*Defunct*] (EA)
Luth .... Lutheran (WDAA)
LUTH .... Lutheran
LUTH .... Luther Medical Products [*NASDAQ symbol*] (SAG)
LUTH .... Luther Medical Products, Inc. (SAUO)
LUTH .... Luther Med Products [*NASDAQ symbol*] (TTSB)
LuthMed ...... Luther Medical Products, Inc. [*Associated Press*] (SAG)
LUTIRO....... Life and Unit Trust Intermediaries Regulatory Organisation [*British*]
LUTIS .... Luton Information Service (NITA)
LUTOM .... Land Use Trade Off Model (DICI)
LUTP........... Land Use and Transport Planning [*British*]

LUT PAR......	Lutetia Parisiorum [Paris] [Imprint] (ROG)
LUTr............	Lighting Unit Trailer (WDAA)
Lut RC	Lutwyche's English Registration Appeal Cases [1843-45] [A publication] (DLA)
LUTS...........	Light Units, Times Square [Electronics]
LUTT...........	Launcher Umbilical Tower Transporter [NASA] (KSC)
Lutw E	Lutwyche's English Common Pleas Reports [A publication] (DLA)
Lutw Reg Cas...	Lutwyche's English Registration Cases [A publication] (DLA)
LUU	Illumination Unit (MCD)
LUU	Laura [Australia] [Airport symbol] [Obsolete] (OAG)
LUU	Louisiana State University, Baton Rouge, LA [OCLC symbol] (OCLC)
LUUG..........	Lunar UNIX Users Group (SAUO)
LUV............	Langgur [Indonesia] [Airport symbol] (OAG)
LUV............	Large Unilamellar Vesicle [Pharmacy] [Biochemistry]
LUV............	Let Us Vote (SAUO)
LUV............	Light Utility Vehicle [Pickup truck]
LU-V	Louisiana State University, School of Veterinary Medicine, Medical Library, Baton Rouge, LA [Library symbol] [Library of Congress] (LCLS)
LUV............	Southwest Airlines [NYSE symbol] (TTSB)
LUV............	Southwest Airlines Co. [NYSE symbol] (SPSG)
LUVO	Lunar Ultraviolet Observatory [NASA]
LUVS	Southwest Airlines Co. (SAUO)
LUW...........	Logical Units of Work [Computer science] (BYTE)
LUW...........	Luwuk [Indonesia] [Airport symbol] (OAG)
LUX...........	Laurens, SC [Location identifier] [FAA] (FAAL)
LUX...........	Lincoln Airlines, Inc. [ICAO designator] (FAAC)
LUX...........	Luxembourg [ANSI three-letter standard code] (CNC)
LUX...........	Luxembourg [Airport symbol] (OAG)
LUX...........	Luxembourg [Seismograph station code, US Geological Survey] (SEIS)
Lux............	Luxembourg (VRA)
LUX...........	Luxottica Group ADS [NYSE symbol] (SPSG)
lux	Luxurious (ADWA)
LUX...........	Luxurious Room [Travel industry] (TVEL)
LUX...........	Luxury [or Luxurious] [Classified advertising] (ADA)
Luxair	Luxembourg Airlines (SAUO)
Luxem	Luxembourg
LuxLBN	Bibliotheque Nationale de Luxembourg, Service du Pret, Luxembourg, Luxembourg [Library symbol] [Library of Congress] (LCLS)
Luxottca.......	Luxottica Group [Associated Press] (SAG)
Luxtec........	Luxtec Corp. [Associated Press] (SAG)
LUXY	Cinemastar Luxury Theaters [NASDAQ symbol] (TTSB)
LUXY	CinemaStar Luxury Theaters, Inc. [NASDAQ symbol] (SAG)
LUXYW	Cinemastar Luxry Theaters Wrrt [NASDAQ symbol] (TTSB)
LUY	Lushoto [Tanzania] [Airport symbol] (AD)
LUZED	Luzon Engineer District [Army] [World War II]
Luzerne Leg Obs (PA)...	Luzerne Legal Observer [Pennsylvania] [A publication] (DLA)
Luzerne Leg Reg R (PA)...	Luzerne Legal Register Reports [Pennsylvania] [A publication] (DLA)
Luzerne LJ (PA)...	Luzerne Law Journal [Pennsylvania] [A publication] (DLA)
Luz Law T....	Luzerne Law Times [Pennsylvania] [A publication] (DLA)
Luz Leg Obs...	Luzerne Legal Observer [Pennsylvania] [A publication] (DLA)
Luz Leg Reg Rep...	Luzerne Legal Register Reports [Pennsylvania] [A publication] (DLA)
Luz LJ.........	Luzerne Law Journal [Pennsylvania] [A publication] (DLA)
Luz LO	Luzerne Legal Observer [Pennsylvania] [A publication] (DLA)
Luz L Reg Rep...	Luzerne Legal Register Reports (Continuation of Kulp) [Pennsylvania] [A publication] (DLA)
Luz LT (NS)...	Luzerne Law Times. New Series [Pennsylvania] [A publication] (DLA)
Luz LT (OS)...	Luzerne Law Times. Old Series [Pennsylvania] [A publication] (DLA)
Lv	Catholic University of Louvain (SAUO)
LV	Laboratory Vehicle (MCD)
LV	Lacrosse Victoria [Australia] [An association]
LV	Lactobacillus Viridescens [Biochemistry] (DAVI)
l/v	Lake View
LV	Lancastrian Volunteers [British military] (DMA)
LV	Landing Vehicle
LV	Land Value (ADA)
LV	Largest Vessel [British] (ADA)
LV	Laryngeal Vestibule [Medicine] (MELL)
LV	LASER Velocimeter
LV	LaserVision [Videodisc system]
LV	Last Vehicle [Railroads] (ROG)
LV	Latch Valve (ACAE)
LV	Latent Variable [Data analysis]
LV	Lateral Ventricle [Neuroanatomy]
LV	Lateral Vestibular Nucleus [Neuroanatomy]
LV	Latino Virus [Medicine] (MELL)
LV	Latvia [Internet country code]
LV	Launch Vehicle (MCD)
LV	Launch Verification [NASA] (IAA)
LV	Lava (WGA)
LV	Laverda SpA [Italy] [ICAO aircraft manufacturer identifier] (ICAO)
LV	Laws of Virginia [A publication] (DLA)
LV	Leaky Valve [Nuclear energy] (NRCH)
LV	Leave (AFM)
lv	Leave (STED)
LV	Leaves (GOBB)
LV	Lecithovitellin (DB)
LV	Leeds Volunteers [British military] (DMA)
LV	Left Ventral Fin [Fish anatomy]
LV	Left Ventricle [Cardiology]
LV	Legal Volt
LV	Lehigh Valley Railroad Co. [Absorbed into Consolidated Rail Corp.] [AAR code]
LV	Leucovorin (DB)
LV	Leukemia Virus [Hematology] (MAE)
LV	Lev [Monetary unit] [Bulgaria]
LV	Level (VLIE)
LV	Level of Study [Online database field identifier]
Lv	Leviticus [Old Testament book]
LV	Licensed Victualer
LV	Lift Vector (NASA)
LV	Light and Variable [Referring to wind]
LV	Light Value [Photography] (DICI)
LV	Light Variegated Maize
LV	Light Vehicle [British military] (DMA)
LV	Light-Vessel [Navigation]
LV	Limited Visibility Study (MCD)
LV	Limit Value
LV	Linear Velocity
LV	Livery
LV	Live Vaccine [Medicine]
LV	Live Virus [Medicine] (MAE)
LV	Livre [Monetary unit] [Obsolete] [French] (ROG)
LV	Loading Valve (MCD)
LV	Load Vertical
L/V	Loan-to-Value Ratio [Business term]
L/V	Local Vertical (KSC)
LV	Logical Volume (SAUO)
LV	Loose Volume
LV	Louis Vuitton [Initials used as a pattern on Vuitton luggage, handbags, etc.]
LV	Low in Volatiles [Commercial grading]
LV	Low Velocity [British military] (DMA)
LV	Low Volatility [Lubricants]
LV	Low Voltage
LV	Low Volume
LV	Lumbar Vertebra [Medicine]
LV	Luncheon Voucher [British]
LV	Lung Volume (MAE)
LV	Valda [France] [Research code symbol]
LVA............	Lancashire Volunteer Artillery [British military] (DMA)
LVA............	Landing Vehicle, Airfoil
LVA............	Landing Vehicle, Assault [Navy symbol]
LVA............	Large Vertical Aperture Antenna [Aviation]
LVA............	Large Vertical Aperture radar (SAUS)
LVA............	Launch Vehicle Availability [NASA]
LVA............	Lava Capital Corp. [Toronto Stock Exchange symbol]
LVA............	Lava Cap Resources Ltd. (SAUO)
LVA............	Left Ventricular Aneurysm [Cardiology]
LVA............	Left Ventricular Aneurysmectomy [Medicine] (STED)
LVA............	Left Ventricular Assistance [Cardiology]
LVA............	Left Vertebral Artery [Medicine] (STED)
LVA............	Left Visual Acuity [Medicine]
LVA............	Literacy Volunteers of America (EA)
LVA............	Local Vendor Agreement (SAUO)
LVA............	Local Virtual Address
LVA............	Logarithmic Video Amplifier (IAA)
LVA............	Low-Velocity Anomaly [Seismology]
LVA............	Low Vision Aid [Ophthalmology]
LVA............	Low-Voltage Activated [Neurochemistry]
LVA............	Low-Voltage Avalanche [Electronics] (IAA)
LVA............	Lucasvarity PLC [NYSE symbol] (SAG)
LV (A) (2)...	Landing Vehicle, Tracked (Armored) (Mark II) ["Water Buffalo," Canopy Type]
LVAD	Left Ventricle Assist Device [Cardiology]
LVAD	Low Velocity Air Drop [Military vehicle specifications]
LVAIC.........	Lehigh Valley Association of Independent College Libraries [Library network]
L-VAM	Leuprolide Acetate, Vinblastine, Adriamycin (Doxorubicin), and Mitomycin (STED)
L-VAM	Lupron, Vinblastine, Adriamycin, Mutamycin [Antineoplastic drug] (CDI)
LVAOO........	Las Vegas Accounting Operations Office (SAUO)
LVAP..........	Launch Vehicle and Propulsion [NASA] (IAA)
LVAR	Launch Vehicle Assessment Report [or Review] [NASA] (KSC)
LVAR	Lithuanian Veterans Association Remove (SAUO)
LVAS	Land Valuation Assessors of Scotland (SAUO)
LVAS	Launch Vehicle Alarm System [NASA] (IAA)
LVAS	Left Ventricle Assist System [Cardiology]
LVAS	Left Ventricular Assist System [Medicine] (STED)
LVAS	Light-Vehicle Animation Simulation [Accident reconstruction] [Automotive engineering]
LVAT..........	Left Ventricular Activation Time [Medicine] (STED)
LVB............	Left Ventricular Bypass [Cardiology]
LVB............	Liquid-Vapor Bubble [Chemical engineering]
LVB............	Livramento [Brazil] [Airport symbol] (OAG)
LVB............	Low-Voltage Bias
LVBLE.........	Laramie Valley Boundary Layer Experiment (SAUO)
LVBP..........	Left Ventricle Bypass Pump [Medicine] (STED)
LVBR..........	Land Valuation Boards of Review [Australia]
LVC............	Decisions of the Lands Tribunal (Rating) [A publication] (DLA)
LVC............	Enid, OK [Location identifier] [FAA] (FAAL)
LVC............	Large Vacuum Chamber [Army]
LVC............	Lebanon Valley College, Annville, PA [OCLC symbol] (OCLC)

LVC	Lillian Vernon [*AMEX symbol*] (TTSB)
LVC	Lillian Vernon Corp. [*AMEX symbol*] (SPSG)
LVC	Log Voltmeter Converter
LVC	Low-Voltage Capacitor
LVC	Low-Voltage Cutoff [*Battery*]
LVC	Lutheran Volunteer Corps (EA)
LVCD	Least Voltage Coincidence Detector
LVCD	Liquid Volume Charge Density [*Automotive fuel systems*]
LVCERI	Luncheon Voucher Catering Education Research Institute (SAUO)
LVCI	Laser Vision Centers [*NASDAQ symbol*] (TTSB)
LVCI	Laser Vision Centers, Inc. [*NASDAQ symbol*] (SAG)
LVCM	Licentiate of the Victoria College of Music [*London*] (ROG)
LVCM	Licentiate of Victoria College of Music (SAUO)
LVCP	Laboratory Vehicle Checkout Procedure
LVCS	Logility Value Chain Solution
LVCS	Low Vertical Caesarean Section [*Medicine*] (STED)
LVCT	Low-Voltage Circuit Tester (MCD)
LVCVA	Las Vegas Convention & Visitors Authority (SAUO)
LVD	Collaboration Validity Date (SAUS)
LVD	Laboratory Vehicle Development
lvd	Leaved
LVD	Left Ventricular Assist Device [*An artificial organ*]
LVD	Left Ventricular Dimension (STED)
LVD	Left Ventricular Dysfunction [*Cardiology*] (DAVI)
LVd	Left Ventricular End-Diastolic Pressure [*Cardiology*] (MAE)
LVD	Level Island, AK [*Location identifier*] [*FAA*] (FAAL)
LVD	Light Valve Display
LVD	Liquid Crystal Visual Display [*Electronics*] (EECA)
LVD	Louvered Door (AAG)
LVD	Low-Velocity Detonation [*or Drop*]
LVD	Low-Voltage Drop (CET)
LVD1	Left Ventricular End-Diastolic Pressure [*Medicine*] (STED)
LVDA	Launch Vehicle Data Adapter [*NASA*]
LVDA	Launch Vehicle Deployment Assembly [*NASA*] (MCD)
LVDC	Launch Vehicle Data Center [*NASA*] (KSC)
LVDC	Launch Vehicle Digital Computer [*NASA*]
LVDC	Low-Voltage Direct Current
LVDd	Left Ventricular Dimension in Enddiastole [*Cardiology*] (DMAA)
LVDE	Large Volume Data Exchange (SAUO)
LVDG	Las Vegas Disc Golf & Tennis [*NASDAQ symbol*] (TTSB)
LVDG	Las Vegas Discount Golf & Tennis [*NASDAQ symbol*] (SAG)
LVDI	Left Ventricular Dimension [*Cardiology*] (DMAA)
LVDIFC	Leroy Van Dyke International Fan Club (EA)
LVDL	Licensed Victuallers' Defence League of England and Wales (BI)
LVDP	Left Ventricular Developed Pressure [*Medicine*] (DMAA)
LVDP	Left Ventricular Diastolic Pressure [*Cardiology*]
LV dp/dt	First Derivation of Left Ventricular Pressure [*Cardiology*] (DAVI)
LVDS	Light-Vehicle Dynamics Simulation [*Accident reconstruction*] [*Automotive engineering*]
LVDS	Liquid, Vee, Diesel-Cycle, Supercharged
LVDS	Low-Voltage Differential Signaling
LVDS	Low Voltage Differential Swing (SAUS)
LVDT	Linear Variable Differential Transducer [*Electronics*]
LVDT	Linear Variable Differential Transformer
LVDT	Linear Variable Displacement Transducer
LVDT	Linear Velocity Displacement Transformer (IEEE)
LVDT	Linear Voltage Differential Transformer (NASA)
LVDT-PRIM	Linear Variable Differential Transformer - Primary
LVDT-SEC	Linear Variable Differential Transformer - Secondary
LVDV	Left Ventricular Diastolic Volume [*Cardiology*] (MAE)
LVE	Launch Vehicle Engine (IAA)
LVE	Leave (WGA)
LVE	Left Ventricular Ejection [*Medicine*] (DMAA)
LVE	Left Ventricular Enlargement [*Cardiology*]
LVE	Linear Vector Equation
LVE	Liquid Vapor Equilibrium
LVEA	Leligh Valley Electronic Association (SAUO)
LVECC	Light Vehicles Energy Consumption Committee (SAUO)
LVED	Left Ventricular End-Diastolic [*Cardiology*]
LVEDC	Left Ventricular End-Diastolic Circumference [*Cardiology*] (MAE)
LVEDD	Left Ventricular End-Diastolic Dimension [*Cardiology*]
LVEDd	Left Ventricular End-Diastolic Dimension [*Medicine*]
LVEDP	Left Ventricular End-Diastolic Pressure [*Cardiology*]
LVEDV	Left Ventricular End-Diastolic Volume [*Cardiology*]
LVEF	Left Ventricular Ejection Fraction [*Time*] [*Cardiology*]
LVEL	Level 8 Systems
LVEN	Las Vegas Entertainment Network [*NASDAQ symbol*] (SAG)
LVEN	Las Vegas Entmt Ntwk [*NASDAQ symbol*] (TTSB)
LVEndo	Left Ventricular Endocardial Half [*Cardiology*] (DAVI)
LVENW	Las Vegas Entmt Ntwk Wrrt'A' [*NASDAQ symbol*] (TTSB)
LVENZ	Las Vegas Entmt Ntwk Wrrt'B' [*NASDAQ symbol*] (TTSB)
LVEP	Left Ventricular End-Diastolic Pressure [*Cardiology*] (MAE)
LVEpi	Left Ventricular Epicardial Half [*Cardiology*] (DAVI)
LVER	Liver Fraction Elevated [*Gastroenterology*] (DAVI)
LVER	Local Veterans Employment Representative [*Department of Labor*]
LVES	Low-Voltage Electrical Stimulation [*Meat treatment*]
LVET	Left Ventricular Ejection Time [*Cardiology*]
LVET	Low Volume Eye Test (DMAA)
LVETI	Left Ventricular Ejection Time Index [*Cardiology*]
LVF	Dallas, TX [*Location identifier*] [*FAA*] (FAAL)
LVF	Left Ventricular Failure [*Cardiology*]
LVF	Left Ventricular Function [*Medicine*] (AMHC)
LVF	Left Visual Field [*Psychometrics*]
LVF	Linear Vector Function
LVF	Low-Voltage Fast [*Electronics*]

LVF	Low-Voltage Foci (MAE)
LVFA	Low Velocity Friction Apparatus (PDAA)
LVFC	Launch Vehicle Flight Control
LVFCS	Launch Vehicle Flight Control System
LVFEL	Low Voltage Free Electron Laser (ACAE)
LVFF	Lloyds Forces Volunteer Fund (WDAA)
LVFMC	Las Vegas Financial Management Center (SAUO)
LVFP	Left Ventricular Filling Pressure [*Cardiology*]
LVFS	Large Volume Filtration System [*Environmental chemistry*]
LVFT2	Left Ventricular Slow Filling Time [*Medicine*] (STED)
LVG	Lauro/Viceroy/Global Joint Service [*Shipping*] (DS)
LVG	Leaving
LVG	Left Ventral Gluteal [*Injection site*]
LVG	Left Ventriculography [*Medicine*]
LVG	Left Ventrogluteal [*Anatomy*] (DAVI)
LVG	Left Visceral Ganglion [*Medicine*]
LVG	Levengood Oil & Gas, Inc. [*Vancouver Stock Exchange symbol*]
LVG	Low Viscosity Gyro (SAUS)
LVGC	Launch Vehicle Guidance Computer [*NASA*]
LVGO	Light Vacuum Gas Oil [*Petroleum technology*]
lvgrm	Living Room (REAL)
LVGSE	Launch Vehicle Ground Support Equipment [*NASA*] (KSC)
LVH	Landing Vehicle, Hydrofoil
LVH	Large Vessel Hematocrit (MAE)
LVH	Left Ventricular Hypertrophy [*Cardiology*]
LVHF	Low Very High Frequency (IAA)
LVHV	Low-Volume High-Velocity (IEEE)
LVHX	Landing Craft, Hydrofoil, Experimental [*Navy symbol*]
LVI	Laus Verbo Incarnato [*Praise to the Incarnate Word*] [*Latin*]
LVI	Lavalin Industries, Inc. [*Toronto Stock Exchange symbol*]
LVI	Left Ventricular Insufficiency [*Cardiology*] (MAE)
LVI	Left Ventricular Ischemia [*Medicine*] (DMAA)
LVI	Lehigh Group, Inc. [*Formerly, LUI Group*] [*NYSE symbol*] (SAG)
LVI	Levi Strauss & Company (SAUO)
LVI	Liquid Vapor Interface
LVI	Livingstone [*Zambia*] [*Airport symbol*] (OAG)
LVI	Local Veterinary Inspector [*British*]
LVI	Low-Viscosity Index (IAA)
LVI	Low-Voltage Inverter [*Electronics*] (AAEL)
LVI	LVI Group, Inc. (SAUO)
LVIA	Lay Volunteers International Association
LVID	Left Ventricle Internal Diameter [*Cardiology*]
LVID	Left Ventricular Internal Diastolic (STED)
LVID	Left Ventricular Internal Dimension [*Cardiology*] (DAVI)
LVIDd	Left Ventricular Internal Dimension Diastole [*Medicine*] (STED)
LVID(ed)	Left Ventricular Internal Diameter, End Diastole [*Medicine*] (STED)
LVID(es)	Left Ventricular Internal Diameter, End Systole [*Medicine*] (STED)
LVIDP	Left Ventricular Initial Diastolic Pressure [*Cardiology*] (AAMN)
LVIDs	Left Ventricular Internal Dimension Systole [*Medicine*] (STED)
L-VIS	LASER Viewdata Information Service (NITA)
LVIS	Launch Vehicle Instrumentation Systems [*NASA*] (KSC)
LVIS	Low Velocity Intense Source
LVIT	Linear Variable Inductance Transducer
LVIV	Left Ventricular Infarct Volume [*Medicine*] (STED)
LVIWIG	Launch Vehicle Integration Working Group (ACAE)
LVJ	Cleveland, OH [*Location identifier*] [*FAA*] (FAAL)
LVK	Livermore, CA [*Location identifier*] [*FAA*] (FAAL)
LVK	Lovelock [*Nevada*] [*Seismograph station code, US Geological Survey*] [*Closed*] (SEIS)
LVL	Laminated-Veneer Lumber
LVL	La Verendrye Line (SAUO)
LVL	Lawrenceville, VA [*Location identifier*] [*FAA*] (FAAL)
LVL	Left Vastus Lateralis [*Anatomy*] (DAVI)
LVL	Level (AAG)
Lvl	Level (TBD)
lvl	Level (VRA)
LVL	Levelland Energy [*Vancouver Stock Exchange symbol*]
LVL	Lex Vehicle Leasing [*British*]
LVL	Linda Vista Library (SAUO)
LVL	Long Vertical Left
LVL	Low-Velocity Layer [*Geophysics*] (OA)
LVL	Universite Laval, Bibliotheque [*UTLAS symbol*]
LVLA	Laser Visual Landing Aid (SAUS)
LVLB	Land Valuers' Licensing Board [*Western Australia*]
LVLD	Very Low-Density Lipoproteins [*Chemistry*] (MEC)
LVLG	Left Ventrolateral Gluteal [*Site of injection*] [*Medicine*]
LVLH	Local Vertical/Local Horizontal (NASA)
LVLO	Local Vehicle Licensing Office [*British*]
LVLOF	Level Off [*Aviation*] (FAAC)
LVLP	Large Virus-Like Particle
LVLSH	Level Shifter (NITA)
LVLT	Level 3 Communications [*NASDAQ symbol*] (SG)
LVM	LaSallian Volunteer Movement (EA)
LVM	LaSallian Volunteers [*An association*] (EA)
LVM	Lateral Vastus Muscle [*Medicine*] (MELL)
LVM	Launch Vehicle Material (MCD)
LVM	Launch Vehicle Monitor
LVM	Left Ventricular Mass [*Cardiology*]
LVM	Light Vehicle Mine [*Military*]
LVM	Line Voltage Monitor
LVM	Literacy Volunteers of Massachusetts
LVM	Livingston, MT [*Location identifier*] [*FAA*] (FAAL)
LVM	Localized Vibrational Mode (PDAA)
LVM	Local Vibrational Mode (SAUS)
LVM	Logical Volume Management (SAUS)

LVM............	Logical Volume Manager (SAUO)
LVM............	Low-Value Materiel (MCD)
LVMA..........	Louisiana Veterinary Medical Association (SRA)
LVMC..........	Low-Variation Medical Condition
LVMF..........	Left Ventricular Minute Flow [*Medicine*] (DB)
LVMH..........	Louis Vuitton Moet-Hennessy [*Commercial firm*] [*Belgium*]
LVMH..........	LVMH Moet-Hennessey Louis Vuitton [*NASDAQ symbol*] (SAG)
LVMHY........	LVMH Most Henn Lou Vttn ADS [*NASDAQ symbol*] (TTSB)
LVMM.........	Left Ventricular Muscle Mass [*Cardiology*] (DAVI)
LVMP..........	Launch Vehicle Mission Peculiar
LVMPD........	Las Vegas Metropolitan Police Department (SAUO)
LVMS..........	LEG [*Liquefied Energy Gas*] Volume Measuring System
LVMS..........	Limb Volume Measuring System
LVMTAS......	Low-Visibility, Moving Target Acquisition and Strike [*Military*]
LVN............	Carnegie Public Library, Las Vegas, NM [*OCLC symbol*] (OCLC)
LVN............	Lakeville, MN [*Location identifier*] [*FAA*] (FAAL)
LVN............	Las Vegas [*Nevada*] [*Seismograph station code, US Geological Survey*] (SEIS)
LVN............	Lateral Ventricular Nerve [*Medicine*] (DB)
LVN............	Lateral Vestibular Nucleus [*Medicine*] (DMAA)
LVN............	Levon Resources Ltd. [*Toronto Stock Exchange symbol*] [*Vancouver Stock Exchange symbol*]
LVN............	Library Video Network [*Video producer*]
LVN............	Licensed Visiting Nurse
LVN............	Licensed Vocational Nurse
LVN............	Light Virgin Naphtha (PDAA)
LVN............	Limiting Viscosity Number
LVN............	Low-Voltage Neon
LVNAT........	Licensed Vocational Nurses Association of Texas (SRA)
LVND..........	LASER Variable Neutral Density
LVNDL........	Licensed Victuallers' National Defence League [*British*] (DI)
LVNG..........	Living
LVNI..........	Laser Video Network [*NASDAQ symbol*] (SAG)
LVNIW........	Laser Video Network Wrrt'A' [*NASDAQ symbol*] (TTSB)
LVNIZ.........	Laser Video Network Wrrt'B' [*NASDAQ symbol*] (TTSB)
LVNJ..........	Long Valley [*New Jersey*] [*Seismograph station code, US Geological Survey*] (SEIS)
LVNM.........	Lava Beds National Monument (SAUO)
LVNP..........	Lassen Volcanic National Park (SAUO)
LVNP..........	Luangwa Valley National Park (SAUO)
LVNTE........	Livent Inc. [*NASDAQ symbol*] (TTSB)
LVNTF........	Livent, Inc. [*NASDAQ symbol*] (SAG)
LVNV..........	Levon Resources Ltd. (SAUO)
LVO............	Launch Vehicle Operations
LVO............	Laverton [*Australia*] [*Airport symbol*] (OAG)
LVO............	Left Ventricle Outflow [*Medicine*] (DMAA)
LVO............	left Ventricular Overactivity [*Cardiology*] (DAVI)
LVO............	Lieutenant of the Royal Victorian Order [*British*] (WDAA)
LVO............	Lieutenant of the Victorian Order [*Canada*] (DD)
LVO............	Lieutenant, Royal Victorian Order [*British*] (WA)
LVO............	Lithiated Vanadium Oxide [*Battery technology*]
LVO............	Louver Opening
LVOA..........	Left Ventricular Overactivity [*Cardiology*] (DAVI)
LVOD..........	Launch Vehicle Operations Division [*NASA*] (IAA)
LVOP..........	Local Vertical and Orbit Plane
LVOR..........	Low-Powered, Very-High-Frequency Omnirange
LVOT..........	Left Ventricular Outflow Tract [*Cardiology*] (CPH)
LVOTO........	Left Ventricular Outflow Tract Obstruction [*Medicine*] (MELL)
LVP............	Large Volume Parenterals [*Medicine*]
LVP............	Left Ventricular Pressure [*Cardiology*]
LVP............	Left Ventricular Pump [*Cardiology*]
LVP............	Light Valve Projector
LVP............	Low-Value Product
LVP............	Low-Voltage Plate
LVP............	Low-Voltage Protection [*Electronics*]
LVP............	Low-Volume Production (TIMI)
LVP............	Lysine Vasopressin [*Antidiuretic hormone*]
LVPD..........	Launch Vehicle Pressure Display [*NASA*] (KSC)
LVpE..........	Evangeline Parish Library, Ville Platte, LA [*Library symbol*] [*Library of Congress*] (LCLS)
LVPFR........	Left Ventricular Peak Filling Rate [*Cardiology*] (DMAA)
LVPG..........	Launch Vehicle Planning Group [*Aerospace*] (AAG)
LVPL..........	Liverpool [*England*]
LVPP..........	Launch Vehicle and Propulsion Program [*NASA*]
LVPS..........	Laboratory Vehicle Procedure Simulator
LVPS..........	Low-Voltage Power Supply
LVPTG........	Lateral Vascularized Patellar Tendon Graft [*Orthopedics*]
LVPW.........	Left Ventricular Posterior Wall [*Cardiology*] (DMAA)
LVPWT........	Left Ventricular Posterior Wall Thickness [*Cardiology*] (DAVI)
LVQ............	Learning Vector Quantization (IDAI)
LVR............	Laboratory of Virology and Rickettsial Diseases
lvr.............	Latvian Soviet Socialist Republic [*MARC country of publication code*] [*Library of Congress*] (LCCP)
LVR............	Lever (MSA)
LVR............	Line Voltage Regulator
LVR............	Liverpool [*England*] [*Seismograph station code, US Geological Survey*] [*Closed*] (SEIS)
LVR............	London Volunteer Regiment [*British military*] (DMA)
LVR............	Longitudinal Video Recording
LVR............	Long Vertical Right
LVR............	Louver (MSA)
LVR............	Low-Voltage Rack
LVR............	Low-Voltage Relay
LVR............	Low-Voltage Release [*Electronics*]
LVR............	Low-Volume Ramjet (MCD)

LVRATS.......	Leave Rations [*Military*] (DNAB)
LVRATS SL...	Leave Rations, Sick Leave [*Military*] (DNAB)
LVRATS SPEC...	Leave Rations, Special Leave [*Military*] (DNAB)
LVRC..........	Lamoille Valley Railroad Co. [*AAR code*]
LVR(CE).......	Low-Voltage Release (Continuous Effect) [*Electronics*] (DNAB)
LVRCN........	Lehigh Valley Regional Computing Network (SAUO)
LVRE..........	Low-Voltage Release Effect [*Electronics*] (MSA)
LV Rep........	Lehigh Valley Law Reporter [*Pennsylvania*] [*A publication*] (DLA)
LVRIS.........	Low-Volume Ramjet Inlet System
LVRJ..........	Low-Volume Ramjet
LVRJ..........	Low Volume Ram Jet (ACAE)
LVRJ..........	Low-Volume Ramjet
LVRLSE.......	Low-Voltage Release [*Electronics*]
LVRO..........	Las Vegas Radiation Operations (SAUO)
LV-ROM.......	LASER Vision Read-Only Memory
LVRR..........	Lehigh Valley Railroad Co. [*Absorbed into Consolidated Rail Corp.*]
LVRS..........	Launch Vehicle Recovery System [*NASA*] (IAA)
LVRS..........	Lightweight Video Reconnaissance System [*Military*] (INF)
LVRS..........	Lung Volume Reduction Surgery [*Medicine*] (ADWA)
LVRT..........	Land and Valuation Review Tribunal [*Northern Territory, Australia*]
LV/RVV........	Local Vertical/Relative Velocity Vector
LVS............	Laboratory Ventilation Data System (SAUO)
LVS............	Large-Volume Sampling (CARB)
LVS............	Las Vegas, NM [*Location identifier*] [*FAA*] (FAAL)
LVS............	Launch Vehicle Simulator [*NASA*] (IAA)
LVS............	Launch Vehicle System (ACAE)
LVS............	Layout Verification of Schematic (AAEL)
LVS............	Leaves (MSA)
LVS............	Left Ventricular Strain [*Cardiology*]
LVs............	Left Ventricular Systolic Pressure Mean [*Cardiology*] (MAE)
LVS............	Light Value System [*Photography*] (BARN)
LVS............	Logistical Vehicle System
LVS............	Logistics Vehicle System
LVS............	London Vegetarian Society (SAUO)
LVS............	Low-Velocity Scanning
LVS............	Low-Volume Sampler (CARB)
LVSB..........	Lakeview Financial [*NASDAQ symbol*] (TTSB)
LVSB..........	Lakeview Financial Corp. [*NASDAQ symbol*] (SAG)
LVSC..........	London Voluntary Service Council [*British*]
LVSE..........	Launch Vehicle Systems Engineer [*NASA*] (SAA)
LVSEM........	Low-Voltage Scanning Electron Microscopy (AAEL)
LVSEMI.......	Left Ventricular Subendocardia Lischemia [*Cardiology*] (DMAA)
LVSF..........	Laboratory Vehicle Support Facility
LVSF..........	Left Ventricular Shortening Fraction [*Medicine*]
LVSG..........	Launch Vehicle Study Group [*NASA*] (KSC)
LVS/ITS.......	LASER Vibration Sensor Inspection Test System [*Army*] (RDA)
LVSO..........	Left Ventricular Systolic Output [*Medicine*] (STED)
LVSP..........	Left Ventricular Systolic Pressure [*Cardiology*]
LVSS..........	Laboratory Vehicle System Segment
LVSS..........	LASER Vector Scoring System (DWSG)
LVSSTS.......	Launch Vehicle Safety System Test Set [*NASA*] (IAA)
LVST..........	Lateral Vestibulospinal Tract [*Medicine*] (DMAA)
LVST..........	Longitudinal Velocity Sorting Tube
LVSTCK.......	Livestock
LVSTK........	Livestock
LVSV..........	Left Ventricular Stroke Volume [*Cardiology*]
LVSW.........	Left Ventricular Septal Wall [*Cardiology*] (DAVI)
LVSW.........	Left Ventricular Stroke Work [*Cardiology*]
LVSWI........	Left Ventricular Stroke Work Index [*Cardiology*]
LVT............	Landing Vehicle, Tracked (Unarmored) [*Navy symbol*]
LVT............	Left Ventricular Tension [*Cardiology*] (MAE)
LVT............	Lexicon Hebraicum et Aramaicum Veteris Testamenti [*Rome*] [*A publication*] (BJA)
LVT............	Licensed Veterinary Technician
LVT............	Linear Velocity Transducer
LVT............	Livingston, TN [*Location identifier*] [*FAA*] (FAAL)
LVT............	Low Voltage Technology (AAEL)
LVT............	Low-Voltage Tubular
LVT............	Lysine Vasotonin [*Adrenergic agent*]
LVT (1).......	Landing Vehicle, Tracked (Unarmored) (Mark I) [*"Alligator"*] [*Navy symbol*]
LVT1..........	Left Ventricular Fast Filling Time [*Medicine*] (STED)
LVT (2).......	Landing Vehicle, Tracked (Unarmored) (Mark II) [*"Water Buffalo"*] [*Navy symbol*]
LVT (3).......	Landing Vehicle, Tracked (Unarmored) (Mark III) [*Navy symbol*]
LVT (4).......	Landing Vehicle, Tracked (Unarmored) (Mark IV)
LVT (A).......	Landing Vehicle, Tracked (Armored) [*Turret Type*]
LVTA..........	London Vintage Taxi Association - American Section (EA)
LVT (A) (1)...	Landing Vehicle, Tracked (Armored) (Mark I) [*"Water Buffalo," Turret Type*]
LVT (A) (4)...	Landing Vehicle, Tracked (Armored) (Mark IV)
LVT (A) (5)...	Landing Vehicle, Tracked (Armored) (Mark V)
LVTC..........	Landing Vehicle, Tracked, Command (NVT)
LVTC..........	Launch Vehicle Test Conductor [*NASA*] (KSC)
LVTCX........	Landing Vehicle, Tracked, Command, Experimental (MCD)
LVTD..........	Las Vegas Mjr League Sports [*NASDAQ symbol*] (TTSB)
LVTE..........	Landing Vehicle, Tracked, Engineer [*Model 1*]
LVTE-1........	Landing Vehicle, Tracked, Engineer, model 1 (SAUO)
LVTH..........	Landing Vehicle, Tracked, Howitzer [*Model 6*]
LVTL..........	Lexicon in Veteris Testameti Libros [*A publication*] (BJA)
LVTP..........	Landing Vehicle, Tracked, Personnel (AABC)
LVTP-CMD...	Landing Vehicle, Tracked Personnel, Command [*Marine Corps*] (VNW)
LVTPX........	Landing Vehicle, Tracked, Personnel, Experimental (MCD)
LVTR..........	Landing Vehicle, Tracked, Recovery (SAUO)

LVTR............	Landing Vehicle, Tracked, Retriever (NVT)
LVT(R).........	Landing Vehicle, Tracked (Rocket) [*British military*] (DMA)
LVTR............	Low-VHF [*Very-High-Frequency*] Transmitter-Receiver
LVTRX..........	Landing Vehicle, Tracked, Recovery, Experimental (MCD)
LVTTL...........	Low Voltage Transistor Transistor Level (SAUS)
LVTU............	Landing Vehicle, Tracked (Unarmored)
LVTX............	Landing Vehicle, Tracked, Experimental (ACAE)
LVUPK.........	Leave and Upkeep Period [*Military*] (NVT)
LVUSA.........	Legion of Valor of the United States of America (EA)
LVV..............	Delavan, WI [*Location identifier*] [*FAA*] (FAAL)
LVV..............	Left Ventricular Volume [*Cardiology*]
LVV..............	Live Varicella Vaccine [*Medicine*] (STED)
LVV..............	Lvov [*Ukraine*] [*Seismograph station code, US Geological Survey*] (SEIS)
LVVC............	Lincolnshire Vintage Vehicle Club [*British*] (DCTA)
LVVP...........	Chlorambucil, Vinblastine, Vincristine, Prednisone [*Antineoplastic drug regimen*] (DAVI)
LVW.............	Landing Vehicle, Wheeled
LVW.............	Las Vegas [*Nevada*] [*Seismograph station code, US Geological Survey*] (SEIS)
LVW.............	Lateral Vaginal Wall [*Medicine*] (STED)
LVW.............	Lateral Ventricular Width (STED)
LVW.............	Left Ventricular Wall [*Anatomy*]
LVW.............	Left Ventricular Work [*Cardiology*]
LVW.............	Linked Vertical Well [*Coal gastification*] (DICI)
LVW.............	Loaded Vehicle Weight
LVW/HW.......	Lateral Ventricular Width to Hemispheric Width (STED)
LVWI...........	Left Ventricular Work Index [*Cardiology*]
LVWM.........	Left Ventricular Wall Motion [*Medicine*] (STED)
LVWMA.......	Left Ventricular Wall Motion Abnormality [*Medicine*] (STED)
LVWT..........	Left Ventricular Wall Thickness [*Cardiology*] (DMAA)
LVX.............	Lily Virus X [*Plant pathology*]
LVY.............	La Verendrye Management Corp. [*Toronto Stock Exchange symbol*]
LVY.............	Levy [*Alaska*] [*Seismograph station code, US Geological Survey*] (SEIS)
LVZ.............	Low-Viscosity Zone
LW..............	Air Nevada [*ICAO designator*] (AD)
LW..............	Griechische und Lateinische Lehnwoerter im Talmud, Midrasch und Targum [*A publication*] (BJA)
LW..............	Lab. Wander [*France*] [*Research code symbol*]
LW..............	Lacerated Wound
LW..............	Lake Erie & Fort Wayne Railroad Co. (SAUO)
LW..............	Landsteiner-Wiener [*Serum*]
L-W.............	Landsverk-Wollan [*Radiation survey meter*]
LW..............	Lane Wood, Inc. (EFIS)
LW..............	Langwelle [*Long Wave*] [*German*] (MCD)
LW..............	Last Word (IAA)
LW..............	Lateral Wall [*Image on transesophageal echocardiography*] [*Cardiology*] (DAVI)
LW..............	Late Warning
LW..............	Launch Window [*Aerospace*] (AAG)
LW..............	Lawrence Welk
Lw..............	Lawrencium [*Symbol changed, 1963, to Lr*] [*Chemical element*]
LW..............	Law Weekly [*A publication*] (DLA)
LW..............	Leave Word [*Telecommunications*] (TEL)
LW..............	Leeway (COE)
LW..............	Lee-White Method [*Hematology*] (MAE)
LW..............	Left Ear, Warm Stimulus [*Medicine*] (MEDA)
LW..............	Left Wing
LW..............	Lethal Weapon [*A motion picture*]
LW..............	Light Wall
LW..............	Light Warning
L/W.............	Light Weathering
LW..............	Light Weight [*Technical drawings*]
LW..............	Lightweight RADAR (NATG)
LW..............	Limited War
LW..............	Limited Warfare (SAUO)
LW..............	Literatures of the World [*A publication*]
LW..............	Liturgisch Woordenboek [*A publication*] (ODCC)
LW..............	Lives With (ADA)
LW..............	Living Worlds (SAUO)
lw..............	Loan Word (BJA)
LW..............	Logical Weakness [*Used in correcting manuscripts, etc.*]
LW..............	Logistics Wing [*Military*]
LW..............	London Waterguard (SAUO)
LW..............	Long Wave [*Radio*]
LW..............	Long Wavelength (ACAE)
LW..............	Long Wire (SAUS)
LW..............	Lotus West (EA)
LW..............	Louisville & Wadley Railway Co. [*AAR code*]
LW..............	Low [*Automotive advertising*]
Lw..............	Lower Hold [*Shipping*] (DS)
LW..............	Low Water [*Tides and currents*]
LW..............	Low Wave (WDAA)
LW..............	Low Wing [*Aviation*] (AIA)
LW..............	Lucas Weinschel, Incorporated (ACAE)
LW..............	Lumens per Watt (ADA)
l/W.............	Lumens per Watt (IDOE)
LW..............	Lung Water
LW..............	United States Law Week [*A publication*] (NTCM)
LW-3...........	Light Weight Three Dimensional Radar (ACAE)
LWA............	Land Withdrawal Act (SAUO)
LWA............	Large Warfighting Aircraft (SAUS)
LWA............	Laser Warning Analyser (SAUS)
LWA............	Last Word Address

LWA............	Liberian World Airlines, Inc. [*ICAO designator*] (FAAC)
LWA............	Lightly Wounded in Action
LWA............	Lightweight Armor
LWA............	Limited Work Authorizations [*Nuclear energy*]
LWA............	Local Welfare Authority [*British*]
LWA............	Long Wire Antenna
LWA............	University of Southwestern Louisiana, Lafayette, LA [*OCLC symbol*] (OCLC)
LWAAM........	Light-Weight Air-to-Air Missile (MCD)
LWADS........	Lightweight Air Defense System (SAUS)
LWAR..........	Lightweight Attack and/or Reconnaissance (NATG)
LWASR........	Letter Writing with Automatic Send-Receive [*Computer science*] (ELAL)
LWASV........	Lightweight Aircraft-to-Surface Vessel [*Military*]
LW/AW........	Light Weight / Air Warning
LWAY..........	Lifeway Foods [*NASDAQ symbol*] (SAG)
LWB............	Greenbrier [*West Virginia*] [*Airport symbol*] (OAG)
LWB............	Laboratory Workbench
LWB............	Lewisburg, WV [*Location identifier*] [*FAA*] (FAAL)
LWB............	Light-Water Breeder [*Reactor*]
LWB............	Lithography Workbench (AAEL)
LWB............	Long Wheelbase
LWB............	Lower Bound [*Computer science*]
LWBR..........	Light-Water Breeder Reactor
LWBS..........	Loyal Wheelwrights' and Blacksmiths' Society [*A union*] [*British*]
LWC............	Last Working Configuration (SAUS)
LWC............	Lawrence [*Kansas*] [*Airport symbol*] (OAG)
LWC............	League of Women Composers [*Later, ILWC*] (EA)
LWC............	Lightweight Coated [*Paper*]
LWC............	Lightweight Concrete [*Technical drawings*]
LWC............	Lindsey Wilson College [*Columbia, KY*]
LWC............	Liquid Water Content
LWC............	Lithuanian World Community (EA)
LWC............	Little Way Circle [*An association*] (EA)
LWC............	Living with Cancer [*An association*] (EA)
LWC............	London Weather Centre (SAUO)
LWC............	London Writers Circle (SAUO)
LWC............	Loop Wiring Concentrator (ELAL)
LWC............	Lost Workday Case (COE)
LWCA..........	Light-Water Critical Assembly [*Nuclear reactor*] [*Japan*]
LWCA..........	Longwave Club of America (EA)
LWCF..........	Land and Water Conservation Fund [*Department of the Interior*]
LWCFA........	Land and Water Conservation Fund Act of 1965 (COE)
LWCG	Lightweight Coated Gravure [*Paper*] (DGA)
LWCH..........	Lightweight Container Handler (MCD)
LWCHW.......	Light-Water-Cooled, Heavy-Water-Moderated Reactor (NRCH)
LWCMD.......	Licentiate of the Welsh College of Music and Drama [*British*] (DBQ)
LWCMS.......	Lightweight Company Mortar System
LWCO.........	Lightweight Coated Offset [*Paper*] (DGA)
LW-COIN.....	Limited War - Counterinsurgency
LWCS..........	Limited War Capabilities Study
LWCSS........	Lightweight Camouflage Screen System (MCD)
LWCT.........	Lachar-Wrobel Critical Items [*Psychology*] (DAVI)
LWCT.........	Lee-White Clotting Time [*Hematology*]
LWD...........	Larger Word [*Computer science*]
LWD...........	Large Woody Debris [*Pisciculture*]
LWD...........	Laser Warning Device (SAUS)
LWD...........	LASER Welder/Driller (PDAA)
LWD...........	Last Work Day (TIMI)
LWD...........	Launch Window Display [*Aerospace*] (MCD)
LWD...........	Left Wing Down [*Aviation*]
LWD...........	Local Work Department (SAUO)
LWD...........	Long-Working Distance [*Microscopy*]
LWD...........	Loomis-Wood Diagram [*Physics*]
LWD...........	Lost Work Day (SAUO)
LWD...........	Low-Water Data [*Marine science*] (OSRA)
LWD...........	Low-Water Datum
LWD...........	Worldwide Airline Services, Inc. [*ICAO designator*] (FAAC)
LWDB..........	Land Warfare Data Base (ACAE)
LWDF..........	Liquid Waste Derived Fuel (EEVL)
LWDF..........	Liquid Waste Disposal Facility (ABAC)
LWDG..........	Lightweight Director Group [*Military*] (CAAL)
LWDII	Lost Workday Injury and Illness (SARE)
LWDM.........	Light Weight Dogfight Missile (ACAE)
LWD/MO......	Lead Writing Device/Manual Option (SAUO)
LWDR.........	Lightweight Designator/ Rangefinder (SAUS)
LWDS	Local Weather Dissemination Systems (SAUO)
LWE...........	Allwe [*Former USSR*] [*FAA designator*] (FAAC)
LWE...........	Lawrence Mining [*Vancouver Stock Exchange symbol*]
LWE...........	Liquid Whole Egg
LWECS........	Low-Wind Energy Conversion System (PDAA)
LWeJ	Welsh Public Library, Welsh, LA [*Library symbol*] [*Library of Congress*] (LCLS)
LWELJ.........	Long Wavelength Expendable Laser Jammer (ACAE)
LWES.........	Longitudinal Work Experience Survey (SAUO)
LWESS........	Lightweight Weapons Engagement Scoring System (ACAE)
LWF...........	Lightweight Fighter [*Air Force*]
LWF...........	Local Welfare Authority Full Time [*British*]
LWF...........	Luminous Wall Firing (DICI)
LWF...........	Lutheran World Federation [*See also FLM*] [*Geneva, Switzerland*] (EAIO)
LWF & C.....	Low Water Full and Change [*Tides and currents*]
LWFC..........	Lloyd Wood Fan Club [*Defunct*] (EA)
LWFCS........	Lightweight Fire Control System [*Military*] (CAAL)
LWFJTF	Lightweight Fighter Joint Test Force [*Air Force*]

LWFUSANC... Lutheran World Federation United States of America National Committee (EA)
LWG............. Corvallis, OR [*Location identifier*] [*FAA*] (FAAL)
LWG............. Lightweight Gun (NG)
LWG............. Logistics Working Group (NAKS)
LWG............. Logistic Work Group [*NATO*] (NATG)
LWG............. Longwood Gardens Library, Kennett Square, PA [*OCLC symbol*] (OCLC)
LWGCR........ Light-Water Moderated, Gas-Cooled Reactor (IAA)
LWGM......... Lightweight Gun Mount [*Military*] (CAAL)
LWGR.......... Light-Water-Cooled, Graphic-Moderated (IAA)
LWH............. Lawn Hill [*Australia*] [*Airport symbol*] [*Obsolete*] (OAG)
LWHS .... Lightweight Headset [*Apollo*] [*NASA*]
LWHSS........ Lightweight Honeycomb Sandwich Structure (ACAE)
LWHVR........ Lightweight High-Velocity Rifle
LWI............... LASER without Inversion
LWI............... Load Wear Index
LWI............... Long Wavelength Infrared (MCD)
LWI............... Low-Water Interval
LWI............... Lutheran World Information [*A publication*]
LWI............... Lwiro [*Zaire*] [*Seismograph station code, US Geological Survey*] (SEIS)
LWIC........... Lightweight Insulating Concrete [*Technical drawings*]
LWII............. Long Wavelength Infrared Illuminator
LWIN........... Leap Wireless International
LWinF.......... Franklin Parish Library, Winnsboro, LA [*Library symbol*] [*Library of Congress*] (LCLS)
LWIR .... Long-Wave Infrared (MUSM)
LWIR .... Long Wavelength Infrared
LWIR .... Long Wavelength Infrared Jammer (ACAE)
LWIRC........ Limited Warfare Intelligence Reduction Complex
LWIRST ...... Lightweight Infra-Red Search & Track system (SAUS)
LWIU.......... Laundry, Dry Cleaning, and Dye House Workers' International Union [*Later, Textile Processors, Service Trades, Health Care, Professional, and Technical Employees International Union*]
LWIU.......... Leather Workers International Union of America (EA)
LWiW.......... Winn Parish Library, Winnfield, LA [*Library symbol*] [*Library of Congress*] (LCLS)
LWJ............. Lucas, William J., Albuquerque NM [*STAC*]
LWK............. Large White Kidney [*Medicine*] (DMAA)
LWK............. Lerwick [*Scotland*] Tingwall Airport [*Airport symbol*] (OAG)
LWK............. Live Weight Killed (EEVL)
LWL............. Lambair Ltd. [*Canada*] [*ICAO designator*] (FAAC)
LWL............. Land Warfare [*formerly, Limited War*] Laboratory [*Army*]
LWL............. Length [*of a boat*] at Waterline
LWL............. Length on the Waterline [*Boating*]
LWL............. Lightweight Launcher (MCD)
LWL............. Lightweight Weapon Launch system (SAUS)
LWL............. Limited War Laboratory [*Military*] (IIA)
LWL............. Liquid Water, Land (ACAE)
LWL............. Load Waterline
LWL............. Long Wavelength (ACAE)
LWL............. Low Waterline
LWL............. Waterline Length [*Navy*]
LWLC.......... Light-Weight Low-Cost (PDAA)
LWLD.......... Lightweight LASER Designator
LWLOJS....... Long Wavelength Optical Jamming Simulator (ACAE)
LWM............. Larrimore, William M., San Francisco CA [*STAC*]
LWM............. Lawrence [*Massachusetts*] [*Airport symbol*] (AD)
LWM............. Lawrence, MA [*Location identifier*] [*FAA*] (FAAL)
LWM............. Leonard Wood Memorial [*American Leprosy Foundation*] (EA)
LWM............. Liquid Waste Monitor [*Nuclear energy*] (IEEE)
LWM............. Low Watermark
LWMB.......... Local Works Managing Budget [*British Armed Forces*]
LWMEL....... Leonard Wood Memorial for the Eradication of Leprosy [*Later, LWM*] (EA)
LWML.......... Light Weight Multiple Launcher (SAUS)
LWML.......... Lutheran Women's Missionary League [*Later, ILWML*] (EA)
LWMP......... Land and Water Management Plan (SAUO)
LWMS......... Light Weight Modular Thermal Sight (SAUS)
LWMS......... Liquid Waste Management System [*Nuclear energy*] (NRCH)
LWN............. Loewen Group Capital Ltd. [*NYSE symbol*] (SAG)
LWN............. Loewen Group, Inc. [*Toronto Stock Exchange symbol*]
LWNA.......... Lumber [*Timber*], Winter, North Atlantic [*Vessel load line mark*]
LWNGF....... Loewen Group [*NASDAQ symbol*] (TTSB)
LWNPr........ Loewen Group Cap Ser'A' 'MIPS' [*NYSE symbol*] (TTSB)
LWNWR...... Lake Woodruff National Wildlife Refuge (SAUO)
LWO............. Layout Work Order (MCD)
LWO............. Limited Warning Operation
LWO............. Limited War Office [*Air Force*] (MCD)
LWO............. Liquid Water, Ocean (ACAE)
LWO............. Long-Wavelength Oscillation [*Astrophysics*]
LWO............. Lubavitch Women's Organization (EA)
LWO............. Lwow [*Former USSR*] [*Airport symbol*] (OAG)
LWOB.......... Lessons Without Borders (SAUO)
LWOFC........ Lindsay Wagner's Official Fan Club (EA)
LWOP.......... Lease with Option to Purchase (COE)
LWOP.......... Leave without Pay
L-word......... Liberal [*Especially in negative political context*]
LWOS.......... Low-Water Ordinary Spring [*Tides*]
LWOST .... Low-Water Ordinary Spring Tides
LWOT......... Left Without Therapy [*Medicine*] (MELL)
LWP............. Langley Working Paper [*NASA*]
LWP............. Leave with Pay (KSC)

LWP............. Lightweight Process (SAUO)
LWP............. Light Window Pintle (SAUS)
LWP............. Limited War Plan
LWP............. Liquid Waste Processing [*Nuclear energy*] (NRCH)
LWP............. Liquid-Water Path [*Meteorology*]
LWP............. Load Water Plane
LWP............. Low Waterplane (PDAA)
LWPF........... Long-Wave Pass Filter (PDAA)
LWPS........... Liquid Waste Processing System [*Nuclear energy*] (NRCH)
LWPW.......... Light-Weight Portable Workstation
LWQ............. Low-Water Quadrature
LWQ............. Walnut Ridge, AR [*Location identifier*] [*FAA*] (FAAL)
LWR............. LASER Warning Receiver (MCD)
LWR............. Launch Warning Receiver [*Electronic countermeasure device*] [*Military*] (VNW)
LWR............. Lawrence Ins. Group [*AMEX symbol*] (TTSB)
LWR............. Lawrence Insurance Group [*AMEX symbol*] (SPSG)
LWR............. Light-Water Reactor
LWR............. Limited War Capability (AAG)
LWR............. Line Width Reduction (AAEL)
LWR............. Liquid Waste Release [*Nuclear energy*] (IEEE)
LWR............. Local Wage Rate
LWR............. Long Wavelength Redundant [*Camera for spectra*]
LWR............. Long-Wave Radiation
LWR............. Lower (AAG)
Lwr.............. Lower (TBD)
lwr.............. Lower
LWR............. Lutheran World Relief (EA)
LWRECCE.... Lightweight Reconnaissance Aircraft (NATG)
LWRENAM... Leading WREN [*Women's Royal Naval Service*] Air Mechanic [*British military*] (DMA)
LWRENCINE... Leading WREN [*Women's Royal Naval Service*] Cinema Operator [*British military*] (DMA)
LWRENDHYG... Leading WREN [*Women's Royal Naval Service*] Dental Hygienist [*British military*] (DMA)
LWRENDSA... Leading WREN [*Women's Royal Naval Service*] Dental Surgery Assistant [*British military*] (DMA)
LWRENEDUC... Leading WREN [*Women's Royal Naval Service*] Education Assistant [*British military*] (DMA)
LWRENMET... Leading WREN [*Women's Royal Naval Service*] Meteorologist [*British military*] (DMA)
LWRENMT ... Leading WREN [*Women's Royal Naval Service*] Motor Transport Driver [*British military*] (DMA)
LWRENPHOT... Leading WREN [*Women's Royal Naval Service*] Photographer [*British military*] (DMA)
LWRENQA.... Leading WREN [*Women's Royal Naval Service*] Quarters Assistant [*British military*] (DMA)
LWRENREM... Leading WREN [*Women's Royal Naval Service*] Radio Electrical Mechanic [*British military*] (DMA)
LWRENRO(M)... Leading WREN [*Women's Royal Naval Service*] Radio Operator (Morse) [*British military*] (DMA)
LWRENS(C)... Leading WREN [*Women's Royal Naval Service*] Stores Assistant (Clothes) [*British military*] (DMA)
LWRENS(S)... Leading WREN [*Women's Royal Naval Service*] Stores Assistant (Stores) [*British military*] (DMA)
LWRENSTD... Leading WREN [*Women's Royal Naval Service*] Steward [*British military*] (DMA)
LWRENS(V)... Leading WREN [*Women's Royal Naval Service*] Stores Assistant (Victualling) [*British military*] (DMA)
LWRENTEL... Leading WREN [*Women's Royal Naval Service*] Telephonist [*British military*] (DMA)
LWRENTSA... Leading WREN [*Women's Royal Naval Service*] Training Support Assistant [*British military*] (DMA)
LWRENWA... Leading WREN [*Women's Royal Naval Service*] Weapon Analyst [*British military*] (DMA)
LWRENWTR(G)... Leading WREN [*Women's Royal Naval Service*] Writer (General) [*British military*] (DMA)
LWRENWTR(P)... Leading WREN [*Women's Royal Naval Service*] Writer (Pay) [*British military*] (DMA)
LWRENWTR(S)... Leading WREN [*Women's Royal Naval Service*] Writer (Shorthand) [*British military*] (DMA)
LWRL .... Light Weight Rail Launcher (ACAE)
LWRM .... Lightweight RADAR Missile (MCD)
LWRO .... Lateral Wheel Run-Out [*Automotive engineering*]
LWRP .... Livermore Water Reclamation Plant (SAUO)
LWRP .... Lukuru Wildlife Research Project (SAUO)
LWRRDC..... Land and Water Resources Research and Development Corporation (SAUO)
LWRRI........ Louisiana Water Resources Research Institute [*Louisiana State University*] [*Department of the Interior*] [*Research center*] (RCD)
LWRS .... Lightweight Weather RADAR Set
LWRU .... Lightweight RADAR Unit (NATG)
LWS............. Large Wafer Study (AAEL)
LWS............. Laser Warning System (SAUO)
LWS............. LASER Weapon System (MCD)
LWS............. Lavage with Saline [*Medicine*] (MELL)
LWS............. Lewiston [*Idaho*] [*Airport symbol*] (OAG)
LWS............. Library Wholesale Services [*Information service or system*] (IID)
LWS............. Lightning Warning Set [*Air Force*]
LWS............. Lightning Warning System [*NASA*] (NASA)
LWS............. Light-Warning RADAR Set (NATG)
LWS............. Lightweight Sight
LWS............. Lightweight Sports [*Concept car*] [*Automotive engineering*]
LWS............. Lightweight System
LWS............. London Wargames Section (SAUO)

LWS.............	Low Water of Spring Tide
LWS.............	Low-Water Sensitivity [Brake fluid designation]
LWS.............	Lutheran Welfare Services [Australia]
LWSC............	Liberian Water and Sewer Corporation (SAUO)
LWSC............	Local Wage Survey Committee (SAUO)
LWSD............	LASER Weapon System Demonstrator [Military]
LWSF............	Lightweight Strike Fighter [NATO Air Forces]
LWSR............	Lightweight Search RADAR (IAA)
LWSR............	Lightweight Strike and Reconnaissance Aircraft (NATG)
LWSR(R)	Lightweight Strike and Reconnaissance Aircraft (Reconnaissance Role) (NATG)
LWSR(S).....	Lightweight Strike and Reconnaissance Aircraft (Strike Role) (NATG)
LWSS............	Letter-Writing Support System (PDAA)
LWST............	Light Waste Storage Tank (IEEE)
LWST............	Lowest (MSA)
LW(STA)......	Light Warning (Station)
LWSTC........	Liquid Waste and Sludge Transporter Council (EA)
Lw Stu H	Law Students' Helper [A publication] (DLA)
LW-SWC.....	Light Weight Sheet Molding Compound
LWT.............	Amphibious Warping Tug [Navy symbol]
LWT.............	Lamb Weather Type [Meteorology]
LWT.............	Launch Window Time (SAUS)
LWT.............	Lewistown [Montana] [Airport symbol] (OAG)
LWT.............	Light Weight Tank (SAUS)
LWT.............	Lightweight Torpedo [Now Mk 50] (DOMA)
LWT.............	Lightweight Transponder
LWT.............	Light Weight Turret (SAUS)
LWT.............	Lightweight Type [Anchor gear]
LWT.............	Liquid Waste Treatment (MCD)
LWT.............	Listen While Talk (IAA)
LWT.............	Local Winter Time [Astronomy] (IAA)
LWT.............	London Weekend Television [England]
LWTA............	LASER Window Test Apparatus [Air Force]
LWTAP........	Food Science and Technology (journ.) (SAUS)
LWTF............	Low-Water-Tolerant Brake Fluid [Automotive engineering]
LWTMA........	Listen While Transmission Multiple Access [Telecommunications] (PDAA)
LWTMA........	London Wool Terminal Market Association (SAUO)
LWTP...........	Light Weight Tracking Pedestal (ACAE)
LWTR...........	Leading Writer [British military] (DMA)
LWTS...........	Laundry Waste Treatment System [Nuclear energy] (NRCH)
LWTS...........	Low-Level Waste Treatment System (ABAC)
LWTT...........	Liquid Waste Test Tank [Nuclear energy] (IEEE)
LWU.............	LASER Welder Unit
LWU.............	Leather Workers International Union of America
LWUI...........	Longshoremen's and Warehousemen's Union International
LWULT.........	Least Widely Used and Least Taught Languages (AIE)
LWV.............	Lackawanna & Wyoming Valley (SAUO)
LWV.............	Lackawanna & Wyoming Valley Railway Co. [Absorbed into Consolidated Rail Corp.] [AAR code]
LWV.............	Landwirtschaftsversorgungsamt [German Land Economic Supply Office] [Post-World War II]
LWV.............	Lawrenceville [Illinois] [Airport symbol] [Obsolete] (OAG)
LWV.............	League of Women Voters of the United States
LWV.............	Light-Weight Van
LWV.............	Longitudinal Wave Velocity (AAEL)
LWVEF.........	League of Women Voters Education Fund (EA)
LWVF...........	League of Woman Voters Foundation (SAUO)
LWVUS	League of Women Voters of the United States (EA)
LWVV...........	League of Women Voters of Victoria [Australia]
LWW............	Launch Window Width [Aerospace]
LWW............	Lightweight Weapon
LWW............	Lippincott Williams & Wilkins
LWWS........	Lightweight Weapons Sight
LWX............	LAN [Linked Access Network]/WAN Exchange [Wide Area Network] [Telecommunications]
LWY.............	Lawas [Malaysia] [Airport symbol] (OAG)
LWYACC	Lithuanian World Youth Association Communications Center [Defunct] (EA)
LWYR	Lawyer
LwyrTitl	Lawyers Title Corp. [Associated Press] (SAG)
LX...............	Crossair [ICAO designator] (AD)
LX...............	dyslexic rebus for excel (SAUS)
LX...............	La Crosse, WI
lx	Larynx (MELL)
LX...............	Linear Executable (SAUS)
LX...............	Liver Extract [Protein/lipid substance] [Immunology]
LX...............	Local Irradiation (MAE)
LX...............	Lower Extremity [Anatomy] (DMAA)
LX...............	Low Expansion Foam (WDAA)
LX...............	Low Index [NWS] (FAAC)
Lx	Lumpectomy [Medicine]
LX...............	Lux [Light] [Latin]
lx	Lux [Symbol] [SI unit of luminance]
LXA.............	Lhasa [China] [Airport symbol] (OAG)
LXA.............	Lipoxin A [Biochemistry]
LXA.............	Load Index from Address
LXAD............	Lexington Army Depot [Kentucky] (AFIT)
lxb	Language Textbook
LXB.............	Lipoxin B [Biochemistry]
LXB.............	Pittsburgh, PA [Location identifier] [FAA] (FAAL)
LXBK............	LSB Bancshares, Inc. North Carolina [NASDAQ symbol] (SAG)
LXBK............	LSB Bancshares(NC) [NASDAQ symbol] (TTSB)
LXC.............	Liquid-Ion Exchange Chromatography (PDAA)
LXD.............	LASER Transceiver Device

LXD.............	Load Index from Decrement
LXE.............	Lightguide Express Entry (VLIE)
LXE.............	LXE, Inc. [Associated Press] (SAG)
LXEI............	LXE, Inc. [NASDAQ symbol] (SAG)
LXFT............	Linear Xenon Flash Tube
LXG.............	Luong Namtha [Laos] [Airport symbol] (AD)
LXGB............	Gibraltar/North Front [Gibraltar] [ICAO location identifier] (ICLI)
LXK.............	Lexmark International Group [NYSE symbol] (SAG)
LXK.............	Lexmark Intl Group'A' [NYSE symbol] (TTSB)
LXL.............	Little Falls, MN [Location identifier] [FAA] (FAAL)
LXM.............	Lintex Minerals [Vancouver Stock Exchange symbol]
LXMAR	Load External Memory Address Register
Lxmbrg........	Luxembourg (SAUO)
LXMO...........	Lexington B & L Financial Corp. [NASDAQ symbol] (SAG)
LXN.............	Lexington, NE [Location identifier] [FAA] (FAAL)
LXN.............	Lexington Resources Ltd. [Vancouver Stock Exchange symbol]
LXP.............	Lexington Corporate Prop [NYSE symbol] (TTSB)
LXP.............	Lexington Corporate Properties [NYSE symbol] (SAG)
LXP.............	Lorain Public Library, Lorain, OH [OCLC symbol] (OCLC)
LXR.............	Airluxor Ltda. [Portugal] [ICAO designator] (FAAC)
LXR.............	Luxor [Egypt] [Airport symbol] (OAG)
LXR.............	LXR Biotechnology [AMEX symbol] (TTSB)
LXR.............	LXR Biotechnology, Inc. [AMEX symbol] (SAG)
LXRBiot........	LXR Biotechnology, Inc. [Associated Press] (SAG)
LXS.............	Lemnos [Greece] [Airport symbol] (OAG)
LX S	Lux Second
LXT.............	Left Exotropia [Ophthalmology]
LXT.............	Linear Xenon Tube
LXU.............	Lukulu [Zambia] [Airport symbol] (AD)
LXU.............	Luxtec Corp. [AMEX symbol] (SAG)
LXV.............	Leadville, CO [Location identifier] [FAA] (FAAL)
LXX.............	Septuagint [Version of the Bible]
LXY.............	Mexia, TX [Location identifier] [FAA] (FAAL)
LY...............	El Al Israel Airlines [ICAO designator] (AD)
LY...............	Lactoalbumin-Yeastolate [Cell growth medium]
LY...............	Langley [Unit of sun's heat]
LY...............	Last Year's Model [Merchandising slang]
LY...............	League for Yiddish [Later, LYI] (EA)
LY...............	Leicestershire Yeomanry (SAUO)
LY...............	Leicestershire Yeomanry (Prince Albert's Own) [British military] (DMA)
LY...............	Lethal Yellowing [Plant pathology]
LY...............	Libya [ANSI two-letter standard code] (CNC)
ly	Libya [MARC country of publication code] [Library of Congress] (LCCP)
LY...............	Light Year
ly	Light-Year
LY...............	Light Yeomanry (SAUO)
LY...............	Linear Yard (AFM)
LY...............	Lucifer Yellow [A dye] [Organic chemistry]
Ly	Lyman [Spectrography]
LY...............	Lynngold Resources, Inc. [Toronto Stock Exchange symbol]
LY...............	Queen's Own Lowland Yeomanry [Military unit] [British]
LYA.............	Lynch, Young & Associates [Newport Beach, CA] [Telecommunications] (TSSD)
LYA.............	Lyon Air [France] [ICAO designator] (FAAC)
LYB.............	Little Cayman [West Indies] [Airport symbol] (OAG)
LYBA............	Beograd [Former Yugoslavia] [ICAO location identifier] (ICLI)
LYBB............	Beograd [Former Yugoslavia] [ICAO location identifier] (ICLI)
LYBE............	Beograd [Former Yugoslavia] [ICAO location identifier] (ICLI)
LYBK............	Banja Luka [Former Yugoslavia] [ICAO location identifier] (ICLI)
LYBNT	Last Year but Not This [Fundraising]
LYC.............	Larchmont Yacht Club (SAUO)
LYC.............	Leicestershire Yeomanry Cavalry (Prince Albert's Own) [British military] (DMA)
LYC.............	Lycoming College, Williamsport, PA [OCLC symbol] (OCLC)
Lyc..............	Lycurgus [of Plutarch] [Fourth century BC] [Classical studies] (OCD)
LYCC...........	Lancashire Yorkshire Canary Club (SAUO)
LYCD	Live Yeast Cell Derivative (DB)
Lycoming....	Lycoming Reporter [Pennsylvania] [A publication] (DLA)
Lycoming R (PA)...	Lycoming Reporter [Pennsylvania] [A publication] (DLA)
Lycoph........	Lycophron [Third century BC] [Classical studies] (OCD)
LYCS...........	Liberia Young Christian Students Movement (SAUO)
Lycurg........	Lycurgus [of Plutarch] [Fourth century BC] [Classical studies] (OCD)
LYD.............	Houston, TX [Location identifier] [FAA] (FAAL)
LYD.............	Lydney [British depot code]
L/yd3	Pounds per Cubic Yard (SAUS)
Lydall...........	Lydall, Inc. [Associated Press] (SAG)
LYDIEA........	Lymphocyte-Detected Immunoglobulin E Antigen [Medicine] (DB)
LYDMA........	Lymphocyte Determined Membrane Antigen [Immunology]
Lydnbg........	Lydenburg Platinum Ltd. [Associated Press] (SAG)
LYDPY.........	Lydenburg Platinum Ltd ADR [NASDAQ symbol] (TTSB)
LYDU...........	Dubrovnik [Former Yugoslavia] [ICAO location identifier] (ICLI)
LYE.............	Lyneham, FTU [British] [FAA designator] (FAAC)
LYES...........	Liver Yang Exuberance Syndrome [Medicine] (DMAA)
LYF.............	Lutheran Youth Fellowship (EA)
LYFT...........	Low-Yield Fallout Trajectory (DNAB)
LYG.............	Lymphomatoid Granulomatosis [Medicine]
LYH.............	Lynchburg [Virginia] [Airport symbol] (OAG)
LyHIF...........	Lymphoblast Human Interferon (DB)
LYI.............	League for Yiddish, Inc. (EA)
LYI.............	Libby, MT [Location identifier] [FAA] (FAAL)
LYL.............	League of Young Liberals [British] (ROG)
LYL.............	Lima, OH [Location identifier] [FAA] (FAAL)
LYLJ	Ljubljana [Former Yugoslavia] [ICAO location identifier] (ICLI)

LYM	Last Year's Model [*Marketing*] (WDAA)
LYM	Lymph [*or Lymphatic*] (WDAA)
LYM	Lymphocyte
LYM	Lympne [*England*] [*Airport symbol*] (AD)
LYMB	Maribor [*Former Yugoslavia*] [*ICAO location identifier*] (ICLI)
LYMBS	Lodzer Young Men's Benevolent Society (EA)
LYMEC	Liberal and Radical Youth Movement of the Euorpean Community (SAUO)
LYMO	Mostar [*Former Yugoslavia*] [*ICAO location identifier*] (ICLI)
LYMP	Lymphocyte (SAUS)
LYMPH	Lymphocyte
Lymphos	Lymphocytes [*Medicine*] (BABM)
Lymphs	Lymphocytes [*Medicine*] (AMHC)
LYN	Atlanta, GA [*Location identifier*] [*FAA*] (FAAL)
LYN	Lamba Youth Network [*An association*] (EA)
LYN	Lehman Brothers, Inc. [*AMEX symbol*] (SAG)
LYN	Lynton Aviation [*British*] [*ICAO designator*] (FAAC)
Lyn	Lynx [*Constellation*]
Lynchburg C.	Lynchburg College (GAGS)
LynchC	Lynch Corp. [*Associated Press*] (SAG)
Lynd	Lyndwood's Provinciales [*A publication*] (DLA)
Lynd Prov	Lyndwood's Provinciales [*A publication*] (DLA)
Lyndw Prov	Lyndwood's Provinciales [*A publication*] (DLA)
Lyne	Lyne's Irish Chancery Cases (Wallis) [*1766-91*] [*A publication*] (DLA)
LyNeF	Lytic Nephritic Factor (DB)
Lyne Lea	Lyne on Leases for Lives [*A publication*] (DLA)
Lyne on Renew	Lyne on Renewals [*A publication*] (DLA)
Lyne (Wall)	Wallis' Select Cases, Edited by Lyne [*1766-91*] [*Ireland*] [*A publication*] (DLA)
LYNX	Bermudas commercial internet (SAUS)
LYO	Lubavitch Youth Organization (EA)
LYO	Lyondell Chemical [*Formerly, Lyondell Petrochem*] [*NYSE symbol*]
LYO	Lyondell Petrochem [*NYSE symbol*] (TTSB)
LYO	Lyondell Petrochemical [*NYSE symbol*] (SPSG)
LYO	Lyons, KS [*Location identifier*] [*FAA*] (FAAL)
LYO	Lyophilized [*Medicine*] (DMAA)
LYOH	Ohrid [*Former Yugoslavia*] [*ICAO location identifier*] (ICLI)
LYON	Liquid-Yield Option Note [*Merrill Lynch & Co.*] [*Finance*]
LYON	Liquid Yield Option Notes (EBF)
Lyon & R BS	Lyon and Redman on Bills of Sale [*A publication*] (DLA)
Lyondl	Lyondell Petrochemical Co. [*Associated Press*] (SAG)
Lyon Ind L	Lyon on the Laws of India [*A publication*] (DLA)
Lyon Just	Lyon's Institutes of Justinian [*A publication*] (DLA)
LYOS	Osijek [*Former Yugoslavia*] [*ICAO location identifier*] (ICLI)
lyot	Layout (VRA)
LYP	Faisalabad [*Pakistan*] [*Airport symbol*] (OAG)
LYP	Lactose, Yeast, and Peptone Agar [*Medicine*] (DMAA)
LYP	Lower Yield Point [*Medicine*] (DMAA)
LYP	Lyallpur [*Pakistan*] [*Airport symbol*] (AD)
Lyp	Lymphosarcoma [*Medicine*]
LYpAS	Logicheskii Yazyk dlia Predstavleniya Algoritmov Sinteza Releinykh Ustroistv [*A Programming Language for Logic and Coding Algorithm*] [*Book title*]
LYPL	Pula [*Former Yugoslavia*] [*ICAO location identifier*] (ICLI)
LYPR	Pristina [*Former Yugoslavia*] [*ICAO location identifier*] (ICLI)
LYPW	Legion of Young Polish Women (EA)
LYPZ	Portoroz [*Former Yugoslavia*] [*ICAO location identifier*] (ICLI)
LYR	Lancashire & Yorkshire Railway [*British*]
LYR	Lancashire & Yorkshire Railway Co. (SAUO)
LYR	Layer (MSA)
lyr	Layer
LYR	Layer Cloud [*Meteorology*] (DA)
LYR	Leeds & York Railway (SAUO)
LYR	Longyear [*Norway*] [*Airport symbol*] (OAG)
Lyr	Lyra [*Constellation*]
LYR	Lyric [*or Lyrical*]
Lyr	Lyrichord [*Record label*]
lyr	Lyricist [*MARC relator code*] [*Library of Congress*] (LCCP)
LYRI	Rijeka [*Former Yugoslavia*] [*ICAO location identifier*] (ICLI)
LYRIC	Language for Your Remote Instruction by Computer [*Computer science*] (MDG)
Lys	De Lysia [*of Dionysius Halicarnassensis*] [*Classical studies*] (OCD)
LYS	Light of Yoga Society (EA)
LYS	Lycksele [*Sweden*] [*Geomagnetic observatory code*]
LYS	Lyon [*France*] [*Airport symbol*] (OAG)
Lys	Lysander [*of Plutarch*] [*Classical studies*] (OCD)
LYS	Lysander Gold [*Vancouver Stock Exchange symbol*]
Lys	Lysias [*Fifth century BC*] [*Classical studies*] (OCD)
LYS	Lysine (DMAA)
lys	Lysine [*An amino acid*] (DOG)
Lys	Lysine [*Also, K*] [*An amino acid*]
Lys	Lysistrata [*of Aristophanes*] [*Classical studies*] (OCD)
LYS	Lysodren (DMAA)
LYS	Lysosome (STED)
LYS	Lysosome [*Cytology*]
LYS	Lysozyme [*Also, LZM*] [*An enzyme*]
LYS	Lysyl [*Enzymology*]
LYS	Lytes Electrolytes [*Medicine*] (DMAA)
LYS	Olean, NY [*Location identifier*] [*FAA*] (FAAL)
LYSA	Sarajevo [*Former Yugoslavia*] [*ICAO location identifier*] (ICLI)
LYSK	Skopje [*Former Yugoslavia*] [*ICAO location identifier*] (ICLI)
LySLk	Lymphoma Syndrome Leukemia [*Medicine*] (STED)
Lyso-PC	Lysophosphatidylcholine [*Also, LPC*] [*Biochemistry*]
LYSP	Split [*Former Yugoslavia*] [*ICAO location identifier*] (ICLI)
LYSV	Leek Yellow Stripe Virus [*Plant pathology*]
LYT	Layout (MSA)
LYTBT	Low-Yield Test Ban Treaty
Lytes	Electrolytes [*Medicine*] (BABM)
LYTES	Electrolytes (STED)
LYTI	Titograd [*Former Yugoslavia*] [*ICAO location identifier*] (ICLI)
LYTS	LSI Industries [*NASDAQ symbol*] (TTSB)
LYTS	LSI Industries, Inc. [*NASDAQ symbol*] (SAG)
LYTT	Lytta [*A Blistering Fly*] [*Pharmacy*] (ROG)
LYTV	Tivat [*Former Yugoslavia*] [*ICAO location identifier*] (ICLI)
LYU	Lehigh University, Bethlehem, PA [*OCLC symbol*] (OCLC)
LYV	Legume Yellows Virus [*Plant pathology*]
LYVR	Vrsac [*Former Yugoslavia*] [*ICAO location identifier*] (ICLI)
LYW	Lyman [*Washington*] [*Seismograph station code, US Geological Survey*] (SEIS)
LYX	Atlantic Rich 9% Exch Nts'97 [*NYSE symbol*] (TTSB)
LYX	Atlantic Richfield Co. [*NYSE symbol*] (SAG)
LYX	Lydd [*England*] [*Airport symbol*]
LYX	Lynx-Canada Explorations Ltd. [*Toronto Stock Exchange symbol*]
Lyx	Lyxose [*Also, l*] [*A sugar*]
LYY	Batesville, AR [*Location identifier*] [*FAA*] (FAAL)
LYYY	Beograd [*Former Yugoslavia*] [*ICAO location identifier*] (ICLI)
LYZ	Lysozyme [*Medicine*] (DMAA)
LYZA	Zagreb [*Former Yugoslavia*] [*ICAO location identifier*] (ICLI)
LYZB	Zagreb [*Former Yugoslavia*] [*ICAO location identifier*] (ICLI)
LYZD	Zadar [*Former Yugoslavia*] [*ICAO location identifier*] (ICLI)
LZ	Balkan [*ICAO designator*] (AD)
LZ	Landing Zone
LZ	Left Zero (IAA)
LZ	Lempel Zev [*Computer science*]
LZ	Leucine Zipper [*Protein structure*]
LZ	Live Zero (IAA)
LZ	Loading Zone
LZ	[*The*] Lubrizol Corp. [*NYSE symbol*] (SPSG)
LZ1	Luftschiff Zeppelin 1
LZA	Labor Zionist Alliance (EA)
LZB	La-Z Boy Chair [*NYSE symbol*] (TTSB)
LZB	La-Z Boy Chair Co. [*NYSE symbol*] (SPSG)
LZC	Landing Zone Construction (SAUO)
LZCC	Landing Zone Control Center [*Air Force*] (IAA)
LZCO	Landing Zone Control Officer [*Air Force*] (AFM)
LZD	Launch Zone Display
LZDF	Launch Zone Display Flag
LZE	Luminous-Zone Emissivity (SAUS)
LZEEBE	Long-Term Zonal Earth Energy Budget Experiment [*Spacecraft*] [*NASA*]
LZF	Launch Zone Flag
LZGF	Lewis Zero Gravity Facility
LZH	Lanchow [*Republic of China*] [*Seismograph station code, US Geological Survey*] (SEIS)
LZIF	Lyudmila Zhivkova International Foundation (EAIO)
LZL	Landing Zone Locator
LZL	Launcher, Zero Length [*British military*] (DMA)
lzm	Lysozyme (STED)
LZM	Lysozyme [*An enzyme*]
LZMT	Landing Zone Marshalling Team (SAUO)
LZO	Launch Zone Override
LZOA	Labor Zionist Organization of America (SAUO)
LZOA	Labor Zionist Organization of America - Poale Zion [*Later, LZA*] (EA)
LZOC	Lincoln Zephyr Owner's Club (EA)
LZP	Landing Zone Preparation (SAUO)
LZP	Latvian Green Party [*Political party*] (EY)
LZP	Left Zero Print (IAA)
LZP	Lorazepam [*Also, L, LOR*] [*Antiepileptic drug*]
LZPC	Lead-Zinc Producers Committee (EA)
LZR	Lazurus Distributors [*Vancouver Stock Exchange symbol*]
LZR	Lizard Island [*Australia*] [*Airport symbol*] (OAG)
LZSA	Landing Zone Support Area (COE)
LZSDCP	Lempel-Ziv-Stac-Data Compression Protocol (SAUS)
LZSU	Leningrad A.A. Zhdanov State University (SAUO)
LZT	Lead Zirconate Titanate [*Ferroelectric material*]
LZT	Local Zone Time
LZU	Lincoln University, Lincoln University, PA [*OCLC symbol*] (OCLC)
LZV	Lazarev [*Later, NVL*] [*Former USSR*] [*Geomagnetic observatory code*]
LZW	Lempel-Zev-Welch [*Compression*] [*Computer science*] (PCM)
LZW	Olney-Noble, IL [*Location identifier*] [*FAA*] (FAAL)
LZY	Greensboro, NC [*Location identifier*] [*FAA*] (FAAL)
LZZ	Lampasas, TX [*Location identifier*] [*FAA*] (FAAL)

M
By Acronym

M................ Absolute Magnitude [*Astronomy*]
M................ All India Reporter, Madras Series [*A publication*] (ILCA)
M................ Angular Momentum [*Symbol*] [*Physics*]
M................ Bending Moment [*Aerospace*] (AAG)
M................ Days before Move Operation [*Usually followed by a number*] [*NASA*] (KSC)
M................ Dynamic Testing Division (SAUO)
M................ Em [*Printing*] (WDMC)
m................ Em [*Printing*] (WDMC)
M................ Emma [*Phonetic alphabet*] [*In use in 1904 and 1914*] (DSUE)
M,............... Experimental & Pit Division (SAUO)
M................ Field Goals Missed [*Football, basketball*]
M................ Figure of Merit (SAUS)
M................ First Sergeant [*Army skill qualification identifier*] (INF)
M................ Ground, Mobile [*JETDS nomenclature*]
M................ Human Being Movement [*Rorschach*] [*Psychology*]
M................ Hungary [*IYRU nationality code*] (IYR)
M................ Imperial Chemical Industries [*Great Britain*] [*Research code symbol*]
M................ Indian Law Reports, Madras Series [*A publication*] (DLA)
M................ Instrumental Magnitude [*Earthquakes*]
M................ Intensity of Magnetization [*Symbol*] (DEN)
m----............ Intercontinental Areas (Eastern Hemisphere) [*MARC geographic area code*] [*Library of Congress*] (LCCP)
M................ J. F. Macfarlan & Co. [*Scotland*] [*Research code symbol*]
M................ Lundi [*French*] (ASC)
M................ Macerare [*Macerate*] [*Pharmacy*]
m................ Mach. (NAKS)
M................ Mach (SHCU)
M................ Machine
M................ Mach Number
M................ MacNeil [*Herman A.*] [*Designer's mark, when appearing on US coins*]
M................ Macpherson's Scotch Session Cases [*1862-73*] [*A publication*] (DLA)
M................ Macrophage (MELL)
M................ Macula (SAUS)
M................ Magenta (WDMC)
m................ Magenta (WDMC)
M................ Magister [*Master*] [*Latin*]
M................ Magistrate
M................ Magistrate Court (SAUO)
M................ Magnaflux
M................ Magnetic
M................ Magnetic Moment [*Symbol*] (DEN)
M................ Magnetic Polarization [*Symbol*] (DEN)
m................ Magnetic Quantum Number [*Atomic physics*] [*Symbol*]
M................ Magnetron (MDG)
M................ Magnification (NTCM)
M................ Magnitude
M................ Maiden
M................ Mail
M................ Main
m................ Main [*Menu*] [*Computer science*] [*Telecommunications*]
M................ Maintainability [*or Maintenance*] (MCD)
m................ Maintainability (NAKS)
M................ Maintenance and Test Assemblies [*JETDS nomenclature*]
M................ Majesty
M................ Major [*Cycle*]
m................ Major Cycle (NAKS)
M................ Make
m................ Maker (SAUO)
m................ Male (DD)
M................ Male [*Electronics*]
M................ Malignant [*Medicine*]
M................ Maloti [*Plural of Loti*] [*Monetary Unit*] [*Lesotho*] (BARN)
M................ Malta (MILB)
M................ Man
M................ Mandatory (KSC)
m................ Mandatory (NAKS)
M................ Mandible (MELL)
M................ Mane [*Morning*] [*Pharmacy*]
M................ Maneuvering Ship [*In speed triangle of relative movement problems*]
M................ Manichaean Middle Persian
M................ Manila [*Rope*]
M................ Manipulus [*A Handful*] [*Pharmacy*]
M................ Mannitol [*Organic chemistry*]
M................ Mano [*Hand*] [*Spanish*]

M................ Mantissa [*Decimal portion of a logarithm*]
m................ Manual (NAKS)
M................ Manual
M................ Manufacturer (SAUO)
M................ Map
M................ March
M................ Mare [*Thoroughbred racing*]
m................ Marginal Propensity to Import [*Economics*]
M................ Maria [*Mary*]
M................ Marijuana (MELL)
M................ Marine [*FCC*] (NTCM)
M................ Marine [*Insurance*]
M................ Marine Corps [*When used as prefix with plane designation*]
M................ Marinus de Caramanico [*Flourished, 1269-85*] [*Authority cited in pre-1607 legal work*] (DSA)
M................ Maritus [*Bridegroom*] [*Latin*]
M................ Mark [*Monetary unit*] [*German*] (GPO)
M................ Marker [*Beacon*] (AFM)
M................ Markka [*Monetary unit*] [*Finland*]
M................ Marksman [*British military*] (DMA)
M................ Marquis [*or Marquess*]
M................ Married
M................ Mars
M................ Marshal
M................ Marshalling Area (SAUO)
M................ Martin Co. Division [*Martin-Marietta Corp.*] [*ICAO aircraft manufacturer identifier*] (ICAO)
M................ Martinus Gosia [*Authority cited in pre-1607 legal work*] (DSA)
M................ Martinus Zamorensis [*Flourished, 13th century*] [*Authority cited in pre-1607 legal work*] (DSA)
M................ Martyr
M................ Marxist [*Politics*]
m................ Masculine (SHCU)
M................ Masculine
m................ masculinum (SAUS)
M................ Masochism (CDAI)
M................ Mason (ROG)
M................ Mass (GOBB)
m................ Mass [*Symbol*] [*IUPAC*]
M................ Massachusetts State Library, Boston, MA [*Library symbol*] [*Library of Congress*] (LCLS)
M................ Massage
M................ Masseur [*Ranking title*] [*British Royal Navy*]
M................ Massive [*Agriculture*]
M................ Master
M................ Mate [*of a ship*]
M................ Mater [*Mother*] [*Latin*]
M................ Maternal (MELL)
M................ Mathematics [*Secondary school course*] [*British*]
M................ Matinee
M................ Matins [*Early morning prayers*]
m................ Matrix (NAKS)
M................ Matrix
M................ Matron [*British military*] (DMA)
M................ Mature
M................ Mature Audiences [*Movie rating*] [*Replaced by GP*]
M................ Matured Bonds [*Investment term*] (DFIT)
M................ Mauthner [*Cell*] [*Neurology*]
M................ Maxilla (MELL)
M................ Maximal [*or Maximum*] [*Medicine*]
M................ Maximum Value [*Electronics*]
M................ Maxwell [*Electronics*] (DEN)
M................ May
m................ Mean (DIPS)
M................ Mean [*Arithmetic average*]
M................ Mean Active Maintenance Downtime [*Computer science*]
M................ Meaningfulness [*Psychology*]
M................ Mean Square
M................ Measles (MELL)
M................ Measure [*Music*]
M................ Measured Ceiling [*Aviation*]
M................ Meatus (MELL)
M................ Mechanical
M................ Mechlorethamine [*Also, HN, HN2, MBA, NM*] [*Mustargen, nitrogen mustard*] [*Antineoplastic drug*]
M................ Medal (ADA)

M .... Media [*Laboratory*] (AAMN)
M .... Medial (DAVI)
(M) .... Median
M .... Mediator
M .... Medical
M .... Medical Service (SAUO)
M .... Medicare (MELL)
M .... Medicinae [*Of Medicine*] [*Latin*]
M .... Medicine
M .... Medieval
M .... Medium [*Size designation for clothing, etc.*]
m .... Medium [*Spectral*]
M .... Medium [*or 2-engine*] Plane
m .... Mega (NAKS)
M .... Mega [*A prefix meaning multiplied by one million*] [*Symbol*]
M .... Megabyte [*Data storage capacity*] [*Computer science*]
M .... Megohm (AAG)
M .... Melendus [*Flourished, 1188-1209*] [*Authority cited in pre-1607 legal work*] (DSA)
M .... Melittin [*Bee venom*]
M .... Melphalan [*Also, A, L-PAM, MPH, MPL*] [*Antineoplastic drug*]
M .... Melts At ____ [*Followed by a temperature*]
M .... Member
M .... Member of (SAUO)
M .... Membrana [*Membrane*] [*Anatomy*]
M .... Memorandum
M .... Memoria [*Memory*] [*Latin*]
M .... Memorial; Journal Officiel du Grand Duche de Luxembourg [*A publication*] (ILCA)
M .... Memory
M .... Meningeal (MELL)
M .... Mensura [*By Measure*] [*Pharmacy*] (ROG)
M .... Mentum [*Chin*]
M .... Menzies' Cape Colony Supreme Court Reports [*A publication*] (DLA)
M .... Meperidine [*Also, MEP*] [*An analgesic*]
M .... Mercaptopurine [*Purinethol*] [*Also, MP, P*] [*Antineoplastic drug*]
M .... Mercury [*Chemical symbol is Hg*] (KSC)
m .... Mercury (NAKS)
M .... Merehurst [*Publisher*] [*British*]
M .... Merge [*Computer science*] (IBMDP)
M .... Merides [*Latin*] [*Noon*] (WDMC)
m .... Meridian (Lower Branch)
M .... Meridian (Upper Branch)
M .... Meridies [*Noon*] [*Latin*]
M .... Meridional Part [*Navigation*]
M .... Mesangium [*Anatomy*]
M .... Mesh
M .... Mesial [*Dentistry*]
M .... Mesomeric [*Organic chemistry*]
M .... Mesophyll [*Botany*]
m .... Meta [*Chemistry*]
M .... Metabolite
M .... Metacenter
M .... Metal
M .... Metalsmith [*Navy*]
M .... Metamorphosis [*Phylogeny*]
M .... Metaproterenol [*Pharmacology*]
M .... Metastasis [*Oncology*]
M .... Meteorological [*JETDS nomenclature*]
M .... Meter (WDMC)
m .... Meter [*SI unit of length*]
M .... Methionine [*One-letter symbol; see Met*]
M .... Method
M .... Methodist
M .... Methotrexate [*Antineoplastic drug*]
m .... Methyl [*As substituent on nucleoside*] [*Biochemistry*]
M .... Metoclopramide [*An antiemetic*]
M .... Metronome
M .... Metropolitan
M .... Mews
M .... Mezzo [*Moderate*] [*Music*]
M .... Michaelmas Term [*British*] [*Legal term*] (ILCA)
m .... Micro (WGA)
M .... Micrococcus [*Genus of bacteria*]
m .... Micrometer (ABAC)
M .... Micrometer
M .... Microphones [*JETDS nomenclature*] [*Military*] (CET)
M .... Microprocessor
M .... Microsporum [*Genus of fungi*]
M .... Microtubule [*Cytology*]
M .... Midazolan [*An anesthetic*]
M .... Midday (ADA)
m .... Middle (NAKS)
M .... Middle
M .... Middle School [*British*]
M .... Middle Term of a Syllogism [*Logistics*] (WDAA)
M .... Midfield [*Men's lacrosse position*]
M .... Midline
M .... Midnight (ROG)
m .... Midship [*Shipping*] (DS)
M .... Midwest Stock Exchange [*Chicago, IL*]
m .... Mihi [*To Me*] [*Latin*] (EES)
M .... Mike [*Phonetic alphabet*] [*International*] [*World War II*] (DSUE)
M .... Mil [*Monetary unit*] [*Cyprus*]
M .... Mild (DAVI)

M .... Mile (WDMC)
m .... mile (WDMC)
M .... Miles
M .... Miles' Pennsylvania Reports [*A publication*] (DLA)
M .... Military
M .... Militia
M .... Milk (ROG)
M .... Mill
M .... Mille [*Thousand*] [*Roman numeral*]
M .... Milli (DFIT)
m .... Milli- [*A prefix meaning divided by 1000*] [*SI symbol*]
M .... Millime [*Monetary unit*] [*Tunisia*]
M .... Millimicrometer (IAA)
M .... Millimicron (DIPS)
M .... Millimicron (IAA)
m .... Million (NAKS)
M .... Million
m .... Mil[*thousand*] (DAVI)
M .... Mine
M .... Minesweeper [*Navy*]
M .... Miniature [*Horticulture*]
M .... Minim
M .... Minimum (ADA)
M .... Ministry
M .... Minor
M .... Mint [*Condition*] [*Numismatics, etc.*]
M .... Minus
M .... Minute
M .... Miotic [*Biology*]
M .... Mira [*A star*] [*Astronomy*] (OA)
M .... Mired (IAA)
M .... Misce [*Mix*] [*Pharmacy*]
M .... Miscellaneous
M .... Miscible
M .... Mishnah [*Basis of the Talmud*] (BJA)
M .... Missile [*Air Force*]
M .... Missile Carrier Aircraft [*Designation for all US military aircraft*]
m .... Missing (NAKS)
M .... Missing [*Data*]
M .... Missing (Weather Reports Only) [*NWS*] (FAAC)
M .... Mission
M .... Mist [*Meteorology*]
M .... Mistura [*Mixture*] [*Pharmacy*]
M .... Mitic Subgroup [*Magnetite, chromite, hematite, ilmenite, titanite, perofskite, rutile*] [*CIPW classification*] [*Geology*]
M .... Mitochondrion [*Cytology*]
M .... Mitomycin [*Also, MC, MT*] [*Antineoplastic drug*]
M .... Mitosis [*Cytology*]
M .... Mitte [*Send*] [*Latin*]
M .... Mix [*or Mixture*]
M .... Mixed School [*British*]
M .... Mobile [*Missile launch environment symbol*] [*Biology*]
M .... Mobilization [*as in M-Day*] [*Military*] (AABC)
M .... Modal (Verb) [*Linguistics*]
M .... Mode
M .... Model [*in military nomenclature*]
M .... MODEM [*Computer science*]
M .... Moderate
M .... Moderate Sea or Swell [*Meteorology*]
M .... Modern [*Post-1920*] [*Deltiology*]
M .... Modification [*FCC*] (NTCM)
m .... Modified [*Regulation or order modified*] [*Used in Shepard's Citations*] [*Legal term*] (DLA)
M .... Modiolus (MELL)
m .... Modulation Coefficient (IDOE)
M .... Modulation Depth [*Broadcasting*]
M .... Modulator (IAA)
M .... Modulus
M .... Moisture
M .... Mol [*or Mole*] [*Measurement*] (DAVI)
m .... Molal [*Solute concentration by weight*] [*Chemistry*]
m .... Molality (MELL)
m .... Molar [*Tooth, deciduous*] [*Dentistry*] (DAVI)
M .... Molar [*Permanent*] [*Dentistry*]
M .... Molar [*Solute concentration by volume*] [*Chemistry*]
M .... Molarity (MELL)
M .... Molar Mass [*Symbol*] [*IUPAC*]
M .... Mole
M .... Molecular Weight [*Also, MOL WT, MW*]
M .... Moment
M .... Moment of Force [*Symbol*] [*IUPAC*]
M .... Monastery
M .... Monday
M .... Money
M .... Monitor (MDG)
m .... Monitor (NAKS)
M .... Monkey [*Phonetic alphabet*] [*Royal Navy*] [*World War I*] [*Pre-World War II*] (DSUE)
M .... Monochrome (IAA)
M .... Monoclonal [*Biochemistry*]
M .... Monocyte [*Hematology*]
M .... Monograph
M .... Monophage [*Biology*]
M .... Monoplane
M .... Monotype (DGA)

M	Monsieur [*Mister*] [*French*]
M	Monsoon
M	Mont [*Monte, etc.*] [*Italy and Sicily only*]
M	Montana (DLA)
M	Montavit Co. [*Austria*] [*Research code symbol*]
m	Month (WDMC)
M	Month
m	Monthly (RION)
M	Monthly
M	Montmorillonite [*A mineral*]
M	Montreal Stock Exchange
M	Monumentum [*Monument*] [*Latin*]
M	Moon
M	Morgan [*George T.*] [*Designer's mark, when appearing on US coins*]
M	Morison's Dictionary of Decisions, Scotch Court of Session [*1540-1808*] [*A publication*] (DLA)
m	Morning (WDMC)
M	Morning
m	Morpha [*Form*] [*Biology*]
M	Morphine [*Slang*]
M	Morphological Rule [*Linguistics*]
M	Morphometric Analysis [*Botany*]
M	Mort [*Dead*] [*French*] (ROG)
M	Mortar
M	Mortgage
M	Mortis [*Of Death*] [*Latin*]
M	Motel
M	Mother
m	Motile [*Sperm*] (MAE)
M	Motivational Ability
M	Motor
M	Motorship (DS)
M	Motorway [*Traffic sign*] [*British*]
M	Moulder [*Navy rating*] [*British*]
M	Mound (MSA)
M	Mountain
M	Mouth
M	Move Being Made [*Computer science*]
M	Movement [*Neurology*]
M	Movement Response [*Used in Rorschach test scoring*] (DIPS)
M	[*Time in Days Before*] Move Operations
M	Mu [*Twelfth letter of the Greek alphabet*] (DAVI)
M	Mucoid
M	Mucoid Colony [*Biochemistry*] (DAVI)
M	Mucus (MELL)
M	Mud
M	Muddy [*Track condition*] [*Thoroughbred racing*]
M	Muddy [*Quality of the bottom*] [*Nautical charts*]
M	Multipara (MAE)
M	Multiplier
M	Municipal Premises [*Public-performance tariff class*] [*British*]
M	Murmur [*Heart*] [*Medicine*]
M	Muscarinic (DB)
M	Musculus [*Muscle*] [*Anatomy*]
M	Music [*Films, television, etc.*]
M	Mustard Gas [*Also, H, HD, HS, HT*] [*Poison gas*] [*US Chemical Corps symbol*]
M	Muster
M	Mutitas [*Dullness*] [*Latin*]
M	Mutual Companies
M	Mutual Inductance [*Symbol*] [*IUPAC*]
M	Mycelium [*Biology*]
M	Mycobacterium [*Genus of microorganisms*]
M	Mycoplasma [*Medicine*] (MAE)
M	Mydriacyl (SAUS)
M	Myopia
M	Myosin [*Muscle physiology*]
M	New York Miscellaneous Reports [*A publication*] (DLA)
M	Nomina [*Names*] [*Probably a misprint for NN, by some supposed to denote St. Mary, patron saint of girls*] [*Latin*] (ROG)
M	Noon [*Meridies*]
M	Ohio Miscellaneous Reports [*A publication*] (DLA)
M	One Thousand [*Roman numeral*]
M	Ordered Multistate [*Botany*]
M	Pole Strength (SAUS)
M	Queen Mary (DLA)
M	Radiant Exitance [*Symbol*] [*IUPAC*]
M	Reckitt & Sons Ltd. [*Great Britain*] [*Research code symbol*]
M	Red Star of Prominent Titanium Oxide Intensity [*Astronomy*] (BARN)
M	Refractive Modulus (IDOE)
m	Response to Human Being Movement [*Rorschach*] [*Psychology*]
M	Strength of Pole [*Chemistry*] (DAVI)
M	Thioinosine [*One-letter symbol; see SIno, Sno*]
/M	Thousand
M-	Time in Days Before Move Operations (SAUS)
M	Time of Maneuver
M	University of Michigan, Ann Arbor (SAUO)
M/0/0/S	Minutes Zero Zero Seconds [*Aerospace*] (AAG)
M/1	Method 1 (NITA)
M_1	Mitral First Sound [*Cardiology*]
M_1	Money Supply of a Country, Consisting of Currency and Demand Deposits [*Economics*]
M_1	Sight Dullness [*on Auscultation*] [*Medicine*] (DAVI)
M1S	Matte One Side [*Aluminum*]
M_2	Insular Segment of Middle Cerebral Artery [*Cardiology*] (DAVI)
M_2	Marked Dullness [*on Auscultation*] [*Medicine*] (DAVI)
M2	Masterspec 2 [*Production Systems for Architects & Engineers, Inc.*] [*Information service or system*] (IID)
M_2	Mitral Second Heart Sound [*Cardiology*] (DAVI)
M2	Moluccan Cockatoo [*Bird*]
M_2	Money Supply of a Country, Including M_1 and Commercial Time Deposits [*Economics*]
m2	Square Meter
M2C	Massachusetts Microelectronics Center [*Research center*] (RCD)
M^2C^2	Multi-Media Communication Control (DOMA)
M2F2	Multimode Fire & Forget (SAUS)
M^2FCS	Multi-Microprocessor Flight Control System (PDAA)
M2FM	Modified Modified Frequency Modulation
M^2H^2	Mary Hartman, Mary Hartman [*Initialism is shortened form of television program title*] [*Also, MH2*]
M2M	Manager-to-Manager (ACRL)
M2M	May Second Movement [*1960s Yale University war protest*] (VNW)
M2S	Matte Two Sides [*Aluminum*]
M^2/S	Square Meters per Second
M_3	Absolute Dullness [*on Auscultation*] [*Medicine*] (DAVI)
m3	Cubic Meter
M3	Mesoscale and Microscale Meteorology division (SAUO)
M/3	Middle Third [*of long bones*] [*Orthopedics*] (DAVI)
M3	Military Manpower Models
M_3	Money Supply of a Country, Including M_2, Savings and Loan Association Deposits, and Certificates of Deposit [*Economics*]
M-3 APD	Military Manpower Models Airborne Personnel Detector [*Device used to collect and test air samples to identify enemy sites*] [*Vietnam*] (VNW)
M3C	MAJCOM Manpower Management Computer (SAUO)
M^3/D	Cubic Meters per Day
M^3/J	Cubic Meters per Joule
M^3/KG	Cubic Meters per Kilogram
$M^3/(M\ A)$	Cubic Meters per Meter Year
$M^3/(M\ D)$	Cubic Meters per Meter Day
M^3/MIN	Cubic Meters per Minute
m3/s	Cubic Meter (or Metre) per Second (SAUS)
M^3/S	Cubic Meters per Second
M-3 TAP	Military Manpower Models Toxicological Agents Protective Suit [*Provided protection from chemical agents*] (VNW)
M-3V	Movimiento 3V [*Nicaragua*] [*Political party*] (EY)
M_4	Cortical Segment of Middle Cerebral Artery [*Cardiology*] (DAVI)
M4	Message from Multiple Media Maximizes [*Communications*] (WDMC)
M5	Manual Five Speed [*DOE*] (TAG)
M/10	Tenth Molar [*Solute concentration by volume*] [*Chemistry*] (DAVI)
M12	M12 [*Hawaii*] [*Seismograph station code, US Geological Survey*] [*Closed*] (SEIS)
M-18-X	Movimiento 18 de Octubre de Accion Revolucionaria Astra [*Astra 18th October Movement of Revolutionary Action*] [*Ecuador*] [*Political party*] (PD)
M-19	April 19 Movement (SAUO)
M-19	Movimiento 19 de Abril [*April 19 Movement*] [*Colombia*]
M-20	Movimiento-20 [*Panama*] [*Political party*] (EY)
M31	Andromeda Galaxy (SAUS)
M-47	Dragon (SAUS)
M50	Mean of 1950 [*Coordinate system*] [*NASA*] (NASA)
M85	85 Percent/15 Percent Unleaded Gasoline [*BTS*] (TAG)
M/100	Hundredth Molar [*Solute concentration by volume*] [*Chemistry*] (DAVI)
MA	Aircraft Stations [*ITU designation*] (CET)
MA	Amherst College, Amherst, MA [*Library symbol*] [*Library of Congress*] (LCLS)
ma---	Arab States [*MARC geographic area code*] [*Library of Congress*] (LCCP)
MA	Commonwealth of Massachusetts (SAUS)
MA	Deputy Commander for Maintenance (SAUO)
MA	Division of Military Application (SAUO)
Ma	Ma'arbae (BJA)
Ma	Ma'aserot (BJA)
MA	Machine Accountant [*Navy*]
Ma	Mach Number [*IUPAC*]
MA	Macroaneurysm (SAUS)
MA	Macronutrient Additives [*Fat substituted for food*]
MA	Madras Artillery [*British military*] (DMA)
MA	Madrid Stock Exchange [*Spain*]
MA	Magister Artium [*Master of Arts*] [*Latin*]
MA	Magma Arizona (SAUO)
MA	Magma Arizona Railroad Co. [*Later, MAA*] [*AAR code*]
MA	Magnesium Association [*Later, IMA*] (EA)
MA	Magnetic Amplifier
MA	Mahogany Association (EA)
MA	Maids of Athena (EA)
MA	Maids of Athens (SAUO)
MA	Main Alarm (IAA)
MA	Main Amplifier (OA)
MA	Maintenance
MA	Maintenance Ability (KSC)
MA	Maintenance Actions
MA	Maintenance Agency (SAUO)
MA	Maintenance Agreement (ELAL)
M/A	Maintenance Analysis (KSC)
MA	Maintenance Area [*Military*] [*British*]
MA	Maintenance Availability
MA	Major (DSUE)
MA	Malayan Airways (SAUO)

Ma	Male (DAVI)
M/A	Male, Altered Animal (DMAA)
MA	Maleic Anhydride [Also, MAH] [Organic chemistry]
MA	Malev Hungarian Airlines (SAUO)
MA	Malicious Damage (MARI)
MA	Malignant Angioendotheliomatosis [Oncology]
MA	Malignant Arrhythmia [Medicine] (DMAA)
MA	Malignant Astrocytoma [Medicine] (MELL)
MA	Malonaldehyde [Organic chemistry]
MA	Malpractice Association (EA)
MA	Malvalic Acid (PDAA)
MA	Mamma (DSUE)
MA	Mammary Adenocarcinoma [Medicine] (DB)
MA	Management Administration [Department of Labor Statistics] (OICC)
MA	Management Adviser
MA	Manager of Aviation
MA	Manager's Assistant (DCTA)
Ma	Manchester Regiment (SAUO)
MA	Mandelic Acid [Organic chemistry] (AAMN)
MA	Manifest Achievement (AAMN)
MA	Manifest Anxiety
MA	Maniilaq Association (EA)
MA	Manpower Administration [Later, Employment and Training Administration] [Department of Labor]
MA	Manual
M/A	Manual or Automatic (NRCH)
MA	Manufacturing Assembly
MA	Manufacturing Authorization (ACAE)
MA	Manure (ROG)
MA	Manx Airlines Ltd.
MA	Map Analysis
MA	Marangoni [Tire retread brand]
MA	March
Ma	March's Action for Slander and Arbitrament [A publication] (DLA)
MA	Margin Account [Investment term]
MA	Marijuana Anonymous (SAUO)
MA	Marine Class
MA	Maritime Administration [Also, MARAD, MARITADMIN] [Department of Transportation]
ma	Maritime Antarctic [Air Mass] [Meteorology] (BARN)
MA	Mark [Coin] (ROG)
MA	Market Administration (HCT)
MA	Market Average [Investment term]
MA	Marketing Assistance (MCD)
MA	Marriage Analysis [Psychology]
Ma	Marsh [Maps and charts]
MA	Marshaling Area [Military]
MA	Martin Ablator (SAUS)
MA	Martin-Albright [Syndrome] [Medicine] (DB)
MA	Martingana [Ship's rigging] (ROG)
Ma	Martinus de Caramanico [Flourished, 1269-85] [Authority cited in pre-1607 legal work] (DSA)
Ma	Martinus Gosia [Authority cited in pre-1607 legal work] (DSA)
MA	Massachusetts [Postal code]
MA	Massachusetts Reports [A publication] (DLA)
MA	Mass Analyzer
MA	Masseter [Medicine] (MELL)
M$_a$	Mass Flow of Air [Aviation] (DA)
Ma	Mass of Atom (DMAA)
MA	Mast Aerial (IAA)
MA	Master (MSA)
MA	Master Alarm
MA	Master Assistant [British military] (DMA)
MA	Master-at-Arms [Navy]
MA	Master of Arts
MA	Master of Arts in Fine Arts (SAUO)
MA	Masurium
MA	Matched Angle (OA)
MA	Mater [Mother] [Latin] (ADA)
MA	Material Authorization (KSC)
MA	Materials Application (SAUO)
MA	Mathematical Association [British] (BI)
Ma	Matheus de Mathesillanis [Flourished, 1381-1402] [Authority cited in pre-1607 legal work] (DSA)
MA	Matrix Antigen [Biochemistry]
MA	Matt Art [Paper] (DGA)
Ma	Mattes [Quality of the bottom] [Nautical charts]
MA	Maturational Age [Also, Development Age] [Medical term] (PAZ)
MA	Mature Adult [Film and video classification]
MA	Mature Australia [An association]
MA	May
MA	May Department Stores Co. [NYSE symbol] (SPSG)
MA	May Dept Stores [NYSE symbol] (TTSB)
MA	Mazdaznan Association (EA)
MA	Mean Arterial Blood Pressure [Medicine] (MAE)
MA	Measurement Accuracy
MA	Mechanical Accessories (MCD)
MA	Mechanical Advantage
MA	Mechanical Ambush (VNW)
MA	Mechanical Atherectomy [Medicine] (MELL)
MA	Mechanically Alloyed [Metallurgy]
MA	Mechanician Apprentice [British military] (DMA)
MA	Mechanoacoustic
MA	Media Alliance (EA)
MA	Medicaid (DLA)
MA	Medical Abbreviation (AAMN)
MA	Medical Assistance [HEW]
MA	Medical Assistant (DAVI)
MA	Medical Audit (MAE)
MA	Medical Authority
MA	Medical Authorization (DAVI)
M/A	Mediterranean/Adriatic [Shipping] (DS)
MA	Mediterranean Area
MA	Medium Artillery
MA	Mega [A prefix meaning multiplied by one million]
Ma	Megaannum (DOG)
MA	Megaloblastic Anemia [Medicine] (MELL)
MA	Megampere (IEEE)
MA	Melanesian Alliance [Papua New Guinea] [Political party] (FEA)
MA	Melodious Accord (EA)
MA	Member of the Academy (SAUO)
MA	Membrane Antigen [Immunology]
MA	Memory Address [Computer science]
MA	Memory Available [Computer science] (IAA)
MA	Menorah Association [Defunct] (EA)
MA	Menstrual Age [Medicine]
MA	Mental Age [Psychology]
MA	Mentum Anterior [In reference to the chin]
MA	Mercenary Association (EA)
MA	Mercer Associates (EA)
MA	Mercury Arc (MSA)
MA	Mercury-Atlas [Spacecraft] [NASA]
MA	Message Assembler
M/A	Mess Attendant
MA	Messies Anonymous [Commercial firm] (EA)
MA	Messing Allowance [British military] (DMA)
MA	Metabolic Acidosis [Medicine] (MELL)
MA	Metabolic Activity
MA	Metabolic Analyzer
MA	Metal Anchor (AAG)
MA	Metallurgistes Unis d'Amerique [United Steelworkers of America] (EAIO)
MA	Meteorological Applications [Branch] [Forecast Systems Laboratory] (USDC)
MA	Meter Amplifier
MA	Meter Angle
M/A	Meters per Year
MA	Methamphetamine [Pharmacology]
MA	Methoxylamine [Organic chemistry]
MA	Methyl Acrylate [Organic chemistry]
MA	Methyl Anthranilate [Organic chemistry]
MA	Methylanthranilic Acid
MA	Metric Association [Later, USMA] (EA)
MA	Metropolitan Area (SAUO)
MA	Mexican-American
MA	Michigan Amber [Variety of wheat]
MA	Microadenoma [Medicine] (MELL)
MA	Microagglutination [Immunochemistry] (DAVI)
MA	Microalloy
MA	Microfilm Address (NITA)
MA	Microphone Amplifier
MA	Microscopic Agglutination [Medicine] (DMAA)
MA	Microwave Associates, Inc. [Later, M/A-Com] (AAG)
MA	Middeck Act
MA	Middeck Aft (MCD)
MA	Middle Ages
MA	Middle Assyrian [Language, etc.] (BJA)
MA	Midland Aluminium Limited (SAUO)
MA	Midmarch Associates (EA)
MA	Midwest Academy (EA)
MA	Mike Amplifier (NASA)
MA	Mikes of America (EA)
MA	Mileage Allowance
MA	Miles Laboratories, Inc. [Research code symbol]
MA	Military Academy
MA	Military Accountant [British military] (DMA)
MA	Military Administration
MA	Military Adviser (SAUO)
MA	Military Aircraft
MA	Military Applications (SAUO)
MA	Military Assistance [or Assistant]
MA	Military Attache [Diplomacy]
MA	Military Aviator
MA	Mill Annealed
MA	Millennium Ecosystem Assessment (SAUO)
MA	Miller-Abbot (Tube) [Medicine]
MA	Milliammeter (IAA)
ma	Milliamp (AEBE)
ma	Milliampere (ELAL)
MA	Milliampere
mA	Milliampere [or Milliamperage]
MA	Milliangstrom [Unit of wavelength of light] (WGA)
Ma	Million Years Ago
MA	Mind Association (EA)
MA	Minimum Aircraft [Powered hang gliders, replicas of early flying machines, etc.] [British]
MA	Mining Association (SAUO)
MA	Ministry of Aviation [British]
MA	Minnesota [Obsolete] (ROG)
MA	Miscellaneous at Anchor [Navy] (NVT)

MA .... Miss Angle
MA .... Missed Appointment
MA .... Missed Approach
MA .... Missile Airframe (AAG)
MA .... Missile Armed (ACAE)
MA .... Missile Away
MA .... Mission Abort (SAUO)
MA .... Mission Accomplished [Air Force]
MA .... Mission Analysis (MCD)
MA .... Missionarius Apostolicus [Missionary Apostolic] [Latin]
MA .... Missionary Apostolic (SAUO)
MA .... Mission Assignment (ACAE)
MA .... Missouri Appeal Reports [A publication] (DLA)
MA .... Mistresses Anonymous (EA)
MA .... Mitomycin-C and Adriamycin [Antineoplastic drug regimen] (DAVI)
MA .... Mitotic Apparatus [Cytology]
MA .... Mitral Annulus [Cardiology] (DAVI)
MA .... Mobile Airlock (MCD)
MA .... Mobile Allocation (CGWS)
MA .... Mobilization Augmentee [Military] (AFM)
MA .... Mobilization for Animals [Defunct] (EA)
MA .... Moderately Advanced (MAE)
MA .... Modern Age [A publication] (BRI)
MA .... Modified Atmosphere [Food technology]
MA .... Modify Address (IEEE)
MA .... Monarchist Alliance (EA)
MA .... Monarticular Arthritis [Medicine]
M/A .... Monetary Allowance
MA .... Monitoring Agency
MA .... Monkeein' Around [An association] (EA)
MA .... Monoamine [Chemistry]
MA .... Monoclonal Antibody [Medicine] (DMAA)
MA .... Monomorphic Adenoma [Medicine] (MELL)
MA .... Monte Carlo Resources [Vancouver Stock Exchange symbol]
MA .... Months After
M/A .... Mood and/or Affect [Psychology] (DAVI)
MA .... Moored Alongside [Navy] (NVT)
MA .... Moral Alternatives [An association] (EA)
MA .... Moreshet Archives [Jerusalem] (BJA)
MA .... Morning After (IIA)
MA .... Morocco [IYRU nationality code] [ANSI two-letter standard code] (CNC)
MA .... Mortuary Affairs [Army] (INF)
MA .... Mother's Aide [Red Cross Nursing Services]
MA .... Mothers of Asthmatics (EA)
MA .... Mountain Artillery
MA .... Mountaineering Association [British] (BI)
MA .... Moving Average [Statistics]
MA .... Multi-chambered Auto-injector (SAUS)
MA .... Multiple Access (NASA)
MA .... Multiple Application [Military] (AFIT)
MA .... Munitionsanstalt [Ammunition Depot] [German military - World War II]
MA .... Munitions Tribunals Appeals, Great Britain High Court of Justice [A publication] (DLA)
MA .... Muscle Activity (MAE)
MA .... Museums' Association (WDAA)
MA .... Musical Appreciation [Record label]
MA .... Music Alliance [Defunct] (EA)
MA .... Muslim Almanac [A publication]
MA .... Mutagenic Activity
MA .... Mutual Age
MA .... My Account [Business term]
MA .... Myanma Airways (EY)
ma .... Myria [A prefix meaning multiplied by 10⁴]
MA .... Office of Management and Administration (SAUO)
MA .... United States Military Academy (AAGC)
MA1 .... Machine Accountant, First Class [Navy]
MA2 .... Machine Accountant, Second Class [Navy]
MA3 .... Machine Accountant, Third Class [Navy]
MAA .... Aerotransportes Mas de Carga SA de CV [Mexico] [ICAO designator] (FAAC)
MAA .... Maastrichtial [Paleontology]
MAA .... Macroaggregated Albumin [Medicine]
MAA .... Madras [India] [Airport symbol] (OAG)
MAA .... Magazine Area A (SAUO)
MAA .... Magma Arizona Railroad Co. [AAR code]
MAA .... Major Aircraft Accident (MCD)
MAA .... Manantiales [Argentina] [Seismograph station code, US Geological Survey] (SEIS)
MAA .... Mandatory Advertising Association [Automotive retailing]
MAA .... Manitoba Association of Architects [1914] [Canada] (NGC)
MAA .... Manufacturers' Agents Association of Great Britain and Ireland (BI)
MAA .... Manufacturers Aircraft Association [Supersedes AMA] [Defunct] (EA)
MAA .... Marina Association of America [Defunct] (EA)
MAA .... Marineartillerieabteilung [Naval Coast Artillery Battalion] [German military - World War II]
MA A .... Massachusetts Appeals Court Reports [A publication] (DLA)
MAA .... Master Army Aviator
MAA .... Master At Arms (SAUS)
MAA .... Master-at-Arms [Navy]
MAA .... Master of Administrative Arts (GAGS)
MAA .... Master of Aeronautics and Astronautics (GAGS)
MAA .... Master of Applied Art (GAGS)
MAA .... Master of Applied Arts

MAA .... Material Access Area [Nuclear energy] (NRCH)
MAA .... Mathematical Association of America (EA)
MAA .... Mature Age Allowance
MAA .... Maximum Acceptance Angle (VLIE)
MAA .... Maximum Authorized Altitude [Aviation]
MAA .... Mecca Minerals Ltd. [Vancouver Stock Exchange symbol]
MAA .... Mechanical Arm Assembly (NASA)
MAA .... Mediaeval Academy of America (EA)
MAA .... Medical Administrative Assistant (DAVI)
MAA .... Medical Artists Association (SAUO)
MAA .... Medical Artists Association of Great Britain (PDAA)
MAA .... Medical Assistance for the Aged
MAA .... Medium Antiaircraft Weapon (NATG)
MAA .... Melanoma-Associated Antigen [Oncology]
MAA .... Member of the Architectural Association (SAUO)
MAA .... Menthoxyacetic Acid [Organic chemistry]
MAA .... Methacrylic Acid [Organic chemistry]
MAA .... Methanearsonic Acid [Organic chemistry]
MAA .... Methyl Acetoacetate [Organic chemistry]
MAA .... Metropolitan Area Acquisition Program (SAUO)
MAA .... Microlight Aircrafts Association [British] (DI)
MAA .... Mid-Amer Apart Communities [NYSE symbol] (TTSB)
MAA .... Mid-America Airlines (SAUO)
MAA .... Mid-America Airways, Inc. (SAUO)
MAA .... [The] Mid-America Apartment Communities [NYSE symbol] (SPSG)
MAA .... Midlands Association for the Arts (SAUO)
MAA .... Military Advisory Assistance (ACAE)
MAA .... Mission Area Analysis (MCD)
MAA .... Mobilization Against AIDS [An association] (EA)
MAA .... Mobilization Automation Appraisal (MCD)
MAA .... Modeling Association of America [Later, MAAI]
MAA .... Moderate Angle of Attack
MAA .... Modified Ames Assay [For toxicology]
MAA .... Monarticular Arthritis [Orthopedics] (DAVI)
MAA .... Monitoring Angle of Attack (SAUS)
MAA .... Moped Association of America [Defunct] (EA)
MAA .... Motel Association of America [Later, National Innkeeping Association]
MAA .... Motor Agents' Association [British]
MAA .... Mouvement Anti-Apartheid [France]
MAA .... Municipal Arborist Association [Later, MAUFS] (EA)
MAA .... Museum of African Art (SAUO)
MAA .... Mutual Aid Agreement (DEMM)
MAA .... Mutual Assistance Association (SAUO)
MAA .... Myositis Association of America (SAUO)
MAAA .... Master of Arts in Arts Administration (PGP)
MAAA .... Member of the American Academy of Actuaries
MAAA .... Memoirs American Anthropological Association (SAUO)
MAAA .... Metropolitan Area Apparel Association (EA)
MAAAA .... Mid-Am Antique Appraisers Association (EA)
MAAAA .... Mid-America Antique Appraisers Association (SAUO)
MAAAP .... macroaggregated Albumin Arterial Perfusion [Medicine] (STED)
MAAAS .... Member of the American Academy of Arts and Sciences (SAUO)
MAAB .... Maintenance Air Abort [Air Force] (AFIT)
MAAB .... Materials Application Advisory Board [NASA] (NASA)
MAABR .... Maintenance Air Abort Rate [Air Force] (AFIT)
MAABS .... Master of Arts in Applied Behavioral Sciences (GAGS)
MAAC .... Mastic Asphalt Advisory Council [British] (BI)
MAAC .... Maximum Allowable Actual Charge [Medicare]
MAAC .... Medical Assistance Advisory Council (SAUO)
MAAC .... Medical Assistants Advisory Council (DAVI)
MAAC .... Metro Atlantic Athletic Conference (PSS)
MAAC .... Metropolitan Area Advisory Committee (SAUO)
MAAC .... Mid-Atlantic Area Council [Regional power council]
MAAC .... Military Assistance Advisory Command (DOMA)
MAAC .... Military Assistance Advisory Committee (SAUO)
MAAC .... Military Assistance Advisory Course (SAUO)
MAAC .... Milliampere Alternating Current (IAA)
MAAC .... Minimum Aft Axial Clearance (ACAE)
MAAC .... Mutual Assistance Advisory Committee
MAACBA ...... Middle Atlantic Association of Colleges of Business Administration
MAACE .... Mississippi Association for Adult and Community Education
MAACL .... Multiple Affect Adjective Check List [of Educational and Industrial Testing Service] [Psychology]
MAACP .... Mediterranean-African Airlift Command Post (SAUO)
MAACP .... Mediterranean Area Airlift Command Post (AFM)
MAACS .... Multi Address Asynchronous Communication System
MA ADAM .... Master of Arts in Alcoholism and Drug Abuse Ministry (PGP)
MAADMA .... Methylaminoacetaldehyde Dimethyl Acetal [Organic chemistry]
MAAE .... Master of Aeronautical and Astronomical Engineering (GAGS)
MAAE .... Master of Arts in Applied Economics (GAGS)
MAAF .... Mediterranean Allied Air Force
MAAF .... Mediterranean Army Air Forces
MAAF .... Michael Army Air Field (MCD)
MAAF .... Museum Association of the American Frontier (EA)
MAA-FDI ...... Museum of African Art - Frederick Douglass Institute [Smithsonian Institution] (EA)
MAAG .... Medical Audit Advisory Group (SAUO)
MAAG .... Military Assistance Advisory Group [Merged with US Military Assistance Command]
MAAGAP ...... Model Analysis of Agricultural Adjustment in the Philippines (SAUO)
MAAGB .... Medical Artists Association of Great Britain (DAVI)
MAAGI .... Military Assistance Advisory Group, Indochina [Later, MAAGV] (VNW)
MAAG-J .... Military Assistance Advisory Group, Japan (SAUO)
MAAGP .... Member, American Academy of General Practice (CMD)

MAAGS	Military Assistants Advisory Groups (SAUO)
MAAGV	Military Assistance Advisory Group, Vietnam [*Formerly, MAAGI*] (VNW)
MAAH	Museum of African American History (EA)
MAAH	Museum of Afro-American History (EA)
MAAI	Modeling Association of America International (EA)
MAAK	Movement for All-Macedonian Action [*Political party*]
MAAL	Massachusetts Alliance of Adult Learners
MAAL	Monthly Adjustment Acceptance List [*Military*] (AFIT)
MAALOX	Magnesium-Aluminum Hydroxide [*Commercial antacid*]
MAALT	Multiple Aircraft Approach and Landing Techniques (MCD)
MAAM	Medium Antiaircraft Missile
MAAMA	Middleton Air Material Agency (SAUO)
MAAMA	Middletown Air Materiel Area (SAA)
MAAMC	Motor Aircraft and Allied Manufacturing Companies (SAUO)
MAAmSt	Master of Arts in American Studies (GAGS)
MAAN	Methyleneaminoacetonitrile [*Organic chemistry*]
MAAN	Mutual Advertising Agency Network [*Grand Forks, ND*] (EA)
MA & D	Mission Analysis and Design
MA & E	Mission Analysis and Engineering [*NASA*]
MA&F	Minister of Agriculture and Fisheries (SAUO)
MA&F	Ministry of Agriculture and Fisheries (SAUO)
MA & P	Maintenance Analysis and Planning (NASA)
MA & T	Manufacturing Assembly and Test (MCD)
MA and T	Missile Assembly and Test [*Building*] (NATG)
MAANPI	Mutual Aid Association of the New Polish Immigration (EA)
MAANS	Midwest Association of Administrative Nursing Supervisors (SAUO)
MAAOM	Master of Arts in Applied Organizational Management (PGP)
MAAP	Maintenance and Administration Panel [*Bell System*]
MAAP	Material Access Authorization Program [*Nuclear energy*] (NRCH)
MAAP	Member, American Association of Physicians (CMD)
MAAP	Milan Army Ammunition Plant (AABC)
MAAP	Minority Association for Animal Protection (SAUO)
MAAP	More Able Autistic Persons
MAAP	More Abled Autistic Persons
MAAP4	Modular Accident Analysis Program (SAUO)
MAAPA	Massachusetts Aggregates and Asphalt Pavement Association (SRA)
MAAPP	Manufacturing Assessment and Planning Package (SPST)
MAAPS	Massachusetts Association of 766 Approved Private Schools (SRA)
MAAPSS	Member of the American Academy of Political and Social Science (SAUO)
MAAR	Maintenance Action Arrival Rate (ACAE)
MAAR	Mandatory Annual Audit Requirement (AAGC)
MAAR	Memoirs of the American Academy in Rome (SAUO)
MAAR	Mojave Antiaircraft Range (SAUO)
MAAR	Monthly Associate Administrator's Review [*NASA*]
MAARA	Midlands Asthma and Allergy Research Association [*British*] (DBA)
MAARC	Magnetic Annular Arc (IEEE)
MA Arch	Master of Arts in Architecture
MAARM	Memory-Aided Antiradiation Missile (MCD)
MAARP	Medium Attack Advanced Readiness Program [*Navy*] (DOMA)
Ma'as	Ma'asroth (BJA)
MAAS	Machine Assisted Assembly System (ACAE)
MAAS	Manpower Allocation and Accounting Subsystem [*Air Force*] (AFM)
MAAS	Manpower Allocations and Accounting System (SAUO)
MAAS	Meet and Assist [*Travel industry*] (TVEL)
MAAS	Michigan Association of Ambulance Services (SRA)
MAAS	Muhammad Ali Amateur Sports
MAAS	Multiple Array Avionics Subsystem
MA-ASE	Multiple Association Application Service Element [*Telecommunications*] (OSI)
MA(AsianStudies)	Master of Arts (Asian Studies)
MAASL	Military Assistance Article and Service List (AFIT)
MAASLA	Movimiento Argentino Antiimperialista de Solidaridad Latinoamericana
Ma'asSh	Ma'aser Sheni (BJA)
MAAST	Multiple Application Addressable Secure Television (ACAE)
MAAT	MAC [*McDonnell Aircraft Corporation*] Acquisition and Attack Trainer (MCD)
MAAT	Management of Advanced Automation Technology Center [*Worcester Polytechnic Institute*] [*Research center*] (RCD)
MAAT	Master of Arts in Applied Theology (PGP)
MAAT	Master of Arts in Art Therapy (GAGS)
MAAT	McCormick Affective Assessment Technique [*Teacher evaluation test*]
MAAT	Member of the Association of Accounting Technicians [*British*] (DCTA)
MAATAG	Mission Area Analysis Test Advisory Group [*Army*]
MAATC	Mobile Antiaircraft Training Center
MAATE	Multiple Application Automatic Test Equipment (ACAE)
MAAU	Mexican-American Affairs Unit [*Office of Education*]
MAAW	Medium Antitank Assault Weapon
MAAWS	Middle Atlantic Association of Women Sailors
MAB	Macroaddress Bus
MAB	Magazine Advertising Bureau [*of MPA*]
MAB	Magazine Area B (SAUO)
MAB	Magnetic Amplifier Bridge
MAB	Mainly about Books [*A publication*]
MAB	Malfunction Analysis Branch [*NASA*]
MAB	Man and the Biosphere Program [*UNESCO*] [*Paris, France*]
MAB	Manganese Alkaline Battery
MAB	Manhay [*Belgium*] [*Geomagnetic observatory code*]
MAB	Manual d'Archeologie Biblique [*A publication*] (BJA)
MAB	Maraba [*Brazil*] [*Airport symbol*] (OAG)
MAB	Maracaibo Oil Exploration Corp. (SAUO)
MAB	Marine Air Base
MAB	Marine Amphibious Brigade
MAB	Master Acquisition Bus [*Computer science*] (MCD)
MAB	Master of Arts in Business (PGP)
MAB	Material Applications Board
MAB	Materials Advisory Board [*Later, NMAB*] [*NAS-NRC*]
MAB	Materials Application Board (SAUS)
MAB	Materials Applications Board (MCD)
MAB	Maximum Androgen Blockade [*Oncology*]
MAB	Mechanical Automation Breadboard (KSC)
MAB	Medical Advisory Board
MAB	Member, Advisory Board
MAB	Memorial Advisory Bureau [*British*] (CB)
MAB	Menswear Association of Britain (PDAA)
MAB	Meteorological Applications Branch (SAUO)
MAB	Methylaminoazobenzene [*Organic chemistry*]
MAB	Metropolitan Asylums Board [*British*]
MAB	Mid-America Bancorp [*AMEX symbol*] (SPSG)
MAB	Millardair Ltd. [*Canada*] [*ICAO designator*] (FAAC)
MAB	Missile Activation Building [*NWA*]
MAB	Missile Assembly Building (MCD)
MAB	Mission Analysis Branch [*Manned Spacecraft Center*]
MAB	Mobile Assault Bridge [*Army*]
MAB	Modular Array Basing (SAUS)
MAB	Monetary Affairs Branch (SAUO)
MAb	Monoclonal Antibody [*Immunochemistry*]
MAB	Multibase Arithmetic Block (ADA)
MAB	Munitions Assignment Board [*Anglo-American*] [*World War II*]
MAB	Mutual Air Board [*Canada*] [*World War II*]
MAB	Nonoclonal Antibody [*Medicine*] (STED)
MABA	Meta-Aminobenzoic Acid [*Organic chemistry*]
MABA	(Methylamino) Benzoic Acid [*Organic chemistry*]
MABAC	Member of the Association of Business and Administrative Computing [*British*] (DBQ)
MABAX	Merrill Lynch: Basic Value CL.A [*Mutual fund ticker symbol*] (SG)
MABB	Maximum Achievable Body Burden (PDAA)
MABCGT	Mutual Adjustment Bureau of Cloth and Garment Trades [*Defunct*] (EA)
MABDG	Marine Aircraft Base Defense Group
MABDW	Marine Air Base Defense Wing
MABE	Master of Agricultural Business and Economics (WGA)
MABE	Master of Arts in Business Education
MABE	Member of the Association of Business Executives (DCTA)
MABE	Mobile Assault Bridge Equipment (SAA)
MABF	Master of Agricultural Business and Finance
MABF	Mobile Assault Bridge/Ferry [*Army*] (RDA)
MABFEX	Marine Amphibious Brigade Field Exercise (NVT)
MABI	Mother's Assessment of the Behavior of Her Infant (STED)
MABIE	Mauna Loa Aerosol Backscatter Intercomparison Experiment (SAUO)
MABIM	Member, American Board of Internal Medicine (CMD)
MABL	Mass Addition Boundary Layer Program [*NASA*]
MABLE	Miniature Autonetics Baseline Equipment
MABLE	Minnesota Atmospheric Boundary Layer Experiments (SAUO)
MABLEX	Marine Amphibious Brigade Landing Exercise (NVT)
MABM	Master of Agribusiness Management (PGP)
MABM	Multilayer Absorbing Bottom Layer
MaBn	Maori Battalion (SAUO)
MABNET	Global Network for Monitoring the Biosphere [*Marine science*] (MSC)
MAB/NSN	MAB Northern Sciences Network (SAUO)
MABO	Marianas-Bonins Group
MABOP	Mustargen [*Nitrogen mustard*], Adriamycin, Bleomycin, Oncovin , Prednisone [*Vincristine*] [*Antineoplastic drug regimen*]
MABOPA	Malaysian Book Publishers' Association (EAIO)
MABP	Mean Arterial Blood Pressure [*Medicine*]
MABPD	Military Assistance Basic Planning Document (CINC)
MABR	Member, American Board of Radiologists (CMD)
MABRON	Marine Air Base Squadron
MABS	Maltese-American Benevolent Society (EA)
MABS	Marine Air Base Squadron
MABS	Maritime Application Bridge System (OA)
MABS	Master of Arts in Behavior Science (GAGS)
MABS	Master of Arts in Biblical Studies (GAGS)
MABS	Methylmethacrylate-Acrylonitrile-Butadiene-Styrene (EDCT)
MABS	Mixed Air Battle Simulation
MABS	Moored Acoustic Buoy System [*Marine science*] (MSC)
MABSC	Management and Behavioral Science Center (SAUO)
MABU	Maschinengewehr-Eisenbeton-Unterstand [*Machine-Gun-Iron-Reinforced Concrete Emplacement*] [*German "pill box," battlefield redoubts*] [*World War I*]
MABUS	Multi-Access Broadcast Unit System (PDAA)
MABX	American Biogenetic Sciences, Inc. [*NASDAQ symbol*] (SAG)
MABX	Military Automatic Branch Exchange (SAUS)
MABXA	Amer Biogenetic Sciences'A' [*NASDAQ symbol*] (TTSB)
MAC	Chief Machine Accountant [*Later, DPC*] [*Navy rating*]
MAC	E. F. MacDonald Company (SAUO)
MAC	Macadam (ADA)
MAC	Macalester College, Weyerhaeuser Library, St. Paul, MN [*OCLC symbol*] (OCLC)
MAC	MacAndrew [*Alcoholism scale*]
Mac	Macassey's New Zealand Reports [*A publication*] (DLA)
MAC	Macau [*ANSI three-letter standard code*] (CNC)
Mac	Macbeth [*Shakespeare work*]
MAC	Maccabees [*Old Testament book*] [*Roman Catholic canon*] (ROG)
MAC	MacConkey [*Agar*] [*Microbiology*]
mac	Macedonian [*MARC language code*] [*Library of Congress*] (LCCP)

MAC............	Macerare [*Macerate*] [*Pharmacy*]
MAC............	Macerated (SAUS)
MAC............	Macerich Co. [*NYSE symbol*] (SAG)
MAC............	Machine-Aided Cognition [*Computer project*] [*Massachusetts Institute of Technology*]
MAC............	MacIntosh [*Blade*] (STED)
Mac	Macintosh [*Computer science*] (WDMC)
MAC............	Mackerel [*Pimp*] [*Slang*] (DSUE)
MAC............	Mackintosh (DSUE)
Mac	Maclean's [*A publication*] (BRI)
Mac	Macnaghten's English Chancery Reports [*A publication*] (DLA)
MAC............	Macon, GA [*Location identifier*] [*FAA*] (FAAL)
MAC............	MacPaint (SAUO)
MAC............	Macro Authentication Code [*Computer science*]
MAC............	Macrocytic Erythrocyte (STED)
MAC............	Macrophage (MELL)
MAC............	Macula (MELL)
MAC............	Macule (STED)
MAC............	Madrid Automated Center (ACAE)
MAC............	Magazine Area C (SAUO)
MAC............	Magistrates' Appeal Cases [*A publication*] (DLA)
MAC............	Magnetic Attitude Control
MAC............	Magnetic Automatic Calculator (DEN)
MAC............	Magyar Athletic Club (SAUO)
MAC............	Main Display Console
MAC............	Maintained Anesthesia Care (MELL)
MAC............	Maintaining Arc Consistency (SAUS)
MAC............	Maintenance Advisory Committee [*NSIA*]
MAC............	Maintenance Allocation Chart [*Military*]
MAC............	Maintenance Analysis Center [*FAA*]
MAC............	Maintenance and Construction [*Computer science*] (IAA)
MAC............	Major Activity Center
MAC............	Major Air Command [*Later, MAJCOM*]
MAC............	Major Ambulatory Categories [*Patient classification system*] (DAVI)
MAC............	Malaysia Accreditation Council (SAUO)
MAC............	Malignancy-Associated Changes [*Cancer*]
MAC............	Malta Air Charter Co. Ltd. [*ICAO designator*] (FAAC)
MAC............	Mammary Carcinoma [*Oncology*]
MAC............	Man Against Computer (SAUO)
MAC............	Management Action Center (SAUO)
MAC............	Management Ad Hoc Committee (SAUO)
MAC............	Management Advisory Committee [*Environmental Protection Agency*] (GFGA)
MAC............	Management Analysis Course (SAUO)
MAC............	Management Assessment Coordinator (SAUO)
MAC............	Man and Computer (DIT)
MAC............	Mandatory Access Control [*Computer science*] (IGQR)
MAC............	Maneuver Analysis and Command
MAC............	Maneuver Area Command [*Army*]
MAC............	Manpower Advisory Committee (OICC)
MAC............	Mapping Advisory Committee (SAUO)
MAC............	Mapping and Analysis Center (SAUO)
MAC............	Mapping Applications Center (SAUO)
MAC............	Maricopa Agricultural Center (SAUO)
MAC............	Marine Affairs Council [*Marine science*] (MSC)
MAC............	Marine Amphibious Corps
MAC............	Marine Artillery Consultant (ACAE)
MAC............	Maritime Advisory Committee [*Terminated, 1968*]
MAC............	Maritime Air Command [*Canada*] [*NATO*] (NATG)
MAC............	Marker and Cell [*Computing technique*] [*NASA*]
MAC............	Market Access and Compliance
MAC............	Mark West Springs [*California*] [*Seismograph station code, US Geological Survey*] (SEIS)
MAC............	Martial Arts Commission [*British*] (DI)
MAC............	Martins Air Charter (SAUO)
MAC............	Mass Absorption Coefficient
MAC............	Massive Algebraic Computation [*Programming language*] [*1958*] [*Computer science*] (CSR)
MAC............	Master Acoustical Console [*Army*]
MAC............	Master Addictions Counselor (SAUO)
MAC............	Master Aperture Card (ACAE)
MAC............	Master Control (MCD)
MAc	Master of Accountancy (SAUO)
M Ac	Master of Accounting
M Ac	Master of Acupuncture (PGP)
MAC............	Master of Arts in Communication (GAGS)
MAC............	Master of Arts in Counseling (PGP)
MAC............	Mastoid Air Cell [*Medicine*] (MELL)
MAC............	Material Accounting Center (ABAC)
MAC............	Material Availability Commitment (AAG)
MAC............	Materials Analysis Co.
MAC............	Materials and Coatings (SSD)
MAC............	Maximal Acid Concentration (STED)
MAC............	Maximal Allowable Concentration (STED)
MAC............	Maximal Allowable Cost (STED)
MAC............	Maximum Acceptable Concentration (LDT)
MAC............	Maximum Acid Concentration [*Clinical chemistry*]
MAC............	Maximum Acquisition Cost (DB)
MAC............	Maximum Admissible [*or Allowable*] Concentration
MAC............	Maximum Allowable Concentration [*Toxicology*]
MAC............	Maximum Allowable Cost [*Medicare, Medicaid*]
MAC............	Maximum Atmospheric Concentration
MAC............	Maximum Concentration of Organics (NAKS)
MAC............	McDonnell Aircraft Co. [*Later, McDonnell Douglas Corp.*] (MCD)
MAC............	McLeod Aerating Cardiac
MAC............	McMaster University [*Hamilton, ON*] (DSUE)
MAC............	Mean Aerodynamic Center
MAC............	Mean Aerodynamic Chord
MAC............	Measurement and Analysis Center [*Telecommunications*] (TEL)
MAC............	Measurement and Control [*A publication*] (IAA)
MAC............	Mechanical Advantage Changer
MAC............	Mechanical Analog Computer (DEN)
MAC............	Media Access Code (RALS)
MAC............	Media Access Control [*Telecommunications*]
MAC............	Media Action Coalition [*Defunct*] (EA)
MAC............	Media Assistance Center (DNAB)
MAC............	Medical Administrative Corps [*Army*] [*World War II*]
MAC............	Medical Advisory Committee [*IATA*] (DS)
MAC............	Medical Alert Center
MAC............	Mediterranean Air Command [*Military*]
MAC............	Mediterranean Air Company (SAUO)
MAC............	Medium Access Control [*Telecommunications*]
MAC............	Medium Armored Car (SAUS)
MAC............	Membership Advisory Committee (SAUO)
MAC............	Membrane Affinity Chromatography
MAC............	Membrane Applications Centre [*University of Bath*] [*British*] (CB)
MAC............	Membrane Attack Complex [*Biochemistry*]
MAC............	Memory Access Command [*Computer science*] (IAA)
MAC............	Memory Access Controller
MAC............	Memory-Address Counter [*Computer science*] (IAA)
MAC............	Men after Christ Band [*R & B recording group*]
MAC............	Merchant Aircraft Carrier [*A ship carrying a cargo of oil or grain and provided with a flight deck for the operation of antisubmarine aircraft*] [*British*] [*World War II*]
MAC............	Message Act Concellation (DA)
MAC............	Message Authentication Code
MAC............	Message Authenticity Check [*Computer science*]
MAC............	Metabolic and Analytical Chemistry
MAC............	Metacarpal Ash per Centimeter
MAC............	Metal Arc Cutting [*Welding*]
MAC............	Methotrexate, Actinomycin D, Cyclophosphamide [*Antineoplastic drug regimen*]
MAC............	Methyl Acetamido Cinnamate [*Organic chemistry*]
MAC............	Methyl Allyl Chloride [*Organic chemistry*]
MAC............	Metric Advisory Committee (SAUO)
MAC............	Miami Aviation Corporation (SAUO)
MAC............	Michigan Apple Committee (EA)
MAC............	Microcystic Adnexal Carcinoma [*Oncology*]
MAC............	Microfilm Aperture Card
MAC............	Microgravity Advisory Committee (SAUO)
MAC............	Microwave-Assisted Curing [*Chemical engineering*]
MAC............	Midair Collision (IIA)
MAC............	Mid-American Conference [*College football*]
MAC............	Midarm Circumference
MAC............	Middle Atlantic Conference, East Riverdale MD [*STAC*]
MAC............	Middle Atmosphere Cooperation (SAUO)
MAC............	Midwest Archives Conference (EA)
MAC............	Military Aid to the Community [*British military*] (DMA)
MAC............	Military Air Command (SAUO)
Mac	Military Aircraft Command [*Airline call sign*]
MAC............	Military Airlift Command [*Formerly, Military Air Transport Service*]
MAC............	Military/Allied Commission [*World War II*]
MAC............	Military and Administrative Committee (SAUO)
MAC............	Military Armistice Commission (KSC)
MAC............	Military Assistance Command (CINC)
MAC............	Mine Action Centre (SAUO)
MAC............	Mine Advisory Committee [*NAS-NRC*] (MCD)
MAC............	Mineralogical Association of Canada
MAC............	Mini-Accommodation Center [*In MAC-1, a low-cost, plastic sleeping module promoted by Texas businessman Charles McLaren*]
MAC............	Minimal Access Coding [*Computer science*] (VLIE)
MAC............	Minimal Alveolar Concentration [*Anesthesiology*]
MAC............	Minimal Auditory Capability Test [*Medicine*]
MAC............	Minimum Alveolar Concentration [*Physiology*]
MAC............	Mining Association of Canada
MAC............	Missile Activation Circuit
MAC............	Missile Advisory Committee [*Pacific Missile Range*] (MUGU)
MAC............	Mission Assignment Code (NATG)
MAC............	Mission Assignment Coordinator (SAUO)
MAC............	Mitomycin C, Adriamycin, Cyclophosphamide [*Antineoplastic drug regimen*]
MAC............	Mitral Annular Calcification [*Cardiology*]
MAC............	MIUW [*Mobile Inshore Undersea Warfare*] Attack Craft [*Navy symbol*]
MAC............	Mixed Armistice Commission [*Arab-Israel borders*] (BJA)
MAC............	Mobil Air Conditioner (EPAT)
MAC............	Mobile Attenuation Code (SAUS)
MAC............	Mobile Automated Correlator (ACAE)
MAC............	Mobile Inshore Undersea Warfare Attack Craft [*Navy*] (MCD)
MAC............	Model Airplane Club
MAC............	Model Algorithmic Control [*Chemical engineering*] [*Computer science*]
MAC............	Modern Arts Criticism [*A publication*]
MAC............	Modern Authors Checklist [*Publication series*]
MAC............	Modulator of Adenylate Cyclase (DB)
MAC............	Monitor and Control [*Computer science*] (IAA)
MAC............	Monitored Anesthesia Care [*Medicine*] (DAVI)
MAC............	Monthly Availability Charge (BUR)
MAC............	Months After Contact (SAUO)
MAC............	Months after Contract Award

MAC............	Moore Action Collectibles (SAUO)
MAC............	Morning-After Call [*Sales*]
MAC............	Mosaic Resources Ltd. [*Vancouver Stock Exchange symbol*]
MAC............	Mothers Against Circumcision (SAUO)
MAC............	Motion Analysis Camera
MAC............	Motor Ambulance Convoy
MAC............	MOUT [*Military Operations on Urbanized Terrain*] Assault Course (INF)
MAC............	Moves, Adds and Changes [*Telecommunications*] (ITD)
MAC............	Movimiento Amplio Colombiano [*Broad-Based Movement of Colombia*] [*Political party*] (PPW)
MAC............	Movimiento Autentico Cristiano [*El Salvador*] [*Political party*] (EY)
MAC............	Movimiento de Autenticidad Colorada [*Paraguay*] [*Political party*] (EY)
MAC............	Mudiad Amdyffyn Cymru [*Welsh Defense Movement*]
MAC............	Multi-Access Computer (VLIE)
MAC............	Multi-Access Computing (NITA)
MAC............	Multiaction Computer
MAC............	Multi-Analyzer Configuration (IAA)
MAC............	Multi-Application Computer (IAA)
MAC............	Multifunctional Automobile Communication System [*Automotive engineering*]
MAC............	Multiphase Atmospheric Chemistry (SAUO)
MAC............	Multiple Access Computer
MAC............	Multiple Access Computing (ELAL)
MAC............	Multiple Access Control [*Computer science*] (DIT)
MAC............	Multiple Access Controller (SAUO)
MAC............	Multiple Address Code
MAC............	Multiple Address Computer (IAA)
MAC............	Multiple Analogue Component [*Satellite Television*]
MAC............	Multiple Aperture Core (VLIE)
MAC............	Multiple Array Correlation (CAAL)
MAC............	Multiplexed Analog Component [*Satellite television*] [*British*]
MAC............	Multiplexed Analog Components [*Satellite television system*]
MAC............	Multiply Accumulate (VLIE)
MAC............	Multiply and Accumulate [*Computer science*] (PCM)
MAC............	Multipurpose Arthritis Center [*Medical University of South Carolina*] [*Research center*]
MAC............	Municipal Assistance Corp. [*New York*] [*Also known as "Big Mac"*]
MAC............	Munitions Assignments Committee [*World War II*]
MAC............	Museum Association of the Caribbean (EAIO)
MAC............	Museums Association of Canada
MAC............	Musical Arts Center (SAUO)
MAC............	Musiciens Amateurs du Canada [*Canadian Amateur Musicians*] (EAIO)
MAC............	Mutual Aid Centre (SAUO)
MAC............	Mycobacterium Avium Complex
MAC............	Mycobacterium Avium-Intracellulare Complex [*Bacteriology*]
MAc............	Russell Memorial Library, Acuhnet, MA [*Library symbol*] [*Library of Congress*] (LCLS)
MACA.........	Mammoth Cave National Park
MACA.........	Management Assistance Corporation of America (AAGC)
MACA.........	Maritime Air Control Authority [*NATO*] (NATG)
MACA.........	Maritime Air Co-ordination Authority (SAUS)
MACA.........	Master of Arts in Communication Arts
MACA.........	Master of Arts in Computer Applications (GAGS)
MAcA.........	Master of the Acupuncture Association [*British*] (DBQ)
MAcA.........	Member of the Acupuncture Association [*British*]
MACA.........	Mental After Care Association [*British*] (EAIO)
MACA.........	Mental After-Care Association (SAUO)
MACA.........	Mexican-American Correctional Association (OICC)
MACA.........	Michigan Association of Children's Alliances (SRA)
MACA.........	Military Air Clearance Authority (SAUO)
MACA.........	Military Airlift Clearance Authority (AABC)
MACA.........	Mini-America's Cup Association (EA)
MACA.........	Modular Automatic Conferencing Arranger (SAUO)
MAC(A).......	Munitions Assignments Committee (Air) [*World War II*]
MACABRE...	Material Ablation with Chemically Active Boundary Layers in Reentry [*NASA*]
MACADS......	MAC Automated Deployment Reporting System [*Military*] (GFGA)
MACAE.......	Minnesota Association of Continuing Adult Education (SAUO)
MACAF........	Mediterranean Allied Coastal Air Forces
MACAF........	Military Airlift Command Numbered Air Force (SAUO)
MacAIMS.....	McDonnell Aircraft Corporation Advanced Interactive Management System (SAUO)
MACAIR.......	Macao Air Transport (SAUO)
MACAIR.......	Munitions Assignments Committee Air (SAUO)
MACAL.......	Military Airlift Command Airlift Operations Report
Macalp Mon L...	Macalpin on Money Lenders [*A publication*] (DLA)
MACALT......	Military Airlift Command Alternate Headquarters (SAUO)
MACAM.......	Military Airlift Command Automated Management
Mac & G......	Macnaghten and Gordon's English Chancery Reports [*A publication*] (DLA)
Mac & H......	Cox, Macrae, and Hertslet's Reports, Crown Cases [*1847-58*] [*England*] [*A publication*] (DLA)
Mac & I.......	Macrae and Hertslet's English Insolvency Cases [*1847-52*] [*A publication*] (DLA)
Mac & Rob...	Maclean and Robinson's Scotch Appeal Cases [*1839*] [*A publication*] (DLA)
MACAP.......	Major Appliance Consumer Action Panel (EA)
Mac A Pat Cas...	MacArthur's Patent Cases [*District of Columbia*] [*A publication*] (DLA)
MAC-API......	Mordechai Anielewicz Circle of Americans for Progressive Israel (EA)
MacAr.........	MacArthur's Patent Cases [*A publication*] (DLA)
MacAr.........	MacArthur's Reports [*8-10 District of Columbia*] [*A publication*] (DLA)
MacAr & M...	MacArthur and Mackey's District of Columbia Supreme Court Reports [*A publication*] (DLA)
MacAr & Mackey...	MacArthur and Mackey's District of Columbia Supreme Court Reports [*A publication*] (DLA)
MACARMS...	Military Airlift Command Aircrew Resources Management System (SAUO)
MACARNET...	Military Airlift Command Airlift Recovery Network (SAUO)
MacAr Pat Cas...	MacArthur's Patent Cases [*District of Columbia*] [*A publication*] (DLA)
MACARS......	Microfilm Aperture Card Automated Retrieval System
MacArth......	MacArthur's Patent Cases [*A publication*] (DLA)
MacArth......	MacArthur's Reports [*8-10 District of Columbia*] [*A publication*] (DLA)
MacArth & M...	MacArthur and Mackey's District of Columbia Supreme Court Reports [*A publication*] (DLA)
MacArth & M (Dist Col)...	MacArthur and Mackey's District of Columbia Supreme Court Reports [*A publication*] (DLA)
MacArth Ct Mar...	MacArthur on Courts-Martial [*A publication*] (DLA)
MacArth Pat Cas...	MacArthur's Patent Cases [*United States*] [*A publication*] (DLA)
MacArthur...	MacArthur's Patent Cases [*A publication*] (DLA)
MacArthur...	MacArthur's Reports [*8-10 District of Columbia*] [*A publication*] (DLA)
MacArthur & M...	MacArthur and Mackey's District of Columbia Supreme Court Reports [*A publication*] (DLA)
MacArthur Pat Cas...	MacArthur's Patent Cases [*United States*] [*A publication*] (DLA)
Macas.........	Macassey's New Zealand Reports [*A publication*] (DLA)
MACAS	Magnetic Capability and Safety System (NVT)
Macask Ex...	Macaskie on Executors, Etc. [*A publication*] (DLA)
MACAT.......	Master of Arts in Counseling Psychology: Art Therapy (PGP)
MACAT.......	Middle School Alternative Classrooms for the Academically Talented [*Education*]
MA(C)AT.....	Motor Accidents (Compensation) Appeal Tribunal [*Northern Territory, Australia*]
MACATS	MATE Automatic Circuit Analyser Test System (SAUS)
Macaulay Hist Eng...	Macaulay's History of England [*A publication*] (DLA)
Macb	Macbeth [*Shakespearean work*] (BARN)
MACB.........	Martial Arts Control Board [*Victoria, Australia*]
MACB.........	Michigan Association of Community Bankers (TBD)
MACB	Missile Assembly Control Building
MACBAA ...	Maine/Anjou Cattle Breeders' Association of Australia
MACBANK...	Machining Data Bank [*PERA*] [*Software package*] (NCC)
MACBASIC...	Measurement and Control BASIC [*Programming language developed by Analog Devices*]
MACBS	Multi-Access Cable Billing System (VLIE)
Macc..........	Maccabees [*Old Testament book*] [*Roman Catholic canon*]
MACC.........	MACC Private Equities [*NASDAQ symbol*] (TTSB)
MACC.........	MACC Private Equities, Inc. [*NASDAQ symbol*] (SAG)
MACC.........	Macro-Ovalocyte [*Biochemistry*] (DAVI)
MACC.........	Madison Academic Computing Center [*University of Wisconsin - Madison*] [*Information service or system*] [*Research center*]
MACC.........	Madison Area Computing Center (SAUO)
MACC.........	Malaysian-American Chamber of Commerce [*Later, AAACC*]
M Acc	Master of Accountancy [*or Accounting*]
MAcc	Master of Accounting (GAGS)
MACC.........	Methotrexate, Adriamycin, Cyclophosphamide, CCNU [*Lomustine*] [*Antineoplastic drug regimen*]
MACC.........	Methotrexate, Adriamycin, Cytoxan, CCNU [*Lomustine*] [*Antineoplastic drug*] (CDI)
MACC.........	Mexican-American Cultural Center (SAUO)
MACC.........	Micro Asynchronous Communications Controller (MHDI)
MACC.........	MidAmerican Communications Corp. [*Telecommunications service*] (TSSD)
MACC.........	Midwest Affiliation of Computer Clubs (SAUO)
MACC.........	Military Aid to Civil Community [*British*]
MACC.........	Military Aid to the Civilian Community (SAUO)
MACC.........	Military Area Control Centre (SAUO)
MACC.........	Military Assistant to the Civil Community
MACC.........	Mobility-Affect-Cooperation-Communication [*Psychiatry*]
MACC.........	Modified Acrylic Clear Coat [*Metal finishing*]
MACC.........	Modified Air Control Center [*Air Force*] (DOMA)
MACC.........	Modular Alter and Compose Console [*Computer science*]
MACC.........	Multiple Applications Control Center (SSD)
MACC.........	Multiple Architecture Control Console (MCD)
MacCarthy ...	MacCarthy's Irish Land Cases [*A publication*] (DLA)
Mac CC	MacGillivray's Copyright Cases [*1901-49*] [*A publication*] (DLA)
Macc Cas...	Maccala's Breach of Promise Cases [*A publication*] (DLA)
Maccl.........	Maccala's Reports [*Modern Reports, Part X*] [*1710-25*] [*A publication*] (DLA)
Maccl Tr	Macclesfield's Trial (Impeachment) [*1725*] [*London*] [*A publication*] (DLA)
Mac CM......	Macomb on Courts-Martial [*A publication*] (DLA)
MACCM2.....	Middle Atmosphere Community Climate Model, Version 2 (SAUO)
MACCM3.....	Middle Atmosphere Community Climate Model, Version 3 (SAUO)
M Acco.......	Master of Accounting
MACCONNET...	Military Airlift Command Contingency Network (SAUO)
M-Accounts...	Merged Accounts (AAGC)
MACCS	Manufacturing and Cost Control System (IAA)
MACCS	Manufacturing Cost Collection System
MACCS	Marine Air Command and Control System (NVT)
M Accs	Master of Accounts
MACCS	Mobile Adaptable Communications Countermeasures System (SAUS)
MACCS	Molecular Access System [*Computer program*]
MAccSc......	Master in Accounting Science (DD)
MACCSU.....	Military Airlift Command Accelerated Command Center System Upgrade (SAUO)
M Acct	Master of Accountancy (PGP)

M Acct........ Master of Accounting (PGP)
MACCT........ Master of Arts in Community College Teaching (GAGS)
MACCT........ Multiple Assembly Cooling Cask Test [*Nuclear energy*] (NRCH)
M ACCUR.... Misce Accuratissime [*Mix Thoroughly*] [*Pharmacy*]
M Accy .... Master of Accountancy (PGP)
MACD .... MacDermid, Inc. [*NASDAQ symbol*] (NQ)
MacD .... MacDevitt's Irish Land Commissioner's Reports [*A publication*] (DLA)
MACD .... Member of the Australasian College of Dermatologists (SAUO)
MACD .... Member of the Australian College of Dentistry (SAUO)
MACD .... Member of the Australian College of Dermatologists (SAUO)
MACDAC...... Machine Communication with Digital Automatic Computer
MACDAC...... Man Communication and Display for an Automatic Computer (PDAA)
MACDAC...... McDonnell Douglas Corp. (KSC)
MACDACsys... MACDAC system (NITA)
MACDATA.... Materials and Components Development and Testing Association [*Paisley College of Technology*] [*British*] (IRUK)
MACDC .... Military Assistance Command Director of Construction
MACDD .... Marine and Coastal Data Directory of Australia (SAUO)
MacDermott Commission... Commission on the Isle Of Man Constitution. Report [*1959*] [*A publication*] (DLA)
MacDev .... MacDevitt's Irish Land Cases [*1882-84*] [*A publication*] (DLA)
MACDIF .... Mapping and Charting Data Interchange Format (SAUO)
MACDIS....... Military Assistance for Civil Disturbance [*Department of Defense*] (DEMM)
Macd Jam ... Macdougall's Jamaica Reports [*A publication*] (DLA)
MACDP .... Metropolitan Atlanta Congenital Defects Program [*Georgia*] (DMAA)
MacDrmd.... MacDermid, Inc. [*Associated Press*] (SAG)
MACDS .... Monitor and Control Display System (MCD)
MACE.......... Mace Security International [*NASDAQ symbol*] (SAG)
MACE.......... Mace Security Intl [*NASDAQ symbol*] (TTSB)
MACE.......... Machine-Aided Composition and Editing
MACE.......... Maintenance Analysis Checkout Equipment
MACE.......... Management Applications in a Computer Environment (IEEE)
MACE.......... Managing Company Expansion [*Manpower Services Commission*] [*British*]
MACE.......... Maneuvering Attack Concept Evaluation (ACAE)
MACE.......... Marginal Absolute Certainty Equivalent [*Statistics*]
MACE.......... Massachusetts Advisory Council on Education (SAUO)
MACE.......... Master Control Executive (IAA)
MACE.......... Master of Air Conditioning Education (NADA)
MACE.......... Master of Air-Conditioning Education (SAUO)
MACE.......... Master of Air Conditioning Engineering
MACE.......... Master of Air-Conditioning Engineering (SAUO)
MACE.......... Master of Arts in Christian Education (PGP)
MACE.......... Master of Arts in Civil Engineering
MACE.......... Master of Arts in Computer Education (PGP)
MACE.......... Mechanical Antenna Control Electronics (MCD)
MACE.......... Member of the Association of Conference Executives [*British*] (DBQ)
MACE.......... Methylchloroform Chloroacetophenone [*Riot-control gas*]
MACE.......... Metropolitan Architectural Consortium for Education (AIE)
MACE.......... Mid-America Commodity Exchange [*Chicago, IL*]
MACE.......... Military Air Cargo Export [*Subsystem*]
MACE.......... Military Airlift Capability Estimator
MACE.......... Military Airlift Center, Europe (MCD)
MACE.......... Military and Computer Electronics Corp. (SAUO)
MACE.......... Minnesota Association for Childhood Education (SAUO)
MACE.......... Minority Advisory Committee on Energy [*Terminated, 1982*] (EGAO)
MACE.......... Mission Adaptive Combat Ensemble (ACAE)
MACE.......... Multi-national Alliance for Criminal Emergencies (SAUO)
MACE.......... Multipurpose Automatic Control Equipment (HEAS)
Maced .... Macedonia
MACED .... Macedonian
MACEF........ Mastic Asphalt Council and Employers Federation [*British*] (DBA)
MACEN .... Air Defense Command & First Air Region (SAUO)
MAC Eng...... Master of Air Conditioning Engineering
MAC Eng...... Master of Air-Conditioning Engineering (SAUO)
MACER .... Macerare [*Macerate*] [*Pharmacy*]
Macerich ..... Macerich Co. [*Associated Press*] (SAG)
MaceSec..... Mace Security International [*Associated Press*] (SAG)
MACEW....... Military Airlift Command Electronic Warfare (ACAE)
MacF .... MacFarlane's Scotch Jury Court Reports [*1838-39*] [*A publication*] (DLA)
MacF .... MacFarlane's Scotch Jury Trials [*A publication*] (DLA)
MACF.......... Mulitple Association Control Function [*Telecommunications*] (OSI)
MACFA........ Mid-Atlantic Collegiate Fencing Association (PSS)
MacFar .... MacFarlane's Scotch Jury Court Reports [*1838-39*] [*A publication*] (DLA)
MacFarl ...... MacFarlane's Scotch Jury Trials [*A publication*] (DLA)
MacFarlane... MacFarlane's Scotch Jury Trials [*A publication*] (DLA)
Macf Cop .... Macfie on Copyright [*A publication*] (DLA)
Macf Min..... Macfarland's Digest of Mining Cases [*A publication*] (DLA)
MacF Pr....... MacFarlane's Practice of the Court of Sessions [*A publication*] (DLA)
MacFrug ..... MacFrugals Bargains Close Outs [*Associated Press*] (SAG)
MACG .... MacGregor Sports & Fitness [*NASDAQ symbol*] (TTSB)
MACG .... MacGregor Sports & Fitness, Inc. [*NASDAQ symbol*] (SAG)
MacG .... MacGregor Sports & Fitness, Inc. [*Associated Press*] (SAG)
MACG .... Maneuver Analysis and Command Group
MACG .... Marine Air Control Group
MACG .... Marshaling Area Control Group [*Military*] (AABC)
MACG .... Military Air Control Group (ACAE)
MAC(G)........ Munitions Assignments Committee (Ground) [*World War II*]
MacG CC ..... MacGillivray's Copyright Cases [*1901-49*] [*A publication*] (DLA)
MacGillivray & Parkington... MacGillivray and Parkington's Insurance Law [*6th ed.*] [*1975*] [*A publication*] (DLA)
MacG S........ MacGregor Sports & Fitness, Inc. [*Associated Press*] (SAG)

MacG Sp....... MacGregor Sports & Fitness, Inc. [*Associated Press*] (SAG)
MACGW ...... MacGregor Sports&Fitness Wrrt [*NASDAQ symbol*] (TTSB)
MACH .... Machabees [*Old Testament book*] [*Douay version*]
mach .... Machine (ELAL)
MACH .... Machine [*or Machinery*]
MACH .... Machinist (WDAA)
MACH .... Master of Arts in Church History (PGP)
MACH .... Measure of Achieving Tendency [*Test*] (TMMY)
MACH .... Military Air Command Hunter [*In MACH 3, a video game by Mylstar Electronics*]
MACH .... Modular Automated Container Handling [*Shipping*] (DS)
MACH .... Multilayer Actuator Head [*Epson America, Inc.*] [*Computer science*] (PCM)
MACH .... Velocity Relative to the Speed of Sound (SAUS)
MACHA .... Member, American College of Hospital Administration (CMD)
Macha .... Michigan Automated Clearing House Association (TBD)
MACHA .... Michigan Automated Clearing House Association
MACHA .... Mid-Atlantic Clearinghouse Association [*Maryland, Virginia, and Washington, DC*]
MACHA .... Midwest Automated Clearing House Association
MACHA .... Military Armistice Commission Headquarters Area (INF)
MACHALT .... Machinery Alteration
MACH D....... Machine Direction Paper (DGA)
MACHDC..... Machinability Data Center [*Computerized search services*] [*Metcut Research Associates, Inc.*]
Macheez...... Macheezmo Mouse Restaurants, Inc. [*Associated Press*] (SAG)
MA Chem..... Master of Applied Chemistry
MACHG .... Machining
MACHGR...... Machine Group
MACH III...... Maintenance Aided Computer-HAWK-[*Homing All The Way Killer*]-Intelligence/Institutional/Instructor [*Military*]
MA(ChildLit/Reading)... Master of Arts in Children's Literature and Reading
MACHIS .... Michigan Association of Consumer Health Information Specialists (SAUO)
MACHO....... Machismo [*Spanish*] (DSUE)
MACHO....... Massive Compact Halo Object [*Astrophysics*]
MACHO....... Massive Compact Halo Objects [*Astronomy*]
MACHO....... Memphians Against Chest Hair at Operas (SAUO)
Macho .... Movimiento Anticomunista Hondureno [*Honduran Anti-Communist Movement*] [*Political party*] (PD)
MACHR .... Machiner
MACH R ...... Machine Ruling (DGA)
m-AChr .... Muscarinic Acetylcholine Receptor [*Biochemistry*]
MACHST ..... Machinist
MachTool ... Machines and Tooling (SAUO)
MACHY .... Machinery
MACI.......... Member of the American Concrete Institute
MACI.......... Military Adaptation of Command [*or Commercial*] Items [*DoD*] (AABC)
MACI.......... Military Adaption of Commercial Items (SAUO)
MACI.......... Millon Adolescent Clinical Inventory (DIPS)
MACI.......... Mine Anti-Char Indetectable (SAUS)
MACI.......... Monitor, Access, and Control Interface (NASA)
MACID........ Media Access Control Identifier (SAUS)
MAC II .... Mica and Chessy [*Acronym is name of interior decorating firm and is taken from first names of owners Mica Ertegun and Chessy Rayner*]
MACII.......... Missouri Aptitude and Career Information Inventory [*Vocational guidance test*]
MACIMS ...... Military Airlift Command Integrated Management System
MACINTER ... International Network of Psychology-Based-Man-Computer Interaction Research (SAUO)
MACINTER ... International Network of Psychology-Based Man-Computer International Research (SAUO)
MACIPS ...... Military Air Command Information Processing System (ACAE)
MACIPS ...... Military Airlift Command Information Processing System (SAUO)
MACIS .... Management and Contracts Information Service
MACISIN ..... Military Airlift Command Information Systems Internetting (SAUO)
MACJC........ Minnesota Association of Community and Junior Colleges (SAUO)
MACJC........ Mississippi Association of Community and Junior Colleges (PSS)
MACJC........ Missouri Association of Community and Junior Colleges (SAUO)
MACK.......... Mackenzie
MAC(K)........ Military Armistice Commission (Korea)
Mack & F Jud A... Mackeson and Forbes' Judicature Acts [*A publication*] (DLA)
Mack BL ..... Mackenzie on Bills of Lading [*A publication*] (DLA)
Mack CL ..... Mackeldey on Modern Civil Law [*A publication*] (DLA)
Mack Crim... Mackenzie's Treatise on Criminal Law [*4 eds.*] [*1678-1758*] [*Scotland*] [*A publication*] (DLA)
Mack Cr L.... Mackenzie's Treatise on Criminal Law [*4th ed.*] [*1678-1758*] [*Scotland*] [*A publication*] (DLA)
Mack Ct Sess... Mackay. Court of Session Practice [*A publication*] (ILCA)
Mackeld....... Mackeldey on Modern Civil Law [*A publication*] (DLA)
Mackeld....... Mackeldey on Roman Law [*A publication*] (DLA)
Mackeld Civil Law... Mackeldey on Modern Civil Law [*A publication*] (DLA)
Mackeld Rom Law... Mackeldey on Roman Law [*A publication*] (DLA)
Mackey........ Mackey's District of Columbia Reports [*12-20 District of Columbia*] [*A publication*] (DLA)
MackFn........ Mackenzie Financial Corp. [*Associated Press*] (SAG)
Mackie........ Mackie Designs, Inc. [*Associated Press*] (SAG)
Mack Inst.... Mackenzie's Institutes of the Law of Scotland [*9 eds.*] [*1684-1758*] [*A publication*] (DLA)
Mack Law of Prop... Mackay's Law of Property [*1882*] [*A publication*] (DLA)
Mack Nat..... Mackintosh's Law of Nature and Nations [*5th ed.*] [*1835*] [*A publication*] (DLA)

Mack Obs .... Mackenzie's Observations on Acts of Parliament [*1675, etc.*] [*Scotland*] [*A publication*]   (DLA)
Mack Rom Law... Mackenzie's Studies in Roman Law [*A publication*]   (DLA)
Macl .... Maclaren on Wills and Successions [*A publication*]   (DLA)
Macl .... Maclaurin's Scotch Criminal Decisions [*A publication*]   (DLA)
MACL......... Master of Arts in Classroom Psychology   (PGP)
MACL......... Maximum Approximate Conditional Likelihood [*Statistics*]
MACL......... Minimum Acceptable Compliance Level   (IAA)
MACL.......... Mood Adjective Check List [*Psychometrics*]
Macl & R..... Maclean and Robinson's Scotch Appeal Cases [*9 English Reprint*] [*A publication*]   (DLA)
Macl & Rob... Maclean and Robinson's Scotch Appeal Cases [*9 English Reprint*] [*A publication*]   (DLA)
MAC layer .. Media Access Control Layer [*Computer science*]   (IGQR)
Macl Bank ... Macleod's Theory and Practice of Banking [*A publication*]   (DLA)
Maclean & R... Maclean and Robinson's Scotch Appeal Cases [*9 English Reprint*] [*A publication*]   (DLA)
Maclean & R (Sc)... Maclean and Robinson's Scotch Appeal Cases [*9 English Reprint*] [*A publication*]   (DLA)
maclib .... Macrolibrary   (MHDI)
MAC LLC ..... Media Access Control Logical Link Control [*Computer science*]
MACLO .... Military Airlift Command Liaison Officer   (SAUO)
MACLOG...... Metropolitan Atlanta Council of Local Governments   (SAUO)
MACLOGFOR... Military Airlift Command Logistics Force Packing System   (SAUO)
MACLOS ...... Manually Commanded to Line-of-Sight   (SAUS)
Macl Rem Cas... Maclaurin's Remarkable Cases [*1670-1773*] [*Scotland*] [*A publication*]   (DLA)
Macl Sh ...... Maclachlan on Merchant Shipping [*A publication*]   (DLA)
Macl Shipp... Maclachlan on Merchant Shipping [*A publication*]   (DLA)
MACM .... Master Chief Machine Accountant [*Later, DPCM*] [*Navy rating*]
MACM .... Master of Arts in Christian Ministries   (PGP)
MACM .... Master of Arts in Church Music   (PGP)
MACM .... Military Aid to Civil Ministries [*British military*]   (DMA)
MA/CM .... Milliamperes per Centimeter
MACM .... Motorized Air Cycle Machine   (MCD)
MACM .... Multi Architecture Cost Model   (ACAE)
MACMA....... Mid-Atlantic Construction Management Association   (SAUO)
MACMA....... Military Airlift Command Minicomputer Acquisition   (SAUO)
MACMA....... Military and Aerospace Connector Manufacturers Association   (EA)
MACMA....... Mutual Aid Centre Managing Agency [*British*]   (CB)
MACMH .... Altona Community Memorial Health Centre, Manitoba [*Library symbol*] [*National Library of Canada*]   (NLC)
MACMIP ...... Military Airlift Command Mainframe Internetting Project   (SAUO)
MACMIS ...... Maintenance and Construction Management Information System [*Computer science*]
MACMIS ...... Major Army Command Management Information System
MACMO .... Mobile Acquisition Career Management Office [*Army*]
MACMOL ...... Macromolecular
MACMS........ Miniature Arms Collectors/Makers Society   (EA)
Macn .... Macnaghten's Hindu Law Cases [*India*] [*A publication*]   (DLA)
Macn .... Macnaghten's Nizamut Adalat Cases [*1805-50*] [*Bengal, India*] [*A publication*]   (DLA)
Macn .... Macnaghten's Select Cases in Chancery Tempore King
Macn .... Macnaghten's Select Cases, Sadr Diwani Adalat [*1791-1858*] [*Bengal, India*] [*A publication*]   (DLA)
MACN .... Mobile Allocation Channel Number   (CGWS)
MAC(N)........ Munitions Assignments Committee (Navy) [*World War II*]
Macn & G..... Macnaghten and Gordon's English Chancery Reports [*A publication*]   (DLA)
Macn & G (Eng)... Macnaghten and Gordon's English Chancery Reports [*A publication*]   (DLA)
Macn CM..... Macnaghten on Courts-Martial [*A publication*]   (DLA)
Macn Cr Ev... Macnaghten's Criminal Evidence [*A publication*]   (DLA)
Macn El Hind L... Macnaghten's Elements of Hindu Law [*A publication*]   (DLA)
Macn Ev ..... Macnally's Rules of Evidence on Pleas of the Crown [*A publication*]   (DLA)
MACNIMAATZ... MacArthur, Nimitz, and Spaatz [*Nickname for World War II command structure of Douglas MacArthur, Chester W. Nimitz, and Carl A. Spaatz*]
Macn NA Beng... Macnaghten's Nizamut Adalat Reports [*Bengal, India*] [*A publication*]   (DLA)
Macn Nul..... Macnamara's Nullities and Irregularities in Law [*1842*] [*A publication*]   (DLA)
MacNSc....... [*The*] MacNeal-Schwendler Corp. [*Associated Press*]   (SAG)
Macn SDA ... Macnaghten's Select Cases, Sadr Diwani Adalat [*1791-1858*] [*Bengal, India*] [*A publication*]   (DLA)
Macn Sel Cas... Select Cases in Chancery Tempore King, Edited by Macnaghten [*1724-33*] [*A publication*]   (DLA)
MACNW ...... Military Airlift Command Northwest   (SAUO)
MACNYC...... Men's Apparel Club of New York City   (EA)
Mac NZ....... Macassey's New Zealand Reports [*A publication*]   (DLA)
MACO .... Major Assembly Checkout [*NASA*]   (NASA)
MAC(O)........ Management Analysis Course (Class O) [*Navy*]   (DNAB)
MACO .... Marshaling Area Control Officer [*Military*]   (AABC)
MACO .... Master of Arts in Counseling   (PGP)
MACOI .... MACV [*Military Assistance Command, Vietnam*] Office of Information   (VNW)
MACOM .... Maintenance Assembly and Check-Out Model   (PDAA)
MACOM .... Major Army Command   (AABC)
MACOM .... Major Commands [*Military*]
M Ac OM .... Master of Arts in Acupuncture and Oriental Medicine   (PGP)
Macomb CM... Macomb on Courts-Martial [*A publication*]   (DLA)
MA Comm .... Master of Arts in Communication   (PGP)
MACOMTELNET... Military Airlift Command Teletype Network   (SAA)

MACON........ Maintenance Console   (MCD)
MACON........ Matrix Connector Punched Card Programmer [*Computer science*]   (IEEE)
MACONS...... Mid-Atlantic Continental Shelf
MACOP........ Methotrexate, Ara-C, Cyclophosphamide, Oncovin [*Vincristine*], Prednisone [*Antineoplastic drug regimen*]
MACOPS...... Military Airlift Command Operational Phone System   (AFM)
MACOPT ...... Machining Optimisation [*PERA*] [*Software package*]   (NCC)
Mac OS....... Macintosh Operating System [*Computer science*]   (CDE)
MACOS .... Man - A Course of Study [*Title of social-studies course*] [*National Science Foundation*]
MACOS .... Military Airlift Combat Operations Staff
MACOV .... Mechanized and Army Combat Operations Vietnam   (AABC)
MACP.......... Macro Control Processor [*Computer science*]   (IAA)
macp .... Macroprocessor   (MHDB)
MACP......... Marine Aviation Campaign Plan
MACP......... Master of Arts in Community Psychology   (PGP)
MACP......... Master of Arts in Counseling Psychology   (PGP)
MACP......... Michigan Association of Cherry Producers   (EA)
MACP......... Michigan Association of Chiefs of Police   (SRA)
MACP......... Military Aid to the Civil Power [*British military*]   (DMA)
MACP......... Mission Analysis Computer Program
MACP......... Mortuary Affairs Collection Point [*Army*]   (INF)
MACP......... Multiple Access Command and Pilot   (ACAE)
MACPA .... Maryland Association of Certified Public Accountants   (SRA)
MACPA .... Michigan Association of Certified Public Accountants   (SRA)
MACPA .... Mid America Crop Protection Association   (SRA)
MAC-PAC.... Manufacturing, Planning, and Control [*Arthur Anderson & Co.*] [*Software package*]   (NCC)
Mac-Paps ... Mackenzie-Papineau Battalion [*Canada*]
Mac Pat Cas... Macrory's Patent Cases [*England*] [*A publication*]   (DLA)
Mac PC....... Macrory's Patent Cases [*England*] [*A publication*]   (DLA)
Macph .... Macpherson, Lee, and Bell's Scotch Session Cases [*A publication*]   (DLA)
Macph .... Macpherson's Scotch Court of Session Cases [*1862-73*] [*A publication*]   (DLA)
Macph Inf .... Macpherson on Infancy [*A publication*]   (DLA)
Macph Jud Com... Macpherson's Practice of the Judicial Committee of the Privy Council [*A publication*]   (DLA)
Macph L & B... Macpherson, Lee, and Bell [*Scotland*] [*A publication*]   (DLA)
Macph Pr C... Macpherson's Practice of the Judicial Committee of the Privy Council [*2nd ed.*] [*1873*] [*A publication*]   (DLA)
Macph Priv Counc... Macpherson's Privy Council Practice [*A publication*]   (DLA)
MACP MACP... Military Aid to the Civil Power   (SAUO)
MACPOL ...... Management, Access Control, Planning & Policy   (SAUO)
Macq .... Macqueen's Scotch Appeal Cases, House of Lords [*A publication*]   (DLA)
Macq D........ Macqueen's Debates on Life-Peerage Questions [*A publication*]   (DLA)
Macq Div ..... Macqueen's Marriage, Divorce, and Legitimacy [*2nd ed.*] [*1860*] [*A publication*]   (DLA)
Macq H & W... Macqueen's Rights and Liabilities of Husband and Wife [*4th ed.*] [*1905*] [*A publication*]   (DLA)
Macq HL Cas... Macqueen's Scotch Appeal Cases, House of Lords [*A publication*]   (DLA)
Macq Mar.... Macqueen's Marriage, Divorce, and Legitimacy [*2nd ed.*] [*1860*] [*A publication*]   (DLA)
Macq Sc App Cas... Macqueen's Scotch Appeal Cases, House of Lords [*A publication*]   (DLA)
Mac R.......... Macdougall's Jamaica Reports [*A publication*]   (DLA)
Mac R.......... Maclean and Robinson's Scotch Appeal Cases [*1839*] [*A publication*]   (DLA)
Macr............ Macrobii [*of Lucian*] [*Classical studies*]   (OCD)
Macr .... MacroChem Corp. [*Associated Press*]   (SAG)
MACR .... Macrocytosis [*Hematology*]   (DAVI)
Macr .... Macromedia, Inc. [*NASDAQ symbol*]   (SAG)
Macr .... Macrory's Patent Cases [*England*] [*A publication*]   (DLA)
MACR .... Materiel Acquisition Control Record   (ACAE)
MACR .... Mean Axillary Count Rate [*Medicine*]   (DMAA)
MACR .... Member of the American College of Radiology
MACR .... Methacrolein [*Also, MAL*] [*Organic chemistry*]
MACR .... Military Airlift Command Regulation   (SAUO)
MACR .... Minneapolis, Anoka and Cuyuna Range Railroad Company   (SAUO)
MACR .... Missing Air Crew Report
MACR .... Multiply, Accumulate, and Round
MAC/RAN .... Measurement Analysis Corporation/Random Data   (ACAE)
Macr & H..... Macrae and Hertslet's English Insolvency Cases [*1847-52*] [*A publication*]   (DLA)
MACRAT ...... Middle-Atmosphere Chemistry, Radiation, and Transport   (SAUS)
MACRAT ...... Middle-Atmosphere Chemistry, Radiation and Transport program   (SAUO)
Macrch .... MacroChem Corp. [*Associated Press*]   (SAG)
MACREC ...... Military Airlift Command Technical Services Company   (SAUO)
MACRES ...... Malaysian Centre for Remote Sensing   (SAUO)
MACRI .... Mercantile Atlantic Coastal Routing Instructions
MACrimStudies... Master of Arts in Criminological Studies
MACRIT .... Manpower Authorization Criteria [*Army*]
Macrmd .... Macromedia, Inc. [*Associated Press*]   (SAG)
MACRO........ Macroassembler   (MHDI)
MACRO........ Macrocytosis [*Hematology*]   (DAVI)
MACRO........ Macroinstruction   (ECII)
MACRO........ Macroprocessor   (MHDI)
MACRO........ Massachusetts Association of Community Rehabilitation Organizations   (SRA)
MACRO........ Merge and Correlate Recorded Output [*Computer science*]   (NASA)

MACRO........ Military Airlift Command Resource Optimization (SAUO)
MACRO........ Monopole, Astrophysics and Cosmic Ray Observatory [*Italy*]
MACRO........ Monopoles, Astrophysics and Cosmic Ray Observatory (SAUO)
Macrob........ Macrobius [*Late fourth and early fifth century AD*] [*Classical studies*] (OCD)
MACROCAL... [*Enhanced*] Macro Version of Common Assembler Language [*Interdata*] (NITA)
MacroCh...... MacroChem Corp. [*Associated Press*] (SAG)
MACROL...... Macro-Based Display Oriented Language [*Raytheon Co.*]
Macr Pat Cas... Macrory's Patent Cases [*England*] [*A publication*] (DLA)
Macr P Cas... Macrory's Patent Cases [*England*] [*A publication*] (DLA)
MACRS........ Modified Accelerated Cost Recovery System [*IRS*]
MacS........... MacSweeney on Mines, Quarries, and Minerals [*5 eds.*] [*1884-1922*] [*A publication*] (DLA)
MACS.......... Magnetic Countermine System (SAUS)
MACS.......... Mainline Automated Clearance System [*Interstate trucking*] [*Highway safety*]
MACS.......... Maintenance Assistance Capability Software (SAUO)
MACS.......... Management Administration Control System
MACS.......... Management & Computer Services, Inc. [*Information service or system*] (IID)
MACS.......... Manned Air Combat Simulation (MCD)
MACS.......... Manufacturing Application Control System (SAUS)
MACS.......... Marine Air Control Squadron
MACS.......... Mass and Charge Spectroscopy
MACS.......... Mastoid Air Cell System [*Anatomy*]
MACS.......... Maximum Aortic Cusp Separation [*Medicine*] (DMAA)
MACS.......... McDonnell Automatic Checkout System [*McDonnell Douglas Corp.*]
MACS.......... Media Account Control System (PDAA)
MACS.......... Medium-Altitude Communications Satellite
MACS.......... Member of the American Chemical Society
MACS.......... Merchant Airship Cargo Satellite (PDAA)
MACS.......... Metering and Accounting System (NITA)
MACS.......... Michigan Association of Christian Schools (SRA)
MACS.......... Michigan Association of Convenience Stores (SRA)
MACS.......... Micro and Anophthalmic Children's Society [*British*] (NRGU)
MACS.......... Micro Anophthalmic Children's Society (WDAA)
MACS.......... Microwave Attitude Control Sensor
MACS.......... Middle Atmosphere in the Climate System (SAUO)
MACS.......... Migrant Advisory Committee
MACS.......... Military Aeronautical Communications Service
MACS.......... Military Airlift Command Service (NATG)
MACS.......... Missile Air-Conditioning System
MACS.......... Mississippi Association of Convenience Stores (SRA)
MACS.......... Mixed Aloha Carrier Sense (SAUO)
MACS.......... Mobile Acoustic Communications System
MACS.......... Mobile Acoustic Communication Study (SAUO)
MACS.......... Mobile Air Conditioning Society (EA)
MACS.......... Modem Access Control System (SAUO)
MACS.......... Modular Application Customizing System [*Computer science*] (ELAL)
MACS.......... Modular Attitude Control Subsystem (SAUS)
MACS.......... Modular Attitude Control System (ACAE)
MACS.......... Monitoring and Control Station
MACS.......... Multi-Access Computer Switch [*Telecommunications*] (TSSD)
MACS.......... Multicenter AIDS [*Acquired Immune Deficiency Syndrome*] Cohort Study [*National Institutes of Health*]
MACS.......... Multiline Automatic Calling System (HGAA)
MACS.......... Multiple Acceleration Control System (SAUS)
MACS.......... Multiple Access Communications System [*West German and Dutch*]
MACS.......... Multiple Application Connector System
MACS.......... Multiple Applications Control System (SAUS)
MACS.......... Multiple-Technique Analytical Computer System
MACS.......... Multiproject Automated Control System
MACS.......... Multipurpose Acquisition and Control System (IAA)
MACS.......... Multipurpose Arcade Combat Simulator [*Marksmanship training*] [*Army*] (INF)
MACS.......... Senior Chief Machine Accountant [*Later, DPCS*] [*Navy rating*]
MACSAM..... Military Airlift Command System Architecture Modernization (SAUO)
MACSAT..... Multiple Access Commercial Satellite (DOMA)
MACSAT..... Multiple Access Communications Satellite (MED)
MACSBUG... Motorola Advanced Computer Symbolic Debugger (SAUS)
MACSCO...... Metropolitan Academic Consultants Sales Corp.
MACSEA..... Military Assistance Command, Southeast Asia
MACSIS...... Multi-Agency Community Services Information System
MAC/SM..... Maintenance Allocation Chart and System Maintenance (MCD)
MACSO........ Military Airlift Command Support Office (SAUO)
MACSOG...... Military Assistance Command Studies and Observation Group (CINC)
MACSQ........ Marine Air Control Squadron
MACSRRPCC... Maxwellian Averaged Cross Section Reactor Physics Computer Code [*Electronics*] (IAA)
MACSS........ Master of Arts in Church Social Services (PGP)
MACSS........ Medium-Altitude Communications Satellite System
MACSS........ Montana Association of County School Superintendents (SAUO)
MACSU........ Maximum Card Study Unit [*An association*] (EA)
MACSV........ Multipurpose Airbmobile Combat-Support Vehicle (SAA)
MACSYM..... Measurement and Control System (MHDB)
MACSYMA... MAC [*Massive Algebraic Computation*] Symbolic Manipulator [*Programming language*] [*1969*] (CSR)
MACT.......... Master of Arts in College Teaching
MACT.......... Maximum Achievable [*or Available*] Control Technology [*Environmental chemistry*]
MACT.......... Military Assistance Command, Thailand (VNW)
MACT.......... Moral Action Choice Test (EDAC)
MACT.......... Multiple-Agent Chemotherapy [*Medicine*] (MELL)

MACTAR...... McMaster-Toronto Arthritis and Rehumatism [*Questionnaire*] [*Medicine*] (DMAA)
MACTEC...... MAC Technical Services Co. (GAAI)
MACTEC...... Military Airlift Command Technical Services Company (SAUO)
MACTELNET... Military Airlift Command Teletype Network (AFM)
MacTEP...... Mac [*Apple's Mackintosh computer*] Terminal Emulation Program
MACTHAI... Military Assistance Command Thailand (SAUO)
MACTIS...... Mine-hunting Action Information Subsystem (SAUS)
MACTM........ Master of Applied Communication Theory and Methodology (PGP)
MACTRAC... Military Airlift Command Traffic Reporting and Control System
MACTU........ Mines and Countermeasures Tactical Unit (SAUO)
MACTU........ Mines and Countermeasures Technical Unit [*Navy*]
MACU.......... Maintenance Assembly Change Unit (SAUS)
MACU.......... Material Cost per Unit (ACAE)
MACU.......... Monitor and Control Unit [*Aerospace*] (IAA)
MACUL........ Michigan Association for Computer Users in Learning (EDAC)
MACV.......... Military Assistance Command, Vietnam
MACV.......... Multipurpose Airmobile Combat-Support Vehicle
MACVD........ Microwave-Assisted Chemical Vapor Deposition [*Coating technology*]
MACVNAG.... Military Assistance Command, Vietnam Naval Advisory Group (VNW)
MACVSOG.... Military Assistance Command Vietnam Special Operations Group (INF)
MACV-SOG... Military Assistance Command, Vietnam Studies and Observations Group (VNW)
MACW........ Midwest Athletic Conference for Women (PSS)
MACW........ Missionary Association of Catholic Women [*Defunct*] (EA)
MACWA...... Mid-Atlantic Council of Watershed Associations (SAUO)
MACWACC... Military Airlift Command Washington Area Computer Center (SAUO)
M Acy.......... Master of Accountancy (PGP)
MACY.......... Master of Arts in Accountancy (PGP)
MACYG........ Mabys Association for the Care of Young Girls (SAUO)
Mad............. All India Reporter, Madras [*A publication*] (DLA)
Mad............. Indian Law Reports, Madras Series [*A publication*] (DLA)
Mad............. Indian Rulings, Madras Series [*A publication*] (DLA)
MAD............ Machine Analysis Display
MAD............ Machine ANSI Data
Mad............. Madagascar
MAD............ Madam
MAD............ Madang [*Papua New Guinea*] [*Seismograph station code, US Geological Survey*] (SEIS)
Mad............. Maddock's English Chancery Reports [*56 English Reprint*] [*1815-22*] [*A publication*] (DLA)
Mad............. Maddock's Reports [*9-18 Montana*] [*A publication*] (DLA)
MAD............ Madeco SA [*NYSE symbol*] (SPSG)
MAD............ Madeco S.A. ADS [*NYSE symbol*] (TTSB)
MAD............ Madison [*Diocesan abbreviation*] [*Wisconsin*] (TOCD)
MAD............ Madison, CT [*Location identifier*] [*FAA*] (FAAL)
MAD............ Madison Fund, Inc. (SAUO)
Mad............. Madras High Court Reports [*India*] [*A publication*] (DLA)
MAD............ Madrid [*Spain*] [*Airport symbol*] (OAG)
MAD............ Magnetic Airborne Detector [*Navy*]
MAD............ Magnetic Anomaly Detection [*or Detector*]
MAD............ Magnetic Azimuth Detector (MCD)
MAD............ Main Assembly Drawing
MAD............ Maintenance Alert Directive [*Aviation*]
MAD............ Maintenance Analysis Data [*or Diagram*] (MCD)
MAD............ Maintenance, Assembly, and Disassembly
MAD............ Major Affective Disorder [*Medicine*] (DMAA)
MAD............ Major Air Disaster (PDAA)
MAD............ Management Analysis Division [*NASA*] (MCD)
MAD............ Management Areas Database (SAUO)
MAD............ Mandibulo-Acral Dysplasia [*Medicine*] (DMAA)
MAD............ Manhunter Assignment Device [*Computer science*]
MAD............ Manufacturing Assembly Drawing
MAD............ Maple Air Services Ltd. [*Canada*] [*ICAO designator*] (FAAC)
MAD............ Marine Air [*or Aviation*] Detachment
MAD............ Marine Air Detection (AFIT)
MAD............ Marine Aviation Detachment (SAUO)
MAD............ Mass Analyzer Detector
MAD............ Master Accession Document [*Computer science*] (BUR)
MAD............ Master Air Data [*Computer*]
M Ad........... Master of Administration (PGP)
MAd............ Master of Arts Administration (GAGS)
MAD............ Material Analysis Data
MAD............ Material Assistance Designated [*Report*] (MCD)
MAD............ Material Availability Date (CET)
MAD............ Materials for the Assyrian Dictionary (BJA)
MAD............ Materiel Acquisition and Delivery [*Military*]
MAD............ Mathematical Analysis of Downtime (DNAB)
MAD............ Maximum Acceptable Deviation
MAD............ Maximum Acid Output [*Biochemistry*] (DAVI)
MAD............ Maximum Allowable Dose [*Medicine*] (DB)
MAD............ Maximum Applicable Dose [*Environmental chemistry*]
MAD............ Mean Absolute Deviation [*Statistics*]
MAD............ MeCCNU [*Semustine*], Adriamycin [*Antineoplastic drug regimen*]
MAD............ Media Access Device [*Telecommunications*]
MAD............ Median Absolute Deviation [*Statistics*]
MAD............ Memory Access Director [*Computer science*] (IAA)
MAD............ Memory Address Driver strength (SAUS)
MAD............ Memphians Against Degeneracy (SAUO)
MAD............ Message Address Directory (SAUO)
MAD............ Methylacridone [*Organic chemistry*]
MAD............ Methylandrostenediol [*Methandriol*] [*Endocrinology*]
MAD............ Michigan Algebraic Decoder (RALS)

MAD............ Michigan Algorithmic Decoder [*IBM Corp.*] [*University of Michigan*] [*Programming language*] [*1961*]
MAD............ Mileage Accumulation Dynamometer
MAD............ Militarischer Abschirmdienst [*Military counterintelligence*] [*Germany*]
MAD............ Military Air Distress (LAIN)
MAD............ Military Assistance Division (SAUO)
MAD............ Milk-Alkali Disease [*Medicine*] (MELL)
MAD............ Mind-Altering Drug
MAD............ Mine Assembly Depot [*Navy*]
MAD............ Mini-Attack Drone
MAD............ Minimal Aural Dose
MAD............ Minimum Absolute Deviation [*Statistics*]
MAD............ Minimum Approach Distance (SAA)
MAD............ Minimum Average Dose [*Medicine*] (DMAA)
MAD............ Missile Assembly Data
MAD............ Mission Analysis Division [*NASA*] (KSC)
MAD............ Mission Area Deficiency [*Army*]
MAD............ Mississippians Against Disposal (SAUO)
MAD............ Mitotic Arrest-Deficient [*Cytology*]
MAD............ Mixed Analog and Digital [*Telecommunications*] (TEL)
MAD............ Model A Drivers (EA)
MAD............ Mongolian Asiatic Development (SAUO)
MAD............ More After Dark [*Screen-saver computer program from Berkeley Systems*] (PCM)
MAD............ Morse Automatic Decoder (IAA)
MAD............ Mortar Air Delivery System [*Military*] (VNW)
MAD............ Mosquito Abatement District (DICI)
MAD............ Motor Assembly and Disassembly
MAD............ Motorsport Advanced Display [*Auto racing*]
MAD............ Multifunction Antenna Development (ACAE)
MAD............ Multiple Access Device
MAD............ Multiple Access Drive (NITA)
MAD............ Multiple-Aperture Device (MUGU)
MAD............ Multiple Audio Distribution [*Communications*]
MAD............ Multiple-Wavelength Anomalous Dispersion [*Crystallography*]
MAD............ Multiply and Add
MAD............ Multiwavelength Anomalous Diffraction [*Physics*]
mAD............ Muscle Adenylate Deaminase (DB)
MAD............ Music and Dance [*American Dance Festival project*]
MAD............ Mutual Ability for Defense [*Pentagon defense policy*]
MAD............ Mutual Assured Destruction [*Nuclear warfare*]
MAD............ Mutually Assured Destruction (SAUS)
MAD............ Myoadenylate Deaminase [*An enzyme*]
MADA .... Multiple Access Demand Assignment (MCD)
MADA .... Multiple Access - Discrete Address [*Navy tactical voice communication*]
MADA .... Muscle Adenylate Deaminase [*Medicine*] (MELL)
madac .... Madrid Air Defense Automated Center (ACAE)
MADAEC ...... Military Application Division of the Atomic Energy Commission
MADAG .... Madagascar (ROG)
Madag .... Madagascar [*Malagasy Republic*] (VRA)
Madag .... Malagasy Republic (VRA)
MADAIR .... Magnetic Anomaly Detection and Identification Ranging (MCD)
MADALINE .... Multi-Adaptive Linear Neuron (PDAA)
MADAM .... Maintenance Diagnostic Assistance Module [*Military*] (CAAL)
MADAM .... Manchester Automatic Digital Machine [*Manchester University*] [*British*] (DEN)
MADAM .... Mangrove Dynamics and Management (SAUO)
MADAM .... Marine Air-Droppable Area Marker (MCD)
MADAM .... Master Data Acquisition Module (SAUS)
MADAM .... Mean and Dispersion Additive Model [*Statistics*]
MADAM .... Moderately Advanced Data Management [*Computer science*]
MADAM .... Multipurpose Automatic Data Analysis Machine
MADAN .... Multimission Attitude Determination/Autonomous Navigation (ACAE)
Mad & B .... Maddox and Bach's Reports [*19 Montana*] [*A publication*] (DLA)
Mad & Gel... Maddock and Geldart's English Chancery Reports [*A publication*] (DLA)
MADAP .... Maastricht Automatic Data Processing and Display System [*Air traffic control*]
MADAR .... Malfunction Analysis, Detection, and Recording [*Computer science*]
MADAR .... Malfunction Analysis, Detection and Reporting (SAUO)
MADAR .... Malfunction and Data Recorder [*Computer science*] (IAA)
MADARS ...... Maintenance Analysis, Detection, and Reporting System [*Computer science*] (AFM)
MADARS ...... Malfunction Analysis, Detection, and Recording Subsystem [*Computer science*]
MADARTS .... Malfunction Detection Analysis, Recording, and Training System
MADB .... Madison Bancshares Group [*NASDAQ symbol*] (TTSB)
Mad Bar ...... Madox's Barona Anglia [*A publication*] (DLA)
MADC .... Machine-Assisted Detection and Classification (NVT)
MADC .... Maritime Administration of the Department of Commerce (SAUO)
MADC .... Milliampere Direct Current [*Electronics*] (IAA)
MADC .... Miniature Air Data Computer (SAUS)
MADC .... Multiplexer Analog-to-Digital Converter (MCD)
MADCAP ...... Mammoth Decimal Arithmetic Program [*NASA*] (KSC)
MADCAP ...... Mobilization and Deployment Capability Assurance Concept [*Military*]
MADCAP ...... Model of Advection, Diffusion, and Chemistry for Air Pollution [*Environmental Protection Agency*] (GFGA)
MADCAR...... Management Data Charting and Review (IAA)
Mad Ch Pr... Maddock's English Chancery Practice [*3rd ed.*] [*1837*] [*A publication*] (DLA)
MADCK........ Marine Aide-de-Camp to the King [*British Admiralty*]
Mad Co........ Madras Code [*India*] [*A publication*] (DLA)
MAD/CO...... Mid-America Dance Company [*St. Louis, MO*]
Madd .... Maddock's English Chancery Reports [*A publication*] (DLA)

Madd .... Maddox's Reports [*9-18 Montana*] [*A publication*] (DLA)
MADD .... Missile Aerosurface Development Device (ACAE)
MADD .... Module for Automatic Dock and Detumble [*Orbital rescue*] [*NASA*]
MADD .... Mothers Against Drunk Driving (EA)
MADD .... Multichannel Analog-to-Digital Data Decoder (IAA)
MADD .... Multiple Acyl-CoA Dehydrogenation Deficiency (STED)
MADDAM...... Macromodule and Digital Differential Analyzer Machine [*Computer science*]
MADDAM..... Multiplexed Analog to Digital, Digital to Analog Multiplexed [*Computer science*]
Madd & B.... Maddox and Bach's Reports [*19 Montana*] [*A publication*] (DLA)
Madd & G.... Maddock and Geldart's English Chancery Reports [*A publication*] (DLA)
Madd & Gel... Maddock and Geldart's English Chancery Reports [*A publication*] (DLA)
Madd Ch...... Maddock's English Chancery Reports [*56 English Reprint*] [*1815-22*] [*A publication*] (DLA)
Madd Ch (Eng)... Maddock's English Chancery Reports [*56 English Reprint*] [*A publication*] (DLA)
Madd Ch Pr... Maddock's English Chancery Practice [*A publication*] (DLA)
MADDDC..... Manufacturers of Aerial Devices and Digger-Derricks Council (EA)
Madden ...... Madden Steven Ltd. [*Associated Press*] (SAG)
MADDIDA..... Magnetic Drum Digital Differential Analyzer
MADDWU..... Mechanics' Assistants' and Dry Dock Workers' Union [*British*]
MADE......... Magnetic Device Evaluator [*Computer science*]
MADE......... Manufacturing and Automated Design Engineering
MADE......... Master of Agricultural Development Economics
MADE......... Microalloy Diffused Electrode
MADE......... Minimum Airborne Digital Equipment
MADE......... Multichannel Analog-to-Digital Data Encoder
MADE......... Multimedia Application Development Environment (SAUS)
Madeco....... Madeco SA [*Associated Press*] (SAG)
M Ad Ed ...... Master of Adult Education (PGP)
MAdEd....... Master of Arts in Adult Education (GAGS)
MADEL........ Medical and Dental Education Levy (SAUO)
Ma de Ma.... Matheus de Mathesillanis [*Flourished, 1381-1402*] [*Authority cited in pre-1607 legal work*] (DSA)
Ma de Math... Matheus de Mathesillanis [*Flourished, 1381-1402*] [*Authority cited in pre-1607 legal work*] (DSA)
MADEN .... Medical and Dental Education Network (SAUO)
MADEP .... Massachusetts Department of Environmental Protection
MADEPSQ.... Marine Air Depot Squadron
MADER .... Management of Atmospheric Data for Evaluation and Research [*Marine science*] (OSRA)
MADERI ...... Mexican-American Documentation and Educational Research Institute
MaderSin..... Maderas y Sinteticos Sociedad Anonima [*Associated Press*] (SAG)
MADEX .... Magnetic Anomaly Detection Exercise (NVT)
Mad Exch .... Madox's History of the Exchequer [*A publication*] (DLA)
MADF......... Maintenance Action Data Form [*Military*] (CAAL)
Mad Fir Burg... Madox's Firma Burgi [*A publication*] (DLA)
Mad Form ... Madox's Formulare Anglicanum [*A publication*] (DLA)
Mad Form Angl... Madox's Formulare Anglicanum [*A publication*] (DLA)
MADG .... Madge NV [*NASDAQ symbol*] (SAG)
Madge .... Madge NV [*Associated Press*] (SAG)
MadGE........ Madison Gas & Electric Co. [*Associated Press*] (SAG)
MADGE........ Malaysian Air Defence Ground Environment (SAUO)
MADGE........ Microwave Aircraft Digital Guidance Equipment [*Helicopters*]
MadgeNt...... Madge NV [*Associated Press*] (SAG)
MADGF........ Madge Networks N.V. [*NASDAQ symbol*] (TTSB)
MADH .... Master of Applied Development and Health (PGP)
MADH .... Methylamine Dehydrogenase [*An enzyme*]
Mad HC ...... Madras High Court Reports [*India*] [*A publication*] (DLA)
Mad Hist Exch... Madox's History of the Exchequer [*A publication*] (DLA)
Madh Pra.... All India Reporter, Madhya Pradesh [*A publication*] (DLA)
Mad I......... Madeira Islands (SAUO)
MADI .... Madison Group Assoc [*NASDAQ symbol*] (TTSB)
MADI .... Management and Distribution of Information (SAUO)
MADI .... Master Data Index
MADIC .... Machinery Acoustic Data Information Center (VLIE)
MADICA ...... Massachusetts Acoustical Drywall-Interior Contractors Association (SRA)
MADICT ...... Modular Advanced Development IC-Tester (VLIE)
MADIS .... Burda-MarketingInfoSystem [*Burda GmbH, Marketing Service Department*] [*Information service or system*] (IID)
MADIS .... Manual Aircraft Data Input System (MCD)
MADIS .... Manual Aircraft Display Information System [*Military*] (CAAL)
MADIS .... Millivolt Analog-Digital Instrumentation System
Mad Isl .... Madeira Islands (SAUO)
Mad Isls ...... Madeira Islands
MADIZ .... Military Air Defense Identification Zone (MCD)
M/ADJ........ Manual Adjusting [*Automotive engineering*]
Mad Jur ...... Madras Jurist [*India*] [*A publication*] (DLA)
MADL......... Maximum Allowable Defect Level (VLIE)
MADL......... Microwave Acoustic Delay Line
Mad Law Rep... Madras Law Reporter [*India*] [*A publication*] (DLA)
MADLR....... Major Assembly Direct Labor Reporting (MCD)
Mad L Rep... Madras Law Reporter [*India*] [*A publication*] (DLA)
MADLS .... Mobile Air Defence Launching System (SAUS)
Mad LT ...... Madras Law Times [*India*] [*A publication*] (DLA)
Mad LW...... Madras Law Weekly [*India*] [*A publication*] (DLA)
MADM .... Maintenance Automated Data Management
MADM .... Manchester Automatic Digital Machine [*Manchester University*] [*British*]
M Adm........ Master of Administration

MADM	Medium Atomic Demolition Munition [*Military*] (AABC)
MADM	Multi-Attribute Decision Making (VLIE)
MADMAN	Magnetic Anomaly Detector Contact Man (NVT)
MADMAN	Master Activity Data Management (DNAB)
M Adm E	Master of Administrative Engineering
MAdmin	Master of Administration
M Admin	Master of Administrative Studies
M Adm J	Master in Administration of Justice (PGP)
M Adm Mgt	Master of Administration Management (PGP)
Madn	Madden Steven Ltd. [*Associated Press*] (SAG)
MADN	Metropolitan Area Digital Network (NTCM)
MAD-N	Mid-America Dance Network [*Kansas City, MO*]
MADN	Mid-American Dance Network
MADO	Mulliken Approximation for Differential Overlap [*Physics*]
MADOC	Medical Analysis of Days of Care [*Report*]
MADOM	Magnetic Acoustic Detection of Mines (DOMA)
Madox	Madox's Formulare Anglicanum [*A publication*] (DLA)
Madox	Madox's History of the Exchequer [*A publication*] (DLA)
MADP	Main Air Display Plot
MADP	Major Acquisition Decision Point [*Military*] (MCD)
MADP	Material Acquisition Decision Process [*Military*] (MCD)
MADP	Mission Area Development Plan [*DoD*]
MADP	Mutual Aid Defence Programme (SAUO)
MADPA	Medicaid Antidiscriminatory Drug Pricing [*and Patient Benefit Restoration*]Act
MADPAC	Materiel Deterioration Prevention and Control [*Program*] [*Army*] (RDA)
Mad Papers	James Madison's Papers [*A publication*] (DLA)
MAD Plan	Mongolian Asiatic Development Plan (SAUO)
MADR	Madras [*India*] (ROG)
MADR	Madritum [*Madrid*] [*Imprint*] [*Latin*] (ROG)
MADR	Master of Arts in Dispute Resolution (PGP)
MADR	Materiel Acquisition Decision Review [*Army*]
MADR	Microprogram Address Register
MAD-R	Multiapertured Device-Resistance (DNAB)
Madr	University of Madras (SAUO)
MA(Drama)	Master of Arts (Drama)
MADRAS	Modular Approach to Definition of RACE Subscriber Premises Network (SAUO)
Madras AgricJ	Madras Agricultural Journal (SAUO)
Madras LJ	Madras Law Journal and Reports [*India*] [*A publication*] (DLA)
MADRE	Magnetic Drum RADAR Equipment
MADRE	Magnetic Drum Receiving Equipment
MADRE	Manufacturing Data Retrieval System (NASA)
MADRE	Martin Automatic Data-Reduction Equipment
MADREC	Malfunction Detection and Recording [*Checkout system for aircraft*] [*Air Force*]
Mad Reg	Madden on Registration of Deeds [*A publication*] (DLA)
Madrid Union	Union for the International Registration of Marks (SAUO)
MADRS	Montgomery-Asberg Depression Rating Scale (STED)
MADS	Machine-Aided Drafting System (IEEE)
MADS	Maintenance and Diagnosis System [*Military*] (CAAL)
MADS	Manned Airborne Defense Station (ACAE)
MADS	Mars Atmosphere Density Sensor
MADS	Meteorological Airborne Data System
MADS	Military Advanced Disk System (SAUS)
MADS	Missile Attitude Determination System [*LASER device*] [*Air Force*]
MADS	Mission Area Deficiency Statement [*Army*] (RDA)
MADS	Mixed Anxiety/Depression Syndrome [*Medicine*] (MELL)
MADS	Mobile Airborne Data System (ACAE)
MADS	Mobile Airborne Defense Station (SAUO)
MADS	Mobile Airborne Defense Station Concept [*Air Force*]
MADS	Mobile Air Defense System
MADS	Modified Air Defence System (SAUS)
MADS	Modular Air Defense System (MCD)
MADS	Modular Army Demonstration System (MCD)
MADS	Modular Auxiliary Data System
MADS	Modular Auxiliary Data Systems (NASA)
MADs	Mothers Against Drugs (SAUO)
MADS	MPS Air Defence Simulator (SAUS)
MADS	Multiple Access Digital System [*Computer science*] (IAA)
MadsBn	Madison Bancshares Group [*Associated Press*] (SAG)
Mad SDAR	Madras Sadr Diwani Adalat Reports [*India*] [*A publication*] (DLA)
Mad Sel Dec	Madras Select Decrees [*A publication*] (DLA)
Mad Ser	Indian Law Reports, Madras Series [*A publication*] (DLA)
MAD-SMS	Movement for Autonomous Democracy-Society for Moravia and Silesia [*Former Czechoslovakia*] [*Political party*] (EY)
MADSPM	Mobilization Against the Draft and Student Peace Mobilization [*An association*] (EA)
MADT	Mean Administrative Delay Time
MADT	Micro-Alloy Diffused Base Transistor (NITA)
MADT	Microalloy Diffused Transistor (MUGU)
MADU	Methylaminodeoxyuridine [*Pharmacology*]
MadUniv	Madison University (SAUO)
MadUniv	Madras University (SAUO)
M Ad VE	Master of Administration in Vocational Education (PGP)
MADVEC	Magnetic Anomaly Detector Vectoring [*Military*] (CAAL)
MADW	Military Air Defense Warning Network
Mad WN	Madras Weekly Notes [*A publication*] (DLA)
MADWN	Military Air Defense Warning Network (IAA)
Mad WNCC	Madras Weekly Notes, Criminal Cases [*India*] [*A publication*] (DLA)
MADYMO	Mathematical Dynamic Modelling (VLIE)
MAE	Macintosh Application Environment [*Software*] (IGQR)
MAE	Madera, CA [*Location identifier*] [*FAA*] (FAAL)
MAE	Maebashi [*Japan*] [*Seismograph station code, US Geological Survey*] (SEIS)
MAE	Maersk Commuter IS [*Netherlands*] [*ICAO designator*] (FAAC)
Mae	Maestro [*Record label*] [*Belgium, etc.*]
MAE	Maine Association of Engineers (SRA)
MAE	Maintenance Engineer
MAE	Malignant Angioendotheliomatosis [*Oncology*]
MAE	Manchester Association of Engineers (SAUO)
MAE	Marine & Aerospace Engineering Pty Ltd. (SAUO)
MAE	Maritime Advisory Exchange (SAUO)
MAE	Master Electric (IAA)
MaE	Master in Engineering (SAUO)
MAE	Master of Aeronautical Engineering (WDAA)
M Ae	Master of Aeronautics
MAE	Master of Aerospace Engineering (PGP)
MAE	Master of Agricultural Economics (PGP)
MAE	Master of Agricultural Education (PGP)
MAE	Master of Agricultural Engineering (GAGS)
MAE	Master of Agricultural Extension (GAGS)
MAE	Master of Art Education
MAE	Master of Arts in Education
MAE	Master of Arts in English (PGP)
MAE	Master of Automotive Engineering (PGP)
MaE	Master of Engineering (SAUO)
MA E	Master of Engineering (WDAA)
MAE	Material and Equipment [*Nuclear energy*] (IAA)
MAE	Matrix Arithmetic Expression
MAE	McDonnell Airborne Evaluator [*McDonnell Douglas Corp.*] (MCD)
MAE	Mean Absolute Error
MAE	Mean Area of Effectiveness (CINC)
MAE	Mechanical and Aerospace Engineering (ACAE)
MAE	Mechanical and Electrical (IAA)
MAE	Medical Air Evacuation
MAE	Medical Association of Eire (SAUO)
MAE	Medium Altitude Endurance (RDA)
MAE	Memory Access Extension [*Computer science*] (ELAL)
MAE	Memory Address Extension [*Computer science*] (CIST)
MAE	Memory Address Register (NITA)
MAE	Merit Access Exchange (SAUS)
MAE	(Methylamino)ethanol [*Organic chemistry*]
MAE	Metropolitan Area Exchange [*Telecommunications*] (ACRL)
MAE	Micro Aided Engineering (NITA)
MAE	Miramar Energy Corp. [*Vancouver Stock Exchange symbol*]
MAE	Missile Airborne Equipment (IAA)
MAE	Missile Assembly Equipment (IAA)
MAE	Mission Accomplishment Estimate [*DoD*]
MAE	Mississippi Association of Educators (SRA)
MAE	Mobile Ammunition Evaluation
MAE	Modified Anglia Engine [*Cosworth racing engines*]
MAE	Monroe Auto Equipment Company (SAUO)
MAE	Motion Aftereffect
MAE	Movement After-Effect (PDAA)
MAE	Moves All Extremities [*Medicine*] (MAE)
MAE	Multilingual Aphasia Examination [*Speech and language therapy*] (DAVI)
MAE	Museum of Atomic Energy (SAUO)
MAE	Mutual Assistance, Executive [*Military appropriation*] (NG)
MAEB	Material Application Evaluation Board [*NASA*] (MCD)
MAEBR	Management of Enlisted Bonus Recipients
MAEC	Manufacturing Analysis of Engineering Change (MCD)
MAEC	Master of Arts in Economics
MAEC	Minimum Adverse Effect Concentration [*Pollution technology*]
MAEC	Missile Attack Emergency Conference (MCD)
MAECAM	Micro-Aided Engineering/Computer Aided Manufacturing [*Micro-Aided Engineering Ltd. and Digital Microsystems Ltd.*] [*Software package*] (NCC)
MAECO	NRA [*National Restaurant Association*] Multi-Unit Architects, Engineers, and Construction Officers (EA)
MA (Econ)	Master of Arts in Economic and Social Studies [*University of Manchester*] [*British*]
MA (Econ)	Master of Arts in Economic Studies [*Universities of Newcastle and Sheffield*] [*British*]
MAECON	Mid-America Electronics Conference
MAECON	Mid-America Electronics Convention (SAUO)
MA(Ed)	Master of Arts in Education (CMD)
MAED	Micro Area Electron Diffraction [*Surface analysis*]
MAEDOS	Micro-Aided Engineering/Drawing Office System [*Micro-Aided Engineering Ltd.*] [*Software package*] (NCC)
MAEDS	Meteosat Argos Extended Dissemination Service (SAUO)
MAEDS	Multisatellite Applications Extended Dissemination Service (SAUO)
MA EdU	Master of Arts in Education (PGP)
MAEE	Marine Aircraft Experimental Establishment
MAeE	Master of Aeronautical Engineering [*Canada*] (ASC)
MAEE	Mid-Atlantic Electrical Exhibition (ITD)
M Ae Eng	Master of Aeronautical Engineering
MAEEW	Moves All Extremities Equally Well [*Neurology*] (DAVI)
MAEF	Mastic Asphalt Employers' Federation [*British*] (BI)
MAEI	Malaysian-American Electronics Industry
MAEL	Marine Aircraft Experimental Laboratory [*British*]
MAEL	Maximum Allowable Emission Level [*Automotive emissions*]
MAELU	Mutual Atomic Energy Liability Underwriters [*Chicago, IL*] (EA)
MAENF	Miramar Mining [*NASDAQ symbol*] (TTSB)
MAENF	Miramar Mining Corp. [*NASDAQ symbol*] (SAG)
MAEO	Master Air Electronics Officer (SAUO)
MAEO	Medium-Altitude Electro-Optical (SAUS)

MAEO	Months after Exercise of Option
M Aeor E	Master of Aeronautical Engineering (SAUO)
MAEP	Measure of Adult English Proficiency (EDAC)
MAEP	Minimum AUTOLAND [*Automatic Landing*] Entry Point (NASA)
MAEPS	Model Adoption Exchange Payment System (EDAC)
MAEQW	Moves All Extremities Quite Well [*Medicine*] (MELL)
MAER	Maximum Allowable Emission Rate [*Environmental Protection Agency*] (ERG)
MAER	Mechanical and Electrical Room (IAA)
MAER	Mobile Ammunition and Reconditioning Unit [*Military*]
MAERC	Minority Access to Energy-Related Careers (SAUO)
M Aero E	Master of Aeronautical Engineering
M Aero E	Master of Aerospace Engineering (PGP)
M Aero Eng	Master of Aeronautical Engineering
MAEROSPOPNSMGT	Masters Aerospace Operations Management [*Air Force*]
MAERP	Mutual Atomic Energy Reassurance Pool
MAERU	Mobile Ammunition Evaluation and Reconditioning Unit
Maes	Maestoso [*Majestic*] [*Music*]
MAES	Maine Agriculture Experiment Station [*University of Maine at Orono*] [*Research center*] (RCD)
MAES	Maintenance Aircraft Engineering Squadron (SAUO)
MAES	Manufacturing and Engineering Support (IAA)
MAES	Massachusetts Agricultural Experiment Station (SAUO)
M Ae S	Master of Aeronautical Science
MAES	Master of Arts in Environmental Sciences (PGP)
MAES	Medical Aid for El Salvador (EA)
MAES	Mexican-American Engineering Society (EA)
MAES	[*Society of*] Mexican American Engineers and Scientists (NTPA)
MAES	Michigan Agricultural Experiment Station [*Michigan State University*] [*Research center*] (RCD)
MAESA	Measurement for Assessing the Effects of Stratospheric Aircraft [*Marine science*] (OSRA)
MAESA	Measurements for Assessing the Effects of Stratospheric Aircraft (USDC)
M Ae Sc	Master of Aeronautical Science
MAESON	Marxist All-Ethiopian Socialist Movement [*Political party*] (PD)
MAESTO	Maestoso [*Majestic*] [*Music*]
MAESTRO	Machine-Assisted Educational System for Teaching by Remote Operation (IEEE)
MAESTRO	Mission Analysis Evaluation and Space Trajectory Operations [*NASA*]
MAET	Master of Arts in English Teaching (PGP)
MAET	Microwave Amplifier Electron Tube
MAET	Missile Accident Emergency Team (AFM)
MAETS	Medical Air Evacuation Transport Squadron [*Army*] [*World War II*]
MAEVIS	Micro-Aided Engineering 3D Visualisation [*Micro-Aided Engineering Ltd. and Micro-Aided Engineering Digital Microsystems Ltd.*] [*Software package*] (NCC)
MAEW	Moves All Extremities Well [*Medicine*] (MEDA)
MAF	Front Militant Autonome [*Autonomous Militant Front*] [*French*] (PD)
MAF	MacAndrews & Forbes Co. (SAUO)
MAF	Macrophage Activating Factor [*Biochemistry*]
MAF	Macrophage-Agglutinating Factor (STED)
MAF	Magnetic Anisotropy Field
MAF	Maintenance Action Form
MAF	Major Academic Field
MAF	Manpower Authorization File
MAF	Manual Acquisition Facility (SAUS)
MAF	Manual Authority File
MAF	Marine Air Facility
MAF	Marine Amphibious Force (AABC)
MAF	Marriage Adjustment Form [*Psychology*]
MAF	Mass Air Flow [*Automotive engineering*]
MAF	Master Address File [*US Census Bureau*]
MAF	Master Appraisal File [*Real estate*]
MAF	Master Audit File (SSD)
MAF	Master Facility Tool (MCD)
MAF	Master of Arts in Finance (PGP)
MAF	Maximum Amplitude Filter
MAF	Medical Assisted Facility (SAUO)
MAF	Medical Awareness Foundation [*Commercial firm*] (EA)
MAF	Mesoscale Analysis Forecasting (SAUS)
MAF	Michoud Assembly Facility [*NASA*] (MCD)
MAF	Middle Atlantic Fisheries (SAUO)
MAF	Midland/Odessa [*Texas*] [*Airport symbol*] (OAG)
MAF	Million Acre Feet [*Hydrology*]
MAF	Mineral Ash Free (ABAC)
MAF	Minimal Audible Field (DIPS)
MAF	Minimum Audible Field
MAF	Minister of Agriculture and Fisheries (SAUO)
MAF	Minister of Armed Forces (NATG)
MAF	Ministry of Agriculture and Fisheries [*British*]
MAF	Missile Assembly Facility
MAF	Mission Aviation Fellowship [*Indonesia*] [*ICAO designator*] (FAAC)
MAF	Mixed Amine Fuel
MAF	Mobile Air Force (NATG)
MAF	Mobile Assault Ferry [*Army*]
MAF	Moisture and Ash Free
MAF	Morris Animal Foundation (EA)
MAF	Mouse Amniotic Fluid [*Veterinary science*] (DB)
MAF	Movable Appendage Factor [*IOR*] [*Yacht racing*]
MAF	Movement Aftereffect [*Optics*]
MAF	Multiple Access Facility [*Computer science*]
MAF	Multiple Access Forward (SSD)
MAF	Multiply-Add-Fused [*Computer science*] (CIST)
MAF	Municipal Advantage Fund [*NYSE symbol*] (SAG)
MAF	Mutual Adjustment Fund (SAUO)
MAF	Mutual Asset Fund (SAUO)
MAFA	Manchester Academy of Fine Arts [*British*]
MAFA	Midarm Fat Area (STED)
MAFA	Middle Atlantic Fencing Association (PSS)
MAFA	Middle Atlantic Fisheries Association (EA)
MAFA	Movement-Associated Fetal Acceleration [*Medicine*] (MELL)
MAFAC	Marine Fisheries Advisory Committee [*Department of Commerce*] [*Washington, DC*] (EGAO)
MAFAP	Minimum Altitude over FAcility on Final Approach Course [*Aviation*] (FAAC)
MAFAS	Marine Automated Flowcharting Analysis System
MAFAs	Movement-Associates Fetal [*Heart rate*] Accelerations [*Obstetrics*] (DAVI)
MAFASA	Marine Amphibious Force Air Support Airfield (MCD)
MAFB	MAF Bancorp [*NASDAQ symbol*] (SPSG)
MAFB	Malmstrom Air Force Base [*Montana*] (KSC)
MAFB	Mitchell Air Force Base
MAF Bcp	MAF Bancorp, Inc. [*Associated Press*] (SAG)
MAFC	MAGTF [*Marine Air Ground Task Force*] All-Source Fusion Center (DOMA)
MAFC	Major Army Field Command (AABC)
MAFC	Master of Arts in Family Counseling (GAGS)
MAFC	Mel Anderson Fan Club [*Defunct*] (EA)
MAFC	Mythadventures Fan Club (EA)
MAFCA	Model A Ford Club of America (EA)
MAFCC	Model A Ford Cabriolet Club (EA)
Mafco	Mafco Consolidated Group [*Associated Press*] (SAG)
MAFCO	Magnetic Field Code
MAFD	Manic Affective Disorder [*Medicine*] (DMAA)
MAFD	Minimum Acquisition Flux Density
MAFE	Maintenance of Air/FMF [*Fleet Marine Force*] Expeditionary Equipment (NG)
MAFEE	Metro Alliance for Engineering Education (TIMI)
MAFES	Mississippi Agricultural and Forestry Experiment Station [*Mississippi State University*] [*Research center*] (RCD)
MAFF	British Ministry of Agriculture, Food and Fisheries (SAUO)
MAFF	Minister of Agriculture, Fisheries and Food (SAUO)
MAFF	Ministry of Agriculture, Fisheries, and Food [*British*]
MAFF	Ministry of Agriculture, Food and Fisheries (SAUO)
MAFF	Ministry of Agriculture, Forestry and Fisheries [*Japan*] (ECON)
MAFFC	Munsters and the Addams Family Fan Club (EA)
MAFFEX	Marine Amphibious Force Field Exercise [*Military*] (NVT)
Maffies	Middle-Aged Affluent Folks [*Lifestyle Classification*]
MAFFS	Modular Airborne Fire Fighting System [*Air Force*]
MAFH	Macroaggregated Ferrous Hydroxide [*Medicine*] (MAE)
MA/FH	Maintenance Actions per Flight Hour (MCD)
MAFH	Multicentric Angiofollicular (Lymph Node) Hyperplasia [*Oncology*]
MAFH	Museum of American Financial History (EA)
MAFI	Medic Alert Foundation International [*Also known as Medic Alert*] (EA)
MAFI	Ministry of Agriculture and Food Industries (SAUO)
MAFI	Ministry of Agriculture, Forestry and Irrigation (SAUO)
MAFIA	Marimba and Fife Inspectors Association [*Women's tongue-in-cheek organization*] [*Defunct*]
MAFIA	Missile Auxiliaries Firing Interlock Assembly (ACAE)
MAFIA	Morte alla Francia Italia Anelo [*Death to the French is Italy's Cry*] [*When used in reference to the secret society often associated with organized crime, "Mafia" is from the Sicilian word for boldness or lawlessness*]
MAFIA	Multiaccess Executive with Fast Interrupt Acceptance [*Computer science*] (MHDI)
MAFIS	Malaysian Aquatic Sciences and Fisheries Information System [*Marine science*] (OSRA)
MAFIS	Management Farm Information Service (PDAA)
MAFIS	Master of Accountancy and Financial Information Systems (PGP)
MAFIS	Mobile Area Field Instrumentation System (SAUO)
MAFIS	Mobile Automated Field Instrumentation System [*TRADOC*] (RDA)
MAFL	Manual of Air Force Law [*British*]
MAFL	Multiaperture Ferrite Logic
MAFLA	Mississippi, Alabama, and Florida [*Oil industry*]
MAFLEX	Marine Amphibious Force Landing Exercise [*Military*] (NVT)
MAFLIR	Modified Advanced Forward-Looking Infrared
MAFLL	Master of Arts in Foreign Language and Literature (PGP)
MAFLS	Memoirs of the American Folklore Society (SAUO)
MAFMIC	Minnesota Association of Farm Mutual Insurance Companies (SRA)
MAFOG	Mediterranean Area Fighter Operations Grid
MAFOR	Marine Forecast [*Pronounced "mayfor"*]
MAFP	Military and Air Force Police [*British military*] (DMA)
MAFPA	Mid-America Food Processors Association (SRA)
MAFR	Major Frame (ACAE)
MAFR	Merged Accountability and Fund Reporting [*Air Force*] (AFM)
MAfr	Missionaries of Africa (TOCD)
mafr	Missionaries of Africa (TOCD)
MAFR	Modified Anarchy Flood Routing (PDAA)
MAfr	Society of Missionaries of Africa (EAIO)
MAFRA	MAF Regulatory Authority (SAUS)
MAFRA	Ministry of Agriculture and Forestry Regulatory Authority (SAUO)
MAFRC	Middle Atlantic Fisheries Research Center [*National Oceanic and Atmospheric Administration*]
MAFREMO	Malawi Freedom Movement (BUAC)
MAFS	Management Arrangements Feasibility Study (HEAS)
MAFS	Manned Aerospace Flight Simulator (ACAE)
MAFS	Memoirs. American Folklore Society [*A publication*]

MAFS.........	Memoirs of the American Folklore Society (SAUO)	MAGB	Maltsters Association of Great Britain (BUAC)
MAFS.........	Mexico-Albania Friendship Society (EAIO)	MAGB	Masectomy Association of Great Britain
MAFS.........	Mobilization Air Force Specialty	MAGB	Microfilm Association of Great Britain
MAFSC......	Mobilization Air Force Specialty Code	MAGB	Microform Association of Great Britain (BUAC)
MAFSI........	Manufacturers' Agents for Food Service Industry (NTPA)	Mag Bl........	Magical Blend [A publication]
MAFSI........	Marketing Agents for Food Service Industry (EA)	MAGBNT......	Museums and Art Galleries Board of the Northern Territory [Australia]
MAFSS.......	Multipoint Airfield Fuel Support System		
MAFSX.......	Merrill Lynch: Federal Secs. Trust Cl.A [Mutual fund ticker symbol] (SG)	MAGBRG......	Magnetic Bearing [Navigation] (DNAB)
		MAG BRIT....	Magna Britannia [Great Britain] [Latin] (ROG)
MAFT.........	Modified-Adopted-Fernald Technique (EDAC)	MagC..........	Magma Copper Co. [Associated Press] (SAG)
MAF/TDC	Maintenance Action Form / Technical Directives Compliance [Military] (DNAB)	MAGCAP......	Magazine Capacity [Military]
		MAGCARD ...	Magnetic Card [Electronics] (ECII)
MAFTEP......	Method for Analysis of Fleet Tactical Effectiveness Performance [Navy] (PDAA)	Mag Cas......	Bittleston, Wise, and Parnell's Magistrates' Cases [England] [A publication] (DLA)
MAFV.........	Mean Ambient Flow Vector [Geology]	Mag Cas......	Magisterial Cases [England] [A publication] (DLA)
MAFVA........	Miniature Armoured Fighting Vehicle Association (EA)	Mag Cas......	Magistrates' Cases [Reprinted from Law Journal Reports] [1892-1910] [A publication] (DLA)
MAG...........	Air Margarita [Venezuela] [ICAO designator] (FAAC)		
MAG...........	Macrogenerator [SEMIS]	Mag Char.....	Magna Charta [or Carta] [Great Charter] [Latin] [A publication] (DLA)
MAG...........	Madang [Papua New Guinea] [Airport symbol] (OAG)	MAGCI........	Magnetic Cast Iron (IAA)
MAG...........	Magadan [Former USSR] [Seismograph station code, US Geological Survey] (SEIS)	mag cit........	Magnesium Citrate [Pharmacy]
		MAGCOM......	Magnetic Contour Matching (MUSM)
mag	Magahi [MARC language code] [Library of Congress] (LCCP)	MAGCON......	Magnetized Concentration [Lunar]
MAG...........	Magazine (AFM)	MagCon	Magnetospheric Constellation (SAUS)
mag	Magazine (VRA)	MagCp........	Magnetech Corp. [Associated Press] (SAG)
Mag	Magazine (DIAR)	MAGCS	Magnetic Cast Steel (IAA)
MAG...........	Magenta (ROG)	Mag Ct.......	Magistrates' Court (DLA)
MAG...........	Maggie Mines [Vancouver Stock Exchange symbol]	MAGD	Magdalen College [Oxford University] (ROG)
Mag	[The] Magistrate [London] [A publication] (DLA)	Magd	Magdalen College, Cambridge (SAUO)
Mag	Magistrate and Municipal and Parochial Lawyer [London] [A publication] (DLA)	Magd	Magdalen College, Oxford (SAUO)
		MAGD	Magdalene College, Cambridge University [England] (ROG)
MAG...........	Magnavox Co. (SAUO)	MAGD	Master of the Academy of General Dentistry (SAUO)
MAG...........	Magnesium [Chemical symbol is Mg]	MAGDA	Mobility Aid and Guide Dog Alliance (BUAC)
MAG...........	MagneTek, Inc. [NYSE symbol] (SPSG)	MAGDARR	Magnavox Doppler and Ranging RADAR (NG)
MAG...........	Magnetic (AFM)	Magd Coll....	Magdalen College, Oxford (SAUO)
mag	Magnetic (WDMC)	MAgDevEc ..	Master of Agricultural Development Economics (ADA)
MAG...........	Magneto (KSC)	Mag Dig.......	Magrath's South Carolina Digest [A publication] (DLA)
MAG...........	Magnetometer [or Magnetometry]	Magdl.........	Magdalenian (VRA)
MAG...........	Magnetosphere Currents (or Fields) (SAUS)	MAGE.........	Map Authoring and Generalisation Expert (SAUO)
MAG...........	Magnetron (CET)	MAGE.........	Marine Aerosol and Gas Exchange [Marine science] (OSRA)
mag	Magnetron	MAGE.........	Marine Aerosol and Gas Exchange Experiment
Mag	Magnificat (GROV)	MAGE.........	Marine Arctic Geological Expedition (SAUO)
MAG...........	Magnification	MAGE.........	Marine Arctic Geological Expedition, Murmansk Association Sevmorgeologia (SAUO)
MAG...........	Magnitude (AFM)		
MAG...........	Magnum (WDAA)	MAGE.........	Marine Gas Emissions (SAUS)
MAG...........	Magnus [Large] [Pharmacy]	MAGE.........	Marine Gas Emissions, Atmospheric Chemistry and Climate (SAUO)
Mag	Magruder's Reports [1, 2 Maryland] [A publication] (DLA)	MAGE.........	Mechanical Aerospace Ground Equipment (TEL)
MAG...........	Magyar [Language, etc.] (ROG)	MAGE.........	Mechanical Assembly Ground Equipment (ACAE)
MAG...........	Main Armament Group	MAGE.........	Multiple Access Ground Equipment (ACAE)
MAG...........	Maintenance Advisory Group (SAUO)	MAGEBT	Tigray Peoples Progressive Association (SAUO)
MAG...........	Management Advisory Group [Environmental Protection Agency] (GFGA)	M Ag Ec......	Master of Agricultural Economics
		M Ag Ed	Master of Agricultural Education
MAG...........	Management Assistance Group [Washington, DC] (EA)	MagelPt......	Magellan Petroleum Corp. [Associated Press] (SAG)
MAG...........	Marine Aircraft [or Aviation] Group	MagelRst.....	Magellan Restauraunt System [Associated Press] (SAG)
MAG...........	Marine Air Group (VNW)	MAGEN	Matrix Generating and Reporting System [Computer science] (PDAA)
MAG...........	Maritime Action Group [Non-carrier naval task group] (DOMA)	MAGERT	Map and Geography Round Table [American Library Association]
MAG...........	Maritime Air Group [Canada]	MAGES	Magnitude Estimation Scaling (MCD)
MAG...........	Marker-Adder Generator	MAgExt	Master of Agricultural Extension (GAGS)
MAG...........	Marketing Aids Group	MAGF.........	Male Accessory Gland Fluid [Medicine] (DB)
M Ag	Master of Agriculture	MAGFET......	Magnetic Metal-Oxide-Semiconductor Field-Effect Transistor (PDAA)
MAG...........	Master of Applied Geography (PGP)		
MAG...........	Maximum Available Gain (IAA)	MAGG	Maggiore [Major] [Music]
MAG...........	Medical Association of Georgia (SRA)	MAGG	Modular Alphanumeric Graphics Generator (IEEE)
MAg	Membrane Antigen (DB)	MAGGE	Medium-Altitude Gravity Gradient Experiment
MAG...........	Metal Active Gas (HEAS)	MAggF........	Macrophage Agglutination Factor [Biochemistry] (MAE)
MAG...........	Military Advisers Group (SAUO)	MAGGI........	Million Ampere Generator [British] (DEN)
MAG...........	Military Advisory Group	MagGp........	Magna Group, Inc. [Associated Press] (SAG)
MAG...........	Military Airlift Group [Air Force]	MAGGS	Modular Advanced Graphics Generation System (IEEE)
MAG...........	Military Assistance Group (SAUO)	Magh	Maghreb (BJA)
MAG...........	Minnesota Attorney General's Office, St. Paul, MN [OCLC symbol] (OCLC)	MAGI	Mackenzie Art Gallery [University of Regina] [Canada] [Research center] (RCD)
MAG...........	Mississippi Air National Guard [FAA designator] (FAAC)	MAGI	Magna Group, Inc. [NASDAQ symbol] (NQ)
MAG...........	Mittelassyrisches Gesetz (BJA)	MAGI	Maryland Automated Geographic Information System [Maryland State Department of State Planning] [Information service or system] (IID)
MAG...........	Mobile Arresting Gear (SAUS)		
MAG...........	Monoammonium Glutamate [Organic chemistry]	MAGI	Master Group Information System [AT & T]
MAG...........	Motorcycle Action Group [British] (DBA)	MAGI	Mathematical Applications Group, Inc. (MCD)
MAG...........	Mutation Activation Gene [Immunology]	MAGI	Microscope Assisted Guided Intervention [Medical technique]
MAG...........	Myelin-Associated Glycoprotein [Biochemistry]	MAGI	Military Gamma Irradiator
MAGA	Medium-Accuracy Gyro Assembly	MAGI	Multiarray Gamma Irradiator
MAGA	Mexican-American Grocers Association (NTPA)	MAGIC	Machine-Aided Graphics for Illustration and Composition [Bell Telephone]
Magal	Magal Security Systems [Commercial firm] [Associated Press] (SAG)		
		MAGIC	Machine for Automatic Graphics Interface to a Computer
Magalog	Magazine-Catalog [Advertising]	MAGIC	Madison Avenue General Ideas Committee [New York City]
magamp.......	Magnetic Amplifier (IDOE)	MAGIC	Magic Foundation for Children's Growth (EA)
MAGAMP.....	Magnetic Amplifier	MAGIC	Magnetically Actuated Grid for Interactive Correspondance (SAUO)
Mag & Con...	Magistrate and Constable [A publication] (DLA)	MAGIC	Magnetic and Germanium Integer Calculator (DEN)
Mag & Const...	Magistrate and Constable [A publication] (DLA)	MAGIC	Magnetic Immunochemistry [Laboratory analysis]
Mag & E Comp...	Magnus and Estrin on Companies [5th ed.] [1978] [A publication] (DLA)	MAGIC	Manual Assisted Gaming of Integrated Combat (PDAA)
		MAGIC	Map and Geographic Information Center (SAUO)
Mag & M & PL...	Magistrate and Municipal and Parochial Lawyer [A publication] (DLA)	MAGIC	Mapping and Geographic Information Centre (SAUO)
		MAGIC	Marine Corps Air-Ground Intelligence Center (MCD)
Mag Antiq....	Magazine Antiques [A publication] (BRI)	MAGIC	Maritime Air-Ground Intelligence Center (SAUO)
Mag Arch.....	Magister Architecturae [Master of Architecture] [Latin]	MAGIC	Market Analysis Guide - Intercity Communications [AT & T]
MAGARLM...	Military Assistance Advisory Group, Army Branch, Logistics-Medical (CINC)	MAGIC	Marketing and Advertising General Information Centre [Datasolve Ltd.] [British] [Information service or system]
MagArt........	Magazine of Art (SAUO)		
MAGB	Maltsters Association [British] (DBA)	MAGIC	Matrix Algebra General Interpretive Coding (IEEE)

MAGIC .... Media Analysis, Grouping, Inventory Control (SAUO)
MAGIC .... Method for Asynchronous Graphics Integral Control [*Computer science*] (PDAA)
MAGIC .... Methods for Advanced Group Technology Integrated with CAD/CAM (SAUO)
MAGIC .... Michigan Automatic General Integrated Computation (MCD)
MAGIC .... Microcomputer Applications of Graphics with Interactive Communications (SAUS)
MAGIC .... Microprobe Analysis Generalized Intensity Corrections
MAGIC .... Microprocessor Application of Graphic with Interactive Communication
MAGIC .... Military Advisory Group in China (SAUO)
MAGIC .... Model of Acidification of Groundwater in Catchment (SAUO)
MAGIC .... Modern Analytical Generator of Improved Circuits [*Computer science*]
MAGIC .... Modified Action Generated Input Control
MAGIC .... Modular Area Graphics Illustrations Composition (DGA)
MAGIC .... Monodisperse Aerosol Generation Interface [*Physics*]
MAGIC .... Motorola Automatically Generated Integrated Circuits
MAGIC .... Mozambique, Angola, and Guine Information Center [*British*]
MAGIC .... Multiple Aperture Gas Imaging Counter (SAUS)
MAGIC .... Multipurpose and Generalized Interface to COBOL [*Computer science*]
Magic Cap ... Magic Communicating Applications Platform [*General Magic*] [*Computer science*]
MAGICS .... Mass Balance of Arctic Glaciers and Ice Sheets in relation to Climate and Sea Level Changes (SAUO)
MAGICS .... Modular Architecture for Graphics & Image Control System (SAUS)
MAGICS .... Multiphase Model for Air, Groundwater, Immiscible Contaminant and Solute Transport [*Computer program for testing water flow*]
MAGIC Telescope... Mayor Atmospheric Gamma-ray Imaging Cherenkov Telescope (SAUO)
MAGID .... Magnetic Intrusion Detector (NVT)
MAGIE .... Midwest Agri Industries Expo [*Illinois Fertilizer and Chemical Association*] (TSPED)
MAGIEC .... Magnavox Government and Industrial Electronics Company (SAUO)
MAGIIC .... Mobile Army Ground Imagery Interpretation Center (MCD)
MAGIIC .... Mobile Army Ground Interpretation Center (SAUO)
MAGIK .... Merit Automated Graphics Interface Kit for simulation system (SAUS)
MAG Inc .... Mathematical Applications Group, Incorporated (SAUO)
Mag Ins .... Magen on Insurance [*A publication*] (DLA)
MAGIS .... Magistrate
MAGIS .... Marine Air Ground Intelligence System
MAGIS .... Megawatt Air-to-Ground Illumination System (MCD)
MAGIS .... Municipal Automated Geographic Information System [*District of Columbia Office of the Mayor*] [*Information service or system*] (IID)
Magis & Const (PA)... Magistrate and Constable [*Pennsylvania*] [*A publication*] (DLA)
Magis Ct ..... Magistrates' Court (DLA)
MAGISIAC.... Marine AirGround Intelligence System Intelligence Analysis Center (SAUO)
MAGL.......... Magna-Lab, Inc. [*NASDAQ symbol*] (SAG)
MAGL.......... Material Acquisition Guidance Letter (MCD)
MAGLA .... Magna-Lab 'A' [*NASDAQ symbol*] (TTSB)
MAGLAD ...... Marksman and Gunnery Laser Device (SAUS)
MAGLAD ...... Marksmanship and Gunnery LASER Device (RDA)
MAGLATCH... Magnetic Latch (MUGU)
MAG-LEV ..... Magnetically-Levitated [*High-speed ground transportation*]
maglev .... Magnetic Levitation (TRID)
MAGLL........ Magna-Lab Wrrt 'E' [*NASDAQ symbol*] (TTSB)
MAGLOC..... Magnetic Logic Computer
maglrv .... Magnetic Levitation (ADWA)
MAGLU .... Magna-Lab Unit [*NASDAQ symbol*] (TTSB)
MAGLW .... Magna-Lab Wrrt 'A' [*NASDAQ symbol*] (TTSB)
MAGLZ........ Magna-Lab Wrrt 'B' [*NASDAQ symbol*] (TTSB)
MAGMA .... Minimal Architecture for Generalized Markup Applications (SAUS)
Magmc .... Magma Copper Co. [*Associated Press*] (SAG)
Mag (MD).... Magruder's Reports [*1, 2 Maryland*] [*A publication*] (DLA)
MAGMOD..... Magnetic Modulator
Mag Mor...... Magna Moralia [*of Aristotle*] [*Classical studies*] (OCD)
Mag Mun Par Law... Magistrate and Municipal and Parochial Lawyer [*A publication*] (DLA)
MAGN .... Magainin Pharmaceuticals [*NASDAQ symbol*] (SPSG)
MAGN .... Magnetic (ROG)
MAGN .... Magnetron [*Electricity*]
MAGN .... Magnus [*Great*] [*Latin*] (ADA)
MAGN .... Monoaminoguanidine Nitrate [*Organic chemistry*]
Magna .... Magna-Lab, Inc. [*Associated Press*] (SAG)
MAGNA .... Materially and Geometrically Non-Linear Analysis (SAUS)
MAGNA 8.... Fourth-Generation Software (SAUS)
MagnaBb .... Magna Bancorp [*Associated Press*] (SAG)
MagnaI .... Magna International, Inc. [*Associated Press*] (SAG)
MagnaL .... Magna-Lab, Inc. [*Associated Press*] (SAG)
Magna Rot Pip... Magnus Rotulus Pipae [*Great Roll of the Pipe*] [*Latin*] [*A publication*] (DLA)
MAGNA-SID... Magnetic Sensing Intrusion Device [*Remote sensor*] [*Also, M-SID*] [*Military*] (VNW)
MAGNETTOR... Magnetic Modulator (SAA)
magnif......... Magnification
MAGNOLIA... Mississippi Alliance for Gaining New Opportunities through Library Information Access
MAGNOX...... Magnesium Oxide [*Magnesium-based alloy*]
MagnPet...... Magnum Petroleum [*Associated Press*] (SAG)
magns .... Magnesium (VRA)
MAGNT .... Museums and Art Galleries of the Northern Territory [*Australia*]

Magntk .... Magnatek, Inc. [*Associated Press*] (SAG)
MAGNUM..... Migraine Awareness Group: A National Understanding for Migraineurs (NRGU)
MAGOX .... Magnesium Oxide [*Acronym is trademark of Basic Chemicals*]
MagP .... Magnum Petroleum [*Associated Press*] (SAG)
MAGP .... Master of Arts in Gerontological Psychology (PGP)
MAGP .... Microfibrillar-Associated Glycoprotein [*Biochemistry*]
MAGp .... Military Airlift Group [*Air Force*] (AFM)
MagPet........ Magnum Petroleum [*Associated Press*] (SAG)
Mag Pharm.. Magister Pharmaciae [*Master of Pharmacy*] [*Latin*]
Mag Phil..... Magister Philosophiae [*Master of Philosophy*] [*Latin*]
Mag Phil Fac Theol... Magister Philosophiae Facultatis Theologicae [*Latin*]
MagPhr........ Magainin Pharmaceuticals [*Associated Press*] (SAG)
MAGPIE ...... Machine Automatically Generating Production Inventory Evaluation [*Computer science*] (IEEE)
MAGPIE ...... Magazine Page Interactive Editor (DGA)
MAGPIE ...... Markov Game Planar Intercept-Evasion Package [*Computer science*]
MAGPIE ...... Mega-Ampere Generator for Plasma Implosion Experiments [*Astrophysics*] (ECON)
MagPt.......... Magnum Petroleum [*Associated Press*] (SAG)
M Agr .... Master of Agriculture
MAGR .... Miniature Airborne GPS Receiver (SAUS)
MAGRAM..... Magnetic Random Access Memory (SAUS)
MAgrDevEc... Master of Agricultural Development Economics
M Agr E ...... Master of Agricultural Engineering
MAgrEc .... Master of Agricultural Economics
M Agr Eng .. Master of Agricultural Engineering
Mag Rer Nat... Magister Rerum Naturalium [*Latin*]
Mag Rer Soc Oec... Magister Rerum Socialium Oeconomicarumque [*Latin*]
M Agric .... Master of Agriculture
MAGROCV ... Military Advisory Group, Government of the Republic of China, Vietnam
Mag Rot ...... Magnus Rotulus [*Great Roll of the Exchequer*] [*Latin*] [*A publication*] (DLA)
M Agr S ...... Master of Agricultural Science
M Agr Sc .... Master of Agricultural Science
MAgrSci ...... Master of Agricultural Science
MAgrSt .... Master of Agricultural Studies (ADA)
Magruder.... Magruder's Reports [*1, 2 Maryland*] [*A publication*] (DLA)
MAGS .... Magal Security Systems [*NASDAQ symbol*] (SAG)
MAGS .... Magistrates (ROG)
MAGS .... Medical Action for Global Security (BUAC)
MAGS .... Midwestern Association of Graduate Schools (SAUO)
MAGS .... Multiple Aminoglycosides [*Antibacterial agents*]
Magsat .... Magnetic Field Satellite (EOSA)
MAGSAT ...... Magnetic Field Satellite [*NASA*] (MCD)
MAGSAT ...... Magnetometer Satellite (NASA)
MAgSc .... Master of Agricultural Science (ADA)
MAgSci........ Master of Agricultural Science
MAGSF .... Magal Security Systems Ltd [*NASDAQ symbol*] (TTSB)
MagSft........ Magic Software Enterprises [*Associated Press*] (SAG)
MAGSI .... Minimum Altitude at Glide Slope Intersection Inbound [*Aviation*] (FAAC)
MAGSIM ...... Magnetic Shield Simulator (PDAA)
MAgSt......... Master of Agricultural Studies
MAGSTR ...... Magistrate
mag sulf...... Magnesium Sulfate [*Pharmacology*] (DAVI)
MAGTAF ...... Marine Air-Ground Task Force (AFM)
MAGTC .... Magnetic Tape Controller (NITA)
MagTch........ Magnetics Technology [*Associated Press*] (SAG)
MAGTD .... Magnitude
MAGTF......... Marine Air-Ground Task Force (NVT)
Mag Theol ... Magister Theologiae [*Master of Theology*] [*Latin*]
MAG-THOR... Magnesium-Thorium [*Inorganic chemistry*]
MAGTOP ...... Management of Traffic Operations [*Federal Highway Administration*]
MAGTRAC... Magnetic Tracker (MUGU)
MAGUK .... Motorcycle Action Group (BUAC)
MAGW .... Maximum Alternate Gross Weight
Magy .... Magyar Muza [*Record label*] [*Hungary*]
Magz........... Magazine
MAH........... Collection des Tablettes Cuneiformes du Musee d'Art et d'Histoire de Geneve (BJA)
MAH........... Findlay, OH [*Location identifier*] [*FAA*] (FAAL)
MAH........... Hampshire College, Amherst, MA [*Library symbol*] [*Library of Congress*] (LCLS)
MAH........... Hanna [*M. A.*] Co. [*NYSE symbol*] (SPSG)
MAH........... Magnesium Aspartate Hydrochloride [*Antihypertensive*]
MAH........... Mahableshwar [*India*] [*Seismograph station code, US Geological Survey*] [*Closed*] (SEIS)
MAH........... M.A. Hanna Co. (EFIS)
MAH........... Mahogany (MSA)
mah........... Mahogany (VRA)
MAH........... Mahommedanism (ROG)
MAH........... Mahon [*Spain*] [*Airport symbol*] (OAG)
MAH........... Maleic Anhydride [*Also, MA*] [*Organic chemistry*]
MAH........... Malev-Hungarian Airlines [*ICAO designator*] (FAAC)
MAH........... Malignancy-Associated Hypercalcemia [*Oncology*]
MAH........... Massachusetts Historical Society, Boston, MA [*OCLC symbol*] (OCLC)
MAH........... Master of Arts in Humanities (GAGS)
mAH........... Milliampere Hour
MAH........... Mothers at Home [*An association*] (PAZ)
MAHA .... Metropolitan Association of Handwriting Analysts (EA)
MAHA .... Microangiopathic Hemolytic Anemia [*Medicine*]

Mah & DRT...	Mahaffy and Dodson's Road Traffic [*3rd ed.*] [*1961*] [*A publication*] (DLA)
Maharashtra LJ...	Maharashtra Law Journal [*India*] [*A publication*] (DLA)
Mahaska..........	Mahaska Investment Co. [*Associated Press*] (SAG)
MAHC	Maximum Allowable Housing Cost [*Army*] (AABC)
MAHCD........	Master of Applied Human and Community Development (PGP)
MAHE..........	Master of Arts in Hebrew Education (BJA)
MAHE..........	Master of Arts in Human Ecology (GAGS)
MAHE..........	Michigan Association for Higher Education (SAUO)
MAHE&FE....	Master of Arts in Home Economics and Family Ecology (GAGS)
Mahedco........	Maharish Heaven on Earth Development Corporation (SAUO)
MAHEFE.......	Master of Arts in Home Economics and Family Ecology (PGP)
MAHH	Malignancy-Associated Humoral Hypercalcemia [*Medicine*] (DMAA)
MAHi	Amherst Historical Society, Amherst, MA [*Library symbol*] [*Library of Congress*] (LCLS)
MAHI	Monarch Avalon [*NASDAQ symbol*] (TTSB)
MAHI	Monarch Avalon, Inc. [*NASDAQ symbol*] (NQ)
MAHL	Master of Arts in Hebrew Letters (PGP)
MAHL..........	Master of Hebrew Literature (BJA)
Mah LJ	Maharashtra Law Journal [*India*] [*A publication*] (DLA)
MAHLOVS...	Middle and High Latitudes Oceanic Variability Study (EOSA)
MAHMA.......	Midwest Assisted Housing Management Association (SRA)
MAHMO.......	Maryland Association of Health Maintenance Organizations (SRA)
MAHN	Mongolian People's Revolutionary Party [*Political party*] (BUAC)
MAHO	Mobile Assisted Hand-Over (CGWS)
MAHOC.......	Manual for Administration of the Hands-On Component (MCD)
MAHOG.......	Mahogany (DSUE)
MA(Hons).....	Master of Arts with Honours (ADA)
MAHP	Member of the Association of Hypnotists and Physiotherapists [*British*]
MAHPVDC..	Magnesium Alloy High-Pressure Die Casting
MAHRM	Master of Arts in Human Resource Management (GAGS)
MAHRS........	Microflex Attitude & Heading Reference System (SAUO)
MAHRSI......	Middle Atmosphere High Resolution Spectrograph Investigation
MAHRU.......	Microflex Attitude & Heading Reference Unit (SAUS)
MAHS	Master of Human Services (GAGS)
MAHSM	Master of Arts in Human Service Management (GAGS)
MAHT	Master of Arts in History Teaching (PGP)
MAI..............	Air Moravia [*Czechoslovakia*] [*ICAO designator*] (FAAC)
MAI..............	Machine-Aided Index (NITA)
MAI..............	Machine-Aided Indexing (KSC)
MAI..............	Magister in Arte Ingeniaria [*Master of Engineering*]
Mai	Maine's Reports [*A publication*] (DLA)
MAI..............	Maintenance Administrative Instruction (SAUO)
mai	Maithili [*MARC language code*] [*Library of Congress*] (LCCP)
MAI..............	Maius [*May*] [*Latin*]
MAI..............	Maizuru [*Japan*] [*Seismograph station code, US Geological Survey*] [*Closed*] (SEIS)
MAI..............	Management Action Indicator (SAUO)
MAI..............	Management Analysis Inc. (SAUS)
MAI..............	Management Analysis Incorporated (SAUO)
MAI..............	Management Assistance, Inc. (EFIS)
MAI..............	Mantle Arm Index
MAI..............	Manufacturers Association of Israel (BUAC)
MAI..............	Mapper Application Interface [*Computer science*]
MAI..............	Marianna [*Florida*] [*Airport symbol*] (AD)
MAI..............	Marianna, FL [*Location identifier*] [*FAA*] (FAAL)
MAI..............	Marriage Adjustment Inventory [*Psychology*]
MAI..............	Master of Fine Arts International [*British*]
MAI..............	Material Annex Item [*Military*]
MAI..............	Maximum Allowable Increase [*Environmental Protection Agency*]
MAI..............	Mean Annual Increment
MAI..............	Media Associates International [*An association*] (EA)
MAI..............	Medical Aid for Indochina [*An association*] (EA)
MAI..............	Medical Aid for Iraq
MAI..............	Medical Assurance [*NYSE symbol*] [*Formerly, MAIC Holdings*] (SG)
MAI..............	Member, Appraisal Institute [*American Institute of Real Estate Appraisers of the National Association of Realtors*] [*Designation awarded by*]
MAI..............	Member of the Anthropological Institute [*British*]
MAI..............	Metropolitan Action Institute [*Formerly, SAI*] (EA)
MAI..............	Micanite and Insulators (IAA)
MAI..............	Microscopic Aggregation Index (DMAA)
MAI..............	Midland Airways Limited (SAUO)
MAI..............	Military Assistance Institute [*Air Force*]
MAI..............	Minimum Annual Income (WDAA)
MAI..............	Ministerium fuer Aussenhandel und Innerdeutschen Handel [*Ministry for Foreign Trade and Domestic German Trade*] [*See also MfAI*]
MAI..............	Ministry of Armament Industry (SAUO)
MAI..............	Mobile Allocation Index (CGWS)
MAI..............	Monash Asia Institute [*Monash University*] [*Australia*]
MAI..............	Movement Assessment of Infants [*Pediatrics*] (DMAA)
MAI..............	Multilateral Agreement of Investment (SAUO)
MAI..............	Multilateral Agreement on Investment [*1998*]
MAI..............	Multilateral Agreement on/of Investment (SAUS)
MAI..............	Multilateral Assistance Initiative (SAUO)
MAI..............	Multilevel Assessment Instrument [*Medicine*] (DMAA)
MAI..............	Multiple Access Interface
MAI..............	Multiple Address Instruction
MAI..............	Museum of the American Indian (SAUO)
MAI..............	Museums Association of India (BUAC)
MAI..............	Music Association of Ireland (DBA)
MAI..............	Mycobacterium Avium-Intracellulare [*Medicine*]
MAI..............	Myobacterium Avium Intercellare (WDAA)
MAIA..........	Magnetic Antibody Immunoassay
MAIA..........	Master of Arts in Industrial Arts (PGP)
MAIA..........	Master of Arts in International Affairs (GAGS)
MAIA..........	Member of the American Institute of Appraisers
MAIAA	Member of the American Institute of Aeronautics and Astronautics [*Formerly, MIAS*]
MAIAA	Mid-America Intercollegiate Athletics Association (PSS)
MAIAC	Maine Athletic Conference (PSS)
MAIADA	Massachusetts Independent Auto Dealers Association (SRA)
Mai Anc L ...	Maine's Ancient Law [*A publication*] (DLA)
MAIAW	Massachusetts Association of Intercollegiate Athletics for Women (PSS)
MAIB	Marine Accident Investigation Board (BUAC)
MAIB	Motor Accidents Insurance Board [*Tasmania, Australia*]
MAIBC	Member of the Architectural Institute of British Columbia [*Canada*] (DD)
MAIBL........	Midland & International Banks Ltd. [*British*]
MAIC..........	MAIC Holdings [*NASDAQ symbol*] (TTSB)
MAIC..........	MAIC Holdings, Inc. [*NASDAQ symbol*] (SAG)
MAIC..........	Maine Aquaculture Innovation Center [*University of Maine*] [*Research center*] (RCD)
MAIC..........	Major Analytical Instrumentation Center [*University of Florida*] [*Research center*] (RCD)
MAIC..........	Michigan Association of Insurance Companies (SRA)
MAIC..........	Mid-America International Agricultural Consortium
MAICE........	Member of the American Institute of Consulting Engineers
MAICh........	Mediterranean Agronomic Institute of Chania (BUAC)
MAIChE.......	Member of the American Institute of Chemical Engineers
MAIC Hld	MAIC Holdings, Inc. [*Associated Press*] (SAG)
MAICS	Master of Arts in Intercultural Studies (PGP)
MAICYA	Major Authors and Illustrators for Children and Young Adults [*A publication*]
MAID	Magnetic Anti-Intrusion Detector (PDAA)
MAID	Maidstone [*Municipal borough in England*]
MAID	Maintenance Automatic Integration Director [*Computer science*]
MAID	Manual Intervention and Display
MAID	Market Analysis and Information Database [*MAID Systems Ltd.*] [*British*] [*Information service or system*] (IID)
MAID	Master Area Interest Decks (MCD)
MAID	Master of Arts in Interior Design (GAGS)
MAID	Master of Arts in International Diplomacy (GAGS)
MAID	Merger Acquisition Improved Decision [*Computer science*]
MAID	Methods Assembly Instruction Development (TIMI)
MAID	Mobile Autonomous Intelligent Device (SAUS)
MAID	Monroe Automatic Internal Diagnosis [*Computer science*]
MAID	Multiple Aircraft Identification Display (PDAA)
MAIDA	Multi-Attribute Identification and Analysis Program [*Jointly developed by Georgia Tech Research Institute and the US Air Force*]
MAID/MILES...	Magnetic Anti-Intrusion Detector/Magnetic Intrusion Line Sensor (MCD)
MAIDS	Machine-Aided Information and Dissemination Systems
MAIDS	Management Automated Information Display System (KSC)
MAIDS	Mouse Acquired Immunodeficiency Syndrome [*Medicine*] (DMAA)
MAIDS	Multipurpose Automatic Inspection and Diagnostic Systems [*Army*]
MAIDS	Murine-Acquired Immunodeficiency Syndrome [*Animal pathology*]
MAIDY	M.A.I.D. ADS [*NASDAQ symbol*] (TTSB)
MAIE..........	Member of the British Association of Industrial Editors (DBQ)
MAIEE	Member of the American Institute of Electrical Engineers
MAIF	Major Analytical Instruments Facility [*Case Western Reserve University*] [*Research center*] (RCD)
MAIG	Matsushita Atomic Industrial Group [*Japan*] (BUAC)
MAIIC	Master of Arts in International Communications (PGP)
Mai Inst	Maine's History of Institutions [*A publication*] (DLA)
MAIL	Mail Boxes Etc. [*NASDAQ symbol*] (NQ)
MAIL	Mail.com
MAIL	MILES [*Multiple Integrated LASER Engagement System*] Action Item Log [*Army*]
MAIL	Multiple Aperture Interlinked (ACAE)
MailBx	Mail Boxes Etc. [*Associated Press*] (SAG)
MAILS	Materiel Acquisition and Integrated Logistics Support
MAILS	Mid-America Interlibrary Services [*Library network*]
MAILS	Mississippi Automated Interlibrary Loan System [*Mississippi State Library Commission*] [*Information service or system*] (IID)
MAILS	Multiple Antenna Instrument Landing System (ACAE)
MailWell.....	Mail-Well, Inc. [*Associated Press*] (SAG)
Maim	Moses Maimonides [*Spanish Talmudist, 1135-1204*] (BJA)
MAIME	Member of the American Institute of Mining and Metallurgical Engineers
MAIME	Member of the American Institute of Mining Engineers (ASC)
MAIMH	Michigan Association for Infant Mental Health (SAUO)
MAIN	Main command post for that echelon (SAUS)
MAIN	Main St. & Main [*NASDAQ symbol*] (TTSB)
MAIN	Main St. & Main, Inc. [*NASDAQ symbol*] (SAG)
MAIN	Maintenance (NASA)
MAIN	Material Automated Information System
MAIN , ...	Material Automated Inventory Network (MCD)
MAIN	Medical Automation Intelligence [*System*]
MAIN	Mid-America Interconnected Network [*Regional power council*]
MAIN	Mid-America Interpool Network (SAUO)
MAIN	Midwest Alliance in Nursing (SRA)
MAIN	Military Authorization Identification Number
MAIN	Multiple Access Internal Network [*Computer science*]
MA, Inc.	Meniere's Australia, Inc. (NRGU)
MA in Comm...	Master of Arts in Communications
MAIND........	Master of Arts in Interior Design (PGP)
MainDta.......	Mainstream Data, Inc. [*Associated Press*] (SAG)

Maine .... Maine Reports [*A publication*] (DLA)
Maine Anc Law... Maine's Ancient Law [*A publication*] (DLA)
Maine PUR... Maine Public Utilities Commission Reports [*A publication*] (DLA)
Maine R .... Maine Reports [*A publication*] (DLA)
Maine Rep... Maine Reports [*A publication*] (DLA)
Mainlobe ..... Major Investigation for Low-Frequency Ocean Bottom Loss Experiment [*Marine science*] (MSC)
MA in LS .... Master of Arts in Liberal Studies (SAUO)
MA in LS .... Master of Arts in Library Science (SAUO)
MAINS .... Marine-Aided Inertial Navigation System (PDAA)
MAINS .... Minehunting Action Information & Navigation System (SAUS)
MAINSITE ... Modular Automated Integrated Systems / Interoperability Test and Evaluation (PDAA)
MainSt.... Main St. & Main, Inc. [*Associated Press*] (SAG)
MainStB.... Main Street BankGroup, Inc. [*Associated Press*] (SAG)
MAINT .... Maintenance (AFM)
maint .... Maintenance (MILB)
Maint.......... Maintenance (TBD)
MA/INT .... Maintenance Actions per Interval (MCD)
MA in T ...... Master of Arts in Teaching (SAUO)
MAINTBN .... Maintenance Battalion (DNAB)
MAINTCE .... Maintenance (ROG)
maintd .... Maintained
Maintex .... Maintenance Conference and Exhibition (SAUO)
MAINTN .... Maintenance [*Automotive advertising*]
MAINTNCE... Maintenance [*Freight*]
MAINTRAIN... Maintenance and Training [*in complex equipment*]
MAINTSUPOFC... Maintenance Supply Office (DNAB)
MAINTSUPP... Maintenance and Support (DNAB)
MAINTSUPPORTOFF... Maintenance Support Office [*Navy*]
MA in Urb Pl... Master of Arts in Urban Planning
MAIO .... Mashhad [*Iran*] [*Seismograph station code, US Geological Survey*] (SEIS)
MAIO .... Mobile Allocation Index Offset (CGWS)
MAIP........... Marine Engineering Improvement Programme (SAUS)
MAIP........... Matrix Algebra Interpretive Program (IEEE)
MAIPP .... Mid-Atlantic Independent Power Producers (SRA)
MAIR .... Manufacturing and Inspection Record (KSC)
MAIR .... Maritime Air (SAUS)
MAIR .... Master of Arts in Industrial Relations
MAIR .... Master of Arts in International Relations (GAGS)
MAIR .... Mesaba Holdings [*NASDAQ symbol*] (TTSB)
MAIR .... Mesaba Holdings, Inc. [*NASDAQ symbol*] (SAG)
MAIR .... Modular Airborne Intercept RADAR (IAA)
MAIR .... Molecular Airborne Intercept RADAR
MAIREASTLANT... Maritime Air, Eastern Atlantic (DNAB)
MAIREASTLANT... Maritime Air, Eastern Atlantic Command (SAUO)
MAIRMAR... Marine Air Depot, Miramar [*California*]
MAIRMED .... Maritime Air Forces Mediterranean [*NATO*] (DNAB)
MAIRMED .... Maritime Air Forces Mediterranean Command (SAUO)
MAIRS .... Military Air Integrated Reporting System (MCD)
MAIRS .... Military Airlift Integrated Reporting System (SAUO)
MAIRU .... Mobile Aircraft Instrument Repair Unit
MAIS .... Maine Association of Independent Schools (SAUO)
MAIS............ Maintenance Analysis Information Sheets (SAUO)
MAIS............ Maintenance Information System [*Military*] (NVT)
MAIS............ Major Automated Information Systems (SAUO)
MAIS............ Management Audit Information System
MAIS............ Master of Accounting Information Systems (PGP)
MAIS............ Master of Arts in Interdisciplinary Studies (GAGS)
MAIS............ Master of Arts in International Studies (GAGS)
MAIS............ Mechanical Aids for the Individual Soldier [*Army*]
MAIS............ Mediterranean Association of International Schools (EA)
MAIS............ Member, Association of Industrial Surgeons (CMD)
MAIS............ Memorandum Approval Information System (SAUO)
MAIS............ Microfilm Alpha Index System
MAIS............ Military Airlift Intelligence System (ACAE)
MAIS............ Minnesota Adaptive Instructional System (EDAC)
MAIS............ Mobile Automated Instrumentation Suite (DWSG)
MAIS............ Mycobacterium Avium-Intracellulare-Scrofulaceum [*Bacteriology*]
MAISA .... Middle Atlantic Intercollegiate Sailing Association
MAISA .... Multiple Analytical Isoelectrofocusing Scanning Apparatus
MAISAC .... Middle Atlantic Inter-Service Athletic Conference (SAUO)
MAISARC.... Major Automated Information System Review Council [*Army*]
MAISE......... Member of the Association of Iron and Steel Engineers (SAUO)
MAISITE....... Modular Automatic Integrated System/Interoperability Test and Evaluation (ACAE)
MAISRC .... Major Automated Information Systems Review Council [*Army*]
MAI Sy........ MAI Systems Corp. [*Associated Press*] (SAG)
MAI Sys....... MAI Systems Corp. [*Associated Press*] (SAG)
MAIT........... Maintenance Assistance and Instruction Team [*Army*] (AABC)
Mait............ Maitland's Select Pleas of the Crown [*A publication*] (DLA)
MAIT........... Matrix Analysis of Insider Threat [*Nuclear energy*] (NRCH)
MAIT........... Methotrexate and Cytosine Arabinoside [*Antineoplastic drug regimen*] (DAVI)
MAIT........... Minimum Autoignition Temperature
MAIT........... Missile Airframe Integration Technology (ACAE)
MAIT........... Mulitdiscipline Accident Investigation Team (SAUO)
MAITA......... Marine and Allied Industries Training Association (AIE)
Mait Gl .... Maitland's Pleas of the Crown, County of Gloucester [*A publication*] (DLA)
Maitland ...... Maitland's Manuscript Session Cases [*Scotland*] [*A publication*] (DLA)
Maitland ..... Maitland's Pleas of the Crown [*1221*] [*England*] [*A publication*] (DLA)
Maitland ...... Maitland's Select Pleas of the Crown [*A publication*] (DLA)

MAIU .... Marine Accident Investigation Unit (BUAC)
MAIWO .... Member of the Austrlaian Institute of Welfare Officers
MAIZ .... Mediterranean Agronomic Institute of Saragossa (BUAC)
MAJ .... Jones Library, Amherst, MA [*Library symbol*] [*Library of Congress*] (LCLS)
MAJ .... Majestic Airlines, Inc. [*ICAO designator*] (FAAC)
MAJ .... Majestic Electronic Stores, Inc. [*Toronto Stock Exchange symbol*]
MAJ .... Majolica [*Ceramics*] (ROG)
maj .... Majolica (VRA)
MAJ .... Major [*Military*] (AABC)
maj .... Major (GEAB)
Maj .... Major (WA)
MAJ .... Majority (KSC)
MAJ .... Majuro [*Marshall Islands*] [*Airport symbol*] (OAG)
MAJ .... Maron [*Java*] [*Seismograph station code, US Geological Survey*] [*Closed*] (SEIS)
MAJ .... Master of Arts in Journalism (GAGS)
MAJ .... Medical Association of Jamaica (BUAC)
MAJ .... Michael Anthony Jewelers [*AMEX symbol*] (TTSB)
MAJ .... Michael Anthony Jewelers, Inc. [*AMEX symbol*] (SPSG)
MAJ .... Model Air Jet
MAJAC........ Maintenance Antijam Console [*Air Force*]
MAJC........... Master of Arts in Journalism and Communication (PGP)
MAJC........... Microprocessor Architecture for Java Computing (SAUS)
MAJC........... Mount Aloysius Junior College [*Pennsylvania*]
MAJC........... Mutual Association of Journeymen Coopers [*A union*] [*British*]
MAJCOM..... Major Command [*Formerly, Major Air Command*] [*Military*]
MAJCON...... Major Air Command Controlled [*Units*]
MAJCS......... Master of Arts in Jewish Communal Service (BJA)
MAJCSSW... Master of Arts in Jewish Communal Studies and Social Work (BJA)
MAJE........... Master of Arts in Jewish Education (BJA)
MAJECA....... Malaysia-Japan Economic Association (SAUO)
MAJ Ed .... Master of Arts in Jewish Education (PGP)
MAJ GEN .... Major General (AFM)
Maj Gen ..... Major General (NTIO)
MAJI............ Magestic Agency for Joint Intelligence
MAJI............ Majority Agency for Joint Intelligence
MAJIC........... Maji Controlled [*A security classification*]
MAJO........... Matsushiro [*Japan*] [*Seismograph station code, US Geological Survey*] (SEIS)
MAJOUR...... Modular Application for Journals (SAUS)
MAJR........... Major Realty [*NASDAQ symbol*] (TTSB)
MAJR........... Major Realty Corp. [*NASDAQ symbol*] (SAG)
MajRty........ Major Realty Corp. [*Associated Press*] (SAG)
MAJS........... Master of Arts in Jewish Studies (PGP)
MAJS........... Master of Arts in Judaic Studies (BJA)
MAJSR......... Major State Register (MHDB)
MAJY .... Majority (ROG)
MAK............ Makedonski Aviotrnasport-Macedonian Airline [*FAA designator*] (FAAC)
MAK............ Makhachkala [*Former USSR*] [*Seismograph station code, US Geological Survey*] (SEIS)
MAK............ Making
MAK............ Makkoth (BJA)
MAK............ Malakal [*Sudan*] [*Airport symbol*] (OAG)
MAK............ Maliair Ltd. [*British*] [*ICAO designator*] (FAAC)
MAK............ Manual Abell-Kendall [*Clinical chemistry*]
mAk............ Maritime Arctic [*Cold Air*] [*Meteorology*] (BARN)
MAK............ Markway Resources Ltd. [*Vancouver Stock Exchange symbol*]
MAK............ Medical Accessories Kit [*Apollo*] [*NASA*]
MAK............ Methyl Amyl Ketone [*Organic chemistry*]
MAK............ Methylated Albumin Kieselguhr [*Chromatography*]
MAK............ Monopulse Antenna Kit
MAKA.......... Major Karyotypic Abnormalities [*Medicine*]
MAKETRANS... Make Necessary Transfer [*Military*] (DNAB)
Makhsh....... Makhshirin (BJA)
MAKHU........ Moskovsky Akademichesky Khoreograficheskly Uchilishche
Makita .... Makita Corp. [*Associated Press*] (SAG)
MAKL........... Markel Corp. [*NASDAQ symbol*] (NQ)
makm .... Makimono (VRA)
MAKO.......... Mako Marine International, Inc. [*NASDAQ symbol*] (SAG)
MAKO.......... Mako Marine Intl. [*NASDAQ symbol*] (TTSB)
MakoM........ Mako Marine International, Inc. [*Associated Press*] (SAG)
MAKOU........ Mako Marine Intl. 'Unit' [*NASDAQ symbol*] (TTSB)
MAKRO........ Management Analysis of Key Resource Operations [*Military*]
Makromol Chem Symp... Makromoleculare Chemie Symposia (MEC)
Maks........... Makhshirin (BJA)
MAKS........... Multipurpose Aero-Space Plane [*Russian delta-wing orbiter*]
Maksh.......... Makhshirin (BJA)
MAKSUTSUB... Make Suitable Substitution
MAL............. Macroassembly Language [*Computer science*] (BUR)
MAL............. Mad Art Lover
MAL............. Magnetic Armature Loudspeaker
MAL............. Maintain at Least (Altitude) [*Aviation*] (FAAC)
Mal............. Malachi [*Old Testament book*]
MAL............. Malachias [*Old testament book*] [*Douay version*]
MAL............. Malaga [*Spain*] [*Seismograph station code, US Geological Survey*] (SEIS)
MAL............. Malan Realty Investors [*NYSE symbol*] (SAG)
MAL............. Malariology Technician [*Navy*]
MAL............. Malaspina College Learning Resources Centre [*UTLAS symbol*]
MAL............. Malate
MAL............. Malay (WDAA)
mal............. Malayalam [*MARC language code*] [*Library of Congress*] (LCCP)
MAL............. Malayan (AABC)

MAL	Malayan Airways Ltd.
Mal	Malaysia (MILB)
MAL	Malaysia (WDAA)
MAL	Malaysian Air Lines
MAL	Malcolm Music [*Publisher*]
Mal	Maleyl [*Biochemistry*]
MAL	Malfunction (KSC)
MAL	Malicious [*FBI standardized term*]
MAL	Malignant (SAUS)
MAL	Malleable (MSA)
mal	Malonate [*Organic chemistry*]
MAL	Malone [*New York*] [*Airport symbol*] (AD)
MAL	Malone College, Canton, OH [*OCLC symbol*] (OCLC)
MAL	Malone, NY [*Location identifier*] [*FAA*] (FAAL)
MAL	Malta (WDAA)
mal	Malum [*Ill*] [*Latin*] (MAE)
Mal	Malus [*Constellation*] (WDAA)
MAL	Man and LASER (MCD)
MAL	Marco Resources [*Vancouver Stock Exchange symbol*]
MAL	Master Authorization List
MAL	Materiel Allowance List [*Military*]
MAL	Maximal Acceptable Load (PDAA)
MAL	McAlpine Aviation Ltd. [*British*] [*ICAO designator*] (FAAC)
MAL	Medullary Thick Ascending Limb [*Anatomy*]
MAL	Memory Access Logic
MAL	Mercury Arc Lamp
MAL	Meta Assembly Language
MAL	Methacrolein [*Also, MACR*] [*Organic chemistry*]
MAL	Midaxillary Line [*Medicine*]
MAL	Middle Assyrian Laws (BJA)
MAL	Mobile Airlock (MCD)
MAL	Modern American Law [*A publication*] (DLA)
MAL	Multiairline [*Type of British pole line construction*]
MAL	Multiple Address Letter (NOAA)
MALA	Malarial Parasites [*Infectious diseases Laboratory and respiratory*] (DAVI)
MALA	Manpower and Logistics Analysis (MCD)
MALA	Master of Arts in Liberal Arts (PGP)
MALA	Master of Arts in Liturgical Arts (PGP)
MAL-AAACE	Media and Adult Learning Section of the American Association for Adult and Continuing Education (EA)
MALAC	Malacology
MALAD	Maladjusted Child [*Social Work*] [*British*] (DSUE)
MALAGOC	Mutual Assistance of the Latin American Government Oil Companies G2 [*See also ARPEL*] (EA)
Malag Rep	Malagasy Republic
MalanR	Malan Realty Investors [*Associated Press*] (SAG)
MALAR	Malaria [*Infectious diseases*] (DAVI)
MALAS	Master of Arts in Latin American Studies (PGP)
MALAS	Midwestern Association for Latin American Studies
Malay	Malaysia (VRA)
Malayan J Trop Geogr	Malayan Journal of Topical Geography (SAUO)
Malayan Nat J	Malayan Nature Journal (SAUO)
Malayan Nat J	Malayan Nature Journal, The (SAUS)
Malaysa	Malaysia Fund, Inc. [*Associated Press*] (SAG)
Malays For	Malaysian Forester (SAUO)
Mal-BSA	Maleated Bovine Serum Albumin [*Medicine*] (DMAA)
MALC	Madison Area Library Council [*Library network*]
MALC	Management of Acquisition Logistics Course (AAGC)
MALC	Midwest Academic Librarians Conference (SAUO)
MALC	Model Aircraft League of Canada (SAUO)
MALCAP	Maryland Academic Library Center for Automated Processing (NITA)
MALCAP	Maryland Library Center for Automated Processing [*Library network*]
MALCD	Matrix-Addressed Liquid Crystal Display
MALCM	Mercantile Adjuster and the Lawyer and Credit Man [*A publication*] (DLA)
Malcolm Ethics	Malcolm's Legal and Judicial Ethics [*A publication*] (DLA)
MALCS	Mujeres Activas en Letras y Cambio Social (EA)
MALD	Master of Arts in Law and Diplomacy
MA(LD)	Master of Arts (Landscape Design), University of Manchester [*British*] (DBQ)
MALD	Modular Analysis of Learning Difficulties (OICC)
MALDEF	Mexican American Legal Defense and Educational Fund (EA)
MALDI	Matrix-Assisted LASER Desorption Ionization [*Spectroscopy*]
Mald Isls	Maldive Islands
MALDMS	Matrix-Assisted LASER Desorption Mass Spectrometry
MALDT	Mean Administrative and Logistics Downtime [*Quality control*] (MCD)
MALE	Military Airlift Estimator (SAUO)
MALE	Multiaperture Logic Element
MALER	Master of Arts in Labor and Employment Relations (PGP)
Malerei u Zeichn	Malerei und Zeichnung [*A publication*] (OCD)
Malev	Hungarian Airlines (BUAC)
MALF	Malfunction (KSC)
MALF	Mobile Aerobee Launch Facility
MALFIRM	Maximum Allowable Level of Fishing Related Mortality (SAUS)
MALG	Minnesota Antilymphoblast Globulin [*Medicine*] (DMAA)
Malg Rep	Malagasy Republic (SAUO)
MALI	Material Annex Line Item [*Military*]
MALI	Matrix-Assisted Laser Ionizaion [*Spectrometry*]
MALI	Michigan Accident Location Index [*Michigan State Police*] [*Information service or system*] (IID)
MALIB	Math Analysis Library (MCD)
MA(LibSc)	Master of Arts (Library Science)
malig	Malignant [*Medicine*]
MALIMET	Master List of Medical Indexing Terms

Malinc	Mallinckrodt Group [*Formerly, IMCERA Group*] [*Associated Press*] (SAG)
Malinckr	Mallinckrodt Group [*Formerly, IMCERA Group*] [*Associated Press*] (SAG)
MALIPR	Material Annex Line Item Progress Report [*Military*] (NG)
MALIS	Master of Arts in Library and Information Science (PGP)
Mal Isl	Maldive Islands (SAUO)
MALL	Creative Computers [*NASDAQ symbol*] (TTSB)
MALL	Creative Computers, Inc. [*NASDAQ symbol*] (SAG)
MALL	Mall [*Postal Service standard*] (OPSA)
MALL	Malleable
MALL	Master of Arts in Liberal Learning (PGP)
MALL	Minnesota Association of Law Libraries [*Library network*]
MALL	Multi-Function Alarm, Locks, and Lighting [*Automotive electronics*]
MALLAR	Manned Lunar Landing and Return (NASA)
Mal Law M	Malynes' Ancient Law Merchant [*A publication*] (DLA)
Mall Ent	Mallory's Modern Entries [*A publication*] (DLA)
Mal Lex Merc	Malynes' Lex Mercatoria [*3 eds.*] [*1622-36*] [*A publication*] (DLA)
Mallon	Mallon Resources Corp. [*Associated Press*] (SAG)
Mallory	Mallory's Irish Chancery Reports [*A publication*] (DLA)
Mal L Rev	Malaya Law Review [*A publication*] (DLA)
MALLS	Multiangle LASER Light-Scattering [*Instrumentation*]
MALM	Maryknoll Associate Lay Missioners (EA)
MALM	Maryknoll Mission Association of the Faithful (EA)
MALM	Master Air Loadmaster (SAUO)
MALMARC	Malaysian MARC (NITA)
MAL MISCH	Malicious Mischief [*Legal term*] (DLA)
MALN	Minimum Air Low Noise (PDAA)
MALN	Mouvement Africain de Liberation Nationale [*African Movement for National Liberation*]
MALODES	Modern Army Logistics Data Exchange System
MALOF	Minimum Accepted Level of Fill [*Military*]
Malone	Editor, 6, 9, and 10, Heiskell's Tennessee Reports [*A publication*] (DLA)
MALOR	Mortar and Artillery Location RADAR (RDA)
MALOS	Maintenance and Logistics Space [*System*]
MALOS	Miniature Optical Laser Sight (SAUS)
MALP	Major Assembly Labor and Performance (MCD)
MALP	Master Alarm Light Panel [*NASA*] (SPST)
MALPAS	Malvern Program Analysis System (NITA)
MAL PROS	Malicious Prosecution [*Legal term*] (DLA)
MALR	Mortar/Artillery Locating RADAR (PDAA)
MALRA	Malaysian Leprosy Relief Association (SAUO)
MALRY	Malaysian Leprosy Relief Association (BUAC)
MALS	Master of Arts in Liberal Studies
MALS	Master of Arts in Library Science
MALS	Master of Arts in Library Service (NADA)
MALS	Median Arcuate Ligament Syndrome [*Medicine*] (MELL)
MALS	Medium-Intensity Approach Lighting System [*Aviation*]
MALS	Members of an Amalgamated Society [*Slang*] [*British*] (DSUE)
MALS	Miniature Air Launcher System (ACAE)
MALS	Multiangle Light Scattering
MALSCE	Massachusetts Association of Land Surveyors and Civil Engineers (SRA)
MALSF	Medium-Intensity Approach Lighting System with Sequenced Flashers [*Aviation*]
MALSF	Medium Intensity Approach Light System with Sequenced Flashing Lights [*FAA*] (TAG)
MALSP	Marine Aviation Logistics Support Program
MALSR	Medium-Intensity Approach Lighting System with Runway Alignment Indicator Lights [*Aviation*]
MALSR	Medium Intensity Approach Light System with Rail [*FAA*] (TAG)
MALS/RAIL	Minimum-Approach Lighting System with Runway Alignment Indicator Lights [*Aviation*] (DNAB)
Mal St	Malay States (SAUO)
MALT	Lion Brewery [*NASDAQ symbol*] (TTSB)
MALT	Lion Brewery, Inc. (The) [*NASDAQ symbol*] (SAG)
MALT	Macosa-Associated Lymphoid Tissue [*Medicine*]
MALT	Male, Altered Animal (DMAA)
MALT	Maltese (DSUE)
MALT	Master of Arts in Language Teaching (GAGS)
MALT	Military Administration of Liberated Territory (SAUO)
MALT	Military Adviser's Language Text
MALT	Military Assistance Language Training
MALT	Mnemonic Assembly Language Translator [*Computer science*] (IEEE)
MALT	Monetary Allowance in Lieu of Transportation [*DoD*]
MALT	Mucosa-Associated Lymphoid Tissue [*Anatomy*]
MALT	Munich Alcoholism Test [*Medicine*] (DMAA)
MALTA	Middle Atlantic Lawn Tennis Association
MALTA SE	Malta Stock Exchange
Malt CM	Maltby on Courts-Martial [*A publication*] (DLA)
MALTL	Mucosa-Associated Lymphoid Tissue Lymphoma [*Medicine*] (MELL)
MALTS	Marine Layer Thickness Study (SAUO)
MALTT	Massachusetts Adult Literacy and Technology Team
MALU	Maine Association of Life Underwriters (SRA)
MALU	Massachusetts Association of Life Underwriters (SRA)
MALU	Michigan Association of Life Underwriters (SRA)
MALU	Minnesota State Association of Life Underwriters (SRA)
MALU	Mississippi Association of Life Underwriters (SRA)
MALU	Missouri Association of Life Underwriters (SRA)
MALU	Mode Annunciator and Logic Unit (PDAA)
MALV	Malva [*Mallow*] [*Pharmacy*] (ROG)
MALVINE	Manuscripts and Letters via Integrated Networks in Europe (TELE)
Malynes	Malynes' Lex Mercatoria [*3 eds.*] [*1622-36*] [*A publication*] (DLA)

MAm .... Amesbury Public Library, Amesbury, MA [*Library symbol*] [*Library of Congress*] (LCLS)
M + Am ...... Compound Myopic Astigmatism [*Ophthalmology*]
MAM .... Joint II March-May Study [*Coastal Upwelling Ecosystems Analysis*] (MSC)
MAM .... Madam (DSUE)
MAM .... Maintenance Assist Module
MAM .... Maintenance Assumes Monitor [*Aviation*] (FAAC)
MAM .... Mambajao [*Philippines*] [*Seismograph station code, US Geological Survey*] [*Closed*] (SEIS)
Mam .... Mammoth
MAM .... Management Analysis Memorandum [*DoD*] (MCD)
MAM .... Management Analysis Model (SAUO)
MAM .... Management and Administration Manual (NRCH)
MAM .... Marquis Academic Media [*Publisher*]
MAM .... Mars Aeronomy Mission (MCD)
MAM .... Master Model (MCD)
MAM .... Master of Agriculture and Management (PGP)
MAM .... Master of Animal Medicine (GAGS)
MAM .... Master of Applied Mechanics (PGP)
MAM .... Master of Arts in Management
MAM .... Master of Arts Management (PGP)
MAM .... Master of Arts - Ministry (PGP)
MAM .... Master of Association Management (PGP)
MAM .... Master of Avian Medicine (PGP)
MAM .... Master of Aviation Management (GAGS)
MAM .... Matamoros [*Mexico*] [*Airport symbol*] (OAG)
MAM .... Material Acquisition Manager [*Army*] (AAGC)
MAM .... Materiel Acquisition Management Program [*Army*] (RDA)
MAM .... Matter-Anti-Matter (PDAA)
MAM .... Maxxim Medical [*NYSE symbol*] (TTSB)
MAM .... Maxxim Medical, Inc. [*NYSE symbol*] (SPSG)
MAM .... Medical Association of Malta (BUAC)
MAM .... Medium-Altitude Missile (MCD)
MAM .... Medium Automotive Maintenance
MAM .... Memory Access Multiplexer (NITA)
MAM .... Memory Allocation Manager
MAM .... Mercury Asset Management [*Commercial firm*] [*British*]
MAM .... Message Access Method [*Honeywell, Inc.*]
MAM .... Meta Aviotransport-Macedonia [*Yugoslavia*] [*ICAO designator*] (FAAC)
MAM .... Methylazoxymethanol (STED)
MAM .... Methylazoxymethanol Acetate [*Organic chemistry*]
MAM .... Microwave Attenuator Monitor (IAA)
MAM .... Military Air Movement
MAM .... Military Assistance Manual (AFM)
MAM .... Milliammeter
mam .... Milliampere-Minute (STED)
MAM .... Milliampere Minutes
MAM .... Missile Alarm Monitor
MAM .... Missile Assembly and Maintenance [*NASA*] (IAA)
MAM .... Mission Air Ministries [*Defunct*] (EA)
MAM .... Mission Area Manager [*Army*]
MAM .... Monoacetylmorphine [*Organic chemistry*]
MAM .... Montclair Art Museum (SAUO)
MAM .... Mot a Mot [*Word for Word*] [*French*]
MAm .... Multiapplication Monitor
MAM .... Multiple Access to Memory [*Computer science*] (IEEE)
MAM .... Munitions Assessment Model (SAUO)
M+Am .... Myopic Astigmatism [*Ophthalmology*] (DAVI)
MAM .... Society of Automotive Engineers, Inc. (AAGC)
MAMA .... Maintenance and Malfunction Analysis (ACAE)
MAMA .... Management Accounting Maintenance Advertising, Inc.
MAMA .... Manual-Automatic Multipoint Apparatus (MCD)
MAMA .... Material Acquisition Management Application [*Suggested name for the Library of Congress computer system*]
MAMA .... Meet-a-Mum Association [*British*] (DI)
MAMA .... Midarm Muscle Area (STED)
MAMA .... Middletown Air Materiel Area [*Air Force*]
MAMA .... Mobile Air Materiel Area (SAUO)
MAMA .... Mobile Automated Metabolic Analyzer [*Aerospace*]
MAMA .... Monoammonium Methanearsonate
MAMA .... Monoclonal Antimalignant Antibody [*Immunochemistry*]
MAMA .... Mothers Against Munchausen Syndrome by Proxy Allegations (SAUO)
MAMA .... Movement for All-Macedonian Action [*Political party*]
MAMA .... Multi-Anode Microchannel Array (PDAA)
MAMAA ...... Mothers Against Murder and Aggression [*An association*] (BUAC)
MAM Ac ..... Methylazoxymethanol Acetate [*Organic chemistry*] (DMAA)
MAMB .... Master of Applied Molecular Biology (PGP)
MAMB .... Military Acquisition Management Branch [*Army*] (RDA)
MAMB .... Military Advisory Mission, Brazil
MAMB .... Missile Assembly and Maintenance Building [*NASA*] (IAA)
MAMB .... Mission Avionics Multiplex Bus (ACAE)
MAMBA ...... Marconi Artillery & Mortar Ballistic Aide (SAUS)
MAMBO ...... Mediterranean Association for Marine Biology and Oceanology [*ICSU*] (EAIO)
MAMBO ...... Mediterranean Association of Marine Biological Oceanography (SAUO)
MAMBO ...... Minuteman Assembly-Maintenance Building, Ogden (SAA)
MAMC .... Altona Medical Centre Library, Manitoba [*Library symbol*] [*National Library of Canada*] (NLC)
MAMC .... Madigan Army Medical Center (AABC)
MAMC .... Master of Arts in Mass Communication (PGP)
MAMC .... Mean Arm Muscle Circumference (STED)

MAMC .... Midarm Muscle Circumference [*Myology*]
MAMDC ...... Multipurpose Arthritis and Musculoskeletal Diseases Center [*University of Alabama, Birmingham*] [*Research center*] (RCD)
MAME .... Master of Arts in Missions/Evangelism (PGP)
MAME .... Michigan Association for Media in Education
MAME .... Michigan Association of Media Educators
MAME .... Missile and Munitions Evaluation
MAME .... Mobile America [*NASDAQ symbol*] (TTSB)
MAME .... Mobile America Corp. [*NASDAQ symbol*] (NQ)
MAME .... Multiple Arcade Machine Emulator (SAUS)
MA Mech .... Master of Applied Mechanics
MAMEE ...... Meyer Ammunition Module - Emerson Electric
MAMEME .... Member of the Association of Mining, Electrical and Mechanical Engineers (SAUO)
MAMFC ...... Master of Arts in Marriage and Family Counseling (GAGS)
MAMFCC .... Master of Arts in Marriage, Family, and Child Counseling (PGP)
MAMFT .... Master of Arts in Marriage and Family Therapy (PGP)
MAmg .... Medial Amygdaloid [*Nucleus*] (STED)
MAMGRAPHY... Mammography
MA Mgt ...... Master of Arts in Management (PGP)
MAmHi .... Amesbury Historical Society, Amesbury, MA [*Library symbol*] [*Library of Congress*] (LCLS)
MAMI .... Machine-Aided Manufacturing Information [*Computer science*]
MAMI .... Modified Alternate Mark Inversion [*Telecommunications*] (TEL)
MAMI .... Multicultural Association of Medical Interpreters of Central New York (SAUO)
MAMI .... Multiple Association Management Institute [*Later, IAMC*] (EA)
MAMIE .... Magnetic Amplification of Microwave Integrated Emissions (IEEE)
MAMIE .... Minimum Automatic Machine for Interpolation and Extrapolation
M Am IMME... Member of the American Institute of Mining and Metallurgical Engineers
MA Min ...... Master of Arts in Ministry (PGP)
MA min ...... Milli-Ampere-Minute (STED)
Ma-Min ...... Milliampere-Minute
MAMIS .... Mandatory Modification and Inspection Summary [*Aviation*] (DA)
MA Missions... Master of Arts in Missions (PGP)
MAML .... Master of Arts in School Media Librarianship (PGP)
MA/ML .... Missile Active/Missile Launch (SAUS)
MAMM .... Master of Arts in Ministry Management (PGP)
MAMMA ...... Men Against the Maxi-Midi Atrocity [*Klosters, Switzerland, group opposing below-the-knee fashions introduced in 1970*]
MAMMAX .... Machine-Made and Machine-Assisted Index [*Computer science*] (IAA)
mammo ...... Mammography [*Gynecology*] (DAVI)
Mamm Rev... Mammal Review (SAUS)
MAM Number... Military Air Movement Number (SAUO)
MAMO .... Advanced Mammography Sys [*NASDAQ symbol*] (TTSB)
MAMO .... Advanced Mammography Systems [*NASDAQ symbol*] (SAG)
MAMOE .... Medical Administration and Miscellaneous Operating Expenses [*Veterans Administration*]
MAMOS ...... Marine Automatic Meteorological Observing Station [*Automatic system*]
MAMOS ...... Missouri Associated Migrant Opportunities Services (EA)
MaMP .... Maine State Planning Office, Augusta, ME [*Library symbol*] [*Library of Congress*] (LCLS)
MAMP .... Mainz Army Maintenance Plant (MCD)
MAMP .... Materiel Acquisition Management Plan
MAMP .... Michigan Army Missile Plant (MCD)
MAMP .... Millampere [*or Milliamperage*] (IAA)
MAMP .... Mission Area Materiel Plan [*Army*]
MAMRC ...... Military Aerospace Maintenance and Regeneration Center (MUSM)
MAMRD ...... Master of Agricultural Management and Resource Development (GAGS)
MAMRON .... Marine Aircraft Maintenance Squadron
MAMS .... Maintenance Activity Management System [*Military*]
MAMS .... Maintenance Assist Modules (MCD)
MAMS .... Marine Meteorological Services [*Marine science*] (MSC)
MAMS .... Master of Applied Mathematical Sciences (PGP)
MAMS .... Master of Associated Medical Sciences (PGP)
MAMS .... Materiel Acquisition Management System
MAMS .... Medical Administration Management System (SAUO)
MAMS .... Medical Administrative Management System
MAMS .... Member of the Association of Medical Secretaries, Practice Administrators, and Receptionists [*British*] (DBQ)
MAMS .... Microgravity Acceleration Measurement System (SAUS)
MAMS .... Military Aircraft Marshaling System
MAMS .... Military Airspace Management System (SAUS)
MAMS .... MIRCOM [*Missile Material Readiness Command*] Automated Microfilm System [*Army*] (IID)
MAMS .... Missile Altitude Measurement System
MAMS .... Missile Assembly and Maintenance Shop [*NASA*]
MAMS .... Missile Assistance Maintenance Structure (IAA)
MAMS .... Mobile Air Movement Squadron (SAUO)
MAMS .... Modern Army Maintenance System
MAMS .... Multiple Access to Memory System [*Computer science*]
MAMS .... Multispectral Atmospheric Mapping Sensor
m-AMSA ..... Acridinyl Ansidide [*Antineoplastic drug*] (DAVI)
m-AMSA ..... Amsacrine [*Antineoplastic drug*] [*Also, AMSA*] (CDI)
MAMSA .... Managing and Marketing Sales Association [*British*] (DBA)
MAM Sc ..... Master of Applied Mathematical Science (PGP)
MAMSER .... Mass Mobilisation for Self Reliance, Social Justice, and Economic Recovery [*Nigeria*] (BUAC)
MAMS-II ..... Maintenance Activity Management System II (SAUO)
M Am Soc CE... Member of the American Society of Civil Engineers

MAmSocHRAE... Member of the American Society of Heating, Refrigeration and Air Conditioning Engineers (SAUO)
MAmSocMechE... Member of the American Society of Mechanical Engineers (SAUO)
MAMSPAR... Member of the Association of Medical Secretaries, Practice Administrators, and Receptionists [British] (DI)
MAMS-R..... Medical Administrative Management System-Revision (SAUO)
MAMSS....... Machine Augmented Manual Scheduling System (MCD)
MAMT......... Mean Active Maintenance Time (MCD)
MAMT......... Mobile Air Movements Team (SAUO)
MAMTC....... Main Administration for Military-Technical Co-operation (SAUO)
MAMTF....... Mobile Automated Microwave Test Facility (PDAA)
MAMTR....... Milliammeter
MA (Mus) .... Master of Arts in Music
MAMV......... Maclura Mosaic Virus [Plant pathology]
MAmW........ Whittier Home Association, Amesbury, MA [Library symbol] [Library of Congress] (LCLS)
MAN.......... Magnetic Automatic Navigation [System] (RDA)
MAN.......... Magnocellular Nucleus [of anterior neostriatum] [Neurology] (DAVI)
MAN.......... Mailorder Association of Nurserymen [Defunct] (EA)
MAN.......... Mainly about Nature [A publication]
MAN.......... Maintenance Alert Network [RCA]
MAN.......... Management (WDAA)
MAN.......... Manager [or Managing] (EY)
man .... Managing (DD)
Man .... Mancando [Dying Away] [Music]
MAN.......... Manchester [England] [Airport symbol] (OAG)
MAN.......... Manchester Regiment (SAUO)
MAN.......... Mandato de Accion y Unidad Nacional [Mandate of Action and National Unity] [Bolivia] [Political party] (PPW)
man .... Mandingo [MARC language code] [Library of Congress] (LCCP)
man .... Mandolin
MAN.......... Mane [Morning] [Pharmacy]
MAN.......... Manege [Horsemanship] [French]
MAN.......... Manhattan
MAN.......... Manifest (AABC)
MAN.......... Manila [Philippines] [Seismograph station code, US Geological Survey] (SEIS)
Man .... Manila (WDAA)
MAN.......... Manilla (ADA)
man .... Manipulate [Medicine] (MAE)
MAN.......... Manipulus [A Handful] [Pharmacy]
Man .... Manitoba [Canada] (DD)
MAN.......... Manitoba [Canadian province]
Man .... Manitoba Law Reports [Canada] [A publication] (DLA)
Man .... Manning's Reports [1 Michigan] [A publication] (DLA)
Man .... Manning's Reports, English Revision Court [1832-35] [A publication] (DLA)
MAN.......... Mannion Air Charter, Inc. [ICAO designator] (FAAC)
MAN.......... Mann Oil Resources, Inc. [Vancouver Stock Exchange symbol]
MAN.......... Mannose (STED)
Man .... Mannose [A sugar]
MAN.......... Manpower, Inc. [NYSE symbol] (SPSG)
MAN.......... Mansfield State College, Mansfield, PA [OCLC symbol] (OCLC)
Man .... Manson's English Bankruptcy Cases [A publication] (DLA)
MAN.......... Manual (KSC)
man .... Manual [A handbook] (WDMC)
MAN.......... Manuel Antonio Noriega [Military commander and de facto ruler of Panama]
MAN.......... Manufacture
Man .... Manufacturer (SAUO)
MAN.......... Manufacturer (WDAA)
MAN.......... Manufacturers Association of Nigeria (BUAC)
MAN.......... Maschinenfabrik Augsburg-Nuernburg [Manufacturer of diesel engines]
MAN.......... Meaningful Assistance in the Neighborhood [of Legal Aid Bureau of George Washington University Law School] (EA)
MAN.......... Methacrylonitrile (EDCT)
MAN.......... Methylammonium Nitrate (EDCT)
MAN.......... Metropolitan Area Network [Telecommunications]
MAN.......... Microwave Aerospace Navigation
MAN.......... Military Aviation Notice [Air Force]
MAN.......... Molecular Anatomy
MAN.......... Molesters Anonymous (EA)
MAN.......... Motorcyclists Against Noise (SAUO)
MAN.......... Mouvement pour une Alternative Non-Violente [Movement for a Nonviolent Alternative] [France] [Political party] (PPE)
MAN.......... Movementu Antiyas Nobo [New Antilles Movement] [Netherlands] [Political party] (EAIO)
MAN.......... Movimentu Antiyas Nobo [New Antilles Movement] [Political party] (EY)
MAN.......... Movimiento de Accion Nacionalista [National Action Movement] [Uruguay] [Political party] (EY)
MAN.......... Muslim Association of Nigeria (SAUO)
MAN.......... University of Manitoba Library [UTLAS symbol]
Man .... Victoria University of Manchester (SAUO)
MAN-6-P..... Mannose-6-Phosphate [Chemistry] (DAVI)
MANA .... Major and National Account (TIMI)
MANA .... Malawi News Agency (BUAC)
MANA .... Manassas National Battlefield Park
MANA .... Manatron, Inc. [NASDAQ symbol] (NQ)
MANA ....sub Mannosidase Alpha (DMAA)
MANA .... Manufacturers Agents National Association (EA)
MANA .... Mexican American Women's National Association (EA)
MANA .... Michigan Association of Nurse Anesthetists (SAUO)

MANA .... Midwives Alliance of North America (EA)
MANA .... Music Advisers' National Association [British]
MANA .... Musicians Against Nuclear Arms [Defunct] (EA)
MAN-AEDS... Manitoba Association for Educational Data Systems [Canada] (EDAC)
MAnaes ...... Master of Anaesthesiology (SAUO)
MANAG ...... Manage
Managem .... Management (SAUO)
MANAM ...... Manual Amendment
Man & G..... Manning and Granger's English Common Pleas Reports [A publication] (DLA)
Man & R..... Manning and Ryland's English King's Bench Reports [1827-30] [A publication] (DLA)
Man & R..... Manning and Ryland's English Magistrates' Cases [1827-30] [A publication] (DLA)
Man & Ry.... Manning and Ryland's English King's Bench Reports [1827-30] [A publication] (DLA)
Man & Ry.... Manning and Ryland's English Magistrates' Cases [1827-30] [A publication] (DLA)
Man & Ry KB... Manning and Ryland's English King's Bench Reports [1827-30] [A publication] (ILCA)
Man & Ry Mag... Manning and Ryland's English Magistrates' Cases [1827-30] [A publication] (DLA)
Man & Ry Mag Cas... Manning and Ryland's English Magistrates' Cases [1827-30] [A publication] (DLA)
Man & Ry MC... Manning and Ryland's English Magistrates' Cases [1827-30] [A publication] (DLA)
Man & S...... Manning and Scott's English Common Bench Reports, Old Series [IX] [A publication] (DLA)
Man & Sask Tax Rep (CCH)... Manitoba and Saskatchewan Tax Reporter (Commerce Clearing House) [A publication] (DLA)
Man & Sc.... Manning and Scott's English Common Bench Reports, Old Series [IX] [A publication] (DLA)
MANAV .... Maneuvering and Navigation System [Military] (IAA)
MANB .... Mannosidase Beta (DMAA)
ManBagel.... Manhattan Bagel Co., Inc. [Associated Press] (SAG)
Manb Coke... Manby's Abridgement of Coke's Reports [A publication] (DLA)
Manb Fines... Manby on Fines [A publication] (DLA)
Man B News... Manitoba Bar News [A publication] (ILCA)
MANC .... Mancando [Decreasing in Loudness] [Music]
MANC .... Mozambique African National Congress (SAUO)
Manc .... Victoria University of Manchester (SAUO)
MANCAN .... Man-Carried Automatic Navigator (MCD)
Man Cas ..... Manumission Cases in New Jersey, by Bloomfield [A publication] (DLA)
MANCH .... Manchester [England]
Manch .... Manchuria
MANCLOS.... Manual Command to Line-Of-Sight (SAUS)
MANCO....... Mancando [Decreasing in Loudness] [Music]
MANCOVA.... Multivariate Analysis of Covariance
MANCPEC.... Malaysia National Committee for Pacific Economic Cooperation
MANCUN...... Mancunium [Signature of the Bishops of Manchester] (ROG)
Mand .... Mandaic (BJA)
MAND .... Mandamus [We Command] [Latin] (ADA)
MAND .... Mandatory (AABC)
Mand .... Mandatory (TBD)
mand .... Mandibar [Dentistry] (DAVI)
MAND .... Mandible
mand .... Mandolin (WDAA)
MAND .... Mandolin [Music]
MAND .... McCarron Assessment of Neuromuscular Development [Psychology] (DHP)
M&A .... Maintenance and Administration (CIST)
M & A......... Maintenance and Assembly (MCD)
M & A......... Management and Administration
M&A .... Mergers and Acquisitions (TDOB)
M & A......... Mergers & Acquisitions Data Base [MLR Publishing Co.] [Information service or system] (CRD)
M & A......... Mississippi & Alabama Railroad (IIA)
M & A......... Missouri & Arkansas Railway Co.
M & A......... Money and Advice
M & A......... Montagu and Ayrton's English Bankruptcy Reports [1833-38] [A publication] (DLA)
M & ABL.... Montagu and Ayrton's Bankrupt Laws [A publication] (DLA)
M&AS........ Music and Art School (SAUO)
MANDATE.... MCCIS Austere Northwood Database & Terminal Equipment (SAUS)
MANDATE.... Multiline Automatic Network Diagnostic and Transmission Equipment [Computer science] (CIST)
M & AW...... Mountain and Arctic Warfare [British military] (DMA)
M & Ayr....... Montagu and Ayrton's English Bankruptcy Reports [1833-38] [A publication] (DLA)
M & B......... Marianna & Blountstown [Railroad] (MHDB)
M & B......... Marianna & Blountstown Railroad Co. (IIA)
M & B......... Matched and Beaded
M&B .... May & Baker (WDAA)
M&B .... May & Baker Ltd. (SAUO)
M & B......... Mild and Bitter [Beer]
M&B .... Mitchells and Butlers Ltd. (SAUO)
M & B......... Montagu and Bligh's English Bankruptcy Reports [1832-33] [A publication] (DLA)
M & BR...... Meridian & Bigbee River Railroad Co. (IIA)
M&BU......... Mother & Baby Unit (WDAA)
M & C........ Maintenance and Checkout (NASA)
M & C........ Maintenance and Cure [Legal shorthand] (LWAP)
M&C.......... Management & Control (SAUS)

M & C..........	Manufacturers and Contractors
M&C...........	Measurement and Control [*The Journal of InstMC*] (ACII)
M & C..........	Monitor and Control Panel [*Computer science*] (NASA)
M & C..........	Montagu and Chitty's English Bankruptcy Reports [*1838-40*] [*A publication*] (DLA)
M&C...........	Morphine and Cocaine [*Medicine*] (DMAA)
M & C..........	Mylne and Craig's English Chancery Reports [*A publication*] (DLA)
M&CA.........	Materials & Chemical Applications (SAUO)
M & C Bills...	Miller and Collier on Bills of Sale [*A publication*] (DLA)
M&CD.........	Metals and Ceramics Division (SAUO)
M & Chit Bankr...	Montagu and Chitty's English Bankruptcy Reports [*1838-40*] [*A publication*] (DLA)
M & Cht Bankr...	Montagu and Chitty's English Bankruptcy Reports [*1838-40*] [*A publication*] (DLA)
M & C Partidas...	Moreau-Lislet and Carleton's Laws of Las Siete Partidas in Force in Louisiana [*A publication*] (DLA)
M&CS.........	Materials & Chemical Sciences Center (SAUO)
M & CSq.....	Mapping and Charting Squadron [*Air Force*]
M & CU......	Monitor and Control Unit [*Aerospace*] (AAG)
M and CW...	Maternity and Child Welfare [*Medicine*] [*British*]
M & D........	Maidstone & District Motor Services Ltd. [*British*] (DCTA)
M&D..........	Maintenance and Diagnostics (SAUO)
M & D........	McCormack & Dodge (NITA)
M & D........	Medicine and Duty [*Marked on a medical report and implying a suspicion of malingering*] [*Military*] [*British*]
M & D........	Mergers and Divestures
M&DOD.......	Mision and Data Operations Directorate (ACAE)
M & DV......	Map and Data Viewer [*NASA*] (KSC)
M&E..........	Machinery and Equipment (ACAE)
M & E........	Maintenance and Equipment (NATG)
M & E........	Maneuvers and Exercises (NATG)
M & E........	Material and Equipment [*Nuclear energy*] (NRCH)
M & E........	Mechanical and Electrical Room (AAG)
M&E..........	Monitoring and Enforcement (SAUS)
M & E........	Monitoring and Evaluation (ECON)
M&E..........	Monitoring and Evaluation (SAUS)
M & E........	Morning and Evening (WDMC)
M & E........	Music and Effects [*Television*]
M & E........	Music and Sound Effects (WDMC)
MANDEC......	Maneuvering Decoy (MCD)
Man Dem.....	Mansel on Demurrer [*1828*] [*A publication*] (DLA)
M & ER......	Mechanical and Electrical Room (AAG)
M&ES.........	Magnetic & Electromagnetic Silencing (SAUS)
M & F........	Male and Female [*Components, as of connecting devices*]
M & F........	Materials and Facilities (MCD)
M & F........	Mother and Father
M&FCS........	Management and Financial Control System (SAUO)
MANDFHAB...	Male and Female Homosexual Association of Great Britain
M & G........	Macnaghten and Gordon's English Chancery Reports [*A publication*] (DLA)
M & G........	Maddock and Geldart's English Chancery Reports [*1815-22*] [*A publication*] (DLA)
M & G........	Manning and Granger's English Common Pleas Reports [*A publication*] (DLA)
M & G........	Mapping and Geodesy [*Army*] (AABC)
M&G..........	Mercantile & General Reinsurance Co. Ltd. (SAUO)
M&G..........	Mobile & Gulf (SAUO)
M & Gel......	Maddock and Geldart's English Chancery Reports [*1815-22*] [*A publication*] (DLA)
M & GN......	Midland and Great Northern Joint Line [*Railway*] [*British*] (ROG)
M&GN........	Midland and Great Northern Joint Railway (SAUO)
M&GNR.......	Midland and Great Northern Railway (SAUO)
M & Gord....	Macnaghten and Gordon's English Chancery Reports [*A publication*] (DLA)
M&GWR.......	Midland and Great Western Railway (SAUO)
M&H..........	Malone & Hyde, Inc. (EFIS)
M&H..........	Mason and Hangar (SAUO)
M & H........	Murphy and Hurlstone's English Exchequer Reports [*1836-37*] [*A publication*] (DLA)
M & HDA.....	Medical and Hospital Department, Army
M&HDA.......	Medical and Hospital Department, U.S. Army (SAUO)
M&I...........	Management and Integration (SAUO)
M & I.........	Manpower and Immigration [*Canada*]
M & I.........	Marine & Industrial
M & I.........	Marshall & Ilsley Bank
M & I.........	Minnesota & International Railway
M & I.........	Modernization and Improvement (AABC)
M & I.........	Modification and Installation (KSC)
M & I.........	Moisture and Impurities [*In fats*]
M & I.........	Movements and Identification [*Military*] (AFM)
M&I...........	Movements and Identification (SAUO)
M & I.........	Municipal and Industrial [*Users of water*]
M&IP.........	Management and Integration Plan (SAUO)
Man Dir......	Managing Director (SAUO)
Man Dir......	Managing Directress (SAUO)
M & IR.......	Manufacturing and Inspection Record (KSC)
M & K........	Mylne and Keen's English Chancery Reports [*A publication*] (DLA)
M and L......	Management and Logistics [*NATO*] (NATG)
mandl.........	Mandorla (VRA)
M&L..........	Matched and Lost [*Investment term*] (DFIT)
M & LA......	Manpower and Logistics Analysis
M&LC........	Mission and Launch Control (ACAE)
M&LS.........	Manistique & Lake Superior (SAUO)
M&M..........	Maintenance Management Committee (SAUO)
M & M........	Make and Mend
M & M........	Manchester & Milford Railway [*Wales*]
M & M........	Martha and the Muffins [*Musical group*]
M & M........	Materials and Maintenance (NASA)
M & M........	Merchants and Manufacturers Association (EA)
M&M..........	Mess and Maintenance [*Marine Corps*] (MUSM)
M & M........	Metals and Minerals Research Services [*British*]
M & M........	Milk and Molasses [*Enema*] [*Medicine*]
M&M..........	Mining & Metallurgy Divisions (ACII)
M & M Bills.....	Montagu and MacArthur's English Bankruptcy Reports [*A publication*] (DLA)
M & M........	Moody and Malkin's English Nisi Prius Reports [*A publication*] (DLA)
M&M..........	Morbidity and Mortality [*Medicine*] (DMAA)
M & M'A.....	Montagu and MacArthur's English Bankruptcy Reports [*A publication*] (DLA)
M & McA....	Montagu and MacArthur's English Bankruptcy Reports [*A publication*] (DLA)
M & M's......	Mass and Meals [*Refers to nuns who appear only at these activities*]
M & N	May and November [*Denotes semiannual payments of interest or dividends in these months*] [*Business term*]
M & N	Medical and Nursing [*Red Cross Disaster Services*]
M & N	Morning and Night [*Medicine*]
M&N...........	Mydriacyl and Neosynephrine [*Medicine*] (MELL)
M & NA.....	Missouri & North Arkansas Railroad [*Nickname: May Never Arrive*]
M & NE......	Manistee & Northeastern Railroad (IIA)
M&NE.........	Manistee and North-Eastern Railway Co. (SAUO)
M & NW.....	Minnesota & Northwestern Railroad
M & O	Machinery and Optics
M & O	Maintenance and Operation (MCD)
m & o	Maintenance and Overhaul (AD)
M & O	Maintenance and Overhaul
M&O...........	Management and Operating (AUEG)
M&O...........	Management and Operations (ABAC)
m & o	Management and Organization (AD)
M & O	Management and Organization
M&O...........	Management and Oversight (SAUO)
MANDO........	Mancando [*Decreasing in Loudness*] [*Music*] (ROG)
M & O	Manpower and Organization [*Military*]
M & O	Materials and Others
M & O	Mobile & Ohio Railroad
M & O	Muscat and Oran (AD)
M & OB	Maintenance and Operations Branch [*BUPERS*]
M & OC	Monitor and Operations Control System [*Space Flight Operations Facility, NASA*]
M&P...........	Maintenance and Process Engineering (SAUO)
M&P...........	Managerial and Professional (DMAA)
M & P.........	Maryland & Pennsylvania Railroad Co. (IIA)
M & P.........	Material and Process
m & p	Materials and Processes (AD)
M&P...........	Materials and Processing (SAUO)
M&P...........	Materials and Producibility (SAUO)
M&P...........	Melphenal and Prednisone [*Medicine*] (MELL)
M & P.........	Moore and Payne's English Common Pleas Reports [*A publication*] (DLA)
M & PE......	Materials and Process Engineering (MCD)
M&PL.........	Materials and Processes List (ACAE)
M & PP......	Manitou & Pike's Peak Railway
M & PP......	Materials and Plant Protection [*Nuclear energy*] (NRCH)
M & P Sh	Maude and Pollock's Law of Merchant Shipping [*A publication*] (DLA)
M&Q..........	Mines and Quarries (AD)
M & R	Maclean and Robinson's Scotch Appeal Cases [*1839*] [*A publication*] (DLA)
m & r	Maintainability and Reliability (AD)
m & r	Maintainability and Repairs (AD)
M & R	Maintenance and Refurbishment (NASA)
M & R	Maintenance and Repair
M & R	Manning and Ryland's English King's Bench Reports [*1827-30*] [*A publication*] (DLA)
M&R..........	Martini & Rossi
M & R	Measure and Record
M & R	Moody and Robinson's English Nisi Prius Reports [*1830-44*] [*A publication*] (DLA)
M & RA.....	Manpower and Reserve Affairs
MANDRA.....	Mid-Atlantic Nostalgia Drag Racing Association
M & RDET ...	Maintenance and Repair Detachment
M & RE.......	Money and Real Estate [*Newspaper section*] (ADA)
M&RF.........	Maintenance and Refurbishing Facility [*Aerospace*] (NAKS)
M & R I & O...	Measure and Record Intake and Output [*Fluid measurement*] [*Medicine*] (CPH)
M & RMC	Manning and Ryland's English Magistrates' Cases [*1827-30*] [*A publication*] (DLA)
M&RO..........	Maintenance and Refurbishment Operations (SAUS)
MANDRO	Mechanically-Alterable Nondestructive Read Out [*Computer science*] (IAA)
M & Rob......	Maclean and Robinson's Scotch Appeal Cases [*1839*] [*A publication*] (DLA)
M & Rob......	Moody and Robinson's English Nisi Prius Reports [*A publication*] (DLA)
M & S.........	Bureau of Medicine and Surgery [*Navy*]
M&S..........	Maintainability and Supportability (ACAE)
M & S.........	Maintenance and Supply
MANDS........	Maintenance and Supply
M & S.........	Manning and Scott's English Common Bench Reports [*IX*] [*A publication*] (DLA)
M & S.........	March and September [*Denotes semiannual payments of interest or dividends in these months*] [*Business term*]

M&S	Marketing & Sales Division (ACII)
M & S	Marks & Spencer [*English department store chain*]
M&S	Marred & Scarred (SAUS)
M & S	Marshall and Swift Cost Index (DICI)
M & S	Materials and Services [*NASA*] (KSC)
M & S	Materials and Structures (SDI)
M&S	Maternity and Surgical (AD)
M & S	Maule and Selwyn's English King's Bench Reports [*A publication*] (DLA)
M & S	McClelland & Stewart [*Canadian publisher*]
M & S	Media and Status [*Code*] [*DoD*]
M&S	Medical and Surgical (AD)
M & S	Medicine and Surgery (AD)
M & S	Methods and Standards
M & S	Microculture and Sensitivity [*Laboratory*] (DAVI)
M & S	Milwaukee & Superior Railroad
M & S	Model and Series (AAG)
m & s	Model and Series (AD)
M & S	Modeling and Simulation
M & S	Moore and Scott's English Common Pleas Reports [*1831-34*] [*A publication*] (DLA)
m & s	Mud and Snow (AD)
M & S	Mud and Snow Tire [*Automotive engineering*]
M & SC	Missile and Space Council [*Defunct*] (EA)
M & Sc	Moore and Scott's English Common Pleas Reports [*1831-34*] [*A publication*] (DLA)
M & Scott	Moore and Scott's English Common Pleas Reports [*1831-34*] [*A publication*] (DLA)
MANDSD	Mean and Standard Deviation
M & SS	Mapping and Survey System (KSC)
M & SSq	Maintenance and Supply Squadron [*Air Force*]
M & StP	Milwaukee & St. Paul Railway
M&T	Main and Trim (COE)
M & T	Maintenance and Test (AAG)
M&T	Monitor and Test (ACAE)
M and T	Movements and Transports (NATG)
M&T	Muscles and Tendons (MELL)
M&TC	Mission and Traffic Control (ACAE)
M & TE	Measurement and Test Equipment (KSC)
M & TP	Manufacturing and Testing Process (KSC)
M & U	Middletown & Unionville Railroad [*Nickname: Miserable and Useless*]
M&V	Magmatism & Volcanoes (SAUS)
M and V	Meat-and-Vegetable [*A canned ration*] [*Military*]
M&W	Marine and War Risks [*Insurance*] (MARI)
M & W	Meeson and Welsby's English Exchequer Reports [*A publication*] (DLA)
M&W	Moore & Wright (WDAA)
M&W	Morecambe & Wise [*Comedians*] (WDAA)
M & WAA	Movers' and Warehousemen's Association of America [*Defunct*]
M & W Abr	Marshall and Wood's Abridgment [*A publication*] (DLA)
M & W Cas	Mining and Water Cases, Annotated [*United States*] [*A publication*] (DLA)
M & WH	Missile and Warhead Magazines
M & W Law Dic	Mozley and Whiteley's Law Dictionary [*A publication*] (ILCA)
M & X	Microscope and X-Ray Inspection
M & Y	Martin and Yerger's Tennessee Reports [*8 Tennessee*] [*1825-28*] [*A publication*] (DLA)
M and Yerger's Rep	Martin and Yerger's Tennessee Reports [*8 Tennessee*] [*1825-28*] [*A publication*] (DLA)
M & YR	Martin and Yerger's Tennessee Reports [*8 Tennessee*] [*1825-28*] [*A publication*] (DLA)
MAN ED	Managing Editor (DGA)
Man El Cas	Manning's English Election Cases (Court of Revision) [*A publication*] (DLA)
M Anesth Ed	Master of Anesthesiology Education (PGP)
MANEX	Management Experten-Nachweis [*Management Experts Data Base*] [*Society for Business Information*] [*Information service or system*] (IID)
Man Exch Pr	Manning's English Exchequer Practice [*A publication*] (DLA)
MANF	Manifold (KSC)
MANF	Manufacturer (WGA)
MANF	May, August, November, and February [*Denotes quarterly payments of interest or dividends in these months*] [*Business term*]
MANFED	Manufacturers Federation (SAUO)
MANFG	Manufacturing (ROG)
MANFIST	Maneuver and Fire Support Team (MCD)
Man For	Management Forum [*A publication*]
MANFOR	Manpower Force Packaging [*Military*]
MANFOR	Manpower Force Packaging System (SAUO)
MANFORCE	Manpower for a Clean Environment [*Water Pollution Control Federation*]
MANFR	Manufacturer
MANFRD	Manufactured
MANFRG	Manufacturing
MANFST	Manifest
MANG	Management
Man G & S	Manning, Granger, and Scott's English Common Bench Reports, Old Series [*I-VIII*] [*A publication*] (DLA)
Man Gaz	Manitoba Gazette [*A publication*] (DLA)
MANGR	Manager
Man Gr & S	Manning, Granger, and Scott's English Common Bench Reports, Old Series [*I-VIII*] [*A publication*] (DLA)
MANGRSS	Manageress (ROG)
MANGT	Management (ROG)
Manhattan C	Manhattan College (GAGS)

Manhattan Sch Music	Manhattan School of Music (GAGS)
Manhattanville C	Manhattanville College (GAGS)
MANHC	Madras Army Native Hospital Corps [*British military*] (DMA)
MAnHi	Andover Historical Society, Andover, MA [*Library symbol*] [*Library of Congress*] (LCLS)
ManhLfe	Manhattan Life Insurance Co. [*Associated Press*] (SAG)
MA-NHP	Massachusetts Natural Heritage Program [*Massachusetts State Division of Fisheries and Wildlife*] [*Information service or system*] (IID)
MANI	Manifold [*Automotive engineering*]
MANI	Midwest Alliance for Nursing Informatics (SAUO)
MANI	Minister of Agriculture for Northern Ireland (SAUO)
MANIAC	Mathematical Analyzer, Numerical Integrator and Computer
MANIAC	Mechanical and Numerical Integrator and Computer (IEEE)
MANICOM	Manned Information and Communications Facility (SAA)
MANIET	Manifest Update (SAUO)
MANIF	Manifest
manif	Manifesto (VRA)
manifest	Manifestation [*Medicine*]
MAnimSc	Master of Animal Science, University of Liverpool [*British*] (DBQ)
Man Int Law	Manning's Commentaries on the Law of Nations [*A publication*] (DLA)
Manip	All India Reporter, Manipur [*A publication*] (DLA)
manip	Manipulation [*Medicine*]
Manip	Manipulus [*A Handful*] [*Pharmacy*]
MANIP	Manual Input [*Computer science*]
MANIS	Modified Atlantic Naval Intelligence Summary
MANIT	Manitoba [*Canadian province*]
Manit	University of Manitoba (SAUO)
ManitDns	Manitoba Dragoons (SAUO)
Manitoba	Armour. Queen's Bench and County Court Reports Tempore Wood [*Manitoba*] [*A publication*] (DLA)
Manitoba	Manitoba Law Reports [*Canada*] [*A publication*] (DLA)
Manitoba L (Can)	Manitoba Law Reports [*Canada*] [*A publication*] (DLA)
Manitw	[*The*] Manitowoc Co., Inc. [*Associated Press*] (SAG)
MANIX	Machine Aids to Nike-X [*Army*] (AABC)
Mankato St U	Mankato State University (GAGS)
M-ANL	Argonne National Laboratory (SAUO)
MANL	Manual (IAA)
MANLA	Malawi National Liberation Army (BUAC)
Man Lim	Mansel on Limitations [*1839*] [*A publication*] (DLA)
MANLOS	Manportable Non-Line-Of-Sight (SAUS)
Man LR	Manitoba Law Reports [*Canada*] [*A publication*] (DLA)
Man LS Chron	Manchester Law Students' Chronicle [*A publication*] (DLA)
Man LSJ	Manchester Law Students' Journal [*A publication*] (DLA)
MANM	Methylated Albumin-Nitrocelluse Membrane [*Analytical biochemistry*]
MANMAM	Manufacturing Management (PDAA)
MANMAN	Manufacturing Management (MHDI)
MANMED	Manual of the Medical Department [*Navy*]
MANMEDDEPT	Manual of the Medical Department [*Navy*]
MANN	Manna [*Pharmacy*] (ROG)
Mann	Manning's Digest of the Nisi Prius Reports [*England*] [*A publication*] (DLA)
Mann	Manning's English Court of Revision Reports [*A publication*] (DLA)
Mann	Manning's Reports [*1 Michigan*] [*A publication*] (DLA)
MANN	Mannlicher Rifle
ManNac	N-Acetylmannosamine [*Biochemistry*]
Mann & G (Eng)	Manning and Granger's English Common Pleas Reports [*A publication*] (DLA)
Mann & R	Manning and Ryland's English King's Bench Reports [*1827-30*] [*A publication*] (DLA)
Mann & R	Manning and Ryland's English Magistrates' Cases [*1827-30*] [*A publication*] (DLA)
Mann & R (Eng)	Manning and Ryland's English King's Bench Reports [*1827-30*] [*A publication*] (DLA)
Mann Bills	Manning on Bills and Notes [*A publication*] (DLA)
Mann Com	Manning's Commentaries on the Law of Nations [*A publication*] (DLA)
Mann EC	Manning's Revision Cases [*1832-35*] [*A publication*] (DLA)
Mann Ex Pr	Manning's English Exchequer Practice [*A publication*] (DLA)
Mann G & S	Manning, Granger, and Scott's English Common Bench Reports [*135-39 English Reprint*] [*1845-56*] [*A publication*] (DLA)
Mann G & S (Eng)	Manning, Granger, and Scott's English Common Bench Reports, Old Series [*I-VIII*] [*A publication*] (DLA)
Manning	Manning's Reports [*1 Michigan*] [*A publication*] (DLA)
Manning	Manning's Unreported Cases [*Louisiana*] [*A publication*] (DLA)
Manning LA	Manning's Unreported Cases [*Louisiana*] [*A publication*] (DLA)
Manning's UC	Manning's Unreported Cases [*Louisiana*] [*A publication*] (DLA)
Manning's Unrep Cases	Manning's Unreported Cases [*Louisiana*] [*A publication*] (DLA)
Mann Nat	Manning's Commentaries on the Law of Nations [*A publication*] (DLA)
Mann Unrep Cas	Manning's Unreported Cases [*Louisiana*] [*A publication*] (DLA)
MANO	Manometer
MANO	Mexican-American Neighborhood Association (SAUO)
MANOP	Manganese Nodule Program [*For sampling on ocean floor*]
MANOP	Manual of Operations
MANOR	Manor [*Commonly used*] (OPSA)
ManorCr	Manor Care, Inc. [*Associated Press*] (SAG)
MANORS	Manors [*Commonly used*] (OPSA)
MANOVA	Multivariate Analysis of Variance [*Statistics*]
MANOVA	Multiway Analysis of Variance (MCD)
MANP	Masai Amboseli National Park (SAUO)
MANP	Mount Apo National Park (SAUO)
MANP	Mount Arayat National Park (SAUO)

MAnP........... Phillips Academy, Andover, MA [Library symbol] [Library of Congress] (LCLS)
MANPAD...... Man-Portable Air Defense (AABC)
MANPADS.... Man-Portable Air Defense System (MCD)
MANPER...... Manpower/Personnel Module (SAUO)
MANPER-B... Manpower and Personnel Module-Base Level (SAUO)
MANPER-M... Manpower and Personnel Module-Major Command Level (SAUO)
MANPLAWS... Manportable Assault Laser Weapons System (ACAE)
MAN PR...... Mane Primo [Early in the Morning] [Pharmacy]
MANPRINT... Manpower and Personnel Integration [Military] (RDA)
MANPRINT... Manpower, Personnel and Training Integration (SAUO)
Manpwl........ Manpower, Inc. [Associated Press] (SAG)
MANPWR..... Manpower (KSC)
MANR.......... Manager (ROG)
Man R .... Manitoba Reports [Maritime Law Book Co. Ltd.] [Information service or system] [A publication] [A publication] (DLA)
MANR.......... Ministry of Agriculture and Natural Resources [Nigeria] (BUAC)
MANR.......... Ministry of Agriculture, Northern Region (SAUO)
Man Ray ..... Emmanuel Radnitsky [American artist, 1890-1976]
MANREQ...... Manpower Requirements System (SAUO)
Man Rev Stat... Manitoba Revised Statutes [Canada] [A publication] (DLA)
MANRRDC ... Manpower Resources Research and Development Center [Army] (RDA)
Man RT Wood... Manitoba Reports Tempore Wood [Canada] [A publication] (DLA)
Mans .... Mansfield College, Oxford (SAUO)
Mans .... Mansfield's Reports [49-52 Arkansas] [A publication] (DLA)
MANS .... Mansiones
MANS .... Mansions
Mans .... Manson's English Bankruptcy and Winding-Up Cases [A publication] (DLA)
MANS .... Map Analysis System [Computer science]
MANS .... Mathematics Applied to novel Situations Test (EDAC)
MANS .... Michigan Association of Non-Public Schools
MANS .... Microcosm Autonomous Navigation System (ADWA)
MANS .... Missile and Nudet Surveillance (SAUS)
MANS .... Mission Analysis for Missile and NUDET Surveillance (SAUO)
MANSA .... Man-Made Soling Association Ltd. [British] (BI)
ManSA .... Manufacturing Society of Australia (SAUO)
MAN/SAFE ... Manual/Automatic Separation and Flotation Equipment (DNAB)
MANSAT .... Manned Satellite
Mans Dem... Mansel on Demurrer [1828] [A publication] (DLA)
Mansf .... Mansfield College, Oxford (SAUO)
Mansf Coll... Mansfield College, Oxford (SAUO)
Mansf Dig.... Mansfield's Digest of Statutes [Arkansas] [A publication] (DLA)
Mansfield U... Mansfield University of Pennsylvania (GAGS)
MANSH........ Manshead [England]
Mans Lim..... Mansel on Limitations [1839] [A publication] (DLA)
Manson....... Manson's English Bankruptcy and Winding-Up Cases [A publication] (DLA)
Manson Bankr Cas... Manson's English Bankruptcy and Winding-Up Cases [A publication] (DLA)
Mans on C... Mansel on Costs [A publication] (DLA)
Manson (Eng)... Manson's English Bankruptcy Cases [A publication] (DLA)
Man Stat...... Manitoba Statutes [Canada] [A publication] (DLA)
MANSWG..... Manpower Systems Work Group
M Ant........... Marcus Antoninus [of Scriptores Historiae Augustae] [Classical studies] (OCD)
MANT........... Master of Arts in New Testament (PGP)
MANTAPS.... Maneuver Arms Tactical Protective System [Army] (RDA)
MANTECH.... Manufacturing Technology
MANTIS .... Man-in-the-loop Target Interdiction System (SAUS)
MANTIS .... Manpack Tactical Intelligence System
MANTIS .... Manual, Alternative, and Natural Therapy Index System (ADWA)
MANTIS .... Manufacturing Team Information Systems (SAUO)
MANTRA....... Middle Atmosphere Nitrogen Trend Assessment
MANTRAC..... Manual Angle Tracking Capability
MANTRAP.... Management Training Program [of Center for Research in Business and Economics, University of Houston]
MANTRAPERS... Manpower, Training, and Personnel (MCD)
Mantrn........ Manatron, Inc. [Associated Press] (SAG)
Man T Wood... Manitoba Reports Tempore Wood [Canada] [A publication] (DLA)
manu .... Manufacture (DAVI)
MANU .... Manugistics Group [NASDAQ symbol] (TTSB)
MANU .... Manugistics Group, Inc. [NASDAQ symbol] (SAG)
MANU .... Mozambique African National Union [Later, FRELIMO]
manuf.......... Manufactured (SHCU)
MANUF........ Manufacturer [or Manufacturing] (ROG)
Manuf.......... Manufactures (DIAR)
Manuf.......... Manufacturing (SAUO)
Manufacturing Mgmt... Manufacturing and Management [A publication]
MANUFD...... Manufactured (ROG)
MANUFG...... Manufacturing (ADA)
ManufHm...... Manufactured Home Communities, Inc. [Associated Press] (SAG)
Manugist ..... Manugistics Group, Inc. [Associated Press] (SAG)
Manum Cas... Bloomfield's Manumission (or Negro) Cases [New Jersey] [A publication] (DLA)
Manum Cases... Bloomfield's Manumission (or Negro) Cases [New Jersey] [A publication] (DLA)
Man Unr Cases... Manning's Unreported Cases [Louisiana] [A publication] (DLA)
Man Unrep Cas... Manning's Unreported Cases [Louisiana] [A publication] (DLA)
Man Unrep Cas (LA)... Manning's Unreported Cases [Louisiana] [A publication] (DLA)
MANUPACS... Manufacturing Planning and Control System (PDAA)
MANUV........ Maneuvering (KSC)
Manvl .... Manville Corp. [Associated Press] (SAG)

Manvlle .... Manville Corp. [Associated Press] (SAG)
MANVOS...... Manual Visas for Overseas System [Australia]
Manw........... Manwood's Forest Laws [1592, 1598, 1615] [A publication] (DLA)
MANWEB...... Merseyside and North Wales Electricity Board (SAUO)
Manw For Law... Manwood's Forest Laws [1592, 1598, 1615] [A publication] (DLA)
Manwood.... Manwood's Forest Laws [1592, 1598, 1615] [A publication] (DLA)
MANX .... Mannion Air Charter, Inc. [Air carrier designation symbol]
MANZ .... Medical Association of New Zealand (BUAC)
MANZ .... Montreal, Australia and New Zealand Shipping Co. Ltd. (SAUO)
MANZ .... Montreal-Australia New Zealand (SAUO)
MANZ .... Motel Association of New Zealand (SAUO)
MANZCP...... Member, Australian & New Zealand College of Psychiatry (CMD)
MAO........... MAC Aviation SL [Spain] [ICAO designator] (FAAC)
MAO........... Magnetic Amplifier Output
MAO........... Mailing Address Only [Military] (AABC)
MAO........... Maintenance and Operation [Army] (AFIT)
MAO........... Major Attack Option [Military] (MCD)
MAO........... Manaus [Brazil] [Airport symbol] (OAG)
MAO........... Manned Apollo Operations [NASA] (KSC)
mao........... Maori [MARC language code] [Library of Congress] (LCCP)
MAO........... Marion, SC [Location identifier] [FAA] (FAAL)
MAO........... Mars Aeronomy Orbiter (MCD)
MAO........... Massive Attack Option (MCD)
MAO........... Master of Art of Oratory
MAO........... Master of the Art of Obstetrics
MAO........... Matair Ltd. [British] [ICAO designator] (FAAC)
MAO........... Material Adjustment Order (MCD)
MAO........... Maximum [or Minimum] Acid Output [Clinical chemistry]
MAO........... Mechanization of Algebraic Operations (PDAA)
MAO........... Medial Ankle Orthosis [Orthopedics] (DAVI)
MAO........... Medical Assistance Only (GFGA)
MAO........... Methylaluminoxane [Organic chemistry]
MAO........... Methyl Aluminoxane Cocatalyst
MAO........... Military Assistance Officer [Army]
MAO........... Monoamine Oxidase [An enzyme]
MAO........... Monoamin Oxidase Inhibitors [An antidepressant]
MAO........... Movement to Arrest Oppressors (EA)
MAO........... Muhammadan Anglo-Oriental
MAOA......... Meteorological Aspects of Ocean Affairs [Marine science] (MSC)
MAOA......... Meyers Aircraft Owners Association (EA)
MAOA......... Mid-America Orthopaedic Association (SAUO)
MAOA......... Monoamine Oxidase A [An enzyme]
MAOA......... Panel of Meteorological Aspects of Ocean Affairs [Marine science] (OSRA)
MAO-B......... Monoamine Oxidase B [An enzyme]
MAODP........ Medic Alert Organ Donor Program (EA)
MAOE.......... Manchester Association of Engineers (SAUO)
MAOE.......... Master of Adult and Occupational Education (PGP)
MAOF.......... Mexican-American Opportunity Foundation (EA)
MA of A .... Motel Association of America (SAUO)
MAOI.......... Monoamine Oxidase Inhibitor [Biochemistry]
MAOM .... Master of Aerospace Operations Management (GAGS)
MAOP .... Maximum Allowable Operating Pressure [In pipelines]
MAOS .... Magnetic Amplifier Output Stage
MAOS .... Metal Alumina Dielectric Oxide Semiconductor (CIST)
MAOS .... Metal-Alumina-Oxide Semiconductor [Computer science] (IAA)
MAOS .... Metal-Aluminum-Oxide Silicon (MSA)
MAOS .... Minimum Aircraft Operating Strips (SAUO)
MAOS .... Minimum Airfield Operating Surface [Military]
MAOT .... Master of Arts in Occupational Therapy
MAOT .... Master of Arts in Old Testament (PGP)
MAOT .... Maximum Allowable Operating Time (NASA)
MAOT .... Medium Aperture Optical Telescope (PDAA)
MAOT .... Member, Association of Occupational Therapists [British]
MAOT .... Member of the Association of Occupational Therapists (SAUO)
MAOT .... Military Assistance Observer Team
MAOT .... Missile Auxiliary Output Tester
MAOT .... Mobile Air Operations Team [Military]
MAOTS .... Missile Auxiliary Output Testers (ACAE)
MAOU .... Member of the American Ornithologists' Union
MAOV .... Mobile Artillery Observation Vehicle (SAUS)
MAP........... Aeronautical Maps and charts (SAUS)
MAP........... Machine Analyzer Package (PDAA)
MAP........... Machinist Apprentice Program (SAUO)
MAP........... Macro Arithmetic Processor [Computer science] (MDG)
MAP........... Macroassembly Program [Computer science]
MAP........... Madeira Abyssal Plain [Geology]
MAP........... Maghreb-Arabe Presse [Maghreb Arab Press Agency] [Morocco]
MAP........... Magnetic-Acoustic-Pressure (NVT)
MAP........... Main Arithmetic Processor (IAA)
MAP........... Maine Public Service [AMEX symbol] (TTSB)
MAP........... Maine Public Service Co. [AMEX symbol] (SPSG)
MAP........... Mainly about People [A publication]
MAP........... Main Memory, Arithmetic Unit, and Post Processor (ACAE)
MAP........... Maintenance Administration Panel (ACRL)
MAP........... Maintenance Analysis Procedure [Computer science]
MAP........... Maintenance Analysis Program [NASA] (KSC)
MAP........... Maintenance and Administration Position (SAUO)
MAP........... Maitre en Administration Publique [Master of Public Administration]
MAP........... Major Point (VLIE)
map........... Malayo-Polynesian [MARC language code] [Library of Congress] (LCCP)
MAP........... Malaysian Alliance Party (SAUO)
MAP........... Mamai [Papua New Guinea] [Airport symbol] (OAG)
MAP........... Management Action Program (ACAE)

MAP............ Management Analysis and Projection (VLIE)
MAP............ Management Analysis [or Assessment] Program
MAP............ Management and Planning Committee [Library of Congress]
MAP............ Management and Programming (IAA)
MAP............ Management Application Protocol (ACRL)
MAP............ Management Assessment Program (SAUO)
MAP............ Management Assistance for Profits
MAP............ Management Assistance Program (SAUO)
MAP............ Management Association of the Philippines (BUAC)
MAP............ Management of an Accounting Practice (SAUO)
MAP............ Manifold Absolute Pressure
MAP............ Manifold Air Pressure
MAP............ Manpower [A publication]
MAP............ Manpower Absorption Plan [Department of Labor]
MAP............ Manpower Analysis Paper
MAP............ Manpower Analysis Procedure (VLIE)
MAP............ Manpower Assistance Project [Department of Labor]
MAP............ Manufacturers' Assistance Program [Michigan State Department of Commerce] [Lansing, MI] [Information service or system] (IID)
MAP............ Manufacturing Activity Projection
MAP............ Manufacturing Automation Protocol [Data communications standards]
MAP............ Map Analysis Package (SAUO)
MAP............ MAP [Medical Assistance Programs] International (EA)
MAP............ Maples, MO [Location identifier] [FAA] (FAAL)
MAP............ Mapping (MSA)
MAP............ Mapping Alliance Program (SAUO)
MAP............ Map section of AIP (SAUS)
MAP............ Marine Advisory Program [Marine science] (MSC)
MAP............ Market Area Planner (SAUO)
MAP............ Marketing Action Planner [National Association of Printers and Lithographers] [A publication]
MAP............ Marketing Assistance Program [Department of Agriculture]
MAP............ Mars Atmosphere Probe
MAP............ Master Activity Programming
MAP............ Master Air Pilot
MAP............ Master Attack Plan [Military] (DOMA)
MAP............ Master Automation Plan (ACAE)
MAP............ Master of Applied Psychology (PGP)
MAP............ Master of Arts in Planning (PGP)
MAP............ Material Acquisition Process [or Program] (MCD)
MAP............ Material Archive Program
MAP............ Materiel Acquisition Plan [Army]
MAP............ Mathematical Analysis without Programming [Computer science]
MAP............ Maxilla Alveolar Process [Medicine] (MELL)
MAP............ Maximal Aerobic Power [Laboratory] (DAVI)
MAP............ Maximum A Posteriori [Statistics]
MAP............ Maximum Average Pressure
MAP............ Maximum Average Price
MAP............ Mean Airway Pressure [Medicine] (DMAA)
MAP............ Mean Aortic Pressure [Medicine]
MAP............ Mean Arterial Pressure [Medicine]
MAP............ Measurement Analysis Program (VLIE)
MAP............ Measurement Assurance Program [National Institute of Standards and Technology]
MAP............ Measure of Academic Progress [Educational test]
MAP............ Mechanized Assignment Processing (VLIE)
MAP............ Mecury All Position (IAA)
MAP............ Media Access Project (EA)
MAP............ Media Analysis Project (EA)
MAP............ Media and People [Information service or system] (IID)
MAP............ Medical Aid for the Palestinians (BUAC)
MAP............ Medical Aid Post
MAP............ Medical Assistace Program [Public human service program] (PHSD)
MAP............ Medical Audit Program [Computerized system of abstracted medical record information]
MAP............ Medicare Advocacy Project
MAP............ Mediterranean Action Plan (BUAC)
MAP............ Megaloblastic Anemia of Pregnancy [Obstetrics] (MAE)
MAP............ Melanesian Alliance Party (SAUO)
MAP............ Melphalan, Adriamycin, Prednisone [Antineoplastic drug regimen]
MAP............ Memory Allocation and Protection
MAP............ Memory Allocation Map (VLIE)
MAP............ Memory Allocation Processor (NITA)
MAP............ Mercapturic Acid Pathway [Biochemistry]
MAP............ Mesenterial Arterial Pressure [Medicine]
MAP............ Message Acceptance Pulse [Aerospace communications]
MAP............ Meta-Aminophenol [Organic chemistry]
MAP............ Meta-Aminopyrimethamine [Biochemistry]
MAP............ Methionyl Aminopeptidase [An enzyme]
MAP............ Methyl Acceptor Protein [Biochemistry] (DAVI)
MAP............ Methylacetoxyprogesterone [Also, MPA] [Endocrinology]
MAP............ Methylacetylene Propadiene [Organic chemistry]
MAP............ Methyl(acetylenyl)putrescine [Biochemistry]
MAP............ Methyl Alcohol Poisoning [Medicine] (MELL)
MAP............ Methyl(amino)propanediol [Organic chemistry]
MAP............ Methylaminopurine (MAE)
MAP............ Microelectronics Application Programme (AIE)
MAP............ Microelectronics Application Project [British] (DCTA)
MAP............ Microlithiasis Alveolarum Pulmonum (DB)
MAP............ Microprocessor Application Project [In manufacturing industry] [Department of the Interior]
MAP............ Microprogrammed Array Processor
MAP............ Microtubule-Associated Protein [Cytology]
MAP............ Microwave Anisotropy Probe [NASA]
MAP............ Microwave Anistropy Probe

MAP............ Middle Atmosphere Programme [International Council of Scientific Unions]
MAP............ Migrant Action Program (OICC)
MAP............ Milestone Analysis Procedure
MAP............ Military Airport Plan [FAA] (TAG)
MAP............ Military Assistance Program [DoD]
MAP............ Military Assistant Program (SAUO)
MAP............ Military Association of Podiatrists [Later, FSPMA] (EA)
MAP............ Military Audit Project
MAP............ Military Awards Profile [Information service or system] (IID)
MAP............ Miller Assessment for Preschoolers
MAP............ Million Annual Passengers (SAUO)
MAP............ MILSTAR Advanced Processor (SAUS)
MAP............ Minimal Audible Pressure (DIPS)
MAP............ Minimum Acceptable Performance [Telecommunications] (TEL)
MAP............ Minimum Annual Premium (MHDW)
MAP............ Minimum Association Price (WDAA)
MAP............ Minimum Attack Parameter [Military]
MAP............ Minimum Audible Pressure
MAP............ Ministry of Aircraft Production [British]
MAP............ Ministry of Aviation Technology (SAUO)
MAP............ Minorities Advancement Plan
MAP............ Missed Approach Point [Aviation] (AFM)
MAP............ Missed Approach Procedure [Aviation]
MAP............ Missile and Package Tester
MAP............ Missile Application Propulsion
MAP............ Missile Assignment Program (SAA)
MAP............ Mission Activity Plan (ACAE)
MAP............ Mission Application Program (NASA)
MAP............ Mission Area Plans (ACAE)
MAP............ Mission Automation Plan (SAUO)
MAP............ Missouri Assessment Program
MAP............ Mitigation Action Plans (COE)
MAP............ Mitogen-Activated Protein [Biochemistry]
MAP............ Mixed Aniline Point
MAP............ Mobile Access Part (CGWS)
MAP............ Model Accreditation Plan (AUEG)
MAP............ Model and Program [Computer science]
MAP............ Modern Aids to Planning (SAUO)
MAP............ Modification Application Plan [Army]
MAP............ Modified American Plan [Travel]
MAP............ Modified Atmosphere Packaging (SAUS)
MAP............ Modified Atmospheric Packaging [Food industry]
MAP............ Modular Acoustic Panel
MAP............ Modular Analysis Processor [Applied Data Research, Inc.]
MAP............ Modular Application Program (VLIE)
MAP............ Modular Application System [Computer science]
MAP............ Modular Array Processor; Hughes Aircraft Co. (SAUO)
MAP............ Modular Assembly Prosthesis [Medicine]
MAP............ Monitoring Attitudes of the Public [ACLI]
MAP............ Monitoring the AIDS Pandemic (SAUO)
MAP............ Monoammonium Phosphate [Inorganic chemistry]
MAP............ Monophasic Action Potential [Electrophysiology] (AAMN)
MAP............ Mothers of AIDS [Acquired Immune Deficiency Syndrome] Patients (EA)
MAP............ Mouse Antibody Production [Test for virus]
MAP............ Movement of the Assemblies of People [Grenada]
MAP............ Multi-Access Pointer (PCM)
MAP............ Multibus Accounting Package (PDAA)
MAP............ Multichannel Astrometric Photometer [Astronomy]
MAP............ Multicoverage Account Program [Insurance]
MAP............ Multicultural Australia Papers [A publication]
MAP............ Multifunction Adaptive Processor (NITA)
MAP............ Multiple Address Processing
MAP............ Multiple Aim Point [ICBM]
MAP............ Multiple Allocation Procedure [PERT]
MAP............ Multiple Antigen Peptide [Medicine] (MELL)
MAP............ Multiple Array Processor
MAP............ Municipal Airport (MCD)
MAP............ Muscle Action Potential
MAP............ Museum Assessment Program [National Foundation on the Arts and the Humanities]
MAP............ Musical Aptitude Profile
MAP............ Mutamycin, Adriamycin, Platinol [Antineoplastic drug] (CDI)
MAP............ Mutual African Press Agency
MAP............ Mutual Assistance Pact
MAP............ Mutual Assistance Plan (NATG)
MAP............ Mutual Assistance Program
MAP............ National Oceanic and Atmospheric Administration [ICAO designator] (FAAC)
MAP3S........ Multistate Atmospheric Power Production Pollution Study [Department of Energy]
MAP3S/PCN... Multistate Atmospheric Power Production Pollution Study/ Precipitation Chemistry Network (SAUO)
MAP27........ Mobile Access Protocol (SAUS)
MAPA......... Malayan Agricultural Producers Association (SAUO)
MAPA......... Malaysian Airlines Pilots Association (SAUO)
MAPA......... Master of Arts in Public Administration (GAGS)
MAPA......... Master of Arts in Public Affairs (GAGS)
MAPA......... Materials and Product Assurance (TIMI)
MAPA......... Mexican-American Political Association
MAPA......... Mooney Aircraft Pilots Association (EA)
MAPA......... Muscle Adenosine Phosphoric Acid [Biochemistry] (DB)
MAPAC....... Marine Pollution Advisory Committee (SAUO)
MAPAC ...... Military Assistance Program Address Code (ACAE)

MAPAD	Military Assistance Program Address Directory
MAPAF	Military Assistance Program Address File
MAPAG	Military Assistance Program Advisory Group
MAPAG	Multi-Association Policy Advisory Group [*An association*]
MAPAI	Mifleget Po'alei Eretz-Yisrael (BJA)
MAPAM	Mifleget Po'alim Me'uhedet (BJA)
MAPAR	Materials and Processes Acceptance Requirement
MAPAS	Master of Arts in Public Administration in Spanish (PGP)
MAPASE	Mobile Application Part-Application Service Elements (SAUS)
MAPBIN	Mauritian Action for Promotion of Breast-Feeding and Infant Nutrition (BUAC)
MAPC	Manpower Model for Control Agencies (SAUO)
MAPC	Master of Arts in Pastoral Counseling (PGP)
MAPC	Maximum Allowable Pevailing Charge [*Medicine*]
MAPC	Migrating Action Potential Complex [*Electrophysiology*]
MAPC	Minnesota Association of Private Colleges (SAUO)
MAPCC	Master of Arts in Pastoral Care and Counseling (PGP)
MAPCC	Military Assistance Program Country Code (AFM)
MAPCHE	Mobile Automatic Programmed Checkout Equipment
MAP/CIO	Military Assistance Program/Common Item Order
MAPCO	Malaysian Association of Private Colleges
MAPCO	Map Code (SAUS)
MAPCO	MAPCO, Inc. [*Associated Press*] (SAG)
MAPCO	Mid-American Pipeline Co.
MAPCON	Microprocessor Applications Consultancy (NITA)
MAPD	Master Part Dimensioned (MCD)
MAPD	Maximum Allowable Percent Defective (PDAA)
MAPDA	Mid-America Periodical Distributors Association
MAPDFA	Media-Advertising Partnership for a Drug-Free America [*Later, DFA*] (EA)
MAPDU	Management Application Protocol Data Unit [*Telecommunications*] (OSI)
MAPE	Master of Arts in Physical Education (GAGS)
MAPE	Master of Arts in Political Economy (PGP)
MAPE	Maximum Absolute Percentage Error [*Statistics*]
MAPE	Mean Absolute Percentage Error [*Statistics*]
MAPE	Microcomputers and Primary Education
MAPES	Management of Personnel Records (SAUO)
MAPESS	Ministry of Public Administration, Employment and Social Security (SAUO)
MAP estimate...	Maximum a Posteriori Estimate
MAPETT	Military Assistance Program Evaluation Team, Thailand (CINC)
MAPEX	Map Exercise [*Military*] (INF)
MAPEX	Mid-America Payment Exchange
MAPEX	Military Articles Pacific Excesses (AFIT)
MAPF	Microatomized Protein Food (MAE)
MAPF	Mobile Aerial Port Flight [*Air Force*]
MAPG	Maximum Available Power Gain (MSA)
MAPG	Monograph Advisory Planning Group (ACAE)
MAP-GA	Military Assistance Program - Grant Aid
MAPGEN	Map Generator (MHDI)
MAPHI	Member of the Association of Public Health Inspectors (SAUO)
MAPHILINDO...	Malaysia, Philippines, Indonesia (SAUO)
MAPI	Machinery and Allied Products Institute (MHDI)
MAPI	Mail Application Programming Interface [*Computer science*] (PCM)
MAPI	Mail Applications Program Interface [*Microsoft Corp.*]
MAPI	Manufacturers Alliance (NTPA)
MAPI	Manufacturers Alliance for Productivity and Innovation (EA)
MAPI	Messaging API [*Application Programming Interface*] [*Computer science*]
MAPI	Microbial Alkaline Protease Inhibitor (DB)
MAPI	Millon Adolescent Personality Inventory [*Personality development test*] [*Psychology*]
MAPI	Mitsubishi Atomic Power Industries (IAA)
MAPICS	Manufacturing, Accounting and Product Information Central System (NITA)
MAPICS	Manufacturing, Accounting, and Production Information Control System [*IBM Corp.*]
MAPID	Machine-Aided Program for Preparation of Instruction Data
MapInfo	Mapinfo Corp. [*Associated Press*] (SAG)
MAPIS	Map Products Information System (SAUO)
MAPK	Mitogen Activated Protein Kinase [*An enzyme*]
MaPKBS	Map Projection Knowledge-based System (SAUO)
MAPL	Manufacturing Assembly Parts List
MAPL	Master Allowance Parts List [*Military*] (CAAL)
MAPL	Military Acquisition Position List (RDA)
MAPLA	Military Assistance Program Logistics Agency [*Merged with Defense Supply Agency*]
MAPLE	Marketing and Product Line Evaluation (PDAA)
MAPLE	Minor Atomic Prolonged Life Equipment (PDAA)
Maple Flag...	Exercise held in Canada (SAUS)
Maple Tech Newsl...	Maple Technical Newsletter (SAUO)
MAPLHGN....	Maximum Average Planar Linear Heat-Generator [*Nuclear energy*] (IAA)
MAPLHGR....	Maximum Average Planar Linear Heat-Generation Rate [*Nuclear energy*] (NRCH)
MAPM	Master of Arts in Pastoral Ministry (PGP)
MAPM	Master of Arts in Pastoral Music (PGP)
M Ap Ma	Master of Applied Mathematics (PGP)
MAP Min	Master of Arts in Pastoral Ministry (PGP)
MAPMIS	Manpower and Personnel Management Information System [*Navy*]
MAPMISMAN...	Manpower and Personnel Management Information System Manual [*Navy*]
MAPMOPP ...	Marine Pollution [*or Petroleum*] Monitoring Pilot Project [*Marine science*] (MSC)
MAPNY	Maritime Association of the Port of New York [*Later, MAPONY/NJ*] (EA)
MAPOLE	Magnetic Dipole Spark Transmitter (NASA)
MAPOM	Military Assistance Program Owned Materiel (AFM)
MAP/One	Manufacturing Automation Protocol/One [*Local area network*] [*Industrial Networking, Inc.*]
MAPONY......	Maritime Association of the Port of New York
MAPONY/NJ..	Maritime Association of the Port of New York/New Jersey (EA)
MAPORD......	Methodology Approach to Planning and Programming Air Force Operational Requirements, Research and Development (IEEE)
MAP/OSP	Military Assistance Program Offshore Procurement (DNAB)
MAPP	Major Accident Prevention Policy (HEAS)
MAPP	Manpower and Personnel Plan [*Army*] (AABC)
MAPP	Manpower and Production Projections [*LIMRA*]
MAPP	Masking Parameter Printout [*Computer science*]
MAPP	MasterCard Automated Point-of-Sale Program
MAPP	Master of Arts in Public Policy (GAGS)
MAPP	Mathematical Analysis of a Perception and Preference
MAPP	Methyl Acetyl Propadrine and Propane (MCD)
MAPP	Mid-Continent Area Power Pool [*Electric power*]
MAPP	Mission Analysis and Performance Program
MAPP	Modern Aids to Planning Program [*Military*] (GFGA)
MApp	Musical Appreciation [*Record label*]
MAppEpidem...	Master of Applied Epidemiology
MAPPER	Maintaining, Preparing, and Processing Executive Reports [*Computer science*] (CDE)
MAPPER	Maintaining, Preparing and Producing Executive Reports (NITA)
MAPPEX	Magazine and Periodical Publishers Exhibition (NITA)
MAPPLE	Macro-Associative Processor Programming Language [*Computer science*] (PDAA)
MAppLing	Master of Applied Linguistics
MApplLit......	Master of Applied Literature (GAGS)
MApplM.......	Master of Applied Mathematics (GAGS)
M Appl Stat...	Master of Applied Statistics (PGP)
MAppPsych...	Master of Applied Psychology
MAPPS	Legislative Council for Photogrammetry (SAUO)
MAPPS	Management Association of Private Photogrammetric Surveyors (EA)
MAppSc	Master of Applied Science
MAppSc-BltEnvir...	Master of Applied Science - Built Environment
MAppSci	Master of Applied Science
MAppSc-MedPhys...	Master of Applied Science - Medical Physics
MAppSc(SocEcol)...	Master of Applied Science in Social Ecology
MAPR	Arm Multiple Antenna Profiler (SAUS)
MAPR	Manufacturing Aids Program Requirements (AAG)
MAPR	Miniature Autonomous Plume Recorder [*Oceanography*]
MAPR	Miniaturization and Automation of Personnel Record (SAUO)
MAPR	Multiple Antenna Profiler Radar (ARMP)
MAPRAT	Maximum Power Ratio (IEEE)
MAPRC	Mediterranean Allied Photographic Reconnaissance Command
MAPRES	Mini Air Passenger Reservation System
MAPRIAL......	Mezhdunarodnaja Assotsiatsija Professorov Russkogo Jazyka i Literatury [*International Association of Teachers of Russian Language and Literature*] (EAIO)
MAPROS......	Maintain Production Schedules
MAPRP	Mesoscale Atmospheric Processes Research Program [*National Oceanic and Atmospheric Administration*]
MAPRS	Master of Arts in Pacific Rim Studies (GAGS)
MAPS	Machine Automated Parts System (MCD)
MAPS	Mail Abuse Prevention System
MAPS	Maintenance Analysis and Procedures System [*Computer science*]
MAPS	Major Assembly Performance System (MCD)
MAPS	Make-a-Picture Story [*Psychological testing*]
MAPS	Management Accounting and Payroll System (NITA)
MAPS	Management Accounting and Performance System
MAPS	Management Analysis and Planning System
MAPS	Management and Planning System (SAUO)
MAPS	Managerial Administrative Problem Solving (ACAE)
MAPS	Manifold Air Pressure Sensor [*Automotive engineering*]
MAPS	Manpower Analysis and Planning Society (EA)
MAPS	Manpower and Personnel System (SAUO)
MAPS	Manpower and Production Survey [*LIMRA*]
MAPS	Manpower Area Planning System [*Under CAMPS*]
MAPS	Manual of Administrative Procedures and Standards (SAUO)
MAPS	Manual of ADP Policies and Procedures (SAUO)
MAPS	Manufacturing and Production System (CIST)
MAPS	Map Analysis Package System (SAUO)
MAPS	Mapinfo Corp. [*NASDAQ symbol*] (SAG)
MAPS	Map Plotting System (SAUS)
MAPS	Maritime Asset Planning System (SAUS)
MAPS	Market-Auction Preferred Stock
MAPS	Marketing, Advertising, and Promotions Solutions Exhibition [*British*] (ITD)
MAPS	Master Activation Phasing Schedule (IAA)
MAPS	Master of Arts in Pastoral Studies (PGP)
MA Ps..........	Master of Arts in Psychology (PGP)
MAPS	Master of Arts in Public Service
MAPS	McGill Action Planning System
MAPS	Measurement of Air Pollution from Satellites
MAPS	Measurement of Atmospheric Pollutants from Space (ACAE)
MAPS	Measurement of Atmospheric Pollution from Satellites (EOSA)
MAPS	Measuring Air Pollution from Space [*Marine science*] (OSRA)
MAPS	Memory-Archives-Programmes-TV (SAUO)
MAPS	Mesoscale Analysis and Prediction System [*Marine science*] (OSRA)
MAPS	Mesoscale Atmospheric Prediction System (SAUO)
MAPS	Meteorological and Aeronautical Presentation System (CTAS)

MAPS	Meteorological Applied Problem Solving
MAPS	Methyl(deazaisoalloxazine)propanesulfonic Acid [*Organic chemistry*]
MAPS	Metropolitan Air Post Society (EA)
MAPS	Microprogramable Arithmetic Processor System (PDAA)
MAPS	MidAmerica Automated Payments Systems [*Banking*] (TBD)
MAPS	Middle Atlantic Planetarium Society (EA)
MAPS	Migratory Animal Pathological Survey (PDAA)
MAPS	Military Academy Preparatory School (SAUO)
MAPS	Military Airlift Command Automated Planning System (SAUO)
MAPS	Military Applications of Photovoltaic Systems
MAPS	Military Aviation Preservation Society (EA)
MAPS	Miller Assessment for Preschoolers (DIPS)
MAPS	Million Adds per Second
MAPS	Millions of Actions per Second (SAUS)
MAPS	Miniature Air Pilot System
MAPS	Minnesota Analysis and Planning System [*University of Minnesota*] [*Research center*] (RCD)
MAPS	Missile Application Propulsion Study
MAPS	Mission Analysis and Planning System (MCD)
MAPS	Mississippi Association of Professional Surveyors (SAUO)
MAPS	Mobile Aerial Port Squadron [*Air Force*]
MAPS	Mobility Analysis and Planning System (SAUO)
MAPS	Mobility Analysis Planning System (MCD)
MAPS	Mobilization Asset Planning System [*Army*]
MAPS	Modern Accounts Payable System (MHDW)
MAPS	Modern American Poetry Site
MAPS	Modular Acoustic Processing System (MCD)
MAPS	Modular Automated Parking System [*Developed by Robotic Parking*] (IDAI)
MAPS	Modular Azimuth Positioning System (SAUS)
MAPS	Modular Azimuth Position System [*Army*] (RDA)
MAPS	Monetary and Payments System [*Committee*] [*American Bankers Association*]
MAPS	Monitoring of Air Pollution by Satellites (KSC)
MAPS	Monoclonal Antibody Purification System
MAPS	Monopropellant Accessory Power Supply [*Aerospace*] (AAG)
MAPS	Muhammad Ali Professional Sports [*Commercial firm*]
MAPS	Multicolor Automatic Projection System (IEEE)
MAPS	Multidimensional Affect and Pain Survey [*Medicine*] (DMAA)
MAPS	Multidisciplinary Association for Psychedelic Studies (EA)
MAPS	Multi-jurisdictional Automated Pre-clearance System
MAPS	Multiple Address Processing System
MAPS	Multiple Agency Processing System
MAPS	Multiple Aim-Point System
MAPS	Multiple Application Phototypesetting System (DGA)
MAPS	Multiple Application Pro-Fan Studies (ACAE)
MAPS	Multiple Assessment Programs and Services
MAPS	Multiple Automated Printing Systems (MCD)
MAPS	Multisatellite Attitude Program System [*NASA*]
MAPS	Multispectral Active Passive Scanner (ACAE)
MAPS	Multistate Atmospheric Power Production Pollution Study (EEVL)
MAPS	Multitarget Automatic Plotting System
MAPS	Multivariate Analysis and Prediction of Schedules
MAPS	Multivariate Analysis, Participation, and Structure
MAPS	Region 2 Environmental Map Catalog System (SAUS)
MAPSAC	Machine-Aided Planning, Scheduling, and Control
MAPSAD	Military Assistance Property Sales and Disposal (AFM)
MAPS/ALPS	Multiple Aim Point System / Alternate Launch Point System (PDAA)
MAP/SAMSR	Joint Army-Air Force Master Plan for the Satisfaction of Army Meteorological Support Requirements (MCD)
MAPSAS	Member of APSAS [*Association of Public Service Administrative Staff*] [*British*]
MApSc	Master of Applied Science (GAGS)
MAPSE	Minimal APSE [*Ada Program Support Environment*] [*Computer science*]
MAPSE	Minimum Implementation ADA Programming Support Environment (NITA)
MAPSEP	Mission Analysis Program for Solar Electric Propulsion [*Computer science*] [*NASA*]
MAPSIM	Mesoscale Air Pollution Simulation Model [*Environmental Protection Agency*] (GFGA)
MAPSP	Map Supply Point (SAUS)
MAPSq	Mobile Aerial Port Squadron [*Air Force*]
M Ap Stat	Master of Applied Statistics (PGP)
MAPsych	Master of Arts in Psychology (GAGS)
MAPT	Military Assistance Program Training (AFM)
MAPT	Military Assistance Program Transfer (AFM)
MAPT	Missed Approach Point [*Aviation*] (FAAC)
MAPT	More Advanced Petrol Tractors [*Germany*]
MAPT	Mothers Are People Too [*Defunct*] (EA)
MAPTA	Metropolitan Association of Professional Travel Agents (TRID)
MAPTAC	Methacrylamidopropyltrimethylammonium Chloride [*Organic chemistry*]
MAPTEL	Maplin Telecommunications (NITA)
MAPTIP	Marine Aerosol Properties & Thermal Imager Performance (SAUS)
MAPTIS	Manpower Personnel and Training Information System [*Navy*]
MAPTIS	Materials and Processes Technical Information Services (SAUO)
MAP-TOE	Management Practices in TOE Units [*Military*] (GFGA)
MAP/TOP	Manufacturing Automation Protocol / Technical Office Protocol (BTTJ)
MAPTOP	Manufacturing Automation Protocol/Technical Office Protocol
MAP/TOP	MAP Technical Office Protocol (SAUO)
MAP-TV	Methods of Assessing the Radiological Impact of Accidents (SAUO)
MAPU	Memory Allocation and Protection Unit (MSA)
MAPU	Movimiento de Accion Popular Unida [*Unified Popular Action Movement*] [*Chile*] [*Political party*] (PD)

MAPU	Multiple Address Processing Unit [*Military*] (AABC)
MAPUC	Member of the Association for Promoting the Unity of Christendom [*British*]
MAPUC	Modified Area Production Urgency Committee [*World War II*]
MAPW	Master of Arts in Professional Writing (PGP)
MAPW	Medical Association for the Prevention of War [*British*] (DBA)
MAQ	MAC Aviation, S.L. [*Spain*] [*FAA designator*] (FAAC)
MAQ	Macquarie Island (SAUO)
maq	Maquette (VRA)
M Aq	Master of Aquaculture (PGP)
MAq	Master of Aquacultures (GAGS)
MAQ	Maximizing Access and Quality (SAUO)
MAQ	Maximum Acceptance Quantity
MAQ	Measures for Air Quality [*Program*] [*National Institute of Standards and Technology*]
MAQ	Monetary Allowance in Lieu of Quarters
MAQ	Monmouthshire Associated Quarries (SAUO)
MAQ	Sena Maduereira [*Brazil*] [*Airport symbol*] (AD)
MAQ Program	Measures for Air Quality Program (SAUO)
MAR	Macroaddress Register
MAR	Magnetic Amplifier Relay
MAR	Main Admitting Room (STED)
MAR	Maintainability Action Request (MCD)
MAR	Maintenance Action Request
MAR	Maintenance Analysis Report (MCD)
MAR	Maintenance and Refurbishment (MCD)
MAR	Maintenance and Repair
MAR	Major Acquisition Review (CTAS)
MAR	Major Aircraft Review [*Navy*]
MAR	Major Area of Responsibility
MAR	Major Assembly Release [*Military*] (AABC)
MAR	Malfunction Array RADAR
MAR	Managed Approach Reservoir [*FAA*] (TAG)
MAR	Management Analysis Report [*DoD*] (MCD)
MAR	Management and Administration Regulations (HEAS)
MAR	Management Assessment Report (MCD)
MAR	Management Assessment Review (MCD)
MAR	Management Assistance Review (SAUO)
MAR	Manistee & Repton R. R. [*AAR code*]
MAR	Manufacturing Action Request (MCD)
MAR	Manufacturing Assembly Report (IAA)
MAR	Maracaibo [*Venezuela*] [*Airport symbol*] (OAG)
MAR	Marasmus (STED)
mar	Marathi [*MARC language code*] [*Library of Congress*] (LCCP)
MAR	March (AFM)
Mar	March (BEE)
MAR	March Helicopters Ltd. [*British*] [*ICAO designator*] (FAAC)
Mar	March's English King's Bench Reports [*1639-42*] [*A publication*] (DLA)
MAR	Maremont Corporation (SAUO)
MAR	Margin (DAVI)
mar	Margin (STED)
MAR	Mar-Gold Resources [*Vancouver Stock Exchange symbol*]
MAR	Marian Minerals [*Vancouver Stock Exchange symbol*]
mar	Marimba (WDAA)
MAR	Marimba [*Music*]
Mar	Marine (DIAR)
MAR	Marine (MSA)
Mar	Marion Laboratories, Inc.
mar	Maritime (SHCU)
MAR	Maritime
MAR	Maritime Administration Report [*Department of Commerce*]
MAR	Maritime Central Airways
Mar	Marius [*of Plutarch*] [*Classical studies*] (OCD)
mar	Marker [*Chromosome*] (STED)
MAR	Market
mar	Maroon [*Philately*]
MAR	Marquette [*Diocesan abbreviation*] [*Michigan*] (TOCD)
MAR	Married
MAR	Marriott International [*NYSE symbol*] (SPSG)
MAR	Marrow (STED)
MAR	Marseilles [*France*] [*Seismograph station code, US Geological Survey*] [*Closed*] (SEIS)
MAR	Marshal (ROG)
Mar	Marshall and Sevestre's Appeals [*1862-64*] [*Bengal, India*] [*A publication*] (DLA)
MAR	Marshall Field Site (SAUO)
Mar	Marshall's Circuit Court Reports [*United States*] [*A publication*] (DLA)
Mar	Marshall's Reports [*Kentucky*] [*A publication*] (DLA)
Mar	Marshall's Reports [*Ceylon*] [*A publication*] (DLA)
Mar	Marshall's Reports [*Bengal*] [*A publication*] (DLA)
MAR	Martial [*Roman poet of the first century AD*] (ROG)
Mar	Martin's Louisiana Reports [*A publication*] (DLA)
Mar	Martin's North Carolina Reports [*1 North Carolina*] [*A publication*] (DLA)
Mar	Marvel's Reports [*Delaware*] [*A publication*] (DLA)
Mar	Mary (Queen of England) (DLA)
MAR	Mass Accumulation Rate [*Geology*]
MAR	Massachusetts College of Art, Boston, MA [*OCLC symbol*] (OCLC)
M-Ar	Massachusetts Secretary of State, Archives Division, Boston, MA [*Library symbol*] [*Library of Congress*] (LCLS)
MAR	Master Angular Reference (IAA)
M Ar	Master of Architecture
MAR	Master of Arts in Religion
MAR	Master of Arts in Research (GAGS)

MA(R)	Master of Arts (Research) (PGP)
MAR	Material Availability Report [*NASA*] (KSC)
MAR	Material Availability Request
MAR	Matrix Attachment Region [*Genetics*]
MAR	Maximal Aggregation Ratio (STED)
MAR	Medication Administration Record [*Medicine*]
MAR	Memory-Address Register [*Computer science*]
MAR	Mercury Arc Rectifier (IAA)
MAR	Microanalytical Reagent
MAR	Microprogram Address Register
MAR	Mid-Air Retrieval (MCD)
MAR	Mid-Atlantic Ridge [*of sea floor*]
MAR	Middeck Accommodations Rack (SAUS)
MAR	Minimal Angle Resolution
MAR	Minimally Attended RADAR (MCD)
MAR	Minimum Acceptable Rate of Return (MHDW)
MAR	Minimum Acceptable Reliability
MAR	Minimum Angle of Resolution (MCD)
MAR	Miscellaneous Apparatus Rack (IAA)
MAR	Missing at Random (IDAI)
MAR	Mission Analysis Report (SAUO)
MAR	Mission Analysis Representative
MAR	Mississippi-Atchafalaya River [*System*] (USDC)
MAR	Mixed Antiglobulin Reaction (STED)
MAR	Modernization and Associated Restructing (SAUO)
MAR	Monoclonal Antibody Resistant [*Immunochemistry*]
MAR	Monoclonal Antibody to Rat (DB)
MAR	Montana Administrative Register [*A publication*] (AAGC)
MAR	Morocco [*ANSI three-letter standard code*] (CNC)
MAR	Movimento di Azione Rivoluzionaria [*Revolutionary Action Movement*] [*Italian*] (PD)
MAR	Movimiento de Accion Revolucionaria [*Revolutionary Action Movement*] [*Mexico*] (PD)
MAR	Multi-Adversity Resistance [*to root rot*] [*Plant pathology*]
MAR	Multifunction Array RADAR
MAR	Multiple Aberration Region [*Genetics*]
MAR	Multiple Access Receiver (ACAE)
MAR	Multiple Access Relay
MAR	Multiple Access Return (SSD)
MAR	Multiple Array RADAR (IAA)
MAR	Municipal Association Record [*A publication*]
MAR	Muscarinic Acetylcholine Receptor [*Biochemistry*]
MaR	Myth and Ritual. Essays on the Myth and Ritual of the Hebrews in Relation to theCulture Pattern of the Ancient East [*A publication*] (BJA)
MAR	Mythology of All Races [*A publication*]
MAr	Robbins Public Library, Arlington, MA [*Library symbol*] [*Library of Congress*] (LCLS)
MAR	Superior Court Mandatory Arbitration Rules (SAUO)
MAR	Tacoma, WA [*Location identifier*] [*FAA*] (FAAL)
MARA	Majority Rule Association (EA)
MARA	Mexican-American Research Association (SAUO)
MARA	Midget Auto Racing Association [*Sanctioning organization*]
MARA	Modular Architecture for Real-time Applications (SAUS)
MARAAWEX	Marine Antiair Warfare Exercise (NVT)
MARAC	Marine Athletic Conference (PSS)
MARAD	Maritime Administration [*Also, MA, MARITADMIN*] [*Department of Transportation*]
MArAd	Master of Archive Administration, University of Liverpool [*British*] (DBQ)
MARAD Program	Maritime Administration Program (SAUO)
MARADVU	Marine Advisory Unit
MARAIRMED	Maritime Air Forces Mediterranean [*NATO*] (NATG)
MARAIRWING	Marine Aircraft Wing
MARALLWEAFITRARON	Marine All Weather Fighter Training Squadron
MarAMA	Marianas Air Materiel Area (SAUO)
MARAMA	Mid-Atlantic Regional Air Management Association
Mar & Yer	Martin and Yerger's Tennessee Reports [*8 Tennessee*] [*1825-28*] [*A publication*] (DLA)
MARAS	Middle Airspace RADAR Advisory Service [*Military*] (DA)
Mar Av	Marvin on General Average [*A publication*] (DLA)
marb	Marble (VRA)
MARB	Marbled [*Edges or sides of cover*] [*Bookbinding*] (ROG)
MARB	Materiel Acquisition Review Board [*Army*]
MARBA	Mid-America Regional Bargaining Association
MARBARGE	Maritime Maintenance Barge
Marbascol	Marine Corps Basic School (SAUO)
MARBASSCOL	Marine Corps Basic School
MarbFn	Marble Financial Corp. [*Associated Press*] (SAG)
MARBI	Machine-Readable Bibliographic Information (AL)
MARBI	Machine-Readable Bibliographic Information Committee (SAUO)
MARBI	Machine-Readable Form of Bibliographic Information [*American Library Association*]
MARBID	Marine Biodiversity Database (SAUO)
Mar Bills	Marius on Bills of Exchange [*A publication*] (DLA)
MarBiol	Marine Biology (SAUO)
MARBKS	Marine Barracks
MARBO	Marianas-Bonins Command
Mar Br	March's Brooke's New Cases [*1651*] [*England*] [*A publication*] (DLA)
MARBRIG	Marine Brigade
MARC	Hruska Meat Animal Research Center [*Department of Agriculture*] (GRD)
MARC	Maastricht Referendum Campaign [*British*] (ECON)
MARC	MAC Airlift Reaction Communications (SAUS)
MARC	Machine Readable card Catalog (SAUO)
MARC	Machine-Readable Cards
MARC	Machine-Readable Catalog (NITA)
MARC	Machine-Readable Cataloging [*Library of Congress*]
MARC	Machine-Readable Code (IAA)
MARC	Magnetic Abrasion Resistant Coating (IAA)
MARC	Management & Applied Research Consultants (SAUO)
MARC	Manpower Allocation Requirement Criteria [*Military*] (RDA)
MARC	Manpower Authorization Request for Change [*Air Force*]
MARC	Manpower Requirements Criteria [*Army*]
MARC	Manufacturers Association of Radiators and Convectors (SAUO)
MARC	Manufacturing Resource Control System [*Deritend Computer Bureau Ltd.*] [*Software package*] (NCC)
Marc	Marcato [*Emphasized*] [*Music*]
Marc	Marcellus [*of Plutarch*] [*Classical studies*] (OCD)
MARC	MARC, Inc. [*NASDAQ symbol*] (SAG)
Marc	Marcus [*of Scriptores Historiae Augustae*] [*Classical studies*] (OCD)
M/A/R/C	Marketing And Research Counselors Inc. [*Irving, TX*] (WDMC)
MARC	Maryland Automotive Reclamation Corp. [*Automotive materials recycling project*]
MARC	Master of Arts in Religious Communication (PGP)
MARC	Matador Automatic RADAR Command
MARC	Material Accountability Recoverability Code
MARC	Materiel Acquisition Resource Committee [*Military*]
MARC	Meat Animal Research Center (SAUO)
MARC	Media Action Research Center (EA)
MARC	Methodist Archives and Research Centre [*John Rylands University Library of Manchester*] [*British*] (CB)
MARC	Methodology for Assessing Radiological Consequences (PDAA)
MARC	Metropolitan Administration for Review and Comment [*Program using regional councils of government to serve as clearinghouses for Federal grants*]
MARC	Metropolitan Applied Research Center (BARN)
MARC	Michigan Aeronautical Research Center (SAUO)
MARC	Micronesian Area Research Center [*University of Guam*] [*Research center*] (RCD)
MARC	Mid-America Regional Council [*Information service or system*] (IID)
MARC	Mid-America Remote Sensing Center (SAUO)
MARC	Military Airlift Command ALCE Reactions Communications (SAUO)
MARC	Mining and Reclamation Council of America (EA)
MARC	Minority Access to Research Careers [*Program*] [*Public Health Service*] [*Bethesda, MD*]
MARC	Missile Annex Review Committee (SAUO)
MARC	Missions Advanced Research and Communication Center (EA)
MARC	Mobile Area Repair Calibration (ACAE)
MARC	Model "A" Restorers Club (EA)
MARC	Modified Azimuth RADAR Correlator
MARC	Monitor and Results Computer (IAA)
MARC	Monitoring and Assessment Research Centre [*Marine science*] (MSC)
MARC	Monitoring and Risk Assessment Centre [*British*]
MARC	Moore Automatic Remote Control
MARC	Mortgage Account Report Compiler (IAA)
MARC	Mouvement d'Action pour la Resurrection du Congo [*Action Movement for the Resurrection of the Congo*] [*Zaire*] (PD)
MARC	Movimiento Agrario Revolucionario del Campesinado Boliviano [*Revolutionary Movement of Bolivian Indian Peasants*] [*Political party*] (PPW)
MARC	Multiaxial Radial Circuit (IAA)
MARC	Multifocal and Recurrent Choroidopathy [*Medicine*] (DMAA)
MARC	Multi-Technology Automated Reader Card (SAUO)
MARC	Mutliple Access Remote Computing (PDAA)
MA(RCA)	Master of Arts, Royal College of Art (Photography) [*British*] (DBQ)
MARCA	Mid-Continent Area Reliability Coordinating Agreement (SAUO)
MARCA	Mid-Continent Area Reliability Coordination Agreement [*Regional power council*]
Mar Cad	Marine Cadet (SAUO)
MARCAD	Marine Corps Aviation Cadet
Marcam	Marcam Corp. [*Associated Press*] (SAG)
MARCAMP	Marine Corps Accrued Military Pay System (NG)
MARCAN	Maneuvering Reentry Control and Ablation Studies
MarCap	Marion Capital Holdings, Inc. [*Associated Press*] (SAG)
MARCAS	Maneuvering Reentry Control and Ablation Studies (MCD)
Mar Cas	Maritime Cases, by Crockford and Cox [*1860-71*] [*A publication*] (DLA)
MARCCO	Master Real-Time Circulation Controller (PDAA)
MARCE	Materiel Asset Redistribution Center Europe [*Military*]
Marcell	Pro Marcello [*of Cicero*] [*Classical studies*] (OCD)
MARCENT	Marine Corps, Central Command (SAUO)
MARCEP	Maintainability and Reliability Cost-Effectiveness Program (IEEE)
MARCH	Marchioness
March	March's English King's Bench and Common Pleas Reports [*A publication*] (DLA)
March	March's Translation of Brooke's New Cases, English King's Bench [*82 English Reprint*] [*A publication*] (DLA)
MArch	Master of Architectural Engineering (GAGS)
M Arch	Master of Architecture
MARCH	Melt-Down Accident Response Characteristics [*Nuclear energy*] (NRCH)
MARCHA	Methodists Associated Representing the Cause of Hispanic Americans [*An association*]
M Arch Des	Master of Architectural Design
M Arch E	Master of Architectural Engineering
M Arch Eng	Master of Architectural Engineering
MArchH	Master of Architectural History (GAGS)
M Arch H	Master of Architectural History (PGP)

M Arch in CP... Master of Architecture in City Planning
MArchivAdmin... Master of Archives Administration (ADA)
March N ...... March's New Cases, English King's Bench and Common Pleas Reports [A publication] (DLA)
March NC .... March's New Cases, English King's Bench [1639-42] [A publication] (DLA)
March NC .... Translation of Brook's New Cases [1515-58] [A publication] (DLA)
March NR .... March's New Cases, English King's Bench [1639-42] [A publication] (DLA)
M Arch Studies... Master of Architectural Studies (PGP)
MArchUD..... Master of Architecture in Urban Design (GAGS)
M Arch UD... Master of Architecture in Urban Design (PGP)
MARCIA....... Mathematical Analysis of Requirements for Career Information Appraisal
MARC II....... Machine-Readable Catalogue (SAUO)
MARC IS....... MARC Israel (NITA)
MARCIVE...... MARC Five (NITA)
MARCKS...... Myristoylated Alanine-Rich C-Kinase Substrate [Biochemistry]
MARC(LC)..... MARC Library of Congress (NITA)
MARCLIP..... Maritime Commands Long-Term Infrastructure Plan (SAUO)
Marc Mant.. Marcus Mantua Benavidius [Deceased, 1582] [Authority cited in pre-1607 legal work] (DSA)
MarcNG ...... Marcum Natural Gas Services, Inc. [Associated Press] (SAG)
MARCO........ Machine Referenced and Coordinated Outline
MARCO........ Marine Construction and Design Company (SAUO)
MARCO........ Microelectronics Advanced Research Corporation (SAUO)
MARCO........ Mid-American Research Corp.
MARCOGAZ... Union of the Gas Industries of the Common Market Countries [Defunct] (EAIO)
MARCOM..... Maritime Command [Canada, since 1964]
MARCOM..... Microwave Airborne Communications Relay (IEEE)
MARCOMM... Maritime Commission (DNAB)
MARCOMMDET... Marine Communications Detachment (DNAB)
MARCOMNAVADGRU... Marine Corps Component Navy Advisory Group (CINC)
MARCON...... Marine Construction Ltd. (SAUO)
MARCON...... Mars Consortium
MARCON...... Micro Archives and Records Online [Developed by AirS, Inc.]
MARCONFOR... Maritime Contingency Force [NATO] (NATG)
MARCONFORLANT... Maritime Contingency Forces, Atlantic [NATO] (NATG)
MARCONP ... Maritime Contingency Plans (NATG)
Mar Conv... Marcy's Epitome of Conveyancing [1881] [A publication] (DLA)
Mar Conv St... Marcy's Conveyancing Statutes [5th ed.] [1893] [A publication] (DLA)
MARCOR...... Marine Corps
MARCORABSCOLLUNIT... Marine Corps Absentee Collection Unit (DNAB)
MARCORADMINDET... Marine Corps Administrative Detachment (DNAB)
MARCORASBCOLLUNITDET... Marine Corps Absentee Collection Unit Detachment (DNAB)
MARCORDISBOF... Marine Corps Disbursing Office
MARCOREP... Marine Corps Representative (DNAB)
MARCORESTRACEN... Marine Corps Reserve Training Center
MARCORHISTCEN... Marine Corps Historical Center (DNAB)
MARCORMAN... Marine Corps Manual
MARCORMEMO... Marine Corps Memorandum (SAUO)
MARCORPERSMAN... Marine Corps Personnel Manual
MARCORPS... Marine Corps
MarCorps...... Marine Corps
MARCORPS... US Marine Corps (SAUS)
MARCORSUPDEP... Marine Corps Supply Depot
MARCORSYSCOM... Marine Corps Systems Command
MARCOT...... Maritime Command Operational Team Training [Canadian Navy]
Mar Crp G ... Marine Corps Gazette [A publication] (BRI)
MARCS........ MAC Airlift Reaction Communications System (SAUS)
MARC-S....... Machine-Readable Cataloguing - Serials (ADA)
MARC(S)....... MARC Serials (NITA)
MARCS .... Marine Computer System (PDAA)
MARCS .... Melcom All Round Adaptive Consolidated Software [Japan]
MARC(UK)... MARC (United Kingdom) (NITA)
Marcus .... [The] Marcus Corp. [Associated Press] (SAG)
Marcus An... Marcus Antonius Blancus [Deceased, 1548] [Authority cited in pre-1607 legal work] (DSA)
Marcus Anto... Marcus Antonius Blancus [Deceased, 1548] [Authority cited in pre-1607 legal work] (DSA)
MARD.......... Marine Assessment Research Division [Marine science] (OSRA)
MA-RD........ Maritime Administration Office of Research and Development [Washington, DC]
MARD.......... Military Aeronautical Research and Development (PDAA)
MARDAC...... Manpower Research and Data Analysis Center [DoD] (NVT)
MARDAN...... Marine Differential Analyzer
MARDATA.... Maritime Data Network [Lloyd's Maritime Data Network Ltd.] [Stamford, CT] [Database]
MARDB........ Mountain Agricultural Resources Development Bureau [Taiwan] (BUAC)
MARDEC...... Malaysian Rubber Development Corp. (BUAC)
Mar de Lau... Martinus Caratti de Laude [Flourished, 1438-45] [Authority cited in pre-1607 legal work] (DSA)
MARDET ..... Marine Detachment
MARDEZ ..... Maritime Defense Zone [Navy] [Coast Guard] (DOMA)
MARDI........ Malaysian Agricultural Research and Development Institute (BUAC)
MARDI........ Mobile Advanced Robotic Defence Initiative (SAUS)
MARDIS....... Modernized Army Research and Development Information System
MARDIV...... Marine Division
MARDO........ Months after Receipt of Delivery Order (MCD)

MARDOS...... Sources of Radioactivity in the Marine Environment and their Relative Contributors to Overall Dose Assessment from Marine Radioactivity (SAUO)
MarDrl........ Marine Drilling Co. [Associated Press] (SAG)
MARDS....... Medium Artillery Delivered Sensor [Army]
MARE.......... Major Accident Response Exercise (MCD)
MARE.......... Major Account Response Evaluation (MCD)
MARE.......... Mare Island Naval Shipyard Island (SAUO)
MARE.......... Maritime Engineering [Canadian Navy]
MARE.......... Master of Arts in Religious Education (PGP)
MARE.......... Miniature Analogue Recording Electronics (SAUS)
MARE.......... Months after Receipt of Equipment [Navy]
MAREA ...... Member of the American Railway Engineering Association
MAREA ...... Middle Leaf Area [Botany]
MAREAC ..... Mallee Agricultural Research and Extension Advisory Committee (SAUO)
MAREC ...... Maritime Reconnaissance radar (SAUS)
MARECEBO... Manned Research on Celestial Bodies Committee [International Academy of Astronautics]
MARECO ...... Marine Radioecology Working Group (SAUO)
MARECS ..... Marine Communications Satellites (NITA)
MARECS ..... Maritime Communications Satellite
MARECS ..... Maritime European Communications Satellite (ACAE)
MARED .... Materiel Acquisition and Readiness Executive Development [Program] [Army] (RDA)
MAREE........ Multiple Access Radio Frequency Equipment (ACAE)
Ma Reg....... Massachusetts Register [A publication] (AAGC)
MAREGSQ.... Marine Air Regulating Squadron
MAREMIC.... Maintenance Repair and Minor Construction [Program] [Air Force]
MAREMICS... Maintenance, Repair and Minor Construction (SAUO)
Mar Eng....... Marine Engineer (PGP)
MARENGRLAB... Marine Engineering Laboratory (SAUO)
MARENTS.... Modified Advanced Research Environmental Test Satellite [Air Force]
MAREP .... Marine Environmental Prediction Task Group [US government] [Terminated, 1969]
MAREP .... Maritime Reporting System (SAUO)
MAREQ .... Military Assistance Requirement (SAUS)
MARES .... Marine Corps Automated Readiness Evaluation System
MARES/FORSTAT... Marine Corps Automated Readiness Evaluation System/Status of Forces
MARESTNG... Marine Corps Reserve Training (NVT)
MAREX .... Marine Array Experiment (SAUS)
MARF.......... Master Area Reference File [Bureau of the Census] (GFGA)
MARF.......... Master Availability Reference File [Army Electronics Command]
MARF.......... Medical Acupuncture Research Foundation (SAUO)
MARF.......... Medical and Actuarial Research Foundation (SAUO)
MARF.......... Metadata Archive Retrieval Facility (SAUO)
Mar Fa........ Martinus de Fano [Deceased circa 1275] [Authority cited in pre-1607 legal work] (DSA)
MARFAIR.... Marine Fleet Air
MARFAIRWEST... Marine Fleet Air, West Coast
Mar Fan....... Martinus de Fano [Deceased circa 1275] [Authority cited in pre-1607 legal work] (DSA)
MARFINCEN... Marine Corps Finance Center (DNAB)
MARFIREX... Marine Firing Exercise (NVT)
MARFOR...... Marine Forces [Element of a Joint Task Force]
MARFS .... Multienvironment Active RF [Radio Frequency] Seeker
MARG .... Margarine (EBF)
Marg........... Margin (WDMC)
marg........... Margin
MARG .... Margin [or Marginal]
MARG .... Marine Amphibious Ready Group (MCD)
MARG .... Market Analysis Report Generator [Computer science]
MARG .... Mediterranean Amphibious Ready Group (MCD)
MARG .... Modern Architectural Research Group (SAUO)
MARGARFOR... Marine Garrison Force
Margate...... Margate Ventures [Associated Press] (SAG)
MARGE........ Margarine (ADA)
MARGEN ..... Management Report Generator [Randolph Data Services, Inc.] [Software package] [Computer science] (IEEE)
MARGEN ..... Mask and Record Generator (TIMI)
MARGI .... Methodology for Analysing Reliability & maintainability Goals (SAUS)
MARGIE...... Memory Analysis, Response Generation, and Interference in English
MARGILSAREA... Marshalls-Gilberts Area
MARGL .... Marginal (ROG)
Margo......... Margo Nursery Farms [Associated Press] (SAG)
MARHELILEX... Marine Helicopter Landing Exercise (NVT)
MARHGN .... Mid-Atlantic Regional Human Genetics Network (SAUO)
MARI .... Marijuana Cigarette [Slang] (DSUE)
Mari........... Marinus de Caramanico [Flourished, 1269-85] [Authority cited in pre-1607 legal work] (DSA)
MARI .... Maros Agricultural Research Institute (SAUO)
MARI .... Medicare Administrative Reform Initiative [Health Care Financing Administration]
MARI .... Mercantile Atlantic Routing Instructions
MARI .... Mexico City Air Quality Research Initiative (SAUO)
MARI .... Microelectronics Applications Research Institute [Newcastle-Upon-Tyne, England]
MARI .... Middle America Research Institute (SAUO)
MARI .... Motivator and Response Indicator
MARIA .... Macroaggregated Radioiodinated Albumin [Radiology] [Pharmacy] (DAVI)
MARIA .... Methods for Assessing the Radiological Impact of Accidents (SAUO)
Marianists ... Society of Mary (SAUO)
Maria Soci... Marianus Socinus [Authority cited in pre-1607 legal work] (DSA)

MARIC .... Marine Resources Information Center [*Massachusetts Institute of Technology*] (NOAA)

MARID .... Mica-Amphibole-Rutile-Ilmenite-Diopside [*Geology*]

MARIDAS .... Maritime Data System (IAA)

MARIE .... Mobile Autonomous Robot in an Industrial Environment (SAUO)

Mariet........... Marietta Corp. [*Associated Press*] (SAG)

MARIF .... Malang Research Institute for Food Crops [*Indonesia*] (BUAC)

Marijuana Rev... Marijuana Review [*A publication*] (DLA)

MARIN .... Marine Industry Application of Broadband Communications (SAUO)

MARIN .... Marine Research Institute Netherlands (SAUO)

MARINALG International... World Association of Seaweed Processors (SAUO)

MARINCO .... Marketing International Consultants (BUAC)

MARINE .... Management Analysis Reporting Information on the Naval Environment System (NG)

Marine Ct R... Marine Court Reporter (McAdam's) [*New York*] [*A publication*] (DLA)

MarinerH ..... Mariner Health Group, Inc. [*Associated Press*] (SAG)

MARINE System... Management Analysis Reporting Information on the Naval Environment System (SAUO)

MARINEX..... Marine Express (AABC)

Marin Frecc... Marinus Freccia [*Flourished, 16th century*] [*Authority cited in pre-1607 legal work*] (DSA)

MARINTRARON... Marine Instrument Training Squadron

MARINTSUM... Maritime Intelligence Summary (SAUS)

MARIP .... Maintenance And Repair Inspection Program [*Military*] (DNAB)

MARIS .... Marine Information Service (SAUO)

MARIS .... Maritime Research Information Service (SAUO)

MARIS .... Materials and Resources Information Service (NITA)

MARIS .... Mississippi Automated Resource Information System (SAUO)

MarisaC....... Marisa Christina, Inc. [*Associated Press*] (SAG)

MARISAT .... Maritime Satellite System [*COMSAT*]

MARISAT .... Maritime Satellite, United States Maritime Administration (SAUO)

MARISP ...... Maritime Strike Plan

Marist Brothers... Little Brothers of Mary (SAUO)

MARIT .... Maritime

MARITA .... Maritime Airfield (NATG)

MARITADMIN... Maritime Administration [*Also, MA, MARAD*] [*Department of Transportation*] (MUGU)

MARITCOM... Maritime Commission

MARITIME ... Maritime-Niddesc Cooperation (SAUO)

MARITIME ... Modelling and Reuse of Information over Time (SAUO)

Maritimes L Rep (CCH)... Maritimes Law Reporter (Commerce Clearing House) [*A publication*] (DLA)

Maritrn .... Maritrans, Inc. [*Associated Press*] (SAG)

MARITZ........ Maritzburg (ROG)

Marius .... Marius. Concerning Bills of Exchange [*4 eds.*] [*1651-84*] [*A publication*] (DLA)

MARK .... Maintenance and Reliability Kit [*Military*] (NVT)

mark .... Market (VRA)

Mark .... Market

MARK .... Material Accountability & Robotic Kitting (SAUS)

MARK .... Mechanized Assignment and Record Keeping [*Database management system*]

MARK .... Mid-Atlantic Ridge Kane

MARKAR ...... Mapping and Reconnaissance Ku-Band Airborne RADAR

MarkCtr........ Mark Centers Trust [*Associated Press*] (SAG)

MARK ED.... Marketing Educational Consortium (SAUO)

Mark El........ Markby's Elements of Law [*6th ed.*] [*1905*] [*A publication*] (DLA)

Markel......... Markel Corp. [*Associated Press*] (SAG)

MarkerI........ Marker International [*Associated Press*] (SAG)

MARKFED.... Punjab State Co-operative Supply and Marketing Federation (SAUO)

MarkIV......... Mark IV Industries, Inc. [*Associated Press*] (SAG)

MarkR......... Markham Review [*A publication*] (ANEX)

MARKS .... Modern Army Record Keeping System (INF)

Marks & Sayre... Marks and Sayre's Reports [*108 Alabama*] [*A publication*] (DLA)

Marks & Sayre's... Marks' and Sayre's Reports [*108 Alabama*] [*A publication*] (DLA)

MarksBr....... Marks Bros. Jewelers, Inc. [*Associated Press*] (SAG)

MARKSIM .... [*A*] Marketing Decision Simulation [*Game*]

MarkSol....... Mark Solutions, Inc. [*Associated Press*] (SAG)

MARKSTRAT... Marketing Strategy [*Simulation package developed by Professors Jean-Claude Larreche and Hubert Gatignon*]

Markup......... Formatierungsmerkmal (SAUS)

MarkVII........ Mark VII, Inc. [*Associated Press*] (SAG)

MarkWst ..... MarkWest Hydrocarbon, Inc. [*Associated Press*] (SAG)

MARL........... Marlboro [*Vermont*] [*Seismograph station code, US Geological Survey*] (SEIS)

MARL........... Master of Arts and Letters

MARL........... Master of Arts in Religious Leadership (PGP)

MARL........... Mobile Acoustics Research Laboratory (MCD)

MarI............. Statute of Marlborough [*A publication*] (DSA)

Mar LA .... Martin's Louisiana Reports [*A publication*] (DLA)

MARLAB...... Mobile Air Research Laboratory (PDAA)

MARLAGS.... Marine Life and Geochemical Studies [*Marine science*] (MSC)

MARLB .... Marlborough (ROG)

Mar LC .... Maritime Law Cases, by Crockford [*1860-71*] [*A publication*] (DLA)

Mar L Cas (NS)... Maritime Law Cases (New Series), by Aspinall [*1870-1940*] [*A publication*] (DLA)

Mar LC NS... Maritime Law Cases, New Series, by Aspinall [*1870-1940*] [*England*] [*A publication*] (DLA)

Mar Leg Bib... Marvin's Legal Bibliography [*A publication*] (DLA)

MARLEX ...... Marine Corps Reserve Landing Exercise (NVT)

MARLF......... Middle Atlantic Regional Library Federation (SAUO)

MARLIB .... An information service based on the Institute of Marine Engineers Library (SAUO)

MAR LIC ...... Marriage License (WDAA)

MarLIN .... Marine Life Information Network for Britain & Ireland

MARLIN .... Middle Atlantic Regional Information Network

MARLIS .... Multi-Agent Relevance Linkage Information System (NITA)

MARLIS ...... Multiaspect Relevance Linkage Information System

Mar LJ .... Maryland Law Journal and Real Estate Record [*A publication*] (DLA)

MARLNO...... Marine Liaison Office (DNAB)

MARLO .... Marine Liaison Officer (DOMA)

MARLOG...... Marine Logistical Command (VNW)

Mar LR .... Maritime Law Cases, First Series, by Crockford [*1860-71*] [*A publication*] (DLA)

Mar LR .... Maritime Law Cases, New Series, by Aspinall [*1870-1940*] [*A publication*] (DLA)

Mar L Rec ... Maryland Law Record [*A publication*] (DLA)

MARLS .... Missouri Association of Registered Land Surveyors (SAUO)

MARLS .... Montana Association of Registered Land Surveyors (SAUO)

MARLSR ...... Manufacturers Association of Robes, Leisurewear, Shirts, and Rainwear [*Defunct*] (EA)

Marlton........ Marlton Technologies, Inc. [*Associated Press*] (SAG)

MarM.......... Marine Midland Banks, Inc. [*Associated Press*] (SAG)

MARM .... Mensa Animal Rights Movement (BUAC)

MARM .... Microprocessor Arithmetic Model

MARM .... Middle Atlantic Regional Meeting [*of American Chemical Society*]

MARM .... Moving Average Rating Method [*Insurance*]

Mar Mant.... Marcus Mantua Benavidius [*Deceased, 1582*] [*Authority cited in pre-1607 legal work*] (DSA)

MARMAP ..... Marine Resources Monitoring, Assessment, and Prediction [*National Oceanic and Atmospheric Administration*]

MARMAP Program... Marine Resources Monitoring, Assessment and Prediction Program (SAUO)

Mar Mech E... Marine Mechanical Engineer

MARMETS .... Marine Meteorological Service

MARMIC ...... Command Level Maintenance Repair and Minor Construction Program Reporting System (SAUO)

MARMOSET... Marconi Mobile Satellite Earth Terminal (SAUS)

MARMOT ..... Colorado libraries electronic system (SAUO)

Marm Par .... Marmor Parium [*Classical studies*] (OCD)

MAR/MSR.... Multifunction Array RADAR / Missile Site RADAR (SAA)

MARN .... Manitoba Association of Registered Nurses (SAUO)

MARN .... Marion Capital Holdings [*NASDAQ symbol*] (NQ)

MARNA........ Marine Navigation (NITA)

MARNAF ...... Marquardt Navair Fuel [*A boron slurry propellant for spacecraft*]

Mar N & Q... Maritime Notes and Queries [*1873-1900*] [*A publication*] (DLA)

MARNAVCOR... Marine Navy Corps (SAUO)

MarNB .... Marine National Bank (California) [*Associated Press*] (SAG)

MarNBk........ Marine National Bank (California) [*Associated Press*] (SAG)

Mar NC........ March's New Cases, English King's Bench [*1639-42*] [*A publication*] (DLA)

Mar NC........ Martin's North Carolina Reports [*1 North Carolina*] [*A publication*] (DLA)

MarnLP........ Marine Ltd. [*Associated Press*] (SAG)

MarnLP........ Marine Ltd. Partnership [*Associated Press*] (SAG)

Mar NR........ March's New Cases [*1639-42*] [*A publication*] (DLA)

Mar NS........ Martin's Louisiana Reports, New Series [*A publication*] (DLA)

MARO .... Maritime Air Radio Organization [*NATO*] (NATG)

MAROPS...... Maritime Operations

MAROPT...... Marine Optical Recording System (SAUO)

MAROTS...... Maritime Orbital Test Satellite

MARP .... Manpower Allocation/Requirements Plan [*Navy*]

MARP .... Manpower Requirements Plan (SAUO)

MARP .... Marine Petroleum Trust [*NASDAQ symbol*] (NQ)

MARP .... Mating and Ranging Program (SAUO)

MARP .... Maximum Authorized for Repair Parts (DNAB)

MARP .... Mobilization Augmentee Revitalization Program [*Military*]

MARP .... Months after Receipt of Problem [*Navy*] (NG)

MARPA .... Mini Automatic Radar Plotting Aid (SAUS)

MARPAC...... Headquarters, Department of the Pacific [*Marine Corps*]

MARPAC...... Maritime Command Pacific [*Canada, since 1964*]

MARPAC...... Maritime Forces, Pacific (SAUO)

MARPAC/ORT... Maritime Forces Pacific Operational Research Team [*Canada*]

MARPDA...... Mid-America Periodical Distributors Association (EA)

MARPE .... Multi-Atom Resonant Photoemission [*Physics*]

MARPEP ...... Marine Physical Environmental Prediction

MarPet........ Marine Petroleum Trust [*Associated Press*] (SAG)

MARPEX ...... Management of Repair Parts Expenditure [*Army*] (PDAA)

MARPIC .... Marine Pollution Information Centre [*Marine Biological Association of the United Kingdom*] (IID)

Marpie......... Middle-Aged Rural Professional [*Lifestyle classification*]

MARPOL...... Convention for the Prevention of Marine Pollution from Ships (SAUS)

MARPOL...... International Convention for the Prevention of Pollution from Ships [*1973*]

MARPOL...... Marine Pollution (SAUO)

MARPOL...... Maritime Pollution Convention [*1978*] (DS)

MarPollutBull... Marine Pollution Bulletin (SAUO)

MARPOLMON... Marine Pollution Monitoring System (SAUO)

MARPOLMON... Sub-Group of Experts on Marine Pollution Monitoring [*Marine science*] (MSC)

MARPRO...... Country Marine Profile Database (SAUS)

MARPRO...... Marine Profile Data Base (GNE)

Mar Prov ..... Maritime Provinces Reports [*Canada*] [*A publication*] (DLA)

MARPS .... Marine Petrol Tr. [*NASDAQ symbol*] (SG)

MARPS .... Mechanized Accounting Reserve Pay System

marq........... Marquetry (VRA)

MARQ .... Marquette Electronics, Inc. [*NASDAQ symbol*] (SPSG)

MARQ .... Marquette Medical Systems, Inc. [*NASDAQ symbol*] (SAG)

MARQ .... Marquis [*or Marquess*]
MARQA .... Marquette Electronics'A' [*NASDAQ symbol*] (TTSB)
MARQA .... Marquette Medical System [*NASDAQ symbol*] [*Formerly, Marquette Electronics*] (SG)
MarqEl .... Marquette Electronics, Inc. [*Associated Press*] (SAG)
MarqG .... Marquee Group, Inc. (The) [*Associated Press*] (SAG)
MarqGrp ...... Marquee Group, Inc. (The) [*Associated Press*] (SAG)
MarqMed ..... Marquette Medical Systems, Inc. [*Associated Press*] (SAG)
Marqst .... Marquest Medical Products, Inc. [*Associated Press*] (SAG)
Marquette Bus Rev... Marquette Business Review [*A publication*] (DLA)
Marquette U... Marquette University (GAGS)
MARQUIS .... Master Remote Query Interface System [*Computer science*]
Marr .... Hay and Marriott's English Admiralty Reports [*A publication*] (DLA)
MARR .... Manpower Authorization Requirement Review (SAUO)
MARR .... Marine Accidents Requiring Rescue (OA)
Mar R .... Maritime Law Reports [*A publication*] (DLA)
Marr .... Marrack's European Assurance Cases [*England*] [*A publication*] (DLA)
Marr .... Marriage (DLA)
MARR .... Maximum Annual Rate of Return [*Finance*]
MARR .... Minimum Attractive Rate of Return [*Economics*]
Marr Adm .... Marriott's English Admiralty Reports [*A publication*] (DLA)
MARRC .... Multi-Channel Automatic Remote Recording
MARRCS ...... Manpower Requirements and Resources Control System [*Navy*] (NVT)
MARRD .... Married (ROG)
MARRE .... Manual RADAR Reconnaissance Exploitation (MCD)
MARRE .... Marriage (ROG)
Mar Rec B ... Martin's Recital Book [*A publication*] (DLA)
Mar Reg ...... Mitchell's Maritime Register [*England*] [*A publication*] (DLA)
MARREP ...... Maritime Report (SAUS)
MARRES ...... Manual RADAR Reconnaissance Exploitation System [*Air Force*]
Marr Form ... Marriott's Formulare Instrumentorum [*Admiralty Court*] [*1802*] [*A publication*] (DLA)
Marriotl .... Marriott International [*Associated Press*] (SAG)
MARRS .... Mechanized Ammunition Recording and Reporting System
MARRS .... Modular Armoured Repair & Recovery System (SAUS)
MARR SETTL... Marriage Settlement [*Legal term*] (DLA)
MARS .... Machine-Activated Recovery System (TIMI)
MARS .... Machine-Aided Realization System
MARS .... Machine-Assisted Reference Section [*American Library Association*] [*Information service or system*] (IID)
MARS .... Machine-Assisted Reference Service [*St. Paul Public Library*] (OLDSS)
MARS .... Machine Automated Realty Service
MARS .... Machine Retrieval System
MARS .... Magnetic Airborne Recording System
MARS .... Magnetic Array Sensor System (SAUS)
MARS .... Maintenance Activities and Resources Simulation [*Computer science*]
MARS .... Maintenance Analysis and Recording Systems
MARS .... Maintenance Analysis Repair Set
MARS .... Maintenance and Repair System (ACAE)
MARS .... Maintenance Assistance and Repair System [*Military*]
MARS .... Major Accident Reporting System [*Engineering*]
MARS .... Management Accounting Reporting System (SAUO)
MARS .... Management Action Reporting System (MCD)
MARS .... Management Analysis Reporting System [*Computer science*]
MARS .... Management and Administrative Reporting Subsystem [*Department of Health and Human Services*] (GFGA)
MARS .... Management Reports and Statistics
MARS .... Man-Hour Accounting and Reporting System [*Military*] (MCD)
MARS .... Manned Aerodynamic Reusable Spaceship
MARS .... Manned Astronautical Research Station [*Space laboratory*]
MARS .... Marconi Automatic Relay System (IEEE)
MARS .... Marine Account Reconciliation Service
MARS .... Marine Aircraft Repair Squadron
MARS .... Marine Corps Ammunition Reporting System (SAUO)
MARS .... Marine Reporting Station [*National Weather Service*]
MARS .... Marine Research Stations network (SAUO)
MARS .... Maritime Mobile Access and Retrieval System (SAUO)
MARS .... Maritime Surface and Subsurface [*Canadian Navy*]
MARS .... Market Analysis and Reference System [*Vancouver stock exchange computer system*] [*Canada*]
MARS .... Marketing and Advertising Reference Service (NITA)
Mars .... Marsden's Select Pleas in the Court of Admiralty [*Selden Society Publications, Vols. 6, 11*] [*A publication*] (DLA)
MARS .... Marsh Supermarkets, Inc. [*NASDAQ symbol*] (NQ)
MARS .... Martin Automatic Reporting System
MARS .... Master Attitude Reference System
MARS .... Master of Arts in Religious Studies (PGP)
MARS .... Material Action Reporting System (MCD)
MARS .... Material Response Study
MARS .... Materials at Risk Survey (SAUO)
MARS .... Materiel Acquisition Resource System [*Military*]
MARS .... Mathematics Anxiety Rating Scale [*Psychology*]
MARS .... Matrix Analysis of Redundant/Routine Structure (ACAE)
MARS .... Maximum Asset Return Strategy [*Allingham, Anderson, Roll & Ross*] [*British*] (ECON)
MARS .... Measuring Accuracy and Repeatability Study
MARS .... Mechanical Accessory Repair Shop (MCD)
MARS .... Media Alert and Response System [*Public relations project devised by Pharmaceutical Manufacturers Association*]
MARS .... Memory-Address Register Storage [*Computer science*]
MARS .... Message Archiving and Retrieval Service (SAUO)
MARS .... Meteorological Airborne Radar Data System (SAUO)
MARS .... Meteorological Automatic Reporting Station [*Canada*]
MARS .... Meteorological Automatic Reporting System (SAUO)
MARS .... Mevinolin Atherosclerosis Regression Study (MEDA)
MARS .... Microprogrammable Accelerator for Rapid Simulations (ACAE)
MARS .... Midair Recovery [*or Retrieval*] System [*Rescue by helicopter*] [*Military*]
MARS .... Mid-Air Retrieval System (SAUO)
MARS .... Migration Agents' Registration Scheme [*Australia*]
MARS .... Military Affiliated Radio System [*or Stations*] [*Amateur-operated radio stations*]
MARS .... Military Airborne RADAR System [*Air Force*] (IAA)
MARS .... Military Amateur Radio Service (SAUO)
MARS .... Military Amateur Radio System (IAA)
MARS .... Military Amphibious Reconnaissance System (RDA)
MARS .... Military Archive & Research Services (SAUO)
MARS .... Millimeter Wave Amplification by Resonance Saturation (IAA)
MARS .... Miniature Attitude Reference System
MARS .... Minimally Attended Radar Station (SAUO)
MARS .... Minimum-Altitude Release and Strafe (MCD)
MARS .... Minolta Automatic Retrieval System (NITA)
MARS .... Mirror Advanced Reactor Study (MCD)
MARS .... Mission Maintenance and Reliability Simulation (MCD)
MARS .... Mitigation and Adaption Research Strategies (SAUO)
MARS .... Mobile Air Defense Radar System (ACAE)
MARS .... Mobile Atlantic Range Stations [*Tracking stations*] (MUGU)
MARS .... Mobile Augmented Reality System
MARS .... Mobile Automatic Reporting Station (SAUO)
MARS .... Mobile Automatic Reporting System (MCD)
MARS .... Model Annotation Search and Retrieval System [*Geological program*]
MARS .... Modern Architectural Research Society (SAUO)
MARS .... Modular Access Random Storage [*Computer science*] (VLIE)
MARS .... Modular Adaptable Radar Simulator (SAUS)
MARS .... Modular Airborne Recorder System (MCD)
MARS .... Modular Airborne Recording System (SAUS)
MARS .... Modular Attack RADAR System (MCD)
MARS .... Monitor and Replenisher System
MARS .... Monitoring Accounting Reporting and Statistical System [*Aviation*]
MARS .... Monograph Acquisitions and Record System [*Library science*] (TELE)
MARS .... Monthly Aerial Reconnaissance Summary (MCD)
MARS .... Motorola Aerial Remote Sensing [*Flying laboratory*]
MARS .... Mouse Antirat Serum (DB)
MARS .... Multi-Access Reservations System [*Travel industry*] (TRID)
MARS .... Multi-Access Reservation System [*Travel industry*] (TVEL)
MARS .... Multiaperture Reluctance Switch [*Data storage unit*]
MARS .... Multicast Address Resolution Server (MLOA)
MARS .... Multicast Address Resolution Service [*Computer science*]
MARS .... Multiple Access Retrieval System [*Control Data Corp.*]
MARS .... Multiple Action Raid Simulation [*France*]
MARS .... Multiple Aerial Refueling System (PDAA)
MARS .... Multiple-Angle Reference System
MARS .... Multiple Aperture Reluctance Switch (VLIE)
MARS .... Multiple Artillery Rocket System [*Army*]
MARS .... Multiuser Archival and Retrieval System [*Computer science*]
MARS .... Multivariate Adaptive Regression Spline (IDAI)
MARS .... Multivariate Adaptive Regression Splines
MARS .... Multivariate Analysis, Retrieval, and Storage [*System*] [*NASA*]
MARS .... PTS Marketing and Advertising Reference Service [*Predicasts, Inc.*] [*Cleveland, OH*] [*Information service or system*] (IID)
MARSA .... Marsh Supermkts'A' [*NASDAQ symbol*] (TTSB)
MARS-A .... Mathematics Anxiety Rating Scale-Adolescents (STED)
MARSA .... Microfilm Association of the Republic of South Africa (BUAC)
MARSA .... Military Accepts Responsibility for Separation of Aircraft (AFM)
Mars Adm.... Marsden's English Admiralty [*A publication*] (DLA)
Mar Sal .... Marius Salomonius [*Deceased, 1557*] [*Authority cited in pre-1607 legal work*] (DSA)
MARSAM ..... Multiple Airborne Reconnaissance Sensors Assessment Model (MCD)
MARSAP ...... Mutual Assistance Rescue and Salvage Plan (SAUO)
MARSAS ...... Marine Search and Attack System (PDAA)
MARSAT ...... Maritime Satellite [*COMSAT*]
MARSATS .... Maritime Satellite System [*COMSAT*]
MARSB .... Marsh Supermkts'B' [*NASDAQ symbol*] (TTSB)
M Ar Sc .... Master of Arts and Sciences
MArSci .... Master of Arts and Sciences (NADA)
Mars Coll..... Marsden's Collisions at Sea [*11th ed.*] [*1961*] [*A publication*] (DLA)
MARSD .... Minimal Attended RADAR Station Display (DWSG)
MARSEN ...... Marine Remote Sensing Experiment (SAUO)
MARSEN ...... Maritime Remote Sensing (MCD)
Marsh .... Marshall and Sevestre's Appeals [*1862-64*] [*Bengal, India*] [*A publication*] (DLA)
Marsh .... Marshall's Circuit Court Decisions [*United States*] [*A publication*] (DLA)
Marsh .... Marshall's English Common Pleas Reports [*1814-16*] [*A publication*] (DLA)
Marsh .... Marshall's High Court Reports [*Bengal*] [*A publication*] (DLA)
Marsh .... Marshall's Reports [*Kentucky*] [*A publication*] (DLA)
Marsh .... Marshall's Reports [*4 Utah*] [*A publication*] (DLA)
Marsh .... Marshall's Reports [*Ceylon*] [*A publication*] (DLA)
MARSH .... Matching Aid to Restore States Habitat (GNE)
Marshall ...... Marshall's Reports [*Bengal*] [*A publication*] (DLA)
Marshall ...... Reports of Cases on Appeal [*Calcutta*] [*A publication*] (DLA)
Marshall U... Marshall University (GAGS)
Marsh Beng... Marshall's Reports [*Bengal*] [*A publication*] (DLA)
Marsh Calc... Marshall's Reports [*Calcutta*] [*A publication*] (DLA)
Marsh Car ... Marshall on Railways as Carriers [*A publication*] (DLA)

Marsh Ceylon... Marshall's Ceylon Reports [*A publication*] (DLA)
Marsh Costs... Marshall on the Law of Costs [*A publication*] (DLA)
Marsh CP..... Marshall's English Common Pleas Reports [*A publication*] (DLA)
Marsh Dec... Marshall on the Federal Constitution [*A publication*] (DLA)
Marsh Dec... Marshall's Circuit Court Decisions, by Brockenbrough [*United States*] [*A publication*] (DLA)
Marsh (Eng)... Marshall's English Common Pleas Reports [*A publication*] (DLA)
MarshFn ...... Marshalltown Financial Corp. [*Associated Press*] (SAG)
Marshl .... Marshall & Isley Corp. [*Associated Press*] (SAG)
Marshlls ...... Marshall & Isley Corp. [*Associated Press*] (SAG)
Marsh Ins ... Marshall on Marine Insurance [*A publication*] (DLA)
Marsh (KY)... Marshall's Reports [*Kentucky*] [*A publication*] (DLA)
MARSHL ...... Marshal (ROG)
Marsh Op...... Marshall's Constitutional Opinions [*A publication*] (DLA)
Marsh Ry...... Marshall on Railways as Carriers [*A publication*] (DLA)
Marsh Ry..... Marshall's Duties and Obligations of Railway Companies [*A publication*] (DLA)
Mar Sill .... Martinus Sillimanus [*Flourished, 13th century*] [*Authority cited in pre-1607 legal work*] (DSA)
MARSIM ...... International Conference on Marine Simulation (PDAA)
MARSIS .... Marine Remote Sensing Information System for Regional European Seas (SAUO)
MARSL .... Machine-Readable Shelf List [*Carleton University*] [*Canada*] (NITA)
Mars Microprobe... Mars Microprobe Project (SAUS)
MARSO .... Marine Corps Shipping Order (NG)
MA/RSO .... Mobilization Augmentee/Reserve Supplement Officer [*Air Force*] (AFM)
MARSPTBN... Marine Support Battalion (DNAB)
MARSREPSYS... Military Affiliate Radio System Repeater System (DNAB)
MARSS .... Meteorological and Range Safety Support (ACAE)
MARSTA ...... Marital Status [*Army*] (AABC)
MARSTELSYS... Military Affiliate Radio System Teletypewriter Relay System (DNAB)
MARSTSIC... Marst on Sicca [*England*]
MARSYAS.... Marshall System for Aerospace Simulation [*Programming language*] [*1966-68*] (CSR)
MArt............ Magazine of Art (SAUO)
MART........... Maintenance Analysis and Review Technique (VLIE)
MART........... Maintenance Analysis Review Technique
Mart............ Martial [*Roman poet, 40-104AD*] [*Classical studies*] (OCD)
Mart............ Martinique (SHCU)
MART.......... Martinique [*West Indies*] (WDAA)
Mart............ Martin's Louisiana Term Reports [*1809-30*] [*A publication*] (DLA)
Mart............ Martin's North Carolina Reports [*1 North Carolina*] [*A publication*] (DLA)
Mart............ Martinus Gosia [*Authority cited in pre-1607 legal work*] (DSA)
MART.......... Martius [*March*] [*Latin*]
MART.......... Martyr
MART.......... Master of Arts in Religion and Theology (PGP)
MART.......... Mathematical Modeling and Reliability Transducer (MCD)
MART.......... Maximising the Market for Telecommunications-Based Rehabilitation Technology (SAUO)
MART.......... Mean Active Repair Time (IEEE)
MART.......... Metropolitan Area Rapid Transit (SAUO)
MART.......... Missile Automation Radiation Test (IAA)
MART.......... Mobile Automatic Radiation Tester
MART.......... Multiplicative Algebraic Reconstruction Technique (DMAA)
MARTA .... Metropolitan Atlanta Rapid Transit Authority [*FTA*] (TAG)
MARTAC ...... Martin Automatic Rapid Test and Control
Mart & Y .... Martin and Yerger's Tennessee Reports [*8 Tennessee*] [*1825-28*] [*A publication*] (DLA)
Mart & Yer... Martin and Yerger's Tennessee Reports [*8 Tennessee*] [*1825-28*] [*A publication*] (DLA)
Mart & Yerg... Martin and Yerger's Tennessee Reports [*8 Tennessee*] [*1825-28*] [*A publication*] (DLA)
Mart & Y (Tenn)... Martin and Yerger's Tennessee Reports [*8 Tennessee*] [*1825-28*] [*A publication*] (DLA)
Mart Ark ...... Martin's Decisions in Equity [*Arkansas*] [*A publication*] (DLA)
MARTC .... Marine Air Reserve Training Command
MartCol........ Martin Color-Fi, Inc. [*Associated Press*] (SAG)
MARTCOM .... Marine Air Reserve Training Command
Mart Cond LA... Martin's Condensed Louisiana Reports [*A publication*] (DLA)
Mart Conv.... Martin's Practice of Conveyancing [*A publication*] (DLA)
MARTD .... Marine Air Reserve Training Detachment
MARTD .... Marine Corps Aviation Reserve Training Depot (SAUO)
Mart Dec ..... United States Decisions in Martin's North Carolina Reports [*A publication*] (DLA)
MARTEC ...... Martin Thin-Film Electronic Circuit
Mar Technol Soc J... Marine Technology Society Journal (SAUO)
Martek........ Martek Biosciences, Inc. [*Associated Press*] (SAG)
MARTEL....... Missile Antiradiation Television [*Military*] (CAAL)
MARTELO .... Maritime Air Telecommunications Organisation (SAUO)
Marten........ Marten Transport Ltd. [*Associated Press*] (SAG)
Mart Ex....... Martin on Executors [*A publication*] (DLA)
Mart GA...... Martin's Reports [*21-30 Georgia*] [*A publication*] (DLA)
MARTHA...... Mobile Autonomous Robots for Transportation and Handling Applications (SAUO)
Marth W Ca... Martha Washington Cases [*A publication*] (DLA)
MARTI .... Maneuverable Reentry Technology Investigation
MARTI .... Mobile Advanced Realtime Image (STED)
Martin.......... Martin's Louisiana Reports [*A publication*] (DLA)
Martin.......... Martin's North Carolina Reports [*1 North Carolina*] [*A publication*] (DLA)
Martin.......... Martin's Reports [*21-30, 54-70 Georgia*] [*A publication*] (DLA)
Mart Ind ...... Martin's Reports [*54-70 Indiana*] [*A publication*] (DLA)

MARTINI ...... Massive Analog Recording Technical Instrument for Nebulous Indications
Martin Index... Martin's Index to Virginia Reports [*A publication*] (DLA)
Martin (Lou) NS... Martin's Louisiana Reports, New Series [*A publication*] (DLA)
Martin's Chy... Martin's Chancery Decisions [*Arkansas*] [*A publication*] (DLA)
Martin's LA Rep... Martin's Louisiana Reports [*A publication*] (DLA)
Martin's LA Rep NS... Martin's Louisiana Reports, New Series [*A publication*] (DLA)
Martin's Louisiana R... Martin's Louisiana Reports [*A publication*] (DLA)
Martin's NS... Martin's Louisiana Reports, New Series [*A publication*] (DLA)
Martin's R NS... Martin's Louisiana Reports, New Series [*A publication*] (DLA)
Martls......... Martyrdom of Isaiah [*Pseudepigrapha*] (BJA)
Martlsa .... Martyrdom of Isaiah [*Pseudepigrapha*] (BJA)
Mart LA ...... Martin's Louisiana Reports, Old and New Series [*A publication*] (DLA)
Mart Laud.... Martinus Caratti de Laude [*Flourished, 1438-45*] [*Authority cited in pre-1607 legal work*] (DSA)
Mart Law Nat... Martens' Law of Nations [*A publication*] (DLA)
Mart MC ...... Martin's Mining Cases [*Canada*] [*A publication*] (DLA)
MartMM...... Martin Marietta Materials [*Associated Press*] (SAG)
Mart NC .... Martin's North Carolina Reports [*1 North Carolina*] [*A publication*] (DLA)
Martnln........ Martin Industries, Inc. [*Associated Press*] (SAG)
MartnL........ Martin Lawrence Ltd. [*Associated Press*] (SAG)
Mart NS ...... Martin's Louisiana Reports, New Series [*A publication*] (DLA)
Mart NS (LA)... Martin's Louisiana Reports, New Series [*A publication*] (DLA)
MARTOS ...... Multiaccess Real-Time Operating System [*AEG Telefunken*] [*Germany*]
Mart OS (LA)... Martin's Louisiana Reports, Old Series [*A publication*] (DLA)
MARTRA & REPLCOMS... Marine Training and Replacement Commands
MArt RCA... Master of Art of the Royal College of Art (SAUO)
M Art (RCA)... Master of Art, Royal College of Art
Mart Rep ...... Martin's Louisiana Reports [*A publication*] (DLA)
Mart Rep NS... Martin's Louisiana Reports, New Series [*A publication*] (DLA)
MARTS .... Advance Monthly Retail Trade Survey (SAUO)
MARTS .... Master RADAR Tracking Station
MARTS .... Master RADAR Training System
MARTS .... Mobile Automatic Radio Telephone System (MCD)
MARTS .... Monthly Advance Retail Trade Survey [*Bureau of the Census*] (GFGA)
MARTS .... MSFC Accounting and Resources Tracking System (SAUS)
Mart USCC ... Martin's Circuit Court Reports [*1 North Carolina*] [*A publication*] (DLA)
MARU .... Medical Architecture Research Unit [*Polytechnic of North London*] [*British*] (IRC)
MARU .... Middle America Research Unit
MARU .... Mobile Aircraft Repair Unit (SAUO)
MARUNET... Maruzen Online Network [*Maruzen Co. Ltd.*] [*Japan*] [*Telecommunications*]
MARUNITNG... Marine Unit Training (NVT)
Maruwhenua... Maori policy section of the Ministry of the Environment (SAUO)
MARV .... Maneuverable AntiRADAR Vehicle (MCD)
MARV .... Maneuverable Reentry Vehicle (AABC)
MaRV .... Maneuvering Reentry Vehicle
MARV .... Marvelous (DSUE)
Marv .... Marvel's Reports [*15-16 Delaware*] [*A publication*] (DLA)
Marv .... Marvetol [*medicine*] (WDAA)
MARV .... Micro Autonomous Robotic Vehicle
MARV .... Mobile Acoustic Recording Vehicle (MCD)
MARV .... Mobile Armored Reconnaissance/Operational Vehicle (MCD)
MARV .... Mobile Armoured Reconnaissance Vehicle (SAUS)
MARV .... Multi-Element Articulated Research Vehicle [*Engineering*] (OA)
Marv Av ...... Marvin on General Average [*A publication*] (DLA)
Marv (Del)... Marvel's Reports [*15-16 Delaware*] [*A publication*] (DLA)
MARVEL ...... Machine-Assisted Realization of the Virtual Electronic Library [*Information service or system*] [*Library of Congress*]
Marvel .... Marvel Entertainment Corp. [*Associated Press*] (SAG)
Marvel .... Marvel's Reports [*15-16 Delaware*] [*A publication*] (DLA)
MARVEL ...... Mississippi Aerophysics Research Vehicle with Extended Latitude
MARVIN....... Mobile Autonomous Robot with Video-Based Navigation (VLIE)
Marv Leg Bib... Marvin's Legal Bibliography [*A publication*] (DLA)
MARVLS ...... MARC Video Disc Library System (NITA)
MARVOR...... French Subsurface Float (SAUO)
MARVS .... Material Acquisition Requirements Validation System (SAUO)
Marv Wr & S... Marvin on Wreck and Salvage [*A publication*] (DLA)
Mar Wr & S... Marvin on Wreck and Salvage [*A publication*] (DLA)
MARX .... Mark Aero [*Air carrier designation symbol*]
Mary .... Maryland Reports [*A publication*] (DLA)
MARY .... Saint Mary Land & Exploration [*NASDAQ symbol*] (SAG)
Marygrove C... Marygrove College (GAGS)
Maryknoll Fathers... Catholic Foreign Missionary Society of America (SAUO)
Maryland ...... Maryland Reports [*A publication*] (DLA)
Maryland Ch Dec... Maryland Chancery Decisions [*A publication*] (DLA)
Maryville U... Maryville University of St. Louis (GAGS)
Marywood C... Marywood College (GAGS)
MAS............ Astronomical Observatory of Cordoba (SAUS)
MAS............ Lithuanian Catholic Youth Association Ateitis (EA)
MAS............ MacDonald Agricultural Services Ltd. [*British*]
MAS............ Machine Accounting School
MAS............ Macintosh Application System [*Computer science*] (CDE)
MAS............ Macroassembler
MAS............ Madang Air Services [*Australia*]
MAS............ Magazine Article Summaries
MAS............ Magic Angle Spinning [*Spectroscopy*]
MAS............ Magnesia-Alumina-Silicate [*Inorganic chemistry*]

MAS	Main Store (VLIE)
MAS	Maintenance Alert System [Truck operations]
MAS	Maintenance and Services (AFIT)
MAS	Maintenance and Supply (AFIT)
MAS	Malabsorption Syndrome (MELL)
MAS	Malaysian Airline System [ICAO designator] (FAAC)
MAS	Managed Airspace (SAUO)
MAS	Managed Application System (VLIE)
MAS	Management Accounting System
MAS	Management Advisory Services
MAS	Management and Administrative Statistics (OICC)
MAS	Management Appraisal Survey [Test]
MAS	Manchester Astronomical Society [England] (BUAC)
MAS	Man-day Account System (SAUO)
MAS	Maneuvering Attack System (MCD)
MAS	Manifest Anxiety Scale [Psychology]
MAS	Manned Aerial Surveillance
MAS	Manual A1 Simplex [Aviation]
MAS	Manufacturing Advisory Service (DCTA)
MAS	Manufacturing Agility Server (VLIE)
MAS	Manufacturing Assembly Specification
MAS	Manufacturing Automation and Support (TIMI)
MAS	Manus [Papua New Guinea] [Airport symbol] (OAG)
MAS	Manus Island [Bismarck Archipelago] [Airport symbol] (AD)
MAS	MAP [Manufacturing Automation Protocol]/One Applications Services [Software] [Automotive engineering]
MAS	Marine Acoustical Services
MAS	Marine Advisory Service [See also NMAS] [National Oceanic and Atmospheric Administration] [Information service or system] (IID)
MAS	Maritime Air Superiority (NVT)
MAS	Marker Assisted Selection (IGSL)
MAS	Market Advisory Service [British Overseas Trade Board] (DS)
MAS	Mars Approach Sensor
MAS	Maryland Academy of Sciences (SAUO)
mas	Masai [MARC language code] [Library of Congress] (LCCP)
MAS	Masco Corp. [NYSE symbol] (SPSG)
MAS	Masculine
MAS	Mason [or Masonry] (ROG)
MAS	Mason Butte [Idaho] [Seismograph station code, US Geological Survey] [Closed] (SEIS)
mas	Masonry (VRA)
Mas	Mason's United States Circuit Court Reports [A publication] (DLA)
Mas	Masorah (BJA)
MAS	Massachusetts Audubon Society, Incorporated (SAUO)
Mas	Massachusetts Reports [A publication] (DLA)
Mas	Massachusetts State Library, Boston, MA [OCLC symbol] (OCLC)
Mas	Masseketh (BJA)
MAS	Master (DSUE)
MAS	Master Activation Schedule (AAG)
MAS	Master Analysis Scheme [Monitoring technique]
MAS	Master Assembly Schedule (SAUO)
MAS	Master of Accounting Science
MAS	Master of Actuarial Science
MAS	Master of Administrative Science (PGP)
MAS	Master of Administrative Studies (ADA)
MAS	Master of Aeronautical Science (GAGS)
MAS	Master of Applied Science
MAS	Master of Applied Spirituality (PGP)
MAS	Master of Applied Statistics (GAGS)
MAS	Master of Archival Studies (GAGS)
MAS	Material Activity Schedule
MAS	Material Application Service [NASA] (IAA)
MAS	Material Availability Schedule
MAS	Mathematics Attitude Scale (EDAC)
MAS	Mature Age Student (ADA)
MAS	Maximum Aerobic Speed [Biology]
MAS	Maximum Amount Subject (MARI)
MAS	McMaster University Library [UTLAS symbol]
MAS	Meconium Aspiration Syndrome [Medicine]
MAS	Media Advisory Service [British]
MAS	Medical Administrative Service (DAVI)
MAS	Medical Advisory Service [British]
MAS	Medical Audit Statistics (PDAA)
MAS	Medical Audit Study (HCT)
MAS	Meiosis-Activating Sterol [Cytology]
MAS	Member of the Arundel Society [British]
MAS	Memory and Auxiliary Storage Subsystem [Space Flight Operations Facility, NASA]
MAS	Mercury Analyzer System [Perkin-Elmer Co. instrument designation]
MAS	Merged Area Schools (OICC)
MAS	Merseyside Archaeological Society (SAUO)
MAS	Merseyside Aviation Society [British] (DBA)
MAS	Mesoatrial Shunt [Medicine] (DMAA)
MAS	Metal-Alumina Semiconductor (IAA)
MAS	Metal-Alumina-Silicon (IEEE)
MAS	Metal Anchor Slots [Technical drawings]
MAS	Metals/Alloy Solidification (SAUS)
MAS	Metastable Atomic State
MAS	Methods and Standards (MCD)
MAS	Methods of Air Sampling and Analysis [Air Pollution Control Association]
MAS	Methods of Analysis Sub-committee (SAUO)
MAS	Mezhdunarodnaya Assotsiatsiya Sudovladeltsev [International Shipowners' Association] [Poland] (EAIO)
MAS	Michigan Academy of Science (SAUO)
MAS	Michigan Audubon Society (SAUO)
MAS	Microage Solutions, Inc. (EFIS)
MAS	Micro-Alloyed Steel [Metallurgical engineering]
MAS	Micro-Assembly System (VLIE)
MAS	Micro Automation System
MAS	Microbeam Analysis Society (EA)
MAS	Microprogram Automation System [Computer science] (IAA)
MAS	Midcourse Active System (MCD)
MAS	Middle Air Space (PDAA)
MAS	Military Agency for Standardization [Brussels, Belgium] [NATO]
MAS	Military Airlift Squadron [Air Force] (CINC)
MAS	Military Antiquarian Society (SAUO)
MAS	Military Area Services (SAUO)
MAS	Military Assistance Sales (MCD)
MAS	Milk-Alkali Syndrome [Medicine] (DMAA)
mAs	Milliampere-Second
MAS	Millimeterwave Atmospheric Sounder (SAUO)
MAS	Milwaukee Astronomical Society (SAUO)
MAS	Mine Avoidance Sonar (SAUS)
MAS	Minimal Access Surgery (SAUO)
MAS	Ministry of Aviation Supply [British]
MAS	Minnesota Academy of Science
MAS	Missile Alignment Set
MAS	Missile Assembly Site (NATG)
MAS	Missile Assigned Switch
MAS	Missile Auxiliaries System
MAS	Mission Area Summary (ACAE)
MAS	Mission Auxiliary Subsystem (ACAE)
MAS	Mississippi Academy of Sciences (BUAC)
MAS	Missouri Academy of Science (SAUO)
MAS	Mobile Access Structure (IGSL)
MAS	Mobile Arm Support [Orthopedics] (DAVI)
MAS	Mobile Atmospheric Spectrometer [Marine science] (OSRA)
MAS	Model Abattoir Society (SAUO)
MAS	Model Assignment Sheet (MCD)
MAS	Modern Army Supply
MAS	Modern Army System
MAS	Modular Accounting System [Computer science] (IAA)
MAS	Modular Application Systems [Martin Marietta Data Systems]
MAS	Monaco Group, Inc. [Toronto Stock Exchange symbol]
MAS	Monetary Allowance in Lieu of Subsistence
MAS	Monetary Authority of Singapore (NUMA)
MAS	Money Advice Scotland (BUAC)
MAS	Monitor and Alarm System (MCD)
MAS	Monmouth Antiquarian Society (EA)
MAS	Monoacetoxylscirpenol [Organic toxin]
MAS	Morgagni-Adam-Stokes (DB)
MAs	Mothers Anonymous (SAUO)
MAS	Mount Alvernia Seminary (SAUO)
MAS	Mount Angel Seminary [Oregon]
MAS	Movement Alarm System [Gynecology]
MAS	Movimiento al Socialismo [Movement towards Socialism] [Argentina] [Political party] (PPW)
MAS	Movimiento al Socialismo [Movement towards Socialism] [Venezuela] [Political party] (PPW)
MAS	Movimiento de Accion Socialista [Peru] [Political party] (EY)
MAS	Movimiento para Accion y Solidaridad [Guatemala] [Political party] (EY)
MAS	Muerte a los Secuestradores [Death to Kidnappers] [Colombia] (PD)
MAS	Mujeres en Accion Sindical [Organizes national and international conferences on women in the economy] [Mexico] (CROSS)
MAS	Multi-Agent System (IDAI)
MAS	Multiaspect Signaling (IEEE)
MAS	Multiple Address System [Telecommunications] (CDE)
MAS	Multiple Aim Structure (MCD)
MAS	Multiple Award Schedule [Government contracting]
MAS	Municipal Analysis Services, Inc. [Information service or system] (IID)
MAS	Municipal Art Society (SAUO)
MAS	Mutually Assured Survival
MAS	Myanmar Agricultural Service (SAUO)
MAS	Society of African Missions (SAUO)
MASA	Mail Advertising Service Association International [Bethesda, MD]
MASA	Malaysian Shipowners Association (SAUO)
MASA	Marine Accessories and Services Association [Later, NAMPS] (EA)
MASA	Master of Advanced Studies in Architecture (PGP)
MASA	Mathematical Association of South Australia
MASA	Medical Acronyms, Symbols & Abbreviations [A publication]
MASA	Medical Association of South Africa (DMAA)
MASA	Medical Association of the State of Alabama (SAUO)
MASA	Member of the Acoustical Society of America (SAUO)
MASA	Men Against Sexual Assault [Australia]
MASA	Mental Retardation-Aphasia-Shuffling Gait-Adducted Thumbs [Syndrome] [Medicine] (DMAA)
MASA	Merged Area Schools Administrators Association (OICC)
MASA	Metals and Alloys Solidification Apparatus (SAUS)
MASA	Michigan Association of School Administrators (SAUO)
MASA	Military Accessories Service Association (EA)
MASA	Military Automotive Supply Agency
MASA	Minnesota Association of School Administrators (SAUO)
MASA	Mission Analysis for reconnaissance-Spanning & Attack (SAUS)
MASA	Mississippi Association of School Administrators (SAUO)
MASA	Modular Avionics Systems Architecture (MCD)
MASA	Montana Association of School Administrators (SAUO)
MASA	Multimedia Services Affiliate Forum (SAUO)

MASA	Multiple Anodic Stripping Analyzer (PDAA)
MASA	Music and Arts Society of America (EA)
MASAAV	Mid-Atlantic States Association of Avian Veterinarians (EA)
MASAC	Master of Arts in Substance Abuse Counseling (PGP)
MASAD	Mission Analysis and Systems Acquisition Division (AAGC)
MASAE	Member of the American Society of Agricultural Engineering
MASAF	Mediterranean Allied Strategic Air Force
MASAI	Mail Advertising Service Association International (EA)
MASAL	Michigan Academy of Science, Arts, and Letters
MASANYC	Mail Advertising Service Association of New York City (SAUO)
MASAP	Michigan Association of Single Adoptive Parents (EA)
MASAQUE	Major Action Significantly Affecting the Quality of the Human Environment (DNAB)
MASAR	Management Assurance of Safety, Adequacy, and Reliability (MHDB)
MASAR	Microwave Accurate Surface Antenna Reflector (PDAA)
MASAR	Multimode Airborne Solid-State Array RADAR System [Military] (PDAA)
MASB	Main Array Signal Band
MASB	MASSBANK Corp. [NASDAQ symbol] (NQ)
MASB	Michigan Association of School Boards (EA)
MA/SB	Motor Antisubmarine Boat [Obsolete] [British]
MASBAL	RCRA Mass Balance System (SAUS)
MASBO	Minnesota Association of School Business Officials (SAUO)
MASC	Magazine Advertising Sales Club (EA)
MASC	Magnetic Attitude Spin Coil
MASC	MAGTF [Marine Air-Ground Task Force] Automated Services Center (GFGA)
MASC	Maintenance Support Concept Model (MCD)
MASC	Management Systems Concept (PDAA)
MASC	Manpower Authorization Standards and Criteria (SAUO)
MASC	Maori Affairs Select Committee (SAUO)
masc	Masculine (SHCU)
MASC	Masculine
MASC	Massachusetts Association of School Committees (SAUO)
masc	Mass Concentration [Medicine] (MAE)
MASc	Master of Agricultural Science (DD)
MA Sc	Master of Applied Science
MASC	Medical Academic Staff Committee (SAUO)
MASC	Medical Advisers Support Centre (SAUO)
MASC	Methylaluminum Sesquichloride [Organic chemistry]
MASC	Microsoft Access Script Command [Computer language]
MASC	Middletown Air Service Command [Air Force]
MASC	Military Automotive Supply Center (MCD)
MASCp	Model to Evaluate Maintenance Support Concepts (MCD)
MASC	Mountain Administration Support Center (SAUO)
MASC	Mountain Administrative Support Center [Marine science] (OSRA)
MASC	Multilayer Aluminium Oxide-Silicon-Dioxide Combination (IAA)
MASC	Multiple Award Schedule Contract [Government contracting]
MASCA	Middle Atlantic States Correctional Association (SAUO)
MASCA	Museum Applied Science Center for Archeology [University of Pennsylvania]
MASCAC	Middle Atlantic States Collegiate Athletic Conference (PSS)
MASCAL	Mass Casualty [Military]
MASCDC	Military Aircraft Storage and Disposition Center (SAUO)
MASCDCS	Madison Avenue Sports Car Driving and Chowder Society (EA)
MASCE	Member of the American Society of Civil Engineers
MASCE	Member of the Australian Society of Civil Engineers (SAUO)
MASCO	Maintenance Schedule Code (PDAA)
Masco	Masco Corp. [Associated Press] (SAG)
MASCO	Mead Access Systems Co.
MASCO	Microprogrammed and Simulated Computer Organization
MASCOM	Master Communications (PDAA)
MASCON	Mass Concentration [of gravitational pull]
MASCOT	Management Advisory System using Computerized Optimization Techniques (PDAA)
MASCOT	Manned Shuttle Comprehensive Optimization and Targeting [NASA]
Mascot	Mascotech [Commercial firm] [Associated Press] (SAG)
MASCOT	Meteorological Auxiliary Sea Current Observation Transmitter
MASCOT	Military Air-Transportable Satellite Communications Terminal
MASCOT	Mobile Air-Transportable Satellite Communications Terminal [Military] (IAA)
MASCOT	Modern Approach to Software Construction, Operation and Test [Ministry of Defence] [British]
MASCOT	Modular Approach to Software Construction Operation and Test (NITA)
MASCOT	Modular Approach to System Construction Operation and Test (MCD)
MASCOT	Motorola Automatic Sequential Computer Operated Tester
Mascotch	Mascotech [Commercial firm] [Associated Press] (SAG)
MasCp	MassMutual Corporate Investors, Inc. [Associated Press] (SAG)
MASCP	Multicultural and Cross-Cultural Supplementation Program [Australia]
MASCP&T	Member, American Society for Clinical Pharmacology & Therapeutics (CMD)
MASCS	Marriage Adjustment Sentence Completion Survey [Psychology]
MASCU	Marine Air Support Control Unit
MASD	Mach Aids to Surface-to-Air Missile Development (IAA)
MASD	Master of Arts in Spiritual Direction (PGP)
MASD	Menstrual-Associatied Sleep Disorder [Medicine] (MELL)
MASD	Mobile Air and Space Defense [Air Force]
MASDC	Military Aircraft Storage and Disposition Center
MASDCMIS	MASDC Management Information System (SAUO)
MASDR	Measurement and Signature Data Requirements (MCD)
MasdSec	Masada Security Holdings, Inc. [Associated Press] (SAG)
MASE	McDonnell Airborne Sidewinder Evaluator [McDonnell Douglas Corp.] (MCD)
MASE	Medical and Scientific Equipment
MASE	Military Assistance Service Fund (AAGC)
MASE	Mission and Systems Engineering (ACAE)
MASE	Moore School Air Space Simulation Effort (MCD)
MASE	Multi-Axis Seat Ejection (SAUS)
MASEA	Midwest Association of Student Employment Administrators [Formerly, MAUSED] (EA)
MASEAN	Medical Association of South East Asian Nations (BUAC)
MASEC	Mid-America Solar Energy Conference (SAUO)
MASEC	Multi-Access Systems Control Terminal (PDAA)
MASEE	Member of the Association of Supervisory and Executive Engineers [British] (DBQ)
MASEFI	Mass Air Sequential Electronic Fuel Injection [Automotive engineering]
MASEG	Microwave Antenna Systems Engineering Group (SAUO)
MASER	Microwave [or Molecular] Amplification by Stimulated Emission of Radiation
maser	Microwave Amplification by Stimulated Emission of Radiation (WDMC)
MASER	Molecular Application by Stimulated Emission of Radiation [Organic chemistry] (DAVI)
MASES	Microcomputer Advice and Selection Expert System (PDAA)
MASEX	Maritime Air Superiority Exercise (NVT)
MASF	Maintenance and Storage Facility (SAUO)
MASF	Marconi Advanced Sample Facility (NITA)
MASF	Military Assistance Service Fund
MASF	Military Assistance Service Funded
MASF	Mobile Aeromedical Staging Facility
MASF	Mobile Aeromedical Staging Flights (SAUS)
MASF	Multiracial American Scholarship Fund
MASFA	Middle Atlantic States Fencing Association (PSS)
MASFC	MAGTF All Source Fusion Center (SAUO)
MASFET	Metal-Alumina-Silicon Field Effect Transistor (IAA)
MASFLEX	Marginal Sea Flux Experiment (SAUO)
MASFLEX	Marginal Sea Flux Experiment in the West Pacific (SAUO)
MASFM	Maintenance and Supply Facility Management (AFIT)
MAS/FS	Mohawk Aerial Surveillance/Flight Simulator (MCD)
MASG	Marine Air Support Group
MASG	Military Airlift Support Group [Air Force]
MASG	Missile Auxiliary Signal Generator
MASG	Monitor and Alarm Subsystem Group (MCD)
MASGC	Mississippi-Alabama Sea Grant Consortium [Sea Grant College] [Research center] (RCD)
MASGP	Military Airlift Support Group [Air Force]
MASH	Manned Antisubmarine Helicopter
MASH	Medical Aid for Sick Hippies [Volunteer medical group]
MASH	Melting-Assimilation-Storage-Homogenization [Geology]
MASH	Memphians Against Social Harassment (SAUO)
MASH	Michigan Area Serial Holdings Consortium [Library network]
MASH	Micro-Analytic Simulation of Households (PDAA)
MASH	Mobile Army Surgical Hospital [Acronym also used as title of a satirical film, 1970, and a TV series]
MASH	Multiple Accelerated Summary Hearing [Deportation of illegal aliens] [Immigration and Naturalization Service]
MASH	Multiple Automated Sample Harvester [for culture systems]
MASH	Mutual Aid Self-Help Group
MASHAE	Member of the American Society of Heating and Air-conditioning Engineers (SAUO)
MASHONLD	Mashonaland (ROG)
MASHRAG	Egypt, Jordan, Lebanon & Syria (SAUS)
MASHVE	Member of the American Society of Heating and Ventilating Engineers (SAUO)
M/ASI	Mach/Airspeed Indicator (GAVI)
MASI	Media Association of the Solomon Islands (BUAC)
MASI	Middle Atmosphere Science Initiative (SAUO)
MASI	Multilevel Academic Skills Inventory [Educational test]
MASI	Multinational Agribusiness Systems, Inc. (SAUO)
MASID	Marine Science Division [Instrument Society of America] (MSC)
MASIIS	Maintenance Analysis Structural Integrity Information System (SAUO)
MASINT	Measurement and Signature Intelligence (MCD)
MASINT	Measuring & Signature Intelligence (SAUS)
MASIS	Management and Scientific Information Service (SAUO)
MASIS	Management and Scientific Information System [Air Force]
MASIS	Maruzen Scientific Information Service Center [Maruzen Co. Ltd.] [Japan] [Telecommunications]
MASIS	Mercury Abort Sensing Instrumentation System [NASA] (AAG)
MASK	Align-Rite International, Inc. [NASDAQ symbol] (SAG)
MASK	Align-Rite Intl. [NASDAQ symbol] (TTSB)
MASK	Maneuvering and Seakeeping
MASK	Medical Anatomy Segmentation Kit (DMAA)
MASK	Mobile Armored Strike Kommand [Game]
MASK	Multilevel Amplitude Shift Keying
maskon	Mass Concentration (BARN)
MAsl	Ashland Public Library, Ashland, MA [Library symbol] [Library of Congress] (LCLS)
masl	Meters above Sea Level
masl	Metres above sea level (SAUS)
MASL	Military Articles and Services List
MASL	Military Assistance Article and Service List (MCD)
MASL	Missouri Association of School Librarian
MASL	Missouri Association of School Librarians
Masland	Masland Corp. [Associated Press] (SAG)
MASLIG	Association of Management Analysts in State and Local Government (EA)
MASLPI	Mexican American State Legislators Policy Institute (CROSS)

MASM.........	Macro Assembler [*Computer language*] (PCM)
MASM.........	Master of Arts in Sacred Music (BJA)
MASM.........	Meta-Assembler (NITA)
MASM.........	Meta-Assembler Language [*Sperry UNIVAC computer language*]
MASM.........	Microsoft Assembler (SAUS)
MASM.........	Military Assistance and Sales Manual (AFIT)
MASM.........	Motorized Antenna Switching Matrix
MASME......	Member of the American Society of Mechanical Engineers
MASME......	Member of the Australian Society of Mechanical Engineers (SAUO)
MAS/MILS ...	Minerals Availability System/Minerals Industry Location Subsystem [*Bureau of Mines*] [*Database*]
MASMOD.....	Mass Model [*Computer program*]
MASMR	Multidimensional Attitude Scale on Mental Retardation (EDAC)
MASN	Machine Accountant, Seaman [*Navy*]
masn	Masonite (VRA)
MASN	Maximum Aggregate Student Number [*Higher Education Funding Council*] (AIE)
MASNC	Minerals Availability System [*Bureau of Mines*] [*Information service or system*] (IID)
Mas NE Pr...	Mason's New England Civil Practice [*A publication*] (DLA)
MASnet.......	Mainframe and Server network (SAUS)
MASNET	Management Support Network (SAUO)
MASNMR.....	Magic Angle Spinning Nuclear Magnetic Resonance [*Spectroscopy*]
Masnte	Maisonette
MASO	Military Assistance Sales Order (CINC)
MASO	Munition Accountable Supply Officer [*Air Force*] (AFM)
MASOA	Master and Slave Oscillator Array (PDAA)
MA (Social Studies)...	Master of Arts (Social Studies)
MA(SocSci)...	Master of Arts (Social Sciences), University of Glasgow [*British*] (DBQ)
MASocStud...	Master of Arts in Social Studies (NADA)
MASON.......	Masonry
Mason	Mason's United States Circuit Court Reports [*A publication*] (DLA)
Mason CCR...	Mason's United States Circuit Court Reports [*A publication*] (DLA)
Mason Circt Ct R...	Mason's United States Circuit Court Reports [*A publication*] (DLA)
MasonDix	Mason-Dixon Bancshares, Inc. [*Associated Press*] (SAG)
Mason R......	Mason's United States Circuit Court Reports [*A publication*] (DLA)
Mason's Code...	Mason's United States Code, Annotated [*A publication*] (DLA)
Mason's R ...	Mason's United States Circuit Court Reports [*A publication*] (DLA)
Mason's Rep...	Mason's United States Circuit Court Reports [*A publication*] (DLA)
Mason US....	Mason's United States Circuit Court Reports [*A publication*] (DLA)
Mason US Circ Ct Rep...	Mason's United States Circuit Court Reports [*A publication*] (DLA)
Mason USR...	Mason's United States Circuit Court Reports [*A publication*] (DLA)
MASP..........	Medical Application Service Provider (SAUO)
MASP..........	Microaerophilus Stationary Phase [*Biochemistry*] (DAVI)
MASP..........	Modular Atmosphere Simulation Program [*NASA*] (KSC)
MASP..........	Multiple Access Signal Processor (ACAE)
MASPAC	Microfilm Advisory Service of the Public Archives of Canada (PDAA)
MAS PIL	Massa Pilularum [*A Pill Mass*] [*Pharmacy*]
MasPrt........	MassMutual Participation Investors [*Associated Press*] (SAG)
MASPS	Minimum Aviation System Performance Standards [*FAA*] (TAG)
MASPSq	Military Airlift Special Squadron [*Air Force*]
MASPTSq	Military Airlift Support Squadron [*Air Force*]
MASq..........	Military Airlift Squadron [*Air Force*] (AFM)
MASQUES...	Medical Application Software Quality Enhancement by Standards (SAUO)
Mas R.........	Massachusetts Reports [*A publication*] (DLA)
MASR	Memory-Address Select Register [*Computer science*] (IAA)
MASR	Microwave Atmosphere Sounding Radiometer (PDAA)
MASR	Miniature Airborne/Spaceborne Reconnaissance (ACAE)
MASR	Multiple-Antenna Moving-Target Surveillance RADAR
MASR	Multiple Antenna Surveillance Radar (SAUS)
MASRC	Major Automated System Review Council [*Military*]
MASRC	Mexican American Studies and Research Center [*University of Arizona*] [*Research center*] (RCD)
Mas Rep......	Massachusetts Reports [*A publication*] (DLA)
MASRO........	Mid-Atlantic Society of Radiation Oncologists (SAUO)
MASRT	Marine Air Support RADAR Teams (IEEE)
MASRU........	Marine Air Support RADAR Unit [*DoD*]
MASS..........	Magic Angle Sample Spinning [*Spectroscopy*]
MASS..........	Manned Activity Scheduling System [*NASA*]
MASS..........	Manned Aircraft Surface to Surface (ACAE)
MASS..........	Manned Aircraft Versus Surface to Surface (ACAE)
MASS..........	MARC [*Machine-Readable Cataloging*] Automated Serials System (PDAA)
MASS..........	MARC-Based Automated Serials System (NITA)
MASS..........	Marine Air Support Squadron
MASS..........	Maritime Air Surveillance Sortie (SAUS)
MASS..........	Maritime Anti-Standing SONAR System (DNAB)
MASS..........	Massa [*A Mass*] [*Pharmacy*]
MASS..........	Massachusetts (AFM)
Mass..........	Massachusetts (BEE)
MASS..........	Massachusetts Association of School Superintendents (SAUO)
MASS..........	Massachusetts Bay (GAAI)
Mass..........	Massachusetts Supreme Judicial Court Reports [*A publication*] (DLA)
mass..........	Massage (DMAA)
MASS..........	Massage
MASS..........	Massive (SAUS)
MA(SS).......	Master of Arts in Social Science (ADA)
MASS..........	Master of Arts in Special Studies (PGP)
M As S	Master of Association Science
MASS..........	Material Accountability and Safeguards System (SAUO)
MASS..........	Materials Acquisition Sub-System [*Computer science*]

MASS..........	Matrix Analysis Subsystem (MCD)
MASS	Maximum Availability and Support Subsystem (VLIE)
MAS/S	Mechanical Arm Sub-System (ACAE)
MASS..........	Mechanically Accelerated Sabot System [*Generation of high-density molecular beams*]
MASS..........	Medicine, Angioplasty, or Surgery Study (DMAA)
MASS..........	Membrane Affinity Separation System
MASS..........	Memorandum Accounts Statement System (DCTA)
MASS..........	MICAP [*Mission Critical Parts*] Asset Sourcing System (DOMA)
MASS..........	Michigan Aging Services System (SAUO)
MASS..........	Michigan Automatic Scanning System (IEEE)
MASS..........	Microsystem Analysis and Simulation System (SAUO)
MAss	Middle Assyrian [*Language, etc.*] (BJA)
MASS..........	Military Agency for Supply and Service (SAUO)
MASS..........	Military Airlift Support Squadron [*Air Force*]
MASS..........	Military Airlift Survivability Study (ACAE)
MASS..........	Military Approach and Surveillance System (SAUO)
MASS..........	Missile and Space Summary (MCD)
MASS..........	Missiles/Ammunition System Study
MASS..........	Mission Avionics Sensor Synergism (SAUS)
MASS..........	Mobility Analysis Support System [*Air Force*]
MASS	Mobilization Automated Support System (SAUO)
MASS..........	Modern Army Supply System
MASS..........	Modular Adaptive Signal Sorter
MASS..........	Modular Aircrew Simulation System (SAUS)
MASS..........	Money Advice Support Services (BUAC)
MASS..........	Monitor and Assembly System [*or Subsystem*] [*Computer science*] (BUR)
MASS..........	Multiple Access Sequential Selection [*Computer science*] (BUR)
MASS..........	Multiple Access Switching System (NITA)
MASS..........	Multiple Array Serial Scan (ACAE)
MASS..........	Multi-role Aid & Support Ship (SAUS)
Mass Acts...	Acts and Resolves of Massachusetts [*A publication*] (DLA)
Mass AD.....	Massachusetts Appellate Decisions [*A publication*] (DLA)
Mass Admin Code...	Code of Massachusetts Regulations [*A publication*] (DLA)
Mass Admin Reg...	Massachusetts Register [*A publication*] (DLA)
Mass ADR...	Massachusetts Appellate Division Reports [*A publication*] (DLA)
Mass Adv Legis Serv...	Massachusetts Advance Legislative Service [*Lawyers Co-Operative Publishing Co.*] [*A publication*] (DLA)
Mass Adv Sh...	Massachusetts Advance Sheets [*A publication*] (DLA)
Mass Adv Sheets...	Massachusetts Advance Sheets [*A publication*] (DLA)
Mass Ann Laws...	Annotated Laws of Massachusetts [*A publication*] (DLA)
Mass Ann Laws...	Annotated Laws of Massachusetts (journ.) (SAUS)
Mass App Ct...	Massachusetts Appeals Court Reports [*A publication*] (DLA)
Mass App Ct Adv Sh...	Massachusetts Appeals Court Advance Sheets [*A publication*] (DLA)
Mass App Dec...	Massachusetts Appellate Decisions [*A publication*] (DLA)
Mass App Div...	Massachusetts Appellate Division Reports [*A publication*] (DLA)
Mass App Rep...	Massachusetts Appeals Court Reports [*A publication*] (DLA)
MASSAR......	Multimode Airborne Solid State Array RADAR
Mass BC & A...	Massachusetts Board of Conciliation and Arbitration Reports [*A publication*] (DLA)
Massbnk......	Massbank Corp. [*Associated Press*] (SAG)
MASSBUS...	Memory Bus [*Digital Equipment Corp.*]
massc.........	Mass Concentration (DMAA)
M As Sc.......	Master of Association Science
MASSCAL	Mass Casualties [*Military*] (AABC)
Mass C Art...	Massachusetts College of Art (GAGS)
MASSCOMP...	Massachusetts Computer Corp. (SAUO)
Mass Cont Election Cushing S & J...	Massachusetts Controverted Election Cases [*A publication*] (DLA)
Mass C Pharmacy...	Massachusetts College of Pharmacy (GAGS)
MASSDAR....	Modular Analysis, Speedup, Sampling, and Data Reduction
MASSDATA...	Mark Sense Source Data Automation Test and Analysis (MCD)
Mass Dent Soc J...	Massachusetts Dental Society Journal (GAGS)
MASSDET ...	Marine Air Support Squadron Detachment (DNAB)
Mass DIA.....	Massachusetts. Department of Industrial Accidents. Bulletin [*A publication*] (DLA)
Mass Dr Com...	Masse. Le Droit Commercial [*A publication*] (DLA)
Mass EC L & R...	Loring and Russell's Election Cases in Massachusetts [*A publication*] (DLA)
Mass Elec Ca...	Massachusetts Election Cases [*A publication*] (DLA)
Mass Elec Cas...	Massachusetts Election Cases [*A publication*] (DLA)
Mass Election Cases...	Loring and Russell's Election Cases in Massachusetts [*A publication*] (DLA)
Mass Election Cases...	Russell's Contested Election Cases [*Massachusetts*] [*A publication*] (DLA)
Mass Gen L...	General Laws of the Commonwealth of Massachusetts (journ.) (SAUS)
Mass Gen Laws...	Massachusetts General Laws [*A publication*] (DLA)
Mass Gen Laws Ann (West)...	Massachusetts General Laws, Annotated (West) [*A publication*] (DLA)
MassHe	Massachusetts Health & Education Tax Exempt Trust [*Associated Press*] (SAG)
MASS HFD...	Multi-Additional SCSI [*Small Computer System Interface*] Subsystem Hot Fix Device [*Computer science*]
Mass IAB	Massachusetts Industrial Accident Board Reports of Cases [*A publication*] (DLA)
MASSIIS	Maintenance Analysis and Structural Integration Information System
Mass LRC Dec...	Massachusetts Labor Relations Commission Decisions [*A publication*] (DLA)
MASSOP.......	Multi-Automatic System for Simulation and Operational Planning (PDAA)
MASSP	Michigan Association of Secondary School Principals (SAUO)
MASSP	Minnesota Association of Secondary School Principals (SAUO)

MASSP	Missouri Association of Secondary School Principals (SAUO)
MASSP	Montana Association of Secondary School Principals (SAUO)
Mass Pil	Massa Pilularum [*A Pill Mass*] [*Pharmacy*]
MassPIRG....	Massachusetts Public Interest Research Group (SAUO)
MASSPO	Manned Space Flight Support Project Office [*NASA*] (IAA)
MASSq	Military Airlift Support Squadron [*Air Force*] (AFM)
Mass R	Massachusetts Reports [*A publication*]
MASSR	Mordovian Autonomous Soviet Socialist Republic (SAUO)
Mass Rep	Massachusetts Reports [*A publication*] (DLA)
MASS SPEC...	Mass Spectrometry (GOBB)
Mass St BC & A..	Massachusetts State Board of Conciliation and Arbitration Reports [*A publication*] (DLA)
Mass Supp...	Massachusetts Reports Supplement [*A publication*] (AAGC)
MASST........	Major Shipboard SATCOM Terminal (MCD)
MASST........	Major Ship Satellite Terminal
MASSTER	Mobile Army Sensor System Test, Evaluation, and Review
MASSTER	Modern Army Selected System Test, Evaluation, and Review
Mass UCC Op...	Massachusetts Unemployment Compensation Commission Opinions [*A publication*] (DLA)
Mass UC Dig...	Massachusetts Division of Unemployment Compensation Digest of Board of Review Decisions [*A publication*] (DLA)
Mass UC Ops...	Massachusetts Division of Unemployment Compensation Opinions [*A publication*] (DLA)
Mass WCC...	Massachusetts Workmen's Compensation Cases [*A publication*] (DLA)
MAST..........	Arousal Seeking Tendency Scale [*Test*] (TMMY)
MAST..........	Machine Automated Speech Transcription (PDAA)
MAST..........	Magnetic Annular Shock Tube
MaST..........	Management and Skills Training (BUAC)
MAST..........	Marine Science and Technology
MAST..........	Marine Science and Technology Programme (SAUO)
MAST..........	Marine Stable Element
MAST..........	Market Structures and Trends on Italy [*Databank Ltd.*] [*British*] (ECON)
MAST..........	Mastech Corp. [*NASDAQ symbol*] (SAG)
MAST..........	Mastectomy [*Medicine*] (AAMN)
MAST..........	Master (ROG)
Mast	Master's Supreme Court Reports [*25-28 Canada*] [*A publication*] (DLA)
MAST..........	Mastoid [*Medicine*]
MAST..........	Measurement and Stimuli System (SSD)
MAST..........	Medical Antishock Trausers (MELL)
MAST..........	Medical Anti-Shock Trousers [*Military*]
MAST..........	Meteorological Automated Sensor and Transceiver [*Military*]
MAST..........	Metro Arson Strike Team (SAUO)
MAST..........	Metropolitan Arson Strike Team (SAUO)
MAST..........	Michelin Americas Small Tires
MAST..........	Michigan Alcoholism Screening Test
MAST..........	Midlevel Positions in Administrative, Staff, and Technical Services [*Civil Service Commission*]
MAST..........	Midwest Agents Selling Travel (TVEL)
MAST..........	Military Antishock Trousers [*Medicine*]
MAST..........	Military Assistance to Safety and Traffic [*Project*] [*Army*] (RDA)
MAST..........	Minimum Abbreviations of Serial Titles [*A publication*]
MAST..........	Missile Automatic Supply Technique
MAST..........	Mobile Aircrew Sustainment Trainer (SAUS)
MAST..........	Mobile Assembly Sterilizer for Testing
MAST..........	Model Assembly Sterilizer for Testing [*NASA*]
MAST..........	Monterey Area Ship Experiment (SAUO)
MAST..........	Monterey Area Ship Track experiment (SAUO)
MAST..........	Multilevel Academic Survey Test [*Educational test*]
MAST..........	Multimission Airborne Surveillance Technology programme (SAUS)
MAST..........	Multiple-Aircraft Simulation Terminal (DA)
MAST..........	Multiple Applications Storage Tube
MAST..........	Multivalued Advanced Simulation Techniques (VLIE)
MAST..........	Munitions Assistance and Standardization Team (MCD)
MASTA........	Medical Advisory Services for Travellers Abroad [*London School of Hygiene and Tropical Medicine*] [*Information service or system*] (IID)
MastAcftCrmnBad...	Master Aircraft Crewman Badge [*Military decoration*] (AABC)
MASTACS	Maneuverability Augmentation System for Tactical Air Combat Simulation (PDAA)
MASTAP	Master System Tape (IAA)
MASTAP	Master Tape (VLIE)
MASTARAV...	Master Army Aviator (AABC)
Mast AR Av Bad...	Master Army Aviator Badge [*Military decoration*]
MASTARS ...	Mechanical and Structural Testing and Referral Service [*National Institute of Standards and Technology*]
MAStat........	Master of Applied Statistics
Mast Div Bad...	Master Diver Badge [*Military decoration*]
MAST-E.......	Multicenter Acute Stroke Trial-Europe [*Neurology*]
Mastec........	Mastec, Inc. [*Associated Press*] (SAG)
Mastech.......	Mastech Corp. [*Associated Press*] (SAG)
Mast El	Masterman's Parliamentary Elections [*1880*] [*A publication*] (DLA)
MASTER	Manuscript Access through Standards for Electronic Records [*Library science*] (TELE)
MASTER	Matching Available Student Time to Educational Resources [*Computer science*]
MASTER	Military Aircraft Satcoms Terminal (SAUS)
MASTER	Miniaturized Sink-Rate Telemetering RADAR
MASTER	Modular Acoustic Stimulator/Emulator (SAUS)
MASTER	Multiple Access Shared Time Executive Routine [*Control Data Corp.*] [*Computer science*]
MASTER KEY...	Managership of Soldier Training, Education, and Readiness with Knowledge and Excellence Year-Round [*Army*] (INF)
MASTEX.......	Mediterranean Aircraft and Ship Transmission Experiment (SAUO)
MASTICH	Mastiche [*Mastic*] [*Pharmacy*] (ROG)
MASTIF........	Multi-Axis Spin Test Inertia Facility [*Training device for astronauts*]
MASTIFF.......	Modular Automated System to Identify Friend from Foe [*Military*] (PDAA)
Mastin Art ...	Masters in Art (SAUO)
Mastin Music...	Masters in Music (SAUO)
MASTIR	Handbook on Marine Scientific and Technological Information Resources (SAUS)
MASTIR	Microfilmed Abstract System for Technical Information Retrieval [*Illinois Institute of Technology*] (IID)
MASTOR	Main Storage (VLIE)
MastPrchtBad...	Master Parachutist Badge [*Military decoration*] (AABC)
MASTS........	Marine Associated Services Technology Systems Exposition [*Canada*] (ITD)
MaSTS........	Marine Strategy for the Torres Strait (SAUO)
MAstS........	Member of the Astronomical Society
MASTT........	MPS Action Speed Tactical Trainer (SAUS)
MASTU	Mobile Antisubmarine Training Unit [*British*]
MASU	Machined Surface
MASU	Mediterranean and African Society for Ultrasound (SAUO)
MASU	Mediterranean and African Society of Ultrasound [*France*] (BUAC)
MASU	Mesoamerican Archaeology Study Unit [*American Topical Association*] (EA)
MASU	Metal Alloy Separation Unit
MASU	Mid-Atlantic State University
MASU	Mobile Army Surgical Unit
MASU	Multiple Acceleration Sensor Unit (PDAA)
MASUA	Mid-America State Universities Association [*Defunct*] (EA)
MASURCA...	Marine Surface Contre Avions (SAA)
MASW	Master of Arts in Social Work
MASW	Master Switch (IAA)
MASW	Military Airlift Support Wing [*Air Force*]
MASW	Mission Application Software (SAUO)
MASWEP	Medium Active Solid Waste Encapsulation Plant [*Nuclear energy*] (NUCP)
MASWg........	Military Airlift Support Wing [*Air Force*] (AFM)
MASWSP	Manager, Antisubmarine Warfare Systems Project [*Navy*]
MASWSPO...	Manager, Antisubmarine Warfare Systems Project Office [*Navy*]
MASWT.......	Mobile Antisubmarine Warfare Target (MCD)
MASWT.......	MPS Anti-Submarine Warfare Trainer (SAUS)
MASX..........	Mastec, Inc. [*NASDAQ symbol*] (SAG)
MAT...........	Machine-Aided Translation (NITA)
MAT...........	Machine Analysis Table (IAA)
MAT...........	Machine-Assisted Translation
MAT...........	Machine Available Time [*Computer science*]
MAT...........	Macro-Alloy Transistor (VLIE)
MAT...........	Maine Air Transport, Inc. (SAUO)
MAT...........	Maine Aviation Corp. [*ICAO designator*] (FAAC)
MAT...........	Maintainability of Software Analysis Tool (MCD)
MAT...........	Maintenance Access Terminal [*Aviation*]
MAT...........	Maintenance Appraisal Team (MCD)
MAT...........	Mammary Ascites Tumor [*Oncology*]
MAT...........	Management Advisory Team (NRCH)
MAT...........	Manifold Air Temperature [*Automotive engineering*]
MAT...........	Manual Arts Therapist
MAT...........	Manufacture and Test (SAUO)
MAT...........	Marine Air Temperature [*Meteorology*]
MAT...........	Maritime, Aviation, and Transport Insurance (DLA)
MAT...........	Marketing Assistance Test
MAT...........	Marksman Advanced Trainer (SAUS)
MAT...........	Master Account Title [*Office of Management and Budget*]
MA(T)	Master of Arts in Teaching (PGP)
MAT...........	Master of Arts in Theology (PGP)
MAT...........	Master Operational Recording Tape Address Table (IAA)
MAT...........	Matachewan Consolidated Mines Ltd. [*Toronto Stock Exchange symbol*]
MAT...........	Matadi [*Zaire*] [*Airport symbol*] [*Obsolete*] (OAG)
MAT...........	Matching Abacus Test [*Parapsychology*]
MAT...........	Material (AFM)
Mat............	Material (DIAR)
mat............	Material (VRA)
MAT...........	Materials Department [*David W. Taylor Naval Ship Research and Development Center*] [*Annapolis, MD*]
MAT...........	Materiel [*Military*] (AFM)
Mat............	Maternal (GEAB)
Mat............	Maternal (STED)
Mat............	Maternity (STED)
MAT...........	Maternity
MAT...........	Mathematical Automata Theory
mat............	Matinee (WDAA)
MAT...........	Matinee
MAT...........	Matins (ROG)
MAT...........	Matrix (MSA)
mat............	Matrix (WDAA)
MAT...........	Matrix Analogies Test [*Intelligence test*]
MAT...........	Matsushiro [*Japan*] [*Seismograph station code, US Geological Survey*] (SEIS)
MAT...........	Mattel, Inc. [*NYSE symbol*] (SPSG)
Mat............	Mattheus de Mathesillanis [*Flourished, 1381-1402*] [*Authority cited in pre-1607 legal work*] (DSA)
MAT...........	Matthew [*New Testament book*]
Mat............	Mature (STED)
MAT...........	Matured
Mat............	Maturity (EBF)

MAT............. Maturity
MAT............. Matutinal (ADA)
MAT............. Mean Absorption Time [Medicine] (MELL)
MAT............. Mean Annual Temperature [Climatology]
MAT............. Measurement of Atmospheric Turbulence
MAT............. Mechanical Aptitude Test
MAT............. Mechanical Assembly Technique (IAA)
MAT............. Mechanically Agitated Tank [Engineering]
MAT............. Medial Axes Transformation (MHDI)
MAT............. Medial Axis Transformation (MHDB)
MAT............. Medical Assessment Tribunal [Queensland, Australia]
MAT............. Medium Artillery Tractor [British military] (DMA)
MAT............. Medium Assault Transport (MCD)
MAT............. Memory Access Table [Computer science]
MAT............. Memory-Address Test
MAT............. Memory Address Translator (NITA)
MAT............. Mercury Amalgamation Trap [Analytical chemistry]
MAT............. Meridian Administration Tools [Telecommunications] (ITD)
MAT............. Meteorological Atmospheric Turbulence (MCD)
MAT............. Methionine Adenosyltransferase [An enzyme]
MAT............. Metropolitan Achievement Test
MAT............. Metropolitan Area Trunk [Telecommunications] (TEL)
MAT............. Microactivity Testing [Catalysis technology]
MAT............. Microagglutination Test [Medicine] (MELL)
MAT............. Microalloy Transistor
MAT............. Microtray Agglutination Test [Clinical chemistry]
MAT............. Microwave Anisotropy Telescope (SAUS)
MAT............. Microwave Antenna Tower
MAT............. Military Aircraft Types
MAT............. Military Air Transport
MAT............. Miller-Abbott Tube [Surgery] [Medicine] (DAVI)
MAT............. Miller Analogies Test [Psychology]
MAT............. Mine Action Team (SAUO)
MAT............. Mine Assembly Team [Navy] (NVT)
MAT............. Minimal Aversion Threshold [to noise]
MAT............. Minimum Allowable Threshold [Chemistry]
MAT............. Missile Acceptance Team (AAG)
MAT............. Missile Acceptance Test
MAT............. Missile Acquisition and Track
MAT............. Missile Adapter Tester
MAT............. Missile Airframe Technology (MCD)
MAT............. Missile Antitank
MAT............. Mobile Advisor Team [Vietnamese team trained by US Army advisors] (VNW)
MAT............. Mobile Aerial Target (AAG)
MAT............. Mobile Arming Tower (KSC)
MAT............. Mobile Assistance Team [Federal disaster planning]
MAT............. Mobile Mine Assembly Team
MAT............. Mobilization Assistance Team (SAUO)
MAT............. Modular Advanced Test (SAUS)
MAT............. Modular Allocation Technique (PDAA)
MAT............. Modular Assembly Technique (IAA)
MAT............. Molecular Analysis Team
MAT............. Monoamine Transporter [Biochemistry]
MAT............. Monocyto-Angiotropin [Biochemistry]
MAT............. Monopulse Angle Tracker (ACAE)
MAT............. Motivation Analysis Test [Psychology]
MAT............. Motor Ambulance Trolley [British]
MAT............. Moving Annual Total [Statistics] (DCTA)
MAT............. Multiallelic Mating-Type Regulatory Gene
MAT............. Multifocal Atrial Tachycardia [Cardiology]
MAT............. Multimedia Access Terminals [Philips] [Electronics]
MAT............. Multiple Access Test
MAT............. Multiple Access Time [Telecommunications] (ECII)
MAT............. Multiple Actuator Test (MCD)
MAT............. Multiple Address Telegrams
MAT............. Multiple-Agent Chemotherapy [Medicine] (DB)
MAT............. Multiple Aptitude Test [Education] (AEBS)
MATA........... Michigan Aviation Trades Association (SAUO)
MATA........... Military Air Transport Association (SAUO)
MATA........... Military Assistance Training Advisor
MATA........... Motorcycle and Allied Trades Association [Later, MIC] (EA)
MATA........... Multiple Answering Teaching Aid (PDAA)
MATA........... Museums Association of Tropical Africa (BUAC)
MATA........... Musical Arena Theatres Association [Later, PAMI] (EA)
MATABE...... Multiple-Weapon Automatic Target and Battery Evaluator (SAA)
MATAC........ Money Advice Trust Advisory Committee (BUAC)
MAT ACCAT... Mobile Access Terminal Advanced Command & Control Architectural Test-bed (SAUS)
MATACQ...... Material Acquisition (NG)
MATADOR... Mobile and Three-Dimensional Air Defense Operations RADAR [Military] (PDAA)
MATADOR... Multi-role Adaptive Tactical Auto-programmable Dynamic Radio System (SAUS)
MATAF........ Mediterranean Allied Tactical Air Force
Mataph........ Metaphysics (SAUO)
Mata Soc..... Mattachine Society (SAUO)
MATB.......... Military Air Transport Board
MATB.......... Missile Auxiliary Test Bench
MATC.......... Maximum Acceptable Tolerance Concentration (GNE)
MATC.......... Maximum Acceptable Toxicant Concentration
MATC.......... Maximum Allowable Toxicant Concentration (EEVL)
MATC.......... Middle Atlantic Conference (PSS)
MATC.......... Military Air Transport Command (MUGU)
MATC.......... Milwaukee Area Technical College (PCM)

MATC.......... Missile Auxiliaries Test Console
MATC.......... Mobilization Army Training Center
MATC.......... Mountain Artillery Training Centre [British military] (DMA)
MATCALS ... Marine Air Traffic and Landing Systems (SAUO)
MATCALS ... Marine Air Traffic Control and Landing System [Navy]
MATCALS ... Mobile Air Traffic Control and All-Weather Landing System (MCD)
MATCAT...... Material Category
MATCen...... Military Air Traffic Center (SAUO)
MATCH .... Manned Anti-submarine Troop-Carrying Helicopter (SAUS)
MATCH .... Manned Attack Torpedo Carrying Helicopter (PDAA)
MATCH .... Manpower and Talent Clearinghouse
MATCH .... Matching Alcoholism Treatments to Client Heterogeneity
MATCH .... Materials and Activities for Teachers and Children
MATCH .... Medium-Range Antisubmarine Torpedo Carrying Helicopter (NATG)
MATCH .... Model for Atmospheric Chemistry and Transport (SAUO)
MATCH .... Mothers Apart from Their Children [British] (DI)
MATCH .... MTMC [Military Traffic Management Command] Automated Transportation Scheduler (GFGA)
MATCH .... Multielement Assured Tracking Chopper
MATCH .... Multimedia Authoring Environments for Children (SAUO)
MATCM....... Master of Acupuncture and Traditional Chinese Medicine (PGP)
MATCO....... Materials Analysis, Tracking, and Control [Johnson Space Center data system] [NASA] (NASA)
MATCO....... Military Air Traffic Coordinating Office [or Officer] [Air Force] (AFM)
MATCOM..... Material and Techniques for Cooperative Management Training (SAUO)
MATCOM..... Materiel Command [Army] (AABC)
MATCOMEUR... Materiel Command, Europe
MATCON..... Microwave Aerospace Terminal Control [Air Force]
MATCon...... Military Air Traffic Control (SAUO)
MATCONOFF... Material Control Officer (MCD)
MatCo-Ord(N)... Material Co-Ordination Division (Naval) [British]
MATCS........ Marine Air Traffic Control Squadron (DNAB)
MATCSDET... Marine Air Traffic Control Squadron Detachment (DNAB)
MATCU....... Marine Air Tactical [later, Traffic] Control Unit [Marine Corps]
MATCU....... Military Air Traffic Coordinating Unit [MTMC] (TAG)
MATCV........ Mobile Air Traffic Control Vehicle [Military]
MATD.......... Mine and Torpedo Detector [SONAR] [Navy]
MATDA........ Methylene-bis-(aminothiadiazole) [Pesticide]
MATDEV ..... Materiel Developer
MATE.......... Machine-Aided Translation Editing (PDAA)
MATE.......... Manual Adaptive TMA [Target Motion Analysis] Estimator [Navy] (ANA)
MATE.......... Manually Aided Tracking Enhancement (MCD)
MATE.......... Marital Attitude Evaluation [Psychology]
MATE.......... Master of Arts in the Teaching of English
Mat E.......... Materials Engineer
MATE.......... Materials for Advanced Turbine Engines (SAUS)
MATE.......... Maternal Attitudes Evaluation (STED)
MATE.......... Matewan BancShares [NASDAQ symbol] (TTSB)
MATE.......... Matewan BancShares, Inc. [NASDAQ symbol] (SAG)
MATE.......... Matrix Automation through EMATS [Military] (MCD)
MATE.......... McDonnell Airborne Trainer and Evaluator [McDonnell Douglas Corp.] (MCD)
MATE.......... Measuring and Test Equipment (IEEE)
MATE.......... Memory-Assisted Terminal Equipment (PDAA)
MATE.......... Meteorological Analog Test and Evaluation (PDAA)
MATE.......... MICOM [Missile Command] Automated Test Equipment
MATE.......... Microprocessor Automatic Testing [ASMAP Electronics Ltd.] [Software package] (NCC)
MATE.......... Missile/Aircraft Test Equipment
MATE.......... Mission Analysis Technique for Experiments
MATE.......... Mobilization and Training Equipment (MCD)
MATE.......... Modular AUTODIN Terminal Equipment (SAUO)
MATE.......... Modular Automated Test Equipment (SAUO)
MATE.......... Modular Automatic Test Equipment
MATE.......... Modular Avionics Test Equipment (ACAE)
MATE.......... Modulated Automatic Test Equipment (SAUS)
MATE.......... Montana Agri-Trade Exposition [Jerry Hanson and Associates, Inc.] (TSPED)
MATE.......... Multiband Automatic Test Equipment
MATE.......... Multiple-Access Time-Division Experiment (IEEE)
MATE.......... Multiple Advanced Technique Evaluation [Military] (CAAL)
MATE.......... Multipurpose Automatic Test Equipment
MATE.......... Multisystem Automatic Test Equipment [British]
MATE.......... Scientific Society of Measurement and Automation (SAUO)
MATEAM...... Manufacturing Process Applications Team (ACAE)
MATEC........ Maintenance Technician (NOAA)
Matec......... MATEC Corp. [Associated Press] (SAG)
MA (T Ed)... Master of Arts in Teacher Education
MAT-EF....... Matrix Analogies Test - Expanded Form [Intelligence test]
MATEL........ Multiplexed Automatic Telephone Equipment (SAUS)
MATELO...... Maritime Air-Radio Telegraph Organization (BUAC)
MATELO...... Maritime Air Telecommunications Organization [NATO] (NATG)
MATEM....... Manual Templating Model (MCD)
MATEP........ Matewan Bancshrs 7.5% Cv'A'Pfd [NASDAQ symbol] (TTSB)
MATER....... Magnetic Tape Event Recorder (ACAE)
MATER....... Material
MATERN..... Maternal (WDAA)
MATERN..... Maternity (WDAA)
Mater Note Aust Aeronaut Res Lab... Australia. Aeronautical Research Laboratories. Materials Note (journ.) (SAUS)
Mater Rep Aust Aeronaut Res lb... Australia. Aeronautical Research Laboratories. Materials Report (journ.) (SAUS)
MATES........ Medium Attack Tactical Employment School [Military] (CAAL)

MATES.........	Mobilization and Training Equipment Site [*Military*] (AABC)
MATES.........	Multi-band Anti-ship Tactical Electronic warfare System (SAUS)
MATES.........	Multimedia Assisted distributed Tele-Engineering Services (SAUO)
MATESL......	Master of Arts in Teaching English as a Second Language (PGP)
MA(TESOL)..	Master of Arts in Teaching English to Speakers of Other Languages
Matewan......	Matewan BancShares, Inc. [*Associated Press*] (SAG)
MATEX........	Macrotext Editor (MHDB)
MATEX........	Massive Air Tracer Experiment (SAUO)
MATEX........	Master of Arts in Textiles (PGP)
MATEX........	Material Expediting [*Program*] (DNAB)
MATFA........	Meat and Allied Trades Federation of Australia (BUAC)
MATFL........	Master of Arts in Teaching Foreign Language (PGP)
Math	Adversus Mathematicos [*of Sextus Empiricus*] [*Classical studies*] (OCD)
MATH..........	Astronomy/Mathematic/Statistics Library (SAUS)
MA(Th)	Master of Arts in Theology
MATH..........	Master of Arts in Therapy (PGP)
Math	Mathematical (SAUO)
Math	Mathematics (AL)
math	Mathematics (ELAL)
MATH..........	Mathematics (EY)
MATH..........	Mathematics Abstracts [*Fachinformationszentrum Karlsruhe GmbH*] [*Information service or system*]
Math	Matheus de Mathesillanis [*Flourished, 1381-1402*] [*Authority cited in pre-1607 legal work*] (DSA)
Math	Mathieu's Quebec Reports [*A publication*] (DLA)
MATH..........	Mathsoft, Inc. [*NASDAQ symbol*] (SAG)
MATH..........	Mobile, Air-Transportable Hospital [*Military*]
MATH..........	Modern Approach to Treatment of Hypertension [*Medicine*] (DMAA)
MathBiosci..	Mathematical Biosciences (SAUO)
MathComput..	Mathematics of Computation (SAUO)
Math D	Doctor of Mathematics
MATHDI	Mathematical Didactics [*Fachinformationszentrum Energie, Physik, Mathematik GmbH*] [*Database*]
Mathe de Afflcti...	Matthaeus de Afflictis [*Deceased, 1528*] [*Authority cited in pre-1607 legal work*] (DSA)
MA Theol.....	Master of Arts in Theology
MATHL........	Mathematical
MATHLAB	Mathematical Laboratory [*Programming language*] (CSR)
MathMo	Mathematical Monthly (SAUO)
MATHN	Mathematician (AFM)
Math N	Matthaeus Nerutius [*Flourished, 16th century*] [*Authority cited in pre-1607 legal work*] (DSA)
MathNotes...	Mathematical Notes (SAUO)
MATHP	Medium Artillery Terminal Homing Projectile
MATHPAC ...	Mathematical Package (IAA)
Math Pres Ev...	Mathews on Presumptive Evidence [*A publication*] (DLA)
MathR..........	Mathematical Reviews (SAUO)
MATHS	Mathematical Access for Technology and Science for visually disabled users (SAUO)
MATHS	Mathematics
Mathsft........	Mathsoft, Inc. [*Associated Press*] (SAG)
MathSystTheory...	Mathematical Systems Theory (SAUO)
Math T	Mathematics Teacher [*A publication*] (BRI)
MathUSSR-Izv...	Mathematics of the USSR-Izvestiya (SAUO)
MathUSSR-Sb...	Mathematics of the USSR-Sbornik (SAUO)
MATI...........	Maldives Association of the Tourism Industry (EY)
MATI...........	Moscow Aviation Technology Institute (SAUO)
MATIC.........	Multiple Area Technical Information Center
MATIC.........	Multi-Strategy Authoring Toolkit for Intelligent Courseware (SAUO)
MATICO	Machine Applications to Technical Information Center Operations
MATICO	Mastic Tile Corporation of America (SAUO)
MATIF.........	Marche a Terme des Instruments Financiere [*French stock exchange*]
MATIF.........	Marche a Terme des Instruments Financiers [*French Financial Futures Market*]
MATILDA	Microwave Analysis Threat Indication and Launch Direction Apparatus [*Military*]
MATINSP	Material Inspection [*Navy*] (NVT)
MATK..........	Martek Biosciences, Inc. [*NASDAQ symbol*] (SAG)
MATL..........	Master of Arts in Teaching of Languages (PGP)
MATL..........	Material (KSC)
MATL..........	Materiel
MATL..........	Middle Atlantic
Mat Lab.......	Material Laboratory (SAUO)
MATLAB	Matrix Laboratory [*Computer science*]
Matlack........	Matlack Systems, Inc. [*Associated Press*] (SAG)
MATLAN	Matrix Language [*Computer science*] (IEEE)
Mat L & T....	Mathews on Landlord and Tenant [*A publication*] (DLA)
MATLC........	Mid-Atlantic Conference (PSS)
MATL REQ ...	Material Requisition
MATL RR	Material Receiving Report
MATM.........	Master of Arts in Teaching of Mathematics (PGP)
MATMO.......	Medical Advanced Technology Management Office
MATMO.......	Military Advanced Technology Management Office (RDA)
MATMOP	Materiel Management Optimization Program [*DoD*]
MATMS.......	Marine Aviation Training Management System (SAUO)
MATMU.......	Mobile Aircraft Torpedo Maintenance Unit
MATNET.......	Mobile Access Terminal Advanced Command & Control Architectural test-bed (SAUS)
MATNO	Material Requested Is Not Available
MATO	Military Air Traffic Operations [*British military*] (DMA)
MATOC	Mobility Air Terminal Operations Center (SAUO)
MATP	Masking Template [*Tool*] (AAG)
MATP..........	Military Assistance Training Program (AABC)
MATP..........	Missile Auxiliary Test Position
MATP..........	Mobilization Assignment Training Plan (SAUO)
Mat Par	Matthew Paris. Historia Minor [*A publication*] (DLA)
Mat Paris....	Matthew Paris. Historia Minor [*A publication*] (DLA)
Mat Part	Mathews on the Law of Partnership [*A publication*] (DLA)
MA-TPM	Maritime Administration Transport Planning Mobilization [*Federal emergency order*]
Mat Por	Mathews on the Law of Portions [*A publication*] (DLA)
MATPS.........	Machine-Aided Technical Processing System [*Yale University Library*] [*New Haven, CT*] [*Computer science*]
MATR..........	Management Access to Records
MATR..........	Matriculate (ROG)
MATR..........	Matron
MATRAC	Military Air Traffic Control Radar Center (SAUO)
MATRAC	Military Air Traffic Control System
MATRACS ...	Military Air Traffic Control System (ACAE)
MATRAS	Manufacturing Technology for Complex Geometries based on Rational Splines (SAUO)
MatrCap......	Matrix Capital Corp. [*Associated Press*] (SAG)
MATRD	Materiel Release Denial [*Army*] (AABC)
MATRE	Material Requested
MATRED	Material Redistribution [*Program*] (DNAB)
matric..........	matriculated (SAUO)
MATRIC	Matriculation
MATRIC	Midwest Agribusiness Trade Research and Information Center [*Iowa State University of Science and Technology*] [*Research center*] (RCD)
MATRIS	Manpower and Training Research Information System [*DoD*] [*Information service or system*] (IID)
MATRIS	Medical Manpower and Training Information Service [*British*] (DAVI)
Matritch......	Matritech, Inc. [*Associated Press*] (SAG)
MATRIX	Management Trial Exercise [*Career orientation simulation*]
MATRIX	Market Trend Index [*Associated Equipment Distributors program*]
Matrl...........	Material
MATRL........	Matrimonial (ROG)
MATRS	Mattress
MATRS	Military Airlift Training Squadron [*Air Force*]
MATRS	Miniature Airborne Telemetry Receiving Station
Matrtc........	Matritech, Inc. [*Associated Press*] (SAG)
MATRW	Military Airlift Training Wing [*Air Force*]
MatrxPh.......	Matrix Pharmaceutical, Inc. [*Associated Press*] (SAG)
MatrxSv.......	Matrix Service Co. [*Associated Press*] (SAG)
MATS..........	Maintenance Analysis Task Sheet
MATS..........	Maintenance Analysis Test Set
MATS..........	Management Action Tracking System (SAUO)
MATS..........	Managers Action Tracking System (SAUO)
MATS.........	Manual Versus Automatic Transmission Study (MCD)
MATS.........	Marconi Acoustic Training System (SAUS)
MATS..........	Master of Arts in Teaching of Science (PGP)
MATS..........	Master of Arts in Theological Studies (PGP)
MATS..........	Material and Toxicology System
MATS..........	Material Transport Segment (AAEL)
MATS..........	Materiel Squadron
MATS..........	Matrimonial Matters [*Slang*] (DSUE)
Mats	Matson's Reports [*22-24 Connecticut*] [*A publication*] (DLA)
MATS..........	Mechanical Accounting for Telephone Service (IAA)
MATS..........	Mechanical Anti-Theft System [*Automotive engineering*]
MATS..........	Mediterranean Air Transport Service
MATS..........	Mesoscale Atmospheric Transport Studies (SAUO)
MATS..........	Midcourse Airborne Target Signature [*Military*] (PDAA)
MATS..........	Military Aircraft Target System (SAUS)
MATS..........	Military Air Transport Service [*Later, Military Airlift Command*]
MATS..........	Miniature Addressable Transceiver (ACAE)
MATS..........	Missile Adapter Test Set (ACAE)
MATS..........	Missile Auxiliaries Test Set
MATS..........	Mission Analysis and Trajectory Simulation (MCD)
MATS..........	Mobile Automatic Telephone System [*Telecommunications*]
MATS..........	Mobile Automatic Test Set (MCD)
MATS..........	Model Aircraft Target System [*British military*] (DMA)
MATS..........	Model Aircrew Training System (SAUS)
MATS..........	Monitoring and Test Subsystem
MATS..........	Multiparticipant Airbattle Training System (ACAE)
MATS..........	Multiple-Access Time Sharing [*Computer science*] (IAA)
MATS..........	Multiple Array Test Set (SAUS)
MATS..........	Multipurpose Automatic Test System (IAA)
MATSA........	Managerial, Administrative, Technical, and Supervisory Association [*British*] (DCTA)
MATSA........	Marek-Associated Tumor-Specific Antigen [*Medicine*] (DMAA)
MATSA........	Marek Associated Tumor-Specified Antigen [*Medicine*] (STED)
MATSB........	Mobile Advance Tactical Support Base [*Navy*] (VNW)
MATSC........	Middletown Air Technical Service Command [*Air Force*]
MatSci........	Material Sciences Corp. [*Associated Press*] (SAG)
MATSCO......	Management and Technical Services Company (AAGC)
MATSE........	Military Air Transport Service in Europe (SAUO)
MAT-SF.......	Matrix Analogies Test - Short Form [*Intelligence test*]
MATSG........	Marine Aviation Training Support Group (DNAB)
MATSO........	Material Requested Being Supplied [*Military*]
Mat Soc......	Mattachine Society (?)
MATSOL......	Massachusetts Association of Teachers of English to Speakers of Other Languages
Matson	Matson's Reports [*22-24 Connecticut*] [*A publication*] (DLA)
MATSR	Military Air Transport Service [*later, Military Airlift Command*] Regulation
MATSS........	Marine Aviation Training Support Squadron (DNAB)

MATSS......... Midwest Automated Technical Services Systems [*Information service or system*] (IID)
MATSTAT.... Materiel Status [*Military*]
MaTSU........ Marine Technology Support Unit (HEAS)
Matsu.......... Matsushita Electric Industrial Co. Ltd. [*Associated Press*] (SAG)
MAtt............ Attleboro Public Library, Attleboro, MA [*Library symbol*] [*Library of Congress*] (LCLS)
Matt............. Matthew [*New Testament book*]
MATT.......... Matthews Studio Equipment Group [*NASDAQ symbol*] (NQ)
MATT.......... Missile ASW [*Antisubmarine Warfare*] Torpedo Target (MCD)
MATT.......... Mobile Acoustic Torpedo Target (NG)
MATT.......... Multimission Advanced Tactical Terminal (DWSG)
Mattel......... Mattel, Inc. [*Associated Press*] (SAG)
Matth Com... Matthews' Guide to Commissioner in Chancery [*A publication*] (DLA)
Matth Cr L... Matthews' Digest of Criminal Law [*A publication*] (DLA)
Matthe de Affli... Matthaeus de Afflictis [*Deceased, 1528*] [*Authority cited in pre-1607 legal work*] (DSA)
Matthews..... Matthews' Reports [*75 Virginia*] [*A publication*] (DLA)
Matthews..... Matthews' Reports [*6-9 West Virginia*] [*A publication*] (DLA)
Matth Exe ... Matthews' Executors and Administrators [*2nd ed.*] [*1839*] [*A publication*] (DLA)
Matth Gribal... Matthaeus Gribaldus [*Deceased, 1564*] [*Authority cited in pre-1607 legal work*] (DSA)
Matth Part ... Matthews on Partnership [*A publication*] (DLA)
Matth Pr Ev... Matthews on Presumptive Evidence [*A publication*] (DLA)
MatthwInt ... Matthews International Corp. [*Associated Press*] (SAG)
MatthwSt .... Matthews Studio Equipment Group [*Associated Press*] (SAG)
MATTS........ Mobile Air Transportable Telecommunications System (SAUO)
MATTS........ Multiple Airborne Target Trajectory System
Mattson ...... Mattson Technology, Inc. [*Associated Press*] (SAG)
MATU.......... Marine Air Traffic Unit
matut........... Matutinus [*In the Morning*] [*Latin*] (STED)
MATUT........ Matutinus [*In the Morning*] [*Pharmacy*]
MATV.......... Master Antenna Television
MATV.......... Matav-Cable Systems Media Ltd. [*NASDAQ symbol*] (SAG)
MatvCab ..... Matav-Cable Systems Media Ltd. [*Associated Press*] (SAG)
MATVY........ Matav-Cable Sys ADS [*NASDAQ symbol*] (SG)
MATW.......... Matthews International Corp. [*NASDAQ symbol*] (SAG)
MATW.......... Matthews Intl. 'A' [*NASDAQ symbol*] (TTSB)
MATW.......... Metal Awning Type Window
MATWAS ..... Marine Automatic Telephone Weather Answering Service [*Marine science*] (MSC)
MATWING.... Medium Attack Wing (NVT)
MATX.......... Matrix Pharmaceutical [*NASDAQ symbol*] (TTSB)
MATX.......... Matrix Pharmaceutical, Inc. [*NASDAQ symbol*] (SAG)
MATZ.......... Military Aerodrome Traffic Zone
MATZ.......... Military Air Traffic Zone (SAUO)
MAU............ Air Mauritius Ltd. [*ICAO designator*] (FAAC)
MAU............ Maghreb Arab Union (SAUO)
MAU............ Maintenance Analysis Unit
MAU............ Maintenance Augmenting Unit (NG)
MAU............ Marine Advisory Unit [*Marine Corps*]
MAU............ Marine Amphibious Unit (NVT)
mau .... Massachusetts [*MARC country of publication code*] [*Library of Congress*] (LCCP)
MAU............ Master Augmentation Unit [*Navy*] (DOMA)
MAU............ Mastung [*Pakistan*] [*Airport symbol*] (AD)
MAU............ Math Acceleration Unit (NITA)
MAU............ Mathematical Advisory Unit [*Ministry of Transport*] [*British*]
MAU............ Matua [*Former USSR*] [*Seismograph station code, US Geological Survey*] (SEIS)
MAU............ Maupiti [*French Polynesia*] [*Airport symbol*] (OAG)
Mau .... Mauricius [*Authority cited in pre-1607 legal work*] (DSA)
MAU............ Mauritius (ROG)
MAU............ Media Access Unit [*Telecommunications*]
MAU............ Medical Assistance Unit [*HEW*]
MAU............ Medium Access Unit [*Computer science*] (BYTE)
MAU............ Medium Attachment Unit [*Computer science*] (TNIG)
MAU............ Memory Access Unit
MAU............ Meyenburg-Altherr-Uehlinger [*Syndrome*] [*Medicine*] (STED)
MAU............ Microalbuminuria [*Medicine*] (MELL)
mAU............ Milliabsorbance Unit [*Spectroscopy*]
MAU............ Million Accounting Units (NASA)
MAU............ Miscellaneous Armament Unit
MAU............ Missile Auxiliary Unit (ACAE)
MAU............ Modern American Usage [*A publication*]
MAU............ Modular Avionics Unit (HLLA)
MAU............ Mount Allison University [*New Brunswick, Canada*]
MAU............ Movement African Union (SAUO)
MAU............ Multiattribute Utility (IEEE)
MAU............ Multiple Access Unit
MAU............ Multiple Aircraft Universal (ACAE)
MAU............ Multistation Access Unit [*Telecommunications*] (PCM)
MAUA.......... Master of Arts in Urban Affairs (GAGS)
Mau & Pol Sh... Maude and Pollock's Law of Merchant Shipping [*A publication*] (DLA)
Mau & Sel... Maule and Selwyn's English King's Bench Reports [*A publication*] (DLA)
MAU/ATU.... Marine Amphibious Unit/Amphibious Task Unit (SAUO)
MAUC.......... Middle Atlantic Underwater Council (SAUO)
MAUD......... Manually-Assisted Universal Deviator
MAUD......... Master of Arts in Urban Design (GAGS)
MAud.......... Master of Audiology
MAUD......... Ministry of Aircraft Uranium Development [*British*] [*World War II*]

MAUD......... Movimento Academico pela Uniao Democrata [*Academic Movement for Democratic Union*] [*Portugal*] [*Political party*] (PPE)
MAUDE....... Morse Automatic Decoder
Maude & P... Maude and Pollock's Law of Merchant Shipping [*A publication*] (DLA)
Maude & P Mer Shipp... Maude and Pollock's Law of Merchant Shipping [*A publication*] (DLA)
Maude & P Shipp... Maude and Pollock's Law of Merchant Shipping [*A publication*] (DLA)
MAUDEP...... Metropolitan Association of Urban Designers and Environmental Planners (EA)
MAUDER...... Metropolitan Association of Urban Designers and Environmental Planners (SAUO)
Maud Ment Res... Maudsley on Mental Responsibility [*A publication*] (DLA)
M Au E .... Master of Automobile Engineering
M Au Eng.... Master of Automobile Engineering
MAUF.......... Multiattribute Utility Function
MAUFS........ Municipal Arborists and Urban Foresters Society (EA)
MAUG .... MicroNet Apple User's Group [*CompuServe*] [*Database*]
Maug Att..... Maugham's Attorneys, Solicitors, and Agents [*1825*] [*A publication*] (DLA)
Maug Att..... Maugham's Statutes Relating to Attorneys, Etc. [*1839*] [*A publication*] (DLA)
Maug Cr L ... Maugham's Outlines of Criminal Law [*2nd ed.*] [*1842*] [*A publication*] (DLA)
Maugh Lit Pr... Maugham's Literary Property [*1828*] [*A publication*] (DLA)
Maugh RP ... Maugham's Outlines of Real Property Law [*1842*] [*A publication*] (DLA)
Maug Jur .... Maugham's Outlines of the Jurisdiction [*1838*] [*A publication*] (DLA)
Maug Law ... Maugham's Outlines of Law [*1837*] [*A publication*] (DLA)
MAUK .... Mining Association of the United Kingdom (BUAC)
Maul & Sel... Maule and Selwyn's English King's Bench Reports [*A publication*] (DLA)
Maule & S... Maule and Selwyn's English King's Bench Reports [*A publication*] (DLA)
MAULEX ..... Marine Amphibious Unit Landing Exercise (NVT)
MauLoa ...... Mauna Loa Macadamia Partners Ltd. [*Associated Press*] (SAG)
MAULT........ Manual or Automatic Ultrasonic Laboratory Test
MAUM .... Movement Against Uranium Mining (SAUO)
Maur........... Mauritania
Maur........... Mauritius
MA Urb Plan... Master of Arts in Urban Planning (SAUO)
MAUR Coy... Maintenance Area Universal Repair Company (SAUO)
Maur Dec.... Mauritius Decisions [*A publication*] (DLA)
Maurit......... Mauritania
MAURP........ Master of Arts in Urban and Regional Planning (GAGS)
Maurti......... Mauritania (VRA)
MAUS .... Mammography Attitudes and Usage Study [*Medicine*] (DMAA)
MAUS .... Mauser Rifle
MAUS .... Messensch Afteliche Autonome Experiment Unter Schewerelosigkeit
MAUS .... Metric Association of the United States (SAUO)
MAUS .... Mobile Automated Scanner
MAUS .... Movimiento de Accion y Unidad Socialista [*Socialist Movement for Action and Unity*] [*Mexico*] [*Political party*] (PPW)
MAUS .... Muensters Apple User Service (SAUO)
MAUSED ...... Midwest Association of University Student Employment Directors [*Later, MASEA*] (EA)
MAusIMM .... Member of the Australasian Institute of Mining and Metallurgy (SAUO)
mauso .... Mausoleum (VRA)
MAUTEL....... Microminiaturized Autonetics Telemetry
MAUU .... Massachusetts Alliance of Utility Unions (SAUO)
MauU.......... University of Mauritius, Reduit, Mauritius [*Library symbol*] [*Library of Congress*] (LCLS)
MAUV .... Multiple Autonomous Vehicle
MAUW .... Modified Advanced Underwater Weapons (MCD)
MAV........... Macrosiphum avenae Virus
MAV........... Magyar Allamvasutak [*Hungarian State Railways*]
MAV........... Maintenance Assistance Vehicle (MCD)
MAV........... Maintenance Assist Vehicle (SAUS)
MAV........... Maloelap [*Marshall Islands*] [*Airport symbol*] (OAG)
MAV........... Manpower Authorization Voucher
MAV........... Mars Ascent Vehicle [*NASA*]
MAV........... Massive Resources Ltd. [*Vancouver Stock Exchange symbol*]
MAV........... Mavesa SA ADS [*NYSE symbol*] (SAG)
MAV........... Max-Aviation [*Canada*] [*ICAO designator*] (FAAC)
MAV........... Maximum Allowable Variation [*Net weight labeling*]
MAV........... McLaren Advanced Vehicles [*Automobile manufacturer*]
MAV........... Mean Absolute Value [*Statistics*]
MAV........... MeCCNU [*Semustine*], Adriamycin, Vincristine [*Antineoplastic drug regimen*]
MAV........... Mechanical Auxiliary Ventricle (PDAA)
MAV........... Micro Air Vehicle [*Remote controlled device*]
MAV........... Military Aerospace Vehicle
mA/V.......... Milliamperes per Volt (DEN)
MAV........... Minimal Apparent Viscosity (STED)
MAV........... Minimum Acceptable Value (MCD)
MAV........... Minimum Apparent Viscosity (DB)
MAV........... Minute Alveolar Volume [*Medicine*] (DAVI)
MAV........... Moscavia [*Former USSR*] [*FAA designator*] (FAAC)
MAV........... Motor Ambulance Van [*British*]
MA(V)......... Motorcycling Australia (Victoria) [*Australia*] [*An association*]
MAV........... Movement Arm Vector (STED)
MAV........... Multi-Appeal Vehicle
MAV........... Myeloblastosis-Associated Virus

MAV	Transmembrane Activation Voltage [*Biochemistry*] (DAVI)
MAVA	Moored Acoustic Vertical Array
MAVA	Multiple Abstract Variance Analysis (STED)
MAVAR	Microwave Amplification by Variable Reactance (IAA)
MAVAR	Mixer Amplification by Variable Reactance (IAA)
MAVAR	Modulating Amplifier Using Variable Resistance
MAVCC	Mid-America Vocational Curriculum Consortium (OICC)
MAVCC	Munich Audio-Visual Communication Center (SAUO)
MAVCS	Multi Axis Vibration Control System (ACAE)
MAVDM	Multiple Application VDM (SAUO)
MAVE	Model for Articulated Vocational Education (EDAC)
MAVE	Multiple Aerial Vehicle Expert [*Army*]
MAV Ed	Master of Administration in Vocational Education (PGP)
MAVERICK	Manufacturers Assistance in Verifying, Identification in Cataloging
MAVES	Manned Mars and Venus Exploration Studies
Mavesa	Mavesa SA ADS [*Associated Press*] (SAG)
MAVI	Microwave Automatic Vehicle Identification (MCD)
MAVICA	Magnetic Video Camera [*Sony Corp.*]
MAVICA	Magnetic Video Card (NITA)
MAVID	Modular Architecture for Video & Image Distribution system (SAUS)
MAVIN	Machine-Assisted Vendor Information Network
MAVIN	Multiple Angle, Variable Interval, Nonorthogonal [*Magnetic resonance imaging*]
MAVIS	Master Vision Screener (PDAA)
MAVIS	McDonnell Douglas Automated Voice Information System (MCD)
MAVIS	Microprocessor-Based Audio Visual Information System (PDAA)
MAVIS	Mobile Armored Vehicle Indigo System [*Radio-controlled tank*]
MAVIS	Mobile Artery and Vein Imaging System [*Medicine*] (STED)
MAVK	Maverick Tube [*NASDAQ symbol*] (TTSB)
MAVK	Maverick Tube Corp. [*NASDAQ symbol*] (SAG)
MAVMA	Massachusetts Veterinary Medical Association (GVA)
MAVMS	MACOM Automated Vehicle Management System (SAUO)
MAVOGA	Malaysian Vocational Guidance Association (SAUO)
MAVPE	Metal Alkyl Vapor-Phase Epitaxy [*Semiconductor technology*]
MAVR	Mitral and Aortic Valve Replacement [*Medicine*] (DMAA)
MAVS	Manned Aerial Vehicle for Surveillance (MCD)
MAVS	Manned Airborne Vehicle Surveillance (ACAE)
MAVS	Modular Advanced Vision System (TIMI)
MavTube	Maverick Tube Corp. [*Associated Press*] (SAG)
MAVU	Modular Audio Visual Unit (PDAA)
MAVUS	Maritime VTOL UAV System (SAUS)
MAVWC	Military Aircraft Voice Weather Code (NATG)
MAW	Machinists and Aerospace Workers (DICI)
MAW	Malden, MO [*Location identifier*] [*FAA*] (FAAL)
MAW	Management Action Workshop (ACAE)
MAW	Management Application Workshop (SAUO)
MAW	Marine Aircraft Wing (SAUO)
MAW	Marine Air Wing (ACAE)
mAw	Maritime Arctic Warm [*Air Mass*] [*Meteorology*] (BARN)
MAW	Master of Arts in Worship (PGP)
MAW	Master of Arts in Writing (GAGS)
MAW	Mauritius Alliance of Women (BUAC)
MAW	Maverick Alternate Warhead (SAUS)
MAW	Mawson [*Antarctica*] [*Seismograph station code, US Geological Survey*] (SEIS)
MAW	Maximum Allowable Weight [*Military*] (INF)
MAW	Mechanically Armed Warhead (ACAE)
MAW	Medium Active Waste [*Nuclear energy*]
MAW	Medium Antiarmor Weapon (INF)
MAW	Medium Antitank Weapon
MAW	Medium Assault Weapon
MAW	Microsoft At Work [*Computer software*] (PCM)
MAW	Mid-American Waste Sys [*NYSE symbol*] (TTSB)
MAW	Mid-American Waste Systems, Inc. [*NYSE symbol*] (SPSG)
MAW	Military Airlift Wing [*Air Force*] (MCD)
MAW	Ministry of Agriculture and Water (SAUO)
MAW	Minor Assist Work
MAW	Missile Approach Warning system (SAUS)
MAW	Mission Adaptive Wing (MCD)
MAW	Mobile Approach Warner (SAUS)
MAW	Mothers for Adequate Welfare (SAUO)
MAW	Mountain & Arctic Warfare (SAUS)
MAW	Multipurpose Assault Weapon (ACAE)
MAW	Mustique Airways [*Barbados*] [*ICAO designator*] (FAAC)
MAWA	Maltese Australian Women's Association
MAWA	Matehematical Association of Western Australia
MAWA	Missile Attack Warning and Assessment [*Military*] (PDAA)
MAWB	Master Air Waybill [*Shipping*] (DS)
MAWC	Marine Air West Coast
MAWCS	Mobile Air Weapons Control System [*ESD*]
MAWD	Mars Atmospheric Water Detection [*NASA*]
MA/WD	Material Annex/Weapons Dictionary [*Military*]
MAWEC	Maritime Aircraft Weather Code (NATG)
MAWFA	Make-a-Wish Foundation of America (EA)
MAWG	Message Attachment Work Group (SAUO)
MAWg	Military Airlift Wing [*Air Force*] (AFM)
MAWG	Mission Analysis Working Group (ACAE)
MAWIA	Mexican American Workers Importation Act
MAWL	Magnetic Aircraft Weapons Link
MAWLOGS	Models of the [*US*] Army Worldwide Logistics System (AABC)
MAWP	Marine Air Wing Pacific
MAWP	Maximum Allowable Working Pressure (PDAA)
MAWR	Ministry of Agriculture Western Region (SAUO)
MAWS	Marine Air Warning Squadron
MAWS	Minimum Additive Waste Stabilization System [*Department of Energy*]
MAWS	Missile Approach Warning System (DOMA)
MAWS	Mobile Aircraft Weighing System (OA)
MAWS	Modular Automated Weather System
MAWste	Mid-American Waste Systems, Inc. [*Associated Press*] (SAG)
MAWTS	Marine Aviation Weapons and Tactics Squadron
MAWTS-1	Marine Aviation Weapons and Tactics Squadron 1
MAWTU	Marine Air Weapons Training Unit (MCD)
MAWU	Montserrat Allied Workers Union (SAUO)
MAX	Cinemax [*Cable television channel*]
MAX	Madrid, Spain [*Spaceflight Tracking and Data Network*] [*NASA*]
MAX	Magic Answer Extractor [*Database*]
max	Manx [*MARC language code*] [*Library of Congress*] (LCCP)
MAX	Matam [*Senegal*] [*Airport symbol*] (OAG)
MAX	Max-Aviation [*Canada*] [*FAA designator*] (FAAC)
MAX	Maxilla [*Jawbone*]
MAX	Maxim (ROG)
MAX	Maxima (WDAA)
MAX	Maximal (SAUS)
MAX	Maximilian Numismatic and Historical Society (EA)
Max	Maximinus [*of Scriptores Historiae Augustae*] [*Classical studies*] (OCD)
max	Maximum (WDMC)
MAX	Maximum
MAX	Maxwell [*Unit of Magnetic Flux*] [*Electronics*] (IAA)
MAX	Media Access Exchange (SAUS)
MAX	Mediterranean Airlines SA [*Greece*] [*ICAO designator*] (FAAC)
MAX	Mercury Air Group [*AMEX symbol*] (TTSB)
MAX	Mercury Air Group, Inc. [*AMEX symbol*] (SPSG)
MAX	Message Automatic Exchange (SAUO)
MAX	Metropolitan Area Communication System (SAUO)
MAX	Metropolitan Area Express [*Railway*] [*Portland, OR*] (ECON)
MAX	Mid-Atlantic Crossroads
MAX	Minerex Resources Ltd. [*Vancouver Stock Exchange symbol*] [*Toronto Stock Exchange symbol*]
MAX	Mobile Automatic Exchange [*Telecommunications*] (NITA)
MAX	Mobile Automatic X-Ray (PDAA)
MAX	Modular Applications Executive [*Modular Computer Systems*]
Maxam	Maxxam Corp. [*Associated Press*] (SAG)
MAXAT	Maximum Aperture Telescope (SAUS)
MAXC	Maxco, Inc. [*NASDAQ symbol*] (NQ)
MAXC	Multiple Access Xerox Computer (NITA)
MAX CLB	Maximum Engine Thrust for Two-Engine Climb (GAVI)
Maxco	Maxco, Inc. [*Associated Press*] (SAG)
MAXCO	Maximum Dynamic Pressure (NASA)
MAXCOL	Maximum Column [*Computer science*] (PCM)
MAXCOM	Modular Applications Executive for Communications [*Modular Computer Systems*]
MaxcrHlt	Maxicare Health Plans, Inc. [*Associated Press*] (SAG)
MAX CRZ	Maximum Engine Thrust for Two-Engine Cruise (GAVI)
Max Dig	Maxwell's Nebraska Digest [*A publication*] (DLA)
MAXE	Max & Erma's Restaurants [*NASDAQ symbol*] (TTSB)
MAXE	Max & Erma's Restaurants, Inc. [*NASDAQ symbol*] (NQ)
Max EP	Maximal Esophageal Pressure [*Medicine*] (MAE)
MaxEr	Max & Erma's Restaurants, Inc. [*Associated Press*] (SAG)
MAXG	Maximum Girth [*Pisciculture*]
MAXI	Maxicare Health Plans [*NASDAQ symbol*] (TTSB)
MAXI	Maxicare Health Plans, Inc. [*NASDAQ symbol*] (NQ)
MAXI	Maximum Potential Licence Period (WDAA)
MAXI	Modular Architecture for the Exchange of Intelligence (SAUO)
MAXID	Maximize Indefinite Delivery Contracts (AFM)
Maxim	Maxim Integrated Products, Inc. [*Associated Press*] (SAG)
MAXIM	Micro Arcsecond X-ray Imaging Mission (SAUS)
MaximGp	Maxim Group [*Associated Press*] (SAG)
MaximPh	Maxim Pharmaceuticals, Inc. [*Associated Press*] (SAG)
Max Int Stat	Maxwell on the Interpretation of Statutes [*A publication*] (DLA)
Maxis	Maxis, Inc. [*Associated Press*] (SAG)
MAXIT	Maximum Interference Threshold [*Telecommunications*] (TEL)
MAX/IT	Modular, Adaptable, Expandable, Intelligent Terminal [*Link Technologies, Inc.*] (PCM)
Max LD	Maxwell's Law Dictionary [*A publication*] (DLA)
MAXM	Maxim Group [*NASDAQ symbol*] (SAG)
MAXMAR	Maximum Mobile Army
Max Mar L	Maxwell's Marine Law [*A publication*] (DLA)
MAX/MIN	Maximum Disclosure / Minimum Delay (DNAB)
MaxmP	Maxim Pharmaceuticals, Inc. [*Associated Press*] (SAG)
MAXNET	Modular Application Executive for Computer Networks (PDAA)
MAXNET	Modular Applications Executive Network (NITA)
MAXNOR	Maximum Number of Runs (MCD)
MAXPAR	Maximum Pain Relief [*Medicine*]
MAXPAX	Maxwell House Coffee Package [*Vendor-machine system for Maxwell House coffee*]
MAXPEN	Maximum Penalty
MAXPID	Maximum Pain Intensity Difference [*Medicine*]
MAX-Q	Maximum Dynamic Pressure (SAUS)
MAXR	Maximum Rate (TVEL)
MAXS	Maxwell Shoe 'A' [*NASDAQ symbol*] (TTSB)
MAXS	Maxwell Shoe Company, Inc. [*NASDAQ symbol*] (SAG)
MAXSECOM	Maximum Security Communications (IAA)
MAXSECON	Maximum Security Communications
Maxserv	Maxserv, Inc. [*Associated Press*] (SAG)
MAX SOCIETY	Maximilian Numismatic and Historical Society (EA)
MAXTOP	Maximum Total Duration Penalty
Maxtor	Maxtor Corp. [*Associated Press*] (SAG)

MAXTTR ...... Maximum Time to Repair [*Navy*] (CAAL)
MAXTWK ..... Maximum Total Work Content
Maxu .... Maxus Energy Corp. [*Associated Press*] (SAG)
MAXUPO...... Maximum Undistorted Power Output (IAA)
Maxus........ Maxus Energy [*Associated Press*] (SAG)
Maxw Cr Proc... Maxwell's Treatise on Criminal Procedure [*A publication*] (DLA)
Maxwel....... Maxwell Laboratories, Inc. [*Associated Press*] (SAG)
Maxwell....... Irish Land Purchase Cases [*1904-11*] [*A publication*] (DLA)
Maxwell....... Maxwell on the Interpretation of Statutes [*A publication*] (DLA)
Maxw Interp St... Maxwell on the Interpretation of Statutes [*A publication*] (DLA)
MaxwllSh .... Maxwell Shoe Co., Inc. [*Associated Press*] (SAG)
MaxwllT....... Maxwell Technologies, Inc. [*Associated Press*] (SAG)
MAXX........ Maximum Access to Diagnosis and Therapy (SAUO)
Maxxim........ Maxxim Medical, Inc. [*Associated Press*] (SAG)
may .... Malay [*MARC language code*] [*Library of Congress*] (LCCP)
MAY.......... Malye Karmakuly [*Former USSR*] [*Geomagnetic observatory code*]
MAY.......... Mangrove Cay [*Bahamas*] [*Airport symbol*] (OAG)
MAY.......... Maya Airways Ltd. [*Belize*] [*ICAO designator*] (FAAC)
MAY.......... Maybelline, Inc. [*NYSE symbol*] (SPSG)
MAY.......... May Department Stores Co., Corporate Information Center, St. Louis, MO [*OCLC symbol*] (OCLC)
MAY.......... Mayfield [*Washington*] [*Seismograph station code, US Geological Survey*] [*Closed*] (SEIS)
MAY.......... Maynard Energy, Inc. [*Toronto Stock Exchange symbol*]
MAY.......... Mayor (ROG)
MAYA.......... Mexican-American Youth Association (SAUO)
MAYA........ Most Advanced, Yet Acceptable [*Industrial design*]
MAYA........ Muslim Arab Youth Association
May Act ...... Mayhew's Action at Law [*1828*] [*A publication*] (DLA)
MAYB.......... Mad About You, Baby (SAUS)
Maybel .... Maybelline, Inc. [*Associated Press*] (SAG)
MAYC.......... Mayflower Conference (PSS)
MAYC.......... Methodist Association of Youth Clubs [*British*] (BI)
May Const Hist... May's Constitutional History of England [*A publication*] (DLA)
MAYCOR...... Maytag Corp. (EFIS)
May Crim Law... May's Criminal Law [*A publication*] (DLA)
May Dam..... Mayne on the Law of Damages [*A publication*] (DLA)
MayDS........ May Department Stores Co. [*Associated Press*] (SAG)
MayflCo ...... Mayflower Co-Operative Bank [*Associated Press*] (SAG)
May Fr Conv... May's Fraudulent Conveyances [*3rd ed.*] [*1908*] [*A publication*] (DLA)
May Ins .... May on Insurance [*A publication*] (DLA)
May Just....... Mayo's Justice [*A publication*] (DLA)
May LR........ Mayurbhani Law Report [*India*] [*A publication*] (DLA)
May Merg.... Mayhew on Merger [*1861*] [*A publication*] (DLA)
Mayn .... Maynard's English Reports, Exchequer Memoranda of Edward I, and Year Books of Edward II [*A publication*] (DLA)
MaynOl........ Maynard Oil Co. [*Associated Press*] (SAG)
MAYO......... Mexican-American Youth Organization (SAUO)
Mayo & Moul... Mayo and Moulton's Pension Laws [*A publication*] (DLA)
Mayo Just.... Mayo's Justice [*A publication*] (DLA)
Mayo Med Sch... Mayo Medicine School (GAGS)
May Parl...... May's Parliamentary Practice [*A publication*] (ILCA)
May Parl Law... May's Parliamentary Law [*A publication*] (DLA)
May Parl Pr... May's Parliamentary Practice [*A publication*] (DLA)
May PL........ May's Parliamentary Practice [*A publication*] (DLA)
MAYPOLE .... May Polarization Experiment [*RADAR storm sensing*]
MAYS.......... Mays [*J. W.*], Inc. [*NASDAQ symbol*] (NQ)
MAYS.......... Mays (JW) [*NASDAQ symbol*] (TTSB)
MaysJ......... Mays [*J. W.*], Inc. [*Associated Press*] (SAG)
MaySpeh ..... May & Speh, Inc. [*Associated Press*] (SAG)
Maytag .... Maytag Corp. [*Associated Press*] (SAG)
MAYW .... Maywood & Sugar Creek [*AAR code*]
MAZ.......... Mayaguez [*Puerto Rico*] [*Airport symbol*] (OAG)
MAZ.......... Mazatlan [*Mexico*] [*Seismograph station code, US Geological Survey*] (SEIS)
MAZ.......... Mazzite [*A zeolite*]
MAZ.......... Mines Air Service Zambia Ltd. [*ICAO designator*] (FAAC)
MAZ.......... Missed Approach Azimuth [*Aviation*]
MAZ.......... Mounting Azimuth [*Weaponry*] (INF)
MazelSt....... Mazel Stores, Inc. [*Associated Press*] (SAG)
MAZH........ Missile Azimuth Heading [*Air Force*]
MAZI.......... Movement for the Advancement of the Zionist Idea [*Israel*] [*Political party*] (EY)
MAZL......... Mazel Stores, Inc. [*NASDAQ symbol*] (SAG)
MAZO......... Missile Azimuth Orientation [*Air Force*] (IAA)
MB.............. All India Reporter, Madhya Bharat [*1950-57*] [*A publication*] (DLA)
MB.............. Bachelor of Medicine [*Other than from Oxford*]
MB.............. Bachelor of Music (WDAA)
mb--- .... Black Sea and Area [*MARC geographic area code*] [*Library of Congress*] (LCCP)
Mb .... Body Wave Magnitude (COE)
MB.............. Boston Public Library and Eastern Massachusetts Regional Public Library System, Boston, MA [*Library symbol*] [*Library of Congress*] (LCLS)
MB.............. Countrywide [*ICAO designator*] (AD)
MB.............. Machine Batch (AAEL)
MB.............. Machine Bolt [*Technical drawings*]
MB.............. MacMillan Bloedel Ltd. [*Associated Press*] (SAG)
MB.............. Magnetic Bearing [*Navigation*]
MB.............. Magnetic Belt (VLIE)
MB.............. Magnetic Brake [*Industrial control*] (IEEE)
MB.............. Magnetron Branch [*Electronics*] (OA)
MBu .... Mailbox (AAG)
MB.............. Main Ballast

MB.............. Main Base [*Air Force*] (AFM)
MB.............. Main Battery [*Guns*]
MB.............. Main Bus (MCD)
MB.............. Maintenance Busy [*Telecommunications*] (TEL)
M-B............. Make-Break
MB.............. Mallory Body [*Medicine*]
MB.............. Mamillary Body [*Medicine*] (DB)
MB.............. Management Baseline (NASA)
MB.............. Management Board (ACII)
MB.............. Manitoba [*Canadian province*] [*Postal code*]
MB.............. Manned Base (SAUO)
MB.............. March-Bender Factor [*Physiology*]
MB.............. Margin Buccal [*Medicine*] (MAE)
MB.............. Marie-Bamberger [*Disease*] [*Medicine*] (DB)
MB.............. Marine Barracks
MB.............. Marine Base
MB.............. Marine Board (EA)
MB.............. Maritime Board (SAUO)
MB.............. Marker Beacon (PIPO)
MB.............. Marketing Board (SAUO)
MB.............. Mark of the Beast [*Disparaging term for 19th century Protestant clerical waistcoats that had Catholic influences*]
MB.............. Marks Banco (ROG)
MB.............. Marsh-Bender [*Factor*] [*Muscle tissue*]
MB.............. Mass Balance
MB.............. Master Block (VLIE)
MB.............. Matchbox [*Mattel*]
MB.............. Material Balance
MB.............. May & Baker Ltd. [*Great Britain*] [*Research code symbol*]
MB.............. MBB-UV, MBB-UD [*Messerschmitt-Boelkow-Blohm*], und Pneuma-Technik [*Germany*] [*ICAO aircraft manufacturer identifier*] (ICAO)
MB.............. Measurement Base [*Military*]
MB.............. Mechanized Battalion [*Army*]
MB.............. Medal of Bravery
MB.............. Medial Bilateral (Neuron) [*Neuroanatomy*]
MB.............. Median Bundle [*Botany*]
MB.............. Medical Board
MB.............. Medical Branch (SAUO)
MB.............. Medical Bulletin
MB.............. Medicare Bureau [*Health Care Financing Administration - Social Security Administration*] (OICC)
MB.............. Medicinae Baccalaureus [*Bachelor of Medicine*] [*Latin*]
MB.............. Medium Bomber
MB.............. Medium Bronze [*Numismatics*]
MB.............. Megabar
Mb.............. Megabase [*A unit of molecular size*]
Mb.............. Megabit [*Computer science*] (WDMC)
MB.............. Megabit [*Binary Digit*] [*Computer science*]
MB.............. Megabuck [*Defense industry colloquialism for one million dollars*] (AAG)
mb.............. Megabyte (ELAL)
MB.............. Megabyte [*Data storage capacity*] [*Computer science*]
Mb.............. Megabyte
MB.............. Melt Back
MB.............. Memorandum Book (ROG)
MB.............. Memory Bank
MB.............. Memory Buffer [*Computer science*]
MB.............. Memory Bus
MB.............. Memoryless Behaviour (VLIE)
MB.............. Mercedes-Benz [*Automobile*]
MB.............. Merchant Bank
MB.............. Merchant Broker (RIMS)
MB.............. Meridian & Bigbee Railroad Co. [*Later, MBRR*] [*AAR code*]
MB.............. Mesiobuccal [*Dentistry*]
MB.............. Message Buffer (ACRL)
MB.............. Message Business
MB.............. Messages of the Bible [*A publication*]
MB.............. Metabisulfite [*Inorganic chemistry*]
MB.............. Metal Box [*Commercial firm*] [*British*]
MB.............. Metal Box Co. Ltd. (SAUO)
MB.............. Methyl Bromide [*Organic chemistry*]
MB.............. Methylene Blue [*Organic chemistry*]
MB.............. Metrication Board [*British*]
MB.............. Metric Board (OICC)
MB.............. Microbeam [*Physics*]
MB.............. Microbiological Assay [*Biochemistry*] (DAVI)
MB.............. Microbody
MB.............. Microelectronics Bibliography [*A publication*]
MB.............. Midbody
MB.............. Mid Byte (ACAE)
MB.............. Middle Babylonian [*Language, etc.*] (BJA)
MB.............. Middle Bronze Age (BJA)
MB.............. Middle Button (VLIE)
MB.............. Middle of Bow [*Music*] (ROG)
MB.............. Militia Bureau [*Superseded in 1933 by National Guard Bureau*]
MB.............. Millibar
mb.............. Millibar [*Unit of pressure*]
mb.............. Millibarn [*Area of nuclear cross-section*]
mb.............. Millibyte [*Computer science*]
MB.............. Million Bytes [*Computer science*] (BUR)
MB.............. Milton Bradley Co. (SAUO)
MB.............. Milton Bradley Ltd. [*British*]
MB.............. Milwaukee Brace [*Medicine*] (MELL)
MB.............. Minimum Bid [*Philately*]
MB.............. Ministry of Blockade (SAUO)

MB	Misce Bene [Mix Well] [Pharmacy]
MB	Miscellaneous Branch, Internal Revenue Bureau [United States] (DLA)
MB	Missed Byte [Computer science] (ECII)
MB	Missile Base [Military]
MB	Missile Body
MB	Missile Bomber
MB	Mixed Bed [Nuclear energy] (NRCH)
MB	Mixing Box (OA)
MB	Mobile Base (DEN)
MB	Model Block (MSA)
MB	Module Balance [Computer science]
MB	Mohelbuch (BJA)
MB	Moisture Balance
MB	Molecular Biosystems [NYSE symbol] (TTSB)
MB	Molecular Biosystems, Inc. [NYSE symbol] (SPSG)
MB	Molybdenum [Chemical element] (ROG)
MB	Momentum Bias (ACAE)
MB	Monthly Breakdown [Used in atmospheric studies]
MB	Monthly Bulletin of Decisions of the High Court of Uganda [A publication] (DLA)
MB	Months Before
MB	Montpelier & Barre Railroad Co. [AAR code]
MB	Mooring Buoy
MB	Morale Branch [Military]
MB	Morrell's English Bankruptcy Reports [A publication] (DLA)
MB	Mortar Board (EA)
M/B	Mother Board (AGLO)
MB	Motor Barge (ADA)
MB	Motor Boat
MB	Mountain Battery [British military] (DMA)
MB	Mucosal Barrier [Medicine] (MELL)
MB	Mucosal Bleeding [Medicine] (MELL)
MB	Multiband (DEN)
MB	Municipal Bond
MB	Municipal Borough
MB	Munitions Board [Abolished 1953, functions transferred to Department of Defense]
MB	Muscle Balance (SAUS)
MB	Museum of Broadcasting
MB	Mushroom Body [Nerve center in insects]
MB	Musicae Baccalaureus [Bachelor of Music]
MB	Music for the Blind [Defunct] (EA)
MB	Muslim Brotherhood [Jordan] (BUAC)
MB	Must Be [Sold] [Classified advertising]
MB	Myocardial Band [Cardiology]
Mb	Myoglobin [Biochemistry, medicine]
Mb	Myoglobin Tritium [Hematology] (DAVI)
MB	Western Airlines [ICAO designator] (AD)
MB-2	Model Boiler-Two [Nuclear energy] (GFGA)
MBA	American Academy of Arts and Sciences, Boston, MA [Library symbol] [Library of Congress] (LCLS)
MBA	Automobilvertriebs Aktiengesellschaft [Austria] [ICAO designator] (FAAC)
MBA	Main Battle Area (AABC)
MBA	Main-Belt Asteroid [Astronomy]
MBA	Mainhardt-Biehl Associates (SAUO)
MBA	Make-or-Buy Authorization (AAG)
MBA	Makers of British Art [A publication]
MBA	Male Bonding Alert [Screenwriter's lexicon]
MBA	Male Bowhunter Aided [International Bowhunting Organization] [Class equipment]
MBA	Malta Broadcasting Authority (BUAC)
MBA	Management Buy-Out Association (BUAC)
MBA	Mantle Bouguer Anomaly [Geology]
MBA	Manufactured Buildings Association [Defunct] (EA)
MBA	Many-Body Alloy [Metallurgy]
MBA	Marching Bands of America (EA)
mba	Marimba
MBA	Marine Biological Association [British]
MBA	Marine Biological Association of the United Kingdom (BUAC)
MBA	Mass Balance Area (NUCP)
MBA	Master Bakers' Association [Australia]
MBA	Master Builders' Association [South Africa] (BUAC)
MBA	Master Business Administration (SAUO)
MBA	Master of Business Administration
MBA	Master of the British Arts Association (DBQ)
MBA	Material Balance Accounting (SAUO)
MBA	Material Balance Area [Nuclear energy]
MBA	Maximum Benefit Amount [Unemployment insurance]
MBA	MB Associates (SAUO)
MBA	Meier Burnout Assessment [Psychology] (DHP)
MBA	Merion Bluegrass Association [Defunct] (EA)
MBA	Methyl Benzyl Alcohol [Organic chemistry]
MBA	Methylbis(beta-chloroethyl)amine [Nitrogen mustard] [Also, HN, NM] [Antineoplastic; war-gas base]
MBA	Methylbovine Albumin (DMAA)
MBA	Methylenebisacrylamide [Organic chemistry]
MBA	Metropolitan Boxing Alliance (SAUO)
MBA	Microbiological Associates, Inc.
MBA	Migratory Bird Act
MBA	Military Base Agreement (CINC)
MBA	Military Benefit Association (EA)
MBA	Milk Bars Association of Great Britain and Ireland Ltd. (BI)
MBa	Miniature Ball [Horticulture]

MBA	Minimum Burst Altitude (AABC)
MBA	Minor Basic Allergens [Immunology]
MBA	Mombasa [Kenya] [Airport symbol] (OAG)
MBA	Monument Builders of America [Later, MBNA]
MBA	Mortar Box Assembly
MBA	Mortgage Bankers Association of America [Washington, DC] (EA)
MBA	Mortgage Brokers Association (SAUO)
MBA	Motor Bearing Assembly (ACAE)
MBA	Motorized Bicycle Association [Later, MAA] (EA)
MBA	Mount Bingar [Australia] [Seismograph station code, US Geological Survey] [Closed] (SEIS)
MBA	Multibeam Antenna
MBA	Multiple Berthing Adaptor (SSD)
MBA	Multiple Birth Association [Australia]
MBA	Rural Municipality of Argyle Public Library, Baldur, Manitoba [Library symbol] [National Library of Canada] (NLC)
MBA	Woodcock-McGrew-Werder Mini-Battery of Achievement [Test] (TMMY)
MBA	Yacht and Motor Boat Association (SAUO)
MBAA	Master Brewers Association of the Americas (EA)
MBAA	Master of Business Administration in Aviation (PGP)
MBAA	Messinian Benevolent Association "Aristomenis" (EA)
MBAA	Methylene Bisacrylamide (PDAA)
MBAA	Mini Bike Association of America (EA)
MBAA	Mortgage Bankers Association of America (SAUO)
MBAA	Mortgage Brokers' Association of Australia
MBAA	Motel Brokers Association of America [Later, AHMB] (EA)
MBAAS	Master of Business Administration in Actuarial Science
MBab	Middle Babylonian [Language, etc.] (BJA)
MBABS	Synod Office, Diocese of Brandon, Anglican Church of Canada, Manitoba [Library symbol] [National Library of Canada] (NLC)
MBAC	Assiniboine Community College, Brandon, Manitoba [Library symbol] [National Library of Canada] (NLC)
MBAC	Marshall Booster Assembly Contractor (MCD)
MBAC	Member of the British Association of Chemists (DAS)
MBACFM	American Board of Commissioners for Foreign Missions, Boston, MA [Library symbol] [Library of Congress] (LCLS)
M-BACOD	Methotrexate (High-Dose) (with Citrovorum Factor Rescue), Bleomycin, Adriamycin,Cyclophosphamide, Oncovin [Vincristine], Dexamethasone [Antineoplastic drug regimen]
M-BACOP	Myelosuppressive Bleomycin, Adriamycin, Cyclophosphamide, Oncovin [Vincristine], Prednisone [Antineoplastic drug regimen]
M-BACOS	Bleomycin, Adriamycin, Cytoxan, Oncovin, Methotrexate with Leucovorin Rescue [Antineoplastic drug] (CDI)
MBACT	Medical Board of the Australian Capital Territory
MBAD	Medical Badge
MB Adm	Master of Business Administration
MBAE	Master of Biological and Agricultural Engineering (PGP)
MBAE	Master of Biosystems and Agricultural Engineering (PGP)
MBAE	Member of the British Association of Electrolysis (DI)
MBA-EP	Master of Business Administration - Experienced Professionals (PGP)
MBAG	Modulated Bayard-Alpert Gauge
MBAG	Research Station, Agriculture Canada [Station de Recherches, Agriculture Canada] Brandon, Manitoba [Library symbol] [National Library of Canada] (NLC)
MBAI	Massachusetts Independent Bankers Association, Inc. (TBD)
MBAI	Mosquito Biting Activity Index [Canada]
MBAIB	Master of Business Administration in International Business (GAGS)
MBAIT	Master of Business Administration in International Trade (PGP)
MBAJ	Magna Bibliotheca Anglo-Judaica (BJA)
MBALs	Minimum Biological Acceptable Levels (SAUO)
MBAM	Main Beam Avoidance Maneuver
MBAMT	Methyl(benzylideneamino)mercaptotriazole [Reagent]
MBANSW	Master Butchers' Association of New South Wales [Australia]
MBANSW	Medical Benevolent Association of New South Wales [Australia]
MBAOT	Member of the British Association of Occupational Therapists (DI)
MBA-PE	Master of Business Administration - Physician's Executive (PGP)
mbar	Millibar [Unit of pressure]
MBAR	Multibeam Acquisition RADAR (MCD)
MBAR	Myocardial Beta Adrenergic Receptor [Cardiology] (DMAA)
MBARI	Monterey Bay Aquarium Research Institute [California]
MBarL	Barnstable Law Library, Barnstable, MA [Library symbol] [Library of Congress] (LCLS)
MBAS	Methylene Blue Active Substance [Organic chemistry]
MBAS	Mutual Benefit and Aid Society [Later, WBF] (EA)
MBASA	Medical Benevolent Association of South Australia
MBASW	Member of the British Association of Social Workers
MBAt	Boston Athenaeum, Boston, MA [Library symbol] [Library of Congress] (LCLS)
MBAT	Multi-Beam Array Transmitter (SAUS)
MBATM	Master of Business in Telecommunication Management (PGP)
MBAUK	Marine Biological Association of the United Kingdom (ARC)
MBAV	Main Battle Air Vehicle [Military] (PDAA)
MBAV	Multi-purpose Base Armoured Vehicle (SAUS)
MBAWS	Marine Base Air Warning System
MBB	Brandeis University, Waltham, MA [OCLC symbol] (OCLC)
MBB	Make-before-Break
MBB	Marble Bar [Australia] [Airport symbol] (OAG)
MBB	Maurer, B. B., Chicago IL [STAC]
MBB	Messerschmitt-Boelkow-Blohm GmbH [West German aircraft company]
MBB	Messerschmitt-Boklow-Blahn (NAKS)
MBB	Miniature Brushless Blower
MBB	Modified Barbiturate Buffer (DMAA)
MBB	Modular Building Block (ACAE)

MBB............	Mortgage-Backed Bonds
MBB............	MSB Bancorp, Inc. [*AMEX symbol*] (SAG)
MBB............	Museum of the Borough of Brooklyn (SAUO)
MBBA..........	Boston Bar Association, Boston, MA [*Library symbol*] [*Library of Congress*] (LCLS)
MBBA..........	Methoxybenzylidene Butylaniline [*Organic chemistry*]
MBBA..........	(Methozybenzylidene)butylaniline [*Organic chemistry*]
MBBA..........	Military Benefit Base Amounts
MBBAQ	Master Boat Builders' Association of Queensland [*Australia*]
MBBC..........	Monterey Bay Bancorp [*NASDAQ symbol*] (TTSB)
MBBC..........	Monterey Bay Bancorp, Inc. [*NASDAQ symbol*] (SAG)
MBBI..........	Babson College, Babson Park, MA [*Library symbol*] [*Library of Congress*] (LCLS)
MBBI..........	Multiple-Bit Binary Input
MBBL..........	Massachusetts Bureau of Library Extension, Boston, MA [*Library symbol*] [*Library of Congress*] (LCLS)
MBBL..........	Thousand Barrels (EG)
MBBLS........	Thousands of Barrels (MCD)
MBbM	Massachusetts Maritime Academy, Buzzards Bay, MA [*Library symbol*] [*Library of Congress*] (LCLS)
MBBO	Multiple-Bit Binary Output
MBBR..........	Brokenhead River Regional Library, Beausejour, Manitoba [*Library symbol*] [*National Library of Canada*] (NLC)
MBBS..........	Bostonian Society, Boston, MA [*Library symbol*] [*Library of Congress*] (LCLS)
MBBS..........	Managed Broad-Band Services (VLIE)
MBBSC	Bachelor of Medicine and Bachelor of Science [*British*] (ROG)
MBC............	American Congregational Association, Boston, MA [*Library symbol*] [*Library of Congress*] (LCLS)
MBC............	Brandon University, Manitoba [*Library symbol*] [*National Library of Canada*] (NLC)
MBC............	Machine Bath Collection
MBC............	Magnetic Bias Coil (IIA)
MBC............	Magnetic Bias Control (DNAB)
MBC............	Mailbox Club [*Later, MCI*] (EA)
MBC............	Main Beam Clutter
MBC............	Male Breast Cancer [*Medicine*] (DB)
MBC............	Malwa Bhil Corps [*British military*] (DMA)
MBC............	Manhattan Bible College [*Kansas*]
MBC............	Manhattan Bowery Corp. (EA)
mbc	Manitoba [*MARC country of publication code*] [*Library of Congress*] (LCCP)
MBC............	Manual Battery Control (AAG)
MBC............	Marine Biomedical Center [*Duke University*] [*Research center*] (RCD)
MBC............	Marine Broadcasting Company (SAUO)
MBC............	Mary Baldwin College [*Virginia*]
MBC............	Massachusetts Biotechnology Council (SAUO)
MBC............	Mass Bias Correction (ABAC)
MBC............	Master Bus Controller [*Computer science*]
MBC............	Master of Beauty Culture
MBC............	Master of Building Construction (PGP)
MBC............	Maximum Bladder Capacity [*Medicine*] (DB)
MBC............	Maximum Breathing Capacity
MBC............	M'Bigou [*Gabon*] [*Airport symbol*] (OAG)
MBC............	McLaughlin-Buick Club of Canada (EAIO)
MBC............	Media Briefing Center (COE)
MBC............	Mediterranean Bombardment Code
MBC............	Mediterranean Burns Club (SAUO)
MBC............	Megabar Diamond Cell [*For high-pressure measurements*]
MBC............	Memory Bus Controller
MBC............	Mercantile Bank of Canada [*Toronto Stock Exchange symbol*] [*Vancouver Stock Exchange symbol*]
MBC............	Mercantile Bankshares Corp. (EFIS)
MBC............	Merchant Banking Company (SAUO)
MBC............	Message Broadcast Controller [*Computer science*] (CIST)
MBC............	Metastatic Breast Cancer [*Medicine*]
MBC............	Meteor Burst Communications [*Military*]
MBC............	Methotrexate, Bleomycin, Cisplatin [*Antineoplastic drug*] (CDI)
MBC............	Methyl Benzimidazolecarbamate [*Organic chemistry*]
MBC............	Methylthymol Blue Complex (BABM)
MBC............	Metropolitan Borough Council [*British*]
MBC............	Mewar Bhil Corps [*British military*] (DMA)
MBC............	Mickelberry Corp. (EFIS)
MBC............	Microcrystalline Bovine Collagen (DB)
MBC............	Middle East Broadcasting Centre (BUAC)
MBC............	Military Budget Committee [*NATO*] (NATG)
MBC............	Military Budget Council (SAUO)
MBC............	Miname Nihon Broadcasting (SAUO)
MBC............	Miniature Bayonet Cap
MBC............	Miniaturized Ballistic Computer
MBC............	Minimum Bactericidal Concentration
MBC............	Minnesota Bible College [*Rochester*]
MBC............	Missile Boresight Correlator (ACAE)
MBC............	Mitsubishi Bank of California (SAUO)
MBC............	Modified Brequet Cruise [*SST*]
MBC............	Monkees Buttonmania Club [*Defunct*] (EA)
MBC............	Mononuclear Blood Cell [*Hematology*]
MBC............	Morris Brown College [*Atlanta, GA*]
MBC............	Morris Brown College, Atlanta, GA [*OCLC symbol*] (OCLC)
MBC............	Mortar Ballistic Computer [*Formerly, MFCC*] [*Army*] (INF)
MBC............	Mother and Baby Care [*Red Cross Nursing Services*]
MBC............	Motorboat Crew [*British military*] (DMA)
MBC............	Mould Bay [*Northwest Territories*] [*Seismograph station code, US Geological Survey*] (SEIS)
MBC............	Mountain Bike Club [*British*] (DBA)
MBC............	Multiple Base Channel (VLIE)
MBC............	Multiple Basic Channel
MBC............	Multiple Board Computer (IAA)
MBC............	Multiple Burst Correcting
MBC............	Munhwa Broadcasting Corp. [*Republic of Korea*] (BUAC)
MBC............	Municipal Borough Council (SAUO)
MBC............	Mutual Broadcasting Company (SAUO)
MBC............	Muzzle/Brake Compensator (SAUS)
MBCA..........	Archives, Brandon University, Manitoba [*Library symbol*] [*National Library of Canada*] (BIB)
MBCA..........	Mechanical Bank Collectors of America (EA)
MBCA..........	Mercedes-Benz Club of America (EA)
MBCA..........	Merchant Bank of Central Africa Ltd.
MBCA..........	Migratory Bird Conservation Act of 1929 (COE)
MBCA..........	Motor Boat Club of America (SAUO)
MBCA..........	Munitions Board Cataloging Agency
MBCAM.......	Commonwealth Air Training Plan Museum, Inc., Brandon, Manitoba [*Library symbol*] [*National Library of Canada*] (NLC)
MBCC..........	Massachusetts Bay Community College [*Wellesley*]
MBCC..........	Matchbox Challenge Cars [*Toy collection*]
MBCC..........	McLaughlin-Buick Club of Canada (EA)
MBCC..........	Medical Benefits Consultative Committee
MBCC..........	Migratory Bird Conservation Commission [*A federal government body*]
MBCD	Modified Binary-Coded Decimal
MBCG	Department of Geography, Brandon University, Manitoba [*Library symbol*] [*National Library of Canada*] (NLC)
MBCI..........	Medical Books for China International (SAUO)
MBCK..........	Mallory Body Cytokeratin [*Medicine*]
MBCM........	Baccalaureus Medicinae, Chirurgiae Magister [*Bachelor of Medicine, Master of Surgery*]
MBCM........	New England Conservatory of Music, Boston, MA [*Library symbol*] [*Library of Congress*] (LCLS)
MBCMA.......	Metal Building Component Manufacturers' Association (EA)
MBCMC.......	Milk Bottle Crate Manufacturers Council [*Defunct*] (EA)
MBCNT	Multilingual Broadcasting Council of the Northern Territory [*Australia*]
MBCo..........	Countway Library of Medicine, Boston, MA [*Library symbol*] [*Library of Congress*] (LCLS)
MBCO	Member of the British College of Ophthalmic Opticians [*British*] (DBQ)
MbCO	Myoglobin, Carboxy [*Biochemistry, medicine*]
MBCP..........	Mauler Battery Command Post (ACAE)
MBCP..........	Missile Base Communications Processor (SAUO)
MBCS..........	Managed Business Consultancy Service (SAUO)
MBCS..........	Medium Bandwidth Compression System
MBCS..........	Member of the British Computer Society (DCTA)
MBCS..........	Meteor Burst Communication System
MBCS..........	Motion Base Crew Station [*NASA*] (NASA)
MBCS..........	Multi-Byte Character Set [*Computer science*] (VLIE)
MBCU..........	Mobile Bombardment Communications Unit [*Military*] (IAA)
MBd	Bedford Free Public Library, Bedford, MA [*Library symbol*] [*Library of Congress*] (LCLS)
MBD............	Episcopal Diocese of Massachusetts, Boston, MA [*Library symbol*] [*Library of Congress*] (LCLS)
MBD............	Machinery Breakdown (MARI)
MBD............	Macroblock Design
MBD............	Magnetic-Bubble Domain Device [*Computer science*] (IEEE)
MBD............	Manual Board [*Telecommunications*] (NITA)
MBD............	Manual Burst Disable (AABC)
MBD............	Maple Bark Disease [*Medicine*] (MELL)
MBD............	Marble Bone Disease [*Medicine*] (MELL)
MBD............	Marchiafava-Bignami Disease [*Medicine*] (MELL)
MBD............	Marie-Bamberger Disease [*Medicine*] (MELL)
MBD............	Materials-by-Design [*Chemical engineering*]
MBD............	Meander Belt Deposit [*Geology*]
MBD............	Metabolic Bone Disease [*Medicine*] (MELL)
MBD............	Methotrexate, Bleomycin, Diamminedichloroplatinum [*Cisplatin*] [*Antineoplastic drug regimen*]
MBD............	Methoxybenzylaminonitrobenzoxadiazole [*Fluorescent probe*] [*Biochemistry*]
MBD............	Methylbutenedial [*Organic chemistry*]
MBD............	Methylene Blue Dye [*Organic chemistry*] (MAE)
MBD............	Meyer-Betz Disease [*Medicine*] (MELL)
MBD............	Million Barrels Daily
MBD............	Minimal Brain Damage [*or Dysfunction*]
MBD............	Minimal Brain Dysfunction [*Neurology*] (DAVI)
MBD............	Minority Business Development Agency (EBF)
MBD............	Mission Baseline Description [*NASA*] (KSC)
MBD............	Moeller-Barlow Disease [*Medicine*] (MELL)
MBD............	Morquio-Brailsford Disease [*Medicine*] (DMAA)
MBD............	Motor Belt Drive (MSA)
M Bd	Munitions Board (SAUO)
MBD............	Muzzle Boresight Device [*Army*] (INF)
MBDA..........	Metal Building Dealers Association [*Later, Systems Builders Association*] (EA)
MBDA	Minority Business Development Agency [*Formerly, OMBE*] [*Department of Commerce*]
MBDAACC...	Milling and Baking Division of American Association of Cereal Chemists (EA)
MBdAF........	United States Air Force, Cambridge Research Center, Bedford, MA [*Library symbol*] [*Library of Congress*] (LCLS)
MBDC	Minority Business Development Center [*Minority Business Development Administration*]
MBdD..........	Document Research Center, Bedford, MA [*Library symbol*] [*Library of Congress*] (LCLS)

MBDET......... Mobile Boarding Detachment [*Coast Guard*]
MBDF.......... Medicare Beneficiaries Defense Fund (EA)
MBDG .... Marine Base Defense Group
MBDG .... Mesiobuccal Developmental Groove [*Medicine*] (DMAA)
MBDG .... Mesiobuccal Development Groove (STED)
MBdgSc ...... Master of Building Science
MBDI .... Major Business Development Initiative
MBDio .... Diocesan Library, Boston, MA [*Library symbol*] [*Library of Congress*] (LCLS)
MBDL .... Missile Battery Data Link (MCD)
MBdM .... Middlesex Community College, Bedford, MA [*Library symbol*] [*Library of Congress*] (LCLS)
MBdMi........ Mitre Corps., Bedford, MA [*Library symbol*] [*Library of Congress*] (LCLS)
MBDOE .... Million Barrels per Day Oil Equivalent (MHDB)
MBDP .... Minority Bank Deposit Program [*Treasury Department*]
MB(DP)AC ... Medical Benefits (Dental Practitioners) Advisory Committee
MBDR .... Make-or-Buy Data Record (KSC)
MBdR.......... Raytheon Co., Missile Systems Division Library, Bedford, MA [*Library symbol*] [*Library of Congress*] (LCLS)
MBDS .... Modular Building Distribution System [*Telecommunications*] (TEL)
MBdV.......... United States Veterans Administration Hospital, Bedford, MA [*Library symbol*] [*Library of Congress*] (LCLS)
MBE .... Bethany Lutheran College, Mankato, MN [*OCLC symbol*] (OCLC)
MBE .... Emerson College, Boston, MA [*Library symbol*] [*Library of Congress*] (LCLS)
MBE .... Mail Boxes Etc. USA [*San Diego, CA*] [*Telecommunications*] (TSSD)
MBE .... Malibu Entmt Intl. [*AMEX symbol*] (SG)
MBE .... Management by Exception
MBE .... Martin-Baker Ltd. [*British*] [*ICAO designator*] (FAAC)
MBE .... Mary Baker Eddy [*Founder of Christian Science*]
MBE .... Master of Bilingual Education (PGP)
MBE .... Master of Business Economics
MBE .... Master of Business Education (GAGS)
MBE .... May Be Elevated [*Medicine*] (DAVI)
MBE .... Medium Below-Elbow [*Cast*] (STED)
MBE .... Member of the [*Order of the*] British Empire [*Facetious translation: "My Bloody Efforts"*]
MBE .... Mennonite Board of Education (EA)
MBE .... Metals-Based Engineering
MBE .... Minority Business Enterprise (MCD)
MBE .... Missile-Borne Equipment
MBE .... Molecular Beam Epitaxy [*Crystallography*]
MBE .... Monbetsu [*Japan*] [*Airport symbol*] (OAG)
MBE .... Monumenta Biblica et Ecclesiastica [*Rome*] [*A publication*] (BJA)
MBE .... Mountasia Entertainment Intl., Inc. [*AMEX symbol*] (SAG)
MBE .... Moving Boundary Electrophoresis [*Analytical biochemistry*]
MBE .... Multiple-Beam Experiment [*In MBE-4, a heavy-ion accelerator at the Lawrence Berkeley Laboratory*]
MBE .... Multistate Bar Examination
MBEA .... Missouri Business Education Association (EDAC)
MBE-ARMS... Multiple Business Entity - Accounts Receivable Management System (MHDB)
MBED.......... Episcopal Diocese of Massachusetts, Diocesan Library and Archives, Boston, MA [*Library symbol*] [*Library of Congress*] (LCLS)
MB Ed .... Master of Business Education
MBehaviouralSc... Master of Behavioural Sciences (ADA)
MBEI .... Member of the Institute of Body Engineers [*British*] (DBQ)
MBEI .... Minnesota Business Educators, Inc (EDAC)
MBELDEF..... Minority Business Enterprise Legal Defense and Education Fund (EA)
MBelm........ Belmont Memorial Library, Belmont, MA [*Library symbol*] [*Library of Congress*] (LCLS)
MBelmM...... McLean Hospital, Belmont, MA [*Library symbol*] [*Library of Congress*] (LCLS)
MBEmm...... Emmanuel College, Boston, MA [*Library symbol*] [*Library of Congress*] (LCLS)
MBEnv .... Master of the Built Environment (ADA)
MBEP.......... Metals-Based Engineering Program
MBEP.......... Minority Business Enterprise Program (SAUO)
MBEP.......... Minority Business Tracking (SAUO)
MBEP.......... Region 4 Minority Business Tracking (SAUS)
MBEPA........ United States Environmental Protection Agency, Region I Library, Boston, MA [*Library symbol*] [*Library of Congress*] (LCLS)
MBER.......... Member
MBER.......... Minority Business Enterprise Representative (COE)
MBER.......... Molecular Beam Electric Resonance [*Physics*]
MBES.......... Member of the Bureau of Engineer Surveyors [*British*] (DBQ)
MBES.......... Mezhdunarodnyi Bank Ekonomicheskovo Sotrudnichestva [*International Bank for Economic Co-Operation - IBEC*] [*Moscow, USSR*] (EAIO)
MBEST........ Modulus Blipped Echo-Planar Single-Pulse Technique (STED)
MBev .... Beverly Public Library, Beverly, MA [*Library symbol*] [*Library of Congress*] (LCLS)
MBev-F........ Beverly Farms Public Library, Beverly, MA [*Library symbol*] [*Library of Congress*] (LCLS)
MBevHi........ Beverly Historical Society, Beverly, MA [*Library symbol*] [*Library of Congress*] (LCLS)
MBevN......... North Shore Community College, Beverly, MA [*Library symbol*] [*Library of Congress*] (LCLS)
MBevT .... Beverly Times, Beverly, MA [*Library symbol*] [*Library of Congress*] (LCLS)
MBE/WBE .... Certification Questionnaire-Minority/ Women Business Enterprise (SAUS)

MBE/WBE .... Certification Questionnaire-Minority/Women Business Enterprise (SAUO)
MBF............ Main Boundary Fault [*Geophysics*]
MBF............ Management by Fear (SAUO)
MBF............ Master Bibliographic File (ADA)
MBF............ Master Builders Federation [*British*] (BI)
MBF............ Materials Business File [*American Society for Metals, The Institute for Metals*] [*Information service or system*] (IID)
MBF............ MBF USA, Inc. [*Associated Press*] (SAG)
MBF............ Meat Base Formula [*Medicine*] (MEDA)
MBF............ Medical Benefits Fund (SAUO)
MBF............ Medullary Blood Flow [*Medicine*] (DMAA)
MBF............ Military Banking Facility
MBF............ Milk Bottlers Federation
MBF............ Missile Beacon Filter
MBF............ Modulator Band Filter (IAA)
MBF............ Molecular Beam Facility [*NASA*]
MBF............ Moving-Bed Filter [*Waste*] (DICI)
MBF............ Multiple Births Foundation (BUAC)
MBF............ Muscle Blood Flow [*Medicine*] (DMAA)
MBF............ Musicians Benevolent Fund [*British*] (BI)
MBF............ Myocardial Blood Flow [*Cardiology*]
MBF............ Thousand Board Feet [*Lumber*]
MBFA.......... Fellowes Athenaeum, Boston, MA [*Library symbol*] [*Library of Congress*] (LCLS)
MBFA.......... MBF USA, Inc. [*NASDAQ symbol*] (SAG)
MBFC.......... Magic of Bewitched Fan Club (EA)
MBFC.......... Medial Brachial Fascial Compartment [*Medicine*] (DMAA)
MBFC.......... Moe Bandy Fan Club (EA)
MBFL.......... Mid-Bergen Federation of Public Libraries [*Library network*]
MBFLB........ Monaural Bifrequency Loudness Balance [*Audiology*] (MAE)
MBFM.......... Massachusetts Grand Lodge, F & AM, Boston, MA [*Library symbol*] [*Library of Congress*] (LCLS)
MBFN.......... Multiple Beam Forming Network [*Military*] (LAIN)
MBFo.......... Forsyth Dental Center, Boston, MA [*Library symbol*] [*Library of Congress*] (LCLS)
MBFP.......... Manufacturing, Build, and Flow Plan (NASA)
MBFR.......... Federal Reserve Bank of Boston, Boston, MA [*Library symbol*] [*Library of Congress*] (LCLS)
MBFR.......... More Better for Russia [*Facetious translation of MBFR - Mutual and Balanced Force Reduction*]
MBFR.......... Mutual and Balanced Force Reduction [*Proposed reduction of forces in central Europe by NATO and Warsaw Pact nations*]
MBFT.......... Multi Band Frequency Translator (ACAE)
MBFUSA...... MBF USA, Inc. [*Associated Press*] (SAG)
MBG........... Gardner Museum, Boston, MA [*Library symbol*] [*Library of Congress*] (LCLS)
MBG........... Marburg [*Disease*] [*Medicine*] (DMAA)
MBG........... Mean Blood Glucose [*Medicine*] (STED)
MBG........... Message Buffer Group (SAUO)
MBG........... Midland Bank Group (SAUO)
MBG........... Missouri Botanical Garden
MBG........... Mobridge, SD [*Location identifier*] [*FAA*] (FAAL)
MBG........... Morphine-Benzedrine Group [*Scale*] [*Medicine*] (DMAA)
MBG & H .... Magna Brittannia, Gallia, et Hibernia [*Great Britain, France, and Ireland*] [*Latin*] (ROG)
MBGE.......... Missile-Borne Guidance Equipment (AFM)
MBGH......... Library Services, Brandon General Hospital, Manitoba [*Library symbol*] [*National Library of Canada*] (NLC)
MBGi .... Gillette Co., Boston R and D Laboratory, Boston, MA [*Library symbol*] [*Library of Congress*] (LCLS)
MBGiI .... Gillette Co., Boston R and D Laboratory, Boston, MA [*Library symbol*] [*Library of Congress*] (LCLS)
MBGS......... Missile-Borne Guidance Set (MCD)
MBGS......... Morphine-Benzedrine Group Scale (STED)
MBGT.......... General Theological Library, Boston, MA [*Library symbol*] [*Library of Congress*] (LCLS)
MBGT.......... Grand Turk [*Turks and Caicos Islands*] [*ICAO location identifier*] (ICLI)
MBGTS .... Missile-Borne Guidance Test Set (AABC)
MBH........... Manual Bomb Hoist
MBH........... Maryborough [*Australia*] [*Airport symbol*] (OAG)
MBH........... Massachusetts Horticultural Society, Boston, MA [*Library symbol*] [*Library of Congress*] (LCLS)
MBH........... Massive Black Hole [*Galactic science*]
MBH........... Maximal Benefit from Hospitalization (STED)
MBH........... Maximum Benefit from Hospitalization (SAUS)
MBH........... Medial Basal Hypothalamus [*Medicine*] (STED)
MBH........... Mediobasal Hypothalamus [*Brain anatomy*]
MBH........... Minard, Bryant H., Pennsauken NJ [*STAC*]
mbH........... Mit Beschraenkter Haftung [*With Limited Liability*] [*German*] (EG)
MBH........... Movimiento de Bases Hayistas [*Movement of Hayista Bases*] [*Peru*] [*Political party*] (PPW)
MBH........... Thousands of BTU per Hour
MBH2.......... Reduced Methylene Blue [*Medicine*] (DMAA)
MBHA.......... Member of the British Hypnotherapy Association (DBQ)
MBHC.......... Boissevain Health Centre, Manitoba [*Library symbol*] [*National Library of Canada*] (NLC)
MBHCM....... Master of Behavioral Health Care Management (PGP)
MBHE.......... Ministries to Blacks in Higher Education (EA)
MBHH......... Handel and Haydn Society, Boston, MA [*Library symbol*] [*Library of Congress*] (LCLS)
MBHI .... Member of the British Horological Institute (DBQ)
MBHI .... Millon Behavioral Health Inventory [*Personality development test*] [*Psychology*]

MBHINST..... Member of the British Horological Institute (ROG)
MBHM .... Harvard Musical Association, Boston, MA [Library symbol] [Library of Congress] (LCLS)
MBHO.......... Managed Behavioral Healthcare Organization (DMAA)
MBHoM....... Houghton Mifflin Co., Boston, MA [Library symbol] [Library of Congress] (LCLS)
MBHPFC ...... [The] Monkees, Boyce and Hart Photo Fan Club (EA)
MBI............. 2-Mercaptobenzimidazol (SAUS)
MBI............. Insurance Library Association of Boston, Boston, MA [Library symbol] [Library of Congress] (LCLS)
MBI............. Major Budget Issue (COE)
MBI............. Management by Initiative [Management technique]
MBI............. Marine Biomedical Institute [University of Texas] [Research center] (RCD)
MBI............. Maritime Bank of Israel (BJA)
MBI............. Maslach Burnout Inventory
MBI............. Masonic Benevolent Institution (SAUO)
MBI............. Master of Biological Illustration (GAGS)
MBI............. Maximal Blink Index [Medicine] (MELL)
MBI............. May Be Issued
MBI............. Mbeya [Tanzania] [Airport symbol] [Obsolete] (OAG)
MBI............. MBIA, Inc. [NYSE symbol] (SPSG)
MBI............. Memory Bank Interface
MBI............. Menan Buttes [Idaho] [Seismograph station code, US Geological Survey] [Closed] (SEIS)
MBI............. Metal Belt Institute [Defunct] (EA)
MBI............. Methylene Bisphenyl Isocyanate [Medicine] (MELL)
MBI............. Methylene Blue Installation [Medicine] (DAVI)
MBI............. Michigan Biotechnology Institute [Michigan State University] [Research center] (RCD)
MBI............. Middle Bronze I [Age]
MBI............. Military Board Instruction
MBI............. Minimal Baryonic Isocurvature [Galactic science]
MBI............. Miscellaneous Babylonian Inscriptions [A publication] (BJA)
MBI............. Modular Building Institute (NTPA)
MBI............. Molecular Biosystems, Inc.
MBI............. Multi Beam Imaging (ACAE)
MBI............. Multibus Interface [Computer science] (MCD)
MBI............. Mycobacterial Infection [Medicine] (MELL)
MBIA........... Malting Barley Improvement Association (EA)
MBIA........... MBIA, Inc. [Associated Press] (SAG)
MBIA........... Merchants Bancorp [NASDAQ symbol] (SAG)
MBIA........... Municipal Bond Insurance Association (EA)
MBIAC .... Missouri Basin Inter-Agency Committee
MBIBTC....... Malting and Brewing Industry Barley Technical Committee [Australia]
MBIC.......... Michigan Bigfoot Information Center [Later, MCBIC]
MBIC.......... Monmouth Biomedical Information Consortium [Library network]
M Bi Ch .... Master of Biological Chemistry
MBiChem..... Master of Biological Chemistry (NADA)
MBID .... Member of the British Institute of Interior Design (DBQ)
M Bi E .... Master of Biological Engineering
MBIE........... Member of the British Institute of Embalmers (DBQ)
MBiEng........ Master of Biological Engineering (NADA)
MBIFCT........ Mgahinga and Bwindi Inpenetrable Forest Conservation Trust (ECON)
MBII............ Masonic Benevolent Institution Ireland (SAUO)
MBII............ Minority Business Information Institute [Defunct] (EA)
MBiIC.......... Cabot Corp., Technical Information Center, Billerica, MA [Library symbol] [Library of Congress] (LCLS)
MBilHi .... Billerica Historical Society, Billerica, MA [Library symbol] [Library of Congress] (LCLS)
MBIM.......... Member of the British Institute of Management [Formerly, MIIA]
MBIO .... Microprogrammable Block Input/Output
M Bio E .... Master of Bioengineering (PGP)
MBioEth....... Master of Bioethics
M Biomath... Master of Biomathematics (PGP)
MBiomedE.... Master of Biomedical Engineering (ADA)
M Biorad ..... Master of Bioradiology
MBiotech ..... Master of Biotechnology
M Bi Phy ..... Master of Biological Physics
MBIS.......... Mackenzie Basin Impact Study (SAUO)
M Bi S .... Master of Biological Sciences
MBIS........... Master of Business Information Systems
MB (IT)........ Master of Business (Information Technology)
MBIT........... MegaBIT [Binary Digit] [Computer science] (MDG)
Mbits/sec.... Megabits per Second [Computer science] (IGQR)
MBIU .... Maintenance Bus Interface Unit (ACAE)
MBIU .... Multiplex Bus Interface Unit (MCD)
MBJ .... Montego Bay [Jamaica] [Airport symbol] (OAG)
MBJ .... Multiple Blinking Jammer (MCD)
MBJI .... Marks Bros Jewelers [NASDAQ symbol] (TTSB)
MBJI .... Marks Bros. Jewelers, Inc. [NASDAQ symbol] (SAG)
MBJT .... Grand Turk [Turks and Caicos Islands] [ICAO location identifier] (ICLI)
MBK........... Bank of Mitsubishi Ltd. [NYSE symbol] (SAG)
MBK........... Bank of Tokyo-MitsubishiADS [NYSE symbol] (TTSB)
MBK........... Madchen-Bibel-Kreise [Bible Reading Circles] [German]
MBK........... Make-Break Keying (IAA)
MBK........... Medications and Bandage kit (NAKS)
MBK........... Methyl Butyl Ketone [Organic chemistry]
MBK........... Missing, Believed Killed (ADA)
MBK........... Mitsubishi Bank Ltd. ADS [NYSE symbol] (SPSG)
MBK........... Multibanc Financial Corp. [Toronto Stock Exchange symbol]
MBK........... Multiple Beam Klystron
MBL .... Main Battle Line [Military] (IAA)

MBL........... Manistee [Michigan] [Airport symbol] (OAG)
MBL........... Mannan-Binding Lectin [Immunology]
MBL........... Marble Bar [Australia] [Seismograph station code, US Geological Survey] (SEIS)
MBL........... Marine Biological Laboratory
MBL........... Marine Boundary Layer [Oceanography]
MBL........... Master Bidders List (NG)
MBL........... Maximum Benefit Level [Health insurance] (GHCT)
MBL........... Measured Blood Loss [Physiology]
MBL........... Mechanical Boundary Layer [Geology]
MBL........... Medium Brightness Laser (ACAE)
MBL........... Medium Brown Loose [Stool] [Gastroenterology] (DAVI)
MBL........... Menstrual Blood Loss [Medicine]
MBL........... Miniature Button Light
MBL........... Minimal Bactericidal Level
MBL........... Missile Baseline
MBL........... Mobile (AFM)
MBL........... Mobile Unit (SAUS)
MBL........... Model Breakdown List
MBL........... Monterey Bay Area Cooperative Library System, Salinas, CA [OCLC symbol] (OCLC)
MBL........... Movimiento Bolivia Libre [Political party] (EY)
MBL........... Multiples of Background Level [Of environmental contaminants]
MBL........... Mutual Benefit Life Insurance Co. (EFIS)
MBLA.......... MBLA Financial Corp. [Associated Press] (SAG)
MBLA.......... Methylbenzyllinoleic Acid [Organic chemistry]
MBLA.......... Mouse Specific Bone-Marrow-Derived Lymphocyte Antigen [Immunology]
MBLA.......... National Mercantile Bancorp [NASDAQ symbol] (NQ)
MBLC.......... Lahey Clinic Foundation, Boston, MA [Library symbol] [Library of Congress] (LCLS)
MBLC.......... Massachusetts Board of Library Commissioners
MBLC.......... Microbore Liquid Chromatography
MBldg......... Master of Building (ADA)
MBldgSc...... Master of Building Science (ADA)
MBldSc....... Master of Building Science
MBLE.......... Mobile Gas Service [NASDAQ symbol] (TTSB)
MBLE.......... Mobile Gas Service Corp. [NASDAQ symbol] (NQ)
MBLF.......... MBLA Financial [NASDAQ symbol] (TTSB)
MBLF.......... MBLA Financial Corp. [NASDAQ symbol] (SAG)
MBLIC......... Mutual Benefit Life Insurance Company (SAUO)
MBLM......... MobileMedia Corp. [NASDAQ symbol] (SAG)
MBLR.......... Madhya Bharat Law Reports [India] [A publication] (DLA)
MblTel........ Mobile Telecommunications & Technology Corp. [Associated Press] (SAG)
MBLY......... Mobley Environmental Services [NASDAQ symbol] (SPSG)
MBM.......... Mac Bride Museum (SAUO)
MBM.......... Magnetic Bubble Memory [Computer science]
MBM.......... Mambone [Mozambique] [Airport symbol] (AD)
MBM.......... Manual Berthing Mechanism [NASA] (SPST)
MBM.......... Market Buy Market [Information service or system] (IID)
MBM.......... Market-by-Market Allocation [Business term] (DOAD)
MBM.......... Master of Brand Management (GAGS)
MBM.......... Master of Building Management (ADA)
MBM.......... Master of Business Management
MBM.......... Meat and Bone Meal
MBM.......... Mennonite Board of Missions (SAUO)
MBM.......... Metal-Barrier-Metal (IEEE)
MBM.......... Mineral Basal Medium [Microbiology]
MBM.......... Modern Black Men [Johnson Publishing Co., Inc.] [A publication]
MBM.......... Mother's Breast Milk [Neonatology] (DAVI)
MBM.......... Multibuoy Mooring [Oil platform]
Mbm.......... Thousand Board (Feet) Measure (WPI)
MBM.......... Thousand Feet Board Measure [Lumber] (GPO)
MBM.......... University of Massachusetts, Joseph P. Healy Library, Boston, MA [Library symbol] [Library of Congress] (LCLS)
MBMA......... Master Boiler Makers' Association (BUAC)
MBMA......... Metal Building Manufacturers Association (EA)
MBMA......... Military Boot Manufacturers Association (EA)
MBMC......... Middle Caicos [Turks and Caicos Islands] [ICAO location identifier] (ICLI)
MBMCC....... Mercedes-Benz Model Car Club
MBMetE...... Metcalf & Eddy, Inc., Boston, MA [Library symbol] [Library of Congress] (LCLS)
MBMF......... Multibeam Multifrequency (CAAL)
MBMG........ Montana Bureau of Mines and Geology [Montana College of Mineral Science and Technology] [Research center] (RCD)
MBMGH-T... Massachusetts General Hospital, Treadwell Library, Boston, MA [Library symbol] [Library of Congress] (LCLS)
MBMH......... Brandon Mental Health Centre, Manitoba [Library symbol] [National Library of Canada] (NLC)
MBMHC ...... Malcolm Bliss Mental Health Center (SAUO)
MBMI......... Mean Body Mass Index
MBMI......... Micro Bio-Medics [NASDAQ symbol] (TTSB)
MBMI......... Micro Bio-Medics, Inc. [NASDAQ symbol] (NQ)
MBMI......... Mind/Body Medical Institute
MBMS......... Bachelor of Medicine, Master of Surgery
MBMS......... Model Base Management Software [Computer science] (IAA)
MBMS......... Molecular Beam Mass Spectrometry (AAEL)
MBMSA....... Massachusetts College of Art, Boston, MA [Library symbol] [Library of Congress] (LCLS)
MBMSE........ Master of Business Management and Software Engineering (PGP)
MBMU........ Mobile Base Maintenance Unit
MBMu .... Museum of Fine Arts, Boston, MA [Library symbol] [Library of Congress] (LCLS)

MBMU	University of Massachusetts, Boston, MA [*Library symbol*] [*Library of Congress*] (LCLS)
MBN	Boston Museum of Science, Boston, MA [*Library symbol*] [*Library of Congress*] (LCLS)
MBN	Metal Building News [*A publication*] (APTA)
MBN	Methylbenzylnitrosamine [*Organic chemistry*]
MBN	Metrobank NA [*AMEX symbol*] (SPSG)
MBN	Mixed Base Notation
MBN	Mombo [*Tanzania*] [*Airport symbol*] (AD)
MBN	Mutual Black Network (NTCM)
MBNA	MBNA Corp. [*Associated Press*] (SAG)
MBNA	Mercedes Benz of North America
MBNA	Methyl(butyl)nitrosamine [*Organic chemistry*]
MBNA	Monument Builders of North America (EA)
MBNAD	Marine Barracks, Naval Ammunition Depot
MBNAS	Marine Barracks, Naval Air Station
MBNBR	Mount Bruce Native Bird Reserve (SAUO)
MBNC	North Caicos [*Turks and Caicos Islands*] [*ICAO location identifier*] (ICLI)
MBNECO	New England College of Optometry, Boston MA [*Library symbol*] [*Library of Congress*] (LCLS)
MBNEH	New England Historic Genealogical Society, Boston, MA [*Library symbol*] [*Library of Congress*] (LCLS)
MBNEL	New England School of Law, Boston, MA [*Library symbol*] [*Library of Congress*] (LCLS)
MBNEN	New England Nuclear Corp., Boston, MA [*Library symbol*] [*Library of Congress*] (LCLS)
MBnet	[*The*] Manitoba Network [*Canada*] [*Computer science*] (TNIG)
MBNMD	Marine Barracks, Naval Mine Depot
MBNMHi	New England Methodist Historical Society, Inc., Boston, MA [*Library symbol*] [*Library of Congress*] (LCLS)
MBNOA	Member of the British Naturopathic and Osteopathic Association
MBNOB	Marine Barracks, Naval Operating Base
MBNQA	Malcolm Baldrige National Quality Award [*Department of Commerce*]
MBNS	Marine Barracks, Naval Station
MBNU	Northeastern University, Boston, MA [*Library symbol*] [*Library of Congress*] (LCLS)
MBNU-L	Northeastern University, Law School, Boston, MA [*Library symbol*] [*Library of Congress*] (LCLS)
MBNY	Merchants Bank of New York [*NASDAQ symbol*] (NQ)
MBNY	Merchants New York Bancorp [*NASDAQ symbol*] (SAG)
MBNY	Merchants NY Bancorp [*NASDAQ symbol*] (TTSB)
MBNYD	Marine Barracks, Navy Yard
MBO	Liberal Bosnian Organization (BUAC)
MBO	Madison, MS [*Location identifier*] [*FAA*] (FAAL)
MBO	Mamburao [*Philippines*] [*Airport symbol*] (OAG)
MBO	Management and Budget Office (MCD)
MBO	Management Buy-Out
MBO	Management by Objectives [*Management technique*] [*Facetious translations: "Management by Oblivion," and "Management by Others"*]
MBO	M'Bour [*Senegal*] [*Seismograph station code, US Geological Survey*] (SEIS)
MBO	Meacham Bridge Oscillator [*Electronics*]
MBO	Mesiobucco-Occlusal [*Dentistry*]
MBO	Million Barrels of Oil (ABAC)
MBO	Mobil Oil Ltd. [*Canada*] [*ICAO designator*] (FAAC)
MBO	Moist Burn Ointment [*Medicine*]
MBO	Monostable Blocking Oscillator [*Electronics*]
MBO	Motor Burnout (AABC)
MBO	Moving Base Operator
MBO	Muslim Bosnian Organization (BUAC)
MBO	Mutual Benefit Organization (SAUO)
MBO	Secondary Vocational Education (SAUS)
MbO$_2$	Myoglobin, Oxy [*Biochemistry, medicine*]
MBOA	Methoxybenzoxazolinone [*Biochemistry*]
MBOA	Motor Barge Owners Association (BUAC)
MBOC	Middle Bay Oil [*NASDAQ symbol*] (TTSB)
MBOC	Middle Bay Oil Co., Inc. [*NASDAQ symbol*] (SAG)
MBOC	Minority Business Opportunity Committee [*Federal interagency group*]
MbOCA	Methylene-bis-Orthochloro Aniline (SAUS)
MBOCA	Methylenebis(ortho-chloroaniline) [*Also, MOCA*] [*Organic chemistry*]
MBOH	Minimum Break-Off Height
MBOL	Motor Burnout Locking (AABC)
MBOM	Boissevain and Morton Regional Library, Boissevain, Manitoba [*Library symbol*] [*National Library of Canada*] (NLC)
Mbone	Multicast Backbone [*Internet terminology*] (CDE)
M-bone	Multicast Backbone [*Computer science*] (DOM)
MBOR	Management by Objectives and Results [*Management technique*] (MCD)
MBOS	Missile Base Operations Supervisor [*Air Force*] (IAA)
MBOS	Multi-User Business Operating System (NITA)
MBou	Jonathan Bourne Public Library, Bourne, MA [*Library symbol*] [*Library of Congress*] (LCLS)
MBOU	Member of the British Ornithologists Union (EY)
MBP	Magneto-Dynamic Positioning
MBP	Major Basic Protein
MBP	Malignant Bone Pain (MELL)
MBP	Maltose-Binding Protein [*Biochemistry*]
MBP	Management by Planning (ACAE)
MBP	Manhattan Bowery Project (EA)
MBP	Manpack Battery Pack
MBP	Massachusetts College of Pharmacy, Boston, MA [*Library symbol*] [*Library of Congress*] (LCLS)
MBP	Master Buy Plan (AAGC)
MBP	Maximum Boiling Point
MBP	MB Brand Present [*Cardiology*] (DAVI)
MBP	Mean Blood Pressure [*Medicine*]
MBP	Mean Brachial Artery Pressure [*Medicine*]
MBP	Mechanical Balance Package (OA)
MBP	Mechanical Booster Pump
MBP	Melitensis, Bovine, Porcine [*Antigen*] (AAMN)
MBP	Mesiobuccopulpal [*Dentistry*]
MBP	Mid-Boiling Point
MBP	Mid Penn Bancorp [*AMEX symbol*] (SG)
MBP	Minnesota Business Partnership (SAUO)
MBP	Modified Bagshawe Protocol [*Medicine*] (MELL)
MBP	Monodibutyl Phosphate [*Organic chemistry*] (NUCP)
MBP	Myelin Basic Protein [*Neurology*]
MBPA	Master of Business and Public Administration
MBPA	Metropolitan Bicycle Polo Association (SAUO)
MBPA	Military Blood Program Agency (AABC)
MBPAS	Monthly Bulk Petroleum Accounting Summary [*Army*] (AABC)
MBP-C	Mannose-Binding Protein C [*Biochemistry*]
MBPC	Model-Based Process Control (AAEL)
MBPC	Munitions Board Petroleum Committee
MBPCX	Merrill Lynch: Pacific Fund Cl.B [*Mutual fund ticker symbol*] (SG)
MBPD	Million Barrels per Day
MBPDA	Metropolitan Bag and Paper Distribution Association (SAUO)
MBPDA	Metropolitan Bag and Paper Distributors Association (EA)
MBPI	Pine Cay [*Turks and Caicos Islands*] [*ICAO location identifier*] (ICLI)
MBPKN	Perry Normal School, Boston, MA [*Library symbol*] [*Library of Congress*] (LCLS)
MBPM	Master of Business and Public Management
MBPM	Maurice Bishop Patriotic Movement [*Grenada*] (BUAC)
MBPO	Military Blood Program Office (AABC)
MBPP	Movimiento Blanco Popular y Progresista [*National Action Movement*] [*Uruguay*] [*Political party*] (EY)
MBPRE	Multitype Branching Process in a Random Environment [*Computer science*]
MBPS	Mechanical Booster Pump System
MBPS	MegaBITS [*Binary Digits*] per Second [*Transmission rate*] [*Computer science*]
Mbps	Megabits per Second (NAKS)
Mbps	Megabytes per Second [*Computer science*] (IGQR)
MBPS	Million BITs [*Binary Digits*] per Second [*Data transmission speed*] [*Computer science*] (NASA)
MBPS	Multigated Blood Pool Scanning [*Medicine*] (DMAA)
MBPS	Munchausen-by-Proxy Syndrome [*Medicine*] (MELL)
MBPT	Many-Body Perturbation Theory [*Physics*]
MBPV	Providenciales [*Turks and Caicos Islands*] [*ICAO location identifier*] (ICLI)
MBPXL	MBPXL Corp. [*Formerly, Missouri Beef Packers - Kansas Beef Industries*]
MBPXL	Missouri Beef Packers Express Line (SAUO)
MBQ	Marine Board of Queensland [*Australia*]
MBQ	Mbarara [*Uganda*] [*Airport symbol*] (OAG)
MBQ	Medical Board of Queensland [*Australia*]
MBQ	Modified Biquinary Code [*Computer science*]
MBR	Maladapted Behavior Record [*Personality development test*] [*Psychology*]
MBR	Management by Results [*Management technique*]
MBR	Marker Beacon Receiver
MBR	Mars Balloon Relay (ACAE)
MBR	Master Bedroom [*Real estate*]
MBR	Master Beneficiary Record [*Social Security Administration*]
MBR	Master Boot Record [*Computer science*] (PCM)
MBR	Material Balance Report [*Nuclear energy*]
MBR	Maximum Base Rent
MBR	Mbout [*Mauritania*] [*Airport symbol*] (AD)
MBR	Mechanical Bag Retriever [*Garbage collector*]
MBR	Mechanical Buffer Register [*Computer science*]
MBR	Member (AFM)
Mbr	Member (AL)
mbr	Member (DD)
MBR	Membrane Bioreactor [*Chemical engineering*]
MBR	Membrane-Bound Ribosomes [*Cytology*]
MBR	Memory Base Register
MBR	Memory Buffer Register [*Computer science*]
MBR	Metal Bulletin Research [*Commercial firm*] [*British*] (ECON)
MBR	Methylene Blue Reduced
MBR	Microwave Background Radiation [*Physics*]
MBR	Mini Badge Reader (IAA)
MBR	Mission Briefing Room [*NASA*] (KSC)
MBR	Modern Business Reports (SAUO)
MBR	Modified Bitumen, Reinforced
MBR	Montebello Resources Ltd. [*Vancouver Stock Exchange symbol*]
MBR	Motivation by Rotation
MBR	Moving Belt Radiator
MBR	Multibomb Rack
MBr	Public Library of Brookline, Brookline, MA [*Library symbol*] [*Library of Congress*] (LCLS)
MBRA	Marathon Boat Racers Association
MBRA	Multibeam Radiometer Antenna
MBradJ	Bradford Junior College [*Later, BC*], Bradford, MA [*Library symbol*] [*Library of Congress*] (LCLS)
MBRBA	Motor Body Repairers and Builders Association (SAUO)
MBRC	Marine Biology Research Centre [*University of Moncton*] [*Canada*] (IRC)

MBRDC .... Medical Bioengineering Research and Development Command [*Army*] (PDAA)

MBRDL .... Medical Bioengineering Research and Development Laboratory [*Army*] (MCD)

MBre .... Brewster Ladies Library, Brewster, MA [*Library symbol*] [*Library of Congress*] (LCLS)

MBR-E .... Memory Buffer Register, Even [*Computer science*] (VLIE)

MBRE .... Memory Buffer Register, Even [*Computer science*]

MBreC .... Cape Cod Museum of Natural History, Brewster, MA [*Library symbol*] [*Library of Congress*] (LCLS)

MBRET .... Middle Breton [*Language, etc.*]

MBRF .... Midbrain Reticular Formation [*Anatomy*]

MBRF .... Mission Bay Research Foundation (SAUO)

MBRG .... Ropes & Gray, Boston, MA [*Library symbol*] [*Library of Congress*] (LCLS)

MBrH .... Hebrew College, Brookline, MA [*Library symbol*] [*Library of Congress*] (LCLS)

MBrHC .... Hellenic College of Arts and Sciences and Holy Cross Greek Orthodox Theological School, Brookline, MA [*Library symbol*] [*Library of Congress*] (LCLS)

MBridT .... Bridgewater State College, Bridgewater, MA [*Library symbol*] [*Library of Congress*] (LCLS)

M Brit IRE ... Member of the British Institution of Radio Engineers [*Later, MIERE*]

M/BRK .... Manual Brake [*Automotive engineering*]

MBRK .... Meadowbrook Rehab Grp'A' [*NASDAQ symbol*] (TTSB)

MBRK .... Meadowbrook Rehabilitation Group [*NASDAQ symbol*] (SAG)

MBRL .... Multiple Ballistic Rocket Launcher

MBRLS .... Multi-Barrel Rocket Launching System (SAUS)

MBRM .... Membrane

MBR-O .... Memory Buffer Register, Odd [*Computer science*] (VLIE)

MBRO .... Memory Buffer Register, Odd [*Computer science*]

MBrock .... Brockton Public Library, Brockton, MA [*Library symbol*] [*Library of Congress*] (LCLS)

MBrockV ...... United States Veterans Administration Hospital, Brockton, MA [*Library symbol*] [*Library of Congress*] (LCLS)

MBRR .... Meridian & Bigbee Railroad Co. [*Formerly, MB*] [*AAR code*]

MBRS .... MemberWorks, Inc. [*NASDAQ symbol*] (SAG)

MBRS .... Minority Biomedical Research Support Program [*Bethesda, MD*] [*National Institutes of Health*] (GRD)

MBRS .... Mount Barker Research Station (SAUO)

MBRSHP ...... Membership

MBRT .... Methylene Blue Reduction Time

MBRUU .... May Be Retained until Unserviceable

MBRV .... Maneuverable Ballistic Reentry Vehicle

MBRW .... Matchbox Regular Wheels [*Toy collection*]

MBRW .... Minnesota Brewing [*NASDAQ symbol*] (TTSB)

MBRW .... Minnesota Brewing Co. [*NASDAQ symbol*] (SAG)

MBrZ .... Zion Research Library, Brookline, Boston, MA [*Library symbol*] [*Library of Congress*] (LCLS)

MBS .... Bay City-Midland-Saginaw [*Michigan*] [*Airport symbol*] (AD)

MBS .... Bethany Lutheran Theological Seminary, Mankato, MN [*OCLC symbol*] (OCLC)

MBS .... Macquarie Broadcasting Service (SAUO)

MBS .... Magnetron Beam Switching

MBS .... Main "Bang" Suppressor

MBS .... Main Buffer Storage (IAA)

MBS .... Mainichi Broadcasting System (SAUO)

MBS .... Maleimidobenzoyl N-Hydroxysuccinimide [*Organic chemistry*]

MBS .... Malta Board of Standards (BUAC)

MBS .... Managed Bandwidth Service

MBS .... Management by System [*Management technique*] (IAA)

MBS .... Manchester Business School [*England*]

MBS .... Marker Board Supplies Limited (SAUO)

MBS .... Market Basket Survey [*Business term*]

MBS .... Martin-Bell Syndrome [*Medicine*] (DMAA)

MBS .... Master Bibliographic System (ADA)

MBS .... Master Boot Sector (SAUS)

MBS .... Master of Basic Science

MBS .... Master of Behavioral Science (GAGS)

MBS .... Master of Building Science (GAGS)

MBS .... Master of Business Science (SAUO)

MBS .... Maximum Burst Size (MLOA)

MBS .... Medborgerlig Samling [*Citizens Rally*] [*Sweden*] [*Political party*] (PPE)

MBS .... Mediterranean Base Section [*Army*] [*World War II*]

MBS .... Medium Bomber Strike (NATG)

MBS .... MedQuist, Inc. [*AMEX symbol*] (SAG)

MBS .... Megabits Per Second (NITA)

mbs .... Megabits per Second (COE)

Mbs .... Megabits per Second [*Computer science*] (IGQR)

M B/S .... Megabits per Second (NAKS)

Mb/s .... Megabits per Second (VLIE)

MBS .... Megabytes Per Second (NITA)

MB/s .... Megabytes per Second (VLIE)

MBS .... Member of the Bibliographical Society (ROG)

MBS .... Menorah Book Service (BJA)

MBS .... Methacrylate Butadiene Styrene [*Plastics technology*]

MBS .... Methionyl Bovine Somatotropin [*Biochemistry*]

MBS .... Methodist Boys' School

MBS .... Miami Beach Symphony (SAUO)

MBS .... Micro Business Systems (NITA)

MBS .... Miniature Book Society (EA)

MBS .... Minimum Basis Sets [*Chemistry*] (MEC)

MBS .... Mission Bit Stream (SAUO)

MBS .... Mission Budget Statement [*Army*]

MBS .... Mobile-Base Simulator (PDAA)

MBS .... Mobile Broadband System (SAUO)

MBS .... Modular Banking System (PDAA)

MBS .... Molecular Beam Scattering (SAUS)

MBS .... Monobutyl Sulfate [*Organic chemistry*]

MBS .... Monumental Brass Society (EA)

MBS .... Morpholine-Based Sulfenamide [*Chemistry*]

MBS .... Mortgage-Backed Securities Information Services [*The Bond Buyer, Inc.*] [*New York, NY*] [*Information service or system*] (IID)

MBS .... Mortgage-Backed Security (DFIT)

MBS .... Mortgage-Backed Security Program [*Government National Mortgage Association*]

MBS .... Motion Base Simulator (MCD)

MBS .... Motor Bus Society (EA)

MBS .... Multibit Shifter (IAA)

MBS .... Multiblade Slurry Saw [*Semiconductor technology*]

MBS .... Multiblock Synchronization Signal Unit [*Telecommunications*] (TEL)

MBS .... Multicore Bar Solder

MBS .... Multilingual Biblioservice of Alberta, Alberta Culture [*UTLAS symbol*]

MBS .... Multiple Batch Station [*Computer science*]

MBS .... Multiple Business System

MBS .... Municipal Broadcasting System (SAUO)

MBS .... Music Broadcasting Society (NADA)

MBS .... Mutual Broadcasting System

MBS .... Muzzle Bore Sight [*British military*] (DMA)

MBS .... Saginaw [*Michigan*] [*Airport symbol*] (OAG)

MBS .... Saginaw, MI [*Location identifier*] [*FAA*] (FAAL)

MBS .... Social Law Library, Boston, MA [*Library symbol*] [*Library of Congress*] (LCLS)

MBSA .... Main Bus-Switching Assembly (SSD)

MBSA .... Maleylated Bovine Serum Albumin [*Biochemistry*]

MBSA .... Manual Business Systems Association [*British*] (DBA)

MBSA .... Medical Board of South Australia

MBSA .... Methylated Bovine Serum Albumin

MBSA .... Model-Based System Analysis (PDAA)

MBSA .... Modular Building Standards Association (EA)

MBSA .... Municipal Board Standards Association (NADA)

MBSA .... Munitions Board Standards Agency

MBSA .... Museum Board of South Australia

MBSB .... Marine Barracks, Submarine Base

MBSC .... Boston State College, Boston, MA [*Library symbol*] [*Library of Congress*] (LCLS)

MBSc .... Master of Behavioural Science

MB Sc .... Master of Business Science

MBSC .... Modular Building Systems Council (EA)

MBSC .... South Caicos [*Turks and Caicos Islands*] [*ICAO location identifier*] (ICLI)

MBSCC .... Mortgage-Backed Securities Clearing Corp. (EMRF)

MBSCSDD .... Master of Back Stabbin', Cork Screwin', and Dirty Dealin' [*Self-conferred degree held by Mordecai Jones in 1967 movie "The Flim-Flam Man"*]

MBSD .... Multi-Barrel Smoke Discharger [*Military*] (PDAA)

MBS Division ... Moore Business Systems Division (SAUO)

MBSE .... Member of Belgian Society of Engineers (SAUO)

MBSF .... Matchbox Superfast [*Toy collection*]

MBSG .... Missouri Basin Systems Group (SAUO)

MBSGM .... Multi-Base Sortie Generation Model (SAUO)

MBSHC .... Mediterranean and Black Seas Hydrographic Commission (SAUO)

MBSI .... Master of Business Information Science (PGP)

MBSI .... Member of the Boot and Shoe Industry [*British*] (DAS)

MBSI .... Member of the British Boot and Shoe Institution (SAUO)

MBSI .... Missile Battery Status Indicator

MBSI .... Musical Box Society, International (EA)

MBSi .... Simmons College, Boston, MA [*Library symbol*] [*Library of Congress*] (LCLS)

MBSJC .... Metropolitan Boroughs Standing Joint Committee (SAUO)

MB-SL .... British Museum - Sloan Herbarium [*London*]

MBSL .... Mobile Surgery Laboratory (SAUO)

MBSL .... Mouse Biochemical Specific Locus [*Test for mutagenesis*]

MBSL .... Multiple-Bubble Sonoluminescence [*Physics*]

MBSM .... Maize Bushy Stunt Mycoplasm [*Plant pathology*]

MBSM .... Mexican Border Service Medal

MBSOGB ...... Musical Box Society of Great Britain

MBSP .... Main Bang Synchronization Pulse (IAA)

MBSP .... Mitchell Bancorp, Inc. [*NASDAQ symbol*] (SAG)

MBSpnea ..... Society for the Preservation of New England Antiquities, Boston, MA [*Library symbol*] [*Library of Congress*] (LCLS)

MBSP-R .... Monitoring Basic Skills Progress-Reading (TES)

MBSQ .... Music Broadcasting Society of Queensland [*Australia*]

MBSS .... Main Beach Signal Station (IAA)

MBSS .... Multi-Band Staring Sensor (ACAE)

MBSS .... Multi-Bank Staring System Sensor (SAUS)

MBSSM .... Maxfield-Buchholz Scale of Social Maturity [*Psychology*]

MBST .... Motor Behavior Screening Test [*Physical education*]

MBST .... Multiple Beam Switching Tube

MBSTA .... Mobilization Station (SAUO)

MBSU .... Multi Bus Switching Unit

MBSuf .... Suffolk University, Boston, MA [*Library symbol*] [*Library of Congress*] (LCLS)

MBSufC .... Suffolk County Court House, Boston, MA [*Library symbol*] [*Library of Congress*] (LCLS)

MBSY .... Salt Cay [*Turks and Caicos Islands*] [*ICAO location identifier*] (ICLI)

MBT .... Main Ballast Tank

MBT .... Main Battle Tank

MBT .... Main Boundary Thrust [*Geology*]

MBT............ Many-Body Theory [Physics] (BARN)
MBT............ Marble Bar - Town [Australia] [Seismograph station code, US Geological Survey] [Closed]
MBT............ Marianna & Blountstown Railroad Co. [AAR code]
MBT............ Masbate [Philippines] [Airport symbol] (OAG)
MBT............ Massive Blood Transfusion [Medicine] (MELL)
MBT............ Master of Business and Technology
MBT............ Master of Business Taxation (GAGS)
MBT............ Mean Body Temperature (WDAA)
MBT............ Mechanical Bathythermograph
MBT............ Memory Block Table [Computer science] (HGAA)
MBT............ Mercaptobenzothiazole [Organic chemistry]
MBT............ Mercury Bombardment Thrustor
MBT............ Metal-Base Transistor [Electronics] (IEEE)
MBT............ Metal Bond Tape
MBT............ Methylenebisthiocyanate [Antimicrobial agent]
MBT............ Methylene Blue Test [Analytical chemistry]
MBT............ Metropolitan Ballet Theatre [Detroit]
MBT............ Midblastula Stage [Embryology]
MBT............ Mid-Blastula Transition [Developmental biology]
MBT............ Minimum Best Torque
MBT............ Mixed Bacterial Toxin
MBT............ Mobile Boarding Team
MBT............ Mobile Telesystems OJSC ADS [NYSE symbol]
MBT............ Modified Boiling Test (PDAA)
MBT............ Mother's Blood Type (ADWA)
MBT............ Motion Base Technologies
MBT............ Motor Burning Time
MBT............ Multimedia-Based Training
MBT............ Murfreesboro, TN [Location identifier] [FAA] (FAAL)
MBT............ Vias Aereas Manabitas CIA Ltds. [Ecuador] [FAA designator] (FAAC)
MBTA.......... Malaysia Baggage Transport Agency (SAUO)
MBTA.......... Massachusetts Bay Transit Authority (ADWA)
MBTA.......... Massachusetts Bay Transportation Authority [Formerly, MTA]
MBTA.......... Metropolitan Boston Transit Authority (BARN)
MBTA.......... Midwest Book Travelers Association (SAUO)
MBTA.......... Migratory Bird Treaty Act (GNE)
MBTA.......... Migratory Bird Treaty Act of 1918 (COE)
MBTC.......... Mercedes-Benz Truck Co.
MBTC.......... Model-Based Temperature Control (AAEL)
MBTCA........ Miniature Bull Terrier Club of America (EA)
MBTD/RP..... Main Battle Tank Distribution/Redistribution Plan (MCD)
MBTFA........ Methylbistrifluoroacetamide [Organic chemistry]
MBTH.......... Methylbenzothiazolinone Hydrazone [Organic chemistry]
MbThSt....... Marburger Theologische Studien (BJA)
MBTI.......... Boston Theological Institute, Learning Development Program, Boston, MA [Library symbol] [Library of Congress] (LCLS)
MBTI.......... Manpower Business Training Institute
MBTI.......... Myers-Briggs Type Indicator [Psychology]
MBTI:AV ..... Myers-Briggs Type Indicator: Abbreviated Version [Personality development test] [Psychology]
MBTS.......... Mercaptobenzothiazole Disulfide [Organic chemistry]
MBTS.......... Meteorological Balloon Tracking System
MBTS.......... Michelin Bead Tension Structure [Tire design]
MBTS.......... Missile Battery Test Set [Military] (IAA)
MBtS.......... Saint John's Seminary, Brighton, MA [Library symbol] [Library of Congress] (LCLS)
MBTT.......... Marine Builders Training Trust (AIE)
MBtu.......... Million British Thermal Units
MBTWK....... Multiple Beam Traveling Wave Klystron
MBU.......... Boston University, Boston, MA [Library symbol] [Library of Congress] (LCLS)
MBU.......... Boston University, School of Medicine, Boston, MA [OCLC symbol] (OCLC)
MBU.......... Hayward Map, CA [Location identifier] [FAA] (FAAL)
MBU.......... Magnetic Bubble Unit (NITA)
MBU.......... Mbambanakira [Solomon Islands] [Airport symbol] (OAG)
MBU.......... Memory Buffer Unit [Computer science]
MBU.......... MIRA [Multifunctional Inertial Reference Assembly] Basic Unit [Air Force] (MCD)
MBU.......... Mission Briefing Unit
MBUC........ Mind Bogglingly Unlikely Coincidence (SAUS)
MBU-E........ Boston University, School of Education, Boston, MA [Library symbol] [Library of Congress] (LCLS)
MBUF........ United Fruit Co., Boston, MA [Library symbol] [Library of Congress] (LCLS)
MBuild........ Master of Building (ADA)
MBUK........ Mercedes-Benz (United Kingdom)
MBU-L........ Boston University, School of Law, Boston, MA [Library symbol] [Library of Congress] (LCLS)
MBU-M .... Boston University, School of Medicine, Boston, MA [Library symbol] [Library of Congress] (LCLS)
MBUMA ...... Mean Time between Unscheduled Maintenance Actions
MBUMR....... MIRA [Multifunctional Inertial Reference Assembly] Basic Unit Mounting Rack [Air Force] (MCD)
MBurPRM .... P. R. Mallory & Co., Burlington, MA [Library symbol] [Library of Congress] (LCLS)
MBus......... Master of Business (ADA)
MBUS......... Memory Bus (TIMI)
MBUS......... Module BUS (SAUS)
MBus-Accy... Master of Business - Accountancy
MBusAd....... Master of Business Administration (ADA)
MBus-Comn... Master of Business - Communication
M Bus Ed..... Master of Business Education

MBUSI .... Mercedes-Benz United States International [Manufacturing operations]
MBus-Mgt.... Master of Business - Management
MBU-T .... Boston University, School of Theology, Boston, MA [Library symbol] [Library of Congress] (LCLS)
MBUUC........ Minnesota Business Utility Users Council [An association] (TSSD)
MBV.......... Main Base Visit (NASA)
MBV.......... Marine Board of Victoria [Australia]
MBV.......... Medical Board of Victoria [Australia]
MBV.......... Mexican Border Veterans (EA)
MBV.......... Minimum Breakdown Voltage
MBV.......... Model-Based Vision (ADWA)
MBV.......... United States Veterans Administration Hospital, Boston, MA [Library symbol] [Library of Congress] (LCLS)
MBV-O........ United States Veterans Administration, Outpatients Clinic, Boston, MA [Library symbol] [Library of Congress] (LCLS)
MBVP.......... Mechanical Booster Vacuum Pump
MBVPS .... Mechanical Booster Vacuum Pump System
MBVT.......... Merchants Banchares, Inc. [NASDAQ symbol] (NQ)
MBVT.......... Merchants Bancshares [NASDAQ symbol] (SAG)
MBVT.......... Merchants Bancshares (VT) [NASDAQ symbol] (TTSB)
MBW.......... Mean Body Weight
MBW.......... Medicine Bow, WY [Location identifier] [FAA] (FAAL)
MBW.......... Medium Black and White [Film] (KSC)
MBW.......... Metropolitan Board of Works [British]
MBW.......... Microbiological Warfare
MBW.......... Moorabbin [Airport symbol]
MBW.......... Mount Baker [Washington] [Seismograph station code, US Geological Survey] (SEIS)
MBW.......... Movement for a Better World (EA)
MBW.......... Munitions Assignment Board (Washington) [World War II]
MBW.......... Western Manitoba Regional Library, Brandon, Manitoba [Library symbol] [National Library of Canada] (NLC)
MBWA .... Management by Walking About [or Wandering Around] [Facetious translation of MBO - Management by Objectives]
MBWA .... Management by Walking Around (SAUO)
MBWA .... Management by Wandering Around (SAUO)
MBWI.......... Wentworth Institute of Technical, Boston, MA [Library symbol] [Library of Congress] (LCLS)
MBWO .... Microwave Backward Wave Oscillator
MBWS .... Wheelock College, Boston, MA [Library symbol] [Library of Congress] (LCLS)
MBX.......... Electronic mailbox (SAUS)
MBX.......... Mailbox (ROAS)
MBX.......... Management by Exception [Management technique] (IAA)
MBX.......... Maribor [Former Yugoslavia] [Airport symbol] (OAG)
MBX.......... Matchbox [Toy collection]
MBX.......... Message Bus Exchange (AAEL)
MBY.......... Make Busy (IAA)
MBY.......... Middleby Corp. [AMEX symbol] (SPSG)
MBY.......... Moberly, MO [Location identifier] [FAA] (FAAL)
MBY & D .... Maintenance, Bureau of Yards and Docks [Budget category] [Obsolete; see FEC] [Navy]
MBYC.......... Manhasset Bay Yacht Club (SAUO)
Mbyte .... Megabyte
Mbyte .... Million Bytes [Computer science]
MBYY.......... Matchbox Models of Yesteryear [Toy collection]
MBZ.......... Magnesia-Buffered Zinc Oxide (PDAA)
MBZ.......... Mandatory Broadcast Zone [Telecommunications] (DA)
MBZ.......... Maues [Brazil] [Airport symbol] (AD)
MBZ.......... Menxel Bouzelfa [Tunisia] [Seismograph station code, US Geological Survey] (SEIS)
MBZ.......... Middle Border Zone [Geology]
MBZ.......... Must Be Zero (IAA)
MBZS.......... Maximum Bandwidth Zero Suppression (VLIE)
MC.......... Aermacchi SpA [Italy] [ICAO aircraft manufacturer identifier] (ICAO)
MC.......... CAA Flying Unit [British] [ICAO designator] (ICDA)
MC.......... Cambridge Public Library, Cambridge, MA [Library symbol] [Library of Congress] (LCLS)
MC.......... Chemists' Club [Formerly, Mining Club] (EA)
MC.......... Consolata Missionary Sisters [Roman Catholic religious order]
MC.......... Department of Mass Communication (SAUO)
MC.......... Macalester College (SAUO)
Mc.......... Maccabees [Old Testament book] [Roman Catholic canon]
M-C.......... MacDonald-Cartier Highway [Canada]
M/C.......... Machine (ROG)
MC.......... Machine Cancellation [Philately]
MC.......... Machine Check [Computer science] (IAA)
MC.......... Machine Code (IAA)
MC.......... Machine Console
MC.......... Machine Cycle (IAA)
MC.......... Machinery Certificate [Shipping]
MC.......... Macula Coloboma [Medicine] (MELL)
MC.......... Madison College (SAUO)
MC.......... Madonna College (SAUO)
MC.......... Magic Circle [An association] (EA)
MC.......... Magister Chirurgiae [Master of Surgery]
MC.......... Magistrates Cases [Legal term] [British]
MC.......... Magistrates Court (SAUO)
MC.......... Magnesium Chlorate [Inorganic chemistry]
MC.......... Magnetic Card [Word processing]
MC.......... Magnetic Clutch
MC.......... Magnetic Core
MC.......... Magnetic Course [Navigation]
M-C.......... Magovern-Cromie [Prosthesis] (AAMN)

MC	Mail Chute (DAC)		MC	Mastercard International [*New York, NY*] (EA)
MC	Mailet College (SAUO)		MC	Master Change (IAA)
MC	Main Cabin		MC	Master Clock (IAA)
M/C	Main Chamber [*NASA*] (KSC)		MC	Master Commandant
MC	Main Channel		MC	Master Commander [*Navy*] [*British*] (ROG)
MC	Main Chute (KSC)		MC	Master Control
MC	Main Cock		MC	Master Controller (SAUS)
MC	Main Color [*Crocheting*]		MC	Master of Ceremonies
MC	Main Condenser [*Nuclear energy*] (NRCH)		MC	Master of Chemistry
MC	Main Coolant (MSA)		MC	Master of Classics
MC	Maine Central (SAUO)		MC	Master of Commerce (GAGS)
M/C	Maintenance and Calibration		MC	Master of Communication (GAGS)
MC	Maintenance Center (MCD)		MC	Master of Congress [*British*] (DAS)
MC	Maintenance Command [*Obsolete*] [*Air Force*] [*British*]		MC	Master of Counseling (GAGS)
MC	Maintenance Console		MC	Master of Criminology (SAUO)
MC	Maintenance Cycle (MCD)		MC	Master of Surgery (SAUO)
MC	Major Component		MC	Matara Cases [*Ceylon*] [*A publication*] (DLA)
MC	Major Critical (ACAE)		MC	Material Center (SAUO)
MC	Major Cycle		MC	Material Code (MCD)
MC	Makers of Canada [*A publication*]		MC	Material Control (AAG)
MC	Making Capacity (IAA)		MC	Materials Committee (MCD)
MC	Malayan Cases [*1908-58*] [*A publication*] (DLA)		MC	Materiel Center (SAUO)
M/C	Male, Castrated Animal (DMAA)		MC	Materiel Change [*Military*]
MC	Malignant Carcinoid [*Medicine*] (MELL)		MC	Materiel Command [*Air Force*]
MC	Malone College (SAUO)		MC	Materiel Concept [*Army*]
MC	Managed Care [*Insurance*] (WYGK)		MC	Mathematical Center (IAA)
MC	Managed Competition		MC	Matsushita Electric Industrial (SAUO)
MC	Management Center (VLIE)		MC	Matsushita Electric Industrial Co. Ltd. [*NYSE symbol*] (SPSG)
MC	Management Committee (IAA)		MC	Matsushita El Ind ADR [*NYSE symbol*] (TTSB)
MC	Management Contents [*Information Access Co.*] [*Information service or system*] (IID)		MC	Mature Cataract (MELL)
MC	Management Council (SAUO)		MC	Maunaolu College (SAUO)
MC	Manatee College (SAUO)		MC	Maury Center for Ocean Science [*Washington, DC*]
M/C	Manchester (ROG)		MC	Maximum Concentration
Mc	Manchester, Chetham Library (SAUO)		MC	Maximum Count Output (IAA)
MC	Manchester College (SAUO)		MC	Mayor's Court (DLA)
Mc	Mandible Coronoid (STED)		MC	Mazda Club (EA)
MC	Manganese Centre (EA)		MC	Measure Code (NITA)
MC	Manhattan College (SAUO)		MC	Mechanical Council (EA)
MC	Manhattanville College (SAUO)		MC	Media Coalition [*Later, MC/ACF*] (EA)
MC	Manhole Cover		MC	Medial Canthus (MELL)
MC	Manned Core (SSD)		MC	Medical Cabinet (SAUO)
MC	Manpower Commission (NADA)		MC	Medical Care, Civilian Source (DNAB)
MC	Manpower Council [*Northern Ireland*] (BUAC)		MC	Medical Center
MC	Mantle Cavity		MC	Medical Certificate (ADA)
MC	Mantle Collar		MC	Medical College (SAUO)
MC	Manual Code (NITA)		MC	Medical Consultant [*Social Security Administration*] (OICC)
MC	Manual Control		MC	Medical Corps [*Navy*]
MC	Manufacturing Center (TIMI)		MC	Medicine Cabinet [*Technical drawings*] (NFPA)
MC	Manufacturing Change (IAA)		MC	Medicines Commission (SAUO)
MC	Mapping Camera		M-C	Medico-Chirurgical
MC	Mapping Center (SAUO)		MC	Medium Capacity [*or Charge*] [*Bomb*]
MC	Maps and Charts [*Interservice*] [*NATO*]		MC	Medium Case bomb (SAUS)
MC	Mare Crisium [*Sea of Crises*] [*Lunar area*]		MC	Medium-Chain [*Triglycerides*] [*Biochemistry*] (MAE)
MC	Marginal Check [*Computer*]		MC	Medium Curing [*Asphalt grade*]
MC	Marginal Checking (NITA)		MC	Medugorje Center (EA)
MC	Marginal Cost [*Business term*]		MC	Medullary Cavity [*Medicine*] (MELL)
M/C	Marginal Credit [*Business term*]		MC	Medullary Cystic Disease [*Medicine*] (AAMN)
MC	Margin Call [*Banking, investments*]		Mc	Megacurie
MC	Maria College (SAUO)		mc	Megacycle (IDOE)
MC	Marian College (SAUO)		Mc	Megacycle
MC	Marietta College (SAUO)		MC	Megacycles (VLIE)
MC	Marine Corps		MC	Megacycles per Second (IAA)
MC	Marine Craft [*British military*] (DMA)		MC	Megalocornea (MELL)
MC	Marion College (SAUO)		MC	Melamine Council [*Defunct*] (EA)
MC	Marist College (SAUO)		MC	Melter Cell (ABAC)
MC	Maritime Commission [*of Department of Commerce*] [*Merged with Federal Maritime Commission*]		MC	Member of Congress
			MC	Member of Council
MC	Mark Cross [*Initials often used as pattern on Mark Cross leather goods*]		MC	Memorandum Club [*Defunct*] (EA)
			MC	Memorandum of Conditions
MC	Marked Capacity [*Freight cars*]		MC	Memorial Commission [*Federal body*]
MC	Market Capacity (ADA)		MC	Memory Charts
MC	Marketing Center [*Veterans Administration*]		MC	Memory Clear [*Computer science*] (PCM)
MC	Mark of the Craft [*Freemasonry*]		MC	Memory Configuration [*Computer science*] (MCD)
MC	Marlboro College (SAUO)		mc	Memory Configuration (NAKS)
MC	Marmon Club (EA)		MC	Memory-Constrained [*Computer science*]
MC	Marque de Commerce [*Trademark*]		MC	Memory Control [*Unit*] [*Computer science*]
MC	Marriage Certificate		MC	Memphis College (SAUO)
MC	Married Couple (ADA)		MC	Menlo College (SAUO)
MC	Marshall College (SAUO)		MC	Mennonite Church (SAUO)
MC	Martin Co. (MCD)		MC	Mercury Club [*Defunct*] (EA)
MC	Martin College (SAUO)		MC	Mercury Contact (IAA)
MC	Mary College (SAUO)		MC	Meredith Corp. (EFIS)
MC	Marycrest College (SAUO)		MC	Merkel Cell [*Anatomy*]
MC	Maryglade College (SAUO)		MC	Mesa College (SAUO)
MC	Marygrove College (SAUO)		MC	Mesenteric Collateral [*Cardiology*] (DAVI)
MC	Maryheart Crusaders (EA)		MC	Mesiocervical [*Dentistry*]
MC	Marylhurst College (SAUO)		MC	Message Center
MC	Marymount College (SAUO)		MC	Message Change (MCD)
MC	Maryville College (SAUO)		MC	Message check (EA)
MC	Marywood College (SAUO)		MC	Message Composer [*Communications, data processing*]
MC	Mass Communication (NTCM)		MC	Mess Call [*Military*]
MC	Mast Cell		MC	Metacarpal [*or Metacarpus*] [*Anatomy*]
MC	Mast Controller (DNAB)		MC	Metal Carbide
MC	MasterCard [*Credit card*]		MC	Metal Case [*Bullet*] (DICI)
			MC	Metal Clad (IAA)

MC	Metaling Clause [Marine insurance]
M/C	Metallic Currency (ROG)
MC	Metatarsocuneiform [Orthopedics] (DAVI)
MC	Meteorological Codes (SAUO)
mc	Meter-Candle (IDOE)
MC	Meter-Candle
MC	Methacholine Challenge [Medicine]
MC	Methodist Chaplain
MC	Methodist Church (WDAA)
MC	Methyl Carbamate [Organic chemistry]
MC	Methylcellulose [Organic chemistry]
MC	Methylchloroform [Organic chemistry]
MC	Methylcholanthrene [Also, MCA] [Organic chemistry]
MC	Methylcystyosine [Biochemistry]
MC	Methylene Chloride [Organic chemistry]
MC	Metric Carat [200 milligrams]
MC	Metrology Center (SAUO)
MC	Metropolitan Counties [British]
MC	Michigan Central (SAUO)
MC	Michigan Central Railroad [Absorbed into Consolidated Rail Corp.] [AAR code]
MC	Michigan Central Railroad Co. (SAUO)
MC	Michigan Chemical Corp.
mc	Micro (SHCU)
MC	Microcarrier [Cell culture technology]
MC	Microcell (SAUS)
MC	Microcephaly [Medicine] (AAMN)
MC	Microchromatographic
MC	Micro Composer (SAUS)
MC	Microcomputer (IAA)
MC	Microcontrol
MC	Microcrystalline Cellulose (DB)
MC	Microfilm Corporation (SAUO)
MC	Microminiature Circuit (IAA)
MC	Micronesia Coalition [Defunct] (EA)
MC	Microphase Corporation (SAUO)
MC	Microstat Corporation (SAUO)
MC	Midcourse
MC	Midcourse Correction (SAA)
MC	Middle Chamber [Freemasonry]
MC	Middle Creek Railroad (IIA)
MC	Midland College (SAUO)
MC	Miles College (SAUO)
MC	Miles on Course
MC	Military Characteristics
MC	Military College [British] (ROG)
MC	Military Committee [NATO]
MC	Military Community (COE)
MC	Military Computer (IEEE)
MC	Military Construction (AFM)
MC	Military Coordination [British]
MC	Military Cross [World War I nickname: Maconochie Cross] [British]
MC	Mill Cutter [Tool] (MCD)
mC	Millicoulomb (MAE)
mc	Millicurie (IDOE)
mC	Millicurie [Also, mCi]
MC	Millicycle [Also, as millihertz] (WGA)
MC	Milligan College (SAUO)
MC	Millipore Corp. [Bedford, MA]
MC	Millipore Corporation (SAUO)
MC	Mills College (SAUO)
MC	Milsaps College (SAUO)
MC	Milton College (SAUO)
MC	Mine Clearance [British military] (DMA)
MC	Mineralocortcoid (LDT)
M-C	Mineralo-Corticoid [Endocrinology]
m/c	Minha Carta [My Respects] [Correspondence] [Portuguese]
m/c	Minha Conta [My Regards] [Correspondence] [Portuguese]
MC	Mini-Cartridge (SAUS)
MC	Minimum Call [Television studio on standby]
MC	Mining Club (EA)
MC	Ministry of Commerce (SAUO)
MC	Minkowski-Chauffard [Syndrome] [Medicine] (DB)
MC	Minor Construction (AFIT)
MC	Minorities in Cable [Defunct] (EA)
MC	Mirror Coil (MCD)
MC	Miscarriage [Obstetrics] (DAVI)
MC	Miserriocordia College (SAUO)
MC	Misionaras Clarisas [Poor Clare Missionary Sisters] [Roman Catholic religious order]
MC	Missile Car (SAA)
MC	Missile Checkout
MC	Missile Code (MUGU)
MC	Missile Command [Army]
MC	Missile Compartment
MC	Missile Container
MC	Missile Control
MC	Missile Controller (SAUS)
MC	Missionaries of Charity [Roman Catholic women's religious order]
MC	Missionary Catechists of the Sacred Hearts of Jesus and Mary [Violetas] [Roman Catholic women's religious order]
MC	Missionary Church (EA)
mc	Mission Capability [NASA] (NAKS)
MC	Mission Capability [NASA] (NASA)
MC	Mission Capable (SAUO)
MC	Mission Completion (MCD)
mc	Mission Completion/Continuation [NASA] (NAKS)
MC	Mission Computer (MCD)
MC	Mission Continuation (MCD)
MC	Mission Control [NASA]
MC	Mission Critical (SAUO)
MC	Mississippi Central [Railroad] (MHDB)
MC	Mississippi Central Railroad (IIA)
MC	Mitchell College (SAUO)
MC	Mitchell Cotts Group Ltd. (SAUO)
MC	Mitochondrial Complementation
MC	Mitomycin [Also, M, MT] [Antineoplastic drug]
MC	Mitotic Cycle [Biochemistry] (DAVI)
MC	Mitoxantrone, Cytarabine [Antineoplastic drug] (CDI)
MC	Mitral Valve Closure [Cardiology]
MC	Mitsubishi Corporation (SAUO)
MC	Mixed Cell [Lymphoma classification]
MC	Mixed Cellularity [Biochemistry] (DAVI)
MC	Mixed Condition [Deltiology]
MC	Mixed Cryoglobulinemia [Medicine]
MC	Mixing Chamber
M/C	Mixture Control [Automobile fuel technology]
MC	Mnemonic Code (AAG)
MC	Mobile Control (DEN)
MC	Mobile Crane (DCTA)
MC	Mobility Control Center (SAUO)
MC	Mobilization Center (SAUO)
MC	Mode Change (CET)
MC	Mode Code
MC	Mode Control (IAA)
MC	Mode Counter
MC	Model Cities (OICC)
MC	Modem Controller [Telecommunications] (IAA)
MC	Modification Center (SAUO)
MC	Modular Computer
MC	Moisture Content
MC	Molded Components (IEEE)
MC	Molecular Contamination [of Clean rooms]
MC	Momentary Contact [Electronics]
MC	Monaco [ANSI two-letter standard code] (CNC)
mc	Monaco [MARC country of publication code] [Library of Congress] (LCCP)
MC	Moneda Corriente [Current Money] [Spanish]
MC	Monetary Committee
MC	Monetary Contact
MC	Monitor and Control [Computer science] (BUR)
MC	Monitor Call [Computer science] (IBMDP)
MC	Monitoring Center (SAUO)
MC	Monkey Cells
MC	Monkey Complement [Immunology]
MC	Monmouth College (SAUO)
MC	Monocomponent Highly Purified Port Insulin [Endocrinology] [Pharmacology] (DAVI)
MC	Monocoupe Club (EA)
MC	Mononuclear Cell [Clinical chemistry] [Also, MNC]
MC	Monopolies Commission [British] (DCTA)
MC	Monotype Caster (DGA)
MC	Monte Carlo [Calculation technique] [Nuclear energy] (NUCP)
MC	Montecatini Mining & Chemical Co. (SAUO)
MC	Montessori Center [Education]
MC	Monticello College (SAUO)
MC	Moravian College (SAUO)
MC	Morehouse College (SAUO)
MC	Morgan Crucible Co. Ltd. (SAUO)
MC	Morris College (SAUO)
MC	Morse Code
MC	Morse Code - Barry Morse Fan Club (EA)
MC	Mortar Carrier [British]
MC	Mortgage Constant (DICI)
MC	Mortgage Credit Condition (EMRF)
MC	Mothercraft Certificate [British] (ADA)
MC	Motor Car (IAA)
MC	Motor Carrier
MC	Motor Chain
MC	Motor Coaches [Public-performance tariff class] [British]
MC	Motor Contact (WGA)
MC	Motor Converter (IAA)
MC	Motor Cortex [Neuroanatomy]
MC	Motorcycle
MC	Motorcycle Driver [British military] (DMA)
MC	Mount Carmel Fraternity (SAUO)
MC	Movement Control [of troops]
MC	Moving Coil [Electronics] (DEN)
MC	Muan Chon [Mass Party] [Political party]
MC	Mucous Cell
MC	Muhlenberg College (SAUO)
MC	Multi Carrier (SAUS)
MC	Multi Cast (SAUS)
MC	Multichip [Circuit] [Electronics]
MC	Multichromatic
MC	Multicomputing (IAA)
MC	Multiconfiguration [Quantum mechanics]
MC	Multipartisan Coalition (EA)
MC	Multiple Choice
MC	Multiple Contact

MC............	Multiple Cyclones (EEVL)
MC............	Multiplex Channel (IAA)
MC............	Multiply-Convolve (SAUS)
MC............	Multnomah College (SAUO)
MC............	Mundelein College (SAUO)
MC............	Munitions Command [Later, Armaments Command] [Army]
MC............	Mushroom Caucus (EA)
MC............	Muskingum College (SAUO)
MC............	Muskogee College (SAUO)
MC............	Mycelial [of fungi] (AAMN)
MC............	Myelocytomatosis [Avian disease]
MC............	Myocarditis [Medicine]
MC............	Myotonia Congenita [Medicine]
MC............	Poor Clare Missionary Sisters (TOCD)
MC............	Rapidair [ICAO designator] (AD)
MC............	Royal Military College (SAUO)
MC............	Saugus Marine Corporation (SAUO)
MC............	Submarine Chaser [Navy symbol]
MC3............	Multi-channel Crypto Controller (SAUS)
MC4............	Medical Communications for Combat Casualty Care [Army]
MC4-R........	Melanocortin-4 Receptor (DIPS)
MC5............	Motor City Five [Rock music group]
MC-130........	Combat Talon (SAUS)
MCA............	Arthur D. Little, Inc., Cambridge, MA [Library symbol] [Library of Congress] (LCLS)
MCA............	Macenta [Guinea] [Airport symbol] (AD)
MCA............	Magic Collectors' Association (EA)
MCA............	Magnetocrystalline Anisotropy [Physics]
MCA............	Mail Control Authority (AFM)
MCA............	Main Console Assembly [NASA] (KSC)
MCA............	Main Coronary Artery [Cardiology] (DAVI)
MCA............	Maintenance Capability Audit [Military] (CAAL)
MCA............	Major Coronary Arteries [Cardiology]
MCA............	Malacca Consumers Association (SAUO)
MCA............	Malaysian Chinese Association [Political party] (PPW)
MCA............	Malaysian Commercial Association (BUAC)
MCA............	Management and Command Ashore (NVT)
MCA............	Management Consultancies Association (SAUO)
MCA............	Management Consultants Association [British] (DCTA)
MCA............	Management Control Activity
MCA............	Management Control Authority (NVT)
MCA............	Maneuvering at Critically Slow Airspeed [Aviation] (PIPO)
MCA............	Manning Control Authority (MCD)
MCA............	Mannlicher Collectors Association (EA)
MCA............	Manufacturers' Consumer Advertising
MCA............	Manufacturing Change Analysis (MCD)
MCA............	Manufacturing Chemists Association [Later, CMA] (EA)
MCA............	Marine Coastguard Agency (SAUO)
MCA............	Marine Corps Association (EA)
MCA............	Marine Cranking Amperes [Battery] [Automotive engineering]
MCA............	Maritime Central Airways (SAUO)
MCA............	Maritime Central Airways, Ltd. (SAUO)
MCA............	Maritime Control Area
MCA............	Market Research Corp. of America
MCA............	Marky Cattle Association (EA)
MCA............	Marquee Contractors Association (BUAC)
MCA............	Mars-Crossing Asteroid [Cosmology]
MCA............	Maserati Club of America (EA)
MCA............	Massachusetts Correctional Association (SAUO)
MCA............	Master Carvers Association [British] (DBA)
MCA............	Master Clock Assembly
MCA............	Master Community Antenna
MCA............	Master Control Assembly [NASA] (NASA)
MCA............	Master Craftsmen's Association [British] (DBA)
MCA............	Master of Commercial Arts
MCA............	Master of Commercial Aviation (PGP)
MCA............	Master of Communication Arts (PGP)
MCA............	Master of Creative Arts
MCA............	Mastiff Club of America (EA)
MCA............	Material Condition and Aging (SAUO)
MCA............	Material Control Adjustment
MCA............	Material Control and Accountability (NRCH)
MCA............	Material Control Area (AAG)
MCA............	Material Coordinating Agency
MCA............	Maternity Center Association (EA)
MCA............	Matrix Case Arrangement (DGA)
MCA............	Maximal Credible Accident [Nuclear technology]
MCA............	Maximum Ceiling Absolute [Aerospace] (AAG)
MCA............	Maximum Credible Accident [Nuclear energy] (NRCH)
MCA............	Maximum Crossing Altitude (MCD)
MCA............	McDonnell Douglas Automation Co., McAuto Campus Library, St. Louis, MO [OCLC symbol] (OCLC)
MCA............	Measurement Capability Analysis (AAEL)
MCA............	Mechanical Contractors Association of America
MCA............	Mechanization Control Area (AAG)
MCA............	Media Communications Association (SAUO)
MCA............	Media Credit Association (EA)
MCA............	Medical Care Administration (STED)
MCA............	Medical Control Agency (SAUO)
MCA............	Medical Correctional Association [Defunct] (EA)
MCA............	Medical Council of Australia (SAUO)
MCA............	Medical Council on Alcoholism [British]
MCA............	Medicines Control Agency [British] (ECON)
MCA............	Megestrol, Cyclophosphamide, and Adriamycin (Doxorubicin) (STED)
MCA............	Merchandising Corp. of America, Inc. (EFIS)

MCA............	Metal Construction Association (EA)
MCA............	Methyl Cation Affinity [Physical chemistry]
MCA............	Methylcholanthrene [Also, MC] [Biochemistry]
MCA............	Methyl Cyanoacrylate [Organic chemistry]
MCA............	Metropolitan Club of America (EA)
MCA............	Metropolitan Cycle Association (SAUO)
MCA............	Microcentrifugal Analyzer [Instrumentation]
MCA............	Micro Channel [Computer science] (CDE)
MCA............	Microchannel Analyzer [Instrumentation]
MCA............	Micro Channel Architecture [Computer hardware]
MCA............	Microfilm Corporation of America (NITA)
MCA............	Microfilming Corp. of America [Information service or system] (IID)
McA............	Microfilming Corp. of America, Glen Rock, NJ [Library symbol] [Library of Congress] (LCLS)
MCA............	Microwave Communications Association (EA)
MCA............	Microwave Control Assembly
MCA............	Mid-Continent Airlines (SAUO)
MCA............	Midcontinent Airlines, Inc. [ICAO designator] (FAAC)
MCA............	Mid-Continental Airlines
MCA............	Middle Cerebral Aneurysm [Cardiology] [Neurology] (DAVI)
MCA............	Middle Cerebral Artery [Anatomy]
MCA............	Midwest Commuter Airlines (SAUO)
MCA............	Mid-West Compensation Association [Superseded by ACA] (EA)
MCA............	Midwest Curling Association [Defunct] (EA)
MCA............	Military Chaplains Association (SAUO)
MCA............	Military Chaplains Association of the USA (EA)
MCA............	Military Civic Action (DOMA)
MCA............	Military Construction Appropriation [or Authorization] (AFM)
MCA............	Military Construction Army (AFIT)
MCA............	Military Coordinating Activity (MCD)
MCA............	Miller Crichton & Associates (SAUO)
MCA............	Millinery Credit Association [Defunct] (EA)
MCA............	Minerals Council of Australia (SAUO)
MCA............	Minimum Crossing Altitude [Aviation]
MCA............	Ministry of Civil Aviation [Later, MTCA] [British]
MCA............	Minnesota Correctional Authority (SAUO)
MCA............	Minnesota Corrections Association (SAUO)
MCA............	Missile Command Amplifier (ACAE)
MCA............	Missing Children of America (EA)
MCA............	Mission Critical Applications (SAUO)
MCA............	Mississippi Code, Annotated [A publication] (DLA)
MCA............	Missouri Corrections Association (SAUO)
MCA............	Mistral Class Association (EA)
MCA............	Mitsubishi Clean Air [Automotive engineering]
MCA............	Mobilisation Combat Aircraft (SAUS)
MCA............	Model Cities Administration [HUD]
MCA............	Modified Cost Approach Document [Department of Housing and Urban Development]
MCA............	Mohair Council of America (EA)
MCA............	Moist Convective Adjustment (SAUS)
MCA............	Monetary Compensation Amount [European Community]
MCA............	Monetary Compensation Amounts (SAUO)
MCA............	Monetary Control Act
MCA............	Monitoring and Control Assembly [NASA] (NASA)
MCA............	Monocarboxylic Acid (STED)
MCA............	Monochloroacetic Acid [Also, MCAA] [Organic chemistry]
MCA............	Monoclonal Antibodies [Microbiology] (DAVI)
MCA............	Montana Code, Annotated [A publication] (DLA)
MCA............	Motion Capture and Analysis (SAUS)
MCA............	Motor Carriers Traffic Association Inc., Greensboro NC [STAC]
MCA............	Motor Control Assembly (MCD)
MCA............	Motorcycle Accident (DAVI)
MCA............	Motor Cycle Industry Association of Great Britain (EAIO)
MCA............	Movement Control Agency [Army]
MCA............	Movers Conference of America
MCA............	Multichannel Analyzer
MCA............	Multi-Criteria Analysis (SAUO)
MCA............	Multiple Classification Analysis [Aviation]
MCA............	Multiple Communications Adapter (DGA)
MCA............	Multiple Congenital Abnormalities [Medicine] (STED)
MCA............	Multiple Congenital Anomaly [Syndrome] [Medicine]
MCA............	Multiplexing Channel Adapter [Telecommunications] (IAA)
MCA............	Multiprocessor (SAUO)
MCA............	Multiprocessor Communications Adapter
MCA............	MuniYield CA Insured Fund II [NYSE symbol] (TTSB)
MCA............	MuniYield California Insured Fund II [NYSE symbol] (SPSG)
MCA............	Muscat Control Agency (SAUO)
MCA............	Musical Corp. of America (NADA)
MCA............	Music Critics Association (EA)
MCA............	Musicians Club of America (EA)
MCA............	Mustang Club of America (EA)
MCAA..........	Marine Corps Aviation Association (EA)
MCAA..........	Mason Contractors Association of America (EA)
MCAA..........	Measurement, Control, and Automation Association (NTPA)
MCAA..........	Mechanical Contractors Association of America (EA)
MCAA..........	Member, Canadian Academy of Allergy (CMD)
MCAA..........	Messenger Courier Association of America (EA)
MCAA..........	Military Civil Affairs Administration (NADA)
MCAA..........	Military Construction Appropriations Act (AAGC)
MCAA..........	Monochloroacetic Acid [Also, MCA] [Organic chemistry]
MCAAA........	Midland Counties Amateur Athletic Association (SAUO)
MCAAC	Medium Caliber Antiarmor Automatic Cannon
MCAAC	Medium Caliber Advanced Automatic Cannon (TIMI)
MCAAC	Medium Caliber Antiarmor Automatic Cannon (MCD)
MCAAF........	Marine Corps Auxiliary Air Facility

MCAAP	McAlester Army Ammunition Plant [*Oklahoma*] (AABC)
MCAAS	Manpower Central Address & AIG System (SAUS)
MCAAS	Marine Corps Auxiliary Air Station
MCAB	Marine Corps Air Base
MCAB	Monoclonal Antibody [*Immunochemistry*]
MCABM	Manner Common among Business Men
MCAC	Machine Accessory [*Tool*] (AAG)
MCAC	Measurement, Control and Automation Conference (SAUO)
MCAC	Midlands Collegiate Athletic Conference (PSS)
MCAC	Military Common Area Control
MCACE	Measurement Characterization and Control of Ambulatory Care in Europe (SAUO)
MC/ACF	Media Coalition/Americans for Constitutional Freedom (EA)
MCACS	Marine Centralized Automatic Control System (PDAA)
MCAD	Marine Corps Air Depot
MCAD	Massachusetts Commission Against Discrimination (SAUO)
MCAD	Mechanical Computer-Aided Design
MCAD	Medium Chain Acyl-CoA Dehydrogenase (DMAA)
MCAD	Medium Chain Acyl-Coenzyme A Dehydrogenase (DB)
MCAD	Military Contracts Administration Department
MCAD	Minneapolis College of Art and Design
McAdam Landl & T...	McAdam on Landlord and Tenant [*A publication*] (DLA)
MCADO	Micronesian Community Action Development Organization (SAUO)
MCAE	Massachusetts Coalition for Adult Education
MCAE	Mechanical Computer-Aided Engineering
MCAE	Mining, Construction, and Agricultural Equipment
MCAF	Macrophage Chemotactic, and Activating Factor (LDT)
MCAF	Marine Corps Air Facility
MCAF	Marine Corps Air Field
MCAF	McAfee Associates [*NASDAQ symbol*] (SAG)
MCAF	Mediterranean Coastal Air Force Headquarters
MCAF	Military Construction, Air Force
MCAFB	McConnell Air Force Base [*Kansas*]
McAfee	McAfee Associates [*Associated Press*] (SAG)
MCA/FYP	Military Construction, Army / Five Year Plan
MCAG	Mapping, Charting, and Geodesy [*Activity*] (MCD)
MCAGCC	Marine Corps Air-Ground Combat Center [*Twenty-nine Palms, Calif.*] (DOMA)
MCAGCTC	Marine Corps Air Ground Combat Training Center (MCD)
MCAG/MGI	Mapping, Charting, and Geodesy/Military Geography Information [*DoD*] (MCD)
MCAI	Maximum Calling Area Indicator (DNAB)
MCAI	Microcomputer-Assisted Instruction (NITA)
MCAIR	McDonnell Aircraft Co. [*Later, McDonnell Douglas Corp.*]
MCAL	Arthur D. Little, Inc., Cambridge, MA [*Library symbol*] [*Library of Congress*] (LCLS)
McAl	McAllister's United States Circuit Court Reports [*A publication*] (DLA)
McA L & Ten...	McAdam on Landlord and Tenant [*A publication*] (DLA)
MCALF	Marine Corps Auxiliary Landing Field
McAll	McAllister's United States Circuit Court Reports [*A publication*] (DLA)
McAll (Cal)	McAllister's United States Circuit Court Reports [*California*] [*A publication*] (DLA)
McAllister US Circ Court R...	McAllister's United States Circuit Court Reports [*A publication*] (DLA)
MCALS	Minnesota Computer-Aided Library System [*University of Minnesota*]
MCAM	Marcam Corp. [*NASDAQ symbol*]
MCAM	Marine Corps Achievement Medal [*Military decoration*]
MCAM	Member of the Communication, Advertising, and Marketing Education Foundation [*British*] (DBQ)
McA Mar Ct...	McAdam's Marine Court Practice [*A publication*] (DLA)
MCA/MR	Multiple Congenital Anomalies/Mental Retardation Syndrome [*Medicine*] (DMAA)
MCA/MR	Multiple Congenital Anomaly/Mental Retardation (SAUO)
Mcan	J. S. Canner & Co., Boston, MA [*Library symbol*] [*Library of Congress*] (LCLS)
MC&A	Material Control and Accountability
MC & A	Material Control and Accounting [*Nuclear energy*] (NRCH)
MC & B	Michigan Contractor & Builder [*A publication*]
MC & C	Measurement, Command, and Control (NASA)
MC&C	Measurement, Command, and Control (SAUS)
MC & G	Mapping, Charting, and Geodesy [*Air Force*] (AFM)
MC & G/MGI	Mapping, Charting, and Geodesy/Military Geography Information [*DoD*]
MC & R	Manufacturing Controls and Requirements
MC&S	Microscopy Culture & Sensitivity [*Medicine*] (WDAA)
MC & W	Master Caution and Warning [*NASA*] (KSC)
M Can L	Master of Canon Law
MCANSW	Medical Consumers' Association of New South Wales [*Australia*]
MCANW	Medical Campaign against Nuclear Weapons (PDAA)
MCAP	Major Command ADP Plan (SAUO)
MCAP	Material Control and Accountability Plan (SAUO)
MCAP	Maximum Calling Area Procedure (SAUO)
MCAP	Medical Commission on Accident Prevention (PDAA)
MCAP	[*The*] MicroCap Fund [*NASDAQ symbol*] (SAG)
MCAP	Microwave Circuit Analysis Package (PDAA)
MCAP	Military Construction Authorized Program
MCAP	Mine Clearance & Armour Protection (SAUS)
MCAP	Ministry of Civil Aviation Publication (SAUO)
MCAP	Minority Contractors Assistance Project [*Jamaica, NY*] (EA)
MCAP	Mobile Consolidated Aerial Port Subsystem (SAUO)
MCAPD	Multiple Channel Analysis Program
MCAPD	Medical Committee against the Abuse of Prisoners by Drugging (SAUO)
MCAPI	Mid-Continent Association of the Pet Industry
MCAR	Machine Check Analysis and Recording (BUR)

MCAR	Machining Arbor [*Tool*] (AAG)
McAr	McArthur's District of Columbia Reports [*A publication*] (DLA)
MCAR	Military Construction, Army Reserve (AABC)
MCAR	Minnesota Code of Agency Rules [*A publication*]
MCAR	Missing Completely at Random (IDAI)
MCAR	Mixed Cell Agglutination Reaction [*Immunology*]
MCAR	Multichannel Acoustic Relay [*Navy*] (ANA)
MCARNG	Military Construction, Army National Guard (AABC)
MCARQUALS...	Marine Carrier Qualifications (NVT)
McArth & M...	MacArthur and Mackey's District of Columbia Reports [*A publication*] (DLA)
MCAS	Machinery Control and Surveillance (SAUS)
MCAS	Marine Corps Air Station
MCAS	Massachusetts Comprehensive Assessment System [*Education*]
MCAS	Master Component Analysis System (TIMI)
MCAS	Material Control Accounting System (SAUO)
MCAS	Middle Cerebral Artery Syndrome [*Medicine*] (DMAA)
MCAS	Minuteman Configuration Accountability System [*Air Force*] (IAA)
MCAS	Modular Component Assembly System (ACAE)
MCAs	Monetary Compensation Amounts (SAUO)
MCASA	Master Cleaners' Association of South Australia [*Australia*]
MCASE	Mechanical Computer-Aided Engineering
MCAS(H)	Marine Corps Air Station (Helicopter) (FAAC)
MCASP	Multiple Constraint Alternative Selector Program [*Bell System*]
MCASTRO	McDonnell Douglas Astronautics Company (SAUO)
MCAT	Maritime Central Analysis Team [*NATO*] (NATG)
MCAT	Master of Creative Arts in Therapy (PGP)
MCAT	Medical College Admissions Test (GAGS)
MCAT	Medical College Admission [*or Aptitude*] Test
MCAT	Middle Cerebral Artery Thrombosis [*Medicine*] (DMAA)
MCAT	Midwest Council on Airborne Television
MCAT	Military Committee Atlantic (SAUO)
MCAT	Monoclonal Antibody Therapy (MELL)
MCATA	Management Council of the American Trucking Association [*Defunct*] (EA)
MCATF	Mechanized Combined Arms Task Force (SAUO)
MCATS	Maneuver Control Automated Test System (SAUO)
MCATS	Marine Corps Automated Test System (DWSG)
MCATS	Marine Corps Aviation Technical School
MCATS	Medium Capacity Automated Telecommunications System (SAUO)
M-CATS	Municipal Certificates of Accrual on Tax-Exempt Securities [*Investment term*] (DFIT)
M-cats	Municipal Certificates of Accumulation on Tax-Exempt Securities (EBF)
MCATT	Multi-weapon Combined Arms Tactical Trainer (SAUS)
MCAU	Main Carrier Acquisition Unit (MCD)
M CAUTE	Misce Caute [*Mix Cautiously*] [*Pharmacy*]
MCAUTO	McDonnell Douglas Automation Co. [*Robotics*]
MCAUTO Company...	McDonnell Douglas Automation Company (SAUO)
MCAV	Modified Constant Angular Velocity (TELE)
MCAVRET	Marine Corps Aviation Refresher Training
MCAWW	Methods for Chemical Analysis of Water and Wastes [*Environmental Protection Agency*]
MCB	Boyne Regional Library, Carman, Manitoba [*Library symbol*] [*National Library of Canada*] (NLC)
MCB	Machine Coated Board (DGA)
MCB	Macrochromatin Body [*Genetics*]
MCB	Main Circuit Breaker (SAUS)
MCB	Main Control Board (NRCH)
MCB	Malaysian Cocoa Butter
MCB	Managing Civilians to Budget [*Army*]
MCB	Manually Controlled Barrier (HEAS)
MCB	Marine Construction Battalion
MCB	Marine Corps Base
MCB	Markings Center Brief (MCD)
MCB	Master Car Builder
MCB	Master Cell Bank [*Cell line*]
MCB	Master of Clinical Biochemistry
MCB	Material Certification Board (SAUO)
MCB	Material Classification Board (DNAB)
MCB	Matheson, Coleman & Bell [*Commercial firm*]
MCB	MC Beverages [*Vancouver Stock Exchange symbol*]
McB	McBurney's [*Point*] [*Medicine*]
MCB	McComb, MS [*Location identifier*] [*FAA*] (FAAL)
MCB	Mechanically Controllable Break [*Junction*] [*In microstructures*]
MCB	Medical Consultative Board (SAUO)
MCB	Membranous Cytoplasmic Body
MCB	Memory Control Block (ROAS)
MCB	Message Control Block [*Computer science*] (CET)
MCB	Metal Corner Bead [*Technical drawings*]
MCB	Methodist College, Belfast [*Northern Ireland*]
MCB	Methylamino(chloro)benzophenone [*Organic chemistry*]
MCB	Metric Conversion Board (NADA)
MCB	Metric Conversion Bureau (NADA)
MCB	Metropolitan Cemeteries Board [*Western Australia*]
MCB	Miami City Ballet
MCB	Microcomputer Board
MCB	Microwave Circuit Board (TIMI)
MCB	Millwork Cost Bureau [*Later, AWI*]
MCB	Miniature Circuit Breaker
MCB	Miscellaneous Change Board (SAUO)
MCB	Miscellaneous Charges Book (SAUO)
MCB	Missouri Concert Ballet
MCB	Mobile Construction Battalion [*Navy*]
MCB	Modular Controllable Booster (MCD)

MCB............ Module Control Block (KSC)
MCB............ Monochlorinated Biphenyl [Organic chemistry]
MCB............ Monochlorobenzene [Organic chemistry]
MCB............ Moose Creek [Alaska] [Seismograph station code, US Geological Survey] [Closed] (SEIS)
MCB............ Mortgage Collateralized Bond
MCB............ Moscow Classical Ballet
MCB............ Motor Cargo Boat
MCB............ Motor Carriers Tariff Bureau Inc., Cleveland OH [STAC]
MCB............ Motor Company of Botswana
MCB............ Multilateral Control Board (SSD)
MCB............ Myocardial Bridging [Cardiology]
MCBA.......... Magnesite and Chrome Brickmakers Association [British] (DBA)
MCBA.......... Master Car Builders' Association [Later, CDOA]
MCBA.......... Mean Cycles Between Assists (AAEL)
MCBA.......... Member of the Certified Bailiffs Association [British] (DI)
MCBD.......... Multi Purpose Chemical Biological Decontaminant (ACAE)
MCBETH...... Military Computer Basic Environment for Test Handling
MCBF.......... Mast Cell Burst Factor (SAUS)
MCBF.......... Mean Countdown Between Failures
MCBF.......... Mean Cycles between Failures [Quality control]
MCBF.......... Microwave Component Business Function (TIMI)
MCBH.......... Multiple Cloud Base Height (ARMP)
MCBI........... Mean Cycles Between Interrupts (AAEL)
MCBIC......... Michigan/Canadian Bigfoot Information Center (EA)
MCBL.......... Motor Cargo Boat (Large) [Coast Guard] (DNAB)
MCBM......... Marine Corps Brevet Medal
MCBM......... Muscle Capillary Basement Membrane [Medicine]
MCBN.......... Mid-Coast Bancorp [NASDAQ symbol] (TTSB)
MCBN.......... Mid-Coast Bancorp, Inc. [NASDAQ symbol] (NQ)
MCBOMF..... Mean Cycles between Operational Mission Failures [Quality control]
MCBP.......... Mean Cycles between Premature Removals [Quality control] (MCD)
MCBP.......... Melphalan, Cyclophosphamide, BCNU [Carmustine], Prednisone [Antineoplastic drug regimen]
MCBP.......... Methylchlorobiphenyl [Organic chemistry]
MCBP.......... Muscle Calcium Binding Parvalbumin [Biochemistry]
McB Pt........ McBurney's Point [Medicine] (CPH)
MCBR......... Master Car Builders' Rules
MCBR......... Minimum Concentration of Bilirubin [Medicine] (MAE)
McBride...... McBride's Reports [1 Missouri] [A publication] (DLA)
MCBs.......... Metacarpal Bone [Medicine] (MELL)
MCBS.......... Micro Computer Business Services
MCBS.......... Mid Continent Bancshares [NASDAQ symbol] (TTSB)
MCBS.......... Mid Continent Bancshares, Inc. [NASDAQ symbol] (SAG)
MCBS.......... Mine-Clearing Blade System [Military] (INF)
MCBS.......... Missionary Congregation of the Blessed Sacrament (TOCD)
mcbs.......... Missionary Congregation of the Blessed Sacrament (TOCD)
MCBS.......... Multicomponent Boot System [Army] (INF)
MCBSE........ Mean Cycles Between Scrap Event (AAEL)
MCBSP........ Multi Channel Buffered Serial Port (SAUS)
MCBU......... Microconfined Bed Unit [Chemical engineering]
MCBW........ Amalgamated Meat Cutters and Butcher Workmen of North America [Later, UFCWIU]
MCC............ Canada-US Military Co-operation Community (SAUO)
MCC............ MacGillivray's Copyright Cases [1901-49] [A publication] (DLA)
MCC............ Machine Control Computer (TIMI)
MCC............ Magdalene College, Cambridge University [England] (ROG)
MCC............ Magnetic Card Code (ELAL)
MCC............ Magnetometer Calibration Coil (ACAE)
MCC............ Mail Classification Center (DNAB)
mcc............ Main Combustion Chamber [NASA] (NAKS)
MCC............ Main Combustion Chamber (NASA)
MCC............ Main Communications Center
MCC............ Main Control Circuit (IAA)
MCC............ Main Control Console [Diving apparatus]
MCC............ Maintenance Control Center [Telecommunications] (AFM)
MCC............ Maintenance Control Circuit (IAA)
MCC............ Maintenance of Close Contact
MCC............ Major Category Code (MCD)
MCC............ Major City Code [IRS]
MCC............ Majority Congress Committee [Defunct] (EA)
MCC............ Management, Command & Control (SAUO)
MCC............ Management Communication Consultants, Inc. [Cincinnati, OH] (TSSD)
MCC............ Management Control Center [Computer science] (BUR)
MCC............ Management Controls Corporation, Inc. (SAUO)
MCC............ Manchester Computing Centre (SAUO)
MCC............ Mandarin Capital Corp. [Vancouver Stock Exchange symbol]
MCC............ Manhattan Chess Club (EA)
MCC............ Manipulative Communications Cover [Military] (ADDR)
MCC............ Manned Control Car [Nuclear energy]
MCC............ Manoeuvre Camber Control (SAUS)
MCC............ Manual Combat Center [Air Force]
MCC............ Manual Control & Counter (SAUO)
MCC............ Manual Control Center [Air Force]
MCC............ Map Collectors' Circle [Defunct] (EA)
MCC............ Marine Corps Commandant
MCC............ Marine Corps Commander (SAUO)
MCC............ Maritime Coordination Center
MCC............ Marked Cocontraction [Medicine]
MCC............ Martin's Mining Cases [British Columbia] [A publication] (DLA)
MCC............ Maryland Committee for Children (EDAC)
MCC............ Marylebone Cricket Club [Governing body for cricket]
MCC............ Massachusetts Council of Churches (SAUO)
MCC............ Master Change Committee

MCC............ Master Control Card [IRS]
MCC............ Master Control Center (NATG)
MCC............ Master Control Code (ELAL)
MCC............ Master Control Console
MCC............ Matchbox Collectors Club [Defunct] (EA)
MCC............ Material Category Code (MCD)
MCC............ Material Characterization Center [For nuclear wastes]
MCC............ Material Control Code
MCC............ Material Control Coordinator (MCD)
MCC............ Materials Characterization Center (SAUO)
MCC............ Materials Control Center (SAUO)
MCC............ Matrimonial Causes Committee (SAUO)
MCC............ Maui Community College [Hawaii]
MCC............ Maxwell Communication Corp. [Formerly, BPCC] [British]
McC............ McCarthy [Panendoscope] [Medicine] (BABM)
McC............ McCoy [Antibodies] [Immunology]
MCC............ Mean Cell [or Corpuscular] Hemoglobin Concentration [Hematology]
MCC............ Mechanical Chemical Codes
MCC............ Mechanically Compensated Crystal
MCC............ Media Center for Children (EA)
MCC............ Media Club of Canada [Formerly, Canadian Women's Press Club]
MCC............ Media Commentary Council [Defunct] (EA)
MCC............ Media Conversion Center [Space Flight Operations Facility, NASA]
MCC............ Medical Council of Canada
MCC............ Melbourne Cricket Club (SAUO)
MCC............ Member of the County Council [British]
MCC............ Memory Cache Controller (SAUO)
MCC............ Memory Control Circuit [Computer science] (IAA)
MCC............ Mennonite Central Committee (EA)
MCC............ Mercury Control Center
MCC............ Mesenchymal Cell Concentration [Medicine] (MELL)
MCC............ Mesoscale Convective Complex [Meteorology]
MCC............ Message Class Code (ACAE)
MCC............ Mesta Machine Company (SAUO)
MCC............ Mestek, Inc. [NYSE symbol] (SPSG)
MCC............ Metacentric Chromosome [Medicine] (MELL)
MCC............ Metacerebral Cell [Neurobiology]
MCC............ Metamorphic Core Complex [Geology]
MCC............ Meteor Communications Corporation (SAUO)
MCC............ Meteorological Communications Center (SAUO)
MCC............ Metrology and Calibration Center [Army] (MCD)
MCC............ Metropolitan Correctional Center (SAUO)
MCC............ Metropolitan County Council [British]
MCC............ Mica Creek [British Columbia] [Seismograph station code, US Geological Survey] [Closed] (SEIS)
MCC............ Microclimatic Conditioning
MCC............ Microclimatic Cooling System [Army]
MCC............ Micro-Computer Chip (VLIE)
MCC............ Micro Concept Car
MCC............ Microcrystalline Cellulose [Organic chemistry]
MCC............ Microcrystalline Chitin
MCC............ Microcrystalline Collagen (DB)
MCC............ Microelectronics & Computer Cooperative (SAUO)
MCC............ Microelectronics and Computer Technology Corp.
MCC............ Microfilm Card Catalog (GEAB)
McC............ Micro Library Canisianum, Maastricht, Holland [Library symbol] [Library of Congress] (LCLS)
MCC............ Midcourse Correction
MCC............ Middlesex Community College [Bedford, MA]
MCC............ Middlesex County Council (SAUO)
MCC............ Middlesex Cricket Club (SAUO)
MCC............ Midwest Climate Center [Marine science] (OSRA)
MCC............ Midwestern Collegiate Conference (PSS)
MCC............ Migrating Combustion Chamber [Increases fuel efficiency]
MCC............ Military Climb Corridor [Aviation]
MCC............ Military Code of Conduct (VNW)
MCC............ Military Colonization Company [British ranch in the Calgary area of Canada]
MCC............ Military Committee (SAUO)
MCC............ Military Communications Center, Inc. [Minneapolis, MN] (TSSD)
MCC............ Military Complements Committee (SAUO)
MCC............ Military Comptrollership Course (MCD)
MCC............ Military Control Center (SAUO)
MCC............ Military Cooperation Committee [US-Canada]
MCC............ Military Co-operation Community (SAUS)
MCC............ Military Coordinating Committee
MCC............ Military Co-ordination Centre (SAUO)
MCC............ Military Coordination Committee (SAUO)
MCC............ Mine Countermeasures Command and Support Ship [Navy]
MCC............ Miniature Center Cap
MCC............ Miniaturized Cassegranian Concentration [Instrumentation]
MCC............ Mini Car Club (SAUO)
MCC............ Mini Car Club, USA (EA)
MCC............ Mini-Channel Communications Control (NITA)
MCC............ Mini-Cylinder Core (SAUS)
MCC............ Minimum Circumscribed Circle [Manufacturing term]
MCC............ Minimum Complete-Killing Concentration (MAE)
MCC............ Mining Commissioner's Cases [Canada] [A publication] (DLA)
MCC............ Ministerial Collecting Center (SAUO)
MCC............ Ministerial Committee on Military Coordination [British] [World War II]
MCC............ Ministerial Council for Corporations [Australia]
MCC............ Minuteman Change Committee [Air Force] (IAA)
MCC............ Miscellaneous Common Carrier
MCC............ Missile Capability Console (MCD)
MCC............ Missile Change Committed (SAA)

MCC............	Missile Checkout Console (SAA)
MCC............	Missile Combat Crew (AAG)
MCC............	Missile Command Coder (AAG)
MCC............	Missile Compensating Control
MCC............	Missile Control Center [Air Force]
MCC............	Missile Control Console
MCC............	Missing in Colon Cancer [Genetics]
MCC.,.........	Mission Control Center [NASA] (MCD)
mcc............	Mission Control Center [NASA] (NAKS)
MCC............	Mission Control Complex [Air Force]
MCC............	Mission Crew Commander (SAUO)
MCC............	Mississippi Chemical Corporation (SAUO)
MCC............	Mississippi College, Law Library, Clinton, MS [OCLC symbol] (OCLC)
MCC............	Mixing Cross-Bar Connector [Telecommunications] (OA)
MCC............	Mobile Command Center
MCC............	Mobile Communications Center (SAUO)
MCC............	Mobile Country Code (CGWS)
MCC............	Mobility Control Center (SAUO)
MCC............	Modem Controller Chip (VLIE)
MCC............	Modern Cereal Chemistry (OA)
MCC............	Modified Close Control [Air Force]
MCC............	Modified Continuous Cooking [Pulp and paper technology]
MCC............	Modulation Coding and Compression (CCCA)
MCC............	Modulation with Constant Control
MCC............	Monier Construction Company Ltd. (SAUO)
MCC............	Monitor Control Console (CAAL)
MCC............	Monitored Command Code [Marine Corps]
MCC............	Monroe Community College (SAUO)
MCC............	Monthly Calibration Check [Automotive emissions]
MCC............	Moody's English Crown Cases Reserved [1824-44] [A publication] (DLA)
MCC............	Morgan Car Club (EA)
MCC............	Morrison Commemorative Stamp Committee (EA)
MCC............	Mortgage Credit Certificate (EMRF)
MCC............	Motor Carrier Cases [ICC]
mcc............	Motor Control Center [NASA] (NAKS)
MCC............	Motor Control Center [NASA]
MCC............	Motor Cycle Club [British]
MCC............	Motorcycle Combination [British]
MCC............	Mount Carmel Confraternity (SAUO)
MCC............	Movement Control Center [Army]
MCC............	Movement Coordination Center (SAUO)
MCC............	Multicell Compound Tire [Automotive engineering]
MCC............	Multichannel Cochlear Implant [Medicine] (MELL)
MCC............	Multichannel Communications Controller
MCC............	Multicomponent Circuits
MCC............	Multiple-Chip Carrier [Computer technology]
MCC............	Multiple Column Control [Computer science] (VLIE)
MCC............	Multiple Communications Control (BUR)
MCC............	Multiple Computer Complex
MCC............	Municipal Corporation's Chronicle [Privately Printed] [A publication] (DLA)
MCC............	Munitions Carriers Conference (EA)
MCC............	Music Critics Circle (SAUO)
MCC............	Muskegon Community College [Michigan]
MCC............	Mutated in Colorectal Cancer [Genetics]
MCC............	Mutual Capital Certificate
MCC............	Ontario Ministry of Culture and Communications (TSSD)
MCC............	Royal Military College Certificate (Senior Department) [British] (ROG)
MCC............	Sacramento, CA [Location identifier] [FAA] (FAAL)
MCCA............	Conference of the Methodist Church in the Caribbean and the Americas (EAIO)
MCCA............	Manufacturers Council on Color and Appearance [Defunct] (EA)
MCCA............	Media Conversion Computer Assembly [Space Flight Operations Facility, NASA]
MCCA............	Medicare Catastrophic Coverage Act [1988]
MCCA............	Michigan Community College Association (SAUO)
MCCA............	Minor Counties Cricket Association [British] (DBA)
MCCA............	Model Car Collectors Association (EA)
MCCA............	Motor Car Collectors of America (EA)
MCCAA............	Michigan Community College Athletic Association (PSS)
MCCAC.........	Massachusetts Community College Athletic Conference (PSS)
McCah.........	McCahon's Kansas Reports [1858-68] [A publication] (DLA)
McCahon.......	McCahon's Kansas Reports [1858-68] [A publication] (DLA)
McCall Nee...	McCall's Needlework [A publication] (BRI)
McCall Pr	McCall's Precedents [A publication] (DLA)
McCanless...	McCanless' Tennessee Reports [A publication] (DLA)
McCar.........	McCarter's New Jersey Equity Reports [A publication] (DLA)
McCart.........	McCarter's New Jersey Equity Reports [A publication] (DLA)
McCart.........	McCarty's New York Civil Procedure Reports [A publication] (DLA)
McCarter......	McCarter's New Jersey Chancery Reports [A publication] (DLA)
McCartney....	McCarty's New York Civil Procedure Reports [A publication] (DLA)
McCarty	McCarty's New York Civil Procedure Reports [A publication] (DLA)
McCarty Civ Proc...	McCarty's New York Civil Procedure Reports [A publication] (DLA)
MC Cas.........	Municipal Corporation Cases, Annotated [11 vols.] [A publication] (DLA)
MCCB.........	Minuteman Change Commitment Board (SAUO)
MCCB.........	Multinational Configuration Control Board (ACAE)
MCCC.........	Macomb County Community College [Michigan]
MCCC.........	Marine Corps Command Center (SAUO)
MCCC.........	Mediacom Communic. 'A' [NASDAQ symbol] (SG)
MCCC.........	Metropolitan Correctional Center (SAUO)
MCCC.........	Middlesex County Cricket Club (SAUO)

MCCC.........	Ministerial Consultative Committee on Curriculum [Queensland, Australia]
MCCC.........	Minnesota Community College Conference (PSS)
MCCC.........	Missile Combat Crew Commander
mccc.........	Mission Control and Computing Center [NASA] (NAKS)
MCCC.........	Mission Control and Computing Center [NASA] (NASA)
MCCC.........	Motor Carrier Claims Commission (SAUO)
MCCC.........	Muskegon County Community College (SAUO)
MCCCA	Marine Corps Combat Correspondents Association (EA)
McC Cl Ass..	McCall's Clerk's Assistant [A publication] (DLA)
MCCD.........	Marine Corps Clothing Depot
MCCD.........	Mechanical Compatibility Control Drawing (MCD)
MCCD.........	Message Cryptographic Check Digits
MCCD.........	Minimal Cumulative Cardiotoxic Dose [Medicine] (STED)
MCCD.........	Minimum Cumulative Cardiotoxic Dose [Medicine] (DMAA)
MCCD.........	Mission Control Console Display (ACAE)
MCCD.........	Multispectral Close Combat Decoy (DWSG)
MCCDC	Marine Corps Combat Development Command [Quantico, VA] (GRD)
MCC-DoD.....	Mission Control Center - Department of Defense [NASA] (NASA)
MCC-DOD.....	Mission Control Center-DOD (SAUS)
MCCDPA	Marine Corps Central Design and Programming Activity (DNAB)
MCCDS	Modified Central Computer Display Set (DNAB)
MCCE.........	Modulation, Coding, Compression and Encryption (CCCA)
MCCE.........	Montana Council for Computers in Education (EDAC)
MCCEd........	Member of the College of Craft Education [British] (DI)
MCCEM.......	Multi-Chamber Concentration and Exposure Model [Environmental Protection Agency] (AEPA)
MCCES........	Marine Corps Communications Electronics School (DNAB)
MCCF.........	Master Class Code File (MCD)
McC F.........	McCall's Forms [A publication] (DLA)
MCCF.........	Michigan Coalition for Clean Forests
MCCF.........	Mission Control Centre France (SAUO)
M/CCFLS.....	Manitowoc Calumet Counties Library System [Library network]
MCC-H........	Mission Control Center - Houston [NASA] (MCD)
McCI.........	Micro-Copy, Inc., Rochester, NY [Library symbol] [Library of Congress] (LCLS)
MCCI.........	MIDCOM Communications [NASDAQ symbol] (TTSB)
MCCI.........	Midcom Communications, Inc. [NASDAQ symbol] (SAG)
MCCI.........	Mucocutaneous Candidiasis [Medicine] (MELL)
MCCIS	Maritime Command, Control & Information System (SAUO)
MCCISWG....	Military Command, Control, and Information Systems Working Group (NATG)
mccj.........	Comboni Missionaries of the Heart of Jesus (TOCD)
MCCJ.........	Comboni Missionaries of the Heart of Jesus (Verona) (TOCD)
McC Just	McCall's New York Justice [A publication] (DLA)
MCC-K	Mission Control Center - Cape Kennedy [NASA] (KSC)
MCC-K	Mission Control Center-Kennedy (SAUS)
MCCL.........	Mason City & Clear Lake R. R. [AAR code]
McCL.........	McCabe Library (SAUO)
MCCL.........	McClain Industries [NASDAQ symbol] (TTSB)
MCCL.........	McClain Industries, Inc. [NASDAQ symbol] (NQ)
McCl.........	McClelland's English Exchequer Reports [A publication] (DLA)
McClain Cr Law...	McClain's Criminal Law [A publication] (DLA)
McClain's Code...	McClain's Annotated Code and Statutes [Iowa] [A publication] (DLA)
McCl & Y.....	McClelland and Younge's English Exchequer Reports [1824-25] [A publication] (DLA)
McClat.........	McClatchy Newspapers, Inc. [Associated Press] (SAG)
McClatN.......	McClatchy Newspapers [Associated Press] (SAG)
McCl Dig......	McClellan's Florida Digest [A publication] (DLA)
McCle.........	McClelland's English Exchequer Reports [A publication] (DLA)
McCle & Yo...	McClelland and Younge's English Exchequer Reports [1824-25] [A publication] (DLA)
McClel.........	McClelland's English Exchequer Reports [A publication] (DLA)
McClel Dig...	McClellan's Digest of Laws [Florida] [A publication] (DLA)
McClell........	McClelland's English Exchequer Reports [A publication] (DLA)
McClell & Y...	McClelland and Younge's English Exchequer Reports [1824-25] [A publication] (DLA)
McCl Ex......	McClellan's Manual for Executors [A publication] (DLA)
McCl IA Co...	McClain's Iowa Code [A publication] (DLA)
McCl Mal.....	McClelland on Civil Malpractice [A publication] (DLA)
McCln.........	McClain Industries, Inc. [Associated Press] (SAG)
MCCLPHEI ...	Mass Conference of Chief Librarians of Public Higher Educational Institutions [Library network]
McCl Pr	McClellan's Probate Practice [A publication] (DLA)
MCCM.........	Mexican Chamber of Commerce of US
MCCM.........	Military Council of Catholic Men (SAUO)
MCC-M	Mission Control Center-Moscow (SAUO)
MCCN.........	Marine and Coastal Community Network (SAUO)
MCCN.........	Midwest Curriculum Coordination Network (OICC)
MCC-NASA...	Mission Control Center-NASA (SAUS)
MCC-NASA...	Mission Control Center - National Aeronautics and Space Administration (NASA)
MCCNSW....	Mini Car Club of New South Wales [Australia]
MCCNU.......	Methylchlorethylcyclakexylinitrosourea (Semustine) [Medicine] (STED)
MCCNU.......	Methyl-(Chloroethyl)-Cyclohexyl-Nitrosourea [Antineoplastic drug regimen] (DAVI)
MCCO	Monaco Coach [NASDAQ symbol] (TTSB)
MCCO	Monaco Coach Corp. [NASDAQ symbol] (SAG)
MC Co	Motor Car Company (SAUO)
MCCOEES....	Michigan Community College Occupational Education Evaluation System (EDAC)
MCCOI........	Multimedia Communications Community of Interest (SAUO)
McCook.......	McCook's Reports [1 Ohio] [A publication] (DLA)

MCCOPO......	Mennonite Central Committee Overseas Peace Office (EA)
McCor..........	McCormick & Co., Inc. [*Associated Press*] (SAG)
MCCOR........	Motion Compensation - Coherent on Receive
McCord........	McCord's South Carolina Law Reports [*1821-28*] [*A publication*] (DLA)
McCord Ch...	McCord's South Carolina Equity Reports [*1825-27*] [*A publication*] (DLA)
McCord Eq...	McCord's South Carolina Chancery Reports [*1825-27*] [*A publication*] (DLA)
McCork........	McCorkle's Reports [*65 North Carolina*] [*A publication*] (DLA)
McCorkle	McCorkle's Reports [*65 North Carolina*] [*A publication*] (DLA)
MCCP..........	Main Communications Control Panel (SAUS)
MCCP..........	Maintenance Console Control Panel
MCCP..........	Manufacturing Cost Control Program [*DoD*]
MCCP..........	Marine Corps Capabilities Plan (DOMA)
MCCP..........	Meta-Chlorophenylpiperazine [*Biochemistry*]
MCCP..........	Microwave Circuit Control Program [*Computer science*]
MCCP..........	Military Consolidated Command Post (SAUO)
MCCP..........	Mission Control Computer Program [*NASA*]
MCCP..........	Mountain Cloud Chemistry Project (SAUO)
MCCP..........	Movement Control Check Point (SAUO)
MCC/PS	Microclimate Conditioning / Power Subsystem [*Army*] (RDA)
MCCQE	Medical Council of Canada's Qualifying Examination
MCCR	Master Change Compliance Record
McCr............	McCrary's United States Circuit Court Reports [*A publication*] (DLA)
MCCR	Medical Committee for Civil Rights [*Defunct*] (EA)
MCCR	Memory Data Capture Cash and Credit Register [*Datacap Systems, Inc.*]
MCCR	Mission-Critical Computer Resource [*Computer science*]
MCCR	Molded Case Circuit Breaker
MCCRA	Medicare Catastrophic Coverage Repeal Act of 1989 (WYGK)
McCrary.......	McCrary's United States Circuit Court Reports [*A publication*] (DLA)
McCrary Elect...	McCrary's American Law of Elections [*A publication*] (DLA)
McCrary's Rep...	McCrary's United States Circuit Court Reports [*A publication*] (DLA)
McCr Elect...	McCrary's American Law of Elections [*A publication*] (DLA)
MCCRES	Marine Corps Combat Readiness Evaluation System
MCCRK	McCormick & Co. [*NASDAQ symbol*] (TTSB)
MCCRK	McCormick & Co., Inc. [*NASDAQ symbol*] (NQ)
MCCRTG	Marine Corps Combat Readiness Training Group
MCCS	Machine Centralized Control System (DWSG)
MCCS	Manual Closed-Loop Control System (VLIE)
MCCS	Marconi Command & Control Systems (SAUS)
MCCS	Master Calendar Control System [*New York City courts' speedup system*]
MCCS	Master Control Communication Station (ACAE)
MCCS	Mechanized Calling Card Service [*Formerly, ABC*] [*Telecommunications*]
MCCs	Metropolitan Correctional Centers (SAUO)
MCCs	Microclimate Cooling System (HEAS)
MCCS	Military Committee in Chiefs of Staff Session [*NATO*] (NATG)
MCCS	Mine Countermeasures Control System (SAUS)
MCCS	Missile Critical Circuit Simulator
mccs...........	Mission Control Center Simulation [*NASA*] (NAKS)
MCCS	Mission Control Center Simulation [*NASA*] (NASA)
MCCS	Mission Control Center System (SAUO)
MCCS	Mission Critical Computer System (DOMA)
MCCS	Mobile Command and Control System (MCD)
MCCSD	Charles Stark Draper Laboratory, Inc., Technical Information Center, Cambridge, MA [*Library symbol*] [*Library of Congress*] (LCLS)
MCCSL	Marconi Command and Control Systems Ltd. (NITA)
MCCSP	Ministerial Council on Common Services Provision [*Australia*]
MCCSS	Mobile Command Center Strategic System (SAUO)
MCCT..........	Multistrip Cesium Contact Thrustor
MCCTA.........	Manufacturing Confectioners' Commercial Travellers Association [*British*] (BI)
MCCTP.........	Manpower and Community College Counselor Training Program (OICC)
MCCU	Micro-Climate Cooling Unit (SAUS)
MCCU	Mobile Coronary Care Unit [*Medicine*]
MCCU	Multiple Channel Control Unit
MCCU	Multiple Communications Control Unit [*Computer science*]
MCCU	Multisystem Channel Communication Unit (SAUS)
McCul Dict...	McCullough's Commercial Dictionary [*A publication*] (DLA)
McCul Pol Econ...	McCulloch's Political Economy [*A publication*] (DLA)
MCCUS	Mexican Chamber of Commerce of the United States (SAUO)
MCCUSCUSRPG...	Military Coordinating Committee, United States Element, Canada-United States Regional Planning Group (AABC)
MCCW	Miami Citizens Crime Watch (SAUO)
MCCW	Military Council of Catholic Women (SAUO)
MCCX..........	Multimedia Communications Exchange (VLIE)
MCD............	Air Medical Ltd. [*British*] [*ICAO designator*] (FAAC)
MCD............	Doctor of Comparative Medicine
MCD............	Dynatech Research/Development Co., Cambridge, MA [*Library symbol*] [*Library of Congress*] (LCLS)
MCD............	Mad Cow Disease [*Medicine*] (MELL)
MCD............	Magistrates' Court Decisions [*New Zealand*] [*A publication*] (DLA)
MCD............	Magna Carta Dames, National Society (EA)
MCD............	Magnetic Circular Dichroism
MCD............	Magnetic Crack Definer [*Aviation*]
MCD............	Maintenance Control Department [*Military*] (DNAB)
MCD............	Malaria Control Detachment [*Army*] [*World War II*]
MCD............	Manipulative Communications Deception [*Military*] (NVT)
MCD............	Manual Control Device
MCD............	Manufacturing and Construction Division (SAUO)

MCD..........	Manufacturing Construction Document (SAA)
MCD..........	Marginal Checking and Distribution
MCD..........	Margin Crease Distance (STED)
MCD..........	Marine Corps District (DNAB)
MCD..........	Marine Craft Detachment (SAUS)
MCD..........	Maritime Commission Decisions
MCD..........	Marr, Cahalan & Dunn [*Law firm*]
MCD..........	Mast Cell Degranulating [*or Destroying*] Peptide [*Biochemistry*]
MCD..........	Mast-Cell Degranulation (STED)
MCD..........	Master Clerical Data [*Management system*]
MCD..........	Master of Civic Design
MCD..........	Master of Communication Disorders (GAGS)
MCD..........	Mathematics and Computer Division [*Supreme Headquarters Allied Powers Europe*] (NATG)
MCD..........	McDonald's Corp. [*NYSE symbol*] [*Toronto Stock Exchange symbol*] (SPSG)
MCD..........	McDonnell Douglas Corp.
MCD..........	Mean Cell [*or Corpuscular*] Diameter [*Hematology*]
MCD..........	Mean Character Difference (EES)
MCD..........	Mean of Consecutive Differences (MAE)
MCD..........	Median Control Death
MCD..........	Medical Care Development, Inc. [*Augusta, ME*] (TSSD)
MCD..........	Medical Crew Director
MCD..........	Medium Corpuscular Density [*Cardiology*] (DAVI)
MCD..........	Medullary Collecting Duct (DB)
MCD..........	Medullary Cystic Disease [*Medicine*] (MAE)
MCD..........	Megawatt Cassegrain Diplexer
MCD..........	Member of the College of Dentists [*British*]
MCD..........	Memory Control Data
MCD..........	Mercy College of Detroit [*Michigan*]
MCD..........	Metabolic Coronary Dilation [*Medicine*] (AAMN)
MCD..........	Metacarpal Cortical Density [*Anatomy*]
MCD..........	Metal-Covered Door [*Technical drawings*]
MCD..........	Metals and Ceramics Division [*Air Force*]
MCD..........	Metaphyseal Chondrodysplasia [*Medicine*]
MCD..........	Microbial Coal Desulfurization
MCD..........	Microelectronic Circuits Division (AAGC)
MCD..........	Mid-Central District [*ATSC*]
MCD..........	Military Contracts Department
MCD..........	Military Coordination Detachment (NATG)
MCD..........	Millicandela
mcD..........	Millicurie-Destroyed
MCD..........	Mines, Countermines, and Demolitions [*Military*] (RDA)
MCD..........	Mine Warfare and Clearance Diving [*Navy*] [*British*]
MCD..........	Minimal Cerebral Dysfunction
MCD..........	Minimal Change Disease [*Nephrology*]
MCD..........	Minimum Cost Design (MCD)
MCD..........	Minister for Coordination of Defence (SAUO)
MCD..........	Minor Civil Division [*Bureau of Census*]
MCD..........	Missile Countermeasure Device (DWSG)
MCD..........	Mission Communication Display (MCD)
MCD..........	Mission Control Directorate [*NASA*]
MCD..........	Mobile Communications Division (SAUO)
MCD..........	Modification of Contract Documents (AAGC)
MCD..........	Modular Capabilities Document (SAUS)
MCD..........	Monitor Criteria Data [*Space Flight Operations Facility, NASA*]
MCD..........	Months for Cyclical Dominance [*Economics*]
MCD..........	Mouse Cytogenetic Database (HGEN)
MCD..........	Movement for Christian Democracy [*Political party*] (WDAA)
MCD..........	Movimiento por el Cambio Democratico [*Mexico*] [*Political party*] (EY)
MCD..........	Multicystic Disease [*Medicine*] (STED)
MCD..........	Multimedia Cartridge Drive (SAUS)
MCD..........	Multiple Carboxylase Deficiency [*Medicine*]
MCD..........	Multiple Concrete Duct [*Telecommunications*] (TEL)
MCD..........	Multiple Cropping Department (SAUO)
MCD..........	Municipal Civil District (GEAB)
MCD..........	Municipal Construction Division [*Environmental Protection Agency*] (GFGA)
MCD..........	Muscle Carnitine Deficiency [*Medicine*] (STED)
MCDA.........	Magna Carta Day Association (SAUO)
MCDA.........	Manpower and Career Development Agency
McDA	McDonnell Aircraft Corporation (SAUO)
MCDA	Micro Channel Developers Association (NTPA)
MCDA	Motor Car Dealers Association (SAUO)
McDAC	McDonnell Aircraft Corporation (SAUO)
MCDARS......	Mechanized Cost Distribution and Reporting System (MCD)
MCDAS	Metropolitan Cities Drug Association Secretaries (EA)
MC-DAS......	Multiple Channel Data Acquisition System (NITA)
MCDB	Master Code Database (MCD)
MCDB	Minimum Cost Design Booster (KSC)
MCDB	Molecular Cellular, and Developmental Biology [*A discipline division*]
MCDBSU......	Master Control and Data Buffer Storage Unit
MCDC	Marine Corps Development Center (SAUO)
MCDC	McDonnell Douglas Corp.
MCDC	Mobilization Concepts Development Center [*Washington, DC*] [*DoD*] (MCD)
MCDC	Montgomery County Detention Center (SAUO)
MCDD	Marine and Coastal Data Directory (SAUO)
MCDD	Monochlorodioxin [*Organic chemistry*]
MCDD	Multichannel Demux/Demod (ACAE)
MCDE..........	Microcide Pharmaceuticals [*NASDAQ symbol*] (TTSB)
MCDE..........	Microcide Pharmaceuticals, Inc. [*NASDAQ symbol*] (SAG)
MCDE..........	Monochlorodimethyl Ether [*Organic chemistry*]
MCDEC	Marine Corps Development and Education Command

MCDEC .... Marine Corps School (SAUO)
McDerI......... McDermott International, Inc. [Associated Press] (SAG)
McDerJ........ McDermott [J. Ray] SA [Associated Press] (SAG)
McDer Land L... McDermot's Irish Land Laws [A publication] (DLA)
MC Det .... Malaria Control Detachment (SAUO)
McDevitt....... McDevitt's Irish Land Commissioner's Reports [A publication] (DLA)
MCDF.......... Methyltrichlorodibenzofuran [Organic chemistry]
MCDF.......... Missile Defense [or Alert] System Control and Display Facility [Air
                  Force] (IAA)
MCDF.......... Mobile Combustion Diagnostic Fixture (MCD)
MCDG .... Monitor Criteria Data Set Generation Processor Assembly [Space
                  Flight Operations Facility, NASA]
MCDH .... Master of Community Dental Health, University of Birmingham
                  [British] (DBQ)
MCDI .... Magneto Capacitor Discharge Ignition
MCDI .... Minnesota Child Development Inventory [Child development test]
                  [Psychology]
McDInv .... McDonald & Co. Investment, Inc. [Associated Press] (SAG)
MCDK .... Multicystic Dysplastic Kidney [Medicine] (DMAA)
MCDM .... Modern College for Distressed Merchants (SAUO)
MCDM .... Multiple Criteria Decision Making
MCDN .... Marine Corps Data Network [Marine Corps] (CIST)
McDn .... McDonald's Corp. [Associated Press] (SAG)
MCDN .... Multi-cellular Data Network [Metricom]
McDn25 .... McDonalds Corp. [Associated Press] (SAG)
McDn36 .... McDonalds Corp. [Associated Press] (SAG)
McDnD........ McDonnell Douglas Corp. [Associated Press] (SAG)
McDnlds....... McDonald's Corp. [Associated Press] (SAG)
McDO.......... McDonald Observatory (SAUO)
MCDOA........ Minewarfare & Clearance Diving Officers' Association (WDAA)
McD Obs...... McDonald Observatory (SAUO)
McDon Jus.... McDonald's Justice [A publication] (DLA)
McDonnell.... McDonnell's Sierra Leone Reports [A publication] (DLA)
McDow Inst... McDowall's Institutes of the Law of Scotland [A publication] (DLA)
MCDP .... Marine Conservation and Development Program (SAUO)
MCDP .... Microprogrammed Communication Data Processor (MCD)
MCDP .... Missionary Catechists of Divine Providence [Roman Catholic
                  women's religious order]
MCDP .... Missionary Catechists of Divine Providence, San Antonio, TX (TOCD)
MCDPrE .... McDonald's Corp. 7.72% Dep Pfd [NYSE symbol] (TTSB)
McDr........... McDermott, Inc. [Associated Press] (SAG)
MCDR .... Multichannel DIFAR [Directional Frequency Analysis and Recording
                  System] Relay (NVT)
MCDS .... Maintenance Control and Display System [NASA] (NASA)
MCDS .... Management Communications and Data System (SSD)
MCDS .... Management Control Data System [Computer science] (IAA)
MCDS .... Mission Control & Display Subsystem (SAUS)
MCDS .... Mission-Critical Defense System [Army]
MCDS .... Modular Cargo Delivery System [MARAD] (TAG)
MCDS .... Multicommand Data System
MCDS .... Multifunction CRT [Cathode-Ray Tube] Display System (NASA)
MCDSH .... Management Communications and Data System Hardware (SSD)
MCD/SLV .... Minimum Cost Design/Space Launch Vehicle [NASA] (KSC)
MCDSP .... Master Combat Data System Plan [Military] (CAAL)
MCDT.......... Mast Cell Degranulation Test [Medicine] (DAVI)
MCDT.......... Mean Corrective Downtime [Computer science]
MCDU .... Multifunction Control & Display Unit (SAUS)
MCDU .... Multifunction CRT [Cathode-Ray Tube] Display Unit (NASA)
MCDU .... Multipurpose Control Display Unit (GAVI)
MCDV .... Maize Chlorotic Dwarf Virus [Plant pathology]
MCDV .... Maritime Coastal Defense Vessel (MILB)
MCDV .... Maximum Cell Delay Variation (SAUS)
MCDW .... Monthly Climate Data for the World (SAUO)
MCDY .... Microdyne Corp. [NASDAQ symbol] (NQ)
MCE .... Episcopal Divinity School, Cambridge, MA [Library symbol] [Library of
                  Congress] (LCLS)
MCE .... MacNeill Industrial, Inc. [Vancouver Stock Exchange symbol]
MCE .... Maintenance Cleaning Equipment (MCD)
MCE .... Management Centre Europe (SAUO)
MCE .... Management Communication Engine (SAUS)
MCE .... Mandatory Continuing Education
MCE .... Manufacturing Cycle Effectiveness
MCE .... Marginal Cost Efficiency [Marketing]
MCE .... Maritime Commission, Emergency Ship
MCE .... Marshall of Cambridge (Engineering) Ltd. [British] [ICAO
                  designator] (FAAC)
MCE .... Master of Chemical Engineering (GAGS)
MCE .... Master of Christian Education
MCE .... Master of Civil Engineering
MCE .... Maximum Capability Envelope
MCE .... MCN Corp. [NYSE symbol] (SAG)
MCE .... MCN Corp. 8.75%'PRIDE' [NYSE symbol] (TTSB)
MCE .... Mean Chance Expectation [Parapsychology]
MCE .... Mechanism Control Electronics (SAUS)
MCE .... Media Conversion Equipment [Space Flight Operations Facility,
                  NASA]
MCE .... Medical Care Evaluation
MCE .... Medicare Code Editor (MEDA)
MCE .... Melbourne Corn Exchange [Australia]
MCE .... Member of Civil Engineering [Canada] (ASC)
MCE .... Membrane Chlorine Expansion [Plastics]
MCE .... Memphis Cotton Exchange (EA)
MCE .... Merced [California] [Airport symbol] (AD)
MCE .... Merced, CA [Location identifier] [FAA] (FAAL)

McE .... Microcard Editions, Inc., Englewood, CO [Library symbol] [Library of
                  Congress] (LCLS)
MCE .... Micro Circuit Engineering Ltd. (SAUO)
MCE .... Microscopically Controlled Excision [Medicine]
MCE .... Mid Course Early (ACAE)
MCE .... Mid Cretaceous Events (SAUO)
MCE .... Military Characteristics Equipment
MCE .... Military Clinical Engineering (DMAA)
MCE .... Military Corrective Establishment
MCE .... Missile Command Electronics (ACAE)
MCE .... Missile Compensating Equipment
MCE .... Mission Control Element (SAUO)
MCE .... Mission Control Equipment [NASA]
MCE .... Mixed Cellulose Esters Membrane Filters
MCE .... Mobile Command Element (NATG)
MCE .... Modular Communications Engine (AGLO)
MCE .... Modular Control Element (MCD)
MCE .... Modular Control Equipment [DoD]
MCE .... Montgomery Cotton Exchange [Defunct] (EA)
MCE .... Moscow Commodity Exchange [Russian Federation] (EY)
MCE .... Multicystic Encephalopathy [Medicine] (DMAA)
MCE .... Multiple Cartilaginous Exostosis [Medicine] (DMAA)
MCE .... Myocardial Contrast Echocardiography [Medicine] (DMAA)
MCE .... Myocardial Embolism [Medicine] (MELL)
MCE .... National Council of Churches, Ministries in Christian Education (EA)
MCEA......... Madison Center for Educational Affairs (EA)
MCEA......... Maryland Classified Employees Association
MCEAC....... Marine Corps Emergency Actions Center
MCEAMS..... Marine Corps Expeditionary Aircraft Maintenance Shelter (SAUO)
MCEB......... Marine Corps Equipment Board
MCEB......... Military Communications-Electronics Board [DoD] [Washington, DC]
MCEC......... Marine Corps Education Center
MCED......... Episcopal Divinity School, Cambridge, MA [Library symbol] [Library of
                  Congress] (LCLS)
MC Ed......... Master of Commercial Education
MCED......... Master of Community Economic Development (PGP)
MC Ed......... Master of Continuing Education (PGP)
MC/EDS...... Mission Control/Electronic Display System (MCD)
M Ce Eng..... Master of Cement Engineering
MCEF......... Mixed Cellulose Ester Filter (GNE)
MCEGGS..... Melbourne Church of England Girls Grammar School (SAUO)
MCEI......... Marketing Communications Executives International [Dallas, TX] (EA)
MCEL......... Machine Check Extended Logout
McEM........ Microfilming Executors & Methods Organization Ltd., Dublin, Ireland
                  [Library symbol] [Library of Congress] (LCLS)
MCEM........ Military Committee Emergency Memorandum (SAUO)
MCE(Melb)... Master of Civil Engineering (Melbourne University)
MCEMS....... Marine Corps Environmentally Controlled Medical System (MCD)
MCen.......... Centerville Public Library, Centerville, MA [Library symbol] [Library of
                  Congress] (LCLS)
MCEN......... Modified Current Expendable Launch Vehicle [NASA] (KSC)
MCENC....... Mid-Central Conference (PSS)
MC Eng....... Master of Civil Engineering
MCEO......... Malayan Council of Employers Organization (SAUO)
MCEP......... Maneuver Criteria Evaluation Program [Army]
MCEPEN .... Midwest Continuing Education Professional Nurses (DHSM)
MCER......... Massachusetts Central [AAR code]
M Cer E ...... Master of Ceramic Engineering
MCES......... Main Condenser Evacuation System [Nuclear energy] (NRCH)
MCES......... Major City Earth Stations [Telecommunications] (TSSD)
MCES......... Marine Corps Exchange System (SAUO)
MCES......... Medical Care Evaluation Study (HCT)
MCES......... Modular Command and Control Evaluation Structure (SAUO)
MCES......... Multiple Cholesterol Emboli Syndrome [Medicine]
MCESS....... Marine Corps Expeditionary Shelter System (MCD)
MCET......... Massachusetts Corporation for Educational Telecommunications
MCET......... Mississippi Center for Educational Television (SAUO)
MCEU......... Mobile Civil Emergency Unit
MCEWG ..... Multinational Communication-Electronics Working Group [Formerly,
                  SGCEC] [NATO] (NATG)
MCF........... Macrophage Chemotactic Factor [Immunochemistry] (MAE)
MCF........... Magic Chef, Inc. (SAUO)
MCF........... Magnetic Confinement Fusion [Physics]
MCF........... Magyar Communion of Friends (EA)
MCF........... Maintenance and Checkout Facility [NASA] (KSC)
MCF........... Maintenance Condemnation Factor (MCD)
MCF........... Maintenance Control Facility (SAUO)
MCF........... Major Component Fail (SAUS)
MCF........... Manual Cervical Fraction [Medicine] (DMAA)
MCF........... Marine Commando Force (SAUO)
MCF........... Master Code File
MCF........... Master Control Facility (ACAE)
MCF........... Master Control File
MCF........... Matched Crystal Filters
MCF........... Maximal Contraction Force [Myology]
MCF........... McFinley Red Lake Mines Ltd. [Toronto Stock Exchange symbol]
MCF........... Mean Carrier Frequency [Radio] (IAA)
MCF........... Measurement Compensation Factor (PDAA)
MCF........... Medical Cybernetics Foundation (EA)
MCF........... Medium Corpuscular Fragility [Hematology]
MCF........... Merced County Free Library, Merced, CA [OCLC symbol] (OCLC)
MCF........... Meta Content File [Netscape] [Computer science]
MCF........... Meta Content Format [Computer science]
MCF........... Metroplex Control Facility [FAA] (TAG)
MCF........... Michigan Colleges Foundation (SAUO)

MCF	Microcomplement Fixation [*Immunochemistry*]
MCF	Middle Cranial Fossa [*Medicine*] (MELL)
MCF	Migrant Children's Fund [*Absorbed by NCEMC*]
MCF	Military Christian Fellowship of Canada (SAUO)
MCF	Military Computer Family (MCD)
MCF	Milled Carbon Fiber
MCF	Million Cubic Feet
MCF	Mine-Clearing Force (SAUO)
MCF	Mink Cell Focus-Inducing [*Virus*]
MCF	Mission Control Facility (MCD)
MCF	Mission Control Forecast (SAUO)
MCF	Mission-Critical Function (PDAA)
MCF	Missouri Colleges Fund (SAUO)
MCF	Mobile Calibration Facility
MCF	Mode Change Flag
MCF	Modular Combustion Facility (SSD)
MCF	Monolithic Crystal Filter
MCF	Mononuclear Cell Factor [*Cytology*]
MCF	Multichannel Fixed
MCF	Multilateral Clearing Facility [*Caribbean Community and Common Market*] (EY)
MCF	Multiple Cassegrain Feed [*Deep Space Instrumentation Facility, NASA*]
MCF	Multiple Cost Factor
MCF	Museum Communication Format (NITA)
MCF	Mutual Coherence Function
MCF	Myocardial Contractile Force [*Cardiology*]
MCF	Myocardial Fascicles [*Medicine*] (MELL)
MCF	Tampa, FL [*Location identifier*] [*FAA*] (FAAL)
MCF	Taurus MuniCalif Hldgs [*NYSE symbol*] (TTSB)
MCF	Taurus Municipal California Holdings [*NYSE symbol*] (SPSG)
MCF	Thousand Cubic Feet
MCF-7	Michigan Cancer Foundation - Seventh Sample [*Strain of rapid-growing breast cancer cells used world-wide in cancer research*]
MCFA	Medium-Chain Fatty Acids [*Organic chemistry*]
MCFA	Miniature Centrifugal Fast Analyzer (DMAA)
MCFA	Mitsubishi Caterpillar Forklift America
MCFA	Monosegmented Continuous Flow Analysis [*Analytical chemistry*]
MCFA	Royal Ministry for Consumer and Family Affairs (SAUO)
McFar	McFarlane's Jury Court Reports [*Scotland*] [*A publication*] (DLA)
McFarl	McFarland Energy, Inc. [*Associated Press*] (SAG)
MCFC	Mary Jo Cattlett Fan Club (EA)
MCFC	Molten Carbonate Fuel Cell [*Energy source*]
MCFC	Motley Crue Fan Club (EA)
MCFD	Malta College of Family Doctors (SAUO)
MCFD	Modular Chaff/Flare Dispenser (PDAA)
MCFD	Thousand Cubic Feet per Day
MCFE	McFarland Energy [*NASDAQ symbol*] (TTSB)
MCFE	McFarland Energy, Inc. [*NASDAQ symbol*] (NQ)
MCFF	Moving Call for Fire [*Military*]
MCFFA	Ministerial Council of/on Forestry, Fisheries and Aquaculture (SAUO)
MCFH	Thousand Cubic Feet per Hour
MCFI	Malaysian Chamber of Film Industries (SAUO)
MCFIM	Microfilm
MCFIX	Ivy Bond Fund Cl.A [*Mutual fund ticker symbol*] (SG)
MCFL	Master Civilian Facilities Listing [*DoD*]
MCFLM	Microfilm (AAG)
MCFMIS	Marine Corps Food Management Information System (SAUO)
MCFO	Marine Corps Freight Office
MCFOS	Military Computer Family Operating System (ACAE)
MCFP	Mean Circulating Filling Pressure (DMAA)
MCFP	Medical Center for Federal Prisoners (SAUO)
MCFP	Member of the College of Family Physicians [*British*]
MCFP(EM)	Member, College of Family Physicians (Emergency Medicine) (CMD)
MCFR	Microframe, Inc. [*NASDAQ symbol*] (SAG)
MCFS	Maneuver Control Functional Segment [*Army*] (RDA)
MCFS	Master Container Freight [*MARAD*] (TAG)
MCFS	Median Cleft Face Syndrome [*Medicine*] (MELL)
MCFS	Middle Cranial Fossa Syndrome [*Medicine*] (MELL)
MCFS	MPS Coastal Fortress Simulator (SAUS)
MCFSA	Minority Caucus of Family Service America (EA)
MCFSAA	Minorities Caucus of Family Service Association of America [*Later, MCFSA*] (EA)
MCFSHE	Microfische
MCFTU	Mauritius Confederation of Free Trade Unions (SAUO)
McFx	Microfax, Universal Information System, Paramus, NJ [*Library symbol*] [*Library of Congress*] (LCLS)
MCG	Magazine Cartoonists Guild [*Later, CG*] (EA)
MCG	Magnetic Compensator Group
MCG	Magnetocardiogram
MCG	Magnetocardiograph (IDOE)
MCG	Magneto Cumulative Generator (MCD)
MCG	Mains Cable Group [*British*] (DBA)
MCG	Man Computer Graphics [*Computer science*] (MCD)
MCG	Mandalay Coral Gardens (SAUO)
MCG	Marine Corps Gazette [*A publication*] (DOMA)
MCG	Master Control Gauge (IAA)
MCG	Master Control Group (SAUO)
MCG	Master of Clinical Gerontology (PGP)
McG	McGill University
MCG	McGill University, Graduate School of Library Science, Montreal, PQ, Canada [*OCLC symbol*] (OCLC)
McG	McGloin's Louisiana Court of Appeal Reports [*A publication*] (DLA)
MCG	McGrath [*Alaska*] [*Airport symbol*] (OAG)
MCG	McGrath, AK [*Location identifier*] [*FAA*] (FAAL)

MCG	Medical College of Georgia [*Augusta*]
MCG	Membrane Coating Granule (DB)
MCG	Memory Character Generator
MCG	Memory Controller Group (DWSG)
MCG	Mesangiocapillary Glomerulonephritis (DB)
MCG	Mesencephalic Central Grey (DB)
MCG	Metric Coordinating Group (MCD)
MCG	Michigan Gas Utilities Company (SAUO)
mcg	Microgram (LDT)
MCG	Microgram [*One millionth of a gram*]
MCG	Microwave Command Guidance
MCG	Midbrain Central Gray [*Brain anatomy*]
MCG	Mid-Canada Gold & Copper [*Vancouver Stock Exchange symbol*]
MCG	Midcourse Guidance [*Navy*] (CAAL)
MCG	Millimeter Wave Contrast Guidance [*Munitions*] (MCD)
MCG	Minimally-Cleaned, Coal-Derived Gas
MCG	Minkowski-Chauffard-Gaeusslen [*Syndrome*] [*Medicine*] (DB)
MCG	Mobile Civilian Group (SAUO)
MCG	Mobile Command Guidance
MCG	Mobile Communications Group [*Air Force*] (MCD)
mCG	Monkey Chorionic Gonadotrophin [*Endocrinology*]
MCG	Monoclonal Gammopathy [*Immunochemistry*] (DMAA)
MCG	Mount Cook Group (SAUO)
MCG	Mount Cook Group of companies (SAUO)
MCG	Movement Control Group (SAUO)
MCG	Moving Coil Galvanometer [*Electronics*]
MCGA	Memory Controller Gate Array [*Computer science*]
MCGA	Multicolor Graphics Adapter [*Computer technology*]
MCGA	Multicolor /Graphics Array [*Computer science*]
McGAP	Mesoscale Climate Model Garmisch-Partenkirchen (SAUO)
MCGC	Metacerebral Giant Cell (DMAA)
MCGC	Michigan Consolidated Gas Co. [*Associated Press*] (SAG)
McGC	Micro Graphic Corp., Garfield, NJ [*Library symbol*] [*Library of Congress*] (LCLS)
MCGCIS	Marine Corps Ground-Controlled Interceptor Squadron (IAA)
MCGCM	Marine Corps Good Conduct Medal
MCGF	Mast Cell Growth Factor (DB)
MCGF	Myeloma Cell Growth Factor [*Biochemistry*]
MCGFP	Maraschino Cherry and Glace Fruit Processors (EA)
MCGH	Marine Corps Gun Howitzer (MCD)
McG-H	McGraw-Hill (SAUO)
MCGI	Morse Construction Group Incorporated (SAUO)
McGill	McGill's Manuscript Decisions, Scotch Court of Session [*A publication*] (DLA)
McGl	McGloin's Louisiana Courts of Appeal Reports [*A publication*] (DLA)
McGl Al	McGlashan. Aliment [*Scotland*] [*A publication*] (DLA)
McGl (LA)	McGloin's Louisiana Courts of Appeal Reports [*A publication*] (DLA)
McGloin	McGloin's Louisiana Courts of Appeal Reports [*A publication*] (DLA)
McGloin Rep (LA)	McGloin's Louisiana Courts of Appeal Reports [*A publication*] (DLA)
McGl Sh	McGlashan's Sheriff Court Practice [*Scotland*] [*A publication*] (DLA)
MCGLX	Ivy Global Fund Cl.A [*Mutual fund ticker symbol*] (SG)
MCGN	Mesangiocapillary Glomerulonephritis [*Medicine*] (AAMN)
MCGN	Minimal-Change Glomerular Nephritis [*Minimal-change glomerulonephritis*] [*Nephrology*] (DAVI)
MCGN	Mixed Cryoglobulinemia-Associated Glomerulonephritis [*Medicine*]
MCGP	Magnavox Code Generation Package (SAUO)
MCGP	Member of the College of General Practitioners [*British*]
MCGp	Mobile Communications Group [*Air Force*] (AFM)
MCGPPC	Manual on the Control of Government Property in the Possession of Contractors
McGrath	McGrath's Mandamus Cases [*Michigan*] [*A publication*] (DLA)
McGrH	McGraw-Hill, Inc. [*Associated Press*] (SAG)
McGrth	McGrath Rent Corp. [*Associated Press*] (SAG)
MCGS	Manual Cover Gas System (SAUO)
MCGS	Microwave Command Guidance System [*RADC*]
McGU	McGill University (SAUO)
McGUL	McGill University Library (SAUO)
MCGW	Maximum Certificated Gross Weight (MCD)
MCGW	Millimeter Wave Contrast Guidance Weapon (ACAE)
MCH	Churchill Public Library, Manitoba [*Library symbol*] [*National Library of Canada*] (NLC)
MCH	Greater Manchester (SAUS)
MCH	Machala [*Ecuador*] [*Airport symbol*] (OAG)
MCH	Machine Channel Handler (ECII)
MCH	Machine Check Handler (NITA)
MCH	Machine-Check Handler [*Computer science*] (MCD)
MCH	Machynlleth [*Welsh depot code*]
M Ch	Magister Chirurgiae [*Master of Surgery*] [*Latin*]
MCH	Mail Chute (AAG)
MCH	March
MCH	Masachapa [*Nicaragua*] [*Seismograph station code, US Geological Survey*] (SEIS)
MCH	Massachusetts Council for the Humanities [*Defunct*] (EA)
MCH	Master of Community Health (GAGS)
MCH	Master of Surgery (SAUO)
MCH	Maternal and Child Health (STED)
MCH	Maternal and Child Health Services [*Generic term*] (DHSM)
MCH	McAlpine Helicopters Ltd. [*British*] [*ICAO designator*] (FAAC)
MCH	Mean Cell [*or Corpuscular*] Hemoglobin [*Hematology*]
MCH	Mean Corpuscular Hemoglobin [*Medicine*] (ADWA)
MCH	Mean Corpuscular Hemoglobin and Red Cell Indices [*Hematology*] (DAVI)
mch	Megacharacter (ELAL)
MCH	Melanin-Concentrating Hormone [*Endocrinology*]

M-Ch............	Memory Channel
MCH.............	Memory Controller Hub
MCH.............	Methacholine [*A cholinergic*]
MCH.............	Methylcyclohexane [*Organic chemistry*]
MCH.............	Methylcyclohexanol [*Organic chemistry*]
MCH.............	Methylcyclohexenone [*Organic chemistry*]
MCH.............	Methylenecyclohexadiene [*Organic chemistry*]
MCH.............	Micham Explorations, Inc. [*Vancouver Stock Exchange symbol*]
Mch.............	Michigan Reports [*A publication*] (DLA)
McH.............	Microeditions Hachette, Paris, France [*Library symbol*] [*Library of Congress*] (LCLS)
MCH.............	Microfibrillar Collagen Hemostat [*Medicine*] (MEDA)
MCH.............	Millenium Chemicals, Inc. [*NYSE symbol*] (SAG)
mc-h............	Millicurie-Hour (STED)
MCH.............	Mission Chapel [*Church of England*]
MCH.............	Moravian Church House (SAUO)
MCH.............	Mother-Child Health
MCH.............	Moveable Cultural Heritage (SAUO)
MCH.............	Muscle Contraction Headache [*Medicine*] (CPH)
MCha..........	Eldredge Public Library, Chatham, MA [*Library symbol*] [*Library of Congress*] (LCLS)
MCHA..........	Moveable Cultural Heritage Act (SAUO)
MCHAN........	Multichannel (AABC)
MChB..........	Boston College, Chestnut Hill, MA [*Library symbol*] [*Library of Congress*] (LCLS)
MChB..........	Magneto-Chiral Birefringence [*Optics*]
MCHB	Maternal and Child Health Bureau (MELL)
MCHb..........	Mean Corpuscular Hemoglobin [*Hematology*] (DAVI)
MCHbC	Mean Cell Hemoglobin Concentration [*Medicine*] (STED)
MCHbC	Mean Corpuscular Hemoglobin Concentration [*Hematology*] (DAVI)
MCHbC	Mean Corpuscular Hemoglobin Count [*Hematology*] (DAVI)
MCHBG........	Maternal and Child Health Block Grant [*Department of Health and Human Services*] (GFGA)
MChB-WO....	Boston College, Weston Observatory, Weston, MA [*Library symbol*] [*Library of Congress*] (LCLS)
MCHC	Marine Corps Historical Center (SAUO)
MCHC	Maternal and Child Health Care (STED)
MCHC	Mean Cell [*or Corpuscular*] Hemoglobin Concentration [*Hematology*]
MCHC	Mean Corpuscular Hemoglobin Concentration [*Medicine*] (STED)
MCHC	Mean Corpuscular Hemoglobin Concentration and Red Cell Indices [*Hematology*] (DAVI)
MCHC	Mean Corpuscular Hemoglobin Count [*Hematology*] (DAVI)
MCHC	Mean Corpusculsar Hemoglobin Concentration [*Physiology*]
MCHC	Metropolitan Collegiate Hockey Conference (PSS)
MCHC	Missing Children...Help Center (EA)
MCHCC	Midwest Christian College Conference (PSS)
MCHCL	Mechanically Cooled
M Ch D	Magister Chirurgiae Dentalis [*Master of Dental Surgery*]
MChD..........	Magneto-Chiral Dichroism [*Optics*]
MChD..........	Master of Dental Surgery (SAUO)
MCHE	Eskimo Museum, Churchill, Manitoba [*Library symbol*] [*National Library of Canada*] (NLC)
M Ch E	Master of Chemical Engineering
MChE	Member of Chemical Engineering (ASC)
MCHEL........	Michigan Community Health Electronic Library (SAUO)
MChelm.......	Adams Library (Chelmsford Public Library), Chelmsford, MA [*Library symbol*] [*Library of Congress*] (LCLS)
MChels	Chelsea Public Library, Chelsea, MA [*Library symbol*] [*Library of Congress*] (LCLS)
MChem........	Master of Chemistry (ADA)
MChemA.......	Master in Chemical Analysis
M Chem E ...	Master of Chemical Engineering
MCHF..........	Marine Corps Historical Foundation (EA)
MCHFR........	Minimum Critical Heat Flux Rates [*Nuclear energy*] (NRCH)
MCHFR	Minimum Critical Heat Flux Ratio [*Nuclear energy*] (NRCH)
MCHg..........	Mean Corpuscular Hemoglobin [*Hematology*] (DAVI)
MCHgb........	Mean Corpuscular Hemogobin [*Hematology*] (DAVI)
MCHGD	Mott Center for Human Growth and Development (EA)
MChi..........	Chicopee Public Library, Chicopee, MA [*Library symbol*] [*Library of Congress*] (LCLS)
MCHI	Mobile Communications Holdings, Inc.
MChiD	Dow Jones & Co., Inc., Chicopee, MA [*Library symbol*] [*Library of Congress*] (LCLS)
MChiL..........	College of Our Lady of the Elms, Chicopee, MA [*Library symbol*] [*Library of Congress*] (LCLS)
M Chir	Magister Chirurgiae [*Master of Surgery*]
MCHJ...........	Maternal and Child Health Journal (SAUO)
MCHL..........	Mayo Clinic Health Letter [*A publication*]
MCHL..........	Mean Corpuscular Hemoglobin [*Count*] [*Hematology*] (DAVI)
MCHM.........	MacroChem Corp. [*NASDAQ symbol*] (NQ)
MCHMAS	Michaelmas [*Feast of St. Michael the Archangel, September 29*] (ROG)
MCHML........	Macrochem Corp. Wrrt'A' [*NASDAQ symbol*] (TTSB)
MCHMM	Macrochem Corp. Wrrt'AA' [*NASDAQ symbol*] (TTSB)
MCHMN	Macrochem Corp. Wrrt'X' [*NASDAQ symbol*] (TTSB)
MCHN	Machine
MCHND........	Machined
M Ch Orth....	Master of Orthopaedic Surgery
M Ch Otol ...	Master of Oto-Rhino-Laryngological Surgery
MCHP	(Methylcinnamylhydrazono)propionate [*Biochemistry*]
MCHP	Microchip Technology [*NASDAQ symbol*] (TTSB)
MCHP	Microchip Technology, Inc. [*NASDAQ symbol*] (SAG)
MChP..........	Pine Manor College, Chestnut Hill, MA [*Library symbol*] [*Library of Congress*] (LCLS)
MCHPE	Manitoba Centre for Health Policy & Evaluation (SAUO)

MCHPRC......	Maternal and Child Health Policy Research Center (ADWA)
MCHQ	Marine Corps Headquarters (SAUO)
M'CHR.........	Manchester [*County in England*] (ROG)
MCHR	Medical Committee for Human Rights [*Defunct*]
mchr	Millicurie Hour (MAE)
M Chr Ed	Master of Christian Education
MCHRF........	Mechanically Refrigerated
MChrLit........	Magazine of Christian Literature (SAUO)
MChrom.......	Master of Chromatics [*British*]
MCHRY........	Machinery (MSA)
MCHS..........	Maternal and Child Health Service (EA)
MChS..........	Member of the Society of Chiropodists
MCHS..........	Microclimate Cooling/Heating System (ACAE)
M chs	Thousands (10^3) of Characters (NITA)
MCHSM.......	Mechanism
MCHST	Machinist (MSA)
MCHT..........	Merchant
MCHTR........	Maintenance Channel Transmit Receiver Register (MHDI)
M'CHTR	Manchester [*County in England*] (ROG)
MCHY..........	Machinery (ROG)
Mchy fwd.....	Machinery Forward (DS)
MCI.............	Data-Media Communications Co. (SAUO)
MCI.............	Kansas City [*Missouri*] [*Airport symbol*] (OAG)
MCI.............	Kansas City, MO [*Location identifier*] [*FAA*] (FAAL)
MCI.............	Machine Check Interrupt (NITA)
MCI.............	Machine Check Interruption [*Computer science*] (BUR)
MCI.............	Major Capital Improvement [*Justification for rent increase*]
MCI.............	Malicious Call Identification [*Telecommunications*] (TEL)
MCI.............	Malleable Cast Iron
MCI.............	Managed Cost Improvement (NRCH)
MCI.............	Management Charter Initiative (SAUO)
MCI.............	Management Consultants International, Inc. [*Information service or system*] (IID)
MCI.............	Management Cost Improvement (SAUO)
MCI.............	Management Counselors International Ltd. (SAUO)
MCI.............	Mandatory Customer Inspection (ACAE)
MCI.............	Manual of Clinical Immunology [*A publication*]
MCI.............	Marine Corps Institute
MCI.............	Marketing Concepts, Inc. [*New York, NY*] [*Telecommunications*] (TSSD)
MCI.............	Massachusetts Correctional Institution (SAUO)
MCI.............	MassMutual Corp. Inv [*NYSE symbol*] (TTSB)
MCI.............	MassMutual Corporate Investors [*NYSE symbol*] (SPSG)
MCI.............	Master Configuration Index (MCD)
MCI.............	Material Concept Investigation (MCD)
MCI.............	Materials Cost Index
MCI.............	Matsushita Communication Industrial [*Japan*]
MCI.............	Maya Carga Internacional SA de CV [*Mexico*] [*ICAO designator*] (FAAC)
MCI.............	MCI Communications Corp. [*Associated Press*] (SAG)
MCI.............	MCI Communications, Incorporated (SAUO)
MCI.............	Mead Carney International Company (SAUO)
MCI.............	Meal, Combat, Individual [*Military*] (AABC)
MCI.............	Mean Cardiac Index
MCI.............	Media Control Interface
MCI.............	Megacurie
MCI.............	Member Canadian Credit Institute (SAUO)
MCI.............	Member of the Concrete Institute (SAUO)
MCI.............	Member of the Credit Institute
MCI.............	Member of the Institute of Commerce [*British*] (DBQ)
MCI.............	Meridian Control Integrator
MCI.............	Methicillin [*Medicine*] (DMAA)
MCI.............	Metropolitan Convalescent Institution (SAUO)
MCI.............	Mexican Coffee Institute (EA)
MCI.............	Microelectronics Computer Corp. (SAUO)
McI	Microfilm Center, Incorporated, Dallas, Texas [*Library symbol*] [*Library of Congress*] (LCLS)
McI	Microplex, Inc., Dallas, TX [*Library symbol*] [*Library of Congress*] (LCLS)
MCI.............	Microwave Communications Inc. (NITA)
MCI.............	Microwave Communications of America, Inc.
MCI.............	MIDAS Component Index (SAUO)
MCI.............	Midland Counties Institution of Engineers (SAUO)
MCI.............	Milk Can Institute [*Defunct*]
mCi.............	Millicurie [*Also, mC*]
MCI.............	Ministry of Commerce and Industry [*Korea*]
MCI.............	Minnesota Counseling Inventory [*Psychology*]
MCI.............	Mission Capability Inspection (SAUO)
MCI.............	Mission Change Indicator [*Air Force*] (AFIT)
MCI.............	Monetary Conditions Index
MCI.............	Monitor Call Instruction (ELAL)
MCI.............	Monte Cassino [*Italy*] [*Seismograph station code, US Geological Survey*] [*Closed*] (SEIS)
MCI.............	Mother and Child International [*Switzerland*] (EAIO)
MCI.............	Motor Coach Industries (SAUO)
MCI.............	Motor Coach Industries International, Inc. (EFIS)
MCI.............	Motor Coach Institute (SAUO)
MCI.............	Motorcycle Industry Association of Great Britain (EAIO)
MCI.............	Mottled Cast Iron
MCI.............	Mucociliary Insufficiency [*Medicine*] (DMAA)
MCI.............	Multichip Integration [*Computer science*] (PDAA)
MCI.............	Muscle Contraction Interference [*Medicine*] (DMAA)
MCIA..........	Methyl Chloride Industry Alliance (SAUO)
MCIA..........	Methyl Chloride Industry Association (EA)
MCIA..........	MicroComputer Investors Association [*Database producer*] (EA)

MCIA............	Mirror Class International Association (SAUO)
MCIAS	Multi-Channel Intelligent/Intercept Announcement System [*Telecommunications*] (DBQ)
MCIBS	Member of the Chartered Institution of Building Services [*British*] (DBQ)
MCIC............	Machine Check Interruption Code [*Computer science*]
MCIC............	Managed Care Information Center (ADWA)
MCIC............	Management Control Information Center (SAUO)
MCIC............	Marine Corps Intelligence Center (DOMA)
MCIC............	MCI Communications [*NASDAQ symbol*] (TTSB)
MCIC............	MCI Communications Corp. [*NASDAQ symbol*] (NQ)
MCIC............	Medical Care Insurance Commission [*Canada*]
MCIC............	Member of the Chemical Institute of Canada
MCIC............	Metals and Ceramics Information Center [*Battelle Memorial Institute*] [*DoD*] [*Information service or system*] (IID)
MCIC............	Micro-Computer Information Center (ACAE)
McIC	Micro Industrial Corp., Bayville, NJ [*Library symbol*] [*Library of Congress*] (LCLS)
MCICU	Medical Coronary Intensive Care Unit (DMAA)
MCID	Malicious Call Identification [*Telecommunications*] (DOM)
MCID	Minimum Clinically Important Difference [*Medicine*] (DMAA)
MCID	Multipurpose Concealed Intrusion Detector [*Army*] (RDA)
McIDAS.......	Man computer Interactive Data Access System (SAUO)
McIDAS.......	Man-Computer Interactive Data Access System
MCIDAS.......	Man-Computer Interactive Data Acquisition System (SAUO)
McIDAS.......	Mancomputer Interactive Data Analysis System (SAUO)
MCIE...........	Midland Counties Institute of Engineers (SAUO)
MCIF	Member of the Canadian Institute of Forestry
mCihr...........	Millicurie Hour (MAE)
MCIM..........	Member Canadian Institute of Mining and Metallurgy (DD)
MCIM..........	Member of the Canadian Institute of Mining
MCIMM.......	Member of the Canadian Institute of Mining and Metallurgy
McIn & E Jud Pr...	McIntyre and Evans' Judicature Practice [*A publication*] (DLA)
McInc...........	MAICO Micrographics, Inc., Wormleysburg, PA [*Library symbol*] [*Library of Congress*] (LCLS)
McInc...........	Microcomfax, Incorporated, Camp Hill, PA [*Library symbol*] [*Library of Congress*] (LCLS)
McINP.........	Mclwaine National Park (SAUO)
MCINS	Minimal Change Idiopathic Nephrotic Syndrome [*Medicine*] (DMAA)
MCInstM......	Member of the Canadian Institute of Marketing (ASC)
McInt...........	McIntosh Music [*Record label*]
MCINTOSH...	Julian & Vera McIntosh Theatre, School of Music (SAUS)
MCIOB	Member of the Chartered Institute of Building [*British*] (DBQ)
MCIP...........	Mated Cast Iron Pair
MCIRA	Microelectronic Replacement Assembly (NG)
MCIS...........	Maintenance Control Information System (IEEE)
MCIS...........	Management Consultancy Information Service (SAUO)
MCIS...........	Management Controlled Information System (VLIE)
MCIS...........	Map and Chart Information System (MHDB)
MCIS...........	Maps and Chart Information System (SAUO)
MCIS...........	Master of Computer and Information Science (PGP)
MCIS...........	Master of Computer Information Systems (GAGS)
MCIS...........	Materials Compatibility in Sodium [*Nuclear energy*] (NRCH)
MCIS...........	Materials Control Information System (MHDB)
MCIS...........	Microsoft Commercial Internet System [*Computer science*]
MCIS...........	Multichannel Initial System (MCD)
MCIS...........	Multiple Corridor Identification System [*Air Force*]
MCISc..........	Master of Clinical Science (CMD)
MCIT	Institute of Traditional Science, Cambridge, MA [*Library symbol*] [*Library of Congress*] (LCLS)
MCIT..........	Member of the Chartered Institute of Transport [*British*] (DCTA)
MCIU	Manipulator Controller Interface Unit (NASA)
MCIU	Maryland Council for International Understanding (SAUO)
MCIU	Master Control and Interface Unit [*NASA*] (NASA)
MCIU	Mission Control and Interface Unit [*NASA*] (NASA)
M Civil E	Master of Civil Engineering (PGP)
MCJ	Maicao [*Colombia*] [*Airport symbol*] (OAG)
MCJ	Master of Comparative Jurisprudence
MCJ	Master of Criminal Justice (GAGS)
MCJ	Memory Control J Bus
MCJ	Michigan Civil Jurisprudence [*A publication*] (DLA)
MCJ	Model Car Journal Association [*Publishing company*] (EA)
MCJA..........	Master of Criminal Justice Administration (GAGS)
MCJC..........	Maryknoll Center for Justice Concerns (EA)
MCJC..........	Mason City Junior College [*Iowa*]
MCJR..........	Multichannel Jezebel [*Sonobuoy System*] Relay [*Military*] (NG)
MCK...........	Maintenance Check (FAAC)
MCK...........	Manson Creek Resources Ltd. [*Vancouver Stock Exchange symbol*]
MCK...........	Marital Check-Up Kit [*Test*] (TMMY)
MCK...........	Master Cook [*Navy*]
MCK...........	McCook [*Nebraska*] [*Airport symbol*] (OAG)
MCK...........	McCook, NE [*Location identifier*] [*FAA*] (FAAL)
MCK...........	McKesson & Robins, Inc. (SAUO)
MCK...........	McKesson Corp. [*Formerly, SP Ventures*] [*NYSE symbol*] (SPSG)
MCK...........	McKinley [*Alaska*] [*Seismograph station code, US Geological Survey*] (SEIS)
MCK...........	Mission/Communication Keyboard (MCD)
MCK...........	Modification Change Kit
MCK...........	M-Type Creatine Kinase (DB)
MCK...........	Multicystic Kidney [*Medicine*] (DMAA)
MCK...........	Muscle Creatine Kinase [*An enzyme*]
MCKA..........	Metal Cutting Knife Association (EA)
McK Consol Laws...	McKinney's Consolidated Laws of New York [*A publication*] (DLA)
MCKD	Multicystic Kidney Disease [*Medicine*]
MCKEES......	Marine Corps Key Experiences Evaluation System (MCD)
McKelvey Ev...	McKelvey on Evidence [*A publication*] (DLA)
McKesson...	McKesson Corp. (Associated Press) (SAG)
McKin Jus ...	McKinney's Justice [*A publication*] (DLA)
McKin Phil Ev...	McKinnon's Philosophy of Evidence [*A publication*] (DLA)
McKS...........	McKenzie Sanctuary (SAUO)
McKVHS	McKee Vocational High School (SAUO)
MCL	Intervega - Movement for Compassionate Living the Vegan Way (EAIO)
MCL	Lesley College, Cambridge, MA [*Library symbol*] [*Library of Congress*] (LCLS)
MCL	Machine Change Levels (SAUS)
MCL	Maintenance Checkoff List
M-CL	Managment List - Consolidated (IID)
MCL	Manchester Central Library (SAUO)
MCL	Manufacturing Control Language [*Computer science*] (MCD)
MCL	Manufacturing Cost Level (ACAE)
MCL	Marine Corps League (EA)
MCL	Mass Change Log (MCD)
MCL	Master Change Log
MCL	Master Clear Line (IAA)
MCL	Master Component List (MCD)
MCL	Master Configuration List
MCL	Master Control List
MCL	Master of Canon Law (PGP)
MCL	Master of Civil Law
MCL	Master of Comparative Law
MCL	Mathematics Computation Laboratory [*General Services Administration*]
MCL	Mature Corpus Luteum [*Medicine*] (MELL)
MCL	Mauritius Congress of Labour (SAUO)
MCL	Maximum Contaminant Level
MCL	Maximum Contaminant Levels
MCL	McClellan Central Laboratory (MCD)
M'Cl	McClelland's English Exchequer Reports [*A publication*] (DLA)
McL	McLaren Micropublishing, Toronto, ON, Canada [*Library symbol*] [*Library of Congress*] (LCLS)
Mc L	McLean's United States Circuit Court Reports [*A publication*] (DLA)
MCL	McNeil River [*Alaska*] [*Seismograph station code, US Geological Survey*] (SEIS)
MCL	Media Communication Lab (SAUS)
MCL	Media Communication Laboratory (SAUO)
MCL	Medial Collateral Ligament [*Anatomy*]
MCL	Medial Cruciate Ligament [*Anatomy*]
MCL	Medical Aviation Services Ltd. [*British*] [*ICAO designator*] (FAAC)
MCL	Medical College of Ohio at Toledo, Toledo, OH [*OCLC symbol*] (OCLC)
MCL	Memory Control and Logging [*Hewlett-Packard Co.*]
MCL	Memory Core Loader (VLIE)
MCL	Mercury Communications Limited (SAUO)
MCL	Message Control Language [*Computer science*]
MCL	Metal Control Laboratories (SAUO)
MCL	Metal Crystal Lattice
MCL	Metropolitan Central Library (SAUO)
MCL	Michigan Compiled Laws (AAGC)
MCL	Micro-Code Language (VLIE)
MCL	Microcomputer Center and Library [*Wisconsin State Department of Public Instruction*] [*Information service or system*] (IID)
MCL	Microcomputer Center/Library (SAUO)
MCL	Microcomputer Language [*Computer science*] (ECII)
MCL	Microprogram Control Logic [*Computer science*] (MDG)
MCL	Microsoft Compatibility Laboratories (VLIE)
MCL	Microwave Cavity Laboratories (SAUO)
MCL	Microwave Cavity Laboratory (IAA)
MCL	Mid-Canada Line [*RADAR warning chain of fence across Canada; sometimes called the McGill Fence*]
MCL	Midclavicular Line [*Medicine*]
MCL	Midcostal Line [*Medicine*]
MCL	Mid Course Late (ACAE)
MCL	Mineral Constitution Laboratories [*Pennsylvania State University*] [*Research center*] (RCD)
MCL	Miniature Cartridge Light
MCL	Mini Circuits Laboratory (IAA)
MCL	Minimal Computer Load
MCL	Minimum Clear Length (ACAE)
MCL	Ministering Children's League [*Australia*]
MCL	Minority Carrier Lifetime [*Solar cell technology*]
MCL	Missile Continuity Loop (MCD)
MCL	Mobilization Cross-Leveling (SAUO)
MCL	Modified Chest Lead [*Medicine*]
MCL	Molten-Caustic-Leaching [*Coal technology*]
MCL	Monitor Control Language [*Computer science*] (ELAL)
MCL	Moore & McCormack Lines, Inc. (SAUO)
MCL	Moore Corp. Ltd. [*NYSE symbol*] [*Toronto Stock Exchange symbol*] (SPSG)
MCL	Moore McCormack Resources, Inc. (SAUO)
MCL	Most Comfortable Level [*Referring to sound level*] [*Otorhinolaryngology*] (DAVI)
MCL	Most Comfortable Loudness Test [*Audiometry*]
MCL	Moving Coil Loudspeaker [*Electronics*]
MCL	Mucocutaneous Leishmaniasis [*Medicine*]
MCL	Multicolor LASER
MCL	Mushroom Canners League (EA)
MCLA	Marine Corps League Auxiliary (EA)
MCLA	Medical Contact Lens Association [*British*]

MCLA	Michigan Compiled Laws, Annotated [*A publication*] (DLA)
MCLA	Microcoded Communications Line Adapter
MCLA	Micro-Coded Communications Link Adaptor (NITA)
MCLA	Monetary Centre for Latin America (SAUO)
MCLA	Motor Carrier Lawyers Association (EA)
MCLAA	Minnesota Computer Literacy and Awareness Assessment (EDAC)
MCLAMS	Measurement, Control, LEID [*Limit of Error of the Inventory Difference*], and MUF Inventory Difference Simulation [*Material Unaccounted For*] [*Nuclear energy*] (NRCH)
McL & R	McLean and Robinson's Scotch Appeal Cases [*1839*] [*A publication*] (DLA)
M'Cl & Y	McClelland and Younge's English Exchequer Reports [*1824-25*] [*A publication*] (DLA)
M'Cl & Yo	M'Clelland and Younge's English Exchequer Reports [*148 English Reprint*] [*A publication*] (DLA)
McLar Tr	McLaren's Trusts in Scotland [*A publication*] (DLA)
McLar W	McLaren's Law of Wills [*Scotland*] [*A publication*] (DLA)
M-CLASS	Mobile CLASS [*Cross-Chain Long-Range Navigation Atmospheric Sounding System*] (USDC)
MCLB	Marine Corps Logistics Base (DOMA)
MCLBA	Marine Corps Logistics Base Albany (SAUO)
MClBiochem	Master of Clinical Biochemistry
MCLC	Lesley College, Cambridge, MA [*Library symbol*] [*Library of Congress*] (LCLS)
MCLC	Main Catalog of the Library of Congress (SAUO)
MCLC	Mine Clearing Line Charge [*Army*]
M Cl D	Master of Clinical Dentistry (PGP)
MCLD	McLeodUSA, Inc. [*NASDAQ symbol*] [*Formerly, McLeod, Inc.*] (SG)
MCLD	Multicolor LASER Display
MCLE	Mandatory Continuing Legal Education [*Australia*] [*A publication*]
M'Cle	M'Clelland's English Exchequer Reports [*148 English Reprint*] [*A publication*] (DLA)
McLean	McLean's United States Circuit Court Reports [*A publication*] (DLA)
M'Cle & Yo	M'Clelland and Younge's English Exchequer Reports [*148 English Reprint*] [*A publication*] (DLA)
McLean's CCR	McLean's United States Circuit Court Reports [*A publication*] (DLA)
McLean's Rep	McLean's United States Circuit Court Reports [*A publication*] (DLA)
M'Clel	M'Clelland's English Exchequer Reports [*148 English Reprint*] [*A publication*] (DLA)
M'Clel & Y	M'Clelland and Younge's English Exchequer Reports [*148 English Reprint*] [*A publication*] (DLA)
M'Clel & Y (Eng)	M'Clelland and Younge's English Exchequer Reports [*148 English Reprint*] [*A publication*] (DLA)
M'Clel (Eng)	McClelland's English Exchequer Reports [*A publication*] (DLA)
MCLFDC	Marine Corps Landing Force Development Center
MCLG	Major Caliber Lightweight Gun [*Navy*] (MCD)
MCLG	Maximum Contaminant Level Goal [*Environmental Protection Agency*]
MCLI	Meiklejohn Civil Liberties Institute (EA)
MCLI5	Manual of Clinical Laboratory Immunology, Fifth Edition (SAUO)
MClinPsych	Master of Clinical Psychology
MClinPsychol	Master of Clinical Psychology (ADA)
MClinSc	Master of Clinical Science (ADA)
MCLJ	Mifflin County Legal Journal [*Pennsylvania*] [*A publication*] (DLA)
MCLK	Master Clock
MCLL	Metrocall, Inc. [*NASDAQ symbol*] (SAG)
MCLL	Missile Compartment, Lower Level
MCLL	Most Comfortable Loudness Level [*On audiometry*] [*Otorhinolaryngology*] (DAVI)
MCLN	Mouvement Centrafricain de Liberation Nationale [*Central African Movement for National Liberation*] (PD)
MCLNS	Mucocutaneous Lymph Node Synrome [*Kawasaki's disease*] (DAVI)
MCLO	Marine Corps Liaison Office (ACAE)
MCLO	Medical Construction Liaison Office [*or Officer*] [*Air Force*] (AFM)
MCLOF	Market Center Limit Order File [*Investment term*] (DICI)
MCLong	Longfellow House, Longfellow National Historic Site, Cambridge, MA [*Library symbol*] [*Library of Congress*] (LCLS)
MCLORA	Marine Corps Level of Repair Analysis
MCLOS	Manual Command-to-Line-of-Sight [*Missile guidance system*] (INF)
MCLOSA	Member of the Continental Law Office Society of America (SAUO)
MCLP	Military Committee Representative Liaison Paper to the International Staff [*North Atlantic Council*] (NATG)
MCLR	Maximum Cell Loss Ratio (SAUS)
MCLR	Midwest Center for Labor Research (EA)
MCLR	Minimum Critical Leaching Rate
MCLS	Maintenance Contractor Logistic Support [*Army*]
MCLS	Metropolitan Cooperative Library System [*Library network*]
MCLS	Monroe County Library System [*Library network*]
MCLS	Mucocutaneous Lymph Node Syndrome [*Medicine*]
MCLSBLANT	Marine Corps Logistic Support Base, Atlantic (MCD)
MCLSBPAC	Marine Corps Logistic Support Base, Pacific (MCD)
MClSc	Master of Clinical Science (ADA)
MClSci	Master Clinical Science (DAVI)
MCLT	Maximum Cruise Level Thrust (MCD)
MCLUB	Mothers Club (SAUO)
MCLV	Missile Control & Launch Vehicle (SAUS)
MCLWG	Major Caliber Lightweight Gun [*Navy*] (NG)
MCM	Circular Mils, Thousands
MCM	Controladora Comercial Mexicana SA de CV [*NYSE symbol*] (SAG)
MCM	Controladora Comer'l Mex GDS [*NYSE symbol*] (SG)
MCM	Cordi-Marian Missionary Sisters [*Roman Catholic religious order*]
MCM	Cordi Marian Sisters (TOCD)
MCM	Heli-Air-Monaco [*ICAO designator*] (FAAC)
MCM	Mac-Am Resources Corp. [*Vancouver Stock Exchange symbol*]
MCM	Machine Control Medium (MCD)
MCM	Machines for Coordinated Multiprocessing
MCM	Macon, MO [*Location identifier*] [*FAA*] (FAAL)
MCM	MADS Control Module (SAUS)
MCM	Magnetic Card Memory [*Computer science*] (IAA)
MCM	Magnetic Core Memory [*Computer science*]
MCM	Maintenance Control Manual [*Canadian Airlines International*]
MCM	Maintenance Control Module [*Telecommunications*] (TEL)
MCM	Management Control Model (VLIE)
MCM	Manned Circumlunar Mission
MCM	Mannes College of Music [*New York, NY*]
MCM	Manual Communication Module [*Telecommunication device for the deaf*]
MCM	Manual Computer Makeready (DGA)
MCM	Manual for Courts-Martial
MCM	Manual of Clinical Microbiology [*A publication*]
MCM	Manufacturing Cycle Management (AAEL)
MCM	Marine Corps Manual
MCM	Massachusetts Institute of Technology, Cambridge, MA [*Library symbol*] [*Library of Congress*] (LCLS)
MCM	Mass Control Module
MCM	Master Control Module
MCM	Master of Christian Ministry (PGP)
MCM	Master of Church Management (PGP)
MCM	Master of Church Music
MCM	Master of Clinical Microbiology (PGP)
MCM	Master of Construction Management (PGP)
MCM	Materiel Change Management
MCM	McCarthy, Crisanti & Maffei, Inc. [*Information service or system*] (IID)
McM	McMaster University (SAUO)
MCM	McMurdo Sound [*Antarctica*] [*Seismograph station code, US Geological Survey*] [*Closed*] (SEIS)
MCM	Mechanical Current Meter [*Marine science*] (OSRA)
MCM	Media and Communication Management (SAUO)
MCM	Medical Corps, Merchant Marine [*USNR officer designation*]
MCM	Mega Cisterna Magna [*Medicine*]
MCM	Megawatt Cassegrain Monopulse
MCM	Melt Compression Molding [*Plastics*]
MCM	Member of the College of Musicians [*British*]
MCM	Memory Control Module
MCM	Meningococcal Meningitis [*Medicine*] (MELL)
MCM	Merged Charge Memory [*Computer science*] (IAA)
MCM	Message Control Module
MCM	Metastatic Carcinomatous Meningitis [*Medicine*] (MELL)
MCM	Microchip Module
MCM	Microcircuit Module
MCM	Microcomputer Machine (IAA)
McM	Micromedia Ltd., Toronto, ON, Canada [*Library symbol*] [*Library of Congress*] (LCLS)
MCM	Microwave Circuit Module [*Computer science*] (IAA)
MCM	Mid-continent Mapping Center (SAUO)
MCM	Mid Course Maneuver (ACAE)
MCM	Military Characteristics Motor Vehicles
MCM	Military Committee Memoranda (SAUO)
MCM	Military Committee Memorandum [*NATO*] (NATG)
MCM	Milli Circular Mil (IAA)
MCM	Million Centimeters (MCD)
Mcm	Million cubic metre (SAUS)
MCM	Mine Countermeasures (NG)
MCM	Mine Countermeasures Ship (SAUO)
MCM	Minichromosome Maintenance [*Cytology*]
MCM	Ministerial Council Meeting (SAUO)
MCM	Minneapolis College of Music
MCM	Miscellaneous Contract Material
MCM	Missile Carrying Missile (AAG)
MCM	Missile Control Module (NVT)
MCM	Missile Coordination Meeting (SAUO)
MCM	Mission Communications Manager (SSD)
MCM	Mission Control Module
MCM	Mississippi College, Clinton, MS [*OCLC symbol*] (OCLC)
MCM	Mitsubishi Common Modules (SAUS)
MCM	Mobile Cinetheodolite Mounts (SAA)
MCM	Mode Control Message (MCD)
MCM	Modular Auxiliary Data System Control Module [*Aerospace*] (NAKS)
MCM	Monolithic Circuit Mask
MCM	Monte Carlo [*Monaco*] [*Airport symbol*] (OAG)
MCM	Monte Carlo Method [*Computer science*]
MCM	Moving Coil Microphone [*Electronics*]
MCM	Moving Coil Motor [*Electronics*] (IAA)
MCM	Multi-Channel Multiplex (VLIE)
MCM	Multichipmodul (SAUO)
MCM	Multichip Module [*Computer science*]
MCM	Multi-Command Manual (SAUS)
MCM	Multilayer Ceramic Multichip [*Electronics*]
MCM	Multinational Computer Models, Inc. [*Information service or system*] (IID)
MCM	Multiple Connected Motor
MCM	Multiple Constant Multiplication (VLIE)
MCM	Multiple Contact Miscible [*Physical chemistry*]
MCM	Multiply-Convolve-Multiply (SAUS)
MCM	Municipal Court of Montreal (DLA)
MCM	Thousand Circular Mils
MCM6	Manual of Clinical Microbiology, 6th Edition (SAUO)
MCMA	Machine Chain Manufacturers Association (EA)

MCMA.........	Marine Corps Mustang Association (EA)
MCMA.........	Metal Cookware Manufacturers Association [*Later, CMA*] (EA)
MCMA.........	Mexico City Metropolitan Area (SAUO)
MCMAI.......	Milton Clinical Multi-Axial Inventory [*Psychology*] (DAVI)
McMas RR...	McMaster's New York Railroad Laws [*A publication*] (DLA)
MCMB.........	Multiple Conductor, Marker Buoy (IAA)
MCMC.........	Marine Corps Memorial Commission
MCMC.........	Markov Chain Monte Carlo (IDAI)
MCMC.........	Markov Chain Monte Carlo Method
MCM-C	MCM-Ceramic (SAUS)
MCMC.........	MCM Corp. [*NASDAQ symbol*] (NQ)
MCMC.........	Medicine Cabinet Manufacturers Council (EA)
MCMC.........	Midwest Committee for Military Counseling (EA)
MCMC.........	Military Construction, Marine Corps (DNAB)
MCMCAT.....	Mine Countermeasures Catamaran [*Military*]
MCMCC.......	Marine Corps Manpower Control Center (SAUO)
MCMCC.......	Marine Corps Movement Coordination Center (DNAB)
MCMCC.......	Mid-Century Mercury Car Club (EA)
McM Com Cas...	McMaster's United States Commercial Cases [*A publication*] (DLA)
McM Com Dec...	McMaster's Commercial Decisions [*A publication*] (DLA)
MCM Cp	MCM Corp. [*Associated Press*] (SAG)
MCM/CS	Mine Countermeasures/Command and Support Ship (MILB)
MCM-D	MCM-Dielectric (SAUS)
McMdL	Micromedia Ltd., Toronto, ON, Canada [*Library symbol*] [*Library of Congress*] (LCLS)
MCMES.......	Member of the Civil and Mechanical Engineering Society
MCMF.........	Marie Curie Memorial Foundation (SAUO)
MCM-F........	Massachusetts Institute of Technology, University Film Study Center, Cambridge, MA [*Library symbol*] [*Library of Congress*] (LCLS)
MCMFA.......	Meeting of Consultation of Ministers of Foreign Affairs
MCMFE.......	Membrane-Covered Mercury Film Electrode [*Electrochemistry*]
MCMG	Man-Carrying Motion Generator [*Space-flight simulation*]
MCMG	Marine Corps Meteorological Group (COE)
MCMG	Military Committee Meteorological Group [*NATO*] (NATG)
MCM-H	Massachusetts Institute of Technology, Francis Russell Hart Nautical Museum, Cambridge, MA [*Library symbol*] [*Library of Congress*] (LCLS)
MCMH	Mine Counter-Measures Hovercraft [*Military*] (PDAA)
MCMHA	Metropolitan College Mental Health Association (EA)
MCMHC	Mine Countermeasures Helicopter Controller (MCD)
MCMI..........	Malleable Chain Manufacturers Institute [*Later, American Chain Association*]
MCMI..........	Millon Clinical Multiaxial Inventory [*Psychology*]
MCMI..........	Minneapolis Center for Microbiological Investigations [*Public Health Service*] (GRD)
MCMI-III	Millon Clinical Multiaxial Inventory-III (DIPS)
MCMIS........	Motor Carrier Management Information System [*BTS*] [*MM*] (TAG)
MCM-L........	Massachusetts Institute of Technology, Lincoln Laboratory, Lexington, MA [*Library symbol*] [*Library of Congress*] (LCLS)
MCML.........	Missile Compartment, Middle Level
MCMLA.......	Midcontinental Chapter of the Medical Library Association (SAUO)
MCMM........	Management Control - Material Management (IEEE)
MCMOPS.....	Mine Countermeasures Operations [*Military*] (NVT)
McMoRn......	McMoRan Oil and Gas Co. [*Associated Press*] (SAG)
MCMOS	Motorola Complementary Metal-Oxide Semi-Conductor [*Electronics*] (IAA)
MCMOV	Maize Chlorotic Mottle Virus [*Plant pathology*]
MCM-P	MCM-Plastic (SAUS)
MCMP........	Middle Constrictor Muscle of Pharynx [*Medicine*] (MELL)
MCMP........	Multi-Channel Multi-Port [*Telecommunications*]
MCMR	Medical Corps, Merchant Marine, General Service [*USNR officer designation*]
MC/MR	Minimum Change/Minimum Risk [*Mask design concept*] [*Army*] (INF)
MCMS	Marin County Medical Society (SAUO)
MCMS.........	Medical Corps, Merchant Marine, Special Service [*USNR officer designation*]
MCMS.........	Midwest Center for Mass Spectrometry [*University of Nebraska - Lincoln*] [*Research center*] (RCD)
M-CM-S	Mobility, Countermobility, and Survivability
MCMS.........	Multichannel Memory System [*Computer science*] (AAG)
MCMS.........	Multiple Countermeasure System
MCMST.......	Montana College of Mineral Science and Technology (SAUO)
MCMTA.......	MCM Tasking Authority (SAUS)
MCMU	Mass Core Memory Unit (MCD)
McMU	McMaster University (SAUO)
McMUL	McMaster University Library (SAUO)
McMul	McMullan's South Carolina Law Reports [*A publication*] (DLA)
McMul Eq	McMullan's South Carolina Equity Reports [*A publication*] (DLA)
McMull Eq (SC)...	McMullan's South Carolina Equity Reports [*A publication*] (DLA)
McMull L (SC)...	McMullan's South Carolina Law Reports [*A publication*] (DLA)
McMUMC....	McMaster University Medical Center (SAUO)
MCMUS	Manual of Courts-Martial, United States
MCMV.........	Maize Chlorotic Mottle Virus [*Plant pathology*]
MCMV.........	Mine Countermeasures Vessel [*or Vehicle*] (NATG)
MCMV.........	Mine Counter-Measure Vessel
MCMV.........	Murine Cytomegalovirus
MCMWTC ...	Marine Corps Mountain Warfare Training Center [*Bridgeport, CA*]
MCN...........	American Journal of Maternal/Child Health Nursing (SAUS)
MCN...........	American Journal of Maternal/Child Nursing (SAUO)
MCN...........	Mac Dan Aviation Corp. [*ICAO designator*] (FAAC)
MCN...........	MACIMS Communication Network (SAUO)
MCN...........	Macon [*Georgia*] [*Airport symbol*] (OAG)
MCN...........	Maintenance Communications Net (MCD)
MCN...........	Maintenance Control Number
MCN...........	Malignant Cystic Neoplasm [*Medicine*] (MELL)
MCN...........	Management Change Notice (MCD)
MCN...........	Management Control Number [*Army*] (AABC)
MCN...........	Manual Control Number
MCN...........	Manufacturing Change Notice
MCN...........	Manufacturing Control Number
MCN...........	Mapping Cylinder Neighborhood
MCN...........	Master Change Notice (KSC)
MCN...........	Master Control Number
MCN...........	Master of Clinical Nutrition
MCN...........	Material Change Notice (MCD)
MCN...........	Material Complaint Notice
MCN...........	MCN Corp. [*Formerly, Michigan Consolidated Gas Co.*] [*Associated Press*] (SAG)
McN...........	McNeil Laboratories, Inc. [*Research code symbol*]
MCN...........	McNeil Mantha, Inc. [*Toronto Stock Exchange symbol*]
MCN...........	MCN Financing [*NYSE symbol*] (SAG)
MCN...........	MCN Michigan LP [*NYSE symbol*] (SAG)
MCN...........	Mercury [*Nevada*] [*Seismograph station code, US Geological Survey*] [*Closed*] (SEIS)
MCN...........	Metropolitan Campus Network (SAUO)
MCN...........	MichCon (EFIS)
MCN...........	Micro Cellular Network [*Computer science*]
MCN...........	Micrococcal Nuclease [*Also, MN*] [*An enzyme*]
MCN...........	Midcourse Navigation [*Navy*] (IAA)
MCN...........	Military Construction, Navy
MCN...........	Minimal Change Nephropathy [*Medicine*] (DMAA)
MCN...........	Missing Children Network [*Defunct*] (EA)
MC-N	Mixed Cell Nodular [*Lymphoma*] [*Medicine*] (STED)
MCN...........	Molecular and Cellular Neuroscience [*A publication*]
MCN...........	Mouvement Congolais National [*Zaire*] [*Political party*] (EY)
MCN...........	Movimiento de Conciliacion Nacional [*National Conciliation Movement*] [*Dominican Republic*] [*Political party*] (PPW)
MCN...........	Musculocutaneous Nerve [*Medicine*] (MELL)
MCN...........	Museum Computer Network (NITA)
MCN...........	Museum Computer Network, Inc. [*American Association of Museums*] [*Research center*] (RCD)
McNagh......	Macnaghten's Select Cases in Chancery Tempore King [*A publication*] (DLA)
McNal Ev	Macnally's Rules of Evidence [*A publication*] (DLA)
MCNC........	Carberry/North Cypress Library, Carberry, Manitoba [*Library symbol*] [*National Library of Canada*] (NLC)
MCNC........	Microcomputer Numerical Control (IAA)
MCNC........	Microelectronics Center of North Carolina [*Research center*] (RCD)
MCNC........	Micromachining Center of North Carolina (SAUO)
MCNE........	Master Certified Netware Engineer (SAUO)
MCNE........	Master Certified Novell Engineer (SAUO)
McNeese St U...	McNeese State University (GAGS)
MCN F	MCN Financing [*Associated Press*] (SAG)
MCNG	Military Construction, National Guard
McN-JR.......	McNeil Laboratories, Inc. [*Research code symbol*]
MCNL.........	Military Committee of National Liberation [*Mali*] [*Political party*] (PPW)
MCNMI.......	MCN Michigan Ltd. [*Associated Press*] (SAG)
MCNP	Mammoth Cave National Park (SAUO)
MCNP	Massachusetts Coalition of Nurse Practitioners (SAUO)
MCNP	Mobile Network Computing Protocol (AEBE)
MCNP	Monitoring Completed Navigation Projects [*Army*]
MCNP	Mount Cook National Park (SAUO)
MCNPB	Marine Corps - Navy Publicity Bureau (SAA)
MCNPrT	MCN Mich L.P.9.375% Pfd [*NYSE symbol*] (TTSB)
MCNR	Military Construction, Naval Reserves
MCNRF.......	Military Construction, Naval Reserve Facilities
MCNRS	Meal Card Number Recording System (MCD)
MCNS	Member, Congress of Neurological Surgeons (CMD)
MCNS	Minimal Change Nephrotic Syndrome [*Medicine*] (DMAA)
MCNS	Multimedia Cable Networking Systems (AEBE)
MCNY	Museum of the City of New York
MCNZ	Medical Council of New Zealand (SAUO)
MCO...........	Aerolineas Marcos SA de CV [*Mexico*] [*ICAO designator*] (FAAC)
MCo...........	Concord Free Public Library, Concord, MA [*Library symbol*] [*Library of Congress*] (LCLS)
MCO...........	Magnetron Cutoff
MCO...........	Main Civilian Occupation
MCO...........	Maintenance Checkoff
MCO...........	Manged Care Organization
MCO...........	Manual Change Order (MSA)
MCO...........	Marine Corps Officer
MCO...........	Marine Corps Order
MCO...........	Mars Climate Orbiter [*NASA*]
MCO...........	Massachusetts College of Optometry
M Co...........	Master of Cosmology
MCO...........	Materials Characterization Organization (SAUO)
MCO...........	Medical Care Organization (STED)
MCO...........	Medicare Carve-Out [*Insurance*] (WYGK)
MCO...........	Merrill Lyn 6.00%'STRYPES' [*NYSE symbol*] (TTSB)
MCO...........	Merrill Lynch & Co. [*NYSE symbol*] (SAG)
MCO...........	Metal Catalyzed Oxidation [*Chemistry*]
MCO...........	Methodist Conference Office (SAUO)
MCO...........	Michigan Corrections Organization (SAUO)
MCO...........	Military City Online [*Computer program*]
MCO...........	Mill Culls Out [*Lumber*]
MCO...........	Mill Cuts Out [*Forest industry*] (WPI)
MCO...........	Minneapolis Community College, Minneapolis, MN [*OCLC symbol*] (OCLC)

MCO............	Miscellaneous Charges Order [*Business term*]
MCO............	Missile Checkout (NG)
MCO............	Missile Control Officer
MCO............	Mission Control Operation [*NASA*]
mco............	Mission Control Operations [*NASA*] (NAKS)
MCO............	Monaco [*ANSI three-letter standard code*] (CNC)
MCO............	Morocco Leather [*Bookbinding*] (DGA)
MCO............	Movement Control Officer [*Army*]
MCO............	Multi Column Option (DGA)
MCO............	Multicystic Ovary [*Medicine*] (MELL)
MCO............	Multiple Channel Oscilloscope
MCO............	Orlando, FL [*Location identifier*] [*FAA*] (FAAL)
MCO............	Orlando [*Florida*] International [*Airport symbol*] (OAG)
MCOA	Mastiff Club of America (EA)
MCOA	Music Center Opera Association [*Los Angeles*]
MCOAG.......	Marine Corps Operations Analysis Group
MCOAM	Material Control Order Additional Material
MCOA/P	Multi-Company Accounts Payable (MHDB)
MCOD.........	Multiple Cause of Death [*Highway safety*]
MCODA.......	Motor Cab Owner Drivers' Association [*British*] (BI)
M-COFT	Mobile Conduct of Fire Trainer [*Combat simulator*]
MCOG.........	Member of the British College of Obstetricians and Gynaecologists (DAS)
MCOGA.......	Mid-Continent Oil and Gas Association (EA)
MCogSc	Master of Cognitive Science
MCOHM	Military Community Oral Health Managers [*Army*]
MCOI	Minority Centers of Influence (DNAB)
MCOLF........	Marine Corps Outlying Landing Field
MCollH	Member of the College of Handcrafts (SAUO)
MCollP	Member of the College of Preceptors [*British*] (DBQ)
MCOM	Marketing Communications (SAUO)
M Com........	Master of Commerce
MCOM	Mathematics of Computation (IEEE)
MCOM	Metricom, Inc. [*NASDAQ symbol*] (SAG)
MCom..........	Minister of Commerce (SAUO)
MCOM	Missile Command [*Army*] (MCD)
MCOM	Mobility Command (SAUO)
M Com Adm...	Master of Commercial Administration
MComm.......	Master of Commerce (ADA)
M Comm......	Master of Commerce and Administration (ROG)
MCOMM	Minimize Communications
MComm.......	Minister of Commerce (SAUO)
M Comm A...	Master of Commerce and Administration (SAUO)
M Comm H...	Master of Community Health
MCommSc...	Master in Commercial Science (DD)
MCommun...	Master in Communication (DD)
M Comp.......	Master of Computing
M Comp E ...	Master of Computer Engineering (PGP)
M Comp L ...	Master of Comparative Law
MCompLaw...	Master of Comparative Law (NADA)
M Com Sc ..	Master of Commercial Science
MComSc......	Master of Computer Science
MCON	EMCON [*NASDAQ symbol*] (TTSB)
MCON	EMCON Associates [*NASDAQ symbol*] (NQ)
MCON	Military Construction
MCON	Military Construction-Navy (SAUO)
MCON	Moment Connections [*Computer Services Consultants Ltd.*] [*Software package*] (NCC)
MConsE	Member of the Association of Consulting Engineers [*British*] (EY)
MCOO	Monte Carlo Opera Orchestra (SAUO)
MCOP	Major Command Orientation Program [*Air Force*] (AFM)
MCOP	Marine Corps Ordnance Publication
mCOP	Measured Colloidal Osmotic Pressure [*Clinical chemistry*]
MCOP	Mission Control Operations Panel [*NASA*] (KSC)
MCOP	Multiple Conductor, Oil-Resistant, Portable [*Cable*]
MCOphth......	Member of the College of Ophthalmologists (SAUO)
MCOPR.......	Major Command of Primary Responsibility [*Air Force*] (AFM)
MCOPS.......	Millions of Complex Operations Per Second (SAUS)
MCOQ	Multiple Choice Objective Question (DA)
MCOR	Methodist Committee for Overseas Relief [*Later, UMCOR*] (EA)
MC/ORB......	Maritime Command Operational Research Branch [*Canada*]
MC/ORD......	Maritime Command Operational Research Division [*Canada*]
MC/ORD......	Military Command Operational Research Division (SAUO)
M'Cord Eq (SC)...	M'Cord's South Carolina Equity Reports [*A publication*] (DLA)
M'Cord L (SC)...	M'Cord's South Carolina Law Reports [*A publication*] (DLA)
MCOS	Microprogrammable Computer Operating System
MCoS	Military College of Science [*British military*] (DMA)
MCOS	Mission Control Operations Section (SAUO)
MCot............	Cotuit Library, Cotuit, MA [*Library symbol*] [*Library of Congress*] (LCLS)
MCOT.........	Missile Checkout Trailer
MCOT.........	Missile Control Officer, Trainer (NG)
MCOTEA	Marine Corps Operational Test and Evaluation Activity (CAAL)
mcoul	Millicoulomb (STED)
Mcoul	Millicoulomb
M Coun.......	Master of Counseling (PGP)
MCouns(Ed)..	Master of Counselling (Education) (ADA)
MCOV	Main Chamber Oxidizer Valve [*NASA*] (KSC)
MCOV	Modified Covariance (DMAA)
MCOW	Medical College of Wisconsin
MCoW..........	Wayside [*Minute Man National Historical Park*], Concord, MA [*Library symbol*] [*Library of Congress*] (LCLS)
MCOwi........	Moody's Corp. [*NYSE symbol*]
MCOY	Military Citizen of the Year (DNAB)
MCP............	Bear Stearns Companies, Inc. [*AMEX symbol*] (SAG)

MCP............	Bear Sterns 5.50%MRK'CHIPS' [*AMEX symbol*] (TTSB)
MCP............	Macapa [*Brazil*] [*Airport symbol*] (OAG)
MCP............	Macrophage-Capping Protein [*Biochemistry*]
MCP............	Main Call Process [*Telecommunications*] (TEL)
MCP............	Main Condensate Pump [*Navy*] (CAAL)
MCP............	Main Coolant Pump (NVT)
MCP............	Maintenance Control Panel [*Navy*] (CAAL)
MCP............	Maintenance Control Point (NG)
MCP............	Malawi Congress Party [*Nyasaland*] [*Political party*] (PPW)
MCP............	Malayan Communist Party [*Political party*]
MCP............	Malaysian Communist Party (SAUO)
MCP............	Male Chauvinist Pig [*Feminist term*]
MCP............	Managed Care Program (MELL)
MCP............	Management and Control of Provisioning (SAUO)
MCP............	Management Control Plan
MCP............	Manual Control Panel
MCP............	Manufacturing Change Point
MCP............	Marcana Petroleum Ltd. [*Vancouver Stock Exchange symbol*]
MCP............	Marine Corps Capabilities Plan (MCD)
MCP............	Maritime Company of Philadelphia (SAUO)
MCP............	Maritime Company of the Philippines (SAUO)
MCP............	Martinique Communist Party [*Political party*]
MCP............	Mary Cheney Library, Manchester, CT [*OCLC symbol*] (OCLC)
MCP............	Massachusetts College of Pharmacy [*Boston*]
MCP............	Master Change Proposal (KSC)
MCP............	Master Computer Program [*NASA*] (KSC)
MCP............	Master COMSEC Plan (SAUO)
MCP............	Master Control Program [*Burroughs Corp.*]
M Cp............	Master of Chiropody
MCP............	Master of City Planning
MCP............	Master of Community Planning (GAGS)
MCP............	Master of Community Psychology (PGP)
MCP............	Master of Counseling Psychology (GAGS)
MCP............	Materials Control Plan (NASA)
MCP............	Materiel Command Procedure [*Military*]
MCP............	Maximal Closure Pressure (STED)
MCP............	Maximal Coverage Problem [*Mathematical modelling*]
MCP............	Maximum Continuous Power
MCP............	Measure and Control Panel (ACAE)
MCP............	Measurements Control Procedure (KSC)
MCP............	Medical College of Pennsylvania
MCP............	Medical Continuation Pay [*Military*] (AABC)
MCP............	MEECN [*Minimum Essential Emergency Communications Network*] Communication Plan (MCD)
MCP............	Melanosis Circumscripta Precancerosa (STED)
MCP............	Melphalan, Cyclophosphamide, Prednisone [*Antineoplastic drug regimen*]
MCP............	Member of the College of Preceptors [*British*]
MCP............	Member of the Colonial Parliament [*British*]
MCP............	Membrane Cofactor Protein [*Biochemistry*]
MCP............	Memory-Centered Processing [*or Processor*] [*System*] [*Computer science*]
MCP............	Message Control Program [*Computer science*]
MCP............	Metacarpal (STED)
MCP............	Metacarpophalangeal [*Anatomy*]
MCP............	Metaclopramide (STED)
MCP............	Meta-Cresol Purple [*Organic chemistry*]
MCP............	Metal Case Profile [*Ammunition*]
MCP............	Metal Casting Pattern (MSA)
MCP............	Meteacarpophalangeal [*Joint*] [*Anatomy*] (DAVI)
MCP............	Meteorological Communications Package (EOSA)
MCP............	Methyl-Accepting Chemotaxis Proteins [*Biochemistry*]
MCP............	Methylchlorophenoxyacetic Acid [*Also, MCPA*] [*Herbicide*]
MCP............	Methylcyclopentane [*Organic chemistry*]
MCP............	Metropolitan and City Police (SAUO)
MCP............	Microchannel Plate [*Computer science*]
MCP............	Microcrystalline Polymer [*Plastics technology*]
McP............	Micro Photo Division, Bell & Howell Co., Wooster, OH [*Library symbol*] [*Library of Congress*] (LCLS)
MCP............	Microsoft Certified Professional (SAUO)
MCP............	Microwave Coupled Plasma [*Spectroscopy*]
MCP............	Midclavicular Plane [*Medicine*] (MELL)
MCP............	Military Construction Plan
MCP............	Military Construction Program (AFIT)
MCP............	Military Construction Project (SAUO)
MCP............	Militia Career Program [*DoD*]
MCP............	Minimum Convex Polygon
MCP............	Missile Control Panel
MCP............	Missile Control Point (NATG)
MCP............	Mission Concept Paper (MCD)
MCP............	Mission Control Processor (ACAE)
MCP............	Mission Control Programmer [*NASA*] (NAKS)
MCP............	Missioneras Catequestas de los Pobres (TOCD)
MCP............	Mitotic-Control Protein [*Cytology*] (MAE)
MCP............	Moca [*Puerto Rico*] [*Seismograph station code, US Geological Survey*] (SEIS)
MCP............	Mode Control Panel
MCP............	Model Cities Program
MCP............	Monitoring and Control Panel (NASA)
MCP............	Monitoring Control Panel (SAUS)
MCP............	Monocalcium Phosphate [*Inorganic chemistry*] [*Food additive*]
MCP............	Monocyte Chemotactic Protein [*Biochemistry*]
MCP............	Monte Capellino [*Italy*] [*Later, ROB*] [*Geomagnetic observatory code*]
MCP............	Mouvement Chretien pour la Paix [*Christian Movement for Peace - CMP*] [*Brussels, Belgium*] (EAIO)

MCP	Movimiento Civico Popular [*Panama*] [*Political party*] (EY)
MCP	Mucin Clot-Prevention [*Test*] [*Medicine*] (STED)
MCP	Mullet-Channel Plate [*Spectrometry*]
MCP	Multibeam Communication Package (SAUS)
MCP	Multicatalytic Proteinase [*An enzyme*]
MCP	Multichannel Communications Program (IEEE)
MCP	Multichip Package (AAEL)
MCP	Multicomponent Plasma
MCP	Multiple-Chip Package
MCP	Multiple Comparison Procedure [*Statistics*]
MCP	Multiple Control Program [*Computer science*]
MCP	Municipal Compliance Plan [*Environmental Protection Agency*] (GFGA)
MCP	Mutation as Cellular Process
MCP	Polaroid Corp., Cambridge, MA [*Library symbol*] [*Library of Congress*] (LCLS)
MCPA	Member of the Canadian Psychological Association
MCPA	Member of the College of Pathologists Australasia
MCPA	Member of the College of Pathologists of Australia (SAUO)
MCPA	Memory Clock Pulse Amplifier
MCPA	Methylchlorophenoxyacetic Acid [*Also, MCP*] [*Herbicide*]
MCPA	Methylenecyclopropylacetic Acid [*Organic chemistry*]
MCPA	Michigan Concrete Paving Association (SAUO)
McPA	Microfilm Corp. of Pennsylvania, Pittsburgh, PA [*Library symbol*] [*Library of Congress*] (LCLS)
MCPA	Midwest College Placement Association
MCPA	Mine Clearance Planning Agency (SAUO)
MCPAC	Military Construction Programs Advisory Committee (AFM)
MCP/AS	Master Control Program / Advanced System (HGAA)
MC Path	Member of the College of Pathologists [*British*]
MCPBA	Meta-Chloroperoxybenzoic Acid [*Organic chemistry*]
MCPC	Manipulator Controller Power Conditioner (MCD)
MCPC	Multiple Channel per Carrier (ACAE)
MCPC	Musee Canadien de la Photographie Contemporaine [*Canadian Museum of Contemporary Photography - CMCP*]
MCPC	Parks Canada [*Parcs Canada*] Churchill, Manitoba [*Library symbol*] [*National Library of Canada*] (NLC)
MCPC	Polaroid Corp. Library, Cambridge, MA [*Library symbol*] [*Library of Congress*] (LCLS)
MCPD	Marine Corps Procurement District
MCPDM	Marine Corps Program Decision Meeting (DOMA)
MCPDP	Meander Channels Plasma Display Panel (IAA)
MCPE	Modular Collective Protection Equipment (RDA)
MCPER	Multiple Critical-Pole Equal-Ripple Rational (MCD)
MCPESCF	Multiconfiguration Paired Excitation Self-Consistent Field [*Physics*]
MCPF	Modular Containerless Processing Facility (SSD)
MCPF	Multichannel Peak Factor (IAA)
MCPG	Media Conversion Program Generator
MCPG	Methycarboxyphenglycine [*Biochemistry*]
MCPH	Metacarpophalangeal [*Anatomy*]
MCPH	Ministry of Concern for Public Health (EA)
McPherson	McPherson, Lee, and Bell's Scotch Session Cases [*A publication*] (DLA)
MCPI	Materiel Command Procurement Inspection (SAUO)
MCPI	Medical Consumer Price Index (DHSM)
MCPJ	Metacarpal Phalangeal [*Medicine*] (STED)
MCPL	Magnetic Circularly Polarized Luminescence [*Spectroscopy*]
MCPL	Mandatory Components Parts List (ACAE)
MCPL	Members of Congress for Peace through Law [*An association*]
MCPL	Middle Country Public Library [*New York*]
MCPL	Multiple-Cue Probability Learning [*Psychology*]
MCPM	Marine Corps Personnel Manual (SAA)
MCPM	Member of the Confederation of Professional Management [*British*] (DBQ)
MCPM	Moncalcium Phosphate Monohydrate [*Inorganic chemistry*]
MCPO	Master Chief Petty Officer [*Navy*]
MCPO	Military Committee Representative Communication to the Private Office of the NATO Secretary General (NATG)
MCPOC	Master Chief Petty Officer of Command [*Navy*]
MCPOF	Master Chief Petty Officer of the Fleet [*or Force*] (DNAB)
MCPOF	Metropolitan and City Police Orphan Fund (SAUO)
MCPON	Master Chief Petty Officer of the Navy
mCPP	M-Chlorophenylpiperazine [*Organic chemistry*]
MCPP	Mecoprop [*Herbicide*]
MCPPR	Marine Corps Program Progress Report
MCPQ	Municipal Code of the Province of Quebec [*A publication*] (DLA)
MCPR	Maximum Critical Power Ratio [*Nuclear energy*] (NRCH)
MCPR	Minimum Critical Power Ratio [*Nuclear energy*] (NRCH)
MC/PRI	Major Claimant/Priority Rating Indicator (MCD)
MCPS	Major Cost Proposal System (MCD)
MCPS	Mechanical Copyright Protection Society [*British*]
MCPS	Megachips per Second (MCD)
mcps	Megacycles per Second (STED)
MCPS	Megacycles per Second [*Megahertz*] [*See also MC/S, MCS, MH, MHz*]
MCPS	Member of the Cambridge Philosophical Society (ROG)
MCPS	Member of the College of Physicians and Surgeons [*British*]
MCPS	Microsoft Certified Product Specialist (SAUO)
MCPS	Military Committee in Permanent Session [*NATO*] (NATG)
MCPS	Mini Core Processing Subsystem (TEL)
MCPS	Missouri Children's Picture Series [*Child development test*] [*Psychology*]
MCPS	Montgomery County Public Schools [*Maryland*]
MCPT	Maritime Central Planning Team [*NATO*] (NATG)
MCPTM	Monte Carlo Particle Trajectory Model [*Physics*]
MCPU	Master Controller Processor Unit (MCD)
MCPU	Mine Clearance and Policy Unit (SAUO)
MCPU	Multiple Central Processing Unit
MCQ	Macquarie Island [*Australia*] [*Seismograph station code, US Geological Survey*] (SEIS)
Mcq	Macqueen's Scotch Appeal Cases, House of Lords [*A publication*] (DLA)
MCQ	Memory Call Queue [*Computer science*] (IAA)
MCQ	Multiple Choice Questions (ADA)
MCQC	Musicassette Quality Committee (NTCM)
MCQP	Milk Carton Quality Performing Council (EA)
MCQS	Member of the Chapter of Quantity Surveyors of the South African Institute of Architects (SAUO)
McQuillin Mun Corp	McQuillin on Municipal Corporations [*A publication*] (DLA)
MCR	Magistrates' Court Reports [*New Zealand*] [*A publication*] (DLA)
MCR	Magnetic Card Reader [*Computer science*]
MCR	Magnetic Character Reader [*Computer science*] (IEEE)
MCR	Magnetic Character Recognition [*Computer science*] (BUR)
MCR	Magnetic Confinement Reactor
MCR	Main Control Room (IEEE)
MCR	Maintenance Control Report
MCR	Management Coaching Relations Test
MCR	Management Consulting & Research Inc. (SAUO)
MCR	Management Control Review (AAGC)
MCR	Manpower Change Request (SAUO)
MCR	Manpower Control Report
MCR	Manual Change Request (MSA)
MCR	Manufacturing Change Request
MCR	Marine Corps Representative (SAA)
MCR	Marine Corps Reserve
MCR	Maryport & Carlisle Railway (SAUO)
MCR	Massachusetts Communications Research (SAUO)
MCR	Master Change Record
MCR	Master Clock Receiver
MCR	Master Control Record System (AABC)
MCR	Master Control Register
MCR	Master Control Relay [*Manufacturing term*]
MCR	Master Control Room (MCD)
MCR	Master Control Routine
MCR	Master of Comparative Religion
M Cr	Master of Criminology
MCR	Matrimonial Causes Rules [*A publication*] (DLA)
MCR	Maximum Combat Readiness [*Military*]
MCR	Maximum Continuous Rating [*Also, MC(S)R*] [*Mechanical engineering*]
MCR	McCloud River Railroad Co. [*AAR code*]
MCR	McCord Corp. (SAUO)
MCR	Medical Corps, General Service [*USNR officer designation*]
MCR	Medical Corps Reserve [*Military*] (DAVI)
MCR	Mediterranean Communications Region [*Air Force*] (MCD)
MCR	Melanocortin Receptor [*Biochemistry*]
MCR	Memory Control Register
MCR	Mercer [*Alaska*] [*Seismograph station code, US Geological Survey*] [*Closed*] (SEIS)
MCR	Message Competition Ratio (MAE)
MCR	Metabolic Clearance Rate
MCR	Methodists for Church Renewal
MCR	Metronome-Conditioned Relaxation
MCR	MFS Charter Income Tr [*NYSE symbol*] (TTSB)
MCR	MFS Charter Income Trust [*NYSE symbol*] (SPSG)
McR	Microcord Sales Corp., Chicago, IL [*Library symbol*] [*Library of Congress*] (LCLS)
MCR	Micro
MCR	Microcarbon Residue [*Petroleum analysis*]
MCR	Micro Copier-Reproducer (VLIE)
MCR	Micrographic Catalog Retrieval
MCR	Micron Industries Ltd. [*Vancouver Stock Exchange symbol*]
MCR	Microwave Cloud Radiometer (ACAE)
MCR	Middle Common Room (SAUO)
MCR	Military Census Report (SAUO)
MCR	Military Characteristics Requirement (MCD)
MCR	Military Command Region (MCD)
MCR	Military Communications Representative (SAUO)
MCR	Military Compact Reactor
MCR	Mine Clearing Roller [*Military*] (INF)
MCR	Minimum Cell Rate [*Telecommunications*] (ACRL)
MCR	Minuteman Change Request [*Air Force*] (IAA)
MCR	Missed Contact Rate (CAAL)
MCR	Missile Clock Receiver
MCR	Missile Computer Room
MCR	Mission Control Room [*Space Flight Operations Facility, NASA*]
MCR	Mission Control Routine [*NASA*]
MCR	Mobile Communication Radio (SAUO)
MCR	Mobile Control Room (DEN)
MCR	Mobilization Contracting Requirement (AFIT)
MCR	Modified Community Rating
MCR	Monacair-Agusta [*Monaco*] [*ICAO designator*] (FAAC)
MCR	Monitor Console Routine (VLIE)
MCR	Montreal Condensed Reports [*A publication*] (DLA)
MCR	Mother-Child Relationship [*Psychology*]
MCR	Motor Conduction Velocity (DB)
MCR	Multichannel Cloud Radiometer (SAUS)
MCR	Multichannel Receiver
MCR	Multi-Contact Relay (IAA)
MCR	Multispectral Cloud Radiometer (MCD)

MCR............. Mutual Climatic Range (QUAC)
MCR............. Myotonia Congenita, Recessive Type [Medicine] (DMAA)
MCR............. Radcliffe College, Cambridge, MA [Library symbol] [Library of Congress] (LCLS)
MCR............. University of Minnesota Technical College, Crookston, MN [OCLC symbol] (OCLC)
MCRA.......... Member of the College of Radiologists Australasia
MCRA.......... Member of the College of Radiologists of Australia (SAUO)
MCRA.......... Mitomycin C Resistance Protein A
McRae......... McRae Industries, Inc. [Associated Press] (SAG)
MCR-Ar........ Radcliffe College, Archives, Cambridge, MA [Library symbol] [Library of Congress] (LCLS)
MCRB.......... Magnetic Compass Record Book
MCRB.......... Market Compilation and Research Bureau, Inc. [North Hollywood, CA] [Information service or system] (IID)
MCRB.......... Military Cost Review Board (MCD)
MCRB.......... Motor Carrier Rate Bureau
MCRBBS....... Marine Corps Reserve Bulletin Board System (DOMA)
MCRBIO....... Microbiology
MCRBLGY.... Microbiology
M Cr C........ Madras Criminal Cases [A publication] (DLA)
MCRC.......... Marine Corps Recruiting Command
MCRC.......... Marketing Communications Research Center [Later, CMC]
MCRC.......... Mass Communications Research Center (SAUO)
MCRC.......... Master Component Rework Capability (MCD)
MCRC.......... Master Control and Reporting Center (SAUO)
McRC.......... Microfilm Recording Co., Weston, ON, Canada [Library symbol] [Library of Congress] (LCLS)
MCRC.......... Mobile Control & Reporting Centre (SAUO)
MCRD.......... Marine Corps Recruit Depot
MCRD.......... Marine Corps Requirements Document (MCD)
MCRD.......... Medullary Cystic Renal Disease [Medicine] (MELL)
MCRDAC....... Marine Corps Research, Development, and Acquisition Command [Quantico, VA] (GRD)
MCRDEP...... Marine Corps Recruit Depot
MCRDT........ Microdata
MCRE.......... MetaCreations Corp. [NASDAQ symbol] (SG)
McRe.......... Micrecord Sales Corp., Lombard, IL [Library symbol] [Library of Congress] (LCLS)
MCRE.......... Mother-Child Relationship Evaluation [Psychology]
MCREGIS.... Motor Carrier Regulation Information System [BTS] (TAG)
MCREL........ Mid-Continent Regional Educational Laboratory [Aurora, CO] [Department of Education]
MCRELCTRNC... Microelectronic
MCREP .... Military Committee Representative [to the North Atlantic Council] (AABC)
MCRep......... Military Committee Representative to the North Atlantic Council (SAUO)
MCRF.......... Master Cross-Reference File
MCRFCH...... Microfiche
MCRFP .... Monitoring of Chemical Residues in Food Products (SAUO)
MCRG .... Medical Career Research Group (SAUO)
MCRG .... Music Copyright Reform Group
MCRH .... Main Control Room Habitability [Nuclear energy] (NRCH)
MCRHS........ Main Control Room Habitability System [Nuclear energy] (NRCH)
MCRHS........ Mid-Continent Railway Historical Society (EA)
MCRI .... Cambridge Research Institute, Inc., Cambridge, MA [Library symbol] [Library of Congress] (LCLS)
MCRI .... Marine Craft Radio Installation
MCRI .... Microcirculation Research Institute [Texas A & M University] [Research center] (RCD)
MCRI .... Monarch Casino & Resort [NASDAQ symbol] (SAG)
MCRI .... Multifactorial Cardiac Risk Index [Cardiology] (DMAA)
MCRIB .... Naval Communications Improvement Review Board (DNAB)
MCrim .... Master of Criminology (GAGS)
MCRL.......... Mapping and Charting Research Laboratory [Ohio State University] (MCD)
MCRL.......... Marine Corrosion Research Laboratory [Navy] (PDAA)
MCRL.......... Master Component Repair List
MCRL.......... Master Cross Reference Library (SAUO)
MCRL.......... Master Cross-Reference List
MCRL.......... Material Cross-Reference List (MCD)
MCRL.......... Micrel, Inc. [NASDAQ symbol] (SAG)
MCRML........ Midcontinental Regional Medical Library (SAUO)
MCRML........ Midcontinental Regional Medical Library Program [University of Nebraska] [Library network] (IID)
MCRMLP ..... Midcontinental Regional Medical Library Program [McGoogan Library of Medicine] [Information service or system] (IID)
MCRN .... Macaroni
MCRN .... Micronics Computers [NASDAQ symbol] (SPSG)
MCRN .... Moscow City Relay Network
MCR (NZ) .... Magistrates' Court Reports (New Zealand) [A publication] (ILCA)
MCRO .... Medical Council and Registration Office (SAUO)
MCROA .... Marine Corps Reserve Officers Association (EA)
MCROC....... Marine Corps Recruit Option Center
MCROSCPY... Microscopy
MCRP .... Maritime Coal, Railway & Power Co. Ltd. [AAR code]
MCRP .... Master of City and Regional Planning (GAGS)
MCRR .... Machine Check Recognition and Recording (VLIE)
MCRR .... Machine Check Research and Recovery [Computer science]
MCRR .... Maine Central Railroad Co. (SAUO)
MCRR .... Maine Central Road Railroad (MHDB)
MCRR .... Marine Corps Reserve Ribbon
MCRR .... Medical Care Research and Review (SAUO)
MCRR .... Michigan Central Railroad (SAUO)

MCRR .... [The] Monongahela Connecting Railroad Co. [AAR code]
MCRRCMPTR... Microcomputer
MCRRD........ Marine Corps Reserve/Recruitment District
MCRS .... Maintenance Computing and Recording System
MCRS .... Marine Corps Recruiting Station
MCRS .... Material Condition Reporting System
MCRS .... Micrographic Catalog Retrieval System
MCRS-S .... Micros Systems, Inc. [NASDAQ symbol] (NQ)
MCR-S .... Radcliffe College, Schlesinger Library, Cambridge, MA [Library symbol] [Library of Congress] (LCLS)
MCRSC........ Marine Corps Reserve Support Center
MCRSCMS.... Marine Corps Reserve Support Center Management System (SAUO)
MCRSS .... Marine Corps Recruiting Substation
MCRT.......... Mean Cell Retention Time (GNE)
MCRT.......... Multichannel Rotary Transformer [Electronics]
MCRU.......... Medical Care Research Unit [University of Sheffield] [British] (ECON)
MCRU.......... Mobile Control and Reporting Unit (IAA)
MCRUD........ Michigan Coalition to Reduce Underage Drinking (SAUO)
MCRV.......... Manned Command/Reconnaissance Vehicle
MCRV .... Mechanised Combat Repair Vehicle (SAUS)
Mcrvsn........ Microvision, Inc. [Associated Press] (SAG)
MCRWV .... Microwave (AAG)
MCS............. esoscale convective system (SAUS)
MCS............. Harvard University, Monographic Cataloging Support Service, Cambridge, MA [OCLC symbol] (OCLC)
MCS............. MacCartney Clan Society (EA)
MCS............. Machine Cancel Society (EA)
MCS............. Machine Control System (VLIE)
MCS............. Machinery Control System (SAUS)
MCS............. Macmillan's Commercial Series [A publication]
MCS............. Madras Civil Service [British]
MCS............. Magnetic Card Selecting (DNAB)
MCS............. Magnetic Card Store [Computer science] (VLIE)
MCS............. Magnetic Character Sensing [Computer science] (VLIE)
MCS............. Magnetic Coupling System (MCD)
MCS............. Main Compution System
MCS............. Main Control Station [Nuclear energy] (IAA)
mcs............. Maintenance and Checkout Station (NAKS)
MCS............. Maintenance and Checkout Station [NASA] (NASA)
MCS............. Maintenance Control Section [DCE]
MCS............. Maintenance Control Subsystem [Computer science] (VLIE)
MCS............. Maintenance Control System [NASA] (IAA)
MCS............. Maintenance Cost System (MCD)
MCS............. Major Component Schedule (AAG)
MCS............. Malayan Civil Service
MCS............. Malignant Carcinoid Syndrome [Medicine] (MELL)
MCS............. Management Computing Services (SAUO)
MCS............. Management Consulting Services (SAUO)
MCS............. Management Control System (MCD)
MCS............. Maneuver Control System [Computer science]
MCS............. Manpower Consultative Service [Canada] (PDAA)
MCS............. Manufacturing and Consulting Services (PCM)
MCS............. Manufacturing Control System
MCS............. Mapping Camera System
MCS............. [The] Marcus Corp. [NYSE symbol] (SPSG)
MCS............. Marcus Island [Japan] [Seismograph station code, US Geological Survey] (SEIS)
MCS............. Marine Casualty Statistics (OA)
MCS............. Marine Conservation Society [British]
MCS............. Marine Cooks and Stewards (SAUO)
MCS............. Marine Cooks and Stewards Union
MCS............. Marine Corps School [Quantico, VA]
MCS............. Marine Corps Schools (SAUO)
MCS............. Marine Corps Station
MCS............. Marine Corps Supply Activity [Obsolete]
MCS............. Maritime Communications System (SAUO)
MCS............. Maritime Communication Subsystem [INTELSAT/INMARSAT]
MCS............. Mass Casualty Supplement [Military]
MCS............. Mast Check System
MCS............. Mast Connection System (SAA)
MCS............. Master Circuit System
MCS............. Master Composite Specification (MCD)
MCS............. Master Control Set (IAA)
MCS............. Master Control Station (NRCH)
MCS............. Master Control System [or Subsystem]
MCS............. Master of Clinical Science (PGP)
MCS............. Master of Commercial Science
MCS............. Master of Communication Studies (PGP)
MCS............. Master of Computer Science (WGA)
MCS............. Material Control Station (SAUO)
MCS............. Material Control System (AAEL)
MCS............. Mathematical Code System
MCS............. Maximal Compatible Set (PDAA)
MCS............. McChip Resources, Inc. [Toronto Stock Exchange symbol]
MCS............. Mean Crew Size (MCD)
MCS............. Measurements Calibration System (KSC)
mcs............. Measurements Calibration System (NAKS)
MCS............. Mechanical Control System [Aviation]
MCS............. Mechanized Characteristics Screening
MCS............. Medical Computer Services (IEEE)
MCS............. Medical Consultant Staff [Social Security Administration] (OICC)
MCS............. Medical Corps, Special Service [USNR officer designation]
MCS............. Medico-Chirurgical Society (SAUO)
MCS............. Medium Close Shot [Photography] (ADA)
MCS............. Meeting Communications Service (VLIE)

MC/s............	Megacycles per Second (VLIE)
MCS............	Megacycles per Second [*Megahertz*] [*See also MCPS, MH, MHz*]
MCS............	Meridian Control Signal
MCS............	Merritt-Chapman & Scott Corp. (SAUO)
MCS............	Merseyside Civic Society (SAUO)
MCS............	Mesocaval Shunt [*Medicine*] (DMAA)
MCS............	Mesoscale Cloud System (SAUO)
MCS............	Mesoscale Convective System [*Meteorology*]
MCS............	Message Control Supervisor [*Computer science*] (MHDI)
MCS............	Message Control System [*Burroughs Corp.*] [*Computer science*] (BUR)
MCS............	Message Conversion System (SAUO)
MCS............	Metachronous Seeding [*Medicine*] (MELL)
MCS............	Meter-Candle Second
MCS............	Method of Constant Stimuli [*Psychophysics*]
MCS............	Methylcholanthrene[*Induced*] Sarcoma [*Medicine*] (DB)
MCS............	Metropolitan Communications Squadron [*British military*] (DMA)
MCS............	Microcirculatory Society (EA)
MCS............	Microcirculatory Society of America (NTPA)
MCS............	Microclimatic Cooling System [*Army*] (DWSG)
MCS............	Microcode Control Storage [*Computer science*] (VLIE)
MCS............	Microcomputer System
MCS............	Microculture and Sensitivity [*Microbiology*] (DAVI)
McS............	Micromation Systems, Inc., Feasterville, PA [*Library symbol*] [*Library of Congress*] (LCLS)
MCS............	Microprocessor Communications System (MCD)
MCS............	Microprogram Certification System (MHDB)
MCS............	Microsoft Consulting Services (CDE)
MCS............	Microwave Carrier Supply
MCS............	Microwave Communication System
MCS............	Milestone Car Society (EA)
MC's............	Military Characteristics [*Technical specification document for nuclear bombs and warheads*]
MCS............	Military Communications Stations
MCS............	Military Communications Systems (SAUO)
MCS............	Miller Communications Systems Ltd. [*Telecommunications service*] (TSSD)
MCS............	Millimeter Wave Contrast Seekers (ACAE)
MCS............	Mine Countermeasures command, control & support Ship (SAUS)
MCS............	Mine Countermeasures Ship [*Navy symbol*]
MCS............	Mine Countermeasure Support [*Obsolete*] [*Military*]
MCS............	Mini-Computer Systems Inc. (NITA)
MCS............	Mini Conference System (PDAA)
MCS............	Minimal Cut Set [*Engineering*]
MCS............	Minimum Chi-Square
MCS............	Mining Certification Service (HEAS)
MCS............	Missile Calibration Station
MCS............	Missile Checkout Set (AAG)
MCS............	Missile Checkout Station
MCS............	Missile Commit Sequence (AAG)
MCS............	Missile Compensating System
MCS............	Missile Controller Set
MCS............	Missile Control System
MCS............	Missionary Sisters of the Sacred Side (TOCD)
MCS............	Mission Control Segment (SSD)
MCS............	Mission Critical Server (SAUS)
MCS............	Mitochondrial Capsule Selenoprotein [*Biochemistry*]
MCS............	Mixture Control Solenoid [*Automotive engineering*]
MCS............	Mobile Calibration Station (IAA)
MCS............	Mobile Checkout Station (AAG)
MCS............	Mobile Coastal Service (SAUO)
MCS............	Mobile Communications System (MCD)
MCS............	Mobile Computer System
MCS............	Mobile Control Station (SAUO)
MCS............	Model-Controlled System [*NASA*]
MCS............	Modular Charge System (SAUS)
MCS............	Modular Composition System [*Diskettes*]
MCS............	Modular Computer System (IEEE)
MCS............	Modulation-Controlled Synchronization (IAA)
MCS............	Module Control Station (ACAE)
MCS............	Moisture Control System (DB)
MCS............	Monitor and Control Software [*FAA*] (TAG)
MCS............	Monitor and Control Subsystem
MCS............	Monitor and Control System [*Deep Space Instrumentation Facility, NASA*]
MCS............	Monitoring Control System (SAUO)
MCS............	Monte Carlo Simulation [*Computer science*] (IAA)
MCS............	Monte Caseros [*Argentina*] [*Airport symbol*] (AD)
MCS............	Monthly Cost Summary (ACAE)
MCS............	Motion Compensation System (ACAE)
MCS............	Motor Circuit Switch
MCS............	Movements Control Section [*British military*] (DMA)
MCS............	Multicast Server (MLOA)
MCS............	Multi-Channel Communications Software (NITA)
MCS............	Multichannel Communication System (IAA)
MCS............	Multichannel Scaling [*Mode*]
MCS............	Multi Channel Seismics (SAUO)
MCS............	Multichannel Seismology [*Geophysics*]
MCS............	Multichannel Switch (IAA)
MCS............	Multichannel System (IAA)
MCS/s............	Multi-Chemical Sensitivity [*Medicine*] (MELL)
MCS............	Multi-Console System (NITA)
MCS............	Multidirectional Category System
MCS............	Multi-media Communications Station (SAUO)
MCS............	Multimedia Conference Service [*Telecommunications*] (CDE)

MCS............	Multiple Character Set (CMD)
MCS............	Multiple Chemical Sensitivities [*Medicine*]
MCS............	Multiple Chemical Sensitivity (SAUO)
MCS............	Multiple Column Selector (IAA)
MCS............	Multiple Combined Sclerosis [*Medicine*] (DB)
MCS............	Multiple Compression Shear (OA)
MCS............	Multiple Computer System
MCS............	Multiple Console Support [*Fujitsu Ltd.*] [*Computer science*] (MCD)
MCS............	Multiplexer Computer Systems (MCD)
MCS............	Multipoint Communication Services (SAUO)
MCS............	Multiprogrammed Computer System (IEEE)
MCS............	Multipurpose Communications and Signaling
MCS............	Multivender Customer Services (SAUO)
MCS............	Multivendor Customer Service [*Computer science*] (CDE)
MCS............	Music Construction Set [*Computer program designed by Will Harvey and published by Electronic Arts*]
MCS............	Myocardial Contractile State [*Cardiology*] (MAE)
MCS............	Residential Model Conservation Standard [*Pacific Northwest Electric Power and Conservation Planning Council*] [*Portland, OR*] (EGAO)
MCSA............	Malta Civil Service Association (SAUO)
MCSA............	Marble Collectors Society of America (EA)
MCSA............	Marine Corps Supply Activity [*Obsolete*] (NVT)
MCSA............	Medical Computer Services Administration (SAUO)
MCSA............	Meritorious Civilian Service Award
MCSA............	Methuen's Commercial Series [*A publication*]
MCSA............	Metropolitan Church Schoolmasters' Association [*A union*] [*British*]
MCSA............	Michigan Council for the Study of Abortion (SAUO)
MCSA............	Microcomputer Software Association - of ADAPSO [*Association of Data Processing Service Organizations*] (EA)
MCSA............	Midwest Collegiate Sailing Association
MCSA............	Military Construction Supply Agency [*Later, Defense Construction Supply Center*]
MCSA............	Minimal Cross-Sectional Area [*Radiology*] (DAVI)
MCSA............	Moloney Cell Surface Antigen [*Medicine*] (DMAA)
MCSA............	Moscow, Camden & San Augustine Railroad [*AAR code*]
MCSA............	Motor Carrier Safety Act of 1984 [*FHWA*] (TAG)
MCSA............	Multichannel Spectrum Analyzer [*Instrumentation*]
MCS-A.........	Multi-Functional Communications System - Asynchronous (HGAA)
MCSA............	Smithsonian Institution, Astrophysical Observatory, Cambridge, MA [*Library symbol*] [*Library of Congress*] (LCLS)
MCS&T.........	Manchester College of Science and Technology (SAUO)
MCSAP.........	Motor Carrier Safety Assistance Program [*Department of Transportation*]
MCSB...........	Milk Cap Statistical Bureau (SAUO)
MCSB...........	Motor Carriers Service Bureau
MCSC...........	Magdalen College School Cadets [*British military*] (DMA)
MCSC...........	Marine Corps Supply Center
MC Sc...........	Master of Commercial Science
MC Sc...........	Master of Computer Science (PGP)
MCSC...........	Materiel Category Structure Code [*Military*]
MCSC...........	Medical College of South Carolina
MCSC...........	Metropolitan Collegiate Swimming Conference (PSS)
MCSC...........	Miami Computer Supply Corp. [*NASDAQ symbol*] (SAG)
MCSC...........	Military College of South Carolina (SAUO)
MCSC...........	Model Codes Standardization Council [*Defunct*]
MCSC...........	Movement Control Sub-Committee [*IATA*] (DS)
MCSCF.........	Multiconfigurational Self-Consistent Field [*Chemical physics*]
MCSCF.........	Multiconfiguration Self-Consistent Field [*Physical chemistry*]
MCS/CHS....	Maneuver Control System / Common Hardware System [*Computer science*]
MCSD.........	Marine Corps Supply Depot (MUGU)
MCSD.........	Mediterranean Commission on Sustainable Development (SAUO)
MCSD.........	Microsoft Certified Solution Developer (SAUS)
MCSD.........	Microsoft Certified Systems Developer (SAUO)
MCSDS.......	Marlowe-Crowne Social Desirability Scale [*Medicine*] (DMAA)
MC Se.........	Master of Commercial Service
MCSE.........	Master of Computer Science and Engineering (GAGS)
MCSE.........	Minimum Critical Size of Ecosystem [*Project*]
MCSEE.......	Member of the Canadian Society of Electrical Engineers (DI)
M-CSF.......	Macrophage-Colony Stimulating Factor [*Biochemistry*]
MCSF.........	Marine Corps Security Force (DNAB)
MCSF.........	Mobile Cryptologic Support Facility (DOMA)
MCSFE.......	Member of the Canadian Society of Forest Engineers (SAUO)
MCSG........	Mathematical and Computational Sciences Group (SAUO)
MCSG........	Mildly Context-Sensitive Grammar [*Artificial intelligence*]
MCSGX.......	Mainstay Government Fund [*Mutual fund ticker symbol*] (SG)
MCSH.........	Manhattanville College of the Sacred Heart (SAUO)
MCSH.........	Maryville College of the Sacred Heart [*Missouri*]
MC Shp.......	MC Shipping, Inc. [*Associated Press*] (SAG)
MCSI...........	Mark Solutions [*NASDAQ symbol*] (TTSB)
MCSI...........	Mark Solutions, Inc. [*NASDAQ symbol*] (SAG)
MCSI...........	Member of the Construction Surveyors' Institute [*British*] (DBQ)
MCSJM.......	Congregation of Missionary Catechists of the Sacred Heart of Jesus and Mary (TOCD)
MCSK.........	Mine Clearance System Kit (SAUS)
MCSK.........	Multiple-Code-Shift Keying (CCCA)
MCSKR.......	Member of the Council, Secretary and Keeper of Records (SAUO)
MCSL.........	Management Control Systems List [*DoD*]
MCSL.........	Marconi Communications Systems Limited (SAUO)
MCSL.........	Marine Corps Stock [*or Supply*] Lists
MCSM.........	Master of Construction Science/Management (PGP)
MCSMAW....	Marine Corps Shoulder-Launched Multipurpose Assault Weapon (MCD)
MCSME.......	Member of the Canadian Society of Mechanical Engineers (SAUO)

MCSMP	Message Conversion System Message Processor (SAUS)
MCSO	Marine Corps Special Orders (SAA)
MCSOII	Multiple-Cause, Systems-Oriented Incident Investigation [Engineering]
MCSP	Maintenance Control and Statistics Process [Telecommunications] (TEL)
MCSP	Member of the Chartered Society of Physiotherapists [British]
MCSP	Member of the Chartered Society of Physiotherapy (SAUO)
MCSP	Mission Completion Success Probability (MCD)
MCSP	Multiple Conductor, Shielded, Pressure-Resistant [Cable]
McSPI	Multicenter Study of Perioperative Ischemia
MCSR	Material Condition Status Report [Military]
MCSR	Materiel Condition Status Reporting System (SAUO)
MC(S)R	Maximum Continuous (Service) Rating [Also, MCR] [Mechanical engineering]
MCSR	Mission Completion Success Rate (SAUS)
MCSR	Motor Carrier Safety Regulations [Department of Transportation]
MCSRP	Management Control Systems Research Project (SAA)
MCSS	Magnetron Compensator Signal Simulator (ACAE)
MCSS	Marine Climatological Summaries Scheme [World Meteorological Organization] [United Nations] (DUND)
MCSS	MATE Control & Support Software (SAUS)
MCSS	Mechanical Circulatory Support System
MCSS	Microscopic Camera Subsystem (KSC)
MCSS	Mid Course Surveillance System (ACAE)
MCSS	Military Clothing Sales Store
MCSS	Military Communications Satellite System
MCSS	Mine Countermeasure Support Ship [Military] (PDAA)
MCSS	Missile Checkout System Selector
MCSS	Missile Control Sub System (ACAE)
MCSS	Mitac Computer Security System (SAUO)
MCSS	Monitor and Control Subsystem [Deep Space Instrumentation Facility, NASA]
MCSSB	Manufacturers Council of Small School Buses (NTPA)
MCSSC	Multi-Color Spin-Scan Camera (ACAE)
MCSSCCJM	Missionary Catechists of the Sacred Hearts of Jesus and Mary (TOCD)
MCSSD	Mobile Combat Service Support Detachment (DOMA)
MCSSG	Military Committee Special Study Group [NATO] (NATG)
MCSSQT	Modified Combat System Ship Qualification Trial [Navy] (CAAL)
MCSST	Multichannel Sea Surface Temperature [Algorithms for oceanography]
MCSST	Multi-Channel SST [Sea Surface Temperature] (USDC)
MCST	Magnetic Card "Selectric" Typewriter [IBM Corp.]
MCST	Member of the College of Speech Therapists [British]
MCST	Ministerial Committee on Science and Technology [South Africa]
MCSTB	Motor Carriers Service Tariff Bureau
MCSTSC	Military Communications System Technical Standards Committee [Army] (AABC)
MCSU	Management Consultation Services Unit [LIMRA]
MCSU	Maximum Card Study Unit (EA)
MCSW	Mining Club of the Southwest (EA)
MCSW	Motor Circuit Switch (MSA)
MCSWG	Multinational Command Systems Working Group (NATG)
MCSX	Managed Care Solutions [NQS] (TTSB)
MCSX	Managed Care Solutions, Inc. [NASDAQ symbol] (SAG)
MCSY	Medic Computer Systems [NASDAQ symbol] (TTSB)
MCSY	Medic Computer Systems, Inc. [NASDAQ symbol] (SAG)
MCSYSCOM	Marine Corps System Command (DOMA)
MCT	Magnetically-Coupled Transformer (IAA)
MCT	Magnetic Card and Tape Unit (IAA)
MCT	Magnetic Character Typewriter (PDAA)
MCT	Magnetic Compass Table (DNAB)
MCT	Magnetic Core Tape
MCT	Magnetic Core Tester
MCT	Main Central Thrust [Geophysics]
MCT	Main Control Tank (MSA)
MCT	Mainstream Corporation Tax
MCT	Managed Change Technique [Management]
MCT	Manchester College of Technology (SAUO)
MCT	Manifold Charge Temperature [Automotive engineering]
MCT	MANPRINT [Manpower and Personnel Integration] Coordination Team [Army]
MCT	Manual Cervical Traction [Medicine] (MELL)
MCT	Maritime Crew Trainer (SAUO)
MCT	Mark Centers Trust [NYSE symbol] (SPSG)
MCT	Mass Culturing Technique [Microbiology]
MCT	Master Cycle Trader (SAUO)
MCT	Master of Christian Training
MCT	Mathematical Cuneiform Texts [A publication] (BJA)
MCT	Mature Cystic Teratoma [Medicine] (MELL)
MCT	Maximum Climb Thrust (NASA)
MCT	Maximum Continuous Thrust [Aviation]
MCT	Maximum Corrective Time (SAUO)
MCT	Maxwell Color Triangle
MCT	Mean Cell [or Corpuscular] Thickness [Hematology]
MCT	Mean Cell [or Corpuscular] Threshold [Hematology] (MAE)
MCT	Mean Circulation Time [Medicine]
MCT	Mean Corpuscular Thickness [Hematology] (CPH)
MCT	Mean Corrective-Maintenance Time (MCD)
MCT	Mean Corrective Time (SAUO)
MCT	Mean Corrective Times (SAUS)
MCT	Mean Correct Time
MCT	Mechanical Comprehension Test
MCT	Medial Canthal Tendon [Medicine] (DMAA)
MCT	Medium-Chain Triglyceride [Biochemistry]
MCT	Medium Combat Truck (SAUS)
MCT	Medullary Cancer of the Thyroid [Medicine]
MCT	Medullary Carcinoma of the Thyroid [Medicine] (AAMN)
MCT	Medullary Collecting Tubules [Anatomy]
MCT	Member of College of Technology (SAUO)
MCT	Member of the College of Technologists (SAUO)
MCT	Memory Cycle Time [Computer science] (MCD)
MCT	Mercury Cadmium Telluride [Photodetector]
MCT	Message Control Task [Computer science]
MCT	Metabolic Control Test (SAUS)
MCT	Metabolic Control Theory [Biochemistry]
MCT	Meta-Chlorotoluene [Organic chemistry]
MCT	Metal-Oxide-Controlled Thyristor (CIST)
MCT	Metric Color Tag [Computer science] (PCM)
MCT	Metrizamide Computed Tomography
MCT	Micro Component Technology Inc. (NITA)
MCT	Microsoft Certified Trainer (SAUS)
MCT	Microstat Development Corp. [Vancouver Stock Exchange symbol]
MCT	Microtoxicity Test [Medicine] (DB)
MCT	Microwave Ceramic Triode
MCT	Mid-Cycle Test [Army training] (INF)
MCT	MILAN Compact Turret (SAUS)
MCT	Military Combat Thrust (SAUS)
MCT	Military Command Technology (AAG)
MCT	Minimum Competency Test [Education]
MCT	Minimum Connecting Time [Travel industry]
MCT	Minnesota Clerical Test
MCT	Missile Compensating Tank
MCT	Mission Control Table (MCD)
MCT	Mobile Communication Terminal
MCT	Mobile Contact Teams [Military] (AABC)
MCT	Mode Coupling Theory [Physics]
MCT	Modified Clinical Technique [Medicine]
MCT	Module and Cell Tester (ACAE)
MCT	Moment to Change Trim (DS)
MCT	Monochlorotriazine [Organic chemistry]
MCT	Mouse Colon Tumor [Pathology]
MCT	Movable Core Transformer [Nuclear energy]
MCT	Movement Control Team [Air Force] (AFM)
MCT	Moving Coil Transducer (SAUS)
MCT	Mucociliary Transport [Physiology]
MCT	Multicell Test (MCD)
MCT	Multiple Compressed Tablet [Pharmacy]
MCT	Multistrip Cesium Thrustor
MCT	Muscat [Oman] [Airport symbol] (OAG)
MCT	United States Department of Transportation, Technical Information Center, Cambridge, MA [Library symbol] [Library of Congress] (LCLS)
MCTA	Metropolitan Commuter Transportation Authority [Greater New York City] [Later, Metropolitan Transportation Authority]
MCTA	Motor Carriers Tariff Association
MCTA	Motor Carriers Traffic Association
MCTA	Motor Carriers Traffic Association Inc. (SAUO)
MCTA	Multiple-Cycle Transient Analysis [Chemistry]
MCTAS	Military/Commercial Transport Aircraft Simulation (PDAA)
MCTB	Motor Carriers Tariff Bureau (EA)
MCTC	Golda Meir Mount Carmel International Training Centre (SAUO)
MCTC	Maritime Cargo Transportation Conference [of MTRB]
MCTC	Metrizamide Computed Tomography Cisternography [Medicine] (DMAA)
MCTC	Metropolitan Collegiate Tennis Conference (PSS)
MCTC	Microelectronics and Computer Technology Corporation (SAUO)
MCTC	Military Corrective Training Centre (SAUO)
MCTC	Movimiento Campesino Tupaj Catari [Bolivia] [Political party] (PPW)
MCTD	Maximum Cell Transfer Delay (SAUS)
MCTD	Medium Capacity Bomb with Temporary Delay Fuse [British military] (DMA)
MCTD	Mixed Connective Tissue Disease [Medicine]
MCTE	Michigan Council of Teachers of English (SAUO)
MCTEX	Marine Continent Thunderstorm Experiment (SAUS)
MCTEX	Maritime Continent Thunderstorm Experiment (SAUO)
MCTF	Monouclear Cell Tissue Factor [Medicine] (DB)
MCTFIST	Marine Corps Tank Full-Crew Interactive Simulator Trainer
MCTFL	Minnesota Council on the Teaching of Foreign Languages (EDAC)
MCTG	Model Change Training Guide
MCTH	MedCath, Inc. [NASDAQ symbol] (SAG)
MCTI	Metal Cutting Tool Institute (EA)
MCTI	Micro Component Tech [NASDAQ symbol] (TTSB)
MCTI	Micro Component Technology, Inc. [NASDAQ symbol] (SAG)
MCTI	Motion Compensated Target Identification (ACAE)
MCTL	Mediterranean Contingency Target List (MCD)
MCTL	Microtel Franchise&Development [NASDAQ symbol] (TTSB)
MCTL	Microtel Franchise & Development Corp. [NASDAQ symbol] (NQ)
MCTL	Microtel International, Inc. [NASDAQ symbol] (SAG)
MCTL	Militarily Critical Technology List [DoD]
MCTLA	Motor Car Traders' Licensing Authority [Victoria, Australia]
MCTNS	Manportable Cannon Thermal Night Sight (MCD)
MCTP	Missile Control Test Panel
MCTR	Mackinac Transportation Co. [AAR code]
MCTR	Message Center
MCTR	Military CTR (SAUS)
MCTRAP	Mechanized Customer Trouble Report Analysis Plan [Telecommunications] (TEL)
MCTRF	Manitoba Cancer Treatment and Research Foundation (SAUO)

MCTS............	Master Central Timing System [*NASA*]
MCT/S............	MILAN Combat Turret on Spartan (SAUS)
MCTS............	Ministerial Correspondence Tracking System [*Australia*]
MCTS............	Moravian College and Theological Seminary (SAUO)
MCTS............	Motor Carriers Tariff Service (EA)
MCTSA............	Military Clothing and Textile Supply Agency [*Merged with Defense Supply Agency*] [*Army*]
MCTSE............	Marine Corps Test Support Element (MCD)
MCTSSA	Marine Corps Tactical Systems and Support Activity [*Camp Pendleton, CA*] (GRD)
MCTT............	Metal-Ceramic Transmitting Tube
MCTV............	Man-Carrying Test Vehicle (MCD)
MCTV............	Manhattan Cable TV, Inc. [*New York, NY*] [*Telecommunications*] (TSSD)
MCU............	Machine Control Unit
MCU............	Machine Tool Control Unit (IAA)
MCU............	Magma Copper Co. [*NYSE symbol*] (SPSG)
MCU............	Magnetic Card Unit [*Computer science*] (IAA)
MCU............	Main Control Unit (IAA)
MCU............	Maintenance Communications Unit [*Environmental science*] (COE)
MCU............	Maintenance Control Unit [*Computer science*]
MCU............	Major Crime Unit [*Elite police squad on television series "Crime Story"*]
MCU............	Malaria Control Unit [*Army*] [*World War II*]
MCU............	Management & Cascade Unit (SAUS)
MCU............	Management Control Unit (PDAA)
MCU............	Manual Control Unit
MCU............	Marangoni Convection Unit (SAUS)
MCU............	Marble Collectors Unlimited (EA)
MCU............	Marine Corps University
MCU............	Marine Craft Unit (SAUS)
MCU............	Master Clock Unit
mcu............	Master Control Unit [*NASA*] (NAKS)
MCU............	Master Control Unit
MCU............	Maximum Care Unit [*Medicine*]
MCU............	Measurement Control Unit (IAA)
MCU............	Mechanism Control Unit (SPST)
MCU............	Median Control Unit (WDAA)
MCU............	Mediterranean Coordination Unit (GNE)
MCU............	Medium Close Up [*A photograph or motion picture sequence taken from a relatively short distance*]
MCU............	Memory Controller Unit (SAUO)
MCU............	Memory Control Unit
MCU............	Message Construction Unit
MCU............	Microcomputer Control Unit
MCU............	Microcontroller Unit (CDE)
MCU............	Micro-Control Unit (NITA)
MCU............	Microprocessor Control Unit
MCU............	Microprogram Control Unit (NITA)
MCU............	Microprogrammed Control Unit [*Navy*]
mcU............	Microunit
MCU............	Micturating Cystourethrography [*Medicine*] (DMAA)
MCU............	Millicurie [*Also, mC, mCI*] (IAA)
MCU............	Miniature Command Unit
MCU............	Minicomputer Unit (IAA)
MCU............	Missile Control Unit (SAUS)
MCU............	Mission Control Unit (MCD)
mcu............	Mission Control Unit [*NASA*] (NAKS)
MCU............	Mobile Calibration Unit
MCU............	Mobile Care Unit [*Emergency medicine*] (DAVI)
MCU............	Modern Churchmen's Union [*British*]
MCU............	Modular Concept Unit (DA)
MCU............	Moment Control Unit
MCU............	Monte Cristo Peak [*Utah*] [*Seismograph station code, US Geological Survey*] (SEIS)
MCU............	Mosquito Conversion Unit [*British military*] (DMA)
MCU............	Motor Cycle Union (SAUO)
MCU............	Mountain Commando Units (CINC)
MCU............	Multi-Chip Unit (SAUO)
MCU............	Multicoupler Unit [*Antenna*] [*Telecommunications*] (TEL)
MCU............	Multiplexer Control Unit
MCU............	Multipoint Control Unit [*Telecommunications*]
MCU............	Multiprocessor Communications Unit
MCU............	Multi-System Communications Unit (NITA)
MCU............	Rochester, NY [*Location identifier*] [*FAA*] (FAAL)
MCUAF	Multi-Corp. [*NASDAQ symbol*] (TTSB)
MCUAF	Multi-Corp, Inc. [*NASDAQ symbol*] (SAG)
MCUB	Marine Corps Uniform Board [*Washington, DC*] (EGAO)
MCUG	Military Computers Users Group
MCUIS	Master Control and User Interface Software Subsystem [*Space Flight Operations Facility, NASA*]
MCUL	Missile Compartment, Upper Level
MCUMP	Multidisciplinary Center for Urban and Minority Problems [*Florida State University*] [*Research center*] [*Defunct*] (RCD)
MCUPA	Medical Committee Under the Poisons Act [*Australia*]
MCurrSt	Master of Curriculum Studies
MCurrStud ..	Master of Curriculum Studies
MCUSR	Memory Control Unit Special Register [*Computer science*] (MHDB)
MCV............	Magnetic Cushion Vehicle (IEEE)
MCV............	Manifold Control Valve [*Automotive engineering*]
MCV............	Manufacturing Council of Victoria [*Australia*]
MCV............	Maritime Commission, Victory Ship
MCV............	Mean Cell [*or Corpuscular*] Volume [*Hematology*]
MCV............	Mean Clinical Value (AAMN)
MCV............	Mean Corpuscular Volume [*Physiology*]

MCV............	Measles-Containing Vaccine
MCV............	Mechanised Combat Vehicle [*British military*] (DMA)
MCV............	Median Cell Volume (DB)
MCV............	Medical Center of Virginia [*University of Virginia*]
MCV............	Medical College of Virginia (SAUO)
MCV............	Meningococcus Vaccine [*Medicine*] (MELL)
MCV............	Mercury [*Nevada*] [*Seismograph station code, US Geological Survey*] (SEIS)
MCV............	Mesabi Community College, Virginia, MN [*OCLC symbol*] (OCLC)
MCV............	Mesoscale Convectively-Generated Vortices [*Marine science*] (OSRA)
MCV............	Method of Composition Velocity [*Physical chemistry*]
MCV............	Microbial Check Valve (PDAA)
MCV............	Middle Cardiac Vein [*Medicine*] (MELL)
MCV............	Missile Corvette (SAUS)
MCV............	Modular Chemical Vessel (TIMI)
MCV............	Molluscum Contagiosum Virus
MCV............	Motor Conduction Velocity (DMAA)
MCV............	Movable Closure Valve (NRCH)
MCV............	Muerto Canyon Virus [*Hantavirus strain*]
MCVD	Metal Chemical Vapor Deposition (AAEL)
MCVD	Modified Chemical Vapor Deposition [*Telecommunications*]
McVey Dig...	McVey's Ohio Digest [*A publication*] (DLA)
MCVF..........	Multichannel Voice Frequency [*Telecommunications*]
MCVFT..........	Multichannel Voice Frequency Telegraphy [*Telecommunications*] (TEL)
MC-V(G)	Medical Officers (Qualified for General Detail) [*USNR designation*]
MCVG	Memory Character Vector Generator
MCVP..........	Materials Control and Verification Program [*NASA*] (NASA)
MCVS	Management and Cost Visibility System (SSD)
MC-V(S)..........	Medical Officers (Qualified for Specialist Duties) [*USNR designation*]
MCVS..........	Multi-Crew Visual System (ACAE)
MCVT..........	Multi-Channel Voice Terminal (SAUS)
MCW..........	Central Missouri State University, Warrensburg, MO [*OCLC symbol*] (OCLC)
MCW..........	Clarence W. Mills, Laurel MD (SAUO)
MCW..........	Mallinckrodt Chemical Works [*Later, Mallinckrodt, Inc.*]
MCW..........	Mason City [*Iowa*] [*Airport symbol*] (OAG)
MCW..........	Mason City, IA [*Location identifier*] [*FAA*] (FAAL)
MCW..........	Maternal and Child Welfare (SAUO)
MCW..........	Maternity and Child Welfare (SAUO)
MCW..........	McDonalds Corp. [*NYSE symbol*] (SAG)
MCW..........	Medical Corps, Women's Reserve [*USNR officer designation*]
MCW..........	Memory Card Writer [*Telecommunications*] (TEL)
MCW..........	Metal Casement Window [*Technical drawings*]
MCW..........	Metro-Cammell Weymaua Ltd. [*British*] (DCTA)
MCW..........	Mills, Clarence W., Laurel MD [*STAC*]
MCW..........	Minimum Clear Width (ACAE)
MCW..........	Modified Continuous Wave [*Telecommunications*] (IAA)
MCW..........	Modulated Carrier Wave [*Telecommunications*] (IAA)
mcw..........	Modulated Continuous Wave (NAKS)
MCW..........	Modulated Continuous Wave [*Radio signal transmission*]
MCW..........	Mount Constitution [*Washington*] [*Seismograph station code, US Geological Survey*] (SEIS)
MCW..........	Weston School of Theology, Cambridge, MA [*Library symbol*] [*Library of Congress*] (LCLS)
MCWA	Malaria Control in War Areas [*Later, Centers for Disease Control*]
MCWA	Massey College Wool Association (SAUO)
MCWA	Mid Continent Wildcatters Association [*Defunct*] (EA)
MCWC	Maternity and Child Welfare Centre (SAUO)
MCWC	World Conservation Monitoring Centre (SAUO)
MCWCS	Ministerial Conference of West and Central African States on Maritime Transportation [*See also CMEAOC*] [*Abidjan, Ivory Coast*] (EAIO)
MCWCS	Ministerial Conference of Western and Central African States on Sea Transport (SAUO)
MCWG	Marine Chemistry Working Group (SAUO)
MCWG	Materiel Center Work Group (SAUO)
McWhrtr	McWhorter Technologies, Inc. [*Associated Press*] (SAG)
McWillie......	McWillie's Reports [*73-76 Mississippi*] [*A publication*] (DLA)
MCWL........	Marine Corps Warfighting Lab
MCWM........	Military Committee Working Memorandum (NATG)
MCWR........	Marine Corps Women's Reserve
MCWR........	Ministry of Communications and Works of the Republic of Cyprus (SAUO)
MCWS........	Minor Caliber Weapon Station (SAUO)
MCWU........	Military Committee of Western European Union (NATG)
MCX..........	Marine Corps Exchange
MCX..........	MC Shipping [*AMEX symbol*] (TTSB)
MCX..........	MC Shipping, Inc. [*AMEX symbol*] (SPSG)
MCX..........	Michelin Capital Ltd. [*Toronto Stock Exchange symbol*]
MCX..........	Minimum-Cost Expediting
MCX..........	Monticello, IN [*Location identifier*] [*FAA*] (FAAL)
MCXD..........	Magnetic Circular X-Ray Dichroism [*Light polarization*]
MCXM..........	Marine Corps Exchange Manual (SAA)
MCXO..........	Microprocessor-Controlled Crystal Oscillator [*Hughes Aircraft Co.*] (ECON)
MCXSERV	Marine Corps Exchange Service Branch (DNAB)
MCY..........	Machinery (IAA)
MCY..........	Maroochydore [*Australia*] [*Airport symbol*] (OAG)
MCY..........	Mercury General [*NYSE symbol*] (SAG)
MCY..........	Mercury, NV [*Location identifier*] [*FAA*] (FAAL)
MCY..........	Mount Calvery Resources Ltd. [*Vancouver Stock Exchange symbol*]
M/CYL..........	Master Cylinder [*Automotive engineering*]
MCZ..........	Maceio [*Brazil*] [*Airport symbol*] (OAG)
MCZ..........	Magnetic Czochralski Process [*Crystallization*]

MCZ	McDonald' Corp. 8.35% 'QUIDS' [*NYSE symbol*] (TTSB)
MCZ	McDonalds Corp. [*NYSE symbol*] (SAG)
mcz	Mechanized (ELAL)
MCZ	Mesoscale Compressible Community Model (SAUO)
MCZ	Museum of Comparative Zoology [*Harvard University*] [*Research center*]
MCZDO	Multicenter Zero Differential Overlap [*Physics*]
MCZNE	Minimum When Control Zone Effective (FAAC)
MD	Air Madagascar [*ICAO designator*] (AD)
MD	Application for Writ of Mandamus Dismissed for Want of Jurisdiction [*Legal term*] (DLA)
MD	Biomedical Office [*Kennedy Space Center Directorate*] (NAKS)
MD	Delalande [*France*] [*Research code symbol*]
MD	Doctor of Medicine (PGP)
MD	Fissile Materials Disposition, Office of (SAUS)
MD	La Maison-Dieu [*Paris*] [*A publication*] (BJA)
MD	Machine Dried Paper (DGA)
MD	Macro Data (IAA)
MD	Macro Directory [*Computer science*] (IAA)
MD	Macular Degeneration [*Ophthalmology*]
Md	Madinhae (BJA)
MD	Madres de los Desamparados [*Mothers of the Helpless*] [*Roman Catholic religious order*]
MD	Magnesium Deficiency [*Medicine*] (DMAA)
MD	Magnetic Deflection [*Cathode-ray tube*] (DEN)
MD	Magnetic Disk [*Computer science*] (BUR)
MD	Magnetic Drum
MD	Mail Drop (COE)
MD	Main Deck [*Naval engineering*]
MD	Main Droite [*With the Right Hand*] [*Music*]
MD	Main Drum (CET)
MD	Main Duct
MD	Maintainability Demonstration (MCD)
M/D	Maintenance/Development [*Effort ratio*]
MD	Maintenance Documentation [*Bell System*] (IAA)
MD	Maintenance Dose [*Medicine*]
M-D	Maiz Dulce [*Race of maize*]
MD	Make Directory [*Computer science*]
MD	Malate Dehydrogenase [*Also, MDH*] [*An enzyme*]
MD	Male Treated with DOC [*Deoxycorticosterone*]
MD	Malfunction Detection (NASA)
MD	Malic Dehydrogenase [*An enzyme*] (MAE)
MD	Malicious Damage (MARI)
MD	Management Data (MCD)
MD	Management Directive
MD	Management Division [*Environmental Protection Agency*] (GFGA)
MD	Managing Director
MD	Managment Domain [*Telecommunications*] (OSI)
M/D	Man Day
M-D	Manic Depression
MD	Manic-Depressive
MD	Manning Department (SAUO)
MD	Mano Destra [*With the Right Hand*] [*Music*]
MD	Mantoux Diameter (MAE)
MCZ	Manual Damper (OA)
MCZ	Manual Data
MD	Manual Direct (NASA)
MD	Manual Disconnect (MCD)
MD	Manu Dextra [*With the Right Hand*] [*Latin*]
MD	Manufacturer Defect
MD	Manufacturing Development (SAUO)
MD	Manufacturing Division (ACAE)
MD	Map Distance (ADA)
MD	Marchand [*Merchant, Trader*] [*French*]
MD	Marek's Disease [*Avian pathology*]
MD	Marine Detachment
MD	Maritime Defense (SAUO)
MD	Market Day [*British*]
MD	Marque Deposee [*Trademark*]
MD	Married
MD	Marshaled Deployability Posture (SAUO)
Md	Maryland (BEE)
MD	Maryland [*Postal code*]
MD	Maryland Reports [*A publication*] (DLA)
Md	Maryland State Library, Annapolis, MD [*Library symbol*] [*Library of Congress*] (LCLS)
MD	Master Diagram (MCD)
MD	Master Dimension (NASA)
MD	Master Directory [*NASA*] [*Information service or system*] (IID)
MD	Master's Decisions (Patents) [*A publication*] (DLA)
MD	Match Dissolve [*Cinematography*] (WDMC)
MD	Material Developer (SAUO)
MD	Material Division (SAUO)
MD	Materiel Developer [*Army*]
MD	Materiels Directorate (SAUO)
MD	Maternal Deprivation (MAE)
MD	Matrimonio Duxit [*Led into Matrimony*] [*Latin*] (ROG)
MD	Maturity Date [*Banking*]
MD	Maximum Degree Allowed to Fit
MD	Maximum Demand (IAA)
MD	Maximum Design Meter
MD	McDonnell Douglas [*NYSE symbol*] (TTSB)
MD	McDonnell Douglas Corp. [*NYSE symbol*] (SPSG)
MD	McDonnell Douglas Corporation (SAUO)

MD	Mean Deviation
M-D	Measured Depth [*Diamonds*]
MD	Measured Discard [*Nuclear energy*] (NRCH)
MD	Measured Drilling [*Diamonds*]
MD	Mechanical Diode [*Mechanical power transmission*]
Md	Median
MD	Mediastinal Disease [*Medicine*] (DB)
MD	Mediation Device (VLIE)
MD	Medical Department [*Army*]
MD	Medical Discharge [*from military service*]
MD	Medical Doctor (AMHC)
MD	Medicinae Doctor [*Doctor of Medicine*] [*Latin*]
M/D	Medicines/Drugs
MD	Mediodorsal [*Anatomy*]
MD	Medium Dosage [*Pharmacology*] (MAE)
MD	Medium Duty
MD	Megadalton
MD	Memorandum of Deposit [*Business term*]
MD	Memory Data Register (DNAB)
MD	Memory Decrement (MHDB)
Md	Mendelevium [*Preferred form, but also see Mv*] [*Chemical element*]
MD	Meniere's Disease [*Medicine*] (DMAA)
MD	Mental Deficiency (DIPS)
MD	Mentally Deficient
MD	Mentally Depressed [*Psychology*] (DB)
MD	Mentally Disabled (OICC)
md	Mercedarious Descalzos (TOCD)
MD	Mesiodistal [*Dentistry*]
Md	Mesoderm [*Botany*]
MD	Message Data
MD	Message Digest (ACRL)
MD	Message-Dropping [*Military*]
MD	Messages per Day
MD	Mess Deck [*Naval*]
MD	Metal Deactivator
MD	Metal Dome [*Watchmaking*] (ROG)
MD	Metals Disintegrating
MD	Metaphors Dictionary [*A publication*]
MD	Meteorological Department (SAUO)
MD	Meteorology Department [*Navy*]
M/D	Meters per Day
MD	Methyldichloroarsine [*Poison gas*]
MD	Methyldopa [*Also, AMD*] [*Antihypertensive compound*]
MD	Metropolitan District [*British*]
MD	Microalloy Diffused
MD	Micro Diagnostics (VLIE)
MD	Microdot (KSC)
MD	Micrometeoroid Detector (ACAE)
MD	Microsoft DoubleSpace [*Computer science*] (PCM)
MD	Microwave Desorber [*Instrumentation*]
MD	Middeck (SAUS)
MD	Middle Deltoid [*Myology*]
MD	Middle Distillate [*Fuel technology*]
MD	Middle District (DLA)
MD	Middle Door [*Theater*]
MD	Middle Dutch [*Language, etc.*]
MD	Midnight Dumping (MHDW)
MD	Migrant with English Language Difficulty
MD	Mildly Diabetic
MD	Military District [*Former USSR*] (NATG)
mD	Millidarcy
MD	Millwall Dock [*British*]
MD	Mine Depot [*Naval*]
MD	Mine Disposal
MD	Mini Disk [*Audio/video technology*]
MD	Minimum Dosage [*Medicine*]
MD	Ministry of Defence (SAUO)
MD	Minute Difference
MD	Miscellaneous Direct (MCD)
MD	Miscellaneous Document
MD	Miss Distance [*Military*]
MD	Missile Defense (SAUO)
MD	Missile Division (AAG)
MD	Missile Driver
MD	Missionary Dentists [*An association*] (EA)
MD	Mission Day
MD	Mission Dependent
MD	Mission Deviation (MCD)
MD	Mission Director [*NASA*] (KSC)
MD	Mitral Disease [*Medicine*]
MD	Mix Design
MD	Mixed Diet (DMAA)
MD	Mobile Depot [*Air Force*] (MCD)
MD	Mobilization Department (SAUO)
MD	Mode [*Grammar*] (ROG)
MD	Moderate Dose [*Medicine*]
MD	Moderately Differentiated
MD	Modernization Division (SAUO)
MD	Modification Document (MCD)
MD	Modified Design [*Cordite*] [*British military*] (DMA)
MD	Modify (VLIE)
MD	Modular Design
M-D	Modulation-Demodulation (HGAA)
M/D	Modulator-Demodulator [*Telecommunications*] (CET)
MD	Modulators [*JETDS nomenclature*] [*Military*] (CET)

MD.............	Moldova [Internet country code]
MD.............	Molecular Diameter
MD.............	Molecular Dynamics
MD.............	Money Down
MD.............	Monitor Displays [Computer science] (BUR)
MD.............	Monochrome Display (VLIE)
MD.............	Monocular Deprivation [Optics]
MD.............	Monroe Doctrine
MD.............	Monsanto Research Co. (SAUO)
md.............	Months after Date (EBF)
MD.............	Months after Date [or Month's Date] [Business term]
md.............	Months' Date (EBF)
MD.............	Mood [Grammar] (ROG)
MD.............	More Dicto [As Directed] [Pharmacy]
MD/.............	More Dirt (SAUS)
M/D.............	Mother/Daughter [Apartment] (BARN)
MD.............	Mothers of the Helpless (TOCD)
MD.............	Motion-Defined (SAUS)
MD.............	Motor Direct
MD.............	Motor Drive
MD.............	Mound Laboratory (SAUO)
MD.............	Movement Directive
MD.............	Movement Disorder (MAE)
MD.............	Movement Distance (SAUO)
MD.............	Multidimensional
MD.............	Multidomain [Grains in rocks] [Geophysics]
MD.............	Multinomial Distribution [Statistics]
MD.............	Multiple Deficiency [Syndrome] [Medicine] (DB)
MD.............	Multiple Dialyzer [Chemical analysis]
MD.............	Multiple Dissemination
MD.............	Multiply-Divide (IAA)
MD.............	Multipurpose Display (MCD)
MD.............	Municipal Docks Railway of the Jacksonville Port Authority [AAR code]
MD.............	Muscular Dystrophy [Medicine]
MD.............	Musicae Doctor [Doctor of Music] (ROG)
MD.............	Musical Director
MD.............	Music Director (NTCM)
MD.............	Myocardial Damage [Cardiology] (MAE)
MD.............	Myocardial Disease [Cardiology]
MD.............	Myotonic Dystrophy [See also MyMD] [Medicine]
MDA.............	Macdonald, Dettwiler & Association Ltd. (SAUO)
MDA.............	Magen David Adom [Israel's Red Cross Service]
MDA.............	Magic Dealers Association [Later, IMDA]
MDA.............	Magnetic Deflection Amplifier
MDA.............	Main Distribution Assembly (NASA)
MDA.............	Maintainability Design Approach
MDA.............	Maintenance Data Analysis (MCD)
MDA.............	Maintenance Depot Assistance [Air Force] (AFM)
MDA.............	Maintenance Design Approach
MDA.............	Malfunction Detector Analyzer (PDAA)
MDA.............	Malondialdehyde [Biochemistry]
MDA.............	Management Development Adviser (AIE)
MDA.............	Mandarian Airlines [ICAO designator] (FAAC)
MDA.............	Manic-Depressive Association (EA)
MDA.............	Manual Dilation of the Anus (AAMN)
MDA.............	Manufacturing Defect Analyzer [Automotive engineering]
MDA.............	MAPCO, Inc. [NYSE symbol] (SPSG)
MDA.............	Marking Device Association (EA)
MD A.............	Maryland Appellate Reports [A publication] (DLA)
MDA.............	Maryland Independent Truckers and Drivers Association (SAUO)
MDA.............	Master Design Award
MDA.............	Master Diversion Airfield (AIA)
MDA.............	Master Drawings Association (EA)
MDA.............	Master Dyers Association (EA)
MDA.............	Master of Development Adminstration (PGP)
MDA.............	Master of Dramatic Art
MDA.............	Material Data Administrator (DNAB)
MDA.............	Material Disposal Area (SAUO)
MDA.............	Material Disposal Authority
MDA.............	Maximum Deficit Amount [Office of Management and Budget] (GFGA)
MDA.............	Maximum Demographic Appeal [Objective of commercial television programming]
MDA.............	Maximum Detachable Activity [Nuclear energy] (NUCP)
MDA.............	McDonald, Dettwiley and Associates (ACAE)
MDA.............	McDonnell-Designed Assembly
MDA.............	McDonnell-Douglas Aerospace (GAVI)
MDA.............	Measurement, Decision, and Actuation [Computer science]
MDA.............	Mechanical Design Automation (TIMI)
MDA.............	Mechanically Despun Antenna (KSC)
MDA.............	Mechanized Directory Assistance [Telecommunications] (TEL)
MDA.............	Media Arts Group [Stock market symbol]
MDA.............	Media Dependent Adapter (SAUS)
MDA.............	Media Device Adapter (SAUS)
MDA.............	Medical Devices Agency (SAUO)
MDa.............	Megadalton (DMAA)
MDA.............	Menthanediamine [Organic chemistry]
MDA.............	Mento-Dextra Anterior [A fetal position] [Obstetrics]
MDA.............	Mentodextroanterior [Medicine] (DB)
MDA.............	Mesocyclone Detection Algorithm [Marine science] (OSRA)
MDA.............	Message Delivery Agent (RALS)
MDA.............	Metal Deactivator [Fuel technology]
MDA.............	Meteoroid Detector-Analyzer
MDA.............	Methyl Diamphetamine

MDA.............	Methyldopamine [Biochemistry]
MDA.............	Methylenedianiline [Also, DAPM, DDM] [Organic chemistry]
MDA.............	Methylenedioxyamphetamine [Biochemistry]
MDA.............	Michigan Dental Association (SAUO)
MDA.............	Microprocessor Development Aid
MDA.............	Middeck Assembly (MCD)
MDA.............	Milestone Decision Authority
MDA.............	Military Damage Assessment
MDA.............	Millinery Distributors Association [British] (BI)
MDA.............	Mine Danger Area (SAUS)
MDA.............	Minimum Decision Altitude (SAA)
MDA.............	Minimum Descent Altitude [Aviation]
MDA.............	Minimum Detectable Activity [Nuclear energy] (NRCH)
MDA.............	Minimum Detectable Amount [of radiation] [Analytical chemistry]
MDA.............	Minnesota Department of Agriculture, St. Paul, MN [OCLC symbol] (OCLC)
MDA.............	Miscellaneous Defense Activities (AAGC)
MDA.............	Miss Distance Analyser (SAUS)
MDA.............	Missile Defense Act (SAUO)
MDA.............	Missilized Driver Assembly (MCD)
MDA.............	Mission Data Assurance (ACAE)
MDA.............	Mission Doctors Association (EA)
MDA.............	Mixed Distribution Analysis [Mathematics]
MDA.............	Mobile Data Association (SAUO)
MDA.............	Mobile Depot Activities [Air Force]
MDA.............	Modified Diffusion Approximation (PDAA)
MDA.............	Modulation-Domain Analysis [Computer science] (CIST)
MDA.............	Monoalythic Design Automation (IAA)
MDA.............	Monochrome Display Adapter [Computer technology]
MDA.............	Monodehydroascorbate [Biochemistry]
MDA.............	Mothers for Decency in Action [Group opposing sex education in schools]
MDA.............	Motorcycling Doctors Association (EA)
MDA.............	Motor Discriminative Acuity [Psychology]
MDA.............	Motor Drive Amplifier
MDA.............	Motorized Door Assembly (SAUS)
MDA.............	Mouvement pour la Democratie en Algerie [Algeria] [Political party] (MENA)
MDA.............	Multidimensional Access
MDA.............	Multidimensional Analysis (IEEE)
MDA.............	Multidimensional Array
MDA.............	Multidocking Adapter (IAA)
MDA.............	Multiple Digit Absorbing [Telecommunications] (TEL)
MDA.............	Multiple Discriminant Analysis [Statistics]
MDA.............	Multiple Docking Adapter [Apollo] [NASA]
MDA.............	Multivariant Discriminant Analysis [Medicine] (DMAA)
MDA.............	Mural Decorators Association (SAUO)
MDA.............	Murray-Darling Association (SAUO)
MDA.............	Muscular Dystrophy Association (EA)
MDA.............	Museum Documentation Association [British] (DBA)
MDA.............	Music Distributors Association (EA)
MDA.............	Mutual Defense Agency (NADA)
MDA.............	Mutual Defense Assistance
MDA.............	San Antonio, TX [Location identifier] [FAA] (FAAL)
MdAA.............	Hall of Records Commission, Annapolis, MD [Library symbol] [Library of Congress] (LCLS)
MDAA.............	Mon-Dak Athletic Association (PSS)
MDAA.............	Muscular Dystrophy Associations of America (EA)
MDAA.............	Mutual Defense Assistance Act
MdAAC.............	Public Library of Annapolis and Anne Arundel County, Annapolis, MD [Library symbol] [Library of Congress] (LCLS)
MDAAQS.............	Miscellaneous Data Analysis and Air Quality Simulation Studies (SAUO)
MDaAr.............	Danvers Archival Center, Peabody Institute, Danvers, MA [Library symbol] [Library of Congress] (LCLS)
MDAC.............	MacDonnell Douglas Aerospace Corp. (SAUS)
MDAC.............	McDonnell Douglas Aircraft Corp.
MDAC.............	McDonnell Douglas Astronautics Co. (NAKS)
MDAC.............	Medical Data Acquisition System
MDAC.............	Methyl(ciethylamino)coumarin [Organic chemistry]
MDAC.............	Microsoft Data Access Component (SAUS)
MDAC.............	Multi-Channel Digital Audio Codec [Intraplex, Inc.]
MDAC.............	Multiplying Digital-to-Analog Converter [Computer science] (IEEE)
MDAC.............	Muscular Dystrophy Association of Canada
MDAC.............	Mutual Defense Assistance-China area (SAUO)
MDAC.............	Mutual Defense Assistance Committee (SAUO)
MDAC.............	Mutual Defense Assistance, General Area of China
MDACA.............	Medical Defense Against Chemical Agents (ACAE)
MDAC/ACDM.............	Muscular Dystrophy Association of Canada/Association Canadienne de la Dystrophie Musculaire (SAUO)
MdaCad.............	ModaCad, Inc. [Associated Press] (SAG)
MDACC.............	Management of Defense Acquisition Contracts Course [DoD] (RDA)
MDACC.............	M. D. Anderson Cancer Center (SAUO)
MdaCd.............	ModaCad, Inc. [Associated Press] (SAG)
MDAC/E.............	McDonnell Douglas Astronautics Company/East (SAUO)
MDAC/W.............	McDonnell Douglas Astronautics Company/West (SAUO)
MDAD.............	Mineral Dust Airway Disease [Medicine] (DMAA)
MDAD.............	Monitoring and Data Analysis Division [Environmental Protection Agency] (GFGA)
MD Admin Code...	Code of Maryland Regulations [A publication] (DLA)
MdAEPA.............	United States Environmental Protection Agency, Annapolis Field Office, AnnapolisScience Center, Annapolis, MD [Library symbol] [Library of Congress] (LCLS)
MDAERP.............	Medical Devices Adverse Experience Reporting Project
MDAF.............	Memoires. Delegation Archeologique Francaise [A publication] (BJA)

MDAFWP......	Motor-Driven Auxiliary Feedwater Pump (IEEE)
MDAGT........	Mutual Defense Assistance, Greece and Turkey
MDAH..........	M. D. Anderson Hospital and Tumor Institute [*Houston, TX*]
MDAI	Marking Device Association International (NTPA)
MDAI	Multidisciplinary Accident Investigation [*National Accident Sampling System*]
MDAIKP	Mutual Defense Assistance, Iran, Republic of Korea, and Philippines
MDAIS	McDonnell Douglas Aerospace Information Services [*Formerly, MCATO*] (MCD)
MD Ala	United States District Court for the Middle District of Alabama (DLA)
MDAN..........	Angelina, Cotui [*Dominican Republic*] [*ICAO location identifier*] (ICLI)
MdAN..........	United States Naval Academy, Annapolis, MD [*Library symbol*] [*Library of Congress*] (LCLS)
MDANAA......	Mutual Defense Assistance, North Atlantic Area
MD & D	Montagu, Deacon, and De Gex's English Bankruptcy Reports [*1840-44*] [*A publication*] (DLA)
MD & DeG...	Montagu, Deacon, and De Gex's English Bankruptcy Reports [*1840-44*] [*A publication*] (DLA)
MD & S	Macon, Dublin & Savannah Railroad (IIA)
MdANE........	United States Navy, Naval Ship Research and Development Laboratory, Annapolis, MD [*Library symbol*] [*Library of Congress*] (LCLS)
MD Ann Code...	Annotated Code of Maryland [*A publication*] (DLA)
MDANSW.....	Muscular Dystrophy Association of New South Wales [*Australia*]
MDAO..........	Mutual Defense Assistance Office (DOMA)
MDA-OSP	Mutual Defense Assistance - Offshore Procurement (SAUO)
MDA-OSP Program...	Mutual Defense Assistance-Offshore Procurement Program (SAUO)
MDAP	Machine and Display Application Program (SAUO)
MDAP	Machover Draw-A-Person Test [*Psychology*]
MDAP	Major Defense Acquisition Program (AAGC)
MDAP	Materiel Deployment/Acceptance Plan (MCD)
MDAP	Military Defense Aid Program (SAUO)
MDAP	Military Defense Assistance Program (SAUO)
MDAP	Military Department Aid Program (ACAE)
MDAP	Morphological Dictionary Adaptor Program (PDAA)
MDAP	Mutual Defense Assistance Pact [*or Program*]
MDaP..........	Peabody Institute, Danvers, MA [*Library symbol*] [*Library of Congress*] (LCLS)
MdApg........	United States Army, Technical Library, Aberdeen Proving Ground, Aberdeen, MD [*Library symbol*] [*Library of Congress*] (LCLS)
MdApgC.......	United States Army, Chemical Systems Laboratory, Aberdeen Proving Ground, Aberdeen, MD [*Library symbol*] [*Library of Congress*] (LCLS)
MdApgO.......	United States Army, Ordnance School, Aberdeen Proving Ground, Aberdeen, MD [*Library symbol*] [*Library of Congress*] (LCLS)
MdApgOB ...	United States Army, Ordnance Board, Aberdeen Proving Ground, Aberdeen, MD [*Library symbol*] [*Library of Congress*] (LCLS)
MdApgP.......	United States Army, Post Library, Aberdeen Proving Ground, Aberdeen, MD [*Library symbol*] [*Library of Congress*] (LCLS)
MD App	Maryland Appellate Reports [*A publication*] (DLA)
MDAR	Malfunction Detection Analysis and Recording [*NASA*] (KSC)
MDAR	Minimum Daily Adult Requirement
MDAR	Mobile Detection Assessment Response System [*USA*]
MDar 1	Dartmouth Public Library, Darmouth, MA [*Library symbol*] [*Library of Congress*] (LCLS)
MDarHi........	Old Dartmouth Historical Society, Dartmouth, MA [*Library symbol*] [*Library of Congress*] (LCLS)
MDARS........	Military Damage Assessment Reporting System (MCD)
MDARS........	Mobile Detection, Assessment, and Response System
MDAS	Manpower Data Automated System (DNAB)
MDAS	Medical Data Acquisition System (KSC)
MDAS	Meteorological Data Acquisition System [*NASA*] (KSC)
MDAS	Miniature Data Acquisition System
MDAS	Mission Data Acquisition System [*NASA*] (NASA)
MDAS	Modular Data Acquisition System (NITA)
MDAS	Multispectral Data Analysis System (ACAE)
MdAS..........	Saint John's College, Annapolis, MD [*Library symbol*] [*Library of Congress*] (LCLS)
MDASA........	Muscular Dystrophy Association of South Australia
MDA-TR	Mutual Defense Assistance - Training Program (SAUO)
MDAU	Maintenance Data Acquisition Unit (HLLA)
MDAV	Medical Defence Association of Victoria (SAUO)
MDAVG........	Mission Duration, Average (MCD)
M (Day).......	Mobilization Day [*Military*] (AFM)
M (Days)......	Metrication Days [*Sponsored by the Metrication Board to educate merchants and public on metric system*] [*British*]
MDB...........	Bren Del Win Centennial Library, Deloraine, Manitoba [*Library symbol*] [*National Library of Canada*] (NLC)
MDB...........	Enoch Pratt Free Library, Baltimore, MD [*OCLC symbol*] (OCLC)
MDB...........	Maintenance Data Bank
MDB...........	Management Database (ACRL)
MDB...........	Master Database
MDB...........	Master Distribution Box [*Missile system*] [*Army*]
MDB...........	Material Distribution Board (DNAB)
MDB...........	MDI Mobile Data International, Inc. [*Toronto Stock Exchange symbol*] [*Vancouver Stock Exchange symbol*]
MDB...........	Medulloblastoma [*Medicine*] (DMAA)
MDB...........	Memory-Data Bank
MDB...........	Mersey Dock Board [*British*] (DAS)
MDB...........	Message Database (MCD)
MDB...........	Methylenedioxybenzene [*Organic chemistry*]
MDB...........	Metrology Data Bank [*GIDEP*]
MDB...........	Microelectronic Data Bank (ACAE)
MDB...........	Minimally Distinct Border [*Color perception*]

MDB...........	Mission Data Book [*NASA*] (NASA)
MDB...........	Mission Display Board Assembly [*Space Flight Operations Facility, NASA*]
MDB...........	Mitglied des Deutschen Bundestages [*Member of the German Federal Parliament*]
MDB...........	Mojave Desert Block [*Geology*]
MDB...........	Movable Deformable Barrier [*Automotive safety*]
MDB...........	Movimento Democratico Brasileiro [*Brazilian Democratic Movement*] [*Political party*] (PPW)
MDB...........	Multichannel Distributed Bridge (CCCA)
MDB...........	Multilateral Development Bank
MDB...........	Multiple Drive Block
MDB...........	Multiplex Data Bus [*Computer science*] (MCD)
MDB...........	Mutual Defense Board [*US-Philippines*] (CINC)
MDB...........	Professional Bancorp [*AMEX symbol*] (SPSG)
MDBA	Murray-Darling Basin Agreement (SAUO)
MdBAE........	United States Army, Corps of Engineers, Baltimore, MD [*Library symbol*] [*Library of Congress*] (LCLS)
MdBaH........	Harford Community College, Bel Air, MD [*Library symbol*] [*Library of Congress*] (LCLS)
MdBaHC	Harford County Library, Bel Air, MD [*Library symbol*] [*Library of Congress*] (LCLS)
MdBAS........	Armco, Inc., Advanced Materials Division, Research Library, Baltimore, MD [*Library symbol*] [*Library of Congress*] (LCLS)
MdBASI.......	Allied Signal, Inc., Baltimore, MD [*Library symbol*] [*Library of Congress*] (LCLS)
MdBASI-C ...	Allied Signal, Inc., Communications Diviaion, Baltimore, MD [*Library symbol*] [*Library of Congress*] (LCLS)
MdBB	Baltimore Bar Library, Baltimore, MD [*Library symbol*] [*Library of Congress*] (LCLS)
MdBb	United States Naval Training Center, Bainbridge, MD [*Library symbol*] [*Library of Congress*] (LCLS)
MdBBC........	Baltimore Conference, Inc., United Methodist Historical Society, Baltimore, MD [*Library symbol*] [*Library of Congress*] (LCLS)
MdBBH	Harford Community College, Bel Air (SAUS)
MdBBJC.......	Community College of Baltimore, Baltimore, MD [*Library symbol*] [*Library of Congress*] (LCLS)
MdBbN	US Naval Training Center, Bainbridge, MD [*Library symbol*] [*Library of Congress*] (LCLS)
MdBBO	[*The*] Baltimore & Ohio Railroad Co., Employees' Library, Baltimore, MD [*Library symbol*] [*Library of Congress*] [*Obsolete*] (LCLS)
MdBBR	Bendix Corp., Baltimore, MD [*Library symbol*] [*Library of Congress*] (LCLS)
MdBBS........	Bon Secours Medical Library, Baltimore, MD [*Library symbol*] [*Library of Congress*] (LCLS)
MDBC	Murray-Darling Basin Commission (SAUO)
MdBCC........	Catonsville Community College, Learning Resources Division, Baltimore, MD [*Library symbol*] [*Library of Congress*] (LCLS)
MdBCH	Baltimore City Court House, Baltimore, MD [*Library symbol*] [*Library of Congress*] (LCLS)
MdBCIC.......	Counter Intelligence Center Corps School, Fort Holabird, Baltimore, MD [*Library symbol*] [*Library of Congress*] (LCLS)
MdBCIC.......	Counter Intelligence Center Corps School, Fort Holabird, Baltimore (SAUS)
MdBCP........	Baltimore County Public Library, Towson, MD [*Library symbol*] [*Library of Congress*] (LCLS)
MdBCPM......	Chemical Pigment Co., Metals Division, Baltimore, MD [*Library symbol*] [*Library of Congress*] (LCLS)
MdBCS........	Coppin State College, Baltimore, MD [*Library symbol*] [*Library of Congress*] (LCLS)
MD-BD........	Major Depression and Bipolar Disorder [*Medicine*] (MELL)
MDBDF........	March of Dimes Birth Defects Foundation (EA)
MdBDH	United States Department of Health and Human Services, Health Care Financing Administration, Office of Research Demonstrations and Statistics, Baltimore, MD [*Library symbol*] [*Library of Congress*] (LCLS)
MdBE	Enoch Pratt Free Library, Baltimore, MD [*Library symbol*] [*Library of Congress*] (LCLS)
MdBeCA.......	Concepts Analysis Agency, Bethesda, MD [*Library symbol*] [*Library of Congress*] (LCLS)
MdBeCl.......	Congressional Information Service, Bethesda, MD [*Library symbol*] [*Library of Congress*] (LCLS)
MdBEs	Essex Community College, Baltimore, MD [*Library symbol*] [*Library of Congress*] (LCLS)
MdBeU........	Uniform Services University of the Health Sciences, Bethesda, MD [*Library symbol*] [*Library of Congress*] (LCLS)
MDBF..........	Mean Distance between Failures [*Quality control*] (MCD)
MdBFamP....	Family Planning Training Institute, Baltimore, MD [*Library symbol*] [*Library of Congress*] (LCLS)
MdBFH........	Fort Holabird Post Library, Baltimore, MD [*Library symbol*] [*Library of Congress*] (LCLS)
MdBFM	Grand Lodge of Ancient Free and Accepted Masons of Maryland, Masonic Library, Baltimore, MD [*Library symbol*] [*Library of Congress*] (LCLS)
MdBFr.........	Friends Meeting, Stony Run, Baltimore, MD [*Library symbol*] [*Library of Congress*] (LCLS)
MdBG..........	Goucher College, Baltimore, MD [*Library symbol*] [*Library of Congress*] (LCLS)
MdBGM-E ...	Manin Marietta Corp., Science and Technology Library, Baltimore (SAUO)
MdBGM-E ...	Martin Marietta Corp., Science and Technology Library, Baltimore, MD [*Library symbol*] [*Library of Congress*] (LCLS)
MdBGM-N ...	Martin Marietta Corp., RIAS Library, Baltimore, MD [*Library symbol*] [*Library of Congress*] (LCLS)

MdBH.......... Baltimore City Hospitals, Doctors' Library, Baltimore, MD [*Library symbol*] [*Library of Congress*] (LCLS)

MDBH......... Barahona [*Dominican Republic*] [*ICAO location identifier*] (ICLI)

MdBHC .... Baltimore Hebrew College, Baltimore, MD [*Library symbol*] [*Library of Congress*] (LCLS)

MdBHC .... Harford County Library, Bel Air (SAUS)

MDBI .... Mean Days between Injuries

MDBI .... Murray Darling Basin Initiative [*Australia*]

MdBJ .... Johns Hopkins University, Baltimore, MD [*Library symbol*] [*Library of Congress*] (LCLS)

MdBJ-A....... Johns Hopkins University, Applied Physics Laboratory, Baltimore (SAUO)

MdBJ-A....... Johns Hopkins University, Applied Physics Laboratory, Silver Spring, MD [*Library symbol*] [*Library of Congress*] (LCLS)

MdBJ-AIS .... Johns Hopkins University, School of Advanced International Studies, Washington, DC [*Library symbol*] [*Library of Congress*] (LCLS)

MdBJ-C....... Johns Hopkins university, Alan Chesney Medical Archives, Baltimore, MD [*Library symbol*] [*Library of Congress*] (LCLS)

MdBJ-G....... Johns Hopkins University, John Work Garrett Library, Baltimore, MD [*Library symbol*] [*Library of Congress*] (LCLS)

MdBJ-H....... Johns Hopkins University, School of Hygiene and Public Health, Maternal and Child Health-Population Dynamics Library, Baltimore, MD [*Library symbol*] [*Library of Congress*] (LCLS)

MdBJ-P....... Johns Hopkins University, George Peabody Library, Baltimore, MD [*Library symbol*] [*Library of Congress*] (LCLS)

MdBJ-W...... Johns Hopkins University, William H. Welch Medical Library, Baltimore, MD [*Library symbol*] [*Library of Congress*] (LCLS)

MDBK .... Madin-Darby Bovine Kidney [*Cell line*]

MDBK .... Medford Bancorp [*NASDAQ symbol*] [*Formerly, Medford Savings Bank*] (SG)

MDBK .... Medford Savings Bank [*NASDAQ symbol*] (SAG)

MdbkIns....... Meadowbrook Insurance Group [*Associated Press*] (SAG)

MDBL .... Maintainability Data Baseline (MCD)

MDBL.......... Maintainability Design Baseline (MCD)

MdBLH........ Lutheran Hospital of Maryland, Baltimore, MD [*Library symbol*] [*Library of Congress*] (LCLS)

MdBLN........ Loyola - Notre Dame Library, Inc., Baltimore, MD [*Library symbol*] [*Library of Congress*] (LCLS)

MdBM .... Medical and Chirurgical Faculty of the State of Maryland, Baltimore, MD [*Library symbol*] [*Library of Congress*] (LCLS)

MDBM .... MULTICS Data Base Manager

MdBMA....... Baltimore Museum of Art, Baltimore, MD [*Library symbol*] [*Library of Congress*] (LCLS)

MdBMC....... Morgan State College [*Later, Morgan State University*] Baltimore, MD [*Library symbol*] [*Library of Congress*] (LCLS)

MDBMC ...... Murray-Darling Basin Ministerial Council [*Australia*]

MdBMH........ Mercy Hospital, McGlannan Memorial Library, Baltimore, MD [*Library symbol*] [*Library of Congress*] (LCLS)

MdBMH-N.... Mercy Hospital, School of Nursing, Baltimore, MD [*Library symbol*] [*Library of Congress*] (LCLS)

MdBMI........ Maryland Institute, School of Fine and Applied Arts, Baltimore, MD [*Library symbol*] [*Library of Congress*] (LCLS)

MDBMS .... Medical Data Base Management System (SSD)

MDBMS .... Megadatabase Management System (SAUS)

MDBMS .... Multidimensional DataBase Management System (SAUS)

MdBMStA .... Mount Saint Agnes College, Baltimore, MD [*Library symbol*] [*Library of Congress*] (LCLS)

MdBNA .... National Institute on Aging, Gerontology Research Center, Baltimore, MD [*Library symbol*] [*Library of Congress*] (LCLS)

MdBo........... Bowie State College, Bowie, MD [*Library symbol*] [*Library of Congress*] (LCLS)

MdBOAS ...... United States Social Security Administration, Baltimore, MD [*Library symbol*] [*Library of Congress*] (LCLS)

MdBP........... Enoch Pratt Free Library, George Peabody Branch, Baltimore, MD [*Library symbol*] [*Library of Congress*] (LCLS)

MDBP .... Mechanically Deboned Broiler Product [*Food technology*]

MDBPB .... Microsoft DoubleSpace BIOS [*Basic Input-Output System*] Parameter Block [*Computer science*] (PCM)

MdBPC......... Peabody Conservatory of Music, Baltimore, MD [*Library symbol*] [*Library of Congress*] (LCLS)

MdBPH .... United States Public Health Service Hospital, Baltimore, MD [*Library symbol*] [*Library of Congress*] (LCLS)

MdBPM........ Peale Museum, Baltimore, MD [*Library symbol*] [*Library of Congress*] (LCLS)

MdBR........... Research Institute for Advanced Study, Baltimore, MD [*Library symbol*] [*Library of Congress*] (LCLS)

MdBREC ...... Engineering Society of Baltimore, Baltimore, MD [*Library symbol*] [*Library of Congress*] (LCLS)

MdbrkRe...... Meadowbrook Rehabilitation Group [*Associated Press*] (SAG)

MDBS .... Micro Data Base Systems (NITA)

MDBS .... Micro Data Base Systems, Inc. (SAUO)

MDBS .... Mobile Data Base Station (SAUO)

MDBS .... Mobile Database Station [*Telecommunications*] (ACRL)

MDBs........... Multilateral Development Banks (SAUO)

MdBS .... Saint Mary's Seminary and University, Baltimore, MD [*Library symbol*] [*Library of Congress*] (LCLS)

MdBSAr .... Sulpician Archives Baltimore, Baltimore, MD [*Library symbol*] [*Library of Congress*] (LCLS)

MdBSet........ Seton Psychiatric Institute, Baltimore, MD [*Library symbol*] [*Library of Congress*] (LCLS)

MdBSH .... Sinai Hospital, Staff Library, Baltimore, MD [*Library symbol*] [*Library of Congress*] (LCLS)

MdBS-P .... Saint Mary's Seminary and University, Philosophy Library, Baltimore, MD [*Library symbol*] [*Library of Congress*] (LCLS)

MdBSP........ Sheppard-Pratt Hospital, Baltimore, MD [*Library symbol*] [*Library of Congress*] (LCLS)

MdBSp........ Sunpapers Library, Baltimore, MD [*Library symbol*] [*Library of Congress*] (LCLS)

MDBSS .... Mischell-Dutton Balanced Salt Solution (STED)

MdBSt.......... Saint Agnes Hospital, Baltimore, MD [*Library symbol*] [*Library of Congress*] (LCLS)

MdBSTS....... Space Telescope Science Institute, Baltimore, MD [*Library symbol*] [*Library of Congress*] (LCLS)

MdBSup....... Sunpapers Library, Baltimore, MD [*Library symbol*] [*Library of Congress*] (LCLS)

MdBT .... Towson State University, Baltimore, MD [*Library symbol*] [*Library of Congress*] (LCLS)

MdBU.......... University of Baltimore, Baltimore, MD [*Library symbol*] [*Library of Congress*] (LCLS)

MdBU-L .... University of Baltimore, Law Library, Baltimore, MD [*Library symbol*] [*Library of Congress*] (LCLS)

MdBUM........ Union Memorial Hospital, Finney Medical Library, Baltimore, MD [*Library symbol*] [*Library of Congress*] (LCLS)

MdBV.......... United States Veterans Administration Hospital, Baltimore, MD [*Library symbol*] [*Library of Congress*] (LCLS)

MDBVHS....... Mabel D. Bacon Vocational High School (SAUO)

MdBWA....... Walters Art Gallery, Baltimore, MD [*Library symbol*] [*Library of Congress*] (LCLS)

MdBWe....... Westinghouse Defense and Space Center, Baltimore, MD [*Library symbol*] [*Library of Congress*] (LCLS)

MdBWesE ... Western Electric Co., Inc., Baltimore, MD [*Library symbol*] [*Library of Congress*] (LCLS)

MdBwiNA..... National Aeronautics and Space Administration, Scientific and Technical Information Facility, Baltimore/Washington International Airport, MD [*Library symbol*] [*Library of Congress*] (LCLS)

MDC........... Atlantic Aero, Inc. [*ICAO designator*] (FAAC)

MDC........... Boston, MA [*Location identifier*] [*FAA*] (FAAL)

MDC........... Dow Chemical Co., Library, Midland, MI [*OCLC symbol*] (OCLC)

MDC........... Machinability Data Center [*Computerized search service*] [*Metcut Research Associates, Inc.*] (IID)

MDC........... Machinery Diagnostic Consultant [*Software program*]

MDC........... Macrophage-Derived Chemokine [*Immunology*]

MDC........... Magnetic Drum Calculator (RALS)

MDC........... Main Display Console

MDC........... Maintenance Data Center (MCD)

MDC........... Maintenance Data Collection [*Military*] (AFM)

MDC........... Maintenance Dependency Chart (IEEE)

MDC........... Major Diagnostic Categories [*Medicine*]

MDC........... Major Distribution Centre (SAUO)

MDC........... Management Data Corporation (SAUO)

MDC........... Management Development Course (MCD)

MDC........... Manhattan Drug Co.

MDC........... Manhattan Drug Corporation (SAUO)

MDC........... Manitoba Development Corporation (SAUO)

MDC........... Manual Direction Center [*Air Force*] (AFM)

MDC........... Manufacturer Declaration of Conformity (SAUO)

MDC........... Manufacturing Development Center (SAUO)

MDC........... Manufacturing Development Council (SAUO)

MDC........... Marshal of the Diplomatic Corps (SAUO)

MDC........... Mason-Dixon Conference (PSS)

MDC........... Master Data Center, Inc. [*Information service or system*] (IID)

MDC........... Master Direction Center [*Air Force*]

MDC........... Master Document Control (ACAE)

MDC........... Materials Dissemination Center [*Institute for Development of Educational Activities*]

MDC........... Max-Delbrueck-Center [*Berlin, Germany*]

MDC........... Maximum Deductible Contribution [*Superannuation*]

MDC........... Maximum Dependable Capacity [*Nuclear energy*] (NRCH)

MDC........... Maximum Depth of Colonization [*Botany*]

MDC........... McAfee Development Center (SAUO)

MDC........... McDonnell Douglas Corp. (MCD)

MDC........... MDC Corp. [*Associated Press*] (SAG)

MDC........... M.D.C Hldgs [*NYSE symbol*] (TTSB)

MDC........... MDC Holdings, Inc. [*NYSE symbol*] (SPSG)

MDC........... Mead Data Central, Inc. [*Dayton, OH*]

MDC........... Mead Data Control (NITA)

MDC........... Mechanical Development Committee (SAUO)

MDC........... Mechanically Deboned Chicken [*Food technology*]

MDC........... Medial Dorsal Cutaneous [*Nerve*] [*Medicine*] (STED)

Md C........... Medical Corps (SAUO)

MDC........... Mediterranean Development Corporation Fund S.A. (SAUO)

MDC........... Medullary Collecting Duct [*Medicine*] (STED)

MDC........... Memory Disk Controller

MDC........... Menado [*Indonesia*] [*Airport symbol*] (OAG)

MDC........... Message conversion system directory Component (SAUS)

MDC........... Message Display Console (MCD)

MDC........... Message Distribution Center (NATG)

MDC........... Meteorological Data Collection

MDC........... Metropolitan District Commission

MDC........... Metropolitan District Council [*British*]

MDC........... Microcomputer Development Center (SAUO)

MDC........... Microprocessor Development Center [*American Microsystems Inc. US*] (NITA)

MDC........... Mild Detonating Cord (MCD)

MDC........... Military District Commander

MDC........... Military District Court (SAUO)

MDC........... Milk Development Council (GVA)

MDC........... Million Dollar Contract [*File*] [*Military*]

MDC........... Milwaukee-Downer College [*Later, Lawrence University*] [*Wisconsin*]

MDC............ Mine Data Centre (SAUO)
MDC............ Mine Dispatch Control
MDC............ Minerals Development Corporation (SAUO)
MDC............ Miniature Detonating Cord (MCD)
MDC............ Minimal Detectable Concentration (STED)
MDC............ Minimobile Data Center [Military]
MDC............ Minimum Detectable Concentration [Analytical chemistry]
MDC............ Ministere des Communications [Department of Communications] [Canada]
MDC............ Minnesota Department of Corrections (SAUO)
MDC............ Missile Development Center [Air Force]
MDC............ Missile Direction Center
MDC............ Missile Display Conference (SAUO)
MDC............ Mission Director Center [NASA] (KSC)
MDC............ Mission Duty Cycle [NASA] (KSC)
MDC............ Mobile Data Center (ACAE)
MDC............ Mobile Defence Corps [British military] (DMA)
MDC............ Mobile Distress Call
MDC............ Modification Detection Code (HGAA)
MDC............ Modified Direct Costs (SAUO)
MDC............ Mongoloid Development Council [Later, NADS] (EA)
MDC............ Montreal Diocesan College [Quebec]
MDC............ Montreux Development [Vancouver Stock Exchange symbol]
MDC............ More Developed Country
MDC............ Mother's Day Council (EA)
MDC............ Motor Dealers' Council [New South Wales, Australia]
MDC............ Motor Direct-Connected
MDC............ Mount Diablo [California] [Seismograph station code, US Geological Survey] (SEIS)
MDC............ Movement Designator Code
MDC............ Muller Data Corp. [Information service or system] (IID)
MDC............ Mullerian Duct Cyst [Medicine] (MELL)
MDC............ Multidimensional Concept [Combines robotic combat vehicles with other unmanned systems] [Army] (RDA)
MDC............ Multilayer Dielectric Coating
MDC............ Multiple Delay Code (AFIT)
MDC............ Multiple Device Controller
MDC............ Multiple Drone Control (MCD)
MDC............ Multistage Depressed Collector (IAA)
MDC............ Radio set control group (SAUO)
MDCA .... Main Distribution Control Assembly (MCD)
MDCA .... Manufacturing Design Change Analysis
MDCA .... Master Diamond Cutters Association (SAUO)
MDCA .... MDC Corp. CI'A' [NASDAQ symbol] (SG)
MDCA .... Mind Development and Control Association (EA)
MDCAC .... Manufacturing Department Change Analysis Commitment (SAA)
MdCam........ Dorchester County Public Library, Cambridge, MD [Library symbol] [Library of Congress] (LCLS)
MdCatSG ..... Spring Grove State Hospital, Catonsville, MD [Library symbol] [Library of Congress] (LCLS)
MDCB .... Moisture Detector Control Box
MDCC .... Master Data Control Console
MDCC .... Molecular Devices [NASDAQ symbol] (TTSB)
MDCC .... Molecular Devices Corp. [NASDAQ symbol] (SAG)
MDCC .... Monaural Detection with Contralateral Cue (PDAA)
MDCD .... Meridian Data [NASDAQ symbol] (TTSB)
MDCD .... Meridian Data, Inc. [NASDAQ symbol] (SAG)
MdCe .... Queen Anne's County Free Library, Centreville, MD [Library symbol] [Library of Congress] (LCLS)
MDCEF........ Medical-Dental Committee on Evaluation of Fluoridation [Defunct] (EA)
MDCGC....... Multidimensional Capillary Gas Chromatography
MD Ch .... Maryland Chancery Reports, by Johnson [4 vols.] [A publication] (DLA)
MDCH .... MDC Holdings, Inc. (MCD)
MDCH .... Michigan Department of Community Health (SAUO)
MDCH .... Middlesex, Duke of Cambridge's Hussars [Military unit] [British]
MD Chan ..... Maryland Chancery Decisions [A publication] (DLA)
MD Chan Dec... Maryland Chancery Decisions [A publication] (DLA)
MD Ch D..... Maryland Chancery Decisions [A publication] (DLA)
MD Ch Dec... Maryland Chancery Decisions [A publication] (DLA)
MdChW....... Washington College, Chestertown, MD [Library symbol] [Library of Congress] (LCLS)
MDCI .... Medical Action Industries [NASDAQ symbol] (TTSB)
MDCI .... Medical Action Industries, Inc. [NASDAQ symbol] (NQ)
MDCI .... Multidisciplinary Counterintelligence (MCD)
MDCK .... Madin-Darby Canine Kidney [Cell line]
MDCL.......... Medical Control [NASDAQ symbol] (SAG)
MDCL.......... MedicalControl Inc [NASDAQ symbol] (TTSB)
MDCLC .... Medical Control, Inc. [NASDAQ symbol] (SG)
MDCLW ...... MedicalControl Wrrt [NASDAQ symbol] (TTSB)
MDCM .... Doctor of Medicine and Master of Surgery (DD)
MDCM .... Medicinae Doctor Chirurgia Magister [Doctor of Medicine and Master of Surgery]
MDCMA ...... Melvil Dui Chowder and Marching Association [Later, MDMCA] (EA)
MDCO .... Consuelo, San Pedro De Macoris [Dominican Republic] [ICAO location identifier] (ICLI)
MDCO .... Marine Drilling [NASDAQ symbol] (TTSB)
MDCO .... Marine Drilling Co. [NASDAQ symbol] (NQ)
MdCoA .... Arctec, Inc., Columbia, MD [Library symbol] [Library of Congress] (LCLS)
MD Code Ann... Annotated Code of Maryland [A publication] (DLA)
MdCoG....... W. R. Grace & Co., Research Library, Columbia, MD [Library symbol] [Library of Congress] (LCLS)

MdCoH........ Hittman Associates, Inc., Columbia, MD [Library symbol] [Library of Congress] (LCLS)
MdConn ...... Mid-Conn Bank [Associated Press] (SAG)
MD Const..... Maryland Constitution [A publication] (DLA)
Mdcore .... Medicore, Inc. [Associated Press] (SAG)
MdCpM....... United States Bureau of Mines, College Park Research Center, College Park, MD [Library symbol] [Library of Congress] (LCLS)
MDCPZ .... Monodesmethylchlorpromazine [Biochemistry]
MDCR .... Cabo Rojo [Dominican Republic] [ICAO location identifier] (ICLI)
MDCR .... Maintenance Data Collection Report (MCD)
MDCR .... Medcross, Inc. [NASDAQ symbol] (NQ)
MDCR .... Michigan Department of Civil Rights
MDCR .... Miller-Dieker Chromosomal Region [Genetics]
MDCR .... Mini Digital Cassette Recorder (VLIE)
MDCRS .... Meteorological Data Collection and Reporting System [FAA] (TAG)
MDCS .... Maintenance Data Collection System [or Subsystem] [Navy]
MDCS .... Malfunction Display and Control System (MCD)
MDCS .... Manufacturing and Distribution Control System
MDCS .... Master Data Control System [Computer science] (IAA)
MDCS .... Master Digital Command System
MDCS .... Material Data Collection System [NASA] (KSC)
MDCS .... Metering and Directional Control System
MDCS .... Mission Data Collection Sheets (CINC)
MDCS .... Mutual Defense Control Staff [Department of State]
MDCS .... Santo Domingo [Dominican Republic] [ICAO location identifier] (ICLI)
MDCSC .... McDonnell Douglas Computer Systems Co. [Formerly, MICRODATA] (MCD)
MDC/SS ...... Multiple Drone Control Strike System (MCD)
MD/CSU ...... Motor Drive Cassette Support Unit
MDCT.......... Mechanical Draft Cooling Tower [Nuclear energy] (NRCH)
MDCT.......... Median Corrective Maintenance Time (MCD)
MDCT.......... Multidimensional Compensatory Task
MdCtr......... Medical Control [Associated Press] (SAG)
MdCu .... Allegany County Library, Cumberland, MD [Library symbol] [Library of Congress] (LCLS)
MDCU .... Magnetic Disk Control Unit
MDCU .... Mobile Dynamic Checkout Unit (AAG)
MDCU .... Multi-Display Control Unit (VLIE)
MdCuAC....... Allegany Community College, Cumberland, MD [Library symbol] [Library of Congress] (LCLS)
MdCvH .... Crownsville State Hospital, Crownsville, MD [Library symbol] [Library of Congress] (LCLS)
MDC-W .... McDonnell Douglas Corporation-West (SAUO)
MDCZ.......... Constanza [Dominican Republic] [ICAO location identifier] (ICLI)
MdD............ Caroline County Public Library, Denton, MD [Library symbol] [Library of Congress] (LCLS)
MDD .... Doctor of Dental Medicine
MDD .... Machine Dependent Data (OA)
MDD .... Madrid [Spain] [Seismograph station code, US Geological Survey] [Closed] (SEIS)
MDD .... Magnetic Disk Drive
MDD .... Maintenance Design Disclosure
MDD .... Maintenance Due Date (NVT)
MDD .... Major Depressive Disorder [Psychiatry]
MDD .... Male Development Disorder (MELL)
MDD .... Management Division Director (SAUO)
MdD............ Mandaic Dictionary [Oxford] [A publication] (BJA)
MDD .... Manic-Depressive Disorder [Medicine] (STED)
MDD .... Marijuana Detection Dog (DNAB)
MDD .... Mate/Demate Device [Aerospace] (NAKS)
MDD .... Maximum Daily Dose (SAUO)
MDD .... McDonald & Co. Invest [NYSE symbol] (TTSB)
MDD .... McDonald & Co. Investments, Inc. [NYSE symbol] (SPSG)
MDD .... Mean Daily Difference [Medicine]
MDD .... Mean Daily Dose
MdD............ Median Deviation [Statistics]
MDD .... Median Droplet Diameter
MDD .... Medical Device Directive (SAUO)
MDD .... Medical Device Directorate (SAUO)
MDD .... Meteorological Data Distribution
MDD .... Midland, TX [Location identifier] [FAA] (FAAL)
MDD .... Milligrams per Square Decimeter per Day
MDD .... Million-Dollar Deal
MDD .... Million Dollar Directory [Dun's Marketing Services] [Parsippany, NJ] [Database]
MDD .... Mineral Deposits Division, Geological Association of Canada (SAUO)
MDD .... Mission Data Display
MDD .... Mission Description Document (SSD)
MDD .... Mouvement Democratique Dahomeen [Dahomean Democratic Movement] [Political party]
MDD .... Multichannel Demultiplexer and Distributor
MDD .... Multidimensional Database
MDD .... Multiple Disk Drive [Computer science] (VLIE)
MDD .... Puerto Maldonado [Peru] [Airport symbol] (AD)
MDDA .... Manic Depressive and Depressive Association [Later, NDMDA] (EA)
MDDA .... Mechanicsburg Defense Depot Activity [AEC]
MDDA .... Minnesota Differential Diagnosis of Aphasia (STED)
MDDB .... Multi-Dimensional Data Base [Computer science] (VLIE)
MDDB .... Multidimensional Database (IDAI)
MDDBMS.... Multi-Dimensional Data Base Management System [Computer science] (VLIE)
MDDC .... Management Decisions Development Corporation [Canada] (NITA)
MDDC .... Manhattan District Declassified Code [AEC]
MDDC .... Military Dependents Dental Clinic (SAUO)
MDDC .... Motor Dealers' Disputes Council [Australia]

MDDCS........	Memorial Dose Distribution Computation Service [*Memorial Sloan-Kettering Cancer Center*] [*Information service or system*] (IID)
MDDD.........	Merrill-Demos DD Scale [*Drug abuse and delinquent behavior test*]
MDDE.........	Maryland & Delaware Railroad Co. [*AAR code*]
MDDF.........	Minimum Delay Data Format (MCD)
MDDI..........	Medical Devices, Diagnostics, & Instrumentation [*Center for Devices and Radiological Health*] [*Also known as The Gray Sheet*] [*A publication*]
MDDJ.........	Dajabon [*Dominican Republic*] [*ICAO location identifier*] (ICLI)
MDDO.........	Maintenance Department (SAUO)
MDDPC........	Methyl Dimethyldihydropyrancarboxylate [*Organic chemistry*]
MDDPM........	Magnetic Drum Data Processing Machine (IAA)
MDDR.........	Maintenance Design Data Report (ACAE)
MDDR.........	Mimimum Distance Decoding Rule (IAA)
MDDS.........	Maintainability Design Data Sheets (MCD)
MDDS.........	Material Directory Data Sheet (MCD)
MDDS.........	Media Documentation Distribution Set (VLIE)
MDDT.........	Master Digital Data Tape (PDAA)
MDDU.........	Manual Data Display Unit [*Computer science*] (VLIE)
MDDUS........	Medical and Dental Defence Union of Scotland (SAUO)
MDDX.........	Middlesex [*Region of London*]
MDE..........	Cincinnati, OH [*Location identifier*] [*FAA*] (FAAL)
MDE..........	Madame (ROG)
MDE..........	Magnetic Decision Element [*Computer science*] (BUR)
MDE..........	Main Distribution Equipment (IAA)
MDE..........	Major Defense Equipment (MCD)
MDE..........	Major Depressive Episode [*Medicine*] (DMAA)
MDE..........	Manufacturing Development Engineering (SAUO)
MDE..........	Master of Developmental Economics (PGP)
MDE..........	Master of Distance Education (PGP)
MDE..........	Master of Domestic Economy (NADA)
MDE..........	Matrix Difference Equation
MDE..........	McDermott, Inc. [*Formerly, Offshore Pipelines*] [*NYSE symbol*] (SAG)
MDE..........	Mechanical Design Environment
MDE..........	Medeea Ltd. [*Romania*] [*FAA designator*] (FAAC)
MDE..........	Medellin [*Colombia*] [*Airport symbol*] (OAG)
MDE..........	Message Distribution Element (SAUO)
MDE..........	Meteoroid Detection Experiment (KSC)
MDE..........	Metina Development [*Vancouver Stock Exchange symbol*]
MDE..........	Middle East (CARB)
MDE..........	Midland Diving Equipment Ltd. (SAUO)
MDE..........	Military Damage Expectancy
MDE..........	Mindy Explorations Ltd. [*Vancouver Stock Exchange symbol*]
MDE..........	Minnesota State Department of Education, Professional Library, St. Paul, MN [*OCLC symbol*] (OCLC)
MDE..........	Missile Display Equipment
MDE..........	Mission Defendent Experiment
MDE..........	Mission Dependent Elements [*NASA*] (KSC)
MDE..........	Mission Dependent Equipment [*NASA*] (KSC)
MDE..........	Mission Dependent Experiment [*NASA*] (NASA)
MDE..........	Mission Display Equipment
MDE..........	Mobile District Engineer (AAG)
MDE..........	Mobile Telemetering Station [*ITU designation*] (DEN)
MDE..........	Modern Drug Encyclopedia [*A publication*]
MDE..........	Modular Design of Electronics (MCD)
MDE..........	Modular Display Electronics (MCD)
MDE..........	Mooring Dynamics Experiment [*Marine science*] (MSC)
MDE..........	Motor Drive Electronics (ACAE)
MdE..........	Mount St. Mary's College, Emmitsburg, MD [*Library symbol*] [*Library of Congress*] (LCLS)
MDE..........	Multidisciplinary Evaluation
MDE..........	National Library of Medicine [*Source file*] [*UTLAS symbol*]
MDEA.........	Marketing and Distributive Education Association [*Later, MEA*] (EA)
MDEA.........	Media 100
MDEA.........	Methyldiethanolamine [*Organic chemistry*]
MDEA.........	Methylenedioxyethamphetamine [*Biochemistry*]
MdEa.........	Talbot County Free Library, Easton, MD [*Library symbol*] [*Library of Congress*] (LCLS)
MDEBP........	Mean Daily Erect Blood Pressure (STED)
MDEC.........	Marine Corps Development and Education Command (SAUO)
MDEC.........	McDonnell Douglas Electronics Company (SAUO)
MDEC.........	Motion Decoder (SAUS)
M Dec S.....	Master of Decision Sciences (PGP)
MdEdgA.......	United States Army, Technical Library, Army Chemical Center, Edgewood, MD [*Library symbol*] [*Library of Congress*] (LCLS)
MDedHi.......	Dedham Historical Society, Dedham, MA [*Library symbol*] [*Library of Congress*] (LCLS)
MDee.........	Dickinson Library, Deerfield, MA [*Library symbol*] [*Library of Congress*] (LCLS)
MDeeD........	Deerfield Academy, Deerfield, MA [*Library symbol*] [*Library of Congress*] (LCLS)
MDeeH........	Historic Deerfield, Inc., Deerfield, MA [*Library symbol*] [*Library of Congress*] (LCLS)
MDeeP........	Pocumtuck Valley Memorial Association, Deerfield, MA [*Library symbol*] [*Library of Congress*] (LCLS)
MDefStudies...	Master of Defence Studies
MDEFWP.......	Motor-Driven Emergency Feedwater Pump [*Nuclear energy*] (NRCH)
MDEL.........	Major Defense Equipment List
M-DEMO.......	Maintenance Demonstration [*DoD*]
MDEN.........	Enriquillo [*Dominican Republic*] [*ICAO location identifier*] (ICLI)
MDEN.........	Males, Density Of [*Ecology*]
MDENDET.....	Mobile Dental Detachment [*Coast Guard*]
M Dent Sc..	Master of Dental Science [*British*]
MDEP.........	Maine Department of Environmental Protection
MDEP.........	Management Decision Package [*DoD*]
MDEP.........	Modernization Development Plan (SAUS)
MDEPrA.......	McDermott Inc $2.20 cm Cv A Pfd [*NYSE symbol*] (TTSB)
MDEPrB.......	McDermott Inc. $2.60 cm Pfd [*NYSE symbol*] (TTSB)
MDEQ.........	Massachusetts Department of Environmental Quality (SAUO)
MDERDA......	Maximum Degree of Emissions Reduction Deemed Achievable [*Environmental Protection Agency*]
M Des........	Master of Design
MDes.........	Mercedarios Descalzos (TOCD)
MDES.........	Multi-Data Entry System [*Computer science*] (VLIE)
MDES.........	Multiple Data Entry System
M Des (RCA)...	Master of Design, Royal College of Art
MDesS........	Master of Design Studies (GAGS)
MDesSt.......	Master of Design Studies
MDET.........	Militarized Digital Element Tester (MCD)
MDEU.........	Material Delivery Expeditor Unit (DNAB)
MDEX.........	Medex, Inc. [*NASDAQ symbol*] (NQ)
MDF..........	Macrodefect Free [*Materials science*]
MDF..........	Macular Degeneration Foundation (SAUO)
MDF..........	Magnetic Direction Finding [*Meteorology*]
MDF..........	Magyar Demokrata Forum [*Hungarian Democratic Forum*] [*Political party*] (EY)
MDF..........	Main Distributing Frame [*Bell System*]
MDF..........	Main Distribution Frame (NITA)
MDF..........	Maintenance Data Form (ACAE)
MDF..........	Maintenance Depot Fabrication
MDF..........	Manipulator Deployment Facility (MCD)
MDF..........	Manipulator Development Facility [*NASA*] (NASA)
MDF..........	Manitoba Development Fund (SAUO)
MDF..........	Manpower Data File (SAUO)
MDF..........	Manual Direction Finder [*Radio*]
MDF..........	Manufacturer's Designated Fuel [*Automotive engineering*]
MDF..........	Map-Dot-Fingerprint Dystrophy (SAUS)
MDF..........	Maritime Defence Force (SAUO)
MDF..........	Market Development Funds [*Business term*]
MDF..........	Master Data File (AFIT)
MDF..........	Master Directory File [*Computer science*]
MDF..........	Master Distribution Frame [*Electronics*] (ECII)
MDF..........	Master Document File [*Computer science*]
MDF..........	Mate/Demate Facility [*NASA*] (NASA)
MDF..........	Mating/Demating Facilities (SAUS)
MDF..........	Mean Dominant Frequency (MAE)
MDF..........	Median Demagnetizing Field [*Geophysics*]
MDF..........	Medium Density Fiberboard
MDF..........	Medium-Frequency Direction Finder [*or Finding*]
MDF..........	Menu Definition File (SAUS)
MDF..........	Metals Datafile [*Materials Information*] [*Information service or system*] (IID)
MDF..........	Metric Data Facility (MCD)
MDF..........	Microcomputer Development Facilities (IEEE)
MDF..........	Micro Defect Free
MDF..........	Micro-Dose-Focusing [*Electron microscopy*]
MDF..........	Midland Doherty Financial Corp. [*Toronto Stock Exchange symbol*]
MDF..........	Midtfly Aps [*Denmark*] [*ICAO designator*] (FAAC)
MDF..........	Midwest Democratic Front (SAUO)
MDF..........	Mild Detonating Fuse
MDF..........	Minimum Detectable Flux
MDF..........	Mission Data File (SAUS)
MDF..........	Mission Degradation Factor (SAUS)
MDF..........	Mixed Dipterocarp Forest
MDF..........	Modify
MDF..........	Monopulse Direction Finding (SAUS)
MDF..........	Mooreland, OK [*Location identifier*] [*FAA*] (FAAL)
MDF..........	Multiband Direction Finder
MDF..........	Myocardial Depressant Factor
MDF/1........	Metals Data File/1 (NITA)
MDFA.........	Magnet Distributors and Fabricators Association (NTPA)
MDFA.........	Mitochondrial Disorders Foundation of America (SAUO)
MDFAT........	Microsoft DoubleSpace File Allocation Table (PCM)
MDFC.........	Mason Dixon International Fan Club (EA)
MDFC.........	Matt Dillon Fan Club (EA)
MDFC.........	McDonnel Douglas Finance Corporation (SAUO)
MDFC.........	McDonnell Douglas Finance Corp. Ltd. [*British*]
MDFCTA......	Metropolitan Drinking Fountain and Cattle Trough Association (SAUO)
MDFD.........	Map-Dot-Fingerprint Dystrophy [*Medicine*] (DMAA)
MdFdBc.......	Maryland Federal Bancorp, Inc. [*Associated Press*] (SAG)
MdFdM........	United States Army Medical Intelligence and Information Agency, Fort Detrick, MD [*Library symbol*] [*Library of Congress*] (LCLS)
MdFhV........	United States Veterans Administration Hospital, Fort Howard, MD [*Library symbol*] [*Library of Congress*] (LCLS)
MD Fla......	United States District Court for the Middle District of Florida (DLA)
MDFLT........	Multi-Directional Forklift Truck (MCD)
MdFmA........	United States Army, Fort George G. Meade Post Recreation Services Library, Fort George G. Meade, MD [*Library symbol*] [*Library of Congress*] (LCLS)
MdFmN.......	National Security Agency, Fort George G. Meade, MD [*Library symbol*] [*Library of Congress*] (LCLS)
MDFMR.......	M-Day Force Materiel Requirement
MDFNA.......	Maximum Density Fuming Nitric Acid
MDFP.........	Mission Data Formats Project [*NASA*] (SSD)
MDFR.........	Make Descent From [*Aviation*] (FAAC)
MDFR.........	Master Data File Record (ACAE)
MDFRC.......	Murray-Darling Freshwater Research Centre (SAUO)
MdFre........	Frederick County Public Library, Frederick, MD [*Library symbol*] [*Library of Congress*] (LCLS)

MdFreCR	Frederick Cancer Research Center, Frederick, MD [*Library symbol*] [*Library of Congress*] (LCLS)
MdFreD	Fort Detrick Technical Library, Frederick, MD [*Library symbol*] [*Library of Congress*] (LCLS)
MdFreFC	Frederick Community College, Frederick, MD [*Library symbol*] [*Library of Congress*] (LCLS)
MdFreH	Hood College, Frederick, MD [*Library symbol*] [*Library of Congress*] (LCLS)
MdFreHi	[*The*] Historical Society of Frederick County, Inc., Frederick, MD [*Library symbol*] [*Library of Congress*] (LCLS)
MdFreSD	Maryland School for the Deaf, Frederick, MD [*Library symbol*] [*Library of Congress*] (LCLS)
MdFroS	Frostburg State College, Frostburg, MD [*Library symbol*] [*Library of Congress*] (LCLS)
MDFRR	Mission Directors Flight Readiness Review [*NASA*] (KSC)
MDG	Air Madagascar, Societe Nationale Malgache de Transports Aeriens [*ICAO designator*] (FAAC)
MDG	Machinery Defective, Government-Furnished (DNAB)
MDG	Machining-Intensive Durable Goods [*Manufacturing*]
MDG	Madagascar [*ANSI three-letter standard code*] (CNC)
Mdg	Madagascar (MILB)
MDG	Madang [*Papua New Guinea*] [*Seismograph station code, US Geological Survey*] (SEIS)
MDG	Major Donors Group (SAUO)
MDG	Marina Development Group [*Commercial firm*] [*British*]
MDG	Marine Data Group (SAUO)
MDG	Mean Diastolic Gradient [*Medicine*] (DMAA)
MDG	Medical Director-General [*Navy*]
MDG	Meridian Gold [*NYSE symbol*] [*Formerly, FMC Gold*] (SG)
MDG	Message Design Guidelines Group (SAUO)
MDG	Metal Density Gauge
MDG	Metasystems Design Group, Inc. [*Arlington, VA*] [*Telecommunications service*] (TSSD)
MDG	Methyladenine Deoxyribonucleic Acid Glycosylase [*Medicine*] (DMAA)
MDG	Mission Data Generation (ACAE)
MDG	Mission Data Generator (SAUO)
MDG	Mission Definition Group (SAUO)
MDG	Molecular Drag Gauge [*Instrumentation*]
MDG	Mono/Diglycerides
MDG	Multi-Disciplinary Group (SAUO)
MDG	Multimedia Development Group (DDC)
MDG	Multiple Diffraction Gratings (ACAE)
MDG	Multiplier Decoder Gate [*Computer science*]
MDG	Multipurpose Display Group (MCD)
MDG	Valdosta, GA [*Location identifier*] [*FAA*] (FAAL)
MDGA	Guerra [*Dominican Republic*] [*ICAO location identifier*] (ICLI)
MD GA	United States District Court for the Middle District of Georgia (DLA)
MDGC	Multidimensional Gas Chromatography
MDGD	Mercury Doped Germanium Detector
MDGF	Macrophage Derived Growth Factor [*Biochemistry*]
MDGGB	Muscular Dystrophy Group of Great Britain (SAUO)
MDGLS	Missouri Division of Geology and Land Survey (SAUO)
MDG(N)	Medical Director-General (Navy) [*British*]
MDGP	Medgroup Inc. Calif [*NASDAQ symbol*] (TTSB)
MDGP	Monash Division of General Practice (SAUO)
MDGR	Multi-Differential GPS Receiver
MDG RCN	Medical Director General of the Royal Canadian Navy (SAUO)
MDGT	Midget (MSA)
MDGWS	Modular Digital Guided Weapon System (ACAE)
MDH	Carbondale [*Illinois*] [*Airport symbol*] (OAG)
MDH	Carbondale/Murphysboro, IL [*Location identifier*] [*FAA*] (FAAL)
MDH	Madison Holdings Ltd. [*Vancouver Stock Exchange symbol*]
MDH	Magnetic Drum Head
MDH	Major Damage History [*Aviation*] (PIPO)
MDH	Malate Dehydrogenase [*Also, MD*] [*An enzyme*]
MDH	Maneuver Director Headquarters [*Military*]
MDH	Maximum Diameter Heat [*Nuclear science*] (OA)
MDH	Mean Dominant Height
MDH	Medullary Dorsal Horn [*Anatomy*]
MDH	Minimum Descent Height [*Aviation*] (FAAC)
MDH	Minnesota Department of Health (SAUO)
MDH	Month-Day-Hour [*Automotive manufacturing*]
MDH	Multidirectional Harassment (PDAA)
MDHA	Masters Deerhounds Association [*British*] (DBA)
MdHag	Washington County Free Library, Hagerstown, MD [*Library symbol*] [*Library of Congress*] (LCLS)
MDHBA	Medical-Dental-Hospital Bureaus of America (EA)
MDHC	McDonnell Douglas Helicopter Co. [*Formerly, HHI*] (MCD)
MDHC	Mersey Docks and Harbour Co. [*British*]
MDHE	Herrera [*Dominican Republic*] [*ICAO location identifier*] (ICLI)
MdHeH	Henryton State Hospital, Henryton, MD [*Library symbol*] [*Library of Congress*] (LCLS)
MdHi	Maryland Historical Society, Baltimore, MD [*Library symbol*] [*Library of Congress*] (LCLS)
Md Hist	Maryland Historical Society (SAUO)
MDHJ	Methyl Dihydrojasmonate [*Organic chemistry*]
MDHL	Modified Hodges-Lehmann Estimator [*Statistics*]
MDHR	Maximum Determined Heart Rate (STED)
MDHR	Methyl Dihydroretinoate [*Biochemistry*]
MDHR	Mini-Decay Heat Removal [*Nuclear energy*] (NRCH)
MDHS	Malate Dehydrogenase, Soluble (STED)
MDHS	McDonnell Douglas Helicopter Systems
MDHTSNAGEJTR	Movement of Dependents and Household Goods to Temporary Station[*s*] Not Authorized at Government Expense, Except as Prescribed in Joint Travel Regulations [*Army*] (AABC)
MDHV	Marek's Disease Herpesvirus [*Medicine*] (DMAA)
MDHY	Higuey [*Dominican Republic*] [*ICAO location identifier*] (ICLI)
MdHyD	De Sales Hall School of Theology, Hyattsville, MD [*Library symbol*] [*Library of Congress*] (LCLS)
MdHyP	Prince George's County Memorial Library, Hyattsville, MD [*Library symbol*] [*Library of Congress*] (LCLS)
MDI	Bemidji, MN [*Location identifier*] [*FAA*] (FAAL)
MDI	C-Methylene-Bisphenol-Isocyanate (SAUS)
MDI	Magnetic Detection Indicator (IAA)
MDI	Magnetic Direction Indicator
MDI	Makurdi [*Nigeria*] [*Airport symbol*] (OAG)
MDI	Management Development Institute (MCD)
MDI	Manic Depression Interval [*Course*]
MDI	Manic Depressive Illness
MDI	Manual Data Input [*SAGE*]
MDI	Manufacturing Development Initiative (SAUO)
MDI	Manufacturing Division Instructions (ACAE)
MDI	Market Decisions, Inc. [*Information service or system*] (IID)
MDI	Market Development Index [*Business term*] (DOAD)
MDI	Master Dimension Information
MDI	Master Direction Indicator
MDI	Master of Didactics
MDI	Material Departmental Instruction
MDI	Mechanical Dynamics Inc. (NITA)
MDI	Media Directions, Inc.
MDI	Media Directors, Incorporated (SAUO)
MDI	Media (or Medium) Dependant (or Dependent) Interface (SAUS)
MDI	Medium Dependent Interface [*Computer science*] (CDE)
MDI	Memotec Data, Inc. [*Toronto Stock Exchange symbol*]
MDI	Mental Development Index [*Bayley Scales of Infant Development*] [*Psychometrics*]
MDI	Meridian Diagnostics, Inc.
MDI	Metered Dose Inhaler [*Medicine*]
MDI	Methylendiphenyldiisocyanat (SAUS)
MDI	Methylenebis (Phenylisocyanate) (GNE)
MDI	Methylene Diisocyanate [*Organic chemistry*]
MDI	Methylene Diphenyl Diisocyanate [*Organic chemistry*]
MDI	Methylene Diphenylene Diisocyanate (SAUS)
MDI	Methylenediphenyl Isocyanate [*Organic chemistry*]
MDI	Michelson Doppler Imager [*Instrumentation*]
MDI	Michigan Disposal, Inc. (EFIS)
MDI	Micro Design International
MDI	Microdosimetric Instrumentation
MDI	Mid America Realty, Inc. [*Formerly, Dial REIT*] [*NYSE symbol*] (SAG)
MDI	Mid-America Realty Inv [*NYSE symbol*] (TTSB)
MDI	Military Decision Items (AFIT)
MDI	Mineral Deposit Inventory Database [*Ontario Geological Survey*] [*Information service or system*] [*Canada*] (CRD)
MDI	Minimum Discrimination Information [*Statistics*]
MDI	Miss-Distance Indicator [*Missiles*] (MUGU)
MDI	Mission Dependent Interface
MDI	Mission to the Deaf, International (EA)
MDI	Mobile Data Initiative (SAUO)
MDI	Mobilization Day Increment [*Military*]
MDI	Mobilization Day Index [*Military*] (NG)
MDI	Modular Devices Inc. (SAUS)
MDI	Monopulse Display Improvement (IAA)
MDI	Monthly Debit Industrial [*Insurance*]
MDI	Mouvement pour la Democratie et l'Independance [*Movement for Democracy and Independence*] [*Central Africa*] (PD)
MDI	Multiple Daily Injection [*Medicine*] (MELL)
MDI	Multiple Design Interface
MDI	Multiple Display Indicator
MDI	Multiple Document Interface [*Computer science*] (PCM)
MDI	Multiple Dosage Insulin [*Medicine*] (STED)
MDI	Multipurpose Display Indicator (ACAE)
MDI	Multiscore Depression Inventory [*Medicine*] (STED)
MDI	Muscular Dystrophy Ireland (NRGU)
MDIA	Mental Development Index, Adjusted (STED)
MDIA	Multidimensional Intraction Analysis (DMAA)
MDIB	Minimum Distribution Incidental Benefit [*Finance*]
MDIBL	Mount Desert Island Biological Laboratory [*Salsbury Cove, ME*] [*Research center*]
MDIC	Malaysian Defence Industries Council (SAUO)
MDIC	Manchester Decoder and Interface Chip (SAUO)
MDIC	Microwave Dielectric Integrated Circuit (IEEE)
MDIC	Multi-Disciplinary Counter Intelligence
MDIC	Multilateral Disarmament Information Centre [*British*]
MDICP	McDonnell Douglas Industrial Control Products (MCD)
M DICT	More Dicto [*As Directed*] [*Pharmacy*]
M Dict	Morison's Dictionary of Decisions, Scotch Court of Session [*1540-1808*] [*A publication*] (DLA)
M Dict	Morrison's Dictionary of Decisions, Scotch Court of Session [*A publication*] (DLA)
M Did	Master of Didactics
M Di E	Master of Diesel Engineering
MDIE	Mother-Daughter Ionosphere Experiment
M Di Eng	Master of Diesel Engineering
MDIF	Manual Data Input Function [*Computer science*]
MDIF & W	Maine Department of Inland Fisheries and Wildlife, Fishery Research Management Division [*Research center*] (RCD)
MDIG	Multiple Display Indicator Group (SAUO)
MDIG	Multipurpose Display Indicator Group (SAUO)
MDII	Management Development II (SAUO)
MDII	Mechanical Dynamics [*NASDAQ symbol*] (TTSB)

MDII	Mechanical Dynamics, Inc. [*NASDAQ symbol*] (SAG)
MDII	Multiple Daily Insulin Injection (STED)
MDIII	Management Development III (SAUO)
MDIN	Medalist Indus [*NASDAQ symbol*] (TTSB)
MDIN	Medalist Industries, Inc. [*NASDAQ symbol*] (NQ)
Md Inst C Art...	Maryland Institute College of Art (GAGS)
MDIO	Maine Debris Information Office [*National Oceanic and Atmospheric Administration*]
M Dip	Master of Diplomacy
M-DIRT	Miss-Distance-Indicator Radioactive Tests [*Missiles*] (MUGU)
MDIS	Maintenance and Diagnostic Information System (ACAE)
MDIS	Manual Data Input Section [*Computer science*]
MDIS	Manual Data Input System [*Computer science*]
M Dis	Marriage Dissolved
MDIS	McDonnell Douglas Information Services
MDIS	McDonnell Information Systems Group (SAUO)
MDIS	Medical Diagnostics Imagery System (SAUS)
MDIS	Medical Digital Imaging Support (RDA)
MDISC	Metadata Interchange Specification [*Computer science*]
MDISC	McDonnell Douglas International Sales Corp. (MCD)
MDISE	Merchandise
MDISI	McDonnell Douglas Information Systems International (SAUO)
MDIT	Mean Disintegration Time (STED)
MDIU	Manned Data Insertion Unit (KSC)
MDIU	Manual Data Input Unit [*Computer science*]
M Div	Master of Divinity
MDIX	Media Dependant Interface Crossed (SAUS)
MDIX	Medium Dependant Interface Crossed (SAUS)
MDJ	Jaro International SA [*Romania*] [*ICAO designator*] (FAAC)
MDJAPAN	McDonnell Douglas Japan Ltd. (SAUO)
MdJC	Maryland House of Corrections, Jessup, MD [*Library symbol*] [*Library of Congress*] (LCLS)
MDJC	Miami-Dade Junior College (SAUO)
MDJC	Mississippi Delta Junior College (SAUO)
MDJCS	Memorandum by the Director, Joint Staff for the Joint Chiefs of Staff (MCD)
Md J Int'l L & Trade...	Maryland Journal of International Law and Trade [*A publication*] (DLA)
MDJL	McDonnell Douglas Japan Ltd. (SAUO)
MDJM	Jainamosa [*Dominican Republic*] [*ICAO location identifier*] (ICLI)
MDK	Mbandaka [*Zaire*] [*Airport symbol*] (OAG)
MDK	Mechanical Disconnect Kit
MDK	Medicore, Inc. [*AMEX symbol*] (SPSG)
MDK	Montana-Dakota Utilities Company (SAUO)
MDK	Multimedia Developers Kit (SAUO)
MDK	Multimedia Development Kit [*Microsoft Corp.*] [*Computer science*]
MDL	Macro Description Language [*Computer science*] (BUR)
MDL	Madill [*S.*] Ltd. [*Vancouver Stock Exchange symbol*]
MDL	Magnetic Delay Line
MDL	Magnetic Double Layer
MDL	Main Defense Line (IAA)
MDL	Maintenance and Diagnostic Logic Display [*Burroughs*] (NITA)
MDL	Maintenance Diagnostic Logic [*Computer science*] (BUR)
MDL	Management Data List (AABC)
MDL	Manager's Discretionary Limit (DCTA)
MDL	Mandala Airlines PT [*Indonesia*] [*ICAO designator*] (FAAC)
MDL	Mandalay [*Burma*] [*Airport symbol*] (AD)
MDL	Mandalay [*Myanmar*] [*Airport symbol*] (OAG)
MDL	Man Days Lost (NUCP)
MDL	Master Data Library [*NASA*]
MDL	Master Deliverables List (AAEL)
MDL	Master Drawing List
MDL	Master Drug List (STED)
MDL	Master of Divine Literature
MDL	Material Deviation List [*Military*]
MDL	Maximum Doping Limit
MDL	Measurement Devices Limited (SAUO)
MDL	Medical Data Limited (SAUO)
MDL	Medulloblastoma [*A type of brain cancer*] (CDI)
MDL	Mercury Delay Line
MDL	Method Detection Limit [*Analytical chemistry*]
MDL	Microprocessor Development Lab (MHDI)
MDL	MicroStation Development Language [*Intergraph Corp.*] (PCM)
MDL	Microwave Delay Line
MDL	Microwave Development Laboratories
MDL	Middle (MSA)
MDL	Military Demarcation Line (CINC)
MDL	Mine Defense Laboratory [*Panama City, Florida*] [*Navy*]
MDL	Miniature Display Light
MDL	Minimum Detectable Level
MDL	Minimum Detection Limit [*Chemistry*]
MDL	Mission Data Load (ACAE)
MDL	Model (ADA)
MDL	Modular Design Language [*Computer science*] (CSR)
MDL	Modular Dummy Load
MDL	Module (MSA)
MDL	Morris Dam Laboratory
MDL	Motor Distal Latency [*Medicine*]
MDL	Muddle [*A computer language*]
MDL	Multi-Disciplinary Laboratory (SAUO)
MDL	Multipurpose Data Link (GAVI)
MDL	S Madill Ltd. [*Vancouver Stock Exchange symbol*]
MDL	University of Baltimore, Law Library, Baltimore, MD [*OCLC symbol*] (OCLC)
MdLA	Maryland Library Association
MD LA	United States District Court for the Middle District of Louisiana (DLA)
MdLaD	Divine Saviour Seminary, Lanham, MD [*Library symbol*] [*Library of Congress*] (LCLS)
MdLapC	Charles County Community College, La Plata, MD [*Library symbol*] [*Library of Congress*] (LCLS)
MD Laws	Laws of Maryland [*A publication*] (DLA)
MDLB	Municipal Development and Loan Board [*Canada*]
MDLC	Material Development and Logistic Command (SAUO)
MDLC	Materiel Development and Logistic Command [*Army - replaced Ordnance, Engineer, Signal, Chemical and Quartermaster Overall Commands*]
MDLC	Mutliple Data Link Controller
MDLD	Midland Financial Group [*NASDAQ symbol*] (SAG)
MDLF	Mobile Drydock Launch Facility
MDLI	MDL Information Sys [*NASDAQ symbol*] (TTSB)
MDLI	MDL Information Systems, Inc. [*NASDAQ symbol*] (SAG)
MDL Info	MDL Information Systems, Inc. [*Associated Press*] (SAG)
Md-LL	Maryland State Law Library, Annapolis, MD [*Library symbol*] [*Library of Congress*] (LCLS)
MDLLE	Mademoiselle
MDLLS	Mediastinal Diffuse Large-Cell Lymphoma with Sclerosis [*Oncology*]
MDLND	Midland
MDLP	Minimum Description Length Principle (IDAI)
MDLP	Mobile Dryer Loan Program
MDLP	Module Data Link Protocol [*Computer science*] (VLIE)
MdLP	United States Department of the Interior, Patuxent Wildlife Research Center, Laurel, MD [*Library symbol*] [*Library of Congress*] (LCLS)
MDLR	La Romana [*Dominican Republic*] [*ICAO location identifier*] (ICLI)
Md-LR	Maryland Department of Legislative Reference, Baltimore, MD [*Library symbol*] [*Library of Congress*] (LCLS)
MDLRC	Mental Disability Legal Resource Center [*Later, MPDLRSDB*] (EA)
MD L Rec	Maryland Law Record [*Baltimore*] [*A publication*] (DLA)
MD L Rep	Maryland Law Reporter [*Baltimore*] [*A publication*] (DLA)
MDLS	Marine Data Logger System
MDLT	Mobile Data Link Terminal (SAUS)
MdLuW	Maryland College for Women, Lutherville, MD [*Library symbol*] [*Library of Congress*] (LCLS)
MDLX	Military Demarkation Line Extended (MCD)
MdLxp	Lexington Park Library, Lexington Park, MD [*Library symbol*] [*Library of Congress*] (LCLS)
Mdm	Madam (WGA)
MDM	Magnetic Disc Memory
MDM	Magnetic Drum Memorex [*Computer science*] (IAA)
MDM	Magneto-Optical Display Memory
MDM	Main Data Memory [*Computer science*] (VLIE)
MDM	Maintenance Depot Material Control
MDM	Maize Dwarf Mosaic Virus [*Plant pathology*]
MDM	Manipulator Deployment Mechanism (MCD)
MDM	Manpower Determination Model [*Military*]
MDM	Manufacturing Data Management (VLIE)
MDM	Maps Distribution Management (SAUO)
MDM	Marketing Data Management (VLIE)
MDM	Marking Diagram Master (MCD)
MDM	Marshall Drummond McCall, Inc. [*Toronto Stock Exchange symbol*]
MDM	Mass Democratic Movement [*Political coalition*] [*South Africa*]
MDM	Master of Development Management
MDM	Maternal Diabetes Mellitus [*Medicine*]
MDM	Maximum Design Meter (MSA)
MDM	Mechanically Deboned Meat [*Food technology*]
MDM	Medical Decision Making (DMAA)
MDM	Medical Monitor (MCD)
MDM	Medium (AABC)
MDM	Medium-Depth Mine (MCD)
MDM	MedPartners/Mullikin [*NYSE symbol*] (TTSB)
MDM	Message Distribution Module (CCCA)
MDM	Metal-Dielectric-Metal [*Filter*]
MDM	Metal Disintegration Machining [*Nuclear energy*] (NRCH)
MDM	Methylenedioxymethamphetamine [*A hallucinogenic drug, also known as "Ecstasy," banned in 1985*] [*Also, MDMA*]
MDM	Michigan-Dartmouth-Massachusetts Institute of Technology [*Observatory*]
MDM	Microdensitometer (IAA)
MDM	Midas Minerals, Inc. [*Toronto Stock Exchange symbol*]
MDM	Mid-Diastolic Murmur [*Medicine*]
MDM	Minor Determinant Mix [*Penicillin*] [*Medicine*] (STED)
MDM	Minor Determinant Mixture [*Medicine*]
MDM	Mission Data Message (SAUO)
MDM	Mission Data Module (ACAE)
MDM	Mixed Dark Matter [*Cosmology*]
MDM	Mobile Depot Maintenance [*Air Force*] (AFM)
MDM	Modified Diffusion Method (NRCH)
MDM	Modular Data Module (HGAA)
MDM	Monolithic Diode Matrix
MDM	Monomethylol Dimethyl (ACAE)
MDM	Movement for a Democratic Military (EA)
MDM	Movimento Democratico de Mocambique [*Democratic Movement of Mozambique*] (AF)
MDM	Multiplexer/Demultiplexer (NASA)
MDM	Multiprocessor Diagnostic Monitor (IAA)
MDM	Working Group on Marine Data Management (SAUO)
MDMA	M-Day Materiel Assets (AFIT)
MDMA	Medical Device Manufacturers Association (NTPA)
MDMA	Methylenedioxymethamphetamine [*A hallucinogenic drug, also known as "Ecstasy," banned in 1985*] [*Also, MDM*]
MDMAA	Mess Deck Master-at-Arms (DNAB)

MDMAF........	Mekong Delta Mobile Afloat Force [*Vietnam*]
Mdmarco.....	Medmarco, Inc. [*Associated Press*] (SAG)
MDMC.........	Medmarco, Inc. [*NASDAQ symbol*] (SAG)
MDMC........	Monte Cristy [*Dominican Republic*] [*ICAO location identifier*] (ICLI)
MDMCA.......	Melvil Dui Marching and Chowder Association (EA)
MdMC-G	Montgomery College, Germantown Campus, Germantown, MD [*Library symbol*] [*Library of Congress*] (LCLS)
MdMC-R	Montgomery College, Rockville Campus, Rockville, MD [*Library symbol*] [*Library of Congress*] (LCLS)
MdMC-T......	Montgomery College, Takoma Park Campus, Takoma Park, MD [*Library symbol*] [*Library of Congress*] (LCLS)
MDMCW	Medmarco Inc. Wrrt'A' [*NASDAQ symbol*] (TTSB)
MDMCZ	Medmarco Inc. Wrrt'B' [*NASDAQ symbol*] (TTSB)
mDMD	Mouse Duchenne Muscular Dystrophy [*Medicine*]
MDME.........	Madame
MDMFM.......	Miniature Digital Matched Filter Module [*Computer science*] (VLIE)
Md-MH	Maryland Department of Mental Hygiene, Baltimore, MD [*Library symbol*] [*Library of Congress*] (LCLS)
MDMH	Methylol Dimethylhydantoin [*Organic chemistry*]
MDML.........	Modified Maximum Likelihood [*Statistics*]
MDMLG	Metropolitan Detroit Medical Library Group (SAUO)
MDMMS	Multidimensional Microscopes and Maize Structures Research Group (SAUO)
MDMN	Modified Posterior Mean [*Statistics*]
MD-MOS......	Multi-Drain Metal-Oxide Semiconductor (AAEL)
MDMR	M-Day Materiel Requirement (AFIT)
MDMR	M-Day Mobilization Requirement
MDMS	Maintenance Data Management Schedule
MDMS	Maintenance Data Management System (SAUO)
MDMS	Marketing Data Management System [*British*]
MDMS	Microbiology Data Management System
MDMS	Miss-Distance Measuring System
MDMS	Moore Data Management Services [*Information service or system*] (IID)
MDMS	Multiple Database Management System (NITA)
MDMS	Multiple Delivery Mine System (SAUS)
MDMSC	McDonnell Douglas Missile Systems Co. (SAUO)
MDMV	Maize Dwarf Mosaic Virus [*Plant pathology*]
MdMwH	Mount Wilson State Hospital, Mount Wilson, MD [*Library symbol*] [*Library of Congress*] (LCLS)
MDN	Madison, IN [*Location identifier*] [*FAA*] (FAAL)
MDN	Maiden Race [*Horse racing*]
MDN	Managed Data Network
MDN	Managed Data Networks (SAUO)
MdN...........	Mandibular Nerve [*Anatomy*]
MDN	Manufacturing Day Number (MCD)
MDN	Mark der Deutschen Notenbank [*Mark of the German Bank of Issue*] [*Later, M*] (EG)
Mdn	Median (DIPS)
MDN	Median (STED)
MDN	Mercury Deposition Network
MDN	Meridian Industrial Trust [*NYSE symbol*] (TTSB)
MDN	Meridian Industrial Trust, Inc. [*AMEX symbol*] (SAG)
MDN	Meta Data Navigator (SAUO)
MDN	Ministere de la Defense Nationale [*Department of National Defense*] [*Canada*]
MDN	Mobilisation pour le Developpement National [*Haiti*] [*Political party*] (EY)
MDN	Movimiento Democratico Nacionalista [*Nationalist Democratic Movement*] [*Guatemala*] [*Political party*]
MDN	Movimiento Democratico Nicaraguense [*Nicaraguan Democratic Movement*] [*Political party*] (PPW)
MDN	Universair [*Spain*] [*ICAO designator*] (FAAC)
MDN.WS......	Meridian Indl Tr Wrrt [*AMEX symbol*] (TTSB)
MDNA	Machinery Dealers National Association (EA)
MDNA	Maximum Density Nitric Acid
MDNA	Mobilehome Dealers National Association (EA)
MDNB	Mean Daily Nitrogen Balance [*Medicine*]
MDNB	Meta-Dinitrobenzene [*Organic chemistry*]
MD/NC........	Mechanical Drafting/Numerical Control (IEEE)
MDNC.........	United States District Court for the Middle District of North Carolina (DLA)
MDNF	Minimal Disjunctive Normal Form (MHDB)
MDNIS........	Machinery Dealers' National Information System
MDNMNA.....	Moorish Divine and National Movement in North America (EA)
MDNP	Methyl Dinitropentanoate [*An explosive*]
Md-NR	Maryland State Department of Natural Resources, Annapolis, MD [*Library symbol*] [*Library of Congress*] (LCLS)
MDNR.........	Michigan Department of Natural Resources
MDNR.........	Minnesota Department of Natural Resources
MDNR.........	Missouri Department of Natural Resources (DOGT)
MDNS.........	Managed Data Network Service (SAUO)
MDNS.........	Managed Data Network Services (NITA)
MDNT	Midnight
MDNX	Modern Air Transport [*Air carrier designation symbol*]
MDO	Macedonia AS [*Yugoslavia*] [*ICAO designator*] (FAAC)
MDO	Maintenance Development Officer (MCD)
MDO	MARC Development Office (NITA)
MDO	Marine Diesel Oil
MdO...........	Masoreten des Ostens (BJA)
MDO	Massive Dark Object [*Galactic science*]
MDO	Mechanized Desert Operations [*Military*] (MCD)
MDO	Medium Density Overlay [*Plywood*]
MDO	Membrane-Derived Oligosaccharide [*Biochemistry*]
MDO	Methylenedioxyphenyl [*Organic chemistry*]

MDO	Middleton Island, AK [*Location identifier*] [*FAA*] (FAAL)
MDO	Mobile District Office [*Army Corps of Engineers*]
MDO	Monthly Debit Ordinary [*Insurance*]
MDO	Moora District Office (SAUO)
MdO...........	Ruth Enlow Library of Garrett County, Oakland, MD [*Library symbol*] [*Library of Congress*] (LCLS)
MDOA	Material Date of Arrival (DNAB)
MDOC	Missouri Department of Conservation
MdOdN	National Plastics Products Co., Odenton, MD [*Library symbol*] [*Library of Congress*] [*Obsolete*] (LCLS)
MdOdS........	Saran Yarn Co., Odenton, MD [*Library symbol*] [*Library of Congress*] [*Obsolete*] (LCLS)
MDOF	Multiple Degree of Freedom [*Acoustics*]
MdOmR	Rosewood Center, Owing Mills, MD [*Library symbol*] [*Library of Congress*] (LCLS)
MDOP........	Malicious Destruction of Property
MDOP........	Maximum Design Operating Pressure [*NASA*]
MDOPA	Methyldopamine [*Biochemistry*]
MDOS	Motorola Disk Operating System
MDOS	Multiprocessor Disk Operating System [*Computer science*] (VLIE)
MDOSIS	Management Data Online Status/Inquiry System (MCD)
MDOT	Department of Transportation (SAUS)
MDOT	Michigan Department of Transportation
MDOT	Modular Digital Output Timer
MDovC........	Chickering House, Dover, MA [*Library symbol*] [*Library of Congress*] (LCLS)
MDovS........	Saint Stephen's College, Dover, MA [*Library symbol*] [*Library of Congress*] (LCLS)
MDP	Coppin State College, Parlett L. Moore Library, Baltimore, MD [*OCLC symbol*] (OCLC)
MDP	Ferrocarril Mexicano del Pacifico [*Mexican Pacific Railroad Co., Inc.*] [*AAR code*]
MDP	Madagascar-Press (SAUO)
MDP	Magyar Dolgozok Partja [*Hungarian Workers' Party*] [*Political party*] (PPE)
MDP	Main Data Path
MDP	Main Display Panel (SAA)
MDP	Maintainability Demonstration Plan (MCD)
MDP	Maintenance Data Panel (SAUS)
MDP	Maintenance Data Program (MCD)
MDP	Maintenance Depot Production
MDP	Maintenance Diagnostic Processor (NITA)
MDP	Maintenance Diagnostic Program [*Computer science*] (IAA)
MDP	Maintenance Display Panel (MCD)
MDP	Malfunction Detection Package
MDP	Malicious Destruction of Property
MDP	Management Development Program (SAUS)
MDP	Management Development Programme [*British*] (DCTA)
MDP	Managing Director Posts [*British*] (DCTA)
MDP	Mandibular Dysostosis and Peromelia (DB)
MDP	Manic Depressive Psychosis
MDP	Manpower Development Program [*Department of Labor*]
MDP	Markov Decision Problem (IDAI)
MDP	Master Data Processing (ACAE)
MDP	Master Decommissioning Plan [*Nuclear energy*] (NRCH)
MDP	Master Design Plan (MCD)
MDP	Master Display Panel (KSC)
MDP	Maximum Diastolic Potential [*Physiology*]
MDP	Mean Datum Plane
MDP	Mean Designation Point (CAAL)
MDP	Mechanically Deboned Poultry [*Food technology*]
MDP	Menthyldiphenyphosphine [*Organic chemistry*]
MDP	Mento-Dextra Posterior [*A fetal position*] [*Obstetrics*]
MDP	Meredith Corp. [*NYSE symbol*] (SPSG)
MDP	Message Discrimination Process [*Telecommunications*] (TEL)
MDP	Meteorological Datum Plane
MDP	Methyldichlorophosphine [*Organic chemistry*]
MDP	Methylene Diphosphonate [*Organic chemistry*]
MDP	Methylenediphosphonic Acid [*Organic chemistry*]
MDP	Microprocessor Debugging Program [*Computer science*] (IAA)
MDP	Milliyetci Demokrasi Partisi [*Nationalist Democracy Party*] [*Turkey*] [*Political party*] (EY)
MDP	Mindiptana [*Indonesia*] [*Airport symbol*] (OAG)
MDP	Minimum Discernible Pulse (MCD)
MDP	Minimum Distance Probability
MDP	Ministry of Defence Police (SAUS)
MDP	Missile Data Processor (OA)
MDP	Mode Products, Inc. [*Vancouver Stock Exchange symbol*]
MDP	Modular Display Processor (SAUS)
MDP	Moslem Democratic Party [*Philippines*] [*Political party*] (PPW)
MDP	Most Dispensable Program [*Television*]
MDP	Motorola Data Processor [*Computer science*] (IAA)
MDP	Mouvement Democratique et Populaire [*Popular Democratic Movement*] [*Senegal*] [*Political party*] (PPW)
MDP	Mouvement Democratique Populaire [*Popular Democratic Party*] [*The Comoros*] [*Political party*] (EY)
MDP	Mouvement des Democrates Progressistes [*Burkina Faso*] [*Political party*] (EY)
MDP	Movimento Democratico Portugues [*Portuguese Democratic Movement*] [*Political party*] (PPE)
MDP	Movimiento Democratico del Pueblo [*Paraguay*] [*Political party*] (EY)
MDP	Movimiento Democratico Peruano [*Peruvian Democratic Movement*] [*Political party*]
MDP	Movimiento Democratico Popular [*Popular Democratic Movement*] [*Chile*] [*Political party*] (PPW)

MDP............ Movimiento Democratico Popular [*Popular Democratic Movement*] [*Ecuador*] [*Political party*] (PPW)
MDP............ Moving Deformable Barrier [*NHTSA*] (TAG)
MDP............ Multi-Designation Protocol (SAUS)
MDP............ Multi-Disciplinary Practice
MDP............ Multi-Divisional Program (SAUO)
MDP............ Multidomain Polymer [*Biology*]
MDP............ Muramyl Dipeptide [*Immunochemistry*]
MDP............ Parkland Regional Library, Dauphin, Manitoba [*Library symbol*] [*National Library of Canada*] (NLC)
MDPA......... Master Data Processing Authorization (ACAE)
MDPA......... Mutual Defense Procurement Authority (SAUO)
MD PA........ United States District Court for the Middle District of Pennsylvania (DLA)
MdPa.......... United States Naval Air Station, Patuxent River, MD [*Library symbol*] [*Library of Congress*] (LCLS)
MDPC........ Mount Diablo Peace Center (EA)
MDPC......... Punta Cana [*Dominican Republic*] [*ICAO location identifier*] (ICLI)
MDPD........ Medical Director
MDPE........ Medium-Density Polyethylene (EDCT)
MDPF......... Metal Diesel Particulate Filter
MDPF......... Methoxy(diphenyl)furanone [*Organic chemistry*]
MDPG........ Magnetic Digital-Pulse Generator
MDPH........ Massachusetts Department of Public Health (SAUO)
MDPHI....... Media Development Project for the Hearing Impaired (NITA)
MDPI......... Mathematics Diagnostic/Prescriptive Inventory (EDAC)
MDPI......... Molecular Diversity Preservation International (SAUO)
MDPL......... Movement for Disarmament, Peace and Liberty (SAUO)
MDPM........ Maintenance Douglas Process Manual
MDPM........ Mechanically Deboned Poultry Meat [*Food technology*]
MdPM........ University of Maryland, Eastern Shore, Princess Anne, MD [*Library symbol*] [*Library of Congress*] (LCLS)
MDPMA...... Member of the Data Processing Managers Association (SAUO)
MDPN......... Midshipman
MDPNE....... Ministry of the Protection of Nature and the Environment (SAUO)
MDPP......... Puerto Plata/La Union [*Dominican Republic*] [*ICAO location identifier*] (ICLI)
MDPPQ....... Mouvement pour la Defense des Prisonniers Politiques du Quebec [*Movement for the Defense of Political Prisoners of Quebec*]
MdPpV........ United States Veterans Administration Hospital, Perry Point, MD [*Library symbol*] [*Library of Congress*] (LCLS)
MDPR......... Madrid Predict [*Orbit identification*]
MDPR......... Manufacturing Development and Process Request (AAG)
MDPS......... Metric Data Processing System [*Air Force*]
MDPS......... Mission Data Planning System (SAUS)
MDPS......... Mission Data Preparations Systems (SAUO)
MDPS......... Mission Data Preparation System [*Military*] (CAAL)
MDPS......... Mission Data Processing System (SAUS)
MDPS......... Mobilization and Deployment Planning System [*Army*]
MDPS......... Mouvement pour la Democratie et le Progres Social [*Benin*] [*Political party*] (EY)
MDPSK....... Multilevel Differential Phase Shift Keying [*Computer science*] (CIST)
MDPT......... Median Preventive Maintenance Time (MCD)
MDPV......... Medium-Duty Passenger Vehicle
MDPVM...... Missionary Daughters of the Most Pure Virgin Mary (TOCD)
MDQ........... Mar Del Plata [*Argentina*] [*Airport symbol*] (OAG)
MDQ........... Market Driven Quality (AAEL)
MDQ........... MDC Communication CI [*AMEX symbol*] [*Formerly, MDC Corp. CI*] (SG)
MDQ........... MDC Communication CI'A' [*AMEX symbol*] (TTSB)
MDQ........... MDC Corp. [*AMEX symbol*] (SAG)
MDQ........... MDE Explorations [*Vancouver Stock Exchange symbol*]
MDQ........... Memory Deviation Quotient (DMAA)
MDQ........... Menstrual Distress Questionnaire [*Medicine*] (DMAA)
MDQ........... Minimum Detectable Quantity
MDQL......... Multidimensional Query Language [*Computer science*]
MDQS......... Management Data Query System [*Computer science*]
MDQW....... Modulation Dope Quantum Well (AAEL)
MDR............ Compania Mexicana de Aeroplanos SA [*Mexico*] [*ICAO designator*] (FAAC)
MDR............ Madras [*India*] [*Seismograph station code, US Geological Survey*] (SEIS)
MDR............ Magnetic Dipole Radiation
MDR............ Magnetic Disc Recorder (NTCM)
MDR............ Magnetic Document Reader (IAA)
MDR............ Magnetic Drum Recorder
MDR............ Magnetic Field Dependent Resistor (IAA)
MDR............ Maintainability Demonstration Report (MCD)
MDR............ Maintenance Data Recorder (ACAE)
MDR............ Maintenance Data Report [*Army*] (AABC)
MDR............ Maintenance Demand Rate (NASA)
MDR............ Maintenance Design Requirement
MDR............ Major Design Review (KSC)
MDR............ Mandatory Device Reporting [*Program*]
MDR............ Manual Data Room
MDR............ Manually Digitized Radar (SAUS)
MDR............ Mark Document Reader [*Trademark*] [*Bell & Howell*]
MDR............ Market Data Retrieval [*Westport, CT*] [*Information service or system*] (IID)
MD R.......... Maryland Reports [*A publication*] (DLA)
MDR............ Master Data Record (NG)
MDR............ Master Discrepancy Report (AAG)
MDR............ Master of Dispute Resolution (PGP)
MDR............ Material Deficiency Reports [*Program*]
MDR............ Materiel Deficiency Report (SAUO)

MDR .... Maximum Desired Result (SAUO)
MDR .... McDermott International, Inc. [*NYSE symbol*] (SPSG)
MDR .... McDermott Intl. [*NYSE symbol*] (TTSB)
MDR .... MD Review [*Social Security Administration*] (OICC)
MDR .... Mechanical Development Report (MCD)
MDR .... Medfra, AK [*Location identifier*] [*FAA*] (FAAL)
MDR .... Median Detection Range (NVT)
MDR .... Medical Department Representative (SAUO)
MDR .... Medical Device Register, Inc. (IID)
MDR .... Medical Device Reporting System
MDR .... Medium Data Rate (DOMA)
MDR .... Medium Deep Recess [*Automotive engineering*]
MDR .... Memory-Data Register
MDR .... Message Detail Recording [*Later, SMDR*] [*Telecommunications*]
MDR .... Metropolitan District Railway [*London*]
MDR .... MicroDesign Resources
MDR .... Microwave Device Reliability (MCD)
MDR .... Milestone Decision Review (MCD)
MDR .... Military Defense Readiness (SAA)
MDR .... Minimum Daily Requirement [*of a vitamin, etc.*] [*Later, Recommended Daily Requirement*] [*FDA*]
MDR .... Minimum Design Requirement (SAUO)
mdr .... Minimum Detectable Radiance (ARMP)
MDR .... Minimum Detectable Radiance (CARB)
MDR .... Minor Discrepancy Repair [*NASA*] (KSC)
MDR .... Minor Discrepancy Review [*NASA*] (GFGA)
MDR .... Missile Deviation Report (AAG)
MDR .... Missing Data Report (NASA)
MDR .... Mission Data Reduction
MDR .... Mock-Up Discrepancy Report [*Aerospace*] (AAG)
MDR .... Monthly Director's Review [*NASA*] (NASA)
MDR .... Morphine-Dependent Rate
MDR .... Morphology Dependent Resonance [*Physics*]
MDR .... Motion Detection Radar [*Hughes Electronics*]
MDR .... Motor-Driven Relay [*or Roter*]
MDR .... Multichannel Data Recorder
MDR .... Multi Disc Reader [*Computer science*] (DGA)
MDR .... Multidrug Resistance [*Medicine*]
MDR .... Multidrug-Resistant
MDR .... Munition Data Requirement
MDRA .... Material Deficiency Report Analysis (SAUO)
MDRA .... Multidrug-Resistance Associated [*Genetics*]
MDRA .... Muscular Dystrophy Research Association (SAUO)
MDRAF .... Mekong Delta Riverine Assault Force [*Vietnam*]
MDRAM .... Multibank DRAM [*Computer science*]
MDRAM .... Multibank Dynamic Random Access Memory [*Computer science*]
MDRC .... Manpower Demonstration Research Corporation (SAUO)
MDRC .... Manual Data Relay Center (MCD)
MDRC .... Materiel Development and Readiness Command [*Formerly, AMC*] [*See also DARCOM*] [*Army*]
MDRCBB ..... Minnesota Dental Research Center for Biomaterials and Biomechanics (SAUO)
MDRD .... Mission Data Requirements Document [*NASA*] (KSC)
MDRE .... Mass Driver Reaction Engine [*Aerospace*]
MD Rep .... Maryland Reports [*A publication*] (DLA)
MDRF .... Materials Dosimetry Reference Facility
MdRFD .... United States Food and Drug Administration, Rockville, MD [*Library symbol*] [*Library of Congress*] (LCLS)
MDRI .... Multidrug-Resistant Infection (MELL)
MDRI .... Multi-purpose Display Repeater Indicator (SAUS)
MDRL .... Mandrel [*Mechanical engineering*]
MDRL .... McDonnell Douglas Research Laboratories (SAUO)
MDRM .... Mouvement Democratique de Renovation Malgache [*Democratic Movement Malagasy Restoration*]
MdRMC........ Montgomery County Department of Public Libraries, Rockville, MD [*Library symbol*] [*Library of Congress*] (LCLS)
MdRNIO....... National Institute for Occupational Safety and Health, Rockville, MD [*Library symbol*] [*Library of Congress*] (LCLS)
MDRO .... Mission Disaster Relief Officer
MDROC........ Mission Design Requirements, Objectives, and Constraints
MDROF........ Managing Director of Royal Ordnance Factories [*British*] (RDA)
MDRP .... Migrant Dropout Reconnection Program [*Board of Cooperative Educational Services Geneseo Migrant Center*] (EA)
MDRP .... Movimiento Democratico Reformista Peruano [*Peruvian Democratic Reformist Movement*] [*Political party*] (PPW)
MDRS .... Management Data Reporting System (MCD)
MDRS .... Manpower Data Relay Station (IAA)
MDRS .... Manufacturing Data Retrieval System (NASA)
MDRS .... Mattis Dementia Rating Scale [*Medicine*] (DMAA)
MDRS .... Mission Data Retrieval System [*NASA*]
MDRS .... Mobilization Designation Reserve Section
MDRS .... Mobilization Designation Reserve Station (SAUO)
MDRS .... Mylar Diaphragm Rupture System
MDRSF .... Multi-Dimensional Random Sea Facility [*Hydraulics Research Station*] (PDAA)
MDRSV .... Maize Dwarf Ringspot Virus [*Plant pathology*]
MDRT .... Million Dollar Round Table [*Des Plaines, IL*] (EA)
MDRTB .... Multidrug-Resistant Tuberculosis (MELL)
MDRTB .... Multidrug-Resistant Tuberculosis [*Medicine*]
MDRTC .... Diabetes Research and Training Center [*University of Michigan*] [*Research center*] (RCD)
MDRUS .... Miniature Donkey Registry of the United States (EA)
MDRX .... Allscripts, Inc. [*NASDAQ symbol*] (SG)
MDRX .... Medicis Pharmaceutical Corp. [*NASDAQ symbol*] (SAG)
MDRX .... Medicis Pharmaceutical 'A' [*NASDAQ symbol*] (TTSB)

MDRY .... Madison Railway Co., Inc. [AAR code]
MDS .... Macintosh Development System [Computer science]
MDS .... Madison [Wisconsin] [Seismograph station code, US Geological Survey] [Closed] (SEIS)
MDS .... Madison Flying Service, Inc. (SAUO)
MDS .... Madison, SD [Location identifier] [FAA] (FAAL)
Mds .... Madrepores [Quality of the bottom] [Nautical charts]
MDS .... Madrona Resources, Inc. [Vancouver Stock Exchange symbol]
MDS .... Magnetic Detection of Submarines [British military] (DMA)
MDS .... Magnetic Disk Storage [Computer science] (IAA)
MDS .... Magnetic Drum Storage [Computer science] (IAA)
MDS .... Magnetic Drum System
MDS .... Mail Distribution Schedule [Air Force] (AFM)
MDS .... Mail Distribution Scheme [Army]
MDS .... Main Device Scheduler (IAA)
MDS .... Main Dressing Station
MDS .... Maintenance Data System (MCD)
MDS .... Maintenance Diagnostic System (MCD)
MDS .... Maintenance Distribution Services Ltd. (EFIS)
MDS .... Maintenance Documentation System [Bell System]
MDS .... Malfunction Detection System [Gemini] [NASA]
MDS .... Management Data System (NASA)
MDS .... Management Decision System (TIMI)
MDS .... Manned Destruct SEAD (SAUS)
MDS .... Manpower Data System (SAUO)
MDS .... Manual Data Supervisor [Computer science] (IAA)
MDS .... Manufacturing Design System (SAUO)
MDS .... Marine Distress Signal (IAA)
MDS .... Market Data System [NYSE]
MDS .... Market Decision System (HGAA)
MDS .... Massachusetts Dental Society (SAUO)
MDS .... Mass Digital Storage
MDS .... Master Delivery Schedule (AAG)
MDS .... Master Development Schedule (KSC)
MDS .... Master Dimension Specification (MSA)
MDS .... Master Drum Sender
MDS .... Master of Decision Sciences (GAGS)
MDS .... Master of Dental Science (GAGS)
MDS .... Master of Dental Surgery
MDS .... Materiel Deployment Schedule
MDS .... Maternal Deprivation Syndrome [Medicine] (DMAA)
MDS .... Mccarron-Dial System (TES)
MDS .... Mechanized Documentation System
MDS .... Medical Dental Service (SAUO)
MDS .... Medical Documentation Service [College of Physicians of Philadelphia] [Information service or system] (IID)
MDS .... Medical Dressing Station
MDS .... Megawatt Demand Setter (NRCH)
MDS .... Memory Disk System [Computer science] (IEEE)
MDS .... Mennonite Disaster Service (EA)
MDS .... Message Distribution Systems
MDS .... Message-Dropping Station [Military] (IAA)
MDS .... Meta Data System (SAUO)
MDS .... Metal-Dielectric Semiconductor [Electronics] (PDAA)
MDS .... Metastable-Atom De-excitation Spectroscopy
MDS .... Meteoroid Detection Satellite [NASA]
MDS .... Meteorological Data System
MDS .... Meteorological Distribution System (SAUO)
MDS .... Methods Development Survey [Bureau of the Census] (GFGA)
MDS .... Metrofiber Multi-Megabit Data Service [Metropolitan Fiber Systems, Inc.]
MDS .... Metropolitan Dairymen's Society [British] (BI)
MDS .... Metropolitan Disposal Services, Inc. (EFIS)
MDS .... "Micky the D" Show [Later, MDS/MMFC] [An association] (EA)
MDS .... Microcomputer Development System (IAA)
MDS .... Microprocessor Development System [Motorola, Inc.]
MDS .... Microsurgery Drill System (DAVI)
MDS .... Microwave Doppler Speed [Electronic engineering]
MDS .... Microwave Multipoint Distribution Systems (EDAC)
MDS .... Midas, Inc. [NYSE symbol] (SG)
MDS .... Middle Caicos [British West Indies] [Airport symbol] (OAG)
MDS .... Middle Distance Swimmer
MDS .... Milestone Description Sheet (ABAC)
MDS .... Milford Docks Air Services Ltd. [British] [ICAO designator] (FAAC)
MDS .... Milk Drinker's Syndrome [Medicine] (DMAA)
MDS .... Miller-Dieker Lissencephaly Syndrome [Medicine]
MDS .... Miller-Dieker Syndrome [Medicine] (DMAA)
MDS .... Mine Detection Set
MDS .... Minerals Data System [Database]
MDS .... Minimal Data Set (SAUS)
MDS .... Minimum Data Set [Computer science]
MDS .... Minimum Detectable Signal
MDS .... Minimum Discernable System
MDS .... Minimum Discernible Signal [Radio]
MDS .... Minimum Discernible System (NASA)
MDS .... Minnesota Dermatological Society (SAUO)
MDS .... Minuteman Defense Study [DoD]
MDS .... Minuteman Defense System [DoD]
MDS .... Miss Distance Sensor (ACAE)
MDS .... Missile Detection System (ACAE)
MDS .... Mission Design and Series [Military] (AFM)
MDS .... Mission Development Simulator [NASA] (NASA)
MDS .... Mission Display System [Navy] (DOMA)
MDS .... Mobile Data Service (DA)
MDS .... Mobile Dental Section (SAUO)

MDS .... Mobile Dental Services
MDS .... Mobile Distribution System (AFM)
MDS .... Mobilization, Deployment and Sustainment (SAUO)
MDS .... Model Designation and Series [Military] (AFIT)
MDS .... Model Design Series (SAUO)
MDS .... Modern Data Systems (IEEE)
MDS .... Modify Device Status (AAEL)
MDS .... Modular Data System
MDS .... Modular Decontamination System (DWSG)
MDS .... Modular Disc Storage (NITA)
MDS .... Modular Dispenser System (SAUS)
MDS .... Modular Display System (ACAE)
MDS .... Modular Distribution System
MDS .... Modulate-Demodulate Subsystem
MDS .... Mohawk Data Sciences [Computer science] (IAA)
MDS .... Mohawk Data Sciences Corp. (SAUO)
MDS .... Mohawk Data Systems Corporation (NITA)
MDS .... Molybdenum Disulfide [Inorganic chemistry]
MDS .... Monitor Distribution System [Television]
MDS .... Montant de Soutien [Amount of Support] [A trade negotiating plan] [EC]
MDS .... Motion Detection System (SAUS)
MDS .... Mouvement Democrate Socialiste [Democratic Socialist Movement] [France] [Political party] (PPW)
MDS .... Mouvement des Democrates Socialistes [Movement of Socialist Democrats] [Tunisia] [Political party] (PPW)
MDS .... Mouvement pour la Democratie Sociale [Burkina Faso] [Political party] (EY)
MDS .... Movement for a Democratic Slovakia [Former Czechoslovakia] [Political party] (EY)
MDS .... Multidimensional Scaling [Statistics]
MDS .... Multiple Dataset System
MDS .... Multiple Deficiency Syndrome [Medicine] (DB)
MDS .... Multiple Deployment System [Military] (IAA)
MDS .... Multipoint Distribution Service [Educational television]
MDS .... Multipoint Distribution Services (ACRL)
MDS .... Multipoint Distribution System [Line-of-sight relay system for electronic signals]
MDS .... Multipoint Microwave Distribution System (WDAA)
MDS .... Multiprocessor Distributed System [Raytheon] (NITA)
MDS .... Municipal Data Service [International City Management Association] [Information service or system] (IID)
MDS .... Myelodysplasia [Medicine]
MDS .... Myelodysplastic Syndrome [Medicine]
MDS .... Myocardial Depressant Substance [Cardiology] (DAVI)
MDS .... Myocardial-Dysplasia Syndrome [Medicine] (MELL)
MDS .... St. Mary's College of Maryland, St. Mary's City, MD [OCLC symbol] (OCLC)
MdSalS .... Salisbury State College, Salisbury, MD [Library symbol] [Library of Congress] (LCLS)
MdSalW .... Wicomico County Free Library, Salisbury, MD [Library symbol] [Library of Congress] (LCLS)
MDSB .... Message Digest Signature Block (HGAA)
MDSC .... Management Data Service Center
MD Sc .... Master of Dental Science [British]
MDSC .... Modular Digital Scan Converter (MCD)
MDSC .... Mohawk Data Sciences Corporation (SAUO)
MDSCB .... Model Data Set Control Block (NITA)
MDSCC .... Madrid Deep Space Communications Complex
MDS Corporation... Mohawk Data Sciences Corporation (SAUO)
MDSD .... Magnetic Disk Storage Device [Computer science]
MDSD .... Mate/Demate Stiff Leg Derrick (MCD)
MDSD .... Monitoring and Data Support Division [Environmental Protection Agency] (GFGA)
MDSD .... Santo Domingo/De las Americas Internacional [Dominican Republic] [ICAO location identifier] (ICLI)
MDSE .... Merchandise (AFM)
Mdse .... Merchandise (EBF)
mdse .... Merchandise (WDAA)
MDSEAD ..... Manned Destruct SEAD (SAUS)
MDSF .... Manipulator Development and Simulation Facility (SAUS)
MDSF .... Mass Data Storage Facility
MDSF .... Mission for Deep Sea Fishermen [British] (DI)
MDSF .... Mission to Deep Sea Fishermen (SAUO)
MDSF .... Mouvement Democrate Socialiste de France [Democratic Socialist Movement of France] [Political party] (PPE)
mdsg .... Merchandising (DD)
MDSG .... Merchandising
MDSG .... Mobilisation Deployment Steering Group (SAUO)
MDSHPMN ... Midshipman
MDSI .... Manufacturing Data Systems Inc. (NITA)
MDSI .... Manufacturing Data Systems International (SAUO)
MDSI .... Modular Display Systems, Incorporated (ACAE)
MDSI .... San Isidro [Dominican Republic] [ICAO location identifier] (ICLI)
MDSIA .... MDS [Multipoint Distribution System] Industry Association [Telecommunications] (EA)
MDSIC .... Metal-Dielectric-Semiconductor Integrated Circuit [Electronics] (PDAA)
MdSim .... Howard County Library, Simpsonville, MD [Library symbol] [Library of Congress] (LCLS)
MDSJ .... San Juan [Dominican Republic] [ICAO location identifier] (ICLI)
MDSL .... Marconi Defence Systems Ltd. (SAUO)
MDSL .... Medis E Ltd. [NASDAQ symbol] (SAG)
MDSL .... Moderate Speed Digital Subscriber Line [Telecommunications] (ACRL)

MDSL............	Multi-Rate Digital Subscriber Line (AEBE)
MDSL............	Multirate DSL (SAUS)
MDSLD..........	Mate/Demate Stiff Leg Derrick
MDSLF..........	Medis El Ltd [NASDAQ symbol] (TTSB)
MDS/MMFC...	"Micky the D" Show/Metal Micky Fan Club (EA)
MDS-MPOLL...	Mail Distribution Scheme / Military Post Office Location List (DNAB)
MDSN..........	Madisn Gas & Elec [NASDAQ symbol] (TTSB)
MDSN..........	Madison Gas & Electric Co. [NASDAQ symbol] (NQ)
MDSN..........	Maximum Dissolved Solids Nebulizer [Product of Applied Research Laboratories]
MDSNG........	Merchandising
MdSnW.........	Worcester County Public Library, Snow Hill, MD [Library symbol] [Library of Congress] (LCLS)
MDSO..........	Medical and Dental Supply Office [Military]
MDSO..........	Mentally Disordered Sex Offender
MDSOR........	Monthly Depot Space and Operating Report
Md-SP..........	Maryland State Planning Commission, Baltimore, MD [Library symbol] [Library of Congress] (LCLS)
MDSP..........	San Pedro De Macoris [Dominican Republic] [ICAO location identifier] (ICLI)
MDSPR........	Mode Suppressor (KSC)
MDSR..........	Malaya District Signal Regiment (SAUO)
MDSRS........	Morphology-Dependent Stimulated Raman Scattering (CARB)
MDSS..........	Magnetic Drum Storage System
MDSS..........	MAGTF [Marine Air-Ground Task Force] Decision-Support System (DOMA)
MDSS..........	Maintenance Decision Support System
MDSS..........	Maritime Pre-Positioned Ships Decision Support System (SAUO)
MDSS..........	Mass Digital Storage System
MDSS..........	McDonnell Douglas Support Services (MCD)
MDSS..........	Medical Decision Support System (DMAA)
MDSS..........	Meteorological Data Sounding System (IEEE)
MDSS..........	Microprocessor Development Support System
MDSS..........	Mission Data Support System [NASA] (KSC)
MDSS..........	Multidimensional Switching System [Instrumentation]
MDSS..........	Multiple Distribution Switching Subsystem (SAUO)
MDSSC........	McDonnell Douglas Space Systems Company (SAUO)
MDSSC........	McDonnell Douglas Space Systems Corporation (SAUO)
MdSsD.........	Library of Dianetics and Scientology, Silver Spring, MD [Library symbol] [Library of Congress] (LCLS)
MdSsFD.......	United States Food and Drug Administration, Bureau of Medical Services, Silver Spring, MD [Library symbol] [Library of Congress] (LCLS)
MdSsGS.......	Church of Jesus Christ of Latter-Day Saints, Genealogical Society Library, Silver Spring Branch, Silver Spring, MD [Library symbol] [Library of Congress] (LCLS)
MDSS-PCT...	Multidimensional Switching System - Packed Column Trap [Instrumentation]
MdSsV.........	Vitro Laboratories, Silver Spring Laboratory Library, Silver Spring, MD [Library symbol] [Library of Congress] (LCLS)
MdSsW........	Washington Theological Coalition, Silver Spring, MD [Library symbol] [Library of Congress] (LCLS)
MdSsX.........	Xaverian College, Silver Spring, MD [Library symbol] [Library of Congress] (LCLS)
MDST..........	Mountain Daylight Saving Time (SSD)
MDST..........	Santiago [Dominican Republic] [ICAO location identifier] (ICLI)
MdStm.........	St. Mary's College of Maryland, St. Mary's City, MD [Library symbol] [Library of Congress] (LCLS)
MDSU..........	Mobile Diving and Salvage Unit (COE)
MdSuFR.......	Washington National Records Center, General Services Administration, Suitland, MD [Library symbol] [Library of Congress] (LCLS)
MDSV..........	Manned Deep Space Vehicle
MdsxWat......	Middlesex Water Co. [Associated Press] (SAG)
MdSyH.........	Springfield State Hospital, Sykesville, MD [Library symbol] [Library of Congress] (LCLS)
MDT............	Compagnie Air Mediterrannee [France] [ICAO designator] (FAAC)
MDT............	Harrisburg [Pennsylvania] [Airport symbol] (OAG)
MDT............	Machine Data Transducer
MDT............	Macro Definition Trailer (VLIE)
MDT............	Maintainability Development Test [Army]
MDT............	Maintenance Demand Time (MCD)
MDT............	Maintenance Downtime (MCD)
MDT............	Mandatory Date of Transportation [Military]
MDT............	Mandatory Drugs Testing (WDAA)
MDT............	Manual Data Technician [Computer science] (IAA)
MDT............	Manufacturers Delegated Testing (NITA)
MDT............	Mass Cell Degeneration Test [Medicine] (DB)
MDT............	Master Data Tape (ACAE)
MDT............	Maximum Dive Time
MDT............	Mean Death Time
MDT............	Mean Delay Time (CAAL)
MDT............	Mean Detonating Time (NASA)
MDT............	Mean Downtime [Computer science]
MDT............	Measurement Descriptor Table (NASA)
MDT............	Mechanical Desktop (VLIE)
MDT............	Mechanically Deboned Turkey [Food technology]
MDT............	Median Detection Threshold (MAE)
MDT............	Median Dorsal Tract [Anatomy]
MDT............	Medium Data Technique [Computer science] (IAA)
MDT............	Med-Tech Systems, Inc. [Vancouver Stock Exchange symbol]
MDT............	Medtronic, Inc. [NYSE symbol] (SPSG)
MDT............	Mento-Dextra Transversa [A fetal position] [Obstetrics]
MDT............	Merchant Deposit Transmittal
MDT............	Mercury Dynamic Test
MDT............	Message Direction Table (MCD)
MDT............	Message Display Terminal (MCD)
MDT............	Message Distribution Terminal (SAUS)
MDT............	Micro Debugging Tool (VLIE)
MDT............	Middletown, PA [Location identifier] [FAA] (FAAL)
MDT............	Mini Disc Terminal [Computer science] (DGA)
MDT............	Minnesota Dance Theatre
MDT............	Mission Data Table (SAUS)
MDT............	Mission Design Team (ACAE)
MDT............	Mobile Data Terminal (MCD)
MDT............	Mobile Display Terminal [Vehicle navigation systems]
MDT............	Moderate (AFM)
MDT............	Modified Data Tag [Computer science] (IAA)
MDT............	Modular Display Tactical
MDT............	Most Demands to Be Traded [Baseball]
MDT............	Mountain Daylight Time
MDT............	Moviment de Defensa de la Terra [Spain] [Political party] (EY)
MDT............	Multidimensional Tasking [Honeywell, Inc.]
MDT............	Multidisciplinary Team
MDT............	Munitions Disposal Technician (SAA)
MDT............	Mutual Defense Treaty
MDT2..........	Martin Marietta, Diehl, Thorn-EMI, Thomson [Army]
MDTA..........	Manpower Development and Training Act [1962] [Later, CETA] [Department of Labor]
MDTA..........	McDonald Deep Test of Articulation [Speech and language therapy] (DAVI)
MDTA..........	Modulation, Demodulation, Terminal, and Associated Equipment
MDTB..........	Milk Distribution Trade Board [British] (DAS)
MDTC..........	MDT Corp. [NASDAQ symbol] (NQ)
MDT Cp.......	MDT Corp. [Associated Press] (SAG)
MDTD..........	Minimum Detectable Temperature Difference (ACAE)
MD Tenn......	United States District Court for the Middle District of Tennessee (DLA)
MDTERP......	Maryland Terrestrial Radiation Package (SAUO)
MDTF..........	Macular Degeneration Task Force [Medicine]
MDTI..........	Missile Director Train Indicator
MDTI..........	Multiple Director Train Indicator (MCD)
MDTL..........	Modified Diode Transistor Logic [Electronics] (IAA)
MDTM.........	Mechanically Deboned Turkey Meat [Food technology]
MDTM.........	Medium-Duty Tank Target Mechanism (SAUS)
MDTP.........	Materiel Developer's Test Program [Military]
MDTP.........	Multidisciplinary Treatment Plan [Medicine] (DAVI)
MDTR.........	Mean Diameter-Thickness Ratio (MAE)
MDTS.........	McDonnell Douglas Training Systems (SAUO)
MDTS.........	MegaBIT [Binary Digit] Digital Troposcatter Subsystem [Communications] (MCD)
MDTS.........	Mission Data Transfer System (SAUO)
MDTS.........	Mobile Doppler Tracking Station
MDTS.........	Modem Diagnostic and Test System (VLIE)
MDTS.........	Modular Data Transaction System
MDTS.........	Multiple Dealer Trading System [Investment term] (DICI)
MDTSA.......	Methods for the Detection of Toxic Substances in Air (HEAS)
MDTSCO......	McDonnell Douglas Technical Services Co. (NAKS)
MDTU.........	Mobile Dockside Transfer Unit
MdTW.........	Washington Missionary College, Tacoma Park, MD [Library symbol] [Library of Congress] [Obsolete] (LCLS)
MDTWN......	Midtown
MDU..........	Maintenance Data Unit (MCD)
MDU..........	Maintenance Diagnostic Unit
MDU..........	Marker Decoder Unit (VLIE)
mdu...........	Maryland [MARC country of publication code] [Library of Congress] (LCCP)
MDU..........	Master Data Unit (IGSL)
MDU..........	Master Driver Unit
MDU..........	MDU Resources Group [NYSE symbol] (TTSB)
MDU..........	MDU Resources Group, Inc. [NYSE symbol] (SPSG)
MDU..........	Medical Defence (or Defense) Union (SAUO)
MDU..........	Medical Defence Union (SAUO)
MDU..........	Medical Defence Union Ltd. [British] (BI)
MDU..........	Memory Drum Unit (ACAE)
MDU..........	Mendi [Papua New Guinea] [Airport symbol] (OAG)
MDU..........	Message Decoder Unit
MDU..........	Message Display Unit [Computer science] (VLIE)
MDu...........	Middle Dutch (BEE)
MDU..........	Middle Dutch [Language, etc.]
MDU..........	Mid-North Resources [Vancouver Stock Exchange symbol]
MDU..........	Mine Disposal Unit
MDU..........	Mine Distributing Unit (SAUS)
MDU..........	Missile Design Unit (SAA)
MDU..........	Mobile Demonstration Unit
MDU..........	Mobile Development Unit [Military] (GFGA)
MDU..........	Mobile Dynamic Unit (AAG)
MDU..........	Modular Dispensing Unit (AAEL)
MDU..........	Montana-Dakota Utilities Co. (SAUO)
MDU..........	Moral Development Unit [Prisoner reform program]
mdu...........	More Dicto Utendus [To Be Used as Directed] [Latin] (WDAA)
MDU..........	Motion Detection Unit [Nuclear energy] (NRCH)
MDU..........	Multidimensional Unfolding [Model] [Statistics]
MDU..........	University of Maryland, Baltimore, Health Sciences Library, Baltimore, MD [OCLC symbol] (OCLC)
MdU..........	University of Maryland, College Park, MD [Library symbol] [Library of Congress] (LCLS)
MDUA.........	Mission Defined Unit Assemblage [Army]
MdU-A........	University of Maryland, Art Library, College Park, MD [Library symbol] [Library of Congress] (LCLS)

MdU-Ar....... University of Maryland, Architecture Library, College Park, MD [Library symbol] [Library of Congress] (LCLS)
MdU-BC....... University of Maryland, Baltimore County Campus, Baltimore, MD [Library symbol] [Library of Congress] (LCLS)
MDUC.......... Meteorological Data Utilization Center (SAUO)
MdU-C......... University of Maryland, Chemistry Library, College Park, MD [Library symbol] [Library of Congress] (LCLS)
MdU-E......... University of Maryland, Engineering and Physical Sciences Library, College Park, MD [Library symbol] [Library of Congress] (LCLS)
MdU-H........ University of Maryland, Health Sciences Library, Baltimore, MD [Library symbol] [Library of Congress] (LCLS)
MDuHi........ Duxbury Rural and Historical Society, Duxbury, MA [Library symbol] [Library of Congress] (LCLS)
MdU-I......... International Piano Archives at Maryland, University of Maryland, College Park, MD [Library symbol] [Library of Congress] (LCLS)
MdU-L........ University of Maryland, School of Law, Baltimore, MD [Library symbol] [Library of Congress] (LCLS)
MDUO......... Myocardial Disease of Unknown Origin [Cardiology]
MDUS......... Medium Data Utilization Station (ACAE)
MDUS......... Meteorological Data Utilization Station (SAUO)
MdU-U........ University of Maryland, Undergraduate Library, College Park, MD [Library symbol] [Library of Congress] (LCLS)
MDV........... Baltimore, MD [Location identifier] [FAA] (FAAL)
MDV........... Doctor of Veterinary Medicine
MDV........... Maldives [ANSI three-letter standard code] (CNC)
MDV........... Map and Data Viewer [NASA] (KSC)
MDV........... Marek's Disease Virus [Avian pathology]
MDV........... Master of Veterinary Medicine
MDV........... Maxim Development Ltd. [Vancouver Stock Exchange symbol]
MDV........... Medeva [AMEX symbol] (SPSG)
MDV........... Medeva ADR [AMEX symbol] (TTSB)
MDV........... Medium-Dollar Value
MDV........... Medouneu [Gabon] [Airport symbol] (OAG)
MDV........... Metropolitan District Valuer (SAUO)
MDV........... Middlebury [Vermont] [Seismograph station code, US Geological Survey] (SEIS)
MDV........... Midivariant [Genetics]
MDV........... Mine Destruction Vehicle (SAUS)
MDV........... Mine Detection Vehicle (SAUS)
MDV........... Mine-Dispensing Vehicle [Army]
MDV........... Minimum Detectable Velocity [Physics]
MDV........... Minimum Domian Velocity (IAA)
MDV........... Mission Development Co. (SAUO)
MDV........... Moldavian Airlines [Macedonia] [FAA designator] (FAAC)
MDV........... Mouvement Democratique Voltaique [Upper Volta Democratic Movement]
MDV........... Mucosal Disease Virus
MDV........... Multiple Dose Vial [Pharmacy]
M-DVD........ Magnetic Digital Versatile Disc
MDVL.......... Medeva plc [LO, exchange symbol] (TTSB)
mdvl.......... Medieval (VRA)
MDVMA....... Maryland Veterinary Medical Association (GVA)
MDW.......... Chicago [Illinois] Midway [Airport symbol] (OAG)
MDW.......... Delta Waterfowl Research Station, Manitoba [Library symbol] [National Library of Canada] (NLC)
MDW.......... Fort Myer Library System and Fort McNair Post Library, Fort Myer, VA [OCLC symbol] (OCLC)
MDW.......... Mars Departure Window [Aerospace]
MdW.......... Masoreten des Westens (BJA)
MDW.......... Mass Destruction Weapons
MDW.......... Meadow [Postal Service standard] (OPSA)
MDW.......... Meadow Mountain [Vancouver Stock Exchange symbol]
MDW.......... Measured Daywork [Payment system]
MDW.......... Midway [Washington] [Seismograph station code, US Geological Survey] (SEIS)
MDW.......... Midway Airlines, Inc. [FAA designator] (FAAC)
MDW.......... Midway Aviation, Inc. [ICAO designator] (FAAC)
MDW.......... Military Defence Works [British]
MDW.......... Military District of Washington [DC]
MDW.......... Mine Disposal Weapon (NATG)
MDW.......... Minnesota, Dakota & Western Railway Co. [AAR code]
MDW.......... Multidimensional Warfare [Military] (CAAL)
MDW.......... Multipair Distribution Wire
MDWAC....... Multiple Drop Wire [Telecommunications] (TEL)
MDWAC....... Midwest Athletic Conference (PSS)
MD WCC...... Maryland Workmen's Compensation Cases [A publication] (DLA)
MdWem....... Carroll County Public Library, Westminster, MD [Library symbol] [Library of Congress] (LCLS)
MdWemC.... Western Maryland College, Westminster, MD [Library symbol] [Library of Congress] (LCLS)
MdWemHi ... Carroll County Historical Society, Westminister, MD [Library symbol] [Library of Congress] (LCLS)
MdwEx........ Midwest Exprss Holding [Associated Press] (SAG)
MDWF........ Midwife
MdwFdl....... Midwest Federal Financial [Associated Press] (SAG)
MDWFY...... Midwifery
MDWP........ Mutual Defense Weapons Program (SAUS)
MDWR........ Mule Deer Winter Ranges (SAUO)
MDWS........ Meadows (MCD)
MDWS........ Missile Detection & Warning System (SAUO)
MdWst........ Med Waste [Associated Press] (SAG)
MDWST....... Midwest
MDWSTRN... Midwestern
MD/WT........ Marine Division/Wing Team (SAUO)
MDWT......... Metric Deadweight Tons (RIMS)

MDWV......... Medwave, Inc. [NASDAQ symbol] (SAG)
MDWY......... Midway
MDX........... Medical Data Exchange [Los Altos, CA] [Commercial firm]
MDX........... Mercedes [Argentina] [Airport symbol] (OAG)
MDX........... Merritech Development [Vancouver Stock Exchange symbol]
MDX........... Middlesex [County in England]
MDX........... Middlesex Regiment (SAUO)
MDX........... Multi-Indexing [Computer science] (CIST)
MDX........... University of Maryland, College of Library and Information Services, College Park, MD [OCLC symbol] (OCLC)
MDXDCR...... Mode Transducer (KSC)
MDXR......... Medar, Inc. [NASDAQ symbol] (NQ)
MDY........... Magnetic Deflection Yoke
MDY........... Middlebury College, Middlebury, VT [OCLC symbol] (OCLC)
MDY........... Midland Gold Corp. [Formerly, Midland Energy Corp.] [Vancouver Stock Exchange symbol]
MDY........... Midway [Midway Islands] [Seismograph station code, US Geological Survey] [Closed] (SEIS)
MDY........... Month, Date, Year
MDY........... Standard & Poor's MidCap 400 Depository Receipts [AMEX symbol] (SAG)
MDY........... Standard & Poor's MidCap Dep Rc [AMEX symbol] (TTSB)
MDYN......... Molecular Dynamics, Inc. [NASDAQ symbol] (SAG)
MDYR......... Model Year
MDZ........... Maritime Defense Zone [Program for drug interdiction]
MDZ........... MDC Corp. [Toronto Stock Exchange symbol]
MDZ........... MDZ, Inc. [NYSE symbol] (SG)
MDZ........... Medford, WI [Location identifier] [FAA] (FAAL)
MDZ........... Mendoza [Argentina] [Seismograph station code, US Geological Survey] (SEIS)
MDZ........... Middle Zero (IAA)
MDZ........... Missile Danger Zone (NVT)
MDZL......... Maritime Defense Zone Atlantic (SAUO)
MDZP......... Maritime Defense Zone Pacific (SAUO)
Me .... C. H. Boehringer Sohn, Ingelheim [Germany] [Research code symbol]
me--- .... Eurasia [MARC geographic area code] [Library of Congress] (LCCP)
ME............. Mache Einkeit (STED)
M/E............ Machine (ROG)
M/E............ Macrocytic/Normochromic [Anemia] [Hematology] (DAVI)
ME............. Macular Edema [Ophthalmology] (DAVI)
ME............. Magic Eye (DEN)
ME............. Magnetic Estimation (OA)
ME............. Magnetoelastic
ME............. Magneto-Electronic (PDAA)
ME............. Magnitude Estimation
Me .... Maine (SHCU)
ME............. Maine [Postal code]
ME............. Main Engine (KSC)
ME............. Main Entry [Library Science] [Online database field identifier]
Me .... Maine Reports (AAGC)
Me .... Maine State Library, Augusta, ME [Library symbol] [Library of Congress] (LCLS)
ME............. Maine Supreme Judicial Court Reports [A publication] (DLA)
ME............. Maintenance Engineering (ACAE)
ME............. Maintenance Equipment
ME............. Maintenance Error (SAUS)
ME............. Maintenance Evaluation (MCD)
ME............. Maitre [Barrister, Advocate] [French] (ROG)
ME............. Majestic Eagles (EA)
ME............. Male Equivalents [Entomology]
ME............. Male Escutcheon [Medicine] (MELL)
ME............. "Malic" Enzyme
ME............. Malt Extract [Microbiology]
ME............. Management Engineering (KSC)
ME............. Management Evaluation [Food Stamp Program] [Department of Agriculture] (GFGA)
ME............. Managing Editor
ME............. Man-Hours Earned
ME............. Manic Episode [Medicine] (MELL)
ME............. Manoeuvre Enhancement mode (SAUS)
ME............. Manpower Estimate (AAG)
ME............. Manson Evaluation [Psychology]
ME............. Manufacturing Engineering (MCD)
ME............. Marbled Edges [Bookbinding]
ME............. Marche de l'Europe [March of Europe] (EAIO)
ME............. March of Europe (SAUO)
ME............. Marine Engine
ME............. Marine Engineer
ME............. Marine Engineering (SAUS)
ME............. Marketing Education
ME............. Marriage Encounter
ME............. Marriage Evaluation [Marital relations test]
M-E............ Martini-Enfield [Rifle]
ME............. Mass Effectiveness (SAUS)
ME............. Master Equatorial
ME............. Master of Education
ME............. Master of Elements
ME............. Master of Engineering
ME............. Master of Mechanical Engineering [Canada] (ASC)
ME............. Materials Evaluation (PDAA)
ME............. Math Error [IRS]
ME............. Mature Equivalent (OA)
ME............. Maximal Efficacy [Medicine] (MELL)
ME............. Maximum Effort

ME	Maximum Energy
ME	Meal
ME	Measurement Engine (IAA)
ME	Measuring Element
ME	Mechanical Efficiency
M/E	Mechanical/Electrical (AAG)
ME	Mechanical Engineer [or Engineering]
ME	Mechanical Equipment
ME	Medial Eminence (DB)
ME	Medial Epicondyle [Medicine]
Me	Median
ME	Median Eminence [of hypothalamus] [Anatomy]
ME	Medical Education (MAE)
ME	Medical Examiner
ME	Medication Error [Medicine] (MELL)
ME	Medication Evaluation (DHP)
ME	Mediterranean
ME	Medium Electroendosmosis [Analytical biochemistry]
ME	Medium Energy
ME	Megacycle (IAA)
Me	Me'ilah (BJA)
Me	Melendus [Flourished, 1188-1209] [Authority cited in pre-1607 legal work] (DSA)
ME	Memory Element [Computer science]
ME	Memory Error (WDAA)
ME	Meningoencephalitis [Medicine] (DB)
ME	Mercaptoethanol [Biochemistry]
ME	Message Element [Telecommunications] (TEL)
ME	Messerschmitt AG [Germany] [ICAO aircraft manufacturer identifier] (ICAO)
ME	Metabolic and Electrolyte Disorders [Medicine] (MEDA)
ME	Metabolism (STED)
ME	Metabolizable Energy
ME	Metairie Site Office (SAUO)
ME	Metal Evaporated [Videotape]
ME	Metalsmith [Navy]
ME	Metamyelocyte (STED)
ME	Meters [JETDS nomenclature] [Military] (CET)
ME	Methionine Enkephalin [Biochemistry]
ME	Methodist
ME	Methodist Episcopal
ME	Methods Engineering (NG)
ME	Methoxyethanol [Organic chemistry]
Me	Methyl [Organic chemistry]
ME	Methyleugenol (STED)
ME	Mexican Stock Exchange
Me	Mexico (SAUO)
ME	Microelectronic
ME	Microemboli [Medicine] (MELL)
ME	Microembolization (STED)
M-E	Microencapsulated
ME	Micrometeoroid Explorer [Satellite]
ME	Microsoft Editor [Computer program] (PCM)
ME	Middle Ear
ME	Middle East [or Middle Eastern]
ME	Middle East Airlines [ICAO designator] (AD)
ME	Middle East Airlines/Air Liban (SAUO)
ME	Middle English [Language, etc.]
ME	Mid-Engine [Automotive engineering]
ME	Military Electronics (MCD)
ME	Military Engineer
ME	Mill Edge (ADA)
ME	Milliequivalent [or Milligram Equivalent] [Also, MEQ]
ME	Mining Engineer
ME	Ministry of Education (SAUO)
ME	Minneapolis Eastern Railway
ME	Miscellaneous Equipment (KSC)
ME	Missile Electrician
ME	Missionary Ecumenical (Rome) (TOCD)
ME	Mission Capital Ltd. [NYSE symbol] (SAG)
ME	Mission Envelope (AAG)
ME	Mistress of English
ME	Miter End [Technical drawings]
ME	Mixture-of-Experts (IDAI)
ME	Mobile Equipment (CGWS)
ME	Mobility Equipment [Military] (AFM)
ME	Modular Electronics (IAA)
ME	Modulation Efficiency
ME	Moessbauer Effect (OA)
ME	Molecular Electronics
ME	Molecular Emission (SARE)
ME	Moment Estimator (PDAA)
ME	Moneta Porcupine Mines, Inc. [Toronto Stock Exchange symbol]
M/E	Month Ending (SAUO)
ME	Montreal Exchange [Canada] (NUMA)
ME	Morristown & Erie Railroad Co. [AAR code]
ME	Most Eminent [Freemasonry] (ROG)
ME	Most Excellent [In titles]
ME	Motion Estimation (TIMI)
ME	Mottled Edges [Bookbinding] (DGA)
ME	Mouse Embryo [Medicine] (DMAA)
ME	Mouse Encephalitis
ME	Mouse Epithelial [Cells] [Hematology] (DAVI)
ME	Mouvement Europeen [European Movement]
ME	Movie Editor

ME	Muhammadan Era
ME	Multiengine
ME	Multiple Embolisms [Medicine] (MELL)
ME	Multiple Exostoses [Medicine] (MELL)
ME	Municipal Engineering (SAUO)
ME	Municipal Engineering and Environmental Technology [A publication] [British]
ME	Munitions Effectiveness
ME	Muscle Examination (STED)
ME	Mutation Engine (SAUO)
ME	Muzzle Energy
ME	Myalgic Encephalomyelitis [Medicine]
ME	Mycobacterial Extracts [Biochemistry]
M:E	Myeloid:Erythroid [Ratio] [Hematology]
ME	Myoepithelium [Cytology]
ME3	Minority Engineering Education Effort [Later, NACME]
MEa	Eastham Public Library, Eastham, MA [Library symbol] [Library of Congress] (LCLS)
MEA	Macae [Brazil] [Airport symbol] (OAG)
MEA	Magnetic Engineering Associates, Inc.
MEA	Main Electronics Assembly (MCD)
MEA	Maine State Library, Augusta, ME [OCLC symbol] (OCLC)
MEA	Maintenance Engineering Analysis
MEA	Major Emergency Actions (SAUO)
MEA	Malaysian Economics Association (SAUO)
MEA	Male-Enhanced Antigen [Medicine] (DMAA)
MEA	Malic Enzyme A (DB)
MEA	Malt Extract Agar [Culture media]
MEA	Manufacturing Engineering Analysis
MEA	Marine Engineering Artificer [Navy rating] [British]
MEA	Marine Engineers' Association [A union] [British]
MEA	Marine Environmental Activities [Marine science] (MSC)
MEA	Maritime Employers Association (NADA)
MEA	Marketing Education Association (EA)
MEA	Master of Engineering Administration
MEA	Master of Engineering Architecture (GAGS)
MEA	Material Experiment Analysis
MEA	Materials Experiment Assembly (ACAE)
MEA	[The] Mead Corp. [NYSE symbol] (SPSG)
MEA	Meanook [Canada] [Geomagnetic observatory code]
MEA	Measurements (NATG)
MEA	Meat Extract Agar [Microbiology]
MEA	Meath [County in Ireland] (ROG)
MEA	Medical Equestrian Association [British] (DBA)
MEA	Medical Exhibitors Association [Later, HCEA] (EA)
MEA	Membrane Electrode Assembly [Fuel cells]
MEA	Memory Inspection Ending Address (MHDB)
MEA	Mercaptoethylamine [Pharmacology]
MEA	Metal Edge Amplifier (MCD)
MEA	Metopon Ethnikis Adadimiourgias [National Regeneration Front] [Greece] [Political party] (PPE)
MEA	Metropolitan Economic Area
MEA	Metropolitan Entertainers' Association [British] (BI)
MEA	Michigan Education Association (SAUO)
MEA	Middle East Airlines - Air Liban [Lebanon]
MEA	Middle East Association [British] (EAIO)
MEA	Migrant Education Agency (SAUO)
MEA	Minimum Energy Absorbed
MEA	Minimum Enroute Altitude
MEA	Minimum en Route IFR Altitude [FAA] (TAG)
MEA	Minister, External Affairs (CINC)
MEA	Ministry of External Affairs, Library Services Division [UTLAS symbol]
MEA	Minnesota Education Association (SAUO)
MEA	Missionary Evangelical Alliance [See also AME] [Switzerland] (EAIO)
MEA	Mission Engagement Area [Military]
MEA	Mission of Economic Affairs (SAUO)
MEA	Modular Engine Analyzer [Automotive engineering]
MEA	Moisture Evaluation Analysis (PDAA)
MEA	Monoethanolamine [Organic chemistry]
MEA	Monoethylamine [Organic chemistry]
MEA	Montana Education Association (SAUO)
MEA	Monteagle [Australia] [Seismograph station code, US Geological Survey] [Closed] (SEIS)
MEA	Multimode Error Analysis
MEA	Multiple Endocrine Abnormalities [Medicine]
MEA	Multiple Endocrine Adenomas [Oncology]
MEA	Multiple Endocrine Adenomatosis [Medicine] (DMAA)
MEA	Multiple Endocrine Adenopathy [Endocrinology] (DAVI)
MEA	Municipal Employees Association (NADA)
MEA	Munitions Effectiveness Assessment (DOMA)
MEA	Musical Educators Association (NADA)
MEA	Music Editors Association (EA)
MEA	Music Education Association (SAUO)
MEA	Myalgic Encephalomyelitis Association [British] (DBA)
MEAB	Maintenance Engineering Analysis Board
MEAC	Manufacturing Engineering Applications Center [Worchester Polytechnic Institute] [Research center] (RCD)
MEAC	Mid-Eastern Athletic Conference
MEAC	Mutual Economic Assistance Council (SAUO)
MEACC	Marine Engineering Artificer Candidate Course (SAUO)
MEACE	Military Engineering Applications of Commercial Explosives [Army] (PDAA)
MEACN	Maintenance Engineering Analyses Control Number [DoD]
MEACON	Masking Beacon (IAA)
MEACONING	Measuring and Confusing (DNAB)

ME Acts .... Acts, Resolves, and Constitutional Resolutions of the State of Maine [*A publication*] (DLA)
MEAD........... Maintenance Engineering Analysis Data
MEAD........... Maintenance Engineering Analysis Division (SAUO)
Mead .... [*The*] Mead Corp. [*Associated Press*] (SAG)
MEAD........... Memphis Army Depot (AABC)
MEAD........... Microbial Evaluation Analysis Device (PDAA)
Mead-J....... Mead Johnson [*Commercial firm*] [*Pharmacology*] (DAVI)
MEADOW..... Meadow [*Commonly used*] (OPSA)
MEADOWS..... Meadows [*Commonly used*] (OPSA)
MEADS .... Maintenance Engineering Analysis Data System
MEADS .... Medium Extended Air Defence System (SAUO)
MEADS .... Medium [*Range*] Extended Air Defense System [*USA-Europe*]
ME/AEROSPACE... Department of Mechanical and Aerospace Engineering (SAUO)
MEAF........... Middle East Air Force [*British*]
MEAF........... Middle Eastern Air Forces (SAUO)
MEAFSA...... Middle East/Southern Asia and Africa South of the Sahara [*Military*]
MeAIB......... (Methylamino)isobutyric Acid [*Biochemistry*]
MEAL.......... Master Equipment Allowance [*or Authorization*] List [*Military*]
MEAL.......... Media Expenditure Analysis Ltd. [*Database producer*]
MEAL.......... Mission for Economic Affairs in London (SAUO)
MEA(L) .... Mission of Economic Affairs in London [*World War II*]
MEAL.......... Mobile Equipment Allowance List (MCD)
MEAM.......... Advisory Committee for Mechanical Engineering and Applied Mechanics [*Washington, DC*] [*Terminated, 1985*] [*National Science Foundation*] (EGAO)
MeAM.......... Augusta Mental Health Institute, Augusta, ME [*Library symbol*] [*Library of Congress*] (LCLS)
MEAM.......... Department of Mechanical Engineering and Applied Mechanics (SAUO)
MEAM.......... Municipal Electric Association of Massachusetts (SAUO)
MeAMH........ Maine State Department of Human Services, Augusta, ME [*Library symbol*] [*Library of Congress*] (LCLS)
MeAMM....... Maine State Museum, Augusta, ME [*Library symbol*] [*Library of Congress*] (LCLS)
MeAMP........ Maine State Planning Office, Augusta, ME [*Library symbol*] [*Library of Congress*] (LCLS)
MEAN.......... Manganese-Enhanced Austenitic Nitrogen Steel
MEAN.......... Microcomputer Education Application Network [*Commercial firm*] (EA)
ME&ES .... Maintenance Environmental and Engineering Services (SAUO)
ME&S .... Management Evaluation & Support (SAUO)
MEANG........ Maine Air National Guard (ACAE)
MEANINGEX... Meaning Extraction [*Programming language*] [*1971*] (CSR)
Means .... Mean's Kansas Reports [*A publication*] (DLA)
MEANT........ Meat Exporters' Association of the Northern Territory [*Australia*]
MEAP.......... Maintenance Engineering Analysis Process (SAUO)
MEAP.......... Maintenance Engineering Analysis Program
MEAP.......... Michigan Educational Assessment Program
MEAP.......... Military Economic Advisory Panel (MCD)
MEAP.......... Multiphasic Environmental Assessment Procedure (DMAA)
MEAPL........ Manufacturing and Engineering Assembly Parts List [*File*]
MEAPO........ Middle East/Africa Projects Office (SAUO)
MEAPS........ Method of Ensemble Average of Periodic Systems
MEAR.......... Maintenance Engineering Analysis Record [*or Report*]
MEAR.......... Maintenance Engineering Analysis Request [*NASA*] (NASA)
MEARS .... Maintenance Engineering Analysis Records (SAUO)
MEARS .... Multi-User Engineering Change Proposal Automated Review System (RDA)
Mears Just... Mears' Edition of Justinian and Gaius [*A publication*] (DLA)
MEAS.......... Marconi-Elliot Avionic Systems (SAUO)
MEAS.......... Measure (AABC)
meas .... Measure (ELAL)
meas .... Measurement (REAL)
MEAS.......... Measurement (ROG)
MEAS.......... Measuring
MEAS.......... Mechanical Engineering Aircraft Squadron (SAUO)
MEAS.......... Middle East Air Staff (SAUO)
MEAs.......... Multilateral Environmental Agreements (SAUO)
MEASAT....... Malaysia East Asia Satellite
MEASCAL .... Measure Calibrate (IAA)
Meas Control (1962-64)... Measurement and Control (1962-64) [*A publication*]
ME Association.. Myalgic Encephalomyelitis Association (NRGU)
Meas Spcl ... Measurement Specialities, Inc. [*Associated Press*] (SAG)
MEAST......... Multi-Echelon Automatic Shop Tester (ACAE)
MeasTech.... Measurement Techniques (SAUO)
MEASURE.... Metrology Automated System for Uniform Recall and Reporting [*Navy*]
MEAT.......... Manpower Employment Assistance Training [*Act*] [*Pennsylvania*]
MEAT.......... Meat Exporters' Association of Tasmania [*Australia*]
MEAT.......... Multiedge Adaptive Tracker (MCD)
MEATR......... Materials, Engineering, and Advanced Test Reactor (SAA)
MeAu .... Auburn Public Library, Auburn, ME [*Library symbol*] [*Library of Congress*] (LCLS)
MeAU.......... University of Maine at Augusta, Augusta, ME [*Library symbol*] [*Library of Congress*] (LCLS)
MeAub......... Auburn Public Library, Auburn, ME [*Library symbol*] [*Library of Congress*] (LCLS)
ME Auto...... Master of Automobile Engineering (SAUO)
ME Auto...... Master of Automotive Engineering (SAUO)
MEAV......... Meat Exporters' Association of Victoria [*Australia*]
MeaVlly .... Meadow Valley Corp. [*Associated Press*] (SAG)
MeaVly .... Meadow Valley Corp. [*Associated Press*] (SAG)
MEAWS........ Maintenance Engineering Analysis Work Sheet (DNAB)
Me B........... Bachelor of Metaphysics

MEB........... Bangor Mental Health Institute, Bangor, ME [*OCLC symbol*] (OCLC)
MeB........... Bowdoin College, Brunswick, ME [*Library symbol*] [*Library of Congress*]
MEB........... Main Electronics Box (NASA)
MEB........... Maine Motor Rate Bureau, Portland ME [*STAC*]
MEB........... Maintenance Evaluation Branch (SAUO)
MEB........... Malic Enzyme B (DB)
MEB........... Manufacturing Evaluation Board (MCD)
MEB........... Marine Expeditionary Brigade
MEB........... Master Electronics Board
MEB........... Maxton, NC [*Location identifier*] [*FAA*] (FAAL)
MEB........... Mechanical Engineering Bulletin [*A publication*] (GFGA)
MEB........... Medial Efferent Bundle [*Neuroanatomy*]
MEB........... Medical Board
MEB........... Medical Evaluation Board [*Military*] (DAVI)
MEB........... Medical Examining Board (SAUO)
MEB........... Melbourne [*Australia*] [*Airport symbol*] (OAG)
MEB........... Memory Expansion Board (SAUO)
MEB........... Mercury Electron Bombardment
MeB........... Methylene Blue [*Organic chemistry*]
MEB........... Microelectronics Bulletin (SAUO)
MEB........... Midlands Electricity Board [*British*]
MEB........... Military Early Bird
MEB........... Modem Evaluation Board (NITA)
MEB........... Moderate Environment Buoy [*Marine science*] (MSC)
MEB........... Muscle-Eye-Brain [*Disease*] [*Medicine*] (DMAA)
MeBa .... Bangor Public Library, Bangor, ME [*Library symbol*] [*Library of Congress*] (LCLS)
MEBA.......... Marine Engineers' Beneficial Association
MEBA.......... Michigan Elk Breeders Association (GVA)
MeBaH........ Husson College, Bangor, ME [*Library symbol*] [*Library of Congress*] (LCLS)
MeBaHi....... Bangor Historical Society, Bangor, ME [*Library symbol*] [*Library of Congress*] (LCLS)
MEBA/NMU... Marine Engineers' Beneficial Association/National Maritime Union (EA)
MeBarhJ....... Jackson Laboratory, Bar Harbor, ME [*Library symbol*] [*Library of Congress*] (LCLS)
MeBaT .... Bangor Theological Seminary, Bangor, ME [*Library symbol*] [*Library of Congress*] (LCLS)
MeBath........ Patten Free Library, Bath, ME [*Library symbol*] [*Library of Congress*] (LCLS)
MeBathM...... Maine Maritime Museum, Bath, ME [*Library symbol*] [*Library of Congress*] (LCLS)
MEBBAS ...... Mission Essential Bare Base Augmentation Sets [*Air Force*]
MeBC.......... Captain John Curtis Memorial Library, Brunswick, ME [*Library symbol*] [*Library of Congress*] (LCLS)
MEBD.......... Medical Evaluation Board [*Military*] (GFGA)
MEBE.......... Middle East Basic Encyclopedia [*A publication*] (MCD)
MEBES........ Manufacturing Electron Beam Exposure System (IAA)
MEBFEX....... Marine Expeditionary Brigade Field Exercise (NVT)
ME-BH .... Medial Eminence-Basal Hypothalamus (DB)
MEBLEX....... Marine Expeditionary Brigade Landing Exercise
MEBO.......... Main Engine Burnout (NASA)
MeBP.......... Pejepscot Historical Society, Brunswick, ME [*Library symbol*] [*Library of Congress*] (LCLS)
Me-BPH .... Maine State Library Service for the Blind and Physically Handicapped, Augusta, ME [*Library symbol*] [*Library of Congress*] (LCLS)
MEBS......... Management Evaluation Guides (SAUO)
MEBS.......... Marketing, Engineering, and Business Services [*Telecommunications*] (TEL)
MEBS.......... Medium Energy Backscattering Spectrometry (AAEL)
MEBS.......... Multicore Extruded Bar Solder
MeBSA......... Methylated Bovine Serum Albumin [*Biochemistry*]
MEBSS........ Materials/Energy Balance Statistical System (SAUO)
MEBU.......... Maschinengewehr-Eisenbeton-Unterstand [*Machine-Gun-Iron-Concrete-Emplacement*] [*German "pill box," battlefield redoubts*] [*World War I*]
MEBU.......... Minimum Essential Back Up (CCCA)
MEBU.......... Mission Essential Backup (MCD)
MEC........... Committee of Ministers on Energy Conservation (SAUO)
MEC........... International Microbiological Education Committee (SAUO)
MEC........... Maine Central (SAUO)
MEC........... Maine Central Railroad Co. [*AAR code*]
MEC........... Main Engine Console (AAG)
MEC........... Main Engine Controller [*NASA*] (NASA)
MEC........... Main Engine Cutoff [*Aerospace*] (AAG)
MEC........... Main Evaluation Center (NVT)
MEC........... Major Events Committee [*Victoria, Australia*]
MEC........... Management Education for Clinicians (SAUO)
MEC........... Manta [*Ecuador*] [*Airport symbol*] (OAG)
MEC........... Manual Emergency Controls [*Aerospace*] (KSC)
MEC........... Manufacturing Engineering Council (EA)
MEC........... Manufacturing Equipment Committee (SAUO)
MEC........... Map Editing Console
MEC........... Marginal Efficiency of Capital [*Economics*]
MEC........... Marine Expeditionary Corps (NVT)
MEC........... Maritime Electric Co. Ltd. [*Toronto Stock Exchange symbol*]
MEC........... Market Economy Country
MEC........... Master Evaluation Center (MCD)
MEC........... Master Event Controller [*NASA*] (NASA)
MEC........... Master Executive Control (ACAE)
MEC........... Master Executive Council (SAUO)
M Ec .... Master of Economics

MEC	Master of Engineering Chemistry
MEC	Materials Engineering Code
MEC	Materials Experiment Carrier (SAUS)
MEC	Maximum Endurable Concentration (NATG)
MEC	Mechanical Fabrication Division (SAUO)
MEC	Mechernich [Federal Republic of Germany] [Seismograph station code, US Geological Survey] [Closed] (SEIS)
MEC	Meconium [Gynecology]
MEC	Median Effective Concentration (DMAA)
MEC	Medical Examination Centre [British] [World War II]
MEC	Medicines Evaluation Committee [Australia]
MEC	Member of Executive Council [British]
MEC	Member of the Executive Committee (SAUO)
MEC	Member of the Executive Council (SAUO)
MEC	Members of the Executive Council (SAUO)
MEC	Mercado Comune Europeo [European Common Market] [Spanish] (DLA)
MEC	Mercury Aircourier Service [ICAO designator] (FAAC)
MEC	Merrimack Education Center [Chelmsford, MA] [Information service or system]
MEC	Meteorological Equipment Change (MCD)
MEC	Meteorology Engineering Center [Navy] (MCD)
MEC	Methodist Episcopal Church
MEC	Methods Engineering Council (SAUO)
MEC	Metrolina Educational Consortium [North Carolina] (EDAC)
MEC	Metrology Engineering Center (SAUO)
MEC	Microelectronics Center
MEC	Microencapsulation [Chemical engineering]
MEC	Microsystems Engineering Corporation (ACAE)
MEC	Microwave Electronics Corp.
MEC	Microwave Electronics Corporation (SAUO)
MEC	MidAmerican Energy [NYSE symbol] (TTSB)
MEC	Mid American Energy Co. [NYSE symbol] (SAG)
MEC	Middle Ear Canal (DMAA)
MEC	Middle Ear Cell (BABM)
MEC	Middle East Centre [University of Cambridge] [British] (CB)
MEC	Middle East Command [Military]
MEC	Milgo Electronics Corporation (SAUO)
MEC	Military Equipment Code (DNAB)
MEC	Military Essentiality Class [or Code]
MEC	Millennium Eco-Communities [Canada]
MEC	Mineral Exploration Company (SAUO)
MEC	Minimum Effective Concentration [Medicine]
MEC	Minimum Energy Curve (IAA)
MEC	Minimum Essential Criteria (MCD)
MEC	Minimum Explosive Concentration [Safety]
MEC	Minnesota Electronic Corporation (SAUO)
MEC	Missile Engagement Console [Military] (CAAL)
MEC	Missile Engagement Controller [Military] (CAAL)
MEC	Missile Equipment Code
MEC	Missile Event Conference (SAUO)
MEC	Mission Events Controller [NASA] (MCD)
MEC	Mitchell Energy Corp. (EFIS)
MEC	Mobile Examination Center [Department of Health and Human Services] (GFGA)
MEC	Mobility Equipment Center (SAUO)
MEC	Mobility Equipment Command [Later, TROSCOM] [Army]
MEC	Model Energy Code [Environmental Protection Agency] (EPAT)
MEC	Modular Electronics Concept (SAUS)
MEC	Molecular Exclusion Chromatography
MEC	Monetary and Economic Council (NADA)
MEC	Monethylcholine [Biochemistry]
MEC	Monolithic Elastic Convolver (TIMI)
MEC	Most Excellent Companion [Freemasonry] (ROG)
MEC	Movimiento Emergente de Concordia [Emerging Movement for Harmony] [Guatemala] [Political party] (PPW)
MEC	Multimedia European Center
MEC	Multiple Element Correlation (ACAE)
MECA	Macedonian Educational and Cultural Association [Australia]
MECA	Main Engine Controller Assembly [NASA] (NASA)
MECA	Maintainable Electronics Component Assembly
MECA	Malfunctioned Equipment Corrective Action
MECA	Manufacturers of Emission Controls Association (EA)
MECA	Map Exercise Computer Assistance (MCD)
MECA	Mars: Evolution of Its Climate and Atmosphere [Planetary science project]
MECA	Matsushita Electric Corp. of America (IAA)
MECA	Measure of Elementary Communication Apprehension (EDAC)
MECA	Medical Emergency Calling Aid (MCD)
MECA	Mercury Evaporation and Condensation Analysis [NASA]
MECA	Micro Education Corp. of America
MECA	Military Educators and Counselors Association (EA)
MECA	Missile Electronics and Computer Assembly [Military] (PDAA)
MECA	Molecular Emission Cavity Analysis [Flame spectrophotometry]
MECA	Multielement Centrifugal Aerowindow
MECA	Multielement Component Array
MECA	Multivalue Electronic Circuit Analysis (IAA)
MECAB	Regional Bureau of the Middle East Committee for the Affairs of the Blind [Saudi Arabia] (EAIO)
MECACON	Middle East Civil Aviation Conference (PDAA)
MECANO	Mechanism of automatic Comparison of Answers with OPACs (SAUO)
Mecano	Mechanotherapy [Physical therapy] (DAVI)
MECAP	Medical Examiners and Coroners Alert Program [Consumer Product Safety Commission]

MECAP	Medical Examiners and Coroners Alert Project (SAUO)
MECAR	Metropolitan Engineers Council on Air Resources
MECAS	Middle East Center for Arab Studies
MECAS	Middle Eastern Center for Arab Studies (SAUO)
MECAS	Middle Eastern College for Arabic Studies (SAUO)
MECAS	Multienergy Californium Assay System [Nuclear energy] (NRCH)
MeCasM	Maine Maritime Academy, Castine, ME [Library symbol] [Library of Congress] (LCLS)
MECAssn	Medical Eye Centre Association [British] (DBA)
MECC	Ecumenical Training Center (SAUO)
MECC	Master Engineering Control Center (SAUO)
MECC	Micellar Electrokinetic Capillary Chromatography
MECC	Middle East Council of Churches (EA)
MECC	Minnesota Educational Computing Consortium (SAUO)
MECC	Minnesota Educational Computing Corp. [NASDAQ symbol] (SAG)
MECC	Muslim Education Co-Ordinating Council (AIE)
MECCA	Management Enlisted Central Career Administration (SAUO)
MECCA	Manufacturing Engineering and Cost Control Applications (NITA)
MECCA	Master Electrical Common Connector Assembly (MCD)
MECCA	Mechanized Catalog (IEEE)
MECCA	Mesoscale Experiment Center for Control and Analysis (SAUO)
MECCA	Milwaukee Exposition and Convention Center and Arena
MECCA	Minnesota Environmental Control Citizens Association (SAUO)
MECCA	Missile Environment Computer Control Analysis (MCD)
MECCA	Missionary and Ecumenical Council of the Church Assembly [Church of England]
MECCA	Modular Electron Column Control and Automation
MECCAS	Microbial Exchanges and Coupling in Coastal Atlantic Systems
MeCCNU	Methyl(chloroethyl)cyclohexylnitrosourea [Semustine] [Antineoplastic drug]
MECD	Military Equipment Characteristics Document (RDA)
MEcDev	Master of Economics of Development
MECDL	Mission Equipment Control Data Link (SAUS)
MECE	Master of Electrical and Computer Engineering (PGP)
MECE	Master of Electrochemical Engineering
MECE	Micellar Electrokinetic Capillary Electrophoresis [Analytical chemistry]
MECE	Movement, Ethyl Chloride, and Elevation [Medicine]
MECEA	Mutual Educational and Cultural Exchange Act of 1961
MEC-ECR	Management Engineering Steering Committee for Embedded Computer Resources (MCD)
MECEd	Master of Early Childhood Education
MECEP	Marine Corps Enlisted Commissioning Education Program (DNAB)
MECF	Main Engine Computational Facilities [NASA] (NASA)
MECF	Micks External Compression Fixator [Instrumentation]
MECG	Material Electrocardiogram (MCD)
MECG	Maternal Electrocardiogram [Cardiology] [Obstetrics] (DAVI)
MECH	Mechanic [or Mechanics] (AFM)
Mech	Mechanica [of Aristotle] [Classical studies] (OCD)
Mech	Mechanical (AL)
mech	Mechanical (DD)
MECH	Mechanical (NAKS)
Mech	Mechanics (BEE)
mech	Mechanics (SHCU)
MECH	Mechanics Savings Bank [NASDAQ symbol] (SAG)
MECH	Mechanism [Automotive engineering]
MECH	Mechanized (DOMA)
mech	Mechanized (MILB)
Mech	Mechanized (VNW)
MECH	MECH Financial [NASDAQ symbol] (SG)
MECH	Methodist Episcopal Church
MECHBAD	Mechanic Badge
MECHBAT	Mechanized Battalion [Army]
MechDy	Mechanical Dynamics, Inc. [Associated Press] (SAG)
ME Ch E	Master of Electrochemical Engineering
Mech E	Mechanical Engineer (PGP)
ME(Chem)	Master of Engineering (Chemical) (ADA)
Mechem	Mechem on Agency [A publication] (DLA)
Mechem	Mechem on Partnership [A publication] (DLA)
Mechem Ag	Mechem on Agency [A publication] (DLA)
Mechem Pub Off	Mechem on Public Offices and Officers [A publication] (DLA)
MECHEN	Mechanical Engineering (NITA)
Mech Eng	Mechanical Engineer
MECHENGR	Mechanical Engineer
MECH/HYD	Mechanical/Hydraulic
MECH I/C	Mechanic in Charge (DCTA)
MECHINF	Mechanized Infantry [Army]
MECHL	Mechanical
MECH L	Mechanic's Lien [Legal term] (DLA)
MECHM	MedChem Products, Inc. (SAUO)
MECHN	Mechanician [Navy] [British]
MECHNL	Mechanical
MECHRIC	Middle East Christian Committee
MECHSFIL	Mechanized Sandbag Filler and Sealer (MCD)
MECHSIM	Mechanical Simulation [of a computer-based directory assistance system]
MECHSM	Mechanism
MechSv	Mechanics Savings Bank [Associated Press] (SAG)
MECHTRAM	Mechanization of Selected Transportation Movement
MECI	Member of the Institute of Employment Consultants [British] (DBQ)
MECI	Mission Essential Contingency Item [Military]
MECIF	Monocyte-Derived Endothelial Cell Inhibitory Factor (DB)
MECK	Mecklermedia Corp. [NASDAQ symbol] (SAG)
Mecklm	Mecklermedia Corp. [Associated Press] (SAG)
MECL	Families of ECL logic (SAUS)
MECL	Minimum Essential Circuit List (SAUO)

2658   Acronyms, Initialisms & Abbreviations Dictionary • 30th Edition

Acronym	Definition
MECL	Mistress of English and Classical Literature (SAUO)
MECL	Motorola Emitter-Coupled Logic (IEEE)
MECL	Multiemitter-Coupled Logic (IAA)
MECM	Meridional Elementary Circulation Mechanism
MECM	Methodist Episcopal Church Mission (SAUO)
MECN	Mecon Inc. [NASDAQ symbol] (TTSB)
MECN	Mobile Extended Corporate Network (SAUO)
MECNY	Municipal Engineers of the City of New York (SAUO)
MECO	Main Engine Cutoff [Aerospace]
MECO	Manual Equipment Checkout (NG)
MECo	Massachusetts Electric Company (SAUO)
Meco	Mechanical Corporation (SAUO)
MECO	Mechanical Equipment Co. Inc. (SAUS)
MECO	Metropolitan Edison Company (SAUO)
MECOBO	Military Export Cargo Offering and Booking Office
MECOD	Member of the College of Dentists (SAUO)
MECOG	Mechatronics Coordination Group (SAUO)
MECOM	Marine Engine Condition Monitor (PDAA)
MECOM	Middle East Command [Military]
MECOM	Middle East Electronic Communications Exhibition (SAUO)
MECOM	Middle East Electronic Communications Show and Conference [Arabian Exhibition Management WLL] [Manama, Bahrain]
MECOM	Mobility Equipment Command [Later, TROSCOM] [Army]
MECOMSAG	Mobility Equipment Command Scientific Advisory Group (MCD)
M Econ	Master of Economics (PGP)
MECON	Metallurgical and Engineering Consultants (SAUO)
MEconS	Master of Economic Science (ADA)
MEconSt	Master of Economic Studies (ADA)
ME Coy	Mechanical Equipment Company (SAUO)
MeCP	Methyl-CCNU, Cytoxan, Prednisone [Antineoplastic drug] (CDI)
MECP	Multielliptical Cavity Pump
MECPr	MidAmer Energy $1.7375 Pfd [NYSE symbol] (TTSB)
MECR	Maintenance Engineering Change Request (MCD)
MEc(Reg Plan)	Master of Economics in Regional Planning (ADA)
MECS	Manufacturing Energy Consumption Survey [Department of Energy] (GFGA)
MECS	Maximal Electroconvulsive Seizure [Neurophysiology]
MECS	Medicus Systems Corp. [NASDAQ symbol] (SAG)
MECS	Medicus Systems Softwr [NASDAQ symbol] (TTSB)
MECS	Middle East Container Service (SAUO)
MECS	Mining Equipment Certification Service (HEAS)
MECS	Mobile Emergency Communication System (CCCA)
MECSIP	Mechanical Subsystems and Equipment Integrity Program (ACAE)
MECSIP	Mechanical Subsystems & equipment Structural Integrity Program (SAUS)
MECSLSI	Mission Equipment Cargo Support Launch Site Installation [NASA] (SPST)
MECT	Mellon Educational and Charitable Trust (SAUO)
MECT	Mission Endurance Cycle Test
MECTAT	Middle East Center for the Transfer of Appropriate Technology (SAUO)
MECTS	Modular Electronic Combat Training System (SAUS)
MECU	Main Engine Control Unit (SAUS)
MECU	Master Engine Control Unit
MECU	Member of the English Church Union
MECU	Municipal Employees Credit Union (NADA)
MECWB	Middle East Committee for the Welfare of the Blind (EA)
MECY	Methotrexate, Cyclophosphamide [Antineoplastic drug regimen]
MECZ	Mechanize (AAG)
MED	Chicago, IL [Location identifier] [FAA] (FAAL)
MED	e-MedSoft.com [AMEX symbol] (SG)
MED	Macro Editor/Debugger [Personics Corp.] [Computer science] (PCM)
MED	Maine Department of Transportation, Augusta, ME [OCLC symbol] (OCLC)
MED	Manhattan Energy District (SAUO)
MED	Manhattan Engineer District [Developed atomic bomb; dissolved, 1946]
MED	Manipulative Electronic Deception (SAUO)
MED	Manipulative Electronics Deception (MCD)
MED	Manual Electron Device
MED	Manual Entry Device
MED	Manufacturing Engineering Document (SAA)
MEd	Master of Education [British] (DET)
M Ed	Master of Education
MED	Master of Education of the Deaf (GAGS)
MED	Master of Elementary Didactics
MED	Master of English Divinity
MED	Master of Environmental Design (GAGS)
MED	Mechanical Equipment Design
MED	Meckeren-Ehlers-Danlos [Syndrome] [Medicine] (DB)
med	Medal (VRA)
MED	Medal [Numismatics]
MED	Medallion Explorations Ltd. [Vancouver Stock Exchange symbol]
MED	Medallist [British] (ROG)
MED	Medan [Sumatra] [Seismograph station code, US Geological Survey] [Closed] (SEIS)
Med	Medea [of Euripides] [Classical studies] (OCD)
MED	Media
med	Medial [Medicine]
MED	Median (AFM)
med	Median (DMAA)
MED	Median Effective Dose [Medicine]
MED	Median Erythrocyte Diameter [Medicine]
Med	Mediator [Legal term] (DLA)
MED	Medical (AFM)

Acronym	Definition
med	Medical (SHCU)
Med	Medical (PHSD)
MED	Medical Department (SAUO)
MED	Medical Engineering Development (IIA)
MED	Medicamenta [Medicaments] [Pharmacy] (ROG)
med	Medication (DMAA)
MED	Medication
MED	Medicine (AABC)
med	Medicine (WDAA)
Med	Medicine (AL)
Med	Medicinical (SAUO)
med	Medieval (BEE)
MED	Medieval
MED	Medina [Saudi Arabia] [Airport symbol] (OAG)
MED	MEDIQ, Inc. [AMEX symbol] (SPSG)
MED	Meditation (ROG)
MED	Mediterranean (AFM)
Med	Mediterranean (SHCU)
MED	Mediterranean Engineer Division [Army Engineers]
MED	Medium (AFM)
med	Medium (DMAA)
MED	Message Element Dictionary (SAUO)
MED	Message Entry Device
MED	Message Exchange Device (SAUS)
MED	Metalworking Equipment Division (SAUO)
MED	Microelectronic Device
MED	Microwave Emission Detector [Instrumentation]
MED	Mid-Continent Ecology Division [Duluth] [Environmental Protection Agency] (AEPA)
MED	Military Electronics Division (SAUO)
MED	Military Energy Depot (SAA)
MED	Minimal Effective Dose [Medicine]
MED	Minimal Erythema Dose [Medicine]
MED	Minimum Effective Dose [Medicine] (LDT)
MED	Minimum Engineering Development (MCD)
MED	Ministry of Education (SAUO)
MED	Minority Enterprise Development
MED	Mobile Energy Depot
MED	Modeling for Equipment Design (AAEL)
MED	Modem Equivalent Device (ACRL)
MED	Modular Evolutionary Development (MCD)
MED	Molecular Electronic Device
MED	Monitor Execution Dump [Computer science]
MED	Multieffect Distillation [Chemical engineering]
MED	Multiformat Electroluminescent Display (PDAA)
MED	Multiple Endocrin Deficiency [Medicine] (MELL)
MED	Multiple Epiphyseal Dysplasia [Medicine] (CPH)
MED	Municipal Electricity Department [New Zealand] (WDAA)
MED	Office of Medical Services (SAUS)
MEDA	Maintenance Error Detection Aid
MEDA	Medaphis Corp. [NASDAQ symbol] (SPSG)
MEDA	Mennonite Economic Development Associates (EA)
MEDA	(Mercaptoethyl)dimethylammonium Chloride [Organic chemistry]
MEDA	Military Emergency Diversion Aerodrome (DA)
MEDA	Military Emergency Diversion Airfield (PIAV)
MEDA	Multiplex Electronic Doppler Analyzer (ACAE)
MEDAAC	Medical Data System for Analysis of Clinical Information (SAUO)
MEDAB	Middle East Database (IID)
MEDAC	Medical Accounting [and Billing Process]
MEDAC	Medical Electronic Data Aquisition and Control
MEDAC	Medical Equipment Display and Conference (IAA)
MEDAC	Military Electronic Data Advisory Committee [NATO] (NATG)
MEDAC	Mouvement de l'Evolution Democratique de l'Afrique Centrale [Central African Democratic Evolution Movement]
MEDAC	Multiple, Endocrine Deficiency - Addison's Disease - Candidiasis [Syndrome] [Endocrinology] (DAVI)
MEDAC	Multiple Endocrine Deficiency, Autoimmune-Candidiasis [Syndrome] [Medicine]
MEDACS	Medical Administrative Control System (IAA)
MedAct	Medical Action Industries, Inc. [Associated Press] (SAG)
MEdAd	Master of Educational Administration (ADA)
MEdAdm	Master of Educational Administration (ADA)
Med Adm C	Medical Administrative Corps [Army] [World War II]
MEdAdmin	Master of Educational Administration
MEDAIR	Medical Environmental Development with Air Assistance (SAUO)
MEDAL	Medallion [Automotive engineering]
MEDAL	Micromechanized Engineering Data for Automated Logistics
MEDAL	Mine warfare Environmental Decision Air Library (SAUO)
MEDALPEX	Mediterranean Alpine Experiment (SAUO)
MEDALS	Military Engineering Data Asset Locator (SAUO)
MEDALS	Modular Engineering Drafting and Library System (IAA)
MEDALSA	Mediterranean Algeria-Sahara Zone [NATO] (NATG)
Medalst	Medalist Industries, Inc. [Associated Press] (SAG)
Medamic	Medamicus, Inc. [Associated Press] (SAG)
Medaph	Medaphis Corp. [Associated Press] (SAG)
Medar	Medar, Inc. [Associated Press] (SAG)
MedArch	Medieval Archaeology (SAUO)
Medarex	Medarex, Inc. [Associated Press] (SAG)
MEDARS	Medical Access and Retrieval System (SAUO)
MED-ART	Medical Automated Records Technology (STED)
Medarx	Medarex, Inc. [Associated Press] (SAG)
MEDAS	Medical Emergency Decisions Assistance System (MCD)
MEDAS	Meteorological Data Acquisition System [NASA] (KSC)
MEDAS	Microfilm Enhanced Data System (PDAA)
MEDASSET	Mediterranean Association to Save the Turtles (SAUO)

MEDAT.........	Multi-Element Discrete Angle Tracker (ACAE)
MedAu.........	Medicine Australia-The Online Journal of Medicine (SAUO)
MEDAUG......	Medical Augmentation (MCD)
MEDAX........	Message Data Exchange Terminal (MCD)
MEDBAD......	Medical Badge
MedBiolEng...	Medical and Biological Engineering (SAUO)
MEDBLD......	Medical and Blood Products Management (SAUO)
MEDBN......	Medical Battalion [Marine Corps]
MEDBO......	Mediterranean Shipping Board [World War II]
MEDBR......	Medical Branch
Med Bull Exxon Corp Affil Co...	Medical Bulletin. Exxon Corporation and Affliated Companies (SAUO)
MEDC...........	[The] Med-Design Corp. [NASDAQ symbol] (SAG)
MEDC...........	Medical Care International, Inc. (SAUO)
Med C........	Medical Corps (SAUO)
MEDC...........	Microelectronics Educational Development Centre [Paisley College] [British] (CB)
MEDC...........	Moessbauer Effect Data Center [University of North Carolina] [Information service or system] (IID)
MEdCA.........	Master of Education in Creative Arts
MED-CAMPUS...	A project for cooperation between higher education institutes around the Mediterranean (SAUO)
MEDCAP......	Medical Civic Action Program (SAUO)
MEDCAP......	Patrol [or Assistance] [or Program] [Military]
MEDCASE....	Medical Care Support Equipment (AABC)
MEDCAT......	Medical Civic Action Teams
MEDCAT......	Medium Altitude Clear-Air Turbulence (MCD)
MEDCAT......	Medium-Altitude Critical Atmospheric Turbulence (MCD)
MedCath......	MedCath, Inc. [Associated Press] (SAG)
MEDCEN......	Medical Center [Army] (AABC)
MEDCEN......	United States Army Medical Center (SAUO)
MEDCENT....	Allied Forces, Central Mediterranean (SAUO)
MEDCENT....	Central Mediterranean Area [NATO]
Med C Georgia...	Medical College of Georgia (GAGS)
MEDCL........	Medical
MedClinNAmer...	Medical Clinics of North America (SAUO)
MEDCMNT...	Medicament
MedCmp......	Medic Computer Systems, Inc. [Associated Press] (SAG)
MEDCN......	Medicine
MEDCO........	Meat Export Development Company (SAUO)
Med Co........	Medical Company (SAUO)
MEDCOAST...	International Conference on the Mediterranean Coastal Environment (SAUS)
Med C Ohio....	Medical College of Ohio at Toledo (GAGS)
MEDCOM.....	Medical Command (MCD)
MEDCOM.....	Mediterranean Communications [Military] (AFM)
MEDCOM.....	Mediterranean Communication System (SAUO)
MEDCOM.....	Mediterranean Planning Committee (SAUO)
MEDCOM....	Mediterranean Regional Committee for START (SAUO)
MEDCOMP...	International Conference on Medical Computer Science (SAUS)
MEDCOMP...	International Congress on Computing in Medicine (SAUO)
MEDCOMP...	Medical Early Direct Commissioning Program (MCD)
MEDCOMPLAN...	Mediterranean Communications Plans [NATO] (NATG)
Medcom System...	Mediterranean Communications System (SAUO)
MEDCON......	Medical Contingency Report [Air Force]
MEDCOOP....	Medical Continuity of Operations Plan [Army] (AABC)
MEDCORE....	Medical Resources Consortium of Central New Jersey [Library network]
MEDCORPS...	Medical Corps [Air Force]
MEDCOS......	Mediterranean Chiefs of Staff [British] [World War II]
Med C Penn...	Medicine College of Pennsylvania (GAGS)
MedcR........	Medco Research, Inc. [Associated Press] (SAG)
Medcross.....	Medcross, Inc. [Associated Press] (SAG)
MedCtr.......	Medical Center (SAUO)
MedCtrl.......	Medical Contol [Associated Press] (SAG)
Med C Wis...	Medicine College of Wisconsin (GAGS)
Medd..........	Meddaugh's Reports [13 Michigan] [A publication] (DLA)
MEDD.........	Medical Device Technol [NASDAQ symbol] (TTSB)
MEDD.........	Medical Device Technologies, Inc. [NASDAQ symbol] (SAG)
MEDDA.......	Mechanized Defense Decision Anticipation [AFSC]
MEDDAC......	Medical Department Activity [Army] (AABC)
MEDDARS....	Medical Display Analysis and Recording System
Meddaugh ...	Meddaugh's Reports [13 Michigan] [A publication] (DLA)
MED-DENT...	Medical Dental Division [Air Force]
Med Dep Co...	Medical Depot Company (SAUO)
Med Devices Rep (CCH)...	Medical Devices Reports (Commerce Clearing House) [A publication] (DLA)
MedDevT.....	Medical Device Technologies, Inc. [Associated Press] (SAG)
MEDDF........	Master Engineering Drawing Data File System
MEdDHi.......	Dukes County Historical Society, Edgartown (SAUO)
MEdDHi.......	Dukes County Historical Society, Edgartown, MA [Library symbol] [Library of Congress] (LCLS)
MEDDIC......	Medical Evidence Disaggregated Direct Input of Costs Database [Social Security Administration] (GFGA)
MEDDOC......	Medical Documentation Systems [Eli Lilly & Co.] [Information service or system] (IID)
MEDDPERSA...	Medical Department Personnel Support Agency [Army] (MCD)
MEDDS........	Mechem Explosives & Drug Detection System (SAUS)
MEDDS........	Medical Data Specialist (AABC)
MedDsg......	[The] Med-Design Corp. [Associated Press] (SAG)
MedDv........	Medical Device Technologies, Inc. [Associated Press] (SAG)
MedDvt.......	Medical Device Technologies, Inc. [Associated Press] (SAG)
MEDDY........	Mediterranean Eddy [Oceanography]
MedDyn......	Medical Dynamics, Inc. [Associated Press] (SAG)
MEDE........	Message Entry & Distribution Equipment (SAUS)

MEDE...........	Military Electronics Defense Exhibition (SAUO)
MEDEA........	International Medical Engineering and Automation Exhibition (SAUO)
MEDEA........	Masters Degree in Energy and Environmental Management and Economics (ECON)
MEDEA........	Material Science Experiment Double Rack for Experiment (SAUS)
MEDEA........	Measurements of Earth Data for Environmental Analysis [Marine science] (OSRA)
MEDEA........	Micro-Electronics Development for European Applications (SAUO)
MEDEA........	Modules and Apparatus (SAUS)
MEDEA........	Multidiscipline Engineering Design, Evaluation, and Analysis (RDA)
MEDEAST	Allied Forces, Southern Europe, Mediterranean East (SAUO)
MEDEAST	Eastern Mediterranean Area [NATO] (NATG)
MEd(Ed/Psych)...	Master of Education (Educational Psychology), University of Birmingham [British] (DBQ)
MEDEF........	Middle East Defence & Security Exhibition (SAUO)
MEDEFLUX...	Mediterranean Flux Measurement Network (SAUO)
MEDEMG	Medical Emergencies [Computerized management course]
Med Eng Phys...	Medical Engineering and Physics (SAUS)
MEDes........	Master of Environmental Design (DD)
Medeva........	Medeva Ltd. [Associated Press] (SAG)
MEDEVAC....	Medical Evacuation Team [Army]
MEDEVAL	Medical Evaluation [Military] (AABC)
MEDEX........	Medecin Extension [Doctors' Aides, or Medics] [French]
Medex	Medex, Inc. [Associated Press] (SAG)
MEDF..........	Maximum Energy Distribution Function
MEDF..........	Midexpiratory Dynamic Flow Rate [Medicine] (DAVI)
MEDFAD.....	Medical Field Assistance Branch (SAUO)
MedfdSv.....	Medford Savings Bank [Associated Press] (SAG)
medfly........	Mediterranean Fruit Fly (SHCU)
MEDFLY......	Mediterranean Fruit Fly
MEDGP	Medical Group [Air Force]
MedGr	Medical Graphics Corp. [Associated Press] (SAG)
MEd(Guid&Coun)...	Master of Education in Guidance and Counselling
MEDH	Maintainability Engineering Design Handbook
MEDHOC.....	Macro-Economic Databank House of Commons (SAUO)
MEDI	Marine Environmental Data Information Referral System [UNESCO] [Paris, France]
medi	Media (VRA)
MEDI	Medicine (DSUE)
MEDI	MedImmune, Inc. [NASDAQ symbol] (SPSG)
MEDI	Missile Error Data Integration [Military] (IAA)
MEDI	Moessbauer Effect Data Index
MEDIA	Magnavox Electronic Data Image Apparatus
MEDIA	Man's Environments - Display Implication and Applications (PDAA)
MEDIA	Manufacturers Educational Drug Information Association
MEDIA	Measures for Encouraging the Development of the Audiovisual Production Industry [EC] (ECED)
Media	Media General, Inc. [Associated Press] (SAG)
MEDIA	Missile Era Data Integration Analysis
MEDIA	Modular Electronic Digital Instrumentation Assemblies (PDAA)
MEDIA	Move to End Deception in Advertising [Student legal action organization]
MediaArt......	Media Arts Group, Inc. [Associated Press] (SAG)
MEDIACULT...	International Institute for Audio-visual Communication and Cultural Development (SAUO)
Media L & P...	Media Law and Practice [A publication] (DLA)
MediaLog	Media Logic, Inc. [Associated Press] (SAG)
Media M.....	Media and Methods [A publication] (BRI)
MEDIA/M.....	Media/Medicine (NITA)
MEDIAS	Mediterranean and Subtropical Africa (SAUO)
MEDIAS	Mediterranean Basin and Sub-tropical Africa (SAUO)
MEDIAS	Regional Research Network for the Mediterranean Basin and Subtropical Africa (SAUS)
MEDIC	Mechanized Design and Integrated Control
MEDIC	Medical Electronic Data Interpretation and Correlation (IAA)
MEDIC	Medical Emergency Development International Committee (SAUO)
Medic	Medicamina Faciei [of Ovid] [Classical studies] (OCD)
MEDICA	Multimedial Medical Diagnostic Assistant (SAUO)
Medicaid	Medical Aid (SHCU)
MEDICAID...	Medical Aid [Federal program providing financial assistance for medical expenses of individual needy citizens]
MEDI-CAL	Medical Aid of California (SAUO)
Medicare	Medical Care (SHCU)
MEDICARE.....	Medical Care [Federal program providing financial assistance for medical expenses of individual senior citizens]
MEDICC	Medical Education Cooperation with Cuba (SAUO)
MEDICEF......	International Center for Medical Environmental Sciences and Future Research (SAUO)
MEDICI	Melodic Dictation Computerized Instruction (EDAC)
Medicinal Chem...	Medicinal Chemistry (MEC)
Medicis........	Medicis Pharmaceutical Corp. [Associated Press] (SAG)
MEDICO	Medical Information Cooperation (DAVI)
MEDICO	Medical International Cooperation
MEDICO	Model Experiment in Drug Indexing by Computer [Rutgers University]
MEDICOM	Medical Communications
MEDICOR.....	Centre for Offshore and Remote Medicine [Memorial University of Newfoundland] [Research center] (RCD)
Medicorp	American Medicorp, Inc. (SAUO)
MEDICOS	Mediterranean Instructions to Convoys [World War II]
MEDICS	Majors Electronic Data Interchange Communications System [Computer science]
MEDICS	Medical Information and Career Service [British] (DAVI)
MEDICS	Medical Information and Communications System (NITA)
MEDICS	Medical Information Computer System (NASA)

MEDICS .... Michael E. DeBakey International Cardiovascular Society [*Later, MEDISS*] (EA)
Medicus....... Medicus Systems Corp. [*Associated Press*] (SAG)
MEDIEV....... Medieval
MEDIF......... Medical Information Form [*British*]
Medigap....... Medicare Supplement Insurance
medi gen..... Media Generated (VRA)
MEDIHC....... Military Experience Directed into Health Careers [*DoD/HEW project*]
MedImun..... MedImmune, Inc. [*Associated Press*] (SAG)
MedInd........ Medical Industries of America [*Associated Press*] (SAG)
MedIndA..... Medical Industries of America [*Associated Press*] (SAG)
MEDINET ..... Medical Information Network [*GTE Telenet Communications Corp.*] [*Telecommunications*]
MEDINFO..... Medical Informatics
MedInn........ Medical Innovations, Inc. [*Associated Press*] (SAG)
MEDINSP..... Medical Inspection [*Military*] (NVT)
MEDINT....... Medical Intelligence (MCD)
MEDIOC....... Mediocris [*Middling*] [*Pharmacy*] (ROG)
MEDIOL....... Mediolanum [*Milan*] [*Imprint*] (ROG)
MEDIPHOR... Monitoring and Evaluation of Drug Interactions in a Pharmacy-Oriented Reporting System [*National Center for Health Services Research*] (DHSM)
MEDIPP....... Medical District Initiated Program Planning [*Veterans Administration*]
MEDIPRO..... Medical District Initiated Peer Review Organization [*Veterans Administration*] (GFGA)
Mediq......... Mediq, Inc. [*Associated Press*] (SAG)
MEDIS .... International Symposium on Medical Information Systems (SAUO)
MEDIS .... Medical Dietary Information System (SAUO)
MEDIS .... Message Diversion Relay System (IAA)
MedisE........ Medis E Ltd. [*Associated Press*] (SAG)
MediSens .... MediSense, Inc. [*Associated Press*] (SAG)
MEDI-SOTA LIBR... Medi-Sota Library Consortium [*Library network*]
MEDISPA ..... Medical Sterile Products Association (SAUO)
MEDISS .... Michael E. DeBakey International Surgical Society (EA)
MEDISTAT ... Banque de Donnees Socio-Economiques des Pays Mediterraneens [*Socioeconomic Data Bank on the Mediterranean Countries*] [*International Center for Advanced Mediterranean Agronomic Studies*] [*Information service or system*] (IID)
Medit.......... Mediterranean (DIAR)
MEDIT........ Mediterranean
MEDITEC...... Dodumentation Medizinische Technik [*Medical Technology Documentation*] [*TechnicalInformation Center*] [*Germany*] [*Information service or system*] (IID)
Meditr......... Meditrust [*Associated Press*] (SAG)
MEDIUM...... Missile Era Data Integration - Ultimate Method
Mediwre...... Mediware Information Systems, Inc. [*Associated Press*] (SAG)
MEDIX .... Medical Data Interchange (RALS)
M Ed J........ Music Educators Journal [*A publication*] (BRI)
Med J Osaka Univ... Medical Journal of Osaka University (SAUO)
MED JUR..... Medical Jurisprudence (ADA)
MEDL......... Marconi Electronic Devices Ltd. [*British*] (IRUK)
MEDL......... Materials Evaluation and Development Laboratory [*General Services Administration*]
MEDL......... Medical
medL.......... medieval Latin (SAUO)
MEDL......... Mission Equipment Development Laboratory (SAUO)
MEDLA........ Molecular Electron Density Lego Assembler [*Modeling technique*] [*Organic chemistry*]
Med L & P... Media Law and Practice [*1980*] [*A publication*] (DLA)
Med L & Pub Pol... Medicine, Law, and Public Policy [*A publication*] (DLA)
MEDLARS .... Medical Literature Analysis and Retrieval System [*National Library of Medicine*] [*Bethesda, MD*] [*Database*]
Med Lat....... Medieval Latin [*Language*]
Med-Legal J... Medico-Legal Journal [*A publication*] (DLA)
Med-Legal Soc'y Trans... Medico-Legal Society. Transactions [*A publication*] (DLA)
Med Leg Pap... Medico-Legal Papers [*A publication*] (DLA)
Med Leg Soc Trans... Transactions. Medico-Legal Society [*A publication*] (ILCA)
Med Leg Vic Proc... Medico-Legal Society of Victoria. Proceedings [*A publication*]
MEDLI......... Motoring Experience for the Disabled by Lions International [*British*]
MEDLINE ..... CD-ROM database equivalent of Index Medicus (SAUS)
MEDLINE ..... Medical Information Online (NITA)
MEDLINE ..... Medical literature analysis and retrieval system (SAUO)
MEDLINE ..... MEDLARS [*Medical Literature Analysis and Retrieval System*] On-Line [*National Library of Medicine*] [*Bibliographic database*]
MEDList....... Master Enumeration District List [*Bureau of Census*]
medln......... Medallion (VRA)
Med LN....... Medico-Legal News [*A publication*] (DLA)
MEDLOC...... Mediterranean Lines of Communication [*Military*] (IAA)
MEDLOC...... Mediterranean Location [*Navy*]
MEDLOG...... Medical Logistics (SAUO)
Med LP........ Medico-Legal Papers [*A publication*] (DLA)
Med L Rptr... Media Law Reporter [*A publication*] (NTCM)
M Ed LS...... Master of Education in Library Science
M ED L SC... Master of Education in Library Science (WDAA)
MEDM......... Medamicus, Inc. [*NASDAQ symbol*] (SAG)
MEDM......... Medium
Medm......... Medmarco, Inc. [*Associated Press*] (SAG)
MEDM......... Med-Mobile, Inc. (SAUO)
MEDMAF...... Mekong Delta Mobile Afloat Force [*Vietnam*] [*Military*] (VNW)
MEDMAILCOORD... Mediterranean Mail Coordinating Office (DNAB)
MEDMAL...... Medical Malpractice Lawsuit Filings [*Medical Malpractice Verdicts, Settlements & Experts*] [*Information service or system*] (CRD)
MEd(Maths).. Master of Education (Mathematics)
MEDMATS ... Medical Materiel Management System [*Army*]
med men..... Medial Meniscectomy [*orthopedics*] (DAVI)

med men..... Medial Meniscus [*Orthopedics*] (DAVI)
MEDMER..... Medical Emergency Report [*Air Force*]
MedMgt...... Medical Management, Inc. [*Associated Press*] (SAG)
MEDMIS ..... Medical Management Information System [*Army*]
Med Moor.... Mediterranean Moor (MUSM)
MEDNET ..... Medical Systems Network (SAUO)
Mednet....... Mednet MPC Corp. [*Associated Press*] (SAG)
MEDNOREAST... Allied Forces, Southern Europe, Mediterranean North East (SAUO)
MEDNOREAST... Northeast Mediterranean Area [*NATO*] (NATG)
MEDNTPS..... Mediterranean Near-Term Prepositioned Ship
MEDO .... Middle East Defense Organization (NATG)
MEDO .... Multipole Expansion of Diatomic Overlap [*Physics*]
MEDOC....... Allied Forces, Southern Europe, Mediterranean West (SAUO)
MEDOC....... Medical Documents [*Eccles Health Sciences Library - University of Utah*] [*Salt Lake City, UT*] [*Bibliographic database*]
MEDOC....... Mediterranean Oceanographic Project [*1969*]
MEDOC....... Western Mediterranean Area [*NATO*] (NATG)
MEDOCHAN... Mary Ellen, Dorothy, Chuck, Ann [*Famous Canadian resort, named for the owners' children*]
MEDOFCOM... Medical Officer-in-Command [*Military*]
MEDOL........ Medically Oriented Language
MEDOWS..... Meadows [*Commonly used*] (OPSA)
MEDP......... Medium Port
MEDP......... MedPlus, Inc. [*NASDAQ symbol*] (SAG)
MEDP......... Mission Essential Data Processing (SAUO)
MedPAC...... Medicare Payment Advisory Commission
MedPAC...... Medicare Payment Assessment Commission
MEDPAR...... Medical Patient Accounting and Reporting (SAUO)
MEDPAR...... Medicare Provider Analysis and Review (GFGA)
MedPart...... MedPartners, Inc. [*Associated Press*] (SAG)
MEDPERFAC... Medical and Personnel Planning Factors Report (SAUO)
MEDPES...... Medical Planning and Execution System (COE)
M EdPh........ Master of Physical Education (SAUO)
MedPlus...... MedPlus, Inc. [*Associated Press*] (SAG)
MEDPOL ...... Coordinated Mediterranean Pollution Monitoring and Research Programme (SAUS)
MEDPOL ...... Mediterranean Action Plan Pollution Monitoring and Research Program (SAUO)
MED POL ..... Mediterranean Pollution Monitoring and Research Programme (SAUO)
MEDPr .... MEDIQ Inc. Cv Pfd [*AMEX symbol*] (TTSB)
MEDPRO...... Medical Education Resources Program (MEDA)
MEDPRP...... Medical Properties, Inc. (SAUO)
MEdPsych.... Master of Educational Psychology (ADA)
MEDQ .... MedQuist Inc. [*NASDAQ symbol*] (TTSB)
MedQst...... MedQuist, Inc. [*Associated Press*] (SAG)
MEDR .... Medco Research, Inc. (SAUO)
MedRA....... Medical Resource Companies of America [*Associated Press*] (SAG)
MEDRAMS... Medical Readiness Assemblage Medical System [*Air Force*] (GFGA)
MEDRC .... Medical Reserve Corps [*Military*] (WDAA)
MEDRECO... Mediterranean Refining Company (SAUO)
MEDRED...... Medical Readiness Report Capability (SAUO)
MEDRED...... Medical Unit Readiness Report [*Air Force*]
MEDREG...... Medical Regulating (SAUS)
MEDREG...... Medical Regulating (or Regulation) (SAUO)
MEDREGREP... Medical Regulating Report (COE)
MEDREQ..... Medical Requirements Model (SAUO)
Med Res Bull Rept Dept... Repatriation Department. Medical Research Bulletin (SAUS)
Med Res C... Medical Reserve Corps (SAUO)
MedResc..... Medical Resources, Inc. [*Associated Press*] (SAG)
MEDRESCO... Medical Research Council (NADA)
MedResEng... Medical Research Engineering (SAUO)
MEDRETES... Medical Readiness Training Exercises [*Army*]
MEDREX...... Medical Readiness Exercise (MCD)
medRNA...... Ribonucleic Acid, Mini-Exon-Derived [*Biochemistry, genetics*]
MEDRTS ..... Medical Requirements Model (SAUO)
MEd(RuralEd)... Master of Education in Rural Education
MEDS......... Maintenance Engineering Data System (SAUO)
MEDS......... Management Engineering Data System (SAUO)
MEDS......... Marine Ecological Database System [*Marine science*] (OSRA)
MEDS......... Marine Embarkation Data System (SAUO)
MEDS......... Marine Environmental Data Service [*Canada*] (NOAA)
MEDS......... Master of Environmental Design Studies [*Canada*] (ASC)
MEDS......... Mechanized Embarkation Data System [*Military*] (NVT)
MEDS......... Medical Electronics and Data Society [*Later, MES*] (EA)
MEDS......... Medical Evaluation Data System (IEEE)
Meds .... Medications [*or Medicines*]
MEDS......... Medstone International, Inc. [*NASDAQ symbol*] (SAG)
MEDS......... Medstone Intl. [*NASDAQ symbol*] (TTSB)
MEDS......... Meteorological and Environmental Data Services (USDC)
MEDS......... Meteorological Data Systems (SAUO)
MEDS......... Meteorological Environmental Data Services [*Marine science*] (OSRA)
MEDS......... Monitoring, Evaluation and Design Support Activity (SAUO)
MEDS......... Multifunction Electronic Display System [*NASA*]
MEDSAC...... Medical Service Activity [*Army*] (AABC)
MEDSARS.... Maintenance Engineering Data Storage and Retrieval System (NG)
Med Sc D.... Doctor of Medical Science [*or the Science of Medicine*]
MEDSCH..... Medical School (ADA)
MedSch(N)... Institute of Naval Medicine [*British*]
Med Sci Sports and Exercise... Medicine and Science in Sports and Exercise (MEC)
MEDSERV .... Medical Service Corps [*Military*] (MCD)

MEDSERVC... Medical Service Corps [Military]
MEDSERWRNT... Medical Service Warrant
MEDSOM..... Medical Supply, Optical, and Maintenance [Army] (RDA)
MEDSOUEAST... Southeast Mediterranean Area [NATO] (NATG)
MEDSOUTHEAST... Allied Forces, Southern Europe, Mediterranean South East (SAUO)
MEDSPA...... Mediterranean Special Programme of Action (SAUO)
MEDSPECC.. Medical Specialist Corps [Military]
MEd(SpecEd)... Master of Education (Special Education)
MEd(SpEd)... Master of Education in Special Education (ADA)
MEDSS........ Multiple Echelon Direct Support System (MCD)
MEdSt......... Master of Educational Studies (ADA)
MEDSTAR.... Medical Staffing and Training to Augment Readiness (MCD)
MEDSTAT .... Medicaid Statistical Reporting and Analysis System (GFGA)
MEDSTATS... Medical Statistics Expert System (DMAA)
med stern.... Median Sternotomy (CPH)
MEDSTOC.... Medical Stock Control System [Army]
MEDSTOCK.. Medical Stock Control System (SAUO)
Medstone .... Medstone International, Inc. [Associated Press] (SAG)
MEdStud...... Master of Educational Studies
MEDSUPDEP... Medical Supply Depot
Medsupp...... Medicare Supplement Insurance
Med Supt...... Medical Superintendent (SAUO)
MedSurg...... Medicine and Surgery (DAVI)
M Ed T........ Master of Education in Teaching (PGP)
MEDT.......... Mean Elapsed Downtime [Computer science] (MCD)
MedT .... Medical Technology Systems, Inc. [Associated Press] (SAG)
MEDT.......... Military Equipment Delivery Team
MEDTC........ Military Equipment Delivery Team Cambodia (VNW)
med tech .... Medical Technician [or Technologist] (AAMN)
Med Tech ... Medical Technologist (SAUO)
Med Tech ... Medical Technology (DAVI)
MedTech...... Medical Technology Systems, Inc. [Associated Press] (SAG)
Med Tox ...... Medical Toxicology and Adverse Drug Experience (MEC)
MEDTRAIN... Medical Literature Training File (NITA)
Medtrnc...... Medtronic, Inc. [Associated Press] (SAG)
MEDU .... Co-ordinating Unit for the MAP (SAUO)
MEDUNSA.... Medical University of Southern Africa (SAUO)
Medusa....... Medusa Corp. [Associated Press] (SAG)
MEDUSA..... Multiple Element Directional Universally Steerable Antenna
Med U So Car... Medical University of South Carolina (GAGS)
MedVat....... MediVators, Inc. [Associated Press] (SAG)
MEDW......... Mediware Information Sys [NASDAQ symbol] (TTSB)
MEDW .... Mediware Information Systems, Inc. [NASDAQ symbol] (SAG)
MedWorld News... Medical World News (SAUO)
MED-WRAP... Medical War Reserve Automated Process (SAUO)
Medwve...... Medwave, Inc. [Associated Press] (SAG)
MEDX.......... Medarex, Inc. [NASDAQ symbol] (SPSG)
MEDXW....... Medarex Inc. Wrrt [NASDAQ symbol] (TTSB)
MEDY.......... Medial Dynamics [NASDAQ symbol] (TTSB)
MEDYN........ Medical Dynamics, Inc. [NASDAQ symbol] (NQ)
MEE............. Maine Office of Energy Resources Library, Augusta, ME [OCLC symbol] (OCLC)
MEE .... Maintenance Engineering Evaluation (MCD)
MEE .... Mare [Loyalty Islands] [Airport symbol] (OAG)
MEE .... Mass Energy Equivalent
MEE .... Massey Energy [NYSE symbol]
MEE .... Master of Electrical Engineering
MEE .... Measured Energy Expenditure (DMAA)
MEE .... Mechanical, Electrical, and Electronic (MCD)
MEE .... Mechanical Evaluation Equipment
MEE .... Meerut [India] [Seismograph station code, US Geological Survey] [Closed] (SEIS)
MEE .... Merrill Lynch & Co., Inc. [NYSE symbol] (SAG)
MEE .... Methyl Ethyl Ether [Organic chemistry]
MEE .... Middle Ear Effusion [Medicine]
MEE .... Middle East Enterprises, Beirut (SAUO)
MEE .... Migration Enhanced Epitaxy (AAEL)
MEE .... Military Engineering Establishment (SAUO)
MEE .... Military Essential Equipment (CINC)
MEE .... Minimum Essential Equipment
MEE .... Mission Essential Equipment [NASA] (KSC)
MEE .... Multilocus Enzyme Electrophoresis (DMAA)
MEE .... Muskogee, OK [Location identifier] [FAA] (FAAL)
MEEC.......... Massachusetts Energy Efficiency Council (SAUO)
MEEC.......... Membrane Enclosed Enzymatic Catalysis
MEEC.......... Middle East Economic Committee (SAUO)
MEECES...... Multi-Experimental Event-Controlled Entry System [Computer science] (VLIE)
MEECN....... Minimal Essential Emergency Communications Network (SAUO)
MEECN....... Minimum Essential Emergency Communications Network [Military]
MEECO....... Metallurgical Equipment Export Company (SAUO)
MEED .... Mechanical and Electrical Engineering Division (SAUO)
MEED .... Medium-Energy Electron Diffraction
MEED .... Microbial Ecology Evaluation Device [NASA] (KSC)
MEED .... Middle East Economic Digest [A publication]
MEED Conferences... Middle East Economic Digest Conferences (SAUO)
ME-EE .... Mechanical Engineer and Electrical Engineer [Academic degree]
MEEF .... Manufacturing Engineering Education Foundation
MEEF .... Mobile Equipment Employment File [Air Force] (AFM)
MEEI .... Manufacturing Engineering Equipment Instruction (SAUO)
MEEL .... Mission Equipment Essentiality List
MeEI .... William Fogg Memorial Library, Eliot, ME [Library symbol] [Library of Congress] (LCLS)
ME(Elec)..... Master of Engineering (Electrical) (ADA)

MEEM .... Master of Environmental Engineering and Management (PGP)
MEEM .... Metastable Electron Emission Microscopy
ME Eng .... Master of Electrical Engineering
MEEP .... Management and Equipment Evaluation Program
MEER .... Mechanical/Electrical Equipment Room (MCD)
MEEREC...... Middle East Environmental Research and Education Committee (SAUO)
MEERS........ Maximum Effective Echo Ranging Speed (NVT)
MEES.......... Marine-Estuarine-Environmental Sciences (PDAA)
MEES.......... Medical Element Engineering and Simulation (DMAA)
MEES.......... Middle East Economic Survey [A publication]
MEES.......... Missile End Game Evaluation System (ACAE)
MEES.......... Multipurpose Electromagnetic Environment Simulator (MCD)
Mees & Ros... Meeson and Roscoe's English Exchequer Reports [A publication] (DLA)
Mees & W ... Meeson and Welsby's English Exchequer Reports [A publication] (DLA)
Mees & Wels... Meeson and Welsby's English Exchequer Reports [A publication] (DLA)
MEET .... Minimum Essential Equipment for Training
MEETA........ Maximum Improvement in Electronics Effectiveness through Advanced Techniques
MEETAT....... Maximum Improvement in Electronics Effectiveness through Advanced Techniques
MEETS........ Minimum Engine Tracking System (SAUO)
MEEV .... Maintenance and Electricity Equipment Vault (MCD)
MEF............. Emerging Mexico Fund [NYSE symbol] (SPSG)
MEF............. Maintenance Efficiency Factor
MEF............. Major Emitting Facility [Environmental Protection Agency]
MEF............. Major Equipment File (MCD)
MEF............. Management Engineering Flight [Air Force]
MEF............. Marine Expeditionary Force
MEF............. Master Edit File [Computer science] (VLIE)
MEF............. Maximal Expiratory Flow [Medicine]
MEF............. Maximum Elevation Figure [Aviation] (PIPO)
MEF............. Meal Export Federation (SAUO)
MEF............. Mechanized Engineering File
MEF............. Median Energy of Fission (NRCH)
MEF............. Mediterranean Expeditionary Force [World War I] [British]
MEF............. Melfi [Chad] [Airport symbol] (AD)
MEF............. Mesopotamian Expeditionary Force [British]
MEF............. Microsoft Easy Fulfillment (VLIE)
MEF............. Middle Ear Fluid
MEF............. Middle East Forces [British]
MEF............. Middle East Forum [Lebanon] (BJA)
MEF............. Mideast File [Tel-Aviv University] [Israel] [Information service or system] (IID)
MEF............. Midexpiratory Flow [Medicine] (DMAA)
MEF............. Migration Enhancement Factor [Biochemistry]
MEF............. Minimum Essential Facilities (SAUO)
MEF............. Minimum Essential Force (CINC)
MEF............. Minimum Essential Functions (SAUO)
MEF............. Ministry for Environment and Forests [India]
MEF............. Ministry of Economy & Finance (SAUO)
MEF............. Mission Equipment Facility (MCD)
MEF............. Mortality Enhancing Factors [Chemical and biological warfare]
MEF............. Mouse Embryo Fibroblast
MEF............. Multiple Effect Flash [Evaporator] [Seawater conversion system]
MEF............. Multi-Purpose Electric Furnace (PDAA)
MEF............. Munitions Equipment Facility (SAUO)
MEF............. Muscle Enhancer Factor [Genetics]
MEF............. Musicians Emergency Fund (EA)
MEF............. Myocyte Enhancing Factor [Genetics]
MEFA.......... Metal Etching and Fabricating Association [Later, National Association of Name Plate Manufacturers] (EA)
MEFA.......... Methyl-CCNU 5-Fluorouracil, Adriamycin [Antineoplastic drug regimen] (DAVI)
MeFarGS ..... Church of Jesus Christ of Latter-Day Saints, Genealogical Society Library, Augusta Branch, Farmingdale, ME [Library symbol] [Library of Congress] (LCLS)
MeFarU........ University of Maine at Farmington, Farmington, ME [Library symbol] [Library of Congress] (LCLS)
MEF/B/U ..... Marine Expeditionary Force/Brigade/Unit (MILB)
MEFC.......... Maximum Economic Finding Cost
MEFC.......... Mister Ed Fan Club (EA)
MEFENET.... Department of Energy Network (SAUS)
MEFEX........ Middle East Food and Equipment Exhibition [Arabian Exhibition Management]
M-EFF.......... Myocardial Efficiency [Cardiology]
MEFFEX....... Marine Expeditionary Force Field Exercise (NVT)
MEFF Renta Fija... derivatives exchange in Barcelona, Spain (SAUS)
MEFF Renta Variable... derivatives exchange in Madrid, Spain (SAUS)
MEFLEX....... Marine Expeditionary Force Landing Exercise (NVT)
MEFPAK....... Manpower and Equipment Force Packaging [Military]
MEFPAK....... Manpower and Equipment Force Packaging System (SAUO)
MEFPMRS.... Marine Expeditionary Force Primary Multi-channel Radio System (SAUS)
MEFR.......... Maximum Expiratory Flow Rate [Medicine]
MEFR.......... Maximum Midexpiratory Flow Rate [Medicine] (DAVI)
MEFS.......... Midterm Energy Forecasting System [Department of Energy] (GFGA)
ME/FS......... Missing/Embryo Fetus Syndrome
MEFSR........ Maximal Expiratory Flow Static Recoil Curve [Medicine] (MAE)
MEFT.......... Minimum Essential Functional Task (SAUO)
MEFTA........ Metalworking Industries in the European Free Trade Association (SAUO)

MeFtkU .... University of Maine at Fort Kent, Fort Kent, ME [*Library symbol*]
                 [*Library of Congress*] (LCLS)
MEFTL .... Middle East Force Target List (MCD)
MEFV .... Maintenance Equipment Floor Valve (NRCH)
MEFV .... Maximal Expiratory Flow Volume [*Medicine*] (AAMN)
MEFV .... Maximum Expiratory Flow Volume (EEVL)
MEG .... Madly Enthusiastic about Grapes
MEG .... Magnetoencephalogram [*Medicine*]
MEG .... Magnetoencephalography [*Medicine*] (ECON)
MEG .... Malange [*Angola*] [*Airport symbol*] (OAG)
MEG .... Management Evaluation Group [*Department of State*]
MEG .... Marketing Executives Group (SAUO)
MEG .... Media General, Inc. [*AMEX symbol*] (SPSG)
MEG .... Mega [*A prefix meaning multiplied by one million*] (AAG)
Meg .... Megabyte (COE)
MEG .... Megabyte [*Computer science*] (DDC)
meg .... Megabyte
MEG .... Megacycle (NTCM)
Meg .... Megakaryocyte [*Hematology*]
meg .... Megaloblastic [*Cytology*] (AAMN)
meg .... Megaron (VRA)
MEG .... Megaton (WDAA)
MEG .... Megawatt (WDAA)
Meg .... Megiddo (BJA)
MEG .... Megillah (BJA)
MEG .... Meglumine (SAUS)
MEG .... Megohm (AAG)
meg .... Megohm (IDOE)
Meg .... Megone's Companies Acts Cases [*1888-90*] [*England*]
                 [*A publication*] (DLA)
MEG .... Mercaptoethylguanidine [*Biochemistry*] (AAMN)
MEG .... Message Entry Generator (NVT)
MEG .... Message Expediting Group (IEEE)
MEG .... Methyl(ethyl)glycine [*Biochemistry*]
MEG .... Midlands Examining Group [*British*] (AIE)
MEG .... Miniature Electronic Group (SAUO)
MEG .... Miniature Electrostatic Gyro
MEG .... Mitsubishi Electric Europe (SAUO)
MEG .... Mobilization Employment Group (SAUO)
MEG .... Monoethylene Glycol [*Chemicals*]
MEG .... Multifocal Eosinophilic Granuloma [*Medicine*] (DMAA)
MEG .... Multimedia Environmental Goals [*Environmental Protection Agency*]
MEG .... NRA [*National Restaurant Association*] Marketing Executives Group
                 [*Chicago, IL*] (EA)
MEGA .... Manoeuvre Enhancement/Gust Alleviation (SAUS)
MEGA .... Megaampere (IAA)
MEGA .... Megakaryocyte [*Hematology*] (DAVI)
MEGA .... Military Evaluation of Geographic Areas
mega- .... Millions (10⁶) (IDOE)
MEGA .... Molecular Evolutionary Genetics Analysis [*Computer software*]
MEGACE ...... Megestrol Acetate [*Antineoplastic drug*]
MEGAFLOPS... Millions of Floating Point Operations per Second (PDAA)
Me-GAG .... Methylglyoxalbis(guanylhydrazone) [*Mitoguazone*] [*Also, MGBG*]
                 [*Antineoplastic drug*]
MeGar .... Gardiner Public Library, Gardiner, ME [*Library symbol*] [*Library of
                 Congress*] (LCLS)
Megarry .... Megarry's The Rent Acts [*A publication*] (DLA)
MEGAS .... Multienergy Gamma Assay System [*Nuclear energy*] (NRCH)
MEGASTAR... Meaning of Energy Growth: An Assessment of Systems,
                 Technologies, and Requirements [*NASA*]
Megatest ..... Megatest Corp. [*Associated Press*] (SAG)
MEGC .... Megacycle (IAA)
MEGC .... Megacycle per Second [*Megahertz*] (IAA)
mEGF .... Mouse Epidermal Growth Factor
mEGF-URO... Mouse Epidermal Growth Factor - Urogastrone [*Endocrinology*]
MEGG .... Merging (FAAC)
Megg Ass .... Meggison's Assets in Equity [*1832*] [*A publication*] (DLA)
Meg-GPA ..... Megakaryocyte Growth-Promoting Activity [*Hematology*]
MEGHP .... Most Excellent Grand High Priest [*Freemasonry*]
MEGI .... Missile Exhaust Gas Ingestion (MCD)
MEGJR .... Middle European Good Templar Youth (SAUO)
MEGLUMINE.. N-Methylglucamine [*USAN*] [*Organic chemistry*]
MEGM .... Most Eminent Grand Master [*Freemasonry*] (ROG)
MEGO .... Mego Financial [*NASDAQ symbol*] (TTSB)
MEGO .... Mego Financial Corp. [*NASDAQ symbol*] (SAG)
MEGO .... Megohm (MSA)
MEGO .... My Eyes Glaze Over [*An article, written about an important subject,
                 that resists reader interest and has a soporific effect*] [*Journalistic
                 slang*]
MegoFin ...... Mego Financial Corp. [*Associated Press*] (SAG)
MegoFinI ..... Mego Financial [*Associated Press*] (SAG)
MegoMrt ...... Mego Mortgage Corp. [*Associated Press*] (SAG)
Megone .... Megone's Companies Acts Cases [*1888-90*] [*England*]
                 [*A publication*] (DLA)
Me Gov't Reg... Maine Government Register [*A publication*] (AAGC)
MEGS .... Male Electronic Genital Stimulator [*Developed by Biosonics, Inc.*]
MEGS .... Market Entry Guarantee Scheme [*Board of Trade*] [*British*] (DI)
MEGS .... Meeting of European Geological Societies (SAUO)
MEGS .... Megasecond (AAG)
MEGS .... Missile End-Game Scoring (SAUS)
MeGS U .... Missile End-Game Scoring System (DWSG)
MEGSSS ...... Mathematics Education for Gifted Secondary School Students
                 Project (EDAC)
MEGT .... Megatest Corp. [*NASDAQ symbol*] (SAG)

MEGT .... Megaton [*Nuclear equivalent of one million tons of high explosive*]
                 (AAG)
MegTa'an ..... Megillat Ta'anit (BJA)
MEGV .... Megavolt (AAG)
MEGW .... Megawatt [*Also, MW*]
MEGWH ...... Megawatt-Hour
MEGX .... Megacards Inc. [*NASDAQ symbol*] (TTSB)
MEGX .... Monoethylglycine Xylidide [*Biochemistry*]
MEH .... Maine State Department of Human Services, Augusta, ME [*OCLC
                 symbol*] (OCLC)
MEH .... Meacham, OR [*Location identifier*] [*FAA*] (FAAL)
MEH .... Medical Eye History (SAUS)
MEH .... Mehamn [*Norway*] [*Airport symbol*] (OAG)
MEH .... Microsomal Epoxide Hydrolase
MEH .... Midwest Express Holdings [*NYSE symbol*] (SAG)
MEH .... Moorfields Eye Hospital (SAUO)
MEH .... Multi-Engined Helicopter (MCD)
Meharry Med C... Meharry Medicine College (GAGS)
MEHDHQ...... Medical Embarkment and Hospital Distribution Headquarters [*World
                 War II*]
MeHi .... Maine Historical Society, Portland, ME [*Library symbol*] [*Library of
                 Congress*] (LCLS)
MEHL .... Mehl Biophile International Corp. [*NASDAQ symbol*] (SAG)
MehlBio...... Mehl Biophile International Corp. [*Associated Press*] (SAG)
MEHP .... Mean Effective Horsepower (IAA)
MEHP .... Monoethylhexyl Phthalate [*Organic chemistry*]
MEHQ .... Monomethyl Ether of Hydroquinone [*Organic chemistry*]
MEHT .... Minimum Eye Height over Threshold [*Aviation*] (FAAC)
MEI .... Main Economic Indicators (NITA)
MEI .... Maine Electronics, Incorporated (ACAE)
MEI .... Main Engine Ignition [*Aerospace*]
MEI .... Maintenance and Engineering Inspection
MEI .... Maintenance Effectiveness Inspection (MCD)
MEI .... Maintenance Engineering Investigation [*DoD*]
MEI .... Maintenance Evaluation Inspection (MCD)
MEI .... Major End Item
MEI .... Management Education Institute [*Arthur D. Little, Inc.*]
MEI .... Management Effectiveness Inspection
MEI .... Management Efficiency Inspection (ACAE)
MEI .... Manpower Education Institute (EA)
MEI .... Manual of Engineering Instructions
MEI .... Manufacturing Engineering Instructions (ACAE)
MEI .... Maps Etc. Incorporated (SAUO)
MEI .... Marginal Efficiency of Investment
MEI .... Marine Ecological Institute (SAUO)
MEI .... Marketing Economics Institute (SAUO)
MEI .... Marketing Economics Institute Ltd. [*New York, NY*]
MEI .... Master Inspection Item [*NASA*] (NAKS)
MEI .... Master of English Literature (SAUO)
MEI .... Mathematics in Education and Industry (SAUO)
MEI .... Matsushita Electronics Incorporated (SAUO)
MEI .... Maximally Exposed Individual
MEI .... Maximum Exposed Individual [*Health risk assessment*]
                 [*Environmental Protection Agency*]
MeI .... Meconium Ileus [*Medicine*]
MEI .... Medicare Economic Index
MEI .... MEI Corporation (SAUO)
Mei .... Meiji Seika Kaisha Ltd. [*Japan*]
MEI .... Meres et Enfants Internationale [*Switzerland*] (EAIO)
MEI .... Meridian [*Mississippi*] [*Airport symbol*] (OAG)
MEI .... Meridian, MS [*Location identifier*] [*FAA*] (FAAL)
MEI .... Metals Engineering Institute (EA)
MEI .... Metastatic Efficiency Index [*Medicine*] (MELL)
MEI .... Middle-Ear Infection (MELL)
MEI .... Middle East Information Service (BJA)
MEI .... Middle East Institute (EA)
MEI .... Military Engineering Item (MCD)
MEI .... Military Environment Inventory [*Rudolf H. Moos*] (TES)
MEI .... [*The*] Ministry of Electronics Industry [*China*]
MEI .... Minnesota Enterprises, Inc. (EFIS)
MEI .... Minnesota Enterprises, Incorporated (SAUO)
MEI .... Minority Educational Institution
MEI .... Mission Essential Item [*Army*]
MEI .... Module Execution Interval [*Computer science*] (VLIE)
MEI .... Morpholinoethylisocyanide [*Organic chemistry*]
MEI .... Most Exposed Individual [*Environmental science*] (FFDE)
MEI .... Multi-Engine Instrument (PIPO)
MEI .... Multivariate ENSO Index (SAUO)
MEI .... Myocardial Efficiency Index [*Cardiology*]
MEIA .... Member of the Institution of Engineers Australia
MEIA .... Microparticle Enzyme Immunoassay
MEIAW ...... Marine Athletic Intercollegiate Association for Women (PSS)
MEIC .... Member of the Engineering Institute of Canada
MEIC .... Middle East Intelligence Center [*World War II*]
Meid .... Against Meidias [*of Demosthenes*] [*Classical studies*] (OCD)
MEIDL .... Manually Entered Identification Library (CAAL)
MEIDS .... Military [*or Miniaturized*] Electronic Information Delivery System
                 (MCD)
MEIDS .... Miniaturized Electronic Information Delivery System (SAUO)
MEIE .... Microcomputer Electronic Information Exchange [*Institute for
                 Computer Science and Technology*]
MEIEA.......... Music and Entertainment Industry Educators Association (NTPA)
MEIEC.......... Metropolitan Electronic Industry Education Council (SAUO)
MEIF .... Mobile Equipment Information File [*Air Force*] (AFM)
MEIG .... Main Engine Ignition [*Aerospace*] (KSC)

MEIGN .... Main Engine Ignition [*Aerospace*]
Meigs .... Meigs' Tennessee Supreme Court Reports [*1838-39*] [*A publication*] (DLA)
Meigs Dig.... Meigs' Digest of Decisions of the Courts of Tennessee [*A publication*] (DLA)
Meigs' R..... Meigs' Tennessee Reports [*A publication*] (DLA)
Me'il .... Me'ilah (BJA)
MEIM .... Minuteman Engineering Instruction Manual (SAA)
MEIMN....... Multiend Item Modification Notice [*NASA*] (KSC)
MEIN .... Medium-Energy Intense Neutron
MEIP .... Marine Engineering Improvement Programme (SAUS)
MEIP .... Mean Effective Injection Pressure [*Diesel engines*]
MEIR .... Mideast Information Resource (BJA)
MEIR .... Minimum Essential Information Requirement (SAUO)
MEIR .... Ministere Federal de l'Expansion Industrielle Regionale [*Department of Regional Industrial Expansion - DRIE*] [*Canada*]
MEIS........... Medium Energy Ion Scattering (MCD)
MEIS........... Middle East Information Service (BJA)
MEIS........... Military Entomology Information Service
MEISER....... Minimum Essential Improvement in System Reliability (ACAE)
Meison .... All-Ethiopia Socialist League (SAUS)
MEISONE .... All Ethiopia Socialist Union
MEISR .... Minimum Essential Improvement in System Reliability (MCD)
meiss........... Melodramma Semiserio [*Music*] (GROV)
MEIT .... Momentum/Energy Integral Technique (MCD)
MEITS......... Mission Effective Information Transmission System
MEITS......... Mission Essential/Effective Information Transmission System (SAUO)
MEIU........... Main Engine Interface Unit (MCD)
MEIU........... Management Education Information Unit, Spastics Society (SAUO)
MEIU........... Middle East Interpretation Unit [*British*]
MEIU........... Mobile Explosives Investigation Unit
MEIVA......... Men's Intercollegiate Volleyball Association (PSS)
MEJ .... Maine Criminal Justice Academy, Waterville, ME [*OCLC symbol*] (OCLC)
MEJ .... Marman Expansion Joint
MEJ .... Maximum Economic Justification
MEJ .... Meade, KS [*Location identifier*] [*FAA*] (FAAL)
MEJ .... Medjet International, Inc. [*ICAO designator*] (FAAC)
MEJ .... Middle East Journal [*A publication*] (BRI)
MEJ .... Movement for Economic Justice (EA)
MEJC .... Miniature Excitatory Junction Potential [*Neurophysiology*]
MEK .... Maine State Library, Bookmobiles, Augusta, ME [*OCLC symbol*] (OCLC)
MEK .... Med-Trans of Florida, Inc. [*ICAO designator*] (FAAC)
MEK .... Meekatharra [*Australia*] [*Seismograph station code, US Geological Survey*] (SEIS)
Mek .... Mekhilta (BJA)
MEK .... Meknes [*Morocco*] [*Airport symbol*] (AD)
MEK .... Methyl Ethyl Ketone [*Organic chemistry*]
MEK .... Salomon, Inc. [*AMEX symbol*] (SPSG)
MEK .... Salomon Inc. 5% MSFI'ELKA' [*AMEX symbol*] (TTSB)
MEKC........... Micellar Electrokinetic Chromatography
MeKh .... Mekhilta (BJA)
MEKO........... Methyl Ethyl Ketoxime [*Organic chemistry*]
MEKP........... Methyl Ethyl Ketone Peroxide [*Organic chemistry*]
MEKTS......... Modular Electronic Kay Telephone System (IAA)
MeL........... Lewiston Public Library, Lewiston, ME [*Library symbol*] [*Library of Congress*] (LCLS)
MEL .... Magnesium Elektron Ltd. [*British*] (IRUK)
MEL .... Maintenance Expenditure Limit (MCD)
MEL .... Maneuvering Element [*Military*] (AABC)
MEL .... Many-Element LASER
MEL .... Marchwood Engineering Laboratories [*Research center*] [*British*] (IRUK)
MEL .... Marine Engineering Laboratory [*Navy*]
MEL .... Master Equipment List [*Military*] (NG)
M EI .... Master of Elements
MEL .... Master of English Language (PGP)
MEL .... Master of English Literature
MEL .... Material Engineering Laboratory
MEL .... Materials Evaluation Laboratory (MCD)
MEL .... Maximum Engagement Line [*Military*] (INF)
MEL .... Maximum Excess Loss
MEL .... Maximum Expenditure Limit (MCD)
MEL .... Maximum Exposure Level [*Hazardous materials*]
MEL .... Maximum Exposure Limit [*Hazardous material control*]
MEL .... Maya Embedded Language (SAUS)
MEL .... Mean Ear Location [*Automotive engineering*]
MEL .... Medium Energy Laser (SAUO)
MEL .... Melamine
MEL .... Melanoma [*Oncology*]
MEL .... Melbourne [*Australia*] [*Airport symbol*] (OAG)
MEL .... Melbourne [*Australia*] [*Seismograph station code, US Geological Survey*] (SEIS)
MEL .... Melbourne [*Later, TOO*] [*Australia*] [*Geomagnetic observatory code*]
mel .... Melena [*Gastroenterology*] (DAVI)
Mel .... Melendus [*Flourished, 1188-1209*] [*Authority cited in pre-1607 legal work*] (DSA)
MEL .... Mellis [*Of Honey*] [*Pharmacy*] (ROG)
MEL .... Mellon Bank Corp. [*NYSE symbol*] (SPSG)
mel .... Melodramma [*Music*] (GROV)
MEL .... Melody
Mel .... Melphalan [*Antineoplastic drug*] (DAVI)
MEL .... Melrose Resources Ltd. [*Vancouver Stock Exchange symbol*]
MEL .... Metabolic Equivalent Level [*Medicine*]

MEL .... Microenergy Logic (IAA)
MEL .... Military Education Level (INF)
MEL .... Minimum Earnings Level
MEL .... Minimum Equipment List
MEL .... Misappropriation of the English Language (SAUO)
MEL .... Missile Ejector Launcher (SAUS)
MEL .... Mistress of English Literature
MEL .... Mobile Erector Launcher [*Military*]
MEL .... Modular Electromagnetic Levitator (SAUS)
MEL .... Moslem Electoral Lobby [*Australia*]
MEL .... Mouse Erythroleukemia
MEL .... Multiengine Land [*Pilot rating*] (AIA)
MEL .... Murine Erythroleukemia [*Oncology*]
MEL .... Music Education League [*Defunct*] (EA)
MEL .... Musika Esperanta Ligo (SAUO)
MEL .... Muzika Esperanto Ligo [*Esperantist Music League*] (EAIO)
MEL .... National Herbarium of Victoria (SAUO)
ME L .... University of Maine. Law Review [*A publication*] (DLA)
MEL 1 .... Military Education Level One [*Army*]
MEL-A........... Marine Engineering Laboratory - Annapolis [*Navy*] (DNAB)
MELA .... Middle East Librarians' Association (EA)
MELAB........... Mechanical Engineering Laboratory [*NASA*] (KSC)
MELAB........... Michigan English Language Assessment Battery (GAGS)
MELABS....... Microwave Engineering Laboratories, Inc. (MCD)
Melami .... Melamine Chemicals, Inc. [*Associated Press*] (SAG)
MELAN......... Melanesia (ROG)
MELAN......... Melanin [*Pigmentation*] (DAVI)
Melanges d'Arch... Melanges d'Archeologie et d'Histoire. Ecole Francaise de Rome [*A publication*] (OCD)
MELAS......... Mitochondrial Myopathy, Encephalopathy, Lactic Acidosis, and Stroke-Like Episod es [*Medicine*]
MELAS......... Mitochrondrial Encephalomyopathy with Acidosis and Stroke [*Medicine*] (MELL)
MeLB........... Bates College, Lewiston, ME [*Library symbol*] [*Library of Congress*] (LCLS)
MELB........... Mission Enhancement-Little Bird [*Military*] (RDA)
Melb........... University of Melbourne (SAUO)
MELBA......... Multipurpose Extended Lift Blanket Assembly (IEEE)
Melbonrne Univ Dep Civ Eng Transp Bull... University of Melbourne. Depament of Civil Engineering. Transport Section. Bulletin (SAUS)
Melb Rpt ..... Melbourne Report [*A publication*]
Melb Stud Ed... Melbourne Studies in Education [*A publication*]
MELC........... Melcombe [*England*]
MELC........... Mouse Erythroleukemia Cell
MELC........... Murine Erythroleukemia Cell [*Medicine*] (STED)
MELCO......... Melville Shoe Corp. (EFIS)
MELCO......... Mitsubishi Electric Company (SAUO)
MELCO......... Mitsubishi Electric Corp. [*Japan*]
MELCOM..... Middle East Libraries Committee
Melcom......... Mitsubishi Electric Company (SPSG)
MELCU......... Multiple External Line Control Unit
MELDI......... Master Equipment List Drawing Index (SAUO)
MeLDL......... Methylated Low-Density Lipoprotein [*Biochemistry*]
MELDOS....... Melioidosis [*Dermatology*] (DAVI)
MELEC......... Microelectronics (IEEE)
M Elec E...... Master of Electrical Engineering (PGP)
ME Legis Serv... Maine Legislative Service [*A publication*] (DLA)
MELEM......... Microelement (IEEE)
MELEO......... Material Exposure in Low Earth Orbit (SAUS)
MELETA....... Mechanical Endurance Load on Environment Test Apparatus (SAUO)
MELF........... Metal Electrode Face Bonding (IAA)
MELF........... Middle East Land Forces [*British*] (NATG)
MELG........... Middle East Liaison Group [*Military*] (AABC)
MELH........... Missile Elevation Heading (IAA)
MELI........... Master Equipment List Identification [*Military*] (IAA)
MELI........... Master Equipment List Index [*Military*] (KSC)
MELI........... Met-Enkaphalin-Like Immunoreactivity [*Medicine*] (STED)
MELI........... Minimum Equipment List Index (NASA)
MELIOS........ Miniature Eyesafe LASER Infrared Observation Set [*A rangefinder*]
MELISR........ National Herbarium of Victoria Specimen Information Register (SAUO)
MELISS........ Mitsubishi Electric Corp. Literature and Information Search Service
MELISS........ Mitsubishi Electric Corporation Literature and Information Search Service (SAUO)
MELISSA....... Meta-Linguistic Syntax Specification Analyzer (VLIE)
MELISSA....... Micro Ecological Life Support Alternative [*European Space Agency*]
Melitco .... Melanesia International Trust Company Limited (SAUO)
MELKONG.... Mechanical Electric Kong [*Robot*]
MELL........... Mellis [*Of Honey*] [*Pharmacy*] (ROG)
MellonBk..... Mellon Bank Corp. [*Associated Press*] (SAG)
MellonP....... Mellon Participating Mortgage Trust Commercial Property Series [*Associated Press*] (SAG)
Mell Parl Pr... Mell's Parliamentary Practice [*A publication*] (DLA)
MELM........... Middle East Lutheran Ministry [*Lebanon*] (EAIO)
MELM........... Minimum Equipment List Manual
Mel Masp .... Melanges Maspero [*A publication*] (OCD)
Meln........... Mellon Bank Corp. [*Associated Press*] (SAG)
MELN........... Metropolitan Electrical League of New Jersey
M Elo .... Master of Elocution
MELO......... Minimum Expected Loss [*Statistics*]
Melon......... Mellon Bank Corp. [*Associated Press*] (SAG)
MELP........... Master English Language Program (ACAE)
MELP........... Measure of Language Proficiency (EDAC)
MELP........... Mid-European Law Project
MELP........... Ministry of Environment, Lands and Parks (SAUO)

MELPrJ....... Mellon Bk 8.50% 'J'Pfd [*NYSE symbol*] (TTSB)
MELPrK....... Mellon Bk 8.20% 'K' Pfd [*NYSE symbol*] (TTSB)
MELPrI....... Mellon Bk 9.60% 'I' Pfd [*NYSE symbol*] (TTSB)
Me-LR .... Law and Legislative Reference Library, Augusta, ME [*Library symbol*]
          [*Library of Congress*] (LCLS)
mels .... Melodramma Serio [*Music*] (GROV)
MELS.......... Microwave and Electronic System (IAA)
MELS.......... Molecularly Engineered Layered Structure
MELSA........ Metropolitan Library Service Agency [*Library network*]
MELSOR ..... Marx, Engels, Lenin, Stalin, October Revolution [*Given name popular
          in Russia after the Bolshevik Revolution*]
MELT .... Mantle Electromagnetic and Tomography [*Geology*]
MELT .... Minimum Equipment Level for Training (MCD)
MELTER ...... Mesosphere/Lower Thermosphere Explorer (SAUS)
MELUS........ Society for the Study of Multi-Ethnic Literature of the United States
          (BARN)
MELV .... Medium Expendable Launch Vehicle (CARB)
MELV .... Melilotus Latent Virus [*Plant pathology*]
MELVA........ Military Electronic Light Valve
Melvile .... Melville Corp. [*Formerly, Melville Shoe Corp.*] [*Associated Press*]
          (SAG)
Melv Tr .... Melvill's Trial (Impeachment) [*London*] [*A publication*] (DLA)
MELVYL...... Melvil Dewey [*Public access online catalog, University of California*]
          (NITA)
Mem .... De Memoria [*of Aristotle*] [*Classical studies*] (OCD)
MEM .... Macrophage Electrophoretic Migration [*Clinical chemistry*] (AAMN)
MEM .... Macrophage Electrophoretic Mobility (STED)
MEM .... Macrophage Electrophoretic Mobility Test (MAE)
MEM .... Magnetic Electron Multiplier (PDAA)
MEM .... Magyar Elet Mozgalma [*Movement of Hungarian Life*] [*Political
          party*] (PPE)
MEM .... Maine State Museum, Augusta, ME [*OCLC symbol*] (OCLC)
MEM .... Malic Enzyme, Mitochondrial (STED)
MEM .... Manufacturing Enterprise Model
MEM .... Marine Engineering Mechanic [*Navy rating*] [*British*]
MEM .... Mars Excursion Mission [*NASA*] (IAA)
MEM .... Mars Excursion Module
MEM .... Master of Ecosystem Management (PGP)
MEM .... Master of Educational Ministry (PGP)
MEM .... Master of Engineering Management
MEM .... Master of Environmental Management (PGP)
Me M........... Master of Metaphysics
MEM .... Materials Experimentation Module (SAUS)
MEM .... Maximum Entropy Method [*Geomagnetism*] [*Computer science*]
MEM .... Mediterranean Air Ambulance, SL [*Spain*] [*FAA designator*] (FAAC)
MEM .... Membach [*Belgium*] [*Seismograph station code, US Geological
          Survey*] (SEIS)
MEM .... Member (EY)
mem .... Member (WDMC)
mem .... Membership (NTIO)
MEM .... MEM Co. [*AMEX symbol*] (TTSB)
MEM .... MEM Co., Inc. [*AMEX symbol*] (SPSG)
MEM .... Memento
mem .... Memoir (WDMC)
MEM .... Memoir
Mem .... Memorabilia [*of Xenophon*] [*Classical studies*] (OCD)
mem .... Memorandum (WDMC)
MEM .... Memorandum
mem .... Memorial (WDMC)
MEM .... Memorial
mem .... Memory (ELAL)
MEM .... Memory (MSA)
MEM .... Memphis [*Tennessee*] [*Airport symbol*] (OAG)
MEM .... Meteoroid Exposure Module (MCD)
MEM .... Methoxyethoxymethyl [*Organic chemistry*]
MEM .... Micro Electro Mechanical (AAEL)
MEM .... Middeck Electronics Module (SAUS)
MEM .... Middle-Ear Muscle [*Anatomy*]
MEM .... Midland Electric Manufacturing Co. (SAUO)
MEM .... Minimal Essential Medium (STED)
MEM .... Minimum Essential Medium [*Culture medium*]
MEM .... Ministry for Energy and Mines (SAUO)
MEM .... Mirror Electron Microscope (PDAA)
MEM .... Missile Engagement Mechanism (MCD)
MEM .... Mission Effectiveness Model (ACAE)
MEM .... Modal Emission Model (EEVL)
MEM .... Model Emission Model [*Environmental Protection Agency*] (GFGA)
MEM .... Module Exchange Mechanism [*NASA*] (NASA)
MEM .... Molecular Exciton Microscopy
MEM .... Mondpaca Esperantista Movada (SAUO)
MEM .... Mondpaca Esperantista Movado [*Esperantist Movement for World
          Peace - EMWP*] [*Tours, France*] (EAIO)
MEM .... Most Efficient/Effective Method [*DoD*]
MEM .... Most Excellent Master [*Freemasonry*]
MEM .... Mount Emily Exploration Ltd. [*Vancouver Stock Exchange symbol*]
MEM .... Multienvironmental Electron Microscope
MEMA .... Marine Engine Manufacturers Association [*Formerly, OMMA*] (EA)
MEMA .... Methyl Methacrylate (STED)
MEMA .... Microelectronic Modular Assembly
MEMa .... Micro-Membranes, Inc. (SAUO)
MEMA .... Middle-Ear Muscle Activity
MEMA .... Motor and Equipment Manufacturers Association (EA)
MEMAC....... Machinery and Equipment Manufacturers Association of Canada
          (SAUO)
MEMAC....... Middle East Medical Advisory Committee [*World War II*]

MeMacU...... University of Maine at Machias, Machias, ME [*Library symbol*]
          [*Library of Congress*] (LCLS)
MemAIEE .... Member of the American Institute of Electrical Engineers (SAUO)
MemAmAnthrAssoc... Memoirs of the American Anthropological Association
          (SAUO)
MemAmerAcadRome... Memoirs of the American Academy in Rome (SAUO)
MemASME.... Member of the American Society of Mechanical Engineers (SAUO)
MEMA/TTC... Motor and Equipment Manufacturers Association's Technical Training
          Council
Memb .... Member (TBD)
MEMB .... Member
Memb .... Membership (AL)
MEMB .... Membranaceous Vellum [*Manuscripts*] (ROG)
MEMB .... Membrane (MSA)
memb .... Membrane (STED)
MEMBERS ... Microprogrammed Experimental Machine with a Basic Executive for
          Real-Time Systems (PDAA)
MEMBIS....... Member Budget Information System [*for House of Representatives*]
MEMBLE ..... Memorable (ROG)
MEMBR....... Middle East Marketing Research Bureau (SAUO)
MEMC........ Marathon Electric Manufacturers Corporation (SAUO)
MEMC........ MEMC Electronic Materials, Inc. [*Associated Press*] (SAG)
MEMC........ Memco Software Ltd. [*NASDAQ symbol*] (SAG)
MEMC........ Methoxyethylmercuric Chloride
MEMC........ Monsanto Electronic Materials Company (SAUO)
MEMC........ Munich Maintenance Equipment Center (SAUO)
MEMCO....... Miller Electric Manufacturing Company (SAUO)
Mem Comm Solar Observ Aust... Memoirs. Commonwealth Solar Observatory.
          Australia [*A publication*]
MEMCON ..... Memorandum of Conversation
MemcoSf ..... Memco Software Ltd. [*Associated Press*] (SAG)
MEMDA....... Memoranda (ROG)
MEMDB....... Medieval and Early Modern Data Bank [*Information service or
          system*] (IID)
MEMDT....... Message Execution Matrix Display Task (SAUO)
MEMDUM ... Memorandum (ROG)
MEME .... Magnetic Environment Measuring Equipment (CAAL)
MEME .... Multiple Entry Multiple Exit
MEME .... Multitasking Extensible Messaging Environment
MEMEC ...... Memory and Electronic Components [*Commercial firm*] [*British*]
ME(Mech)... Master of Engineering (Mechanical) (ADA)
MEM ERR .... Memory Error [*Information retrieval*]
Mem Fac Ed Shiga Univ Natur Sci... Shiga University. Faculty of Education
          Memoirs. Natural Science (SAUS)
Mem Geol Survey Vic... Memoirs. Geological Survey of Victoria [*Australia*]
          [*A publication*]
MEMI .... Master Equipment Management Index [*Air Force*] (AFM)
MeMi .... Millinocket Memorial Library, Millinocket, ME [*Library symbol*] [*Library
          of Congress*] (LCLS)
MEMIC........ Medical Microbiology Interdisciplinary Committee [*International
          Council of Scientific Unions*]
MEMIC........ Mobile Eletromagnetic Incompatibility (PDAA)
MemIMD...... Memoirs of the India Meteorological Department (SAUO)
MEMIS........ Maintenance and Engineering Management Information System
          (SAUO)
MEMISTOR... Memory Resistor (DEN)
MEML .... Master Equipment Management List [*Air Force*] (AFM)
Meml .... Memorial (PROS)
MEML .... Memorial
MEML .... Molecular Engineering and Materials Laboratory [*MIT*] (MCD)
MEMLACTV... Memorial Activities [*Military*] (AABC)
Mem LJ ...... Memphis Law Journal [*Tennessee*] [*A publication*] (DLA)
MEMLZ .... Memorialize (ABBR)
MEMLZD...... Memorialized (ABBR)
MEMLZG..... Memorializing (ABBR)
MEMLZN..... Memorialization (ABBR)
MEMLZR..... Memorializer (ABBR)
MEMMA ...... Mining Electromechanical Maintenance Association (IAA)
MEMMDLE... Memory Module (IAA)
MEMO......... Marine Environmental Management Office [*Marine science*] (MSC)
MEMO......... Maryland Educational Media Organization
MEMO......... Medical Equipment Management Office [*Air Force*] (AFM)
memo......... Memorandum (WDMC)
MEMO......... Memorandum
MEMO......... Middle East Money [*London-Beirut*] (BJA)
MEMO......... Minnesota Educational Media Organization (EDAC)
MEMO......... Mission Essential Maintenance Only (MCD)
MEMO......... Mission Essential Maintenance Operation (MCD)
MEMO......... Model for Evaluating Missile Observation
MEMO......... More Education - More Opportunities (DNAB)
MEMO......... Voice It Worldwide [*NASDAQ symbol*] (TTSB)
MEMO......... Voice It Worldwide, Inc. [*NASDAQ symbol*] (SAG)
MEMOCS...... Mitsubishi Electric Corp. Multiterm Out-of-Context System
MEMO/MAINT... Medical Equipment Management Office/Maintenance (SAUO)
Memo Mgmt... Memo to Management [*Australian Institute of Management,
          Queensland Division*] [*A publication*]
Memorex ..... Memorex Telex NV [*Associated Press*] (SAG)
MEMOREX ... Memory Excellence [*Brand name*]
MEMOS....... Manufacturing Engineering Management Operations System (MCD)
MEMP .... Maximization of Expected Maximum Profit [*Econometrics*]
MEMP .... Mechanical Engineering and Motive Power (SAUO)
Memphis LJ.. Memphis Law Journal [*Tennessee*] [*A publication*] (DLA)
Memphis St U... Memphis State University (GAGS)
Memp LJ ..... Memphis Law Journal [*Tennessee*] [*A publication*] (DLA)
MEMPP....... Morpholinoethylmethylphenylpyridazone [*An analgesic*]

MEMPR......	Ministry of Energy, Mines and Petroleum Resources (SAUO)
MEMPT......	Memory Point
MEMQ......	Married Enlisted Men's Quarters
ME (MR).....	Medical Evidence (Medical Report or Record) (OICC)
MEMR.........	Memory Read [*Computer science*] (VLIE)
MEMR.........	Multiple Exostoses-Mental Retardation Syndrome [*Medicine*] (DMAA)
MEMR.........	Ramtron Australia Ltd. (SAUO)
MEMRA.........	Mechanical Equipment Manufacturers Representatives Association (EA)
MEMRAC	Mission Essential Material Readiness and Condition (MCD)
MEMRB......	Middle East Marketing Research Bureau (SAUO)
memrl.........	Memorial (VRA)
MEMS.........	Master of Emergency Medical Service (PGP)
MEMS.........	Master of Engineering in Manufacturing Systems (GAGS)
MEMS.........	Michelin Earthmover Management System [*Tire design*]
MEMS.........	Microbial Ecological Monitoring System [*Apollo*] [*NASA*]
MEMS.........	Microelectromechanical System [*Materials science and technology*]
MEMS.........	Micro Electro Mechanical Systems
MEMS.........	Mineral Economics and Management Society
MEMS.........	Missile Equipment Maintenance Sets (MUGU)
MEMS.........	Modular Engine Management System [*Automotive engineering*]
MEMS.........	Multieffect, Multistage
MEMSEL......	Memory Select [*Computer science*] (MHDI)
Mem Soc Assn...	Memorial Society Association (SAUO)
MEMSPO	Michigan Elementary and Middle School Principals Organization (SAUO)
Mem St UL Rev...	Memphis State University. Law Review [*A publication*] (DLA)
Memtec......	Memtec Ltd. [*Associated Press*] (SAG)
MEMTRB......	Mechanical Engineering and Machine Tools Requirements Board (SAUO)
MEMU.........	Manned Extravehicular Manipulating Unit (MCD)
MEMW.........	Memory Write [*Computer science*] (MHDB)
MemWks	MemberWorks, Inc. [*Associated Press*] (SAG)
MEMX.........	Memorex Telex NV [*NASDAQ symbol*] (SAG)
MEMXY.........	Memorex Telex ADS [*NASDAQ symbol*] (TTSB)
MEMY.........	Memory (ROG)
MEN............	Master Equipment Number [*Military*] (NG)
M En............	Master of English
Men	Menaechmi [*of Plautus*] [*Classical studies*] (OCD)
Men	Menahot (BJA)
Men	Menander [*Fourth century BC*] [*Classical studies*] (OCD)
MEN............	Menasco Manufacturing Co. (SAUO)
men	Mende [*MARC language code*] [*Library of Congress*] (LCCP)
MEN............	Mendoza [*Argentina*] [*Seismograph station code, US Geological Survey*] [*Closed*] (SEIS)
men	Meningeal (STED)
MEN............	Meningitis [*Medicine*] (MELL)
MEN............	Mennonite (ABBR)
MEN............	Meno [*Slower*] [*Music*]
MEN............	Menology
Men	Menorah: Australian Journal of Jewish Studies [*A publication*] (APTA)
Men	Mensa [*Constellation*]
MEN............	Mense [*or Menses*] (ABBR)
MEN............	Men's Equality Now International (EA)
MEN............	Menstruation (ABBR)
MEN............	Mensuration (ABBR)
MEN............	Mention
Men	Menzies' Cape Of Good Hope Reports [*1828-49*] [*A publication*] (DLA)
MEN............	Methylethylnitrosamine (STED)
MEN............	Middle-East News Agency (SAUO)
MEN............	Mistozen Electronic Nebulizer
MEN............	Multiple Earthed Neutral (IAA)
MEN............	Multiple Endocrine Neoplasia [*Medicine*]
MEN............	Multiple Endocrine Neoplasia/Neoplasms (STED)
MEN............	Multiple Event Network
MEN............	MuniEnhanced Fund [*NYSE symbol*] (SPSG)
MENA.........	Middle East and North Africa [*A publication*]
MENA.........	Middle East News Agency
MENA.........	Mission Element Need Analysis (MCD)
MENA.........	Mitsubishi Engine North America
MENA.........	Mitsubishi Engine North America, Inc.
MENC.........	Music Educators National Conference (EA)
MENCAP......	Royal Society for Mentally Handicapped Children & Adults [*England*]
Mence Lib ...	Mence's Law of Libel [*1824*] [*A publication*] (DLA)
MEND	Massive Economic Neighborhood Development [*New York City*]
MEND	Maximum Entropy Noise Deconvolution [*Statistics*]
MEND	Medical Education for National Defense
MEND	Mendelism
MEND	Mothers Embracing Nuclear Disarmament [*An association*] (EA)
MENDAP......	Melbourne Network Dimensioning and Analysis Programmes (SAUO)
Mendl Lib ...	Mendelssohn Library (SAUO)
MENEV......	Menevensis [*Signature of the Bishops of St. David's*] [*British*] (ROG)
MENEX.......	Maintenance Engineering Exchange
Menex	Menexemus [*of Plato*] [*Classical studies*] (OCD)
M Eng.........	Master of Engineering
M Eng.........	Master of English
MENG	Meaning (ABBR)
M Eng.........	Mechanical Engineer
MEng.........	Member of Environmental Sciences/Studies [*Canada*] (ASC)
MEng.........	Mining Engineer (SAUO)
M-ENG.........	Multiengined
M Eng&PA ..	Master in Engineering and Public Administration (SAUO)
M Eng & PA...	Master in Engineering and Public Administration
MENGF........	Meaningful (ABBR)
MENGFY	Meaningfully (ABBR)
MENGLS	Meaningless (ABBR)
MENGLSY ...	Meaninglessly (ABBR)
M Eng Mgt..	Master of Engineering Management (PGP)
MEngPA	Master of Engineering and Public Administration (NADA)
M Engr........	Master of Engineering (PGP)
MEngrg	Master of Engineering (SAUO)
MEngS	Master of Engineering Science
M Eng Sc ..	Master of Engineering Science
MEngSt........	Master of Engineering Studies (ADA)
MENI	Ministry of Education in Northern Ireland (SAUO)
ME(NI)........	Ministry of Education (Northern Ireland)
MENI	Multiple Endocrine Neoplasia Type I [*Medicine*] (DMAA)
MENIC	Middle East Network Information Center [*Internet resource*]
MENIT	Mennonite
MENJ	Menley & James, Inc. [*NASDAQ symbol*] (SPSG)
Menken.......	Menken's Civil Procedure Reports [*30 New York*] [*A publication*] (DLA)
MenleyJ......	Menley & James, Inc. [*Associated Press*] (SAG)
Menn	Menninger [*Karl Augustus*] [*American psychiatrist*] (DAVI)
MENNON......	Mennonite (ABBR)
MENNS	Meanness (ABBR)
MENO	Menopause (DSUE)
MENO	Menorrhoea (ABBR)
MENP.........	Menopause (ABBR)
MENP.........	Mount Elgon National Park (SAUO)
MENPL........	Menopausal (ABBR)
Men Rel	Menandri Reliquiae [*A publication*] (OCD)
MENRIS	Mountain Environment and Natural Resources Information System (SAUO)
MENS.........	K&G Men's Center [*NQS*] (TTSB)
MENS.........	K & G Mens Center, Inc. [*NASDAQ symbol*] (SAG)
M En S	Master of Environmental Science (PGP)
Mens	Mensa [*Constellation*]
MENS.........	Mensis [*Month*] [*Latin*]
MENS.........	Mensura [*By Measure*] [*Pharmacy*]
MENS.........	Microamperage Electrical Nerve Stimulation [*Medicine*] (MELL)
MENS.........	Middle East Neurosurgical Society (EAIO)
MENS.........	Missile Element Need Statement
MENS.........	Mission Element Needs Statement (MCD)
MENS.........	Mission Essential Needs Statement (SAUO)
MENS IIB	Multiple Endocrine Neoplasia Syndrome IIB (SAUS)
Men's J	Men's Journal [*A publication*] (BRI)
menst	Menstrual [*or Menstruate*] (AAMN)
MENSTD	Menstruated (ABBR)
MENSTG	Menstruating (ABBR)
MENSTL.....	Menstrual (ABBR)
MENSTN	Menstruation (ABBR)
MENSUR	Mensuration (ROG)
M Ent..........	Master of Entomology
MENT.........	Mental
MENT.........	Mentalis (ABBR)
MENT.........	Mentioned
MENT.........	Mentor Graphics [*NASDAQ symbol*] (TTSB)
MENT.........	Mentor Graphics Corp. [*NASDAQ symbol*] (NQ)
Mental & Physical Disab L Rep...	Mental and Physical Disability Law Reporter [*A publication*] (DLA)
MENTD	Mentioned
MentGr	Mentor Graphics Corp. [*Associated Press*] (SAG)
MENTH	Mentha [*Mint*] [*Pharmacy*] (ROG)
MENTH	Menthol (SAUS)
Ment Hlth Aust...	Mental Health in Australia [*A publication*]
MentInc	Mentor Income Fund [*Associated Press*] (SAG)
MENTL	Mental
MentlHlt	Mental Health Management, Inc. [*Associated Press*] (SAG)
MENTLY.......	Mentally
MENTN	Mention (ROG)
MENTNB	Mentionable (ABBR)
MENTND	Mentioned (ABBR)
MENTNG	Mentioning (ABBR)
MENTNR	Mentioner (ABBR)
Mentor	Mentor Corp. [*Associated Press*] (SAG)
MENTOR	Mobile Electrical Network Testing, Observation, and Recording (PDAA)
MENTOR	[*A*] Programming Language [*1963*] (CSR)
MENTT	Mentality (ABBR)
MENTY.......	Mentally (ABBR)
M Env	Master of Environment (PGP)
MEnv	Master of Environmental Studies (DD)
M Env Des...	Master of Environmental Design (PGP)
M Env E.....	Master of Environmental Engineering (PGP)
MENVEGR ...	Master of Environmental Engineering (PGP)
M Envir E....	Master of Environmental Engineering (PGP)
MEnvPlan ...	Master of Environmental Planning
MEnvS	Master of Environmental Science (GAGS)
MEnvS	Master of Environmental Studies
MEnvSc.......	Master of Environmental Science (ADA)
M Env Sc ..	Master of Environmental Science (PGP)
MEnvSt.......	Master of Environmental Studies (ADA)
MEnvStud ...	Master of Environmental Studies (ADA)
MEnvStudies...	Master of Environmental Studies
MenWre.......	Mens Warehouse [*Associated Press*] (SAG)
MeNwS.......	Saint Joseph's College, North Windham, ME [*Library symbol*] [*Library of Congress*] (LCLS)

Menz............	Menzies' Cape Of Good Hope Reports [1828-49] [A publication] (DLA)
Menz Conv...	Menzies' Conveyancing [A publication] (DLA)
Menzies.......	Menzies' Cape Of Good Hope Reports [1828-49] [A publication] (DLA)
Menzingen Sisters...	Sisters of the Holy Cross (SAUO)
MEO..............	Jefferson City, MO [Location identifier] [FAA] (FAAL)
MEO..............	Maintenance Engineering Order [NASA] (KSC)
MEO..............	Major Engine Overhaul
MEO..............	Management Engineering Office (SAUO)
MEO..............	Manned Earth Orbit
MEO..............	Manned Extravehicular Operation
MEO..............	Marine Engineer Officer [British]
MEO..............	Mass in Earth Orbit [NASA]
MEO..............	Medical Education Online (SAUO)
MEO..............	Medical Emergency Officer (DAVI)
MEO..............	Medium Earth Orbit (SSD)
MEO..............	Message Exchange Occurrence (SAUO)
MEO..............	Military Electronics Office (SAUO)
MEO..............	Military Equal Opportunity (MCD)
MEO..............	Mining Engineering Officer [British military] (DMA)
MEO..............	Montello Resources Ltd. [Vancouver Stock Exchange symbol]
MEO..............	Most Efficient/Effective Organization [DoD]
MEO..............	Scandinavian Aviation Center AS [Denmark] [ICAO designator] (FAAC)
MEOC...........	Marine Emergency Operations Center [Western Australia]
MEOC...........	Marine Environmental Quality Committee [Marine science] (OSRA)
MEOC...........	Medium Earth Orbit, Circular (ACAE)
MEOD...........	Maximum Extended Operating Domain (SAUO)
MEOER	Member of the European Osteopathic Register
MEOF...........	Marine Environmental Observation and Forecasting (NOAA)
MEOH	Methanex Corp. [NASDAQ symbol] (SAG)
MEOH	Methyl Alcohol
MEOHF	Methanex Corp. [NASDAQ symbol] (TTSB)
MEOL...........	Manned Earth Orbit Laboratory (IAA)
MEOM..........	Manned Earth Orbit Mission
MEOM..........	Medium Earth Orbit, Molniya (ACAE)
MEOOW........	Marine Engineer Officer of the Watch [British]
MEOP...........	Maximum Engine Operating Pressure
MEOP...........	Maximum Expected Operating Pressure
MEOPT.........	Multi-Engine Operations & Procedures Trainer (SAUS)
MEOR...........	Microbial Enhanced Oil Recovery [Petroleum technology]
MEOs...........	Mass Education Officers (SAUO)
MEOS...........	Medium Earth Orbit Satellites (ACRL)
MEOS...........	Microsomal Ethanol-Oxidizing System [Biochemistry]
MEOS...........	Mode/Energy Offset
MEOSAB	Missile Explosive Ordnance Safety Advisory Board [Pacific Missile Range] (MUGU)
MEOSS.........	Mobile Electro-Optical Surveillance System (SAUS)
MEOTBF.......	Mean Engine Operating Time between Failures [Quality control]
MEOV...........	Maximum Expected Operating Value [FCC]
MEOW	Marine Engineer Officer's Writer [British military] (DMA)
MEOW	Mono-Extraction Orthophoto Workstation (SAUO)
MEOW	[The] Moral Equivalent of War [Phrase used by President Jimmy Carter to describe his energy bill]
MEOW	Multiple Engineering Order Wire (SAUS)
MEOWS	Multimode Electro-Optical Weapon System
MEP.............	Magnetic Energy Product
MEP.............	Magyar Elet Partja [Party of Hungarian Life] [Political party] (PPE)
MEP.............	Mahajana Eksath Peramuna [People's United Front] [Sri Lanka] [Political party] (PPW)
MEP.............	Main Enable Plug (ACAE)
MEP.............	Main Engine Propellant (MCD)
MEP.............	Main Entry Point (NASA)
MEP.............	Main European Port (SAUO)
MEP.............	Maintainability Evaluation Process (MCD)
MEP.............	Maintenance Engineering Program (SAUO)
MEP.............	Major Electronics Procurement
MEP.............	Major Extinction Position [Polarizer-Analyzer]
MEP.............	Management Engineering Plan (CCCA)
MEP.............	Management Engineering Program [Air Force] (AFM)
MEP.............	Management Evaluation Program (AAG)
MEP.............	Manual Entry Panel [Military] (CAAL)
MEP.............	Manuals of Engineering Practice [ASCE]
MEP.............	Manufacturing Engineering Plan
MEP.............	Manufacturing Extension Partnership [National Institute for Science and Technology]
MEP.............	Mars Entry Probe
MEP.............	Master Environmental Plan (BCP)
MEP.............	Master Evaluation Plan [Army]
MEP.............	Master of Engineering Physics
MEP.............	Master of Environmental Planning (GAGS)
MEP.............	Maximal Expiratory Pressure [Medicine] (DB)
MEP.............	Maximum Economic Potential
MEP.............	Maximum Entropy Principle (PDAA)
MEP.............	Maximum Escape Performance [Ejection seat] (MCD)
MEP.............	Maximum Expiratory Pressure [Medicine] (DMAA)
MEP.............	Maxwell Electronic Publishing [Information service or system] (IID)
mep.............	Mean Effective Pressure (ADWA)
MEP.............	Mean Effective Pressure
Mep.............	Mean Effective Pressure
MEP.............	Medical Education Program [Air Force]
MEP.............	Medium External Pintle (SAUS)
MEP.............	Member of the European Parliament
MEP.............	Meperidine [Also, M] [An analgesic]

MEP.............	Mersing [Malaysia] [Airport symbol] (OAG)
MEP.............	Methanol Environmental Performance [Automotive engineering]
MEP.............	Methods Engineering Program [Navy] (NVT)
MEP.............	Methyl(ethyl)pyridine [Organic chemistry]
MEP.............	Methyl Parathion [Also, MP, MPN] [Pesticide]
MEP.............	Microcircuit Emulation Program
MEP.............	Micro-Electronics Education Programme (NITA)
MEP.............	Microelectronics Package (SAUS)
MEP.............	Microelectronics Programme [British]
MEP.............	Microfile Enlarger Printer (NITA)
MEP.............	Middle East Policy [A publication] (BRI)
MEP.............	Midwest Express Airlines, Inc. [ICAO designator] (FAAC)
MEP.............	Migrant Education Projects
MEP.............	Minimum Energy Path [Physical chemistry]
MEP.............	Minimum Entry Point (MCD)
MEP.............	Minority Engineering Program (SAUO)
MEP.............	Minority Entrepreneurship Program [Small Business Administration]
MEP.............	Minuteman Education Program [Air Force] (AFM)
MEP.............	Mission Effects Projector [Lunar exploration]
MEP.............	Mission Equipment Package
MEP.............	Mitochondrial Encephalopathy [Medicine] (DMAA)
MEP.............	Mobile Electric Power (NG)
MEP.............	Mobil Exploration & Producing Services, Inc., Dallas, TX [OCLC symbol] (OCLC)
MEP.............	Mogul End Prong [Lamp base] (NTCM)
MEP.............	Molecular Electrostatic Potentials [Physical chemistry]
MEP.............	Monitoring Environmental Progress (SAUO)
MEP.............	Moon-Earth-Plane (SAA)
MEP.............	Motor End Plate
MEP.............	Motor-Evoked Potential (OA)
MEP.............	Motor Evoked Potentials (SAUS)
MEP.............	Mouvement d'Ecologie Politique [Ecology Political Movement] [France] [Political party] (PPW)
MEP.............	Movimiento Electoral del Pueblo [People's Electoral Movement] [Venezuela] [Political party] (PPW)
MEP.............	Movimiento Electoral del Pueblo [People's Electoral Movement] [Netherlands Antilles] [Political party] (PPW)
MEP.............	Mucoid Exopolysaccharide [Biochemistry]
MEP.............	Multielliptical Pump
MEP.............	Multimodality Evoked Potential [Neurophysiology]
MEP.............	Multiple Equipment Package (SAUS)
MEP.............	Multiple-Exposure Photography
MEP.............	Multiple Extraction Procedure (GNE)
MEP.............	Paris Foreign Mission Society (TOCD)
mep.............	Paris Foreign Mission Society (TOCD)
MeP.............	Portland Public Library, Portland, ME [Library symbol] [Library of Congress] (LCLS)
MEP.............	Societas Parisiensis Missionum ad Exteros [Paris Foreign Missions Society] [Roman Catholic men's religious order]
MEP-91........	Mesoscale Evolution Project-1991 [Marine science] (OSRA)
MEPA...........	Marine and Estuarine Protected Area
MEPA...........	Master in Engineering and Public Administration
MEPA...........	Master of Engineering and Public Administration (SAUO)
MEPA...........	Masters Electro-Plating Association (SAUO)
MEPA...........	Meteorology and Environmental Protection Administration (SAUO)
MEPA...........	Meterological and Environmental Protection Administration (SAUO)
MEPARC.....	Middle East Policy and Research Center (EA)
MEPAS.........	Multimedia Environmental Pollutant Assessment System (SAUO)
MEPC...........	Marine Environment Protection Committee [IMCO] (MSC)
MEPC...........	Maritime Environment Protection Committee (NADA)
MEPC...........	Master of Environmental Pollution Control (GAGS)
MEPC...........	MEPC International Capital LP [Associated Press] (SAG)
MEPC...........	Metropolitan Estate and Property Corporation Munich Ltd. (SAUO)
MEPC...........	Metropolitan Estate and Property International N.V. (SAUO)
MEPC...........	Miniature End Plate Current
MEPC BMCM...	Marine Environment Protection Committee Baltic Maritime Coordinating Meeting (SAUO)
MEPCOM......	Military Enlistment Processing Command [DoD]
MEPCOM.....	Military Entrance Processing Command (SAUO)
MEPD...........	Master of Education - Professional Development (PGP)
MEPDP	Meander Electrodes Plasma Display Panel (IAA)
MEPED.........	Medium-Energy Proton and Electron Detector
MEPES.........	Medical Planning and Execution System (DOMA)
MEPES.........	Medical Planning and Execution System (Model)
MEPEX.........	Middle East Ports Exhibition (SAUO)
MEPF...........	Multiple Experiment Processing Furnace
MEPF-GCF ...	Mutiple Experiment Processing Facility-Crystal Growth Furnace (SAUS)
MEPF-MAS...	Multiple Experiment Processing Facility-Metal Alloy Solidification (SAUS)
MEPGS	Mobile Electric Power Generator Set (MCD)
MEPH...........	Master of Public Health Engineering (NADA)
MEPH...........	Mephobarital [A sedative and anticonvulsant] [Pharmacology] (DAVI)
MEPHISTO...	Mephistopheles [Foreman] [Slang] [British] (DSUE)
ME Phy........	Master of Engineering Physics
MEPIS..........	Management Engineering Program Information System (SAUO)
MEPL...........	Master Engineering Parts Library (TIMI)
MePM..........	Maine Charitable Mechanic Association, Portland, ME [Library symbol] [Library of Congress] (LCLS)
MEPM..........	Medium-Term Energy Policy Model
MePMC........	Maine Medical Center, Portland, ME [Library symbol] [Library of Congress] (LCLS)
MEPOL.........	Metropolitan Police Officers [British]
MePoSS	United Society of Shakers, Shaker Library, Poland Spring, ME [Library symbol] [Library of Congress] (LCLS)

MEPP...........	Marine Electric Power Plant (PDAA)
MEPP...........	Middle East Peace Process (SAUO)
MEPP...........	Middle East Peace Project (EA)
MEPP...........	Miniature End Plate Potential
MEPP...........	Mobile Electric Power Plant (NG)
MEPR...........	Medical Expense and Performance Report (SAUO)
MEPrA..........	Mission Capital 9.875%'MIPS' [NYSE symbol] (TTSB)
MEPrB..........	Mission Capital 8.50% 'MIPS' [NYSE symbol] (TTSB)
MEPRD........	Ministry of Environmental Protection and Regional Development (SAUO)
MePriU	University of Maine at Presque Isle, Presque Isle, ME [Library symbol] [Library of Congress] (LCLS)
MEPROB......	Meprobamate [Mythyl propyltrimethylene carbamate] [Tranquilizer] (DAVI)
MEPROBAMATE...	Methyl Propyltrimethylene Carbamate [Tranquilizer]
MEPRS	Medical Expense and Performance Reporting System (SAUO)
MEPRS	Military Entrant-Processing and Reporting System (GFGA)
MEPRS/DDS...	Medical Expense and Performance Reporting System/Dental Data System [Air Force] (GFGA)
MePS...........	Maine Public Service Co. [Associated Press] (SAG)
MEPS...........	Means-End Problem-Solving Procedure [or Test] [Psychology]
MEPS...........	Medium-Energy Particle Spectrometer (MCD)
MEPS...........	Members of the European Parliament (ECON)
MEPS...........	Message Editing and Preparation Service (SAUO)
MEPS...........	Message Editing and Processing Station (SAUO)
MEPS...........	Message Editing and Processing System (MCD)
MEPS...........	Military Entrance and Processing Station
MEPS...........	Military Entrance Processing Stations (SAUO)
MEPS...........	Military Express and Passenger Bus Service (SAUO)
MEPS...........	Modular Electrical Power Station
MEPS...........	Monochrome Electronic Prepress Systems (DGA)
MEPS...........	Multimedia Environmental Pollutant Assessment System (COE)
MEPSA.........	Middle East Peace and Stability Act [1957]
mEPSC........	Miniature Excitory Postsynaptic Currents [Neurobiology]
MEPSCAT	Military Entrance Physical Strength Capacity Test (INF)
MEPSDU	Module Experimental Process System Development Unit [Photovoltaic energy systems]
MEPSI.........	Mexico-Elmhurst Philatelic Society, International (EA)
MEPSP.........	Miniature Excitatory Postsynaptic Potential [Neurophysiology]
MEPU..........	Ministry of Pre-University Education (SAUO)
MEPU..........	Monofuel Emergency Power Unit
MEPW.........	Ministry of Economic Planning Western Region (SAUO)
MEQ...........	Marine Environmental Quality [Marine science] (MSC)
MEQ...........	Married Enlisted Quarters
MEQ...........	Middle East Quarterly [A publication] (BRI)
mEq	Milliequavalent (ADWA)
meq	Milliequivalent [Gram equivalent weight] (DOG)
MEQ...........	Milliequivalent [or Milligram Equivalent] [Also, ME]
MEQ...........	Mission Equities Corporation (SAUO)
MEQ...........	Modified Examination Question (SAUO)
MEQA.........	Mechanized Equipment Assignment [AT & T]
MEQC.........	Marine Environmental Quality Committee (SAUO)
MEQC.........	Medicaid Eligibility Quality Control (GFGA)
MEQ/L.........	Milliequivalent per Liter
MEQPT........	Major Equipment (COE)
MEQPT........	Major Equipment ID Code (SAUO)
MER...........	Ethamoxytriphetol [An antiestrogen] (DAVI)
MER...........	Madras European Regiment [British military] (DMA)
MER...........	Magneto-Elastic Resonance (PDAA)
MER...........	Main Engine Room [Navy] (CAAL)
MER...........	Maine State Department of Environmental Protection and Department of Conservation, Augusta, ME [OCLC symbol] (OCLC)
MER...........	Maintenance Engineering Report (MCD)
MER...........	Maintenance Evaluation Report (SAUO)
MER...........	Management Expense Ratio
MER...........	Manager, External Relations (SAUO)
MER...........	Mandatory Experience Regulation (DB)
MER...........	Manned Earth Reconnaissance [Naval Air Electronic Systems Command project]
MER...........	Manpower Estimate Report (AAGC)
MER...........	Manpower Estimating Relationships (MCD)
MER...........	Manpower Evaluation Report [Military]
MER...........	Marine Environmental Response [USCG] (TAG)
MER...........	Market Exchange Rates [Monetary conversion rate] (ECON)
MER...........	Mass Energy Relationship
MER...........	Master Employee Record [DoD]
MER...........	Master of Energy Resources (GAGS)
MER...........	Maximum Effective Range
MER...........	Maximum Efficient Rate [Oil]
MER...........	Maximum Energy Recovery [Chemical engineering]
MER...........	Mean Ejection Rate [Medicine]
MER...........	Mechanical Equipment Room (DAC)
MER...........	Mechanics, Electrical, and Radio (MCD)
MER...........	Medical Emergency Room (DMAA)
MER...........	Medical Error Reduction (MELL)
MER...........	Medication Errors Reporting
MER...........	Mercantile
MER...........	Merced, CA [Location identifier] [FAA] (FAAL)
MER...........	Merchandise (ADA)
MER...........	Merchant (AFM)
MER...........	Merchant Ship (SAUO)
MER...........	Mercurial (WDAA)
MER...........	Mercury (ADA)
Mer...........	Mercury [Record label]

MER...........	Merida [Mexico] [Seismograph station code, US Geological Survey] (SEIS)
MER...........	Meridian (KSC)
mer...........	Meridian (SHCU)
MER...........	Meridional [Geology]
Mer...........	Merivale's English Chancery Reports [A publication] (DLA)
MER...........	Merlinoite [A zeolite]
MER...........	Merrell-National Laboratories [Research code symbol]
MER...........	Merrill Lynch [NYSE symbol] (TTSB)
MER...........	Merrill Lynch & Co. [NYSE symbol] (SAG)
MER...........	Merrill Lynch & Co. Preferred Capital Trust I [NYSE symbol] (SAG)
MER...........	Message Error Rate (SAUO)
MER...........	Metal Etch Resist
MER...........	Metal Evaporated Resistor
MER...........	Methanol Extraction [or Extruded] Residue [Immunology]
MER...........	Methow Aviation, Inc. [ICAO designator] (FAAC)
MER...........	Metropolitan Elevated Railroad (SAUO)
MER...........	Middle East Record [A publication] (BJA)
MER...........	Minimum Energy Requirements
MER...........	Ministry of Energy Resources (SAUO)
MER...........	Mission Evaluation Room [NASA] (NASA)
MER...........	Mitteleuropaeisches Reisebuero [Middle European Travel Bureau] [German]
MER...........	Monthly Energy Review [Department of Energy] [Database]
MER...........	Most Economical Rating
MER...........	Multielement RADAR
MER...........	Multiple Ejection Rack (SAUO)
MER...........	Multiple Ejector Rack (NG)
MER...........	Murmur/Energy Ratio (DMAA)
MER...........	Museum Education Roundtable (EA)
MER...........	Myeloid-Erythrocyte [or Erythroid] [Hematology] (DAVI)
MER-29........	Triparanol [Pharmacology] [A cholesterol biosynthesis inhibitor removed from market due to side effects] (DAVI)
MERA..........	Maeventec Employers Rated Almanac [Maeventec] [Information service or system] (CRD)
MERA..........	Michigan Educational Research Association (SAUO)
MERA..........	Microelectronic Radar (ACAE)
MERA..........	Microelectronics for RADAR Application (MCD)
MERA..........	Molecular Electronics for RADAR Applications (IEEE)
MERA..........	Mormons for ERA (EA)
MERADCOM...	Mobility Equipment Research and Development Command [Army]
MERADO......	Mechanical Engineering Research and Development Organisation
MERAG........	Middle-East Research and Action Group (SAUO)
MERALCO	Manila Electric Railroad & Light Company [Still known by acronym, although official name now Manila Electric Company]
MERALT.......	Meridian Altitude [Navigation]
Mer & St Corp...	Merewether and Stephen's Municipal Corporations [A publication] (DLA)
MERASEX	Mesoscale Rain and Snowfall Experiment (SAUO)
MERB..........	Mechanical Engineering Research Board (SAUO)
MERB..........	Medical Examiniation and Review Board [DoD] (DAVI)
MerBkNY......	Merchants New York Bancorp [Associated Press] (SAG)
MerBNY	Merchants New York Bancorp [Associated Press] (SAG)
MERC..........	Chicago Mercantile Exchange (EBF)
MERC..........	Meat Export Research Center [Iowa State University] [Research center] (RCD)
MERC..........	Medical Equipment Repair Center (SAUO)
MERC..........	Mercantile (ROG)
Merc..........	Mercator [of Plautus] [Classical studies] (OCD)
MERC..........	Mercedes [Automobile] (DSUE)
MERC..........	[A] Mercenary
MERC..........	Mercurial (ABBR)
MERC..........	Mercury
MERC..........	Mercury Project [NASA] (KSC)
MERC..........	Middle-Atlantic Educational and Research Center
MERC..........	Middle East Regional Cooperation [U.S. Agency for International Development]
MERC..........	Middle East Regional Cooperation Program (SAUO)
MERC..........	Middle East Resource Center [Defunct] (EA)
MERC..........	Minimum Electrical Resistance Condition (PDAA)
MERC..........	Minority Economic Resource Center [Howard University, Washington, DC]
MERC..........	Mobile Equipment Replacement Cask [Nuclear energy] (NUCP)
MERC..........	Morgantown Energy Research Center (SAUO)
MERC..........	Multi-Racial Education Resources Centre [British] (AIE)
MERC..........	Music Education Research Council (EA)
Merc Ad & Law & Credit Man...	Mercantile Adjuster and Lawyer and Credit Man [A publication] (DLA)
MercAir.......	Mercury Air Group, Inc. [Associated Press] (SAG)
MERCASREP...	Merchant Ship Casualty Report [Navy] (NVT)
MERCAST	Merchant Ship Broadcast [Navy]
MERCAST	Merchant Shop Broadcast System (SAUO)
MERCASUM...	Merchant Ship Casualty Summary [Navy] (NVT)
MercBcp......	Mercantile Bancorp [Associated Press] (SAG)
Merc Cas.....	Mercantile Cases [A publication] (DLA)
MERCE........	Mercedes [Automobile] (DSUE)
Mercedarians...	Order of Our Lady of Mercy (SAUO)
Mercer........	Mercer County Law Journal [Pennsylvania] [A publication] (DLA)
Mercer........	Mercer International [Associated Press] (SAG)
Mercer Beasley L Rev...	Mercer Beasley Law Review [A publication] (DLA)
Mercer BL Rev...	Mercer Beasley Law Review [A publication] (DLA)
Mercer U	Mercer University (GAGS)
MercFn	Mercury Finance Co. [Associated Press] (SAG)
MercGn........	Mercury General Corp. [Associated Press] (SAG)
Merch..........	Merchant (TBD)

MERCH .... Merchantable
MERCHANT... Methods in Electronic Retail Cash Handling (SAUO)
Merch Dict... Merchants' Dictionary [A publication] (DLA)
Merc (Hob)... Mercury (Hobart) [A publication]
MERCHT ...... Merchant
Merch V....... [The] Merchant of Venice [Shakespearean work] (BARN)
MERCI .... Multimedia European Research Conferencing Integration (SAUO)
MercInt........ Mercury Interactive Corp. [Associated Press] (SAG)
Merck .... Merck & Co., Inc. [Associated Press] (SAG)
Merc LJ .... Mercantile Law Journal [New York or Madras] [A publication] (DLA)
MERCM .... Mercantilism (ABBR)
MERCO .... Mercantile Communications [Shipping]
MERCO .... Merchant Ship Control [Navy]
MERCOFORM... Merchant Ship Communications Formatted (MCD)
MERCOMMS... Merchant Marine Communications System (DNAB)
MERComP ... New England Regional Computing Program (SAUO)
MERCON ..... Universal Transversal Mercator Converter [Computer program]
MERCOS ..... Merchant Codes [Shipping]
MERCOSUR... Common Market of the South
MERCPAC ... Mercury Enthusiast Restorer Custom Performance Auto Club (EA)
MERCRy ...... Mercury [Chemistry] (DAVI)
MERCS .... Mercer International SBI [NASDAQ symbol] (SPSG)
MERCS .... Mercer Intl. SBI [NASDAQ symbol] (TTSB)
MercSt........ Mercantile Stores Co., Inc. [Associated Press] (SAG)
MERCT .... Mercantilist (ABBR)
MERCTL....... Mercantile
MerctlBk ...... Mercantile Bankshares Corp. [Associated Press] (SAG)
MERCY .... Medical Emergency Relief Care for Youth
MERDC .... Mobility Equipment Research and Development Center [Army] (MCD)
MERDI .... Montana Energy and Magneto-Hydrodynamics Research Institute [Later, Montana Energy Research and Development Institute] [Research center]
MERDIFF ..... Meridian Difference
MerdIns .... Meridian Insurance Group, Inc. [Associated Press] (SAG)
MERDL .... Medical Equipment Research and Development Laboratory [Army]
MerdrNt .... Meridian National Corp. [Associated Press] (SAG)
Merdth .... Meredith Corp. [Associated Press] (SAG)
MERE .... Mortar Elevation & Ranging Equipment (SAUS)
MEREA .... Member of the American Electrical Railway Engineering Association
MERECEN .... Movimiento Estable Republicano Centrista [El Salvador] [Political party] (EY)
MEREP........ Merchant Ship Arrival and/or Departure Report (NATG)
MEREP........ Merchant Ship Report [Navy]
MERERCAC... Middle Eastern Regional Radioisotope Centre for the Arab Countries (SAUO)
ME(Res) ...... Master of Engineering (Research)
MERES .... Matrix of Environmental Residuals for Energy Systems [Computerized information system]
ME Rev Stat... Maine Revised Statutes [A publication] (DLA)
ME Rev Stat Ann... Maine Revised Statutes, Annotated [A publication] (DLA)
MERF.......... Medical Education Research Foundation [San Diego]
MERG .... Macular Electroretinogram (DB)
MERGE .... Mechanized Retrieval for Greater Efficiency [Computer science]
MERGE .... Model for Evaluating Regional and Global Effects of GHG reduction policies (SAUO)
MERGV .... Martian Exploratory Rocket Glide Vehicle
MERI.......... Medical Education Research and Information Database
MERI.......... Medical Research Institute (SAUO)
MERI.......... Meritrust Federal Savings Bank [NASDAQ symbol] (SAG)
MERI.......... Meritrust Fed Svg Bk Morgan [NASDAQ symbol] (TTSB)
MERI.......... Mineral Exploration Research Institute [See also IREM] [Canada] [Research center] (RCD)
MERI.......... Mining and Excavation Research Institute [Research center] (RCD)
MERI.......... Moderate Resolution Imaging Spectrometer (ACAE)
MERIC .... Michigan Education Resources Information Center [Michigan State Library] [Information service or system] [Defunct] (IID)
MERID .... Meridian (ABBR)
MeridDia ...... Meridian Diagnostics, Inc. [Associated Press] (SAG)
MeridDta ...... Meridian Data, Inc. [Associated Press] (SAG)
MeridI......... Meridian Industrial Trust, Inc. [Associated Press] (SAG)
Meridn........ Meridian [A publication]
MeridSpt...... Meridian Sports, Inc. [Associated Press] (SAG)
MERIE .... Magnetically Enhanced Reactive Ion Etching [By plasmas]
MeriFdl....... Meritrust Federal Savings Bank [Associated Press] (SAG)
MerilCp........ Merrill Corp. [Associated Press] (SAG)
MERINT .... Merchant Intelligence Report [Navy]
MERINT .... Merchant Ship Intelligence (NVT)
MERINTREP... Merchant Ship Arrival and/or Departure Intermediate Report (NATG)
MERINTREP... Merchant Shipping Intelligence Report (SAUO)
Merions ...... Merionethshire (DIAR)
MERIONS..... Merionethshire [County in Wales]
MERIP .... Middle East Research and Information Project (EA)
MERIS .... European Medium Resolution Imaging Spectrometer (SAUO)
MERIS .... Medium Resolution Imaging Spectrometer (SSD)
Merisel....... Merisel, Inc. [Associated Press] (SAG)
MerisL........ Meris Laboratories, Inc. [Associated Press] (SAG)
MERIT .... Maastricht Economic Research Institute on Innovation and Technology
MERIT .... Mechanical Engineers Reading Improvement Techniques (SAUO)
MERIT .... Medical Relief International (SAUO)
MERIT .... Method to Extend Research in Time [National Institutes of Health]
MERIT .... Military Exploitation of Reconnaissance and Intelligence Technology (SAUO)
MERIT .... Monitor the Earth Rotation and Intercompare Techniques [by means of radio telescope measurements]

MERIT......... Multiple RADAR-Integrated Tracking [Military] (PDAA)
MERIT......... [The] The Michigan Educational Research Network [Computer science] (TNIG)
MeritH .... Merit Holding Corp. [Associated Press] (SAG)
MERITOC ..... Meritocracy (ABBR)
MERITOC ..... Meritocrat (ABBR)
Meriv .... Merivale's English Chancery Reports [A publication] (DLA)
Meriv (Eng)... Merivale's English Chancery Reports [A publication] (DLA)
Merix Cp...... Merix Corp. [Associated Press] (SAG)
MERK.......... Merkert American [NASDAQ symbol] (SG)
MERL .... Marine Ecosystem Research Laboratory [University of Rhode Island] [Research center]
MERL .... Massachusetts Institute of Technology Electronic Research Laboratory (SAUO)
MERL .... Materials Engineering Research Laboratory [NASA] (NASA)
MERL .... Materials Engineering Research Laboratory Ltd. [British] (IRC)
MERL .... Materials Equipment Requirements List (NASA)
MERL .... Mechanical Engineering Research Laboratory (SAUO)
MerL .... Merrill Lynch & Co., Inc. [Associated Press] (SAG)
MerL .... Merrill Lynch & Co. Preferred Capital Trust I [Associated Press] (SAG)
MERL .... Mobile Emergency Radiological Laboratory (DEMM)
MERL .... Municipal Environmental Research Laboratory [Environmental Protection Agency] (GRD)
MerLEur....... Merrill Lynch & Co., Inc. [Associated Press] (SAG)
MERLIN .... Machine Readable Library Information [British Library] [Information service or system] (IID)
MERLIN .... Management of Expenditure and Resident-Linked Information Network [Computer science]
MERLIN .... Medical Emergency Relief International (MELL)
MERLIN .... Medium-Energy Reactor Light-Water Industrial Neutron [British] (DEN)
MERLIN .... Modular Ejection-Rated Low-profile Imaging for Night (SAUS)
MERLIN .... Multielement Radio-Linked Interferometer Network [Astronomy]
Mer LJ........ Mercantile Law Journal [Madras, India] [A publication] (DLA)
MERM......... Masters of Earth Resources Management (PGP)
MERM......... Material Evaluation Rocket Motor
MERM......... Multilateral Exchange Rate Model (ADA)
MERMAID ... Marine Environment Remote-Controlled Measuring and Integrated Detection (SAUO)
MERMAID ... Metrication and Resource Modelling Aid (SAUO)
MERMAIDS... Mediterranean Eddy Resolving Modelling and Interdisc Studies (SAUO)
Mermic........ Merrimac Industries, Inc. [Associated Press] (SAG)
MERMLS..... Mid-Eastern Regional Medical Library Service [Library network]
MERMUT..... Mobile Electronic Robot Manipulator and Underwater Television (IEEE)
MERN .... Medical Ethics Resource Network of Michigan (SAUO)
MEROD .... Message Entry & Read Out Device (SAUS)
MERP.......... Marine Ecosystem Response Project (SAUO)
MERP.......... Maximum Effective Radiated Power [Telecommunications] (OTD)
MERP.......... Miniature Electronic Repair Program (DNAB)
MerP6......... Meridian Point Realty Trust VI Co. [Associated Press] (SAG)
MERPASS.... Meridian Passage [Navigation]
MERPL........ Mission Essential Repair Parts List (MCD)
MerPnt 8 ..... Meridian Point Realty Trust VIII [Associated Press] (SAG)
MERPrA ...... Merrill Lynch 9% Sr'A'Dep Pfd [NYSE symbol] (TTSB)
MERPS .... Multiple Event Record and Playback System (NTCM)
MerPt4....... Meridian Point Realty Trust IV [Associated Press] (SAG)
MerPt6....... Meridian Point Realty Trust VI [Associated Press] (SAG)
MerPt7....... Meridian Point Realty Trust VII [Associated Press] (SAG)
MerPt 8 ...... Meridian Point Realty Trust VIII Co. [Associated Press] (SAG)
MerPt83...... Meridian Point Realty Trust 1983 [Associated Press] (SAG)
MERQ .... Mercury Interactive [NASDAQ symbol] (TTSB)
MERQ .... Mercury Interactive Corp. [NASDAQ symbol] (SAG)
MerR .... Mercuric Ion Receptor [Biochemistry]
MERR .... Minor Equipment Relocations, Replacements (DNAB)
MERRA .... Michigan Energy and Resources Research Association (SAUO)
MERRA .... Middle East Relief and Rehabilitation Administration [World War II]
Merr Att...... Merrifield on Attorneys [1830] [A publication] (DLA)
MERRC .... Middle Eastern Regional Radioisotope Centre for the Arab Countries [Cairo, Egypt] (WND)
Merr Costs... Merrifield's Law of Costs [A publication] (DLA)
MERRECT.... Mercury Rectifier (IAA)
MERRF .... Myoclonic Epilepsy Associated with Ragged Red Fibres [Medicine]
Merrimack ... Smith's New Hampshire Reports [A publication] (DLA)
MerrLyn ...... Merrill Lynch & Co., Inc. [Associated Press] (SAG)
MERRT .... Medical Emergency Radiological Response Team (SAUO)
Merry W ..... [The] Merry Wives of Windsor [Shakespearean work] (BARN)
MERS......... Mechanical Engineering in Radar Symposium (SAUO)
MERS......... Medical Equipment Reporting System [Veterans Administration]
MERS......... Medium Resolution Imaging Spectrometer (CARB)
MERS......... Meris Laboratories [NASDAQ symbol] (SPSG)
MERS......... Mobile Emergency Response Support
MERS......... Mobile Emergency Response System (DEMM)
MERS......... Mobility Environmental Research Studies
MERS......... Mobility Environmental Research Study (SAUO)
MERS......... Most Economical Route Selection [Also, ARS] [Bell System] [Telecommunications]
MERS......... Movimiento de Estudiantes Revolucionarios Salvadorenos [Revolutionary Movement of Salvadoran Students] (PD)
MERS......... Multielement Radiometer System
MERS......... Mysore Engineering Research Station (SAUO)
MERSAP ..... Merchant Ship Auxiliary Program (DNAB)
MERSAR ..... Merchant Ship Search and Rescue (PDAA)

MERSAR...... Merchant Ship Search and Rescue Manual (SAUO)
MERSAT...... Meteorology and Earth Observation Satellite (NASA)
MERSEX...... Merchant Ship Code Systems [*NATO*] (NATG)
Mersey .... Merseyside [*County in England*] (WGA)
MERSHIP.... Merchant Ship [*Navy*] (NVT)
MERSHIP.... Merchant Shipping system (SAUO)
MERSIGS..... Merchant Signals [*Shipping*]
MERSSAR.... Merchant Ship Search and Rescue (SAUO)
MERT.......... Maintenance Engineering Review Team [*Navy*] (NG)
Mert............ Merten's Law of Federal Income Taxation [*A publication*] (DLA)
MERT.......... Merton College [*Oxford University*] (ROG)
Mert............ Merton College, Oxford (SAUO)
MERT.......... Milwaukee Electric Railway & Transport Co. [*AAR code*]
MERT.......... Modified Effective-Range Theory (PDAA)
Mert Coll .... Merton College (SAUO)
MER/TER ..... Multiple Ejection Rack/Triple Ejection Rack (MCD)
MertMd....... Merit Medical Systems, Inc. [*Associated Press*] (SAG)
MERTS........ Micropound Extended Range Thrust Stand [*NASA*]
MERTU........ Medical Entomology Research and Training Unit, University de Valle (SAUO)
MERU .... Milliearth Rate Unit [*NASA*] (KSC)
MERX.......... Mercer Enterprises [*Air carrier designation symbol*]
MERX.......... Merix Corp. [*NASDAQ symbol*] (SAG)
MeryL......... Merry Land & Investment Co., Inc. [*Associated Press*] (SAG)
MeryLd....... Merry Land & Investment Co., Inc. [*Associated Press*] (SAG)
MERZONE.... Merchant Shipping Control Zone [*NATO*] (NATG)
MERZONES... Merchant shipping Zones (SAUS)
MES............ Maharashtra Ekikaran Samithi [*India*] [*Political party*] (PPW)
MES............ Main Engine Start [*NASA*] (KSC)
MES............ Main Equipment Supplier (NATG)
MES............ Maine State Planning Office, Augusta, ME [*OCLC symbol*] (OCLC)
MES............ Mainly English-Speaking
MES............ Maintenance Electrolyte Solution [*Physiology*]
MES............ Major Equipment Supplier (ACAE)
MES............ Malaysian Economic Society (SAUO)
MES............ Management Engineering Squadron [*Air Force*]
MES............ Managing Editor Software, Inc. (SAUO)
MES............ Manned Exploration Site (MCD)
MES............ Manual Entry System [*or Subsystem*] (IEEE)
MES............ Manuals of Elementary Science [*A publication*]
MES............ Manufaturing Execution System [*Engineering*]
MES............ Mapping and Earth Science (ELAL)
MES............ Marine Environmental Services (SAUO)
MES............ Marine Evacuation System (SAUO)
MES............ Marketable Equity Securities [*Investment term*] (DICI)
MES............ Mass Expulsion System (MCD)
MES............ Master, Environmental Studies (CMD)
MES............ Master Erection Schedule (DNAB)
MES............ Master of Engineering Science (SAUO)
MES............ Master of Engineering Sciences
MES............ Master of Engineering Studies
MES............ Master of Environmental Science (DD)
MES............ Master of Environmental Studies (PGP)
MES............ Master of Special Education (PGP)
MES............ Mated Elements [*or Events*] Simulator [*NASA*] (MCD)
MES............ Mated Events Simulator
MES............ Maximal Electroshock [*Physiology*]
MES............ Maximum Electroshock Seizure [*Medicine*]
MES............ Mechanical Engineering Society (SAUO)
MES............ Medan [*Indonesia*] [*Airport symbol*] (OAG)
MES............ Medical Electronics Society [*Defunct*] (EA)
MES............ Medical Equipment Set [*Army*]
MES............ Medium Energy Source (SAUS)
MES............ Medium Energy Source Program [*Air Force*]
MES............ Medsource Systems, Inc. [*Vancouver Stock Exchange symbol*]
MES............ Melville Corp. [*Formerly, Melville Shoe Corp.*] [*NYSE symbol*] (SPSG)
MES............ Mesaba Aviation [*ICAO designator*] (FAAC)
Mes............ Mesencephalic (DB)
MES............ Mesozoic [*Period, era, or system*] [*Geology*]
MES............ Message Entry Subsystem (SAUO)
MES............ Message Entry System (MCD)
MES............ Messina [*Italy*] [*Seismograph station code, US Geological Survey*] (SEIS)
MES............ Mesylate [*Organic chemistry*]
ME(S) .... Methodist Episcopal, South
MES............ Mexican Epigraphic Society (EA)
MES............ Michigan Engineering Society (SAUO)
MES............ Midwest Electronic Society (SAUO)
MES............ Military Engineer Services [*British*]
MES............ Minerals Engineering Society [*British*]
MES............ Miniature Edison Screw
MES............ Minimum Efficiency Scale
MES............ Minor Earth Stations (ACAE)
MES............ Miscellaneous Equipment Specification (HGAA)
MES............ Missile Electrical Simulator
MES............ Missile Engineering Station
MES............ Mission Events Sequence (MCD)
MES............ Mobile Earth Station (DA)
M-ES........... Mobile End System (ACRL)
MES............ Modal Emission Model (SAUO)
MES............ Moessbauer Emission Spectroscopy
MES............ MOL [*Manned Orbiting Laboratory*] Environmental Shelter
MES............ Monitoring Energy Systems
MES............ More Effective Schools [*Program*] [*Defunct*]

MES............ Morpholinoethanesulfonic Acid [*A buffer*]
MES............ Motor End Support
MES............ Movimento de Esquerda Socialista [*Movement of the Socialist Left*] [*Portugal*] [*Political party*] (PPE)
MES............ Moving Earth Simulator (MCD)
MES............ Multiengine Sea [*Pilot rating*] (AIA)
MES............ Multilinear Events Sequencing [*Engineering*]
MES............ Multiple Earning Statement [*Banking*] (MHDW)
MES............ Multiple Endocrine Syndrome [*Endocrinology*]
MES............ Myoelectric Signal
MES............ South Methodist Episcopal Church (SAUO)
MESA.......... Maintenance Engineering Support Analysis [*Military*] (CAAL)
MesA .... Maitre es Arts [*Master of Arts*] [*French*]
MESA.......... Malaria Eradication Special Account
MESA.......... Manned Environmental Systems Assessment [*NASA*]
MESA.......... Marine Ecosystems Analysis [*Pollution-monitoring project*]
MESA.......... Marine Education Society of Australia (SAUO)
MESA.......... Marshall Engineers and Scientists Association (SAUO)
MESA.......... Mathematics, Engineering, and Science Achievement (ABAC)
MESA.......... Maximum Entropy Spectrum Analysis
MESA.......... Mechanics Educational Society of America (EA)
MESA.......... Medical Emergency Service Associates (EA)
MESA.......... Medium Power-Switching Application (IAA)
MESA.......... Men to End Spouse Abuse (EA)
MESA.......... Mesa Air Group [*NASDAQ symbol*] (TTSB)
MESA.......... Mesa Air Group, Inc. [*NASDAQ symbol*] (SAG)
MESA.......... Mesa Airlines, Inc. [*NASDAQ symbol*] (NQ)
MESA.......... Meta Email Search Agent [*Computer science*]
MESA.......... Microsurgical Epididymal Sperm Aspiration
ME/SA........ Middle East/Southern Asia
MESA.......... Middle East Studies Association of North America (EA)
M ESA .... Miniature Electrostatic Accelerometer (NAKS)
MESA.......... Miniature Electrostatically Suspended Accelerometer (MCD)
MESA.......... Minimum Essential Support Analysis (MCD)
MESA.......... Mining Enforcement and Safety Administration [*Terminated, 1978; functions transferred to Mine Safety and Health Administration, Department of Labor*]
MESA.......... Mobile Entertainments, Southern Area [*British military*] (DMA)
MESA.......... Model Experimental Systems Analysis [*In-depth study of sewage outfall in the New York Bight*] [*Inactive*] (OSRA)
M ESA .... Modular Equipment Stowage Assembly [*Aerospace*] (NAKS)
MESA.......... Modularized Equipment Storage [*or Stowage*] Area [*or Assembly*] [*Apollo*] [*NASA*]
MESA.......... Module Tool Set Evaluation Strategic Achitectures (ACAE)
MESA.......... MSFC Engineering Support Area (SAUS)
MESA.......... Multi-Ethnic Study of Atherosclerosis
MESA.......... Multiple Engagement Simulation Analyzer [*Military*]
MESA.......... Multiplexed Electronic Synthetic Array (ACAE)
MESA.......... Multi-role Electronically Scanned Array (SAUS)
MESA.......... Music Editor, Scorer, and Arranger [*Computer program*] (PCM)
MESA.......... Myoepithelial Sialadenitis [*Medicine*] (DMAA)
MesaAir...... Mesa Air Group, Inc. [*Associated Press*] (SAG)
MesaAr....... Mesa Airlines, Inc. [*Associated Press*] (SAG)
MESAB........ Medical Education for South African Blacks [*An association*] (EA)
Mesab........ Mesabi Trust [*Associated Press*] (SAG)
Mesaba....... Mesaba Holdings, Inc. [*Associated Press*] (SAG)
MesabaH..... Mesaba Holdings, Inc. [*Associated Press*] (SAG)
MeSaco ...... Dyer Library, Saco, ME [*Library symbol*] [*Library of Congress*] (LCLS)
MeSacoT .... Thornton Academy, Saco, ME [*Library symbol*] [*Library of Congress*] (LCLS)
MesaInc...... Mesa, Inc. [*Associated Press*] (SAG)
MesaLb....... Mesa Laboratories, Inc. [*Associated Press*] (SAG)
MESAMAC .. Engine Status Accounting System (SAUO)
MESAN .... Mouvement de l'Evolution Sociale de l'Afrique Noire [*Black African Social Evolution Movement*]
MESANA ...... Middle East Studies Association of North America (SAUO)
MesaR .... Mesa Royalty Trust [*Associated Press*] (SAG)
MESAR .... Minimum-Essential Security Assistance Requirements (COE)
MESAR .... Multifunction Electric Scan Adaptive RADAR [*Military*] [*British*]
MESAR .... Multi-function Electronically Scanned Adaptive Radar (SAUS)
MESB .... Mechanical Standards Board (SAUO)
MESB .... Michigan Environmental Science Board
MESBIC....... Minority Enterprise Small Business Investment Company
MESC.......... Marine Environmental Sciences Consortium [*Library network*]
MESC.......... Master Event Sequence Controller (KSC)
ME Sc .... Master of Engineering Science
MESC.......... Mescaline
MESC.......... Middle East Service Command [*Army*] [*World War II*]
MESC.......... Middle East Supercomputer Centre [*Bahrain Centre for Studies and Research*] (ECON)
MESC.......... Middle East Supply Center [*World War II*]
MESC.......... Middle East Supply Centre (SAUO)
MESC.......... Middle East Supply Council [*World War II*]
MESC.......... Miniature Excitatory Synaptic Current [*Neurophysiology*]
MESC.......... Mission Events Sequence Controller [*NASA*] (KSC)
MESC.......... Modular Equipment Standards Committee (AAEL)
MESC.......... Modular Equipment Sub-Committee for Communications (SAUO)
MESCAL....... United States Biological Cruise of Baja California (SAUS)
MESCH .... Multi-Environment Scheme [*Medicine*] (DMAA)
MESCH .... Multi-WAIS Engine for Searching Commercial Hosts (SAUS)
MESCO .... Message Electronic Switching Computer (IAA)
MESCO .... Middle East Science Cooperation Office (SAUO)
MESCPL....... Mess Corporal [*Marine Corps*]
MESC(W)..... Middle East Supply Committee (Washington) [*World War II*]

MESD............	Mesdames [Plural of Mrs.] [France]
MESDIS..........	Message Distribution System (SAUO)
MESEC..........	Multi-Cultural Environmental Science Education Centers (ABAC)
MESEEC........	Methodologies to Estimate Social, Environmental and Economic Consequences (SAUO)
MeSepPM....	Penobscot Marine Museum, Searsport, ME [Library symbol] [Library of Congress] (LCLS)
MESF	Minimum Engineered Safety Features (NRCH)
MESF	Mobile Earth Station Facility
MESFET......	Metal-Semiconductor Field-Effect Transistor
MESFET......	Metal Silicon Field-Effect Transistor (VLIE)
MESG..........	Maximum Experimental Safe Gap (IEEE)
MESG..........	Mediterranean Shipping Group [NATO] (NATG)
mesg	Message (ELAL)
MESG..........	Microelectrostatic Gyro
MESGA	Microelectrostatic Gyro-Accelerometer
MESGE........	Message (ABBR)
MESGER	Messenger (ABBR)
MESH..........	Macintosh Enhanced SCSI Hardware (SAUS)
MESH..........	Marine Aspects of Earth System History [Research programs]
MeSH..........	Medical Subject Headings (ADWA)
MESH..........	Medical Subject Headings (NITA)
MeSH..........	Medical Subject Headings Vocabulary File [National Library of Medicine] [Information service or system] (CRD)
MESH..........	Multiple Electronically Synopsing Hierarchy (RDA)
MESH..........	Museum Exchange for System's Help [National Museum of Natural History] (IID)
MESI...........	Modified, Exclusive, Shared, and Invalid Data (PCM)
MESIM..........	Mission Essential Subsystem Inoperative Maintenance
MeSk	Skowhegan Free Public Library, Skowhegan, ME [Library symbol] [Library of Congress] (LCLS)
MeSkS	Margaret Chase Smith Library Center, Skowhegan, ME [Library symbol] [Library of Congress] (LCLS)
MESL..........	Marine Environment Studies Laboratory [Marine science] (OSRA)
MESL..........	Membrane-Enveloped Soil Layer
MESL..........	Merchants' Exchange of St. Louis (EA)
MESL..........	Microwave Electronic Systems Ltd.
MESL..........	Minimum Essential Subsystem List (SAUO)
MESL..........	Mission Essential Subsystems List (NVT)
MESM..........	Master of Environmental Science (PGP)
MESM..........	Mission Essential Subsystem Matrix [Navy] (ANA)
MESM..........	Multiechelon Supply Model (AABC)
MesoAm	Meso American (VRA)
MESOL..........	Management Education Scheme by Open Learning (SAUO)
Mesol	Mesolithic (VRA)
MesoNet......	Mesoscale Network (SAUS)
Mesop..........	Mesopotamia (VRA)
MESOP	Mesopotamia
MESOPAC ...	Mesoscale Meteorological Preprocessor Program (COE)
MESOPUFF...	Mesoscale Puff Model (EEVL)
MESOSOFT...	Mesoscale Data Management Facility (SAUO)
MESP..........	Management Engineering Scheduling Program (SAUO)
MESP..........	Minuteman Extended Survivable Power (DWSG)
MESPA..........	Minnesota Elementary School Principals Association (SAUO)
MESPF	Malayan Estates Staff Provident Fund (SAUO)
MesPGN	Mesangial Proliferative Glomerulonephritis [Nephrology] (DMAA)
MESPOT	Mesopotamia (DSUE)
MESPREP	Message Preparation (SAUO)
MeSprN	Nasson College, Springvale, ME [Library symbol] [Library of Congress] (LCLS)
MESq..........	Management Engineering Squadron [Air Force]
MESRF	Middle East Special Requirement Fund
MESROM	Materials-Evaluation Subcaliber Rocket Motor (SAA)
Mesrx..........	Measurex Corp. [Associated Press] (SAG)
MESS..........	Magnetic Emulsion Spectrometer
MESS..........	Mangled Extremity Severity Score [Medicine] (MELL)
MESS..........	Master of Exercise and Sport Sciences (PGP)
MESS..........	Maximum Effective SONAR Speed (NVT)
MESS..........	Maximum Efficiency Structural System (IAA)
MESS..........	Mechanical Electronic Subassembly Simulator
MESS..........	Messenger (MSA)
MESS..........	Messerschmitt [German fighter aircraft] (DSUE)
MESS..........	Military Equipment Support Subsystem (SAUO)
MESS..........	Misalignment Estimation Software System (MCD)
MESS..........	Mixed Evolutionarily Stable Strategy [Breeding selection]
MESS..........	Model Evaluation Support System (COE)
MESS..........	Monitor Event Simulation System (IEEE)
MESSAGE ...	Modular Electronic Solid-State Aerospace Ground Equipment
MESSCPL	Mess Corporal [Marine Corps]
MESSE..........	Messuage (ROG)
MESSENGER...	Mercury Surface, Space Environment, Geochemistry and Ranging Mission [NASA launch date proposed for March 2004]
MESSER	Messerschmitt [German fighter aircraft] (DSUE)
MESSR	Multispectrum Electronic Self-Scanning Radiometer (MCD)
MESSRS	Messieurs [Plural of Mister] [French]
Messrs.........	Monsieurs (SHCU)
MESSSGT ...	Mess Sergeant [Marine Corps]
MESST..........	Eucharistic Missionaries of the Most Holy Trinity (TOCD)
MEST	Eucharistic Missionaries of St. Theresa (Mexico) (TOCD)
MEST	Maintenance Engineering Support Team (MCD)
MEST	Matter, Energy, Space and Time (SAUO)
MEST	Mestizo (ABBR)
MEST	Ministere d'Etat, Sciences et Technologie [Ministry of State for Science and Technology - MOSST] [Canada]
MEST	Missile Electrical System Test (NG)

MEST	Mouse Ear Swelling Test [Analytical biochemistry]
MESTA..........	Marine Ecosystem Study in Tropical Areas [Marine science] (MSC)
Mestek..........	Mestek, Inc. [Associated Press] (SAG)
MESTIND	Measurement Standards Instrumentation Division (SAUO)
MESTS..........	Missile Electric System Test Set [Military] (PDAA)
MESU..........	Microelectronics Support Unit [for the Microelectronics Education Programme] [British]
MESUCORA...	International Exhibition of Measurement, Control, Regulation and Automation (SAUO)
MESUCORA...	Measurement, Control, Regulation, and Automation (IEEE)
MESUR..........	Mars Environmental Survey [NASA]
MESW..........	Meta-Software [NASDAQ symbol] (TTSB)
MESW..........	Meta-Software, Inc. [NASDAQ symbol] (SAG)
ME/SWA	Middle East/Southwest Asia (SAUO)
MESYLATE...	Methansulfonate (ACAE)
MET	East Tennessee State University, Medical Library, Johnson City, TN [OCLC symbol] (OCLC)
MET	Magic Eye Tube
MET	Maintenance Engineering Technique
MET	Maintenance Evaluation Team
MET	Management Engineering Team [Air Force] (AFM)
MET	Manufacturer's Excise Tax
MET	Marksmanship Expert Trainer (SAUS)
MET	Master Events Timer (MCD)
MET	Master of Education in Teaching (GAGS)
MET	Materials-Energy-Toxics [Recycling]
MET	Maximal Exercise Test (DMAA)
MET	Mean Elapsed Time (MCD)
met	Measurement (DS)
MET	Mechanical Engineering Technician
MET	Medium Energy Telescope
MET	Medium Equipment Transporter (MCD)
MET	Memphis [Tennessee] [Seismograph station code, US Geological Survey] (SEIS)
MET	Metabolic Equivalent [Medicine]
MET	Metabolic Equivalent of the Task (DMAA)
MET	Metal [or Metallic] (AAG)
met	Metallic [Referring to breath sounds] [Medicine] (DAVI)
MET	Metallic [Automotive advertising]
met	Metallophone
MET	Metallurgical
MET	Metalore Resources Ltd. [Toronto Stock Exchange symbol]
Met	Metamorphoses [of Ovid] [Classical studies] (OCD)
Met	Metamorphoses [of Apuleius] [Classical studies] (OCD)
MET	Metaphor
MET	Metaphysics
Met	Metastasis [Medicine] (AMHC)
MET	Metastasis [Medicine]
MET	Metatarsus [Flamenco dance term]
Met	Metcalfe's Reports [58-61 Kentucky] [A publication] (DLA)
Met	Metcalf's Reports [Rhode Island] [A publication] (DLA)
Met	Metcalf's Reports [Massachusetts] [A publication] (DLA)
MET	Meteorological (NAKS)
MET	Meteorological Broadcast (IAA)
MET	Meteorological Committee (SAUO)
MET	Meteorological Office [British] (DSUE)
MET	Meteorological Research Flight [British] [ICAO designator] (FAAC)
MET	Meteorology (AFM)
MET	Methionine (DB)
met	Methionine [An amino acid] (DOG)
Met	Methionine [Also, M] [An amino acid]
MET	Metronome [Music]
MET	Metropolis (ROG)
MET	Metropolitan (AAG)
Met	Metropolitan (DIAR)
met	Metropolitan (ELAL)
Met	Metropolitan Correction Center (SAUO)
MET	Metropolitan Electric Tramways [British] (ROG)
Met	Metropolitan Museum of Art (SAUO)
MET	Metropolitan Music Hall [London] [British] (DSUE)
Met	Metropolitan Opera (SAUO)
Met	[New York] Metropolitan Opera House
Met	Metropolitan Police [British] (WDAA)
MET	[The] Metropolitan Railway [British] (ROG)
MET	Metropolitan Realty [AMEX symbol] (TTSB)
MET	Metropolitan Realty Corp. [AMEX symbol] (CTT)
MET	Metropolitan Transport Authority (SAUO)
MET	Metuchen [Diocesan abbreviation] [New Jersey] (TOCD)
MET	Micro-Electronic Technology (ADA)
MET	Middle European Time (SAUO)
MET	Mid-European Time (SAUO)
MET	Midexpiratory Time [Medicine]
MET	Midshipman Embarkation Team [Navy]
MET	Minimum Energy Trajectory
MET	Minimum Essentials Test [Educational test]
MET	Minimum Exposure Time
MET	Minor Expendable Tool (MCD)
MET	Missile Electrical Technician [Aerospace] (IAA)
MET	Missile Escort Team [Air Force] (AFM)
MET	Mission Elapsed Time [NASA] (NAKS)
MET	Mission Entry Time
MET	Mission Environment Tape
MET	Mission Equipment Team (ACAE)
MET	Mission Event Timer [NASA] (KSC)
MET	Mobile Engineering Team [Navy]

MET .... Mobile Environmental Teams (SAUO)
MET .... Mobile Equipment Transporter [NASA]
MET .... Mobile Examining Team (SAUO)
MET .... Modality Examination Terminal (DMAA)
MET .... Modesto & Empire Traction Co. [Formerly, METC] [AAR code]
MET .... Modified Expansion Tube (IEEE)
MET .... Modular Equipment Transporter [NASA]
MET .... Molecular Electronic Technique
MET .... Mond Excavation at Thebes [London] [A publication] (BJA)
MET .... Monitoring & Enforcement Teams (SAUO)
MET .... Motorola Environmental Telemetry
MET .... Multibutton Electronic Telephone (NITA)
MET .... Multi-Element Tracker (ACAE)
MET .... Multiemitter Transistor
MET .... Multi-Environment Trainer (MCD)
MET .... Multiple Employer Trust [Insurance]
MET .... Multistage Exercise Test (DMAA)
MET .... Multistage Exercise Testing (DB)
MET .... Sensor Meteorological Satellite Sensor (SAUS)
META .... Computer series [Digital Scientific]
META .... Maintenance Engineering Training Agency (SAUO)
META .... Management Engineering Training Agency (SAUO)
META .... Maritime Education and Training Act of 1980
META .... Maryland Electronics Technicians Association (SAUO)
META .... Megachannel Extraterrestrial Array [For receiving possible radio signals from non-earth civilizations]
META .... Megachannel Extra-Terrestrial Assay
meta .... Metacarpal [Anatomy] (DAVI)
META .... metamyelocyte [Hematology] (DAVI)
meta .... Metatarsal [Anatomy] (DAVI)
META .... Metatec Corp. [NASDAQ symbol] (SAG)
META .... Methods of Extracting Text Automatically [Programming language] [General Electric Co.] [Computer science] (IEEE)
META .... Metropolitan Educational Television Association [Canada]
META .... Model Engineering Trade Association [British] (BI)
META 1 .... Metabolic Profile 1 [Biochemistry] (DAVI)
METAB .... Metabolism
METABC .... Metabolic (ABBR)
Metabol .... Metabolism: Clinical and Experimental (MEC)
METABZ .... Metabolize (ABBR)
METABZD .... Metabolized (ABBR)
METABZG .... Metabolizing (ABBR)
METAC .... Medium Tactical Transport Aircraft [Military]
METAC .... Methacryloyloxyethyltrimethylammonium Chloride [Organic chemistry]
METADEX .... Metal Abstracts Index Data Base [Bibliographic database] [British] (IID)
METADEX .... Metals Abstracts Inex (NITA)
METADS ...... Meteorological Acquisition and Display System (PDAA)
METAF ...... Meteorological Terminal Aviation Weather Forecast [FAA] (TAG)
METAG .... Meteorological Advisory Group [ICAO] (DA)
MetaGp .... Meta Group, Inc. [Associated Press] (SAG)
META II .... Megachannel Extra Terrestrial Array II (SAUS)
METAL .... Machine Evaluation & Translation Language (SAUO)
METAL .... Meta-Language (VLIE)
Metal .... Metallurgy (DIAR)
METAL .... Metallurgy
METAL .... Militarily Significant Emergent Technologies Awareness List [Proposed] [DoD]
MetalcId .... Metaclad Corp. [Associated Press] (SAG)
MetalcId .... Metalclad Corp. [Associated Press] (SAG)
Metall .... Metallurgy (BEE)
METALL .... Metallurgy
METALLOG ... Metallography (DGA)
Metall Rep Aeronaut Res Lab Aust ... Australia. Aeronautical Research Laboratories. Metallurgy Report (journ.) (SAUS)
Metall Tech Memo Aust Aeronaut Res Lab ... Australia. Aeronautical Research Laboratories Metallurgy Technical Memorandum (journ.) (SAUS)
MetalR .... Metallica Resources, Inc. [Associated Press] (SAG)
META M .... Metaphysical Magazine [A publication] (ROG)
Metamin .... Metals and Minerals Investment Corp. Ltd. (SAUO)
MET & E ...... Medical Equipment Test and Evaluation [Army Medical Material Agency] (PDAA)
MET&E .... Medical Equipment Test and Evaluation Division (SAUO)
METAPH .... Metaphorical (ROG)
Metaph .... Metaphysica [of Aristotle] [Classical studies] (OCD)
METAPH .... Metaphysical [or Metaphysics] (ROG)
METAPH .... Metaphysician (ABBR)
metaph .... Metaphysics [Parapsychology] (DAVI)
METAPHYS ... Metaphysic (ABBR)
METAPLAN ... Methods of Extracting Text Automatically Programming - Language [General Electric Co.] [Computer science] (IEEE)
METAR .... Aviation Route Weather Report (SAUO)
METAR .... Aviation Routine Weather Report [ICAO] (FAAC)
METAR .... Meteorological Actual Report (WEAT)
METAR .... Meteorological Aviation Report (SAUO)
METAR .... Meteorological Terminal Aviation Routine Weather Report [FAA] (TAG)
METAS .... Metastasize [Medicine]
MetaSft .... Meta-Software, Inc. [Associated Press] (SAG)
METASYMBOL ... Metalanguage Symbol
Metatec .... Metatec Corp. [Associated Press] (SAG)
METATH .... Metathesis
METB .... Metal Base
METB .... MetroBanCorp [NASDAQ symbol] (SAG)
METB .... Metropolitan Borough

METBX .... Mgn. Stanley D. Witter Precious Metals & Min. [Mutual fund ticker symbol] (SG)
METC .... Medesto & Empire Traction Co. (MHDB)
METC .... Metal Curb (AAG)
METC .... Metallic (VLIE)
Metc .... Metcalfe's Reports [58-61 Kentucky] [A publication] (DLA)
Metc .... Metcalf's Reports [Massachusetts] [A publication] (DLA)
Metc .... Metcalf's Reports [Rhode Island] [A publication] (DLA)
METC .... Metropolitan Conference (PSS)
METC .... Military Equipment Test Center (CAAL)
METC .... Modesto & Empire Traction Co. [Later, MET] [AAR code]
METC .... Monthly Estimate to Completion (MCD)
METC .... Morgantown Energy Technology Center [Morgantown, WV] [Department of Energy] (GRD)
METC .... Mouse Embryo Tissue Culture
METCA .... Merchant Token Collectors Association (EA)
METCAL ...... Metrology and Calibration [Air Force] (AFIT)
METCAN ...... Metal Matrix Composite Analyzer [Organic chemistry]
MET-CAR ...... Metallo-Carbohedrene [Organic chemistry]
Metc Cont ... Metcalf on the Law of Contracts [A publication] (DLA)
METCHEM ...... Metals/Materials, Fabricating and Testing Conference and Show for the Petrochemical Industry (SAUO)
METCIR .... Metropolitan Circuits, Inc. (SAUO)
Metc KY ...... Metcalfe's Reports [58-61 Kentucky] [A publication] (DLA)
Metc Mass ... Metcalf's Reports [Massachusetts] [A publication] (DLA)
Met Co .... Meteorological Company (SAUO)
METCO .... Meteorological Coordinating Committee (SAUO)
METCO .... Meteorological Coordination Office (SAUO)
METCO .... Meteorological Coordination Officer (MUGU)
METCO .... Metropolitan Council for Educational Opportunity (EA)
METCO .... Mobile Engine Tester, Computer-Operated (DNAB)
MetCoil .... Met Coil Systems Corp. [Associated Press] (SAG)
METCON ...... Metropolitan Consortium for Minorities in Science and Engineering (USDC)
Metc Yelv ... Metcalf's Edition of Yelverton [A publication] (DLA)
METD .... Management Education Training and Development (AIE)
METD .... Mean Effective Temperature Difference [Refrigeration]
METD ...... Metal Door
METD ...... Metastatic Disease [Oncology]
METDLGY ...... Methodology
MetDR .... Metropolitan District Railway (SAUO)
METDST .... Middle European Time Daylight Saving Time (SAUO)
METE .... Hungarian Scientific Society for the Food Industry (SAUO)
Met E .... Metallurgical Engineer
Mete .... Meteorologica [of Aristotle] [Classical studies] (OCD)
METE .... Multiple ECM [Electronic Countermeasures] Threat Environment [Military] (CAAL)
METE .... Multiple Engagement Test Environment [Military] (PDAA)
METE .... Multiple Environment Threat Emitter (MCD)
METEC .... Meteoroid Technology [Satellite] [NASA]
METEC .... Meteorologist Technician (NOAA)
MetEC .... Metropolitan Edison Capital Ltd. [Associated Press] (SAG)
METEI .... Medical Expedition to Eastern Island (SAUO)
MetEng .... Metallurgical Engineering (DD)
METEOR ...... Manned Earth-Satellite Terminal Evolving from Earth-to-Orbit Ferry Rockets (SAA)
METEOR ...... Marine Environmental Testing and Electro-Optical Radiation (MCD)
METEOR ...... Meteorological Event Oriented Reporting System (SAUO)
METEOR ...... Meteorological Satellite [Former USSR]
METEOR ...... Meteorology
Meteor .... Meteorology
METEOR ...... Multiple Experiment Transporter into Earth Orbit and Return (SAUS)
METEOR ...... Operational Weather Satellite (SAUO)
METEORIT ... Meteoritical
Meteorol .... Meteorological (SAUO)
meteorol ...... Meteorology (ADWA)
Meteorol ...... Meteorology (BEE)
METEOROL ...... Meteorology
Meteorol Atmos Phys ... Meteorology and Atmospheric Physics (SAUO)
METEOROLO ...... Meteorology (ABBR)
METEOSAT ...... ESA Geostationary Meteorological Satellite (SAUS)
METEOSAT ...... European earth resources and meteorological satellite of the ESA program (SAUS)
METEOSAT ...... European Geostationary Meteorological Satellite (SAUO)
Meteosat ...... European Geostationary Meteorological Satellite operated by EUMETSAT (SAUS)
METEOSAT ...... European Space Agency Meteorological Satellite (SAUS)
METEOSAT ...... Geosynchronous Meteorology Satellite (EOSA)
METEOSAT ...... Meteorological Satellite [European Space Agency]
METEOSAT ...... Meteorology Satellite (SAUO)
METEOSAT-3 ... European Space Agency geostationary meteorological satellite (SAUS)
METEOSTAT ...... European Meteorological Satellite (SAUO)
METEPA ...... Tris(methylethylene)phosphoric Triamide [Organic chemistry]
METER ...... Machine Examination Teaching, Evaluation, and Re-education (PDAA)
METF .... Metal Flashing
MetFACS ...... Metropolitan Life Insurance Co. Financial and Administrative Customer Services System (HGAA)
METG .... META Group [NASDAQ symbol] (TTSB)
METG .... Meta Group, Inc. [NASDAQ symbol] (SAG)
METGX .... Metal Grill
METG .... Middle East Task Group (DNAB)
METG .... Military Effects Test Group (SAUO)
METGL .... Meteorological (WGA)

MetGlob........	Metro Global Media, Inc. [*Associated Press*] (SAG)
Meth	Mercaptoethanol [*Organic chemistry*]
METH	Methadone (ABBR)
METH	Methamphetamine (ABBR)
meth	Methamphetamine (ADWA)
METH	Methane (AAG)
Meth	Methaphetamine Hydrochloride [*An amphetamine, commonly known as speed*] (VNW)
Meth	Methedrine [*Stimulant*]
METH	Methicillin [*An antibiotic*]
METH	Method (ROG)
METH	Methode Electronics, Inc. [*NASDAQ symbol*] (NQ)
Meth	Methodist (WDAA)
METH	Methodist
meth	Methyl [*Organic chemistry*] (DAVI)
METH	Methylated (ADA)
METH	Methylated Spirit (DSUE)
METH	Methylmeth (ABBR)
METH	Methyprylon (ABBR)
METHA	Methode Electronics 'A' [*NASDAQ symbol*] (TTSB)
Methanx	Methanex Corp. [*Associated Press*] (SAG)
MetHb	Methemoglobin [*Biochemistry, medicine*]
METHB	Methode Electronics 'B' [*NASDAQ symbol*] (TTSB)
METH BL	Methylene Blue (SAUS)
METHC	Methodic (ABBR)
MethCh	Methodist Chaplain [*Navy*] [*British*]
MeThCh	Methylthiocholine [*Biochemistry*]
Meth Ch Ca...	Report of Methodist Church Cases [*A publication*] (DLA)
Methd	Methode Electronics, Inc. [*Associated Press*] (SAG)
METHDST ...	Methodist
METHEN	Methenamine (SAUS)
METHEN MAN...	Methenamine Mandelate (SAUS)
METHEN SULF...	Methenamine Sulfate (SAUS)
METHEN SULFOSAL...	Methenamine Sulfosalicylate (SAUS)
Meth Epis	Methodist Episcopal (SAUO)
MeTHF	Methyltetrahydrofolic Acid [*Biochemistry*]
met hgh	Methemoglobin [*Biochemistry*] (DAVI)
METHIMAZOLE...	Methylmercaptoimidazole [*Also, MMI*] [*Thyroid inhibitor*]
METHO	Methodology (ABBR)
METHOG	Methodology (ABBR)
METHOGL ...	Methodological (ABBR)
METHS	Methylated Spirits (ADA)
METH SAL	Methyl Salicylate (SAUS)
methyl-CCNU...	Methyl-1-(2-chloroethyl)-3-cyclohexyl-1 Nitrosourea [*Antineoplastic drug regimen*] (DAVI)
Methyl-GAG...	Methylglyoxal-bis-guanylhydrazone [*Antineoplastic drug*] (CDI)
METHYLPRED ACE...	Methylprednisolone Acetate (SAUS)
METHYL TEST...	Methyltestosterone (SAUS)
METHZ	Methodize (ABBR)
METHZD	Methodized (ABBR)
METI	Major Engineering Test Item (AAG)
METI	Medical Education Technologies, Inc.
METIC	Meticulous (ABBR)
METIMP	Meteorological Equipment Improvement Program (NG)
METIS	Meteorological Information System (SAUO)
METJ	Metal Jalousie
METJET	Meteorological Sounding Rocket, Ramjet-Powered [*NASA*] (SAA)
METKIT	Metrics Education Toolkit
METL	Materials and Ecological Testing Laboratory [*Research center*] (RCD)
METL	Metal
METL	Metallica Resources, Inc. [*NASDAQ symbol*] (SAG)
METL	Metallurgy (VLIE)
METL	Mission Essential Task List [*Army*] (INF)
METL	Multielement Two-Layer (AAEL)
METL	Region 4 Metals System (SAUS)
METLA	Finnish Forest Research Institute (SAUO)
Met Lab.......	Metabolic Laboratory [*Colorado State University*] (RCD)
MET LAB.....	Metallurgical Laboratory (SAUO)
METLAND	Metropolitan Landscape Planning Model (SAUO)
METLC	Metallic
Met Lith Assn...	Metropolitan Lithographers Association (SAUO)
METLLRGCL..	Metallurgical
METLLRGST..	Metallurgist
METLO	Metrological Equipment and Technical Liaison Officer [*Navy*] (NG)
METM	Master of Engineering and Technology Management (PGP)
METM	Metal Mold
MET/M	Missile Engine Technician/Mechanic (AAG)
Metmail.......	Metromail Corp. [*Associated Press*] (SAG)
Met Man......	Metro Manila (SAUO)
metMb	Metmyoglobin [*Medicine*] (MEDA)
METMF	Marine Corps Meteorological Mobile Facility (SAUO)
m et n	Mane et Nocte [*Morning and night*] [*Latin*] [*Pharmacy*] (DAVI)
M et N	Mane et Nocte [*Morning and Night*] [*Pharmacy*]
METNO	Advance telegraphic notification relating to the operation of WWW (SAUS)
METO	Maximum Engine Takeoff [*Power*] [*Air Force*]
METO	Maximum Except during Takeoff
METO	Maximum Except Take-Off (SAUS)
METO	Mediterranean Treaty Organization (SAUO)
METO	Meteorological Office [*or Officer*] [*Air Force*]
METO	Meteorological Officer (SAUO)
METO	Metro Capital Corp. [*NASDAQ symbol*] (SAG)
METO	Middle East Treaty Organization
METOB	Meteorologist Observation (NOAA)
METOC........	Bureau of Meteorology and Oceanographic Services (SAUS)
METOC........	Meteorological and Oceanographic (SAUO)
METOF	Meteorological Office
Met Off	Meteorological Office [*British*] (AIA)
METOFOR	Methodology for Total Force Concept [*Military*]
METON	Measured Tons Discharged or Loaded [*Shipping*]
meton	metonymice (SAUS)
METON	Metonymy
METOP	Maximum Expected Takeoff Power (AFM)
METOP	Meteorological Operation (SAUO)
METOP	Meteorological Operational Satellite (SAUS)
METOP	Meteorological Orbiting Platform (SAUS)
Metopera	Metropolitan Opera Association (EA)
MeToV	United States Veterans Administration Center, Togus, ME [*Library symbol*] [*Library of Congress*] (LCLS)
METOXI........	Military Effectiveness in a Toxin Environment (AABC)
METP	Metal Partition
METP	Metal Portion
MetPro........	Met-Pro Corp. [*Associated Press*] (SAG)
metpt	Metalpoint (VRA)
METR	Metal Roof
METR	Meteorology (NG)
Metr	Metropolitan (RION)
METR	Metropolitan
MetR	Metropolitan Railway [*British*]
METR	Minimum Essential Training Requirements
METRA	Media Education Training (SAUO)
METRA	Metal RADAR
METRA	Multiple-Event Time Recording Apparatus (PDAA)
MetraB	Metra Biosystems [*Associated Press*] (SAG)
MetrBcp	MetroBancorp [*Associated Press*] (SAG)
Metrbk	Metrobank North America [*Associated Press*] (SAG)
MetrCap	Metro Capital Corp. [*Associated Press*] (SAG)
Metrcm	Metricom, Inc. [*Associated Press*] (SAG)
METREX	Metropolitan Centrex [*Telephone network*]
METRG	Metering (VLIE)
METRI	Military Essentiality through Readiness Indices
METRIA	Metropolitan Tree Improvement Alliance (EA)
METRIC........	Multiechelon Technique for Recoverable Item Control (MCD)
MetrisCo......	Metris Companies, Inc. [*Associated Press*] (SAG)
METRL........	Meteorology (NG)
METRL........	Metrology Requirements List [*DoD*]
METRLGST...	Meteorologist
MetRlt	Metropolitan Realty Corp. [*Associated Press*] (SAG)
MetrNet	Metro Networks, Inc. [*Associated Press*] (SAG)
METRO	Materiel Essential to Reconstitution Operations [*Air Force*] (AFM)
METRO	Messenger Transport Organizer [*Developmental biology*]
METRO	Meteorological (SAUO)
METRO	Meteorological Equipment Terminal and Representative Observation (MCD)
METRO	Meteorology
METRO	Metering and Traffic Recording with Offline Processing (PDAA)
Metro..........	Metro-Goldwyn-Mayer (WDMC)
Metro..........	Metropolitan (AL)
metro	Metropolitan (SHCU)
METRO	Metropolitan
METRO	Metropolitan Collegiate Athletic Conference (EA)
METRO	Metropolitan Reference and Research Library Organization (SAUO)
METRO	Michigan Effectuation, Training, and Research Organization [*Computer-programmed simulation game*]
METRO	New York Metropolitan Reference and Research Library Agency [*Brooklyn, NY*] [*Library network*]
MetroBcp	Metropolitan Bancorp [*Associated Press*] (SAG)
METROC	Meteorological Rocket
Metrocall	Metrocall, Inc. [*Associated Press*] (SAG)
MetroFn	Metro Financial Corp. [*Associated Press*] (SAG)
Metrogs	Metrogas SA [*Associated Press*] (SAG)
METROL	Metrology
Metrolog	Metrologic Instruments, Inc. [*Associated Press*] (SAG)
Metromda	Metromedia International Group [*Associated Press*] (SAG)
METROMEX...	Metropolitan Meteorological Experiment
METROP	Metropol (WDAA)
METROP	Metropolis (ADA)
METROP	Metropolitan
METROPOL...	Metropolis [*or Metropolitan*] (ABBR)
Metropolis ...	World Association of the Major Metropolises (SAUO)
Metrotrn	Metrotrans Corp. [*Associated Press*] (SAG)
MetroV........	MetroVision of North America, Inc. [*Associated Press*] (SAG)
METRRA	Metal Re-Radiation RADAR [*Mine detection system*] [*Army*] (RDA)
MetRS	Methionyl-Transfer Ribonucleic Acid Synthetase [*An enzyme*]
MetrTl	Metro-Tel Corp. [*Associated Press*] (SAG)
MetrV..........	MetroVision of North America, Inc. [*Associated Press*] (SAG)
METS	Maintainability Evaluation and Tracking System (MCD)
METS	Maintenance Equipment Transport System (SAUO)
METS	Materials and Equipment Trading Service (AAEL)
METS	Mechanized Export Traffic System [*Army*] (AABC)
METS	Metabolic Equivalents [*Medicine*] (DMAA)
METS	Metal Strip
mets	metastases (SAUS)
Mets	Metastasis [*Oncology*] (MAE)
METS	Met-Coil Systems [*NASDAQ symbol*] (TTSB)
METS	Met-Coil Systems Corp. [*NASDAQ symbol*] (NQ)
METS	Metropolitan Emergency Telephone System (COE)
METS	Mining and Earthmoving Technology System
METS	Missile Electrical Technician Specialist (SAUO)
MET/S	Missile Electrical Technician/Specialist (AAG)

METS	Missile Environmental Testing Study
METS	Mobile Electronic Test Set (MCD)
METS	Mobile Engine Test Stand
METS	Modified Engineered Time Standards
METS	Modular Engine Test System (MCD)
METS	Modularized Equipment Transport System [NASA]
METS	Multiple Exposure Testing System [Advertising analysis]
METSAAT	Meteorological Satellite (USDC)
MET/SAT	Meteorological Satellite
METSATS	Multi-Echelon Tester Standard Analog Test Set (ACAE)
METSATT	Meteorological Satellite [Marine science] (OSRA)
Met Serv	Meteorological Service (SAUO)
m et sig	Misce et Signa [Mix and write a label] [Latin] [Pharmacy] (DAVI)
M et Sig	Misce et Signa [Mix and Label] [Pharmacy]
m et sign	Misce et Signa [Mix and Label] [Latin] (WDAA)
METSII/ACI	Military Export Traffic System II-Enhanced/Automated Carrier Interface (SAUO)
METT	Manned, Evasive Target Tank [Army]
METT	Maximum Exercise Tolerance Test (DMAA)
METT	Microwave Energy Transmission Test (SSD)
METT	Mission, Enemy, Terrain and Troops (SAUO)
METT	Mission, Enemy, Terrain and Weather, Troops and Firepower Available
Met Tec	Meteorologist Technician (SAUO)
METTM	Mission, Enemy, Terrain and Weather, Troops and Firepower Available, and Maneuver Space (MCD)
Met Tr J	Metal Trades Journal [A publication]
METT-T	Mission, Enemy, Terrain and Weather, Troops and Firepower Available and Time (INF)
METT-T	Mission, Enemy, Terrain, Troops, and Time [Military]
METTW	Mission, Enemy, Terrain, Tactics, Weather [Criteria for establishing military strategy] [Army] (VNW)
METU	Marine Electronic Technical Unit (MUGU)
METU	Mobile Electronics Technical Unit
METU	Mobile Electronics Training Unit
METVC	Main Engine Thrust Vector [Aerospace] (NAKS)
METVC	Main Engine Thrust Vector Control (MCD)
METW	Military Emergency Travel Warrant [MTMC] (TAG)
METW	Municipality of East Troy, Wisconsin [AAR code]
MET Watch	Meteorological Watch (SAUO)
metwk	Metalwork (VRA)
Metz	Metzenbaum [Instruments] [Surgery] (DAVI)
meu	Maine [MARC country of publication code] [Library of Congress] (LCCP)
MEU	Main Electronics Unit (SAUS)
MEU	Main Electronic Unit (INF)
MEU	Marine Expeditionary Unit
MEU	Marromeu [Mozambique] [Airport symbol] (AD)
MEU	Maximum Expected Utility (DMAA)
MEU	Memory Expansion Unit
MEU	Message Encoder Unit
MEU	Methylumbelliferone [Biochemistry]
MEU	Mind Extension University [Cable television channel]
MEU	Mission Essential Unit (SAUO)
MEU	Modern English Usage (WDAA)
MEU	Multiplexer Encoder Unit
MEU	Municipal Electricity Undertaking
MeU	University of Maine, Orono, ME [Library symbol] [Library of Congress] (LCLS)
MEUA	Million European Units of Account (PDAA)
MEUF	Micellar-Enhanced Ultrafiltration [Chemical engineering]
MEUG	Major Energy Users' Group [British]
MeU-G	University of Maine at Portland/Gorham, Gorham, ME [Library symbol] [Library of Congress] (LCLS)
MeU-L	University of Maine, Law Library, Portland, ME [Library symbol] [Library of Congress] (LCLS)
MEULEX	Marine Expeditionary Unit Landing Exercise (NVT)
MeUmb	Methylumbelliferyl [Biochemistry]
MeU-P	University of Maine at Portland/Gorham, Portland, ME [Library symbol] [Library of Congress] (LCLS)
MEU/SOC	Marine Expeditionary Unit/Special Opperations Capable (MUSM)
MEV	Manned Entry Vehicle
MEV	Mars Excursion Vehicle (SAUO)
MEV	Maximal Exercise Ventilation (MELL)
MEV	Medical Evacuation Vehicle (MCD)
MeV	Mega-Electronvolt (ODBW)
MEV	Mega [or Million] Electron Volts
MEV	Middle Ear Ventilation (MELL)
MEV	Million Electron Volts (MCD)
MeV	Million Electronvolts (COE)
MEV	Minden, NV [Location identifier] [FAA] (FAAL)
MEV	Murine Erythroblastosis Virus [Medicine] (DB)
MEvA	Avco-Everett Research Laboratory, Everett, MA [Library symbol] [Library of Congress] (LCLS)
MEVE	Mesa Verde National Park
MeVEMsJ	Mercury, Venus, Earth, Mars, Jupiter (PDAA)
MEVMA	Maine Veterinary Medical Association (GVA)
MEvP	Parlin Memorial Library, Everett, MA [Library symbol] [Library of Congress] (LCLS)
MEW	Maintenance Equipment Wing (SAUO)
MEW	Manitoba Department of Environment, Workplace Safety, and Health [UTLAS symbol]
MEW	Manufactures Empty Weight (MCD)
MEW	Marine Early Warning
MEW	Mean Equivalent Wind [Meteorology] (DA)

MEW	Measure of Economic Welfare
MEW	Microwave Early Warning [Radio] [Air Force]
MEW	Microwave Early Warning Radar (SAUO)
MEW	Middle East Watch [An association] (EA)
MEW	Minimum Envelope Weight (MCD)
MEW	Ministry of Economic Warfare [British]
MEW	Missionaries of the Eternal Word [Formerly, CFMA] (EA)
MEW	Mobile Early Warning
MEW	Modern English Writers [A publication]
MeW	Waterville Public Library, Waterville, ME [Library symbol] [Library of Congress] (LCLS)
MEWA	Ministry of Education, Western Australia
MEWA	Missile Electronics Warfare Area (ACAE)
MEWA	Motor and Equipment Wholesalers Association [Later, ASIA]
MEWA	Multiple Employer Welfare Arrangement
MEWA	Multiple-Employer Welfare Association (WYGK)
MEWAC	Mediterranean Europe, West Africa Conference (SAUO)
MeWC	Colby College, Waterville, ME [Library symbol] [Library of Congress] (LCLS)
MEWC	Middle East Section of the War Cabinet [British] [World War II]
MEWC	Middle East War Council [British military] (DMA)
MEWD	Missile Electronic Warfare Division [White Sands Missile Range] (AAG)
MEWDS	Multifocal Evanescent White Dot Syndrome (SAUS)
MeWe	Wells Public Library, Wells, ME [Library symbol] [Library of Congress] (LCLS)
MeWebr	Walker Memorial Library, Westbrook, ME [Library symbol] [Library of Congress] (LCLS)
MEWES	Mobile Electronic Warfare Environment Simulator (ACAE)
MEWETS	Multiple Electronic Warfare Emitter Target System (ACAE)
MEWG	Maintenance Engineering Working Group [NASA] (NASA)
MEWO	Manufacturing Engineering Work Order (MCD)
MEWPP	Modular Electronic Warfare Pre-Processor (SAUS)
MEWS	Mews [Postal Service standard] (OPSA)
Mews	Mews' Digest of English Case Law [A publication] (DLA)
MEWS	Microwave Electronic Warfare System
MEWS	Missile Early Warning Station (AFM)
MEWS	Missile Early Warning System (ACAE)
MEWS	Missile Electronic Warfare System [Army]
MEWS	Mission Essential Weapon System [Military] (CAAL)
MEWS	Mobile Electronic Warfare Simulator (MCD)
MEWS	Modular Electronic Warfare Simulator [Navy]
MEWS	Modular Electronic Warfare System (ACAE)
MEWS	Modular EW Simulator (SAUS)
MEWS	Mono-Extraction Workstation (SAUO)
Mews	[The] Reports [1893-95] [England] [A publication] (DLA)
Mews Dig	Mews' Digest of English Case Law [A publication] (DLA)
MEWSG	Maritime Electronic Warfare Support Group (SAUO)
MEWSG	Multinational Electronic Warfare Support Group (SAUO)
MEWSG	Multiservice Electronic Warfare Support Group [Originally Maritime Electronic Warfare Support Group] [NATO] (DOMA)
MEWSS	Mobile Electronic Warfare Support System [Military] (LAIN)
MEWT	Matrix Electrostatic Writing Technique
MEWT	Microelectronic Weld Tester
MEWTA	Missile Electronic Warfare Technical Area [White Sands Missile Range] (AABC)
MEWU	Metal and Engineering Workers Union (SAUO)
MEWUSA	Metal and Electrical Workers Union of South Africa (SAUO)
MEX	Mariner Explorations [Vancouver Stock Exchange symbol]
M Ex	Master of Expression
MEx	Mekhilta Exodus (BJA)
MEX	Memorex Corp., Memorex Technical Information Library, Santa Clara, CA [OCLC symbol] (OCLC)
MEX	Metro Express II, Inc. [ICAO designator] (FAAC)
Mex	Mexican (DIAR)
MEX	Mexican (ROG)
MEX	Mexico [ANSI three-letter standard code] (CNC)
Mex	Mexico (VRA)
MEX	Mexico City [Mexico] [Airport symbol] (OAG)
MEX	Microcell Extender (SAUS)
MEX	Microelectronics (SAUS)
MEX	Military Engineering Experimental Establishment [British]
MEX	Military Exchange
MEX	Mississippi Export Railroad (IIA)
MEX	Mobile Exercise
MEX	MODEM Executive [Computer telecommunications program]
MEX	Temporary Rank [Army slang]
Mexamerican	Mexican-American (SHCU)
MEXAMS	Metals Exposure Analysis Modeling System (EEVL)
MExB	Motor Explosive Boat [British military] (DMA)
MEXE	Military Engineering Experimental Establishment [British]
MexEqt	Mexico Equity & Income Fund [Associated Press] (SAG)
MexFd	[The] Mexico Fund, Inc. [Associated Press] (SAG)
MexG	Gulf of Mexico (SAUS)
MEXH	Multi-Energy X-Ray Holography [Physics]
MEXnet	Mexico Network
MexP	Mexican Pharmacopoeia [A publication]
MExSt	Master of Experimental Statistics (GAGS)
MEXT	Maximal Exercise Testing
MExtEd	Master of Extension Education (GAGS)
MEY	Mapleton, IA [Location identifier] [FAA] (FAAL)
MEY	Maximum Economic Yield [Fishery management] (MSC)
MEY	Meghauli [Nepal] [Airport symbol] (OAG)
Meyer Des Inst Judiciares	Meyer's Des Institutiones Judiciares [A publication] (DLA)

MeYoO .... Old York Historical Society, York, ME [*Library symbol*] [*Library of Congress*] (LCLS)
MEZ .... Augusta Mental Health Institute, Augusta, ME [*OCLC symbol*] (OCLC)
MEZ .... Maritime Exclusion Zone (SAUO)
MEZ .... Mena, AR [*Location identifier*] [*FAA*] (FAAL)
MEZ .... Merces [*Brazil*] [*Airport symbol*] (AD)
Mez. .... Mezuzah (BJA)
MEZ .... Mezzo [*Moderate*] [*Music*]
Mez. .... Mezzo-Soprano (GROV)
mez. .... Mezzotint (VRA)
MEZ .... Mezzotinto [*Medium Tint, Half Tone*] [*Engraving*] (ROG)
MEZ .... Missile Engagement Zone (NVT)
MEZ .... Mittel Europaeische Zeit [*Central European Time*] [*German*]
MEZN .... Mezzanine (ABBR)
mezn .... Mezzanine (VRA)
Mezrabpom... International Workers Aid (SAUO)
Mezsovprof... International Council of Trade and Industrial Unions (SAUO)
MEZT .... Mezzotint [*Printing*] (ABBR)
MEZZ .... Mezzanine (KSC)
MEZZ .... Mezzotint [*Printing*] (ABBR)
MEZZO .... Mezzosoprano (ABBR)
MEZZO .... Mezzotint [*Printing*] (ROG)
MF .... 5-Methyltetrahydrofolate [*Biochemistry*] (DAVI)
MF .... Fall River Public Library, Fall River, MA [*Library symbol*] [*Library of Congress*] (LCLS)
MF .... Le Maitre Phonetique [*A publication*] (BJA)
MF .... Machine Finish [*Paper*]
mf .... Machine-Finish Paper (WDMC)
MF .... Magazines for Friendship [*An association*] (EA)
MF .... Magnetic Field
MF .... Magnetic Fluid [*Physics*]
MF .... Magnetic Focus [*of cathode-ray tube*] (DEN)
MF .... Magneto [*or Magnetic*] Field Generators [*JETDS Nomenclature*] [*Military*] (CET)
MF .... Magnetomotive Force (KSC)
MF .... Main Feed [*Technical drawings*]
MF .... Main Force [*Military*]
M/F .... Mainframe (NITA)
MF .... Mainframe (TIMI)
MF .... Maintenance Facility (ACAE)
MF .... Maintenance Factor
MF .... Maintenance Float [*Military*]
MF .... Maintenance Fuel
M/F .... Maintenance to Flight [*Ratio*]
MF .... Maisonneuve Fracture [*Medicine*] (MELL)
MF .... Major Facilitator [*Biochemistry*]
MF .... Major Function (MCD)
M/F .... Make From (SAA)
MF .... Malaysia Fund [*NYSE symbol*] (TTSB)
MF .... Malaysia Fund, Inc. [*NYSE symbol*] (SPSG)
M/F .... Male or Female
MF .... Male to Female [*Ratio*]
MF .... Mali Franc [*Monetary unit*]
MF .... Mallet Finger (MELL)
MF .... Mallet Fracture [*Medicine*] (MELL)
MF .... MAM Aviation Ltd. [*British*] [*ICAO designator*] (ICDA)
MF .... Management Group (SAUO)
MF .... Mandatory Frequency (DA)
MF .... Mandibular Foramen [*Medicine*] (MELL)
MF .... Mantle Floor
MF .... Manufacture (WGA)
MF .... March Fracture [*Medicine*] (MELL)
MF .... Mare Feccunditatis [*Sea of Fertility*] [*Lunar area*]
M/F .... Marked For
MF .... Mark Forward [*Papers*] [*British*]
MF .... Marshall Field & Co. (SAUO)
MF .... Martinus de Fano [*Deceased circa 1275*] [*Authority cited in pre-1607 legal work*] (DSA)
MF .... Masculinity-Femininity (AEBS)
M-F .... Massey-Ferguson (SAUO)
MF .... Massey-Ferguson GmbH (SAUO)
MF .... Massey-Ferguson, Inc. (EFIS)
M$_f$ .... Mass Flow of Fuel [*Aviation*] (DA)
MF .... Mass Fraction (ACAE)
MF .... Massora Finalis (BJA)
M/F .... Master File
MF .... Master Frame
MF .... Master of Finance
MF .... Master of Forestry
MF .... Mastic Floor [*Technical drawings*]
MF .... Matching Funds (OICC)
MF .... Mate and Ferry [*NASA*] (NASA)
MF .... Material Factor
MF .... Maurice-Farman [*British military*] (DMA)
mf .... Mauritius [*MARC country of publication code*] [*Library of Congress*] (LCCP)
MF .... Maximum Flowering Day [*Botany*]
MF .... Measurement Facility [*Computer science*] (IBMDP)
MF .... Meat Free [*Diet*]
MF .... Mechanical Flap [*Aviation*]
MF .... Meclofenamate [*Organic chemistry*]
MF .... Medal of Freedom [*Military decoration*]
MF .... Media Filter (ACRL)
MF .... Media Forum (EA)

MF .... Medical Foundation [*Australia*]
MF .... Mediterranean Fleet (SAUO)
mf .... Medium Frequency (WDMC)
MF .... Medium Frequency [*Radio electronics*]
MF .... Melamine-Formaldehyde [*Plastics technology*]
MF .... Melomanes Francais [*Record label*] [*France*]
MF .... Membrane Filter
MF .... Merck Frosst Laboratories [*Canada*]
MF .... Merthiolate-Formaldehyde [*Solution*]
MF .... Message Format (ECII)
MF .... Metal Factor [*Geophysical measurement*]
MF .... Metallic Film
MF .... Meter Fix (CTAS)
MF .... Methotrexate, Fluorourcil, Calcium Leucovorin Rescue [*Antineoplastic drug*] (CDI)
MF .... Methyl Farnesoate [*Organic chemistry*]
MF .... Methylformamide (ACAE)
MF .... Methyl Formate [*Organic chemistry*]
MF .... Methylfuran [*Organic chemistry*]
mf .... Mezzo Forte (NTIO)
MF .... Mezzo Forte [*Moderately Loud*] [*Music*] (ROG)
MF .... Microfarad
MF .... Microfiche [*Sheet microfilm*]
MF .... Microfilament (MELL)
mf .... Microfilaria (STED)
Mf .... Microfilariae
MF .... Microfilm
MF .... Microfiltration
MF .... Microflocculation [*Biochemistry*] (DAVI)
MF .... Microform
MF .... Microscopic Factor
MF .... Midcavity Forcep [*Medicine*] (DMAA)
MF .... Middeck Forward (MCD)
MF .... Middle Fork [*AAR code*]
MF .... Middle French [*Language, etc.*]
MF .... Middling Fair (IAA)
mf .... Mid-Frequency (IDOE)
MF .... Mid Fuselage
MF .... Midfuselage (SAUS)
MF .... Mi Favor [*My Favor*] [*Spanish*]
MF .... Mike Force [*Indigenous personnel trained and commanded jointly by US and Vietnamese forces, and used as a reaction and/or reinforcing unit*]
MF .... Milk Foundation [*National Dairy Council*] (EA)
MF .... Millard Filmore [*US president, 1800-1874*]
MF .... Miller-Fischer [*Syndrome*] [*Medicine*] (DB)
MF .... Mill Finish
MF .... Mill Fixture (MCD)
MF .... Millifarad (GPO)
mF .... Millifarad (IDOE)
MF .... Millipore Filter [*Intravenous therapy*] (CPH)
MF .... Mind Freedom
MF .... Minister [*or Ministry*] of Food [*British*]
MF .... Ministry of Food (SAUO)
M/F .... Minorities/Females
MF .... Missile Failure (AAG)
MF .... Mitogenic Factor [*Cytology*]
MF .... Mitomycin, Fluorouracil [*Antineoplastic drug regimen*]
MF .... Mitotic Figure [*Genetics*]
MF .... Mixed Flow (AAG)
MF .... Mobile Facility (MCD)
MF .... Modern Fiction
MF .... Modifying Factor [*Toxicology*]
MF .... Modulated Frequency (SAUS)
MF .... Modulation Factor
MF .... Molecular Formula (NITA)
MF .... Mole Fraction [*Chemistry*]
M-F .... Monday through Friday (CDAI)
MF .... More Follows [*Newspaper copy*] (DGA)
mf .... More Follows [*Copyediting*] (WDMC)
MF .... More Fragments (ACRL)
MF .... Morningstar Foundation (EA)
MF .... Morphogenetic Furrow [*Cell differentiation*]
MF .... Morris Foundation [*British*] (DBA)
MF .... Mossy Fiber [*Neuroanatomy*]
MF .... Mother Fooler [*Bowdlerized version*]
MF .... Motor Field
MF .... Motor Freight
MF .... Mound Facility (SAUO)
MF .... Mucosal Fluid (DB)
MF .... Multifactorial (DIPS)
MF .... Multifamily (PA)
MF .... Multifrequency [*Telecommunications*]
MF .... Multi-Function (SAUO)
MF .... Multifunctional (MCD)
MF .... Multiple Feedback (MED)
MF .... Multiplying Factor [*Microscopy*]
MF .... Munitions Facility (ACAE)
MF .... Muscle Fiber
MF .... Musicians Foundation (EA)
MF .... Mutation Frequency [*Medicine*] (DMAA)
MF .... Mutual Fund [*Business term*]
MF .... Mycosis Fungoides [*Dermatology*]
MF .... Myelinated Fiber [*Neuroanatomy*]
MF .... Myelin Figure [*Medicine*]

MF	Myelofibrosis [*Medicine*] (DB)
M/F	My Favor (ADA)
MF	Myocardial Fibrosis [*Cardiology*]
MF	Myofibrillar [*Anatomy*]
MF	Red Carpet Flying Service [*ICAO designator*] (AD)
MF	Royal Munster Fusiliers [*Military unit*] (DMA)
MF	SAAB-Scania AB [*Sweden*] [*ICAO aircraft manufacturer identifier*] (ICAO)
MF	Spofa Ltd. [*Czechoslovakia*] [*Research code symbol*]
MF/1	Measurement Frequency/1 [*IBM*] (NITA)
MF²K	Medical Force 2000 [*Army*] (DOMA)
MF2K	Medical Force 2000 (SAUO)
MFA	America First Mtg Investments [*NYSE symbol*] (SG)
MFA	Macrofollicular Adenoma [*Medicine*] (MELL)
MFA	Mafia Islands [*Tanzania*] [*Airport symbol*] (OAG)
MFA	Malfunction Alert [*Computer science*] (BUR)
MFA	Malicious False Alarm [*Firefighting*]
MFA	Malta Fencible Artillery [*British*]
MFA	Managed Futures Association (NTPA)
MFA	Manned Flight Awareness [*NASA*] (NASA)
MFA	Marconi-Franklin Antenna
MFA	Marine Fabricators Association (NTPA)
M Fa	Martinus de Fano [*Deceased circa 1275*] [*Authority cited in pre-1607 legal work*] (DSA)
MFA	Master Fencers Association (NADA)
MFA	Master File Activities [*Computer science*]
MFA	Master Fine Arts (SAUO)
MFA	Master of Fine Arts
MFA	Material Fielding Agreement [*Army*]
MFA	Materiel Fielding Agreement (SAUO)
MFA	Mauritius Freeport Authority
MFA	McAlpin(e) Family Association (EA)
MFA	Meningitis Foundation of America (NRGU)
MFA	Menningar- og Fraedslusamband Althydu [*Workers' Educational Association*] [*Iceland*] (EY)
MFA	Men's Fashion Association of America (EA)
MFA	Mercantile Fleet Auxiliary [*British*]
MFA	Metal Finishing Association [*British*] (DBA)
MFA	Methyl Fluoracetate [*Organic chemistry*]
MFA	Miami, FL [*Location identifier*] [*FAA*] (FAAL)
MFA	Microelectronics for All Kit (NITA)
MFA	Military Flying Area [*Canadian*]
MFA	Military Functions Appropriation (AABC)
MFA	Minimum Flight Altitude [*Aviation*] (DA)
MFA	Minister for Foreign Affairs [*British*]
MFA	Miscellaneous Federal Agencies (SAUO)
MFA	Mississippi Forestry Association (WPI)
MFA	Missouri Farmers Association (EFIS)
MFA	Mitchell Field [*Alaska*] [*Seismograph station code, US Geological Survey*] [*Closed*] (SEIS)
MFA	Mobilization for Animals (EA)
MFA	Modify Field Attribute [*Computer science*] (DCDG)
MFA	Monofluoroacetate [*Organic chemistry*]
MFA	Motor Factors Association [*British*] (BI)
MFA	Movement for Federation of the Americas (EA)
MFA	Movimento das Forcas Armadas [*Armed Forces Movement*] [*Portugal*] [*Political party*] (PPE)
MFA	Multi-Fiber Arrangement [*International trade*]
MFA	Multi-Fibre Agreement (SAUO)
MFA	Multifocal Functional Autonomy [*Medicine*] (DMAA)
MFA	Multifunctional Acrylate [*Organic chemistry*]
MFA	Multifunction Antenna
MFA	Multiple Factor Analysis (DB)
MFA	Multiple Filer Audit Program
MFA	Mumpower Family Association (EA)
MFA	Museum of Fine Arts [*Boston*] (BJA)
MFAA	Masters of Foxhounds Association of America [*Later, American Master of Foxhounds Association*] (EA)
MFAA	Monuments, Fine Arts and Archives Section (SAUO)
MFA & A.....	Monuments, Fine Arts, and Archives [*SHAEF*] [*World War II*]
MFA Art and Arch...	Master of Fine Arts in Art and Archaeology (SAUO)
MFAB	Museum of Fine Arts, Boston
MFAB-F..........	Mobile Floating Assault Bridge-Ferry [*Military*]
MFABI..........	Metal Fixing Association for Building Insulation (SAUO)
MFAC..........	Magnetic Fusion Advisory Committee [*Department of Energy*] [*Washington, DC*]
MFAC..........	Market Facts [*NASDAQ symbol*] (TTSB)
MFAC..........	Market Facts, Inc. [*NASDAQ symbol*] (NQ)
M Fac Hom...	Member of the Faculty of Homeopathy (SAUO)
MFAD..........	Maneuver Force Air Defense
MFAG..........	Medical First Aid Guide for use in Accidents Involving Dangerous Goods (SAUO)
MFAH..........	Museum of Fine Arts of Houston (SAUO)
MFai..........	Millicent Library, Fairhaven, MA [*Library symbol*] [*Library of Congress*] (LCLS)
MFAIRWEST...	Marine Fleet Air, West Coast
MFal	Falmouth Public Library, Falmouth, MA [*Library symbol*] [*Library of Congress*] (LCLS)
MFALDA	Marginal Farmers and Agricultural Labourers Development Agency (SAUO)
MFalHi..........	Falmouth Historical Society, Falmouth, MA [*Library symbol*] [*Library of Congress*] (LCLS)
MFAMUS	Master of Fine Arts in Music (WDAA)
MFAMW.......	Modern Free and Accepted Masons of the World (EA)
MF&A	Monuments, Fine Arts and Archives (SAUO)

MF & P......	Materials Finishes and Processes (MCD)
MF & R......	Manpower Forces and Readiness [*Military*]
MF & S......	Magazine Flooding and Sprinkling
MFANSW......	Master Farriers' Association of New South Wales [*Australia*]
MFAP..........	Manned Flight Awareness Program [*NASA*] (KSC)
MFAR..........	Meter Fix Acceptance Rate (CTAS)
MFAR..........	Michigan Foundation for Advanced Research (SAUO)
MFAR..........	Modernized Fleet Accounting and Reporting
MFAR..........	Multi-Function Array RADAR (MCD)
MFARCS	Member of the Faculty of Anaesthetists of the Royal College of Surgeons (SAUO)
MFARS	Defense Mapping Agency Federal Acquisition Regulation Supplement [*A publication*] (AAGC)
MFAS..........	Master of Fisheries and Aquatic Science (PGP)
MFASMR......	Multifrequency Aperture Synthesis Microwave Radiometer (ACAE)
MFAST..........	Mwave Folded Array Signal Transform (SAUS)
MFAT..........	Multifocal Atrial Tachycardia [*Cardiology*] (DAVI)
MFAW..........	Master of Fine Arts in Writing (PGP)
MFB..........	Bristol Community College, Fall River, MA [*Library symbol*] [*Library of Congress*] (LCLS)
MFB..........	Mammal Fibroblast (DB)
MFB..........	Mass Fraction Burn [*Automotive engine combustion analysis*]
MFB..........	Master of Finance and Banking (PGP)
MFB..........	Medial Forebrain Bundle [*Medicine*]
MFB..........	Message from Base
MFB..........	Metallic Foreign Body
MFB..........	Metropolitan Fire Brigade [*British*]
MFB..........	MFB Mutual Insurance Co. [*from Manufacturers Mutual Fire Insurance Co., Firemen's Mutual Insurance Co., Blackstone Mutual Insurance Co.*]
MFB..........	Mill Fixture Base (MCD)
MFB..........	Mixed Functional Block (IEEE)
MFB..........	Moisture Free Basis
MFB..........	Motional Feedback
MFB..........	Motor Freight Tariff Bureau, Springfield IL [*STAC*]
MFBAR	Multifunction Band Airborne Radio
MFBARS	Multifunction-Multiband Airborne Radio System (ACAE)
MFBB..........	Mexican Food and Beverage Board (EA)
MFBC..........	MFB Corp. [*NASDAQ symbol*] (SAG)
MFB Cp......	MFB Corp. [*Associated Press*] (SAG)
MFBE..........	Minority/Female Business Enterprise
MFBF..........	Mean Flights between Failures [*Military*] (CAAL)
MFBF..........	Minimum Film Boiling Flux
MFBF..........	Multi-Function Bomb Fuze (SAUS)
MFBI..........	Major Fuel Burning Installation (GFGA)
MFBI..........	Major Industrial Fuel-Burning Installations (SAUO)
MFBM..........	Thousand Feet Board Measure [*Lumber*]
MFBMP..........	Project Manager, Fleet Ballistic Missile [*Navy*]
MFBP..........	Main Feed Booster Pump (NVT)
MFBP..........	Manufacturing Flow and Building Plan (NASA)
MFBS..........	Marine and Freshwater Biomedical Science (GNE)
MFBS..........	McKinney Functional Board Shop (TIMI)
MFBTE	Midland Federation of Building Trades Employees (SAUO)
MFC..........	Magnesium Flat Cell
MFC..........	Magnetic Film Counter
MFC..........	Magnetic Tape Field Scan [*Computer science*]
MFC..........	Main Fuel Control (MCD)
MFC..........	Manual Frequency Control
MFC..........	Maritime Fruit Carriers [*Steamship*] (MHDW)
MFC..........	Maritime Fruit Carriers Company (SAUO)
MFC..........	Mass Flow Controller [*Engineering*]
MFC..........	Master File Copy [*Computer science*] (KSC)
MFC..........	Master Flow Controller [*Nuclear energy*] (NRCH)
MFC..........	Master of Forest Conservation (PGP)
MFC..........	Mastership in Food Control [*British*] (DBQ)
MFC..........	Mean Frequency of Compensation (STED)
MFC..........	Median Femoral Condyle [*Anatomy*]
MFC..........	Medicated Face Conditioner [*Brand manufactured by Mennen*]
MFC..........	Membrane Fecal Coliform (PDAA)
m-FC..........	Membrane Focal Coli [*Broth*] (STED)
MFC..........	Merrell's Fan Club (EA)
MFC..........	Message Formatting Committee (SAUO)
MFC..........	Metal-Finishing Category (GNE)
MFC..........	Meteorological and Oceanographic Forecast Center (COE)
MFC..........	Microfibrillated Cellulose (DB)
MFC..........	Microfilm Frame Card
MFC..........	Microfunctional Circuit
MFC..........	Microsoft Foundation Classes [*Computer science*] (PCM)
MFC..........	Microsoft Foundation Class Library [*Computer science*] (PCM)
MFC..........	Military Forces of the Crown (SAUO)
MFC..........	Military Frequency Changer
MFC..........	Minimal Flight Forecasting Charts [*Air Force*]
MFC..........	Minimal Fungicidal Concentration [*Medicine*] (DMAA)
MFC..........	Mirinda's Friendship Club (EA)
MFC..........	Missile Fire Control (MCD)
MFC..........	Mission Football Conference (PSS)
MFC..........	Mississippi Flyway Council
MFC..........	Modern Foods Council [*Defunct*] (EA)
MFC..........	Moncton Flying Club [*Canada*] [*ICAO designator*] (FAAC)
MFC..........	Morrison Fresh Cooking [*NYSE symbol*] (TTSB)
MFC..........	Morrison Fresh Cooking, Inc. [*NYSE symbol*] (SAG)
MFC..........	Mortar Fire Controller [*British*]
MFC..........	Mortgage Funding Corp. [*British*]
MFC..........	Most-Favored Customer (AAGC)

MFC .... Motor Freight Controller [*National Accounting and Finance Council*] [*A publication*]
MFC .... Motorized Flow Control
MFC .... Movimiento Familiar Cristiano (EA)
MFC .... Multi-Frequency Code [*Telecommunications*] (DA)
MFC .... Multifrequency Signaling, Compelled [*Telecommunications*] (TEL)
MFC .... Multifunctional Chipcard (SAUO)
MFC .... Multifunctional Concentrate (EDCT)
MFC .... Multi-Function Console (SAUS)
MFC .... Multiple File Concept (DNAB)
MFC .... Multiple Flight Computer (NASA)
MFC .... Multiple Flight Controller (NASA)
MFC .... Municipal Financial Corp. [*Toronto Stock Exchange symbol*]
MFC .... Music Feature Card (SAUS)
MFCA .... Master File Change Activity [*Computer science*] (MCD)
MFCA .... Master Fruit Carriers Association (SAUO)
MFCA .... Miniature Figure Collectors of America (EA)
MFCA .... Multi-Function Communications Adaptor (NITA)
MFCA .... Mutlifunction Communications Adapter
MFCAE .... Masters of Foxhounds Club of America and England [*Defunct*] (EA)
MFCB .... Michigan Financial Corp. [*NASDAQ symbol*] (SAG)
MFCB .... Michigan Finl Corp. [*NASDAQ symbol*] (TTSB)
MFCC .... Marriage and Family Counseling Certificate (PGP)
MFCC .... Marriage, Family, and Child Counseling (PGP)
MFCC .... Marriage, Family, and Child Counselor [*Psychology*] (DAVI)
MFCC .... Maximum Free Carrier Concentration (AAEL)
MFCC .... McFarland Cascade Company (SAUO)
MFCC .... Minimum Functional Combat Capability
MFCC .... Missile Fire Control Computer [*Military*] (CAAL)
MFCC .... Missile Flight Caution Corridor (AFM)
MFCC .... Mission Flight Control Center (SAUO)
MFCC .... Mortar Fire Control Calculator [*Later, MBC*] [*Military*] (INF)
MFCC .... Mortar Fire Direction Center Data Calculator [*Army*]
MFCC .... Multi-Function Common Console (SAUS)
MFCCA .... Master Floorcovering Contractors Association (SAUO)
MFCD .... Microgravity Fluids and Combustion Diagnostics (SAUS)
MFCD .... Modular Flare Chaff Dispenser [*Military*] (PDAA)
MFCD .... Multifunction Colour Display (SAUS)
MFCDU .... Multi-Function Control and Display Unit
MFCF .... Multinational Fuel Cycle Facility
MFCI .... Molten Fuel Coolant Interaction [*Nuclear energy*] (NRCH)
MFCL .... Master Fund Control List [*Air Force*] (AFM)
MFC/LB .... Multi-Frequency / Local Battery [*Telecommunications*] (DA)
MFCM .... Member of the Faculty of Community Medicine [*British*]
MFCM .... Multifunction Card Machine (BUR)
MFCMA .... Magnuson Fishery Conservation and Management Act [*1976*] [*Also, FCMA*]
MFCO .... Manual Fuel Cutoff (AAG)
MFCO .... Microwave Filter [*NASDAQ symbol*] (TTSB)
MFCO .... Microwave Filter Co., Inc. [*NASDAQ symbol*] (NQ)
MFCP .... Multifunction Control/Panel (MCD)
MFCRS .... Multifunction Flight Control Reference System (ACAE)
MFCS .... Magnetic Field Calibration System
MFCS .... Manual Flight Control System [*NASA*]
MFCS .... Mason Fracture Classification System [*Medicine*] (MELL)
MFCS .... Master of Family and Consumer Sciences (PGP)
MFCS .... Mathematical Foundation of Computer Science (PDAA)
MFCS .... Maximum Flat Control System
MFCS .... Medical Function Control System (PDAA)
MFCS .... Microprocessor Flight Control System (DOMA)
MFCS .... Missile Fire Control System (NG)
MFCS .... Modified Fire Control System (SAUS)
MFCS .... Mortar Fire Control System [*Military*] (INF)
MFCSB .... Missile Fire Control Status Board (SAUO)
MFCT .... Major Fraction Thereof
MFCT .... Modular Furnace Component Technology (SAUS)
MFCU .... Multifunction Card Unit
MFCV .... Modulating Flow Control Valve (MCD)
MFCV .... Muscle Fibre Conduction Velocity (DMAA)
MFCX .... Marshalltown Financial [*NASDAQ symbol*] (TTSB)
MFCX .... Marshalltown Financial Corp. [*NASDAQ symbol*] (SAG)
MFD .... Canadian Department of Fisheries and Oceans, Marine Fish Division [*Research center*] (RCD)
MFD .... Magic Foods, Inc. [*Vancouver Stock Exchange symbol*]
MFD .... Magnetic Frequency Detector
MFD .... Magnetofluiddynamic
MFD .... Main Feed (MCD)
MFD .... Malfunction Detection (NASA)
MFD .... Malfunctioning Display (DA)
MFD .... Mandibulofacial Dysostosis (STED)
MFD .... Manifold [*Paper*] (DGA)
MFD .... Mansfield [*Ohio*] [*Airport symbol*] (OAG)
MFD .... Mansfield, OH [*Location identifier*] [*FAA*] (FAAL)
mfd .... Manufactured (WDAA)
MFD .... Manufactured
MFD .... Massachusetts Financial Development Fund, Inc. (SAUO)
MFD .... Master File Directory [*Computer science*]
MFD .... Maximum Frequency Difference [*Statistics*]
MFD .... Mechanical-Front-Drive [*Tractor*]
MFD .... Memory-for-Designs [*Test*] [*Psychology*]
MFD .... Message Format Designator
MFD .... Metal Floor Deck [*Technical drawings*]
MFD .... Microfarad
MFD .... Midflight Deck (SAUS)
MFD .... Midforceps Delivery [*Obstetrics*]

MFD .... Military First Destination (SAUO)
MFD .... Military Forwarding Depot [*British military*] (DMA)
MFD .... Milk-Free Diet (STED)
MFD .... Millifarad (MCD)
MFD .... Minimal Fatal Dose [*Medicine*] (STED)
MFD .... Minimum Fatal Dose
MFD .... Minimum Focusing Distance [*Optics*]
MFD .... Monteggia Fracture-Dislocation [*Medicine*] (MELL)
MFD .... Multifunction Display (MCD)
MFD .... Multiple Family Dwelling [*Real estate*]
MFD .... Multistage Flash Distillation (PDAA)
MFD .... Multivariable Frequency Domain
MFD .... Municipal Facilities Division [*Environmental Protection Agency*] (GFGA)
MFDB .... Manufacturing Data Base (TIMI)
MFDC .... Main Facility Device Controller [*Telecommunications*] (CIST)
MFDC .... Mortar Fire Data Computer (SAUS)
MFDC .... Morzen Mortar Fire Data Computer [*Military*] [*British*] (INF)
MFDC .... Mouvement des Forces Democratiques de la Casamance [*Senegal*] [*Political party*]
MFDCC .... Marine Fire Detection Control Center
MFDE .... Midflight Deck Experiment (SAUS)
MF/DF .... Medium-Frequency Direction Finder [*or Finding*] (NVT)
MFDO .... Member of the Faculty of Dispensing Opticians [*British*] (DBQ)
MFDP .... Maintenance Float Distribution Point [*Computer science*] (NATG)
MFDP .... Mississippi Freedom Democratic Party
MFDS .... Modular Fuel Delivery Station [*Shipboard installation*] [*Navy*] (DOMA)
MFDSG .... Multifunction Display Symbol Generator (MCD)
MFDSUL .... Multifunction Data Set Utility Language
MFDT .... Memory-for-Designs Test [*Psychology*]
MFDT .... Multiple False Doppler Target
MFDU .... Multifunction Display Unit [*Aviation*]
MFE .... Machinery and Fixed Equipment [*British*]
MFE .... Magnetic Field Energy
MFE .... Magnetic Field Experiment (SAUO)
MFE .... Magnetic Field Explorer [*NASA*]
MFE .... Maison de la Fondation Europeenne (EAIO)
MFE .... Major Fleet Escort
MFE .... Manpower Force Element (SAUO)
MFE .... Manual of Field Engineering [*British military*] (DMA)
MFE .... Master of Financial Economics (PGP)
MFE .... Master of Forest Engineering
MFE .... McAllen [*Texas*] [*Airport symbol*] (OAG)
MFE .... McAllen, TX [*Location identifier*] [*FAA*] (FAAL)
MFE .... Mean Fibre Extent (PDAA)
MFE .... Mercury Film Electrode [*Electrochemistry*]
MFE .... Microabrasion Foil Experiment [*For cosmic dust retrieval*]
MFE .... Mid-Frequency Execution
MFE .... Mid-Frequency Executive (NASA)
MFE .... Military Forwarding Establishment (SAUO)
MFE .... Ministry for the Environment (SAUO)
MFE .... Mischief Enterprises Ltd. [*Vancouver Stock Exchange symbol*]
MFE .... Moire Fringe Effect (PDAA)
MFE .... Mouvement Federaliste Europeen [*European Federalist Movement*] [*France*]
MFEA .... Magnetic Fusion Engineering Act
MFEA .... Mutual Fund Education Alliance (NTPA)
MFECC .... Magnetic Fusion Energy Computing Center (ACAE)
MFECS .... Mediterranean Far East Container Service (SAUO)
MFED .... Manned Flight Engineering Division [*NASA*]
MFED .... Maximum Flat Envelope Delay
MFed .... Miners' Federation of Great Britain (DAS)
MFED .... Multifunctional Exercise Device (SPST)
MFEIP .... Ministry of Food Education and Information Practice [*British*]
MFEL .... Manpower Force Element Listing (SAUO)
MFEL .... Medical Free Electron LASER
MFEM .... Magnetic Field Explorer Mission (SAUO)
MFEM .... Maximal Forced Expiratory Maneuver [*Medicine*] (DAVI)
MFE/MAGNOLIA ... MFE /Magnetic Field Experiment (SAUO)
MFEnet .... Magnetic Fusion Energy Network
MFENET .... Magnetic Fusion Energy Research Network [*Department of Energy*]
MFENET .... National Magnetic Fusion Energy Network (SAUO)
MF Eng .... Master of Forest Engineering
MFEQ .... Mechanical Facilities and Equipment (SAA)
MFER .... Ministry of Foreign Economic Relations (SAUO)
MFES .... Main Fixed Earth Station [*NASA*] (PDAA)
MFES .... Major Fleet Escort Study [*Navy*] (CAAL)
MFF .... Flin Flon Public Library, Manitoba [*Library symbol*] [*National Library of Canada*] (NLC)
MFF .... MacFadden Foundation (SAUO)
MFF .... Magnetic Flip-Flop [*Computer science*]
MFF .... Mariposa Folk Foundation (EAIO)
MFF .... Master Freight File
MFF .... Match Flip Flop [*Computer science*] (MHDI)
MFF .... Matching Familiar Figures [*Psychology*]
MFF .... MDM [*Manipulator Deployment Mechanism*] Flight Forward [*NASA*] (GFGA)
MFF .... Melbourne Film Festival [*Australia*]
MFF .... Mezzo Fortissimo [*Rather Loud*] [*Music*] (ADA)
MFF .... Military Free Fall [*Parachute jump*] (MCD)
MFF .... Mixed Fighter Force (SAUO)
MFF .... Moanda [*Gabon*] [*Airport symbol*] (OAG)
MFF .... Munitions Filling Factory (ADA)
MFF .... St. Martin Du Fouilloux [*France*] [*Seismograph station code, US Geological Survey*] (SEIS)

MFFC .... Milton Federal Financial [*NASDAQ symbol*] (TTSB)
MFFC .... Milton Federal Financial Corp. [*NASDAQ symbol*] (SAG)
MFFC .... Mixed Fighter Force Concept (SAUS)
MFFGH .... Flin Flon General Hospital, Manitoba [*Library symbol*] [*National Library of Canada*] (NLC)
MFF/HALO ... Military Free Fall / High Altitude Low Opening Parachute
MFFHB .... Hudson Bay Mining & Smelting Co. Ltd., Flin Flon, Manitoba [*Library symbol*] [*National Library of Canada*] (NLC)
MFFLR .... Muffler [*Automotive advertising*]
MFFO .... Mixed Force Fighter Operations (SAUO)
MFFR .... Modified Field Fire Range (MCD)
MFFS .... Microsoft Flash File System (VLIE)
MFFT .... Matching Familiar Figures Test [*Education*]
MFFT .... Minimum Film Formation Temperature [*Coating technology*]
MFG .... Magnetic Field Gradient (MELL)
MFG .... Major Functional Group [*NASA*] (KSC)
Mfg .... Manufacturer (SAUO)
MFG .... Manufacturing (AFM)
mfg .... Manufacturing (DD)
Mfg .... Manufacturing (PROS)
MFG .... McQuay-Norris Manufacturing Co. (SAUO)
MFG .... Message Flow Graph
MFG .... Metropolitan Fire Brigade (SAUO)
MFG .... Milk Fat Globule
MFG .... Modified Heat-Degraded Gelatin [*Medicine*] (MEDA)
MFG .... Molded Fiberglass
MFG .... More Friendly Garbage (VLIE)
MFG .... Multi-Function Gateway (SAUS)
MFG .... Multi-Function Generator (NITA)
MFG .... Munitions Family Group
MFGA .... Master Furriers Guild of America (EA)
MFGDP .... Manual of Federal Geographic Data Products (SAUO)
MfgDTF .... Manufacturing Domain Task Force (SAUO)
MFGM .... Milk Fat Globule Membrane
MFGR .... Manufacturer
MFH .... Magnetic Film Handler (CMD)
MFH .... Malignant Fibrous Histiocytoma [*Oncology*]
MFH .... Markel Financial Holdings Ltd. [*Toronto Stock Exchange symbol*]
MFH .... Master of Fox Hounds
MFH .... Master of Foxhounds (SAUO)
MFH .... Master of the Fox Hunt (DD)
MFH .... Membrane-Free Hemolystate [*Hematology*] (DAVI)
MFH .... Military Family Housing (AFM)
M/F/H .... Minorities, Females, Handicapped
MFH .... Mobile Field Hospital
MFHA .... Master of Foxhounds Association (SAUO)
MFHA .... Masters of Foxhounds Association [*British*] (BI)
MFHA .... Medal for Humane Action [*Berlin Airlift, 1948-9*] [*Military decoration*]
MFHBF .... Mean Flight Hours between Failures [*Quality control*] (MCD)
MFHBMA ..... Mean Flight Hours between Maintenance Actions [*Quality control*] (NVT)
MFHBUMA... Mean Flight Hour between Unscheduled Maintenance Actions [*Quality control*] (MCD)
MFHC .... Missile Flight Hazard Corridor (AFM)
MFHD .... Multi-Function Head-down Display (SAUS)
MFHD .... My First Hard Drive [*Computer science*]
MFHF .... Mobile Fuel Handling Flight (SAUS)
MFHFS .... Multifunction High-Frequency SONAR (MCD)
MFHom .... Member of the Faculty of Homeopathy (SAUO)
MF Hom ...... Member of the Faculty of Homoeopathy [*British*]
MFHR .... Media Fund for Human Rights (EA)
MFHS .... Mobile Fuel Handling Squadron (SAUO)
m/f/h/v .... Male, Female, Handicapped, Veteran (BARN)
MFi .... Fitchburg Public Library and Regional Center for Central Massachusetts, RegionalLibrary System, Fitchburg, MA [*Library symbol*] [*Library of Congress*] (LCLS)
MFI .... MacFrugal's Bargains [*Formerly, Pic'n'Save Corp.*] [*NYSE symbol*] (SPSG)
MFI .... MacFrugals Bargains Closeouts [*NYSE symbol*] (TTSB)
MFI .... Magazines for Industry [*An association*]
MFI .... Magnetic Field Indicator
MFI .... Magnetic Field Intensity
MFI .... Major Force Issues [*Army*] (AABC)
MFI .... Marketfax Infoservices Ltd. [*Vancouver Stock Exchange symbol*]
MFI .... Marketing Freedom Index [*OPEC*] [*Business term*]
MFI .... Marshfield [*Wisconsin*] [*Airport symbol*] (OAG)
MFI .... Marshfield, WI [*Location identifier*] [*FAA*] (FAAL)
MFI .... Master Facility Inventory [*Department of Health and Human Services*] (GFGA)
MFI .... Mean Flourescence Intensity [*Biochemistry*]
MFI .... Melt-Flow Index [*of plastics*]
MFI .... Metal Fabricating Institute (EA)
MFI .... Metal-Finishing Industy
MFI .... MicroFinancial, Inc. [*NYSE symbol*] (SG)
MFI .... Military Financial Instruction
MFI .... Mobile Fuel Irradiator [*IEEE*]
MFI .... Multifunction Interpreter (SAUS)
MFI .... Multipoint Flexible Injection [*Automotive fuel systems*]
MFI .... Multi-point Fuel Injection
MFI .... Multiport Fuel Injection [*Automotive technology*]
MFI .... Musicians Foundation Incorporated (SAUO)
MFI .... Myofibril Fragmentation Index [*Food technology*]
MFIA .... Member, Fundraising Institute-Australia, Inc. (NFD)
MFIA .... Municipal Finance Industry Association (NTPA)
MFIANE ..... Mutual Fire Insurance Association of New England (SAUO)

MFIBNE ...... Mutual Fire Inspection Bureau of New England (SAUO)
MFIC .... Microfluidics International [*NASDAQ symbol*] (TTSB)
MFIC .... Microfluidics International Corp. [*NASDAQ symbol*] (SAG)
MFIC .... Military Flight Information Center
MFIC .... Missile Flight Information Center (SAUO)
MFIC .... Mutual Federation of Independent Cooperatives [*Later, Northeast Dairy Cooperative Federation*] (EA)
MFID .... Multiple-Electrode Flame Ionization Detector
MFIE .... Magnetic Field Integral Equation (PDAA)
MF-IFGR ..... Michael Fund (International Foundation for Genetic Research) (EA)
MFin .... Master of Finance
MFIN .... Metro Financial Corp. [*NASDAQ symbol*] (SAG)
MFinStud ..... Master of Financial Studies
MFIOP .... Multifunction I/O Processor (SAUS)
MFIP .... Microforms in Print [*Database*]
MFIP .... Multi-Function Interoperability Processor (SAUS)
MFIS .... Magnetic Field-Induced Superconductivity
MFisc .... Maitrise en Fiscalite (DD)
MFish .... Ministry of Fisheries (SAUO)
MFISH .... Multiplex Fluorescence in Situ Hybridization
MFIST DMD... Modified FIST DMD (SAUS)
MFiT .... Fitchburg State College, Fitchburg, MA [*Library symbol*] [*Library of Congress*] (LCLS)
MFIT .... Manual Fault Isolation Test
MFIT .... Modified Flight Intersection Tape (SAA)
MFIV .... Mainwater Feed Isolation Valve [*Nuclear energy*] (NRCH)
MFJ .... Minister for Justice (SAUO)
MFJ .... Moala [*Fiji*] [*Airport symbol*] (OAG)
MFJ .... Modified Final Judgment [*Telecommunications*]
MFJ .... Movement for Freedom and Justice [*Ghana*] [*Political party*] (EY)
MFJC .... Memorial Foundation for Jewish Culture (EA)
MFJSA .... Mass Finishing Job Shops Association (EA)
MFK .... Mafeking [*South Africa*] [*Airport symbol*] (OAG)
MFK .... Mill Fixture Key [*Tool*]
MFKP .... Multifrequency Key Pulsing
MFKT .... Mobile Field Kitchen Trailer (MCD)
MFKY .... Maxey Flats, Kentucky [*Commercial waste site*] (GAAI)
MFL .... Magnetic Field Line
MFL .... Main Feedwater Line [*Nuclear energy*] (NRCH)
MFL .... Maintain Flight Level [*Aviation*]
MFL .... Maintenance Fault List (ACAE)
MFL .... Maintenance-Free Lifetime (PDAA)
MFL .... Master Force List [*DoD*]
MFL .... Master of Family Life
MFL .... Matrimonial and Family Law [*New York, NY*] [*A publication*]
MFL .... Matrimonial and Family Life [*A publication*]
MFL .... Maximum Foreseeable Loss [*Insurance*]
MFL .... Methodists for Life [*Defunct*] (EA)
MfL .... Microfile (Pty.) Ltd., Johannesburg, South Africa [*Library symbol*] [*Library of Congress*] (LCLS)
MFL .... Midland Forensic Laboratory (SAUO)
MFL .... Million Fibers per Liter (EEVL)
MFL .... Missile Firing Laboratory (KSC)
MFL .... Mobile Field Laboratory
MFL .... Mobile Field Laundry [*Military*]
MFL .... Modern Foreign Language
MFL .... Motor Freight Line
MFL .... Multiple Fragment Laceration [*Shrapnel wound*] [*Military*] (VNW)
MFL .... Mutual Funds Limited (SAUO)
MFLA .... Midwest Federation of Library Associations
m flac .... Membrana Flaccida [*Flaccid Membrane*] [*Latin*] [*Medicine*] (MAE)
MFLB .... Motor Fuel Licensing Board [*Australia*]
MFLC .... Mid-Florida Conference (PSS)
MFLD .... Male-Female Longevity Difference
MFLD .... Manifold (KSC)
MFLD .... Message Field [*Computer science*]
MFLDA .... Malaysian Federal Land Development Authority (SAUO)
MFlem .... Middle Flemish [*Language*] (BARN)
MFLFd .... MuniVest Florida Fund [*Associated Press*] (SAG)
MFLIC .... Modified Fluid in Cell [*Automotive engine combustion analysis*]
MFLOP .... Mega-Floating Point Operation
MFLOP .... Mega Floating-Point Operations per Second [*Computer science*]
MFLOP .... Million Floating Point Operations (SAUO)
MFLOPS ...... Million Floating Point Instructions per Second (AAEL)
Mflops .... Million Floating-Point Operations per Second [*Computer science*] (ODBW)
MFLOPS ...... Million Floating-Point Operations per Second [*Processing power units*] [*Computer science*]
MFLOPS ...... Millions of Floating Point Operations Per Second [*Telecommunications*] (ACRL)
MFLP .... Mattel Family Learning Program
MFLP .... Multifile Linear Programming
MFLR .... Mayflower Co-Operative Bank [*NASDAQ symbol*] (NQ)
MFLT .... Mathematics Functional Literacy Test (EDAC)
MFLT .... Mean Fault Location Time (DNAB)
MFLT .... Mean First Lesions Time [*Immunochemistry*]
MFLZ .... Mejdunarodna Fondatzia Lyudmila Zhivkova [*Lyudmila Zhivkova International Foundation*] (EAIO)
MFm .... Framingham Town Library, Framingham, MA [*Library symbol*] [*Library of Congress*] (LCLS)
MFM .... Glenair [*British*] [*FAA designator*] (FAAC)
MFM .... Magnetic-Field Modulation [*Computer science*] (PCM)
MFM .... Magnetic Field Monitor [*NASA*]
MFM .... Magnetic Force Microscope
MFM .... Magnetic Forming Machine

MFM	Magnetofluid Mechanic
MFM	Mass Flow Meter (AAEL)
MFM	Master File Maintenance [Computer science]
MFM	Master of Financial Management (ADA)
MFM	Materials Flow Management [Manufacturing]
MFM	Maternal-Fetal Medicine (MELL)
MFM	Maximally Flat Magnitude
MFM	Meals for Millions Foundation [Later, MFM/FFH] (EA)
MFM	MFC Mining Finance Corp. [Toronto Stock Exchange symbol] [Vancouver Stock Exchange symbol]
MFM	MFS Municipal Income Trust [NYSE symbol] (SPSG)
MFM	MFS Municipal Inc. Tr [NYSE symbol] (TTSB)
MFM	Micrometer Frequency Meter
MFM	Minced Fish Meat [Food technology]
MFM	Mine Firing Mechanism
MFM	Miniature Fluxgate Magnetometer
MFM	Minneapolis-St. Paul [Minnesota] [Seismograph station code, US Geological Survey] (SEIS)
MFM	Missile Farm Monitor [Army] (AABC)
MFM	Missile Fatigue Monitor
MFM	Mississippi State University, Mississippi State, MS [OCLC symbol] (OCLC)
MFM	Modified Frequency Modulation [Electronics]
MFM	Morrissey, Fernie & Michel Railway [AAR code]
MFM	Mouvement pour le Pouvoir Proletarien [or aux Petits] [Movement for Proletarian Power] [Malagasy] [Political party] (PPW)
MFM	Movable Fine Mesh
MFM	Multi-Faith Meal [Army] (INF)
MFM	Multifunctional Monomer [Organic chemistry]
MFM	Multistage Frequency Multiplexer
MFM	Municipal Finance and Management (SAUO)
MFMA	Maple Flooring Manufacturers Association (EA)
MFMA	Master Fish Merchants Association (SAUO)
MFMA	Metal Farming Manufacturers Association (SAUO)
MFMA	Metal Findings Manufacturers Association (EA)
MFMA	Metal Framing Manufacturers Association (EA)
MFMA	Midwest Feed Manufacturers Association [Later, AFMA] (EA)
MFMA	Monolithic Ferrite Memory Array
MFMA	Multi-Function Microwave Aperture (SAUS)
MF/MAGNOLIA	Magnetic Field Experiment (SAUO)
MFMANSW	Master Fish Merchants' Association of New South Wales [Australia]
MFMBARS	Multi-Function, Multi-Band Airborne Radio System (PDAA)
MFmcM	Marist College and Seminary, Framingham Center, MA [Library symbol] [Library of Congress] (LCLS)
MFMD	MonofluoromethylIDOPA (DB)
MFM/FFH	Meals for Millions/Freedom from Hunger Foundation (EA)
MFMH	Monofluoromethylhistidine [Antineoplastic drug]
MFmHi	Framingham Historical society, Framingham, MA [Library symbol] [Library of Congress] (LCLS)
MFMI	Men for Missions International (EA)
MFMIS	Metal Ferroelectric Metal Insulator Semiconductor
MFMM	Microwave Frequency Measurement Module
MFMMA	Metal Forming Machinery Makers' Association (HEAS)
MFMR	Multifrequency Microwave Radiometer (MCD)
MFMS	Military Flight Management System (SAUS)
MFMS	Mobile Flight Mission Simulator [Army]
MFmT	Framingham State College, Framingham, MA [Library symbol] [Library of Congress] (LCLS)
MFMT	Maryland Functional Mathematics Test (EDAC)
MFMT	Microwave Frequency Modulation Transmitter
MFMT	National Federation of Meat Traders (SAUO)
MF/MWS	Male/Female - Married/Widow [or Widower]/Single
MFN	MDC Financial, Inc. [Vancouver Stock Exchange symbol]
MFN	Mercury Finance [NYSE symbol] (TTSB)
MFN	Mercury Finance Co. [NYSE symbol] (SPSG)
MFN	Metabolic Fecal Nitrogen (PDAA)
MFN	Milford Sound [New Zealand] [Airport symbol] (OAG)
MFN	Most-Favored-Nation [Trading status]
MFN	Muffin (ABBR)
MFNG	Motion for a Finding of Not Guilty
MFNO	Midland Federation of Newspaper Owners (SAUO)
MFNP	Mount Field National Park (SAUO)
MFNP	Murchison Falls National Park (SAUO)
MFNS	Millard Fillmore National Society [Defunct] (EA)
MFNX	Metromedia Fiber Network'A' [NASDAQ symbol] (SG)
MFNZ	Music Federation of New Zealand (SAUO)
MFO	Mafco Consolidated Group [NYSE symbol] (SAG)
MFO	Major Function Overlay (MCD)
MFO	Marine Fuel Oil
MFO	Master Frequency Oscillator (NG)
MFO	Material Fielding Operations (MCD)
MFO	Medium Frequency Oscillator (DMAA)
MFO	Member of the Faculty of Ophthalmologists (SAUO)
MFO	Military Forwarding Officer
MFO	Military Forwarding Organization
MFO	Missile Field Office (AAG)
MFO	Missile Firing Order
MFO	Missile Flight Office (SAUO)
MFO	Mixed-Function Oxidase [Biochemistry]
MFO	Multi-Functional Optimization
MFO	Multinational Force and Observers [Eleven-nation peace-keeping force for the Sinai]
MFO	Multiple Facility Organization
MFOA	Municipal Finance Officers Association (SAUS)

MFOA	Municipal Finance Officers Association of US and Canada [Later, GFOA] (EA)
MFOC	Military and Government Fiber Optics and Communications [Conference] (TSSD)
MFOccM	Member of the Faculty of Occupational Medicine (SAUO)
MFOD	Manned Flight Operations Directive [NASA] (KSC)
MFOE	Mixed-Function Oxidase Enzyme System
MFOI	Major Force Oriented Issue [Military] (AFM)
MFOM	Master, Faculty of Occupational Medicine (DAVI)
MFOM	Member, Faculty of Occupational Medicine (CMD)
MFOM	MLRS Family of Munitions (SAUS)
MFON	Missile Firing Order Normal [Military] (CAAL)
MFOPP	Missile Firing Order Patch Panel
MFor	Master of Forestry
MForSc	Master of Forest Science (ADA)
MFOT	Mean Forced Outage Time (PDAA)
MFOV	Medium Field-Of-View (SAUS)
MFOW	Pacific Coast Marine Firemen, Oilers, Watertenders, and Wipers Association
MFOWW	Marine Firemen, Oilers, Watertenders and Wipers (SAUO)
MFOX	Multipurpose Fiber Optic Transceiver (ACAE)
MFP	Franciscan Missionaries Our Lady of Peace (TOCD)
MFP	Magnetic Field Perturbation
MFP	Main Feed Power [Nuclear energy] (NRCH)
MFP	Main Feed Pump (NVT)
MFP	Main Feedwater Pump [Nuclear energy] (NRCH)
MFP	Main Force Patrol [In movie "Mad Max"]
MFP	Main Fuel Pump (SAUS)
MFP	Major Force Program [Air Force] (AFIT)
MFP	Management Framework Plan
MFP	Master File Program [Computer science]
MFP	Master Personnel File (SAUO)
MFP	Matched Filter Performance
MFP	Materiel Fielding Plan
MFP	Maximum Fluoride Protection [Colgate-Palmolive Co.]
MFP	Maximum Freezing Point
MFP	Mean Free Path
MFP	Meat, Fish and Poultry
MFP	Medium Floor Pintle (SAUS)
MFP	Melphalan, Fluorouracil, Farlutal (Medroxyprogesterone acetate) [Antineoplastic drug regimen]
MF(P)	Microfiche (Positive)
MFP	Middle Free Path
MFP	Military Foot Police (SAUO)
MFP	Minimal Flight Path
MFP	Minimum Facility Plan (ACAE)
MFP	Minister of Fuel and Power (SAUO)
MFP	Ministry of Fuel and Power [British]
MFP	Mixed Fission Products [Nuclear energy]
MFP	Mobile Flux Platform (USDC)
MFP	Moca [Fernando Poo] [Equatorial Guinea] [Seismograph station code, US Geological Survey] (SEIS)
MFP	Molecular Free Path
MFP	Monofluorophosphate [Inorganic chemistry]
MFP	Movement for a Free Philippines (EA)
MFP	Multi-Factor Productivity
MFP	Multiform Printer
MFP	Multifrequency Pulsing (MSA)
MFP	Multifunction Peripheral [Chip] [Computer science]
MFP	Multifunction Polis
MFP	Multifunction Printers (PS)
MFP	Multi-Purpose Facility (SAUO)
MFP	Myofascial Pain [Medicine]
MFPA	Massachusetts Forest and Park Association (SAUO)
MFPA	Michigan Forest and Park Association (SAUO)
MFPA	Monolithic Focal Plane Array (PDAA)
MFPA	Mosaic Focal Plane Array (ACAE)
MFPA	Multi-Function Peripheral Association (SAUO)
MFPB	Mineral Fiber Products Bureau
MFPC	Man-Made Fibres Producers Committee [British] (DBA)
MFPC	Multifunction Protocol Converter
MFPD	Modern Federal Practice Digest [A publication] (DLA)
MFPE	Minimum Final Prediction Error (MHDI)
MFPE	Minimum Foundation Program for Education (SAUO)
MFPE	Misson From Planet Earth (SAUO)
MFPF	Minefield Planning Folder [Navy] (DOMA)
MFPG	Mechanical Failures Prevention Group
MFPG	Mixed Fission Products Generator [Nuclear energy]
MFPh	Member of the Faculty of Physiotherapists [British]
MFPharmM	Member of the Faculty of Pharmaceutical Medicine (SAUO)
MFPHM	Member, Faculty of Public Health Medicine (CMD)
MFPhys	Member of the Faculty of Physiatrists [British]
MFPK	Multifunction Program Keyboard (MCD)
mfpm	Made from Purchased Materials [Manufacturing]
MFP/MTP	Materiel Fielding Plan/Materiel Transfer Plan [Army] (RDA)
MFPS	Materiel Fielding Plans (ACAE)
MFPS	Member of the Faculty of Physicians and Surgeons [Glasgow]
MFPS	Mobile Field Photographic Section (NATG)
MFPS	Modular Force Planning System (MCD)
MFPT	Machinery Failure Prevention Technology (RDA)
MFPT	Main Feedwater Pump Turbine [Nuclear energy] (NRCH)
MFPT	Mean First-Passage Time [Biochemistry]
MFPTC	Main Feed Pump Turbine Condenser [Nuclear energy] (NRCH)
MFPU	Mobile Field Photographic Unit (SAUS)
MFP-UK	Mothers for Peace - UK (EAIO)

MFPUL........	Mississippi Forest Products Utilization Laboratory [*Mississippi State University*] [*Research center*] (RCD)
MFPVC.......	Multifocal Premature Ventricular Contractions [*Medicine*] (MEDA)
MFQ............	Maradi [*Niger*] [*Airport symbol*] (OAG)
M'F R	MacFarlane's Scotch Jury Court Reports [*1838-39*] [*A publication*] (DLA)
MFR............	Macfie Resources [*Vancouver Stock Exchange symbol*]
MFR............	Machine Feature Recognition
MFR............	Mail File Requirement [*Code*] [*Computer science*]
MFR............	Malfunctional Review
MFR............	Malfunction Rate
MFR............	Malfunction Receiver
MFR............	Manipulator Foot Restraint (NASA)
MFR............	Manufacture [*or Manufacturer*] (AFM)
mfr.............	Manufacture (DD)
mfr.............	Manufacturer (ELAL)
Mfr.............	Manufacturer (PROS)
MFR............	Manufacturer
MFr............	Mare Frigoris [*Sea of Cold*] [*Lunar area*]
MFR............	Marine Fishery Reserve
MFR............	Master Facility Register [*Nuclear energy*]
MFR............	Master Frame Recognize (MCD)
MFR............	Master Frequency Record [*FCC list*] (NTCM)
MFr............	Master of Forest Resources (GAGS)
M Fr	Master of French (PGP)
MFR............	Maximum Flight Rate (NASA)
MFR............	Mean Firing Rate [*Neurophysiology*]
MFR............	Mean Flow Rate (DB)
MFR............	Medford [*Oregon*] [*Airport symbol*] (OAG)
MFR............	Medford, OR [*Location identifier*] [*FAA*] (FAAL)
MFr............	Melomanes Francais [*Record label*] [*France*]
MFR............	Melt-Flow Rate [*of plastics*]
MFR............	Memorandum for Record [*Military*]
MFR............	Memorandum for the Record (SAUO)
MfR............	Microform Review, Inc., Weston, CT [*Library symbol*] [*Library of Congress*] (LCLS)
MFR............	Middle French [*Language, etc.*]
MFR............	Mid-Forceps Rotation [*Obstetrics*] (DAVI)
MFR............	Military Field Representative (SAA)
MFR............	Minimum Funding Requirement
MFR............	Missile Firing Range (AAG)
MFR............	Mission Fired Report (SAUO)
MFR............	Model Form and Record
MFR............	Mucus Flow Rate (MAE)
MFR............	Multifilter Radiometer (ARMP)
MFR............	Multifrequency Receiver [*Telecommunications*]
MFR............	Multifunctional Receiver (NASA)
MFR............	Multifunctional Review (NASA)
MFR............	Multifunction RADAR
MFR............	Mutual Force Reductions
MFran........	Ray Memorial Library, Franklin, MA [*Library symbol*] [*Library of Congress*] (LCLS)
MFRC..........	Manufacturer Code [*Automotive emissions*]
MFRC..........	Maritimes Forest Research Centre [*Research center*] (RCD)
MFRC..........	Master of Forest Resources and Conservation (PGP)
MFRD	Manufactured (ABBR)
MFRE..........	Manufacture (ADA)
MFREA........	Multiple Food Retailers Employers' Association [*British*]
MFRF..........	Mean-Family Replacement Factor
MFRG	Manufacturing
MFRG	Medical Functional Requirements Group (MCD)
MFRI..........	MFRI, Inc. [*NASDAQ symbol*] (SPSG)
MFRI..........	Migratory Fish Research Institute [*University of Maine*] [*Research center*] (RCD)
MFRN	Manufacturer Name [*Automotive emissions*]
MFRN	Manufacturers Number
MFRP.........	Midwest Fuel Recovery Plant [*AEC*]
MFRP.........	Multigrade Functional Rehabilitation Platform [*Medicine*]
MFRPA	Maxey Flats Radioactive Protective Association (EA)
MFRR	Manufacturer (ABBR)
MFRS..........	Maritime Force Requirements Study (SAUO)
MFRS..........	Master File Replacement System [*Computer science*]
MFRS..........	Multifunction Receiver System
MFRSR........	Multifilter Rotating Shadowband Radiometer (CARB)
MFRT..........	Maryland Functional Reading Test (EDAC)
MFRT..........	Modulated Frequency Radio Telephone (PDAA)
MFRY.........	Manufactory (ABBR)
MFS............	Fleet Minesweeper (Steel-Hulled) [*Navy symbol*]
MFS............	Frostburg State College, Library, Frostburg, MD [*OCLC symbol*] (OCLC)
MFS............	Macintosh File Structure [*Apple Computer, Inc.*] [*Computer science*] (CIST)
MFS............	Macintosh File System [*Computer science*]
MFS............	Magnetic Field Strength
MFS............	Magnetic Tape Field Search [*Computer science*]
MFS............	Maine Forest Service (SAUO)
MFS............	Major Frame Synchronization (ACAE)
MFS............	Malleable Founders' Society [*Later, Iron Castings Society - ICS*]
MFS............	Maltese Falcon Society [*Defunct*] (EA)
MFS............	Manned Flying System (MCD)
MFS............	Manufactures
MFS............	Marble Falls, TX [*Location identifier*] [*FAA*] (FAAL)
MFS............	Marfan Syndrome [*Medicine*]
MFS............	Marine-Finish Slate (MSA)
MFS............	Massachusetts Financial Services

MFS............	Master Fabrication Schedule (DNAB)
MFS............	Master of Family Studies (GAGS)
MFS............	Master of Food Science
MFS............	Master of Foreign Service
MFS............	Master of Foreign Study
MFS............	Master of Forensic Science (GAGS)
MFS............	Master of Forest Science (GAGS)
MFS............	Master of Forest Studies (PGP)
MFS............	Master of French Studies (PGP)
MFS............	Material False Statement [*Nuclear energy*] (NUCP)
MFS............	Maxillofacial Surgery [*Medical specialty*] (DHSM)
MFS............	McCloud Flat South [*California*] [*Seismograph station code, US Geological Survey*] (SEIS)
MFS............	Medal Field Service [*Canada*]
MFS............	Medicare Fee Schedule
MFS............	Medicated Feeding Stuff (GVA)
MFS............	Member of the Faraday Society (SAUO)
MFS............	Mercury Feed System
MFS............	Message Format Service
MFS............	Metropolitan Fiber Systems, Inc.
MfS............	Microfilm Systems, Colorado Springs, CO [*Library symbol*] [*Library of Congress*] (LCLS)
MFS............	Microfuel Systems [*Vancouver Stock Exchange symbol*]
MFS............	Military Flight Service
MFS............	Miller Flying Services, Inc. [*ICAO designator*] (FAAC)
MfS............	Ministerium fuer Staatssicherheit [*Ministry for State Security*] [*See also MISTAI, MSS*] [*Germany*] (EG)
MFS............	Minnesota Follow-Up Study Rehabilitation Rating Scale
MFS............	Miraflores [*Colombia*] [*Airport symbol*] (OAG)
MFS............	Missile Firing Simulator (NATG)
MFS............	Missile Firing Station [*Army*]
MFS............	Missile Fuse Set Servo
MFS............	Missing from Shelf (ADA)
MFS............	Missouri Followback Survey [*Department of Health and Human Services*] (GFGA)
MFS............	Mitral First Sound [*Cardiology*] (CPH)
MFS............	Mobile File Sync (SAUS)
MFS............	Mobilization for Survival (SAUO)
MFS............	Modern Fiction Studies [*A publication*] (BRI)
MFS............	Modified Filing System [*Computer science*] (PCM)
MFS............	Modified Full Spray
MFS............	Modular Flexible Scheduling [*Education*]
MFS............	Mountain Fuel Supply Co. (SAUO)
MFS............	Multi-Frequency Signalling [*Telecommunications*] (NITA)
MFS............	Multifunction Sensor (MCD)
MFS............	Multi-Function Switch [*Automotive engineering*]
MFS............	Multiple-Frequency Synthesizer
MFS............	Multiple Sclerosis Foundation (EA)
MFS............	Municipal Ferrous Scrap
MFS............	Museum of Fisheries and Shipping (SAUO)
MFS............	National Mobilization for Survival (EA)
MFSA..........	Master Floor Sanders Association (NADA)
MFSA..........	Metal Finishing Suppliers' Association (EA)
MFSA..........	Methodist Federation for Social Action (EA)
MFSA..........	Missile Flight Safety Approval (ACAE)
MFSB..........	Mother, Father, Sister, Brother [*Musical group*]
MFSB..........	Mutual Bancompany [*NASDAQ symbol*] (TTSB)
MFSB..........	Mutual Bancompany, Inc. [*NASDAQ symbol*] (SAG)
MFSc..........	Master of Fisheries Science
MFS C	MFS Communication Co. [*Associated Press*] (SAG)
MFSC..........	Missile Flight Safety Center [*Pacific Missile Range*] (MUGU)
MFS Cm	MFS Communication Co. [*Associated Press*] (SAG)
MFSD..........	Maritime Fire Support Demonstrator
MFSE..........	Main Fire Support Element (AABC)
MFSF..........	Magazine of Fantasy and Science Fiction [*A publication*] (BRI)
MFSFU........	Matt-Finish Structural Facing Units [*Technical drawings*]
MFSG..........	Microbiological Food Surveillance Group (SAUO)
MFSG..........	Missile Firing Safety Group (MUGU)
MFSK..........	Multiple-Frequency Shift Keying
MFSL..........	Maryland Fed Bancorp [*NASDAQ symbol*] (TTSB)
MFSL..........	Maryland Federal Bancorp, Inc. [*NASDAQ symbol*] (NQ)
MFSL..........	Mathematical and Functional Subroutine Library (MHDB)
MFSO..........	Missile Flight Safety Officer
MFSOA........	Missile Flight Safety Officer Assistant (MUGU)
MFSOC	Missile Flight Safety Officer Console (MUGU)
MF SOL	Merthiolate-Formaldehyde [*Stock*] Solution (BABM)
MFSOP	Missile Flight Safety Operations Plan
MFSP..........	Macro Function Signal Processor (SAUS)
MFSR..........	Magnetic Film Strip Recorder
MFSS..........	Medical Field Service School [*Army*]
MFSS..........	Missile Flight Safety System (AAG)
MFSS..........	Multi-Frequency Signalling System [*Telecommunications*] (EECA)
Mfst	Manifest (EBF)
MFST..........	Manifest
mfst	Manifest (ELAL)
MFST..........	Medical Field Service Technician (BABM)
MFST..........	MFS Communications [*NASDAQ symbol*] (TTSB)
MFST..........	MFS Communication Co. [*NASDAQ symbol*] (SAG)
MFST..........	Mobile Fire Safety Team
MFSTB........	Manifestable (ABBR)
MFSTD........	Manifested (ABBR)
MFSTG........	Manifesting (ABBR)
MFSTN........	Manifestation (ABBR)
MFSTO........	Manifesto (ABBR)
MFSTP........	MFS Commun 8% Cv Dep'A'Pfd [*NASDAQ symbol*] (TTSB)

MFSU..........	Mobile Field Service Unit
MFSW..........	Membrane-Filtered Sea Water
MFT.............	Drury Military Extension, Springfield, MO [*OCLC symbol*] (OCLC)
MFT.............	Magnetic Flow Transmitter
MFT.............	Mail for Tots (EA)
MFT.............	Mainframe Termination [*Telecommunications*] (TEL)
MFT.............	Major Fraction Thereof
MFT.............	Manson Finance Trust Ltd. (SAUO)
MFT.............	Manufacturing (SAUO)
MFT.............	Manufacturing Fit Test
MFT.............	Marconi Fast Tuning (MCD)
MFT.............	Marriage and Family Therapist [*Psychology*]
MFT.............	Master File Table
MFT.............	Master File Tax [*Code*] [*IRS*]
MFT.............	Master Fitness Trainer [*Army*] (INF)
MFT.............	Master of Family Therapy (GAGS)
MFT.............	Master of Foreign Trade
MFT.............	Materiel Fielding Team [*Army*] (RDA)
MFT.............	Materiel Field Test (MCD)
MFT.............	Mean Flight Time (KSC)
MFT.............	Mean Free Time
MFT.............	Mechanized Flame Thrower
MFT.............	Medical Field Service Technician [*Navy*]
MFT.............	Melter Feed Tank (ABAC)
MFT.............	Meson Field Theory
MFT.............	Metal Film Resistor
MFT.............	Metallic Facility Terminal [*Telecommunications*] (TEL)
MFT.............	Meter Fix Crossing Time (CTAS)
MFT.............	Meter Fix Time/Slot Time [*FAA*] (TAG)
MFT.............	Mine Fuse Train
MFT.............	Minimum Film-Forming Temperature [*Wax polishes*]
MFT.............	Minimum Flexible Targeting (SAUO)
MFT.............	Minuteman Flexible Targeting (ACAE)
MFT.............	Missile Flight Time
MFT.............	Mission Flight Trainer [*Navy*]
M FT............	Mistura Fiat [*Let a Mixture Be Made*] [*Pharmacy*]
MFT.............	Mobile Foot Restraint (SSD)
MFT.............	Molecular Field Theory [*Physical chemistry*]
MFT.............	Monolayer Formation Time [*Physical chemistry*] (OA)
MFT.............	Morgan Financial Corp. [*Toronto Stock Exchange symbol*]
MFT.............	Most-Favorable Term (MHDW)
MFT.............	Motor Freight Tariff [*Business term*] (ADA)
MFT.............	Motor Freight Terminal
MFT.............	Multifocal Atrial Tachycardia [*Cardiology*] (DMAA)
MFT.............	Multilingual Forestry Terminology
MFT.............	Multiple Family Therapy (DHP)
MFT.............	Multiposition Frequency Telegraphy [*Telecommunications*] (OA)
MFT.............	Multiprogramming (NITA)
MFT.............	Multiprogramming with a Finite Amount of Trouble [*Computer science*]
MFT.............	Multiprogramming with Fixed Number of Tasks [*Computer science*] (BUR)
MFT.............	MuniYield FL Insured Fund [*NYSE symbol*] (TTSB)
MFT.............	MuniYield Florida Insured Fund [*NYSE symbol*] (SPSG)
MFT.............	Muscle Function Test
MFTA...........	Managed Futures Trade Association (EA)
MFTA...........	Multiduct Fuel Test Assembly [*Nuclear energy*] (NRCH)
MFTA...........	Multi-Function Towed Array
MFTAD........	Master Flight Test Assignment Document (NASA)
MFTAD........	Master Flight Test Assignments Document [*NASA*]
MFTB..........	Motor Freight Tariff Bureau
MFTC..........	Metalworking Fair Trade Coalition [*Later, MTC*] (EA)
MFTCom.......	Member of the Faculty of Teachers in Commerce [*British*] (DBQ)
MFTD..........	Mobile Field Training Detachment [*Military*] (AFM)
MF-TDA.......	Multiple-Feedback, Time-Division Multiple Access (MED)
MFTDMA.....	Multiple Frequency Time Division Multiple Access (LAIN)
MFTF..........	Mirror Fusion Test Facility [*For study of new energy source*]
MFTF..........	Missionary Flight Training Foundation [*Defunct*]
MFTGS........	Midcourse Fix and Terminal Guidance System (MCD)
MFTHBA......	Missouri Fox Trotting Horse Breed Association (EA)
MFT L..........	Millifoot Lamberts (DEN)
MFTL..........	Modular Field Test Laser (ACAE)
MFTL..........	My Favorite Toy Language [*Computer hacker terminology*] (NHD)
M FT M........	Misce Fiat Mistura [*Mix to Make a Mixture*] [*Pharmacy*]
m ft mist.....	Misce Flat Mistura [*Mix and Let a Mixture be Made*] [*Latin*] (WDAA)
MFTP..........	Modified Federal Test Procedure [*EPA engine test*]
MFTRS........	Magnetic Flight Test Recording System
MFTS..........	Medial Femorotibial Space [*Anatomy*]
MFT/S.........	Missile Facilities Technician/Specialist (AAG)
MFTT..........	Multi-Function Tanker Transport (SAUS)
MFTT..........	Multi-Function Telephone Terminal [*Telecommunications*] (VLIE)
MFTU.........	Macao Federation of Trade Unions
MFTU.........	Macau Federation of Trade Unions (SAUO)
MFTU.........	Multi-Function Tape Unit (VLIE)
MFTV.........	Mechanical Fit Test Vehicle
MFTVP........	Motor-Free Test of Visual Perception [*Psychology*] (DAVI)
MFU...........	Magnetic Force Upset [*Metals*]
MFU...........	Marine Forecast Unit [*National Weather Service*]
MFU...........	Medical Follow up (SAUS)
MFU...........	Mfuwe [*Zambia*] [*Airport symbol*] (OAG)
MFU...........	Military Foul-Up [*Bowdlerized version*] (DSUE)
MFU...........	MIRA [*Multifunctional Inertial Reference Assembly*] Fighter Unit [*Air Force*] (MCD)
MFU...........	Myoclonus Families United (EA)

MFU...........	Pacific Coast Marine Firemen, Oilers, Watertenders, and Wipers Association [*Also known as Marine Firemen's Union*] (EA)
MFUA..........	Medical Follow-Up Agency [*National Research Council*]
MFUI..........	Mechanics Friendly Union Institution [*British*]
MFUMR.......	MIRA [*Multifunctional Inertial Reference Assembly*] Fighter Unit Mounting Rack [*Air Force*] (MCD)
MFUN.........	Morgan Funshares [*NASDAQ symbol*] (TTSB)
MFUN.........	Morgan Funshares, Inc. [*NASDAQ symbol*] (SAG)
MFURB.......	Maryland Fire Underwriters Rating Bureau (SAUO)
Mfurers Mon...	Manufacturers' Monthly [*A publication*]
MFUSYS.....	Microfiche File Update System [*Computer science*] (PDAA)
MFUW........	Magnetic Force Upset Welding [*Metals*]
MFV...........	Forward Visibility More than ___ Miles [*Aviation*] (FAAC)
MFV...........	Magnetic Field Vector
MFV...........	Main Feedwater Valve [*Nuclear energy*] (NRCH)
MFV...........	Main Fuel Valve [*Aerospace*] (NAKS)
MFV...........	Maintenance Floor Valve (NRCH)
MFV...........	Mars Flyby Vehicle [*Aerospace*]
MF V..........	Materiel Division, Western Military Region Command (SAUO)
MFV...........	Melfa, VA [*Location identifier*] [*FAA*] (FAAL)
MFV...........	Methanol-Fueled Vehicle [*Automotive engineering*]
MFV...........	MFS Special Value Trust [*NYSE symbol*] (SPSG)
MFV...........	Microfilm Viewer
MFV...........	Military Flight Vehicles
MFV...........	Motor Fishing Vessel [*British military*] (DMA)
MFVA..........	Main Fuel Valve Actuator (SAUS)
MFVD..........	Maximum Forward Voltage Drop
MFVP.........	Mauler Feasibility Validation Program
MFVPT.......	Motor-Free Visual Perception Test
mfVSG........	Membrane Form of Variant Surface Glycoprotein [*Biochemistry*]
MFVT.........	Mixed-Flow Vectored Thrust (SAUS)
MFW.........	Main Feedwater [*Nuclear energy*] (NRCH)
MFW.........	M&F Worldwide [*NYSE symbol*] (SG)
MFW.........	Maritime Federation of the World (NADA)
MFW.........	Metres of Fresh Water
MFW.........	Migrant Farm Worker (OICC)
MFW.........	Milton-Freewater [*Oregon*] [*Seismograph station code, US Geological Survey*] (SEIS)
MFW.........	Ms. Foundation for Women (EA)
MFW.........	Multi-Function Wheel [*Automotive classified advertising*]
MFW.........	Multi-Function Workstation (SAUO)
MFW.........	Multiple Fragment Wound (MAE)
MFW.........	Multiple Fragment Wounds (SAUS)
MFWC.........	Marine Fleet Air, West Coast
MFWCS........	Main Feedwater and Condensate System [*Environmental science*] (COE)
MFWD	Mechanical Front Wheel Drive [*Off-highway equipment*]
MFWG	Mechanical Failures Working Group (SAUO)
MFWLB.......	Main Feedwater Line Break [*Nuclear energy*] (NRCH)
MFWP.........	Maryland Functional Writing Program (EDAC)
MFWV........	Main Feedwater Valve [*Nuclear energy*] (NRCH)
MFX...........	Mirror Fusion Experiment [*Nuclear energy*]
MFXT..........	Meter Fix Time [*Aviation*] (FAAC)
MFY...........	Manufactory (ABBR)
MFY...........	Mobilization for Youth
MFY...........	Music for Youth
MFZ...........	Mezzo Forzando [*Music*]
MFZ...........	Missile Firing Zone
MFZ...........	Mofaz Air [*Malawi*] [*FAA designator*] (FAAC)
MG.............	Geometric Mean [*Psychology*]
MG.............	Groundswell, Inc. of Minnesota (EA)
mg.............	Guadalupe Missioners (TOCD)
MG.............	Gudalupe Missioners (TOCD)
MG.............	Machine-Glazed [*Poster paper*]
MG.............	Machine Group (SAUO)
MG.............	Machine Gun (MUGU)
MG.............	Machine Gunner [*British military*] (DMA)
MG.............	Machinery of Government [*British*]
MG.............	Madagascar [*ANSI two-letter standard code*] (CNC)
mg.............	Mafic Granulite [*Geology*]
MG.............	Magenta (ROG)
MG.............	Maggioni & C. [*Italy*] [*Research code symbol*]
Mg.............	Maghemite [*A mineral*]
MG.............	Magna International, Inc. [*Toronto Stock Exchange symbol*]
Mg.............	Magnesium [*Chemical element*]
MG.............	Magnetic Armature (MSA)
MG.............	Maharashtrawadi Gomantak [*India*] [*Political party*] (PPW)
MG.............	Main Gauche [*With the Left Hand*] [*Music*]
MG.............	Main Generator (IAA)
MG.............	Main Group (SAUO)
MG.............	Maintainability Group (SAUO)
MG.............	Major General
Mg.............	Major General
MG.............	Make Good
MG.............	Malachite Green [*A dye*]
mg.............	Malagasy Republic [*Madagascar*] [*MARC country of publication code*] [*Library of Congress*] (LCCP)
MG.............	Mammary Gland [*Anatomy*]
MG.............	Management Group (SAUO)
MG.............	Management Guide (SAUO)
MG.............	Managerial Grid
MG.............	Manager's Guide
Mg.............	Mangrove [*Maps and charts*]
MG.............	Manual Group (NRCH)
MG.............	Manufactured Goods (AAEL)

MG...............	Manufacturing
MG...............	Maof Airlines [*Israel*] [*ICAO designator*] (ICDA)
MG...............	Marcus Gunn (Pupil) [*Ophthalmology*]
MG...............	Margin (DAVI)
MG...............	Marginal (AAG)
MG...............	Margun Music [*Publisher*]
MG...............	Marine Gunner
MG...............	Martinus Gosia [*Authority cited in pre-1607 legal work*] (DSA)
MG...............	Master-General [*Military*] [*British*]
MG...............	Master Generator [*Telecommunications*] (OA)
MG...............	Master Group (VLIE)
mg...............	Master-Group (SAUO)
MG...............	Matrix Glass [*Geology*]
MG...............	Meaning (ROG)
MG...............	Measurements Group (SAUO)
MG...............	Medal for Gallantry
MG...............	Media General Financial Services [*Information retrieval*]
MG...............	Media Guide
MG...............	Medial Gastrocnemius [*Anatomy*]
MG...............	Medium Grain [*Lumber*]
MG...............	Mega-Gauss
Mg...............	Megagram (COE)
MG...............	Megagram
MG...............	Membranous Glomerulopathy [*Nephrology*]
MG...............	Menopausal Gonadotropin [*Endocrinology*]
MG...............	Mesiogingival [*Dentistry*]
MG...............	Message Generator
MG...............	Metal Glass (IAA)
MG...............	Metal Goods [*Department of Employment*] [*British*]
MG...............	Metallgesellschaft [*German commodities and futures contractor*] (ECON)
MG...............	Metallurgical Grade
MG...............	Meteorological Group [*Range Commanders Council*] [*White Sands Missile Range, NM*]
MG...............	Methylene Glutamine
MG...............	Methylglucoside [*Organic chemistry*]
MG...............	Methylglyoxal [*Also, MGLY*] [*Organic chemistry*]
MG...............	Methyl Green [*A dye*]
MG...............	MG Car Club (EA)
MG...............	MGM Grand Air [*ICAO designator*] (AD)
MG...............	Michaelis-Gutmann Bodies (MAE)
mg...............	Microgram (DAVI)
MG...............	Microwave Generator
MG...............	Middle Gimbal [*Yaw*]
M/G.............	Miles per Gallon
MG...............	Military Government [*or Governor*]
MG...............	Millard-Gubler [*Syndrome*] [*Medicine*] (DB)
MG...............	Millennium Guild (EA)
MG...............	Mill Glazed [*Paper*]
MG...............	Milligauss (ABBR)
MG...............	Milli Gram (ACAE)
Mg...............	Milligram (DIPS)
mg...............	Milligram
mg%...........	Milligram per 100 ml (SAUS)
MG...............	Millwright Group (EA)
MG...............	Minister General (SAUO)
MG...............	Minister of the Gospel (GEAB)
MG...............	Minnesota Groundswell (EA)
MG...............	Minority Group
MG...............	Miracle of Grace [*Pseudonym used by William Smith*]
MG...............	Misioneros de Guadalupe [*Missionaries of Guadelupe*] [*Mexico*] (EAIO)
MG...............	Missile Gas
MG...............	Missile Guidance
MG...............	Mixed Grain
MG...............	[*The*] Mobile & Gulf Railroad Co. [*Formerly, MGU*] [*AAR code*]
MG...............	Mobile Generator (KSC)
MG...............	Modified Guaranteed [*Securities trading*]
MG...............	Moeso-Gothic [*Language, etc.*] (ROG)
MG...............	Monoglyceride [*An enzyme*] (MAE)
MG...............	Monogram Industries, Inc. (SAUO)
MG...............	Morgan Group [*AMEX symbol*] (TTSB)
MG...............	[*The*] Morgan Group, Inc. [*AMEX symbol*] (SAG)
MG...............	Morning
MG...............	Morris Garages [*British automobile manufacturer; initialism used as name of sports car it produces*]
MG...............	Motion for Mandamus Granted [*Legal term*] (ILCA)
MG...............	Motor Generator
MG...............	Mug (ABBR)
MG...............	Multigauge
MG...............	Muncie-Getrag [*Refers to an automotive transmission designed by Getrag, a West German company, and built by General Motors in Muncie, IN*]
MG...............	Muscle Group (MAE)
MG...............	Myasthenia Gravis [*Medicine*]
MG...............	Myasthenia Gravis Foundation (EA)
MG...............	Mycoplasma Gallisepticum (DB)
MG...............	Myoglobin [*Medicine*] (DMAA)
MG...............	Myriagram [*Ten Thousand Grams*] (ROG)
MG...............	Pompano Airways [*ICAO designator*] (AD)
Mg/₁............	Milligrams per Liter (GNE)
MGA............	Madras Geographical Association (SAUO)
MGA............	Magna International, Inc. [*NYSE symbol*] (SPSG)
MGA............	Major-General i/c Administration (SAUO)
MGA............	Major-General in Charge of Administration [*British*]

MGA............	Mammary Gland Adenoma [*Medicine*] (MELL)
MGA............	Managing General Agency [*Insurance*]
MGA............	Managing General Agent [*Insurance*]
MGA............	Managua [*Nicaragua*] [*Airport symbol*] (OAG)
MGA............	Marble and Granite Association [*British*] (BI)
MGA............	Martin Goffman Associates (IID)
MGA............	Master Gemology Association (EA)
MGA............	Master of General Administration (DMAA)
MGA............	Master of Government Administration (GAGS)
MGA............	Matrox Graphics Architecture [*Matrox Eletronics Systems Ltd.*] (PCM)
MGA............	Medium-Gain Antenna
MGA............	Megaline Resources [*Vancouver Stock Exchange symbol*]
MGA............	Melengestrol Acetate [*Endocrinology*]
MGA............	Member of the General Assembly (SAUO)
MGA............	Mercantile Gold [*Vancouver Stock Exchange symbol*]
MGA............	Middle Gimbal Angle (NASA)
MGA............	Middle Gimbal Assembly (KSC)
MGA............	Middle Gimbal Axis (KSC)
MGA............	Milagra Ridge [*California*] [*Seismograph station code, US Geological Survey*] (SEIS)
MGA............	Military Government Association
MGA............	Module Generator Assembly (DWSG)
MGA............	Monochrome Graphics Adapter [*Hercules*] [*Computer science*] (PCM)
MGA............	[*The*] Monongahela Railway Co. [*AAR code*]
MGA............	Monongahela Railway Company (SAUO)
MGA............	Mother Guardian Allowance
MGA............	Multimedia Graphics Architecture [*Computer science*] (PCM)
MGA............	Multiple Gas Analyzer
MGA............	Mushroom Growers Association [*Commercial firm*] (EA)
MGA............	Mushroom Growers Cooperative Association [*Defunct*] (EA)
MGAA.........	Major-General, Anti-Aircraft Artillery (SAUO)
MGAA.........	Medium-Gain Autotrack Antenna
MGAA.........	Miniature Golf Association of America (EA)
MGAB.........	Maintenance Ground Abort [*Air Force*] (AFIT)
MGABR.......	Maintenance Ground Abort Rate [*Air Force*] (AFIT)
MGAC.........	Monongahela Connecting Railroad (SAUO)
MGACG.......	Missile Guidance Alignment Checkout Group (SAUO)
MGAD.........	Machine-Gun Artillery Division [*Former USSR*]
mgal...........	Milligal [*Unit of acceleration*]
MGAL.........	Thousand Gallons (EG)
MGAL/D.....	Million Gallons per Day
mgallon......	Million Gallons (COE)
MGALS........	Milligals (ABBR)
MGAM........	Member Get a Member [*Prodigy Services Co.*]
MGAM........	Morgan Grenfell Asset Management [*Investment management firm*] [*British*]
MGAM........	Multimedia Games [*NASDAQ symbol*] (TTSB)
MGAM........	Multimedia Games, Inc. [*NASDAQ symbol*] (SAG)
MGAMS/CDTR...	Microgravity Accelerometer Measurement System/Cassette Data Tape Recorder (SAUS)
MGaMW......	Mount Wachusett Community College, Gardner, MA [*Library symbol*] [*Library of Congress*] (LCLS)
MG&E.........	Madison Gas & Electric Co. (EFIS)
MG&E.........	Michigan Gas and Electric Co. (SAUO)
MG & L........	Measurement of Gains and Losses (DICI)
MG & S.......	Manning, Granger, and Scott's English Common Pleas Reports [*1845-56*] [*A publication*] (DLA)
MGAO.........	Minority Graphic Arts Organization (EA)
MGAP.........	Magnetic Attitude Prediction
MGAP.........	Micro-Grain Array Processor [*Electronics*]
MGARJS.....	Mobile Ground-to-Air RADAR Jamming System
MGAS.........	Marcum Natural Gas Service, Inc. [*NASDAQ symbol*] (SAG)
MGAS.........	Marcum Natural Gas Svcs [*NASDAQ symbol*] (TTSB)
MGAS.........	Motor Gasoline [*Military*]
MGAT.........	Manchester General Ability Test [*Education*] (AEBS)
MGAWA......	Market Gardeners' Association of Western Australia
MGAWD......	Make Good All Works Distributed [*Legal term*] (BARN)
MGB............	Main Gear Box (MCD)
MGB............	Manageable (ABBR)
MGB............	Medial Geniculate Body (DIPS)
MGB............	Medium-Girder Bridge (RDA)
MGB............	Ministerstvo Gosudarstvennoy Bezopasnosti [*Ministry of State Security*] [*Former USSR*] (LAIN)
MGB............	Missile Gunboat (SAUS)
MGB............	Mississippi Bureau of Geology (SAUO)
MGB............	Mobile Garbage Bin
MGB............	Morgan Stan Global Opt Bd Fd [*NYSE symbol*] (TTSB)
MGB............	Morgan Stanley Global Opportunities Bond Fund, Inc. [*NYSE symbol*] (SAG)
MGB............	Motor Gunboat [*British*]
MGB............	Mount Gambier [*Australia*] [*Airport symbol*] (OAG)
MGBC.........	Maranatha Gospel Bottle Crusade [*Later, CEM*] (EA)
MGBC.........	Modelling Global Biogeochemical Cycles (SAUO)
MGBCS........	Murray Grey Beef Cattle Society [*Australia*]
MGBG.........	Methylglyoxalbis(guanylhydrazone) [*Mitoguazone*] [*Also, Me-GAG*] [*Antineoplastic drug*]
MGBG.........	Methylglyoxal-Bis[*guanylhydrazone*] (DB)
MGBN.........	Bananera [*Guatemala*] [*ICAO location identifier*] (ICLI)
MGBNVCP...	Murray Geological Basin Native Vegetation Clearance Policy (SAUO)
MGBT.........	Manageability (ABBR)
MGBY.........	Manageably (ABBR)
MGC............	Machine-Gun Car [*or Carrier*] [*British*]
MGC............	Machine-Gun Co. [*or Corps*]
MGC............	Machine-Gun Combination [*British*]
MGC............	Machine Gun Corps (SAUO)

MGC............	Magec Aviation Ltd. [British] [ICAO designator] (FAAC)
MGC............	Magic (ABBR)
MgC............	Magnocellular Neuroendocrine Cell [Medicine] (DMAA)
MGC............	Major Gain Control
MGC............	Major General Commandant [Marine Corps]
MGC............	Management Group Codes (MCD)
MGC............	Manual Gain Control
MGC............	Manufactured Goods Collection (AAEL)
MGC............	Marriage Guidance Council [British]
MGC............	Marriage Guidance Counsellor (SAUO)
MGC............	Metacerebral Giant Cell [Cytology]
MGC............	Metallized Glass Coil
MGC............	Michigan City [Indiana] [Airport symbol] (OAG)
MGC............	Michigan City, IN [Location identifier] [FAA] (FAAL)
MGC............	Midcourse Guidance and Control
MGC............	Middle Georgia College [Cochran]
MGC............	Minimal Glomerular Change [Nephrology]
MGC............	Minimum Gelling Concentration [Hematology]
MGC............	Missile Guidance and Control
MGC............	Missile Guidance Computer (MCD)
MGC............	Montgomery County Community College, Blue Bell, PA [OCLC symbol] (OCLC)
MGC............	Morgan Grenfell Smallcap [NYSE symbol] (TTSB)
MGC............	Morgan Grenfell Smallcap Fund, Inc. [NYSE symbol] (SPSG)
MGC............	Mouse Genome Conference (HGEN)
MGC............	Movers Association of Greater Chicago, Chicago, IL [STAC]
MGC............	Museums and Galleries Commission [Government body] [British]
MGCA	Men's Garden Clubs of America (EA)
MGCA	Mobile Ground-Controlled Approach [Aviation]
MGCA	Mushroom Growers Cooperative Association [Defunct]
MG CARB....	Magnesium Carbonate (SAUS)
MGCAX	Managers Capital Appreciation Fund
MGCB	Coban [Guatemala] [ICAO location identifier] (ICLI)
MGCB	Master Gate Control Block [Computer science] (VLIE)
MGCC	Medical Graphics [NASDAQ symbol] (TTSB)
MGCC	Medical Graphics Corp. [NASDAQ symbol] (NQ)
MGCC	MG [Morris Garage]Car Club
MGCC	Missile Guidance and Control Computer
MGCD	Maximum Gapless Coverage Distance (NG)
MGCE	Multifocal Giant Cell Encephalitis [Medicine] (MELL)
MGCI	Master Ground-Controller Interception RADAR (NATG)
MGCI	Most General Common Instance (IDAI)
MGCL..........	Magical (ABBR)
MGCLY	Magically (ABBR)
mg/cm	Milligram per Centimeter (COE)
MGCN	Magician (ABBR)
MGCO	Mars Geoscience/Climatology Orbiter
MGCOA.......	National Golf Course Owners Association (NTPA)
MGCP	Media Gateway Control Protocol [Computer science] (VLIE)
MGCP	Media-Gateway Control Protocol [Computer science] (AGLO)
MGCR	Carmelita [Guatemala] [ICAO location identifier] (ICLI)
MGCR	Maritime Gas-Cooled Reactor
MGCRB.......	Medicare Geographic Classification Review Board
MGCR-CX ...	Maritime Gas-Cooled Reactor Critical Experiment
MGCS	Manual Gas Control Station (SAUO)
MGCS	Meteosat Ground Computer System [Aviation] (DA)
MGCS	Meteosat Ground Computing Station (SAUO)
MGCS	Missile Guidance and Control System (MCD)
MGCS	Missile Guidance Cooling System (DWSG)
MGCS	Mobile Ground Control Station (SAUO)
MGCT..........	Coatepeque [Guatemala] [ICAO location identifier] (ICLI)
MGCT..........	Mixed Germ Cell Tumor [Medicine] (MELL)
MGCYL	Megacycle (ABBR)
MGD	Machine Gaming Division [Queensland, Australia]
MGD	Magadan [Later, FUR] [Former USSR] [Geomagnetic observatory code]
MGD	Magadan 1 [Former USSR] [Seismograph station code, US Geological Survey] (SEIS)
MGD	Magnetogasdynamic
MGD	Managed
MGD	Master of Graphic Design (PGP)
MGD	Maternal Genetic Disease (MELL)
MGD	Maximal Glucose Disposal [Medicine] (DMAA)
MGD	McGregor-Doniger, Inc. (SAUO)
MGD	Mean Gain Deviation (IEEE)
MG/D	Megagrams per Day
MGD	Mercury Germanium Detector
MGD	Miehle-Goss-Dexter [Rockwell International Corp.]
MGD	Military Geographic Documentation (AABC)
mg/d	Milligrams per Deciliter
MGD	Million Gallons per Day
MGD	Millions of Gallons per Day (COE)
MGD	Minority Group Designator [Office of Personnel Management] (GFGA)
MGD	Mixed Gonadal Dysgenesis [Medicine]
MGD	Molybdopterin Guanine Dinucleotide [Biochemistry]
MGD	Mouse Genome Database
MGD	Mugged (ABBR)
MGD	Murgold Resources, Inc. [Toronto Stock Exchange symbol]
MGD	North-East Cargo Airlines [Russian Federation] [ICAO designator] (FAAC)
MGDC	Morgan Grenfell Development Capital (WDAA)
MgdCare.....	Managed Care Solutions, Inc. [Associated Press] (SAG)
MGDF	Megakaryocyte Growth and Development Factor [Cytology]
MGDF	Modified Granular Diffusion Flame [Propellant]

MGdHi........	Managed High-Income Income Portfolio [Associated Press] (SAG)
mg/dl	milligrams per 100 milliliters (SAUS)
MGdMun.....	Managed Municipals Portfolio [Associated Press] (SAG)
MGdMun2 ...	Managed Municipals Portfolio II [Associated Press] (SAG)
MGDS	Member in General Dental Surgery (DMAA)
MGDS	Mines Geologic Disposal System (SAUO)
MGDSRCS Eng...	Membership in General Dental Surgery, Royal College of Surgeons of England [British] (DBQ)
MGE............	Evergreen Regional Library, Gimli, Manitoba [Library symbol] [National Library of Canada] (NLC)
MGE............	Maintenance Ground Equipment [Formerly, GSF]
MGE............	Manage (ABBR)
MGE............	Marge Enterprises [Vancouver Stock Exchange symbol]
MGE............	Marietta, GA [Location identifier] [FAA] (FAAL)
MGE............	Master of Geological Engineering (NADA)
MGE............	Megaloblastic Erythropoiesis [Medicine] (MELL)
MGE............	Message (ADA)
MGE............	Micro-Station Foundation and Modular GIS Environment (SAUO)
MGE............	Milwaukee Grain Exchange [Defunct]
MGE............	Minneapolis Grain Exchange (EA)
MGE............	Missile Guidance Element
MGE............	Modular Geographic Environment
MGE............	Modular Gis Environment (SAUO)
MGEB..........	Manageable (ABBR)
MGEBT........	Manageability (ABBR)
MGEBY	Manageably (ABBR)
MGED..........	Managed (ABBR)
M Ge E	Master of Geological Engineering
M Ge Eng ...	Master of Geological Engineering
MGEG.........	Managing (ABBR)
mg-el..........	Milligram-Element (MAE)
MGEM.........	Modern Gun Effectiveness Model (MCD)
M GEN	Major General
MGEN.........	Micro General [NASDAQ symbol] (TTSB)
MGEN E	Micro General Corp. [NASDAQ symbol] (NQ)
M Gen E	Master of General Engineering (PGP)
MGenStud...	Master of General Studies (ADA)
MGENT.......	Management (ABBR)
M Geo E	Master of Geological Engineering (PGP)
M Geol E	Master of Geological Engineering
MGeolEng...	Master of Geological Engineering (NADA)
MGER.........	Manager (ABBR)
MGERL.......	Managerial (ABBR)
MGES..........	Esquipulas [Guatemala] [ICAO location identifier] (ICLI)
MGES..........	Maintenance Ground Equipment Section
MGES..........	Multiple-Gated Equilibrium Scintigraphy (DB)
MGEUS.......	Maintenance Ground Equipment Utilization Sheets
Mgf.............	Free Magnesium
MGF............	Macrophage Growth Factor (PDAA)
MGF............	Magnify (MSA)
MGF............	Maringa [Brazil] [Airport symbol] (OAG)
MGF............	Mast-Cell Growth Factor [Cytology]
MGF............	Maternal Grandfather (AAMN)
MGF............	Metallised Glass-Fibre chaff (SAUS)
MGF............	MFS Government Markets Income Trust [NYSE symbol] (SPSG)
MGF............	MFS Gvt Mkts Income Tr [NYSE symbol] (TTSB)
MGF............	Missionary Gospel Fellowship (EA)
MGF............	Mobile Guerrilla Force [Vietnam]
MGF............	Moment-Generating Function [Mathematics]
MGF............	Motor-Generator Flywheel (MCD)
MGF............	Multipotent Growth Factor [Medicine] (MELL)
MGF............	Myasthenia Gravis Foundation
MGF............	Myoblast Growth Factor [Biochemistry]
MGF............	Myxoma Growth Factor [Biochemistry]
MGFA..........	Myasthenia Gravis Foundation of America (SAUO)
MGFC..........	Mickey Gilley Fan Club [Defunct] (EA)
MGFE..........	Moment-Generating Function Estimator
MGFEL........	Master Government-Furnished Equipment List (NVT)
MGFG	Magnifying
MGFL..........	Flores [Guatemala] [ICAO location identifier] (ICLI)
MGFS..........	Media General Financial Services, Inc. [Information service or system] (IID)
MGFY..........	Magnify (VLIE)
MGFZB........	Mein Gott, Fueg Es zum Besten [My God, Order It for the Best] [Motto of Sophie, consort of Georg Friedrich, Margrave of Brandenburg-Anspach (1563-1639)] [German]
MGG	Machine Gun Guards [British military] (DMA)
MGG	Managing (ABBR)
MGG	Marine Geology and Geophysics (SAUO)
MGG	Marine Geology and Geophysics Report (SAUO)
MGG	May-Gruenwald-Giemsa [A stain] [Hematology]
MGG	Mega Gold Resources Ltd. [Vancouver Stock Exchange symbol]
MGG	Memory Gate Generator [Computer science]
MGG	Metropolitan Greetings, Incorporated (SAUO)
MGG	MGM Grand [NYSE symbol] (TTSB)
MGG	MGM Grand, Inc. [NYSE symbol] (SPSG)
MGG	Military Government for Germany (SAUO)
MGG	Missile Guidance Group
MGG	Molecular and General Genetics (SAUO)
MGG	Monopropellant Gas Generator (PDAA)
MGG	Mouse Gamma-Globulin
MGG	Mugging (ABBR)
MGG	Musik in Geschichte und Gegenwart [A publication]
MGGB..........	Modular Guided Glide Bomb (MCD)
MGGH..........	Methylglyoxal Guanylhydrazone [Antineoplastic drug] (MAE)

MGGM .... Mars General Circulation Model [For planetary weather study]
MGGM .... Maternal Great Grandfather (SAUS)
MGGS .... Major General, General Staff
MGGT .... Guatemala/La Aurora [Guatemala] [ICAO location identifier] (ICLI)
MGH .... Madigan General Hospital (SAUO)
MGH .... Mammogenic Hormone [Medicine] (MELL)
MGH .... Margate [South Africa] [Airport symbol] (OAG)
MGH .... Massachusetts General Hospital (DAVI)
MGH .... Massachusetts General Hospital, Treadwell Library, Boston, MA [OCLC symbol] (OCLC)
mgh .... Milligram Hour [Pharmacy]
MGH .... Monoglyceride Hydrolase [An enzyme] (MAE)
MGH .... Monosodium Glutamate Headache [Medicine] (MELL)
MGH .... Monumenta Germaniae Historica [A publication] (ODCC)
MGH .... Morden & Helwig Group, Inc. [Toronto Stock Exchange symbol]
MGH .... Museum of Garden History [British]
MgHiYld ...... Managed High Yield Fund [Associated Press] (SAG)
MGHT .... Huehuetenango [Guatemala] [ICAO location identifier] (ICLI)
MG HYDROX... Magnesium Hydroxide (SAUS)
MGI .... Gillam Municipal Library, Manitoba [Library symbol] [National Library of Canada] (NLC)
MGI .... Macrophage and Granulocyte Inducer [Biochemistry]
MgI .... Magazine Index
MGI .... Magnetics International Ltd. [Toronto Stock Exchange symbol]
MGI .... Management Games Institute [Raytheon Co.]
MGI .... Mapping and Geography Institute (SAUO)
MGI .... Marine Geological Institute [Indonesia] [Marine science] (OSRA)
MGI .... Matagorda Island, TX [Location identifier] [FAA] (FAAL)
MGI .... Mavtech Holdings, Inc. [Toronto Stock Exchange symbol]
MGI .... Media Group Inc. (SAUO)
MGI .... Medial Giant Interneuron [Neurobiology]
MGI .... Member of the Gas Institute [British]
MGI .... Member of the Institute of Certificated Grocers [British]
MGI .... Member of the Institute of Certified Grocers (SAUO)
MGI .... Metal Grating Institute [Defunct]
MGI .... MGIC Investment Corp. (SAUO)
MGI .... MGI Properties [NYSE symbol] (SPSG)
MGI .... Microbial Genome Initiative (HGEN)
MGI .... Military Geographic Information [or Intelligence] (MCD)
MGI .... Mobile Gamma Irradiator [Nuclear energy]
MGI .... Multi-Function Interpreter (SAUS)
MGI .... Multigraphic Interface [XOR Systems]
MGIB .... Management and Graduate Item Bank [Reasoning skills test]
MGIB .... Montgomery GI Bill (INF)
MGIC .... Magic Software Enterprises, Inc. [NASDAQ symbol] (SAG)
MGIC .... MGIC Investment Co. [Associated Press] (SAG)
MGIC .... Mortgage Guaranty Insurance Corp. [Subsidiary of MGIC Investment Corp.]
MGICA .... Mortgage Guaranteed Insurance Corporation of Australia (SAUO)
MGICF .... Magic Software Enterprises [NASDAQ symbol] (TTSB)
MGID .... Military Geographic Information and Documentation (AABC)
MGIKQ .... Magic Restaurants [NASDAQ symbol] (TTSB)
MGIN .... Margin (ROG)
MGINS .... Mugginess (ABBR)
MGI Phr ...... MGI PHARMA, Inc. [Associated Press] (SAG)
MGI Prp .... MGI Properties [Associated Press] (SAG)
MGIR .... Motor Glider Instructor Rating [Aviation] (DA)
MGIS .... Micro Geographic Information System (SAUO)
MGIS .... Military Geographic Information System (SAUO)
MGIWQ .... Magic Restaurants Wrrt [NASDAQ symbol] (TTSB)
MGJ .... Montgomery, NY [Location identifier] [FAA] (FAAL)
MGK .... Michele Gold Mountain Ltd. [Vancouver Stock Exchange symbol]
MGk .... Middle Greek [Language] (BARN)
MGK .... Modern Greek [Language, etc.]
mg/kg .... Milligrams per Kilogram (AAMN)
mg/kg/day ... milligram per kilogram per day (SAUS)
mg/kg/hr .... milligram per kilogram per hour (SAUS)
MGI .... Gloucester Lyceum and Sawyer Free Public Library, Gloucester, MA [Library symbol] [Library of Congress] (LCLS)
MGL .... Machine Group Listing (SAUO)
MGL .... Machine Gun LASER (MCD)
MGL .... Magalia [California] [Seismograph station code, US Geological Survey] (SEIS)
MGL .... Magellan Health Svcs [AMEX symbol] (TTSB)
MGL .... Magnanimous Green Leprechaun
MGL .... Malachite Green Leucocyanite (OA)
MGL .... Management Guidance Letter (SAUO)
MGL .... Marginal (MSA)
MGL .... Matrix Generator Language [Computer science] (BUR)
MGL .... Michigan General Corporation (SAUO)
mg/l .... Milligram per Liter (COE)
mg/L .... Milligrams per Liter (MEC)
MG/L .... Milligrams per Liter
MGL .... Mingle (ABBR)
MGL .... Missouri Gravity Low [Geology]
MGL .... Mogul
Mgl .... Mongolia (MILB)
MGL .... Mongolian Airlines [ICAO designator] (FAAC)
MGL .... Mongrel (ABBR)
MGL .... Mono Gold Mines, Inc. [Vancouver Stock Exchange symbol]
MGL .... Monteagle, TN [Location identifier] [FAA] (FAAL)
MGL .... Morris Geneological Library (SAUO)
MGL .... Move-Grow-Learn [Program for visual perception development]
MGLA .... Massachusetts General Laws Annotated [A publication]
M GLAM ...... Mid Glamorgan [County in Wales]

MGLC .... Misty Mountain Gold Ltd. [NASDAQ symbol] (SAG)
MGLD .... Mild General Learning Disability
MGLD .... Mingled (ABBR)
MGLG .... Mingling (ABBR)
MGIHi .... Cape Ann Historical Association, Gloucester, MA [Library symbol] [Library of Congress] (LCLS)
MGLL .... La Libertad [Guatemala] [ICAO location identifier] (ICLI)
MGLMNA .... Megalomania (ABBR)
MGLMNAC... Megalomaniac (ABBR)
MGLP .... Methylglucose Lipopolysaccharide [Biochemistry]
MGLPS .... Megalopolis (ABBR)
MGLY .... Methylglyoxal [Also, MG] [Organic chemistry]
MGM .... Mailgram
MGM .... Master Group Multiplexer
MGM .... Maternal Grandmother (AAMN)
MGM .... Mayer's Ganz Mispocheh [Mayer's Whole Family] [A Yiddish nickname for Metro-Goldwyn-Mayer, it reflects the tendency of early studio chiefs to hire their relatives and friends]
MGM .... Mechanics of Granular Materials
MGM .... Medical Group Management Journal (SAUO)
MGM .... Medical Group Missions of the Christian Medical and Dental Society (EA)
MGM .... Member-Get-a-Member [Marketing] (WDMC)
MGM .... Memory Grant Manager (SAUS)
MGM .... Metro-Goldwyn-Mayer [Record label] [USA, Great Britain, etc.]
MGM .... MGM Grand Air, Inc. [ICAO designator] (FAAC)
MGM .... Milligram (DFIT)
mgm .... Milligram
MGM .... Mobile-Launched Ground-Attack Missile
MGM .... Molecular and Genetic Medicine
MGM .... Montgomery [Alabama] [Airport symbol] (OAG)
MGM .... Morgain Minerals, Inc. [Vancouver Stock Exchange symbol]
MGM .... Mother's Grandmother (MAE)
MG/M² .... Megagrams per Square Meter
MG/M³ .... Megagrams per Cubic Meter
mg/m₃ .... Milligrams of Material per Cubic Meter of Air (GNE)
MGMA .... Magma (ABBR)
MGMA .... Medical Group Management Association (EA)
MGMA .... Metro Global Media [NASDAQ symbol] (TTSB)
MGMA .... Metro Global Media, Inc. [NASDAQ symbol] (SAG)
MG-MA .... Motor Generator-Motor Alternator (COE)
MGMC .... Multiple Gun Motor Carriage
MGMD .... Ministerial Group on the Misuse of Drugs [British]
MGMG .... MGM Grand, Inc. [Associated Press] (SAG)
MG/MGI .... Mapping, Geodesy and Military Geographic Intelligence (SAUO)
MGMGMG.... Milwaukee and Greatlakes MG [Morris Garage] Motorcar Group
MGMI .... Metallgezellschaft Metals Index [British] (NUMA)
mg/min .... milligrams per minute (SAUS)
MGMIS .... Medical Group Management Information Service [Medical Group Management Association] (DHSM)
MGML .... Malacatan [Guatemala] [ICAO location identifier] (ICLI)
MGML .... Minimal Generalized Markup Language (SAUS)
MGMM........ Melchor De Mencos [Guatemala] [ICAO location identifier] (ICLI)
MGMNT ...... Management
MGMR .... Ministry of Geology and Mineral Resources [China]
MGMS .... Manchester Geological and Mining Society (SAUO)
MGMT .... Make Good a Magnetic Track of (Degrees) [Aviation] (FAAC)
mgmt .... Management (DD)
Mgmt .... Management (TBD)
MGMT .... Management
Mgmt Forum... Management Forum [A publication]
MGN .... Magangue [Colombia] [Airport symbol] (AD)
MGN .... Magazine (ABBR)
MGN .... Magneto [Generator]
MGN .... Margin [Accounting]
MGN .... Marine Guidance Note (SAUO)
MGN .... Medial Geniculate Nucleus [Medicine]
MGN .... Membranous Glomerulonephritis [Nephrology]
MGN .... Mendial Geniculate Nucleus (PDAA)
MGN .... Mengen [Turkey] [Seismograph station code, US Geological Survey] (SEIS)
MGN .... Micrograin (ABBR)
MGN .... Mirror Group Newspapers [British]
MGN .... Morgan Aviation Services Ltd. [Nigeria] [ICAO designator] (FAAC)
MGN .... Morgan Products Ltd. [NYSE symbol] (SPSG)
MGN .... Multigrounded Neutral [Telecommunications] (TEL)
Mgna .... Magna-Lab, Inc. [Associated Press] (SAG)
MGNAN .... Margination (ABBR)
MGNES .... Metal Goods Not Elsewhere Specified [Department of Employment] [British]
MGNETC ...... Magnetic (ABBR)
MGNETCY ... Magnetically (ABBR)
MGNETMTR.. Magnetometer (ABBR)
MGNETSM ... Magnetism (ABBR)
MGNETZ ...... Magnetization (ABBR)
MGNETZ ...... Magnetize [or Magnetized] (ABBR)
MGNFI .... Magnify (ABBR)
MGNFIB....... Magnifiable (ABBR)
MGNFID....... Magnified (ABBR)
MGNFIG....... Magnifying (ABBR)
MGNFIN....... Magnification (ABBR)
MGNFIR....... Magnifier (ABBR)
MGNFNC...... Magnificence (ABBR)
MGNFNT...... Magnificent (ABBR)
MGNFTY ...... Magnificently (ABBR)

MGNIA	Marginalia (ABBR)
MGNL	Magna Bancorp [*NASDAQ symbol*] (SAG)
MGNLT	Marginality (ABBR)
MGNLY	Marginally (ABBR)
MGNMT	Magnanimity (ABBR)
MGNMU	Magnanimous (ABBR)
MGNSM	Magnesium [*Chemical symbol is Mg*]
MGNT	Magnate (ABBR)
MGNT	Magnet (ABBR)
MGNTC	Magnetic
MGNTO	Magneto
MGNTUD	Magnitude (ABBR)
MGNTZD	Magnetized
MGO	Machine Gun Officer [*British military*] (DMA)
MGO	Main Geophysical Observatory [*Russia*] (CARB)
MGO	Management by Goals and Objectives (MCD)
MGO	Marine Gas Oil (SAUS)
MGO	Master General of the Ordnance [*Army*] [*British*]
MGO	Master of Gynaecology and Obstetrics (ADA)
MGO	Mato Grosso [*Brazil*] [*Airport symbol*] (AD)
MGO	Megagauss-Oersted [*Magnetic field strength*]
MGO	Military Government Officer
MGO	Million Gauss Oersted [*Unit of energy density*]
MGO	Mortgage Insurance Co. of Canada [*Toronto Stock Exchange symbol*]
MGOCC	Morris Garage Octagon Car Club [*British*] (EAIO)
MGOe	Megagauss-Oersted [*Also, MGO*] [*Magnetic field strength*]
MGOS	Metal-Glass-Oxide-Silicon (PDAA)
MGOT	Maggot (ABBR)
M GOTH	Moeso-Gothic [*Language, etc.*] (ROG)
MGovt	Military Government (SAUO)
MGP	Application for Mandamus Granted in Part [*Legal term*] (DLA)
MGP	Macarthur Gruen Party [*Political party*] [*Australia*]
MG(P)	Machinery of Government, Parliamentary Procedure [*British*]
MGP	Maguayo [*Puerto Rico*] [*Seismograph station code, US Geological Survey*] (SEIS)
MGP	Maharastrawadi Gomantak Party (SAUO)
MGP	Maintenance Ground Point
MGP	Manga [*Papua New Guinea*] [*Airport symbol*] (OAG)
MGP	Manufactured Gas Plant [*Environmental biotechnology*]
MGP	Marcus Garvey Park (SAUO)
MGP	Marginal Granulocyte Pool [*Hematology*]
MGP	Mary Glawgow Publications [*Publisher*] [*British*]
MGP	Membranous Glomerulopathy [*Medicine*] (DB)
MGP	Merchants Group [*AMEX symbol*] (TTSB)
MGP	Merchants Group, Inc. [*AMEX symbol*] (SPSG)
MGP	Meteorology/Geophysics Package (ACAE)
MGP	Methylglucose Polysaccharide [*Biochemistry*]
MGP	Methyl Green Pyronine [*A stain*]
MGP	Micro-G Physics and Chemistry Experiments Group [*NASA*] (SSD)
MGP	Monochrome Graphics Printer [*Computer science*] (CDE)
MGP	Morrison-Grey Enterprises [*Vancouver Stock Exchange symbol*]
MGP	Mountain Gorilla Project (EA)
MGP	Mouvement Gaulliste Populaire [*Popular Gaullist Movement*] [*France*] [*Political party*] (PPW)
MGP	Mucous Glycoproteins [*Biochemistry*]
MGP	Multiple Goal Programming
MGP	Museum of the Great Plains [*Lawton, OK*]
MGPB	Puerto Barrios [*Guatemala*] [*ICAO location identifier*] (ICLI)
MGPC	Grandview Personal Care Home, Manitoba [*Library symbol*] [*National Library of Canada*] (NLC)
MGPC	Medical Group Practice Council (SAUO)
MGPCU	Missile Ground Power Control Unit (AAG)
M-GPD	Million US Gallons per Day [*AEC, OSW*]
MGPF	Multiprogram General-Purpose Facilities [*Oak Ridge National Laboratory*]
MGPGP	Master of Group Process and Group Psychotherapy (PGP)
MGPHN	Megaphone (ABBR)
MGPL	Marine Gene Probe Laboratory [*Dalhousie University*] [*Canada*]
MGPP	Poptun [*Guatemala*] [*ICAO location identifier*] (ICLI)
MGPPL	Motor Glider Private Pilot's Licence [*British*] (AIA)
MGPR	M.G. Products [*NASDAQ symbol*] (TTSB)
MGPR	MG Products, Inc. [*NASDAQ symbol*] (SAG)
MG Prod	MG Products, Inc. [*Associated Press*] (SAG)
MGQ	Maximum Guarantee Quality (SAUO)
MGQ	Mogadishu [*Somalia*] [*Airport symbol*] (OAG)
MGQC	Quiche [*Guatemala*] [*ICAO location identifier*] (ICLI)
MGQZ	Quezaltenango [*Guatemala*] [*ICAO location identifier*] (ICLI)
MGR	Machine Gun Regiment [*British military*] (DMA)
mgr	Magister [*Master*] [*Latin*]
MGR	Manager (AFM)
mgr	Manager (NTIO)
Mgr.	Manager (ODBW)
MGR	Marrow Graft Rejection [*Medicine*] (MELL)
MGR	Marrow Granulocyte Reserves [*Hematology*]
MGR	Matusadona Game Reserve (SAUO)
MGR	McGraw-Edison Co. (SAUO)
MGR	Medieval Greek [*Language, etc.*]
MGR	Merry-Go-Round Entertainment (EFIS)
MGR	Metal Glaze Resistor
MGR	Method of Generated Responses [*Psychology*]
MGR	Micro-Graphic Reporting (PDAA)
MGR	Middlegate Resources, Inc. [*Vancouver Stock Exchange symbol*]
M GR	Middle Greek [*Language, etc.*] (ROG)
MGR	Minimum Government Requirements (SAUO)
MGR	Mixed Gas Rebreather
MGR	Mobile-Launched Ground-Attack Rocket
MGR	Modified Gain Ratio [*Medicine*] (MAE)
MGR	Modular Gas-Cooled Reactor [*Developed by MIT*] [*Nuclear energy*]
Mgr.	Monsignor (ODBW)
MGR	Monsignor
MGR	Moraga Resources Ltd. [*Vancouver Stock Exchange symbol*]
MGR	Moultrie, GA [*Location identifier*] [*FAA*] (FAAL)
MGR	Moultrie/Thomasville [*Georgia*] [*Airport symbol*] (OAG)
MGR	Mouvement de la Gauche Reformatrice [*Movement of the Reformist Left*] [*France*] [*Political party*] (PPW)
MGR	Mugger (ABBR)
MGR	Multiple Gas Rebreathing [*Medicine*] (DMAA)
MGR	Murmurs, Gallops, or Rubs [*Cardiology*] (DAVI)
MGRA	Major-General, Royal Artillery [*Army*] [*British*]
MGRA	Master Geographical Reference Area (SAUO)
MGRA	Migrate (ABBR)
MGRAD	Migrated (ABBR)
MGRAG	Migrating (ABBR)
MGRAN	Migration (ABBR)
MGranbyS...	Saint Hyacinth College and Seminary, Granby, MA [*Library symbol*] [*Library of Congress*] (LCLS)
MGRATR	Migrator (ABBR)
MGRATRY....	Migratory (ABBR)
MGRC	McGrath RentCorp [*NASDAQ symbol*] (NQ)
MGRC	Melbourne Greyhound Racing Club [*Australia*]
mgrd	Middleground (VRA)
MGREC	Magnetic Recorder [*or Recording*] (IAA)
MGrefC	Greenfield Community College, Greenfield, MA [*Library symbol*] [*Library of Congress*] (LCLS)
MGRESS......	Manageress (ROG)
MGRGT	Modular Gas-Cooled Reactor Gas Turbine [*Developed by MIT*] [*Nuclear energy*]
MGRHS	May God Rest His Soul
MGRI	Mobile Ground Radio Installation
MGRL	Managerial (ABBR)
MGRM	Major-General, Royal Marines [*British military*] (DMA)
MGRM	Metallgesellschaft Refining & Marketing [*American subsidiary of the German commodities and futures contractor*] (ECON)
MGRM	Milligram (ROG)
MGRMTRSF...	MGRM Training, Reserve & Special Forces (SAUO)
MGRN	Migration (ABBR)
MGRNL	Migrational (ABBR)
MGRP	Minimum-Gradient Reaction Path [*Chemical kinetics*]
MGRS	Ferrocarriles Nacionales de Mexico [*AAR code*]
MGrS	Groton School, Groton, MA [*Library symbol*] [*Library of Congress*] (LCLS)
MGRS	Meter Gauge Rolling-Stock [*British*]
MGRs..........	Microbial Genetic Resources (SAUS)
MGRS	Military Grid Reference System (AABC)
MGRT	Migrant (ABBR)
MGRT	Retalhuleu [*Guatemala*] [*ICAO location identifier*] (ICLI)
MGRTY	Migratory (ABBR)
MGRW	Matrix Generator and Report Writer [*Computer science*]
MGRY	Milgray Electronics [*NASDAQ symbol*] (TTSB)
MGRY	Milgray Electronics, Inc. [*NASDAQ symbol*] (NQ)
MGS...........	Machine Gun School [*British military*] (DMA)
MGS...........	Magellan Resources Corp. [*Vancouver Stock Exchange symbol*]
MGS...........	Maine Geological Survey (SAUO)
MGS...........	Manchester Geographical Society (SAUO)
MGS...........	Mangaia [*Cook Islands*] [*Airport symbol*] (OAG)
MGS...........	Marine Geophysical Survey (NOO)
MGS...........	Mars Global Surveyor [*NASA*]
MGS...........	Maryland Geological Survey (SAUO)
MGS...........	Master Gemology Society [*Defunct*] (EA)
MGS...........	Master of General Studies (GAGS)
MGS...........	Master of Gerontological Studies (GAGS)
MGS...........	Memoirs of the Geological Survey (SAUO)
MG's..........	Memphis Group [*In name of singing group "Booker T and the MG's"*]
MGS...........	Metal Gravel Stop
MGS...........	Metre-Gram-Second
MGS.\........	Metrogas SA [*NYSE symbol*] (SAG)
MGS...........	MetroGas S.A. CI'B'ADS [*NYSE symbol*] (TTSB)
MGS...........	Microcomputer Graphic System
MGS...........	Middleton Gardens [*South Carolina*] [*Seismograph station code, US Geological Survey*] (SEIS)
MGS...........	Midwestern Gilbert and Sullivan Society (EA)
MGS...........	Military Government Section [*World War II*]
MGS...........	Minnesota Geological Survey (SAUO)
MGS...........	Missile Guidance Section [*or Set, or System*]
MGS...........	Mission Ground Station (MCD)
MGS...........	Mobile Gas Service Corp. (EFIS)
MGS...........	Mobile Ground Station (SAUO)
MGS...........	Mobile Ground System
MGS...........	Moment Gyro System
MGS...........	Motor Generator Set (CAAL)
MGS...........	Moveable Ground Station (ACAE)
MgS04	Magnesium Sulfate (SAUS)
MGSA	Marriage Guidance South Australia
MGSA	Melanoma Growth Stimulatory Activity [*Biochemistry*]
MGSA	Memoirs of the Geological Society of America (SAUO)
MGSA	Military General Supply Agency [*Merged with Defense General Supply Center*]
MGSA	Modern Greek Studies Association (EA)
MG SAL	Magnesium Salicylate (SAUS)

MGSC	Missile Guidance Set Control
MGSCD	Martha Graham School of Contemporary Dance [*New York, NY*]
MGSch	Machine Gun School (SAUO)
MGSD	Michigan Geological Survey Division (SAUO)
MGSE	Maintenance Ground Support Equipment
MGSE	Mechanical Ground Support Equipment
MGSE	Missile Ground Support Equipment
MGSE	Mobile Ground Support Equipment
MGSE-ECM...	Maintenance Ground Support Equipment-Environmental Controls and Mechanisms (SAA)
MGSGT	Master Gunnery Sergeant [*Marine Corps*] (DNAB)
MGSI	Memoirs of the Geological Survey of India (SAUO)
MGSIUF	Marquis Giuseppe Scicluna International University Foundation (EA)
MGSJ	San Jose [*Guatemala*] [*ICAO location identifier*] (ICLI)
MGSL	Memoirs of the Geological Society of London (SAUO)
MGSM	Medium Ground Station Module (SAUS)
MGSM	San Marcos [*Guatemala*] [*ICAO location identifier*] (ICLI)
MGSMTC	Mid-Gulf Seaports Marine Terminal Conference (SAUO)
MGSpS	Guadalupan Missionaries of the Holy Spirit (TOCD)
MGSS	Manned Geosynchronous Spacecraft Servicer (SSD)
MGST	Miles [*Multiple Integrated Laser Engagement System*] Gunnery Skills Test [*USA*]
MGST	Military Geography Specialist Team
MGSTL	Magisterial (ABBR)
MGSTRA	Magistrate (ABBR)
MGT	Magenta Development Corp. [*Vancouver Stock Exchange symbol*]
MGT	Major Ground Test (NASA)
MGT	Management (AFM)
Mgt	Management (AL)
mgt	Management (ELAL)
MGT	Margate Air Services [*South Africa*] [*ICAO designator*] (FAAC)
MGT	Master-Group Translator [*Telecommunications*] (TEL)
MGT	Master of Gas Technology (GAGS)
MGT	Megaton [*Nuclear equivalent of one million tons of high explosive*] (AAG)
MGT	Meteorological and Geoastrophysical Titles
MGT	Millingimbi [*Airport symbol*]
MGT	Mobile [*Truck-Mounted*] Ground Terminal
MGT	Movie Going Time
MGT	Multiple Glomus Tumor [*Medicine*] (MELL)
MGT	Multiplex Genetic Testing [*Medicine*] (MELL)
MG/TA	Map Graphic and Terrain Analysis (SAUO)
MG/TA	Map Graphic and Terrain Analysis (SAUS)
MGTANALYSO...	Management Analysis Officer [*Air Force*]
MGTAV	Modern Greek Teachers' Association of Victoria [*Australia*]
MGTB	Mexican Government Tourist Bureau (SAUO)
MGTC	Morgan Guaranty Trust Company (SAUO)
MGTD	Mexican Government Tourist Delegation (SAUO)
MGTENGR...	Management Engineer [*Air Force*]
MGTG	Moving Ground Target Detection
MGTI	Member of the Gymnastic Teachers' Institute [*British*] (ROG)
MGTIR	Mightier (ABBR)
mgtis	Meningitis [*Medicine*] (MAE)
MGTIST	Mightiest (ABBR)
MGTMTR	Magnetometer
MGTNS	Mightiness (ABBR)
MGTO	Mexican Government Tourism Office (EA)
MGTO	Mexican Government Tourist Office (SAUO)
MG TRISIL...	Magnesium Trisilicate (SAUS)
MgtTch	Management Technologies, Inc. [*Associated Press*] (SAG)
MGTY	Mighty (ABBR)
MGU	Main-Group Ureilite [*Meteorite component*]
MGU	MGM Resources Corp. [*Vancouver Stock Exchange symbol*]
MGU	Midcourse Guidance Unit [*Navy*] (CAAL)
MGU	Military Government Unit
MGU	[*The*] Mobile & Gulf Railroad Co. [*Later, MG*] [*AAR code*]
MGU	Moscow State University (SAUO)
MGU	Moskovskiy Gosudarstvenniy Universitet [*Moscow State University*] [*Former USSR*] (MSC)
MGU	Most General Unifier (IDAI)
MGUN..........	Marine Gunner
M Gun Sgt...	Master Gunnery Sergeant (SAUO)
MGUS	Monoclonal Gammopathies of Undetermined Significance [*Medicine*] (DMAA)
MGV...........	Mechanically-Guided Vehicle
MGV...........	Miniature Gate Valve
MGV...........	Monogram Oil & Gas, Inc. [*Vancouver Stock Exchange symbol*]
MGVC	Manual Governing Valve Control [*Nuclear energy*] (NRCH)
MGVT..........	Mated Ground Vibration Test (NASA)
MGVT..........	Montgomery [*Vermont*] [*Seismograph station code, US Geological Survey*] (SEIS)
MGW	G. W. Murphy Industries, Inc. (SAUO)
MGW	Magnesium Sulfate, Glycerine, and Water (Enema) [*Medicine*]
MGW	Maximum Gross Weight (WDAA)
MGW	Midland Great Western (SAUO)
MGW	Mission Gross Weight
MGW	Morgantown [*West Virginia*] [*Airport symbol*] (OAG)
MGW	Morgantown, WV [*Location identifier*] [*FAA*] (FAAL)
MGWA	Marriage Guidance Western Australia
MGWR	Midland Great Western Railway [*British*] (ROG)
MGWS	Modular Guided Weapon System (MCD)
MGWU	Malta General Workers Union, Valetta (SAUO)
MGX...........	Moabi [*Gabon*] [*Airport symbol*] (OAG)
MGX...........	Mossimo, Inc. [*NYSE symbol*] (SAG)
MGXI	Micrografx, Inc. [*NASDAQ symbol*] (SAG)

M-GXT	Multistage Graded Exercise Test [*Cardiology*] (DAVI)
MGY............	Dayton, OH [*Location identifier*] [*FAA*] (FAAL)
MGY............	Mega-Dyne Industrial Corp. [*Vancouver Stock Exchange symbol*]
MGY............	Muggy (ABBR)
MGyn and Obs...	Master of Gynaecology and Obstetrics (SAUO)
MGYSGT	Master Gunnery Sergeant [*Marine Corps*]
MGZ...........	Maschinengewehr-Zieleinrichtung [*Machine-Gun Sighting Mechanism*] [*German military - World War II*]
MGZ...........	Mayaguez [*Diocesan abbreviation*] [*Puerto Rico*] (TOCD)
MGZ...........	Mergui [*Myanmar*] [*Airport symbol*] (OAG)
MGZF.........	Maschinengewehr-Zielfernrohr [*Machine-Gun Telescopic Sight*] [*German military - World War II*]
MH.............	Air-Cushion Vehicle built by Mitsubishi [*Japan*] [*Usually used in combination with numerals*]
MH.............	Fe3O4-Fe2O3 buffer (SAUS)
MH.............	[*A*] Grammar of Masoretic Hebrew [*A publication*] (BJA)
MH.............	Ha-Mo'atsah ha-Hakla'it (BJA)
MH.............	Harvard University, Cambridge, MA [*Library symbol*] [*Library of Congress*] (LCLS)
mh	Macao [*MARC country of publication code*] [*Library of Congress*] (LCCP)
MH.............	Magdalen Hospital (SAUO)
MH.............	Magnetic Head [*or Heading*]
MH.............	Magnetite-Hematite [*Geology*]
MH.............	Mail Handler [*Computer science*]
MH.............	Main Hatch
MH.............	Maintenance Handbook
MH.............	Maintenance Hemodialysis [*Nephrology*] (CPH)
MH.............	Makkabi Hazair (BJA)
MH.............	Malaysia Airlines [*Airline flight code*] (ODBW)
MH.............	Malaysian Airline System [*ICAO designator*] (AD)
MH.............	Malden Hospital [*Malden, MA*]
MH.............	Maleic Hydrazide [*Plant growth regulator*]
MH.............	Malignant Histiocytosis [*Medicine*]
MH.............	Malignant Hyperpyrexia [*Medicine*]
MH.............	Malignant Hypertension [*Medicine*] (DMAA)
MH.............	Malignant Hyperthermia [*Medicine*]
MH.............	Malt House
MH.............	Mammotropic Hormone [*Endocrinology*]
MH.............	Manhole (AAG)
MH.............	Man-Hour (MCD)
MH.............	Mannoheptulose (DB)
MH.............	Manual Hold [*Telecommunications*]
MH.............	Manufactured Housing (PA)
MH.............	Manufacturers Hanover Corp. (EFIS)
MH.............	Manufacturers Hanover Trust Co. (SAUO)
MH.............	Mare Humorum [*Sea of Moisture*] [*Lunar area*]
MH.............	Marital History
MH.............	Marshall Islands [*ANSI two-letter standard code*] (CNC)
M-H............	Martini-Henry [*Rifle*]
MH.............	Masonic Hall (ROG)
MH.............	Master Herbalist
MH.............	Master Hosts [*An association*] [*Defunct*] (EA)
MH.............	Master of Hamburgerology [*McDonald's Corp. Hamburger University*]
MH.............	Master of Harriers [*British*] (WDAA)
MH.............	Master of Health (GAGS)
MH.............	Master of Horticulture
MH.............	Master of Hounds [*British*]
MH.............	Master of Humanics
MH.............	Master of Humanities (GAGS)
MH.............	Master of Hygiene
MH.............	Master of the Horse [*British*] (ROG)
MH.............	Master of the Hunt
MH.............	Materials Handling (NATG)
MH.............	Maximum Height [*Ballistics*]
M-H............	McGraw-Hill (NITA)
MH.............	Mechanical Handling [*Describes type of produce; for example, MH-1 refers to a kind of tomato*]
MH.............	Medal of Honor [*Often erroneously called Congressional Medal of Honor*] [*Military decoration*]
MH.............	Medal of Honour (SAUO)
MH.............	Medial Hypothalamus [*Medicine*] (DMAA)
MH.............	Medical History
MH.............	Medium Power Homing (PIPO)
MH.............	Megahertz [*Megacycles per second*] [*See also MCPS, MCS, MC/S, MHZ*] (NATG)
Mh	Mehri (BJA)
MH.............	Melanophore Hormone [*Also, MSH*] [*Endocrinology*]
MH.............	Melanophore-Stimulating Hormone [*Medicine*] (DMAA)
MH.............	Mended Hearts (EA)
MH.............	Menstrual History [*Medicine*]
MH.............	Mental Health
MH.............	Mental Hygiene (DMAA)
MH.............	Mentally Handicapped (AIE)
MH.............	Merchants Haulage (DS)
MH.............	Mercurihematoporphyrin [*Pharmacology*]
MH.............	Meristem Height [*Botany*]
MH.............	MeSH Heading [*Online database field identifier*]
MH.............	Message Handler [*Computer science*]
MH.............	Metal Halide (MCD)
M/H............	Meters per Hour
M/H............	Microcytic/Hypochromic [*Anemia*] [*Hematology*] (DAVI)
MH.............	Microhematuria [*Medicine*]
mH.............	Microhenry
MH.............	Middlesex Hussars (Duke of Cambridge's) [*British military*] (DMA)

MH	Migraine Headache (MELL)
M/H	Miles per Hour [*Also, MPH*]
MH	Military History (AABC)
MH	Military Hospital (ADA)
mh	Millihenry (AEBE)
mH	Millihenry (GPO)
mH	Millihour [*One-thousandth of an hour*] (AAG)
MH	Minehunter (SAUS)
MH	Ministry of Health [*British*]
MH	Ministry of Housing (SAUO)
M-H	Minneapolis-Honeywell Regulator Co. [*Later, HON*]
MH	Miscellaneous Hardware
MH	Mishnaic Hebrew [*Language, etc.*] (BJA)
MH	Mitsubishi Heavy Industries Ltd. [*Japan*] [*ICAO aircraft manufacturer identifier*] (ICAO)
MH	Mobile High-Power [*Reactor*] [*Proposed*] (NRCH)
MH	Mobile Home (WGA)
MH	Mobile Host (SAUS)
MH	Mobility Haiti (EA)
MH	Modified Huffman (SAUO)
MH	Moist Heat (STED)
MH	Molting Hormone [*Endocrinology, entomology*]
MH	Monosymptomatic Hypochondriasis [*Medicine*] (DMAA)
MH	Morgagni Hernia [*Medicine*] (MELL)
MH	Most High [*Freemasonry*]
MH	Most Honorable
MH	Mostly Harmless (SAUS)
MH	Mount Hood Railway Co. [*AAR code*]
M-H	Mueller-Hinton [*Agar*] [*Microbiology*]
MH	Mulberry Heart (OA)
MH	Multihandicapped
MH	Multiple Handicapped (STED)
MH	Murine Hepatitis
MH	Music Hall [*Record label*]
MH	Mutant Hybrid [*Medicine*] (DMAA)
MH	Muzzle Hatch
MH	Myocardial Hypertrophy [*Medicine*] (MELL)
MH	Myohyoid [*Medicine*] (DMAA)
MH2	Mary Hartman, Mary Hartman [*Initialism is shortened form of television program title*] [*Also, M²H²*]
MHA	Canadian Malignant Hyperthermia Association (SAUO)
MHA	Hamline University, St. Paul, MN [*OCLC symbol*] (OCLC)
MH-A	Harvard University, Arnold Arboretum, Cambridge, MA [*Library symbol*] [*Library of Congress*] (LCLS)
MHa	Haverhill Public Library, Haverhill, MA [*Library symbol*] [*Library of Congress*] (LCLS)
MHA	Machinery Haulers Association (SAUO)
MHA	Machinery Haulers Association Agent, Saint Paul MN [*STAC*]
MHA	Madonna House Apostolate [*Combermere, ON*] (EAIO)
MHA	Mahdia [*Guyana*] [*Airport symbol*] (OAG)
MHA	Maintenance Hazard Analysis (MCD)
MHA	Man-Hour Accounting (NVT)
MHA	Manila Hemp Association [*British*] (DBA)
MHA	Mansion House Association on Transport (SAUO)
MHA	Mansion House Association on Transport, Inc. [*British*] (BI)
MHA	Marine Historical Association [*Later, MSM*] (EA)
MHA	Masonry Heather Association of North America (NTPA)
MHA	Master in Health Care Administration (CPGU)
MHA	Master of Health Administration
MHA	Master of Hospital Administration
MHA	Material Handling Area
MHA	Maximum Hypothetical Accident [*Nuclear energy*] (IEEE)
MHA	Mean Horizontal Acceleration
MHA	Meat Hygiene Authority [*Australia*]
MHA	Medal for Humane Action [*Berlin Airlift, 1948-9*] [*Military decoration*]
MHA	Medical Hospitals Association (SAUO)
MHA	Member of House of Assembly [*British*]
MHA	Mennonite Health Assembly (SAUO)
MHA	Mennonite Health Association (EA)
MHA	Mental Health Abstracts [*Database*] [*IFI/Plenum Data Co.*] [*Information service or system*] (CRD)
MHA	Mental Health Administration [*Later, ADAMHA*]
MHA	Mental Health Analysis [*Psychology*] (AEBS)
MHA	Mental Health Association [*Later, NMHA*] (EA)
MHA	Mental Health Authority (NADA)
MHA	Mental Hospitals Association (SAUO)
MHA	Mervyn Hughes Associates Ltd. (SAUO)
MHA	Methemalbumin [*Medicine*] (MAE)
MHA	Methionine Hydroxy Analog [*Poultry feed*]
MHA	Methodist Homes for the Aged [*British*] (BI)
MHA	Metlakatla Housing Authority (SAUO)
MHA	Michigan Health & Hospital Association (SAUO)
MHA	Microangiopathic Hemolytic Anemia [*Medicine*]
MHA	Microhemagglutination [*Test for Syphilis*] [*Immunochemistry*] (DAVI)
MHA	Military Health Affairs (DOMA)
MHA	Minehunter, Auxiliary [*Navy symbol*] [*Obsolete*]
MHA	Minimum Holding Altitude [*Aviation*]
MHA	Ministry of Home Affairs (SAUO)
MHA	Mixed Hemadsorption Assay [*Clinical chemistry*]
MHA	Modified Handling Authorized [*Air Force*]
MHA	Mormon History Association (EA)
MHA	Mountain High Aviation [*ICAO designator*] (FAAC)
MHA	Mueller Hinton Agar [*Microbiology*] (OA)
MHA	Multiple Handicapped Association (NADA)

MHA	Multiple Hazard Analysis [*Department of Emergency Management*] (DEMM)
MHA	Multiple Headset Adapter [*Aerospace*] (NAKS)
MHA	Mutual Households Associations Ltd. [*British*] (BI)
MH-AA	Harvard University, Afro-American Studies, Lamont Undergraduate Library, Cambridge, MA [*Library symbol*] [*Library of Congress*] (LCLS)
MHAC	Man-Hour Accounting Card
MHAC	Mental Health Act Commission (SAUO)
MHAC	Midwest Hispanic AIDS Coalition (SAUO)
MHAC	Multifrequency High-Gain Antenna Configuration (SSD)
MHadP	Porter-Phelps-Hunting Foundation, Hadley, MA [*Library symbol*] [*Library of Congress*] (LCLS)
MH-AH	Harvard University, Andover-Harvard Theological Library, Cambridge, MA [*Library symbol*] [*Library of Congress*] (LCLS)
MHAM	Amapala [*Honduras*] [*ICAO location identifier*] (ICLI)
MHAM	Multiple Hamartoma [*Medicine*] (DMAA)
MHAMS	Master of Historical Administration and Museum Studies (GAGS)
MHaNE	Northern Essex Community College, Haverhill, MA [*Library symbol*] [*Library of Congress*] (LCLS)
MHansAF	United States Air Force Research Library, Hanscom Air Force Base, Hanscom, MA [*Library symbol*] [*Library of Congress*] (LCLS)
MH-AO	Harvard University, Oakes Ames Orchid Library, Cambridge, MA [*Library symbol*] [*Library of Congress*] (LCLS)
MHAO	Mental Health Association of Oregon
MHAQ	Material Handling Association of Quebec (AC)
MHar	Brooks Free Library, Harwich, MA [*Library symbol*] [*Library of Congress*] (LCLS)
MH-Ar	Harvard University Archives, Cambridge, MA [*Library symbol*] [*Library of Congress*] (LCLS)
MHARCT	Mansion House Association on Railway and Canal Traffic (SAUO)
MH-AS	Harvard University, George R. Agassiz Station, Cambridge, MA [*Library symbol*] [*Library of Congress*] (LCLS)
MHAS	Man-Hour Accounting System (DNAB)
MHathD	Danvers State Hospital, Hathorne, MA [*Library symbol*] [*Library of Congress*] (LCLS)
MHA-TP	Microhemagglutination Assay Treponema Pallidum [*Immunochemistry*]
MHA-TP	Micro-Hemagglutination-Treponema pallidum (SAUS)
MHAU	Major Hazards Assessment Unit (HEAS)
MHAUS	Malignant Hyperthermia Association of the United States (EA)
MHAWA	Master Hairdressers' Association of Western Australia
MHB	Maintenance Handbook
MHB	Mary Hardin-Baylor College, Belton, TX [*OCLC symbol*] (OCLC)
MHB	Master Horizontal Bomber
MHB	Material Handling Bureau (SAUO)
MHB	Maximum Hospital Benefit [*Medicine*] (DMAA)
MHb	Medial Habenular [*Neuroanatomy*]
MHB	Mental Health Branch (SAUO)
MHB	Methemoglobin [*Immunochemistry*] (DAVI)
MHb	Methemoglobin [*Biochemistry, medicine*]
MHB	Military History Branch [*USMACV*]
MHB	Mine-Hauling Bogie [*Mining engineering*]
MHB	Mueller-Hinton Base (DMAA)
MHB	Mueller-Hinton Broth [*Cell growth medium*]
MHb	Myohemoglobin [*Hematology*]
MH-BA	Harvard University, Graduate School of Business Administration, Boston, MA [*Library symbol*] [*Library of Congress*] (LCLS)
MHBA	Medical-Dental-Hospital Bureaus of America (SAUO)
MHBA	Morgan Horse Breeders Association [*Defunct*] (EA)
MH-BH	Harvard University, Blue Hill Meteorological Observatory, Cambridge, MA [*Library symbol*] [*Library of Congress*] (LCLS)
MH-BL	Harvard University, Biological Laboratories, Cambridge, MA [*Library symbol*] [*Library of Congress*] (LCLS)
MH-BM	Harvard University, George David Birkhoff Mathematics Library, Cambridge, MA [*Library symbol*] [*Library of Congress*] (LCLS)
MHBM	Modern Heavy Ballistic Missile (ADA)
MHBN	Mothers' Home Business Network (EA)
MH-BR	Harvard University, Busch-Reisinger Museum of Germanic Culture, Cambridge, MA [*Library symbol*] [*Library of Congress*] (LCLS)
MH-BS	Harvard University, Biochemical Sciences Tutorial Library, Cambridge, MA [*Library symbol*] [*Library of Congress*] (LCLS)
MHBSS	Modified Hank's Balanced Salt Solution [*Cell culture*]
MHC	Coastal Minehunter (SAUS)
MH-C	Harvard University, Chemistry Library, Cambridge, MA [*Library symbol*] [*Library of Congress*] (LCLS)
MHC	Historical Committee of the Mennonite Church (EA)
MHC	MAD [*Magnetic Anomaly Detector*] Hunting Circle (NVT)
MHC	Madras High Court Reports [*India*] [*A publication*] (DLA)
MHC	Major Histocompatibility Complex [*Immunology*]
MHC	Managed Health Care (SAUO)
MHC	Manipulator Hand Controller [*Aerospace*] (NAKS)
MHC	Manipulator Handset Controller (MCD)
MHC	Manufactured Home Communities [*NYSE symbol*] (SPSG)
MHC	Manufacturers Hanover Corp. (EFIS)
MHC	Mars Hill College [*North Carolina*]
MHC	Mary Holmes College, West Point, MS [*OCLC symbol*] (OCLC)
MHC	Mason & Hanger Corp.
MHC	Material Handling Crane [*Autocrane*] (MCD)
MHC	Materials Handling Crane (SAUS)
MHC	Mauritian Housing Corporation (SAUO)
MHC	Mean Horizontal Candle [*Aerospace*]
MHC	Mechanical-Hydraulic Control [*Nuclear energy*] (NRCH)
MHC	Mediterranean Committee for Thalassemia (SAUO)
MHC	Mental Health Care [*British*] (DAVI)

MHC............	Mental Health Center (MEDA)
MHC............	Mental Health Clinic (DAVI)
MHC............	Mental Health Commission (SAUO)
MHC............	Mental Health Course [British]
MHC............	Mild Hydrocracking [Petroleum technology]
MHC............	Minehunter, Coastal [Navy symbol]
MHC............	Mobile Housing Carriers Conference Inc., Arlington VA [STAC]
MHC............	Modified Huffman Coding (NITA)
MHC............	Moisture Holding Capacity
MHC............	Morgan Horse Club [Later, American Morgan Horse Association] (EA)
MHC............	Morris Harvey College [West Virginia]
MHC............	Mount Hamilton [Lick Observatory] [California] [Seismograph station code, US Geological Survey] (SEIS)
MHC............	Mount Holyoke College [South Hadley, MA]
MHC............	Multiphasic Health Checkup [Medicine] (AAMN)
MHC............	Myosin Heavy Chain [Muscle biology]
MHCA	Catacamas [Honduras] [ICAO location identifier] (ICLI)
MHCA	Master of Health Care Administration (GAGS)
MHCA	Tumor Histocompatibility Antigen [Medicine] (MELL)
MHC & W ...	Mississippi, Hill City & Western Railroad
MHCAT	Minehunter Catamaran [Military]
MHCC	Mobile Housing Carriers Conference [Defunct] (EA)
MHCC	Multipak Heliax Coaxial Cable
MH/CD	Mental Health/Chemical Dependency
MH-CE	Harvard University, Commission on Extension Courses, Cambridge, MA [Library symbol] [Library of Congress] (LCLS)
MH-CE	Materials Handling and Construction Equipment (DNAB)
MHCG	Comayagua [Honduras] [ICAO location identifier] (ICLI)
MHCH	Choluteca [Honduras] [ICAO location identifier] (ICLI)
MH-CI	Harvard University, Center for International Affairs, Semitic Museum, Cambridge, MA [Library symbol] [Library of Congress] (LCLS)
MHCI	Master of Human-Computer Interaction [PGP]
MHCI	Member of the Hotel and Catering Institute (SAUO)
MHCIMA	Member of the Hotel, Catering, and Institutional Management Association [British] (DBQ)
MHC/I/O	Minehunter, Coastal/Inshore/Offshore (MILB)
MH-CL	Harvard University, Career Reference Library, Cambridge, MA [Library symbol] [Library of Congress] (LCLS)
MH-CM	Harvard University, Child Memorial and English Tutorial Library, Cambridge, MA [Library symbol] [Library of Congress] (LCLS)
MHCO	Marquette & Huron Mountain Railroad Co., Inc. [AAR code]
MHCO	Mine-Hunting Control Officer (NATG)
MHCO	Moore-Handley, Inc. [Birmingham, AL] [NASDAQ symbol] (NQ)
MHCOA	Motor, Hearse, and Car Owners Association (EA)
MH-CP	Harvard University, Center for Population Studies, Boston, MA [Library symbol] [Library of Congress] (LCLS)
MHCP	Mean Horizontal Candlepower
MHCR	Madras High Court Reports [India] [A publication] (DLA)
MH-CS	Harvard University, Godfrey Lowell Cabot Science Library, Cambridge, MA [Library symbol] [Library of Congress] (LCLS)
MHCS	Mental Hygiene Consultation Service
MHCS	Multicultural Health Communication Service (SAUO)
M/hct	Microhematocrit [Clinical chemistry]
MHCT..........	Modified Human Calcitonin (DB)
MHCT..........	Puerto Castilla [Honduras] [ICAO location identifier] (ICLI)
MHCU	Mental Health Care Unit [Medicine]
MHD	Magnetohydrodynamic [Simulation] [Marine science] (OSRA)
MHD	Magnetohydrodynamics [Electric power]
MHD	Maintenance Hemodialysis [Medicine] (DMAA)
MHD	Mashhad [Iran] [Airport symbol] (OAG)
MHD	Master of Human Development (PGP)
MHD	Masthead (MSA)
MHD	Mean Hemolytic Dose [Pharmacology] (MAE)
MHD	Mechanized Hebrew Dictionary [A publication] (BJA)
MHD	Medical and Health Department (SAUO)
MHD	Medical Holding Detachment
MHD	Medium Hard Drawn (MSA)
MHD	Mental Health Department [Medicine]
MHD	Mental Health Digest
MHD	Meshed [Iran] [Airport symbol] (AD)
MHD	Meter Heading Differential
MHD	Military History Detachment
MHD	Minimal Hemolytic Dose [Medicine] (LDT)
MHD	Minimum Hamming Distance [Computer science]
MHD	Minimum Hemolytic Dilution [Medicine] (DMAA)
MHD	Minimum Hemolytic Dose
MHD	Movable Head Disc (NITA)
MHD	Moving Head Disk [Computer science] (TEL)
MHD	Multihead Disk (NASA)
MHD	Multiple Head Disc (NITA)
MHDA	Modified High-Density Acid (MCD)
MHDA	Multiplex Heteroduplex Analysis [Medicine] (MELL)
MHDC	Magnetohydrodynamic Conversion [Nuclear energy] (NRCH)
MHDDE	Medium Heavy-Duty Diesel Engine [Motor vehicle specifications]
MHDDV	Medium Heavy-Duty Diesel Vehicle (EPAT)
MHDF	Medium- and High-Frequency Direction-Finding Station
MHDG	Magnetohydrodynamic Generator (PDAA)
MHDI	Morgan Horse Development Institute [Defunct] (EA)
MH-DJ	Harvard University, Documentation Center on Contemporary Japan, Cambridge, MA [Library symbol] [Library of Congress] (LCLS)
MHDL	Magnetohydrodynamic LASER (PDAA)
MHDL	Microwave Hardware Design Language
MHDNA........	Mobile Home Dealers National Association [Defunct]
MH-DO........	Harvard University, Harvard University Development Office, Cambridge, MA [Library symbol] [Library of Congress] (LCLS)
MHDPA	Monohexadecylphosphoric Acid [Organic chemistry]
MHDSRIP	May His Departed Soul Rest in Peace (BJA)
MHDU	Medical Hemodialysis Unit [Nephrology] (DAVI)
MHE...........	Maintenance and Handling Equipment
MHE...........	Manufactured Home Estates
MHE...........	Mass Health & Education Tax-Exempt [AMEX symbol] (SPSG)
MHE...........	Mass Hlth & Edu Tax-Exempt Tr [AMEX symbol] (TTSB)
MHE...........	Master of Health Education (GAGS)
MHE...........	Master of Higher Education (GAGS)
MHE...........	Master of Highway Engineering (NADA)
MHE...........	Master of Home Economics (GAGS)
MHE...........	Master of Home Economics Engineering (NADA)
MHE...........	Master of Human Ecology (PGP)
MHE...........	Materials Handling Equipment [Military] (AFM)
MHE...........	Materiel Handling Equipment [Army] (INF)
MHE...........	Mean Hook Extent (PDAA)
MHE...........	Mechanical Handling Equipment (MCD)
MHE...........	Mental Health Enquiry [Medical/computing registers] [British]
MHE...........	Message Handling Element (SAUO)
MHE...........	Ministry of Higher Education (SAUO)
MHE...........	Missile Handling Equipment
MHE...........	Mitchell [South Dakota] [Airport symbol] (OAG)
MHE...........	Mitchell, SD [Location identifier] [FAA] (FAAL)
MHE...........	Multiple Headspace Extraction [Analytical chemistry]
MHE...........	Munitions Handling Equipment (MCD)
MHE...........	Muzzle Hatch Electrical
MHE...........	Myddleton Hotels & Estates Limited (SAUO)
MH-EA	Harvard University, East Asian Research Center, Cambridge, MA [Library symbol] [Library of Congress] (LCLS)
MHEA.........	Material Handling Engineers Association (SAUO)
MHEA.........	Mechanical Handling Engineers' Association [British] (BI)
MHealthAdmin...	Master of Health Administration (ADA)
MHEANA	Masonic Homes Executives' Association of North America (EA)
MH-EB	Harvard University, Oakes Ames Library of Economic Botany, Cambridge, MA [Library symbol] [Library of Congress] (LCLS)
MHeb..........	Middle Hebrew [Language, etc.] (BJA)
MH Ec	Master of Home Economics (PGP)
MHEC.........	Midwestern Higher Education Commission
MHEC.........	Muzzle Hatch Electrical Control
MH-Ed	Harvard University, Graduate School of Education, Cambridge, MA [Library symbol] [Library of Congress] (LCLS)
MHEd.........	Master of Health Education (GAGS)
MHEd.........	Master of Higher Education
MHEDA	Material Handling Equipment Distributors Association (EA)
MHEE.........	Master of Home Economics Education (NADA)
MHEEd........	Master of Home Economics Education (NADA)
MHEF.........	Milton H. Erickson Foundation (EA)
MHEG.........	Multimedia and Hypermedia Expert Group (TELE)
MHEO.........	Migrant Health Education Officer [Australia]
MHEOWS.....	Multicolored High Energy Outgoing Wavefront Sampling (ACAE)
MH-ER	Harvard University, East Asian Studies Reading Room, Cambridge, MA [Library symbol] [Library of Congress] (LCLS)
MH-ES	Harvard University, Center for European Studies, Cambridge, MA [Library symbol] [Library of Congress] (LCLS)
MHET.........	Monolithic Hot Electron Transistor (NITA)
MHEX.........	Methohexital [An anesthetic]
MH-F	Harvard University, Farlow Reference Library, Cambridge, MA [Library symbol] [Library of Congress] (LCLS)
M-H-F	Massey-Harris-Ferguson (SAUO)
MHF...........	Master History File
MHF...........	Medium-High Frequency
MHF...........	Mental Health Foundation (SAUO)
MHF...........	Meridian House Foundation [Later, MHI]
MHF...........	Message Handling Facility (SAUO)
MHF...........	Microsillon et Haute-Fidelite [Record label] [France]
MHF...........	Mirror Furnace (SAUS)
MHF...........	Mixed Hydrazine Fuel
MHF...........	Municipal High Care [NYSE symbol] (TTSB)
MHF...........	Municipal High Income Fund, Inc. [NYSE symbol] (CTT)
MHF...........	Muni High Income Fund (EFIS)
MHF...........	Myosin Head Fragment [Biochemistry]
MHF...........	Smith Point, TX [Location identifier] [FAA] (FAAL)
MH-FA	Harvard University, Fine Arts Library, Cambridge, MA [Library symbol] [Library of Congress] (LCLS)
MHFA.........	Multiple Conductor, Heat and Flame Resistant, Armor [Cable]
MHFB.........	Mental Health Film Board (EA)
MHFC.........	Merle Haggard Fan Club (EA)
MHFES........	Materials Handbook for Fusion Energy Systems (SAUO)
MH/FH	Man-Hours per Flying Hour [Air Force] (DNAB)
MHFNZ	Mental Health Foundation of New Zealand (SAUO)
MHFPR	Maximum Hypothetical Fission Product Release [Nuclear energy] (NRCH)
MHFR	Maximum Hypothetical Fission Product Release [Nuclear energy] (NRCH)
MHF(V)........	Mental Health Foundation (Victoria) [Australia]
MHFWPR.....	Mental Health Fieldwork Performance Report [Occupational therapy]
MH-G	Harvard University, Gray Herbarium, Cambridge, MA [Library symbol] [Library of Congress] (LCLS)
MHG..........	Mahogany (WGA)
MHG..........	Malartic Hygrade Gold Mines Ltd. (MHDW)
MHG..........	Mannheim [Germany] [Airport symbol] (OAG)
MHG..........	MDS Health Group Ltd. [Toronto Stock Exchange symbol]
MHG..........	Message Header Generator (PDAA)

MHG	Metropolitan Health Group (DMAA)
MHG	Middle High German [*Language, etc.*]
MHG	Midrash ha-Gadol (BJA)
mHg	Millimeters of Mercury [*A measurement of pressure*] (MAE)
MHG	Miniature Hydrogen Generator
MHG	Modern High German [*Language, etc.*] (ROG)
MH-GG	Harvard University, Committee on Experimental Geology and Geophysics, Hoffman Laboratory, Cambridge, MA [*Library symbol*] [*Library of Congress*] (LCLS)
MH-GI	Harvard University, Hamilton A. R. Gibb Islamic Seminar, Cambridge, MA [*Library symbol*] [*Library of Congress*] (LCLS)
MH-GM	Harvard University, Gordon McKay Library, Cambridge, MA [*Library symbol*] [*Library of Congress*] (LCLS)
MH-GS	Harvard University, Geological Sciences Library, Cambridge, MA [*Library symbol*] [*Library of Congress*] (LCLS)
MH-H	Harvard University, Houghton Library, Cambridge, MA [*Library symbol*] [*Library of Congress*] (LCLS)
MHH	Mandala Holistic Health [*Defunct*] (EA)
MH-H	Mare Humorum-Helmet [*Lunar area*]
MHH	Marsh Harbour [*Bahamas*] [*Airport symbol*] (OAG)
MH-HD	Harvard University, History Department Library, Cambridge, MA [*Library symbol*] [*Library of Congress*] (LCLS)
MH-HF	Harvard University, Harvard Forest Library, Petersham, MA [*Library symbol*] [*Library of Congress*] (LCLS)
MHHFC	Machine and Hull History File Card (DNAB)
MH-Hi	Harvard University, Hilles Library of Radcliffe College, Cambridge, MA [*Library symbol*] [*Library of Congress*] (LCLS)
MHHI	Multihandicapped Hearing-Impaired
MH-HJ	Harvard University, Arnold Arboretum, Horticultural Library, Jamaica Plain, MA [*Library symbol*] [*Library of Congress*] (LCLS)
MH-HO	Harvard University, Lucien Howe Library of Ophthalmology, Boston, MA [*Library symbol*] [*Library of Congress*] (LCLS)
MH-HP	Harvard University, Center for Analysis of Health Practices, Cambridge, MA [*Library symbol*] [*Library of Congress*] (LCLS)
MHHPA	Methylhexahydrophthalic Anhydride [*Organic chemistry*]
MH-HS	Harvard University, History of Science Library, Cambridge, MA [*Library symbol*] [*Library of Congress*] (LCLS)
MHHS	Medal of Honor Historical Society (EA)
MHHW	Mean Higher High Water [*Tides and currents*]
MHHWS	Mean Higher High-Water Springs [*Tides and currents*]
MH-HY	Harvard University, Harvard-Yenching Library, Cambridge, MA [*Library symbol*] [*Library of Congress*] (LCLS)
MHHZO	Move High-to-High Zone (VLIE)
MHI	Malignant Histiocytosis of Intestine [*Medicine*] (DMAA)
MHI	Malone & Hyde, Incorporated (SAUO)
MHI	Manual Hit Indicator (SAUS)
MHI	Manufactured Housing Insitute (WPI)
MHI	Manufactured Housing Institute (EA)
MHI	Marine Hydrophysical Institute
MHI	Mashhad [*Iran*] [*Seismograph station code, US Geological Survey*] (SEIS)
MHi	Massachusetts Historical Society, Boston, MA [*Library symbol*] [*Library of Congress*] (LCLS)
MHI	Material Handling Institute (EA)
MHI	Material Hazard Index (AAEL)
MHI	Materials Handling Institute, Inc.
MHI	Meat Hygiene Inspector (GVA)
MHI	Mended Hearts, Inc. [*Affiliated with the American Heart Association*] (NRGU)
MHI	Mental Health Index (DMAA)
MHI	Mental Health Institute (OICC)
MHI	Mental Health Inventory (DMAA)
MHI	Meridian House International (EA)
MHI	Meridian International Center [*Washington, D.C.*] (EA)
MHI	Metal Hydrides Incorporated (SAUO)
MHI	Military Health Institute
MHI	Military History Institute [*Army*] (MCD)
MHI	Ministry of Health Inspectorate (SAUO)
MHI	Minor Head Injury (MELL)
MHI	Minority Health Initiative (SAUO)
mhi	misc.health.infertility newsgroup (SAUO)
MHI	Mitsubishi Heavy Industries
MHI	Mitsubishi Heavy Industries Ltd.
MHI	Morgan Hydrocarbons, Inc. [*Toronto Stock Exchange symbol*]
MHI	Morrison Health Care, Inc. [*NYSE symbol*] (SAG)
MHI	Morrison Management Specialists [*NYSE symbol*] (SG)
MHIA	Material Handling Industry Association (NTPA)
MHIA	Mitsubishi Heavy Industries America, Inc.
MHIBL	Mile High Intercollegiate Baseball League (PSS)
MH-IC	Harvard University, Collection of Historic Scientific Instruments Collection, Cambridge, MA [*Library symbol*] [*Library of Congress*] (LCLS)
MHIC	Islas Del Cisne O Santanilla [*Honduras*] [*ICAO location identifier*] (ICLI)
MH-ID	Harvard University, Harvard Institute for International Development, Cambridge, MA [*Library symbol*] [*Library of Congress*] (LCLS)
MHID	Medical and Health Information Directory [*A publication*]
MHIDAS	Major Hazard Incident Data Service [*Atomic Energy Authority*] [*British*] [*Information service or system*] (IID)
MHIDAS	Modular High Integration Distributed Architecture databus System (SAUS)
M Hi E	Master of Highway Engineering
M Hi Eng	Master of Highway Engineering
MHIFC	Michael Harding International Fan Club (EA)
MHIFM	Milton Helpern Institute of Forensic Medicine (EA)

MHII	Material Handling Institute Incorporated (SAUO)
MHILC	Hampshire Inter-Library Center, Inc., Amherst, MA [*Library symbol*] [*Library of Congress*] [*Obsolete*] (LCLS)
MHingM	Hingham Marine Museum, Hingham, MA [*Library symbol*] [*Library of Congress*] (LCLS)
MHIP	Missile Homing Improvement Program (DWSG)
MHISL	Mile High Intercollegiate Softball League (PSS)
MHJ	Microwave Hybrid Junction
MHJC	Mary Holmes Junior College (SAUO)
MHJU	Juticalpa [*Honduras*] [*ICAO location identifier*] (ICLI)
MHK	Manhattan [*Kansas*] [*Airport symbol*] (OAG)
MHK	Manhattan, KS [*Location identifier*] [*FAA*] (FAAL)
MHK	Master of Human Kinetics (GAGS)
MHK	Member of the House of Keys [*Isle Of Man*] [*British*]
MHK	Military History of Korea
MH/K	Mine Hunter/Killer [*Military*]
MHK	Mohawk Industries [*NYSE symbol*] (SG)
MHK	Morgan Stanley Group, Inc. [*AMEX symbol*] (SAG)
MH-KG	Harvard University, Kennedy School of Government, Cambridge, MA [*Library symbol*] [*Library of Congress*] (LCLS)
MH-KM	Harvard University, Kennedy Inter-Faculty Program in Medical Ethics, Cambridge, MA [*Library symbol*] [*Library of Congress*] (LCLS)
MHKVLY	Mohawk Valley (FAAC)
MHL	Hamline University, School of Law, St. Paul, MN [*OCLC symbol*] (OCLC)
MH-L	Harvard University, Law School, Cambridge, MA [*Library symbol*] [*Library of Congress*] (LCLS)
M (HL)	House of Lords' Appeals, in Macpherson's Court of Sessions Cases, Third Series [*1862-73*] [*Scotland*] [*A publication*] (DLA)
MHL	Manaus Harbour Limited (SAUO)
MHL	March Resources [*Vancouver Stock Exchange symbol*]
MHL	Marshall Islands [*ANSI three-letter standard code*] (CNC)
MHL	Marshall, MO [*Location identifier*] [*FAA*] (FAAL)
MHL	Master of Hebrew Letters (BJA)
MHL	Master of Hebrew Literature
MHL	Master of Humane Letters
MHL	Mast Hull Loop
MHL	Metastable Helium Level
MHL	Microprocessor Host Loader (TIMI)
MHL	Minimum Helium Loss [*System*]
MHL	Mission Hills Library (SAUO)
MHl	Morrison Health Care [*NYSE symbol*] (TTSB)
MHLA	McGraw-Hill Learning Architecture
MHLB	Ministry of Health, Legal Branch (SAUO)
MHLC	La Ceiba/Goloson Internacional [*Honduras*] [*ICAO location identifier*] (ICLI)
MHLC	Multidimensional Health Locus of Control [*Diagnostic scale*]
MHLE	La Esperanza [*Honduras*] [*ICAO location identifier*] (ICLI)
MHLF	Mutual Home Loan Funds (SAUO)
MHLG	Ministry of Housing and Local Government (SAUO)
MHLH	Myogenic Helix-Loop-Helix [*Genetics*]
MH-Li	Harvard University, Linguistics Library, Cambridge, MA [*Library symbol*] [*Library of Congress*] (LCLS)
MHLLDA	Mobile Home Landscapers and Landscape Designers Association (EA)
MH-Lm	Harvard University, Lamont Undergraduate Library, Cambridge, MA [*Library symbol*] [*Library of Congress*] (LCLS)
MHLM	San Pedro Sula/La Mesa Internacional [*Honduras*] [*ICAO location identifier*] (ICLI)
MHLN	McGraw-Hill Learning Network
MHLOS	Mega High Level Language Operations per Second (CCCA)
MHLP	Mental Health Law Project (EA)
MHLS	Metabolic Heat Load Simulator
MHLS	Mid-Hudson Library System [*Library network*]
MHLTA	Men's Hat Linings and Trimmings Association [*Defunct*] (EA)
MHLW	Major Hazards Legislation Working Party (HEAS)
MHLW	Mean Higher Low Water [*Tides and currents*]
MHLZO	Move High-to-Low Zone (VLIE)
MHM	Master of Hotel Management (PGP)
MHM	Mental Health Management [*AMEX symbol*] (SPSG)
MHM	Metal-Hydrogen-Metal [*Chemical bond*]
MHM	MHM Services [*AMEX symbol*] (SAG)
mhm	Mill Hill Missionaries (TOCD)
MHM	Mill Hill Missionaries [*Roman Catholic men's religious order*]
MHM	Minchumina, AK [*Location identifier*] [*FAA*] (FAAL)
MHM	Minimum Hardware Modification [*Aircraft landing*]
MHM	Mount Hope Mineral Railroad Co. [*Absorbed into Consolidated Rail Corp.*] [*AAR code*]
MHM	Muzzle Hatch Mechanical
MH/MA	Manhours/Maintenance Action (ACAE)
MHMA	Marcala [*Honduras*] [*ICAO location identifier*] (ICLI)
MHMA	Master House Movers' Association [*Australia*]
MHMA	Mobile Home Manufacturers Association [*Later, Manufactured Housing Institute*]
MHMB	Ministry of Health, Medical Branch (SAUO)
MHMC	Mental Health Materials Center (EA)
MHMC	Mercy Hospital and Medical Center (SAUO)
MHMC	Montefiore Hospital and Medical Center (SAUO)
MH-ME	Harvard University, Center for Middle Eastern Studies, Cambridge, MA [*Library symbol*] [*Library of Congress*] (LCLS)
MHME	More Heart More Edge [*Screenwriter's lexicon*]
MHMey	Meyerson [*M.H.*] & Co. [*Associated Press*] (SAG)
MHMeyer	Meyerson [*M.H.*] & Co. [*Associated Press*] (SAG)
MH-MH	Harvard University, John Peabody Monks Library, Cambridge, MA [*Library symbol*] [*Library of Congress*] (LCLS)

MH-ML .... Harvard University, Ticknor Library of Modern Languages, Cambridge, MA [*Library symbol*] [*Library of Congress*] (LCLS)
MHMP .... Moving Head Multiple Platter (RALS)
MH/MR .... Mental Health and Mental Retardation (DAVI)
MHMS .... Master of Health Management Systems (PGP)
MHMS .... Master of Human Movement Studies (ADA)
MHMS .... Material Handling and Management Society (EAIO)
MHMS .... Middlesex Hospital Medical School (SAUO)
MHMS .... Modular Hydrologic Modeling System [*Marine science*] (OSRA)
MHM Serv ... MHM Services [*Associated Press*] (SAG)
MH-Mu .... Harvard University, Music Library, Cambridge, MA [*Library symbol*] [*Library of Congress*] (LCLS)
MHMY .... Meyerson [*M.H.*] & Co. [*NASDAQ symbol*] (SAG)
MHMY .... M.H. Meyerson & Co. [*NASDAQ symbol*] (TTSB)
MHMYW ...... M H Meyerson & Co. Wrtt [*NASDAQ symbol*] (TTSB)
MHN .... Manhattan Mineral [*Vancouver Stock Exchange symbol*]
MHN .... Mannitol Hexanitrate [*Organic chemistry*]
MHN .... Massive Hepatic Necrosis [*Medicine*] (MAE)
MHN .... McGraw-Hill News [*Database*] (IT)
MHN .... Mental Health Net (SAUO)
MHN .... Morbus Hemolyticus Neonatorum [*Medicine*] (MELL)
MHN .... Moving Haven (SAUS)
MHN .... Mullen, NE [*Location identifier*] [*FAA*] (FAAL)
MHN .... Musical Heritage Network [*Internet resource*]
MHN .... Mylohyoid Nerve [*Medicine*] (MELL)
MHNAMT ..... Methyl(hydroxylnaphthalamino)mercaptotriazole [*Organic chemistry*]
MH-NE .... Harvard University, Near Eastern Languages and Literatures Library, Cambridge, MA [*Library symbol*] [*Library of Congress*] (LCLS)
MHNGS .... Marble Hill Nuclear Generating Station (NRCH)
MHNJ.......... Guanaja [*Honduras*] [*ICAO location identifier*] (ICLI)
MH-NJ .... Harvard University, Nieman Collection of Contemporary Journalism, Cambridge, MA [*Library symbol*] [*Library of Congress*] (LCLS)
MHNPS .... Marble Hill Nuclear Power Station (NRCH)
MHNV .... Nuevo Ocotepeque [*Honduras*] [*ICAO location identifier*] (ICLI)
MH-O .... Harvard University, Harvard College Observatory, Cambridge, MA [*Library symbol*] [*Library of Congress*] (LCLS)
MHO .... Manchester Resources Corp. [*Vancouver Stock Exchange symbol*]
MHO .... Medical House Officer (MELL)
MHO .... Microsomal Heme Oxygenase (DB)
MHO .... Millhouse Developments Ltd. [*British*] [*ICAO designator*] (FAAC)
MHO .... Minehunter Ocean [*Navy*] (ANA)
MHO .... M/I Schottenstein Homes, Inc. [*NYSE symbol*] (SPSG)
MHO .... Modern Human Origins
MHO .... Mohanbari [*India*] [*Airport symbol*] (AD)
MHO .... Mount Hopkins Observatory [*Later, FLWO*] [*Smithsonian Institution*] (GRD)
mho .... Reciprocal Ohm [*Unit of conductance*]
MHOA .... Mutual Help and Occupancy Agreement [*Department of Housing and Urban Development*] (GFGA)
MHOA .... Olanchito [*Honduras*] [*ICAO location identifier*] (ICLI)
M Ho Ec ..... Master of Household Economy
MHOF .... Mobile Home Owners Federation [*NFMHO*] [*Superseded by*] (EA)
MH/OH......... Man Hours per Operating Hour [*Maintenance*] (RDA)
MHoly.......... Holyoke Public Library, Holyoke, MA [*Library symbol*] [*Library of Congress*] (LCLS)
MHolyC........ Holyoke Community College, Holyoke, MA [*Library symbol*] [*Library of Congress*] (LCLS)
M Hor .... Master of Horticulture
MHort(RHS)... National Diploma in Horticulture (Royal Horticultural Society) [*British*] (DBQ)
MHortSc ...... Master of Horticultural Science
M Ho Sc ...... Master of Household Science
MHOTY .... My Hat's Off To You (VLIE)
MH-P .... Harvard University, Peabody Museum, Cambridge, MA [*Library symbol*] [*Library of Congress*] (LCLS)
MHp............. Harwich Port Library Association, Harwich Port, MA [*Library symbol*] [*Library of Congress*] (LCLS)
MHP............ Maclean Hunter Ltd. [*Toronto Stock Exchange symbol*]
MHP............ Master of Health Planning (ADA)
MHP............ Master of Health Professions (PGP)
MHP............ Master of Heritage Preservation (GAGS)
MHP............ Master of Historical Preservation (GAGS)
MHP............ Master of Humanities in Philosophy (PGP)
MHP............ McGraw-Hill Companies [*NYSE symbol*] (TTSB)
MHP............ McGraw-Hill, Inc. [*NYSE symbol*] (SPSG)
MHP............ Medium-High Pressure (MSA)
MHP............ Mental Health Project
MHP............ Mercurihydroxypropane [*Clinical chemistry*]
MHP............ Message Handling Processor
MHP............ Metabolic Heat Production [*Physiology*]
MHP............ Military Health Plan [*DoD*]
MHP............ Milli Hedef Partisi [*National Goal Party*] [*Turkish Cyprus*] [*Political party*] (PPE)
MHP............ Mississippi Highway Patrol (SAUO)
MHP............ Missouri Highway Patrol (SAUO)
MHP............ Mobile Host Protocol (SAUS)
MH-PA .... Harvard University, Littauer Library of the Kennedy School of Government, Cambridge, MA [*Library symbol*] [*Library of Congress*] (LCLS)
MHPA .... Palmerola [*Honduras*] [*ICAO location identifier*] (ICLI)
MH-PC .... Harvard University, Palaeography Library, Cambridge, MA [*Library symbol*] [*Library of Congress*] (LCLS)
MHPCC .... Maui High Performance Computer Center (SAUO)
MHPCC .... Maui High Performance Computing Center (SAUO)
MHPD .... Masonite Hydropress Die (MSA)

MHPE.......... Master of Health Professions Education (PGP)
MHPE.......... Methoxy-Hydroxyphenylethanol [*Organic chemistry*] (MAH)
MHPE.......... Progreso [*Honduras*] [*ICAO location identifier*] (ICLI)
MH PE & R... Master of Health, Physical Education, and Recreation
MHPE Conj... Methoxy-Hydroxyphenylethanol Conjugate [*Organic chemistry*] (DAVI)
MHPEd........ Master of Health Personnel Education (ADA)
MHPG......... (Methoxyhydroxyphenyl)ethyleneglycol [*Also, MOPEG*] [*Organic chemistry*]
MHPG Conj... Methoxyhydrophony Gylcol Conjugate [*Organic chemistry*] (DAVI)
MHPH......... Man-Hours per Flying Hour [*Air Force*] (AFIT)
MHPI .... Military Housing Privatization Initiative [*1996*]
MH-PL .... Harvard University, Milman Parry Collection of Oral Literature, Cambridge, MA [*Library symbol*] [*Library of Congress*] (LCLS)
MHPL.......... Puerto Lempira [*Honduras*] [*ICAO location identifier*] (ICLI)
MH-PO........ Harvard University, Personnel Office Library, Cambridge, MA [*Library symbol*] [*Library of Congress*] (LCLS)
MH-PP......... Harvard University, Public Policy Program, Cambridge, MA [*Library symbol*] [*Library of Congress*] (LCLS)
MH-PR........ Harvard University, Physics Research Library, Cambridge, MA [*Library symbol*] [*Library of Congress*] (LCLS)
MH-Ps .... Harvard University, Psychology Research Library, Cambridge, MA [*Library symbol*] [*Library of Congress*] (LCLS)
MHPU .... Puerto Cortes [*Honduras*] [*ICAO location identifier*] (ICLI)
MH-Pv .... Harvard University, Preservation Center, Cambridge, MA [*Library symbol*] [*Library of Congress*] (LCLS)
MHQ .... Mariehamn [*Finland*] [*Airport symbol*] (OAG)
MHQ .... Maritime Headquarters (NVT)
MHQ .... Mediterranean Headquarters (SAUO)
MH-R .... Harvard University, Russian Research Center, Cambridge, MA [*Library symbol*] [*Library of Congress*] (LCLS)
MHR .... Magnum Hunter Resources [*AMEX symbol*] (SG)
MHR .... Major Histocompatibility Region [*Immunology*]
MHR .... Major Homology Region [*Biochemistry*]
MHR .... Malignant Hyperthermia Resistance [*Medicine*] (DMAA)
MHR .... Man-Hour
MHR .... Master of Human Resources (GAGS)
MHR .... Maternal Heart Rate (MELL)
MHR .... Maximal Heart Rate (SAUS)
MHR .... Maximum Heart Rate
MHR .... McGraw-Hill Ryerson Ltd. [*Toronto Stock Exchange symbol*]
MHR .... Measurement Handicap Rule [*Sailing*]
MHR .... Medical Humanities Review [*A publication*] (BRI)
MHR .... Member of the House of Representatives
MHR .... Methemoglobin Reductase [*Hematology and laboratory*] (DAVI)
MHR .... Microwave Hologram RADAR
MHR .... Mile High Radar (SAUS)
MHR .... Miniature Helium Refrigerator
MHR .... Missile Hazard Report (AFM)
MHR .... Mount Hamilton Road [*California*] [*Seismograph station code, US Geological Survey*] (SEIS)
MHr .... Myohemerythrin [*Biochemistry*]
MHR .... Sacramento, CA [*Location identifier*] [*FAA*] (FAAL)
MHR .... United States Army Military History Institute, Carlisle Barracks, PA [*OCLC symbol*]
MH-RA .... Harvard University, Harvard Radio Astronomy Center, Fort Davis, TX [*Library symbol*] [*Library of Congress*] (LCLS)
MHRA .... Medical and Health Research Association of New York City (SAUO)
MHRA .... Modern Humanities Research Association, American Branch [*Defunct*] (EA)
MHRA .... Morab Horse Registry of America (EA)
MHRAC .... Mine Health Research Advisory Committee [*National Institute for Occupational Safety and Health*] [*Morgantown, WV*] (EGAO)
MH-RB........ Harvard University, Rubel Asiatic Research Bureau, Fogg Art Museum, Cambridge, MA [*Library symbol*] [*Library of Congress*] [*Obsolete*] (LCLS)
MHRB .... Mental Health Review Board [*Victoria, Australia*]
MH-RC........ Harvard University, Fred N. Robinson Celtic Seminar, Cambridge, MA [*Library symbol*] [*Library of Congress*] (LCLS)
MHRC .... Manitoba Health Research Council [*Canada*]
MHRD......... Master in Human Resource Department (PGP)
MHRF .... Mental Health Research Fund (SAUO)
MH-RI .... Harvard University, RISM-US Project Center, Cambridge, MA [*Library symbol*] [*Library of Congress*] (LCLS)
MHRI .... Mental Health Research Institute [*University of Michigan*] [*Research center*]
MHRI .... Miami Heart Research Institute (SAUO)
MHRIM .... Master of Hotel, Restaurant, and Institutional Management (PGP)
MHRIR .... Master of Human Resources and Industrial Relations (PGP)
MHRM .... Master of Human Resources Management (PGP)
MHRM .... Microcomputers in Human Resource Management [*Advanced Personnel Systems*] [*Information service or system*] (CRD)
MHROD....... Master of Human Resources and Organization Development (PGP)
MH-RP........ Harvard University, Robbins Library of Philosophy, Cambridge, MA [*Library symbol*] [*Library of Congress*] (LCLS)
MHRR .... MSAD Hardware Reflight Review (SAUS)
MHRS .... Magnetic Heading Reference System
MHRS .... Million Hours (SAUO)
MHRS .... Modified Hazard Ranking System (ABAC)
MHRST .... Medical and Health Related Sciences Thesaurus [*A publication*] (IEEE)
MHRT .... Mental Health Review Tribunal [*British*]
MHRTA .... Masters in Hotel, Restaurant, Tourism, and Administration (PGP)
MHRU .... Ruinas De Copan [*Honduras*] [*ICAO location identifier*] (ICLI)
MHRV .... Movement for Human Rights in Vietnam [*Defunct*] (EA)

MH-S	Harvard University, Statistics Library, Cambridge, MA [Library symbol] [Library of Congress] (LCLS)
MHS	Machined Hemispherical Shell
MHS	Magnetic Hand Scanner [Computer science] (ELAL)
MHS	Magnetic Heading System (AAG)
MHS	Magnetomotive Hammer System
MHS	Maher, Inc. [Toronto Stock Exchange symbol]
MHS	Mail Handling Service (SAUO)
MHS	Mail Handling System [Computer science]
MHS	Major Histocompatibility System [Immunology]
MHS	Malignant Hyperthermia Susceptible [Medicine]
MHS	Malignant Hypothermia Susceptible [Patients] [Emergency medicine] (DAVI)
MHS	Mammoth Hot Springs [Wyoming] [Seismograph station code, US Geological Survey] (SEIS)
MHS	Man-Hours per Sortie [Air Force] (AFIT)
MHS	Marine Hospital Service [Public Health Service]
MHS	Massachusetts Historical Society (SAUO)
MHS	Massachusetts Horticultural Society (SAUO)
MHS	Master Hotel Supplier [Educational Institute of the American Hotel and M otel Association] [Designation awarded by]
MHS	Master of Health Sciences (PGP)
MHS	Master of Health Services (GAGS)
MHS	Master of Hispanic Studies (PGP)
MHS	Master of Humane Studies (PGP)
MHS	Master of Human Services (GAGS)
MHS	Maximum Histalog Stimulation [Gastroenterology] (DAVI)
MHS	McMaster University Health Sciences Library [UTLAS symbol]
MHS	Measurement Handicapping System [Yacht racing]
MHS	Meat Hygiene Service (GVA)
MHS	Mechanical Handling System
MHS	Member of the Historical Society
MHS	Message Handling Service [Telecommunications] (PCM)
MHS	Message Handling System [Computer science]
MHS	Methylhydrazine Sulfate [Organic chemistry]
MHS	Microwave Humidity Sounder (EOSA)
M/H/S	Miles per Hour per Second
MHS	Military Health System (SAUO)
MHS	Military Heraldry Society (SAUO)
MHS	Military Historical Society [Defunct] (EA)
MHS	Ministry of Home Security [British]
MHS	Minnesota Historical Society, St. Paul, MN [OCLC symbol] (OCLC)
MHS	Missile Hazard Space (AFM)
MHS	Modular Hardware System [Computer science] (VLIE)
MHS	Modulated Hybrid System [Electric vehicles]
MHS	Moravian Historical Society (EA)
MHS	Morris High School (SAUO)
MHS	Mount Shasta, CA [Location identifier] [FAA] (FAAL)
MHS	Multiple Hospital System
MHS	Multiple Host Support
MHS	Musical Heritage Society [Commercial firm] (EA)
MHS	Sisters of the Most Holy Sacrament [Roman Catholic religious order]
MHSA	Master of Health Services Administration (GAGS)
MHSA	Master of Human Services Administration (PGP)
MH/SA	Mental Health/Substance Abuse
MH-SC	Harvard University, Herbert Weir Smyth Classical Library, Cambridge, MA [Library symbol] [Library of Congress] (LCLS)
MHSC	Manipulator Handset Controller (MCD)
MHSc	Master of Health Sciences (CMD)
MH Sc	Master of Home Science (SAUO)
MHSc	Master of Household Science (SAUO)
MHSC	Mental Health Study Center [National Institute of Mental Health] (GRD)
MHSCP	Mean Hemispherical Candlepower
MH-SD	Harvard University, Graduate School of Design, Cambridge, MA [Library symbol] [Library of Congress] (LCLS)
MHSDC	Multiple High-Speed Data Channel
MHSE	Master of Health Science Education (PGP)
MH-SF	Harvard University, Schering Foundation Library, Boston, MA [Library symbol] [Library of Congress] (LCLS)
MHSF	Metropolitan Hospital Sunday Fund (SAUO)
MHSH	Mental Health Services for the Homeless [Department of Health and Human Services] (GFGA)
MHSH	Mission Helpers of the Sacred Heart [Roman Catholic women's religious order]
MH-SI	Harvard University, Program for Science and International Affairs Library, Cambridge, MA [Library symbol] [Library of Congress] (LCLS)
MHSIP	Mental Health Statistics Improvement Program [Department of Health and Human Services] (GFGA)
MH-SL	Harvard University, Sanskrit Library, Cambridge, MA [Library symbol] [Library of Congress] (LCLS)
MHSLA	Michigan Health Sciences Libraries Association (SAUO)
MHSLN	Midwest Health Science Library Network [Library network]
MHSM	Mason & Hanger-Silas Mason Co., Inc. (RDA)
MHSM	Mental Hygiene Society of Maryland (SAUO)
MHSO	Masada, the Holocaust Survivors Organization (EA)
MHSO	Minehunter Sweeper Ocean [Navy] (ANA)
MH-SP	Harvard University, Science and Public Police Program Library, Cambridge, MA [Library symbol] [Library of Congress] (LCLS)
MHSP	Moving Head Single Platter (RALS)
MHSP	Municipal Health Services Program [Department of Health and Human Services] (GFGA)
MHSP	San Pedro Sula [Honduras] [ICAO location identifier] (ICLI)

MH-SR	Harvard University, Social Relations Library, Cambridge, MA [Library symbol] [Library of Congress] (LCLS)
MHSR	Santa Rosa De Copan [Honduras] [ICAO location identifier] (ICLI)
MHSS	Materials Handling Support System [Military] (AFM)
MHSS	Mental Health Special Interest Section [American Occupational Therapy Association]
MHSS	Message Handling System Service (NITA)
MHSS	Military Health Service System
MHSS	Ministry of Home Security Schools (SAUO)
MHSS(NI)	Ministry of Health and Social Services (Northern Ireland)
MHSSRI	Michigan Health and Social Security Research Institute [Detroit, MI] [Research center] (RCD)
MHST	Multiphasic Health Screen Test (DAVI)
MHSTB	Mental Handicap Staff Training Board [British]
MHSV	Multipurpose High-Speed Vehicle (MCD)
MHSZ	Santa Barbara [Honduras] [ICAO location identifier] (ICLI)
MHT	Maghemite, Inc. [Vancouver Stock Exchange symbol]
MHT	Main Himalayan Thrust [Geology]
MHT	Manchester [New Hampshire] [Airport symbol] (OAG)
MHT	Manchester, NH [Location identifier] [FAA] (FAAL)
MHT	Manhattan [Kansas] [Seismograph station code, US Geological Survey] [Closed] (SEIS)
MHT	Manhattan Industries, Inc. (SAUO)
MHT	Manufacturers Hanover Trust Co. [of Manufacturers Hanover Corp.] [Nickname: "Manny Hanny"]
MHT	Mean High Tide [Tides and currents]
MHT	Methyl(hydroxyethyl)thiazole [Organic chemistry]
MHT	Meyer Hydraulic Theory
MHT	Mild Heat Treatment (IEEE)
MHT	Missile Handling Trailer (AAG)
MHT	Missile Height Target [Military]
MHT	Museum of History and Technology [Smithsonian Institution]
MHTA	Molten High-Temperature Alloy
MHTC	Manufacturers Hanover Trust Company (SAUO)
MHTD	Missouri Highway and Transportation Department (SAUO)
MHTE	Tela [Honduras] [ICAO location identifier] (ICLI)
MHTF	Manhattan Homicide Task Force (SAUO)
MHTF	Manufactured Housing Task Force [Defunct] (EA)
MHTG	Marine Helicopter Training Group (NVT)
MHTG	Tegucigalpa/Toncontin Internacional [Honduras] [ICAO location identifier] (ICLI)
MHTGR	Modular High-Temperature Gas Reactor [Nuclear energy]
MHTJ	Trujillo [Honduras] [ICAO location identifier] (ICLI)
MHTL	Motorola High-Threshold Logic
MHTS	Main Heat Transport System [Nuclear energy] (NRCH)
MH/TS	Manhours/Troubleshooting Action (ACAE)
MHTS	Message Handling Test System [Computer science] (VLIE)
MHTS	Multiphasic Health Testing Services (DMAA)
MHTTA	Member of the Highway and Traffic Technicians Association [British] (DBQ)
MHTV	Manned Hypersonic Test Vehicle (MCD)
M Hu	Master of Humanities
MHU	Material Handling Unit (AFIT)
MHU	MIIX Group [NYSE symbol] (SG)
MHUC	Mid-Hudson Conference (PSS)
MHUD	Monocular Heads-Up Display [Aviation]
MHuGH	John H. Glenn High School, Huntington, NY [Library symbol] [Library of Congress] (LCLS)
M Hum	Master of Humanities
M Hum Svcs	Master of Human Services (PGP)
MH-UR	Harvard University, Ukrainian Research Institute Reference Library, Cambridge, MA [Library symbol] [Library of Congress] (LCLS)
MHV	Magnetic Heart Vector [Cardiology]
MHV	Manned Hypersonic Vehicle
MHV	Mean Horizontal Velocity
MHV	Mill Hill Virus [Medicine] (DB)
MHV	Mill Hill Vocabulary Scale [Test] (TMMY)
MHV	Mine Hunting Vessel (SAUS)
MHV	Miniature Homing Vehicle [Missile]
MHV	Mojave, CA [Location identifier] [FAA] (FAAL)
MHV	Mouse Hepatitis Virus
MHV	Murine Hepatitis Virus
MHVD	Marek's Herpesvirus Disease [Avian pathology] (MAE)
MHVDF	Medium-, High-, and Very-High-Frequency Direction-Finding Station
MHVPS	Manual High-Voltage Power Supply
MHW	H. W. Morgan, Los Angeles (SAUO)
MHW	Mean High Water [Tides and currents]
MHW	Medial Heel Wedge [Orthopedics] (DAVI)
MHW	Mental Health Worker (SAUO)
MHW	Merrill Lynch & Co. [AMEX symbol] (SAG)
MHW	Ministry of Health and Welfare [Japan] (ECON)
MHW	Morgan, H. W., Los Angeles CA [STAC]
MHW	Multihundred Watt
MH-WA	Harvard University, Charles Warren Center for Studies in American History, Cambridge, MA [Library symbol] [Library of Congress] (LCLS)
MHWI	Mean High-Water Lunitidal Interval [Tides and currents]
MHWL	Mean High Water Level (QUAC)
MHWLR	Mobile Hostile Weapon Locating RADAR (NATG)
MHWN	Mean High-Water Neap [Tides and currents]
MHW-RTG	Multi-Hundred-Watt Radioisotope Thermoelectric Generator (PDAA)
MHWS	Mean High-Water Springs [Tides and currents]
M Hx	Medical History (MAE)
MHX	MeriStar Hospitality [Formerly, CapStar Hotel] [NYSE symbol]
MHX	Mine Hunter Experimental

MHy	Hyannis Public Library, Hyannis, MA [*Library symbol*] [*Library of Congress*] (LCLS)
MHY	Managed High Income Portfolio [*NYSE symbol*] (SPSG)
MHY	Managed High Inc. Portfolio [*NYSE symbol*] (TTSB)
M Hy	Master of Hygiene
MHY	Morehead [*Papua New Guinea*] [*Airport symbol*] (OAG)
M Hyg	Master of Hygiene
MHyT	State Teachers' College, Hyannis, MA [*Library symbol*] [*Library of Congress*] [*Obsolete*] (LCLS)
MH-Z	Harvard University, Museum of Comparative Zoology, Cambridge, MA [*Library symbol*] [*Library of Congress*]
MHz	Megahertz [*Megacycles per Second*] [*See also MCPS, MCS, MC/S, MH*]
MHZ	Millihertz (WDAA)
MI	Lab. Miquel [*Spain*] [*Research code symbol*]
MI	Mach Indicated
MI	Machine Independent
MI	Machine Intelligence (RDA)
MI	Mackey International Airlines [*ICAO designator*] (AD)
MI	Mackey International, Inc. [*USA*] [*ICAO designator*] (OAG)
MI	Madras Infantry [*British*]
MI	Magazine Index [*Information Access Corp.*] [*Information service or system*] (IID)
MI	Magnetic Instability (ELAL)
MI	Maintenance Indicator (SAUO)
MI	Maintenance Instruction (AAG)
MI	Major Issue (MCD)
MI	Major Item [*Military*]
MI	Malachi [*Old Testament book*] (BJA)
MI	Malleable Iron
MI	Management Indicator (SAUO)
MI	Management Information (CAAL)
mi	Management Information (NAKS)
MI	Management Intern
MI	Management International Review (SAUO)
MI	Mandatory Investigation (HEAS)
MI	Manhattan Industries, Inc. (EFIS)
MI	Manual Individual [*Nuclear energy*] (NRCH)
MI	Manual Input [*Computer science*]
MI	Manufacturer Inquiry
MI	Manufacturing Index (MCD)
MI	Manufacturing Industries [*Department of Employment*] [*British*]
MI	Manufacturing Inspector (FAAC)
MI	Manufacturing Instruction (MSA)
MI	Marconi Industries [*General Electric Co.*] [*British*]
MI	Marconi Instruments Ltd. (SAUO)
MI	Mare Imbrium [*Sea of Showers*] [*Lunar area*]
MI	Mare Island, California [*Site of naval base*]
MI	Marginal Income [*Economics*]
MI	Mariana Islands (ACAE)
MI	Marine Insurance
MI	Marine Investigation (LAIN)
MI	Maritime Interdiction (SAUS)
MI	Market Identifiers [*Dun's Marketing Services*] [*Database*]
MI	Marketing Improvements Ltd. (SAUO)
MI	Market Investigation [*Army*]
MI	Marshall Indus [*NYSE symbol*] (TTSB)
MI	Marshall Industries [*NYSE symbol*] (SPSG)
MI	Marshall Islands
MI	Massa Intermedia (DB)
MI	Master Index
MI	Master Item (MSA)
MI	Master of Instruction (PGP)
MI	Master of Insurance (GAGS)
MI	Match Institute [*Defunct*] (EA)
MI	Material Inspection [*Navy*]
MI	Maturation Index (MAE)
MI	Mauritius Institute (SAUO)
MI	Measurement Incorporated (SAUO)
MI	Meat Inspection (SAUO)
MI	Meat Inspection Division [*of ARS, Department of Agriculture*]
MI	Mechanical Impedance
M/I	Mechanical Impulse (KSC)
MI	Mechanical Incontinence [*Medicine*] (MELL)
MI	Meconium Ileus [*Medicine*]
MI	Medical Illustrator
MI	Medical Improvement [*Social Security Administration*]
MI	Medical Inspection
MI	Medium Intensity (MSA)
MI	Melanophore Index [*Biology*]
MI	Mellon Institute [*Carnegie-Mellon University*] [*Research center*] (RCD)
MI	Meloidogyne incognita [*A nematode*]
MI	Melt Inclusions [*Geology*]
MI	Member of the Institute (SAUO)
MI	Member of the Institution (SAUO)
MI	Memorial Inscription
MI	Memory Interface [*Computer science*] (ELAL)
MI	Mensa International [*British*] (EAIO)
MI	Menstrual Induction [*Medicine*]
MI	Mental Illness
MI	(Mercaptoethyl)trimethylammonium Iodide [*Pharmacology*]
MI	Mercaptoimidazole [*Organic chemistry*] (MAE)
MI	Merit Increase (MHDW)
MI	Merritt Island [*Florida*] [*NASA*] (KSC)
MI	Mesha Inscription (BJA)
MI	Mesioincisal [*Dentistry*]
MI	Meso-Inositol [*or Myoinositol*] [*Organic chemistry*]
MI	Metabolic Index
MI	Metal Industries (SAUO)
MI	Metal-to-Insulator [*Transition*]
MI	Metastases below the Head and Neck [*Oncology*]
MI	Method Index [*British police term*]
MI	Methods Instruction (DNAB)
MI	Methylindole [*Organic chemistry*]
M-I	Metro-International Program Services of New York (EA)
MI	Mexican Isthmus [*Crude oil*]
MI	Mica [*A mineral*]
MI	Micah [*Old Testament book*]
MI	Michelin [*Tire casing code*]
MI	Michelson Interferometer (PDAA)
MI	Michigan [*Postal code*]
MI	Michigan Reports [*A publication*] (DLA)
Mi	Michigan State Library, Lansing, MI [*Library symbol*] [*Library of Congress*] (LCLS)
MI	Microbiological Inputs [*Canning*] (DICI)
MI	Microinch (IAA)
MI	Microinstruction [*Computer science*]
MI	Microwave Imager (ACAE)
MI	Micru International (EA)
MI	Middle Initial
MI	Middle Iron Age (BJA)
MI	Middlesex Regiment (SAUO)
MI	Migration Index [*Immunology*]
MI	Migration Inhibition [*Cytology*]
MI	Mil [*Former USSR*] [*ICAO aircraft manufacturer identifier*] (ICAO)
MI	Mile
mi	Mile
mi	Miles (SHCU)
MI	Military Institute
MI	Military Intelligence [*Army*]
MI	Military Internee
MI	Military Item
MI	Militia Mariae Immaculatae [*Militia of the Immaculate*] (EAIO)
MI	Mill
MI	Miller Integrator
MI	Mineral Insulated [*Cable*] (NRCH)
MI	Miniaturized Instrumentation (MCD)
M/I	Minimum Impulse (KSC)
MI	Mining Inspectorate (HEAS)
MI	Ministry of Information [*British*] [*World War II*]
MI	Minor (ROG)
MI	Minority Institution
MI	Minority Interest [*Business term*]
MI	Minute (ADA)
MI	Miscellaneous Income (MHDW)
MI	Mishnah [*Basis of the Talmud*] (BJA)
MI	Missed Interception [*Military*]
MI	Missile (CINC)
MI	Missile Industry (AAG)
MI	Missionary Internship [*An association*] (EA)
MI	Mission Independent [*NASA*]
MI	Mississippi [*Obsolete*] (ROG)
M-I	Missouri-Illinois Railroad (SAUO)
MI	Missouri-Illinois Railroad Co. [*AAR code*]
Mi	Mitomycin C [*Also, MMC, MTC*] [*Antineoplastic drug*]
MI	Mitosis Index [*Medicine*] (MELL)
MI	Mitotic Indices [*Cytology*]
MI	Mitral Incompetence [*Cardiology*]
MI	Mitral Insufficiency [*Cardiology*]
MI	Mixed Income
MI	Mobility Impairment (NVT)
MI	Mobility International (EA)
MI	Mode Indicator (HGAA)
MI	Moderately Included [*Colored gemstone grade*]
MI	Modification Instructions (KSC)
MI	Moment of Inertia
MI	Monetary Incentive
MI	Money Stock [*British*] (DCTA)
MI	Monitoring Information (NITA)
MI	Monitor Inspection (AFM)
MI	Monitor International (ASF)
MI	Mononucleosis Infectiosa [*Medicine*] (DB)
MI	Monument Inscription [*Genealogy*]
MI	Mooseheart, International
MI	Moose, International (EAIO)
MI	Morphologic Index [*Volume of trunk divided by length of limbs*]
MI	[*The*] Mortgage Index [*Hale Systems, Inc.*] [*Information service or system*] (CRD)
MI	Mortgage Insurance (EMRF)
MI	Motility Index [*Of intestine*] [*Gastroenterology*]
MI	Motion Imagery
MI	Motorola Interconnect [*Electronics*]
MI	Mounted Infantry
MI	Move In (WDMC)
MI	Movement Instruction [*British military*] (DMA)
MI	Multi-Industry Interest
MI	Multiple Instruction (HGAA)
MI	Multiple-Intelligences
MI	Murphy International Transport [*Commercial firm*] [*British*]

MI	Muskies, Inc. (EA)
MI	Mutual Inductance
MI	Mutual Interference
MI	Myocardial Infarction [Cardiology]
MI	Myo-Inositol [Chemistry] [Dietetics] (DAVI)
MI	Office of Minority Economic Impact (SAUO)
MI	Writ of Mandamus Will Issue [Legal term] (DLA)
mi²	Square Mile (CDAI)
MI³MS	Minolta Integrated Information and Image Management System [Optical disc] (IT)
MI5	Military Intelligence [State security] [British] (ODBW)
MI6	Military Intelligence [Espionage] [British] (ODBW)
MiA	Alma Public Library, Alma, MI [Library symbol] [Library of Congress] (LCLS)
MIA	AMI (Air Mercury International) [Belgium] [ICAO designator] (FAAC)
MIA	[An] Introduction to the Apocrypha [B. Metzger] [A publication] (BJA)
MIA	Malaysian Institute of Art (SAUO)
MIA	Management Information Analysis (SAUO)
MIA	Manager, Internal Audit (SAUO)
MIA	Manchester International Airport [British] (DS)
MIA	Manila International Airport
MIA	Manitoba Institute of Agrologists (SAUO)
MIA	Marble Institute of America (EA)
MIA	Marine Industries Association (SAUO)
MIA	Marine Insurance Act (MARI)
MIA	Maritime Information Association [British] (EAIO)
MIA	Master of Industrial Arts
MIA	Master of Intercultural Administration (PGP)
MIA	Master of Internal Affairs (NADA)
MIA	Master of International Administration (PGP)
MIA	Master of International Affairs
MIA	Meat Industry Authority (SAUO)
MIA	Medical Indemnity of America, Inc. (DHSM)
MIA	Medically Indigent Adult (MEDA)
MIA	Meetings Industry Association (COBU)
MIA	Member of the Institute of Arbitrators [British]
MIA	Member of the South African Institute of Architects (SAUO)
MIA	Metal Interface Amplifier
MIA	Methylisatoic Anhydride [Organic chemistry]
MIA	Metropolitan Intercollegiate Association (PSS)
MIA	Miami [Florida] [Seismograph station code, US Geological Survey] [Closed] (SEIS)
Mia	Miami Dolphins [National Football League] [1966-present] (NFLA)
MIA	Miami International Airport (SAUO)
MIA	Miami University, Oxford, OH [OCLC symbol] (OCLC)
MIA	Mica Industry Association [Defunct] (EA)
MIA	Military Inspection Agency (NATG)
MIA	Military Intelligence Agency (MCD)
MIA	Millinery Institute of America [Later, MIB] (EA)
MIA	Minimum IFR Altitude [FAA] (TAG)
MIA	Minimum Instrument Altitude [Aviation] (AFM)
MIA	Minor Acknowledgment (VLIE)
MIA	Missile Intelligence Agency (AABC)
MIA	Missing in Action [Military]
MIA	Mission Implementation Agreement (SAUO)
MIA	Mission-Independent Area [NASA]
MIA	Monoiodoacetic Acid [Organic chemistry]
MIA	Montgomery Improvement Association (SAUO)
MIA	Moore's Indian Appeals [A publication] (DLA)
MIA	Mouse in Able (SAUO)
MIA	"Mouse in Able" Program
MIA	Multiflex Interface Adapter
MIA	Multiplexer Interface Adapter (NASA)
MIA	Multiplex Interface Adapter (NASA)
MIA	Murrumbidgee Irrigation Area [Australia] (BARN)
MIA	Music Industries Association [British] (DBA)
MIA	Mutual Improvement Association [Mormon Youth Movement] (BARN)
MIA	Mythmaking in America [A publication]
MiAa	Ann Arbor Public Library, Ann Arbor, MI [Library symbol] [Library of Congress] (LCLS)
MIAA	Medical Industry Association of Australia
MIAA	Meetings Industry Association of Australia
MIAA	Member of the Incorporated Association of Architects and Surveyors [British] (DBQ)
MIAA	Member of the Institute of Affiliate Accountants (ADA)
MIAA	Member of the Institute of Automobile Assessors [British]
MIAA	Michigan Intercollegiate Athletics Association (PSS)
MIAA	Miniatures Industry Association of America (EA)
MIAA	Mutual Insurance Advisory Association [Defunct] (EA)
MiAaC	Concordia Lutheran College, Ann Arbor, MI [Library symbol] [Library of Congress] (LCLS)
MiAaE	Environmental Research Institute of Michigan, Ann Arbor, MI [Library symbol] [Library of Congress] (LCLS)
MiAaF	Gerald R. Ford Library, Ann Arbor, MI [Library symbol] [Library of Congress] (LCLS)
MiAaFL	Great Lakes Fisheries Laboratory, Ann Arbor, MI [Library symbol] [Library of Congress] (LCLS)
MIAAHC	Michigan Alliance Against Hate Crimes
MiAaI	Inter-University Consortium for Political and Social Research, Ann Arbor, MI [Library symbol] [Library of Congress] (LCLS)
MiAaK	KMS Fusion, Inc., Ann Arbor, MI [Library symbol] [Library of Congress] (LCLS)
MiAaP	Parke, Davis & Co., Research Library, Ann Arbor, MI [Library symbol] [Library of Congress] (LCLS)
MIA(APS)	Meat Inspectors' Association (Australian Public Service)

MIAASM	Member, International Academy of Aviation & Space Medicine (CMD)
MiAaW	Washtenaw County Library, Ann Arbor, MI [Library symbol] [Library of Congress] (LCLS)
MiAaWC	Washtenaw Community College, Ann Arbor, MI [Library symbol] [Library of Congress] (LCLS)
MIAB	Magnetically Impelled Arc Butt [Welding] (MCD)
MIAB	Modular Interchangeable Ambulance Body [Military] [British]
MiAC	Alma College, Alma, MI [Library symbol] [Library of Congress] (LCLS)
MIAC	Maintenance Information and Control [Environmental science] (COE)
MIAC	Manufacturing Industries Advisory Council (NADA)
MIAC	Material Identification Accounting Code
MIAC	Metals Information Analysis Center (IID)
MIAC	Minimum Automatic Computer (IEEE)
MIAC	Minnesota Intercollegiate Athletic Conference (PSS)
MIAC	Multipoint Interactive Audio-Visual Communication (NITA)
MIACF	Meander Inverted Autocorrelated Function
MIA-CHI	Miami-Chicago (SAUO)
MIACS	Manufacturing Information and Control System
MiAd	Adrian Public Library, Adrian, MI [Library symbol] [Library of Congress] (LCLS)
MiAdC	Adrian College, Adrian, MI [Library symbol] [Library of Congress] (LCLS)
MiAdL	Lenawee County Library, Adrian, MI [Library symbol] [Library of Congress] (LCLS)
MIADMB	Murrumbidgee Irrigation Area and Districts Management Board (SAUO)
MIADS	Map Information Assembly and Display System
MIADS	Minot Air Defense Sector [ADC]
MiAdS	Siena Heights College, Adrian, MI [Library symbol] [Library of Congress] (LCLS)
MIAE	Member of the Institute (or Institution) of Automobile Engineers (SAUO)
MIAE	Member of the Institution of Agricultural Engineers (SAUO)
MIAE	Member of the Institution of Automobile Engineers [British]
MIAEA	Member of the Institute of Automotive Engineer Assessors [British] (DBQ)
MIAEA	Member of the Institute of Automotive Engineers of America (SAUO)
MI Ae E	Member of the Institute of Aeronautical Engineers [British]
MIAEF	Missed Interception Due to Airborne Equipment Failure [Air Force]
MIAeS	Member of the Institute of Aeronautical Science (SAUO)
MIAeS	Member of the Institute of Aeronautical Sciences
MIAESR	Melbourne Institute of Applied Economic and Social Research [Australia]
MIAFTR	Motor Insurance Anti-Fraud and Theft Register [Database] [British]
MIAG	Management Information and Analysis Group (MCD)
MIAgrE	Member of the Institution of Agricultural Engineers [British]
MiAhO	Oakland Community College, Auburn Heights, MI [Library symbol] [Library of Congress] (LCLS)
MIAIF	Meteorological Information for Aircraft in Flight
MIAK	Methyl Isoamyl Ketone [Organic chemistry]
MIAL	Maine Image Analysis Laboratory (SAUO)
MiAlb	Albion Public Library, Albion, MI [Library symbol] [Library of Congress] (LCLS)
MiAlbC	Albion College, Albion, MI [Library symbol] [Library of Congress] (LCLS)
MiAlbW	Woodlands Library Cooperative, Albion, MI [Library symbol] [Library of Congress] (LCLS)
MiAld	Helena Township Public Library, Alden, MI [Library symbol] [Library of Congress] (LCLS)
MiAll	Allendale Township Library, Allendale, MI [Library symbol] [Library of Congress] (LCLS)
MiAlle	Allegan Public Library, Allegan, MI [Library symbol] [Library of Congress] (LCLS)
MiAllG	Grand Valley State College, Allendale, MI [Library symbol] [Library of Congress] (LCLS)
MiAlmo	Henry Stephens Memorial Library, Almont, MI [Library symbol] [Library of Congress] (LCLS)
MiAln	Alanson Public Library, Alanson, MI [Library symbol] [Library of Congress] (LCLS)
MiAlp	Alpena County Library, Alpena, MI [Library symbol] [Library of Congress] (LCLS)
MiAlpC	Alpena Community College, Alpena, MI [Library symbol] [Library of Congress] (LCLS)
MIALS	Medium Intensity Approach Light System [Aviation] (DA)
MIAM	Major Items Automated Management (AAGC)
MIAM	Mid-Am, Inc. [NASDAQ symbol] (NQ)
MIAMA	Member of the Incorporated Advertising Managers' Association [British] (DAS)
MIAME	Member of the Institute of Automotive Mechanical Engineers (ADA)
MIAMI	Metoprolol in Acute Myocardial Infarction [Cardiology study]
MIAMI	Microwave Ice Accretion Measurement Instrument (MCD)
MiamiCm	Miami Computer Supply Corp. [Associated Press] (SAG)
Miami LQ	Miami Law Quarterly [A publication] (DLA)
Miami L Rev	Miami Law Review [Florida] [A publication] (DLA)
Miami U (Ohio)	Miami University (Ohio) (GAGS)
MIAMP	Mid Am $1.8125 Cv'A'Pfd [NASDAQ symbol] (TTSB)
MiamSb	Miami Subs Corp. [Associated Press] (SAG)
MIAMSI	Mouvement International d'Apostolat des Milieux Sociaux Independants [International Movement of Apostolate in the Independent Social Milieux] [Vatican City] (EAIO)
MI & RR	Material Inspection and Receiving Report [Military] (KSC)
MI and SInst	Member of the Iron and Steel Institute (SAUO)
MIANG	Michigan Air National Guard (MUSM)
MIA-NY	Miami-New York (SAUO)

MIAO .... Master Index Assembly Outline [*Paper*]
MiAp .... Allen Park Public Library, Allen Park, MI [*Library symbol*] [*Library of Congress*] (LCLS)
MIAP .... International Movement for Peace Action (SAUO)
MIAP .... Member of the Institution of Analysts and Programmers [*British*] (DBQ)
MIAP .... Miami International Airport (SAUO)
MIAP .... Military Incentive Analysis Program (MCD)
MIAPD .... Mid-Central Air Procurement District
MiApDB .... Detroit Baptist Divinity School, Allen Park, MI [*Library symbol*] [*Library of Congress*] (LCLS)
MIAPL .... Master Index of Allowable Parts Lists [*Navy*]
MiApV .... United States Veterans Administration Hospital, Allen Park, MI [*Library symbol*] [*Library of Congress*] (LCLS)
MIAQ .... Music Industry Association of Queensland [*Australia*]
MIAR .... Microaddress Register [*Computer science*] (MHDI)
MI Arch ...... Master of Interior Architecture (PGP)
M I Arch Eng... Master of Interior Architectural Engineering
MiArm .... Armada Free Public Library, Armada, MI [*Library symbol*] [*Library of Congress*] (LCLS)
MIARS .... Maintenance Information Automated Retrieval System [*DoD*]
MIARS .... Microfilm Information and Retrieval System (DNAB)
MIAS .... Maintenance Information Authorizing System (MCD)
MIAS .... Major Item Automated System [*Army Materiel Command*] (AABC)
MIAS .... Marine Information and Advisory Service [*Institute of Oceanographic Sciences*] [*Databank*] [*British*] (IID)
MIAS .... Member of the Incorporated Association of Architects and Surveyors [*British*] (DBQ)
MIAS .... Member of the Institute of Aeronautical Science [*Later, MAIAA*]
MIAS .... Mobile Intelligence Analysis Center (ACAE)
MIAS .... Monroe Institute of Applied Sciences [*Later, TMI*] (EA)
MIAS .... Muhyiddin Ibn Arabi Society
MIASA .... Motorcycle Industry Association of South Australia
MIA-SFO ..... Miami-San Francisco (SAUO)
MIASI .... Moore Institute of Art, Science and Industry (SAUO)
MIAT .... Mean Interarrival Time (MHDB)
MIAT .... Member of the Institute of Asphalt Technology [*British*] (DBQ)
MiAt .... Montmorency County Public Library, Atlanta, MI [*Library symbol*] [*Library of Congress*] (LCLS)
MIAT .... Music Industry Association of Tasmania [*Australia*]
MIATA .... Murrumbidgee Irrigation Area Tourist Association [*Australia*]
MIATCO ...... Mid-America International Agri-Trade Council
MiAth .... Athens Township Library, Athens, MI [*Library symbol*] [*Library of Congress*] (LCLS)
MIA-TOR ..... Miami-Toronto (SAUO)
MiAu .... Augusta-Ross Township District Library (McKay Library), Augusta, MI [*Library symbol*] [*Library of Congress*] (LCLS)
MIAW .... Movie in a Window (SAUS)
MIAWA .... Member of the International Association of Wood Anatomists (SAUO)
MIAX .... McCulloch International Airlines [*Air carrier designation symbol*]
MIB .... Management Improvement Board (AAG)
MIB .... Management Information Base
MIB .... Management Information Block [*Computer science*]
MIB .... Management Information Database (CGWS)
MIB .... Manual Input Buffer [*Computer science*]
MIB .... Marine Index Bureau
MIB .... Maritime Index Bureau (NADA)
MIB .... Marketing of Investments Board [*Finance*] [*British*]
MIB .... Master Instruction Book
MIB .... Master Interconnect Board (MCD)
MIB .... Master of International Business (GAGS)
MIB .... Meat Inspection Branch (SAUO)
MIB .... Mechanized Infantry Battalion (MCD)
MIB .... Medical Impairment Bureau [*Insurance*]
MIB .... Medical Information Bureau [*Databank*]
MIB .... Medical Information Bus (RALS)
MIB .... Medium Industry Bank [*South Korea*] (IMH)
MIB .... Member Information Bank [*Computer science*] (ELAL)
MiB .... Men in Black [*UFO mythology*]
MiB .... Men in Black [*UFO mythology*]
MIB .... Mental Information Bureau (SAUO)
MIB .... Metal Information Bureau (SAUO)
MIB .... Mexican Investment Board [*Public relations and investor assistance*] [*Mexico*] (CROSS)
MIB .... Mezhdunarodnyi Investitsionnyi Bank [*International Investment Bank - IIB*] [*Moscow, USSR*] (EAIO)
MIB .... Michigan Inspection Bureau (SAUO)
MIB .... Michigan Intra-State Motor Tariff Bureau Inc., Lansing MI [*STAC*]
MIB .... Microinstruction Bus [*Computer science*]
MIB .... Midland Bancorp [*NYSE symbol*] (SPSG)
MIB .... Midland Bank PLC [*NYSE symbol*] (SAG)
MIB .... Military Intelligence Battalion (MCD)
MIB .... Military Intelligence Board (MCD)
MIB .... Military Intelligence Branch (SAUO)
MIB .... Military Intelligence Bureau (SAUO)
MIB .... Millinery Information Bureau (EA)
MIB .... Minimum Impulse BIT [*Binary Digit*] [*Computer science*] (MCD)
MIB .... Minot, ND [*Location identifier*] [*FAA*] (FAAL)
MIB .... Mint in the Box [*Doll collecting*]
MIB .... Missile Interceptor Base (SAUO)
MIB .... Missionary Information Bureau
MIB .... Missouri Inspection Bureau (SAUO)
MIB .... Montana Independent Bankers (TBD)
MIB .... Motor Inspection Building
MIB .... Motor Insurers' Bureau Ltd. [*British*] (ILCA)

MIB .... Mouvement d'Insoumission Bretonne [*Breton Insubordination Movement*] [*France*] (PD)
MIB .... Multibanc NT Financial Corp. [*Toronto Stock Exchange symbol*]
MIB .... Multilayer Interconnection Board
MIB .... Mustard Information Bureau (EA)
MIB .... Mutual Inductance Bridge
MiBa .... Bad Axe Public Library, Bad Axe, MI [*Library symbol*] [*Library of Congress*] (LCLS)
MIBA .... Malta International Business Authority (EY)
MIBA .... Master of International Business Administration (GAGS)
MIBA .... Member of the Institute of British Architects (ROG)
MIBA .... Metropolitan Intercollegiate Basketball Association (EA)
MIBA .... Miniere de Bakwanga [*Zaire*]
MIBA .... Missouri Independent Bankers Association (TBD)
MiBaC .... Battle Creek College (SAUS)
MiBal .... Pathfinder Community Library, Baldwin, MI [*Library symbol*] [*Library of Congress*] (LCLS)
MiBar .... Barryton Public Library, Barryton, MI [*Library symbol*] [*Library of Congress*] (LCLS)
MiBar .... Burr Oak Township Library, Burr Oak, MI [*Library symbol*] [*Library of Congress*] (LCLS)
MIBAR .... Multi-Channel In-Band Airborne Relay (PDAA)
MIBARS ...... Mechanized Infantry Battalion Air Reconnaissance Support (ACAE)
MIBARS ...... Military Intelligence Battalion (SAUO)
MIBARS ...... Military Intelligence Battalion Aerial Reconnaissance and Support [*Army*] (AFM)
MiBat .... Battle Creek Public School, Battle Creek, MI [*Library symbol*] [*Library of Congress*] (LCLS)
MiBatC .... Battle Creek College, Battle Creek, MI [*Library symbol*] [*Library of Congress*] [*Obsolete*] (LCLS)
MiBatK .... Kellogg Community College, Battle Creek, MI [*Library symbol*] [*Library of Congress*] (LCLS)
MiBatV .... United States Veterans Administration Hospital, Battle Creek, MI [*Library symbol*] [*Library of Congress*] (LCLS)
MiBatW ...... Willard Public Library, Battle Creek, MI [*Library symbol*] [*Library of Congress*] (LCLS)
MiBay .... Bay City Public Library, Bay City, MI [*Library symbol*] [*Library of Congress*] (LCLS)
MiBayM ...... Bay Medical Center, Bay City, MI [*Library symbol*] [*Library of Congress*] (LCLS)
MiBayS .... Bay County Library System, Bay City, MI [*Library symbol*] [*Library of Congress*] (LCLS)
MiBay-S ...... Bay County Library System, Sage Branch Library (SAUS)
MiBayS-A .... Bay County Library System, Auburn Branch Library, Auburn, MI [*Library symbol*] [*Library of Congress*] (LCLS)
MiBayS-B .... Bay County Library System, Broadway Branch Library, Bay City, MI [*Library symbol*] [*Library of Congress*] (LCLS)
MiBayS-L .... Bay County Library System, Linwood Branch Library, Linwood, MI [*Library symbol*] [*Library of Congress*] (LCLS)
MiBayS-P .... Bay County Library System, Pinconning Branch Library, Pinconning, MI [*Library symbol*] [*Library of Congress*] (LCLS)
MiBayS-S .... Bay County Library System, Sage Branch Library, Bay City, MI [*Library symbol*] [*Library of Congress*] (LCLS)
MIBB .... Missouri & Illinois Bridge & Belt Railroad [*AAR code*] [*Terminated*]
MIBC .... Methyl Cap. Isobutyl Carbinol [*Also, MIC*] [*Organic chemistry*]
MIBCO .... Member of the Institution of Building Control Officers [*British*] (DBQ)
MIBE .... Member of the Institution of British Engineers (SAUO)
MiBeiM .... Beaver Island Mormon Colony Library, St. James, Beaver Island, MI [*Library symbol*] [*Library of Congress*] [*Obsolete*] (LCLS)
MiBel .... Bellevue Township Library, Bellevue, MI [*Library symbol*] [*Library of Congress*] (LCLS)
MiBela .... Bellaire Public Library, Bellaire, MI [*Library symbol*] [*Library of Congress*] (LCLS)
MiBen .... Benzonia Public Library, Benzonia, MI [*Library symbol*] [*Library of Congress*] (LCLS)
MiBes .... Bessemer Public Library, Bessemer, MI [*Library symbol*] [*Library of Congress*] (LCLS)
MiBeu .... Beulah Public Library, Beulah, MI [*Library symbol*] [*Library of Congress*] (LCLS)
MIBF .... Member of the Institute of British Foundrymen
MIBF .... Member of the Institution of British Foundrymen (SAUO)
MIBF .... Montreal International Book Fair
MIBG .... Meta-Iodobenzylguanidine [*Biochemistry*]
MiBh .... Benton Harbor Public Library, Benton Harbor, MI [*Library symbol*] [*Library of Congress*] (LCLS)
MiBhL .... Lake Michigan College, Benton Harbor, MI [*Library symbol*] [*Library of Congress*] (LCLS)
MiBhW .... Whirlpool Corp., Technical Information Center, Benton Harbor, MI [*Library symbol*] [*Library of Congress*] (LCLS)
MiBicr .... Thomas Fleschner Memorial Library, Birch Run, MI [*Library symbol*] [*Library of Congress*] (LCLS)
Mibid .... Madrid Interbank Bid Rate [*Spain*] (NUMA)
MI Biol .... Member of the Institute of Biology [*British*] (EY)
MiBir .... Baldwin Public Library, Birmingham, MI [*Library symbol*] [*Library of Congress*] (LCLS)
MIBK .... Methyl Isobutyl Ketone [*Also, MIK*] [*Organic chemistry*]
MIBL .... Molecular Imaging and Bioinformatics Laboratory (SAUO)
MiBla .... Rolland Township Library, Blanchard, MI [*Library symbol*] [*Library of Congress*] (LCLS)
MiBloA .... Cranbrook Academy of Art, Bloomfield Hills, MI [*Library symbol*] [*Library of Congress*] (LCLS)
MiBloC .... Cranbrook Institute of Science, Bloomfield Hills, MI [*Library symbol*] [*Library of Congress*] (LCLS)

MiBloCAr..... Cranbrook Eductional Community, Archives and Historical Collections, Bloomfield Hills, MI [Library symbol] [Library of Congress] (LCLS)

MiBloGS ...... Church of Jesus Christ of Latter-Day Saints, Genealogical Society Library, Bloomfield Hills Branch, Bloomfield Hills, MI [Library symbol] [Library of Congress] (LCLS)

MIBNAU....... Instituut voor Toegepast Biologisch Onderzoek in de Natuur. Mededeling (journ.) (SAUS)

MIBOC .... Marketing of Investments Board Organising Committee [British]

MIBOC .... Marketing of Investments Board Organizing Committee (SAUO)

MIBOR .... Madrid Interbank Offered Rate (MHDW)

MIBOS .... Measurement of Ingratiatory Behaviours in Organisational Settings (WDAA)

MiBoy .... Boyne City Public Library (SAUS)

MiBoy .... Boyne City Public Library, Boyne City, MI [Library symbol] [Library of Congress] (LCLS)

MiBoyf .... Boyne Falls Public Library (SAUS)

MiBoyf .... Boyne Falls Public Library, Boyne Falls, MI [Library symbol] [Library of Congress] (LCLS)

MIBPA .... Methyliminobispropylamine [Organic chemistry]

Mi-BPH .... Michigan Department of Education, State Library Services, Blind and Physically Handicapped Library, Lansing, MI [Library symbol] [Library of Congress] (LCLS)

MIBPrA .... Midland Bank A1/A2 Unit ADS [NYSE symbol] (TTSB)

MIBPrB .... Midland Bank B1/B2 Unit ADS (TTSB)

MIBPrC .... Midland Bank C1/C2 Unit ADS [NYSE symbol] (TTSB)

MiBr............. Big Rapids Community Library, Big Rapids, MI [Library symbol] [Library of Congress] (LCLS)

MIBRAG....... Mitteldeutschen Brunkohle (ECON)

MiBrc........... Brown City Public Library, Brown City, MI [Library symbol] [Library of Congress] (LCLS)

MiBre........... Howe Memorial Library, Breckenridge, MI [Library symbol] [Library of Congress] (LCLS)

MiBrF.......... Ferris State College, Big Rapids, MI [Library symbol] [Library of Congress] (LCLS)

MiBrid .... Bridgeport Public Library, Bridgeport, MI [Library symbol] [Library of Congress] (LCLS)

MiBridm ...... Bridgman Public Library, Bridgman, MI [Library symbol] [Library of Congress] (LCLS)

MiBrig .... Brighton City Library, Brighton, MI [Library symbol] [Library of Congress] (LCLS)

MIBritE .... Member of the Institute of British Engineers (EY)

MIBritE .... Member of the Institute of British Engineers (SAUO)

MIBritishE.... Member of the Institute of British Engineers

MI British E... Member of the Institution of British Engineers (SAUO)

MIBs .... Management Information Bases [Compaq] [Computer science]

MIBS............ Master of International Business Studies

MIBS............ Miami International Boat Show and Sailboat Show (ITD)

MiBs .... Sparks Memorial Library, Berrien Springs, MI [Library symbol] [Library of Congress] (LCLS)

MiBsA.......... Andrews University, Berrien Springs, MI [Library symbol] [Library of Congress] (LCLS)

MIBT............ Methyl Isatin-beta-thiosemicarbazone

MiBu............ Taymouth Township Library, Burt, MI [Library symbol] [Library of Congress] (LCLS)

MiBur........... Burr Oak Township Library, Burr Oak, MI [Library symbol] [Library of Congress] (LCLS)

MiBurl .... Burlington Township Library, Burlington, MI [Library symbol] [Library of Congress] (LCLS)

MIBURN....... Mississippi Burning [Code name of FBI investigation]

MIBWG .... Military Intelligence Board Working Group

MIC.............. Aerolineas de Michoacan [Mexico] [ICAO designator] (FAAC)

MIC.............. Congregatio Clericorum Regularium Marianorum sub titulo Immaculatae ConceptionisBeatae Mariae Virginis [Marian Fathers] [Roman Catholic religious order]

MIC.............. Congregation of Marians of the Immaculate Conception (TOCD)

mic.............. Congregation of Marians of the Immaculate Conception (TOCD)

MIC.............. IEEE Medical Imaging Committee (EA)

MIC.............. Itasca Community College, Grand Rapids, MN [OCLC symbol] (OCLC)

MIC.............. Machine Intelligence Corporation (SAUO)

MIC.............. Machinery Installation Certificate

MIC.............. Made in Canada [Business term]

MIC.............. Magnesium Industry Council [British] (BI)

MIC.............. Magnetic Ink Character [Computer science] (HGAA)

MIC.............. Maintenance Identification Code [Military] (CAAL)

MIC.............. Maintenance Index Code (DNAB)

MIC.............. Maintenance Information Center [Navy] (NG)

MIC.............. Maintenance Information Chart [DoD]

MIC.............. Maintenance Inventory Center [Air Force] (AFIT)

MIC.............. Major Immunogene Complex [Genetics] (DOG)

MIC.............. Malayan Indian Congress (SAUO)

MIC.............. Malaysian Indian Congress [Political party] (PPW)

MIC.............. Management & Industrial Consultants

MIC.............. Management Indicator Code (MCD)

mic.............. Management Information Center (NAKS)

MIC.............. Management Information Center

MIC.............. Management Information Corp. [Cherry Hill, NJ] [Information service or system] (IID)

MIC.............. Management Integration Consortium

MIC.............. Manchester Information Committee (SAUO)

MIC.............. Marine Information Centre [Information service or system] (IID)

MIC.............. Market Impact Clearance

MIC.............. Marketing Intelligence Corp. [Information service or system] (IID)

MIC.............. Marketing International Corp. [Washington, DC] (TSSD)

MIC.............. Marshall Islands Congress (SAUO)

MIC.............. Martinello Importing Co. Ltd. (SAUS)

MIC.............. Maruman Integrated Circuits (NITA)

MIC.............. Maruzen International Co., Inc. [Information service or system] (IID)

MIC.............. Masonry Industry Committee (EA)

MIC.............. Master Interrupt Control [Computer science] (OA)

MIC.............. Match Indicator Code (MCD)

MIC.............. Material Identification and Control (DNAB)

MIC.............. Material Inventory Control

MIC.............. Materials Irradiation Chamber

MIC.............. Maternal and Infant Care [Medicine]

MIC.............. Maximum Inscribed Circle [Manufacturing term]

MIC.............. Meat Importers' Council [Later, MICA] (EA)

MIC.............. Meat Industry Council [Australia]

MIC.............. Mechanized Information Center [Information service or system]

MIC.............. Media Information Control (SAUO)

MIC.............. Media Interface Connector (SAUO)

MIC.............. Medical Imaging Committee (NTPA)

MIC.............. Medical Industrial Complex

MIC.............. Medical Information Centre (NITA)

MIC.............. Medical Intensive Care

MIC.............. Medical Interfraternity Conference (EA)

MIC.............. Medium-Intensity Conflict [Military]

MIC.............. Medium Interface Connector [Optics] (CDE)

MIC.............. Medugorje Information Center (EA)

MIC.............. Mellonics Information Center [Information service or system] (IID)

MIC.............. Mellon InvestData Corp. [New York, NY] [Information service or system] (IID)

MIC.............. Memory in Cassette

MIC.............. Memory Interface Connection [Computer science]

MIC.............. Merseyside Innovation Centre Ltd. [Research center] [British] (CB)

MIC.............. Message Identification Code [Computer science] (BUR)

MIC.............. Meteorological Information Committee [NATO] (NATG)

MIC.............. Meteorologist-In-Charge [Marine science] (OSRA)

MIC.............. Methylisobutyl Carbinol [Also, MIBC] [Organic chemistry]

MIC.............. Methyl Isocyanate [Organic chemistry]

MIC.............. Metro Industrial [Vancouver Stock Exchange symbol]

Mic .... Micah [Old Testament book]

MIC.............. Michigan Information Center [Michigan State Department of Management and Budget] [Information service or system] (IID)

MIC.............. Michigan Instructional Computer

MIC.............. Michilla [Chile] [Seismograph station code, US Geological Survey] (SEIS)

mic .... Micmac [MARC language code] [Library of Congress] (LCCP)

MIC.............. Microbiologically-Influenced Corrosion [Metallurgical engineering]

MIC.............. Microcomputer Index [Information service or system] (IID)

MIC.............. Microcytosis [Biochemistry] (DAVI)

MIC.............. Microelectronic Integrated Circuit (MCD)

mic .... Micrometer (WDMC)

MIC.............. Micrometer [A "mike"]

MIC.............. Microphone (AABC)

mic .... Microphone (WDMC)

MIC.............. Microscopic (DAVI)

MIC.............. Microscopic Findings in Centrifugal Urinary Sediment [Biochemistry] (DAVI)

Mic .... Microscopium [Constellation]

MIC.............. Microscopy

MIC.............. Microsoft Internet Chat (SAUS)

MIC.............. Microwave Integrated Circuitry

MIC.............. Microwave Integrated Circuits (NITA)

MIC.............. Microwave Interference Coordination

MIC.............. Microwave International Corporation (SAUO)

MIC.............. Middle-in-Chain (ELAL)

MIC.............. Middle Income Country [Category of developing country]

MIC.............. Mid-Intensity Conflict [Military] (INF)

MIC.............. Midwest Intercollegiate Conference (PSS)

MIC.............. Milgo Electronics Corporation (SAUO)

MIC.............. Military Indoctrination Center

MIC.............. Military-Industrial Complex (ADWA)

M-IC............. Military-Industrial Complex

MIC.............. Military Information Center [Defunct] (EA)

MIC.............. Military Intelligence Corps (SAUO)

MIC.............. Military Introductory Letter

MIC.............. Millicm International Cellular S.A. [Commercial firm] [Luxembourg]

MIC.............. Mineral Industries Census

MIC.............. Minimal [or Minimum] Inhibitory Concentration

MIC.............. Minimal Isorrheic Concentration [Medicine]

MIC.............. Minimum Ignition Current (IEEE)

MIC.............. Minimum Inhibitory Concentration [Bactericidal characteristic]

MIC.............. Minneapolis, MN [Location identifier] [FAA] (FAAL)

MiC.............. Minocycline [Antibiotic compound] (AAMN)

MIC.............. Minor Care Clinic [Medicine]

MIC.............. Missile Identification Code [Military] (CAAL)

MIC.............. Missing Interruption Character (NITA)

MIC.............. Missing Interruption Checker (MCD)

MIC.............. Missionary Sisters of the Immaculate Conception [Roman Catholic religious order]

MIC.............. Missionary Sisters of the Immaculate Conception (Canada) (TOCD)

MIC.............. Mississippi Industrial College [Holly Springs]

MIC.............. Mitsubishi International Corporation (SAUO)

MIC.............. MLRS International Corp. (SAUS)

MIC.............. Mobile Incident Center (WDAA)

MIC.............. Mobile Information Center [An association]

MIC.............. Mobile Intelligence Center (SAUO)

MIC.............. Mobile Intensive Care [Medicine] (DHSM)

MIC	Model Immune Complex [*Medicine*] (DMAA)
MIC	Monaco Information Centre (SAUO)
MIC	Monitoring, Identification, and Correlation
MIC	Monolithic Integrated Circuit
MIC	Mononuclear Inflammatory Cell (DMAA)
MIC	Morphology-Immunology-Cytogenetics [*Classification of Leukemias*]
MIC	Mortgage Insurance Certificate (EMRF)
MIC	Mortgage Insurance Co.
MIC	Motorcycle Industrial Council (SAUO)
MIC	Motorcycle Industry Council (EA)
MIC	Motors Insurance Corporation (SAUO)
MIC	Mountain Instructor's Certificate [*British*] (DI)
MIC	Movimiento de Integracion Colorada [*Paraguay*] [*Political party*] (EY)
MIC	Multichip Integrated Circuit (NITA)
MIC	Multifield Identification Chip (ACAE)
MIC	Multimedia Interactive Control
MIC	Multinational Intelligence Cell (MCD)
MIC	Multiperil Insurance Conference
MIC	Multiple Input Change (VLIE)
MIC	Multiple Interface Connection (SAUS)
MIC	MuniYield CA Insured Fund [*NYSE symbol*] (TTSB)
MIC	MuniYield California Insured Fund [*NYSE symbol*] (SPSG)
MIC	Music Industry Conference (EA)
MIC	Music Industry Council [*Later, Music Industry Conference*] (EA)
MIC	Music Information Center (TELE)
MIC	Mutual Improvement Class [*British railroad term*]
MIC	Mutual Interference Chart (IEEE)
MiCa	Indianfields Public Library, Caro, MI [*Library symbol*] [*Library of Congress*] (LCLS)
MICA	Macroinstruction Compiler Assembler [*Computer science*]
MICA	Major Incidents Computer Application (PDAA)
MICA	Management Improvement Corporation of America (SAUO)
MICA	Maternity and Infant Care Association (SAUO)
MICA	Meat Importers' Council of America (EA)
MICA	Mentally Ill Chemical Abuser
MICA	MicroAge, Inc. [*NASDAQ symbol*] (SAG)
MICA	Midwest Insulation Contractors Association
MICA	Mobile Industrial Caterers' Association (EA)
MICA	Mortgage Insurance Companies of America (EA)
MICA	Moscow Institute for Complex Automation (SAUO)
MiCac	Rawson Memorial Library, Cass City, MI [*Library symbol*] [*Library of Congress*] (LCLS)
MiCad	Cadillac-Wexford Public Library, Cadillac, MI [*Library symbol*] [*Library of Congress*] (LCLS)
MICAD	Micro-Installation, Inc. (SAUO)
MICAD	Multipurpose Integrated Chemical Agent Alarm [*Army*] (DOMA)
MiCadCS	Cadillac Public School, Cadillac, MI [*Library symbol*] [*Library of Congress*] (LCLS)
MiCadM	Mid-Michigan Library League, Cadillac, MI [*Library symbol*] [*Library of Congress*] (LCLS)
MiCadPS	Wexford Public Schools, Cadillac, MI [*Library symbol*] [*Library of Congress*] (LCLS)
MICAF	Measuring Improved Capabilities of Army Forces (SAUO)
MICAF	Measuring Improved Capability of Army Forces
MiCal	Calumet Public-School Library, Calumet, MI [*Library symbol*] [*Library of Congress*] (LCLS)
MICALL	Microprocedure Call [*Computer science*] (MHDB)
MiCam	Camden Township Library, Camden, MI [*Library symbol*] [*Library of Congress*] (LCLS)
MICAM	Microammeter [*Electronics*]
MICAM	Micro Camera (NITA)
MICAM	Micro-Connection Assembly Method
MICAM	Mid-Function Integral Control Alarm Module [*Electronics systems*] [*Automotive engineering*]
MICAM	Module Integrated Connection and Assembly Method (ACAE)
MICAP	Measuring Improved Capability [*Army*]
MICAP	Mission Capability
MICAP	Mission Capability Analysis System (SAUO)
MICAP	Mission Capable (SAUS)
MICAP	Mission Impaired Capability Awaiting Parts (SAUO)
MICAP	Mission Incapable, Awaiting Parts (MCD)
MICAP	Multi-National Investigations Cooperative on Aerial Phenomena
MICAPS	Mine/Countermine Casualty Assessment Producing System (MCD)
MICAS	Military Intelligence Co., Aerial Surveillance (MCD)
MICAS	Military Intelligence Company (SAUO)
MiCassC	Cass County Library, Cassopolis, MI [*Library symbol*] [*Library of Congress*] (LCLS)
MICB	Meck Island Control Building [*Army*] (AABC)
MICBM	Mobile Intercontinental Ballistic Missile
MiCc	Carson City Public Library, Carson City, MI [*Library symbol*] [*Library of Congress*] (LCLS)
MICC	Malaysian International Chambers of Commerce (SAUO)
MICC	Maritime International Cooperation Centre (SAUO)
MICC	Metal Interconnect Cascade Cell [*Photovoltaic energy systems*]
MICC	Military Information Control Committee (CINC)
MICC	Millicom International Cellular [*NASDAQ symbol*] (SAG)
MICC	Mineral Insulated Conductor Cable (VLIE)
MICC	Mineral Insulated, Copper Covered [*Cable*]
MICC	Mitogen-Induced Cellular Cytotoxicity [*Medicine*] (DB)
MICC	Mortgage Insurance Co. of Canada
MICCF	Millicom Intl Cellular S.A. [*NASDAQ symbol*] (TTSB)
MICCI	Malaysia International Chamber of Commerce and Industry (EAIO)
MICCLE	Michigan Interorganizational Committee on Continuing Library Education (EDAC)
MICCO	Model Inner City Community Organization [*Washington, DC*]
MICCS	Management Information and Commitment Control System (SAUO)
MICCS	Minuteman Integrated Command and Control System [*Missiles*]
Mic D	Doctor of Microbiology
MICD	Mechanical, Thermal, and Optical Interface Control Document (MCD)
MICDS	Movable In-Core Detector System [*Nuclear energy*] (NRCH)
MICE	Management Information Capability for Enforcement [*Environmental Protection Agency*] (GFGA)
MICE	Man's Impact on Coastal and Estuarine Ecosystems [*Marine science*] [*United Nations*] (OSRA)
MICE	Material Transfer, Information Transfer, Control Transfer, Energy Transfer
MICE	Member of the Institute of Civil Engineers (SAUO)
MICE	Member of the Institution of Chemical Engineers (SAUO)
MICE	Member of the Institution of Civil Engineers [*Formerly, AMICE*] [*British*]
MICE	Methods Information Communication Exchange Service (AEPA)
MICE	Methods Information Communications Exchange (SAUO)
MICE	Microelectronic Integrated Checkout Equipment
MICE	Missile Intercept Computer Evaluation (ACAE)
MICE	Modular Integrated Communications Environment (VLIE)
MICE	Money, Ideology, Compromise, Ego [*CIA acronym for possible explanations for spy defections*]
MICE	Morphological Image Complexity Evaluation (ACAE)
MICE	Multi-Interface Computer Equipment (SAUS)
MICE	Multi-Media, Information, Communication, and Entertainment [*Automotive electronics*]
MICE	Multimedia Integrated Conferencing for Europe (SAUO)
MICE	Multimedia Integrated Conferencing for European Researchers (SAUO)
MICE	Mutual Insurance Council of Editors [*Later, PICA*] (EA)
MiCe	Nottawa Township Library, Centerville, MI [*Library symbol*] [*Library of Congress*] (LCLS)
MiCeG	Glen Oaks Community College, Centreville, MI [*Library symbol*] [*Library of Congress*] (LCLS)
MICEI	Member of the Institution of Civil Engineers India (SAUO)
MICEI	Member of the Institution of Civil Engineers Ireland (SAUO)
MICEI	Member of the Institution of Civil Engineers of Ireland
MICELEM	Microphone Element (IEEE)
MiCen	Leslie R. Foss Public Library, Center Line, MI [*Library symbol*] [*Library of Congress*] (LCLS)
MiCenl	Central Lake Township Library, Central Lake, MI [*Library symbol*] [*Library of Congress*] (LCLS)
MiCES	Microcomputer-Controlled Electroanalysis System [*Interactive Microwave*]
MiCf	Crystal Falls Community Library, Crystal Falls, MI [*Library symbol*] [*Library of Congress*] (LCLS)
MicFocu	Micro Focus Group PLC [*Associated Press*] (SAG)
Micfrm	Microframe, Inc. [*Associated Press*] (SAG)
MICG	Macromolecular Insoluble Cold Globulin (DMAA)
MICG	Management Information Coordinating Group [*Navy*]
MICG	Mercury Iodide Crystal Growth
MICG	Microfield Graphics [*NASDAQ symbol*] (TTSB)
MICG	Microfield Graphics, Inc. [*NASDAQ symbol*] (SAG)
MICH	Michaelmas [*Feast of St. Michael the Archangel, September 29*]
Mich	Michaelmas Term [*British*] [*Legal term*] (DLA)
MICH	Michaels [*J.*], Inc. [*NASDAQ symbol*] (NQ)
MICH	Michaels J [*NASDAQ symbol*] (TTSB)
MICH	Micheas [*Old Testament book*] [*Douay version*]
Mich D	Michigan (ODBW)
MICH	Michigan
Mich	Michigan Supreme Court Reports [*A publication*] (DLA)
MiCha	Chase Public Library, Chase, MI [*Library symbol*] [*Library of Congress*] (LCLS)
Mich Admin Code	Michigan Administrative Code [*A publication*] (DLA)
Mich Adv	Michigan Reports Advanced Sheets [*A publication*] (DLA)
MICHANT	Michael Anthony Jewelels, Inc. (SAUO)
MichAnt	Michael Anthony Jewelers, Inc. [*Associated Press*] (SAG)
Mich App	Michigan Court of Appeals Reports [*A publication*] (DLA)
MiChar	Charlotte Public Library, Charlotte, MI [*Library symbol*] [*Library of Congress*] (LCLS)
Mich AS	Michigan Audubon Society (SAUO)
Mich Att'y Gen Biennial Rep	Biennial Report of the Attorney General of the State of Michigan [*A publication*] (DLA)
MichBr	Michigan Brewery, Inc. [*Associated Press*] (SAG)
MichBrw	Michigan Brewery, Inc. [*Associated Press*] (SAG)
Mich Calidon	Michael Calidonius [*Flourished, 16th century*] [*Authority cited in pre-1607 legal work*] (DSA)
Mich CCR	Michigan Circuit Court Reporter [*A publication*] (DLA)
Mich Comp L Ann	Michigan Compiled Laws, Annotated [*A publication*] (DLA)
Mich Comp Laws	Michigan Compiled Laws [*A publication*] (DLA)
Mich Comp Laws	Michigan Compiled Laws Annotated [*West*] [*A publication*] (AAGC)
Mich Comp Laws Ann	Michigan Compiled Laws, Annotated [*A publication*] (DLA)
Mich Cr Ct Rep	Michigan Circuit Court Reporter [*A publication*] (DLA)
Mich Ct Cl	Michigan Court of Claims (AAGC)
Mich Ct Cl	Michigan Court of Claims Reports [*A publication*] (DLA)
MiChe	Cheboygan Area Public Library, Cheboygan, MI [*Library symbol*] [*Library of Congress*] (LCLS)
MiChel	McKune Memorial Library, Chelsea, MI [*Library symbol*] [*Library of Congress*] (LCLS)
MIChemE	Member of the Institution of Chemical Engineers [*British*] (EY)
MiChes	Chesaning Public Library, Chesaning, MI [*Library symbol*] [*Library of Congress*] (LCLS)
MichFncl	Michigan Financial Corp. [*Associated Press*] (SAG)
Michie's GA Repts Ann	Georgia Reports, Annotated [*A publication*] (DLA)

Michie's Jur...	Michie's Jurisprudence of Virginia and West Virginia [*A publication*] (DLA)
MichJ..........	Michaels [*J.*], Inc. [*Associated Press*] (SAG)
Mich Jur......	Michigan Jurisprudence [*A publication*] (DLA)
Mich L.........	Michigan Lawyer [*A publication*] (DLA)
Mich Legis Serv...	Michigan Legislative Service [*A publication*] (DLA)
Mich Leg News...	Michigan Legal News [*A publication*] (DLA)
MichlF.........	Michael Foods, Inc. [*Associated Press*] (SAG)
Mich LJ	Michigan Law Journal [*A publication*] (DLA)
MichLRev......	Michigan Law Review (SAUO)
Mich Nisi Prius...	Brown's Michigan Nisi Prius Reports [*A publication*] (DLA)
Mich NP	Brown's Michigan Nisi Prius Reports [*A publication*] (DLA)
Mich Pub Acts...	Public and Local Acts of the Legislature of the State of Michigan [*A publication*] (DLA)
Mich PUC Ops...	Michigan Public Utilities Commission Orders and Opinions [*A publication*] (DLA)
Mich R.........	Michigan Reports [*A publication*] (DLA)
Mich RC Dec...	Michigan Railroad Commission Decisions [*A publication*] (DLA)
MICHS........	Michaelmas [*Feast of St. Michael the Archangel, September 29*]
Mich SBA Jo...	Michigan State Bar Association. Journal [*A publication*] (DLA)
Mich Stat Ann...	Michigan Statutes, Annotated [*A publication*] (DLA)
MichStr........	Michael Stores [*Associated Press*] (SAG)
Mich St U	Michigan State University (GAGS)
Mich Supr Ct Rep...	Michigan Reports [*A publication*] (DLA)
Mich T........	Michaelmas Term [*British*] [*Legal term*] (DLA)
Mich Tech U...	Michigan Technological University (GAGS)
MiChv.........	Charlevoix Public Library, Charlevoix, MI [*Library symbol*] [*Library of Congress*] (LCLS)
Mich Vac	Michaelmas Vacation [*British*] [*Legal term*] (DLA)
Mich WCC ...	Michigan Industrial Accident Board, Workmen's Compensation Cases [*A publication*] (DLA)
MICI..........	Metadata Information Clearinghouse Interactive
MICIM........	Methodology for the Introduction of CIM (SAUO)
MICIS........	Material Information Control and Information System (MCD)
MiCiS........	Material Information Control and Information System (NAKS)
MICIS........	Material Inventory Control and Inventory System (NASA)
MICIS........	Microbial Culture Information Service [*Department of Trade and Industry*] [*British*] [*Information service or system*]
MICIS........	Midwestern Climate Information System [*Marine science*] (OSRA)
MICK.........	Manufacturers Item Correlation Key
MICL.........	Mid Infrared Chemical Laser (ACAE)
MICL.........	Missile In-Commission Level
MiCla.........	Garfield Memorial Public Library, Clare, MI [*Library symbol*] [*Library of Congress*] (LCLS)
MICLE........	Institute of Continuing Legal Education, University of Michigan (DLA)
MICLE........	Michigan Institute of Continuing Legal Education (SAUO)
MICLIC.......	Mine Clearing Line Charge [*Army*] (INF)
MiClin........	Clinton Public Library, Clinton, MI [*Library symbol*] [*Library of Congress*] (LCLS)
MICLO	Management Information Control Liaison Officers (MCD)
MICLP........	Medical Informatics Cultural Literacy Project (ADWA)
MICM.........	Associate Member of the Institute of Credit Management [*British*] (DBQ)
MICM.........	Member of the Institute of Credit Management (SAUO)
MICM.........	MICOM Communications [*NASDAQ symbol*] (TTSB)
MICM.........	Micom Communications Corp. [*NASDAQ symbol*] (SAG)
MICM.........	Monolithic Integrated Circuit Mask
MICMD	Milwaukee Contract Management District (SAA)
MICMPTR	Microcomputer (MSA)
MICN	Medical Intensive Care Nurse (DAVI)
MICN	Micrion Corp. [*NASDAQ symbol*] (SAG)
MICN	Mobile Intensive Care Nurse [*Emergency Medicine*] (DAVI)
MICNIA	Modular Integrated Communication, Navigation & Identification Avionics (SAUS)
MICNS	Modular Integrated Communications and Navigation System (RDA)
MICO	Management Information Systems Control Officer (MCD)
MICO	Mankato Industrial Corp. [*Automotive industry supplier*]
MICO	Member of the Institute of Careers Officers [*British*] (DBQ)
MICO	Midland Continental R. R. [*AAR code*] [*Obsolete*]
MICo.........	Military Intelligence Company (SAUO)
MICO	MLV Integration and Checkout (MCD)
MICOFT.......	Mutual Insurance Committee on Federal Taxation (EA)
MiCol.........	Coloma Public Library, Coloma, MI [*Library symbol*] [*Library of Congress*] (LCLS)
MiCole........	Coleman Area Library, Coleman, MI [*Library symbol*] [*Library of Congress*] (LCLS)
MiCole........	Coleman Art Library (SAUS)
MiColo........	Colon Township Library, Colon, MI [*Library symbol*] [*Library of Congress*] (LCLS)
MiCom........	Comstock Township Library, Comstock, MI [*Library symbol*] [*Library of Congress*] (LCLS)
Micom........	Microwave Communications of America Inc. (SAUO)
MICOM	Missile Command [*Redstone Arsenal, AL*] [*Army*]
MICOM	Mission Command (SAUO)
MICOM	US Army Missile Command (AAGC)
MicomC.......	Micom Communications Corp. [*Associated Press*] (SAG)
MICOM-RDEC...	Missile Command Research, Development, and Engineering Center [*Army*] (RDA)
MICOMS.......	Maintenance Information Concerning [*the repair and operation of*] Missile Systems
MiCon........	Constantine Township Library, Constantine, MI [*Library symbol*] [*Library of Congress*] (LCLS)
MICON	Military Construction Program (MUGU)
micon	Motion Icon [*Computer science*] (WDMC)

MICONEX.....	Multinational Instrumentation Conference and Exposition [*China Instrument Society*]
MiCoop........	Coopersville District Library, Coopersville, MI [*Library symbol*] [*Library of Congress*] (LCLS)
MI-COPICS...	Management Information for COPICS [*Communications Oriented Production Information and Control System*] Users [*IBM Corp.*]
MICORE.......	Management Improvement/Cost Reduction Program (SAUO)
MICorrST.....	Member of the Institute of Corrosion Science and Technology [*British*] (DBQ)
MICOS	Mini Computer Systems (NITA)
MICOS	Multifunctional Infra-red Coherent Optical Scanner (SAUS)
MICOS	Multi Functional Infrared Coherent Optical Sensor (ACAE)
MICOT	Minimum Completion Time (VLIE)
MICOTOWS...	Minister in Charge of Treaty of Waitangi Settlements (SAUO)
MICP	Management and Investment Companies Program
MICP	Military Inventory Control Point (MCD)
MICPAC	Microelectronic Integrated Circuit Package (MCD)
MICPAK	Modular Integrated Circuit Package
MIC PAN	Mica Panis [*Crumb of Bread*] [*Pharmacy*]
MicPwr	Microwave Power Devices, Inc. [*Associated Press*] (SAG)
MICR	Magnetic Ink Character Recognition [*Banking*] [*Computer science*]
MICR	Management Improvement and Cost Reduction Project Reporting System
MIC/R	Media Interface Connector/Receptacle [*Computer science*] (AGLO)
MICR	Microenergy, Inc. [*NASDAQ symbol*] (SAG)
MICR	Microscope (MSA)
Micr	Microscopium [*Constellation*]
MICRA	Medical Injury Compensation Reform Act
MICRA	Microelectronic Integrated Circuit Replaceable (ACAE)
MICRA	Miniature Insulated Contact Range (PDAA)
MICRAD	Microwave Radiometry (MCD)
MICRADS	Microwave Radiation System (PDAA)
MICRAM	Microminiature Individual Components Reliable Assembled Modules
MicrBi........	Micro Bio-Medics, Inc. [*Associated Press*] (SAG)
Micrdy	Microdyne Corp. [*Associated Press*] (SAG)
Micrel	Micrel, Inc. [*Associated Press*] (SAG)
Micrenr.......	Microenergy, Inc. [*Associated Press*] (SAG)
MicrFlt.......	Microwave Filter Co., Inc. [*Associated Press*] (SAG)
Micrgfx.......	Micrografx, Inc. [*Associated Press*] (SAG)
MicrGn.......	Micro General Corp. [*Associated Press*] (SAG)
Micrion.......	Micrion Corp. [*Associated Press*] (SAG)
Micrl	Microleague Multimedia, Inc. [*Associated Press*] (SAG)
Micrleag......	Microleague Multimedia, Inc. [*Associated Press*] (SAG)
MICR/MIMR...	Magnetic Ink Character Recognition / Magnetic Ink Mark Recognition (BTTJ)
MIC-RN.......	Mobile Intensive Care Registered Nurse [*Emergency medicine*] (DAVI)
Micrnics	Micronics Computers, Inc. [*Associated Press*] (SAG)
MicrnT	Micron Technology [*Associated Press*] (SAG)
micro	Extremely Small (IDOE)
MICRO........	Microcomputer
MICRO........	Microelectronics Innovation and Computer Science Research Program [*University of California*] [*Research center*] (RCD)
MICRO........	Microprocessor
micro	Microscopic
MICRO........	Multiple Indexing and Console Retrieval Operations (NITA)
MICRO........	Multiple Indexing and Console Retrieval Options [*Information retrieval*] [*Computer science*]
MICROACE...	Microminiature Automatic Checkout Equipment
MicroAge.....	MicroAge, Inc., [*Associated Press*] (SAG)
Micro-AIDS...	Micro-Aircraft Integrated Data System (SAUS)
MICROBIOL...	Microbiological [*or Microbiology*]
MicroCap.....	[*The*] MicroCap Fund [*Associated Press*] (SAG)
MICROCAT...	Micro-Catalogue (NITA)
Microchip	Microchip Technology, Inc. [*Associated Press*] (SAG)
Microcm	Microcom, Inc. [*Associated Press*] (SAG)
MICROCON...	Microcomputer Based Services for Retrospective Conversions (NITA)
microcryst...	Microcrystalline (BARN)
MicroCSI.....	MicroStation Customer Support Library [*Intergraph Corp.*] (PCM)
MicroCT......	Micro Component Technology, Inc. [*Associated Press*] (SAG)
MICROD......	Council for Microphotography and Document Reproduction (SAUO)
MICRODIS...	Microform Document of Information System (MCD)
MICRO-DISC...	Microcomputer-Videodisc
MICRODOC...	Council for Microphotography and Document Reproduction [*British*]
Microfd......	Microfield Graphics, Inc. [*Associated Press*] (SAG)
MicrofdG.....	Microfield Graphics, Inc. [*Associated Press*] (SAG)
Microflu......	Microfluidics International Corp. [*Associated Press*] (SAG)
MICROFX.....	Intelligence Data Processing Set (SAUO)
MICROG......	Microgram [*One millionth of a gram*]
MicroIntg	Micro-Integration Corp. [*Associated Press*] (SAG)
MICROLAB...	Microfabrication Laboratory [*University of California, Berkeley*] [*Research center*] (RCD)
Microlg.......	Microlog Corp. [*Associated Press*] (SAG)
MicroLin......	Micro Linear Corp. [*Associated Press*] (SAG)
MICROM.....	Microinstruction Read-Only Memory [*Computer science*]
MICROMIN...	Microminiature (IEEE)
MICRON.....	Micronavigator [*Air Force*]
MICRON.....	Micron Products, Inc. (SAUO)
MicronEl......	Micron Electronics, Inc. [*Associated Press*] (SAG)
Micrones	Micronesian (DIAR)
MICRONET...	Microcomputer Network (NITA)
Micront.......	Micronetics, Inc. [*Associated Press*] (SAG)
Microp........	Micropolis Corp. [*Associated Press*] (SAG)
MICROPAC...	Micromodule Data Processor and Computer (IEEE)
MicroPh.......	Microcide Pharmaceuticals, Inc. [*Associated Press*] (SAG)

MICROPOWER SOURCES... Design, Study and Construction of Micropower Sources and Their Use in Microelectronics and Communication Technologies (SAUO)

Micro Proc Ann Workshop Microprogram... Micro Proceedings. Annual Workshop on Microprogramming (SAUO)

MICROPSI.... Microcomputer Printed Subject Indexes (NITA)

MICROS ..... Microscopy

Micros .... Micros Systems, Inc. [*Associated Press*] (SAG)

MICROSECS... Microfilm Sequential Coding System [*Bell System*]

Microsft ..... Microsoft Corp. [*Associated Press*] (SAG)

MICROSID ... Small Seismic Intrusion Detector (PDAA)

MicroSIFT .... Microcomputer Software and Information for Teachers [*Northwest Regional Educational Laboratory*] [*Information service or system*] (IID)

MICROSIM... Microinstruction Simulator [*Computer science*] (MHDI)

Microsoft ..... Microsoft Corp. [*Associated Press*] (SAG)

microSQUID... Microscopy, Microscopic Superconducting Quantum Interference Devices

MicrosTo ..... Micros-To Mainframe, Inc. [*Associated Press*] (SAG)

MICROTEL ... Microsoft/Intel (SAUS)

Microtel ..... Microtel International, Inc. [*Associated Press*] (SAG)

Microtl .... Microtel Franchise & Development Corp. [*Associated Press*] (SAG)

MicroTo ...... Micros-To Mainframe, Inc. [*Associated Press*] (SAG)

MICRO TR ... Microwave Tower [*Nautical charts*]

MICRO-VERS... Microcomputer Vocational Education Reporting System (EDAC)

MicroWre..... Micro Warehouse, Inc. [*Associated Press*] (SAG)

MicrPck ...... Microelectronic Packaging, Inc. [*Associated Press*] (SAG)

MICRS .... Main Instrument Console and Readout Stations (NATG)

MicrtcRs ...... Microtec Research, Inc. [*Associated Press*] (SAG)

Micrtek .... Microtek Medical, Inc. [*Associated Press*] (SAG)

Micrtest ...... Microtest, Inc. [*Associated Press*] (SAG)

MICRU .... MICRU International (EA)

Micrvisn ...... Microvision, Inc. [*Associated Press*] (SAG)

MICS........... Machine Inventory Control System [*Computer science*] (VLIE)

MICS........... Macro Interpretive Commands [*Computer science*] (VLIE)

MICS........... Macro Interpretive Command System (SAUO)

MICS........... Maintenance Inventory Control System [*Bell System*]

MICS........... Management Information and Control System [*Navy*]

MICS........... Management Integrated Control System

MICS........... Manned Interactive Control Stations (MCD)

MICS........... Manufacturing Information and Control System (OA)

MICS........... Material Inventory Control System [*NASA*] (SSD)

MICS........... Materiel Intransit Control System (SAUO)

MICS........... Medical Instrument Calibration System (PDAA)

MICS........... Microprocessor Inertia and Communication System

MICS........... Military Integrated Communications System (CINC)

MICS........... Mineral-Insulated Copper-Sheathed [*Cable*] (IEEE)

Mics........... Miscellaneous (SAUO)

MICS........... Missile Inspection Completion Sheet (MCD)

MICS........... Mitsubishi Intelligent Cockpit System [*Automotive engineering*]

MICS........... Mobile Integrated Communications System (SAUS)

MICS........... Multiman Intermittent Cooling System (SAUS)

MICS........... Multiplex Interior Communications (NG)

MICS........... Museum of the International College of Surgeons (NADA)

MICS........... MVS Integrated Control System (NITA)

MICSA .... Maine Indian Claims Settlement Act [*1980*]

MicSem .... Microsemi Corp. [*Associated Press*] (SAG)

Micsft .... Microsoft Corp. [*Associated Press*] (SAG)

MICSLP....... Maintenance Inventory Control Stock Levels Projection (SAUO)

MICTAR ...... Minnesota Center for Twin and Adoption Research (ECON)

MictchS .... Microtouch Systems, Inc. [*Associated Press*] (SAG)

MictchSy...... Microtouch Systems, Inc. [*Associated Press*] (SAG)

MICU .... Medical Intensive Care Unit [*Medicine*]

MICU .... Mobile Intensive Care Unit [*Medicine*]

MICU(N)...... Mobile Intensive Care Unit [*or Nurse*] (GNE)

MIC UNESCO-IOC/MIC... Marine Information Centre (SAUO)

MICV.......... Mechanized Infantry Combat Vehicle [*Army*]

MICV-FPW... Mechanized Infantry Combat Vehicle - Firing Port Weapon (MCD)

MICVS .... Mechanized Infantry Combat Vehicle Systems [*Army*] (RDA)

MiCw .... Coldwater Public Library, Coldwater, MI [*Library symbol*] [*Library of Congress*] (LCLS)

MICW........... Member of the Institute of Clerks of Works of Great Britain, Inc. (DBQ)

Micware ...... Microware Systems Corp. [*Associated Press*] (SAG)

MiCwB .... Branch County Library, Coldwater, MI [*Library symbol*] [*Library of Congress*] (LCLS)

MICWU .... Motor Industry Combined Workers Union (SAUO)

MiD............. Detroit Public Library, Detroit, MI [*Library symbol*] [*Library of Congress*] (LCLS)

MID............. Magnetically Insulated Diode [*Physics*]

MID............. Maintenace Index Page (DNAB)

MID............. Manpower Information Division [*Navy*]

MID............. Mare Island Division [*San Francisco Bay Naval Shipyard, Vallejo, CA*]

MID............. Marginally Indigent Defendant

MID............. Master of Industrial Design

MID............. Master of Interior Design (GAGS)

MID............. Material Identification (AAEL)

MID............. Maximum Inhibiting Dilution [*Medicine*] (MAE)

MID............. Maximum Inhibiting Duration [*Medicine*] (DAVI)

MID............. Measure of Intellectual Development (EDAC)

MID............. Meat Inspection Division [*of ARS, Department of Agriculture*]

MID............. Mechanical Inertia Dynamometer [*Automotive emissions*]

MID............. Median Incisal Diastema [*Medicine*] (MELL)

MID............. Median Infective Dose [*Bacteriology*]

MID............. Mentioned in Dispatches (ADA)

MID............. Merida [*Mexico*] [*Airport symbol*] (OAG)

MID............. Mesioincisodistal [*Dentistry*]

MID............. Message Identification [*Computer science*]

MID............. Message Identifier (ACRL)

MID............. Message Input Description

MID............. Message Input Device (AABC)

MID............. Mid Airways [*France*] [*FAA designator*] (FAAC)

MID............. Midbody

MID............. Midcon Oil & Gas Ltd. [*Toronto Stock Exchange symbol*]

MID............. Mid-Continent Telephone Corp. (SAUO)

MID............. Middle (AFM)

mid............. Middle (VRA)

MID............. Middleton Island [*Alaska*] [*Seismograph station code, US Geological Survey*] (SEIS)

MID............. Middling Space [*Typesetting*] (DGA)

Mid............. Middoth (BJA)

Mid............. Midland [*Topography*] (ROG)

MID............. MIDLNET [*Midwest Regional Library Network*], St. Louis, MO [*OCLC symbol*] (OCLC)

MID............. Midnight

Mid............. Midrash [*Interpretation of Old Testament writings*] (BJA)

Mid............. Midshipman (WDAA)

MID............. Midshipman [*Navy*]

MID............. Midway Railroad Co. [*AAR code*]

MID............. Midwest Stock Exchange [*Chicago, IL*] (CDAI)

MID............. Midwifery (ROG)

MID............. Military Information Division (SAUO)

MID............. Military Intelligence Department (SAUO)

MID............. Military Intelligence Detachment (AABC)

MID............. Military Intelligence Division [*War Department*] [*World War II*]

MID............. Mines Inspection Department (SAUO)

MID............. Minimal Infecting Dose [*Medicine*] (MELL)

MID............. Minimal Inhibiting Dose [*Medicine*]

MID............. Minimal Irradiation Dose [*Medicine*] (MELL)

MID............. Minimum Infective Dose [*Bacteriology*]

MID............. Ministerstvo Inostrannykh Del [*Ministry of Foreign Affairs*] [*Former USSR*]

MID............. Missile Intelligence Directorate [*Army*] (AABC)

MID............. Missile Intelligence Directory

MID............. Missing Insects Department

MID............. Modified Ionization Detector (MCD)

MID............. Mortgage Interest Differential

MID............. Movimiento de Integracion Democratica [*Democratic Integration Movement*] [*Dominican Republic*] [*Political party*] (PPW)

MID............. Movimiento Independiente Democratico [*Independent Democratic Movement*] [*Panama*] [*Political party*] (PPW)

MID............. Multi-Information Display [*Automotive engineering*]

MID............. Multinfarct Dementia (DIPS)

MID............. Multiple Individually Designated (ACAE)

MID............. Multiple Infant Dementia [*Neurology*] (CPH)

MID............. Multiple Infarct Dementia [*Neurology*]

MID............. Multiple Ion Detection

MID............. Multiplex Identification (SAUS)

MID............. Multiplexing Identifier [*Telecommunications*] (ACRL)

MID............. Munitions Inventions Department [*British military*] (DMA)

MID............. Musically Intelligent Device [*Electronic musical instruments*]

MiDA .... Detroit Institute of Arts, Detroit, MI [*Library symbol*] [*Library of Congress*] (LCLS)

MIDA .... Major Item Data Agency (SAUO)

MIDA .... Major Items Data Agency [*Military*]

Mida .... Malaysian Industrial Development Authority (SAUO)

MIDA .... Message Interchange Distributed Application [*Telecommunications*] (OSI)

MIDA .... Mid-American International Development Association [*Nigeria*]

MIDA .... Moviemiento de Integracion Democratica [*The Dominican Republic*] [*Political party*] (EY)

MIDA .... Myocardial Ischemia Dynamic Analysis [*Medicine*] (DMAA)

MiDAA .... Catholic Archdiocese of Detroit, Archives, Detroit, MI [*Library symbol*] [*Library of Congress*] (LCLS)

MidAAprt...... Mid America Apartment Communities, Inc. [*Associated Press*] (SAG)

MidABc .... Mid-America Bancorp [*Associated Press*] (SAG)

MIDAC .... Management Information for Decision and Control

MIDAC .... Michigan [*University of*] Digital Automatic Computer

MiDACI .... American Concrete Institute, Detroit, MI [*Library symbol*] [*Library of Congress*] (LCLS)

MIDADE ...... Mouvement International d'Apostolat des Enfants [*International Movement of Apostolate of Children*] [*France*]

MidAE .... Mid American Energy Co. [*Associated Press*] (SAG)

MidAg .... Midrash Aggadah (BJA)

Mid-Am .... Mid-America: An Historical Review [*A publication*] (BRI)

MIDAM .... Midamerica Commodity Exchange (EA)

MidAm .... Mid-Am, Inc. [*Associated Press*] (SAG)

MiDAMA ...... Automobile Manufacturers Association, Inc., Detroit (SAUS)

MiDAMA ...... Automobile Manufacturers' Association, Inc., Detroit, MI [*Library symbol*] [*Library of Congress*] (LCLS)

MidAmEn...... Mid American Energy Co. [*Associated Press*] (SAG)

MidAmIn....... Mid-Am, Inc. [*Associated Press*] (SAG)

MidAmR ..... Mid America Realty, Inc. [*Formerly, Dial REIT*] [*Associated Press*] (SAG)

MIDAN .... Microprocessor Data Analyzer [*Instrumentation*]

MIDANET .... Mortgage Information Direct Access Network [*FHLMC*] (EMRF)

MidAp......... Mid America Apartment Communities [*Associated Press*] (SAG)

MIDAR .... Microwave Detection and Ranging

MIDAR .... Motion Indicating RADAR (MCD)

MID-ARK...... Mid-Arkansas Regional Library [Library network]
MIDARM...... Microdynamic Angle and Rate Monitoring System
MIDAS......... Mainline Information Display and Automation System [Salford Electrical Instruments] (NITA)
MIDAS .... Maintenance Integrated Data Access System (MCD)
MIDAS .... Management Information and Development Aids System (SSD)
MIDAS .... Management Information, Data & Accounting System (SAUS)
MIDAS .... Management Information Dissemination Administrative System (SAUO)
MIDAS .... Management Integrated Data Accumulating System
MIDAS .... Management Interactive Data Accounting System [Computer science] (CIST)
MIDAS .... Man-Machine Integration Design and Analysis System (GAVI)
MIDAS .... Manufacturing Information Distribution and Acquisition System (ACAE)
MIDAS .... Marine Inclination Differential Alignment System (SAUS)
MIDAS .... Maritime Industrial Development Area [Navy]
MIDAS .... Materiel Inventory Data Acquisition System
MIDAS .... Measurement Information Data Analysis System [or Subsystem] (IEEE)
MIDAS .... Mechanism Integration Design and Analysis System [Computer-assisted engineering]
MIDAS .... Medical Information Dissemination Using ASSASSIN (NITA)
MIDAS .... Memory Implemented Data Acquisition Systems
MIDAS .... Meteorological Information and Dose Acquisition System [Nuclear energy] (NRCH)
MIDAS .... Meteorological Integrating Data Acquisition System [Marine science] (MSC)
MIDAS .... Microcomputer-Interfaced Data Acquisition System [Computer science]
MIDAS .... Micro-Diagnostics for Analysis and Repair (NITA)
MIDAS .... Microimaged Data Addition System [CAPS Equipment Ltd.]
MIDAS .... Microprogrammable Integrated Data Acquisition System
MIDAS .... Microprogramming Design Aided System [RCA]
MIDAS .... Microscopic Image Digital Acquisition System (PDAA)
MIDAS .... Mine & Ice Detection/Avoidance System (SAUS)
MIDAS .... Mine Detection and Avoidance System (MCD)
MIDAS .... Miniature Data Acquisition System
MIDAS .... Missile Defense Alarm [or Alert] System [Air Force]
MIDAS .... Missile Detection and Alarm System [Army] (AABC)
MIDAS .... Missile Detection and Surveillance (CAAL)
MIDAS .... Missile Intercept Data Acquisition System
MIDAS .... Mobile Integrated Digital Automatic System (SAUS)
MIDAS .... Model for Interheater Deployment by Air and Sea [DoD]
MIDAS .... Model for Intertheater Deployment and Scheduling (SAUO)
MIDAS .... Modified Integration Digital Analog Simulator [Computer science] (MCD)
MIDAS .... Modular Integrated Design Automated System
MIDAS .... Modular Interactive Data Acquisition System [National Institute of Standards and Technology]
MIDAS .... Modular International Dealing and Accounting System (NITA)
MIDAS .... Modulator Isolation Diagnostic Analysis System (IEEE)
MIDAS .... Monopoly Information and Data Analysis System
MIDAS .... Multicenter Isradipine Diuretic Atherosclerosis Study
MIDAS .... Multi-Discipline Data Analysis System (GAVI)
MIDAS .... Multi-Mode International Data Acquisition Service (NITA)
MIDAS .... Multioptional Interactive Display and Analytic System (MCD)
MIDAS .... Multiple Index Data Access System [Prime Computer, Inc.]
MIDAS .... Multiple Input Data Acquisition System [Bell System]
MIDAS .... Multiple Integrated Document Assembly System [Computer science] (BYTE)
MIDAS .... Multitier Distributed Application Services [Computer science]
MIDAS .... Munich Image Data Analysis System
MID/ASIA..... Middle East/Asia Region [USTTA] (TAG)
MIDATA ...... Marconi Integrated Design and Test Automation [Marconi Industries] [Telecommunications] [British]
MIDATL....... Mid-Atlantic (DNAB)
MidAtlan...... Mid-Atlantic Medical Services, Inc. [Associated Press] (SAG)
MidatRty...... Midatlantic Realty Trust [Associated Press] (SAG)
MIDATS ...... Modular Intermediate Depot Automatic Test System (ACAE)
MiDb........... Dearborn Public [Henry Ford Centennial] Library, Dearborn, MI [Library symbol] [Library of Congress] (LCLS)
MiDB .... Detroit Bar Association, Detroit, MI [Library symbol] [Library of Congress] (LCLS)
MiD-B......... Detroit Public Library, Burton Historical Collection, Detroit, MI [Library symbol] [Library of Congress] (LCLS)
MIDB .... Major Item Data Base (SAUO)
MIDB .... Misr Iran Development Bank
MiDBA .... Detroit Bar Association, Detroit, MI [Library symbol] [Library of Congress] (LCLS)
MidBay....... Middle Bay Oil Co., Inc. [Associated Press] (SAG)
MiDbEI........ Edison Institute [Henry Ford Museum and Greenfield Village] Library, Dearborn, MI [Library symbol] [Library of Congress] (LCLS)
MiDbF......... Ford Motor Co., Dearborn, MI [Library symbol] [Library of Congress] (LCLS)
MiDbGS....... Church of Jesus Christ of Latter-Day Saints, Genealogical Society Library, Dearborn Stake Branch, LDS Chapel, Dearborn, MI [Library symbol] [Library of Congress] (LCLS)
MiDbHi........ Dearborn Historical Museum, Dearborn, MI [Library symbol] [Library of Congress] (LCLS)
MidBk........ Midland Bank PLC [Associated Press] (SAG)
MiDbME...... Society of Manufacturing Engineers, Dearborn, MI [Library symbol] [Library of Congress] (LCLS)
MidbO......... Oakwood Hospital, Dearborn, MI [Library symbol] [Library of Congress] (LCLS)

MiDbU .... University of Michigan, Dearborn Campus, Dearborn, MI [Library symbol] [Library of Congress] (LCLS)
MIDBX .... Mgn. Stanley D. Witter Mid-Cap Growth Cl.B [Mutual fund ticker symbol] (SG)
MiDC .... Detroit Chancery [Catholic Church] Archives, Detroit, MI [Library symbol] [Library of Congress] (LCLS)
MIDC .... MidConn Bank [NASDAQ symbol] (NQ)
MIDC .... Movement for an Independent and Democratic Cuba (EA)
MIDCAB ...... Minimally Invasive Direct Coronary Artery Bypass [Medicine] (MELL)
MiDCh .... Children's Hospital of Michigan, Detroit, MI [Library symbol] [Library of Congress] (LCLS)
MiDChryE.... Chrysler Corp., Engineering Division, Detroit, MI [Library symbol] [Library of Congress] (LCLS)
MiDCL .... Detroit College of Law, Detroit, ME [Library symbol] [Library of Congress] (LCLS)
Midcom .... Midcom Communications, Inc. [Associated Press] (SAG)
MidContB..... Mid Continent Bancshares, Inc. [Associated Press] (SAG)
MIDCRU...... Midshipman Cruise [Navy] (NVT)
MidCst........ Mid-Coast Bancorp, Inc. [Associated Press] (SAG)
MidcstE....... Midcoast Energy Resources, Inc. [Associated Press] (SAG)
MIDD .... Middleby Corp. [NASDAQ symbol] (TTSB)
MIDDLE .... Microprogram Design Description Language [1977] [Computer science] (CSR)
Middlebury C... Middlebury College (GAGS)
MiDDS .... Duns Scotus College, Detroit, MI [Library symbol] [Library of Congress] (LCLS)
MIDDS .... Meteorological Interactive Data Display System (ACAE)
MIDDS/MEIDAS... Meteorological Interactive Display Data System/Man Computer Interactive Data Access System (SAUS)
Middx .... Middlesex [County in England] (ODBW)
MIDDX........ Middlesex [County in England]
Middx Sit..... Sittings for Middlesex at Nisi Prius [A publication] (DLA)
MIDEASTFOR... Middle East Force [Military] (AABC)
Mid East L Rev... Middle East Law Review [A publication] (DLA)
MIDEAST MI LIB... Mideastern Michigan Library Cooperative [Library network]
MiDec.......... Van Buren County Library, Decatur, MI [Library symbol] [Library of Congress] (LCLS)
MiDecD....... Decatur Township Library, Webster Memorial Library Building, Decatur, MI [Library symbol] [Library of Congress] (LCLS)
MiDeck........ Deckerville Public Library, Deckerville, MI [Library symbol] [Library of Congress] (LCLS)
MiDecV........ Van Buren County Library, Webster Memorial Library Building, Decatur, MI [Library symbol] [Library of Congress] (LCLS)
MiDEd........ Detroit Edison Co., Detroit, MI [Library symbol] [Library of Congress] (LCLS)
MIDEF......... Microprocedure Definition
MIDEFO....... Mission Debrief Forms (CINC)
MIDEH........ Indigenous Humanist Democratic Movement (SAUO)
MiDelD........ Delton District Library, Delton, MI [Library symbol] [Library of Congress] (LCLS)
MIDELEC...... Midlands Electricity Board (SAUO)
MIDES .... Missile Detection System
MiDet.......... De Tour Area School and Public Library, De Tour Village, MI [Library symbol] [Library of Congress] (LCLS)
MIDET........ Military Intelligence Detachment (ACAE)
MiDew .... De Witt Public Library, De Witt, MI [Library symbol] [Library of Congress] (LCLS)
MiDex......... Dexter District Library, Dexter, MI [Library symbol] [Library of Congress] (LCLS)
MIDEX .... Medium-Class Explorer
MIDF .... Major Item Data File (AABC)
MIDF .... Malaysian Industrial Development Finance Co. (SAUO)
MIDF .... Multiple Input Describing Function (PDAA)
MIDFC .... Malaysian Industrial Development Finance Company (SAUO)
MiDG .... Gale Research Co., Detroit, MI [Library symbol] [Library of Congress] (LCLS)
Mid G .... Graduate Midwife
MIDGET ...... Modular Integrated Digital Equipment Tester (ACAE)
MiDGH......... Detroit General Hospital, Medical Library, Detroit, MI [Library symbol] [Library of Congress] (LCLS)
MiDGM-L..... General Motors World Headquarters, General Motors Law Library, Detroit, MI [Library symbol] [Library of Congress] (LCLS)
MiDGrH........ Grace Hospital, Detroit, MI [Library symbol] [Library of Congress] (LCLS)
MIDH .... Middletown & Hummelstown Railroad Co. [AAR code]
MIDH .... Mouvement pour l'Instauration de la Democratie en Haiti [Political party] (EY)
MidHag........ Midrash ha-Gadol (BJA)
MiDHF .... Henry Ford Hospital, Detroit, MI [Library symbol] [Library of Congress] (LCLS)
MiDHH........ Harper Hospital, Department of Libraries, Detroit, MI [Library symbol] [Library of Congress] (LCLS)
MiDHi .... Detroit Historical Society, Detroit, MI [Library symbol] [Library of Congress] (LCLS)
MIDI .... Manufacturer Association (SAUO)
MIDI .... Midisoft Corp. [NASDAQ symbol] (SAG)
MIDI .... Minnesota Infant Development Inventory [Child development test] [Psychology]
MIDI .... Miss Distance Indicator (MCD)
MIDI .... Musical Instrument Digital Interface [Port] [Socket on an electronic synthesizer that permits a direct computer connection]
MiDi........... Windsor Township Library, Dimondale, MI [Library symbol] [Library of Congress] (LCLS)
MIDIRS .... Midwives Information and Resource Service [British] (EAIO)
Midisoft .... Midisoft Corp. [Associated Press] (SAG)

MIDIST	Mission Interministerielle de l'Information Scientifique et Technique [*Interministerial Mission for Scientific and Technical Information*] [*France*] [*Information service or system*] (IID)
MiDIT	Detroit Institute of Technology, Detroit, MI [*Library symbol*] [*Library of Congress*] (LCLS)
MidIwa	Mid Iowa Financial Corp. [*Associated Press*] (SAG)
MIDIZ	Mid-Canada Identification Zone
MidJob	Midrash Job (BJA)
MidJonah	Midrash Jonah (BJA)
MiDL	Michigan Library Consortium, Wayne State University, Detroit, MI [*Library symbol*] [*Library of Congress*] (LCLS)
MIDL	Midland [*English dialect*] (ROG)
MIDL	Midlantic Corp. [*NASDAQ symbol*] (NQ)
MIDL	Miniature Interoperable Data Link (ACAE)
MIDL	Modular Interoperable Data Link (ACAE)
MIDLAT	Middle Latitude [*Navigation*]
MidIBk	Midland Bank PLC [*Associated Press*] (SAG)
MidIby	Middleby Corp. [*Associated Press*] (SAG)
MidICp	Midlantic Corp. [*Associated Press*] (SAG)
MidLekTov...	Midrash Lekah Tov (BJA)
MidIFn	Midland Financial Group [*Associated Press*] (SAG)
MIDLIS	Multifamily Insurance and Direct Loan Information System [*Department of Housing and Urban Development*] (GFGA)
MidInd	Midland Co. [*Associated Press*] (SAG)
MIDLNET	Midwest Regional Library Network
MidIRs	Midland Resources, Inc. [*Associated Press*] (SAG)
MiDM	Marygrove College, Detroit, MI [*Library symbol*] [*Library of Congress*] (LCLS)
MiDMC	Mercy College of Detroit, Detroit, MI [*Library symbol*] [*Library of Congress*] (LCLS)
MiDMch	Mariners' Church, Detroit, MI [*Library symbol*] [*Library of Congress*] (LCLS)
MID-MO	Mid-Month [*Amount of pay to be received by payee on the 15th day of the month*] (AABC)
MiDMP	Merrill-Palmer Institute, Detroit, MI [*Library symbol*] [*Library of Congress*] (LCLS)
MIDMS	Machine Independent Data Management System [*Defense Intelligence Agency*] (MCD)
MiDMtC	Mount Carmel Mercy Hospital, Medical Library, Detroit, MI [*Library symbol*] [*Library of Congress*] (LCLS)
MIDN	Midshipman [*Navy*]
MIDNET	Midland Network (NITA)
MIDnet	[*The*] Midwest Network [*Computer science*] (TNIG)
midnoc	Midnight (DAVI)
MiDo	Dorr Township Library, Dorr, MI [*Library symbol*] [*Library of Congress*] (LCLS)
MIDOC	Mildew-Induced Defacement of Organic Coatings
MidOcn	Mid Ocean Ltd. [*Associated Press*] (SAG)
MiDolb	Osceola Township Public and School Library, Dollar Bay, MI [*Library symbol*] [*Library of Congress*] (LCLS)
MIDOP	Missile Doppler
MIDOR	Miss Distance Optical Recorder [*Military*] (PDAA)
MIDORI	Modern Information and Documentation Organizing and Rearrangement, Incorporated (SAUO)
MIDOT	Multiple Interferometer Determination of Trajectories
MiDow	Dowagiac Public Library, Dowagiac, MI [*Library symbol*] [*Library of Congress*] (LCLS)
MIDP	Major Item Distribution Plan (AABC)
MIDP	Microbiology and Infectious Diseases Program [*Bethesda, MD*] [*National Institute of Allergy and Infectious Diseases*] [*Department of Health and Human Services*] (GRD)
MIDP	Microwave Induced Delayed Phosphorescence (AAEL)
MIDP	Motor Industry Development Program
MiDP	Providence Hospital, School of Nursing, Detroit, MI [*Library symbol*] [*Library of Congress*] (LCLS)
MIDPAC	Mid-Pacific
MIDPAC	US Army Forces, Middle Pacific [*Name commonly used for AFMIDPAC*] [*World War II*]
MiDPD	Parke, Davis & Co., Detroit, MI [*Library symbol*] [*Library of Congress*] (LCLS)
MIDPM	Member of the Institute of Data Processing Management [*British*] (DCTA)
MidProv.......	Midrash Proverbs (BJA)
MidPs	Midrash Tehillim [*or The Midrash on Psalms*] (BJA)
MIDPT	Midpoint (FAAC)
MidQ	Midwest Quarterly: A Journal of Contemporary Thought [*A publication*] (ANEX)
MIDR	Mandatory Incident and Defect Reporting (NATG)
MidR...........	Midland Resources, Inc. [*Associated Press*] (SAG)
Midr............	Midrash [*Interpretation of Old Testament writings*] (BJA)
MIDR	Mosaicked Image Data Record (SAUS)
MID-RATS.....	Midnight Rations [*Navy*]
MiDRI	Rehabilitiation Institute, Detroit, MI [*Library symbol*] [*Library of Congress*] (LCLS)
MidrR	Midrash Rabbah (BJA)
MidrSong.....	Midrash to the Song of Songs (BJA)
MiDry..........	Dryden Township Library, Dryden, MI [*Library symbol*] [*Library of Congress*] (LCLS)
MIDS	Management Information and Data Systems (NVT)
MIDS	Management Information and Decision System (VLIE)
MIDS	Management Information Decision Support [*Computer science*] (CIST)
MIDS	Management Information Decision System [*Computer science*] (CIST)
MIDS	Management Information Display System (MCD)
MIDS	Marketing Information Data Systems, Inc. [*Information service or system*] (IID)
MIDS	Matrix Information and Directory Services
MIDS	Matrix Information and Directory Services, Inc.
MIDS	Mid-South Insurance Co. [*NASDAQ symbol*] (NQ)
MIDS	Miniature Integrated Data System (MCD)
MIDS	Miscarriage Infant Death Stillbirth Support Group
MIDS	Missile Ignition and Destruct Simulator
MIDS	Mission Information Dispensing System (VLIE)
MIDS	Movable Instrument Drive System [*Nuclear energy*] (NRCH)
MIDS	Movement Information Distribution Station
MIDS	MPAC Information Data System (SAUO)
MIDS	Multifunctional Information Distribution System [*NATO*] (MCD)
MIDS	Multimode Information Distribution System
Midsag........	Midsagittal [*Medicine*]
MidSam.......	Midrash Samuel (BJA)
MIDSD	Management Information and Data Systems Division [*Environmental Protection Agency*] (GFGA)
MiDSH	Sacred Heart Seminary, Detroit, MI [*Library symbol*] [*Library of Congress*] (LCLS)
MIDSIM	Maxwell International Development Simulation
MIDSIM	Midcourse Simulation (ACAE)
MiDSn	Sinai Hospital, Detroit, MI [*Library symbol*] [*Library of Congress*] (LCLS)
Mids ND	[*A*] Midsummer Night's Dream [*Shakespearean work*] (BARN)
MidSou	Mid-South Insurance Co. [*Associated Press*] (SAG)
MIDSR	Midsummer (ROG)
MidStat.......	Mid-States PLC [*Associated Press*] (SAG)
Midsth........	Midsouth Bancorp, Inc. [*Associated Press*] (SAG)
MidsthB.......	Midsouth Bancorp, Inc. [*Associated Press*] (SAG)
MIDTA	Member of the International Dance Teachers' Association [*British*] (DBQ)
MidTan	Midrash Tanna'im on Deuteronomy (BJA)
Mid'Tehil.....	Midrash Tehillim [*or The Midrash on Psalms*] (BJA)
Mid Tenn St U...	Middle Tennessee State University (GAGS)
MIDTRARON...	Midshipman Training Squadron [*Navy*] (NVT)
MIDU	Malfunction Insertion and Display Unit [*Aviation*]
MIDU	Missile Ignition Delay Unit (SAUS)
MiDU	University of Detroit, Detroit, MI [*Library symbol*] [*Library of Congress*] (LCLS)
MiDU-C........	University of Detroit, Colombiere Campus, Clarkston, MI [*Library symbol*] [*Library of Congress*] (LCLS)
MiDU-D........	University of Detroit, Dental Library, Detroit, MI [*Library symbol*] [*Library of Congress*] (LCLS)
MiDU-L........	University of Detroit, Law Library, Detroit, MI [*Library symbol*] [*Library of Congress*] (LCLS)
MIDW	Midwestern (AFM)
MiDW	Wayne State University, Detroit, MI [*Library symbol*] [*Library of Congress*] (LCLS)
MiDW-AL.....	Wayne State University, Walter P. Reuther Library of Labor and Urban Affairs, Archivesof Labor History and Urban Affairs, Detroit, MI [*Library symbol*] [*Library of Congress*] (LCLS)
MidwBn	Midwest Bancshares [*Associated Press*] (SAG)
MiDWc.........	Wayne County Records, Court House, Wayne County, Detroit, MI [*Library symbol*] [*Library of Congress*] (LCLS)
MiDWcC	Wayne County Community College, Detroit, MI [*Library symbol*] [*Library of Congress*] (LCLS)
MIDWEEK	Manager Integrated Dictionary Week [*Manager Software Products*] (EA)
MIDWEST	Midwest Automated Clearing House Association (TBD)
MIDWESTNAVFACENGCOM...	Midwest Division Naval Facilities Engineering Command
Midwest S U...	Midwestern State University (GAGS)
MidwGm......	Midway Games, Inc. [*Associated Press*] (SAG)
MidwGr.......	Midwest Grain Products, Inc. [*Associated Press*] (SAG)
MiDW-L	Wayne State University, Law Library, Detroit, MI [*Library symbol*] [*Library of Congress*] (LCLS)
MiDW-M	Wayne State University, Medical Library, Detroit, MI [*Library symbol*] [*Library of Congress*] (LCLS)
MiDW-Mi......	Wayne State University, Miles Manuscript Collection, Detroit, MI [*Library symbol*] [*Library of Congress*] [*Obsolete*] (LCLS)
MiDW-P	Wayne State University, School of Pharmacy, Detroit, MI [*Library symbol*] [*Library of Congress*] (LCLS)
MidwRE	Midwest Real Estate Shopping Centers Ltd. [*Associated Press*] (SAG)
MiDW-S	Wayne State University, Kresge-Hooker Science Library, Detroit, MI [*Library symbol*] [*Library of Congress*] (LCLS)
MIE	Aero Premier de Mexico, SA de CV [*Mexico*] [*FAA designator*] (FAAC)
MiE	East Lansing Public Library, East Lansing, MI [*Library symbol*] [*Library of Congress*] (LCLS)
MIE	European Federation for Medical Informatics [*Sweden*] (EAIO)
MIE	Hungarian Association for the Protection of Industrial Property (SAUO)
MIE	Magnetic Isotope Effect [*Physics*]
MIE	Magnetron Ion Etching [*Semiconductor technology*]
MIE	Major Items of Equipment
MIE	Management Improvement and Evaluation
MIE	Management Information Element [*Telecommunications*] (OSI)
MIE	Maserati Information Exchange (EA)
MIE	Mass Inertia Excitation
MIE	Master of Industrial Engineering
MIE	Master of Irrigation Engineering
MIE	Medical Improvement Expectation (MELL)
MIE	Member of the Institute of Engineers (SAUO)

MIE	Member of the Institution of Mechanical Engineers (SAUO)
MIE	Merrill Lynch & Co. "MITTS" 98 [*NYSE symbol*] (SPSG)
MIE	Meteor Ionizing Efficiency
Mi-E	Michigan State Library, Escanaba Branch, Escanaba, MI [*Library symbol*] [*Library of Congress*] (LCLS)
MiE	Minimum Effect [*Pharmacology*]
MIE	Minimum Ignition Energy
MIE	Mission-Independent Equipment [*NASA*]
MIE	Mobile Inspection Equipment (SAA)
MIE	Modal Identification Experiment [*NASA*] (SPST)
MIE	Monitor Inertial Electronics (ACAE)
MIE	Muncie [*Indiana*] [*Airport symbol*] (OAG)
MIE	Muncie, IN [*Location identifier*] [*FAA*] (FAAL)
MIEA	Master Information Exchange Agreement (SAUS)
MIEA	Member of the Institution of Engineers, Australia (SAUO)
MIEA	Music Industry Educators Association (EA)
MiEad	East Detroit Memorial Library, East Detroit, MI [*Library symbol*] [*Library of Congress*] (LCLS)
MiEat	Eaton Rapids Public Library, Eaton Rapids, MI [*Library symbol*] [*Library of Congress*] (LCLS)
MIEAWA	Meat Industries Employers' Association of Western Australia
MIEC	Branche Africaine du Mouvement International des Etudiants Catholiques [*African International Movement of Catholic Students - AIMCS*] (EAIO)
MiEc	Eau Claire District Library, Eau Claire, MI [*Library symbol*] [*Library of Congress*] (LCLS)
MIEC	Meteorological Information Extraction Center
MIEC	Military Intelligence Exchange Center (CINC)
MIEC	Mixed Ionic and Electronic Conducting [*Polymers*]
MIEC	[*Meteorological Information Extraction Center*] Operator Guide
MIEC	Pax Romana, Mouvement International des Etudiants Catholiques [*Pax Romana, International Movement of Catholic Students - IMCS*] [*Paris, France*] (EAIO)
MIECO	Marshall Islands Import-Export Company (SAUO)
MIED	Member of the Institution of Engineering Designers [*British*] (DBQ)
MIEE	Mechanical, Instrument, and Electrical Engineering [*Department of Employment*] [*British*]
MIEE	Member of the Institution of Electrical Engineers [*Formerly, AMIEE*] [*British*] (EY)
MIEEE	Member of the Institute of Electrical and Electronic Engineers
MIEETAT	Major Improvements in Electronic Effectiveness through Advanced Technology (MCD)
MIEF	Master Imagery Exchange Format (MCD)
MIEI	Member of the Institution of Engineering Inspection [*British*]
MIE(Ind)	Member of the Institution of Engineers, India
MiElb	Elberta Public Library, Elberta, MI [*Library symbol*] [*Library of Congress*] (LCLS)
MIEIecIE	Corporate Member of the Institution of Electrical and Electronics Incorporated Engineers [*British*] (DBQ)
MiElk	Elk Rapids District Library, Elk Rapids, MI [*Library symbol*] [*Library of Congress*] (LCLS)
MiEm	Glen Lake Community Library, Empire, MI [*Library symbol*] [*Library of Congress*] (LCLS)
MIEM	Master in International Economics and Management (ECON)
MIEM	Master Member of the Institute of Executives and Managers [*British*] (DBQ)
MIEM	Masters Degree in International Economics and Management (ECON)
MiEM	Michigan State University, East Lansing, MI [*Library symbol*] [*Library of Congress*] (LCLS)
MIE Mgmt	Master of Industrial Engineering Management (PGP)
MiEmp	Glen Lake Community Library, Empire, MI [*Library symbol*] [*Library of Congress*] (LCLS)
MI Eng	Master of Industrial Engineering
MIER	Management-Initiated Early Retirement (ADA)
MIER	Military Intelligence Enlisted Reserve (SAUO)
MIERE	Member of the British Institute of Electronic and Radio Engineers (SAUO)
MIERE	Member of the Institution of Electronic and Radio Engineers [*Formerly, M Brit IRE*] [*British*]
MIERS	Modernized Imagery Exploitation and Reporting System (MCD)
MIES	Member of the Institution of Engineers and Shipbuilders, Scotland
MIES	Metastable Impact Electron Spectroscopy (SAUS)
MIES	Modernised-Imagery Exploitation System (SAUS)
MIES	Multi-Imagery Exploitation System
MiEsc	Escanaba Public Library, Escanaba, MI [*Library symbol*] [*Library of Congress*] (LCLS)
MiEscB	Bay De Noc Community College, Escanaba, MI [*Library symbol*] [*Library of Congress*] (LCLS)
MIESR	Matrix Isolation and Electron Spin Resonance [*Analytical chemistry*]
MIESS	Member of the Institution of Engineers and Shipbuilders, Scotland (SAUO)
MiEv	Evart Public Library, Evart, MI [*Library symbol*] [*Library of Congress*] (LCLS)
MiEw	McMillan Township Library, Ewen, MI [*Library symbol*] [*Library of Congress*] (LCLS)
MI Ex	Member of the Institute of Export [*British*]
MIExE	Member of the Institute of Executive Engineers and Officers [*British*] (DBQ)
MIEx(Grad)	Member of the Institute of Export [*British*] (DBQ)
MIExpE	Member of the Institute of Explosives Engineers [*British*] (DBQ)
MIF	International Falcon Movement (SAUO)
MIF	Macrophage Inhibitory Factor [*Immunology*]
MIF	Maker Interchange Format [*Computer science*] (CDE)
MIF	Malfunction Investigations File (MCD)
MIF	Management Information File [*Computer science*] (PCM)
MIF	Management Information Format [*Computer science*]
MIF	Manual Intervention Facility
MIF	MARC [*Machine-Readable Cataloging*] International Format
MIF	Maritime Interception Force (DOMA)
MIF	Maritime Interdiction Force (SAUO)
MIF	Marker Interchange Format (SAUO)
MIF	Mass-Independent Fractionation [*Chemistry*]
MIF	Master Index File
MIF	Master Inventory File (AFIT)
MIF	Master Item File (MCD)
MIF	Maximal Inspiratory Flow [*Medicine*]
MIF	Maximum Inspiratory Force [*Medicine*] (MELL)
MIF	Medina, OH [*Location identifier*] [*FAA*] (FAAL)
MIF	Melanocyte-Inhibiting Factor [*Endocrinology*]
MIF	Melanocyte-Stimulating-Hormone Release Inhibiting Factor [*Also, MRIF*] [*Endocrinology*]
MIF	Melanotropin Inhibiting Factor [*Biochemistry*]
MIF	Melbourne International Festival [*Australia*]
MIF	Member of the Institute of Fuel (SAUO)
MIF	Membrane Immunofluorescence [*Analytical biochemistry*]
MIF	Merthiolate-Iodine-Formaldehyde [*Technique*]
MIF	Mesoderm-Inducing Factor [*Embryology*]
MIF	Midinspiratory Flow [*Medicine*] (DMAA)
MIF	Migration Inhibition [*or Inhibitory*] Factor [*Cytology*]
MIF	Milk Industry Foundation (EA)
MIF	Milk in First [*Tea-pouring procedure*]
MIF	Miners' International Federation [*See also FIM*] [*Brussels, Belgium*] (EAIO)
MIF	Minimum Internetworking Functionality (VLIE)
MIF	Missile-in-Flight
MIF	Mixed Immunofluorescence [*Medicine*] (MAE)
MIF	Mobile Instrument Facility
MIF	Modernization and Implementation Facility (SAUO)
MIF	Module Integration Facility (SSD)
MIF	Monopulse Interference Filter
MIF	Mortgage Indemnity Fund [*Veterans Administration*]
MIF	Multisource Intelligence File (MCD)
MIF	MuniInsured Fund Inc. [*AMEX symbol*] (SPSG)
MIF	MuniInsred Fund [*AMEX symbol*] (TTSB)
MIF	Myocardial Infarction [*Cardiology*] (DHSM)
MIFA	Member of the Institute of Foresters of Australia (SAUO)
MIFA	Mitomycin C, Fluorouracil, Adriamycin [*Antineoplastic drug regimen*]
MIFACS	Medical Institutions' Financial Accounting System
MI-FA-MI	Misery, Famine, Misery [*Said to be "earth's song," in theory that all planets emit musical sounds governed by their paths around the sun*]
MIFAS	Mechanized Integrated Financial Accounting System [*Department of State*]
MIFASS	Marine Integral (or Integrated) Fire and Air Support System (SAUO)
MIFASS	Marine Integrated Fire and Air Support System
MiFaw	Farwell Public Library, Farwell, MI [*Library symbol*] [*Library of Congress*] (LCLS)
MIFC	Madonna International Fan Club [*Defunct*] (EA)
MIFC	Merthiolate-Iodine Formalin Concentration
MIFC	Mid Iowa Financial Corp. [*NASDAQ symbol*] (SAG)
MIFC	Mid-Iowa Finl [*NASDAQ symbol*] (TTSB)
MIFCT	Moscow Institute of Fine Chemical Technology (SAUO)
MIFD	Material Information Flow Device [*Military*] (AFM)
MIFE	Manila International Futures Exchange [*Philippines*] (NUMA)
MIFE	Minimum Independent Failure Element
MIFERSO	Eastern Senegal Iron Ore Mining Co. (SAUO)
MIFERSO	Eastern Senegal Iron Ore Mining Company (SAUS)
MIFF	Management Information Format File [*Computer science*]
MIFF	Member of the Institute of Freight Forwarders [*British*] (ODBW)
MiFg	Fairgrove Township Library, Fairgrove, MI [*Library symbol*] [*Library of Congress*] (LCLS)
MIFG	Micro Focus Group Ltd. [*NASDAQ symbol*] (SAG)
MIFG	Patches of Shallow Fog not Deeper Than Two Meters [*NWS*] (FAAC)
MIFGY	Micro Focus Grp ADS [*NASDAQ symbol*] (TTSB)
MIFI	Missile In-Flight Indicator
MiFil	Fife Lake Public Library, Fife Lake, MI [*Library symbol*] [*Library of Congress*] (LCLS)
MIFIR	Microwave Instantaneous Frequency Indication Receiver (MCD)
MIFirE	Member of the Institution of Fire Engineers [*British*] (DCTA)
MIFireE	Member of the Institution of Fire Engineers [*British*] (EY)
MIFL	Master International Frequency List
MiFli	Flint Public Library, Flint, MI [*Library symbol*] [*Library of Congress*] (LCLS)
MiFliACS	AC Spark Plug Co., General Motors Corp., Flint, MI [*Library symbol*] [*Library of Congress*] (LCLS)
MiFliC	University of Michigan at Flint, and Charles Stewart Mott Community College, Flint, MI [*Library symbol*] [*Library of Congress*] (LCLS)
MiFliG	GMI Engineering and Management Institute, Flint, MI [*Library symbol*] [*Library of Congress*] (LCLS)
MiFos	Watertown Township Library, Fostoria, MI [*Library symbol*] [*Library of Congress*] (LCLS)
MiFow	Fowlerville Public Library, Fowlerville, MI [*Library symbol*] [*Library of Congress*] (LCLS)
MIFR	Master International Frequency Register
MIFR	Maximal Inspiratory Flow Rate [*Medicine*]
MIFR	Minor Frame (ACAE)
MIFR	Monitored International Frequency Register (NITA)
MIFR	Mullerian Inhibiting Factor [*Medicine*] (MELL)
MIFR	Multiband Infrared Filter Radiometer

MiFra	Frankfort City Library, Frankfort, MI [*Library symbol*] [*Library of Congress*] (LCLS)
MiFram	James E. Wickson Memorial Library, Frankenmuth, MI [*Library symbol*] [*Library of Congress*] (LCLS)
MiFras	Fraser Public Library, Fraser, MI [*Library symbol*] [*Library of Congress*] (LCLS)
MiFrem	Fremont Public Library, Fremont, MI [*Library symbol*] [*Library of Congress*] (LCLS)
MIFS	Material Information Flow System [*Military*] (AFM)
MIFS	Multiplex Interferometric Fourier Spectroscopy
MIFS	Myanmar-IRRI Farming Systems (SAUO)
M/IFS	VM/Interactive File Snaring (SAUS)
MIFSA	Missile In-Flight Safety Approval (MUGU)
MIFT	Manchester International Freight Terminal [*British*] (DS)
MIFV	Mechanised Infantry Fighting Vehicle (SAUS)
Mig	De Migratione Abrahami [*Philo*] (BJA)
MIG	Mach Interface Generator (SAUS)
MIG	Magnetic Injection Gun (IEEE)
MIG	Magnetized Ionized Gas
MIG	Malaria Immune Globulin
MIG	Management Information Guide [*Reference series*]
MIG	Marine Industry Group (SAUO)
MIG	Mars Investigation Group [*Defunct*] (EA)
MIG	MCE Interface Group (SAUO)
MIG	Meadowbrook Insurance Group [*NYSE symbol*] (SAG)
MIG	Meadowbrook Insurance Grp [*NYSE symbol*] (TTSB)
MIG	Measles Immune Globulin [*Immunology*]
MIG	Meat Innovation Grant
MIG	Medial Inferior Geniculate Artery [*Anatomy*]
MIG	Medical Information Group (SAUO)
MIG	Medicare Insured Group (HCT)
M-Ig	Membrane Immunoglobulin [*Immunology*]
MIG	Message Identification Group (SAUO)
MIG	Metal-Inert-Gas [*Underwater welding*]
MIG	Metallic Inert Gas (SAUS)
MIG	Methane Inert Gas (MCD)
Mig	Mignon [*Horticulture*]
MIG	Migration (SAUO)
MIG	Mikoyan and Gurevich [*Acronym used as designation for a Russian aircraft and is formed from the names of the aircraft's designers*]
MIG	Military Intelligence Group (MCD)
MIG	Military Intelligence Guide (MCD)
MIG	Millington, TN [*Location identifier*] [*FAA*] (FAAL)
MIG	Ming Mines Ltd. [*Vancouver Stock Exchange symbol*]
MIG	Miniature Integrating Gyroscope
MIG	Minimum Income Guarantee
MIG	Moody's Investment Grade
MIG	Mortgage Indemnity Guarantee (WDAA)
MIG	Multilevel Interconnect Generator
MIG-1	Moody's Investment Grade (DFIT)
MIGA	Multilateral Investment Guarantee Agency [*World Bank*]
MIGA	Multinational Investment Guarantee Agency (SAUO)
MiGal	Galesburg Memorial Library, Galesburg, MI [*Library symbol*] [*Library of Congress*] (LCLS)
MI/GAL	Miles per Gallon (WDAA)
MiGali	Galien Township Public Library, Galien, MI [*Library symbol*] [*Library of Congress*] (LCLS)
MIGasE	Member of the Institution of Gas Engineers [*British*]
MiGay	Gaylord-Otsego County Public Library, Gaylord, MI [*Library symbol*] [*Library of Congress*] (LCLS)
MIGB	Millinery Institute of Great Britain (BI)
MiGc	Garden City Public Library, Garden City, MI [*Library symbol*] [*Library of Congress*] (LCLS)
MIGCAP	MIG [*Mikoyan and Gurevich*] Combat Air Patrol (DNAB)
MIGD	Member of the Institute of Grocery Distribution [*British*] (DBQ)
MIGE	Missile Impact and Gaseous Explosions (HEAS)
MIGeol	Member of the Institution of Geologists [*British*] (DBQ)
MIGET	Miniature Interface General-Purpose Economy Terminal [*Computer science*] (MHDB)
MIgG	Monkey Immunoglobulin G [*Immunology*]
MIGG	MRA Implementation Guide Group (SAUO)
MiGh	Loutit Library, Grand Haven, MI [*Library symbol*] [*Library of Congress*] (LCLS)
MIGI	Meridian Insrance Gp [*NASDAQ symbol*] (TTSB)
MIGI	Meridian Insurance Group, Inc. [*NASDAQ symbol*] (NQ)
MIGITS	Miniature Integrated GPS/INS Tactical System (SAUS)
MiGl	Gladstone Public Library, Gladstone, MI [*Library symbol*] [*Library of Congress*] (LCLS)
MiGlad	Gladwin County Library, Gladwin, MI [*Library symbol*] [*Library of Congress*] (LCLS)
MiGlad-B	Gladwin County Library, Beaverton Branch Library, Beaverton, MI [*Library symbol*] [*Library of Congress*] (LCLS)
MIGN	Michigan Northern Railway Co., Inc. [*AAR code*]
MiGp	Grosse Pointe Public Library, Grosse Pointe, MI [*Library symbol*] [*Library of Congress*] (LCLS)
MiGr	Grand Rapids Public Library, Grand Rapids, MI [*Library symbol*] [*Library of Congress*] (LCLS)
MiGrA	Aquinas College, Grand Rapids, MI [*Library symbol*] [*Library of Congress*] (LCLS)
MiGran	Grant Public Library, Grant, MI [*Library symbol*] [*Library of Congress*] (LCLS)
MiGray	Crawford County Library, Grayling, MI [*Library symbol*] [*Library of Congress*] (LCLS)
MiGrB	Grand Rapids Baptist College, Grand Rapids, MI [*Library symbol*] [*Library of Congress*] (LCLS)
MiGrC	Calvin College and Seminary, Grand Rapids, MI [*Library symbol*] [*Library of Congress*] (LCLS)
MiGre	Greenville Public Library, Greenville, MI [*Library symbol*] [*Library of Congress*] (LCLS)
MiGrJC	Grand Rapids Junior College, Grand Rapids, MI [*Library symbol*] [*Library of Congress*] (LCLS)
MiGrl	Grand Ledge Public Library, Grand Ledge, MI [*Library symbol*] [*Library of Congress*] (LCLS)
MiGrL	Grand Rapids Law Library, Grand Rapids, MI [*Library symbol*] [*Library of Congress*] (LCLS)
MiGrlP	Grand Ledge Public Library, Grand Ledge, MI [*Library symbol*] [*Library of Congress*] (LCLS)
MiGrMtM	Mount Mercy Academy, Grand Rapids, MI [*Library symbol*] [*Library of Congress*] (LCLS)
MiGrW	Western Michigan Genealogical Society, Grand Rapids, MI [*Library symbol*] [*Library of Congress*] (LCLS)
MIGS	MASnet Internet Gateway Server (SAUS)
MIGS	Metal-Induced Gap States (AAEL)
MIGS	Miniature Infrared Guidance Sensor (ACAE)
MIGS	Music Industries Golfing Society [*British*] (BI)
MiGw	Forsythe Township Public Library, Gwinn, MI [*Library symbol*] [*Library of Congress*] (LCLS)
MIH	Brownsville, TX [*Location identifier*] [*FAA*] (FAAL)
MIH	Master of Industrial Health
MIH	Melanocyte-Stimulating Hormone-Inhibitory Hormone [*Endocrinology*] (DAVI)
MIH	Melanotropin Release Inhibiting Hormone (SAUS)
MIH	Member of the Institute of Housing [*British*] (DBQ)
MIH	Member of the Institute of Hygiene [*British*]
MIH	Migraine with Interparoxysmal Headache [*Neurology*] (DAVI)
MIH	Migraine with Interval Headache (MELL)
MIH	Miles in the Hour [*Rate of military march*]
MIH	Minimal Intermittent [*Dosage of*] Heparin [*Pharmacology*] (DAVI)
MIH	Missing Interruption Handler [*Computer science*] (IBMDP)
MIH	Molecule-Induced Homolysis [*Chemistry*]
MIH	Molt Inhibitory Hormone
MIH	Multiplex Interface Handler
MiHa	Hart Public Library, Hart, MI [*Library symbol*] [*Library of Congress*] (LCLS)
MIHA	Move-In Housing Allowance
MiHaf	Hartford Public Library, Hartford, MI [*Library symbol*] [*Library of Congress*] (LCLS)
MiHal	Cromaine Library, Hartland, MI [*Library symbol*] [*Library of Congress*] (LCLS)
MiHam	Hamtramck Public Library, Hamtramck, MI [*Library symbol*] [*Library of Congress*] (LCLS)
MiHamb	Hamburg Township Library, Hamburg, MI [*Library symbol*] [*Library of Congress*] (LCLS)
MiHan	Hancock Public-School Library, Hancock, MI [*Library symbol*] [*Library of Congress*] (LCLS)
MiHanS	Suomi College, Hancock, MI [*Library symbol*] [*Library of Congress*] (LCLS)
MiHars	Harrison Public Library, Harrison, MI [*Library symbol*] [*Library of Congress*] (LCLS)
MiHarsM	Mid-Michigan Community College, Harrison, MI [*Library symbol*] [*Library of Congress*] (LCLS)
MiHarv	Alcona County Library, Harrisville, MI [*Library symbol*] [*Library of Congress*] (LCLS)
MiHas	Hastings Public Library, Hastings, MI [*Library symbol*] [*Library of Congress*] (LCLS)
MiHb	Harbor Beach Public Library, Harbor Beach, MI [*Library symbol*] [*Library of Congress*] (LCLS)
Mi-HC	Michigan Historical Commission, State Archives Library, Lansing, MI [*Library symbol*] [*Library of Congress*] (LCLS)
MIHC	M. I. Hummel Club (EA)
MiHe	Hesperia Public Library, Hesperia, MI [*Library symbol*] [*Library of Congress*] (LCLS)
MIHE	Member of the Institute of Health Education [*British*]
MIHE	Member of the Institution of Highway Engineers (SAUO)
MIHEc	Member of the Institute of Home Economics [*British*] (DBQ)
MiHem	Mary C. Rauchholz Memorial Library, Hemlock, MI [*Library symbol*] [*Library of Congress*] (LCLS)
MIHIC	Mile High Conference (PSS)
MiHil	Mitchell Public Library, Hillsdale, MI [*Library symbol*] [*Library of Congress*] (LCLS)
MiHilC	Hillsdale College, Hillsdale, MI [*Library symbol*] [*Library of Congress*] (LCLS)
MiHilm	Hillman Public Library, Hillman, MI [*Library symbol*] [*Library of Congress*] (LCLS)
MiHl	Houghton Lake Public Library, Houghton Lake, MI [*Library symbol*] [*Library of Congress*] (LCLS)
MIHL	MIH Limited 'A' [*NASDAQ symbol*] (SG)
MIHM	Master of International Health Management (PGP)
MiHM	Michigan Technological University, Houghton, MI [*Library symbol*] [*Library of Congress*] (LCLS)
MIHO	Miles Homes [*NASDAQ symbol*] (TTSB)
MIHO	Miles Homes, Inc. [*NASDAQ symbol*] (SAG)
MiHol	Herrick Public Library, Holland, MI [*Library symbol*] [*Library of Congress*] (LCLS)
MiHolH	Hope College, Holland, MI [*Library symbol*] [*Library of Congress*] (LCLS)
MiHolW	Western Theological Seminary, Holland, MI [*Library symbol*] [*Library of Congress*] (LCLS)
MiHom	Homer Public Library, Homer, MI [*Library symbol*] [*Library of Congress*] (LCLS)

MiHow .... Howell Carnegie Library, Howell, MI [*Library symbol*] [*Library of Congress*] (LCLS)

MiHp .... McGregor Public Library, Highland Park, MI [*Library symbol*] [*Library of Congress*] (LCLS)

MiHP .... Portage Lake District Library, Houghton, MI [*Library symbol*] [*Library of Congress*] (LCLS)

MiHpDH .... Detroit Osteopathic Hospital, Highland Park, MI [*Library symbol*] [*Library of Congress*] (LCLS)

MIHPED .... Microwave-Induced Helium Plasma Emission Detection (NATG)

MiHPL .... Portage Lake District Library, Houghton, MI [*Library symbol*] [*Library of Congress*] (LCLS)

MIHS .... Marshall Islands High School (SAUO)

MIHT .... Member of the Institution of Highways and Transportation [*British*] (DBQ)

MIHT .... Moscow Institute of Heat Technology (IGSL)

MiHu .... Hudson Public Library, Hudson, MI [*Library symbol*] [*Library of Congress*] (LCLS)

MiHudv .... Hudsonville Public Library, Hudsonville, MI [*Library symbol*] [*Library of Congress*] (LCLS)

MIHVE .... Member of the Institution of Heating and Ventilating Engineers [*British*]

MII .... Caddo Mills, TX [*Location identifier*] [*FAA*] (FAAL)

MII .... Management Interest Inventory [*Test*]

MII .... Manufacturing Impact Item (MCD)

MII .... Marilia [*Brazil*] [*Airport symbol*] (OAG)

MII .... Medical Imaging Informatics (RALS)

MI/I .... Microinches per Inch (KSC)

MII .... Microsoft, IBM, Intel (SAUO)

MII .... Military Intelligence Interpreter

MII .... Military Intelligence Interrogation

MII .... Mineral Information Institute (EA)

MII .... Ministry of Industry Information (SAUO)

MII .... Minnesota Interlibrary Telecommunications Exchange, Minneapolis, MN [*OCLC symbol*] (OCLC)

MII .... Modular Image Interpretation (ACAE)

MII .... Morton International [*NYSE symbol*] (TTSB)

MII .... Morton International, Inc. [*NYSE symbol*] (SPSG)

MII .... Motorists Information, Inc. [*Defunct*] (EA)

MIIA .... Medical Information and Intelligence Agency (SAUO)

MIIA .... Medical Intelligence and Information Agency [*Formerly, MIO*] [*DoD*]

MIIA .... Member of the Institute of Industrial Administration [*Later, MBIM*] [*British*]

MIIA .... Merritt Island Industrial Area [*NASA*] (KSC)

MIIA .... Mine Inspectors' Institute of America (EA)

MIIC .... International Catholic Movement for Intellectual and Cultural Affairs (SAUO)

MIIC .... Pax Romana, Mouvement International des Intellectuels Catholiques [*Pax Romana, International Catholic Movement for Intellectual and Cultural Affairs - ICMICA*] [*Geneva, Switzerland*] (EAIO)

MIICS .... Master Item Identification Control System

MiId .... Idlewild Public Library, Idlewild, MI [*Library symbol*] [*Library of Congress*] (LCLS)

MIID .... Media Institutes for Institute Directors

MIIDS .... Military Intelligence Integrated Data System (SAUO)

MIIDS .... Missile Interior Intrusion Detection System (DWSG)

MIIDS/IDB .... Military Intelligence Integrated Data System/Integrated Database (SAUS)

MIIE .... Member of the Institution of Industrial Engineers (SAUO)

MIIF .... Maintenance of Inactive Industrial Facilities

MIIF .... Master Item Intelligence File

MIIFC .... Michigan Intercollegiate Football Conference (PSS)

MIIL .... Master Item Identification List

MIIM .... Master of International and Intercultural Management (PGP)

MIIM .... Member of the Institution of Industrial Managers [*British*] (DCTA)

MI Inf Sc ...... Member of the Institute of Information Scientists [*British*]

MiInr .... Indian River Public Library, Indian River, MI [*Library symbol*] [*Library of Congress*] (LCLS)

MI insuf ...... Mitral Insufficiency [*Cardiology*] (DAVI)

MiInt .... Interlovhen Public Library, Interlochen, MI [*Library symbol*] [*Library of Congress*] (LCLS)

MIIR .... Mellon Institute of Industrial Research (SAUO)

MiIrmD .... Dickinson County Library, Iron Mountain, MI [*Library symbol*] [*Library of Congress*] (LCLS)

MiIrmD-N ..... Dickinson County Library, Norway Branch, Norway, MI [*Library symbol*] [*Library of Congress*] (LCLS)

MiIrmM .... Mid-Peninsula Library Federation Headquarters, Iron Mountain, MI [*Library symbol*] [*Library of Congress*] (LCLS)

MiIrmV .... United States Veterans Administration Hospital, Iron Mountain, MI [*Library symbol*] [*Library of Congress*] (LCLS)

MiIrr .... West Iron District Library, Iron River, MI [*Library symbol*] [*Library of Congress*] (LCLS)

MIIRS .... Modular Imagery Interpretation & Reporting System (SAUS)

MiIrw .... Ironwood Carnegie Library, Ironwood, MI [*Library symbol*] [*Library of Congress*] (LCLS)

MiIs .... Ishpeming Carnegie Library, Ishpeming, MI [*Library symbol*] [*Library of Congress*] (LCLS)

MIIS .... Marshall Islands Intermediate School (SAUO)

MIIS .... Member of the Institute of Industrial Supervisors (SAUO)

MIIS .... Miscellaneous Inputs Information Subsystem [*Computer science*]

MIIS .... Modular Imagery Interpretation System

MIIS .... Monterey Institute of International Studies (ECON)

MIISA .... Management Information and Instructional Systems Activity (DNAB)

MIISADET .... Management Information and Instructional Systems Activity Detachment (DNAB)

MIISAU .... Management Information and Instructional Systems Activity Unit (DNAB)

MIISE .... Member of the International Institute of Social Economics [*British*] (DBQ)

MIISec .... Member of the Institute of Industrial Security [*British*] (DBQ)

MIIT .... Manned Interceptor Integration Team (SAA)

Milt .... Thompson Home Library, Ithaca, MI [*Library symbol*] [*Library of Congress*] (LCLS)

MIIU .... Marine Incident Investigation Unit (SAUO)

MIJ .... Dugway/Tooele, UT [*Location identifier*] [*FAA*] (FAAL)

MIJ .... Maatschappij [*Joint Stock Company*] [*Netherlands*]

MIJ .... Master of International Journalism (PGP)

MIJ .... Member of the Institution of Journalists

MIJ .... Metal Insulator Junction

MIJ .... Mili [*Marshall Islands*] [*Airport symbol*] (OAG)

MiJa .... Jackson Public Library, Jackson, MI [*Library symbol*] [*Library of Congress*] (LCLS)

MiJaC .... Jackson County Library, Jackson, MI [*Library symbol*] [*Library of Congress*] (LCLS)

MiJaCc .... Jackson Community College, Jackson, MI [*Library symbol*] [*Library of Congress*] (LCLS)

MiJaCP .... Consumers Power Co., Parnall Technical Library, Jackson, MI [*Library symbol*] [*Library of Congress*] (LCLS)

MIJAL .... Memoirs, International Journal of American Linguistics (SAUO)

MiJam .... Jamestown Township Library, Jamestown, MI [*Library symbol*] [*Library of Congress*] (LCLS)

MIJARC .... Mouvement International de la Jeunesse Agricole et Rurale Catholique [*International Movement of Catholic Agricultural and Rural Youth - IMCARY*] [*Louvain, Belgium*] (EAIO)

MIJC .... Mouvement International des Juristes Catholiques, Pax Romana [*France*]

MiJen .... Georgetown Township Library, Jenison, MI [*Library symbol*] [*Library of Congress*] (LCLS)

MIJI .... Meaconing, Interference, Jamming and Intrusion (SAUO)

MIJI .... Meaconing, Intrusion, Jamming, Interference [*Military*] (NVT)

MIJO .... Missile Joint Optimization

MiK .... Kalamazoo Public Library, Kalamazoo, MI [*Library symbol*] [*Library of Congress*] (LCLS)

MIK .... Meerblick, SA [*Spain*] [*FAA designator*] (FAAC)

MIK .... Methyl Isobutyl Ketone [*Also, MIBK*] [*Organic chemistry*]

MIK .... Mikkeli [*Finland*] [*Airport symbol*] (OAG)

Mik .... Mikva'ot (BJA)

MIK .... Minitrack [*Alaska*] [*Seismograph station code, US Geological Survey*] [*Closed*] (SEIS)

MIK .... Missile Installation Kit (ACAE)

MIK .... More in the Kitchen [*Family dinner-table expression*]

MiKa .... Kalkaska County Library, Kalkaska, MI [*Library symbol*] [*Library of Congress*] (LCLS)

MIKA .... Medical Imaging Centers of America (EFIS)

MIKA .... Minor Karyotypic Abnormalities [*Medicine*]

MIKADOS ..... Mini Instant Keyboard Assembler, Debug, and Operating System [*Computer science*] (MHDI)

Mikasa .... Mikasa, Inc. [*Associated Press*] (SAG)

MiKB .... Borgess Hospital, Medical Library, Kalamazoo, MI [*Library symbol*] [*Library of Congress*] (LCLS)

MiKC .... Kalamazoo College, Kalamazoo, MI [*Library symbol*] [*Library of Congress*] (LCLS)

MiKCS .... Institute of Cistercian Studies, Western Michigan University, Kalamazoo, MI [*Library symbol*] [*Library of Congress*] (LCLS)

MIKE .... Manipulator Interactive Kinematics Evaluator (SSD)

MIKE .... Mass-Analyzed Ion Kinetic Energy

MIKE .... Measurement of Instantaneous Kinetic Energy (IEEE)

MIKE .... Michael Stores [*NASDAQ symbol*] (SAG)

MIKE .... Micro Interpreter for Knowledge Engineering [*Computer science*]

MIKE .... Microphone (CET)

mike .... Microphone (IDOE)

MIKE .... Multiwave Italian Key System (NITA)

MIKER .... Microbalance Inverted Knudsen Effusion Recoil

MIKES .... Mass-Analyzed Ion Kinetic Energy Spectrometry

MikGed .... Mikra'ot Gedolot (BJA)

MiKin .... Kingston Community Public Library, Kingston, MI [*Library symbol*] [*Library of Congress*] (LCLS)

MiKins .... Kingsley Public Library, Kingsley, MI [*Library symbol*] [*Library of Congress*] (LCLS)

MIKK .... Medjunarodni Institut za Kucnu Knjizevnost [*International Institute for Home Literature - IIHL*] [*Belgrade, Yugoslavia*] (EAIO)

MiKL .... Kalamazoo Library System, Kalamazoo, MI [*Library symbol*] [*Library of Congress*] (LCLS)

MIKL .... Michael Foods [*NASDAQ symbol*] (TTSB)

MIKL .... Michael Foods, Inc. [*NASDAQ symbol*] (NQ)

MIKN .... Mikohn Gaming [*NASDAQ symbol*] (TTSB)

MIKN .... Mikohn Gaming Corp. [*NASDAQ symbol*] (SAG)

Mikohn .... Mikohn Gaming Corp. [*Associated Press*] (SAG)

MiKPSc .... Kalamazoo Public School District, Kalamazoo, MI [*Library symbol*] [*Library of Congress*] (LCLS)

MIKR .... Mikron Instr [*NASDAQ symbol*] (TTSB)

MIKR .... Mikron Instrument Co., Inc. [*NASDAQ symbol*] (NQ)

Mikron .... Mikron Instrument Co., Inc. [*Associated Press*] (SAG)

MiKUp .... Upjohn Co., Kalamazoo, MI [*Library symbol*] [*Library of Congress*] (LCLS)

MiKUp_B ...... Upjohn Co., Business Library, Kalamazoo, MI [*Library symbol*] [*Library of Congress*] (LCLS)

MiKV .... Kalamazoo Valley Community College, Kalamazoo, MI [*Library symbol*] [*Library of Congress*] (LCLS)

Mikv .... Mikva'ot (BJA)

MiKW	Western Michigan University, Kalamazoo, MI [*Library symbol*] [*Library of Congress*] (LCLS)
MiKWUp	W. E. Upjohn Institute for Employment Research, Kalamazoo, MI [*Library symbol*] [*Library of Congress*] (LCLS)
miky	Milky [*Philately*]
MiL	Lansing Public Library, Lansing, MI [*Library symbol*] [*Library of Congress*] (LCLS)
MIL	Machine Independent Language (VLIE)
MIL	Machine Interface Layer [*Computer science*] (VLIE)
MIL	Macro-Instruction Link [*Computer science*] (VLIE)
MIL	Magnetic Indicator Loop (NVT)
MIL	Malaya Indonesia Line (SAUO)
MIL	Malfunction Indicator Light [*Automotive engineering*]
MIL	Malfunction Investigation Laboratory
MIL	Map and Imagery Laboratory (SAUO)
MIL	Marine Instrumentation Laboratory [*Marine science*] (OSRA)
MIL	Market Investigations Limited (SAUO)
MIL	Master Index List (MCD)
MIL	Master Instrumentation List
MIL	Master Item Identification List (AABC)
MIL	Material
MIL	Matrox Imaging Library (SAUS)
MIL	Meat Import Law (SAUO)
MIL	Member of the Institute of Linguists [*British*]
MIL	Mensa International [*British*] (EAIO)
MIL	Merrit Island (SAUO)
MIL	Merritt Island Tracking Station [*Florida*]
MIL	Microimplementation Language [*Burroughs Corp.*]
MIL	Microsystems International Limited (SAUO)
MIL	Milan [*Italy*] [*Seismograph station code, US Geological Survey*] [*Closed*] (SEIS)
MIL	Mileage
MIL	Miles Laboratories, Inc. (SAUO)
Mil	Miles' Pennsylvania Reports [*A publication*] (DLA)
mil	Military (BEE)
MIL	Military (CMD)
MIL	Military (EY)
MIL	Military Instrumentation List
MIL	Military in the Loop (ACAE)
MIL	Military Specification [*Followed by a single capital letter and numbers*] (IEEE)
mil	Militia (WDAA)
MIL	Militia
Mil	Miller's Reports [*1-5 Louisiana*] [*A publication*] (DLA)
Mil	Miller's Reports [*3-18 Maryland*] [*A publication*] (DLA)
MIL	Millieme [*Monetary unit*] [*Egypt, Sudan*]
mil	Milli-Inch
MIL	Milliliter
MIL	Milling
MIL	Million
MIL	Millipore Corp. [*NYSE symbol*] (SPSG)
Mil	Mills' New York Surrogate's Court Reports [*A publication*] (DLA)
Mil	Mill's South Carolina Constitutional Reports [*A publication*] (DLA)
MIL	Milwaukee [*Wisconsin*]
MIL	Minnesota Instructional Language [*Computer science*] (CSR)
MIL	Missile Industry Liaison (SAA)
MIL	Module Interconnection Language
MIL	Mothers-in-Law Club International (EA)
MIL	Movimiento Iberico Libertario [*Spain*] [*Political party*]
MIL	Moving Inspection Lot
MIL	Office of Public Library and Interlibrary Cooperation, St. Paul, MN [*OCLC symbol*] (OCLC)
Mil	Pro Milone [*of Cicero*] [*Classical studies*] (OCD)
MILA	Merritt Island Launch Area [*NASA*]
Mila	Militia [*British military*] (DMA)
MILAA	Milstar Corp. [*NASDAQ symbol*] (NQ)
MiLac	Missaukee County Library, Lake City, MI [*Library symbol*] [*Library of Congress*] (LCLS)
MiLacES	Lake City Elementary School, Lake City, MI [*Library symbol*] [*Library of Congress*] (LCLS)
MiLacHS	Lake City High School, Lake City, MI [*Library symbol*] [*Library of Congress*] (LCLS)
MILAD	Military Advisor [*SEATO or ANZUS Council*] (CINC)
MILADGOVT	Military Advisory Government
MILADGRU	Military Advisory Group
MILADREP	Military Advisors Representative (CINC)
MiLai	Laingsburg Public Library, Laingsburg, MI [*Library symbol*] [*Library of Congress*] (LCLS)
MiLakv	Cato Township Public Library, Lakeview, MI [*Library symbol*] [*Library of Congress*] (LCLS)
MiLal	Lake Linden-Hubbell Public School Library, Lake Linden, MI [*Library symbol*] [*Library of Congress*] (LCLS)
MiLan	L'Anse Township School and Public Library, L'Anse, MI [*Library symbol*] [*Library of Congress*] (LCLS)
MILAN	Missile d'Infanterie Leger Antichar
MILAN	Missile, Infantry Light Antiarmor [*Antitank system*] (INF)
Mil & Vet C	Military and Veterans Code [*A publication*] (DLA)
MILAP	Maintenance Information Logically Analyzed and Presented (SAUO)
MILAP	Modified Industry and Labour Adjustment Program (SAUO)
MILAS	Micrometer Low-Approach System
MilATCC	Military Air Traffic Control Centre (SAUO)
Mil Av	Military Aviator [*Army*]
MiLaw	Lawton Public Library, Lawton, MI [*Library symbol*] [*Library of Congress*] (LCLS)
MILBA	Military Base Agreement (CINC)

MiLC	Lansing Community College, Lansing, MI [*Library symbol*] [*Library of Congress*] (LCLS)
MILC	Metal Ion Liquid Chromatography
MILC	Midwest Interlibrary Center [*Later, CRL*]
MILC	Military Characteristics
MILC	Modified Intermediate Low Cycle (SAUS)
MILCAP	Military Civic Action Program
MILCAP	Military Standard Contract Administration Procedures [*DoD*]
MILCAPSYS	Measuring Military Capability & Constraints Information System (SAUS)
MILCEST	Military Communications Electronic Systems Technology (MCD)
MilcmIn	Millicom International Cellular [*Associated Press*] (SAG)
MilColl	Military College (SAUO)
MILCOM	Military Command (DNAB)
MILCOM	Military Committee Communication [*NATO*]
MILCOMP	Military Computer
MILCOMSAT	Military Communications Satellite
MILCON	Military Construction
MILCON-DA	Military Construction, Defense Agencies
MILCONF	Military Confinement
MILCS	Metropolitan Interlibrary Cooperative System [*New York Public Library*] [*Information service or system*]
MILD	Magnetic-Intrusion Line Detector (SAUS)
MILDAT	Military Damage Assessment Team (AABC)
MILDDU	Military-Industry Logistics Data Development Unit
MILDEC	Military Decision (NATG)
MILDEP	Military Department (COE)
MILDEPS	Military Departments (AABC)
MILDEPT	Military Department
MILDET	Military Detachment
MILDIP	Military-Industry Logistics Data Interchange Procedures
MILDIS	Military-Industry Logistics Data Interchange System
MILDOC	Military Document (AAGC)
MiLe	Leland Township Public Library, Leland, MI [*Library symbol*] [*Library of Congress*] (LCLS)
MILE	Member of the Institution of Locomotive Engineers (SAUO)
MILE	Minuteman Integrated Life Extension [*Telecommunications*] (LAIN)
MIL-E-CON	Military Electronic Conference
MileH	Miles Homes, Inc. [*Associated Press*] (SAG)
MileHme	Miles Homes, Inc. [*Associated Press*] (SAG)
MilePr	Milestone Properties [*Associated Press*] (SAG)
MiLer	LeRoy Public Library, LeRoy, MI [*Library symbol*] [*Library of Congress*] (LCLS)
MILES	Magnetic Intrusion Line Sensor (PDAA)
Miles	Miles' District Court Reports [*1825-41*] [*Philadelphia, PA*] [*A publication*] (DLA)
MILES	Military Implications of LASER Employment by the Soviets
MILES	Multiple Integrated LASER Engagement Simulation [*or System*] [*Army*]
MILES	Multiple Integrated LASER Engagement System (COE)
MILES/AGES	Multiple-Integrated LASER Engagement Simulation / Air Ground Engagement Simulator
Miles (PA)	Miles' Pennsylvania Reports [*A publication*] (DLA)
Miles R	Miles' Pennsylvania Reports [*A publication*] (DLA)
Miles R & O	Miles' Rules and Orders [*A publication*] (DLA)
Miles Rep	Miles' Pennsylvania Reports [*A publication*] (DLA)
MilestnSci	Milestone Scientific, Inc. [*Associated Press*] (SAG)
MiLew	Lewiston Public Library, Lewiston, MI [*Library symbol*] [*Library of Congress*] (LCLS)
MiLex	Moore Public Library, Lexington, MI [*Library symbol*] [*Library of Congress*] (LCLS)
MILF	Moro Islamic Liberation Front [*Philippines*] [*Political party*]
MiLG	Great Lakes Bible College, Lansing, MI [*Library symbol*] [*Library of Congress*] (LCLS)
MILGA	Member of the Institute of Local Government Administrators [*British*] (ODBW)
MiLGH	Lansing General Hospital Library, Lansing, MI [*Library symbol*] [*Library of Congress*] (LCLS)
MILGOV	Military Government (SAUO)
Mil Govt	Military Government (SAUO)
MILGP	Military Group
Milgray	Milgray Electronics, Inc. [*Associated Press*] (SAG)
MILGRP	Military Group (DNAB)
MILGRU	Military Group (DNAB)
MiLGS	Church of Jesus Christ of Latter-Day Saints, Genealogical Society Library, Lansing Branch, Stake Center, Lansing, MI [*Library symbol*] [*Library of Congress*] (LCLS)
MIL GSFC	Spaceflight Tracking and Data Network Station (SAUO)
MIL-HDBK	Military Handbook
MIL-I	Military Instruction (AAGC)
MIL-I	Military Specification on Interference (IEEE)
MILI	Multilevel Informal Language Inventory [*Test*]
MILIC	Microwave Insular Line Integrated Circuit (IEEE)
MILIC	Millimeter Insular Line Integrated Circuit (PDAA)
MILIC	Ministerial Libraries and Information Centers
MiLIM	Ingham Medical Center, John W. Chi Memorial Library, Lansing, MI [*Library symbol*] [*Library of Congress*] (LCLS)
MILIMETS	Military Meteorological System (SAUO)
MILINREP	Military Incident Report (MCD)
MILIRAD	Millimeter RADAR (MCD)
MILIRAD	Millimeter Wave RADAR Fuze (MCD)
MILIS	Multicenter Investigation of the Limitation of Infarct Size (MEDA)
MiLit	Litchfield District Library, Litchfield, MI [*Library symbol*] [*Library of Congress*] (LCLS)
milit	Military (WDAA)

MILIT........... Military
Military LJ... Military Law Journal [*A publication*] (DLA)
MILITRAN.... Military in Transition Database [*Information service or system*] (IID)
MiLivM......... Madonna College, Livonia, MI [*Library symbol*] [*Library of Congress*] (LCLS)
MiLivPS........ Livonia Public Schools, Livonia, MI [*Library symbol*] [*Library of Congress*] (LCLS)
Mil Jur Cas & Mat... Military Jurisprudence, Cases and Materials [*A publication*] (DLA)
MILJUSDOCFILE... Military Justice Docket File (DNAB)
MILK........... Moments of Intimacy, Laughter and Kinship
Mill............ Millenium (DIAR)
MILL........... Miller Industries, Inc. [*NASDAQ symbol*] (SAG)
Mill............ Miller's Reports [*3-18 Maryland*] [*A publication*] (DLA)
Mill............ Miller's Reports [*1-5 Louisiana*] [*A publication*] (DLA)
MILL........... Million
Mill............ Mills' New York Surrogate's Court Reports [*A publication*] (DLA)
Mill............ Mill's South Carolina Constitutional Reports [*A publication*] (DLA)
Mill & C Bills... Miller and Collier on Bills of Sale [*A publication*] (DLA)
Mill & F Pr... Miller and Field's Federal Practice [*A publication*] (DLA)
Mill & V Code... Milliken and Vertrees' Tennessee Code [*A publication*] (DLA)
Mill Civ L ... Miller's Civil Law of England [*1825*] [*A publication*] (DLA)
Mill Code..... Miller's Iowa Code [*A publication*] (DLA)
Mill Const... Mill's South Carolina Constitutional Reports [*A publication*] (DLA)
Mill Const (SC)... Mill's South Carolina Constitutional Reports [*A publication*] (DLA)
Mill Dec ...... Miller's Circuit Court Decisions (Woolworth) [*United States*] [*A publication*] (DLA)
Mill Dec ...... Miller's United States Supreme Court Decisions [*Condensed, Continuation of Curtis*] [*A publication*] (DLA)
Mill El .... Miller's Elements of the Law of Insurances [*A publication*] (DLA)
MillenCh...... Millenium Chemicals, Inc. [*Associated Press*] (SAG)
Millenia .... Millenia, Inc. [*Associated Press*] (SAG)
Mill Eq M .... Miller's Equitable Mortgages [*1844*] [*A publication*] (DLA)
Miller.......... Miller's Reports [*3-18 Maryland*] [*A publication*] (DLA)
Miller.......... Miller's Reports [*1-5 Louisiana*] [*A publication*] (DLA)
Miller Const... Miller on the Constitution of the United States [*A publication*] (DLA)
MillerIn........ Miller Indusries, Inc. [*Associated Press*] (SAG)
Miller's Code... Miller's Revised and Annotated Code [*Iowa*] [*A publication*] (DLA)
Millersville U... Millersville University of Pennsylvania (GAGS)
MILLIE......... Maximum Interchange of the Latest Logistic Information Is Essential
milli IU/ml... Milli-International Unit per Milliliter (DAVI)
Millin.......... Petty Sessions Cases [*1875-98*] [*Ireland*] [*A publication*] (DLA)
Mill Ins........ Miller's Elements of the Law of Insurances [*A publication*] (DLA)
Millipore...... Millipore Corp. [*Associated Press*] (SAG)
Millipre........ Millipore Corp. [*Associated Press*] (SAG)
millisec .... Millisecond
Mill LA .... Miller's Reports [*1-5 Louisiana*] [*A publication*] (DLA)
Mill Log....... Mill's Logic [*A publication*] (DLA)
Mill MD .... Miller's Reports [*3-18 Maryland*] [*A publication*] (DLA)
Mill Op .... Miller's Circuit Court Decisions (Woolworth) [*United States*] [*A publication*] (DLA)
Mill Part...... Miller on Partition [*A publication*] (DLA)
MillPhar ...... Millennium Pharmaceuticals, Inc. [*Associated Press*] (SAG)
Mill Pl & Pr... Miller's Iowa Pleading and Practice [*A publication*] (DLA)
MillrHr........ Miller [*Herman*], Inc. [*Associated Press*] (SAG)
MILLS.......... Mills [*Commonly used*] (OPSA)
Mills .... Mills' New York Surrogate's Court Reports [*A publication*] (DLA)
Mills Ann St... Mills' Annotated Statutes [*Colorado*] [*A publication*] (DLA)
Mills C .... Mills College (GAGS)
MillsCp........ Mills Corp. [*Associated Press*] (SAG)
Mills Em D... Mills on Eminent Domain [*A publication*] (DLA)
Mills Em Dom... Mills on Eminent Domain [*A publication*] (DLA)
Mills (NY).... Mills' New York Surrogate's Court Reports [*A publication*] (DLA)
Mills' Surr Ct... Mills' New York Surrogate's Court Reports [*A publication*] (DLA)
MIllumES..... Member of the Illuminating Engineers Society (SAUO)
MIL-M......... Military Manual (MCD)
MILMO......... Military Motorcycle [*Army*] (INF)
MILNET........ Military Network
MILNRY .... Millinery
MILO........... Magnetically Insulated Line Oscillator (ADWA)
MILO........... Mainframe Interface to Libraries Online [*Illinois Library Computer Systems Office online union catalog*]
MILO........... Maryland Interlibrary Loan (NITA)
MILO........... Maryland Interlibrary Organization [*Information service or system*] (IID)
MILO........... Miami Valley Library Organization [*Library network*]
MILO........... Microphone Locator (ACAE)
MILO........... Military Intelligence Liaison Officer (SAUO)
MILO........... Most Input for the Least Output [*Business term*]
MILOC......... Military Oceanography (PDAA)
MILocoE ...... Member of the Institution of Locomotive Engineers [*British*] (EY)
MILOGS .... Marine Integrated Logistic System (SAUO)
MIL OPS ...... Military Operations [*USCG*] (TAG)
MIL/OS........ Military/Ordnance Specification (MCD)
MILOX .... Mid-Latitude Ecosystems and Photochemical Oxidants (SAUO)
MIL P.......... Military Police (SAUO)
Mil P .... Military Post
MILP.......... Mixed Integer Linear Program [*Statistics*]
MILPAC........ Military Personnel Accounting Activity [*Army*] (AABC)
MILPAS........ Miscellaneous Information Listing Program Apollo Spacecraft [*NASA*] (KSC)
MILPAY........ Military Pay (SAUO)
MILPER........ Military Personnel
MILPERCEN... Military Personnel Center [*Alexandria, VA*] [*Army*] (AABC)
MILPERS ...... Military Personnel

MILPERSINS... Military Personnel Information System
MILPERSINST... Military Personnel Instructions (MCD)
MILPERSIS.... Military Personnel Information Subsystem (MCD)
MILPHAP...... Military Provincial Health Assistance Program (AABC)
MILPINS ...... Military Police Information System (DNAB)
MILPO .... Military Personnel Office (AABC)
MILPOD .... Mixed Integer and Linear Programming Open Deck (PDAA)
MilPr........... Milestone Properties [*Associated Press*] (SAG)
MILR........... Maintenance Incident Log Report [*Navy*] (CAAL)
MILR........... Master of Industrial and Labor Relations
MilrBld .... Miller Building Systems, Inc. [*Associated Press*] (SAG)
MILREP........ Military Representative (NATG)
Mil Rep ...... Militia Reporter [*Boston*] [*A publication*] (DLA)
MILREPC ...... Military Representatives Committee (SAUO)
Mil Rev ...... Military Review [*A publication*] (BRI)
MILRIS .... Military Routing Identifier System
MILS .... Marine Integrated Logistics System
MILS .... Master of Information and Library Science (GAGS)
MILS .... Medication Information Leaflet for Seniors [*Medicine*] (DMAA)
MILS .... Member of the Incorporated Law Society [*British*]
MILS .... Microcomputer Integrated Library System
MILS .... Microwave Instrument Landing System
MILS .... Military Standard Logistics System (MCD)
MILS .... Milliradians (KSC)
MILS .... Mineral Industry Location System [*Bureau of Mines*] [*Information service or system*] (IID)
MILS .... Missile Impact Locating [*or Location*] System
MiLS .... Sparrow (E.W.) Hospital Library, Lansing, MI [*Library symbol*] [*Library of Congress*] (LCLS)
MILSAT....... Military Satellite
MILSATCOM... Military Satellite Communications [*Systems*]
MILSBILLS.... Military Standard Billing System
MILSCAP ..... Military Standard Administrative Procedure (ACAE)
MILSCAP .... Military Standard Contract Administration Procedures [*DoD*]
MILSICCS ... Military Standard Item Characteristics Coding Structure (SAA)
MILSIMDS... Military Standard Item Management Data System
MILSIMS..... Military Standard Inventory Management System
MILSO .... Military Standard Logistics Systems Office [*DoD*] (MCD)
MILS/PAC... Missile Impact Location System, Pacific (SAA)
MILSPEC..... Military Specification
MILSPEC..... Military Specifications (GAVI)
Mil-Specs ... Military Specifications (WDAA)
MILSPETS.... Military Standard Petroleum System (MCD)
MIL SPOT .... Military Standard Procurement Operations Technique
MILSPOT .... Military Standard Purchase Operating Technique
MILSPRED .... Military Standard for Providing Research and Exploratory Development Data
MILSTAAD ... Military Standard Activity Address Directory
MILSTAC.... Military Staff Communication (NATG)
MILSTAG .... Military Standardization Agreement (CINC)
MILSTAM ... International Military Staff Memorandum [*NATO*] (NATG)
MILSTAMP... Military Standard Movement Procedures (SAUO)
MILSTAMP... Military Standard Requisitioning and Issue Procedure (SAUO)
MILSTAMP... Military Standard Transportation and Movement Procedure
MILSTAN ... Military Agency for Standardization [*NATO*]
MILSTAN ... Military Standard (SAUO)
MILSTAR ... Military Satellite Tracking and Reconnaissance (ACAE)
MILSTAR .... Military Strategic and Tactical Relay Satellite (SAUO)
MILSTAR .... Military Strategic and Tactical Relay System [*Satellite communications*]
MILSTAR .... Military Strategic Tactical (SAUO)
MILSTARAP... Military Standard Transportation Action Report and Accounting Procedures (MCD)
MIL STD .... Military Standard
MILSTD....... Military Standard
MILSTEP..... Military Standard Evaluation Procedure
MILSTEP..... Military Supply and Transportation Evaluation Procedures (AFM)
MILSTICC... Military Standard Item Characteristics Coding
MILSTICCS... Military Standard Item Characteristics Coding Structure
MILSTIICS ... Military Standard Item Identification Coding System
MiLStL........ Saint Lawrence Hospital Medical Library, Lansing, MI [*Library symbol*] [*Library of Congress*] (LCLS)
MILSTRAMP... Military Standard Transportation and Movement Procedure
MILSTRAP ... Military Standard Requisition and Accounting Procedures (MCD)
MILSTRAP ... Military Standard Transaction Reporting and Accounting Procedures
MILSTRAP ... Military Standard Transaction Reports and Accounting Procedures (SAUO)
MILSTRIP .... Military Standard Requisitioning and Issue Procedure
MILSTRIP .... Military Standard Transportation and Movement Procedure (SAUO)
MILSVC....... Military Services
Mil Sym ..... Milwaukee Symphony (SAUO)
MILT .... Military Language Tutor
MILT .... Milton [*England*]
MILT .... Miltope Group [*NASDAQ symbol*] (TTSB)
MILT .... Miltope Group, Inc. [*NASDAQ symbol*] (NQ)
MILTAG....... Military Technical Assistance Group
MILTAM...... Misrad Isre'eli Li-tevi'ot Mi-Germanyah (BJA)
MiLTC......... Thomas M. Cooley Law School, Lansing, MI [*Library symbol*] [*Library of Congress*] (LCLS)
MILTELCOMM... Military Telecommunications
MiltonF....... Milton Federal Financial Corp. [*Associated Press*] (SAG)
MILTOP....... Man-in-the-Loop Trajectory Optimization Program [*NASA*]
Miltope....... Miltope Group, Inc. [*Associated Press*] (SAG)
MILTOSS ..... Military Transportation of Small Shipments (NVT)
MIL TRA ...... Military Training [*USCG*] (TAG)

MILTRACS ...	Military Air Traffic Control System (SAUO)
Mil Trib	Military Tribunal (SAUO)
MILU............	Missile Interface & Logic Unit (SAUS)
MiLud	Ludington Public Library, Ludington, MI [*Library symbol*] [*Library of Congress*] (LCLS)
MiLut...........	Luther Public Library, Luther, MI [*Library symbol*] [*Library of Congress*] (LCLS)
MiLv	Mink Endogenous Virus (DB)
MILVAN	Military Van (MCD)
MIL VIG	Military Vigilance (SAUO)
MILW...........	Chicago, Milwaukee, St. Paul & Pacific Railroad Co. [*AAR code*]
Milw	Milward's Irish Ecclesiastical Reports [*1819-43*] [*A publication*] (DLA)
Milw	Milwaukee [*Wisconsin*]
Milwaukee Law...	Milwaukee Lawyer [*A publication*] (DLA)
Milwau Sch Eng...	Milwaukee School of Engineering (GAGS)
Milw Ir Ecc Rep...	Milward's Irish Ecclesiastical Reports [*1819-43*] [*A publication*] (DLA)
MilwLnd	Milwaukee Land Co. [*Associated Press*] (SAG)
MiLy	Lyons Public Library, Lyons, MI [*Library symbol*] [*Library of Congress*] (LCLS)
MIM	Magnetic Interaction Mechanism
MIM	Maintenance Instructions Manual [*DoD*]
MIM	Maintenance Interface Machine (NITA)
MIM	Manufacturing Information Memorandum
MIM	Map Image Metafile (SAUS)
MIM	Marine Information Management [*Marine science*] (MSC)
MIM	Marine Information Management and Metadata (SAUO)
MIM	Master of Industrial Management
MIM	Master of International Management
MIM	Member of the Institute of Management (DD)
MIM	Member of the Institution of Metallurgists [*British*] (DBQ)
MIM	Memory-Intensive Modules (TIMI)
MIM	Mendelian Inheritance in Man [*Genetics*]
MIM	Merimbula [*Australia*] [*Airport symbol*] (OAG)
MIM	Message Input Module [*Telecommunications*] (TEL)
MIM	Metal Injection Molding [*Metal fabrication*]
MIM	Metal Insulator Metal [*Light detector*]
MIM	Microion Mill
MIM	Micro Isolation Mount (SAUS)
MIM	Microwave Interface Module
MIM	Mid Mountain Mining [*Vancouver Stock Exchange symbol*]
MIM	Military Iranian Mission [*World War II*]
MIM	Milo [*Maine*] [*Seismograph station code, US Geological Survey*] (SEIS)
Mim	Mimeograph (AAGC)
MIM	Mimeographed (ADA)
MIM	Mimino [*Former USSR*] [*FAA designator*] (FAAC)
MIM	Mindanao Independence Movement [*Philippines*] [*Political party*]
MIM	Minimum (DA)
MIM	Minorities in Media (EA)
MIM	Minorities in Medicine [*Eastern Michigan University Macy Scholarship*]
MIM	Misappropriation, Interference and Misrepresentation
MIM	Missile Identification Module [*Military*] (CAAL)
MIM	Mobile-Launched Interceptor Missile
MIM	Mobile-launched surface-to-air Missile (SAUS)
MIM	MODEM Interface Modules [*Computer science*]
MIM	Modified Index Method (IEEE)
MIM	Montagu Investments Management [*Commercial firm*] [*British*]
MIM	Morality in Media (EA)
MIM	Mouvement Independantiste Martiniquais [*Martinique Independence Movement*] [*Political party*] (PD)
MIM	Multilateral Initiative in Malaria
MIM	Multilateral Initiative on Malaria [*International coordination effort*]
MIM	Multilayer Interference Mirror [*Optical instrumentation*]
MIM	Multiple Ion Monitoring [*Mass spectrometry*]
MIM	Multiplex Interface Module (ACAE)
Mim	United States Internal Revenue Bureau, Commissioner's Mimeographed Published Opinions [*A publication*] (DLA)
MIMA...........	Member, Industrial Medical Association (CMD)
MIMA...........	Metal Injection Molding Association (NTPA)
MIMA...........	Mineral Insulation Manufacturers Association (EA)
MIMA...........	Minor Machine Accessory (MCD)
MIMA...........	Minute Man National Historical Park
MIMA...........	Music Industry Manufacturers Association [*Defunct*] (EA)
MIMAA.........	Motor Inn, Motel and Accommodation Association [*Australia*]
MIMAC.........	Measurement and Improvement of Manufacturing Capacity
MiMaci	Mackinac Island Public Library, Mackinac Island, MI [*Library symbol*] [*Library of Congress*] (LCLS)
MiMack........	Mackinaw City Public Library, Mackinaw City, MI [*Library symbol*] [*Library of Congress*] (LCLS)
MIMAF.........	Musicians International Mutual Aid Fund
MiMan	Manchester Township Library, Manchester, MI [*Library symbol*] [*Library of Congress*] (LCLS)
MiManc	Mancelona Township Library, Mancelona, MI [*Library symbol*] [*Library of Congress*] (LCLS)
MIM&GE......	Member of the Institute of Mechanical & General Engineers (SAUO)
MIManf........	Member of the Institute of Manufacturing [*British*] (DBQ)
MiMani	Manistee County Library, Manistee, MI [*Library symbol*] [*Library of Congress*] (LCLS)
MiMant........	Manton Public Library, Manton, MI [*Library symbol*] [*Library of Congress*] (LCLS)
MiMar..........	M. Alice Chapin Memorial Library, Marion, MI [*Library symbol*] [*Library of Congress*] (LCLS)
MiMarc........	Marcellus Township Library, Marcellus, MI [*Library symbol*] [*Library of Congress*] (LCLS)
MIMarE.......	Member of the Institute of Marine Engineers [*British*] (EY)
MI Mar E	Member of the Institute (or Institution) of Marine Engineers (SAUO)
MiMarl........	Marlette Township Library, Marlette, MI [*Library symbol*] [*Library of Congress*] (LCLS)
MiMaRP	Maple Rapids Public Library, Maple Rapids, MI [*Library symbol*] [*Library of Congress*] (LCLS)
MiMarq........	Peter White Public Library, Marquette, MI [*Library symbol*] [*Library of Congress*] (LCLS)
MiMarqAS ...	Marquette-Alger Intermediate School District, Learning Materials Center, Marquette, MI [*Library symbol*] [*Library of Congress*] (LCLS)
MiMarqHi	Marquette County Historical Society, John M. Longyear Memorial Library, Marquette, MI [*Library symbol*] [*Library of Congress*] (LCLS)
MiMarqN	Northern Michigan University, Marquette, MI [*Library symbol*] [*Library of Congress*] (LCLS)
MiMarqNA ...	Northern Michigan University, University Archives and Historical Collections, Marquette, MI [*Library symbol*] [*Library of Congress*] (LCLS)
MiMarqS......	Superiorland Library Cooperative System, Marquette, MI [*Library symbol*] [*Library of Congress*] (LCLS)
MiMars........	Marshall Public Library, Marshall, MI [*Library symbol*] [*Library of Congress*] (LCLS)
MiMary	Marysville Public Library, Marysville, MI [*Library symbol*] [*Library of Congress*] (LCLS)
MiMas	Ingham County Library, Mason, MI [*Library symbol*] [*Library of Congress*] (LCLS)
MIMAS........	Magnetically Insulated Macroparticle Accelerator System
MIMAS........	Multifield Integrated Meltdown Analysis System (SAUO)
MiMay	Mayville District Public Library, Mayville, MI [*Library symbol*] [*Library of Congress*] (LCLS)
MIMB	Malaysia International Merchant Bankers (SAUO)
MIMB	Mint in a Mint Box [*Collectibles*]
MIMBD	Meeting on the Interconnection of Molecular Biological (or Biology) Databases (SAUO)
MIMBD	Meeting on the Interconnection of Mology Biology Databases (SAUS)
MIMBM.......	Member of the Institute of Municipal Building Management [*British*] (DBQ)
MIMC..........	Management Inventory on Managing Change [*Test*]
MIMC..........	Marconi International Marine Communication Company (SAUO)
MIMC..........	Massachusetts Interactive Media Council
MimC..........	Maxwell International Microforms Corporation, Fairview Park, Elmsford, NY [*Library symbol*] [*Library of Congress*] (LCLS)
MIMC..........	Maxwell International Microforms Corporation Incorporated (SAUO)
MIMC..........	Member of the Institute of Management Consultants
MIMC..........	Microforms International Marketing Corp. [*Pergamon*]
MIMC..........	Multivariable Internal Model Control [*Control engineering*]
MIMCO	McGraw-Hill Information Management Co. [*Database producer*] (IID)
MiMD..........	Dorsch Memorial Public Library, Monroe, MI [*Library symbol*] [*Library of Congress*] (LCLS)
MIMD..........	Management Information of Metrology Data (AAEL)
MIMD..........	Multiple Instruction/Multiple Data (NITA)
MIMD..........	Multiple Instruction, Multiple Data Processor [*Computer science*] (CIST)
MIMD..........	Multiple Instruction Stream, Multiple Data Stream (MCD)
MIME	Member of the Institute of Mining Engineers
MIME	Member of the Institution of Mechanical Engineers [*Formerly, AMIMechE*] [*British*]
MIME	Member of the Institution of Mining Engineers (SAUO)
MIME	Microcomputers in Mathematics Education (AIE)
MIME	Ministry of Information Middle East [*British*] [*World War II*]
MIME	Minor Machine Equipment (MCD)
MIME	Multimedia Internet Mail Extension
MIME	Multipurpose Internet Mail Extension [*Computer science*]
MIME	Multipurpose Internet Mail Extensions [*Computer science*] (ACRL)
MiMe	Spies Public Library, Menominee, MI [*Library symbol*] [*Library of Congress*] (LCLS)
MiMec	Morton Township Library, Mecosta, MI [*Library symbol*] [*Library of Congress*] (LCLS)
MIMechE	Member of the Institution of Mechanical Engineers [*Formerly, AMIMechE*] [*British*] (EY)
MiMen	Mendon Township Library, Mendon, MI [*Library symbol*] [*Library of Congress*] (LCLS)
MIMEO........	Mimeographed (ADA)
MIMEO........	Multiple Input Memo Engineering Order (MCD)
MiMer.........	Merrill District Library, Merrill, MI [*Library symbol*] [*Library of Congress*] (LCLS)
MiMes	Mesick Public Library, Mesick, MI [*Library symbol*] [*Library of Congress*] (LCLS)
MIMEX........	Major Item Material Excess [*Air Force*] (AFIT)
MIMF	Member of the Institute of Metal Finishing [*British*] (DBQ)
MIMGTechE...	Member of the Institution of Mechanical Engineers and General Technician Engineers [*British*] (DBQ)
MIMH..........	Member of the Institute of Materials Handling [*British*] (DBQ)
MIMI	Magnetospheric Imaging Instrument (ACAE)
MIMI	Medical Workstations for Intelligent Interactive Acquisition and Analysis of Digital Medical Images (SAUO)
MIMI	Member of the Institute of Motor Industry [*British*]
MIMI	Member of the Institute of the Motor Industry (SAUO)
MIMI	Micro Miniature Compact Harness (MCD)
MIMIC..........	Measure and Inspection Masks for Integrated Circuits (MCD)
MIMIC..........	Method of Micromolding in Capillaries [*Materials science*]
MIMIC..........	Microfilm Information Master Image Converter (PDAA)

MIMIC.........	Micromoulding in Capillaries [*Plastics technology*]
MIMIC.........	Microwave and Millimeter-Wave Monolithic Integrated Circuits Project [*DoD*]
MIMIC.........	Microwave Monolithic Integrated Circuit [*Used in wireless communication*]
MIMIC.........	Millimetric Wave Monolithic Integrated Circuit (SAUS)
MIMIC/CUS...	Michigan Metropolitan Information Center/Center for Urban Studies [*Wayne State University*] [*Information service or system*] (IID)
MIMIC model...	Multiple Indicator Multiple Cause Model
MIMICS.........	Micromodule Microprogrammed Computer System (PDAA)
MiMid.........	Grace A. Dow Memorial [*Public*] Library, Midland, MI [*Library symbol*] [*Library of Congress*] (LCLS)
MiMidD.........	Dow Chemical Co., Midland, MI [*Library symbol*] [*Library of Congress*] (LCLS)
MiMidDC.....	Dow Corning Corp., Midland, MI [*Library symbol*] [*Library of Congress*] (LCLS)
MiMidDG.....	Dow Gardens, Midland, MI [*Library symbol*] [*Library of Congress*] (LCLS)
MiMidGS.....	Church of Jesus Christ of Latter-Day Saints, Genealogical Society Library, Midland Stake Branch, Midland, MI [*Library symbol*] [*Library of Congress*] (LCLS)
MiMidN.........	Northwood Institute, Midland, MI [*Library symbol*] [*Library of Congress*] (LCLS)
MiMil.........	Milan Public Library, Milan, MI [*Library symbol*] [*Library of Congress*] (LCLS)
MiMill.........	Millington Township Library, Millington, MI [*Library symbol*] [*Library of Congress*] (LCLS)
MI MIN.........	Miles per Minute (WDAA)
MIMinE.........	Member of the Institution of Mining Engineers [*British*] (EY)
MiMio.........	Oscoda County Public Library, Mio, MI [*Library symbol*] [*Library of Congress*] (LCLS)
MIMIS.........	Major Item Management Information System (SAUO)
MIMIS.........	Municipal Improvement Management Information System (ACAE)
MIMIT.........	Member of the Institute of Musical Instrument Technology [*British*] (DBQ)
MIMJ.........	Metal Insulator - Metal Junction
MIMM.........	Management Inventory on Modern Management [*Test*]
MIMM.........	Master of Mining and Metallurgy (DD)
MIMM.........	Member of the Institute of Mining and Metallurgy [*British*] (EY)
MIMM.........	Member of the Institution of Mining and Metallurgy (SAUO)
MIMM.........	Mexican Institution of Mining and Metallurgy (SAUO)
MIMMIS......	Marine Corps Integrated Manpower Management Information System
MIMMS.......	Marine Corps Integrated Maintenance Management System
MIMO.........	Man In, Machine Out [*Computer science*]
MIMO.........	Modified Input - Modified Output [*Computer science*]
MiMo.........	Monroe County Library System, Monroe, MI [*Library symbol*] [*Library of Congress*] (LCLS)
MIMO.........	Multi-Input, Multi-Output [*Electronics*] (AAEL)
MIMO.........	Multiple-Input/Multiple-Output [*Computer science*]
MiMoHi.......	Monroe County Historical Museum, Archives, Monroe, MI [*Library symbol*] [*Library of Congress*] (LCLS)
MIMOLA.....	Machine Independent Microprogramming Language
MiMor.......	Stair Public Library, Morenci, MI [*Library symbol*] [*Library of Congress*] (LCLS)
MiMory.......	Morley-Stanwood Community Library, Morley, MI [*Library symbol*] [*Library of Congress*] (LCLS)
MIMOS........	Malaysian Institute of Microelectronic Systems (SAUO)
MIMOSA......	Mission Modes and Space Analysis (NASA)
MIMOSA......	Mission Modes and Systems Analysis (ACAE)
MIMOT.......	Master of International Management of Technology (PGP)
MIMP.........	Magazine Industry Market Place [*A publication*]
MIMP.........	Mint in Manufacturer's Packaging [*Collectibles*]
MIMP.........	Mint in Mint Package [*Collectibles*]
MIMR.........	Magnetic Ink Mark Recognition
MIMR.........	May Institute of Medical Research
MIMR.........	Minimal Inhibitor Mole Ratio [*Biochemistry*]
MIMR.........	Multi-Frequency Imaging Microwave Radiometer (EOSA)
MIMS.........	Major Item Management System (AABC)
MIMS.........	Manifest Information Management System (GAAI)
MIMS.........	Master of Integrated Manufacturing Systems (PGP)
MIMS.........	Material Information Management System (MCD)
MiMS.........	Medical Information Management System (NAKS)
MIMS.........	Medical Information Management System [*NASA*]
MIMS.........	Medical Inventory Management System
MIMS.........	Member of the Institute of Management Specialists [*British*] (DBQ)
MIMS.........	Metal Impact Monitoring System [*Nuclear energy*] (NRCH)
MIMS.........	MIM Corp. [*NASDAQ symbol*] (SG)
MIMS.........	Mincom Information Management System (SAUS)
MIMS.........	Mineral Insulated, Metal Sheathed [*Cable*]
MIMS.........	Missile Maintenance Squadron [*Air Force*]
MIMS.........	Mitrol Industrial Management System [*Mitrol, Inc.*] [*Information service or system*] (IID)
MIMS.........	Mobile Information System (SAUO)
MIMS.........	Modular Isodrive Memory Series
MIMS.........	Monthly Index of Medical Specialties [*A publication*] (DB)
MIMS.........	Multi-Item Multisource (IEEE)
MIMS.........	Multiple Independently Maneuvering Submunitions (MCD)
MIMS.........	Multiple Independent Maneuvering Submissile (ACAE)
MIMSA......	Minority Institutions in Marine Sciences Association (SAUO)
MIMSE......	Microwave-Infrared Mesoph-eric-Stratospheric Experiment (SAUO)
MIMSO......	Military Indoctrination for Medical Service Officers (SAUO)
MIMSq......	Missile Maintenance Squadron [*Air Force*] (AFM)
MIMT.........	Member of the Institute of Music Teachers (ADA)
MIMT.........	Member of the Institute of the Motor Trade (SAUO)

MiMtc.........	Mount Clemens Public Library, Mount Clemens, MI [*Library symbol*] [*Library of Congress*] (LCLS)
MiMtcM.......	Macomb County Library, Mount Clemens, MI [*Library symbol*] [*Library of Congress*] (LCLS)
MiMtp.........	Mount Pleasant Public Library, Mount Pleasant, MI [*Library symbol*] [*Library of Congress*] (LCLS)
MiMtpC.......	Chippewa Library League, Mt. Pleasant, MI [*Library symbol*] [*Library of Congress*] (LCLS)
MiMtpT.......	Central Michigan University, Mount Pleasant, MI [*Library symbol*] [*Library of Congress*] (LCLS)
MiMu.........	Hackley Public Library, Muskegon, MI [*Library symbol*] [*Library of Congress*] (LCLS)
MIMU.........	Miniature Inertial Measurement Unit
MIMU.........	Miniaturization Inertial Measurement Unit (TIMI)
MiMuB.......	Muskegon Business College, Muskegon, MI [*Library symbol*] [*Library of Congress*] (LCLS)
MIMUG.......	Meetings Industry Microcomputer Users Group [*Defunct*] (EA)
MiMul.........	Mulliken District Library, Mulliken, MI [*Library symbol*] [*Library of Congress*] (LCLS)
MiMuM.......	Muskegon County Library, Muskegon, MI [*Library symbol*] [*Library of Congress*] (LCLS)
MIMUN.......	Marine Institute of Memorial University (SAUO)
MiMun........	Munising Public Library, Munising, MI [*Library symbol*] [*Library of Congress*] (LCLS)
MIMunE.......	Member of the Institute of Municipal Engineers [*British*] (EY)
MIMUSA......	Matrix Iteration Method of Unfolding Spectra [*Computer science*]
MIMV.........	Mirabilis Mosaic Virus [*Plant pathology*]
MIN.........	Business European Airways Ltd. [*British*] [*FAA designator*] (FAAC)
MIN.........	Marketing Information Network [*Information service or system*] (IID)
MIN.........	Master of Insurance
MIN.........	Media Industry Newsletter [*A publication*]
MIN.........	Medial Interlaminar Nucleus (DMAA)
MIN.........	Meeting Individual Needs [*Educational publishing*]
MIN.........	Member Information Network [*for House of Representatives*]
MIN.........	Member of the Institute of Navigation [*British*]
MIN.........	Metabolic Information Network [*Founded in 1989*] (NRGU)
MIN.........	MFS Intermediate Income SBI [*NYSE symbol*] (SPSG)
MIN.........	MFS Intermediate Income Trust [*Associated Press*] (SAG)
MIN.........	MFS Interm Incme SBI [*NYSE symbol*] (TTSB)
min.........	Microinch (BARN)
Min.........	Minaean [*or Minean*] (BJA)
MIN.........	Mine [*or Minecraft*] [*Navy*]
MIN.........	Mine Identification and Neutralization (PDAA)
MIN.........	Mineral [*California*] [*Seismograph station code, US Geological Survey*] (SEIS)
Min.........	Mineralogical (SAUO)
MIN.........	Mineralogy
MIN.........	Miniature
MIN.........	Minim
MIN.........	Minimal (SAUS)
MIN.........	Minimum (AFM)
min.........	Minimum [*A minim measurement*] (DAVI)
Min.........	Minimum (DFIT)
min.........	Mining (DD)
MIN.........	Mining
MIN.........	Minion [*Typography*] (DGA)
MIN.........	Minister [*or Ministry*]
Min.........	Minister [*or Ministry*] (ODBW)
MIN.........	Ministry (SAUO)
Min.........	Minnesota Reports [*A publication*] (DLA)
Min.........	Minnesota Vikings [*National Football League*] [*1961-present*] (NFLA)
min.........	Minor (SHCU)
MIN.........	Minor
MIN.........	Minority
Min.........	Minor's Alabama Reports [*A publication*] (DLA)
MIN.........	Minto Resources [*Vancouver Stock Exchange symbol*]
MIN.........	Minute (AFM)
min.........	Minute (IDOE)
Min.........	Minutes (DIAR)
MIN.........	Mobile Identification Number (ACRL)
MIN.........	Mobile Intelligent Network (SAUO)
MIN.........	Mobilization Identification Number [*Military*]
MIN.........	Molasses Information Network (EA)
MIN.........	Most in Need Population
MIN.........	Motor Interneuron (MELL)
MIN.........	Movimiento de Integracion Nacional [*National Integration Movement*] [*Venezuela*] [*Political party*] (PPW)
MIN.........	Movimiento de Integracion Nacional [*National Integration Movement*] [*Ecuador*] [*Political party*] (PPW)
MIN.........	Movimiento de Izquierda Nacional [*National Left-Wing Movement*] [*Bolivia*] [*Political party*] (PPW)
M-IN.........	Multimedia Intelligent Networking (SAUO)
MIN.........	Multipath Interconnection Network (VLIE)
MIN.........	Multistage Interconnection Network (RALS)
MINA.........	Member of the Institution of Naval Architects [*British*]
MINA.........	Monoisonitrosoacetone [*Biochemistry*]
MINA.........	Multiplexed Input NHRE [*National Hail Research Experiment*] Averager
MINABB......	Minimum Abbreviations [*of MAST*]
MINAC.........	Miniature Navigation Airborne Computer
MINAC.........	Minuteman Action Committee (SAA)
MINAGE......	Minimum Seed-Bearing Age [*Botany*]
MinAgric......	Ministry of Agriculture, Fisheries and Food (SAUO)
MiNas.........	Putnam Public Library, Nashville, MI [*Library symbol*] [*Library of Congress*] (LCLS)

minat.......... Miniature (VRA)
MINAT .... Miniature
MINATOM .... Ministry for Atomic Energy Issues (SAUO)
MiNazC........ Nazareth College, Nazareth, MI [*Library symbol*] [*Library of Congress*] (LCLS)
MiNb.......... New Buffalo Public Library, New Buffalo, MI [*Library symbol*] [*Library of Congress*] (LCLS)
MINBATFOR... Minecraft Battle Force, Pacific Fleet
MINBL .... Minimum Balance (VLIE)
Min B/L....... Minimum Bill of Lading (DS)
M-in-C........ Matron-in-Chief [*Navy*] [*British*]
MINC .... Minicomputer
MINC .... Modular Instrumentation Computer (VLIE)
MINC .... Module Interconnect (SAUS)
MINCOM ...... Miniaturized Communications [*Navy*] (DNAB)
MINCOMS .... Multiple Interior Communications System (MCD)
MINCONMAR... Ministerial Conference of West and Central African States on Maritime Transport [*Ivory Coast*] (EAIO)
MINCOS .... Modular Inventory Control System [*Computer science*] (VLIE)
MIND .... Magnetic Integrator Neuron Duplicator
MIND .... Management Institute for National Development
MIND .... Management of Information through Natural Discourse (SAUO)
MIND .... Method in Natural Development [*Mental diet plan*]
MIND .... Methods of Intellectual Development [*National Association of Manufacturers*]
MIND .... Microsoft Internet Developer (SAUO)
MIND .... Mining Item Name Directory [*A publication*]
MIND .... Mitcham Indus [*NASDAQ symbol*] (TTSB)
MIND .... Mitcham Industries [*NASDAQ symbol*] (SAG)
MIND .... Modular Interactive Network Designer
MIND .... Multidisciplinary Institute for Neuropsychological Development (EA)
MIND .... Multiple Infrared Naval Decoy
MINDAC .... Marine Inertial Navigation Data Assimilation Computer (IEEE)
MIndAdm ..... Master of Industrial Administration (GAGS)
MINDAL .... Meat Importers National Defence Association (SAUO)
MINDAP .... Microwave-Induced Nitrogen Discharge at Atmospheric Pressure [*Spectrometry*]
MINDAT .... Minerals Data Base [*of the Law of the Sea*] (GNE)
MINDD .... Minimum Due Date per Order
MIndE .... Master of Industrial Engineering (SAUO)
MIndEd .... Master of Industrial Education
Min Def ...... Ministry of Defence (SAUO)
MIN-DEF ...... Ministry of Defence [*British*]
Min Dig .... Minot's Digest [*Massachusetts*] [*A publication*] (DLA)
MIND/INDUS... Automation of Proofs by Mathematical Induction (SAUO)
MinDirig ...... Ministerialdirigent (SAUO)
MINDIV .... Mine Division [*Navy*]
MINDO .... Modified Intermediate Neglect of Diatomic Overlap (AAEL)
MINDO .... Modified Intermediate Neglect of Differential Overlap [*Quantum mechanics*]
MIndR .... Master of Industrial Relations (CPGU)
MINDS .... Mental Illness Nervous Disorders Society [*Australia*]
MindSpr....... MindSpring Enterprises, Inc. [*Associated Press*] (SAG)
MINE .... Medical Improvement not Expected (DHP)
MINE .... Mesna, Ifosfamide, Mitoxantrone, Etoposide [*Antineoplastic drug*] (CDI)
MINE .... Microbial Information Network Europe [*EEC*]
Min E .... Mineral Engineer
Min E.......... Mining Engineer
MINE .... Minneapolis Eastern Railway Co. [*AAR code*]
MINE .... Minnesota Information Network for Educators (SAUO)
MINE .... Montana Information Network Exchange [*Library network*]
MINE .... Multi-Indenture NORS [*Not Operationally Ready Status*] Evaluator (MCD)
MINEAC .... Miniature Electronic Auto-Collimator
MINEASYFAC... Mine Assembly Facilities
MINEC .... Military Necessity
MINECTRMEASSTA... Mine Countermeasure Station [*Military*]
MINECTRMEASTA... Mine Countermeasures Station [*Military*] (DNAB)
M In Ed....... Master of Industrial Education (PGP)
MINEDAF ..... Conference of Ministers of Education and Those Responsible for Economic Planing in African Member States (SAUO)
MINEDAP ..... Regional Conference of Ministers of Education and Those Responsible for Economic Planning in Asia and the Pacific (SAUO)
MINEDARAB... Conference of Ministers of Education and Those Responsible for Economic Planning in Arab States (SAUO)
MINEDEFLAB... Mine Defense Laboratory [*Navy*]
MINEDEUROPE... Conference of Ministers of Education of Member States of the Europe Region (SAUO)
MINEDLAC ... Conference of Ministers of Education and those Responsible for Economic Planning in Latin America and Caribbean (SAUO)
MiNeg.......... Negaunee Public Library, Negaunee, MI [*Library symbol*] [*Library of Congress*] (LCLS)
MINELCO ..... Miniature Electronic Component (WDAA)
MINEPACSUPPGRU... Mine Force, Pacific Fleet, Support Group Unit (DNAB)
miner........... Minerology (DD)
Mineral........ Mineralogical (SAUO)
Mineral........ Mineralogy (BEE)
MINERAL ..... Mineralogy
MINERALOG... Mineralogical
Mineralog Mag... Mineralogical Magazine (SAUS)
Mineral Soc... Mineralogical Society (SAUO)
MINERVA ..... Minimization of Earthworks for Vertical Alignment (PDAA)
MineSf........ Mine Safety Appliances Co. [*Associated Press*] (SAG)

MINESLA ..... Conference of Ministers of Education and those Responsible for the Promotion of Science and Technology in Relation to Development in Latin American and the Caribbean (SAUO)
MINET.......... Medical Information Network [*GTE Telenet Communications Corp.*] [*Reston, VA*] [*Telecommunications*]
MINET.......... Metropolitan Information Network
MINET.......... Movement Information Network (SAUO)
MIN EV .... Minutes of Evidence [*Legal term*] (DLA)
MINEVDET ... Mine Warfare Evaluation Detachment
MiNew........ Newaygo Carnegie Public Library, Newaygo, MI [*Library symbol*] [*Library of Congress*] (LCLS)
MINEWARCOM... Mine Warfare Command [*Navy*]
MiNew-C...... Croton Public Library, Newaygo, MI [*Library symbol*] [*Library of Congress*] (LCLS)
MINEX .... Minelaying, Minesweeping, and Mine-Hunting Exercise [*NATO*] (NATG)
MINEX .... Mine Warfare Exercise (NVT)
MINFLOT ..... Mine Flotilla [*Navy*]
MInfoTech ... Master of Information Technology and Communication
MInfSys ...... Master of Information Systems
Min Fuel ..... Ministry of Fuel and Power (SAUO)
MING .... Magnetic Induction Nuclear Gyroscope
MIng .... Maitre en Ingenierie [*Master of Engineering*] [*French*]
Ming .... Maitrise en Ingenierie [*Master of Engineering*] (DD)
MING .... Middle Class, Intelligent, Nice Girl [*Lifestyle classification*]
MINGSE ...... Minimum Ground Support Equipment Concept (MCD)
MiNhL.......... Lenox Township Library, New Haven, MI [*Library symbol*] [*Library of Congress*] (LCLS)
MinHous ..... Ministry of Housing and Local Government (SAUO)
MINI.......... Method of Implicit Nonstationary Iteration (PDAA)
MINI.......... Miniature (KSC)
MINI.......... Minicomputer (VLIE)
MINI.......... Minicomputer Industry National Interchange [*An association*] (EA)
MINI.......... Minimize Individually Negotiated Instruments (AFM)
MINI.......... Minimum (DSUE)
MINI.......... Mobile Mini [*NASDAQ symbol*] (TTSB)
MINI.......... Mobile Mini, Inc. [*NASDAQ symbol*] (SAG)
MiNi.......... Niles Community Library, Niles, MI [*Library symbol*] [*Library of Congress*] (LCLS)
MINIA .... Monkey Intranuclear Inclusion Agent (MAE)
MINIAC .... Minimal Automatic Computer (VLIE)
MINIACT ...... Minimum Acquisition Tracking System (MUGU)
MINIAPS ...... Miniature Accessory Power Supply
MINIBIB ...... Danish government libraries catalogue (SAUS)
MINIBIB ...... Government libraries catalogue (SAUO)
MINICATS ... Miniaturization of Federal Catalog System Publications
MINICOM ..... Minimum Communications
MINI COMP... Miniature Compact (MCD)
MINICS .... Minimal-Input Cataloguing System [*Loughborough University of Technology*]
MINICS/PDS... MINICS Periodicals Data System (NITA)
MINIDAU..... Miniature Data Acquisition Unit
MINIDOS...... Mini Disk Operating System (IDOE)
MINI-ELS ..... Mini-Emitter Location System (MCD)
MINI-IR....... Minimum Incident Report (VLIE)
Miniluv .... Ministry of Love [*From George Orwell's novel, "1984"*]
Mini-MADS... Minimodular Auxiliary Data System (SAUS)
MiniMd .... MiniMed, Inc. [*Associated Press*] (SAG)
MINI-MEG.... Mini Message Entry Generator (ACAE)
MINI MUX.... Miniaturized Multiplexes (MCD)
MiNiN .... National Standard Information Resources, Niles, MI [*Library symbol*] [*Library of Congress*] (LCLS)
Mining Chem Engng Rev... Mining and Chemical Engineering Review [*A publication*]
Mining Engng Rev... Mining and Engineering Review [*A publication*]
MiningS....... Mining Services International Corp. [*Associated Press*] (SAG)
Min Inst....... Minor's Institutes of Common and Statute Law [*A publication*] (DLA)
MIN INVEST... Minimum Investment [*Finance*]
Minipax ...... Ministry of Peace [*From George Orwell's novel, "1984"*]
MINIPERT.... Mini Program Evaluation and Review Technique (VLIE)
Miniplenty ... Ministry of Plenty [*From George Orwell's novel, "1984"*]
Mini-POPs ... Mini Points of Presence
MINIRAD...... Minimum Radiation (CAAL)
MINIRAR...... Minimum Radiation Requirements [*Missiles*] (IEEE)
MINIS .... Mini Intraport Network Information System (SAUO)
MINISID...... Miniature Seismic Intrusion Detector [*DoD*]
MINISINS..... Miniature Ship Inertial Navigation System (MCD)
MINI-STE .... Mini-Special Test Equipment (ACAE)
MiniSTEP .... Mini Satellite Test of the Equivalence Principle (SAUS)
MINISTREL... Models for Information Storage and Retrieval (SAUO)
MINI-SUBLAB... Miniature Submarine Laboratory
MINIT.......... Minimum Interference Threshold [*Telecommunications*] (TEL)
MINITAS ..... Miniature True Airspeed Computer
MINITECH ... Ministry of Technology (SAUO)
MINITEX ...... Minnesota Interlibrary Telecommunications Exchange [*Library cooperative*] [*Minnesota Higher Education Coordinating Board*] [*Minneapolis, MN*]
MINITEX ...... Minnesota Interlibrary Teletex Experiment (SAUO)
MINITRACK... Minimum-Weight Tracking [*System*] (MUGU)
Minitrue...... Ministry of Truth [*From George Orwell's novel, "1984"*]
MINIVAR...... Minimum Variance Orbit Determination (MCD)
MINIW .... Mobile Mini Wrrt [*NASDAQ symbol*] (TTSB)
MINK .... Missouri-Iowa-Nebraska-Kansas (SAUO)
MINK .... Missouri-Iowa-Nebraska-Kansas League [*Old baseball league*]
MINL.......... Minimum Licence Period (WDAA)

MINL .... Minnetonka Corp. (SAUO)
MINLANT ..... Mine Warfare Forces, Atlantic [*Navy*]
Minl E.......... Mineral Engineer (PGP)
MINLP .... Mixed-Integer Nonlinear Program [*Computer science*]
MINMAC-PC... Mini-Macroeconomic Personal Computer Model [*Department of Energy*] (GFGA)
MIN/MAX ..... Minimum/Maximum (RIMS)
MINMB .... Mint in a Near Mint Box [*Collectibles*]
MIN MC .... Minimum Material Condition [*Computer science*]
MINMP .... Mint in Near Mint Package [*Collectibles*]
MINN .... Minnesota (AFM)
Minn .... Minnesota (ODBW)
Minn .... Minnesota Supreme Court Reports [*A publication*] (DLA)
Minn Admin Reg... Minnesota State Register [*A publication*] (DLA)
MinNauki..... Ministry of Science and Technical Policy (SAUO)
MinnBrw...... Minnesota Brewing Co. [*Associated Press*] (SAG)
Minn Code Agency... Minnesota Code of Agency Rules [*A publication*] (DLA)
Minn Code Ann... Minnesota Code, Annotated [*A publication*] (DLA)
Minn Ct Rep... Minnesota Court Reporter [*A publication*] (DLA)
Minn DL & I Comp... Minnesota Department of Labor and Industries. Compilation of Court Decisions [*A publication*] (DLA)
MINN DPW LIB... Minnesota Department of Public Welfare Library Consortium [*Library network*]
MinnEd .... Minnesota Educational Computing Corp. [*Associated Press*] (SAG)
MINNEMAST... Minnesota School Mathematics and Science Teaching Project [*University of Minnesota*] (AEE)
Minn Gen Laws... Minnesota General Laws [*A publication*] (DLA)
Minn (Gil).... Minnesota Reports (Gilfillan Edition) [*A publication*] (DLA)
Minn (Gill)... Minnesota Reports (Gilfillan Edition) [*A publication*] (DLA)
Minn Hist Soc... Minnesota Historical Society (SAUO)
Minn Law J... Minnesota Law Journal [*A publication*] (DLA)
Minn Laws... Laws of Minnesota [*A publication*] (DLA)
Minn LJ .... Minnesota Law Journal [*St. Paul*] [*A publication*] (DLA)
MINNLP .... Minnesota Linear Programming (SAUO)
MinnMul ...... Minnesota Municipal Income Trust [*Associated Press*] (SAG)
MinnMuT ..... Minnesota Municipal Term Trust [*Associated Press*] (SAG)
Minn Orch ... Minnesota Orchestra (SAUO)
MinnPL........ Minnesota Power & Light Co. [*Associated Press*] (SAG)
Minn R & WCAT Div... Minnesota Railroad and Warehouse Commission. Auto Transportation Co. Division Reports [*A publication*] (DLA)
Minn Reg..... Minnesota Register [*A publication*] (AAGC)
Minn Rep..... Minnesota Reports [*A publication*] (DLA)
Minn Reps... Minnesota Reports [*A publication*] (DLA)
Minn Sess Law Serv (West)... Minnesota Session Law Service (West) [*A publication*] (DLA)
Minn Stat..... Minnesota Statutes [*A publication*] (AAGC)
Minn Stat Ann... Minnesota Statutes, Annotated [*A publication*] (DLA)
Minn Stat Ann (West)... West's Minnesota Statutes, Annotated [*A publication*] (DLA)
Minntc .... Minntech Corp. [*Associated Press*] (SAG)
MinnTr2........ Minnesota Term Trust, Inc. II [*Associated Press*] (SAG)
Minn WCD... Minnesota Workmen's Compensation Decisions [*A publication*] (DLA)
MINOD......... Miniaturized Infrared Night Observation Device (ACAE)
MIN OIL....... Mineral Oil (SAUS)
MiNop.......... Leelanau Township Library, Northport, MI [*Library symbol*] [*Library of Congress*] (LCLS)
Minor........... Minor's Alabama Supreme Court Reports [*1820-26*] [*A publication*] (DLA)
Minor........... Minor's Institutes [*A publication*] (DLA)
Minor (Ala)... Minor's Alabama Reports [*A publication*] (DLA)
Minor (Ala)... Minor's Institutes [*Alabama*] [*A publication*] (DLA)
Minorc......... Minorco [*Formerly, Minerals & Resources Corp. Ltd.*] [*Associated Press*] (SAG)
MINORCO .... Minerals & Resources Corporation (SAUO)
Minor Inst.... Minor's Institutes of Common and Statute Law [*A publication*] (DLA)
Minor's Alabama Rep... Minor's Alabama Reports [*A publication*] (DLA)
Minor's Ala R... Minor's Alabama Reports [*A publication*] (DLA)
Minor's Ala Rep... Minor's Alabama Reports [*A publication*] (DLA)
Minor's R .... Minor's Alabama Reports [*A publication*] (DLA)
Minor's Rep... Minor's Alabama Reports [*A publication*] (DLA)
MINOS......... Main Injector Neutrino Oscillation Search [*Particle Physics*]
MINOS......... Manual Intervention and Observation Simulator (AAG)
MINOS......... Marconi Integrated Naval Operations System (SAUS)
MINOS......... Mine Operating System (PDAA)
MINOS......... Mixed Integer Operational Scheduling (PDAA)
MINOS......... Modular Input/Output System
Minot St U... Minot State University (GAGS)
MINOX......... Minimum Oxidizer (KSC)
MINP .... Mallacoota Inlet National Park (SAUO)
MinP............ Minnesota Power & Light Co. [*Associated Press*] (SAG)
MINPAC........ Mine Warfare Forces, Pacific [*Navy*]
MinPBW ...... Ministry of Public Building and Works (SAUO)
MIN PLEN..... Minister Plenipotentiary (WDAA)
Min Plenit ... Minister Plenipotentiary (SAUO)
MINPOREN... National Association of Commercial Broadcasters in Japan (EY)
MinPres....... Minister President
MINPRIRODI... Ministry of Protection of the Environment and Natural Resources of the Russian Federation (SAUO)
MINPROC .... Mineral Processing Technology [*Canada Department of Energy, Mines, and Resources*] [*Information service or system*] (CRD)
MINPRT....... Minimum Processing Time per Operation
Min PW .... Ministry of Public Works (SAUO)
MINQU......... Minimum Norm Quadratic Unbiased [*Statistics*]
MINQUE....... Minimum Norm Quadratic Unbiased Estimation [*Statistics*] (PDAA)
MINR .... Minimum Rate [*Travel industry*] (TRID)
MINR .... Minimum R Factor [*Spectrometry*]
Min R .... Minnesota Reports [*A publication*] (DLA)
MINRA......... Miniature International Racing Association
MINRAD....... Minimum Radiation (MCD)
Min Rep ...... Minnesota Reports [*A publication*] (DLA)
MINRL .... Mineral
MINRON ...... Mine Squadron [*Navy*]
MINRTY....... Minority
MINS .... Mare Island Naval Shipyard [*Also, MINSY*] [*Later, MID*]
MINS .... Marine Integrated Navigation System (SAUS)
MINS .... Miniature Inertial Navigation System
MINS .... Minors in Need of Supervision [*Classification for delinquent children*]
MINSA......... Ministry of Health (SAUO)
MINSAT....... Minimum Safe Air Travel (SAA)
MINSD......... Minimum Planned Start Date per Operation
Minsec......... Mineral Securities Australia Ltd. (SAUO)
MINSK......... [A] Russian digital computer [*Moscow University*]
MINSOP....... Minimum Slack Time per Operation
MINSQ......... Minimum Squares [*Mathematical statistics*]
MInstAEA..... Member of the Institute of Automotive Engineer Assessors [*British*] (DBQ)
M Inst AM ... Member of the Institute of Administrative Management [*British*] (DCTA)
MInstBB....... Member of the Institute of British Bakers (DBQ)
MInstBCA..... Member of the Institute of Burial and Cremation Administration [*British*] (DBQ)
MInstBE .... Member of the Institution of British Engineers
MInstBRM.... Member of the Institute of Baths and Recreation Management [*British*] (DBQ)
MInstBRMDip... Diploma Member of the Institute of Baths and Recreation Management [*British*] (DBQ)
MInstBTM .... Member of the Institute of Business and Technical Management [*British*] (DBQ)
MInstCE .... Member of the Institution of Civil Engineers [*Later, MICE*] [*British*] (EY)
M Inst CM ... Member of the Institute of Commercial Management [*British*] (DCTA)
MInstD......... Member of the Institute of Directors [*British*] (DI)
MInstE......... Member of the Institute of Energy [*British*] (DBQ)
MInstE......... Member of the Institution of Engineers [*British*] (EY)
MInstF......... Member of the Institute of Fuel [*British*]
MInstFF .... Member of the Institute of Freight Forwarders [*British*] (DBQ)
MInstGasE ... Member of the Institution of Gas Engineers [*British*] (EY)
MInstHE....... Member of the Institution of Highway Engineers [*British*]
M INST J ...... Member of the Institute of Journalists [*British*] (DGA)
M Inst Jour... Member of the Institute of Journalists [*British*] (ROG)
MInstM .... Member of the Institute of Marketing [*British*]
MInstM .... Member of the Institute of Metals (SAUO)
MInstMC...... Member of the Institute of Measurement and Control [*British*] (DBQ)
MInstME ...... Member of the Institution of Mining Engineers [*British*]
MInstMet ..... Member of the Institute of Metals [*British*]
MInstMM ..... Member of the Institute of Mining and Metallurgy (SAUO)
MInstMM ..... Member of the Institution of Mining and Metallurgy [*British*]
MInstMO ..... Member of the Institute of Market Officers [*British*] (DI)
MInstMSM... Member of the Institute of Marketing and Sales Management (SAUO)
MInstNA...... Member of the Institution of Naval Architects [*British*] (EY)
MInstNDT ... Member of the British Institute of Non-Destructive Testing (DBQ)
MInstP .... Member of the Institute of Physics (ADA)
MInstPC...... Member of the Institute of Public Cleansing (SAUO)
MInstPE ...... Member of the Institute of Petroleum Engineers (ADA)
MInstPet ..... Member of the Institute of Petroleum [*British*] (EY)
MInstPI........ Member of the Institute of Patentees and Inventors [*British*] (EY)
MInstPI........ Member of the Institute of Patentees Inc. (SAUO)
MInstPkg .... Member of the Institute of Packaging [*British*] (DI)
M Inst PS .... Member of the Institute of Purchasing and Supply [*British*] (DCTA)
MInstPT ...... Member of the Institute of Petroleum Technologists (SAUO)
MInstR......... Member of the Institute of Refrigeration [*British*] (DBQ)
MINSTR ...... Minister
MInstRA....... Member of the Institute of Registered Architects [*British*]
MInstRadE... Member of Institute of Radio-Engineers (SAUO)
M Inst RE .... Member of the Institute of Radio Engineers (SAUO)
MINSTREL ... Management Information Software Tool-Research in Libraries (SAUO)
MInstSM...... Member of the Institute of Sales Management (SAUO)
MInstSMM ... Member of the Institute of Sales and Marketing Management [*British*] (DBQ)
MInstSP....... Member Institution of Sewage Purification [*Ecology*] (DAVI)
MInstSP....... Member of the Institution of Sewage Purification (SAUO)
MInstStructE... Member of the Institution of Structural Engineers (ADA)
MInstSWM... Member of the Institute of Solid Waste Management [*British*] (DI)
MInstT .... Member of the Institute of Technology [*British*] (EY)
MInstT .... Member of the Institute of Transport [*British*]
M Inst TA..... Member of the Institute of Transport Administration [*British*] (DCTA)
MInstTM ...... Member of the Institute of Travel Managers in Industry and Commerce [*British*] (ODBW)
MInstW .... Member of the Institute of Welding [*British*]
MInstWE ...... Member of the Institution of Water Engineers [*British*]
MInstWHS ... Member of the Institute of Works and Highways Superintendents [*British*] (DI)
MInstWPC.... Member of the Institution of Water Pollution Control [*British*] (DI)
MINSY .... Mare Island Naval Shipyard [*Also, MINS*] [*Later, MID*]
MINT............ Bank of Montreal, Canadian Imperial Bank of Commerce, Bank of Nova Scotia, and Toronto-Dominion Bank
MINT............ Major International Narcotics Traffickers [*Register*] [*Drug Enforcement Administration*]
MINT............ Management Information Network for Training (SAUO)

MINT	Managing the Integration of New Technology (SAUO)
MINT	Materiel Identification and New Item Control Technique [*AFLC*]
MINT	Media Integration [*Computer science*]
MINT	Micro-Integration [*NASDAQ symbol*] (TTSB)
MINT	Micro-Integration Corp. [*NASDAQ symbol*] (SAG)
MINT	Minorities International Network for Trade (EA)
MINT	Municipal Insured National Trust
MINT	Mutual Interference (SAUS)
MinTch	Minerals Technologies, Inc. [*Associated Press*] (SAG)
MINTEC	Mining Technology Abstracts [*Canada Centre for Mineral and Energy Technology*] [*Information service or system*] (CRD)
MINTECH	Ministry of Technology [*British*]
MINTEK	Council for Mineral Technology (SAUO)
MINTEL	Market Intelligence Report
MINTEQ	Geochemical Model (SAUS)
MINTER	Ministerio do Interior [*Ministry of the Interior*] [*Information service or system*] (IID)
MINTERM	Miniature Terminal (SAUS)
MINTEX	M International Inc. (SAUO)
MINTIE	Minimum Test Instrumentation Equipment
MIntLaw	Master of International Law
M Int Med	Master of Internal Medicine (SAUO)
MIntMed	Master of International Medicine (NADA)
MinTopEnergo	Ministry of Fuel and Energy (SAUO)
MINTR	Miniature (MSA)
MINTS	Mutual Institutions National Transfer System, Inc. [*Banking*]
MINTS	Mutual Insurance National Transfer System, Inc.
MINTSS	Military Airlift Command Intelligence Support System (SAUO)
MINTWK	Minimum Total Work Content
MINU	Mobile Instrument Investigation Unit
MINucE	Member of the Institution of Nuclear Engineers [*British*]
MI Nucl E	Member of the Institution of Nuclear Engineers [*British*]
MINUET	Minimum Energy Trajectory Model [*Army*] (AABC)
MINUET	Minnesota Internet User's Essential Tool (VLIE)
MINUGUA	United Nations Verification Mission for/in Guatemala (SAUO)
MiNun	Crockery Township Library, Nunica, MI [*Library symbol*] [*Library of Congress*] (LCLS)
MINUS	Modular Integrated Utility Systems (MCD)
MinutInt	Minuteman International [*Associated Press*] (SAG)
MINW	Master Interface Network (MCD)
MINWARCOM	Mine Warfare Command (SAUO)
MINWARTECH	Mine Warfare Technician [*Navy*] (DNAB)
MINWR	Merritt Island National Wildlife Refuge (SAUO)
MINWR	Minimum Weapon Radius (SAA)
MIN WT	Minimum Weight (WDAA)
MINX	Mines in the New Century programme (SAUS)
MINX	Multimedia Information Network Exchange [*Computer science*]
MINY	Mineralogy (ROG)
MINY	Minority (ROG)
MinZdravMedProm	Ministry of Public Health and Medical Industry (SAUO)
MIO	Management Improvement and Operating Plan [*Department of Housing and Urban Development*] (GFGA)
MIO	Management Information Office [*or Officer*] [*Air Force*] (AFM)
mio	Management Integration Office (NAKS)
MIO	Management Integration Office [*NASA*] (NASA)
MIO	Map Information Office [*US Geological Survey*]
MIO	Marine Inspection Office [*Coast Guard*]
MIO	Marine Inspection Operations [*USCG*] (TAG)
MIO	Maritime Interception Operations [*Coast Guard*] (DOMA)
MIO	Maritime Interdiction Operations
MIO	Medical Intelligence Office [*Later, MIIA*] [*DoD*]
MIO	Meteoritic Impact Origin (AAG)
MIO	Metric Information Office [*National Institute of Standards and Technology*]
MIO	Miami, OK [*Location identifier*] [*FAA*] (FAAL)
MIO	Midas Commuter Airlines CA [*Venezuela*] [*ICAO designator*] (FAAC)
MIO	Military Industrial Organization (ACAE)
MIO	Military Intelligence Officer [*British military*] (DMA)
MIO	Military Interviewing Officer (SAUO)
MIO	Minimal Identifiable Odor
MIO	Mobile Ionospheric Observatory [*Boston University*]
MIO	Mobile Issuing Office [*Navy*]
MIO	Modular Input/Output [*Telecommunications*]
MIO	Motility Indol Ornithine [*Medium*] [*Medicine*] (BABM)
MIO	Movements Identification Officer [*Air Force*]
MIO	Movements Identification Order (SAUO)
MIO	Movements Integration Office
MIO	Multi-Institutional Organization [*Generic term*] (DHSM)
MIO	Multiple Input/Output (NITA)
MIO	Multiple Input/Output Stream [*Computer science*]
MIOA	Medical Industries of America [*NASDAQ symbol*] (SAG)
MIOAC	Military Intelligence Officer Advanced Course (DOMA)
MIOB	Member of the Institute of Building [*British*]
MIOB	Member of the Institute (or Institution) of Builders (or Building) (SAUO)
MiOC	Olivet College, Olivet, MI [*Library symbol*] [*Library of Congress*] (LCLS)
MIOCA	Monolithic Integrated Optics for Customer Access Applications (SAUO)
MIOD	Message Input-Output Devices (MCD)
MIOG	Manual of Investigative and Operational Guidelines [*FBI*]
MIOK	Magyar Izraelitak Orszagos Kepviselete (BJA)
MiOIA	Alumni Memorial Library, Orchard Lake, MI [*Library symbol*] [*Library of Congress*] (LCLS)
MIOM	Member, Institute of Office Management (SAUO)

MIoM	Member of the Institute of Metals (SAUO)
MIONP	Microwave-Induced Optical Nuclear Polarization [*Physics*]
MiOnt	Ontonagon Township Library, Ontonagon, MI [*Library symbol*] [*Library of Congress*] (LCLS)
MIOP	Magnetic Iron Oxide Particle (DMAA)
MIOP	Master Input/Output Processor (NITA)
MIOP	Member of the Institute of Osteopathy and Physiotherapy [*British*]
MIOP	Member of the Institute of Printing [*British*] (DBQ)
MIOP	Multiplexing Input-Output Processor [*Computer science*] (BUR)
MIOS	Modular Input-Output System (TEL)
MIOS	Multi-IMU [*Internal Measuring Unit*] Operation System [*NASA*]
MIOSH	Member of the Institution of Occupational Safety and Health [*British*] (DCTA)
MIOSHA	Michigan Occupational Safety and Health Act (SAUO)
MIOT	Member of the Institute of Operating Theatre Technicians [*British*]
MIOT	Municipal Income Opportunities Trust [*Associated Press*] (SAG)
MiOt	Otsego District Public Library, Otsego, MI [*Library symbol*] [*Library of Congress*] (LCLS)
MIOT2	Municipal Income Opportunities Trust II [*Associated Press*] (SAG)
MIOT3	Municipal Income Opportunities Trust III [*Associated Press*] (SAG)
MiOv	Ovid Public Library, Ovid, MI [*Library symbol*] [*Library of Congress*] (LCLS)
MIOW	Member of the Institute of Welding (SAUO)
MiOw	Owosso Public Library, Owosso, MI [*Library symbol*] [*Library of Congress*] (LCLS)
MiOwJW	John Wesley College, Owosso, MI [*Library symbol*] [*Library of Congress*] (LCLS)
MIP	Machine Independent Package (DGA)
MIP	Machine Instruction Processor [*Computer science*] (BUR)
MIP	Macrophage-Induced Protein [*Biochemistry*]
MIP	Macrophage Inflammatory Protein [*Biochemistry*]
MIP	Magnetic Index Pulse (ACAE)
MIP	Mainframe Internetting Project (SAUO)
MIP	Main Instrument Panel (MCD)
MIP	Maintainer Instructional Package (MCD)
MIP	Maintenance Implementation Plan [*FAA*] (TAG)
MIP	Maintenance Improvement Program
MIP	Maintenance Index Page
MIP	Major Intrinsic Protein [*Biochemistry*]
MIP	Malleable Iron Pipe
MIP	Management Implementation Plan (MCD)
MIP	Management Improvement Plan
MIP	Management Improvement Program [*Military*]
MIP	Management Incentive Program
MIP	Management Information Protocol [*Telecommunications*] (OSI)
MIP	Management Intern Program
MIP	Mandatory Inspection Point (KSC)
MIP	Manual Index Page [*SNMMMS*]
MIP	Manual Input Processing [*or Program*] [*Computer science*]
MIP	Manufacturers of Illumination Products (EA)
MIP	Marche International des Programmes de Television International [*International Marketplace for Buyers and Sellers of Television Programs*] (NTCM)
MIP	Marine Insurance Policy
MIP	Master Improvement Program (AFIT)
MIP	Master Index Pulse (ACAE)
MIP	Master Information Paper [*Military*] (CAAL)
MIP	Master Insurance Program
MIP	Master of Intellectual Property (PGP)
MIP	Material Improvement Plan [*or Program*] [*Aviation*]
MIP	Material in Process [*Computer science*] (CIST)
MIP	Materiel Improvement Project [*Military*]
MIP	Matrix Inversion Program [*Computer science*] (BUR)
MIP	Maximum Inspiratory Pressure [*Medicine*]
MIP	Maximum Integration Phone (SAUO)
MIP	Maximum Investment Plan (WDAA)
MIP	Mean Incubation Perios (MELL)
MIP	Mean Indicated Pressure
MIP	Mean Intravascular Pressure [*Cardiology*] (MAE)
MIP	Measuring Instruments Pullin Ltd. (SAUO)
MIP	Mechanized Infantry Program [*United States Army, Europe*] (MCD)
MIP	Medicaid Interim Payments
MIP	Member of the Institute of Petroleum (SAUO)
MIP	Member of the Institute of Plumbing [*British*] (DBQ)
MIP	Membrane-Intercalated Particles [*Cytology*]
MIP	Membrane Isolation Process [*Food technology*]
MIP	Merfin Hygienic [*Vancouver Stock Exchange symbol*]
MIP	Message Input Processor
MIP	Methodology Investigation Proposal (MCD)
MIP	Methods Improvement Program [*IBM Corp.*]
MIP	Microelectronic Integrated Processing [*Symposium*]
MIP	Microwave-Induced Plasma [*Spectrometry*]
MIP	Microwave Interference Protection
MIP	Middle Interphalangeal Joint [*Anatomy*] (DAVI)
MIP	Military Improvement Program
MIP	Military Information Program
MIP	Military Interdepartmental Purchase
MIP	Military International Police (SAUO)
MIP	Million Instructions per Second
MIP	Milton, PA [*Location identifier*] [*FAA*] (FAAL)
MIP	Minimal Inspiratory Pressure [*Medicine*] (DB)
MIP	Minimum Import Prices [*Economics*]
MIP	Minimum Impulse Pulse
MIP	Ministry of Irrigation and Power (SAUO)
MIP	Mint in Package [*Doll collecting*]

MIP	Missile Impact Prediction (SAUO)
MIP	Missile Impact Predictor [Air Force]
MIP	Missile Instrumentation Package [Military] (CAAL)
MIP	Mission Integration Panel [NASA] (SSD)
MIP	Missouri Institute of Psychiatry (SAUO)
MIP	Missouri Institute of Psychiatry Library, St. Louis, MO [OCLC symbol] (OCLC)
MIP	Mixed Integer Programming [Computer science]
MIP	MMU [Manned Maneuvering Unit] Integration Plan [NASA] (GFGA)
MIP	Mobilization Improvement Program [MTMC] (TAG)
MIP	Model Implementation Plan
MIP	Model Improvements Program [TRADOC] (MCD)
MIP	Model Installation Program (AAGC)
MIP	Modern Irish Printer [A publication] [British] (DGA)
MIP	Modest Improvement Program [Military] (NVT)
MIP	Modification Instruction Package (KSC)
MIP	Modulated Interframe Plan
MIP	Molecularly Imprinted Polymer [Biotechnology]
MIP	Monthly Intelligence Production (MCD)
MIP	Monthly Investment Plan [Stock exchange term] (SPSG)
MIP	Mortgage Insurance Premium
MIP	Mortgage Investments Plus, Inc. (MHDW)
MIP	Most Important Person
MIP	Motivation Indoctrination Program [Military]
MIP	Mouvement Independent Populaire [Popular Independent Movement] [Luxembourg] [Political party] (PPE)
MIP	Mouvement Islamique Progressiste [Islamic Progressive Movement] [Tunisia] [Political party] (PD)
MIP	Movimiento Independiente Peruano [Peruvian Independent Movement] [Political party]
MIP	Multi-Island Programme (SAUO)
MIP	Multipurpose Information Processor [Computer science] (MHDB)
MIP	Museums Informatics Project (SAUO)
MIP	Mycorrhiza Inoculum Potential [Soil science]
MIP	Myo-inositolphosphate [Biochemistry]
MIPA	Macrophage Inflammatory Protein Alpha (DMAA)
MIPA	Master of International Public Administration (GAGS)
MIPA	Member of the Institute of Practitioners in Advertising [British]
MIPA	Member of the Institute of Public Administration (ADA)
MIPA	Methylisopropylaniline [Organic chemistry]
MIPA	Missile Procurement, Army (AABC)
MIPA	Monoisopropylamine [Organic chemistry]
MiPa	Port Austin Township Library, Port Austin, MI [Library symbol] [Library of Congress] (LCLS)
MIPAC	Motamar International Peace Advancement Campaign (SAUO)
Mipad	Multimodal, Interactive Note Pad
MIP-AES	Microwave-Induced Plasma-Atomic Emission Spectroscopy
MiPal	Richmond Township Public Library, Palmer, MI [Library symbol] [Library of Congress] (LCLS)
MiPar	Parchment Community Library, Parchment, MI [Library symbol] [Library of Congress] (LCLS)
MIPAS	Management Information Planning and Accountancy Service (MHDI)
MIPAS	Michelson Interferometric Passive Atmosphere Sounder (EOSA)
MiPaw	Paw Paw Public Library, Paw Paw, MI [Library symbol] [Library of Congress] (LCLS)
MIPB	Macrophage Inflammatory Protein Beta (DMAA)
MIPB	Material Improvement Project Board (SAUO)
MIPB	Monoisopropylbiphenyl (PDAA)
MIPC	Manifold Ignition Primary Charge
MIPC	Master Index Pulse Corrected (ACAE)
MIPC	Member of the Institute of Production Control [British] (DBQ)
MIPC	Metropolitan Information Processing Conference (MCD)
MIPD	Manpower Intelligence and Planning Division (AIE)
MIPD	Manufacturing Industry Products Division (MCD)
MIPDS	Minuteman Instrumented Payload Delivery System (ACAE)
MIPE	Magnetic Induction Plasma Engine
MIPE	Member of the Institution of Production Engineers [British] (DAS)
MIPE	Men's International Peace Exchange (EA)
MIPE	Mobile Intelligence Processing Element (DOMA)
MIPE	Modular Information Processing Equipment
MIPE	Moscow Institute of Power Engineering (SAUO)
MiPec	Elk Township Library, Peck, MI [Library symbol] [Library of Congress] (LCLS)
MiPel	Pellston Public Library, Pellston, MI [Library symbol] [Library of Congress] (LCLS)
MiPen	Pentwater Township Library, Pentwater, MI [Library symbol] [Library of Congress] (LCLS)
MiPet	Member of the Institute of Petroleum (SAUO)
MiPet	Petoskey Public Library, Petoskey, MI [Library symbol] [Library of Congress] (LCLS)
MiPetN	North Central Michigan College, Petoskey, MI [Library symbol] [Library of Congress] (LCLS)
MIPEX	Model Improvement Experiment (MCD)
MIPG	Master Index Pulse Generator
MiPh	Saint Clair County Library System, Port Huron, MI [Library symbol] [Library of Congress] (LCLS)
MIPHE	Member of the Institute of Public Health Engineers [British] (DBQ)
MIPHE	Member of the Institution of Public Health Engineers (SAUO)
MiPhM	Saint Clair County Community Mental Health Services, Port Huron, MI [Library symbol] [Library of Congress] (LCLS)
MiPhS	Saint Clair Community College, Port Huron, MI [Library symbol] [Library of Congress] (LCLS)
MIPI	Medicine in the Public Interest (EA)
MIPI	Member of the Institute of Professional Investigators [British] (DBQ)
MiPi	Pigeon District Library, Pigeon, MI [Library symbol] [Library of Congress] (LCLS)
MIPIE	Michigan Products Information Exchange [Interchange Plus, Inc.] [Information service or system] (IID)
MiPin	Pinckney Community Public Library, Pinckney, MI [Library symbol] [Library of Congress] (LCLS)
MIPIR	Missile Precision Instrumentation RADAR
MIPIR	Multimission Imagery Photographic Interpretation Report (MCD)
MiPit	Pittsford Township Library, Pittsford, MI [Library symbol] [Library of Congress] (LCLS)
MIPK	Methyl Isopropyl Ketone [Organic chemistry]
MiPl	Charles A. Ransom Public Library, Plainwell, MI [Library symbol] [Library of Congress] (LCLS)
MIPL	Master Indentured Parts List
MIPL	Mauritius Institute Public Library (SAUO)
MIPL	Monthly Intelligence Production Listing (MCD)
MIPL	Multimission Image Processing Laboratory (SAUO)
MIPlantE	Member of the Institution of Plant Engineers [British]
MIPLOGS	Marine Integrated Personnel and Logistics Subsystem
MiPIS	State Technical Institute and Rehabilitation Center, Plainwell, MI [Library symbol] [Library of Congress] (LCLS)
MiPlySJ	Saint John's Provincial Seminary, Plymouth, MI [Library symbol] [Library of Congress] (LCLS)
MIPM	Member of the Institute of Personnel Management [British]
MIP/MA	Missile in Place/Missile Away
MIPMS	Microwave-Induced Plasma Mass Spectrometry
MIPO	Multiple Item Purchase Order (AAG)
MiPon	Pontiac Public Libraries, Pontiac, MI [Library symbol] [Library of Congress] (LCLS)
MiPonO	Oakland County Law Library, Clark J. Adams-Philip Pratt Library, Pontiac, MI [Library symbol] [Library of Congress] (LCLS)
MiPonSJ	Saint Joseph Mercy Hospital, General Medical Library, Pontiac, MI [Library symbol] [Library of Congress] (LCLS)
MiPor	Portage Public Library, Portage, MI [Library symbol] [Library of Congress] (LCLS)
MIPORN	Miami Pornography [FBI undercover investigation, 1977-80]
MiPorPS	Portage Public Schools, Portage, MI [Library symbol] [Library of Congress] (LCLS)
MiPorS	Seventh Day Adventists Junior Academy, Portage, MI [Library symbol] [Library of Congress] (LCLS)
MiPot	Benton Township - Potterville District Library, Potterville, MI [Library symbol] [Library of Congress] (LCLS)
MIPP	Maintainability Index Prediction Procedure
MIPP	Master of International Public Policy (GAGS)
MIPP	Milk Indemnity Payment Program
MiPPT	McMaster Institute for Polymer Production Technology [McMaster University] [Canada] (IRC)
MIPR	Manhattan Institute for Policy Research (EA)
MIPR	Master Index Pulse Reference (ACAE)
MIPR	Medical Intelligence Production Requirements (MCD)
MIPR	Member of the Institute of Public Relations [British]
MIPR	Military Interagency Procurement Requisition (SAUO)
MIPR	Military Interagency Purchase Request (SAUO)
MIPR	Military Interdepartmental Procurement [or Purchase] Request
MIPR	Military Intergovernmental Purchase Request (NASA)
MIPR	Monthly Interim Progress Report
MIPRCS	Microprocessor (MSA)
MIPRG	Master Index Pulse Reference Generator (ACAE)
Mipro	Manufactures Import Promotion Organization (SAUO)
MIProdE	Member of the Institution of Production Engineers [British] (EY)
MIPS	Maintenance Index Pages (ACAE)
MIPS	Management Information Progress Sheets (MCD)
MIPS	Marine Integrated Personnel System (MCD)
MIPS	Martinsried Institute for Protein Sequences [Database producer]
MIPS	Master Installment Purchase System (ACAE)
MIPS	Meaningless Information per Second (SAUS)
MIPS	Medium Integrated Propulsion System (SAUS)
MIPS	Member of the Phonographic Society [British] (ROG)
MIPS	Membership Information Processing System [AARP]
MIPS	Merritt Island Press Site [NASA] (NASA)
MIPS	Microprocessor with Interlocked Pipeline Stages (RALS)
MIPS	Microprocessor Without Interlocked Pipeline Stages (NITA)
MIPS	Microwave-Induced Plasma Spectroscopy (MEC)
MIPS	Microwave Pulse Storage System [or Subsystem] (MCD)
MIPS	Military Information Processing System
mips	Million Instructions Per Second [Computer science] (WDMC)
MIPS	Million Instructions per Second (ACAE)
MIPS	Millions of Instructions per Second [Facetious translations: "Meaningless Indication of Performance"; "Meaningless Instructions per Second"; "Meaningless Indicator of Processor Speed"] [Computer science]
mips	Millions of Instructions per Second
MIPS	Millon Index of Personality Styles [Test] (TMMY)
MIPS	Miniature Implantable Power System
MIPS	Missile Impact Prediction System
MIPS	Missile Information Processing System (MCD)
MIPS	Mission and Information Planning System (ACAE)
MIPS	Modular Instrumentation Package System (MCD)
MIPS	Modular Integrated Pallet System [Tank monitoring] [Army] (RDA)
MIPS	Multi Instruction Processing System (SAUO)
MIPS	Multimission Image Processing Subsystem (SAUS)
MIPS	Multiple Index Processing System (MCD)
MIPS	Munich Information Center for Protein Sequences (SAUO)
MIPS	Myocardial Isotopic Perfusion Scan [Cardiology] (DAVI)

MiPs	Sanilac Township Library, Port Sanilac, MI [Library symbol] [Library of Congress] (LCLS)
MIPsiMed	Member of the Institute of Psionic Medicine [British]
MIPSL	Manufacturing Indentured Parts Summary List (ACAE)
MIPSM	Member of the Institute of Purchasing and Supply Management (ADA)
MIPSNY	Metro-International Program Services of New York (EA)
MIPTC	Men's International Professional Tennis Council [Defunct] (EA)
MI PTG M	Member of the Institute of Printing Management [British] (DGA)
MiPtl	Portland District Library, Portland, MI [Library symbol] [Library of Congress] (LCLS)
MIPTV	Marche International des Programmes de Television [Cannes Film Festival] [France]
MIPVCE	Multiple-Input Phase-Variable Canonical Form (PDAA)
MIQ	Maiquetia [Venezuela] [Airport symbol] (AD)
MIQ	Maniwaki [Quebec] [Seismograph station code, US Geological Survey] (SEIS)
MIQ	Member of the Institute of Quarrying [British] (DBQ)
MIQ	Minimum Identifiable Quantity [Analytical chemistry]
MIQ	Minnesota Importance Questionnaire [Vocational test]
Miq	Miqva'ot [or Miqwa'ot] (BJA)
MIQA	Member of the Institute of Quality Assurance [British] (DBQ)
MIQPS	Member of the Institute of Qualified Private Secretaries [British] (DI)
Mir	Horne's Mirror of Justice [A publication] (DLA)
MIR	Magnetic Ink Read
MIR	Main Immunogenic Region [Immunology]
MIR	Maintenance Infusion Rate [Medicine]
MIR	Maintenance Inspection Report
MIR	Major Impact Report (SAUO)
MIR	Malfunction Investigation Report [NASA] (KSC)
MIR	Management Information Report
MIR	Management Information Repository [Computer science] (CIST)
MIR	Management Information Requirement [Production management]
MIR	Manager, Iwi Relationships (SAUO)
MIR	Mandatory Inspection Report (MCD)
MIR	Manual Input Room (SAA)
MIR	Master Index of Repairables (MCD)
MIR	Master Inventory Record
MIR	Master of Industrial Relations
MIR	Material Inspection Report [Navy]
MIR	Material Investigators Reactor [NASA]
MIR	Maverick Interim Report
MIR	Maximum Incremental Reactivity [Exhaust emissions] [Automotive engineering]
MIR	Maximum Individual Risk [Environmental science] (FFDE)
MIR	Maximum Information Rate (SAUO)
MIR	Medical Incident Report
MIR	Member of the Institute of Population Registration [British] (DBQ)
MIR	Memory-Information Register [Computer science]
MIR	Memory Input Register [Computer science]
MIR	Method Improvement Request (MCD)
MIR	Method of Integral Relations
MIR	Microinstruction Register
MIR	Micropower Impulse RADAR [For fluid level sensing]
MIR	Midday Intelligence Report (SAUO)
MIr	Middle Irish (ADWA)
MIR	Middle Irish [Language, etc.]
MIR	Mid Infrared (ACAE)
MIR	Mid-Infrared Spectrum [Spectroscopy]
MIR	Military Intelligence, Research [World War II]
MIR	Millimeter-Wave Imaging Radiometer (ARMP)
MIR	Mineta Resources Ltd. [Vancouver Stock Exchange symbol]
MIR	Minimum Income Requirements (OICC)
MIR	Minneapolis Industrial Railway Co. [AAR code]
MIR	Mirage Resorts [NYSE symbol] (SPSG)
MIR	Miramichi Air Services Ltd. [Canada] [ICAO designator] (FAAC)
MIR	MIRLYN [Michigan Research Library Network]
MIR	Mirny [Antarctica] [Seismograph station code, US Geological Survey] (SEIS)
MIR	Mirror (KSC)
MIR	Mishap Investigation Report (MCD)
MIR	Missile Identification Record
MIR	Missile Intelligence Report
MIR	Mission Inherent Reliability
MIR	Mitochondrial Import Receptor [Biochemistry]
MIR	Model Incident Report [Telecommunications] (TEL)
MIR	Modular Integrated Rack (MCD)
MIR	Moisture Insulation Resistance [Electronics] (AAEL)
MIR	Molded-In Electronics [Automotive engineering]
MIR	Monastir [Tunisia] [Airport symbol] (OAG)
MIR	Mouvement International de la Reconciliation [International Fellowship of Reconciliation]
MIR	Mouvement pour l'Independance de la Reunion [Movement for the Independence of Reunion] [Political party] (PD)
MIR	Movement for International Reconciliation (SAUO)
MIR	Movimiento de Izquierda Revolucionario [Movement of the Revolutionary Left] [Bolivia] [Political party] (PPW)
MIR	Movimiento de Izquierda Revolucionario [Movement of the Revolutionary Left] [Chile] [Political party]
MIR	Movimiento de Izquierda Revolucionario [Movement of the Revolutionary Left] [Venezuela] [Political party]
MIR	Multiband Infrared Radiometer
MIR	Multiple Instrumentation RADAR (MCD)
MIR	Multiple Internal Reflectance (EDCT)
MIR	Multiple Internal Reflection [Spectroscopy]

MIR	Multiple Isomorphous Replacement [Crystallography]
MIR	Multiple-target Instrumentation Radar (SAUS)
MIR	Multiplex Intensity Rules
MIR	Multitarget Instrumentation RADAR [Military] (CAAL)
MIR	Music Information Retrieval [Computer science]
MIR	Mutual Interference Report (MCD)
MIR	Orbital System (SAUS)
MIR	Russian Space Station (SAUO)
MIRA	Management Information Research Associates (SAUO)
MIRA	Massachusetts Immigrant and Refugee Advocacy Coalition
MIRA	Member of the Institute of Registered Architects (SAUO)
MIRA	Merchants Instant Response Authorization (SAA)
MIRA	MILAN Infra-Red Attachment (SAUS)
MIRA	Miniature Infrared Alarm
MIRA	Monterey Institute for Research in Astronomy
MIRA	Monthly Index of Russian Accessions [Library of Congress]
MIRA	Motor Industry Research Association [British] (DCTA)
MIRA	Movimiento de Independencia Revolucionaria en Armas [Puerto Rican independence group] [Political party]
MIRA	Movimiento Independentista Armado [Armed Pro-Independence Movement] [Puerto Rico] [Political party] (PD)
MIRA	Multifunctional Inertial Reference Assembly [Air Force] (MCD)
MIRAC	Management Information Research Assistance Center (AABC)
MIRAC	Master Index Remote Access Capability (MHDI)
MIRAC	Microfilmed Reports and Accounts (PDAA)
MIRACL	Management Information Report Access without Computer Languages [Computer science] (IEEE)
MIRACL	Mid-Infrared Advanced Chemical LASER
MIRACLE	Mokum Industrial Research Automatic Calculator for Laboratory and Engineering
MIRACLE	Multidisciplinary Integrated Research Activities in Complex Laboratory Environments [National Science Foundation]
MIRACLE	Music and Image Resources Assisted Computer Library Exchange (TELE)
MIRACL/SLBD	MIRACL/Sea Lite Beam Director (SAUS)
MIRACODE	Microfilm Information Retrieval Access Code
MIRAD	Monostatic Infrared Intrusion Detector (WDAA)
MIRADCOM	Missile Research and Development Command [Army]
MIRADOR	Minefield Reconnaissance and Detector System [Army]
MIRADS	Management Information and Display System [NASA]
MIRADS	Marshall [Space Flight Center] Information Retrieval and Display System [NASA] (PDAA)
MIRAGE	Megacity Impact on Regional and Global Environments (SAUO)
MIRAGE	Microelectronic Indicator for RADAR Ground Equipment (MCD)
MIRAGE	Migration of Radioisotopes in the Geosphere (SAUO)
MIRAGE	Moessbauer Isotopic Resonant Absorption of Gamma Emission [Physics]
MIRAGE	Multi-disciplinary Interest in Rural and General Health Education (SAUO)
MIRAID	Maintenance Information Retrieval Aid
MIRAID	Maritime Institute for Research and Industrial Development [Washington, DC] (EA)
MIRAMO	Missionary Radio Monitors (SAUO)
Miramr	Miramar Mining Corp. [Associated Press] (SAG)
MIRAN	Miniature Infrared Analyzer [Spectrometer]
MIRAN	Missile Ranging
MIRAS	Mortgage Interest Relief at Source [British] (DCTA)
MIRAS	Multiple Isomorphous Replacement with Anomalous Scattering [Crystallography]
MIRAT	MILPERCEN Initial Recruiting and Training Plan (MCD)
MIRB	Mutual Insurance Rating Bureau [Defunct] (EA)
MIRBM	Medium Intermediate-Range Ballistic Missile (MCD)
MIRC	Market Intelligence Research Co. [Palo Alto, CA] (TSSD)
MIRC	Member of the Idle Rich Class (SAUO)
MIRC	Michael-Initiated Ring Closure [Organic chemistry]
MIRC	Microtubuloreticular Complex (DMAA)
MIRC	Missile-in-Range Computer (MCD)
MIRc	Reed City Public Library, Reed City, MI [Library symbol] [Library of Congress] (LCLS)
MIRCEN	Microbial Resources Centres Network (SAUO)
MIRCEN	Microbiological Resource Center [UNESCO]
Mirch D & S	Mirchall's Doctor and Student [A publication] (DLA)
MIRCLE	Mid-Infrared Chemical Laser (ACAE)
MIRCOM	Missile Materiel Readiness Command [Army]
MIRCOM	Missile Research Command (SAUO)
MIRCS	Mechanical Instrument Repair and Calibration Shop (DNAB)
MIRD	Medical Internal Radiation Dose [Committee] [Society of Nuclear Medicine]
MIRD	Medium Internal Radiation Dose (WDAA)
MIRD	Minor Irregularities and Deficiencies
MIRd	Seville Township Library, Riverdale, MI [Library symbol] [Library of Congress] (LCLS)
MIRE	Media Information Research Exchange (SAUO)
MIRE	Member of the Institution of Radio Engineers [British] (EY)
MIRE	Mine Identification, Recovery & Exploitation (SAUS)
MiRea	Reading Community Library, Reading, MI [Library symbol] [Library of Congress] (LCLS)
MIRECC	Mental Illness Research, Education, and Clinical Center [Department of Veterans Affairs]
MIRED	Microreciprocal Degrees
Mireh Advow	Mirehouse on Advowsons [1824] [A publication] (DLA)
Mireh Ti	Mirehouse on Tithes [2nd ed.] [1822] [A publication] (DLA)
MiRem	Wheatland Township Library, Remus, MI [Library symbol] [Library of Congress] (LCLS)

MiRep............ Republic-Michigamme Public Library, Republic, MI [*Library symbol*] [*Library of Congress*] (LCLS)
MIREQ .... Minimum Requirements Specified
MiRes........... Reading Community Library, Reading, MI [*Library symbol*] [*Library of Congress*] (LCLS)
MIRF............ Major Item Removal Frequency [*Army Aviation Systems Command*]
MIRF............ Multiple Instantaneous Response File
MIRF............ Myopia International Research Foundation (EA)
MIRFAC ...... Mathematics in Recognizable Form Automatically Compiled [*Computer science*]
MIRIAM ...... Major Incident Room Index and Action Management [*Police computer*] [*British*]
MIRIAM ...... Model Scheme for Information on Rural Development Initiatives and Agree Markets (SAUO)
MiRic........... Richmond Public Library, Richmond, MI [*Library symbol*] [*Library of Congress*] (LCLS)
MiRicl.......... Richland Community Library, Richland, MI [*Library symbol*] [*Library of Congress*] (LCLS)
MIRICLE ..... Mirrored Ions Closed-Loop Electrons (MCD)
MIRID .... Miniature RADAR Illumination Detector (MCD)
MIRID .... Mobile Infrared Inspection and Diagnostic (ACAE)
MIRID .... Monostatic Infrared Intrusion Detector (PDAA)
MIRINZ .... Meat Industry Research Institute of New Zealand
MIR-IR........ Multiple Internal Reflectance Infrared Spectroscopy (MCD)
MIRIS .... Michigan Inventory and Resource Information System (SAUO)
MIRIS .... Modified Infrared Interferometer Spectrometer
Mir Just ...... Horne's Mirror of Justice [*A publication*] (DLA)
MIRL............ Macrophage Ia Recruiting Factor (SAUS)
MIRL............ Medium Intensity Runway Edge Lights [*Aviation*] (FAAC)
MIRL............ Mineral Industry Research Laboratory
MIRLS .... Miniature Infra-Red Linescan (SAUS)
MIRLTD .... Mid-Infrared Laser Target Designator (ACAE)
MIRLYN .... Michigan Research Library Network
MIRN .... Movimento Independente da Reconstrucao Nacional [*Independent Movement of National Reconstruction*] [*Portugal*] (PPE)
MIRN-PDP ... Movimento Independente de Reconstrucao Nacional - Partido da Derecha Portuguesa [*Independent Movement for National Reconstruction - Party of the Portuguese Right*] [*Political party*] (PPW)
MIRO .... Malaysia Inter-Religious Organization (SAUO)
MIRO .... Mineral Industry Research Organisation [*British*] (DBA)
MIRO .... Mining Industry Research Organisation [*British*]
MiRochOU ... Oakland University, Rochester, MI [*Library symbol*] [*Library of Congress*] (LCLS)
MiRog.......... Presque Isle County Library, Rogers City, MI [*Library symbol*] [*Library of Congress*] (LCLS)
MiRom......... Romeo District Library, Romeo, MI [*Library symbol*] [*Library of Congress*] (LCLS)
MIROS .... Modulation Inducing Retrodirective Optical System [*NASA*]
MiRos.......... Roseville Public Library, Roseville, MI [*Library symbol*] [*Library of Congress*] (LCLS)
MiRosc .... Gerrish-Higgins School District Public Library, Roscommon, MI [*Library symbol*] [*Library of Congress*] (LCLS)
MiRoscK ...... Kirtland Community College, Roscommon, MI [*Library symbol*] [*Library of Congress*] (LCLS)
MiRoy.......... Royal Oak Public Library, Royal Oak, MI [*Library symbol*] [*Library of Congress*] (LCLS)
MiRoyWB .... William Beaumont Hospital, Royal Oak, MI [*Library symbol*] [*Library of Congress*] (LCLS)
MIRP .... Manipulated Information Rate Processor
MIRP .... Myocardial Infarction Rehabilitation Program [*Cardiology*] (DAVI)
Mir Parl .... Mirror of Parliament, London [*A publication*] (DLA)
Mir Pat Off... Mirror of the Patent Office [*Washington, DC*] [*A publication*] (DLA)
MIR-Peru ..... Movimiento de Izquierda Revolucionaria [*Movement of the Revolutionary Left of Peru*] [*Political party*] (PPW)
MIRPF .... Micro Image Relative Position Formula [*Computer science*]
MIRPL .... Major Item Repair Parts List (NATG)
MIRPS .... Multiple Information Retrieval by Parallel Selection
Mirr .... Horne's Mirror of Justice [*A publication*] (DLA)
MIRR .... Material Inspection and Receiving Report [*Military*]
MIRR .... Materiel Inspection and Receiving Report (SAUO)
mirr .... Mirror (VRA)
MIRR .... Mitsubishi Research Reactor [*Japan*]
MIRRC .... Motor Insurance Repair Research Centre [*British*] (CB)
MIRRER ...... Microwave Identification Railroad Encoding Reflector (DNAB)
MIRROR ...... Management Information Reporting and Review of Operational Resources System
MIRROS....... Modulation Inducing Reactive Retrodirective Optical System [*NASA*]
MirRsrt .... Mirage Resorts [*Associated Press*] (SAG)
MIRS .... Management Information and Reporting System (VLIE)
MIRS .... Management Information Retrieval System (TIMI)
MIRS .... Manpower Information Retrieval System (IEEE)
MIRS .... Marketing Information Retrieval System (SAUO)
MIRS .... Medical Information Retrieval Service (NITA)
MIRS .... Micro-Interactive Retrieval System (DNAB)
MIRS .... Mid-America Interventional Radiological Society (SAUO)
MIRS .... Mid-Infrared Source (ACAE)
MIRS .... Military Intelligence Research Section [*Navy*]
MIRS .... Military Intelligence Research Service (SAUO)
MIRS .... Military Intelligence Reserve Society (SAUO)
MIRS .... Millimeter Wave Instrumentation Radar Station (ACAE)
MIRS .... Miniaturized Imagery Receive System (SAUS)
MIRS .... Modular Integrated Radar System (ACAE)
MIRS .... MOTS [*Module Test Set*] Information Retrieval System
MIRS .... Multimedia Information Retrieval Services (SAUO)

MIRS .... Multiple Internal Reflection Spectroscopy
MIRS .... Multi-purpose Infrared Sight (PDAA)
MIRS .... Musical Information Retrieval System (TELE)
MiRsc........... Ogemaw District Library, Rose City, MI [*Library symbol*] [*Library of Congress*] (LCLS)
MIRSE .... Member of the Institution of Railway Signal Engineers [*British*] (DBQ)
MIRSE .... Multipurpose Imaging Radiometer Spectrometer Equipment
MIRSI .... Monthly Inventory Report of Special Items
MIRSIM .... Mineral Resource Simulation Model (PDAA)
MirSIP .... Mirage System Improvement Programme (SAUS)
MIRSL .... Microwave Remote Sensing Laboratory (CARB)
MIRST .... Multiple Infrared Scattered Light Recorder
MIRT............ Member, Institute of Reprographic Technicians (SAUO)
MIRT............ Molecular Infrared Track (IEEE)
MIRTAK ...... Martin Infrared Tracker
MIRTE.......... Member of the Institute of Road Transport Engineering [*British*] (DBQ)
MIRTE.......... Member of the Institute of Road Transport Engineers (SAUO)
MIRTOS ...... Minimum Real Time Operating System (NITA)
MIRTRAC ... Missile Infrared Tracking System (DNAB)
MIRTRAK ... Martin Infrared Tracker (SAA)
MIRTS .... Modular Infra-Red Transmitting System (SAUS)
MIRU .... Missile Inertial Reference Unit (ACAE)
MIRU .... Myocardial Infarction Research Unit [*Cardiology*] (DAVI)
MiRud.......... Rudyard School Public Library, Rudyard, MI [*Library symbol*] [*Library of Congress*] (LCLS)
MIRV .... Multiple Independently-Guided Re-entry Vehicle [*NASA*] (PDAA)
MIRV .... Multiple Independently-Targetable Reentry Vehicle [*Military*]
MIS.............. Machine Instruction Set (VLIE)
MIS.............. Magnetic Isolation System (SAUS)
MIS.............. Maintenance Indicator System [*TACOM*] [*Army*] (RDA)
MIS.............. Maintenance Information System (SAUO)
MIS.............. Managed Internet Service [*Computer science*]
MIS.............. Management Indicator Species (SAUO)
MIS.............. Management Information Science
MIS.............. Management Information Service
MIS.............. Management Information Services (SAUO)
MIS.............. Management Information Specialist
MIS.............. Management Information Strategy
mis.............. Management Information System [*NASA*] (NAKS)
MIS.............. Management Information System [*Generic term*]
MIS.............. Management Information Systems [*Corporation for Public Broadcasting*] [*Information service or system*] (IID)
MIS.............. Management Integrated System (TEL)
MIS.............. Manifold Interest Schedule
MIS.............. Man in Space
MIS.............. Manpower Information System (MCD)
MIS.............. Manson Impact Structure [*Iowa*] [*Geology*]
MIS.............. Manufacturing Information System [*Computer science*] (BUR)
MIS.............. Map Information System (SAUO)
MIS.............. Marine Information System (NITA)
MIS.............. Marine Isotope Stage [*Climatology*]
MIS.............. Market Impact Study
MIS.............. Marketing Information System
MIS.............. Mary Immaculate Seminary [*Pennsylvania*]
MIS.............. Master Implementation Schedule [*NATO Air Defense Ground Environment*] (NATG)
MIS.............. Master Integrated Schedule (AAG)
MIS.............. Master of Individualized Studies (GAGS)
MIS.............. Master of Industrial Safety (SARE)
MIS.............. Master of Information Science (PGP)
MIS.............. Master of Information Services (GAGS)
MIS.............. Master of Information Systems (PGP)
MIS.............. Master of Interdisciplinary Studies (GAGS)
MIS.............. Master of International Service
MIS.............. Master of International Studies (PGP)
MIS.............. Material Inspection Service [*Navy*]
MIS.............. Maturation-Inducing Substance [*Endocrinology*]
MIS.............. Mechanical Impact System [*Aerospace*]
MIS.............. Mechanical Inertia Simulation [*Automotive emissions*]
MIS.............. Mechanical Insulation Services, Inc. (EFIS)
MIS.............. Mechanical Interruption Summary [*FAA*]
MIS.............. Mechanically Induced Stress [*Agriculture*]
MIS.............. Media and Information Services [*Queensland, Australia*]
MIS.............. Median Iris Society (EA)
MIS.............. Medical Information Science
MIS.............. Medical Information System (COE)
MIS.............. Medical Information Systems (SAUO)
MIS.............. Medical Inspector of Seamen (SAUO)
MIS.............. Meiosis-Inducing Substance (DB)
MIS.............. Member of the Institute of Statisticians [*Formerly, AIS*] [*British*]
MIS.............. Member of the Institute of Surveyors (ADA)
MIS.............. Merchandise Information System (PDAA)
MIS.............. Message Input Segment (SAUS)
MIS.............. Metal Insulated Semiconductor (VLIE)
MIS.............. Metal Insulated Structure
MIS.............. Metal-Insulator-Semiconductor (MCD)
MIS.............. Metal Insulator Silicon (AAEL)
MIS.............. Meteorological Impact Statement [*FAA*] (TAG)
MIS.............. Metering Information System [*Telecommunications*] (OA)
MIS.............. Metrology Information Service [*GIDEP*]
MIS.............. MICOM [*Missile Command*] Specification [*Army*]
MIS.............. MicroServe Information Systems
MIS.............. Microwave Imager and Sounder (ACAE)
MIS.............. Midstate Airlines, Inc. [*ICAO designator*] (FAAC)

MIS	Migrant Information Service (SAUO)
MIS	Milieu Information Service (EA)
MIS	Military Information System (SAUO)
MIS	Military Intelligence Section [South Africa]
MIS	Military Intelligence Services [Army]
MIS	Military Intelligence Summary [Defense Intelligence Agency]
MIS	Military Interim Specification [Army] (MCD)
MIS	Military Interpreter Service (SAUO)
MIS	Mine Issuing Ship
MIS	Mineral Industry Survey [Department of Commerce] (GFGA)
MIS	Mineral Industry Surveys (SAUO)
MIS	Mineral Information Section [Natural Environment Research Council] (IID)
MIS	Minicube System, Inc., Carlisle PA [STAC]
MIS	Minority Institutions (COE)
MIS	Minstrel Instruction Service (NADA)
MIS	Minstrel Instruction Society (SAUO)
MIS	Miscarriage (DSUE)
mis	Miscellaneous [MARC language code] [Library of Congress] (LCCP)
MIS	Miscellaneous (NATG)
MIS	Miserable (DSUE)
MIS	Mishima [Japan] [Seismograph station code, US Geological Survey] (SEIS)
MIS	Misima [Papua New Guinea] [Airport symbol] (OAG)
Mis	Misopogon [of Julian] [Classical studies] (OCD)
MIS	Missile
MIS	Missile Interim Specification [Army]
MIS	Missile Specification
MIS	Missile Squadron (SAUO)
MIS	Missing (AABC)
MIS	Mission College, Santa Clara, CA [OCLC symbol] (OCLC)
mis	Mission Information Subsystem [NASA] (NAKS)
mis	Mission Information System [or Subsystem]
Mis	Mississippi Reports [A publication] (DLA)
MIS	Mississippi River Corporation (SAUO)
MIS	Missouri
Mis	Missouri Reports [A publication] (DLA)
MIS	Mistico [Ship's rigging] (ROG)
MIS	Mobile Telephone Service (SAUO)
MIS	Mobility Information Service [British]
MIS	Modified in Situ [Experimental technique for converting shale into oil]
MIS	Modular Injection System [Plastics]
MIS	Monte-Carlo Inelastic Scattering [Code] [Computer science] (NRCH)
MIS	Month-in-Sample [Bureau of the Census] (GFGA)
MIS	Months in Service
MIS	Moody Institute of Science (EA)
MIS	Moody's Investor Service [A publication] (MHDW)
MIS	Motor Inert Storage
MIS	Muellerian Inhibiting Substance [Embryology] [Biochemistry]
MIS	Multicultural Information Strategy
MIS	Multilingual Information System (SAUO)
MIS	Multimedia Information Sources (VLIE)
MIS	Multistage Information System [Computer science] (ELAL)
Mis	New York Miscellaneous Reports [A publication] (DLA)
MIS	NRA [National Restaurant Association] Management Information Services [Defunct] (EA)
MiS	Saginaw Public Libraries, Saginaw, MI [Library symbol] [Library of Congress] (LCLS)
MISA	Maritime Industry Seagoing Award (SAUO)
MISA	Maxwell International Subscription Agency
MISA	Meat Industry Suppliers Association (EA)
MISA	Military Impacted Schools Association (NTPA)
MISA	Military-Industrial Supply Agency
MISA	Motorists Information Services Association (EA)
MISA	Municipal and Industry Strategy for Abatement
MISAA	Middle Income Student Assistance Act [1978]
MISAC	Member of the Incorporated Society of Advertisement Consultants [British] (DAS)
MiSal	Saline Public Library, Saline, MI [Library symbol] [Library of Congress] (LCLS)
MISAM	Multiple Index Sequential Access Method
MiSan	Sandusky Public Library, Sandusky, MI [Library symbol] [Library of Congress] (LCLS)
MISAR	Microfilm Information Storage and Retrieval (MCD)
MISAR	Microprocessed Sensing and Automatic Regulation [Engine control system] [Automotive industry]
MISAR	Miniature Information Storage and Retrieval (PDAA)
MiSaS	Spring Arbor College, Spring Arbor, MI [Library symbol] [Library of Congress] (LCLS)
Mis Astig	Mixed Astigmatism [Ophthalmology] (DAVI)
MiSb	Bingham Township Library, Suttons Bay, MI [Library symbol] [Library of Congress] (LCLS)
MiS-B	Saginaw Public Libraries, Butman-Fish Library, Saginaw, MI [Library symbol] [Library of Congress] (LCLS)
MISC	Malaysian International Shipping Corp. (DS)
MISC	Malaysian International Shipping Corporation (SAUO)
MiSc	Mason County Library, Scottville, MI [Library symbol] [Library of Congress] (LCLS)
MISC	Military Intelligence Service Center (SAUO)
MISC	Minimum Instruction Set Computer (CIST)
MISC	Minimum Instruction Set Computing (SAUO)
MISC	Miscarriage [Medicine]
MISC	Miscellaneous (AFM)
Misc.	Miscellaneous (DFIT)
misc.	Miscellaneous (WDMC)
MISC	Miscellaneous and Other Operations [USCG] (TAG)
Misc	Miscellaneous Reports [New York] [A publication] (DLA)
MISC	Movement for an Independent Socialist Canada
MiS-C	Saginaw Public Libraries, Claytor Branch Library, Saginaw, MI [Library symbol] [Library of Congress] (LCLS)
Misc 2d	Miscellaneous Reports, Second Series [New York] [A publication] (DLA)
MisCa	Mission Capital Ltd. [Associated Press] (SAG)
MISCAP	Mission Capability (COE)
MISCAP	Mission Capability Statement (MCD)
Misc Dec	Ohio Miscellaneous Decisions (Gottschall) [1865-73] [A publication] (DLA)
Misc Doc	Miscellaneous Document [US. House of Representatives of Senate] (BARN)
Miscel	Miscellaneous Reports [New York] [A publication] (DLA)
MISCEND	Miscendus [To Be Mixed] [Pharmacy]
MISCEX	Miscellaneous Exercise [Military] (NVT)
MISchott	Schottenstein [M. I.] Homes, Inc. [Associated Press] (SAG)
MISCL	Miscellaneous
Misc New York	Miscellaneous New York Reports [A publication] (AAGC)
Misc (NY)	Miscellaneous Reports [New York] [A publication] (DLA)
MISCO	McCall Information Systems Co.
MISCO	Microchemical Specialties Company (SAUO)
MISCON	Misconduct
Misc Publ Univ KY Co-Op Ext Serv Agr Home Econ HE	Miscellaneous Publication. University of Kentucky. Cooperative Extension Service. Agriculture and Home Economics HE (SAUO)
Misc Rep	Miscellaneous Reports [New York] [A publication] (DLA)
Misc Reports	New York Miscellaneous Reports [A publication] (DLA)
Misc Repts	New York Miscellaneous Reports [A publication] (DLA)
MiScW	West Shore Community College, Scottville, MI [Library symbol] [Library of Congress] (LCLS)
MISD	Management Information Systems Directorate [Army Missile Command] [Redstone Arsenal, AL]
MISD	Misdemeanor [FBI standardized term]
MISD	Multiple Instruction, Single Data [Processor configuration] (IEEE)
MISDAS	Mechanical Impact System Design for Advanced Spacecraft (IEEE)
MISDM	Misdemeanor [Legal shorthand] (LWAP)
MISDM	Misdemeanor and Cure [Legal shorthand] (LWAP)
MISDMR	Misdemeanor (ROG)
MISDO	Management Information System Development Office (DNAB)
MISE	Mechanized Infantry in a Smoke Environment (MCD)
MISE	Member of the Institution of Structural Engineers (SAUO)
MISE	Miniature Sample (AAG)
MiSe	Sebewaing Township Library, Sebewaing, MI [Library symbol] [Library of Congress] (LCLS)
MISEA	Management Information Systems Economic Analysis
MISEA	Meat Industry Supply and Equipment Association [Later, MISA] (EA)
MISED	Machine Independent Systems Effectiveness Data System (MCD)
MISEG	Management Information System Executive Group (DNAB)
MISEP	Mutual Information System on Employment Policies (SAUO)
MISEP	Mutual Information System on Employment Policies in Europe (IID)
MISER	Management Information System for Expenditure Reporting (PDAA)
MISER	Manned Interceptor SAGE Evaluation Routine (MCD)
MISER	Mean Integral Square Error (PDAA)
MISER	Media Insertion Schedule Evaluation Report [Advertising]
MISER	Microwave Space Electronics Relay
MISER	Militant Society for the Eradication of Rounds [British] (DI)
MISER	Miniature, Indicating and Sampling Electronic Respirometer (PDAA)
MISER	Minimum Size Executive Routines
MISES	Merchandises (ROG)
MiSf	Southfield Public Library, Southfield, MI [Library symbol] [Library of Congress] (LCLS)
MiSfB	Bendix Corp., Engineering Development Center, Bendix Center, Southfield, MI [Library symbol] [Library of Congress] (LCLS)
MiSfE	Eaton Corp. Engineering Research Center, Southfield, MI [Library symbol] [Library of Congress] (LCLS)
MISFET	Metal-Insulator-Semiconductor Field-Effect Transistor
MiSfL	Lawrence Institute of Technology, Southfield, MI [Library symbol] [Library of Congress] (LCLS)
MiSfM	Midrasha College of Jewish Studies, Southfield, MI [Library symbol] [Library of Congress] (LCLS)
MiSfP	Providence Hospital Library, Southfield, MI [Library symbol] [Library of Congress] (LCLS)
MISFROR	Multiple Investment Sinking Fund Rate of Return (ADA)
MISG	Mental Illness Specific Grant (SAUO)
MISG	Missing (VLIE)
MISG	Modified Immune Serum Globulin [Medicine] (MELL)
MISG-C	Maintenance Interservice Support Group Center (MCD)
Mish	Mishnah [Basis of the Talmud] (BJA)
MiSh	Shelby Public Library, Shelby, MI [Library symbol] [Library of Congress] (LCLS)
MISHAP	Missiles High-Speed Assembly Program
MISHAP	Much Increased Salary, Hardly Any Pension [Lifestyle classification]
MiShep	Coe Township Library, Shepherd, MI [Library symbol] [Library of Congress] (LCLS)
MiSHS	Saginaw Health Sciences Library, Saginaw, MI [Library symbol] [Library of Congress] (LCLS)
MISI	Member of the Iron and Steel Institute [British]
MISI	Metro Information Services [Stock market symbol]
MISI	Metro Information Svcs. [NASDAQ symbol] (SG)
MISI	Micro Imaging Systems, Incorporated (SAUO)
MISI	Micro Information Systems, Incorporated (SAUO)
MISI	Multipath Intersymbol Interference (PDAA)

MISIAS	Management Information Systems Inventory and Analysis System [*Navy*]
MISICC	Management Information System Input to Command and Control (SAUO)
MIS/IL	Metal-Insulator-Semiconductor Inversion Layer [*Photovoltaic energy systems*]
MISIM	Metal-Insulator-Semiconductor Insulator Metal (MCD)
MIS/INAS	MIS for Industrial Naval Air Stations (SAUO)
MIS(India) ...	Member of the Institution of Surveyors of India
MISIP	Management Information System Improvement Plan
MISIP	Merck Infrared Spectral Interpretation Package [*For minicomputers*] [*Analytical chemistry*]
MISIP	Minority Institutions Science Improvement Program [*National Science Foundation*]
MISIS	Micro Integrated Storm Information System [*Marine science*] (OSRA)
MISJ	Medical Instrument Society of Japan (SAUO)
MISL	Major Indoor Soccer League [*Defunct*] (EA)
MISL	Malfunction Investigation Support Laboratory [*NASA*] (KSC)
MISL	Management Information System Laboratory
MISL	Missile
MiSl	South Lyon Public Library, South Lyon, MI [*Library symbol*] [*Library of Congress*] (LCLS)
MIS LABS	Midwest Integrated Systems Laboratories, Inc. [*Watertown, WI*] (TSSD)
MISLIC	Mid- and South Staffordshire Libraries in Cooperation (NITA)
MISLIC	Mid-Staffordshire Libraries in Co-operation (SAUO)
MISLPA	Major Indoor Soccer League Players Association (EA)
MISM	MAJCOM Information System Manager (SAUO)
MISM	Member of the Institute of Supervisory Management [*British*] (DBQ)
MISM	Metal-Insulator-Semiconductor Metal (MCD)
MiSM	Michigan Lutheran Seminary, Saginaw, MI [*Library symbol*] [*Library of Congress*] (LCLS)
MISMA	Major Item Supply Management Agency
MISMA	Member of the Incorporated Sales Managers Association [*British*] (DAS)
MISMA	Model Improvement and Study Management [*Army*]
MISMAC	Missile and Munitions Materiel Center (MCD)
MISMD	Medical Illustration Service for Museum Design [*Armed Forces Institute of Pathology*] (RDA)
MISMDS	Multiple Instruction Streams Multiple Data Steams
MISMO	Maintenance Interservice [*or Intersupport*] Management Office [*DARCOM*] (AFIT)
MISMO	MAJCOM Information Systems Management Office (SAUO)
MISMR	Michigan Society for Medical Research (GVA)
Mis Mus	Mistress of Music
MISN	Misnumbered (WGA)
MISO	Maintenance Interservice Office [*Air Force*] (AFIT)
MISO	Management Information Systems Office (AABC)
MISO	Military Intelligence Service Organization (NADA)
MISO	Misonidazole [*Azomycin*] [*Oncology, Radiosensitizer*]
MiSod	Sodus Township Library, Sodus, MI [*Library symbol*] [*Library of Congress*] (LCLS)
Misonix	Misonix, Inc. [*Associated Press*] (SAG)
Misonx	Misonix, Inc. [*Associated Press*] (SAG)
MISP	Maintenance Integrated Support Plan (SAUO)
MISP	MAJCOM Information Systems Plan (SAUO)
MISP	Management Information System Plan
MISP	Manned Interceptor Simulation Program
MISP	Mathematics in Society Project (AIE)
MISP	Medical Information Systems Program [*Computer science*] (BUR)
MISP	Member of the Institute of Sales Promotion [*British*] (DI)
MISP	Member of the Institution of Sewage Purification (SAUO)
MISP	Microelectronics Industry Support Programme (NITA)
MISP	Microprocessor Industry Support Programme [*British*] (DCTA)
MISPC	Mechanized Infantry Squad Proficiency Course [*Army*]
MISPE	Monopulse Information Signal Processing Element (ACAE)
MiSpl	Warner Baird Library, Spring Lake (SAUS)
MiSpl	Warner Baird Library, Spring Lake, MI [*Library symbol*] [*Library of Congress*] (LCLS)
MIS-Q	Maintenance Information System for Quality (MCD)
MISR	Machine Supply Requisition (VLIE)
MISR	Major Item Status Report
MISR	Makerere Institute of Social Research (SAUO)
MISR	Mars In-situ-utilization Sample Return [*Computer science*]
MISR	Matrix Ion Species Ratio [*Spectroscopy*]
MISR	Minimum Industrial Sustaining Role (NG)
Mis R	Missouri Reports [*A publication*] (DLA)
MISR	Modular Industrial Solar Retrofit Program [*Department of Energy*]
MISR	Mosler Information Storage and Retrieval System (MCD)
MISR	Multi-Angle Imaging Spectrometer [*Marine science*] (OSRA)
MISR	Multi-Angle Imaging Spectroradiometer (EOSA)
MISR	Multi-Impact Signature Register (PDAA)
MISR	Multiple Input Signal Register (NITA)
MISRAN	Missile Range
MISRC	Management Information Systems Research Center [*University of Minnesota*] [*Research center*] (RCD)
MISRE	Microwave Space Relay [*Electronics*]
MISREP	Joint Tactical Air Reconnaissance/Surveillance Mission Report (SAUO)
MISREP	Misrepresentation [*Legal shorthand*] (LWAP)
MISREP	Mission Report [*Air Force*] (AFM)
Mis Rep	Missouri Reports [*A publication*] (DLA)
MISS	Major Item Special Study [*Army Aviation Systems Command*]
MISS	Management and Information System Staff [*United Nations Development Program*]

MISS	Man in Space Simulator
MISS	Man in Space Soonest
MISS	Manpower Information Systems Support (SAUO)
MISS	Mechanical Interruption Statistical Summary (IEEE)
MISS	Mecklenburg Internet Service System (SAUO)
MISS	Medical Information Science Section [*National Institutes of Health*] [*Information service or system*] (IID)
MISS	Microwave Imager Sensor Study (MCD)
MISS	Mid-Course Surveillance System (MCD)
MISS	Miniature SOFAR [*Sound Fixing and Ranging*] System
MISS	Minicomputer Interfacing Support System [*Computer science*]
MISS	Missile Intercept Scoring System (SAUS)
MISS	Missile Intercept Simulation System
Miss	Mission (DIAR)
MISS	Mission
miss	Missionary
MISS	Mississippi (AFM)
Miss	Mississippi (ODBW)
MISS	Mississippian [*Period, era, or system*] [*Geology*]
MISS	Mississippian [*Railway*] [*AAR code*]
MISS	Mississippi Chemical [*NASDAQ symbol*] (TTSB)
MISS	Mississippi Chemical Corp. [*NASDAQ symbol*] (SAG)
Miss	Mississippi Supreme Court Reports [*A publication*] (DLA)
MISS	Mobile Instrumentation Support System
MISS	Mobile Integrated Support System (MCD)
MISS	Modular Infrared Sensor System (ACAE)
MISS	Multiband Image Scanning System
MISS	Multi-Input-Safety-Shutdown (PDAA)
MISS	Multi-Item Single Source (IEEE)
MiS-S	Saginaw Public Libraries, South Jefferson Branch, Saginaw, MI [*Library symbol*] [*Library of Congress*] (LCLS)
MiSs	Sault Ste. Marie Carnegie Public Library, Sault Ste. Marie, MI [*Library symbol*] [*Library of Congress*] (LCLS)
MISSA	Management Information System Support Agency (SAUO)
MiSsB	Baylis Public Library, Sault Ste. Marie, MI [*Library symbol*] [*Library of Congress*] (LCLS)
Miss C	Mississippi College (GAGS)
MissChm	Mississippi Chemical Corp. [*Associated Press*] (SAG)
Miss Code Ann ...	Mississippi Code, Annotated [*A publication*] (DLA)
MISS-D	Minuteman Integrated Schedules Status and Data Systems [*Missiles*]
Miss Dec	Mississippi Decisions [*A publication*] (DLA)
MIS-SDS	Multiple Instruction Streams - Single Data Streams [*Computer science*] (MHDB)
MISSI	Multilevel Information System Security Initiative (SAUO)
MISS-IDA	Meteorology Interactive Software System for Image Data Analysis (ACAE)
MISSIL	Management Information System Symbolic Interpretive Language [*Computer science*] (MCD)
MISSILEX	Missile Firing Exercise (NVT)
MISSIO	Internationales Katholisches Missionswerk [*Pontifical Mission Society*] [*Aachen, Federal Republic of Germany*] (EAIO)
MISSION	Manufacturing Information System Support Integrated Online [*Computer science*] (MHDI)
MISSION	Mission [*Commonly used*] (OPSA)
MISSIS	Mississippi Student Information System (EDAC)
MiSsL	Lake Superior State College, Sault Ste. Marie, MI [*Library symbol*] [*Library of Congress*] (LCLS)
Miss Law	Mississippi Lawyer [*A publication*] (DLA)
Miss Law Rev ...	Mississippi Law Review [*A publication*] (DLA)
Miss Laws ..	General Laws of Mississippi [*A publication*] (DLA)
Miss Laws ..	General Laws of Mississippi (journ.) (SAUS)
Miss Lawyer ...	Mississippi Lawyer [*A publication*] (DLA)
Miss L Rev ...	Mississippi Law Review [*A publication*] (DLA)
MISSN	Mission [*Commonly used*] (OPSA)
MissnW	Mission West Properties [*Associated Press*] (SAG)
Misso	Missouri Reports [*A publication*] (DLA)
MISSOPH	Man in Space Sophisticated (MUGU)
Misso R	Missouri Reports [*A publication*] (DLA)
Misso Rep ..	Missouri Reports [*A publication*] (DLA)
Missouri	Missouri Reports [*A publication*] (DLA)
Missouri R...	Missouri Reports [*A publication*] (DLA)
Missouri Rep...	Missouri Reports [*A publication*] (DLA)
Missour Rep...	Missouri Reports [*A publication*] (DLA)
MissPw	Mississippi Power Co. [*Associated Press*] (SAG)
MissQ	Mississippi Quarterly [*A publication*] (ANEX)
MISSR	Missioner (ROG)
Miss R	Mississippi Reports [*A publication*] (DLA)
Miss RC	Mississippi Railroad Commission Reports [*A publication*] (DLA)
Miss Reg	Mississippi Register [*A publication*] (AAGC)
Miss Rep	Mississippi Reports [*A publication*] (DLA)
Miss Serv W...	Missionary Service With
Miss St Ca ...	Morris' Mississippi State Cases [*1818-72*] [*A publication*] (DLA)
Miss St Cas..	Morris' Mississippi State Cases [*1818-72*] [*A publication*] (DLA)
Miss St U	Mississippi State University (GAGS)
Miss St U Women...	Mississippi State University for Women (GAGS)
MISST	Missile-Supersonic Transport
MIS Sulf U...	End Uses of Sulfur and Sulfuric Acid. Mineral Industry Survey (journ.) (SAUS)
MissVly	Mississippi Valley Bancshares, Inc. [*Associated Press*] (SAG)
MissVw	Mississippi View Holding Co. [*Associated Press*] (SAG)
MISSY	Missionary
MIST	Avalon Capital [*NASDAQ symbol*] (TTSB)
MIST	Avalon Capital, Inc. [*NASDAQ symbol*] (SAG)
MIST	Magnetosphere, Ionosphere and Solar Terrestrial (SAUO)
MIST	Manchester Institute of Science and Technology (SAUO)

MI St .... Master of Information Studies (PGP)
MIST .... Maximum Isothermal System Temperature [*Nuclear energy*] (NRCH)
MIST .... Medical Information System via Telephone [*University of Alabama*]
MIST .... Member of the Institute of Science Technology [*British*] (DBQ)
MIST .... Metal-Insulator-Semiconductor Transistor (CCCA)
MIST .... Metal Insulator Silicon Field-Effect Transistor [*Also, MISFET*] (EECA)
MIST .... Microburst and Severe Thunderstorm Experiment (or Project) (SAUO)
MIST .... Microburst and Severe Thunderstorm Project (SAUS)
MIST+ .... Microbursts in Severe Thunderstorms
MIST+ .... Microcomputer Information Support Tools [*2B Enterprises*] [*Washington, DC*] (TSSD)
MIST .... Minimum Structure Module
MIST .... Minor Isotopes Safeguards Techniques [*Nuclear energy*]
MIST .... Mistura [*Mixture*] [*Pharmacy*]
MIST .... MIUS [*Modular Integrated Utility Systems*] Integration and Subsystems Test (MCD)
MIST .... Modular Interoperable Surface Terminal (SAUS)
MIST .... Mosaic Infrared Sensor Technology (ACAE)
MIST .... Multi-Input Standard Tape
MIST .... Multiloop Integral System Test [*Nuclear energy*] (NRCH)
MIST .... Multipurpose In-Space Throttleable Engine (MCD)
MIST .... Music Information System for Theorists (PDAA)
MISTAF .... Management Information Systems Task Force (SAA)
MiStan .... Stanton Public Library, Stanton, MI [*Library symbol*] [*Library of Congress*] (LCLS)
MISTC .... Member of the Institute of Scientific and Technical Communicators [*British*] (DBQ)
MISTC .... Men's International Squash Tournament Council [*Cardiff, Wales*] (EAIO)
MISTC .... Multiple Information Set Tracking Correlator System (SAUO)
MiStc .... Saint Clair Shores Public Library, Saint Clair Shores, MI [*Library symbol*] [*Library of Congress*] (LCLS)
MiStch .... Saint Charles Public Library, Saint Charles, MI [*Library symbol*] [*Library of Congress*] (LCLS)
MiSte .... Lincoln Township Public Library, Stevensville, MI [*Library symbol*] [*Library of Congress*] (LCLS)
MISTE .... Military Intelligence Special Training Element (DOMA)
MISTEL .... Delft Monograph Document Delivery And Catalogue (SAUS)
MiStep .... Menominee County Library, Stephenson, MI [*Library symbol*] [*Library of Congress*] (LCLS)
MISTER .... Mobile Integrated System Trainer, Evaluator, and Recorder [*Navy*]
MIST-FOAL ... Multi-Stage Force Allocation (SAA)
MiSth .... Sterling Heights Public Library, Sterling Heights, MI [*Library symbol*] [*Library of Congress*] (LCLS)
MiSthe .... Richfield Township Public Library, St. Helen, MI [*Library symbol*] [*Library of Congress*] (LCLS)
MISTI .... Multipurpose International Securities Trading Information (MHDW)
MiSti .... St. Ignace Public Library, St. Ignace, MI [*Library symbol*] [*Library of Congress*] (LCLS)
MISTIC .... Michigan State Integral Computer
MISTIC .... Missile System Target Illuminator Controlled (MCD)
MISTIC .... Model Interstate Scientific and Technical Information Clearinghouse
MISTIC .... Multiple Information Set Tracking Correlation (ACAE)
MISTIGRI ..... Mobile Integrated Surveillance of Tactical Information Gathered (SAUS)
MISTIR .... Multifunction Imaging Search/Track Infrared
MiStjo .... Bement Public Library, St. Johns (SAUS)
MiStjo .... Bement Public Library, St. Johns, MI [*Library symbol*] [*Library of Congress*] (LCLS)
MiStjW .... Whirlpool Corp., Research Library, St. Joseph, MI [*Library symbol*] [*Library of Congress*] (LCLS)
MiStlo .... Theodore Austin Cutler Memorial Library, St. Louis, MI [*Library symbol*] [*Library of Congress*] (LCLS)
MISTM .... Member of the Institute of Sales Technology and Management [*British*] (DBQ)
MISTR .... Management of Items Subject to Repair [*Air Force*] (AFM)
MISTRA .... Minnesota Study of Twins Reared Apart
MISTRAM ..... Missile Trajectory Measurement [*Air Force*]
MISTRANS ... Mistranslation (ADA)
MISTRAULANT ... Missile Weapons System Training Unit, Atlantic (DNAB)
MISTRAUPAC ... Missile Weapons System Training Unit, Pacific (DNAB)
MistrJay ...... Mister Jay Fashions International, Inc. [*Associated Press*] (SAG)
MIStructE .... Member of the Institution of Structural Engineers [*British*] (EY)
MISTT .... Midwest Interstate Sulfur Transformation and Transport [*Meteorology*]
MiStu .... Sturgis Public Library, Sturgis, MI [*Library symbol*] [*Library of Congress*] (LCLS)
MISTY .... Missile System for Tactical Telephony (ACAE)
MistyM .... Misty Mountain Gold Ltd. [*Associated Press*] (SAG)
MISU .... Meteorological Institute Stockholm University (SAUO)
MiSun .... Sunfield District Library, Sunfield, MI [*Library symbol*] [*Library of Congress*] (LCLS)
MISURA .... Miskito, Sumo, and Rama [*Nicaraguan Indian coalition*]
MISURASATA ... Miskito, Sumo, and Rama [*Nicaraguan Indian coalition*]
MiSV .... United States Veterans Administration Hospital, Saginaw, MI [*Library symbol*] [*Library of Congress*] (LCLS)
MISVAL .... Missile Evaluation (ACAE)
MISVE .... Management Information Systems for Vocational Education (OICC)
MISW .... Member of the Institute of Shorthand Writers, practising in High Court of Justice (SAUO)
MISW .... Member of the Institute of Social Welfare [*British*] (DBQ)
MiSW .... White Pine Library System, Saginaw, MI [*Library symbol*] [*Library of Congress*] (LCLS)
M-ISWS .... Illinois State Water Survey (SAUO)
MISX .... Metered Services Information Exchange (SAUO)

MiS-Z .... Saginaw Public Libraries, Zauel Memorial Library, Saginaw, MI [*Library symbol*] [*Library of Congress*] (LCLS)
MIT .... Advanced Magnetics, Inc. (SAUO)
MIT .... Machine Interface Terminal [*Tangram Computer Aided Engineering*] [*Software package*] (NCC)
MIT .... Macrotrends International [*Vancouver Stock Exchange symbol*]
MIT .... Made in Taiwan (SAUO)
MIT .... Madras Institute of Technology (SAUO)
MIT .... Makari Intradermal Test [*Medicine*] (DB)
MIT .... Male Impotence Test [*Medicine*] (DMAA)
MIT .... Management Information Tree [*Telecommunications*] (OSI)
MIT .... Mandatory Independent Taxation [*British*] (DI)
MIT .... Manual Inputs-Tracks (SAA)
MIT .... Mara Institute of Technology (SAUO)
MIT .... Maritime Institute of Technology (SAUO)
MIT .... Marked If Touched (VLIE)
MIT .... Market if Touched [*Stock exchange term*]
MIT .... Market if Touched order (SAUO)
MIT .... Marrow Iron Turnover [*Medicine*] (DMAA)
MIT .... Massachusetts Institute of Technology (GAGS)
MIT .... Massachusetts Investors Trust
MIT .... Master Instruction Tape [*Computer science*]
MIT .... Master in Teaching (PGP)
MIT .... Master of Industrial Technology (PGP)
MIT .... Master of Initial Teaching (PGP)
MIT .... Material Improvement Team (MCD)
MIT .... Material in Transit (MCD)
MIT .... Material Introduction Team
MIT .... Materials Interaction Test (ABAC)
MIT .... Medium Intertheater Transport (MCD)
MIT .... Melodic Intonation Therapy (DMAA)
MIT .... Mercury Integrated Test
MIT .... Mercury Ion Thruster
MIT .... Merrill Lynch & Co., Inc. [*NYSE symbol*] (SPSG)
MIT .... Merrill Lynch & Co'MITTS' 2001 [*NASDAQ symbol*] (TTSB)
MIT .... Metabolism Inhibition Test [*Medicine*] (DMAA)
MIT .... Metal Insulator Transition [*Electronics*] (AAEL)
MIT .... Middle Italian [*Language, etc.*]
MIT .... Miles in-Trail [*FAA*] (TAG)
MIT .... Military Intelligence Translator
MIT .... Milled in Transit [*Commodities*]
MIT .... Miller Air Transporters [*ICAO designator*] (FAAC)
MIT .... Milwaukee Institute of Technology [*Wisconsin*]
MIT .... Minimum Individual Training
MIT .... Ministry of Industry and Trade [*Israel*]
MIT .... Minnesota Institute of Technology (SAUO)
MIT .... MIPS Technologies Inc. (SAUO)
MIT .... Miracidal Immobilization Test [*Parasitology*]
MIT .... Miscellaneous Tool (SAA)
MIT .... Missouri-Illinois Traffic Service, East Saint Louis IL [*STAC*]
Mit .... Mitannian (BJA)
MIT .... Miter
MIT .... Mitigate
MIT .... Mito [*Japan*] [*Seismograph station code, US Geological Survey*] (SEIS)
MIT .... Mitomycin [*Medicine*] (DMAA)
MIT .... Mitsubishi Electric Corporation (NITA)
MIT .... Mitte [*Send*] [*Latin*]
MIT .... Mobile Instructor Team (MCD)
MIT .... Mobile Instructor Training [*Army*]
MIT .... Modern Investment Theory [*Finance*] (MHDB)
MIT .... Modular Industrial Terminal
MIT .... Modular Intelligent Terminal
MIT .... Monoiodotyrosine [*Biochemistry*]
MIT .... Motorist Inclusive Tour [*British*] (DCTA)
MIT .... Movements Identification Technican (SAA)
MIT .... Multiple Incidence Technique [*Structure testing*]
MIT .... Multiple Insert Tooling
MIT .... Municipal Investment Trust
MIT .... Myocardial Infarction Triage [*Medicine*] (MELL)
MIT .... Shafter, CA [*Location identifier*] [*FAA*] (FAAL)
MIT .... Society of Management Information Technology [*British*]
MiT .... Traverse City Public Library, Traverse City, MI [*Library symbol*] [*Library of Congress*] (LCLS)
MITA .... Maine Island Trail Association
MITA .... Member of the Industrial Transport Association [*British*]
MITA .... MetLife's Intelligent Text Analyzer [*Textual analysis of life insurance applications*] (IDAI)
MITA .... Microcomputer Industry Trade Association
MITA .... Minority Information Trade Annual [*A publication*]
MITAG .... Minority Affairs Task Group (DNAB)
MITAGS .... Maritime Institute of Technology and Graduate Studies (SAUO)
MITAN .... Microwave Technology as Applied to Air Navigation (ADA)
MITAS .... Missile Threat Analysis Simulator (ACAE)
MITAS .... Multi-sensor Imaging Technology for Airborne Surveillance (SAUS)
MITASK .... Mission Tasking (COE)
MITB .... Missile Interface Test Bench
MiTc .... Iosco-Arenac Regional Library, Tawas City, MI [*Library symbol*] [*Library of Congress*] (LCLS)
MITC .... Magdalen Island Transportation Company (SAUO)
MITC-Z .... Methylisothiocyanate [*Pesticide*]
MITC .... Microfilm and Information Technology Center
MiTc-A .... Iosco-Arenac Regional Library, AuGres Branch Library, AuGres, MI [*Library symbol*] [*Library of Congress*] (LCLS)

MiTc-E......... Iosco-Arenac Regional Library, East Tawas Branch Library, East Tawas, MI [*Library symbol*] [*Library of Congress*] (LCLS)
Mitch.......... Mitcham Industries [*Associated Press*] (SAG)
Mitcham...... Mitcham Industries [*Associated Press*] (SAG)
Mitch B & N... Mitchell on Bills, Notes, Etc. [*1829*] [*A publication*] (DLA)
Mitchell's Mar Reg... Mitchell's Maritime Register [*England*] [*A publication*] (DLA)
Mitch Mod Geog... Mitchell's Modern Geography [*A publication*] (DLA)
Mitch MR..... Mitchell's Maritime Register [*England*] [*A publication*] (DLA)
Mit Ch Pl.... Mitford on Equity Pleading [*A publication*] (DLA)
MiTc-O........ Iosco-Arenac Regional Library, Oscoda Township Branch Library, Oscoda, MI [*Library symbol*] [*Library of Congress*] (LCLS)
MiTc-P........ Iosco-Arenac Regional Library, Plainfield Township Branch Library, Hale, MI [*Library symbol*] [*Library of Congress*] (LCLS)
MiTc-S........ Iosco-Arenac Regional Library, Standish Branch Library, Standish, MI [*Library symbol*] [*Library of Congress*] (LCLS)
MiTc-T........ Iosco-Arenac Regional Library, Tawas City Branch Library, Tawas City, MI [*Library symbol*] [*Library of Congress*] (LCLS)
MiTc-W........ Iosco-Arenac Regional Library, Whittemore Branch Library, Whittemore, MI [*Library symbol*] [*Library of Congress*] (LCLS)
MITD.......... Member of the Institute of Training and Development [*British*] (DBQ)
MITDA......... Maryland Independent Truckers and Drivers Association [*Later, ITDA*] (EA)
MIT DIC....... Massachusetts Institute of Technology, Division of Industrial Cooperation (SAUO)
Mit Drunk.... Mittermaier's Effect of Drunkenness on Criminal Responsibilty [*A publication*] (DLA)
MITE.......... Magnetic Insulation Test Experiment
MITE.......... Master Instrumentation Timing Equipment (CET)
MITE.......... Mathematics Institute for Teacher Enhancement (SAUO)
MITE.......... Meetings and Incentive Travel Exposition [*Trade show*]
MITE.......... Microelectronic Integrated Test Equipment
MITE.......... Microelectronics Test and Evaluation [*Raytheon Co.*]
MITE.......... Microprocessor Industrial Terminal [*Computer science*] (MHDB)
MITE.......... Miniaturized Integrated Telephone Equipment
MITE.......... Missile Integration Terminal Equipment [*Computer science*]
MITE.......... Mission Training and Evaluation (ACAE)
MITE.......... Multiple Input Terminal Equipment
MiTe.......... Tecumseh Public Library, Tecumseh, MI [*Library symbol*] [*Library of Congress*] (LCLS)
MITEC........ Machine Intelligent Technical Controller (SAUO)
MITECS....... Multi-International Teacher Education Cooperatives (EDAC)
MiTek........ Tekonsha Public Library, Tekonsha, MI [*Library symbol*] [*Library of Congress*] (LCLS)
MitekS........ Mitek Systems, Inc. [*Associated Press*] (SAG)
MITEL........ Mike and Terry's Lawnmowers [*Commercial firm*] [*canada*]
Mitel......... Mitel Corp. [*Associated Press*] (SAG)
MITER........ Modular Installation of Telecommunications Equipment Racks (TEL)
MITF.......... Municipal Investment Trust Fund
MITF.......... Musser International Turfgrass Foundation (EA)
MITFA........ Metropolitan Intercollegiate Track & Field Association (PSS)
Mitf & Ty Eq Pl... Tyler's Edition of Mitford's Equity Pleading [*A publication*] (DLA)
Mitf Eq Pl... Mitford on Equity Pleading [*A publication*] (DLA)
MITGS........ Marine Institute of Technology and Graduate Studies [*Baltimore*]
MITH.......... Marble-in-the-Hole [*Game used in psychometrics*]
MITH.......... Mithracin [*Antineoplastic drug*] (CDI)
Mith.......... Mithramycin [*Antineoplastic drug*] (DAVI)
MiTho........ Betsie Valley District Library, Thompsonville, MI [*Library symbol*] [*Library of Congress*] (LCLS)
MiThr......... Three Rivers Public Library, Three Rivers, MI [*Library symbol*] [*Library of Congress*] (LCLS)
MITI.......... Ministry of International Trade and Industry [*Japan*]
MITI.......... Ministry of International Trade and Investment (SAUO)
MITI.......... Moms in Touch International (EA)
MITI.......... Multilingual Intelligence Interface (SAUO)
MITI.......... Myocardial Infarction, Triage, and Intervention Project [*or Trial*] [*Cardiology study*]
MITIC......... Myanmar International Trust and Investment Co. (ECON)
MITIL......... Massachusetts Institute of Technology Instrumentation Laboratory (SAA)
MITILAC....... Massachusetts Institute of Technology Information Laboratory Automatic Coding
Mit Insuf.... Mitral Insufficiency [*Cardiology*]
MITJ.......... Member of the Institute of Technical Journalists [*British*] (DGA)
MITK.......... Mitek Systems [*NASDAQ symbol*] (TTSB)
MITK.......... Mitek Systems Inc. [*NASDAQ symbol*] (SAG)
MITKA........ Movimiento Indio Tupaj Katari [*Tupaj Katari Indian Movement*] [*Bolivia*] [*Political party*] (PPW)
MITL.......... Man-in-the-Loop [*Army*]
MITLA........ Microcircuit Technology in Logistics Applications [*Defense Logistics Agency*]
MIT/LIN....... Massachusetts Institute of Technology, Lincoln Laboratory (SAUO)
MIT/LL........ Massachusetts Institute of Technology/Lincoln Laboratory (AAG)
MITLS......... Man-in-the-Loop Simulator [*Military*]
MITM.......... Management Inventory on Time Management [*Test*]
MITM.......... Military-Industry Technical Manual
MITMA........ Man in the Middle Attack (SAUS)
MITMA........ Member, Institute of Trade Mark Agents (SAUO)
MITMA........ Member of the Institute of Trade Mark Agents [*British*]
MITMA........ Military Traffic Management Agency [*Later, DTMS*]
MIT/MAT...... Missile Interface Test/Missile Auxiliary Test (ACAE)
Mit MR....... Mitchell's Maritime Register [*England*] [*A publication*] (ILCA)
MITMS........ Military-Industry Technical Manual Specifications
MITN.......... Michigan Information Technology Network
MiTN.......... Northwestern Michigan College, Traverse City, MI [*Library symbol*] [*Library of Congress*] (LCLS)

MITNJ......... Member of the Industrial Team of New Jersey (SAUO)
MIT/NSL....... Massachusetts Institute of Technology/Naval Supersonic Laboratory (AAG)
MITO.......... Meat Industry Training Organisation (AIE)
MITO.......... Member of the Institute of Training Officers [*International Institute of Social Economics*] [*British*] (DI)
MITO.......... Minimum Interval Takeoff
mito.......... mitochondria (SAUS)
Mito.......... Mitomycin-C [*Antineoplastic drug*] (DAVI)
MITO-C....... Mitomycin-C [*Antineoplastic drug*] (DAVI)
MITOC........ Multiple Intercommunications Technical Operations Communications [*NASA*] (KSC)
MITOCS....... Missile Technical Operations Communications System (MCD)
MITOL........ Machine-Independent Telemetry-Oriented Language [*Computer science*] (IEEE)
MiTop........ Topinabee Public Library, Topinabee, MI [*Library symbol*] [*Library of Congress*] (LCLS)
MITP.......... Master Intern Training Plan [*Military*]
MITP.......... Measurement and Instrumentation Technology Panel (ACII)
MITP.......... Miniature Template [*Tool*]
MiTP.......... Peninsula Community Library, Traverse City, MI [*Library symbol*] [*Library of Congress*] (LCLS)
MITR.......... Massachusetts Institute of Technology Reactor
MITR.......... Mortgage Interest Tax Relief [*British*]
MiTr.......... Troy Public Library, Troy, MI [*Library symbol*] [*Library of Congress*] (LCLS)
MITRA......... Management Institute for Training and Research in Asia (SAUO)
MitrArd....... Mitropolia Ardealului [*Sibiu, Rumania*] (BJA)
MitrBan....... Mitropolia Banatului [*Timisoara, Rumania*] (BJA)
MITRE........ Massachusetts Institute of Technology, Research and Engineering (SAUO)
MIT-RE........ Massachusetts Institute of Technology, Research and Engineering Group (SAUO)
MITRE........ Massachusetts Institute of Technology Research Establishment (NATG)
MITRE........ Miniature Individual Transmitter-Receiver Equipment (MCD)
MITRE........ MITRE Corp. (SAUO)
MitrMoldSuc... Mitropolia Moldovei si Sucevei [*Jassy, Rumania*] (BJA)
MiTrWB....... William Beaumont Hospital, Troy, MI [*Library symbol*] [*Library of Congress*] (LCLS)
MITS.......... Management Information and Text System
MITS.......... Management Information Tracking System (COE)
MITS.......... Man-in-the-Sea Program [*Navy*]
MITS.......... Man in the Street [*The average man*] [*Usually "Mr. Mits"*] [*See also T C MITS*]
MITS.......... Marshall Integrated Telecommunications System (SAUO)
MITS.......... Master's Intelligent Terminal System [*Software package*] [*Nippon Kokan*]
MITS.......... Michigan Information Transfer Source [*University of Michigan*] (IID)
MITS.......... Michigan Travel System
MITS.......... Microfiche Image Transmission System (MCD)
MITS.......... Micro Instrumentation and Telemetry Systems (NITA)
MITS.......... Military Air Lift Command Imagery Transmission System (ACAE)
MITS.......... Military Airlift Command Intra-Theater Transmission System (SAUO)
MITS.......... Missile Ignition Test Simulator
MITS.......... Missile Interface Test Set
MITS.......... Mission Integrated Transparency System (ACAE)
MITS.......... Missouri-Illinois Traffic Service
MITS.......... Mitsui & Co. Ltd. [*NASDAQ symbol*] (NQ)
MITS.......... Mobile Independent Target System (INF)
MITS.......... Model Instrumentation Telemetry System (SAUO)
MITS.......... Monthly International Terrorist Summary (MCD)
MITS.......... Multiple Inward-Turning Scoop (MCD)
MITS.......... Multiplex Information Transfer System (PDAA)
MITSA........ Member of the Institute of Trading Standards Administration [*British*] (DBQ)
mit sang..... Mitte Sanguinem [*Take Away Blood*] [*Latin*] (MAE)
MitsbBk...... Mitsubishi Bank Ltd. [*Associated Press*] (SAG)
mitse........ Made in the Same Establihment [*Manufacturing*]
MITSG........ Massachusetts Institute of Technology Sea Grant Program (NOAA)
MIT/SL........ Massachusetts Institute of Technology/Sloan Laboratory (AAG)
MIT/SmL...... Massachusetts Institute of Technology/Servomechanisms Laboratory (AAG)
MIT/SpL...... Massachusetts Institute of Technology/Spectroscopy Laboratory (AAG)
Mitsui........ Mitsui & Co. Ltd. [*Associated Press*] (SAG)
MITSY........ Memory Interface Test System (ACAE)
MITSY........ Mitsui & Co ADR [*NASDAQ symbol*] (TTSB)
MITT.......... Member of the Institute of Travel and Tourism [*British*] (ODBW)
MITT.......... Mitte [*Send*] [*Latin*]
MITT.......... Mobile Imagery Transmission Terminal (DOMA)
MITT.......... Mobile Integrated Tactical Terminal (DOMA)
MITTAT........ Mittatur [*Let Be Sent*] [*Pharmacy*] (ROG)
Mitte Sang... Mitte Sanguinem [*Bleed*] [*Pharmacy*] (BABM)
mitte sang... Mitte Sanguinem [*Bleed*] [*Latin*] (DAVI)
MITTINS...... Michigan Travel Trade Information Service
MITTS........ Minutes of Telecommunications Traffic [*Measure of voice, fax, and data transmission*]
MITTS........ Mobile IGOR [*Intercept Ground Optical Recorder*] Tracking Telescope System [*Air Force*]
MITT SANG ad UNC SALTEM... Mitte Sanguinem ad Uncias ___ Saltem [*Take Away ___ Ounces of Blood at Least*] [*Pharmacy*] (ROG)
MITT TAL..... Mitte Tales [*Send Such*] [*Pharmacy*]
MiTu.......... Tustin Public Library, Tustin, MI [*Library symbol*] [*Library of Congress*] (LCLS)

MITY	Mity Lite, Inc. [*NASDAQ symbol*] (SAG)
MityLite	Mity Lite, Inc. [*Associated Press*] (SAG)
MIU	Machine Interface Unit (HGAA)
MIU	Maharishi International University, Fairfield, IA [*OCLC symbol*] (OCLC)
MIU	Maiduguri [*Nigeria*] [*Airport symbol*] (OAG)
MIU	Malfunction Insertion Unit [*Aviation*]
MIU	Message Interface Unit (CAAL)
MIU	Methylisourea [*Organic chemistry*]
miu	Michigan [*MARC country of publication code*] [*Library of Congress*] (LCCP)
MIU	Microalgae International Union (EA)
MIU	Micronesian Insurance Underwriters (SAUO)
mIU	Milli-International Unit
MIU	Missile Interface Unit
MIU	Mobile Inspection Unit [*Military*] (AFM)
MIU	Model Interface Unit (NITA)
MIU	Modem Interface Unit [*Computer science*] (ELAL)
MIU	Moisture, Insolubles, and Unsaponifiables [*Fat analysis*]
MIU	Motor Impeller Unit
MIU	Multi-Input Unit [*Testing equipment*]
miu	Multiplex Interface Unit (NAKS)
MIU	Multiplex Interface Unit (NASA)
MIU	Multistation Interface Unit [*Computer science*]
MiU	University of Michigan, Ann Arbor, MI [*Library symbol*] [*Library of Congress*] (LCLS)
MiU	University of Michigan, Physics-Astronomy Library (SAUO)
MiU-A	University of Michigan, Asia Library, Ann Arbor, MI [*Library symbol*] [*Library of Congress*] (LCLS)
MiUb	Sleeper Public Library, Ubly, MI [*Library symbol*] [*Library of Congress*] (LCLS)
MiU-BA	University of Michigan, Graduate School of Business Administration, Ann Arbor, MI [*Library symbol*] [*Library of Congress*] (LCLS)
MiU-C	University of Michigan, William L. Clements Library, Ann Arbor, MI [*Library symbol*] [*Library of Congress*] (LCLS)
MiUcD	Delta College, University Center, MI [*Library symbol*] [*Library of Congress*] (LCLS)
MiUcS	Saginaw Valley College, University Center, MI [*Library symbol*] [*Library of Congress*] (LCLS)
MIU/FCO	Mobile Inspection Unit / Functional Checkout (SAA)
MiU-G	University of Michigan, Bureau of Government Library, Ann Arbor, MI [*Library symbol*] [*Library of Congress*] (LCLS)
MiU-H	University of Michigan, Michigan Historical Collection, Ann Arbor, MI [*Library symbol*] [*Library of Congress*] (LCLS)
MiU-Ho	University of Michigan, Avery and Julie Hopwood Room, Ann Arbor, MI [*Library symbol*] [*Library of Congress*] (LCLS)
MiU-L	University of Michigan, Law Library, Ann Arbor, MI [*Library symbol*] [*Library of Congress*] (LCLS)
MiU-M	University of Michigan, Medical Center, Ann Arbor, MI [*Library symbol*] [*Library of Congress*] (LCLS)
MiUnv	Columbia Township Library, Unionville, MI [*Library symbol*] [*Library of Congress*] (LCLS)
MiU-RE	University of Michigan, Center for Research on Economic Development, Ann Arbor, MI [*Library symbol*] [*Library of Congress*] (LCLS)
MIUS	Modular Integrated Utility System [*HUD*]
MIUSA	Mobility International USA (EA)
MiU-T	University of Michigan, Transportation Library, Ann Arbor, MI [*Library symbol*] [*Library of Congress*] (LCLS)
MiUt	Utica Public Library, Utica, MI [*Library symbol*] [*Library of Congress*] (LCLS)
MIUTC	Military Intelligence Unit Training Center (AABC)
MiUtS	Shelby Township Library, Utica, MI [*Library symbol*] [*Library of Congress*] (LCLS)
MIUU	Meteorological Institute of the University of Uppsala [*Sweden*] (USDC)
MIUU	Meterorological Institute of the University of Uppsala, Sweden [*Marine science*] (OSRA)
MIUW	Mobile Inshore Undersea Warfare [*Navy*] (NG)
MIUWG	Mobile Inshore Undersea War Group [*Navy*] (VNW)
MIUWS	Mobile Inshore Undersea Warfare Surveillance [*Navy*] (NVT)
MIUWSU	Mobile Inshore Undersea Warfare Surveillance Unit [*Navy*] (CINC)
MIV	Main Instrumentation Van [*NASA*]
MIV	Mi-Avia [*Russian Federation*] [*ICAO designator*] (FAAC)
MIV	MICC Investments Ltd. [*Toronto Stock Exchange symbol*]
MIV	Millville, NJ [*Location identifier*] [*FAA*] (FAAL)
MIV	Mobile Instrumentation Van (KSC)
MIV	Moving Ion Voltmeter
MiVa	Bullard-Sanford Public Library, Vassar, MI [*Library symbol*] [*Library of Congress*] (LCLS)
MIVA	Midwestern Intercollegiate Volleyball Association (PSS)
MIVA	Missionary Vehicle Association (EA)
MIVA-America	Missionary Vehicle Association of America (EA)
MIVAC	Microwave Vacuum [*Dryer*] (MCD)
MIVC	Magnetically Induced Velocity Charge [*Southwest Research Institute*]
MIVEC	Mitsubishi Innovative Valve Timing and Lift Electronic Control System [*Automotive engineering*] (PS)
MiVer	Vermontville Public Library, Vermontville, MI [*Library symbol*] [*Library of Congress*] (LCLS)
MiVes	Vestaburg Public Library, Vestaburg, MI [*Library symbol*] [*Library of Congress*] (LCLS)
MIVI	Mississippi View Holding [*NASDAQ symbol*] (TTSB)
MIVI	Mississippi View Holding Co. [*NASDAQ symbol*] (SAG)
MiVi	Vicksburg Community Library, Vicksburg, MI [*Library symbol*] [*Library of Congress*] (LCLS)
MIVPO	Modified Inside Vapor Phase Oxidation (EECA)
MIW	Airborne of Sweden AB [*ICAO designator*] (FAAC)
MIW	Marshalltown, IA [*Location identifier*] [*FAA*] (FAAL)
MiW	Med in Web (SAUO)
MIW	Microinstruction Word
MIW	Milk Ingredient Water (OA)
MIW	Mine Warfare (NVT)
MiWaC	Wayne County Federated Library System, Wayne, MI [*Library symbol*] [*Library of Congress*] (LCLS)
MiWaC-B	Wayne County Federated Library System, Department for the Blind and Physically Handicapped, Wayne, MI [*Library symbol*] [*Library of Congress*] (LCLS)
MIWACS	Modular Integrated Weapon Aiming & Control System (SAUS)
MiWak	Wakefield Public Library, Wakefield, MI [*Library symbol*] [*Library of Congress*] (LCLS)
MiWal	Melrose Township Public Library, Walloon Lake, MI [*Library symbol*] [*Library of Congress*] (LCLS)
MiWald	Waldron District Library, Waldron, MI [*Library symbol*] [*Library of Congress*] (LCLS)
MiWalv	Walkerville Public Library, Walkerville, MI [*Library symbol*] [*Library of Congress*] (LCLS)
MiWar	Warren Public Library, Warren, MI [*Library symbol*] [*Library of Congress*] (LCLS)
MiWarBH	Bi-County Community Hospital, Warren, MI [*Library symbol*] [*Library of Congress*] (LCLS)
MiWarGME	General Motors Corp., Engineering Library and Information Services, Warren, MI [*Library symbol*] [*Library of Congress*] (LCLS)
MiWarGMR	General Motors Corp., Research Laboratories Division, Warren, MI [*Library symbol*] [*Library of Congress*] (LCLS)
MiWarGMR-E	General Motors Corp., Engineering Staff Library, Warren, MI [*Library symbol*] [*Library of Congress*] (LCLS)
MiWarM	Macomb County Community College, Warren, MI [*Library symbol*] [*Library of Congress*] (LCLS)
MiWatv	Watervliet Public Library, Watervliet, MI [*Library symbol*] [*Library of Congress*] (LCLS)
MiWbH	Holocaust Memorial Center, West Bloomfield, MI [*Library symbol*] [*Library of Congress*] (LCLS)
MIWE	Member of the Institution of Water Engineers [*British*] (EY)
MiWe	West Branch Public Library, West Branch, MI [*Library symbol*] [*Library of Congress*] (LCLS)
MiWeld	Gladys MacArthur Memorial Library, Weidman, MI [*Library symbol*]
MIWES	Member of the Institution of Water Engineers and Scientists [*British*] (DI)
MIWG	Military Airlift Command Interoperability Working Group (SAUO)
MiWh	White Pigeon Township Library, White Pigeon, MI [*Library symbol*] [*Library of Congress*] (LCLS)
MiWhc	E. Jack Sharpe Public Library, White Cloud, MI [*Library symbol*] [*Library of Congress*] (LCLS)
MIWHR	Melpomene Institute for Women's Health Research (EA)
MIWHTE	Member of the Institution of Works and Highways Technician Engineers [*British*] (DBQ)
MiWin	Fremont Township Library, Winn, MI [*Library symbol*] [*Library of Congress*] (LCLS)
MIWM	Member of the Institution of Works Managers [*British*]
MIWMA	Member of the Institute of Weights and Measures Administration [*British*]
MiWol	Wolverine Community Library, Wolverine, MI [*Library symbol*] [*Library of Congress*] (LCLS)
MiWp	Carp Lake Township Library, White Pine, MI [*Library symbol*] [*Library of Congress*] (LCLS)
MIWPC	Member of the Institute of Water Pollution Control [*British*]
MIWS	Multipurpose Individual Weapon System (MCD)
MIWSP	Member of the Institute of Work Study Practitioners [*British*]
MIWT	Member of the Institute of Wireless Technology [*British*]
MiWy	Bacon Memorial Public Library, Wyandotte, MI [*Library symbol*] [*Library of Congress*] (LCLS)
MIX	Magnetic Ionization Experiment
MIX	McGraw-Hill Information Exchange for Educators
MIX	Member Information Exchange [*American Society for Training and Development - ASTD*] [*Alexandria, VA*] [*Information service or system*] (IID)
MIX	Merrill Lynch & Co. [*NYSE symbol*] (SAG)
MIX	Merrill Lynch & Co'MITTS' 2001 [*NYSE symbol*] (TTSB)
MIX	Methylisobutylxanthine [*Also, IBMX*] [*Biochemistry*]
MIX	Metropolis, IL [*Location identifier*] [*FAA*] (FAAL)
MIX	Microprogram Index Register [*Computer science*] (CIST)
MIX	Mix Canyon Road [*California*] [*Seismograph station code, US Geological Survey*] (SEIS)
MIX	Mixed Schedule of Reinforcement (DIPS)
MIX	Mixing
MIX	Mixture (KSC)
mix	Mixture (MEC)
MIX	Mores Island [*Bahamas*] [*Airport symbol*] (AD)
mix mon	Mixed Monitor [*Obstetrics*] (DAVI)
MIXT	Mixtura [*Mixture*] [*Pharmacy*]
MIXX	Medical Innovations [*NASDAQ symbol*] (TTSB)
MIXX	Medical Innovations, Inc. [*NASDAQ symbol*] (NQ)
MIY	Miyako [*Japan*] [*Seismograph station code, US Geological Survey*] (SEIS)
MIY	Montgomeryshire Imperial Yeomanry [*British military*] (DMA)
MIY	MuniYield Michigan Insured Fund [*NYSE symbol*] (SPSG)
MiY	Ypsilanti Area Public Library, Ypsilanti, MI [*Library symbol*] [*Library of Congress*] (LCLS)

MiYCC .... Cleary College, Ypsilanti, MI [*Library symbol*] [*Library of Congress*] (LCLS)

MiYEM .... Eastern Michigan University, Ypsilanti, MI [*Library symbol*] [*Library of Congress*] (LCLS)

MIZ .... Marginal Ice Zone [*Oceanography*]

MIZ .... Missile Interception Zone [*Military*]

Miz. .... Mizrachi [*or Mizrahi*] (BJA)

MIZ .... Mizusawa [*Japan*] [*Seismograph station code, US Geological Survey*] (SEIS)

MiZ .... Zeeland Public Library, Zeeland, MI [*Library symbol*] [*Library of Congress*] (LCLS)

Mizar .... Mizar, Inc. [*Associated Press*] (SAG)

MIZEX .... Marginal Ice Zone Experiment [*Oceanography*]

MIZPAC ...... Marginal Sea Ice Zone Pacific [*Marine science*] (MSC)

MIZR .... Mizar, Inc. [*NASDAQ symbol*] (SAG)

MJ .... Lineas Aereas Privadas Argentinas [*ICAO designator*] (AD)

MJ .... Madras Jurist [*India*] [*A publication*] (DLA)

MJ .... Main Jet [*Automotive engineering*]

MJ .... Major Subject Descriptor [*Online database field identifier*]

MJ .... Manual Jack (VLIE)

MJ .... Manufacturers' Junction Railway Co. [*AAR code*]

MJ .... Marijuana

MJ .... Marine Jet

MJ .... Master of Journalism

MJ .... Master of Jurisprudence

MJ .... Mastic Joint [*Technical drawings*]

MJ .... Mead Johnson & Co. [*Research code symbol*]

MJ .... Mechanical Joint (NASA)

MJ .... Megajoule

MJ .... Michael Joseph [*Commercial firm*] [*British*]

MJ .... Microturbo [*France*] [*ICAO aircraft manufacturer identifier*] (ICAO)

MJ .... Military Judge (AFM)

MJ .... Military Justice Reporter (West) [*A publication*] (DLA)

MJ .... Milwaukee Journal [*A newspaper*]

MJ .... Minerva Jacket [*Medicine*] (MELL)

MJ .... Ministry of Justice (SAUO)

mj .... Missionaries of St. Joseph (TOCD)

mj .... Missionaries of St. Joseph (Mexico) (TOCD)

MJ .... Missionary Sisters of Jesus (TOCD)

MJ .... Modular Jack (VLIE)

mj .... Montserrat [*MARC country of publication code*] [*Library of Congress*] (LCCP)

MJA .... Manja [*Madagascar*] [*Airport symbol*] (OAG)

MJA .... Master of Justice Administration (PGP)

MJA .... Medical Journalists Association [*British*] (DBA)

MJA .... Merchant Jewellers' Association Ltd. [*British*] (BI)

MJA .... Midstates Jeepster Association (EA)

MJAA .... Messianic Jewish Alliance of America (EA)

MJAJ .... Maanpuolustuksen ja Turvallisuuden Ammattijaerjestoet [*Defence and Security Employees Union*] [*Finalnd*] (EY)

MJAO .... Mediterranean Joint Air Orders

MJB .... Master Jet Base [*Navy*] (NVT)

MJB .... Mejit [*Marshall Islands*] [*Airport symbol*] (OAG)

MJB .... Missile Junction Box

MJB .... Moore Jig Borer

MJC .... Junior College District, Kansas City, MO [*OCLC symbol*] (OCLC)

MJC .... Majestic Contractors Ltd. [*Toronto Stock Exchange symbol*]

MJC .... Man [*Ivory Coast*] [*Airport symbol*] (OAG)

MJC .... Manatee Junior College (SAUO)

MJC .... Manitoba Journal of Counselling [*A publication*]

MJC .... Marshalltown Junior College [*Iowa*]

MJC .... Marymount Junior College (SAUO)

MJC .... Massachusetts Job Council

MJC .... Masters and Johnson Center (SAUO)

MJC .... Medieval Jewish Chronicles [*A publication*] (BJA)

MJC .... Mercy Junior College [*Missouri*] [*Closed, 1971*]

MJC .... Metropolitan Junior College (SAUO)

MJC .... Miami-Jacobs College [*Ohio*]

MJC .... Midway Junior College [*Kentucky*]

MJC .... Military Junior College (AABC)

MJC .... Moberly Junior College [*Missouri*]

MJC .... Modesto Junior College [*California*]

MJC .... Montgomery Junior College [*Maryland*]

MJC .... Morse Junior College [*Connecticut*]

MJC .... Morton Junior College [*Later, Morton College*] [*Cicero, IL*]

MJC .... Muscatine Junior College [*Iowa*]

MJC .... Muslim Judicial Council (SAUO)

MJCA .... Midbody Jettison Control Assembly (NASA)

MJCA .... Mississippi Junior College Association (SAUO)

MJCAA .... Mississippi Junior College Athletic Association (PSS)

MJCAC .... Midwest Junior College Athletic Conference (PSS)

MJCC .... Maryland Junior College Athletic Conference (PSS)

MJCC .... Melbourne Junior Chamber of Commerce [*Australia*]

MJCOM ...... Major Command (SAUO)

MJCS .... Joint Chiefs of Staff Memorandum (SAUO)

MJCS .... Memorandum for the Joint Chiefs of Staff (MCD)

MJD .... Doctor of Medical Jurisprudence

MJD .... Management Job Description (PDAA)

MJD .... Modified Julian Date [*Astronomy*] (TEL)

MJD .... Mohenjo Daro [*Pakistan*] [*Airport symbol*] (OAG)

MJD .... Mouvement de la Jeunesse Djiboutienne [*Political party*] (EY)

MJDQ .... Minnesota Job Description Questionnaire [*Research test*]

MJ Ed ...... Master of Jewish Education (PGP)

MJEMS .... Modular Jet Engine Management Simulator (SAUO)

MJF .... Greenville, TX [*Location identifier*] [*FAA*] (FAAL)

MJF .... Medical Journal Finder (SAUO)

MJF .... Multiple Juxtapositional Fixedness [*Tongue-in-cheek description of unusually strong bonding between metal ions and some ligands*]

MJF .... Muslim Janbaz Force (SAUO)

MJG .... Mayajigua [*Cuba*] [*Airport symbol*] (AD)

MJG .... Moore Jig Grinder

MJGA .... Manufacturing Jewelers Golf Association (EA)

MJGA .... Midwest Job Galvanizers Association [*Defunct*] (EA)

MJH .... Majma [*Saudi Arabia*] [*Airport symbol*] (AD)

MJI .... Maji [*Ethiopia*] [*Airport symbol*] (AD)

MJI .... Masters and Johnson Institute [*St. Louis, MO*] [*Formerly, Reproductive Biology Research Foundation*] [*Research center*]

MJI .... Member of the Journalists Institute

MJI .... MuniYield New Jersey Insured Fund [*NYSE symbol*] (SPSG)

MJI .... MuniYield NJ Insured Fund [*NYSE symbol*] (TTSB)

MJIE .... Member of the Junior Institute of Engineers [*British*]

MJInstE ...... Member of the Junior Institution of Engineers (SAUO)

MJL .... Medial Joint Line [*Orthopedics*] (DAVI)

MJL .... Meyer, Jr., L. Agnew, Washington DC [*STAC*]

MJL .... Mouila [*Gabon*] [*Airport symbol*] (OAG)

MJL .... Murray's Jat Lancers [*British military*] (DMA)

MJM .... Man-Job Match [*Military*]

MJM .... Mbuji-Mayi [*Zaire*] [*Airport symbol*] (OAG)

MJMA .... Mechanical Jack Manufacturers Association [*Defunct*] (EA)

MJMI .... Messianic Jewish Movement International (EA)

MJMJ .... Missionaries of Jesus, Mary, and Joseph [*Roman Catholic women's religious order*]

MJMT .... Mean Job Mill Time [*Quality control*] (MHDB)

MJN .... Majunga [*Madagascar*] [*Airport symbol*] (OAG)

MJN .... Royal Air Force of Oman (Air Transport) [*ICAO designator*] (FAAC)

MJNMM ...... Master of Journalism in New Media Management (GAGS)

MJNPE .... Mobile Joint Nuclear Planning Element (SAUO)

MJO .... Madden-Julian Oscillation (SAUO)

MJO .... Mariner Jupiter Orbit [*NASA*]

MJO .... Owens Technical College, Learning Resource Media Center, Toledo, OH [*OCLC symbol*] (OCLC)

MJOC .... Maritime Joint Operations Centre (SAUO)

MJP .... Jackson Metropolitan Library System, Jackson, MS [*OCLC symbol*] (OCLC)

MJP .... Master of Jewish Pedagogy

MJP .... Mastuj [*Pakistan*] [*Airport symbol*] (AD)

MJP .... Military Justice Procedure (SAUO)

MJP .... Mount John Pukaki [*New Zealand*] [*Seismograph station code, US Geological Survey*] (SEIS)

MJP .... Multiple Job Processing [*Computer science*] (VLIE)

M-JPEG .... Motion-Joint Photographic Expert Group [*Computer science*] (DCDG)

MJPM .... Master of Justice Policy and Management (PGP)

MJPS .... Mouvement des Jeunesses Progressistes Soudanaises [*Sudanese Progressive Youth Movement*] [*Mali*]

MJQ .... Jackson, MN [*Location identifier*] [*FAA*] (FAAL)

MJQ .... Modern Jazz Quartet [*Musical group*]

MJR .... Maintenance Job Request

MJR .... Major

Mjr. .... Major [*Record label*]

MJR .... Management Job Review [*LIMRA*]

MJS .... Maintenance Jettison System [*NASA*]

MJS .... Manipulator Jettison System [*or Subsystem*] (MCD)

MJS .... Mariner Jupiter-Saturn [*NASA*]

MJS .... Master of Japanese Studies (ADA)

MJS .... Master of Judaic Studies (PGP)

MJS .... Master of Juridical Science (DLA)

MJS .... Member of the Japan Society

MJS .... Movimiento Juvenil Salesiano [*Salesian Youth Movement - SYM*] (EAIO)

MJSA .... Manufacturing Jewelers and Silversmiths of America (EA)

MJSA .... Manufacturing Jewelers Sales Association

MJSA .... Mouvement des Jeunesses Socialistes Africaines [*African Socialist Youth Movement*]

MJSD .... March, June, September, and December [*Denotes quarterly payments of interest or dividends in these months*] [*Business term*]

MJSG .... Medem Jewish Socialist Group [*Defunct*] (EA)

MJSTC .... Majestic

MJT .... Magic Johnson Theaters

MJT .... Maintenance Job Tracking (ACAE)

MJT .... Maintenance Job Tracking System (SAUO)

MJT .... Majorteck Industries [*Vancouver Stock Exchange symbol*]

MJT .... Materials Joining Tool

MJT .... Mead Johnson Tube [*Medicine*] (DMAA)

MJT .... Multijet Transport

MJT .... Multi-Job Terminal [*Computer science*] (VLIE)

MJT .... Museum of Jurassic Technology

MJT .... Mytilene [*Greece*] [*Airport symbol*] (OAG)

MJTG .... Mitigation Joint Test Group (SAUO)

MJU .... Jackson State University, Jackson, MS [*OCLC symbol*] (OCLC)

MJU .... Mamuju [*Indonesia*] [*Airport symbol*] (OAG)

MJU .... Mariner Jupiter-Uranus [*Mission*] [*NASA*]

MJu .... Medica Judaica [*A publication*] (BJA)

MJU .... Multijunction Unit [*Computer science*] (BUR)

MJUO .... Mount John University Observatory [*New Zealand*]

MJUPG .... Movimiento da Juventude da Uniao Popular da Guine [*Youth Movement of Guinean People's Union*]

MJUPS .... Mouvement des Jeunes de l'Union Progressiste Senegalaise [*Youth Movement of the Senegalese Progressive Movement*]

MJur .... Master of Jurisprudence

MJV	Mojud Hosiery Company (SAUO)
MJV	Murcia [Spain] [Airport symbol] (OAG)
MJW	J. W. Mays, Inc. (SAUO)
MJW	Madison Junction [Wyoming] [Seismograph station code, US Geological Survey] [Closed] (SEIS)
MJWG	MANPRINT [Manpower and Personnel Integration] Joint Working Group [Army]
MJX	Masjed Soleyman [Iran] [Airport symbol] (AD)
MJX	Toms River, NJ [Location identifier] [FAA] (FAAL)
MJY	Majesty Resources [Vancouver Stock Exchange symbol]
MJZ	Mahfid [South Arabia] [Airport symbol] (AD)
MJZ	Mount John [New Zealand] [Seismograph station code, US Geological Survey] (SEIS)
MK	Air Mauritius [ICAO designator] (AD)
MK	Macedonia [Internet country code]
MK	Magic Kingdom [Walt Disney World]
MK	Malawi Kwacha [Monetary unit]
MK	Manual Clock [Computer science] (MDG)
MK	Mark [Ammunition] (NATG)
mk	Mark (WDMC)
Mk	Mark [New Testament book]
MK	Markka [Monetary unit] [Finland] (GPO)
MK	Marschkolonne [March Column] [German military - World War II]
MK	Mask [Computer science]
MK	Master Key [Locks] (ADA)
MK	Mebyon Kernow [Sons of Cornwall] [National liberation party] [Political party]
MK	Megakaryocyte (DMAA)
MK	Member of Knesset (BJA)
M/K	Member of the Knesset (SAUO)
MK	Menaquinone [Vitamin K] [Also, MQ] [Biochemistry]
MK	Merck & Co., Inc. [Research code symbol]
MK	Metarrithmistikon Komma [Reformist Party] [Greece] [Political party] (PPE)
MK	Microphone (MDG)
MK	Middle Kingdom [Egyptology] (ROG)
mK	Millikelvin
MK	Milton Keynes [Russian city]
MK	Miscellaneous Kits [JETDS nomenclature] [Military] (CET)
MK	Mit Kappe [With Cap] [German military - World War II]
MK	Mit Kern [With Core] [German military - World War II]
MK	Modification Kit (AAG)
MK	Mo'ed Katan (BJA)
MK	Monk
MK	Monkey Kidney
MK	More-Kraepelin [Disease] [Medicine] (DB)
MK	Morgan Keenan [System] [Astronomy]
M-K	Morrison-Knudsen Co., Inc. [Boise, ID] (TSSD)
MK	Morrison Knudsen Corp. (SAUO)
MK	Morse Key (DEN)
MK	Mounier-Kuhn [Syndrome] [Medicine] (DB)
MK	Multiple Kill [Aerospace]
mk	Muscat and Oman [Oman] [MARC country of publication code] [Library of Congress] (LCCP)
MK	Myokinase (DMAA)
MKA	Machine Knife Association (EA)
MKA	Makaopuhi [Hawaii] [Seismograph station code, US Geological Survey] (SEIS)
MKA	Marine-Kuestenartillerie [Naval Coast Artillery] [German military - World War II]
MKA	Master Kennel Association [Commercial firm] (EA)
MKA	Metrika Systems [AMEX symbol] (SG)
MKA	Miller, SD [Location identifier] [FAA] (FAAL)
MKA	MK Aircargo [British] [ICAO designator] (FAAC)
MKAS	Meyer-Kendall Assessment Survey [Interpersonal skills and attitudes test]
MKATA	Machine Knife and Allied Trades Association (SAUO)
MKAU	MK Gold [NASDAQ symbol] (TTSB)
MKAU	MK Gold Co. [NASDAQ symbol] (SAG)
MKB	Mary Kathryn Bonk [Editor]
MKB	Mary K. Bonk [Editor]
MKB	Megakaryoblast [Hematology]
MKB	Mekambo [Gabon] [Airport symbol] (OAG)
MKBF	Mean Kilometers between Failures
MKBWU	Machine Knife and Bayonet Workers' Union [British]
MKC	Kansas City [Missouri] [Airport symbol] (OAG)
MKC	Magic Kingdom Club [Walt Disney Productions]
MKC	Mammal Kidney Cell (DB)
MKC	Marion Laboratories, Inc. (SAUO)
MKC	Mark Resources, Inc. [Toronto Stock Exchange symbol]
MKC	McCormick & Co. [NYSE symbol] (SG)
MKC	McKeesport Connecting Railroad Co. [AAR code]
MKC	Megakaryocyte [Medicine] (MELL)
MKC	Moncks Corner [South Carolina] [Seismograph station code, US Geological Survey] [Closed] (SEIS)
MKC	Monkey Kidney Cell (DMAA)
MKC	University of Health Sciences, Kansas City, MO [OCLC symbol] (OCLC)
MKD	Marked (MSA)
MKDIR	Make Directory [Computer science]
MKDS	Master Key Data Set [Computer science] (VLIE)
MKE	Arthur G. McKee & Co. (SAUO)
MKE	Association of the Hungarian Librarians (SAUO)
MKE	General Mitchell International Airport [FAA] (TAG)
MKE	Hungarian Chemical Society (SAUO)

MKE	Milwaukee [Wisconsin] [Airport symbol] (OAG)
MKE	Molecular Kinetic Energy
MKF	Mackenzie Financial Corp. [Toronto Stock Exchange symbol]
MKFC	Mackenzie Financial Corp. [NASDAQ symbol] (SAG)
MKFCF	Mackenzie Financial [NASDAQ symbol] (TTSB)
MKG	K.G. Munson (SAUO)
MKG	Magnetocardiogram
MKG	Making
MKG	Mallinckrodt Group [Formerly, IMCERA Group] [NYSE symbol] (SAG)
MKG	Marking
MKG	Maurer Kunst Geselle [Fellowcraft] [Freemasonry] [German]
M-KG	Meteor-Kilogram
M-KG	Meter-Kilogram (KSC)
MKG	Munson, K. G., Weyers Cave VA [STAC]
MKG	Muskegon [Michigan] [Airport symbol] (OAG)
MK Gold	MK Gold Co. [Associated Press] (SAG)
MKgP	Posse School, Inc., Kendal Green, MA [Library symbol] [Library of Congress] [Obsolete] (LCLS)
MKGPr	Mallincrodt Group 4% Pfd [NYSE symbol] (TTSB)
MKGS	Markings
MKH	Mackintosh-Hemphill Co. (SAUO)
MKH	Mauna Kea [Hawaii] [Seismograph station code, US Geological Survey] (SEIS)
MKH	Million of Kilowatt Hours (MCD)
MKH	Mokhotlong [Lesotho] [Airport symbol] (OAG)
MKH	Multiple Key Hashing
MKHS	Menkes' Kinky Hair Syndrome [Medicine] (DMAA)
MKI	M-Corp Inc. [Formerly, Mike's Submarines] [Toronto Stock Exchange symbol]
MKIE	Mackie Designs [NASDAQ symbol] (TTSB)
MKIE	Mackie Designs, Inc. [NASDAQ symbol] (SAG)
M Kin	Master of Kinesiology (PGP)
MkIS	Marketing Information System
MKJ	Makoua [Congo] [Airport symbol] (OAG)
MKJK	Kingston [Jamaica] [ICAO location identifier] (ICLI)
MKJM	Montego Bay [Jamaica] [ICAO location identifier] (ICLI)
MKJP	Kingston/Norman Manley International [Jamaica] [ICAO location identifier] (ICLI)
MKJS	Montego Bay/Sangster International [Jamaica] [ICAO location identifier] (ICLI)
MKK	Kaunakakai, HI [Location identifier] [FAA] (FAAL)
Mkk	Markka [Monetary unit] [Finland]
MKK	Molokai/Kaunakakai [Hawaii] [Airport symbol] (OAG)
MkK	Monkey Kidney [Medicine] (DMAA)
MKK	Morgan, Keenan, Kellman [System] [Astronomy]
MKL	Jackson [Tennessee] [Airport symbol] (OAG)
MKL	Jackson, TN [Location identifier] [FAA] (FAAL)
MKL	Lakeland Regional Library, Killarney, Manitoba [Library symbol] [National Library of Canada] (NLC)
MKL	Markel Corp. [NYSE symbol] (SG)
MKL	Maskali [Djibouti] [Seismograph station code, US Geological Survey] (SEIS)
MKL	Megakaryocytic Leukemia [Hematology]
MKLP	Mitotic Kinesin-Like Protein [Biochemistry]
MKM	Kansas City, MO [Location identifier] [FAA] (FAAL)
MKM	Manawatu Knitting Mills (SAUO)
MKM	Marksman [Marine Corps]
MKM	Mink Minerals Resources, Inc. [Vancouver Stock Exchange symbol]
MKM	Mukah [Malaysia] [Airport symbol] (OAG)
MKM	Myopic Keratomileusis [Ophthalmology]
MKMA	Machine Knife Manufacturers Association (EA)
MkmQualBad ...	Marksman Qualification Badge [Military decoration] (AABC)
MKN	Malekolon [Papua New Guinea] [Airport symbol] (OAG)
MKN	Mouvement Cooperatif National [Haiti] [Political party] (EY)
MKN	Northeast Missouri State University, Kirksville, MO [OCLC symbol] (OCLC)
MKNP	Malawi Kasungu National Park (SAUO)
MKNP	Mount Kenya National Park (SAUO)
MKO	Makung Airlines [Taiwan] [ICAO designator] (FAAC)
MKO	Mauna Kea Observatory [Hawaii] (BARN)
MKO	Mikado Resources Ltd. [Vancouver Stock Exchange symbol]
MKO	Modification Kit Order
MKO	Munafiqeen Khalq Organization (SAUO)
MKO	Muskogee, OK [Location identifier] [FAA] (FAAL)
MKP	Magyar Kommunista Part [Hungarian Communist Party] [Political party] (PPE)
MKP	Makemo [French Polynesia] [Airport symbol] (OAG)
MKP	McKeesport, PA [Location identifier] [FAA] (FAAL)
MkP	Mikropress GmbH, Bonn, Germany [Library symbol] [Library of Congress] (LCLS)
mkp	misc.kids.pregnancy newsgroup (SAUO)
MKP	Myokinetic Psychodiagnosis [Psychology] (AEBS)
MKPL	Computer Marketplace [NASDAQ symbol] (TTSB)
MKPL	Computer Marketplace, Inc. [NASDAQ symbol] (SAG)
MKPLW	Computer Marketplace Wrrt'A' [NASDAQ symbol] (TTSB)
MKPLZ	Computer Marketplace Wrrt'B' [NASDAQ symbol] (TTSB)
MKQ	Merauke [Indonesia] [Airport symbol] (OAG)
MKQCP	Member of the King's and Queen's College of Physicians [Ireland]
MKR	Glasgow, MT [Location identifier] [FAA] (FAAL)
mkr	Maker (VRA)
MKR	Maker
MKR	Marker [Beacon]
MKR	Meekatharra [Australia] [Airport symbol] (OAG)
MKR	Mkuzi Game Reserve (SAUO)

MKRADC	Middle Kentucky River Area Development Council (SAUO)
MK Rail	MK Rail Corp. [*Associated Press*] (SAG)
mKRB	Modified Krebs-Ringer Bicarbonate [*Solution*]
MKRL	MK Rail [*NASDAQ symbol*] (TTSB)
MKRL	MK Rail Corp. [*NASDAQ symbol*] (SAG)
MKS	Makassar [*Celebes*] [*Seismograph station code, US Geological Survey*] (SEIS)
MKS	Marks & Spencer Canada, Inc. [*Toronto Stock Exchange symbol*]
MKS	Marksman [*Marine Corps*]
MKS	Mekane [*Ethiopia*] [*Airport symbol*] (OAG)
mks	Meter-Kilogram-Second (IDOE)
MKS	Meter-Kilogram-Second [*System of units*]
MKS	Microwave Keying Switch
MKS	Mikasa, Inc. [*NYSE symbol*] (SAG)
MKS	Moncks Corner, SC [*Location identifier*] [*FAA*] (FAAL)
MKS	Mortice Kern Systems, Inc. [*Waterloo, ON Canada*] [*Commercial firm*] (CDE)
MKS	Pimichikamac Air Ltd. [*Canada*] [*FAA designator*] (FAAC)
MKSA	Absolute MKS (SAUS)
mksa	Meter, Kilogram, Second, Ampere (VLIE)
MKSA	Meter-Kilogram-Second-Ampere [*System of units*]
MKSAP	Medical Knowledge Self-Assessment Program (SAUO)
MKSI	MKS Instruments [*NASDAQ symbol*] (SG)
MKSS	Microwave Keying Switching Station
MKSTNG	Marksmanship Training (NVT)
MKT	Mankato, MN [*Location identifier*] [*FAA*] (FAAL)
Mkt	Market (EBF)
mkt	Market (WDMC)
MKT	Market
MKT	Market order (SAUO)
MKT	Missouri-Kansas-Texas Railroad Co. [*AAR code*]
MKT	Mobile Kitchen Trailer [*Military*] (INF)
MKT	Mu Kappa Tau (EA)
MKTA	Makita Corp. [*NASDAQ symbol*] (SAG)
MKTAY	Makita Corp. [*NASDAQ symbol*] (TTSB)
MKTC	Monkey Kidney Tissue Culture (DB)
MktFct	Market Facts, Inc. [*Associated Press*] (SAG)
Mktg	Marketing (TBD)
mktg	Marketing (WDMC)
MKTG	Marketing
MKTI	Mission Kit Technical Instruction
MKTI	Morrison-Knudsen Technologies, Inc. [*Boise, ID*] [*Telecommunications*] (TSSD)
MKTL	MarketLink, Inc. [*NASDAQ symbol*] (SAG)
MKTLH	Tri-Lake Health Centre, Killarney, Manitoba [*Library symbol*] [*National Library of Canada*] (NLC)
MktLink	MarketLink, Inc. [*Associated Press*] (SAG)
Mkt Mgr	Marketing Manager (SAUO)
MKTNG	Marketing
MKTP	Market Planning (SAUO)
MKTP	Mark Template [*Tool*]
MKTT	Missouri-Kansas-Texas Railroad Co. (of Texas) [*AAR code*]
MKTT	Modification Kit Tank Telephone (SAUS)
MKTU	Marksmanship Training Unit (AABC)
MKTW	MarketWatch.com [*NYSE symbol*] (SG)
MkTwain	Mark Twain Bancshares, Inc. [*Associated Press*] (SAG)
MKU	Makokou [*Gabon*] [*Airport symbol*] (OAG)
MKU	Mary Kathleen Uranium (SAUO)
MKU	Mock-Up
MKUP	Makeup
MKV	Killed-Measles Vaccine [*Immunology*] (MAE)
MKV	Marksville, LA [*Location identifier*] [*FAA*] (FAAL)
MKV	Miniature Kill Vehicle [*Military*] (SDI)
MKV	Multiple Kill Vehicle
MKVNV	Muskmelon Vein Necrosis Virus [*Plant pathology*]
MKW	Magnetokinetic Wave
MKW	Manokwari [*Indonesia*] [*Airport symbol*] (OAG)
MKW	Mikawa [*Japan*] [*Seismograph station code, US Geological Survey*] (SEIS)
MKW	Military Knight of Windsor [*British*]
MKW	Munitionskraftwagen [*Ammunition Truck*] [*German military - World War II*]
MKX	Mukalla [*South Arabia*] [*Airport symbol*] (AD)
MKY	Mackay [*Australia*] [*Airport symbol*] (OAG)
MKY	Makeyevka [*Former USSR*] [*Seismograph station code, US Geological Survey*] [*Closed*] (SEIS)
MKY	Marco Island, FL [*Location identifier*] [*FAA*] (FAAL)
MKY	Monky Aerotaxis SA [*Mexico*] [*ICAO designator*] (FAAC)
MKYFC	Mike and Kathy Yager Fan Club [*Later, MYFC*] (EA)
MKZ	Los Angeles, CA [*Location identifier*] [*FAA*] (FAAL)
MKZ	Malacca [*Malaysia*] [*Airport symbol*] (OAG)
ML	Aviation Services [*ICAO designator*] (AD)
ML	Holder of a Major Licence (SAUO)
ML	Land Mobile Station [*ITU designation*] (NATG)
ML	Licentiate in Medicine
ML	Licentiate in Midwifery
ML	Machine Language [*Computer science*]
ML	Macro Library (VLIE)
ML	Macula Lutea (MELL)
ML	Madras Lancers [*British military*] (DMA)
ML	Magic Lantern Society of the United States and Canada (EA)
ML	Magnetic Latching [*Electronics*] (OA)
ML	Magnetogasdynamics Laboratory [*MIT*] (MCD)
ML	Magnitude Local (COE)
ML	Mail
ML	Mail Label
ML	Mail List (SAUS)
ML	Mainland (MUGU)
ML	Main Line [*Business term*]
ML	Main Lobe
ML	Maintained Load (WDAA)
ML	Maintenance Laboratory (MUGU)
ML	Maintenance Level (VLIE)
M/L	Maintenance Loop (MCD)
ML	Major League [*Baseball*]
ML	Major Lobe (MSA)
ML	Malachi [*Old Testament book*]
Ml	Malaysia (SAUO)
ML	Mali [*ANSI two-letter standard code*] (CNC)
ml	Mali [*MARC country of publication code*] [*Library of Congress*] (LCCP)
ML	Malignant Lymphoma [*Oncology*]
M:L	maltase-to-Lactase [*Ratio*] [*Biochemistry*] (DAVI)
ML	Management Level
ML	Management List
ML	Mandibular Line [*Jaw anatomy*]
ML	Manipulation Language (NITA)
ML	Manipulator Language [*Computer science*]
ML	Mantle Length
ML	Mantle Lip
ML	Manual Loader (AAG)
ML	Manual Local (IAA)
ML	Manufacturing License (NRCH)
ML	Maple Leaf Gardens Ltd. [*Toronto Stock Exchange symbol*]
ML	March for Life (EA)
ML	Marie-Leri [*Syndrome*] [*Medicine*] (DB)
ML	Marine Limit (QUAC)
ML	Mark-Up Language [*Computer science*]
Ml	Marl [*Quality of the bottom*] [*Nautical charts*]
M-L	Martin-Lewis [*Medium*] [*Microbiology*]
M/L	Mass to Luminosity [*Ratio*] [*Astronomy*]
ML	Master of Laws
ML	Master of Letters
ML	Master of Librarianship (GAGS)
ML	Master of Literature
ML	Material List (MSA)
ML	Materials Laboratory (SAUO)
ML	Mater Lectionis (BJA)
ML	Maule Aircraft Corp. [*ICAO aircraft manufacturer identifier*] (ICAO)
ML	Maurice Lacroix
ML	Maximum Likelihood [*Statistics*]
ML	Maximum to Left (SAUS)
ML	Mean Level
ML	Medial Lemniscus [*Neuroanatomy*]
ML	Medical Laboratory (SAUO)
ML	Medical Letter (EA)
ML	Medical Logistics (SAUO)
ML	Medieval Latin [*Language, etc.*]
ML	Medium Lorry [*British*]
ML	Megaliter
ML	Member Library [*OCLC or RLIN*]
ML	Member's Liability [*Health insurance*] (GHCT)
ML	Memory Layout [*Computer science*] (ELAL)
ML	Memory Location [*Computer science*]
ML	Memory Loss (MELL)
ML	Merrill Lynch & Co., Inc. (EFIS)
ML	Mesa Laboratory (SAUO)
ML	Mesiolingual [*Dentistry*]
ML	Metabolic Loss [*Physiology*]
M-L	Metallic-Longitudinal (IEEE)
ML	Meteorological Devices [*JETDS nomenclature*] [*Military*] (CET)
ML	Meteorology Laboratory (GNE)
ML	Methods of Limits (IEEE)
ML	Metromail Corp. [*NYSE symbol*] (SAG)
ML	Mexican League [*Baseball*]
ML	Microprogramming Language
ML	Microwave Laboratory [*Stanford University*] (MCD)
ML	Middeck Left (MCD)
ML	Middle Compass Locator (PIPO)
ML	Middle Latin [*Language, etc.*]
ML	Middle Left (WDAA)
ML	Middle Lobe [*Of lung*]
ML	Midlife (DAVI)
ML	Midline
ML	Migne Series [*Latina*] [*A publication*] (BJA)
ML	Milan Stock Exchange (SG)
ml	Mile (IDOE)
ML	Milieu
ML	Military Law
ML	Military Leave (GFGA)
ML	Military Liaison
ML	Military Payroll Money List
ML	Milk Letdown (MELL)
ML	Mill
ml	Millilambert (DIPS)
mL	Millilambert
ml	Milliliter (AEBE)
ML	Milliliter (GOBB)
ML	Milliliter
ML	Mine Layer (WDAA)

ML	Mineral Lease (ADA)
ML	Minerva Library [A publication]
ML	Minilab
ML	Minimum Level (EEVL)
ML	Mining and Logging [Tires]
ML	Ministry of Labour (SAUO)
ML	Missile Launcher
ML	Missile Layout
ML	Missile Lethality [Military]
M/L	Missile-Lift [Aerospace] (AAG)
ML	Missile Liner
ML	Mission Life [Aerospace]
ML	Mission Load (AABC)
ML	Mixed Lengths
ML	Mobile Launcher [NASA] (KSC)
ML	Mobile Low-Power [Reactor] (NRCH)
ML	Mode-Locked [Laser technology]
ML	Moderate Load service [Automotive engineering]
ML	Moderately Long [Botany]
ML	Modern Languages (AIE)
ML	Modern Lithographer [A publication] (DGA)
ML	Modified License [FCC] (NTCM)
ML	Molder [Navy rating]
ML	Mold Line [Technical drawings]
ML	Molecular Layer [of the hippocampus] [Neurology]
ML	Monarchist League [Defunct] (EA)
ML	Moneda Legal [Legal Tender] [Spanish] [Business term]
ML	Money List
M/L	Monocyte-Lymphocyte [Ratio] [Clinical chemistry]
ML	Monolayer [Physical chemistry]
ML	Monolithic
ML	More Later (SAUS)
ML	Morocco Lined [Covers] [Bookbinding] (ROG)
ML	Motherwell [Postcode] (ODBW)
ML	Motor Launch
ML	Mountain Leader [British military] (DMA)
ML	Mouse Laminin
ML	Mouse Lysozyme [Biochemistry]
ML	Mucolipidosis [Medicine]
ML	Mucrones Length [Of Crustacea]
ML	Multilayer [Pharmacy]
ML	Multiple-Line [Insurance]
ML	Multiple Location [Insurance]
ML	Multiple-Locus [Light flashes]
ML	Munitions List
ML	Music Library Records [Record label]
ML	Muslim League [Bangladesh] [Political party] (FEA)
ML	Mutual Inductance [Symbol] (DEN)
ML	Muzzle-Loading
ML	Myelogenous Leukemia [Oncology]
ML	Myeloid Leukemia [Medicine] (DB)
ML	Myrialiter [Unit of measurement] (ROG)
ML1	Small Minesweeper [Navy symbol]
ML1	Molder, First Class [Navy rating]
ML2	Molder, Second Class [Navy rating]
ML3	Molder, Third Class [Navy rating]
MLA	Auxiliary Motor Launches (NATG)
MLA	Forty-Mile Air [ICAO designator] (FAAC)
MLA	Macedonian Literary Association [Australia]
MLA	Magic Lantern Adaption (SAUS)
MLA	Magnetic Lens Assembly
MLA	Mail List Agent (SAUS)
MLA	Maine Library Association (SAUO)
MLA	Maine Lobstermen's Association (EA)
mla	Malagasy [MARC language code] [Library of Congress] (LCCP)
MLA	Malaspina [Alaska] [Seismograph station code, US Geological Survey] (SEIS)
MLA	Malta [Airport symbol] (OAG)
MLA	Mandatory Liquid Assets [Finance]
MLA	Maneuver Limited Altitude (GAVI)
MLA	Maneuver Load Alleviation [Aviation]
MLA	Manitoba Library Association (SAUO)
MLA	Manpack Loop Antenna
MLA	Manufacturing License Agreement
MLA	Marine Librarians Association (EA)
MLA	Maritime Law Association of the US (EA)
MLA	Marker-Labelled Antigen (DB)
MLA	Marlat Resources Ltd. [Vancouver Stock Exchange symbol]
MLA	Martin Landau Aficionados [An association]
MLA	Maryland Library Association (SAUO)
MLA	Massachusetts Library Association (SAUO)
MLA	Master Locksmiths Association [British] (BI)
MLA	Master of Landscape Architecture
MLA	Master of Liberal Arts (GAGS)
MLA	Matching Logic and Adder
MLA	MDM [Manipulator Deployment Mechanism] Launch Aft [NASA]
MLA	Mean Line of Advance [Military] (NVT)
MLA	Mechanical Lubricator Association
MLA	Medial Left Abdomen [Injection site]
MLA	Medical Library Association (EA)
MLA	Member of Legislative Assembly (SAUO)
MLA	Member of the Legislative Assembly
MLA	Member of the Library Association [British] (ROG)
MLA	Mento-Laeval Anterior [A fetal position] [Obstetrics]
MLA	Mercantile Library Association (SAUO)
MLA	Merritt Island Tracking Station [Florida]
MLA	Mesiolabial [Dentistry]
MLA	Metal Lath Association [Later, ML/SFA] (EA)
MLA	Metrolina Library Association [Library network]
MLA	Michigan Library Association (SAUO)
MLA	Microprocessor Language Assembler [Computer science]
MLA	Microwave Linear Accelerator
MLA	Microwave Link Analyzer (ACAE)
MLA	Midland Co. [AMEX symbol] (SPSG)
MLA	Midwest Lacrosse Association (PSS)
MLA	Military Liaison Assistant (DOMA)
MLA	Minimal Lactose-Arabinose [Culture medium]
MLA	Mining Lease Application
MLA	Minnesota Library Association
MLA	Mississippi Library Association (SAUO)
MLA	Missouri Library Association (SAUO)
MLA	Mistress of Liberal Arts
MLA	Mixed Lead Alkalis (EDCT)
MLA	Mixed Lead Alkyl [Organic chemistry]
MLA	MLA International Biography of Books & Articles on the Modern Languages and Lit.
MLA	Modern Language Association (NADA)
MLA	Modern Language Association of America (EA)
MLA	Modern Languages Association (SAUO)
MLA	Monochrome Lens Assembly (MCD)
MLA	Monocytic Leukemia, Acute (MAE)
MLA	Monophosphoryl Lipid A [Medicine] (MELL)
MLA	Montana Library Association (SAUO)
MLA	Motor Launch, Auxiliary [NATO]
MLA	Multi-Housing Laundry Association (EA)
MLA	Multi Letter Acronym (ACAE)
MLA	Multilinear Array [In earth scanning]
MLA	MultiLink Advanced [Local area network] [The Software Link, Inc.]
MLA	Multiple Line Adaptor (NITA)
MLA	Multiplex Line Adapter
MLA	Multispectral Linear Array (SSD)
MLA	Music Library Association (EA)
MLA	Muzzle Loaders' Association of Great Britain
MLA	Valetta [Malta] [Airport symbol] (AD)
MLAA	Medical Library Assistance Act [1965]
MLAA	Modern Language Association of America (SAUO)
MLA/ATG	Modern Language Association/ Association of Teachers of German (SAUO)
MLAB	Mesa Laboratories [NASDAQ symbol] (TTSB)
MLAB	Mesa Laboratories, Inc. [NASDAQ symbol] (SAG)
MLAB	Modeling Laboratory [Programming language] [1970] (CSR)
MLAB	Multilingual Aphasia Battery [Medicine] (DMAA)
M Lab R	Monthly Labor Review [A publication] (BRI)
MLAF	Missile Loading Alignment Fixture
MLAGB	Muzzle Loaders Association of Great Britain (BI)
MLAI	Mesiolabioincisal [Dentistry]
M La L	Master of Latin Letters
MLaI	Mesiolabioincisal [Medicine] (MEDA)
MLAMH	Mona Lisas and Mad Hatters [Defunct] (EA)
MLAN	Midland Co. [NASDAQ symbol] (SG)
MLANA	Melkite Laymen's Association of North America (EA)
MLanc	Lancaster Town Library, Lancaster, MA [Library symbol] [Library of Congress] (LCLS)
MLandArch	Master of Landscape Architecture [Canada] (DD)
MLandEc	Master in Land Economy
ML&T	Master of Law and Taxation (GAGS)
MLAP	Mean Left Atrial Pressure [Cardiology]
MLaP	Mesiolabiopulpal [Dentistry]
MLAP	Migrant Legal Action Program (EA)
MLAP	Muslim League Assembly Party [Pakistan] [Political party] (FEA)
MLAPU	Marxist-Leninist Armed Propaganda Unit [Turkey]
MLAR	Mill Arbor
MLAR	Multilayer Antireflection [Coating]
ML Arch	Master of Landscape Architecture
MLAS	Master of Laboratory Animal Science (PGP)
MLASES	Molasses [Freight]
MLA-SMHL	Medical Library Association, Section on Mental Health Libraries (EA)
MLA/SWIR	Multispectral Linear Array Short Wave Infrared (ACAE)
MLAT	Mean Latitude
MLAT	Modern Language Aptitude Test [Military] (AFM)
MLATD	Mediterranean League Against Thromboembolic Diseases (SAUO)
MLAUD	Master of Landscape Architecture in Urban Development (GAGS)
MLAUK	Member of the Library Association, United Kingdom (ROG)
M'Laur	M'Laurin's Scotch Judiciary Cases [1774] [A publication] (DLA)
MLAUS	Maritime Law Association of the United States (SAUO)
MLaw	Lawrence Free Public Library, Lawrence, MA [Library symbol] [Library of Congress] (LCLS)
MLb	Macrolymphoblast (DB)
MLB	Magnetic Linear Birefringence (MCD)
MLB	Major League Baseball
MLB	Malabar [Java] [Seismograph station code, US Geological Survey] [Closed] (SEIS)
MLB	Manufacturing Load Boards (MCD)
MLB	Marginal Lands Board (SAUO)
MLB	Maritime Labor Board [Terminated, 1942]
MLB	Maritime Law Book Key Number Data Base [Maritime Law Book Co. Ltd.] [Canada] [Information service or system] (CRD)
MLB	Medallion Books Ltd. [Vancouver Stock Exchange symbol]
MLB	Melbourne [Florida] [Airport symbol] (OAG)
MLB	Merrill Lynch & Co. [NYSE symbol] (SAG)

MLB	Metallic Link Belt (AABC)
MLB	Metropolitan Toronto Library Board, Systems Unit [*UTLAS symbol*]
MLB	Micro-Laryngobronchoscopy [*Medicine*] (DMAA)
MLB	Middle Linebacker [*Football*]
MLB	Mini Landbridge [*MARAD*] (TAG)
MLB	Mobile Logistics Support Base (NVT)
MLB	Monaural Loudness Balance [*Audiology*]
MLB	Motor Lifeboat
MLB	Multilayer Board
MLB	Multiple Listing Board (BARN)
MLB	Multiple Listing Bureau (SAUO)
MLBC	ML Bancorp. [*NASDAQ symbol*] [*Formerly, MLF Bancorp.*] (SG)
MLBC	ML Bancorp, Inc. [*NASDAQ symbol*] (SAG)
MLBM	Modern Large Ballistic Missile
ML Bncp	ML Bancorp, Inc. [*Associated Press*] (SAG)
MLBP	Major League Baseball Properties (NDBD)
MLBP	Mechanical Low Back Pain (MELL)
MLBPA	Mailing List Brokers Professional Association [*Defunct*] (EA)
MLBPA	Major League Baseball Players Association (EA)
MLBPAA	Major League Baseball Players Alumni Association (NDBD)
MLBR	Medium Low-BIT [*Binary Digit*] Rate [*Computer science*]
MLBS	Multi Layer Boards (ACAE)
MLBU	Mobile Laundry and Bath Unit [*Military*] [*British*]
MLBW	Moderately Low Birth Weight (MELL)
MLC	Machine Cornering Limit [*Equipment design*]
MLC	Machine Level Control [*Computer science*]
MLC	Madras Light Cavalry [*British military*] (DMA)
MLC	Magnetic Ledger Card (CMD)
MLC	Main Lobe Cancellation (ACAE)
MLC	Main Lobe Clutter
MLC	Major Landing Craft
MLC	Major Legislation of Congress [*Data processing system*] [*Congressional Research Service*]
MLC	Major Line Component [*of NOAA*] (NOAA)
MLC	Management Level Chart [*Military*] (AFIT)
MLC	Management Level Code [*Military*] (AFIT)
ML-C	Management List - Consolidated
MLC	Maneuver Load Control [*Aviation*]
MLC	Manhattan National Corp. [*NYSE symbol*] (SPSG)
MLC	Mansfield Law Club (SAUO)
MLC	Manufacturers Life Capital Corp., Inc. [*Toronto Stock Exchange symbol*]
MLC	Manzanita Lake [*California*] [*Seismograph station code, US Geological Survey*] (SEIS)
MLC	Maori Land Court (SAUO)
MLC	Maple Leaf Club (EA)
MLC	Master Labor Contract (AABC)
MLC	McAlester, OK [*Location identifier*] [*FAA*] (FAAL)
MLC	Meat and Livestock Commission [*British*] (ARC)
MLC	Median Lethal Concentration [*Toxiclogy*] (LDT)
MLC	Medical Liability Commission [*Defunct*] (EA)
MLC	Medical Library Center (DIT)
MLC	Medium Level Center (ELAL)
MLC	Member of the Legislative Council
MLC	Memphis Library Council [*Library network*]
MLC	Mergenthaler Linotype Company, Brooklyn (SAUO)
MLC	Merrill Lynch & Co., Inc. [*NYSE symbol*] (SAG)
MLC	Merrill Lyn GI'MITTS'98 [*NYSE symbol*] (TTSB)
MLC	Mesh Level Control
MLC	Metropolitan Toronto Library Board, Cataloguing Department [*UTLAS symbol*]
MLC	Micellar Liquid Chromatography
MLC	Michigan Library Consortium [*Lansing, MI*] [*Library network*]
MLC	Microelectric Logic Circuit
MLC	Microprogram Location Counter
MLC	Midlife Conversion
MLC	Miles College, Birmingham, AL [*OCLC symbol*] (OCLC)
MLC	Military Landing Craft
MLC	Military Liaison Committee [*Energy Research and Development Administration*]
MLC	Military Load Class (RDA)
MLC	Minimum Lethal Concentration
MLC	Missile Launch Car (SAUS)
MLC	Missile Logistics Center [*Army*]
MLC	Mississippi-Louisiana Conference (PSS)
MLC	Mississippi State Library Commission [*Information service or system*] (IID)
MLC	Mixed Leukocyte Culture [*Hematology*]
MLC	Mixed Ligand Chelate (DB)
MLC	Mixed Lymphocyte Culture [*Hematology*]
MLC	Mobile Launch Center
MLC	Mobile Launcher Computer [*NASA*] (NASA)
MLC	Modern Language Caucus [*of New University Conference*]
MLC	Modern Language Centre [*Ontario Institute for Studies in Education*] [*Canada*] (IRC)
MLC	Modular Load Carrier (SAUS)
MLC	Molder, Chief [*Navy rating*]
MLC	MOL [*Manned Orbiting Laboratory*] Launch Complex (MCD)
MLC	Monarchist League of Canada (EAIO)
MLC	Money Laundering Control Act (GOBB)
MLC	Morphine-Like Compound [*Immunology*]
MLC	Motor Launch, Cabin
MLC	Motor Load Control
MLC	Mountain Leadership Certificate [*British*] (DI)
MLC	Multilamellar Cytosome [*Biochemistry*] (MAE)
MLC	Multilayer Capacitor [*Electronics*]
MLC	Multilayer Ceramic [*Materials technology*]
MLC	Multilayer Ceramic Capacitor (NITA)
MLC	Multilayer Circuit
MLC	Multilens Camera
MLC	Multi-Level Cell (AAEL)
MLC	Multiline Communications Controller (SAUO)
MLC	Multiline Control (BUR)
MLC	Multilink Control Field [*Telecommunications*] (ACRL)
MLC	Multilumen Catheter [*Medicine*] (MELL)
MLC	Multiplanar Link Chain
MLC	Municipal Leasing Corp.
MLC	Myelomonocytic Leukemia, Chronic (MAE)
MLC	Myosin Light Chain [*Muscle biology*]
MLC	Myth, Legend, Custom in the Old Testament [*A publication*] (BJA)
MLCA	Modified Life Cycle Assessment [*Recycling*]
MLCAD	Maintenance and Logistics Factors in Computer Aided Design (SAUO)
MLCAEC	Military Liaison Committee to the Atomic Energy Commission (IEEE)
MLCB	Missile Launch Control Blockhouse
MLCB	Moored Limited Capability Buoy [*Marine science*] (MSC)
MLCB	Multilayer Circuit Board
ML/CB-CC	Malignant Lymphoma/Centroblastic-Centrocytic [*Oncology*]
ML/CC	Malignant Lymphoma/Centrocytic [*Oncology*]
MLCC	Mined Land Conservation Conference [*Later, BCR*]
MLCC	Modular Life Cycle Cost (ACAE)
MLCC	Multilayer Ceramic Capacitor [*Electronics*]
MLCD	Multi-Line Call Detail (ROAS)
MLCG	Missile Launcher Control Group
MLCH	Major Logistical Control Headquarters (MCD)
MLCH	MLC Holdings, Inc. [*NASDAQ symbol*] (SAG)
MLC Hld	MLC Holdings, Inc. [*Associated Press*] (SAG)
MLCI	Multi-Link Channel Interface [*Computer science*] (VLIE)
MLCIM	Marquette League for Catholic Indian Missions [*Defunct*] (EA)
MLCK	Myosin Light Chain Kinase [*An enzyme*]
MLCM	Molder, Master Chief [*Navy rating*]
MLCN	Multilocular Cystic Nephroma (DMAA)
MLCNY	Medical Library Center of New York [*Information service or system*] (IID)
MLCO	Member of the London College of Osteopathy [*British*] (DI)
MLCOM	Member of the London College of Osteopathic Medicine [*British*] (DBQ)
MLCox99n	Merrill Lynch & Co. [*Associated Press*] (SAG)
MLCP	Machine Level Control Program (VLIE)
MLCP	Mobile Land Command Post (AABC)
MLCP	Multilayer Ceramic Package [*Electronics*]
MLCP	Multiline Communications Processor
MLCP	Myosin Light-Chain Phosphatase (DB)
MLCPX	Merrill Lynch: Capital Fund Cl.A [*Mutual fund ticker symbol*] (SG)
MLCR	Medical Laboratories Army Chemical Center [*Maryland*]
MLCR	Medical Laboratory Contract Reports [*Army*] (MCD)
MLCR	Mixed Lymphocyte Culture Reaction [*Hematology*] (AAMN)
MLCRO	Ministry of Labour Claims and Records Office (SAUO)
MLCS	Molder, Senior Chief [*Navy rating*]
MLCS	Multilayer Ceramic Substrates [*Electronic circuit boards*]
MLCSP	Multi-Level Continuous Sampling Plan (VLIE)
MLCT	Metal-to-Ligand Charge Transfer [*Physical chemistry*]
MLCU	Magnetic Ledger Card Unit [*Computer science*] (MHDB)
MLCU	Mill Cutter [*Tool*]
MLCur	Merrill Lynch & Co. [*Associated Press*] (SAG)
MLD	Air Moldova [*ICAO designator*] (FAAC)
MLD	Legislative Reference Library - Minnesota Document Collection, St. Paul, MN [*OCLC symbol*] (OCLC)
MLD	Machine Language Debugger [*National Computer Sharing Service*]
MLD	Main Line of Defense
MLD	MAJCOM Level Data (SAUO)
MLD	Malad City, ID [*Location identifier*] [*FAA*] (FAAL)
MLD	Malden [*Missouri*] [*Seismograph station code, US Geological Survey*] [*Closed*] (SEIS)
MLD	Marginally Learning Disabled
MLD	Masking Level Difference [*Hearing*]
MLD	Master Layout Duplicate (MSA)
MLD	Master of Landscape Design
MLD	Maximum Lateral Damage (PDAA)
MLD	Maximum Likelihood Detection (MCD)
MLD	Mean Level Detector (ACAE)
MLD	Mean Low-Water Datum [*Nuclear energy*] (NRCH)
MLD	Medial Lethal Dose [*Genetics*] (DOG)
MLD	Median Lethal Dose [*Also, LD_{50}*] [*Lethal for 50%*] [*Medicine*]
MLD	Mesencephalicus Lateralis Dorsalis (DB)
MLD	Metachromatic Leukodystrophy [*Medicine*]
MLD	Middle Landing
MLD	Midland [*AAR code*]
MLD	Mild (WGA)
MLD	Military Liaison Department (SAUO)
MLD	Minimal Lesion Disease
MLD	Minimum Lethal Dose
MLD	Minimum Line of Detection [*Air Force*]
MLD	Missile Launch Detector (MCD)
MLD	Mixed Layer Depth (MCD)
MLD	Mixed Liaison Detachment (SAUO)
MLD	Moderate Learning Difficulties (AIE)
mld	Mold (VRA)
MLD	Molded (KSC)
MLD	Molding [*Technical drawings*]

MLD............ Mouvement pour la Liberation de Djibouti [*Movement for the Liberation of Djibouti*] (PD)
MLD............ Ocean Mixed Layer Depth (SAUS)
MLDAS........ Meteorological and Lighting Data Acquisition System [*NASA*] (KSC)
MLDB.......... Regional Library, Lac Du Bonnet, Manitoba [*Library symbol*] [*National Library of Canada*] (NLC)
MLDC.......... Miner's Legal Defense Committee [*Defunct*] (EA)
MLDD.......... Moderately Lightly Doped Drains (NITA)
MLDD.......... Mooring Leg Deployment Device (PDAA)
ML Des........ Master of Landscape Design
MLDG.......... Molding (KSC)
MLDI........... Meter List Display Interval [*FAA*] (TAG)
ML Dig & R... Monthly Law Digest and Reporter [*Canada*] [*A publication*] (DLA)
ML Direct...... ML Direct, Inc. [*Associated Press*] (SAG)
MLDL........... Mooring Line Data Line [*Environmental buoy cable*]
MLDLP......... Mailing Label and Directory Lookup Package (PDAA)
MLDNG........ Moulding
MLDR.......... ML Direct, Inc. [*NASDAQ symbol*] (SAG)
MLDR.......... Molder (ADA)
MLDS.......... Motor Launch, Double Shelter
MLD/S......... Multi-Legend Display Switch (MCD)
MLDT........... Mean Logistic Delay Time [*Military*] (CAAL)
MLDT........... Mean Logistic Down Time
MLDU.......... Marriage Law Defence Union [*British*]
MLE............ Magazine Lee-Enfield [*British military*] (DMA)
MLE............ Male [*Maldives*] [*Airport symbol*] (OAG)
MLE............ Manned Lunar Exploration [*NASA*] (AAG)
MLE............ Mariner-Like Elements [*Genetics*]
MLE............ Martin Lawrence Limited Editions [*NYSE symbol*] (SAG)
MLE............ Maryland Law Encyclopedia [*A publication*] (DLA)
MLE............ Master of Applied Linguistics and Exegesis (PGP)
MLE............ Master of Land Economy
MLE............ Maximum Likelihood Estimate [*or Estimator*] [*Statistics*]
MLE............ Maximum Loss Expectancy [*Insurance*]
MLE............ Medium Local Exchange [*Telecommunications*] (TEL)
MLE............ Merrill Lynch Economics (NITA)
MLE............ Mesoscale Lightning Experiment (ACAE)
MLE............ Meta-Language Extension (VLIE)
MLE............ Microprocessor Language Editor [*Computer science*]
MLE............ Mid-Latitude Ecosystem (SAUO)
MLE............ Midline Episiotomy [*Obstetrics*] (DAVI)
MLE............ Mile
MLE............ Mileto [*Italy*] [*Seismograph station code, US Geological Survey*] [*Closed*] (SEIS)
MLE............ Millenium Language Extension (SAUS)
MLE............ Missile Launch Envelope
MLE............ Mobile Launcher Equipment [*NASA*] (SAA)
MLE............ Module Resources, Inc. [*Vancouver Stock Exchange symbol*]
MLE............ Molecular Layer Epitaxy [*Coating technology*]
MLE............ Muconate Lactonizing Enzyme
MLE............ Multi-Line Editor (SAUS)
MLE............ Myocardial Lactate Extraction [*Clinical chemistry*]
MLE............ Omaha, NE [*Location identifier*] [*FAA*] (FAAL)
MLEA.......... Metal Lath Export Association (SAUO)
MLEA.......... Multiple-Line Exclusive Agent [*Insurance*]
M'Lean's R... McLean's United States Circuit Court Reports [*A publication*] (DLA)
MLED.......... Maximum Likelihood Estimator Deconvolution [*Statistics*]
MLegS........ Master of Legal Studies
MLEL.......... Malignant Lymphoepithelial Lesion [*Medicine*] (DMAA)
MLEM......... Multi-Language Environment (VLIE)
MLenB........ Berkshire Christian College, Lenox, MA [*Library symbol*] [*Library of Congress*] (LCLS)
ML Eng........ Master of Landscape Engineering
MLeo........... Leominster Public Library, Leominster, MA [*Library symbol*] [*Library of Congress*] (LCLS)
MLeoHi........ Leominster Historical Society, Inc., Leominster, MA [*Library symbol*] [*Library of Congress*] (LCLS)
MLEP.......... Manned Lunar Exploration Program [*NASA*] (KSC)
MLEP.......... Minority Legislative Education Program
MLEP.......... Multipurpose Long Endurance Plane
MLES.......... Multiple-Line Encryption System (AABC)
MLEV.......... Manned Lifting Entry Vehicle (MCD)
MLex........... Cary Memorial Library, Lexington, MA [*Library symbol*] [*Library of Congress*] (LCLS)
MLexHi........ Lexington Historical Society, Lexington, MA [*Library symbol*] [*Library of Congress*] (LCLS)
MLexK......... Kennecott Copper Corp., Ledgemont Laboratory, Lexington, MA [*Library symbol*] [*Library of Congress*] (LCLS)
MLexM........ Museum of Our National Heritage, Lexington, MA [*Library symbol*] [*Library of Congress*] (LCLS)
MLexSC....... Scottish Rite of Freemasonry, Northern Jurisdiction USA, Supreme Council Library, Lexington, MA [*Library symbol*] [*Library of Congress*] (LCLS)
MLF............. Fast Motor Launches (NATG)
MLF............. Maintenance Level Function
MLF............. Male Liberation Foundation (EA)
MLF............. Malolactic Fermentation
MLF............. Maple Leaf Foods [*Toronto Stock Exchange symbol*] (SPSG)
MLF............. Maximum Load Factor
MLF............. MDM [*Manipulator Deployment Mechanism*] Launch Forward [*NASA*]
MLF............. Media Language and Format (CET)
MLF............. Medial Longitudinal Fasciculus [*Medicine*]
MLF............. Medical Liberation Front (EA)
M/LF........... Medium/Low Frequency (NATG)
MLF............. Micro Louver Film [*Adhesives*]

MLF............. Milford [*Ohio*] [*Seismograph station code, US Geological Survey*] (SEIS)
MLF............. Milford, UT [*Location identifier*] [*FAA*] (FAAL)
MLF............. Mobile Land Force
MLF............. Mobile Launcher Facility [*NASA*] (KSC)
MLF............. Modelling Language and Formalism (VLIE)
MLF............. MOL [*Manned Orbiting Laboratory*] Launch Facilities (MCD)
MLF............. Morphine-Like Factor [*Medicine*] (DB)
MLF............. Motor Launch, Fast [*NATO*]
MLF............. Multilaminar Film (SAUS)
MLF............. Multi-Lateral Fleet (SAUO)
MLF............. Multilateral Force [*NATO*]
MLFA.......... Fireman Apprentice, Molder, Striker [*Navy rating*]
MLFA.......... Machine-Learned Fragment Analysis (AGLO)
MLFA.......... Maine Lobster Fishermen's Association (EA)
MLFA.......... Merrill Lynch Financial Advantage
MLFAT........ MOL [*Manned Orbiting Laboratory*] Launch Facilities Acceptance Team (MCD)
MLFB.......... MLF Bancorp [*NASDAQ symbol*] (TTSB)
MLFB.......... MLF Bancorp, Inc. [*NASDAQ symbol*] (SAG)
MLF Bc....... MLF Bancorp, Inc. [*Associated Press*] (SAG)
MLFC.......... Michele Lee Fan Club (EA)
MLFC.......... Michigan Library Film Circuit [*Library network*]
MLFC.......... Mike Lunsford Fan Club (EA)
MLFC.......... Moses Lake Flight Center [*Washington*] (SAA)
MLFN.......... Fireman, Molder, Striker [*Navy rating*]
MLFN.......... Malfunction (VLIE)
MLFS.......... Magic Lantern Film Society [*An association*]
MLFS.......... Master Library File System (VLIE)
MLFS.......... Modular Lightweight FLIR System (SAUS)
MLFX.......... Mill Fixture [*Tool*]
MLG........... Mailing
MLG........... Main Landing Gear [*Aerospace*] (NAKS)
MLG........... Malang [*Indonesia*] [*Airport symbol*] (OAG)
mlg............ malignant (SAUS)
MLG........... Metalgesellschaft Canada Investment [*Toronto Stock Exchange symbol*]
MLG........... Middle Low German [*Language, etc.*]
MLG........... Milling [*Freight*]
MLG........... Mission Liaison Group [*Military*]
MLG........... Mitochondria Lipid Glucogen [*Cytology*] (AAMN)
MLG........... Moulage
MLG........... Multiple Line Group [*Radiation*]
MLG........... Musicland Stores [*NYSE symbol*] (SAG)
MLGCV....... Movement for the Liberation of Portuguese Guinea and the Cape Verde Islands
MLGN......... Minimal Lesion Glomerulonephritis [*Medicine*] (DMAA)
MLGP.......... Movimento de Libertacao da Guine Portuguesa [*Movement for the Liberation of Portuguese Guinea*]
MLGS.......... Microwave Landing Guidance System [*FAA*]
MLGSCA..... Medical Library Group of Southern California and Arizona (SAUO)
MLGT98...... Merrill Lynch & Co., Inc. [*Associated Press*] (SAG)
MLGW........ Maximum Landing Gross Weight
ML-H.......... Malignant Lymphoma, Histiocytic [*Medicine*] (DB)
MLH........... Mauna Loa [*Hawaii*] [*Seismograph station code, US Geological Survey*] (SEIS)
MLH........... Medium Lift Helicopter (MCD)
MLH........... Merlin Resources Ltd. [*Vancouver Stock Exchange symbol*]
MLH........... Minimum List Heading [*Standard Industrial Classification*] (PDAA)
MLH........... Mulhouse/Basel [*France*] [*Airport symbol*] (OAG)
MLHA.......... Master Ladies Hairdressers Association (SAUO)
MLHCP........ Mean Lower Hemispherical Candlepower (IAA)
MLHGR....... Maximum Linear Heat Generation Ratio (NRCH)
MLHIX........ Merrill Lynch: Corp. Bond: Hi Inc. CL.A [*Mutual fund ticker symbol*] (SG)
MLHK......... Merrill Lynch & Co. [*Associated Press*] (SAG)
MLHR......... Master of Labor and Human Resources (PGP)
MLHR......... Miller (Herman) [*NASDAQ symbol*] (TTSB)
MLHR......... Miller [*Herman*], Inc. [*NASDAQ symbol*] (NQ)
MLHW........ Mean Lower High Water [*Tides and currents*]
MLHYX....... Merrill Lynch: Muni Bond National Cl.A [*Mutual fund ticker symbol*] (SG)
MLHZO....... Move Low-to-High Zone (VLIE)
MLI............. Machine Language Instruction
MLI............. Magnetic Level Indicator
MLI............. Maislin Industries Ltd. [*Toronto Stock Exchange symbol*]
MLI............. Malad Range [*Idaho*] [*Seismograph station code, US Geological Survey*] (SEIS)
MLI............. Mali [*ANSI three-letter standard code*] (CNC)
MLI............. Maltese Light Infantry [*British military*] (DMA)
MLI............. Marine Light Infantry [*Navy*] [*British*] (ROG)
MLI............. Marker Light Indicator
MLI............. Master Listing Index
MLI............. Master of Literary Interpretation
MLI............. Mean Linear Intercept
MLI............. Measurement Layer Interface (SAUS)
MLI............. Mesiolinguoincisal [*Dentistry*]
MLI............. Message Level Interface (NITA)
MLI............. Mid-Life Improvement (SAUS)
MLI............. Minimum Line of Interception [*Air Force*]
MLI............. Mixed Lymphocyte Interaction [*Immunology*]
MLI............. Moline, IL [*Location identifier*] [*FAA*] (FAAL)
MLI............. Mollie Gibson Mines [*Vancouver Stock Exchange symbol*]
MLI............. Mueller Industries [*NYSE symbol*] (SPSG)
MLI............. Muller Industries [*NYSE symbol*] (SAG)

MLI .... Multilayer Insulation
MLI .... Multi-Leaving Interface [*Computer science*] (VLIE)
MLI .... Multiple Link Interface [*Computer science*]
MLI .... Munitions List Item (MCD)
MLIA .... Multiplex Loop Interface Adapter
MLib .... Master of Librarianship
M Libr .... Master of Librarianship (PGP)
M Lib Sc ..... Master of Library Science (BARN)
MLibSci ...... Master of Library Science (NADA)
MLIC .... Manhattan Life Insurance [*NASDAQ symbol*] (TTSB)
MLIC .... Manhattan Life Insurance Co. [*NASDAQ symbol*] (SAG)
MLID .... Multiple Link Interface Drive [*Telecommunications*] (PCM)
MLID .... Multiple Link Interface Driver [*Telecommunications*] (ACRL)
MLIFC .... Mark Lindsay International Fan Club [*Defunct*] (EA)
MLIFC .... Michelle Lynn International Fan Club (EA)
MLIGL01 ..... Merrill Lynch & Co. [*Associated Press*] (SAG)
MLIM .... Matrix Log-In Memory
MLIN .... Micro Linear [*NASDAQ symbol*] (TTSB)
MLIN .... Micro Linear Corp. [*NASDAQ symbol*] (SAG)
MLing .... Master of Languages [*British*] (DBQ)
MLIP .... Message Level Interface Port (NITA)
MLIR .... Master of Labor and Industrial Relations (GAGS)
MLIRB .... Multi-Line Insurance Rating Bureau [*Later, ISO*]
MLIS .... Master of Library and Information Science
MLIS .... Measurement Laboratory Information Service [*Battelle Memorial Institute*]
MLIS .... Metal-Liquid-Insulator Semiconductor [*Electronics*] (PDAA)
MLIS .... Micropolis Corp. [*NASDAQ symbol*] (NQ)
MLIS .... Molecular LASER Isotope Separation
MLIS .... Multilingual Information Society (SAUO)
MLIS .... Multiple Level Indexing Scheme [*Computer science*]
MLISP .... Meta LISP [*List Processor*] [*Programming language*] [*Computer science*] (CSR)
M Lit .... Master of Letters
M Lit .... Master of Literature
MLitl .... Inforonics Inc., Littleton, MA [*Library symbol*] [*Library of Congress*] (LCLS)
MLitM .... Master of Liturgical Music (GAGS)
MLitSt .... Master of Literary Studies (ADA)
M Litt .... Master of Letters
MLitt .... Master of Literature
ML IV .... Mucolipidosis IV [*A genetic disease*]
MLJ .... Memphis Law Journal [*A publication*] (DLA)
MLJ .... Milledgeville, GA [*Location identifier*] [*FAA*] (FAAL)
MLJ .... Modern Language Journal [*A publication*] (BRI)
MLK .... Malta, MT [*Location identifier*] [*FAA*] (FAAL)
MLK .... Martin Luther King, Jr.
MLK .... Matlack Systems [*NYSE symbol*] (TTSB)
MLK .... Matlack Systems, Inc. [*NYSE symbol*] (CTT)
MLK .... Milford [*Kansas*] [*Seismograph station code, US Geological Survey*] (SEIS)
MLKCNSC ... Martin Luther King, Jr., Center for Nonviolent Social Change (EA)
MLKCSC ..... Martin Luther King, Jr., Center for Social Change [*Later, MLKCNSC*] (EA)
MLKIII .... Martin Luther King III
MLL .... Manchester Lines Ltd. (SAUO)
MLL .... Mandella Resources Ltd. [*Vancouver Stock Exchange symbol*]
MLL .... Manned Lunar Landing [*NASA*]
MLL .... Marshall [*Alaska*] [*Airport symbol*] (OAG)
MLL .... Marshall, AK [*Location identifier*] [*FAA*] (FAAL)
MLL .... Master Lines Layout (MSA)
MLL .... Master of Latin Literature
MLL .... Master of Law Librarianship (ILCA)
MLL .... Maynard Listener Library [*Defunct*] (EA)
MLL .... MDM [*Manipulator Deployment Mechanism*] Launch Left [*NASA*]
MLL .... Mean Lesion Length [*Pathology*]
MLL .... Middle Lobe of Lung (MELL)
mL/L .... Milliliters per Liter (EEVL)
ML/L .... Milliliters per Liter (EG)
MLL .... Minimum Level of Living (SAUO)
MLL .... Mistress of Liberal Learning
MLL .... Mixed Lineage Leukemia [*Medicine*] (DMAA)
MLL .... Modify Lot Location (AAEL)
MLL .... Music Lovers League (NADA)
MLL .... University of Minnesota, Law Library, Minneapolis, MN [*OCLC symbol*] (OCLC)
MLLA .... Mineral Lands Leasing Act of 1920 (COE)
MLLAA .... Modern Language Association of America (NADA)
ML/LB .... Malignant Lymphoma/Lymphoblastic [*Oncology*]
MLLDI .... Multi-Level Laser Designator Illuminator (ACAE)
MLLE .... Mademoiselle (ACAE)
MLLE .... Mademoiselle [*Miss*] [*French*] (EY)
Mlle .... Mademoiselle [*Miss*] [*French*] (WA)
MLLE .... Medium Large Local Exchange [*Telecommunications*] (TEL)
Mlles .... Mesdemoiselles [*Misses*] [*French*]
MLLFT .... Modified Lensless Fourier Transform (PDAA)
ML Libr .... Master of Law Librarianship
MLLM .... Microminiature Low Level Multicoders (ACAE)
MLLP .... Manned Lunar Landing Program [*NASA*]
ML/LPC .... Malignant Lymphoma/Lymphoplasmacytoid [*Oncology*]
MLLV .... Medium-Lift Launch Vehicle (SAUS)
MLLW .... Mean Lower Low Water [*Tides and currents*]
MLLW .... Medium Level Liquid Waste [*Nuclear energy*] (NUCP)
MLLW .... Mixed Low-Level Waste (GAAI)
MLLWK .... Millwork

MLLWL .... Mean Lower Low Water Line [*Tides and currents*] (PDAA)
MLLWS .... Mean Lower Low-Water Springs [*Tides and currents*]
MLM .... Magazine Lee-Metford [*British military*] (DMA)
MLM .... Mailing-List Manager [*Type of database*]
MLM .... Martin Marietta Materials [*NYSE symbol*] (SAG)
MLM .... Massive Liver Metastasis [*Oncology*]
MLM .... Master of Landscape Management
MLM .... Master of Library Media (PGP)
MLM .... Maximum Likelihood Method [*Statistics*]
MLM .... Membrane Light Modulator (PDAA)
MLM .... Mesa Lucera [*New Mexico*] [*Seismograph station code, US Geological Survey*] (SEIS)
MLM .... Metall Mining Corp. [*Toronto Stock Exchange symbol*]
MLM .... Microbial Load Monitor (MCD)
MLM .... Middle Limiting Membrane (SAUS)
MLM .... Military Liaison Mission [*Germany*]
MLM .... Minesweeper, River [*Navy symbol*] (VNW)
MLM .... Mixed Level Matrix
MLM .... Modern Labelling Methods Ltd. (SAUO)
MLM .... Moody Literature Ministries (EA)
MLM .... Morelia [*Mexico*] [*Airport symbol*] (OAG)
MLM .... Mound Laboratory, Miamisburg [*AEC*] (MCD)
MLM .... Multilayer Metalization (IEEE)
MLM .... Multilevel Marketing
MLM .... Multilevel Metal (AAEL)
MLM .... Multi-Longitudinal Mode (ACRL)
MLM .... Multipurpose Lightweight Missile
MLM .... Multnomah Literature Ministries [*Publisher*] [*Portland, OR*]
MLM .... Muslim League of Malaya, Kuala Lumpur (SAUO)
MLMA .... Metal Ladder Manufacturers Association
MLMA .... Metal Lath Manufacturers Association [*Later, ML/SFA*]
MLMA .... Miners' Lamp Manufacturers' Association [*British*] (BI)
MLMA .... Moss Litter Manufacturers Association (SAUO)
MLMA .... Multilevel Multiaccess
MLMBX .... Merrill Lynch: Muni Bond: Insured Cl.A [*Mutual fund ticker symbol*] (SG)
MLMGIC98.. Merrill Lynch & Co. [*Associated Press*] (SAG)
MLMI .... Microleague Multimedia [*NASDAQ symbol*] (TTSB)
MLMI .... Microleague Multimedia, Inc. [*NASDAQ symbol*] (SAG)
MLMIA .... Multi-Level Marketing International Association [*Irvine, CA*] (EA)
MLMIC .... Minnesota Land Management Information Center (SAUO)
ml/min/m² ... Milliliters per Minute per Square Meter (CPH)
MLMIS .... Minnesota Land Management Information System (SAUO)
MLMIW .... Microleague Multimedia Wrrt [*NASDAQ symbol*] (TTSB)
MLML .... Moss Landing Marine Laboratories [*San Jose State University*] [*Research center*] (RCD)
MLMR .... Multi-Level Message Release (SAUS)
MLMS .... Member of the London Mathematical Society
MLMS .... Multipurpose Lightweight Missile System
MLMTT .... Marxism-Leninism-Mao Tse-Tung Thought [*Ideologies guiding the New People's Army, a guerrilla movement in the Philippines*]
MLN .... Management List - Navy (NVT)
MLN .... Mediastinal Lymph Node [*Medicine*] (MELL)
MLN .... Melilla [*Spain*] [*Airport symbol*] (OAG)
MLN .... Membranous Lupus Nephropathy [*Medicine*] (MELL)
MLN .... Mesenteric Lymph Node [*Medicine*] (STED)
MLN .... Message Ledger Number (SAUO)
MLN .... Metropolitan Library Network [*Library network*]
MLN .... Mid-Lateral Nerve
MLN .... Milan Resources & Development [*Vancouver Stock Exchange symbol*]
MLN .... Minuteman Library Network [*Information service or system*] (IT)
MLN .... MLN (Modern Language Notes) [*A publication*] (BRI)
MLN .... Mobile Large Node (SAUS)
MLN .... Mouvement de Liberation Nationale [*National Liberation Movement*] [*Burkina Faso*] [*Banned, 1974*] [*Political party*]
MLN .... Movimiento de Liberacion Nacional [*National Liberation Movement*] [*Guatemala*] [*Political party*] (PPW)
MLN .... Movimiento de Liberacion Nacional [*National Liberation Movement*] [*Uruguay*] [*Political party*]
MLN .... Multiple Length Number
MLN .... Mulungwishi [*Zaire*] [*Seismograph station code, US Geological Survey*] (SEIS)
MLN .... Museum Loan Network
MLNAC .... Mesa Laboratory Network Access Completion (SAUO)
MLNC .... Missouri Library Network Corp. [*Information service or system*] (IID)
MInd .... Maximum Landing Weight [*Aviation*] (DA)
MLNG .... Melange
MLNik 97 .... Merrill Lynch & Co. [*Associated Press*] (SAG)
MLNIS .... Modified Atlantic Naval Intelligence Summary (MCD)
MLNM .... Millennium Pharmaceuticals [*NASDAQ symbol*] (TTSB)
MLNM .... Millennium Pharmaceuticals, Inc. [*NASDAQ symbol*] (SAG)
MLNP .... Malawi Lengwe National Park (SAUO)
MLNR .... Milliner (WGA)
MLNR .... Ministry of Land and Natural Resources (SAUO)
mLNRc........ Mouse Lymph Node Homing Receptor
MLNS .... Ministry of Labour and National Service [*British*] [*World War II*]
MLNS .... Mucocutaneous Lymph Node Syndrome [*Medicine*] (STED)
MLNSC .... Manual Lujan Jr. Neutron Scattering Center (SAUO)
MLNWR .... Medicine Lake National Wildlife Refuge (SAUO)
MLNYX .... Merrill Lynch: N.Y. Muni Bond Cl.B [*Mutual fund ticker symbol*] (SG)
MLO .... Main Lube Oil [*System*] (NRCH)
MLO .... Manipulative Learning Operation [*in laboratory work*]
MLO .... Manned Lunar Orbiter [*NASA*]

MLO	Marxisten-Leninisten Oesterreichs [*Marxists-Leninists of Austria*] [*Political party*] (PPE)
MLO	Master Layout Original (MSA)
MLO	Mauna Loa Observatory [*Hawaii*] [*National Weather Service*]
MLO	Mechanized Letter Office (DCTA)
MLO	Media Liaison Officer
MLO	Medio-Lateral Oblique [*Medicine*] (AMHC)
MLO	Mesiolinguo-Occlusal [*Dentistry*]
MLO	Midland Light Orchestra (SAUO)
MLO	Military Landing Officer
MLO	Milos [*Greece*] [*Airport symbol*] (OAG)
MLO	Mine-Like Objects (SAUS)
MLO	Missile Launch Officer (AAG)
MLO	Missile Lift-Off (AAG)
MLO	M. L. Cass Petroleum [*Vancouver Stock Exchange symbol*]
MLO	Mortgage Loan Officer [*Banking*] (TBD)
MLO	Movement Liaison Officer (NATG)
MLO	Mycoplasma-Like Organisms [*Microbiology*]
MLOC	Million Lines of Code (ACAE)
MLOG	Microlog Corp. [*NASDAQ symbol*] (NQ)
MLOI	Master List of Outstanding Items [*Military*] (DNAB)
MLon	Richard Salter Storrs Library, Longmeadow, MA [*Library symbol*] [*Library of Congress*] (LCLS)
MLonHi	Longmeadow Historical Society, Longmeadow, MA [*Library symbol*] [*Library of Congress*] (LCLS)
MLOPEX	Mauna Loa Observatory Photochemical Experiment (SAUO)
MLOPEX	Mauna Loa Observatory Photochemistry Experiment (SAUO)
MLOPEX II	Mauna Loa Observatory Photochemical Experiment II (SAUO)
MLOR	Maintenance/Logistics Observer Report
MLow	Lowell City Library, Lowell, MA [*Library symbol*] [*Library of Congress*] (LCLS)
MLowT	Lowell Technological Institute, Lowell, MA [*Library symbol*] [*Library of Congress*] [*Obsolete*] (LCLS)
MLowTC	Lowell State College, Lowell, MA [*Library symbol*] [*Library of Congress*] [*Obsolete*] (LCLS)
MLowU	University of Lowell, Lowell, MA [*Library symbol*] [*Library of Congress*] (LCLS)
MLowU-N	University of Lowell - North Campus, Alumni/Lydon Memorial Library, Lowell, MA [*Library symbol*] [*Library of Congress*] (LCLS)
MLP	Machine Language Program [*Computer science*]
MLP	Major Late Promoter [*Genetics*]
MLP	Major Late Promotor [*Biochemistry*]
MLP	Malabang [*Philippines*] [*Airport symbol*] (OAG)
MLP	Malaspina [*Alaska*] [*Seismograph station code, US Geological Survey*] (SEIS)
MLP	Malfunction-Linked People
MLP	Malta Labor Party [*Political party*] (PPW)
MLP	Master Limited Partnership
MLP	Master Logistics Plan (AABC)
MLP	Maui Land & Pineapple [*AMEX symbol*] (SG)
MLP	Mauritius Labor Party [*Political party*] (PPW)
MLP	Maximum Likelihood Program
MLP	Mentoleva Posterior [*A fetal position*] [*Obstetrics*]
MLP	Mesa Limited Partnership (EFIS)
MLP	Mesiolinguopulpal [*Dentistry*]
MLP	Message Link Protocol (SAUO)
MLP	Metal Lath and Plaster [*Technical drawings*]
MLP	Michigan Law and Practice [*A publication*] (DLA)
MLP	Microsomal Lipoprotein [*Immunochemistry*]
MLP	Millipore Corp., Bedford, MA [*OCLC symbol*] (OCLC)
MLP	Minimum Latency Programming
MLP	Mirror Landing Procedures (MCD)
MLP	Mobile Launcher Platform [*NASA*] (NASA)
MLP	Modified Longest Path
MLP	Monitored Line Program (SPST)
MLP	Mortgage Loan Partnership [*Investment term*]
MLP	Movimiento de Liberacion del Pueblo [*People's Liberation Movement*] [*El Salvador*] [*Political party*] (PD)
MLP	Movimiento de Liberacion Proletaria [*Proletarian Liberation Movement*] [*Mexico*] [*Political party*]
MLP	Mullan Pass, ID [*Location identifier*] [*FAA*] (FAAL)
MLP	Multi-Layered Packaging (PDAA)
MLP	Multilayer Link Protocol (SAUS)
MLP	Multi-Layer Perceptron (AAEL)
MLP	Multilevel Precedence
MLP	Multilevel Procedure (MCD)
MLP	Multilevel Programmer
MLP	Multilink Point-to-Point protocol (SAUS)
MLP	Multilink Procedure [*Computer science*] (TNIG)
MLP	Multilink Protocol [*Telecommunications*] (ACRL)
MLP	Multiple Layer Perceptron (IDAI)
MLP	Multiple Line Printing (CMD)
MLP	Multi-Step Products [*Toronto Stock Exchange symbol*]
MLPA	Modified Link Pack Area (MCD)
MLPC	Management-Labor Policy Committee
MLPC	Mouvement de Liberation du Peuple Centrafricain [*Movement for the Liberation of the Central African People*] (PD)
MLPC	Multilayer Printed Circuit
MLPCB	Machine Language Printed Circuit Boards [*Computer science*] (IEEE)
MLPD	Maximum Likelihood Predictive Density [*Statistics*]
ML-PDL	Malignant Lymphoma, Poorly Differentiated Lymphocytic [*Medicine*] (STED)
MLPED	Mobile Launcher Pedestal [*NASA*] (NASA)
MLPF	Miniature Low Pass Filter
MLPFS	Merrill Lynch, Pierce, Fenner & Smith [*of Merrill Lynch & Co., Inc.*] [*Stockbrokers*] [*Wall Street slang name: "Thundering Herd"*]
MLPI	Maximum Likelihood Parameter Identification (ACAE)
MLPN	Maintenance Planning (SAUS)
MLPNPP	Mobile Low-Power Nuclear Power Plant
MLPP	Multilevel Precedence and Preemption [*Telecommunications*] (TEL)
ML-PPP	Multilink Point-to-Point Protocol [*Telecommunications*] (ACRL)
MLPRF	Modular Low Power Radio Frequency (SAUS)
MLPS	Manchester Literary and Philosophical Society (SAUO)
MLPS	Multilingual Publishing Software
MLPS	Multilink Processing System (SAUS)
MLPS	Myxoid Liposarcoma [*Genetics*]
MLP USA	Marxist-Leninist Party of the United States of America (SAUO)
MLP USA	Marxist-Leninist Party of the USA (EA)
MLPWB	Multilayer Printed-Wiring Board (IEEE)
MLQ	Malabar Law Quarterly [*A publication*] (DLA)
MLQ	Malalaua [*Papua New Guinea*] [*Airport symbol*] (OAG)
MLQ	Modern Language Quarterly [*A publication*] (ANEX)
MLR	Leaf Rapids Public Library, Manitoba [*Library symbol*] [*National Library of Canada*] (NLC)
MLR	Machine Location Report (VLIE)
MLR	Magnetic Latching Relay (MCD)
MLR	Mailer
MLR	Main Line of Resistance
M/LR	Maintenance Loop Recorder (MCD)
MLR	Malayan Law Reports [*1950-54*] [*A publication*] (DLA)
MLR	Manitoba Law Reports [*Canada*] [*A publication*] (DLA)
MLR	Marginal Lending Rate [*Finance*]
MLR	Marine Life Resources [*Program*]
MLR	Maryland Law Record [*A publication*] (DLA)
MLR	Master-Locating RADAR (AABC)
MLR	Matched Logistic Regression [*Statistics*]
MLR	Mauritius Law Reporter [*A publication*] (DLA)
MLR	Maximum Logical Records [*Computer science*] (VLIE)
MLR	MDM [*Manipulator Deployment Mechanism*] Launch Right [*NASA*]
MLR	Mean Length Response (DMAA)
MLR	Mean Lethal Radius
MLR	Mechanized Line Records [*Later, LMOS*] [*Bell System*]
MLR	Medium Lift Replacement programme (SAUS)
MLR	Medium-Lift Requirement [*Helicopter/VSTOL*] [*Marine Corps*] (DOMA)
MLR	Memory Lockout Register [*Computer science*]
MLR	Message Log Report (AAEL)
MLR	Meston Lake Resources, Inc. [*Toronto Stock Exchange symbol*] [*Vancouver Stock Exchange symbol*]
MLR	Middle Latency Response [*Medicine*]
MLR	Miller Industries [*NYSE symbol*] (TTSB)
MLR	Millersburg, OH [*Location identifier*] [*FAA*] (FAAL)
MLR	Minimum Latency Routine
MLR	Minimum Lending Rate
MLR	Minnesota Legislative Reference Library, St. Paul, MN [*OCLC symbol*] (OCLC)
MLR	Missile Launch Response [*Navy*] (CAAL)
MLR	Mixed Leukocyte Reaction [*Analytical biochemistry*]
MLR	Mixed Lymphocyte [*or Leukocyte*] Reaction [*or Response*] [*Immunology*]
MLR	Modern Language Review [*A publication*] (BRI)
MLR	Modular Laser Rangefinder (ACAE)
MLR	Monodisperse Latex Reactor
MLR	Monotone Likelihood Ratio [*Statistics*]
MLR	Monthly Letter Report
MLR	Montreal Law Reports [*A publication*] (DLA)
MLR	Mortar Locating RADAR (MCD)
MLR	Multichannel Linear Recording (VLIE)
MLR	Multi-Disperse Latex Reactor
MLR	Multilayer Resist [*Lithography*]
MLR	Multilevel Resist [*For microlithography*]
MLR	Multiple Linear Regression [*Mathematics*]
MLR	Multiple Linear Regression Analysis (SAUO)
MLR	Multiple Line Reading [*Computer science*] (ELAL)
MLR	Multiple Location Risk [*Insurance*]
MLR	Multiply and Round
MLR	Muntele Rosu [*Romania*] [*Seismograph station code, US Geological Survey*] (SEIS)
MLR	Muzzle-Loading Rifle
MLRA	Major Land Resource Area [*USDA topographic characterization*]
MLRA	Marriage Law Reform Association [*British*]
MLRA	Multivariate Linear Regression Analysis [*Advertising marketing*]
MLRB	Master Logistics Review Board (AAG)
MLRB	Mutual Loss Research Bureau [*Later, Property Loss Research Bureau*] (EA)
MLRC	Mallon Resources [*NASDAQ symbol*] (TTSB)
MLRC	Mallon Resources Corp. [*NASDAQ symbol*] (CTT)
MLRC	Master Logistics Review Committee
MLRC	Mickey Leland National Urban Air Toxics Research Center (COE)
MLRC	Minor League Research Committee (EA)
MLRC	Multilevel Rail Car
MLRCA	Mini Lop Rabbit Club of America (EA)
MLR CS	Montreal Law Reports, Superior Court [*Canada*] [*A publication*] (DLA)
MLRF	Mini Laser Range Finder (ACAE)
MLRG	Marine Life Research Group [*Scripps Institution of Oceanography*]
MLRG	Muzzle-Loading Rifled Gun
MLRHR	Master of Labor Relations and Human Resources (PGP)
MLRP	Marine Corps Long-Range Plans
MLRP	Marine Life Research Program

MLRP..........	Minuteman Long Range Plan [*Telecommunications*] (LAIN)
MLRQB........	Montreal Law Reports, Queen's Bench [*A publication*] (DLA)
MLRS..........	Manual Launch - RADAR Search
MLRS..........	McDonald Laser Ranging System [*For observations*]
MLRS..........	Monodisperse Latex Reactor System
MLRS..........	Multiple Launch Rocket System [*DoD*] (MCD)
MLRSC	Montreal Law Reports, Superior Court [*Canada*] [*A publication*] (DLA)
MLRS ER	Multiple Launch Rocket System Extended Range Rocket [*Military*]
MLRS FDS...	Mobile Launch Rocket System Fire Direction System (SAUO)
MLRS-PGM...	Multiple Launch Rocket System Precision Guided Munitions (RDA)
MLRS-TGW...	Multiple Launch Rocket System Terminally Guided Warhead
MLRTP.........	Multileaving Remote Terminal Processor [*Computer science*] (MHDI)
MLRus98	Merrill Lynch & Co. [*Associated Press*] (SAG)
MLRV..........	Manned Lunar Roving Vehicle [*NASA*] (PDAA)
MLRV..........	Myrobalan Latent Ringspot Virus [*Plant pathology*]
MLS............	Machine Literature Searching [*Computer science*] (DIT)
MLS............	Mac Library System [*Computer Advanced Software Products - CASPR*] [*Cupertino, CA*] [*Information service or system*] (IID)
MLS............	Macrolide/Lincosamide/Streptogramine (DB)
MLS............	Magnetically-Linked Solenoid (MCD)
MLS............	Maintenance Loading Sheet (MCD)
MLS............	Major League Soccer
MLS............	Mall Airways, Inc. [*ICAO designator*] (FAAC)
MLS............	Manistique & Lake Superior R. R. [*AAR code*]
MLS............	Manned Lunar Surface [*NASA*]
MLS............	Master Laboratory Station
MLS............	Master of Legal Studies (GAGS)
MLS............	Master of Liberal Studies (GAGS)
MLS............	Master of Librarianship
MLS............	Master of Library Science
MLS............	Master of Library Services (PGP)
MLS............	Master of Library Studies
MLS............	Master of Life Science (GAGS)
MLS............	Maximized LOD [*Logarithm of the Odds*] Score [*Statistics*]
MLS............	Maximum Life-Span
MLS............	Maxwell Library Systems [*Information service or system*] (IID)
MLS............	Mean Lifespan (AAMN)
MLS............	Mechanical Limit Stop
MLS............	Mechanical Limit Switch
MLS............	Median Life Span [*Oncology*] (DAVI)
MLS............	Median Longitudinal Section
MLS............	Medico-Legal Society (SAUO)
MLS............	Medium Life Span
MLS............	Medium Long Shot [*A photograph or motion picture sequence taken from a relatively great distance*]
MLS............	Member of the Linnean Society (SAUO)
MLS............	Metal Slitting
MLS............	Metropolitan Libraries Section [*Public Library Association*]
MLS............	Microprocessor Line Set (VLIE)
MLS............	Microwave Landing System [*Aviation*]
MLS............	Microwave Limb Sounder
MLS............	Microwave Line Stretcher
MLS............	Middle Lobe Syndrome [*Medicine*] (STED)
MLS............	Miles City [*Montana*] [*Airport symbol*] (OAG)
MLS............	Miles City, MT [*Location identifier*] [*FAA*] (FAAL)
MLS............	Military Labor Service
MLS............	Military Labour Service (SAUO)
MLS............	Military Sealift Command
ML/S...........	Milliliters per Second
MLS............	Mills (MCD)
MLS............	Mills Corp. [*NYSE symbol*] (SAG)
MLS............	Miniature Linguistic Systems
MLS............	Minimum Launch Speed [*British military*] (DMA)
MLS............	Minimum Legal Size [*Pisciculture*]
MLS............	Minor Lymphocyte Stimulating [*Genetics*]
MLS............	Missile-Launching System (NG)
MLS............	Missile Lift System (AAG)
MLS............	Missile Location System (IEEE)
MLS............	Mississippi County Library System, Blytheville, AR [*Inactive*] [*OCLC symbol*] (OCLC)
MLS............	Mixed Language System (PDAA)
MLS............	Mobile Library Service [*British*]
MLS............	Mobile Logistic Support (CINC)
MLS............	Modern Language Studies [*A publication*] (ANEX)
MLS............	MOL [*Manned Orbiting Laboratory*] Launch Site (MCD)
MLS............	Moulis [*France*] [*Seismograph station code, US Geological Survey*] (SEIS)
MLS............	Movement for the Liberation of the Sanwi (SAUO)
MLS............	Movimento per le Liberta Statuarie [*Movement for Statutory Liberty*] [*Sanmarinese*] (PPE)
MLS............	Movimiento de Liberacion Sebta [*Ceuta Liberation Movement*] [*Spain*] (PD)
MLS............	Multifrequency LASER Sounding (MCD)
MLS............	Multilanguage System [*Computer science*] (IEEE)
MLS............	Multilayered Structure [*Botany*]
MLS............	Multi-Layer Steel [*Engine gaskets*] [*Automotive engineering*]
MLS............	Multilevel Security (MCD)
MLS............	Multiline Selection [*Asahi Glass of Japan*]
MLS............	Multiparameter Light Scattering [*Physics*]
MLS............	Multiple Level Security (CCCA)
MLS............	Multiple Link Support (SAUO)
MLS............	Multiple Listing Service [*Real estate*]
MLS............	Music Learning System [*Trademark*]
MLS............	Myelomonocytic Leukemia, Subacute (MAE)
MLSA..........	Ministry of Labour Staff Association [*British*]
MLSA..........	Modified Launch Services Agreement (ACAE)
MLSAA........	Middle Level Student Activities Association
ML SAI99....	Merrill Lynch & Co. [*Associated Press*] (SAG)
MLSB..........	Major League Scouting Bureau [*Baseball*]
MLSB..........	Member of the London School Board
MLSB..........	Migrating Long Spike Burst (DMAA)
ML Sc	Master of Library Science
MLSC..........	Measured Logistics Support Cost (SAUS)
MLSC..........	Member of the London Society of Compositors
MLSC..........	Micronesian Legal Services Corp. (EA)
MLSC..........	Multiple Loop Sidelobe Canceller (CCCA)
MLS/CP.......	Microwave Landing System / Curved Path [*Aviation*]
MLS DDN....	Multi-Level Secure Defense Data Network (SAUO)
MLSE..........	Malformed Low-Set Ears (MELL)
MLSE..........	Maximum Likelihood Sequence Estimation (VLIE)
MLSE..........	Mechanical Launch Support Equipment [*NASA*] (KSC)
MLSF..........	Mobile Laboratory Storage Facility (SAUO)
MLSF..........	Mobile Logistic Support Forces (MCD)
ML/SFA.......	Metal Lath/Steel Framing Association Division of National Association of Architectural Metal Manufactureres (EA)
MLSG..........	Mobile Logistics Support Group (NVT)
MLSI..........	Mulitple Line Scan Imaging (DMAA)
MLSI..........	Multilevel Large-Scale Integration
MLSIS.........	Major License Silviculture Information System (SAUO)
MLSIT.........	Master of Library Science and International Technology (PGP)
MLSJ..........	Macquarie Law Students Journal [*A publication*]
MLSK..........	Master Lock, Skeleton Key
MLSO..........	Mauna Loa Solar Observatory (SAUO)
MLSO..........	Medical Laboratory Scientific Officer (SAUO)
MLSO..........	Mode-Locked Surface-Acoustic Wave Oscillator [*Telecommunications*] (TEL)
ML Society...	Magic Latern Society of the United States and Canada (EA)
MLSOP	Movement for the Liberation of Soa Tome and Principe [*Political party*]
MLSP..........	Master of Law and Social Policy (GAGS)
MLSP..........	Multiple-Link Satellite Program
MLSP97.......	Merrill Lynch & Co., Inc. [*Associated Press*] (SAG)
MLSP98.......	Merrill Lynch & Co., Inc. [*Associated Press*] (SAG)
M-L-S-R......	Missing, Lost, Stolen, or Recovered [*Government property*] (DNAB)
MLSR..........	Molder, Ship Repair [*Navy rating*]
MLSRC	Molder, Ship Repair, Cupola Tender [*Navy rating*]
MLSRF	Molder, Ship Repair, Foundryman [*Navy rating*]
MLSRM	Molder, Ship Repair, Molder [*Navy rating*]
MLSS..........	Mechanized Letter Sorting System [*Hong Kong Post Office*]
MLSS..........	Military and Federal Specifications and Standards [*Information Handling Services*] [*Information service or system*] (CRD)
MLSS..........	Mixed-Liquor Suspended Solid [*Water pollution*]
MLST..........	Medico-Legal Society of Tasmania [*Australia*]
MLST..........	Merrill Language Screening Test [*Educational test*]
MLST..........	Milstead [*AAR code*]
MLSTP........	Movimento de Libertacao de Sao Tome e Principe [*Movement for the Liberation of Sao Tome and Principe*] [*Portugal*] (PPW)
MLSU..........	Moscow Lomonosov State University (SAUO)
MLSU..........	Multiple Listening Station Unit (VLIE)
MLSW/SSNCC..	Ministry of Labour and Social Welfare/Social Services National Coordination Council (SAUO)
MLSW/SSNCC..	Molsw/Social Services National Coordination Council (SAUO)
MLSW/SWC...	Ministry of Labour and Social Welfare/Social Welfare Council (SAUO)
MLSW/SWC...	Molsw/Social Welfare Council (SAUS)
ML SYP98 ...	Merrill Lynch & Co. [*Associated Press*] (SAG)
MLT............	Madras Law Times [*India*] [*A publication*] (DLA)
MLT............	Magnetic Levitation Transportation
MLT............	Magnetic Local Time
MLT............	Malta [*ANSI three-letter standard code*] (CNC)
mlt............	Maltese [*MARC language code*] [*Library of Congress*] (LCCP)
MLT............	Manned Lunar Test [*NASA*] (KSC)
MLT............	Manufacturing Lead Time
MLT............	Mass Loaded Transducer
MLT............	Master Library Tape [*Computer science*]
MLT............	Master Lower Tester (SAUS)
MLT............	Master of Law and Taxation
MLT............	Maximum Lethal Time [*of radiation exposure*] (DEN)
MLT............	Mean Latency Time (DB)
MLT............	Mean Length per Turn
MLT............	Mean Level Tracker (ACAE)
MLT............	Mean Life Time (NATG)
MLT............	Mean Logistical Time (IEEE)
MLT............	Mean Low Tide [*Tides and currents*]
MLT............	Mechanized Line Testing [*Telecommunications*] (TEL)
MLT............	Mechanized Loop Testing (MCD)
MLT............	Median Lethal Time (DB)
MLT............	Medical Laboratory Technician [*or Technologist*]
MLT............	Medium Level Tripod [*British military*] (DMA)
MLT............	Melatonin
MLT............	Mentolaeva Transverse [*A fetal position*] [*Obstetrics*] (AAMN)
MLT............	Microlayer Transistor
MLT............	Millinocket, ME [*Location identifier*] [*FAA*] (FAAL)
MLT............	Misallat [*Egypt*] [*Geomagnetic observatory code*]
MLT............	Missile Loader Transport (SAUS)
MLT............	Mitel Corp. [*NYSE symbol*] [*Toronto Stock Exchange symbol*] (SPSG)
MLT............	Mixing-Length Theory [*Physics of convection*] [*Chemical engineering*]
MLT............	Mobile Laboratory Table

MLT .... Mobile Launch Tower
MLT .... Modulated Lapped Transform [*Telecommunications*]
MLT .... Monolithic Logic Technology (ELAL)
MLT .... Muexins-Length Theory
MLT .... Multi-Level Transition (SAUO)
MLT .... Multiple Logical Terminal (SAUS)
MLT .... Munitions Lift Trailer (SAUS)
MLTA .... Maine Land Title Association (SAUO)
MLTA .... Modern Languages Teachers Association (SAUO)
MLTA .... Multiple Line Terminal Adapter [*Computer science*] (BUR)
MLT-AD ...... Medical Laboratory Technology-Associate Degree
MLT (AMT)... Medical Laboratory Technician (American Medical Technologists) (DAVI)
MLT(ASCP)... Medical Laboratory Technician (American Society of Clinical Pathologists) (DMAA)
MLTC .... Mixed Lymphocyte-Tumor Culture [*Immunology*]
MltcPrt......... Multicanal Participacoes [*Associated Press*] (SAG)
ML Tech01... Merrill Lynch & Co. [*Associated Press*] (SAG)
MLTF .... Major Late Transcription·Factor [*Genetics*]
MLTF .... Military Law Task Force (EA)
MLTG .... Melting
MLTG .... Missile Launch Tube Group
MLTG .... Multi-Link Transmission Group (SAUO)
MLTI .... Mixed Lymphocyte Target Interaction (DMAA)
MLTI .... Mixed Lymphocyte-Tumor [*Cell*] Interaction [*Immunology*]
ML/TL .... Mucrones Length to Total Body Length Ratio [*Of Crustacea*]
MLTLVL....... Melting Level [*NWS*] (FAAC)
MltmdG........ Multimedia Games, Inc. [*Associated Press*] (SAG)
MLTMS........ Multileg Tanker Mooring System (MCD)
MLTN .... Molten Metal Technology [*NASDAQ symbol*] (TTSB)
MLTN .... Molten Metal Technology, Inc. [*NASDAQ symbol*] (SAG)
MLTP .... Ministers Leadership Training Program [*Defunct*] (EA)
MLTPL .... Multiplane
MLTRY........ Military
MLTS .... Military Land Transportation Service (SAUO)
MLTSL......... Multiple Sail [*Navy*] (NVT)
MLTU .... Missile Loop Test Unit
MLTY .... Military (MDG)
MLU .... Major League Umpires Association
MLU .... Malka Resources Ltd. [*Vancouver Stock Exchange symbol*]
MLU .... Mean Length of Utterance [*Linguistics*]
MLU .... Memory Loading Unit [*of FADAC*] [*Military*]
MLU .... Memory Logic Unit [*Computer science*]
MLU .... Mid-Life Update
MLU .... Miscellaneous Live Unit [*Military*] (AFM)
MLU .... Mobile Laundry Unit
MLU .... Mobile Living Unit [*Mobile home*]
MLU .... Monitor & Logic Unit (SAUS)
MLU .... Monroe [*Louisiana*] [*Airport symbol*] (OAG)
MLU .... Monroe, LA [*Location identifier*] [*FAA*] (FAAL)
MLU .... Montlucon Air Service [*France*] [*ICAO designator*] (FAAC)
MLU .... Multiple Logical Unit
MLUA.......... Major League Umpires Association (EA)
MLURI .... Macaulay Land Use Research Institute, Aberdeen [*British*] (IRUK)
MLUS.......... Merrill Lynch & Co. [*Associated Press*] (SAG)
ML/USA .... Mailing List User and Supplier Association [*Defunct*] (EA)
MLV .... Air Moldova International, SA [*FAA designator*] (FAAC)
MLV .... Magnetic Levitation Vehicle (BARN)
MLV .... Main LOX [*Liquid Oxygen*] Valve [*NASA*] (KSC)
MLV .... Malvaux [*France*] [*Seismograph station code, US Geological Survey*] (SEIS)
MLV .... Matrix Light Valve
MLV .... Maximum Lung Volume [*Physiology*]
MLV .... McDonnell Launch Vehicle [*McDonnell Douglas Corp.*] (MCD)
MLV .... Medium Launch Vehicle
MLV .... Medium Lift Vehicle (ACAE)
MLV .... Membrane Light Valve [*Optics*]
MLV .... Memory Loader Verifier (DWSG)
MLV .... Mobile Launch Vehicle [*Air Force*]
MLV .... Modify Logging Versions (AAEL)
MLV .... Moloney Leukemia Virus [*Medicine*] (DMAA)
MLV .... Mouse Leukemia Virus (MAE)
MLV .... Mulberry Latent Virus [*Plant pathology*]
MLV .... Multilamellar Large Vesicle [*Pharmacy*] [*Biochemistry*]
MLV .... Multilamellar Lipid Vesicle (DB)
MLV .... Multilaminar Phospholipid Vesicle [*Immunology*]
MLV .... Multilaminar Vesicle [*Medicine*] (DMAA)
MLV .... Murine Leukemia Virus [*Also, MuLV*]
MLV(A) .... Murine Leukemia Virus (Abelson)
MLVDP .... Maximum Left Ventricular Developed Pressure [*Cardiology*] (DMAA)
MLV(M) ...... Murine Leukemia Virus (Moloney)
MLVP.......... Manned Lunar Vehicle Program [*NASA*] (AAG)
MLVPS........ Manual Low-Voltage Power Supply
MLV(R) .... Murine Leukemia Virus (Rauscher)
MLVS.......... Mill Vise
MLVS.......... Multilevel Voltage Select (MCD)
MLVSS........ Mixed-Liquor Volatile Suspended Solids [*Chemical engineering*]
MLVT .... Mobile Launch Vehicle Transporter [*Air Force*]
MLVW........ Maximum Loaded Vehicle Weight
MLVW........ Medium Logistic Vehicle, Wheeled (SAUS)
MLW .... Madras Law Weekly [*India*] [*A publication*] (DLA)
Mlw .... Malawi (MILB)
MLW .... Master of Labour Welfare (SAUO)
MLW .... Master Warning Light (IAA)
MLW .... Maximum Landing Weight [*Aviation*]

MLW .... Mean Low Water [*Tides and currents*]
MLW .... Medium-Level Radioactive Waste (NUCP)
MLW .... Military Land Warrant (GEAB)
MLW .... Milwaukee [*Wisconsin*] [*Seismograph station code, US Geological Survey*] [*Closed*] (SEIS)
MLW .... Monrovia [*Liberia*] [*Airport symbol*] (OAG)
MLW .... Multiple Logical Windowing [*Computer science*]
MLWA .... Maximum Landing Weight Authorized [*Aviation*] (DA)
MLWG .... Modern Languages Working Group (AIE)
MLWI .... Mean Low-Water Lunitidal Interval [*Tides and currents*]
MLWL......... Mail-Well, Inc. [*NASDAQ symbol*] (SAG)
MLWL......... Mean Low Water Level (QUAC)
MLWMS...... Miscellaneous Liquid Waste Management System (NRCH)
MLWN .... Mean Low-Water Neap [*Tides and currents*]
MLWS......... Mean Low-Water Spring [*Tides and currents*]
MLWS......... Miniature LASER Weapon Simulator (MCD)
MLWS......... Minimum Level Water Stand (NATG)
MLX .... Malatya [*Turkey*] [*Airport symbol*] (OAG)
MLX .... Mauna Loa 2 [*Hawaii*] [*Seismograph station code, US Geological Survey*] (SEIS)
MLX .... Merritt Island, Florida [*Spaceflight Tracking and Data Network*] [*NASA*]
MLX .... MLX Corp. [*Associated Press*] (SAG)
MLX01 .... Magnetically-levitated Linear Motor Vehicle
MLXR .... MLX Corp. [*NASDAQ symbol*] (SAG)
MLy .... Lynn Public Library, Lynn, MA [*Library symbol*] [*Library of Congress*] (LCLS)
MLY .... Manley Hot Springs [*Alaska*] [*Airport symbol*] (OAG)
MLY .... Manley Hot Springs, AK [*Location identifier*] [*FAA*] (FAAL)
MLY .... Moly Mite Resources [*Vancouver Stock Exchange symbol*]
MLY .... Multiply (MDG)
Mly .... National Library of Malaysia, Kuala Lumpur, Malaysia [*Library symbol*] [*Library of Congress*] (LCLS)
MLYC .... Moosehead Lake Yacht Club (SAUO)
MlyKA......... Arkib Negara [*National Archives of Malaysia*], Federal Government Building,Kuala Lumpur, Malaysia [*Library symbol*] [*Library of Congress*] (LCLS)
MlyKgM...... Sarawak Museum, Kuching, Malaysia [*Library symbol*] [*Library of Congress*] (LCLS)
MlyKU........ University of Malaya, Kuala Lumpur, Malaysia [*Library symbol*] [*Library of Congress*] (LCLS)
MLyL .... Lynn Public Library, Lynn, MA [*Library symbol*] [*Library of Congress*] (LCLS)
MlyPS........ Universiti Sains Malaysia (University of Science, Malaysia), Minden, Penang, Malaysia [*Library symbol*] [*Library of Congress*] (LCLS)
MLZ .... Melo [*Uruguay*] [*Airport symbol*] (OAG)
MM .... Machine Made Paper (DGA)
MM .... Machine-Made Snow [*Skiing*]
MM .... Machinery
MM .... Machinist's Mate [*Navy rating*]
M/m .... Made Merchandise (EBF)
MM .... Made Merchantable
MM .... Maelzel's Metronome [*Music*]
MM .... Magister Melendus [*Flourished, 1188-1209*] [*Authority cited in pre-1607 legal work*] (DSA)
mm .... Main Memory (NAKS)
MM .... Main Memory
mm .... Main Module (NAKS)
MM .... Main Module (NASA)
MM .... Maintenance Manual
MM .... Maintenance Monitor
MM .... Majesties
MM .... Major Medical [*Insurance*]
MM .... Major Mode (KSC)
mm .... Major Mode (NAKS)
MM .... Malignant Melanoma [*Oncology*]
mm .... Malta [*MARC country of publication code*] [*Library of Congress*] (LCCP)
MM .... Management Manual (KSC)
MM .... Man Machine (CGWS)
M/M .... Man/Machine
MM .... Manmade [*Diamonds*]
MM .... Man-Month (AFM)
mm .... Man-Month (NAKS)
MM .... Manual Maximal Displacement [*Sports medicine*]
MM .... Manual Morse (MCD)
MM .... Manual of Movement (SAUO)
MM .... Manufacturing Management
MM .... Manufacturing Manual (AAG)
MM .... Manufacturing Methods (AAEL)
MM .... Marilyn Monroe [*American motion picture star, 1926-1962*]
MM .... Mariner Mars Project [*NASA*]
MM .... Maritime Mobile
MM .... Mark Mason (ROG)
MM .... Mark Master [*Freemasonry*]
MM .... Marshall Manual (SSD)
MM .... Marshall-Marchetti Procedure [*Medicine*] (MAE)
MM .... Martha Movement (EA)
M-M .... Martin Marietta Corp.
MM .... Martyres [*Martyrs*]
mm .... Maryknoll Fathers, Catholic Foreign Mission Society of America (TOCD)
MM .... Maryknoll Missionary (SAUO)
MM .... Maryknoll Missioners [*Catholic Foreign Mission Society*] [*Roman Catholic religious order*]

MM	Maryknoll Sisters of St. Dominic (TOCD)
mm	Mass Memory (NAKS)
MM	Mass Memory (NASA)
MM	Massorah Magna [or Massora Magna] (BJA)
MM	Master Mason [Freemasonry]
MM	Master Mechanic
MM	Master Monitor
MM	Master of Management
MM	Master of Mathematics (GAGS)
MM	Master of Medicine
MM	Master of Ministry (PGP)
MM	Master of Modern Studies (PGP)
MM	Master of Music (GAGS)
MM	Masters
MM	Material Manufacturer (SAUO)
MM	Materials Management [Nuclear energy]
MM	Materials Measurement (IEEE)
MM	Materia Medica (ROG)
MM	Mathematics Model
MM	Math Model (KSC)
mm	Math Model (NAKS)
MM	Matrimonium [Matrimony] [Latin]
M/M	Maximum and Minimum (KSC)
MM	Measure for Measure [Shakespearean work]
MM	Mechanical Maintenance
MM	Medal for Merit [Military decoration]
MM	Medial Malleolus [Anatomy] (AAMN)
MM	Medial Meniscus [Anatomy]
MM	Media Manager (SAUO)
MM	Median Method [Mathematics]
MM	Medical Man (ROG)
mm---	Mediterranean Sea and Area [MARC geographic area code] [Library of Congress] (LCCP)
MM	Medium Maintenance
MM	Med Mera [And So Forth] [Latin] (ILCA)
MM	Megamega [A prefix meaning multiplied by one trillion] (DEN)
MM	Megameter
MM	Melanotic Melanoma [Medicine] (DB)
MM	Melaveh Malka (BJA)
MM	Melbourne Marathon [Australia]
MM	Melody Maker [A publication] (WDAA)
MM	Membranes [Leaves of parchment] (ROG)
MM	Memory Module (MCD)
MM	Memory Multiplexer [Computer science] (MDG)
MM	Mercantile Marine (SAUO)
MM	Merchant Marine
MM	Mesoscale Model [Marine science] (OSRA)
MM	Messageries Maritimes [Forwarding agents] [French]
MM	Messieurs [Plural of Mister] [French]
MM	Metal Manufacture [Department of Employment] [British]
MM	Metered Market Service [A. C. Nielsen Co.] (NTCM)
MM	Methadone Maintenance [Medicine] (DHP)
MM	Methylmalonyl-CoA Mutase [An enzyme]
MM	Methyl Mercaptan [Organic chemistry]
MM	Methyl Methacrylate [Also, MMA] [Organic chemistry]
MM	Metronome Mark (ROG)
MM	Metropolitan Museum (SAUO)
MM	Microfilm
MM	Micromanipulator [Instrumentation]
MM	Micromodule (AAG)
MM	Micro Mole (ACAE)
MM	Midcourse Mode [Navy] (CAAL)
MM	Middle Manager
MM	Middle Marker [in an instrument landing system]
MM	Middle Minoan [Archaeology] (BJA)
MM	Military Macaw [Bird]
MM	Military Medal [World War I nickname: Maconochie Medal] [British]
MM	Military Medicine
MM	Military Message (SAUO)
MM	Military Mission (SAUO)
MM	Milla Wa-Milla (BJA)
MM	Millimeter (DFIT)
mm	Millimeter [Metric]
mM	Millimole [Mass]
mm	Million (WDMC)
MM	Minelayer Fleet [Navy symbol] [Obsolete]
MM	Minimal Medium [Microbiology]
M/M	Minimum/Maximum
MM	Minister of Munitions [British] [World War II]
MM	Ministry of Mines [British] (DAS)
MM	Ministry of Munitions (SAUO)
MM	Mint Mark [Numismatics]
MM	Minuteman [Missile] (AABC)
Mm	Misch Metal [A commercial mixture of rare earth metals]
MM	Mismated [Merchandising slang]
MM	Missile Master [Fire direction and coordination system]
MM	Missile Monitor (MCD)
MM	Missile Motion
MM	Missionary of Maryknoll (SAUO)
mm	Mission Manager [NASA] (NAKS)
MM	Mission Manager [NASA/USAF]
MM	Mission Module
MM	Mission Monitor (MCD)
M/M	Mister or Mrs. [In addresses] [Correspondence]
MM	Mistress of Music
MM	Mitochondrial Myopathy [Medicine]
MM	Mitral Murmur [Medicine] (MELL)
mm	Mixed Media (VRA)
MM	Mixed Monitor [External Tocotransducer and internal scalp exectrode] [Neonatology] [Obstetrics] (DAVI)
MM	Mobile Management (SAUO)
MM	Mobility Management (SAUO)
MM	Moderation Management
MM	Modern Motor [A publication]
MM	Modification or Maintenance [Aircraft]
MM	Modified Mercalli [Scale measuring earthquake intensity] [Seismology]
MM	Modigliani-Miller Propositions [Corporate finance] (ECON)
MM	Mois Maconnique [Masonic Month] [Freemasonry] [French]
MM	Molecular Mechanics [Physical chemistry]
MM	Money Market [Investment term]
MM	Monmouthshire Regiment (SAUO)
MM	Mononeuritis Multiplex [Inflammation of nerves] [Medicine] (TAD)
MM	Monostable Multivibrator [Electronics] (OA)
MM	Monthly Meetings [Quakers]
MM	Morality in Media (EA)
MM	Moral Majority [An association] (EA)
MM	Morbidity and Mortality [Medicine] (DMAA)
MM	Morel-Morgagni [Syndrome] [Medicine] (DB)
MM	More Moderate Service [Automotive engineering]
MM	Morrison-Maierle, Inc. (EFIS)
MM	Moslem Mosque (EA)
MM	Mothers Matter [Commercial firm] (EA)
MM	Motor Magnet
MM	Motor Maintenance [Army]
MM	Motor Maintenance Aptitude Area [Army]
MM	Motor Meal [Medicine] (MEDA)
MM	Motor Mechanic [British military] (DMA)
MM	Motor Movement (SAUO)
MM	Mould Made Paper (DGA)
MM	Mouse Myoblast [Cell line]
MM	Moving Magnet [Stereo equipment]
MM	Mozambique Metical [Monetary unit] (IMH)
M/M	Mr. & Mrs. (VRA)
MM	Much Married [Slang]
MM	Mucous Membrane
MM	Multi-Media (OICC)
MM	Multimeter
MM	Multi Mission Surveillance System (ACAE)
MM	Multimode
MM	Multiple Master [Computer science] (CDE)
MM	Multiple Myeloma [Medicine]
MM	Multipolar Magnetic [Sun] (DICI)
MM	Munitions Maintenance (MCD)
mm	Murmur [Cardiology] (DAVI)
MM	Muscles [Medicine]
MM	Muscularis Mucosa [Medicine] (MAE)
MM	Museum Media [A publication]
MM	Musical Majority [Defunct] (EA)
MM	Mutatis Mutandis [With the Necessary Changes] [Latin]
MM	Mutual Risk Management [NYSE symbol] (SPSG)
MM	Myanmar [Internet country code]
MM	Myeloid Metaplasia [Medicine]
MM	Myelomeningocele [Medicine]
MM	Myriameters [Metric system] (ROG)
MM	Program Maintenance Manual (SAUO)
MM	SAM Colombia [Airline flight code] (ODBW)
MM	Sociedad Aeronautica Medellin [ICAO designator] (AD)
MM	Xaverian Missionary Society of Mary, Inc. [Roman Catholic women's religious order]
MM1	Machinist's Mate, First Class [Navy rating]
MM2	Machinist's Mate, Second Class [Navy rating]
MM²	Square Millimeter
MM³	Cubic Millimeter
mm3	Cubic Millimeter (or Millimetre) (SAUS)
MM3	Machinist's Mate, Third Class [Navy rating]
MM4	Mesoscale Meteorological Model-Version 4 [Marine science] (OSRA)
MM5	Fifth Generation of Penn State/NCAR Mesoscale Model (SAUS)
MM5	Mesoscale Model Version 5 [Marine science] [Pennsylvania State University] (OSRA)
MMA	Average Male Mass
MMA	Caltech Millimeter Array (SAUS)
MMA	MacRobertson Miller Airline Services [Australia]
MMA	Magnetotactic Multicellular Aggregate [Microbiology]
MMA	Maine Maritime Academy (SAUO)
MMA	Maine Medical Association (SAUO)
MMA	Main Mission Antennas
MMA	Major Machine Accessory (MCD)
MMA	Major Maintenance Availability (MHDB)
MMA	Malmo [Sweden] [Airport symbol] (OAG)
MMA	Management and Marketing Abstracts [PIRA] [Bibliographic database] [British]
MMA	Manchester Mathematics Association (SAUO)
MMA	Maneuver Motor Array (MCD)
MMA	Manitoba Medical Association (SAUO)
MMA	Manual Metal Arc [Welding]
MMA	Maria Mitchell Association (EA)
MMA	Marine Mammal Act [1972] (MSC)
MMA	Marine Maritime Academy
MMA	Marine Motor Association (ROG)

MMA............	Married Man's Allowance [*Taxes*] [*British*]
MMA............	Martin Marietta Aerospace (ACAE)
MMA............	Massachusetts Maritime Academy [*Buzzards Bay*]
MMA............	Massachusetts Maritime Academy, Captain C. H. Hurley Library, Buzzards Bay, MA [*OCLC symbol*] (OCLC)
MMA............	Massachusetts Military Academy
MMA............	Mass Memory Assembly (SAUS)
MMA............	Master of Management and Administration, Cranfield Institute of Technology [*British*] (DBQ)
MMA............	Master of Manpower Administration (GAGS)
MMA............	Master of Marine Affairs (GAGS)
MMA............	Master of Media Arts (PGP)
MMA............	Master of Medical Art (GAGS)
MMA............	Master of Municipal Administration
MMA............	Master of Musical Art (GAGS)
MMA............	Master of Musical Arts
MMA............	Masters of Medicine [*A publication*]
MMA............	Mastitis-Metritis-Agalactia Syndrome [*Medicine*] (DMAA)
MMA............	Material Management Activity (SAUO)
MMA............	Material Manufacturing Authorization (AAG)
MMA............	Materials Marketing Associates [*Hartford, CT*] (EA)
MMA............	Maymac Petroleum Corp. [*Vancouver Stock Exchange symbol*]
MMA............	Mazda Motors of America
MMA............	Medical Management Analysis System (HCT)
MMA............	Medical Marketing Association (NTPA)
MMA............	Medical Materiel Account [*Military*] (AABC)
MMA............	Medical Mutual Aid (GNE)
MMA............	Memory-to-Memory Adapter [*Computer science*]
MMA............	Merchandise Marks Act (ROG)
MMA............	Merchant Marine Academy (SAUO)
MMA............	Merchants and Manufacturers Association
MMA............	Mercy Medical Airlift (EA)
MMA............	Merrill's Marauders Association (EA)
MMA............	Meter Manufacturers' Association (IAA)
MMA............	Methylmalonic Acid [*Organic chemistry*]
MMA............	Methylmalonic Acidemia [*Medicine*]
MMA............	Methyl Methacrylate [*Also, MM*] [*Organic chemistry*]
MMA............	Metro Manila Airways International, Inc. [*Philippines*] [*ICAO designator*] (FAAC)
MMA............	Metropolitan Magazine Association [*Later, Magazine Publishers Association*] (EA)
MMA............	Metropolitan Museum of Art [*New York*] (BJA)
MMA............	Microcomputer Managers Association (HGAA)
MMA............	Micro Manager's Association (AGLO)
MMA............	Microminiature Mixer Amplifier
MMA............	Microtome Manufacturers Association [*British*] (DBA)
MMA............	Middle Meningeal Artery [*Neuroanatomy*]
MMA............	Military Medical Academy [*Armed forces medical college*]
MMA............	Millimeter Array [*Astronomy*]
MMA............	Minelayer Auxiliary Ship [*Navy symbol*] [*Obsolete*]
MMA............	Minor Motor Aphasia [*Medicine*] (MELL)
MMA............	Mirror Manufacturers Association
MMA............	Missile Maintenance Area (AAG)
MMA............	Mitomycin A [*Antineoplastic drug*]
MMA............	Modified Motorcycle Association
MMA............	Momentum Management Assembly (ACAE)
MMA............	Monomethylamine [*Organic chemistry*]
MMA............	Monomethyl Arsonic Acid [*Organic chemistry*]
MMA............	Monorail Manufacturers Association (EA)
MMA............	Monosil Manufacturers Association
MMA............	Monovalent Metal Azide [*Inorganic chemistry*]
MMA............	Mothers and Midwives Action [*Australia*] [*An association*]
MMA............	Motoring in Miniature Association (EA)
MMA............	Motorsports Marketing Association [*Langhorne, PA*] [*Defunct*] (EA)
MMA............	MSFC Management Association (SAUO)
MMA............	Multifunction Microwave Aperture
MMA............	Multi-Megabit-Anpassung (SAUS)
MMA............	Multimission Aircraft (SAUS)
MMA............	Multiple Module Access
MMA............	Multiplexed Matrix Array
MMA............	Mummy Mountain [*Arizona*] [*Seismograph station code, US Geological Survey*] [*Closed*] (SEIS)
MMA............	Municipal Mortgage & Equity LLC [*AMEX symbol*] (SAG)
MMA............	Museum of Modern Art (SAUO)
MMA............	Music Masters' Association [*British*]
MMA............	Music of Modern Art (NADA)
MMAA..........	Acapulco/General Juan N. Alvarez Internacional [*Mexico*] [*ICAO location identifier*] (ICLI)
MMAA..........	Man/Machine Assembly Analysis (MCD)
MMAA..........	Merchandise Mart Apparel Association [*Defunct*]
MMAA..........	Mini-Microaggregates of Albumin (DMAA)
MMAA..........	Monomethylarsonic Acid [*Organic chemistry*]
MMAA..........	Mono-N-methylacetoacetamide [*Organic chemistry*]
MMAC..........	Material Management Aggregation Code (MCD)
MMAC..........	Medical Materiel Advice Code [*Military*] (AFM)
MMAC..........	Multi-Media Access Center [*Cabletron Systems, Inc.*]
MMAC..........	Multimedia Mobile Access Communications (SAUO)
MMAC..........	Multiple Model Adaptive Control [*Flight control*]
MMAC-FNB...	Multi-Media Access Center with Flexible Network Bus [*Cabletron Systems, Inc.*]
MMACS........	Maintenance Management and Control System (MCD)
MMACS........	Maintenance, Mechanical Arm, and Crew System Engineer (SAUS)
MMACS........	Medicaid/Medicare Automated Certification System (GFGA)
MMAD	Mass-Median Aerodynamic Diameter [*of particles*]
MMAD	Millimeter Wave Active Decoy (ACAE)

MM Adm.....	Master of Municipal Administration
M Ma E.......	Master of Marine Engineering
MMAE........	Master of Mechanical and Aerospace Engineering (PGP)
M Ma Eng...	Master of Marine Engineering
MMAG........	Martin Marietta Astronautics Group (SAUO)
MMal..........	Malden Public Library, Malden, MA [*Library symbol*] [*Library of Congress*] (LCLS)
MMAL........	Mitsubishi Motors Australia, Limited (SAUO)
M-MALS	Multimode Aircraft Landing System (MCD)
MMam........	Marstons Mills Public Library, Marstons Mills, MA [*Library symbol*] [*Library of Congress*] (LCLS)
MMAN	Aeropuerto del Norte [*Mexico*] [*ICAO location identifier*] (ICLI)
MMAN	Minuteman International [*NASDAQ symbol*] (SAG)
MMAN	Minuteman Int'l [*NASDAQ symbol*] (TTSB)
MM & F.......	Merchant Marine and Fisheries Committee [*Congressional committee*] (MSC)
MM&M	Manning, Maxwell & Moore, Incorporated (SAUO)
MM & M.....	Material Manual and Memorandum (AAG)
MM & M.....	Minerals, Mining, and Metallurgy
MM & M Soc of Am...	Member of the Mining and Metallurgical Society of America
MM&P........	Masters, Mates and Pilots (SAUO)
MM & SC....	Major Mission and Support Category
MM & T.......	Manufacturing Methods and Technology [*Program*] [*Army Materiel Command*] (RDA)
MManHi......	Manchester Historical Society, Manchester, MA [*Library symbol*] [*Library of Congress*] (LCLS)
MMAO	Monomethylamine Oxidase (DB)
MMAP........	Marine Mammal Action Plan (SAUO)
MMAP........	Microgravity Measurement and Analysis Project (SAUS)
MMAP........	Microwave Multi-Application Payload [*NASA*] (PDAA)
MMAP........	Multi Media Access Profile (SAUS)
MMAR	Main Memory Address Register
MMar..........	Marlborough Public Library, Marlborough, MA [*Library symbol*] [*Library of Congress*] (LCLS)
MMAR	Money Management Analytical Research Group
M-MARP	Mobilization Manpower Allocations/Requirements Plan [*Military*]
MMARS	Military Middle Airspace Radar Service (PIAV)
MMarsW	Historic Winslow House, Marshfield, MA [*Library symbol*] [*Library of Congress*] (LCLS)
MMART.......	Mobile Medical Augmentation Readiness Team (DNAB)
MMAS........	Aguascalientes [*Mexico*] [*ICAO location identifier*] (ICLI)
MMAS........	Manufacturing Management Accounting System (PDAA)
MMAS........	Master of Military Art and Science (MCD)
MMAS........	Material Management Accountability System (NASA)
MMAS........	Material Management and Accounting System (AAGC)
MMAS........	Medical Materiel Accounting System (SAUO)
MmAS........	Minerva Mikrofilm A/S, Hellerup, Denmark [*Library symbol*] [*Library of Congress*] (LCLS)
MMAS........	Mini-Manned Aircraft System (PDAA)
MMASC......	Major Mission and Support Category
MMat..........	Free Public Library, Mattapoisett, MA [*Library symbol*] [*Library of Congress*] (LCLS)
MMAT........	Mobile Mine Assembly Team (NG)
MMath........	Master of Mathematics
MMATP........	Methadone Maintenance and Aftercare Treatment Program [*Medicine*] (DMAA)
M Mat SE ...	Master of Material Science and Engineering (PGP)
MMAU........	Master Multiattribute Utility (IEEE)
MMAU........	Millimass Unit (IAA)
MMAXc	Maximum Corrective Maintenance Down-Time (SAUO)
MMAXCT....	Maximum Corrective Time (SAUO)
MMB..........	Marine Midland Banks, Inc. [*NYSE symbol*] (SPSG)
MMB..........	Master Menu Board [*Military*]
MMB..........	Master of Medical Biochemistry (GAGS)
MMB..........	Mast Mounting Bracket (SAUS)
MMB..........	Memanbetsu [*Japan*] [*Geomagnetic observatory code*]
MMB..........	Membrane [*Medicine*]
MMB..........	Mercedarian Missionaries of Berriz [*Also, OMerc*] [*Roman Catholic women's religious order*]
MMB..........	Method of Mass Balance [*Physical chemistry*]
MMB..........	Methylmercury Bromide [*Organic chemistry*]
MMB..........	Metropolitan Milk Board [*South Australia*]
MMB..........	Midwest Motor Carriers Bureau, Inc., Oklahoma City OK [*STAC*]
MMB..........	Milk Marketing Board (SAUO)
MMB..........	Milk Marketing Board for England and Wales
MMB..........	Million Barrels
MMB..........	Minimum Monthly Balance [*Finance*]
MMB..........	Mitsui Manufacturers Bank (SAUO)
MMB..........	Mixer Manufacturers Bureau [*Defunct*] (EA)
MMB..........	Mouth-to-Mouth Breathing (MELL)
MMB..........	Multi-Mission Bus (ACAE)
MMB..........	Multiport Memory Bank [*Computer science*] (MHDB)
MMB..........	Sisters Mercedarian Missionaries of Berriz (SAUO)
MMBA........	Money Market Deposit Account (EBF)
MMBAT.......	Main Missile Battery
MMBB........	Molecular Marine Biology and Biotechnology [*A publication*]
MMBC........	Maryland Motor Boat Club (SAUO)
MMB/D	Million Barrels per Day
MMBEMD ...	Mean Miles between Essential Maintenance Demand [*Quality control*]
MMBF........	Mean Miles between Failures [*Quality control*]
MMBF........	Million Board Feet (WPI)
MMBI KNC RAN...	Murmansk Marine Biological Institute, Kola Scientific Centren Academy of Sciences (SAUS)
MMBI KNC RAN...	Murmansk Marine Biological Institute, Kola Scientific Centre, Russian Academy of Sciences (SAUO)

MMBL......... MacMillan Bloedel Ltd. [*NASDAQ symbol*] (NQ)
MMBLF....... MacMillan-Bloedel [*NASDAQ symbol*] (TTSB)
MMBM....... Mammalian Meat and Bone Meal (SAUS)
MMBMF..... Mean Miles between Mission Failures [*Quality control*] (MCD)
MMBOMF .... Mean Miles between Operational Mission Failures [*Quality control*] (MCD)
MMBP......... Military Medical Benefits Property (AABC)
MMBR .... Mean Miles between Removals [*Quality control*] (MCD)
MMBR .... Microbiology and Molecular Biology Reviews [*A publication*]
MMBR .... Multipurpose Supersonic Beamrider (ACAE)
MMBSF....... Mean Miles between System Failures [*Quality control*] (MCD)
MMBTU....... Million British Thermal Units (MENA)
MMBUMA .... Mean Miles between Unscheduled Maintenance Actions [*Quality control*] (MCD)
MMC........... Ciudad Mante [*Mexico*] [*Airport symbol*] (AD)
MMC........... Machinist's Mate, Chief [*Navy rating*]
MMC........... Magical Mystery Chip (VLIE)
MMC........... Magnesium Methyl Carbonate [*Organic chemistry*]
MMC........... Main Memory Controller [*Computer science*] (CIST)
MMC........... Maintenance Management Center
MMC........... Maintenance Management Course [*Army*]
MMC........... Maintenance Monitor Console (CTAS)
MMC........... Malaya Military College (SAUO)
MMC........... Malaysian Marketing Corporation (SAUO)
MMC........... Malaysian Mining Corporation (SAUO)
MMC........... Manifold-Mounted Converter [*Automotive emissions*]
MMC........... Man Machine Communication (SAUO)
MMCP......... Man-Machine Communication [*Computer science*]
MMC........... Man Marketing Council [*New York City*]
MMC........... Manufacturing Methods Committee
MMC........... Manufacturing Methods Council (AAEL)
MMC........... Marine Mammal Commission [*Marine science*] (MSC)
MMC........... Marsh & McLennan Companies, Inc. [*NYSE symbol*] (SPSG)
MMC........... Martin Marietta Corp. (KSC)
mmc........... Martin Marietta Corp. (NAKS)
MMC........... Martin's Reports of Mining Cases [*Canada*] [*A publication*] (DLA)
MMC........... Mary Morstan's Companions [*An association*]
MMC........... Marymount Manhattan College [*New York, NY*]
MMC........... Massachusetts Microelectronics Center [*Research center*] (RCD)
MMC........... Master of Mass Communication (GAGS)
MMC........... Matched Memory Cycle [*Computer science*]
MMC........... Materiel Management Center [*Military*] (AABC)
MMC........... Materiel Management Code [*Military*] (AFM)
MMC........... Maximum Material Condition
MMC........... Maximum Metal Concept
MMC........... Maximum Metal Condition (IEEE)
MMC........... Maximum Miscibility Composition [*Physical chemistry*]
MMC........... Mazda Motor Corp.
MMC........... Mean Meridional Circulation [*Climatology*]
MMC........... Medical Milk Commission (SAUO)
MMC........... Meet Me Conference [*Telecommunications*] (DOM)
MMC........... Meharry Medical College (SAUO)
MMC........... Melbourne Magistrates Court [*Australia*]
MMC........... Memory Management Controller (IEEE)
MMC........... Meningomyelocele [*Medicine*] (MELL)
MMC........... Merchant Marine Council [*Coast Guard*]
MMC........... Metabolic Measurement Cart [*Beckman Instruments, Inc.*]
MMC........... Metal-Matrix Composite
MMC........... Metropolitan Motor Carriers Conference Inc., Dover NJ [*STAC*]
MMC........... Microcar and Minicar Club (EA)
MMC........... Microcomputer Marketing Council [*Direct Marketing Association*] (PCM)
MMC........... Micrometeoroid Capsule (OA)
MMC........... Micronesian Minerals [*Vancouver Stock Exchange symbol*]
MMC........... Microsoft Management Console
MMC........... Microsoft Management Control
MMC........... Midcourse Measurement Correction
MMC........... Middle Cape [*Alaska*] [*Seismograph station code, US Geological Survey*] (SEIS)
MMC........... Middle Management Council (SAUO)
MMC........... Mid Motor Controller [*Aerospace*] (NAKS)
MMC........... Migrating Myoelectric Complexes [*Electrophysiology*]
MMC........... Military Microwave Components (TIMI)
MMC........... Millsaps College, Jackson, MS [*OCLC symbol*] (OCLC)
MMC........... Minelayer, Coastal [*Navy symbol*] [*Obsolete*]
MMC........... Minerals Marketing Corporation (SAUO)
MMC........... Minicar and Microcar Club (EA)
MMC........... Minicomputer Maintenance Center (VLIE)
MMC........... Minimal Medullary Concentration [*Medicine*] (MAE)
MMC........... Missile Maintenance Crew (AFM)
MMC........... Missile Measurements Center
MMC........... Missile Motion Computer
mmc........... Mission Management Center [*NASA*] (NAKS)
MMC........... Mission Management Center [*NASA*] (NASA)
MMC........... Mission Management Computer (SAUS)
MMC........... Mission Monitoring Center [*Army*]
MMC........... Mitomycin C [*Mutamycin*] [*Also, Mi, MTC*] [*Antineoplastic drug*]
MMC........... Mitsubishi Motors Corp.
MMC........... Mixed Medical Commission (SAUO)
MMC........... Modular Mission Computer (SAUS)
MMC........... Money Management Council [*British*]
MMC........... Money Market Certificate [*Investment term*]
MMC........... Monopolies and Mergers Commission [*British*]
MMC........... Monthly Maintenance Charge (VLIE)
MMC........... Mortar Motor Carrier

MMC........... Mount Marty College [*South Dakota*]
MMC........... Mount Mary College [*Wisconsin*]
MMC........... Mount Mercy College [*Iowa; Pennsylvania*]
MMC........... Movements Monitoring Center (SAUO)
MMC........... Mucosal Mast Cell [*Medicine*]
MMC........... Multimedia Marketing Council (DOM)
MMC........... Multipart Memory Controller (NITA)
MMC........... Multiport Memory Controller
MMCA........ Cananea [*Mexico*] [*ICAO location identifier*] (ICLI)
MMCA........ Methyl Monochloroacetate [*Organic chemistry*]
MMCA........ Midbody Motor Control Assembly (NASA)
MMCA........ Mid Motor Controller Assembly [*Aerospace*] (NAKS)
MMCA........ Minor Military Construction, Army
M McA........ Montague and McArthur's English Bankruptcy Reports [*A publication*] (DLA)
MM Cas....... Martin's Reports of Mining Cases [*Canada*] [*A publication*] (DLA)
MMCB........ Cuernavaca [*Mexico*] [*ICAO location identifier*] (ICLI)
MMCB........ Methods in Molecular and Cellular Biology [*A publication*]
MMCB........ Midwest Motor Carriers Bureau, Inc.
MMCBE....... Machinist's Mate, Construction Battalion, Equipment Operator [*Navy rating*]
MMCC........ Ciudad Acuna [*Mexico*] [*ICAO location identifier*] (ICLI)
MMCC........ Manhattan Miniature Camera Club (EA)
MMCC........ Medicare Managed Care Contract (SAUO)
MMCC........ Mid-Century Mercury Car Club (EA)
MMCC........ Military Manpower Claimant Code (DNAB)
MMCC........ Mission Management and Control Centre (SAUO)
MMCC........ Moscow Mission Control Center (SAUO)
MMCC........ Multimini Computer Compiler (MHDI)
MMCCS....... MILSTAR [*Military Strategic and Tactical Relay System*] Mobile Consolidation and Control Station (DWSG)
MMCD .... Master Monitor Criteria Data File
MMCD .... Multimedia CD [*Computer science*]
MMCD .... Multimedia Compact Disc
MMCE......... Ciudad Del Carmen [*Mexico*] [*ICAO location identifier*] (ICLI)
MMCF......... Million Cubic Feet
MMCF......... Multimedia Communications Forum (DDC)
MMCFD....... Million Cubic Feet a Day
MMCG .... Mid-Murray Citrus Growers [*Australia*]
MMCG .... Nuevo Casas Grandes [*Mexico*] [*ICAO location identifier*] (ICLI)
MMCH .... Chilpancingo [*Mexico*] [*ICAO location identifier*] (ICLI)
MMCI......... Mopar Muscle Club International (EA)
MMCI......... MultiMedia Concepts International, Inc. [*NASDAQ symbol*] (SAG)
MMCI......... MultiMedia Concepts Intl. [*NASDAQ symbol*] (TTSB)
MMCIAC..... Metal Matrix Composites Information Analysis Center [*DoD*] [*Information service or system*] (IID)
MMCIL........ Majhuee Multipurpose Cooperative Institution Limited (SAUO)
MMCIL........ Majhuee Multipurpose Cooperative Institution Ltd. (SAUS)
MMCIW....... MultiMeda Concepts Intl-Wrrt [*NASDAQ symbol*] (TTSB)
MMCIW....... MultiMedia Concepts International, Inc. [*NASDAQ symbol*] (SAG)
MMcKNP..... Mount McKinley National Park (SAUO)
MMCL......... Culiacan [*Mexico*] [*ICAO location identifier*] (ICLI)
MMCL......... Major Missile Component List
MMCL......... Master Measurement and Control List (MCD)
MMCM....... Chetumal [*Mexico*] [*ICAO location identifier*] (ICLI)
MMCM....... Machinist's Mate, Master Chief [*Navy rating*]
MMCM....... Master of Music in Church Music (PGP)
MMCMP....... Mobilization, Military and Civilian Manpower Program (AABC)
MMCN....... Ciudad Obregon [*Mexico*] [*ICAO location identifier*] (ICLI)
MMCN....... MMC Networks [*NASDAQ symbol*] (SG)
MMCNA...... Moto Morini Club of North America (EA)
MMCNY...... Marine Museum of the City of New York (SAUO)
MMCO....... Maintenance Material Control Officer (DNAB)
MMCOI .... Multimedia Communications Community of Interest (SAUO)
MMCP........ Campeche [*Mexico*] [*ICAO location identifier*] (ICLI)
MMCP........ Medicaid Managed Care Program (SAUO)
MMCP........ Micro-Master Control Processor (NITA)
M/MCRP..... AUTODIN Memory/Memory Control Replacement Program (MCD)
MMCS........ Ciudad Juarez/Abraham Gonzalez Internacional [*Mexico*] [*ICAO location identifier*] (ICLI)
MMCS........ Machinist's Mate, Senior Chief [*Navy rating*]
MMCS........ Manufacturing Management Control System (VLIE)
MMCS........ Mass Memory Control Subsystem (TEL)
MMCS........ Mauritius Marine Conservation Society (SAUO)
MMCS........ McCullough/McCulloch Clan Society (EA)
MMCS........ Minimum Modified Chi-Squared [*Statistics*]
MMCS........ Missile and Munitions Center and School [*Army*] (RDA)
MMCS........ Mitsubishi Multi-Communication System [*Driver information system*]
MMCS........ Modernization Management and Control System [*Social Security Administration*]
MMCS........ Multidimensional-Multiattributional Causality Scale (EDAC)
MMCS........ Multiple-Mission Command System [*NASA*]
MMCSA....... Microwave Microminiature Communications System for Aircraft (DNAB)
MMCSEER ... Marjorie Mayrock Center for CIS [*Commonwealth of Independent States*] and East European Research [*Israel*] (EAIO)
MMCSRS..... MACOM Materiel Condition Status Reporting System (SAUO)
MMCT........ Maritime Mobile Coastal Telegraphy
MMCT........ Metal-to-Metal Charge Transfer [*Physical chemistry*]
MMCT........ Microcell-Mediated Chromosome Transfer [*Genetics*]
MMCT........ Mobile Maintenance Contact Team (MCD)
MMCTS....... Material Management Center Theater Supply [*Army*]
MMCU .... Chihuahua/Internacional [*Mexico*] [*ICAO location identifier*] (ICLI)
MMCV........ Ciudad Victoria [*Mexico*] [*ICAO location identifier*] (ICLI)
MMCX........ Multimedia Communication Exchange (SAUO)

MMCY	Celaya [Mexico] [ICAO location identifier] (ICLI)
MMCZ	Cozumel/Internacional [Mexico] [ICAO location identifier] (ICLI)
MMD	Magical Mystery Disease (WDAA)
MMD	Magnetic Mirror Device
MMD	Maintenance Management Division [Army] (INF)
MMD	Manual of the Medical Department [Navy]
MMD	Mass Median Diameter
MMD	Master Makeup and Display
MMD	Master Monitor Display
MMD	Material, Maintenance, and Distribution (MCD)
MMD	Materiel Management Decision [Military]
MMD	Materiel Management Division [Army]
MMD	Maximum Mixing Depths [Meteorology]
MMD	Mean Mass Density
MMD	Mean Mass Diameter
MMD	Mean Measure of Divergence [Statistics]
MMD	Mean Missile [or Mission] Duration (KSC)
MMD	Mercantile Marine Department (SAUO)
MMD	Merchang Mariner's Document [Navy]
MMD	Merchant Marine Detail
MMD	Microlithographic Mask Development [Program] (AAEL)
MMD	Microwave Mixer Diode
MMD	Middle Management Development
MMD	Milkmaid's Dislocation [Medicine] (MELL)
MMD	Minami Daito Jima [Volcano Islands] [Airport symbol] (OAG)
MMD	Minelayer, Fast [Navy symbol]
MMD	Minimal Morbidostatic Dose [Medicine] (MAE)
MMD	Mini-Module Drive (PDAA)
MMD	Missile Miss Distance [Military] (CAAL)
MMD	Mission Management and Dissemination (MCD)
MMD	Mobile Multi-function Device (SAUS)
MMD	Mobile Servicing Center, Maintenance Department [Canada]
MMD	Molecular Mass Distribution [Organic chemistry]
MMD	Money Market Directories, Inc. [Also, an information service or system] (IID)
MMD	Moore Medical Corp. [AMEX symbol] (SPSG)
MMD	Movement for Multi-Party Democracy [Zambia] [Political party]
MMD	Moving Map Display
MMD	Moyamoya Disease [Medicine] (DMAA)
MMD	MSC [Mobile Servicing Center] Maintenance Depot (SSD)
MMD	MSFC [Marshall Space Flight Center] Management Directive [NASA]
MMD	Multi-Effect Multistage Distillation (PDAA)
MMD	Multimode Display
MMD	Myotonic Muscular Dystrophy [Medicine] [Medicine] (DMAA)
MMD	Servite Missionary Sisters of the Sorrowful Mother (TOCD)
MMDA	Martin Marietta Denver Aerospace (ACAE)
MMDA	Mass Merchandising Distributors' Association (EA)
MMDA	(Methoxy)methylenedioxyamphetamine [A hallucinogen]
MMDA	Money Market Deposit Account [Investment term]
MMDA	Myristicin [or glyceryl trimyristate] [Chemical dependency] (DAVI)
MMDB	Mass Memory Database (NASA)
MMDB	Master Measurement Database (NASA)
MMDB	Molecular Modelling Database (SAUO)
MMDC	Manual Master Direction Center
MMDC	Master Message Display Console (MCD)
MMDC	Mount Misalignment Data Collection Routine
MMDDS	Mucous Membrane Drug Delivery System [Medicine] (DB)
mmddyy	Month, Day, Year (HGAA)
MMDF	Mission Mode Data File
MMDF	Mission Model Data File [NASA] (NASA)
MMDF	Multichannel Memorandum Distribution Facility (SAUO)
MMDG	Mark Morris Dance Group
MMDI	Middle Management Development Initiative
MMDI	Momentum Distribution (EFIS)
MMDL	Microminiature Delay Line
MMDM	Ciudad Mante [Mexico] [ICAO location identifier] (ICLI)
MMDM	Mobile Mixed Deployment Minuteman (SAA)
MMDMTI	Multi Mode Display Moving Target Indicator (ACAE)
MMDO	Durango [Mexico] [ICAO location identifier] (ICLI)
MMDO	Magnetic Modulation Direct Overwrite (SAUS)
MMDOC	Merchant Mariners Documentation [BTS] (TAG)
MMDP	Middle Management Development Program
MMDR	Microcircuit Module, Driver/Receiver
MMDS	Maintenance Management Data System [Military] (CAAL)
MMDS	Martin Marietta Data Systems
MMDS	Moving Map Display Equipment (SAUS)
MMDS	Multichannel Memorandum Distribution Facility (SAUO)
MMDS	Multichannel Multipoint Distribution Service [Broadcasting term]
MMDS	Multichannel, Multipoint Distribution System [Telecommunications] (ACRL)
MMDS	Multi-Mode Seeker Demonstration project (SAUS)
MMDS	Multipoint Microwave Distribution System (WDAA)
MMDS	Multipoint Multichannel Distribution Service (SAUS)
MME	Machinist's Mate, Engineman [Navy rating]
Mme	Madame (WA)
MME	Major Machine Equipment (MCD)
MME	Major Movable Equipment (MEDA)
MME	Man Month Equivalents (SPST)
MME	Manned Mars Expedition (SAUO)
MME	Master of Manufacturing Engineering (PGP)
MME	Master of Material Engineering (GAGS)
MME	Master of Mathematics for Educators (PGP)
MME	Master of Mechanical Engineering (GAGS)
M Me	Master of Metaphysics
MME	Master of Mineral Engineering (GAGS)
MME	Master of Mining Engineering
MME	Master of Music Education
MME	Material Military Establishment [Formerly, OSRD] (MCD)
MME	Maximum Maintenance Effort [Military] (AFM)
MMe	Medford Public Library, Medford, MA [Library symbol] [Library of Congress] (LCLS)
MME	Mediterranean Medical Entente (EAIO)
MME	Methylmethacrylate [Organic chemistry]
MME	Micrometeoric Erosion (AAG)
MME	Mid-Atlantic Medical Services, Inc. [NYSE symbol] (SAG)
MME	Middlesborough [England] [Airport symbol] (AD)
MME	Military Message Experiment (SAUO)
MME	Milkmaid's Elbow [Medicine] (MELL)
MME	Million Market Edition [US News and World Report]
MME	Minimum Mean Estimate
MME	Missile Maintenance Equipment (AABC)
MME	M-Mode Echocardiography [Medicine] (DB)
MME	Mobile Meteorological Equipment (SAUO)
MME	Montessori Method of Education (WDAA)
MME	Tees-Side [England] [Airport symbol] (OAG)
MMEA	Maryland Music Educators Association (SAUO)
MMEA	Massachusetts Music Educators Association (SAUO)
MMEA	Michigan Music Educators Association (SAUO)
MMEA	Minnesota Music Educators Association (SAUO)
MMEA	Mississippi Music Educators Association (SAUO)
MMEA	Montana Music Educators Association (SAUO)
MMEC	Machinery Maintenance Engineering Center (AFIT)
MMEC	Machinery-Metals Export Club [Later, International Industrial Marketing Club] (EA)
MMEC	Migrating Myoelectric Complex [Physiology]
M Mech E	Master of Mechanical Engineering
MMechEng	Master of Mechanical Engineering (NADA)
MMECT	Multimonitored Electroconvulsive Treatment (DIPS)
MMECT	Multiple-Monitored Electroconvulsive Therapy [Schizophrenia]
MMED	Mass Median Equivalent Diameter [of airborne particles]
M Med	Master of Medicine
MM Ed	Master of Music Education
MMed	Moore Medical Corp. [Associated Press] (SAG)
MMED	Multimedia, Inc. [NASDAQ symbol] (SAG)
MMedAnaes	Master of Medicine (Anaesthesia)
MMEDC	Multimedia, Inc. (MHDW)
MMedCardiol	Master of Medicine (Cardiology)
MMed(CM)	Master of Medicine (Community Medicine)
MMedEd	Master of Medical Education
MMedPaed	Master of Medicine (Paediatrics)
MMedPath	Master of Medicine (Pathology)
MMedRadD	Master of Medicine (Diagnostic Radiology)
M Med Sc	Master of Medical Science
MMedVen	Master of Medicine (Venereology)
MMEE	Medicare, Medicaid, Education and the Environment [President Clinton political agenda]
MMEF	Maximal Midexpiratory Flow [Also, MMF] [Medicine]
MMEFR	Maximal Midexpiratory Flow Rate [Medicine]
MMEI	Mass Media Exposure Index (SAUO)
MMEI	Military Medicine Education Institute [DoD] (DOMA)
MMEL	Master Minimum Equipment List (DA)
MMel	Melrose Public Library, Melrose, MA [Library symbol] [Library of Congress] (LCLS)
MM Eng	Master of Mechanical Engineering
MMEP	Marine Mammal Events Program (EA)
MMEP	Minuteman Education Program [Air Force] (AFM)
MMEP	Missouri Mathematics Effectiveness Project (EDAC)
MMEP	Multiple Modality Evoked Potential [Neurophysiology]
MMEP	Tepic [Mexico] [ICAO location identifier] (ICLI)
MMER	Marine Models Electronic Record (SAUO)
MMES	Ensenada [Mexico] [ICAO location identifier] (ICLI)
MMES	Maritime Mobile Earth Station (ACAE)
MMES	Martin Marietta Energy Systems, Inc. (SAUO)
MMES	Master Material Erection Schedule [Shipbuilding] (NG)
Mmes	Mesdames [Ladies] [French]
MMES	MSFC [Marshall Space Flight Center] Mated Element Systems [NASA] (NASA)
MMES	Southwestern Manitoba Regional Library, Melita, Manitoba [Library symbol] [National Library of Canada] (NLC)
MMET	Maintenance Management Engineering Team [Military]
M Met	Master of Metallurgy
MMeT	Tufts University, Medford, MA [Library symbol] [Library of Congress] (LCLS)
M Met E	Master of Metallurgical Engineering
MMetEng	Master of Metallurgy and Engineering, University of Sheffield [British] (DBQ)
MMeT-EP	Tufts University, Eliot Pearson Department of Child Study, Medford, MA [Library symbol] [Library of Congress] (LCLS)
MMeT-F	Tufts University, Fletcher School of Law and Diplomacy, Medford, MA [Library symbol] [Library of Congress] (LCLS)
MMeT-Hi	Tufts University, Universalist Historical Society, Medford, MA [Library symbol] [Library of Congress] (LCLS)
MMeT-M	Tufts University, Medical and Dental School, Boston, MA [Library symbol] [Library of Congress] (LCLS)
MMEX	Map Maneuver Exercise (MCD)
MMEX	Mexico [Mexico] [ICAO location identifier] (ICLI)
MMF	Fleet Minelayer [Navy symbol]
MMF	Machine Master File (ACAE)
mmf	Magnetomotive Force
MMF	Make Money Fast (SAUS)

MMF	Mamfe [*Cameroon*] [*Airport symbol*] (OAG)
MMF	Maritime Life Assurance Co. [*Toronto Stock Exchange symbol*]
MMF	Maximum Midexpiratory Flow [*Also, MMEF*] [*Medicine*]
MMF	Meals for Millions Foundation (SAUO)
MMF	Mean Maximum Flow [*Medicine*]
MMF	Mechanical Machine-Finished Paper (DGA)
MMF	Member of the Medical Faculty
MMF	Memory Mapped File (SAUS)
MMF	Microelectronics Manufacturing Facility [*Philco-Ford Corp.*] (MCD)
MMF	Micromation Microfilm
MMF	Micromembrane Filter
mmf	Micromicrofarad (IDOE)
MMF	Micromicrofarad (MUGU)
MMF	Milbank Memorial Fund (SAUO)
MMF	Minelayer, Fleet [*Navy symbol*] [*Obsolete*]
MMF	Missile Maintenance Facility (ACAE)
MMF	Mobile Magnetic Field
MMF	Mobile Missile Facility (MCD)
MMF	Mobility Maintenance Facility (NVT)
mmf	Modern Maid Food Products, Inc. (SAUO)
MMF	Module Maintenance Facility
MMF	Money Market Fund [*Investment term*]
MMF	Moravian Music Foundation (EA)
MMF	Moving Magnetic Feature [*Astronomy*] (OA)
MMF	Multimode Fiber (ACRL)
MMF	MultiMode Fiberoptic Cable [*Telecommunications*] (DDC)
MMF	Mutual Musicians Foundation (EA)
MMF	National Association of Master Mechanics and Foremen of Naval Shore Establishments
MMFA	Fireman Apprentice, Machinist's Mate, Striker [*Navy rating*]
MMFA	Montreal Museum of Fine Arts (SAUO)
MMFAB	Metals and Machine Fabricators (SAUO)
MMFC	Michael Murphy Fan Club (EA)
MMFCC	Master of Marriage, Family and Child Counseling (GAGS)
MMFCG	Maintenance Management Functional Coordinating Group [*Army*]
MMFC-MF	Marilyn Monroe Fan Club - Marilyn Forever (EA)
MMFCS	Multi-Missile Fire Control System [*Military*]
MMFD	Micromicrofarad (GPO)
MMFF	Modular Multizone Furnace Facility (SAUS)
MMFF	Multimode Fire & Forget (SAUS)
MMFFS	Multi-Modular Fluid Filtration System
MMFI	Moravian Music Foundation, Incorporated (SAUO)
MMFITB	Man-Made Fibres Producing Industry Training Board [*British*] (BI)
MMFL	Mobile Maintenance Facility Liaison (ACAE)
MMFM	Modified Modified Frequency Modulation (NITA)
MMFN	Fireman, Machinist's Mate, Striker [*Navy rating*]
MMFO	Maintenance Management Field Office [*Military*] (MCD)
MMFO	Material Management Field Office
MMFPA	Man-Made Fiber Producers Association [*Later, MMFPAI*] (EA)
MMFPAI	Man-Made Fiber Producers Association, Inc. (EA)
MMFPB	Mill Mutual Fire Prevention Bureau [*Defunct*] (EA)
MMFPI	Man-Made Fiber Producers Institute (SAUO)
MMFR	Maximal Midflow Rate [*Medicine*] (MAE)
MMFR	Maximum Midexpiratory Flow Rate [*Physiology*]
MMFS	Manufacturing Message Format Service (NITA)
MMFS	Manufacturing Messaging Format Standards [*Automotive engineering*]
MMFT	Master of Marriage and Family Therapy (GAGS)
MMFV	Manned Mars Flyby Vehicle [*Aerospace*]
MMG	Machinist's Mate, Industrial Gas Generating Mechanic [*Navy rating*]
MMG	MacMillan Gold [*Vancouver Stock Exchange symbol*]
MMG	Magdalena Milpas Altas [*Guatemala*] [*Seismograph station code, US Geological Survey*] (SEIS)
MMG	Magnetomyogramm (SAUS)
MMG	Mean Maternal Glucose [*Clinical chemistry*]
MMG	Mechanomyography [*Medicine*]
MMG	Medium Machine Gun
MMG	Metromedia International Group [*AMEX symbol*] (SAG)
MMG	Motor Machine Gun Corps [*British military*] (DMA)
MMG	Motor-Motor Generator [*Nuclear energy*] (NRCH)
MMG	Mount Magnet [*Australia*] [*Airport symbol*] (OAG)
MMG	Movie Makers Guild (EA)
MMG	Multimedia Management Group (SAUO)
MMG	Multimode Guidance (MCD)
MMGA	Mannequin and Models' Guild of Australia
MMGB	Motor Machine Gun Battalion [*British military*] (DMA)
MMGC	Mego Mortgage Corp. [*NASDAQ symbol*] (SAG)
MMGI	Medical Marketing Group (EFIS)
MMGI	Member of the Mining, Geological, and Metallurgical Institute of India
MMGL	Guadalajara/Miguel Hidalgo Y Costilla Internacional [*Mexico*] [*ICAO location identifier*] (ICLI)
MMGM	Guaymas/General Jose Maria Yanez Internacional [*Mexico*] [*ICAO location identifier*] (ICLI)
M Mgmt	Master of Management (PGP)
MMGR	Masai Mara Game Reserve (SAUO)
MMGS	Motor Machine Gun Service [*British military*] (DMA)
MMGS	Mount Muhavura Gorilla Sanctuary (SAUO)
MMGT	Guanajuato [*Mexico*] [*ICAO location identifier*] (ICLI)
MMgt	Master of Management
MMGT	Medical Management, Inc. [*NASDAQ symbol*] (SAG)
MMGT	Microwave Magneto-Transconductance (ACAE)
MMGT	Multimastergroup Translator (SAUO)
MMgtEng	Master of Management Engineering (NADA)
MMh	Abbot Public Library Marblehead, Ma [*Library symbol*] [*Library of Congress*] (LCLS)

MMH	Macromicromodular Hyperplasia [*Medicine*]
MMH	Maintenance Man-Hours (NG)
MMH	Mammoth Lakes [*California*] [*Airport symbol*] (OAG)
MMH	Mammoth Lakes, CA [*Location identifier*] [*FAA*] (FAAL)
MMH	Maplex Management & Holdings Ltd. [*Toronto Stock Exchange symbol*]
MMH	Master of Management in Hospitality (PGP)
MMH	Master of Medical Humanities (PGP)
MMH	Meristar Hotels & Resorts [*NYSE symbol*] (SG)
MMH	Methylmercuric Hydroxide [*Organic chemistry*]
MMH	Mikromatika Air Cargo Ltd. [*Hungary*] [*ICAO designator*] (FAAC)
MM/H	Millimeters per Hour
MMH	Mismatched Hand Holes [*Tire maintenance*]
MMH	Monomethylhydrazine [*Organic chemistry*]
MMH	Multimode Hydrophone [*Military*] (CAAL)
MMHA	Metropolitan Mutual Housing Association [*Defunct*] (EA)
MMHC	Tehuacan [*Mexico*] [*ICAO location identifier*] (ICLI)
MMH/FH	Maintenance Man-Hours per Flight Hours
mmHg	Millimeters of Mercury [*A measurement of pressure*] (KSC)
MMhHi	Marblehead Historical Society, Marblehead, MA [*Library symbol*] [*Library of Congress*] (LCLS)
MMHi	Milton Historical Society, Milton, MA [*Library symbol*] [*Library of Congress*] (LCLS)
MMHIO	Midwest Migrant Health Information Office (EA)
MMH/MA	Mean Manhours per Maintenance Action
MMHO	Hermosillo/Internacional [*Mexico*] [*ICAO location identifier*] (ICLI)
MMH/OH	Maintenance Man-Hours per Operating Hours (MCD)
MMHQ	Meta-Methoxyhydroquinone [*Organic chemistry*]
MMHR	Maintenance Man-Hours
MMHR/FH	Maintenance Man-Hours per Flight Hours (MCD)
MMH/S	Maintenance Man-Hours per Sortie [*Aerospace*] (MCD)
MMHS	Mechanized Materials Handling System [*Air Force*]
MMHS	Military Message Handling System (SAUO)
MMHSRA	Marine Mammal Health and Stranding Response Act
MMH/UH	Maintenance Man-Hours per Utilization Hour (ACAE)
MMI	Athens, TN [*Location identifier*] [*FAA*] (FAAL)
MMI	Macrophage Migration Inhibition [*Cytology*]
MMI	Main Memory Interface (NITA)
MMI	Major Market Index
MMI	Malaysian Marine Industries (SAUO)
MMI	Management and Maintenance Inspection (NVT)
MMI	Management of Motives Index [*Test*]
MMI	Man-Machine Interaction (NITA)
MMI	Man-Machine Interface
MMI	Manpower Management Information
MMI	Manufacturing Message Interface [*Data communications standards*]
MMI	Marshall Management Instruction (SAUO)
MMI	Martin Marietta International
MMI	Materials Management Institute
MMI	Materials Management International (SAUO)
MMI	Mature Market Institute [*An association*] [*Defunct*] (EA)
MMI	Mean Motility Index [*For intestine*]
MMI	Mechanized Manufacturing Information
MMI	Medicus Mundi Internationalis [*International Organization for Cooperation in Health Care - IOCHC*] [*Nijmegen, Netherlands*] (EAIO)
MMI	Methylmercaptoimidazole [*Also, METHIMAZOLE*] [*Thyroid inhibitor*]
MMI	Michigan Molecular Institute, Inc. [*Formerly, Midland Macromolecular Institute*] [*Research center*] (RCD)
MMI	Micromagnetic Industries
MMI	Middle Management Institute [*Special Libraries Association*]
MMI	Midland Macromolecular Institute [*Midland, MI*]
MMI	Mild [*or Minimal*] Memory Impairment [*Medicine*]
MMI	Minnesota Mining & Manufacturing Co., St. Paul, MN [*OCLC symbol*] (OCLC)
MMI	MMI Companies [*NYSE symbol*] (SPSG)
MMI	Mode-Media Interaction (MCD)
MMI	Mode-Medium Instability (SAUS)
MMI	Modified Mercalli Intensity [*Earthquake magnitude*] [*Seismology*]
MMI	Money Management Institute [*Commercial firm*] (EA)
MMI	Monolithic Memories, Inc. [*Computer science*]
MMI	Montana Myotis Leukoencephalitis [*Virus*]
MMI	Monthly Management Information Report (SAUO)
MMI	Moslem Mosque Incorporated (SAUO)
MMI	MSFC [*Marshall Space Flight Center*] Management Instruction [*NASA*]
MMI	Multi-Media Integration (AGLO)
MMI	Multi-Message Interface (NITA)
MMI	Multiport Memory Interface [*Computer science*] (MHDB)
MMI	Mutual Mortgage Insurance Fund [*FHA*] (EMRF)
MMIA	Colima [*Mexico*] [*ICAO location identifier*] (ICLI)
MMIA	Medical Malpractice Insurance Association
MMIA	Military Mission to the Italian Army [*World War II*]
MMI&CS	Martin Marietta Information and Communication System (ACAE)
MMIB	Man-Machine Integration Branch [*Ames Research Center*] [*NASA*]
MMIC	Maintenance Management Information and Control (MCD)
MMIC	Marinduque Mining and Industrial Corporation (SAUO)
M Mic	Master of Microbiology
MMIC	Millimeter/Microwave Integrated Circuit
MMIC	Miniature Microwave Integrated Circuit
MMIC	Monolithic Microwave Integrated Circuit
MMI CoS	MMI Companies [*Associated Press*] (SAG)
MMICRO-LANGUAGE ARTS	Microcomputer Managed Information for Criterion Referenced Objectives-Language Arts [*Educational Development Corp.*] (TES)

MMICRO-MATH... Microcomputer Managed Information for Criterion Referenced Objectives-Math [*R. Hambleton*] (TES)
MMICS......... Maintenance Management Information and Control System
MMID......... Merida [*Mexico*] [*ICAO location identifier*] (ICLI)
MMidwif Master of Midwifery
M Mi E Master of Mining Engineering
MMiEng......... Master of Mining Engineering (NADA)
MMIF......... Macrophage Migration Inhibitory Factor (DMAA)
MMIF......... Mutual Mortgage Insurance Fund [*Federal Housing Administration*]
MMIFC......... Marilyn Monroe International Fan Club (EA)
MMIHS .... Megacystis-Microcolon-Intestinal Hypoperistalsis Syndrome [*Medicine*] (DMAA)
MMII......... Mass Marketing Insurance Institute (EA)
MMII......... Multimedia Individualized Instruction [*Army*]
MMIIL......... Multi-Input Multi-Output Integrated Injection Logic (IAA)
MMIIP......... Multimedia Individualized Instructional Package [*Army*]
MMIIS......... Material Management Integrated Information System (ACAE)
MMIJ .... Mining and Materials Processing Institute of Japan
MMIJ .... Mining and Metallurgical Institute of Japan (SAUO)
M Mil......... Master of Military Science (SAUO)
MMilt......... Milton Public Library, Milton, MA [*Library symbol*] [*Library of Congress*] (LCLS)
MMiltC......... Curry College, Milton, MA [*Library symbol*] [*Library of Congress*] (LCLS)
MMIM......... Isla Mujeres [*Mexico*] [*ICAO location identifier*] (ICLI)
MMIMS......... Modular Multi-Influence Minesweeping System (SAUS)
M Min......... Master of Ministries (PGP)
MMinMgt..... Master of Mining Management
MMINTERFACE... Multimedia Assisted Teleoperation (SAUO)
MMIO......... Saltillo [*Mexico*] [*ICAO location identifier*] (ICLI)
MMIP......... Maintenance Management Improvement Program (MCD)
MMIP......... Manual of Meat Inspection Procedures [*of the USDA*]
MMIPS......... Man-Machine Interactive Processing System (PDAA)
MMIPS......... Multiple Mode Integrated Propulsion System (PDAA)
MMIR......... Multispectral Microwave Imaging Radiometer (ACAE)
MMIRA......... Multi-Mission Intermeshing Rotor Aircraft (SAUS)
MMIRC .... Mind-Machine Interaction Research Center [*University of Florida*] [*Research center*] (RCD)
MMIS......... Maintenance Management Information System [*Military*] (AFM)
MMIS......... Manpower Maneuvering Information System (SAUS)
MMIS......... Master of Management Information Systems (GAGS)
MMIS......... Materials Management Information System (SAUO)
MMIS......... Materials Manager Information System (SAUO)
MMIS......... Medicaid Management Information System [*HEW*]
MMIS......... Member of the Mining Institute of Scotland (SAUO)
MMIS......... Mortgage Market Information Service
MMIS......... Multinational Meetings Information Services BV [*Netherlands*] [*Information service or system*] (IID)
MMIS......... Municipal Management Information System [*Civil Defense*]
M Miss .... Master of Missiology (PGP)
MMIT......... Iztepec [*Mexico*] [*ICAO location identifier*] (ICLI)
MMIT......... Man-Machine Interrogation Technique
MMITI......... Martin Marietta Information Technology Institute (ACAE)
MMITS......... Modular Multifunction Information Transfer System (SAUO)
MMIU......... Multi-Part Memory Interface Unit (NITA)
MMIU......... Multiport Memory Interface Unit
MMJ......... Main Metering Jet [*Automotive engineering*]
MMJ......... Matsumoto [*Japan*] [*Airport symbol*] (OAG)
MMJ......... Modified Modular Jack (SAUO)
MMJ......... Pittsburgh, PA [*Location identifier*] [*FAA*] (FAAL)
MMJA......... Jalapa [*Mexico*] [*ICAO location identifier*] (ICLI)
MMJC......... Meridian Municipal Junior College [*Mississippi*]
MMJP......... Main Metering Jet-Primary [*Automotive engineering*]
MMJS......... Main Metering Jet-Secondary [*Automotive engineering*]
MMK......... Loparskaya [*Formerly, Murmansk*] [*Former USSR*] [*Geomagnetic observatory code*]
MMK......... Maison Master Keyed [*Locks*] (ADA)
MMK......... Marshall-Marchetti-Krantz [*Procedure*] [*Medicine*] (MEDA)
MMK......... Material Mark
MMK......... Meriden, CT [*Location identifier*] [*FAA*] (FAAL)
MMK......... Murmansk [*Former USSR*] [*Airport symbol*] (OAG)
MMKR .... Middle Marker [*in an instrument landing system*]
MML......... Maintenance Management Level [*Military*]
MML......... Maker Markup Language [*Computer science*] (AGLO)
MML......... Managing the Modern Laboratory [*A publication*]
MML......... Man-Machine Language [*Computer science*] (TEL)
MML......... Manual of Military Law [*British*]
MML......... Marshall [*Minnesota*] [*Airport symbol*] (OAG)
MML......... Marshall, MN [*Location identifier*] [*FAA*] (FAAL)
MML......... Marx Memorial Library (SAUO)
MML......... Massachusetts Mutual Life Insurance Co. (EFIS)
MML......... Mass Mutual Mortgage and Realty Investors (SAUO)
MML......... Master Measurements List (NASA)
MML......... Master of Modern Languages
MML......... Mathematics Markup Language (SAUS)
MML......... McKinley Memorial Library, Niles, OH [*OCLC symbol*] (OCLC)
MML......... Menika Mining Ltd. [*Vancouver Stock Exchange symbol*]
MML......... Merrill Lyn 6.50%'STRYPES' [*NYSE symbol*] (TTSB)
MML......... Merrill Lynch & Co. [*NYSE symbol*] (SAG)
MML......... Metal-Metal Laminate
MML......... Micromedia Ltd. [*ACCORD*] [*UTLAS symbol*]
mM/L......... Millimole/Liter [*Chemistry*]
MML......... Minimum Message Length (IDAI)
MML......... Missouri Municipal League (SAUO)
MML......... Mobile Media Line

MML......... Moloney Murine Leukemia [*Medicine*] (DMAA)
MML......... Monomethyllysine (DB)
MML......... Mote Marine Laboratory (NOAA)
MML......... Motor Movement Latency
MML......... Multimaterial Laminate
MML......... Myelomonocytic Leukemia [*Medicine*] (DMAA)
MMLA......... Midwest Modern Language Association (BARN)
MMLA......... Military Mission of Liaison Administration [*World War II*]
MMLAN......... Multi Media Local Area Network (ACAE)
MMLC......... Lazaro Cardenas [*Mexico*] [*ICAO location identifier*] (ICLI)
MMLC......... Medium Mobility Load Carrier (SAUS)
MMLD......... Merchant Mariners Licensing and Documentation [*BTS*] (TAG)
MMLE......... Modified Maximum Likelihood Estimates [*Statistics*]
MMLEC......... Munitions Management and Labour Efficiency Committee [*British*] [*World War II*]
MMLES......... Map-Matching Location - Estimation System [*Aviation*]
MMLL......... Michigan Regional Libraries Film Program at Cadillac [*Library network*]
MMLM......... Los Mochis [*Mexico*] [*ICAO location identifier*] (ICLI)
MMLME......... Mediterranean, Mediterranean Littoral, and/or Middle East
MMLO......... Leon [*Mexico*] [*ICAO location identifier*] (ICLI)
MMLP......... La Paz/General Manuel Marquez de Leon Internacional [*Mexico*] [*ICAO location identifier*] (ICLI)
MMLRF......... Micro Modular Laser Range Finder (ACAE)
MMLS......... Military Microwave Landing System (MCD)
MMLS......... Mobile Microwave Landing System (SAUS)
M-M-L-S... Model-Modes-Loads-Stresses [*Aerospace*] (NAKS)
MMLSA......... Military Microwave Landing System, Avionics (DWSG)
MMLT......... Loreto [*Mexico*] [*ICAO location identifier*] (ICLI)
MMLV......... Moloney Murine Leukaemia Virus [*Medicine*] (BABM)
MMLV......... Moloney Murine Leukemia Virus [*of mice*] [*Veterinary medicine*] (DAVI)
MMM......... Aviation Co. Meridian [*Former USSR*] [*FAA designator*] (FAAC)
MMM......... International Association of Margaret Morris Method (SAUO)
MMM......... Magnetism and Magnetic Materials
MMM......... Maine Maritime Academy, Castine, ME [*OCLC symbol*] (OCLC)
MMM......... Maintenance and Material Management [*Navy*]
MMM......... Maintenance Management Manual
MMM......... Maintenance Man-Minute
MMM......... Manned Maneuvering Module [*Aerospace*] (IIA)
MMM......... Manned Mars Mission [*NASA*]
MMM......... Margaret Morris Movement [*British*] (BI)
MMM......... Marine & Aviation Management International [*British*] [*ICAO designator*] (FAAC)
MMM......... Marine Multipurpose Missile (DNAB)
MMM......... Mariner Mission to Mars (ACAE)
MMM......... Mark Master Mason [*Freemasonry*]
MMM......... Mars Mission Module
MMM......... Mass Media Ministries [*An association*]
MMM......... Master in Media Management
MMM......... Master of Management in Manufacturing (PGP)
MMM......... Master of Medical Management (PGP)
MMM......... Master of Ministry Management (PGP)
MMM......... Material Maintenance Management (MCD)
MMM......... Material Movement Management (AAEL)
MMM......... Materials Management Manual (SAUO)
MMM......... Mauritian Militant Movement (SAUO)
MMM......... McAdam Resources, Inc. [*Toronto Stock Exchange symbol*]
MMM......... Meaningful Measures of Merit (SAUO)
MMM......... Measuring Monitoring Module (KSC)
MMM......... Medical Materiel Manager [*Military*] (AABC)
MMM......... Medical Missionaries of Mary [*Roman Catholic women's religious order*]
MMM......... Member of the Order of Military Merit [*Canada*] (DD)
MMM......... Memory Mapper Modul (SAUO)
MMM......... Mesocale and Microscale Meteorology (GNE)
MMM......... Micro Macro Magician (SAUS)
mmm......... Micromillimeter (WGA)
MMM......... Microsome-Mediated Mutagenesis (DB)
MMM......... Middle Management Module
MMM......... Middlemount [*Australia*] [*Airport symbol*] (OAG)
MMM......... Militia Mea Multiplex [*Pseudonym used by William Tooke*]
mmm......... Millimicron [*Microscopy*] (CPH)
MMM......... Minnesota Mining & Manufacturing Co. [*Also known as 3M Co.*] [*Associated Press*] (SAG)
MMM......... Mobile Media Mode (SAUS)
MMM......... Mode Management Module (SAUO)
MMM......... Modern Music Management (SAUO)
MMM......... Modern Music Masters Society
MMM......... Money Market Monitor [*Financial Products Group*] [*Information service or system*] (IID)
MMM......... Monomethylmetoxuron [*Organic chemistry*]
MMM......... Montana Myotis Meningoencephalitis [*Medicine*] (DB)
MMM......... Mormon Mesa, NV [*Location identifier*] [*FAA*] (FAAL)
MMM......... Mouvement Militant Mauricien [*Mauritian Militant Movement*] [*Political party*] (PPW)
MMM......... Mouvement Mondial des Meres [*World Movement of Mothers - WMM*] [*Paris, France*] (EAIO)
MMM......... Multigrid Modulator Multiplier
MMM......... Multi-Mission Missile (ACAE)
MMM......... Multimission Module [*Aerospace*]
MMM......... Multimode Mode Matrix (MCD)
MMM......... Myelofibrosis and Myeloid Metaplasia [*Hematology*]
MMM......... Myelosclerosis with Myeloid Metaplasia [*Medicine*] (MAE)
MMM......... Mysteria Mystica Maxima (SAUO)

MMMA.........	Maine Merchant Marine Academy (SAUO)
MMMA.........	Matamoros Internacional [*Mexico*] [*ICAO location identifier*] (ICLI)
MMMA.........	Metalforming Machinery Makers Association [*British*] (DBA)
MMMA.........	Milking Machine Manufacturers Association [*British*] (DBA)
MMMA.........	Music Masters and Mistresses Association (AIE)
MMM&SA	Master Monumental Masons and Sculptors Association (SAUO)
MMMC.........	Machine Material Movement Component (AAEL)
MMMC.........	Medical Materiel Management Center [*Military*] (AABC)
MMMC.........	Milking Machine Manufacturers Council (EA)
MMMC.........	Minimum Monthly Maintenance Charge (MHDW)
MMMD.........	Merida/Lic. Manuel Crecencio Rejon Internacional [*Mexico*] [*ICAO location identifier*] (ICLI)
MMMDCS	Multi-National Maintenance Management Data Collection System (SAUO)
MMME.........	Martin Marietta Missile Electronics Division [*Military*]
MMME.........	Master of Metallurgical and Materials Engineering (PGP)
MMMEP.......	Military Manpower Management Evaluation Project (NG)
MMMF.........	Man-Made Mineral Fiber
MMMF.........	Money Market Mutual Fund [*Investment term*]
MMMF.........	Multinational Mixed Manned Force (NATG)
MMMFS.......	Money Market Mutual Fund Shares [*Investment term*]
MMMFTP.....	Matched Maturity Marginal Fund Transfer Pricing (EBF)
MMMI.........	Meat Machinery Manufacturers Institute (EA)
MMMIS........	Maintenance and Material Management Information System
MMML.........	Mexicali/General Rodolfo Sanchez Taboada Internacional [*Mexico*] [*ICAO location identifier*] (ICLI)
MMMLTG.....	Mixed Media Multi-Link Transmission Group (SAUO)
MMMM........	Man, Material, Machinery, Methods [*Statistical process control*]
MMMM........	Morelia [*Mexico*] [*ICAO location identifier*] (ICLI)
MMMN........	[*The*] Memorial of Moses on Mount Nebo [*A publication*] (BJA)
MMMOS.......	Mobile Micrometeorological Observation System
MMMPC.......	Maintenance and Material Management Project Center [*Navy*]
MMMR.........	Medical Material Mission Reserve [*Military*] (AABC)
MMMS.........	Maintenance and Material Management System (KSC)
MMMS.........	Martin Marietta Manned Space System (SAUO)
MMMS.........	Martin Marietta Missile System [*Military*]
MMMS.........	Material Movement Management Standard (AAEL)
MMMS.........	Medical Materiel Management System (SAUO)
MMMS.........	Merck Molecular Modelling System (DB)
MMMS.........	Militarized Multimission Modular Spacecraft (SAUS)
MMMS.........	Minerals, Metals, and Materials Society (EA)
MMMS.........	Modern Music Masters Society (SAUO)
MMMS.........	Multi-Mission Management System (SAUS)
MMMS-OL...	Medical Materiel Management System-On Line [*Air Force*] (GFGA)
MMMSP......	Mouvement Militant Mauricien Socialiste Progressiste [*Mauritius Militant Socialist Progressive Movement*] (PPW)
MMMT.........	Malignant Mixed Mesodermal Tumor [*Medicine*] (MELL)
MMMT.........	Malignant Mixed Muellerian Tumor [*Oncology*]
MMMT.........	Metastatic Mixed Mullerian Tumor [*Medicine*] (MELL)
MMMT.........	Minatitlan [*Mexico*] [*ICAO location identifier*] (ICLI)
MMMTF.......	Mobilization Materiel Management Task Force
MMM/UH	Maintenance Man-Minutes per Utilization Hour (ACAE)
MMMV.........	Monclova [*Mexico*] [*ICAO location identifier*] (ICLI)
MMMX.........	Mexico/Lic. Benito Juarez Internacional [*Mexico*] [*ICAO location identifier*] (ICLI)
MMMY.........	Monterrey/General Mariano Escobedo Internacional [*Mexico*] [*ICAO location identifier*] (ICLI)
MMMZ.........	Mazatlan/General Rafael Buelna [*Mexico*] [*ICAO location identifier*] (ICLI)
MMn...........	Elizabth Taber Library, Marion, MA [*Library symbol*] [*Library of Congress*] (LCLS)
MMN...........	Maintenance Module Node (ACAE)
MMN...........	Marathon Minerals [*Vancouver Stock Exchange symbol*]
MMN...........	Medial Muscle Motoneuron [*Neuroanatomy*]
MMN...........	Miami, FL [*Location identifier*] [*FAA*] (FAAL)
MMN...........	Mismatch Negativity [*Neurophysiology*]
MMN...........	Modified Melin-Norkram's Agar [*Microbiology*]
MMN...........	Morbus Maculosus Neonatorum [*Medicine*] (DMAA)
MMN...........	Museum of Man and Nature (SAUO)
MMNA	Moto Morini Club of North America (EA)
MMNAFWB..	Master's Men of the National Association of Free Will Baptists (EA)
MMNC........	Marrow Mononuclear Cell (DMAA)
MMNG........	Nogales/Internacional [*Mexico*] [*ICAO location identifier*] (ICLI)
MMNIC	Main Mediterranean Naval Intelligence Center [*Navy*]
MMNL.........	Nuevo Laredo [*Mexico*] [*ICAO location identifier*] (ICLI)
MMNOM......	Monmouths Nominal [*Software engineering cost model*]
MMNP........	Mount McKinley National Park (SAUO)
MM(NSW)....	Milk Marketing (New South Wales) [*Australia*]
MMNU........	Nautla [*Mexico*] [*ICAO location identifier*] (ICLI)
MMO...........	Intel Mobile Module [*Computer science*]
MMO...........	Mach Max Operating (GAVI)
MMO...........	Main Meteorological Office
MMO...........	Maintenance Management Office (SAUO)
MMO...........	Maio [*Cape Verde Islands*] [*Airport symbol*] (OAG)
MMO...........	Marseilles, IL [*Location identifier*] [*FAA*] (FAAL)
Mmo	Maximum operating (SAUS)
M$_{mo}$	Maximum Operating Mach Number [*Aviation*] (DA)
MMO...........	Medio Mundo [*Nicaragua*] [*Seismograph station code, US Geological Survey*] (SEIS)
MMO...........	Medium Machine Oil (BARN)
MMO...........	Mercantile Marine Office [*or Officer*] [*British*]
MMO...........	Methane Monooxygenase [*An enzyme*]
MMO...........	Micrographics Management Officer (MCD)
MMO...........	Minuteman Ordnance (SAA)
MMO...........	MIPR [*Military Interdepartmental Purchase Request*] Management Office (AFIT)
MMO...........	Mismatched Outer Diameter [*Tire maintenance*]
MMO...........	Mission Management Office (ACAE)
MMO...........	Mission Management Office Meeting (SAUO)
MMO...........	MMT Resources [*Vancouver Stock Exchange symbol*]
MMO...........	Mobile Module [*Computer science*]
MMO...........	Monarch Machine Tool Co. [*NYSE symbol*] (SPSG)
MMO...........	Multimodel Optimization (AAEL)
MMO...........	Music Minus One [*Recording label*]
MMOA........	Martin Marietta Orlando Aerospace (ACAE)
MMOA........	Maxillary Mandibular Odentectomy Alveolectomy [*Dentistry*] (DAVI)
MMOA	Mobile Modular Office Association (EA)
MMOAG......	Research Station, Agriculture Canada [*Station de Recherches, Agriculture Canada*] Morden, Manitoba [*Library symbol*] [*National Library of Canada*] (NLC)
MMOB	Military Money Order Branch (AFM)
MMOBCD....	Millions of Octane-Barrels per Calendar Day [*Petroleum industry*]
MMOC	Modified Method of Characteristics [*Environmental Protection Agency*] (AEPA)
MMOC	Multimissions Operations Center (ACAE)
MMOD	Micromodule (IEEE)
M Mod A	Museum of Modern Art (SAUO)
MMODE......	Mirror Mode (MCD)
MMODS	Master Material Ordering and Delivery Schedule (DNAB)
MMOECB	Maintenance Mode Operational Equipment Checkout Box (MCD)
MMOG	Merchant Marine Officers Guild [*Defunct*] (EA)
MMOL.........	Manned Orbital Laboratory (SAUO)
mmol	micromole (SAUS)
mmol	Millimole [*Mass*]
MMoL.........	Myelomonoblastic Leukemia [*Medicine*] (DMAA)
mmol/l	Millimole per Liter [*Measurement*] (DAVI)
MMONS	Methyl-methoxy-nitrostilbene [*Organic chemistry*]
MMOS	Message Multiplexer Operating System
MMOS	Mobile Micrometeorological Observation System (KSC)
MMOS	Modified Metal-Oxide Semiconductor (AAEL)
MMOS	Multicomputing Multitasking Operating System (NITA)
MMOS	Multi-Modal Organ Modeling System (SAUO)
mmos	Multimode Optical Sensor (NAKS)
MMOS	Multimode Optical Sensor (NASA)
MMOU	Multilateral Memorandum of Understanding
MMOW	Morden-Winkler Regional Library, Morden, Manitoba [*Library symbol*] [*National Library of Canada*] (NLC)
MMOW	South Central Regional Library, Morden, Manitoba [*Library symbol*] [*National Library of Canada*] (NLC)
MMOX	Oaxaca [*Mexico*] [*ICAO location identifier*] (ICLI)
MMP...........	AMP, Inc. [*FAA designator*] (FAAC)
MMP...........	International Organization of Masters, Mates, and Pilots (EA)
MMP...........	Machined Metal Part
MMP...........	Machine Main Performance (VLIE)
MMP...........	Magnetospheric Multiprobe (SSD)
MMP...........	Magnetotactic, Many-Celled Prokaryote [*Biology*]
MMP...........	Magyar Megujulas Partja [*Party of Hungarian Renewal*] [*Political party*] (PPE)
MMP...........	Main Micro-Processor (VLIE)
MMP...........	Maintenance and Modernization Program (ACAE)
MMP...........	Maintenance Management Plan
MMP...........	Maintenance Management Program (SAUO)
MMP...........	Maintenance Message Process [*Telecommunications*] (TEL)
MMP...........	Maintenance Monitor Panel (MCD)
MMP...........	M & M Porcupine Gold Mines [*Vancouver Stock Exchange symbol*]
MMP...........	Manufacturing Methods Procedure (MCD)
MMP...........	Marian Movement of Priests (EA)
MMP...........	Marilyn Monroe Productions, Inc. (SAUO)
MMP...........	Maritime Mobile Phone
MMP...........	Mashonaland Mounted Police [*British military*] (DMA)
MMP...........	Massively Multi-Processing [*Computer science*] (VLIE)
MMP...........	Master Mobilization Plan [*DoD*]
MMP...........	Master Music Printers and Engravers Association (DGA)
MMP...........	Master of Marine Policy (GAGS)
MMP...........	Master of Museum Practice (GAGS)
MMP...........	Master of Music Performance (PGP)
MMP...........	Masters in Management Program (SAUO)
MMP...........	Matabeleland Mounted Police [*British military*] (DMA)
MMP...........	Materials Management Plan (ABAC)
MMP...........	Matrix Metalloproteinase [*An enzyme*]
MMP...........	Maxim Pharmaceuticals, Inc. [*AMEX symbol*] (SAG)
MMP...........	Mean Maximum Pressure (SAUS)
MMP...........	Medical Mission Planner (SAUO)
MMP...........	Merchant Marine Personnel Division [*Coast Guard*]
MMP...........	Meteorological Monitoring Plan (SAUO)
MMP...........	Methadone Maintenance Program
MMP...........	Methyl-D-Mannopyranoside [*Organic chemistry*]
MMP...........	Microprogrammable Multiprocessor (MCD)
MMP...........	Microsatellite Mutator Phenotype [*Cytology*]
MMP...........	Military Microprocessor (ACAE)
MMP...........	Military Mounted Police
MMP...........	Minimum Miscibility Pressure [*Physical chemistry*]
MMP...........	Missile Mode Panel (MCD)
mmp	Mixed Melting Point [*Chemistry*]
MMP...........	Modernization Management Plan
MMP...........	Modes in Math Project [*National Science Foundation*]
MMP...........	Modular Midcourse Package [*DoD*]
MMP...........	Modular Mission Payload (SAUS)
MMP...........	Momentum Management Program [*NASA*] (KSC)

MMP............ Mompos [*Colombia*] [*Airport symbol*] (OAG)
MMP............ Money Market Preferred Stock [*Investment term*]
MMP............ Money Market Premium (AGLO)
MMP............ Monitoring/Metering Panel [*Telecommunications*] (OA)
MMP............ Mortar Master Plan [*Military*] (INF)
MMP............ Mount Mary [*New Zealand*] [*Seismograph station code, US Geological Survey*] (SEIS)
MMP............ Multiplexed Message Processor
MMP............ Munich Military Post (SAUO)
MMPA........ Magnetic Materials Producers Association (EA)
MMPA........ Magnetic Materials Products Association (AAGC)
MMPA........ Marine Mammals Protection Act [*1972*]
MMPA........ Mining and Mineral Policy Act of 1970 (COE)
MMPA........ Poza Rica [*Mexico*] [*ICAO location identifier*] (ICLI)
MMPAS...... Mobilization Manpower Policy Analysis [*Military*]
MMPB........ Manpower Management Planning Board
MMPB........ Puebla [*Mexico*] [*ICAO location identifier*] (ICLI)
MMPC........ Maritime Mobile Phone Coastal
MMPC........ Market Milk Producers' Council [*Australia*]
MMPC........ Mobilization Material Procurement Capability
MMPC........ Multi Message Package Chaffing (SAUS)
MMPC........ Pachuca [*Mexico*] [*ICAO location identifier*] (ICLI)
MMPD .... Material Movement Priority Designator (DNAB)
MMPD .... Methoxy-Meta-Phenylenediamine [*Organic chemistry*]
MMPD .... Money Manager Profile Diskettes [*Investment Management Institute*] [*Information service or system*] (IID)
MMPDABC ... Medical Materiel Program for Defense Against Biological and Chemical Agents [*Army*] (AABC)
MMPDABC ... Prepositioned Materiel Program for Defense Against Biological and Chemical Agents (SAUO)
MMPDC ...... Maritime Mobile Phone Distress and Calling
MMPDS...... Methoxy-Meta-Phenylenediamine Sulfate [*Organic chemistry*]
MMPE........ Punta Penasco [*Mexico*] [*ICAO location identifier*] (ICLI)
MMPF........ Master Military Pay File (AABC)
MMPF........ Microgravity and Materials Processing Facility
MMPG........ Piedras Negras [*Mexico*] [*ICAO location identifier*] (ICLI)
MMPGS...... Massively Multi-Player Games
MMPI.......... Marquest Medical Products, Inc. [*NASDAQ symbol*] (NQ)
MMPI.......... McGill-Melzack Pain Index [*Questionnaire and Home Life Change Index*] (DAVI)
MMPI.......... Minnesota Multiphasic Personality Inventory [*Psychology*]
MMPI.......... Montgomery Medical and Psychological Institute (EA)
MMPI-2....... Minnesota Multiphasic Personality Inventory-2 (DIPS)
MMPI-A....... Minnesota Multiphasic Personality Inventory-Adolescent (DIPS)
MMPI-D....... Depression scale of the Minnesota Multiphasic Personality Inventory (SAUS)
MMPM........ Marine Management Programming Model (SAUO)
MMPM........ Multimedia Presentation Manager [*IBM Corp.*] (PCM)
MMPN........ Uruapan [*Mexico*] [*ICAO location identifier*] (ICLI)
MMPNC ...... Medical Materiel Program for Nuclear Casualties [*Army*] (AABC)
MMPO........ Mission Management and Planning Office (SAUO)
MMPP.......... Mechanized Market Programming Procedures [*Computer science*] (TEL)
mmpp.......... Millimeters Partial Pressure
MMPP.......... Moose Mountain Provincial Park (SAUO)
MMPPPA...... Medicare and Medicaid Patient and Program Protection Act
MMPR .... Methylmercaptopurine Ribose [*Biochemistry*]
MMPR .... Missile Manufacturer's Planning Report
MMPR .... Puerto Vallarta/Lic. Gustavo Dias Ordaz Internacional [*Mexico*] [*ICAO location identifier*] (ICLI)
MMPS........ Manpower Mobilization Planning System (SAUO)
MMPS........ Manufacturing Material Planning System (MHDB)
MMPS........ Manufacturing Message Format System
MMPS........ Medical Media Production Service [*Commercial firm*] (DAVI)
MMPS........ Money Market Preferred Stock (EBF)
MMPS........ Puerto Escondido [*Mexico*] [*ICAO location identifier*] (ICLI)
MMPSE...... Multiuse Mission Payload Support Equipment (MCD)
MMPT........ Man-Machine Partnership Translation [*Telecommunications*] (IEEE)
MMPT........ Modem Media.Poppe Tyson'A' [*NASDAQ symbol*] (SG)
MMPT........ Monitored and Modulated Periodontal Therapeutics [*Dentistry*]
mm-PTH...... Mid-Molecule Parathyroid Hormone [*Endocrinology*] (DAVI)
MMPU........ Memory Manager and Protect Unit (IEEE)
MMPVS...... Modified Military Pay Voucher System (AABC)
MMQ........... Market Milk Quota (SAUO)
MMQ........... Minimum Manufacturing Quality
MMQT........ Queretaro [*Mexico*] [*ICAO location identifier*] (ICLI)
MMR........... Austin, TX [*Location identifier*] [*FAA*] (FAAL)
MMR........... Machinist's Mate, Refrigeration [*Navy rating*]
MMR........... Mach Meter Reading (MCD)
MMR........... Magnetically-Modulated Microwave Reflection [*Spectrometer*]
MMR........... Magnetic Memory Record (NITA)
MMR........... Maine State Department of Marine Resources, West Boothbay Harbor, ME [*OCLC symbol*] (OCLC)
MMR........... Main Memory Register
MMR........... Maintenance Management Report (SAUO)
MMR........... Maintenance Management Review (ACAE)
MMR........... Management Milestone Records [*Navy*] (NG)
MMR........... Mass Migration Response (DEMM)
MMR........... Mass Miniature Radiography
MMR........... Master Microfiche Record
MMR........... Master of Marketing Research (GAGS)
MMR........... Materiel Management Review [*DoD*]
MMR........... Maternal Mortality Rate [*Gynecology*]
MMR........... Maternal Mortality Ratio (SAUO)
MMR........... McMoRan Exploration [*NYSE symbol*] (SG)

MMR........... Mean Motion Resonance [*Astrophysics*]
MMR........... Measles-Mumps-Rubella [*Immunology*]
MMR........... Merchant Marine Reserve (DNAB)
MMR........... Method of Mixed Ranges (PDAA)
MMR........... Midline Malignant Reticulosis [*Hematology*] (DAVI)
MMR........... Mild Mental Retardation (MELL)
MMR........... Military Media Review [*A publication*] (DNAB)
MMR........... Miniature Micropower Resistor
MMR........... Minimum Marginal Return
MMR........... Minimum Military Requirement (SAUS)
MMR........... Minnedosa Regional Library, Minnedosa, Manitoba [*Library symbol*] [*National Library of Canada*] (NLC)
MMR........... Mismatch Repair [*Genetics*]
MMR........... Missed Message Rate (CAAL)
MMR........... Mitchell's Maritime Register [*England*] [*A publication*] (DLA)
MMR........... Mixed Municipal Refuse
MMR........... Mobile Mass X-Ray (MAE)
MMR........... Mobilization Materiel Requirement [*Military*]
MMR........... Moderate Mental Retardation (DIPS)
MMR........... Modular Multiband Radiometer
MMR........... Monomethylolrutin [*Organic chemistry*]
MMR........... Monroe Mendelsohn Research, Inc. [*Information service or system*] (IID)
MMR........... Monthly Management Review (ACAE)
MMR........... Monthly Meteorological Records (DNAB)
MMR........... Monthly Musical Record (SAUO)
MMR........... Monumental Maintenance Requirements (MCD)
MMR........... Morris Minor Registry (EA)
MMR........... Motorized Microfilm Reader
MMR........... Mouth-to-Mouth Resuscitation (MELL)
MMR........... Multi-Market Radio
MMR........... Multi Mission Radar (ACAE)
MMR........... Multimode RADAR
MMR........... Multimode Radiometer (MCD)
MMR........... Multi-Mode Receiver [*Navigation systems*]
MMR........... Multiple Match Resolver
MMR........... Mustang Motorcycle Registry [*Defunct*] (EA)
MMR........... Myocardial Metabolic Rate [*Cardiology*] (MAE)
MMRA........ Maritime Marshland Rehabilitation Administration (SAUO)
MMRA........ Maritime Marshland Rehabilitation Association (SAUO)
MMRA .... Mobilization Materiel Requirement Adjustment [*Military*] (NG)
MMR & S... Military Medical Research and Services Program (CINC)
MMRB........ Maintenance Management Review Board (MCD)
MMRB........ Master Material Review Board (NADA)
MMRB........ Materiel Management Review Board (AFIT)
MMRB........ MOS [*Military Occupational Specialty*] Medical Retention Board [*Army*]
MMRBM...... Mobile Medium-Range Ballistic Missile [*Air Force*]
MMRC........ Materials and Mechanics Research Center [*Army*] (MCD)
MMRC........ Materiel Management Review Committee (SAUO)
MMRC........ Mature Market Resource Center (EA)
MMRC........ Mental Retardation Research Center
MMRC........ Mountain Meadow Research Center [*Colorado State University*] [*Research center*] (RCD)
M-MRCP..... Multi-Management Resolution Control Processor
MMRD........ Materials and Molecular Research Division [*Lawrence Berkeley Laboratory*] [*Research center*] (RCD)
MMRD........ Miniature Multipurpose RADIAC Device (MCD)
MMRD........ Multi Mode Radar Display (ACAE)
MMRDDP..... Multi Mode Radar Digital Doppler Processor (ACAE)
MMRE......... Materials Methods Research and Engineering (MCD)
MMRF......... Marshfield Medical Research Foundation (HGEN)
MMRFS...... Multi Mode Radar Feasibility Study (ACAE)
MMRI......... Macheezmo Mouse Restaurants, Inc. [*NASDAQ symbol*] (SAG)
MMRI......... Metallurgy and Materials Science Research Institute [*Thailand*] (BUAC)
MMRI......... Mississippi Mineral Resources Institute [*University of Mississippi*] [*Research center*] (RCD)
MMRIM....... Mat Molding Reaction Injection Molding [*Plastics technology*]
MMRI......... Macheezmo Mouse Restaurants [*NASDAQ symbol*] (TTSB)
MMRP........ Marine Corps Midrange Objectives Plan (MCD)
MMRP .... Minerals and Materials Research Programs [*North Carolina State University*] [*Research center*] (RCD)
MMRP........ Missile Master Replacement Program
MMRPV ...... Multi Mission Remotely Piloted Vehicle (ACAE)
MMRPV...... Multimission RPV (SAUS)
MMRR........ Military Manpower Requirements Report (MCD)
MMRRI....... Mining and Minerals Resources Research Institute (SAUO)
MMRRI....... Utah Mining and Minerals Resources Research Institute [*University of Utah*] [*Research center*] (RCD)
MMRS .... Manned Military Recovery System (SAA)
MMRS .... Metal and Minerals Research Service (BUAC)
MMRX .... Mecdet MPC Corp. [*NASDAQ symbol*] (SAG)
MMRX .... Mednet MPC [*NASDAQ symbol*] (TTSB)
MMRX .... Mednet MPC Corp. [*NASDAQ symbol*] (SAG)
MMRX .... Reynosa/General Lucio Blanco Internacional [*Mexico*] [*ICAO location identifier*] (ICLI)
MMS .... Macbride Museum Society (EA)
MMS .... Machinist's Mate, Shop Mechanic [*Navy rating*]
MMS .... Macmillan's Manuals for Students [*A publication*]
MMS .... Magnetic Minesweeping (MSA)
MMS .... Maintenance Management Software
MMS .... Maintenance Management System
MMS .... Manager, Ministerial Services (SAUO)
MMS .... Man-Machine System (MCD)

MMS	Manpower Management Staff [*NATO*] (NATG)
MMS	Manpower Management System [*Marine Corps*]
MMS	Manufacturing Management Sciences, Inc. (SAUO)
MMS	Manufacturing Message [*or Messaging*] Specification [*or Standard*] [*Computer science*]
MMS	Manufacturing Monitoring System [*Computer science*] (IBMDP)
MMS	Marist Missionary Sisters (BUAC)
MMS	Marks, MS [*Location identifier*] [*FAA*] (FAAL)
MMS	Massachusetts Medical Society (BUAC)
MMS	Mass Mammographic Screening [*Medicine*] (DMAA)
MMS	Mass Memory Store [*Computer science*] (IEEE)
MMS	Mass Memory Subsystem [*Aviation*]
MMS	Master of Management Science (GAGS)
MMS	Master of Management Studies
MMS	Master of Marine Science (GAGS)
MMS	Master of Marketing Science (PGP)
MMS	Master of Materials Science (GAGS)
MMS	Master of Mechanical Science
MMS	Master of Medical Science
MMS	Master of Modern Studies (PGP)
MMS	Mast Mounted Sight
MMS	Mast-Mounted Sight
MMS	Mast Mounted Signal (MCD)
MMS	Matam [*Senegal*] [*Seismograph station code, US Geological Survey*] [*Closed*] (SEIS)
MMS	Maternity and Maternity Services [*British*]
MMS	MAXIMUS, Inc. [*NYSE symbol*] (SG)
MMS	Medical Mission Sisters (EA)
MMS	Medicus Mundi Switzerland (SAUO)
MMS	Meetings Management Society (NTPA)
MMS	Megacystis-Megaureter Syndrome [*Medicine*] (MELL)
MMS	Member of the Institute of Management Services [*British*] (DBQ)
MMS	Memory Management System
MMS	Merchant Marine Safety
MMS	Message Management System [*Computer science*] (CIST)
MMS	Metabolic Monitoring System
MMS	Metacaine Methanesulfonate [*Local anesthetic*]
MMS	Metastable Metal Surface [*Catalyst science*]
MMS	Meteorological Measuring System
MMS	Methodist Missionary Society [*British*]
MMS	Methyl Methanesulfonate [*Experimental mutagen*]
MMS	Metropolitan Map Series [*Bureau of the Census*] (GFGA)
MMS	Mexican Mathematical Society (BUAC)
MMS	Mexican Meteorological Service
MMS	Michigan Multispectral Scanner
MMS	Microfiche Management System
MMS	Micro Measurement System [*3D Digital Design & Development Ltd.*] [*Software package*] (NCC)
MMS	Micromembrane Suppressor [*Ion chromatography*]
MMS	Micro Memory Systems (NITA)
MMS	Microscale Meteorology Section (SAUO)
MMS	Middle Meningeal System [*Neuroanatomy*]
MMS	Military Message Service [*British military*] (DMA)
MMS	Milkman's Syndrome [*Medicine*] (MELL)
MM/S	Millimeters per Second
MMS	Minerals Management Service [*Department of the Interior*] [*Washington, DC*]
MMS	Mini-Mental State [*Psychometric testing*]
MMS	Minimum Manned Satellite (ACAE)
MMS	Minimum Mean Square (PDAA)
MMS	Minimum Methadone Service [*Medicine*] (MELL)
MMS	Missile Maintenance Squadron (SAA)
MMS	Missile Management System (SAUS)
MMS	Missile Mix Study [*NAVAIR*] (NG)
MMS	Missile Monitor System [*Army*]
MMS	Mission Modular Spacecraft (MCD)
mms	Mission Modular Spacecraft [*NASA*] (NAKS)
MMS	Mississippi County Community College Library, Blytheville, AR [*OCLC symbol*] (OCLC)
MMS	Mobile Monitoring Station
MMS	Modular Measuring System
MMS	Modular Modeling System
MMS	Modular Multiband Scanner (MCD)
mms	Modular Multiband Scanner (NAKS)
MMS	Modular Multimission Spacecraft [*NASA*]
MMS	Modular Multispectral Scanner
MMS	Module Making System (SAUS)
MMS	Module Management System [*Computer science*] (CIST)
MMS	Mohs' Micrographic Surgery
MMS	Momentum Management System [*NASA*] (SSD)
MMS	Money Management System
MMS	Money Market Services, Inc. [*Belmont, CA*] [*Database producer*]
MMS	Moravian Missionary Society
MMS	Motor Minesweeper
MMS	Movement Monitoring System (SAUO)
MMS	Multilevel Mail Server (SAUS)
MMS	Multimedia Messaging Service (SAUO)
MMS	Multimedia System
mms	Multimission Modular Spacecraft [*NASA*] (NAKS)
MMS	Multimission Modular Spacecraft [*NASA*] (NASA)
MMS	Multimission Ship [*DoD*]
MMS	Multi-Mission Spacecraft
MMS	Multimode Seeker (MCD)
MMS	Multimodular Mission Spacecraft (ACAE)
MMS	Multi-Part Memory System [*Perkin-Elmer*] (NITA)
MMS	Multiple Microprocessor System (ACAE)
MMS	Multiplex Modulation System
MMS	Municipal Management System (HGAA)
MMS	Munitions Maintenance and Storage
MMS	Munitions Maintenance Squadron [*Air Force*]
MMS	Musical Masterpiece Society [*Record label*] [*USA, Europe*]
MMS	Mycon Marketing Services Ltd. (SAUO)
MMS	Myeloma Morphology Score [*Oncology*]
MMS1	US Minerals Management Services (SAUS)
MMS1	Mobile Mast Spectrometer 1 (SAUS)
MMSA	Man-Machine System Analysis [*Engineering*]
MMSA	Manual Molder Shielded Arc
MMSA	Master of Midwifery, Society of Apothecaries
MMSA	Materials and Methods Standards Association (EA)
MMSA	Medical Mycological Society of the Americas (EA)
MMSA	Member, Medical Specialists' Association (CMD)
MMSA	Mercantile Marine Service Association [*British*]
MMSA	Methods and Materials Standards Association (EA)
MMSA	Military Medical Supply Agency [*Later, Defense Medical Supply Center*]
MMSA	Mining and Metallurgical Society of America (EA)
MMSA	Mistress of Midwifery, Society of Apothecaries (SAUO)
MMSA	Mitsubishi Motor Sales of America, Inc.
MMSA	Multiple-Mission Support Area [*Space Flight Operations Facility, NASA*]
MMSAA	Metals and Minerals Shippers Association of Australia
MMSAC	Medical Manpower Standing Advisory Committee (SAUO)
MMSB	Methyl(methionine)sulfonium Bromide [*Organic chemistry*]
MMSBC	Master, Medical Science in Biomedical Communication (CMD)
MMSc	Master of Management Science (GAGS)
MMSc	Master of Marine Science (GAGS)
MM Sc	Master of Mechanical Science
MMSc	Master of Medical Science (GAGS)
MMSC	Mediterranean Marine Sorting Center
MMSC	Minnesota Metropolitan State College
MMSC	Multimode SONAR Console
MMSCFD	Million Standard Cubic Feet per Day
MMSCV	Manned Military System Capability Vehicle
MMSD	Mass Memory Storage Device (DWSG)
MMSD	Mixed Motor and Sensory Deficits [*Neurology*]
MMSD	Multimode Seeker Deduction (DWSG)
MMSD	Multiple Minor Symptoms Day [*Environmental medicine*]
MMSD	San Jose Del Cabo [*Mexico*] [*ICAO location identifier*] (ICLI)
MMSE	Master of Manufacturing Systems Engineering (PGP)
MMSE	Mini-Mental State Examination [*Psychometrics*]
MMSE	Minimum Mean Squared Error
MMSE	Minimum Mean Square Error
MMSE	Mission Module Simulation Equipment (MCD)
MMSE	Molecular Monitor Shuttle Experiment (ACAE)
MMSE	Multiple-Mission Support Equipment [*NASA*]
MMSE	Multiuse Mission Support Equipment [*NASA*] (NAKS)
MMSG	Molecular Manufacturing Shortcut Group (BUAC)
MMSI	Maritime Mobile Service Identity (SAUO)
MMSI	Merit Medical Systems, Inc. [*NASDAQ symbol*] (SAG)
MMSI	Multi-Medium Scale Integration (SAA)
MMSIP	Maintenance Management Systems Improvement Project [*Air Force*] (DOMA)
MMSJ	Medical Mobilization for Soviet Jewry (EA)
MMSI	Merit Medical Systems [*NASDAQ symbol*] (TTSB)
MMSL	Microgravity Materials Science Laboratory [*NASA*]
MMSM	Santa Lucia [*Mexico*] [*ICAO location identifier*] (ICLI)
MMSP	Malignant Melanoma of Soft Parts [*Medicine*] (DMAA)
MMSP	San Luis Potosi [*Mexico*] [*ICAO location identifier*] (ICLI)
MMSQ	Munitions Maintenance Squadron [*Air Force*]
MMSR	Machinist's Mate, Ship Repair [*Navy rating*]
MMSR	Master Materiel Support Record
MMSR	Monthly Materiel Status Report
MMSR	Multiple-Mission Support Recording [*NASA*]
MMSRC	Mediterranean Maritime Surveillance and Reconnaissance Center (DNAB)
MMSRE	Machinist's Mate, Ship Repair, Engine Operator [*Navy rating*]
MMSRI	Machinist's Mate, Ship Repair, Instrument Maker [*Navy rating*]
MMSRO	Machinist's Mate, Ship Repair, Outside Machinist [*Navy rating*]
MMSRS	Machinist's Mate, Ship Repair, Inside Machinist [*Navy rating*]
MMSS	Manned Maneuverable Space System
MMSS	Manual Mode Space Simulator
MMSS	Marine Meteorological Services System [*WMO*] (MSC)
MMSS	Maritime Mobile Satellite Service (ACAE)
MMSS	Massachusettensis Medicinae Societatis Socius [*Fellow of the Massachusetts Medical Society*]
MMSS	Mast Mounted Sight System (MCD)
M/MSS	Medicare and Medicaid Statistical Systems (GFGA)
MMSS	Missile Motion Subsystem
MMSS	Multi Mission System Study (ACAE)
MMSS	Multimodule Space Station [*NASA*] (KSC)
MMSSF	Man Machine System Simulation Facility (ACAE)
MM St	Master of Museum Studies (PGP)
MMST	Microelectronics Manufacturing Science and Technology (AAEL)
MMST	Mini-Mental State Test (SAUS)
MMST	Multimode Storage Tube
MM ST	Muscle Strength (BABM)
mm st	Muscle Strength [*Neurology*] (DAVI)
MMSTP	Master Missile System Training Program (SAA)
MMSU	Mariano Marcos State University (SAUO)
MMSV	Mouse Moloney Sarcoma and Leukemia Virus [*Medicine*] (DB)

MMSW......... International Union of Mine, Mill, and Smelter Workers [*Later, USWA*]
MMT........... Alpha-Methyl-m-tyrosine [*Pharmacology*]
MMT........... Columbia, SC [*Location identifier*] [*FAA*] (FAAL)
MMT........... Macmillan's Manuals for Teachers [*A publication*]
MMT........... Main Mantle Thrust [*Geology*]
MMT........... Malignant Mixed Tumor [*Medicine*] (MELL)
MMT........... Manportable MILSTAR [*Military Strategic and Tactical Relay*] Terminal [*Army*]
MMT........... Manual Muscle Test
MMT........... Manufacturing Methods Technology (AAGC)
MMT........... Marine Minerals Technology [*National Oceanic and Atmospheric Administration*]
MMT........... Maritime Mobile Telegraph
MMT........... Mass Memory Test (NASA)
MMT........... Master of Medical Technology
MMT........... Master of Movement Therapy (GAGS)
MMT........... Master of Music Teaching (GAGS)
MMT........... Math Model Test (MCD)
MMT........... Medial Meniscus Tear [*Medicine*] (MELL)
MMT........... Merchant Marine Technical Division [*Coast Guard*]
MMT........... Metal Mount
MMT........... Methadone Mainetnance Treatment [*Medicine*] (MELL)
MMT........... Methylcyclopentadienyl Manganese Tricarbonyl [*Organic chemistry*]
MMT........... MFS Multimarket Income [*NYSE symbol*] (SPSG)
MMT........... MFS Multimarket Income Trust [*Associated Press*] (SAG)
MMT........... Midland Mortgage Investors Trust (SAUO)
MMT........... Military Mail Terminal (AFM)
MMT........... Military Maintenance Technician
MMT........... Million Metric Tons (IMH)
MMT........... Miniature Mobile Target (SAUS)
MMT........... Miniature Moving Target (MCD)
MMT........... Miniaturized Munitions Technology
MMT........... Mini Mobile Target [*Military*] (CAAL)
MMT........... Missile Maintenance Technician (AABC)
MMT........... Missile Mate Test
MMT........... Mobile Maintenance Team (MCD)
MMT........... Modernization Management Team [*Military*] (CAAL)
MMT........... Molten Metal Technology [*Waste management*] (ECON)
MMT........... Monolithic Mirror Telescope
mmt........... Monomethoxytrityl [*As substituent on nucleoside*] [*Biochemistry*]
MMT........... Monthly Mean Temperature [*Meteorology*]
MMT........... Monument Resources [*Vancouver Stock Exchange symbol*]
MMT........... Morse Mission Trainer
mMT........... Mouse Metallothionein [*Biochemistry*]
MMT........... Muenchner Mode-Tage [*Germany*]
MMT........... Multimodal Therapy [*Arnold Lazarus*] (DIPS)
MMT........... Multimode Tonotron
MMT........... Multi Mode Transponder (ACAE)
MMT........... Multiple Mirror Observatory
MMT........... Multiple-Mirror Telescope [*Mount Hopkins, AZ*] [*Jointly operated by Smithsonian Institution and the University of Arizona*] [*Astronomy*]
MMT........... Multiple-Mission Telemetry [*NASA*]
MMT........... Murine Metallothionein [*Biochemistry*]
MMTA......... Mercantile Marine Trawlermen's Association [*A union*] [*British*]
MMTA......... Methylmetatyramine (DB)
MMTA......... Minor Metals Traders' Association [*British*]
MMTA......... MultiMedia Telecommunications Association (DDC)
MMTA......... Tlaxcala [*Mexico*] [*ICAO location identifier*] (ICLI)
MMTB......... Tuxtla Gutierrez [*Mexico*] [*ICAO location identifier*] (ICLI)
MMTC......... Marine Minerals Technology Center [*National Oceanic and Atmospheric Administration*]
MMTC......... Maritime Mobile Telegraphy Calling
MMTC......... Materiel Management Training Center [*Military*]
MMTC......... Memtec Ltd. [*NASDAQ symbol*] (SAG)
MMTC......... Midwest Manufacturing Technology Council (SAUO)
MMTC......... Minerals and Metals Trading Corp. (BUAC)
MMTC......... Mouvement Mondial des Travailleurs Chretiens [*World Movement of Christian Workers - WMCW*] [*Brussels, Belgium*] (EAIO)
MMTC......... Torreon [*Mexico*] [*ICAO location identifier*] (ICLI)
MMTCY....... Memtec Ltd ADS [*NASDAQ symbol*] (TTSB)
MMTD......... Multimode Tonotron Display
MMTDC....... Maritime Mobile Telegraph Distress and Calling
MMTE......... Manufacturing Methods Technology Engineering (ACAE)
MMTF......... Military Manpower Task Force
MMTG......... Tuxtla Gutierrez [*Mexico*] [*ICAO location identifier*] (ICLI)
MMTI......... Member of the Metal Treating Institute (SAUO)
MMTIC....... Murphy-Meisgeier Type Indicator for Children [*Test*] (TES)
MMTJ......... Tijuana/General Abelardo L. Rodriguez Internacional [*Mexico*] [*ICAO location identifier*] (ICLI)
MMTL......... Tulancingo [*Mexico*] [*ICAO location identifier*] (ICLI)
M Mtl E...... Master of Materials Engineering (PGP)
M Mtl E...... Master of Metal Engineering (PGP)
MMTLN....... Map Margin Top Line (SAA)
MMT/M....... Missile Maintenance Technician/Mechanic (AAG)
MMTM........ Multimedia Training Material
MMTM........ Tampico/General Francisco Javier Mina Internacional [*Mexico*] [*ICAO location identifier*] (ICLI)
MMTN........ Tamuin [*Mexico*] [*ICAO location identifier*] (ICLI)
MMTO........ Missiles Made to Order [*Military*] (RDA)
MMTO........ Multiple Mirror Telescope Observatory [*Research center*] (RCD)
MMTO........ Toluca [*Mexico*] [*ICAO location identifier*] (ICLI)
MMTP........ Methadone Maintenance Treatment Program (AAMN)
MMTP........ Methyl(methylthio)phenol [*Organic chemistry*]
MMTP........ Microwave Temperature Profiler (SAUS)

MMTP......... Tapachula [*Mexico*] [*ICAO location identifier*] (ICLI)
MMTPS....... Maintenance Materiel Transaction Processing System (SAUO)
MMTQ........ Tequesquitengo [*Mexico*] [*ICAO location identifier*] (ICLI)
MMTR........ Mean-Maintenance-Man-Hours to Repair (MCD)
MMTR........ Military Manpower Training Report (MCD)
M/MTRG...... Main Metering [*Automotive engineering*]
MMTS........ Maximum Minimum Temperature System
MMTS........ Methyl Methanethiolsulfonate [*Organic chemistry*]
MMTS........ MILAN Moving Target System (SAUS)
MMTS........ Multi-Media Tutorial Services, Inc. [*NASDAQ symbol*] (SAG)
MMTS........ Multiple-Mission Telemetry System [*NASA*]
MMTSF....... Million Metric Tons of Standard Fuel
MMTSW...... Multi-Media Tutorial Wrrt [*NASDAQ symbol*] (TTSB)
MMTT........ Mechanised Moving Target Trainer (SAUS)
MMTT........ Mobile Minuteman Train Test (SAA)
MMTT........ Multimechanical Thermal Treatment
MMTTU....... Modular Magnetic Tape Transport Units (MCD)
MMTV........ Mouse Mammary Tumor Virus
MMTX........ Tuxpan [*Mexico*] [*ICAO location identifier*] (ICLI)
MMTY........ Monterrey [*Mexico*] [*ICAO location identifier*] (ICLI)
MMU.......... Main Memory Unit
MMU.......... Managed Municipal Portfolio [*NYSE symbol*] (SPSG)
MMU.......... Manchester Metropolitan University [*British*] (AIE)
mmu.......... Manned Maneuvering Unit [*NASA*] (NAKS)
MMU.......... Manned Maneuvering Unit [*Aerospace*]
mmu.......... Mass Memory Unit (NAKS)
MMU.......... Mass Memory Unit
MMu.......... Master of Music (GAGS)
MMU.......... McMaster University (SAUO)
MMU.......... Medical Maintenance Unit [*Army*] [*World War II*]
MMU.......... Memory Management Unit [*Computer chip*]
MMU.......... Memory Mapping Unit (NITA)
MMU.......... Mercaptomethyl Uracil [*Pharmacology*] (MAE)
MMU.......... Metered Message Unit [*Telecommunications*] (TEL)
MMU.......... Midcourse Maneuvering Unit [*Aerospace*] (MCD)
MMU.......... Midcourse Measurement Unit [*Aerospace*] (KSC)
MMU.......... Millimass Unit (DEN)
MMU.......... Million Monetary Units (PDAA)
MMU.......... Missile Motion Unit
MMU.......... Mobile Monitoring Unit
MMU.......... Modular Maneuvering Unit [*Aerospace*]
MMU.......... Monolithic Memory Unit
MMU.......... Morristown, NJ [*Location identifier*] [*FAA*] (FAAL)
MMU.......... Multimessage Unit [*Telecommunications*] (TEL)
MMU.......... University of Missouri, Columbia, Health Sciences Library, Columbia, MO [*OCLC symbol*] (OCLC)
MMUA........ Major Mail Users of Australia
MMUAV...... Multi-Mission Unmanned Aerial Vehicle
MMUC........ Mazda Motor Manufacturing USA Corp.
MMUC........ Midwest Medical Union Catalog
MMUD........ Monolithic Memory Unit Diagnostic
M Mu Ed..... Master of Music Education (PGP)
M'Mul Ch SC... M'Mullan's South Carolina Equity Reports [*1840-42*] [*A publication*] (DLA)
M'Mul LSC... M'Mullan's South Carolina Law Reports [*1840-42*] [*A publication*] (DLA)
MMuLv....... Moloney Murine Leukemia Virus [*Medicine*] (DB)
MMuLV....... Moloney Murine Leukemia Virus [*Medicine*] (DMAA)
MMUN........ Cancun [*Mexico*] [*ICAO location identifier*] (ICLI)
MMus......... Master of Music (GAGS)
M Mus Ed.... Master of Music Education
M Mus (Mus Ed)... Master of Music in Music Education
M Mus (Mus Lit)... Master of Music in Music Literature
M Mus (PSM)... Master of Music in Public School Music
MMusRCM... Master of Music of the Royal College of Music (SAUO)
M Mus (RCM)... Master of Music, Royal College of Music
M Mus (W Inst)... Master of Music in Wind Instruments
MMV.......... Maize Mosaic Virus [*Plant pathology*]
MMV.......... Mandatory Minute Ventilation (DMAA)
MMV.......... Mandatory Minute Volume (DMAA)
MMV.......... Mast Mount Visionics (MCD)
MMV.......... Maubois, Mocquot, and Vassal [*Cheesemaking*]
MMV.......... McMinnville, OR [*Location identifier*] [*FAA*] (FAAL)
MMV.......... Minimale Mandatory Ventilation (SAUS)
MMV.......... Modular Military Vehicle (SAUS)
mmv.......... Monostable Multivibrator (IDOE)
MMV.......... Monostable Multivibrator
MMV.......... Multi-Mission Vehicle (SAUS)
MMVA........ Villahermosa [*Mexico*] [*ICAO location identifier*] (ICLI)
MMVD........ Mixed Mitral Valve Disease [*Medicine*] (DMAA)
MMVF........ Multimedia Video File [*Computer science*]
MMVR........ Veracruz/General Heriberto Jara [*Mexico*] [*ICAO location identifier*] (ICLI)
MMVS........ Mast Mount Visionics System (MCD)
MMW......... Main Magnetization Winding [*Telecommunications*] (OA)
MMW......... Mean Maximum Weight
MMW......... Medium Multi-purpose Wheeled (SAUS)
MMW......... Miami, OK [*Location identifier*] [*FAA*] (FAAL)
MMW......... Multimegawatt (SDI)
mmwave...... Millimeter Wave (AAEL)
MMWCS...... Multimission Weapons Control System
MMWE....... Millimeter Wave Experiment
MMWEC...... Massachusetts Municipal Wholesale Electric Company (SAUO)
MMWG....... Military Mobilization Working Group
MMWM...... Multimedia Window Manager (SAUS)

MMWR	Millimetric Wave Radar (SAUS)
MMWR	Morbidity and Mortality Weekly Report [*A publication*] (DMAA)
MMWW	Metamor Worldwide [*NASDAQ symbol*] [*Formerly, COREstaff, Inc.*]
MMX	Magma Copper Co. (SAUO)
MMX	Mastergroup Multiplex [*AT & T*]
MMX	Matrix Math Extensions (PCM)
MMX	Memory Multiplexer [*Computer science*]
MMX	Micron's Millenia XKU [*Computer science*]
MMX	Miracema do Norte [*Brazil*] [*Airport symbol*] (AD)
MMX	Multimedia Extensions (PCM)
MMXI	Media Metrix [*NASDAQ symbol*] (SG)
MMY	Many, LA [*Location identifier*] [*FAA*] (FAAL)
MMY	Mental Measurements Yearbook [*Psychology*] [*A publication*]
MMY	Military Man-Years (AABC)
MMY	Miyakojima [*Japan*] [*Airport symbol*] (OAG)
MMYD	Mental Measurements Yearbook Database [*University of Nebraska, Lincoln*] [*Database*]
MMZ	Maimana [*Afghanistan*] [*Airport symbol*] [*Obsolete*] (OAG)
MMZC	Zacatecas [*Mexico*] [*ICAO location identifier*] (ICLI)
MMZH	Zihuatanejo [*Mexico*] [*ICAO location identifier*] (ICLI)
MMZM	Zamora [*Mexico*] [*ICAO location identifier*] (ICLI)
MMZO	Manzanillo [*Mexico*] [*ICAO location identifier*] (ICLI)
MMZP	Zapopan [*Mexico*] [*ICAO location identifier*] (ICLI)
MMZT	Mazatlan [*Mexico*] [*ICAO location identifier*] (ICLI)
MN	Machinery Numeral [*Marine insurance*] (DS)
MN	Madeleine Mines Ltd. [*Toronto Stock Exchange symbol*]
MN	Magnetic North
MN	Main (AAG)
MN	Main Network [*Telecommunications*] (TEL)
MN	Making of the Nations [*A publication*]
MN	Malignant Nephrosclerosis [*Medicine*] (DB)
MN	Management Network (MCD)
Mn	Manganese [*Chemical element*]
MN	Mansion
MN	Mantle Nerve
MN	Manual
MN	Manufacturer's Name (NITA)
MN	Manx Airlines Ltd.
MN	Mare Nectaris [*Sea of Nectar*] [*Lunar area*]
MN	Marketspan Corp. [*NYSE symbol*] [*Formerly, Long Island Lighting*]
MN	Master Navigator [*Air Force*]
MN	Master of Nursing
MN	Material Number
MN	Materiel Needs [*Army*]
MN	Maxim Nordenfelt Gun
Mn	Mean Range [*Difference in height between mean high water and mean low water*] [*Tides and currents*]
MN	Measurement Name (NITA)
MN	Mecanorma [*Graphic artist products*] [*British*]
MN	Medial Interlaminar Nucleus [*Neurology*] (DAVI)
MN	Media Network (EA)
MN	Median Nerve [*Anatomy*]
MN	Meeting Number (NITA)
MN	Meetings Name (NITA)
MN	Meganewton
MN	Melanocytic Nevus [*Medicine*] (MELL)
MN	Melena Neonatorum (DB)
MN	Membranous Nephropathy [*Medicine*] (MELL)
MN	Meniere's Network [*An association*] (EA)
MN	Meningopneumonitis [*Medicine*]
Mn	Merchant Navy (WDAA)
MN	Merchant Navy
M-N	Merrell-National [*Commercial firm*] (DAVI)
MN	Message Number (ACAE)
MN	Message Number [*Computer science*] (ELAL)
MN	Metanephrine [*Medicine*] (DMAA)
m-N	Meter-Newton
MN	Michigan [*Obsolete*] (ROG)
MN	Micrococcal Nuclease [*Also, MCN*] [*An enzyme*]
M/N	Microcytic/Normochromic [*Anemia*] [*Hematology*] (DAVI)
MN	Microneutralization [*Chemistry*]
MN	Midnight
MN	Migrating Neuron [*Neuroanatomy*]
mN	Millinormal [*One one-thousandth of normal*]
MN	Mineman [*Navy rating*]
MN	Minnesota [*Postal code*]
Mn	Minnesota State Law Library, St. Paul, MN [*Library symbol*] [*Library of Congress*] (LCLS)
MN	Minor Descriptor (SAUS)
MN	Minor Subject Descriptor [*Online database field identifier*]
MN	Minus (VLIE)
MN	Mission Need
MN	Mnemonic
Mn	Modern [*Linguistics*]
M/N	Moneda Nacional [*National Money*] [*Spanish*]
MN	Mongolia [*ANSI two-letter standard code*] (CNC)
MN	Mononuclear [*Hematology*]
MN	Mononuclear Lymphocytes (SAUS)
MN	Monthly Notices of the Royal Astronomical Society (SAUO)
MN	Month Name (BJA)
MN	Moon (ROG)
MN	Moreh Nebukhim [*Maimonides*] (BJA)
M-N	Motility Nitrate [*Medium*] [*Microbiology*] (DAVI)
MN	Moto Nave [*Motor ship*] [*Latin*] (IIA)
MN	Motor Neuron [*Anatomy*]

MN	Mouvement National [*Morocco*] [*Political party*] (EY)
MN	Movimiento Nacional [*Costa Rica*] [*Political party*] (EY)
MN	Multinodular [*or Multinodulate*] [*Medicine*]
MN	Mutato Nomine [*The Name Being Changed*] [*Latin*]
MN	Myoneural [*Medicine*]
MN1	Mineman, First Class [*Navy rating*]
MN2	Mineman, Second Class [*Navy rating*]
MN3	Mineman, Third Class [*Navy rating*]
MnA	Aitken Public Library, Aitken, MN [*Library symbol*] [*Library of Congress*] (LCLS)
MNA	Augsburg College, Minneapolis, MN [*OCLC symbol*] (OCLC)
MNA	Management Network Architecture (SAUO)
MNA	Massachusetts Nurses Association (SAUO)
MNA	Master Negative Assembly [*Monophoto*] (DGA)
M Na	Master of Navigation
MNA	Master of Nonprofit Administration (GAGS)
MNA	Master of Nurse Anesthesia (PGP)
MNA	Master of Nursing Administration
MN(A)	Material Need (Abbreviated) (MCD)
MNA	Maximum Noise Area
MNA	Melanguane [*Indonesia*] [*Airport symbol*] (OAG)
MNA	Melinga Resources Ltd. [*Vancouver Stock Exchange symbol*]
MNA	Member of the National Assembly [*British*]
MNA	Merpati Nusantara Airlines PT [*Indonesia*] [*ICAO designator*] (FAAC)
MNA	Meta-Nitroaniline [*Organic chemistry*]
MNA	Methoxynaphthylamine [*Organic chemistry*]
MNA	Methylnadic Anhydride [*Organic chemistry*]
MNA	Methylnitroaniline [*Organic chemistry*]
MNA	Michigan Nurses Association (SAUO)
MNA	Mina [*Nevada*] [*Seismograph station code, US Geological Survey*] (SEIS)
MNA	Minnesota Municipal Term Trust [*NYSE symbol*] (SPSG)
MNA	Minnesota Nurses Association (SAUO)
MNA	Missing, Not Enemy Action
MNA	Mississippi Nurses Association (SAUO)
MNA	Mouvement d'Action Politique et Sociale [*Political and Social Action Movement*] [*Switzerland*] [*Political party*] (PPW)
MNA	Mouvement National Algerien [*National Algerian Movement*]
MNA	Multinetwork Area [*Term used in TV ratings*]
MNA	Multiple Newsagents Association [*British*] (DBA)
MNA	Multishare Network Architecture [*Mitsubishi Corp.*] (BUR)
MNA	Myanmar News Agency (EY)
MNAA	Molecular Neutron Activation Analysis
MnAbnE	Alborn Elementary School, Alborn, MN [*Library symbol*] [*Library of Congress*] (LCLS)
MnAd	Annandale Public Library, Annandale, MN [*Library symbol*] [*Library of Congress*] (LCLS)
Mn-Ad	Minnesota State Department of Administration, Budget Library, St. Paul, MN [*Library symbol*] [*Library of Congress*] (LCLS)
MNAD	Multi-National Airmobile Division (SAUO)
MnAda	Ada Public Library, Ada, MN [*Library symbol*] [*Library of Congress*] (LCLS)
MNAdaE	Ada Elementary School, Ada, MN [*Library symbol*] [*Library of Congress*] (LCLS)
MnAdaH	Ada High School, Ada, MN [*Library symbol*] [*Library of Congress*] (LCLS)
MnAdBE	Bendix Elementary School Annandale, MN [*Library symbol*] [*Library of Congress*] (LCLS)
MnAdH	Annandale High School, Annandale, MN [*Library symbol*] [*Library of Congress*] (LCLS)
MnADM	Depot Museum, Aitken, MN [*Library symbol*] [*Library of Congress*] (LCLS)
MnAdMS	Annandale Middle School, Annandale, MN [*Library symbol*] [*Library of Congress*] (LCLS)
MNAEA	Member of the National Association of Estate Agents [*British*] (DBQ)
Mn-Ag	Minnesota Department of Agriculture, St. Paul, MN [*Library symbol*] [*Library of Congress*] (LCLS)
MnAJ	Aitken Jr.-Sr. High School Media Center, Aitken, MN [*Library symbol*] [*Library of Congress*] (LCLS)
MnAkE	Akeley Elementary School, Akeley, MN [*Library symbol*] [*Library of Congress*] (LCLS)
MnAkH	Akeley High School, Akeley, MN [*Library symbol*] [*Library of Congress*] (LCLS)
MnAl	Albany Public Library, Alabany, MN [*Library symbol*] [*Library of Congress*] (LCLS)
MnAlb	Albert Lea Public Library, Albert Lea, MN [*Library symbol*] [*Library of Congress*] (LCLS)
MnAlbeCH	Chokio-Alberta High School, Alberta, MN [*Library symbol*] [*Library of Congress*] (LCLS)
MnAle	Alexandria Public Library, Alexandria, MN [*Library symbol*] [*Library of Congress*] (LCLS)
MnAleCJ	Central Junior High School, Alexandria, MN [*Library symbol*] [*Library of Congress*] (LCLS)
MnAleDH	Douglas County Hospital, Health Science Library, Alexandria, MN [*Library symbol*] [*Library of Congress*] (LCLS)
MnAleJH	Jefferson High School, Alexandria, MN [*Library symbol*] [*Library of Congress*] (LCLS)
MnAleLE	Lincoln Elementary School, Alexandria, MN [*Library symbol*] [*Library of Congress*] (LCLS)
MnAleR	Alexandria Runestone Museum, Alexandria, MN [*Library symbol*] [*Library of Congress*] (LCLS)
MnAleSM	St. Mary's School, Alexandria, MN [*Library symbol*] [*Library of Congress*] (LCLS)
MnAleTI	Alexandria Technical Institute, Alexandria, MN [*Library symbol*] [*Library of Congress*] (LCLS)

MnAleWE..... Washington Elementary School, Alexandria, MN [*Library symbol*] [*Library of Congress*] (LCLS)

MnAlFE........ Farming Elementary School, Albany, MN [*Library symbol*] [*Library of Congress*] (LCLS)

MnAlH .... Holy Family School, Albany, MN [*Library symbol*] [*Library of Congress*] (LCLS)

MnAlJ .... Albany Jr. H.S./Elementary Library, Albany, MN [*Library symbol*] [*Library of Congress*] (LCLS)

MnAlmA....... Amador Heritage Center, Almelund, MN [*Library symbol*] [*Library of Congress*] (LCLS)

MnAlS.......... Albany Senior High School, Albany, MN [*Library symbol*] [*Library of Congress*] (LCLS)

MnAlSP........ St. Pius V School, Albany, MN [*Library symbol*] [*Library of Congress*] (LCLS)

MnAlvE .... Albertville Elementary School, Albertville, MN [*Library symbol*] [*Library of Congress*] (LCLS)

MNAM .... Military North African Mission [*World War II*]

MNam.......... Nantucket Atheneum, Nantucket, MA [*Library symbol*] [*Library of Congress*] (LCLS)

MnAnA........ Anoka-Ramsey Community College, Anoka, MN [*Library symbol*] [*Library of Congress*] (LCLS)

MN & ALOA... Merchant Navy and Air Line Officers' Association [*A union*] [*British*] (DS)

MNANG........ Minnesota Air National Guard (MUSM)

MnAnGS...... Anoka County Genealogical Society, Anoka, MN [*Library symbol*] [*Library of Congress*] (LCLS)

MnAnHi........ Anoka County Historical Society, Anoka, MN [*Library symbol*] [*Library of Congress*] (LCLS)

MNanHi .... Nantucket Historical Association, Nantucket, MA [*Library symbol*] [*Library of Congress*] (LCLS)

MNanMM..... Nantucket Maria Mitchell Association, Nantucket, MA [*Library symbol*] [*Library of Congress*] (LCLS)

MnAnVT....... Anoka Area Vocational Technical Institute, Anoka, MN [*Library symbol*] [*Library of Congress*] (LCLS)

MNanW........ Nantucket Whaling Museum, Nantucket, MA [*Library symbol*] [*Library of Congress*] (LCLS)

MNAO .... Mobile Naval Airfield Organization

MNAOA........ Merchant Navy and Air Line Officers' Association [*A union*] [*British*] (DCTA)

MnAp .... Appleton Public Library, Appleton, MN [*Library symbol*] [*Library of Congress*] (LCLS)

MNAP .... Manager of National Antarctic Programme (SAUO)

MNAP .... Mixed Nerve Action Potential [*Medicine*] (DMAA)

MnApH........ Appleton Municipal Hospital, Appleton, MN [*Library symbol*] [*Library of Congress*] (LCLS)

MnApPS...... Appleton Public Schools, Appleton, MN [*Library symbol*] [*Library of Congress*] (LCLS)

MN Arch ..... Master of Naval Architecture

MnARE........ Rippleside Elementary School, Rippleside Elementary IMC, Aitken, Mn [*Library symbol*] [*Library of Congress*] (LCLS)

MnArS .... Argyle School, Argyle, MN [*Library symbol*] [*Library of Congress*] (LCLS)

MNAS .... Member of the National Academy of Sciences

MNAs........... Members of the National Assembly (SAUO)

MNASc........ Memoirs of the National Academy of Sciences (SAUO)

MnAsHi........ Pine County Historical Reference Library, Askov, MN [*Library symbol*] [*Library of Congress*] (LCLS)

MnAshS ...... Ashby Public School, Ashby, MN [*Library symbol*] [*Library of Congress*] (LCLS)

MNASSA...... Monthly Notes. Astronomical Society of Southern Africa [*A publication*]

MNASTD ..... Multicultural Network of the American Society for Training and Development (EA)

MnAt........... Atwater Public Library, Atwater, MN [*Library symbol*] [*Library of Congress*] (LCLS)

MnAtPS........ Atwater-Grove City Public Schools, Atwater, MN [*Library symbol*] [*Library of Congress*] (LCLS)

MNatQ .... United States Quartermaster Research and Development Center, Natick, MA [*Library symbol*] [*Library of Congress*] (LCLS)

MNatRes...... Master of Natural Resources (ADA)

MNatSci....... Master of Natural Science (GAGS)

MnAtSJS...... St. John's Lutheran School, Atwater, MN [*Library symbol*] [*Library of Congress*] (LCLS)

MnAu.......... Austin Public Library, Austin, MN [*Library symbol*] [*Library of Congress*] (LCLS)

MNAU .... Mobile Naval Airfield Unit

MnAudS....... Audubon Public School, Audubon, MN [*Library symbol*] [*Library of Congress*] (LCLS)

MnAuH........ Hormel Institute, University of Minnesota, Austin, MN [*Library symbol*] [*Library of Congress*] (LCLS)

MnAuPS...... Austin Public Schools Media, Austin, MN [*Library symbol*] [*Library of Congress*] (LCLS)

MnAur.......... Aurora Public Library, Aurora, MN [*Library symbol*] [*Library of Congress*] (LCLS)

MnAurH ...... Mesabi East High School, Aurora,MN [*Library symbol*] [*Library of Congress*] (LCLS)

MnAuS......... Austin State Junior College, Austin, MN [*Library symbol*] [*Library of Congress*] (LCLS)

MnAuV......... Austin Vocational Technical Institute, Austin, MN [*Library symbol*] [*Library of Congress*] (LCLS)

MnAvoE ...... Avon Elementary School, Avon, MN [*Library symbol*] [*Library of Congress*] (LCLS)

MnAvZ .... Minnesota Zoological Garden, Apple Valley, MN [*Library symbol*] [*Library of Congress*] (LCLS)

MnB .... Becker Public Library, Becker Elementary School, Becker, MN [*Library symbol*] [*Library of Congress*] (LCLS)

MNB............ Bemidji State University, Bemidji, MN [*OCLC symbol*] (OCLC)

MNB............ Maldives News Bureau (EY)

MNB............ Mandibular Nerve Block [*Medicine*] (MELL)

MNB............ Mannosidase Beta (DMAA)

MNB............ Maverick Naturalite Beef Corp. [*Vancouver Stock Exchange symbol*]

MNB............ Median Neuroblast [*Cytology*]

MNB............ Medical Negligence Board (WDAA)

MNB............ Minnesota Muni Term Tr-II [*AMEX symbol*] (TTSB)

MNB............ Minnesota Term Trust, Inc. II [*AMEX symbol*] (SAG)

MNB............ Mint No Box [*Doll collecting*]

MNB............ Moanda [*Zaire*] [*Airport symbol*] (OAG)

MNB............ Mobile Naval Base [*British military*] (DMA)

MNB............ Moscow Narodny Bank Ltd. [*Former USSR*]

MNB............ Multinozzle Base

MNB............ Murine Neuroblastoma (DB)

MNB............ Texte de Louvre [*Paris*]: Monuments de Ninive et de Babylone [*A publication*] (BJA)

MnBa.......... Balaton Public Library, Balaton, MN [*Library symbol*] [*Library of Congress*] (LCLS)

MNBA .... Minimum Normal Burst Altitude

MNBA .... Mono-normal-butylamine [*Organic chemistry*]

MNBA .... Multinational Business Association (BUAC)

MnBab .... Babbitt Public Library, Babbitt, MN [*Library symbol*] [*Library of Congress*] (LCLS)

MnBabE ...... J.F. Kennedy Elementary School, Babbit, MN [*Library symbol*] [*Library of Congress*] (LCLS)

MnBabH....... J.F. Kennedy High School, Babbitt, MN [*Library symbol*] [*Library of Congress*] (LCLS)

MnBacS ...... Backus School, Backus, MN [*Library symbol*] [*Library of Congress*] (LCLS)

MnBadS ...... Badger School, Badger, MN [*Library symbol*] [*Library of Congress*] (LCLS)

MnBag .... Bagley Public Library, Bagley, MN [*Library symbol*] [*Library of Congress*] (LCLS)

MnBagE ...... Bagley Elementary School, Bagley, MN [*Library symbol*] [*Library of Congress*] (LCLS)

MnBaPS...... Balaton Public Schools, Balaton, MN [*Library symbol*] [*Library of Congress*] (LCLS)

MnBar......... Barnesville Public Library, Barnesville, MN [*Library symbol*] [*Library of Congress*] (LCLS)

MnBarFe...... Florence Atkinson Elementary School, Barnesville, MN [*Library symbol*] [*Library of Congress*] (LCLS)

MnBarH ...... Barnesville High School, Barnesville, MN [*Library symbol*] [*Library of Congress*] (LCLS)

MnBaSPL..... St. Peter's Lutheran School, Balaton, MN [*Library symbol*] [*Library of Congress*] (LCLS)

MnBatS........ Battle Lake Public School, Battle Lake, MN [*Library symbol*] [*Library of Congress*] (LCLS)

MnBau .... Baudette Public Library, Baudette, MN [*Library symbol*] [*Library of Congress*] (LCLS)

MnBauLH..... Lake of the Woods High School, Baudette, MN [*Library symbol*] [*Library of Congress*] (LCLS)

MnBaxE ...... Baxter Elementary School, Baxter, MN [*Library symbol*] [*Library of Congress*] (LCLS)

MNBB .... MNB Bancshares [*NASDAQ symbol*] (SAG)

MNB Bn ...... MNB Bancshares [*Associated Press*] (SAG)

MNBCCS...... Multi-Nevoid Basal-Cell Carcinoma Syndrome [*Medicine*] (MELL)

MNBDF........ Meta-Nitrobenzenediazonium Tetrafluoroborate [*Organic chemistry*]

MNBDO........ Mobile Naval Base Defence Organization [*British*] [*World War II*]

MnBE .... Becker Elementary School, Becker, MN [*Library symbol*] [*Library of Congress*] (LCLS)

MnBeaPS...... Beardlsey-Brown Valley Public Schools, Beardlsey, MN [*Library symbol*] [*Library of Congress*] (LCLS)

MnBeB .... Bertha-Hweitt School, Bertha, MN [*Library symbol*] [*Library of Congress*] (LCLS)

MNBedf........ New Bedford Free Public Library, New Bedford, MA [*Library symbol*] [*Library of Congress*] (LCLS)

MNBedfHi.... Old Dartmouth Historical Society, New Bedford Whaling Museum, New Bedford, MA [*Library symbol*] [*Library of Congress*] (LCLS)

MnBelPS...... Bellingham Public Schools, Bellingham, MN [*Library symbol*] [*Library of Congress*] (LCLS)

MnBem .... Bemidji Public Library, Bemidji, MN [*Library symbol*] [*Library of Congress*] (LCLS)

MnBemCE..... Central Elementary School, Bemidji, MN [*Library symbol*] [*Library of Congress*] (LCLS)

MnBemDE..... Deer Lake Elementary School, Bemidji, MN [*Library symbol*] [*Library of Congress*] (LCLS)

MnBemH...... Bemidji High School, Bemidji, MN [*Library symbol*] [*Library of Congress*] (LCLS)

MnBemHE..... Horace May Elementary School, Bemidji, MN [*Library symbol*] [*Library of Congress*] (LCLS)

MnBemJE .... J.W. Smith Elementary School, Bemidji, MN [*Library symbol*] [*Library of Congress*] (LCLS)

MnBemLE..... Lincoln Elementary School, Bemidji, MN [*Library symbol*] [*Library of Congress*] (LCLS)

MnBemMS..... Benidji Middle School, Bemidji, MN [*Library symbol*] [*Library of Congress*] (LCLS)

MnBemNE.... Northern Elementary School, Bemidji, MN [*Library symbol*] [*Library of Congress*] (LCLS)

MnBemOH.... Oak Hills Bible College, Bemidji, MN [*Library symbol*] [*Library of Congress*] (LCLS)

MnBemPE.... Paul Bunyan Elementary School, Bemidji, MN [*Library symbol*] [*Library of Congress*] (LCLS)

MnBemS...... Bemidji State College [*Later, Bemidji State University*], Bemidji, MN [*Library symbol*] [*Library of Congress*] (LCLS)

MnBemSE.... Solway Elementary School, Bemidji, MN [*Library symbol*] [*Library of Congress*] (LCLS)

MnBemSP... St. Philips School, Bemidji, MN [*Library symbol*] [*Library of Congress*] (LCLS)

MnBenPS..... Benson Public Schools, Benson, MN [*Library symbol*] [*Library of Congress*] (LCLS)

MnBenSF..... St. Francis Xavier School, Benson, MN [*Library symbol*] [*Library of Congress*] (LCLS)

MnBevPS..... Belview Public School, Bleview, MN [*Library symbol*] [*Library of Congress*] (LCLS)

MnBf............ Buffalo Public Library, Buffalo, MN [*Library symbol*] [*Library of Congress*] (LCLS)

MnBfaE......... Big Falls Elementary School, Big Falls, MN [*Library symbol*] [*Library of Congress*] (LCLS)

MnBfH .... Buffalo Memorial Hospital, Medical Library, Buffalo, MN [*Library symbol*] [*Library of Congress*] (LCLS)

MnBfHi .... Wright County Historical Society, Buffalo, MN [*Library symbol*] [*Library of Congress*] (LCLS)

MnBfl............ Buffalo Intermediate School, Buffalo, MN [*Library symbol*] [*Library of Congress*] (LCLS)

MnBfJ .... Buffalo Junior High School, Buffalo, MN [*Library symbol*] [*Library of Congress*] (LCLS)

MnBfoS........ Bigfork School, Bigford, MN [*Library symbol*] [*Library of Congress*] (LCLS)

MnBfP.......... Buffalo Primary Library, Buffalo, MN [*Library symbol*] [*Library of Congress*] (LCLS)

MnBfS.......... Buffalo Senior High School, Buffalo, MN [*Library symbol*] [*Library of Congress*] (LCLS)

MnBfSF........ St. Francis Xavier School, Buffalo, MN [*Library symbol*] [*Library of Congress*] (LCLS)

MnBfW......... Wright Vocational Coop Center, Buffalo, MN [*Library symbol*] [*Library of Congress*] (LCLS)

MnBg .... Myrtle Mabee Library, Belgrade, MN [*Library symbol*] [*Library of Congress*] (LCLS)

MnBgE......... Belgrade Elementary School, Belgrade, MN [*Library symbol*] [*Library of Congress*] (LCLS)

MnBgH......... Belgrade High School, Media Center, Belgrade, MN [*Library symbol*] [*Library of Congress*] (LCLS)

MnBH........... Becker High School, Becker, MN [*Library symbol*] [*Library of Congress*] (LCLS)

MnBHi .... Sherbourne County Historical Society, Becker, MN [*Library symbol*] [*Library of Congress*] (LCLS)

MnBhM........ Braham Middle School, Braham, MN [*Library symbol*] [*Library of Congress*] (LCLS)

MnBhSE....... Southview Elementary School, Braham, MN [*Library symbol*] [*Library of Congress*] (LCLS)

MnBhWH .... Westview High School, Media Center, Braham, MN [*Library symbol*] [*Library of Congress*] (LCLS)

MnBi............ Bird Island Public Library, Bird Island, MN [*Library symbol*] [*Library of Congress*] (LCLS)

MnBirlS .... Indus School, Birchdale, MN [*Library symbol*] [*Library of Congress*] (LCLS)

MnBiSM....... St. Mary's School, Bird Island, MN [*Library symbol*] [*Library of Congress*] (LCLS)

MnBiwE .... Bray Elementary School, Biwabik, MN [*Library symbol*] [*Library of Congress*] (LCLS)

MnBiwH....... V.L. Reishus High School, Biwabik, MN [*Library symbol*] [*Library of Congress*] (LCLS)

MNBK.......... Marine National Bank (California) [*NASDAQ symbol*] (SAG)

MNBK.......... Marine Nat'l Bank [*NASDAQ symbol*] (TTSB)

MnBkES .... Blomkest Elementary School, Blomkest, MN [*Library symbol*] [*Library of Congress*] (LCLS)

MNBKW...... Marine Natl Bk Irvine CA Wrrt [*NASDAQ symbol*] (TTSB)

MnBl............ Big Lake Public Library, Big Lake, MN [*Library symbol*] [*Library of Congress*] (LCLS)

MNBL........... Bluefields [*Nicaragua*] [*ICAO location identifier*] (ICLI)

MnBla.......... Blackduck Public Library, Blackduck, MN [*Library symbol*] [*Library of Congress*] (LCLS)

MnBlaE........ Blackduck Elementary School, Blackduck, MN [*Library symbol*] [*Library of Congress*] (LCLS)

MnBlaH........ Blackduck High School, Blackduck, MN [*Library symbol*] [*Library of Congress*] (LCLS)

MnBlE......... Big Lake Elementary School, Big Lake, MN [*Library symbol*] [*Library of Congress*] (LCLS)

MNBLE........ Modified Nearly Best Linear Estimator [*Statistics*]

MnBlH .... Big Lake High School, Big Lake, MN [*Library symbol*] [*Library of Congress*] (LCLS)

MnBloPS...... Bloomington Public Schools, Bloomington, MN [*Library symbol*] [*Library of Congress*] (LCLS)

MnBmE........ Barnum Elementary School, Barnum, MN [*Library symbol*] [*Library of Congress*] (LCLS)

MnBmH........ Barnum High School, Barnum, MN [*Library symbol*] [*Library of Congress*] (LCLS)

MNBO .... Management Buy-Out

MnBov .... Bovey Public Library, Bovey, MN [*Library symbol*] [*Library of Congress*] (LCLS)

MnBovM...... Connor-Jasper Middle School, Bovey, MN [*Library symbol*] [*Library of Congress*] (LCLS)

MnBovS .... Balsam School, Bovey, MN [*Library symbol*] [*Library of Congress*] (LCLS)

MnBr............ Brainerd Public Library, Brainerd, MN [*Library symbol*] [*Library of Congress*] (LCLS)

MNBR .... Los Brasiles/Carlos Ulloa [*Nicaragua*] [*ICAO location identifier*] (ICLI)

MnBraS........ Brandon Public School, Brandon, MN [*Library symbol*] [*Library of Congress*] (LCLS)

MnBrC......... Brainerd Community College, Brainerd, MN [*Library symbol*] [*Library of Congress*] (LCLS)

MnBre.......... Breckenridge Public Library, Breckenridge, MN [*Library symbol*] [*Library of Congress*] (LCLS)

MnBreE........ Breckenridge Elementary School, Breckenridge, MN [*Library symbol*] [*Library of Congress*] (LCLS)

MnBreH ...... Breckenridge High School, Breckenridge, MN [*Library symbol*] [*Library of Congress*] (LCLS)

MnBrFJ .... Franklin Junior High School, Brainerd, MN [*Library symbol*] [*Library of Congress*] (LCLS)

MnBrGE .... Garfield Elementary School, Brainerd, MN [*Library symbol*] [*Library of Congress*] (LCLS)

MnBrHE ...... Harrison Elementary School, Brainerd, MN [*Library symbol*] [*Library of Congress*] (LCLS)

MnBrHS .... Brainerd High School, Brainerd, MN [*Library symbol*] [*Library of Congress*] (LCLS)

MnBrLE .... Lincoln Elementary School, Brainerd, MN [*Library symbol*] [*Library of Congress*] (LCLS)

MnBrLoE...... Lowell Elementary School, Brainerd, MN [*Library symbol*] [*Library of Congress*] (LCLS)

MnBro.......... Browntown Public Library, Browntown, MN [*Library symbol*] [*Library of Congress*] (LCLS)

MnBroPS ..... Brownton Public Schools, Brownton, MN [*Library symbol*] [*Library of Congress*] (LCLS)

MnBrRE .... Riverside Elementary School, Brainerd, MN [*Library symbol*] [*Library of Congress*] (LCLS)

MnBruE .... Bruno Elementary School, Bruno, MN [*Library symbol*] [*Library of Congress*] (LCLS)

MnBrv .... Carnegie Public Library, Browns Valley, MN [*Library symbol*] [*Library of Congress*] (LCLS)

MnBrvPS ..... Beardsley-Browns Valley Public Schools, Browns Valley, MN [*Library symbol*] [*Library of Congress*] (LCLS)

MnBrWE ...... Whittier Elementary School, Brainerd,MN [*Library symbol*] [*Library of Congress*] (LCLS)

MnBrwES ..... Brewster Elementary School, Brewster, MN [*Library symbol*] [*Library of Congress*] (LCLS)

MnBrWM ..... Washington Middle School, Brainerd, MN [*Library symbol*] [*Library of Congress*] (LCLS)

MnBtH .... Brooten High School, Brooten, MN [*Library symbol*] [*Library of Congress*] (LCLS)

MnBul.......... Buhl Public Library, Buhl, MN [*Library symbol*] [*Library of Congress*] (LCLS)

MnBulR........ Range Geneaological Society, Buhl, MN [*Library symbol*] [*Library of Congress*] (LCLS)

MnBuS......... St. Michael School, Buckman, MN [*Library symbol*] [*Library of Congress*] (LCLS)

MnBvC......... Christ the King School, Browerville, MN [*Library symbol*] [*Library of Congress*] (LCLS)

MnBvP......... Browerville Public School, Browerville, MN [*Library symbol*] [*Library of Congress*] (LCLS)

MNBWS .... Miami Nature Biotechnology Winter Symposium (HGEN)

MNBZ........... Bonanza [*Nicaragua*] [*ICAO location identifier*] (ICLI)

MNC............ Concordia College, St. Paul, MN [*OCLC symbol*] (OCLC)

MNC............ Magnocellular Neurosecretory Cells

MNC............ Major NATO Command [*or Commander*] (NATG)

MNC............ Manager, National Clients (SAUO)

MNC............ Masonite Corporation (SAUO)

MNC............ Media News Corporation (SAUO)

MNC............ Mental Nurses' Cooperation (ROG)

MNC............ Microcomputer Numerical Control (MCD)

MNC............ Mineman, Chief [*Navy rating*]

MNC............ Ministerial Nomination Committee [*Australia*]

Mn-C........... Minnesota State Department of Corrections, St. Paul, MN [*Library symbol*] [*Library of Congress*] (LCLS)

MNC............ MIT Airlines Ltd. [*ICAO designator*] (FAAC)

MNC............ Mobile Network Code (CGWS)

MNC............ Monaco Coach [*NYSE symbol*] (SG)

MNC............ Moncalieri [*Italy*] [*Seismograph station code, US Geological Survey*] [*Closed*] (SEIS)

MNC............ Monica Resources [*Vancouver Stock Exchange symbol*]

MNC............ Mononuclear Cell (DB)

MNC............ Mononucleated Cell [*Clinical chemistry*] [*Also, MC*]

MNC............ Mouvement National Congolais [*Congolese National Movement*]

MNC............ Mouvement National du Congo-Lumumba [*Congo National Movement-Lumumba*] [*Zaire*] (PD)

MNC............ Movement for a New Congress (SAUO)

MNC............ Movimiento Nacional Conservador [*National Conservative Movement*] [*Colombia*] [*Political party*] (EY)

MNC............ Multinational Company [*Business term*]

MNC............ Multinational Corp.

MNC............ Multinucleated Cell [*Medicine*] (MELL)

MNC............ Multiplicative Noise Compensator [*Telecommunications*] (TEL)

MNC............ Nacala [*Mozambique*] [*Airport symbol*] (AD)

MNC............ Shelton, WA [*Location identifier*] [*FAA*] (FAAL)

MnCaCC...... Cambridge Community College, Cambridge, MN [*Library symbol*] [*Library of Congress*] (LCLS)

MnCaE........ East Central Regional Library, Cambridge, MN [*Library symbol*] [*Library of Congress*] (LCLS)

MnCaES .... Cambridge Elementary School, Media Center, Cambridge, MN [*Library symbol*] [*Library of Congress*] (LCLS)

MnCaH......... Cambridge Memorial Hospital, Health Sciences Library, Cambridge, MN [*Library symbol*] [*Library of Congress*] (LCLS)

MnCaHi — Isanti County Historical Society, Cambridge, MN [*Library symbol*] [*Library of Congress*] (LCLS)

MnCaHS — Cambridge High School, Media Center, Cambridge, MN [*Library symbol*] [*Library of Congress*] (LCLS)

MnCalE — Callaway Elementary School, Callaway, MN [*Library symbol*] [*Library of Congress*] (LCLS)

MnCaM — Cambridge Middle School, Media Center, Cambridge, MN [*Library symbol*] [*Library of Congress*] (LCLS)

MnCamE — Campbell-Tintah Elementary School, Campbell, MN [*Library symbol*] [*Library of Congress*] (LCLS)

MnCamH — Campbell-Tintah High School, Campbell, MN [*Library symbol*] [*Library of Congress*] (LCLS)

MnCan — Canby Public Library, Canby, MN [*Library symbol*] [*Library of Congress*] (LCLS)

MnCanH — Canby Community Hospital, Canby, MN [*Library symbol*] [*Library of Congress*] (LCLS)

MnCanHS — Canby High School, Canby, MN [*Library symbol*] [*Library of Congress*] (LCLS)

MnCarE — Carlos Elementary School, Carlos, MN [*Library symbol*] [*Library of Congress*] (LCLS)

MnCas — Cass Lake Community Library, Lake, MN [*Library symbol*] [*Library of Congress*] (LCLS)

MnCasCB — Chief Bug-O-Nay-Ge-Shig Library, Cass Lake, MN [*Library symbol*] [*Library of Congress*] (LCLS)

MnCaSD — Cambridge Seventh Day Adventist Library, Cambridge, MN [*Library symbol*] [*Library of Congress*] (LCLS)

MnCasE — Cass Lake Elementary School, Cass Lake, MN [*Library symbol*] [*Library of Congress*] (LCLS)

MnCaSH — Cambridge State Hospital, Staff Library, Cambridge, MN [*Library symbol*] [*Library of Congress*] (LCLS)

MnCasHS — Cass Lake High School, Cass Lake, MN [*Library symbol*] [*Library of Congress*] (LCLS)

MNCC — Multinational Coordination Center [*NATO*]

MnCcH — Hazelden Foundation, Staff library, Center City, MN [*Library symbol*] [*Library of Congress*] (LCLS)

MNCF — Merchant Navy Comforts Fund (SAUO)

MnCgL — Lakeside Intermediate Media Center, Chisago City, MN [*Library symbol*] [*Library of Congress*] (LCLS)

MnCgP — Chisago Lakes Primary School, Chisago City, MN [*Library symbol*] [*Library of Congress*] (LCLS)

MnCh — Carver County Library, Chaska, MN [*Library symbol*] [*Library of Congress*] (LCLS)

MNCH — Chinandega/German Pomares [*Nicaragua*] [*ICAO location identifier*] (ICLI)

MnChaHS — Chandler-Lake Wilson High School, Chandler, MN [*Library symbol*] [*Library of Congress*] (LCLS)

MnChi — Chisholm Public Library, Chisholm, MN [*Library symbol*] [*Library of Congress*] (LCLS)

MnChiE — Vaughan-Steffensrud Elementary School, Chisholm, MN [*Library symbol*] [*Library of Congress*] (LCLS)

MnChiJ — Chisholm Junior High School, Chisholm, MN [*Library symbol*] [*Library of Congress*] (LCLS)

MnChiI — Iron Range Research Library, Chisholm, MN [*Library symbol*] [*Library of Congress*] (LCLS)

MnChiSH — Chisholm Senior High School, Chisholm, MN [*Library symbol*] [*Library of Congress*] (LCLS)

MnChoE — Chokio-Alberto Elementary School, Chokio, MN [*Library symbol*] [*Library of Congress*] (LCLS)

MNCI — Corn Island [*Nicaragua*] [*ICAO location identifier*] (ICLI)

MNCI — Neepawa Collegiate Institute, Manitoba [*Library symbol*] [*National Library of Canada*] (NLC)

MNCIS — Management Numerical Control Information System (MCD)

MNC-K — Mouvement National Congolais - Kalonji [*Congolese National Movement*] [*Kalonji Wing*]

MnCl — Cloquet Public Library, Cloquet, MN [*Library symbol*] [*Library of Congress*] (LCLS)

MNCL — Monoclonal Gammopathy Identified [*Immunology*] (DAVI)

MNC-L — Mouvement National Congolais - Lumumba [*Congolese National Movement*] [*Lumumba Wing*]

MnClaE — Clarissa Elementary School, Clarissa, MN [*Library symbol*] [*Library of Congress*] (LCLS)

MnCLaH — Clarissa High School, Clarissa, MN [*Library symbol*] [*Library of Congress*] (LCLS)

MnClc — Clara City Public Library, Clara City, MN [*Library symbol*] [*Library of Congress*] (LCLS)

MnClCE — Churchill Elementary School, Cloquet, MN [*Library symbol*] [*Library of Congress*] (LCLS)

MnClcPS — Clara City Public Schools, Clara City, MN [*Library symbol*] [*Library of Congress*] (LCLS)

MnCleS — Clearbrook Public School, Clearbrook, MN [*Library symbol*] [*Library of Congress*] (LCLS)

MnClHi — Carlton County Historical Society, Cloquet, MN [*Library symbol*] [*Library of Congress*] (LCLS)

MnClim — Climax Public Library, Climax, MN [*Library symbol*] [*Library of Congress*] (LCLS)

MnClimS — Climax-Shelly School, Climax, MN [*Library symbol*] [*Library of Congress*] (LCLS)

MnClkE — Clearview Elementary School, Clear lake, MN [*Library symbol*] [*Library of Congress*] (LCLS)

MnClM — Cloquet Middle School, Cloquet, MN [*Library symbol*] [*Library of Congress*] (LCLS)

MnClOS — Fond du Lac Ojibway School, Cloquet, MN [*Library symbol*] [*Library of Congress*] (LCLS)

MnCls — Cold Spring Community Library, Cold Spring, MN [*Library symbol*] [*Library of Congress*] (LCLS)

MnClsE — Cold Spring Elementary/Rocori Junior School, Cold Spring, MN [*Library symbol*] [*Library of Congress*] (LCLS)

MnClSH — Cloquet Senior High School, Cloquet, MN [*Library symbol*] [*Library of Congress*] (LCLS)

MnClsR — Rocori High School, Cold Spring, MN [*Library symbol*] [*Library of Congress*] (LCLS)

MnClsS — St. Boniface Elementary School, Cold Spring, MN [*Library symbol*] [*Library of Congress*] (LCLS)

MnClWE — Washington Elementary School, Cloquet, MN [*Library symbol*] [*Library of Congress*] (LCLS)

MnCm — Calumet Public Library, Calumet, MN [*Library symbol*] [*Library of Congress*] (LCLS)

MNCM — Mineman, Master Chief [*Navy rating*]

MNCMPTR — Minicomputer (MSA)

MnCo — Cokato Public Library, Cokato, MN [*Library symbol*] [*Library of Congress*] (LCLS)

MnCoD — Dassel-Cokato Jr./Sr. High School, Cakoto, MN [*Library symbol*] [*Library of Congress*] (LCLS)

MnCoE — Cokato Elementary School, Media Center, Cokato, MN [*Library symbol*] [*Library of Congress*] (LCLS)

MnCohS — Cohasset School, Cohasset, MN [*Library symbol*] [*Library of Congress*] (LCLS)

MnCol — Coleraine Public Library, Coleraine, MN [*Library symbol*] [*Library of Congress*] (LCLS)

MnColH — Greenway High School, Coleraine, MN [*Library symbol*] [*Library of Congress*] (LCLS)

MnCoM — Cokato Museum, Cokato, MN [*Library symbol*] [*Library of Congress*] (LCLS)

MnCoo — Cook Public Library, Cook, MN [*Library symbol*] [*Library of Congress*] (LCLS)

MnCooS — Cook Public School, Cook, MN [*Library symbol*] [*Library of Congress*] (LCLS)

MnCosPS — Cosmos Public School, Cosmos, MN [*Library symbol*] [*Library of Congress*] (LCLS)

MnCotS — Cotton Public School, Cotton, MN [*Library symbol*] [*Library of Congress*] (LCLS)

MNCP — Math Network Curriculum Project (EDAC)

MNCP — Mbandzeni National Convention Party [*Swaziland*] (BUAC)

MNCPL — Municipal

MNCPPC — Maryland-National Capital Park and Planning Commission

MNCPPLTY — Municipality

MnCr — Crookston Public Library, Crookston, MN [*Library symbol*] [*Library of Congress*] (LCLS)

MNCR — Material Nonconformance Report (COE)

MnCr — Polk County Library, Crookston, MN [*Library symbol*] [*Library of Congress*] (LCLS)

MnCrCH — Central High School, Crookston, MN [*Library symbol*] [*Library of Congress*] (LCLS)

MnCrHE — Highland Elementary School, Crookston, MN [*Library symbol*] [*Library of Congress*] (LCLS)

MnCrLE — Lincoln Elementary School, Crookston, MN [*Library symbol*] [*Library of Congress*] (LCLS)

MnCrMS — Mount St. Benedict, Crookston, MN [*Library symbol*] [*Library of Congress*] (LCLS)

MnCroE — Crosby-Ironton Elementary School, Crosby, MN [*Library symbol*] [*Library of Congress*] (LCLS)

MnCroH — Crosby-Ironton High School, Crosby, MN [*Library symbol*] [*Library of Congress*] (LCLS)

MnCrpM — Mercy Medical Center, Coon Rapids, MN [*Library symbol*] [*Library of Congress*] (LCLS)

MNCRR — Metro-North Commuter Railroad (SAUO)

MnCrU — University of Minnesota Technical College, Crookston, MN [*Library symbol*] [*Library of Congress*] (LCLS)

MnCrWE — Washington Elementary School, Crookston, MN [*Library symbol*] [*Library of Congress*] (LCLS)

MnCrwHS — Cromwell High School, Cromwell, MN [*Library symbol*] [*Library of Congress*] (LCLS)

MNCS — Master Net Control Station (SAUO)

MNCS — Merchant Navy Comforts Service (SAUO)

MNCS — Mineman, Senior Chief [*Navy rating*]

MNCS — Multipoint Network-Control System

MnCS — St. John's University, Collegeville, MN [*Library symbol*] [*Library of Congress*] (LCLS)

MnCt — Carlton Public Library, Carlton, MN [*Library symbol*] [*Library of Congress*] (LCLS)

MnCtE — South Terrace Elementary School, Carlton, MN [*Library symbol*] [*Library of Congress*] (LCLS)

MnCtH — Carlotn High School, Carlton, MN [*Library symbol*] [*Library of Congress*] (LCLS)

MnCtwPS — Cottonwood Public School, Cottonwood, MN [*Library symbol*] [*Library of Congress*] (LCLS)

MNCV — Motor Nerve Conduction Velocity [*Medicine*]

MnCyS — Cyrus Public School, Cyrus, MN [*Library symbol*] [*Library of Congress*] (LCLS)

MND — Mandalay [*Burma*] [*Seismograph station code, US Geological Survey*] [*Closed*] (SEIS)

MND — Marlin Developments [*Vancouver Stock Exchange symbol*]

MND — Martin Nuclear Division [*AEC*] (MCD)

MND — Material Need Document [*DoD*]

MND — Mean Narrow Dose [*Radiation therapy*] (DAVI)

MND — Medial Nuclear Division [*Cytology*]

MND — Mendenhall, AK [*Location identifier*] [*FAA*] (FAAL)

MND — Midsummer Night's Dream [*Shakespearean work*]

MND — Minimum Necrosing Dose

MND — Minister of National Defence [*Canada*]

MND .... Ministry of National Defence [*British*] (MCD)
MND .... Minor Neurological Dysfunction
MND .... Mission Need Determination (DOMA)
MND .... Mission Need Document [*DoD*]
MND .... Mission Non-Delivery (MCD)
MND .... Mitchell Energy & Development Corp. [*NYSE symbol*] (SAG)
MND .... Modified Neck Dissection [*Medicine*] (DMAA)
MND .... Motor Neuron Disease [*Medicine*]
MND .... Mound
MND .... Movimento Nacional Democratico [*National Democratic Movement*] [*Portugal*] [*Political party*] (PPE)
MND .... Multi-National Division (SAUO)
MND .... University of Minnesota-Duluth, Duluth, MN [*OCLC symbol*] (OCLC)
MNDA .... Missionary Sisters of Notre Dame des Anges [*Roman Catholic religious order*]
MNDA .... Missionary Sisters of Our Lady of the Angels (BUAC)
MND A .... Mitchell Energy/Dev'A' [*NYSE symbol*] (TTSB)
MNDA .... Motor Neurone Disease Association [*British*] (DBA)
MND Association... Motor Neurone Disease Association (NRGU)
MnDaw .... Carnegie Library, Dawson, MN [*Library symbol*] [*Library of Congress*] (LCLS)
MNDAWA ...... Motor Neurone Disease Association of Western Australia
MnDawJH .... Johnson Memorial Hospital and Nursing School, Dawson, MN [*Library symbol*] [*Library of Congress*] (LCLS)
MnDawPS.... Dawson-Boyd Public Library, Dawson, MN [*Library symbol*] [*Library of Congress*] (LCLS)
MND B .... Mitchell Energy/Dev'B' [*NYSE symbol*] (TTSB)
MND-C........ Multi-National Division, Centre (SAUO)
MND-C........ Multi-National Division, Centre. To be formed between October (SAUS)
MNDD .... Mouvement National pour la Democratie et le Developpement [*Benin*] [*Political party*] (EY)
MnDe .... Delano Public Libbrary, Delano, MN [*Library symbol*] [*Library of Congress*] (LCLS)
MnDeE .... Delano Elementary School, Delano, MN [*Library symbol*] [*Library of Congress*] (LCLS)
MnDeH .... Delano High School, Delano, MN [*Library symbol*] [*Library of Congress*] (LCLS)
MnDeM........ Delano Middle School, Delano, MN [*Library symbol*] [*Library of Congress*] (LCLS)
MNDEP .... Mineral Deposits Data Base (SAUO)
MnDerE........ King Elementary School, Deer River, MN [*Library symbol*] [*Library of Congress*] (LCLS)
MnDerH .... Deer River High School, Deer River, MN [*Library symbol*] [*Library of Congress*] (LCLS)
MnDES .... Dassel Elementary School, Media Center, Dassel, MN [*Library symbol*] [*Library of Congress*] (LCLS)
MnDeSP ...... St. Peter's School, Delano, MN [*Library symbol*] [*Library of Congress*] (LCLS)
MnDI........... Detroit Lakes Public Library, Detroit Lakes, MN [*Library symbol*] [*Library of Congress*] (LCLS)
MnDIH .... Community High School, Detroit Lakes, MN [*Library symbol*] [*Library of Congress*] (LCLS)
MnDIHi........ Becker County Historical Society, Detroit Lakes, MN [*Library symbol*] [*Library of Congress*] (LCLS)
MnDIJ.......... Community Junior High School, Detroit Lakes, MN [*Library symbol*] [*Library of Congress*] (LCLS)
MnDILe........ Lincoln Elementary School, Detroit Lakes, MN [*Library symbol*] [*Library of Congress*] (LCLS)
MnDIRE .... Rossman Elementary School, Detroit Lakes, MN [*Library symbol*] [*Library of Congress*] (LCLS)
MnDITI......... Detroit Lakes Technical Institute, Detroit Lakes, MN [*Library symbol*] [*Library of Congress*] (LCLS)
MnDIWE ...... Washington Elementary School, Detroit Lakes, MN [*Library symbol*] [*Library of Congress*] (LCLS)
MNDO .... Merchant Navy Discipline Organisation [*British*] (DS)
MNDO .... Modified Neglect of Diatomic Overlap (AAEL)
MNDO .... Modified Neglect of Differential Overlap [*Quantum mechanics*]
MNDP .... Bibliotheque Pere Champagne [*Pere Champagne Library*], Notre-Dame-De-Lourdes, Manitoba [*Library symbol*] [*National Library of Canada*] (BIB)
MNDP .... Multinational Data Processing (MHDB)
MND-S......... Multi-National Division, South (SAUO)
MND-S......... Multi-National Division, South. Due to become operational in (SAUS)
MNDTH .... Minimum Depth (NOAA)
MNDTS .... Member of the Non-Destructive Testing Society of Great Britain
MnDu .... Duluth Public Library, Duluth, MN [*Library symbol*] [*Library of Congress*] (LCLS)
MnDuBE .... Birchwood Elementary School, Duluth, MN [*Library symbol*] [*Library of Congress*] (LCLS)
MnDuBVE .... Bay View Elementary School, Duluth, MN [*Library symbol*] [*Library of Congress*] (LCLS)
MnDuCE....... Cobb Elementary Library, Duluth, MN [*Library symbol*] [*Library of Congress*] (LCLS)
MnDuCH ...... Central High School, Duluth, MN [*Library symbol*] [*Library of Congress*] (LCLS)
MnDuCOE .... Congdon Park Elementary School, Duluth, MN [*Library of Congress*] (LCLS)
MnDuCPE .... Chester Park Elementary School, Duluth, MN [*Library symbol*] [*Library of Congress*] (LCLS)
MnDuDH ...... Denfeld High School, Duluth, MN [*Library symbol*] [*Library of Congress*] (LCLS)
MnDuEH ...... East High School, Duluth, MN [*Library symbol*] [*Library of Congress*] (LCLS)

MnDuEPA .... United States Environmental Protection Agency, National Water Quality Laboratory, Duluth, MN [*Library symbol*] [*Library of Congress*] (LCLS)
MnDuGE ...... Grant Elementary School, Duluth, MN [*Library symbol*] [*Library of Congress*] (LCLS)
MnDuHE ...... Homcroft Elementary School, Duluth, MN [*Library symbol*] [*Library of Congress*] (LCLS)
MnDuHi .... Northeast Minnesota Historical Center Library, Duluth, MN [*Library symbol*] [*Library of Congress*] (LCLS)
MnDuHS ...... Hermantown High School, Duluth, MN [*Library symbol*] [*Library of Congress*] (LCLS)
MnDuLE ...... Lincoln Elementary School, Duluth, MN [*Library symbol*] [*Library of Congress*] (LCLS)
MnDuLOE .... Lowell Elementary School, Duluth, MN [*Library symbol*] [*Library of Congress*] (LCLS)
MnDuLPE .... Lester Park Elementary School, Duluth, MN [*Library symbol*] [*Library of Congress*] (LCLS)
MnDuLWE.... Lakewood Elementary School, Duluth, MN [*Library symbol*] [*Library of Congress*] (LCLS)
MnDuM........ Miller-Dawn Hospital and Medical Center, Duluth, MN [*Library symbol*] [*Library of Congress*] (LCLS)
MnDuME ...... Merritt Elementary School, Duluth, MN [*Library symbol*] [*Library of Congress*] (LCLS)
MnDuMPJ .... Morgan Park Junior High School, Duluth, MN [*Library symbol*] [*Library of Congress*] (LCLS)
MnDuMS...... Marshall School, Duluth, MN [*Library symbol*] [*Library of Congress*] (LCLS)
MnDuMWE... MacArthue/West Elementary School, Duluth MN [*Library symbol*] [*Library of Congress*] (LCLS)
MnDuNE ...... Nettleton Elementary School, Duluth, MN [*Library symbol*] [*Library of Congress*] (LCLS)
MnDuNR...... Natural Resources Research Institute, Duluth, MN [*Library symbol*] [*Library of Congress*] (LCLS)
MnDuNSE .... North Shore Elementary School, Duluth, MN [*Library symbol*] [*Library of Congress*] (LCLS)
MnDuOJ....... Ordean Junior High School, Duluth, MN [*Library symbol*] [*Library of Congress*] (LCLS)
MnDuPC ...... Duluth Prison Camp, Duluth, MN [*Library symbol*] [*Library of Congress*] (LCLS)
MnDuPE ...... Piedmont Elementary School, Duluth, MN [*Library symbol*] [*Library of Congress*] (LCLS)
MnDuSE....... Stowe Elementary School, Duluth, MN [*Library symbol*] [*Library of Congress*] (LCLS)
MnDuSLH .... St. Louis County Helth Dept., Duluth, MN [*Library symbol*] [*Library of Congress*] (LCLS)
MnDuStL...... Saint Luke's Hospital, Duluth, MN [*Library symbol*] [*Library of Congress*] (LCLS)
MnDuStM .... Saint Mary's Hospital, Duluth, MN [*Library symbol*] [*Library of Congress*] (LCLS)
MnDuStS .... College of Saint Scholastica, Duluth, MN [*Library symbol*] [*Library of Congress*] (LCLS)
MnDuTI........ Duluth Technical Institute, Duluth, MN [*Library symbol*] [*Library of Congress*] (LCLS)
MnDuTRC .... Teachers' Resource Center, Duluth, MN [*Library symbol*] [*Library of Congress*] (LCLS)
MnDuU .... University of Minnesota, Duluth, MN [*Library symbol*] [*Library of Congress*] (LCLS)
MnDuWE ...... Washburn Elementary School, Duluth, MN [*Library symbol*] [*Library of Congress*] (LCLS)
MnDuWJ...... Washington Junior High School, Duluth, MN [*Library symbol*] [*Library of Congress*] (LCLS)
MnDuWJH ... Woodland Junior High School, Duluth, MN [*Library symbol*] [*Library of Congress*] (LCLS)
MNDX .... Mobile Non-Director Exchange [*Telecommunications*] (NITA)
MNE .... College of St. Catherine, St. Paul, MN [*OCLC symbol*] (OCLC)
Mne .... Marine [*British military*] (DMA)
MNE .... Master of Naval Engineering
MNE .... Master of Nuclear Engineering
MNE .... Mentone [*France*] [*Airport symbol*] (AD)
MNE .... Merchant Navy Establishment [*British*] (DS)
MNE .... Methylallyl Nitrophenyl Ether [*Organic chemistry*]
MNE .... Methylnorepinephrine [*Also, Normetanephrine*] [*Biochemistry*]
MNE .... Minden, LA [*Location identifier*] [*FAA*] (FAAL)
MNE .... Mineo [*Sicily*] [*Seismograph station code, US Geological Survey*] [*Closed*] (SEIS)
MNE .... Minimum Number of Elements
Mn-E .... Minnesota State Department of Education, St. Paul, MN [*Library symbol*] [*Library of Congress*] (LCLS)
MNE .... Modern English [*Language, etc.*]
MNE .... Moneygram Payment Systems [*NYSE symbol*] (SAG)
MNE .... Multinational Enterprise
MNe .... Newburyport Public Library, Newburyport, MA [*Library symbol*] [*Library of Congress*] (LCLS)
MNEA.......... Merchant Navy Establishment Administration [*British*] (DS)
MnEb .... Eagle Bend Public Library, Eagle Bend, MN [*Library symbol*] [*Library of Congress*] (LCLS)
MnEbS .... Eagle Bend School, Eagle Bend, MN [*Library symbol*] [*Library of Congress*] (LCLS)
MnEcES ...... Echo-Wood Lake Elementary School, Echo, MN [*Library symbol*] [*Library of Congress*] (LCLS)
MNECInst of E&S... Member of North East Coast Institution of Engineers & Shipbuilders (SAUO)
MNECP .... Mobile National Emergency Command Post [*Air Force*]
MN Ed .... Master of Nursing Education
MN ED .... Material Need Engineering Development (MCD)

MnEdS.........	Southdale-Hennepin Area Library, Edina, MN [*Library symbol*] [*Library of Congress*] (LCLS)
MNEE..........	Mission Nonessential Equipment [*NASA*] (KSC)
MNeeS.........	GTE-Sylvania, Electric Systems Group, Needham, MA [*Library symbol*] [*Library of Congress*] (LCLS)
MnEfAE.......	Adams Elementary School, Fergus Falls, MN [*Library symbol*] [*Library of Congress*] (LCLS)
MnEfS.........	Effie School, Effie, MN [*Library symbol*] [*Library of Congress*] (LCLS)
MnEgfCE......	Crestwood Elementary School, East Grand Forks, MN [*Library symbol*] [*Library of Congress*] (LCLS)
MnEgfH.......	East Grand Forks High School, East Grand Forks, MN [*Library symbol*] [*Library of Congress*] (LCLS)
MnEgfJ.......	Central Junior High School, Grand Forks, MN [*Library symbol*] [*Library of Congress*] (LCLS)
MnEgfRE.....	River Heights Elementary School, East Grand Forks, MN [*Library symbol*] [*Library of Congress*] (LCLS)
MnEgfTI......	East Grand Forks Technical Institute, East Grand Forks, MN [*Library symbol*] [*Library of Congress*] (LCLS)
MnEgfVE.....	Valley Elementary School, East Grand Forks, MN [*Library symbol*] [*Library of Congress*] (LCLS)
MNeHi........	Newburyport Historical Society, Newburyport, MA [*Library symbol*] [*Library of Congress*] (LCLS)
MNEIMME....	Member of the North of England Institute of Mining and Mechanical Engineers (SAUO)
MnElb........	Thorsen Memorial Public Library, Elbow Lake, MN [*Library symbol*] [*Library of Congress*] (LCLS)
MnElbE.......	West Central Elementary School, Elbow Lake, MN [*Library symbol*] [*Library of Congress*] (LCLS)
MnElbH.......	West Central High School, Elbow Lake, MN [*Library symbol*] [*Library of Congress*] (LCLS)
MnEly.........	Ely Public Library, Ely, MN [*Library symbol*] [*Library of Congress*] (LCLS)
MnElyJS......	Memorial Junior/Senior High School, Ely, MN [*Library symbol*] [*Library of Congress*] (LCLS)
MnElyV.......	Vermillion Community College, Ely, MN [*Library symbol*] [*Library of Congress*] (LCLS)
MnElyWE.....	Washington Elementary School, Ely, MN [*Library symbol*] [*Library of Congress*] (LCLS)
Mnemos.....	Mnemosyne [*A publication*] (OCD)
MN Eng.....	Master of Naval Engineering
MnEr..........	Elk River Public Library, Elk River, MN [*Library symbol*] [*Library of Congress*] (LCLS)
MNERAM.....	Members of New England Regional Art Museum
MnErHE......	Handke Elementary School, Elk River, MN [*Library symbol*] [*Library of Congress*] (LCLS)
MnErPE......	K.G. Parker Elementary School, Elk River, MN [*Library symbol*] [*Library of Congress*] (LCLS)
MnErS.........	Elk River Senior High School, Elk River, MN [*Library symbol*] [*Library of Congress*] (LCLS)
MnErSA.......	St. Andrew's School, Elk River, MN [*Library symbol*] [*Library of Congress*] (LCLS)
MnErSJ......	Salk Junior High School, Elk River, MN [*Library symbol*] [*Library of Congress*] (LCLS)
MnErSJL.....	St. John's Lutheran School, Elk River, MN [*Library symbol*] [*Library of Congress*] (LCLS)
MnErsS.......	Erksine Public School, Erkskine, MN [*Library symbol*] [*Library of Congress*] (LCLS)
MnErVJ......	Vandenberge Junior High School, Elk River, MN [*Library symbol*] [*Library of Congress*] (LCLS)
MNES..........	Median Nerve Entrapment Syndrome [*Medicine*] (MELL)
MNES..........	Mine Safety Appl [*NASDAQ symbol*] (TTSB)
MNES..........	Mine Safety Appliances Co. [*NASDAQ symbol*] (NQ)
MnEskH......	Esko High School, Esko, MN [*Library symbol*] [*Library of Congress*] (LCLS)
MnEskWE....	Winterquist Elementary School, Esko, MN [*Library symbol*] [*Library of Congress*] (LCLS)
MNET..........	Mission and Data Operations Directorate Network (MCD)
MNET..........	Multicom Publishing [*NASDAQ symbol*] (SAG)
MNEV..........	Musica Nostra et Vostra, National Corp. of America (EA)
MnEvaE.......	Evansville Elementary School, Evansville, MN [*Library symbol*] [*Library of Congress*] (LCLS)
MnEvaH......	Evansville High School, Evansville, MN [*Library symbol*] [*Library of Congress*] (LCLS)
MnEvH........	Eden Valley-Watkins High School, Eden Valley, MN [*Library symbol*] [*Library of Congress*] (LCLS)
MnEvl........	Eveleth Public Library, Eveleth, MN [*Library symbol*] [*Library of Congress*] (LCLS)
MnEvlFE.....	Franklin Elementary School, Eveleth, MN [*Library symbol*] [*Library of Congress*] (LCLS)
MnEvlSH.....	Eveleth-Gilbert Senior High School, Eveleth, MN [*Library symbol*] [*Library of Congress*] (LCLS)
MnF...........	Buckham Memorial Library, Faribault, MN [*Library symbol*] [*Library of Congress*] (LCLS)
MNF...........	College of St. Benedict, St. Joseph, MN [*OCLC symbol*] (OCLC)
MNF...........	Forbes Library, Northampton, MA [*Library symbol*] [*Library of Congress*] (LCLS)
MNF...........	Mana [*Fiji*] [*Airport symbol*] (OAG)
MNF...........	Manager, National Finance (SAUO)
MNF...........	Manitou Reef Resources [*Vancouver Stock Exchange symbol*]
MNF...........	Maritime Nuclear Forces (SAUO)
MNF...........	Menagasha National Forest (SAUO)
MNF...........	Millers' National Federation (EA)
MNF...........	Mizo National Front [*India*] (PD)
MNF...........	Morehead & North Fork R. R. [*AAR code*]
MNF...........	Mountain View, MO [*Location identifier*] [*FAA*] (FAAL)
MNF...........	Multilateral Nuclear Force
MNF...........	Multinational Force [*Eleven-nation peace-keeping force for the Sinai*]
MNF...........	Multinational Peace-Keeping Force (SAUO)
MNF...........	Multisystem Networking Facility
MNF...........	Myelinated Nerve Fiber [*Medicine*] (MELL)
MnFa	Martin County Library, Fairmont, MN [*Library symbol*] [*Library of Congress*] (LCLS)
MNFD	Manifold (ECII)
MnFE	Missile Not Fully Equipped (AAG)
MnFer.........	Fertile Public Library, Fertile, MN [*Library symbol*] [*Library of Congress*] (LCLS)
MnFerS.......	Fertile-Betrami School, Fertile, MN [*Library symbol*] [*Library of Congress*] (LCLS)
MnFf	Fergus Falls Public Library, Fergus Falls, MN [*Library symbol*] [*Library of Congress*] (LCLS)
MNFF..........	Magyar Nemzeti Fueggetlensegi Front [*Hungarian National Independence Front*] [*Political party*]
MnFfC.........	Fergus Falls Community College, Fergus Falls, MN [*Library symbol*] [*Library of Congress*] (LCLS)
MnFfCE.......	Cleveland Elementary School, Fergus Falls, MN [*Library symbol*] [*Library of Congress*] (LCLS)
MnFfEC.......	West Central Educational Cooperative Service Unit, Fergus Falls, MN [*Library symbol*] [*Library of Congress*] (LCLS)
MnFfH.........	Lake Region Hospital, Fergus Falls, MN [*Library symbol*] [*Library of Congress*] (LCLS)
MnFfHA.......	Hillcrest Academy, Fergus Falls, MN [*Library symbol*] [*Library of Congress*] (LCLS)
MnFfHi........	Otter Tail County Historical Society, Fergus Falls, MN [*Library symbol*] [*Library of Congress*] (LCLS)
MnFfL.........	Lutheran Brethren Schools, Fergus Falls, MN [*Library symbol*] [*Library of Congress*] (LCLS)
MnFfM........	Fergus Falls Middle School, Fergus Falls, MN [*Library symbol*] [*Library of Congress*] (LCLS)
MnFfME.......	McKinley Elementary School, Fergus Falls, MN [*Library symbol*] [*Library of Congress*] (LCLS)
MnFfO........	Otter Tail Power Co., Fergus Falls, MN [*Library symbol*] [*Library of Congress*] (LCLS)
MnFfRT.......	Fergus Falls Regional Treatment Center, Fergus Falls, MN [*Library symbol*] [*Library of Congress*] (LCLS)
MnFfSH.......	Fergus Falls Senior High School, Fergus Falls, MN [*Library symbol*] [*Library of Congress*] (LCLS)
MnFfV.........	Viking Library System, Fergus Falls, MN [*Library symbol*] [*Library of Congress*] (LCLS)
MNFI..........	Michigan Natural Features Inventory [*Michigan State Department of Natural Resources*] [*Information service or system*] (IID)
MnFiE.........	Finlayson Elementary School, Finlayson, MN [*Library symbol*] [*Library of Congress*] (LCLS)
MnFiH.........	Finlayson High School, Finlayson, MN [*Library symbol*] [*Library of Congress*] (LCLS)
MnFisS	Fisher Public School, Fisher, MN [*Library symbol*] [*Library of Congress*] (LCLS)
MNFLD	Manifold (KSC)
MnFILS	Lincoln School, Floodwood, MN [*Library symbol*] [*Library of Congress*] (LCLS)
MnFo	Foley Community Library, Foley, MN [*Library symbol*] [*Library of Congress*] (LCLS)
MnFoE	Foley Elementary School, Foley, MN [*Library symbol*] [*Library of Congress*] (LCLS)
MnFoH	Foley High School, Foley, MN [*Library symbol*] [*Library of Congress*] (LCLS)
MnFoS	St. John's School, Foley, MN [*Library symbol*] [*Library of Congress*] (LCLS)
MNFP..........	Magyar Nemzeti Fueggetlensegi Part [*Hungarian National Independence Party*] [*Political party*] (PPE)
MNFP..........	Multinational Fighter Program [*Air Force*]
MNFP..........	Multiple Number of Faults per Pass (PDAA)
MnFpS	Sacred Heart School, Freeport MN [*Library symbol*] [*Library of Congress*] (LCLS)
MnFraE.......	Frazee Elementary School, Frazee, MN [*Library symbol*] [*Library of Congress*] (LCLS)
MnFraHS	Frazee-Vergas High School, Frazee, MN [*Library symbol*] [*Library of Congress*] (LCLS)
MNFRM	Main Frame
MnFrnCES....	Cedar Mt. Elementary School, Franklin, MN [*Library symbol*] [*Library of Congress*] (LCLS)
MnFrUH......	Unity Hospital, Fridley, MN [*Library symbol*] [*Library of Congress*] (LCLS)
MNFS..........	Minor Frame Synchronization (ACAE)
MnFS	Seabury Divinity School, Faribault, MN [*Library symbol*] [*Library of Congress*] (LCLS)
MnFt..........	Fosston Public Library, Fosston,MN [*Library symbol*] [*Library of Congress*] (LCLS)
MnFtH.........	Fosston High School, Fosston, MN [*Library symbol*] [*Library of Congress*] (LCLS)
MnFtME	Magelssen Elementary School, Fosston, MN [*Library symbol*] [*Library of Congress*] (LCLS)
MnFu	Fulda Public Library, Fulda, MN [*Library symbol*] [*Library of Congress*] (LCLS)
MNFU.........	Manx National Farmers Union [*British*] (DBA)
MnFuES	Fulda Elementary School, Fulda, MN [*Library symbol*] [*Library of Congress*] (LCLS)
MnFuJSH	Fulda Junior-Senior High School, Fulda, MN [*Library symbol*] [*Library of Congress*] (LCLS)
MnFuStP	St. Paul's Lutheran School, Fulda, MN [*Library symbol*] [*Library of Congress*]

MNG .... Gustavus Adolphus College, St. Peter, MN [*OCLC symbol*] (OCLC)
MNG .... Managing (MSA)
Mng .... Managing (TBD)
MNG .... Mangahao [*New Zealand*] [*Seismograph station code, US Geological Survey*] (SEIS)
MNG .... Maningrida [*Australia*] [*Airport symbol*] [*Obsolete*] (OAG)
mng .... Meaning
MNG .... Microwave Negative Grid
MNG .... Minimal No-Good (SAUS)
MNG .... Modulated Noise Generator (PDAA)
MNG .... Mongolia [*ANSI three-letter standard code*] (CNC)
MNG .... Morning
MNG .... Mourning (ROG)
MNG .... Multinodular Goiter [*Endocrinology*] (DAVI)
MnGarE .... Garfield Elementary School, Garfield, MN [*Library symbol*] [*Library of Congress*] (LCLS)
MnGBES ...... Helen Baker Elementary School, Glencoe, MN [*Library symbol*] [*Library of Congress*] (LCLS)
MnGc .... Grove City Public Library, Grove City, MN [*Library symbol*] [*Library of Congress*] (LCLS)
MnGcJH .... Atwater-Grove City Junior High School, Grove City, MN [*Library symbol*] [*Library of Congress*] (LCLS)
MnGeH .... Grey Eagle High School, Grey Eagle, MN [*Library symbol*] [*Library of Congress*] (LCLS)
MnGf .... Granite Falls Public Library, Granite Falls, MN [*Library symbol*] [*Library of Congress*] (LCLS)
MnGfH .... Granite Falls Municipal Hospital, Granite Falls, MN [*Library symbol*] [*Library of Congress*] (LCLS)
MnGfODS ..... Open Door Bible School, Granite Falls, MN [*Library symbol*] [*Library of Congress*] (LCLS)
MnGfPS .... Granite Falls Public School, Granite Falls, MN [*Library symbol*] [*Library of Congress*] (LCLS)
MnGfTC .... Southwest Technical College, Granite Falls, MN [*Library symbol*] [*Library of Congress*] (LCLS)
MnGGH .... Glencoe Hospital, Glencoe, MN [*Library symbol*] [*Library of Congress*] (LCLS)
MnGHS .... Glencoe Public High School, Glencoe, MN [*Library symbol*] [*Library of Congress*] (LCLS)
MnGi .... Gilbert Public Library, Gilbert, MN [*Library symbol*] [*Library of Congress*] (LCLS)
MNGIE .... Mitochrondrial Neurogastrointestinal Encephalomyopathy
MnGiHi .... Iron Range Historical Society, Gilbert MN [*Library symbol*] [*Library of Congress*] (LCLS)
MnGiJH .... Gilbert-Eveleth Junior High School, Gilbert, MN [*Library symbol*] [*Library of Congress*] (LCLS)
MnGiNSE ..... Nelle Shean Elementary School, Gilbert, MN [*Library symbol*] [*Library of Congress*] (LCLS)
MnGle .... Glenwood Public Library, Glenwood, MN [*Library symbol*] [*Library of Congress*] (LCLS)
MnGLES ...... Lincoln Elementary School, Glencoe, MN [*Library symbol*] [*Library of Congress*] (LCLS)
MnGleSH ..... Glenwood Senior High School, Glenwood, MN [*Library symbol*] [*Library of Congress*] (LCLS)
MNGLX .... Montgomery Global Long-Short Fund [*Investment term*]
MnGlyE .... Glyndon Elementary School, Glyndon, MN [*Library symbol*] [*Library of Congress*] (LCLS)
MnGlyHS .... Glyndon-Felton High School, Glyndon, MN [*Library symbol*] [*Library of Congress*] (LCLS)
MnGm .... Grand Marais Public Library, Grand Marais, MN [*Library symbol*] [*Library of Congress*] (LCLS)
MnGmFT ...... United States National Park Service, Grand Portage Northern Minnesota Fur Trade Library, Grand Marais, MN [*Library symbol*] [*Library of Congress*] (LCLS)
MnGmH .... Cook County High School, Grand Marais, MN [*Library symbol*] [*Library of Congress*] (LCLS)
MnGMS .... Glencoe Middle School, Glencoe, MN [*Library symbol*] [*Library of Congress*] (LCLS)
MnGmSE ..... Sawtooth Elementary School, Grand Marais, MN [*Library symbol*] [*Library of Congress*] (LCLS)
MNGMT ...... Management (ADA)
MNGNG .... Managing
MnGonS ...... Gonvick-Trail Community School, Gonvick, MN [*Library symbol*] [*Library of Congress*] (LCLS)
MnGoos ...... Goodridge Public School, Goodridge, MN [*Library symbol*] [*Library of Congress*] (LCLS)
MNGP .... Monticello Nuclear Generating Plant (NRCH)
MnGpE .... Grand Portage Elementary School, Grand Portage, MN [*Library symbol*] [*Library of Congress*] (LCLS)
MnGr .... Grand Rapids Public Library, Grand Rapids, MN [*Library symbol*] [*Library of Congress*] (LCLS)
mngr .... Manager (SHCU)
MNGR .... Manager
MNGR .... Monsignor
MnGra .... Graceville Public Library, Graceville, MN [*Library symbol*] [*Library of Congress*] (LCLS)
MnGraBS .... Big Stone Hutterite Colony School, Graceville, MN [*Library symbol*] [*Library of Congress*] (LCLS)
MnGraCHS ... Clinton-Graceville High School, Graceville, MN [*Library symbol*] [*Library of Congress*] (LCLS)
MnGraH .... Holy Trinity Hospital, Graceville, MN [*Library symbol*] [*Library of Congress*] (LCLS)
MnGre .... Greenbush Public Library, Greenbush, MN [*Library symbol*] [*Library of Congress*] (LCLS)
MnGrEMS .... Edna I. Murphy School, Grand Rapids, MN [*Library symbol*] [*Library of Congress*] (LCLS)

MnGreS .... Greenbush Public School, Greenbush, MN [*Library symbol*] [*Library of Congress*] (LCLS)
MnGrFLS .... Forrest Lake School, Grand Rapids, MN [*Library symbol*] [*Library of Congress*] (LCLS)
MnGrFW ..... Forest Wildlife Population and Research Group, Grand Rapids, MN [*Library symbol*] [*Library of Congress*] (LCLS)
MnGrl .... Itasca Community College, Grand Rapids, MN [*Library symbol*] [*Library of Congress*] (LCLS)
MnGrM .... Grand Rapids Middle School, Grand Rapids, MN [*Library symbol*] [*Library of Congress*] (LCLS)
MNGRM .... Monogram
MnGrRS .... Riverview School, Grand Rapids, MN [*Library symbol*] [*Library of Congress*] (LCLS)
MnGrSH ...... Grand Rapids Senior HighSchool, Grand Rapids, MN [*Library symbol*] [*Library of Congress*] (LCLS)
MnGrSS ..... Southwest School, Grand Rapids, MN [*Library symbol*] [*Library of Congress*] (LCLS)
MnGryS .... Grygla Public School, Grygla, MN [*Library symbol*] [*Library of Congress*] (LCLS)
Mngt .... Management
MnGvH .... Golden Valley Health Center, Golden Valley, MN [*Library symbol*] [*Library of Congress*] (LCLS)
MNH .... Magnum Resources [*Vancouver Stock Exchange symbol*]
MNH .... Makers of National History [*A publication*]
MNH .... Maternal and Neonatal Health (SAUO)
Mn-H .... Minnesota State Department of Health, St. Paul, MN [*Library symbol*] [*Library of Congress*] (LCLS)
MNH .... Mint Never Hinged [*Philately*]
MNH .... Monarch Airlines [*ICAO designator*] (FAAC)
MNH .... Munich [*Germany*] [*Seismograph station code, US Geological Survey*] [*Closed*] (SEIS)
MNH .... Museum of National History (SAUO)
MNH .... Museum of Natural History [*Smithsonian Institution*]
MNH .... University of Minnesota-Duluth, Health Science Library, Duluth, MN [*OCLC symbol*] (OCLC)
MnHaH .... Norman County West High School, Halstad, MN [*Library symbol*] [*Library of Congress*] (LCLS)
MnHal .... Hallock Public Library, Hallock, MN [*Library symbol*] [*Library of Congress*] (LCLS)
MnHalH .... Hallock High School, Hallock, MN [*Library symbol*] [*Library of Congress*] (LCLS)
MnHan .... Hancock Community Library, Hancock, MN [*Library symbol*] [*Library of Congress*] (LCLS)
MnHanE .... Hancock Elementary School, Hancock, MN [*Library symbol*] [*Library of Congress*] (LCLS)
MnHanH .... Hancock High School, Hancock, MN [*Library symbol*] [*Library of Congress*] (LCLS)
MnHaw .... Hawley Public Library, Hawley, MN [*Library symbol*] [*Library of Congress*] (LCLS)
MnHawE .... Hawley Elementary School, Hawley, MN [*Library symbol*] [*Library of Congress*] (LCLS)
MnHawH ...... Hawley High School, Hawley, MN [*Library symbol*] [*Library of Congress*] (LCLS)
MnHcS .... Hill City School, Hill City, MN [*Library symbol*] [*Library of Congress*] (LCLS)
MnHe .... Hector Public Library, Hector, MN [*Library symbol*] [*Library of Congress*] (LCLS)
MnHE .... Hinckley Elementary School, Hinckley, MN [*Library symbol*] [*Library of Congress*] (LCLS)
MnHel .... Heron Lake Public Library, Heron Lake, MN [*Library symbol*] [*Library of Congress*] (LCLS)
MnHelES ...... Heron Lake Elementary School, Heron Lake, MN [*Library symbol*] [*Library of Congress*] (LCLS)
MnHendH .... Hendricks Community Hospital, Hendricks, MN [*Library symbol*] [*Library of Congress*] (LCLS)
MnHendPS .. Hendircks Public School, Hendricks, MN [*Library symbol*] [*Library of Congress*] (LCLS)
MnHenE .... West Elementary School, Hendrum, MN [*Library symbol*] [*Library of Congress*] (LCLS)
MnHennS ..... Henning Public School, Henning, MN [*Library symbol*] [*Library of Congress*] (LCLS)
MnHePS .... Hector Public School, Hector, MN [*Library symbol*] [*Library of Congress*] (LCLS)
MnHH .... Hinckley High School, Hinckley, MN [*Library symbol*] [*Library of Congress*] (LCLS)
MnHi .... Minnesota Historical Society, St. Paul, MN [*Library symbol*] [*Library of Congress*] (LCLS)
MnHi-Ar .... minnesota Historical Society, Division of Archives and Manuscripts, St. Paul, MN [*Library symbol*] [*Library of Congress*] (LCLS)
MnHib .... Hibbing Public Library, Hibbing, MN [*Library symbol*] [*Library of Congress*] (LCLS)
MnHibC .... Hibbing Community College, Hibbing, MN [*Library symbol*] [*Library of Congress*] (LCLS)
MnHibM .... Central Mesabi Medical Center, Hibbing, MN [*Library symbol*] [*Library of Congress*] (LCLS)
MnHilCS ...... Hills Christian School, Hills, MN [*Library symbol*] [*Library of Congress*] (LCLS)
MnHilES ...... Hills-Beaver Creek Elementary School, Hills, MN [*Library symbol*] [*Library of Congress*] (LCLS)
MnHilHS ...... Hills-Beaver Creek High School, Hills, MN [*Library symbol*] [*Library of Congress*] (LCLS)
MnHitE .... Ulen-Hitterdal Elementary School, Hitterdal, MN [*Library symbol*] [*Library of Congress*] (LCLS)
MnHl .... Howard Lake Public Library, Howard Lake, MN [*Library symbol*] [*Library of Congress*] (LCLS)

MNHLA .... Musicians National Hot Line Association (EA)

MnHldSDS ... Seventh Day Adventist School, Holland, MN [*Library symbol*] [*Library of Congress*] (LCLS)

MnHlE .... Howard Lake-Waverly Elementary School, Howard Lake, MN [*Library symbol*] [*Library of Congress*] (LCLS)

MnHlH .... Howard Lake-Waverly High School, Howard Lake, MN [*Library symbol*] [*Library of Congress*] (LCLS)

MnHlS .... St. James Lutheran School, Howard Lake, MN [*Library symbol*] [*Library of Congress*] (LCLS)

MnHoE .... Holdingford Elementary School, Holdingford, MN [*Library symbol*] [*Library of Congress*] (LCLS)

MnHofS .... Hoffman Public School, Hoffman, MN [*Library symbol*] [*Library of Congress*] (LCLS)

MnHoH .... Holdingford Jr./Sr. High School, Holdingford, MN [*Library symbol*] [*Library of Congress*] (LCLS)

MnHol .... Hoyt Lakes Public Library, Hoyt Lakes, MN [*Library symbol*] [*Library of Congress*] (LCLS)

M-NHSS ...... Modified New Haven Schizophrenic Scale

MnHu .... Hutchinson Public Library, Hutchinson, MN [*Library symbol*] [*Library of Congress*] (LCLS)

MnHuHMS ... Hutchinson Middle School, Hutchinson, MN [*Library symbol*] [*Library of Congress*] (LCLS)

MnHumS ...... Humbolt School, Humbolt, MN [*Library symbol*] [*Library of Congress*] (LCLS)

MnHuPES .... Park Elementary School, Hutchinson, MN [*Library symbol*] [*Library of Congress*] (LCLS)

MnHuSH ...... Hutchinson Senior High School, Hutchinson, MN [*Library symbol*] [*Library of Congress*] (LCLS)

MnHuStA ..... St. Anastasis School, Hutchinson, MN [*Library symbol*] [*Library of Congress*] (LCLS)

Mn-Hw .... Minnesota State Department of Transportation, St. Paul, MN [*Library symbol*] [*Library of Congress*] (LCLS)

MNI .... Mach Number Indicated (MCD)

MNI .... Madras Native Infantry [*British*]

MNI .... Maina Air Ltd. [*Nigeria*] [*FAA designator*] (FAAC)

MNI .... Malaysian National Insurance (SAUO)

MNI .... Manado [*Celebes*] [*Seismograph station code, US Geological Survey*] (SEIS)

MNI .... Manning, SC [*Location identifier*] [*FAA*] (FAAL)

MNI .... Many [*Amanteur radio shorthand*] (WDAA)

MNI .... Masoneilan International (SAUO)

MNI .... McClatchy Newspapers, Inc. [*NYSE symbol*] (SPSG)

MNI .... Media Networks, Inc.

MNI .... Member of the Nautical Institute [*British*]

MNI .... Meridian Technologies, Inc. [*Toronto Stock Exchange symbol*]

MnI .... Mille lacs Lake Community Library, Isle, MN [*Library symbol*] [*Library of Congress*] (LCLS)

MNI .... Minimum Number of Individuals [*Statistics*]

MNI .... Ministry of National Insurance [*British*]

MNI .... Montserrat [*West Indies*] [*Airport symbol*] (OAG)

MNI .... Movimiento Nacionalista de Izquierda [*Bolivia*] (PPW)

MNI .... Winona State University, Winona, MN [*OCLC symbol*] (OCLC)

MNIA .... Member of the National Institute of Accountants [*Australia*]

MNIA .... Multinational Nuclear Incident Agreement (SAUO)

MNIC .... Mnemonic Instruction Code (VLIE)

Mnlf .... International Falls Public Library, International Falls, MN [*Library symbol*] [*Library of Congress*] (LCLS)

MnlfBC .... Boise Cascade Corp., Research Library, International Falls, MN [*Library symbol*] [*Library of Congress*] (LCLS)

MnlfE .... International Falls Elementary School, International Falls, MN [*Library symbol*] [*Library of Congress*] (LCLS)

MnlfH .... International Falls High School, International Falls, MN [*Library symbol*] [*Library of Congress*] (LCLS)

MnlfM .... A.B. Middle School, International Falls, MN [*Library symbol*] [*Library of Congress*] (LCLS)

MnlfRC .... Rainy River Community College, International Falls, MN [*Library symbol*] [*Library of Congress*] (LCLS)

MnIgS .... Inver Hills State Junior College, Inver Grove Heights, MN [*Library symbol*] [*Library of Congress*] (LCLS)

MnIH .... Isle High School/Elementary School, Isle, MN [*Library symbol*] [*Library of Congress*] (LCLS)

MNIH .... Member of the National Institute of Hardware [*British*] (DBQ)

MNIMH .... Member of the National Institute of Medical Herbalists [*British*]

MNIND .... Mineral Industry Data Base (SAUO)

MnIrCS .... Cherry Public School, Iron, MN [*Library symbol*] [*Library of Congress*] (LCLS)

MNIS .... Manning & Napier Information Services

MnIsE .... Isanti Elementary School, Isanti, MN [*Library symbol*] [*Library of Congress*] (LCLS)

MnIsM .... Isnati Middle School, Isanti, MN [*Library symbol*] [*Library of Congress*] (LCLS)

MNIT .... Mobile Networks Integration Technology (SAUO)

Mnlv .... Ivanhoe Public Library, Ivanhoe, MN [*Library symbol*] [*Library of Congress*] (LCLS)

MnlvEHS ...... Lincoln Elementary-High School, Ivanhoe, MN [*Library symbol*] [*Library of Congress*] (LCLS)

MnJ .... Jackson County Library System, Jackson, MN [*Library symbol*] [*Library of Congress*] (LCLS)

MNJ .... Mananjary [*Madagascar*] [*Airport symbol*] (OAG)

MNJ .... Microelectronic Noise Jammer

MNJ .... Middletown & New Jersey Railway Co., Inc. [*AAR code*]

MNJ .... Movimiento Nacionalista Justicialista [*Justicialist Nationalist Movement - JNM*] [*Argentina*] (PPW)

MNJ .... Myoneural Junction [*Medicine*]

MNJ .... St. John's University, Collegeville, MN [*OCLC symbol*] (OCLC)

MnJaPS .... Jasper Public Schools, Jasper, MN [*Library symbol*] [*Library of Congress*] (LCLS)

MnJeJSH ...... Storden-Jeffers Junior Senior High School, Jeffers, MN [*Library symbol*] [*Library of Congress*] (LCLS)

MnJES .... Jackson Elementary School, Jackson, MN [*Library symbol*] [*Library of Congress*] (LCLS)

MnJoTS .... Trinity Lutheran School, Johnson, MN [*Library symbol*] [*Library of Congress*] (LCLS)

MnJPS .... Jackson Public Schools, Jackson, MN [*Library symbol*] [*Library of Congress*] (LCLS)

MNJTS .... Mouvement National des Jeunes Travailleurs du Senegal [*National Movement of Young Workers of Senegal*]

MNK .... Bethel College, Learning Resources Center, St. Paul, MN [*OCLC symbol*] (OCLC)

MnK .... Kimball Public Library, Kimball, MN [*Library symbol*] [*Library of Congress*] (LCLS)

MNK .... Maiana [*Kiribati*] [*Airport symbol*] (OAG)

MNK .... Mankoya [*Zambia*] [*Airport symbol*] (AD)

MNK .... Pleshenitzi [*Formerly, Minsk*] [*Former USSR*] [*Geomagnetic observatory code*]

MNK .... Rochester, MN [*Location identifier*] [*FAA*] (FAAL)

MNKA .... Minimum Number of Animals Known Alive [*Ecology*]

MnKaES .... Kandiyohi Elementary School, Kandiyohi, MN [*Library symbol*] [*Library of Congress*] (LCLS)

MnKarE .... Karlstad Elementary School, Karlstad, MN [*Library symbol*] [*Library of Congress*] (LCLS)

MnKarH .... Tri-County High School, Karlstad, MN [*Library symbol*] [*Library of Congress*] (LCLS)

MnKE .... Kimball Elementary School, Kimball, MN [*Library symbol*] [*Library of Congress*] (LCLS)

MnKee .... Keewatin Public Library, Keewatin, MN [*Library symbol*] [*Library of Congress*] (LCLS)

MnKeEs .... Kerkhoven-Murdoch-Sunberg Elementary School, Kerkhoven, MN [*Library symbol*] [*Library of Congress*] (LCLS)

MnKeHS .... Kerkhoven-Murdoch-Sunberg High School, Kerkhoven, MN [*Library symbol*] [*Library of Congress*] (LCLS)

MnKenS .... Kensington Public School, Kensington, MN [*Library symbol*] [*Library of Congress*] (LCLS)

MnKeP .... Kerkoven Public Library, Kerkoven, MN [*Library symbol*] [*Library of Congress*] (LCLS)

MnKH .... Kimball High School, Kimball, MN [*Library symbol*] [*Library of Congress*] (LCLS)

MnKHC .... Holy Cross School, Kimball, MN [*Library symbol*] [*Library of Congress*] (LCLS)

MnKin .... Kinney Public Library, City Hall, Kinney, MN [*Library symbol*] [*Library of Congress*] (LCLS)

MNL .... Mangla [*New Mirpur*] [*Pakistan*] [*Seismograph station code, US Geological Survey*] (SEIS)

MNL .... Manila [*Philippines*] [*Airport symbol*] (OAG)

MNL .... Manual (MSA)

MNL .... Marine Navigating Light

MNL .... Marine Navigation Levy (SAUO)

MNL .... Marked Neutrophilic Leukocytosis [*Medicine*] (DMAA)

MNL .... Maximum Number of Lamellae (DMAA)

MNI .... McClatchy Newspapers'A' [*NYSE symbol*] (TTSB)

MNL .... McConnell Peel Resources [*Vancouver Stock Exchange symbol*]

MNL .... Medical Nutrition Laboratory [*Army*]

MNL .... Mesenteric Node Lymphocyte

MNL .... Minerals Officer [*Foreign service*]

MNL .... Miniliner SRL [*Italy*] [*ICAO designator*] (FAAC)

MNL .... Minnesota National Laboratory

MNL .... Molecular Neurobiology Laboratory [*Salk Institute for Biological Studies*]

MNL .... Mononuclear Leukocyte [*Hematology*]

MNL .... Montgomery County-Norristown Public Library, Norristown, PA [*OCLC symbol*] (OCLC)

MNL .... Movement for National Liberation [*Barbados*] [*Political party*] (PPW)

MNL .... Multinomial Logit [*Statistics*]

MNL .... National Liberation Movement [*Guatemala*] [*Political party*] (PD)

MNL .... Valdez, AK [*Location identifier*] [*FAA*] (FAAL)

MNLA .... Malayan National Liberation Army (SAUO)

MNLA .... Mon National Liberation Army [*Myanmar*] [*Political party*] (EY)

MnLaiL .... Lake Itasca Forestry and Biological Station, Lake Itasca, MN [*Library symbol*] [*Library of Congress*] (LCLS)

MnLam .... Lamberton Public Library, Lamberton, MN [*Library symbol*] [*Library of Congress*] (LCLS)

MnLamS .... Lamberton School, Lamberton, MN [*Library symbol*] [*Library of Congress*] (LCLS)

MnLanS .... Lancaster Public School, Lancaster, MN [*Library symbol*] [*Library of Congress*] (LCLS)

MnLapS .... Laporte Public School, Laporte, MN [*Library symbol*] [*Library of Congress*] (LCLS)

MnLb .... Lake Benton Public Library, Lake Benton, MN [*Library symbol*] [*Library of Congress*] (LCLS)

MnLbBa .... Buffalo Ridge Baptist Academy, Lake Benton, MN [*Library symbol*] [*Library of Congress*] (LCLS)

MnLbPS .... Lake Benton Public Schools, Lake Benton, MN [*Library symbol*] [*Library of Congress*] (LCLS)

MNLCA .... Methylnorlaudanosolinecarboxylic Acid [*Biochemistry*]

MNLD .... Mainland (FAAC)

Mn-Leg .... Minnesota State Legislative Library, St. Paul, MN [*Library symbol*] [*Library of Congress*] (LCLS)

MnLeoCS ..... Leota Christian School, Leota, MN [*Library symbol*] [*Library of Congress*] (LCLS)

MnLepPS..... Lester Prairie Public School, Lester Prairie, MN [*Library symbol*] [*Library of Congress*] (LCLS)

MnLeW........ Washington County Library, Lake Elmo, MN [*Library symbol*] [*Library of Congress*] (LCLS)

MnLf.......... Carnegie City Library, Little Falls, MN [*Library symbol*] [*Library of Congress*] (LCLS)

MNLF......... Malayan National Liberation Front [*Singapore*] [*Political party*] (PD)

MNLF......... Moro National Liberation Front [*Philippines*] [*Political party*] (PD)

MnLfCL....... Charles Lindbergh Elementary School, Little Falls, MN [*Library symbol*] [*Library of Congress*] (LCLS)

MnLfH......... Little Falls Community High School, Little Falls, MN [*Library symbol*] [*Library of Congress*] (LCLS)

MnLfLE....... Lincoln Elementary School, Little Falls, MN [*Library symbol*] [*Library of Congress*] (LCLS)

MnLfM........ Little Falls Community Middle School, Little Falls, MN [*Library symbol*] [*Library of Congress*] (LCLS)

MnLfMS...... Mid-State Educational Cooperative, Little Falls, MN [*Library symbol*] [*Library of Congress*] (LCLS)

MnLfN........ North Star Christian Academy, Little Falls, MN [*Library symbol*] [*Library of Congress*] (LCLS)

MnLfO........ Our Lady of Lourdes School, Little Falls, MN [*Library symbol*] [*Library of Congress*] (LCLS)

MnLfoE....... Littlefork Elementary School, Littlefork, MN [*Library symbol*] [*Library of Congress*] (LCLS)

MnLfoH....... Littlefork High School, Littlefork, MN [*Library symbol*] [*Library of Congress*] (LCLS)

MnLfS........ St. Francis Convent, Little Falls, MN [*Library symbol*] [*Library of Congress*] (LCLS)

MnLfSG....... St. Gabriel's Hospital, Little Falls, MN [*Library symbol*] [*Library of Congress*] (LCLS)

MnLfSM...... St. Mary's School, Little Falls, MN [*Library symbol*] [*Library of Congress*] (LCLS)

MnLfW........ Weyerhauser Memorial Museum, Little Falls, MN [*Library symbol*] [*Library of Congress*] (LCLS)

MnLi........... Lindstrom Public Library, Lindstrom, MN [*Library symbol*] [*Library of Congress*] (LCLS)

MnLiJ .... Chisago Lakes Area Junior High School, Lindstrom, MN [*Library symbol*] [*Library of Congress*] (LCLS)

MnLiS .... Chisago Lakes Senior High School, Lindstrom, MN [*Library symbol*] [*Library of Congress*] (LCLS)

MnLit .... Litchfield Public Library, Litchfield, MN [*Library symbol*] [*Library of Congress*] (LCLS)

MnLitSH ...... Litchfield Senior High School, Litchfield, MN [*Library symbol*] [*Library of Congress*] (LCLS)

MnLitSP....... St. Philip's School, Litchfield, MN [*Library symbol*] [*Library of Congress*] (LCLS)

MnLitWES.... Wagner Elementary School, Litchfield, MN [*Library symbol*] [*Library of Congress*] (LCLS)

MnLkpE........ Lake Park Elementary School, Lake Park, MN [*Library symbol*] [*Library of Congress*] (LCLS)

MnLkpH .... Lake Park High School, Lake Park, MN [*Library symbol*] [*Library of Congress*] (LCLS)

MnLl............ Lake Lillian Public Library, Lake Lillian, MN [*Library symbol*] [*Library of Congress*] (LCLS)

MNLL......... Malaysian National Liberation League (NADA)

MNLN .... Leon/Fanor Urroz [*Nicaragua*] [*ICAO location identifier*] (ICLI)

MNLO .... Merchant Navy Liaison Officer (SAUO)

MnLon .... Margaret Welch Memorial Library, Longville, MN [*Library symbol*] [*Library of Congress*] (LCLS)

MnLp .... Long Prairie Public Library, Long Prairie, MN [*Library symbol*] [*Library of Congress*] (LCLS)

MnLpCHi...... Christie Home Historical Society, Long Prairie, MN [*Library symbol*] [*Library of Congress*] (LCLS)

MnLpE .... Long Prairie Elementary School, Long Prairie, MN [*Library symbol*] [*Library of Congress*] (LCLS)

MnLpH .... Long Prairie High School, Long Prairie, MN [*Library symbol*] [*Library of Congress*] (LCLS)

MnLpHi........ Todd County Historical Society, Long Prairie, MN [*Library symbol*] [*Library of Congress*] (LCLS)

MnLpM .... Meadowview School, Long Prairie, MN [*Library symbol*] [*Library of Congress*] (LCLS)

MnLpS .... St. Mary of Mt. Carmel, Long Prairie, MN [*Library symbol*] [*Library of Congress*] (LCLS)

MnLpT .... Trinity Lutheran School, Long Prairie, MN [*Library symbol*] [*Library of Congress*] (LCLS)

MNLS.......... Marine Navigating Light System

MNLS.......... Modified New Least Square (PDAA)

MnLS.......... St. John Nepomuk School, Lastrup, MN [*Library symbol*] [*Library of Congress*] (LCLS)

MnLsG .... Green Giant Corp., Le Sueur, MN [*Library symbol*] [*Library of Congress*] (LCLS)

MnLucOLS ... Our Lady of Victory School, Lucan, MN [*Library symbol*] [*Library of Congress*] (LCLS)

MNLY.......... Mainly (FAAC)

MnLyPS .... Lynd Public Library, Lynd, MN [*Library symbol*] [*Library of Congress*] (LCLS)

MNM.......... Mankato State University, Mankato, MN [*OCLC symbol*] (OCLC)

MNM.......... Master of Nonprofit Management (PGP)

MNM.......... Menominee [*Michigan*] [*Airport symbol*] (OAG)

MNM.......... Metal Nonmetal [*Materials science*]

MNM.......... Military Necessity Modification

mnm........... Minimum (AD)

MNM.......... Minimum

MNM.......... Minneapolis [*Minnesota*] [*Seismograph station code, US Geological Survey*] (SEIS)

MnM........... Minneapolis Public Library and Information Center, Minneapolis, MN [*Library symbol*] [*Library of Congress*] (LCLS)

mnm........... Mnemonic (AD)

MNM.......... Motile with Normal Morphology [*Medicine*] (MELL)

MNM.......... Museum of New Mexico [*Research center*] (RCD)

MnMA......... Augsburg College and Seminary, Minneapolis, MN [*Library symbol*] [*Library of Congress*] (LCLS)

MnMAb........ Abbott-Northwestern Hospitals, Inc., Minneapolis, MN [*Library symbol*] [*Library of Congress*] (LCLS)

MnMAC....... Anoka County Library, Minneapolis, MN [*Library symbol*] [*Library of Congress*] (LCLS)

MnMaE........ Mahnomen Elementary School, Mahnomen, MN [*Library symbol*] [*Library of Congress*] (LCLS)

MnMah .... Mahnomen High School, Mahnomen, MN [*Library symbol*] [*Library of Congress*] (LCLS)

MnMAM....... American Medical Systems, Inc., Minneapolis, MN [*Library symbol*] [*Library of Congress*] (LCLS)

MnManBC.... Bethany Lutheran College, Mankato, MN [*Library symbol*] [*Library of Congress*] (LCLS)

MnManBS.... Bethany Lutheran Theological Seminary, Mankato, MN [*Library symbol*] [*Library of Congress*] (LCLS)

MnManM...... Minnesota Valley Regional Library, Mankato, MN [*Library symbol*] [*Library of Congress*] (LCLS)

MnManS...... Mankato State College [*Later, Mankato State University*], Mankato, MN [*Library symbol*] [*Library of Congress*] (LCLS)

MnManTD.... Traverse des Sioux Library System, Mankato, MN [*Library symbol*] [*Library of Congress*] (LCLS)

MNMANY..... Men's Neckwear Manufacturers Association of New York [*Defunct*] (EA)

MnMAR....... American Rehabilitation Foundation Minneapolis, MN [*Library symbol*] [*Library of Congress*] (LCLS)

MnMar......... Marshall-Lyon County Library, Marshall, MN [*Library symbol*] [*Library of Congress*] (LCLS)

MnMarb........ Marble Public Library, Marble, MN [*Library symbol*] [*Library of Congress*] (LCLS)

MnMarC....... Marshall-Lyon County Library, Marshall, MN [*Library symbol*] [*Library of Congress*] (LCLS)

MnMarH .... Weiner Memorial Hospital, Marshall, MN [*Library symbol*] [*Library of Congress*] (LCLS)

MnMarLS..... Samuel Lutheran School, Marshall, MN [*Library symbol*] [*Library of Congress*] (LCLS)

MnMarPE..... Parkside Elementary School, Marshall, MN [*Library symbol*] [*Library of Congress*] (LCLS)

MnMarS....... Southwest Minnesota State College, Marshall, MN [*Library symbol*] [*Library of Congress*] (LCLS)

MnMarWES... West Side Elementary School, Marshall, MN [*Library symbol*] [*Library of Congress*] (LCLS)

MnMay .... Maynard Public Library, Maynard, MN [*Library symbol*] [*Library of Congress*] (LCLS)

MnMayPS .... Maynard Public Schools, Maynard, MN [*Library symbol*] [*Library of Congress*] (LCLS)

MnMBL....... Bakken Library of Electricity in Life, Minneapolis, MN [*Library symbol*] [*Library of Congress*] (LCLS)

MNMC........ Medical Network for Missing Children (EA)

MnMc .... Monticello Public Library, Monticello, MN [*Library symbol*] [*Library of Congress*] (LCLS)

MnMCA....... Minneapolis College of Art and Design, Minneapolis, MN [*Library symbol*] [*Library of Congress*] (LCLS)

MnMCC....... Minneapolis Community College, Minneapolis, MN [*Library symbol*] [*Library of Congress*] (LCLS)

MnMcgE....... McGrath Elementary School, McGrath, MN [*Library symbol*] [*Library of Congress*] (LCLS)

MnMcgr........ McGregor Public Library, McGregor, MN [*Library symbol*] [*Library of Congress*] (LCLS)

MnMcgrS...... McGregor School, McGregor, MN [*Library symbol*] [*Library of Congress*] (LCLS)

MnMcgrSL... Sandy Lake Visitor Center, McGregor, MN [*Library symbol*] [*Library of Congress*] (LCLS)

MnMcH .... Monticello-Big Lake Community Hospital Library, Monticello, MN [*Library symbol*] [*Library of Congress*] (LCLS)

MnMci .... McInotosh Public Library, McIntosh, MN [*Library symbol*] [*Library of Congress*] (LCLS)

MnMciE .... McIntosh Elementary School, McIntosh, MN [*Library symbol*] [*Library of Congress*] (LCLS)

MnMciH .... McIntosh-Winger High School, McIntosh, MN [*Library symbol*] [*Library of Congress*] (LCLS)

MnMcJ......... Monticello Junior High School, Monticello, MN [*Library symbol*] [*Library of Congress*] (LCLS)

MnMck........ McKinley Public Library, McKinley, MN [*Library symbol*] [*Library of Congress*] (LCLS)

MnMcPE ...... Pinewood East Elementary School, Monticello, MN [*Library symbol*] [*Library of Congress*] (LCLS)

MnMcPW .... Pinewood West Elementary School, Monticello, MN [*Library symbol*] [*Library of Congress*] (LCLS)

MnMcR........ Rivercrest Christian School, Monticello, MN [*Library symbol*] [*Library of Congress*] (LCLS)

MnMcS........ Monticello Senior High School, Monticello, MN [*Library symbol*] [*Library of Congress*] (LCLS)

MnMcSR...... St. Henry Catholic Church, School of Religion Library, Monticello, MN [*Library symbol*] [*Library of Congress*] (LCLS)

MNMD........ MiniMed, Inc. [*NASDAQ symbol*] (SAG)

MnMe .... Melrose Public Library, Melrose, MN [*Library symbol*] [*Library of Congress*] (LCLS)

MnMeaS...... Toivola-Meadowlands School, Meadowlands, MN [*Library symbol*] [*Library of Congress*] (LCLS)

MnMeE....... Melrose, New Munich, Spring Hill Elementary School, Melrose, MN [*Library symbol*] [*Library of Congress*] (LCLS)

MnMeH....... Melrose High School, Melrose, MN [*Library symbol*] [*Library of Congress*] (LCLS)

MnMeJ....... Melrose Junior High School, Melrose, MN [*Library symbol*] [*Library of Congress*] (LCLS)

MnMenE....... Menahga Elementary School, Menagha, MN [*Library symbol*] [*Library of Congress*] (LCLS)

MnMenH....... Menagha High School, Menagha, MN [*Library symbol*] [*Library of Congress*] (LCLS)

MnMeS....... St. John-St. Andrew School, Melrose, MN [*Library symbol*] [*Library of Congress*] (LCLS)

MnMeSM....... St. Mary's Elementary School, Melrose, MN [*Library symbol*] [*Library of Congress*] (LCLS)

MnMF......... Fairview Hospital, Minneapolis, MN [*Library symbol*] [*Library of Congress*] (LCLS)

MnMFL....... Association of Free Lutheran Congregation and Seminary Headquarters, Minneapolis, MN [*Library symbol*] [*Library of Congress*] (LCLS)

MnMFR....... Federation Reserve Bank of Minneapolis, Minneapolis, MN [*Library symbol*] [*Library of Congress*] (LCLS)

MnMG......... Golden Valley Lutheran College, Minneapolis, MN [*Library symbol*] [*Library of Congress*] (LCLS)

MNMG .... Managua/Augusto Cesar Sandino [*Nicaragua*] [*ICAO location identifier*] (ICLI)

MnMGM....... General Mills, Inc., Minneapolis, MN [*Library symbol*] [*Library of Congress*] (LCLS)

MnMGS....... Church of Jesus Christ of Latter-Day Saints, Genealogical Society Library, Minneapolis Branch, Minneapolis, MN [*Library symbol*] [*Library of Congress*] (LCLS)

MnMH......... Hennepin County Medical Society, Minneapolis, MN [*Library symbol*] [*Library of Congress*] (LCLS)

MnMHCL....... Hennepin County Library, Minneapolis, MN [*Library symbol*] [*Library of Congress*] (LCLS)

MnMHen....... Henkel Corp., Minneapolis, MN [*Library symbol*] [*Library of Congress*] (LCLS)

MnMHH....... Hennepin County General Hospital, Minneapolis, MN [*Library symbol*] [*Library of Congress*] (LCLS)

MnMHLL....... Hennepin County Law Library, Minneapolis, MN [*Library symbol*] [*Library of Congress*] (LCLS)

MnMI.......... Interlutheran Theological Seminary and Bible School, Minneapolis, MN [*Library symbol*] [*Library of Congress*] (LCLS)

MNMIA........ Men's Neckwear Manufacturers Institute of America (EA)

MNMIC........ Modernized National Military Intelligence Center

MNMIC........ Modernized NMIC [*National Military Intelligence Center*] (MCD)

MnMiE......... Milaca Elementary School, Milaca, MN [*Library symbol*] [*Library of Congress*] (LCLS)

MnMiH......... Milaca High School, Milaca, MN [*Library symbol*] [*Library of Congress*] (LCLS)

MnMiIE....... Miltona Elementary School, Miltona, MN [*Library symbol*] [*Library of Congress*] (LCLS)

MnMiM........ Milaca Middle School, Milaca, MN [*Library symbol*] [*Library of Congress*] (LCLS)

MnMIn........ Interstudy, Minneapolis, MN [*Library symbol*] [*Library of Congress*] (LCLS)

MnMinPS..... Minneota Public Schools, Minneota, MN [*Library symbol*] [*Library of Congress*] (LCLS)

MnMinSE..... St. Edward School, Minneota, MN [*Library symbol*] [*Library of Congress*] (LCLS)

MnMirS....... Middle River School, Middle River, MN [*Library symbol*] [*Library of Congress*] (LCLS)

MnMK......... Kenny Rehabilitation Institute, Minneapolis, MN [*Library symbol*] [*Library of Congress*] (LCLS)

MNMKT........ Money Market (NITA)

MnMLD....... Lutheran Deaconess Hospital, Minneapolis, MN [*Library symbol*] [*Library of Congress*] (LCLS)

MNMIE........ Maple Lake Elementary School, Maple Lake, MN [*Library symbol*] [*Library of Congress*] (LCLS)

MnMIH......... Maple Lake High, Maple Lake, MN [*Library symbol*] [*Library of Congress*] (LCLS)

MnMIn........ Milan Public Library, Milan, MN [*Library symbol*] [*Library of Congress*] (LCLS)

MnMInES..... Milan Elementary School, Milan, MN [*Library symbol*] [*Library of Congress*] (LCLS)

MnMIS........ St. Timothy School, Maple Lake, MN [*Library symbol*] [*Library of Congress*] (LCLS)

MnMlyPS..... Milroy Public Schools, Milan, MN [*Library symbol*] [*Library of Congress*] (LCLS)

MnMMC....... Metropolitan State Community College, Minneapolis, MN [*Library symbol*] [*Library of Congress*] (LCLS)

MnMMe....... Medtronic, Inc., Minneapolis, MN [*Library symbol*] [*Library of Congress*] (LCLS)

MnMMeH..... Methodist Hospital, Minneapolis, MN [*Library symbol*] [*Library of Congress*] (LCLS)

MnMMet..... Metropolitan Medical Center, Medical Library, Minneapolis, MN [*Library symbol*] [*Library of Congress*] (LCLS)

MnMMet-H... Metropolitan Medical Center, Hospital Services Library, Minneapolis, MN [*Library symbol*] [*Library of Congress*] (LCLS)

MnMMetS.... Metropolitan State Junior College, Minneapolis, MN [*Library symbol*] [*Library of Congress*] (LCLS)

MnMMH....... Minneapolis-Honeywell Regulator Co., Minneapolis, MN [*Library symbol*] [*Library of Congress*] (LCLS)

MnMMSC...... MTS Systems Corporation, Minneapolis, MN [*Library symbol*] [*Library of Congress*] (LCLS)

MnMMSP..... Minnesota School of Professional Psychology, Minneapolis, MN [*Library symbol*] [*Library of Congress*] (LCLS)

MnMMtS...... Mount Sinai Hospital, Minneapolis, MN [*Library symbol*] [*Library of Congress*] (LCLS)

MnMN......... Normandale Community College, Minneapolis, MN [*Library symbol*] [*Library of Congress*] (LCLS)

MnMNC....... North Central Bible College, Minneapolis, MN [*Library symbol*] [*Library of Congress*] (LCLS)

MnMnCMS... Cedar Mountain School, Morgan, MN [*Library symbol*] [*Library of Congress*] (LCLS)

MnMNH....... North Memorial Hospital, Minneapolis, MN [*Library symbol*] [*Library of Congress*] (LCLS)

MnMNHe..... North Hennepin Community College, Minneapolis, MN [*Library symbol*] [*Library of Congress*] (LCLS)

MnMnI........ Mountain Lake Public Library, Mountain Lake, MN [*Library symbol*] [*Library of Congress*] (LCLS)

MnMnICS.... Mountain Lake Christian School, Mountain Lake, MN [*Library symbol*] [*Library of Congress*] (LCLS)

MnMnIHS.... Mountain Lake Public High School, Mountain Lake, MN [*Library symbol*] [*Library of Congress*] (LCLS)

MnMnIMB.... Mt. Bethany Christian School, Mountain Lake, MN [*Library symbol*] [*Library of Congress*] (LCLS)

MnMnP....... Morgan Pubic Library, Morgan, MN [*Library symbol*] [*Library of Congress*] (LCLS)

MnMo......... Morris Public Library, Morris, MN [*Library symbol*] [*Library of Congress*] (LCLS)

MnMoE........ Morris Elementary School, Morris, MN [*Library symbol*] [*Library of Congress*] (LCLS)

MnMoh....... Moorhead Public Library, Moorhead, MN [*Library symbol*] [*Library of Congress*] (LCLS)

MnMohC..... Concordia College, Moorhead, MN [*Library symbol*] [*Library of Congress*] (LCLS)

MnMohEE.... Edison Elementary School, Moorhead, MN [*Library symbol*] [*Library of Congress*] (LCLS)

MnMohHi.... Clay County Historical Society, Library and Archives, Moorhead, MN [*Library symbol*] [*Library of Congress*] (LCLS)

MnMohJ...... Moorhead Junior High School, Moorhead, MN [*Library symbol*] [*Library of Congress*] (LCLS)

MnMohL...... Lake Agassiz Regional Library, Moorhead, MN [*Library symbol*] [*Library of Congress*] (LCLS)

MnMohPS... Moorhead Public Schools System, Moorhead, MN [*Library symbol*] [*Library of Congress*] (LCLS)

MnMohS..... Moorhead State College, Moorhead, MN [*Library symbol*] [*Library of Congress*] (LCLS)

MnMohSA... St. Ansgar Hospital, Health Science Library, Moorhead, MN [*Library symbol*] [*Library of Congress*] (LCLS)

MnMohSH... Moorhead Senior High School, Moorhead, MN [*Library symbol*] [*Library of Congress*] (LCLS)

MnMohSJ... St. Joseph School, Moorhead, MN [*Library symbol*] [*Library of Congress*] (LCLS)

MnMohWE... Washington Elementary School, Moorhead, MN [*Library symbol*] [*Library of Congress*] (LCLS)

MnMoI........ Moose Lake Public Lake, Moose Lake, MN [*Library symbol*] [*Library of Congress*] (LCLS)

MnMoIS...... Moose Lake Public School, Moose Lake, MN [*Library symbol*] [*Library of Congress*] (LCLS)

MnMoM....... Morris Middle School, Morris, MN [*Library symbol*] [*Library of Congress*] (LCLS)

MnMoMHS... Morris High School, Morris, MN [*Library symbol*] [*Library of Congress*] (LCLS)

MnMotS....... Motley School, Motley, MN [*Library symbol*] [*Library of Congress*] (LCLS)

MnMoU........ University of Minnesota, Morris, MN [*Library symbol*] [*Library of Congress*] (LCLS)

MnMov .... Chippewa County Library System, Montevideo, MN [*Library symbol*] [*Library of Congress*] (LCLS)

MnMovCH... Chippewa County-Montevideo Hospital, Montevideo, MN [*Library symbol*] [*Library of Congress*] (LCLS)

MnMovMS... Montevideo Middle School, Montevideo, MN [*Library symbol*] [*Library of Congress*] (LCLS)

MnMovRE.... Ramsey Elementary School, Montevideo, MN [*Library symbol*] [*Library of Congress*] (LCLS)

MnMovSE.... Sanford Elementary School, Montevideo, MN [*Library symbol*] [*Library of Congress*] (LCLS)

MnMovSEC... Southwest-West Central Educational Cooperative Service Unit, Montevideo, MN [*Library symbol*] [*Library of Congress*] (LCLS)

MnMovSH... Montevideo Senior High School, Montevideo, MN [*Library symbol*] [*Library of Congress*] (LCLS)

MnMP......... Pillsbury Co., Minneapolis, MN [*Library symbol*] [*Library of Congress*] (LCLS)

MnMrFE....... Fairview Elementary Library, Mora, MN [*Library symbol*] [*Library of Congress*] (LCLS)

MnMrH .... Mora High School, Mora, MN [*Library symbol*] [*Library of Congress*] (LCLS)

MnMrHi....... Kanabec County Historical Society, Mora, MN [*Library symbol*] [*Library of Congress*] (LCLS)

MnMrMS..... Mora Fairview Central Middle School, Mora, MN [*Library symbol*] [*Library of Congress*] (LCLS)

MnMrR .... Rum River Vocational Center, Mora, MN [*Library symbol*] [*Library of Congress*] (LCLS)

MnMS......... Saint Louis Park Medical Center, Minneapolis, MN [*Library symbol*] [*Library of Congress*] (LCLS)

MnMSMC..... Saint Mary's Junior College, Minneapolis, MN [*Library symbol*] [*Library of Congress*] (LCLS)

MnMSMH ....   Saint Mary's Hospital, Minneapolis, MN [*Library symbol*] [*Library of Congress*] (LCLS)

MNMT.........   Monument

MnMtE ....   Montrose Elementary School, Montrose, MN [*Library symbol*] [*Library of Congress*] (LCLS)

MnMti ....   Mountain Iron Public Library, Mt. Iron, MN [*Library symbol*] [*Library of Congress*] (LCLS)

MnMtiE ....   Merritt Elementary School, Mt. Iron, MN [*Library symbol*] [*Library of Congress*] (LCLS)

MnMtiHS ......   Mt. Iron High School, Mt. Iron, MN [*Library symbol*] [*Library of Congress*] (LCLS)

Mnmtl ....   Monumental (DIAR)

MnMuKS ......   Kerkhover-Murdock-Sunberg School, Murdock, MN [*Library symbol*] [*Library of Congress*] (LCLS)

MnMULS .....   University of Minnesota Union List of Serials, Minneapolis, MN [*Library symbol*] [*Library of Congress*] (LCLS)

MnMVA ....   United States Veterans Administration Hospital, Minneapolis, MN [*Library symbol*] [*Library of Congress*] (LCLS)

MnMW ....   Walker Art Center, Minneapolis, MN [*Library symbol*] [*Library of Congress*] (LCLS)

MNN ....   Carleton College, Northfield, MN [*OCLC symbol*] (OCLC)

MNN ....   Madness Network News (EA)

MNN ....   Main Network Node [*Computer science*] (CIST)

MNN ....   Marion, OH [*Location identifier*] [*FAA*] (FAAL)

MNN ....   Median Nerve Neuropathy [*Medicine*] (MELL)

MNN ....   Minneapolis [*Minnesota*] [*Seismograph station code, US Geological Survey*] (SEIS)

Mn-N ....   Minnesota State Department of Natural Resources, St. Paul, MN [*Library symbol*] [*Library of Congress*] (LCLS)

MNN ....   Monenco Ltd. [*Toronto Stock Exchange symbol*]

MnNaSH ......   Nashwauk-Keewatin Senior High School, Nashwauk, MN [*Library symbol*] [*Library of Congress*] (LCLS)

MnNbU ....   United Theological Seminary of the Twin Cities, New Brighton, MN [*Library symbol*] [*Library of Congress*] (LCLS)

MnNC..........   Carleton College, Northfield, MN [*Library symbol*] [*Library of Congress*] (LCLS)

MnNeS.........   Nevis Public School, Nevis, MN [*Library symbol*] [*Library of Congress*] (LCLS)

MnNeuL ....   Doctor Martin Luther College, New Ulm, MN [*Library symbol*] [*Library of Congress*] (LCLS)

MNNG ....   Methylnitronitrosoguanidine [*Biochemistry*]

MnNHi ....   Norwegian-American Historical Association, Northfield, MN [*Library symbol*] [*Library of Congress*] (LCLS)

MnNisE ....   Nisswa Elementary School, Nisswa, MN [*Library symbol*] [*Library of Congress*] (LCLS)

MnNI..........   New London Public Library, New London, MN [*Library symbol*] [*Library of Congress*] (LCLS)

MnNIES.......   New London Elementary School, New London, MN [*Library symbol*] [*Library of Congress*] (LCLS)

MnNIJSH .....   New London-Spicer Junior Senior High School, New London, MN [*Library symbol*] [*Library of Congress*] (LCLS)

MnNIPES .....   Prairie Woods Elementary School, New London, MN [*Library symbol*] [*Library of Congress*] (LCLS)

MnNmT........   Mankato Area Vocational-Technical Institute, North Mankato, MN [*Library symbol*] [*Library of Congress*] (LCLS)

MnNob.........   North Branch Area Library, North Branch, MN [*Library symbol*] [*Library of Congress*] (LCLS)

MnNobH ......   North Branch High School, North Branch, MN [*Library symbol*] [*Library of Congress*] (LCLS)

MnNobM......   North Branch Middle School, North Branch, MN [*Library symbol*] [*Library of Congress*] (LCLS)

MnNoS.........   Northome School, Northome, MN [*Library symbol*] [*Library of Congress*] (LCLS)

MNNP ....   Malawi Nyika National Park (AD)

MNNR ....   Marine National Nature Reserve (SAUO)

MnNS..........   Saint Olaf College, Northfield, MN [*Library symbol*] [*Library of Congress*] (LCLS)

MnNS-K ....   Saint Olaf College, Kierkegaard Library, Northfield, MN [*Library symbol*] [*Library of Congress*] (LCLS)

MnNym........   New York Mills Public Library, New York Mills, MN [*Library symbol*] [*Library of Congress*] (LCLS)

MnNymH......   New York Mills High School, New York Mills, MN [*Library symbol*] [*Library of Congress*] (LCLS)

MNO ....   Maddona Resources Corp. [*Vancouver Stock Exchange symbol*]

mno ....   Manobo [*MARC language code*] [*Library of Congress*] (LCCP)

MNO ....   Manono [*Zaire*] [*Airport symbol*] (OAG)

MNO ....   Master of Nonprofit Organization (PGP)

MNO ....   Mauritanian Nationalist Organisation (BUAC)

MNO ....   Mobile Network Operators (SAUO)

MnO............   Owatonna Free Public Library, Owatonna, MN [*Library symbol*] [*Library of Congress*] (LCLS)

MNO ....   Refugio, TX [*Location identifier*] [*FAA*] (FAAL)

MNO ....   Saint Olaf College, Northfield, MN [*OCLC symbol*] (OCLC)

MNoadT.......   North Adams State College, North Adams, MA [*Library symbol*] [*Library of Congress*] (LCLS)

MNoanM......   Merrimack College, North Andover, MA [*Library symbol*] [*Library of Congress*] (LCLS)

MNoanMV.....   Merrimack Valley Textile Museum, North Andover, MA [*Library symbol*] [*Library of Congress*] (LCLS)

MNodS........   Southeastern Massachusetts University, North Dartmouth, MA [*Library symbol*] [*Library of Congress*] (LCLS)

MNoeS........   Stonehill College, North Easton, MA [*Library symbol*] [*Library of Congress*] (LCLS)

MnOgS........   Ogilvie Public School, Ogilvie, MN [*Library symbol*] [*Library of Congress*] (LCLS)

MnOkaHJH...   Huron Lake-Okabena-Lakefield Junior High School, Okabena, MN [*Library symbol*] [*Library of Congress*] (LCLS)

MnOkS.........   Oklee Public School, Oklee, MN [*Library symbol*] [*Library of Congress*] (LCLS)

MnOl..........   Olivia Public Library, Olivia, MN [*Library symbol*] [*Library of Congress*] (LCLS)

MnOlES.......   Olivia Elementary School, Olivia, MN [*Library symbol*] [*Library of Congress*] (LCLS)

MnOlStA ......   St. Aloysious School, Olivia, MN [*Library symbol*] [*Library of Congress*] (LCLS)

MNOMU ......   Mobile Nuclear Ordnance Maintenance Unit (MCD)

MnOnC........   Crosier Seminary Library, Onamia, MN [*Library symbol*] [*Library of Congress*] (LCLS)

MnOnE ....   Onamia Elementary School, Onamia, MN [*Library symbol*] [*Library of Congress*] (LCLS)

MnOnG ....   Galloway Boy's Ranch School, Onamia, MN [*Library symbol*] [*Library of Congress*] (LCLS)

MnOnH ....   Onamia High School, Onamia, MN [*Library symbol*] [*Library of Congress*] (LCLS)

MNOPF ....   Merchant Navy Officers' Pension Fund [*British*] (DS)

MNOR..........   Missile Not Operationally Ready (SAA)

MNORM.......   Missile Not Operationally Ready - Maintenance [*Air Force*]

MNORP........   Missile Not Operationally Ready - Parts [*Air Force*]

MnOrS ....   Orr Public School, Orr, MN [*Library symbol*] [*Library of Congress*] (LCLS)

MnOrv.........   Ortonville Public Library, Ortonville, MN [*Library symbol*] [*Library of Congress*] (LCLS)

MnOrvH ....   Ortonville Hospital, Ortonville, MN [*Library symbol*] [*Library of Congress*] (LCLS)

MnOrvPS .....   Ortonville Public School, Ortonville, MN [*Library symbol*] [*Library of Congress*] (LCLS)

mnos ....   Metallic Nitrogen-Oxide Semiconductor (AD)

MNOS ....   Metal Nitride Oxide Semiconductor (SAUO)

MNOS ....   Metal-Nitride-Oxide Silicon [*or Semiconductor*]

MNOSFET ....   Metal-Nitride-Oxide-Semiconductor Field-Effect Transistor

MnOsS........   Osakis School, Osakis, MN [*Library symbol*] [*Library of Congress*] (LCLS)

MNOS/SOS...   Metal-Nitride Oxide Semiconductor / Silicon-on-Sapphire

MNot...........   Cobb Memorial Library, North Truro,MA [*Library symbol*] [*Library of Congress*] (LCLS)

MNoW ....   Wheaton College, Norton, MA [*Library symbol*] [*Library of Congress*] (LCLS)

MNP............   Malay National Party [*Political party*] (AD)

MNP............   Marsabit National Park [*Kenya*] (AD)

MNP............   Maximum Negative Pressure [*Nuclear energy*] (NRCH)

MNP............   Median Nerve Palsy [*Medicine*] (MELL)

MNP............   Meru National Park [*Equatorial Kenya*] (AD)

MNP............   Meta-Nitrophenol [*Organic chemistry*]

MNP............   Microcom Networking Protocol [*Telecommunications*] (ACRL)

MNP............   Microcom Network Protocol (ADWA)

MNP............   Microcomputer Networking Protocol

MNP............   Microcone Networking Protocol

MNP............   Midnapore (1979) Resources, Inc. [*Vancouver Stock Exchange symbol*]

MNP............   Mikumi National Park [*Tanzania*] (AD)

Mn-P..........   Minnesota State Department of Planning, St. Paul, MN [*Library symbol*] [*Library of Congress*] (LCLS)

MNP............   Mononuclear Phagocyte (DMAA)

MNP............   Moravian National Party [*Czech Republic*] [*Political party*] (BUAC)

MNP............   More Nearly Perfect [*Microsoft Corp.*] [*Computer science*]

MNP............   Morton-Norwich Products, Inc. (SAUO)

MNP............   Mouvement Nationale Patriotique [*Haiti*] [*Political party*] (EY)

MNP............   Movimiento Nacionalista Popular [*Popular Nationalist Movement*] [*Chile*] [*Political party*] (PD)

MNP............   Movimiento Nacional y Popular [*Paraguay*] [*Political party*] (EY)

MNP............   Movimiento No Partidarizado [*Peru*] [*Political party*] (EY)

MNP............   Multinomial Probit [*Statistics*]

MNP............   Multiple Networking Protocol (SAUO)

MNP............   Municipal Partners Fund [*NYSE symbol*] (SPSG)

MNP............   Mushandike National Park [*Rhodesia*] (AD)

MNP............   Northern Mariana Islands [*ANSI three-letter standard code*] (CNC)

MnP............   Princeton Community Library, Princeton, MN [*Library symbol*] [*Library of Congress*] (LCLS)

MNP............   University of Minnesota, St. Paul, MN [*OCLC symbol*] (OCLC)

MNP-4.........   Microcon Network Protocol-4 [*Computer science*] (DDC)

MNP5..........   Microcom Networking Protocol, Class Five [*Computer science*]

MNP-5.........   Microcom Network Protocol-5 [*Computer science*] (DDC)

MNPA ....   Malaysian Newspaper Publishers Association (EAIO)

MNPA ....   Mono-normal-propylamine [*Organic chemistry*]

MnPapH.......   Parkers Prairie High School, Parkers Prairie, MN [*Library symbol*] [*Library of Congress*] (LCLS)

MnParFE......   Frank White Elementary School, Park Rapids, MN [*Library symbol*] [*Library of Congress*] (LCLS)

MnParH ....   Park Rapids Area High School, Park Rapids, MN [*Library symbol*] [*Library of Congress*] (LCLS)

MnParM.......   Park Rapids Middle School, Park Rapids, MN [*Library symbol*] [*Library of Congress*] (LCLS)

MnPc ....   Pine City Pubic Library, Pine City, MN [*Library symbol*] [*Library of Congress*] (LCLS)

MNPC ....   Puerto Cabezas [*Nicaragua*] [*ICAO location identifier*] (ICLI)

MnPcE ....   Pine City Elementary School, Pine City, MN [*Library symbol*] [*Library of Congress*] (LCLS)

MnPcH.........   Pine City High School, Pine City, MN [*Library symbol*] [*Library of Congress*] (LCLS)

MnPcS......... St. Mary's School, Pine City, MN [*Library symbol*] [*Library of Congress*]

MnPcT........ Pine Technical Institute Learning Resource Center, Pine City, MN [*Library symbol*] [*Library of Congress*] (LCLS)

MNPD......... Missile and Nuclear Programming Data (AABC)

MnPeC....... Pease Community Christian School, Pease, MN [*Library symbol*] [*Library of Congress*] (LCLS)

MnPeIE....... Pequot Lakes Elementary School, Pequot Lakes, MN [*Library symbol*] [*Library of Congress*] (LCLS)

MnPeIH....... Pequot Lakes High School, Pequot Lakes MN [*Library symbol*] [*Library of Congress*] (LCLS)

MnPerH....... Pelican Rapids High School, Pelican Rapids, MN [*Library symbol*] [*Library of Congress*] (LCLS)

MnPerVE..... Viking Elementary School, Pelican Rapids, MN [*Library symbol*] [*Library of Congress*] (LCLS)

MnPH......... Princeton High School, Princeton, MN [*Library symbol*] [*Library of Congress*] (LCLS)

MnPhE........ Perham Elementary School, Perham, MN [*Library symbol*] [*Library of Congress*] (LCLS)

MnPhP........ Perham Public Library, Perham, MN [*Library symbol*] [*Library of Congress*] (LCLS)

MNPI.......... Microcom, Inc. [*NASDAQ symbol*] (NQ)

MnPi........... Pierz Public Library, Pierz, MN [*Library symbol*] [*Library of Congress*] (LCLS)

MnPiH........ Healy High School, Pierz, MN [*Library symbol*] [*Library of Congress*] (LCLS)

MnPiHE....... Harding Elementary School, Pierz, MN [*Library symbol*] [*Library of Congress*] (LCLS)

MnPiIS........ Pillager Public School, Pillager, MN [*Library symbol*] [*Library of Congress*] (LCLS)

MnPiS......... St. Joseph's Elementary School, Pierz, MN [*Library symbol*] [*Library of Congress*] (LCLS)

MnPJ.......... Princeton Junior High School, Princeton, MN [*Library symbol*] [*Library of Congress*] (LCLS)

MNPL......... Machinists Non-Partisan Political League (EA)

MnPluS....... Pershing Public School, Plummer, MN [*Library symbol*] [*Library of Congress*] (LCLS)

MnPNE....... Princeton North Elementary School, Princeton, MN [*Library symbol*] [*Library of Congress*] (LCLS)

mnpo.......... Main Port (AD)

MnPO......... Median Preoptic Area (DB)

MNPO......... Median Preoptic Area [*Brain anatomy*]

MNPO......... Mobile Navy Post Office

MNPO......... Multi National Program Office (ACAE)

MNPP......... Midland Nuclear Power Plant (NRCH)

MnPpBES..... Dr. Brown Elementary School, Pipestone, MN [*Library symbol*] [*Library of Congress*] (LCLS)

MnPpHES.... Hill Elementary School, Pipestone, MN [*Library symbol*] [*Library of Congress*] (LCLS)

MnPpHS...... Pipestone Cental High School, Pipestone, MN [*Library symbol*] [*Library of Congress*] (LCLS)

MN-PPL...... Machinists Non-Partisan Political League (EA)

MnPpTC...... Southwest Technical College, Pipestone, MN [*Library symbol*] [*Library of Congress*] (LCLS)

MnPr.......... Kitchigami Regional Library, Pine River, MN [*Library symbol*] [*Library of Congress*] (LCLS)

MnPrbMCS... Central Minnesota Christian School, Prinsburg, MN [*Library symbol*] [*Library of Congress*] (LCLS)

MnPrbPS..... Prinsburg Public Schools, Prinsburg, MN [*Library symbol*] [*Library of Congress*] (LCLS)

MnPrE......... Pine River Elementary School, Pine River, MN [*Library symbol*] [*Library of Congress*] (LCLS)

MnPrH........ Pine River High School, Pine River, MN [*Library symbol*] [*Library of Congress*] (LCLS)

MnProJ........ Jedlicka Junior High School, Proctor, MN [*Library symbol*] [*Library of Congress*] (LCLS)

MnProSH..... Proctor Senior High School, Proctor, MN [*Library symbol*] [*Library of Congress*] (LCLS)

MnPrP........ Pine River Public Library, Pine River, MN [*Library symbol*] [*Library of Congress*] (LCLS)

MNPS......... Millstone Nuclear Power Station (NRCH)

MNPS......... Minimum Navigation Performance Specification [*Aviation*] (FAAC)

MNPS......... Minimum Navigation Performance Specification Airspace (PIPO)

MNPS......... Movimiento Nazionale Pan-Somalo [*Pan-Somali National Movement*] [*Political party*]

MNPSA....... Minimum Navigation Performance Specification Airspace [*Aviation*] (FAAC)

MnPSE........ Princeton South Elementary School, Princeton, MN [*Library symbol*] [*Library of Congress*] (LCLS)

MNPT......... Meta-Nitro-para-toluidine [*Organic chemistry*]

MnPv.......... Paynesville Public Library, Paynesville, MN [*Library symbol*] [*Library of Congress*] (LCLS)

MnPvEM...... Paynesville Elementary & Middle School, Paynesville, MN [*Library symbol*] [*Library of Congress*] (LCLS)

MnPvH........ Paynesville Hospital, Medical Staff Library, Paynesville, MN [*Library symbol*] [*Library of Congress*] (LCLS)

MnPvHi....... Paynesville Historical Society, Paynesville, MN [*Library symbol*] [*Library of Congress*] (LCLS)

MnPvHS...... Paynesville, High School, Paynesville, MN [*Library symbol*] [*Library of Congress*] (LCLS)

MNPWR...... Manpower (AFM)

MNPZ......... Mononitrosopiperazine [*Biochemistry*]

mnpz.......... Monopolize (AD)

mnpzd........ Monopolized (AD)

mnpzg......... Monopolizing (AD)

mnpzn......... Monopolization (AD)

MNQ.......... Manicouagan [*Quebec*] [*Seismograph station code, US Geological Survey*] (SEIS)

MNQ......... Manifest Needs Questionnaire (EDAC)

MNQ......... Methylnaphthoquinone [*Organic chemistry*]

MNQ......... Monto [*Australia*] [*Airport symbol*] (OAG)

MNQ......... Montoro Resources [*Vancouver Stock Exchange symbol*]

MNQ......... University of Minnesota, Waseca, Waseca, MN [*OCLC symbol*] (OCLC)

MNR......... James J. Hill Reference Library, St. Paul, MN [*OCLC symbol*] (OCLC)

MNR.......... Maintenance/Nonconformance Record (MCD)

MNR......... Manor (MCD)

MNR......... Manor Care, Inc. [*NYSE symbol*] (SPSG)

MNR......... Marrow Neutrophil Reserve [*Medicine*]

MNR......... Massive Nuclear Retaliation (AAG)

mnr.......... Massive Nuclear Retaliation (AD)

MNR......... Maximum Number of Records (MHDB)

MNR......... McMaster Nuclear Reactor [*Canada*]

MNR......... McNellen Resources, Inc. [*Vancouver Stock Exchange symbol*] [*Toronto Stock Exchange symbol*]

MNR......... Mean Neap [*Tide*] Rise [*Tides and currents*]

mnr.......... Mean Neap Rise (AD)

Mnr.......... Mijnherr [*Mr.*] [*Dutch*] (AD)

MNR......... Mines Road [*California*] [*Seismograph station code, US Geological Survey*] (SEIS)

MNR......... Minimum Noise Routes

MNR......... Ministry of Natural Resources (SAUO)

MNR......... Monair SA [*Switzerland*] [*ICAO designator*] (FAAC)

MNR......... Mongu [*Zambia*] [*Airport symbol*] (OAG)

MNR......... Morphine-Naive Rats

MNr......... Morrill Memorial Library, Norwood, MA [*Library symbol*] [*Library of Congress*] (LCLS)

MNR......... Mouvement Nationaliste Revolutionnaire [*Revolutionary Nationalist Movement*] [*France*] [*Political party*] (PD)

MNR......... Movimiento Nacionalista Revolucionario [*National Revolutionary Movement*] [*Bolivia*] [*Political party*] (PPW)

MNR......... Movimiento Nacional Reformista [*National Reformist Movement*] [*Honduras*] [*Political party*]

MNR......... Movimiento Nacional Revolucionario [*National Revolutionary Movement*] [*El Salvador*] [*Political party*] (PPW)

MNR......... Mozambique National Resistance [*Political party*] (AD)

MNR......... Mozambique National Resistance Movement

MnR......... Rochester Public Library, Rochester, MN [*Library symbol*] [*Library of Congress*] (LCLS)

MnRa......... Raymond Public Library, Raymond, MN [*Library symbol*] [*Library of Congress*] (LCLS)

MnRaKE...... Knight Elementary School, Randall, MN [*Library symbol*] [*Library of Congress*] (LCLS)

MNRAS....... Monthly Notices of the Royal Astronomical Society (SAUO)

MNRC......... Minorco [*Formerly, Minerals & Resources Corp. Ltd.*] [*NASDAQ symbol*] (NQ)

MnRc......... Rush City Public Library, Rush City, MN [*Library symbol*] [*Library of Congress*] (LCLS)

MnRcE........ Rush City Elementary School, Rush City, MN [*Library symbol*] [*Library of Congress*] (LCLS)

MnRcH........ Rush City High School, Rush City, MN [*Library symbol*] [*Library of Congress*] (LCLS)

MNRCS....... Median Normalized RADAR Cross Section

MNRCY....... Minorco ADR [*NASDAQ symbol*] (TTSB)

MnRelE........ Redlake Elementary School, Redlake, MN [*Library symbol*] [*Library of Congress*] (LCLS)

MnRelH .... Redlake High School, Redlake, MN [*Library symbol*] [*Library of Congress*] (LCLS)

MnRemE....... Remer Elementary School, Remer, MN [*Library symbol*] [*Library of Congress*] (LCLS)

MnRemH ...... Northland High School, Remer, MN [*Library symbol*] [*Library of Congress*] (LCLS)

MnRen........ Renville City Library, Renville, MN [*Library symbol*] [*Library of Congress*] (LCLS)

MnRenBPS... Bird Island-Danube-Renville-Sacred Heart (BDRSH) Public Schools, Renville, MN [*Library symbol*] [*Library of Congress*] (LCLS)

MNRF......... Moonroof [*Automotive advertising*]

MnRfE........ Rockford Elementary School, Rockford, MN [*Library symbol*] [*Library of Congress*] (LCLS)

MnRfH .... Rockford High School, Rockford, MN [*Library symbol*] [*Library of Congress*] (LCLS)

MnRfM........ Rockford Middle School, Rockford, MN [*Library symbol*] [*Library of Congress*] (LCLS)

MnRgE........ Rogers Elementary School, Rogers, MN [*Library symbol*] [*Library of Congress*] (LCLS)

MnRgS........ St. Martin's School, Rogers, MN [*Library symbol*] [*Library of Congress*] (LCLS)

MNRH........ Movimiento Nacionalista Revolucionario Historico [*Historic Revolutionary Nationalist Movement*] [*Bolivia*] [*Political party*] (PPW)

MnRiE........ Rice Elementary School, Rice, MN [*Library symbol*] [*Library of Congress*] (LCLS)

MNRJ......... Museo Nacional de Rio de Janeiro [*National Museum of Rio de Janeiro*] [*Portugal*] (AD)

MNRL......... Mineral (MSA)

mnrl.......... Mineral (VRA)

MNrL......... Morrill Memorial Library, Norwood, MA [*Library symbol*] [*Library of Congress*] (LCLS)

MnRIF.......... Red Lake Falls Public Library, Red Lake Falls, MN [*Library symbol*] [*Library of Congress*] (LCLS)

MnRlfHE...... J.A. Hughes Elementary School, Red Lake Falls, MN [*Library symbol*] [*Library of Congress*] (LCLS)

MnRIPS... Sioux Valley-Round Lake-Brewster Public School, Round Lake, MN [*Library symbol*] [*Library of Congress*] (LCLS)

MNRM Master of Natural Resource Management (PGP)

MnRM.......... Mayo Clinic, Rochester, MN [*Library symbol*] [*Library of Congress*] (LCLS)

MnRmE........ Richmond Elementary School, Richmond, MN [*Library symbol*] [*Library of Congress*] (LCLS)

MnRMeH..... Rochester Methodist Hospital, Rochester, MN [*Library symbol*] [*Library of Congress*] (LCLS)

MnRmP........ Richmond Public Library, Richmond, MN [*Library symbol*] [*Library of Congress*] (LCLS)

MnRmS........ Sts. Peter and Paul Elementary School Library, Richmond, MN [*Library symbol*] [*Library of Congress*] (LCLS)

MNRO Monroe Muffler Brake [*NASDAQ symbol*] (SPSG)

MNRO.......... Monro Muffler Brake, Inc. [*NASDAQ symbol*] (SAG)

MnRoN........ Northwestern College, Roseville, MN [*Library symbol*] [*Library of Congress*] (LCLS)

MnRoP........ Minnesota State Pollution Control Agency, Roseville, MN [*Library symbol*] [*Library of Congress*] (LCLS)

MnRos........ Roseau Public Library, Roseau, MN [*Library symbol*] [*Library of Congress*] (LCLS)

MnRosE....... Roseau Elementary School, Roseau, MN [*Library symbol*] [*Library of Congress*] (LCLS)

MnRosH....... Roseau High School, Roseau, MN [*Library symbol*] [*Library of Congress*] (LCLS)

MnRosMS.... Malung School, Roseau, MN [*Library symbol*] [*Library of Congress*] (LCLS)

MnRothS...... Rothsay Public School, Rothsay, MN [*Library symbol*] [*Library of Congress*] (LCLS)

MnRoy........ Royalton Public Library, Royalton, MN [*Library symbol*] [*Library of Congress*] (LCLS)

MnRoyS....... Royalton School, Royalton, MN [*Library symbol*] [*Library of Congress*] (LCLS)

MNRP.......... Movimiento Nacionalista Revolucionario del Pueblo [*Nationalist Revolutionary People's Movement*] [*Bolivia*] [*Political party*] (PPW)

MNRPM....... Malay Nationalist Revolutionary Party of Malaya [*Partai Kebangsaan Melayu Revolusioner Malaya*] [*Political party*] (PPW)

MnRPS........ Rochester Public Schools, Rochester, MN [*Library symbol*] [*Library of Congress*] (LCLS)

MnRR.......... Rochester State Junior College, Rochester, MN [*Library symbol*] [*Library of Congress*] (LCLS)

MNRS.......... Manors [*Postal Service standard*] (OPSA)

MNRS.......... Midwest Nursing Research Society (SAUO)

MNRS.......... Mobile Neutron Radiographic System

MnRS.......... Southeastern Libraries Cooperating [*SELCO*], Rochester Public Library, Rochester, MN [*Library symbol*] [*Library of Congress*] (LCLS)

Mnrsm......... Mannerism (VRA)

MnRStM...... Saint Mary's Hospital, Rochester, MN [*Library symbol*] [*Library of Congress*] (LCLS)

mnrt............ Minaret (VRA)

MNRT......... Minister of State for Research and Technology (SAUO)

MNRT......... Monmouth Real Estate Investment Trust [*NASDAQ symbol*] (NQ)

MNRTA....... Monmouth R.E. Inv CL'A' [*NASDAQ symbol*] (TTSB)

MNRU......... Medical Neuropsychiatric Research Unit (AD)

MNRU......... Modulated Noise Reference Unit [*Telecommunications*] (TEL)

MnRuPS...... Ruthton Public Schools, Ruthton, MN [*Library symbol*] [*Library of Congress*] (LCLS)

MnRusPS.... Russell Public Schools, Russell, MN [*Library symbol*] [*Library of Congress*] (LCLS)

MNRV......... Movimiento Nacionalista Revolucionario - Vanguardia Revolucionaria 9 de Abril [*Bolivia*] [*Political party*] (EY)

MnRvJ........ John Clark Elementary School, Rockville, MN [*Library symbol*] [*Library of Congress*] (LCLS)

MnRw......... Red Wing Public Library, Red Wing, MN [*Library symbol*] [*Library of Congress*] (LCLS)

MnRwf........ Redwood Falls Public Library, Redwood Falls, MN [*Library symbol*] [*Library of Congress*] (LCLS)

MnRwfGES... Reede Gray Elementary School, Redwood Falls, MN [*Library symbol*] [*Library of Congress*] (LCLS)

MnRwfH....... Redwood Falls Hospital, Redwood Falls, MN [*Library symbol*] [*Library of Congress*] (LCLS)

MnRwfJSH... Redwood Falls-Morton Junior Senior High School, Redwood Falls, MN [*Library symbol*] [*Library of Congress*] (LCLS)

MnRwfSJL ... St. John's Lutheran School, Redwood Falls, MN [*Library symbol*] [*Library of Congress*] (LCLS)

MNS.......... College of Saint Scholastica Library, Duluth, MN [*OCLC symbol*] (OCLC)

MNS.......... MacNeal-Schwendler [*AMEX symbol*] (TTSB)

MNS.......... Malayan Nature Society (BUAC)

MNS.......... Managed Network Services (SAUS)

MNS.......... Management Need Statement (AAGC)

Mns .... Manaus (AD)

MNS.......... Manitoba Naturalists Society [*Canada*] (BUAC)

MNS.......... Mansa [*Zambia*] [*Airport symbol*] (OAG)

MNS.......... Martin's Louisiana Reports, New Series [*A publication*] (DLA)

MNS.......... Master of Natural Sciences (GAGS)

MNS.......... Master of Nuclear Science (GAGS)

MNS.......... Master of Nursing Science

MNS.......... Master of Nutritional Science

MNS.......... Materiel Need Statement [*Army*]

MNS.......... Maturity News Service

MNS.......... McGuire Nuclear Station (NRCH)

MNS.......... Mechanical Neutral Start [*Automotive engineering*]

MNS.......... Medial Nuclear Stratum (DB)

MNS.......... Member of the Numismatical Society [*British*]

mns .... Metal-Nitride-Semiconductor (AD)

MNS.......... Meta-Nitride Semiconductor (MCD)

MNS.......... Microband National System, Inc. [*New York, NY*] [*Telecommunications*] (TSSD)

MNS.......... Microneurography Society (EA)

MNS.......... Mine Neutralization System [*Military*] (CAAL)

Mns .... Mines (AD)

MNS.......... Mines

MNS.......... Ministic Air [*Canada*] [*ICAO designator*] (FAAC)

MNS.......... Ministry of National Service [*World War I*] [*British*]

MNS.......... Minneapolis, Northfield & Southern Railway [*AAR code*]

MNS.......... Minneapolis, Northfield & Southern Railway Co. (SAUO)

MNS.......... Minutes [*International telex abbreviation*] (WDMC)

MNS.......... Mission Needs Statement [*Army*] (RDA)

MNS.......... Molded Nylon Screw

MNS.......... Moravian National Party [*Political party*] (BUAC)

MNS.......... Movement for a New Society [*Defunct*] (EA)

MNS.......... Movimiento Nacional de Salvacion [*National Movement of Salvation*] [*Dominican Republic*] [*Political party*] (PPW)

MNS.......... Smith College, Northampton, MA [*Library symbol*] [*Library of Congress*] (LCLS)

MnS .... St. Paul Public Library, St. Paul, MN [*Library symbol*] [*Library of Congress*] (LCLS)

MnSa.......... Sandstone Public Library, Sandstone, MN [*Library symbol*] [*Library of Congress*] (LCLS)

MNSA .... Seaman Apprentice, Mineman, Striker [*Navy rating*]

MnSaE........ Sandstone Elementary School, Sandstone, MN [*Library symbol*] [*Library of Congress*] (LCLS)

MnSaF........ Federal Correctional Institute Library, Sandstone, MN [*Library symbol*] [*Library of Congress*] (LCLS)

MnSAG....... Minnesota Attorney General's Office, St. Paul, MN [*Library symbol*] [*Library of Congress*] (LCLS)

MnSagHS ... Albrook High School, Saginaw, MN [*Library symbol*] [*Library of Congress*] (LCLS)

MnSaH........ Sandstone Area Hospital/Nursing Home, Sandstone, MN [*Library symbol*] [*Library of Congress*] (LCLS)

MnSaJS....... Sandstone Junior/Senior High School, Sandstone, MN [*Library symbol*] [*Library of Congress*] (LCLS)

MnSanLS.... Zion Lutheran School, Sanborn, MN [*Library symbol*] [*Library of Congress*] (LCLS)

MnSanPS.... Sanborn Public School, Sanborn, MN [*Library symbol*] [*Library of Congress*] (LCLS)

MnSarH....... Sartell High School, Sartell, MN [*Library symbol*] [*Library of Congress*] (LCLS)

MnSarM....... Sartell Middle School, Sartell, MN [*Library symbol*] [*Library of Congress*] (LCLS)

MnSarS....... St. Francis Xavier School, Sartell, MN [*Library symbol*] [*Library of Congress*] (LCLS)

MNSaS .... Swift River Valley Historical Society, New Salem, MA [*Library symbol*] [*Library of Congress*] (LCLS)

MnSB.......... Bethel College, St. Paul, MN [*Library symbol*] [*Library of Congress*] (LCLS)

MNSBC....... Minnesota North Stars Booster Club (EA)

MnSBH....... Bethesda Lutheran Hospital, St. Paul, MN [*Library symbol*] [*Library of Congress*] (LCLS)

MNSC .... Main Network Switching Center [*Telecommunications*] (TEL)

MN Sc .... Master of Nursing Science

MNSC .... San Carlos/San Juan [*Nicaragua*] [*ICAO location identifier*] (ICLI)

MnSc .... Sauk Centre Public Library, Sauk Centre, MN [*Library symbol*] [*Library of Congress*] (LCLS)

MnSCC........ Concordia College, St. Paul, MN [*Library symbol*] [*Library of Congress*] (LCLS)

MnSCH .... Children's Hospital, St. Paul, MN [*Library symbol*] [*Library of Congress*] (LCLS)

MnScHF....... Holy Family School, Sauk Center, MN [*Library symbol*] [*Library of Congress*] (LCLS)

MNSCL....... Miniscule

MnScL .... Sinclair Lewis Foundation, Sauk Centre, MN [*Library symbol*] [*Library of Congress*] (LCLS)

MnScM........ Meadow View School, Sauk Centre, MN [*Library symbol*] [*Library of Congress*] (LCLS)

MnScML...... Mary Lyon School, Minnesota Correctional Facility, Sauk Centre, MN [*Library symbol*] [*Library of Congress*] (LCLS)

MnScP........ Sauk Centre Public Schools, Sauk Centre, MN [*Library symbol*] [*Library of Congress*] (LCLS)

MnScSM...... St. Michael's Hospital and Convalescent and Nursing Center, Sauk Centre, MN [*Library symbol*] [*Library of Congress*] (LCLS)

MnSCU....... Minnesota State Colleges and Universities

MNSD......... Mouvement National pour une Societe de Developpement [*Niger*] [*Political party*] (EY)

MnSEA........ Minnesota Energy Agency, St. Paul, MN [*Library symbol*] [*Library of Congress*] (LCLS)

MnSebS....... Sebeka School, Sebeka, MN [*Library symbol*] [*Library of Congress*] (LCLS)

MNSER .... Mean Normalized Systolic Ejection Rate [*Cardiology*]

MNSF.......... Monoclonal-Nonspecific Suppressor Factor [*Immunology*]

MnSG.......... Gillette State Hospital for Crippled Children, St. Paul, MN [*Library symbol*] [*Library of Congress*] (LCLS)

MnSGC .... Minnesota Governor's Commission on Crime Prevention and Control, St. Paul, MN [*Library symbol*] [*Library of Congress*] (LCLS)

MnSGH .... Group Health, Inc., St. Paul, MN [*Library symbol*] [*Library of Congress*] (LCLS)

MnSH .... Hamline University, St. Paul, MN [*Library symbol*] [*Library of Congress*] (LCLS)

MnSheS .... Shelly School, Shelly, MN [*Library symbol*] [*Library of Congress*] (LCLS)

MnSH-L .... Hamline University, School of Law, St. Paul, MN [*Library symbol*] [*Library of Congress*] (LCLS)

MnShS .... Scott County Library, Shakopee, MN [*Library symbol*] [*Library of Congress*] (LCLS)

MNSI .... Siuna [*Nicaragua*] [*ICAO location identifier*] (ICLI)

MnSib .... Silver Bay Public Library, Silver Bay, MN [*Library symbol*] [*Library of Congress*] (LCLS)

MnSibHS ..... Wm. Kelley High School, Silver Bay, MN [*Library symbol*] [*Library of Congress*] (LCLS)

MnSibME .... Mary MacDonald Elementary School, Silver Bay, MN [*Library symbol*] [*Library of Congress*] (LCLS)

MnSifE .... Holler Elementary School, South International Falls, MN [*Library symbol*] [*Library of Congress*] (LCLS)

MnSJ .... James J. Hill Reference Library, St. Paul, MN [*Library symbol*] [*Library of Congress*] (LCLS)

MnSL .... Luther Theological Seminary, St. Paul, MN [*Library symbol*] [*Library of Congress*] [*Obsolete*] (LCLS)

MNSL........... Mainsail

MNSL.......... Maintenance Non-Significant Lists (ACAE)

MnSLBF ...... Lutheran Brotherhood Foundation Reformation Library, St. Paul, MN [*Library symbol*] [*Library of Congress*] (LCLS)

MnSLN .... Luther-Northwestern Seminary, St. Paul, MN [*Library symbol*] [*Library of Congress*] (LCLS)

MnSly .... Slayton Public Library, Slayton, MN [*Library symbol*] [*Library of Congress*] (LCLS)

MnSlyES ...... Slayton Elementary School, Slayton, MN [*Library symbol*] [*Library of Congress*] (LCLS)

MnSlyJSH ... Slayton Junior-Senior High School, Slayton, MN [*Library symbol*] [*Library of Congress*] (LCLS)

MnSM .... Macalester College, St. Paul, MN [*Library symbol*] [*Library of Congress*] (LCLS)

MnSmH........ St. Michael-Albertville High School, St. Michael, MN [*Library symbol*] [*Library of Congress*] (LCLS)

MnSmM .... St. Michael-Albertville Middle School, St. Michael, MN [*Library symbol*] [*Library of Congress*] (LCLS)

MnSMMfg... Minnesota Mining & Manufacturing Co., Technical Library, St. Paul, MN [*Library symbol*] [*Library of Congress*] [*Obsolete*] (LCLS)

MnSMN........ Mounds-Midway School of Nursing, St. Paul, MN [*Library symbol*] [*Library of Congress*] (LCLS)

MnSmP........ St. Michael Parish School, St. Michael, MN [*Library symbol*] [*Library of Congress*] (LCLS)

MnSN........... Northwestern Lutheran Theological Seminary, St. Paul, MN [*Library symbol*] [*Library of Congress*] [*Obsolete*] (LCLS)

MNSN .... Seaman, Mineman, Striker [*Navy rating*]

MnSOD .... Manganese Superoxide Dismutase

MnSOEO ...... Minnesota Office of Economic Opportunity, St. Paul, MN [*Library symbol*] [*Library of Congress*] (LCLS)

MnSP........... Saint Paul Public Library, St. Paul, MN [*Library symbol*] [*Library of Congress*] (LCLS)

MNSPE .... Member of the National Society of Physical Education (SAUO)

MnSpES....... Spicer Elementary School, Spicer, MN [*Library symbol*] [*Library of Congress*] (LCLS)

MnSpP......... Spicer Public Library, Spicer, MN [*Library symbol*] [*Library of Congress*] (LCLS)

MNSQ .... Motor Neurone Society of Queensland [*Australia*]

MnSqlS........ Squaw Lake School, Squaw Lake, MN [*Library symbol*] [*Library of Congress*] (LCLS)

MnSrB .... Benton County Historical Museum, Sauk Rapids, MN [*Library symbol*] [*Library of Congress*] (LCLS)

MnSRC .... Ramsey County Public Library, St. Paul, MN [*Library symbol*] [*Library of Congress*] (LCLS)

MnSrH .... Sauk Rapids High School, Sauk Rapids, MN [*Library symbol*] [*Library of Congress*] (LCLS)

MnSrHJ........ Hillside Junior High School, Sauk Rapids, MN [*Library symbol*] [*Library of Congress*] (LCLS)

MnSRM........ Ramsey County Medical Society, St. Paul, MN [*Library symbol*] [*Library of Congress*] (LCLS)

MnSrPE........ Pleasantview Elementary School, Sauk Rapids, MN [*Library symbol*] [*Library of Congress*] (LCLS)

MnSrS .... Sacred Heart School, Sauk Rapids, MN [*Library symbol*] [*Library of Congress*] (LCLS)

MnSrT.......... Trinity Lutheran School, Sauk Rapids, MN [*Library symbol*] [*Library of Congress*] (LCLS)

MNSS .... Modified Need Satisfaction Schedule

MNS-S .... Smith College, Sophia Smith Collection, Northampton, MA [*Library symbol*] [*Library of Congress*] (LCLS)

MnSS........... St. Paul Seminary, St. Paul, MN [*Library symbol*] [*Library of Congress*] (LCLS)

MNSSA .... Motor Neurone Society of South Australia

MnSSC......... College of St. Catherine, St. Paul, MN [*Library symbol*] [*Library of Congress*] (LCLS)

MnSSEP....... Median Nerve Somatosensory Evoked Potential [*Neurology*] (DAVI)

MnSSJ......... St. John's Hospital, St. Paul, MN [*Library symbol*] [*Library of Congress*] (LCLS)

MnSSJos ...... St. Joseph's Hospital, St. Paul, MN [*Library symbol*] [*Library of Congress*] (LCLS)

MnSSM........ Science Museum of Minnesota, Louis S. Headley Memorial Library, St. Paul, MN [*Library symbol*] [*Library of Congress*] (LCLS)

MnSSP......... St. Paul Ramsey Hospital, St. Paul, MN [*Library symbol*] [*Library of Congress*] (LCLS)

MnSSpU ...... Sperry UNIVAC, St. Paul, MN [*Library symbol*] [*Library of Congress*] (LCLS)

MnSST......... College of St. Thomas, St. Paul, MN [*Library symbol*] [*Library of Congress*] (LCLS)

MNST .... Motor Neurone Society of Tasmania [*Australia*]

MnSt............ Staples Public Library, Staples, MN [*Library symbol*] [*Library of Congress*] (LCLS)

MNSTB .... Monostable (MSA)

MNSTBMV .. Monostable Multivibrator (MSA)

MnStbSP...... Saint Paul Bible College, Saint Bonifacius, MN [*Library symbol*] [*Library of Congress*] (LCLS)

MnStclA....... Appollo High School, St. Cloud, MN [*Library symbol*] [*Library of Congress*] (LCLS)

MnStclBS.... Benton/Stearns Special Education Professional Library, St. Cloud, MN [*Library symbol*] [*Library of Congress*] (LCLS)

MnStclCF..... Minnesota Corrections Facility Library, St. Cloud, MN [*Library symbol*] [*Library of Congress*] (LCLS)

MnStclCH ... St. Cloud Cathedral High School, St. Cloud, MN [*Library symbol*] [*Library of Congress*] (LCLS)

MnStclD....... Diocese of St. Cloud, St. Cloud, MN [*Library symbol*] [*Library of Congress*] (LCLS)

MnStclEC..... Central Minnesota Educational Cooperative Service Unit, St. Cloud, MN [*Library symbol*] [*Library of Congress*] (LCLS)

MnStclER..... Central Minnesota Educational Research and Development Council, Film Library, St. Cloud, MN [*Library symbol*] [*Library of Congress*] (LCLS)

MnStclG....... Great River Regional Library, St. Cloud, MN [*Library symbol*] [*Library of Congress*] (LCLS)

MnStclGP ... Green Pastures Christian School, St. Cloud, MN [*Library symbol*] [*Library of Congress*] (LCLS)

MnStclH....... St. Cloud Hospital, Health Sciences Library, St. Cloud, MN [*Library symbol*] [*Library of Congress*] (LCLS)

MnStclHi...... Stearns County Historical Society, St. Cloud, MN [*Library symbol*] [*Library of Congress*] (LCLS)

MnStclIHS .... Holy Spirit School, St. Cloud, MN [*Library symbol*] [*Library of Congress*] (LCLS)

MnStclJ .... Jefferson Elementary School, St. Cloud, MN [*Library symbol*] [*Library of Congress*] (LCLS)

MnStclL....... Lincoln Elementary School, St. Cloud, MN [*Library symbol*] [*Library of Congress*] (LCLS)

MnStclM....... Madison Elementary School, St. Cloud, MN [*Library symbol*] [*Library of Congress*] (LCLS)

MnStclMc..... McKinley Elementary School, St. Cloud, MN [*Library symbol*] [*Library of Congress*] (LCLS)

MnStclMS.... St. Cloud Media Services, St. Cloud, MN [*Library symbol*] [*Library of Congress*] (LCLS)

MnStclN....... St. Cloud School of Nursing Library, St. Cloud, MN [*Library symbol*] [*Library of Congress*] (LCLS)

MnStclP....... Sts. Peter & Paul Primary School, St. Cloud, MN [*Library symbol*] [*Library of Congress*] (LCLS)

MnStclR....... Roosevelt Elementary School, St. Cloud, MN [*Library symbol*] [*Library of Congress*] (LCLS)

MnStclS....... St. Cloud State University, St. Cloud, MN [*Library symbol*] [*Library of Congress*] (LCLS)

MnStclSA..... St. Anthony School, St. Cloud, MN [*Library symbol*] [*Library of Congress*] (LCLS)

MnStclSC..... Stearns/Benton Counties Law Library, St. Cloud, MN [*Library symbol*] [*Library of Congress*] (LCLS)

MnStclSE..... St. Cloud South Elementary School, St. Cloud, MN [*Library symbol*] [*Library of Congress*] (LCLS)

MnStclSM.... St. Mary Help of Christians School, St. Cloud, MN [*Library symbol*] [*Library of Congress*] (LCLS)

MnStclSP..... Sts. Peter & Paul Middle Schol, St. Cloud, MN [*Library symbol*] [*Library of Congress*] (LCLS)

MnStclSt...... St. Augustine School, St. Cloud, MN [*Library symbol*] [*Library of Congress*] (LCLS)

MnStclV....... United States Veterans Administration Hospital, St. Cloud, MN [*Library symbol*] [*Library of Congress*] (LCLS)

MnStclVT..... St. Cloud Area Vo-Tech Institute, St. Cloud, MN [*Library symbol*] [*Library of Congress*] (LCLS)

MnStclW...... Westwood Elementary School, St. Cloud, MN [*Library symbol*] [*Library of Congress*] (LCLS)

MnSteE........ Stephen Elementary School, Stpehen, MN [*Library symbol*] [*Library of Congress*] (LCLS)

MnSteH........ Stephen High School, Stephen, MN [*Library symbol*] [*Library of Congress*] (LCLS)

MnStH .... United District Hospital, Staples, MN [*Library symbol*] [*Library of Congress*] (LCLS)

MnStHS ...... Staples High School, Staples, MN [*Library symbol*] [*Library of Congress*] (LCLS)

MnStj........... Watonwan County Library, St. James, MN [*Library symbol*] [*Library of Congress*] (LCLS)

MnStjoKE..... Kennedy Elementary School, St. Joseph, MN [*Library symbol*] [*Library of Congress*] (LCLS)

MnStjoL....... St. Joseph Lab School, St. Joseph, MN [*Library symbol*] [*Library of Congress*] (LCLS)

MnStjoS....... College of St. Benedict, St. Joseph, MN [*Library symbol*] [*Library of Congress*] (LCLS)

MnStLE........ Lincoln Model Elementary School, Staples, MN [*Library symbol*] [*Library of Congress*] (LCLS)

MnSTM .... Three M (3M) Co., St. Paul, MN [*Library symbol*] [*Library of Congress*] (LCLS)

MnSTM-A .... Three M (3M) Co., St. Paul, MN [*Library symbol*] [*Library of Congress*] (LCLS)

MnSTM-B ... Three M (3M) Co., Business Information Service, St. Paul, MN [*Library symbol*] [*Library of Congress*] (LCLS)

MnSTM-E ..... Three M (3M) Co., Engineering Information Services, St. Paul, MN [*Library symbol*] [*Library of Congress*] (LCLS)

MnSTM-G .... Three M (3M) Co., St. Paul, MN [*Library symbol*] [*Library of Congress*] (LCLS)

MnSTM-H .... Three M (3M) Co., Health Care Library, St. Paul, MN [*Library symbol*] [*Library of Congress*] (LCLS)

MnSTM-M .... Three M (3M) Co., St. Paul, MN [*Library symbol*] [*Library of Congress*] (LCLS)

MnSTM-P .... Three M (3M) Co., St. Paul, MN [*Library symbol*] [*Library of Congress*] (LCLS)

MnSTM-T ..... Three M (3M) Co., St. Paul, MN [*Library symbol*] [*Library of Congress*] (LCLS)

MnStNE .... North Elementary School, Staples, MN [*Library symbol*] [*Library of Congress*] (LCLS)

MnStoES ...... Storden-Jeffers Elementary School, Storden, MN [*Library symbol*] [*Library of Congress*] (LCLS)

MnStpeG ...... Gustavus Adolphus College, St. Peter, MN [*Library symbol*] [*Library of Congress*] (LCLS)

Mnstr .... Munster (AD)

MNSTRY ...... Ministry

MnStS .... Sacred Heart School, Staples, MN [*Library symbol*] [*Library of Congress*] (LCLS)

MnStT .... Staples Technical Institute, Staples, MN [*Library symbol*] [*Library of Congress*] (LCLS)

MnStwPS ...... Stewart Public Schools, Stewart, MN [*Library symbol*] [*Library of Congress*] (LCLS)

MnSU .... University of Minnesota, St. Paul, MN [*Library symbol*] [*Library of Congress*] (LCLS)

MnSU-Bc ..... University of Minnesota, Biochemistry Library, St. Paul, MN [*Library symbol*] [*Library of Congress*] (LCLS)

MnSuES .... Sunberg Elementary School, Sunberg, MN [*Library symbol*] [*Library of Congress*] (LCLS)

MnSU-Et ...... University of Minnesota, Entomology Library, St. Paul, MN [*Library symbol*] [*Library of Congress*] (LCLS)

MnSU-F .... University of Minnesota, Forestry Library, St. Paul, MN [*Library symbol*] [*Library of Congress*] (LCLS)

MnSUH .... United Hospitals, Inc., St. Paul, MN [*Library symbol*] [*Library of Congress*] (LCLS)

MnSU-PP ..... University of Minnesota, Plant Pathology Library, St. Paul, MN [*Library symbol*] [*Library of Congress*] (LCLS)

MnSUSF ...... United States Forest Service, North Central Forest Experiment Station, St. Paul, MN [*Library symbol*] [*Library of Congress*] (LCLS)

MnSU-V .... University of Minnesota, Veterinary Medicine Library, St. Paul, MN [*Library symbol*] [*Library of Congress*] (LCLS)

MNSV .... Motor Neurone Society of Victoria [*Australia*]

MnSw .... Swanville Public Library, Swanville, MN [*Library symbol*] [*Library of Congress*] (LCLS)

MnSwE .... Swanville Elementary School, Swanville, MN [*Library symbol*] [*Library of Congress*] (LCLS)

MnSwH .... Swanville High School, Swanville, MN [*Library symbol*] [*Library of Congress*] (LCLS)

MnSWM .... William Mitchell College of Law, St. Paul, MN [*Library symbol*] [*Library of Congress*] (LCLS)

MNT .... College of St. Thomas, St. Paul, MN [*OCLC symbol*] (OCLC)

M/N/T .... Main/Satellite/Tributary Network [*Telecommunications*] (ACRL)

MNT .... Maintained [*Automotive advertising*]

MNT .... Maternal and Neonatal Tetanus [*Medicine*]

mnt .... Mean Neap Tide (AD)

MNT .... Medical Nutrition Therapy (ADWA)

MNT .... Minnesota and Ontario Paper [*Stock exchange symbol*] (AD)

Mn-T .... Minnesota State Department of Taxation, St. Paul, MN [*Library symbol*] [*Library of Congress*] (LCLS)

MNT .... Minto [*Alaska*] [*Airport symbol*] (OAG)

MNT .... Minute [*Angle*]

MNT .... Modern Network Theory [*Electrical engineering computer*]

MNT .... Moffatt New Testament Commentary [*A publication*] (BJA)

MNT .... Monitor

MNT .... Mononitrotoluene [*Organic chemistry*]

MNT .... Montedison SpA [*NYSE symbol*] (SPSG)

MNT .... Montoro Gold, Inc. [*Vancouver Stock Exchange symbol*]

MNT .... Montreal [*Quebec*] [*Seismograph station code, US Geological Survey*] (SEIS)

MNT .... Montserrat Airways Ltd. [*Antigua and Barbuda*] [*ICAO designator*] (FAAC)

MNT .... Morton's Neuroma of Toe [*Medicine*] (MELL)

MNT .... Mount (KSC)

MNT .... Mountain

MNT .... Mouse Infection Neutralization Test [*Medicine*] (MELL)

MNt .... Newton Free Library, Newton, MA [*Library symbol*] [*Library of Congress*] (LCLS)

MNTA .... Minnesota Telephone Association (CGWS)

MNTAIN ...... Mountain [*Commonly used*] (OPSA)

MnTalE .... North Elementary School, Talmoon, MN [*Library symbol*] [*Library of Congress*] (LCLS)

MntasiaE ..... Mountasia Entertainment International, Inc. [*Associated Press*] (SAG)

MNTB .... Medial Nucleus of Trapezoid Body [*Neuroanatomy*]

MNTB .... Merchant Navy Training Board [*British*] (DS)

MNTC .... Mexican National Tourist Council (EA)

MNTC .... Moffatt New Testament Commentary [*A publication*] (BJA)

MNtcA .... Andover Newton Theological School, Newton Center, MA [*Library symbol*] [*Library of Congress*] (LCLS)

MnTcFW ...... United States Fish and Wildlife Service, Science Reference Library, Twin Cities, MN [*Library symbol*] [*Library of Congress*] (LCLS)

MnTcM .... United States Bureau of Mines, Twin Cities, MN [*Library symbol*] [*Library of Congress*] (LCLS)

MNTD .... Maximum Non-Toxic Dose [*Toxicology*] (LDT)

MnTEC .... Northwest Education Cooperative Service Unit, Thief River Falls, MN [*Library symbol*] [*Library of Congress*] (LCLS)

MnTf .... Taylor Falls Public Library, Taylor Falls, MN [*Library symbol*] [*Library of Congress*] (LCLS)

MnTFM .... Franklin Middle School, Thief River Falls, MN [*Library symbol*] [*Library of Congress*] (LCLS)

MnTfS .... Taylor Falls School, Taylor Falls, MN [*Library symbol*] [*Library of Congress*] (LCLS)

MNTG .... Mounting

MnTh .... Two Harbors Public Library, Two Harbors, MN [*Library symbol*] [*Library of Congress*] (LCLS)

MnThE .... John A. Johnson Elementary School, Two Harbors, MN [*Library symbol*] [*Library of Congress*] (LCLS)

MnThHS .... Two Harbors High School, Two Harbors, MN [*Library symbol*] [*Library of Congress*] (LCLS)

MNTHLY ...... Monthly

MnThM .... Minnehaha Middle School, Two Harbors, MN [*Library symbol*] [*Library of Congress*] (LCLS)

MNTHZ .... Methylnitrosothiazolidine [*Organic chemistry*]

MNTK .... Mezhotraslevoi Naucho-Tekhni-Cheskii Kompleks [*Interdisciplinary Scientific-Technological Complex*] [*Russian*]

MNTK .... Movimiento Nacional Tupaj Katari [*Bolivia*] [*Political party*] (PPW)

MnTKS .... Knox School, Thief River Falls, MN [*Library symbol*] [*Library of Congress*] (LCLS)

MNTL .... Manufacturers National (EFIS)

MNTL .... Mental

MnTLH .... Lincoln High School, Thief River Falls, MN [*Library symbol*] [*Library of Congress*] (LCLS)

mntmp .... Minimum Temperature (AD)

MNTMP .... Minimum Temperature (NOAA)

MnTMT .... Mark Twain School, Thief River Falls, MN [*Library symbol*] [*Library of Congress*] (LCLS)

mntn .... Maintain (AD)

MNTN .... Maintain

MNTN .... Mountain

MnTN .... Northland State Junior College, Thief River Falls, MN [*Library symbol*] [*Library of Congress*] (LCLS)

mntnc .... Maintenance (AD)

MNTNC .... Maintenance

mntnd .... Maintained (AD)

mntng .... Maintaining (AD)

MnTNo .... Northrop Resource Room, Thief River Falls, MN [*Library symbol*] [*Library of Congress*] (LCLS)

MnTNR .... Northwest Regional Library, Thief River Falls, MN [*Library symbol*] [*Library of Congress*] (LCLS)

MNTNS .... Mountains [*Commonly used*] (OPSA)

MNTO .... Moroccan National Tourist Office (AD)

MnToS .... Togo School, Togo, MN [*Library symbol*] [*Library of Congress*] (LCLS)

MnTP .... Thief River Falls Public Library, Thief River Falls, MN [*Library symbol*] [*Library of Congress*] (LCLS)

MnTPC .... Pennington County Extension Office, Thief River Falls, MN [*Library symbol*] [*Library of Congress*] (LCLS)

MnTPPS .... Manganese Tetraphenylporphine Sulfonate [*Organic chemistry*]

MNTPr .... Montedison Bearer Svg Pfd ADS [*NYSE symbol*] (TTSB)

MNTR .... Mentor Corp. [*NASDAQ symbol*] (NQ)

mntr .... Monitor (AD)

MNTR .... Monitor (MDG)

MnTrES .... Tracy Elementary School, Tracy, MN [*Library symbol*] [*Library of Congress*] (LCLS)

MnTrJSH ...... Trace Junior-Senior High School, Tracy, MN [*Library symbol*] [*Library of Congress*] (LCLS)

MNTRNG ...... Monitoring

MnTrStM ...... St. Mary's School, Tracy, MN [*Library symbol*] [*Library of Congress*] (LCLS)

MNTS .... Medial Nucleus Tractus Solitarius [*Neuroanatomy*]

MNTS .... Methyl(Nitroso) Toluenesulphonamide [*Organic chemistry*]

MNTS .... Mountains

MNtS .... Swedenborg School of Religion, Newton, MA [*Library symbol*] [*Library of Congress*] (LCLS)

MnTSB .... St. Bernard's School, Thief River Falls, MN [*Library symbol*] [*Library of Congress*] (LCLS)

MNtSH .... Newton College of the Sacred Heart [*Later, Newton College*], Newton, MA [*Library symbol*] [*Library of Congress*] (LCLS)

MNTV .... Mercury Network Test Vehicle (MUGU)

MNTVC .... Movable Nozzle Thrust-Vector Control (IGSL)

MnTW .... Washington School, Thief River Falls, MN [*Library symbol*] [*Library of Congress*] (LCLS)

MnTwvE .... Twin Valley Elementary School, Twin Valley, MN [*Library symbol*] [*Library of Congress*] (LCLS)

MnTwvH .... Twin Valley High School, Twin Valley, MN [*Library symbol*] [*Library of Congress*] (LCLS)

MNTX .... Minntech Corp. [*NASDAQ symbol*] (NQ)

MnTy .... Tyler Public Library, Tyler, MN [*Library symbol*] [*Library of Congress*] (LCLS)

MnTyHS .... Russell-Tyler-Ruthon High School, Tyler, MN [*Library symbol*] [*Library of Congress*] (LCLS)

MNU .... Maniti Sugar [*Stock exchange symbol*] (AD)
MNu .... Mare Nubium [*Sea of Clouds*] [*Lunar area*]
MNU .... Methylnitrosourea [*Also, NMU*] [*Organic chemistry*]
MNU .... Middle Name Unknown (MCD)
MNU .... Milford North [*Utah*] [*Seismograph station code, US Geological Survey*] (SEIS)
MNU .... Minimum Number of Units [*Chemical engineering*]
mnu .... Minnesota [*MARC country of publication code*] [*Library of Congress*] (LCCP)
MNU .... Moulmein [*Myanmar*] [*Airport symbol*] (OAG)
MNU .... Movement for National Unity [*St. Vincent*] (BUAC)
MNU .... Mundee Mines Ltd. [*Vancouver Stock Exchange symbol*]
MnU .... University of Minnesota, Minneapolis, MN [*Library symbol*] [*Library of Congress*] (LCLS)
MNU .... University of Minnesota, Minneapolis, MN [*OCLC symbol*] (OCLC)
MnU-Ar .... University of Minnesota, Archives, Minneapolis, MN [*Library symbol*] [*Library of Congress*] (LCLS)
MnU-B .... University of Minnesota, Biomedical Library, Minneapolis, MN [*Library symbol*] [*Library of Congress*] (LCLS)
MNucSc .... Master of Nuclear Science (GAGS)
MnU-Fb .... University of Minnesota, Freshwater Biological Institute, Navarre, MN [*Library symbol*] [*Library of Congress*] (LCLS)
MnU-IA .... University of Minnesota, Immigration History Research Center, St. Paul, MN [*Library symbol*] [*Library of Congress*] (LCLS)
MnU-K .... University of Minnesota, Kerlan Children's Books Collection, Minneapolis, MN [*Library symbol*] [*Library of Congress*] (LCLS)
MnU-L .... University of Minnesota, Law Library, Minneapolis, MN [*Library symbol*] [*Library of Congress*] (LCLS)
MnUIH .... Ulen-Hitteral High School, Ulen, MN [*Library symbol*] [*Library of Congress*] (LCLS)
MnU-MS ...... University of Minnesota, Manuscript Collection, Minneapolis, MN [*Library symbol*] [*Library of Congress*] (LCLS)
MnUnS .... Underwood Public School, Underwood, MN [*Library symbol*] [*Library of Congress*] (LCLS)
MnUpE .... Upsala Elementary School, Upsala, MN [*Library symbol*] [*Library of Congress*] (LCLS)
MnU-Ph .... University of Minnesota, Pharmacy Library, Minneapolis, MN [*Library symbol*] [*Library of Congress*] (LCLS)
MnUpH .... Upsala High School, Upsala, MN [*Library symbol*] [*Library of Congress*] (LCLS)
MNUR .... Mouvement National pour l'Union et la Reconciliation au Zaire [*National Movement for Union and Reconciliation in Zaire*] [*Political party*] (PD)
MnU-Rb .... University of Minnesota, Rare Book Division, Minneapolis, MN [*Library symbol*] [*Library of Congress*] (LCLS)
MNurs .... Master of Nursing (NADA)
MNursing ..... Master of Nursing
MnU-SW ...... University of Minnesota, Social Welfare History Archives Center, St. Paul, MN [*Library symbol*] [*Library of Congress*] (LCLS)
MNUT .... Methylnitrosourethane [*Organic chemistry*]
MNutrSc ...... Master of Nutritional Science
MNV .... Madisonville, TN [*Location identifier*] [*FAA*] (FAAL)
MNV .... Marginal Net Value
MNV .... Marion Power Shovel [*Stock exchange symbol*] (AD)
MNV .... Mina [*Nevada*] [*Seismograph station code, US Geological Survey*] (SEIS)
MNV .... Mine-Neutralization Vehicle [*Military*] (MCD)
Mn-V .... Minnesota State Vocational Rehabilitation Library, St. Paul, MN [*Library symbol*] [*Library of Congress*] (LCLS)
MNV .... Modular Nuclear Vehicle
MNV .... Southwest State University, Marshall, MN [*OCLC symbol*] (OCLC)
MNV .... United States Veterans Administration Hospital, Northampton, MA [*Library symbol*] [*Library of Congress*] (LCLS)
MnV .... Virginia Public Library, Virginia, MN [*Library symbol*] [*Library of Congress*] (LCLS)
MnVA .... Arrowhead Library System, Virginia, MN [*Library symbol*] [*Library of Congress*] (LCLS)
MnVePS ...... Verdi Public School, Verdi, MN [*Library symbol*] [*Library of Congress*] (LCLS)
MnVerS .... Verndale Public School, Verndale, MN [*Library symbol*] [*Library of Congress*] (LCLS)
MnVHS .... Virginia Junior-Senior High School, Virginia, MN [*Library symbol*] [*Library of Congress*] (LCLS)
MnVilS .... Villard Public School, Villard, MN [*Library symbol*] [*Library of Congress*] (LCLS)
MnVM .... Mesabi Community College, Virginia, MN [*Library symbol*] [*Library of Congress*] (LCLS)
MNVM .... Million Nighttime Vehicle Mile
MnVME .... James Madison Elementary School, Virginia, MN [*Library symbol*] [*Library of Congress*] (LCLS)
MNVR .... Maneuver
MnVRE .... Roosevelt Elementary School, Virginia, MN [*Library symbol*] [*Library of Congress*] (LCLS)
MnVRM .... Virginia Regional Medical Center, Virginia, MN [*Library symbol*] [*Library of Congress*] (LCLS)
Mn-W .... Minnesota State Department of Public Welfare, St. Paul, MN [*Library symbol*] [*Library of Congress*] (LCLS)
MNW .... Moneywise Resources [*Vancouver Stock Exchange symbol*]
MNW .... Monowai [*New Zealand*] [*Seismograph station code, US Geological Survey*] (SEIS)
MNW .... Northwest Missouri State University, Maryville, MO [*OCLC symbol*] (OCLC)
MnWa .... Wabasso Public Library, Wabasso, MN [*Library symbol*] [*Library of Congress*] (LCLS)

MnWad .... Wadena City Library, Wadena, MN [*Library symbol*] [*Library of Congress*] (LCLS)
MnWadE ...... Wadena Elementary School, Wadena, MN [*Library symbol*] [*Library of Congress*] (LCLS)
MnWadH ...... Wadena High School, Wadena, MN [*Library symbol*] [*Library of Congress*] (LCLS)
MnWadJ ...... Wadena Junior High School, Wadena, MN [*Library symbol*] [*Library of Congress*] (LCLS)
MnWaES ...... Wabasso Elementary School, Wabasso, MN [*Library symbol*] [*Library of Congress*] (LCLS)
MnWaHS .... Wabasso High School, Wabasso, MN [*Library symbol*] [*Library of Congress*] (LCLS)
MnWal .... Walker Public Library, Walker, MN [*Library symbol*] [*Library of Congress*] (LCLS)
MnWalC .... Cass County Extension Office, Walker, MN [*Library symbol*] [*Library of Congress*] (LCLS)
MnWalH ...... Walker-Hackensack High School, Walker, MN [*Library symbol*] [*Library of Congress*] (LCLS)
MnWalHi ..... Cass County Historical Society, Walker, MN [*Library symbol*] [*Library of Congress*] (LCLS)
MnWanS ...... Wannaska School, Wannaska, MN [*Library symbol*] [*Library of Congress*] (LCLS)
MnWar .... Godell Memorial Library, Warren, MN [*Library symbol*] [*Library of Congress*] (LCLS)
MnWarE ...... Warren Elementary School, Warren, MN [*Library symbol*] [*Library of Congress*] (LCLS)
MnWarJS ..... Warren Junior/Senior High School, Warren, MN [*Library symbol*] [*Library of Congress*] (LCLS)
MnWarr .... Warroad Public Library, Warroad, MN [*Library symbol*] [*Library of Congress*] (LCLS)
MnWarrE ..... Warroad Elementary School, Warroad, MN [*Library symbol*] [*Library of Congress*] (LCLS)
MnWarrH ..... Warroad High School, Warroad, MN [*Library symbol*] [*Library of Congress*] (LCLS)
MnWas .... Le Sueur-Waseca Regional Library, Waseca, MN [*Library symbol*] [*Library of Congress*] (LCLS)
MnWaStA ..... St. Anne School, Wabasso, MN [*Library symbol*] [*Library of Congress*] (LCLS)
MnWasU ...... University of Minnesota Technical College, Waseca, MN [*Library symbol*] [*Library of Congress*] (LCLS)
MnWatSA ..... St. Anthony School, Watkins, MN [*Library symbol*] [*Library of Congress*] (LCLS)
MnWauWE ... Waubon-Ogema-White Earth School, Waubon, MN [*Library symbol*] [*Library of Congress*] (LCLS)
MnWayC ..... Cargill Instructional Center, Wayzata, MN [*Library symbol*] [*Library of Congress*] (LCLS)
MnWblL .... Lakewood Community College, White Bear Lake, MN [*Library symbol*] [*Library of Congress*] (LCLS)
MnWbS .... Warba School, Warba, MN [*Library symbol*] [*Library of Congress*] (LCLS)
MnWE .... Isle-Wahkon Elementary School, Wahkon, MN [*Library symbol*] [*Library of Congress*] (LCLS)
MNWEB .... Merseyside and North Wales Electricity Board [*British*] (AD)
MNWEB .... Midlands & North Western Electricity Board (SAUO)
MnWeCS ...... Westbrook Christian School, Westbrook, MN [*Library symbol*] [*Library of Congress*] (LCLS)
MnWeP .... Westbrook Public Library, Westbrook, MN [*Library symbol*] [*Library of Congress*] (LCLS)
MnWePS ...... Westbrook Public School, Westbrook, MN [*Library symbol*] [*Library of Congress*] (LCLS)
MnWgMS .... Westbrook-Walnut Grove Middle School, Walnut Grove, MN [*Library symbol*] [*Library of Congress*] (LCLS)
MNWH .... Mojo Nixon World Headquarters (EA)
MnWhe .... Wheaton Community Library, Wheaton, MN [*Library symbol*] [*Library of Congress*] (LCLS)
MnWheH ...... Wheaton Community Hospital, Wheaton, MN [*Library symbol*] [*Library of Congress*] (LCLS)
MnWheHS ... Wheaton-Dumont High School, Wheaton, MN [*Library symbol*] [*Library of Congress*] (LCLS)
MnWhePE ... J.E. Pearson Elementary School, Wheaton, MN [*Library symbol*] [*Library of Congress*] (LCLS)
MnWil .... Lawson Memorial Library, Willmar, MN [*Library symbol*] [*Library of Congress*] (LCLS)
MnWilCS ...... Christian Community School, Willmar, MN [*Library symbol*] [*Library of Congress*] (LCLS)
MNWiLES .... Lafayette Elementary School, Willmar, MN [*Library symbol*] [*Library of Congress*] (LCLS)
MnWilGES ... Garfield Elementary School, Willmar, MN [*Library symbol*] [*Library of Congress*] (LCLS)
MnWilH .... Rice Memorial Hospital, Willmar, MN [*Library symbol*] [*Library of Congress*] (LCLS)
MnWilIL .... Immanuel Lutheran School, Willmar, MN [*Library symbol*] [*Library of Congress*] (LCLS)
MnWilJES .... Jefferson Elementary School, Willmar, MN [*Library symbol*] [*Library of Congress*] (LCLS)
MnWilJS ...... Willmar Junior High School, Willmar, MN [*Library symbol*] [*Library of Congress*] (LCLS)
MnWilLiS ..... Lincoln Elementary School, Willmar, MN [*Library symbol*] [*Library of Congress*] (LCLS)
MnWilPS .... Willmar Public Schools, Willmar, MN [*Library symbol*] [*Library of Congress*] (LCLS)
MnWilRC ..... Willmar Regional Treatment Center, Staff Library, Willmar, MN [*Library symbol*] [*Library of Congress*] (LCLS)
MnWilRE ..... Roosevelt Elementary School, Willmar, MN [*Library symbol*] [*Library of Congress*] (LCLS)

MnWilRL	Crow River Regional Library, Willmar, MN [*Library symbol*] [*Library of Congress*] (LCLS)
MnWilS	Willmar State Junior College, Willmar, MN [*Library symbol*] [*Library of Congress*] (LCLS)
MnWilSH	Willmar Senior High School, Willmar, MN [*Library symbol*] [*Library of Congress*] (LCLS)
MnWilTC	Willmar Technical Center, Willmar, MN [*Library symbol*] [*Library of Congress*] (LCLS)
MnWilWES	Washington Elementary School, Willmar, MN [*Library symbol*] [*Library of Congress*] (LCLS)
MnWin	Windom Public Library, Windom, MN [*Library symbol*] [*Library of Congress*] (LCLS)
MnWinH	Windom Area Hospital, Windom, MN [*Library symbol*] [*Library of Congress*] (LCLS)
MnWinHS	Windom Area High School, Windom, MN [*Library symbol*] [*Library of Congress*] (LCLS)
MnWino	Winona Public Library, Winona, MN [*Library symbol*] [*Library of Congress*] (LCLS)
MnWinoCT	College of Saint Teresa, Winona, MN [*Library symbol*] [*Library of Congress*] (LCLS)
MnWinoS	Winona State College [*Later, Winona State University*], Winona, MN [*Library symbol*] [*Library of Congress*] (LCLS)
MnWinoSM	Saint Mary's College, Winona, MN [*Library symbol*] [*Library of Congress*] (LCLS)
MnWinWES	Winfair Elementary School, Windom, MN [*Library symbol*] [*Library of Congress*] (LCLS)
MnWlHS	Echo-Wood Lake High School, Wood Lake, MN [*Library symbol*] [*Library of Congress*] (LCLS)
MnWlSJ	St. John's School, Wood Lake, MN [*Library symbol*] [*Library of Congress*] (LCLS)
MnWnSJL	St. John's Lutheran School, Winsted, MN [*Library symbol*] [*Library of Congress*] (LCLS)
MnWoCCS	Calvary Christian School, Worthington, MN [*Library symbol*] [*Library of Congress*] (LCLS)
MnWoCES	Central Elementary School, Worthington, MN [*Library symbol*] [*Library of Congress*] (LCLS)
MnWoH	Worthington Regional Hospital, Worthington, MN [*Library symbol*] [*Library of Congress*] (LCLS)
MnWoJH	Worthington Junior High, Worthington, MN [*Library symbol*] [*Library of Congress*] (LCLS)
MnWoLS	Lakeview School, Worthington, MN [*Library symbol*] [*Library of Congress*] (LCLS)
MnWoN	Nobles County Library, Worthington, MN [*Library symbol*] [*Library of Congress*] (LCLS)
MnWoP	Plum Creek Library System, Worthington, MN [*Library symbol*] [*Library of Congress*] (LCLS)
MnWoS	Worthington State Junior College [*Later, Worthington Community College*], Worthington, MN [*Library symbol*] [*Library of Congress*] (LCLS)
MnWoSH	Worthington Senior High School, Worthington, MN [*Library symbol*] [*Library of Congress*] (LCLS)
MnWoSMS	St. Mary's School, Worthington, MN [*Library symbol*] [*Library of Congress*] (LCLS)
MnWoWCS	Worthington Christian School, Worthington, MN [*Library symbol*] [*Library of Congress*] (LCLS)
MnWoWES	West Elementary School, Worthington, MN [*Library symbol*] [*Library of Congress*] (LCLS)
MnWp	Waite Park Public Library, Waite Park, MN [*Library symbol*] [*Library of Congress*] (LCLS)
MnWpS	St. Joseph's School, Waite Park, MN [*Library symbol*] [*Library of Congress*] (LCLS)
MNWR	Malheur National Wildlife Refuge [*Oregon*] (AD)
MNWR	Mattamuskeet National Wildlife Refuge [*North Carolina*] (AD)
MNWR	Merced National Wildlife Refuge [*California*] (AD)
MNWR	Mingo National Wildlife Refuge [*Missouri*] (AD)
MNWR	Minidoka National Wildlife Refuge [*Idaho*] (AD)
MNWR	Mississiquoi National Wildlife Refuge [*Vermont*] (AD)
MNWR	Modoc National Wildlife Refuge [*California*] (AD)
MNWR	Montezuma National Wildlife Refuge [*New York*] (AD)
MNWR	Moosehorn National Wildlife Refuge [*Maine*] (AD)
MnWrC	Willow River Camp Library, Willow River, MN [*Library symbol*] [*Library of Congress*] (LCLS)
MnWreS	Wrenshall Public School, Wrenshall, MN [*Library symbol*] [*Library of Congress*] (LCLS)
MnWriLE	Lincoln Elementary School, Wright, MN [*Library symbol*] [*Library of Congress*] (LCLS)
MnWrS	Willow River School, Willow River, MN [*Library symbol*] [*Library of Congress*] (LCLS)
MnWs	Winsted Public Library, Winsted, MN [*Library symbol*] [*Library of Congress*] (LCLS)
MnWsHT	Holy Trinity School, Winsted, MN [*Library symbol*] [*Library of Congress*] (LCLS)
MNWSL	Merchant Navy War Service League [*Australia*]
MnWspD	Dakota County Library, West St. Paul, MN [*Library symbol*] [*Library of Congress*] (LCLS)
MnWsPS	Winsted Public School, Winsted, MN [*Library symbol*] [*Library of Congress*] (LCLS)
MNX	Manx Airlines Ltd. [*British*] [*ICAO designator*] (FAAC)
Mnx	Manx Gaelic (AD)
MNX	University of Minnesota, Morris, Morris, MN [*OCLC symbol*] (OCLC)
MNY	Money
MNY	Mono Island [*Solomon Islands*] [*Airport symbol*] (OAG)
MNY	Monteynard [*France*] [*Seismograph station code, US Geological Survey*] (SEIS)
MNY	MONY Group [*NYSE symbol*] (SG)
MNY	Saint Mary's College, Winona, MN [*OCLC symbol*] (OCLC)
MNY	Taurus Municipal New York Holdings [*NYSE symbol*] (SPSG)
MNY	Taurus MuniNewYork Hldgs [*NYSE symbol*] (TTSB)
MNYRC	Metropolitan New York Rugby Conference (PSS)
MNZ	College of Saint Teresa, Winona, MN [*OCLC symbol*] (OCLC)
MNZ	Manassas [*Virginia*] [*Airport symbol*] (OAG)
MNZ	Manzanillo [*Mexico*] [*Seismograph station code, US Geological Survey*] (SEIS)
MnZE	Zimmerman Elementary School, Zimmerman, MN [*Library symbol*] [*Library of Congress*] (LCLS)
MNZIE	Member of the New Zealand Institution of Engineers (SAUO)
Mnzlo	Manzanillo (AD)
MO	Abbott Laboratories [*Research code symbol*]
MO	Calm Air International [*ICAO designator*] (AD)
MO	Macau [*ANSI two-letter standard code*] (CNC)
MO	Machine Operation (AFM)
Mo	Maestro GG1MasterGG2 [*Italian*] (AD)
MO	Magneto-Optic [*Computer science*]
MO	Magneto-Optical [*Physics*]
mo	Mail Order (AD)
MO	Mail Order [*Business term*]
MO	Maintenance and Operating [*Factor*] (NG)
MO	Maintenance Officer (MCD)
M/O	Maintenance/Organization (MCD)
M/O	Maintenance to Operation [*Ratio*]
m/o	Maintenance-to-Operation (AD)
MO	Maize Oil (PDAA)
MO	Major Objective (KSC)
mo	Major Objective (NAKS)
MO	Make Offer
MO	Making Objects [*Research test*] [*Psychology*]
MO	Malaoxon (LDT)
m/O	Male Oriental (AD)
MO	Managed Object [*Telecommunications*] (OSI)
MO	Management Object (SAUO)
MO	Management Office
MO	Management Operations (SPST)
MO	Management Order (NOAA)
MO	Managing Owner (RIMS)
M/O	Manned and Operational (MUGU)
MO	Manned Orbiter (MCD)
mo	Manned Orbiter [*NASA*] (NAKS)
MO	Manually Operated
mo	Manual Operation (AD)
MO	Manual Orientation (MCD)
mo	Manual Orientation (NAKS)
MO	Manual Output
MO	Manufacturer's Output
mo	Manufacturing Order (NAKS)
MO	Manufacturing Order (NASA)
MO	Manufacturing Outline
MO	March Order [*Military*]
MO	Marketing Organization (AD)
MO	Mark Off
MO	Mars Observer Mission (MCD)
MO	Mars Orbiter [*NASA*] (KSC)
mo	Masonry Opening (AD)
MO	Masonry Opening [*Technical drawings*]
mo	Mass Observation (AD)
MO	Mass Observation
MO	Master of Obstetrics
MO	Master of Oratory
MO	Master of Osteopathy
mo	Master Oscillator (AD)
MO	Master Oscillator [*Radio*]
MO	Mature Outlook (EA)
MO	Mechanical Obstruction (MELL)
MO	Medial Oblique [*View*] [*Radiology*] (DAVI)
MO	Medical Officer [*Military*]
MO	Medical Orderly (WDAA)
MO	Medium Oocyte
MO	Medulla Oblongata [*Medicine*] (MELL)
MO	Member Organisation (ACII)
MO	Memory Operation
MO	Memory Output [*Computer science*]
MO	Mesio-Occlusal [*Dentistry*]
MO	Mesityl Oxide [*Also, MSO*] [*Organic chemistry*]
MO	Metal-Organic (AAEL)
MO	Meteorological Office [*British*]
MO	Meteorology Officer (MUGU)
mo	Method of Operation (AD)
MO	Method of Operation
MO	Methoxime [*Organic chemistry*]
MO	Methyl Orange [*Organic chemistry*]
MO	Micro-Opaque
mo	Microoperation (MHDB)
MO	Micro-Osmometer
MO	Microwave Oven (PDAA)
MO	Middeck Overhead (MCD)
mo	Middeck Overhead (NAKS)
mO	Mid-Oxygen [*Beta-alumina crystallography*]
MO	Military Observer (WDAA)
MO	Military Operations [*British military*] (DMA)
MO	Military Orders Issued by the President as Commander in Chief of the Armed Forces [*A publication*] (DLA)

MO.............	Military Services [Diocesan abbreviation] [Maryland] (TOCD)
Mo.............	Mineral Oil (DB)
MO.............	Mineral Oil
MO.............	Mineral Order [Defense Minerals Exploration Administration] [Department of the Interior] [A publication] (DLA)
MO.............	Ministerstvo Oborony [Ministry of Defense] [Former USSR]
MO.............	Ministry Outstanding (SAUO)
MO.............	Minor-Oppenheim [Syndrome] [Medicine] (DB)
MO.............	Minute Output [Of heart]
m/o............	Mi Orden [My Order] [Spanish] (AD)
MO.............	Miscellaneous Operation (MUGU)
MO.............	Missile Officer (AAG)
mo.............	Mission Operations [NASA] (NAKS)
MO.............	Mission Operations [NASA]
MO.............	Mission Oriented
MO.............	Missouri [Postal code] (AFM)
Mo.............	Missouri (BEE)
Mo.............	Missourian (AD)
Mo.............	Missouri Reports [A publication] (AAGC)
Mo.............	Missouri State Library, Jefferson City, MO [Library symbol] [Library of Congress] (LCLS)
MO.............	Missouri Supreme Court Reports [1821-1956] [A publication] (DLA)
MO.............	Mitral Valve Opening [Cardiology]
MO.............	Mixed Oxide (NRCH)
MO.............	Mobile Object [Telecommunications] (OA)
MO.............	Mobile Station [Air Force]
Mo.............	Mode [Statistics]
MO.............	Moderato [Moderate Speed] [Music] (ADA)
MO.............	Moderator
Mo.............	Modern Orthodox (BJA)
Mo.............	Modern Reports [England] [A publication] (DLA)
MO.............	Modification Order (AFIT)
MO.............	Modulate Open [Nuclear energy] (NRCH)
MO.............	Modus Operandi [Police term for distinctive techniques used by criminals]
MO.............	Mohawk [Tire retread brand]
MO.............	Mohawk Airlines, Inc. [Obsolete]
MO.............	Molded [Construction]
mo.............	Molecular Orbital (AD)
MO.............	Molecular Orbital [Atomic physics]
Mo.............	Moloney [Strain] [Medicine] (DB)
Mo.............	Molybdenum [Chemical element]
mo.............	Moment (AD)
MO.............	Moment (DSUE)
MO.............	Monaco [IYRU nationality code] (IYR)
Mo.............	Monaldus [Flourished, 13th century] [Authority cited in pre-1607 legal work] (DSA)
Mo.............	Monday (CDAI)
MO.............	Money Order
MO.............	Monitor Output
MO.............	Monooxygenase [An enzyme]
MO.............	Month (AFM)
mo.............	Month (WDMC)
MO.............	Monthly Order [Navy]
m-o............	Months Old (AD)
MO.............	Months Old (MEDA)
Mo.............	Montreal Stock Exchange [Canada]
MO.............	Mooney Aircraft, Inc. [ICAO aircraft manufacturer identifier] (ICAO)
Mo.............	Moore's English Privy Council Reports [1836-62] [A publication] (DLA)
Mo.............	Moore's Indian Appeals [A publication] (DLA)
MO.............	Moral Obligation (MHDW)
MO.............	Moravian
MO.............	Morning
MO.............	Morphin (SAUS)
Mo.............	Morphine [Medicine] (WDAA)
M-O............	Morris-Oxford (AD)
MO.............	Morse Code Light [or Fog Signal] [Navigation signal]
mo.............	Moth Eaten (AD)
mo.............	Mother (GEAB)
MO.............	Mother
M/O............	Mother of (SAUS)
MO.............	Motion for Mandamus Overruled [Legal term] (DLA)
mo.............	Motor Operated (AD)
MO.............	Motor Operated (MSA)
MO.............	Moustache (DSUE)
MO.............	Mouth
mo.............	Move (NAKS)
MO.............	Move (NASA)
MO.............	Movement Orders
MO.............	Move Out (WDMC)
MO.............	Multi-Option (MCD)
MO.............	Mumps Orchitis [Medicine] (MELL)
MO.............	Municipal Offices (ROG)
MO.............	Murphy Oil Co. Ltd. [Toronto Stock Exchange symbol]
mo.............	Mustered Out (AD)
MO.............	Mustered Out [of military service]
MO.............	No Evidence of Distal Metastasis [Oncology] (DAVI)
MO.............	Philip Morris Companies, Inc. [NYSE symbol] (SPSG)
MO$_2$.........	Mixed Oxides
MO$_2$.........	Myocardial Oxygen Consumption [Cardiology] (MAE)
MO7............	Magneto-Optic 7 (IGQR)
MOA............	Made on Assembly
MOA............	Magnetic Optical Activity
MOA............	Mail Order Association of America (NTPA)

MOA............	Make on Arrival (NASA)
MOA............	Management Operations Audit [Navy] (NG)
MOA............	Manual-Off-Automatic (KSC)
MOA............	Marine Office of America (AD)
MOA............	Marine Officer's Attendant [British military] (DMA)
MOA............	Massachusetts Orthopaedic Association (SAUO)
MOA............	Matrix Output Amplifier
MOA............	McDonald's Operators' Association (EA)
MOA............	Mechanism of Action [Medicine] (DAVI)
MOA............	Medical Outreach for Armenians (EA)
moa............	Medium Observation Aircraft (AD)
MOA............	Medium Observation Aircraft
M o A.........	Memorandum of Agreement (AD)
MOA............	Memorandum of Agreement
MOA............	Memorandum of Assistance
MoA............	Memorandum of Association (WDAA)
MOA............	Method of Accomplishment (AFIT)
MOA............	Method of Adjustment [Aviation]
MOA............	Methods of Administration [Department of Education] (OICC)
MOA............	Metropolitan Opera Association (AD)
MOA............	Metropolitan Opera Auditions (AD)
MOA............	Michigan Optometric Association (SAUO)
MOA............	Microlensing Observations in Astrophysics (SAUS)
MOA............	Microwave Oven Association (BUAC)
MOA............	Military Assistance Program Order Amendment (AFM)
MOA............	Military Operations Area [FAA] (TAG)
MoA............	Ministry of Agriculture [British] (AD)
MOA............	Ministry of Aviation [British]
MOA............	Minnesota Orchestral Association (AD)
moa............	Minute of Angle (AD)
MOA............	Minute of Angle
MOA............	Misr Overseas Airways [Egypt]
moa............	Missile Optical Alignment (AD)
MOA............	Missile Optical Alignment
MOA............	Missouri Botanical Garden, St. Louis, MO [OCLC symbol] (OCLC)
MOA............	Moa [Cuba] [Airport symbol] (OAG)
MOA............	Modern Operating Agreement [Labor negotiations]
MOA............	Molln [Austria] [Seismograph station code, US Geological Survey] (SEIS)
MOA............	Monoamine Oxidase (MELL)
MOA............	Mountain Lake Resources, Inc. [Vancouver Stock Exchange symbol]
moa............	Mud on Airstrip (AD)
MOA............	Municipality of Anchorage (SAUO)
MOA............	Municipal Officers' Association (ROG)
MoA............	Museum of Australia (BUAC)
MOA............	Music Operators of America [Later, AMOA] (EA)
MOAA...........	Mail Order Association of America (EA)
MOAA...........	Marina Operators Association of America (NTPA)
MOAA...........	Municipal Officers' Association of Australia
MOA/ACD.......	Ministry of Agriculture/ Agriculture Communication Division (SAUO)
MOA/AIC.......	Ministry of Agriculture/ Agricultural Inputs Corp. (SAUS)
MOA/AIC.......	Ministry of Agriculture/ Agricultural Inputs Corporation (SAUO)
MOA/APROSC...	Ministry of Agriculture/ Agricultural Projects Service Centre (SAUO)
MoAB..........	Monoclonal Antibody [Immunochemistry]
MOABWEPO...	Members of Anything Bill [Clinton] Was Ever Part Of [Pronounced "Mo-ab-wee-po"]
MOAC..........	Ministry of Agriculture and Cooperatives [Thailand] (BUAC)
MOACA.........	Ministry of Aviation Cataloguing Authority (SAUO)
MOA/CDB.......	Ministry of Agriculture/Cotton Development Board (SAUO)
MOAD..........	Methotrexate, Oncovin [Vincristine] L-asparaginase, Dexamethasone [Antineoplastic drug regimen] (DAVI)
MOA/DDC.......	Ministry of Agriculture/Dairy Development Corp. (SAUO)
MOA/DFAMS...	Ministry of Agriculture/ Department of Food and Agricultural Marketing Services (SAUO)
MOA/DLDAH...	Ministry of Agriculture/ Department of Livestock Development & Animal Health (SAUO)
MO Admin Code...	Missouri Code of State Regulations [A publication] (DLA)
MO Admin Reg...	Missouri Register [A publication] (DLA)
MOA/DOA.......	Ministry of Agriculture/ Department of Agriculture (SAUO)
MOA/DOAD...	DEPARTMENT OF AGRICULTURE DEVELOPMENT (SAUS)
MOA/DOAD...	Ministry of Agriculture/ Department of Agriculture Development (SAUO)
MOA/DOF.......	Ministry of Agriculture/ Department of Fisheries (SAUO)
MOA/DOH.......	Ministry of Agriculture/ Department of Horticulture (SAUO)
MOA/DOI.......	Ministry of Agriculture/ Department of Irrigation (SAUO)
MOA/DOL.......	Ministry of Agriculture/ Department of Livestock (SAUO)
MOADS.........	Maneuver Oriented Ammunition Distribution System (SAUS)
MOADS.........	Montgomery Air Defense Sector [of SAGE] (MUGU)
MOAE..........	Mitigation of Adverse Effect [Environmental science] (COE)
MOAF..........	Meteorological and Oceanographic Analyst/Forecaster [Course] (DNAB)
MOAF..........	Ministry of Agriculture and Forests [Republic of Korea] (BUAC)
MOA/JDTC...	Ministry of Agriculture/Jute Development and Trading Corp. (SAUS)
MOA/JDTC...	Ministry of Agriculture/Jute Development and Trading Corporation (SAUO)
Moak..........	Moak's English Reports [A publication] (DLA)
Moak (Eng)...	Moak's English Reports [A publication] (DLA)
Moak Eng Rep...	Moak's English Reports [A publication] (DLA)
Moak Und....	Moak's Edition of Underhill on Torts [A publication] (DLA)
Moak Underh Torts...	Moak's Edition of Underhill on Torts [A publication] (DLA)
Moak Van S Pl...	Moak's Edition of Van Santvoord's Equity Pleading [A publication] (DLA)
MOAL..........	Mail-Order Action Line [Direct marketing association] (WDMC)
MOALC........	Mobile Air Logistics Center [Air Force]
MOAMA........	Mobile Air Materiel Area

MOA/NARC...	Ministry of Agriculture/ National Agricultural Research Centre (SAUO)
MO&DA.......	Mission Operations and Data Analysis (ACAE)
MO&DS.......	Mission Operations and Data System (SAUO)
MO & DSD...	Mission Operations and Data Systems Directorate (SSD)
MO & G	Master of Obstetrics and Gynaecology
MO & O	Memorandum Opinion and Order (NTCM)
Mo & P........	Moore and Payne's English Common Pleas Reports [*A publication*] (DLA)
Mo & R........	Moody and Robinson's English Nisi Prius Reports [*A publication*] (DLA)
Mo & S........	Moore and Scott's English Common Pleas Reports [*1831-34*] [*A publication*] (DLA)
Mo & Sc	Moore and Scott's English Common Pleas Reports [*1831-34*] [*A publication*] (DLA)
MOANG.......	Missouri Air National Guard (MUSM)
MO Ann Stat (Vernon)...	Vernon's Annotated Missouri Statutes [*A publication*] (DLA)
MOA/NTDC..	Ministry of Agriculture/Nepal Tea Development Corp. (SAUS)
MOA/NTDC..	Ministry of Agriculture/ Nepal Tea Development Corporation (SAUO)
MOAP	Management Observation Assessment Program (SAUO)
MO Ap	Missouri Appeal Reports [*A publication*] (DLA)
MO App	Missouri Appeal Reports [*A publication*] (DLA)
MO Appeals...	Missouri Appeal Reports [*A publication*] (DLA)
MO App (KC)...	Missouri Appeal Reports [*Kansas City*] [*A publication*] (DLA)
MO App Rep...	Missouri Appeal Reports [*A publication*] (DLA)
MO Apps......	Missouri Appeal Reports [*A publication*] (DLA)
MO App (St L)...	Missouri Appeal Reports [*St. Louis*] [*A publication*] (DLA)
MO AR........	Missouri Appellate Reporter [*A publication*] (DLA)
MOARS	Mobilization Assignment Reserve Section [*Military*]
moAt	Mainstream of American Thought (AD)
MOAT..........	Methods of Appraisal and Test (MHDB)
MOAT..........	Minewarfare Operational Analysis Tool (SAUS)
MOAT..........	Missile on Aircraft Test
moat	Missile-on-Aircraft Testing [*Military*] (AD)
MOAT..........	Mission Opportunities for Airship Technology (ACAE)
MOATL.........	Modal Acoustic Transmission Loss (MCD)
MOATRS	MAJCOM On-Line Aerospace Vehicle Training Report System (SAUO)
MOATS	Message Originating and Terminating Station (ACAE)
MOB............	Mail Order Buyer (WDMC)
MOB............	Main Olfactory Bulb [*Anatomy*]
MOB............	Main Operating Base
MOB............	Main Operations Base (SAUO)
mob	Make or Buy (AD)
MOB............	Make or Buy [*Economics*]
MOB............	Man-Overboard
MOB............	Master of Organizational Behavior (GAGS)
MOB............	Medical Office Building (DAVI)
MOB............	Menlo Park [*California*] [*Seismograph station code, US Geological Survey*] (SEIS)
MOB............	Methane-Oxidizing Bacteria
MOB............	Military Order of Battle (SAUO)
MOB............	Missile Order of Battle (AFM)
MOB............	Mobil Corp. [*NYSE symbol*] [*Toronto Stock Exchange symbol*] (SPSG)
mob	Mobile (AD)
MOB............	Mobile [*Alabama*] [*Airport symbol*]
Mob	Mobile, Alabama [*Maritime abbreviation*] (AD)
MOB............	Mobile Operating Base (ACAE)
mob	Mobile Vulgus [*Disorderly Group of People*] [*Latin*] (AD)
MOB............	Mobility [*MTMC*] (TAG)
MOB............	Mobility Status (SAUO)
MOB............	Mobilization [*or Mobilize*] (AFM)
Mob	Mobley's Contested Election Cases, United States House of Representatives [*1882-89*] [*A publication*] (DLA)
MOB............	Mock-Up Board [*Navy*] (AFIT)
MOB............	Modification of Benefits [*Health insurance*] (GHCT)
MOB............	Money-Order Business
MOB............	Montreux-Oberland-Bernois [*Railway*] [*Canada*] (AD)
MOB............	Municipals over Bonds [*Investment term*]
MOB............	Mustargen [*Nitrogen mustard*], Oncovin , Bleomycin [*Vincristine*] [*Antineoplastic drug regimen*]
Mob	National Mobilization Committee to end the War in Viet-Nam (SAUO)
MOB............	Southwest Baptist College, Bolivar, MO [*OCLC symbol*] (OCLC)
MOBA	Military Operations in Built-Up Areas
MOBA	Museum of Bad Art (ADWA)
MOBAC........	Monterey Bay Area Cooperative Library System [*Library network*]
MOBAS	Model Basin
MOBAT	Mobile Battalion Antitank Gun [*British military*] (DMA)
Mo' Bay	Mobile Bay, Alabama [*Montego Bay, Jamaica*] (AD)
MOBC2	Mobilization Command and Control (SAUO)
MOBCOM......	Mobile Command [*Canada*] (AD)
mobcom	Mobile Communications (AD)
MOBCOM.....	Mobile Communications
Mob Con......	Mobilising Control (WDAA)
MOBCON.....	Mobilization Construction Plan [*Military*] (NVT)
MOBCON.....	Mobilization Movement Control [*MTMC*] (TAG)
MOBCONBAT..	Mobile Construction Battalion [*Navy*] (DNAB)
MOBCTR	Mobilization Center (DNAB)
MOBD	Mediterranean Oceanic Data Base (SAUO)
MOBDES......	Mobilization Designation [*or Designee*]
MOBDET......	Mobility Deployment Planning System (SAUO)
MOBDIC.......	Mobile Digital Computer
MOBED	Mobile Education Demonstration
MoBeHi........	Scott County Historical Society, Benton, MO [*Library symbol*] [*Library of Congress*] (LCLS)
MOBERS	Mobilization Equipment Redistribution System
mobeu	Mobile Emergency Unit (AD)
MOBEU	Mobile Emergency Unit (NOAA)
MOBEX	Mobile Excursion (MCD)
MOBEX	Mobile Exploration [*NASA*]
MOBEX	Mobility Test Exercise [*Military*]
MOBIC	Mobility of Blind and elderly people Interacting with Computers (SAUO)
MOBIDA.......	Mobile Data Acquisition System (MCD)
MOBIDAC.....	Mobile Data Acquisition System
MOBIDACS...	Mobile Data Acquisition System (AD)
mobidic	Mobile Digital Computer (AD)
MOBIDIC......	Mobile Digital Computer [*Sylvania Electric Products Co.*]
MOBIDICK....	Multivariable On-Line Bilingual Dictionary Kit (SAUO)
MOB-III........	Methotrexate, Oncovin [*Vineristine*], Bleomycin [*Antineoplastic drug regimen*] (DAVI)
MOB-III........	Mitomycin C, Oncovin [*Vincristine*], Bleomycin, Cisplatin [*Antineoplastic drug regimen*]
Mobil	Mobil Corp. [*Associated Press*] (SAG)
mobil	Mobility (AD)
MOBIL	Mobility
MOBILAB	Mobile Rapid Photo Processing Laboratory (ACAE)
Mobilarian....	Mobile Branch Librarian (AD)
mobilary	Mobile Library (AD)
MOBILE.......	Mobile Source Emissions Model (SAUO)
MOBILE5A	Mobile Source Emission Factor Model (SAUO)
MOBILESAT...	Mobile Satellite Corp. [*King Of Prussia, PA*] [*Telecommunications*] (TSSD)
MOBILHY	Hydrological Atmospheric Pilot Experiment (SAUO)
MOBIS	Management-Oriented Budget Information System
mobl	Macro-Oriented Business Language [*Computer science*] (AD)
MOBL..........	Macro-Oriented Business Language [*Computer science*]
MOBL..........	Main Operating Base LASER
Mobl	Mobley's Contested Election Cases, United States House of Representatives [*1882-89*] [*A publication*] (DLA)
mobl	Mopliert [*Furnished*] [*German*] (AD)
MobIAm	Mobile America Corp. [*Associated Press*] (SAG)
MOBLAS	Mobile Laser (ACAE)
moblas	Mobile LASER Satellite Tracking Station (AD)
Mobley	Mobley Environmental Services [*Associated Press*] (SAG)
MobIGs	Mobile Gas Service Corp. [*Associated Press*] (SAG)
mob lib	Mobile Librarian (AD)
MobIM	Mobile Mini, Inc. [*Associated Press*] (SAG)
MobIMin	Mobile Mini, Inc. [*Associated Press*] (SAG)
mob lt..........	Man Overboard and Breakdown Light (AD)
MOBMAN......	Mobilization Manpower Planning System [*DoD*]
MobMda	MobileMedia Corp. [*Associated Press*] (SAG)
MOBMDR......	Mobilization Master Data Record [*Army*]
Mob O	Mobilising Officer (WDAA)
MOBO	Mother Board (VLIE)
MOBOL	Mohawk Business-Oriented Language [*Mohawk Data Systems*]
MoBoIS	Southwest Baptist College, Bolivar, MO [*Library symbol*] [*Library of Congress*] (LCLS)
MOBOT	Mobile Remote-Controlled Robot
mobot	Mobile Robot (AD)
MOBOT	Mobile Robot (VLIE)
MOBOT	Modular Robot
MOBPERS....	Mobilization Personnel Processing System (SAUO)
MOBPERSACS...	Mobilization Personnel Structure and Composition System [*DoD*]
MOBPLANS...	Mobility Plans (SAUO)
MoBr..........	Brentwood Public Library, Brentwood, MO [*Library symbol*] [*Library of Congress*] (LCLS)
MOBRASOP...	Mobilization Requirements in Support of the Army Strategic Objectives Plan
MOBREM	Mobilization Base Requirements Model (SAUO)
MOBS	Mobile Hospitals [*Military slang*]
MOBS	Mobile Ocean Basing System (PDAA)
MOBS	Moebius Syndrome [*Medicine*] (DMAA)
MOBS	Multiple-Orbit Bombardment System
MOBSCOPE...	Mobilization Shipments Configured for Operation Planning and Execution [*MTMC*] (TAG)
MOBSF	Mobility Support Flight [*Military*]
MOBSS	Mobility Support Squadron [*Air Force*]
MOBSS	Mobilization Support System [*MTMC*] (TAG)
MOBSSL-UAF...	Merritt and Miller's Own Block Structured Simulation Language, Unpronounceable Acronym For [*1969*] [*Computer science*] (CSR)
MOBSSq	Mobility Support Squadron [*Air Force*]
MOBSUPPGRU...	Mobile Support Group [*Military*] (DNAB)
MOBTA	Mobilization Table of Distribution and Allowances (AD)
MOBTB	Mobilization Troop Basis [*Army*] (AABC)
MOBTDA	Mobilization Table of Distribution and Allowances [*Military*] (AABC)
MOBTR	Mobile Trainer
MOBTRAN....	Mobilization and Deployment Transportability (SAUO)
MOBU	Mobilization Base Units
MOBULA	Model Building Language [*Programming language*] (IEEE)
mobula	Model-Building Language (AD)
Mob Wkshp...	Mobile Workshop (SAUO)
MOBY	Marine Optical Buoy (ROAS)
MOBYC	My Own Bloody Yacht Club [*Founded in England; registered with Lloyds of London*]
MOC............	Magnetic Optic Converter
MOC............	Maintenance Operational Check
MOC............	Maintenance Operations Center [*Military*]

MOC............	Maintenance Operations Control [*Canadian Airlines International*]
MOC............	Makapuu Oceanic Center [*Hawaii*] (AD)
MOC............	Management and Operating Contractor (ODBW)
MOC............	Management of Change
MOC............	Management-Oriented Computing (MHDB)
MOC............	Manual Operations Control
moc	Manufacturing Other Charges (AD)
MOC............	Manufacturing Outreach Center
MOC............	Marcos Owners Club [*Formerly, Marcos Club*] (EA)
MOC............	Margin of Control [*Environmental science*] (COE)
MOC............	Margin of Criticality [*Environmental science*] (COE)
moc	Marine Operation Center (NAKS)
MOC............	Marine Operation Center [*NASA*] (NASA)
MOC............	Market on Close [*Investment term*] (NUMA)
MOC............	Marlin Owners' Club (EA)
MOC............	Mars Observer Camera
MOC............	Mars Orbiter Camera
MOC............	Massachusetts Oilheat Council (SAUO)
MOC............	Master Operational Computer [*or Controller*]
moc	Master Operation Control (AD)
MOC............	Master Operations Center
MOC............	Master Operations Console
MOC............	Master Operations Control
MOC............	Master Ordnance Configuration File [*Navy*]
MOC............	Materials Operations Center (SAUO)
MOC............	Materiel Obligation Code (ACAE)
MOC............	Mathematical Operations Computer
MOC............	Mauna Olu College [*Maui*] (AD)
MOC............	Maximum Operational Capacity [*Chemical engineering*]
MOC............	Maximum Oxygen Consumption
MOC............	Mechanical Off-Machine Coated Paper (DGA)
MOC............	Memorandum of Conditions
MOC............	Memorandum of Cooperation (SAUO)
MOC............	Memory Operating Characteristic [*Computer science*] (IEEE)
MOC............	Meridional Overturning Cell (SAUS)
MOC............	Merland Explorations Ltd. [*Toronto Stock Exchange symbol*]
MOC............	Messerschmitt Owners Club (EA)
MOC............	Method of Characteristics [*Equilibrium flow*]
MOC............	Metropolitan Owners' Club [*Woking, Surrey, England*] (EAIO)
MOC............	Microelectronics and Computer (SAUO)
MOC............	Microwave Oven Control (TIMI)
MOC............	Mid Ocean Limited [*NYSE symbol*] (SAG)
MOC............	Mid Ocean Ltd [*NYSE symbol*] (TTSB)
MOC............	Mid-Ohio Conference (PSS)
MOC............	Military Occupation Code (MCD)
MOC............	Military Order of the Carabao (EA)
MOC............	Minimal Oxygen Consumption
MOC............	Minimum Obstacle Clearance [*Aviation*] (FAAC)
MOC............	Minimum Operating Capability (SAUO)
MOC............	Minimum Operational Characteristics
MOC............	Minister of Conservation (SAUO)
MOC............	Ministry of Communications (CINC)
MOC............	Ministry of Construction [*Republic of Korea*] (BUAC)
MOC............	Missile Operation Center [*Air Force*]
MOC............	Missionaries of Charity [*Australia*]
MOC............	Mission Operation Computer
MOC............	Mission Operations Complex [*NASA*] (KSC)
moc	Mission Operations Computer (AD)
MOC............	Missions Operations Center (or Centre) (SAUO)
MOC............	Mobile Oil Cooler
MOC............	Mobile Operations Center [*Air Force*] (DOMA)
MOC............	Mobile-Originated Call (CGWS)
moc	Mocassin (AD)
MOC............	Moccasin
MOC............	Modern Operating Contract [*Automibile industry labor relations*]
MOC............	Modular Operations Centre (SAUS)
MOC............	Modular Organization Charting (PDAA)
MOC............	Montes Claros [*Brazil*] [*Airport symbol*] (OAG)
MOC............	Morris College, Sumter, SC [*Inactive*] [*OCLC symbol*] (OCLC)
MOC............	Mother of the Chapel [*Unions*] [*British*] (DI)
MOC............	Multifunction Operator Console (SAUS)
MOC............	Multiple Ocular Coloboma [*Medicine*] (DMAA)
MoC.............	Museum of the Confederacy (SAUO)
MOC............	Mustang Owners Club (EA)
MOC............	Myanma Oil Corporation (SAUO)
MOC............	Supreme Pup Tent, Military Order of the Cootie (EA)
MOCA	Merisel Open Computing Alliance (SAUO)
MOCA	Methotrexate, Oncovin [*Vincristine*], Cyclophosphamide, Adriamycin [*Antineoplastic drug regimen*]
MOCA	Methylenebis(ortho-chloroaniline) [*Also, MBOCA*] [*Organic chemistry*]
moca	Minimum Obstruction Clearance Altitude (AD)
MOCA	Minimum Obstruction Clearance Altitude [*Aviation*]
MOCA	Missouri Classical Association (SAUO)
MOCA	Mitsubishi Owner's Club of America
MOCA	Mixed Object Document Content Architecture [*Computer science*] (CIST)
MOCA	Montezuma Castle National Monument
MOCA	Museum of Contemporary Art [*Los Angeles*]
MOCAM	Mobile Checkout and Maintenance (AAG)
mocamp	Motor Camp (AD)
MOCAN.......	Motor Can
MoCanC.......	Culver-Stockton College, Canton, MO [*Library symbol*] [*Library of Congress*] (LCLS)
MOCAPT	Missouri Center for Agricultural Products Technology (BUAC)
MOCAS	Mechanization of Contract Administration Service (MCD)
MOCAT	Measurement and Observation of Clear Air Turbulence (ACAE)
MOCC	Master Operations Control Center (SAA)
MOCC	Memory-Operating Characteristic Curve (DIPS)
MOCC	Metal-Oxygen Cluster Compounds [*Chemistry*]
MOCC	MG Octagon Car Club [*Formerly, Octagon Car Club*] (EA)
MOCC	Miniature Operations Control Center (SAUO)
MOCC	Mission Operations Control Center (SSD)
MOCC	Mobile Operations Command Center (DOMA)
MOCC	Mobile Operations Control Centre (SAUO)
MOCCA	, Cyclophosphamide, Alkeran [*Lomustine*] [*Melphalan*] [*Antineoplastic drug regimen*]
MOCCA	Mobile Computing & Communication Appliance [*Digital Equipment Corp.*]
MoCCA.........	Mobile Computing and Communication Appliance [*Digital Equipment Corp.*]
MOCCA	Mobile Operations Center for Communication and Analysis (SAUO)
MOCCAC	Missouri Community College Athletic Conference (PSS)
MOCCC	Massachusetts Organized Crime Control Council (AD)
MOccThy......	Master of Occupational Therapy (ADA)
MOcE	Master of Oceanographic Engineering (GAGS)
MOCEM.......	Meteorological and Oceanographic Equipment Maintenance Course (DNAB)
MOCERT	Motorcycle Certification Data (SAUO)
MOCF..........	Maintenance Operations Control File (MCD)
MOCF..........	Manchester Open College Federation [*British*] (AIE)
MOCF..........	Mission Operations Computational Facilities [*NASA*] (NASA)
MoCg	Cape Girardeau Public Library, Cape Girardeau, MO [*Library symbol*] [*Library of Congress*] (LCLS)
MoCgS.........	Southeast Missouri State University, Cape Girardeau, MO [*Library symbol*] [*Library of Congress*] (LCLS)
MoCheL	Logan College of Chiropractic, Chesterfield, MO [*Library symbol*] [*Library of Congress*] (LCLS)
mochwr........	Mochaware (VRA)
MOCI	Ministry of Commerce and Industry [*British*] (AD)
MOCI	Ministry of Commerce and Industry [*Republic of Korea*] (BUAC)
MOCI	Mound City Group National Monument
MOCI	Mustang Owners Club International (EA)
MOCIC	Molecular Orbital Constraint of Interaction Coordinates [*Atomic physics*]
MOCL	Metz Owners Club Library (EA)
MoCli..........	Henry County Library, Clinton, MO [*Library symbol*] [*Library of Congress*] (LCLS)
MoCIS.........	Saint Louis Junior College, Clayton, MO [*Library symbol*] [*Library of Congress*] [*Obsolete*] (LCLS)
MOCM	Missile Out of Commission for Maintenance (MUGU)
MOCN	Mid Ocean Ltd. [*NASDAQ symbol*] (SAG)
MOCN	Modern Controls, Inc. [*Associated Press*] (SAG)
MOCNA	Maserati Owners Club of North America (EAIO)
MOCNA	Metropolitan Owners Club of North America (EA)
MOCNESS....	Multiple Opening-Closing Net and Environmental Sensing System [*For collecting marine samples*]
MOCO	Machinery Overhaul Co.
MOCO	Missile Operations Control Officer (AAG)
MOCO	MOCON, Inc. [*NASDAQ symbol*] (SG)
MOCO	Modern Controls [*NASDAQ symbol*] (TTSB)
MOCO	Modern Controls, Inc. [*NASDAQ symbol*] (NQ)
MoCoC.........	Christian College, Columbia, MO [*Library symbol*] [*Library of Congress*] (LCLS)
MOCOCO.....	Movement Coordinating Committee (SAUO)
Mo Code Regs...	State of Missouri Code of State Regulations Annotated [*A publication*] (AAGC)
MOCODES....	Mobile Coastal Defense System (MCD)
MoCoGS	Church of Jesus Christ of Latter-Day Saints, Genealogical Society Library, Columbia Missouri Branch, Columbia, MO [*Library symbol*] [*Library of Congress*] (LCLS)
MoCoJ	Joint Collection, Western Historical Manuscript Collection and State Historical,Columbia, MO [*Library symbol*] [*Library of Congress*] (LCLS)
MoCom........	Mobile Command (AD)
MOCOM	Mobility Command [*AMC*]
MOCOMMDOPS...	DEPARTMENT OF POSTAL SERVICES (SAUS)
MOCOMMDOPS...	Ministry of Communications Department of Postal Services (SAUO)
MOCOMMDOPS...	Ministry of Communications/Department of Postal Services (SAUS)
MOCOMM/NTC...	Ministry of Communications/Nepal Telecommunications Corp. (SAUS)
MOCON.......	Mobile Repair Parts Container
MoConA.......	Conception Abbey and Seminary, Conception, MO [*Library symbol*] [*Library of Congress*] (LCLS)
MoCoS.........	Stephens College, Columbia, MO [*Library symbol*] [*Library of Congress*] (LCLS)
MoCoV........	Harry S Truman Memorial Veterans Hospital, Columbia, MO [*Library symbol*] [*Library of Congress*] (LCLS)
mocp	Missile Out of Commission for Parts [*Military*] (AD)
MOCP	Missile Out of Commission for Parts (AFM)
MOCP	Mission Operational Computer Program (SAUO)
MOCR	Metz Owners Club Register (EA)
mocr	Mission Operation Control Room (AD)
MOCR	Mission Operations Control Room
MOCR	Moores Creek National Military Park
MOCS	MacPhail Operant Chambers (SAUO)
MOCS	Managed Object Conformance Statement [*Telecommunications*] (OSI)
MOCS	Master Operations Control System (KSC)

MOCS	Microsoft Official Curriculum Seminar (SAUO)
MOCS	Military Order of Columbia's Shield (EA)
MOCS	Missile Operational Communications Systems (ACAE)
MOCS	Mission Operation and Control Subsystem (ACAE)
MOCS	Mons Officer Cadet School (SAUO)
MOCS	Multichannel Ocean Color Scanner (ACAE)
mocs	Multichannel Ocean Color Sensor (NAKS)
mocs	Multichannel Ocean Color Sensor [*NASA*]
MOCS	Multiple Output Control System (ECII)
MoCStP	Saint Paul's College, Concordia, MO [*Library symbol*] [*Library of Congress*] (LCLS)
MOCSW	Monitor and Operations Control Software Subsystem [*Space Flight Operations Facility, NASA*]
MOCT	Mean Overhaul Cycle Time [*Quality control*] (MCD)
MOC/TPC	Ministry of Commerce/Trade Promotion Centre (SAUO)
MOCV	Manual Oxygen Control Valve (NASA)
MO-CVD	Metal-Organic Chemical Vapor Deposition [*Also, MO-VPE, OM-CVD, OM-VPE*] [*Semiconductor technology*]
MOD	Drury College, Springfield, MO [*OCLC symbol*] (OCLC)
Mod	Made Over Democrat [*Facetious translation referring to Mods - Moderate Republicans*]
MOD	Magnetic Optical Display
MOD	Magneto-Optical Disc [*Digital audio technology*]
MOD	Magneto-Optic Disk [*Computer science*] (CIST)
MOD	Mail-Order Delivery
MOD	Mail Order Department [*Business term*]
MOD	Maintenance of Deception
MOD	Maintenance of Defense (ACAE)
MOD	Management and Organization Division [*Environmental Protection Agency*] (GFGA)
MOD	Manager on Duty
MOD	Manned Orbital Development Station [*See also MODS, MOSS, MTSS*] [*Air Force/NASA*]
MOD	Manpower and Organization Division [*Air Force*]
MOD	Manual Overdrive [*Automotive engineering*]
MOD	Manufacturers Operations Division [*Environmental Protection Agency*] (GFGA)
MOD	Mapping of Disease
MOD	March of Dimes (HGEN)
MOD	March on Drugs [*An association*]
MOD	Marine Operations Division [*Environmental Protection Agency*] (GFGA)
Mod	Marxist on Drugs [*Mods - Facetious translation referring to Moderate Republicans*]
MOD	Master of Organizational Development (GAGS)
MoD	Masters of Deception (SAUS)
MOD	Masters of Disaster [*Computer hacker gang*]
MOD	Masters of Downloading [*Computer science*] (VLIE)
MOD	Maturity Onset Diabetes [*Medicine*]
MOD	Maximum Operating Depth (SAUO)
MOD	Medical Officer of the Day [*Military*]
MOD	Medical Officer on Duty (DAVI)
MOD	Medicine, Osteopathy, and Dentistry [*HEW program*]
MOD	Memorandum of Decision (COE)
MOD	Mesial, Occlusal, and Distal [*Describes location of openings in a carious tooth*] [*Dentistry*]
m-o-d	Mesial-Occlusal-Distal [*Dentistry*] (AD)
MOD	Message Output Description [*Computer science*]
MOD	Message Output Descriptor [*Computer science*] (CIST)
MOD	Metallo-Organic Deposition [*Materials technology*]
MOD	Method of Delivery
MOD	Microfilm-Output Device
MOD	Microsoft Office 2000 Developer [*Microsoft*]
MOD	Microwave Oscillating Diode (MCD)
MOD	Military Airlift Command Operational Directive (SAUO)
MOD	Military Obligation Designator
MOD	Military Orbital Development System [*See also MODS, MOSS, MTSS*] [*Air Force/NASA*]
Mod	Mindless Operative of the Devil [*Mods - Facetious translation referring to Moderate Republicans*]
MOD	Ministry of Defence [*British*]
MOD	Ministry of Overseas Development [*British*] (ILCA)
MOD	Minuteman Operating Directive (SAA)
MOD	Miscellaneous Obligation Document
MOD	Mission Objectives Document (MCD)
MOD	Mission Operating Directive (SAUO)
MOD	Mission Operations Director [*NASA*] (KSC)
MOD	Mission Operations Directorate (SAUO)
MOD	Mobile Obstacle Detachment (MCD)
MOD	Mobility Opportunity and Development
mod	modality [*Physical therapy*] (DAVI)
MOD	Modal (Verb) [*Linguistics*]
MOD	Modatech Systems, Inc. [*Vancouver Stock Exchange symbol*]
mod	Model (AD)
MOD	Model (KSC)
MOD	Modem (SAUO)
MOD	Moderate [*or Moderator*] (AABC)
mod	Moderate (AD)
MOD	Moderate Room [*Travel industry*] (TRID)
mod	Moderato (SHCU)
MOD	Moderato [*Moderate Speed*] [*Music*]
Mod	Modern (AD)
mod	Modern (AD)
MOD	Modern
Mod	Modernist (DIAR)

Mod	Modern Reports [*England*] [*A publication*] (DLA)
MOD	Modesto [*California*] [*Airport symbol*] (OAG)
mod	Modification (AD)
MOD	Modification [*or Modify*] (AFM)
MOD	Modifier [*Linguistics*]
MOD	Modiim [*Israel*] [*Later, AMT*] [*Geomagnetic observatory code*]
mod	Modular (AD)
MOD	Modular Observation Device (RDA)
MOD	Modulation [*Telecommunications*] (KSC)
MOD	Modulator (CET)
mod	Modulator (IDOE)
MOD	Modulator-Demodulator [*Telecommunications*] (MCD)
mod	Modulo [*Mathematics*] (CDE)
mod	Modulus (IDOE)
MOD	Modulus
MOD	Money-Order Department
MOD	Month of Detachment
MOD	Motor-Operated Disconnect [*Nuclear energy*] (NRCH)
MOD	Moving Domain Memories [*Computer science*] (MDG)
Mod	Style's English King's Bench Reports [*1646-55*] [*A publication*] (DLA)
MOD	Supreme Industries [*AMEX symbol*] (SAG)
MOD10	Modulus 10 Check Digit [*Computer science*]
MODA	Ministry of Defense and Aviation (MCD)
MODA	ModaCad, Inc. [*NASDAQ symbol*] (SAG)
MODA	Motion Detector and Alarm [*Army*]
MODABUND	Mosquito Data Bank of the University of Notre Dame
MODAC	Meteorological Observation and Data Assimilation Center (SAUO)
MODAC	Mountain System Digital Automatic Computer
MODACOM	Mobile Data Communication (SAUO)
MODACS	Modular Data Acquisition and Control System [*or Subsystem*] [*Modular Computing Systems, Inc.*]
MOD(AD)	Ministry of Defence (Army Department) [*British*]
Mod Am Law	Modern American Law [*A publication*] (DLA)
MODAP	Modified Apollo [*NASA*] (MCD)
MODAP	Multiple Operational Data Acquisition Program [*Computer science*]
MODAPS	Maintenance and Operational Data Presentation Study (AAG)
MODAPS	Modal Data Acquisition and Processing System
MODAPTS	Modular Arrangement of Predetermined Time Standards
Modarco	Modern Art Collection S.A. (SAUO)
MODARI	Methods of Defeating Advanced RADAR Threats [*NASA*] (NAKS)
MODART	Methods of Defeating Advanced RADAR Threats (NASA)
MODAS	Maintenance and Operational Data Access Subsystem (SAUO)
MODAS	Maintenance and Operational Data Access System (ACAE)
MODAS	Model for Intertheater Deployment by Air & Sea (SAUO)
MODAS	Modular Data Acquisition System (SAUS)
MODAS	Multidirectional Osmotic Drug Absorption System [*Medicine*]
modasm	Modular Air-to-Surface Missile [*Military*] (AD)
MODASM	Modular Air-to-Surface Missile (MCD)
MODATS	Mohawk Data Transmission System (MCD)
MODAW	ModaCAD Inc. Wrrt [*NASDAQ symbol*] (TTSB)
MODB	Master Object Data Base (SAUS)
m-o-d-b	Mesial-Occlusal-Distal-Buccal [*Dentistry*] (AD)
MODB	Military Occupational Data Bank [*Later, AOSP*] (AABC)
MODBSC	Modular Boresight Computer (ACAE)
MODCA	Mixed Object Document Content Architecture [*Computer science*] (BTTJ)
MO:DCA	Mixed Object: Document Content Architecure [*Computer science*] (CDE)
MODCAR	Modified Owners and Drivers Corp. for the Advancement of Racing (EA)
Mod Cas	Modern Cases [*6 Modern Reports*] [*1702-45*] [*A publication*] (DLA)
Mod Cas L & Eq	Modern Cases at Law and Equity [*8, 9 Modern Reports*] [*1721-55*] [*A publication*] (DLA)
Mod Cas per Far	Modern Cases Tempore Holt, by Farresley [*7 Modern Reports*] [*A publication*] (DLA)
Mod Cas T Holt	Modern Cases Tempore Holt, by Farresley [*7 Modern Reports*] [*A publication*] (DLA)
MOD CIS	Ministry of Defence Communication Information System (SAUO)
MOD CIS	Ministry of Defense Communication Information System (SAUS)
modcom	Modernity Commercialized (AD)
MODCOM	Modular Computer System
MODCOMP	Modular Computer Systems Inc. (NITA)
MODCON	Man Machine System for the Optimum Design and Construction of Buildings (PDAA)
MOD CON	Modern Convenience (DSUE)
mod-cons	Modern-Construction Houses (AD)
mod cons	Modern Conveniences (AD)
MODCPS	Multiple Output Direct Current Power Supply
MODC-USA	United States Army Modification Center (SAUO)
MODD	Meteorological and Omega Data Digitizer (SAUS)
MODD	Military Order of Devil Dogs (EA)
Modd	Modern Medical Modalities Corp. [*Associated Press*] (SAG)
moddem	Modulator-Demodulator (AD)
mod/demod	Modulate-Demodulate (AD)
MODDF	Military Order, Devil Dog Fleas (EA)
MOD DICT	In the Manner Directed [*Abbreviation from the Latin*] [*Pharmacy*] (ROG)
MOD DIG	Modular Digital Image Generator (SAUS)
MODE	Management of Objectives with Dollars through Employees [*Department of Agriculture*]
MODE	Merchant Oriented Data Entry
MODE	Methoxy(O-desmethyl)encainide [*Biochemistry*]
MODE	Middeck Zero-Gravity Dynamics Experiment (SAUO)
MODE	Mid-Ocean Dynamics Experiment [*National Science Foundation*]
ModE	Modern English (AD)

MODE	Monitor Data Equipment
MODE	Monitoring Overseas Direct Employment (DNAB)
MODE	Music on Demand (TELE)
MODE 4	Refueling (SAUS)
MODE C	Altitude Reporting Mode of Secondary Radar [FAA] (TAG)
MO Dec	Missouri Decisions [A publication] (DLA)
MODEC	Motor Optimization Design Evaluation Code (MCD)
Model Bus Corp Act Anno 2d	American Bar Association Model Business Corporation Act, Annotated, Second Series [A publication] (DLA)
Model Business Corp Act	American Bar Association Model Business Corporation Act, Annotated [A publication] (DLA)
MODELH/PRDH	Mouvement pour la Liberation d'Haiti/Parti Revolutionnaire d'Haiti [Political party] (EY)
ModelImp	Model Imperial, Inc. [Associated Press] (SAG)
Model Land Dev Code	American Law Institute Model Land Development Code [A publication] (DLA)
Model R	Model Railroader [A publication]
MODELS	Modernization of the Defense Logistics Standard System (SAUO)
MODEM	Modelling of Emission and Consumption in Urban Areas (SAUO)
MODEM	Modulate/Demodulate [or Modulation/Demodulation or Modulator-Demodulator] [Computer science]
modem	Modulating-Demodulating (AD)
Mod (Eng)	English King's Bench Modern Reports [86-88 English Reprint] [A publication] (DLA)
MOD ENT	Modern Entries [Legal term] (DLA)
Modern Lib	Modern Library (AD)
MODES	Mode Optimization and Delivery Estimation System (SAUO)
MODEST	Missile Optical Destruction Technique
MODESTI	Mould Design and Manufacturing Optimization (SAUO)
Modest Pistor	Modestinus Pistoris [Deceased, 1565] [Authority cited in pre-1607 legal work] (DSA)
MODET	Mortar Detection
MODEX	Mobilization Deployment Exercise (MCD)
modf	Modification (AD)
MODF	Modify (AAG)
MODFET	Modulation-Doped Field-Effect Transistor [Solid-state physics]
MODFLIR	Modular Forward-Looking Infrared Seeker
MODFN	Modification (AAG)
MODFR	Modifier (AAG)
Mod'g	Modifying [Legal term] (DLA)
ModGr	Modern Greek [Language]
MODHATR	Modified Hatrack [Cyclone forecasting] [Navy]
ModHeb	Modern Hebrew (AD)
MODHIWAY	Modified Highway Program (SAUO)
MODI	Major Oversea Depot and Installation Method [Army]
MODI	Modified Distribution
MODI	Modine Manufacturing Co. [NASDAQ symbol] (NQ)
MODI	Modine Mfg [NASDAQ symbol] (TTSB)
MODI	Modular Optical Digital Interface
MODIA	Method of Designing Instructional Alternatives (PDAA)
MODICON	Modular-Dispersed-Control
MODIF	Modification (KSC)
MODIG	Modular Digital Image Generation [Computer science]
MODIGSI	Modular Digital Simulation (MCD)
MODIL	Manufacturing Operations Development and Integration Laboratory
MODILS	Modular Instrument Landing System
MODIM	MOTS [Module Test Set] Design Information Memorandum
Modine	Modine Manufacturing Co. [Associated Press] (SAG)
Mod Int	Brown's Modus Intrandi [A publication] (DLA)
Modio	MODEM and Radio [Telecommunications]
MODIR	Modulated Infra-Red jammer (SAUS)
mod/iran	Modification, Inspection, and Repair as Necessary (AD)
MOD/IRAN	Modification/Inspection and Repair as Necessary
MODIS	Moderate Resolution Imaging Spectroradiometer (EOSA)
MODIS	Mode Shape Display [Module]
MODISCO	Mechanization of Defense Industrial Security Clearance Office [DoD]
MODIS-N	Moderate Resolution Imaging Spectrometer-Nadir (EOSA)
MODIS-T	Moderate Resolution Imaging Spectrometer-Tilt (EOSA)
MODL	Model [Automotive emissions]
MODL	Model Imperial, Inc. [NASDAQ symbol] (SAG)
ModL	Modern Latin [Language]
ModLA	Modern Language Association, New York, NY [Library symbol] [Library of Congress] (LCLS)
MODLAN	Mission Operations Division Local Area Network (SAUO)
Mod L & Soc'y	Modern Law and Society [A publication] (DLA)
ModLA-R	Modern Language Association Research in Progress Program, New York NY [Library symbol] [Library of Congress] (LCLS)
MOD LITH	Modern Lithographer [A publication] (DGA)
MODLOC	Modified Location
MODLOG 77	Modernization of Logistics 1977 [Army]
MODM	Magneto-Optical Display Memory
MODM	Major Oversea Depot Method [Army]
MODM	Manned One-Day Mission [NASA]
MODM	Mature-Onset Diabetes Mellitus (MAE)
MODM	Modern Medical Modalities Corp. [NASDAQ symbol] (SAG)
MODM	Modern Medl Modalities [NASDAQ symbol] (TTSB)
MODMATS	Modified Missile Auxiliary Test Set (ACAE)
ModMd	Modern Medical Modalities Corp. [Associated Press] (SAG)
ModMed	Modern Medical Modalities Corp. [Associated Press] (SAG)
Mod Med Aust	Modern Medicine of Australia [A publication]
MODMW	Modern Med Modalities Wrrt'A' [NASDAQ symbol] (TTSB)
MODMZ	Modern Med Modalities Wrr'B' [NASDAQ symbol] (TTSB)
MOD(N)	Ministry of Defence (Navy) [British]
MODNET	Mission Operations Directorate Network (SAUO)
MoDNM	Morpholinodaunomycin [Also, MRD] [Antineoplastic drug]
MODO	Moderato [Moderate Speed] [Music] (ROG)
modo	Moderato [Moderately] [Italian] (AD)
Mod Off Dat Man	Modern Office and Data Management [A publication]
Mod Office Data Mgmt	Modern Office and Data Management [A publication]
MOD/OP	Maintenance of Deception/Operation
MODOP	Mobil Oil Direct Oxidation Process [Gas desulfurization process]
MODOR	Molecularized Doppler RADAR
MODP	Modern Programming Practice
MODPAC	Modular Restraint, Recovery, and Survival Package
MOD(PE)	Ministry of Defence (Procurement Executive) [British]
MODPLAN	Model Planning (TIMI)
MODPOT	Model Potential [Physics]
Mod Pract Comm	Modern Practice Commentator [A publication] (DLA)
mod praes	Modo Praescripto [In the manner prescribed] [Latin] [Pharmacy] (BARN)
MOD PRAESC	Modo Praescripto [In the Manner Prescribed] [Latin] [Pharmacy] (MAH)
MOD PRAESCRIPT	Modo Praescripto [In the Manner Prescribed] [Pharmacy]
mod pres	Modo Prescripto [In the Manner Prescribed] [Latin] (AD)
MOD PRESCR	Modo Praescripto [In the Manner Prescribed] [Pharmacy] (ROG)
mod pst	Modeling Paste (VRA)
MODR	Microwave Optical Double Resonance (PDAA)
MODR	Moderate Rate [Travel industry] (TRID)
modr	Moderate Room Rate Desired (AD)
MODR	Monodetail Drawing (MSA)
MODREFTRA	Modified Refresher Training [Navy] (NVT)
Mod Rep	Modern Reports [England] [A publication] (DLA)
Mod Rep	Style's English King's Bench Reports [1646-55] [A publication] (DLA)
MODS	Major Operations Data System (NVT)
MODS	Manned Orbital Development Station [See also MOD, MOSS, MTSS] [Air Force/NASA]
MODS	Manpower Operations Data System [Employment and Training Administration] [Department of Labor]
MODS	Material Ordering and Delivery Schedule (DNAB)
MODS	Medically Oriented Data System (MCD)
MODS	Medium Ocean Data Station
mods	Mesial-Occlusal-Distal [Dentistry] (AD)
MODS	Military Orbital Development System [See also MOD, MOSS, MTSS] [Air Force/NASA]
MODS	Missile Offense/Defense System
MODS	Mission Operations and Data System (SAUO)
MODS	Mission Operations Design Support
MODS	Mobility-Planning Data System [Military] (GFGA)
MODS	Mobilization Planning Data System (SAUO)
MODS	Models (MCD)
MODS	Models for Organizational Design and Staffing (DNAB)
Mods	Moderates [Reference to political philosophy of some members of the Republican party]
MODS	Moderations [First public Oxford examination] (ROG)
MODS	Modifications
MODS	Modular Oriented Direct Support (MCD)
MODS	Multiple Organ Dysfunction Syndrome [Medicine]
MODSA	Ministry of Defence Staff Association (BUAC)
ModSAF	Modular Semi-Automated Forces (SAUS)
MODSAF	Modular Semi-Automatic Forces
MODSC	Magnetooptically Detected Spin Conversion [Physics]
ModStealth	Modular Stealth (SAUS)
MODT	Mean Operational Delay Time
MODT	Modtech, Inc. [NASDAQ symbol] (SAG)
Modtec	Modtech, Inc. [Associated Press] (SAG)
MODTEPS	Modular Toxic Environment Protective Suit [NASA]
MODTLE	Mobilization on Development, Trade, Labor, and Environment [An association]
MODTO	Moderato [Moderate Speed] [Music]
modto	Moderato [Moderately] [Italian] (AD)
MODU	Mobile Offshore Drilling Unit
MODU Code	Code for the Construction and Equipment of Mobile Offshore Drilling Units (SAUO)
MODUK	Ministry of Defence UK (SAUS)
MODUK	Ministry of Defence United Kingdom (SAUO)
MODULA	Modular Programming Language (CSR)
Modula-2	Modular Language-2 [Computer science]
MODULAB	Modular Clinical Laboratory [Military] (CAAL)
MOD/UM	Modulated/Unmodulated (SSD)
Mod Un	Modern Unionist [A publication]
Mod Unionist	Modern Unionist [A publication]
MODUS	Modular One Dynamic User System [Computer science] (MHDI)
MODUSSE	Manufacturers of Domestic Unvented Supply Systems Equipment [British] (DBA)
MODWORS	Modification Work Order Report Status
MODWT	Maximal Overlap Discrete Wavelet Transform (SAUS)
MODY	Maturity Onset Diabetes of the Young [Medicine] (DMAA)
MOE	Evangel College, Springfield, MO [OCLC symbol] (OCLC)
MOE	MAD Operational Effectiveness (DNAB)
MOE	Maintenance of Effort [Medicare Act]
MOE	Major Organizational Entity (MCD)
MOE	Margin of Exposure [Toxicology]
MOE	Mars Orbit Ejection (MCD)
MOE	Master of Ocean Engineering (GAGS)
MOE	Master of Oral English
MOE	Maximum Output Entropy (PDAA)
moe	Measure of Effectiveness (AD)
MOE	Measure of Effectiveness
MoE	Ministry of Education [British] (AD)
MOE	Ministry of Education [British] (DAS)

M o E............ Ministry of Energy [*British*] (AD)
MOE............. Ministry of Environment [*Canada*]
MOE............. Ministry of the Environment [*Bulgaria*] (BUAC)
MOE............. Mission-Oriented Equipment
MOE............. Model Operational Environment (SAA)
MOE............. Modulus of Elasticity [*Mechanics*]
MOE............. Moli Energy Ltd. [*Toronto Stock Exchange symbol*] [*Vancouver Stock Exchange symbol*]
MOE............. Momeik [*Myanmar*] [*Airport symbol*] (OAG)
MOE............. Mu Phi Epsilon [*An association*] (NTPA)
MOE............. Mythical Operational Environment (SAA)
MOE............. Ontario Ministry of Education, Information Centre, Research Branch [*UTLAS symbol*]
MOE............. Telemetering Mobile Station [*ITU designation*]
MOEA........... Ministry of Economic Affairs [*British*] (AD)
MOEC........... Ministry of Education and Culture (SAUO)
MOEC/AES ... Ministry of Education and Culture/Adult Education Section (SAUO)
MOEC/CTSDC... Ministry of Education and Culture/Curriculum, Textbook, Supervision Development Centre (SAUO)
MOEC/DOA... Ministry of Education and Culture/Department of Archaeology (SAUO)
MOEC/LDT ... Ministry of Education and Culture/Lumbini Development Trust (SAUO)
MOECSW...... Ministry of Education, Culture and Social Welfare (SAUO)
MOECSW/SWC... Ministry of Education, Culture and Social Welfare/Social Welfare Council (SAUO)
MOED .... Molecular Orbital Energy Diagram
MOED .... Morristown-Edison National Park Service Group
MOEDA .... Measures of Effectiveness, Development, and Application (MCD)
MOEH .... Medical Officer for Environmental Health (WDAA)
MOELP......... Ministry of Environment, Lands and Parks (SAUO)
MOEP........... Meteorological and Oceanographic Equipment Program (NG)
MOER .... MACOM [*Major Command*] Outstanding Excess Report
MOERO........ Medium Orbiting Earth Resources Observatory (IEEE)
MOES........... Mathematics Olympiads for Elementary Schools (EDAC)
MOET.......... Multiple Ovulation and Embryo Transfer (SAUO)
MOETLO ...... Meteorological and Oceanographic Equipment Technical Liaison Officer
MoExGS....... Excelsior Springs Genealogical Society, Excelsior Springs, MO [*Library symbol*] [*Library of Congress*] (LCLS)
MOF............. Fontbonne College, St. Louis, MO [*OCLC symbol*] (OCLC)
MOF............. Mal-Union of Fracture [*Medicine*] (MELL)
MOF............. Manned Orbital Flight [*NASA*] (NASA)
MOF............. Marine Oxidation/Fermentation
MOF............. Mature Ovarian Follicle [*Medicine*] (MELL)
MOF............. Maumere [*Indonesia*] [*Airport symbol*] (OAG)
mof............. Maximum Observed Frequency (AD)
MOF............. Maximum Observed Frequency [*Radio*]
MOF............. Maximum Operating Frequency
MOF............. MeCCNU [*Semustine*], Oncovin , Fluorouracil [*Vincristine*] [*Antineoplastic drug regimen*]
MOF............. Member of the Force (LAIN)
mof............. Member of the Police Force (AD)
mof............. Metal Oxide Film (AD)
MOF............. Metal-Oxide Film
MOF............. Methotrexate, Oncovin [*Vincristine*] 5-Fluorouracil [*Antineoplastic drug regimen*] (DAVI)
MOF............. Methoxyflurane [*Anesthetic*] (AAMN)
MOF............. Methylo-CCNU, Vineristine, Fluorouracil [*Antineoplastic drug regimen*] (DAVI)
MOF............. Michoud Operations Facility [*NASA*] (AAG)
MoF............. Ministry of Finance [*British*] (AD)
MOF............. Ministry of Finance [*Japan*] (ECON)
MOF............. Ministry of Food [*British*]
MOF............. Ministry of Forests (SAUO)
MOF............. Mission Operations Facility [*NASA*] (KSC)
MOF............. Modified Olefin Film [*Plastics*]
MOF............. Moffat Communications Ltd. [*Toronto Stock Exchange symbol*]
MOF............. Months of Operational Flying (DNAB)
MOF............. Multi-Option Facility
MOF............. Multioption Fuze (MCD)
MOF............. Multiple Organ Failure [*Medicine*]
M of A .... Ministry of Agriculture, Fisheries and Food (SAUO)
MOFA.......... Multi-Option Fuze, Artillery
M of A&F.... Ministry of Agriculture and Fisheries (SAUO)
MOFAB .... Mobile Floating Assault Bridge-Ferry [*Military*] (MCD)
MOFACS....... Multiorder Feedback and Compensation Synthesis
MOF/ADBN.. Ministry of Finance/ Agriculture Development Bank of Nepal (SAUO)
M of AP .... Ministry of Aircraft Production (SAUO)
MOFAP........ Ministry of Fuel and Power [*British*]
M of Arch .... Master of Architecture
MOFARS...... Maintenance Overload Factor Reporting System
MOFAST...... Mechanization of Freight and Shipping Terminal [*DoD*]
MOFAT........ Multi Phase Flow and Transport (SAUO)
MoFC.......... Central Methodist College, Fayette, MO [*Library symbol*] [*Library of Congress*] (LCLS)
M of C .... Master of Commerce
MOFC.......... Michael O'Leary Fan Club [*Defunct*] (EA)
M of D .... Ministry of Defence [*British*]
M of E .... Ministry of Education [*British*]
M of E .... Minutes of Evidence
MOFE/DNPWC... Ministry of Forests and Environment/Department of National Parks & Wildlife Conservation (SAUO)
MOFE/DOF ... Ministry of Forests and Environment/Department of Forests (SAUO)
MOFE/DOMP... Ministry of Forests and Environment/Department of Medicinal Plants (SAUO)

MOFE/DOSC... Ministry of Forests and Environment/Department of Soil Conservation (SAUO)
MOFE/FPDB... Ministry of Forests and Environment/Forest Products Development Board (SAUO)
Mofert......... Ministry of Foreign Economic Relations and Trade [*China*] (BUAC)
MOFERT ..... Ministry of Foreign Economic Relations and Trade [*China*]
MOFE/TCN .. Ministry of Forests and Environment/Timber Corporation of Nepal (SAUO)
M of F .... Ministry of Food (SAUO)
MOFF........... Multiple Options Funding Facility [*Euronotes*]
M of F&P .... Ministry of Fuel and Power (SAUO)
MOFFS......... Multi-Megabit Operation Flexible Frame Synchronizer (ACAE)
M of HA...... Matrons of Hospitals Association (ROG)
M of Hist .... Magazine of History [*A publication*] (BRI)
M of I .... Ministry of Information (SAUO)
M of I .... Moment of Inertia
MoFIM........ Mark Twain Shrine, Mark Twain State Park, Florida, MO [*Library symbol*] [*Library of Congress*] (LCLS)
MoFloSS..... Saint Stanislaus Seminary, Florissant, MO [*Library symbol*] [*Library of Congress*] (LCLS)
M of M .... Maintenance of Membership [*Labor unions*]
M of M .... Museum of Man (SAUO)
MOFN .... MovieFone CI'A' [*NASDAQ symbol*] (TTSB)
MOFN .... MovieFone, Inc. [*NASDAQ symbol*] (SAG)
M of P .... Ministry of Pensions and National Insurance (SAUO)
M of P .... Ministry of Power (SAUO)
M of R .... Minister of Reconstruction [*British*] (AD)
M of R .... Ministry of Reconstruction (SAUO)
MOF/RATC... Ministry of Finance/Revenue Administration Training Centre (SAUO)
MOFS.......... Maintenance of Flying Skills (ACAE)
M of S .... Ministry of Supply (SAUO)
MOFS.......... Multiple Organ Failure Syndrome [*Medicine*] (DMAA)
MOF-STREP... MeCCNU [*Semustine*], Oncovin , Fluorouracil, Streptozotocin [*Vincristine*] [*Antineoplastic drug regimen*]
MOFTEC...... Ministry of Foreign Trade & Economic Cooperation [*China*]
Moftec .... Ministry of Foreign Trade and Economic Co-Operation [*China*] (BUAC)
MOFTU .... MIG Operational Fighter Training Unit [*India*] [*Air Force*]
MoFuWC..... Westminster College, Fulton, MO [*Library symbol*] [*Library of Congress*] (LCLS)
M of V .... [*The*] Merchant of Venice [*Shakespearean work*]
M of W .... Maintenance of Way [*Railroading*]
MOFW .... Military Order of Foreign Wars of the United States (EA)
MOG .... Assemblies of God Graduate School, Springfield, MO [*OCLC symbol*] (OCLC)
MOG .... Machinery of Government
MOG .... Managed Object Group (SAUO)
MOG .... Mannville Oil & Gas Ltd. [*Toronto Stock Exchange symbol*]
Mog............ Margaret (AD)
MOG .... Master of Obstetrics and Gynecology (AD)
MOG .... Material Ordering Guide [*Shipbuilding*]
MOG .... Material Other than Grape [*Wine making*]
MOG .... Medical Oncology Group
MOG .... Metropolitan Opera Guild (EA)
MOG .... Micro-Optic Gyroscope
MOG .... Milicias Obreras Guatemaltecas [*Guatemalan Workers' Militia*] (PD)
MOG .... Minicomputer Operations Group (SAUO)
MOG .... Mogadishu [*Somalia*] [*Seismograph station code, US Geological Survey*] [*Closed*] (SEIS)
MOG .... Monghsat [*Myanmar*] [*Airport symbol*] (OAG)
MOG .... Montague, CA [*Location identifier*] [*FAA*] (FAAL)
MOG .... Moog, Inc. [*AMEX symbol*] (SPSG)
MOG .... Morgan [*Automobile*]
MOG .... Municipal Officers' Guild (ROG)
MOG .... Myelin Oligodendrocyte Glycoprotein [*Biochemistry*]
MOGA .... Management of Officer Grade Authorization (MCD)
MOGA .... Microwave and Optical Generation and Amplification (MCD)
MOGA .... Mid-Continent Oil and Gas Association (SAUO)
MOGA .... Ministry of General Administration (SAUO)
MOGA .... Montana Outfitters and Guides Association (EA)
MOGA/NASC... Ministry of General Administration/Nepal Administrative Staff College (SAUO)
mogas .... Motor Gasoline (AD)
MOGAS........ Motor Gasoline [*Military*]
MOGN .... MGI PHARMA, Inc. [*NASDAQ symbol*] (NQ)
MOGN .... Molecular Genetics, Inc. (MHDW)
MOGUL....... Modular Gun Laying System (SAUS)
MOGUNTIA... Model of the Global Universal Tracer Transport in the Atmosphere [*Marine science*] (OSRA)
Moguyde...... Mouvement Guyanais de Decolonisation [*Guiana Decolonization Movement*] [*France*] [*Political party*] (PPW)
MoGvS........ Grain Valley Associated School District, Grain Valley, MO [*Library symbol*] [*Library of Congress*] (LCLS)
MoH............ Hannibal Free Public Library, Hannibal, MO [*Library symbol*] [*Library of Congress*] (LCLS)
MOH........... Hydrological and Meteorological Mobile Station [*ITU designation*]
MOH........... Master, Occupational Health (CMD)
MOH........... Master of Occupational Health (PGP)
MOH........... Master of Otter Hounds
MOH........... Master of Otter-hounds (SAUO)
moh .... Material Overhead (AD)
moh .... Maximum Operating Hours (AD)
MOH........... Maximum Operating Hours (MCD)
MOH........... Medal of Honor [*Often erroneously called Congressional Medal of Honor*] [*Military decoration*]

MOH	Medical Officer of Health [*British*]
MOH	Metropolitan Opera House (SAUO)
MOH	Ministry of Health [*British*]
MoH	Ministry of Housing and Local Government (SAUO)
MOH	Moche Resources, Inc. [*Vancouver Stock Exchange symbol*]
MOH	Mohasco Corp. (SAUO)
moh	Mohawk [*MARC language code*] [*Library of Congress*] (LCCP)
MOH	Mohawk Airlines, Inc. [*Obsolete*]
MOH	Museum of Holography [*New York City*]
MOH	Music on Hold (ITD)
MOH	New York, NY [*Location identifier*] [*FAA*] (FAAL)
MOH	St. Louis Priory School, St. Louis, MO [*OCLC symbol*] (OCLC)
MOH	Tigerfly [*British*] [*ICAO designator*] (FAAC)
MoHam	Hamilton Public Library, Hamilton, MO [*Library symbol*] [*Library of Congress*] (LCLS)
Moham	Mohammedan (AD)
MOHAM	Mohammedan (ROG)
MoHarC	Cass County Public Library, Harrisonville, MO [*Library symbol*] [*Library of Congress*] (LCLS)
MOHAT	Modular Handling and Transport
MOHATS	Mobile Overland Hauling and Transport System [*Air Force*]
MOHAVE	Measurement of Haze and Visual Effects [*Study*] [*Marine science*] (OSRA)
MOHAVE	Measurement of Haze and Visusal Effects [*Study*] (USDC)
Mohawk	Mohawk Industries, Inc. [*Associated Press*] (SAG)
MOHE	Ministry of Health (SAUO)
MOHE/APH	Ministry of Health/Amp Pipal Hospital (SAUO)
MOHEC	Maintenance of Hercules Capability (SAA)
MOHE/CHL	Ministry of Health/Central Health Laboratory (SAUO)
MOHE/DAU	Ministry of Health/ Department of Ayurveda (SAUO)
MOHE/DWSS	DEPARTMENT OF WATER SUPPLY AND SANITATION (SAUS)
MOHE/DWSS	Ministry of Health/ Department of Water Supply and Sanitation (SAUO)
MOHE/HICC	Ministry of Health/Health Education, Information and Communication (SAUS)
MOHE/HICC	Ministry of Health/National Health Education, Information and Communication (SAUO)
MOHE/NCAID	Ministry of Health/ National Centre For Aid & Standard Control (SAUS)
MOHE/NCAID	Ministry of Health/ National Centre For Aid & Std Control (SAUO)
MOHE/NFPMC	Ministry of Health/ Nutritious Food Programme Management Committee (SAUO)
MOHE/OH	Ministry of Health/ Okhaldhunga Hospital (SAUO)
MOHE/PA	Ministry of Health/Patan Hospital (SAUO)
MOHE/PHD	Ministry of Health/Public Health Division (SAUS)
MOHE/RDRL	Ministry of Health/Royal Drugs Research Laboratory (SAUO)
MOHE/TS	Ministry of Health/Tansen Hospital (SAUO)
MOHE/WRH	Ministry of Health/Western Regional Hospital (SAUO)
MoHi	Missouri State Historical Society, Columbia, MO [*Library symbol*] [*Library of Congress*] (LCLS)
MoHig	Robertson Memorial Library, Higginsville, MO [*Library symbol*] [*Library of Congress*] (LCLS)
MoHigH	Habilitation Center, Higginsville, MO [*Library symbol*] [*Library of Congress*] (LCLS)
MOHILL	Machine-Oriented High-Level Language [*Computer science*] (HGAA)
MOHK	Mohawk Industries [*NASDAQ symbol*] (SAG)
MOHLG	Ministry of Housing and Local Government [*British*] (AD)
MOH(LHA)	Medical Officer of Health (Local Health Authority) [*British*]
MOHLL	Machine Oriented High Level Language (SAUS)
MoHM	Mark Twain Museum, Hannibal, MO [*Library symbol*] [*Library of Congress*] (LCLS)
mohms	Milliohms (AD)
MOHMS	Milliohms (WDAA)
moho	Mohorovicic Discontinuity [*Geology*] (AD)
Moho	Mohorovicic Discontinuity (ADWA)
MOHO	Mohorovicic Discontinuity [*Geology*]
MOHOL	Machine-Oriented Higher Order Language [*Computer science*] (MHDI)
MOHOME	Ministry of Home (SAUO)
MOH/PHD	Ministry of Health/public Health Division (SAUO)
MOHPP/DHM	Ministry of Housing and Physical Planning/Department of Hydrology and Meteorology (SAUO)
MOHPP/DHUD	Ministry of Housing and Physical Planning/Department of Housing and Urban Development (SAUO)
MOHPP/DOA	Ministry of Housing and Physical Planning/Department of Archaeology (SAUO)
MOHPP/DOB	Ministry of Housing and Physical Planning/Department of Buildings (SAUO)
MOHPP/DWSS	Ministry of Housing and Physical Planning/Department of Water Supply and Sewerage (SAUO)
MOHPP/NWSC	Ministry of Housing and Physical Planning/Nepal Water Supply Corp. (SAUS)
MOHPP/NWSC	Ministry of Housing and Physical Planning/Nepal Water Supply Corporation (SAUO)
MOHS	Master of Occupational Health and Safety
mohs	Mud, Oil, Hooks, Slings [*Insurance*] (AD)
MOHSLG	Health Sciences Library [*Library network*]
MoHu	Huntsville Public Library, Huntsville, MO [*Library symbol*] [*Library of Congress*] (LCLS)
MOI	Main-d'Oeuvre Indigene [*Indigenous Manpower*] [*Congo - Leopoldville*]
MOI	Maintenance Operating Instruction [*Air Force Logistics Command*]
MOI	Make on Installation (SAA)
MOI	Marine Officer Instructor (DOMA)
MOI	Mars Orbit [*or Orbital*] Insertion [*Aerospace*]

moi	Maximum Obtainable Irradiance (AD)
MOI	Maximum Obtainable Irradiance
MOI	Maximum Oxygen Intake [*Medicine*] (DB)
MOI	Mechanism of Injury (SAUO)
MOI	Memorandum of Information (SAUO)
MOI	Memorandum of Instruction (INF)
MOI	Memorandum of Intent (COE)
MOI	Memorandum of Interest (MCD)
MOI	Message of Operational Intent (NVT)
MOI	Methods of Instruction
MOI	Military Occupational Information (AABC)
moi	Military Occupational Information (AD)
MOI	Military Operations and Intelligence
MOI	Minimum Operating Inventory [*Business term*]
MOI	Ministry of Information [*British*] [*World War II*]
MoI	Ministry of the Interior [*British*] (AD)
MOI	Mission Oriented Items (SAUO)
MOI	Mitiaro [*Cook Islands*] [*Airport symbol*] (OAG)
MOI	Molco Industries [*Vancouver Stock Exchange symbol*]
MOI	Moment of Inertia
MOI	Monaco Oceanographic Institute
MOI	Mouvement Ouvrier International (BJA)
moi	Multiplicity of Infection (AD)
MOI	Multiplicity of Infection
MOI	William Jewell College, Liberty, MO [*OCLC symbol*] (OCLC)
MOIA	Mission Oriented Item Activity (SAUO)
Mo IA	Moore's Indian Appeals [*A publication*] (DLA)
MOIAA	Missouri Intercollegiate Athletic Association (PSS)
MOI/BLSF	Ministry of Industry/Bansbari Leather and Shoe Factory (SAUO)
MOIC	Medical Officer-in-Charge [*Military*]
MOIC	Medical Officer in Command (AD)
MOIC	Military Oceanographic Information Center (NATG)
MOIC	Missile Ordnance Inhibit Circuit (ACAE)
MOI/CIDB	Ministry of Industry/Cottage Industry Development Board (SAUO)
MOI/CIDB	Ministry of Information and Communication/Cottage Industry Development Board (SAUS)
MOIC/NTC	Ministry of Information and Communication/Nepal Telecommunication Corp. (SAUS)
MOIC/NTC	Ministry of Information and Communication/Nepal Telecommunication Corporation (SAUO)
MOI/DCVSSI	Ministry of Industry/ Department of Cottage, Village & Small Scale Industries (SAUO)
MOI/DCVSSI	Ministry of Information and Communication/Department of Cottage, Village & Small Scale Industries (SAUS)
MOIDE	Military Occupational Information Data Bank
MOI/DMG	Ministry of Industry/ Department of Mines and Geology (SAUO)
MOI/DMG	Ministry of Information and Communication/Department of Mines and Geology (SAUS)
MOI/FIPD	Ministry of Industry/Foreign Investment Promotion Division (SAUO)
MOI/FIPD	Ministry of Information and Communication/Foreign Investment Promotion Division (SAUS)
MOIG	Master of Occupational Information and Guidance
MOI/HCC	Ministry of Industry/Himal Cement Company (SAUO)
MOI/HCC	Ministry of Information and Communication/Himal Cement Company (SAUS)
MOI/HCI	Ministry of Industries/Hetauda Cement Industries Ltd. (SAUO)
MOIL	Marine Operations and Instrumentation Laboratory [*Marine science*] (OSRA)
MOIL	Maynard Oil [*NASDAQ symbol*] (TTSB)
MOIL	Maynard Oil Co. [*NASDAQ symbol*] (NQ)
MOIL	Motor Oil
MOI/LICC	Ministry of Industry/Leather Industries Coordination Cell (SAUO)
MOI/LICC	Ministry of Information and Communication/Leather Industries Coordination Cell (SAUS)
MoIM	Mid-Continent Public Library Service, Independence, MO [*Library symbol*] [*Library of Congress*] (LCLS)
MoIMC	Independence Medical Center, Independence, MO [*Library symbol*] [*Library of Congress*] (LCLS)
MOI/NBR	Ministry of Industry/Nepal Bureau of Standards (SAUO)
MOI/NIDC	Ministry of Industry/Nepal Industrial Development Corporation (SAUO)
MOI/NIDC	Ministry of Information and Communication/Nepal Industrial Development Corp. (SAUS)
MOI/NTDC	Ministry of Industry/Nepal Tea Development Corporation (SAUO)
MOI/NTDC	Ministry of Information and Communication/Nepal Tea Development Corp. (SAUS)
MOIP	Mandatory Oil Import Program
moip	Missile on Internal Power [*Military*] (AD)
MOIP	Missile on Internal Power
MOIPI	Multi-Purpose Offshore Industrial Port Islands (NOAA)
MoIPS	Independence Public School District, Independence, MO [*Library symbol*] [*Library of Congress*] (LCLS)
MOIR	Maximum Ozone Incremental Reactivity [*Environmental science*]
MOIR	Movimiento Obrero Independiente Revolucionario [*Independent Revolutionary Workers' Movement*] [*Colombia*] [*Political party*] (PPW)
MOIR	Movimiento Obrero Izquierdista Revolucionario [*Colombia*] [*Political party*] (PPW)
MOIRA	Model of International Relations in Agriculture (PDAA)
MoIRC	Reorganized Church of Jesus Christ of Latter-Day Saints, Independence, MO [*Library symbol*] [*Library of Congress*] (LCLS)
Moir Cap Pun	Moir on Capital Punishment [*A publication*] (DLA)
MoIS	Independence Sanitarium and Hospital, Independence, MO [*Library symbol*] [*Library of Congress*] (LCLS)
MOIS	Maritime Operational Intelligence Summary

MOIS .... Michigan Occupational Information System [*Michigan State Department of Education*] [*Lansing*] [*Information service or system*] (IID)

MOIS .... Mission Operations Intercommunication System [*NASA*]

Moish .... Moishe (AD)

MOIST .... Macro Output System [*NASA*] (KSC)

MOISTR ...... Moisture

MoIT .... Harry S Truman Library, Independence, MO [*Library symbol*] [*Library of Congress*] (LCLS)

moiv .... Mechanically Operated Inlet Valve (AD)

MOIV .... Mechanically Operated Inlet Valve (ADA)

MOJ .... Material on Job Date [*Telecommunications*] (TEL)

MOJ .... Metering over Junction [*Network administration*] [*Telecommunications*] (TEL)

MOJ .... Ministry of Jute [*Bangladesh*]

MOJ .... Muong Sing [*Laos*] [*Airport symbol*] (AD)

MOJA .... Movement for Justice in Africa [*Liberia*] [*Political party*] (PPW)

MOJAC .... Mood, Orientation, Judgment, Affect, Content (AAMN)

MOJA-G ...... Movement for Justice in Africa-Gambia [*Political party*]

MoJc .... Thomas Jefferson Library System, Jefferson City, MO [*Library symbol*] [*Library of Congress*] (LCLS)

MoJcL .... Lincoln University, Jefferson City, MO [*Library symbol*] [*Library of Congress*] (LCLS)

MOJMRP ..... Meteorological Office, Joint Meteorological Radio Propagation Sub-Committee (BUAC)

MoJo .... Joplin Public Library, Joplin, MO [*Library symbol*] [*Library of Congress*] (LCLS)

MoJoM .... Missouri Southern State College, Joplin, MO [*Library symbol*] [*Library of Congress*] (LCLS)

MOJT .... Managed On-the-Job Training (DNAB)

Mo Jur .... Monthly Jurist [*A publication*] (DLA)

MoK .... Kansas City Public Library, Kansas City, MO [*Library symbol*] [*Library of Congress*] (LCLS)

MOK .... Mohawk Carpet Mills [*Stock exchange symbol*] (AD)

MOK .... Mokapu [*Hawaii*] [*Seismograph station code, US Geological Survey*] (SEIS)

Mok .... Mokpo (AD)

MoKA .... American Nurses' Association, Kansas City, MO [*Library symbol*] [*Library of Congress*] (LCLS)

MOKA .... Coffee People, Inc. [*NASDAQ symbol*] (SAG)

MoKAI .... Kansas City Arts Institute, Kansas City, MO [*Library symbol*] [*Library of Congress*] (LCLS)

MoKAr .... Avila College, Kansas City (SAUS)

MoKAv .... Avila College, Kansas City, MO [*Library symbol*] [*Library of Congress*] (LCLS)

MoKB .... Bar Library Association of Kansas City, Kansas City, MO [*Library symbol*] [*Library of Congress*] (LCLS)

MoKBa .... Barstow School, Kansas City, MO [*Library symbol*] [*Library of Congress*] (LCLS)

MoKBen ...... Bendix Corp., Technical Information Center, Kansas City, MO [*Library symbol*] [*Library of Congress*] (LCLS)

MoKBH .... Baptist Memorial Hospital, Kansas City, MO [*Library symbol*] [*Library of Congress*] (LCLS)

MoKBM .... Burns and McDonnell Engineering Co., Kansas City, MO [*Library symbol*] [*Library of Congress*] (LCLS)

MoKBV .... Black & Veatch Consulting Engineers, Central Library, Kansas City, MO [*Library symbol*] [*Library of Congress*] (LCLS)

MoKCH .... Children's Mercy Hospital, Kansas City, MO [*Library symbol*] [*Library of Congress*] (LCLS)

MoKChe ...... Chemagro, Kansas City, MO [*Library symbol*] [*Library of Congress*] (LCLS)

MoKCO .... Kansas City College of Osteopathic Medicine, Kansas City, MO [*Library symbol*] [*Library of Congress*] (LCLS)

MoKCoH ...... Jackson County Public Hospital, Kansas City, MO [*Library symbol*] [*Library of Congress*] (LCLS)

MOKE .... Magneto-Optic Kerr Effect

MoKEP .... United States Environmental Protection Agency, Kansas City, MO [*Library symbol*] [*Library of Congress*] (LCLS)

MoKF .... Farmland Industries Inc., Communications Services, Kansas City, MO [*Library symbol*] [*Library of Congress*] (LCLS)

MoKFR .... Federal Reserve Bank of Kansas City, Kansas City, MO [*Library symbol*] [*Library of Congress*] (LCLS)

MOKG .... Morgan, Olmstead, Kennedy & Gardner Corp. (SAUO)

MoKGH .... Kansas City General Hospital, Kansas City, MO [*Library symbol*] [*Library of Congress*] (LCLS)

MoKGS .... Church of Jesus Christ of Latter-Day Saints, Genealogical Society Library, Kansas City Branch, Kansas City, MO [*Library symbol*] [*Library of Congress*] (LCLS)

MoKHA .... Kansas City Area Hospital Association, Kansas City, MO [*Library symbol*] [*Library of Congress*] (LCLS)

MoKHC .... Hallmark Cards, Inc., Kansas City, MO [*Library symbol*] [*Library of Congress*] (LCLS)

MoKiCO .... Kirksville College of Osteopathy and Surgery, Kirksville, MO [*Library symbol*] [*Library of Congress*] (LCLS)

MoKiU .... Northeast Missouri State University, Kirksville, MO [*Library symbol*] [*Library of Congress*] (LCLS)

MoKJ .... Jackson County Medical Society, Kansas City, MO [*Library symbol*] [*Library of Congress*] (LCLS)

MoKKM .... Martin Luther King Memorial Hospital, Kansas City, MO [*Library symbol*] [*Library of Congress*] (LCLS)

MoKL .... Linda Hall Library, Kansas City, MO [*Library symbol*] [*Library of Congress*] (LCLS)

MoKLH .... Lakeside Hospital, Kansas City, MO [*Library symbol*] [*Library of Congress*] (LCLS)

MoKLo .... Loretto in Kansas City, Kansas City, MO [*Library symbol*] [*Library of Congress*] (LCLS)

MoKMB .... Midwestern Baptist Theological Seminary, Kansas City, MO [*Library symbol*] [*Library of Congress*] (LCLS)

MoKMC .... Midwest College of Medical Assistants, Kansas City, MO [*Library symbol*] [*Library of Congress*] (LCLS)

MoKMI .... Missouri Institute of Technology, Kansas City, MO [*Library symbol*] [*Library of Congress*] (LCLS)

MoKML .... Marion Laboratories, Inc., Kansas City, MO [*Library symbol*] [*Library of Congress*] (LCLS)

MoKMM ...... Menorah Medical Center, Kansas City, MO [*Library symbol*] [*Library of Congress*] (LCLS)

MoKMoC ...... Mobay Chemical Corp., Kansas City, MO [*Library symbol*] [*Library of Congress*] (LCLS)

MoKMR .... Midwest Research Institute, Kansas City, MO [*Library symbol*] [*Library of Congress*] (LCLS)

MoKMW ...... Maple Woods Community College, Kansas City, MO [*Library symbol*] [*Library of Congress*] (LCLS)

MoKN .... Nazarene Theological Seminary, Kansas City, MO [*Library symbol*] [*Library of Congress*] (LCLS)

MoKNA .... Nelson-Atkins Museum of Art, Spencer Art Reference Library, Kansas City, MO [*Library symbol*] [*Library of Congress*] (LCLS)

MoKNE .... Newman Ecumenical Seminary, Kansas City, MO [*Library symbol*] [*Library of Congress*] (LCLS)

MoKNG .... Nelson Art Gallery, Art Reference Library, Kansas City, MO [*Library symbol*] [*Library of Congress*] (LCLS)

MoKNT .... Saint Paul School of Theology, Kansas City, MO [*Library symbol*] [*Library of Congress*] (LCLS)

MoKP .... Penn Valley Junior College, Kansas City, MO [*Library symbol*] [*Library of Congress*] (LCLS)

MoKPC .... Pembroke County Day School, Kansas City, MO [*Library symbol*] [*Library of Congress*] (LCLS)

MoKPh .... Park Hill North Junior High School, Kansas City, MO [*Library symbol*] [*Library of Congress*] (LCLS)

MoKphJH ..... Park Hill North Junior High School, Kansas City, MO [*Library symbol*] [*Library of Congress*] (LCLS)

MoKPHS ...... Pembroke Hill School, Kansas City, MO [*Library symbol*] [*Library of Congress*] (LCLS)

MoKPhSD ... Park Hill School District, Kansas City, MO [*Library symbol*] [*Library of Congress*] (LCLS)

MoKPi .... Pioneer Community College Library, Kansas City, MO [*Library symbol*] [*Library of Congress*] (LCLS)

MoKR .... Rockhurst College, Kansas City, MO [*Library symbol*] [*Library of Congress*] (LCLS)

MoKRes .... Research Hospital and Medical Center, Kansas City, MO [*Library symbol*] [*Library of Congress*] (LCLS)

MoKRh .... Rockhurst High School, Kansas City, MO [*Library symbol*] [*Library of Congress*] (LCLS)

MoKSH .... Sunset Hill School, Kansas City, MO [*Library symbol*] [*Library of Congress*] (LCLS)

MoKStJ .... Saint Joseph's Hospital, Kansas City, MO [*Library symbol*] [*Library of Congress*] (LCLS)

MoKStL .... Saint Luke's Hospital of Kansas City, Kansas City, MO [*Library symbol*] [*Library of Congress*] (LCLS)

MoKStM ...... Saint Mary's Hospital, Kansas City, MO [*Library symbol*] [*Library of Congress*] (LCLS)

MoKStP .... Saint Paul Theological Seminary, Kansas City, MO [*Library symbol*] [*Library of Congress*] (LCLS)

MoKStT .... Saint Theresa's Academy, Kansas City, MO [*Library symbol*] [*Library of Congress*] (LCLS)

MoKT .... Teachers College of Kansas City, Kansas City, MO [*Library symbol*] [*Library of Congress*] [*Obsolete*] (LCLS)

MoKTrL .... Trinity Lutheran Hospital, Kansas City, MO [*Library symbol*] [*Library of Congress*] (LCLS)

MoKU .... University of Missouri at Kansas City, Kansas City, MO [*Library symbol*] [*Library of Congress*] (LCLS)

MoKU-D ...... University of Missouri at Kansas City, Dental School, Kansas City, MO [*Library symbol*] [*Library of Congress*] (LCLS)

MoKU-I .... University of Missouri at Kansas City, Instructional Materials Center, Kansas City, MO [*Library symbol*] [*Library of Congress*] (LCLS)

MoKu-L .... University of Missouri at Kansas City, Law Library, Kansas City, MO [*Library symbol*] [*Library of Congress*] (LCLS)

MoKU-M ...... University of Missouri at Kansas City, Medical Library, Kansas City, MO [*Library symbol*] [*Library of Congress*] (LCLS)

MoKU-Mus. ... University of Missouri at Kansas City, Music Conservatory, Kansas City, MO [*Library symbol*] [*Library of Congress*] (LCLS)

MoKVA .... United States Veterans Administration Hospital, Kansas City, MO [*Library symbol*] [*Library of Congress*] (LCLS)

MoKW .... Western Missouri Mental Health Center, Kansas City, MO [*Library symbol*] [*Library of Congress*] (LCLS)

MOL .... John Morrell & Co. (SAUO)

mol .... Machine-Oriented Language (AD)

MOL .... Machine-Oriented Language [*Programming language*]

MOL .... Manned Orbital Laboratory (SAUO)

MOL .... Manned Orbiting Laboratory [*NASA*]

MOL .... Master of Organizational Leadership (PGP)

MOL .... Master of Oriental Languages

MOL .... Master of Oriental Learning

MOL .... Maximum Operating Level

MOL .... Maximum Order Limitation (AAGC)

mol .... Maximum Output Level (AD)

MOL .... Maximum Output Level

MOL .... Maximum Overall Length (DAC)

MOL .... Metallo-Organic LASER

MOL .... Method of Lines [*Mathematics*]

MOL............	Microsoft Open License (SAUS)
MOL............	Microtel International, Inc. [*AMEX symbol*] (SAG)
MOL............	Middle of Life (ACAE)
MOL............	Minimum Oxygen Concentration [*at which ignition occurs*]
MOL............	Ministry of Labour [*Later, DE*] [*British*]
MOL............	Missouri State Library, Jefferson City, MO [*OCLC symbol*] (OCLC)
mol............	Moldavian [*MARC language code*] [*Library of Congress*] (LCCP)
MOL............	Molde [*Norway*] [*Airport symbol*] (OAG)
Mol............	Moldova (MILB)
mol............	Mole [*Amount of substance*] [*SI unit*]
mol............	Molecular (AD)
MOL............	Molecular (DMAA)
MOL............	Molecular Layer
MOL............	Molecule [*or Molecular*] (AAG)
mol............	Molecule (SHCU)
MOL............	Molesting [*FBI standardized term*]
MOL............	Moliere [*Pseudonym of French actor and dramatist Jean Baptiste Poquelin, 1622-1673*] (ROG)
Mol............	Mollendo (AD)
mol............	Mollis [*Soft*] [*Latin*] (AD)
Mol............	Molloy's De Jure Maritimo [*A publication*] (DLA)
Mol............	Molloy's Irish Chancery Reports [*1827-31*] [*A publication*] (DLA)
MOL............	Molodezhnaya [*Former USSR*] [*Geomagnetic observatory code*]
MOL............	Molson Companies Ltd. [*Toronto Stock Exchange symbol*] [*Vancouver Stock Exchange symbol*]
MOL............	Montebello, VA [*Location identifier*] [*FAA*] (FAAL)
MOL............	Multiple On-Line Programming [*Computer science*] (EECA)
M-O-L	My Old Lady [*Wife*] [*Slang*]
MOL............	Universite de Moncton, Law Library [*UTLAS symbol*]
MOLA............	Mars Observer Laser Altimeter
MOLA............	Mars Orbiter LASER Alitmeter
MOLA............	Mars Orbiter LASER Altimeter
MOLA............	Midwest Open Land Association (EA)
molab............	Mobile Laboratory (AD)
MOLAB............	Mobile Laboratory [*NASA*]
MOLAB............	Mobile Lunar Laboratory (AD)
MOL/ACTS ...	Manned Orbiting Laboratory / Altitude Control and Transmission System (DNAB)
MOLAP	Multidimensional Online Analytical Processing (RALS)
MOLAR	Mortar/Artillery Locating Radar (SAUS)
MOLARA	Motoring Organisations Land Access and Rights Association [*British*] (DBA)
MOLARS	Meteorological Office Library Accessions and Retrieval System (NITA)
MOLAS	Mono Lake APIPS Study (SAUO)
Mo Law Rep...	Monthly Law Reporter [*A publication*] (DLA)
MO Laws	Laws of Missouri [*A publication*] (DLA)
MOLB............	Majestic Circle, Military Order of Lady Bugs of USA (EA)
MolBio.........	Molecular Biosystems, Inc. [*Associated Press*] (SAG)
molc............	Molar Concentration [*Chemistry*] (MAE)
MOLC...........	Multiple Operational Launch Complex (MUGU)
MOLCAB	Mobile Landing Craft Advanced Base
MOLCHOP....	More or Less Charterer's Option (RIMS)
Mol Crys Liq Crys...	Molecular Crystals and Liquid Crystals (AD)
MOLD...........	Model of Light Diode
Moldav	Moldavian (DIAR)
Mol De Jure Mar...	Molloy's De Jure Maritimo et Navali [*A publication*] (DLA)
Moldov	Moldovan (DIAR)
MOLD/RADC...	Ministry of Local Development/Remote Area Development Committee (SAUO)
MOLDS	Institute for Modernization of Land Data Systems (SAUO)
MOLDS	Management On-Line Data System [*University of Syracuse*]
MOLDS	Modernization of Land Data Systems [*North American Institute for the Modernization of Land Data Systems*] [*Falls Church, VA*]
MOLDS	Multiple Online Debugging System [*Computer science*] (IEEE)
Moldv	Moldavia (AD)
MOLD/WDD...	Ministry of Local Development/Women Development Division (SAUO)
MOLE...........	Market Odd-Lot Execution System [*Computer science*] (MHDI)
mole............	Molecular (AD)
MOLE...........	Molecular Ecology (SAUO)
MOLE...........	Molecular Optics LASER Examiner [*Spectrometry*]
MOLEC.........	Molecular
MolecDev ...	Molecular Devices Corp. [*Associated Press*] (SAG)
MolecDy	Molecular Dynamics, Inc. [*Associated Press*] (SAG)
Mol Ecol	Molecular Ecology (SAUO)
molecom	Molecularized Computer (AD)
MOLECOM ...	Molecularized Digital Computer
MOLED	Molecule Organic Light Emitting Display (SAUS)
MoLeeH	Lee's Summit Hospital, Lee's Summit, MO [*Library symbol*] [*Library of Congress*] (LCLS)
MoLeeL	Longview Community College, Lee's Summit, MO [*Library symbol*] [*Library of Congress*] (LCLS)
MoLeeS	Lees Summit Public School District, Lees Summit, MO [*Library symbol*] [*Library of Congress*] (LCLS)
MoLeeU	Unity School Library, Lee's Summit, MO [*Library symbol*] [*Library of Congress*] (LCLS)
Mo Leg Exam...	Monthly Legal Examiner [*New York*] [*A publication*] (DLA)
MO Legis Serv (Vernon)...	Missouri Legislative Service (Vernon) [*A publication*] (DLA)
MOLEM........	Mobile Lunar Excursion Module [*NASA*] (PDAA)
MOLETRONICS...	Molecular Electronics
MOLEVATOR...	Motor Elevator [*Mechanical lifting stand for arc lamps*]
MOLEX.........	Molecular Executive [*Graphic substructure chemical search system*]
Molex	Molex, Inc. [*Associated Press*] (SAG)

MOLF...........	Modular Laser Fire Control (SAUS)
molfr...........	Mole Fraction [*Chemistry*] (DMAA)
MOLGEN	Molecular Genetics [*Program*] [*Computer science*]
MOLI............	Microsoft Online Institute (SAUO)
MOLIDER......	Movimiento Liberal Democratico Revolucionario [*Revolutionary Democratic Liberal Movement*] [*Honduras*] [*Political party*]
Molink	Moscow Link (AD)
MOLINK.......	Moscow-Washington Direct Communications Link (SAUO)
MOLINK.......	Moscow/Washington Emergency Communications Link (MCD)
MoLiPS........	Liberty Public Schools District, Liberty, MO [*Library symbol*] [*Library of Congress*] (LCLS)
Molirena......	Movimiento Liberal Republicano Nacionalista [*Nationalist Liberal Republican Movement*] [*Panama*] [*Political party*] (PPW)
MOLIS	Minority On-Line Information Service
MOLISV	Movement for Liberation and Development [*Italy*] Political party] (EAIO)
MoLiWJ	William Jewell College, Liberty, MO [*Library symbol*] [*Library of Congress*] (LCLS)
Mol JM	Molloy's De Jure Maritimo et Navali [*A publication*] (DLA)
moll	Metallo-Organic Liquid LASER (AD)
MOLL...........	Metallo-Organic Liquid LASER
mol/l...........	Molecules per Liter [*Measurement*] (DAVI)
Moll	Moller Organ Co. [*Record label*]
MOLL...........	Mollis [*Soft*] [*Pharmacy*]
Moll	Molloy's De Jure Maritimo [*A publication*] (DLA)
Moll	Molloy's Irish Chancery Reports [*1827-31*] [*A publication*] (DLA)
MOLLE........	Modular Light-Weight Load-Carrying Equipment [*Army*]
MOLLI.........	Micro OnLine Library Information [*Nichols Advanced Technologies, Inc.*]
mollie.........	Mollienisia (AD)
MOLLUS	Military Order of the Loyal Legion of the United States (EA)
Mollus	Mollusca (AD)
MOLLUSA	Military Order of the Loyal Legion of the USA (AD)
MOL/M³	Moles per Cubic Meter
Mo L Mag...	Monthly Law Magazine [*London*] [*A publication*] (DLA)
MOLNS	Ministry of Labour and National Service [*World War II*] [*British*] (DAS)
MOLO	Mideastern Ohio Library Organization [*Library network*]
MOLOC........	Ministry of Labour Occupational Classification [*Later, CODOT*] [*British*]
MOLOO	More or Less Owner's Option (RIMS)
MOLP..........	Microsoft Open License Pak (SAUO)
MOLP..........	Multiple Objective Linear Programming [*Computer science*] (PDAA)
Mol Pharmacol...	Molecular Pharmacology (MEC)
Mol Phys	Molecular Physics (AD)
Mol Plant-Microbe Interact...	Molecular Plant-Microbe Interactions (SAUO)
MOLR/DOS...	Ministry of Land Reforms/ Department of Survey (SAUS)
MOLR/DOS...	Ministry of Land Reforms/Department of Survey (SAUO)
MOLS..........	Magnetic-Operated Limit Switch
MOLS..........	Mirror Optional Landing System [*Aviation*] (NG)
MOLS..........	Mobile Object Location System
MOLS..........	Multiple Object Location System [*Army*]
MOLS..........	Mutually Orthogonal Latin Square
Mol Screen News...	Molecular Screening News (SAUO)
MOLSINK.....	Molecular Sink of Outer Space [*Vacuum testing chamber for spacecraft systems*]
MOLSW/DOL...	Ministry of Labour and Social Welfare/Department of Labour (SAUO)
MolT...........	Hany S Truman Library, Independence (SAUS)
MOLT..........	Manually-Operated Lift Truck (DWSG)
molt...........	Molten (AD)
MOLT..........	Molten
MoltenM......	Molten Metal Technology, Inc. [*Associated Press*] (SAG)
MOLTOL	Manned Orbiting Laboratory Test-Oriented Language [*NASA*] (MCD)
MOLTS........	Model Output Location Time Series (SAUO)
mol wt	Molecular Weight (AD)
Mol wt........	Molecular Weight (DB)
MOL WT	Molecular Weight [*Also, M, MW*]
MOLX..........	Molex, Inc. [*NASDAQ symbol*] (NQ)
MOLXA........	Molex Inc'A' [*NASDAQ symbol*] (TTSB)
MOLY..........	Molecular Analysis [*by a computer graphics system*] [*Chemistry*]
moly	Molybdenum (AD)
Moly	Molyneaux's Reports. English Courts, Tempore Car. I [*A publication*] (DLA)
MOLY..........	Mouse Lymphoma Cells [*Oncology*]
MOM............	Macro Observation Module [*Microscopy*]
MOM............	Main Outcome Measure [*Medicine*] (MELL)
MOM............	Maintenance Operations Management (MCD)
MOM............	Management of Migration [*of wastewaters*]
MOM............	Manager of Managers (SAUO)
MOM............	Manned Orbiting Mission [*NASA*]
MOM............	Man-on-the-Move [*Military slang*] (DNAB)
MOM............	Man Overboard Module [*Boating*]
MOM............	Manufacturing Operations Management (SAUO)
MOM............	Many on Many (ACAE)
MoM............	Map oriented Machine (SAUO)
MOM............	Mark XII Output and Monitoring System (SAA)
m/ o m/.......	Mas o Menos [*More or Less*] [*Spanish*] (AD)
MOM............	Master of Manufacturing (PGP)
MOM............	Measure of Merit (MCD)
MOM............	Medical Opportunities in Michigan (SAUO)
MOM............	Men Our Masters (SAUO)
MOM............	Message-Oriented Middleware [*Computer science*]
MOM............	Message Output Module [*Telecommunications*] (TEL)
MOM............	Metal-Oxide Metal (MCD)
MOM............	Method of Moments (SAUS)

MOM............ Methods of Moderation [*An association*] (EA)
MOM............ Methoxymethyl [*Organic chemistry*]
mom............ Micromation Online Microfilmer [*Computer science*] (AD)
MOM............ Micromation Online Microfilmer
MOM............ Microsoft Office Manager [*Microsoft Corp. computer program*] (PCM)
m-o-m........ Middle of Month (AD)
MOM............ Middle of the Month
MOM............ Military Official Mail (AABC)
MOM............ Military Ordinary Mail (AABC)
mom............ Military Ordinary Mail (AD)
MOM............ Military Overseas Mail [*An association*] (EA)
mom............ Milk of Magnesia (AD)
MOM............ Milk of Magnesia
MOM............ Ministry of Munitions (SAUO)
MOM............ Minutes of Meeting
MOM............ Missile Operations Manager (MUGU)
MOM............ Missionary Sisters of Our Lady of Mercy [*Roman Catholic religious order*]
MOM............ Mission Operations Manager (EOSA)
MOM............ Mitochondrial Outer-Membrane [*Biochemistry*]
MOM............ Modified Operational Missile
MOM............ Modular Ocean Model (USDC)
mom............ Moment (NAKS)
MOM............ Moment
MOM............ Momentary (MSA)
MOM............ Momentum
Mom............ Momma (AD)
MOM............ Momote [*Admiralty Islands*] [*Seismograph station code, US Geological Survey*] (SEIS)
MOM............ Mother's Restaurants Ltd. [*Toronto Stock Exchange symbol*]
MOM............ Mucoid Otitis Media [*Medicine*] (DMAA)
MOM............ Multipurpose Office Machine (VLIE)
MOM............ Multirole OTO Munition (SAUS)
MOM............ Musee Oceanographique Monaco [*Monaco Oceanographic Museum*] [*France*] (AD)
M-O-M........ My Old Man [*Husband*] [*Slang*]
MOMA........ Madagasikara Otronin'ny Malagasy [*Formerly, MONIMA*] [*Madagascar Led by Malagasy*]
MOMA........ Message-Oriented Middleware Association (SAUO)
MOMA........ Methoxyhydroxymandelic Acid [*Organic chemistry*]
MoMA........ Museum of Modern Art [*New York*] (AD)
MOMA........ Museum of Modern Art [*New York*]
MOMAC....... Monkey Mountain Advisory Center [*Military*] (CINC)
MOMAG...... Mobile Mine Assembly Group [*Military*] (CAAL)
MOMAGDET... Mobile Mine Assembly Group Detachment (DNAB)
MOMAGU..... Mobile Mine Assembly Group Unit (DNAB)
MoManW.... Laura Ingalls Wilder - Rose Wilder Lane Home and Museum, Mansfield, MO [*Library symbol*] [*Library of Congress*] (LCLS)
momau........ Modern Mobile Army (AD)
MOMAR...... Modern Mobile Army [*Military*]
MoMaryU.... Northwest Missouri State University, Maryville, MO [*Library symbol*] [*Library of Congress*] (LCLS)
MOMAT...... Mobile Mine Assembly Team
MOMATLANT... Mobile Mine Assembly Team, Atlantic (DNAB)
MOMATPAC... Mobile Mine Assembly Team, Pacific (DNAB)
momau........ Mobile Mine Assembly Unit (AD)
MOMAU...... Mobile Mine Assembly Unit (NVT)
MOMAULANT... Mobile Mine Assembly Unit, Atlantic (DNAB)
MOMAULANTDETKEF... Mobile Mine Assembly Unit, Atlantic, Keflavik Detachment (DNAB)
MOMAUPAC... Mobile Mine Assembly Unit, Pacific (DNAB)
MO-MB....... Mail-out/Mail-back (SAUS)
MOMB........ Mombasa [*Island near Kenya*] (ROG)
MOMBE...... Metallo-Organic Molecular Beam Epitaxy [*Solid state physics*]
MOMC........ Mint on a Mint Card [*Collectibles*]
MOMC........ Mint on Mint Card [*Toy collection*]
MOMC........ Mount McKinley National Park
MOMCOMS... Man-On-the-Move Communications System (SAUS)
MOMCOMS... Mobile Mine Countermeasures Command (DNAB)
MoMex....... Mexico-Audrain County Library, Mexico, MO [*Library symbol*] [*Library of Congress*] (LCLS)
MOMI......... Museum of the Moving Image [*London*] (ECON)
MOMIMTS ... Military and Orchestral Musical Instrument Makers' Trade Society [*A union*] [*British*] (DCTA)
m-o-m in am if no bm by pm... Milk-of-Magnesia in the Morning if No Bowel Movement by Evening [*Medicine*] (AD)
MOMISMAINTU... Mobile, Missile Maintenance Unit (DNAB)
MomI......... Moslem Meal (AD)
MOML........ Moslem Meal [*Airline notation*] (ADA)
MoMLV....... Moloney Murine Luekemia Virus [*Used for gene transfer protocols*] (DOG)
MoMM....... Missouri Valley College, Marshall, MO [*Library symbol*] [*Library of Congress*] (LCLS)
MOMM....... Motor Machinist's Mate [*Navy rating*]
MOMMSR.... Motor Machinist's Mate, Ship Repair [*Navy rating*]
MOMO........ Macrosomia-Obesity-Macrocephaly-Ocular Abnormalities [*Syndrome*] [*Medicine*] (DMAA)
MOMP........ Major Outer Membrane Protein [*Biochemistry*]
MOMP........ Michigan Ordnance Missile Plant [*Army*]
MOMP........ Mid-Ocean Meeting Place
MOMP........ Mustargen [*Nitrogen mustard*], Oncovin , Methotrexate, Prednisone [*Vincristine*] [*Antineoplastic drug regimen*]
MOMR........ Mayor's Office of Manpower Resources (AD)
MOMS........ Manganese Oxide Mesoporous Structure [*Inorganic Chemistry*]
MOMS........ Measure of Mission Success [*Military*] (CAAL)

MOMS .... Member of the Organisation and Methods Society [*British*] (DI)
moms .... Mervaerdiomsaetningsskat [*Value-Added Tax*] [*Danish*] (AD)
MOMS .... Meteorological and Oceanographic Measurements System [*Chevron Oil Co.*]
MOMS .... Meteorological Optic Measuring System (MCD)
MOMS .... Michigan-University Own Mathematical System (SAUO)
MOMS .... Micro-Opto-Mechanical Systems
moms .... Missile Operate Mode Simulator (AD)
MOMS .... Missile Operate Mode Simulator
MOMS .... Modified Operational Missile System (DNAB)
MOMS .... Modular Optoelectronic Multispectral Scanner (MCD)
MOMS .... Modular Optoelectronic Stereo Scanner (SAUS)
MOMS .... Mothers for Moral Stability [*Group opposing sex education in schools*]
MOMS .... Mothers Offering Maternal Support [*An association*] (MELL)
MOMS .... Mothers of Men in Service [*World War II*]
MOMS .... Multimegabit Operation Multiplexer System
MOMS .... Multiple Orbit - Multiple Satellite
MOMS .... Multiple Organ Malrotation Syndrome [*Medicine*] (DMAA)
MOM's .... Multiples over the Median [*Statistics*]
MoMSV...... Moloney Mouse Sarcoma Virus
MOMTD..... Metal on Metal Tunnel Diode (ACAE)
MoMuLV .... Moloney Murine Leukemia Virus [*Also, MLV*]
MOMV....... Manned Orbital Maneuvering Vehicle
MOM/WOW... Men Our Masters/Women Our Wonders [*Antifeminist group*] (EA)
MON........... Above Mountains [*ICAO*] (FAAC)
mon........... Maison [*House*] [*French*] (AD)
MON........... Member of the Order of the Niger [*Nigeria*]
MON........... Memorandum of Need
MON........... Memorandum of Negotiation (MCD)
MON........... Missouri Valley College, Marshall, MO [*Inactive*] [*OCLC symbol*] (OCLC)
MON........... Mixed Oxides of Nitrogen
Mon........... Monaco (AD)
MON........... Monaco [*Monaco*] [*Seismograph station code, US Geological Survey*] (SEIS)
MON........... Monaghan [*County in Republic of Ireland*] (ROG)
Mon........... Monaghan's Unreported Cases (Pennsylvania Superior Court) [*A publication*] (DLA)
Mon........... Monarch [*Record label*] [*British*]
MON........... Monarch Airlines Ltd. [*British*] [*ICAO designator*] (FAAC)
MON........... Monarch Investments Ltd. [*Toronto Stock Exchange symbol*]
mon........... Monastery (SHCU)
MON........... Monastery
Mon........... Monday (AD)
Mon........... Monday (AFM)
Mon........... Monegasque (AD)
mon........... Monetary (AD)
MON........... Monetary (AFM)
Mon........... Mongol [*One affected with Down's syndrome*] [*Medicine*] (DAVI)
mon........... Mongol [*MARC language code*] [*Library of Congress*] (LCCP)
MON........... Mongolian (AABC)
Mon........... Moniteur Belge [*A publication*] (ILCA)
Mon........... Monitor (AD)
mon........... Monitor (WDMC)
MON........... Monitor [*Navy ship symbol*]
mon........... Monitor/Contractor [*MARC relator code*] [*Library of Congress*] (LCCP)
Mon .... Monmouthshire (AD)
MON........... Monmouthshire [*County in Wales*]
Mon .... Monoceros [*Constellation*]
Mon .... Monoclinic [*Crystallography*]
Mon .... Monoclonal Antibodies, Inc.
MON........... Monocyte [*Hematology*]
Mon .... Monogram [*Numismatics*]
mon........... Monograph (BJA)
MON........... Monomoy Surfboat [*Coast Guard*] (DNAB)
MON........... Monon [*Railroad*] (MHDW)
Mon .... Monongahela
MON........... Monsanto Co. [*NYSE symbol*]
Mon .... Monsieur [*Mister*] [*French*]
Mon .... Monsignor (WGA)
mon........... Monsoon (AD)
Mon .... Montag [*Monday*] [*German*] (AD)
Mon .... Montana
Mon .... Montana Reports [*A publication*] (DLA)
Mon .... Montana Supreme Court Reports [*A publication*] (DLA)
MON........... Month
MON........... Monticello, AR [*Location identifier*] [*FAA*] (FAAL)
MON........... Monument (AAG)
Mon .... Monument (AD)
mon........... Monument (AD)
MON........... Monument Still Exists [*Genealogy*] (ROG)
mon........... Motor Octane Number (AD)
MON........... Motor Octane Number [*Fuel technology*]
MoN........... Mountain Name (BJA)
MON........... Mount Cook [*New Zealand*] [*Airport symbol*] (OAG)
MoN........... North Kansas City Public Library, North Kansas City, MO [*Library symbol*] [*Library of Congress*] (LCLS)
MON........... Universite de Moncton, Bibliotheque [*UTLAS symbol*]
Mona........ Madonna [*Our Lady*] [*Italian*] (AD)
MONA......... Marche des Options Negociables sur Actions [*Options exchange*] [*France*] (EY)
MONA......... Missouri Nurses Association (SAUO)
MONA......... Modular Navigation [*Aviation*]

Mona	Monaco (VRA)
Mona	Monaghan's Reports [147-165 Pennsylvania] [A publication] (DLA)
MONA	Monitor Assembly [Ground Communications Facility, NASA]
MONAB	Mobile Naval Advanced Base [British military] (DMA)
MONAB	Mobile Noise Analysis Barge
MONAB	Mobile Operating Naval Air Base
Monac	Monaco Finance [Associated Press] (SAG)
MonacoC	Monaco Coach Corp. [Associated Press] (SAG)
MonacoF	Monaco Finance [Associated Press] (SAG)
Monag	Monaghan (AD)
Monag	Monaghan's Reports [147-165 Pennsylvania] [A publication] (DLA)
MONAGH	Monaghan [County in Republic of Ireland] (ROG)
Monaghan	Monaghan's Reports [147-165 Pennsylvania] [A publication] (DLA)
Monaghan (PA)	Monaghan's Reports [147-165 Pennsylvania] [A publication] (DLA)
MONAGN	Monaghan [County in Republic of Ireland]
MONAL	Mobile Nondestructive Assay Laboratory [AEC]
MONALISA	Modelling Natural Images for Synthesis and Animation (SAUS)
Mon Anc	Monumentum Ancyranum [Classical studies] (OCD)
Mon Angl	Monasticon Anglicanum [A publication] (DLA)
Monare	Movement for National Redemption (SAUO)
Monas	Monastic (AD)
Monash U	Monash University (SAUO)
Monash Univ Law Rev	Monash University. Law Review [A publication]
MonAvl	Monarch Avalon, Inc. [Associated Press] (SAG)
monbas	Monobasic (AD)
MONBUSHO	Ministry of Education, Science and Culture Japan (SAUO)
MONC	Metropolitan Opera National Council
MonCap	Monmouth Capital Corp. [Associated Press] (SAG)
MonCasn	Monarch Casino & Resort [Associated Press] (SAG)
monch	Monochrome (VRA)
Monc Inn	Moncrieff's Liability of Innkeepers [1874] [A publication] (DLA)
MOND	Mondavi [Robert] [NASDAQ symbol] (SAG)
MOND	Monday (ROG)
MOND	Robert Mondavi 'A' [NASDAQ symbol] (TTSB)
Mondavi	Mondavi [Robert] [Associated Press] (SAG)
MON/DIR	Mission Monitoring Direction
mon/dir	Monitoring Direction (AD)
MONE	MatrixOne, Inc. [NASDAQ symbol] (SG)
MONE	Money Store [NASDAQ symbol] (TTSB)
MONE	[The] Money Store, Inc. [NASDAQ symbol] (SAG)
MONECA	Motor Network Calculator
MONEG	Monsoon Numerical Experimental Group (SAUO)
MONEG	Monsoon Numerical Experimentation Group (SAUO)
MONEP	Marche des Options Negotiables de Paris [French Traded Options Market] (ODBW)
MONES	Molecular Nonthermal Excitation Spectrometry
MONET	High Data Rate Mobile Internet (SAUS)
MONET	Managing Open Networks (AGLO)
MONET	Mobile Networks Integration [Telecommunications]
MONET	Monetary
MONET	Multi-Wavelength Optical Network (AAEL)
MONEVAL	Monthly Evaluation Report [Military]
monex	Monsoon Experiment (AD)
MONEX	Monsoon Experiment [Also, MONSOONEX]
Moneygr	Moneygram Payment Systems [Associated Press] (SAG)
MoneySt	[The] Money Store, Inc. [Associated Press] (SAG)
MONF	Monaco Finance [NASDAQ symbol] (SAG)
MONFA	Monaco Finance 'A' [NASDAQ symbol] (TTSB)
Mong	Mongol (AD)
Mong	Mongolia (SHCU)
MONG	Mongolian [Language, etc.]
mong	Mongolisch [Mongolian] [German] (AD)
MONG	Mongrel (DSUE)
MONG	Moning [Tea trade] (ROG)
Mongo	Mongolia (VRA)
Mongol	Mongolian (DIAR)
MONG SOCK	Mongolia Society (SAUO)
mon-H	Monohydrogen (AD)
MoNHI	Missouri Natural Heritage Inventory [Missouri State Department of Conservation] [Information service or system] (IID)
MONICA	Monitoring of Trends and Determinants in Cardiovascular Disease
MONICA	Multilateral Monitoring of Trends and Determinants in Cardiovascular Disease (SAUO)
monik	Moniker (AD)
MONIL	Mobile Non-Destructive Inspection Laboratory (DNAB)
MONIMA	Mouvement National pour l'Independance de Madagascar [National Movement for the Independence of Madagascar] [Political party] (PPW)
MONITOR	Strategic Analysis, Forecasting and Evaluation in Research and Technology (SAUO)
Mon Law Mag	Monthly Law Magazine [London] [A publication] (DLA)
Mon Law Rep	Monthly Law Reporter [A publication] (DLA)
Mon Leg R (PA)	Monroe Legal Reporter [Pennsylvania] [A publication] (DLA)
Mon LR	Monash University Law Review (SAUO)
MONM	Monmouth Capital [NASDAQ symbol] (TTSB)
MONM	Monmouth Capital Corp. [NASDAQ symbol] (SAG)
MONMC	Mint on Near Mint Card [Collectibles]
Mon Meth	Monahan's Method of the Law [1878] [A publication] (DLA)
MoNMH	North Kansas City Memorial Hospital, North Kansas City, MO [Library symbol] [Library of Congress] (LCLS)
Monmouth C	Monmouth College (GAGS)
MONMS	Monmouthshire [County in Wales]
Mon Not Roy Soc Tas	Monthly Notices. Royal Society of Tasmania [A publication]
MONO	Monaural (KSC)
Mono	Monoceros [Constellation]
MONO	Monochrome (DSUE)
mono	Monocyte [Hematology]
Mono	Monogram [Record label]
mono	Mononucleosis [Medicine] (AD)
MONO	Mononucleosis [Medicine]
mono	Monophonic (AD)
MONO	Monophonic
mono	Monopoly (AD)
mono	Monopropellant (AD)
mono	Monorail (AD)
MONO	Monorail (WDAA)
MONO	Monotone (DOAD)
mono	Monotype (AD)
MONO	Monotype (ADA)
monob	Mobile Noise Barge (AD)
MONOB	Mobile Noise Barge
MONOC	Monocoque (MSA)
monocl	Monoclinic (AD)
MONOCL	Monoclinic
monocot	Monocotyledon [Biology] (BARN)
Monod	Monon Railroad (AD)
monog	Monogram (AD)
monog	Monograph (AD)
MONOG	Monograph
Monogr Soc Res Child Dev	Monographs of the Society for Research in Child Development (SAUO)
MONOHUD	Monocular Head-Up Display (SAUS)
MONOK	Monitor Resumed Normal Operation [Aviation communications]
MONOLIN	Mobile Node Logistics and Industrial Network (SAUO)
MONOP	Monopoly [Legal shorthand] (LWAP)
monos	Monitor Out of Service (AD)
MONOS	Monitor Out of Service [Aviation communications]
monot	Monotonous (AD)
monot	Monotype (AD)
MonP	Monongahela Power Co. [Associated Press] (SAG)
MonP25	Monongahela Power Co. [Associated Press] (SAG)
monpl	Monopoly (AD)
monpr	Monoprint (VRA)
MonPw	Montana Power Co. [Associated Press] (SAG)
Monrch	Monarch Machine Tool Co. [Associated Press] (SAG)
MoNRDEP	Ministry of Natural Resources Development and Environmental Protection [Ethiopia] (ECON)
MonRE	Monmouth Real Estate Investment Corp. [Associated Press] (SAG)
Mon River	Monongahela River (AD)
Monro	Acta Cancellariae [England] [A publication] (DLA)
Monro AC	Monro's Acta Cancellariae [1545-1625] [A publication] (DLA)
Monroc	Monroc, Inc. [Associated Press] (SAG)
Monroe	Monroe Legal Reporter [Pennsylvania] [A publication] (DLA)
Monroe LR	Monroe Legal Reporter [Pennsylvania] [A publication] (DLA)
MonroM	Monro Muffler Brake, Inc. [Associated Press] (SAG)
MONS	Monastery
Mons	Monmouthshire (DIAR)
MONS	Monmouthshire [County in Wales]
MONS	Monsieur [In France this form is considered contemptuous] [Preferred form is M]
Mons	Monsieur [Mister] [French] (AD)
Monsan	Monsanto Co. [Associated Press] (SAG)
Monsanto Res Corp Mound Lab Res Dev Rep	Monsanto Research Corporation. Mound Laboratory. Research and Development Report (SAUO)
Mons Cur	Monsoon Current (AD)
MONSE	Modified Navier-Stokes Equations for Numerical Investigation of 3D Unsteady Viscous Flows (SAUO)
MONSEE	Monitoring of the Sun Earth Environment [International Council of Scientific Unions] (MCD)
Monsig	Monseigneur [My Lord] [French] (AD)
MONSIG	Monsignor [Lord, Sir] [French]
MONSOONEX	Monsoon Experiment [Also, MONEX]
MonSt	Montgomery Street Income Securities, Inc. [Associated Press] (SAG)
monstro	Monstrosity (AD)
MONSTRY	Monastery
MONSU	Movement for National Student Union (SAUO)
Mont	Montagu's English Bankruptcy Reports [A publication] (DLA)
Mont	Montana (AD)
MONT	Montana (AFM)
Mont	Montana Supreme Court Reports [A publication] (DLA)
Mont	Monterrey (AD)
Mont	Montevideo (AD)
Mont	Montgomery (AD)
MONT	Montgomeryshire [County in Wales]
Mont	Montilla [Record label] [USA, Spain, etc.]
MONT	Montmorillonite [Mineralogy]
Mont	Montpelier (AD)
Mont	Montreal (AD)
Mont	Montriou's Bengal Reports [A publication] (DLA)
MONT	Montrose District Office (SAUO)
mont	Monument (VRA)
Mont Admin R	Administrative Rules of Montana [A publication] (DLA)
Mont Admin Reg	Montana Administrative Register [A publication] (DLA)
MonTal	Monumenta Talmudica (BJA)
Mont & A	Montagu and Ayrton's English Bankruptcy Reports [1833-38] [A publication] (DLA)
Mont & Ayr	Montagu and Ayrton's English Bankruptcy Reports [1833-38] [A publication] (DLA)

Mont & Ayr Bankr...   Montagu and Ayrton's English Bankruptcy Reports [1833-38] [*A publication*] (DLA)

Mont & Ayr Bankr (Eng)...   Montagu and Ayrton's English Bankruptcy Reports [1833-38] [*A publication*] (DLA)

Mont & Ayr BL...   Montagu and Ayrton's Bankrupt Laws [*A publication*] (DLA)

Mont & B.....   Montagu and Bligh's English Bankruptcy Reports [1832-33] [*A publication*] (DLA)

Mont & B Bankr...   Montagu and Bligh's English Bankruptcy Reports [1832-33] [*A publication*] (DLA)

Mont & B Bankr (Eng)...   Montagu and Bligh's English Bankruptcy Reports [1832-33] [*A publication*] (DLA)

Mont & Bl....   Montagu and Bligh's English Bankruptcy Reports [1832-33] [*A publication*] (DLA)

Mont & C.....   Montagu and Chitty's English Bankruptcy Reports [1838-40] [*A publication*] (DLA)

Mont & C Bankr...   Montagu and Chitty's English Bankruptcy Reports [1838-40] [*A publication*] (DLA)

Mont & C Bankr (Eng)...   Montagu and Chitty's English Bankruptcy Reports [1838-40] [*A publication*] (DLA)

Mont & Ch...   Montagu and Chitty's English Bankruptcy Reports [1838-40] [*A publication*] (DLA)

Mont & Chitt...   Montagu and Chitty's English Bankruptcy Reports [1838-40] [*A publication*] (DLA)

Mont & M....   Montagu and MacArthur's English Bankruptcy Reports

Mont & MacA...   Montagu and MacArthur's English Bankruptcy Reports [*A publication*] (DLA)

Mont & M Bankr (Eng)...   Mantagu and MacArthur's English Bankruptcy Reports [1826-30] [*A publication*] (DLA)

Mon T B ......   T. B. Monroe's Kentucky Reports [17-23 Kentucky] [*A publication*] (DLA)

Mont Bankr (Eng)...   Montagu's English Bankruptcy Reports [*A publication*] (DLA)

Mont Bank Rep...   Montagu's English Bankruptcy Reports [*A publication*] (DLA)

MontBB........   Monterey Bay Bancorp, Inc. [*Associated Press*] (SAG)

Mont BC .....   Montagu's English Bankruptcy Reports [*A publication*] (DLA)

Mont Bk L....   Montagu's Bankrupt Law [4th ed.] [1827] [*A publication*] (DLA)

MONTBLEX...   Monsoon Trough Boundary Layer Experiment (SAUO)

Mont Cas....   Montriou's Cases in Hindoo Law [*A publication*] (DLA)

Montclair St C..   Montclair State College (GAGS)

Mont CMS&T...   Montana College of Mineral Science and Technology (GAGS)

Mont Code Ann...   Montana Code, Annotated [*A publication*] (DLA)

Mont Comp...   Montagu on Composition [1823] [*A publication*] (DLA)

Mont Cond Rep...   Montreal Condensed Reports [*A publication*] (DLA)

Mont D & DeG...   Montagu, Deacon, and De Gex's English Bankruptcy Reports [1840-44] [*A publication*] (DLA)

Mont Dig .....   Montagu's Digest of Pleadings in Equity [*A publication*] (DLA)

Monte ....   Montebianco (AD)

Monte ....   Monte Carlo (AD)

Monte ....   Montefiore (AD)

Monte ....   Montevideo (AD)

Monte ....   Montgomery (AD)

Monted ....   Montedison SpA [*Associated Press*] (SAG)

Monten ....   Montenegro

Mont Eq Pl...   Montagu's Digest of Pleadings in Equity [*A publication*] (DLA)

Monterey Inst...   Monterey Institute of Foreign Studies (GAGS)

Montfort Fathers...   Missionaries of the Company of Mary (SAUO)

montg ....   Montage (VRA)

MONTG ....   Montgomeryshire [*County in Wales*]

Montgom ...   Montgomeryshire [*England*] (AD)

MONTGOM...   Montgomeryshire [*County in Wales*]

Montgoms ...   Montgomeryshire (DIAR)

Month Dig Tax Articles...   Monthly Digest of Tax Articles [*A publication*] (DLA)

Month JL .....   Monthly Journal of Law [*A publication*] (DLA)

Month Jur....   Monthly Jurist [*Bloomington, IL*] [*A publication*] (DLA)

Month Law Bul...   Monthly Law Bulletin [*New York*] [*A publication*] (DLA)

Month Law Rep...   Law Reporter [*Boston*] [*A publication*] (DLA)

Month L Bull (NY)...   Monthly Law Bulletin (New York) [*A publication*] (DLA)

Month Leg Ex...   Monthly Legal Examiner [*New York*] [*A publication*] (DLA)

Month Leg Exam...   Monthly Legal Examiner [*New York*] [*A publication*] (DLA)

Month Leg Exam (NY)...   Monthly Legal Examiner (New York) [*A publication*] (DLA)

Month LJ .....   Monthly Journal of Law [*Washington*] [*A publication*] (DLA)

Month LM....   Monthly Law Magazine [*London*] [*A publication*] (DLA)

Month L Rep...   Monthly Law Reporter [*Boston*] [*A publication*] (DLA)

Month L Rep...   Monthly Law Reports [*Canada*] [*A publication*] (DLA)

Month L Rev...   Monthly Law Review [*A publication*] (DLA)

Monthly Lab Rev...   Monthly Labor Review [*A publication*] (DLA)

Monthly L Bul...   New York Monthly Law Bulletin [*A publication*] (DLA)

Month West Jur...   Monthly Western Jurist [*A publication*] (DLA)

Mont Ind......   Monthly Index to Reporters [*A publication*] (DLA)

Mont Inst....   Montriou's Institutes of Jurisprudence [*A publication*] (DLA)

Mont Law ....   Montana Lawyer [*A publication*] (DLA)

Mont Laws...   Laws of Montana [*A publication*] (DLA)

Mont Leg News...   Montreal Legal News [*A publication*] (DLA)

Mont Liens...   Montagu on Liens [*A publication*] (DLA)

Mont LR ......   Montreal Law Reports, Queen's Bench [*A publication*] (DLA)

Mont LR ......   Montreal Law Reports, Superior Court [*A publication*] (DLA)

Mont LRQB...   Montreal Law Reports, Queen's Bench [*A publication*] (DLA)

Mont LRSC...   Montreal Law Reports, Superior Court [*A publication*] (DLA)

Mont Merc Law...   Montefiore's Synopsis of Mercantile Law [*A publication*] (DLA)

montp ....   Monotype (VRA)

Montparno ...   Montparnasse (AD)

Mont Part ...   Montagu's Digest of the Law of Partnership [*A publication*] (DLA)

MontPas ......   Monterey Pasta [*Associated Press*] (SAG)

MONT-PEA...   Montana Public Employees Association

Montpellier MAI...   Mediterranean Agronomic Institute of Montpellier (SAUO)

Montr..........   Montreal [*Canada*] (AD)

MONTR........   Montreal [*Canada*]

Montr..........   Montriou's Bengal Reports [*A publication*] (DLA)

Montr..........   Montriou's Supplement to Morton's Reports [*A publication*] (DLA)

Montr Cond Rep...   Montreal Condensed Reports [*A publication*] (DLA)

Montreal LQB (Can)...   Montreal Law Reports, Queen's Bench [*Canada*] [*A publication*] (DLA)

Montreal LRQB...   Montreal Law Reports, Queen's Bench [*Canada*] [*A publication*] (DLA)

Montreal LRSC...   Montreal Law Reports, Superior Court [*Canada*] [*A publication*] (DLA)

Montreal LSC (Can)...   Montreal Law Reports, Superior Court [*Canada*] [*A publication*] (DLA)

Mont Rep.....   Montriou's Reports, Supreme Court [1846] [*Bengal, India*] (DLA)

Mont Rev Code Ann...   Montana Revised Code, Annotated [*A publication*] (DLA)

MONTRG......   Monitoring (AABC)

montrg ....   Monitoring (AD)

Montr Leg N..   Montreal Legal News [*A publication*] (DLA)

Montr QB....   Montreal Law Reports, Queen's Bench [*A publication*] (DLA)

Montr Super...   Montreal Law Reports, Superior Court [*A publication*] (DLA)

MontryH........   Monterey Homes Corp. [*Associated Press*] (SAG)

MontryR........   Monterey Resources, Inc. [*Associated Press*] (SAG)

Mont S.........   Montreal Star [*A publication*] (AD)

MONTSAME...   Mongolyn Tsahilgaan Medeeniy Agentlag [*Press agency*] [*Mongolia*]

Mont SO........   Montagu. Set-Off [2nd ed.] [1828] [*A publication*] (DLA)

Mont Sp L....   Montesquieu's Spirit of Laws [*A publication*] (DLA)

Mont St U....   Montana State University (GAGS)

Mont Super...   Montreal Law Reports, Superior Court [*A publication*] (DLA)

MONT TER...   Montana Territory

Monty ....   Montgomery (AD)

Monty ....   Montmorency (AD)

MONUA........   United Nations Angola Observation Mission (SAUO)

MONUC........   United Nations Organization Mission in the Democratic Republic of the Congo (SAUO)

Mon ULR ...   Monash University. Law Review [*A publication*]

MoNvC.........   Cottey College, Nevada, MO [*Library symbol*] [*Library of Congress*] (LCLS)

Mon Weather Rev...   Monthly Weather Review (SAUO)

Mon WJ.......   Monthly Western Jurist [*A publication*] (DLA)

Mony ....   Monastery (AD)

MONY ....   Music Operators of New York (AD)

MONY ....   Mutual of New York [*Insurance company*]

MONZ ....   Museum of New Zealand (SAUO)

MOO ....   Management Operations Officer [*Social Security Administration*]

MOO ....   Milkbottles Only Organization (EA)

MOO ....   Missile Operations Officer [*NASA*] (KSC)

MOO ....   Money-Order Office

Moo ....   Moody's English Crown Cases [168, 169 English Reprint] [*A publication*] (DLA)

MOO ....   Moomba [*Australia*] [*Airport symbol*] [*Obsolete*] (OAG)

MOO ....   Moongold Resources [*Vancouver Stock Exchange symbol*]

MOO ....   Moorlands [*Tasmania*] [*Seismograph station code, US Geological Survey*] (SEIS)

MOO ....   MUD [*Multi-User Dungeon*] Object-Oriented [*Computer science*] (DOM)

MOO ....   Multiple-User Dimension Object Oriented [*Computer technology*]

MOO ....   School of the Ozarks, Point Lookout, MO [*OCLC symbol*] (OCLC)

Moo A ....   Moore's Reports [*Bosanquet and Puller*] [*England*] [*A publication*] (DLA)

Moo & M.....   Moody and Malkin's English Nisi Prius Reports [*A publication*] (DLA)

Moo & Mal...   Moody and Malkin's English Nisi Prius Reports [*A publication*] (DLA)

Moo & P......   Moore and Payne's English Common Pleas Reports [*A publication*] (DLA)

Moo & Pay...   Moore and Payne's English Common Pleas Reports [*A publication*] (DLA)

Moo & R......   Moody and Robinson's English Nisi Prius Reports [*A publication*] (DLA)

Moo & Rob...   Moody and Robinson's English Nisi Prius Reports [*A publication*] (DLA)

Moo & S......   Moore and Scott's English Common Pleas Reports [1831-34] [*A publication*] (DLA)

Moo & Sc....   Moore and Scott's English Common Pleas Reports [1831-34] [*A publication*] (DLA)

Moo CC........   Moody's English Crown Cases Reserved [1824-44] [*A publication*] (DLA)

MOO C of S...   Management Office, Office, Chief of Staff

Moo CP........   Moore's English Common Pleas Reports [*A publication*] (DLA)

Moo Cr C...   Moody's English Crown Cases Reserved [1824-44] [*A publication*] (DLA)

Mood.........   Moody's English Crown Cases Reserved [1824-44] [*A publication*] (DLA)

Mood & M...   Moody and Malkin's English Nisi Prius Reports [*A publication*] (DLA)

Mood & Malk...   Moody and Malkin's English Nisi Prius Reports [*A publication*] (DLA)

Mood & R...   Moody and Robinson's English Nisi Prius Reports [*A publication*] (DLA)

Mood & Rob...   Moody and Robinson's English Nisi Prius Reports [*A publication*] (DLA)

Mood CC......   Moody's English Crown Cases Reserved [1824-44] [*A publication*] (DLA)

MOODS........   Music Object-Oriented Distributed System

Moody ....   Moody's English Crown Cases [168, 169 English Reprint] [*A publication*] (DLA)

Moody & M...   Moody and Malkin's English Nisi Prius Reports [*A publication*] (DLA)

Moody & M (Eng)... Moody and Malkin's English Nisi Prius Reports [*A publication*] (DLA)

Moody & R... Moody and Robinson's English Nisi Prius Reports [*A publication*] (DLA)

Moody & R (Eng)... Moody and Robinson's English Nisi Prius Reports [*A publication*] (DLA)

Moody CC (Eng)... Moody's English Crown Cases [*168, 169 English Reprint*] [*A publication*] (DLA)

Moody Cr C... Moody's English Crown Cases [*168, 169 English Reprint*] [*A publication*] (DLA)

Moody Cr Cas... Moody's English Crown Cases [*168, 169 English Reprint*] [*A publication*] (DLA)

Moog........... Moog, Inc. [*Associated Press*] (SAG)

Moo GC....... Moore's Gorham Case, English Privy Council [*A publication*] (DLA)

Moo Ind App... Moore's Reports, Privy Council, Indian Appeals [*1836-72*] [*A publication*] (DLA)

MOON......... Management of Optical Networks (SAUO)

MOON......... Meeting Our Operational Needs

Moon......... Moon's Reports [*133-144 Indiana*] [*6-14 Indiana Appeals*] [*A publication*] (DLA)

moop........... Mechlorethamine, Vincristine, Procarbazine, Prednisone [*Medicine*] (AD)

MOOP......... Ministerstvo Okhrany Obshchestvennogo Poryadka [*Ministry for Maintenance of Public Order*] [*Former USSR*] (LAIN)

MOOP......... Missile Out of Order for Parts (MCD)

Moo PC....... Moore's English Privy Council Cases, Old and New Series [*A publication*] (DLA)

Moo PCC..... Moore's English Privy Council Cases [*A publication*] (DLA)

Moo PC Cas NS... Moore's English Privy Council Cases, New Series [*A publication*] (DLA)

Moo PCC NS... Moore's English Privy Council Cases, New Series [*A publication*] (DLA)

Moo PC (NS)... Moore's English Privy Council Cases, New Series [*A publication*] (DLA)

Moor........... Dartmoor Prison [*Devon, England*] (AD)

Moor........... English King's Bench Reports, by Sir Francis Moore [*1512-1621*] [*A publication*] (DLA)

Moore......... Moore Corp. Ltd. [*Associated Press*] (SAG)

Moore......... Moore's English Common Pleas Reports [*A publication*] (DLA)

Moore......... Moore's English Privy Council Reports [*A publication*] (DLA)

Moore......... Moore's Reports [*Texas*] [*A publication*] (DLA)

Moore......... Moore's Reports [*Alabama*] [*A publication*] (DLA)

Moore......... Moore's Reports [*Arkansas*] [*A publication*] (DLA)

Moore A ...... Moore's Reports [*Bosanquet and Puller*] [*England*] [*A publication*] (DLA)

Moore Abs... Moore's Abstracts of Title [*6th ed.*] [*1925*] [*A publication*] (DLA)

Moore & P... Moore and Payne's English Common Pleas Reports [*A publication*] (DLA)

Moore & P (Eng)... Moore and Payne's English Common Pleas Reports [*A publication*] (DLA)

Moore & S... Moore and Scott's English Common Pleas Reports [*1831-34*] [*A publication*] (DLA)

Moore & S (Eng)... Moore and Scott's English Common Pleas Reports [*1831-34*] [*A publication*] (DLA)

Moore & W... Moore and Walker's Reports [*22-24 Texas*] [*A publication*] (DLA)

Moore & Walker... Moore and Walker's Reports [*22-24 Texas*] [*A publication*] (DLA)

Moore CP .... Moore's English Common Pleas Reports [*A publication*] (DLA)

Moore Cr Law... Moore's Criminal Law and Procedure [*A publication*] (DLA)

Moore EI... Moore's East Indian Appeals [*A publication*] (DLA)

Moore Fed Practice... Moore's Federal Practice [*A publication*] (DLA)

Moore GC.... Moore's Gorham Case, English Privy Council [*A publication*] (DLA)

MooreHd...... Moore-Handley, Inc. [*Associated Press*] (SAG)

Moore Ind App... Moore's Indian Appeals [*A publication*] (DLA)

Moore Ind App (Eng)... Moore's Indian Appeals [*England*] [*A publication*] (DLA)

Moore Indian App... Moore's Indian Appeals [*England*] [*A publication*] (DLA)

Moore Int L... Moore's Digest of International Law [*A publication*] (DLA)

MooreP....... Moore Products Corp. [*Associated Press*] (SAG)

Moore PC .... Moore's English Privy Council Reports [*A publication*] (DLA)

Moore PCC... Moore's English Privy Council Cases [*A publication*] (DLA)

Moore PCC (Eng)... Moore's English Privy Council Cases [*A publication*] (DLA)

Moore PCC NS... Moore's English Privy Council Cases, New Series [*A publication*] (DLA)

Moore PCC NS (Eng)... Moore's English Privy Council Cases, New Series [*A publication*] (DLA)

Moore PC NS... Moore's English Privy Council Reports, New Series [*A publication*] (DLA)

Moore Presby Dig... Moore's Presbyterian Digest [*A publication*] (DLA)

Moore QB .... Moore's English Queen's Bench Reports [*A publication*] (DLA)

Moore's Adj... Moore's International Adjudications [*Legal term*] (AD)

Moore's Arb... Moore's International Arbitrations [*Legal term*] (AD)

Moore's Dig... Moore's Digest [*Legal term*] (AD)

Moorhead St U... Moorhead State University (GAGS)

MOORNG ..... Mooring [*Freight*]

MOOS .... Modular Ocean Observation System [*Marine science*] (MSC)

MoOs........... Saint Clair County Library, Osceola, MO [*Library symbol*] [*Library of Congress*] (LCLS)

MOOSE .... Man [*or Manual*] Orbital Operations Safety Equipment [*Space life raft*] [*NASA*]

MOOSE .... Man Out of Space Easiest

MOOSE .... Method for Object-Oriented Software Engineering [*Computer science*] (VLIE)

MOOSE .... Move Out of Saigon Expeditiously [*or Earliest*] [*Army project, Vietnam*]

MOOSEMUSS... Maneuver, Objective, Offensive, Surprise, Economy of Force, Mass, Unity of Command, Simplicity, Security [*Basic principles of war*] [*See also MOSS MOUSE*]

Moo Sep Rep... Moore's Separate Report of Westerton Versus Liddell [*A publication*] (DLA)

MOOSSE...... Manned Orbital Oceanographic Survey System Experiment

moot........... Moved Out of Town (AD)

MOOT .... Move Out of Town [*Reduction of troop concentrations in cities*] [*Military*]

Moot Ct Bull... University of Illinois. Moot Court Bulletin [*A publication*] (DLA)

Moo Tr......... Moore's Divorce Trials [*A publication*] (DLA)

MOOTW .... Military Operations Other than War (RDA)

MOOV......... Moovies, Inc. [*NASDAQ symbol*] (SAG)

Moovie .... Moovies, Inc. [*Associated Press*] (SAG)

MOOW........ Medical Officer of the Watch

MOP.......... Machine Operating Processing (ACAE)

MOP.......... Magnetized Orange Pipe [*Minesweeping device*] [*Navy*]

MOP.......... Maintenance of Property

MOP.......... Maintenance Operating Procedure (MCD)

MOP.......... Maintenance Operations Protocol (ACRL)

MOP.......... Maintenance Outline Procedure [*Nuclear energy*] (NRCH)

MOP.......... Major Organ Profile [*Medicine*] (DMAA)

MOP.......... Major Overhaul Program [*Navy*]

MOP.......... Make or Purchase [*Engineering design*]

MOP.......... Management Oversight Practices (SAUO)

MOP.......... Management Overview Program (SAUO)

MOP.......... Manned Orbital Platform

MOP.......... Manner of Performance [*Officer rating*]

MOP.......... Manual of Practice (GNE)

MOP.......... Manual Operations Panel

MOP.......... Manual Override Panel (AAG)

MOP.......... Manufacturers Output Policy [*Insurance*]

MOP.......... Manuscript on Paper

MOP.......... Margin of Profit [*Accounting*]

MOP.......... Master Operating Panel (CAAL)

MOP.......... Matrix Operations Programming

MOP.......... Measures of Performance (MCD)

mop.......... Medical Outpatient (AD)

MOP.......... Medical Outpatient

MoP.......... Meeting of the Parties to the Kyoto Protocol (SAUO)

M o P.......... Member of Parliament [*British*] (AD)

MOP.......... Member of Parliament [*British*]

MOP.......... Memorandum of Participation (ARMP)

MOP.......... Memorandum of Policy

MOP.......... Memory Organization Packet [*Artificial intelligence*]

MOP.......... Message Output Processing

MOP.......... Meta Object Protocol (SAUS)

MOP.......... Meteorological Operational Programme (SAUO)

MOP.......... Methallyloxyphenol

MOP.......... Method of Procedure [*Telecommunications*] (ITD)

MOP.......... Methoxypsoralen [*Also, MP*] [*Pharmacology*]

MOP.......... Migrant Opportunity Program [*Department of Labor*]

MOP.......... Military Operation (GFGA)

MOP.......... Minimum Ordered Partition

MOP.......... Ministerio de Obras Publicas [*Ministry of Public Works*] [*Spanish*] (AD)

M o P.......... Minister of Pensions [*British*] (AD)

M o P.......... Minister of Power [*British*] (AD)

M o P.......... Minister of Production [*British*] (AD)

MOP.......... Ministry of Pensions [*British*]

MOP.......... Ministry of Pensions and Social Insurance (SAUO)

MOP.......... Ministry of Power [*British*]

MOP.......... Ministry of Production [*British*]

MOP.......... Minute of Program [*Broadcasting*] (NTCM)

MOP.......... Mission Operations Plan (MCD)

MOP.......... Mobile Offshore Production (SAUS)

MOP.......... Mobility Operating Procedure [*Military*] (AFM)

MOP.......... Model Office Project

MOP.......... Model Operational Plan

MOP.......... Mode of Operation

MOP.......... Modify Operating Procedures (AAEL)

MOP.......... Modular Operating Procedure (MUGU)

MOP.......... Modulation on the Pulse (NG)

MOP.......... Monarch Peak [*California*] [*Seismograph station code, US Geological Survey*] (SEIS)

MOP.......... Monthly Obligation Plan (SAUO)

mop.......... Mother of Pearl (AD)

MOP.......... Mother-of-Pearl

MOP.......... Mount Pleasant, MI [*Location identifier*] [*FAA*] (FAAL)

MOP.......... Mouvement d'Organisation du Pays [*Haiti*] [*Political party*] (EY)

MOP.......... Mouvement Ouvriers-Paysans [*Workers' and Peasants' Movement*] [*Haiti*] (PD)

MOP.......... Mouvement pour l'Ordre et la Paix [*Movement for Order and Peace*] [*New Caledonia*] [*Political party*] (PD)

MOP.......... Multiple Online Processing (NITA)

MOP.......... Multiple Online Programming [*Computer science*] (DIT)

MOP.......... Multiple Oocytes per Disk [*Medicine*] (MELL)

MOP.......... Multiple Output Program (MCD)

MOP.......... Muriate of Potash [*Fertilizer*]

MOP.......... Mustard, Onions, Pickles [*Restaurant slang*]

MOP.......... Mustargen [*Nitrogen mustard*], Oncovin , Prednisone [*Vincristine*] [*Antineoplastic drug regimen*]

mop.......... Mustering-Out Pay (AD)

MOP.......... Mustering-Out Pay [*Military*]

MOP.......... Myositis Ossificans Progressiva [*Medicine*] (MELL)

MOP............. , Procarbazine [Vincristine] [Antineoplastic drug regimen]
MOP............. St. Louis College of Pharmacy, St. Louis, MO [OCLC symbol] (OCLC)
MOPA .... Mail Order Publisher Authority (PDAA)
mopa .... Master Oscilator Power Amplifier (AD)
MOPA .... Master Oscillator Power Amplifier [Radio]
MOPA .... Method of Physical Action [Acting technique] (WDAA)
MOPA .... Methoxyphenylacetic Acid [Herbicide]
MOPA .... Methoxypropylamine [Organic chemistry]
MOPA .... Modus Operandi - Personal Appearance [FBI computer procedure]
MOPA .... Museum of Photographic Arts [San Diego] (AD)
MOPAC .... Methoxyhydroxyphenylacetic Acid [Organic chemistry]
MOPAC .... Missouri Pacific Railroad Co.
Mo-Pac .... Missouri-Pacific Railroad Company (SAUO)
MoPac .... Missouri Pacific - Texas & Pacific (AD)
MOPAC .... Mixed Oligonucleotide Primed Amplification of cDNA [Biochemistry]
MoPacRR .... Missouri-Pacific Railroad Company (SAUO)
MOPALI ...... Movimiento Paraguayo de Liberacion [Political party] (EY)
MOPAR .... Management of Post Attack Resources (ACAE)
MOPAR .... Master Oscillator Power Amplifier RADAR
mopar .... Master Oscillator-Power Amplifier RADAR (AD)
MOPAR .... Motor Parts [Chrysler Corp.]
MoParkC ..... Park College, Parkville, MO [Library symbol] [Library of Congress] (LCLS)
mopb .... Manually Operated Plotting Board (AD)
MOPB .... Manually Operated Plotting Board
MOPB .... Metallo-Organic Petroleum-Based Coating [Materials science]
MOP-BAP .... Mustargen [Nitrogen mustard], Oncovin , Procarbazine, Bleomycin, Adriamycin, Prednisone [Vincristine] [Antineoplastic drug regimen]
Mo PC .... Moore's English Privy Council Reports [A publication] (DLA)
MOPC .... Mouse Plasmocytoma [Cell line]
MOPCOM ..... Matrix Operations Programming Combination of Estimates
MOPD .... Maximum Operating Pressure Differential (ECII)
MOPE.......... Method of Personnel Evaluation
MOPE.......... Multiple Object Parameter Estimation
MOPED .... Ministry of Planning and Economic Development [Ethiopia] (ECON)
MOPED .... Motor/Pedal [Motorized bicycle]
mopeds....... Motorized Pedals (AD)
MOPEG .... (Methoxyhydroxyphenyl)ethyleneglycol [Also, MHPG] [Organic chemistry]
MoPeS .... Saint Mary's Seminary, Perryville, MO [Library symbol] [Library of Congress] (LCLS)
MOPET....... Methoxyhydroxyphenylethanol [Organic chemistry]
mopf.......... Missile Onloading Prism Fixture (AD)
MOPF.......... Missile Onloading Prism Fixture
MOPF.......... Mobile Optical Propagation Facility
MOPH .... Military Order of the Purple Heart of the United States of America (EA)
MOPH .... Ministry of Public Health (SAUO)
MOPI .... Maximum Rate Output Initiator (NASA)
MOPIC .... Motion Picture [Army] (AABC)
mopic .... Motion Picture [Military] (WDMC)
MOPIMS ...... Mathematical, Optical, and Philosophical Instrument Makers' Society [A union] [British]
MOPITT....... Measurements of Pollution in the Troposphere
MOPIX .... Motion Pictures
MoPL .... Map oriented Programming Language (SAUO)
MOPLN .... Mission Orbit Planning (ACAE)
MoPIS.......... School of the Ozarks, Point Lookout, MO [Library symbol] [Library of Congress] (LCLS)
MOPMS .... Modular Pack Mine System (RDA)
MOPN .... Methoxypropionitrile [Organic chemistry]
MoPobT .... Three Rivers Community College, Poplar Bluff, MO [Library symbol] [Library of Congress] (LCLS)
MoPobV .... United States Veterans Administration Hospital, Medical Library, Poplar Bluff, MO [Library symbol] [Library of Congress] (LCLS)
MOPOCO...... Movimiento Popular Colorado [Colorado Popular Movement] [Paraguay] [Political party] (PD)
MOPP .... Material Operations and Parts Procurement (ACAE)
MOPP .... Mechlorethamine, Oncovin, Procarbazine, Prednisone [Medicine] (MEDA)
MOPP .... Methotrexate, Oncomycin, Prednisone, Procarbazine [Antineoplastic drug regimen] (DAVI)
MOPP .... Military Operational Protective Posture [Chemical warfare] (RDA)
MOPP .... Military-Oriented Protective Posture
MOPP .... Mission Objective Protective Posture (SAUO)
MOPP .... Mission-Oriented Protection Posture [Army] (AABC)
MOPP .... Mission Oriented Protective Posture [Gear] [USA]
MOPP .... Modular Operating Procedure (MUGU)
MOPP .... Mustargen hydrochloride, Oncovin [Vincristine], Procarbazine, Prednisone [Antineoplastic drug regimen]
MOPP .... Mustargen [Nitrogen mustard], Oncovin , Procarbazine, Prednisone [Vincristine] [Antineoplastic drug regimen]
MOPP .... Mustine, Oncovin [Vincristine] Procarbazine, Prednisone [Antineoplastic drug regimen] (DAVI)
MOPP .... nitrogen Mustard, Oncovin, Prednisone, Procarbazine (SAUS)
MOPP/ABV... Mustargen [Nitrogen mustard], Oncovin , Procarbazine, Prednisone, Adriamycin, Bleomycin, Vinblastine [Vincristine] [Antineoplastic drug regimen]
MOPP/ABVD... Mechlorethamine, Oncovin [Vincristine] Procarbazine, Prednisone, Doxo rubicin, Bleomycin, Vinblastine, Dacarbazine [Antineoplastic drug regimen] (DAVI)
MOPP-BLEO... Mustargen [Nitrogen mustard], Oncovin , Procarbazine, Prednisone, Bleomycin [Vincristine] [Antineoplastic drug regimen]

MOPPCPF.... Mustargen [Nitrogen mustard], Oncovin , Procarbazine, Prednisone (for Patients with Compromised Pulmonary Function) [Vincristine] [Antineoplastic drug regimen]
MOPPE .... Modified Operational Propulsion Plan Examination [Navy] (NVT)
MOPPHDB ... Mustargen [Nitrogen mustard], Oncovin , Procarbazine, Prednisone, High-Dose Bleomycin [Vincristine] [Antineoplastic drug regimen]
MOPPLDB.... Mustargen [Nitrogen mustard], Oncovin , Procarbazine, Prednisone, Low-DoseBleomycin [Vincristine] [Antineoplastic drug regimen]
MOPP-LO BLEO... Mechlorethamine [Vincristine] Procarbazine, Prednisone, Bleomycin [Antineoplastic drug regimen] (DAVI)
MOPPS .... Modelling and Prototyping of a Clinical Support System (SAUO)
mopr........... Manner of Performance Rating (AD)
MOPR .... Manner of Performing Rating
MOPR .... Mission Operations Planning Review [NASA] (NASA)
MOPR .... Mission Operations Planning Room (MCD)
mopr.......... Mop Rack (AD)
MOPR .... Mop Rack
MOPr .... Mustargen [Nitrogen mustard], Oncovin , Procarbazine [Vincristine] [Antineoplastic drug regimen]
MOPr.......... , Prednisone [Vincristine] [Antineoplastic drug regimen]
Mo Prec...... Moile's Precedents [A publication] (DLA)
moprl......... Mother-of-Pearl (VRA)
MOPS .... Mail-Order Protection Scheme [British]
MOPS .... Maneuver Operations Program System [NASA]
MOPS .... Man-Operated Propulsion System
MOPS .... Marine Oil Pickup Service [Marine science] (MSC)
MOPS .... Maritime Officer Production Study [Canadian Navy]
MOPS .... Mechanization Outside Plant Scheduling System (MHDB)
MOPS .... Mechanized Outdoor Planning System
MOPS .... Merchandise Ordering Processing System (AD)
MOPS .... Message Output Processing System (SAUO)
MOPS .... Microwave Optical-Photoselection Microscopy
MOPS .... Military Operation Phone System
MOPS .... Million Operations per Second [Processing power units] [Computer science]
MOPS .... Minimum Operational Performance Standard [Aviation] (DA)
MOPS .... Missile Operations
MOPS .... Missile Operations Paging [or Phone] System [NASA]
MOPS .... Missile Operations System (AD)
MOPS .... Mission Operations Planning System [NASA] (KSC)
MOPS .... Morpholinopropanesulfonic Acid [A buffer]
MOPS .... Mothers of Preschoolers International (PAZ)
MOPS .... Multispectral Opium Poppy Sensor System
MO PSC ...... Missouri Public Service Commission Reports [A publication] (DLA)
MO PSC (NS)... Missouri Public Service Commission Reports (New Series) [A publication] (DLA)
MO PSCR ..... Missouri Public Service Commission Reports [A publication] (DLA)
MOPSS .... Management & Operation of Public Services Section [Reference and User Services Association] [American Library Association]
MOPSS .... Multispectral Opium Poppy Sensor System (AD)
MOPSY .... Multi-Programming Operating System [Computer science] (PDAA)
MOpt........... Master of Optometry (GAGS)
MOPT......... Mean One Way Propagation Time [Telecommunications] (TEL)
MOPTAR ..... Multiobject Phase Tracking and Ranging [FAA]
MOPTARS.... Multi-Object Phase-Tracking and Ranging System [FAA] (PDAA)
MOPTE........ Measure of Potential Training Effectiveness [Army]
MOptom....... Master of Optometry (ADA)
MOPTS .... Mobile Photographic Tracking Station (IEEE)
MO PUR ..... Missouri Public Utility Reports [A publication] (DLA)
MOPV .... Monovalent Oral Polio Vaccine [Immunology]
MOPW .... Ministry of Population Welfare [Pakistan] (ECON)
MOQ .... Fort Stewart (Hinesville), GA [Location identifier] [FAA] (FAAL)
MOQ .... Lindenwood College, St. Charles, MO [OCLC symbol] (OCLC)
MOQ .... Married Officer Quarters
MOQ .... Minimum Order Quantity (MCD)
MOQ .... Morocco Explorations [Vancouver Stock Exchange symbol]
MOQ .... Morondava [Madagascar] [Airport symbol] (OAG)
MOR .... AS Morefly [Norway] [ICAO designator] (FAAC)
MOR .... Magneto-Optical Rotation
MOR .... Main Operating Room (MELL)
MOR .... Management Operating Ratios (NG)
MOR .... Mandatory Occurrence Reporting
MOR .... Manually Operated Rifle (GOBB)
MOR .... Manufacturing Operation Record (NASA)
MOR .... Marital Opportunity Ratio (DIPS)
MOR .... Market Opinion Research, Inc. [Information service or system] (IID)
MOR .... Mars Orbital Rendezvous
MOR .... Master of Operations Research (PGP)
M Or .... Master of Oratory
MOR .... Maximum Ozone Reactivity [Exhaust emissions] [Automotive engineering]
MOR .... Medical Officer Report [Navy] (NG)
MOR .... Memorandum of Record (COE)
MOR .... Memory Output Register [Computer science]
MOR .... Merchandising and Operating Results
MOR .... Meteorological Optical Range (PDAA)
mor.......... Middle of the Road (AD)
MOR .... Middle of the Road [Broadcasting]
MOR .... Mid-Oceanic Ridge
MOR .... Military Operational Requirement (SAUO)
MOR .... Military Operations Research
M o R .... Ministry of Reconstruction [British] (AD)
MOR .... Missile Operationally Ready [Air Force]
MOR .... Mission Operations Room (MCD)
MOR .... Missions Operations Report [NASA] (KSC)

MO R	Missouri Reports [*A publication*] (DLA)
MOR	Modulus of Rupture [*Mechanics*]
MOR	Monthly Operating Report (IEEE)
MOR	Monthly Operating Review (USDC)
Mor	Moral (DIAR)
MOR	Moral (ROG)
Mor	Moralia [*of Plutarch*] [*Classical studies*] (OCD)
MOR	Moravian College, Bethlehem, PA [*OCLC symbol*] (OCLC)
MOR	Moray [*County in Scotland*] (ROG)
MOR	Mordenite [*A zeolite*]
Mor	Morelia (AD)
Mor	Morelos (AD)
MOR	Morendo [*Gradually Softer*] [*Music*]
mor	Morendo [*Dying Away*] [*Italian*] (AD)
MOR	Morgan Keegan & Co., Inc. [*NYSE symbol*] (SPSG)
MOR	Morgan Keegan Inc. [*NYSE symbol*] (TTSB)
MOR	Morgan Owners Register (EA)
MOR	Mori [*Japan*] [*Seismograph station code, US Geological Survey*] [*Closed*] (SEIS)
Mor	Morisco (AD)
Mor	Morison's Dictionary of Decisions, Scotch Court of Session [*1540-1808*] [*A publication*] (DLA)
MOR	Morning Star Resources [*Vancouver Stock Exchange symbol*]
Mor	Moroccan (AD)
mor	Morocco (AD)
Mor	Morocco (SHCU)
MOR	Morocco
MOR	Morocco Leather [*Bookbinding*] (ROG)
MOR	Morphine [*A narcotic*]
MOR	Morpholine [*Organic chemistry*]
MOR	Morphology (MELL)
Mor	Morris' Reports [*Jamaica*] [*A publication*] (ILCA)
MOR	Morristown, TN [*Location identifier*] [*FAA*] (FAAL)
MOR	Mortality Odds Ratio
mor	Mortar (AD)
MOR	Mortar
MOR	Movimiento Obrero Revolucionario Salvado Cayetano Carpio [*El Salvador*] [*Political party*] (EY)
MOR	Museum of the Rockies [*Montana, USA*]
MORA	Mandibular Orthopedic Repositioning Appliance [*Dentistry*]
MORA	Mimimum Off-Route Altitude [*Aviation*] (DA)
MORA	Mount Rainier National Park
MORAB	Morgan and Arabian [*Type of horse developed from these two breeds*] [*Acronym is also said to stand for "Muscular, Outstanding, Refined, Athletic, Beautiful," the horse's distinguishing characteristics*]
MORAL	Massachusetts Organization for the Repeal of Abortion Laws
MORAN	Management of Resources, Accesses & Network (SAUO)
Mor & Carl	Moreau-Lislet and Carleton's Laws of Las Siete Partidas in Force in Louisiana [*A publication*] (DLA)
MoRAP	Missouri Resource Assessment Partnership (SAUO)
MORASS	Modern Ramjet System Synthesis (MCD)
Morav	Moravia (AD)
MORB	Mid-Ocean Ridge Basalt [*Geology*]
Morb	Morbihan (AD)
MORBREPT	Morbidity Report
MORBTGREPT	Morbidity Telegraphic Report
MORC	Medical Officers' Reserve Corps
MORC	Midget Ocean Racing Class [*or Club*]
Mor Chy Acts	Morgan's Chancery Acts and Orders [*6th ed.*] [*1885*] [*A publication*] (DLA)
MORCO	Morrison, Inc. (EFIS)
Mor Comp	Morris on Compensations [*A publication*] (DLA)
Mor Corp	Morawetz on Private Corporations [*A publication*] (DLA)
MORCOS	Mortar Computer System (SAUS)
MORD	Magneto-Optic Rotary Dispersion (PDAA)
MORD	Medical Operations Requirements Document (MCD)
MORD	Military Operations Research Department
MORD	Ministry of Revolutionary Development [*Vietnam*]
MORD	Mission Operations Requirements Document [*NASA*] (NASA)
Mord	Mordehai (AD)
Mordhy	Mordehai (AD)
Mor Dic	Morison's Dictionary of Decisions, Scotch Court of Session [*1540-1808*] [*A publication*] (DLA)
mor dict	More Dicto [*As Directed*] [*Latin*] (AD)
Mor Dict	Morison's Dictionary of Decisions, Scotch Court of Session [*1540-1808*] [*A publication*] (DLA)
MOR DICT	Moro Dicto [*As Directed*] [*Pharmacy*]
Mor Dig	Morley's Digest of the Indian Reports [*A publication*] (DLA)
Mor Dig	Morrison's New Hampshire Digest [*A publication*] (DLA)
Mor Dil	Morris on Dilapidations [*2nd ed.*] [*1871*] [*A publication*] (DLA)
MORDS	Manned Orbital Research and Development System
MORDT	Mobilization Operational Readiness Deployment Test [*DoD*]
Mordy	Mordechai (AD)
MORE	Management of Radiographic Environments [*Radiology*] (DAVI)
MORE	Meal, Ordered Ready-to-Eat [*Army*] (RDA)
MORE	Microbial Oil Recovery Enhancement [*Petroleum technology*]
MORE	Midwest Organization for Research in Education (AEBS)
MORE	Military Officer Record Examination
MORE	Minority Officer Recruitment Effort
MORE	Minority Outreach Research and Education (SAUO)
MORE	Mission for Outreach, Renewal, and Evangelism (AD)
MORE	Money, Opportunity, Responsibility, and Equality [*Of organization "MORE for Women"*]
MORE	Multioptical Reconnaissance Equipment [*Military*] (CAAL)

Mor E & RD Law	Morice's English and Roman Dutch Law [*A publication*] (DLA)
Mor Eas	Morris on the Law of Easements [*A publication*] (DLA)
Moreau & Carleton's Partidas	Moreau-Lislet and Carleton's Laws of Las Siete Partidas in Force in Louisiana [*A publication*] (DLA)
MORE DICT	More Dicto [*As Directed*] [*Pharmacy*] (ROG)
Morehead St U	Morehead State University
Morehouse Sch of Med	Morehouse School of Medicine (GAGS)
MOREL	Michigan-Ohio Regional Educational Laboratory
More Lect	More's Lectures on the Law of Scotland [*A publication*] (DLA)
MORENA	Mouvement de Redressement National [*Gabon*] [*Political party*] (EY)
MORENA	Movimiento de Renovacion Nacional [*National Renewal Movement*] [*Venezuela*] [*Political party*] (PPW)
MORENA	Movimiento de Restauracion Nacional [*National Restoration Movement*] [*Colombia*] [*Political party*] (EY)
MORENET	Missouri Research and Education Network
MO Rep	Missouri Reports [*A publication*] (DLA)
MOREP	Monthly Report
moreps	Monitor Station Reports (AD)
MOREPS	Monitor Station Reports
MORES	Minerals, Oils, and Resources Shares Fund [*British*]
MORE SOL	More Solito [*In the Usual Way*] [*Pharmacy*] (ROG)
MOREST	Mobile Arresting Gear [*Navy*]
More St	More's Notes on Stair's Institutes of Scotland [*A publication*] (DLA)
MORET	Moreton [*England*]
MO Rev Stat	Missouri Revised Statutes [*A publication*] (DLA)
Morey Out Rom Law	Morey's Outlines of Roman Law [*A publication*] (DLA)
MORF	Male or Female (NHD)
MorF	Male or Female
MORF	Manned Orbital Research Facility [*NASA*] (MCD)
mor fib	Moral Fiber (AD)
MORFLOT	Ministry of the Merchant Marine of the Soviet Union (SAUO)
MORG	Morgan Financial Corp. [*NASDAQ symbol*] (SAG)
MORG	Morgan Finl (Del) [*NASDAQ symbol*] (TTSB)
Morg	Morgan's Chancery Acts and Orders [*6th ed.*] [*1885*] [*A publication*] (DLA)
MORG	Movements Reports Generator (DNAB)
MORG	Museo Oceanografico de Rio Grande [*Oceanographic Museum of Rio Grande*] [*Brazil*] (AD)
MORGA	Municipal Organization Act (DICI)
Morgan	Morgan [*J. P.*] & Co., Inc. [*Associated Press*] (SAG)
Morgan	Morgan's Digest [*Ceylon*] [*A publication*] (DLA)
Morg & Ch Jud Acts	Morgan and Chute on the Judicature Acts [*A publication*] (DLA)
Morg & WLJ	Morgan and Williams' Law Journal [*London*] [*A publication*] (DLA)
Morgan LM	Morgan's Legal Miscellany [*Ceylon*] [*A publication*] (DLA)
Morgan St U	Morgan State University (GAGS)
Morg Ch	Morgan's Chancery Acts and Orders [*6th ed.*] [*1885*] [*A publication*] (DLA)
MorgFn	Morgan Financial Corp. [*Associated Press*] (SAG)
MorgFun	Morgan Funshares, Inc. [*Associated Press*] (SAG)
MorgGr	Morgan Grenfell Smallcap Fund, Inc. [*Associated Press*] (SAG)
MorgK	Morgan Keegan [*Associated Press*] (SAG)
MorgKeg	Morgan Keegan & Co., Inc. [*Associated Press*] (SAG)
Morg Lit	Morgan on the Law of Literature [*A publication*] (DLA)
morg mar	Morganatic Marriage (AD)
Morgn	Morgan [*J. P.*] & Co., Inc. [*Associated Press*] (SAG)
MorgnF	Morgan's Foods, Inc. [*Associated Press*] (SAG)
MorgnP	Morgan Products Ltd. [*Associated Press*] (SAG)
MorgSt	Morgan Stanley Group, Inc. [*Associated Press*] (SAG)
Morg Tar	Morgan on the United States Tariff [*A publication*] (DLA)
Mor Hors	Morrell on the Law of Horses [*A publication*] (DLA)
MORI	F. Maros Research Institute for Food Crops (SAUO)
Mori	Market and Opinion Research International [*Polling organization*] (ODBW)
MORI	Market and Opinion Research International [*Polling organization*]
Mor IA	Morris' Iowa Reports [*1839-46*] [*A publication*] (DLA)
MORIE	Metalorganic Reactive Ion Etching (AAEL)
MORIF	Microprogram Optimization Technique Considering Resource Occupancy and Instruction Formats (MHDB)
MoRih	Richmond Heights Memorial Library, Richmond Heights, MO [*Library symbol*] [*Library of Congress*] (LCLS)
moritzer	Mortar Howitzer (AD)
MORITZER	Mortar Howitzer (NATG)
MorKnd	Morrison-Knudsen Co., Inc. [*Associated Press*] (SAG)
MORL	Manned Orbital [*or Orbiting*] Research Laboratory [*NASA*]
MORL	Medium-Sized Orbital Research Laboratory (SAA)
Morl Dig	Morley's East Indian Digest [*A publication*] (DLA)
Mor Lib	Morgan Library (AD)
Mor M	Master Mortician
Morm	Mormon (AD)
MORM	Mormon (WDAA)
MoRM	University of Missouri at Rolla, Rolla, MO [*Library symbol*] [*Library of Congress*] (LCLS)
Mor Maj	Moral Majority (AD)
Mor Min Rep	Morrison's Mining Reports [*A publication*] (DLA)
Mor Miss	Morris' Reports [*Mississippi*] [*A publication*] (DLA)
morn	Morning (AD)
MORN	Morning
MornGp	Morningstar Group [*Associated Press*] (SAG)
Morningside C	Morningside College (GAGS)
Moro	Book of Moroni (AD)
MORO	Moon Orbiting Observatory (SAUS)
Moro	Morocco (VRA)
MORO	Morocco Leather [*Bookbinding*] (ROG)
Moroc	Moroccan (AD)

MOROCLANT...   Maritime Forces Morocco (SAUO)
MORP ....   Medical and Occupational Radiation Program [HEW]
MORP ....   Meteorite Observation and Recovery Project [Canada]
MORP ....   Mid-Ocean Ridge Peridotite [Geology]
MORP ....   Moore Products [NASDAQ symbol] (TTSB)
MORP ....   Moore Products Co. [NASDAQ symbol] (NQ)
morph ....   Morphine (AD)
MORPH ....   Morphine (WDAA)
morph ....   Morphology (AD)
MORPH ....   Morphology
Morphing .....   Metamorphosizing [Video technology]
MORPHOL ...   Morphology
morphophysio...   Morphophysiological (AD)
MORPHS.....   Minicomputer-Operated Retrieval (Partially Heuristic) System [Computer science]
Mor Pr ....   Morehead's Practice [A publication] (DLA)
Mor Priv Corp...   Morawetz on Private Corporations [A publication] (DLA)
MORPS ....   Maritime Other Ranks Production Study [Canadian Navy]
MorR ....   Bibliotheque Generale et Archives, Rabat, Morocco [Library symbol] [Library of Congress] (LCLS)
Morr............   Morrell's English Bankruptcy Reports [A publication] (DLA)
Morr............   Morris' Iowa Reports [1839-46] [A publication] (DLA)
Morr............   Morris' Jamaica Reports [A publication] (DLA)
Morr............   Morris' Reports [Bombay, India] [A publication] (DLA)
Morr............   Morris' Reports [Oregon] [A publication] (DLA)
Morr............   Morris' Reports [California] [A publication] (DLA)
MORR..........   Morristown National Historical Park
Morr Bankr Cas...   Morrell's English Bankruptcy Cases [A publication] (DLA)
Morr BC ....   Morrell's English Bankruptcy Reports [A publication] (DLA)
Morr Bomb...   Morris' Reports [Bombay, India] [A publication] (DLA)
Morr Cal ......   Morris' Reports [California] [A publication] (DLA)
Morr Dict .....   Morrison's Dictionary of Decisions, Scotch Court of Session [A publication] (DLA)
Morr Dig .....   Morrison's Digest of Mining Decisions [A publication] (DLA)
Morr Dig .....   Morrison's New Hampshire Digest [A publication] (DLA)
Morrell Bankr Cas...   Morrell's English Bankruptcy Cases [A publication] (DLA)
Morrell BC...   Morrell's English Bankruptcy Cases [A publication] (DLA)
Morrell (Eng)...   Morrell's English Bankruptcy Cases [A publication] (DLA)
Mor Rep ......   Morris' Law of Replevin [A publication] (DLA)
Morris..........   Morris' Iowa Reports [1839-46] [A publication] (DLA)
Morris..........   Morris' Jamaica Reports [A publication] (DLA)
Morris..........   Morris' Reports [California] [A publication] (DLA)
Morris..........   Morris' Reports [Oregon] [A publication] (DLA)
Morris..........   Morris' Reports [Bombay, India] [A publication] (DLA)
Morris..........   Morris' Reports [Mississippi] [A publication] (DLA)
Morris..........   Morrissett's Reports [80, 98 Alabama] [A publication] (DLA)
Morris & Har...   Morris and Harrington's Reports [Bombay, India] [A publication] (DLA)
Morris (IA)...   Morris' Iowa Reports [1839-46] [A publication] (DLA)
Morris (Iowa)...   Morris' Iowa Reports [1839-46] [A publication] (DLA)
Morrison......   Morrison Restaurants, Inc. [Associated Press] (SAG)
Morrison Min Rep...   Morrison's Mining Reports [United States] [A publication] (DLA)
Morris R ......   Morris' Jamaica Reports [A publication] (DLA)
Morris Repl...   Morris on Replevin [A publication] (DLA)
Morris St Cas...   Morris' Mississippi State Cases [1818-72] [A publication] (DLA)
Morr Jam.....   Morris' Jamaica Reports [A publication] (DLA)
MorrKn.......   Morrison Knudsen Corp. [Associated Press] (SAG)
MorrKnud ....   Morrison Knudsen Corp. [Associated Press] (SAG)
Morr Mines...   Morrison's Digest of Mining Decisions [A publication] (DLA)
Morr Min R...   Morrison's Mining Reports [United States] [A publication] (DLA)
Morr Min Rep...   Morrison's Mining Reports [A publication] (DLA)
Morr Miss....   Morris' Reports [Mississippi] [A publication] (DLA)
Morr MR.....   Morrison's Mining Reports [United States] [A publication] (DLA)
MorrowSn....   Morrow Snowboards, Inc. [Associated Press] (SAG)
Morr Repl....   Morris' Law of Replevin [A publication] (DLA)
Morr St Cas...   Morris' Mississippi State Cases [1818-72] [A publication] (DLA)
Morr Trans...   Morrison's Transcript of United States Supreme Court Decisions [A publication] (DLA)
Mor Ry Com...   Morris on Railway Compensations [A publication] (DLA)
MORS ....   Group of Experts Monitoring of Radioactive Substances in the Baltic Sea (SAUO)
MORS ....   Midland Operational Research Society (AD)
MORS ....   Military Operations Research Society (EA)
MORS ....   Military Operations Research Symposia (MCD)
MORS ....   Military Operations Research Symposium (SAUO)
MORS ....   Minefield & Ordnance Recovery Management System (SAUS)
MORS ....   Multi-Outlet Reservoir Study [Department of the Interior] (GRD)
MORSA.......   Movement Requirements for Staff Planning and Special Studies Applications (SAUO)
mor sal........   More Solito [In the Usual Manner] [Latin] (AD)
M Or Sc.......   Master of the Science of Oratory
MORSEAFRON...   Moroccan Sea Frontier [Navy] [World War II]
Morse Arb ...   Morse on the Law of Arbitration and Award [A publication] (DLA)
Morse Banks...   Morse on the Law of Banks and Banking [A publication] (DLA)
Morse Bk.....   Morse on the Law of Banks and Banking [A publication] (DLA)
Morse Exch Rep...   Morse's Exchequer Reports [Canada] [A publication] (DLA)
MorSEm.......   Morgan Stanley Emerging Markets [Associated Press] (SAG)
Morse Tr......   Morse's Famous Trials [A publication] (DLA)
MORSL ....   Mobilization Reserve Stockage List [Army] (AABC)
MorsnFr.......   Morrison Fresh Cooking, Inc. [Associated Press] (SAG)
MorsnHl.......   Morrison Health Care, Inc. [Associated Press] (SAG)
mor sol........   More Solito [In the usual manner] [Latin] [Pharmacy] (DAVI)
MOR SOL.....   More Solito [In the Usual Way] [Pharmacy]
MORST........   Ministry of Research, Science and Technology (SAUO)

Mor St Ca....   Morris' Mississippi State Cases [1818-72] [A publication] (DLA)
Mor St Cas...   Morris' Mississippi State Cases [1818-72] [A publication] (DLA)
Mor Supp.....   Morison's Dictionary of Decisions, Scotch Court of Session, Supplement [1620-1768] [A publication] (DLA)
Mor Syn.......   Morison's Synopsis, Scotch Session Cases [1808-16] [A publication] (DLA)
moRt...........   Mainstream of Republican Thought (AD)
MORT ....   Management Oversight and Risk Tree (NASA)
MORT ....   Master Operational Recording Tape [SAGE]
MORT ....   Ministry of Research and Technology (SAUO)
MORT ....   Ministry of Roads and Trees (SAUO)
MORT ....   Missile Operation [or Ordnance] Readiness Test [or Testing]
mor t ....   Morse Taper (AD)
MORT ....   Morse Taper
mort............   Mortal (AD)
mort............   Mortality
MORT ....   Mortar (AABC)
mort............   Mortar (AD)
Mort...........   Mortemart (AD)
mort............   Mortgage (AD)
MORT ....   Mortgage (ADA)
mort............   Mortician (AD)
MORT ....   Mortician
Mort...........   Mortimer (AD)
Mort...........   Morton (AD)
MORT ....   Mortuary (ADA)
MORTAL ......   Mortality (BABM)
mortal.........   Mortality [Statistics] (DAVI)
MORTG ....   Mortgage
MortnRst.....   Mortons Restaurant Group [Associated Press] (SAG)
Morton.........   Morton's Reports, Calcutta Superior Court [India] [A publication] (DLA)
Morton Int ...   Morton International, Inc. [Associated Press] (SAG)
Mor Tran.....   Morrison's Transcript of United States Supreme Court Decisions [A publication] (DLA)
MORTREP....   Mortar Bombing Report
Mort Vend...   Morton's Vendors and Purchasers [1837] [A publication] (DLA)
MORU.........   Mount Rushmore National Memorial
MORV ....   Mobile Overpass Roadway-Repair Vehicle
Mor Wills ...   Morrell on the Law of Wills [A publication] (DLA)
Mos ....   Book of Mosiah (AD)
Mos ....   De Vita Mosis [Philo] (BJA)
MOS............   Machinery and Occupational Safety Act [Environmental science]
MOS............   Macula of Saccule [Medicine] (MELL)
MOS............   Magneto-Optical System (AD)
MOS............   Mail-Order Sales (WDAA)
MOS............   Maintenance Operations Section [Marine Corps] (DOMA)
MOS............   Major Operating System [Army] (AABC)
MOS............   Malta Ornithological Society (SAUO)
MOS............   Management Operating System
MOS............   Management Operations Staff [Environmental Protection Agency] (GFGA)
MOS............   Management Orientation School [LIMRA]
MOS............   Manned Orbital Station (AAG)
MOS............   Man on the Street (WDMC)
MOS............   Man-on-the-Street Interview [Journalism]
MOS............   Manual Override Switch
MOS............   Manufacturing Operating System [IBM Corp.]
MOS............   Manufacturing Operations Survey (MCD)
MOS............   Margin of Safety [Business term]
MOS............   Marine Observation Satellite [Japan]
MOS............   Marine Occupational Standard (DNAB)
MOS............   Maritime Operational Intelligence Summary (MCD)
MOS............   Marking of Overseas Shipments
MOS............   Mass On-Line Storage (SAUO)
MOS............   Master Operating System [Sperry UNIVAC]
MOS............   Material Ordering Schedule
MOS............   Mathematical Off-Print Service [American Mathematical Society]
MOS............   Mean Opinion Score
MOS............   Measurement of Skill (AEBS)
MOS............   Measure of Suitability (CAAL)
MOS............   Mechanical Oblique Sketcher
MOS............   Medial Orbital Sulcus (DB)
MOS............   Medical Outcomes Study (DMAA)
MOS............   Member of the Opposite Sex (SAUS)
MOS............   Memorandum of Support (SAUO)
MOS............   Memory Operating Software [Computer science]
MOS............   Memory-Oriented System
MOS............   Mercantile Open Stock
MOS............   Meridian Ocean Systems (SAUS)
MOS............   Mesa Offshore Trust (EFIS)
MOS............   Metal Oxide on a Substrate (MCD)
mos ....   Metal-Oxide Semiconductor (AD)
MOS............   Metal-Oxide Semiconductor
mos ....   Metal-Oxide Silicon (AD)
MOS............   Metal-Oxide-Silicon [Integrated circuit] [Electronics]
MOS............   Metal Oxide Software Similarity (AGLO)
MOS............   Microprogram Operating System
MOS............   Microsomal Ethanol-Oxidizing System (DMAA)
MOS............   Military Occupational Skill (SAUO)
mos ....   Military Occupational Specialty (AD)
MOS............   Military Occupational Specialty [Army]
MOS............   Military Occupational Specification Serial Number [British] [World War II]

MOS............	Military Oceanography Subcommittee [*National Security Industrial Association*] (USDC)
MOS............	Military Overseas Supply [*British*]
mOs............	Milliosmole [*or Milliosmolar*] (AAMN)
MOS............	Minimum Operating Strip (SAUO)
MOS............	Minimum Operating System [*Sperry Univac*] (NITA)
MOS............	Ministry of Sound (SAUO)
MOS............	Ministry of State [*British*]
MOS............	Ministry of Supply [*Also, MS*] [*British*]
MOS............	Minus Optical Sound [*Film industry*]
mos	Missile On Stand (AD)
MOS............	Missile on Stand
MOS............	Missile Operations Station
MOS............	Mission Operations Software (ACAE)
MOS............	Mission Operations Strategy [*NASA*]
MOS............	Mission Operations System [*NASA*]
MOS............	Mit Out Sound [*i.e., "without sound"*] [*Film industry*]
mos	Mit-Out Sound (AD)
MOS............	Mitral Opening Sound [*Cardiology*]
MOS............	Model Output Statistics [*Meteorology*]
MOS............	Mode of Shipment (ACAE)
MOS............	Modular Operating System (BUR)
MOS............	Moloney Murine Sarcoma [*Medicine*] (DMAA)
MOS............	Monitor Only crew Station (SAUS)
MOS............	Monolithic Oxide Silicon (SAUO)
mos	Months (AD)
MOS............	Months
MOS............	Morton Air Services Ltd.
mos	Mosaic (VRA)
MOS............	Mosaic
Mos	Moscow (AD)
MOS............	Moscow [*Russia*] [*Seismograph station code, US Geological Survey*] (SEIS)
Mos	Moseley's English Chancery Reports [*25 English Reprint*] [*A publication*] (DLA)
Mos	Mosella [*of Ausonius*] [*Classical studies*] (OCD)
MOS............	Moses Point, AK [*Location identifier*] [*FAA*] (FAAL)
Mos	Moshe (AD)
Mos	Moslem (AD)
MOS............	Mosport Park Corp. [*Vancouver Stock Exchange symbol*]
mos	Mossi [*MARC language code*] [*Library of Congress*] (LCCP)
MOS............	Multiple Object Spectroscopy (PDAA)
MOS............	Multiprogramming Operating System
MoS.............	Museum of Sydney [*Australia*]
MOS............	Myelofibrosis Osteosclerosis [*Medicine*] (DMAA)
MOS............	Myocardial Oxygen Supply [*Medicine*] (MELL)
MOS............	Springfield-Greene County Library, Springfield, MO [*OCLC symbol*] (OCLC)
MoS.............	St. Louis Public Library, St. Louis, MO [*Library symbol*] [*Library of Congress*] (LCLS)
MOS-1	Marine Observations Satellite-1 (SAUO)
MOSA	Medical Officers of Schools Association (SAUO)
MOSA	Medical Officers of Schools Associations [*British*]
MOSA	Method of Standard Addition [*Statistics*]
MOSA	Michigan Optometric Student Association (SAUO)
MOSA	Minimum Operational Safe Altitude (DOMA)
MOSA	Ministry of Science and Arts [*US and Israel*]
MoSAB.........	Anheuser-Busch, Inc., St. Louis, MO [*Library symbol*] [*Library of Congress*] (LCLS)
MOSAIC	Macro Operation Symbolic Assembler and Information Compiler [*Computer science*] (IEEE)
MOSAIC	Metal-Oxide-Semiconductor Advanced Integrated Circuit [*Electronics*] (IEEE)
MOSAIC	Method of Scenic Alternative Impacts by Computer (PDAA)
MOSAIC	Ministry of Supply Automatic Integrator and Computer [*British*] (DEN)
MOSAIC	Mobile SONAR Automatic Information Classifier (TIMI)
MOSAIC	Mobile System for Accurate ICBM Control (MCD)
MOSAIC	Modular Open System Architecture for Industrial Motion Control (SAUO)
MOSAIC	Multifunctional on-the-Move Secure Adaptive Integrated Communications [*Military*]
MOSAIC	Multi-User, On-Line System for Automated Information Communication (SAUO)
MOSAICC	Micro-organisms Sustainable Use and Access Regulation (SAUO)
MOSAICC	Micro-organisms Sustainable Use and Access Regulation, an International Code of Conduct (SAUS)
MOSAICS	Melcom Optical Software Applications for Integrated Commercial Systems (PDAA)
MOSAP	Marine Oil Spills Action Plan (SAUO)
MOSAR	Modulation Scan Array RADAR [*or Receiver*]
MOSART	Monolithic Signal Processor and Detector Array (ACAE)
MOSASR	Metal Oxide Semiconductor Analogue Shift Register [*Electronics*] (PDAA)
MoSavHi......	Andrew County Historical Society, Savannah, MO [*Library symbol*] [*Library of Congress*] (LCLS)
MOSAW	Medium Operating Speed Automatic Weapon [*Military*]
MOSB	Military Order of the Stars and Bars (EA)
MoSB	Missouri Botanical Garden, St. Louis, MO [*Library symbol*] [*Library of Congress*] (LCLS)
Mosbas........	Moscow Basin (AD)
MOSC	Management Orientation Study Course [*LIMRA*]
mosc	Manned Orbital Systems Concept (AD)
MOSC	Manned Orbital Systems Concepts [*NASA*]
MOSC	Marine Oil Spills Committee (SAUO)
MOSC	Maritime Operations Support Center (SAUO)
MOS-C	Metal-Oxide Semiconductor Capacitor (AAEL)
MOSC	Midland-Odessa Symphony and Chorale (AD)
MOSC	Military Occupational Specialty Code (AABC)
MOSC	Military Oil Subcommittee [*of North African Economic Board*] [*World War II*]
MOSC	Mission Operations System Center (ACAE)
MOSC	Mosaic
MOSCA	McNamara-O'Hara Service Contract Act of 1965 (WYGK)
MOSCAP	Modified Service Contract and Procedures [*DoD*]
MoSCC........	St. Louis Community College, Instructional Resource Technical Services, St. Louis, MO [*Library symbol*] [*Library of Congress*] (LCLS)
MoSCEx......	Christ Seminary-Seminex, St. Louis, MO [*Library symbol*] [*Library of Congress*] (LCLS)
MoSCH	Concordia Historical Institute, St. Louis, MO [*Library symbol*] [*Library of Congress*] (LCLS)
MOSCH.......	Moschus [*Musk*] [*Pharmacology*] (ROG)
MoSCo........	St. Louis County Library, St. Louis, MO [*Library symbol*] [*Library of Congress*] (LCLS)
Moscom......	Moscom Corp. [*Associated Press*] (SAG)
Mos Cont	Moseley's Contraband of War [*1861*] [*A publication*] (DLA)
MOSCOW....	Museum of Soviet Calculators on the Web [*Computer science*]
MoSCP........	St. Louis College of Pharmacy, St. Louis, MO [*Library symbol*] [*Library of Congress*] (LCLS)
MoSCRR	Center for Reformation Research, St. Louis, MO [*Library symbol*] [*Library of Congress*] (LCLS)
MoSCS........	Concordia Seminary, St. Louis, MO [*Library symbol*] [*Library of Congress*] (LCLS)
MoSCT........	Covenant Theological Seminary, St. Louis, MO [*Library symbol*] [*Library of Congress*] (LCLS)
MOSD	Military Occupational Specialty Division (SAUO)
MoSDM.......	United States Air Force, Defense Mapping Agency Aerospace Center, St. Louis, MO [*Library symbol*] [*Library of Congress*] (LCLS)
Mose	Moises (AD)
Mose	Moseley (AD)
Mose	Mosen (AD)
Mose	Moses (AD)
MoSe	Sedalia Public Library, Sedalia, MO [*Library symbol*] [*Library of Congress*] (LCLS)
MoSE	United States Army, Corps of Engineers, District Library St. Louis, St. Louis, MO [*Library symbol*] [*Library of Congress*] (LCLS)
MoSed	Sedalia Public Library, Sedalia, MO [*Library symbol*] [*Library of Congress*] (LCLS)
MOSEL.......	Molten-Salt Epithermal Reactor
Moseley......	Moseley's English Chancery Reports [*25 English Reprint*] [*A publication*] (DLA)
Mos El L	Moseley's Elementary Law [*2nd ed.*] [*1878*] [*A publication*] (DLA)
Mosely (Eng)...	Moseley's English Chancery Reports [*25 English Reprint*] [*A publication*] (DLA)
MOSES	Major Open Systems Environment Standards (SAUO)
MOSES	Manned Open Sea Experiment Station (NOAA)
MOSES	Manufacturing Operations Short Event Scheduling
MOSES	Massive Open Systems Environment Standard [*Computer science*]
MOSES	Meteorological Observing Station (SAUO)
MOSES	Mobile Station for Environmental Services (SAUO)
MOSES	Molecular Orbital Self-Consistent Energy System (PDAA)
MOSES	Motor-Operated Sled Ejection System (MCD)
MOSES	Movable Search System (MCD)
MOSES	Multioccupant Sealed Environment Simulator
MoSF	Fontbonne College, St. Louis, MO [*Library symbol*] [*Library of Congress*] (LCLS)
MOSF	Multiple Organ System Failure [*Medicine*] (MELL)
MOSFET.......	Metal Oxide Semiconductor Field Effect Transformer (NITA)
mosfet	Metal-Oxide Semiconductor Field-Effect Transistor (AD)
MOSFET.......	Metal-Oxide-Semiconductor [*or Silicon*] Field-Effect Transistor
MOSFETS ...	Metal Oxide Substrate Field Effect Transistor
MoSFi..........	Eugene Field House, St. Louis, MO [*Library symbol*] [*Library of Congress*] (LCLS)
MoSFRR	Foundation for Reformation Research, St. Louis, MO [*Library symbol*] [*Library of Congress*] [*Obsolete*] (LCLS)
MoSGS	Church of Jesus Christ of Latter-Day Saints, Genealogical Society Library, St. Louis Branch, St. Louis, MO [*Library symbol*] [*Library of Congress*] (LCLS)
MOsH	Medical Officers of Health (SAUO)
Mosh	Moshav [*or Moshava*] (BJA)
MoSHi..........	Missouri Historical Society, St. Louis, MO [*Library symbol*] [*Library of Congress*] (LCLS)
MoSHS	Harris-Stowe State College Library, St. Louis, MO [*Library symbol*] [*Library of Congress*] (LCLS)
MoSHT	Harris Teachers College, St. Louis, MO [*Library symbol*] [*Library of Congress*] (LCLS)
MOSI	Mosinee Paper [*NASDAQ symbol*] (TTSB)
MOSI	Mosinee Paper Corp. [*NASDAQ symbol*] (NQ)
mosic..........	Metal-Oxide-Semiconductor Integrated Circuit (AD)
MOSID	Ministry of Supply Inspection Department [*British*] (AD)
MoSIG	International Graduate School, St. Louis, MO [*Library symbol*] [*Library of Congress*] (LCLS)
Mosine	Mosinee Paper Co. [*Associated Press*] (SAG)
MoSIO	International Library, Archives, and Museum of Optometry, St. Louis, MO [*Library symbol*] [*Library of Congress*] (LCLS)
MoSIP..........	Missouri Institute of Psychiatry, St. Louis, MO [*Library symbol*] [*Library of Congress*] (LCLS)
MOSIS	Monolithic Silicon Detector (ACAE)
MOSIS	MOS Implementation Service (NITA)

MOSIX .... Multicomputer Operating System for UNIX (SAUO)
Mosk........... Moscovici (AD)
Mosk........... Moscowitz (AD)
Mosk........... Moskowitz (AD)
MOSK .... Multimode Operation Support Services (ACAE)
MoSL .... Law Library Association of St. Louis, St. Louis, MO [*Library symbol*] [*Library of Congress*] (LCLS)
MOSLS .... Military Occupational Specialty Level System
MOS/LSI ...... Metal Oxide Silicon/Large Scale Integration [*Electronics*]
MOSM .... Metal-Oxide Semimetal (IEEE)
mosm .... Milliosmol (AD)
mOsm .... Milliosmol [*or Milliosmole*] [*Chemistry*]
MOSM .... Mission Operations System Manager [*NASA*]
MoSM .... St. Louis Mercantile Library Association, St. Louis, MO [*Library symbol*] [*Library of Congress*] (LCLS)
MoSMa .... Maryville College, St. Louis, MO [*Library symbol*] [*Library of Congress*] (LCLS)
MoSMal ...... Mallinckrodt Chemical Works [*Later, Mallinckrodt, Inc.*], St. Louis, MO [*Library symbol*] [*Library of Congress*] (LCLS)
Mos Man ..... Moses on the Law of Mandamus [*A publication*] (DLA)
MoSMc .... McDonnell Douglas Corp., Corporate Library, St. Louis, MO [*Library symbol*] [*Library of Congress*] (LCLS)
MoSMcA ...... McDonnell Douglas Automation Co., St. Louis, MO [*Library symbol*] [*Library of Congress*] (LCLS)
MoSMed ...... St. Louis Medical Society, St. Louis, MO [*Library symbol*] [*Library of Congress*] (LCLS)
mOsmol .... Milliosmole [*Measurement*] (DAVI)
MoSMon ...... Monsanto Chemical Co., St. Louis, MO [*Library symbol*] [*Library of Congress*] (LCLS)
MOSNAG..... Mossine Nagant Rifle
MOS/NFC .... Ministry of Supplies/Nepal Food Corp. (SAUS)
MOS/NFC .... Ministry of Supplies/Nepal Food Corporation (SAUO)
MOS/NOC ... Ministry Of Supplies/Nepal Oil Corp. (SAUS)
MOS/NOC ... Ministry Of Supplies/Nepal Oil Corporation (SAUO)
MOSOP .... Missouri Sexual Offender Program (AD)
MOSOP .... Movement for the Survival of Ogoni People
MOSOP .... Movement for the Survival of the Ogoni People
MOSP .... Master Ordnance Systems Pattern File [*Navy*]
MOSP .... Medical and Osteopathic Scholarship Program (DNAB)
MOSP .... Microsoft Online Services Partnership (SAUO)
MOSP .... Multi-mission Optronic Stabilised Payload (SAUS)
MoSp .... Public Libraries of Springfield and Greene County, Springfield, MO [*Library symbol*] [*Library of Congress*] (LCLS)
MoSpA .... Assemblies of God Graduate School, Springfield, MO [*Library symbol*] [*Library of Congress*] (LCLS)
MoSpBB ...... Baptist Bible College, Springfield, MO [*Library symbol*] [*Library of Congress*] (LCLS)
MoSpCB ...... Central Bible College, Springfield, MO [*Library symbol*] [*Library of Congress*] (LCLS)
MoSpD .... Drury College, Springfield, MO [*Library symbol*] [*Library of Congress*] (LCLS)
MoSPD .... St. Louis Post-Dispatch, St. Louis, MO [*Library symbol*] [*Library of Congress*] (LCLS)
MoSpDC ...... Drury College, Springfield, MO [*Library symbol*] [*Library of Congress*] (LCLS)
MoSpE .... Evangel College, Springfield, MO [*Library symbol*] [*Library of Congress*] (LCLS)
MOSPF .... Multicast Open Shortest Path First (SAUS)
MoSPI .... Pet, Inc., St. Louis, MO [*Library symbol*] [*Library of Congress*] (LCLS)
MOSPO .... Mobile Satellite Photometric Observatory [*NASA*] (NASA)
MOS Poland... Ministerstwo Opieki Spotecznes [*Ministry of Social Welfare*] [*Poland*] (AD)
MOSPOR ..... Movement for the Struggle for Political Rights [*Uganda*] (PD)
MoSpS .... Southwest Missouri State College, Springfield, MO [*Library symbol*] [*Library of Congress*] (LCLS)
MoSPS........ St. Louis Priory School, St. Louis, MO [*Library symbol*] [*Library of Congress*] (LCLS)
MoSPSc .... Saint Louis Priory School, St. Louis, MO [*Library symbol*] [*Library of Congress*] (LCLS)
MoSR .... City Art Museum of St. Louis, St. Louis, MO [*Library symbol*] [*Library of Congress*] (LCLS)
MoSR .... Saint Louis Art Museum, Richardson Memorial Library, St. Louis, MO [*Library symbol*] [*Library of Congress*] (LCLS)
MOSRAM..... Metal-Oxide Semiconductor Random-Access Memory (EECA)
MOSRD........ Motor Machinist's Mate, Ship Repair, Diesel Engineering Mechanic [*Navy rating*]
MOSRG........ Motor Machinist's Mate, Ship Repair, Gasoline Engine Mechanic [*Navy rating*]
MOSROM..... Metal-Oxide Semiconductor Read-Only Memory [*Computer science*] (CIST)
MOSROM..... Metal-Oxide-Silicon Read-Only Memory (IDOE)
moss........... Maintenance-Operations Support Set (AD)
MOSS .... Maintenance-Operations Support Set (AFM)
MOSS .... Management and Organisation in Secondary Schools (AIE)
MOSS .... Manned Orbital Space Station [*or System*] [*See also MOD, MODS, MTSS*] [*Air Force/NASA*]
MOSS .... Map Overlay Statistical System (SAUO)
MOSS .... Market Opening Sector Specific (AD)
MOSS .... Market-Oriented, Sector-Selective [*or Specific*] [*Trade negotiations between United States and Japan*]
MOSS .... Market Oversight Surveillance System
MOSS .... Mathematical Optimization Subroutine System (VLIE)
MOSS .... Measure of Semiconductor (AGLO)

MOSS .... Middle-Aged, Overstressed, Semiaffluent Suburbanite [*Lifestyle classification*]
MOSS .... Military Orbital Space System [*See also MOD, MODS, MTSS*] [*Air Force/NASA*]
MOSS .... Military Overseas Shelter Survey [*Civil Defense*]
MOSS .... Mission Operations Support Satellites (ACAE)
MOSS .... Mission Operation Support Services (ACAE)
MOSS .... Mobile Oceanography Support System (SAUO)
MOSS .... Mobile Submarine Simulator (NVT)
MOSS .... Mobility Support Set [*or System*] [*for aircraft*] (MCD)
MOSS .... Modelling Systems [*Moss Systems Ltd.*] [*Software package*] (NCC)
MOSS .... Monitor Output Signal Strength
MOSS .... Mothers of Sons in Service [*World War II*]
MOSS .... Mutually Owned Society for Songwriters
MOSSA .... Mine Officials and Salaried Staff Association (SAUO)
MOSSA .... Northern Rhodesia Mine Officials and Salaried Staff Association
Mossies....... Middle-Aged, Overstressed Semiaffluent Suburbanites [*Lifestyle Classification*]
Mossimo...... Mossimo, Inc. [*Associated Press*] (SAG)
MoSSJ........ St. John Cantius Seminary, St. Louis, MO [*Library symbol*] [*Library of Congress*] (LCLS)
MOSS MOUSE... Maneuver, Objective, Security, Surprise, Mass, Offensive, Unity of Command, Simplicity, Economy of Force [*Basic principles of war*] [*See also MOOSEMUSS*] (MCD)
MOSSRS...... Management Order Ship Status Reporting System (MCD)
MOSST .... Ministry of State for Science and Technology [*Canada*]
MOST.......... Management Operation System Technique
MOST.......... Manned Orbital Solar Telescope
MOST.......... Mass Optical Storage Technologies [*Computer science*]
MOST.......... Mediterranean Oak Forest (SAUS)
most .... Metal-Oxide Semiconductor Transistor (AD)
MOST.......... Metal-Oxide-Semiconductor Transistor
MOST.......... Metal-Oxide-Silicon Transistor (IDOE)
MOST.......... Michigan Opportunities and Skills Training (AD)
MOST.......... Ministry of Science and Technology (SAUO)
MOST.......... Missile on Shipboard Test (ACAE)
MOST.......... Mission-Orientated Simulator Training (SAUS)
MOST.......... Mission Oriented Systems Tape [*Military*] (CAAL)
MOST.......... Mobile Open Systems Technologies (SAUO)
MOST.......... Mobile Optical Surveillance Tracker
MOST.......... Mobile Oversnow Transport
MOST.......... Mobile SONAR Technology [*Marine science*] (MSC)
MOST.......... Modified OECD [*Organization for Economic Cooperation and Development*] Screening Test [*Biodegradability Test*]
MOST.......... Modular Office System Terminal [*Computer science*] (VLIE)
MOST.......... Molonglo Observatory Synthesis Telescope
MOST.......... Mothers of Super Twins [*Military*]
MOST.......... Motorcycle Operator Skill Test
MOST.......... Multipulse Observation Sizing Technique [*Southwest Research Institute*]
MOSTA .... Midwest Old Settlers and Threshers Association (EA)
MOSTAB ..... Modular Stability [*Derivative program*]
MO St Ann... Missouri Statutes, Annotated [*A publication*] (DLA)
MoStc .... St. Charles City-County Library, St. Charles, MO [*Library symbol*] [*Library of Congress*] (LCLS)
MoStcL .... Lindenwood College, St. Charles, MO [*Library symbol*] [*Library of Congress*] (LCLS)
MOSTE........ Ministry of Science, Technology and Environment (SAUO)
Mostell .... Mostellaria [*of Plautus*] [*Classical studies*] (OCD)
MoStgA .... Sainte Genevieve Archives, Sainte Genevieve County Court, Ste. Genevieve, MO [*Library symbol*] [*Library of Congress*] (LCLS)
MoStj .... St. Joseph Public Library, St. Joseph, MO [*Library symbol*] [*Library of Congress*] (LCLS)
MoStjM........ Methodist Medical Center, St. Joseph, MO [*Library symbol*] [*Library of Congress*] (LCLS)
MoStjMW .... Missouri Western State College, St. Joseph, MO [*Library symbol*] [*Library of Congress*] (LCLS)
MoStjS......... St. Joseph State Hospital, St. Joseph, MO [*Library symbol*] [*Library of Congress*] (LCLS)
mostl .... Metal-Oxide Semiconductor Transistor Logic (AD)
MOSTL......... Metal-Oxide-Semiconductor Transistor Logic (CET)
MOSTT........ Mosaic Optical Sensor Technology Testbed (ACAE)
MOST/TDIS... Mobile SONAR Technology/Technical Document Information System [*Marine science*] (MSC)
MoSU .... Mobile Ordnance Service Unit
MoSU .... St. Louis University, St. Louis, MO [*Library symbol*] [*Library of Congress*] (LCLS)
MoSU-C .... St. Louis University, School of Commerce and Finance, St. Louis, MO [*Library symbol*] [*Library of Congress*] (LCLS)
MoSU-D .... St. Louis University, School of Divinity, St. Louis, MO [*Library symbol*] [*Library of Congress*] (LCLS)
MoSUE........ Union Electric Co., St. Louis, MO [*Library symbol*] [*Library of Congress*] (LCLS)
MoSU-L .... St. Louis University, School of Law, St. Louis, MO [*Library symbol*] [*Library of Congress*] (LCLS)
MoSU-M .... St. Louis University, School of Medicine, St. Louis, MO [*Library symbol*] [*Library of Congress*] (LCLS)
MoSU-P .... St. Louis University, School of Philosophy, St. Louis, MO [*Library symbol*] [*Library of Congress*] (LCLS)
MOSUPPU ... Mobile Support Unit (DNAB)
MoSV.......... Catholic Central Union of America, St. Louis, MO [*Library symbol*] [*Library of Congress*] (LCLS)
MoSVA........ United States Veterans Administration Hospital, St. Louis, MO [*Library symbol*] [*Library of Congress*] (LCLS)

MoSW..........	Washington University, St. Louis, MO [*Library symbol*] [*Library of Congress*] (LCLS)
MoSW-D	Washington University, School of Dentistry, St. Louis, MO [*Library symbol*] [*Library of Congress*] (LCLS)
MoSW-F	Washington University, School of Fine Arts, St. Louis, MO [*Library symbol*] [*Library of Congress*] (LCLS)
MoSW-L	Washington University, School of Law, St. Louis, MO [*Library symbol*] [*Library of Congress*] (LCLS)
MoSW-M	Washington University, Medical School, St. Louis, MO [*Library symbol*] [*Library of Congress*] (LCLS)
MOSZ..........	Massive Offshore Surf Zone
MOSZK	Central Union of Hungarian Cooperative Societies (SAUO)
MOT...........	Aeromonterrey SA [*Mexico*] [*ICAO designator*] (FAAC)
MOT...........	Magneto-Optical Trap [*Physics*]
MOT...........	Management of Technology
MOT...........	Manned Orbital Telescope [*NASA*]
MOT...........	Manufacturing Operation and Tooling
MOT...........	[*The*] March of Time [*Radio and motion picture series*]
MOT...........	Marine Oil Transportation [*AAR code*]
MOT...........	Mark on Top (NVT)
MOT...........	Master of Occupational Therapy (GAGS)
MOT...........	Master Operability Test (CAAL)
MOT...........	Maximum Operating Time (NG)
MOT...........	Maximum Overhaul Time (SAUS)
MOT...........	McDonald Observatory [*Texas*] [*Seismograph station code, US Geological Survey*] (SEIS)
mot..........	Mean Operating Time (AD)
MOT...........	Mean Operating Time
MOT...........	Means of Testing [*Telecommunications*] (OSI)
mot..........	Mechanical Operability Test (AD)
MOT...........	Mechanical Operability Test
MOT...........	Medial Olfactory Tract [*Anatomy*]
mot	Member of Our Tribe (AD)
MOT...........	Member of Our Tribe [*Jewish slang*]
MOT...........	Men of the Trees [*Australia*] [*An association*]
MOT...........	Method of Testing (MCD)
mot	Middle of Target (AD)
MOT...........	Military Ocean Terminal (AABC)
MOT...........	Mineral-Oil Tolerance [*of resin solutions*]
M o T..........	Minister of Transport [*British*] (AD)
MOT...........	Ministry of Tourism [*Philippines*] (DS)
MOT...........	Ministry of Trade (SAUO)
MOT...........	Ministry of Transport [*British or Canadian*]
MOT...........	Ministry of Transportation (SAUO)
MOT...........	Minot [*North Dakota*] [*Airport symbol*] (OAG)
MOT...........	Missile Operability Test (MCD)
MOT...........	Molecular-Orbital Theory [*Physical chemistry*]
MOT...........	Monalta Resources, Inc. [*Vancouver Stock Exchange symbol*]
MOT...........	Monthly Overtime (RIMS)
MOT...........	Month of Travel [*Military*]
MOT...........	Motion
MOT...........	Motor (AAG)
mot	Motor (AD)
MOT...........	Motorized
MOT...........	Motorola, Inc. [*NYSE symbol*] (SPSG)
MOT...........	Motor Operating Time
MOT...........	Mouse Operating Table [*Research instrumentation*]
MOT...........	Mouse Ovarian Tumor [*Veterinary science*] (DB)
MOT...........	Murine Ovarian Teratocarcinoma [*Animal pathology*]
MOT...........	Tarkio College, Tarkio, MO [*OCLC symbol*] (OCLC)
MOTA..........	Mail Order Traders Association (MHDB)
MOTA..........	Manitoba Oculo-Tricho-Anal [*Syndrome*] [*Medicine*] (DMAA)
MOTA..........	Materials Open-Test Assembly [*Nuclear energy*] (NRCH)
MOTA..........	Michigan Ohio Telecommunications Association (TSSD)
MOTA..........	Mid-Ocean Target Array (AAG)
MOTA..........	Museum of Temporary Art [*Washington, DC*]
MoTaC..........	Tarkio College, Tarkio, MO [*Library symbol*] [*Library of Congress*] (LCLS)
MOTACC......	Manufacturers of Telescoping and Articulating Cranes Council (EA)
MOTA-IC......	Alloy Test (SAUS)
MOTAM.......	Moving Target Attack Missile (ACAE)
MOT & E.....	Multinational Operational Test and Evaluation
MOTAR........	Modular Thermal Analyzer Routine [*Computer science*]
MOTARDES...	Moving Target Detection System (IEEE)
MOTARDIV...	Mobile Target Division [*Mine Force*] [*Navy*]
MOTARDS....	Moving Target Detection System
MOTAS	Member of the Appropriate Sex (NHD)
MOTAT........	Museum of Transport and Technology (AD)
MOTBA	Military Ocean Terminal, Bay Area [*Oakland, CA*] (AABC)
MOTBY	Military Ocean Terminal, Bayonne (AABC)
MOTC..........	Ministry of Transit and Communications [*Philippines*] (AD)
MOTC..........	Montreal Tramways [*AAR code*]
Motcc..........	Motility with correction (SAUS)
MotClb..........	Motor Club of America [*Associated Press*] (SAG)
M o TCP	Ministry of Town and Country Planning [*British*] (AD)
MOTD	Maintenance and Operating Technical Data (ACAE)
MOTD	Message of the Day (SAUS)
MOT/DCA	Ministry of Tourism/ Department of Civil Aviation (SAUO)
MOTE..........	Measure of Training Effectiveness [*Military*]
MOTEC........	Maritime Operations Tactical Evaluation Centre (SAUO)
MOTECS	Mobile Tactical Exercise Control System (DNAB)
MOTEL........	Motor Hotel
MOTESZ.......	Magyar Orvostudomanyi Tarsasagok Szovetsege [*Federation of Hungarian Medical Societies*] (EAIO)
MOTET........	Mother Tongue and English Teaching (AIE)
MOTF..........	Manganese Oxide Thin Film
MOTG	Marine Operational Training Group
MOTG	Morally Obliged to Go [*British*] [*Slang*]
moth..........	Mother (AD)
moth-in-law...	Mother-in-Law (AD)
Moth Jones...	Mother Jones [*A publication*] (BRI)
MothrWk......	Mothers Work, Inc. [*Associated Press*] (SAG)
MOTI..........	Message Oriented Text Interchange [*Telecommunications*] (OSI)
MOTIF.........	Maui Optical Tracking and Identification Facility [*Hawaii*] [*Air Force*]
MOTION.......	Model for Transforming, Identifying and Optimising Core Processes (SAUO)
MOTIS	Message Oriented Text Interchange System [*Telecommunications*] (OSI)
MOTIS	Missile on Stand Timing Simulator (MCD)
MOTIS	MOS Timing Simulator Software (NITA)
MOT-key	Modified One-Time key (SAUS)
MOTKI	Military Ocean Terminal, King's Bay (AABC)
MOTM.........	Member of the Month (SAUO)
MOTN.........	Motion
MOTNAC......	Manual of Tumor Nomenclature [*Medicine*] (DHSM)
MOTNE	Meteorological Operational Telecommunications Network Europe
MOTNEG	Meteorological Operational Telecommunication Network in Europe, Regional Planning Group [*ICAO*] (PDAA)
MOTO	Moto Photo [*NQS*] (TTSB)
MOTO	Moto Photo, Inc. [*NASDAQ symbol*] (NQ)
motoboard	Motorized Skateboard (AD)
motocross.....	Motorcycle Cross Country Race (AD)
MOTOGAS ...	Motor Gasoline [*Military*]
mot op........	Motor Operated (AD)
MotoPh........	Moto Photo, Inc. [*Associated Press*] (SAG)
MOTOR........	Mobile Oriented Triangulation of Reentry
MOTOR	Monthly Throughput Observation Report (DNAB)
motorcade	Motorized-Vehicle Parade (AD)
motorcross.....	Motorcycle Cross (AD)
MOTOREDE...	Movement to Restore Decency [*Group opposing sex education in schools*]
MOTORWAY...	Motorway [*Commonly used*] (OPSA)
MOTOS	Member of the Opposite Sex [*Electronic mail language*]
MOTOUR/DCA...	Ministry of Tourism/ Department of Civil Aviation (SAUO)
MOTOUR/DCA...	Ministry of Tourism/Department of Civil Aviation (SAUS)
MOTOUR/HMT...	Ministry of Tourism/ Hotel Management and Tourism Training Centre (SAUO)
MOTP..........	Manufacturing or Testing Process (KSC)
MOTP..........	Medical Officer Training Plan [*Canada*]
MOTP..........	Minuteman Operational Targeting Program (ACAE)
MOTPICT	Motion Picture
MOTPT........	Ministry of Transport (SAUO)
MoTr..........	Grundy County-Jewett Norris Library, Trenton, MO [*Library symbol*] [*Library of Congress*] (LCLS)
MOTR	Motor Club of America [*NASDAQ symbol*] (NQ)
MOTR	Multiple Object-Tracking RADAR (MCD)
MotrPrt	Motorcar Parts & Accessories, Inc. [*Associated Press*] (SAG)
MOTS..........	Mend Our Tongues Society (EA)
MOTS..........	Metal Oxide Threshold Switches (MCD)
MOTS..........	Military off the Shelf (ACAE)
MOTS..........	Minitrack Optical Tracking Station [*or System*] [*NASA*]
mots	Minitrack Optical Tracking System (AD)
MOTS..........	Missile Operability Test Station (MCD)
MOTS..........	Mobile Optical Tracking System
MOTS..........	Module Test Set
Motsc..........	Motility without correction (SAUS)
MOTSS	Member of the Same Sex [*Electronic mail language*]
MOTSS	More of the Sameold Sameold (SAUS)
MOTSU	Military Ocean Terminal, Sunny Point (AABC)
MOTT..........	Men of the Trees (SAUO)
MOTT..........	Mycobacteria Other Than Tubercle Bacilli
MOTU	Mobile Operating Technical Unit (SAUO)
MOTU	Mobile Operational Training Unit (MCD)
MOTU	Mobile Optical Tracking Unit (MCD)
MOTU	Mobile Ordnance Technical Unit [*Military*] (CAAL)
MOTU	Mobile Technical Unit (NG)
MOTUDET....	Mobile Ordnance Technical Unit Detachment (DNAB)
MOTV..........	Manned Orbit Transfer Vehicle (MCD)
MotV..........	Motor Nucleus of the Trigeminal Nerve [*Medicine*] (DB)
MOU	Macula of Utricle [*Medicine*] (MELL)
MOU	Maximum Oxygen Uptake
MoU	Memorandum of Understanding (AD)
mou	Memorandum of Understanding (AD)
MOU	Memorandum of Understanding
mou	Missouri [*MARC country of publication code*] [*Library of Congress*] (LCCP)
MOU	Mountain States Telephone & Telegraph Co. (SAUO)
MOU	Mountain Village [*Alaska*] [*Airport symbol*] (OAG)
Mou	Mouse [*Computer science*] (PCM)
MOU	Southwest Missouri State University, Springfield, MO [*OCLC symbol*] (OCLC)
MoU	University of Missouri, Columbia, MO [*Library symbol*] [*Library of Congress*] (LCLS)
MoU-D	University of Missouri, School of Dentistry, Kansas City, MO [*Library symbol*] [*Library of Congress*] (LCLS)
MOUG..........	Map Online Users Group (EA)
MOUG..........	Maryland Online User Group (NITA)
Moult Ch......	Moulton's New York Chancery Practice [*A publication*] (DLA)
Moult Ch P...	Moulton's New York Chancery Practice [*A publication*] (DLA)

MoU-M .... University of Missouri, Medical Library, Kansas City, MO [*Library symbol*] [*Library of Congress*] (LCLS)
MOUND....... Mound Plant [*Department of Energy*] [*Miamisburg, OH*] (GAAI)
MOUNT....... Mount [*Commonly used*] (OPSA)
MOUNTAIN... Mountain [*Commonly used*] (OPSA)
MOUNTAINS... Mountains [*Commonly used*] (OPSA)
Mountbtn...... Mountbatten, Inc. [*Associated Press*] (SAG)
MOUNTIN .... Mountain [*Commonly used*] (OPSA)
MountPr...... Mountain Province Mining, Inc. [*Associated Press*] (SAG)
Mounty .... Member of the Royal Canadian Mounted Police (SAUO)
MOURAD ..... Mouvement pour la Renovation et l'Action Democratique [*The Comoros*] [*Political party*] (EY)
MOUS .... Multiple Occurrences of Unexplained Symptoms [*Medicine*]
MOUSE....... Manager Owner User Systems Engineer (OA)
MOUSE....... Minimum Orbital Unmanned Satellite (AD)
MOUSE....... Minimum Orbital Unmanned Satellite of the Earth
MOUSS .... Management and Operation of User Services Section
MOUSS .... Management and Operations of User Services Section [*American Library Association*]
MoU-St .... University of Missouri at St. Louis, St. Louis, MO [*Library symbol*] [*Library of Congress*] (LCLS)
MOUT .... Mobile Operation in Urban Terrain (SAUS)
MOUTH....... Modular Output Unit for Talking to Humans
MOUTRE ...... Mission Oriented Unit Training by Echelon [*Military*] (INF)
MoU-V .... University of Missouri, Veterinary Medicine Library, Columbia, MO [*Library symbol*] [*Library of Congress*] (LCLS)
mov .... Apple QuickTime [*Computer science*]
MOV............ Main Oxidizer Valve (KSC)
mov .... Main Oxidizer Valve (NAKS)
MOV............ Manned Orbiting Vehicle [*NASA*]
MOV............ Manuscript on Vellum
MOV............ Margin of Victory [*Automobile racing*]
MOV............ Mass of Vehicle
MOV............ Materiel Obligation Validation (AFIT)
MOV............ Metal-Oxide Varistor
MOV............ Method of Validation
MOV............ Military-Owned Vehicle
MOV............ Minimal Occlusive Volume (DMAA)
MOV............ Monclova, MX [*Location identifier*] [*FAA*] (FAAL)
MOV............ Monument Valley, UT [*Location identifier*] [*FAA*] (FAAL)
MOV............ Moranbah [*Australia*] [*Airport symbol*] (OAG)
MOV............ Morovis [*Puerto Rico*] [*Seismograph station code, US Geological Survey*] (SEIS)
MOV............ Moshassuck Valley Railroad Co. [*AAR code*]
MOV............ Motor Oil Volatility
MOV............ Motor-Operated Valve (NRCH)
mov .... Movable (AD)
MOV............ Movable [*Technical drawings*]
mov .... Moved (GEAB)
MOV............ Movement (AABC)
MOV............ Movie
mov .... Movimento [*Movement*] [*Italian*] (AD)
mov .... Multiple-Orifice Valve (AD)
MOV............ Stephens College, Columbia, MO [*OCLC symbol*] (OCLC)
MOVA .... Main Oxidizer Valve Actuator (SAUS)
MOVA .... Microprocessor Optimized Vehicle Actuation
MOVA .... Movado Group, Inc. [*NASDAQ symbol*] (SAG)
MOVAD .... Movement Adaptability (SAUO)
MOVAD .... Movement and Delivery (SAUO)
Movado....... Movado Group, Inc. [*Associated Press*] (SAG)
M-OVAL....... Macrovalocytes [*Microbiology*] (DAVI)
MOVCO .... Movement Control Organisation [*British military*] (DMA)
MOVCORD ... Movement Coordinator
MOVDHHG... Movement of Dependents and Household Goods in Advance of Permanent Change of Station Orders is Authorized [*Army*] (AABC)
MOVE.......... Cinema Ride Inc. [*NASDAQ symbol*] (TTSB)
MOVE.......... Management of Value Engineering
MOVE.......... Manage Old Vehicles Easily [*Performance Data Services, Inc.*] [*Software*]
MOVE.......... Microprocessor Open Vision Environment (SAUO)
MOVE.......... Microsoft Overlay Virtual Environment (SAUS)
MOVE.......... Mobility Opportunities Via Education (SAUO)
move .... Movement (WDAA)
MOVE.......... Moving
MOVE.......... Multiple Occupancy Vehicles (DICI)
MOVECAP ... Movement Capabilities [*Military*] (CINC)
MOVEET...... Ministers of Vocational Education, Employment and Training (SAUO)
MOVEM....... Movement Overseas Verification of Enlisted Members [*Army*] (AABC)
movem........ Movement Overseas Verification of Enlisted Members (AD)
moverep ...... Movement Report (AD)
MOVEREP .... Movement Report [*Military*] (NATG)
Move Short Soc... Movement Shorthand Society (AD)
MOVEW .... Cinema Ride Wrrt [*NASDAQ symbol*] (TTSB)
movi .... Movie (AD)
MOVI .... Movie Gallery [*NASDAQ symbol*] (TTSB)
MOVI .... Movie Gallery, Inc. [*NASDAQ symbol*] (SAG)
MOVIEBYU... Colored Movie Software produced by Brigham Young University (SAUO)
MovieFn ...... MovieFone, Inc. [*Associated Press*] (SAG)
MovieGal..... Move Gallery, Inc. [*Associated Press*] (SAG)
MovieGal..... Movie Gallery, Inc. [*Associated Press*] (SAG)
MovieStr...... Movie Star, Inc. [*Associated Press*] (SAG)
MOVIMS ...... Motor Vehicle Information Management System [*Bell System*]
MOVL.......... Moving Left (VLIE)

MOVLAS ...... Manually Operated Visual Landing Aid System (NG)
MOVMT....... Movement
movord .... Movement Order (AD)
MOVORD ..... Movement Order [*Military*] (NVT)
MOVP .... Military-Owned Vehicle Plan (AFM)
MO-VPE ...... Metal-Organic Vapor Phase Epitaxy [*Also, MO-CVD, OM-CVD, OM-VPE*] [*Semiconductor technology*]
MOVPE .... Metal Oxide Vapour Phase Epitaxy (SAUS)
MOVPER...... Supreme Council, Mystic Order Veiled Prophets of Enchanted Realm (EA)
MOVR......... Moving Right (VLIE)
MOVREP...... Movement Report [*Military*] (NVT)
MOVREP...... Movement Reporting (SAUO)
MOVREP System... Movement Reports System (SAUO)
MOVS .... Manual Overseas Visa System
MOVS .... Military-Owned Vehicle Service (AABC)
MOVSUM .... Movement Summary (SAUO)
Movt.......... Movement (DIAR)
movt........... Movement (GROV)
MOVT......... Movement [*Music*] (ROG)
MOVTAS ...... Modified Visual Target Acquisition System (ACAE)
MOW .... Catskill Airways, Inc. [*FAA designator*] (FAAC)
MOW .... Meals on Wheels
M o W .... Minister of Works [*British*] (AD)
MOW .... Ministry of Works [*British*] (MCD)
MoW.......... Ministry of Works (SAUO)
mow........... Mission Operations Wing [*NASA*] (NAKS)
MOW .... Mission Operation Wing [*NASA*] (KSC)
MOW .... Mohawk Airlines [*ICAO designator*] (FAAC)
MOW .... Montana Western Railway [*AAR code*]
MOW .... Moscow [*Former USSR*] [*Airport symbol*] (OAG)
MOW .... Movement for the Ordination of Women [*British lobbying group*] (ECON)
MOW .... Movie of the Week [*Television programming*]
MOW .... Westminster College, Fulton, MO [*OCLC symbol*] (OCLC)
MOWA .... Meals-on-Wheels America [*An association*]
MOWA .... Michigan Outdoor Writers Association
MOWAM ..... Mobile Water Mine (MCD)
MoWarbT..... Central Missouri State University, Warrensburg, MO [*Library symbol*] [*Library of Congress*] (LCLS)
MoWarbTR... Trails Regional Library, Johnson County-Lafayette County Library, Warrensburg, MO [*Library symbol*] [*Library of Congress*] (LCLS)
MOWASP..... Mechanization of Warehousing and Shipment Procedures [*or Processing*] [*Defense Supply Agency*]
mowasp....... Mechanization of Warehousing and Shipment Processing (AD)
MOWB .... Ministry of Works and Buildings [*British*]
MOWBC....... Winnipeg Bible College, Otterburne, Manitoba [*Library symbol*] [*National Library of Canada*] (NLC)
MoWD .... Ministry of Works and Development [*British*] (AD)
MOWG .... Mission Operations Working Group (SAUO)
MoWgK....... Saint Louis Roman Catholic Theological [*Kenrick*] Seminary, Webster Groves,MO [*Library symbol*] [*Library of Congress*] (LCLS)
MoWgT........ Eden Theological Seminary, Webster Groves, MO [*Library symbol*] [*Library of Congress*] (LCLS)
MoWgW....... Webster College, Webster Groves, MO [*Library symbol*] [*Library of Congress*] (LCLS)
MoWhAF...... United States Air Force, Whiteman Air Force Base Library, Whiteman AFB, MO [*Library symbol*] [*Library of Congress*] (LCLS)
MoWitt........ Mobile Window Thermal Test Facility [*Berkeley, CA*] [*Lawrence Berkeley Laboratory*] [*Department of Energy*] (GRD)
Mo W Jur .... Monthly Western Jurist [*A publication*]
MOWOG...... Morris Wolseley Group [*Automobile manufacturing organization*]
MOWOS....... Meteorological Office Weather Observing System (PDAA)
MOWR/DOI... Ministry of Water Resources/ Department of Irrigation (SAUO)
MOWR/DOI... Ministry of Water Resources/Department of Irrigation (SAUS)
MOWR/DOMH... Ministry of Water Resources/Department of Meteorology and Hydrology (SAUO)
MOWR/GROUND... Ministry of Water Resources/Water Resources Development Board (SAUS)
MOWR/GWRDB... Ministry of Water Resources/Ground Water Resources Development Board (SAUO)
MOWR/MHDB... Ministry of Water Resources/Marsyangdi Hydroelectric Development Board (SAUO)
MOWR/NEA... Ministry of Water Resources/Nepal Electricity Authority (SAUO)
MOWR/SHDP... Ministry of Water Resources/Small Hydro Power Department (SAUO)
MOWS .... Manned Orbital Weapon Station [*or System*]
Mow St........ Mowbray's Styles of Deeds [*A publication*] (DLA)
M o WT .... Minister of War Transport [*British*] (AD)
MOWT .... Ministry of War Transport [*Terminated, 1956*] [*British*]
MOWT/DOR... Ministry of Works and Transport/Department of Roads (SAUO)
MOWT/NTRC... Ministry of Works and Transport/Nepal Transport Corp. (SAUS)
MOWT/NTRC... Ministry of Works and Transport/Nepal Transport Corporation (SAUO)
MOWT/SBC... Ministry of Works and Transport/Sajha Bus Corp. (SAUS)
MOWT/SBC... Ministry of Works and Transport/Sajha Bus Corporation (SAUO)
MOWW .... Military Order of the World Wars (EA)
MOX........... Manually-Operated Changeover [*Computer science*]
MOX........... Mars Oxident Experiment [*NASA*]
MOX........... Mixed Oxide [*Fuel*]
mox .... Mixed Oxides (AD)
MOX........... Mixed Uranium Plutonium Oxide
MOX........... Morris, MN [*Location identifier*] [*FAA*] (FAAL)
MOX........... Moxa [*German Democratic Republic*] [*Seismograph station code, US Geological Survey*] (SEIS)

MOX............	Moxalactam [*An antibiotic*]
mox	Oxidized Metal Explosive (AD)
MOXB	Moxham Bank [*NASDAQ symbol*] (TTSB)
MOXB	Moxham Bank Corp. [*NASDAQ symbol*] (SAG)
MOXE...........	All sky monitor on Spectrum-X-Gamma (SAUS)
Moxham	Moxham Bank Corp. [*Associated Press*] (SAG)
MOXIE	Men Organized to X-press Indignant Exasperation [*Seattle group opposing below-the-knee fashions introduced in 1970*]
MOXY	McMoRan Oil & Gas [*NASDAQ symbol*] (TTSB)
MOXY	McMoRan Oil and Gas Co. [*NASDAQ symbol*] (SAG)
MOXY	Model X-Y [*AEC computer code*]
MOY.............	Mahogany Minerals [*Vancouver Stock Exchange symbol*]
MOY.............	Matchbox Models of Yesteryear [*Toy collection*]
MOY.............	Mondy [*Former USSR*] [*Seismograph station code, US Geological Survey*] (SEIS)
moy	Money (AD)
MOY.............	Money
MOY.............	Monterrey [*Colombia*] [*Airport symbol*] (AD)
MOY.............	Salt Lake City, UT [*Location identifier*] [*FAA*] (FAAL)
MOYA	Ministry of Youth Affairs (SAUO)
MOYC..........	Moyco Technologies [*NASDAQ symbol*] (TTSB)
MOYC..........	Moyco Technologies, Inc. [*NASDAQ symbol*] (SAG)
MoycoT........	Moyco Technologies, Inc. [*Associated Press*] (SAG)
Moyle	Moyle's Criminal Circulars [*India*] [*A publication*] (DLA)
Moyle	Moyle's Entries [*1658*] [*England*] [*A publication*] (DLA)
MOZ............	Aerocharter GmbH [*Austria*] [*ICAO designator*] (FAAC)
MOZ............	Mezhdunarodnaya Organizacia Zhurnalistov [*International Organization of Journalists*] [*Russian*] (AD)
MOZ............	Missouri Southern State College, Library, Joplin, MO [*OCLC symbol*] (OCLC)
MOZ............	Mittlere Ortszeit (SAUO)
MOZ............	Moorea Island [*French Polynesia*] [*Airport symbol*] (OAG)
Moz.............	Mozambique (AD)
MOZ............	Mozambique [*ANSI three-letter standard code*] (CNC)
MOZAIC	Measurement of Ozone by Airbus-in-Service Aircraft
Mozam........	Mozambique (AD)
Moz & W	Mozley and Whiteley's Law Dictionary [*A publication*] (DLA)
Moz Cur.......	Mozambique Current (AD)
MOZL..........	Military Order of the Zouave Legion of the United States (EA)
Mozley & W...	Mozley and Whiteley's Law Dictionary [*A publication*] (DLA)
Mozley & Whiteley...	Mozley and Whiteley's Law Dictionary [*A publication*] (DLA)
MOZLUS	Military Order of the Zouave Legion of the US (EA)
MOZMVUS...	Military Order of Zouaves, Militia and Volunteers of the United States (EA)
mozza	Mozzarella (AD)
MP..............	All India Reporter, Madhya Pradesh [*A publication*] (DLA)
MP..............	Atlantis Airlines [*ICAO designator*] (AD)
Mp..............	Import [*Economics*]
MP..............	Machine Pistol [*Military*] (IIA)
MP..............	Machine Pressed
MP..............	Macrophage (MELL)
MP..............	Macroprocessor
MP..............	Madonna Plan (EA)
MP..............	Magic Packet (SAUS)
MP..............	Magnetic Particle
MP..............	Magnetic Pressure (NVT)
MP..............	Magnetopause [*In a magnetic field*]
MP..............	Magnifying Power (IIA)
mp..............	Mail Payment (AD)
MP..............	Mail Payment (EBF)
M/P.............	Main Parachute (MCD)
MP..............	Main Phase (IEEE)
MP..............	Main Propulsion (DNAB)
MP..............	Mains Propres [*Personal Delivery*] [*French*]
MP..............	Maintainability Plan
MP..............	Maintenance Panel (AAG)
mp..............	Maintenance Part (AD)
MP..............	Maintenance Period
MP..............	Maintenance Plan
MP..............	Maintenance Planning (SAUO)
MP..............	Maintenance Point
MP..............	Maintenance Prints
MP..............	Maintenance Procedure (MCD)
MP..............	Maintenance Program
MP..............	Major Payload (SAUS)
MP..............	Major Program (CAAL)
MP..............	Major Project (SAUO)
MP..............	Mallinckrodt, Inc. [*Research code symbol*]
MP..............	Malpractice (MELL)
MP..............	Management Package (NASA)
MP..............	Management Plan
MP..............	Management Policy (SAUO)
MP..............	Management Process (SAUO)
MP..............	Managing Printer [*A publication*] (DGA)
MP..............	Manganese Poisoning [*Medicine*] (MELL)
mp..............	Manifold Pressure (AD)
MP..............	Manifold Pressure
MP..............	Manoeuvre Programmer (SAUO)
MP..............	Manpower
MP..............	Manpower and Personnel (MCD)
MP..............	Manpower Plan (SAUO)
MP..............	Mansfield Park [*Novel by Jane Austen*]
MP..............	Manual Proportional [*Attitude control system of Mercury spacecraft*]
MP..............	Manual Pulser
MP..............	Manufacturing Process
MP..............	Manufacturing-Use Product (EEVL)
MP..............	Manu Propria [*In documents, after king's signature*] [*Italian*]
MP..............	Marbled Paper (DGA)
MP..............	Marching Pack (DNAB)
MP..............	Marginal Physical Product [*Economics*]
MP..............	Marginal Product
MP..............	Marine Police
MP..............	Marine Pollution
MP..............	Marine Provost [*British military*] (DMA)
MP..............	Maritime Patrol (NATG)
MP..............	Maritime Polar Air Mass
MP..............	Maritime Policy [*British*] (ROG)
MP..............	Market Price [*Business term*]
MP..............	Marshall's Posse (EA)
MP..............	Maschinenpistole [*Submachine Gun*] [*German*] (AD)
MP..............	Massa Pilularum [*A Pill Mass*] [*Pharmacy*] (ROG)
MP..............	Massively Parallel (AAEL)
MP..............	Massorah Parva [*or Massora Parva*] (BJA)
MP..............	Mass Properties (MCD)
MP..............	Master of Painting
MP..............	Master of Pharmacy (GAGS)
MP..............	Master of Planning (GAGS)
MP..............	Master Pointer [*Computer science*] (BYTE)
MP..............	Master Printer (DGA)
MP..............	Master Printers Annual [*A publication*] (DGA)
MP..............	Mastoid Process [*Medicine*] (MELL)
MP..............	Match Problems [*Research test*] [*Psychology*]
MP..............	Material Pass (AAG)
MP..............	Material Professional [*Army*]
MP..............	Mathematical Programming [*Computer science*]
MP..............	Matrix Protein (DB)
MP..............	Matthew Pelosi [*Designer's mark when appearing on US coins*]
MP..............	Maturity Phase
MP..............	Maxillary Process
MP..............	Maximum Flowering Period [*Botany*]
M/P.............	Maximum Performance [*Automotive engineering*]
MP..............	McIntyre Porcupine Mines, Ltd. (SAUO)
MP..............	Mean Pressure (MAE)
MP..............	Measurement Pipette
MP..............	Measurement Pragmatic [*Computer science*] (OA)
MP..............	Measuring Point (NASA)
MP..............	Mechanical Paper
MP..............	Mechanical Part
MP..............	Mechanical Printer
MP..............	Medial Pallium [*Neuroanatomy*]
MP..............	Media Processor [*Computer science*] (BUR)
MP..............	Media Project (EA)
MP..............	Medical Payment [*Insurance*]
MP..............	Medium Energy Physics Division (SAUO)
mp..............	Medium Pressure (AD)
MP..............	Medium Pressure
mp..............	Meeting Point (AD)
MP..............	Meeting Point [*Military*]
MP..............	Melchor Developments Ltd. [*Toronto Stock Exchange symbol*]
MP..............	Melphalan, Prednisone [*Antineoplastic drug regimen*]
MP..............	Melrose Place [*Television program title*]
mp..............	Melting Point (AD)
MP..............	Melting Point
MP..............	Melting Pot
MP..............	Member of Parliament [*British*]
MP..............	Member of Police
MP..............	Membrane Production (SSD)
M/P.............	Memorandum of Partnership [*Business term*]
MP..............	Menstrual Period [*Medicine*]
MP..............	Mental Process [*Work-factor system*]
MP..............	Mentum Posterior [*In reference to the chin*]
MP..............	Mercaptopurine [*Purinethol*] [*Also, M, P*] [*Antineoplastic drug*]
MP..............	Mercator's Projection (BARN)
MP..............	Mercury Poisoning [*Medicine*] (MELL)
MP..............	Meridional Part [*Navigation*]
MP..............	Merzbacher-Pelizaeus [*Disease*] [*Medicine*] (DB)
MP..............	Mesiopulpal [*Dentistry*]
MP..............	Message Processing (SAUO)
MP..............	Message Processor
MP..............	Metacarpophalangeal [*Anatomy*]
M-P.............	Metal or Plastic (AAG)
MP..............	Metal Particle
MP..............	Metal-Piercing (SAUS)
m-p.............	Metal-Point (AD)
MP..............	Metal-Powder [*Videotape*]
MP..............	Metatarsophalangeal [*Anatomy*]
MP..............	Meteorology Panel (MCD)
MP..............	Methodist Protestant
MP..............	Methoxypsoralen [*Also, MOP*] [*Pharmacology*]
MP..............	Methyl Palmoxirate [*Organic chemistry*]
MP..............	Methyl Parathion [*Also, MEP, MPN*] [*Pesticide*]
MP..............	Methylphenidate [*Central Nervous system stimulant*]
MP..............	Methylprednisolone [*Endocrinology*]
MP..............	Methylprednisolone Sodium Succinate [*Medicine*] (DAVI)
MP..............	Methylpurine [*Organic chemistry*]
MP..............	Metra Potential (NITA)
MP..............	Metropolitan Police
MP..............	Mexican Peso [*Monetary unit*]
MP..............	Mezzo Piano [*Moderately Soft*] [*Music*]
mp..............	Mezzo-Piano [*Moderately Soft*] [*Italian*] (AD)

MP	Michoud Plant [*NASA*] (MCD)
M(P)	Microfilm (Positive)
MP	Micronized Progesterone
MP	Microprint
mp	Microprocessor (ELAL)
MP	Microprocessor [*Instrumentation*]
MP	Microprogram
MP	Middle phalanx [*Anatomy*] (DAVI)
MP	Middle Point
MP	Midland Plant [*Nuclear energy*] (NRCH)
MP	Midline Precursor [*Cytology*]
MP	Mid-Phase
MP	Midpoint (DIPS)
MP	Mile-Post
mp	Milepost (AD)
MP	Military Pay (AFM)
MP	Military Police [*Army*]
MP	Military Post (SAUO)
MP	Military Prohibitionist [*Slang*]
MP	Military Property (MCD)
M/P	Milk/Plasma [*Ratio*] [*Physiology*]
m/p	Milk Powder (AD)
MP	Minimum Phase (IEEE)
MP	Minimum Premium [*Insurance*]
MP	Mining Permit (AD)
MP	[*The*] Mini Page [*A newspaper supplement*]
MP	Minister Plenipotentiary
MP	Minister Provincial (AD)
MP	Minuteman Platform
MP	Minutes Played [*Hockey*]
MP	Miscellaneous Paper [*or Publication*]
MP	Miscellaneous Proposal (AD)
MP	Missile Platform
MP	Missile Positioning
MP	Missile Possessed (SAA)
M/P	Missing Parts
MP	Missing Perforation [*Philately*]
MP	Missing Person
MP	Mission Payload (MCD)
MP	Mission Planner (MCD)
MP	Mission Profile (MCD)
MP	Mississippi Power Co. [*NYSE symbol*] (SPSG)
MP	Missouri Pacific Railroad Co. [*AAR code*]
MP	Mistress of Philosophy
MP	Mitsubishi Plastics [*Japan*] (PDAA)
MP	Mixed Pattern
MP	Mixed Population
MP	Mobilization Plan
MP	Modern Philology [*A publication*] (BRI)
MP	Modification Package
MP	Modified Construction Permit [*FCC*] (NTCM)
MP	Modo Praescripto [*In the Manner Prescribed*] [*Pharmacy*]
MP	Mod Package (SAUS)
MP	Modus Ponens [*Rule of inference*] [*Logic*] [*Latin*]
MP	Molecular Pair [*Physical Chemistry*]
MP	Molecular Pathology (SAUO)
MP	Monetary Policy
mp	Mongolia [*MARC country of publication code*] [*Library of Congress*] (LCCP)
MP	Monitor Panel
MP	Monitor Printer (CET)
MP	Monophosphate [*Chemistry*] (MAE)
MP	[*The*] Month in Parliament [*A publication*] [*British*]
MP	Months after Payment (EBF)
MP	Montreal Protocol (SAUO)
MP	Monumentum Posuit [*Erected a Monument*] [*Latin*]
MP	Mooring Pipe [*or Post*] (ADA)
M/P	Morjumiid-Pterocephalid Boundary [*Paleogeologic boundary*]
MP	Morning Prayer (WGA)
MP	Mortgage-Participation Certificate [*Investment term*]
MP	Mortgage Payment in Full
MP	Motherland Party [*Anatavan Partisi*] [*Turkey*] [*Political party*] (PPW)
mp	Motion Picture (AD)
MP	Motion Picture Production [*Navy*]
MP	Motor Potential
MP	Mounted Police
MP	Mouth Pressure [*Dentistry*] (DAVI)
MP	Mouvement Populaire [*Popular Movement*] [*Morocco*] [*Political party*] (PPW)
MP	Mouvement Progressif [*Cameroon*] [*Political party*] (EY)
MP	Movement Protein [*Cytology*]
MP	Mucopeptide [*Biochemistry*]
MP	Mucopolysaccharide [*Also, MPS*] [*Clinical chemistry*]
MP	Mucopurulent [*Biochemistry*] (DAVI)
MP	Multilink PPP [*Point-to-Point Protocol*] (PCM)
MP	Multiparous [*Obstetrics*]
MP	Multiperil [*Insurance*]
MP	Multiphase [*Physics*]
MP	Multi Phonon (AAEL)
MP	Multiple Processor [*or Multiprocessing*] [*Computer science*] (BUR)
MP	Multiple Punch (DNAB)
MP	Multiplex (VLIE)
MP	Multiplier Phototube
MP	Multipoint (VLIE)
mp	Multipole (AD)

MP	Multipole
MP	Multiprocessing [*Computer science*] (CDE)
mp	Multipurpose (AD)
MP	Multipurpose
MP	Municipal Police
M/P	Muscle Plasma [*Ratio*]
MP	Mycoplasma Pneumonia [*Medicine*]
MP	Mycoplasma Pulmonis [*A bacterium*]
mp	Myeloma Protein [*Oncology*] (DAVI)
MP	My Pal [*Slang*]
MP	Northern Mariana Islands [*ANSI two-letter standard code*] (CNC)
MP	Pinawa Public Library, Manitoba [*Library symbol*] [*National Library of Canada*] (NLC)
MP2D	Multipart, Two Dimensional
MP3	MPEG Audio Layer 3 (SAUS)
MPA	Magazine Publisher's Association (NTCM)
MPA	Magazine Publishers of America [*New York, NY*] [*Database producer*] (IID)
MPA	Maine Pharmaceutical Association (SAUO)
MPA	Main Political Administration [*of the Army and Navy*] [*Russian*] (DOMA)
MPA	Main Propulsion Assistant
MPA	Main Pulmonary Artery [*Anatomy*]
MPA	Maintenance Planning Analysis (MCD)
MPA	Major Projects Association [*British*] (DBA)
MPA	Management Professionals Association [*Madras, India*] (EA)
MPA	Manager, Public Awareness (SAUO)
MPA	Maneuver Propulsion Assembly (MCD)
MPA	Manpower and Personnel Administration [*Military*] [*British*]
MPA	Man-Powered Aircraft
MPA	Marine Physician Assistant (AD)
MPA	Marine Preservation Association
MPA	Marine Protected Area
mpa	Maritime Patrol Aircraft (AD)
MPA	Maritime Patrol Aircraft (NATG)
MPA	Marketing and Promotion Association [*British*]
MPA	Maryland & Pennsylvania Railroad Co. [*AAR code*]
MPA	Maryland Pharmaceutical Association (SAUO)
mpa	Maryland Port Authority (AD)
MPA	Mass Processing Analysis (SAUS)
M Pa	Master of Painting
MPA	Master of Physician Assistant (PGP)
MPA	Master of Professional Accountancy [*or Accounting*]
MPA	Master of Professional Accounting (NADA)
MPA	Master of Professional Arts
MPA	Master of Public Accounting (SAUO)
MPA	Master of Public Administration
MPA	Master of Public Affairs
MPA	Master Pastrycooks' Association [*Australia*]
MPA	Master Personnel Administration
MPA	Master Photographers Association (AD)
MPA	Master Photographers Association of Great Britain (BI)
MPA	Master Printers of America (EA)
MPA	Master Project Assignment (MCD)
MPA	Materiel Project Administration (ACAE)
MPA	Mechanical Packing Association [*Later, Fluid Sealing Association*] (EA)
MPA	Medical Prescibing Adviser (SAUO)
MPA	Medical Procurement Agency
MPA	Medium Performance Amplifier (ACAE)
MPA	Medroxyprogesterone [*Medicine*] (AD)
MPA	Medroxyprogesterone Acetate [*Also, MAP*] [*Endocrinology*]
mpa	Megapascal (AD)
MPa	Megapascal
MPA	Member of Parliamentary Assembly (SAUO)
MPA	Mercaptopropionic Acid [*Organic chemistry*]
MPA	Metal Powder Association [*Later, MPIF*]
MPA	Methacrylate Producers Association (EA)
MPA	Methoxypropylamine [*Organic chemistry*]
MPA	Methylphosphoric Acid [*Organic chemistry*]
MPA	Methylprednisolone Acetate [*A glucocorticoid*] (MAE)
MPA	Metropolitan Pensions Association (SAUO)
MPA	Metropolitan Pensions Associations (AD)
MPA	Michigan Paraoptometric Association (SAUO)
MPA	Michigan Prevention Association (SAUO)
MPA	Micropattern Analyzer (DB)
MPA	Microwave Power Absorption (AAEL)
MPA	Microwave Power Amplifier
MPA	Mid Pacific Air Corp. [*ICAO designator*] (FAAC)
MPA	Midwestern Psychological Association (MCD)
MPA	Military Pay Account
MPA	Military Pay and Allowance
MPA	Military Pay Area (AFM)
MPA	Military Personnel Appropriation (AFM)
MPA	Military Personnel, Army
MPA	Military Police Association [*Defunct*] (EA)
MPA	Military Proposal and Analysis
mPa	Millipascal [*Unit of pressure*]
MPA	Mines Police Association (SAUO)
MPA	Miniature Pendulum Accelerometer (SAA)
MPA	Miniature Photocell Activator
MPA	Miniature Piston Actuator (MCD)
MPA	Missile Procurement, Army (AABC)
MPA	Missionary Pilots Association [*Defunct*] (EA)
MPA	Mission Payload Assessment [*Air Force*] (DOMA)

MPA............	Mission Performance Assessment [*NASA*] (KSC)
MPA............	Mission Phase Analysis
MPA............	Mission Profile Analysis
MPA............	Missouri Pharmaceutical Association (SAUO)
MPA............	Mixer/Power Amplifier [*Telecommunications*]
MPA............	Mobile Press Association (EA)
MPA............	Models and Photographers of America (EA)
MPA............	Modern Poetry Association (EA)
MPA............	Modern Professional Army (SAUO)
MPA............	Modification Proposal and Analysis (MCD)
MPA............	Modulated Pulse Amplifier [*Telecommunications*] (IAA)
MPA............	Molybdeophosphoric Acid [*Inorganic chemistry*]
MPA............	Monthly Product Announcement [*Bureau of the Census*] (GFGA)
MPA............	Moose Pass [*Alaska*] [*Seismograph station code, US Geological Survey*] (SEIS)
MPA............	Mortar Package Assembly
MPA............	Mortar Producers Association [*British*] (DBA)
MPA............	Motion Picture Alliance
MPA............	Motion Picture Association (NTPA)
MPA............	Motion Picture Association of America (SAUO)
MPA............	Motoring Press Association
MPA............	Multimode Processing Array (ACAE)
MPA............	Multiplant Action [*Nuclear energy*] (NRCH)
MPA............	Multiple Parameter Analysis
MPA............	Multiple Peptide Analysis [*Biochemistry*]
MPA............	Multiple-Period Average (IEEE)
MPA............	Multiple Peripheral Adapter
mpa............	Multiple Product Announcement (AD)
MPA............	Multiple Product Announcement (NTCM)
MPA............	Multiple Project Assurance
MPA............	Multiple Protocol Architecture [*Computer science*] (PCM)
MPA............	Multiple-Use Planning Area
MPA............	Multi-Point Asynchronous (NITA)
MPA............	Multiprecision Arithmetic
MPA............	Multipurpose Additive (EDCT)
MPA............	Multi-Purpose Aircraft (SAUS)
MPA............	MuniYield Pennsylvania Fund [*NYSE symbol*] (SPSG)
MPA............	Museum Publications of America
MPA............	Music Publishers Association (NADA)
MPA............	Music Publishers' Association of the United States (EA)
MPA............	Mycophenolic Acid [*Biochemistry*]
MPA............	Nampa, ID [*Location identifier*] [*FAA*] (FAAL)
MPA............	Premenstrual Asthma [*Medicine*] (DAVI)
MPAA..........	Motion Picture Association of America (EA)
MPAA..........	Motorcar Parts & Accesories, Inc. [*NASDAQ symbol*] (SAG)
MPAA..........	Multi-beam Phased-Array Antenna (SAUS)
MPAA..........	Multifunctional Phased-Array Antenna (SAUS)
MPAA..........	Musical Performing Arts Association (NTCM)
MPAB..........	Military Petroleum Advisory Board
MPAC..........	Impact Systems, Inc. [*NASDAQ symbol*] (NQ)
MPAC..........	Master Plan for Academic Computing (AD)
MPAC..........	Materials and Parts Availability Control (SAUO)
MPAC..........	Military Pay and Allowance Committee (AFM)
MPAC..........	Multipurpose Application Console (SSD)
MP Acc.......	Master of Professional Accountancy (PGP)
MP Acc.......	Master of Professional Accounting (PGP)
MPAcc........	Master of Public Accounting (GAGS)
MP Acct.......	Master of Professional Accounting (PGP)
MPACS........	Management Planning and Control System [*IBM Corp.*]
MPACT........	Microprocessor Application to Control-Firmware Translator [*Computer science*] (MHDI)
MPAD	Manpower Personnel Assignment Document (AFM)
MPAD	Maximum Permissible Accumulated Dose [*of radiation*] (ADA)
mpad	Maximum Permissible Annual Dose (AD)
MPAD	Menlo Park Applications Development [*IBM Corp.*]
MPAD	Mission Planning and Analysis Division [*NASA*]
MP Adm	Master of Public Administration
MPAE..........	Max-Planck-Institut fur Aeronomie [*An association*]
MPAEA........	Mountain Plains Adult Education Association (AEBS)
MPaed........	Master of Paediatrics
MPAFD	Multiple Pulse Arm Fire Device (MCD)
MP Aff	Master of Public Affairs (PGP)
MPAG	Maxwell Pensioners' Action Group (WDAA)
MPAGB	Modern Pentathlon Association of Great Britain (DBA)
MPAI..........	Master Plan for Army Intelligence (SAUO)
mpai...........	Maximum Permissible Annual Intake (AD)
MPAI..........	Maximum Permissible Annual Intake [*Radiation*] (NRCH)
MPAIAC	Movimiento para la Autodeterminacion y Independencia del Archipielago Canario [*Movement for the Self-Determination and Independence of the Canary Archipelago*] [*Canary Islands*] [*Spanish*] (PD)
MPAJA........	Malayan People's Anti-Japanese Army [*World War II*]
MPAJU........	Malayan People's Anti-Japanese Union [*World War II*]
MPAK..........	Middeck Payload Accommodation Kit (SAUS)
mpam	Maritime Polar Air Mass (AD)
MPAM.........	Maritime Polar Air Mass (MSA)
MPAMA.......	Milk Products Advertising-Merchandising Association (EA)
MPAN.........	Macrosopic Polyarteritis Nodosa [*Medicine*] (MELL)
MP&C.........	Maintenance Planning and Control
MP & CS	Management Planning and Control System
MP & IS	Material Process and Inspection Specification (AAG)
MP&L..........	Minnesota Power and Light Co. (SAUO)
MP&L..........	Mississippi Power and Light Co. (SAUO)
MP&L Company...	Minnesota Power & Light Company (SAUO)
MP & MAC...	Marine Petroleum and Minerals Advisory Committee [*Terminated, 1976*] [*National Oceanic and Atmospheric Administration*] (NOAA)
MP&MTD.....	Motion Picture & Medical Television Department (SAUO)
MP&QA.......	Manufacturing, Production, and Quality Assurance
mp & rs.......	Motive Power and Rolling Stock (AD)
MP & TF.....	Motion Picture and Television Fund
MPANSW.....	Master Patternmakers' Association of New South Wales [*Australia*]
MPANSW.....	Master Poulterers' Association of New South Wales [*Australia*]
MPAP.........	Mean Pulmonary Artery Pressure [*Cardiology*]
MPAPS	Motivation and Potential for Adoptive Parenthood Scale [*Psychology*]
MPAQ	McGill Pain Assessment Questionnaire (MELL)
MPAR	Maintenance Program Analysis Report
MPAR	Microprogram Address Register
MPAR	Multicanal Participacoes [*NASDAQ symbol*] (SAG)
m part	Movable Partition (AD)
MPAS.........	Maritime Patrol Airship Study
MPAS.........	Maryland Parent Attitude Survey [*Psychology*]
MPAS.........	Master of Physical Activity Studies (PGP)
MPAS.........	Master of Physician Assistant Studies (PGP)
MPAS.........	Mild Perioxic Acid Schiff [*Reaction*] [*Medicine*] (DMAA)
mpas	Millipascal Second (AD)
MPASK	Multi-Phase and Amplitude-Shift-Keying [*Computer science*] (PDAA)
MPASS	Modular Processing and Support System
MPASS	Multi-Purpose Amphibious Support Ship (SAUS)
MPast.........	Master in Pastoral Studies
MPAT..........	Management Postition Analysis Test [*William J. Reddin*] (TES)
MPAT..........	Multipurpose All-Terrain Vehicle
MPAT..........	Multi-Purpose Anti-Tank (SAUS)
MPATI.........	Midwest Program for Airborne Television Instruction [*Defunct*]
MPAU	Mahatma Phule Agricultural University (SAUO)
MPA-URP	Master of Public Affairs and Urban and Regional Planning (PGP)
MPAUS	Music Publishers' Association of the United States (DGA)
m payl	Maximum Payload (AD)
MPB..........	Berkshire Athenaeum, Pittsfield, MA [*Library symbol*] [*Library of Congress*] (LCLS)
MPB..........	Machine-Pressed Bales
MPB..........	Magnetic Particle Brake
MPB..........	Maine Potato Board (EA)
MPB..........	Maintenance Parts Breakdown (KSC)
mpb..........	Male Pattern Baldness (AD)
MPB..........	Male-Pattern Baldness
MPB..........	Master of Physical Biology
MPB..........	Material Performance Branch [*Air Force*]
MPB..........	Materials Properties Branch [*Army*] (RDA)
MPB..........	Matrix Program Board
MPB..........	Maximum Participation Base (IIA)
MPB..........	Mechanically Processed Beef [*Food technology*]
MPB..........	Mephobarbital [*Antiepileptic drug*]
MPB..........	Meprobamate (DMAA)
MPB..........	Merit Promotion Bulletin [*Military*]
MPB..........	Miami [*Florida*] Public Seaplane Base [*Airport symbol*] (OAG)
MPB..........	Military Personnel Branch (SAUO)
MPB..........	Miniature Precision Bearing, Inc.
MPB..........	Missing Persons Bureau
MPB..........	Montpelier & Barre Railroad Co. [*Later, MB*] [*AAR code*]
MPB..........	Motorized Pontoon Bridge (MCD)
MPB..........	Mouvement Progressiste de Burundi [*Progressive Movement of Burundi*]
MPB&MTD.....	Mucopurulent Bronchitis [*Medicine*] (MELL)
MPB..........	Multilayer Printed Board
MPB..........	Munitions Packaging Branch [*Picatinny Arsenal*] [*Army*] (RDA)
MPB..........	Musica Popular Brasileira [*Pop music*]
MPBA..........	Machine Printers' Beneficial Association [*Later, MPEA*]
MPBA..........	Model Power Boat Association [*British*] (DBA)
MPBA..........	Multiple Practice Bomb Adapter (SAUS)
MPB and W...	Ministry of Public Buildings and Works (SAUO)
MPBB..........	Maximum Permissible Body Burden [*Radiation*]
mpbb..........	Maximum Permissible Body Burden [*of Radiation*] (AD)
MPBB..........	Methyl(phenyl)(butyl)barbituric (Acid) [*Biochemistry*]
MPBC..........	Berkshire Community College, Pittsfield, MA [*Library symbol*] [*Library of Congress*] (LCLS)
MPBC..........	Memphis Power Boat Club [*Tennessee*] (AD)
MPBDS	Material Properties Bibliographic Data System [*Purdue University*] [*Database*]
MPBE..........	Molten Plutonium Burn-Up Experiment [*Nuclear energy*] (IEEE)
MPBEA........	Mountain Plains Business Education Association (AEBS)
MPBI..........	Multiple Post Boost Intercept Study (ACAE)
MPBL..........	Berkshire Law Library Association, Pittsfield, MA [*Library symbol*] [*Library of Congress*] (LCLS)
MPBMA.......	Munitions Production Base Modernization Agency (SAUO)
MPBME.......	Munitions Production Base Modernization, Expansion (RDA)
MPBN.........	Military Police Battalion
MPBO.........	Bocas Del Toro [*Panama*] [*ICAO location identifier*] (ICLI)
MPBP.........	Mechanically Processed Beef Product [*Food technology*]
MPBP.........	Metal Polishers, Buffers, Platers, and Allied Workers International Union (EA)
mp br........	Multipunch Bar (AD)
MPBR........	Multipunch Bar
MPBRS	Maintenance Production/Backlog Reporting System (SAUO)
MPBS........	Medical Pocket-Book Series [*A publication*]
MPBS........	Multipurpose Bayonet System [*Army*] (INF)
MPBS........	Mutual Permanent Building Society (AD)
MPBW........	Ministry of Public Building and Works [*Later, DOE*] [*British*]
MPC..........	Machine Punch Card

MPC	Magellan Petroleum [*Exchange Symbol*] (TTSB)
MPC	Magnetic Particle Clutch
MPC	Maharashtra Prajatantra Congress [*India*] [*Political party*] (PPW)
MPC	Maharashtra Progressive Congress [*India*] [*Political party*] (PPW)
MPC	Maidstone Paper Converters [*Commercial firm*] [*British*]
MPC	Maine Potato Council [*Later, MPB*] (EA)
MPC	Maintenance Parts Catalog
MPC	Maintenance Policy Council [*DoD*] [*Washington, DC*]
MPC	Maintenance Priority Code
MPC	Maintenance Procedure Chart
MPC	Mandatory Product Control
MPC	Manpower and Personnel Center (SAUO)
MPC	Manpower & Personnel Centre (SAUO)
MPC	Manpower and Personnel Council [*DoD*]
MPC	Manpower Planning Council
MPC	Manpower Policy Committee (SAUO)
MPC	Manpower Priorities Committee
MPC	Manual Pointing Controller (MCD)
MPC	Manufacturing Plan Change
MPC	Manufacturing, Planning, and Control
MPC	Marco Polo Club (EA)
MPC	Marginal Producers Cost [*Engineering economics*]
mpc	Marginal Propensity to Consume (AD)
MPC	Marginal Propensity to Consume [*Economics*]
MPC	Marine Policy Center (GNE)
MPC	Marine Pollution Control, Inc. (EFIS)
mpc	Marine Protein Concentrate (AD)
MPC	Marine Protein Concentrate [*See also FPC*] (MSC)
MPC	Marker Pulse Conversion [*Telecommunications*] (TEL)
MPC	Market Performance Committee [*of NYSE*]
MPC	Master Control Program [*Computer science*] (ECII)
MPC	Master of Pastoral Counseling (PGP)
MPC	Master of Personnel Counseling (GAGS)
MPC	Master of Professional Counseling (PGP)
MPC	Master of Public Communication (PGP)
MPC	Master Parts Card
MPC	Master Phasing Chart (MCD)
MPC	Master Program Chart (MCD)
MPC	Materials Policy Commission (SAUO)
MPC	Materials Preparation Center [*Ames, IA*] [*Ames Laboratory*] [*Department of Energy*] (GRD)
MPC	Materials Processing Center [*Massachusetts Institute of Technology*] [*Research center*] (RCD)
mpc	Materials Program Code (AD)
MPC	Materials Properties Council (EA)
MPC	Materiel Program Code [*Air Force*] (AFM)
MPC	Materiel Program Costs (ACAE)
mpc	Mathematics, Physics, Chemistry (AD)
mpc	Maximum Permissible Concentration (AD)
MPC	Maximum Permissible Concentration [*Later, RCG*] [*Radiation*]
MPC	Mean Plasma Concentration [*Medicine*] (MELL)
MPC	Mechanical Positioning Control
MPC	Mechanized Production Control
MPC	Medical Practices' Committee (WDAA)
MPC	Medium Processing Channel [*Carbon*] (DICI)
MPC	Megaparsec
MPC	Member of Parliament of Canada
MPC	Member of Provincial Council (SAUO)
MPC	Member Pickwick Club [*From "The Pickwick Papers" by Charles Dickens*]
MPC	Membrane Protein Complex [*Cytology*]
MPC	Memory Protection Check (MCD)
MPC	Meningococcal Protein Conjugate [*Medicine*] (MELL)
MPC	Meperidine, Promethazine, and Chlorpromazine [*Drug regime*]
MPC	Merleau-Ponty Circle (EA)
MPC	Message Processing Center
MPc	Metallophthalocyanine [*Organic chemistry*]
MPC	Metal Properties Council (SAUO)
MPC	Meteorological Prediction Center (KSC)
MPC	Metromedia Producers Corp.
MPC	Metropolitan Police College (AD)
MPC	Metropolitan Police Commissioner (AD)
MPC	Microcircuit Power Converter
MPC	Microparticle Concentration [*Analytical chemistry*]
MPC	Microprocessor [*Computer science*] [*Unit*] (ECII)
MPC	Micro-Processor Controller [*Computer science*] (AGLO)
MPC	Microprogram Control
MPC	Micropurulent Cervicitis [*Medicine*]
MPC	Midbody Pyro Controller (NASA)
MPC	Midpalmar Crease [*Medicine*] (MELL)
MPC	Mid Power Controller [*Aerospace*] (NAKS)
MPC	Midwest Parentcraft Center (EA)
mpc	Military Payment Certificate (AD)
MPC	Military Payment Certificate
MPC	Military Personnel Center (AFM)
MPC	Military Pioneer Corps [*British*]
MPC	Military Police Corps
MPC	Military Police Force (AD)
MPC	Military Postal Clerk (AFM)
MPC	Military Property Custodian (AFIT)
Mpc	Million Parsecs [*Interstellar space measure*]
MPC	Mineral Policy Center (EA)
MPC	Miniature Protector Connector [*Telecommunications*] (TEL)
MPC	Minimal Flight Planning Charts [*Air Force*]
MPC	Minimum Mycoplasmacidal Concentration [*Medicine*] (MAE)
mpc	Minimum Planning Chart (AD)
MPC	Minimum Protozoacidal Concentration
MPC	Ministry Partnership Committee (SAUO)
MPC	Minor Planet Center [*Smithsonian Institution*]
MPC	Missile Practice Camp (SAUO)
MPC	Mission Planning Center (MCD)
MPC	Mission Profile Course (MCD)
MPC	Mississippi Library Commission, Jackson, MS [*OCLC symbol*] (OCLC)
MPC	Mitsubishi Petrochemical Co. Ltd. (SAUO)
MPC	Mobile Processing Center (MCD)
MPC	Mode and Power Control [*Aviation*]
MPC	Model Penal Code (AD)
MPC	Model Predictive Control [*Chemical engineering*]
MPC	Model Procurement Code [*for State and Local Governments*] (AAGC)
MPC	Modular Peripheral Interface Converter
MPC	Monagas Pipeline Crude [*Petrochemical engineering*]
MPC	Monetary Policy Committee [*France*] (ECON)
MPC	Monetary Policy Committee [*Bank of England*]
MPC	Monitor Proportional Counter (MCD)
MPC	Monolayer-Protected Metal Cluster [*Materials science*]
MPC	Montana Power Company (SAUO)
MPC	Monterey Peninsula College [*California*]
MPC	Montreal Presbyterian College
MPC	Moore's English Privy Council Cases [*A publication*] (DLA)
MPC	Morphine Positive Control [*Epidemiology*]
MPC	Mortgage-Participation Certificate [*Investment term*] (GFGA)
MPC	Most Probable Cost (AAGC)
MPC	Mother-of-Pearl Clouds [*Meteorology*] (PDAA)
MPC	Motion Picture Camera (MCD)
MPC	Motion Picture Control Panel (MSA)
MPC	Motorized Pressure Control [*Hydraulics*]
MPC	Mountain Pacific Air Ltd. [*Canada*] [*ICAO designator*] (FAAC)
MPC	Mouse Myeloma Cell [*Cell biology*]
MPC	Mouvement Patriotique Congolais [*Congo Patriotic Movement*] [*Political party*]
MPC	Movable Platform Configuration
MPC	Mucopurulent Cervicitis [*Medicine*] (MELL)
MPC	Multicultural Psychiatric Center [*Australia*]
MPC	Multielectron Photoactive Center [*Physical chemistry*]
MPC	Multimedia Personal Computer
MPC	Multimedia Personal Computer Group [*Subsidiary of Software Publishers Association*] (IGQR)
MPC	Multi-Party Conference [*Namibia*] [*Political party*] (PPW)
MPC	Multipath Core
MPC	Multiple Payload Carrier (SSD)
MPC	Multiple Process Chart
MPC	Multiple-Profile Configuration (MCD)
MPC	Multiple-Purpose Communications (NG)
MPC	Multipolar Cell [*Medicine*] (MELL)
MPC	Multiprocessor Computer
MPC	Multiprogram Control [*Computer science*]
MPC	Multi-Protocol Cartridge [*Automotive diagnosis*]
mpc	Multipurpose Carrier (AD)
MPC	Multipurpose Center
MPC	Multipurpose Computer (CMD)
MPC	Multi-Purpose Concept (SAUS)
MPC	Multi-Purpose Console (SAUS)
MPC	Multispectral Photographic Camera (KSC)
MPC	Myeloblastpromyelocyte Compartment [*Hematology*] (DAVI)
MPC	Thousand Pieces (EG)
MPCA	Magnetic Powder Core Association (EA)
MPCA	Marine and Ports Council of Australia (AD)
MPCA	Markham Prayer Card Apostolate (EA)
MPCA	Master Pastry Cooks Association (AD)
MPCA	Melanin-Producing Cell Autoantibody [*Endocrinology*]
MPCA	Microbial Pest Control Agent (EPAT)
MPCA	Mid Power Controller Assembly [*Aerospace*] (NAKS)
MPCA	Miniature Pinscher Club of America (EA)
MPCA	Minnesota Pollution Control Agency
MPCA	Multiway Principal Components Analysis [*Mathematics*]
MPCABS	Michigan Project for Computer-Assisted Biblical Studies [*University of Michigan*] [*Information service or system*] (IID)
MPCAG	Military Parts Control Advisory Group [*DoD*]
MPCASS	Modernization Parts Control Automated Support System (SAUO)
MPCASS	Modernized Parts Control Automated Support System
MPCB	Manufacturing Plan Control Board (AD)
MPCB	Minuteman Parts Control Board [*Missiles*]
MPCB	Motion Picture Code Board (SAUO)
MPCB	Multilayer Printed Circuit Board
MPCblack	Medium Processing Channel Black (EDCT)
mpc black	Medium-Processing Channel Black (AD)
MPCC	Manufacturing Planning Change Coordination (MCD)
MPCC	Material Purchase Contracts Control
MPCC	Microprogrammable Communications Controller [*Computer science*] (MHDI)
MPCC	Minnesota Private College Council (AD)
MPCC	Multiprocessor Computer Complex
MPCC	Multiprotocol Communications Controller
MPCCC	Metropolitan Post Card Collectors Club (EA)
MPCD	Major Program Components Document (SAUO)
MPCD	Manufacturing Process Control Document (KSC)
MPCD	Minimum Perceptible Color Difference

MPCD	Mouvement Populaire Constitutionnel Democratique [*Popular Democratic Constitutional Movement*] [*Morocco*] [*Political party*] (PPW)
MPCD	Multipurpose Color Display
MPCE	Music Publishers Contact Employees
MPCF	Campo De Francia/Enrique A. Jimenez [*Panama*] [*ICAO location identifier*] (ICLI)
MPCF	Millions of Particles per Cubic Foot (PDAA)
MPCFP	Canadian Food Products Development Center, Portage La Prairie, Manitoba [*Library symbol*] [*National Library of Canada*] (NLC)
MPCH	Changuinola/Cap. Manuel Nino [*Panama*] [*ICAO location identifier*] (ICLI)
MPCH	Methodist Protestant Church
MPCI	Mandatory Product Control Items (MCD)
MPCI	Microsoft Press Computer Dictionary
MPCI	Military Police Criminal Investigation
MPCI	Multiport Programmable Communications Interface
MPCI	Multi-Purpose Chemical Laser (ACAE)
MPCID	Military Police Criminal Investigation Detachment
MPCL	Monolithical Peltier Cooled LASER (MCD)
MPCL	Mooney Problem Check List [*Psychology*]
MPCL	Movimiento Patriotico Cuba Libre [*Free Cuba Patriotic Movement*] [*Political party*] (AD)
MPCL(G)	Maximum Permissible Contaminent Level (Goal) (GNE)
MPCLP	Mental Patient Civil Liberties Project (EA)
MPCM	Microprogram Control Memory
MPCM	Multi-Purpose Central Mount/Module [*Military*] (LAIN)
MPCMC	Multimedia PC Marketing Council (SAUO)
MPCMP	Mass Properties Control and Management Plan (ACAE)
MPCO	Colon [*Panama*] [*ICAO location identifier*] (ICLI)
MPCO	Micropolycystic Ovary [*Syndrome*] [*Medicine*] (DMAA)
MPCO	Military Police Commanding Officer (MCD)
MPCO	Military Police Company
MPCP	Mid-Peninsula Conversion Project [*Later, CEC*] (EA)
MP/CP	Military Personnel/Civilian Personnel
MPCP	Missile Power Control Panel (AAG)
mpcp	Missile Power Control Panel (AD)
MPCPA	Music Publishers Contact Personnel Association [*British*] (DBA)
MPCR	Memorandum Program Change Request [*Military*] (CAAL)
MPCR	Microprogram Count Register [*Computer science*] (MHDB)
MPCRI	Mercantile Pacific Coastal Routing Instructions
MPCS	Machinery, Plant Control System [*Navy*]
MPCS	Manual Propositional Control System (AAG)
MP/CS	Manufacturing Planning and Control System (SAUO)
MPCS	Master Plan for Computing Services (AD)
MPCS	Mission Planning and Control Software (SAUS)
MPCS	Mission Planning and Control Station
MPCS	Multiparty Connection Subsystem [*Telecommunications*] (TEL)
MPCS	Multiprocessing Control System [*Computer science*]
MPCS	Multi-Protocol Communications Subsystem (SAUS)
MPCSOT	Machinery, Plant Control System Operator Trainer [*Navy*]
MPCSW	Multipurpose Close Support Weapon [*Military*] (AABC)
MPCTNS	Manportable Common Thermal Night Sight (ACAE)
MPCU	Marine Pollution Control Unit [*Department of Transportation*]
MPCU	Maximum Permissible Concentration of Unidentified Radionuclides in Water
mpcur	Maximum Permissible Concentration of Unidentified Radionuclides (AD)
MPD	Disability Ministries [*Formerly, Ministry with Persons with Disabilities*] (EA)
MPD	Magnetoplasmadynamic
MPD	Magnetospheric Particle Detector (MCD)
MPD	Main DC [*Direct Current*] Power Distributor Assembly (MCD)
MPD	Main Pancreatic Duct [*Anatomy*]
MPD	Maintenance Policy Document [*Deep Space Instrumentation Facility, NASA*]
MPD	Make per Drawing (SAA)
MPD	Management Policy and Directives
MPD	Map Pictorial Display
MPD	Marlborough Productions Ltd. [*Vancouver Stock Exchange symbol*]
M Pd	Master of Pedagogy
MPD	Master of Product Design (GAGS)
MPD	Master Planned Community (PA)
MPD	Material Property Damage (DNAB)
MPD	Materials Physics Division [*Air Force*]
MPD	Materials Proximity Detector
MPD	Maximum Packing Depth (NG)
mpd	Maximum Permissible Dose (AD)
MPD	Maximum Permissible Dose [*Radiation*]
MPD	Maximum Permitted Dose (SAUS)
MPD	Maximum Possible Dose [*Medicine*] (WDAA)
MPD	Mean Phenetic Distance
MPD	Mean Photon Flux Density
MPD	Mean Population Doubling [*Cytology*]
MPD	Medical Pay Date
MPD	Medusa Portland Cement Company (SAUO)
MPD	Membrane Polarographic Detector [*Instrumentation*]
MPD	Membrane Potential Difference [*Medicine*] (DMAA)
MPD	Meridian Point Realty IV [*AMEX symbol*] (SPSG)
MPD	Message Preparation Directory (SAUS)
MPD	Meta-Phenylenediamine [*Organic chemistry*]
MPD	Methane Phophonyl Dichloride [*Nerve gas intermediate*] [*Organic chemistry*]
MPD	Methylpentanediol [*Organic chemistry*]
MPD	Methylphosphonic Diamide [*Flame retardant*] [*Organic chemistry*]

MPD	Metropolitan Park District (AD)
MPD	Metropolitan Police Department (AD)
MPD	Metropolitan Police District [*London*]
MPD	Microprocessor Developments (NITA)
MPD	Microwave Plasma Detector [*Instrumentation*]
MPD	Midwest Presenters Directory [*Information service or system*] (IID)
MPD	Military Pay Division (AD)
MPD	Military Pay Division, Finance Center, US Army
MPD	Military Personnel Division (SAUO)
MPD	Military Position Description
MPD	Military Priority Date
MPD	Military Prisons Department [*British military*] (DMA)
MPD	Mines and Petroleum Department (SAUO)
MPD	Minimal Perceptible Difference (DMAA)
MPD	Minimal Phototoxic Dose [*Medicine*] (DMAA)
MPD	Minimum Permissible Dose
MPD	Minimum Premarket [*Health and Safety*] Data [*OEEC*]
MPD	Mini Port Driver (SAUS)
MPD	Minnesota Percepto-Diagnostic Test
mpd	Missile Purchase Description (AD)
MPD	Missile Purchase Description [*Army*]
MPD	Missing Pulse Detector (MHDI)
MPD	Mode-Power Distribution [*Electronics*]
MPD	Modification Program Directive (AFIT)
MPD	Movement for Democratic Process [*Zambia*] [*Political party*] (EY)
MPD	Movement Priority Designator (DNAB)
MPD	Movimento para Democracia [*Cape Verde*] [*Political party*] (EY)
MPD	Movimiento Popular Democratico [*Popular Democratic Movement*] [*Ecuador*] [*Political party*] (PPW)
MPD	Movimiento Popular Dominicano [*Dominican Popular Movement*] [*Dominican Republic*] [*Political party*] (PPW)
MPD	Mpanda [*Tanzania*] [*Airport symbol*] (AD)
MPD	m-Phenylenediamine [*Also, MPDA*] [*Organic chemistry*]
MPD	Multiperson Prisoner's Dilemma [*Statistics*]
MPD	Multiphoton Dissociation [*Physical chemistry*]
mpd	Multiple Personality Disorder (AD)
MPD	Multiple Personality Disorder
MPD	Multipurpose Diffractometer
MPD	Multipurpose Display (MCD)
MPD	Myeloprofiferative Disorder [*Medicine*] (MELL)
MPD	Myeloproliferative Disease [*Medicine*] (DMAA)
MPD	Myofascial Pain Dysfunction [*Neurology*]
MPDA	David/Enrique Malek [*Panama*] [*ICAO location identifier*] (ICLI)
MPDA	Monitor-Printer-Diskette Adapter
MPDA	Motion Picture Distributors Association (AD)
MPDA	m-Phenylenediamine [*Also, MPD*] [*Organic chemistry*]
MPDA	Multiplatform Disk Array (SAUS)
MPDAA	Motion Picture Distributors' Association of Australia
MPDATA	Multidimensional Positive Definite Advection Algorithm (SAUS)
MPDB	Main Power Distribution Box (SSD)
MPD-C	Manpack Personnel Detector-Chemical [*Officially the Olfractronic Personnel Detector*] [*Military*] (VNW)
MPDC	Mechanical Properties Data Center [*Defense Logistics Agency*] [*Information service or system*]
MPDC	Missile Prelaunch Data Computer (MCD)
MPDD	Meteorological Penetration Detection Development
MPDE	Maximum Permissible Dose Equivalent (ERG)
MPDES	Microprocessor Data Extraction System [*Military*] (CAAL)
MPDFA	Master Photo Dealers' and Finishers' Association [*Later, PMA*] (EA)
MPDG	Multi-Purpose Display Generator (ACAE)
MPDGP	Mornington Peninsula Division of General Practice (SAUO)
MPDGP	Murray Plains Division of General Practice (SAUO)
MPDI	Marine Products Development Irradiator
MPDI	Microwave Power Devices [*NASDAQ symbol*] (TTSB)
MPDI	Microwave Power Devices, Inc. [*NASDAQ symbol*] (SAG)
mp di	Multipunch Die (AD)
MPDI	Multipunch Die
MPDL	Mission Profile Development List
MPDL	Movimiento Pro-Democracia y Libertad [*Panama*] [*Political party*] (EY)
MPDLRSDB	Commission on the Mentally Disabled [*Formerly, Mental and Physical Disability Legal Research Services and Data Bases*] (EA)
MPDM	Maintenance Planning Data Manual (MUGU)
MPDP	Manpower Development Program [*Department of Labor*]
MPDPIS	Master Plan for Data Processing and Information Systems (AD)
MPDS	Mandibular Pain Dysfunction Syndrome [*Medicine*] (DMAA)
MPDS	Mechanical Provisioning Data System
MPDS	Message Processing and Distributing System [*Navy*] (NVT)
MPDS	Message Processing Display System (CCCA)
MPDS	Metropolitan Police Detective School (SAUO)
MPDS	Missile Piercing Discarding Sabot (PDAA)
MPDS	Mission Planning Debriefing Station (MCD)
MPDS	Monitored Professional Development Scheme (WDAA)
MPDS	Multi-Purpose Decontamination System (SAUS)
MPDS	Multi-Purpose Display System (DA)
MPDS	Myofascial Pain Dysfunction Syndrome [*Neurology*] (DAVI)
MPDSA	Master Painters, Decorators, and Signwriters Association (AD)
MPDSANSW	Master Painters, Decorators and Signwriters' Association of New South Wales [*Australia*]
MPDT	Magnetoplasmadynamic Thruster [*Electric thruster type*]
MPDT	Mean Preventive Downtime [*Computer science*]
MPDT	Minnesota Perception Diagnostic Test (AD)
MPDT	Minnesota Percepto-Diagnostic Test [*Psychology*]
MPDTL	Medium-Power Diode-Transistor Logic (ECII)

MPDU	Message Protocol Data Unit [*Telecommunications*] (OSI)
MPDU	Mobile Power Distribution Unit (DWSG)
MP-DV	Multiply-Divide (NITA)
MPE	Malignant Pericardial Effusion [*Medicine*] (MELL)
MPE	Management Program for Executives (ECON)
MPE	Manual Plot Entry (MCD)
MPE	Master of Physical Education
MPE	Mathematical and Physical Sciences and Engineering (IEEE)
MPE	Maximum Permissible Exposure [*Radiation*]
mpe	Maximum Permissible Exposure [*to Radiation*] (AD)
MPE	Maximum Possible Error
MPE	Max-Planck-Institut fur Extraterrestrische Physik [*Germany*]
MPE	Meat Promotion Executive [*British*]
MPE	Mechanized Production of Electronics
MPE	Meeting Planners Expo (ITD)
MPE	Memory Parity Error
MPE	Metallocene Polyethylenes (SAUS)
MPE	Metaphenoxylene [*Analytical chemistry*]
MPE	Methidiumpropyl Ethylenediaminetetraacetic Acid [*Analytical biochemistry*]
MPE	Midi Provence Electronique (SAUS)
MPE	Minimum Perceptible Erythema [*Dermatology*]
MPE	Minimum Performance Envelope (MCD)
MPE	Minimum Potential Energy [*Fission*]
MPE	Ministry of Planning and Environment (SAUO)
MPE	Missile Positioning Equipment (KSC)
MPE	Mission and Performance Envelope
MPE	Mission-Peculiar Equipment
MPE	Mission to Planet Earth (USDC)
MPE	Modern Programming Environment (ACAE)
MPE	Monthly Project Evaluation
MPE	Moving Paper Electrophoresis
MPE	Multiphoton Excitation [*Physics*]
MPE	Multipion Exchange
MPE	Multiple Phase Ejector
MPE	Multiple Protective Earthing (IAA)
MPE	Multiprogramming Executive [*Hewlett-Packard Co.*]
MPEA	Machine Printers and Engravers Association of the United States (EA)
MPEA	Meat and Poultry Export Association
MPEA	Motion Picture Exhibitors Association (AD)
MPEA	Motion Picture Export Association (SAUO)
MPEA	Mouvement Populaire d'Evolution Africaine [*African People's Evolution Movement*]
MPEAA	Motion Picture Export Association of America (EA)
MPeaHi	Peabody Historical Society, Peabody, MA [*Library symbol*] [*Library of Congress*] (LCLS)
MPeal	Peabody Institute, Peabody, MA [*Library symbol*] [*Library of Congress*] (LCLS)
MPEAUS	Machine Printers and Engravers Association of the United States (DGA)
MPEAUS	Master Printers and Engravers Association of the United States (AD)
MPEC	Miniature Piano Enthusiast Club (EA)
MPEC	Minor Planet Electronic Circular [*A publication*]
MPEC	Minor Planets Electronic Circular
MPEC	Molt Periosteal Elevator [*Medicine*] (MELL)
MPEC	Multicultural Publishing and Education Council (NTPA)
MPEC	Multipolar Electrocoagulation [*Medicine*] (MELL)
MPECC	Multiprocessor Experimental Computer Complex
MPECS	Multi-Pass Expert Control System (VLIE)
MPed	Master of Pedagogy (CPGU)
MPed	Master of Physical Education
MPED	Minimal Phototoxic Erythema Dose [*Medicine*] (MELL)
M Pe E	Master of Petroleum Engineering
M Pe Eng....	Master of Petroleum Engineering
MPEG	Methoxypolyethylene Glycol [*Organic chemistry*]
MPEG	Military Police Escort Guard
MPEG	Motion Picture Experts Group
mpeg	Motion Picture Experts Group [*Computer science*]
MPEG	Moving [*or Motion*] Pictures Experts Group [*Motion video standard*] (PCM)
MPEG-1	Motion picture Experts Group, video compression standard (SAUO)
MPEG II	Motion Pictures Expert Group II (SAUO)
MPEH	Methylphenylethylhydantoin [*Organic chemistry*] (MAE)
MPEIR	Molecular Pathogenesis of Eye Infection Research Center (SAUO)
MPE/iX........	Multiprogramming Executive / POSIX [*Portable Operating System Interface for Unix*] [*Computer science*] (CDE)
MPEL	Maximum Permissible Exposure Levels [*Radiation*]
M Pen..........	Minister of Pensions [*British*] (AD)
M Pen	Ministry of Pensions [*British*] (AD)
MPen	Ministry of Pensions and Social Insurance (SAUO)
MPEP	Manual of Patent Examining Procedures
MPEP	Metalworking Processes and Equipment Program
MPEP	Model Performance Evaluation Program [*Centers for Disease Control*]
MPER..........	Master of Personnel and Employee Relations (GAGS)
MPER..........	Material-in-Process Engineering Request
MP-ER	Multiple Punch, Error Release (DNAB)
M Perf A	Master of Performing Arts (PGP)
MPERR	Master Personnel Record
MPers..........	Middle Persian (AD)
MPES..........	Management Planning and Evaluation Staff [*Environmental Protection Agency*] (GFGA)
MPE/S..........	Maritime Prepositioned Equipment and Supplies [*Navy*] (ANA)
MPES..........	Mass Properties Engineering Section

MPES..........	Mathematical, Physical, and Engineering Science (AD)
MPES..........	Maximum Performance Ejection Seat [*Navy*]
MPES..........	Medical Planning and Execution System (DOMA)
MPES..........	Multi-Programming Executive System (VLIE)
MPESS..........	Mission Peculiar Experiment Support Structure
MPET..........	Magellan Petroleum Corp. [*NASDAQ symbol*] (NQ)
MPetE..........	Master of Petroleum Engineering (GAGS)
MP Ex	Modern Practice of the Exchequer [*A publication*] (DLA)
MPF..........	Machine Parts Fabrication
MPF..........	Major Project Funding
MPF..........	Malaya Police Federation (SAUO)
MPF..........	Malaysian Peasants Front [*Political party*] (AD)
MPF..........	Mapping Field (ACRL)
MPF..........	Map Predicted Fire (SAUS)
MPF..........	Marematlou Freedom Party (SAUO)
MPF..........	Maritime Patrol Force (MCD)
MPF..........	Maritime Prepositioning Force (DOMA)
MPF..........	Master Parts File (MCD)
MPF..........	Materials Processing Facility [*NASA*] (KSC)
MPF..........	Maturation-Promoting Factor [*Cytology*]
MPF..........	Maximum Probably Flood (ABAC)
MPF..........	Mean Power Frequency [*of myoelectric signals*]
MPF..........	Median and Paired Fins [*Ichthyology*]
MPF..........	Medical Passport Foundation [*Defunct*] (EA)
MPF..........	Medium Payload Fairing (IGSL)
MPF..........	Melamine-Phenol-Formaldehyde (EDCT)
MPF..........	Meridian Point Realty VI [*AMEX symbol*] (SPSG)
MPF..........	Metallurgical Plantmakers Federation (AD)
MPF..........	Metal Parts Furnace (MCD)
MPF..........	Methodist Peace Fellowship [*Defunct*] (EA)
MPF..........	Metropolitan Police Force [*Scotland Yard*] [*London, England*]
MPF..........	Mexico Pilgrims Foundation (EA)
MPF..........	Micellar Polymer Flooding [*Petroleum technology*]
MPF..........	Michigan Parkinson Foundation (SAUO)
MPF..........	Micro Professor (NITA)
MPF..........	Million Pair Feet [*Telecommunications*] (TEL)
MPF..........	Missile Pressure Fuel (AAG)
MPF..........	Missile Procurement Fund (AAGC)
MPF..........	Mission Planning Facility (SAUO)
MPF..........	Mission Planning Forecast
MPF..........	Mitosis-Promoting Factor [*Cytology*]
MPF..........	Mizrachi Palestine Fund (EA)
MPF..........	Modern Polar Front [*Climatology*]
MPF..........	Momentary Power Failure (SAUO)
mpf..........	Motion-Picture Film (AD)
MPF..........	M-Phase Promoting Factor [*Cytology*]
MPF..........	Multiple Primary Feed [*Deep Space Instrumentation Facility, NASA*]
MPF..........	Multipurpose Facility (DOMA)
mpf..........	Multi-Purpose Food (AD)
MPF..........	Multipurpose Food [*Refers to a specific combination of ingredients used in a food relief program*]
MPF..........	Multispectral Photographic Facility
MPF..........	Murine Pathogen Free [*Rats or mice*]
MPF..........	Religious Teachers, Filippini [*Roman Catholic women's religious order*]
MPFASAF	Military Police Functional Automation System for the Army in the Field (MCD)
MPFC..........	Mamas and the Papas Fan Club (EA)
MPFC..........	Mobile Petrol Filling Centre [*British military*] (DMA)
MPFC..........	Morgan Plus Four Club (EA)
MPFC..........	Mountain Parks Financial Corp. [*NASDAQ symbol*] (SAG)
MPFC..........	Mountain Parks Fin'l [*NASDAQ symbol*] (TTSB)
MPFC..........	Multipurpose Fire Control System
MPFCS..........	Multi Purpose Fire Control System (ACAE)
MPFE..........	Motion Picture Film Editors [*Defunct*] (EA)
MPFF..........	Multi-Purpose Fighter Facility (SAUS)
MPFI..........	Multi-Point Fuel Injection [*Automotive engineering*]
MPFP..........	Melt-Processable Fluoropolymers [*Plastics technology*]
MPFS..........	Fuerte Sherman [*Panama*] [*ICAO location identifier*] (ICLI)
MPFS..........	MACRIT [*Manpower Authorization Criteria*] Planning Factors Study [*Army*]
MPFS..........	Microwave Position-Fixing System (NOAA)
MPFS..........	Multiple Primary Feed System [*Deep Space Instrumentation Facility, NASA*]
MPFW..........	Multishot Portable Flame Weapon (MCD)
MPG..........	General Electric Co., Pittsfield, MA [*Library symbol*] [*Library of Congress*] (LCLS)
MPG..........	Georgetown University, Medical Library Processing Center, Washington, DC [*OCLC symbol*] (OCLC)
MPG..........	Magazine Promotion Group [*Defunct*] (EA)
MPG..........	Magnetic Porous Glass [*Materials science*]
MPG..........	Magnetopneumogram [*Medicine*]
MPG..........	Main Professional Grade (WDAA)
MPG..........	Manhattan Publishing Group (EA)
MPG..........	Marine and Ports Group (SAUO)
MPG..........	Maritime Patrol Group
MPG..........	Matched Power Gain
MPG..........	Mathematics Products Group (SAUO)
MPG..........	Max-Planck-Gesellschaft [*West German research organization*]
MPG..........	McArthur, OH [*Location identifier*] [*FAA*] (FAAL)
MPG..........	Meridian Point Realty VII [*AMEX symbol*] (SPSG)
MPG..........	Micrograms per Gram
MPG..........	Microwave Products Group (SAUO)
MPG..........	Microwave Pulse Generator
MPG..........	Mid Plate Gyre [*Nuclear energy*] (NUCP)

mpg	Miles per Gallon (SHCU)
Mpg	Miles per Gallon
MPG	Miles per Gallon
MPG	Military Products Group
MPG	Milk Protein Hydrolysate [*Biochemistry*] (DAVI)
MPG	Miniature Precision Gyrocompass (IEEE)
MPG	Mobile Protected Gun [*Army*] (RDA)
MPG	Molecular Presentation Graphics [*Software program*]
MPG	Monopropylene Glycol [*Chemicals*]
MPG	MPG Investment Corp. Ltd. [*Toronto Stock Exchange symbol*] [*Vancouver Stock Exchange symbol*]
MPG	Multi Channel Pulse Generator (ACAE)
MPG	Multimedia Publishers Group (EA)
MPG	Multiple Point Ground (NAKS)
MPG	Museum of Practical Geology (SAUO)
MPG	Patrologia Graeca [*J. P. Migne*] [*Paris*] [*A publication*] (BJA)
MPGA	Maine Personnel and Guidance Association (AD)
MPGA	Maryland Personnel and Guidance Association (AD)
MPGA	Metropolitan Public Gardens Association [*British*] (BI)
MPGA	Michigan Personnel and Guidance Association (AD)
MPGA	Ministry of Pensions General Administration (SAUO)
MPGA	Minnesota Personnel and Guidance Association (AD)
MPGA	Missouri Personnel and Guidance Association (AD)
MPGF	Male Pronucleus Growth Factor [*Biochemistry*]
MPGHM	Mobile Payload Ground Handling Mechanism (MCD)
MPGI	Mouvement Populaire pour la Guadeloupe Independante [*Popular Movement for Independent Guadeloupe*] (PD)
MPGM	Monophosphoglycerate Mutase [*Biochemistry*] (DAVI)
mpgn	Membrano Proliferative Glomerulonephritis [*Medicine*] (AD)
MPGN	Membranoproliferative Glomerulonephritis [*Nephrology*]
MPGN	Mesangioproliferative Glomerulonephritis [*Nephrology*] (DAVI)
MPG News	Maine Potato Growers Inc. News (SAUO)
MPG-NT	Mobile Protected Gun, Near-Term (ACAE)
MPGR	Mana Pools Game Reserve [*Rhodesia*] (AD)
MPGS	Microprogram Generating System
MPGS	Microprogramming Generating System (NITA)
MPGS	Mobile Protected Gun System [*Army*] (MCD)
MPGS	Multi-Purpose Graphic System [*Computer science*]
MPGT	Mediastinal Paraganglionic Tumor [*Medicine*] (MELL)
MPH	Championship Auto Racing [*NYSE symbol*] (SG)
MPH	G. C. Murphy Co. (SAUO)
MPH	Maintenance Parts Handbook
MPH	Male Pseudohermaphroditism [*Medicine*] (DB)
MPH	Martinair Holland NV [*Netherlands*] [*ICAO designator*] (FAAC)
M Ph	Master of Philosophy
MPH	Master of Physical Education and Health
MPH	Master of Public Health
MPH	McGregor Point, HI [*Location identifier*] [*FAA*] (FAAL)
MPH	Meat Packing House (AD)
MPH	Medium Pintle Head (SAUS)
MPH	Melphalan [*Also, A, L-PAM, M, MPL*] [*Antineoplastic drug*]
MPH	Mentally and Physically Handicapped (OICC)
MPH	Meridian Point Realty [*AMEX symbol*] (SPSG)
MPH	Meridian Point Rlty VIII [*AMEX symbol*] (TTSB)
MPH	Mesh Plug Hernioplasty [*Medicine*] (MELL)
MPH	Methodist Publishing House (DGA)
MPH	Methylphenidate [*Pharmacology*] (DAVI)
MPH	Micro-Phonics Technology International Corp. [*Vancouver Stock Exchange symbol*]
mph	Miles per Hour (IDOE)
Mph	Miles per Hour
MPH	Miles per Hour [*Also, M/H*]
MPH	Military Public Health (SAUO)
MPH	Milk Protein Hydrolysate (BABM)
MPH	Missionary Sisters of Our Lady of Perpetual Help (TOCD)
M Ph	Mistress of Philosophy
MPH	Multiple Probe Head [*Laboratory technology*]
MPHA	Michigan Public Health Association (SAUO)
MPHA	Minnesota Public Health Association (SAUO)
MPH&TM	Master of Public Health and Tropical Medicine (GAGS)
M Phar	Master of Pharmacy
M Phar C	Master of Pharmaceutical Chemistry
M Pharm	Master of Pharmacy
M Ph C	Master of Pharmaceutical Chemistry
MPHC	Metal-Skinned, Paper-Honeycomb Cored (PDAA)
MPh(D)	Master of Philosophy (CPGU)
MPHD	Multiple Pituitary Hormone Deficiency [*Medicine*] (MELL)
MPHE	Master of Public Health Education (PGP)
MPHE	Master of Public Health Engineering
MPHE	Material and Personnel Handling Equipment (NASA)
MPHEC	Maritime Provinces Higher Education Commission (AD)
MPH Ed	Master of Public Health Education
MPH Eng	Master of Public Health Engineering
MPHI	Michigan Public Health Institute (SAUO)
M Phil	Master of Philosophy
M Phil F	Master of Philosophical Foundations (PGP)
MPHN	Master of Public Health Nursing
MPHO	Howard Air Force Base [*Panama*] [*ICAO location identifier*] (ICLI)
M Pho	Master of Photography
MPHP	Maximal Predicted Heart Rate [*Medicine*] (MELL)
MPHP	Multiple-Pass Heuristic Procedure (PDAA)
MPHPr	Meridian Point Rlty VIII Pfd [*AMEX symbol*] (TTSB)
mphps	Miles Per Hour Per Second (AD)
MPHPS	Miles per Hour per Second
MPHR	Maximum Predicted Heart Rate [*Cardiology*]

M Ph S	Master of Physical Science
M Ph Sc	Master of Physical Science
MPHT	Missile Potential Hazard Team (SAUO)
MPHTM	Master of Public Health and Tropical Medicine
MPhty	Master of Physiotherapy [*British*] (ADA)
M Phy	Master of Physics
M Phys A	Member of the Physiotherapists' Association [*British*]
MPhysics	Master of Physics (DD)
mpi	Magnetic Particle Inspection (AD)
MPI	Magnetic Particle Inspection
MPI	Magnetic Peripherals Inc. (NITA)
MPI	Magnetic Press, Inc. [*Information service or system*] (IID)
MPI	Malaria Philatelists International (EA)
MPI	Mamitupo [*Panama*] [*Airport symbol*] (OAG)
MPI	Management Partnerships International, Inc. (IID)
MPI	Mandsley Personality Inventory [*Psychology*] (DB)
MPI	Manitoba Properties, Inc. [*Toronto Stock Exchange symbol*] [*Vancouver Stock Exchange symbol*]
MPI	Mannosephosphate Isomerase [*An enzyme*]
MPI	Man-Portable Illuminator
MPI	Manufacturing Process Instructions
mpi	Marginal Propensity to Invest (AD)
MPI	Marginal Propensity to Invest [*Economics*]
MPI	Marine Pollution Incident [*Marine science*] (OSRA)
MPI	Marriage-Personality Inventory [*Psychology*]
MPI	Martin Processing, Incorporated (SAUO)
MPI	Mass Psychogenic Illness
MPI	Master Patient Index (MEDA)
MPI	Masterpiece Theatre [*Public television*]
MPI	Material Process Instruction (AD)
MPI	Matter of Public Importance (ADA)
MPI	Maudsley Personality Inventory [*Psychology*]
MPI	Maximal Permitted Intake [*Medicine*]
mpi	Maximum Point of Impulse (AD)
MPI	Maximum Point of Impulse
MPI	Maximum Potential Intensity
MPI	Maximum Precipitation Intensity [*Meteorology*] (PDAA)
MPI	Max Planck Institute (AD)
MPI	Max-Planck Institute for Meteorology [*Marine science*] [*Germany*] (OSRA)
MPI	Max-Planck-Institut fuer Astronomie [*Max Planck Institute for Astronomy*] [*Germany*]
mpi	Mean Point of Impact (AD)
MPI	Mean Point of Impact [*Air Force*]
MPI	Medicare Provider Identifier (SAUO)
MPI	Medicine in the Public Interest (AD)
MPI	Medi-Physica, Inc. (DAVI)
MPI	Meeting Planners International (EA)
MPI	Meeting Professionals International (NTPA)
MPI	Message Passing Interface [*Software program conducted at Mississippi State University*]
MPI	Message Pattern Indicator
MPI	Message Processing Interactive (MCD)
MPI	Metal Powder Industries Federation
MPI	Metropolitan Property Investments (SAUO)
MPI	Michelson Polarizing Interferometer [*Instrumentation*]
MPI	Microprocessor Interface
MPI	Middle Path International (SAUO)
MPI	Milestone Properties [*NYSE symbol*] (SPSG)
MPI	Military Police Investigator [*or Investigation*] (AABC)
MPI	Military Procurement Instruction
MPI	Miltarpsykologiska Institutet [*Military Psychology Institute*] [*Sweden*] (PDAA)
MPI	Ministry of Public Information (SAUO)
MPI	Minneapolis Public Library and Information Center, Minneapolis, MN [*OCLC symbol*] (OCLC)
MPI	Minnesota Prekindergarten Inventory [*Ireton and Thwing*] (TES)
MPI	Minnesota Preschool Inventory [*Child development test*]
MPI	Missile Periodic Inspection (AAG)
MPI	Missing Persons International (EA)
MPI	Mission Payload Integration (MCD)
MPI	Mitsui Petrochemical Industries (AD)
MPI	Molded Plastic Insulation
MPI	Molecular Parameter Index
MPI	Monographs of the Peshitta Institute [*A publication*] (BJA)
MPI	Monsoon Pollen Index [*Paleoceanography*]
MPI	Morris Pratt Institute Association (EA)
MPI	Movimiento Patriotico Institucional [*Panama*] [*Political party*] (EY)
MPI	Movimiento pro Independencia de Puerto Rico (EA)
MPI	Multibus Peripheral Interface [*Intel Corp.*] [*Computer science*] (CIST)
MPI	Multiphase Ionization [*Chemical physics*]
mpi	Multiphasic Personality Inventory (AD)
MPI	Multiphasic Personality Inventory
mpi	Multiphoton Ionization (AD)
MPI	Multiphoton Ionization [*Spectrometry*]
MPI	Multiple Power Input (RDA)
MPI	Multiple Protocol Interface [*Computer science*]
MPI	Multipoint-Electronic Fuel Injection [*Automotive engineering*]
MPI	Multi-Port Injection [*Automobile term*] (GOBB)
MPI	Multiprecision Integer (SAUS)
MPI	Multiprocessor Interconnect Bus (SAUS)
MPI	Multi-Protocol Interchange (SAUS)
MPI	Multiprotocol Interface (SAUS)
MPI	Municipal Price Index (SAUO)
MPI	Museum of the Plains Indians (AD)

MPI	Mutagenic Potency Index [*For toxicology*]
MPI	Myocardial Perfusion Imaging [*Cardiology*]
MPIA	Master in Political and Institutional Administration
MPIA	Master of Pacific International Affairs (GAGS)
MPIA	Master of Public and International Affairs (GAGS)
MPIA	Max-Planck-Institut fuer Astronomie [*Max Planck Institute for Astronomy*] [*Germany*]
MPIAD	MOD [*Maintenance of Deception*] Personnel Interceptor Assembly/Disassembly
MPIAS	Max Planck Institute for the Advancement of Science (SAUO)
MPIC	Message Processing Interrupt Count
MPIC	Mobile Phase Ion Chromatography
MPIC	Motion Picture Industry Controllers (EA)
MPIC	Motion Picture Industry Council (EA)
MPIC	Motion Picture Institute of Canada
MPIES	Medicare Physician Identification and Eligibility System (SAUO)
MPIF	Message Passing Interface Forum (USDC)
MPIF	Metal Powder Industries Federation (EA)
MPIIN	Modification Procurement Instrument Identification Number [*NASA*] (NASA)
M-pill	Menstruation Pill [*Medicine*] (AD)
MPIM	Max-Planck-Institute fuer Meteorologie [*Marine science*] [*Germany*] (OSRA)
MPIM	Multipurpose Individual Munition [*Weapon*]
MPIM/SRAW	Multi-Purpose Individual Munition/Short Range Assault Weapon [*Military*] (RDA)
MPIO	Mission and Payload Integration Office [*NASA*]
MPIP	Machine Parts Inspection Plans (MCD)
MPIP	Maintenance Posture Improvement Program (MCD)
MPIP	Meat and Poultry Inspection Program [*Department of Agriculture*]
MPIP	Miniature Precision Inertial Platform (OA)
MPIPrA	Milestone Properties Cv $0.78Pfd [*NYSE symbol*] (TTSB)
MPIR	Missile Precision Instrumentation RADAR (MSA)
MPIRO	Multiple Peril Insurance Rating Organization [*Later, Multiperil Insurance Conference*]
MPIW	Multi-Purpose Individual Weapon (SAUS)
MPIX	Microelectronic Packaging [*NASDAQ symbol*] (TTSB)
MPIX	Microelectronic Packaging, Inc. [*NASDAQ symbol*] (SAG)
MPJ	Member of the Profession of Journalism [*British*] (DGA)
MPJ	Metacarpophalangeal Joint [*Anatomy*]
MPJ	Morrilton, AR [*Location identifier*] [*FAA*] (FAAL)
MPJ	Mouvement Panafricain de la Jeunesse [*Pan-African Youth Movement - PYAM*] [*Algeria*]
MPJE	Jaque [*Panama*] [*ICAO location identifier*] (ICLI)
MP-JFI	Managerial and Professional Job Functions Inventory [*Test*]
mPK	Cold Maritime Polar Air Mass [*Meteorology*] (BARN)
MPK	Maintenance Parts Kit (MSA)
mpk	Manpack
MPK	Martis Peak [*California*] [*Seismograph station code, US Geological Survey*] (SEIS)
MPK	McKinley Park [*Alaska*] [*Airport symbol*] (AD)
MPK	Methyl Propyl Ketone (EDCT)
MPK	Microphone Probe Kit
mPK	Polar Maritime Air Colder than Underlying Surface (AD)
MPKC	Management Problem-Knowledge Coupler
MPL	Macro Programming Language [*Computer application*] (PCM)
MPL	Magnesium Pemoline [*Pharmacology*]
MPL	Magneto Photo Luminescence
MPL	Maintenance Parts Lists
MPL	Mandatory Parts List [*DoD*]
MPL	Manipulation Positioning Latches [*Aerospace*] (NAKS)
MPL	Manipulator Positioning Latches (MCD)
MPL	Man Position Locator
MPL	Manufacturing Parts List (AAG)
mpl	Maple (DAC)
MPL	Maple
MPL	Maple Technology Ltd. [*Vancouver Stock Exchange symbol*]
MPL	Marine Physical Laboratory [*Research center*] (RCD)
MPL	Marine Physics Laboratory [*Scripps*]
MPL	Mars Probe Lander [*Aerospace*]
MPL	Master of Patent Law
MPI	Master of Planning
MPL	Master of Polite Literature
MPL	Master of Public Law
MPL	Master Parts List
MPL	Master Planner, Inc. [*ICAO designator*] (FAAC)
MPL	Material Processing Laboratory (SSD)
mpl	Mathematical Programming Language [*Computer science*] (AD)
MPL	Mathematical Programming Language [*Computer science*] (PDAA)
MPL	Mavis, Paul A., South Bend IN [*STAC*]
MPL	Maxillofacial Prosthesis Laboratory [*WRAMC*] (RDA)
mpl	Maximum Payload (AD)
MPL	Maximum Penalized-Likelihood [*Statistics*]
mpl	Maximum Permissible Language (AD)
mpl	Maximum Permissible Level (AD)
MPL	Maximum Permissible Level [*Radiation*] (DEN)
MPL	Maximum Possible Loss (COE)
MPL	Maximum Probable Loss [*Insurance*]
MPL	Maximum Procurement Level (AFIT)
MPL	Mechanical Parts List (NASA)
MPL	Mechanical Properties Loop [*Nuclear energy*] (NRCH)
MPL	Megneto Photo Luminescence (AAEL)
MPL	Melphalan [*Also, A, L-PAM, M, MPH*] [*Antineoplastic drug*]
MPL	Memphis Public Library (AD)
MPL	Mesiopulpolingual [*Dentistry*] (MAE)
mpl	Message Processing Language [*Computer science*] (AD)
MPL	Message Processing Language [*Burroughs Corp.*]
MPL	Metals Processing Laboratory [*MIT*] (MCD)
MPL	Metering Pumps Limited
MPL	Metropolitan Police Laboratory (AD)
MPL	Metropolitan Property & Liability Insurance Co. (EFIS)
MPL	Miami Public Library (AD)
MPL	Micro Power Light [*Automotive lighting*]
MPL	Microprocessor [*or Motorola's*] Programming Language [*1975*] [*Computer science*] (CSR)
MPL	Microprogramming Language (NITA)
MPL	Milwaukee Public Library (AD)
MPL	Mine Planter (NATG)
MPL	Minimum Power Level [*Aerospace*] (NAKS)
MPL	Minnesota Power [*NYSE symbol*] [*Formerly, Minnesota Power & Light*]
MPL	Minnesota Power & Light Co. [*NYSE symbol*] (SPSG)
MPL	Mission Planning Laboratory [*NASA*] (KSC)
MPL	Mississippi Power and Light (SAUO)
MPL	Missouri Pacific Lines (AD)
MPL	Mistress of Patent Law (SAUO)
MPL	Mistress of Polite Literature
MPL	Mixer/Preamplifier/Local Oscillator (ACAE)
MP/L	Modified Construction Permit and License [*FCC*] (NTCM)
MPL	Monessen Public Library, Monessen, PA [*OCLC symbol*] (OCLC)
MPL	Monkey Placental Lactogen
MPL	Monophosphoryl Lipid [*Biochemistry*]
MPL	Montoneros Patria Libre [*Guerrilla group*] [*Ecuador*] (EY)
MPL	Montpellier [*France*] [*Airport symbol*] (OAG)
MPL	Montreal Public Library [*Canada*] (AD)
MPL	Motion Picture Laboratories [*Commercial firm*]
MPL	Motivated Productivity Level [*Quality control*]
MPL	Mouvement Politique Lulua [*Lulua Political Movement*] [*Political party*]
MPL	Movimento Politica dei Lavoratori [*Workers' Political Movement*] [*Italy*] [*Political party*] (PPE)
MPL	Movimiento Popular de Liberacion "Cinchoneros" [*"Cinchoneros" Popular Liberation Movement*] [*Honduras*] [*Political party*]
MPL	Mozilla Public License (SAUO)
MPL	Multilevel Pass transistor Logic (SAUS)
MPL	Multi-Platform Launcher (SAUS)
MPL	Multiple Payload Launcher
mpl	Multiple-Position Lock (AD)
MPL	Multiple-Pulsed Laser (ACAE)
MPL	Multipurpose Limousine
MPL	Multischedule Private Line
MPL	Multi-Services, Inc. [*FAA designator*] (FAAC)
MPL	Patrologia Latina [*J. P. Migne*] [*Paris*] [*A publication*] (BJA)
MPI	Plymouth Public Library, Plymouth, MA [*Library symbol*] [*Library of Congress*] (LCLS)
MPIA	Antiquarian House, Plymouth, MA [*Library symbol*] [*Library of Congress*] (LCLS)
MPLA	Malayan People's Liberation Army
MPLA	Mask Programmable Logic Array (NITA)
MPLa	Mesiopulpolabial [*Dentistry*] (MAE)
MPLA	Metropolitan Public Libraries Association [*New South Wales, Australia*]
MPLA	Monophosphoryl Lipid A [*Biochemistry*]
MPLA	Mountain Plains Library Association (AEBS)
MPLA	Movimento Popular de Libertacao de Angola [*Popular Movement for the Liberation of Angola*] [*Political party*]
MPLA	Popular Movement for the Liberation of Angola (SAUO)
MPlan	Master of Planning
MPlanStud	Master of Planning Studies
MPlanStudies	Master of Planning Studies
MPLA-PT	Movimento Popular de Libertacao de Angola - Partido do Trabalho [*Popular Movement for the Liberation of Angola - Party of Labor*] [*Political party*] (PPW)
MPLAW	Melamine Paper Laminate (PDAA)
MPLAW	Modified Programmers Language [*Computer science*] (PDAA)
MPLAW	Moving Part Logic (PDAA)
MPLAW	Multipulse Scaling-Law Code using Data Base Interpolation (PDAA)
MPLB	Balboa/Albrook [*Panama*] [*ICAO location identifier*] (ICLI)
MPLB	Maximum Permissible Lung Burden [*Industrial hygiene*]
MPLC	Medium-Pressure Liquid Chromatography
MPLC	Mid-Peninsula Library Cooperative [*Library network*]
MPLC	Movimento Popular de Libertacao de Cabinda [*Popular Movement for the Liberation of Cabinda*] [*Angola*] [*Political party*] (PD)
MPLC	Movimiento Popular de Liberacion Cinchonero [*Guerrilla forces*] [*Honduras*] (EY)
MPLC	Multi-Platform Launch Controller
MPLCC	Most Probable Life Cycle Cost (ACAE)
MPLCC	Most-Probable Life Cycle Cost
MPLD	Mouvement Populaire pour la Liberation de Djibouti [*Political party*] (EY)
MPLE	Multipurpose Long Endurance [*Aircraft*]
MPLEJ	Military Police Law Enforcement Journal (SAUO)
MPLG	Materials Processing in Low Gravity (SAUS)
MPLG	Multi-Purpose Lithium Grease
MPLH	Multipurpose Light Helicopter (DOMA)
MPLI	Michigan Picture Language Inventory (EDAC)
MPLL	Malayan People's Liberation League
MPLM	Machine-Prepared List of Materials (ACAE)
MPLM	Mini-Pressurized Logistic Modules [*Space technology*]
MPLN	Maintenance Planning [*Database*] (NASA)

MPLO	Military Postal Liaison Office
MPLP	La Palma [*Panama*] [*ICAO location identifier*] (ICLI)
MPLP	Marxist Progressive Labor Party [*Political party*] (AD)
MPLP	Mental Patients Liberation Projects
MPIP	Plimoth Plantation, Inc., Plymouth, MA [*Library symbol*] [*Library of Congress*] (LCLS)
MPLP	Portage Plains Regional Library, Portage La Prairie, Manitoba [*Library symbol*] [*National Library of Canada*] (NLC)
MPLPC	Multipulse Linear Productive Coding (PDAA)
MPLPDC	MDC Library, Manitoba Developmental Centre, Portage La Prairie [*Library symbol*] [*National Library of Canada*] (BIB)
MPLPM	Manitoba School, Portage La Prairie, Manitoba [*Library symbol*] [*National Library of Canada*] (NLC)
MPLPr	MP&L Cap I 8.05% 'QUIPS' [*NYSE symbol*] (TTSB)
MPLPrA	Minn Pwr & Lt 5% cm Pfd [*AMEX symbol*] (TTSB)
MPL + PRED	Melphalan and Prednisone [*Antineoplastic drug regimen*] (DAVI)
MPL + PRED(MP)	Melphalan and Prednisone [*Antineoplastic drug regimen*] (DAVI)
MPIPS	Pilgrim Society, Plymouth, MA [*Library symbol*] [*Library of Congress*] (LCLS)
MPLR	Medium Power Loop Range
MPLR	Movement for the Liberation of Reunion (SAUO)
MPLS	Maximal Principle Least Squares
Mpls	Minneapolis (AD)
MPLS	Multi-Protocol Label Switching (MLOA)
MPLSM	Multiple Position Letter Sorting Machine (PDAA)
MPLSM	Multiple Position Letter Sort Machine
MPLSS	Marketing of Public Library Services Section [*Public Library Association*]
MPLU	Most Probable Library User
MPLX	Multiplexer
MPLXR	Multiplexer
MPM	Magnetic Phase Modulator
MPM	Magnum Petroleum [*AMEX symbol*] (SAG)
MPM	Mahorais Peoples Movement (SAUO)
MPM	Main Propulsion Motor
MPM	Maintenance and Peripheral Module (SAUS)
MPM	Maintenance Planning Manual (NG)
MPM	Maintenance Program Management [*Military*] (AABC)
MPM	Major Program Memorandum [*Military*]
MPM	Major Project Manager
MPM	Malignant Papillary Mesothelioma [*Medicine*]
MPM	Malignant Pleural Mesothelioma (ADWA)
MPM	Manipulator Positioning Mechanism [*Aerospace*] (NAKS)
MPM	Manpower Planning Model
MPM	Manufacture Procedure Manual (KSC)
MPM	Maputo [*Mozambique*] [*Airport symbol*] (OAG)
MPM	Marginal Propensity to Import [*Economics*]
MPM	Marshall Plan of the Mind [*BBC radio program*] (ECON)
MPM	Master of Personnel Management (GAGS)
MPM	Master of Pest Management (DD)
MPM	Master of Professional Management (PGP)
MPM	Master of Project Management (PGP)
MPM	Master of Psychological Management
MPM	Master of Psychological Medicine (ADA)
MPM	Master of Public Management
MPM	Materials Properties Manual (SAUO)
MPM	Mauritian Patriotic Movement (SAUO)
MPM	Maximum Permitted Mileage [*Airlines*]
MPM	Maximum Pionization Method (OA)
MPM	Medical Planning Module (DOMA)
MPM	Message Processing Modules (MCD)
MPM	Metal-Plastic Metal [*Automotive engineering*]
mpm	Meters Per Minute (AD)
MPM	Meters per Minute
MPM	Metra-Potential Method [*Graph theory*]
MPM	Microprogram Memory
MPM	Microscope-Photometer
MPM	Microwave Power Meter
MPM	Microwave Power Module (SAUS)
MPM	Mid-Pacific Mountains [*Geology*]
MPM	Miles per Minute
MPM	Milestone Planning Meeting (MCD)
MPM	Milk Plant Monthly (SAUO)
MPM	Milwaukee Public Museum (AD)
MPM	Miniaturized Pointing Mount [*Spacelab*] [*NASA*]
MPM	Missile Power Monitor (AAG)
mpm	Missile Power Monitor (AD)
MPM	Modest Petrovich Mussorgsky [*1839-1881*] (AD)
mpm	Mole-Percent Metal (AD)
MPM	Monoclonal Paratopic Molecule (DB)
MPM	Monocycle Position Modulation
MPM	Mortality Probability Models [*Medicine*]
MPM	Mouse Peritoneal Macrophages
MPM	Mouvement Populaire Mahorais [*Mayotte People's Movement*] [*Comoros*] [*Political party*] (PPW)
MPM	Movement Planning Module (SAUO)
MPM	Moving Presentation Mode
MP/M	Multiprocessing Monitor Control Program [*Computer science*]
MP/M	Multiprogramming Control Program for Microcomputers
MP/M	Multiprogramming Control Program for Microprocessors (NITA)
MPM	Multiprogramming Monitor
mpm	Multipurpose Meal (AD)
MPM	Multipurpose Meal
MPM	Multipurpose Missile (MCD)
MP-M	Museum Plantin Moretus [*Belgium*] (AD)
MPM2	Multimedia Presentation Manager/2 (SAUS)
MPMA	Master of Public Management and Administration
MPMA	Metal Packaging Manufacturers Association [*British*] (DBA)
MPMA	Methylphorbol Myristate Acetate [*Organic chemistry*]
MPMA	Montford Point Marine Association (EA)
MPMA	Motion Picture Museum Association [*British*] (BI)
MPM&PH	Master of Preventive Medicine and Public Health (GAGS)
MPMC	Microprogram Memory Control (NITA)
MPMC	Military Personnel, Marine Corps
MPMCANSW	Master Plumbers and Mechanical Contractors Association of New South Wales [*Australia*]
MPMCAV	Master Plumbers and Mechanical Contractors' Association of Victoria [*Australia*]
MPMCAWA	Master Plumbers and Mechanical Contractors' Association of Western Australia
MPMD	Methylpentemethylenediamine [*Plastics*]
MPMD	Multiple Processor Multiple Data Architecture (RALS)
MPMG	Marine Pollution Management Group [*British*]
MPMG	Melt-Powder Melt-Growth [*Materials Science*]
MPMG	Multi-Purpose Molybdenum Grease
MPMG	Panama/Paitilla, Marco A. Gelabert [*Panama*] [*ICAO location identifier*] (ICLI)
MPMH	Mean Preventive Maintenance Hours
MPMI	Magazine and Paperback Marketing Institute (EA)
MPMIC	Mechanical Properties of Materials Information Center (MCD)
MPMIS	Military Personnel Management Information System (SAUO)
MPMIS	Military Police Management Information System
MPML	Main Profile-Main Level (SAUS)
MPML	Mid-Pacific Marine Laboratory (MSC)
MP/ML	Modified Construction Permit and Modified License [*FCC*] (NTCM)
MPML	MPM Technologies, Inc. [*NASDAQ symbol*] (SAG)
MPMLE	MPM Technologies [*NASDAQ symbol*] (TTSB)
MPMLQ	Multipulse Maximum Likelihood Quantization (SAUS)
MPMM	Monthly Project Management Meetings (SAUO)
MPMMG	Marine Pollution Monitoring Management Group (ASF)
MPMO	Motion Picture Machine Operator [*A union*] (NTCM)
MPMP	Mass Properties Management Plan (NASA)
MPMP	Master Program Management Plan (SAUO)
MPMP	(Methylpiperidyl)methylphenothiazine [*Sedative*]
MPMP	Modification Program Management Plan (MCD)
MPMPR	Metropolitan Police Missing Persons Register [*British*]
MPMPrEC	Magnum Pete $1.10 Cv'C'Pfd [*AMEX symbol*] (TTSB)
MPMR	Movimiento Patriotica Manuel Rodriguez [*Manuel Rodriguez Patriotic Movement*] [*Chile*] [*Political party*] (EY)
MPMRP	Master Petroleum Material Requirements Plan (MCD)
MPMS	Mattress and Palliasse Makers' Society [*A union*] [*British*]
MPMS	Missile Performance Measurement System (SAUO)
MPMS	Missile Performance Measuring System (MCD)
MPMS	Multiple-Pressure Measuring System
MPMSE	Multiuse Payload and Mission Support Equipment (MCD)
MPMT	Mean Preventive Maintenance Time (MCD)
MPMT	Mellon Participating Mortgage Trust Commercial Properties Series [*NASDAQ symbol*] (NQ)
MPMT	Multiple Primary Malignant Tumor [*Oncology*]
MPM Tch	MPM Technologies, Inc. [*Associated Press*] (SAG)
MPMUL	Military Production Master Urgency List
MPMV	Mason-Pfizer Monkey Virus
MPN	Manpower Personnel, Navy (DOMA)
MPN	Manufacturers Part Number (MCD)
MPN	Manufacturer's Productivity Network [*Hewlett-Packard Co.*]
MPN	Mariner Post-Acute Network [*Formerly, Paragon Health Network*] [*NYSE symbol*]
MPN	Master in Psychiatric Nursing (GAGS)
MPN	Master Part Number (MCD)
MPN	Maximum Possible Number (EPAT)
MPN	Maximum Probable Number (EEVL)
MPN	Mean Probable Number (MCD)
MPN	Medial Preoptic Nucleus [*Brain anatomy*]
MPN	Methyl Parathion [*Also, MEP, MP*] [*Pesticide*]
MPN	Microwave Product News (SAUO)
MPN	Military Pay, Navy [*An appropriation*]
MPN	Military Personnel, Navy
MPN	Military Procurement, Navy (MCD)
MPN	Mobility Position Number (SAUO)
MPN	Monongahela Power Co. [*AMEX symbol*] (SPSG)
mpn	Most Probable Number (AD)
MPN	Most Probable Number
MPNA	Midwest Professional Needlework Association [*Later, APNRA*] (EA)
MPNA	Working Group on Pollution Baseline and Monitoring Studies in the North Atlantic (SAUO)
MPNC	Mouvement pour le Progres National Congolais [*Movement for National Congolese Progress*]
MPNDS	Material Properties Numerical Data System [*Purdue University*] [*Database*]
MPNE	Manpower Needs [*Military*]
MPNF	Manpower-Needs Forecasting (MCD)
MPNI	Ministry of Pensions and National Insurance [*Later, MSS*] [*British*]
MPNPrA	Monogahela Pwr 4.4% Pfd [*AMEX symbol*] (TTSB)
MPNPrC	Monongah Power 4/50%cm C Pfd [*AMEX symbol*] (TTSB)
MPNST	Malignant Peripheral Nerve Sheath Tumor
MPN-XX	Next Generation Mobile Ground Radar (SAUS)
MPO	Macedonian Patriotic Organization of US and Canada (EA)
MPO	Main Production Order (SAUO)
MPO	Major Program Objective (MCD)

MPO............	Management and Personnel Office (ODBW)
MPO............	Managerial & Professional Officers (WDAA)
MPO............	Managers, Proprietors, and Officials
MPO............	Manual Purchase Orders (SAUO)
MPO............	Manufacturer's Point of Origin (TIMI)
MPO............	Manufacturing Production Order (NRCH)
MPO............	Maputo [Mozambique] [Geomagnetic observatory code]
MPO............	Material Project Office (ACAE)
MPO............	Maximum Power Output
MPO............	Medial Preoptic [Brain anatomy]
MPO............	Member of the Post Office [British]
MPO............	Memorandum Purchase Order (AD)
mpo	Memory Printout (AD)
MPO............	Memory Printout [Computer science]
MPO............	Memory Protect Override
MPO............	Mercury Project Office [NASA] (SAA)
MPO............	Metropolitan Planning Organization
MPO............	Metropolitan Police Office [Familiarly called "Scotland Yard" from its site at New Scotland Yard] [British]
MPO............	Miami Philharmonic Orchestra (AD)
MPO............	Military Pay Order
MPO............	Military Permit Office [or Officer]
MPO............	Military Personnel Office
MPO............	Military Planning Office [SEATO] (CINC)
MPO............	Military Post Office
MPO............	Minimal Perceptible Odor (MELL)
MPO............	Misconduct Policy Officer [National Institutes of Health]
MPO............	Missile Processing Operation (MCD)
MPO............	Mission Planning Officer (SAUO)
MPO............	Mobile Post Office
MPO............	Mobile Printing Office (AD)
MPO............	Modular Personnel Office (SSD)
MPO............	Motion Picture Operator
MPO............	MotivePower Indus. [NYSE symbol] (SG)
MPO............	Mount Pocono, PA [Location identifier] [FAA] (FAAL)
MPO............	Mustering Petty Officer
MPO............	Myeloperoxidase [An enzyme]
MPOA	Medial Preoptic Area [Medicine]
MPOA	Medical Power of Attorney (MELL)
MPOA	Multiprotocol over Asynchronous Transfer Mode [Computer science] (IGQR)
MPOA	Puerto Obaldia [Panama] [ICAO location identifier] (ICLI)
MPOAH	Medial Preoptic-Anterior Hypothalamic [Brain anatomy]
MPOC	Mini-Pilot Open Chamber [Automotive engineering]
MPOC	Multipurpose Operators Console (SAUS)
MPOD	Mean Planned Outage Duration [Electronics] (IEEE)
MP-OES	Multi-Point Optical Emission Spectroscopy (AAEL)
MPOI	Master Program of Instruction [Army] (AABC)
MPOIS	Military Police Operations and Information System [Army] (MCD)
M-POL	Maritime Policy Division (SAUO)
MPol	Master of Policy
M Pol	Master of Political Science (PGP)
MPolAdmin...	Master of Policy and Administration
MPolEcon	Master of Political Economy [British] (ADA)
MPol Econ ...	Mistress of Political Economy (SAUO)
MPOLL	Military Post Office Location List (AFM)
MPolLaw	Master of Policy and Law
M Pol Sc	Master of Political Science
MPOM	Maintenance Program Operations Management [Military] (AABC)
MPOR	Maintenance Plant at Ober Ramstadt [Army] (MCD)
MPOS	Manportable Office System [Army] (RDA)
MPOS	Military Plans and Operations Staff
MPOS	Mobile Post Office Society (EA)
MPOS	Movie Projector Operator's School (DNAB)
MPOS	Multipurpose Optimization System [Computer science]
MPOSC	Master of Polar and Ocean Science
MPOT	Master in Psychiatric Occupational Therapy (GAGS)
M-POTS	Mobile Psychological Operations Transmitter (DOMA)
MPOW	Multiple Purpose Operator Workstation (SAUO)
MPP	Mailer's Postmark Permit
MPP	Maintainability Program Plan
MPP	Major Program Proposal (AAG)
MPP	Malleable Penile Prosthesis [Medicine] (MELL)
MPP	Manipur People's Party [India] [Political party] (PPW)
mpp	Marginal Physical Product (AD)
MPP	Marginal Physical Product [Agriculture]
MPP	Marine Power Plant (PDAA)
MPP	Market Promotion Program (WPI)
MPP	Martens Polarization Photometer [Physics]
MPP	Massively Parallel Processor [Image processing]
MPP	Massive Periretinal Proliferation [Ophthalmology] (DAVI)
MPP	Master in Public Policy [National University of Singapore]
MPP	Master of Physical Planning (NADA)
MPP	Master of Public Policy
MPP	Master Patch Panel [Air Force] (MCD)
MPP	Master Program Plan (NG)
MPP	Master's Degree in Public Policy
MPP	Material Processing Platform (SPST)
MPP	Material Processing Procedure (NASA)
MPP	Materials Preparation Program (SAA)
MPP	Materiel Performance Package [Military] (AFM)
MPP	Matrix Processing Peptidase [An enzyme]
MPP	Maximum Performance Penalty (ACAE)
MPP	Maximum Perfusion Pressure [Cardiology] (DAVI)
MPP	Maximum Positive Pressure [Nuclear energy] (NRCH)
MPP	Medial Pterygoid Plate [Medicine] (MELL)
MPP	Medical Personnel Pool
MPP	Medical Planning Program (SAUO)
MPP	Medical Properties (EFIS)
MPP	Medical Provisioning Point (SAUS)
MPP	Melanesian Progressive Parti [Vanuatu] [Political party] (EY)
MPP	Melphalan, Prednisone, Procarbazine [Antineoplastic drug regimen]
MPP	Member of Provincial Parliament [British]
MPP	Memory Parity and Protect (NITA)
MPP	Mercaptopyrazidopyrimidine [Antineoplastic drug] (MAE)
MPP	Merit Promotion Plan [or Program] [NASA] (NASA)
MPP	Message Posting Protocol (SAUO)
MPP	Message Processing Program [Computer science]
MPP	Meta Postprocessor [Software program] [Symbolic Control, Inc.]
MPP	Methyl(phenyl)pyridine [Biochemistry]
MPP	Methylpiperazine [Organic chemistry]
MPP	Microfilm Printer/Plotter
MPP	Microprogrammable Processor (MCD)
MPP	Miles per Pound [NASA] (KSC)
MPP	Military Pay Procedures
MPP	Minimum Premium Plans [Insurance]
MPP	Minority Procurement Policy (AAGC)
MPP	Miscellaneous Personal Property [Legal term] (DLA)
MPP	Missile Power Panel (AAG)
MPP	Mission Payload Package (ACAE)
MPP	Mission-Planning Program [Gerospace] (BARN)
MPP	Mistress of Physical Planning (SAUO)
MPP	Mitochondrial Processing Peptidase [Biochemistry]
MPP	Modern Programming Practice
MPP	Molypermalloy Powder [Metallurgy] (EECA)
MPP	Mongol People's Party [Mongolia] [Political party] (FEA)
MPP	Monodisperse Polymer Particle
MPP	Mono Power Pack (HGAA)
mpp	Most Probable Position (AD)
MPP	Most Probable Position [Navigation]
MPP	Mothers in Prison Projects (EA)
MPP	Motion Picture Pioneers (EA)
MPP	Motion Picture Projector (MSA)
MPP	Mount Pasian [Philippines] [Seismograph station code, US Geological Survey] (SEIS)
MPP	Mulatupo [Panama] [Airport symbol] (OAG)
MPP	Multiphase Printing (AAEL)
MPP	Multiple Particle Plasma
MPP	Multiple Payload Program [Military]
MPP	Multiple-Product Pricing [Business term] (MHDB)
MPP	Multi-Programmable Processor (VLIE)
MPP	Multiprogrammable Processor Port (VLIE)
MPP	Multi-Purpose Platform (SAUS)
MPP	Programme of Mass Privatisation [Poland] (ECON)
MPPA	Management Plans for Protected Areas (SAUO)
MPPA	Master of Public Policy Administration (GAGS)
MPPA	Metal Powder Producers Association (EA)
MPPA	Michigan Press Photographers Association (SAUO)
MPPA	Motion Picture Producers Association (SAUO)
MPPA	Music Publishers' Protective Association [Later, NMPA] (EA)
MPPAA	Multiemployer Pension Plan Amendments Act [1980] (GFGA)
MPPAR	Mouse Peroxisome Proliferator-Activated Receptor [Biochemistry]
MPPAV	Master Poultry Processors' Association of Victoria [Australia]
MPPB	Meeting of Presidents of Professional Bodies (SAUO)
MPPB	Methyl(phenyl)(propyl)barbituric (Acid) [Biochemistry]
MPPC	Mailer's Postmark Permit Club (EA)
MPPC	Master Program Phasing Chart (MCD)
MPPC	Medical Personnel (Priority) Committee [World War II]
MPPC	Microsoft Point to Point Compression [Microsoft Corp.] [Computer science] (PCM)
MPPC	Military Pay Procedure Committee
MPPC	Multipotent Hematopoietic Progenitor Cell [Biochemistry]
MPPC	Panama [Panama] [ICAO location identifier] (ICLI)
MPPCA	Maryland Probation, Patrol and Corrections Association (AD)
MPPCF	Million Particles per Cubic Foot [in air]
mppcf	Millions of Particles per Cubic Foot of Air (AD)
MPPCS	Manpower and Personnel Contingency Support System (SAUO)
MPPD	Maximum Probable Property Damage [Hazard analysis]
MPPD	Military Personnel Procurement Division (SAUO)
MPPD	Multi-Purpose Peripheral Device (VLIE)
MPPDA	Medicine-Pediatrics Program Directors Association (SAUO)
MPPEAS	GEF/UNDP/IMO Regional Programme for the Prevention and Management of Marine Pollution in the East Asian Seas (SAUO)
MPPEAS	Regional Programme for the Prevention and Management of Marine Pollution in the East Asian Seas (SAUS)
MPPEC........	Mean Peak Plasma Ethanol Concentration [Medicine] (DMAA)
MPPF	Malayan Planters Provident Fund (SAUO)
MPPG	Magnesium Pyridoxal Phosphate Glutamate [Biochemistry]
MPPH	(Methylphenyl)phenylhydantoin [Organic chemistry]
MPPH	Motion Picture Phonographic Unit
MPPHA	Multiparameter Pulse Height Analyzer
MPPhS........	Member of the Royal Pharmaceutical Society [Canada] (DD)
MPPL	Mobilization Procurement Planning List (SAUO)
mp pl..........	Multipunch Plate (AD)
MPPL	Multipunch Plate
MPPL	Multipurpose Processing Language [Computer science] (IEEE)
MPPL	Multipurpose Programming Language
MPPLT........	Military Police Platoon (DNAB)
MPPM........	Master of Public and Private Management
MPPM........	Materials-Process-Product Model (PDAA)

MPPM..........	Military Personnel Procurement Manual
MPPM..........	Mission Prediction and Performance Module [*Aerospace*]
MPPN	Malignant Persistent Positional Nystagmus [*Medicine*] (DMAA)
MPPO	Modified Polyphenylene Oxide [*Plastics technology*]
MPPP..........	Mechanically Processed Pork Product [*Food technology*]
MPPP..........	Methyl(phenyl)(propionoxy)piperidine [*Organic chemistry*]
MPPP..........	Money-Purchase Pension Plan [*Human resources*] (WYGK)
MPPP..........	MP3.com, Inc. [*NASDAQ symbol*] (SG)
MPPP..........	Multilink Point-to-Point Protocol (SAUS)
MPPPM........	Master of Plant Protection and Pest Management (GAGS)
MPPR	Mobilization Production Planning Requirements [*Military*]
MPPR	Modification Program Progress Report (AFIT)
MPPR	Monthly Production Progress Reports (MCD)
MPPrA.........	Mississippi Pwr 7.25% Dep Pfd [*NYSE symbol*] (TTSB)
MPPRB	Materiel Procurement Priorities Review Board [*Army*] (AABC)
MPPrB	Mississippi Pwr 6.65% Dep Pfd [*NYSE symbol*] (TTSB)
MPPRC	Materiel Procurement Priorities Review Committee [*Army*] (RDA)
MPPrC	Mississippi Pwr 6.32% Dep Pfd [*NYSE symbol*] (TTSB)
MPPRCA.......	Marine Plastic Pollution Research and Control Act
MPPS	Mammary Gland Physiology and Pathology Society (GVA)
MPPS	Master Production Planning Schedule [*Air Force*] (AFIT)
MPPS	Master Program Planning Schedule
MPPS	Medicare Prospective Payment System
MPPS	Military Personnel Procurement Service (SAUO)
mpps	Million Pulses per Second (AD)
MPPS	Moroccan Party of Progress and Socialism [*Political party*]
MPPS	Multipurpose (AABC)
MPPSE........	Multipurpose Payload Support Equipment (NASA)
MPPT	Maximum Power Point Tracking [*Power system*]
MPPT	Message Preparation Processing Task (SAUO)
MPPT	Methylprednisolone Pulse Therapy [*Medicine*]
MPPT	Moller-Plesset Perturbation Theory [*Physical chemistry*]
MPPU	Multi-Purpose Processor Unit (SAUS)
MPPUP	Master of Public Policy and Urban Planning (PGP)
MPPWCOM...	Military Police Prisoner of War Command (AABC)
MPQ.............	Manchester Personality Questionnaire [*Test*] (TMMY)
MPQ.............	Manpower Planning Quota (PDAA)
mpq	Manpower-Planning Quota (AD)
MPQ.............	McGill Pain Questionnaire [*Dentistry*]
MPQ.............	Morgan Stanley Group [*AMEX symbol*] (SAG)
MPQ.............	Multidimensional Personality Questionnaire [*Personality development test*] [*Psychology*]
MPQA	Minuteman Production Quality Assurance (MCD)
MPQP	Multi-Protocol Quad Port [*Computer science*] (VLIE)
MPQ/T	Mean Personnel Quantity per Task (MCD)
MPQT	Missile Performance Qualification Test (TIMI)
MPR.............	Machined Part Requisition (MCD)
MPR.............	Maculopapular Rash [*Medicine*]
MPR.............	Madjelis Permusiawaratan Rakat [*People's Deliberative Assembly*] [*Indonesia*] (AD)
MPR.............	Maintainability Problem Report (NASA)
MPR.............	Maintainability Program Requirements (AD)
MPR.............	Maintenance Personnel Roster
MPR.............	Major Project Report (SAUS)
MPR.............	Make Pages Resident (VLIE)
MPR.............	Management Policies and Requirements (SAUO)
MPR.............	Management Program Review [*NASA*] (NASA)
MPR.............	Manager Profile Record [*Test*] [*Richardson, Bellows, Henry, and Co. Inc.*] (TES)
MPR.............	Mane Primo [*Early in the Morning*] [*Pharmacy*] (ROG)
MPR.............	Mannose Phosphate Receptor [*Biochemistry*]
MPR.............	Manpack Radio (SAUS)
MPR.............	Manpower (AABC)
MPR.............	Manpower Policy and Requirements Branch [*Department of Defence*] [*Australia*]
MPR.............	Manufacturing Parts Record (KSC)
MPR.............	Manufacturing Planning Review (MCD)
MPR.............	Mariposa Resources, Inc. [*Vancouver Stock Exchange symbol*]
MPR.............	Maritime Provinces Reports [*Canada*] [*A publication*] (DLA)
MPR.............	Marked Page Reader (VLIE)
MPR.............	Marrow Production Rate [*Hematology*]
MPR.............	Master Personnel Records (ACAE)
MPR.............	Master Power Regulator
MPR.............	Material Purchase Requisition
MPR.............	Materials and Process Requirement [*Navy*]
MPR.............	Mauritanian Party for Renewal [*Political party*] (EY)
MPR.............	Maximal Pulse Rate [*Medicine*] (MELL)
MPR.............	Maximum Performance Reward (ACAE)
MPR.............	Maximum Potential Representation (MUGU)
MPR.............	Maximum Practical Rate [*Aviation*]
MPR.............	Mayaguez [*Puerto Rico*] [*Seismograph station code, US Geological Survey*] (SEIS)
MPR.............	McPherson, KS [*Location identifier*] [*FAA*] (FAAL)
MPR.............	Mechanical Pressure Regulator (NRCH)
MPR.............	Medium Power RADAR (NATG)
mpr.............	Medium-Power RADAR (AD)
MPR.............	Melt-Processible Rubber
MPR.............	Mercaptopurine Ribonucleoside [*Antineoplastic drug*]
MPR.............	Mercury Plunger Relay
MPR.............	Message Processing Region [*IBM Corp.*]
MPR.............	Met-Pro Corp. [*AMEX symbol*] (SPSG)
MPR.............	Microprogram Register (MHDI)
MPR.............	Milepost Review (ACAE)
MPR.............	Military Pay Record
MPR.............	Military Personnel Record (AFM)
MPR.............	Military Photo-Reconnaissance (PDAA)
MPR.............	Military Power Reserve (SAUO)
MPR.............	Mine Production Report
MPR.............	Minimum Processing Requirement
MPR.............	Mission Planning Room (SAUS)
MPR.............	Mock-Up Purchase Request [*NASA*] (NASA)
MPR.............	Model Parts Release (VLIE)
MPR.............	Mongolian Peoples Republic
MPR.............	Monoclonal Antibody Production Rate
MPR.............	Monopulse RADAR (MSA)
MPR.............	Monthly Program Review (USDC)
MPR.............	Monthly Progress Report
MPR.............	Monthly Project Report
MPR.............	Mouvement Populaire de la Revolution [*Popular Revolutionary Movement*] [*Zaire*] [*Political party*] (PD)
MPR.............	Mouvement Populaire Revolutionnaire [*Popular Revolutionary Movement*] [*Tunisia*] [*Political party*] (PD)
MPR.............	Movimento Popolare Rivoluzionario [*Popular Revolutionary Movement*] [*Italy*] [*Political party*] (PD)
MPR.............	Multi-band Pulsed Radar (SAUS)
MPR.............	Multi-Part Repeater (VLIE)
MPR.............	Multiple-Pass Radiator [*Automotive engineering*]
MPR.............	Multiple Provider Router [*Computer science*] (ACRL)
MPR.............	Multi-Port Repeater [*Computer science*] (CIST)
MPR.............	MultiProtocol Router [*Novell, Inc.*] (PCM)
MPR.............	Multipurpose Recorder
MPR.............	Music Power Rating
MPR.............	Myeloproliferative Reaction [*Medicine*] (MELL)
M Pr A........	Master of Professional Accountancy (PGP)
MPRA.........	Military Police Regimental Association (EA)
MPRC	Maryland Psychiatric Research Center [*University of Maryland*] [*Research center*] (RCD)
MPRC	Mayday Pain Resource Center (SAUO)
MPRC	Medical Program Review Committee [*DoD*] [*Washington, DC*] (EGAO)
MPRC	Military Personnel Records Center (MCD)
MPRC	Motion Picture Research Council
MPRC	Multipurpose Range Complex [*Army*] (INF)
MPRC-H......	Multipurpose Range Complex - Heavy [*Army*]
MPRC-L......	Multipurpose Range Complex - Light [*Army*]
MPRE.........	Medium Power Reactor Experiment
MPRE.........	Minimum Pure Radium Equivalent (MCD)
MPRES	Modular Plasma Reactor Simulator (AAEL)
mpress	Medium Pressure (AD)
MPRESS	Medium Pressure
MPRF.........	Master Parts Record File (VLIE)
mPRF.........	Median Pontine Reticular Formation [*Neurophysiology*]
MPRF.........	Medium Pulse Recurrence Frequency (MCD)
MPRF.........	Motion Picture Relief Fund [*Later, MPTF*] (EA)
M Pr Gph....	Master in Professional Geophysics
MPRH.........	Rio Hato [*Panama*] [*ICAO location identifier*] (ICLI)
MPRI	Member of the Plastics and Rubber Institute [*British*] (DBQ)
MPRI	Merchant Pacific Routing Instructions [*Shipping*]
MPRI	Mount Prat [*Italy*] [*Seismograph station code, US Geological Survey*] (SEIS)
MPRI	Multiphoton Resonance Ionization [*Spectrometry*]
MPRJ	Military Personnel Records Jacket [*Army*] (AABC)
MPRL..........	Manpower and Personnel Research Laboratory [*Army Research Institute for the Behavioral and Social Sciences*] (RDA)
MPRL..........	Master Parts Reference List
MPRL..........	Military Physics Research Laboratory [*University of Texas*] (MCD)
MPRM.........	Marine Pollution Research and Monitoring (SAUO)
M Pr M.......	Master of Preventive Medicine
MPRMAC	Military Participation Ratio of the Military Age Cohorts
MPrMet........	Master of Professional Meteorology (GAGS)
MPRO.........	Machine Processing Section [*National Security Agency*]
M Prob S	Master of Probability and Statistics (PGP)
MProcEng....	Master of Process Engineering, University of Sheffield [*British*] (DBQ)
M Prof Acc ..	Master of Professional Accountancy
MProfAcc....	Master of Professional Accounting (GAGS)
M Prof Past...	Master of Professional Pastoral (PGP)
MPROM.......	Mask Programmed Read-Only Memory [*Computer science*]
MPRP.........	Mean Prioritized Replacement Position (SAUO)
MPRP.........	Mercaptopurine Ribonucleotide [*Antineoplastic drug*]
MPRP.........	Mongolian People's Revolutionary Party [*Mongol Ardyn Khuv'sgalt Nam*] [*Political party*] (PPW)
MPRP.........	Muslim Peoples Republican Party [*Political party*] (AD)
MPRR.........	Management Program Review Report [*NASA*] (MCD)
MPRR.........	Missouri-Pacific Railroad Company (SAUO)
MPRR.........	Mobility Personnel Resource Roster (SAUO)
MPRS.........	Management Planning and Reporting System (COE)
MPRS.........	Marine Pollution Retrieval System [*BTS*] (TAG)
MPRS.........	Microform Personnel Records System (NVT)
MPRSA	Marine Protection, Research, and Sanctuaries Act [*1972*]
MPRST	Maximum Probability Ratio Sequential Test (PDAA)
MPRT.........	Multipurpose Rail Transport (NRCH)
MPRTM.......	Master of Park, Recreation, and Tourism Management (GAGS)
MPRT/R	Missile Pneudraulic Repair Technician/Repairman (AAG)
MPS...........	Macular Photocoagulation Study (SAUS)
MPS...........	Magazine Printers Section (EA)
MPS...........	Magnetic Pole Strength
MPS...........	Mail Preference Service [*Direct Mail Advertising Association*]
MPS...........	Main Power Switch
MPS...........	Main Propulsion System [*or Subsystem*] [*NASA*] (KSC)
MPS...........	Maintenance Performance System [*DoD*]

MPS	Maintenance Problem Summary
MPS	Maitrise en Psychologie Industrielle [*French*] (CPGU)
MPS	Management of Parts Shortages (SAUO)
MPS	Management Policy Statement
MPS	Managerial Philosophies Scale [*Test*]
MPS	Manpower Planning System (SAUO)
MPS	Manpower System (NRCH)
MPS	Manual Phase Shifter
MPS	Manufacturing Process Specification (AAG)
MPS	Marbled Paper Sides (AD)
mps	Marbled Paper Sides [*Bookbinding*]
MPS	Marginal Propensity to Save [*Economics*]
MPS	Marine Polymetalic Sulfide
MPS	Marine Prepositioned Ships Program
MPS	Maritime Postmark Society [*Later, USCS*] (EA)
MPS	Maritime Prepositioning Ship (MCD)
MPS	Maritime Prepositioning Squadron (DOMA)
MPS	Marriage Prediction Schedule [*Psychology*]
MPs	Master in/of Psychology (SAUO)
MPS	Master of Pastoral Studies (PGP)
MPS	Master of Personnel Service (GAGS)
MPS	Master of Policy Sciences (PGP)
MPS	Master of Political Science (GAGS)
MPS	Master of Professional Studies (PGP)
MPS	Master of Professional Studies in Human Relations
M Ps	Master of Psychology
MPS	Master of Public Service (GAGS)
MPS	Master Performance System
MPS	Master Phasing Schedule (ACAE)
MPS	Master Planning Schedule (MCD)
MPS	Master Production Schedule
MPS	Master Program Schedule (NASA)
MPS	Master Project Summary [*Civil Defense*]
MPS	Material Planning Study
MPS	Material Planning System [*Manufacturing management*]
MPS	Material Processing Specification (NASA)
MPS	Material Processing System
MPS	Materials Processing in Space [*NASA*]
MPS	Materiel Planning Study [*Army*]
MPS	Mathematical Programming Society [*Voorburg, Netherlands*] (EAIO)
MPS	Mathematical Programming System [*Computer science*]
MPS	Maximum Performance Escape System (MCD)
MPS	Max Planck Society [*Germany*]
MPS	Mean Prognostic Score [*Medicine*] (MELL)
MPS	Mechanical Phase Shifter
MPS	Mechanical Power Systems
MPS	Median Period of Survival
MPS	Medical Practice Study
MPS	Medical Products Sales (SAUO)
MPS	Medical Protection Society [*British*] (DBA)
MPS	Medical Provider Survey [*Department of Health and Human Services*] (GFGA)
MPS	Medical Publishing Standard (DB)
MPS	MegaBITS [*Binary Digits*] per Second [*Transmission rate*] [*Computer science*] (MCD)
mps	Megacycles per Second (AD)
MPS	Meiosis-Preventing Substance [*Cyctology*]
MPS	Member of the Pharmaceutical Society [*British*]
MPS	Member of the Philogical Society (SAUO)
MPS	Member of the Philological Society [*British*]
MPS	Member of the Physical Society [*British*]
MPs	Members of Parliament (SAUO)
MPS	Memory Processor Switch
MPS	Mercury Procedures Simulator [*NASA*]
MPS	Merit Pay System (MCD)
MPS	Merrill-Palmer School (SAUO)
MPS	Mervyn Peake Society (EA)
MPS	Mesoscale Prediction Section (SAUO)
MPS	Message Processing Service (SAUS)
MPS	Message Processing Subsystem (SAUO)
MPS	Message Processing System (NVT)
mps	Meters per Second (AD)
MPS	Meters per Second
MPS	Methodist Philatelic Society (EA)
MPS	Methyl Phenyl Sulfide [*Organic chemistry*]
MPS	Michigan Picture Stories [*Psychology*] (DAVI)
MPS	Microbial Profile System [*Microbiology*]
MPS	Microlensing Planet Search (SAUS)
MPS	Microphone Power Supply
MPS	Microprocessor Series [*or System*] (MDG)
MPS	Micro Processor Systems A/S (SAUO)
MPS	Microwave Phase Shifter
MPS	Microwave Pressure Sounder (MCD)
MPS	Microwave Pulse Source
mps	Miles per Second (IDOE)
MPS	Miles per Second
MPS	Military Planning Staff (CINC)
MPS	Military Postal Service (AFM)
MPS	Military Postal System (SAUO)
mpsh	Military Production Specifications
MPS	Milwaukee Public Museum (AD)
MPS	Minimum Performance Specification (DA)
MPS	Minimum Piecework Standard [*British*]
MPS	Minimum Property Standards [*FHA*]
MPS	Minister of Public Security [*British*]
MPS	Ministry of Posts and Telecommunications (SAUO)
MPS	Ministry of Public Security (SAUO)
MPS	Minnesota Pathological Society (SAUO)
MPS	Misioneras del Perpetual Socorro (TOCD)
MPS	Missionary Sisters of Our Lady of Perpetual Help (TOCD)
MPS	Mission Parcels Society [*British*]
MPS	Mission Payload Subsystem (SAUS)
MPS	Mission Planning System (SAUO)
MPS	Mission Preparation Sheet
MPS	Mission-Processing Subsystem (MCD)
MPS	Mission Profile Simulator [*NASA*]
MPS	Miss Porter's School [*Farmington, CT*]
MPS	Mixed Potential System (PDAA)
MPS	Mixed-Propellant System (SAUS)
MPS	Mobile Pointing Station (ACAE)
MPS	Mobile Positioning Ship (DNAB)
MPS	Modis Professional Svcs. [*NYSE symbol*] (SG)
MPS	Modular Power Subsystem
MPS	Modular Power System (MCD)
MPS	Modular Processor System [*Computer science*] (PCM)
MPS	Molecular Photoemission Spectroscopy
MPS	Mononuclear Phagocyte System [*Hematology*]
MPS	Mont Pelerin Society (EA)
MPS	Montreal Platelet Syndrome [*Medicine*] (DMAA)
MPS	Motion Picture Service [*Department of Agriculture*]
mps	Motor Parts Stock (AD)
MPS	Motor Products Corporation (SAUO)
MPS	Motor Pump Set (SAUS)
MPS	Motor Pump System (MCD)
MPS	Mount Pleasant [*Texas*] [*Airport symbol*] [*Obsolete*] (OAG)
MPS	Mouvement Patriotique du Salut [*Chad*] [*Political party*] (EY)
MPS	Mouvement Populaire Senegalais [*Senegalese Popular Movement*] [*Political party*]
MPS	Movement-Produced Stimuli
MPS	Movimiento de Patria Socialista [*Venezuela*] [*Political party*] (EY)
MPS	Mucopolysaccharide [*Also, MP*] [*Clinical chemistry*]
MPS	Mucopolysaccharidosis [*Medicine*]
MPS	Multi-Format Photointerpretation System (SAA)
MPS	Multiparticle Spectrometer [*Brookhaven National Laboratory*]
MPS	Multiphasic Screening [*Medicine*]
MPS	Multi-Plane Programming System (NITA)
MPS	Multiple Peptide Synthesis [*Biochemistry*]
MPS	Multiple Protective Shelter (SAUS)
MPS	Multiple Protective Structure [*Missile bases*]
MPS	Multiple Vertical Protective Shelter [*for missiles*]
MPS	Multiprocessing System [*Computer science*]
MPS	Multiprogramming Periodic Tasking System (NITA)
MPS	Multiprogramming System [*Computer science*]
MPS	Multi-Protocol Support [*Computer science*] (AGLO)
MPS	Multipurpose Ship (AABC)
MPS	Muzzle Position Sensor (MCD)
MPS	Myeloma Progression Score [*Oncology*]
MPS	Myocardial Perfusion Scintigraphy [*Medicine*] (DB)
MPS2	Society for Mucopolysaccharide Diseases (EA)
MPS2	Region 2 Merit Pay System (SAUS)
MPSA	Master of Public School Art
MPSA	Metropolitan Pharmaceutical Secretaries Association (EA)
MPSA	Military Petroleum Supply Agency [*Later, Defense Petroleum Supply Center*]
MPSA	Military Postal Service Agency
MPSA	Military Production Supply Agency (SAUO)
MPSA	Santiago [*Panama*] [*ICAO location identifier*] (ICLI)
MPSB	Military Production and Supply Board (SAUO)
MPSB-PWS	Permanent Working Staff of the Military Production and Supply Board (SAUO)
MPSC	Marianas Political Status Commission
MPSC	Material Planning Schedule and Control [*Division of Inspection Offices, Navy*]
MPSC	Michigan Public Services Commission (SAUO)
MPSC	Military Personnel Security Committee
MPSC	Military Provost Staff Corps [*British*]
MPSC	Movimiento Popular Socialcristiano [*Christian Social Popular Movement*] [*El Salvador*] [*Political party*] (PD)
MPSCL	Mathematical Programming System Control Language [*1974*] [*Computer science*] (CSR)
MP/SCM	Multiport Semiconductor Memory (MHDI)
MPSCOA	Military Pay Service Center Overseas Areas (SAUO)
MPSE	Moreless Payload Specialist Experiment (SAUS)
MPSE	Motion Picture Sound Editors (EA)
MPSE	Multipurpose Payload Support Equipment (MCD)
MPSF	Mountain Pacific Sports Federation (PSS)
MPSF	Multi-Purpose Special Fund [*Asian Development Bank*] [*United Nations*] (EY)
MPSG	Marketing Programs and Services Group, Inc. [*Gaithersburg, MD*] [*Information service or system*] [*Telecommunications*] (TSSD)
MPSG	Multi-Band Portable Signal Generator (PDAA)
MPSGB	Member of the Pharmaceutical Society of Great Britain (SAUO)
MPSH	Mean Pressure Suction Head (AAG)
mpsh	Mean Pressure Suction Head (AD)
MPS-HHSA	Master of Professional Studies-Hospital and Health Services Administration
MPSI	Message Processing Systems, Inc. [*Charlotte, NC*] [*Telecommunications service*] (TSSD)
MPSI	MPSI Systems, Inc. [*NASDAQ symbol*] (SAG)

MPS I	Mucopolysaccharidoses [*Hurler Syndrome*] [*Also, Scheie Syndrome and Hurler/Scheie Syndrome*] (PAZ)
MPSIG	Monty Python Special Interest Group (EA)
MPS II	Mucopolysaccharidoses [*Hunter Syndrome*] (PAZ)
MPS IV	Mucopolysaccaridoses [*Morquio Syndrome*] (PAZ)
MPSK	Multiple Phase Shift Keying [*Computer science*] (TEL)
MPSL	Materials and Process Specification List (SAUS)
MPSM	Master of Public School Music
MPSM	Master Problem Status Manual
MPSM	MODEM Pooling Service Module [*Telecommunications*]
MPSM	Multipurpose Submunition (RDA)
MPSMT	Merrill-Palmer Scale of Mental Tests [*Psychology*] (DAVI)
MPSN	Microwave Pulse Shaping Network
MPSNY	Montserrat Progressive Society of New York (EA)
MPsO	Master of Psychology Orientation (NADA)
MPsO	Master of Psychology-Orientation (SAUO)
MPsO	Mistress of Psychology Orientation (SAUO)
MPSOC	Multi Purpose Satellite Operations Center (ACAE)
MP SOV GR COM	Most Puissant Sovereign Grand Commander [*United States*] [*Freemasonry*] (ROG)
MPSP	Mathematical Problem-Solving Project [*National Science Foundation*]
MP(S)P	Mechanically Processed (Species) Product (DICI)
MPSP	Micro Programmable Scene Processor (ACAE)
MPSP	Military Personnel Security Program
MPSP	Modular Programmable Scene Processor (ACAE)
MPSR	Military Petroleum Stocks Report (SAUO)
MPSR	Mission Profile Storage and Retrieval [*NASA*] (NASA)
MPSR	Multipurpose Support Room (MCD)
MPSRE	Master of Professional Studies in Real Estate (PGP)
MPSRON	Maritime Prepositioning Ship Squadron (DOMA)
MPSRT	Matched-Pairs Signed-Rank Test [*Statistics*]
MPSS	Main Parachute Support Structure (NASA)
MPSS	Maryland Preschool Self-Concept Scale (EDAC)
MPSS	Master Production Scheduling System (TIMI)
MPSS	Message Processing Subsystem (ACAE)
MPSS	Mission Payload System Segment
MPSS	Mission Planning and Scheduling System (SAUS)
MPSS	Multiple Payload Support Structure (SAUS)
MPSS	Multiple Protective Structure System (AD)
MPSS	Multipurpose Sampling System
M Ps Sc	Master of Physic Sciences
MPsSc	Master of Psychological Science (GAGS)
MPST	Minimum Performance Standard Test [*Military*] (CAAL)
MPST	Multipurpose Support Team [*NASA*] (NAKS)
M Ps Th	Master of Psycho-Therapy
MPSTWG	Mission Planning System Test Working Group [*Military*] (CAAL)
MPSU	Missile Pressure Status Unit (AAG)
MPSV	Myeloproliferative Sarcoma Virus
MPSW	Master of Psychiatric Social Work (NADA)
MP SWAT	Military Police Special Weapons and Tactics Team (VNW)
MPSX	Mathematical Programming System Extended [*IBM Corp.*] [*Computer science*]
MPsych	Master of Psychology
MPsych	Mistress of Psychology (SAUO)
MPsychApp	Master of Applied Psychology (ADA)
MPsych(Clin)	Master of Psychology (Clinical)
MPsych(Ed)	Master of Psychology (Education)
MPsychMed	Master of Psychological Medicine, University of Liverpool [*British*] (DBQ)
MPsychol	Master of Psychology
MPsychTh	Master of Psychotherapy
M Psy Med	Master of Psychological Medicine
MPT	Alpha-Methyl-p-tyrosine [*Also, AMPT*] [*Pharmacology*]
MPT	Magnetic Particle Testing [*Nuclear energy*] (NRCH)
MPT	Main Propulsion Test [*NASA*] (NASA)
mpt	Male Pipe Thread (AD)
MPT	Male Pipe Thread (MSA)
MPT	Maneuver Planning Table [*NASA*]
MPT	Manpower and Training (DOMA)
MPT	Manpower, Personnel, and Training
MPT	Manpower Target (SAUS)
MPT	Marginal Propensity to Tax [*Economics*]
MPT	Marquis Public Theater (SAUO)
MPT	Maryland Public Television [*Owings Mills*] [*Information service or system*] [*Telecommunications*] (TSSD)
Mpt	Maryport (AD)
MPT	Master of Pastoral Theology (PGP)
MPT	Master of Physical Therapy (GAGS)
MPT	Matupit Island [*New Britain*] [*Seismograph station code, US Geological Survey*] (SEIS)
MPT	Maximum Part Time (SAUO)
MPT	Maximum Power Transfer (IDOE)
MPT	Mean Preventive Maintenance Time (MCD)
MPT	Mean Pulse Time
MPT	Mechanical Power Transmission
MPT	Medical Proficiency Training (SAUO)
mpt	Melting Point (AD)
M PT	Melting Point (ROG)
MPT	Memory Point Track (SAUS)
MPT	Memory Processing Time
MPT	Mercury Procedures Trainer
MPT	Message Processing Task [*Computer science*] (ECII)
MPT	Message Processing Time (SAUO)
MPT	Metal-Phthalocyanine Tetramine [*Organic chemistry*]
MPT	Methyl-para-Tyrosine [*Biochemistry*]

MPT	Michigan Picture Test [*Psychology*]
mpt	Microprocessing Programmable Terminal [*Computer science*] (AD)
MPT-SD	Microprogramming Technique
mpt	Midpoint (AD)
MPT	Miles per Tankful (AD)
mpt	Miles per Tankful (AD)
MPT	Military Potential Test (AABC)
MPT	Milk Pasteurization Tribunal [*Australia*]
MPT	Minimum Pressurization Temperature [*Nuclear energy*] (NRCH)
MPT	Minimum Process Time
MPT	Ministry of Post and Telegraph (SAUO)
MPT	Ministry of Posts and Telecommunications [*People's Republic of China*] (ECON)
MPT	Missile Preflight Tester
MPT	Missile Procedure Trainer
MPT	Mission Planning Table [*NASA*] (KSC)
MPT	Mission Planning Terminal (MCD)
MPT	Mixed Parotid Gland Tumor [*Oncology*]
MPT	Modern Poetry in Translation [*A publication*] (WDAA)
MPT	Modern Portfolio Theory [*Finance*]
MPT	Molydopterin [*Biochemistry*]
MPT	Morphine Provocative Test [*Gastroenterology*] (DAVI)
MPT	MOS [*Military Occupational Specialty*] Proficiency Training [*DoD*]
MPT	Motional Pickup Transducer (MCD)
MPT	Mouvement Populaire Tchadien [*Chadian Popular Movement*] [*Political party*]
MPT	Mouvement Populaire Togolais [*Togolese Popular Movement*] [*Political party*]
MPT	Mouvement pour le Progres et la Tolerance [*Burkina Faso*] [*Political party*] (EY)
MPT	Multilateral Preparatory Talks (NATG)
mpt	Multiple Pure Tone (AD)
MPT	Multiple Pure Tone [*Sound*]
MPT	Multiple-Purpose Telescope
mpt	Multipower Transmission (AD)
MPT	Multi-Purpose Tracer (SAUS)
MPT	Municipal Partners Fund II [*NYSE symbol*] (TTSB)
MPT 1327	European hybrid digital trunked radio (SAUS)
MPTA	Machine Power Transmission Association (AD)
mpta	Main Propulsion Test Article (AD)
MPTA	Main Propulsion Test Article [*Aerospace*] (NAKS)
MPTA	Manpower, Personnel, and Training Analysis
MPTA	Mechanical Power Transmission Association (EA)
MPTA	Municipal Passenger Transport Association, Inc. [*British*] (BI)
MPTAO	Military Personnel and Transportation Assistance Office (MCD)
MPTB	Meridian Point Realty Trust [*NASDAQ symbol*] (SAG)
MPTB	Monophosphate Tungsten Bronze [*Metallurgy*]
MPTB	Multisolid Pneumatic Transport Bed [*Chemical engineering*]
MPTBS	Meridian Point Rlty Tr 83 [*NASDAQ symbol*] (TTSB)
MPTCA	Motion Picture and Television Credit Association (EA)
MPTCC	Most Probable Total Contract Cost (AAGC)
MPTCMA	Motion Picture and Television Credit Managers Association [*Later, MPTCA*] (EA)
MPTD	Metropolitan Police, Thames Division (SAUO)
MPTDS	Multi-Purpose Tactical Display Set (ACAE)
MPTE	Manual Peculiar Test Equipment (ACAE)
MPTE	Multipurpose Test Equipment
MPTEDA	Mechanical Power Transmission Equipment Distributors Association [*Later, Power Transmission Distributors Association*] (EA)
MPTER	Multiple Point Source Model with Terrain [*Environmental Protection Agency*] (GFGA)
MPTF	Main Propulsion Test Facility [*NASA*] (NASA)
MPTF	Mission Planning Task Force (KSC)
MPTF	Motion Picture and Television Fund (EA)
MPTF	Multiple Protocol Transport Feature (SAUO)
MPTF	Music Performance Trust Funds (EA)
MPTH	Methylphenothiazine [*Organic chemistry*]
MPTH	Mpath Interactive [*NASDAQ symbol*] (SG)
MPTIS	Manpower, Personnel and Training Integration System (ACAE)
MPTL	Materials Processing Technology Laboratory (SSD)
MPTMH	Major Peace Treaties of Modern History, 1648-1967 [*A publication*] (DLA)
MPTN	Multiprotocol Transport Network [*Telecommunications*] (ACRL)
MPTO	Methods and Procedures Technical Orders
MPTO	Tocumen/General Omar Torrijos H. [*Panama*] [*ICAO location identifier*] (ICLI)
MPTP	1-Methyl-4-Phenyl-1,2,3,6-Tetrahydropyridin (SAUS)
MPTP	Main Propulsion Test Program (MCD)
MPTP	Methyl(phenyl)tetrahydropyridine [*Organic chemistry*]
MPTP	Music Preference Test of Personality [*Psychology*]
MPTR	MedPartners, Inc. [*NASDAQ symbol*] (SAG)
MPTR	Mobile Position Tracking RADAR
MPTR	Motor, Pain, Touch, Reflex [*Neurology*] (DAVI)
MPTR	Multipurpose Training Range [*Army*]
MPTS	Manpower, Personnel, and Training Support [*Military*] (CAAL)
MPTS	Manpower, Personnel, Training, and Safety [*Army*]
MPTS	Metal Parts (AABC)
MPTS	Metropolitan Police Training School (SAUO)
MPTS	Mobile Photographic Tracking Station
MPTS	Multi-Protocol Transport Service [*Telecommunications*]
MPTS	Multipurpose Test Set (DWSG)
MPTS	Multipurpose Tool Set (MCD)
MP-T-SD	Multi-Purpose Tracer, Self-Destroying (SAUS)
MPT-SD	Multipurpose, Tracer, Self-Destruct [*Army*]
MP(TSWG)	Military Police Tripartite Standing Working Group (AABC)

MPTT.......... Maintenance Part Task Trainer [Army]
MPTUS........ Marble Polishers' Trade Union Society [British]
MPTUSU...... Malayan Postal and Telecommunications Uniformed Staff Union (SAUO)
MPTV.......... MPTV, Inc. [NASDAQ symbol] (SAG)
MPTWT....... Medium Power Traveling Wave Tube
MPU............ Magnetic Pickup [Electronics]
MPU............ Main Power Unit
MPU............ Main Propulsion Unit
MPU............ Maintenance Processor Unit (VLIE)
MPU............ Malayan Planning Unit [World War II]
MPU............ Malposition of Uterus [Medicine] (MELL)
MPU............ Manpack Unit (MCD)
MPU............ Mapua [Papua New Guinea] [Airport symbol] [Obsolete] (OAG)
MPU............ Medical Practitioners' Union [Later, Medical Practitioners' Section - MPS] [British] (DCTA)
MPU............ Memory Protection Unit
MPU............ Mental Parents Union (AD)
MPU............ Message Picking-Up
MPU............ Microphone Preamplifier Unit (ACAE)
mpu............ Microprocessor Unit (AD)
MPU............ Microprocessor Unit [CPU of microcomputer] [Computer science]
MPU............ MIDI [Musical Instrument Digital Interface] Processing Unit [Computer technology]
MPU............ Miniature Portable Unit
MPU............ Minutes per Unit
MPU............ Missile Power Unit (DNAB)
MPU............ Missing Persons Unit (AD)
MPU............ Mission Programming Unit (SAUS)
MPU............ Mixing and Pumping Unit [Bulk explosives] (MCD)
MPU............ Mobile Production Unit [On-site television recording] (NTCM)
mpu............ Monitor Printing Unit (AD)
MPU............ Monitor Printing Unit [Computer science]
MPU............ Motorola Processor Unit
MPU............ Motor Pressurization Unit
MPU............ Multi-Processor Unit (VLIE)
MPU401....... MIDI Processing Unit 401 (SAUS)
MPUA.......... Military and Police Uniform Association (EA)
M Pub......... Master of Publishing (PGP)
M Pub Adm... Master of Public Administration
MPubAdmin... Master of Public Administration
MPubLaw .... Master of Public Law
MPubPol...... Master of Public Policy
MPUL.......... Military Production Urgencies List (NG)
MPUS.......... Military Production Urgencies System
MPU/VPU..... Modem Processor Unit/Voice Processor Unit (SAUS)
MPV............ Magistrae Piae Venerini [Religious Venerini Sisters] [Roman Catholic religious order]
MPV............ Magnetic Polarization Vector
MPV............ Main Portal Vein [Medicine] (DMAA)
MPV............ Man-Powered Vehicle
M-P v......... Mason-Pfizer Virus [Medicine] (AD)
MPV............ Mass Mutual Participating Investors [NYSE symbol] (CTT)
MPV............ MassMutual Participation Investors [NYSE symbol] (SAG)
MPV............ Mean Platelet Volume [Hematology]
MPV............ Meerwein-Ponndorf-Verley [Organic chemistry]
MPV............ Metatarsus Primus Varus [Orthopedics] (DAVI)
MPV............ Methane-Powered Vehicle
MPV............ Military Pay Voucher
MPV............ Missouri Public Service Company (SAUO)
MPV............ Mitral Valve Prolapse [Medicine] (DMAA)
MPV............ Montpelier [Vermont] [Airport symbol] (OAG)
MPV............ Mountain Province [Vancouver Stock Exchange symbol]
MPV............ Multipurpose Passenger Vehicle
MPV............ Multi-Purpose Variant (SAUS)
mpv............ Multipurpose Vehicle (AD)
MPV............ Multipurpose Vehicle [Automotive engineering]
MPVA.......... Main Propellant Valve Actuator (MCD)
MP/VAP....... Maritime Patrol/Reconnaissance Attack Aircraft (NATG)
MPVI.......... Mountain Province Mining, Inc. [NASDAQ symbol] (SAG)
MPVIF......... Mountain Province Mining [NASDAQ symbol] (TTSB)
MPVM......... Master of Preventive Veterinary Medicine (GAGS)
MPVP......... Mean Pulmonary Venous Pressure [Cardiology]
MPVPC....... Montreal Paint and Varnish Production Club (SAUO)
MPVR .... El Porvenir [Panama] [ICAO location identifier] (ICLI)
MPVSCS ..... Military Pay Voucher Summary and Certification Sheet
MPVT.......... Montpelier [Vermont] [Seismograph station code, US Geological Survey] (SEIS)
MPVU .... Multi-Plot Variable Updating (SAUS)
MPW........... Macintosh Programmers Workbench (SAUO)
MPW........... Macintosh Programmer's Workshop [Computer science] (BTTJ)
mPw .... Maritime Polar [Air Mass] Warm [Meteorology] (BARN)
MPW........... Master of Public Works (PGP)
MPW........... Minneapolis-Moline [Stock exchange symbol] (AD)
MPW........... Modified Plane Wave (IEEE)
MPW........... Multi-Product Wafer (AAEL)
MPW........... Whiteshell Nuclear Research Establishment, Atomic Energy of Canada [Etablissement de Recherche Nucleaire Whiteshell, L'Energie Atomique du Canada] Pinawa,Manitoba [Library symbol] [National Library of Canada] (NLC)
MPWB......... Multilayer Printed-Wiring Board
MPWBS ...... Master Plan Works Breakdown Structure (AD)
MPWC .... Michigan Pure Water Council (EA)
MPWC .... Multiprocess Wet Cleaning (EPAT)
MPWD .... Machine-Prepared Wiring Data [Telecommunications] (TEL)

MPWG .... Mechanical Properties Working Group (SAUO)
MPWG .... Minuteman Parts Working Group [Missiles]
MPWG .... MPW Industrial Svcs. [NASDAQ symbol] (SG)
MPWP .... Maximum Permissible Working Pressure (HEAS)
MPWS .... Mobile Protected Weapon System (RDA)
MPWU .... Movement for Political World Union [Blommenslyst, Fyn, Denmark] (EA)
MPWUPH..... Ministry of Public Works, Urban Planning and Housing (SAUO)
MPX............ Aeromexpress, SA de CV [Mexico] [FAA designator] (FAAC)
MPX............ Magazine Page Exposure [Publishing] (WDMC)
MPX............ Mapped Programming Executive [Systems Engineering Laboratories U.S.] (NITA)
MPX............ Microprocessor Exchange [Computer science]
MPX............ Mid-America Payment Exchange [Banking] (TBD)
mpx .... Multiplex (AD)
mpx .... Multiplex [or Multiplexer] [Telecommunications]
MPX............ Multiprocessor Extension (PCM)
MPX............ Multiprogramming Executive [Computer science]
MPXR .... Multiplexer
mpxr .... Multiplexor (AD)
Mpy .... Maatschappij [Company] [Dutch] (AD)
MPY........... Milli-Inches per Year [Corrosion technology]
mpy .... Mils per Year (ABAC)
MPY........... Multiple Problem Youth
mpy .... Multiply (AD)
MPY........... Multiply (MDG)
MPY........... Multiprobe Yield (TIMI)
MPZ............ Mid-Continent Petroleum [Stock exchange symbol] (AD)
MPZ............ Modified Protamine Zinc [Insulin]
MPZ............ Mount Pleasant, IA [Location identifier] [FAA] (FAAL)
MPZ............ Myelin Protein, Zero (DMAA)
MPZL.......... Panama [Panama] [ICAO location identifier] (ICLI)
MQ............. Mack Trucks, Inc. (SAUO)
MQ............. Magnum Airlines [ICAO designator] (AD)
MQ............. Management Quarterly Magazine [A publication] (EAAP)
MQ............. MARC [Machine-Readable Cataloging] Quebecois [Source file] [UTLAS symbol]
MQ............. Marketing Quota
MQ............. Martinique [ANSI two-letter standard code] (CNC)
mq .... Martinique [MARC country of publication code] [Library of Congress] (LCCP)
MQ............ Mayflower Quarterly [A publication] (GEAB)
mq .... Memory Quotient (AD)
MQ............. Memory Quotient
MQ............. Menaquinone [Vitamin K] [Also, MK] [Biochemistry]
MQ............. Merit Quotient
MQ............. Message Queue [Computer science] (VLIE)
mq .... Metol-Quinol [Medicine] (AD)
MQ............. Metol-Quinol [Developer] [Photography] (ROG)
MQ............. Metol-Quinone [Medicine] (AD)
mq .... Metol-Quinone [Medicine] (AD)
MQ............. Mining and Quarrying [Department of Employment] [British]
MQ............. Mo'ed Qatan [or Qattan] (BJA)
Mq............. Mosque (AD)
mq .... Mosque (BARN)
MQ............. Mothering Quotient
mq .... Multiple Quotient (AD)
MQ............. Multiplier Quotient [Computer science]
MQ............. Musical Quarterly [A publication] (BRI)
MQ............. Simmons Airlines [ICAO designator] (AD)
MQ............. Thomas Crane Public Library, Quincy, MA [Library symbol] [Library of Congress] (LCLS)
MQA........... Adams Mansion, Quincy, MA [Library symbol] [Library of Congress] (LCLS)
MQA........... Manual of Qualification for Advancement
MQA........... Manufacturing Quality Assurance
MQA........... Manufacturing Quality Audit
MQA........... Measurement Quality Assurance
MQA........... Medical Quality Assurance (AD)
MQA........... Multiple Queue Assignment [Computer science] (ITD)
MQA........... Murrayaquinone-A [Biochemistry]
MQAB .... Medical Quality Assurance Board (AD)
MQAD .... Materials Quality Assurance Directorate [Ministry of Defence] [British]
MQB........... Macomb, IL [Location identifier] [FAA] (FAAL)
MQB........... Mining Qualifications Board [British] (BI)
MQC........... Macroscopic Quantum Coherence [Physics]
MQC........... Mammography Quality Control
MQC........... Manufacturing Quality Control (MCD)
MQC........... Marquette Company (SAUO)
MQC........... Microbiologic Quality Control (DMAA)
MQCL.......... Master Quality Characteristic List (MCD)
MQD........... Manhattan, KS [Location identifier] [FAA] (FAAL)
MQD........... Metallurgical Quenching Dilatometry
MQD........... Milner. Questions de Droit [A publication] (DLA)
MQD........... Monolithic Quad Device
MQDT .... Multichannel Quantum Defect Theory [Physics]
MQE........... Managed Query Environment [Computer science] (ITCA)
Mqe........... Martinique (AD)
MQE........... Martinique [West Indies] (WDAA)
MQE........... Message Queue Element [Computer science]
MQEM......... Michigan Quarterly Economic Model (NITA)
mqf .... Mobile Quarantine Facility (AD)
MQF........... Mobile Quarantine Facility [NASA]
MQG .... General Dynamics, Quincy Shipbuilding Division, Quincy, MA [Library symbol] [Library of Congress] (LCLS)

MQG	Milgarra [*Queensland*] [*Airport symbol*] (AD)
MQHi	Quincy Historical Society, Quincy, MA [*Library symbol*] [*Library of Congress*] (LCLS)
MQI	Macquarie Island [*Australia*] [*Seismograph station code, US Geological Survey*] [*Closed*] (SEIS)
MQI	Maiquetia [*Venezuelan airport*] (AD)
MQI	Manteo, NC [*Location identifier*] [*FAA*] (FAAL)
MQI	Message Queuing Interface [*Computer science*] (VLIE)
MQID	Message Queue Identification [*Computer science*] (VLIE)
MQIFX	Mutual Qualified Fund [*Mutual fund ticker symbol*] (SG)
mqil	Miniature Quartz Incandescent Lamp (AD)
MQIL	Miniature Quartz Incandescent Lamp
MQJ	Indianapolis, IN [*Location identifier*] [*FAA*] (FAAL)
MQK	Youngstown, OH [*Location identifier*] [*FAA*] (FAAL)
MQL	Mean Queue Length [*Computer science*] (VLIE)
MQL	Method Quantification Limits (COE)
MQL	Mildura [*Australia*] [*Airport symbol*] (OAG)
mql	Miniature Quartz Lamp (AD)
MQL	Miniature Quartz Lamp
MQLF	Mobile Quick-Look Facility (SAUS)
MQM	Master of Quality Management (PGP)
MQM	Master of the Queen's Music [*British*] (AD)
MQM	Message Queue Manager [*Computer science*] (MCD)
MQM	Mohajir Qami Movement [*Pakistan*] [*Political party*]
MQM	Monida, MT [*Location identifier*] [*FAA*] (FAAL)
MQM	Muhajir Qaumi Movement [*Pakistan*] [*Political party*] (ECON)
MQM	University of New Mexico, Medical Center Library, Albuquerque, NM [*OCLC symbol*] (OCLC)
MQN	Magnetic Quantum Number [*Atomic physics*]
MQN	Message Queue Name [*Computer science*] (VLIE)
MQ-NMR	Multiple Quantum Nuclear Magnetic Resonance (AAEL)
MQO	Marksmanship Qualification Order [*Marine Corps*]
MQO	Mosquito Creek Gold Mining [*Vancouver Stock Exchange symbol*]
MQP	Mandatory Quote Period (NUMA)
MQP	Military Qualification Program (NG)
MQP	Mineral Wells, TX [*Location identifier*] [*FAA*] (FAAL)
MQP	Motor Qualification Program (NG)
MQQ	Moundou [*Chad*] [*Airport symbol*] (AD)
MQR	Michigan Quarterly Review [*A publication*] (BRI)
MQR	Miscellaneous Quote Request (MCD)
MQRNS	Multiplier Quotient Register [*Computer science*]
MQRNS	Modified Quadratic Residue Number System (MCD)
MQS	Coatesville, PA [*Location identifier*] [*FAA*] (FAAL)
MQS	Maintenance Quality Specialist (MCD)
MQS	Manufacturing Quality System (TIMI)
MQS	Master of Quantitative Systems
MQS	Military Qualification Standard
MQS	Mobile Quality Services (AD)
MQS	Motion to Quash Subpoena (NRCH)
MQS	Multiprogrammed Queued Tasking System (NITA)
MQS	Mustique [*Windward Islands*] [*Airport symbol*] (OAG)
MQSA	Mammography Quality Standards Act
MQSA	Mammography Quality Standards Act of 1992
MQSS	Mary Queen of Scots Society (EAIO)
MQST	MapQuest.com, Inc. [*NASDAQ symbol*] (SG)
MQT	Macquest Resources Ltd. [*Toronto Stock Exchange symbol*]
MQT	Macroscopic Quantum Tunneling [*Quantum mechanics*]
MQT	Marquette [*Michigan*] [*Airport symbol*] (OAG)
MQT	Military Qualification Test (NG)
MQT	Mission Qualification Training
MQT	Model Qualification Test
MQT	Motor Qualification Test (NG)
MQT	MuniYield Quality Fund II [*NYSE symbol*] (SPSG)
MQU	Beckley, WV [*Location identifier*] [*FAA*] (FAAL)
MQU	Makus Resources, Inc. [*Vancouver Stock Exchange symbol*]
MQU	Mariquita [*Colombia*] [*Airport symbol*] (OAG)
MQU	Media Quality Unit [*Communications*]
MQU	Multiplier Quotient Unit [*Computer science*]
MQUAD	Metal Quad
MQUIPS	Million Quality Improvements Per Second (SAUS)
MQV	Ministere de la Qualite de la Vie [*Ministry of the Quality of Life*] [*France*] (AD)
MQW	McRae, GA [*Location identifier*] [*FAA*] (FAAL)
MQW	Multiple Quantum Well [*Switch for an optical computer*]
MQW	Multiquantum Well (NITA)
MQWL	Multiquantum Well Lasers (NITA)
MQX	Makale [*Ethiopia*] [*Airport symbol*] (OAG)
MQY	MuniYield Quality Fund [*NYSE symbol*] (SPSG)
MQY	Smyrna, TN [*Location identifier*] [*FAA*] (FAAL)
mqyco	Minimum Quantity Yards per Color (AD)
mqyds	Minimum Quantity Yards per Design (AD)
MR	Air Mauritanie [*Mauritania*] [*ICAO designator*] (ICDA)
MR	Application for Writ of Mandamus Refused [*Legal term*] (DLA)
M/R	Machine Receipt
mr	Machine Record (AD)
MR	Machine Records
mr	Machine Rifle (AD)
MR	Machine Rifle
MR	Machinery Repairman [*Navy rating*]
MR	Macrophage Rich
MR	Magister [*Master*] [*Latin*] (ROG)
MR	Magnetic Recorder (DEN)
MR	Magnetic Resonance
MR	Magnetic Resonating (AD)
MR	Magnitude of Rotation

MR	Mail and Records Group (SAUO)
MR	Main Ring (SAUS)
MR	Maintainability Report
M+R	Maintenance and Refurbishment
M+R	Maintenance and Repair
MR	Maintenance Ratio (MCD)
MR	Maintenance Request (TIMI)
MR	Maintenance Review
MR	Management Requirements (MCD)
MR	Management Reserve (MCD)
MR	Management Review (SAUO)
MR	Mandatory Reporting (HEAS)
MR	Mandelate Racemase [*An enzyme*]
MR	Maneuver Radius (ACAE)
MR	Manifest Refraction (SAUS)
MR	Manitoba Law Reports [*Canada*] [*A publication*] (DLA)
MR	Mannose Resistant [*Biochemistry*]
MR	Manpower Requirements
MR	Manual Removal [*Medicine*]
MR	Manufacturer's Representative
MR	Manufacturing Requisition
m/r	Map Reading (AD)
MR	Map Reading
mr	Map Reference (AD)
mr	Map Reference
MR	Marble (AAG)
MR	Marca Registrada [*Registered Trademark*] [*Spanish*]
Mr.	March (RION)
MR	March
MR	Marginal Return [*Army*] (AABC)
mr	Marginal Revenue (AD)
MR	Marginal Revenue [*Economics*]
MR	Marianist Sisters (TOCD)
MR	Mariner (ACAE)
MR	Maritime Reconnaissance (NATG)
MR	Maritime Regiment
MR	Marker Ranger (SAUS)
MR	Marketing Research Division [*of AMS, Department of Agriculture*]
MR	Market Rate (SAUO)
MR	Mark Russell (AD)
MR	Marston Radiators Ltd. (SAUO)
MR	Mask Register
MR	Massachusetts Review: A Quarterly of Literature, the Arts and Public Affairs [*A publication*] (ANEX)
Mr	Master (AD)
MR	Master [*British military*] (DMA)
MR	Master of the Rolls
MR	Master Relay [*Electrical*] (DICI)
MR	Master Reset (MCD)
MR	Master Routing (SAA)
MR	Material Request [*or Requisition*] (MCD)
MR	Material Review [*Aviation*] (AAG)
MR	Materiel Readiness [*Army*]
MR	Mate's Receipt
m/r	Mates' Receipt (RIMS)
MR	Mathematical Review (SAUO)
MR	Mauritania [*ANSI two-letter standard code*] (CNC)
MR	Mauritius Decisions [*A publication*] (DLA)
MR	Mauritius Reports [*A publication*] (DLA)
MR	Maximal Response
MR	Maximum Range (IAA)
MR	Maximum to Right (SAUS)
MR	May Repeat [*Medicine*]
MR	McCloud River [*Railroad*] (MHDW)
MR	McCloud River Railroad Co. (SAUO)
MR	Mean Radius (MCD)
MR	Mean Rate (SAUS)
MR	Measles, Rubella [*Immunology*]
MR	Measured Rating [*IOR*] [*Yacht racing*]
MR	Mechanical Restraint [*for mental patients*] [*British*]
MR	Medial Rectus [*Eye anatomy*]
MR	[*The*] Media Report [*A publication*] (NTCM)
MR	Medical Record
MR	Medical Rectus [*Muscle*] [*Anatomy*]
MR	Medical Report
mr	Medium Range (AD)
MR	Medium Range
MR	Medium-Range Planes [*Navy*]
MR	Medium Reduction (NITA)
MR	Medium Release (WDAA)
MR	Medium Resolution
MR	Medullary Ray [*Botany*] (BARN)
mr	Meester [*Master*] [*Dutch*] (AD)
MR	Megarayleigh [*Optics*]
MR	Melkersson-Rosenthal [*Syndrome*] [*Medicine*] (DB)
MR	Memorandum for Record [*Military*] (AFM)
MR	Memorandum Receipt [*Military*] (MUGU)
MR	Memory Read [*Computer science*]
MR	Memory Recall [*Computer science*] (PCM)
MR	Memory Reclaimer
MR	Memory Register [*Computer science*]
mr	Mentally Retarded (AD)
MR	Mental Retardation
MR	Mental Retardation Program [*Public human service program*] (PHSD)
MR	Mercury-Redstone [*NASA*]

MR	Message Register (AAG)
MR	Message Repeat
mr	Metabolic Rate (AD)
MR	Metabolic Rate
MR	Metal Removing Co. (SAUO)
MR	Meter
MR	Methacholine Response [Medicine]
MR	Methane Recovery (CARB)
MR	Methane Response [Automotive emissions]
MR	Methodist Review (SAUO)
mr	Methyl Red (AD)
MR	Methyl Red [A dye]
MR	Methyl Reductase [An enzyme]
MR	Metropolitan Railway [British]
MR	Metropolitan Railway Co. (SAUO)
MR	Michael Resources Ltd. [Vancouver Stock Exchange symbol]
MR	Michigan Reformatory (AD)
MR	Microfilm Review (SAUO)
MR	Microminiature Relay
MR	Microplate Reader [Computer science]
MR	Microwave Radiometer (ACAE)
MR	Middle Repetitive [Genetics]
m/r	Middle Right (AD)
MR	[The] Middlesex Regiment [British]
MR	Mid-Engine, Rear-Drive [Automotive engineering]
MR	Midland Railway [British]
MR	Midland Railway Co. (SAUO)
MR	Midland Red Bus Co. (SAUO)
MR	Midrib [Botany]
MR	Migration Ratio (DNAB)
MR	Military Railroad (AD)
MR	Military Readiness
MR	Military Region [Viet Cong term]
MR	Military Regulation
MR	Military Representative (NATG)
MR	Military Requirement
M/R	Military Reserve (CINC)
MR	Military Review (MCD)
MR	Militia Reserve [British military] (DMA)
MR	Milk-Ring [Test] [Medicine] (MEDA)
MR	Milliradian (DEN)
MR	Millirem (DEN)
mR	Milliroentgen (AD)
mr	Milliroentgen
mr	Mill Run (AD)
MR	Mill Run [Unselected lot of a manufactured product]
MR	Milrinone [Biochemistry]
MR	Mine Rake (DWSG)
MR	Mineralo-Corticoid Receptor [Endocrinology]
MR	Mineral Range Railroad (IIA)
mr	Mineral Rubber (AD)
MR	Mineral Rubber
mr	Mine Run (AD)
MR	Mine-Run
MR	Miniatures Rules (VLIE)
MR	Minimum Required
MR	Mining Reports, Edited by R. S. Morrison [Chicago] [A publication] (DLA)
MR	Mining Review [A publication]
MR	Mini Registry (EA)
MR	Minister of Reconstruction (SAUO)
MR	Minister-Residentiary [Diplomacy]
MR	Ministry of Reconstruction [World War I] [British]
MR	Minnesota Review [A publication] (BRI)
MR	Minor Repair (MCD)
MR	Mi Remesa [My Remittance] [Spanish] [Business term]
MR	Miscellaneous Report
MR	Missed Recognition (SAA)
MR	Missile RADAR [Military] (CAAL)
MR	Missile Receiver
MR	Missile Reference
MR	Missile Rounds (MCD)
M/R	Missiles and Rockets [A publication]
MR	Missionarius Rector [Missionary Rector] [Latin]
MR	Mission Radius (MCD)
MR	Mission Ready [Aircraft]
MR	Mission Reliability
MR	Mission Report [NASA]
MR	Mission Requirements (ACAE)
Mr	Mister (WDAA)
MR	Mister
MR	Mistura [Mixture] [Pharmacy] (ROG)
MR	Mitochondriarich [Cytology]
MR	Mitral Reflux [Cardiology] (MAE)
MR	Mitral Regurgitation [Cardiology]
MR	Mittleres Reich in Aegypten [A publication] (BJA)
M/R	Mixture Radio (SAUS)
MR	Mixture Ratio (KSC)
Mr	Mobile Revertant [Bacteriology]
MR	Mobility Required [Civil Service]
MR	Mobilizacion Republicana [Republican Mobilization] [Nicaragua] [Political party] (AD)
MR	Mobilization Regulation [Army]
MR	MODEM Ready [Computer science]
MR	Moderately Resistant [Plant pathology]
MR	[The] Modern Reader's Bible (1907) [A publication] (BJA)
M-R	Modification and Restriction [of DNA] [Biochemistry, genetics]
MR	Modification Request [or Requirement]
MR	Modified Road (SAUO)
MR	Modular Redundancy
MR	Modulation Rate (DB)
MR	Modulation Response
MR	Moisture Resistant (IEEE)
MR	Molar Refraction
MR	Molecular Replacement [Crystallography]
MR	Moment of Resistance
MR	Mondcivitan Republic [Defunct] (EAIO)
MR	Monitor Recorder
MR	Monon Railroad (AD)
MR	Monthly Rental (VLIE)
MR	Monthly Report
MR	Monthly Review
MR	Moon Rise (DNAB)
MR	Morgan Refractories Limited (SAUO)
MR	Morgan's Foods, Inc. [AMEX symbol] (SPSG)
MR	Morning Report [Army]
mr	Morocco [MARC country of publication code] [Library of Congress] (LCCP)
MR	Moro's Reflex [Medicine] (MELL)
MR	Morris Register [An association] (EAIO)
MR	Mortality Rates
MR	Mortality Ratio (MAE)
Mr	Mother (AD)
mr	Motivational Research (AD)
MR	Motivation Research
MR	Motormannes Riksforbund [Motorists' Association] [Swedish] (AD)
MR	Motor Reduction
MR	Motor Rifle (CCCA)
MR	Mounted Rifles (SAUO)
MR	Mounted Route (TBD)
MR	Movement Region (SAUO)
MR	Multifamily Residential Zone (AD)
MR	Multi-Mirror Reflector [Lamp]
MR	Multiple Requesting [IBM Corp.]
MR	Multiplier Register
MR	Multi-Reflecton [Lighting]
MR	Multi-Role (SAUS)
MR	Municipal Reform [or Reformer]
MR	Municipal Reform Party (SAUO)
MR	Muscle Receptor [Medicine] (DMAA)
MR	Muscle Relaxant [Medicine] (DMAA)
MR	Music Records [Record label]
MR	Muster Report
MR	Mutual Recognition
MR	Mutual Responsibility [Movement within Anglican Communion to make its mission more efficacious]
MR	Mycorrhizal Roots [Botany]
MR	Radiolocation Mobile Station [ITU designation]
MR	Reading Public Library, Reading, MA [Library symbol] [Library of Congress] (LCLS)
mr---	Red Sea and Area [MARC geographic area code] [Library of Congress] (LCCP)
Mr	Relative Molecular Mass (DOG)
MR1	Machinery Repairman, First Class [Navy rating]
MR2	Machinery Repairman, Second Class [Navy rating]
MR3	Machinery Repairman, Third Class [Navy rating]
MR-13	Movimiento Revolucionario 13 de Noviembre [November 13 Revolutionary Movement] [Guatemala]
MR-13 Movement of 13 NoGuatemala...	Movimiento Revolucionario de 13 de Noviembre [Revolutionary Movement of 13 November] [Guatemala] [Political party] (AD)
MRA	Golden Myra Resources, Inc. [Toronto Stock Exchange symbol]
MRA	Machine Readable Archives Division [Public Archives of Canada] [Information service or system] (IID)
MRA	Machine Records Activity
MRA	Magnetic Reaction Analyzer (PDAA)
MRA	Magnetic Resonance Angiography [Medicine] (DMAA)
MRA	Main Renal Artery [Medicine] (DB)
MRA	Main Ring Assembly (SAUS)
MRA	Maneuver Right Area [Army]
MRA	Manufacturers Representatives of America (EA)
MRA	Marine Reserves Act (SAUO)
MRA	Maritime Royal Artillery [British military] (DMA)
MRA	Marketing Research Association [Chicago, IL] (EA)
MRA	Marrow Repopulating Activity [Medicine] (DB)
MRA	Martinaire [ICAO designator] (FAAC)
MRA	Masonic Relief Association of USA and Canada (EA)
MRA	Master of Recreation Administration (GAGS)
MRA	Master of Rehabilitation Administration (GAGS)
MRA	Master of Resource Administration (GAGS)
MRA	Master Retailers Association (AD)
MRA	Material Review Activity
MRA	Materials Requirement Analysis (PDAA)
MRA	Materials Review Area (AAG)
MRA	Matrix Reducibility Algorithm (PDAA)
MRA	Maximum Rendezvous Altitude
MRA	Mazda Research & Development of North America
MR-A	Mean Reference Axis (MCD)
MRA	Mean Right Atrial [Cardiology]
MRA	Mechanical Readiness Assessment (NASA)

MRA	Medial Right Abdomen [*Injection site*]
MRA	Medical Record Administrator
MRA	Medical Record Analyst (HCT)
MRA	Medical Resource Co. of America [*AMEX symbol*] (SPSG)
mra	Medium-Powered Radio Range (AD)
MRA	Medium-Powered Radio Range (Adcock)
MRA	Men's Rights Association (EA)
MRA	Menswear Retailers of America (EA)
MRA	Messtechnik, Regelungstechnik, Automatik [*Hoppenstedt Wirtschaftsdatenbank GmbH*] [*Germany*] [*Information service or system*] (CRD)
mra	Metro Rating Area (AD)
MRA	Metro Rating Area [*Arbitron television ratings*] (NTCM)
MRA	Microgravity Research Associates
MRA	Midwest Resources Association [*Defunct*]
mra	Minimum Reception Altitude (AD)
MRA	Minimum Reception Altitude [*Aviation*]
MRA	Minimum Reserve Authorization
MRA	Minimum Resolvable Angle
MRA	Minimum Retirement Age (GFGA)
MRA	Ministry for Rural Affairs [*British*] (WDAA)
MRA	Missile RADAR Altimeter (MCD)
MRA	Mission Ready and Available (ACAE)
MRA	Misurata [*Libya*] [*Airport symbol*] (OAG)
MRA	Mixed Refrigerant Autocascade [*Cryogenic system*]
MRA	Model Reporting Area [*for Blindness Statistics*] [*HEW*]
MRA	Module Rack Assembly
MRA	Moral Re-Armament (EA)
MRA	Motorcycle Retailers of America [*Later, NMRA*] (EA)
MRA	Mountain Rescue Association (EA)
MRA	Multiple Recording Accelerometer
MRA	Multiple Regression Analysis
MRA	Multiple Resource Area Nomination [*National Register of Historic Places*]
MRA	Multi Resolutions Analysis (SAUS)
MRA	Multivariate Regression Analysis [*Medicine*] (DMAA)
MRA	Mutual Recognition Agreement (SAUO)
MRA	Mycelium Radius Atrovirens [*A fungus*]
MRA	Rapid City Regional Library, Manitoba [*Library symbol*] [*National Library of Canada*] (NLC)
MRAA	Marine Retailers Association of America (EA)
MRAA	Mental Retardation Association of America (EA)
MRAALS	Marine Corps Remote Area Approach and Landing System (MCD)
mraam	Medium-Range Air-to-Air Missile [*Military*] (AD)
MRAAM	Medium-Range Air-to-Air Missile (MCD)
MRA&L	Manpower Accounting System (SAUO)
MRA & L	Manpower, Reserve Affairs and Logistics (MCD)
mrac	Manifold-Regulator Accumulator Charging (AD)
MRAC	Manifold-Regulator Accumulator Charging [*Formerly, NCP*] (AAG)
MRAC	Member of the Royal Agricultural College [*British*]
MRAC	Meter-Reading Access Circuit [*Bell Laboratories*]
MRAC	Model Reference Adaptive Control (VLIE)
MRACGP	Member of the Royal Australasian College of General Practice (BABM)
MRACO	Member of the Royal Australasian College of Ophthalmologists [*British*] (BABM)
MRACP	Member of Royal Australasian College of Physicians
MRACR	Member of Royal Australasian College of Radiologists [*British*] (BABM)
MRACS	Model Reference Adaptive Control System (VLIE)
MRAD	Mass Random Access Disk [*Computer science*]
M Rad	Master of Radiology
mrad	Megarad (AD)
MRAD	Microwave Radiometer (ACAE)
mrad	Millirad (AD)
mrad	Milliradian (IDOE)
MRAD	Milliradians (KSC)
MRAD	Minor Restricted Activity Day [*Environmental medicine*]
MRAD	Multiple Range Alignment Device [*Army*] (INF)
MRadA	Member of the Radionic Association [*British*]
M Rad (D)	Master of Radiology (Radiodiagnosis)
MRAD/IN	Milliradians per Inch
MRADS	Mass Random Access Data Storage [*Computer science*]
M Rad (T)	Master of Radiology (Radiotherapy)
M Ra E	Master of Radio Engineering
M Ra Eng	Master of Radio Engineering
MRAeS	Member of the Royal Aeronautical Society [*British*] (ADA)
MRAF	Marshal of the Royal Air Force [*British*]
MRAF	Missile Round Assembly Facility
M-RAG	Moderately Repressive Authoritarian Government
MRAIC	Member of the Royal Architectural Institute of Canada
MRAJ	Aranjuez [*Costa Rica*] [*ICAO location identifier*] (ICLI)
MRaK	Myth, Ritual, and Kingship. Essays on the Theory and Practice of Kingship in theAncient Near East and in Israel [*A publication*] (BJA)
MRAL	Alajuela [*Costa Rica*] [*ICAO location identifier*] (ICLI)
MRAL	Mandatory Retirement Age Law of 1978 (WYGK)
MRAL	Materiel Readiness Authorization List [*Military*]
MRAL	Mobile Radionuclide Analysis Laboratory (SAUO)
MRAM	Amubri [*Costa Rica*] [*ICAO location identifier*] (ICLI)
MRAM	Magnetic Random-Access Memory [*Computer science*] (PS)
MRAM	Member of the Royal Academy of Music [*British*]
MRAM	Multi-Mission Redeye Air-Launched Missile [*Military*] (PDAA)
MRAN	Medical Resident Admitting Note (MEDA)
MR & A	Market Research and Analysis

MR & D	Material Redistribution and Disposal
MR & DA	Material Redistribution and Disposal Administration
MR & DC	Medical Research and Development Command [*Army*] (AD)
MR&DF	Malleable Research and Development Foundation (AD)
MR&E	Mobile Reclamation & Repair (SAUS)
MR & S	Materials Research and Standards (AD)
MR & T	Mississippi River and Tributaries [*Flood-control project*]
MRANZCP	Member of the Royal Australian and New Zealand College of Psychiatrists [*British*] (BABM)
MRAO	Mobilization Reserve Acquisition Objective [*Military*]
MRAO	Mullard Radio Astronomy Observatory (USDC)
MRAP	Management Review and Analysis Program (AD)
MRAP	Marginal Revenue/Average Physical Product [*Economics*]
MRAP	Mean Right Atrial Pressure [*Cardiology*]
MRAP	Mortgage and Rental Assistance Program [*Australia*]
MRAP	Mouvement Contre le Racisme et pour l'Amitie Entre les Peuples [*Movement Against Racism and for Friendship between People*] (EAIO)
MRAP	Movement Against Racism and for Friendship between Peoples (SAUO)
MRAP	Movimiento de Resistencia Armada Puertorriquena [*Puerto Rican Armed Resistance Movement*] [*Political party*] (PD)
MRAPCON	Mobile RADAR Approach Control (AFM)
MRAPM	Materials Research and Protection Methods (SAA)
MRAR	Atirro [*Costa Rica*] [*ICAO location identifier*] (ICLI)
MRAR	Manpower Requirements Analysis Report [*Military*]
MRAS	Main Renal Artery Stenosis [*Medicine*] (DMAA)
MRAS	Management Resources Accounting System
MRAS	Manpower Resources Accounting System [*Air Force*]
MRAS	Member of the Royal Academy of Science [*British*]
MRAS	Member of the Royal Asiatic Society [*British*]
MRAS	Member of the Royal Astronomical Society [*British*] (DI)
MRAS	Model Reference Adaptive System (PDAA)
MRASB	Member of the Royal Asiatic Society of Bengal
MRASE	Member of the Royal Agricultural Society of England
mrasm	Medium-Range Air-to-Surface Missile [*Military*] (AD)
MRASM	Medium-Range Air-to-Surface Missile (MCD)
MRASTU	Marine Reserve Aviation Supply Training Unit (DNAB)
MRAT	Altamira De San Carlos [*Costa Rica*] [*ICAO location identifier*] (ICLI)
mrat	Medium-Range Applied Technology (AD)
MRAT	Mobile Radiation Tester (IAA)
MRATE	Money Market Rates [*I. P. Sharp Associates*] [*Canada*] [*Information service or system*] (CRD)
MRATGW	Medium Range ATGW (SAUS)
MR ATOMIC	Multiple Rapid Automatic Test of Monolithic Integrated Circuits (PDAA)
MRAUSCAN	Masonic Relief Association of the United States and Canada (AD)
MRB	Magnetic Recording Boresight [*or Borescope*]
MRB	Magnetospheric Radio Burst
MRB	Maintenance Review Board (MCD)
MRB	Malaysian Rubber Bureau (EA)
MRB	Management Reserve Budget (SAUO)
MRB	Management Review Board (SAUO)
MRB	Marble [*Technical drawings*]
MRB	Marble Base (AAG)
mrb	Marble Base (AD)
MRB	Martinsburg, WV [*Location identifier*] [*FAA*] (FAAL)
MRB	Master Reference Buoy [*Navy*] (NVT)
MRB	Material Review Board [*Aviation*] (MCD)
MRB	Medium Range Blast (SAUS)
MRB	Mersey River Board (SAUO)
MRB	Metals Reserve Board [*of the Reconstruction Finance Corp.*]
MRB	Method Request Broker (SAUO)
MRB	Microcircuit Reliability Bibliography (NITA)
MRB	Mileage Rationing Board [*World War II*]
MRB	Missile Review Board (SAUO)
MRB	Mission Review Board [*NASA*]
MRB	Mister Build Industry, Inc. [*Vancouver Stock Exchange symbol*]
MRB	Mobile Radio Broadcasting (SAUO)
MRB	Mobile Riverine Base [*Navy*]
MRB	Modification Requirements Board [*NASA*] (KSC)
MRB	Modification Review Board (AFM)
MRB	Mortgage Revenue Bond
MRB	Mortgage Review Board (SAUO)
MRB	Motorized Rifle Battalion [*Former USSR*]
MRB	Motor Rescue Boat
MRB	Motor Surfboat [*Coast Guard*] (DNAB)
MRB	Motor Truck Rate Bureau Inc., Columbia SC [*STAC*]
MRB	Multi-Role Boat (SAUS)
MRB	Multi-Role Bomber [*Program*] [*DoD*]
MRB	Mutual Reinsurance Bureau (EA)
MRBA	Buenos Aires [*Costa Rica*] [*ICAO location identifier*] (ICLI)
MRBA	Marimba, Inc. [*NASDAQ symbol*] (SG)
MRBA	Mississippi River Bridge Authority (AD)
MRBB	Babilonia [*Costa Rica*] [*ICAO location identifier*] (ICLI)
MRBC	Barra Del Colorado [*Costa Rica*] [*ICAO location identifier*] (ICLI)
MRBC	Missouri River Basin Commission
MRBC	Molded Rubber Blended Cover
MRBC	Monkey Red Blood Cells
MRBC	Mouse Red Blood Cell [*Medicine*] (DMAA)
MRBC	Multiple Resolution Bitmap Compiler (SAUS)
MRBCMA	Mean Rounds between Corrective Maintenance Actions [*Quality control*] (MCD)
MR-BD	Mercury-Redstone Booster Development [*Spacecraft*] [*NASA*]
MRBF	Mean Renal Blood Flow [*Nephrology*]

MRBF..........	Mean Rounds between Failures [*Military*] (CAAL)
MRBI	Market Research Bureau Ireland (SAUO)
MRBIR	Municipal Registered Bond Interest Record [*Standard & Poor's Corp.*] [*Information service or system*] (CRD)
MRBK	Mercantile Bankshares [*NASDAQ symbol*] (TTSB)
MRBK	Mercantile Bankshares Corp. [*NASDAQ symbol*] (NQ)
MRBL..........	Marble
MRBL	Marble Financial Corp. [*NASDAQ symbol*] (NQ)
MRBM	Bremen [*Costa Rica*] [*ICAO location identifier*] (ICLI)
MRBM	Medium [*or Mid*]-Range Ballistic Missile
mrbm..........	Medium-Range Ballistic Missile [*Military*] (AD)
MRBN	Bataan [*Costa Rica*] [*ICAO location identifier*] (ICLI)
MRBNA	Member of the Royal British Nursing Association (ROG)
MRBO	Boca Naranjo [*Costa Rica*] [*ICAO location identifier*] (ICLI)
MRBOMF	Mean Rounds between Operational Mission Failures [*Quality control*] (MCD)
MRBP	Barra De Parismina [*Costa Rica*] [*ICAO location identifier*] (ICLI)
MRBP	Missouri River Basin Project
MRBS	Mean Rounds between Stoppages [*Quality control*] (MCD)
MRBS	Medium Range Bit Synchronizer (ACAE)
MRBS	Modified Road Brigade Slice (MCD)
MRBT	Barra De Tortuguero [*Costa Rica*] [*ICAO location identifier*] (ICLI)
MRBT	Multirod Burst Test [*Nuclear energy*] (NRCH)
MRC............	Columbia/Mt. Pleasant, TN [*Location identifier*] [*FAA*] (FAAL)
MRC............	Graduate Center for Materials Research [*University of Missouri - Rolla*] [*Research center*] (RCD)
MRC............	Interdepartmental Committee on Manpower Requirements [*British*] [*World War II*]
MRC............	Machine-Readable Code
MRC............	Machinery Repairman, Chief [*Navy rating*]
mrc............	Magnetic Rectifier Control (AD)
MRC............	Magnetic Rectifier Control
MRC............	Magnetic Research Corp. (MCD)
MRC............	Magneto-Resistive Cluster (SAUS)
MRC............	Mail Reminder Card (SAUS)
MRC............	Maintenance and Repair Craft [*Military*]
MRC............	Maintenance and Repair Cycle
MRC............	Maintenance Requirement Card
MRC............	Major Readiness Command (MCD)
MRC............	Major Reality Corp. (EFIS)
MRC............	Major Regional Conflict (SAUO)
MRC............	Major Regional Contingency (DOMA)
MRC............	Major Renal Calix [*Medicine*] (MELL)
MRC............	Major Retail Center
MRC............	Malaria Research Centre [*India*]
MRC............	Management Research Center [*University of Wisconsin - Milwaukee*] [*Research center*] (RCD)
MRC............	Management Research Corp. [*Shelbyville, IN*] [*Information service or system*] (IID)
MRC............	Manitoba Research Council [*Research center*] (RCD)
MRC............	Manpower Requirements Change [*Military*] (GFGA)
MRC............	Manufacturing Resource Control [*Kongsberg Vaapenfabrikk*] [*Software package*] (NCC)
MRC............	Manufacturing Rules Checker (TIMI)
MRC............	Maracas
MRC............	Marietta College, Marietta, OH [*OCLC symbol*] (OCLC)
MRC............	Marine Research Committee
MRC............	Marine Research Corp. [*Marine science*] (OSRA)
MRC............	Marine Resources Council
MRC............	Marketing Research Council (NTPA)
MRC............	Market Research Council
MRC............	Marlin-Rockwell Corp. (AD)
MRC............	Massachusetts Rehabilitation Commission (SAUO)
MRC............	Master of Rehabilitation Counseling
MRC............	Master Requirements Code
MRC............	Master Routing Control (SAA)
MRC............	Material Redistribution Center
MRC............	Materials Research Center [*Lehigh University*] (RCD)
MRC............	Materials Research Center [*Northwestern University*] (RCD)
MRC............	Materials Research Corp.
MRC............	Materials Review Crib (AAG)
MRC............	Materiel Readiness Command [*Military*]
MRC............	Materiel Release Confirmation [*Army*] (AABC)
MRC............	Mathematics Research Center (MCD)
Mrc............	Mauricio [*Mauritius*] [*Spanish*] (AD)
MRC............	Maximum Recycling Capacity (DMAA)
MRC............	Maximum Reverse Current
MRC............	Measurement Requirements Committee [*NASA*] (NASA)
MRC............	Measurement Research Center [*University of Iowa*]
MRC............	Media Resource Center [*Adelaide, Australia*]
MRC............	Media Resource Controller (ACAE)
MRC............	Medical Registration Council [*British*] (DAVI)
MRC............	Medical Research Center (SAUO)
MRC............	Medical Research Committee
MRC............	Medical Research Council [*Research center*] [*British*] (IRC)
MRC............	Medical Research Council of South Africa (SAUO)
MRC............	Medical Reserve Corps
MRC............	Mekong River Commission [*Thailand*]
MRC............	Memorial Research Center [*University of Tennessee*] [*Research center*] (RCD)
MRC............	Memory Request Controller
MRC............	Men's Republican Club (NADA)
MRC............	Men's Resource Center (EA)
MRC............	Men's Resource Connection [*An association*] (EA)
MRC............	Message-based Reliable Channel (SAUS)

MRC............	Metabolic Clearance Rate (DB)
MRC............	Metals Reserve Co. [*World War II*]
MRC............	Metals Reserve Company (SAUO)
MRC............	Meteorological Research Committee [*British*]
MRC............	Methods Research Corp. (AD)
MRC............	Methylrosaniline Chloride [*Also, GV*] [*A dye*]
MRC............	Metrics Research Corp. [*Information service or system*] (IID)
MRC............	Microwave Radio Corp. (SAUS)
MRC............	Mid-Roll Change Capability
MRC............	Mid-Roll Interchange [*Advanced photo system*]
MRC............	Midwestern Relay Co. [*Milwaukee, WI*] [*Telecommunications*] (TSSD)
MRC............	Military Reform Caucus (EA)
MRC............	Military Region Command (MCD)
MRC............	Military Representatives Committee [*NATO*] (NATG)
MRC............	Military Reunions Council (EA)
MRC............	Military Revolutionary Council (CINC)
MRC............	Miniature Rifle Club (SAUO)
MRC............	Minnesota Restitution Center (AD)
MRC............	Minorco Canada Ltd. [*Toronto Stock Exchange symbol*]
MRC............	Minor Renal Calix [*Medicine*] (MELL)
MRC............	Missile Research Corp.
MRC............	Mission Requirements Change [*NASA*] (KSC)
MRC............	Mission Research Corporation (SAUO)
MRC............	Mission Resources Center [*Sydney, Australia*]
MRC............	Mississippi River Commission [*Vicksburg, MS*] [*Army*]
MRC............	Mobile Radio Communications
MRC............	Model Railway Club [*British*]
MRC............	Modern Railroad Club (AD)
MRC............	Modified River Compatible Alteration (SAUO)
MRC............	Monterey Resources, Inc. [*NYSE symbol*] (SAG)
MRC............	Monthly Recurring Charge (SAUO)
MRC............	Montrose [*Colorado*] [*Seismograph station code, US Geological Survey*] [*Closed*] (SEIS)
MRC............	Moon's RADAR Coordinates
MRC............	Morning Readiness Check
MRC............	Motorized Rifle Co. (INF)
MRC............	Motor Racing Club (AD)
MRC............	Mouvement des Renovateurs Communistes [*France*] [*Political party*] (EY)
MRC............	Movement Report Center [*Military*]
MRC............	Mueller-Ribbing-Clement [*Syndrome*] [*Medicine*] (DB)
MRC............	Multiple Register Counter (IEEE)
MRC............	Multiple Regression/Correlation [*Statistical analysis*]
MRCA	Canas [*Costa Rica*] [*ICAO location identifier*] (ICLI)
MRCA	Market Research Corp. of America (AD)
MRCA	Member of the Royal College of Anaesthetists (SAUO)
MRCA	Most Recent Common Ancestor
mrca	Multirole Combat Aircraft (AD)
MRCA	Multirole Combat Aircraft
MRCAS	Monetary Ration Credit Allowance System [*Military*] (AFM)
MRCAT	Miniature Radio-Controlled Aerial Target (MCD)
MrcBnc	Merchants Bancshares [*Associated Press*] (SAG)
MRCC	Coto 47 [*Costa Rica*] [*ICAO location identifier*] (ICLI)
MRCC	Maritime Rescue Coordination Center [*Australia*]
MRCC	Material Review Central Control [*Aviation*] (MCD)
MRCC	Medical Research Council of Canada (BARN)
MRCC	Member of the Royal College of Chemistry [*British*]
MRCC	Mercury Recovery Control Center
MRCC	Molded Rubber Coupling Cushion
MRCC	Movement Report Control Center [*Military*]
MRCC	Multibus Remote Channel Controller (TIMI)
MRCCC	Medical Research Council, Collaborative Centre [*British*] (CB)
MRCD	Caledonia [*Costa Rica*] [*ICAO location identifier*] (ICLI)
MRCD	Memory Raster Colour Display (PDAA)
MRCD	Movement for Responsible Coastal Development (SAUO)
MRCE..........	Carate [*Costa Rica*] [*ICAO location identifier*] (ICLI)
MRCE..........	Marginal Relative Certainty Effect [*Statistics*]
MRCF..........	Martin Color-Fi, Inc. [*NASDAQ symbol*] (SAG)
MRCF..........	Mayo Biotechnology Research Computer Facility [*Mayo Clinic*] [*Research center*] (RCD)
MRCF..........	Microsoft Real-Time Compression Format [*Microsoft Corp.*] (PCM)
MRCF..........	Missile Recycle Facility (SAA)
MRCF..........	Module Repair Calibration Facility
MRCGP........	Member of the Royal College of General Practitioners [*British*]
MRCGP........	Member, Royal College of General Practice [*British*] (CMD)
MRCH	Chacarita [*Costa Rica*] [*ICAO location identifier*] (ICLI)
MrchBcp	Merchants Bcp. [*Associated Press*] (SAG)
MrchBnc	Merchants Bancshares, Inc. [*Associated Press*] (SAG)
MrchGp	Merchants Group, Inc. [*Associated Press*] (SAG)
MRCHNT......	Merchant
MRCI	Ciruelas [*Costa Rica*] [*ICAO location identifier*] (ICLI)
MRCI	Maximum Rescue Coverage Intercept [*Environmental science*] (COE)
MRCI	Medical Registration Council of Ireland (AD)
MRCI	Medical Research Council of Ireland (SLS)
MRCI	Microsoft Real-Time Compression Interface [*Microsoft Corp.*] (PCM)
MRCI	Mine Readiness/Certification Inspection (MCD)
MRCI	Modular Re-configurable C4I Interface (SAUS)
MRCI	Multireference Configuration Interaction [*Quantum chemistry*] (MCD)
MRCL..........	Master Cross-Reference List
MRCL..........	Medical Research Council Laboratories (SAUO)
MRCL..........	Mercurial
MRCLOS	Missile Reference Command-to-Line-Of-Sight (SAUS)
MRCM	Machinery Repairman, Master Chief [*Navy rating*]
MRCMC	Murrumbidgee Regional Catchment Management Committee (SAUO)
MRCMCCR...	Medical Responsibility Center Manager Cost Center Report (SAUO)

MRCN	Minuteman Requirement Control Number (SAA)
MRCo	Malaysian Refrigerator Co. (AD)
MRCO	Manufacturing Research Corp. of Ontario [*Research center*] [*Canada*] (RCD)
MRCO	Member of the Royal College of Ophthalmologists (SAUO)
MRCO	Member of the Royal College of Organists [*British*]
MRCO	Meridian National Corp. [*NASDAQ symbol*] (NQ)
MRCOA	Medical Research Council Trial in Older Adults
MRCOG	Member of the Royal College of Obstetricians and Gynaecologists [*British*]
MRCOL	Meridian Natl Wrrt'A' [*NASDAQ symbol*] (TTSB)
MRCOP	Meridan Natl $3.75 Cv'B'Pfd [*NASDAQ symbol*] (TTSB)
MRCOZ	Meridian Natl Wrrt [*NASDAQ symbol*] (TTSB)
MRCP	Maoist Revolutionary Communist Party [*Political party*] (AD)
MRCP	Master of Regional and City Planning (PGP)
MRCP	Master of Regional and Community Planning (GAGS)
MRCP	Member of the Royal College of Physicians [*British*]
MRCP	Member of the Royal College of Preceptors [*British*]
MRCP	Microfilm Research Centers Project [*Defunct*] (EA)
MRCP	Mobile RADAR Control Post
MRCPA	Mobilization Reserve Components Program of the Army (AABC)
MRC Path	Member of the Royal College of Pathologists [*British*]
MRCPCH	Member of the Royal College of Paediatrics and Child Health (SAUO)
MRCPE	Member of the Royal College of Physicians, Edinburgh
MRCPEd	Member of the Royal College of Physicians of Edinburgh
MRCP Edin	Member of the Royal College of Physicians of Edinburgh
MRCPGlas	Member of the Royal College of Physicians of Glasgow
MRCP (Glasg)	Member of the Royal College of Physicians and Surgeons of Glasgow (AAMN)
MRCP Glasg	Member of the Royal College of Physicians of Glasgow
MRCPI	Member of the Royal College of Physicians of Ireland
MRCP Ire	Member of the Royal College of Physicians of Ireland (SAUO)
MRCP Irel	Member of the Royal College of Physicians of Ireland
MRC Psych	Member of the Royal College of Psychiatrists [*British*]
MRCPUK	Member of the Royal College of Physicians of the United Kingdom [*British*] (AD)
MRCP UK	Member of the Royal Colleges of Physicians of the United Kingdom
MRCR	Carrillo [*Costa Rica*] [*ICAO location identifier*] (ICLI)
MRCR	Measurement Requirement Change Request [*NASA*] (KSC)
MRCR	Member of the Royal College of Radiologists (SAUO)
MRCRR	Machine-Readable Collections Reading Room [*Library of Congress*] (IT)
MRCS	Machinery Repairman, Senior Chief [*Navy rating*]
MRCS	Mechanoreceptor Cueing Subsystem (MCD)
MRCS	Medium Resolution Camera System (MCD)
MRCS	Member of the Royal College of Surgeons [*British*]
MRCS	Missile Range Calibration Satellite
MRCS	Mobile Reporting & Control System (SAUS)
MRCS	Multiple Report Creation System
MRCS	Multiple RPV [*Remotely Piloted Vehicle*] Control System (PDAA)
MRCSA	Migrant Resource Center of South Australia
MRCSE	Member of the Royal College of Surgeons, Edinburgh
MRCSI	Member of the Royal College of Surgeons, Ireland (ROG)
MRCTS	Missile Round Cable Test System
MRCU	Mini-Remote Control Unit (MHDI)
MRCV	Cabo Velas [*Costa Rica*] [*ICAO location identifier*] (ICLI)
MRCV	Mixture Ratio Control Valve (KSC)
MRCV	Multi-Role Combat Vehicle (SAUS)
MRCVS	Member of the Royal College of Veterinary Surgeons [*British*] (EY)
MRCWA	Midland Railway Company of Western Australia (AD)
MRCY	Mercury General [*NASDAQ symbol*] (TTSB)
MRCY	Mercury General Corp. [*NASDAQ symbol*] (NQ)
MRCZ	Carrizal [*Costa Rica*] [*ICAO location identifier*] (ICLI)
MRCZ	Medical Research Council of Zimbabwe (SAUO)
MRD	MacDermid, Inc. [*NYSE symbol*] (SG)
MRD	Main Roads Department (SAUO)
MRD	Maintenance Requirements Documents (CTAS)
MRD	Management Review Division (SAUO)
MRD	Mandatory Retirement Date [*Army*] (AABC)
MRD	Manual Ringdown [*Telecommunications*] (TEL)
MRD	Margin-Reflex Distance (SAUS)
MRD	Maritime Research Department [*An association*] [*Inactive*] (EA)
MRD	Marketing Requirement Document
MRD	Master Requirements Directory [*Military*] (AFM)
MRD	Material Required Date
MRD	Material Requirement Document (SAUO)
MRD	Material Requirements Deck (AAG)
MRD	Material Requirements Drawing (MCD)
MRD	Material Review Disposition [*Aviation*]
MRD	Materials Required Data (SAUO)
MRD	Materiel Redistribution Division [*Army*] (AFIT)
MRD	Materiel Release Denial [*Military*] (AABC)
MRD	Materiel Requirements Document [*Army*]
MRD	McCloud Ranger District (SAUO)
MRD	Measuring & Reference Device (SAUS)
MRD	Media Review Digest
MRD	Medical Records Department (DAVI)
MRD	Medical Reference Department (AD)
MRD	Medical Research Division
MRD	Medium Rate Demodulator (ACAE)
MRD	Melcor Developments Ltd. [*Toronto Stock Exchange symbol*]
MRD	Memorandum for Regional Directors (AAGC)
MRD	Memory Raster Display [*Computer science*]
MRD	Memory Read [*Computer science*] (MHDI)
MRD	Merida [*Venezuela*] [*Airport symbol*] (OAG)
MRD	Meridian Air Cargo, Inc. [*ICAO designator*] (FAAC)
MRD	Mesoscale Research Division [*National Severe Storms Laboratory*] (USDC)
MRD	Metabolic Renal Disease [*Medicine*] (MELL)
mrd	Metal Rolling Door (AD)
MRD	Metal Rolling Door [*Technical drawings*]
mrd	Metal Roof Deck (AD)
MRD	Metal Roof Deck [*Technical drawings*]
MRD	Methane Response Definition [*Automotive emissions*]
MRD	Microbiological Research Department (AD)
MRD	Milestone Review Documentation [*Army*]
MRD	Military Reference Data
MRD	Military Requirements Determination
mrd	Millirutherford
MRD	Minimal Renal Disease [*Medicine*] (MELL)
MRD	Minimal Residual Disease [*Medicine*]
mrd	Minimum Reacting Dose (AD)
MRD	Minimum Reacting Dose
MRD	Mission Rehearsal Device (SAUS)
MRD	Mission Requirements Document [*NASA*] (KSC)
MRD	Mississippi River Division [*Army Corps of Engineers*]
MRD	Missouri River Division [*Army Corps of Engineers*]
MRD	Mobil Research & Development Corp., Engineering Information Center, Princeton, NJ [*OCLC symbol*] (OCLC)
MRD	Monostable Relay Driver
MRD	Morpholinodaunorubicin [*Also, MoDNM*] [*Antineoplastic drug*]
MRD	Mortality Rate to Double
MRD	Motorized Rifle Division [*Military*] (AD)
MRD	Motor Racing Developments
MRD	Motor Receiving Dolly
MRD	Movement for the Restoration of Democracy [*Pakistan*] [*Political party*] (PD)
MRD	Movement for the Restoration of Democracy [*Nepal*] [*Political party*]
MRD	Multireference Double Excitation [*Physics*]
MRD	Russell and District Regional Library, Russell, Manitoba [*Library symbol*] [*National Library of Canada*] (NLC)
MRDA	Maintenance Requirement Development Activity [*Military*] (CAAL)
MRDA	Media Research Directors Association (EA)
MRDA	Mission Requirements Definition and Analysis (SAUO)
MRDA	Mundri Relief and Development International Committee (SAUO)
MRDAC	Manpower Research and Data Analysis Center [*DoD*] (DNAB)
MRDB	Materiel Returns Data Base (SAUO)
MRDB	Mission Requirements Data Base [*NASA*] (SSD)
MRDC	Medical Research and Development Command [*Frederick, MD*] [*Army*]
MRDC	Microelectronic Research and Development Center (SAUO)
MRDC	Military Requirement and Development Committee (NATG)
MRDC	Military Research and Development Center [*US-Thailand*]
MRDC	Missile Research and Development Command [*Army*] (MCD)
MRDC	Module RADAR Display Console
MRDCC	Metropolitan Refuse Disposal Consultative Committee [*Melbourne, Australia*]
MRDD	Don Diego [*Costa Rica*] [*ICAO location identifier*] (ICLI)
MR/DD	Mentally Retarded and Developmentally Disabled
MRDD	Mental Retardation and Developmental Disabilities [*National Institutes of Health*]
MRDE	Mining Research and Development Establishment [*National Coal Board*] [*British*]
MRDEC	Missile Research Development and Engineering Center [*Formerly, Army Missile Laboratory*] (RDA)
mrdf	Machine-Readable Data Files [*Computer science*] (AD)
MRDF	Machine-Readable Data Files
MRDF	Marine Resources Development Foundation
MRDF	Maritime Radio Direction Finding
MRDF	Metals Research and Development Foundation [*Defunct*] (EA)
MRDFS	Manpack Radio Direction Finding System (SAUO)
MRDFS	Man-Portable Radio Direction-Finding System
MRDG	Manufacturing Research and Design Group [*McMaster University*] [*Canada*] [*Research center*] (RCD)
MRDGP	Mackay Region Division of General Practice (SAUO)
mrdhd	Maximum Recommended Daily Human Dose (AD)
MRDIS	Message Reproduction and Distribution System [*Military*] (CAAL)
MRDL	Mean Reciprocal Detection Latency
MRDL	Mineral Resurces Development Laboratory [*Australia*]
MRDL	Missouri River Division Laboratory [*Army Corps of Engineers*]
MRDM	Malnutrition Related Diabetes Mellitus (SAUS)
MRDN	Material Receipt Discrepancy Notice (AD)
MRDN	Meridian Bancorp, Inc. [*NASDAQ symbol*] (NQ)
MrdN	Meridian National Corp. [*Associated Press*] (SAG)
MRDN	Mouvement Revolutionnaire pour la Democratie Nouvelle [*Revolutionary Movement for New Democracy*] [*Senegal*] (PD)
MrdN 99	Meridian National Corp. [*Associated Press*] (SAG)
MrdnBc	Meridian Bancorp, Inc. [*Associated Press*] (SAG)
MRDNL	Meridional
MRDO	Dieciocho [*Costa Rica*] [*ICAO location identifier*] (ICLI)
MRDOS	Mapped Real-Time Disk Operating System [*Computer science*] (MDG)
MRDR	Material Receipt Discrepancy Record
MRDR	Material Review Disposition Record (NASA)
MRDS	Maintenance Ratio at Direct Support level (SAUO)
MRDS	Maintenance Requirements Data Systems (SAUO)
MRDS	Malfunction Rate Detection System (DNAB)
MRDS	MARC [*Machine-Readable Cataloging*] Records Distribution Service [*National Library of Canada*] (IID)
MRDS	Member of the Royal Drawing Society [*British*] (ROG)

MRDS .... Message Reproduction and Distribution System [*Military*] (MCD)
MRDS .... Mineral Resources Data System [*US Geological Survey*] [*Information service or system*] (IID)
MRDS .... Mission Recorder Display Set (MCD)
MRDS .... Modular Responsive Defense System
MRDS .... Molded Rubber Duct System
MRDT .... Mortality Rate Doubling Time
MRDTI .... Metal Roof Deck Technical Institute [*Later, Steel Deck Institute*] (EA)
MRDV .... Maize Rough Dwarf Virus [*Plant pathology*]
MRDY .... Message Ready [*Computer science*] (MHDI)
MRE .... Major Research Equipment
MRE .... Malayan Royal Engineers (SAUO)
MRE .... Manicore [*Brazil*] [*Airport symbol*] (AD)
MRE .... Mara Lodges [*Kenya*] [*Airport symbol*] (OAG)
MRE .... Maritime Radio Executive [*British*]
MRE .... Market Research Extracts Report (JAGO)
M Re .... Master of Religion
MRE .... Master of Religious Education
MRE .... Materiel Readiness Expediter [*Army*]
MRE .... Matter (ROG)
MRE .... Maximal Relative Error [*Mathematical statistics*]
MRE .... Maximal Resistive Exercise (DMAA)
MRE .... Maximal Respiratory Effectiveness (DMAA)
MRE .... Mazda Research of Europe [*Automobile manufacturer operations*]
mre .... Meal Ready to Eat (AD)
MRE .... Meal, Ready-to-Eat [*Army rations designation, replaces C-rations*]
MRE .... Meals Rejected by Everyone
mre .... Mean Radial Error (AD)
MRE .... Mean Radial Error
MRE .... Medco Research, Inc. [*AMEX symbol*] (SAG)
MRE .... Melissa Resources, Inc. [*Vancouver Stock Exchange symbol*]
MRE .... Memory Register Exponent [*Computer science*] (MHDI)
MRE .... Metal Regulatory Element [*Genetics*]
MRE .... Metal-Responsive Element [*Genetics*]
MR-E .... Methemoglobin Reductase [*An enzyme*] (MAE)
MRE .... Microbiological Research Establishment [*British*]
MRE .... Microrocket Engine
MRE .... Mid-Range Estimate
MRE .... Militia Royal Engineers [*British military*] (DMA)
MRE .... Missile Recertification Equipment
MRE .... Missile Recycle Equipment (SAA)
MRE .... Mobil Research & Development Corp., Paulsboro, NJ [*OCLC symbol*] (OCLC)
MRE .... Modern Ramjet Engine (MCD)
MRE .... Monopropellant Rocket Engine (SAUS)
MRE .... Morally Repugnant Elite [*Lifestyle classification*] (ECON)
MRE .... Motor Requirement Evaluation (SAUS)
MRE .... Movimiento Revolucionario Espartaco [*Bolivia*] [*Political party*] (PPW)
MRE .... Movimiento Revolucionario Estudantil [*Colombia*] [*Political party*] (EY)
MRE .... Multiple-Response Enable (IEEE)
MREA .... Estero Azul [*Costa Rica*] [*ICAO location identifier*] (ICLI)
MREAC .... Mon Repos Est au Ciel [*My Rest Is in Heaven*] [*Motto of Ludwig Philipp, Count of the Palatinate of Simmern (1602-1654)*] [*French*]
MREAC ...... Murmansk Regional Environmental Affairs Committee (SAUO)
MREC .... El Carmen [*Costa Rica*] [*ICAO location identifier*] (ICLI)
MREC .... Medical Research Ethics Committee
MREC .... Multicentre Research Ethics Committee (SAUO)
MRECM .... Master of Real Estate and Construction Management (GAGS)
MRED .... Master of Real Estate Development (GAGS)
MREd .... Master of Recreation Education (GAGS)
MR Ed .... Master of Religious Education
MREDA .... Marine Resources and Engineering Development Act [*1966*] (MSC)
M Re E .... Master of Refrigeration Engineering
M Re Eng .... Master of Refrigeration Engineering
MREF .... Medical Research Endowment Fund
MRefEng ..... Master of Refrigeration Engineering (NADA)
MREGAD ..... Multiplexer Regenerator Address [*Computer science*] (MHDI)
MRegSc ...... Master of Regional Science (ADA)
MReh .... Blanding Free Public Library, Rehoboth, MA [*Library symbol*] [*Library of Congress*] (LCLS)
MREHIS ...... Member of the Royal Environmental Health Institute of Scotland (DBQ)
MREI .... Marriage Role Expectation Inventory [*Psychology*]
M-REIT .... Mutual Real Estate Investment Trust
M Rel .... Master of Religion (PGP)
MREL .... Mining Resource Engineering Ltd. (SAUO)
MRELB .... Malaysian Rubber Exchange and Licensing Board (AD)
MRelEd ...... Master of Religious Education (GAGS)
mrem .... Millirem
mrem .... Milliroentgen Equivalent Man (AD)
MREM .... Milliroentgen Equivalent Man [*Radiation measurement*]
mrem/h ...... Millirem per Hour (DS)
MREmpS ..... Member of the Royal Empire Society [*British*]
MREM/YR .... Millirems per Year (SAUO)
MREP .... Maneuvering Room Equipment Panel (DNAB)
MREP .... Medical Remedial Enlistment Program (DNAB)
mrep .... Milliroentgen Equivalent Physical (MAE)
MRER .... El Ron Ron [*Costa Rica*] [*ICAO location identifier*] (ICLI)
MRERF .... Manufacturers Representatives Educational Research Foundation [*Rolling Meadows, IL*] (EA)
MRES .... Material Requirements Estimation System [*Navy*]
MRES .... Member of the Royal Entomological Society [*British*] (ROG)
MRES .... Military Requirements Estimation System

MRES .... Missing Research and Enquiry Service (SAUO)
MResEnvS ... Master of Resource and Environmental Studies
MResEnvSt... Master of Resource and Environmental Studies
MRESS .... Marine Recreational Fishing Statistics Survey [*Marine science*] (OSRA)
MResSc ...... Master of Resource Science
MRET .... Esterillos [*Costa Rica*] [*ICAO location identifier*] (ICLI)
M Ret .... Master of Retailing
MRET .... Merit Holding [*NASDAQ symbol*] (TTSB)
MRET .... Merit Holding Corp. [*NASDAQ symbol*] (SAG)
M REV .... Most Reverend
MRev .... Revere Public Library, Revere, MA [*Library symbol*] [*Library of Congress*] (LCLS)
MRF .... Magnetorheological Finishing [*Optics manufacturing*] (RDA)
MRF .... Maintenance and Refurbishment Facility [*NASA*] (KSC)
MRF .... Maintenance Repair Facility
MRF .... Maintenance Repair Frequency
mrf .... Maintenance Replacement Factor (AD)
mrf .... Maintenance Replacement Factor (NG)
MRF .... Maintenance Responsibility File (MCD)
MRF .... Mankind Research Foundation (EA)
MRF .... Marble Floor (AAG)
mrf .... Marble Floor (AD)
MRF .... Marfa, TX [*Location identifier*] [*FAA*] (FAAL)
MRF .... MariFarms, Inc. [*Later, Marine Harvest International*] [*AMEX symbol*] (SPSG)
MRF .... Marine Recreational Fishing [*Marine science*] (MSC)
MRF .... Markov Random Field [*Mathematics*]
MRF .... Materials Recovery Facility [*for recycling of glass, plastics, etc.*]
MRF .... Maternal Resistance Factor (BARN)
MRF .... Maximum Retarding Force (NASA)
MRF .... Mayo Research Foundation (AD)
MRF .... Measurements/Stimuli Request Form [*NASA*] (NASA)
MRF .... Medical Record File (DMAA)
MRF .... Medical Red Flag (SAUS)
MRF .... Medium-Range Forecast [*Model*] [*Marine science*] (OSRA)
MRF .... Megawatt Receiver Filter
MRF .... Melanocyte-Stimulating Hormone Releasing Factor [*Endocrinology*]
MRF .... Melanotropin Releasing Factor [*Biochemistry*]
MRF .... Mental Retardation Facility
MRF .... Mentor Income Fund [*Formerly, RAC Income Fund*] [*NYSE symbol*] (SPSG)
MRF .... Merfin Resources Ltd. [*Vancouver Stock Exchange symbol*]
MRF .... Mesencephalic [*or Midbrain*] Reticular Formation [*Anatomy*]
MRF .... Message Refusal [*Telecommunications*] (TEL)
MRF .... Metal Regulatory Factor [*Genetics*]
MRF .... Meteorological Radar Facility (ACAE)
MRF .... Meteorological Research Flight
MRF .... Meteorological Rocket Facility
MRF .... Metering Research Facility [*Research center*] (RCD)
MRF .... Methodist Relief Fund [*British*]
MRF .... Midbrain Reticular Formation [*Brain anatomy*]
MRF .... Milestone Reference File [*Military*] (CAAL)
MRF .... Military Reconnaissance Force [*British military*] (DMA)
MRF .... Miraflores [*Peru*] [*Seismograph station code, US Geological Survey*] (SEIS)
MRF .... Missile Reconstitution Force [*Air Force*] (DOMA)
MRF .... Mission Readiness Flying
MRF .... Mission Reliability Factor [*Military*] (AABC)
MRF .... Mitral Regurgitant Flow [*Medicine*]
MRF .... Mobile Reaction Force (SAUO)
MRF .... Mobile Riverine Force [*Navy*] (NVT)
MRF .... Moderate Renal Failure [*Medicine*] (DMAA)
MRF .... Modular Rigid Frame (PDAA)
MRF .... Module Release Form (ACAE)
MRF .... Module Repair Facility (DNAB)
MRF .... Monoclonal Rheumatoid Factor [*Medicine*] (DB)
mRF .... Monoclonal Rheumatoid Factor [*Medicine*] (MELL)
MRF .... Motorcycle Riders Foundation (SAUO)
MRF .... Movement for Rights and Freedoms [*Bulgaria*] [*Political party*]
MRF .... MSH [*Melanophore-Stimulating Hormone*] Releasing Factor [*Medicine*] (DAVI)
MRF .... Muellerian Regression Factor [*Embryology*] (DAVI)
MRF .... Muellerian Repressor Factor [*Embryology*]
MRF .... Multipath Reduction Factor [*Electronics*]
MRF .... Multirole Fighter [*Replacement for the F-16*] [*Air Force*] (DOMA)
MRF .... Multi-Role Fuze (SAUS)
MRF .... Muscle Regulatory Factor [*Physiology*]
MRF .... Music Research Foundation
MRF .... Myopia Research Foundation [*Later, MIRF*]
MRFA .... Fireman Apprentice, Machinery Repairman, Striker [*Navy rating*]
MRFAC .... Manufacturers Radio Frequency Advisory Committee (EA)
MRFB .... Malayan Rubber Fund Board (AD)
MRFC .... Malawi Rural Finance Co. Ltd.
MRFC .... Mouse Rosette-Forming Cell (DMAA)
MRFCA .... Mental Residual Functional Capacity Assessment [*Social Security Administration*]
MRFD .... Finca Delicias [*Costa Rica*] [*ICAO location identifier*] (ICLI)
MRFDK .... Mechanical Remote Fuze Disassembly Kit [*Military*] (CAAL)
MRFI .... Finca 10 (Nuevo Palmar Sur) [*Costa Rica*] [*ICAO location identifier*] (ICLI)
MRFI .... Mutually Responsible Facilitation Inventory [*Personality development test*] [*Psychology*]
MRFIT .... Multiple Risk Factor Intervention Trial [*Cardiology*]
MRFL .... Flamengo [*Costa Rica*] [*ICAO location identifier*] (ICLI)

MRFL............	Master Radio Frequency List (NATG)
mr flight	Meteorological Research Flight (AD)
MRFN	Fireman, Machinery Repairman, Striker [*Navy rating*]
MRFP..........	Finca La Promesa [*Costa Rica*] [*ICAO location identifier*] (ICLI)
MRFR	Mobilization Reserve for Retention [*Military*]
MRFS..........	Finca 63 [*Costa Rica*] [*ICAO location identifier*] (ICLI)
MRFS..........	Mid-Range Force Study [*DoD*]
MRFSS	Marine Recreational Fishing Statistics Survey (USDC)
MRFT..........	Missile Ready for Test (MCD)
MRFT..........	Modified Rapid Fermentation Test
MRFU	Multiple Rocket Firing Unit
MRFV..........	Maize Rayado Fino Virus [*Plant pathology*]
mrg.............	Magnetic Radiation Generator (AD)
MRG	Magnetic Radiation Generator
MRG	Magnetic Resonance Gyro (MCD)
MRG	Main Repair Group [*British military*] (DMA)
MRG	Maintainability Requirements Group (AD)
MRG	Maintenance Requirements General (MCD)
MRG	Management Requirement General (ACAE)
MRG	Management Research Group (SAUO)
MRG	Management Research Groups [*British*]
MRG	Management Review Group (SAUO)
MRG	Mandatory Resource Group (MCD)
MRG	Manridge Explorations Ltd. [*Toronto Stock Exchange symbol*]
mrg.............	Margin (AD)
mrg.............	Marginalia (AD)
MRG	Master of Religious Guidance
MRG	Master Reference Gyro (PDAA)
MRG	Material Review Group [*Aviation*]
MRG	Medium Range
MRG	Merge [*Computer science*]
MRG	Mesters Vig [*Greenland*] [*Airport symbol*] (AD)
MRG	Methane Rich Gas
mrg.............	Methane-Rich Gas (AD)
MRG	Military Research Group (SAUO)
MRG	Minimum Revenue Guarantee (SAUO)
MRG	Minorities Research Group (AD)
MRG	Minority Rights Group (EAIO)
MRG	Mission Rules Guidelines [*NASA*] (KSC)
MRG	Mobile River Group [*Navy*] (VNW)
MRG	Modelling Research Group [*University of Southern California*] [*Research center*] (RCD)
MRG	Modern Rythmic Gymnastics (EDAC)
MRG	Mooring (MSA)
MRG	Morgantown [*West Virginia*] [*Seismograph station code, US Geological Survey*] (SEIS)
MRG	Mortons Restaurant Group [*NYSE symbol*] (SAG)
MRG	Mouvement des Radicaux de Gauche [*Left Radical Movement*] [*Wallis and Futuna Islands*] [*Political party*] (EY)
MRG	Mouvement des Radicaux de Gauche [*Left Radical Movement*] [*France*] [*Political party*] (PPE)
MRG	Movement Requirements Generator
MRG	Multinational Recruitment Group (SAUO)
MRG	Municipal Reform Group [*Tasmania, Australia*]
MRG	Murmurs, Rubs, and Gallops [*Cardiology*] (DAVI)
MRGA	Garza [*Costa Rica*] [*ICAO location identifier*] (ICLI)
MRGA	Manhattan Ryegrass Growers Association (EA)
MRGF	Golfito [*Costa Rica*] [*ICAO location identifier*] (ICLI)
MRGI	Minority Rights Group International [*British*] (EAIO)
MRGITF	Machine-Readable Government Information Task Force [*Government Documents Round Table*] [*American Library Association*]
MRGO..........	Margo Nursery Farms [*NASDAQ symbol*] (TTSB)
MRGO..........	Margo Nursery Farms, Inc. [*NASDAQ symbol*] (NQ)
MRGO..........	Mississippi River Gulf Outflow (AD)
MR-GO........	Mississippi River-Gulf Outlet
MRGP..........	Guapiles [*Costa Rica*] [*ICAO location identifier*] (ICLI)
MRGR	Mean Relative Growth Rate [*Physiology*]
MRGS..........	Member of the Royal Geographical Society [*British*]
MrgS...........	Morgan Stanley Group, Inc. [*Associated Press*] (SAG)
MrgSHY.......	MorgaN Stanley High Yield Fund [*Associated Press*] (SAG)
MRGT..........	Guatuso [*Costa Rica*] [*ICAO location identifier*] (ICLI)
MRGU	Guanacaste [*Costa Rica*] [*ICAO location identifier*] (ICLI)
MRGV	Marine Research Group of Victoria [*Australia*]
MRH	Beaufort, NC [*Location identifier*] [*FAA*] (FAAL)
MRH	Hinds Junior College, Raymond, MS [*OCLC symbol*] (OCLC)
MRH	Magnetic Recording Head
MRH	Mango Resources [*Vancouver Stock Exchange symbol*]
MRH	Master of Russian History
MRH	Mechanical Recording Head
MRH	Melanocyte-Releasing Hormone [*Endocrinology*]
MRH	Member of the Royal Household [*British*] (AD)
mr/h...........	Microroentgon per Hour (COE)
MRH	Mild Resid Hydrocracking [*M. W. Kellogg Co. process*]
mr/h...........	Milliroentgens per Hour (DS)
MRH	Mission-Related Hardware
MRH	Mobile Remote Handler
MRH	Monitoring River Health (SAUO)
MRH	MSH [*Melanophore-Stimulating Hormone*] Releasing Hormone [*Laboratory Science*] (DAVI)
MRH	Rossburn District Hospital, Rossburn, Manitoba [*Library symbol*] [*National Library of Canada*] (NLC)
MRHA..........	Mannose-Resistant Hemagglutination
MRHD	Mounted Ration Heating Device [*Army*] (INF)
MR head......	Magneto-Resistive Head [*Computer science*] (DDC)
MRHG..........	Hacienda Rancho Grande [*Costa Rica*] [*ICAO location identifier*] (ICLI)
MRHI	Monitoring River Health Initiative (SAUO)
MRHIB	Multiantimicrobial Resistant Hemophilus Influenza B
MRHJ..........	Hacienda Jaco (Harbor Land) [*Costa Rica*] [*ICAO location identifier*] (ICLI)
mrhm..........	Milliroentgens per Hour at One Meter
MRHMC	Michael Reese Hospital and Medical Center (AD)
MRHO	Hacienda Rio Cuarto [*Costa Rica*] [*ICAO location identifier*] (ICLI)
MRHP	Hacienda Platanar [*Costa Rica*] [*ICAO location identifier*] (ICLI)
mr/hr	Milliroentgens per Hour
MRHS	Hacienda La Suerte [*Costa Rica*] [*ICAO location identifier*] (ICLI)
MRHS	Materiel Request History and Status
MRHS	Member of the Royal Historical Society [*British*] (ROG)
MRHS	Midwest Railway Historical Society (EA)
MRHSF	Materiel Request History and Storage File
MRI	Anchorage, AK [*Location identifier*] [*FAA*] (FAAL)
MRI	Information Dynamics Corp., Reading, MA [*Library symbol*] [*Library of Congress*] (LCLS)
MRI	Machine Records Installation [*Military*]
MRI	Magazine Research, Inc. (AD)
mri.............	Magnetic-Resonance Imager (AD)
MRI	Magnetic Resonance Imagery (SHCU)
MRI	Magnetic Resonance Imaging [*Medicine*] (AMHC)
mri.............	Magnetic Rubber Inspection (AD)
MRI	Malt Research Institute [*Later, NMRI*]
MRI	Management Recruiters International (HGAA)
MRI	Management Resources International (SAUO)
MRI	Manufacturing Run-In
MRI	Marine Research Institute
MRI	Marital Roles Inventory [*Psychology*]
MRI	Mass Retailing Institute [*Formerly, Mass Merchandising Research Institute*] [*Later, NMRI*]
MRI	Material Receiving Instruction [*Bechtel*] [*Nuclear energy*] (NRCH)
MRI	Material Review Item [*Aviation*]
MRI	Mauritius Island [*Mascarene Islands*] [*Seismograph station code, US Geological Survey*] [*Closed*] (SEIS)
MRI	McRae Industries, Inc. [*AMEX symbol*] (SPSG)
mri.............	Mean Rise Interval (AD)
MRI	Mean Rise Interval [*Tides and currents*]
MRI	Measurement Requirements and Interface (MCD)
MRI	Meat Research Institute [*British*]
MRI	Mediamark Research, Inc. [*Database producer and database*] [*Information service or system*] (IID)
MRI	Mediator Release Inhibitor [*Biochemistry*]
MRI	Medical Records Index (AD)
MRI	Medical Research Institute [*Florida Institute of Technology*] [*Research center*] (RCD)
mri.............	Medium-Range Interceptor (AD)
MRI	Medium-Range Interceptor
MRI	Member of the Royal Institution [*British*]
MRI	Memory Reference Instruction
MRI	Mental Research Institute (EA)
MRI	Mesoscale Research Initiative (SAUO)
MRI	Message Routing Indicator (COE)
MRI	Meteorological Research, Incorporated (SAUO)
MRI	Meteorological Research Institute (AD)
MRI	Microwave Research Institute [*Polytechnic Institute of Brooklyn*] (MCD)
MRI	Midwest Research Institute
MRI	Military Reform Institute (AD)
mri.............	Milstrip Routing Identifier (AD)
MRI	Mineral Resources Institute [*University of Alabama*] [*Research center*] (RCD)
MRI	Mineral Resources International Ltd. [*Toronto Stock Exchange symbol*]
MRI	Minimum Release Interval (DNAB)
MRI	Ministry of Radio Industry (SAUO)
MRI	Minority Research Initiation (SAUS)
MRI	Minority Research Institution [*Program*] [*National Science Foundation*]
MRI	Miscellaneous RADAR Input
MRI	Missile Range Index
MRI	Modeling, Rendering, and Interaction (RALS)
MRI	Moderate Renal Insufficiency [*Medicine*]
MRI	Moderate Resolution Imager (SAUS)
MRI	Modified River Incompatible Alteration (SAUO)
mri.............	Monopulse Resolution Improvement (AD)
MRI	Monopulse Resolution Improvement
MRI	Motor Repair Insurance (AD)
MRI	Multiple RADAR Interrogator (MUGU)
MRI.A	McRae Indus'A' [*AMEX symbol*] (TTSB)
MRI.B	McRae Indus Cv 'B' [*AMEX symbol*] (TTSB)
MRIA	Magnetic Recording Industry Association [*Later, Electronic Industries Association*] (EA)
MRIA	Member of the Royal Irish Academy (EY)
MRIA	Model Railroad Industry Association (EA)
MRIAI	Member of the Royal Institute of the Architects of Ireland
MRIAS	Manchester Region Industrial Archaeology Society (SAUO)
MRIBA	Member of the Royal Institute of British Architects (ROG)
MRIC	Mandatory Recovery Items Code (MCD)
M-RIC	Manpower Resource Identification Code [*Military*]
MRIC	Member of the Royal Institute of Chemistry [*British*]
MRIC	Morning Report Indicator Code [*Army*] (AABC)

MRIC .... Revolutionary Movement of the Christian Left [*Ecuador*] [*Political party*] (PPW)

MRICC .... Missile and Rockets Inventory Control Center [*Army*]

MRICD .... Medical Research Institute of Chemical Defense (RDA)

MRICS .... Member of the Royal Institution of Chartered Surveyors [*British*]

MRID .... Master Record Identification Number (EPAT)

MRIF .... Maintenance Ratio Intermediate Forward

MRIF .... Melanocyte-Stimulating-Hormone Release Inhibiting Factor [*Also, MIF*] [*Endocrinology*]

MRIF .... MSH [*Melanophore-Stimulating Hormone*] Release Inhibiting Factor [*Laboratory science*] (DAVI)

MRIH .... Melanocyte-Stimulating Hormone-Release-Inhibiting Hormone [*Endocrinology*] (MAE)

MRII .... Medical Resources [*NASDAQ symbol*] (TTSB)

MRII .... Medical Resources, Inc. [*NASDAQ symbol*] (SAG)

MRIID .... Medical Research Institute of Infectious Diseases [*Army*] (RDA)

MRIL .... Mandatory Recovery Items List (MCD)

MRIL .... Master Repairable Item List

MRIN .... Member of the Royal Institute of Navigation [*British*] (DBQ)

MRINA .... Member of the Royal Institution of Naval Architects [*British*]

MR INC .... Men's Rights, Inc. (EA)

MRINDO ...... Modified Rydberg Intermediate Neglect of Differential Overlap [*Physics*]

MRINZ .... Meat Research Institute of New Zealand (AD)

MRIO .... Multiregional Input-Output

MRIP .... Imperio [*Costa Rica*] [*ICAO location identifier*] (ICLI)

MRIP .... Management Review and Improvement Program [*Department of Labor*]

MRIP .... Prairie Crocus Regional Library, Rivers, Manitoba [*Library symbol*] [*National Library of Canada*] (NLC)

MRIPA .... Member of the Royal Institute of Public Administration (ADA)

MRIPHH ...... Member of the Royal Institute of Public Health and Hygiene [*British*]

MRIPS .... Multi-modality Radiological Image Processing System (SAUO)

MRIPWC ...... Member of the Royal Institute of Painters in Water Colours [*British*] (ROG)

mrir .... Medium Resolution Infrared (AD)

MRIR .... Medium-Resolution Infrared Radiometer [*NASA*]

MRIR .... Modification and Retrofit Installation Report (ACAE)

MRIRBM ...... Medium-Range and Intermediate-Range Ballistic Missile (MCD)

MRIS .... Maritime Research Information Service [*National Academy of Sciences*]

MRIS .... Market Research Information System [*Bell System*]

MRIS .... Marshall & Isley Corp. [*NASDAQ symbol*] (NQ)

MRIS .... Material Readiness Index System [*Military*]

MRIS .... Media Relations & Information Services (SAUO)

MRIS .... Medical Research Information System [*Veterans Administration*]

MRIS .... Mobile Range Instrumentation System

MRIS .... Modernization Resource Information Submission [*Army*] (RDA)

MRISAN ...... Maintenance Requirement Interim Support Asset Notice (MCD)

MRIT .... Marine RADAR Interrogator-Transponder (PDAA)

MRIT .... Mean Re-Initialization Time

MRIT .... Merit Software, Inc. [*NASDAQ symbol*] (SAG)

MRIT .... Mobile Remote Intelligence Terminal (ACAE)

MRITC .... Methylrhodamine Isothiocyanate [*Organic chemistry*]

MRIU .... Missile Round Interface Unit

MRIW .... Medical Research Institute of Worcester (SAUO)

MRIX .... Midland Resources [*NASDAQ symbol*] (SPSG)

MRIXZ .... Midland Res Inc. Wrrt [*NASDAQ symbol*] (TTSB)

MRJ .... Microwave Rotary Joint

MRJ .... Mineral Point, WI [*Location identifier*] [*FAA*] (FAAL)

MRJ .... Miniature Revolving Joint

MRJE .... Multileaving Remote Job Entry [*IBM Corp.*]

MRJE .... Multiple Remote Job Entry (NITA)

MRJSDK ...... Macintosh Runtime for Java Software Developer Kit (SAUS)

MRJY .... Mister Jay Fashions International, Inc. [*NASDAQ symbol*] (SAG)

MRJY .... Mr Jay Fashions Intl [*NASDAQ symbol*] (TTSB)

MRK .... Marco Island [*Florida*] [*Airport symbol*] (OAG)

mrk .... Mark (VRA)

MRK .... Mark

MRK .... Markair, Inc. [*ICAO designator*] (FAAC)

MRK .... Merck & Co. [*NYSE symbol*] (TTSB)

MRK .... Merck & Co., Inc. [*NYSE symbol*] (SPSG)

MRK .... Merrimack College, McQuade Library, North Andover, MA [*OCLC symbol*] (OCLC)

MRK .... Millrock Development Corp. [*Vancouver Stock Exchange symbol*]

MRK .... Modified Redlich-Kwong [*Chemical equation*]

MRK .... Morioka [*Japan*] [*Seismograph station code, US Geological Survey*] (SEIS)

MRK .... Myth, Ritual, and Kingship [*A publication*] (BJA)

MRK .... Rayville, LA [*Location identifier*] [*FAA*] (FAAL)

mrkd .... Marked (AD)

MRKD .... Marked [*Computer science*] (MDG)

mrkg .... Marking (AD)

MRKHS .... Mayer-Rokitansky-Kuester-Hauser Syndrome [*Medicine*] (MELL)

mrkr .... Marker (AD)

MRKR .... Marker (WGA)

MRKR .... Marker International [*NASDAQ symbol*] (SAG)

MRKR .... Marker Intl. [*NASDAQ symbol*] (TTSB)

MRKTPLC .... Marketplace

MRKTR .... Marketer

Mrkts .... Markets (AD)

MRL .... Aeromorelos SA de CV [*Mexico*] [*ICAO designator*] (FAAC)

MRL .... Machine Representation Language

MRL .... Magnovox Research Laboratories (CCCA)

MRL .... Main Rail Launcher (DWSG)

MRL .... Maintenance Repair Level (MCD)

MRL .... Maintenance Requirements List (MCD)

MRL .... Manipulator Retention Latch [*or Lock*] (NASA)

MRL .... Manipulator Retention Lock (SAUS)

MRL .... Manufacturing Reference Line

MRL .... Manufacturing Research Laboratory

MRL .... Marine Drilling [*NYSE symbol*]

MRL .... Marine Research Laboratory (SAUO)

MRL .... Maritime Rear Link (MCD)

MRL .... Marketing Research Library

MRL .... Martel Oil & Gas [*Vancouver Stock Exchange symbol*]

MRL .... Master Repair List (AFIT)

MRL .... Master Report List

MRL .... Master Requirements List (SAUO)

MRL .... Material Requirements Lists

MRL .... Materials Research Laboratories [*National Science Foundation*] [*Research center*]

MRL .... Materiel Requirements List [*Military*]

MRL .... Maximized Relative Likelihood (PDAA)

MRL .... Maximum Recording Level

MRL .... Maximum Residue Level (SAUO)

MRL .... Maximum Residue Limit (PDAA)

MRL .... Meaning-Representation Language [*Computer science*]

MRL .... Medical Record Librarian

MRL .... Medical Records Library (AD)

MRL .... Medical Research Laboratory [*Navy and Air Force*] (MCD)

MRL .... Merrell-National Laboratories [*Research code symbol*]

MRL .... Minerals Research Laboratory (MCD)

MRL .... Minimal Response Level [*Audiometry*]

MRL .... Minimum Residue Level

MRL .... Minimum Residues Limit (SAUO)

MRL .... Minimum-Risk Level [*Environmental science*] (COE)

MRL .... Ministers Referral Letters (SAUO)

MRL .... Missionary Research Library (EA)

MRL .... Mobile Replenishment List (AFIT)

MRL .... Modular Rocket Launcher (SAUS)

MRL .... Motor Refrigeration Lighter (ADA)

mrl .... Motor Refrigerator Lighter (AD)

mrl .... Multiple Rocket Launcher (AD)

MRL .... Multiple Rocket Launcher

MRL .... Multiple Ruby LASER

MRL .... Multipoint Recorder/Logger

MRLA .... La Paquita [*Costa Rica*] [*ICAO location identifier*] (ICLI)

MRLA .... Malayan Races Liberation Army

MRLB .... Liberia/Tomas Guardia Internacional [*Costa Rica*] [*ICAO location identifier*] (ICLI)

MRLC .... Los Chiles [*Costa Rica*] [*ICAO location identifier*] (ICLI)

MRLC .... Maintenance Repair Level Code (ACAE)

MRLC .... Multi-Resolution Land Cover Characterization (SAUS)

MRLDC .... Milton Roy Laboratory Data Control (SAUO)

MRLE .... Laurel [*Costa Rica*] [*ICAO location identifier*] (ICLI)

MRLF .... La Flor [*Costa Rica*] [*ICAO location identifier*] (ICLI)

MRLF .... Monthly Report on the Labor Force (OICC)

MRLG .... La Garroba [*Costa Rica*] [*ICAO location identifier*] (ICLI)

MRLI .... La Ligia [*Costa Rica*] [*ICAO location identifier*] (ICLI)

MRLL .... Las Lomas [*Costa Rica*] [*ICAO location identifier*] (ICLI)

MRLL .... Merrill Corp. [*NASDAQ symbol*] (NQ)

MRLM .... Limon/Limon Internacional [*Costa Rica*] [*ICAO location identifier*] (ICLI)

MRLOGAEUR... Minimum Required Logistics Augmentation Europe (MCD)

MRLP .... Monster Raving Loony Party (WDAA)

MRLPC .... Mouvement de Regroupement et de Liberation du Peuple Congolais [*Movement for the Regroupment and Liberation of the Congolese People*]

MRLR .... La Roca [*Costa Rica*] [*ICAO location identifier*] (ICLI)

MRLS .... Mini Raman Lidar System

MRLS .... Multiple Rocket Launcher System (SAUS)

MRLT .... Las Trancas [*Costa Rica*] [*ICAO location identifier*] (ICLI)

MRLU .... La Maruca [*Costa Rica*] [*ICAO location identifier*] (ICLI)

MRLV .... La Cueva [*Costa Rica*] [*ICAO location identifier*] (ICLI)

MRLV .... Mobile Raman Lidar Van

MRLY .... La Yolanda [*Costa Rica*] [*ICAO location identifier*] (ICLI)

MRM .... Aerocharter, Inc. [*Canada*] [*ICAO designator*] (FAAC)

MRM .... Magnetic Resonance Microscopy

mrm .... Mail Readership Measurement (AD)

MRM .... Mail Readership Measurement

MRM .... Maintenance, Reporting, and Management [*Military*] (MCD)

MRM .... Management Responsibility Matrix

MRM .... Management Review Meeting (AFIT)

MRM .... Manari [*Papua New Guinea*] [*Airport symbol*] (OAG)

MRM .... Master of Resource Management (GAGS)

MRM .... Materiel Readiness and Modernization (SAUO)

mrm .... Mechanically Recovered Meat (AD)

MRM .... Mechanically Removed Meat

MRM .... Medical Record Manager

MRM .... Medical Repair Technician [*Navy*]

MRM .... Medium-Range Missile (MCD)

MRM .... Merrimac Industries, Inc. [*AMEX symbol*] (SPSG)

MRM .... Metabolic Rate Monitor [*Trademark*]

MRM .... Metastable Reaction Monitoring [*Analytical chemistry*]

MRM .... Michelson Rotating Mirror

mrm .... Miles of Relative Movement (AD)

MRM .... Miles of Relative Movement [*Navigation*]

MRM .... Miscellaneous Radioactive Material (GAAI)

MRM .... Modified Radical Mastectomy [*Medicine*] (MELL)

MRM	Most Recently Used Master [*Computer science*]
MRM	Motif Resource Manager [*Computer science*] (AGLO)
MRM	Movement for the Redemption of Liberian Muslims [*Political party*] (EY)
MRM	Movimento da Resistencia de Mozambique [*Mozambique Resistance Movement*]
MRM	Multiple Reaction Monitoring [*Chemistry*]
MRM	Multiple Residue Method [*Medicine*] (MELL)
MRM	Music for the Rights of Man (EA)
MRMA	Montealto [*Costa Rica*] [*ICAO location identifier*] (ICLI)
MRMC	Medical Research and Materiel Command [*Army*]
MRMC	Medical Research Modernization Committee (EA)
MRMC	Murcielago [*Costa Rica*] [*ICAO location identifier*] (ICLI)
MRMDF	Multi-Use Remote Manipulator Development Facility [*NASA*] (SPST)
MRMJ	Mojica [*Costa Rica*] [*ICAO location identifier*] (ICLI)
MRML	Medium-Range Missile Launcher
MRML	Montelimar O Los Sitios [*Costa Rica*] [*ICAO location identifier*] (ICLI)
MRMO	Mobilization Reserve Materiel Objective [*Army*]
MRMO-A	Mobilization Reserve Materiel Objective - Acquisition [*Army*] (AFIT)
MRMP	Marginal Revenue/Marginal Physical Product [*Economics*]
MRMPO	Mobilization Reserve Materiel Procurement Objective [*Army*]
MRMR	Mining Rock-Mass Rating [*Mining technology*]
MRMR	Mobilization Reserve Materiel Requirement [*Army*]
MRMS	MARC [*Machine-Readable Cataloging*] Record Management System
MRMS	Maritime Resources Management Service (SAUO)
MRMS	Metabolic Rate Measuring System
MRMS	Mobile/Tracked Remote Manipulator System (SSD)
MRMS	Monetary Ration Management System [*Military*] (AFM)
MRMS	Mount Rushmore Memorial Society (EA)
MRMU	Mobile Radiological Measuring Unit
MRMU	Mobile Remote Manipulating Unit [*Air Force*]
MRMVA	Master Retail Milk Vendors Association (AD)
MRMW	Memory Write [*Computer science*] (MHDI)
MRN	Malignant Renal Neoplasm [*Medicine*] (MELL)
MRN	Marion [*South Africa*] [*Geomagnetic observatory code*]
MRN	Maritime Radionavigation
MRN	Material Recorder Notice (AD)
MRN	Median Raphe Nucleus [*Medicine*]
MRN	Medium-Round Nose [*Diamond drilling*]
MRN	Meteorological Rocket Network [*NASA*]
MRN	Minimum Rejection Number
MRN	Missions Gouvernementales Francaises [*France*] [*ICAO designator*] (FAAC)
MRN	Modified Random Network [*Crystallography*]
MRN	Moran Resources Corp. [*Vancouver Stock Exchange symbol*]
MRN	Morganton, NC [*Location identifier*] [*FAA*] (FAAL)
MRN	Morning (ROG)
MRN	Morrison Knudsen [*NYSE symbol*] (TTSB)
MRN	Morrison-Knudsen Co., Inc. [*NYSE symbol*] (SPSG)
MRN	Motor Racing Network
MRN	Mouvement pour la Reconstruction Nationale [*Haiti*] [*Political party*] (EY)
MRN	Movimiento de Renovacion Nacional [*Movement for National Renovation*] [*Colombia*] [*Political party*] (PPW)
MRNA	Marina
mRNA	Ribonucleic Acid, Messenger [*Biochemistry, genetics*]
MRNC	Marine Ltd. Partnership [*NASDAQ symbol*] (SAG)
MRNC	Meteorological Rocket Network Committee [*NASA*] (SAA)
MRNC	Nicoya [*Costa Rica*] [*ICAO location identifier*] (ICLI)
MRNCZ	Marina Ltd Partnership [*NASDAQ symbol*] (TTSB)
MRND	Maintenance Required Not Developed (MSA)
MRND	Mouvement Revolutionnaire National pour le Developpement [*National Revolutionary Movement for Development*] [*Rwanda*] [*Political party*] (PPW)
MRNE	Marine
MRNet	[*The*] Minnesota Regional Network [*Computer science*] (TNIG)
mrng	Mooring (AD)
mrng	Morning (AD)
MRNG	Morning
MRNJ	Naranjo (Seveers) [*Costa Rica*] [*ICAO location identifier*] (ICLI)
MRNL	Medical Research and Nutrition Laboratory [*Army*] (MCD)
MRNP	Mount Rainier National Park [*Washington*] (AD)
MRNP	Mount Revelstoke National Park [*British Columbia*] (AD)
mRNP	Ribonucleoprotein, Messenger [*Biochemistry*]
MRNPF	Member, Royal Nurses Pension Fund [*British*] (ROG)
MRNR	Mariner Health Group [*NASDAQ symbol*] (TTSB)
MRNR	Mariner Health Group, Inc. [*NASDAQ symbol*] (SAG)
MRNS	Marine Radar & Navigation Simulator (SAUS)
MRNS	Modular Reusable Nuclear Shuttle
MRNS	Nosara [*Costa Rica*] [*ICAO location identifier*] (ICLI)
Mro	Maestro (AD)
mro	Maintenance, Repair, and Operating (AD)
MRO	Maintenance, Repair, and Operation
MRO	Maintenance, Repair, and Overhaul
MRO	Maintenance Report Order (SAA)
MRO	Management and Resources Office (SAUO)
MRO	Management Review Officer
MRO	Mandatory Requirements Office (SAUO)
MRO	Mandatory Router Option (SAUS)
MRO	Manufacturing Rework Order
MRO	Master Reference Oscillator (DMAA)
MRO	Masterton [*New Zealand*] [*Airport symbol*] (OAG)
MRO	Materiel Readiness Officer (MCD)
MRO	Materiel Release Order [*Air Force*]
MRO	Mechanized RADAR Observer

MRO	Media Resources Officer (AIE)
MRO	Medical Regulating Office [*or Officer*] [*Army*] (AABC)
MRO	Medical Research Organization [*Generic term*]
MRO	Medical Review Officer (GFGA)
MRO	Member of the Register of Osteopaths [*British*]
MRO	Meridor Resources Ltd. [*Vancouver Stock Exchange symbol*]
MRO	Message Releasing Officer
MRO	Message Review Officer (MCD)
MRO	Mid-Range Objectives
MRO	Military Release Orders
MRO	Mine Radiographic Outfit [*Military*] (PDAA)
MRO	Minimal Recognizable Odor [*Medicine*] (DMAA)
MRO	Minority Recruiting Officer (DNAB)
MRO	Morrison Flying Service, Inc. [*ICAO designator*] (FAAC)
MRO	Motor Routing Order
MRO	Movement Report Office [*Military*]
MRO	Multi-Region Operation (SAUO)
MRO	Multi-Region Option (HGAA)
MRO	Muscle Receptor Organ [*Neurophysiology*]
MRO	Rossburn Regional Library, Manitoba [*Library symbol*] [*National Library of Canada*] (NLC)
MRO	USX-Marathon Group [*NYSE symbol*] (SPSG)
MROA	Magnetic Raman Optical Activity [*Spectrometry*]
MROAR	Modification and Repair Order and Acceptance Record (AD)
MROC	Mobile Range Operation Center (NVT)
MROC	Monroc, Inc. [*NASDAQ symbol*] (SAG)
MROC	Multi-Command Required Operational Capability (ACAE)
MROC	Multiple-Command Required Operational Capability (SAUO)
MROC	Multi-Role Operations Cabin (SAUS)
MROC	San Jose/Juan Santamaria Internacional [*Costa Rica*] [*ICAO location identifier*] (ICLI)
MROCC	Medical Review Officer Certification Council (SAUO)
MROD	Medical Research and Operations Directorate [*NASA*] (KSC)
MROF	Maintenance, Repair, and Operation of Facility (KSC)
MROFIE	Mission Requirements on Facilities/Instruments/Experiments (SAUS)
MROL	Minimum Resolvable Object Length
MROM	Macro Read-Only Memory [*Computer science*]
MROM	Masked Read-Only Memory [*Computer science*]
MROP	Major Reconstruction of Obsolete Public Housing (SAUO)
MRORG	Maintenance Ratio at Organizational Level (SAUO)
MROS	Material Requirements and Operating Standards (SAUO)
MROS	Multirole Operations Cabin (SAUS)
mrov	Moreover (AD)
M-ROVER	Michigan's Remote Operated Vehicle for Education and Research
MROW	Manufacture, Repair & Overhaul Wing (SAUS)
MRoxH	Hebrew Teachers College, Roxbury, MA [*Library symbol*] [*Library of Congress*] (LCLS)
MRP	Application for Writ of Mandamus Refused in Part [*Legal term*] (DLA)
MRp	Carnegie Library, Rockport, MA [*Library symbol*] [*Library of Congress*] (LCLS)
mrp	Machine-Readable Passport (AD)
MRP	Machine-Readable Passport (DA)
MRP	Magnum Rifle Powder (DICI)
MRP	Maintenance Rally Point [*Military*] (INF)
MRP	Maintenance Real Property (NVT)
MRP	Maintenance Repair Part (ACAE)
MRP	Malfunction Reporting Program [*Navy*]
MRP	Management Readiness Profile [*London House, Inc.*] (TES)
MRP	Management Requirements and Practices (SAUO)
MRP	Management Requirements & Procedures (SAUO)
mrp	Manned Reusable Payload (AD)
MRP	Manned Reusable Payload
mrp	Manned Reusable Product (AD)
MRP	Manned Rotating Platform
MRP	Manpower Requirements & Personnel (SAUO)
MRP	Manual Repair Point (SAUS)
MRP	Manual Reporting Post (NATG)
MRP	Manufacturer's Recommended Price (ODBW)
MRP	Manufacturing Requirements Planning [*Purchasing computer program*] (PCM)
MRP	Manufacturing Resource Planning [*Computer science*]
mrp	Marginal Revenue Product (AD)
MRP	Marginal Revenue Product [*Economics*]
MRP	Markov Renewal Program
MRP	Marla [*Australia*] [*Airport symbol*] (OAG)
MRP	Mass Resolving Power [*Physics*]
MRP	Master in Regional Planning (DD)
MRP	Master of Regional Planning
MRP	Master Restationing Plan [*DoD*]
MRP	Material Reliability Program [*Military*] (AFIT)
MRP	Material Requirements Planning [*Pronounced "merp"*]
MRP	Material Reserve Planning
MRP	Material Resource Planning (ACII)
MRP	Materiel Returns Program [*Military*] (AFIT)
MRP	Mathematics Resources Project [*National Science Foundation*]
MRP	Maximum Rated Power
mrp	Maximum Resolving Power (AD)
MRP	Maximum Resolving Power
mrp	Maximum Retail Price (AD)
MRP	Maximum Retail Price [*British*]
MRP	Medical Record Practitioner [*Medicare*] (DHSM)
MRP	Medical Reimbursement Plan
MRP	Medical Removal Protection (SARE)
MRP	Members Retirement Plan [*of the American Medical Association*] (DAVI)

MRP............ Merapi [*Java*] [*Seismograph station code, US Geological Survey*] [*Closed*] (SEIS)
MRP............ Message Routing Process [*Telecommunications*] (TEL)
MRP............ Mid-Range Plan [*1969-70*] [*Military*]
MRP............ Militarism Resource Project (EA)
MRP............ Military Rated Power (NG)
MRP............ Military Representatives of Associated Pacific Powers [*World War II*]
MRP............ Military Requirements Plan (NATG)
MRP............ Minimum Reaction Posture (NVT)
MRP............ Miscellaneous Relay Panel (MCD)
MRP............ Mississippi River Plume [*Marine science*] (OSRA)
MRP............ Mitochondrial RNA [*Ribonucleic Acid*] Processing [*Cytology*]
MRP............ Mobile RADAR Post
MRP............ Mobile Repair Party (MCD)
MRP............ Mobile Reporting Post (SAUS)
MRP............ Modern Religious Problems [*A publication*]
MRP............ Molybdate-Reactive Phosphorus [*Analytical chemistry*]
MRP............ Monthly Report of Progress
MRP............ Morley Library, Painesville, OH [*OCLC symbol*] (OCLC)
MRP............ Morrison Petroleums Ltd. [*Toronto Stock Exchange symbol*]
MRP............ Motor Racing Publications [*Publisher*] [*British*]
MRP............ Mouvement Republicain Populaire [*Popular Republican Movement*] [*France*] [*Political party*] (PPE)
MRP............ Mouvement Revolutionnaire du Peuple [*Chad*] [*Political party*] (EY)
MRP............ Movimiento Republicano Progresista [*Progressive Republican Movement*] [*Venezuela*] [*Political party*]
MRP............ Movimiento Revolucionario del Pueblo - Ixim [*People's Revolutionary Movement - Ixim*] [*Guatemala*] [*Political party*] (PD)
MRP............ Movimiento Revolucionario Popular [*Venezuela*] [*Political party*] (EY)
MRP............ Multimode Radar Processor (ACAE)
MRP............ Multiple-Rate Processor (CCCA)
MRP............ Multiplex Recording Photography
MRP............ Multi-Racial Party [*Zambia*] [*Political party*] (EY)
MRP............ Multi-Roller Press (EEVL)
MRP............ Reston and District Regional Library, Reston, Manitoba [*Library symbol*] [*National Library of Canada*] (NLC)
MR/PA........ Make Ready / Put Away (DNAB)
MRPA .... Master of Recreation and Parks Administration (GAGS)
MRPA .... Metropolitan Region Planning Authority (AD)
MRPA .... Modified Random Phase Approximation
MRPA .... Punta Burica [*Costa Rica*] [*ICAO location identifier*] (ICLI)
MRPARABAD... Master Parachutist Badge [*Military decoration*]
MRPB .... Playa Blanca [*Costa Rica*] [*ICAO location identifier*] (ICLI)
MRPC .... Mercury Rankine Power Conversion [*Nuclear energy*]
MRPC .... Mouvement de Regroupement des Populations Congolaises [*Movement for the Regroupment of the Congolese People*] [*Political party*]
MRPC .... Paso Canoas [*Costa Rica*] [*ICAO location identifier*] (ICLI)
MRPD .... Medium Repetition-Rate Pulsed Doppler (ACAE)
MRPD .... Pandora [*Costa Rica*] [*ICAO location identifier*] (ICLI)
MRPE......... Palo Verde [*Costa Rica*] [*ICAO location identifier*] (ICLI)
MRPF......... Maintenance of Real Property Facilities (AABC)
MRPG .... Potrero Grande [*Costa Rica*] [*ICAO location identifier*] (ICLI)
MRPhS .... Member of the Royal Pharmaceutical Society [*Canada*] (DD)
MRPI .... Paissa [*Costa Rica*] [*ICAO location identifier*] (ICLI)
MRP II .... Manufacturing Resource Planning (SAUO)
MRPJ......... Puerto Jimenez [*Costa Rica*] [*ICAO location identifier*] (ICLI)
MRPL......... Main Ring Path Length (SAUO)
MRPL......... Material Requirements Planning List [*Navy*]
MRPL......... Portalon [*Costa Rica*] [*ICAO location identifier*] (ICLI)
MRPM .... Material Research and Production Methods (MCD)
MRPM .... Palmar Sur [*Costa Rica*] [*ICAO location identifier*] (ICLI)
MRPN .... Pelon Nuevo [*Costa Rica*] [*ICAO location identifier*] (ICLI)
MRPP .... Maoist Reorganization Movement of the Party of the Proletariat [*Political party*] (AD)
MRPP .... Mortgage Rate Protection Program [*Canada*]
MRPR .... Parrita [*Costa Rica*] [*ICAO location identifier*] (ICLI)
MRPRA........ Malaysian Rubber Producers' Research Association [*Research center*] [*British*] (IRC)
MRPS .... Manufacturing and Resource Planning System [*Cincom Systems Ltd.*] [*Software package*] (NCC)
MRPS .... Marine Petrol Tr [*NASDAQ symbol*] (TTSB)
MRPS .... Materials Requirement Planning System (HGAA)
M rps .... Maurituis Rupee [*Monetary unit*] (AD)
MRPS .... Midline Retroperitoneal Syndrome [*Medicine*] (MELL)
MRPS .... Paissa [*Costa Rica*] [*ICAO location identifier*] (ICLI)
MRPV .... Mini-Remotely Piloted Vehicle (PDAA)
MRPV .... San Jose/Tobias Bolanos Internacional [*Costa Rica*] [*ICAO location identifier*] (ICLI)
MRQ .... Marinduque [*Philippines*] [*Airport symbol*] (OAG)
MRQ .... Marquardt Corp. [*Stock exchange symbol*] (AD)
MRQ .... Maximum Release Quantity [*DoD*]
MRQE........ Marquee Group, Inc. (The) [*NASDAQ symbol*] (SAG)
MRQP........ Quepos (La Managua) [*Costa Rica*] [*ICAO location identifier*] (ICLI)
MRR .... Macara [*Ecuador*] [*Airport symbol*] (OAG)
MRR .... Machine-Readable Record (MCD)
MRR .... [*The*] Magistrates of the Roman Republic [*A publication*] (OCD)
MRR .... Mail Return Rate (SAUS)
MRR .... Maintenance, Repairs, and Replacements [*Military*]
MRR .... Maintenance, Replacement, Removal (AFIT)
MRR .... Mandatory Removal Roster [*Army*]
MRR .... Manila Railroad (SAUO)
MRR .... Manistee Railroad
MRR .... Manufacturing Readiness Review (ACAE)
MRR .... Marrow Release Rate [*Hematology*]

MRR .... Master Record Repository (MCD)
MRR .... Material Readiness Report (MCD)
MRR .... Material Receiving [*Inspection*] Report [*Nuclear energy*] (NRCH)
MRR .... Material Rejection Report
MRR .... Material Release Point (SAUO)
MRR .... Material Reliability Report (MCD)
MRR .... Material Removal Rate (MCD)
MRR .... Material Review Record [*or Reports*] [*Aviation*] (MCD)
MRR .... Material Review Request
MRR .... Materiel Readiness Report [*Army*] (AABC)
MRR .... Maximal Relaxation Rate [*Medicine*]
MRR .... Maximum Rate of Rise [*Biometrics*]
MRR .... Mechanical Reliability Report [*FAA*]
MRR .... Mechanical Research Report
mrr............ Medical Research Reactor (AD)
MRR .... Medical Research Reactor
MRR .... Medium-Range RADAR (NG)
MRR .... Medium-Range Recovery
MRR .... Metal Removal Rate
MRR .... Microelectronic Radio Receiver
MRR .... Microfilm Reader Recorder
MRR .... Mid-Atlantic Realty Trust [*AMEX symbol*] (SPSG)
MRR .... Middlesborough & Redcar Railway (SAUO)
MRR .... Milestone Readiness Review [*NASA*] (KSC)
MRR .... Military Renegotiation Regulation
MRR .... Miniature Reed Relay
MRR .... Minimum Rediscount Rate
MRR .... Minimum Reporting Requirement [*NASA*] (KSC)
MRR .... Minimum Residual Radiation (SAUS)
MRR .... Minimum Risk Route (MCD)
MRR .... Missile Reliability Restoration (SAUS)
MRR .... Missile Restraint Release
MRR .... Mission Readiness Review (SAUS)
MRR .... Mission Reconfiguration Request (MCD)
MRR .... Mission Requirements Review (ACAE)
MRR .... Molecular Rotational Resonance
MRR .... Monomer Reactivity Ratio (PDAA)
MRR .... Monthly Review Report
MRR .... Motorized Rifle Regiment [*Former USSR*]
MRR .... Multiple Response Resolver
MRR .... Multi-Role Radar (ACAE)
MRR .... Muroran [*Japan*] [*Seismograph station code, US Geological Survey*] (SEIS)
MRRA .... Master of Recreation Resources (F6) Administration (PGP)
MRRA .... Military Retirement Reform Act
MRRAS........ Murder Release Risk Assessment Scale (AD)
MRRB .... Maintenance Requirements Review Board [*Military*] (AFIT)
MRRB .... Manual Remote Rebroadcast Box (SAUS)
MRRB .... Materiel Release Review Board [*Military*]
MRRB .... Materiel Requirements Review Board [*Military*] (AFIT)
MRRC .... Materiel Requirements Review Committee [*Military*]
MRRC .... Mechanical Reliability Research Center
MRRC .... Mental Retardation Research Center [*University of California, Los Angeles*] [*Research center*] (RCD)
MRRC .... Ralph L. Smith Mental Retardation Research Center [*University of Kansas*] [*Research center*] (RCD)
MRRD .... Marine Resources Research Division [*Now Ocean Environment Research Division*] (USDC)
MRRDB....... Malaysian Rubber Research and Development Board (AD)
MRRF .... Monitor Research and Recovery Foundation
MRRF .... Rio Frio O Progreso [*Costa Rica*] [*ICAO location identifier*] (ICLI)
MRRI .... Marine Resources Research Institute [*South Carolina Wildlife and Marine Resources Department*] [*Research center*] (RCD)
MRRL .... Materiel Repair Requirement List [*Military*] (AFIT)
MRRL .... Metabolism and Radiation Research Laboratory [*North Dakota State University*] [*Research center*] (RCD)
MRRM .... Rancho Del Mar [*Costa Rica*] [*ICAO location identifier*] (ICLI)
MRRN .... Rancho Nuevo [*Costa Rica*] [*ICAO location identifier*] (ICLI)
MRRP .... Maintenance and Repair of Real Property [*Military*]
MRRP .... Medical Radioisotopes Research Program (SAUO)
MRRP .... Motorways, Roads, and Road Programmes [*British*]
MR-RPV....... Mid Range Remotely Piloted Vehicle (ACAE)
MRRS .... Magnetic Reed Rotary Switch
MRRS .... Materiel Readiness Reporting System [*Army*]
MRRS .... Military Route Reconnaissance Staff (SAUO)
MRRS .... Mobile Rail Repair Shop (MCD)
MRRS .... Multiple Railroad System
MRRS .... Multi-Rail Rocket System (PDAA)
MRRT .... Maintenance Requirements Review Team (MUGU)
MRRTC .... Maligaya Rice Research and Training Center (SAUO)
MRRV .... Manoeuvring Re-entry Research Vehicle (SAUS)
MRRW........ Morrow Snowboards [*NASDAQ symbol*] (TTSB)
MRRW........ Morrow Snowboards, Inc. [*NASDAQ symbol*] (SAG)
MRRX........ Roxana Farms [*Costa Rica*] [*ICAO location identifier*] (ICLI)
MRS........... Airline of the Marshall Islands [*ICAO designator*] (FAAC)
MRS........... Maars [*Alaska*] [*Seismograph station code, US Geological Survey*] (SEIS)
MRS........... Mado Robin Society [*Defunct*] (EA)
MRS........... Magnetic Reed Switch
MRS........... Magnetic-Resonance Spectroscopy [*Biochemistry*] (ECON)
MRS........... Magnetic Resonance Spectrum
MRS........... Maintenance Repair and Service (ACAE)
MRS........... Maintenance Reporting System [*Army*]
MRS........... Maintenance Requirement Substantiated (MSA)
MRS........... Malfunction Reporting System [*Boeing*]

MRS............ Management Relations Survey [*Test*]
MRS............ Management Reporting System
MRS............ Management Review System (NASA)
MRS............ Manipulator Repair Shop (NRCH)
MRS............ Manned Reconnaissance Satellite [*Air Force*]
MRS............ Manned Repeater Station [*Telecommunications*] (OA)
MRS............ Manufacturers Railway Co. [*AAR code*]
MRS............ Marches (ROG)
mrs............ Marginal Rate of Substitution (AD)
MRS............ Marginal Rate of Substitution [*Economics*]
MRS............ Mariah Resources Ltd. [*Vancouver Stock Exchange symbol*]
MRS............ Market Research Society [*British*]
MRS............ Marseille [*France*] [*Airport symbol*] (OAG)
MRS............ Master Radar Station (SAUO)
MRS............ Master Repair Schedule [*Air Force*] (AFM)
MRS............ Material Request [*or Requirement*] Summary
MRS............ Material Research Society Meeting (SAUO)
MRS............ Material Returned to Store [*NASA*] (KSC)
MRS............ Material Routing Slip
MRS............ Materials Research Society (EA)
MRS............ Materiel Repair System [*Air Force*] (AFM)
MRS............ Media Recognition System [*Computer science*] (PCM)
MRS............ Media Report Service (NITA)
MRS............ Media Resource Service [*Scientists' Institute for Public Information*] [*Information service or system*] (IID)
MRS............ Medical Readiness System (SAUO)
MRS............ Medical Receiving Station
MRS............ Medical Reception Station [*Military*]
MRS............ Medical Research Society [*British*]
MRS............ Medical Resupply Set Model (SAUO)
MRS............ Medium Range Search
MRS............ Medium-Range SONAR (NVT)
MRS............ Medium Range Surveillance (SAUS)
MRS............ Melkersson-Rosenthal Syndrome [*Medicine*] (DMAA)
MRS............ Memo Routing Slip
MRS............ Meritor Automotive [*NYSE symbol*] (SG)
MRS............ Mesoscale Research Section (SAUO)
MRS............ Metals Removal System [*Petroleum refining*]
MRS............ Metastasis Research Society (SAUO)
MRS............ Methicillin-Resistant Staphylococcus [*Qureus*] [*Medicine*] (DAVI)
MRS............ Methicillin-Resistant Staphylococcus Aureus [*Antimicrobial therapy*] (MEDA)
MRS............ Metro Recovery Systems (EFIS)
MRS............ Michigan Radiological Society (SAUO)
MrS............ Microfilm Records System, Inc., Mamaroneck, NY [*Library symbol*] [*Library of Congress*] (LCLS)
MRS............ Microfilm Replacement System [*Computer science*]
MRS............ Micro Reflective Structure [*Computer science*]
MRS............ Midcoast Energy Resources, Inc. [*AMEX symbol*] (SAG)
MRS............ Midlands Research Station [*British Gas*] (WDAA)
MRS............ Migration and Refugee Services (EA)
MRS............ Military Radar Stations (ACAE)
MRS............ Military Railway Service [*Army*]
MRS............ Military Requirements Study (AAGC)
MRS............ Military Retirement System
MRS............ Minimum Radial Separation [*Manufacturing term*]
MRS............ Minimum Reporting Standard [*Broadcasting*] (NTCM)
MRS............ Minimum Residual Shutdown (IGSL)
MRS............ Mini-Reconstruction System (MCD)
MRS............ Ministry of Recreation and Sport [*British*] (AD)
MRS............ Missile Reentry Systems (AFIT)
MRS............ Missile Round Simulator
MRS............ Mission de Ras Shamra [*A publication*] (BJA)
MRS............ Mission Radio System (SAUO)
MRS............ Mission Rehearsal System (SAUS)
MRS............ Mission-Related Software
Mrs............ Missus (AD)
Mrs............ Mistress (AD)
MRS............ Mistress (DAVI)
MRS............ Mixed Reproductive Strategy [*Avian biology*]
MRS............ Mobile Radio Service (DA)
MRS............ Mobile Reception System (SAUS)
MRS............ Mobile Remote Servicer (SSD)
MRS............ Mobility Requirements Study [*DoD*]
MRS............ Mobilization Requirement Study
MRS............ Mobilization Reserve Stocks [*Army*]
MRS............ Moderator Recovery System (COE)
MRS............ Modification Record Sheet [*NASA*] (KSC)
MRS............ Monitored Retrievable Storage [*of nuclear waste*]
MRS............ Monitored Retrievable Storage Facility [*Environmental science*] (COE)
MRS............ Monorail System
MRS............ Moore-Rott-Sears [*Theory*]
MRS............ Mortgage-Related Security (EMRF)
MRS............ Mothers Return to School
MRS............ Motor Rotation Stand
MRS............ Mountain Rescue Service (AD)
MRS............ Mouvement Republicain Senegalais [*Senegalese Republican Movement*] [*Political party*] (PPW)
MRS............ Movement and Reinforcement Study (MCD)
MRS............ Movement Report Sheet [*Military*]
MRS............ Movement Report System [*Military*]
MRS............ Multilateral RADAR Strike System [*Air Force*] (MCD)
MRS............ Multilateral RADAR Surveillance System [*Air Force*] (MCD)
MRS............ Multiple Representative Sections [*Pathology*] (DAVI)

MRS............ Multiple Rocket System (SAUS)
MRS............ Multipurpose Research System
MRS............ Multipurpose Reusable Spacecraft (IIA)
MRS............ Multirole System (SAUS)
MRS............ Multispectral Resource Scanner (ACAE)
MRS............ Music Reading Software (PCM)
MRS............ Muzzle Reference System (MCD)
MRS3.......... Multilateral RADAR Surveillance/Strike System [*Air Force*]
MRSA.......... Machinery Repairman, Seaman Apprentice [*Navy rating*]
MRSA.......... Maine Revised Statutes, Annotated [*A publication*] (DLA)
MRSA.......... Mandatory RADAR Service Area
MRSA.......... Marisa Christina, Inc. [*NASDAQ symbol*] (SAG)
MRSA.......... Materiel Readiness Support Activity [*Army*] (RDA)
MRSA.......... Materiel Readiness Support Agency [*Navy*]
MRSA.......... Medium Range Surveillance Aircraft [*Military*] (PDAA)
mrsa.......... Medium-Range Surveillance Aircraft (AD)
MRSA.......... Member of the Royal Society of Arts [*British*]
MRSA.......... Merrimack River Study Act of 1990 (COE)
MRSA.......... Metal Roofing Systems Association (NTPA)
MRSA.......... Methicillin-Resistant Staphylococcus Aureus [*Antimicrobial therapy*]
MRSA.......... Microwave Radiometer, Scatterometer, and Altimeter (MCD)
MRSA.......... Military RADAR Service Area [*Aviation*] (AIA)
MRSA.......... San Alberto [*Costa Rica*] [*ICAO location identifier*] (ICLI)
MRSAM ...... Medium-Range Surface-to-Air Missile (SAUS)
MR San A.... Member of the Royal Sanitary Association of Scotland
MRSanAS.... Member of the Royal Sanitary Association of Scotland (SAUO)
MR San Asn... Member of the Royal Sanitary Association [*British*] (AD)
MRSB.......... Material Requirements for Stock Balance
MRSB.......... San Cristobal [*Costa Rica*] [*ICAO location identifier*] (ICLI)
Mr SBA ...... Maryland State Bar Association, Report [*A publication*] (DLA)
MRSC .... Maritime Rescue Sub-Center [*Canada*]
MRSc .... Master of Rural Science [*British*] (ADA)
MRSC .... Member of the Royal Society of Canada
MRSC .... Member of the Royal Society of Chemistry [*British*] (DBQ)
MRSC .... Mississippi Remote Sensing Center [*Mississippi State University*] [*Research center*] (RCD)
MRSC .... Municipal Research & Services Center of Washington (SAUO)
MRSC .... Santa Cruz [*Costa Rica*] [*ICAO location identifier*] (ICLI)
MRSD .... Maximum Rated Standard Deviation [*Statistics*]
MRSD .... Mission Requirements on System Design [*NASA*]
MRSE .... Microwave Remote Sensing Experiment (ACAE)
MRSG .... Santa Clara De Guapiles [*Costa Rica*] [*ICAO location identifier*] (ICLI)
MRSGB ...... Member of the Radio Society of Great Britain (SAUO)
MRSH .... Marsh (ADA)
MRSH .... Member of the Royal Society of Health [*British*]
MRSh.......... Modern Red Schoolhouse
MRSH .... Shiroles [*Costa Rica*] [*ICAO location identifier*] (ICLI)
MRSHLL ...... Marshall
MrshllInd...... Marshall Industries [*Associated Press*] (SAG)
MrshMc ...... Marsh & McLennan Companies, Inc. [*Associated Press*] (SAG)
MrshS .... Marsh Supermarkets, Inc. [*Associated Press*] (SAG)
MrshSu ...... Marsh Supermarkets, Inc. [*Associated Press*] (SAG)
MRSI .... Maintenance and Repair Support Items
MRSI .... Maintenance Repair Spares Instruction (MCD)
MRSI .... Medium-Range SOF [*Special Operations Forces*] Insertion (DOMA)
MRSI .... Member of the Royal Sanitary Institute [*British*] (ROG)
MRSI .... Michigan Recovery Systems, Inc. (EFIS)
MRSI .... Mobilization Requirements, Secondary Items
MRSI .... MRS Technology, Inc. [*NASDAQ symbol*] (SAG)
MRSI .... Multi-Round Simultaneous Impact (SAUS)
MRSI .... San Isidro De El General [*Costa Rica*] [*ICAO location identifier*] (ICLI)
MRSID .... Multi-Resolution Seamless Image Database
MRSJ .... Commission for Racial Justice (EA)
MRSJ .... San Jose [*Costa Rica*] [*ICAO location identifier*] (ICLI)
MRSJ .... United Church of Christ Ministers for Racial and Social Justice (EA)
MRSL .... Member of the Royal Society of Literature [*British*]
MRSM .... Maintenance and Reliability Simulation Model (PDAA)
MRSM .... Member of the Royal Society of Medicine [*British*] (DI)
MRSM .... Member of the Royal Society of Musicians [*British*] (DI)
MRSM .... Mississippi River Suspended Matter
MRSM .... Santa Marta [*Costa Rica*] [*ICAO location identifier*] (ICLI)
MRSMA ...... Member of the Royal Society of Marine Artists [*British*] (DI)
MRSMGB .... Member of the Royal Society of Musicians of Great Britain (SAUO)
MRSMP ...... Member of the Royal Society of Miniature Painters [*British*] (DI)
MRSN .... Machinery Repairman, Seaman [*Navy rating*]
MRSN .... Sirena [*Costa Rica*] [*ICAO location identifier*] (ICLI)
MRSO .... Mobilization Reserve Stockage Objective [*Army*]
MRSO .... Santa Maria De Guacimo [*Costa Rica*] [*ICAO location identifier*] (ICLI)
MRSP .... Multifunction RADAR Signal Processor (MCD)
MRSP .... Myakka River State Park [*Florida*] (AD)
MRSP .... San Pedro [*Costa Rica*] [*ICAO location identifier*] (ICLI)
MRSPE ...... Member of the Royal Society of Painters and Etchers [*British*] (DI)
MRSPH ...... Member of the Royal Society for the Promotion of Health (SAUO)
MRSPP ...... Member of the Royal Society of Portrait Painters [*British*]
MRSPWC .... Member of the Royal Society of Painters in Water Colours [*British*]
MRSR .... Magazine Ready Service Rings (SAUS)
MRSR .... Mars Rover Sample Return (ACAE)
MR-SR ...... Material Review - Ships Record (MCD)
MRSR .... Multi-Role Survivable Radar [*Army*] (DOMA)
MRSR .... Samara [*Costa Rica*] [*ICAO location identifier*] (ICLI)
MRSRM ...... Mars Rover and Sample Return Mission (SAUO)
MRSS .... Main and Reheat Steam System [*Nuclear energy*] (NRCH)

MRSS .... Manned Rovolving Simulated Space Station (SAA)
MRSS .... Master Remote Slave Station (MCD)
MRSS .... Missile Response Simulation Software
MRSS .... San Joaquin de Abangares [*Costa Rica*] [*ICAO location identifier*] (ICLI)
mrsss........... Manned Revolving Space Systems Simulator (AD)
MRST........... Member of the Royal Society of Teachers [*British*]
MRST........... Minimum Remaining Slack Time (PDAA)
MRST........... San Agustin [*Costa Rica*] [*ICAO location identifier*] (ICLI)
MRS Tch...... MRS Technology, Inc. [*Associated Press*] (SAG)
MRSV .... Maneuverable Recoverable Space Vehicle
MRSV .... Military Railway Service Veterans (EA)
MRSV .... San Vito De Jaba [*Costa Rica*] [*ICAO location identifier*] (ICLI)
MRSW .... Member of the Royal Society of Scottish Painters and Watercolours [*British*] (DAS)
MRSX .... Sixaola [*Costa Rica*] [*ICAO location identifier*] (ICLI)
MRT............. Air Mauritanie [*Mauritania*] [*ICAO designator*] (FAAC)
MRT............. Machine-Readable Tapes [*Computer science*]
MRT............. Maintainability Review Team [*Navy*] (NG)
MRT............. Maintenance Readiness Training (DNAB)
MRT............. Maintenance Recovery Team (SAUO)
MRT............. Maintenance Response Team (SAUO)
MRT............. Major Role Therapy [*Schizophrenia*]
MRT............. Malignant Rhabdoid Tumor [*Oncology*]
MRT............. Manpack Radio Telephone (SAUO)
MRT............. Marble Threshold (AAG)
MRT............. Marietta Resources [*Vancouver Stock Exchange symbol*]
Mrt............... Martinique (AD)
MRT............. Marysville, OH [*Location identifier*] [*FAA*] (FAAL)
MRT............. Mass Rapid Transit (AD)
MRT............. Mass Rapid Transport [*British*]
MRT............. Material Review Tag [*Aviation*] (MCD)
MRT............. Mauritania [*ANSI three-letter standard code*] (CNC)
MRT............. Mauritius Radio Telescope (SAUO)
MRT............. Maximum Rated Thrust (MCD)
MRT............. Maximum Repair Time (PDAA)
MRT............. Maze-Running Time [*Psychology*]
mrt.............. Mean Radiant Temperature (AD)
MRT............. Mean Radiant Temperature
MRT............. Mean Radiative-Transfer [*Meteorology*]
MRT............. Mean Ready Time (MCD)
MRT............. Mean Repair Time
MRT............. Mean Residence Time [*Kinetics*]
MRT............. Mean Resolvable Temperature (ACAE)
MRT............. Mean Retention Time [*Physiology*]
MRT............. Measured Rate of Time (PDAA)
MRT............. Median Reaction Time (MELL)
MRT............. Median Recognition Threshold (MAE)
MRT............. Median Relapse Time (MELL)
MRT............. Medical Records Technician (DAVI)
MRT............. Medium Range Truck [*Military*]
MRT............. Medium-Range Typhon [*Missile*] (NG)
MRT............. Meridional Ray Trace
Mrt............... Merit [*Record label*]
MRT............. Metropolitan Readiness Test
mrt.............. Mid-Range Trajectory (AD)
mrt.............. Mildew-Resistant Thread (AD)
MRT............. Mildew-Resistant Thread
MRT............. Milestones Reporting Techniques
MRT............. Military Rated Thrust (NG)
mrt.............. Military-Rated Thrust (AD)
MRT............. Military Reserve Technician (GFGA)
MRT............. Military Review Team (AD)
MRT............. Milk Ring Test (PDAA)
MRT............. Miniature Receiver Terminal
MRT............. Minimal Resolvable Temperature
MRT............. Minimum Resolvable Temperature (MCD)
MRT............. Missile Round Trainer (MCD)
MRT............. Missile Round Transporter (MCD)
mrt.............. Mission Readiness Tester (AD)
MRT............. Mobile RADAR Target
MRT............. Mobile Radio Terminal (SAUO)
MRT............. Mobile Repair Team (SAUO)
MRT............. Modified Rhyme Test
MRT............. Modulus of Rupture Test (AD)
MRT............. Mortgage & Realty Trust (EFIS)
MRT............. Movimento Revolucionario Tiradentes [*Revolutionary Tiradentes Movement*] [*Brazil*] [*Political party*] (PD)
MRT............. Multiple Requests Terminal [*Computer science*] (HGAA)
MRT............. Multi-Radar Tracking (SAUS)
MRT............. Murotomisaki [*Japan*] [*Seismograph station code, US Geological Survey*] (SEIS)
MRT............. Muscle Response Test
MRT............. Reformed Theological Seminary, Jackson, MS [*OCLC symbol*] (OCLC)
MRT 6 .... Metropolitan Readiness Tests-Sixth Edition [*J. R. Nurss*] (DIPS)
MRTA.......... Maintenance Requirements Task Analysis (AD)
MRTA.......... Marietta Corp. [*NASDAQ symbol*] (NQ)
MRTA.......... Marketing Research Trade Association [*Later, MRA*] (EA)
MRTA.......... Mechanical Response Tissue Analyzer [*For measuring bone strength*]
MRTA.......... Movimiento Revolucionario Tupac Amaru [*Peru*] [*Political party*] (EY)
MRTA.......... Tamarindo de Bagaces [*Costa Rica*] [*ICAO location identifier*] (ICLI)
MRTAF........ Marshal of the Royal Air Force (SAUO)
MRTB.......... Metallic Return Transfer Breaker (ACAE)

MRTB.......... Missile Research Test Building (ACAE)
MRTB.......... Ticaban [*Costa Rica*] [*ICAO location identifier*] (ICLI)
MRTC.......... Marine Corps Reserve Training Center
MRTC.......... Medical Replacement Training Center (SAUO)
MRTC.......... Military Real-Time Computer (AAG)
MRTC.......... Multiple Real-Time Commands (NASA)
MRTCB........ Machine Ruling Trade Conciliation Board (SAUO)
MRTCS........ Miniaturized Real Time Computational System (ACAE)
MRTD .... Minimum Resolvable Temperature Difference (PDAA)
MRTE.......... Master of Radio and Television Engineering
MRTE.......... Missile Round Test Equipment
MRT Eng..... Master of Radio and Television Engineering
MRTF.......... Mean Rounds To Failure (SAUS)
MRTF/A....... Manual Radar Terrain Following/Avoidance (ACAE)
MRTFB........ Major Range and Test Facility Base [*Military*] (CAAL)
MRTFL........ Medium Rough Terrain Forklift (SAUS)
MRTFM....... Mean Rounds to First Maintenance [*Army*]
MRTG.......... Mortgage
MRTG.......... Multi Router Traffic Grapher (SAUS)
MRTG .... Taboga [*Costa Rica*] [*ICAO location identifier*] (ICLI)
MRTHN........ Marathon
MRTI........... Moscow Radio Technical Institute (SAUO)
MRTI........... Multirole Thermal Imager [*Defense electronics*]
MRTK.......... Movimiento Revolucionario Tupaj Katari [*Tupaj Katari Revolutionary Movement*] [*Bolivia*] [*Political party*] (PPW)
mrtm........... Maritime (AD)
MRTM.......... Maritime
MRTM.......... Tamarindo de Santa Cruz [*Costa Rica*] [*ICAO location identifier*] (ICLI)
MRTN.......... Marten Transport [*NASDAQ symbol*] (TTSB)
MRTN .... Marten Transport Ltd. [*NASDAQ symbol*] (NQ)
Mrtnz .... Martinez (AD)
mrto............ Miscellaneous Reference Tool (AD)
MRTP.......... Master of Regional and Town Planning
MRTP.......... Master of Rural and Town Planning (GAGS)
MRTP.......... Military Reliable Tube Program
MRTPI .... Member of the Royal Town Planning Institute [*British*]
MRTR .... Mortar [*Technical drawings*] (DAC)
MRTR .... Tambor [*Costa Rica*] [*ICAO location identifier*] (ICLI)
MRTRY .... Mortuary
mrts............ Marginal Rate of Technical Substitution (AD)
MRTS.......... Marginal Rate of Technical Substitution [*Ecology*]
MRTS.......... Mass Rapid Transit System (AD)
MRTS.......... Master RADAR Tracking Station
Mrts .... Mauritius (AD)
MRTS.......... Member of the Royal Television Society (SAUO)
MRTS.......... Meteorological Real-Time System [*Computer science*] (KSC)
MRTS.......... Microwave Repeater Test Set (DA)
MRTS.......... Missile Round Test Set
MRTS.......... Monthly Retail Trade Survey (SAUO)
MRTS.......... Multi-Media Remote Teaching System [*AT & T Co., Illinois Institute of Technology*]
MRT-S .... Multi-Role Turret System (SAUS)
MRTT........... Modified Rushton Towed Target (SAUS)
MRTT........... Modular Record Traffic Terminal [*Formerly, COED*] [*Army*] (MCD)
MRTT........... Multi-Role Tanker Transport (SAUS)
MRTU .... Multiple Remote Terminal Unit (SAUS)
MRTU .... Multiplex Remote Terminal Unit (MCD)
MRU .... Machine Records Unit [*Computer science*]
MRU .... Main Resource Unit
MRU .... Maintenance Recorder Unit (SAUS)
MRU .... Maintenance Replaceable Unit (MCD)
MRU .... Mano River Union [*See also UFM*] (EAIO)
MRU .... Maritime Reconnaissance Unit [*British military*] (DMA)
mru .... Mass Radiography Unit (AD)
MRU .... Mass Radiography Unit
MRU .... Material Recovery Unit
MRU .... Mauritius [*Airport symbol*] (OAG)
MRU .... Medical Rehabilitation Unit (AD)
MRU .... Message Retransmission Unit
MRU .... Meteorological Research Unit
MRU .... Microfilm Recording Unit
MRU .... Microwave Relay Unit
MRU .... Military RADAR Unit [*Aviation*] (FAAC)
mru .... Minimal Reproductive Unit (AD)
MRU .... Minimal Reproductive Units [*Bacteriology*]
MRU .... Minimum Replacement Unit
mru .... Mobile Radio Unit (AD)
MRU .... Mobile Radio Unit [*Air Force*]
MRU .... Mobile Receiving Unit (SAUS)
MRU .... Mobile Refrigeration Unit (KSC)
MRU .... Mobile Remote Unit [*From computer game "Hacker II"*]
MRU .... Most Recently Used Data [*Computer science*] (PCM)
MRU .... Motion Reference Unit (MCD)
MRU .... Mountain Rescue Unit (COE)
MRU .... Movement Release Unit [*MTMC*] (TAG)
MRU .... Much Regret, I Am Unable
MRU .... Multifunction Reference Unit (MCD)
MRUA .... Mobile Radio Users' Association (IAA)
MRUASTAS... Medium-Range Unmanned Aerial Surveillance and Target Acquisition System (NATG)
MR-UAV ...... Medium Range UAV (SAUS)
M Ru E .... Master of Rural Engineering
M Ru Eng .... Master of Rural Engineering
MRUP .... Upala [*Costa Rica*] [*ICAO location identifier*] (ICLI)

MRurSc.......	Master of Rural Science [*British*] (ADA)
MRUSI........	Member of the Royal United Service Institution [*British*]
MRV...........	Maintenance-Recovery Vehicle (SAUS)
MRV...........	Maneuvering Reentry Vehicle
MRV...........	Mark V Petroleums & Mines [*Vancouver Stock Exchange symbol*]
MRV...........	Mars Roving Vehicle [*NASA*] (PDAA)
MRV...........	Marvel Entertainment Group [*NYSE symbol*] (SPSG)
mrv...........	Material Receipt Voucher (AD)
MRV...........	Middlesex Rifle Volunteers [*Military*] [*British*] (ROG)
MRV...........	Mineral Nyye Vody [*Former USSR*] [*Airport symbol*] (OAG)
MRV...........	Mini-Rotary Viscometer [*Mechanical engineering*]
MRV...........	Minute Respiratory Volume
MRV...........	Miravia Ltd. [*Romania*] [*FAA designator*] (FAAC)
MRV...........	Missile Recovery Vessel (AD)
mrv...........	Missile Re-Entry Vehicle (AD)
MRV...........	Missouri River Division (SAUO)
mrv...........	Mixed Respiratory Vaccine [*Medicine*] (AD)
MRV...........	Mixed Respiratory Vaccine
MRV...........	Mouvement de Regroupement Voltaique [*Upper Volta Regroupment Movement*] [*Political party*]
MRV...........	Mulberry Ringspot Virus [*Plant pathology*]
MRV...........	Multiple Re-entry Vehicle (SAUO)
MRVA	Member of the Rating and Valuation Association [*British*] (DI)
MRVA	Minimum Radar Vectoring Altitude (SAUS)
MRVC	Member of the Royal Veterinary College [*British*]
MRVC	MRV Communications, Inc. [*NASDAQ symbol*] (SAG)
MRVC	Multiple Rate Voice Card (SAUS)
MRV Cm	MRV Communications, Inc. [*Associated Press*] (SAG)
MRVI	Monte Reale Valcellina [*Italy*] [*Seismograph station code, US Geological Survey*] (SEIS)
MRVL..........	Marvell Technology Group [*NASDAQ symbol*]
MRVLP	Maneuvering Reentry Vehicle for Low-Level Penetration (MCD)
MRVP	Mean Right Ventricular Pressure [*Cardiology*]
mrV-P	Methyl Red Voges-Proskauer [*Bacteriology*] (AD)
MRVP	Methyl-Red, Voges-Proskauer [*Medium*] [*Bacteriology*]
MRVR	Mechanised Repair & Recovery Vehicle (SAUS)
MRVT..........	Miravant [*NASDAQ symbol*]
MRVT..........	Miravant Medical Technologies
MRVT..........	Multiple Rate Voice Terminal [*Telecommunications*] (LAIN)
MRVTB	Maximally Restrictive Verifiable Test Ban [*For nuclear bombs*]
MRW	Maximum Ramp Weight (SAUO)
mrw	Morale, Recreation, and Welfare (AD)
MRW	Morale, Recreation, and Welfare [*Military*] (AFM)
MRW	Morioka [*Japan*] [*Airport symbol*] (OAG)
mr/w	Multiple Read/Write (AD)
MRWA	Midland Railway of Western Australia (AD)
mrwc	Multiple Reading, Writing, Compiling (AD)
MRWC	Multiple Read-Write Compute
MRWG	Mission Requirements Working Group (ACAE)
MRWS	Mobile RADAR Weather System (DNAB)
MRWS	Monoscopic Revision Workstation (SAUO)
MRX...........	Hermens/Markair Express [*ICAO designator*] (FAAC)
MRX...........	Magnetoresistive Extended [*Computer science*]
MRX...........	Medicis Pharmaceutical "A" [*NYSE symbol*]
MRX...........	Memorex Corp. (IAA)
MRX...........	Mineiros [*Brazil*] [*Airport symbol*] (AD)
MRX...........	Mobil Oil Corp., Toxicology Division, Information Center, Princeton, NJ [*OCLC symbol*] (OCLC)
MRX...........	Movement Research Exchange
MRX...........	Riverside, CA [*Location identifier*] [*FAA*] (FAAL)
MRXS	Mental Retardation, X-Linked, Syndrome [*Medicine*] (DMAA)
MRY...........	Marilyn Resources [*Vancouver Stock Exchange symbol*]
MRY...........	Mary [*Former USSR*] [*Seismograph station code, US Geological Survey*] [*Closed*] (SEIS)
MRY...........	Merry Land & Invest [*NYSE symbol*] (TTSB)
MRY...........	Merry Land & Investment [*NYSE symbol*] (SAG)
MRY...........	Monterey [*California*] [*Airport symbol*] (OAG)
MRYPr........	Merry Land & Inv Sr'A'Cv Pfd [*NYSE symbol*] (TTSB)
MRYPrC......	Merry Land & Inv Sr'C'Cv Pfd [*NYSE symbol*] (TTSB)
mrytm........	Must Have Reply Here by Tomorrow Morning (AD)
mrz	Marzo [*March*] [*Spanish*] (AD)
MRZ...........	Moree [*Australia*] [*Airport symbol*] (OAG)
MRZ...........	Syracuse, NY [*Location identifier*] [*FAA*] (FAAL)
MRZP..........	Zapotal De Guanacaste [*Costa Rica*] [*ICAO location identifier*] (ICLI)
MS..............	Brody Medical Science Building (SAUS)
MS..............	Egyptair [*ICAO designator*] (AD)
MS..............	IEEE Magnetics Society (EA)
MS..............	Ma'aser Sheni (BJA)
MS..............	Machinery Survey [*Shipping*]
ms	Machine Screw (AD)
MS..............	Machine Screw
MS..............	Machine Selection (IEEE)
ms	Machine Steel (AD)
MS..............	Machine Steel
MS..............	Machining System (IAA)
MS..............	Macromodular System [*Computer science*] (IEEE)
MS..............	Macro Society (EA)
MS..............	Magnetic South
MS..............	Magnetic Stirrer [*Biotechnology*]
MS..............	Magnetic Storage [*Computer science*]
MS..............	Magnetic Strip (IAA)
MS..............	Magnetic Susceptibility (SAUS)
MS..............	Magnetic Synchron (IAA)
MS..............	Magnetostatic [*Telecommunications*] (IAA)
MS..............	Magnetostriction
M/S	Mail Station (ACAE)
MS..............	Mail Station (ACAE)
MS..............	Mail Steamer
M/S	Mail Stop
MS..............	Main Sequence [*Astronomy*]
M/S	Mainstage [*NASA*] (KSC)
MS..............	Main Station (SAUS)
MS..............	Main Steam (NRCH)
MS..............	Main Storage
ms	Main Switch (AD)
MS..............	Main Switch
ms	Maintenance and Service (AD)
MS..............	Maintenance and Service
MS..............	Maintenance Schedule (DA)
MS..............	Maintenance Squadron
MS..............	Maintenance Standard
MS..............	Maintenance Superintendent [*Military*] (AFIT)
MS +..........	Maintenance Support Positive
MS..............	Maintenance System (ACII)
MS..............	Majority Stockholder
ms	Major Subject (AD)
MS..............	Major Subject [*Military*]
MS..............	Maladjustment Score [*Psychology*]
MS..............	Male Servant
MS..............	Malone Society (EA)
MS..............	Mammal Society (EAIO)
MS..............	Management Science [*Computer science*] (BUR)
MS..............	Management Services (KSC)
MS..............	Management Staff [*Environmental Protection Agency*] (GFGA)
MS..............	Management System (OICC)
MS..............	Manic State [*Medicine*] (DB)
MS..............	Manned Station (IAA)
M/S	Mannlicher-Schoenauer (AD)
MS..............	Mannose Sensitive [*Biochemistry*]
MS..............	Mano Sinistra [*With the Left Hand*] [*Music*]
M/S	Manslaughter
MS..............	Man Station [*Military*]
MS..............	Man System (SAUS)
MS..............	Manual Sequential (NRCH)
MS..............	Manual Supplement
MS..............	Manual System (DCTA)
MS..............	Manufacturing in Space
MS..............	Manufacturing Specification (AAG)
MS..............	Manufacturing Standard
MS..............	Manufacturing Status (AAG)
MS..............	Manufacturing Support
Ms	Manuscript (AL)
ms	Manuscript (VRA)
MS..............	Manuscript (WDAA)
MS..............	Manuscript Reports [*A publication*] (DLA)
MS..............	Manuscript Society (EA)
MS..............	Manuscriptum [*Manuscript*] [*Latin*]
MS..............	Mare Serenitatis [*Sea of Serenity*] [*Lunar area*]
ms	Margin of Safety (AD)
MS..............	Margin of Safety [*Engineering*]
MS..............	Marian Sisters of the Diocese of Lincoln (TOCD)
MS..............	Marie-See [*Syndrome*] [*Medicine*] (DB)
MS..............	Marie-Struempell [*Disease*] [*Medicine*] (DB)
MS..............	Marijuana Smoke
Ms	Mariners [*Seattle Baseball Team*] (AD)
MS..............	Marine Status (ARMP)
MS..............	Marital Status
MS..............	Maritime Surveillance (SAUS)
MS..............	Marker Switch (IAA)
MS..............	Marketing Society (COBU)
m/s	Marking and Stenciling (AD)
MS..............	Mark Sense (NITA)
MS..............	Mark Sensing (MSA)
MS..............	Marquandia Society (EA)
MS..............	Marshall Steel Ltd. [*Toronto Stock Exchange symbol*]
MS..............	Mass Spectrography
MS..............	Mass Spectrometer (AAEL)
Ms	Mass Spectrometer (NAKS)
ms	Mass Spectrometric (AD)
MS..............	Mass Spectrometry
MS..............	Mass Spectroscopy
MS..............	Mass Storage [*Computer science*]
MS..............	Master of Science (GAGS)
MS..............	Master of Sociology
MS..............	Master of Surgery
MS..............	Master Scene [*Major script sequence*] (NTCM)
MS..............	Master Scheduler (CMD)
MS..............	Master Sequencer (AAG)
MS..............	Master Sergeant
M-S	Master-Servant [*Legal shorthand*] (LWAP)
MS..............	Master Shot [*Film production*] (NTCM)
MS..............	Master-Slave [*Computer science*] (MHDI)
ms	Master Switch (AD)
MS..............	Master Switch
MS..............	Master Synchronizer (CET)
MS..............	Mast Section (IAA)
ms	Matched Set (AD)
MS..............	Matched Set [*Philately*]
MS..............	Match Station (VLIE)
Ms	Material Specification (NAKS)

MS	Materials Science
MS	Material Standard (AD)
MS	Material Support
MS	Mathis Society [Defunct] (EA)
Ms	Mating Sequence and Control [NASA] (NAKS)
MS	Mating Sequence and Control (NASA)
MS	Matrix Spike
Ms	Mature Motion Pictures (AD)
Ms	Mauritius (MILB)
Ms	Mauritius
MS	Maxillary Sinus [Medicine] (MELL)
ms	Maximum Stress (AD)
MS	Maximum Stress
ms	Mean Square (AD)
MS	Mean Square
MS/	Measured Service Pricing [Telecommunications] (TEL)
M/S	Measurement Stimuli (NASA)
MS	Measurement Systems Inc. (SAUS)
MS	Measuring Set
MS	Measuring System
MS	Mechanical Seal
MS	Mechanical Stimulation (DB)
MS	Mechanized Scheduling [Telecommunications] (TEL)
MS	Meckel Syndrome [Medicine] (DMAA)
MS	Medial Septum [Anatomy]
MS	Media-Service GmbH [Database producer] (IID)
MS	Media Society [British] (DBA)
MS	Medical Science (DAVI)
MS	Medical Services [Navy] [British]
MS	Medical Staff [British military] (DMA)
MS	Medical Student (DAVI)
MS	Medical Supplies [Military]
MS	Medical Survey [Navy]
MS	Medicine and Surgery [Navy] (IEEE)
MS	Medium-Scale (IAA)
MS	Medium Set [Adhesives]
MS	Medium Setting [Asphalt grade]
ms	Medium Shot (AD)
MS	Medium Soft (IAA)
MS	Medium-Speed (IAA)
ms	Medium Steel (AD)
MS	Medium Steel
MS	Meeting of Signatories [INTELSAT]
MS	Meeting Series [Online database field identifier]
MS	Megalosperm [Medicine] (MELL)
MS	Megasecond (IAA)
MS	Mega Society (EA)
MS	Megasporocyte [Botany]
MS	Melville Society (EA)
M/S	Member State (DCTA)
M/S	Memorandum Slip [for informal interoffice communications]
MS	Memoriae Sacrum [Sacred to the Memory Of] [Latin]
MS	Memory Store [Computer science] (PCM)
MS	Memory System
MS	Mencken Society (EA)
Ms	Mendes (AD)
MS	Menkes' Syndrome [Medicine] (MELL)
MS	Men of the Stones (EA)
MS	Mental Status [Psychology]
MS	Merchant Shipping
MS	Mercury-Scout [Spacecraft] [NASA]
MS	Merit System (OICC)
MS	Mesa [Type of transistor] (MDG)
Ms	Mesothorium (AD)
MS	Message Store [Telecommunications] (OSI)
MS	Message Switch (SAUS)
MS	Message Switching [Telecommunications] (IAA)
MS	Messaging Services (VLIE)
MS	Mess Management Specialist [Military] (MUSM)
MS	Mestome Sheath [Botany]
Ms	Mesyl [Organic chemistry]
MS	Metallurgical Society (NADA)
m/s	Metal Shank (AD)
MS	Metals Society [Later, IOM] (EAIO)
MS	Metal Stamping
MS	Meteoritical Society (EA)
MS	Meteoroid Shield (KSC)
MS	Meteor Scatter (PDAA)
ms	Meters per Second (AD)
M/S	Meters per Second
MS	Methionine Synthase [An enzyme]
MS	Method of Sale
MS	Methyl Salicylate [Organic chemistry]
MS	Metric Size (IAA)
ms	Metric System (AD)
MS	Metric System
MS	Mezzo Soprano [Music] (ROG)
MS	Michigan State University of Agriculture and Applied Sciences (AD)
MS	Microbial Susceptibility [Medicine] (DB)
MS	Microcirculatory Society (EA)
MS	Microprogram Storage [Computer science] (MDG)
MS	Microscope Slide (DMAA)
MS	Microscopic System
ms	Microsecond (VLIE)
ms	Microseismic (AD)
MS	Microsoft Corporation (WDMC)
MS	Microsphere
M/S	Microwave Scanner [Marine science] (OSRA)
MS	Microwave Spectrum
MS	Mid-Shot
ms	Mild Steel (AD)
MS	Mild Steel
m/s	Milestone (AD)
MS	Milestone (KSC)
Ms	Milestone (NAKS)
MS	Milestone Scientific [AMEX symbol] (SG)
MS	Military Science (AABC)
MS	Military Secretary [British]
MS	Military Service
MS	Military Service Act [British]
MS	Military Specification (AAG)
MS	Military Staff [British military] (DMA)
MS	Military Standard (NAKS)
MS	Military Standard [Parts designation]
MS	Military Survivors (EA)
MS	Milk Sugar (MELL)
MS	Millennium Society (EA)
Ms	Millisecond (NAKS)
ms	Millisecond
MS	Milliseconds (ACAE)
mS	Millisiemens
MS	Minesweeper [or Minesweeping]
MS	Miniature Screw [Lamp base] (NTCM)
m/s	Miniature Sheet of Stamps (AD)
MS	Minimal Support (DAVI)
ms	Minimum Stress (AD)
MS	Minister of State [British]
MS	Ministry of Shipping [British]
MS	Ministry of Supply [Also, MOS] [British]
MS	Minority Stockholder
M/S	Minor Support (KSC)
MS	Minor Surgery (SAUS)
ms	Mint State (AD)
MS	Mint State
MS	Minus
MS	Minutes (AAG)
MS	Miscellaneous
MS	Miscellaneous Services [Department of Employment] [British]
MS	Missile Station (AAG)
MS	Missile Support (SAUS)
MS	Missile System
ms	[The] Missionaries of Our Lady La Salette (TOCD)
MS	Missionaries of Our Lady of LaSalette [Roman Catholic religious order]
MS	Missionary Sisters of Our Lady of Africa [White Sisters] [Roman Catholic religious order]
MS	Missionary Society [British]
MS	Mission Sequencer (SAA)
MS	Mission Simulator
MS	Mission Specialist (MCD)
Ms	Mission Specialist [NASA] (NAKS)
MS	Mission Station (MCD)
Ms	Mission Station [NASA] (NAKS)
MS	Missions to Seamen (EA)
MS	Mission Support
MS	Mississippi [Postal code]
Ms	Mississippi State Library, Jackson, MS [Library symbol] [Library of Congress] (LCLS)
Ms	Mistress (DAVI)
ms	Mitral Stenosis (AD)
MS	Mitral Stenosis [Cardiology]
MS	Mittelsatz [Middle Movement] [Music]
M-S	Mitte-Seite [Stereo] (IEEE)
MS	Mobile Searchlight [British]
MS	Mobile Service [Telecommunications] (TEL)
MS	Mobile Station (VLIE)
MS	Mobile Surgery [British]
MS	Mobilization Station [DoD]
MS	Modal Sensation [Psychology]
MS	Modal Sensitivity [Medicine]
MS	Model Station
MS	Modem Sharing (ACAE)
MS	Moderately Susceptible [Plant pathology]
MS	Modern Science [A publication]
MS	Modulation Sensitivity
MS	Moessbauer Spectroscopy
MS	Molar Degree of Substitution [Organic chemistry]
MS	Molar Solution [Dentistry]
MS	Molar Substitution (DB)
m/s	Molecular Sieve (MCD)
MS	Molecular Staffing [Optics] (EECA)
MS	Molecular Stuffing (VLIE)
MS	Molecular Substitution
M-S	Monday through Saturday (AD)
MS	Money Supply
MS	Mongolian Spot [Medicine]
MS	Monitor Station
MS	Monorail Society (EA)
m/s	Month after Sight (AD)
ms	Months after Sight (AD)

MS	Months after Sight [*or Month's Sight*] [*Business term*]
MS	Montserrat [*ANSI two-letter standard code*] (CNC)
MS	Morel Syndrome [*Medicine*] (MELL)
MS	More of the Same (SAUS)
MS	More Segments (VLIE)
MS	More Significant [*Statistics*]
MS	Morgan Stanley Group, Inc. [*NYSE symbol*] (SPSG)
MS	Morphine Sulfate [*Narcotic*]
MS	Morquio-Silverkioeld [*Syndrome*] [*Medicine*] (DB)
MS	Morse Tape (IAA)
MS	Most Severe [*Automotive engineering*]
MS	Most Significant
MS	Motile Sperm
MS	Motion Sensitivity (KSC)
MS	Motor Ship
m/s	Motorskib [*Motorship*] [*Norwegian*] (AD)
MS	Motor Starting (IAA)
MS	Motor Supports
MS	Mucosubstance (MAE)
MS	Multilateral Staff [*Environmental Protection Agency*] (GFGA)
ms	Multiple Sclerosis (AD)
MS	Multiple Sclerosis [*Medicine*]
MS	Multiple Section (MSA)
ms	Multiple Starters (AD)
MS	Multiplexer Section (SAUS)
MS	Multiplexer Storage (IAA)
MS	Multistart [*Optimization method*]
Ms	Multistring (NAKS)
MS	Multistring (NASA)
MS	Munchausen's Syndrome [*Medicine*] (MELL)
MS	Murashige-Skoog [*Medium*] [*Botany*]
Ms	Murmurs [*Medicine*] (DMAA)
MS	Murphy-Sturm [*Lymphosarcoma*] [*Medicine*] (DB)
MS	Muscle Shortening [*Medicine*]
ms	Muscle Strength (AD)
MS	Muscle Strength
MS	Musculactive Substance [*Medicine*]
MS	Musculoskeletal [*Medicine*]
MS	Music Sales Corporation [*Publisher*]
Ms	Mussels [*Quality of the bottom*] [*Nautical charts*]
MS	Mustard Seed (EA)
MS	Mycoplasma Synoviae [*A pathogen*]
MS	Myelosclerosis [*Medicine*] (MELL)
MS	Mythopoeic Society (EA)
MS	Ship Station [*ITU designation*] (CET)
MS	Somerset Library [*Bibliotheque Somerset*], Manitoba [*Library symbol*] [*National Library of Canada*] (BIB)
MS	Springfield City Library, Springfield, MA [*Library symbol*] [*Library of Congress*] (LCLS)
MS1	Mess Management Specialist, First Class [*Navy rating*] (DNAB)
MS-2	Mare Serenitatis [*Sea of Serenity*] [*Lunar area*]
MS2	Mess Management Specialist, Second Class [*Navy rating*] (DNAB)
M/S²	Meters per Second Squared
MS2	Micro-Set System 2 (NITA)
MS3	Mess Management Specialist, Third Class [*Navy rating*] (DNAB)
MS-3	Military Staffing Standards System
MS3	Munitions Support Structure Study [*Army*]
MS3	Munitions System Support Structure
MS3-X	Munitions System Support Structure - Extended [*Army*]
MS04	Morphine Sulfate (SAUS)
mS-222	Tricaine Methane Sulphonate [*Chemistry*] (DAVI)
MSA	Magazine Shippers Association
MSA	Mahri, Suqutri, and Shahri (BJA)
MSA	Main Store Allocator
MSA	Maintenance Support Activity
MSA	Major Serologic Antigen [*Medicine*] (MELL)
MSA	Major System Acquisition (COE)
MSA	Malaysia-Singapore Airlines
MSA	Male Specific Antigen (PDAA)
MSA	Malta Standardisation Authority (SAUS)
MSA	Management Science Associates, Inc. [*Information service or system*] (IID)
MSA	Management Science of America (HGAA)
MSA	Management Service Architecture (SAUS)
MSA	Management System Analysis
MSA	Management System Audits (EEVL)
MSA	Mandusa Resources Ltd. [*Vancouver Stock Exchange symbol*]
MSA	Manitoba Society of Artists [*1925*] [*Canada*] (NGC)
MSA	Mannitol Salt Agar (MAE)
MSA	Marigold Society of America (EA)
MSA	Marine Safety Agency (WDAA)
MSA	Marine Science Activities [*Program*] [*Coast Guard*]
MSA	Marine Stewards' Association [*Australia*]
MSA	Mariological Society of America (EA)
MSA	Maritime Safety Agency (NADA)
MSA	Maritime Safety Authority (SAUS)
MSA	Marker Signal Attenuation
MSA	Market Science Associates, Inc. [*Information service or system*] (IID)
MSA	Marlowe Society of America (EA)
MSA	Marquetry Society of America (EA)
MSA	Marshal Sprayable Ablative [*NASA*]
MSA	Masonic Service Association of the United States (EA)
MSA	Massachusetts School of Art
MSA	Mass-Separating Agent [*Chemical engineering*]
MSA	Mass Storage Adapter
MSA	Master of School Administration (PGP)
MSA	Master of Science Administration (PGP)
MSA	Master of Science and Arts
MSA	Master of Science in Accountancy
MSA	Master of Science in Accounting (GAGS)
MSA	Master of Science in Administration (GAGS)
MSA	Master of Science in Agriculture
MSA	Master of Science in Anesthesia (PGP)
MSA	Master of Science in Anthropology (PGP)
MSA	Master of Scientific Agriculture
MSA	Master of Sport Administration (GAGS)
MSA	Material Service Area
MSA	Material Stores Area (KSC)
MSA	Material Surveillance Assembly [*Nuclear energy*] (NRCH)
MSA	Matrix Scheme for Algorithms (PDAA)
MSA	Mature Students' Association [*British*] (BI)
MSA	Mean Spherical Approximation [*Physical chemistry*]
MSA	Measure of Sampling Adequacy Index (EDAC)
MSA	Mechanical Signature Analysis
MSA	Media Studies Association [*British*]
MSA	Medical Savings Account
MSA	Medical Scientists' Association [*Australia*]
MSA	Medical Service Agency (WYGK)
MSA	Medical Services Account
MSA	Medical Services Administration [*HEW*]
MSA	Medusa Corp. [*NYSE symbol*] (CTT)
MSA	Member of the Society of Apothecaries [*British*]
MSA	Member of the Society of Architects [*British*] (DAS)
MSA	Member of the Society of Arts [*British*]
MSA	Membrane-Stabilizing Activity [*Cardiology*]
MSA	Membrane Surface Area [*Cytology*]
MSA	Merchant Shipping Act
MSA	Mercury Singapore Airlines
MSA	Mermaid Series [*A publication*]
MSA	Mesa Public Library, Mesa, AZ [*OCLC symbol*] (OCLC)
MSA	Metaphysical Society of America (EA)
MSA	Meteorological Satellite Activity (IAA)
MSA	Meteorological Support Activity [*Army Electronics Command*]
MSA	Methacrylate Structural Adhesive
MSA	Methanesulfonic Acid [*Organic chemistry*]
MSA	Method of Standard Additions
MSA	Methyltrimethylsilylacetamide [*Organic chemistry*]
MSA	Metropolitan Service Area [*Telecommunications*] (TSSD)
MSA	Metropolitan Statistical Area [*Census Bureau*]
MSA	Metropolitan Statistical Area Standard
MSA	Michigan Statutes Annotated [*A publication*] (AAGC)
MSA	Microcomputer Software Association (EA)
MSA	Microgravity Science and Applications
MSA	Microscopy Society of America (NTPA)
MSA	Microsomal Antibody
MSA	Microwave System Analyzer (ACAE)
MSA	Middle Sacral Artery [*Medicine*] (MELL)
MSA	Middle States Association (NADA)
MSA	Middle States Association of Colleges and Schools (EA)
MSA	Middle Stone Age [*Anthropology*]
MSA	Midsystolic Click [*Medicine*] (DB)
MSA	Military Service Act [*British*] (DMA)
MSA	Military Subsistence Agency [*Merged with Defense Supply Agency*]
MSA	Millennium Star Atlas [*A publication*]
MSA	Milton Society of America (EA)
MSA	Mineralogical Society of America (EA)
MSA	Mine Safety Appliance
MSA	Minesweeper, Auxiliary [*Navy symbol*] [*Obsolete*]
MSA	Minimum Safe Altitude [*Aviation*]
MSA	Minimum Sector Altitude [*Aviation*] (PIPO)
MSA	Minimum Surface Area (KSC)
MSA	Minimun Sector Altitude [*Aviation*] (PIAV)
MSA	Minnesota Statutes, Annotated [*A publication*] (DLA)
MSA	Misce Secundum Artem [*Mix Pharmaceutically*] [*Latin*]
MSA	Missile Support Activity (MCD)
MSA	Missile System Analyst (SAA)
MSA	Missile System Availability (MCD)
MSA	Missionary Sisters of the Assumption [*Roman Catholic religious order*]
MSA	Mission Services Association (EA)
MSA	Mission Support Area [*NASA*]
MSA	Mistral Air SRL [*Italy*] [*ICAO designator*] (FAAC)
MSA	Mobile Subscriber Access (MCD)
MSA	Modern Studies Association [*British*] (DBA)
MSA	Monitor and Switching Assembly
MSA	Morale Support Activities [*Military*] (AABC)
MSA	Most Seriously Affected [*Food-deficient nations*]
MSA	Motor Schools' Association of Great Britain (BI)
MSA	Mount Pleasant, TX [*Location identifier*] [*FAA*] (FAAL)
MSA	Mount San Antonio [*New Mexico*] [*Seismograph station code, US Geological Survey*] (SEIS)
MSA	Mouse Serum Albumin [*Clinical chemistry*]
MSA	Mouvement Socialiste Africain [*African Socialist Movement*] [*Political party*]
MSA	Mouvement Souverainete Association [*Canada*] (PPW)
MSA	Multichannel Signal Averager [*Computer science*]
MSA	Multiple System Atrophy [*Medicine*]
MSA	Multiplication Stimulating Activity [*Cytochemistry*]
MSA	Multisubsystem Adapter [*Sperry UNIVAC*]
MSA	Multivariate Survival Analysis [*Statistics*]

MSA............	Municipal Saleyards Association [*Victoria, Australia*]
MSA............	Muscle Sympathetic Activity [*Medicine*] (DMAA)
MSA............	Museum Store Association (EA)
MSA............	Muslim Students' Association of the US and Canada (EA)
MSA............	Mutual Security Act [*1954*]
MSA............	Mutual Security Agency [*Functions transferred to Foreign Operations Administration, 1953*]
MSA............	Mutual Society of Arts (NADA)
MSA............	Mycological Society of America (EA)
MSa............	Salem Public Library, Salem, MA [*Library symbol*] [*Library of Congress*] (LCLS)
MSA-1........	Marshall Sprayable Ablator (SAUS)
MSA-2........	Improved Marshall Sprayable Ablator (SAUS)
MSAA........	Master of Science in Astronautics and Aeronautics (PGP)
MSAA........	Membrane Structures Association of Australasia
MSAA........	Microsoft Active Accessibility [*Computer science*]
MSAA........	Moderately Severe Aplastic Anemia [*Hematology*]
MSAA........	Multiple-Sclerosis-Associated Agent [*A virus*]
MSAA........	Multiple Sclerosis Association of America
MSAAB......	Military Services Ammunition Allocation Board (AABC)
MSAAC......	Mower Specialists' Association of Australia Cooperative
MSAAE......	Master of Science in Aeronautical and Astronautical Engineering (GAGS)
MSAAP......	Mississippi Army Ammunition Plant (AABC)
MSAAT......	Member of the Society of Architectural and Allied Technicians [*British*] (DI)
MSAb..........	Evans Memorial Library, Aberdeen, MS [*Library symbol*] [*Library of Congress*] (LCLS)
MS/AB........	Massenet Society/American Branch (EA)
MSAc..........	Master of Science in Accounting
MSAC.........	Mid-State Athletic Conference (PSS)
MSAC.........	Missile System Analyst Console (AAG)
MSAC.........	Moore School of Automatic Computers [*University of Pennsylvania*]
MSAC.........	Mount Saint Agnes College [*Maryland*] [*Merged with Loyola College*]
MSAC.........	Murray State Agricultural College [*Oklahoma*]
MSAC.........	Sonsonate/Acajutla [*El Salvador*] [*ICAO location identifier*] (ICLI)
MSACC.......	Master of Science in Accounting (PGP)
MS Acct......	Master of Science in Accounting (PGP)
MS/Accy......	Master of Science in Accountancy
MSACHA......	Mid-South Automated Clearing House Association
MSACM.......	Master of Science in Acquisition and Contract Management (PGP)
MSACS........	Middle States Association of Colleges and Schools (DHP)
MSAD.........	Materials Summary Acceptance Document (MCD)
MSAD.........	Microgravity Science and Applications Division (SAUS)
MSAD.........	Motor Safe and Arm Device
MSAD.........	Multisatellite Attitude Determination [*NASA*]
MS Admin....	Master of Science in Administration (PGP)
MSADY.......	Mid-States plc ADS [*NASDAQ symbol*] (TTSB)
MSaE.........	Essex Institute, Salem, MA [*Library symbol*] [*Library of Congress*] (LCLS)
MSAE........	Master of Science in Aeronautical Engineering
MSAE........	Master of Science in Aerospace Engineering (GAGS)
MSAE........	Master of Science in Agricultural Engineering (PGP)
MSAE........	Master of Science in Architectural Engineering (PGP)
MSAE........	Master of Science in Art Education (PGP)
MSAE........	Member of the Society of Automotive Engineers
MSAER......	Master of Science in Aerospace Engineering (PGP)
MSAF........	Meconium Stained Amniotic Fluid [*Neonatology*] (DAVI)
MSafetySc..	Master of Safety Science
MSAFP.......	Maternal Serum Alpha Fetoprotein [*Clinical chemistry*]
MSAfrica.....	Morgan Stanley Africa Investment Fund [*Associated Press*] (SAG)
MSafSc......	Master of Safety Science
MS (Ag)......	Master of Science in Agriculture
MSAG.........	MEECN Senior Advisory Group (SAUS)
MSAG.........	Multifunction Self-Aligned Gate (SAUS)
MS (Ag E)....	Master of Science in Agricultural Engineering
MS Agr.......	Master of Science in Agriculture
MSAgrEng....	Master of Science in Agricultural Engineering (NADA)
MSAH.........	Michigan Sportsmen Against Hunger
MSAI..........	American International College, Springfield, MA [*Library symbol*] [*Library of Congress*] (LCLS)
MSAI..........	Master of Science in Artificial Intelligence (GAGS)
MSAICE......	Member of the South African Institution of Civil Engineers
MSAInstMM...	Member of the South African Institute of Mining and Metallugy
MSAL.........	Mammal Serum Albumin (DB)
MSALAS......	Medical Sickness Annuity & Life Assurance Society (WDAA)
MSALT........	Mean Sea Level Altitude (ACAE)
MsAM........	Alcorn Agricultural and Mechanical College, Lorman, MS [*Library symbol*] [*Library of Congress*] (LCLS)
MSAM........	Master of Science in Applied Mechanics
MSAM........	Medium-range Surface-to-Air Missile (SAUS)
M-SAM........	Medium Surface-to-Air Missile [*Army*]
MSAM........	Microsoft Screen Access Model (SAUS)
MSAM........	Mobile Surface-to-Air Missile
MSAM........	Morgan Stanley Asset Management [*Commercial firm*]
MSAM........	Morpholinomethyl Salicyclamide [*Analgesic compound*]
MSAM........	Multi-Indexed Sequential Access Method [*Computer science*]
MSAM........	Multiple Sequential Access Method (NITA)
MSAMP.......	Master Ship Acquisition Milestone Plan
MSAMS.......	Mobile Surface-to-Air Missile System (MCD)
M San........	Master of Sanitation
MSAN.........	Microwave Steerable Null Antenna Array (ACAE)
MS & C.......	Marley, Scrooge, and Cratchit [*Accounting agency*]
MS & E.......	Materials Science and Engineering
MS & FR	Missile Stability and Frequency Response

MS & LR	Manchester, Sheffield & Lincolnshire Railway [*Later, Great Central*] [*British*] (ROG)
MS & NI	Michigan Southern & Northern Indiana Railroad
MS & P.......	Materials Synthesis and Processing [*National Science Foundation*]
MS & R	Merchant Shipbuilding and Repairs
MS & W	Maintenance Shop and Warehouse (NRCH)
MSanHi.......	Sandwich Historical Society, Sandwich, MA [*Library symbol*] [*Library of Congress*] (LCLS)
MSANS........	Multiple Small-Angle Neutron Scattering [*Surface analysis*]
M San Sc.....	Master of Sanitary Science
MSanSc&PH...	Master of Sanitary Science and Public Health (GAGS)
MSAO	Medical Services Accountable Officer
MSAO	Morale Support Activities Office
MSAP	Master of Science in Applied Physics (PGP)
MSAP.........	Master of Science in Applied Psychology (PGP)
MSAP.........	Master Space Allocation Plan (MCD)
MSAP.........	Mean Systemic Arterial Pressure [*Cardiology*]
MSAP.........	Military Security Assistance Projection [*Military*]
MSAP.........	Multisatellite Attitude Prediction [*NASA*]
MSaP.........	Peabody Museum of Salem, Salem, MA [*Library symbol*] [*Library of Congress*] (LCLS)
MSApSc......	Master of Science in Applied Science (GAGS)
MSAR	Microwave Spectrometer and Radiometer (ACAE)
MSAR	Mines Safety Appliance Research (IEEE)
MSAR	Miniature Synthetic Aperture Radar (SAUS)
Ms-Ar..........	Mississippi Department of Archives and History, Jackson, MS [*Library symbol*] [*Library of Congress*] (LCLS)
MSARC	Marine Systems Acquisition Review Council (MCD)
MS Arch	Master of Science in Architecture
MS Arch St...	Master of Architectural Studies (PGP)
MSAS........	Malaysia Singapore Australia Society
MSAS........	Mandel Social Adjustment Scale [*Psychology*]
MSAS........	Marine Sciences Affairs Staff [*A publication*]
MSAS........	Master of Science in Architectural Studies (GAGS)
MSa/s........	MegaSamples per Second (CDE)
MSAS........	Microwave Signature Acquisition System (MCD)
MSAS........	Military Sponsored Air Service
MSAS........	Minnesota School Attitude Survey [*Educational test*]
MSAS........	Modal Suppression Augmentation System [*Aerospace*]
M Sa Sc	Master of Sacred Sciences
MSAsia........	Morgan Stanley Asia Pacific Fund [*Associated Press*] (SAG)
MSAT.........	Master of Science in Advanced Technology (PGP)
MSAT.........	Minnesota Scholastic Aptitude Test
MSAT.........	Missile System Analyst Technician (SAA)
MSaT.........	Salem State College, Salem, MA [*Library symbol*] [*Library of Congress*] (LCLS)
MSATA........	Motorcycle, Scooter, and Allied Trades Association [*Later, MIC*]
MSAT-A	Multisensor Aided Targeting-Air [*Army*] (DOMA)
MSAT-Air.....	Multi-Sensor Aided Targeting-Airborne (SAUS)
MSATF........	Missile Site Activation Task Force (SAA)
MSATS........	Marksman Small Arms Training System (SAUS)
MSATT........	Martian Surface and Atmosphere through Time [*NASA*]
MSAT-X	Mobile Satellite Experiment (MCD)
MSAU.........	Multistation Access Unit [*Telecommunications*] (TSSD)
MSAUSC.....	Muslim Students' Association of the United States and Canada (EA)
MSAutE.......	Member of the Society of Automobile Engineers [*British*]
MSAV.........	Medical Scientists' Association of Victoria [*Australia*]
MSAV.........	Microsoft Anti-Virus [*Microsoft Corp.*] [*Computer science*] (PCM)
MSAW	Minimum Safe Altitude Warning [*Aviation*]
MSAWA........	Migrant and Seasonal Agricultural Worker Act of 1983 (WYGK)
MSAWS	Mobile Surface-to-Air Weapon System (MCD)
MsB...........	Biloxi Public Library, Biloxi, MS [*Library symbol*] [*Library of Congress*] (LCLS)
MSB............	Iola, KS [*Location identifier*] [*FAA*] (FAAL)
MSB............	Magnetic Susceptibility Bridge
MSB............	Main Steamline Break [*Nuclear energy*] (NRCH)
MSB............	Main Support Base [*Air Force*] (AFM)
MSB............	Main Support Battalion [*Army*] (DOMA)
MSB............	Main Switchboard
MSB............	Maintenance Standard Book
MSB............	Maintenance Support Base [*Military*]
MSB............	Male Sexual Biomass [*Botany*]
MSB............	Manpower Services Branch [*Military*] (MCD)
MSB............	Maritime Subsidy Board [*Maritime Administration*] [*Department of Commerce*]
MSB............	Martin's Scarlet Blue [*Histologic stain*]
MSB............	Mass Spectrometry Bulletin [*Mass Spectrometry Data Centre*] [*Bibliographic database*] [*British*]
Ms B............	Master of Bacteriology
MSB............	Master of Science in Business
MSB............	Material Support Branch [*NASA*] (KSC)
MSB............	Mediterranean Shipping Board [*World War II*]
MSB............	Member of the School Board [*British*] (ROG)
MSB............	Memory Storage Buffer [*Computer science*] (CAAL)
MSB............	Mesabi Tr Ctfs SBI [*NYSE symbol*] (TTSB)
MSB............	Mesabi Trust [*NYSE symbol*] (SAG)
MSB............	Methylstyrylbenzene [*Fluorescent compound*]
MSB............	Metropolitan Separate School Board [*UTLAS symbol*]
MSB............	Michael Stanley Band [*Musical group*]
MSB............	Mid-Small Bowel [*Gastroenterology*] (DAVI)
MSB............	Military Security Board
MSB............	Military Service Branch [*World War I*] [*Canada*]
MSB............	Mine Subsidence Board [*New South Wales, Australia*]
MSB............	Minesweeping Boat [*Navy symbol*]
MSB............	Minority Small Business (BARN)

MSB............ Missile Storage Building (NATG)
MSB............ Missile Support Base (SAA)
MSB............ Mission Simulator Building (MCD)
MSB............ Mobile Support Base (DNAB)
MSB............ Montadale Sheep Breeders Association (EA)
MSB............ Most Significant BIT [Binary Digit] [Computer science]
MSb............ Most Significant Bit (RALS)
MSB............ Motor Surfboat
MSB............ Multi-Step Industries [Vancouver Stock Exchange symbol]
MSB............ Multnomah School of the Bible [Oregon]
MSB............ Municipal Securities Board [Approved by Congress May 22, 1975] [Securities and Exchange Commission]
MSB............ Museum of Southwestern Biology [University of New Mexico] [Research center] (RCD)
MSB............ Music Sound Books [Record label]
MSB............ Mutual Savings Bank
MSBA.......... Malaysia, Singapore, and Brunei Association [British] (DBA)
MSBA.......... Master of Science in Business Administration
MSBA.......... Military School Band Association (EA)
MSBAE........ Master of Science in Biological and Agricultural Engineering (PGP)
MSBAE........ Master of Science in Biosystems and Agricultural Engineering (PGP)
MsBB.......... Beauvoir, the Jefferson Davis Shrine, Biloxi, MS [Library symbol] [Library of Congress] (LCLS)
MSBB.......... MSB Bancorp [NASDAQ symbol] (TTSB)
MSBB.......... MSB Bancorp, Inc. [NASDAQ symbol] (SAG)
MSB Bcp...... MSB Bancorp, Inc. [Associated Press] (SAG)
MSBC.......... MainStreet BankGroup [NASDAQ symbol] (TTSB)
MSBC.......... MainStreet BankGroup, Inc. [NASDAQ symbol] (SAG)
MSBC.......... Master of Science in Building Construction
MSBC.......... Steinbach Bible College, Manitoba [Library symbol] [National Library of Canada] (BIB)
MSBCA .... Maryland State Board of Contract Appeals (AAGC)
MSB-COD .... Minority Small Business-Capital Ownership Development Program [Small Business Administration]
MSBE.......... Master of Science in Biomedical Engineering (GAGS)
MSBE.......... Master of Science in Business Education (PGP)
MSBE.......... Molten-Salt Breeder Experiment [Nuclear energy]
MsBel......... Humphreys County Library, Belzoni, MS [Library symbol] [Library of Congress] (LCLS)
MSBENG ...... Master of Science in Bioengineering (PGP)
MSBF.......... Mean Sorties between Flights (MCD)
MSBF.......... MSB Financial [NASDAQ symbol] (TTSB)
MSBF.......... MSB Financial, Inc. [NASDAQ symbol] (SAG)
MSB Fn........ MSB Financial, Inc. [Associated Press] (SAG)
MSBIC .... Minority Small Business Investment Company (AAGC)
MSBK .... Mutual Savings Bank [NASDAQ symbol] (TTSB)
MSBK .... Mutual Savings Bank FSB [NASDAQ symbol] (SAG)
MSBL.......... Member of the School Board, London [Defunct] [British] (ROG)
MSBLA........ Mouse Specific B Lymphocyte Antigen [Immunology]
MSBLK........ Mild Steel, Black Finish (IAA)
MSBLMS...... Multi Station Boundary Layer Model System (PDAA)
MSBLS........ Microwave Scanning Beam Landing Station [or System] [NASA] (NASA)
MSBLS........ Microwave Scanning Beam Land Station [NASA]
MSBLS-GS.... Microwave Scanning Beam Landing System Ground Station [NASA]
MsBm .... Blue Mountain College, Blue Mountain, MS [Library symbol] [Library of Congress] (LCLS)
MSBM.......... Master of Science in Business Management (PGP)
MSBME........ Master of Science in Biomedical Engineering (PGP)
MSBMS........ Master of Science in Basic Medical Science (PGP)
MSBNSW..... Maritime Services Board of New South Wales [Australia]
MSBO .... Mooring and Salvage Officer [Navy] [British]
MSBP .... Munchausen Syndrome by Proxy [Medicine]
Ms-BPH .... Mississippi Library Commission, Services for the Handicapped, Jackson, MS [Library symbol] [Library of Congress] (LCLS)
MsBr........... Lincoln-Lawrence-Franklin Regional Library, Brookhaven, MS [Library symbol] [Library of Congress] (LCLS)
MSBR .... Maximum Storage Bus Rate
MSBR .... Military Strength Balance Report (AFM)
MSBR .... Molten-Salt Breeder Reactor
MSbrA .... American Optical Corp., Southbridge, MA [Library symbol] [Library of Congress] (LCLS)
MSBRT .... Mild Steel, Bright Finish (IAA)
MsBs .... City-County Memorial Library, Bay St. Louis, MS [Library symbol] [Library of Congress] (LCLS)
MSBS.......... Minimum Social Behavior Scale [Psychology]
MsBsNA....... National Aeronautics and Space Administration, NASA/NSTL Research Library, NSTL Station, Bay St. Louis, MS [Library symbol] [Library of Congress] (LCLS)
MsBsNO....... United States Naval Oceanographic Office NSTL Station, Bay St. Louis, MS [Library symbol] [Library of Congress] (LCLS)
MsBsS .... Divine Word Seminary, Bay St. Louis, MS [Library symbol] [Library of Congress] (LCLS)
MSBT.......... Missionary Servants of the Most Blessed Trinity [Roman Catholic women's religious order]
MSBTh........ Member of the Society of Health and Beauty Therapists [British] (DBQ)
MSBu.......... Thousand Standard Bushels (EG)
MS Bus........ Master of Science in Business
MSBV.......... Mooring Salvage and Boom Vessel (PDAA)
MSBVW .... Magnetostatic Backward Volume Wave [Telecommunications] (TEL)
MSBY.......... Most Significant Byte [Computer science]
MSC............ Chief Mess Management Specialist [Formerly, CSC, CST, SDC] [Navy rating]

MSC............ College de St.-Boniface, Manitoba [Library symbol] [National Library of Canada] (NLC)
MSC............ Congregation of the Marianites of the Holy Cross (TOCD)
MSC............ Congregation of the Sisters Marianites of Holy Cross [Roman Catholic religious order]
.... [The] MacNeal-Schwendler Corp.
MSC............ Macro Selection Compiler [Computer science] (BUR)
MSC............ Madras Staff Corps [British]
MSC............ Magnetically Settable Counter
MSC............ Magnetic Surface Current
MSC............ Magnitude Square of the Complex Coherence (PDAA)
MSC............ Maharashtra Socialist Congress [India] [Political party] (PPW)
MSC............ Mailstop Code
MSC............ Maine Sardine Council (EA)
MSC............ Main Storage Control [Computer science] (BUR)
MSC............ Main Switching Centre [Telecommunications] (NITA)
MSC............ Maintenance Support Center (MCD)
MSC............ Maisach [Federal Republic of Germany] [Geomagnetic observatory code]
MSC............ Major Subcontract (MCD)
MSC............ Major Subordinate Command [Military]
MSC............ Major Subordinate Commander (SAUS)
MSC............ Malaysian Multimedia Super Corridor
MSC............ Management Service Center [Marine science] (OSRA)
MSC............ Management Services Contractor [INTELSAT]
MSC............ Manchester Ship Canal
MSC............ Mandatory Settlement Conference [Insurance]
MSC............ Mandatum sine Clausula [Authority without Restriction] [Latin]
MSC............ Mankato State College [Later, Mankato State University] [Minnesota]
MSC............ Manned Spacecraft (ACAE)
msc............ Manned Spacecraft Center [NASA] (NAKS)
MSC............ Manned Spacecraft Center [Later, Johnson Space Center] [NASA]
MSC............ Manpower Services Commission [British]
MSC............ Maple Syrup Council (EA)
MSC............ Marine Safety Committee (SAUS)
MSC............ Marine Safety Council [Coast Guard]
MSC............ Marine Science Center [Oregon State University] [Research center] (RCD)
MSC............ Marine Science Council [Marine science] (MSC)
MSC............ Marine Stewardship Council
MSC............ Marital Status Code [IRS]
MSC............ Maritime Safety Committee [Advisory Committee on Pollution of the Sea]
MSC............ Maritime Service Committee [New York, NY] (EA)
MSC............ Maritime Surveillance Capability (CCCA)
MSC............ Marketing Services Conference [LIMRA]
MSC............ Marquise [Marchioness] [French] (ROG)
MSC............ Marrow Stromal Cell [Biochemistry]
MSC............ Maryland State College [Merged with University of Maryland]
MSC............ Mass Storage Control [Computer science] (BUR)
MSC............ Mass Storage Controller (NITA)
MSc............ Master of Science [Academic degree] (AIE)
MSC............ Master of Science in Commerce (DD)
MSC............ Master of Science in Communication (PGP)
MSC............ Master of Science in Counseling (GAGS)
MSc............ Master of Science in Epidemiology & Biostatistics (CMD)
MSC............ Master of Speech Communication (GAGS)
msc............ Master Sequence Controller (NAKS)
MSC............ Master Sequence Controller (NASA)
MSC............ Master Status Chart
MSC............ Material Sciences [NYSE symbol] (TTSB)
MSC............ Material Sciences Corp. [NYSE symbol] (SPSG)
MSC............ Material Source Code
MSC............ Materials Science Center [Cornell University]
msc............ Materials Service Center (NAKS)
MSC............ Materials Service Center [NASA] (NASA)
MSC............ Materiel Screening Code [DoD] (AFIT)
MSC............ Materiel Status Committee [Military] (AABC)
MSC............ Materiel Support Center (MCD)
MSC............ Materiel Support Command (MCD)
MSC............ Mathematics, Science, and Computer [Education]
MSC............ Mathematics/Science/Computer
MSC............ Mean Spherical Candlepower [Computer science] (IAA)
MSC............ Mechanical Super-Calendered Paper (DGA)
MSC............ Medical Service Commission [Canada]
MSC............ Medical Service Corps [Military]
MSC............ Medical Social Coordinator
MSC............ Medical Specialist Corps [Military]
MSC............ Medical Staff Corps [British]
MSC............ Mediterranean Society of Chemotherapy (EAIO)
MSC............ Mediterranean Sub-Commission [Silva Mediterranea] [FAO]
MSC............ Medium-Scale Computer (IAA)
MSC............ Memory Storage Control [Computer science]
MSC............ Memphis Service Center [IRS]
MSC............ Mesa [Arizona] [Airport symbol] [Obsolete] (OAG)
MSC............ Mesitylenesulfonyl Chloride [Biochemistry]
MSC............ Message Sequence Chart [Telecommunications] (TEL)
MSC............ Message Switching Center [Telecommunications]
MSC............ Message Switching Computer [Telecommunications] (TEL)
MSC............ Message Switching Concentration
MSC............ Metal Shielded Cabinet
MSC............ Meteorological Satellite Center [Aerospace] (IAA)
MSC............ Methane Sulfonyl Chloride [Organic chemistry]
MSC............ Metric System - Conversion (NATG)
MSC............ Metropolitan State College [Denver, CO]

MSC............	Microgravity Smoldering Combustion Experiment (SAUS)
MSC............	Micronesia Support Committee [*Later, MC*] (EA)
MSC............	Microscale Cloud [*Module*] [*Air Force*]
MSC............	Microsystems Centre (NITA)
MSC............	Microwave Semiconductors Corporation (ACAE)
MSC............	Microwave Stripline-Circuit (PDAA)
MSC............	Mid-South Conference (PSS)
MSC............	Midwestern Simulation Council
MSC............	Migent Software [*Vancouver Stock Exchange symbol*]
MSC............	Mile of Standard Cable
MSC............	Milestone Schedule Charts (MCD)
MSC............	Military Scout Car [*British*]
msc............	Military Sealift Command (NAKS)
MSC............	Military Sealift Command [*Formerly, MSTS, NTS*] [*Navy*] (NOAA)
MSC............	Military Staff Committee [*United Nations*] (DLA)
MSC............	Military Studies Center (EA)
msc............	Millisecond (WGA)
MSC............	Milliwatts per Square Centimeter
MSC............	Minesweeper, Coastal [*Nonmagnetic*] [*Navy symbol*]
MSC............	Minor Suma Corp. [*Kansas City, MO*] (TSSD)
MSC............	Mirror Sign Convention
MSC............	Mirror Streak Camera
MSC............	Miscellaneous (ADA)
MSC............	Missile and Space Council [*Defunct*] (AAG)
MSC............	Missile Sequence Charts (AAG)
MSC............	Missile Support Co. [*Army*]
MSC............	Missile System Checkout (AAG)
MSC............	Missionaries of the Sacred Heart (TOCD)
msc............	Missionaries of the Sacred Heart (TOCD)
MSC............	Missionarii Sacratissimi Cordis [*Missionaries of the Most Sacred Heart*] [*Roman Catholic men's religious order*]
MSC............	Missionarii Sancti Caroli [*Missionaries of St. Charles*] [*Roman Catholic men's religious order*]
msc............	Missionary Servants of Christ (TOCD)
MSC............	Missionary Sisters of the Most Sacred Heart of Jesus [*Roman Catholic religious order*]
MSC............	Missionary Sisters of the Most Sacred Heart of Jesus of Hiltrup (TOCD)
MSC............	Missionary Sisters of the Sacred Heart [*Cabrini Sisters*] [*Roman Catholic religious order*]
MSC............	Mississippi Central R. R. [*AAR code*]
Ms-C............	Mississippi Library Commission, Jackson, MS [*Library symbol*] [*Library of Congress*] (LCLS)
MSC............	Mississippi Southern College
MSC............	Mixing Smoke Chamber (MCD)
MSC............	Mobile Servicing Center [*Canada*]
MSC............	Mobile Switching Center (ACRL)
MSC............	Mode Selector Controller (MCD)
MSC............	Modified Stirling Cycle (ACAE)
MSC............	Moding Sequencing and Control (MCD)
msc............	Moding Sequencing and Control (NAKS)
MSC............	Modular Spacecraft Computer (ACAE)
MSC............	Mono-Stereo Compatible (PDAA)
MSC............	Montana State College (MCD)
MSC............	Moorhead State College [*Minnesota*]
MSC............	Morgan State College [*Later, Morgan State University*] [*Baltimore, MD*]
MSC............	Moscow Airways [*Russian Federation*] [*ICAO designator*] (FAAC)
MSC............	Most Significant Character [*Computer science*] (MDG)
MSC............	Motor Speed Changer (IAA)
MSC............	Motor Speed Control
MSC............	Motor Starting Contractor
MSC............	Motor Submersible Canoe [*British Marines' Special Forces*] [*World War II*]
MSC............	Mountain Safety Council (SAUS)
MSC............	Moved, Seconded, and Carried
MSC............	Multimedia Super Corridor [*Proposed, Malaysia*]
MSC............	Multiple Scan Correlator
MSC............	Multiple Spindle Chucker
MSC............	Multiple Systems Coupling [*Computer science*]
MSC............	Multipotential Stem Cells [*Hematology*]
MSC............	Multisensor Correlator (CAAL)
MSC............	Multiservice Center
MSC............	Multistrip Coupler [*Telecommunications*] (TEL)
MSC............	Multisystem Coupling [*Computer science*]
MSC............	Murray State College [*Later, MSU*] [*Kentucky*]
MSC............	Museum Support Center [*Smithsonian Institution*]
MSC............	Muskingum College, New Concord, OH [*OCLC symbol*] (OCLC)
Msc............	New York Miscellaneous Reports [*A publication*] (DLA)
MSC............	Springfield College, Springfield, MA [*Library symbol*] [*Library of Congress*] (LCLS)
Msc 2d........	New York Miscellaneous Reports. Second Series [*A publication*] (DLA)
MsCa...........	Canton Public Library, Canton, MS [*Library symbol*] [*Library of Congress*] (LCLS)
MScA...........	Maitre es Sciences Appliquees [*Master of Applied Science*] [*French*]
MScA...........	Make or Subcontract Authorization (AAG)
MScA...........	Master of Applied Science (DD)
M Sc A	Master of Science (Applied) (PGP)
MScA...........	Master of Science in Agriculture (CPGU)
MScA...........	Master of Social Administration (GAGS)
MSCA...........	McCarthy Scales of Children's Abilities [*Education*]
MSCA...........	Mechanical Service Contractors of America (NTPA)
MSCA...........	Microwave Switch Control Assembly
MSCA...........	Military Support to Civil Authorities (AABC)

MSCA...........	Missile Site Construction Agency [*Army*]
msca...........	Missing Cargo (DS)
MSCA...........	Mixed Spectrum Critical Assembly [*Nuclear energy*]
MSCA...........	M.S Carriers [*NASDAQ symbol*] (TTSB)
MSCA...........	MS Carriers, Inc. [*NASDAQ symbol*] (NQ)
MSCA...........	Multi-Site Cooperative Agreement (COE)
MSCAC........	Massachusetts State Collegiate Athletic Conference (PSS)
MSc(Acoustics)...	Master of Science (Acoustics) (ADA)
MSc(AeroMed)...	Master of Science (Aeromedicine)
MSc(Ag).......	Master of Science (Agriculture)
MScAgri.......	Master of Science in Agriculture
MSc(Agric)...	Master of Science in Agriculture
MSc(AgricE)...	Master of Science (Agricultural Economics) (ADA)
MSc(AgricEc)...	Master of Science (Agricultural Economics) (ADA)
MSCAJC........	Martin Steinberg Center of the American Jewish Congress (EA)
MsCaM.........	Madison County Library, Canton, MS [*Library symbol*] [*Library of Congress*] (LCLS)
MSc(Appl) ...	Master of Science (Applied) (ADA)
MsCar.........	Leake County Library, Carthage, MS [*Library symbol*] [*Library of Congress*] (LCLS)
MSc(Arch) ...	Master of Science (Architecture)
MSc(Arch)(Cons)...	Master of Science (Architectural) (Conservation)
M Sc (Architecture)...	Master of Science in Architecture
MS Carr.......	MS Carriers, Inc. [*Associated Press*] (SAG)
MSCAT........	Minesweeper Catamaran [*Military*]
MSCB...........	Missile Site Control Building (AABC)
MsCba.........	Shelby Memorial Library, Columbia, MS [*Library symbol*] [*Library of Congress*] (LCLS)
MSc(Biochem)...	Master of Science (Biochemistry)
MSc(Biotech)...	Master of Science (Biotechnology) (ADA)
M Sc BMC ...	Master of Science in Biomedical Communications (PGP)
MSc(BuildServ)...	Master of Science (Building Services) (ADA)
MSCC...........	Major Subcontract Change Coordination (MCD)
MSCC...........	Manned Space Flight Control Center [*Air Force*]
MSCC...........	Master of Science in Christian Counseling (PGP)
MScC...........	Master of Science in Commerce (DD)
MSCC...........	Master Simulator Control Console (MCD)
MSCC...........	Microsemi Corp. [*NASDAQ symbol*] (NQ)
MSCC...........	Midstream Clean Catch [*Urine Sample*] (DAVI)
MSCC...........	Military Space Surveillance Control Center (IAA)
MSCC...........	Missile Site Control Center (MCD)
MSCC...........	Morgan Sports Car Club (EA)
MSCCC........	Minimum Shuffle Control Cell Core [*Nuclear energy*] (NUCP)
M Sc CE	Master of Science in Chromo-Electronic Science
MScCE........	Master of Science in Civil Engineering [*British*] (ADA)
MSc(Cer).....	Master of Science in Ceramics (ADA)
MScChemTech...	Master of Science in Chemical Technology [*British*] (ADA)
MScCom........	Master in Commercial Sciences
MScComm........	Master in Commercial Science (DD)
MSc(CommMed)...	Master of Science (Community Medicine)
M Sc CS	Master of Science in Computer Science (PGP)
MScD...........	Doctor of Medical Science (DAVI)
MScD...........	Doctor of Science in Medicine (DAVI)
M Sc D	Doctor of the Science of Medicine
MScD...........	Magister Scientia Dentalis [*Master of Dental Science*] [*British*]
MScD...........	Master of Dental Science
MSCD...........	Master of Science in Communication Disorders (PGP)
MScD	Master of Science in Dentistry (GAGS)
MSCD	Military Support of Civil Defense (AABC)
MSCD	Mobile Source Control Division
MSCDC........	Missouri State Census Data Center [*Information service or system*] (IID)
MSc(Dent) ...	Master of Science in Dentistry
MSCDEX........	Microsoft Compact Disc Extension [*Computer science*] (DOM)
MSCDEX	MicroSoft Compact Disc Read Only Memory Extensions [*Computer science*] (IGQR)
MSCDEX	MS-DOS, CD-ROM Extension [*Computer science*]
MSCDIS	Master of Science in Communication Disorders (PGP)
MSCDR........	Minimum Standardized Crash Data Reporting
MSCDR........	Mohawk Synchronous Communication Data Recorder [*Military*] (PDAA)
MSCE...........	Main Storage Control Element [*Computer science*] (IEEE)
MSCE...........	Master of Science in Civil Engineering
MSCE...........	Master of Science in Clinical Engineering (PGP)
MSCE...........	Master of Science in Clinical Epidemiology (PGP)
MSCE...........	Master of Science in Computer Engineering (GAGS)
MScE...........	Master of Science in Engineering (DD)
MSCE...........	Microsoft Site Commerce Edition (VLIE)
MSCE...........	Modular, Standard Control Electronics (SAUS)
M Sc (Econ)...	Master of Science in Economics
MSCEd........	Master of Science in Continuing Education (GAGS)
M Sc Ed......	Master of Science in Education
MSc(EdPsych)...	Master of Science in Educational Psychology (CMD)
MSCEE........	Master of Science in Civil and Environmental Engineering (PGP)
M Sc EE......	Master of Science in Electrical Engineering
MSc(Elec)...	Master of Science in Electronics [*British*] (ADA)
M Sc (Elec Eng)...	Master of Science in Electrical Engineering
MSCELM........	Military Sealift Command, Eastern Atlantic and Mediterranean (DNAB)
MSCEM........	Master of Science in Civil Engineering Management (PGP)
M Sc (Eng)...	Master of Science (Engineering)
MSc(Engg)...	Master of Science (Engineering)
M Sc Engr ...	Master of Science in Engineering (PGP)
MSc(Epid)...	Master of Science (Epidemiology)
MS (Cer E)...	Master of Science in Ceramic Engineering

MSCF..........	Master of Science in Computational Finance (PGP)
MScF..........	Master of the Science of Forestry [or Master of Science in Forestry]
MSCF..........	Millions of Standard Cubic Feet (AAG)
MSCF..........	Multisource Correlation Facility (MCD)
MSCFAM......	Royal Canadian Army Museum, Canadian Forces Base, Shilo, Manitoba [Library symbol] [National Library of Canada] (NLC)
MSCFD........	Thousand Standard Cubic Feet per Day (SAUS)
M Sc FE.......	Master of Science in Forest Engineering (PGP)
MSCFE........	Military Sealift Command, Far East (DNAB)
MSCFH........	Thousand Standard Cubic Feet per Hour (SAUS)
MSCFM........	Thousand Standard Cubic Feet per Minute (SAUS)
M Sc (For)....	Master of Science in Forestry
MSCGpe	Missionaries of the Sacred Heart of Jesus and of Our Lady of Guadalupe (TOCD)
msch..........	Microscheduler (MHDI)
MSCH	Mode Switch Chassis
MsCh	Tallahatchie County Library, Charleston, MS [Library symbol] [Library of Congress] (LCLS)
MSCHAP......	Microsoft Challenge Handshake Authentication Protocol (SAUS)
MSChE........	Master of Science in Chemical Engineering
M Sch Mus...	Master of School Music
MSc(HomeScience)...	Master of Science (Home Science)
MSc(Hort)....	Master of Science in Horticulture [British] (ADA)
MSCI..........	Madrid Stock-Exchange Index [Spain] (ECON)
MSCI..........	Master Ships Configuration Index (MCD)
MSCI..........	Mediterranean Secret Convoy Instructions [World War II]
MSCI..........	Military Science
MSCI..........	Missile Status Control Indicator [Military] (CAAL)
M/SCI..........	Mission/Safety Critical Item [NASA] (NASA)
MSCI..........	Mission Scientist (SAUS)
MSCI..........	Molten Steel Coolant Interaction (NRCH)
MSCI..........	Morgan Stanley Capital Index (NUMA)
MSCI..........	Morgan Stanley Capital International
MSCI-EAFE...	Morgan-Stanley Capital International - Europe, Australia, Far East [Free] [Index - Financial]
M Sci Mil	Master of Military Science
M Sc in Agr Eng...	Master of Science in Agricultural Engineering
M Sc in Agr Ex...	Master of Science in Agricultural Extension
MSC(IndDes)...	Master of Science (Industrial Design) (ADA)
M Sc in ME...	Master of Science in Mechanical Engineering
MSC/I/O/R...	Minesweeper, Coastal/Inshore/Offshore/Riverine (MILB)
MSCIS	Master of Science in Computer Information Science (PGP)
MSCIS	Master of Science in Computer Information Systems
MSCIS	Model Spinal Cord Injury Systems (SAUS)
MScitHi........	Scituate Historical Society, Scituate, MA [Library symbol] [Library of Congress] (LCLS)
MSCJ..........	Master of Science in Criminal Justice (WGA)
MSCJA........	Master of Science in Criminal Justice Administration (PGP)
MSCJA-AJC...	Martin Steinberg Center for Jewish Artists - American Jewish Congress [Defunct] (EA)
MSCK..........	Missionary Sisters of Christ the King (TOCD)
MSCKC........	Measurement of Self Concept in Kindergarten Children [Psychology]
M Sc L.......	Master of the Science of Law
MSCL..........	Master Ships Configuration List (MCD)
MSCL..........	Mississippi State Chemical Laboratory [Mississippi State University] [Research center] (RCD)
MSCL..........	Springlfied City Library, Springfield, MA [Library symbol] [Library of Congress] (LCLS)
MSCLANT	Military Sealift Command, Atlantic (DNAB)
MSCLANTDET...	Military Sealift Command, Atlantic Detachment (DNAB)
MsCld	Carnegie Public Library, Clarksdale, MS [Library symbol] [Library of Congress] (LCLS)
MsCle	Bolivar County Library, Cleveland, MS [Library symbol] [Library of Congress] (LCLS)
MSCLE........	Maximum Space Charge Limited Emission (IAA)
MsCleD........	Delta State College, Cleveland, MS [Library symbol] [Library of Congress] (LCLS)
MsCleP........	Presbyterian Church Library, Cleveland, MS [Library symbol] [Library of Congress] (LCLS)
MsCliBHi	Mississippi Baptist Historical Society, Clinton, MS [Library symbol] [Library of Congress] (LCLS)
MsCliM........	Mississippi College, Clinton, MS [Library symbol] [Library of Congress] (LCLS)
MSC LNO.....	Major Subordinate Command Liaison Officer
M Sc (Lond)...	Master of Science, London
MSCLS........	Master of Science in Clinical Laboratory Science (PGP)
MSCLS........	Master of Science in Clinical Laboratory Studies (PGP)
MSCM..........	Master Chief Mess Management Specialist [Formerly, SDCM] [Navy rating]
M Sc M.......	Master of the Science of Medicine
MSCM..........	Mobile Station Class Mark (CGWS)
MSCM..........	Mobile Surface Contamination Monitor
MSCM..........	MOSCOM Corp. [NASDAQ symbol] (NQ)
M Sc (Mech Eng)...	Master of Science in Mechanical Engineering
M Sc Med....	Master of Medical Science
MScMed......	Master of Science in Medicine [British] (ADA)
MSc(Med)....	Master of Science (Medical)
M Sc Met....	Master of Science in Metallurgy
MSc(Min)	Master of Science in Mining [British] (ADA)
MSCN	Manned Satellite Communication Network (ACAE)
MScN	Master of Science in Nursing
MSCN	Misconnection [Travel industry] (TRID)
MSc(NatResMgt)...	Master of Science in Natural Resources Management
MSc(NeuChem)...	Master of Science (Neurochemistry)
MSCNU........	Master of Science in Clinical Nutrition (PGP)
MSc(Nut)	Master of Science (Nutrition)
MSc(Nutr)...	Master of Science in Nutrition [British] (ADA)
MSCNY	Marine Society of the City of New York (EA)
MSCO	Manned Spacecraft Operations [NASA] (KSC)
MSCO	Manual Sustainer Cutoff [NASA] (KSC)
M Sc O	Master of the Science of Oratory
MSC(O)........	Minesweeper, Coastal (Old) [Navy symbol]
MSc(OccMed)...	Master of Science (Occupational Medicine)
MsCol	Lowndes County Library System, Columbus, MS [Library symbol] [Library of Congress] (LCLS)
MsColS........	Mississippi State College for Women, Columbus, MS [Library symbol] [Library of Congress] (LCLS)
MS Cons......	Master of Science in Conservation
MSCOP	Missile Systems Checkout Program [Aerospace] (IAA)
MSc(Ophth)...	Master of Science (Ophthalmology)
MScOptom....	Master of Science in Optometry (ADA)
MsCor..........	Northeast Regional Library, Corinth, MS [Library symbol] [Library of Congress] (LCLS)
M Sc (Ost)...	Master of Science in Osteopathy
MSCOTSG....	Medical Service Corps, Office of the Surgeon General
MS Coun......	Master of Science in Counseling (PGP)
MSCP..........	Mass Storage Control Protocol (NITA)
MSCP..........	Master of Science in Community Planning
MSCP..........	Master of Science in Counseling Psychology (PGP)
M Sc P	Master of Science in Planning (PGP)
MSCP..........	Mean Spherical Candlepower
MSCP..........	Member of the Society of Certified Professionals [British] (DBQ)
MSCP..........	Missile Systems Checkout Programmer [Aerospace] (IAA)
MSCP..........	Motor Short-Circuit Protector (IAA)
MSCPAC	Military Sealift Command, Pacific (DNAB)
MS Cp E	Master of Science in Computer Engineering (PGP)
MScPhm......	Master of Science in Pharmacy (ADA)
M Sc Pl	Master of Science in Planning (PGP)
M/S CPO	Master/Senior Chief Petty Officer (SAUS)
M/S/CPO......	Master/Senior/Chief Petty Officer of the Command (DNAB)
MSCPR	Mixed-Suspension, Classified-Product Removal [Crystallizer] [Chemical engineering]
M Sc PT	Master of Science in Physical Therapy (PGP)
MSCR	Machine Screw
MSCR	Measurement/Stimuli Change Request (MCD)
MSCR	Multilayer Side-Cladded Ridge Waveguide (PDAA)
MSCR/A	Major Subcontract Change Request/Approval (MCD)
MSc(Rehab)...	Master of Science (Rehabilitation Medicine)
MSCREP	Military Sealift Command Representative (DNAB)
MSCRP	Master of Science in City and Regional Planning (PGP)
MSCRP	Master of Science in Community and Regional Planning (PGP)
MsCs	Crystal Springs Library, Crystal Springs, MS [Library symbol] [Library of Congress] (LCLS)
MSCS..........	Management Scheduling and Control System [Telecommunications] (TEL)
MSCS..........	Manual SHORAD [Short Range Air Defense] Control System (RDA)
MSCS..........	Mass Storage Control System [Computer science] (IAA)
MSCS..........	Master of Science in Computer Science
MSCS..........	Merchant Ship Control Service [Navy]
MSCS..........	Microsoft Clustering Server [Computer science]
MSCS..........	Microsoft Cluster Server
MSCS..........	Microsoft Commerce Server (AGLO)
MSCS..........	Miner Sentence Completion Scale [Psychology]
MSCS..........	Mobile Service Communications Satellite (ACAE)
MSCS..........	Multiple Satellite Communications System (ACAE)
MSCS..........	Multiservice Communications Systems (RDA)
MSCS..........	Senior Chief Mess Management Specialist [Formerly, CSCS, SDCS] [Navy rating]
MS CSCO....	Morgan Stanley Group, Inc. [Associated Press] (SAG)
MSCSD........	Master of Science in Communication Sciences and Disorders (PGP)
MSCSE........	Master of Science in Computer and Systems Engineering (PGP)
MSCSE........	Master of Science in Computer Science and Engineering (PGP)
MScSoc	Master of Social Science (CPGU)
M Sc (Social Sciences)...	Master of Science in the Social Sciences
M Sc (Soc Sci)...	Master of Science (Social Science)
MSCSO-M & R...	Military Sealift Command Service Office - Maintenance and Repair (DNAB)
MSCSO-OCPO...	Military Sealift Command Service Office - Operations Cargo Passenger Office (DNAB)
MSCSO-SA...	Military Sealift Command Service Office - Supply Assistant (DNAB)
MScSt..........	Master of Scientific Studies (ADA)
MSCT..........	Malignant Small Cell Tumor [Oncology]
MScT	Master of Science in Teaching (GAGS)
MScT	Master of Science Teaching (GAGS)
MSCT..........	Member of the Society of Cardiological Technicians [British]
MSCT..........	Miniature Synaptic Calcium Transient [Neurophysiology]
MSCTC........	Mass Storage Control Table Create [Computer science] (MHDI)
M Sc Tech ...	Master of Science in Technology
M Sc Tech ...	Master of Technical Science
MSCTRANSU...	Military Sealift Command Transportation Unit (DNAB)
MSCU	Medical Special Care Unit (DMAA)
MSCU	Military Sealift Command Unit (DNAB)
MSCU	Modular Store Control Unit
MSCU	Multistation Control Unit [Telecommunications] (IAA)
MSC(UN)......	Military Staff Committee of the United Nations
MSCV..........	Connecticut Valley Historical Museum, Springfield, MA [Library symbol] [Library of Congress] (LCLS)
MSCVAN......	[An] MSC [Military Sealift Command] Leased/Controlled Seavan or Milvan
MSCW	Marked Stack Control Word

MSCW	Mississippi State College for Women [*Columbus*]
MSD	Doctor of Medical Science
Ms D	Doctor of Metaphysics
MsD	Holmes County Library, Durant, MS [*Library symbol*] [*Library of Congress*] (LCLS)
MSD	Magnetic Storage Drum [*Computer science*]
MSD	Major Seismic Disturbance
MSD	Management Services Department [*British*] (DCTA)
MSD	Management Systems Division [*Environmental Protection Agency*] (EPA)
MSD	Mansfield, LA [*Location identifier*] [*FAA*] (FAAL)
MSD	Manual SHORAD [*Short Range Air Defense*] Control System [*Army*]
MsD	Manuscript Decisions [*Comptroller General*] [*United States*] [*A publication*] (DLA)
MSD	Maple-Syrup Disease [*Medicine*] (MELL)
MSD	Marginal Support Date (COE)
MSD	Marine Sanitation Device
MSD	Marine Sciences Directorate [*Canada*] (MSC)
MSD	Marine Signal Detachment (SAA)
MSD	Maritime-Self-Defense
MSD	MARS [*Modular Airborne Recorder System*] Supplemental Data (GFGA)
MSD	Mass Selector Detector [*Gas chromatography*]
MSD	Mass Sensor Demonstration
MSD	Mass Spectral Detector (ABAC)
MSD	Mass Storage Device [*Computer science*]
MSD	Master of Dietetics (GAGS)
MSD	Master of Science in Dentistry
MSD	Master of Science in Design (PGP)
MSD	Master of Science in Dietetics (PGP)
MSD	Master of Scientific Didactics
MSD	Master Resources & Developments Ltd. [*Vancouver Stock Exchange symbol*]
MSD	Master Standard Data
MSD	Master Surgeon Dentist
MSD	Material Safety Data
MSD	Materials and Structures Division [*NASA*]
MSD	Material Support Data (MCD)
MSD	Material Support Date (DOMA)
MSD	Matrix Spike Duplicate
MSD	McNaney Spectroelectric Device
MSD	Mean Solar Day
MSD	Mean Squared Distance [*Data analysis*]
MSD	Mean Square Deviation [*or Difference*]
MSD	Mean-Square Displacement [*Statistical graphing*]
MSD	Mechanical Setting Device
MSD	Medical Stores Department [*Tanzania*]
MSD	Medium Screen Display (SAUS)
MSD	Metal Sensor Detection
MSD	Metering Suction Differential (NG)
MSD	Method of Steepest Descent
MSD	Metropolitan Sewer District (GNE)
MSD	Microdata Software Development (MCD)
MSD	Microelectronics Systems Division (ACAE)
MSD	Microsoft Diagnostics [*Microsoft Corp.*] [*Computer science*] (PCM)
MSD	Microsoft System Diagnostics (VLIE)
MSD	Microsurgical Discectomy [*Medicine*] (MELL)
MSD	Mid-Summer Drought (SAUS)
MSD	Mild Sickle Cell Disease (AAMN)
MSD	Military Sales Department
MSD	Military Store Department [*British military*] (DMA)
MSD	Military Support Division [*of Materiel Testing Directorate*] (RDA)
MSD	Minesweeper, Drone [*Navy symbol*]
MSD	Minimal Steric Difference [*Organic chemistry*]
MSD	Minimum Safe Distance (AABC)
MSD	Misce, Signa, Da [*Mix, Write (the Directions), and Give (to the Patient)*] [*Pharmacy*] (ROG)
MSD	Missiles and Space Division [*NASA*] (KSC)
MSD	Missile Support Days (AAG)
MSD	Missile Systems Development (AAG)
MSD	Mission Sensor Data (ACAE)
MSD	Mission Systems Data (SAA)
MSD	Mixed Service Drive [*Tire design*]
MSD	Mobilization Stores Depot (SAUS)
MSD	Molecular Size Distribution [*Chemistry*]
MSD	Molecular Structures and Dimensions [*A publication*]
MSD	Molten Salt Destruction [*Incineration process*]
MSD	Monorail and Suspension Device [*British*]
MSD	Morale Support Detachment [*Army*]
MSD	Morgan Stanley Emerging Markets Debt Fund, Inc. [*NYSE symbol*] (SAG)
MSD	Morgan Stanley Emer'g Mkt Debt [*NYSE symbol*] (TTSB)
MSD	Mossoro [*Brazil*] [*Airport symbol*] (AD)
MSD	Most Significant Decade (IAA)
MSD	Most Significant Digit [*Computer science*]
MSD	Motor Storage Dolly
MSD	Mount Pleasant [*Utah*] [*Airport symbol*] (OAG)
MSD	Movimento Social Democrata [*Social Democrat Movement*] [*Portugal*] [*Political party*] (PPE)
MSD	Moving Scene Display
MSD	Multifrequency Signal Detector [*Telecommunications*]
MSD	Multimode Silent Digital (SAUS)
MSD	Multiple Sensor Discrimination (ACAE)
MSD	Multiple Spark Discharge [*Autotronic Controls Corp.*] [*Automotive engineering*]
MSD	Multiple Sulfatase Deficiency [*Medicine*] (AAMN)
MSD	Multisatellite Dispenser (MCD)
MSD	Multisensor Display
MSD	Multisensory Disorder
MSD	Multi-Site Damage (SAUS)
MSD	Munitions Systems Division (SAUS)
MSDA	Maryland State Dental Association (SAUS)
MSDA	Masada Security Holdings, Inc. [*NASDAQ symbol*] (SAG)
MSDAC	Minnesota State Drafting Advisory Committee (EDAC)
MSDB	Main Storage Database
MSDBP	Mean Squared Distance Between Pairs [*Statistics*] (PDAA)
MSDC	Maintenance Signal Data Cassette (MCD)
MSDC	Maintenance Signal Data Converter (MCD)
MSDC	Manual Slave Direction Center [*RADAR site*]
MSDC	Mass Spectrometry Data Centre [*Royal Society of Chemistry*] (IID)
MSDC	Microwave Spectra Data Center [*National Institute of Standards and Technology*]
MSDC	Molten Salts Data Center [*Rensselaer Polytechnic Institute*] [*National Institute of Standards and Technology*] [*Research center*] (IID)
MSDD	Master of Science in Design and Development (PGP)
MSDD	Milli-Second Delay Detonator [*Military*] (PDAA)
MSDD	Multi-Sensory Developmental Delays
MSDE	Microsoft Data Engine (VLIE)
MSde	Tilton Library, South Deerfield, MA [*Library symbol*] [*Library of Congress*] (LCLS)
MSDE-BSNT ...	Department of Education-Business Services (SAUS)
MSDE-CA	Department of Education-C & A (SAUS)
MSDE-DORS ...	Department of Education-Rehabilitation (SAUS)
MSDEF	Missile System Development and Evaluation Facility (MCD)
MSDE-LBRY ...	Department of Education-Libraries (SAUS)
MS Dent	Master of Science in Dentistry
MSDE-PRIM ...	Department of Education-Planning, Results (SAUS)
MSDEQ	Mothers' Sensory Developmental Expectation Questionnaire [*Occupational therapy*]
MSDerm	Master of Science in Dermatology (NADA)
MS Des	Master of Science in Design
MSDE-SCO	Department of Education-Community Outreach (SAUS)
MSDE-SIS	Department of Education-Improvement (SAUS)
MSDF	Maritime Self-Defense Force [*Japan*]
MSDF	Maritime Staff Defense Force (CINC)
MSDF	Multi-Sensor Data Fusion (ACAE)
MSDFF	Master Slave D Flip Flop (NITA)
MSDG	Multiple Sensor Display Group (MCD)
MSDHS	Mission System Data Handling Subsystem (SAUS)
MSDI	Mainstream Data, Inc. [*NASDAQ symbol*] (SAG)
MSDI	Martin Suicide Depression Inventory (MELL)
MS Di	Master of Scientific Didactics
MSDI	Mayonnaise and Salad Dressings Institute [*Later, Association for Dressings and Sauces*] (EA)
MSDIF	Modeling and Simulation Data Interchange Format (SAUS)
MSDIG	McGuire Safe Driver Interview Guide (AEBS)
MSDL	Magnetostrictive Delay Line
MSDL	Microsoft Download [*Computer science*] (AGLO)
MSD licence ...	Music, Singing & Dancing Licence (WDAA)
MSDM	Medium-Speed DynaBIT [*Binary Digit*] Memory [*Computer science*]
MSDM	Morgan Stanley Group, Inc. [*Associated Press*] (SAG)
MSDN	Microbial Strain Data Network [*Information service or system*] (IID)
MSDN	Microsoft Developer's Network [*Computer science*] (PCM)
MSDNA	Multicopy Single-Stranded Deoxyribonucleic Acid [*Biochemistry, genetics*]
MSDO	Management Systems Development Office
MSDOS	Microsoft Disk Operating System [*Computer science*] (AGLO)
MS-DOS	Microsoft Disk Operating System [*IBM Corp.*] [*Computer science*]
MSDP	Missile Site Data Processor (AABC)
MSDPS	Missile Site Data Processing System (AABC)
MSDPSS	Missile Site Data Processing Subsystem (AABC)
MSDR	Main Storage Data Register [*Computer science*] (IAA)
MSDR	Maintenance Signal Data Recorder (MCD)
MSDR	Master Sensor Data Record [*For spacecraft*]
MSDR	Materials Science Double Rack
MSDR	Multiplexer Storage Data Register [*Computer science*] (IAA)
MSDR	Multi-Spectral Scanner Data Redundancy (ACAE)
MSDRS	Maintenance Signal Data Recording Set [*or System*] (MCD)
MSDS	Magnetic Storage Drum System [*Computer science*]
MSDS	Maintenance Safety Data Sheets (MCD)
MSDS	Manufacturer's Safety Data Sheet (WDAA)
MSDS	Marconi Space and Defence Systems (MUSM)
MSDS	Master Simulation Data System (Model) [*Army*]
MSDS	Material Safety Data Sheets [*Occupational Health Services, Inc.*] [*Information service or system*]
MSDS	McGuire Safe Driver Scale (AEBS)
MSDS	Message Switching Data Service
MSDS	Microsoft Developer Support (VLIE)
MSDS	Missile Static Development Site (AAG)
MSDS	Missile System Development Stand (AAG)
MSDS	Mission Specific Data Set [*Army*]
MSDS	Multisolvent Delivery System
MSDS	Multispectral Scanner and Data System
MSDT	Maintenance Strategy Diagraming Technique (IEEE)
MSDT	Mean Supply Downtime (CAAL)
MSDT	Meshless Storage Display Tube
MSDX	Mason-Dixon Bancshares [*NASDAQ symbol*] (TTSB)
MSDX	Mason-Dixon Bancshares, Inc. [*NASDAQ symbol*] (SAG)
MSE	Magnetic Strain Energy

MSE...........	Maintenance Support Equipment [*Deep Space Instrumentation Facility, NASA*]
MSE...........	Major Source of Employment
MSE...........	Major Support Element (DOMA)
MSE...........	Malaysia Shipyard & Engineering (SAUS)
MSE...........	Manned Spacecraft Engineer (MCD)
MSE...........	Manston [*England*] [*Airport symbol*] (AD)
MSE...........	Manufacturing Support Equipment (ACAE)
MSE...........	Manufacturing Systems Engineering
MSE...........	Marshall Energy Ltd. [*Vancouver Stock Exchange symbol*]
MSE...........	Mask Superposition Error [*Computer science*] (IAA)
MSE...........	Massachusetts Studies in English [*A publication*] (ANEX)
MSE...........	Mass Storage Editor [*Computer science*] (MCD)
MSE...........	Master of Sanitary Engineering
MSE...........	Master of Science in Chemical Engineering
MSE...........	Master of Science in Education
MSE...........	Master of Science in Engineering
MSE...........	Master of Software Engineering (GAGS)
MSE...........	Master of Systems Engineering
MSE...........	Materials Science and Engineering (ACAE)
MSE...........	Materiel Status Evaluation [*Army*] (AABC)
MSE...........	Mean Square Error [*Statistics*]
MSE...........	Measuring and Stimuli Equipment (NASA)
MSE...........	Mechanical Support Equipment (KSC)
MSE...........	Medical Support Equipment (NASA)
MSE...........	Member of the Society of Engineers [*British*]
MSE...........	Mental Status Examination [*Neurology*] (DAVI)
MSE...........	Merck, Sharp & Dohme [*Later, Merck & Co., Inc.*] Research Laboratory, Rahway , NJ [*OCLC symbol*] (OCLC)
MSE...........	Merit Students Encyclopedia [*A publication*]
MSE...........	Metaphloem Sieve Element [*Botany*]
MSE...........	Mexican Stock Exchange (MHDW)
MSE...........	Microsoft Exchange server (SAUS)
MSE...........	Mid-Song Element [*Ornithology*]
MSE...........	Midwest Stock Exchange [*Chicago, IL*] (EA)
MSE...........	Military Specification Exception (RDA)
MSE...........	Military Standard Engines
MSE...........	Milk-Sensitive Enteropathy [*Medicine*]
MSE...........	Milwaukee School of Engineering [*Wisconsin*]
MSE...........	Minus Sense (SAA)
MSE...........	Missile Support Element (AABC)
MSE...........	Missile Support Equipment
MSE...........	Mission Staff Engineer (MCD)
MSE...........	Mission Support Element (MCD)
MSE...........	Mississippi Export Railroad Co. [*AAR code*]
MSE...........	Mobile Subscriber Equipment [*Military*]
MSE...........	Modern Ship Equivalent
MSE...........	Montreal Stock Exchange (CDAI)
MSE...........	Moose
MSE...........	Morgan Stan Fin 8.40% Cp Uts [*NYSE symbol*] (TTSB)
MSE...........	Morgan Stanley Finance PLC Capital Unit [*NYSE symbol*] (SAG)
MSE...........	Multiple Sample Exchanger (SAUS)
MSE...........	Multiple Simultaneous Engagement (MCD)
MSE...........	Multi-Position Small Engine [*Automotive engineering*]
MSE...........	Muscle-Specific Enhancer [*Genetics*]
MSE...........	Muscle-Specific Enolase [*Medicine*] (DMAA)
MSE...........	Muscle Strengthening Exercise (MELL)
MSEA...........	M & S [*Modeling and Simulation*] Executive Agent [*Army*]
M Se A	Master of Secretarial Arts
MSEA...........	Medical Society Executives Association [*Later, AAMSE*] (EA)
MSEA...........	Metropolitan Bancorp [*NASDAQ symbol*] (TTSB)
MSEA...........	Metropolitan Bancorp Seattle [*NASDAQ symbol*] (SAG)
MSEC...........	Maintenance Support Equipment Center
MSEC...........	Master of Science in the Economic Aspects of Chemistry
MSEC...........	Master Separation Events Controller (MCD)
MSEC...........	Materials Science and Engineering Commission [*British*]
MSEC...........	Message Security (ACAE)
MSEC...........	Michelin Stress Equilibrium Casing [*Tire design*]
MSEC...........	Millisecond (GOBB)
msec...........	Millisecond
MSECE...........	Master of Science in Electrical and Computer Engineering (PGP)
MS Eco	Master of Science in Economics (PGP)
MS Econ......	Master of Science in Economics (PGP)
MSecSchSci...	Master of Secondary School Science (GAGS)
MsecSP	Managed Security Service Provider
MS Ed......	Master of Sanitary Education
MSEd...........	Master of Science Education (GAGS)
MS Ed...........	Master of Science in Education
MSED...........	Minimum Signal Element Duration [*Telecommunications*] (TEL)
MSED...........	Ministry of State for Economic Development [*Canada*]
MSED...........	Mobile Source Enforcement Division [*Environmental Protection Agency*]
MS EdU......	Master of Science in Education (PGP)
MSEE...........	Major Source Enforcement Effort [*Environmental Protection Agency*] (GFGA)
MSEE...........	Master of Science in Electrical Engineering
MSEE...........	Master of Science in Environmental Engineering (GAGS)
MSEE...........	Mean Square Error Efficiency [*Statistics*]
MSE (Elec)...	Master of Science in Engineering - Electrical
MSEF...........	Missile System Evaluation Flight (MUGU)
MSEG...........	Medical Service Group [*Military*]
MSEG...........	Memory-Segment [*Computer science*]
MSEG...........	Missile Systems Evaluation Group (CINC)
MSEH...........	Master of Science in Environmental Health (PGP)
MSEI...........	Mean Square Error Inefficiency [*Statistics*]

MSEIS...........	Microgravity Systems Engineering Information System (SAUS)
MSEL...........	Lord Selkirk Regional School, Selkirk, Manitoba [*Library symbol*] [*National Library of Canada*] (NLC)
MSEL...........	Master of Science and English Literature
MSEL...........	Master of Science in Environmental Law (PGP)
MSEL...........	Master Scenario Events List (MCD)
MSEL...........	Merisel, Inc. [*NASDAQ symbol*] (SPSG)
MSEL...........	Mullen Scales of Early Learning [*Child development test*] [*Psychology*]
MSEL...........	Selkirk Community Library, Manitoba [*Library symbol*] [*National Library of Canada*] (NLC)
MS Elect E...	Master of Science in Electrical Engineering
MSEM...........	Mainstreamed Special Educator Model (EDAC)
MSEM...........	Master of Science in Engineering and Mining (GAGS)
MSEM...........	Master of Science in Engineering Management (PGP)
MSEM...........	Master of Science in Engineering Mechanics
MSEM...........	Master of Science in Engineering of Mines (PGP)
MSEM...........	Master of Science in Environmental Management (PGP)
MSEM...........	Metrology Specific Equipment Model (AAEL)
MSEM...........	Mission Status and Evaluation Module
MS EMD......	Morgan Stanley Emerging Markets Debt Fund, Inc. [*Associated Press*] (SAG)
MSEMech...	Master of Science in Engineering Mechanics (GAGS)
MSEMgt...	Master of Science in Engineering Management (GAGS)
MSEMH...........	Selkirk Mental Health Centre, Manitoba [*Library symbol*] [*National Library of Canada*] (NLC)
MS/EMI...........	Mission Sequence/Electromagnetic Interference
MSEMPR...........	Missile Support Equipment Manufacturers Planning Reports (MCD)
MS En E......	Master of Science in Environmental Engineering (PGP)
MS Eng.......	Master of Sanitary Engineering
MS Eng.......	Master of Science in Engineering
MS Engr......	Master of Science in Engineering (PGP)
MS Engr Sci...	Master of Science in Engineering Science (PGP)
MS Ent...........	Master of Science in Entomology
MS Env E.....	Master of Science in Environmental Engineering (PGP)
MSEnvrE...........	Master of Science in Environmental Engineering (GAGS)
MSEO...........	Marine Services Engineer Officer [*Navy*] [*British*]
MSEP...........	Maintenance Standardization Evaluation Program [*Air Force*] (AFM)
MSEP...........	Mean Square Error of Prediction [*Statistics*] (PDAA)
MSEP...........	Mercury Scientific Experiment Panel
MSEP...........	Military Standard Evaluation Program
MSEPN...........	School of Psychiatric Nursing, Selkirk, Manitoba [*Library symbol*] [*National Library of Canada*] (NLC)
MSEPS...........	Modular Space Electrical Power Station
M/SEQ...........	Master Sequencer
MSER...........	Management System Evaluation Review (NG)
MSER...........	Master of Science in Energy Resources (GAGS)
MSER...........	Mean Systolic Ejection Rate [*Cardiology*]
MSER...........	Mental Status Examination Report (DIPS)
MSER...........	Multiple Stores Ejection Rack [*For munitions*] (MCD)
MSERD...........	Ministry of State for Economic and Regional Development [*Canada*]
MSERT...........	Member of the Society of Electronic and Radio Technicians [*British*] (DBQ)
MSES...........	Marine Scientific Equipment Service [*British*]
MSES...........	Master of Science in Engineering Science (PGP)
MSES...........	Master of Science in Environmental Studies (PGP)
MSES...........	Medical School Environmental Stress
MSES...........	Medical Service Squadron [*Military*]
MSES...........	Mobile Status Entry System
M Se Sc	Master of Secretarial Science
MSESM...........	Master of Science in Engineering Science and Mechanics (PGP)
MSESS...........	Master of Science in Exercise and Sport Studies (GAGS)
M Se St	Master of Secretarial Studies
MSET...........	Maintenance Standardization and Evaluation Team (MCD)
MSET...........	Multistage Exercise Test [*Medicine*] (CPH)
MSETM...........	Master of Science in Environmental Technology Management (PGP)
MSE TPN.....	Mobile Subscriber Equipment Tactical Packet Network [*Computer science*] [*Military*] (RDA)
MSEUE...........	Mouvement Socialiste pour les Etats Unis d'Europe
MSEuro...........	Morgan Stanley European Emerging Markets Ltd. [*Associated Press*] (SAG)
MSEVM...........	Master of Science in Environmental Management (PGP)
MSEW...........	Medical Service Wing [*Military*]
MSEX...........	Middlesex Water [*NASDAQ symbol*] (TTSB)
MSEX...........	Middlesex Water Co. [*NASDAQ symbol*] (NQ)
MS Exp Surg...	Master of Science in Experimental Surgery (PGP)
MSF...........	Congregatio Missionariorum a Sancta Familia [*Congregation of the Missionaries of the Holy Family*] [*Roman Catholic men's religious order*]
MSF...........	Construction Education Foundation [*Formerly, Merit Shop Foundation*] (EA)
MSFU...........	Macrophage Spreading Factor [*Hematology*]
MSF...........	Magnetic Silencing Facility [*Kingsburg, GA*] (DWSG)
MSF...........	Maintenance Source File (MCD)
MSF...........	Manned Space Flight [*NASA*] (KSC)
MSF...........	Manufacturing, Science, and Finance Union [*British*] (WA)
MSF...........	Mark Sense Form (MCD)
MSF...........	Mass Storage Facility [*Computer science*] (IBMDP)
MSF...........	Master of Science in Finance
MSF...........	Master of the Science of Forestry
MSF...........	Master Source File [*Computer science*] (BUR)
MSF...........	Matched Spatial Filter [*Optics*]
MSF...........	Maximum Shear Force
MSF...........	Max Sea Food SA de CV [*El Salvador*] [*ICAO designator*] (FAAC)

MSF............. Medecins sans Frontieres [*Doctors without Borders - DWB*] [*France*] (EAIO)
MSF............. Medium Standard Frequency (DEN)
MSF............. Member of the Society of Floristry [*British*] (DI)
MSF............. Merit Shop Foundation [*Washington, DC*] (EA)
MSF............. Metal Space-Frame (MCD)
MSF............. MetaScience Foundation (EA)
MSF............. Metastasis-Stimulating Factor [*Immunosuppressant*]
MSF............. Methanesulfonyl Fluoride [*Organic chemistry*]
MSF............. Migration Stimulating Factor [*Cytology*]
MSF............. Militarily Significant Fallout (SAUS)
MSF............. Military Support Fund (MCD)
MSF............. Mind Science Foundation (EA)
MSF............. Minesweeper, Fleet [*Steel hull*] [*Navy symbol*]
MSF............. Minimum Sustaining Field [*Atomic reactor*]
MSF............. Missionary Sisters of the Holy Family (TOCD)
MSF............. Mission Simulator Facility
MSF............. Mobile Striking Force [*Military*]
MSF............. Mobility Support Forces [*Military*]
MSF............. Moisture Seekers Foundation [*Later, Sjogren's Syndrome Foundation - SSF*] (EA)
MSF............. Month-Second-Foot [*Measurement*]
MSF............. Morale Support Funds (MCD)
MSF............. Morgan Stanley Emerging Market [*NYSE symbol*] (SPSG)
MSF............. Moroccan Sea Frontier [*Navy*] [*World War II*]
MSF............. Motorcycle Safety Foundation (EA)
MSF............. Mott Scattering Formula [*Physics*]
MSF............. Multiaxial Stress Field
MSF............. Multi-Sensor Fusion (ACAE)
MSF............. Multi-Stage Filter [*Automotive engineering*]
MSF............. Multistage Flash [*Desalination method*]
MSF............. Muscle Shock Factor
MsFa .... Jefferson County Library, Fayette, MS [*Library symbol*] [*Library of Congress*] (LCLS)
MSFA........... Mid-States Football Association (PSS)
MSFAM....... Master of Science in Family Studies (PGP)
MSFB........... Multi-Solids Fluidized Bed [*Chemical engineering*]
MSFC........... George C. Marshall Space Flight Center (SAUS)
MSFC........... Mark Slade Fan Club (EA)
MSFC........... Marshall Space Flight Center [*Also known as GCMSC*] [*NASA*]
MSFC........... McCarver Sisters Fan Club (EA)
MSFC........... Medical Students for Choice
MSFC........... Mid-South Football Conference (PSS)
MSFC........... Mobile Strike Force Command [*Military*] (VNW)
MSFC........... Morale Support Fund Council [*Military*] (AABC)
MSFC........... Mutual Society of the French Community (EA)
MSFCV....... Main Stream Flow Control Valve [*Nuclear energy*] (NUCP)
MSFD.......... Millimeter Wave Seeker Feasibility Demonstration
MSFDC....... Microsoft and First Data Corp.
MSFDPS ...... Manned Space Flight Data Processing System [*NASA*]
MSFE........... Mechanisms of Soil Formation and Evolution (SAUS)
MSFEB......... Manned Space Flight Experiments Board [*NASA*] (KSC)
MSFET........ Metal-on-Silicon Field-Effect Transistor [*Electronics*] (IAA)
MSFET........ Metal Schottky Gate Field Effect Transistor [*Electronics*] (IAA)
MSFF.......... Master Slave Flipflop [*Nuclear energy*] (IAA)
MSFH.......... Manned Space Flight Headquarters [*NASA*]
MSFI........... MS Financial [*NASDAQ symbol*] (TTSB)
MSFI........... MS Financial Corp. [*NASDAQ symbol*] (SAG)
MS Fin........ Morgan Stanley Finance PLC Capital Unit [*Associated Press*] (SAG)
MSFIS......... Microsoft Fax Information Service (SAUS)
MSFL........... Manned Space Flight Laboratory [*NASA*] (IAA)
MSFLS......... Microwave Scanning Beam Landing System (SAUS)
MSFLS......... Microwave Scanning Beam Land Station (SAUS)
MSFLV......... Manned Space Flight and Launch Vehicles [*Panel*]
MSFM.......... Master of Financial Management (PGP)
MSFM.......... Master of Science in Forest Management
MSFN.......... Manned Space Flight Network [*NASA*]
MSFn.......... Morgan Stanley Finance PLC Capital Unit [*Associated Press*] (SAG)
MS Fncl....... MS Financial, Inc. [*Associated Press*] (SAG)
MSFNOC...... Manned Space Flight Network Operations Center [*NASA*] (KSC)
MSFO.......... Manned Space Flight Operations [*NASA*] (KSC)
MSFOR........ Master of Science in Forestry (PGP)
MS For .... Master of Science in Forestry
MSFP.......... Manned Space Flight Program [*NASA*] (KSC)
MSFP.......... Migrant and Seasonal Farmworkers Program [*Title III*] (OICC)
MSFP.......... Mosaic-Staring Focal Plane (SAUS)
MSFRSP ...... Male Sterile-Facilitated Recurrent Selection Population [*Plant breeding*]
MSFS........... Main Steam and Feed Water System (IEEE)
MSFS........... Manned Space Flight Subcommittee [*NASA*] (AAG)
MSFS........... Manned Space Flight System [*NASA*] (IAA)
MSFS........... Master of Science in Family Studies (PGP)
MSFS........... Master of Science in Financial Services (PGP)
MSFS........... Master of Science in Foreign Service (GAGS)
MSFS........... Master of Science in Forensic Science (GAGS)
MSFS........... Missionaries of St. Francis of Sales [*Roman Catholic religious order*]
MSFSG .... Manned Space Flight Support Group (MCD)
MSFSRD...... Manned Space Flight Support Requirements Documentation [*NASA*]
MSFT.......... Microsoft Corp. [*NASDAQ symbol*] (NQ)
MSFU.......... Merchant Service Fighter Unit [*Air Force*] [*British*]
MSFVW........ Magnetostatic Forward Volume Wave [*Telecommunications*] (TEL)
MSFW......... Migrant and Seasonal Farmworkers
MSFX.......... Master Fixture
MSG............. [*The*] Imperial Merchant Service Guild [*British*]
MSG............. Madison Square Garden [*New York, NY*] (NADA)

MSG............. Madison Square Garden Network [*Cable-television system*]
MSG............. Maintenance Steering Group (MCD)
MSG............. Management Steering Group (AAEL)
MSG............. Manufacturers Standard Gauge
MSG............. Mapper Sweep Generator
MSG............. Mapping Supervisor Gap Filler (SAA)
MSG............. Marine Security Guard
MSG............. Maritime Studies Group [*Military*] (VNW)
MSG............. Mascot Gold Mines Ltd. [*Toronto Stock Exchange symbol*] [*Vancouver Stock Exchange symbol*]
MSG............. Massage (DAVI)
MSG............. Master of Science in Gerontology (GAGS)
MSG............. Master Sergeant [*Army*] (AABC)
MSG............. Maximum Stable Gain (IAA)
MSG............. Mechanical Subsystem Group [*NASA*] (NASA)
MSG............. Message (AFM)
msg............. Message (IDOE)
MSG............. Methysergide [*A serotonin antagonist*] [*Pharmacology*] (DAVI)
MSG............. Microcephaly Support Group [*British*] (NRGU)
MSG............. Microcomputer Support Group
MSG............. Microwave Signal Generator
MSG............. Miners' Support Group (WDAA)
MSG............. Ministry of Solicitor General [*Canada*]
MSG............. Ministry of the Solicitor General Library [*UTLAS symbol*]
MSG............. Miscellaneous Simulation Generator
MSG............. Missile Systems Group [*of General Motors Corp.*]
MSG............. Missing [*Military*]
MSG............. Mission Support Groups (MCD)
MSG............. Mobile Support Group [*Military*] (NVT)
MSG............. Modular Steam Generator (NRCH)
MSG............. Modulation Signal Generator (NITA)
MSG............. Moessingen [*Federal Republic of Germany*] [*Seismograph station code, US Geological Survey*] (SEIS)
MSG............. Monosodium Glutamate [*Food additive*] [*Pharmacology*]
MsG............. William Alexander Percy Memorial Library, Greenville, MS [*Library symbol*] [*Library of Congress*] (LCLS)
MSGA .... Master Gauge
MSGA .... Merchant Service Guild of Australia
MSGB .... Manorial Society of Great Britain (EAIO)
MSGB .... Muslim Society in Great Britain
MSGBI .... Mineralogical Society of Great Britain and Ireland (EAIO)
MSGC .... Master of Science in Genetic Counseling (PGP)
MSGC .... Multinucleated Stromal Giant Cell
MSGCEN...... Message Center
MSGCTR...... Message Center [*Aviation*] (FAAC)
MSGDPU...... Message-Drop and Pick-Up [*Military*] (IAA)
MSGE.......... Master of Science in Geological Engineering (NADA)
MS Geo E .... Master of Science in Geological Engineering (PGP)
MSGFLG....... Message Flag [*Computer science*] (MHDI)
MSGFM....... Message Form (MUGU)
MS-GFW ...... Memory for Sequence Subtest of the Goldman-Fristoe-Woodcock Auditory Skills TestBattery (EDAC)
MSGG .... Message Generator (MSA)
MSGI .... Marketing Services Group
MSGID........ Message Identifier
MSGL.......... Multi-Salvo Grenade Launcher (SAUS)
MSGL.......... Multishot Grenade Launcher (RDA)
MSGL.......... Thousand Square Feet of Single Glueline (WPI)
MSGlobl ...... Morgan Stanley Global Opportunities Bond Fund, Inc. [*Associated Press*] (SAG)
MSGM .... Master of Science in Government Management
MSG Mgt ..... Master of Science in Game Management
MSGO .... Mediterranean Secret General Orders
MSGO .... Miskimins Self-Goal-Other Discrepancy Scale [*Psychology*] (DHP)
MSGoH........ Holmes Junior College, Goodman, MS [*Library symbol*] [*Library of Congress*] (LCLS)
MSGP .... Mobile Support Group [*Military*]
MSGR .... Messenger (AFM)
MSGR .... Mobile Support Group [*Military*]
MSGR .... Monseigneur
Msgr .... Monsignor (SHCU)
MSGR .... Monsignor
MsGren........ Grenada County Library, Grenada, MS [*Library symbol*] [*Library of Congress*] (LCLS)
M Sgt........... Master Sergeant (NTIO)
MSGT.......... Master Sergeant
MsGu .... Gulfport-Carnegie-Harrison County Library, Gulfport, MS [*Library symbol*] [*Library of Congress*] (LCLS)
MSGV.......... Mouse Salivary Gland Virus [*Medicine*] (DMAA)
MsGW......... Washington County Library System, Greenville, MS [*Library symbol*] [*Library of Congress*] (LCLS)
MSGWA .... Military and Sporting Gun Workers' Association [*A union*] [*British*]
MsGwL .... Greenwood-Leflore Public Library, Greenwood, MS [*Library symbol*] [*Library of Congress*] (LCLS)
MSG/WTG...... Message Waiting (MDG)
MSh............ Ma'aser Sheni (BJA)
MSH............ Magnetoelastic Static Hysteresis (MCD)
MSH............ Management Sciences for Health
MSH............ Mashhad [*Iran*] [*Seismograph station code, US Geological Survey*] [*Closed*] (SEIS)
MSH............ Master of Science in Horticulture (NADA)
MSH............ Master of Science in Hospice (PGP)
MSH............ Master of Science in Hygiene (NADA)
MSH............ Master of Staghounds
MSH............ Mauler Seeker Head

MSH............	Medical Self-Help [*Defunct*]
MSH............	Melanocyte-Stimulating Hormone [*Also, MH*] [*Endocrinology*]
MSH............	Melanophore-Stimulating Hormone [*Endocrinology*] (AAMN)
MSH............	Men of the Sacred Hearts (EA)
MSH............	Metastable Helium (MCD)
MSH............	Metropolitan Cooperative Library System, Pasadena, CA [*OCLC symbol*] (OCLC)
MSH............	Minesweeper Hunter Vessel
MSH............	Mishibishu Resources [*Vancouver Stock Exchange symbol*]
MSH............	Missionaries of the Sacred Heart [*Roman Catholic men's religious order*]
Ms-H............	Mississippi State Board of Health, Jackson, MS [*Library symbol*] [*Library of Congress*] (LCLS)
MSH............	Mont Saint-Hilaire
MSH............	Mount St. Helens [*Washington*] [*Geology*]
MSH............	US Marshal Service [*Department of Justice*] [*ICAO designator*] (FAAC)
MsHa............	Hattiesburg Public Library, Hattiesburg, MS [*Library symbol*] [*Library of Congress*] (LCLS)
MSHA	Mannose-Sensitive Hemagglutination [*Medicine*] (DMAA)
MSHA	Master of Science in Health Administration (PGP)
MSHA	Master of Science in Hospital Administration
MSHA	Mine Safety and Health Administration [*Department of Labor*]
MSha	Sharon Public Library, Sharon, MA [*Library symbol*] [*Library of Congress*] (LCLS)
MSHAA	Member of the Society of Hearing Aid Audiologists [*British*] (DBQ)
MSHAA	Morocco Spotted Horse Association of America [*Defunct*] (EA)
MShaK.........	Kendall Whaling Museum, Sharon, MA [*Library symbol*] [*Library of Congress*] (LCLS)
MSH & Ph Ed...	Master of Science in Health and Physical Education
MsHaP.........	[*The*] Library-Hattiesburg, Petal Forrest County, Hattiesburg, MS [*Library symbol*] [*Library of Congress*] (LCLS)
MsHaU.........	University of Southern Mississippi, Hattiesburg, MS [*Library symbol*] [*Library of Congress*] (LCLS)
MsHaW........	William Carey College, Hattiesburg, MS [*Library symbol*] [*Library of Congress*] (LCLS)
MSHB	Minimum Safe Height of Burst [*Military*]
MSHCS	Master of Science in Human and Consumer Science (PGP)
MsHe	First Regional Library, Hernando, MS [*Library symbol*] [*Library of Congress*] (LCLS)
MSHE..........	Master of Science in Home Economics
MSHE..........	Master of Science in Hydraulic Engineering
MSH Ec........	Master of Science in Home Economics
MSH Ed	Master of Science in Health Education (PGP)
MSHES	Master of Science in Human Environmental Sciences (PGP)
MSHG	Meshing
MSHI	Medium Scale Hybrid Integration [*Computer science*] (IAA)
MSH-IF	Melanocyte-Stimulating Hormone-Inhibiting Factor [*Endocrinology*] (MAE)
MSH-IF	Melanophore-Stimulating Hormone [*Intermedin*] Inhibiting Factor [*Laboratory science*] (DAVI)
MSHJ..........	Medical Staff Hospital Joint Venture
MSHK	Megadata Corp. (MHDW)
MSHK	Morgan Stanley Group, Inc. [*Associated Press*] (SAG)
Mshl	Marshal (BARN)
MShM..........	Mount Holyoke College, South Hadley, MA [*Library symbol*] [*Library of Congress*] (LCLS)
MS Hort.......	Master of Science in Horticulture
MsHos	Marshall County Library, Holly Springs, MS [*Library symbol*] [*Library of Congress*] (LCLS)
MsHosR.......	Rust College, Holly Springs, MS [*Library symbol*] [*Library of Congress*] (LCLS)
MsHou	Houston Carnegie Public Library, Houston, MS [*Library symbol*] [*Library of Congress*] (LCLS)
Mshp	Machine Shop (MHDB)
MSHP	Maintain System History Program [*IBM Corp.*]
MSHP	Master of Science in Health Professions (PGP)
MSHP	Missionary Sisters of the Holy Family (Poland) (TOCD)
MSHR	Master of Science in Human Resources (PGP)
MSHR	Melanocyte Stimulating Hormone Receptor [*Medicine*] (DMAA)
MSHR	Missionary Sisters of Our Lady of the Holy Rosary [*Blackrock, County Dublin, Republic of Ireland*] (EAIO)
MSHRF	Melanocyte-Stimulating Hormone Releasing Factor (DB)
MSHRM	Master of Science in Human Resources Management (PGP)
MSHS	Master of Science in Health and Safety (GAGS)
MSHS	Master of Science in Health Science (PGP)
MSHS	Master of Science in Health Systems (GAGS)
MSHS	Medical Sciences History Society [*British*] (DBA)
MSHSA	Master of Science in Human Service Administration (PGP)
MSHSE	Master of Science in Health Science Education (PGP)
mshsks	Mesh Sacks
MSHy..........	Master of Science in Hygiene (DAVI)
MS Hyg.	Master of Science in Hygiene
MsHz	Copiah-Jefferson Regional Library, Hazelhurst, MS [*Library symbol*] [*Library of Congress*] (LCLS)
MSI............	Magnetic Source Imaging [*Neuroscience*]
msi	Maintenance Significant Item (NAKS)
MSI............	Maintenance Significant Items (NASA)
MSI............	Maintenance Supply Item
MSI............	Maintenance Support Index
MSI............	Management Style Inventory [*Test*] (TMMY)
MSI............	Manned Satellite Inspector
MSI............	Man System Integration (IAA)
MSI............	Manufacturing Standing Instructions (ACAE)
MSI............	Manufacturing Support Item

MSI............	Marine Science Institute [*University of California, Santa Barbara*] [*Research center*] (RCD)
MSI............	Marine Science Institute [*Philippines*]
MSI............	Marine Specialty Inc. (SAUS)
MSI............	Marital Satisfaction Inventory [*Psychology*]
MSI............	Marketing Science Institute [*Cambridge, MA*] (EA)
MSI............	Master of Science in Instruction (PGP)
MSI............	Master of Science in Insurance
MSI............	Mathematical Sciences Institute [*Cornell University*] [*Research center*] (RCD)
MSI............	Maximum Speed Indicator
MSI............	Maxwell Scientific International [*Inc.*]
MSI............	Mean Spleen Index
MSI............	Medical Seminars International (EA)
msi	Medium Scale Integration (NAKS)
MSI............	Medium-Scale Integration [*Circuit packaging*]
MSI............	Megapounds per Square Inch
MSI............	Member of the Sanitary Institute [*British*] (ROG)
MSI............	Member of the Surveyors' Institution [*British*] (ROG)
MSI............	Mentoring Style Indicator [*Test*] (TMMY)
MSI............	Meritorious Service Increase (SAUS)
MSI............	Messina ING [*Istituto Nazionale Geodetico*] [*Sicily*] [*Seismograph station code, US Geological Survey*] (SEIS)
MSI............	Metal Support Interaction [*Catalysis*]
MSI............	Micorsoft Installer [*Computer science*]
MSI............	Microbiological Safety Index (DB)
MSI............	Micro-Star International (SAUS)
MSI............	Microwave Services International, Inc. [*Denville, NJ*] [*Telecommunications*] (TSSD)
MSI............	Middle-Scale Integration [*Computer science*] (IAA)
MSI............	Military Service Indicator (MCD)
MSI............	Military Standard Item (MCD)
MSI............	Military Static Inverter
MSI............	Mill Service, Inc. (EFIS)
MSI............	Minesweeper, Inshore [*Navy symbol*]
MSI............	Missile Status Indicator
MSI............	Missile Subsystem Integration (SAA)
MSI............	Mission Success Indicator (MCD)
MSI............	Moderate Scale Integration [*Electronics*]
MSI............	Molecular Sciences Institute
MSI............	Molecular Surface Ionization
MSI............	Money Store (EFIS)
MSI............	Moon Sphere of Influence (KSC)
MSI............	Moshi [*Tanzania*] [*Airport symbol*] (AD)
MSI............	Mother Symptom Inventory [*Psychology*]
MSHG	Motor Sich [*Ukraine*] [*FAA designator*] (FAAC)
MSI............	Motor Skills Inventory [*Sensorimotor skills test*]
MSI............	Movie Star, Inc. (SPSG)
MSI............	Movimento Sociale Italiano [*Italian Social Movement*] [*Political party*] (PPE)
MSI............	Multicomm Sciences International, Inc. [*Denville, NJ*] (TSSD)
MSI............	Multiple Spark Igniter
MSI............	Multiple Subcutaneous Injections [*Medicine*] (MELL)
MSI............	Multiple Subcutaneous Insulin [*Medicine*]
MSI............	Multisensor Imagery
MSI............	Multi Sensor Integration (ACAE)
MSI............	Multispectral Imagery (DOMA)
MSI............	Multispectral Scan Imaging (ACAE)
MSI............	Multisystem Involvement [*Medicine*]
MSI............	Museum of Science and Industry [*Chicago, IL*]
MSI............	Museum Services Institute [*Department of Education*] (OICC)
MSI............	Mustang Software International [*California*] [*Bulletin board system*]
MSI............	Second Independence Movement [*Ecuador*] [*Political party*] (PPW)
MSIA..........	Church of the Movement for Spiritual Inner Awareness (ECON)
MSIA..........	Mass Spectrometric Immunoassay
MSIA..........	Master of Institutional Administration (GAGS)
MSIA..........	Master of Science in Industrial Administration
MSIA..........	Master of Science in International Adminstration (PGP)
MSIA..........	Master of Science in International Affairs (GAGS)
MSIA..........	Member of the Society of Industrial Artists [*British*]
MSIA..........	Multispectral Image Analyzer (ACAE)
MSIAD	Member of the Society of Industrial Artists and Designers [*British*] (DBQ)
MSIB..........	Master of Science in International Business (PGP)
MSIB..........	Modular Systems Interface Bus (NITA)
MSIBK	Master of Science in International Banking (PGP)
MsIbM	Mississippi Valley State College, Itta Bena, MS [*Library symbol*] [*Library of Congress*] (LCLS)
MSIC..........	Mid-South Independent Conference (PSS)
MSIC..........	Missile and Space Intelligence Center [*DoD*]
MSIC..........	Mixed-Signal Integrated Circuit [*Electronics*]
MSIC..........	Mobile Subscriber Indentification Number (CGWS)
M-SID.........	Magnetic Sensing Intrusion Device [*Remote sensor*] [*Also, MAGNA-SID*] [*Military*] (VNW)
MSID..........	Mass Spectrometric Isotope Dilution
MSID..........	Measurement Stimulation Identification (MCD)
MSID	Medium-Scale Integration Device [*Circuit packaging*]
MSI-DN.......	Movimento Sociale Italiano-Destra Nazionale [*Italian Social Movement-National Right*] [*Political party*] (EY)
MSIE..........	Master of Science in Industrial Engineering
MSIE..........	Master of Science in International Economics (PGP)
MSIEOR	Master of Science in Industrial Engineering and Operations Research (GAGS)
MSIF..........	Multi-Systems Integration Facility (SSD)
MSIG	Most Significant (IAA)

MSIGM	Macintosh Special Interest Group of Mensa (EA)
MS IGT	Morgan Stanley Group, Inc. [*Associated Press*] (SAG)
MSIGX	Oppenheimer Main Street Inc. & Growth [*Mutual fund ticker symbol*] (SG)
MSIIP	Missile System Installation Interrupted for Parts (NVT)
MS IIS	Microsoft Internet Information Server (SAUS)
MSIL	Master of Science in International Logistics (PGP)
MSIM	Master of Science in Industrial Management
MSIM	Master of Science in Information Management (GAGS)
MSIMC	Master of Science in Information Management and Communication (PGP)
MSIMD	Multiple Single Instruction, Multiple Data (MCD)
MsIn	Henry M. Seymour Library, Indianola, MS [*Library symbol*] [*Library of Congress*] (LCLS)
MSIN	Mail Stop Identification Number (ABAC)
MS in Aero E...	Master of Science in Aeronautical Engineering
MS in Ag	Master of Science in Agriculture
MS in Ag E...	Master of Science in Agricultural Education
MS in Ag Ec...	Master of Science in Agricultural Economics
MS in Agr....	Master of Science in Agriculture
MS in Agr Ed...	Master of Science in Agricultural Education
MS in AN.....	Master of Science in Agricultural Engineering
MS in Aud & Sp...	Master of Science in Audiology and Speech
MS in BA.....	Master of Science in Business Administration
MS in Bl Sc...	Master of Science in Biological Sciences
MS in C	Master of Science in Commerce
MS in C & BA...	Master of Science in Commercial and Business Administration
MS in CE....	Master of Science in Civil Engineering
MS in Cer....	Master of Science in Ceramics
MS in Cer E...	Master of Science in Ceramic Engineering
MS in Cer Tech...	Master of Science in Ceramic Technology
MS in Ch....	Master of Science in Chemistry
MS in Ch E...	Master of Science in Chemical Engineering
MS in Ch Eng...	Master of Science in Chemical Engineering
MS in Con ...	Master of Science in Conservation
MS in CRP...	Master of Science in City and Regional Planning
MS Ind E	Master of Science in Industrial Engineering
MSIndEng...	Master of Science in Industrial Engineering (NADA)
MS in Derm...	Master of Science in Dermatology
MS India......	Morgan Stanley India Investment Fund [*Associated Press*] (SAG)
MS in Dt....	Master of Science in Dietetics
MS in E	Master of Science in Education
MS in E	Master of Science in Engineering
MS in Ed	Master of Science in Education
MS in EE....	Master of Science in Electrical Engineering
MS in EM....	Master of Science in Engineering Mechanics
MS in EM....	Master of Science in Engineering of Mines
MS in E Mgt...	Master of Science in Engineering Management
MS in EP....	Master of Science in Engineering Physics
MS in ES....	Master of Science in Engineering Science [*or Sciences*]
MS in For....	Master of Science in Forestry
MS in GE....	Master of Science in General Engineering
MS in Gp Engr...	Master of Science in Geophysical Engineering
MS in GSM...	Master of Science in General Science and Mathematics
MS in HE....	Master of Science in Home Economics
MS in H Ec...	Master of Science in Home Economics
MS in HR....	Master of Science in Human Relations
MS in ID.....	Master of Science in Industrial Design
MS in IE....	Master of Science in Industrial Engineering
MS in IM.....	Master of Science in Industrial Management
MS in Ind Ed...	Master of Science in Industrial Education
MS in LS.....	Master of Science in Library Science
MS in ME....	Master of Science in Mechanical Engineering
MS in Mech...	Master of Science in Engineering Mechanics
MS in Med...	Master of Science in Medicine
MS in Met ...	Master of Science in Metallurgy
MS in Met E...	Master of Science in Metallurgical Engineering
MS in Mus...	Master of Science in Music
MS in Mus Ed...	Master of Science in Music Education
MS in N......	Master of Science in Nursing
MS in NE....	Master of Science in Nursing Education
MS in N Ed...	Master of Science in Nursing Education
MS in Nr Ed...	Master of Science in Nursing Education
MS in NT.....	Master of Science in Nuclear Technology
MS in Nucl E...	Master of Science in Nuclear Engineering
MS in PA.....	Master of Science in Public Administration
MS in PE....	Master of Science in Petroleum Engineering
MS in PE....	Master of Science in Physical Education
MS in P Ed...	Master of Science in Physical Education
MS in Pet E...	Master of Science in Petroleum Engineering
MS in PH.....	Master of Science in Public Health
MS in Phar...	Master of Science in Pharmacy
MS in Phy ...	Master of Science in Physics
MS in PRE...	Master of Science in Petroleum Refining Engineering
MS in PSM...	Master of Science in Public School Music
MS in Py Sc...	Master of Science in Poultry Science
MS in Rad ...	Master of Science in Radiology
MS in Rec ...	Master of Science in Recreation
MS in Ret...	Master of Science in Retailing
MS in Sp ...	Master of Science in Speech
MS in SS.....	Master of Science in Sanitary Science
MS in SS.....	Master of Science in Social Service
MS in SW....	Master of Science in Social Work
MS in T & I...	Master of Science in Trade and Industrial Education
MS in Trans E...	Master of Science in Transportation Engineering

MSINZ	Member of the Surveyors' Institute of New Zealand
MSIO	Mass Storage Input-Output [*Computer science*] (IEEE)
MSIO	Medical Systems Integration Office [*Army*] (RDA)
MSIP...........	Mechanical Stress Improvement Process [*Nuclear energy*] (NUCP)
MSIP...........	Minority Science Improvement Program [*Department of Education*] (GFGA)
MSIP...........	Modeling and Simulation Investment Plan [*Army*]
MSIP...........	Multinational Staged Improvement Program (MCD)
MSIP...........	Multistage Improvement Program (DOMA)
MSIPC	Master of Science in Information Processing and Communications (PGP)
MSIR	Machine Survey and Installation Report
MSIR	Master of Science in Industrial Relations (GAGS)
MSIR	Master of Social and Industrial Relations
MSIR , ...	Master Stock Item Record
MSIS	Main Steam Isolation Signal [*Nuclear energy*] (NRCH)
MSIS	Manned Satellite Inspection System
MSIS	Man-Systems Integration Standard (SSD)
MSIS	Marine Safety Information System [*Coast Guard*] (MSC)
MSIS	Mask Shop Information System [*Bell Laboratories*]
MSIS	Mass Spectral Information System
MSIS	Mass Spectrometer and Incoherent Scatter (SAUS)
MSIS	Mass Spectrometer Incoherent Scatter (ACAE)
MSIS	Master of Science in Computer-Based Information Systems
MSIS	Master of Science in Information Science (GAGS)
MSIS	Master of Science in Information Systems (PGP)
MSIS	Master of Science in Interdisciplinary Studies (PGP)
MSIS	Model State Information System [*Environmental Protection Agency*] (GFGA)
MSIS	Multi-Sensor Integrated Surveillance (SAUS)
MSIS	Multi-sensor Stabilised Integrated Sensor (SAUS)
MSIS	Multisensor Stabilized Integrated System
MSIS	Multistate Information System [*Patient records*]
MSISDN	Mobile Station Integrated Service Digital Network Number (CGWS)
MSISL	Moore School Information Systems Laboratory
Ms IT	Manuscript, Inner Temple [*A publication*] (DLA)
MSIT	Master of Science in Industrial Technology (PGP)
MSIT	Member of the Society of Instrument Technology [*British*]
MSIT	Missile Subsystem Integration Technology (ACAE)
MSITTL	Medium Scale Integration Transistor-Transistor Logic (CIST)
MSIV	Main Steam Isolation Valve [*Nuclear energy*] (NRCH)
MSIVLCS	Main Steam Isolation Valve Leakage Control System [*Nuclear energy*] (NRCH)
MS/IWS	Master of Science/Industry Work Study
MSIX	Mining Services International Corp. [*NASDAQ symbol*] (NQ)
MSIX..........	Mining Svcs Intl [*NASDAQ symbol*] (TTSB)
MsJ............	Jackson Municipal Library, Jackson, MS [*Library symbol*] [*Library of Congress*] (LCLS)
MSJ	Machine Screw Jack
MSJ	Master of Science in Journalism
MSJ	Medical Sisters of St. Joseph (TOCD)
MSJ	Misawa [*Japan*] [*Airport symbol*] (OAG)
MSJ	Mission San Jose [*California*] [*Seismograph station code, US Geological Survey*] (SEIS)
MSJ	Multiple Subsonic Jet
MSJ96	Morgan Stanley Group, Inc. [*Associated Press*] (SAG)
MSJA	Master of Science in Judicial Administration (GAGS)
MsJB	Belhaven College, Jackson, MS [*Library symbol*] [*Library of Congress*] (LCLS)
MSJBS........	Master of Science in Japanese Business Studies (PGP)
MsJG	Mississippi Bureau of Geology, Jackson, MS [*Library symbol*] [*Library of Congress*] (LCLS)
MsJMC	Millsaps College, Jackson, MS [*Library symbol*] [*Library of Congress*] (LCLS)
MsJPED.......	Episcopal Diocese of Mississippi, Jackson, MS [*Library symbol*] [*Library of Congress*] (LCLS)
MSJPS........	Master of Science in Justice and Public Safety (PGP)
MSJPS........	Master of Science in Justice and Public Service (GAGS)
MsJRD........	Research and Development Center Library, Jackson, MS [*Library symbol*] [*Library of Congress*] (LCLS)
MsJRT	Reformed Theological Seminary, Jackson, MS [*Library symbol*] [*Library of Congress*] (LCLS)
MsJS	Jackson State College [*Later, Jackson State University*], Jackson, MS [*Library symbol*] [*Library of Congress*] (LCLS)
MSJS	Master of Science in Jewish Studies (PGP)
MsJV	United States Veterans Administration Hospital, Jackson, MS [*Library symbol*] [*Library of Congress*] (LCLS)
MsJW	Wesley Biblical Seminary, Jackson, MS [*Library symbol*] [*Library of Congress*] (LCLS)
MSK...........	Grupo Indl Maseca ADS [*NYSE symbol*] (TTSB)
MSK...........	Grupo Industrial Maseca SA de CV [*NYSE symbol*] (SAG)
MSK...........	Magyar Statisztikai Kozlemenyek [*Hungary*]
MSK...........	Major Subcontractor
MSK...........	Manual Select Keyboard [*Computer science*] (KSC)
MSK...........	Mask [*Computer science*] (IAA)
MSK...........	Master of Science in Kinesiology (GAGS)
MSK...........	Mastic Point [*Andros Islands, Bahamas*] [*Airport symbol*] (AD)
MSK...........	Medullary Sponge Kidney [*Anatomy*] (MAE)
MSK...........	Medvedev, Sponheuer, Karnick [*Earthquake intensity scale*]
MSK...........	Memorial Sloan-Kettering Cancer Center [*New York*] (AGLO)
MsK...........	Mid-Mississippi Regional Library, Kosciusko, MS [*Library symbol*] [*Library of Congress*] (LCLS)
MSK...........	Minimal Shift Keying (NITA)
MSK...........	Minimum Shift Keying
MSK...........	Minimum Spares Kit (ACAE)

MSK............ Misaki [Japan] [Seismograph station code, US Geological Survey] [Closed] (SEIS)
MSK............ Mission Support Kit
MSK............ Mobility Support Kit
MSK............ Mostek Corporation (NITA)
MSK............ Musculoskeletal [Orthopedics] (DAVI)
MSKB.......... Microsoft Knowledge Base [Computer science] (PCM)
MSKC.......... Memorial Sloan-Kettering Cancer Center [Research center] (RCD)
MSKCC........ Memorial Sloan-Kettering Cancer Center [New York]
MSKCP........ Missionary Sisters of Christ the King of Polonia (TOCD)
MSKM.......... Minimum Shift Keyed Modulation (NITA)
MSKP.......... Management Skills - Knowledge Profile [Business term]
MSKP.......... Medical Sciences Knowledge Profile (DAVI)
MsL............. Laurel Library Association, Laurel, MS [Library symbol] [Library of Congress] (LCLS)
MSL............. Machine Specification Language
MSL............. Magnetic Surfaces Laboratory
MSL............. Main Sea Level (AAG)
MSL............. Main Steam Line [Nuclear energy] (NRCH)
MSL............. Maintenance Supply Liaison [Air Force] (AFM)
MSL............. Major Soccer League (BARN)
MSL............. Management Selection Ltd.
MSL............. Management Systems Laboratories [Virginia Polytechnic Institute and State University] [Research center] (RCD)
MSL............. Manned Space Laboratory [NASA] (IAA)
MSL............. Manpower Source Listing (MCD)
MSL............. Marine Systems Laboratory [Smithsonian Institution]
MSL............. Master of Sacred Literature
MSL............. Master of Science in Language
MSL............. Master of Science in Librarianship (PGP)
MSL............. Master of Science in Limnology (PGP)
MSL............. Master of Science in Linguistics
MSL............. Master of Studies in Law (PGP)
MSL............. Master Save List [Military] (AFIT)
MSL............. Master Scheduling Letter
MSL............. Masterseal [Record label]
MSL............. Master Support List (MCD)
MSL............. Master Symbol List (SAUS)
MSL............. Materialien zum Sumerischen Lexikon. B. Landsberger. Patrologiae Cursus Completus. Series Latina [A publication] (BJA)
MSL............. Materials and Structures Laboratory [Texas A & M University] [Research center] (RCD)
MSL............. Materials Science Laboratory (TIMI)
MSL............. Maximum Service Life [or Limit] (AAG)
MSL............. Maximum Stillwater Level [Nuclear energy] (NRCH)
MSL............. Maximum Street Load (CTAS)
msl............. Mean Sea Level (PIAV)
MSL............. Mean Sea Level
MSL............. Measurement Standards Laboratory
MSL............. Measurement System Laboratory (MCD)
MSL............. Mechanical Systems Laboratory [NASA] (NASA)
MSL............. Message Switched Line (MCD)
MSL............. Meteorological Satellite Laboratory
MSL............. Methuen's Standard Library [A publication]
MSL............. Microcomputer Sales and Leasing, Inc.
MSL............. Microgravity Science Laboratory [NASA]
MSL............. Microstar Software Ltd. [Nepean, ON] [Telecommunications] (TSSD)
MSL............. Microwave Systems Laboratory (ACAE)
MSL............. Midsouth Bancorp, Inc. [AMEX symbol] (SAG)
MSL............. Midsternal Line
MSL............. Military Shipping Label
MSL............. Military Side Loader [Air transport] [British]
MSL............. Military Support List (MCD)
MSL............. Minesweeping Launch [Navy ship symbol]
MSL............. Minimum Size Limit [Pisciculture]
MSL............. Minneapolis & St. Louis [Railroad] (MHDB)
MSL............. Minnesota State Law Library, St. Paul, MN [OCLC symbol] (OCLC)
MSL............. Missile (AFM)
msL............. Missile (MILB)
MSL............. Missile Sea Level
MSL............. Missile Site Load (MCD)
MSL............. Modify System Logging (AAEL)
MSL............. Moisture Sensitivity Level (AGLO)
MSL............. Molecular Spectroscopy Laboratory [Fisk University] [Research center] (RCD)
MSL............. Mouvement des Sociaux-Liberaux [Movement of Social Liberals] [France] [Political party] (PPW)
MSL............. Multiple Stinger Launcher
MSL............. Multiple Symmetric Lipomatosis [Medicine] (DMAA)
MSL............. Municipal Savings & Loan Corp. [Toronto Stock Exchange symbol]
MSL............. Muscle Shoals [Alabama] [Airport symbol] (OAG)
MSL............. Snow Lake Community Library, Manitoba [Library symbol] [National Library of Canada] (NLC)
MSIA........... Atlantic Union College, South Lancaster, MA [Library symbol] [Library of Congress] (LCLS)
MSLA.......... Main Steam Line Accident [Nuclear energy] (NRCH)
MSLA.......... Manitoba School Library Association
MSLA.......... Master of Science in Legal Administration (PGP)
MSLA.......... Missionary Sisters of Our Lady of the Angels [Lennoxville, PQ] (EAIO)
MSLA.......... Mouse Specific Lymphocyte Antigen [Immunology]
MSLA.......... Multisample Luer Adapter [Medicine] (MEDA)
MSLAET....... Member of the Society of Licensed Aircraft Engineers and Technologists [British] (DBQ)

MsLb.......... Long Beach Public Library, Long Beach, MS [Library symbol] [Library of Congress] (LCLS)
MSLB.......... Main Steam Line Break [Nuclear energy] (NRCH)
MsLbU........ University of Southern Mississippi, Gulf Park, Richard G. Cox Library, Long Beach, MS [Library symbol] [Library of Congress] (LCLS)
MSLC.......... Master Synchronizer and Load Control [Electrical generation]
MSLC.......... Minnesota Short Lines Co. [AAR code]
MSLC.......... Missile Sites Labor Commission [A federal government body] [Abolished 1967; functions transferred to Federal Mediation and Conciliation Service]
MSLC.......... Multi-Loop Sidelobe Cancellation (SAUS)
MSLCOMD... Missile Command [Army]
MSLD.......... Masland Corp. [NASDAQ symbol] (SAG)
MSLD.......... Mass Spectrometer Leak Detector (NRCH)
MsLE.......... Lauren Rogers Library and Museum of Art, Laurel, MS [Library symbol] [Library of Congress] (LCLS)
MSLEX........ Missile Exercise (DOMA)
MSLF.......... Mountain States Legal Foundation (EA)
MSLFM........ Massenet Society and Lovers of French Music [Later, MSAB] (EA)
MSLG.......... Maintenance Support Logistics Group [Military] (CAAL)
Ms LI.......... Manuscript, Lincoln's Inn [A publication] (DLA)
MsLi........... Microfilm Services Ltd., Auckland, New Zealand [Library symbol] [Library of Congress] (LCLS)
MSLIR .... Master of Science in Labor and Industrial Relations
MS Litt .... Master of Sacred Letters
MSLIVSS ..... Main Steam Line Isolation Valve Sealings System [Nuclear energy] (NRCH)
MSLM......... Microchannel Spatial Light Modulator [Electronics]
MSLMAINTSq... Missile Maintenance Squadron [Air Force]
MSLN......... Mari Sandoz Library Network [Library network]
MSLO......... Master Layout
MSLO......... Medical Service Liaison Officer [Air Force]
MSLOUG...... Medium-Sized Libraries/OCLC [Online Computer Library Center] Users Group
MSLP.......... Malawi Socialist Labour Party [Political party] (EY)
MSLP.......... Master of Speech-Language Pathology (PGP)
MSLP.......... Mean Sea Level Pressure (WEAT)
MSLP.......... San Salvador/El Salvador Internacional [El Salvador] [ICAO location identifier] (ICLI)
MSLPr .... MidSouth Bancorp Sr'A'Cv Pfd [AMEX symbol] (TTSB)
MSLQ.......... Motivated Strategies for Learning Questionnaire [Test] (TMMY)
MSLR.......... Mixed Skin Cell-Leukocyte Reaction [Medicine] (DMAA)
MSLS.......... Maneuverable Satellite Landing System (MUGU)
MSLS.......... Master of Science in Law and Society (DLA)
MSLS.......... Master of Science in Library Science
MSLS.......... Master of Science in Logistics Systems (PGP)
MSLS.......... Missile Site Location System (MCD)
MSLS.......... Modular Site Location System (ACAE)
MSLS.......... Multi-Slice Least Squares [Software for crystallography]
MSLSc........ Master of Science in Library Science
MSLT.......... Military Solid Logic Technology (IAA)
MSLT.......... Multiple Sleep Latency Test
MSLWARNINGSq... Missile Warning Squadron [Air Force]
MSLY.......... Mostly (MSA)
MSM............ Maastricht School of Management [Netherlands]
MSM............ Major System Mode (CAAL)
MSM............ Manhattan School of Music
msm............ Manned Support Module [NASA] (NAKS)
MSM............ Manned Support Module [NASA] (NASA)
MSM............ Manufacturing Shop Manual (SAA)
MSM............ Manufacturing Standards Manual
MSM............ Marine Safety Manual [Coast Guard] [A publication] (DLA)
MSM............ Mars Surface Module (MCD)
MSM............ Mass Scatterable Mine (RDA)
MSM............ Master of Medical Science
MSM............ Master of Sacred Ministry (PGP)
MSM............ Master of Sacred Music
MSM............ Master of Science in Management
MSM............ Master of Science in Music
MSM............ Master of Service Management (PGP)
MSM............ Master Scheduling Manager
MSM............ Master Slave Manipulator [Nuclear energy]
MSM............ Mauritian Socialist Movement [Political party]
MSM............ Meal Semiconductor Metal (IAA)
MSM............ Mechanically Separated Meat [Food technology]
MSM............ Medium Minesweeper (NATG)
MSM............ Memory Seat Module
MSM............ Memory Storage Module
MSM............ Men Who Have Sex with Men [Australia] [An association]
MSM............ Mercury Specialist Management [Commercial firm] [British]
MsM............ Meridian Public Library, Meridian, MS [Library symbol] [Library of Congress] (LCLS)
MSM............ Meritorious Service Medal [Military decoration]
MSM............ Message Switching Multiplexing (RALS)
MSM............ Messman
MSM............ Metal-Semiconductor-Metal (IEEE)
MSM............ Methyl Sulfonylmethane [Biochemistry]
MSM............ Micro Surface Mapping [Software package] (NCC)
MSM............ Microwave Switch Matrix (LAIN)
MSM............ Mid-Systolic Murmur [Medicine] (MELL)
MSM............ Millimeter and Submillimeter Conference (MCD)
MSM............ Mineral Salts Medium [Medicine] (DMAA)
MSM............ Minesweeper, River [Navy symbol] [Obsolete]
MSM............ Missile Standards Manual [Military] (IAA)
MSM............ Mission Simulation Model

MSM............ Mission Support Manager (ACAE)
MSM............ Missouri School of Mines
MSM............ Modified Source Multiplication (NRCH)
MSM............ Montana School of Mines
MSM............ Morehouse School of Medicine [Atlanta, GA]
MSM............ Motorized Switching Matrix
MSM............ Motorsteuermonolith
MSM............ Mount St. Mary's College, Emmitsburg, MD [OCLC symbol] (OCLC)
MSM............ Mouvement Social Mohutu [Mohutu Social Movement]
MSM............ Mouvement Solidaire Muluba [Muluba Solidarity Movement] [Political party]
MSM............ MSC Industrial Direct'A' [NYSE symbol] (TTSB)
MSM............ Multi-Speed Module [Automotive ignition systems]
MSM............ Muscat Securities Market
MSM............ Mystic Seaport Museum (EA)
MSM............ Thousand Feet Surface Measure [Lumber]
MSMA......... Mail Systems Management Association [New York, NY] (EA)
MSMA......... Major Symphony Managers Association (EA)
MSMA......... Margarine and Shortening Manufacturers Association (EAIO)
MSMA......... Master Sign Makers' Association (NADA)
MSMA......... Medical-Surgical Manufacturers Association [Later, HIMA]
MSMA......... Metal Sink Manufacturers Association [British] (DBA)
MSMA......... Meteorological Services to Marine Activities [WMO] (MSC)
MSMA......... Metropolitan Symphony Managers Association (EA)
MSMA......... Monosodium Methyl Arsonate [Herbicide]
MSMA......... Monosodium Salt of Methylarsonic Acid [Agriculture]
MsMac........ Noxubee County Library, Macon, MS [Library symbol] [Library of Congress] (LCLS)
MSMAE....... Master of Science in Materials Engineering (PGP)
MSMAN....... Master Sign Makers' Association [British] (BI)
MsMar........ Quitman County Library, Marks, MS [Library symbol] [Library of Congress] (LCLS)
MSMAS....... Master of Science in Media Arts and Sciences (PGP)
MS Mat....... Master of Science in Materials Engineering (PGP)
MS Mat E.... Master of Science in Materials Engineering (PGP)
MS Mat SE.. Master of Science in Material Science and Engineering (PGP)
MSMatSE.... Master of Science in Materials Science Engineering (GAGS)
MSMAV....... Master Stone Masons' Association of Victoria [Australia]
MSMB......... Mortgage Secondary Market Board [Australia]
MSMC......... Master of Science in Marketing Communication (GAGS)
MSMC......... Master of Science in Mass Communication (GAGS)
MSMC......... Master Schedule and Milestone Chart (MCD)
MSMC......... Member of the Spectacle Makers Co. [British] (ROG)
MSMC......... Migrant Studies and Media Center [Australia]
MSMC......... Military Subsistence Market Center (MUGU)
MsMc.......... Pike-Amite Library System, McComb, MS [Library symbol] [Library of Congress] (LCLS)
MSMCS....... Master of Science in Management and Computer Science (PGP)
MSMD........ Madras Subordinate Medical Department [British military] (DMA)
MSMDA...... Mutual Sewing Machine Dealers Association (EA)
MSME......... Master of Science in Mathematics Education (PGP)
MSME......... Master of Science in Mechanical Engineering
MSMEA....... Multiwall Sack Manufacturers Employers Association [British] (DBA)
MS Mech E.. Master of Science in Mechanical Engineering
MSMed....... Master of Medical Science (NADA)
MS Met E.... Master of Science in Metallurgical Engineering
MS Metr...... Master of Science in Meteorology (PGP)
MSMF......... Maintenance Support Management File (MCD)
MSMFE....... Master of Science in Manufacturing Engineering (PGP)
MS Mfg E.... Master of Science in Manufacturing Engineering (PGP)
MsMFM...... Masonic Library, Meridian, MS [Library symbol] [Library of Congress] (LCLS)
MS Mf SE... Master of Science in Manufacturing Systems Engineering (PGP)
MSMG........ Missionary Sisters of the Mother of God [Roman Catholic religious order]
MSMgt........ Master of Science in Management (GAGS)
MS Mgt E.... Master of Science in Management Engineering
MSMI......... Master of Science in Medical Illustration (GAGS)
MSMIA........ Medical and Sports Music Institute of America (EA)
MS Min....... Master of Science in Mining (PGP)
MS Min E.... Master of Science in Mining Engineering (PGP)
MSMIS....... Master of Science in Management Information Systems (PGP)
MS/MIS...... Master of Science/Management Information Systems
MSML........ Minesweeping Motorlaunch [Navy]
MSMLCS..... Mass Service Mainline Cable Systems
MSMM........ Master of Science in Manufacturing Management (PGP)
MsMM........ Meridian Junior College, Meridian, MS [Library symbol] [Library of Congress] (LCLS)
MsMo.......... Lawrence County Public Library, Monticello, MS [Library symbol] [Library of Congress] (LCLS)
MS Mot....... Master of Science in Management of Technology (PGP)
MSMP......... Master Sensitized Material Print (MSA)
MSMP......... Modeling and Simulation Master Plan [Army]
MSMP......... Multispectral Measurements Program (MCD)
MSMPR....... Mixed-Suspension, Mixed-Product Removal [Crystallizer] [Chemical engineering]
MSMQ........ Microsoft Message Queue Server [Computer science]
MSMR........ Massachusetts Society for Medical Research (GVA)
MSMR........ Missouri School of Mines Reactor
MSMS........ Machine Strap Makers' Society [A union] [British]
MSMS........ Magnetic Signature Measurement System (SAUS)
MSMS........ Marine Safety Management System [BTS] (TAG)
MSMS........ Master of Science in Management Science (PGP)
MSMS........ Master of Science in Medical Sciences (PGP)
MS/MS........ Materials Science and Manufacturing in Space [Program] [NASA]

MSMS........ Max Steiner Memorial Society (EA)
MSMS........ Membership Section for Multihospital Systems [Later, HCS] (EA)
MSMS........ Meteorological Systems Management Section
MSMS........ Michigan State Medical Society (SAUS)
MSMS........ Microwave Self-Mixing Sensor (ACAE)
MSMS........ Mutual Security Military Sales
MS-MS........ Tandem Mass Spectroscopy
MSMSA........ Master of Science in Management Systems Analysis (PGP)
MSMSE....... Master of Science in Manufacturing Systems Engineering (PGP)
MSMSE....... Master of Science in Material Science Engineering (PGP)
MSMSEd..... Master of Science in Mathematics and Science Education (GAGS)
MSMSP....... Project Manager, Surface Missile Systems [Navy]
MsMStA...... Saint Aloysius Academy, Meridian, MS [Library symbol] [Library of Congress] (LCLS)
MS MT........ Manuscript, Middle Temple [A publication] (DLA)
MSMT........ Master of Science in Medical Technology (GAGS)
MSMT......... Measurement (KSC)
MS Mt E...... Master of Science in Materials Engineering (PGP)
MSMTH....... Metalsmith [Navy]
MsMU........ Mississippi State University, Meridian Branch, Meridian, MS [Library symbol] [Library of Congress] (LCLS)
MSMU .... Mobile Spectrum Monitoring Unit
MSMus....... Master of Science in Music (NADA)
MSMusEd ... Master of Science in Music Education (NADA)
MSMV......... Monk Seal Morbillivirus
MSMV......... Monostable Multivibrator
MSMW........ Magnetically Suspended Momentum Wheel
MSN........... Dane County Regional-Truax Field [FAA] (TAG)
MSN........... Emerson Radio Corp. [AMEX symbol] (SAG)
MSN........... Madison [Wisconsin] [Airport symbol] (OAG)
MSN........... Main-Stem Node [Botany]
MSN........... Maintenance and Support Network
MSN........... Manned Space Network [NASA] (MCD)
MSN........... Manufacturing Sequence Number (TIMI)
MSN........... Mason
MSN........... Master of Science in Nursing
MSN........... Master Serial Number (AAG)
MSN........... Material Supply Notice (AAG)
MSN........... Median Sample Number (PDAA)
MSN........... Merchant Shipping Notice (SAUS)
MSN........... Message Sequence Number (CAAL)
MSN........... Microsoft Network [Microsoft Corp.]
MSN........... Mildly Subnormal [Medicine] (MAE)
MSN........... Military Serial Number
MSN........... Military Service Number
MSN........... Mission (AFM)
MSN........... Mobil Showcase Network [Television]
MSN........... Modern Satellite Network [Cable-television system]
MSN........... Morrison Minerals Ltd. [Toronto Stock Exchange symbol]
MSN........... Movimiento de Salvacion Nacional [National Salvation Movement] [Colombia] [Political party] (EY)
MSN........... Mozambique Support Network (EA)
MSN........... Multiple Subscriber Number [Telecommunications] (DOM)
MSN........... Music, Sport, News [Radio broadcasting format]
MsN........... Public Library of Natchez and Adams County, Natchez, MS [Library symbol] [Library of Congress] (LCLS)
MsNa.......... Jennie Belle Stephens Smith Library, New Albany, MS [Library symbol] [Library of Congress] (LCLS)
MSNA......... Master of Science in Nurse Anesthesia (GAGS)
MSNA......... Master of Science in Nursing Administration (GAGS)
MSNA......... Mission Accomplished [Military] (AABC)
MSNAP....... Merchant Ship Naval Augmentation Program [Navy]
MSNAP....... Microwave Steerable Null Antenna Processor (MCD)
MSNBC....... Microsoft Corp. National Broadcasting Co. [Cable news channel]
MSNC .... Masonic
MSNCDRFAIRECONRON... Mission Commander, Fleet Air Reconnaissance Squadron (DNAB)
MSND......... Mercury Substitution and Nucleonic Detection (PDAA)
MSND.......... Mouvement Social pour la Nouvelle Democratie [Cameroon] [Political party] (EY)
MSNE......... Master of Science in Nuclear Engineering (GAGS)
MsNe.......... Newton Public Library, Newton, MS [Library symbol] [Library of Congress] (LCLS)
MsNeC........ Clarke Memorial College, Newton, MS [Library symbol] [Library of Congress] (LCLS)
MSNEd........ Master of Science in Nursing Education (NADA)
MS-Net .... Microsoft Network [Computer science] [Also, MSN] (CDE)
MSNET....... Microsoft Network [Computer science] (HGAA)
MSNF......... Milk Solids - Not Fat [Food industry]
MSNF......... Multisystem Networking Facility [Computer science]
MSNGR....... Messenger (ADA)
MSNHP....... Mississippi Natural Heritage Program [Mississippi State Department of Wildlife Conservation] [Jackson, MS] [Information service or system] (IID)
MSNI .... (Mesitylenesulfonyl)nitroimidazole [Organic chemistry]
MSNik 97..... Morgan Stanley Group, Inc. [Associated Press] (SAG)
MSN(R)....... Master of Science in Nursing (Research) (PGP)
MSNRY....... Masonry (MSA)
MSNS .... Master of Science in Natural Science (PGP)
MSNS .... MediSense, Inc. [NASDAQ symbol] (SAG)
MSN/SSN.... Military Service Number / Social Security Number (DNAB)
MS Nsurg ... Master of Science in Neurosurgery (PGP)
MSNT......... (Mesitylenesulfonyl)nitrotriazolide [Biochemistry]
MSNuclEng... Master of Science in Nuclear Engineering (NADA)

MSNY	Massena [*New York*] [*Seismograph station code, US Geological Survey*] (SEIS)
MSNY	Mattachine Society of New York [*Defunct*] (EA)
MSO............	Main Signal Office [*British*]
MSO............	Maintenance Standard Order
MSO............	Maintenance Support Office [*Navy*]
MSO............	Malaysian Students' Organization [*Australia*]
MSO............	Managed Service Organization [*Health Insurance*]
MSO............	Management Science Office
MSO............	Management Service Organization
MSO............	Management Systems Office [*NASA*]
MSO............	Management Systems Operations (ACAE)
MSO............	Mandatory Second Surgical Opinion [*Health insurance*] (GHCT)
MSO............	Manned Solar Observatory (MCD)
MSO............	Manned Spacecraft Operations [*NASA*] (KSC)
MSO............	Manufacturer's Statement of Origin
MSO............	Manufacturing Sequence Outline (MCD)
MSO............	Marginally Stable Orbit [*Physics*]
MSO............	Marine Safety Office (MCD)
MSO............	Marine Staff Officers (EA)
MSO............	Maritime Staff Office (ACAE)
MSO............	Marketing Service Office (SAUS)
MSO............	Marketing Services Officer [*Insurance*]
MSO............	Mars Surface Operation
MSO............	Mass Spectrometer Outgasing (KSC)
MSO............	Master of Science in Orthodontics (GAGS)
M So............	Master of Sociology
MSO............	Master of the Science of Oratory
MSO............	Master Specification Officer (SAUS)
MSO............	Material Sales Order
MSO............	Materiel Status Office (MCD)
MSO............	Medial Superior Olive [*Brain anatomy*]
MSO............	Medical Staff Organization (HCT)
MSO............	Member of the Society of Osteopaths [*British*]
MSO............	Mentally Stable and Oriented (MELL)
MSO............	Mesityl Oxide [*Also, MO*] [*Organic chemistry*]
MSO............	Methionine Sulfoxime [*Biochemistry*]
MSO............	Military Satellite Organization
MSO............	Military Service Obligation (AFM)
MSO............	Military Supply Officer (AFM)
MSO............	Minesweeper, Ocean [*Nonmagnetic*] [*Navy symbol*]
MSO............	Missabe Southern Railroad
MSO............	Missile Safety Officer (AFM)
MSO............	Missoula [*Montana*] [*Seismograph station code, US Geological Survey*] (SEIS)
MSO............	Mixed Services Organisation [*British Armed Services*]
MSO............	Mobile Switching Office [*Bell System*]
MSO............	Model for Spare Optimization (MCD)
MSO............	Morale Support Officer [*Military*] (AABC)
MSO............	Moss Resources Ltd. [*Vancouver Stock Exchange symbol*]
MSO............	Mouvement Socialiste Occitan [*Occitanian Socialist Movement*] [*France*] [*Political party*] (PPE)
MSO............	Mozambique Solidarity Office (EA)
MSO............	Multiple System Operator [*Cable television*]
MSO............	Multiple Systems Operator (ACRL)
MSO............	Multistage Operation (MHDI)
MSo............	Public Library of the City of Somerville, Somerville, MA [*Library symbol*] [*Library of Congress*] (LCLS)
MSOA	Military Studies and Operational Analysis (ADA)
MSOA	Missouri State Orthopaedic Association (SAUS)
MSOB	Manned Spacecraft Operations Building [*NASA*] (KSC)
MSOB	Master of Science in Organizational Behavior
MSobPR	New England Regional Primate Research Center, Harvard University, Southborough, MA [*Library symbol*] [*Library of Congress*] (LCLS)
MSOC	MANPRINT [*Manpower and Personnel Integration*] Staff Officer Course [*Military*] (RDA)
MSOC	Marine Systems Operational Compiler
MSOC	Maritime Sector Operations Center [*NATO*] (NATG)
MSoc	Master of Sociology (ADA)
MSOC	Mechanized Smoke Obscurants Carrier (SAUS)
MSocAdmin...	Master of Social Administration
msocc	Multisatellite Operations Control Center [*NASA*] (NAKS)
MSOCC	Multisatellite Operations Control Center [*NASA*]
M Soc E......	Member of the Society of Engineers [*British*]
MSocPol	Master of Social Policy
M Soc Sc.....	Master of Social Science (PGP)
MSocSc	Master of Social Sciences
MSocSci	Master of Social Sciences
MSocSt	Master of Social Studies
MSocStud ...	Master of Social Studies (ADA)
MSocWk	Master of Social Work
MSOD	Master of Science in Organizational Development (GAGS)
MSOD	Military Service Obligation Date (AFM)
MSOD	Mobile Source Operations Division
MSOE..........	Master of Science in Ocean Engineering (PGP)
MSOE..........	Milwaukee School of Engineering [*Wisconsin*]
MSOE..........	Multiband Spectral Observation Equipment
MSOF..........	Multisystem Organ Failure [*Medicine*] (CPH)
MSOG	Glenwood and Souris Regional Library, Souris, Manitoba [*Library symbol*] [*National Library of Canada*] (NLC)
MSOG	Molecular Sieve Oxygen Generating (PDAA)
MSohG........	Gordon-Conwell Theological Seminary Library, South Hamilton, MA [*Library symbol*] [*Library of Congress*] (LCLS)
MSOINST....	Maintenance Support Office Instructions [*Navy*]
MSOL..........	Manned Scientific Orbital Laboratory [*NASA*] (IAA)
MSOLA	Missionary Sisters of Our Lady of Africa (TOCD)
MSOM	Master of Science in Organization and Management (PGP)
MSOM	Modernized Systems Operations Manual [*Computer science*]
MSom	Somerset Public Library, Somerset, MA [*Library symbol*] [*Library of Congress*] (LCLS)
MSON	Misonix, Inc. [*NASDAQ symbol*] (SAG)
MSonHi.......	South Natick Historical, Natural History, and Library Society, South Natick, MA [*Library symbol*] [*Library of Congress*] (LCLS)
MSONW.......	Misonix Inc. Wrrt [*NASDAQ symbol*] (TTSB)
MSOP	Measurement System Operating Procedure (NG)
MSOP	Medical School Objectives Project (DMAA)
MSOP	Mezzo Soprano [*Music*]
MSOP	Mutual Security Objectives Plan (CINC)
MSOPF	Multicast Open Shortest Path First (SAUS)
MSOphthal...	Master of Ophthalmological Surgery (NADA)
M Sopr	Mezzo Soprano [*Music*]
MSOR	Master of Science in Operations Research (GAGS)
MSOR	Maximum System Operational Range
MSOR	Missile Systems Operational Report [*Military*] (IAA)
MS Orn Hort...	Master of Science in Ornamental Horticulture
MSORS	Mechanized Sales Office Record System [*Telecommunications*] (TEL)
MS(Orth).....	Master of Surgery (Orthopedic)
MSOS	Mass Storage Operating System [*Control Data Corp.*] [*Computer science*] (NVT)
M So Sc	Master of Social Science
M So Se	Master of Social Service
MSOT.........	Master of Science in Occupational Technology (PGP)
MSOT.........	Master of Science in Occupational Therapy (GAGS)
MS Otol	Master of Science in Otolaryngology (PGP)
M So W	Master of Social Work
MSOW	Modular Standoff Weapon [*Ballistic missile*]
MsP	Jackson County - Pascagoula City Library, Pascagoula, MS [*Library symbol*] [*Library of Congress*] (LCLS)
MSP............	Macrophage Stimulating Protein [*Biochemistry*]
MSP............	Magnetic Scalar Potential
MSP............	Maintenance Service Plan
MSP............	Maintenance Support Plan [*or Program*] [*Army*]
MSP............	Maintenance Surveillance Procedure (IEEE)
MSP............	Management Service Provider
MSP............	Management System Programmers Ltd. (NITA)
MSP............	Manager Software Products Ltd. (NITA)
MSP............	Manager Support Programs (MCD)
MSP............	Manual Switching Position (IAA)
MSP............	Manufacturing Systems Products (ACAE)
MSP............	Marine Security Program [*FHWA*] (TAG)
MSP............	Marine Shale Processors, Inc. (EFIS)
MSP............	Maritime Shore Patrol
MSP............	Market Stabilization Price [*Department of Agriculture*]
MSP............	Mark-Sensed Punching (SAUS)
MSP............	Mass Storage Processor [*Honeywell, Inc.*]
MSP............	Master of School Psychology (PGP)
MSP............	Master of Science in Pharmacy
MSP............	Master of Science in Planning (PGP)
MSP............	Master of Social Psychology (PGP)
M Sp...........	Master of Speech
MSP............	Master of Speech Pathology (PGP)
MSP............	Master Shuttle Verification Plan (MCD)
MSP............	Master Simulator Program (NVT)
MSP............	Matched Sale-Purchase Agreement [*Business term*]
MSP............	Material Support Plan [*or Program*]
MSP............	Maximum Silo Price [*Farming terminology*]
MSP............	Maximum Sound Pressure
MSP............	Measurement Sensitive Products (DICI)
MSP............	Mededelingen Spinozahuis [*A publication*] (BJA)
MSP............	Media Signal Processor (SAUS)
MSP............	Media Suite Pro [*Computer software*] (CDE)
MSP............	Medical Specialist
MSP............	Medium Side Prong [*Lamp base type*] (NTCM)
MSP............	Medium-Speed Printer (AABC)
MSP............	Medium Stressed Platform
MSP............	Merozoite Surface Protein [*Of protozoa*]
MSP............	Message Security Protocol (SAUS)
MSP............	Metal Splash Pan (AAG)
MSP............	Microsoft Paint [*Computer science*] (CDE)
MSP............	Microsoft Solution Provider [*Computer science*] (CDE)
MSP............	Microspectrophotometry
MSP............	Microsuspension Seeded Polymerization (DICI)
MSP............	Military Space Program (AAG)
MSP............	Millisecond Pulsar [*Astronomy*]
MSP............	Minesweeper, Patrol [*Navy*] (DNAB)
MSP............	Miniature Series of Painters [*A publication*]
MSP............	Minimum Service Period (TIMI)
MSP............	Minimum Sustaining Power
MSP............	Minneapolis-St. Paul [*Minnesota*] [*Airport symbol*]
MSP............	Miscellaneous Small Parts
MSP............	Missile Setting Panel [*Military*] (CAAL)
MSP............	Missile Simulator Plug
MSP............	Missile Status Panel (ACAE)
MSP............	Missile Support Plan
MSP............	Missionaries of St. Paul (TOCD)
msp	Missionaries of St. Paul (TOCD)
MSP............	Mission Support Plan (MCD)
MSP............	Mobile Support Package (MCD)

MSP .... Moderata Samlingspartiet [*Moderate Unity Party*] [*Sweden*] [*Political party*] (PPE)
MSP .... Mode Select Panel (IAA)
MSP .... Modular Switching Peripheral (ACAE)
MSP .... Modular System Programs [*IBM Corp.*]
MSP .... Monosodium Orthophosphate [*Inorganic chemistry*]
MSP .... Monosodium Phosphate (EDCT)
MSP .... Morgan Stan Fin 8.20% Cp Uts [*NYSE symbol*] (TTSB)
MSP .... Morgan Stanley Finance PLC Capital Unit [*NYSE symbol*] (SAG)
msp .... Mortuus sine Prole [*Dead without Issue*] [*Latin*] (WGA)
MSP .... Mosaic Sensor Program (MCD)
MSP .... Most Significant Position (CMD)
MSP .... Motorized Set Point (IAA)
MSP .... Mount St. Thomas [*Philippines*] [*Seismograph station code, US Geological Survey*] (SEIS)
MSP .... Mouse Serum Protein [*Biochemistry*] (DAVI)
MSP .... Movement Support Plans (ACAE)
MSP .... Movimento Socialista Popular [*Popular Socialist Movement*] [*Portugal*] [*Political party*] (PPE)
MSP .... Multicamera Synthesizing Projector (ACAE)
MSP .... Multiprocessing Server Pack [*Computer science*] (CDE)
MSP .... Multipurpose Semi-Submersible Platform (DNAB)
MSP .... Multisensor Processor (CAAL)
MSP .... Multi-Tech Supervisory Protocol [*Telecommunications*] (PCM)
MSP .... Munchausen Syndrome by Proxy [*Child abuse*] (DIPS)
MSP .... Mutual Security Program
MSP .... Mutual Support Program
MSP .... Servicio de Vigilancia Aerea del Ministerio de Seguridad Publica [*Costa Rica*] [*ICAO designator*] (FAAC)
MSPA .... Maine Sardine Packers Association (EA)
MSPA .... Marin Self-Publishers Association (EA)
MSPA .... Master of Science in Professional Accountancy (PGP)
MSPA .... Master of Science in Public Administration (GAGS)
MSPA .... Master of Speech Pathology and Audiology (PGP)
MSPA .... Member, Society of Pension Actuaries [*American Society of Pension Actuari es*] [*Designation awarded by*]
MSPA .... Migrant and Seasonal Worker Protection Act (WPI)
MSPA .... Modified Sodium Polyacrylate [*Organic chemistry*]
MSP & SSM... Minneapolis, St. Paul & Sault Ste. Marie Railway Co. (IIA)
MSPAP .... Maryland School Performance Assessment Program
MSPAW ...... Miedzynarodowe Stowarzyszenie Przyjaciele Angkor Wat [*International Association of Friends of Angkor Wat*] [*Multinational association based in Poland*] (EAIO)
MSPB .... Medical Specialist Preference Blank
MSPB .... Merit Systems Protection Board [*Formerly, Civil Service Commission*]
MSPC .... Manufacturer Standard Paint Color [*Motor vehicle specification*]
MSPC .... Medical Specialist Corps [*Military*]
MSPC .... MOPAR Scat Pack Club (EA)
MSPC .... Multivariate Statistical Process Control
MSPCL .... Lower Fort Garry National Historic Park, Parks Canada [*Parc Historique National Lower Fort Garry, Parcs Canada*] Selkirk, Manitoba [*Library symbol*] [*National Library of Canada*] (NLC)
MSPCP .... Mobile Source Pollution Control Program [*Environmental Protection Agency*]
MSPD .... Master of Social Planning and Development (ADA)
MSPD .... Matrix Solid-Phase Dispersion [*Analytical chemistry*]
MSPD .... Maximum Speed
MSPD .... Mulheres Portuguesas Social-Democratas [*An association*] (EAIO)
MSPE .... Maintenance Safety and Protection Equipment (AFIT)
MSPE .... Master of Science in Petroleum Engineering (PGP)
MSPE .... Master of Science in Physical Education
MSPE .... Master Plate [*Tool*] (AAG)
MSpecEd .... Master of Special Education
MSpEd .... Master of Special Education
MsPeM .... Mississippi Gulf Coast Junior College, Perkinston, MS [*Library symbol*] [*Library of Congress*] (LCLS)
MSPEQ .... Morgan Stanley Group [*Associated Press*] (SAG)
MSpeSJ ...... Saint Joseph's Abbey, Spencer, MA [*Library symbol*] [*Library of Congress*] (LCLS)
MSPetE....... Master of Science in Petroleum Engineering (GAGS)
MSPetEng... Master of Science in Petroleum Engineering (NADA)
MSP Ex ...... Master of Science in Exercise Physiology (PGP)
MSPEx .... Master of Science in Physiology of Exercise (GAGS)
MSPF .... Maritime Special Purpose Force (COE)
MSPF .... Multispectral Photographic Facility
MSPFW ...... Multishot Portable Flame Weapon (DNAB)
MSPG .... Magnetic Shock Pulse Generator (IAA)
MSPG .... Master of Science in Psychology (PGP)
MSPG .... Materiel Support Planning Guidance [*Military*] (AABC)
MSPG .... Measure Specific Performance Guarantee [*Calculation*] (AAGC)
MSPG .... MindSpring Enterprises [*NASDAQ symbol*] (TTSB)
MSPG .... MindSpring Enterprises, Inc. [*NASDAQ symbol*] (SAG)
MSPGN ...... Mesangial Proliferative Glomerulonephritis [*Nephrology*]
MSPH .... Master of Science in Poultry Husbandry
MSPH .... Master of Science in Public Health
MsPh .... Neshoba County Library, Philadelphia, MS [*Library symbol*] [*Library of Congress*] (LCLS)
MSPharm .... Master of Science in Pharmacy (NADA)
MSPHE ...... Master of Science in Public Health Engineering
MSPH Ed .... Master of Science in Public Health Education
MS Phr .... Master of Science in Pharmacy (PGP)
MS Phys Op... Master of Science in Physiological Optics (PGP)
MsPi .... Crosby Memorial Library, Picayune, MS [*Library symbol*] [*Library of Congress*] (LCLS)
MSPI........... M&T Software Partner International (SAUS)

MSPI .... Modified Ship Plan Index
MSPIR .... Master of Science in Personnel and Industrial Relations
MSPLT .... Master Source Program Library Tape [*Computer science*] (BUR)
MsPMF .... United States Department of Commerce, National Marine Fisheries Service, Pascagoula, MS [*Library symbol*] [*Library of Congress*] (LCLS)
MSPM Rehab... Master of Science in Physical Medicine and Rehabilitation (PGP)
MSPN .... Medical Student's Progress Note (DMAA)
MSPNGE ..... Master of Science in Petroleum and Natural Gas Engineering (PGP)
MSPO .... Mercury Support Planning Office (MUGU)
MSPO .... Meridian Sports [*NASDAQ symbol*] (TTSB)
MSPO .... Meridian Sports, Inc. [*NASDAQ symbol*] (SAG)
MSPO .... Military Support Planning Officer [*Civil Defense*]
MSPO .... Mission System Project Office [*Military*] (CAAL)
MsPog .... Harriette Person Memorial Library, Port Gibson, MS [*Library symbol*] [*Library of Congress*] (LCLS)
MSPoly........ Master of Science in Polymers (GAGS)
MsPon .... Dixie Regional Library, Pontotoc, MS [*Library symbol*] [*Library of Congress*] (LCLS)
MsPop .... Poplarville Public Library, Poplarville, MS [*Library symbol*] [*Library of Congress*] (LCLS)
MSPP .... Merit System Protection Plan
MSPP.......... Michigan Screening Profile of Parenting [*Psychology*]
MsPr .... Jefferson Davis County Library, Prentiss, MS [*Library symbol*] [*Library of Congress*] (LCLS)
MSPR .... Master Spares Positioning Resolver [*Data processing*]
MSPR .... Medical System Program Review [*Army*] (RDA)
MSPR .... Model State Packaging Regulation [*National Institute of Standards and Technology*]
MSPr .... Morgan Stanley 9.36% Pfd [*NYSE symbol*] (TTSB)
MSPRB .... Meteorological Satellite Program Review Board [*NOAA and NASA*]
MSPrB .... Morgan Stanley 8.88% Dep Pfd [*NYSE symbol*] (TTSB)
MSPrC .... Morgan Stanley 8.75% Dep Pfd [*NYSE symbol*] (TTSB)
MSPrD .... Morgan Stanly 7.375% Dep Pfd [*NYSE symbol*] (TTSB)
MSPRS .... Multispectral Photographic Reconnaissance (MCD)
MSPS .... Maneuvering Satellite Propulsion System (MCD)
MSPS .... Master of Science in Planning Studies (PGP)
MSPS .... Master of Science in Psychological Services (GAGS)
MSPS .... Megasample per Second (IAA)
MSPS .... Mega Symbols per Second (MCD)
MSpS .... Misioneros del Espiritu Santo [*Missionaries of the Holy Spirit*] [*Mexico*] (EAIO)
MSpS .... Missionaries of the Holy Spirit (TOCD)
msps .... Missionaries of the Holy Spirit (TOCD)
MSPS .... Mobilization Station Planning System [*MTMC*] (TAG)
MSPS .... Modular Self-Protection System (SAUS)
MSPS .... Modular Space Power Station
MSPS .... Multisource Processing System (MCD)
MSPS .... Multi-Spectral Point Scanner (ACAE)
MSPS .... Myocardial Stress Perfusion Scintigram [*Medicine*]
MSPT .... Marine Silent Power Transmission (SAUS)
MSPT .... Master of Science in Physical Therapy (GAGS)
MSpThy ...... Master of Speech Therapy (ADA)
MS Pw .... Mississippi Power Co. [*Associated Press*] (SAG)
MSPWS ...... Microsoft Personal Web Server [*Computer science*] (AGLO)
Msq .... Masque [*Record label*]
MSQ........... Minnesota Satisfaction Questionnaire
MSQ........... Minsk [*Former USSR*] [*Airport symbol*] (OAG)
MSQ........... Mosquito Construction Gold [*Vancouver Stock Exchange symbol*]
MSQL......... Multilevel Structured Query Language (SAUS)
MSQT......... Missile Ship Qualification Test [*Navy*] (NVT)
MSQT......... Modified Ship Qualification Test
MsR............ Capital Area Regional Library, Raymond, MS [*Library symbol*] [*Library of Congress*] (LCLS)
MSR........... Egypt Air [*ICAO designator*] (FAAC)
MSR........... Machine Specific Register (SAUS)
MSR........... Machine Status Register [*Computer science*] (OA)
MSR........... Machine Stress Rated
MSR........... Macrophage Scavenger Receptor [*Immunology*]
MSR........... Magnetic Shift Register
MSR........... Magnetic Silencing Range [*Navy*] (DOMA)
MSR........... Magnetic Silencing Ranger (DWSG)
MSR........... Magnetic Storage Ring [*Computer science*]
MSR........... Magnetic Stripe Reader (IAA)
MSR........... Magnetic Superresolution
MSR........... Main Status Register [*Computer science*] (VLIE)
MSR........... Main Supply Road [*or Route*]
MSR........... Makassar [*Sulawesi, Indonesia*] [*Airport symbol*] (AD)
MSR............ Male Seniors [*International Bowhunting Organization*] [*Class equipment*]
MSR........... Mammalian Selectivity Ratio (FFDE)
MSR........... Management Summary Report (ABAC)
MSR........... Management Systems Representative (MCD)
MSR........... Manual Sliding Roof [*Automotive accessory*]
MSR........... Manufacturing Service Request (MCD)
MSR........... Manufacturing Specification Request (AAG)
MSR........... Marketing Service Representative
MSR........... Marketing Support Representative
MSR........... Market Share Reporter [*A publication*]
MSR........... Mark Sense Reading
MSR........... Mark Sheet Reader [*Computer science*] (BUR)
MSR........... Mark-to-Space Ratio (VLIE)
MSR........... Mass Storage Resident [*Computer science*] (IEEE)
MS (R)........ Master of Science in Research
MSR........... Master Stock Record (DNAB)

MSR	Material Status Report [*AEC*]
MSR	Maximum Steam Rate [*Nuclear energy*] (NRCH)
MSR	McDonnell Simulator Recorder [*McDonnell Douglas Corp.*] (MCD)
MSR	Mean Spring Rise [*Tides and currents*]
MSR	Mean Square Residual
MSR	Mean Square Root (IAA)
MSR	Mechanically Steered Radar (ACAE)
MSR	Mechanized Storage and Retrieval [*Computer science*]
MSR	Medium Stocking Rate [*Agriculture*] (OA)
MSR	Member of the Society of Radiographers [*British*]
MSR	Membrane-Spanning Region [*Cytology*]
MSR	Memory Select Register (NITA)
MSR	Merchant Ship Reactor [*Navy*]
MSR	Message Has Been Misrouted [*Communications*]
MSR	Metal Seal Ring
MSR	Metalsmith, Ship Repair [*Navy*]
MSR	Meteorological Sounding Rocket
MSR	Microsoft Research Center
MSR	Micro Support Resource Corp. [*Atlanta, GA*]
MSR	Microwave Scanning Radiometer (ACAE)
MSR	Midwest Sunbeam Registry (EA)
MSR	Milestone Status Report [*Military*] (AFIT)
MSR	Mineral-Surface Roof [*Technical drawings*]
MSR	Mine Smelter and Refinery Databank [*Commodities Research Unit Ltd.*] [*Information service or system*] (CRD)
MSR	Minesweeper, Patrol [*Navy symbol*] [*Obsolete*]
MSR	Minesweeper River [*Navy symbol*] (VNW)
MSR	Minimum Sales Responsibility [*Automotive sales quotas*]
MSR	Minimum Security Requirement
MSR	Minimum Sustaining Rate (MCD)
MSR	Missile Scoring Reliability (MCD)
MSR	Missile Simulation Round (ACAE)
MSR	Missile Site RADAR [*Army*] (MCD)
MSR	Missile Site Range
MSR	Missile Surface RADAR (MCD)
MSR	Mission Success Ratio [*Military*] (CAAL)
MSR	Mission Support Recording [*Deep Space Instrumentation Facility, NASA*]
MSR	Mission Support Room [*NASA*] (KSC)
MSR	Mobile Sea Range (NVT)
MSR	Mobile Support Router (SAUS)
MSR	Mode Status Register (IAA)
MSR	Modification Status Report (KSC)
MSR	Modular Survivable Radar (SAUS)
MSR	Module Support Rack (NASA)
MSR	Moisture Separator Reheater (NRCH)
MSR	Molten-Salt Reactor
MSR	Monthly Status Report [*Navy*]
MSR	Montserrat [*ANSI three-letter standard code*] (CNC)
MSR	Movimiento Socialista Revolucionario [*Revolutionary Socialist Movement*] [*Panama*] [*Political party*] (PPW)
MSR	MSR Exploration [*AMEX symbol*] (TTSB)
MSR	MSR Exploration Ltd. [*Associated Press*] (SAG)
MSR	Multi-Carrier Station Radio [*or Remote*] Control Equipment (PDAA)
MSR	Multicomet Sample Return [*Space science*]
MSR	Multijunction Semiconductor Rectifier
MSR	Multisensor Reconnaissance (SAUS)
MSR	Multispeed Repeater
MSR	Multitrack Serpentine Recording (VLIE)
MSR	Munster [*Germany*] [*Airport symbol*] (OAG)
MSR	Muscle Stretch Reflexes [*Medicine*] (DAVI)
MSR	Musicians for Social Responsibility (EA)
MSR	St. Louis Art Museum, St. Louis, MO [*OCLC symbol*] (OCLC)
MSRA	Master of Science in Recreation Administration (PGP)
MSRA	Middle States Regatta Association (EA)
MSRA	Midwest Ski Representatives Association (EA)
MSRA	Multiple Shoe Retailers' Association [*British*] (BI)
MSRadSc	Master of Science in Radiation Science (GAGS)
MSR/ASR	Main Supply Route/Alternative Supply Route (MCD)
MSRB	Margaret Sanger Research Bureau [*Defunct*] (EA)
MSRB	Metalsmith, Ship Repair, Blacksmith [*Navy*]
MSRB	Metrology Standards Requirements Board (ACII)
MSRB	Municipal Securities Rulemaking Board [*Securities and Exchange Commission*]
MSRC	Marine Sciences Research Center [*State University of New York at Stony Brook*] [*Research center*] (RCD)
MSRC	Marine Spill Response Corp. [*An association*]
MSRC	Master of Science in Resource Conservation (PGP)
MSRC	Materiel Studies Review Committee [*Army*]
MSRC	Medical and Surgical Relief Committee [*Defunct*] (EA)
MSRC	Membre, Societe Royale du Canada [*French*] (CPGU)
MSRC	Metalsmith, Ship Repair, Coppersmith [*Navy*]
MSRD	Marine Services Research Division [*Now Coastal and Arctic Research Division*] (USDC)
MSRD	Mean Square Relative Displacement [*Spectra*]
MSRD	Mobile Service & Repair Depot (SAUS)
MSRD	Mobile Servicing and Repair Detachment [*Military*] [*British*]
MSRE	Master of Science in Real Estate and Urban Affairs
MSRE	Master of Science in Religious Education (PGP)
MSRE	Mir Sample Return Experiment [*NASA*] (SPST)
MSRE	Molten Salt Reactor Experiment
MSRE	Moon Signal Rejection Equipment (AFM)
MSRec	Master of Science in Recreation (NADA)
MSRet	Master of Science in Retailing (NADA)
MSRF	Metalsmith, Ship Repair, Forger-Anglesmith [*Navy*]

MSRF	Microwave Space Research Facility
MSRFT	Minesweeper Refresher Training [*Navy*] (NVT)
MSRG	Medieval Settlement Research Group [*British*] (DBA)
MSRG	Member of the Society of Remedial Gymnasts [*British*]
MSRG	Moated Sites Research Group (EA)
MSRG	Modular Shift Register Generator
MSRGSN	Mountain States Regional Genetic Services Network (SAUS)
MsRH	Hinds Junior College, Raymond, MS [*Library symbol*] [*Library of Congress*] (LCLS)
MSRI	Mathematical Sciences Research Institute [*University of California, Berkeley*] (PDAA)
MSRI	Mathematical Sciences Research Institute [*University of Minnesota*] (PDAA)
MsRi	Pine Forest Regional Library, Richton, MS [*Library symbol*] [*Library of Congress*] (LCLS)
MSRIS	Molten-Salt Reactor Information System
MSRJE	Multiple Session Remote Job Entry [*Computer science*] (VLIE)
MSRK	Mathias-Soave-Redlich-Kwong [*Equation of state*]
MSRL	Marine Sciences Research Laboratory [*Canada*] (MSC)
MSRL	Materials Science Research Laboratory (TIMI)
MSRL	Mobile Secondary Reference Laboratory
MSRM	Main Steam Radiation Monitor (IEEE)
MSRM	Mars Sample Return Mission [*NASA*]
MSRMNT	Measurement
MSRMP	Master of Science in Radiological Medical Physics (PGP)
MSRN	Mobile Station Roaming Number (CGWS)
MSRNW	North-West Regional Library, Swan River, Manitoba [*Library symbol*] [*National Library of Canada*] (NLC)
MSRO	Missile System Requirements Outline (MCD)
MSRP	Management Sciences Research Project [*University of California*] (MCD)
MSRP	Manufacturer's Suggested Retail Price
MSRP	Massive Selective Retaliatory Power (NATG)
MSRP	Meteorological Sounding Rocket Program [*NASA*]
MSRP	Missile, Space and Range Pioneers (EA)
MSRP	Mission Support Real Property [*NASA*] (KSC)
MSRP	Multi Stage Retrofit Program (ACAE)
MSRPC	Microsoft Remote Procedure Call (SAUS)
MSRPP	Multidimensional Scale for Rating Psychiatric Patients
MSRPS	State Retirement & Pension System (SAUS)
MS(R)PT	Master of Science (Research) in Physical Therapy (PGP)
MSR (R)	Member of the Society of Radiographers (Radiography) [*British*]
MSRR	Mission and System Requirements Review [*NASA*]
MSRR	Modeling and Simulation Resource Repository (SAUS)
MSRS	Main Steam Radiation System (IEEE)
MSRS	Master of Science in Recreational Studies (PGP)
MSRS	Materiel System Requirements Specification [*Military*]
MSRS	Metalsmith, Ship Repair, Sheet Metal Worker [*Navy*]
MSRS	Meteoroid Shield Release System (MCD)
MSRS	Military Spending Research Services, Inc. [*Information service or system*] (IID)
MSRS	Military System Requirement Specification (ACAE)
MSRS	Miniature Sonobuoy Receiver System (SAUS)
MSRS	Missile Strike Reporting System
MSRS	Multiple Stylus Recording System (OA)
MSRSIM	Missile Site RADAR Simulation [*Missile system evaluation*] (RDA)
MSRT	Master Standard Reference Tape [*Computer science*] (VLIE)
MSRT	Mean Supply Response Time
MSR (T)	Member of the Society of Radiographers (Radiotherapy) [*British*]
MSRT	Mini System Real-Time (VLIE)
MSRT	Minnesota Spatial Relations Test (DIPS)
MSRT	Missile System Readiness Test (IEEE)
MSRT	Mobile Subscriber Radio Terminal [*Army*]
MSRT	Mobile Subscriber Receiver/Transmitter (SAUS)
MSRTE	Misroute
MS-RTP	Micelle-Stabilized Room-Temperature Phosphorescence
MSRTS	Migrant Student Records Transfer System (GFGA)
MS Russ	Morgan Stanley Russia & New Europe Fund, Inc. [*Associated Press*] (SAG)
MSRV	Main Steam Relief Valve [*Nuclear energy*] (NRCH)
MSRY	Masonry
MSS	Magnetic Spark Spectrometer (PDAA)
MSS	Magnetic Stereotaxis System [*Surgery*]
MSS	Magnetic Storm Satellite [*Air Force/NASA*]
MSS	Magnetic Strip Storage [*Computer science*] (VLIE)
MSS	Main Steam System [*Nuclear energy*] (NRCH)
MSS	Main Support Structure (NRCH)
MSS	Maintenance Standards Study (MCD)
MSS	Maintenance Status System (MCD)
mss	Maintenance Status System (NAKS)
MSS	Maintenance Support Schedule [*Air Force*] (AFM)
MSS	Major Stationary Source [*Environmental Protection Agency*]
MSS	Make Suitable Substitution
MSS	Managed Security Services
MSS	Management Science Systems (IEEE)
MSS	Management Statistics Subsystem (TEL)
MSS	Management Summary Sheets (MCD)
MSS	Management Supplier Selection (AAG)
MSS	Management Support Services (ACAE)
MSS	Management Support Staff [*Social Security Administration*]
MSS	Management Support System (USDC)
MSS	Management Systems Study (MCD)
MSS	Manned Space Station [*NASA*]
MSS	Manual Safety Switch
MSS	Manufacturers Standardization Society (AAGC)

mss............	Manufacturers Standardization Society (NAKS)
MSS............	Manufacturers Standardization Society of the Valve and Fittings Industry (EA)
MSS............	Manuscripta [Manuscripts] [Latin]
MSS............	Manuscript, Signed
MSS............	MAP [Manufacturing Automation Protocol]/One System Software [Industrial Networking, Inc.]
MSS............	Marine Safety Services [British] (DCTA)
MSS............	Marital Satisfaction Scale [Psychology] (DAVI)
MSS............	Maritime Support Service
MSS............	Mary Stuart Society of America (EA)
MSS............	Massage
MSS............	Massena [New York] [Airport symbol] (OAG)
MSS............	Mass Storage Service [Computer science]
MSS............	Mass Storage System [Computer science]
MSS............	Mastergroup Surveillance System [AT & T]
MSS............	Master of Sanitary Science
MSS............	Master of Science in Safety (GAGS)
MSS............	Master of Selected Studies (PGP)
MSS............	Master of Social Science
MSS............	Master of Social Service
MSS............	Master of Social Studies
MSS............	Master of Sport Science (GAGS)
MSS............	Master Station Subsystem
MSS............	Master Surveillance Station [Air Force]
MSS............	Master Switching Station (MCD)
MSS............	Master System Schedule (MCD)
MSS	Matrix Switch System [Electronics]
MSS............	Maximum Segment Size [Computer science] (VLIE)
MSS............	Mayo Smith Society (EA)
MSS............	Mean Solar Second (IAA)
MSS............	Measurement Specialities, Inc. [AMEX symbol] (SAG)
MSS............	Measurement Specialties [AMEX symbol] (TTSB)
MSS............	Measurement Standard Sensitivity (DICI)
MSS............	Mechanical and Structural Subsystems (MCD)
MSS............	Mechanically Separated Spleen [Food technology]
MSS............	Mechanical Speed Switch
MSS............	Mechanical Support System (MCD)
mss............	Mechanical Support Systems (NAKS)
MSS............	Medical Service School [Air Force] (AFM)
MSS............	Medical Social Services
MSS............	Medical Superintendents' Society (DAVI)
MSS............	Medical Supply Section (SAUS)
MSS............	Medium Survey Ship [Marine science] (MSC)
MSS............	Megasample per Second (IAA)
MSS............	Member of the Statistical Society [British] (ROG)
MSS............	Memory System Security [Computer science] (ECII)
MSS............	Men's Social Services [Salvation Army]
MSS............	Mental Status Schedule [Psychology]
MSS............	Message Support Subsystem (MCD)
MSS............	Message Switching Station [Telecommunications] (CET)
MSS............	Message Switching System
MSS............	Messtetten [Federal Republic of Germany] [Seismograph station code, US Geological Survey] (SEIS)
MSS............	Metal Silicone Silicon (VLIE)
MSS............	Metal Spring Seal
MSS............	Metastable State (IAA)
MSS............	Meteorological Satellite Section
MSS............	Meter Stamp Society (EA)
MSS............	Methylprednisolone Sodium Succinate [Antirheumatoid compound]
MSS............	Metropolitan Speleological Society [Australia]
MSS............	Metropolitan Switching System (VLIE)
MSS............	Mexican-Spanish Speaking (OICC)
MSS............	Microwave Switching Station
MSS............	Midcourse Surveillance System (MCD)
MSS............	Midwest Sociological Society (AEBS)
MSS............	Military Security Service [RVNAF]
MSS............	Military Supply Standards [DoD] (MCD)
MSS............	MIMOLA Software System (SAUS)
MSS............	Mine Search System [Navy] (DOMA)
MSS............	Minesweeper, Special [Device] [Navy symbol]
MSS............	Miniature Signaling System [Railway term] (DCTA)
MSS............	Miniature Stepping Switch
MSS............	Miniature Surveillance System (SAUS)
MSS............	Ministry of Social Security [British]
MSS............	Minnesota Satisfactoriness Scale [Job performance test]
MSS............	Minor Surgery Suite [Medicine] (DAVI)
MSS............	Missile Safety Set (IAA)
MSS............	Missile Security Squadron
MSS............	Missile Select Switch
MSS............	Missile Sensor Study (ACAE)
MSS............	Missile Sight System [Army]
MSS............	Missile Stabilization System
MSS............	Missile Station Select
MSS............	Missile Subsystem
MSS............	Missile Support Stand (MCD)
MSS............	Missile Support Subsystem (SAUS)
MSS............	Mission Simulator System
mss............	Mission Specialist Station [NASA] (NAKS)
MSS............	Mission Specialist Station [NASA] (NASA)
MSS............	Mission Status Summary (MCD)
mss............	Mission Status Summary [NASA] (NAKS)
MSS............	Mission Support Site [Army]
MSS............	Mission Support System (ACAE)
MSS............	Mission System Simulator (MCD)
MSS............	Mississauga Public Library [UTLAS symbol]
MSS............	Mixed Spectrum Superheater [Nuclear energy]
MSS............	Mobile Satellite Service
MSS............	Mobile Satellite System (DA)
MSS............	Mobile Service Structure (KSC)
mss............	Mobile Service Structure (NAKS)
MSS............	Mobile Servicing System [For space station]
MSS............	Mobile Subscriber Equipment System (SAUS)
MSS............	Mobile Subscriber Subsystem (ACAE)
MSS............	Mobility Subsystem (KSC)
MSS............	Modelling and Simulation Studies [Marine science] (MSC)
MSS............	Model Skin Surface [Artificial skin]
MSS............	Modern Satellite Systems, Inc. [Whitehouse Station, NJ] [Telecommunications] (TSSD)
MSS............	Mode Selection Switch (KSC)
MSS............	Mode Sickness Susceptibility (KSC)
MSS............	Modified Scram System [Nuclear energy] (NRCH)
MSS............	Modify System State (AAEL)
MSS............	Modularized Simulation System (ACAE)
MSS............	Modular Space Station
MSS............	Modulation Semiconductor Structure
MSS............	Moored Sonobuoy System (MCD)
MSS............	Moored Surveillance System [To detect and destroy enemy submarines] [Navy]
MSS............	Morris Air Service [ICAO designator] (FAAC)
MSS............	Motion Sickness Susceptibility (MCD)
MSS............	Motor Surveillance Service [MTMC] (TAG)
MSS............	Movement Shorthand Society [Later, Center for Sutton Movement Writing] (EA)
MSS............	Mucus-Stimulating Substance
MSS............	Multibeam Steering System
MSS............	Multimedia Systems Services (RALS)
MSS............	Multiple Sclerosis Society [British]
MSS............	Multiple Selling Service (OA)
MSS............	Multiple Steady States [Chemical engineering]
MSS............	Multi-Satellite System (ACAE)
MSS............	Multispectral Scanner [or Sensor]
MSS............	Multispectral Scanner System
MSS............	Multispectral/Spin Scanner (SAUS)
MSS............	Multistatic Sonar System (SAUS)
MSS............	Multitask Single Stream System (NITA)
MSS............	Muscular Subaortic Stenosis [Cardiology]
MSS............	Music Story Series [A publication]
MSS............	Special Minesweeper [Navy symbol]
MSs............	Swansea Free Public Library, Swansea, MA [Library symbol] [Library of Congress] (LCLS)
MSSA............	Maintenance Supply Services Agency (NATG)
MSSA............	Manchester Scales of Social Adaptation [Psychology]
MSSA............	Master of Science in Social Administration (GAGS)
MSSA............	Master Safeguards and Security Agreements (DOMA)
MSSA............	Midland Steel Stockholders Association [British] (DBA)
MSSA............	Military Selective Service Act (OICC)
MSSA............	Military Subsistence Supply Agency [Later, Defense Subsistence Supply Center]
mssa............	Missionaries of the Holy Apostles (TOCD)
MSsA............	Missionaries of the Holy Apostles [Roman Catholic men's religious order]
MSSA............	Missionary Servants of St. Anthony [Roman Catholic women's religious order]
MSSA............	Modification of Special Service Authorization [FCC] (NTCM)
MSSA............	Multi-Sensor Surveillance Aircraft (SAUS)
MSS & H.....	Master of Science in Speech and Hearing
MSSanE.........	Master of Science in Sanitary Engineering
MSS AS.......	Multistatic Sonar System Acoustic Source (DOMA)
MSSB............	Mid-State Federal Savings Bank (EFIS)
MSSB............	Missile Servicing and Storage Building [Military] (IAA)
MSSBR............	Multi-Purpose Supersonic Beamrider (ACAE)
MSSC............	Main Storage Stock Control [Computer science] (IAA)
MSSC............	Management System for Support Contracts [Social Security Administration]
MSSC............	Maritime Surface Surveillance Capability (SAUS)
MSSC............	Mass Storage System Communications (NITA)
MSSC............	Mass Storage System Communicator [Computer science] (IBMDP)
MSSC............	Mass Storage System Control [Computer science] (BUR)
MS Sc............	Master of Sanitary Science
MS Sc............	Master of Social Science
MSSc............	Master of Surgical Science, University of Dundee [British] (DBQ)
MSSC............	Medium SEAL [Sea, Air, and Land] Support Craft [Navy symbol]
MSSC............	Metropolitan School Study Council [Columbia University] (AEE)
MSSC............	Military Standard and Specification Committee
MSSC............	Military Store Staff Corps [British military] (DMA)
MSSC............	Missile System Software Center
MSSC............	Missionary Society of St. Columban (EAIO)
MSSC............	Mobile Service Switching Center
MSSC............	Multiple Sclerosis Society of Canada
MSSC............	Multi-Spectral Scanning Camera (ACAE)
MSSCB........	Missionary Sisters of St. Charles Borromeo (TOCD)
MSSCC	Military Space Surveillance Control Center (MUGU)
MSSCC	Missionaries of the Sacred Hearts of Jesus and Mary (TOCD)
msscc	Missionaries of the Sacred Hearts of Jesus and Mary (TOCD)
MSSCC	Missionarii a Sacris Cordibus Jesus et Mariae [Missionaries of the Sacred Hearts of Jesus and Mary] [Roman Catholic men's religious order]
MSSCC	Multicolor Spin-Scan Cloudcover Camera
MSSCE........	Mixed Spectrum Superheater Critical Experiment [Nuclear energy]

MSSCS	Manned Space Station Communications System [*NASA*]
MSSD	Model Secondary School for the Deaf (EA)
MSSE..........	Master of Science in Sanitary Engineering
MSSE..........	Master of Science in Secondary Education of Students (who are Deaf or Hard of Hearing)
MSSE..........	Missile System Support Equipment
MSSE..........	Multi-Sensor Situation Elaboration (SAUS)
MSS/EC.......	Missile System Supervisor/Engagement Controller [*Military*] (CAAL)
MSSEng.......	Master of Science in Sanitary Engineering (NADA)
MSSFA........	Michigan Steelhead and Salmon Fisherman's Association
MSSG	Marine Expeditionary Unit Service Support Group (DOMA)
MSSG	Message
MSSG	Multiple Sclerosis Susceptibility Gene [*Medicine*] (DB)
MSSG	Stanford Medical Student Survival Guide (SAUS)
MSSH	Master of Science in Speech and Hearing (PGP)
MSSH	Springfield Hospital, Medical Center Library, Springfield, MA [*Library symbol*] [*Library of Congress*] (LCLS)
MSSI..........	Master of Science in Strategic Intelligence (PGP)
MSSJ.........	Missionary Servants of St. Joseph [*Roman Catholic women's religious order*]
MSSJ..........	Multiple Subsonic Jet
MSSL..........	Management Systems Summary List
MSSL..........	Master of Science in Speech and Language (PGP)
MSSL..........	Missile System Stockage List (AFIT)
MSSL..........	Mullard Space Science Laboratory [*University of London*] (PDAA)
MSSM.........	Mars Spinning Support Module [*NASA*] (KSC)
MSSM.........	Master of Science in Science Management (PGP)
MSSM.........	Master of Science in Systems Management (PGP)
MSSM.........	Missionary Sisters of the Society of Mary [*Italy*] (EAIO)
MsSM.........	Mississippi State University, State College, MS [*Library symbol*] [*Library of Congress*] (LCLS)
MSSM.........	Mount Sinai School of Medicine [*New York*] (PDAA)
MSSM.........	Multiple-Sine-Slit Microdensitometer (PDAA)
MSSMS.......	Munitions Section of Strategic Missile Squadron (AAG)
MSSN	Mean Square Signal-to-Noise (IAA)
MSSN	Mission
MSSNRY.....	Missionary
MSSNSW.....	Multiple Sclerosis Society of New South Wales [*Australia*]
MSSP..........	Miscellaneous Small Special Projects (AAG)
MSSP..........	Missionary Society of Saint Paul [*Australia*]
MSSp..........	Mission Sisters of the Holy Spirit [*Roman Catholic religious order*]
MSSP..........	Model Seafood Surveillance Project [*National Marine Fisheries Service*]
MSSPA	Master of Speech Pathology and Audiology (GAGS)
MSSPA	Missionary Society of St. Paul the Apostle (EA)
MSSPC	Missionary Sisters of St. Peter Claver (EA)
MS Sp Ed	Master of Science in Special Education (PGP)
MS-SPRING...	Multiplex-Section, Shared-Protection Rings
MSSQ	Mission Support Squadron
MSSQ	Multiple Sclerosis Society of Queensland [*Australia*]
MSSR	Mars Soil [*or Surface*] Sample Return
MSSR	Medical Society for the Study of Radiesthesia (EA)
MSSR	Mixed Spectrum Superheat Reactor
MSSR	Mobility, Survivability, Sizing Recommendations (MCD)
MSSR	Monopulse Secondary Surveillance RADAR (DA)
MSSS..........	Main Steam Supply System [*Nuclear energy*] (NRCH)
MSSS..........	Maintenance and Service Subsystem (IAA)
MSSS..........	Maintenance Supply Services System (NATG)
MSSS..........	Manned Space Station Simulator [*NASA*] (MUGU)
MSSS..........	Manned Static Space Simulator
MSSS..........	Manuscripts, Signed
MSSS..........	Mass Spectral Search System [*National Bureau of Standards, Environmental Protection Agency, and National Institutes of Health*] [*Database*]
MSSS..........	Master of Science in Social Science
MSSS..........	Midcourse Surveillance Satellite Study (ACAE)
MSSS..........	Missionary Sisters of the Most Blessed Sacrament [*Roman Catholic religious order*]
MSSS..........	Mobile Spectrum Search System
MSSS..........	Mobile Submarine Simulator System (DWSG)
MSSS..........	Multiple-Start Systematic Sampling [*Statistics*]
MSSS..........	San Salvador/Ilopango Internacional [*El Salvador*] [*ICAO location identifier*] (ICLI)
MSSSM-MMS...	Missionary Sisters of the Society of Saint Mary - Marist Missionary Sisters (EA)
MSSST........	Meeting Street School Screening Test [*Used to detect learning disabilities*]
MSSSW	Mass Spectral Search System-Wiley [*Cornell University*] [*Database*]
MSST..........	Manufacturing Standards and Specifications for Textbooks
MSST..........	Master of Science in Science Teaching
MSST..........	Mean Sea Surface Temperature
MSST..........	Meldesammelstelle [*Message Center*] [*German military - World War II*]
MSST..........	Member of the Society of Surveying Technicians [*British*] (DBQ)
MSST..........	Ministry of State for Science and Technology [*Canada*]
MSST..........	Missionary Servants of the Most Holy Trinity [*Roman Catholic men's religious order*]
MSST..........	Multiple Sclerosis Society of Tasmania [*Australia*]
MsSt..........	Oktibbeha County Library System, Starkville, MS [*Library symbol*] [*Library of Congress*] (LCLS)
MSST..........	Springfield Technical Community College, Springfield, MA [*Library symbol*] [*Library of Congress*] (LCLS)
MSSTA........	Multispectra Solar Telescope Array (SAUS)
MSStat........	Master of Science in Statistics (GAGS)
MSSTC........	Mobile Service Structure Test Conductor (KSC)
MSStEng......	Master of Science in Structural Engineering (NADA)
MsStL	Oktibbeha County Library System, Starkville, MS [*Library symbol*] [*Library of Congress*] (LCLS)
MSSTM.......	Military Space Systems Technology Model (MCD)
MSSTS........	McMurdo Sound Sediment and Tectonic Studies (SAUS)
MSSU	Meteorology on Stamps Study Unit [*American Topical Association*] (EA)
MSSU	Midstream Specimen of Urine [*Medicine*]
MSSU	Mississippi State University (PDAA)
MsSu	Sunflower County Library, Sunflower, MS [*Library symbol*] [*Library of Congress*] (LCLS)
MS Surg	Master of Science in Surgery (PGP)
MSSV.........	Maize Sterile Stunt Virus [*Plant pathology*]
MSSV.........	Maximum Safe Sampling Volume [*Analytical chemistry*]
MSSV.........	Multiple Sclerosis Society of Victoria [*Australia*]
MSSVD	Medical Society for the Study of Venereal Diseases [*Leeds, England*] (EAIO)
MSSVFI.......	Manufacturers Standardization Society of the Valve and Fittings Industry (EA)
MSSW	Magnetostatic Surface Wave [*Telecommunications*] (TEL)
MSSW	Master of Science in Social Work
MSSWA	Multiple Sclerosis Society of Western Australia
MS Sy Sc....	Master of Science in Systems Science (PGP)
MST	Aeroamistad SA de CV [*Mexico*] [*ICAO designator*] (FAAC)
MST	Association of Maximum Service Telecasters (EA)
MsT	Lee-Itawamba Regional Library, Tupelo, MS [*Library symbol*] [*Library of Congress*] (LCLS)
MST	Maastricht [*Netherlands*] [*Airport symbol*] (OAG)
MST	Machinery Safety Tag
MST	Machine Shock Test
MST	Machine Steel
MST	Magnetostrictive Transducer
MST	Maintenance Standard Tests [*Military*]
MST	Maintenance Support Team (MCD)
MST	Management Survey Team (AAG)
MST	Manifold Surface Temperature [*Automotive engineering*]
MST	Marconi Self-Tuning (IAA)
MST	Marine Science Technician [*Coast Guard*] (MUSM)
MST	Mass Spectrometer Tube
MST	Mass Storage Task [*Computer science*] (NOAA)
MST	Master (MCD)
MST	Master of Sacred Theology
MST	Master of Science in Taxation (GAGS)
MST	Master of Science in Teaching
MST	Master of Science in Tourism (GAGS)
MST	Master of Science Teaching (GAGS)
MST	Master of Science Technology (PGP)
MST	Master of Secondary Teaching (GAGS)
MST	Master of Speech Therapy (GAGS)
M St...........	Master of Statistics
MSt...........	Master of Studies, University of Oxford [*British*] (DBQ)
MST	Master of Systems Technology (PGP)
MST	Master of Teaching
MST	Maximal Stimulation Test (DMAA)
MST	Maximum Service Telecasters
MST	Maximum Summer Temperature [*Climatology*]
MST	McCarthy Screening Test [*Intended to diagnose academic potentials and disabilities*] (DIPS)
MST	Mean Selected Temperature
MST	Mean Service Time (CIST)
MST	Mean Solar Time
MST	Mean Survival Time
MST	Mean Swell Time [*Botulism test*] [*Food analysis*]
MST	Measurement
MST	Measurement Status Table (NASA)
MST	Mechanics Support Team [*Military*] (GFGA)
MST	Medial Superior Temporal [*Brain Anatomy*]
MST	Median Survival Time
MST	Media Systems Technology (HGAA)
MST	Medium-Scale Technology
MST	Medium STOL [*Short Takeoff and Landing*] Transport [*Aircraft*]
MST	Memotron Storage Tube
MST	Mercantile Stores Co., Inc. [*NYSE symbol*] (SPSG)
MST	Mercury System Test [*NASA*]
MST	Mesosphere-Stratosphere-Troposphere [*Marine science*] (OSRA)
MST	Message Status Table (MCD)
MST	Microprocessor Simulation Technology (SAUS)
MST	Microsecond Trip
MST	Micro System Technology (AAEL)
MST	Microwave Satellite Technologies, Inc. [*Wellington, NJ*] (TSSD)
MST	Midsummer Time
MST	Military Science Training
MST	Military Shipping Tag
MST	Military Support Team (SAUS)
MST	Miniature Situations Test (EDAC)
MST	Minimal Spanning Tree [*Computer science*]
MST	Minimum Spawning Time [*Pisciculture*]
MST	Ministry, Society, and Theology [*A publication*] (APTA)
MST	Missile Surveillance Technology (MCD)
MST	Missile System Test
MST	Mission Sequence Test (SAUS)
MST	Mission Simulator Test (MCD)
MST	Mission Support Team (MCD)
MST	Mistral Resources Ltd. [*Vancouver Stock Exchange symbol*]
MST	Mobile Service Tower [*Aerospace*]

MST............ Mobile Strike Team
MST............. Mobile Support Team (NVT)
MST............. Mobile Systems Technology (SAUS)
MST............. Modal Survey Test (MCD)
MST............. Module Service Tool (NASA)
MST............. Module Systems Trainer (SAUS)
MST............. Moisture-Proof Heat-Sealing Transparent [Flexography] (DGA)
MST............. Monolithic Systems Technology
M St............. More's Notes on Stair's Institutes of Scotland [A publication] (ILCA)
MST............. Morphine Sulphate [Medicine] (WDAA)
MST............. Mostar [Yugoslavia] [Seismograph station code, US Geological Survey] [Closed] (SEIS)
MST............. Mountain Standard Time
MST............. Movement of Landless Rural Workers [Brazil]
MST............. Movimento Sem Terra [Political party] [Brazil]
MST............. Multimode Storage Tube
MST............. Multi Sensor Track (ACAE)
MST............. Multi-Sensor Tracking (SAUS)
MST............. Multisystem Test [Military]
MST............. Mutual Security Treaty (MCD)
MST............. St. Cloud State University, St. Cloud, MN [OCLC symbol] (OCLC)
MST............. Therapeutic Massage Therapist (NUJO)
MST3K......... Mystery Science Theater 3000 [Cable television program]
MSTA.......... Manufacturers Surgical Trade Association [Later, HIMA] (EA)
MSTA.......... Master of Science in Statistics (PGP)
MSTA.......... Master Tape (AAG)
MSTA.......... Member of the Swimming Teachers' Association [British] (DBQ)
MSTA.......... Mumps Skin Test Antigen [Clinical chemistry]
MSTAB......... Manufacturing Systems Technical Advisory Board (AAEL)
MSTACCMB... Master Aircraft Crewman Badge [Military decoration] (GFGA)
MSTAN......... Modal Stamen Number per Flower [Botany]
MST & E...... Multiservice Test and Evaluation [Military]
MSTAR........ Manportable Surveillance & Target Acquisition Radar (SAUS)
MSTAR .... MLRS [Multiple Launch Rocket System] Smart Tactical Rocket [USA]
MSTARAVB... Master Army Aviator Badge [Military decoration] (GFGA)
MSTART ...... Missile System to Attack Relocatable Targets (ACAE)
MSTAT........ Marine Safety Training and Assistance Team [RSPA] (TAG)
M Stat........ Master of Statistics (PGP)
mstb .... Mastaba (VRA)
MSTB.......... Mission Simulator and Training Building
MS TBR ...... Morgan Stanley Group [Associated Press] (SAG)
MSTC.......... Management Systems Training Council [British]
MSTC.......... Manned Spacecraft Test Center [NASA] (KSC)
MSTC.......... Manufacturing Systems and Technology Center [Baltimore, MD] [Westinghouse Electric Corp.]
MSTC.......... Maryland State Teachers College
MSTC.......... Massachusetts State Teachers College
MSTC.......... Master of Science in Telecommunications (PGP)
MSTC.......... Mastic
MSTC.......... Microwave Sensitivity Time Control [Circuit]
MSTC.......... Midwest Securities Trust Co.
MSTC.......... Multi-Spectral Target Cueing (ACAE)
MSTCS(GB)... Member of the Society of Thoracic and Cardiovascular Surgeons (Great Britain)
MSTD.......... Master Steward [Marine Corps]
MSTD.......... Member of the Society of Typographic Designers (DGA)
MSTDIVB .... Master Diver Badge [Military decoration] (GFGA)
MSTE.......... Master of Science in Technical Education (GAGS)
MSTE.......... Master of Science in Transportation Engineering (GAGS)
M St E .... Master of Structural Engineering
MSTE.......... Steinbach Public Library, Manitoba [Library symbol] [National Library of Canada] (NLC)
MS (T Ed).... Master of Science in Teacher Education
MSTEd........ Master of Science in Technical Education (GAGS)
MSTEL........ Member of the Society of Telegraph Engineers, London [British] (ROG)
M St Eng ..... Master of Structural Engineering
MSTEODBAD... Master Explosive Ordnance Disposal Badge [Military decoration] (GFGA)
M-STEP....... Multi-State Teacher Education Project
MSText........ Master of Science in Textiles (GAGS)
MS Text Chem... Master of Science in Textile Chemistry (PGP)
MSTFA......... (Methyl)trimethylsilyltrifluoroacetamide [Organic chemistry]
MSTFLSB..... Master Flight Surgeon Badge [Military decoration] (GFGA)
MSTG.......... Mass Storage Task Group [CODASYL]
MstG........... Master Glaziers Karate International [Associated Press] (SAG)
MSTG.......... Material Safety Task Group [Air Force] (AFM)
MSTG.......... Melbourne Screen and Theatre Guild [Australia]
MSTG.......... Mustang Software [NASDAQ symbol] (TTSB)
MSTG.......... Mustang Software, Inc. [NASDAQ symbol] (SAG)
MSTGA .... Library Allard, St. Georges, Manitoba [Library symbol] [National Library of Canada] (BIB)
MstGlaz ...... Master Glaziers Karate International [Associated Press] (SAG)
MSTGP .... Material Safety Task Group [Air Force]
MSTh.......... Mesothorium [Radioelement]
MsTI........... Itawamba Junior College, Tupelo Campus, Tupelo, MS [Library symbol] [Library of Congress] (LCLS)
MSTI.......... Miniature Sensor Technology Integration [Orbital satellites]
MSTI.......... Multiple Soft Tissue Injuries [Medicine]
M ST J........ Ordinary Member of the Order of St. John of Jerusalem
MSTJ.......... Public Library, St. James-Assiniboia, Manitoba [Library symbol] [National Library of Canada] (NLC)
MSTK.......... MOS Specific Tool Kit (SAUS)
MSTL.......... Military Subvention Type Lorry [British]

MSTL.......... Minneapolis & St. Louis Railway Co. [Later, MSL Industries, Inc.] [AAR code]
MSTLAB....... Materials and Science Toxicology Laboratory [University of Tennessee] [Research center] (RCD)
MSTLY........ Mostly [NWS] (FAAC)
mstly .... Mostly
MSTM......... Master of Science in Teaching Mathematics (PGP)
MSTM......... Master of Science in Technology Management (GAGS)
MSTM......... Master of Science in Tropical Medicine (GAGS)
MSTM......... Mennonite Village Museum, Steinbach, Manitoba [Library symbol] [National Library of Canada] (NLC)
MSTM......... Missile Service Test Model [Military] (IAA)
MS TMX ..... Morgan Stanley Group, Inc. [Associated Press] (SAG)
MSTO......... Main-Sequence Turnoff [Stellar physics]
MSTO......... Military System Training Organization (SAA)
MStoc......... Stockbridge Library Association, Stockbridge, MA [Library symbol] [Library of Congress] (LCLS)
MStocA....... Austen Riggs Center, Inc., Stockbridge, MA [Library symbol] [Library of Congress] (LCLS)
MSTOL....... Medium-Slow Takeoff and Landing
MSTOS....... South Interlake Regional Library, Stonewall, Manitoba [Library symbol] [National Library of Canada] (NLC)
MsToT .... Tougaloo College, Tougaloo, MS [Library symbol] [Library of Congress] (LCLS)
MSTP......... Maintenance Support Test Package [Military]
MStp.......... Maize Stripe [Plant pathology]
MSTP......... Manual System Training Program (SAA)
MSTP......... Master Template
MSTP......... Medical Scientist Training Program [National Institutes of Health]
MSTP......... Multimission Software Transmission Project (SAUS)
MStP & A.... Minneapolis, St. Paul & Ashland Railway
MSTP & SSM... Minneapolis, St. Paul & Sault Ste. Marie Railway Co.
MSTPHC..... Multistop Time-to-Pulse Height Converter [NASA]
MSTPJ......... Jolys Regional Library, St. Pierre, Manitoba [Library symbol] [National Library of Canada] (NLC)
MSTPRCHT... Master Parachutist Badge [Military decoration] (GFGA)
MStpV........ Maize Stripe Virus [Plant pathology]
MSTR......... [The] Massena Terminal Railroad Co. [AAR code]
mstr .... Master (VRA)
MSTR......... Master
MSTR......... MicroStrategy Inc'A' [NASDAQ symbol] (SG)
MSTR......... Moisture [NWS] (FAAC)
MSTR......... Morningstar Group [NASDAQ symbol] (SAG)
MSTR......... Multivariable Self-Tuning Regulator [Control technology]
MSTR......... Ste-Rose Regional Library, Manitoba [Library symbol] [National Library of Canada] (NLC)
MSTrans ..... Master of Science in Transportation (NADA)
MSTransE.... Master of Science in Transportation Engineering (NADA)
MSTRE........ Moisture (MSA)
MSTS......... Manifold Surface Temperature Sensor [Automotive engineering]
MSTS......... McDonnell Scrap Tool System [McDonnell Douglas Corp.] (MCD)
MSTS......... Mean Standard Toxicity Score (MCD)
MSTS......... Microprocessor Spark Timing System
MSTS......... Microsoft Terminal Server (SAUS)
MSTS......... Midcourse Surveillance Tracking System (SAUS)
MSTS......... Military Sea Transportation Service [Later, MSC] [Navy]
MSTS......... Minuteman System Test Station (ACAE)
MSTS......... Missile Simulator Test Set (MCD)
MSTS......... Missile Static Test Site [Air Force]
MSTS......... Missile Station Test Set (MCD)
MSTS......... Missile Subsystem Test Set [Military] (CAAL)
MSTS......... Multi-Source Tactical Systems (SAUS)
MSTS......... Multisubscriber Time-Sharing Systems [Computer system]
MSTS......... Multisystem Training System
MSTSFE...... Military Sea Transport Service, Far East
MSTSL....... Master of Science in Teaching a Second Language (GAGS)
MSTSO .... Military Sea Transportation Service Office [Obsolete]
MSTT......... Multi-Spectral Tracking Telescope (ACAE)
MSTU......... Military Sea Transport Union
MStuO .... Old Sturbridge Village Library, Sturbridge, MA [Library symbol] [Library of Congress] (LCLS)
MSTV......... Maize Stripe Virus [Plant pathology]
MSTV......... Manned Supersonic Test Vehicle (MCD)
MSTV......... Master-Scale Television
MSTV......... Multi-Spectral Television (ACAE)
MsTy.......... Walthall County Library, Tylertown, MS [Library symbol] [Library of Congress] (LCLS)
MSu........... Goodnow Library, Sudbury, MA [Library symbol] [Library of Congress] (LCLS)
MSU........... Main Storage Unit [Computer science]
MSU........... Main Switching Unit [Telecommunications] (NITA)
MSU........... Maintenance and Status Unit [Telecommunications] (TEL)
MSU........... Maintenance Service Unit (IAA)
MSU........... Maintenance Signal Unit [Telecommunications] (TEL)
MSU........... Maintenance Station Unit (ACAE)
MSU........... Malaria Survey Unit [Army] [World War II]
MSU........... Management Signal Unit [Telecommunications] (TEL)
MSU........... Management Support Unit
MSU........... Management Systems Unit
MSU........... Maple Sugar (or Syrup) Urine [Medicine] (DMAA)
MSU........... Marysvale [Utah] [Seismograph station code, US Geological Survey] (SEIS)
MSU........... Maseru [Lesotho] [Airport symbol] (OAG)
MSU........... Masonic Study Unit [American Topical Association] (EA)
msu .... Mass Storage Unit (NAKS)

MSU............. Mass Storage Unit [Computer science] (NASA)
MSU............. Material Salvage Unit
MSU............. Mathematical Study Unit [American Topical Association] (EA)
MSU............. Measurable System Unit (TIMI)
msu .... Measuring Stimuli Unit (NAKS)
MSU............. Measuring Stimuli Units (NASA)
MSU............. Medical Service Unit [Air Force] (AFM)
MSU............. Medical Studies Unit (DAVI)
MSU............. Medical Subjects Unit [American Topical Association] (EA)
MSU............. Medical Support Unit [Department of Emergency Management] (DEMM)
MSU............. Memory Service Unit [Computer science]
MSU............. Memphis State University [Tennessee]
MSU............. Message Switching Unit
MSU............. Meteorology on Stamps Study Unit [American Topical Association] (EA)
MSU............. Michigan State University [East Lansing]
MSU............. Microelectronics Support Unit [Department of Education and Science] (NITA)
MSU............. Microwave Sounding Unit [Telecommunications] (TEL)
MSU............. Midstream Specimen of Urine [Medicine]
MSU............. Mid-Stream Urine [Medicine] (DMAA)
MSU............. Mill Sawyers' Union [British]
MSU............. Ministerial Services Unit (SAUS)
MSU............. Mission Systems Update (SAUS)
msu .... Mississippi [MARC country of publication code] [Library of Congress] (LCCP)
MSU............. Mobile Signals Unit [British military] (DMA)
MSU............. Modern Sharing Unit [Computer science] (OA)
MSU............. Mode Selector Unit
MSU............. Monitored Stroke Unit (SAUS)
MSU............. Monosodium Urate [Organic chemistry]
MSU............. Montana State University [Bozeman]
MSU............. Morgan Stan Fin 7.82% Cp Uts [NYSE symbol] (TTSB)
MSU............. Morgan Stanley Financial [NYSE symbol] (SPSG)
MSU............. Morgan State University, Baltimore, MD [OCLC symbol] (OCLC)
MSU............. Motor-Switching Unit (MCD)
MSU............. Multiblock Synchronization Signal Unit [Telecommunications] (TEL)
MSU............. Multiple Signal Unit [Telecommunications] (TEL)
MSU............. Murray State University [Kentucky]
MSU............. Myocardial Substrate Uptake [Medicine] (DMAA)
MsU............. University of Mississippi, University, MS [Library symbol] [Library of Congress] (LCLS)
MSUAG .... Michigan State University Advisory Group [Contracted with the Government of South Vietnam to provide-civilian training] (VNW)
MSU Business Topics... Michigan State University Business Topics [A publication] (DLA)
MSUCLE ...... Missouri State University Continuing Legal Education (DLA)
MSUD .... Maple Syrup Urine Disease Family Support Group [Founded in 1982] (NRGU)
MSUD .... Master of Science in Urban Design (GAGS)
MSUDC........ Michigan State University Discrete Computer
MSUDFSG.... MSUD [Maple Syrup Urine Disease] Family Support Group (EA)
MSUESM ..... Master of Science in Urban Environmental Systems Management (PGP)
MSuL........... Goodnow Library, Sudbury, MA [Library symbol] [Library of Congress] (LCLS)
MSUL........... Medical Schools of the University of London (DAS)
MsU-L......... University of Mississippi, Law School, University, MS [Library symbol] [Library of Congress] (LCLS)
MSUM .... Mission Society for United Methodists (EA)
MSUM .... Monosodium Urate Monohydrate [Organic chemistry]
MsU-M......... University of Mississippi, Medical Center, Jackson, MS [Library symbol] [Library of Congress] (LCLS)
MSUP .... Mouvement pour la Solidarite, l'Union et le Progres [Benin] [Political party] (EY)
MsU-P .... University of Mississippi, School of Pharmacy, University, MS [Library symbol] [Library of Congress] (LCLS)
MSU-PVMA.. Michigan State University Pre-Veterinary Medical Association (GVA)
M Sur .... Master of Surgery
MSurg.......... Master of Surgery (BABM)
MSurgery..... Master of Surgery (NADA)
MSurv......... Master of Surveying
MSurvMap ... Master of Surveying and Mapping
MSurvSc ..... Master of Surveying Science
MSUS .... Mouvement Socialiste d'Union Senegalaise [Senegalese Socialist Movement] [Political party]
MSUSM .... Medical Society of the United States and Mexico (EA)
MSUS/PALS... Minnesota State Universities System Project for Automated Library Systems [Mankato State University Library] [Mankato, MN] [Information service or system]
MSuSR .... Sperry Rand Research Center, Sudbury, MA [Library symbol] [Library of Congress] (LCLS)
MSV............. Catskills/Sullivan County [New York] [Airport symbol] [Obsolete] (OAG)
MSV............. Magnetically Supported Vehicle
MSV............. Maintenance Support Vessel
MSV............. Maize Streak Virus [Plant pathology]
MSV............. Manned Space Vehicle [NASA] (AAG)
MSV............. Manufacturers Services [NYSE symbol]
MSV............. Martian Surface Vehicle
MSV............. Mass Stimulated Vehicles (MCD)
MSV............. Mass Storage Volume
MSV............. Materials Screening Vehicle (SAUS)
MSV............. Maximal Sustained Level of Ventilation [Medicine]

MSV............. Mean Square Velocity
MSV............. Mean Square Voltage (NRCH)
MSV............. Medical Society of Virginia (SAUS)
MSV............. Meteor Simulation Vehicle (SAA)
MSV............. Micro Surveillance system (SAUS)
mSv............. Millisievert [Radiation dose]
MSV............. Miniature Solenoid Valve
MSV............. Missionary Sisters of Verona [Roman Catholic religious order]
MSV............. Mississippi & Skuna Valley Railroad Co. [AAR code]
MSV............. Mobile Surface Vehicle (AAG)
MSV............. Modular Support Vehicle (SAUS)
MSV............. Molecular Solution Volume
MSV............. Molinia Streak Virus
MSV............. Moloney Sarcoma Virus (AAMN)
MSV............. Monitored Sine Vibration [Test] (MCD)
msv............. Monitored Sine Vibration [Test] (NAKS)
MSV............. Monticello, NY [Location identifier] [FAA] (FAAL)
MSV............. Morgan Stan Fin 9% Cp Uts [NYSE symbol] (TTSB)
MSV............. Morgan Stanley Finance Markets Ltd. Capital Units [NYSE symbol] (SAG)
MSV............. Mouse Sarcoma Virus
MSV............. Multifunctional Service Vessel [Off-shore drilling technology]
MSV............. Multipurpose Support Vessel [Offshore drilling]
MSV............. Multi-Service Vendor (VLIE)
MSV............. Murine Sarcoma Virus
MsV............. Vicksburg Public Library, Vicksburg, MS [Library symbol] [Library of Congress] (LCLS)
MSVA.......... Magnetic Speed Variable Assist [General Motors] [Power steering]
MSVA.......... Magnetic Steering Variable Assist [Automotive engineering]
MSVC.......... Mass Storage Volume Control [Computer science] (BUR)
MSVC.......... Master of Vocational Counseling (GAGS)
MSVC.......... Maximal Sustained Ventilatory Capacity [Medicine] (DMAA)
MSVC.......... Meta-Signalling Virtual Channel (VLIE)
MSVC.......... Mount St. Vincent College [New York]
MSVCS .... Missile Sight Video Camera Systems (MCD)
MSVD.......... Missile and Space Vehicle Department [NASA] (KSC)
MsVE.......... United States Army, Corps of Engineers, Waterways Experiment Station, Vicksburg,MS [Library symbol] [Library of Congress] (LCLS)
MSVI........... Mass Storage Volume Inventory [Computer science] (IAA)
MSV(M)....... Murine Sarcoma Virus (Moloney)
MSVO .... Missile and Space Vehicle Office [NASA] (IAA)
MsVO .... Old Court House Museum Library, Vicksburg, MS [Library symbol] [Library of Congress] (LCLS)
MSVP.......... Master Shuttle Verification Plan (MCD)
MSVR .... Mandatory Securities Valuation Reserve [National Association of Insurance Commissioners]
MSW........... Machine Status Word [Computer science]
MSW........... Magnetostatic Waves [Telecommunications] (TEL)
MSW........... Mammal Species of the World (SAUS)
MSW........... Massawa [Ethiopia] [Airport symbol] (OAG)
MSW........... Master of Social Welfare
MSW........... Master of Social Work
MSW........... Master's in Social Work
MSW........... Master Switch
MSW........... Maximum Shipping Weight [MTMC] (TAG)
MSW........... Mean Sea Water
MSW........... Mean Shallow Water
MSW........... Medical Social Worker [British]
MSW........... Medical Solid Waste (EEVL)
MSW........... Meters of Seawater [Deep-sea diving]
MSW........... Microswitch
MSW........... Microwave Spectrometer (TEL)
MSW........... Mikheyev-Smirnov-Wolfenstein Theory [Oscillation effect] [Particle physics]
MSW........... MI Software Co. [Vancouver Stock Exchange symbol]
MSW........... Mission West Properties [AMEX symbol] (SPSG)
MSW........... Modified Sinewave (SAUS)
MSW........... Multiple Shrapnel Wounds
MSW........... Multiple Stab Wounds [Emergency medicine] (DAVI)
MSW........... Municipal Solid Waste
MSW........... Western Massachusetts Regional Public Library System, Springfield, MA [Library symbol] [Library of Congress] (LCLS)
MSWAP .... Master of Social Welfare and Administration Planning
MSWD .... Mean Square Weighted Deviation [Statistics]
MSWD .... Multisystem Weapon Delivery [Air Force]
M Sw En ...... Master of Software Engineering (PGP)
MSWG .... Manpower Systems Work Group
MSWG .... Materials Science Working Group (SAUS)
MSWG .... Military Spending Working Group
MSWG .... Military Strategy Working Group (SAUS)
MSWG .... Modeling and Simulation Working Group
MS/WG .... Module Select/Write Gate [Computer science] (VLIE)
MsWJ .... Jefferson College, Washington, MS [Library symbol] [Library of Congress] [Obsolete] (LCLS)
MSWJ.......... Midland and South Western Junction Railway [British]
MSWL......... Municipal Solid Waste Landfill
MSWLF........ Municipal Solid Waste Landfill
MSWLFS...... Municipal Solid Wast Landfills (BCP)
MSWM........ Men Who Have Sex With Men [AIDS transmission group]
MsWov .... Wilkinson County Library System, Woodville, MS [Library symbol] [Library of Congress] (LCLS)
MsWp.......... Tombigbee Regional Library, West Point, MS [Library symbol] [Library of Congress] (LCLS)

MsWpCt....... Court House Library, West Point, MS [*Library symbol*] [*Library of Congress*] (LCLS)
MsWpMH..... Mary Holmes College, West Point, MS [*Library symbol*] [*Library of Congress*] (LCLS)
MSWREE ...... Master of Science in Water Resources and Environmental Engineering (PGP)
MSWT......... Minimum-Speed Wind Tunnel (MCD)
MsWv .... Water Valley Public Library, Water Valley, MS [*Library symbol*] [*Library of Congress*] (LCLS)
MSWYE....... Modified Seawater Yeast Extract [*Agar*] [*Microbiology*] (DAVI)
MSX........... Mascota [*Mexico*] [*Airport symbol*] (AD)
MSX........... MascoTech, Inc. [*NYSE symbol*] (SPSG)
MSX........... MicroSoft Extended [*Computer science*] (VLIE)
MSX........... Microsoft Extended Basic (NITA)
MSX........... Midcourse Space Experiment (MCD)
MSX........... Minesweeper, Experimental [*Navy symbol*]
MSX........... Mossendjo [*Congo*] [*Airport symbol*] (OAG)
MSX........... Multinucleate Nature, Spherical Shape, Unknown History
MSXPr........ Masco Tech Inc. Cv Pfd [*NYSE symbol*] (TTSB)
MSY........... Massey University School of Aviation [*New Zealand*] [*ICAO designator*] (FAAC)
MSY........... Maximum Sustainable Yield
MSY........... Minimum Sustainable Yield [*Pisciculture*]
MSY........... Morgan Stanley High Yield Fund [*NYSE symbol*] (SPSG)
MSY........... Morgan Stanley Hi Yld Fd [*NYSE symbol*] (TTSB)
MSY........... New Orleans [*Louisiana*] [*Airport symbol*]
MsY........... Yazoo-Sharkey Library System, Yazoo City, MS [*Library symbol*] [*Library of Congress*] (LCLS)
MSYN .... Master Synchronization (VLIE)
MSYNC .... Master Synchronization [*Telecommunications*] (TEL)
MSYNC .... Master Synchronizer (MSA)
MSYS......... Medical Technology Systems, Inc. [*NASDAQ symbol*] (NQ)
M-SysFD...... M-Systems Flash Disk Pioneers Ltd. [*Associated Press*] (SAG)
M Sy Th ..... Master of Systematic Theology
MSZ........... Massive Surf Zone
MSZ........... Milford Sound [*New Zealand*] [*Seismograph station code, US Geological Survey*] (SEIS)
MSZ........... Moga Stan Fin 7.80% Cp Uts [*NYSE symbol*] (TTSB)
MSZ........... Morgan Stanley Finance Markets Ltd. Capital Unit [*NYSE symbol*] (SAG)
MSZ........... Mossamedes [*Angola*] [*Airport symbol*] (OAG)
MSZDP .... Magyar Szocial Demokrata Part [*Hungarian Social Democratic Party*] [*Political party*] (PPE)
MSZMP....... Magyar Szocialista Munkaspart [*Hungarian Socialist Workers' Party*] [*Political party*] (PPE)
MSzP .... Magyar Szocialista Part [*Hungarian Socialist Party*] [*Political party*] (EY)
MT .... Core Melt Through [*Nuclear energy*] (IEEE)
MT .... Empty [*Slang*]
MT .... Flame Tight
MT .... Internacia Asocio Monda Turismo [*International Association for World Tourism*] (EAIO)
MT .... Internal Revenue Bureau Miscellaneous Tax Ruling [*United States*] [*A publication*] (DLA)
MT .... Machine Tool
MT .... Machine Tool Technology Program [*Association of Independent Colleges and Schools specialization code*]
MT .... Machine Translation [*Computer science*]
MT .... Mac Knight Airlines [*ICAO designator*] (AD)
M-T............ Macroglobulin-Trypsin [*Complex*] (DAVI)
M-T............ Macroglobulin-Trypsin Complex [*Medicine*] (BABM)
MT .... Magic Tee (IAA)
MT .... Magnetic
MT .... Magnetic Particle Testing [*Nuclear energy*] (IEEE)
MT .... Magnetic Tape
MT .... Magnetic Tube
mt .... Magnetite [*CIPW classification*] [*Geology*]
MT .... Magnetotelluric [*Geological surveying*]
MT .... Mail Transfer
MT .... Mail Tray (AAG)
MT .... Main Telescope
MT .... Maintenance Technician (MUGU)
MT .... Maintenance Time
MT .... Maintenance Trailer
MT .... Maintenance Trainer (MCD)
MT .... Malaria Therapy [*British*]
MT .... Malignant Teratoma [*Oncology*]
MT .... Malta [*IYRU nationality code*] [*ANSI two-letter standard code*] (CNC)
MT .... Mammary Tumor [*Medicine*]
MT .... Mammilothalamic Tract [*Anatomy*]
MT .... Management Team
MT .... Mandated Territory
MT .... Mannesman Tally (NITA)
MT .... Mantle Tentacle
MT .... Manual Test
MT .... Manual Traction (SAUS)
M/T............ Manual Transmission [*Automotive engineering*]
MT .... Manufacturing Technology (RDA)
MT .... Marathoner's Toe (MELL)
MT .... Mare Tranquillitatis [*Sea of Tranquility*] [*Lunar area*]
MT .... Maritime Tropical Air Mass
MT .... Market Town [*Geographical division*] [*British*]
MT .... Mark Trunk (IAA)
MT .... Masking Template (MCD)
MT .... Masoretic Text [*of the Bible*] [*Hebrew tradition*]

M/T............ Masses or Tumors [*Medicine*] (CPH)
MT .... Mast (IAA)
MT .... Master of Taxation (GAGS)
MT .... Master of Teaching (GAGS)
MT .... Master of Technology (GAGS)
MT .... Master of Textiles (PGP)
MT .... Master Teacher (ADA)
MT .... Master Timer
MT .... Master Tool (NASA)
MT .... Mat
MT .... Materials Test (IEEE)
MT .... Material Test (IAA)
MT .... Material Transfer (NRCH)
MT .... Mathematics Teacher [*A publication*]
Mt .... Matthew [*New Testament book*]
MT .... Maximal Therapy [*Medicine*]
MT .... Maximum Torque
MT .... Maximum Total (VLIE)
MT .... Maximum Traction [*Tire design*]
MT .... Mean Tide [*Tides and currents*]
MT .... Mean Time
MT .... Measured Time
MT .... Measurement (IAA)
MT .... Measurement Ton (MUGU)
M/T............ Measurement Tons (COE)
MT .... Measuring Transformer (IAA)
MT .... Mechanical Technician (KSC)
MT .... Mechanical Test (MCD)
MT .... Mechanical Time [*Fuse*] (AABC)
MT .... Mechanical Traction [*British military*] (DMA)
MT .... Mechanical Translation [*Computer science*]
MT .... Mechanical Transport
MT .... Mediaeval Towns [*A publication*]
MT .... Medial Triceps Brachii [*Medicine*]
MT .... MediaTel [*Database*] [*British*]
MT .... Medical Technician [*British military*] (DMA)
MT .... Medical Technologist
MT .... Medical Transcriptionist (DAVI)
MT .... Medical Transfer (WDAA)
MT .... Meditrust Corp. [*NYSE symbol*] [*Formerly, Meditrust SBI*] (SG)
MT .... Meditrust SBI [*NYSE symbol*] (SPSG)
MT .... Medium Truck [*British*]
MT .... Megaton [*Nuclear equivalent of one million tons of high explosive*] (AFM)
MT .... Megatron (CET)
Mt .... Meitnerium [*Proposed name and symbol for recently-discovered element*]
MT .... Melatonin (MELL)
MT .... Melt Through [*Nuclear energy*] (NRCH)
MT .... Membrana Tympani [*Anatomy*]
MT .... Mesenteric Traction [*Medicine*]
MT .... Mesotocin [*Endocrinology*]
MT .... Message Table [*Computer science*] (OA)
MT .... Message Transfer [*Computer science*] (VLIE)
MT .... Message Type (CGWS)
MT .... Metallothionein [*Biochemistry*]
MT .... Metal Threshold (AAG)
MT .... Metatarsal [*Anatomy*]
MT .... Meteor Construzioni Aeronautiche & Elettroniche SpA [*Italy*] [*ICAO aircraft manufacturer identifier*] (ICAO)
MT .... Meter (MCD)
MT .... Metering Truss (SAUS)
MT .... Methoxytryptamine [*Biochemistry*]
MT .... Methoxytyramine [*Biochemistry*]
MT .... Methyltryptophan [*Biochemistry*]
MT .... Methyltyrosine [*Biochemistry*]
Mt .... Metical (ODBW)
mt .... Metric Ton (SHCU)
MT .... Metric Ton [*1,000 kilograms*]
MT .... Michaelmas Term [*British*] [*Legal term*] (ROG)
MT .... Microptic Theodolite
MT .... Microsyn Torquer (SAA)
MT .... Microthrombus [*Hematology*]
MT .... Microtome [*Instrumentation*]
MT .... Microtubule [*Cytology*]
MT .... Microwave Thermograph [*Medical instrumentation*]
MT .... Middle Temple [*London*] [*One of the Inns of Court*]
MT .... Middle Temporal [*Anatomy*]
MT .... Middle Temporal Lobe [*of the brain*]
MT .... Middle Turbinate [*Otorhinolaryngology*] (DAVI)
MT .... Midland Terminal Railroad (IIA)
MT .... Midrash Tanna'im (BJA)
MT .... Midship Deep Tank
MT .... Might
MT .... Migratory Trout
MT .... Military Tanker [*British*]
MT .... Military Technician
MT .... Military Tractor [*British*]
MT .... Military Train [*British military*] (DMA)
MT .... Military Training
M/T............ Military Transport
MT .... Million Tonne (CARB)
mt .... Millitesla
MT .... Miniature Tube (NTCM)
MT .... Minimum Temperature (DS)

MT	Minimum Threshold [*Medicine*] (DB)
MT	Minimum Transfer (DCTA)
MT	Ministry of Transport [*Later, DOE*] [*British*]
MT	Mishneh Torah [*Maimonides*] (BJA)
MT	Missile Target (SAUS)
MT	Missile Technician [*Navy rating*]
MT	Missile Test
MT	Missile Tilt
MT	Mission Time (MCD)
MT	Mission Trainer (ACAE)
MT	Mission Trajectory (MCD)
mt	Mitochrondrial [*Medicine*]
MT	Mitomycin [*Also, M, MC*] [*Antineoplastic drug*]
MT	Mitotic Time (DB)
MT	Mitral [*Valve*] [*Cardiology*]
MT	Mobile Target (SAUS)
MT	Mobile Team
MT	Mobile Terminal (DA)
MT	Mobile Termination (SAUS)
MT	Mobile/Transportable (CCCA)
MT	Mobile Traveler [*Recreational vehicle*]
MT	Mode Transducer
MT	Modified Tape Armor [*Telecommunications*] (TEL)
MT	Modus Tolens [*Rule of inference*] [*Logic*] [*Latin*]
MT	Moluccas Time (SAUS)
MT	Monroe Tidal Drainage [*Medicine*] (DMAA)
MT	Montana [*Postal code*]
MT	Montana Reports [*A publication*] (DLA)
Mt	Montana State Library, Helena, MT [*Library symbol*] [*Library of Congress*] (LCLS)
MT	More Than
MT	Morse Taper (IAA)
MT	Morton Toe (MELL)
MT	Moscow Time (SAUS)
MT	Most (WGA)
MT	Motilin [*Biochemistry*]
MT	Mo Time [*An association*] (EA)
MT	Motor Driver [*British military*] (DMA)
MT	Motor Tanker
MT	Motor Terminal (IAA)
MT	Motor Threshold [*Medicine*]
MT	Motor Transport [*Military*]
MT	Motor Trend Magazine [*A publication*]
MT	Mount [*Maps and charts*] (KSC)
Mt	Mount (ODBW)
Mt	Mountain (SHCU)
mt	Mountain (VRA)
MT	Mountain [*Board on Geographic Names*]
MT	Mountain Time
MT	Mounted [*Technical drawings*]
MT	Mountings [*JETDS nomenclature*] [*Military*] (CET)
MT	Mounting Tray
MT	Movement Time [*Physical education*]
MT	Moxalactam/Ticarcillin (DB)
MT	MTC Electronic [*Vancouver Stock Exchange symbol*]
MT	Muertos Trough [*Geology*]
MT	Multi-frequency Transducer (SAUS)
MT	Multiple Tics (MELL)
MT	Multiple Transfer
MT	Multiple Twin (IAA)
MT	Multitasking
MT	Muscle and Tendon [*Medicine*] (MAE)
MT	Muscles and Tendons (SAUS)
MT	Muscle Testing (MELL)
MT	Muscle Trauma (MELL)
mt	Music-Theatre Piece (GROV)
MT	Music Therapist [*or Therapy*]
MT	MUX [*Multiplex*] Terminal (MCD)
Mt	Mycobacterium Tuberculosis [*Bacteriology*]
MT	Myelotomography [*Medicine*]
MT	Transcona Public Library, Manitoba [*Library symbol*] [*National Library of Canada*] (NLC)
MT	Traverse City Public Library (SAUS)
MT1	Missile Technician, First Class [*Navy rating*]
MT2	Missile Technician, Second Class [*Navy rating*]
MT3	Missile Technician, Third Class [*Navy rating*]
MT6	Mercaptomerin [*Pharmacology*] (DAVI)
MTA	Mackenzie Tribbeck Associates Ltd. (SAUS)
MTA	MAC [*Military Airlift Command*] Transportation Authorization (AFM)
MTA	Magnetic Tape Accessory [*General Electric Co.*]
MTA	Magnetic Torquer Assembly (SAUS)
MTA	Magyar TavKozlesi ADS [*NYSE symbol*] (SG)
MTA	Mail Transfer Agent [*Computer science*]
MTA	Maintenance Task Analysis
MTA	Maintenance Training Aid (SAUS)
MTA	Major Test Article (NASA)
MTA	Major Trading Area (CGWS)
MTA	Major Training Area [*Army*]
MTA	Malignant Teratoma, Anaplastic [*Medicine*] (DMAA)
MTA	Mammary Tumor Agent (DOG)
MTA	Managed Thermactor Air [*Automotive engineering*]
MTA	Management by Talking Around [*Business term*]
MTA	Management Transactions Audit [*Test*]
MTA	Manpower Training Association (AEBS)
MTA	Man-Tended Approach (SSD)
MTA	Manual Target Acquisition (MCD)
MTA	Manufacturing Technical Assistance
MTA	Marine Trades Association [*British*] (DBA)
MTA	Maritime Training Association (EA)
MTA	Market Technicians Association (NADA)
MTA	Mark Twain Association (EA)
MTA	Marshall Trowelable Ablator (SAUS)
MTA	Mass Thermal Analysis (MCD)
MTA	Master of Tax Accounting (GAGS)
MTA	Master of Teaching Arts (GAGS)
MTA	Master of Theater Arts (GAGS)
MTA	Master Timer Assembly
MTA	Materials Testing Activity (MCD)
MTA	Materiel Transfer Agreement [*DoD*]
MTA	Mean Tryptic Activity (PDAA)
MTA	Measurement Tolerance Allowed (ACAE)
MTA	Media Technology Associates Ltd. [*Bethesda, MD*] [*Telecommunications service*] (TSSD)
MTA	Medical Technical Assistant (DMAA)
MTA	Medical Technology Assessment (DMAA)
MTA	Melamine Tableware Association (EA)
MTA	Message Terminal Area (MCD)
MTA	Message Transfer Agent [*Telecommunications*] (PCM)
MTA	Message Transfer Architecture [*Computer science*]
MTA	Message Transport Agent [*Telecommunications*] (PCM)
MTA	Meta Communications Group, Inc. [*Toronto Stock Exchange symbol*]
MTA	Metatarsus Adductus [*Anatomy*] (DAVI)
MTA	MetaTechnologies Associates [*Oakland, CA*] [*Telecommunications service*] (TSSD)
MTA	Methods-Time Analysis [*Industrial engineering*]
MTA	Methylthionadenosine [*Biochemistry*]
MTA	Metric Tons per Annum
MTA	Metropolitan Transit Authority [*Later, MBTA*] [*Initialism also title of folk song about Boston's transit system*]
MTA	Metropolitan Transportation Authority [*Greater New York City*]
MTA	Metropolitan Travel Agents [*Inactive*] (EA)
MTA	Midterm Availability
MTA	Mid-West Truckers Association (EA)
MTA	Military Technical Advisor (DNAB)
MTA	Military Testing Association (MCD)
MTA	Military Training Airspace (NATG)
MTA	Military Training Area (DA)
MTA	Military Transportation Authorization [*Air Force*]
MTA	Miniature Truck Association [*Defunct*] (EA)
MTA	Minimum Terms Agreement
MTA	Minimum Terrain-Clearance Altitude [*Aviation*]
MTA	Minimum Time Ashore (SAUS)
MTA	Minor Task Authorization [*Navy*]
MTA	Missile Transfer Area (IAA)
MTA	Missile Tube Air
MTA	Mississippi Test Area [*Aerospace*] (AAG)
MTA	Mitchell Aero, Inc. [*ICAO designator*] (FAAC)
MTA	Mobile Training Assistance (CINC)
MTA	Mobility Test Article [*Lunar-surface rover*] [*NASA*]
MTA	Modified Tape Armor [*Telecommunications*] (IAA)
MTA	Monopulse Tracking Antenna
MTA	Motion-Time Analysis
MTA	Motorhome Travelers Association [*Defunct*] (EA)
MTA	Motor Trade Association (NADA)
MTA	Mount Allison University Library [*UTLAS symbol*]
MTA	Mount Auburn Hospital, Cambridge, MA [*OCLC symbol*] (OCLC)
MTA	Movimiento Teresiano de Apostolado [*Teresian Apostolic Movement - TAM*] [*Italy*] (EAIO)
MTA	M Technology Association
MTA	Multilateral Trade Agreement (AAGC)
MTA	Multiple Tailors Association [*British*] (BI)
MTA	Multiple-Terminal Access [*Computer science*] (IBMDP)
MTA	Multiterminal Adapter (IEEE)
MTA	Multitumor Antibody [*Clinical chemistry*]
MTA	Municipal Treasurers Association of the United States and Canada
MTA	Museum Trustee Association (EA)
MTA	Musical Theatres Association
MTA	Music Teachers' Association [*British*] (BI)
MTA	Music Trades' Association [*British*] (BI)
MTA	Muslim Teachers' Association (AIE)
MTA	Myoclonic Twitch Activity [*Neurology*] (DAVI)
MTA	Reference My Talk Address [*Military*] (IAA)
MTa	Taunton Public Library, Taunton, MA [*Library symbol*] [*Library of Congress*] (LCLS)
MTA 4	Medical Technician, Acting, 4th Class [*British military*] (DMA)
MTAA	Mopar Trans-Am Association [*Commercial firm*] (EA)
MTaB	Bristol County Law Library, Taunton, MA [*Library symbol*] [*Library of Congress*] (LCLS)
MTAB	Marginal Terrain Assault Bridge [*Military*] (RDA)
MTAB	Military Technical Acceptance Board (MCD)
MTAC	Mailers Technical Advisory Committee (EA)
MTAC	Mathematical Tables and Other Aids to Computation
MTAC	Michigan Test of Aural Comprehension [*J. Upshur*] (TES)
MTAC	Mid-Atlantic Technology Applications Center [*University of Pittsburgh*] [*Research center*] (RCD)
MTAC	Multiple Test Acceptance Code [*Lubricants testing*] [*Automotive engineering*]
MTAC	Multiple Test Acceptance Criteria
MTAC	Multiple Time Around Clutter
MTACC	Modular Tactical Air Control Centre (SAUS)

MTACCS	Marine Tactical Command and Control System (MCD)
MTACLS.......	Marine Tactical Air Control and Landing System
MTACP	Magnetic Tape Ancillary Control Process [*Computer science*] (CIST)
MTACS.........	Marine Tactical Air Control System (SAUS)
MTAD	Multi-Trace Analysis Display (SAUS)
MTAD	N-methyl-triazolinedione
MTADS	Marine Corps Tactical Data System (AFIT)
MTADS	Mass Tactical Aerial Delivery System (SAUS)
MTAE	Message Transfer Agent Entity [*Telecommunications*] (OSI)
MTAE	Multiple-Time-Around Echoes (SAUS)
MTAE	Multiple Time Around Elimination (ACAE)
MTAF	Mediterranean Tactical Air Force Headquarters
MTAG..........	Manufacturing Technology Advisory Group [*DoD*] (RDA)
MTAG..........	Mission Theological Advisory Group (WDAA)
MTaHi..........	Old Colony Historical Society, Taunton, MA [*Library symbol*] [*Library of Congress*] (LCLS)
MtAHS..........	Alberton High School, Alberton, MT [*Library symbol*] [*Library of Congress*] (LCLS)
MTAI............	Meal Tickets Authorized and Issued [*Army*] (AABC)
MTAI............	Member of the Institute of Travel Agents [*British*]
MTAI............	Minnesota Teacher Attitude Inventory
MTAIF..........	Member of the Australasian Institute for Fundraising (NFD)
MTAK..........	Magyar Tudomanyos Akademia Konyvtara [*Hungarian Academy of Sciences Library*] (IID)
mTAL..........	Medullary Thick Ascending Limb [*Anatomy*]
MTAM..........	Maritime Tropical Air Mass (MSA)
MTAM..........	Multileaving Telecommunications Access Method (VLIE)
MT(AMT)	Medical Technologist (American Medical Technologists) (DAVI)
MT & AETF...	Missile Tilt and Azimuth Error Test Fixture
MT & CE.....	Missile Test and Checkout Equipment
MT&RC......	Marine Training and Replacement Command (SAA)
MT & SE.....	Maintenance Test and Support Equipment
MTANSW	Motor Trades Association of New South Wales [*Australia*]
MTANSW	Music Teachers' Association of South Australia
MTAP..........	Machine Timing Analysis Program (VLIE)
MTAP..........	Management Technical Applications Plan (MCD)
MTAP..........	Methylthioadenosine Phosphorylase [*An enzyme*]
MTAP..........	Multifunction Target Acquisition Processor (ACAE)
MTAR..........	Manual Terrain Avoidance RADAR
MTAR..........	Moving Target Acquisition RADAR (MCD)
MTAS..........	Membrana Tympana Auris Sinistrae [*Medicine*] (DMAA)
MTAS..........	Microwave Transistor Amplifiers (ACAE)
MTAS..........	Modular Target Acquisition System (TIMI)
MTAS..........	Multisensor Target Acquisition System [*Military*] (RDA)
MTASA........	Motor Trade Association of South Australia
MT(ASCP)....	Registered Medical Technologist (American Society of Clinical Pathologists)
MT(ASCP)SBB...	Medical Technologist (American Society of Clinical Pathologists) Specialist in Blood Bank [*Technology*] (DAVI)
MTase	Methyltransferase [*An enzyme*]
MTA/SME.....	Machining Technology Association of the Society of Manufacturing Engineers (EA)
MTAT	Mean Turn-Around Time [*Quality control*]
MTAT	Mixing Tee Acceptance Test [*Automotive emissions*]
MTA US & C...	Municipal Treasurers Association of the US and Canada (EA)
MTAWA........	Motor Trade Association of Western Australia
M Tax	Master of Taxation (PGP)
MtB.............	Bozeman Pubic Library, Bozeman, MT [*Library symbol*] [*Library of Congress*] (LCLS)
MTB.............	Maintenance of True Bearing
MTB.............	Maintenance Time Budget
MTB.............	Main Terminal Board
MTB.............	Main Time Base [*Electronics*]
MTB.............	Malaysian Tin Bureau [*Defunct*] (EA)
MTB.............	M&T Bank [*NYSE symbol*] [*Formerly, First Empire State*]
MTB.............	Maori Trust Board (SAUS)
MTB.............	Marcaptan Terminated Polybutadiene (PDAA)
MTB.............	Marine Test Boat
MTB.............	Mark Twain Bancshares, Inc. [*NYSE symbol*] (SAG)
MTB.............	Materials Testing Branch [*NASA*]
MTB.............	Materials Transportation Bureau [*Department of Transportation*]
MTB.............	Maximum Theoretical Bandwidth (MHDI)
MTB.............	Mechanical Time Base
MTB.............	Medium Tank Battalion
MTB.............	Message to Base
MTB.............	Methantheline [*or Methanthine*] Bromide [*Pharmacology*]
MTB.............	Methoxy(trifluoromethyl)butyrophenone [*Biochemistry*]
MTB.............	Methylthymol Blue [*An indicator*] [*Chemistry*]
MTB.............	Missile Torpedo Boat (SAUS)
MTB.............	Mobility Test-Bed (SAUS)
MTB.............	Modified Tyrode's Buffer [*Clinical chemistry*]
MTB.............	Module Test Bed [*Military*] (CAAL)
MTB.............	Monte Libano [*Colombia*] [*Airport symbol*] (OAG)
MTB.............	Monterey, CA [*Location identifier*] [*FAA*] (FAAL)
MTB.............	(Morpholinylthio)benzothiazole [*Organic chemistry*]
MTB.............	Motor Tariff Bureau, Charleston WV [*STAC*]
MTB.............	Motor Torpedo Boat
MTB.............	Multichannel Triple Bridge
MTB.............	Seaplane Bomber [*Russian symbol*]
MTBA..........	Machine Tool Builders' Association
MTBA..........	Master Test Bed Aircraft (ACAE)
MTBA..........	Mean Time Between Assists (AAEL)
MTBA..........	Melbourne Tenpin Bowling Association [*Australia*]
MTBA..........	Methyl-tert-butylaniline [*Organic chemistry*]
MTBA..........	Multi-Threat Body Armor [*Army*]

MtBaF	Fallon County Library, Baker MT [*Library symbol*] [*Library of Congress*] (LCLS)
MtBaHS	Baker High School, Baker, MT [*Library symbol*] [*Library of Congress*] (LCLS)
MTBAMA.....	Mean Time between Any Maintenance Actions [*Quality control*] (MCD)
MTBAP........	Mean Productive Time Between Assists
MTBASIC ...	Multitasking BASIC [*Computer science*]
MTBC.........	Mean Time Between Calls [*Computer science*] (ELAL)
MtBC..........	Montana State University at Bozeman, Bozeman, MT [*Library symbol*] [*Library of Congress*] (LCLS)
MTBCA	Mean Time between Corrective Action (MCD)
MTBCA	M.T. Bottle Collectors Association (EA)
MTBCD	Mean Time Between Confirmed Defects [*Quality control*] (MHDI)
MTBCF	Mean Time between Confirmed Failures [*Quality control*]
MTBCF	Mission Time between Critical Failures
MTBCMA.....	Mean Time Between Corrective Maintenance (ACAE)
MTBCME.....	Mean Time between Corrective Maintenance Events [*Quality control*] (CAAL)
MTBCMI.....	Mean Time between Corrective Maintenance Interrupts [*Quality control*] (CAAL)
MTBD.........	Mean Time between Defects [*Quality control*] (PDAA)
MTBD.........	Mean Time between Degradations [*Quality control*] [*Telecommunications*] (TEL)
MTBD.........	Mean Time between Demands [*Quality control*] (MCD)
MTBD.........	Mean Time between Discrepancies [*Quality control*]
MTBD.........	Methyl(triazabicyclo)decene [*Organic chemistry*]
MTBDE........	Mean Time between Downing Events [*Quality control*]
MTBDR........	Mean Time between Depot Repair [*Quality control*] (PDAA)
MTBE.........	Mean Time between Errors [*Quality control*]
MTBE.........	Mean Time between Events [*Quality control*]
MTBE.........	Meningeal Tick-Borne Encephalitis [*Medicine*] (DMAA)
MTBE.........	Methyl Tertiary Butyl Ether [*Fuel additive*]
MTBEF........	Mean Time Between Equipment Failures (ACAE)
MtBeHS	Rocky Boy Tribal High School, Box Elder, MT [*Library symbol*] [*Library of Congress*] (LCLS)
MTBEMA......	Mean Time between Essential Maintenance Actions [*Quality control*]
MTBER........	Mean Time between Engine Removal [*Quality control*] (DNAB)
MTBERA......	Mean Time between Essential Replacement Actions [*Quality control*]
MtBeS.........	Stone Child Community College, Box Elder, MT [*Library symbol*] [*Library of Congress*] (LCLS)
MTBETF	Methyl Tertiary Butyl Ether Task Force (EA)
MTBF	Mean Time Between Failures (DMAA)
MTBFA........	Mean Time between False Alarms [*Quality control*] (AABC)
MTBFC........	Mean Time between Failures, Critical [*Military*]
MTBFC........	Mean Time between Flight Cancellations [*Quality control*]
MTBFEC......	Motor Truck, Bus, and Fire Engine Club [*Defunct*] (EA)
MTBFL........	Mean Time between Function Loss [*Quality control*]
MTBFMI......	Mean Time Between False Maintenance Indicators (ACAE)
MTBFP........	Mean Productive Time Between Failures
MTBFRO......	Mean Time between Failures Requiring Overhaul [*Quality control*]
MTBHA	Mark Twain Boyhood Home Associates (EA)
MTBHMF.....	Maintenance between Hardware Mission Failures [*Quality control*]
MTBHQ.......	Mono-Tertiarybutylhydroquinone [*Also, TBHQ*] [*Organic chemistry*]
MTBI..........	Mean Time Between Incident
MTBI..........	Mean Time between Interrupts [*Quality control*]
MTBI..........	Mild Traumatic Brain Injury
MtBil...........	Billings Public Library, Billings, MT [*Library symbol*] [*Library of Congress*] (LCLS)
MtBilB	Bureau of Land Management, Billings, MT [*Library symbol*] [*Library of Congress*] (LCLS)
MtBilBH	Big Sky Hospice, Billings, MT [*Library symbol*] [*Library of Congress*] (LCLS)
MtBilC	Billings Clinic, Billings, MT [*Library symbol*] [*Library of Congress*] (LCLS)
MtBilD	Deaconess Medical Center, Billings, MT [*Library symbol*] [*Library of Congress*] (LCLS)
MtBilE	Eastern Montana College, Billings, MT [*Library symbol*] [*Library of Congress*] (LCLS)
MtBilFW	United States Fish and Wildlife, Billings, MT [*Library symbol*] [*Library of Congress*] (LCLS)
MtBilGS	Church of Jesus Christ of Latter-Day Saints, Genealogical Society Library, Billings Branch, Billings, MT [*Library symbol*] [*Library of Congress*] (LCLS)
MtBilMH	Billings Mental Health Center, Billings, MT [*Library symbol*] [*Library of Congress*] (LCLS)
MtBilNC	Northern Rockies Cancer Center, Billings, MT [*Library symbol*] [*Library of Congress*] (LCLS)
MtBilPP	Planned Parenthood of Billings, Billings, MT [*Library symbol*] [*Library of Congress*] (LCLS)
MtBilR	Rocky Mountain College, Billings, MT [*Library symbol*] [*Library of Congress*] (LCLS)
MtBilRF	Rimrock Foundation Library, Billings, MT [*Library symbol*] [*Library of Congress*] (LCLS)
MtBils	Billings Public Schools, Billings, MT [*Library symbol*] [*Library of Congress*] (LCLS)
MtBilSV	Saint Vincents Hospital, Billings, MT [*Library symbol*] [*Library of Congress*] (LCLS)
MtBilY	Yellowstone Treatment Center, Billings, MT [*Library symbol*] [*Library of Congress*] (LCLS)
MtBilYH	Yellowstone City-County Helth Department, Billings, MT [*Library symbol*] [*Library of Congress*] (LCLS)
MTblack.......	Medium Thermal Black (EDCT)
MTBM.........	Mean Time between Maintenance [*Quality control*] (AFM)
MTBM.........	Mean Time between Malfunctions [*Quality control*]

MTBM........... Microtunneling Boring Machine (RDA)
MTBMA...... Mean Time between Maintenance Actions [*Quality control*]
MTBMAF...... Mean Time between Mission Affecting Failures [*Quality control*]
MTBMCF...... Mean Time between Mission Critical Failure [*Quality control*]
MTBME........ Mean Time between Malfunction Events [*Quality control*] (CAAL)
MTBN........... Motor Transportation Battalion [*Military*]
MTBN........... Mountbatten, Inc. [*NASDAQ symbol*] (SAG)
MTBO........... Mean Time Before Obsolescence [*Navy*] (DOMA)
MTBO........... Mean Time between Outages [*Quality control*]
                    [*Telecommunications*] (TEL)
MTBO........... Mean Time between Overhauls [*Quality control*] (MCD)
MTBO........... Minimum Time before Overhaul [*Quality control*]
MTBOF........ Mean Time between Operational Failures [*Quality control*]
MTBOMF...... Mean Time between Operational Mission Failures [*Quality control*]
                    (MCD)
MTBPER ...... Mean Time between Permanent Engine Removal [*Quality control*]
                    (DNAB)
MTBPM....... Mean Time Between Planned Maintenance [*Engineering*]
MtBr............ Broadus Public Library, Broadus, MT [*Library symbol*] [*Library of
                    Congress*] (LCLS)
MTBR........... Mean Time between Removal [*or Repair or Replacement*] [*Quality
                    control*]
MTBR........... Mean Time Between Replacement
MTBRDR...... Mean Time between Removal for Depot Repair [*Quality control*]
                    (MCD)
MTBRON...... Motor Torpedo Boat Squadron [*Navy*]
MTBS........... Mean Time between Service [*Quality control*] (MCD)
MTBS........... Mean Time Between Stops [*Quality control*] (IAA)
MTBS........... Methuen's Text-Books of Science [*A publication*]
MTBSD........ Mean Time between Supply Demands [*Quality control*] (MCD)
MTBSE........ Mean Time Between Software Errors [*Quality control*] (MHDI)
MTBSF........ Mean Time between Software Failures [*Quality control*] (CAAL)
MTBSF........ Mean Time between System Failures [*Quality control*]
MTBSHF...... Mean Time between System Hardware Failures [*Quality control*]
                    (MCD)
MTBSOF...... Mean Time between System Operational Failures [*Quality control*]
                    (MCD)
MTBSP........ Mobilization Troop Basic Stationing Plan (MCD)
MTBSTC...... Motor Torpedo Boat Squadrons Training Center [*Melville, RI*] [*Navy*]
MTBT........... Miniature Thermal Bar Torch [*Army*] (RDA)
MTBTF........ Mean Time between Testable Failures [*Quality control*]
MtBu.......... Butte Free Public Library, Butte, MT [*Library symbol*] [*Library of
                    Congress*] (LCLS)
MtBuE.......... Montana Energy Research and Development Institute, Butte, MT
                    [*Library symbol*] [*Library of Congress*] (LCLS)
MTBUF......... Mean Time Between Undetected Failures [*Quality control*] (IAA)
MtBULM...... Union List of Montana Serials, Bozeman, MT [*Library symbol*]
                    [*Library of Congress*] (LCLS)
MTBUM........ Mean Time Between Unscheduled Maintenance [*Quality control*]
                    (MHDI)
MtBuM......... Montana College of Mineral Science and Technology, Butte, MT
                    [*Library symbol*] [*Library of Congress*] (LCLS)
MTBUMA ..... Mean Time between Unscheduled Maintenance Actions [*Quality
                    control*]
MTBUR .... Mean Time between Unscheduled Removals [*or Replacements*]
                    [*Quality control*]
MtBwB .... Blackfeet Community College Library, Browning, MT [*Library symbol*]
                    [*Library of Congress*] (LCLS)
MTC .... Carroll College, Library, Helena, MT [*OCLC symbol*] (OCLC)
MTC .... Machine Tool Control
MTC .... Machine Trim Compensator (AAG)
MTC .... Magnetic Tape Cassette [*Computer science*]
MTC .... Magnetic Tape Channel [*Computer science*]
MTC .... Magnetic Tape Command [*Computer science*] (IAA)
MTC .... Magnetic Tape Control [*Computer science*]
MTC .... Magnetic Tape Controller (NITA)
MTC .... Magnetization Transfer Contrast [*Imaging technique*]
MTC .... Maintenance Task Cycle
MTC .... Maintenance Time Constraint (IEEE)
MTC .... Main Trunk Circuit [*World Meteorological Organization*]
                    [*Telecommunications*] (TEL)
MTC .... Majestic Resources [*Vancouver Stock Exchange symbol*]
MTC .... Make Today Count (EA)
MTC .... Maneuver Training Command [*Army*] (AABC)
MTC .... Manhattan Theater Club
MTC .... Man-Tended Capability (SSD)
MTC .... Man-Tended Committee (SSD)
MTC .... Manual Traffic Control (MCD)
MTC .... Manufacturing Technology Center
MTC .... Manufacturing Technology Centre of New Brunswick [*Research
                    center*] (RCD)
MTC .... Marcus Tullius Cicero [*Roman orator and author, 106-43 BC*]
MTC .... Maritime Transport Committee [*OECD*] (DS)
MTC .... Mass Transfer Coefficient
MTC .... Master of Textile Chemistry
MTC .... Master Table of Contents (IAA)
MTC .... Master Tape Control
MTC .... Master Test Component (SAUS)
MTC .... Master Thrust Control [*or Controller*] [*NASA*] (NASA)
MTC .... Master Training Concept [*Problem solving*]
MTC .... Material Testing Center
MTC .... Materiel Testing Command [*Merged with Weapons and Mobility
                    Command*] [*Army*]
MTC .... Maximum Tolerable Concentration [*Toxicology*]
MTC .... Maximum Toxic Concentration [*Medicine*]

MTC .... Maximum Track Capacity
MTC .... Mechanical Torpedo Countermeasure [*Military*] (CAAL)
MTC .... Mechanical Training Centre (SAUS)
MTC .... Mechanical Transport Corps
MTC .... Medical Test Cabinet
MTC .... Medical Training Center [*Later, Academy of Health Sciences*] [*Army*]
MTC .... Medium Terminal Complexes (MCD)
MTC .... Medullary Thyroid Carcinoma [*Medicine*]
MTC .... Meet the Composer (EA)
MTC .... Member of Technical College [*British*] (DI)
MTC .... Memory Test Computer [*SAGE*]
MTC .... Message Table of Contents (MCD)
MTC .... Message Transmission Controller
MTC .... Meteorological Training Center
Mtc .... Methylthiocarbamoyl [*Biochemistry*]
MTC .... Metocurine [*A muscle relaxant*]
MTC .... MIDI [*Musical Instrument Digital Interface*] Time Code
MTC .... Military Tactical Computer (MCD)
MTC .... Military Training Cadets [*A boys' World War II organization*]
MTC .... Military Transportation Command
MTC .... Military Transportation Committee [*NATO*] (NATG)
mtC .... Million Tonnes Carbon (EES)
MTC .... Mini Tele-Copter (SAUS)
MTC .... Minor Transaction Code (VLIE)
MTC .... Missile Technician, Chief [*Navy rating*]
MTC .... Missile Test Center
MTC .... Missile Transfer Car
MTC .... Missile Tube Control
MTC .... Mission and Test Computer
MTC .... Mission and Traffic Control
MTC .... Mitomycin C [*Mutamycin*] [*Also, Mi, MMC*] [*Antineoplastic drug*]
MTC .... Mitsui Toatsu Chemicals, Inc. [*Japan*]
MTC .... Mobile Tactical Computer (PDAA)
MTC .... Mobile Target Carrier
MTC .... Mobile Terminated Call (CGWS)
MTC .... Moderator Temperature Coefficient (NRCH)
MTC .... Modulation Transfer Curve (OA)
MTC .... Monostable Trigger Circuit (VLIE)
MTC .... Monsanto Co. [*NYSE symbol*] (SPSG)
MTC .... Morgan Territory [*California*] [*Seismograph station code, US
                    Geological Survey*] (SEIS)
MTC .... Morse Telegraph Club (EA)
MTC .... Motor Transport Corps [*Military*]
MTC .... Mount Clemens, MI [*Location identifier*] [*FAA*] (FAAL)
MTC .... MOUT [*Military Operations on Urbanized Terrain*] Training Complex
                    [*Army*] (INF)
MTC .... Mouvement Traditionaliste Congolais [*Congolese Traditionalist
                    Movement*]
MTC .... Moving Target Carrier (MCD)
MTC .... Multicomm Telecommunications Corp. [*Formerly, Mutual Satellite
                    Services*]
MTC .... Multiple Tube Counts
MTC .... Multistate Tax Commission (EA)
MTC .... Music Teacher's Certificate [*British*] (DI)
MTC .... Mutating Transformation Converter (IAA)
MTC .... Mystic Terminal Co. [*AAR code*]
MTC .... Ontario Ministry of Transportation and Communications [*Canada*]
                    (TSSD)
MTCA .... Cayes [*Haiti*] [*ICAO location identifier*] (ICLI)
MTCA .... Methyltetrahydrocarbolinecarboxylic Acid [*Organic chemistry*]
MTCA .... Methylthiazolidinecarboxylic Acid [*Organic chemistry*]
MTCA .... Military Terminal Control Area
MTCA .... Minimum Terrain-Clearance Altitude [*Aviation*]
MTCA .... Ministry of Transport and Civil Aviation [*Later, MT*] [*British*] (MCD)
MTCA .... Monitor and Test Control Area [*NASA*] (NASA)
MTCA .... Multiple-Terminal Communication Adapter [*Computer science*]
MtCaC........ Little Big Horn College, Crow Agency, MT [*Library symbol*] [*Library of
                    Congress*] (LCLS)
MTCACS ..... Marine Corps Tactical Command and Control System (MCD)
MTCAS........ Marine Corps Tactical Command and control System (SAUS)
MTCB .... Master Timer Control Block [*Computer science*] (VLIE)
MTCB .... Metropolitan Taxicab Board (NADA)
MTCC .... Magnetics Technology [*NASDAQ symbol*] (SAG)
MTCC .... Magnetic Technologies [*NASDAQ symbol*] (TTSB)
MTCC .... Master Timing and Control Circuit
MTCC .... Military Air Transport Service [*later, Military Airlift Command*]
                    TransportControl Center
MTCC .... Modular Tactical Communications Center
MTCD .... Microvolume Thermal Conductivity Detector [*Instrumentation*]
MTCE .... Maintenance [*Telecommunications*] (TEL)
MTCE .... Million Tonnes of Carbon Equivalent (CARB)
MTCE .... Million Tons of Coal Equivalent [*A comparative unit of energy content
                    widely used in the oil industry*]
MTCF .... Mean Time to Catastrophic Failure [*Quality control*]
MTCF .... Missile Tube Comparator Fixture
MtCG .... Glacier County Library, Cut Bank, MT [*Library symbol*] [*Library of
                    Congress*] (LCLS)
MtCh .... Blaine County library, Chinook, MT [*Library symbol*] [*Library of
                    Congress*] (LCLS)
MTCH.......... Cap Haitien Internacional [*Haiti*] [*ICAO location identifier*] (ICLI)
MTCH.......... Magnetic Tape Channel (NITA)
MT Ch.......... Master of Textile Chemistry
MTCH.......... Mining Technology Clearing House [*British*] [*Information service or
                    system*] (IID)
MtchBnc ...... Mitchell Bancorp, Inc. [*Associated Press*] (SAG)

MtChe.......... Liberty County Library, Chester, MT [*Library symbol*] [*Library of Congress*] (LCLS)

MtchIE .... Mitchell Energy & Development Corp. [*Associated Press*] (SAG)

MtCi............. George McCone Memorial County Library, Circle, MT [*Library symbol*] [*Library of Congress*] (LCLS)

MTCI............. Magnetic Tape Control Interface (MCD)

MTCI............. Management Technologies [*NASDAQ symbol*] (TTSB)

MTCI............. Management Technologies, Inc. [*NASDAQ symbol*] (NQ)

MTCI............. Member of the Trust Companies Institute (DD)

MTCL............. Motorcycle

MTCM.......... Master of Traditional Chinese Medicine (PGP)

MTCM.......... Missile Technician, Master Chief [*Navy rating*]

MTCN.......... Minimum Throughput Class Negotiation (VLIE)

MTCNOLD .... Minimum Tax Credit Net Operating Loss Deduction [*Business term*]

MTCO............ Macon Terminal Co. [*AAR code*]

MTCOECD .... Maritime Transport Committee of the Organization for Economic Cooperation and Development [*France*] (EAIO)

MtCoHS .... Columbus High School, Columbus, MT [*Library symbol*] [*Library of Congress*] (LCLS)

MtCol........... Colstrip Bicentennial Library, Colstrip, MT [*Library symbol*] [*Library of Congress*] (LCLS)

MtCon.......... Conrad Public Library, Conrad, MT [*Library symbol*] [*Library of Congress*] (LCLS)

MTCON .... Microwave Aeropace Terminal Control [*Air Force*] (IAA)

MTCP........... Master of Town and Country Planning (ADA)

MTCP........... Ministry of Town and Country Planning [*British*]

MTCR........... Million Tonnes of Coal Replacement (CARB)

MTCR........... Missile Technology Control Regime [*US, Canada, Britain, France, West Germany, Japan*]

MTCS........... Madelian Thomas Completion Stories [*Psychology*] (DAVI)

MTCS........... Mean Time to Cycle Slip (ACAE)

MTCS........... Melbourne Theatre Cooperative Society [*Australia*]

MTCS........... Meteor Trail Communications System

MTCS........... Minimal Terminal Communications System (NVT)

MTCS........... Minimum Teleprocessing Commmunications System

MTCS........... Missile Technician, Senior Chief [*Navy rating*]

MTCT............ Manipulator/Teleoperator Control Technology (SSD)

MTCU........... Magnetic Tape Control Unit [*Computer science*]

MTCU........... Mobile Temperature Conditioning Units (ACAE)

MTCV........... Main Turbine Control Valve (IEEE)

MTCV........... Modified Total Containment Vessel (SAUS)

MTCW.......... Major 20th-Century Writers [*A publication*]

MTD............. Macknight Airlines [*Australia*] [*ICAO designator*] (FAAC)

MTD............. Magnetic Tape Disk (MCD)

MTD............. Main Technical Directorate (RDA)

MTD............. Maintenance Task Demand File (MCD)

MTD............. Maintenance Tasks Distribution

MTD............. Maintenance Technical Directive (SAA)

MTD............. Maintenance Technology Development

MTD............. Maintenance Training Department

MTD............. Manager, Traffic Department

MTD............. Manager, Transportation Department

MTD............. Maneuvering Technology Demonstrator (ACAE)

MTD............. Manufacturing and Test Documentation (ACAE)

MTD............. Manufacturing Technology Development (RDA)

MTD............. Manufacturing Technology Directorate [*Army*] (RDA)

MTD............. Manufacturing Technology Division [*Air Force*]

MTD............. Marine Technology Directorate [*British*]

MTD............. Maritime Trades Department, AFL-CIO [*American Federation of Labor and Congress of Industrial Organizations*] (EA)

MTD............. Mass Tape Duplicator/Verifier [*Computer science*] (MCD)

MTD............. Master of Textile Dyeing

MTD............. Master of Transport Design

MTD............. Master Tape Data

MTD............. Master Time Display

MTD............. Master Tracking Data [*NASA*]

MTD............. Materiel Testing Directorate [*Army*] (RDA)

MTD............. Maximum Tolerated Dose [*Medicine*]

MTD............. Mean Temperature Difference

MTD............. Mean Therapeutic Dose [*Medicine*]

MTD............. Mean Time Down [*Computer science*] (VLIE)

MTD............. Mean Tolerated Dose [*Medicine*]

MTD............. Mean Total Dose [*Medicine*] (DMAA)

MTD............. Mean Tubular Diameter

MTD............. Mechanical Road Transport Driver [*British military*] (DMA)

MTD............. Metacarpal Total Density [*Anatomy*]

MTD............. Metal Trades Department, AFL-CIO [*American Federation of Labor and Congress of Industrial Organizations*] (EA)

MTD............. Metastatic Trophoblastic Disease [*Medicine*] (AAMN)

MTD............. Meta-Toluenediamine [*Organic chemistry*]

MTD............. Methyltriazolinedione [*Organic chemistry*]

MTD............. Mettler-Toledo Intl. [*NYSE symbol*] (SG)

MTD............. Microwave Target Designator

MTD............. Midwife Teacher's Diploma [*British*]

MTD............. Military Test Directorate [*Program*] [*Army*] (RDA)

MTD............. Minimal Toxic Dose (IEEE)

MTD............. Mintel International Development Corp. [*Vancouver Stock Exchange symbol*]

MTD............. Mitte Tales Doses [*Send Such Doses*] [*Pharmacy*]

MTD............. Mobile Target Division [*Mine Force*] [*Navy*]

MTD............. Mobile Training Detachment

MTD............. Mobilization Table of Distribution [*Military*]

MTD............. Monroe Tidal Drainage [*Urology*] (DAVI)

MTD............. Month to Date (VLIE)

MTD............. Mount Darwin [*Zimbabwe*] [*Seismograph station code, US Geological Survey*] (SEIS)

mtd............. Mounted (VRA)

MTD............. Mounted

MTD............. Moving Target Detector [*RADAR*]

MTD............. Multimodal Transport Document [*Computer science*] (VLIE)

MTD............. Multiple Target Deception (MCD)

MTD............. Multiple Target Discrimination (MCD)

MTD............. Multiple Tile Duct [*Telecommunications*] (TEL)

MTDA........... Marine Tactical Data (IAA)

MTDA........... Methyl Trimethylsilyl Dimethylketene Acetal [*Organic chemistry*]

MTDA........... Modification Table of Distribution and Allowances [*Army*] (AABC)

MTDB........... Machine Type Data Base [*Computer science*] (VLIE)

MTDB........... Metropolitan Transit Development Board (NADA)

MTDC........... Modified Total Direct Costs [*Economics*]

MTDDA........ Minnesota Test for Differential Diagnosis of Aphasia [*Psychology*]

MTDDIS........ Mesoscale Transport Diffusion and Deposition Model for Industrial Sources [*Environmental Protection Agency*] (GFGA)

MTDE........... Maritime Tactical Data Exchange (NATG)

MTDe........... Modern Technology Demonstration Engine

MT Des........ Master of Textile Design

MtDeSP .... Montana State Prison, Conley Lake, Deer Lodge, MT [*Library symbol*] [*Library of Congress*] (LCLS)

MTDF........... Master Tracking Data File [*NASA*]

MTDF........... Mobile Tank Depermer Facility (DWSG)

MtDi............ Dillon City Library, Dillon, MT [*Library symbol*] [*Library of Congress*] (LCLS)

MtDiGS........ Church of Jesus Christ of Latter-Day Saints, Genealogical Society Library, ButteStake Branch, Dillon Chapel, Dillon, MT [*Library symbol*] [*Library of Congress*] (LCLS)

MtDiW .... Western Montana College, Dillon, MT [*Library symbol*] [*Library of Congress*] (LCLS)

MTDL........... Maintenance Task Description List (ACAE)

MTDL........... Multiple Tap Delay Line

mtDNA........ Deoxyribonucleic Acid, Mitochondrial [*Biochemistry, genetics*]

mtDNA........ Mitochondrial DNA [*Deoxyribonucleic acid*] (USDC)

MTDP........... Medium Term Defense Plan (NATG)

MTDP........... Medium Term Development Plan [*Economics*] (FEA)

MTDP........... Mid-Term Defence build-up Project (SAUS)

MTDS........... Manufacturing Test Data System (IEEE)

MTDS........... Marine Tactical Data System

MTDS........... Marine Toebreak Data System (NG)

MTDS........... Metallurgical and Thermochemical Data Service [*Department of Trade and Industry*] [*Information service or system*] (IID)

MTDS........... Missile Trajectory Data System (MUGU)

MTDSK........ Magnetic Tape Disk [*Computer science*] (NASA)

MTDT........... Modified Tone Decay Test (MAE)

MTE............. AirTran Airways, Inc. [*FAA designator*] (FAAC)

MtE............. Ekalaka Public Library, Ekalaka, MT [*Library symbol*] [*Library of Congress*] (LCLS)

MTE............. Machine Transaction Entry [*Computer science*] (VLIE)

MTE............. Magnetic Tape Encoder [*Computer science*] (IAA)

MTE............. Magnetosphere-Thermosphere Explorer [*NASA*]

MTE............. Maintenance Test Equipment (MCD)

MTE............. Maintenance Training Equipment (MCD)

MTE............. Manteigas [*Portugal*] [*Seismograph station code, US Geological Survey*] (SEIS)

MTE............. Manual Test Equipment (ACAE)

MTE............. Mass Transport Experiment (SAUS)

MTE............. Master of Teacher Education (PGP)

MTE............. Master of Textile Engineering

MTE............. Maximum Temperature Engine

MTE............. Maximum Tracking Error

MTE............. Maximum Tractive Effort [*Equipment design*]

MTE............. Measurement and Test Equipment [*Environmental science*] (COE)

MTE............. Megaton-Equivalent (SAUS)

MTE............. Member of the Telegraph Engineers [*British*] (ROG)

MTE............. Merit Technologies Ltd. [*Vancouver Stock Exchange symbol*]

MTE............. Mesophere-Thermosphere Explorer (ACAE)

mte............. Metal-Engraver [*MARC relator code*] [*Library of Congress*] (LCCP)

MtE............. Metropolitan Edison Co. [*Associated Press*] (SAG)

MTE............. Microwave Test Equipment

MTE............. Missile Test Engineer (MUGU)

MTE............. Missing Time Experience

MTE............. Mitre Corp., Bedford Operations Library, Bedford, MA [*OCLC symbol*] (OCLC)

MTE............. Mobile Telephone Exchange [*Nordic Mobile Telephone*]

MTE............. Modern Technology Engine

MTE............. Modular Threat Emitter (DWSG)

MTE............. Module Table Entry [*Computer science*] (BYTE)

MTE............. Monte Alegre [*Brazil*] [*Airport symbol*] (AD)

MTE............. Multiple Terminal Emulator

MTE............. Multiple Terminator Emulator (NITA)

MTE............. Multiple Trace Elements [*Medicine*] (MELL)

MTE............. Multipurpose Test Equipment

MTE............. Multisystem Test Equipment [*Military*]

MTE............. Multithreshold Element (IAA)

MTE-5.......... Multielectrolyte Concentrate [*Pharmacology*] (DAVI)

MTEA........... Maintenance Training Effectiveness Analysis [*Army*]

MTEA........... Metal Trades Employers Association (NADA)

MTEA........... Minimum Target Elevation Angle (MCD)

MTEAA......... (Methylthio)ethyl Acetoacetate [*Organic chemistry*]

MTEC........... Maintenance Test Equipment Catalog (MCD)

MTEC........... Meridian Medical Tech. [*NASDAQ symbol*] (SG)

MTec........... Metric Tons Energy Consumption

MTEC	Microtec Research, Inc. [*NASDAQ symbol*] (SAG)
MTEC	Monash Timber Engineering Center [*Australia*]
MTEC	Motorola Training and Education Center (SAUS)
M Tech	Master of Technology
MTECP	Maintenance Test Equipment Certification Procedure (SAA)
MTECR	Maintenance Test Equipment Certification Requirement (SAA)
MTEE	Maintenance Test Equipment, Electrical (NASA)
MTEE	Mean Transverse Emission Energy (PDAA)
MTEE	Mission Time Extreme Environment [*NASA*] (KSC)
MTEEC	Maintenance Test Equipment, Electronic (NASA)
MTEF	Maintenance Test Equipment, Fluid (NASA)
MTEG	Mickey Thompson Entertainment Group [*Auto racing*]
MTEG	Port-Au-Prince [*Haiti*] [*ICAO location identifier*] (ICLI)
MTEL	Manning Table and Equipment List
MTEL	Maximum Tolerable Exposure Level [*Toxicology*]
MTEL	Methyltriethyllead [*Organic chemistry*]
MTEL	Mobile Telecommunications & Technology Corp. [*NASDAQ symbol*] (SAG)
MTEL	Mobile Telecommun Tech [*NASDAQ symbol*] (TTSB)
MTelEng	Master of Telecommunications Engineering (NADA)
MtELH	Lincoln County Senior High School, Eureka, MT [*Library symbol*] [*Library of Congress*] (LCLS)
MTELP	Michigan Test of English Language Proficiency [*J. Upshur*] (TES)
MTEM	Magnetosphere-Thermosphere Explorer Mission (SAUS)
MTEM	Maintenance Test Equipment Module (MCD)
MTEM	Mechanical Maintenance Test Equipment (NASA)
MTEM	Mesosphere-Thermosphere Explorer Mission (SAUS)
MT Eng	Master of Textile Engineering
MTEO	Maintenance Test Equipment, Optical (NASA)
M'TER	Manchester [*City in England*] (ROG)
MTER	Multitest Evaluation Report [*Nuclear energy*] (NRCH)
MTES	Metastable Transfer Emission Spectroscopy
MTES	Methyltriethoxysilane [*Organic chemistry*]
MTESL	Master in Teaching English as a Second Language (PGP)
MTET	Maximal Treadmill Exercise Test
Mtewan	Matewan BancShares [*Associated Press*] (SAG)
MTEWS/AD	Mobile Tactical Early Warning System for Air Defense [*NATO*]
MTEX	Mission Template Expert (SSD)
MText	Master of Textiles (NADA)
MTF	Fairbanks, AK [*Location identifier*] [*FAA*] (FAAL)
MTF	Machine Tool Forum
MTF	Maintenance Test Facility [*Telecommunications*] (OTD)
MTF	Maintenance Test Flight (MCD)
MTF	Maintenance Training Flight [*Military*]
MTF	Manufacturing Technology Facility [*US Army Communications-Electronics Command*] [*Fort Monmouth, NJ*] (RDA)
MTF	Matrix Test Facility (MCD)
MTF	Maximum Terminal Flow (MAE)
MTF	Mean Time to Failure [*Quality control*]
MTF	Mechanical Time Fuze
MTF	Medical Treatment Facility (AABC)
MTF	Medical Treatment Faculty (DAVI)
MTF	Megawatt Transmitter Filter
MTF	Men's Tie Foundation [*Later, NAA*] (EA)
MTF	Message Text Formatting
MTF	Message Transfer Facility [*Telecommunications*] (OSI)
MTF	Metal Trades Federation (NADA)
MTF	Metastable Time of Flight
MTF	Meteorological Task Force (MCD)
MTF	Microsoft Tape Format [*Microsoft Corp.*] [*Computer science*] (PCM)
MTF	Microwave Test Facility
MTF	Mild Thyroid Failure [*Medicine*] (MELL)
MTF	Military Treatment Facility [*DoD*]
MTF	Minimum Toggle Frequency [*Computer science*] (ELAL)
MTF	Missile Track File (ACAE)
MTF	Mississippi Test Facility [*Later, NSTL*] [*NASA*]
MTF	Mizan Teferi [*Ethiopia*] [*Airport symbol*] [*Obsolete*] (OAG)
MTF	Mock-Up Test Facility (MCD)
MTF	Modulation Transfer Function [*Resolution measure*]
MtF	Monitoring the Future [*University of Michigan project*]
mtf	More to Follow [*Copyediting*] (WDMC)
MTF	Motif
MTF	Moulded Fiber Technology
MTF	Multiple Tube Fermentation
MTF	Multitarget Frequency
MTF	Murine Typhus Fever [*Medicine*] (MELL)
MTFA	Medium-Term Financial Assistance
MTFA	Modulation Transfer Function Analyzer
MTFA	Modulation Transfer Function Area (ACAE)
MtFb	Chouteau County Free Library, Fort Benton, MT [*Library symbol*] [*Library of Congress*] (LCLS)
MTFC	Masters Track and Field Committee (EA)
MTFCA	Model "T" Ford Club of America (EA)
MTFCI	Model T Ford Club International (EA)
MTFD	Minimum Tracking Flux Density
MTFE	Mercury Thin Film Electrode [*Electrochemistry*]
MTFEX	Mountain Field Exercise [*Military*] (NVT)
MTFF	Man-Tended Free Flyer (MCD)
MTFF	Mean Time to First Failure [*Quality control*] (AAG)
MTFhV	United States Veterans Administration Center, Fort Harrison, MT [*Library symbol*] [*Library of Congress*] (LCLS)
MTFL	Mean Time to Fault Locate [*Quality control*] (CAAL)
MTFMPP	Meta-Trifluoromethylphenylpiperazine [*Biochemistry*]
MTFO	Modular Training Field Option (NASA)
MTFP	Marema Tlou Freedom Party [*Lesotho*]

MTFR	Mean Time for Repair [*Quality control*] (IAA)
MTFR	Message Text Formatting Reporting
MTFR	Metal Furring [*Technical drawings*]
MTFR	[*The*] Minnesota Transfer Railway Co. [*AAR code*]
MtFR	Rosebud County Library, Forsyth, MT [*Library symbol*] [*Library of Congress*] (LCLS)
MtFrHS	Frenchtown High School, Frenchtown, MT [*Library symbol*] [*Library of Congress*] (LCLS)
MTFS	Marine Terminal Fuel Separator (MCD)
MTFS	Medium-Term Financial Strategy
MTFSC	Ministerial Task Force on Soil Conservation [*Australia*]
MTFT	Mean Time to Functional Test (ACAE)
MTFTS	Marine Terminal Fuel Tankage System (MCD)
MTG	Aviation Co. Mostransgas [*Former USSR*] [*FAA designator*] (FAAC)
MtG	Glendive Public Library, Glendive, MT [*Library symbol*] [*Library of Congress*] (LCLS)
MTG	Main Tank Gun [*Army*]
MTG	Main Traffic Group [*Telecommunications*] (TEL)
MTG	Main Turbogenerator
MTG	Media Task Group [*Environmental Protection Agency*] (GFGA)
MTG	Meeting (AFM)
mtg	Meeting (BEE)
MTG	Melt-Textured Growth [*Chemistry*]
MTG	Methanol-to-Gasoline [*Process*] [*Mobil Oil Corp.*]
MTG	Methoxytriglycol [*Organic chemistry*]
MTG	Methyl Tetradecylglycidate [*Biochemistry*]
MTG	(Methyl)thiogalactoside [*Biochemistry*]
MTG	MGIC Investment [*NYSE symbol*] (TTSB)
MTG	MGIC Investment Co. [*NYSE symbol*] (SPSG)
MTG	Microsyn Torque Generator (SAA)
MTG	Montague Island [*Alaska*] [*Seismograph station code, US Geological Survey*] (SEIS)
Mtg	Mortgage (EBF)
mtg	Mortgage (GEAB)
MTG	Mortgage [*Finance*] (SPSG)
MTG	Motorsports Technology Group [*General Motors Corp.*]
MTG	Motor-Torque Generator
MTG	Mounting
MTG	Multiple-Trigger Generator
MTG	Multipurpose Target Generator
MTGAS	Mechanical Transport Gasoline [*Military*] [*British*]
MTGBKT	Mounting Bracket (IAA)
MTGC	Mounting Center (MSA)
MTGCF	Mobile Transportation Ground Command Facility (MCD)
MtGD	Dawson College, Glendive, MT [*Library symbol*] [*Library of Congress*] (LCLS)
MTGD	Mortgaged (ROG)
MtGDH	Dawson County High School, Glendive, MT [*Library symbol*] [*Library of Congress*] (LCLS)
mtge	Mortgage (DD)
Mtge	Mortgage (TBD)
MTGE	Mortgage
MTGEE	Mortgagee
MTGF	Mouse Transforming Growth Factor [*Biochemistry*]
MTGHS	Magnetic, True, and Grid Heading Select (MCD)
MtGl	Glasgow City-County Library, Glasgow, MT [*Library symbol*] [*Library of Congress*] (LCLS)
MTGOR	Mortgagor
MTGP	Monitor Table Generator Program (MCD)
MtGr	Great Falls Public Library, Great Falls, MT [*Library symbol*] [*Library of Congress*] (LCLS)
MtGrCE	College of Great Falls, Great Falls, MT [*Library symbol*] [*Library of Congress*] (LCLS)
MtGrCH	Columbus Hospital, Health Sciences Library, Great Falls, MT [*Library symbol*] [*Library of Congress*] (LCLS)
MtGrGS	Church of Jesus Christ of Latter-Day Saints, Genealogical Society Library, GreatFalls Branch, Great Falls, MT [*Library symbol*] [*Library of Congress*] (LCLS)
MtGrPS	Great Falls Public Schools, Great Falls, MT [*Library symbol*] [*Library of Congress*] (LCLS)
MTGS	Metal-to-Glass Seal
MTGS	Midcourse and Terminal Guidance System [*NASA*]
MTGU	Australian Master Tax Guide Updater [*A publication*]
MTGU	Main Turbine / Gearing Unit (PDAA)
MTGW	Maximum Total Gross Weight (MCD)
MTG/WESS	Main Tank Gunfire/Weapon Effects Signature Simulator (MCD)
MtH	Helena Public Library, Helena, MT [*Library symbol*] [*Library of Congress*] (LCLS)
MTH	Magnetic Tape Handler [*Computer science*]
MTH	Marathon [*Florida*] [*Airport symbol*] (OAG)
MTH	Massachusetts Institute of Technology [*ICAO designator*] (FAAC)
M Th	Master of Theology
MTH	Master of Tropical Health
MTH	Meath [*County in Ireland*] (ROG)
MTH	Meritage Corp. [*Formerly, Monterey Homes Corp.*] [*NYSE symbol*]
MTH	Metharbital [*An anticonvulsant*] [*Pharmacology*] (DAVI)
MTH	Methylthiohydantoin [*Organic chemistry*]
MTH	Microptic Theodolite
MTH	Mithramycin [*Medicine*] (DMAA)
MTH	Mithramycin (Aureolic acid, mithracin) [*Antineoplastic drug*]
MTH	Monterey Homes Corp. [*NYSE symbol*] (SAG)
MTH	Month
MTH	Mount Holyoke College, South Hadley, MA [*OCLC symbol*] (OCLC)
MTH	Mount Hood Railway Co. [*Later, MH*] [*AAR code*]
Mth	Mouth [*Maps and charts*]

MTH............ Thompson Public Library, Manitoba [*Library symbol*] [*National Library of Canada*] (NLC)

MtHa............ Havre Hill County Library, Havre, MT [*Library symbol*] [*Library of Congress*] (LCLS)

MThA............ Master of Theatre Arts

MtHam......... Bitter Root Public Library, Hamilton, MT [*Library symbol*] [*Library of Congress*] (LCLS)

MtHamRL .... United States National Institute of Health, Rocky Mountain Laboratory Library, Hamilton, MT [*Library symbol*] [*Library of Congress*] (LCLS)

MtHaN .... Northern Montana College, Havre, MT [*Library symbol*] [*Library of Congress*] (LCLS)

MtHar .... Big Horn County Public Library, Hardin, MT [*Library symbol*] [*Library of Congress*] (LCLS)

MtHarC .... Fort Belknap College, Harlem, MT [*Library symbol*] [*Library of Congress*] (LCLS)

MtHarlF .... Fort Belknap Community College, Harlem, MT [*Library symbol*] [*Library of Congress*] (LCLS)

MTHB............ Mark Twain Home Board (EA)

MTHBD.......... Motherboard (MSA)

MtHC .... Carroll College, Helena, MT [*Library symbol*] [*Library of Congress*] (LCLS)

MtHCE .... Montana Census and Economic Information Center, Helena, MT [*Library symbol*] [*Library of Congress*] (LCLS)

MTHD .... Method (MSA)

MtHe........... Laurie Hill Library, Heron, MT [*Library symbol*] [*Library of Congress*] (LCLS)

M Theol....... Master of Theology

MTHF........... Methyltetrahydrofolate [*or Methyltetrahydrofolic*] [*Biochemistry*]

MTHF........... Methyltetrahydrofuran [*Organic chemistry*]

MTHFR........ Methylene Tetrahydrofolate Reductase [*An enzyme*]

MtHG .... United States Geological Survey, Water Resources Division, Helena, MT [*Library symbol*] [*Library of Congress*] (LCLS)

MThGH........ Metallothionein-Human Growth Hormone [*Endocrinology*]

MtHGS......... Church of Jesus Christ of Latter-Day Saints, Genealogical Society Library, Helena Branch, Helena, MT [*Library symbol*] [*Library of Congress*] (LCLS)

MTHHF........ Methyltetrahydrohomofolate [*Biochemistry*]

MtHHS......... Helena High School, Helena, MT [*Library symbol*] [*Library of Congress*] (LCLS)

MtHi............ Montana Historical Society, Helena, MT [*Library symbol*] [*Library of Congress*] (LCLS)

MTHL........... Medial Thyrohyoid Ligament [*Medicine*] (MELL)

Mthly .... Monthly (DLA)

MTHM........... Metric Ton of Heavy Metal (NUCP)

MTHM........... Million Tons Heavy Metal

MtHMv........ Mountain View School, Helena, MT [*Library symbol*] [*Library of Congress*] (LCLS)

Mt Holyoke C... Mount Holyoke College (GAGS)

MTHPA .... Methyltetrahydrophthalic Anhydride [*Organic chemistry*]

MThPast....... Maitre en Theologie Pastorale [*Master in Pastoral Theology*] [*French*]

M Th Past.... Master of Pastoral Theology (PGP)

MtHPI .... Montana Office of Public Instruction, Resource Center, Helena, MT [*Library symbol*] [*Library of Congress*] (LCLS)

MTHR .... Merthyr [*Cardiff*] [*Welsh depot code*]

MTHR .... Mother

MTHRD .... Male Threaded

MtHs .... Hot Springs Public Library, Hot Springs, MT [*Library symbol*] [*Library of Congress*] (LCLS)

MTHS........... Middle Turbinate Headache Syndrome [*Medicine*] (MELL)

MtHS .... Shodair Children's Hospital, Helena, MT [*Library symbol*] [*Library of Congress*] (LCLS)

MtHSH........ Shodair Hospital, Helena, MT [*Library symbol*] [*Library of Congress*] (LCLS)

MtHsHS .... Hot Springs High School, Hot Springs, MT [*Library symbol*] [*Library of Congress*] (LCLS)

MtHSP......... Saint Peter's Community Hospital, Helena, MT [*Library symbol*] [*Library of Congress*] (LCLS)

MTHWL....... Motherwell [*Scotland*]

mthy .... Monthly [*Publishing*] (WDMC)

MTI............. Arturo Rodriguez Martinez [*Mexico*] [*FAA designator*] (FAAC)

MTI............. Machine Tools Industry (MCD)

MTI............. Maeventec Travel Information [*Maeventec*] [*Information service or system*] (CRD)

MTI............. Magyar Tavviati Iroda [*Hungarian News Agency*] (BARN)

MTI............. Main Tank Injection

MTI............. Maintenance Team Inspection [*Environmental science*] (COE)

MTI............. Malignant Teratoma Intermediate [*Oncology*] (MAE)

MTI............. Manitoba Technical Institute [*Canada*]

MTI............. Manpower Training Institute

MTI............. Manufacturing Technologies Inc. (SAUS)

MTI............. Manufacturing Technology Initiative (ACAE)

MTI............. Marked Temperature Inversion [*Aviation*] (DA)

MTI............. Marketing and Training Institute (EA)

MTI............. Materials Technology Institute of the Chemical Process Industries (EA)

MTI............. Material Thickness Indicator

MTI............. Maximum Therapeutic Index (EDCT)

MTI............. Mechanical Technology, Inc.

MTI............. Mechanical Tolerance Index [*Food technology*]

MTI............. Media Technology International [*British*]

MTI............. Medium Tip-In [*Automotive testing*]

MTI............. Member of the Trust Institute (DD)

MTI............. Metal Treating Institute (EA)

MTI............. Methylthioinosine [*Biochemistry*]

MTI............. Methyltransferase I [*An enzyme*]

MTI............. Military Training Instructor (AFM)

MTI............. Minimum Time Interval [*Medicine*]

MTI............. Ministry of Trade and Industry [*Canada*]

MTI............. MIPS Technologies Inc. (SAUS)

MTI............. Missile Training Installation (NATG)

MTI............. Mission Training International (EA)

MTI............. Mobile Training Institute [*Klamath Falls, OR*] [*Telecommunications service*] (TSSD)

MTI............. Modern Telecommunications, Inc. [*New York, NY*] (TSSD)

MTI............. Morton Thiokol, Inc. (SAUS)

MTI............. Mosteiros [*Cape Verde Islands*] [*Airport symbol*] (OAG)

MTI............. Mouvement de la Tendance Islamique [*Islamic Trend Movement*] [*Tunisia*] (PD)

MTI............. Moving Target Indicator

MTI............. Multichannel Time Intervalometer (VLIE)

MTI............. Multigraphics, Inc. [*AMEX symbol*] (SG)

MTI............. Multiple Target Interception (SAUS)

MTI............. Multispectral Thermal Imager

MTI............. Multi-Spectral Thermal Imager Spacecraft [*Department of Energy*]

MTI............. Multi-Terminal Interface [*Computer science*] (VLIE)

MTI............. MuniYield Insured Fund II [*NYSE symbol*] (SPSG)

MTIA........... Metal Trades Industry Association (NADA)

MTIAA......... Metal Trades Industry Association of Australia

MTIAC......... Manufacturing Technology Information Analysis Center [*DoD*] [*Information service or system*] (IID)

MTIC........... Malaysia Tourist Information Center (EA)

MTIC........... Moving Target Indicator Coherent (IEEE)

MTIC........... MTI Technology

MTICFAR .... Moving Target Indicator Constant False Alarm Rate (CET)

MTID........... Machine Type Identification Data [*Computer science*] (VLIE)

MTID........... Master of Technology for International Development (PGP)

MTIE........... Microthrust Ion Engine

Mties .... Empties (SAUS)

MTIF........... Maritime Technical Information Facility [*Maritime Administration*] [*Database producer*] (IID)

MTIF........... Master Tailored Interest File [*Navy*] (NG)

MTIF........... Mission Time Improvement Factor (VLIE)

MTIG........... MTI Technology [*NASDAQ symbol*] (TTSB)

MTIHM........ Metric Tons Initial Heavy Metal (GAAI)

MTIK........... Miller Building Sys [*NASDAQ symbol*] (TTSB)

MTIK........... Miller Building Systems, Inc. [*NASDAQ symbol*] (NQ)

MTIK........... Missile Test Installation Kit

MTIK........... Moving Target Indicator Kit

MTIL........... Maximum Tolerable Insecurity Level (OA)

MTIM........... Manual Trim in Motion [*Aviation*]

MTIN........... Martin Industries [*NASDAQ symbol*] (TTSB)

MTIN........... Martin Industries, Inc. [*NASDAQ symbol*] (SAG)

MTIN........... Mountain [*Commonly used*] (OPSA)

MTIP........... Moving Target Indication Processor (ACAE)

MTIRA .... Machine Tool Industry Research Association [*Research center*] [*British*]

MTIRI.......... Multispectral Thermal Infrared Imager (SSD)

MTIS........... Maintenance Task Information System (NG)

MTIS........... Manufacturing and Trade Inventories and Sales (SAUS)

MTIS........... Material Turned into Stores

MTIS........... Mean Time in Shop [*Quality control*] (MCD)

MTIS........... Multimodal Traveler Information Systems [*FTA*] (TAG)

MTIS........... Multiplex Transmitter Input Signals (PDAA)

MTI Tch .... MTI Technology Corp. [*Associated Press*] (SAG)

MTIX........... Mechanical Technology (EFIS)

MTIX........... Micro Therapeutics

MTJ............. Mark Twain Journal [*A publication*] (ANEX)

MTJ............. Mesifta Tifereth Jerusalem (BJA)

MTJ............. Midtarsal Joint [*Anatomy*] (DAVI)

MTJ............. Missile Track Jamming [*Military*] (CAAL)

MTJ............. Montrose [*Colorado*] [*Airport symbol*] (OAG)

MTJ............. Mount Tsukuba [*Japan*] [*Seismograph station code, US Geological Survey*] (SEIS)

MTJA........... Jacmel [*Haiti*] [*ICAO location identifier*] (ICLI)

MTJE .... Jeremie [*Haiti*] [*ICAO location identifier*] (ICLI)

MtJG........... Garfield County Library, Jordan, MT [*Library symbol*] [*Library of Congress*] (LCLS)

MTK............ Camp Ripley/Little Falls, MN [*Location identifier*] [*FAA*] (FAAL)

MtK............ Flathead County Free Library, Kalispell, MT [*Library symbol*] [*Library of Congress*] (LCLS)

MTK............ Makin [*Kiribati*] [*Airport symbol*] (OAG)

MTK............ Mechanical Time Keeping (NASA)

MTK............ Medium Tank

MTK............ Mintek Resources [*Vancouver Stock Exchange symbol*]

MTK............ Mitaka [*Japan*] [*Seismograph station code, US Geological Survey*] [*Closed*] (SEIS)

mtk............ Tropical Maritime Cold Air Mass [*Meteorology*] (BARN)

MtKF........... Flathead Valley Community College, Kalispell, MT [*Library symbol*] [*Library of Congress*] (LCLS)

MtKFH .... Flathead Senior High School, Kalispell, MT [*Library symbol*] [*Library of Congress*] (LCLS)

MtKGS .... Church of Jesus Christ of Latter-Day Saints, Genealogical Society Library, Kalispell Branch, Kalispell, MT [*Library symbol*] [*Library of Congress*] (LCLS)

MtKH .... Kalispell Regional Hospital, Kalispell, MT [*Library symbol*] [*Library of Congress*] (LCLS)

MTL............ Magnetic Tape Loader

MTL............ Main Transfer Line (MCD)

MTL............ Maitland [*Australia*] [*Airport symbol*] (OAG)

MTL	Mantle Zone Lymphoma [*Medicine*] (DMAA)
MTL	Manufacturing and Technology Laboratory
MTL	Mass-Transport-Limited [*Chemical engineering*]
MTL	Master Tape Loading
MTL	Matched Transmission Line
MTL	Material (KSC)
MTL	Materials Technology Laboratory [*Watertown, MA*] [*Army*] (RDA)
MTL	Materials Test Loop [*Nuclear energy*] (NRCH)
MTL	Mean Tide Level [*Tides and currents*]
MTL	Mean Time Level
MTL	Medial Temporal Lobe [*Brain anatomy*]
MTL	Median Threshold Limit (EEVL)
MTL	Median Tolerance Limit [*Toxicity*]
MTL	Medium Term Loan (DCTA)
MTL	Mercantile Bancorp, Inc. [*NYSE symbol*] (SPSG)
MTL	Merged-Transistor Logic
MTL	Message Transfer Layer [*Telecommunications*] (OSI)
MTL	Metal (AAG)
MTL	Microelectronic Test Laboratory (IAA)
MTL	Minimum Time Limit
MTL	Minimum Triggering Level [*Aviation*] (DA)
MTL	Mobilization Training Loss [*Military*]
MTL	Mobiltherm Light (NRCH)
Mt-L	Montana State Law Library, Helena, MT [*Library symbol*] [*Library of Congress*] (LCLS)
MTL	Motel
MTL	Motivation and Training Laboratory [*Army*] (RDA)
MTL	Mount Taylor [*New Mexico*] [*Seismograph station code, US Geological Survey*] (SEIS)
MTL	Multiple Conductor Transmission Line (PDAA)
MTL	Raf-Avia [*Latvia*] [*ICAO designator*] (FAAC)
MTLA	Micropublishers' Trade List Annual [*A publication*]
MTLC	Mass Transfer Limiting Current (PDAA)
MTLC	Metalclad Corp. [*NASDAQ symbol*] (SAG)
MTLC	Metallic (MSA)
MTLD	Mouvement pour le Triomphe des Libertes Democratiques [*Movement for the Triumph of Democratic Liberties*] [*Algeria*]
MtLdD	Dull Knife Memorial College Library, Lame Deer, MT [*Library symbol*] [*Library of Congress*] (LCLS)
MtLe	Lewistown City Library, Lewistown, MT [*Library symbol*] [*Library of Congress*] (LCLS)
MTLG	Metrologic Instruments [*NASDAQ symbol*] (TTSB)
MTLG	Metrologic Instruments, Inc. [*NASDAQ symbol*] (SAG)
Mtlg	Mitteilung [*Report*] [*German*] (BJA)
MTLGY	Metallurgy
MTLI	MTL, Inc. [*NASDAQ symbol*] (SAG)
MtLib	Lincoln County Free Library, Libby, MT [*Library symbol*] [*Library of Congress*] (LCLS)
MtLibH	Libby High School, Libby, MT [*Library symbol*] [*Library of Congress*] (LCLS)
MtLibJ	Libby Junior High School, Libby, MT [*Library symbol*] [*Library of Congress*] (LCLS)
MTL Inc	MTL, Inc. [*Associated Press*] (SAG)
MTLM	Metal Management [*NASDAQ symbol*] (TTSB)
MTLNG	Metallizing
MTLP	Master Tape Loading Program
MTLP	Metabolic Toxemia of Late Pregnancy [*Medicine*]
MTLP	Monitor Table Listing Program (NASA)
MTLR	Moving Target Locating RADAR (AABC)
MTLS	Magazine Torpedo Launch System (SAUS)
MTLS	Mesial Temporal Lobe Seizure [*Medicine*]
MTLS	MetaTools Inc. [*NASDAQ symbol*] (TTSB)
MTLS	Munitions Transfer [*or Transporter*] and Loading System (MCD)
MtLv	Livingston Public Library, Livingston, MT [*Library symbol*] [*Library of Congress*] (LCLS)
MTLV	Missile Transport & Loading Vehicle (SAUS)
MtLvHS	Park High School, Livingston, MT [*Library symbol*] [*Library of Congress*] (LCLS)
MtLvMS	Livingston Middle School, Livingston, MT [*Library symbol*] [*Library of Congress*] (LCLS)
MtLvSD	Livingston Elementary Schools, Livingston, MT [*Library symbol*] [*Library of Congress*] (LCLS)
M-TLX	Mitsubishi Transfer-Line Heat Exchanger
MTLZ	Metallize (MSA)
MTM	Machine Type Model (VLIE)
MTM	Magnetic Tape Message
MTM	Maintenance Task Monitor (MCD)
MTM	Maintenance Test Module
MTM	Manpower Tradeoff Methodology [*Military*]
MTM	Mark-to-Market [*Securities*]
MTM	Mark Twain Memorial (EA)
MTM	Marlborough Technical Management [*British*]
MTM	Mary Tyler Moore [*Actress after whom film studio MTM Enterprises is named*]
MTM	Masked Terrain Map [*Military*]
MTM	Master in the Teaching of Mathematics (PGP)
MTM	Master of Theology and Ministry (PGP)
MTM	Master of Transport Management
MTM	Master of Tropical Medicine
MTM	Matsumoto [*Japan*] [*Seismograph station code, US Geological Survey*] (SEIS)
MTM	Mean Time Measurement
MTM	Mechanical Road Transport Mechanic [*British military*] (DMA)
MTM	Mechanical Test Model
MTM	Methods-Time Measurement [*Industrial engineering*]
MTM	Methylthiomethyl [*Organic chemistry*]
MTM	Metlakatla [*Alaska*] [*Airport symbol*] (OAG)
MTM	Metlakatla, AK [*Location identifier*] [*FAA*] (FAAL)
MTM	Metric Ton of Metal (ABAC)
MTM	Michelin Tire Monitor [*System*] [*Automotive engineering*]
MTM	Million Ton Miles
MTM	Million Train Miles
MTM	Mission Test Module (IAA)
MTM	Mobile Transfer Method (AAG)
MTM	Model Test-Model (VLIE)
MTM	Modified Thayer-Martin [*Medium*] [*Microbiology*]
MTM	Modular Torque Motor
MTM	Moving Target Mechanism (SAUS)
MTM	Moving Terrain Model
MTM	Mt. Grant Mines Ltd. [*Vancouver Stock Exchange symbol*]
MTM	MTM [*Methods-Time Measurement*] Association for Standards and Research (EA)
MTM	MTM Aviation GMBH Munchen [*Federal Republic of Germany*] [*FAA designator*] (FAAC)
MTM	MTM Productions, Inc. [*Named for actress Mary Tyler Moore*]
MTM	Multiple Terminal Manager (NITA)
MTM	Multiple Threat Modulation [*Military*] (CAAL)
MTM	Multiple Time Measurement (VLIE)
MTM	Multi-Taper Method [*Spectroscopy*]
MTM	Multi-Tasking Monitor (NITA)
MTM	Multi-Terminal Monitor (NITA)
MTM	Myotubular Myopathy [*Medicine*] (DMAA)
MTM	Thayer-Martin, Modified [*Agar*] (DMAA)
MTMA	Methods Time-Measurement Association (IAA)
MTMA	Military Terminal Major Aerodromes (NATG)
MTMA	Military Terminal Manoeuvring Area (SAUS)
MTMA	Military Traffic Management Agency [*Later, DTMS*]
MtMa	Phillips County Library, Malta, MT [*Library symbol*] [*Library of Congress*] (LCLS)
MTMAINTCO	Motor Maintenance Company (DNAB)
MTMASR	MTM [*Methods-Time Measurement*] Association for Standards and Research [*Later, MTM*] (EA)
MTMB	Military Traffic Management Bulletin (SAA)
MTMC	(Methylthio)-meta-Cresol [*Organic chemistry*]
MTMC	Micros-To Mainframe, Inc. [*NASDAQ symbol*] (SAG)
MTMC	Micros To Mainframes [*NASDAQ symbol*] (TTSB)
MtMc	Miles City Public Library, Miles City, MT [*Library symbol*] [*Library of Congress*] (LCLS)
MTMC	Military Traffic Management Command [*DoD*]
MtMcC	Miles Community College, Miles City, MT [*Library symbol*] [*Library of Congress*] (LCLS)
MTMCEA	Military Traffic Management Command, Eastern Area [*Bayonne, NJ*]
MTMC-OA	Military Traffic Management Command Operations Analysis Division [*Newport News, VA*]
MtMcPh	Pine Hill School, Miles City, MT [*Library symbol*] [*Library of Congress*] (LCLS)
MTMCTEA	Military Traffic Management Command Transportation Engineering Agency (AABC)
MTMCTTC	Military Traffic Management Command Transportation Terminal Command, Europe [*MTMC*] (TAG)
MTMCTTU	Military Traffic Management Command Transportation Terminal Unit (AABC)
MTMCWA	Military Traffic Management Command, Western Area [*Oakland, CA*]
MTM/D	Million Ton Miles/Day (MCD)
MTM/D	Million Ton Miles per Day (ACAE)
MT/MF	Magnetic Tape to Microfilm
MTMF	Multiple Task Management Feature (NITA)
MTM-GPD	Methods Time Measurement and General Purpose Data (PDAA)
MTMH	Master of Tropical Medicine and Hygiene (GAGS)
MTMI	Microtek Medical [*NASDAQ symbol*] (TTSB)
MTMI	Microtek Medical, Inc. [*NASDAQ symbol*] (SAG)
MtMis	Missoula Public and Missoula County Free Library, Missoula, MT [*Library symbol*] [*Library of Congress*] (LCLS)
MtMisGS	Church of Jesus Christ of Latter-Day Saints, Genealogical Society Library, Missoula Branch, Missoula, MT [*Library symbol*] [*Library of Congress*] (LCLS)
MtMisSP	Saint Patrick Hospital, Missoula, MT [*Library symbol*] [*Library of Congress*] (LCLS)
MtMisW	Western Montana Clinic, Missoula, MT [*Library symbol*] [*Library of Congress*] (LCLS)
MTMM	Multitrait-Multimethod Model
MTMOD	Magnetic Tape Module (IAA)
MTMP	MACOM [*Major Command*] Telephone Modernizations Program
MTMR	Military Traffic Management Regulation
mt mRNA	Mitochondrial Messenger RNA [*Ribonucleic Acid*] [*Genetics*] (DOG)
MTMS	Machine Tool Management System (VLIE)
MTM's	Magnetic Tape Transmissions (CET)
MTMS	Memorex Tape Management System [*Computer science*] (IAA)
MTMS	Metal-to-Metal Seal
MTMS	Methyltrimethoxysilane [*Organic chemistry*]
MTMS	Military Traffic Management Service (MCD)
MTMS	Mobilization Training Management System [*DoD*]
MTMS	Multi-Terminal Modular System (DGA)
MTMT	Mail and Telephone Mode Test (SAUS)
MTMT	Multiple Target & Missile Tracker (SAUS)
MTMT	Multiple Terminal Monitor Task [*Computer science*] (VLIE)
MTMTS	Military Traffic Management and Terminal Service [*Later, MTMC*] [*Army*]
MTMTS-TSP	Military Traffic Management and Terminal Service Transportation Strike Plan (DNAB)

MTN............	Baltimore, MD [*Location identifier*] [*FAA*] (FAAL)
MTN............	Main Telecommunication Network [*United Nations*] (EY)
MTN............	Manton [*Australia*] [*Seismograph station code, US Geological Survey*] (SEIS)
MTN............	Medical Television Network (BARN)
MTN............	Medium-Term Note [*Finance*]
MTN............	Message Transport Network [*Computer science*] (VLIE)
MTN............	Metatolylnitrile [*Organic chemistry*]
MTN............	Mirtone International, Inc. [*Toronto Stock Exchange symbol*]
MTN............	Mizlou Television Network
MTN............	Mobil Producing TX & NM, Inc., Houston, TX [*OCLC symbol*] (OCLC)
MTN............	Motion (MSA)
mtn............	Mountain (MILB)
Mtn............	Mountain (TBD)
MTN............	Mountain
MTN............	Mountain Air Cargo, Inc. [*FAA designator*] (FAAC)
MTN............	Move Trace Number (TIMI)
MTN............	Multilateral Trade Negotiations
MTN............	Multinational Trade Negotiations (IAA)
MTNA..........	Music Teachers National Association (EA)
MTND..........	Mercury Tube Nutation Damper
MTNFC.........	Mel Tillis National Fan Club (EA)
MTNHP........	Montana Natural Heritage Program [*Helena, MT*] [*Information service or system*] (IID)
MTNK..........	Main Tank [*Automotive emissions*]
MT-NMR.......	Magnetic Transfer Nuclear Magnetic Resonance (DB)
MtnPkFn......	Mountain Parks Financial Corp. [*Associated Press*] (SAG)
MTNS..........	Manportable Thermal Night Sight (ACAE)
MTNS..........	Metal-Thick Nitride Semiconductor (IAA)
MTNS..........	Metal-Thick Nitride-Silicon (IAA)
MTNS..........	Metal-Thick Oxide-Nitride-Silicon
MTNS..........	Mountains [*Postal Service standard*] (OPSA)
MTNT..........	Metro Networks, Inc. [*NASDAQ symbol*] (SAG)
MtNxPS........	Noxon Public School, Noxon, MT [*Library symbol*] [*Library of Congress*] (LCLS)
MTO............	Made to Order (ODBW)
MTO............	Magnetic Tape Operator (MCD)
MTO............	Maintenance Technology Office [*Air Force Logistics Command*]
MTO............	Manitoulin Air Services Ltd. [*Canada*] [*ICAO designator*] (FAAC)
MTO............	Man-Tended Operation (SSD)
MTO............	Manufacturing Technical Order (SAA)
MTO............	Manufacturing Technology Objective
MTO............	Master Terminal Operator (IAA)
MTO............	Master Timing Oscillator (MCD)
MTO............	Mattoon [*Illinois*] [*Airport symbol*] (OAG)
MTO............	Maximum Time Out (MCD)
MTO............	Medical Transport Officer [*Navy*]
MTO............	Mediterranean Theater of Operations (ADWA)
MTO............	Mediterranean Theater of Operations, United States Army [*Shortened form of MTOUSA*] [*World War II*]
MTO............	Message Template Object [*Computer science*] (AGLO)
MTO............	Message Terminal Operation [*Military*] (CAAL)
MTO............	Message to Observer (SAUS)
MTO............	Methanol-to-Olefin [*Process*]
MTO............	Mid Term Objective (ACAE)
MTO............	Missile Test Operator (SAA)
MTO............	Mission, Task, Objective
MTO............	Mission Type Order (DOMA)
MTO............	Mississippi Test Operations [*NASA*]
MTO............	Modification Task Outline (KSC)
MTO............	Motor Transport Officer [*Military*]
MTO............	Mouvement Togolais pour la Democratie [*Togolese Movement for Democracy*] [*Political party*] (PD)
MTO............	Movement Transfer Order (MCD)
MTO............	Muffin-Tin Orbital [*Physics*]
MTO............	Multilateral Trading Organization (ECON)
MTO............	Multimodal Transport Operator
MTOAL........	Mobilization Table of Allowance Listing [*Military*] (DNAB)
MTOB..........	Manned Test Operations Board [*NASA*]
MTOC..........	Microtubular Organizing Complex [*Physiology*]
MTOC..........	Microtubule Organizing Center [*Cytology*]
MTOC..........	Mitotic Organizing Center [*Cytology*]
MTOC..........	Monitoring Transport of Ocean Currents [*Project*] [*Marine science*] (OSRA)
MTOCs........	Microtubule Organizing Centers (DOG)
MTOE..........	Mid-Term Operations Estimate (SAUS)
MTOE..........	Million Tons of Oil Equivalent
MTOE..........	Modification Table of Organization and Equipment [*Army*] (AABC)
MTOGW.......	Maximum Takeoff Gross Weight [*Aviation*] (MCD)
MTOL..........	Mean Time off Line (AAEL)
MTOL..........	Mean Time on Line (AAEL)
MTOM.........	Master of Traditional Oriental Medicine (PGP)
MTOM.........	Maximum Take-Off Mass (SAUS)
MTON.........	Measurement Ton
MTON.........	Metro One Telecommunications, Inc. [*NASDAQ symbol*] (SAG)
MTONS........	Metal-Thick Oxide-Nitride-Silicon (MSA)
MTONS........	Metric Tonnes (RIMS)
MTOP..........	Molecular Total Overlap Population (IEEE)
MTOPS........	Million Theoretical Operations per Second [*Computer science*]
MTORQ........	Maximum Torque
MTOS..........	Magnetic Tape Operating System (NITA)
MTOS..........	Magnetic Tape Operations System [*Computer science*] (NRCH)
MTOS..........	Major Trauma Outcome Study [*American College of Surgeons Committee on Trauma*]
MTOS..........	Metal-Thick Oxide Semiconductor (IAA)

MTOS..........	Metal-Thick Oxide-Silicon
MTOS..........	Multi-Tasking Operating System (NITA)
MTOSFET.....	Metal-Thick Oxide Semiconductor Field Effect Transistor (IAA)
MTOUSA......	Mediterranean Theater of Operations, United States Army [*Sometimes shortened to MTO*] [*World War II*]
MTOW	Maximum Takeoff Weight [*Aviation*] (MCD)
MTox	Master of Toxicology (GAGS)
MTP............	Island Helicopters, Inc. [*ICAO designator*] (FAAC)
MTP............	Magnetic Tape Processor (NITA)
MTP............	Maintenance Test Package (MCD)
MTP............	Manual Troubleshooting Procedures [*Army*]
MTP............	Manufacturing Technical Procedure [*NASA*] (NASA)
MTP............	Manufacturing Technology Program [*Aviation Systems Command*] (RDA)
MTP............	Manufacturing Technology Projects [*Manufacturing Technology Information Analysis Center*] [*Information service or system*] (CRD)
MTP	Manufacturing Test Procedure
MTP	Master of Town and Country Planning
MTP	Master of Town Planning
MTP	Master of Transpersonal Psychology (PGP)
MTP	Master Test Plan (KSC)
MTP	Master Training Plan [*Navy*] (ANA)
MTP	Master Transportation Plan (AAG)
MTP	Master Typography Program (DNAB)
MTP	Materiel Test Procedure [*Army*]
MTP	Materiel Transfer Plan [*Army*]
MTP	Maximum Tire Pressure (ADA)
MTP	Maximum Tolerated Pressure (MELL)
MTP	Maximum Total Trihalomethane Potential (EG)
MTP	Mechanical Thermal Pulse (IEEE)
MTP	Medical Termination of Pregnancy (MELL)
MTP	Message Transfer Protocol [*Telecommunications*] (OSI)
MTP	Message Transmission Part [*Telecommunications*] (TEL)
MTP	Metatarsophalangeal [*Anatomy*]
MTP	Methods Test Panel [*Bureau of the Census*] (GFGA)
MTP	(Methylthio)phenol [*Organic chemistry*]
MTP	Microsomal Triglyceride Transfer Protein [*Biochemistry*]
MTP	Microtubule Protein [*Cytology*]
MTP	Microwave Temperature Profiler (ARMP)
MTP	Military Type Property
MTP	Miniature Trimmer Potentiometer
MTP	Minimum Time Path (OA)
MTP	Missile Transfer Panel (AAG)
MTP	Missile Tube Pressurization
MTP	Mission Tailored Product
MTP	Mission Tasking Package (COE)
MTP	Mission Test Plan (KSC)
MTP	Mission Training Plan [*Military*] (INF)
MTP	Mobilization Training Program [*Military*]
MTP	Mobilization Troop Program [*Army*]
MTP	Modular Terminal Processor (NITA)
MTP	Montana Power Co. [*NYSE symbol*] (SPSG)
MTP	Montauk Point [*New York*] [*Airport symbol*] [*Obsolete*] (OAG)
MTP	Monte Pirata [*Puerto Rico*] [*Seismograph station code, US Geological Survey*] (SEIS)
MTP	MOS [*Military Occupation Specialty*] Training Plan
MTP	Mother Tongue Project (AIE)
MTP	Movimiento Todos par la Patria [*Argentina*] [*Political party*] (EY)
MTP	Multiple-Task Performance
MTP	Multiply Twinned Particles (DICI)
MTP	Multipoint (DNAB)
MTP	Muramyl Tripeptide (DB)
MtP	Plains Public Library, Plains, MT [*Library symbol*] [*Library of Congress*] (LCLS)
MTP	[*The*] Pas Public Library, Manitoba [*Library symbol*] [*National Library of Canada*] (NLC)
MTPA..........	Master Textile Printers Association (EA)
MTPA..........	(Methoxy)trifluoromethylphenylacetic Acid [*Organic chemistry*]
MTPA..........	Mobile Transponder Performance Analyzer [*Aviation*] (DA)
MtPaS.........	Salish Kootenai College Library, Pablo, MT [*Library symbol*] [*Library of Congress*] (LCLS)
MtPaTS........	Two Eagle School, Pablo, MT [*Library symbol*] [*Library of Congress*] (LCLS)
MTPB..........	Malaysia Tourism Promotion Board (EA)
MTPC..........	Metal Tube Packaging Council of North America [*Later, TCNA*] (EA)
MTPC..........	Minimal Total Processing Time (NITA)
MTPCNA......	Metal Tube Packaging Council of North America [*Later, TCNA*]
MTPE..........	Mission to Planet Earth [*Proposed NASA satellite*]
MTPF..........	Maximum Total Peaking Factor [*Nuclear energy*] (NRCH)
MTP FET......	Metal/Tunnelling-Nitride Polysilicon Gate FET (NITA)
MTPH..........	Maximum Temperature of Previous Heating [*Archaeology*]
MTPI...........	Member of the Town Planning Institute [*British*]
MTPJ..........	Metatarsophalangeal Joint [*Medicine*] (DMAA)
MTPK..........	Keewatin Community College, The Pas, Manitoba [*Library symbol*] [*National Library of Canada*] (NLC)
MTPM.........	Mean Time to Provide Manpower (DNAB)
MT/PMP......	Mobile Transporter/Permanent Manned Presence (SAUS)
MtPoF.........	Fort Peck Community College, Poplar, MT [*Library symbol*] [*Library of Congress*] (LCLS)
MtPol..........	Polson City Library, Polson, MT [*Library symbol*] [*Library of Congress*] (LCLS)
MTPP..........	Material Test Procedure Pamphlet
MTPP..........	Missile-to-Target Patch Panel
MTPP..........	Port-Au-Prince/Internacional [*Haiti*] [*ICAO location identifier*] (ICLI)

MTP-PE........	Muramyl Tripeptide Phosphatidylethanolamine [*Antineoplastic drug*] (CDI)
MTPPI............	Medical Technology and Practice Patterns Institute (SAUS)
MtPPS	Plains Public School Library, Plains, MT [*Library symbol*] [*Library of Congress*] (LCLS)
MTPR............	Miniature Temperature Pressure Recorder [*Marine science*] (OSRA)
MTPS............	Magnetic Tape Programming System [*Computer science*] (IEEE)
MTPS............	Maintenance Test Packages (ACAE)
MTPS............	Modern Talking Picture Service, Inc. [*Funded by U.S. Department of Education*] (PAZ)
MTPSI............	Master Test Program Set Index (ACAE)
MTPT............	Minimal Total Processing Time (IEEE)
MTPU............	Missile Tank Pressurization Unit (AAG)
MTPUG.........	Pascal/MT Users Group [*Defunct*] (EA)
MTPW..........	Master of Technical and Professional Writing (GAGS)
MtPw	Sheridan County Free Library, Plentywood, MT [*Library symbol*] [*Library of Congress*] (LCLS)
MTPX............	Port-De-Paix [*Haiti*] [*ICAO location identifier*] (ICLI)
MTPY............	Millions of Tons per Year [*of solids, e.g., coal*]
MTQ.............	CAAA Air Martinique [*France*] [*ICAO designator*] (FAAC)
MTQ.............	Greenville, MS [*Location identifier*] [*FAA*] (FAAL)
MTQ.............	Martinique [*ANSI three-letter standard code*] (CNC)
MTQ.............	Methaqualone [*or Methyltolylquinazolone, or Metolquizolone*] [*Sedative*]
MTQ.............	Mitchell [*Australia*] [*Airport symbol*] (OAG)
MTQ.............	Mount Allard Resources [*Vancouver Stock Exchange symbol*]
MTQAS	Methadone Treatment Quality Assurance System [*National Institute on Drug Abuse*]
MTQM..........	Master of Total Quality Management (PGP)
MTR.............	Magic-Tone Records [*Record label*]
MTR.............	Magnetic Core Transistor Relay (IAA)
MTR.............	Magnetic Tape Reader (NITA)
MTR.............	Magnetic Tape Recorder
MTR.............	Magnetisation Transfer Ratio (SAUS)
MTR.............	Main Timing Register
MTR.............	Major Trouble Report (MCD)
MTR.............	Marked Target Receiver (SAUS)
MTR.............	Mass, Tenderness, Rebound [*On abdominal examination*] [*Gastroenterology*] (DAVI)
MTR.............	Mass-Transfer Rate [*Chemical engineering*]
MTR.............	Mass Transit Railway (DS)
MTR.............	Master Tool Record (SAA)
MTR.............	Materials Testing Reactor
MTR.............	Materials Testing Report
MTR.............	Material Transfer Recorder [*LASER*] [*Army*]
MTR.............	Maximum Tracking Range
MT/R............	Maximum Traction/Reinforced [*Automotive tires*]
MTR.............	Mean Time to Removal [*Quality control*]
MTR.............	Mean Time to Restore [*Quality control*] (IAA)
MTR.............	Measa Royalty Trust [*NYSE symbol*] (SAG)
MTR.............	Meinicke Turbidity Reaction [*Obsolete test for syphilis*]
MTR.............	Mental Treatment Rules [*British*]
MTR.............	Mesa Royaty Tr UBI [*NYSE symbol*] (TTSB)
MTR.............	Meter [*or Metering*] (AAG)
mtr.............	Meter (IDOE)
MTR.............	Methylthioribose [*Biochemistry*]
MTR.............	Metroflight, Inc. [*ICAO designator*] (FAAC)
Mtr.............	Metronome [*Record label*] [*Scandinavia, Germany, etc.*]
MTR.............	Mid-Term Review
MTR.............	Migration Traffic Rate (OA)
MTR.............	Military Technical Revolution (DOMA)
MTR.............	Military Temperature Range
MTR.............	Military Training Route [*Aviation*] (FAAC)
MTR.............	Milliammeter (IAA)
MTR.............	Miniature Temperature Recorder (USDC)
MTR.............	Minimum Technological Requirement
MTR.............	Minimum Time Rate
MTR.............	Miscellaneous Tax Ruling [*IRS*] (AAGC)
MTR.............	Missile Track [*or Tracking*] RADAR [*Air Force*]
MTR.............	MITRE Corp., Library Department, McLean, VA [*OCLC symbol*] (OCLC)
MTR.............	Mobile Test Rig (SAUS)
MTR.............	Mobile Tracking Range [*Military*] (CAAL)
MTR.............	Modification Traceability Record (MCD)
MTR.............	Modular Tree Representation (MHDI)
MTR.............	Monitor [*Computer science*] (BUR)
mtr.............	Monitor (ELAL)
MTR.............	Monopulse Tracking Receiver
MTR.............	Monteria [*Colombia*] [*Airport symbol*] (OAG)
MTR.............	Monterrey [*California*] [*Seismograph station code, US Geological Survey*] (SEIS)
MTR.............	Montour Railroad Co. [*AAR code*]
MTR.............	Motor (AABC)
MTR.............	Moving Target Reactor
MTR.............	Moving Target Resolver (MCD)
MT-R	Mud Traction-Reinforced [*Truck tires*]
MTR.............	Multiple Thermocouple Reference
MTR.............	Multiple Token Ring [*Telecommunications*] (OSI)
MTR.............	Multiple Tracking Range
MTR.............	Multiple Track RADAR
MTR.............	Museum of Television and Radio [*New York*]
MTR.............	Mutual Resources [*Vancouver Stock Exchange symbol*]
MTR.............	Universite de Montreal, Bibliotheque [*UTLAS symbol*]
MTRA..........	Machine Tools Research Association (WDAA)
MTRA..........	Meta Biosystems [*NASDAQ symbol*] (SAG)
MTRA..........	Metra Biosystems [*NASDAQ symbol*] (SAG)
MTRACS	Multiple input Tracking Control System (SAUS)
M/TRANS	Manual Transmission [*Automotive engineering*]
MTransEc.....	Master of Transport Economics
MTRAT........	Maverick Target Recognition and Acquisition Trainer (ACAE)
MTRB..........	Man-Tended Review Board (SSD)
MTRB..........	Maritime Transportation Research Board [*National Research Council*]
MTRB..........	Motor Truck Rate Bureau
MTRC..........	Man-Tended Reference Configuration (SSD)
MTRC..........	Metric
MTRCL........	Motorcycle (AABC)
Mtrclt..........	Motorcyclist [*Army*]
MTRCYL.......	Motorcycle
MtRd..........	Community Library, Roundup, MT [*Library symbol*] [*Library of Congress*] (LCLS)
MtRd-E	Roundup Central Elementary School Library, Roundup, MT [*Library symbol*] [*Library of Congress*] (LCLS)
MTRDN........	Motor-Driven
MTRE.........	Magnetic Tape Recorder End
MTRE.........	Missile Test and Readiness Equipment
MTRE.........	Missile Test and Readiness Evaluation [*Military*] (IAA)
Mt Res Dev...	Mountain Research and Development (SAUS)
MT REVD	Most Reverend (ROG)
MTRF..........	Mark Twain Research Foundation (EA)
MTRF..........	Master Training File [*Computer science*]
MTRG..........	Masses, Tenderness, Rebound, Guarding (SAUS)
MTRG..........	Metering (MSA)
MTRI...........	Missile Test Range Instrumentation
MTRK..........	Minitrack (KSC)
MTRL..........	Material
MTRM..........	Modulated Throat-Rocket Motor (MCD)
MTRN..........	Metrotrans Corp. [*NASDAQ symbol*] (SAG)
mtRNA........	Ribonucleic Acid, Mitochondrial [*Biochemistry, genetics*]
MTRNTY	Maternity
MTRO..........	Metro-Tel Corp. [*NASDAQ symbol*] (NQ)
MtRo..........	Ronan City Library, Ronan, MT [*Library symbol*] [*Library of Congress*] (LCLS)
MtroOne......	Metro One Telecommunications, Inc. [*Associated Press*] (SAG)
MTR OP.......	Motor Operated [*Freight*]
MTRP..........	Machine Tool Retrofit Program
MTRP..........	Master of Town and Regional Planning [*British*] (ADA)
MTRP..........	Maximum Transfer Rate Performance (SAUS)
mtrRNA........	Mitochondrial Ribosomal RNA[*Ribonucleic Acid*] [*Genetics*] (DOG)
MTRS..........	Magnetic Tape Recorder Set
MTRS..........	Magnetic Tape Recorder Start
MTRS..........	Magnetic Tape Reformatting System [*Hewlett-Packard Co.*]
MTRS..........	Mattress (MSA)
MTRS..........	Metris Companies, Inc. [*NASDAQ symbol*] (SAG)
MTRS..........	Multimode Tactical Radar Simulator (ACAE)
MT Rulings...	Miscellaneous Tax Rulings [*Australia*] [*A publication*]
MTRUW.......	Mixed Transuranic Waste (GAAI)
MtrVac........	MotorVac Technologies, Inc. [*Associated Press*] (SAG)
MTRX..........	Matrix Service [*NASDAQ symbol*] (TTSB)
MTRX..........	Matrix Service Corp. [*NASDAQ symbol*] (NQ)
MTRY..........	Momentary (FAAC)
MTS...........	Machine-Tractor Stations
MTS...........	Magnetic Tape Station [*Computer science*] (CET)
MTS...........	Magnetic Tape Storage [*Computer science*] (IAA)
MTS...........	Magnetic Tape System [*Computer science*]
MTS...........	Magnetic Type System [*Computer science*] (IAA)
MTS...........	Mainsborne Telecontrol System (NITA)
MTS...........	Maintenance Training Set (MCD)
MTS...........	Maintenance Transmittal Sheet
MTS...........	Main Trunk System [*Telecommunications*] (TEL)
MTS...........	Management Tracing System (COE)
MTS...........	Management Tracking System [*Environmental Protection Agency*] (EPA)
MTS...........	Manager, Technical Support (SAUS)
MTS...........	Manitoba Telephone System [*Telecommunications service*] (TSSD)
MTS...........	Manned Teller System
MTS...........	Manpower Training Services
MTS...........	Mantrust Asahi Airways PT [*Indonesia*] [*ICAO designator*] (FAAC)
MTS...........	Manual Testing System [*Sports medicine*]
MTS...........	Manufacturing Technology Section [*Navy*]
MTS...........	Manzini [*Swaziland*] [*Airport symbol*] (OAG)
MTS...........	Mardan Test Set
MTS...........	Marine Tactical System (SAUS)
MTS...........	Marine Technology Society (EA)
MTS...........	Maritime Tactical Schools (MCD)
MTS...........	Marked Target Seeker (SAUS)
MTS...........	Marketing and Transportation Situation [*Series*] [*A publication*]
MTS...........	Marketing Technical Services
MTS...........	Mark Twain Society [*Defunct*] (EA)
MTS...........	MARS [*Military Affiliate Radio System*] Technical Service (CET)
MTS...........	Mass Target Sensor
MTS...........	Mass Termination System [*Computer science*] (IEEE)
MTS...........	Master of Teaching of Science (GAGS)
MTS...........	Master of Theological Studies (WGA)
MTS...........	Master Test Station
MTS...........	Master Timing Schedule
MTS...........	Master Timing System
MTS...........	Material Test Specification (MSA)
MTS...........	Material Tracking Standard (AAEL)
MTS...........	Matsue [*Japan*] [*Seismograph station code, US Geological Survey*] (SEIS)

MTS	Medical Testing Systems [*Commercial firm*]
MTS	Medicare Transaction System (DMAA)
MTS	Member of the Technical Staff [*A generic term*]
MTS	Memory Test System
MTS	Meridian Telecommunication Services [*Indianapolis, IN*] (TSSD)
MTS	Merlin Training System (SAUS)
MTS	Message Telecommunications Service
MTS	Message Telephone Service (NITA)
MTS	Message Toll Service [*Communications*]
MTS	Message Traffic Study
MTS	Message Transfer Service
MTS	Message Transfer System [*Telecommunications*] (OSI)
MTS	Message Transmission Subsystem [*Telecommunications*] (TEL)
MTS	Meteoroid Technology Satellite [*NASA*]
MTS	Methods-Time Study [*Industrial engineering*]
MTS	Methyltrichlorosilane [*Organic chemistry*]
MTS	Metric Time System (NASA)
MTS	Metropolitan Transportation System (PA)
MTS	Michigan Terminal System [*Computer science*]
MTS	Microprocessor Training System [*Integrated Computer Systems*] (NITA)
MTS	Microsoft Transaction Server [*Computer science*]
MTS	Microtubule-Stabilizing Solution [*Cytology*]
MTS	Microwave Temperature Sounder (EOSA)
MTS	Microwave Test Set (MCD)
MTS	Military Tactical Systems (SAUS)
MTS	Military Test Satellite
MTS	Military Training Standard (AFM)
MTS	Million (10^6) Transitions Per Second [*Of magnetic storage*] (NITA)
MTS	Missile Test Set
MTS	Missile Test Stand
MTS	Missile Test Station
MTS	Missile Tracking Station [*DoD*]
MTS	Missile Tracking System (IEEE)
MTS	Missile Training Squadron
MTS	Missile Tube Supply
MTS	Missions to Seamen [*British*]
MTS	Mississippi Test Site [*Aerospace*] (AAG)
MTS	Mobile Telephone Service
MTS	Mobile Terminal System [*IBM Corp.*]
MTS	Mobile Tracking Station [*NASA*]
MTS	Mobile Training Set (AFM)
MTS	Mobil-Trac System [*MTMC*] (TAG)
MTS	Modem Test Set (NITA)
MTS	Moderate Tactile Stimulus [*Neurology*] (DAVI)
MTS	Modernization through Spares [*Army program*]
MTS	Modular Tactical Switch (SAUS)
MTS	Modular Television System [*Telecommunications*] (CDE)
MTS	Modular Terminal System (NITA)
MTS	Module Test Set (MCD)
MTS	Module Test System (IAA)
MTS	Module Tracking System (NRCH)
MTS	Money Transfer System (IAA)
MTS	Monosyllable, Trochee, Spondee Test [*Of speech discrimination*] (DAVI)
MTS	Montgomery Street Income Securities, Inc. [*NYSE symbol*] (SPSG)
MTS	Monthly Treasury Statement [*Government*] (AFM)
MTS	Morale Tendency Score (AEE)
MTS	Motion-Time Standards [*Industrial engineering*]
MTS	Motor-Operated Transfer Switch
MTS	Motor Tariff Service
MTS	Motor Turbine Ship (IIA)
MTS	Mountains [*Board on Geographic Names*]
MTS	Moving Target Screen (MCD)
MTS	Moving Target Simulator (RDA)
MTS	Moving Time Series
MTS	MTS Systems Corp. [*Associated Press*] (SAG)
MTS	Multicellular Tumor Spheroid [*Medicine*] (DB)
MTS	Multichannel Television Sound [*or Stereo*]
MTS	Multichannel TV Sound (WDMC)
MTS	Multichannel TV Stereo (WDMC)
MTS	Multimedia Teleschool (SAUS)
MTS	Multiple Target Screen
MTS	Multiple Terminal System (NITA)
MTS	Multiple Time Scale
MTS	Multiple Tumor Suppressor [*Oncology*]
MTS	Multipoint Terminal Software [*Computer science*] (VLIE)
MTS	Muscle Testing System [*Myology*]
MTS	Musculotendinous Structure (DMAA)
MTS	State Law Library of Montana, Helena, MT [*OCLC symbol*] (OCLC)
MTS1	Multiple Tumour Suppressor 1 [*Genetics*] (ECON)
MTSA	Mantissa (VLIE)
MTSA	Seaman Apprentice, Missile Technician, Striker [*Navy rating*]
MTSAA	Multidiscipline Technical Safety Assurance Appraisal [*Environmental science*] (COE)
MTSAT	Multi-functional Transport Satellite
MTSB	Meridial Trans-Sonic Boundary-Layer [*Aerodynamics*]
MtSc	Daniels County Free Library, Scobey, MT [*Library symbol*] [*Library of Congress*] (LCLS)
MTSC	Magnetic Tape Selectric Composer [*IBM Corp.*]
MTSC	Master of Teaching Speech Communication (GAGS)
MTSC	Master of Technical and Scientific Communication (GAGS)
MTSC	Master of Theological Studies Counseling (PGP)
MTSC	MTS Systems [*NASDAQ symbol*] (TTSB)
MTSC	MTS Systems Corp. [*NASDAQ symbol*] (NQ)

MTSD	Military Transmission Systems Department [*NORAD*]
MTSE	Magnetic Trap Stability Experiment (IEEE)
MTSE	Message Transfer Service Element [*Computer science*] (VLIE)
MTSF	Mean Time to System Failure [*Quality control*] (PDAA)
MTS/GMS	Module Test Set / Guided Missile System (DWSG)
MTSGT	Master Technical Sergeant [*Marine Corps*]
MTSGT(C)	Master Technical Sergeant (Commissary) [*Marine Corps*]
MtSh	Toole County Free Library, Shelby, MT [*Library symbol*] [*Library of Congress*] (LCLS)
MTSI	Mean Time to System Interrogation (VLIE)
MTSI	Micro Touch Systems [*NASDAQ symbol*] (TTSB)
MTSI	Microtouch Systems, Inc. [*NASDAQ symbol*] (SAG)
MtSid	Sidney Public Library, Sidney, MT [*Library symbol*] [*Library of Congress*] (LCLS)
Mt Sinai Sch Med	Mount Sinai School of Medicine of The City University of New York (GAGS)
MTSL	Message Transfer Sublayer [*Telecommunications*] (OSI)
MTSL	Monitoring and Technical Support Laboratory [*Environmental Protection Agency*] (GFGA)
MTSN	Machine Type and Serial Number (VLIE)
MTSN	Mattson Technology [*NASDAQ symbol*] (TTSB)
MTSN	Mattson Technology, Inc. [*NASDAQ symbol*] (SAG)
MTSN	Seaman, Missile Technician, Striker [*Navy rating*]
MTSO	Mean Time to Switch-Over (VLIE)
MTSO	Mobile Telephone Switching Office [*Telecommunications*]
MTSO	Multiprogramming Time-Sharing Operating System [*Computer science*] (VLIE)
MTSP	Maintenance Test Support Package [*Army*]
MTSP	Microelectronics Technology Support Program (SAUS)
MTSP	Microelectronic Technology Support Program (ACAE)
MTSPS	Multiple Transducer Seismic Profiling System
MTSQ	Mechanical Time, Superquick [*Fuse*] [*Weaponry*]
MTSQF	Mechanical Time, Superquick Fuze [*Weaponry*] (MCD)
MTSR	Maximal Temperature of the Synthesis Reaction [*Chemical engineering*]
MTSR	Mean Time to Service Restoral [*Quality control*] [*Telecommunications*] (TEL)
MTSR	Mean Time to System Restoration [*Computer science*] (VLIE)
MTSR	Mid-Term Status Reports
MTSS	Magnetic Tape Storage System
MTSS	Manned Test Space System [*See also MOD, MODS, MOSS*] [*Air Force/NASA*]
MTSS	Medial Tibial Stress Syndrome [*Medicine*] (MELL)
MTSS	Military Test Space Station [*See also MOD, MODS, MOSS*] [*Air Force/NASA*]
MTSS	Mine Warfare Tactical Support System (SAUS)
MTSS	Modular Torpedo Support System (SAUS)
MTSSL	Methanethiosulphonate Spin Label [*Analytical chemistry*]
MTST	Magnetic Tape Selectric Typewriter [*IBM Corp.*]
MTST	Maximal Treadmill Stress Test [*Medicine*] (DMAA)
MTST	Microtest, Inc. [*NASDAQ symbol*] (SAG)
Mt St Mary's C	Mount St. Mary's College (GAGS)
MtStrS	St. Regis School, St. Regis, MT [*Library symbol*] [*Library of Congress*] (LCLS)
MTSU	Magnetic Tape Search Unit [*Computer science*]
MTSU	Middle Tennessee State University
MtSu	Mineral County Public Library, Superior, MT [*Library symbol*] [*Library of Congress*] (LCLS)
MTS/VO	Motor Transportation Supervisor/Vehicle Operator (AAG)
MTT	Magnetic Tape Terminal [*Computer science*]
MTT	Magnetic Tape Transport [*Computer science*] (IEEE)
MTT	Maintenance Training Team (MCD)
MTT	Malignant Trophoblastic Teratoma [*Oncology*] (MAE)
MTT	Mammillothalamic Tract [*Neuroanatomy*]
MTT	Manned Target Tank (SAUS)
MTT	Maritime Telegraph & Telephone Co. Ltd. [*Toronto Stock Exchange symbol*]
MTT	Masked Terrain Trainer [*Military*]
MTT	Master of Textile Technology
MTT	Material Testing Technology (MCD)
MTT	Maximal Treadmill Test (CPH)
MTT	Maximum Touch Temperature (MCD)
MTT	Mean Transit Time
MTT	Mediterranean Tours and Travel [*Egypt*]
MTT	Medium Tactical Transport [*Army*]
MTT	Medium Tactical Truck [*Army*] (RDA)
MTT	Message Transfer Time (NITA)
MTT	Methyl(thio)tetrazole [*Biochemistry*]
MTT	Metropolitan Edison Co. [*NYSE symbol*] (SPSG)
MTT	Microprogram Trace Tape [*Computer science*] (VLIE)
MTT	Microsoft Travel Technologies [*Computer science*] (VLIE)
MTT	Microwave Theory and Technique (MCD)
MTT	Military Training Team (MCD)
MTT	Minatitlan [*Mexico*] [*Airport symbol*] (OAG)
MTT	Missionary Tech Team (EA)
MTT	Mi-Tsiyon Tetse Torah [*Tel Aviv*] (BJA)
MTT	Mobile Training Team
MTT	Mobile Travel Team (MCD)
MTT	Monetta Fire Tower [*South Carolina*] [*Seismograph station code, US Geological Survey*] (SEIS)
MTT	Monotetrazolium [*Medicine*] (MAE)
MTT	Moving Target Tracking (ACAE)
MTT	Moving Turning Target (SAUS)
MTT	Multiple Target Tracker
MTT	Munitions Transfer Truck (MCD)

MTT	Orion SpA [*Italy*] [*ICAO designator*] (FAAC)
MtT	Prairie County Library, Terry, MT [*Library symbol*] [*Library of Congress*] (LCLS)
MTTA	Machine Tool Technologies Association [*British*] (EAIO)
MTTA	Machine Tool Trades Association (ACII)
MTTA	Mean Time to Accomplish [*Quality control*] (NASA)
MTTA	Mean Time to Arrive [*Computer science*] (ELAL)
MTTA	Mean Time to Assist (AAEL)
MTTA	Multi-Tenant Telecommunications Association (EA)
MTTB	Mean Time to Bench [*Repair*] [*Quality control*]
MTTC	Manufacturing Technology Technical Council
MTTC	Mean Time to Change Parts [*Quality control*] (MCD)
MTTC	Mean Time to Correct (AAEL)
MTTC	Mechanised Transport Training Corps [*British military*] (DMA)
MtTcES	Trout Creek Elementary School, Trout Creek, MT [*Library symbol*] [*Library of Congress*] (LCLS)
MTTD	Mean Time to Detect [*Quality control*] (MCD)
MTTD	Mean Time to Diagnosis [*Quality control*] (BUR)
MTTE	Magnetic Tape Terminal Equipment [*Computer science*] (CET)
MTTE	Mean Time to Exchange [*Quality control*] (MCD)
MTTEA	Marine Towing and Transportation Employers Association [*Defunct*] (EA)
MTTF	Mean Time to Failure [*Quality control*]
MTTF	Microbuoy Transportable Test Facility (SAUS)
MtTf	Thompson Falls Public Library, Thompson Falls, MT [*Library symbol*] [*Library of Congress*] (LCLS)
MTTFF	Mean Time to First Failure [*Quality control*]
MtTfS	Thompson Falls Schools, Thompson Falls, MT [*Library symbol*] [*Library of Congress*] (LCLS)
MTTFSF	Mean Time to First System Failure [*Quality control*] (PDAA)
MTTFSR	Mean Time to First System Repair [*Quality control*] (PDAA)
MTTHS	Modern Transport Technical and Historical Society [*Later, SFCH*] (EA)
MTTI	Magnetic Tape Transport Interface [*Computer science*] (MCD)
MTTI	Mean Time to Inspect [*Quality control*] (CAAL)
MTTI	Modified Tension Time Index [*Cardiology*]
MTTL	Motorola Transistor-Transistor Logic (IAA)
MTTM	Magnetic Tape and Telemetry (MCD)
MTTM	Mean Time to Maintain [*Quality control*] (CMD)
MTTN	Multi-Tranche Tap Note [*Finance*] [*British*]
MTTO	Minuetto [*Slow Air*] [*Music*] (ROG)
MTTOP	Machine Tool Trigger Order Program (MHDB)
MTTP	Materials Testing and Technology Program
MTTP	Maximum Total Trihalomethane Potential (FFDE)
MTTPO	Mean Time to Planned Outage (IEEE)
MTTPrC	Metropol Ed 3.90% cm Pfd [*NYSE symbol*] (TTSB)
MTTPrZ	Met-Ed Capital L.P. 'MIPS' [*NYSE symbol*] (TTSB)
MTTR	Magnetic Tape Transport Replacement (DWSG)
MTTR	Maximum Time to Repair (MCD)
MTTR	Maximum Time to Replace [*Navy*] (IAA)
MTTR	Mean Time to Removal [*Quality control*]
MTTR	Mean Time to Repair [*Quality control*] (CAAL)
MTTR	Mean Time to Replacement [*Quality control*]
MTTR	Mean Time to Restore [*Quality control*] (IEEE)
MTTR	Missile Target Tracking RADAR (MCD)
MTTR	Multi-Target Tracking Radar (SAUS)
MTTRF	Mission Time to Restore Function
mttRNA	Mitochondrial Transfer RNA[*Ribonucleic Acid*] [*Genetics*] (DOG)
MTTRS	Mean Time to Restore Software [*Quality control*] (CAAL)
MTTRS	Mean Time to Restore System [*Quality control*]
MTTS	Marine Terminal Tankage System (MCD)
MTTS	Mean Time to Service [*Quality control*]
MTTS	Mean Time to Trouble Shoot (ACAE)
MTT-S	Microwave Theory and Techniques Society (ACAE)
MTTS	Mobile Target Tracking System
MTTS	Multiple Target Tracking System
MTTS	Multiplexed Tactical Telephone System (SAUS)
MTTS	Multitask Terminal System
MTTS	Multi-Task Training System (SAUS)
MTTSF	Mean Time to System Failure [*Quality control*] (PDAA)
MTTT	Mean Time to Test (MCD)
MTTU	Modular Timing Terminal Unit
MTTUO	Mean Time to Unplanned Outage (IEEE)
MTTV	Maneuvering Target Test Vechicle
MTTW	Mean Time to Wait for Parts [*Quality control*] (MCD)
MtTyrSH	Troy Senior High School, Troy, MT [*Library symbol*] [*Library of Congress*] (LCLS)
MTU	Magnetic Tape Unit [*Computer science*]
MTU	Magnetometer Test Unit (ACAE)
MTU	Maintenance Training Unit
MTU	malignant Teratoma Undifferentiated [*Oncology*] (DAVI)
MTU	Managed Municipal Portfolio II [*NYSE symbol*] (SPSG)
MTU	Managed Muni Portfolio II [*NYSE symbol*] (TTSB)
MTU	Manchester Terminal Unit (NITA)
MTU	Master Terminal Unit [*Instrumentation*]
MTU	Master Time Unit
MTU	Master Timing Unit [*Aerospace*] (NAKS)
MTU	Master Trigger Unit (IAA)
MTU	Maximum Transmission Unit [*Computer science*] (IGQR)
MTU	Medical Therapy Unit (DMAA)
MTU	Memory Transfer Unit (NITA)
MTU	Methylthiouracil [*Pharmacology*]
MTU	Metric Tons of Uranium
MTU	Metric Ton Unit
MTU	Metric Units (DFIT)
MTU	Michigan Technological University [*Houghton*]
MTU	Microwave Transmission Unit (ACAE)
MTU	MIRA [*Multifunctional Inertial Reference Assembly*] Transport Unit [*Air Force*] (MCD)
MTU	Missile Tracking Unit (MCD)
MTU	Missile Training Unit [*Air Force*]
MTU	Mist Therapy Unit [*Medicine*]
MTU	Mobile Technical Unit (MCD)
MTU	Mobile Test Unit [*Army*] (RDA)
MTU	Mobile Training Unit
MTU	Mobile Treatment Unit [*Environmental Protection Agency*] (GFGA)
MTU	Module Test Unit [*Nuclear energy*] (NRCH)
mtu	Montana [*MARC country of publication code*] [*Library of Congress*] (LCCP)
MTU	Montreal Trustco, Inc. [*Toronto Stock Exchange symbol*]
MTU	Mosquito Training Unit [*British military*] (DMA)
MTU	Motorinen Turbo-Union [*Germany*]
MTU	Multiplexer and Terminal Unit
MTU	Multiterminal Unit (TEL)
MTU	Myton, UT [*Location identifier*] [*FAA*] (FAAL)
MtU	University of Montana at Missoula, Missoula, MT [*Library symbol*] [*Library of Congress*] (LCLS)
M TUBERC	Mycobacterium Tuberculosis [*Bacteriology*] (CPH)
MtU-L	University of Montana at Missoula, Law School, Missoula, MT [*Library symbol*] [*Library of Congress*] (LCLS)
MTUMR	MIRA [*Multifunctional Inertial Reference Assembly*] Transport Unit MountingRack [*Air Force*] (MCD)
MTUOP	Mobile Training Units Out for Parts
MTUR	Mean Time between Unscheduled Removals [*or Replacements*] [*Quality control*] (IIA)
MTUR	Mean Time to Unscheduled Replacement [*Quality control*] (PDAA)
MTV	Conference des Ministres Europeens du Travail [*Conference of European Ministers of Labour*] (EAIO)
MTV	Mammary Tumor Virus
MTV	Management Television [*Air Force*] (AFM)
MTV	Maneuvering Technology Vehicle
MTV	Manifold Tuning Valve [*Automotive engineering*]
MTV	Marginal Terrain Vehicle
MTV	Martinsville, VA [*Location identifier*] [*FAA*] (FAAL)
M TV	Master of Television
MTV	Mean Transformed Value
MTV	Media Transforming Virus [*Alleged virus causing immunodeficiency disease*]
MTV	Medium Tactical Vehicle [*Army*] (RDA)
MTV	Metatarsus Varus [*Anatomy*] (DAVI)
MTV	Miniature Test Vehicle (ACAE)
MTV	Missile Test Vehicle
MTV	Missile Training Vehicle
MTV	Mobile Test Vehicle (SAUS)
MTV	Modulated Throttle Valve [*Automotive engineering*]
MTV	Molecular Tagging Velocimetry
MTV	Mota Lava [*Vanuatu*] [*Airport symbol*] (OAG)
MTV	Motor Test Vehicle (IAA)
MTV	Motor Torpedo Vessel [*British*]
MTV	Motor Transport Volunteers [*Military unit*] [*British*]
MTV	Mountain Valley Air Service, Inc. [*ICAO designator*] (FAAC)
MTV	Mount Tassie [*Australia*] [*Seismograph station code, US Geological Survey*] [*Closed*] (SEIS)
MTV	Mouse Mammary Tumor Virus (DMAA)
MTV	Multicultural Television (ADA)
MTV	Munitions Tow Vehicle (MCD)
MTV	Munition Test Vehicle
MTV	Music Television [*Warner Amex Satellite Entertainment Co.*] [*Cable-television system*]
MTV	Mutatur Terminatio Versiculi [*The Termination of the Little Verse Is Changed*]
MTVAL	Master Tape Validation
MTVC	Main Thrust Vector Control (SAUS)
MTVC	Manned [*or Manual*] Thrust Vector Control (MCD)
MTVP	Moving Target Video Processor
MTVS	Mission Test and Video System
MTVT	Medium Tactical Vehicle Trailer (SAUS)
MTVU	Module Thruster Valve Unit
MTW	Machine Tool Wire
MTW	Main Trawl Winch
MTW	Manitowoc [*Wisconsin*] [*Airport symbol*] (OAG)
MTW	Manitowoc Co. [*NYSE symbol*] (SPSG)
MTW	Marinette, Tomahawk & Western Railroad Co. [*AAR code*]
MTW	Maximum Taxi Weight [*Aviation*]
MTW	Mean Tumor Weight [*Medicine*] (DB)
MTW	Military Transport Wagon [*British*]
MTW	Mission to the World (EA)
MTW	Mobile Training Wing [*Air Force*]
MTW	Mountain Waves (WEAT)
MTW	Music Treasures of the World [*Record label*]
mtw	Tropical Maritime Warm Air Mass [*Meteorology*] (BARN)
MtW	Wibaux Public Library, Wibaux, MT [*Library symbol*] [*Library of Congress*] (LCLS)
MTWA	Maximum Total Weight Authorized [*Aviation*] (AIA)
MTWC	Morgan Three-Wheeler Club (EA)
MTWF	Metal Thru-Wall Flashing [*Technical drawings*]
MtWfSH	Whitefish Senior High School, Whitefish, MT [*Library symbol*] [*Library of Congress*] (LCLS)
MTWLW	Manufacturer's Treadwear Limited Warranty [*Tire marketing*]
MTWN	Mark Twain Bancshares, Inc. [*NASDAQ symbol*] (NQ)

MTWN	Mark Twain Bancshrs [*NASDAQ symbol*] (TTSB)
MTWO	Material Test Work Order (SAA)
MTWO	Melamine Chemicals [*NASDAQ symbol*] (TTSB)
MTWO	Melamine Chemicals, Inc. [*NASDAQ symbol*] (NQ)
M-T WP	Medium-Term Work Programme (SAUS)
MTWP	Multiplier Traveling Wave Phototube (IAA)
MtWp	Roosevelt County Library, Wolf Point, MT [*Library symbol*] [*Library of Congress*] (LCLS)
MTWR	Micro-Thrust Water Rocket (ACAE)
MTWS	MAGTF [*Marine Air-Ground Task Force*] Tactical Warfare Simulation [*DoD*]
MTWS	Manual Track While Scan
MtWs	Montana State Hospital, Patient Library, Warm Springs, MT [*Library symbol*] [*Library of Congress*] (LCLS)
MTWV	Metawave Communications [*NASDAQ symbol*] (SG)
MTWX	Mechanized Teletypewriter Exchange (TEL)
MTWY	Motorway [*Postal Service standard*] (OPSA)
MTX	Fairbanks [*Alaska*] Metro Field [*Airport symbol*] [*Obsolete*] (OAG)
MTX	Manual Transaxle
MTX	Manual Transmission
MTX	Master of Taxation
MTX	Matrix (IAA)
MTX	Message Text Format (COE)
MTX	Methotrexate [*Antineoplastic drug*]
MTX	Microwave TOKAMAK [*Toroidal Kamera Magnetic*] Experiment [*Plasma physics*]
MTX	Military Traffic Expediting Service (AABC)
MTX	Minerals Technologies [*NYSE symbol*] (SPSG)
MTX	Mobile Telephone Exchange (CGWS)
MTX	Morrell Tank Line [*AAR code*]
MTX	Multi-Tasking Executive [*Computer science*] (VLIE)
MTX	Multi-Terminal Executive [*Computer science*] (VLIE)
MTXC	Matrix Capital Corp. [*NASDAQ symbol*] (SAG)
MTX-CF	Methotrexate with Citrovorum Factor Rescue [*Antineoplastic drug regimen*]
MTX + MP	Methotrexate and Mercaptopurine [*Antineoplastic drug regimen*] (DAVI)
MTX + MP + CTX	Methotrexate, Mercaptopurine, and Cytoxan [*Cyclophosphamide*] [*Antineoplastic drug regimen*] (DAVI)
MTY	Empty
MTY	Marlton Technologies [*AMEX symbol*] (TTSB)
MTY	Marlton Technologies, Inc. [*AMEX symbol*] (SPSG)
MTY	Matsuyama [*Japan*] [*Seismograph station code, US Geological Survey*] (SEIS)
Mty	Maturity (EBF)
MTY	Maturity [*Business term*]
MTY	Mekhon ha-Tekanim ha-Yisre'eli (BJA)
MTY	Million Tons per Year
MTY	Monterrey [*Mexico*] [*Airport symbol*] (OAG)
mtydm	Martyrdom (VRA)
MTZ	Mass Transfer Zone [*Chemical engineering*]
MTZ	MasTec, Inc. [*NYSE symbol*] (SG)
MTZ	Montezuma [*Chile*] [*Seismograph station code, US Geological Survey*] [*Closed*] (SEIS)
MTZ	Motorized (AAG)
MTZ	Tuskegee, AL [*Location identifier*] [*FAA*] (FAAL)
MU	Akaflieg Muenchen Mitsubishi Heavy Industries [*Germany*] [*Japan*] [*ICAO aircraft manufacturer identifier*] (ICAO)
MU	China Eastern Airlines [*ICAO designator*] (AD)
Mu	Mache Unit [*Measure of radium emanation from solutions*] (AAMN)
MU	Machine Unit
MU	Mail Unit (KSC)
MU	Maintenance Unit [*Military*]
MU	Makeup (NRCH)
MU	Management Unit [*Aviation*]
MU	Maneuvering Unit (KSC)
mu	Map Unit (DOG)
MU	Marginal Utility [*Economics*]
MU	Markup
MU	Marvel Universe
MU	Mass Units
mu	Master Unit (NAKS)
MU	Master Unit (NASA)
mu	Mauritania [*MARC country of publication code*] [*Library of Congress*] (LCCP)
MU	Mauritius [*ANSI two-letter standard code*] (CNC)
MU	Measurement Unit
MU	Memory Unit [*Computer science*] (MCD)
MU	Mental Units of Growth [*Psychology*]
MU	Mescaline Unit (DB)
MU	Message Unit [*Telecommunications*]
MU	Methylene Unit
MU	Methylumbelliferone [*Biochemistry*]
MU	Methylurea [*Organic chemistry*]
MU	Micro [*One millionth*] (WDAA)
mu	Micron [*Micrometer*] (AAMN)
MU	Micron Technology, Inc. [*NYSE symbol*] (SPSG)
MU	Microwave Unit (CARB)
MU	Midcourse Update (ACAE)
mu	Millimicro- [*Now nano*] (IDOE)
Mu	Millimicron (AAG)
mu	Millimicron [*Nanometer*] (IDOE)
MU	Million Units
mU	Milliunit (AAMN)
MU	Misrair [*ICAO designator*] (AD)

MU	Missing Upper (VLIE)
mu	Mobile Unit (NAKS)
MU	Mobile Unit
MU	Mock-Up (AAG)
mu	Mockup (NAKS)
MU	Modular Unit (IAA)
MU	Monetary Unit (ADA)
M/U	Monitor Unit [*Telecommunications*] (TEL)
MU	Montevideo Units [*Of uterine activity*]
MU	Mothers' Union [*Episcopalian*]
MU	Motor Union
MU	Motor Unit
MU	Mouse Unit [*Medicine*] (DMAA)
mu	Mouse Unit (LDT)
MU	Mueller Cell [*Eye anatomy*]
MU	Mulching [*Environmental science*] (COE)
MU	Multidestination [*Carrier*]
mu	Multiple Unit (NAKS)
MU	Multiple Unit
MU	Multiple Use (IAA)
MU	Multiplexing Unit
MU	Multi-Unit (SAUS)
mu	Multiuser [*Computer science*] (ELAL)
MU	Munitions Command [*Later, Armaments Command*] [*Army*] (MCD)
Mu	Muscle [*Anatomy*] (DAVI)
MU	Musical Union [*Oberlin College*] [*Ohio*]
MU	Musician [*Navy rating*]
MU	Musicians' Union [*British*] (DCTA)
MU	Music Program [*Association of Independent Colleges and Schools specialization code*]
MU	Muster [*Business term*] (DCTA)
Mu	Mutator [*A bacteriophage*]
MU	University of Massachusetts, Amherst, MA [*Library symbol*] [*Library of Congress*] (LCLS)
MU1	Musician, First Class [*Navy rating*]
MU2	Musician, Second Class [*Navy rating*]
MU3	Musician, Third Class [*Navy rating*]
MUA	Machinery Users' Association [*British*] (BI)
MUA	Mail User Agent [*Computer science*] (DCDG)
MUA	Mail Users' Association [*British*]
MUA	Manipulation Under Anesthesia [*Medicine*] (DMAA)
MUA	Manned Undersea [*or Underwater*] Activity [*Marine science*]
MUA	Maritime Union of Australia
MUA	Master of Urban Affairs (GAGS)
MUA	Master of Urban Architecture (GAGS)
MUA	Materials Usage Agreement (NASA)
MUA	Material Utilization Agreement (SAUS)
MUA	Maximum Usable Altitude [*Aviation*]
MUA	Memorandum of Understanding and Agreement
MUA	Metallurgistes Unis d'Amerique [*United Steelworkers of America - USWA*]
MU A	Microampere (WDAA)
MUA	Middle Uterine Artery [*Medicine*] (DMAA)
MUA	Military Utility Assessment
MUA	Ministry of State for Urban Affairs [*Canada*]
MUA	Mixed Underachievers [*Education*]
MUA	Monotype Users' Association (NADA)
MUA	Mothers' Union in Australia
MUA	Motor Unit Activity (DMAA)
MUA	Multiple Unit Activity [*Neurophysiology*]
MUA	Munda [*Solomon Islands*] [*Airport symbol*] (OAG)
MUA	Muniassets Fund [*NYSE symbol*] (SPSG)
MUA	Murray Aviation, Inc. [*ICAO designator*] (FAAC)
MUAA	Major Unit Assembly Area (MCD)
MUAC	Mid Upper Arm Circumference [*Anatomy*]
MUACS	Manpower Utilization and Control System
MUADEE	[*The*] Mars Upper Atmosphere Dynamics, Energetics and Evolution Spacecraft [*NASA*] (ECON)
MUAG	Central Agramonte [*Cuba*] [*ICAO location identifier*] (ICLI)
MU/AG	Mid-Upper [*Turret*] Air Gunner [*British military*] (DMA)
MU & P	Makeup and Purification [*Nuclear energy*] (NRCH)
MUAP	Motor Unit Action Potential [*Physiology*]
MUARC	Monash University Accident Research Center [*Australia*]
MUART	Microprocessor Universal Asynchronous Receiver Transmitter (IAA)
MUAT	Antilla [*Cuba*] [*ICAO location identifier*] (ICLI)
MUAT	Mobile Underwater Acoustic Unit (NATG)
MUB	Maun [*Botswana*] [*Airport symbol*] (OAG)
MUB	University of Maryland, Baltimore County Campus, Catonsville, MD [*OCLC symbol*] (OCLC)
MUBA	Baracoa/Oriente [*Cuba*] [*ICAO location identifier*] (ICLI)
MU BAR	Microbar (WDAA)
MUBE	El Caribe [*Cuba*] [*ICAO location identifier*] (ICLI)
MUBI	Cayo Mambi [*Cuba*] [*ICAO location identifier*] (ICLI)
MUBIS	Multiple Beam Interval Scanner
MUBO	Batabano [*Cuba*] [*ICAO location identifier*] (ICLI)
MUBR	Mean Units between Replacement [*Quality control*]
MUBUS	Microprocessor Bus [*Computer science*] (VLIE)
MUBY	Bayamo [*Cuba*] [*ICAO location identifier*] (ICLI)
MUC	Maximum Urinary Concentration [*Medicine*]
MUC	Meritorious Unit Citation [*Military decoration*]
MUC	Meritorious Unit Commendation [*Military decoration*] (AFM)
MUC	Missionary Union of the Clergy [*British*] (BI)
MUC	Mount Union College [*Alliance, OH*]
MUC	Mucilaginous (ROG)
MUC	Mucosal Ulcerative Colitis [*Medicine*]

MUC............	Multicoupler
MUC............	Multiple Use Counter (IAA)
MUC............	Munich [Germany] [Airport symbol] (OAG)
MUC............	Musician, Chief [Navy rating]
MUCA	Ciego De Avila [Cuba] [ICAO location identifier] (ICLI)
MuCA2	Muniyield California Insured Fund II [Associated Press] (SAG)
MuCAIns	MuniYield California Insured Fund [Associated Press] (SAG)
MUCB	Caibarien [Cuba] [ICAO location identifier] (ICLI)
MUCC	Cunagua [Cuba] [ICAO location identifier] (ICLI)
MUCC	Michigan United Conservation Clubs
MUCF..........	Cienfuegos [Cuba] [ICAO location identifier] (ICLI)
MUCG	Macquarie University Caving Group [Australia]
MUCG	Management/Union Consultative Group [Australia]
Much D & S...	Muchall's Doctor and Student [A publication] (DLA)
MUCHFET	Multichannel Field Effect Transistor (IAA)
MUCIA	Midwest Universities Consortium for International Activities [University of Indiana]
MUCILAG	Mucilaginous (ROG)
MUCK	Multi-User Chat Kingdom (SAUS)
MUCL..........	Cayo Largo Del Sur [Cuba] [ICAO location identifier] (ICLI)
MUCL..........	Mycological Collection of the UCL (SAUS)
MUCM	Camaguey/Ignacio Agramonte [Cuba] [ICAO location identifier] (ICLI)
MUCM	Musician, Master Chief [Navy rating]
MUCN	Ciego De Avila Norte [Cuba] [ICAO location identifier] (ICLI)
MUCO	Colon [Cuba] [ICAO location identifier] (ICLI)
MUCO	Materiel Utilization Control Office (AFIT)
MUCOM	Munitions Command [Later, Armaments Command] [Army]
Mu Corp Ca...	Municipal Corporation Cases [United States] [A publication] (DLA)
Mu Corp Cir...	Municipal Corporation Circular [England] [A publication] (DLA)
MUCROMAF...	Multiple Critical Root Maximally Flat (PDAA)
MUCS	Central Noel Fernandez [Cuba] [ICAO location identifier] (ICLI)
MUCS	Musician, Senior Chief [Navy rating]
MUCU	Santiago De Cuba/Antonio Maceo [Cuba] [ICAO location identifier] (ICLI)
MUCUSA......	Missionary Union of the Clergy in the United States of America [Later, PMUPR] (EA)
MUCV	Las Clavellinas [Cuba] [ICAO location identifier] (ICLI)
MUCY	Cayajabo [Cuba] [ICAO location identifier] (ICLI)
MUD	Macromind Utility Disk
MUD	Master of Urban Design (GAGS)
MUD	Master User Directory (MHDI)
MUD	Matched Unrelated Donor [Medicine] (MELL)
MUD	Memory Unit Drum [Computer science]
MUD	Mercaptoundecanol [Organic chemistry]
MUD	Middle, Up, Down [in game of bridge]
MUD	Minimum Urticarial Dose [Medicine] (DMAA)
MUD	Mouvement pour l'Unite et la Democratie [Djibouti] [Political party] (EY)
MUD	Mouvement Union Democratique [Democratic Union Movement] [Monaco] [Political party] (PPE)
MUD	Multiple User Dimension [Computer science]
MUD	Multiple-User Domain (SAUS)
MUD	Multiple User Dungeon [Computer science]
MUD	Multi-User Device (ABAC)
MUD	Multiuser Dialogue [Computer science] (IGQR)
MUD	Multi-User Domain [Computer science]
MUD	Multi-User Dungeon [Computer game]
MUD	Municipal Utility District [Investment term] (DFIT)
MUD	Murchison Falls [Uganda] [Airport symbol] (AD)
MUDAID.......	Multivariate, Univariate, and Discriminant Analysis of Irregular Data [Statistics] (IAA)
MUDAR........	Mulheres por um Desenvolvimento Alternativo [Development Alternatives with women for a New Era - DAWN] [Brazil] (EAIO)
MUDAS........	Modular Universal Data Acquisition System (SAUS)
MUDD	Multisource Unified Data Distribution (PDAA)
MUDDC........	Multiunit Direct Digital Control (IAA)
MUDET	Militarized Universal Digital Element Tester (MCD)
MUDL	Microwave Ultrasonic Delay Line
MUDPAC	Modular Unit Deployable Package (SAUS)
MUDPIE	Museum and University Data Processing Information Exchange (IAA)
MUDR.........	Multidetail Drawing (MSA)
MUDS	Multiple Usage Data Sheet (MCD)
MUDSS	Mobile Underwater Debris Survey System
Mudst	Mudstone Soil [Agronomy]
MUDWNT......	Makeup Demineralizer Waste Neutralizer Tank (IEEE)
MUE...........	Kamuela [Hawaii] [Airport symbol] (OAG)
MUE...........	Medication Use Evaluated (MELL)
MUE...........	Meritorious Unit Emblem [Military decoration]
MUE...........	Microcomputer Users in Education (AIE)
MUE...........	Motor Unit Estimate (DB)
MUE...........	Motor Unit Estimated (DMAA)
MUEI..........	Micron Electronics, Inc. [NASDAQ symbol] (SAG)
MUEI..........	Micron Electronics [NASDAQ symbol] (TTSB)
MUEL	Mueller [Paul] Co. [NASDAQ symbol] (NQ)
Mueller........	Mueller Industries [Associated Press] (SAG)
MuellerInd...	Muller Industries [Associated Press] (SAG)
MuellerP......	Mueller [Paul] Co. [Associated Press] (SAG)
MUERI.........	Murdoch University Energy Research Institute [Australia]
MUEW	eW MonopolUEbertragungsWeg (SAUS)
MUEXEC......	Multi-User Executive [Computer science] (VLIE)
MUF..........	Makeup Feed [Boiler]
MUF...........	Marksmanship Under Fire (SAUS)
MUF...........	Material Unaccounted For [Nuclear energy]
MUF...........	Maximum Usable Frequency [Signal transmission]
MU F	Microfarad (WDAA)

MUF...........	Muffler
MUF...........	Muting [Indonesia] [Airport symbol] (OAG)
MuFAR........	Multi-target Field Artillery Radar (SAUS)
MUFC.........	Central Amancio Rodriguez [Cuba] [ICAO location identifier] (ICLI)
MUFD.........	Makeup Feed [Boiler]
MUFFIN	Multi-Use Interagency News [FSS database] (AAGC)
MUFFLIR	Multi-Function Forward Looking Infrared (ACAE)
MUFFS........	Multiple Frequency Firing System (ACAE)
MUFL.........	Florida [Cuba] [ICAO location identifier] (ICLI)
MuFLIn	MuniYield Florida Insured Fund [Associated Press] (SAG)
MUFLNG	Mouvement pour l'Unification des Forces de Liberation de la Guadeloupe [Movement for the Unification of National Liberation Forces of Guadeloupe] [Political party] (PD)
MUFLR	Muffler
MUFM........	Mouvement Universal pour une Federation Mondiale [World Association of World Federalists - WAWF] [Netherlands]
MUFON........	Mutual UFO [Unidentified Flying Object] Network (EA)
MUFON........	Mutual UFO Network, Inc.
MUFT.........	Multigroup Fourier Transform [Code] [Nuclear energy] (NRCH)
MUFTI.........	Minimum Use of Force Tactical Intervention [British police]
MUG	Macintosh User Group [Computer science] (WDMC)
MUG	Make-Up Gas [Chemical engineering]
MUG	Manning Unit Group [Air Force] (AFM)
MUG	Marcive Users Group [Library network]
MUG	MARC Users Group (NITA)
MUG	Maximum Unilateral Gain (IAA)
MUG	Maximum Usable Gain [Bell System]
MUG	Methylumbelliferylglucuronide [Biochemistry]
MUG	Microcomputer User's Group (ACAE)
MU G	Microgram (WDAA)
MUG	Ministry of Useless Gestures [Organization to increase number of voters] [British]
MUG	Mitosis with Unreplicated Genome [Cytology]
MUG	Mulege [Mexico] [Airport symbol] [Obsolete] (OAG)
MUG	Multiset Users Group (EA)
MUG	MUMPS [Massachusetts General Hospital Utility Multiprogramming System] Users' Group (EA)
MUG	Murgor Resources, Inc. [Vancouver Stock Exchange symbol]
MUGA	Multigated Angiogram [Cardiology] (DAVI)
MUGA	Multiple Gate Acquisition Analysis [Scan] (DAVI)
MUGA	Multiple-Gated Acquisition [Nuclear medicine]
MU-GAL.......	Methylumbelliferyl-B-Galactosidase [Biochemistry] (MAE)
MUGA scan...	Multiple-Gated Arteriography Scan [Medicine] (WDAA)
MUGB.........	Methylumbelliferyl Guanidinobenzoate [Biochemistry]
MUGD.........	MUMPS User Group Deutschland (SAUS)
MUGEx........	Multigated Blood Pool Image during Exercise [Hematology] (DMAA)
MUGM	Guantanamo, US Naval Air Base [Cuba] [ICAO location identifier] (ICLI)
MUGN	Giron [Cuba] [ICAO location identifier] (ICLI)
MUGR	Multigated Blood Pool Image at Rest [Medicine] (DMAA)
MUGSE	Multimission-Unique Ground Support Equipment (MCD)
MUGT	Guantanamo [Cuba] [ICAO location identifier] (ICLI)
MUGX.........	Multiple Gated Acquisition Exercise [Scan] [Cardiology] (DAVI)
MUH..........	Memorial University of Newfoundland, Health Sciences Library [UTLAS symbol]
MUH..........	Mersa Matruh [Egypt] [Airport symbol] (AD)
MU H	Microhenry (WDAA)
MUHA.........	Habana/Jose Marti [Cuba] [ICAO location identifier] (ICLI)
MUHG.........	Holguin [Cuba] [ICAO location identifier] (ICLI)
MUI...........	Fort Indiantown Gap (Annville), PA [Location identifier] [FAA] (FAAL)
MUI...........	Machine Utilization Index [Computer science]
MUI...........	Mashhad University [Iran] [Seismograph station code, US Geological Survey] (SEIS)
MUI...........	Mass Unbalance Input [Computer science]
MUI...........	Metals USA [NYSE symbol] (SG)
MUI...........	Mode-Independent Unnumbered Information
MUI...........	Monsoonal Upwelling Index [Paleoceanography]
MUI...........	Movement for the Unity of the Left [Ecuador] [Political party] (PPW)
MUI...........	Trans Air [FAA designator] (FAAC)
MUIFX	Nationwide Fund [Mutual fund ticker symbol] (SG)
MUIG	Minicomputer Users Interest Group [Later, Mini/Micro Special Interest Group] (EA)
MU IN	Microinch (WDAA)
MuInII.........	Muniyield Insured Fund [Associated Press] (SAG)
MUIR.........	Microinstruction Register (MHDI)
Muir Gai	Muirhea's Institutes of Gaius [A publication] (DLA)
MUIS	Isabella [Cuba] [ICAO location identifier] (ICLI)
MulT	Municipal Income Trust [Associated Press] (SAG)
MulT2	Municipal Income Trust II [Associated Press] (SAG)
MulT3	Municipal Income Trust III [Associated Press] (SAG)
MUJ..........	Mui [Ethiopia] [Airport symbol] (OAG)
MUJA.........	Majana [Cuba] [ICAO location identifier] (ICLI)
MUK..........	Alamogordo, NM [Location identifier] [FAA] (FAAL)
MUK..........	Mauke [Cook Islands] [Airport symbol] (OAG)
MUK..........	MEPC International Capital LP [NYSE symbol] (SAG)
MUK..........	Muk Air Taxi [Denmark] [ICAO designator] (FAAC)
MUK..........	Mukerian [India] [Seismograph station code, US Geological Survey] [Closed] (SEIS)
MUKPrA......	MEPC Intl Cap 9.125%'QUIPS' [NYSE symbol] (TTSB)
MUL..........	Manned Underwater Laboratories [Marine science] (MSC)
MUL..........	Manufacturing under Licence [British] (DS)
MUL..........	Master Urgency List [Navy]
MUL..........	Mobile-Moored Undersea Laboratory
MUL..........	Mobile User Link (SAUS)
MUL..........	Modify User Login (AAEL)

MUL............	Moultrie, GA [*Location identifier*] [*FAA*] (FAAL)
MUL............	Mullan [*Idaho*] [*Seismograph station code, US Geological Survey*] (SEIS)
MUL............	MULS [*Minnesota Union List of Serials*], Minneapolis, MN [*OCLC symbol*] (OCLC)
MUL............	Multicare Cos. [*NYSE symbol*] (TTSB)
mul............	Multilingual [*MARC language code*] [*Library of Congress*] (LCCP)
MUL............	Multiplexer
MUL............	Multiply (MDG)
MULASSS...	Multiple LASER Source Signature Simulator (MCD)
MULB............	Habana [*Cuba*] [*ICAO location identifier*] (ICLI)
MULDEM......	Multiplexer/Demultiplexer [*Bell Laboratories*]
MULDEX......	Multiplexer/Demultiplexer
MULDEX......	Multipoint Cross-Reference Index
MULE............	Manned-Unmanned Lunar Explorer
MULE............	Modular Universal LASER Equipment (MCD)
MULE............	Multilingual Enhancement of GNU EMACS (SAUS)
MULE............	Multiple-Use Linear Energizer [*Automotive engineering*]
MULE............	Multi-Use Lightsat Environment (SAUS)
MULH............	Habana [*Cuba*] [*ICAO location identifier*] (ICLI)
Mu LJ........	Municipal Law Journal [*A publication*] (DLA)
MULL............	Modern Uses of Logic in Law
MULL............	Mullion [*Technical drawings*]
MULM............	La Coloma [*Cuba*] [*ICAO location identifier*] (ICLI)
MuIMR........	Multi-Market Radio, Inc. [*Associated Press*] (SAG)
MuIMRad......	Multi-Market Radio, Inc. [*Associated Press*] (SAG)
MULO............	Multipurpose Lightweight Overboot [*Army*]
MULQUAL....	Multiple Goal Water Quality Model (PDAA)
MULR............	Malayan Union Law Reports [*1946-47*] [*A publication*] (ILCA)
MULR............	Muller
MULS............	Mobile Unit Launch Site (IAA)
MULSF............	Signed Multiplication [*Computer science*]
MULSF............	Macquarie University Law School Foundation [*Australia*]
MULSP........	Missouri Union List of Serial Publications [*St. Louis Public Library*] [*Missouri*] [*Information service or system*] (IID)
MULT............	Multiple
MULT............	Multiple Schedule of Reinforcement (DIPS)
MULT............	Multiply (NASA)
MULTA........	Multiple-Use Land Alliance (EA)
MULTACK....	Multiple Target Attack (ACAE)
MULTACK....	Multiple Target Attack System Integration and Simulation (ACAE)
MULTACKS...	Multi-Attack System (ACAE)
MULTAM......	Multiple Target Assessment Model (ACAE)
MultClr........	Multi-Color Corp. [*Associated Press*] (SAG)
MULTEWS ..	Multiple Electronics Warfare Surveillance [*DoD*]
MULTEWS ...	Multitarget Electronic Warfare System
MULTH........	Multilith
multi............	Multicolored [*Philately*]
MULTI............	Multiple (DAVI)
multi............	Multiple (ELAL)
MULTI............	Multiplexer
Multicne........	Multicare Companies [*Associated Press*] (SAG)
MULTICOR...	Multinational Finance Corp. [*Indonesia*] (EY)
MultiCp........	Multi-Corp, Inc. [*Associated Press*] (SAG)
Multicre........	Multicare Companies [*Associated Press*] (SAG)
MULTICS......	Multiplexed Information and Computing Service [*Honeywell, Inc.*]
MultiCul R...	MultiCultural Review [*A publication*] (BRI)
Multilink PPP...	Multichannel Connection Protocol Based on the Point-to-Point Protocol [*Computer science*]
Multilink PPP...	Multilink Point-to-Point Protocol [*Computer science*]
MultiMC......	MultiMedia Concepts International, Inc. [*Associated Press*] (SAG)
MultiMed....	MultiMedia Concepts International, Inc. [*Associated Press*] (SAG)
MULTIMED...	Multimedia Exposure Assessment Model [*Environmental Protection Agency*] (AEPA)
multip............	Multiparous [*Obstetrics*]
MULTIPAC...	Multiple Pool Processor and Computer (PDAA)
MULTIPLE....	Multipurpose Program that Learns [*Computer science*] (PDAA)
MULTI-SDF...	Multiple Signal Direction Finder (ACAE)
MULTIV........	Multivibrator (IAA)
multivits......	Multivitamins [*Pharmacy*]
MultM........	Multi-Market Radio, Inc. [*Associated Press*] (SAG)
MultMC......	MultiMedia Concepts International, Inc. [*Associated Press*] (SAG)
Multmd........	Multimedia Concepts International, Inc. [*Associated Press*] (SAG)
MultMT........	Multi-Media Tutorial Services, Inc. [*Associated Press*] (SAG)
MULTOS......	Multimedia Office Server (SAUS)
MULTOTS...	Multiple Units Link 11 Test and Operational Training System [*Navy*] (NVT)
MULTP........	Multiplier (NITA)
MultPb........	Multicom Publishing [*Associated Press*] (SAG)
MULTR........	Multimeter (AAG)
MULTR........	Multiplier
MULTS........	Mobile Universal Link 11 Translator System (SAUS)
MultZns	Multiple Zones International, Inc. [*Associated Press*] (SAG)
MULU............	Unsigned Multiplication [*Computer science*]
MuLv............	Murine Leukemia Virus [*Medicine*] (DB)
MuLV............	Murine Leukemia Virus [*Also, MLV*]
Mum............	Chrysanthemum [*Horticulture*]
MUM............	Mass Memory Unit Manager (SAUS)
MUM............	Maximum Useful Magnification (MCD)
MUM............	Method of Unweighted Means [*Statistics*]
MUM............	Methodology for Unmanned Manufacture [*Robotics project*] [*Japan*]
MUM............	Multiple Unit Message [*Telecommunications*] (IEEE)
MUM............	Multiuse Manuscript
MUM............	Multiuse Mnemonics (IAA)
MUM............	Multi-User Message (NITA)
MUM............	Multiuser Monitor
MUM............	Mumias [*Kenya*] [*Airport symbol*] [*Obsolete*] (OAG)
MUM............	University of Mississippi, University, MS [*OCLC symbol*] (OCLC)
MU M²	Square Micrometer (WDAA)
MU M³	Cubic Micrometer (WDAA)
MUMA............	Punta De Maisi [*Cuba*] [*ICAO location identifier*] (ICLI)
MUMAD......	Museum Angkatan Darat [*Indonesia*]
Mumf............	Mumford's Jamaica Reports [*A publication*] (DLA)
MUMG	Managua [*Cuba*] [*ICAO location identifier*] (ICLI)
MUMH	Matahambre [*Cuba*] [*ICAO location identifier*] (ICLI)
MUMI............	Manzanillo [*Cuba*] [*ICAO location identifier*] (ICLI)
MUMJ............	Mayajigua [*Cuba*] [*ICAO location identifier*] (ICLI)
Mum Jam	Mumford's Jamaica Reports [*A publication*] (DLA)
MUMLIB	Multimedia Technology in Libraries (TELE)
MUMM............	Management Unit of the Mathematical Model of the North Sea and Scheldt Estuary (SAUS)
MUMMERS...	Manned-Unmanned Environmental Research Station (MSC)
MUMMS	Marine Corps Unified Materiel Management System
Mummy	Mature Upwardly Mobile Mommy [*Lifestyle classification*]
MUMO	Moa [*Cuba*] [*ICAO location identifier*] (ICLI)
MUMP	Marshall - University of Michigan Probe [*Rocket flight*]
MUMPS	Massachusetts General Hospital Utility Multiprogramming System [*Programming language*]
MUMPS	Multiple-Unit, Moving-Projectile System (MCD)
MUMS	Mobile Utility Module System (IEEE)
MUMS	Modular Underwater Measurement System (SAUS)
MUMS	Mothers United for Moral Support
MUMS	Multiple Unguided Mine System (MCD)
MUMS	Multiple-Use MARC [*Machine-Readable Cataloging*] System [*Online retrieval system*] [*Information service or system*] [*Library of Congress*]
MUMSU	Monash University Malaysian Students' Union [*Australia*]
MUMT	Matanzas [*Cuba*] [*ICAO location identifier*] (ICLI)
MuMTV	Murine Mammary Tumor Virus
MUMZ..........	Manzanillo [*Cuba*] [*ICAO location identifier*] (ICLI)
MUN	Aeromundo Ejecutivo, SA de CV [*Mexico*] [*FAA designator*] (FAAC)
MUN	Maturin [*Venezuela*] [*Airport symbol*] (OAG)
MUN	Memorial University of Newfoundland [*Marine science*] (MSC)
MUN	Memorial University of Newfoundland Library [*UTLAS symbol*]
MUN	Mundaring [*Australia*] [*Seismograph station code, US Geological Survey*] (SEIS)
Mun	Munford's Reports [*15-20 Virginia*] [*A publication*] (DLA)
mun	Municipal (SHCU)
Mun	Municipal (TBD)
MUN	Municipal
Mun	Municipal Law Reporter [*A publication*] (DLA)
MUN	Munitions (AFM)
Mun	Munitions Appeals Reports [*England*] [*A publication*] (DLA)
MUN	Munsingwear, Inc. [*NYSE symbol*] (SPSG)
MUNA	La Cubana [*Cuba*] [*ICAO location identifier*] (ICLI)
MUNA	United Nations Association of Mauritius (EAIO)
MunAdv	Municipal Advantage Fund [*Associated Press*] (SAG)
MUNAF	Movimento de Unidade Nacional Antifascista [*National United Antifascist Movement*] [*Portugal*] [*Political party*] (PPE)
Mun & El Cas...	Municipal and Election Cases [*India*] [*A publication*] (DLA)
Mun App	Munitions Appeals Reports [*England*] [*A publication*] (DLA)
Mun App Rep...	Munitions Appeals Reports [*England*] [*A publication*] (DLA)
Mun App Sc...	Munitions of War Acts, Appeal Reports [*1916-20*] [*Scotland*] [*A publication*] (DLA)
MUNB	San Nicolas De Bari [*Cuba*] [*ICAO location identifier*] (ICLI)
MUNBG..........	Munitions Building [*Washington, DC*] [*Obsolete*]
MUNBLDG....	Munitions Building [*Obsolete*] [*Washington, DC*] (DNAB)
MUNC	Munitions Command [*Later, Armaments Command*] [*Army*]
MUNC	Nicaro [*Cuba*] [*ICAO location identifier*] (ICLI)
MunCA	MuniYield California Fund [*Associated Press*] (SAG)
Mun Corp Cas...	Municipal Corporation Cases [*A publication*] (DLA)
Mun Ct	Municipal Court (DLA)
Mun Ct App Dist Col...	Municipal Court of Appeals for the District of Columbia (DLA)
Mund	De Mundo [*of Aristotle*] [*Classical studies*] (OCD)
MUND	Model Urban Neighborhood Demonstration
Mundy	Abstracts of Star Chamber Proceedings [*1550-58*] [*A publication*] (DLA)
MUNE	Multiple Negative [*Circuit*] (AAG)
MUNEX	Munitions Allocation and Expenditure Tracking System (ACAE)
Munf	Munford's Reports [*15-20 Virginia*] [*A publication*] (DLA)
MunFL	MuniYield Florida Fund [*Associated Press*] (SAG)
MUNFLA	Memorial University of Newfoundland Folklore and Language Archive [*Research center*] [*Canada*] (RCD)
Munf (VA)....	Munford's Reports [*15-20 Virginia*] [*A publication*] (DLA)
MUNG	Mush until No Good [*Describes destruction of computer software*]
MUNG..........	Nueva Gerona [*Cuba*] [*ICAO location identifier*] (ICLI)
MUNGE........	Movimiento para la Unificacion Nacional de Guinea Ecuatorial [*Movement for National Unification of Equatorial Guinea*] [*Political party*] (EY)
Mung Pay	Munger on Application of Payments [*A publication*] (DLA)
MunHi..........	Municipal High Income Fund, Inc. [*Associated Press*] (SAG)
MUNI	Municipal (AFM)
Muni	Municipal (EBF)
muni	Municipal (ELAL)
muni	Municiple (SHCU)
Muniast	Muniassets Fund, Inc. [*Associated Press*] (SAG)
MUNIC..........	Municipal
Munic & PL...	Municipal and Parish Law Cases [*England*] [*A publication*] (DLA)
Munic LR (PA):.	Municipal Law Reporter [*Pennsylvania*] [*A publication*] (DLA)

MUNIDB...... Municipal Bonds Databank (NITA)
MuniFd...... MuniEnhanced Fund [Associated Press] (SAG)
MuniIn...... Muni Insured Fund, Inc. [Associated Press] (SAG)
MUNIMT...... Muniment (ROG)
MuniMtg...... Municipal Mortgage & Equity LLC [Associated Press] (SAG)
MunIns...... MuniYield Insured Fund [Associated Press] (SAG)
MUNIREP..... Munitions Report [Worldwide report of location and status of air munitions] [Military]
MUniv...... Master of the University
Muniv2...... Munivest Fund II [Associated Press] (SAG)
MuniYld...... MuniYield Fund, Inc. [Associated Press] (SAG)
MuNJIn...... MuniYield New Jersey Insured Fund [Associated Press] (SAG)
Munk Emp Liab... Munkman's Employer's Liability at Common Law [8th ed.] [1975] [A publication] (DLA)
Mun LJ...... Municipal Law Journal [A publication] (DLA)
Mun LR...... Municipal Law Reporter [Pennsylvania] [A publication] (DLA)
Mun LR...... Municipal Law Reports [1903-13] [Scotland] [A publication] (DLA)
Mun L Rep... Chrostwaite's Pennsylvania Municipal Law Reporter [A publication] (DLA)
MunMI...... MuniYield Michigan Fund [Associated Press] (SAG)
MunMIIn...... MuniYield Michigan Insured Fund [Associated Press] (SAG)
MunNJ...... MuniYield New Jersey Fund [Associated Press] (SAG)
MunNY...... MuniYield New York Insured Fund [Associated Press] (SAG)
MunPA...... MuniYield Pennsylvania Fund [Associated Press] (SAG)
MunPrt...... Municipal Partners Fund [Associated Press] (SAG)
MunPrt2...... Municipal Partners Fund 2 [Associated Press] (SAG)
MunQI2...... Muniyield Quality Fund II, Inc. [Associated Press] (SAG)
MunQlty...... MuniYield Quality Fund, Inc. [Associated Press] (SAG)
Mun Rep...... Municipal Reports [Canada] [A publication] (DLA)
Munsng...... Munsingwear, Inc. [Associated Press] (SAG)
MUNSS...... Munition Support Squadron
Mun Tort Lib... Municipal, School, and State Tort Liability [A publication] (DLA)
MUNU...... Central Brasil [Cuba] [ICAO location identifier] (ICLI)
Munvst...... MuniVest Fund, Inc. [Associated Press] (SAG)
MuNY2...... Muniyield New York Insured Fund II [Associated Press] (SAG)
MuNY3...... Muniyield New York Insured Fund III [Associated Press] (SAG)
MunyAZ...... Muniyield Arizona Fund II [Associated Press] (SAG)
MunyIAZ...... Muniyield Arizona Fund [Associated Press] (SAG)
MUO...... Maximum Undistorted Output
MUO...... Mountain Home, ID [Location identifier] [FAA] (FAAL)
MUO...... Municipal University of Omaha [Later, University of Nebraska at Omaha]
MUO...... Myocardiopathy of Unknown Origin [Cardiology]
MUO...... Pioneer Interest Shares [Formerly, Mutual of Omaha Interest Shares, Inc.] [NYSE symbol] (SPSG)
MUO...... Pioneer Interest Shs [NYSE symbol] (TTSB)
MUOD...... Mean Unplanned Outage Duration (IEEE)
MUON...... Mu-Meson [An elementary particle]
MUP...... Major Urinary Protein (DB)
MUP...... Make-Up Pay (MHDB)
MUP...... Manchester University Press [Manchester, England]
MUP...... Manufacturing-Use Product (EEVL)
MUP...... Master of Urban Planning
MUP...... Maximal Urethral Pressure [Medicine] (MELL)
MUP...... Metalworking under Pressure (PDAA)
MUP...... Modify User Password (AAEL)
MUP...... Molded Urea Plastics
MUP...... Motor Unit Potential
MUP...... Mouse Urine Protein [Biochemistry] (DAVI)
MUP...... Mouvement de l'Unite Populaire [Popular Unity Movement] [Tunisia] [Political party] (PD)
MUP...... Movimiento da Unidade Progressiva [Brazil] [Political party] (EY)
MUP...... Multiple Utility Peripheral (NITA)
MUPA...... Punta Alegre [Cuba] [ICAO location identifier] (ICLI)
MUPAD...... Multi Processing Algebra Data (SAUS)
MuPAIns...... MuniVest Pennsylvania Insured Fund [Associated Press] (SAG)
MUPB...... Baracoa Playa/Habana [Cuba] [ICAO location identifier] (ICLI)
MUPDD...... Master of Urban Planning, Design, and Development (PGP)
MUPEJARS... Multiple Peanut-Butter Jars [Unconventional musical instrument used in performance by the "Music for Homemade Instruments" ensemble]
MUPF...... Modified Ultrapherical Polynominal Filter (IAA)
MUPID...... Multiple Universally Programmable Intelligent Decoder [Telecommunications] (TSSD)
MUPID...... Multi-Purpose Universal Programmable Intelligent Decoder (NITA)
MuPIT...... Municipal Premier Income Trust [Associated Press] (SAG)
MUPL...... Military Urgency Planning List (NG)
MUPL...... Mock-Up Planning
MUPL...... Pilon [Cuba] [ICAO location identifier] (ICLI)
MUPO...... Maximum Undistorted Power Output
MUPO...... Multiple Positive [Circuit] (AAG)
MUPP...... Master of Urban Planning and Policy (GAGS)
MUPPATS... Multiparticle Position- and Time- Sensitive Detector
MUPPET...... Marionette and Puppet
Muppie...... Mennonite Urban Professional [Lifestyle classification]
Muppie...... Middle-Aged Urban Pinhead [Lifestyle classification]
Muppie...... Middle-Aged Urban Professional [Lifestyle classification]
Muppy...... Male Urban Professional [Lifestyle classification]
MUPR...... Pinar Del Rio [Cuba] [ICAO location identifier] (ICLI)
MUPROF...... Multiple Projected Fibonacci [Microwave circuit]
MUPS...... Central Guatemala [Cuba] [ICAO location identifier] (ICLI)
MUPS...... Manpower Utilisation and Payment Structure [Imperial Chemical Industries] [British]
MUPS...... Mechanized Unit Property System [Telecommunications] (TEL)
MUPS...... Metastases with Unknown Primary Site [Medicine] (MELL)

MUPS...... Minimum Universal Pension System [Proposed to reform pension coverage]
MUPS...... Multiple Utility Peripheral System [Computer science]
MUPT...... Patria [Cuba] [ICAO location identifier] (ICLI)
MuPV...... Murine Polyomavirus [Medicine]
MUR...... Aerolinea Muri [Mexico] [ICAO designator] (FAAC)
MUR...... Management Update and Retrieval System (NRCH)
MUR...... Manpower Utilization Report (MCD)
MUR...... Marudi [Malaysia] [Airport symbol] (OAG)
MUR...... Mock-Up Reactor [NASA]
MUR...... Montana Utilities Reports [A publication] (DLA)
MUR...... Movimiento de Unidad Revolucionaria [Guerrilla forces] [Honduras] (EY)
mur...... Mural (VRA)
Mur...... Muramic Acid [Also, MurA] [Biochemistry]
MUR...... Murder [FBI standardized term]
MUR...... Murgab [Former USSR] [Seismograph station code, US Geological Survey] [Closed] (SEIS)
Mur...... Murlyn [Record label]
Mur...... Murphey's Reports [5-7 North Carolina] [A publication] (DLA)
MUR...... Murphy Oil [NYSE symbol] (TTSB)
MUR...... Murphy Oil Corp. [NYSE symbol] (SPSG)
Mur...... Murray's Ceylon Reports [A publication] (DLA)
Mur...... Murray's Jury Court Cases [1815-30] [Scotland] [A publication] (DLA)
MUR...... Mustang Resources, Inc. [Vancouver Stock Exchange symbol]
Mur...... Pro Murena [of Cicero] [Classical studies] (OCD)
MUR...... Radio Relay Message Unit [Telecommunications] (TEL)
MURA...... Midwestern Universities Research Association
MurA...... Muramic Acid [Also, Mur] [Biochemistry]
Mur & H...... Murphy and Hurlstone's English Exchequer Reports [1836-37] [A publication] (DLA)
Mur & Hurl... Murphy and Hurlstone's English Exchequer Reports [1836-37] [A publication] (DLA)
MURAT...... Munitions a Risques Atenues (SAUS)
Murat Antiq Med Aevi... Muratori's Antiquitates Medii Aevi [A publication] (DLA)
MURATREC... Multi-RADAR Track Reconstitution [Aviation] (DA)
MURB...... Multiple Unit Residential Building [Canada]
MUrbDes(Arch)... Master of Urban Design
MUrbRegPlg... Master of Urban and Regional Planning
MURC...... Measurable Undesirable Respiratory Contaminants [Pollution index] [Superseded by PSI]
MURC...... Murdock Communications Corp. [NASDAQ symbol] (SAG)
MURCO...... Murphy Oil Corp. (EFIS)
MURD...... Multi-Use Ranger/Designator (ACAE)
MURD...... Murder (ROG)
Murdck...... Murdock Communications Corp. [Associated Press] (SAG)
Murd Epit..... Murdoch's Epitome Canada [A publication] (DLA)
MURDER...... Murray basin Disposal by Evaporation Resource (SAUS)
Murdock...... Murdock Communications Corp. [Associated Press] (SAG)
MURF...... Material Utilization Reference File [Military]
MURFAAM... Mutual Reduction of Forces and Armaments and Associated Measures
MURFAAMCE... Mutual Reduction of Forces and Armaments and Associated Measures in Central Europe
Murfree Off Bonds... Murfree on Official Bonds [A publication] (DLA)
MURG...... Machine Utilization Report Generator
MURI...... Mild Upper Respiratory Illness [Virus] [Obsolete usage]
MURIEL...... Multimedia Remote Interactive Electronic Documents (TELE)
MURL...... Major Urban Resource Library [Department of Education] (GFGA)
MURL...... Mock-Up Release
MurNAc...... N-Acetylmuramate [Laboratory science] (DAVI)
MURP...... Manned Upperstage Reusable Payload
MURP...... Master of Urban and Regional Planning
MURP...... Master of Urban and Rural Planning (GAGS)
Murp & H.... Murphy and Hurlstone's English Exchequer Reports [1836-37] [A publication] (ILCA)
Murph...... Murphey's Reports [5-7 North Carolina] [A publication] (DLA)
Murph & H... Murphy and Hurlstone's English Exchequer Reports [1836-37] [A publication] (DLA)
Murph (NC)... Murphey's Reports [5-7 North Carolina] [A publication] (DLA)
MURPL...... Master of Urban and Regional Planning (PGP)
MurpO...... Murphy Oil Corp. [Associated Press] (SAG)
Murr...... Murray's Ceylon Reports [A publication] (DLA)
Murr...... Murray's Jury Court Cases [1815-30] [Scotland] [A publication] (DLA)
Murr...... Murray's Laws and Acts of Parliament [Scotland] [A publication] (DLA)
MURR...... University of Missouri Research Reactor
Murray...... Murray's Scotch Jury Court Reports [A publication] (DLA)
Murray (Ceylon)... Murray's Ceylon Reports [A publication] (DLA)
Murray (Scot)... Murray's Scotch Jury Trials [A publication] (DLA)
Murray's Eng Dict... Murray's English Dictionary [A publication] (DLA)
Murray St U... Murray State University (GAGS)
Murr Over Cas... Murray's Overruled Cases [A publication] (DLA)
MURS...... Machine Utilization Reporting System (PDAA)
MURS...... Machine Utilization Report System [Computer science] (IAA)
MURS...... Minority Undergraduate Research Support
MURS...... Mouvement Universel de la Responsabilite Scientifique [Universal Movement for Scientific Responsibility - UMSR] (EAIO)
MURS...... Mursley [England]
Mur Tab Cas... Murray's Table of United States Cases [A publication] (DLA)
MURTF...... Nur Advanced Technologies [NASDAQ symbol] (TTSB)
MURTS...... Multiple User Remote Terminal Supervisor (MHDI)
Mur Us...... Murray's History of Usury [A publication] (DLA)

Mur US Ct ...	Murray's Proceedings in the United States Courts [*A publication*] (DLA)
MURXF.........	International Murex Technologies [*NASDAQ symbol*] (SAG)
MURXF.........	Intl Murex Technologies [*NASDAQ symbol*] (TTSB)
MUS..............	A. G. Ruthven Museums Building (SAUS)
MUS..............	Magnetic Unloading System
MUS..............	Maintenance Utilization Sheet
MUS..............	Major Use Stations (ACAE)
MUS..............	Manned Underwater Station
MUS..............	Manual Update Service (NITA)
MUS..............	Mass Unbalance Spin
MUS..............	Master of Urban Studies (ADA)
MUS..............	Mauritius [*ANSI three-letter standard code*] (CNC)
MUS..............	Methylumbelliferone Sulfate [*Biochemistry*]
MU S	Microsecond (WDAA)
MUS..............	Midstream Urine Specimen [*Medicine*] (MELL)
MUS..............	Mission Upgrade System (SAUS)
MUS..............	Monetary Unit Sampling (ADA)
MUS..............	Mouse Urologic Syndrome (DMAA)
MUS..............	Multiprogramming Utility System [*Regnecentralen*] [*Denmark*]
MUS..............	Multiutility System (MCD)
Mus	Musca [*Constellation*]
MUS..............	Muschocho Explorations Ltd. [*Toronto Stock Exchange symbol*]
MUS..............	Muscimol [*Biochemistry*]
MUS..............	Muscle (SAUS)
mus	Musee (VRA)
mus	Museen (VRA)
mus	Museo (VRA)
Mus	Museum (AL)
mus	Museum (VRA)
MUS..............	Museum
mus	Music (SHCU)
MUS..............	Music
MUS..............	Musician (GOBB)
MUS..............	Muskinabad [*Former USSR*] [*Seismograph station code, US Geological Survey*] [*Closed*] (SEIS)
mus	Muskogee [*MARC language code*] [*Library of Congress*] (LCCP)
Mus	Muslim
MUS..............	University of Southern Mississippi, Hattiesburg, MS [*OCLC symbol*] (OCLC)
MUSA	Manufacturing USA [*A publication*]
MUSA	Mentoring USA
MUSA	Multiple Unit Steerable Antenna [*Electronics*]
MUSA	Multiple Unit Steerable Array (NITA)
MUSA	San Antonio De Los Banos [*Cuba*] [*ICAO location identifier*] (ICLI)
MUSA	Seaman Apprentice, Musician, Striker [*Navy rating*]
Mus AD........	Doctor of Musical Arts
MUS & T	Manned Undersea Science and Technology [*Marine science*] (MSC)
MUSAP........	Multisatellite Augmentation Program [*NASA*]
MUSARC......	Major United States Army Reserve Command (AABC)
MUSAT	Multiple Station Analytical Triangulation (PDAA)
MUSAT	Multipurpose UHF [*Ultra High Frequency*] Satellite (IAA)
MUSB	Mobile Unit Support Base (AAG)
Mus B	Musicae Baccalaureus [*Bachelor of Music*] [*Latin*]
Mus Bac	Musicae Baccalaureus [*Bachelor of Music*] [*Latin*]
Mus Bach	Musicae Baccalaureus [*Bachelor of Music*] [*Latin*]
Mus Belge ...	Musee Belge [*A publication*] (OCD)
MUSC	Medical University of South Carolina
MUSC	Memphis Union Station Co. [*AAR code*]
MUSC	Multiunit Supervisory Control (IAA)
Musc............	Musca [*Constellation*]
MUSC	Muscarine [*Alkaloid*]
MUSC	Muscles [*or Muscular*]
MUSC	Music
MUSC	Santa Clara [*Cuba*] [*ICAO location identifier*] (ICLI)
MUSCL	Musical
MUSCLE	Millions of Unusual Small Creatures Lurking Everywhere [*Toy by Mattel, Inc.*]
MUSCM	Missile Unit Simulated Combat Mission (SAA)
muscm.........	Musical Comedy (GROV)
MUSCO........	Muhoroni Sugar Co. Ltd.
Mus D	Doctor of Music (SAUS)
Mus D	Musicae Doctor [*Doctor of Music*] [*Latin*]
Mus Doc......	Doctor of Music (SAUS)
Mus Doc	Musicae Doctor [*Doctor of Music*] [*Latin*]
MUSE...........	Mace Utilities Sector Editor [*Computer science*]
MUSE...........	Machine User Symbiotic Environment (PDAA)
MUSE...........	Machine User Symbolic Environment (IAA)
MUSE...........	Medical Urethral System for Erection
MUSE...........	Medical Use of Simulation Electronics
MUSE...........	Microcomputer Users in Education
MUSE...........	Micromuse, Inc. [*NASDAQ symbol*] (SG)
MUSE...........	MIDI [*Musical Instrument Digital Interface*] Users Sequencer/Editor [*Roland International Corp.*]
MUSE...........	Mobile Utilities Support Equipment [*Navy*] (NG)
MUSE...........	Model to Understand Simple English (PDAA)
MUSE...........	Modular Utilities for Systems Education (IAA)
MUSE...........	Monitor of Ultraviolet Solar Energy
MUSE...........	Multimedia User Environment [*Computer science*]
MUSE...........	Multiple Sub-Nyquist Subsampling Encoding [*Digital recording system introduced 1984*]
MUSE...........	Multiuser Shared Environment [*Computer science*] (IGQR)
MUSE...........	Multi-User-Simulated Environment (PS)
MUSE...........	Musicians United for Safe Energy (EA)
MUSE...........	Musicians United to Stop Exclusion [*Defunct*] (EA)
Mus Ed B....	Bachelor of Music Education
Mus Ed D....	Doctor of Music Education
MUSEDET	Mobile Utilities Support Equipment Detachment [*Navy*] (DNAB)
Mus Ed M....	Master of Music Education
MUSF...........	Habana/Santa Fe [*Cuba*] [*ICAO location identifier*] (ICLI)
MUSG..........	Sagua La Grande [*Cuba*] [*ICAO location identifier*] (ICLI)
Mus G Paed	Musicae Graduatus Paedagogus [*Graduate Teacher in Music*]
MUSH..........	Mail Users Shell [*Computer science*] (VLIE)
MUSH..........	Multiuser Shared Hallucination [*Computer science*] (IGQR)
MusH..........	Music Hall [*Record label*] [*Argentina*]
MUSHes	Multiuser Shared Hallucinations [*Computer game players*]
MUSI	Mexico-United States Institute (EA)
MUSI	Multi User Shared Illusion [*Computer science*] (VLIE)
musi	Musical (GROV)
MUSIC	Machine Utilization Statistical Information Collection (IAA)
MUSIC	Mass Unity Sounding in Concert [*Duke Ellington definition of music*]
MUSIC	McGill University System for Interactive Computing
MUSIC	Multiple Signal Classification (VLIE)
MUSIC	Multiple System Intelligent Controller [*Computer science*]
MUSIC	Multisensor Intelligence Correlator (IAA)
MUSIC	Multi-Spectral Infrared Camera (ACAE)
MUSIC	Multi-User System for Integrated Control [*Computer science*] (VLIE)
Music...........	Musicology (DIAR)
MUSICAM	Masking Pattern Universal Sub-Band Integrated Coding and Multiplexing [*Broadcasting*]
MusicLd.......	Musicland Stores [*Associated Press*] (SAG)
MUSICOL.....	Musical Instruction Composition Oriented Language (NITA)
MUSICOMP...	Music Composition
MUSIL	Multiprogramming Utility System Interpretive Language [*Regnecentralen*] [*Denmark*]
MUSJ...........	San Julian (Escuela de Aviacion) [*Cuba*] [*ICAO location identifier*] (ICLI)
MUSL...........	Marconi Underwater Systems Ltd. [*British*]
MUSL...........	Multiple Stinger Launcher
MUSL...........	Musician's Library [*A publication*]
MUSL...........	Muslin (ROG)
musl............	Muslin (VRA)
MUSL...........	Santa Lucia [*Cuba*] [*ICAO location identifier*] (ICLI)
MUSLE.........	Modified Universal Soil Loss Equation [*Agricultural Research Service*]
MUSLO.........	Morocco-United States Liaison Office (AFM)
musm	Museum (BEE)
Mus M	Musicae Magister [*Master of Music*] [*Latin*]
MusMComp...	Master of Music Composition, University of Manchester [*British*] (DBQ)
MusMPerf....	Master of Music Performance, University of Manchester [*British*] (DBQ)
Musn...........	Musician [*British military*] (DMA)
MUSN	Seaman, Musician, Striker [*Navy rating*]
MUSN	Siguanea, Isla De La Juventud [*Cuba*] [*ICAO location identifier*] (ICLI)
MUSR	Simon Reyes [*Cuba*] [*ICAO location identifier*] (ICLI)
MUSRP........	McGill University Savanna Research Project (MCD)
MUSS	Manchester University Software System (NITA)
MUSS	Missile Unit Support System
MUSS	Mobile Unit Support System (IAA)
muss...........	Module Utility Support Structure (NAKS)
MUSS	Module Utility Support Structure (NASA)
MUSS	Musical Series [*A publication*]
MUSS	Sancti Spiritus [*Cuba*] [*ICAO location identifier*] (ICLI)
MUST	Machine Utilization Report Generator (DNAB)
MUST	Malaysian University of Science and Technology
MUST	Manned Undersea Science and Technology [*Marine science*] (OSRA)
MUST	Manned Undersea Station
MUST	Manpower Utilization System and Techniques [*Department of State*]
MUST	Maximum Utilization of Skills and Training [*Civil Service Commission*]
MUST	Medical Unit Self-Contained Transportable [*Field hospital*] [*Army*]
MUST	Meeting Updates in Skill Training [*International Labor Organization*] [*Information service or system*] [*United Nations*] (DUND)
MUST	Message User Service Transcriber (IAA)
MUST	Mobile Undersea Systems Test (ACAE)
MUST	Mobile Underwater Surveillance Team (MCD)
MUST	Mobile Unit Sanitation Trailer
MUST	Multi-Mission UHF [*Ultra High Frequency*] SATCOM [*Satellite Command*] Terminal
MUST	Multiple Source Technique
MUST	Multipurpose User-Oriented Software Technology (MHDI)
MUSTA	Mock-Up Spallation Target Assembly (PDAA)
MUSTARD....	Multi-Racial Union of Squatters to Alleviate Racial Discrimination [*British*] (DI)
MUSTARD....	Multiunit Space Transport and Recovery Device (MCD)
MUSTARD....	Museum and University Storage and Retrieval of Data (NITA)
MUSTPAC-1...	Medical Ultrasound, Three-Dimensional and Portabel with Advanced Communications [*An imaging device*] (INF)
MUSTRAC....	Multiple-Simultaneous-Target Steerable Telemetry Tracking System [*Navy*]
MUSTRAN....	Music Translation (NITA)
MUSTRS......	Multi-Sensor Target Recognition System (SAUS)
MustSft........	Mustang Software, Inc. [*Associated Press*] (SAG)
MUSYA........	Multiple-Use Sustained-Yield Act of 1960
MU Sys E....	Master of Urban Systems Engineering (PGP)
Mut	De Mutatione Nominum [*Philo*] (BJA)
MUT.............	Makeup Tank [*Nuclear energy*] (NRCH)
MUT.............	Master Upper Tester (SAUS)
MUT.............	Mean Up Time [*NASA*] (KSC)
MUT.............	Mercury Unit Test

MUT............	Mock-Up Template
MUT............	Modular Universal Terminal (IAA)
MUT............	Module under Test
MUT............	Monitor Under Test (VLIE)
MUT............	Multinational Resources [*Vancouver Stock Exchange symbol*]
MUT............	Multiservicios Aeronauticos SA de CV [*Mexico*] [*ICAO designator*] (FAAC)
MUT............	Muntinlupa [*Philippines*] [*Geomagnetic observatory code*]
MUT............	Muscatine, IA [*Location identifier*] [*FAA*] (FAAL)
MUT............	Mutagen (DMAA)
MUT............	Mutilated
MUT............	Mutual (ADA)
Mut............	Mutual (TBD)
Mut............	Mutukisna's Ceylon Reports [*A publication*] (DLA)
MUTA..........	Made-Up Textiles Association [*British*] (DBA)
MUTA..........	Military Upper Traffic Control Area (DA)
MUTA..........	Multiple Unit Training Assembly [*Army*] (AABC)
MUTACI	Mutuelle des Autochtones de la Cote d'Ivoire [*Mutual Association of the Natives of the Ivory Coast*]
MUTCD	Manual on Uniform Traffic Control Devices [*Highway engineering*] [*A publication*]
MUTCD	Manual on Uniform Traffic Control Traffic Control Devices [*Federal Housing Adminstration*]
MUTD	Trinidad [*Cuba*] [*ICAO location identifier*] (ICLI)
MUTE..........	Mobile Universal Test Equipment (PDAA)
MUTE..........	Multiple Unit for Transmission Elimination [*Military*] (CAAL)
MUTES.........	Multiple Threat Emitter System [*Air Force*]
MUTEX.........	Multiuser Terminal Executive (MHDI)
MUTEX.........	Multi-User Transaction Executive (NITA)
MUTEX.........	Mutually Exclusive (VLIE)
MUTHX........	Mutual Shares Fund [*Mutual fund ticker symbol*] (SG)
MUTI...........	Manati [*Cuba*] [*ICAO location identifier*] (ICLI)
MUTL..........	Mutual (ROG)
MUTR	Makai Undersea Test Range (DNAB)
MutRisk	Mutual Risk Management Ltd. [*Associated Press*] (SAG)
MUTS..........	Manual Unit Test Set
MUTS..........	Multiple Target Simulation (MCD)
MutSvg	Mutual Savings Bank FSB [*Associated Press*] (SAG)
MUTT..........	Military Utility Tactical Transport
MUTT..........	Military Utility Tactical Truck
MUTT..........	Mobile Utility Transfer Tank [*To collect used oils*]
MUTT..........	Multiuse Terminal Translator (MHDI)
mutt...........	Mutton [*An em space*] [*Typesetting*] (WDMC)
MUTT/JEFF...	Multi-Use Tactical Terminal/Judiciary Efficient Fixed Frame (ACAE)
MUTTS........	Multiple Unit Terminal Test Set (MCD)
MutualB	Mutual Bancompany, Inc. [*Associated Press*] (SAG)
Mutukisna...	Mutukisna's Ceylon Reports [*A publication*] (DLA)
MUU	Main User Unit (SAUS)
MUU	Mount Union, PA [*Location identifier*] [*FAA*] (FAAL)
MUU	Mouse Uterine Unit [*Gynecology*] (MAE)
MUU	University of Missouri, Columbia, Columbia, MO [*OCLC symbol*] (OCLC)
MUV...........	Marine Unit Vietnam (VNW)
MUV...........	Mechanized Utility Vehicle (MCD)
MU V	Microvolt (WDAA)
MUV...........	Middle Ultraviolet
MUV...........	Mobile Underwater Vehicle
MUV...........	Philadelphia, PA [*Location identifier*] [*FAA*] (FAAL)
MUVA	Central Primero De Enero [*Cuba*] [*ICAO location identifier*] (ICLI)
MuvCAIn	Munivest California Insured Fund [*Associated Press*] (SAG)
MuvMIIn	MuniVest Michigan Insured Fund [*Associated Press*] (SAG)
MuvNJFd	MuniVest New Jersey Fund [*Associated Press*] (SAG)
MuvNYIn	MuniVest New York Insured Fund [*Associated Press*] (SAG)
MUVR	Varadero [*Cuba*] [*ICAO location identifier*] (ICLI)
MUVT	Las Tunas [*Cuba*] [*ICAO location identifier*] (ICLI)
MUW	Mascara [*Algeria*] [*Airport symbol*] (OAG)
MU W	Microwatt (WDAA)
MUW	Music Wire
MUW	Mutarara [*Mozambique*] [*Airport symbol*] (AD)
MUW	University of Mississippi, School of Law Library, University, MS [*OCLC symbol*] (OCLC)
MUWO	Muir Woods National Monument
MUWS	Manned Underwater Station
MUWU	Mouse Uterine Weight Unit [*Gynecology*]
MUX...........	Multan [*Pakistan*] [*Airport symbol*] (OAG)
mux...........	Multiplex (NAKS)
MUX...........	Multiplex [*or Multiplexer*] [*Telecommunications*]
Mux...........	Multiplexer (AAEL)
MUX...........	Multiplexer (PIPO)
MUX...........	Musto Explorations Ltd. [*Toronto Stock Exchange symbol*]
MUXARC.......	Multiplexing Automatic Error Correction (IAA)
MUXART	Multiplexed Asynchronous Receiver/Transmitter (MCD)
MUX/DEMUX...	Multiplexer and Demultiplexer
MUXER	Multiplexer
MUXES	Multiplexes [*or Multiplexers*] [*Telecommunications*]
MUXIC	Multiplex/Multiple Voice Interior Communications (DNAB)
MUXMOD.....	Multiplex Modulation
MUX/PRI/SEC..	Multiplexer/Priority/Second
MUY...........	Lehman Br Micron'YEELD'97 [*AMEX symbol*] (TTSB)
MUY...........	Lehman Brothers, Inc. [*AMEX symbol*] (SAG)
MUY...........	Toolik, AK [*Location identifier*] [*FAA*] (FAAL)
MUZ...........	Musoma [*Tanzania*] [*Airport symbol*] (OAG)
Muza...........	Muza and Other Labels [*Record label*] [*Poland*]
MUZAK	Music and Kodak [*Terms combined to coin brand name for canned music*]
MUZG	Zaragoza [*Cuba*] [*ICAO location identifier*] (ICLI)
MUZH	Muzzle Hatch
MUZM.........	Makerere-University Zoology Museum [*Uganda*]
MV.............	Airlines of Western Australia [*Australia*] [*ICAO designator*] (ICDA)
MV.............	MacRobertson-Miller Airline Service [*ICAO designator*] (AD)
M/V...........	Magnetic Variation (MCD)
MV.............	Mahzor Vitry [*A publication*] (BJA)
MV.............	Maintenance Version (IAA)
MV.............	Main Verb [*Linguistics*]
MV.............	Majority-Vote Technique [*Parapsychology*]
MV.............	Maldives [*ANSI two-letter standard code*] (CNC)
MV.............	Manifold Vacuum [*Automotive engineering*]
MV.............	Manned Vehicle
MV.............	Manpower Voucher [*Army*] (AABC)
MV.............	Mantle Vessel
MV.............	Manual Valve (MCD)
mv.............	Manual Valve (NAKS)
mv.............	Manufacturing Verification (NAKS)
MV.............	Manufacturing Verification (NASA)
MV.............	Mare Vaporum [*Sea of Vapor*] [*Lunar area*]
MV.............	Mariner Venus Project [*NASA*]
MV.............	Market Value
MV.............	Mauve [*Philately*] (ROG)
MV.............	Mean Value
MV.............	Mean Variation
MV.............	Mean Voltage (IAA)
MV.............	Measles Virus
MV.............	Measured Value
MV.............	Mechanical Ventilation [*Medicine*]
MV.............	Medial Vestibular Nucleus [*Neuroanatomy*]
MV.............	Medicus Veterinarius [*Veterinary Physician*]
MV.............	Medium Voltage
MV.............	Medium Volume
MV.............	Megavolt
Mv.............	Mendelevium [*Symbol is Md*] [*Chemical element*]
MV.............	Mentor Exploration & Development Co. Ltd. [*Toronto Stock Exchange symbol*]
MV.............	Merchant Vessel
MV.............	Mercury Vapor
MV.............	Methyl Violet [*A dye*]
MV.............	Methyl Viologen [*Organic chemistry*]
MV.............	Mezza Voce [*Half the Power of the Voice*] [*Music*]
MV.............	Microvilli [*Cytology*]
mV.............	Microvolt
MV.............	Microwave [*Physics*] (DAVI)
MV.............	Midland Valley R. R. [*AAR code*]
MV.............	Military Vehicle
MV.............	Military Vigilance (NATG)
MV.............	Million Volts
mv.............	Millivolt (NAKS)
mV.............	Millivolt
MV.............	Miniature Vehicle (MCD)
MV.............	Minimal Variant (IAA)
MV.............	Minimum Viscosity
MV.............	Minute Ventilation [*Medicine*]
MV.............	Minute Volume [*Medicine*]
MV.............	Mitoxantrone, VePesid [*Antineoplastic drug*] (CDI)
MV.............	Mitral Valve [*Cardiology*]
MV.............	Mixed Venous [*Blood*]
MV.............	Modern Varieties [*Agriculture*]
MV.............	Modus Vivendi [*Way of Living*] [*Latin*]
MV.............	Molar Volume [*Chemistry*]
MV.............	Money Velocity [*Economics*]
MV.............	Monochromatic Vision (WDAA)
MV.............	Montevideo [*City in Uruguay*] (ROG)
MV.............	Mostly Verbatim [*FAR clauses*] (AAGC)
MV.............	Motorized Valve (KSC)
MV.............	Motor Vehicle (CDAI)
MV.............	Motor Vehicle Mishap (DNAB)
mv.............	Motor Vessel (ODBW)
MV.............	Motor Vessel
MV.............	Motor Volunteers [*British military*] (DMA)
MV.............	Move [*Telecommunications*] (TEL)
MV.............	Multiconverter Vector [*Computer science*] (IAA)
MV.............	Multivessel [*Medicine*] (DB)
MV.............	Multivibrator
MV.............	Multivitamins [*Nutrition*]
mv.............	Multivolt (ELAL)
MV.............	Musica Viva (ADA)
MV.............	Muzzle Velocity [*Ballistics*]
MV.............	Mycoplasmatales Virus
MV-678.......	Agricultural Research Service (SAUS)
MVA..........	Machine Vision Association [*Later, MVA/SME*] (EA)
MVA..........	Machining Variation Analysis
MVA..........	Machinists Vise Association [*Later, HTI*] (EA)
MVA..........	Main Valve Actuator (NASA)
MVA..........	Malignant Ventricular Arrhythmias [*Cardiology*] (DAVI)
MVA..........	Manifold Vacuum Assist [*Automotive engineering*]
MVA..........	Manufacturing Value Added
MVA..........	Marginal Value Analysis (MCD)
MVA..........	Market-Value Accounting [*Banking*] (ECON)
MVA..........	Market Value Added
MVA..........	Market Value Appraiser (DD)
MVA..........	Master of Visual Arts (GAGS)
MVA..........	Mean Vertical Acceleration

MVA............	Mechanical Ventricular Assistance [*Medicine*] (DMAA)
MVA............	Megavolt-Ampere
MVA............	Mercury Volatilizing Activity
MVA............	Merrimack Valley College Library, Manchester, NH [*OCLC symbol*] (OCLC)
MVA............	Mevalonic Acid [*Organic chemistry*]
MVA............	Million Volt Amperes
MVA............	Millivolt Ampere [*Nuclear energy*] (IAA)
MVA............	Mina, NV [*Location identifier*] [*FAA*] (FAAL)
MVA............	Minimum Vectoring Altitude [*FAA*] (TAG)
MVA............	Minnova, Inc. [*Toronto Stock Exchange symbol*] (SPSG)
MVa............	Minute Ventilatory Volume for Experimental Animal Species
MVA............	Mississippi Valley Airlines, Inc. [*ICAO designator*] (FAAC)
MVA............	Missouri Valley Authority
MVA............	Mitral Valve Area [*Cardiology*]
MVA............	Modern Volunteer Army
MVA............	Monovinylacetylene [*Organic chemistry*]
MVA............	Motor Vehicle Accident [*Medicine*] (AFM)
MVA............	Motor Vehicle Allowance
MVA............	Motor Vehicle Assembly [*Military*] [*World War II*]
MVA............	Multivariate Analysis (GFGA)
MVA............	Music Video Association (EA)
MVA............	Myvatn [*Iceland*] [*Airport symbol*] [*Obsolete*] (OAG)
M-VAC.........	Methotrexate, Vinblastine, Adriamiacin [*Doxorubicin*] Cisplatin [*Antineoplastic drug regimen*] (DAVI)
MVAC..........	Methotrexate, Vinblastine, Adriamycin, Cisplatin [*Antineoplastic drug*] (CDI)
MVAC..........	MotorVac Technologies [*NASDAQ symbol*] (TTSB)
MVAC..........	MotorVac Technologies, Inc. [*NASDAQ symbol*] (SAG)
MVAC..........	Motor Vehicle Air Conditioner (EEVL)
MVACS........	Mars Volatiles and Climate Survey [*NASA*]
MVAK..........	Module Vertical Access Kit [*NASA*] (SPST)
MVal..........	Market Value [*Insurance*]
MV & P.......	Morton's Vendors and Purchasers [*1837*] [*A publication*] (DLA)
MVAP..........	Modern Volunteer Army Program (AABC)
MVAPCA......	Motor Vehicle Air Pollution Control Act (GFGA)
MVAR..........	Megavar
MVAR..........	Megavolt-Ampere Reactive [*Nuclear energy*] (IAA)
MVARH........	Megavar-Hour
MVAS..........	Multipurpose Ventricular Actuating System (NASA)
MVAS..........	Murray Valley Air Service [*Australia*]
MVA/SME	Machine Vision Association [*Society of Manufacturing Engineers*] (EA)
MVAT..........	MediVators, Inc. [*NASDAQ symbol*] (SAG)
MVAT..........	Metacyclic Variant Antigen Type [*Immunology*]
MVAT..........	Multiple Vandal Assembly Terminal (ACAE)
MVAU..........	Maximum Volt-Ampere Utilization [*Electronics*]
MVB............	Martin Van Buren [*US president, 1782-1862*]
MVB............	Mechanical Vacuum Booster
MVB............	Mississippi Valley Motor Freight Bureau, Saint Louis MO [*STAC*]
MVB............	Mixed Venous Blood [*Medicine*] (DAVI)
MVB............	Motor V-Belt
MVB............	Motor Vessel Boat
MVB............	Multimedia Viewer Book (VLIE)
MVB............	Multivesicular Body
MVB............	Multivibrator
MVB............	Mvengue [*Gabon*] [*Airport symbol*] (OAG)
MVBD..........	Multiple V-Belt Drive
MVBF..........	Motor Vehicle Brake Fluid [*Automotive engineering*]
MVBFC........	Martin Van Buren Fan Club (EA)
MVBI..........	Mississippi Valley Bancshares [*NASDAQ symbol*] (TTSB)
MVBI..........	Mississippi Valley Bancshares, Inc. [*NASDAQ symbol*] (SAG)
MVBL..........	Movable (MSA)
MVBR..........	Motor Vehicle Body Repair (HEAS)
MVBR..........	Multivibrator
MVC............	Management Verification Consortium (AIE)
mvc............	Manual Volume Control (NAKS)
MVC............	Manual Volume Control
MVC............	Maryville College, St. Louis, MO [*OCLC symbol*] (OCLC)
MVC............	Master Vellum Center [*Jet Propulsion Laboratory, NASA*]
mvc............	Master Volume Control (NAKS)
MVC............	Master Volume Control (NASA)
MVC............	Maui Volcanic Complex [*Geology*]
MVC............	Maximal Voluntary Contraction
MVC............	Maximum Vital Capacity [*Medicine*] (DAVI)
MVC............	Mechanical Vapor Compressor [*Engineering*]
MVC............	Micro Ventures Ltd. [*Vancouver Stock Exchange symbol*]
MVC............	Mississippi Vocational College
MVC............	Missouri Valley College
MVC............	Missouri Valley Conference [*Sports*]
MVC............	Mitral Valve Cusps [*Medicine*] (MELL)
MVC............	Model-View-Controller [*Computer science*]
MVC............	Monroeville, AL [*Location identifier*] [*FAA*] (FAAL)
MVC............	Motor vehicle Collision (or Crash) (SAUS)
MVC............	Motor Volunteer Corps [*British military*] (DMA)
MVC............	Move Character [*Computer science*] (VLIE)
MVC............	Multiple Variate Counter (IEEE)
MVC............	MuniVest California Insured Fund [*NYSE symbol*] (SPSG)
MVC............	Myocardial Vascular Capacity [*Cardiology*] (MAE)
MVCC..........	Military Vehicle Collectors Club [*Later, MVPA*] (EA)
MVCC..........	Mountain Valley Collegiate Conference (PSS)
MVCM.........	Millivolt per Centimeter [*Nuclear energy*] (IAA)
MVCMB.......	Murray Valley Citrus Marketing Board [*Australia*]
MVCN.........	Multi-Vendor Computer Networks (AGLO)
MVCO.........	Meadow Valley [*NASDAQ symbol*] (TTSB)

MVCO	Meadow Valley Corp. [*NASDAQ symbol*] (SAG)
MVCOW	Meadow Valley Wrrt [*NASDAQ symbol*] (TTSB)
MVCS..........	Marine Vapor Control System
MVCS..........	Motor Vehicle Certification System
MVCU	Multivariable Control Unit [*Computer science*]
MVD............	Doctor of Veterinary Medicine
MVD............	Map and Visual Display
MVD............	Metal Vapor Deposition (EDCT)
MVD............	Microvascular Decompression [*Medicine*] (MELL)
MVD............	Mineralny Vody Department of Cibil Aviation [*Former USSR*] [*FAA designator*] (FAAC)
MVD............	Minimum-Variance Deconvolution (MCD)
MVD............	Mission Variation Drawing (MCD)
MVD............	Mitral Valve Disease [*Cardiology*]
MVD............	Montevideo [*Uruguay*] [*Airport symbol*] (OAG)
MVD............	Motor Vehicle Department (DLA)
MVD............	Motor Vehicle Distributing [*Military*]
MVD............	Motor Vehicle Driver Selection Battery [*Army*]
MVD............	Motor Voltage Drop (IAA)
mvd............	Moved (GEAB)
MVDA.........	Motor Vehicle Dealers Act
MVDA.........	Motor Vehicles Dismantlers Association [*British*] (BI)
MVDA,........	Multivariate Variance and Discriminant Analysis [*Mathematics*]
MVDC.........	Megavolt Direct Current [*Nuclear energy*] (IAA)
MVDC.........	Millivolt Direct Current [*Nuclear energy*] (IAA)
MVDF.........	Medium- and Very-High-Frequency Direction-Finding Station
MVDFC	Mamie Van Doren Fan Club (EA)
MVDI..........	Microfield Virtual Device Interface [*Computer science*] (HGAA)
MVDLB	Motor Vehicle Dealers' Licensing Board [*Western Australia*]
MVDM.........	Multiple Virtual DOS [*Disk Operating System*] Machine [*Computer science*] (PCM)
MVD-MGB..	Ministerstvo Vnutrennikh Del-Ministerstvo Gosudarstvennoe Bezopasnosti [*Later, KGB*]
MVDr	Medicus Veterinarius Doctor [*Doctor of Veterinary Medicine*]
MVDS	Modular Vault Dry Store [*Nuclear energy*] (NUCP)
MVDS	Modular Video Data System [*Sperry UNIVAC*]
MVDS	Multipoint Video Distribution Service (AAEL)
MVE............	Maple Valley Explorations Ltd. [*Vancouver Stock Exchange symbol*]
MVE............	Master of Vocational Education (NADA)
MVE............	Mauve [*Philately*] (ROG)
MVE............	Methyl Vinyl Ether [*Organic chemistry*]
MVE............	Mitral Valve Echogram [*Cardiology*]
MVE............	Mobile Vocational Evaluation [*Vocational guidance test*]
MVE............	Montevideo, MN [*Location identifier*] [*FAA*] (FAAL)
MVE............	Multivariate Exponential Distribution [*Statistics*]
MVE............	Murray Valley Encephalitis [*Virus*]
MVE............	Virden-Elkhorn Regional Library, Virden, Manitoba [*Library symbol*] [*National Library of Canada*] (NLC)
MVEA..........	Missouri Valley Electric Association
MV Ed.........	Master of Vocational Education
MVEE..........	Military Vehicles and Engineering Establishment [*Research center*] [*British*]
MVEFS........	Motor Vehicle Emission and Fuel Standards (COE)
MVEL..........	Motor Vehicle Emission Laboratory [*Environmental Protection Agency*]
MVEMJSUNP...	My Very Excellent Mother Just Served Us Nine Pies [*Mnemonic guide to the nine planets: Mercury, Venus, Earth, Mars, Jupiter, Saturn, Uranus, Neptune, Pluto*]
MVetClinStud...	Master of Veterinary Clinical Studies
MVetMed	Master of Veterinary Medicine (NADA)
M Vet Sc	Master of Veterinary Science (PGP)
MVetSci.......	Master of Veterinary Science (NADA)
MVetSt........	Master of Veterinary Studies
MVF............	Manned Vertical Flight (MCD)
MVF............	Missile Verification Firing
MVF............	Mitral Valve Flow [*Medicine*] (DMAA)
MVF............	Moisture Volume Fraction (PDAA)
MVF............	MuniVest Fund [*AMEX symbol*] (TTSB)
MVF............	MuniVest Fund, Inc. [*AMEX symbol*] (SPSG)
MVFC..........	Mack Vickery Fan Club (EA)
MVFC..........	Mr. V Fan Club [*Defunct*] (EA)
MVFC..........	Municipal Valuation Fees Committee [*Victoria, Australia*]
MVFV..........	Manned Venus Flyby Vehicle
MVG............	Mengenverbrauchsguttern [*Mass Consumption Goods*] [*German*]
MVG............	Minven Gold Corp. [*Toronto Stock Exchange symbol*]
MVG............	Most Valuable Girl
MVG............	Moving
MVG............	Mycoplasmatales Virus [*from*] Goat
MVGA.........	Monochrome Video Graphics Array [*Computer science*] (CDE)
MVGF.........	Myxoma Virus Growth Factor [*Biochemistry*]
MV Grad......	Mitral Valve Gradient [*Cardiology*] (MAE)
MVGVT	Mated Vertical Ground Vibration Test [*NASA*] (NASA)
MVH...........	Massive Vitreous Hemorrhage [*Medicine*] (DMAA)
MVH...........	Methotrexate, VP-16 Hyxamethylmelamine [*Antineoplastic drug regimen*] (DAVI)
MVh...........	Minute Ventilatory Volume for Human
MVH...........	Mohave Gold, Inc. [*Vancouver Stock Exchange symbol*]
MVH...........	Mountain View [*Hawaii*] [*Seismograph station code, US Geological Survey*] (SEIS)
MVh...........	Vineyard Haven Public Library, Vineyard Haven, MA [*Library symbol*] [*Library of Congress*] (LCLS)
MVHD	Hospital District Number 10, Virden, Manitoba [*Library symbol*] [*National Library of Canada*] (NLC)
MVho..........	Minute Ventilatory Volume for Human in an Occupational Environment

MVI............. Macrotrends Ventures, Inc. [*Vancouver Stock Exchange symbol*]
MvI............. Marcive, Inc., San Antonio, TX [*Library symbol*] [*Library of Congress*] (LCLS)
MVI............. Maximum Visual Impact (DNAB)
MVI............. Medium Value Item (NATG)
MVI............. Medium Viscosity Index (PDAA)
MVI............. Melt Volume Index [*Materials science*]
MVI............. Merchant Vessel Inspection Division [*Coast Guard*]
MVI............. Mercury Vapor Isolator
MVI............. Metal Ventilator Institute (EA)
MV/I............. Millivolt to Current [*Converter*] [*Nuclear energy*] (NRCH)
MVI............. Minami Daito Jima [*Volcano Islands*] [*Seismograph station code, US Geological Survey*] (SEIS)
MVI............. Miniature Variable Inductor
MVI............. Motion Video Instructions (SAUS)
MVI............. Motor Vehicle Inspection
MVI............. Multiple Vitamin Infusion [*Pharmacology*] (DAVI)
MVI............. Multivalvular Involvement [*Medicine*] (DMAA)
MVI............. Multivitamin (AMHC)
MVI............. Multivitamins Intravenously [*Pharmacology*] (DAVI)
MVIACSA...... Motor Vehicle Information and Cost Saving Act (EEVL)
MVIC.......... Mitsubishi Variable Intake System [*Automotive engine design*]
MVICSA........ Motor Vehicle Information and Cost Saving Act
MVICSA........ Motor Vehicle Information and Cost Savings Act (EG)
MVII............. Mark VII [*NASDAQ symbol*] (TTSB)
MVII............. Mark VII, Inc. [*NASDAQ symbol*] (SAG)
MVII............. Minnesota Vocational Interest Inventory
MVIJC........ Motor Vehicle Industry Joint Council [*British*] (DCTA)
MVI/M......... Motor Vehicle Inspection/Maintenance (GFGA)
MVIN.......... Medium Viscosity Index-Naphthenic (PDAA)
MVIP.......... Medium Viscosity Index-Paraffinic (PDAA)
MVIP.......... Multi-Vendor Integration Protocol [*Computer science*]
MVIS.......... Maximum Voluntary Isometric Strength
MVIS.......... Microvision, Inc. [*NASDAQ symbol*] (SAG)
MVIS.......... Murrumbidgee Irrigation Area Vine Improvement Society [*Australia*]
MVJ............. Mandeville [*Jamaica*] [*Airport symbol*] [*Obsolete*] (OAG)
MVJ............. MuniVest New Jersey Fund [*NYSE symbol*] (SPSG)
MVJ............. MuniVest NJ Fund [*NYSE symbol*] (TTSB)
MVJC.......... Mount Vernon Junior College [*Washington, DC*]
MVK............. Maverick Tube [*NYSE symbol*]
MVK............. Methyl Vinyl Ketone [*Organic chemistry*]
MVK............. Mulka [*Australia*] [*Airport symbol*] [*Obsolete*] (OAG)
MVL............. Magadan Airlines [*Russian Federation*] [*ICAO designator*] (FAAC)
MVL............. Man-Vehicle Laboratory [*Massachusetts Institute of Technology*] [*Research center*] (RCD)
MVL............. Manville Corp. [*NYSE symbol*] (CTT)
MVL............. Marley Vehicle Leasing [*Commercial firm*] [*British*]
MVL............. Marvel Enterprises [*NYSE symbol*] (SG)
MVL............. Mercury Vapor Lamp
MVL............. Metal Vapor LASER
MVL............. Mitral Valve Leaflet (DMAA)
MVL............. Moderate Visual Loss (SAUS)
MVL............. Morrisville, VT [*Location identifier*] [*FAA*] (FAAL)
MVL............. Mountain Valley Library System, Sacramento, CA [*OCLC symbol*] (OCLC)
MVL............. Multiple-Valued Logic [*Computer science*]
MVL............. Multiple Virtual Line [*Developed by Paradyne Corporation*] (DCDG)
MVL............. Murray Valley League [*Australia*]
MVL............. Mycoplasmatales Virus [*from*] Acholeplasma laidlawii
MVL............. Mylan Ventures Ltd. [*Vancouver Stock Exchange symbol*]
MVL............. Naval
MVLA.......... Mount Vernon Ladies' Association of the Union (EA)
MVLD.......... Man Worn Laser Detector (SAUS)
MVLDC........ Murray Valley League for Development and Conservation [*Australia*]
MVLS.......... Magic Valley Regional Library System [*Library network*]
MVLS.......... Mandibular Vestibulolingual Sulcoplasty [*Surgery*]
MVLS.......... Meecham Verbal Language Scale (DAVI)
MVLT.......... Morse/Voice Language Trainer (SAUS)
MVLU.......... Minimum Variance Linear Unbiased [*Statistics*]
MVLUE........ Minimum Variance Linear Unbiased Estimator [*Statistics*] (OA)
MVM............. Air Cargo America, Inc. [*ICAO designator*] (FAAC)
MVM............. Manager Virtual Machine [*Computer science*] (CIST)
mvm............. Mariner Venus/Mercury (NAKS)
MVM............. Mariner Venus-Mercury Project [*NASA*]
MVM............. Massachusetts Volunteer Militia (HGAA)
MVM............. Master of Veterinary Medicine
MVM............. Medium-Voltage Mode
MVM............. Microvillous Membrane [*Cytology*] (MAE)
MVM............. Million Vehicle Miles
mV/m............. Millivolts per Meter (DEN)
MVM............. Minimum Virtual Memory
MVM............. Minute Virus of Mice
MVM............. Multiple Virtual Modem [*Computer science*] (CIST)
MVM............. Multivolume Monographs
MVM............. MuniVest Michigan Insured Fund [*NYSE symbol*] (SPSG)
MVMA.......... Motor Vehicle Manufacturers Association (NADA)
MVMA.......... Motor Vehicle Manufacturers Association of the United States (EA)
MVMC.......... Motor Vehicle Maintenance Course
MVMF.......... Ministerstvo Voenno-Morskogo Flota [*Ministry of the Navy*] [*1950-53; merged into the MO*] [*Former USSR*]
MVMFB........ Mississippi Valley Motor Freight Bureau
MVMNT........ Movement
MVMT.......... Movement (AFM)
MVN............. Magna Ventures Ltd. [*Vancouver Stock Exchange symbol*]
MVN............. Marvin Ltd. [*British*] [*ICAO designator*] (FAAC)

MVN............. Medial Ventromedial Nucleus [*Medicine*] (DMAA)
MVN............. Median Ventricular Nerve [*Medicine*]
MVN............. Mount Vernon [*Illinois*] [*Airport symbol*] (OAG)
MVNT.......... Movement (SAUS)
MVO............. Maximum Venous Outflow [*Medicine*]
MVO............. Member of the Royal Victorian Order [*British*]
MVO............. Military Vehicles Operation [*of General Motors Corp.*]
MVO............. Mitral Valve Opening [*Medicine*] (DMAA)
MVO............. MMC Video One Canada Ltd. [*Toronto Stock Exchange symbol*] [*Vancouver Stock Exchange symbol*]
MVO............. Money Value Only (AFIT)
MVO............. Mongo [*Chad*] [*Airport symbol*] (AD)
MVO$_2$......... Myocardial Oxygen Consumption [*Cardiology*] (DAVI)
MVO$_2$......... Myocardial Oxygen Ventilation Rate [*Cardiology*] (MAE)
MVOA.......... Mitral Valve Orifice Area [*Cardiology*] (DMAA)
MVOC.......... Microbial Volatile Organic Compounds (SAUS)
MVP............. Machine Vision Processor
MVP............. Magnetic Vector Potential
MVP............. Maintenance Verification Plan
MVP............. Manpower Validation Program
MVP............. Marginal Value of Product [*Agriculture*]
MVP............. Master Verification Plan (MCD)
MVP............. Mechanical Vacuum Pump
MVP............. Methylvinylpyridine [*Organic chemistry*]
MVP............. Methyl-Violet Paper (MSA)
MVP............. Microvascular Pressure [*Medicine*] (DMAA)
MVP............. Micro Vector Processor (TIMI)
MVP............. Millivolt Potentiometer (IDOE)
MVP............. Minimum Viable Population [*Demographics*]
MVP............. Minority Vendors Program
MVP............. Mitral Valve Prolapse [*Cardiology*]
MVP............. Mitu [*Colombia*] [*Airport symbol*] (OAG)
MVP............. Modular Voice Processor (SAUS)
MVP............. Most Valuable Player [*Athletics*] [*Facetious translation: "Most Volatile Player"*]
MVP............. Most Valuable Princess [*Princess Diana*] [*British*] [*Slang*]
MVP............. Most Valuable Product (PCM)
MVP............. Motor Vehicle Plant (SAUS)
MVP............. Mountain View Public Library, Mountain View, CA [*OCLC symbol*] (OCLC)
MVP............. Multimedia Video Processor [*Texas Instruments*] (PS)
MVP............. Multiple Virtual Processing (NITA)
MVP............. Multivalue Program [*Computer science*]
MVP............. Multivariable Program [*Computer science*] (IAA)
MVP............. MuniVest Pennsylvania Insured Fund [*NYSE symbol*] (SPSG)
MVP............. MVP Capital Corp. [*Toronto Stock Exchange symbol*]
MVPA.......... Military Vehicle Preservation Association (EA)
MVPA.......... Motor Vehicle Plan Administration
MVPC.......... Motor Vehicle Personal Computer [*Mobile communications*]
MVPCB........ Motor Vehicle Pollution Control Board (NADA)
MVPCCS...... Motor Vehicle Post Crash Communications System (PDAA)
MVPD-26 .... metrotrexate, Citrovorum Factor, VM-26, Procarbazine, Dexamethasone [*Antineoplastic drug regimen*] (DAVI)
MVPE.......... Market Value of Portfolio Equity
MVPP.......... Mechlorethamine/Vinblastine/Procarbazine/Prednisone (DB)
MVPP.......... Mustargen [*Nitrogen mustard*], Vinblastine, Procarbazine, Prednisone [*Antineoplastic drug regimen*]
MVPp.......... Mustine, Vinblastine, Procarbazine, prednisone [*Antineoplastic drug regimen*] (DAVI)
MVPR.......... Master Verification Process Requirement (SSD)
MVPS.......... Manually Variable Phase Shifter
MVPS.......... Mechanical Vacuum Pump System
MVPS.......... Medicare Volume Performance Standard
MVPS.......... Medium-Voltage Power Supply (IAA)
MVPS.......... Mitral Valve Prolapse Syndrome [*Cardiology*]
MVPS.......... Multiple Vertical Protective Shelter [*for missiles*] (MCD)
MVPT.......... Motor-Free Visual Perception Test
MVPTG........ Medial Vascularized Patellar Tendon Graft [*Sports medicine*]
MVQ............. Malvern, AR [*Location identifier*] [*FAA*] (FAAL)
MVR$_2$......... Malabar Volunteer Rifles [*British military*] (DMA)
MVR............. Maneuver (AABC)
MVR............. Maroua [*Cameroon*] [*Airport symbol*] (OAG)
MVR............. Massive Vitreous Retraction (MAE)
MVR............. Massive Vitreous Retractor [*Blade*] [*Ophthalmology*] (DAVI)
MVR............. Master Verification Requirement (SSD)
MVR............. Maverick Airways Corp. [*FAA designator*] (FAAC)
MVR............. Maximum Ventilation Rate [*Medicine*] (DAVI)
MVR............. Mean Value Reference [*Mathematics*]
MVR............. Mechanical Vapor Recompression [*For evaporators*]
MVR............. Microvitreoretinal (DMAA)
MVR............. Minimal Vascular Resistance [*Medicine*] (DMAA)
MVR............. Minisatellite Variant Repeat [*Genetics*]
MVR............. Missing Volume Report
MVR............. Mitral Valve Regurgitation [*Cardiology*] (DAVI)
MVR............. Mitral Valve Replacement [*Cardiology*]
mvr............. Moldavian Soviet Socialist Republic [*MARC country of publication code*] [*Library of Congress*] (LCCP)
MVR............. Mondavi Resources Ltd. [*Vancouver Stock Exchange symbol*]
MVR............. Monthly Variance Report (ABAC)
MVR............. Motor Vehicle Repair (HEAS)
MVR............. Motor Vehicle Report
MVR............. Mover
MVR............. Mussoorie Volunteer Rifles [*British military*] (DMA)
MVRA.......... Metropolitan Visiting and Relief Association [*British*]
MVRCA........ Magnalink Variable Resource Compression Algorithm (SAUS)

MVRDC........	Motor Vehicle Repair Disputes Committee [*New South Wales, Australia*]
MVRG	Medieval Village Research Group (EA)
MVRI	Mixed Vaccine, Respiratory Infection [*Medicine*]
MVRIAG.......	Murray Valley Rural Industry Assistance Group [*Australia*]
MVRIC	Motor Vehicle Repair Industry Council [*New South Wales, Australia*]
MVRO	Minimum-Variance Reduced-Order [*Statistics*] (PDAA)
MVRS	Marine Vapor Recovery System (GNE)
MVRS	Mechanical Vapor Recovery System [*Engineering*]
MVRS	Mystic Valley Railway Society (EA)
MVRT	Multivoltage Radiation Therapy (MELL)
MVS	Magnetic Valve System [*Diesel engines*]
MVS	Magnetic Voltage Stabilizer
MVS	Manifold Vacuum Sensor [*Automotive engineering*]
MVS	Master of Valuation Sciences (GAGS)
MVS	Master of Veterinary Studies
MVS	Master of Veterinary Surgery
MVS	Mature Vesicular Follicle [*Medicine*] (MELL)
MVS	Mechanical Vibration System
MVSc	Megastar Ventures [*Vancouver Stock Exchange symbol*]
MVS	Mennonite Voluntary Service
MVS	Mesenteric Venous System [*Medicine*] (MELL)
MVS	Metal Vapour Synthesis [*Chemistry*]
MVS	Metering Valve Sensor [*Automotive engineering*]
mvs	Middle Value Select (NAKS)
MVS	Middle Valve Select (MCD)
MVS	Midvoid Stream [*Medicine*] (MELL)
MVS	Military Vehicle Systems (ACAE)
MVS	Millersville State College, Millersville, PA [*OCLC symbol*] (OCLC)
MVS	Mine Ventilation System [*Engineering*]
MVS	Miniature Vehicle Sensor (ACAE)
MVS	Minimum Visual Signal
MVS	Ministerstvo Vooruzhennykh Sil [*Ministry of the Armed Forces*] [*1946-50; superseded by VM, MVMF*] [*Former USSR*]
MVS	Missile Velocity Servo
MVS	Mission Verification System (SAUS)
MVS	Mission Video System [*NASA*]
MVS	Mitral Valve Stenosis [*Cardiology*] (DAVI)
MVS	Mobile Video Services Ltd. [*Washington, DC*] [*Telecommunications*] (TSSD)
MVS	Modular 8mm Video System [*Eastman Kodak Co.*]
MVS	Modularized Vehicle Stimulation [*Program*]
MVS	Most Valued Supplier [*Mazda Motor Corp.*]
MVS	Multiple Vibration System
mvs	Multiple Virtual Storage (NAKS)
MVS	Multiple Virtual Storage [*IBM Corp.*] [*Computer science*]
MVS	Multiple Virtual System [*Computer science*]
MVS	Multiprogramming with Virtual Storage [*Computer science*] (ECII)
MVS	Multivariable Storage [*Computer science*]
MVS	Multivendor Service (DMAA)
MVS	MuniVest Florida Fund [*NYSE symbol*] (SPSG)
MVS	Muzzle Velocity System (SAUS)
MVSB..........	Motor Vehicle Storage Building
MVSc..........	Master of Veterinary Science [*Canada*] (ASC)
MVS/ESA	Multiple Virtual Storage/Enterprise System Architecture [*Computer science*] (VLIE)
MVSESASP...	Multiple Virtual Storage/ Extended System Architecture System Product (SAUS)
MVSI..........	MVSI, Inc. [*NASDAQ symbol*] (SAG)
MVSL..........	Mouse Visible Specific Locus [*Test for mutagenesis*]
MVSMA.......	Mechanical Vibrating Screen Manufacturers Association [*Later, Vibrating Screen Manufacturers Association*] (EA)
MVSN	Milizia Volontaria per la Sicurezza Nazionale [*Italian Voluntary Militia for National Security*] (WDAA)
MVSP.........	Maintain Visual Separation [*Aviation*]
MVSPC........	Multi-Variate Statistical Process Control [*Computer science*] (VLIE)
MVSR.........	Monthly Vital Statistics Report [*A publication*] (DHSM)
MVSRF.......	Man-Vehicle Systems Research Facility (SAUS)
MVSS..........	Motor Vehicle Safety Standard
MVSS..........	Motor Vehicle Storage Shed [*Army*] (AABC)
MVSSE........	Multiple Virtual Storage System Extension
MVS/SE.......	MVS/System Extension (NITA)
MVS/SP	MVS/System Product (NITA)
MVSt..........	Master of Veterinary Studies (ADA)
MVS/TSO	Multiple Virtual Storage/Time Sharing Option (SAUS)
MVS/TSO	Multiple Virtual Storage/Time-Sharing Option [*Computer science*] (VLIE)
MVS/XA	MVS/Extended Architecture (NITA)
MVSZGA......	Mein Vertrauen Steht zu Gott Allein [*My Trust Is in God Alone*] [*Motto of Johann Adolf II, Duke of Saxony-Weissenfels (1649-97)*] [*German*]
MVT...........	Malfunction Verification Test (MCD)
MVT...........	Marginal Value Theorem [*Mathematical model developed by Dr. Eric Charnov*]
MVT...........	Market-Value Transmission [*Pricing concept*]
MVT...........	Mataiva [*French Polynesia*] [*Airport symbol*] (OAG)
MVT...........	Maximal Ventilation Time [*Medicine*] (DAVI)
MVT...........	Miscellaneous Vector Table
MVT...........	Mission Verification Test [*NASA*] (NASA)
MVT...........	Mississippi Valley Type [*Ore deposits*] [*Geology*]
MVT...........	Moisture Vapor Transmission (EDCT)
MVT...........	Moisture Vapor Transmission Rate
MVT...........	Monte Vettore [*Italy*] [*Seismograph station code, US Geological Survey*] (SEIS)
MVT...........	Motor Vehicle Theft (GOBB)
MVT	Motor Vehicle Title
MVT	Mount Vernon Terminal [*AAR code*]
MVT	Movement (MSA)
MVT	Multinational Volunteer Teams
MVT	Multiprogramming with a Variable Number of Tasks [*IBM Corp.*] [*Control program*] [*Computer science*]
MVT	Multivariable Task (MCD)
MVT	Munivest Fund II [*NYSE symbol*] (SAG)
MVT	MuniVest Fund, Inc. [*NYSE symbol*] (SPSG)
MVTE	Master of Vocational-Technical Education (GAGS)
MVT Ed........	Master of Vocational and Technical Education (PGP)
MVTL..........	Modified Variable-Threshold Logic [*Computer science*]
MVTLEA.......	Motor Vehicle Theft Law Enforcement Act [*1984*]
MVTR..........	Moisture Vapor Transmission Rate
MVTS..........	Motor Vehicle Tampering Survey (EEVL)
MVTS..........	Motor Vehicle Test Station (COE)
MVT/TSO	MVT/Time Sharing Option (NITA)
MVTV	MetroVision of North America, Inc. [*NASDAQ symbol*] (SAG)
MVU	Minimum Variance Unbiased [*Statistics*]
MVU	Mulege [*Mexico*] [*Airport symbol*] (AD)
MVU	Musgrave [*Australia*] [*Airport symbol*] [*Obsolete*] (OAG)
MVUE	Man/Vehicular User Equipment
MVUE..........	Minimum Variance Unbiased Estimate [*Statistics*]
MVULE........	Minimum Variance Unbiased Linear Estimator [*Statistics*]
MVV	Maximum Volume Ventilation (SAUS)
MVV	Maximum Voluntary Ventilation
MVV	Maximum Voluntary Volume [*Medicine*] (DAVI)
MVV	Mean Vertical Velocity
MVV	Mitsubishi Vertical Vortex [*Automotive engineering*]
MVV	Mixed Vespid Venom [*Pharmacology*] (DAVI)
MVV_1	Maximal Ventilatory Volume (MAE)
MVVPP	Mustargen [*Nitrogen mustard*], Vincristine, Vinblastine, Procarbazine, Prednisone [*Antineoplastic drug regimen*]
MVW	Minot-Von Willebrand [*Syndrome*] [*Medicine*] (DB)
MVW	Missile Viewing Window
MVW	Mount Vernon [*Washington*] [*Airport symbol*] (OAG)
MVW	Mud Volcano [*Wyoming*] [*Seismograph station code, US Geological Survey*] (SEIS)
MVWDU	Missile Viewing Window Deicing Unit
MVWGS	Multi-Vintage Wine Growers Society [*British*] (DBA)
MVX	Media Videotex [*Vancouver Stock Exchange symbol*]
MVX	Minvoul [*Gabon*] [*Airport symbol*] (OAG)
MVX	Multiplex
MVY	Martha's Vineyard [*Massachusetts*] [*Airport symbol*] (OAG)
MVY	MuniVest New York Insured Fund [*NYSE symbol*] (SPSG)
MVY	MuniVest NY Insured Fund [*NYSE symbol*] (TTSB)
MVZ	Move Zones (VLIE)
MVZ	Museum of Vertebrate Zoology [*University of California, Berkeley*]
MVZG..........	Mein Verlangen zu Gott [*My Desires (I Give) to God*] [*Motto of Anna Marie, Margravine of Brandenburg (1609-80)*] [*German*]
MVZS..........	Manifold Vacuum Zone Switch [*Automotive engineering*]
MW	Machine Word (IAA)
MW	Magnesiowustite [*Mineralogy*]
MW	Malawi [*ANSI two-letter standard code*] (CNC)
mw	Malawi [*MARC country of publication code*] [*Library of Congress*] (LCCP)
M-W	Mallory-Weiss Syndrome [*Medicine*] (MEDA)
MW	Management World [*Administrative Management Society*] [*A publication*]
MW	Manual Word
MW	Manufacturing Week (MCD)
MW	Man Watchers (EA)
mw	Man Week (NAKS)
MW	Man-Week (NASA)
MW	Marginal Wage [*Economics*]
MW	Marginal Wings [*Botany*]
MW	Master of Wine [*Bestowed by the Worshipful Company of Vintners, one of the ancient guilds in the City of London*]
M/W	Mate With (MCD)
MW	Maya Airways [*ICAO designator*] (AD)
MW	Media Watch [*An association*] (EA)
MW	Medium Wall
MW	Medium Wave (WA)
MW	Medium Wave Band
MW	Meetings Word (NITA)
MW	Megawatt [*Also, MEGW*]
MW	Memory Write [*Computer science*]
MW	Men's Wearhouse [*NYSE symbol*]
M-W	Merriam-Webster [*Publisher*]
MW	Message Waiting
MW	Metachrondral Wave [*Physiology*]
MW	Metalworker [*British military*] (DMA)
M/W	Methanol/Water
mW	Microwatt
mw	Microwave (NAKS)
MW	Microwave
MW	Middle Ware (VLIE)
MW	Middle Welsh [*Language, etc.*]
MW	Midwife (MELL)
MW	Midwing [*Aviation*] (AIA)
MW	Migratory Worker (OICC)
MW	Milliwatt (ACAE)
mw	Milliwatt (NAKS)
mW	Milliwatt
MW	Mine Warfare

MW	Mine Warning (NATG)
MW	Ministry of Works [*British*]
MW	Minnesota Western Railroad (IIA)
MW	Mixed Wastes [*Environmental science*] (COE)
mw	Mixed Widths [*Forest industry*] (WPI)
MW	Mixed Widths
MW	Mobile Workshop [*British*]
MW	Modulated Wave (IAA)
MW	Moewe Flugzeugbau, Heini Dittmar [*Germany*] [*ICAO aircraft manufacturer identifier*] (ICAO)
MW	Molecular Weight [*Also, M, MOL WT*]
MW	Money Wages [*Economics*]
MW	Monier-Williams Method (RDA)
MW	Montana Western Railway (IIA)
MW	Mosaic Wart [*Medicine*] (MELL)
MW	Most Worshipful [*Freemasonry*]
MW	Most Worthy
MW	Motor Wagon [*British*]
MW	Mud Weight [*Well drilling technology*]
MW	Multiple Warts [*Medicine*] (MELL)
MW	Multiple Wounds
MW	Multipurpose Weapon (MCD)
MW	Multi-Wink (VLIE)
MW	Multiwire (IAA)
MW	Music of the World [*American Forces Radio and Television Service*] (DNAB)
MW	Music Wire
Mw	Weighted Mean [*Psychology*]
MW	Winnipeg Centennial Library, Manitoba [*Library symbol*] [*National Library of Canada*] (NLC)
MW	Worcester Public Library and Central Massachusetts Regional Library System Headquarters, Worcester, MA [*Library symbol*] [*Library of Congress*] (LCLS)
MWA	American Antiquarian Society, Worcester, MA [*Library symbol*] [*Library of Congress*] (LCLS)
MWA	Major World Authors [*A publication*]
MWA	Management by Walking Around
MWA	Manitoba Department of Agriculture, Winnipeg, Manitoba [*Library symbol*] [*National Library of Canada*] (NLC)
MWA	Manufacturing Work Authority
MWA	Marion [*Illinois*] [*Airport symbol*] (OAG)
MWA	Married Women's Association [*British*] (DBA)
MWA	Mayflower Warehousemen's Association (EA)
MWA	Media Women's Association
MWA	Meteorological Watch Advisory
MWA	Mid-West Abrasive Co. (EFIS)
MWA	Midwest Area (SARE)
MWA	Mineral Workings Act [*Town planning*] [*British*]
MWA	Modern Woodmen of America (EA)
MWA	Momentum-Wheel Assembly
MWA	Movers' & Warehousemen's Association of America Inc., Washington DC [*STAC*]
MWA	Multiple Weapons Adapter (SAUS)
MWA	Munitions of War Act [*British*]
MWA	Mystery Writers of America (NADA)
MW/AA	Missile Warning/Attack Assessment (MCD)
MWAA	Movers' and Warehousemen's Association of America [*Defunct*] (EA)
MWAC	Air Command Headquarters, Canadian Forces Base, Westwin, Manitoba [*Library symbol*] [*National Library of Canada*] (NLC)
MWAC	Assumption College, Worcester, MA [*Library symbol*] [*Library of Congress*] (LCLS)
MWAC	Midwest Archeological Center [*National Park Service*] (GRD)
MWAD	Alcohol and Drug Education Service, Winnipeg, Manitoba [*Library symbol*] [*National Library of Canada*] (NLC)
MWAE	Minimum-Weighted-Absolute Error [*Statistics*] (PDAA)
MWAF	Alcoholism Foundation of Manitoba, Winnipeg, Manitoba [*Library symbol*] [*National Library of Canada*] (NLC)
MWAG	Research Station, Agriculture Canada [*Station de Recherches, Agriculture Canada*] Winnipeg, Manitoba [*Library symbol*] [*National Library of Canada*] (NLC)
MWAI	Mystery Writers of America Inc. (NADA)
MWal	Waltham Public Library, Waltham MA [*Library symbol*] [*Library of Congress*] (LCLS)
MWalA	American Jewish Historical Society, Waltham, MA [*Library symbol*] [*Library of Congress*] (LCLS)
MWalAF	African Studies Association, Brandeis University, Waltham, MA [*Library symbol*] [*Library of Congress*] (LCLS)
MWalB	Brandeis University, Waltham, MA [*Library symbol*] [*Library of Congress*] (LCLS)
MWalBe	Bentley College, Waltham, MA [*Library symbol*] [*Library of Congress*] (LCLS)
MWalFAR	Federal Archives and Records Center, General Services Administration, Waltham, MA [*Library symbol*] [*Library of Congress*] (LCLS)
MWalG	General Telephone & Electronics Laboratories, Inc., Waltham Research Center Library, Waltham, MA [*Library symbol*] [*Library of Congress*] (LCLS)
MWalK	John F. Kennedy Library, Waltham, MA [*Library symbol*] [*Library of Congress*] (LCLS)
MWalMT	Mobil Tyco Solar Energy Corp., Waltham, MA [*Library symbol*] [*Library of Congress*] (LCLS)
MWAMA	Administration Branch, Manitoba Department of Municipal Affairs, Winnipeg, Manitoba [*Library symbol*] [*National Library of Canada*] (NLC)

MWAMT	Aikins, MacAulay, and Thorvaldson Law Firm, Winnipeg, Manitoba [*Library symbol*] [*National Library of Canada*] (NLC)
MWAR	Microware Systems Corp. [*NASDAQ symbol*] (SAG)
MWAR	Microwave Systems [*NASDAQ symbol*] (TTSB)
MWar	Wareham Free Library, Wareham, MA [*Library symbol*] [*Library of Congress*] (LCLS)
MWARA	Major World Air Route Area
MWARN	Manitoba Association of Registered Nurses, Winnipeg, Manitoba [*Library symbol*] [*National Library of Canada*] (NLC)
MWARS	Major Command Worldwide Ammunition Reporting System [*Army*]
MWARS	Synod Office, Diocese of Rupert's Land, Anglican Church of Canada, Winnipeg, Manitoba [*Library symbol*] [*National Library of Canada*] (NLC)
MWAS	Arthritis Society, Winnipeg, Manitoba [*Library symbol*] [*National Library of Canada*] (NLC)
MWASD	Assiniboine South School Division No. 3, Winnipeg, Manitoba [*Library symbol*] [*National Library of Canada*] (NLC)
MWat	Watertown Free Public Library, Watertown, MA [*Library symbol*] [*Library of Congress*] (LCLS)
MWatM	Massachusetts Bay Community College, Watertown, MA [*Library symbol*] [*Library of Congress*] (LCLS)
MWatP	Perkins School for the Blind, Watertown, MA [*Library symbol*] [*Library of Congress*] (LCLS)
MWatP-BP	Massachusetts Regional Library for the Blind and Physically Handicapped, PerkinsSchool for the Blind, Watertown, MA [*Library symbol*] [*Library of Congress*] (LCLS)
MWatP-BPH	Regional Library for the Blind and Physically Handicapped, Perkins School for the Blind, Watertown, MA [*Library symbol*] [*Library of Congress*] (LCLS)
MWAV	M-Wave, Inc. [*NASDAQ symbol*] (SAG)
MWAVE	Microwave
M-Wave	M-Wave, Inc. [*Associated Press*] (SAG)
MWAX	Mountain West Airline [*Air carrier designation symbol*]
M-Way	Motorway [*British*]
MWayR	Raytheon Co., Wayland, MA [*Library symbol*] [*Library of Congress*] (LCLS)
MWB	Master Work Book (NASA)
MWB	Maxwell-Wien Bridge [*Electronics*]
MWB	Metropolitan Water Board [*British*]
MWB	Middlewest Motor Freight Bureau, Kansas City MO [*STAC*]
MWB	Military War Book (SAUS)
MWB	Ministry of Works and Buildings [*British*]
MWB	Motor Whale Boat
MWB	Multilayer Wiring Board
MWBA	Bristol Aerospace Ltd., Winnipeg, Manitoba [*Library symbol*] [*National Library of Canada*] (NLC)
MWBAS	Mail Will Be Addressed to Show
MWBC	Mean Wafers Between Cleans (AAEL)
MWBC	Technical Library, Boeing of Canada Ltd., Winnipeg, Manitoba [*Library symbol*] [*National Library of Canada*] (NLC)
MWBe	Becker Junior College, Worcester, MA [*Library symbol*] [*Library of Congress*] (LCLS)
MWBH	Bethel Hospital, Winkler, Manitoba [*Library symbol*] [*National Library of Canada*] (NLC)
MWBI	Midwest Bacshares Del [*NASDAQ symbol*] (TTSB)
MWBI	Midwest Bancshares [*NASDAQ symbol*] (SAG)
MWBL	Mounted Warfighting Battlespace Laborarory [*Army*] (RDA)
MWBM	Bethania Mennonite Personal Care Home, Winnipeg, Manitoba [*Library symbol*] [*National Library of Canada*] (NLC)
MWBMT	Mint with Both Mint Tags [*Collectibles*]
MWBP	Missile Warning Bypass (DWSG)
MWbriM	Massasoit Community College, West Bridgewater, MA [*Library symbol*] [*Library of Congress*] (LCLS)
MWC	Clark University, Worcester, MA [*Library symbol*] [*Library of Congress*] (LCLS)
MWC	Mad World Campaign [*An association*] [*Defunct*] (EA)
MWC	Magnetoionic Wave Component
MWC	Major Wingfield Club (EA)
MWC	Mary Washington College [*University of Virginia*]
MWC	Maxwell Communication Corp. [*Toronto Stock Exchange symbol*]
MWC	Medium Weight Coated Paper (DGA)
MWC	Melbourne Walking Club [*Australia*]
MWC	Midwest Conference (PSS)
MWC	Miltonvale Wesleyan College [*Kansas*]
MWC	Milwaukee, WI [*Location identifier*] [*FAA*] (FAAL)
MWC	Minister for [*or Ministry of*] War Communications [*British*] [*World War II*]
MWC	Missile Warning Center (ACAE)
MWC	Missile Weapons Control (MCD)
MWC	Monod-Wyman-Changeux [*Model*] [*Enzymology*]
MWC	Mount Wilson [*California*] [*Seismograph station code, US Geological Survey*] (SEIS)
MWC	Moving-Withdrawal Chromatography
MWC	Multiple Water Connector (KSC)
MWC	Multi-Wire Cable (VLIE)
MWC	Municipal Waste Combustor (GFGA)
MWC	Music and Record Library, Canadian Broadcasting Corp. [*Musicotheque et Discotheque, Societe Radio-Canada*] Winnipeg, Manitoba [*Library symbol*] [*National Library of Canada*] (NLC)
MWCA	Monetary Working Capital Adjustment [*British*]
MWCA	Monterey Wine Country Association (EA)
MWCAC	Midwest Collegiate Athletic Conference (PSS)
MWCB	Cayman Brac/Gerrard Smith [*Cayman Islands*] [*ICAO location identifier*] (ICLI)
MWCB	Manufacturer's Working Cell Bank [*Cell line*]

MWCC .... Metropolitan Wrestling Coach's Conference (PSS)
MWCC .... Mineral Water Co. of Canada (ECON)
MWCCA .... Manitoba Department of Consumer and Corporate Affairs, Winnipeg, Manitoba [*Library symbol*] [*Obsolete*] [*National Library of Canada*] (NLC)
MWCCAC ..... Midwest Community College Athletic Conference (PSS)
MWCCI .... Manitoba Consumer's Bureau, Winnipeg, Manitoba [*Library symbol*] [*National Library of Canada*] (NLC)
MWCCIR ...... Central Region Information Resources Center, Canada Department of Communications[*Centre de Documentation Region du Centre, Ministere des Communications*] Winnipeg, Manitoba [*Library symbol*] [*National Library of Canada*] (NLC)
MWC/CS ...... Mechanized Wire Centering/Cross Section [*AT & T*] [*Telecommunications*] (TEL)
MWCE .... Controlled Environments Ltd., Winnipeg, Manitoba [*Library symbol*] [*National Library of Canada*] (NLC)
MWCE .... Millimeter Wave Communications Experiment
MWCF .... Canadian Forces Aerospace and Navigation School, Canadian Forces Base Winnipeg, Westwin, Manitoba [*Library symbol*] [*National Library of Canada*] (NLC)
MWCG .... Grand Cayman [*Cayman Islands*] [*ICAO location identifier*] (ICLI)
MWCH .... Concordia Hospital, Winnipeg, Manitoba [*Library symbol*] [*National Library of Canada*] (NLC)
MWCHA .... Charles Howard & Associates, Winnipeg, Manitoba [*Library symbol*] [*National Library of Canada*] (NLC)
MWCHD .... Charleswood Public Library, Winnipeg, Manitoba [*Library symbol*] [*National Library of Canada*] (NLC)
MWCI .... Canertech, Inc., Winnipeg, Manitoba [*Library symbol*] [*National Library of Canada*] (NLC)
MWCL .... Little Cayman/Boddenfield [*Cayman Islands*] [*ICAO location identifier*] (ICLI)
MWCL .... Worcester County Law Library Association, Worcester, MA [*Library symbol*] [*Library of Congress*] (LCLS)
MWCLC .... Midwest Classic Conference (PSS)
MWCM .... Canadian Mennonite Bible College, Winnipeg, Manitoba [*Library symbol*] [*National Library of Canada*] (NLC)
MWCM .... Milliwatt per Square Centimeter (IAA)
MWCMS ...... Centre for Mennonite Brethren Studies in Canada, Winnipeg, Manitoba [*Library symbol*] [*National Library of Canada*] (NLC)
MWCO .... Medium Weight Coated Offset Paper (DGA)
MWCO .... Molecular Weight Cutoff [*Chemistry*]
MWCR .... Georgetown/Owen Roberts International [*Cayman Islands*] [*ICAO location identifier*] (ICLI)
MWCR .... Mercury-Wetted Contact Relay
MWCS .... Marine Wing Communication Squadron
MWCS .... Mental Welfare Commission for Scotland
MWCS .... Midwest Cable & Satellite, Inc. [*Minneapolis, MN*] [*Telecommunications*] (TSSD)
MWCS .... Millimeter Wave Contrast Seeker (MCD)
MWCS .... Missile Weapons Control System (MCD)
MWCS .... Mobile Weapons Control System
MWCSC .... Midwest Collegiate Ski Conference (PSS)
MWCSCC ..... Midwest Council of Sports Car Clubs
MWCSJ .... Minimum Wage Coalition to Save Jobs [*Defunct*] (EA)
MWCSS .... Mine Warfare Command Support System (SAUS)
MWCT .... Manitoba Cancer Treatment and Research Foundation, Winnipeg, Manitoba [*Library symbol*] [*National Library of Canada*] (NLC)
MWCU .... Credit Union Central of Manitoba, Winnipeg, Manitoba [*Library symbol*] [*National Library of Canada*] (NLC)
MWCU .... Molecular Weight Cut-Off [*Metallurgy*]
MWCWB ...... Canadian Wheat Board [*Commission Canadienne du Ble*] Winnipeg, Manitoba [*Library symbol*] [*National Library of Canada*] (NLC)
MWD .... Magnetostatic Wave Device (ACAE)
MWD .... Measurement-While Drilling [*Drilling technology*]
MWd .... Megawatt-Day (ABAC)
MWD .... Megawatt-Day
MWD .... Megaword
MWD .... Metering Water Dispenser [*Apollo*] [*NASA*]
MWD .... Meters Water Depth
MWD .... Metropolitan Water District
MWD .... Microwave Diathermy [*Physical therapy*] (DAVI)
MWD .... Military Working Dog (DOMA)
MWD .... Millimeter Wave Device
MWD .... Molecular Weight Distribution
MWD .... Morgan Stanley Dean Witter [*NYSE symbol*] [*Formerly, Dean Witter Discover & Co.*] (SG)
MWD .... Moving Window Display (MCD)
MWD .... Rochester, NY [*Location identifier*] [*FAA*] (FAAL)
MWDAC .... Mountain West Desegregation Assistance Centers (EDAC)
MWDCA .... Midwest Decoy Collectors Association (EA)
MWDDEA .... Mutual Weapons Development Data Exchange Agreement [*NATO*]
MWDDEP .... Mutual Weapons Development Data Exchange Procedures [*NATO*]
MWDEA .... Mutual Weapons Development Data Exchange Agreement (TIMI)
MWDGP .... Manly Warringah Division of General Practice (SAUS)
MWDGP .... Mid West Division of General Practice (SAUS)
MWDI .... Master Water Data Index [*US Geological Survey*] [*Information service or system*] (CRD)
MWDL .... Deer Lodge Hospital, Winnipeg, Manitoba [*Library symbol*] [*National Library of Canada*] (NLC)
MWD/MTU ... Megawatt-Days per Metric Ton of Uranium
MWDO .... Minewarfare Tactical Development Group (SAUS)
MWDP .... Master Warning Display Panel (SAUS)
MWDP .... Mutual Weapons Development Program [*NATO*]
MWDRR .... Manitoba Department of Renewable Resources, Winnipeg, Manitoba [*Library symbol*] [*National Library of Canada*] (NLC)

MWDS .... Man-Worn Detector System (SAUS)
MWDS .... Med/Waste Inc. [*NASDAQ symbol*] (TTSB)
MWDS .... Missile Warning and Display System [*or Subsystem*] (MCD)
MWDSW ...... Med/Waste Inc. Wrrt'A' [*NASDAQ symbol*] (TTSB)
MWD/T .... Megawatt-Days per Ton
MWDT .... Mutual Weapons Development Team [*Military*]
MWDU .... Ducks Unlimited, Winnipeg, Manitoba [*Library symbol*] [*National Library of Canada*] (NLC)
MWE .... Manitoba Department of Education, Winnipeg, Manitoba [*Library symbol*] [*National Library of Canada*] (NLC)
MWE .... Manufacturer's Weight Empty (DA)
MWE .... Megawatt Electric (IAA)
MWe .... Megawatts of Electric Power
MWE .... Merowe [*Sudan*] [*Airport symbol*] (OAG)
MWE .... Meters of Water Equivalent
MWE .... Millimeter Wave Experiment
MWeA .... Westfield Athenaeum, Westfield, MA [*Library symbol*] [*Library of Congress*] (LCLS)
MWEAE .... Central Region Headquarters, Atmospheric Environment Service, Environment Canada[*Quartier-General de la Region Centrale, Service de l'Environnement Atmosphe rique, Environnement Canada*] Winnipeg, Manitoba [*Library symbol*] [*National Library of Canada*] (NLC)
MWeba .... Whelden Memorial Library, West Barnstable, MA [*Library symbol*] [*Library of Congress*] (LCLS)
MWebaC ...... Cape Cod Community College, West Barnstable, MA [*Library symbol*] [*Library of Congress*] (LCLS)
MWECW ...... Canadian Wildlife Service, Environment Canada [*Service Canadien de la Faune, Environnement Canada*] Winnipeg, Manitoba [*Library symbol*] [*National Library of Canada*] (NLC)
MWEE .... Mechanised Warfare Experimental Establishment [*British military*] (DMA)
MWEEP .... Environmental Protection Service, Environment Canada [*Service de la Protection de l'Environnement, Environnement Canada*] Winnipeg, Manitoba [*Library symbol*] [*National Library of Canada*] (NLC)
MWEIA .... Montessori World Educational Institute Australia
MWelC .... Wellesley College, Wellesley, MA [*Library symbol*] [*Library of Congress*] (LCLS)
MWelD .... Dana Hall School Library, Wellesley, MA [*Library symbol*] [*Library of Congress*] (LCLS)
MWeldi .... Member of the Welding Institute [*British*] (DBQ)
MWEM .... Major Work Element Manager (ACAE)
MWEM .... Manitoba Environmental Management Division, Winnipeg, Manitoba [*Library symbol*] [*National Library of Canada*] (NLC)
MWEM .... Mine Warfare Evaluation Model
MWEMM ...... Manitoba Energy and Mines, Winnipeg, Manitoba [*Library symbol*] [*National Library of Canada*] (NLC)
MWenhG ...... Gordon College, Wenham, MA [*Library symbol*] [*Library of Congress*] (LCLS)
MWenhHi ..... Wenham Historical Society and Museum, Wenham, MA [*Library symbol*] [*Library of Congress*] (LCLS)
MWES .... Member of the Women's Engineering Society [*British*] (DBQ)
MWESM .... Special Materials Services, Manitoba Department of Education, Winnipeg, Manitoba [*Library symbol*] [*National Library of Canada*] (NLC)
MWesR .... Regis College, Weston, MA [*Library symbol*] [*Library of Congress*] (LCLS)
MWestonGS... Church of Jesus Christ of Latter-Day Saints, Genealogical Society Library, Boston Branch, Weston, MA [*Library symbol*] [*Library of Congress*] (LCLS)
MWestonR... Regis College, Weston, MA [*Library symbol*] [*Library of Congress*] (LCLS)
MWeT .... Westfield State College, Westfield, MA [*Library symbol*] [*Library of Congress*] (LCLS)
MWEU .... Moving Wall Electrophoresis Unit (SAUS)
MWEWSH ... Manitoba Department of Environment, Workplace Safety and Health, Winnipeg, Manitoba [*Library symbol*] [*National Library of Canada*] (NLC)
MWeyAA...... Abigail Adams Historical Society, Weymouth, MA [*Library symbol*] [*Library of Congress*] (LCLS)
MWF .... Make-a-Wish Foundation [*Later, MWFA*] (EA)
MWF .... Marine General Workers' Federation
MWF .... Medical Women's Federation [*British*] (DAS)
MWF .... Medical Working File (DOMA)
MWF .... Military Works Force (SAUS)
MWF .... Monday, Wednesday, Friday (BARN)
MWFA .... Make-a-Wish Foundation of America (EA)
MWFC .... Mary Wilson Fan Club (EA)
MWFC .... Midwest Football Conference (PSS)
MWFCA .... Motor Wheel and Flyer Club of America [*Defunct*] (EA)
MWFCS .... Multiweapons Fire Control System (DNAB)
MWFD .... Fred Douglas Lodge Nursing Home, Winnipeg, Manitoba [*Library symbol*] [*National Library of Canada*] (NLC)
MWFD .... Midwest Federal Financial [*NASDAQ symbol*] (SAG)
MWFD .... Midwest Fed Finl [*NASDAQ symbol*] (TTSB)
MWFG .... Fort Garry Public Library, Winnipeg, Manitoba [*Library symbol*] [*National Library of Canada*] (NLC)
MWFI .... Manitoba Department of Finance, Winnipeg, Manitoba [*Library symbol*] [*National Library of Canada*] (NLC)
MWFM .... Microwave Window Failure Mechanism
MWfo .... J. V. Fletcher Library, Westford, MA [*Library symbol*] [*Library of Congress*] (LCLS)
MWFOPS ..... Mine Warfare Operations (NVT)

MWFP.........	Winnipeg Free Press Co. Ltd., Manitoba [*Library symbol*] [*National Library of Canada*] (NLC)
MWFRS	Manitoba Department of Fitness, Recreation and Sport, Winnipeg, Manitoba [*Library symbol*] [*National Library of Canada*] (NLC)
MWFS.........	Marine Wing Facilities Squadron
MWFS.........	Maritime Warfare School [*Canadian Navy*]
MWFSD	Frontier School Division, Winnipeg, Manitoba [*Library symbol*] [*National Library of Canada*] (NLC)
MWFW........	Freshwater Institute, Fisheries and Oceans Canada [*Institut des Eaux Douces, Peches et Oceans Canada*] Winnipeg, Manitoba [*Library symbol*] [*National Library of Canada*] (NLC)
MWG	Maintenance Analyzer Working Group (MCD)
MWG	Maintenance Working Group (VLIE)
MWG	Management Working Group [*Army*] (RDA)
MWG	Maternal Weight Gain (MELL)
MWG	Meteorological Working Group
MWG	Missile-Warning Group [*Military*]
MWG	Model Work Group [*Environmental Protection Agency*] (GFGA)
MWG	Muenster-Westfalen [*Federal Republic of Germany*] [*Seismograph station code, US Geological Survey*] (SEIS)
MWG	Music Wire Gauge
MWGBP.......	Guertin Brothers Paint Library, Winnipeg, Manitoba [*Library symbol*] [*National Library of Canada*] (NLC)
MWGC........	Midwestern Governors Conference
MWGCP	Most Worthy Grand Chief Patriarch
MWGH........	Grace Hospital, Winnipeg, Manitoba [*Library symbol*] [*National Library of Canada*] (NLC)
MWGHA.......	Gunn Hoffer & Associates Law Firm, Winnipeg, Manitoba [*Library symbol*] [*National Library of Canada*] (NLC)
MWGM	Most Worshipful [*or Worthy*] Grand Master [*Freemasonry*]
MWGP	Midwest Grain Products [*NASDAQ symbol*] (TTSB)
MWGP	Midwest Grain Products, Inc. [*NASDAQ symbol*] (CTT)
MWGR	Canadian Grain Commission, Agriculture Canada [*Commission Canadienne des Grains, Agriculture Canada*] Winnipeg, Manitoba [*Library symbol*] [*National Library of Canada*] (NLC)
MWGW	Great West Life Assurance Co., Winnipeg, Manitoba [*Library symbol*] [*National Library of Canada*] (NLC)
MWH	Baycorp Holdings [*AMEX symbol*] (SG)
MWH	College of the Holy Cross, Worcester, MA [*Library symbol*] [*Library of Congress*] (LCLS)
MWH	Main Wiring Harness [*Automotive engineering*]
MWH	Manitoba Hydro, Winnipeg, Manitoba [*Library symbol*] [*National Library of Canada*] (NLC)
Mwh...........	Megawatt Hour
MWh...........	Megawatt-Hour (MCD)
MW(H)........	Megawatts (Heat) (IEEE)
MWH	Milliwatt Hour
MWH	Model Wave Height
MWH	Mokuaweoweo [*Hawaii*] [*Seismograph station code, US Geological Survey*] (SEIS)
MWH	Moses Lake [*Washington*] [*Airport symbol*] (OAG)
MWHB	Hudson's Bay House, Winnipeg, Manitoba [*Library symbol*] [*National Library of Canada*] (NLC)
MWhB..........	Marine Biological Laboratory, Woods Hole, MA [*Library symbol*] [*Library of Congress*] (LCLS)
MWHF	Michigan Wildlife Habitat Foundation
MWHG	Marine Wing Headquarters Group
MWHGL	Multiple Wheel Heavy Gear Loading [*Aviation*]
MWHi	Worcester Historical Society, Worcester, MA [*Library symbol*] [*Library of Congress*] (LCLS)
MWhN	United States National Marine Fisheries Service, Northeast Fisheries Center, Woods Hole, MA [*Library symbol*] [*Library of Congress*] (LCLS)
MWHO	Manitoba Health Organizations, Winnipeg, Manitoba [*Library symbol*] [*National Library of Canada*] (NLC)
MWHP	Information Resources Center, Manitoba Health, Winnipeg, Manitoba [*Library symbol*] [*National Library of Canada*] (NLC)
MWHQ	Mobile War Headquarters (SAUS)
MWHR	Henderson Regional Library, Winnipeg, Manitoba [*Library symbol*] [*National Library of Canada*] (NLC)
MWHS	Library Services, Health Sciences Centre, Winnipeg, Manitoba [*Library symbol*] [*National Library of Canada*] (NLC)
MWHS	Marine Wing Headquarters Squadron (NVT)
MWHS	Micro Warehouse [*NASDAQ symbol*] (TTSB)
MWHS	Micro Warehouse, Inc. [*NASDAQ symbol*] (SAG)
MWHS	Modified Warhead Section (MCD)
MWHSC	Manitoba Health Services Commission, Winnipeg, Manitoba [*Library symbol*] [*National Library of Canada*] (NLC)
MWHSDET...	Marine Wing Headquarters Squadron Detachment (DNAB)
MWHT	Miscellaneous Waste Holdup Tank [*Nuclear energy*] (NRCH)
MWHX	MarkWest Hydrocarbon, Inc. [*NASDAQ symbol*] (SAG)
MWI...........	Insurance Institute of Winnipeg, Manitoba [*Library symbol*] [*National Library of Canada*] (NLC)
MWI...........	Malawi [*ANSI three-letter standard code*] (CNC)
MWI...........	Mantle Width Index
MWI...........	Many Worlds Interpretation [*Term coined by authors John Barrow and Frank Tipler in their book, "The Anthropic Cosmological Principle"*]
MWI...........	Master Weavers Institute (EA)
MWI...........	Measured Workload Index [*Aviation*]
MWI...........	Medical Waste Incinerator (EEVL)
MWI...........	Message-Waiting Indicator
MWI...........	Missionary Women International (EA)
MWI...........	Montserrat [*West Indies*] [*Seismograph station code, US Geological Survey*] (SEIS)
MWI...........	Motor-Ways Inc., Des Moines IA [*STAC*]
MWIA.........	Medical Women's International Association [*See also AIFM*] [*Cologne, Federal Republic of Germany*] (EAIO)
MWIAP	Prairie Regional Office, Parks Canada [*Bureau Regional des Pres, Parcs Canada*] Winnipeg, Manitoba [*Library symbol*] [*National Library of Canada*] (NLC)
MWIC.........	Manitoba Department of Economic Development, Winnipeg, Manitoba [*Library symbol*] [*National Library of Canada*] (NLC)
MWiCA	Sterling and Francine Clark Art Institute, Williamstown, MA [*Library symbol*] [*Library of Congress*] (LCLS)
MWIDE	IDE Engineering Co., Winnipeg, Manitoba [*Library symbol*] [*National Library of Canada*] (NLC)
MWIE.........	Indus Electronic, Winnipeg, Manitoba [*Library symbol*] [*National Library of Canada*] (NLC)
MWIF.........	Ivan Franko Museum & Library, Winnipeg, Manitoba [*Library symbol*] [*National Library of Canada*] (NLC)
MWIFC........	Midwest Intercollegiate Football Conference (PSS)
MWIN.........	Indian and Northern Affairs Canada [*Affaires Indiennes et du Nord Canada*],Winnipeg, Manitoba [*Library symbol*] [*National Library of Canada*] (BIB)
MWIP.........	Mixed Waste Integrated Program [*Department of Energy*]
MWIR	Medium-Wavelength Infrared
MWIR	Midwave Infrared Sensor (MCD)
MWIR	Mixed Waste Inventory Report [*Department of Energy*]
MWIS.........	National Network of Minority Women in Science (EA)
MWIV.........	Mean Wildlife Index Value [*Statistics*] (PDAA)
MWIVA	Midwest Intercollegiate Volleyball Association (PSS)
MWiW	Williams College, Williamstown, MA [*Library symbol*] [*Library of Congress*] (LCLS)
MWiW-C......	Williams College, Chapin Library, Williamstown, MA [*Library symbol*] [*Library of Congress*] (LCLS)
MWJ	Canada Department of Justice [*Ministere de la Justice*] Winnipeg, Manitoba [*Library symbol*] [*National Library of Canada*] (NLC)
MWJ	Matthews Ridge [*Guyana*] [*Airport symbol*] (OAG)
MWJC.........	Marjorie Webster Junior College [*Washington, DC*]
MWJCAC......	Midwestern Junior College Athletic Conference (PSS)
MWJHS........	Jewish Historical Society of Western Canada, Winnipeg, Manitoba [*Library symbol*] [*National Library of Canada*] (NLC)
MWJP.........	Jewish Public Library, Winnipeg, Manitoba [*Library symbol*] [*National Library of Canada*] (NLC)
MWK..........	Kelvin High School, Winnipeg, Manitoba [*Library symbol*] [*National Library of Canada*] (NLC)
MWK..........	Mill Work [*Technical drawings*]
MWK..........	Milwaukee Land [*AMEX symbol*] (TTSB)
MWK..........	Milwaukee Land Co. [*AMEX symbol*] (SPSG)
MWK..........	Mount Airy, NC [*Location identifier*] [*FAA*] (FAAL)
MWL..........	Law Society of Manitoba, Winnipeg, Manitoba [*Library symbol*] [*National Library of Canada*] (NLC)
MWL..........	Mail-Well, Inc. [*NYSE symbol*] (SG)
MWL..........	Malawi Women's League
MWL..........	Mean Water Level
MWL..........	Meteoric Water Line [*Geology*]
MWL..........	Milled-Wood Lignin
mWL..........	Milliwatt Logic
MWL..........	Mineral Wells [*Texas*] [*Airport symbol*] (AD)
MWL..........	Mineral Wells, TX [*Location identifier*] [*FAA*] (FAAL)
MWL..........	Miniature Warning Light (HEAS)
MWL..........	Minimum Wage Laws (OICC)
MWL..........	Motor Water Lighter (ADA)
MWL..........	Municipal Waste Leachate (GNE)
MWL..........	Muslim World League (BJA)
MWL..........	Mutual Welfare League (NADA)
MWLAE.......	Millimeter Wave Large Antenna Experiment [*NASA*] (PDAA)
MWLCC.......	Lutheran Council in Canada, Winnipeg, Manitoba [*Library symbol*] [*National Library of Canada*] (NLC)
MWLD	Man Worn LASER Detector [*Assembly*] (MCD)
MWLD	Man-Worn LASER Device [*Army*]
MWLDA	Maine Wholesale Lobster Dealers Association [*Defunct*] (EA)
MWLG	Midwest Women's Legal Group (EA)
MWLMV.......	Maize White Line Mosaic Virus [*Plant pathology*]
MWLR	Labour Research Library, Manitoba Department of Labour and Manpower, Winnipeg, Manitoba [*Library symbol*] [*National Library of Canada*] (NLC)
MWLS.........	Faculty of Law, University of Manitoba, Winnipeg, Manitoba [*Library symbol*] [*National Library of Canada*] (NLC)
MWM.........	Maxwell-Wagner Mechanism [*Physics*]
MWM.........	Medical Library, University of Manitoba, Winnipeg, Manitoba [*Library symbol*] [*National Library of Canada*] (NLC)
MWM.........	Millimeter Wave Mixer
MWM.........	Minskoff, Wiseman, Minskoff [*Program for the development of language abilities*]
MWM.........	Mode-Woche-Muenchen [*Munich Fashion Week - International Fashion Fair*] [*Germany*] (TSPED)
MWM.........	Moments with Meredith - Meredith Baxter-Birney Fan Club [*Defunct*] (EA)
MWM.........	Morfee Wheel Manufacturing [*Vancouver Stock Exchange symbol*]
MWM.........	Motif Window Manager [*Computer science*] (VLIE)
MWM.........	Windom, MN [*Location identifier*] [*FAA*] (FAAL)
MWM.........	Worcester Art Museum, Worcester, MA [*Library symbol*] [*Library of Congress*] (LCLS)
MWMA........	Manitoba Department of Municipal Affairs, Winnipeg, Manitoba [*Library symbol*] [*National Library of Canada*] (NLC)
MWMA........	Multiple Wine Merchants Association [*British*] (BI)
MWMA........	Municipal Waste Management Association (NTPA)
MWM & R ...	Metal-Working Machine and Robot

MWMBC ...... Mennonite Brethren Bible College, Winnipeg, Manitoba [*Library symbol*] [*National Library of Canada*] (NLC)
MWMC .... Metropolitan Waste Management Council [*Melbourne, Australia*]
MwMC .... Midwest Microfilm Service, Co., Springfield, IL [*Library symbol*] [*Library of Congress*] (LCLS)
MWMCA ...... Michigan Women for Medical Control of Abortion (EA)
MWME .... Maclaren Engineering, Winnipeg, Manitoba [*Library symbol*] [*National Library of Canada*] (NLC)
MWMF .... Mixed Waste Management Facility [*Environmental science*] (COE)
MWMFB ...... Middlewest Motor Freight Bureau
MWMFOC ... Multiwavelength Multifield of View (SAUS)
MWMG .... Misericordia General Hospital, Winnipeg, Manitoba [*Library symbol*] [*National Library of Canada*] (NLC)
MWMH .... Winnipeg Municipal Hospital, Manitoba [*Library symbol*] [*National Library of Canada*] (NLC)
MWMHC ...... Mennonite Heritage Centre, Winnipeg, Manitoba [*Library symbol*] [*National Library of Canada*] (NLC)
MWMM .... Manitoba Museum of Man & Nature, Winnipeg, Manitoba [*Library symbol*] [*National Library of Canada*] (NLC)
MWMMP ...... Meadowood Manor Personal Care Home, Winnipeg, Manitoba [*Library symbol*] [*National Library of Canada*] (NLC)
MWMP .... City of Winnipeg Metro Planning Division, Manitoba [*Library symbol*] [*National Library of Canada*] (NLC)
MWMPE .... Manitoba Pool Elevators Library, Winnipeg, Manitoba [*Library symbol*] [*National Library of Canada*] (NLC)
MWMR .... Multiple Write, Multiple Read (SAUS)
MWMRC ...... Manitoba Research Council, Winnipeg, Manitoba [*Library symbol*] [*National Library of Canada*] (NLC)
MWMRTL ..... Milliwatt Motorola Resistor Transistor Logic (IAA)
MWMSE .... Minimum-Weighted Mean Square Error (IAA)
MWMT .... Metal-Working Machine Tool
MWMT .... Mint with Mint Tag [*Collectibles*]
MWMTC .... Manitoba Theater Center, Winnipeg, Manitoba [*Library symbol*] [*National Library of Canada*] (NLC)
MWMTS .... Manitoba Teachers Socity, Winnipeg, Manitoba [*Library symbol*] [*National Library of Canada*] (NLC)
MWMU .... University of Massachusetts, Medical Center, Worcester, MA [*Library symbol*] [*Library of Congress*] (LCLS)
MWn .... GAR Memorial Library, West Newbury, MA [*Library symbol*] [*Library of Congress*] (LCLS)
MWN .... Gordon College, Wenham, MA [*Inactive*] [*OCLC symbol*] (OCLC)
MWN .... Madras Weekly Notes [*India*] [*A publication*] (DLA)
MWN .... Message Waiting Notification (SAUS)
MWN .... Mount Washington, NH [*Location identifier*] [*FAA*] (FAAL)
MWNCC .... Madras Weekly Notes, Criminal Cases [*India*] [*A publication*] (DLA)
MWNT .... Multi-Walled Carbon Nanotube
MWNT .... Multiwalled Nanotube [*Materials science*]
MWNT .... Multiwall Nanotube [*Materials science*]
MWO .... Maintenance Work Order
MWO .... Manufacturing Work Order
MWO .... Master Warrant Officer [*Canadian Forces, since 1964*]
MWO .... Master Work Order (AAG)
MWO .... Mental Welfare Officer [*British*]
MWO .... Middletown, OH [*Location identifier*] [*FAA*] (FAAL)
MWO .... Millimeter Wavelength Oscillator
MWO .... Millimeter Wave Observatory [*University of Texas at Austin*] [*Research center*] (RCD)
MWO .... Modification Work Order
MWO .... Mount Wilson Observatory (NADA)
MWO .... Rev. Peres Oblats, Winnipeg, Manitoba [*Library symbol*] [*National Library of Canada*] (NLC)
MWo .... Woburn Public Library, Woburn, MA [*Library symbol*] [*Library of Congress*] (LCLS)
MWOA .... Mizrachi Women's Organization of America [*Later, AMW*] (EA)
MWOC .... Mothers without Custody (EA)
MWOFP .... Modification Work Order Fielding Plan
MWollE .... Eastern Nazarene College, Wollaston, MA [*Library symbol*] [*Library of Congress*] (LCLS)
MWOP .... Mixed Waste Office Paper [*Pulp and paper technology*]
MWOT .... Master Warrant Officer Training [*DoD*]
MWP .... Legislative Library of Manitoba, Winnipeg, Manitoba [*Library symbol*] [*National Library of Canada*] (NLC)
MWP .... Malta Workers Party [*Political party*] (PPE)
MWP .... Maneuvering Work Platform [*NASA*]
MWP .... Mangla [*Pakistan*] [*Airport symbol*] (AD)
MWP .... Master of Welfare Policy
MWP .... Maximum Working Pressure
MWP .... Mean Wedge Pressure (DMAA)
MWP .... Mechanical Wood Pulp [*Paper*]
MWP .... Medieval Warm Period [*Geoscience*]
MWP .... Membrane Waterproofing
MWP .... Metabolic Waste Production
MWP .... Meteorological Weather Processor (GAVI)
MWP .... Meteorologist Weather Processor [*FAA*] (TAG)
MWP .... Mexican Water Plan [*Land use*]
MWP .... Millimeter Wave Propagation
MWP .... Ministry of Works and Planning [*British*]
MWP .... Missile Warning Position (MCD)
MWP .... Mixed Waste Project (ABAC)
MWP .... Momentum Wheel Platform (ACAE)
MWP .... Most Worthy Patriarch
MWP .... Worcester Polytechnic Institute, Worcester, MA [*Library symbol*] [*Library of Congress*] (LCLS)
MWPA .... Married Women's Property Act [*1882*] [*British*] (AIA)

MWPA .... Provincial Archives of Manitoba, Winnipeg, Manitoba [*Library symbol*] [*National Library of Canada*] (NLC)
MWPC .... Moorepark Whey Protein Concentrate (OA)
MWPC .... Multiple Wire Proportional Counter
MWPC .... Multiwire Proportional Chamber (IAA)
MWPCPA ..... Archaeology Subsection Office, Prairie Region Library, Parks Canada [*Recherches Archeologiques, Bibliotheque de la Region des Pres, Parcs Canada*] Winnipeg, Manitoba [*Library symbol*] [*National Library of Canada*] (NLC)
MWPCPH ..... Historic Resources Conservation Subsection Office, Prairie Region Library, ParksCanada [*Ressources et Conservation Historiques, Bibliotheque de la Region de s Pres, Parcs Canada*] Winnipeg, Manitoba [*Library symbol*] [*National Library of Canada*] (NLC)
MWPCR .... Riding Mountain National Park, Parks Canada [*Parc National Riding Mountain, Parcs Canada*] Wasagaming, Manitoba [*Library symbol*] [*National Library of Canada*] (NLC)
MWPE .... Mental Workload and Performance (SAUS)
MWPF .... Marine Wildlife Preservation Fund
MWPI .... Munson-Williams-Proctor Institute [*Utica, NY*]
MWPL .... Public Library Services, Manitoba Department of Culture, Heritage and Recreation, Winnipeg, Manitoba [*Library symbol*] [*National Library of Canada*] (NLC)
MWPNR .... Park Management Library, Manitoba Department of Natural Resources, Winnipeg, Manitoba [*Library symbol*] [*National Library of Canada*] (NLC)
MWPO .... Mine Warfare Project Office [*Naval Material Command*]
MWpP .... Westport Free Public Library, Westport, MA [*Library symbol*] [*Library of Congress*] (LCLS)
MWPPH .... Provincial Public Health Nursing Services, Winnipeg, Manitoba [*Library symbol*] [*National Library of Canada*] (NLC)
MWPR .... Monthly Work Package Report [*NASA*] (NASA)
MWPS .... Manitoba Probation Services, Winnipeg, Manitoba [*Library symbol*] [*National Library of Canada*] (NLC)
MWPS .... Master of Wood and Paper Science (GAGS)
MWPS .... Multimeter Wave Power Source
MWQ .... Magwe [*Myanmar*] [*Airport symbol*] (OAG)
MWQ .... Quinsigamond Community College, Worcester, MA [*Library symbol*] [*Library of Congress*] (LCLS)
MWQCG ...... Media and Information Services, Quadraplegic Communications Group, Inc., Winnipeg, Manitoba [*Library symbol*] [*National Library of Canada*] (NLC)
MWR .... Magnetic Tape Write [*Computer science*] (VLIE)
MWR .... Maintenance Work Request [*or Requirement*]
MWR .... Man-Worn Receiver (MCD)
mwr .... Marwari [*MARC language code*] [*Library of Congress*] (LCCP)
MWR .... Mean Width Ratio
MWR .... Metal Whisker Reinforcement
MWR .... Method of Weighted Residual
MWR .... Microwave Radiation (MELL)
MWR .... Microwave Radiometer (CARB)
MWR .... Millimeter-Wave Radar (DOMA)
MWR .... Mine Warfare Range (SAUS)
MWR .... Mine Watching RADAR (NATG)
MWR .... Mini Web Reel (DGA)
MWR .... Missile-Warning Receiver (MCD)
MWR .... Morale, Welfare, and Recreation [*DoD*]
MWR .... Mountain-West Resources [*Vancouver Stock Exchange symbol*]
MWR .... Mower
MWR .... Muncie & Western Railroad Co. [*AAR code*]
MWR .... Royal Winnipeg Ballet, Manitoba [*Library symbol*] [*National Library of Canada*] (NLC)
MWRA .... Master of Water Resources Administration (PGP)
MWRA .... Morale, Welfare, and Recreation Activity [*DoD*] (AFIT)
MWRAILS .... Microwave Remote Area Instrument Landing System (IAA)
MWRC .... Maintain Well to Right of Course [*Aviation*] (FAAC)
MWRC .... Melbourne Western Region Commission [*Australia*]
MWRC .... Mount Washington Railway Co. [*AAR code*]
MWRC .... RCMP [*Royal Canadian Mounted Police*] Crime Laboratory, Winnipeg, Manitoba [*Library symbol*] [*National Library of Canada*] (NLC)
MWRCC .... Roman Catholic Chancery Office, Winnipeg, Manitoba [*Library symbol*] [*National Library of Canada*] (NLC)
MWRK .... Mothers Work [*NASDAQ symbol*] (TTSB)
MWRK .... Mothers Work, Inc. [*NASDAQ symbol*] (SAG)
MWroxV ...... United States Veterans Administration Hospital, West Roxbury, MA [*Library symbol*] [*Library of Congress*] (LCLS)
MWRR .... Learning Resources Centre, Red River Community College, Winnipeg, Manitoba [*Library symbol*] [*National Library of Canada*] (NLC)
MWRRC .... Montana Water Resources Research Center [*Montana State University, University ofMontana, and Montana College of Mineral Science and Technology*] [*Research center*] (RCD)
MWRRL .... Library Technician Program, Red River Community College, Winnipeg, Manitoba, LS [*National Library of Canada*] (NLC)
MWRS .... Millimeter Wave Radio System (MCD)
MWRS .... Richardson Securities of Canada, Winnipeg, Manitoba [*Library symbol*] [*National Library of Canada*] (NLC)
MWRT .... Mobile Wing Reconnaissance Technical [*Squadron*]
mWRTL .... Milliwatt Resistor-Transistor Logic (IDOE)
MWS .... Major Weapon System [*Manager*] (MCD)
MWS .... Mallory-Weiss Syndrome [*Medicine*] (MELL)
MWS .... Management Work Station (BUR)
MWS .... Manned Weapons Station (ACAE)
MWS .... Marden-Walker Syndrome [*Medicine*] (DMAA)
MWS .... Marine Weather Service (NOAA)

MWS............ Master of Women's Studies (PGP)
MWS............ Master Warning System (SAUS)
MWS............ Mawashi [*Ryukyu Islands*] [*Seismograph station code, US Geological Survey*] [*Closed*] (SEIS)
MWS............ Maximum Wind Speed
MWS............ Medium Wide Shot [*Photography*]
MWS............ Megawatt Waveguide Switch
MWS............ Member of the Wernerian Society [*British*] (ROG)
MWS............ Meridional Wind Stress (SAUS)
MWS............ Microwave Scatterometer [*Telecommunications*] (TEL)
MWS............ Microwave Station
MWS............ Microwave Wind Spectrometer
MWS............ Mikity-Wilson Syndrome [*Neonatology*] (DAVI)
MWS............ Mini Weapon Sight (SAUS)
MWS............ Mini Workstation (SSD)
MWS............ Missile Warning Set (SAUS)
MWS............ Missile Warning Squadron
MWS............ Missile Warning System (SAUS)
MWS............ Missile Weapon System [*Military*] (CAAL)
MWS............ Missouri Western State College, St. Joseph, MO [*OCLC symbol*] (OCLC)
MWS............ Mobile Weapon System
MWS............ Modular Weapons System (MCD)
MWS............ Modular Workstation (SAUS)
MWS............ Moersch-Woltman Syndrome [*Medicine*] (DMAA)
MWS............ Molecular Wake Shield (SAUS)
MWS............ Most Wise Sovereign [*Freemasonry*]
MWS............ Most Worshipful Scribe [*Freemasonry*] (ROG)
MWS............ Mount Wilson, CA [*Location identifier*] [*FAA*] (FAAL)
MWS............ Muckle-Wells Syndrome [*Medicine*] (MELL)
MWS............ Multiwork Station
MWSA .... St. Andrew's College, Winnipeg, Manitoba [*Library symbol*] [*National Library of Canada*] (NLC)
MWSAC .... St. Amant Center, Winnipeg, Manitoba [*Library symbol*] [*National Library of Canada*] (NLC)
MWSACB .... Salvation Army Catherine Booth Bible College, Winnipeg, Manitoba [*Library symbol*] [*National Library of Canada*] (BIB)
MWSB .... Saint Boniface Public Library, Winnipeg, Manitoba [*Library symbol*] [*National Library of Canada*] (NLC)
MWSBM ...... Saint Boniface General Hospital Medical Library, Winnipeg, Manitoba [*Library symbol*] [*National Library of Canada*] (NLC)
MWSBN .... Saint Boniface General Hospital School of Nursing Library, Winnipeg, Manitoba [*Library symbol*] [*National Library of Canada*] (NLC)
MWSC .... American Men and Women of Science [*Database*] [*R. R. Bowker Co.*] [*Information service or system*] (CRD)
MWSC .... Midwestern Simulation Council
MWSC .... Mine Warfare Support Centre (SAUS)
MWSC .... Mine Warfare Systems Centre (SAUS)
MWSC .... Society for Manitobans with Disabilities, Inc., Winnipeg, Manitoba [*Library symbol*] [*National Library of Canada*] (NLC)
MWSCS .... Midwestern Signal Corps School
MWSD .... Missile and Weapons Systems Division [*Military*] (IAA)
MWSD .... Teachers' Library and Resource Centre, Winnipeg School Division No. 1, Manitoba [*Library symbol*] [*National Library of Canada*] (NLC)
MWSE.......... Midwest Stock Exchange, Inc. (HGAA)
MWSF.......... Molecular Wake Shield Facility (SAUS)
MWSG .... Marine Wing Support Group (NVT)
MWSGDET ... Marine Wing Support Group Detachment (DNAB)
MWSGR....... Marine Wing Staff Ground (MCD)
MWSH .... Worcester State Hospital, Worcester, MA [*Library symbol*] [*Library of Congress*] (LCLS)
MWSJ.......... St. John's College, Winnipeg, Manitoba [*Library symbol*] [*National Library of Canada*] (NLC)
MWSM......... Stony Mountain Institution Library, Winnipeg, Manitoba [*Library symbol*] [*National Library of Canada*] (NLC)
MWSOGH .... Educational Services, Seven Oaks General Hospital, Winnipeg, Manitoba [*Library symbol*] [*National Library of Canada*] (NLC)
MWSP .... St. Paul's College, Winnipeg, Manitoba [*Library symbol*] [*National Library of Canada*] (NLC)
MWSPA .... Spiece Associates, Winnipeg, Manitoba [*Library symbol*] [*National Library of Canada*] (NLC)
MWSPC ...... Social Planning Council of Winnipeg, Manitoba [*Library symbol*] [*National Library of Canada*] (NLC)
MW Sprg ..... Mid-West Spring Manufacturing Co. [*Associated Press*] (SAG)
MWSR .... Magnetic Wire Shift Register
MWSR .... Microwave Water Substance Radiometer [*Marine science*] (OSRA)
MWSS .... Manitoba Regional Library, Secretary of State Canada [*Bibliotheque Regionale du Manitoba, Secretariat d'Etat*], Winnipeg, Manitoba [*Library symbol*] [*National Library of Canada*] (NLC)
MWSS .... Marine Wing Support Squadron [*Navy*] (ANA)
MWSS .... Metropolitan Waterworks and Sewerage System [*Philippines*]
MWSS .... Metwork Six [*NASDAQ symbol*]
MWSS .... Mid-West Spring Manufacturing Co. [*NASDAQ symbol*] (SAG)
MWSS .... Millimeter Wave Signal Source (ACAE)
MWSSE....... Mid-West Spring Mfg [*NASDAQ symbol*] (TTSB)
MWST .... Mean Weighted Skin Temperature
MWST .... Miscellaneous Waste Storage Tank [*Nuclear energy*] (NRCH)
MWST .... Missile Warning System Test (MCD)
MWSV .... St. Vital Public Library, Winnipeg, Manitoba [*Library symbol*] [*National Library of Canada*] (NLC)
MWT............ Maintenance of Wakefulness Test (MELL)
MWT............ Makeup Water Treatment (IEEE)
MWT............ Marconi Wireless Telegraph [*Telecommunications*] (IAA)
MWT............ Master of Wood Technology

MWT............ McWhorter Technologies, Inc. [*NYSE symbol*] (SAG)
MWT............ Mean Water Temperature
MWT............ Medium Wheeled Tractor (SAUS)
MWT............ Megawatt Thermal [*Nuclear energy*] (NRCH)
MWT............ Michigan Walleye Tour
MWT............ Midwest Aviation [*Southwest Aviation, Inc.*] [*ICAO designator*] (FAAC)
MWT............ Millimeter Wave Technology (ACAE)
MWT............ Millimeter Wave Tube
MWT............ Ministry of War Transport [*Terminated, 1956*] [*British*]
MWt............. Molecular Weight [*Also, M, MOL WT, MW*] (AAMN)
MWT............ Monitor Wafer Turner (AAEL)
MWT............ Moolawatana [*Australia*] [*Airport symbol*] [*Obsolete*] (OAG)
MWT............ Mountain War Time
MWT............ Myocardial Wall Thickness [*Cardiology*] (DMAA)
Mwt............. Thermal Megawatt [*Also, TMW*]
MWT............ Winnipeg Tribune, Manitoba [*Library symbol*] [*National Library of Canada*] (NLC)
MWTA......... Airworthiness Library, Central Region, Transport Canada [*Bibliotheque de la Navigabilite Aerienne, Region Centrale, Transports Canada*], Winnipeg, Manitoba [*Library symbol*] [*National Library of Canada*] (NLC)
MWTA......... Medical Waste Tracking Act [*1988*] (FFDE)
MWTA......... Medical Waste Treatment Act
MWTC......... Ministry of War Time Communications [*British*] [*World War II*]
MWTC......... Teshmount Consultants, Winnipeg, Manitoba [*Library symbol*] [*National Library of Canada*] (NLC)
MWTCR ...... Central Regional Library, Transport Canada [*Bibliotheque Regionale du Centre, Transports Canada*], Winnipeg, Manitoba [*Library symbol*] [*National Library of Canada*] (NLC)
MWTCS....... Modernized Weather Teletypewriter Communications System (FAAC)
MWTE......... Interdisciplinary Engineering, Winnipeg, Manitoba [*Library symbol*] [*National Library of Canada*] (NLC)
MWTE......... Modern Weapons Training Exercises (MCD)
MWTGM .... Milimeter Wage Terminal Guided Missile (ACAE)
MW(th) .... Megawatts (Thermal)
MWTHA....... Michigan Wild Turkey Hunters Association
MWTP......... Mixed Waste Treatment Project
MWTR .... Mean Waiting Time for Supply Replacement (DNAB)
MWTR .... Monthly Wholesale Trade Report [*A publication*]
MWTS......... Manitoba Telephone System, Winnipeg, Manitoba [*Library symbol*] [*National Library of Canada*] (NLC)
MWTS......... Millimeter Wave Transmitting Subsystem (ACAE)
MWTS......... Monthly Wholesale Trade Survey (SAUS)
MWTU......... Marble Workers' Trade Union [*British*]
MWU .... Maccabi World Union [*Ramat Gan, Israel*] (EAIO)
MWU .... Mercer University, Southern School of Pharmacy, Atlanta, GA [*OCLC symbol*] (OCLC)
MWU .... Mine Workers Union [*South Africa*] (IMH)
MWU .... Modified Wohlgemuth Unit [*Of hydrolytic enzyme activity*]
MWU .... Mussau [*Papua New Guinea*] [*Airport symbol*] (OAG)
MWU .... University of Manitoba, Winnipeg, Manitoba [*Library symbol*] [*National Library of Canada*] (NLC)
MWUA .... Ukrainian Academy of Arts and Science, Winnipeg, Manitoba [*Library symbol*] [*National Library of Canada*] (NLC)
MWUAF ...... Architecture and Fine Arts Library, University of Manitoba, Winnipeg, Manitoba [*Library symbol*] [*National Library of Canada*] (NLC)
MWUC........ University of Winnipeg, Manitoba [*Library symbol*] [*National Library of Canada*] (NLC)
MWUCE ...... Ukrainian Cultural and Educational Centre, Winnipeg, Manitoba [*Library symbol*] [*National Library of Canada*] (NLC)
MWUD .... Dental Library, University of Manitoba, Winnipeg, Manitoba [*Library symbol*] [*National Library of Canada*] (NLC)
MWUG .... Department of Geography, University of Manitoba, Winnipeg, Manitoba [*Library symbol*] [*National Library of Canada*] (NLC)
MWUGG....... United Grain Growers, Winnipeg, Manitoba [*Library symbol*] [*National Library of Canada*] (NLC)
MWUM .... Map and Atlas Collection, University of Manitoba, Winnipeg, Manitoba [*Library symbol*] [*National Library of Canada*] (NLC)
MWUML ...... Underwood McLellan Ltd., Winnipeg, Manitoba [*Library symbol*] [*National Library of Canada*] (NLC)
MWUSA ...... Minute Women of the United States of America (EA)
MWV............ Maximum Working Voltage [*Electronics*]
MWV............ Mexican War Veteran
MWV............ Milkweed Virus
MWV............ Minor War Vessels (SAUS)
MWV............ Modulated Wavy Vortex [*Fluid mechanics*]
MWV............ Motor Tariff Bureau of West Virginia, Charleston WV [*STAC*]
MWV............ Multifit Weapons Vehicle (SAUS)
MWVGH....... Victoria General Hospital, Winnipeg, Manitoba [*Library symbol*] [*National Library of Canada*] (NLC)
MWVP......... Minor War Vessels Programme (SAUS)
MWVS......... Branch Library, Manitoba Veterinarian Services, Winnipeg, Manitoba [*Library symbol*] [*National Library of Canada*] (NLC)
MWVS......... Mission Weapon Visionics System (SAUS)
MWW.......... Majestic Wine Warehouses [*Commercial firm*] [*British*]
MWW.......... Manual Wire Wrap
MWW.......... Mark's Work Wearhouse Ltd. [*Toronto Stock Exchange symbol*]
MWW.......... Marquis Who's Who [*Marquis Who's Who, Inc.*] [*Information service or system*] [*A publication*]
MWW.......... [*The*] Merry Wives of Windsor [*Shakespearean work*] (BARN)
MWW.......... Municipal Wastewater
MWW.......... William Ave. Branch, Winnipeg Public Library, Manitoba [*Library symbol*] [*National Library of Canada*] (NLC)

MWW........... Worcester State College, Worcester, MA [*Library symbol*] [*Library of Congress*] (LCLS)

MWWA .... Winnipeg Art Gallery, Manitoba [*Library symbol*] [*National Library of Canada*] (NLC)

MWWC .... Military Weather Warning Center (NOAA)

MWWC .... Winnipeg Clinic, Manitoba [*Library symbol*] [*National Library of Canada*] (NLC)

MWWF......... Manual Wire Wrap Fixture

MWWII .... Mothers of World War II

MWWK .... West Kildonan Public Library, Winnipeg, Manitoba [*Library symbol*] [*National Library of Canada*] (NLC)

MWWLW ..... W. L. Wardrop & Associates, Winnipeg, Manitoba [*Library symbol*] [*National Library of Canada*] (NLC)

MWWR .... Water Resources Division, Manitoba Department of Natural Resources, Winnipeg, Manitoba [*Library symbol*] [*National Library of Canada*] (NLC)

MWWSH ...... Manitoba Workplace Safety and Health Division, Winnipeg, Manitoba [*Library symbol*] [*National Library of Canada*] (NLC)

MWWU .... Marine Wing Weapon Unit

MWWV .... Movement of Working Women and Volunteers [*Tel Aviv, Israel*] (EAIO)

MWX........... Montpelier, VT [*Location identifier*] [*FAA*] (FAAL)

MWY........... Midway Games, Inc. [*NYSE symbol*] (SAG)

MWY........... Miranda Downs [*Australia*] [*Airport symbol*] [*Obsolete*] (OAG)

MWYE......... Megawatt Year of Electricity (IAA)

MWyr.......... Megawatt-Year (ABAC)

MWZ........... Mwanza [*Tanzania*] [*Airport symbol*] (OAG)

MX............. Compania Mexicana de Aviacion [*ICAO designator*] (OAG)

MX............. Magnavox (SAUS)

MX............. Mail Exchange [*Computer science*]

mx .... Management (DAVI)

MX............. Master Agility Excellent

MX............. Matrix (BUR)

Mx .... Maxwell [*Unit of magnetic flux*] [*Also, abWb*]

MX............. Measurex Corp. [*NYSE symbol*] (SPSG)

MX............. Metaxylene

MX............. Mexicana [*Airline*] (DS)

MX............. Mexicana de Aviacion [*ICAO designator*] (AD)

MX............. Mexican L & P Co. Ltd. [*Toronto Stock Exchange symbol*]

MX............. Mexico [*ANSI two-letter standard code*] (CNC)

mx .... Mexico [*IYRU nationality code*] [*MARC country of publication code*] [*Library of Congress*] (LCCP)

MX............. Middlesex [*Region of London*]

MX............. Missile, Experimental

MX............. Mix

MX............. Motocross (WGA)

MX............. Multiple Address

mx .... Multiplex (NAKS)

MX............. Multiplex [*or Multiplexer*]

MX............. Murexide [*An indicator*] [*Chemistry*]

MX............. Mutually Exclusive (ACAE)

MX............. Peacekeeper Missile (SAUS)

MXA............ Compania Mexicana de Aviacion SA [*Mexico*] [*ICAO designator*] (FAAC)

MXA............ Manila, AR [*Location identifier*] [*FAA*] (FAAL)

MXA............ Minnesota Municipal Income Portfolio [*AMEX symbol*] (SPSG)

MXA............ Minnesota Muni Inc. Portfolio [*AMEX symbol*] (TTSB)

MXA............ Mobile Exercise Area [*Military*] (NVT)

MXAL.......... Mercury Xenon Arc Lamp

MXB............ Masamba [*Indonesia*] [*Airport symbol*] (OAG)

MXB............ Medix Resources [*AMEX symbol*] (SG)

MXB............ Multimedia Extension Board (SAUS)

MXC............ MATEC Corp. [*AMEX symbol*] (SPSG)

MXC............ Maxon Computer Systems, Inc. [*Toronto Stock Exchange symbol*]

MXC............ Mexair SA [*Switzerland*] [*ICAO designator*] (FAAC)

MXC............ Monticello [*Utah*] [*Airport symbol*] (OAG)

MXC............ Multimedia Extension Connector (SAUS)

MXC............ Multiplexer Channel [*Computer science*]

MXC............ University of Cincinnati, Medical Center, Cincinnati, OH [*OCLC symbol*] (OCLC)

MxChGS...... Church of Jesus Christ of Latter-Day Saints, Genealogical Society Library, Colonia Juarez Branch, Chihuahua, Mexico [*Library symbol*] [*Library of Congress*] (LCLS)

MXCPEC ..... Mexico National Committee for Pacific Economic Cooperation

MXD........... Marion Downs [*Queensland*] [*Airport symbol*] (AD)

MXD........... Maximum-Latewood-Density

MXD........... Mixed

mxd .... Mixed

MXD........... Mixed Artillery [*Military*] (VNW)

MXD........... Mixed Use Development (PA)

MXD........... Multiple Transmitter Duplicator

MXDA .... Meta-Xylenediamine [*Organic chemistry*]

MXD CL ...... Mixed Carload [*Freight*]

MXDCR .... Mode Transducer (MSA)

MXDTH .... Maximum Depth (NOAA)

MXE........... Manx Airlines (Europe) Ltd. [*British*] [*ICAO designator*] (FAAC)

MXE........... Mexico Eqty & Income Fd [*NYSE symbol*] (TTSB)

MXE........... Mexico Equity & Income Fund [*NYSE symbol*] (SPSG)

MXE........... Modena, PA [*Location identifier*] [*FAA*] (FAAL)

MXF........... Mexico Fund [*NYSE symbol*] (TTSB)

MXF........... [*The*] Mexico Fund, Inc. [*NYSE symbol*] (SPSG)

MXF........... Montgomery, AL [*Location identifier*] [*FAA*] (FAAL)

MXFL.......... Mixed Flow

MXG........... Mixing (MSA)

MxGuBF....... Biblioteca Benjamin Franklin, Guadalajara, Mexico [*Library symbol*] [*Library of Congress*] (LCLS)

MXIC.......... MX Information Center [*Defunct*] (EA)

MXICY .... Macronix Intl ADR [*NASDAQ symbol*] (TTSB)

MXIM .... Maxim Integrated Prod [*NASDAQ symbol*] (TTSB)

MXIM .... Maxim Integrated Products, Inc. [*NASDAQ symbol*] (NQ)

MXIS.......... Maxis, Inc. [*NASDAQ symbol*] (SAG)

MXK........... Camp Springs, MD [*Location identifier*] [*FAA*] (FAAL)

MXK........... Metekel [*Ethiopia*] [*Airport symbol*] (AD)

MXK........... Multiple-Frequency X- and K-Band

MXL........... Mexicali [*Mexico*] [*Airport symbol*] (OAG)

MXL........... Mixed Workload [*Computer science*] (PCM)

MXLU.......... Malcolm X Liberation University

MXM.......... Matrix Memory (MHDI)

MXM.......... Maximum (ADA)

MXM.......... MAXXAM, Inc. [*AMEX symbol*] (SPSG)

MXM.......... Morombe [*Madagascar*] [*Airport symbol*] (OAG)

MxMBF....... Biblioteca Benjamin Franklin, Mexico City, Mexico [*Library symbol*] [*Library of Congress*] (LCLS)

MxMBN....... Biblioteca Nacional de Mexico, Mexico City, Mexico [*Library symbol*] [*Library of Congress*] (LCLS)

MxMC........ Centro de Investigacion y de Estudios Avanzados, Instituto Politecnico Nacional, Mexico City, Mexico [*Library symbol*] [*Library of Congress*] (LCLS)

MxMCM...... Colegio de Mexico, Mexico, Mexico City, Mexico [*Library symbol*] [*Library of Congress*] (LCLS)

MxMGS....... Church of Jesus Christ of Latter-Day Saints, Genealogical Society Library, Mexico City Branch, Mexico City, Mexico [*Library symbol*] [*Library of Congress*] (LCLS)

MxMI .... Universidad Iberoamericana, Mexico [*Library symbol*] [*Library of Congress*] (LCLS)

MX/MM .... Missile X/Minuteman Missile

MxMoT .... Instituto Tecnologico y de Estudios Superiores de Monterrey, Monterrey, Mexico [*Library symbol*] [*Library of Congress*] (LCLS)

MX/MPS ...... Missile X [*Deploy In*] Multiple Protective Shelters

MxN .... Maxillary Nerve [*Neuroanatomy*]

MXN.......... Morlaix [*France*] [*Airport symbol*] (OAG)

MX-NM .... Matrix - National Module

MXO.......... Monticello, IA [*Location identifier*] [*FAA*] (FAAL)

MXP.......... May Air Xpress, Inc. [*ICAO designator*] (FAAC)

MXP.......... Mesa, Inc. [*NYSE symbol*] (SAG)

MXP.......... Milan [*Italy*] Malpensa Airport [*Airport symbol*] (OAG)

MXPST....... Maximum Possible Storm (NOAA)

MXQ.......... Modular X-Ray Quantometer

MXQ.......... Wilmington, OH [*Location identifier*] [*FAA*] (FAAL)

MXR.......... Mask Index Register

MXR.......... Mass X-Ray

MXR.......... Merrix Air Ltd. [*British*] [*ICAO designator*] (FAAC)

MXR.......... Mixer (MSA)

MXR.......... Moussoro [*Chad*] [*Airport symbol*] (AD)

MXR.......... Raton, NM [*Location identifier*] [*FAA*] (FAAL)

MXRAN .... Maximum Rainfall (NOAA)

M-X/RES ..... M-X [*Missile*] Renewable Energy System

MXRV .... Middlesex Rifle Volunteers [*Military*] [*British*] (DMA)

MXS.......... Max Minerals, Inc. [*Vancouver Stock Exchange symbol*]

MXS.......... Maxus Energy Corp. [*NYSE symbol*] (SPSG)

MXSBP .... Maxus Energy [*NASDAQ symbol*] (SAG)

MXSBP .... Maxus Energy $4 Cv Pfd [*NASDAQ symbol*] (TTSB)

MXSPrA ...... Maxus Energy $2.50 Pfd [*NYSE symbol*] (TTSB)

MXSV.......... Maxserv, Inc. [*NASDAQ symbol*] (SAG)

MXT.......... Chicago, IL [*Location identifier*] [*FAA*] (FAAL)

MXT.......... Maintirano [*Madagascar*] [*Airport symbol*] (OAG)

MXT.......... Message Exchange Terminal

MXT.......... Metris Cos. [*NYSE symbol*] (SG)

MXT.......... Mixture

MXT.......... Morgan StanGp 6.00% Tele'PERQS' [*AMEX symbol*] (TTSB)

MXT.......... Morgan Stanley Group, Inc. [*AMEX symbol*] (SAG)

MXTMP....... Maximum Temperature (NOAA)

MXTR.......... Maxtor Corp. [*NASDAQ symbol*] (NQ)

MXU.......... Mobile Exhibition Unit (NITA)

MXU.......... Mullewa [*Australia*] [*Airport symbol*] [*Obsolete*] (OAG)

MXU.......... Multiplexer Unit [*Telecommunications*]

MxU.......... Universidad Nacional Autonoma de Mexico, Mexico City, Mexico [*Library symbol*] [*Library of Congress*] (LCLS)

MXVRC .... Middlesex Volunteer Rifle Corps [*British military*] (DMA)

MXW.......... Maxwell, CA [*Location identifier*] [*FAA*] (FAAL)

MXWL.......... Maxwell Laboratories, Inc. [*NASDAQ symbol*] (NQ)

MXWL.......... Maxwell Labs [*NASDAQ symbol*] (TTSB)

MXWL.......... Maxwell Technologies, Inc. [*NASDAQ symbol*] (SAG)

MXWND....... Maximum Wind (NOAA)

MXX.......... International Murex Technologies (SAUS)

MXX.......... Merchant Express Aviation [*Nigeria*] [*ICAO designator*] (FAAC)

MXX.......... Mora [*Sweden*] [*Airport symbol*] (OAG)

MXY.......... McCarthy [*Alaska*] [*Airport symbol*] (OAG)

MXY.......... McCarthy, AK [*Location identifier*] [*FAA*] (FAAL)

MXY.......... [*The*] Yarumal Foreign Mission Institute (Colombia) (TOCD)

MY............ Air Mali [*ICAO designator*] (AD)

My............ All India Reporter, Mysore Series [*A publication*] (ILCA)

MY............ Machine Yield [*Agriculture*] (OA)

MY............ Mahzor Yanai (BJA)

MY............ Malaysia [*IYRU nationality code*] [*ANSI two-letter standard code*] (CNC)

my............ Malaysia [*MARC country of publication code*] [*Library of Congress*] (LCCP)

MY............ Man-Year (AFM)

M/Y............	Marshaling Yards [Military]
My..............	May (RION)
MY..............	May
my..............	Mayer [A unit of heat capacity]
MY..............	Mean Year (IAA)
MY..............	Mean Yield [Agriculture]
MY..............	Miller-Yoder Language Comprehension Test
MY..............	Million Years
M/Y............	Model Year
MY..............	Model Year [Automotive industry]
MY..............	Montgomeryshire Yeomanry [British military] (DMA)
MY..............	Motorized Yacht (TRID)
MY..............	Motor Yacht
MY..............	Muddy [Track condition] [Thoroughbred racing]
My..............	Myanmar (Burma) (MILB)
My..............	Myopia (DIPS)
MY..............	Myopia
MY..............	Myria [A prefix meaning multiplied by 10⁴]
MY..............	Myxedematous [Endocrinology] (DAVI)
MYA..........	Million Years Ago
MYA..........	Model Yachting Association [British] (DBA)
MYA..........	Moruya [Australia] [Airport symbol] (OAG)
MYA..........	Myasishchev [Aircraft] [Commonwealth of Independent States]
MYA..........	Myflug HF [Iceland] [ICAO designator] (FAAC)
mya..........	Myiare (BARN)
MYAB........	Clarence Bain, Andros Island [Bahamas] [ICAO location identifier] (ICLI)
MYAF........	Andros Town, Andros Island [Bahamas] [ICAO location identifier] (ICLI)
MYAG	Gorda Cay, Abaco Island [Bahamas] [ICAO location identifier] (ICLI)
MYAK........	Congo Town, Andros Island [Bahamas] [ICAO location identifier] (ICLI)
MYAM........	Marsh Harbour, Abaco Island [Bahamas] [ICAO location identifier] (ICLI)
MYAN	San Andros, Andros Island [Bahamas] [ICAO location identifier] (ICLI)
My & C	Mylne and Craig's English Chancery Reports [A publication] (DLA)
My & Cr......	Mylne and Craig's English Chancery Reports [A publication] (DLA)
My & K	Mylne and Keen's English Chancery Reports [A publication] (DLA)
MYAO	Moores Island, Abaco Island [Bahamas] [ICAO location identifier] (ICLI)
MYAP........	Spring Point [Bahamas] [ICAO location identifier] (ICLI)
MYAPP......	Main Yankee Atomic Power Plant (NRCH)
MYAS........	Sandy Point, Abaco Island [Bahamas] [ICAO location identifier] (ICLI)
MYAT........	Treasure Cay, Abaco Island [Bahamas] [ICAO location identifier] (ICLI)
MYAW	Walker Cay, Abaco Island [Bahamas] [ICAO location identifier] (ICLI)
MYB...........	Aerolineas Del Mayab, SA de CV [Mexico] [FAA designator] (FAAC)
MYB...........	Mayoumba [Gabon] [Airport symbol] (OAG)
MYBC........	Chub Cay, Berry Island [Bahamas] [ICAO location identifier] (ICLI)
MYBC........	Myosin-Binding Protein C (DMAA)
MYBG	Bullocks Harbour/Great Harbour Cay, Berry Island [Bahamas] [ICAO location identifier] (ICLI)
MYBO	Ocean Cay, Bimini Island [Bahamas] [ICAO location identifier] (ICLI)
MYBP..........	Million Years before Present [Geology]
MYBS........	Alice Town/South Bimini, Bimini Island [Bahamas] [ICAO location identifier] (ICLI)
MYBT........	Cistern Cay, Berry Island [Bahamas] [ICAO location identifier] (ICLI)
MYBW	Big Whale Cay, Berry Island [Bahamas] [ICAO location identifier] (ICLI)
MYBX........	Little Whale Cay, Berry Island [Bahamas] [ICAO location identifier] (ICLI)
MYC..........	Malartic Hygrade Gold Mines Ltd. [Vancouver Stock Exchange symbol]
MYC..........	Maracay [Venezuela] [Airport symbol] (OAG)
MYC..........	Massenya [Chad] [Airport symbol] (AD)
MYC..........	Middlesex Yeomanry Cavalry [British military] (DMA)
MYC..........	Montgomeryshire Yeomanry Cavalry [British military] (DMA)
MYC..........	Multiyear Contract
MYC..........	MuniYield California Fund [NYSE symbol] (SPSG)
MYC..........	Mycology (WGA)
MYCA........	Arthur's Town, Eleuthera Island [Bahamas] [ICAO location identifier] (ICLI)
MYCB........	New Bight, Cat Island [Bahamas] [ICAO location identifier] (ICLI)
MYCH	Hawks Nest Creek/Hawks Nest, Cat Island [Bahamas] [ICAO location identifier] (ICLI)
MYCI..........	Colonel Hill, Crooked Island [Bahamas] [ICAO location identifier] (ICLI)
MYCI..........	Mirrer Yeshiva Central Institute (EA)
MYCO	Mycobacterium
MYCO	Mycogen Corp. [NASDAQ symbol] (NQ)
Myco..........	Mycoplasma [A bacterium] (DAVI)
Mycogn......	Mycogen Corp. [Associated Press] (SAG)
MYCOL	Mycology
Mycol Res ..	Mycological Research (SAUS)
MYCOS........	My Compact Operating System [Toshiba]
MYCOS/SS...	MYCOS Support System (NITA)
MYCP..........	Pittsdown, Crooked Island [Bahamas] [ICAO location identifier] (ICLI)
MYCS..........	Cay Sal [Bahamas] [ICAO location identifier] (ICLI)
MYCX..........	Cutlass Bay, Cat Island [Bahamas] [ICAO location identifier] (ICLI)
MYD............	Malindi [Kenya] [Airport symbol] (OAG)
MYD............	Miyadu [Japan] [Seismograph station code, US Geological Survey] [Closed] (SEIS)
MYD............	MuniYield Fund [NYSE symbol] (SPSG)

MYD............	Myotonic Muscular Dystrophy [Medicine] (DB)
MYDP	Multi-Year Development Plan [Environmental Protection Agency] (ERG)
MYDW	Multiple Yield Defense Weapon
MYE	Man Year Equivalent (SPST)
MYE	Mary Ellen Resources Ltd. [Vancouver Stock Exchange symbol]
MYE	Miyake Jima [Japan] [Airport symbol] (OAG)
MYE	Myers Indus [AMEX symbol] (TTSB)
MYE	Myers Industries, Inc. [AMEX symbol] (SPSG)
MYEC..........	Cape Eleuthera, Eleuthera Island [Bahamas] [ICAO location identifier] (ICLI)
MYEG..........	George Town, Exuma Island [Bahamas] [ICAO location identifier] (ICLI)
MYEH..........	North Eleuthera, Eleuthera Island [Bahamas] [ICAO location identifier] (ICLI)
MYEL	Mulitple Myeloma [Hematology] (DAVI)
MYEL	Myelin [or Myelinated] [Medicine]
MYEL	Myelocyte [Hematology]
MYEL	Myelogram [Medicine] (AAMN)
MYEL	Staniel Cay, Exuma Island [Bahamas] [ICAO location identifier] (ICLI)
myelo	Myelocyte [Hematology]
Myelo	Myelogram (AMHC)
MYEM..........	Governor's Harbour, Eleuthera Island [Bahamas] [ICAO location identifier] (ICLI)
MYEN..........	Norman's Cay, Exuma Island [Bahamas] [ICAO location identifier] (ICLI)
MYER..........	Rock Sound/International, Eleuthera Island [Bahamas] [ICAO location identifier] (ICLI)
Myer Dig	Myer's Texas Digest [A publication] (DLA)
Myer Fed Dec...	Myer's Federal Decisions [A publication] (DLA)
MyerL	[The] Myers [L. E.] Co. Group [Associated Press] (SAG)
Myer's Fed Dec...	Myer's Federal Decisions [United States] [A publication] (DLA)
MyersInd	Myers Industries, Inc. [Associated Press] (SAG)
MYES..........	Lee Stocking Island, Exuma Island [Bahamas] [ICAO location identifier] (ICLI)
MYEY..........	Hog Cay, Exuma Island [Bahamas] [ICAO location identifier] (ICLI)
MYF............	Methodist Youth Fellowship
MYF............	MuniYield Florida Fund [NYSE symbol] (SPSG)
MYF............	Myogenic Factor (DMAA)
MYF............	San Diego [California] Montgomery Field [Airport symbol] [Obsolete] (OAG)
MYFC..........	Mike Yager Fan Club (EA)
MYFV..........	Melandrium Yellow Fleck Virus [Plant pathology]
MYG............	Massachusetts Institute of Technology, Cambridge, MA [OCLC symbol] (OCLC)
MYG............	Matka [Yugoslavia] [Seismograph station code, US Geological Survey] (SEIS)
MYG............	Mayaguana [Bahamas] [Airport symbol] (OAG)
MYG............	Maytag [NYSE symbol] (SAG)
MYG............	Maytag Corp. [NYSE symbol] (TTSB)
MyG............	Myasthenia Gravis [Medicine] (MELL)
MYG............	Myriagram [Ten Thousand Grams]
MYGD	Deep Water Cay, Grand Bahama Island [Bahamas] [ICAO location identifier] (ICLI)
MYGF..........	Freeport/International, Grand Bahama Island [Bahamas] [ICAO location identifier] (ICLI)
MYGM........	Grand Bahama Auxiliary Air Force Base, Grand Bahama Island [Bahamas] [ICAO location identifier] (ICLI)
MYGN	Myriad Genetics [NASDAQ symbol] (TTSB)
MYGN	Myriad Genetics, Inc. [NASDAQ symbol] (SAG)
MYGW	West End, Grand Bahama Island [Bahamas] [ICAO location identifier] (ICLI)
MYH............	Rosh-Pina [Israel] [Airport symbol] (AD)
MYHEC	Michigan Youth Hunter Education Challenge
MY I	First Multiyear Contract [Military] (RDA)
MYI............	Magical Youths International (EA)
MYI............	Metallic Yarns Institute [Defunct]
MYI............	MuniYield Insured Fund [NYSE symbol] (SPSG)
MYIG	Matthew Town, Great Inagua Island [Bahamas] [ICAO location identifier] (ICLI)
MY II	Second Multiyear Contract [Military] (RDA)
MYIM..........	Mylar Insulation Material
MYJ............	Matsuyama [Japan] [Airport symbol] (OAG)
MYJ............	MuniYield New Jersey Fund [NYSE symbol] (SPSG)
MYK............	May Creek [Alaska] [Airport symbol] (OAG)
MYK............	May Creek, AK [Location identifier] [FAA] (FAAL)
MYK............	Miyakojima [Ryukyu Islands] [Seismograph station code, US Geological Survey] (SEIS)
MYL............	Aeromyl SA de CV [Mexico] [ICAO designator] (FAAC)
MYL............	McCall, ID [Location identifier] [FAA] (FAAL)
MYL............	Mylan Laboratories, Inc. [NYSE symbol] (SPSG)
MYL............	Mylan Labs [NYSE symbol] (TTSB)
MYL............	Myrialiter [Unit of measurement]
Mylan	Mylan Laboratories, Inc. [Associated Press] (SAG)
Myl & C	Mylne and Craig's English Chancery Reports [A publication] (DLA)
Myl & C (Eng)..	Mylne and Craig's English Chancery Reports [A publication] (DLA)
Myl & Cr......	Mylne and Craig's English Chancery Reports [A publication] (DLA)
Myl & K	Mylne and Keen's English Chancery Reports [A publication] (DLA)
Myl & K (Eng)...	Mylne and Keen's English Chancery Reports [A publication] (DLA)
MYLD..........	Deadman's Cay, Long Island [Bahamas] [ICAO location identifier] (ICLI)
Mylex..........	Mylex Corp. [Associated Press] (SAG)

My LJ	Mysore Law Journal [*India*] [*A publication*] (DLA)
Mylne & K...	Mylne and Keen's English Chancery Reports [*A publication*] (DLA)
MYLR............	Diamond Roads, Long Island [*Bahamas*] [*ICAO location identifier*] (ICLI)
MYLS............	Mid-York Library System [*Library network*]
MYLS............	Stella Maris, Long Island [*Bahamas*] [*ICAO location identifier*] (ICLI)
MYLX............	Mylex Corp. [*NASDAQ symbol*] (NQ)
MYM.............	Managing Your Money [*MECA Software, Inc.*] (PCM)
MYM.............	Marley Mines Ltd. [*Vancouver Stock Exchange symbol*]
MYM.............	Monkey Mountain [*Guyana*] [*Airport symbol*] (OAG)
MYM.............	Muniyield Michigan Fund [*NYSE symbol*] (SAG)
MYM.............	Myriameter
MyMD..........	Myotonic Muscular Dystrophy [*See also MD*] [*Medicine*]
MYMD	New York Military District (SAUS)
MYMM........	Mayaguana Auxiliary Air Force Base, Mayaguana Island [*Bahamas*] [*ICAO location identifier*] (ICLI)
MYMS........	Mothers of Young Mongoloids [*Later, PODSC*] (EA)
MYMV........	Mungbean Yellow Mosaic Virus [*Plant pathology*]
MYN...........	Mareb [*Yemen*] [*Airport symbol*] [*Obsolete*] (OAG)
myn	Mayan [*MARC language code*] [*Library of Congress*] (LCCP)
MYN...........	Mayan Energy, Inc. [*Vancouver Stock Exchange symbol*]
MYN...........	MuniYield New York Insured Fund [*NYSE symbol*] (SPSG)
MYN...........	MuniYield NY Insured Fund [*NYSE symbol*] (TTSB)
MYNA	Nassau [*Bahamas*] [*ICAO location identifier*] (ICLI)
MYNN.........	Nassau/International, New Providence Island [*Bahamas*] [*ICAO location identifier*] (ICLI)
MYO...........	Myocardial [*or Myocardium*] [*Cardiology*] (AAMN)
MYO...........	Myoglobin (DB)
MYOB.........	Mind Your Own Business [*Slang*]
MYOBB........	Mind Your Own Business, Buster [*Slang*]
MYOC-A.......	Myocarditis, Pericarditis [*Cardiology*] (DAVI)
MYOGLB......	Myoglobin [*hematology*] (DAVI)
MYOP	Multiyear Operational Plan [*Long-range forecast produced by the Canadian government*]
myop	Myopia [*Ophthalmology*] (DAVI)
MYP...........	Mannito-Egg Yolk Polymyxin (OA)
MY/P............	Mean Yield/Plants [*Agriculture*]
MYP............	Montgomery [*Pakistan*] [*Airport symbol*] (AD)
MYP............	Multiyear Procurement [*DoD*]
MYPO	Multiyear Procurement Objective [*DoD*]
MYQ...........	Windsor Locks, CT [*Location identifier*] [*FAA*] (FAAL)
MYR.............	Maximum Yield Research [*Agricultural technology*]
m/yr............	Milli-Inches per Year [*Corrosion technology*]
Myr	Million Years
MYR.............	Million Years [*Also, MY*]
MYR.............	Miriadair [*France*] [*ICAO designator*] (FAAC)
MYR.............	[*The*] Myers [*L. E.*] Co. Group [*NYSE symbol*] (SPSG)
MYR.............	MYR Group [*NYSE symbol*] (TTSB)
Myr	Myrick's California Probate Court Reports [*1872-79*] [*A publication*] (DLA)
myr.............	Myrtle [*Philately*]
MYR.............	Myrtle Beach [*South Carolina*] Myrtle Air Force Base [*Airport symbol*] (OAG)
MYRA	Multiyear Rescheduling Agreement [*Banking*]
MYRAA	Model Yacht Racing Association of America (EA)
Myr Cal Prob...	Myrick's California Probate Court Reports [*1872-79*] [*A publication*] (DLA)
MYRD..........	Duncan Town, Exuma Island [*Bahamas*] [*ICAO location identifier*] (ICLI)
Myriad	Myriad Genetics, Inc. [*Associated Press*] (SAG)
Myrick (Cal)...	Myrick's California Probate Court Reports [*1872-79*] [*A publication*] (DLA)
Myrick Prob (Cal)...	Myrick's California Probate Court Reports [*1872-79*] [*A publication*] (DLA)
Myrick's Prob Rep...	Myrick's California Probate Court Reports [*1872-79*] [*A publication*] (DLA)
MYRP	Port Nelson, Exuma Island [*Bahamas*] [*ICAO location identifier*] (ICLI)
Myr Prob	Myrick's California Probate Court Reports [*1872-79*] [*A publication*] (DLA)
Myr Prob Rep...	Myrick's California Probate Court Reports [*1872-79*] [*A publication*] (DLA)
Mys.............	All India Reporter, Mysore [*A publication*] (DLA)
MYS.............	Maderas y Sinteticos [*NYSE symbol*] (SPSG)
MYS.............	Maderas y Sinteticos ADS [*NYSE symbol*] (TTSB)
MYS.............	Malaysia [*ANSI three-letter standard code*] (CNC)
MYS.............	Man-Year-Space [*Army*] (AABC)
MYS.............	Masisa S.A. ADS [*Formerly, Maderas y Sinteticos ADS*] [*NYSE symbol*]
MYS.............	Myasthenic Syndrome [*Neurology*]
MYS.............	Mystery Mountain Minerals [*Vancouver Stock Exchange symbol*]
MYS.............	Mystic, KY [*Location identifier*] [*FAA*] (FAAL)
MYS.............	Mystic Marinelife Aquarium, New London, CT [*OCLC symbol*] (OCLC)
Mys Ch Ct...	Mysore Chief Court Reports [*India*] [*A publication*] (DLA)
Mys HCR	Mysore High Court Reports [*India*] [*A publication*] (DLA)
Mys LJ	Mysore Law Journal [*India*] [*A publication*] (DLA)
Mys LR	Mysore Law Reports [*India*] [*A publication*] (DLA)
MYSM..........	Cockburn Town, San Salvador Island [*Bahamas*] [*ICAO location identifier*] (ICLI)
MySoft.........	MySoftware Co. [*Associated Press*] (SAG)
MYSOLN......	Mysoline [*An anticonvulsant*] [*Wyeth-Ayerst Laboratorie*] (DAVI)
Mysore	Mysore Law Reports [*India*] [*A publication*] (DLA)
Mysore LJ ...	Mysore Law Journal [*India*] [*A publication*] (DLA)
Mys R (R)....	Mysore Reports (Reprint) [*1878-1923*] [*India*] [*A publication*] (DLA)

MYST...........	Mystery
MYSTIC.......	Mystic
MYSTIC STAR...	Presidential Support AirGround Communications System (SAUS)
MYSW.........	MySoftware Co. [*NASDAQ symbol*] (SAG)
Mys WN......	Mysore Weekly Notes [*1891-92*] [*India*] [*A publication*] (DLA)
MYT.............	MuniYield New York Insured Fund II [*NYSE symbol*] (SPSG)
MYT.............	MuniYield NY Insured Fund II [*NYSE symbol*] (TTSB)
MYT.............	Myitkyina [*Myanmar*] [*Airport symbol*] (OAG)
MYT.............	Mytec Technology, Inc. [*Vancouver Stock Exchange symbol*]
MYT.............	Mythology
MYTA...........	Maintainability Task Analyses (NASA)
MYTAB.........	Myristyltrimethylammonium Bromide [*Organic chemistry*]
MYTD.........	Model Year to Date
MYTGC	Miller-Yoder Test of Grammatical Comprehension [*Speech and lanaguage therapy*] (DAVI)
MYTH..........	Mythical (GOBB)
Myth..........	Mythology (BEE)
myth..........	Mythology (ELAL)
MYTH..........	Mythology
MYTHOL	Mythology (WGA)
Myth Vat...	Mythographi Vaticani [*A publication*] (OCD)
MYTK...........	Mitek Surgical Products (EFIS)
MYU...........	Mekoryuk [*Alaska*] [*Airport symbol*] (OAG)
MYV...........	Malva Yellows Virus [*Plant pathology*]
MYV...........	Marysville [*California*] [*Airport symbol*] (AD)
MYV...........	Marysville, CA [*Location identifier*] [*FAA*] (FAAL)
MYVAL.........	Maintainability Evaluation (NASA)
MYW...........	Mtwara [*Tanzania*] [*Airport symbol*] (OAG)
MYW...........	Multiple Yield Weapon
MYWF.........	Masonic Youth Welfare Fund [*Australia*]
MYX...........	Marion, VA [*Location identifier*] [*FAA*] (FAAL)
MYX...........	Menyamya [*Papua New Guinea*] [*Airport symbol*] (OAG)
MYX...........	Methotrexate [*Antineoplastic drug*] (CDI)
MYXO	Myxomatosis (DSUE)
MYY...........	Miri [*Malaysia*] [*Airport symbol*] (OAG)
MYY...........	MuniYield MY Insured Fund III [*NYSE symbol*] (TTSB)
MYY...........	MuniYield New York Insured Fund III [*NYSE symbol*] (SPSG)
MYY...........	Philadelphia, PA [*Location identifier*] [*FAA*] (FAAL)
MYZ...........	Marysville, KS [*Location identifier*] [*FAA*] (FAAL)
MYZ...........	Mayoko [*Gabon*] [*Airport symbol*] (AD)
MYZ...........	Miyazaki [*Japan*] [*Seismograph station code, US Geological Survey*] (SEIS)
MZ	Mantle Zone
MZ	Marginal Zone [*Neurology*]
m-z	Mass to Charge Ratio
MZ	Merpati Nusatnara Airlines [*ICAO designator*] (AD)
Mz..............	Methoxyphenylazobenzyloxycarbonyl [*Biochemistry*]
MZ	Mezzo [*Moderate*] [*Music*] (ROG)
Mz..............	Mezzo Soprano
MZ	Middle Zone (HEAS)
MZ	Midzone Phenomenon [*Immunology*]
MZ	Miesiecznik Zydowski (BJA)
MZ	Milacron, Inc. [*NYSE symbol*] (SG)
MZ	Minus Zero (IAA)
MZ	Monozygotic [*Genetics*]
MZ	Monozygotic Twins (DIPS)
MZ	Mozambique [*ANSI two-letter standard code*] (CNC)
mz..............	Mozambique [*MARC country of publication code*] [*Library of Congress*] (LCCP)
MZ	Museum of Zoology (NADA)
MZA............	Air Zory [*Bulgaria*] [*FAA designator*] (FAAC)
MZA............	Mariazell [*Austria*] [*Seismograph station code, US Geological Survey*] (SEIS)
MZA............	Monozygotic Twins Reared Apart [*Genetics*]
MZa............	Monozygotic Twins Reared or Raised Apart (DIPS)
MZA............	MuniYield Arizona Fund [*AMEX symbol*] (TTSB)
MZA............	MuniYield Arizona Fund, Inc. [*AMEX symbol*] (SPSG)
MZAD..........	Mains Army Depot [*Germany*]
MZB............	Mocimboa da Praia [*Mozambique*] [*Airport symbol*] (AD)
MZB............	San Diego, CA [*Location identifier*] [*FAA*] (FAAL)
MZBZ..........	Belize/International [*Belize*] [*ICAO location identifier*] (ICLI)
MZC............	Mitzic [*Gabon*] [*Airport symbol*] (OAG)
MZCP..........	Mean Zonal Candlepower (IAA)
MZE............	Multifunctional Zone Evaluation (ACAE)
MZF............	Manganese Zinc Ferrite
MZF............	Mazirat [*France*] [*Seismograph station code, US Geological Survey*] (SEIS)
MZFR..........	Mehrzweck Forschungs [*Reactor*] [*Germany*] (NRCH)
MZFW..........	Maximum Zero Fuel Weight [*Aviation*] (MCD)
MZG...........	Makung [*Taiwan*] [*Airport symbol*] (OAG)
MZI............	Mopti [*Mali*] [*Airport symbol*] (OAG)
MZJ............	Marana, AZ [*Location identifier*] [*FAA*] (FAAL)
MZK...........	Marakei [*Kiribati*] [*Airport symbol*] (OAG)
MZL............	Aerovias Montes Azules, SA de CV [*Mexico*] [*FAA designator*] (FAAC)
MZL............	Manizales [*Colombia*] [*Airport symbol*] (OAG)
MZL............	Muzzle (MSA)
MZM...........	Metz [*France*] [*Airport symbol*] (OAG)
MZM...........	Movado Zenith Mondia
MZN...........	Maruzen Co. Ltd. [*UTLAS symbol*]
MZN...........	Minj [*New Guinea*] [*Airport symbol*] (AD)
MZN...........	Mount Vernon Nazarene College, Mount Vernon, OH [*OCLC symbol*] (OCLC)
MZO...........	Manzanillo [*Cuba*] [*Airport symbol*] (OAG)

MZO............ Mazie Landing [*Oklahoma*] [*Seismograph station code, US Geological Survey*] (SEIS)

MZOA........... Masada of the Zionist Organization of America (EA)

MZON .... Multiple Zones International, Inc. [*NASDAQ symbol*] (SAG)

M-ZONE...... Manufacturing Zone (MHDB)

MZP............. Meta-Azidopyrimethamine [*Biochemistry*]

MZP............. Modulated Zone Plate (PDAA)

MZPI............ Microwave Zone Position Indicator (IAA)

MZQ............. Mozambique [*Mozambique*] [*Airport symbol*] (AD)

MZR............. Mazar-I-Sharif [*Afghanistan*] [*Airport symbol*] (OAG)

MZR............. Monroe, LA [*Location identifier*] [*FAA*] (FAAL)

MZR............. Multi-Zone Recording (CIST)

MZS............. Mahfooz Aviation [*Gambia*] [*FAA designator*] (FAAC)

MZS............ Master of Zoology Science (GAGS)

MZS............. Spokane, WA [*Location identifier*] [*FAA*] (FAAL)

MZ Sc......... Master of Zoological Science

MZSCS......... Martinek-Zaichkowsky Self-Concept Scale for Children [*Child development test*]

MZSH........... Missionary Zelatrices of the Sacred Heart [*Roman Catholic women's religious order*]

MZsL .... Magyar Zsido Lexikon [*A publication*] (BJA)

MZT............. Mazatlan [*Mexico*] [*Airport symbol*] (OAG)

MZt............. Monozygotic Twins Reared or Raised Together (DIPS)

MZT............. Monozygotic Twins Reared Together [*Genetics*]

MZU............. Muzaffarpur [*India*] [*Airport symbol*] (AD)

MZV .... Magyar Zsidok Vilagszovetsege [*World Federation of Hungarian Jews*] (EAIO)

MZV .... Moline, IL [*Location identifier*] [*FAA*] (FAAL)

MZX............. Augusta, GA [*Location identifier*] [*FAA*] (FAAL)

MZX............. Massio [*Ethiopia*] [*Airport symbol*] (AD)

MZY............. Mzimba [*Malawi*] [*Airport symbol*] (AD)

MZZ............. Marion [*Indiana*] [*Airport symbol*] (AD)

MZZ............. Marion, IN [*Location identifier*] [*FAA*] (FAAL)

M~of~M....... Ministry of Munitions (SAUO)

N
By Acronym

N................. All India Reporter, Nagpur Series [*A publication*] (ILCA)
n................. Amino [*As substituent on nucleoside*] [*Biochemistry*]
n................. Amount of Substance [*Molecular quantity*] [*Symbol*] [*IUPAC*]
N................. Asparagine [*Biochemistry*] (DAVI)
N................. Asparaginyl (SAUS)
N................. Avogadro Number [*Number of molecules in one gram-molecular weight of a substance*]
N................. Carbon Star [*Astronomy*] (BARN)
N................. Cementex [*Research code symbol*]
N................. Clearance Hot Delivered (SAUS)
N................. Cranial Nerve (DIPS)
N................. Digestum Novum [*A publication*] [*Authority cited in pre-1607 legal work*] (DSA)
N................. Dr. Karl Thomae GmbH [*Germany*] [*Research code symbol*]
N................. Dumb [*Auxiliary craft suffix*] [*British*] [*Navy*]
N................. Educational Premises [*Public-performance tariff class*] [*British*]
N................. Efficiency [*Physics*] (BARN)
N................. Electron N-Type Semiconductor Material
N................. Employment [*Economics*]
N................. En [*Typography*] (WDAA)
n................. En [*Printing measurement*] (WDMC)
N................. Flying Boat [*Russian aircraft symbol*]
n................. Footnote (DLA)
N................. Haploid Chromosome Number (DOG)
N................. Haploid Number [*Genetics*]
N................. H. Lundbeck [*Denmark*] [*Research code symbol*]
N................. INCO Ltd. [*Formerly, International Nickel Co. of Canada Ltd.*] [*NYSE symbol*] [*Toronto Stock Exchange symbol*] (SPSG)
n................. [*An*] Indefinite Quantity [*Mathematics*] (ROG)
n................. index of refraction (SAUS)
N................. Knight [*Chess*]
N................. Magnetic Flux [*Symbol*] (ROG)
N................. Nail
N................. Name
N................. Nan [*Phonetic alphabet*] [*World War II*] (DSUE)
n................. Nano [*A prefix meaning divided by one billion*] [*SI symbol*]
N................. Naringenin [*Organic chemistry*]
N................. Naris [*Nostril*] [*Pharmacy*]
N................. Narrow
N................. Nasal
N................. Nasion (MELL)
N................. National [*Screw threads*]
N................. Nationalist (ROG)
N................. Nationalist Party [*British*] [*Political party*]
N................. National League [*Baseball*]
N................. Native [*Ecology*]
N................. Natural Division [*Geography*]
N................. Naturalization (DNAB)
N................. Natural Number (IDOE)
N................. Natus [*Birth*] [*Latin*]
N................. Nautical
N................. Naval [*British military*] (DMA)
N................. Navigation
N................. Navigational Aids [*JETDS nomenclature*]
N................. Navy
N................. Nay [*Vote*]
N................. Near [*Optics*] (WDAA)
N................. Near the Nut (or Heel) of the Bow [*Music*] (ROG)
N................. Necrotic
n................. Need (DIPS)
N................. Need [*Psychology*]
N................. Negative (PIPO)
n................. Negative [*Crystal*]
N................. Negro
N................. Neisseria [*Medicine*]
N................. Nematic Phase [*Physical chemistry*]
N................. Nematocyst [*Zoology*]
N................. Nepal (MILB)
N................. Neper [*A unit on a natural logarithmic scale*] (DEN)
n................. Nephew (GEAB)
N................. Nephew
N................. Nepos [*Grandson*] [*Latin*]
N................. Nervus [*Nerve*] [*Anatomy*]
N................. Nested [*Freight*]
N................. Nesting [*Ornithology*]
N................. Net

N................. Network [*FCC program source designation*] (NTCM)
n................. Network (WDMC)
N................. Neuraminidase [*An enzyme*]
N................. Neurogenic Element
N................. Neurology
N................. Neuropathy [*Medicine*] (DAVI)
N................. Neuroticism
N................. Neuroticism Index (SAUS)
N................. Neuter
n................. Neutral (MEC)
N................. Neutral
n................. Neutrino (SAUS)
N................. Neutron (NAKS)
n................. Neutron [*A nuclear particle*]
N................. Neutron Number [*Physics*] (DAVI)
N................. Neutrophil [*Hematology*]
N................. Nevus (MELL)
N................. New [*Stock exchange term*] (SPSG)
N................. New Issue [*Investment term*] (DFIT)
N................. New Persian
n................. News (WDMC)
N................. News
N................. Newspaper
N................. News Program (NTCM)
N................. Newton [*Symbol*] [*SI unit of force*]
N................. New York State Library, Albany, NY [*Library symbol*] [*Library of Congress*] (LCLS)
N................. New York Stock Exchange [*New York, NY*]
n................. Next [*Computer science*] [*Telecommunications*]
N................. Ngultrum [*Monetary unit*] [*Bhutan*] (BARN)
N................. Nichrome (IAA)
N................. Nickel (NTIO)
n................. Nickel (SHCU)
N................. Nicolaus Furiosus [*Flourished, 12th century*] [*Authority cited in pre-1607 legal work*] (DSA)
N................. Nicotinamide [*Also, NAA*] [*Vitamin*]
N................. Niece (ADA)
N................. Nifedipine [*Pharmacology*]
n................. Night (WDMC)
N................. Night [*Approach and landing charts*] [*Aviation*]
N................. Night [*Broadcasting term*]
N................. Night Fighter [*When suffix to plane designation*] [*Navy*]
N................. Night Game [*Baseball*]
N................. Nighttime (NTCM)
N................. Nitrogen [*Chemical element*]
N................. Nitrogen Peroxide (SAUS)
N................. Nitrogen Tetroxide (SAUS)
N................. No
N................. Nocardia [*Genus of bacteria*] (MAE)
N................. Nocte [*At Night*] [*Pharmacy*]
N................. Nodal [*Oncology*]
N................. Node [*Lymphatic*] [*Anatomy*]
N................. Noise [*Broadcasting*]
N................. Nomen [*Name*] [*Latin*]
N................. Nominal [*Stock exchange term*] (SPSG)
N................. Nominally Labeled [*Compound, with radioisotope*]
N................. Nominative
N................. None
N................. Nonmalignant [*Of tumors*] [*Medicine*]
N................. Nonne [*Globulin test*]
N................. Nontactical [*Military*]
N................. Noon (WDMC)
N................. Noon
N................. Norein [*Geology*]
N................. Norland Potato
N................. Norm (WDAA)
N................. Normal [*Solute concentration*] [*Chemistry*]
n................. Normal [*Molecular structure*] [*Chemistry*]
N................. Normal Depth [*Earthquakes*]
N................. Normal Horsepower
N................. Normality (SAUS)
N................. Normal Solution (DOG)
N................. Norse [*Language, etc.*]
N................. Norske Veritas [*Norwegian ship classification society*] (ROG)
N................. North [*or Northern*]

n----	North America [*MARC geographic area code*] [*Library of Congress*] (LCCP)
N	Northeastern Reporter [*Commonly cited NE*] [*A publication*] (DLA)
N	Northern Ireland Law Reports [*A publication*] (DLA)
N	Northern latitude (SAUS)
N	Northgate Exploration Ltd. [*Gold producer*] [*Canada*]
N	Northing (SAUS)
N	North London [*Postcode*] (ODBW)
N	Northwestern Reporter [*Commonly cited NW*] [*A publication*] (DLA)
N	Norway [*IYRU nationality code*]
N	Noster [*Our*] [*Latin*]
N	Nostril (AAMN)
N	Not (DAVI)
N	Notative Speed (WDAA)
n	Note (WDMC)
N	Note
n	Noun (WDMC)
N	Noun
N	No Uniform [*For schoolgirls*] [*British*]
N	Novellae [*Novels*] [*New Constitutions of Justinian*] [*A publication*] (DLA)
N	Novelty [*Insulation*]
N	November [*Phonetic alphabet*] [*International*] (DSUE)
N	Novice Slope [*Skiing*]
N	Nu [*Thirteenth letter of the Greek alphabet*] (DAVI)
N	Nuclear
N	Nuclear Propelled [*When following vessel classification, as CAG(N)*] [*Navy*]
N	[*A*] Nucleoside [*One-letter symbol; see Nuc*]
N	Nucleus [*of a cell*] [*Biology*]
n	Nucleus [*Psychology*]
N	Nucleus (of Syllable) [*Linguistics*]
N	Nullity [*Divorce cases*] [*British*] (ROG)
n	Number [*Usually integer*] (IDOE)
N	Number
N	Number Factor (DIPS)
N	Number (of Bits) [*Computer science*] (ECII)
N	Number of Molecules [*Symbol*] [*IUPAC*]
n	Number of Observations [*Statistics*] (DAVI)
n	Number (of Turns) [*Electronics*] (ECII)
N	Numeric
N	Numerical Ability (DIPS)
N	Nun [*Buoy*]
N	Nunnery
N	Nupta [*Married*] [*Latin*]
N	Nurse (ADA)
N	Nuts [*Phonetic alphabet*] [*Royal Navy*] [*World War I*] [*Pre-World War II*] (DSUE)
N	Nylon (AAG)
N	Nymph [*Entomology*]
N	Nystatin [*Antifungal antibiotic*]
N	Population Size [*Symbol*] (MAE)
n	Principal Quantum Number [*Atomic physics*] (DEN)
N	Probe [*Missile vehicle type symbol*]
n	Refractive Index [*Symbol*] [*Physics*]
N	Rockwell International Corp. [*ICAO aircraft manufacturer identifier*] (ICAO)
N	Size of Sample [*Statistics*] (DAVI)
N	Sound in Air [*JETDS nomenclature*]
N	South African Law Reports, Natal Province Division [*1910-46*] [*A publication*] (DLA)
N	Special Test, Permanent [*Aircraft classification letter*]
N	Stauffer Chemical Co. [*Research code symbol*]
N	Tilt Correction
N1E	Nosed One Edge [*Lumber*] (DAC)
N_2	Molecular Nitrogen [*Chemistry*] (DAVI)
N2	Nitrogen
N2E	Nosed Two Edges [*Lumber*] (DAC)
N2H04	Nitrogen Peroxide (NAKS)
N2H4	Hydrazine (NAKS)
N2N	Neighbor to Neighbor [*An association*] (EA)
N2N	Project Neighbor to Neighbor (EA)
N2O	Distickstoffoxid (SAUS)
N_2O	Nitrous Oxide [*An Anesthetic*] (DAVI)
$N_2O:O_2$	Nitrous Oxide to Oxygen Ratio [*Anesthesiology*] (DAVI)
N3	Cyclophosphamide, Vincristine, Triflurothymidine, Papaverine [*Antineoplastic drug regimen*] (DAVI)
N3F	National Fantasy Fan Federation (EA)
N4A	National Academic Athletic Advisors' Association (NTPA)
N4A	National Association of Academic Advisors for Athletics (EA)
N4A	National Association of Area Agencies on Aging [*Also, NAAAA*] (EA)
N4-HC	National 4-H Council (EA)
N4WDA	National 4 Wheel Drive Association (EA)
N/30	Net in Thirty Days
N204	Nitrogen Tetroxide (NAKS)
NA	Academician of the National Academy of Design, New York [*1825*] (NGC)
Na	Avogadro's Number [*Chemistry*] (DAVI)
NA	De Natura Animalium [*of Aelianus*] [*Classical studies*] (OCD)
Na	Exchangeable Body Sodium (AD)
NA	Nabisco Holdings 'A' [*NYSE symbol*] (TTSB)
Na	Nabisco Holdings Corp. [*NYSE symbol*] (SAG)
Na	Nachrichten
NA	Nachrichtenabteilung [*Signal battalion*] [*German military - World War II*]
NA	Nachrichten-Aufklaerung [*Signal intelligence*] [*German military - World War II*]
NA	Nadir (WGA)
Na	Nahum [*Old Testament book*]
NA	Nailable [*Technical drawings*]
Na	Naira [*Monetary unit*] [*Nigeria*]
N/A	Name and Address
NA	Namibia [*ANSI two-letter standard code*] (CNC)
nA	Nanoampere [*One billionth of an ampere*]
NA	Naphthalene Dicarboxylic Acid
NA	Naphthylacetamide [*Organic chemistry*]
NA	Naphthylamine [*Organic chemistry*]
NA	Napoleonic Association [*Enfield, Middlesex, England*] (EAIO)
NA	Narcolepsy Association [*British*] (DBA)
NA	Narcotics Anonymous (EA)
NA	Narrow Angle
NA	Nasal Allergy (MELL)
NA	Nash Papyrus (BJA)
NA	National Academician
NA	National Academy (ROG)
NA	National Acme [*Thread*]
NA	National Action [*Australia*]
NA	National Aerospace Standards Committee (AAGC)
NA	National Airlines, Inc. [*ICAO designator*]
NA	National Airport [*Under control of BAA*] [*British*]
NA	National Alliance (EA)
NA	National Ambucs (EA)
NA	[*The*] National Archives [*of the United States*]
NA	National Army
NA	National Assistance [*British*]
NA	National Association [*National Bank*]
NA	National Bank of Canada [*Toronto Stock Exchange symbol*] [*Vancouver Stock Exchange symbol*]
NA	Nationale Aktion fuer Volk und Heimat [*National Action for People and Homeland*] [*Switzerland*] [*Political party*] (PPE)
NA	Native American (GOBB)
Na	Natrium [*Sodium*] [*Chemical element*]
NA	Natural Axis
na	Naturalized (GEAB)
NA	Naturally Aspirated [*Diesel engines*]
NA	Nautical Almanac
NA	Nautical Archaeology [*Oceanography*]
NA	Naval Academy
NA	Naval Accounts [*British*]
NA	Naval Adviser (SAUS)
NA	Naval Aircraft
NA	Naval Airman [*Navy rating*] [*British*]
NA	Naval Air Systems Command Manual
NA	Naval Architect
NA	Naval Assistant [*Navy rating*] [*British*]
NA	Naval Attache [*Diplomacy*]
NA	Naval Auxiliary
NA	Naval Aviator
NA	Navigation Aid (IAA)
NA	Navion Aircraft Co. [*ICAO aircraft manufacturer identifier*] (ICAO)
NA	Navy Aircraft (IAA)
NA	Needle Aspiration [*Surgery*]
NA	Needs Assessment (OICC)
NA	Nelson Associates [*Also, an information service or system*] (IID)
NA	Neo-Assyrian [*or New Assyrian*] [*Language, etc.*] (BJA)
NA	Net Absolutely (MARI)
NA	Net Assessment Organization [*Navy*]
NA	Net Assets [*Banking*]
na	Netherlands Antilles [*MARC country of publication code*] [*Library of Congress*] (LCCP)
NA	Network Adapter (MCD)
NA	Network Administrator (DMAA)
NA	Neuraminidase (DMAA)
NA	Neuraminidase Activity [*An enzyme*]
NA	Neurologic Age (DMAA)
NA	Neuropathology [*Medicine*] (DHSM)
NA	Neurotics Anonymous (NADA)
NA	Neutral Axis
NA	Neutrality Act (SAUS)
NA	Neutralizing Antibody [*Immunochemistry*]
NA	Neutron Absorption (SAUS)
NA	Neutrophil Antibody [*Immunology*] (DAVI)
NA	New Account
NA	New African [*A publication*]
NA	New Age [*Later, LR*] [*An association*] (EA)
NA	New Alternative Party [*Venezuela*] [*Political party*]
NA	New Associations [*Later, NAP*] [*A publication*]
NA	Newsletter Association (EA)
NA	Newton Abbot [*British depot code*]
NA	Next Action (NASA)
NA	Next Address (VLIE)
NA	Next Assembly
NA	Ney-Allen [*Astronomy*]
NA	Nickel Alloy (SAUS)
NA	Nicotinic Acid [*Biochemistry*]
NA	Night Alarm [*Telecommunications*] (TEL)
NA	Night Answer (WDMC)
NA	Niro Atomizer Ltd., Copenhagen (SAUS)
NA	Nitric Acid (SAUS)
NA	Nitrobenzene Association [*Defunct*] (EA)

NA.............. Nizamut Adalat Reports [India] [A publication] (DLA)
NA.............. No Abnormalities (SAUS)
NA.............. No Abnormality [Medicine] (MAE)
NA.............. No Access [Telecommunications] (TEL)
NA.............. No Account [Banking]
N/A.............. No Action
NA.............. No Activity (ELAL)
N/A.............. No Advice [Business term]
N/A.............. No Alternative (DAVI)
NA.............. No Answer (WDMC)
NA.............. No Approval Required (MHDW)
NA.............. No Assets (AFIT)
NA.............. Noctes Atticae [of Gellius] [Classical studies] (OCD)
NA.............. Nomina Anatomica [System of anatomical terminology]
NA.............. Nonabrasive (SAUS)
N/A.............. Nonacceptance [Business term]
NA.............. Nonacosadiynoic Acid (SAUS)
NA.............. Nonacquiescence [Legal term] (DLA)
NA.............. Nonactivated
NA.............. Nonagglomerating (SAUS)
NA.............. Nonalcoholic
NA.............. Non Allocatur [Legal] [Latin] (ROG)
NA.............. Nonaqueous (SAUS)
NA.............. Non-Attached [European political movement] (ECON)
NA.............. Nonattainment (COE)
NA.............. Nonattendance
NA.............. Non-Australian (SAUS)
NA.............. Nora Alice [DoD satellite]
NA.............. Noradrenaline [Also known as NE: Norepinephrine] [Biochemistry]
NA.............. Normal Adult
NA.............. Normal Alarm (SAA)
NA.............. Normalized Air (SAUS)
NA.............. Normally Aspirated [Automotive engineering]
NA.............. North Africa
NA.............. North African (SAUS)
NA.............. North America
NA.............. Northanger Abbey [Novel by Jane Austen]
NA.............. North Atlantic Industries
NA.............. North Australia (SAUS)
NA.............. North Australian (SAUS)
NA.............. Northern Alberta Railways Co. (IIA)
NA.............. Norwegian metrology and Accreditation service (SAUS)
NA.............. Nostra Aetate [Declaration on the Relationship of the Church to the
                 Non-Christian Religions] [Vatican II document]
NA.............. Nostro Account [Our Account] [An account maintained by a bank
                 with a bank in a foreign country]
N/A.............. Not Above
NA.............. Not Absolutely (SAUS)
NA.............. Not Accurate (CIST)
NA.............. Not Active (ELAL)
NA.............. Not Actual (ELAL)
NA.............. Not Adjustable (SAUS)
NA.............. Not Adjusted (SAUS)
NA.............. Not Admitted [Medicine] (MAE)
N/A.............. Not Affected (AAG)
NA.............. Not Allowed
NA.............. Not And [Logical operator] [Computer science]
n/a.............. Not Applicable (WA)
NA.............. Not Applicable
NA.............. Not Apply (ACAE)
NA.............. Not Appropriated
NA.............. Not Assigned
NA.............. Not Authorized
n/a.............. Not Available (WA)
NA.............. Not Available
NA.............. Noticias Argentinas SA [News agency] [Argentina] (EY)
NA.............. Novice Agility
NA.............. Nozzle Assembly
NA.............. Nuclear Antibody (DMAA)
NA.............. Nuclear Antigen (MELL)
NA.............. Nuclear Assessment (SAUS)
NA.............. Nucleic Acid [Biochemistry]
NA.............. Nucleus Accumbens [Neuroanatomy]
NA.............. Nucleus Ambiguus [Neuroanatomy]
NA.............. Nueva Alternativa [Venezuela] [Political party] (EY)
NA.............. Number of Aimpoints [Military]
NA.............. Numerical Analysis [Computer science] (BUR)
NA.............. Numerical Aperture [Microscopy]
NA.............. Nurse Anesthetist (AAMN)
NA.............. Nurse's Aide
NA.............. Nurses Almanac
NA.............. Nursing Assistant
NA.............. Nursing Auxiliary [British]
NA.............. Nurturant-Authoritative [Psychotherapy]
NA.............. Nutrient Agar [Microbiology]
NA.............. Organon, Inc. [Research code symbol]
Na.............. Sodium [Chemical element] (AAMN)
nA.............. Transitional Antarctic Coastal Air Mass [Meteorology] (BARN)
NA 1SL........ Naval Assistant to the First Sea Lord [British military] (DMA)
Na5 DTPA.... Pentasodium Diethylenetriaminepentaacetic Acid (SAUS)
NAA.......... 1-Naphthaleneacetic Acid (LDT)
NAA.......... Naalehu [Hawaii] [Seismograph station code, US Geological Survey]
                 [Closed] (SEIS)
NAA.......... N-Acetyl Aspartate (MELL)
NAA.......... Name and Address (VLIE)

NAA.......... Nanny Academy of America [Defunct] (EA)
NAA.......... Naphthaleneacetic Acid [Biochemistry] (DAVI)
NAA.......... Naphthylacetic [or Napthaleneacetic] Acid [Organic chemistry]
NAA.......... Narrabri [Australia] [Airport symbol] (OAG)
NAA.......... Narrow-Angle Acquisition
NAA.......... National Academy of Arbitrators (EA)
NAA.......... National Academy of Astrology [Defunct] (EA)
NAA.......... National Aeronautic Association (NADA)
NAA.......... National Aeronautic Association of the USA (EA)
NAA.......... National Aeronautics and Space Administration, Washington, DC
                 [OCLC symbol] (OCLC)
NAA.......... National Aeronca Association (EA)
NAA.......... National Aerosol Association (EA)
NAA.......... National Aftermarket Audit Co.
NAA.......... National Aggregates Association (NTPA)
NAA.......... National Airspace Analysis [FAA] (TAG)
NAA.......... National Aldrich Association (EA)
NAA.......... National Alumni Association (EA)
NAA.......... National Apartment Association (EA)
NAA.......... National Aphasia Association (NRGU)
NAA.......... National Arborist Association (AGLO)
NAA.......... National Archery Association of the United States (EA)
NAA.......... National Ash Association (EA)
NAA.......... National Association of Accountants [Montvale, NJ] (EA)
NAA.......... National Auctioneers Association (EA)
NAA.......... National Automobile Association (NADA)
NAA.......... National Oceanic and Atmospheric Administration [Department of
                 Commerce] [ICAO designator] (FAAC)
NAA.......... Natural Areas Association (EA)
NAA.......... Naval Air Arm [British]
NAA.......... Naval Airship Association (EA)
NAA.......... Naval Attache for Air
NAA.......... Neckwear Association of America (EA)
NAA.......... Network Analysis Area [Space Flight Operations Facility, NASA]
NAA.......... Neuron Activation Analysis [Neurology] (DAVI)
NAA.......... Neutral Amino Acid [Biochemistry]
NAA.......... Neutron Activation Analysis
NAA.......... Neutrophil Aggregation Activity (MELL)
NAA.......... New Art Association (EA)
NAA.......... Newsletter Association of America (EA)
NAA.......... Newspaper Association of America [Reston, VA] (WDMC)
NAA.......... Nicotinic Acid Amide [Also, N]
NAA.......... Nigerian-American Alliance (EA)
NAA.......... Nitroanthranilic Acid [Organic chemistry]
NAA.......... No Apparent Abnormalities [Medicine]
NAA.......... Nocturnal Acid Accumulation [Botany]
NAA.......... Noise Analysis Approach (ELAL)
NAA.......... Nonattainment Area [Environmental Protection Agency] (EPA)
NAA.......... Nord Africa Aviazione
NAA.......... North American Aviation, Inc. [Later, Rockwell International Corp.]
NAA.......... North Atlantic Alliance
NAA.......... North Atlantic Area (SARE)
NAA.......... North Atlantic Assembly
NAA.......... Northeast Atlantic Airlines, Inc. (SAUS)
NAA.......... Northern Attack Area
NAA.......... Norway-America Association (EA)
NAA.......... Notable Asian Americans [A publication]
naa.......... Not Always Afloat [Shipping] (ODBW)
NAA.......... Not Always Afloat [Shipping]
NAA.......... Not at All (SAUS)
NAA.......... Nuclear Accidents Agreement (SAUS)
NAA.......... Nuclear Activation Analysis (PDAA)
NAA.......... Nurses Auxiliaries Association (SAUS)
NAAA.......... National Agricultural Aviation Association (EA)
NAAA.......... National Alarm Association of America (EA)
NAAA.......... National Alliance of Athletic Associations [Defunct] (EA)
NAAA.......... National Association of American Academicians (NADA)
NAAA.......... National Association of Arab Americans (EA)
NAAA.......... National Auto Auction Association [Lincoln, NE] (EA)
NAAAA.......... National Association for the Advancement of Aardvarks in America
                 [Defunct] (EA)
NAAAA.......... National Association of Area Agencies on Aging [Also, N4A] (EA)
NAAACC.......... National Association of Antique Automobile Clubs of Canada
NAAACPA..... National Association of Asian American Certified Public
                 Accountants (EA)
NAAAID........ National Association of Americans of Asian Indian Descent (EA)
NAAAP........ National Association of Asian-American Professionals (EA)
NAAAP........ North American Association of Alcoholism Programs [Later, ADPA]
                 (EA)
NAAAS........ National Association for Applied Arts and Sciences (EA)
NAAAS........ National Association of African American Studies (NTPA)
NAAAS........ National Association of Air Ambulance Services (SAUS)
NAAASL....... National Association of African American Students of Law (EA)
NAAB.......... National Architectural Accrediting Board (EA)
NAAB.......... National Archival Appraisal Board [Canada]
NAAB.......... National Association of Animal Breeders (EA)
NAABA.......... National Association for the Advancement of the Black Aged (EA)
NAABAVE.... National Association for the Advancement of Black Americans in
                 Vocational Education (EA)
NAABC.......... National Association American Business Clubs [High Point, NC]
NAABCV....... National Association American Balloon Corps Veterans (EA)
NAABI.......... National Association of Alcoholic Beverage Importers [Later, NABI]
                 (EA)
NAABSA....... Not Always Afloat but Safe Aground [Shipping]
NAAC.......... National Adoption Assistance Center (EA)

NAAC	National Agricultural Advisory Commission (NADA)
NAAC	National Air Access Council (NTPA)
NAAC	National Association for Ambulatory Care (EA)
NAAC	National Association of Agricultural Contractors [British] (BI)
NAAC	National Association of Avon Collectors (EA)
NAAC	Navy Aeroballistics Advisory Committee (MCD)
NAAC	No Apparent Anesthesia Complication [Medicine] (MELL)
NAAC	North American Adoption Congress (EA)
NAACC	National Association for American Composers and Conductors (EA)
NAACC	National Association of Angling and Casting Clubs [Later, ACA]
NAACC	Northwest Athletic Association of Community Colleges (PSS)
NAACCR	North American Association of Central Cancer Registries
NAACE	National Association of Advisers in Computer Education (AIE)
NAACLS	National Accrediting Agency for Clinical Laboratory Sciences (EA)
NAACO	National Association of American Community Organizations (EA)
NAACO	North American Arms Corporation of Canada (SAUS)
NAACOG	NAACOG: the Organization for Obstetric, Gynecologic, and Neonatal Nurses [Formerly, Nurses Association of the American College of Obstetricians and Gynecologists] (EA)
NAACOG	Nurses Association of the American College of Obstetrics and Gynecology (SAUS)
NAACP	National Association for the Advancement of Colored People (EA)
NAACP	Neoplasia, Allergy, Addison's Disease, Collagen Disease, and Parasites [Medicine]
NAACPA	National Association of Asian American Certified Public Accountants (MHDB)
NAACS	National Association of Accredited Cosmetology Schools (EA)
NAACS	National Association of Adult College Students (EA)
NAACS	National Association of Aircraft and Communications Suppliers [Defunct] (EA)
NAACSS	National Association for the Accreditation of Colleges and Secondary Schools (EA)
NAACSW	North American Association of Christians in Social Work [Later, NACSW] (EA)
NAACT	National Association of Assessors and Collectors of Taxes [A union] [British]
NAAD	National Association of Aluminum Distributors (EA)
NAAD	Navajo Army Depot [Arizona] (AABC)
NAAD	Nicotine Acid Adenine Dinucleotide (SAUS)
NAAD	Nicotinic Acid Adenine Dinucleotide [Biochemistry]
NAAD	North American Association for the Diaconate (EA)
NAADAA	National Antique and Art Dealers Association of America (EA)
NAADAC	National Association of Alcoholism and Drug Abuse Counselors (EA)
NAADC	National Association of Art and Design Companies (EA)
NAADC	North American Aerospace Defense Command (SAUS)
NAADC	North American Air Defense Command (AAG)
NAADC	North American Area Defense Command (SAUS)
NAADD	National Association of Athletic Development Directors
NAADD	National Association on Alcohol, Drugs & Disability (SAUS)
NAADI	National Association of Approved Driving Instructors [British] (DBA)
NAADM	North American Air Defense Modernization (SAUS)
NAADM	North American Defense Modernization (SAUS)
NAADMP	North American Air Defense Master Plan (CCCA)
NAADS	New Army Authorization Documents System (AABC)
NAADS	New Army Automatic Data System
NAAE	National Association of Aeronautical Examiners (EA)
NAAE	National Association of Afro-American Educators
NAAE	National Association of Agriculture Employees (EA)
NAAE	Nordic Association for Adult Education (EAIO)
NAAE	North American Academy of Ecumenists (EA)
NAAEC	North American Agreement on Environmental Cooperation (EPAT)
NAAEE	North American Association of Environmental Educators
NAAF	National Alopecia Areata Foundation (EA)
NAAF	Naval Auxiliary Air Facility
NAAF	New Amino Acid Formula [Nutrition]
NAAF	North African Air Force [World War II]
NAAFA	National Association of Agricultural Fair Agencies (NTPA)
NAAFA	National Association to Advance Fat Acceptance (EA)
NAAFETEE	North American Association For Exports To Eastern Europe (SAUS)
Naafi	Navy, Army & Air Force Institute (WDAA)
NAAFI	Navy, Army, and Air Force Institutes [Responsible for clubs, canteens, and provision of some items for messing of British armed forces]
NAAFW	National Association of Air Forces Women
NAAG	N-Acetylaspartylglutamic Acid [Biochemistry]
NAAG	National Association of Attorneys General (EA)
NAAG	NATO Army Advisory Group (NATG)
NAAG	NATO Army Armaments Group (AABC)
NAAG	Nordic Association of Applied Geophysics (EA)
NAAG	North African Adjutant General [World War II]
NAAGA	North African Adjutant General, Analysis and Control Division [World War II]
NAAGC	North African Adjutant General, Casualty Branch [World War II]
NAAG-DPG	North Atlantic-Arctic Gateways Detailed Planning Group (SAUS)
NAAGE	North African Adjutant General, Personnel Division [World War II]
NAAGG	North African Adjutant General, Executive Division [World War II]
NAAGO	North African Adjutant General, Operations Division [World War II]
NAAGP	North African Adjutant General, Postal Division [World War II]
NAAGS	North African Adjutant General, Statistical Division [World War II]
NAAHE	National Association for the Advancement of Humane Education [LA NAHEE] (EA)
NAAHL	National Association of Affordable Housing Lenders (NTPA)
NAAHP	National Association of Advisors for the Health Professions (EA)
NAAHSC	North American Association of Hunter Safety Coordinators
NAAI	National Alliance of Arts and Industry

NAAI	National Association of Accountants in Insolvencies (EA)
NAA-ICIF	North American Association of the ICIF [International Cooperative Insurance Federation] [Detroit, MI] (EA)
NAAIS	National Aircraft Accident Investigation School [FAA]
NAAIS	North American Association of Inventory Services [Greensboro, NC] (EA)
NAAJ	National Association of Agricultural Journalists (NTPA)
NAAJHHA	North American Association of Jewish Homes and Housing for the Aging (EA)
NAAJS	National Academy for Adult Jewish Studies (EA)
NAAK	Nerve Agent Antidote Kit [Military] (RDA)
NAAL	National Alliance for Animal Legislation [Defunct] (EA)
NAAL	North American Academy of Liturgy (EA)
NAAL	North American Aerodynamic Laboratory [Wind tunnel] (NASA)
NAALA	North American Aviation Los Angeles (SAUS)
NAALBWV	National Association for the Advancement of Leboyer's Birth Without Violence (EA)
NAALC	National Afro-American Labor Council [Later, NALC]
NAALS	Navigational Aids and Landing Systems (MCD)
NAAM	National Association of Anvil Makers [A union] [British]
NAAM	National Association of Architectural Metal Manufacturers (IAA)
NAAM	North American Aliyah Movement (EA)
NAAMA	National Agricultural Advertising and Marketing Association [Later, NAMA]
NAAMACC	National Association for the Accreditation of Martial Arts Colleges and Curriculum (EA)
NAAMIC	National Association of Automotive Mutual Insurance Companies [Later, American Insurers Highway Safety Alliance] (EA)
NAAMM	National Association of Architectural Metal Manufacturers (EA)
NAAMM	North American Academy of Musculoskeletal Medicine (EA)
NAAMO	National Association Agricultural Marketing Officials (NTPA)
NAAN	National Advertising Agency Network [New York, NY] (EA)
NAAN	North American Advertising Agency Network (NTPA)
NAAN	Nuclear Arms Alert Network [Defunct] (EA)
NAANACM	National Association for the Advancement of Native American Composers and Musicians
NAANAD	National Association of Anorexia Nervosa and Associated Disorders (DHP)
NAANBW	National Amalgamated Association of Nut and Bolt Workers [A union] [British]
NAAND	North American Association for the Diaconate (EA)
NA & D C & O	Selection of Cases Decided in the Native Appeal and Divorce Court, Cape and Orange Free State [A publication] (DLA)
NA & DT & N	Transvaal and Natal Native Appeal and Divorce Court Decisions [A publication] (DLA)
NA&G	Norgulf Lines (SAUS)
NA & G	Norgulf Lines (North Atlantic & Gulf) (AD)
NA & G	North Atlantic & Gulf Steamship Co. (MHDW)
Na & K	Sodium and Potassium [Urine test] [Biochemistry] (DAVI)
Na & KSP	Sodium and Potassium Spot [Urine Test] (DAVI)
NAANGHT	National Association of Air National Guard Health Technicians (EA)
NAANP	National Alliance for the Advancement of Nodnarbian Philosophy (EA)
NAAO	National Association of Amateur Oarsmen [Later, USRA] (EA)
NAAO	National Association of Artists' Organizations (EA)
NAAO	National Association of Assessing Officers [Later, IAAO]
NAAO	Navy Area Audit Office [London]
NAAO	North America Aircraft Operations (SAUS)
NAAO	North American Aircraft Operations (SAUS)
NAAO	North American Automotive Operations [Ford Motor Co.]
NAAOJ	National Association for the Advancement of Orthodox Judaism (EA)
NAAOP	National Association for the Advancement of Older People (EA)
NAAOSE	National Association of Advisory Officers Special Education [British] (DBA)
NAAP	N-Acetylaminophenazone [Organic chemistry]
NAAP	National Association for Accreditation in Psychoanalysis (EA)
NAAP	National Association fot the Advancement of Psychoanalysis (NTPA)
NAAP	National Association of Activity Professionals (EA)
NAAP	National Association of Advertising Publishers [Later, AFCP] (EA)
NAAP	National Association of Apnea Professionals (EA)
NAAP	Netherlands Antarctic Programme (SAUS)
NAAP	Newport Army Ammunition Plant (AABC)
NAAPABAC	National Association for the Advancement of Psychoanalysis and the American Boards for Accreditation and Certification (EA)
NAAPABAP	National Association for the Advancement of Psychoanalysis and the American Board for Accreditation in Psychoanalysis (EA)
NAAPAE	National Association for Asian and Pacific American Education (EA)
NAAPHE	National Association for the Advancement of Private Higher Education [Later, United Student Association]
NAAPI	National Association of Accountants for the Public Interest [Later, API] (EA)
NAAPM	National Association for the Advancement of Perry Mason (EA)
NAAPPA	North American Association for the Protection of Predatory Animals (SAUS)
NAAPPB	National Association of Amusement Parks, Pools, and Beaches [Later, IAAPA]
NAAPS	Nozzle Actuator Auxiliary Power Supply (SAA)
NAAQS	National Ambient Air Quality Standards [Environmental Protection Agency]
NAAR	National Alliance for Autism Research (NRGU)
NAAR	National Association of Advertising Representatives (DGA)
NAAR	Night Air-to-Air Refueling (SAUS)
NAARD	North American Aviation Rocketdyne Division (SAA)
Naar Elec	Naar on Suffrage and Elections [A publication] (DLA)
NAARFC	National Association of Auto Racing Fan Clubs

NAARMC...... National Association of Auto Racing Memorabilia Collectors (EA)
NAARPR ..... National Alliance Against Racist and Political Repression (EA)
NAARS......... National Association of Radio Reading Services (SAUS)
NAARS......... National Automated Accounting Research System [*American Institute of Certified Public Accountants*] [*Database*] [*Information service or system*] (IID)
NAAS .... National Academy of American Scholars (EA)
NAAS .... National Agricultural Advisory Service [*Later, ADAS*] [*British*]
NAAS .... National Air Audit System [*Environmental Protection Agency*] (GFGA)
NAAS .... National Anorexic Aid Society (EA)
NAAS .... National Association of Academies of Science (EA)
NAAS .... National Association of Art Services [*Later, NAADC*] (EA)
NAAS .... National Aviation Assistance
NAAS .... Naval Area Audit Service
NAAS .... Naval Auxiliary Air Station
NAAS .... Navy Aircraft Accounting System
NAAS .... Navy Area Audit Service (DNAB)
NAAS .... New Academic Appointments Scheme (SAUS)
NAAS .... Newsletter of the Association for Asian Studies (SAUS)
NAAS .... Nordic Association for American Studies (EAIO)
NAAS .... North American Apiotherapy Society (EA)
NAAS .... North American Automated Systems co. (SAUS)
NAA S&ID... North American Aviation Space and Information Division (SAUS)
NAASC........ North American Aviation Science Center (SAA)
NAASC........ Northwest African Air Service Command [*World War II*]
NaAsc......... Sodium Ascorbate (SAUS)
NAASD........ North American Aviation Space Division (SAA)
NAASER...... National Association of American School Employees and Retirees (EA)
NAASERLDC... National Association of American School Employees and Retirees Legal Defense Counsel (EA)
NAASFEP .... National Association of Administrators of State and Federal Education Programs (EA)
NAASL .... North American Academy of the Spanish Language (EA)
NAASLANT... Navy Auxiliary Air Stations, Atlantic
NAASLN....... National Association for Adults with Special Learning Needs (EA)
NAASMWB... National Amalgamated Association of Sheet Metal Workers and Blaziers [*A union*] [*British*]
NAASPAC.... Navy Auxiliary Air Stations, Pacific
NAASPL ...... North American Association of State and Provincial Lotteries (EA)
NAASR .... National Association for Armenian Studies and Research (EA)
NAASR........ North American Association for the Study of Jean-Jacques Rousseau (EA)
NAASS .... North American Association of Summer Sessions (EA)
NAASTOR .... Non-Addressable Auxiliary Storage [*Computer science*] (VLIE)
NAASW .... Nonacoustic Antisubmarine Warfare [*Military*]
NAASW .... Non-Acoustic ASW (SAUS)
NAAT .... National Association of Agricultural Teachers [*Australia*]
NAAT .... Naval Air Advance Training (SAA)
NAATA .... National Asian American Telecommunications Association (EA)
NAATC .... Naval Air Advanced Training Command
NAATD .... North-American Association of Telecommunications Dealers (NTPA)
NAATP .... National Association of Addiction Treatment Providers (EA)
NAATP .... National Association of Alcoholism Treatment Programs (EA)
NAATP .... New African Air Transport Policy (SAUS)
NAATPWB.... National Amalgamated Association of Tin Plate Workers and Blaziers [*A union*] [*British*]
NAATS .... National Association of Air Traffic Specialists (EA)
NAATS .... National Association of Auto Trim Shops (EA)
NAATTFO .... National Association of Alcohol and Tobacco Tax Field Officers
NAAUG....... North American Autocad User's Group [*Computer science*] (VLIE)
NAAUS....... National Archery Association of the United States (NADA)
NAAUSA....... National Association of Assistant United States Attorneys (NTPA)
NAAUTC....... National Amateur Athletic Union Taekwondo Committee [*Later, NAAUTUUSA*] (EA)
NAAUTUUSA... National AAU [*Amateur Athletic Union*] Taekwondo Union of the United Statesof America [*Formerly, NAAUTC*] (EA)
NAAV .... National Alliance Against Violence (EA)
NAAV .... National Association of Atomic Veterans (EA)
NAAV .... North American Association of Ventriloquists (EA)
NAAW .... National Association of Accordion Wholesalers [*Defunct*] (EA)
NAAWER...... National Association of Arc Welding Equipment Repairers [*British*] (DBA)
NAAWFS...... Naval Air All Weather Flight Squadron
NAAWP....... National Association for the Advancement of White People [*Defunct*] (EA)
NAAWS....... NATO Anti-Air Warfare System (DOMA)
NAAWS....... North American Association of Wardens and Superintendents (EAIO)
NAAWUL...... National Agricultural and Allied Workers' Union of Liberia (IMH)
NAB .... Mina Airline Company [*Egypt*] [*FAA designator*] (FAAC)
Nab............. Nabatean (BJA)
NAB .... National Accreditation Board (SAUS)
NAB .... National Acoustics Board (MUGU)
NAB .... National Advisory Board (ACII)
NAB .... National Advisory Body [*British*]
NAB .... National Aircraft Beacon
NAB .... National Alliance of Business [*Washington, DC*] (EA)
NAB .... National Alliance of Businessmen (NADA)
NAB .... National Apex Body [*India*] (BUAC)
NAB .... National Associated Businessmen [*Defunct*] (EA)
NAB .... National Association of Bioengineers [*Defunct*] (EA)
NAB .... National Association of Boards of Examiners for Nursing Home Administrators (EA)
NAB .... National Association of Bookmakers Ltd. [*British*] (BI)
NAB .... National Association of Broadcasters

NAB .... National Audience Board [*An association*] (NTCM)
NAB .... National Australia Bank ADS [*NYSE symbol*] (SPSG)
NAB .... Naval Advanced Base
NAB .... Naval Air Base
NAB .... Naval Amphibious Base
NAB .... Navigational Aid to Bombing [*Air Force*]
NAB .... Needle Aspiration Biopsy [*Surgery*]
NAB .... Net Asset Backing
NAB .... Netware Asynchronous Board (SAUS)
Nab............. Neutralizing Antibodies [*Medicine*] (MELL)
NAB .... New American Bible
NAB .... News Agency of Burma
NAB .... Newspaper Advertising Bureau [*New York, NY*] (EA)
NAB .... Nickel Alkaline Battery
NAB .... Nigeria-Arab Bank Ltd.
NAB .... Nitric Acid Burns [*Medicine*] (MELL)
NAB .... Nitrosoanabasine [*Organic chemistry*]
NAB .... Non-A, Non-B [*Hepatitis*] [*Infectious diseases*] (DAVI)
NAB .... None of the Above
NAB .... North American Biologicals, Inc.
NAB .... North American Blastomycosis [*Medicine*] (MELL)
NAB .... North Atlantic Base (SAUS)
NAB .... Not Above [*Aviation*]
NAB .... Not at Bedside [*Medicine*] (MELL)
NAB .... Novarsenobenzene (DMAA)
NAB .... Nuclear Air Burst
NAB .... Nuclear Assembly Building
NAB .... Nut and Bolt
NAB$2CC..... National Association of Bicentennial $2 Cancellation Collectors (EA)
NAB A......... NAB Asset Corp. [*Associated Press*] (SAG)
NABA......... National Alliance of Black Americans
NABA......... National Amateur Basketball Association (EA)
NABA......... National Association of Black Accountants [*Washington, DC*] (EA)
NABA......... National Association of Breweriana Advertising (EA)
NABA......... Naval Amphibious Base Annex
NABA......... Nitro-(amino)butyric Acid
NABA......... North American Ballet Association [*Defunct*] (EA)
NABA......... North American Benefit Association [*Port Huron, MI*] (EA)
NABA......... North American Broadcasters Association (SAUS)
NABA......... North American Bungee Association (EA)
NABA......... North American Butterfly Association
NABA......... Woman's Life Insurance Society
NABAC....... National Association for Bank Auditors and Comptrollers [*Later, BAI*] (EA)
NABADA...... Association of Container Reconditioners
NABARD..... National Bank for Agricultural and Rural Development [*India*] (BUAC)
NABAS........ National Association of Ballon Suppliers (BUAC)
NABAS........ National Association of Balloon Artists and Suppliers [*Great Britain*]
NABATRA..... Naval Air Basic Training Center
NABB .... National Association for Better Broadcasting (EA)
NABB .... National Association of Barber Boards (EA)
NABB .... National Association of Business Brokers (EA)
NABBA........ National Amateur Body Building Association [*British*] (BI)
NABBA........ North American Brass Band Association (EA)
NABBEA...... National Association of Boards of Barbers Examiners of America [*Later, NABB*] (EA)
NABBP........ National Association of Base Ball Players (NDBD)
NABBS........ National Association of Bench and Bar Spouses (EA)
NABC......... NAB Asset Corp. [*NASDAQ symbol*] (SAG)
NABC......... National Association of Basketball Coaches of the United States (EA)
NABC......... National Association of Bingo Clubs [*British*] (BI)
NABC......... National Association of Boys' Clubs [*British*]
NABC......... Normative Adaptive Behavior Checklist (TES)
NABC......... North American Blueberry Council (EA)
NABC......... North American Bridge Championships (SAUS)
NABC......... North American Broadcasting Corp. (SAUS)
NABCA........ National Alcoholic Beverage Control Association (EA)
NABCA........ National Association for Bank Cost Analysis (EA)
NABCA........ National Association for Bank Cost and Management Accounting (EA)
NABCA........ National Association of Black Catholic Administrators (EA)
NABCE........ National Association of Black Consulting Engineers (EA)
NABCJ........ National Association of Blacks in Criminal Justice (EA)
NABCM....... National Association of Baby Carriage Manufacturers (EA)
NABCM....... National Association of Brattice Cloth Manufacturers (EA)
NABCO........ National Alliance of Breast Cancer Organizations (EA)
NABCO........ National Association of Black County Officials (EA)
NABCO........ National Association of Building Cooperatives [*Ireland*] (BUAC)
NABCO........ Nippon Air Brake Co. Ltd. [*Tokyo, Japan*]
NAB curve ... National Association of Broadcasters Curve (MED)
NABD......... National Association of Bank Directors [*Later, ASBD*] (EA)
NABD......... National Association of Blood Donors (BUAC)
NABD......... National Association of Brick Distributors (EA)
NABD......... Naval Advanced Base Depot
NABD......... North American Band Directors (SAUS)
NABDC........ National Association of Blueprint and Diazotype Coaters [*Later, ARMM*]
NABDCC...... North American Band Directors Coordinating Committee (EA)
NABE .... National Association for Bilingual Education (EA)
NABE .... National Association for Business Economics (EA)
NABE .... National Association of Bar Executives (EA)
NABE .... National Association of Biological Engineering
NABE .... National Association of Boards of Education (EA)
NABE .... National Association of Book Editors [*Defunct*] (EA)
NABE .... National Association of Business Economists (EA)

NABE .... National Association of Business Education (IAA)
nabe .... Neighborhood (ADWA)
NABE .... North Atlantic Bloom Experiment (SAUS)
NABE .... Nuclear Air Burst Effect
NABEA .... North American Bicycle Exhibitor Association [*Defunct*] (EA)
NABER .... National Association of Business and Educational Radio (EA)
NABESS .... National Association of Business Education State Supervisors [*Stillwater, OK*] (EA)
NABET .... National Association Broadcast Employees and Technicians (EA)
NABEWD .... North American Board for East-West Dialogue (SAUS)
NABF .... National Alliance of Black Feminists (EA)
NABF .... National Amateur Baseball Federation (EA)
NABF .... North American Baptist Fellowship (EA)
NABF .... North American Boxing Federation (EA)
NABG .... National Association of Blacks within Government (EA)
NABGG .... National Association of Black Geologists and Geophysicists (EA)
NABHP .... National Association of Black Hospitality Professionals (EA)
NABI .... NABI, Inc. [*NASDAQ symbol*] (SAG)
NABI .... National Association of Beverage Importers (EA)
NABI .... National Association of Biblical Instructors [*Later, American Academy of Religion*] (EA)
NABI .... National Association of Bunco Investigators
NABI .... North American Biologicals, Inc. (EFIS)
NABIL .... Nepal Arab Bank Ltd. (BUAC)
NABIM .... National Association of Band Instrument Manufacturers (EA)
NABIM .... National Association of British and Irish Millers [*Incorporated*] (DBA)
NABIN .... North Alabama Biomedical Information Network (SAUS)
NABio .... North American Biologicals, Inc. [*Associated Press*] (SAG)
NABIPB .... National Association of Blacks in Public Broadcasting (SAUS)
NABIR .... Natural and Accelerated Bioremediation Research [*Department of Energy*]
NABIS .... National Association of Business and Industrial Saleswomen [*Denver, CO*] (EA)
NABIS .... National Biological Survey
NABIS .... Northern Alberta Brain Injury Society (SAUS)
NABISCO .... National Biscuit Co. [*Acronym now used as company name*]
NabisH .... Nabisco Holdings Corp. [*Associated Press*] (SAG)
NABJ .... National Association of Black Journalists (EA)
NAB-JOBS .... National Alliance of Business - Job Opportunities in the Business Sector (OICC)
NABL .... National Accreditation Board for Testing and Calibration Laboratories (SAUS)
NABL .... National Association of Bond Lawyers (EA)
NABL .... National Association of Builders' Labourers [*A union*] [*British*]
NABLOC .... Brussels Tariff Nomenclature for the Latin American Free Trade Association (BARN)
NABLT .... National Association of Business Law Teachers [*Later, NBLC*] (EA)
NABM .... National Association of Bedding Manufacturers [*Later, ISPA*] (EA)
NABM .... National Association of Biscuit Manufacturers (BUAC)
NABM .... National Association of Black Manufacturers (EA)
NABM .... National Association of Blouse Manufacturers (EA)
NABM .... National Association of Boating Magazines [*Defunct*] (EA)
NABM .... National Association of Boat Manufacturers (EA)
NABM .... National Association of Book Manufacturers [*Defunct*] (EA)
NABM .... National Association of British Manufacturers
NABM .... National Association of Building Manufacturers [*Later, HMC*] (EA)
NABMA .... National Association of British Market Authorities
NABMCC .... National Association of Black and Minority Chambers of Commerce [*Later, NBCC*] (EA)
NABMO .... NATO Bullpup Management Office [*Missiles*] (NATG)
NABMP .... National Association of Black Media Producers
NABN .... EMSL-RTP National Atmospheric Background Network (SAUS)
NABO .... National Alliance of Black Organizations (EA)
NABO .... National Association of Boat Owners (BUAC)
NABO .... North Atlantic Biocultural Organization [*A research cooperative*]
NABOB .... National Association of Black Owned Broadcasters (EA)
NABOM .... National Association of Building Owners and Managers [*Later, BOMA*] (EA)
NABOR .... National Association of Bank Club Organization
Nabors .... Nabors Industries, Inc. [*Associated Press*] (SAG)
NABP .... National Association of Black Professors (EA)
NABP .... National Association of Boards of Pharmacy (EA)
NABP .... National Association of Book Publishers (NADA)
NABPAC .... National Association of Business Political Action Committees (EA)
NABPARS .... Navy Automatic Broadcasting, Processing, and Routing System (NG)
NABPLEX .... National Association of Boards of Pharmacy Licensure Examination
NABPO .... NATO Bullpup Production Organization [*Missiles*] (NATG)
NABPP .... National Association of Black Procurement Professionals (NTPA)
NABPR .... National Association of Baptist Professors of Religion (EA)
NABPS .... National Association of Business and Industrial Saleswomen (NTPA)
NABPULP .... National Book Pulping Centre (BUAC)
NABR .... National Association for BioMedical Research (EA)
NABR .... National Association of Baby Sitter Registries [*Later, NASR*] (EA)
NABR .... National Association of Basketball Referees (EA)
NABR .... National Association of Beverage Retailers (NTPA)
NABR .... Natural Bridges National Monument
NaBr .... Sodium Bromide [*Pharmacology*] (DAVI)
NABREP .... National Association of Black Real Estate Professionals (EA)
NABRT .... National Association for Better Radio and Television (NADA)
NABRTI .... National Association of Bar-Related Title Insurers [*San Diego, CA*] (EA)
NABS .... National Advertising Benevolent Society [*British*]
NABS .... National AIDS Behavioral Survey
NABS .... National Alliance of Blind Students (EA)
NABS .... National Association of Bank Servicers (EA)
NABS .... National Association of Barber Schools [*Later, NABSS*] (EA)
NABS .... National Association of Bereavement Services (BUAC)
NABS .... National Association of Black Students (EA)
NABS .... National Association of Breeders Services (DBA)
NABS .... National Association of Business Services [*Baldwin, NY*] (EA)
NABS .... National Association of Buying Services (EA)
NABS .... NATO Airborne SATCOM (MCD)
NABS .... Nordic Association for British Studies (BUAC)
NABS .... Normal Abdominal Bowel Sound [*Medicine*] (CPH)
NABS .... Normoactive Bowel Sounds [*Gastroenterology*] (DAVI)
NABS .... North American Benthological Society (EA)
NABS .... North American Blue-Bird Society (EA)
NABS .... Nuclear-Armed Bombardment Satellite [*Study*] [*Air Force*] (AAG)
NABSC .... National Association of Building Service Contractors [*Later, BSCA*]
NABSCAN .... National Advertised Brands Scanning Reports [*Research project*]
NABSE .... National Alliance of Black School Educators (EA)
NABSE .... Norwegian Artillery Battery Survey Equipment (SAUS)
NABS/GMF .... NATO Airbase Satellite/Ground Mobile Force (MCD)
NABSMSW .... National Alliance of Black Salesmen and Saleswomen (NTPA)
NABSP .... National Association of Blue Shield Plans [*Later, BCBSA*] (EA)
NABSS .... National Alliance of Black School Superintendents (AEE)
NABSS .... National Association of Barber Styling Schools (EA)
NABST .... National Advisory Board on Science and Technology [*Canada*]
NABSTP .... Navy Adult Basic Skills Training Program (NVT)
NABSW .... National Association of Black Social Workers (EA)
NABT .... National Association of Bankruptcy Trustees (EA)
NABT .... National Association of Biology Teachers (EA)
NABT .... National Association of Black Professors (BUAC)
NABT .... National Association of Blind Teachers (EA)
NABTA .... National Association of Business Travel Agents (EA)
NABTC .... National Associated Building Trades Council [*A union*] [*British*]
NABTC .... Naval Air Base Training Command
NABTC .... North American Brain Tumor Coalition (SAUS)
NABTE .... National Association for Business Teacher Education [*Reston, VA*] (EA)
NABTFP .... National Association of Black Television and Film Producers (NTCM)
NABTO .... National Association of Bar and Tavern Owners (NTPA)
NABTRACOM .... Naval Air Basic Training Command (DNAB)
NABTS .... National Alliance Building Trades Society [*A union*] [*British*]
NABTS .... National Association of Broadcast Transmission Standards (PCM)
NABTS .... North American Basic Teletext Specification (WDMC)
NABTS .... North American Broadcasting Teletext Standard (SAUS)
NABTS .... North American Broadcast Teletext Specification (SAUS)
NABTS .... North American Broadcast Teletext Standard (NTCM)
NABTTI .... National Association of Business Teacher-Training Institutions
NABU .... Naval Advanced Base Unit
NABU .... Nonadjusting Ball-Up [*A hopeless state of confusion*] [*Military slang*]
NABUG .... National Association of Broadcast Unions and Guilds (EA)
NABV .... National Association for Black Veterans (EA)
NABVICU .... National Association of Blind and Visually Impaired Computer Users [*Defunct*] (EA)
NABW .... National Association of Bank Women [*Chicago, IL*] (EA)
NABWA .... National Association of Black Women Attorneys (EA)
NABWE .... National Association of Black Women Entrepreneurs [*Detroit, MI*] (EA)
NABWMT .... National Association of Black and White Men Together: A Gay Multiracial Organiz ation for All People (EA)
NABWS .... National Amalgamated Brass Workers' Society [*A union*] [*British*]
NABWU .... North American Baptist Women's Union (BUAC)
NABX .... Needle Aspiration Biopsy [*Medicine*] (MELL)
NAC .... Association of Chiropodists (NADA)
NAC .... CDC National AIDS Clearinghouse (EA)
NAC .... Nacelle [*Aviation*]
NAC .... N-Acetyl-L-Cysteine [*Biochemistry*]
NAC .... Naples Alcofuel Club [*Defunct*] (EA)
NAC .... NASA Advisory Council (SAUS)
NAC .... National Ability Center (EA)
NAC .... National Abortion Campaign [*British*] (DBA)
NAC .... National Academy of Conciliators (EA)
NAC .... National Accelerator Center [*South Africa*] [*Research center*]
NAC .... National Access Center [*Defunct*] (EA)
NAC .... National Accreditation Council (SAUS)
NAC .... National Accreditation Council for Agencies Serving the Blind and Visually Handicapped (EA)
NAC .... National Achievement Clubs (EA)
NAC .... National Action Committee on the Status of Women [*Canada*] (CROSS)
NAC .... National Adoption Center [*Information service or system*] (IID)
NAC .... National Advertising Campaign [*Army*]
NAC .... National Advisory Committee
NAC .... National Advisory Council
NAC .... National Aero Club (EA)
NAC .... National Aeronautical Corp.
NAC .... National Agency Check [*Security clearance*]
NAC .... National Agricultural Centre [*British*] (CB)
NAC .... National Agricultural Council (BUAC)
NAC .... National Air Carrier Association (MCD)
NAC .... National Air Charters [*Zambia*] (BUAC)
NAC .... National Air Communications [*British*]
NAC .... National Alumni Council of the United Negro College Fund (EA)
NAC .... National Amusements Council (BUAC)
NAC .... National Anglers' Council [*British*]
NAC .... National Anxiety Center (EA)
NAC .... National Aquaculture Council (EA)
NAC .... National Archives Council (BUAC)

NAC	National Arts Centre [Canada]
NAC	National Arts Club (EA)
NAC	National Asbestos Council (EA)
NAC	National Association for the Childless [British] (DBA)
NAC	National Association of Cemeteries [Later, ACA] (EA)
NAC	National Association of Choirs [British] (BI)
NAC	National Association of Composers, USA (EA)
NAC	National Association of Concessionaires (EA)
NAC	National Association of Conveyancers [British] (DBA)
NAC	National Association of Coopers [A union] [British]
NAC	National Association of Coroners (EA)
NAC	National Association of Counselors (EA)
NAC	National Association of Counties
NAC	National Asthma Campaign (BUAC)
NAC	National Asthma Center [Later, NJCIRM]
NAC	National Audience Composition [Nielsen Television Index] (NTCM)
NAC	National Audiovisual Center [General Services Administration]
NAC	National Automotive Center [Army] (RDA)
NAC	National Aviation Club (EA)
NAC	National Aviation Corp.
NAC	Native American Church (ECON)
NAC	Native Appeal Courts [South Africa] [A publication] (DLA)
NAC	NATO Alert Committee (SAUS)
NAC	Natural Area Council (EA)
NAC	Naval Academy
NAC	Naval Air Center
NAC	Naval Air Command [British]
NAC	Naval Aircraftman [British]
NAC	Naval Amyloid Component [Medicine]
NAC	Naval Avionics Center (MCD)
NAC	Navy Acquisition Circular (AAGC)
NAC	Navy Activity Control (DNAB)
NAC	Navy Advanced Concept (CAAL)
NAC	NCAR Administrators Committee (SAUS)
NAC	Nebraska Administrative (Code) Rules and Regulations [A publication] (AAGC)
NAC	Negative Acknowledge Character [Computer science] (VLIE)
NAC	Negative Air Cushion [Aviation] [Air Force]
NAC	Neighbourhood Advice Council
NAC	Neo-American Church (EA)
NAC	Net Advertising Circulation (DOAD)
NAC	Network Access Center [Telecommunications]
NAC	Network Access Controller
NAC	Network Adapter Card [Computer science] (VLIE)
NAC	Network Administration Center [Computer science] (VLIE)
NAC	Network Advisory Committee [to Library of Congress and Council on Library Resources]
NAC	Network Analysis Center [Contel, Inc.] [Telecommunications service] (TSSD)
NAC	Network Analysis Corporation (CCCA)
NAC	Network Appliance Corp. [Commercial firm]
NAC	Networks and Communications (SAUS)
NAC	Nevada Administrative Code (SAUS)
NAC	New American Community (MHDB)
NAC	New Apostolic Church
NAC	New Assembly of Churches (BUAC)
NAC	Nielson Audience Composition
NAC	Nipple Areolar Complex [Oncology]
NAC	Nitric Acid Concentrator (MCD)
NAC	Nitrogen Mustard [Mustargen], Adriamycin, CCNU [Lomustine] [Antineoplastic drug regimen]
NAC	NMCS [Nuclear Material Control System] Automatic Control
NAC	No Action (SAUS)
NAC	No Action Taken on Communication [Travel industry] (TRID)
NAC	No Additional Charge
NAC	No Apparent Change (MCD)
NAC	Noise Advisory Council [British]
NAC	Nonairline Carrier [Aerospace]
NAC	Nordic Academic Council [Defunct] (EA)
NAC	Nordic Actors' Council (EAIO)
NAC	Nordic Association for Campanology (EA)
NAC	Normal Approach Course [Navy] (NVT)
NAC	North American Collectors (EA)
NAC	North American Committee [An association] (EA)
NAC	North American Mortgage Co. [NYSE symbol] (SPSG)
NAC	North Atlantic Coast
NAC	North Atlantic Conference (PSS)
NAC	North Atlantic Council
NAC	North Atlantic Current [Oceanography]
NAC	North Atlantic Shipping Conference (DS)
NAC	Northeast Air Command
NAC	Northern Air Cargo, Inc. [ICAO designator] (FAAC)
NAC	Norwegian-American Council (SAUS)
NAC	Norwegian American Cruises (SAUS)
NAC	Nozzle Area Control
NAC	Nuclear Assurance Corp.
NAC	Null Attached Concentrator (SAUS)
NAC	Null Attachment Concentrator (SAUS)
NAC	Nursing Audit Committee (MEDA)
NAC	US Catholic Bishops' National Advisory Council (EA)
NACA	National Academy of Code Administration (EA)
NACA	National Acoustical Contractors Association [Later, CISCA] (EA)
NACA	National Advisory Committee for Aeronautics [Functions transferred to NASA, 1958]
NACA	National Advisory Committee on Aeronautics [OST] (TAG)

NACA	National Advisory Council on Aging (SAUS)
NACA	National Agricultural Chemicals Association (EA)
NACA	National Air Carrier Association (EA)
NACA	National Animal Control Association (EA)
NACA	National Armored Car Association (EA)
NACA	National Association for Campus Activities (EA)
NACA	National Association for Children of Alcoholics (DHP)
NACA	National Association for Clean Air [South Africa] (BUAC)
NACA	National Association for Court Administration (EA)
NACA	National Association of Catastrophe Adjusters [Comfort, TX] (EA)
NACA	National Association of Cellular Agents (EA)
NACA	National Association of Child Advocates (EA)
NACA	National Association of Childbirth Assistants (EA)
NACA	National Association of Christians in the Arts (EA)
NACA	National Association of Consumer Advocates (EA)
NACA	National Association of Cost Accountants [Later, NAA]
NACA	National Association of County Administrators (EA)
NACA	National Association of Cuban Architects (in Exile) [Defunct] (EA)
NACA	National Athletic and Cultural Association [Ireland] (EAIO)
NACA	National Athletic and Cycling Association (BUAC)
NACA	National Autosound Challenge Association [Later, IASCA] (EA)
NACA	Naval Aviation Cadet Act of 1942
NACA	Netherlands-America Community Association (EA)
NACA	Network of Aquaculture Centres in Asia (BUAC)
NACA	North American Center on Adoption [Defunct] (EA)
NACA	North American College of Acupuncture
NACA	North American Comente Association (SAUS)
NACA	North American Corriente Association (EA)
NACA	North American Currach Association (EA)
NACA	North Australian Canine Association
NACAA	National Assembly of Community Arts Agencies (EA)
NACAA	National Association of Community Action Agencies (EA)
NACAA	National Association of Computer-Assisted Analysis (IAA)
NACAA	National Association of Consumer Agency Administrators (EA)
NACAA	National Association of County Agricultural Agents (EA)
NACAB	National Accreditation Council for Agencies Serving the Blind and Visually Handicapped [New York, NY]
NACAB	National Agricultural Centre Advisory Board (BUAC)
NACAB	National Association of Citizens Advice Bureaus [British] (DBA)
NACA BCA	Nationalo Advisory Commission for Aeronautics Board of Contract Appeals (AAGC)
NACAC	National Association of Catholic Alumni Clubs [Later, CACI] (EA)
NACAC	National Association of College Admission Counselors (EA)
NACAC	North African Antiaircraft Section [World War II]
NACAC	North American Council on Adoptable Children (EA)
NACACP	National Cash Register Applied COBOL [Common Business-Oriented Language] Package (IAA)
NACADA	National Academic Advising Association (EA)
NACAE	National Advisory Council on Adult Education [Washington, DC]
NACAE	National Advisory Council on Art Education (BUAC)
NACAF	Northwest African Coastal Air Force [World War II]
NACAL	Navy Air Cooperation and Liaison Committee
NACAM	National Association of Corn and Agricultural Merchants (BUAC)
NAC & O	Cape and Orange Free State Native Appeal Court, Selected Decisions [A publication] (DLA)
NACAO	National Association of County Arts Officers (BUAC)
NACAP	National Association of Claims Assistance Professionals (EA)
NACAP	National Association of Co-Op Advertising Professionals [Defunct] (EA)
NACAR	National Advisory Committee on Aeronautical Research [South Africa] (BUAC)
NACARM	Northwest America Civil Air Routes Manual
NACAS	National Advisory Committee on Agricultural Services [Canada] (BUAC)
NACAS	National Association of College Auxiliary Services (EA)
NACAT	National Association of College Automotive Teachers (EA)
NACAT	North American Council of Automotive Teachers (NTPA)
NACATS	North American Clear Air Turbulence Tracking System [Aviation]
NACAWM-USA	National Association of Cuban Women and Men of the United States (EA)
NACAW-USA	National Association of Cuban-American Women of the USA (EA)
NACB	National Academy of Clinical Biochemistry (NTPA)
NACB	National Association of Catering Butchers [British] (DBA)
NACB	National Association of College Broadcasters (EA)
NACB	National Association of Convention Bureaus (NADA)
NACB	Native American Community Board (EA)
NACB	Navy and Army Canteen Board [British military] (DMA)
NACBA	National Association of Church Business Administration (EA)
NACBC	Natinal Advisory Centre on the Battered Child (BUAC)
NACBFAA	National Association of Customs Brokers and Forwarders Association of America
NACBO	National Association of Cosmetic Boutique Owners (EA)
NACBP	No-Adjust Car Building Process [Ford Motor Co.] [Automotive engineering]
NACBS	National Affiliation of Concerned Business Students [Defunct] (EA)
NACBS	National Association and Council of Business Schools
NACBS	North American Conference on British Studies (EA)
NACBT	National Association of Cognitive-Behavioral Therapists (SAUS)
NACC	National Aboriginal Consultative Committee [Australia] (BUAC)
NACC	National Advisory Cancer Council
NACC	National Agency Check Center (AFM)
NACC	National Air Conservation Commission (EA)
NACC	National Alliance of Czech Catholics (EA)
NACC	National Association for Colitis and Crohn's Disease (BUAC)
NACC	National Association for Core Curriculum (EA)

NACC .... National Association of Catholic Chaplains (EA)
NACC .... National Association of Childbearing Centers (EA)
NACC .... National Association of Collegiate Commissioners [*Later, CCA*] (EA)
NACC .... National Association of Counsel for Children (EA)
NACC .... National Automatic Controls Conference
NACC .... Naval Academy Computer Center
NACC .... Nigerian-American Chamber of Commerce (NTPA)
NACC .... North America Control Committee (SAUS)
NACC .... North American Calibration Cooperation (SAUS)
NACC .... North American-Chilean Chamber of Commerce (EA)
NACC .... North Atlantic Christian Conference (PSS)
NACC .... North Atlantic Co-operation Council (SAUS)
NACC .... North Atlantic Council for Cooperation (SAUS)
NACC .... Norwegian American Chamber of Commerce
NACC .... Novel Architectures Computing Committee [*British*]
NAC (C) .... Selected Decisions of the Native Appeal Court (Central Division) [*1948-51*] [*South Africa*] [*A publication*] (DLA)
NACCA .... National Association for Creative Children and Adults (EA)
NACCA .... National Association of Claimants' Counsel of America [*Also known as NACCA Bar Association*] [*Later, ATLA*]
NACCA .... National Association of Consumer Credit Administrators (EA)
NACCA .... National Association of County 4-H Club Agents [*Later, NAE4-HA*] (EA)
NACCA .... National Association of County Civil Attorneys (EA)
NACCA .... North American Council of Chemical Associations (SAUS)
NACCAC ...... National Community College Athletic Conference (PSS)
NACCALJ ..... National Association of Claimants' Compensation Attorneys. Law Journal [*A publication*] (DLA)
NACCAM ...... National Coordinating Committee for Aviation Meteorology
NACCAN ...... National Association of Christian Councils and Networks (BUAC)
NAC (C & O)... Reports of the Decisions of the Native Appeal Courts, Cape Province and the Orange Free State [*South Africa*] [*A publication*] (ILCA)
NACCAS ...... National Accrediting Commission of Cosmetology Arts and Sciences (EA)
NACCB .... National Accreditation Council for Certification Bodies (AIE)
NACCB .... National Association of Computer Consultant Businesses (EA)
NACCC .... National Association of Citizens Crime Commissions (EA)
NACCC .... National Association of Congregational Christian Churches [*Later, CCCNA*] (EA)
NACCC .... Network of Access and Child Contact Centres (BUAC)
NACCC .... North American-Chilean Chamber of Commerce (NTPA)
NACCCA ...... National Association of Civilian Conservation Corps Alumni (EA)
NACCCAN ... National Centre for Christian Communities and Networks [*Westhill College*] [*British*] (CB)
NACCD .... National Advisory Commission on Civil Disorders (NADA)
NACCDD ...... National Association of County Community Development Directors (EA)
NACCE .... National Advisory Council on Continuing Education (OICC)
NACCE .... North American Conference on Christianity and Ecology (EA)
NACCED ...... National Association for County Community and Economic Development (NTPA)
NACCES ...... Naval Air Crew Combat Ejection Seat (DWSG)
NACCG .... National Association of Crankshaft and Cylinder Grinders [*British*] (BI)
NACCHO ...... National Aboriginal Community-Controlled Health Organization [*Australia*]
NACCHO ...... National Association of County and City Health Officials (NTPA)
NACCIC .... National Association of County Intergovernmental Relations Officials (NTPA)
NACCIMA.... Nigerian Association of Chambers of Commerce, Industry, Mines and Agriculture (SAUS)
NACCM .... National Association for Child Care Management [*Defunct*] (EA)
NACCMHC... National Academy of Certified Clinical Mental Health Counselors (DHP)
NACCO .... NACCO Industries, Inc. [*Associated Press*] (SAG)
NACCO .... North American Coal Corp. (EFIS)
NACCP .... North American Cambridge Classics Project (SAUS)
NACCRRA .... National Association of Child Care Resource and Referral Agencies (EA)
NACCRT ...... North America Coordinating Center for Responsible Tourism (EA)
NACCS .... National Association for Chicana and Chicano Studies (NTPA)
NACCSMA.... NATO Command and Control Systems Management Agency (PDAA)
NACCSS ...... National Association of Commodity Cargo Superintendents and Suveyors [*British*] (DBA)
NACCT .... North American Congress of Clinical Toxicology (SAUS)
NACCU .... National Association of Canadian Credit Unions (BUAC)
NACCW .... National Advisory Centre on Careers for Women [*British*] (CB)
NACCWO...... National Association of Civil Court Welfare Officers (BUAC)
NACD .... National Academy for Child Development (SAUS)
NACD .... National Alliance of Cleaning Distributors [*Commercial firm*] (EA)
NACD .... National Association for Cave Diving [*Inactive*]
NACD .... National Association for Community Development [*Defunct*] (EA)
NACD .... National Association of Chemical Distributors (EA)
NACD .... National Association of Computer Dealers (ROAS)
NACD .... National Association of Conservation Districts
NACD .... National Association of Container Distributors (EA)
NACD .... National Association of Corporate Directors [*Washington, DC*] (EA)
NACD .... Not Acidified [*Biochemistry*] (DAVI)
NACDA........ National Archive for Computerized Data on Aging [*Department of Health and Human Services*] (GFGA)
NACDA........ National Arts and Cultural Development Act of 1964
NACDA........ National Association of Collegiate Directors of Athletics (EA)
NACDAC...... National Association for City Drug and Alcohol Coordination [*Defunct*] (EA)

NACDAP....... National Advisory Council for Drug Abuse Prevention [*Terminated, 1975*] (EGAO)
NACDC .... National Association of Career Development Consultants (EA)
NACDD........ National Advisory Council on Services and Facilities for the Developmentally Disabled [*Terminated, 1978*] [*HEW*] (EGAO)
NACDE .... National Association for Child Development and Education [*Later, NACCM*] (EA)
NACDET ...... National Association of Colleges in Distributive Education and Training (BUAC)
NACDFB ...... National Association of Canada Dry Franchise Bottlers (EA)
NACDFLM ... National Association of Catholic Diocesan Family Life Ministers [*Later, NACFLM*] (EA)
NACDL .... National Association of Criminal Defense Lawyers (EA)
NACDLF ...... National Association of Community Development Loan Funds (EA)
NACDPA...... National Association of County Data Processing Administrators (EA)
NAC/DPC..... North Atlantic Council/Defense Planning Committee (SAUS)
NACDR........ National Association of College Deans and Registrars [*Later, NACDRAO*] (EA)
NACDRAO .... National Association of College Deans, Registrars, and Admissions Officers (EA)
NACDS .... National Association of Chain Drug Stores (EA)
NACDS .... North American Clinical Dermatologic Society (EA)
NACE .... Nace International
NACE .... National Advisory Committee for Electronics
NACE .... National Advisory Committee on Electronics [*India*] (BUAC)
NACE .... National Association for Career Education (EA)
NACE .... National Association for Curriculum Enrichment and Extension [*British*] (EAIO)
NACE .... National Association of Catering Executives (EA)
NACE .... National Association of Childbirth Education [*Defunct*] (EA)
NACE .... National Association of Corrosion Engineers (EA)
NACE .... National Association of Counsellors in Education (AIE)
NACE .... National Association of County Engineers (EA)
NACE .... National Autobody Congress and Exposition [*Precision Planning and Sales, Inc.*] (TSPED)
NACE .... Native Americans for a Clean Environment (EA)
NACE .... Neutral Atmospheric Composition Experiment [*Geophysics*]
NACE .... North American Commission on the Environment
NACE .... North American Cycle Exhibitor Association (EA)
NACEBE ...... National Association of Classroom Educators in Business Education [*Cambridge City, IN*] (EA)
NACEC .... National Association of Charitable Estate Counselors (EA)
NACEC .... North American Center for Emergency Communications (EA)
NACEC .... North American Commission for Environmental Cooperation (SAUS)
NACEC .... North American Committee of Enamel Creators (EA)
NACECE ...... National Advisory Council on Extension and Continuing Education
NACED .... National Advisory Committee on the Education of the Deaf [*Terminated, 1973*] [*HEW*] (EGAO)
NACED .... National Advisory Council on the Employment of Disabled People (BUAC)
NACED .... National Advisory Council on the Employment of the Disabled [*British*]
NACEDC ...... National Advisory Council on Education of Disadvantaged Children (OICC)
NAC/EDP...... National Advisory Council on Education Professions Development [*HEW*] (EGAO)
NAC-EDTA.... N-Acetyl-L-Cysteine Ethylenediaminetetra-Acetic Acid [*Biochemistry*] (MAE)
NACEEO .... National Advisory Council on Equality of Educational Opportunity [*Termina ted, 1979*] [*HEW*] (EGAO)
NACEHC....... National Accreditation Council for Environmental Health Curricula (EA)
NACEIC .... National Advisory Council on Education for Industry and Commerce (MCD)
NACEL .... Navy Air Crew Equipment Laboratory [*Philadelphia, PA*]
NACEO .... National Advisory Council on Economic Opportunity (EA)
NACEPD....... National Advisory Council on Education Professions Development [*Terminate d, 1976*] [*HEW*] (OICC)
NACEPE .... National Association of Creamery Proprietors and Wholesale Dairymen (BUAC)
NACEPT .... National Advisory Committee for Environmental Policy and Technology [*Environmental Protection Agency*]
NACERI........ National Advisory Council for Educational Research and Improvement [*Washington, DC*] [*Department of Education*] (GRD)
NACES .... National Association of Credential Evaluation Services (EA)
NACES .... Navy Aircrew Common Ejection Seat [*British*]
NACESW ...... National Association of Chief Education Social Workers (AIE)
NACETA .... National Association of County Employment and Training Administrators [*Later, NACTEP*] (EA)
NACEW .... National Advisory Council on the Employment of Women [*New Zealand*] (BUAC)
NACF .... National Agricultural Cooperative Federation [*Republic of Korea*] (BUAC)
NACF .... National Art-Collectors' Fund [*British*]
NACF .... National Association of Church Furnishers [*British*] (BI)
NACF .... Navy Air Combat Fighter (MCD)
NACFA .... North American Clun Forest Association (EA)
NACFE .... National Association of Certified Fraud Examiners (EA)
NACFFA ...... National Advisory Committee for the Flammable Fabrics Act
NACFI .... North American Council on Fishery Investigations (SAUS)
NACFL .... National Advisory Committee on Farm Labor [*Defunct*] (EA)
NACFLM ...... National Association of Catholic Family Life Ministers (EA)
NACFR .... National Association of Casual Furniture Retailers (EA)
NACFRC....... North Atlantic Coastal Fisheries Research Center (SAUS)

NACFRC.......	North Atlantic Coastal Fisheries Research Centre (BUAC)
NACFT........	National Academy of Counselors and Family Therapists (EA)
NACFT........	National Association of Cattle Foot Trimmers (GVA)
NACG..........	National Association of Conservative Graduates (AIE)
NACG..........	National Association of County Governments (OICC)
NACG..........	North African Commanding General [*World War II*]
NACGC........	National Association of Collegiate Gymnastics Coaches (Men) (EA)
NACGC........	National Association of Colored Girls Clubs [*Later, NAGC*] (EA)
NACGG........	North American Commercial Gladiolus Growers [*Later, CGD-NAGC*] (EA)
NACGM.......	National Association of Chewing Gum Manufacturers (EA)
NACGS........	North American Cottage Garden Society
NACGT........	National Association of Careers and Guidance Teachers [*British*] (DBA)
NACH..........	National Academy of Clinicians and Holistic Health (EA)
NACH..........	National Advisory Committee on the Handicapped
NACH..........	National Advisory Council for the Handicapped (NADA)
NACH..........	National Association for the Craniofacially Handicapped (EA)
NACH..........	National Association of Clergy Hypnotherapists (EA)
NACH..........	National Association of Coal Haulers [*Defunct*] (EA)
nAch	Need for Achievement
NACHA........	National Automated Clearing House Association [*Washington, DC*] (EA)
NACHA........	National Collegiate Hockey Association (PSS)
NACHC........	National Advisory Committee on Handicapped Children [*Terminated, 1973*] [*HEW*] (EGAO)
NACHC........	National Association of Christian Colleges (PSS)
NACHC........	National Association of Community Health Centers (EA)
Nach Chem Tech...	Nachrichten aus Chemie, Technik und Laboratorium (MEC)
NACHES.......	Association of Jewish Family, Children's Agency Professionals (EA)
NACHFA.......	National Association of County Health Facility Administrators (EA)
NACHGR......	National Advisory Council for Human Genome Research (HGEN)
NACHM.......	Nachmittags [*Afternoon*] [*German*]
NACHO........	National Association of Chemical Hygiene Officers (SARE)
NACHO........	National Association of County Health Officials (EA)
NACHP........	National Association of Counsellors, Hypnotherapists and Psychotherapists (BUAC)
NACHP........	North African Chaplain's Section [*World War II*]
NAChR........	Nicotinic Acetylcholine Receptor [*Immunology*]
NACHRI.......	National Association of Children's Hospitals and Related Institutions (EA)
NACHRK......	North American Coalition for Human Rights in Korea (EA)
NACHSA......	National Association of County Human Services Administrators (EA)
NACHVRO....	National Air Conditioning, Heating, Ventilating, and Refrigeration Officials (EA)
NACI..........	Naphthenic Acid Corrosion Index
NACI..........	National Agency Check and Written Inquiries
NACI..........	National Association for the Cottage Industry (EA)
NACIA........	National Association of Crop Insurance Agents [*Anoka, MN*] (EA)
NACIE........	National Advisory Council on Indian Education (OICC)
NACIFO.......	National Association of Church and Institutional Financing Organizations [*Atlanta, GA*] (EA)
NACIME......	North American Committee for IME [*Institut Medical Evangelique*] [*Defunct*] (EA)
NACIO........	National Association of County Information Officers (EA)
NACIO........	Naval Air Combat Information Office [*or Officer*]
NACIP........	Navy Assessment and Control of Installation Pollutants
NACIS.........	National Credit Information Service [*TRW, Inc.*] [*Long Beach, CA*] [*Credit-information databank*] (IID)
NACIS.........	Naval Air Combat Information School
NACIS.........	Navy Air Control and Identification System
NACIS.........	Networking Analytical and Computing Information Systems [*National Aeronautics and Space Administration*]
NACIS.........	North American Cartographic Information Society (EA)
NACISA.......	North Atlantic Communications and Information Systems Agency [*NATO*]
NACISO.......	NATO Communications and Information Systems Organization (EAIO)
NACITA.......	National Association of County Information Technology Administrators (NTPA)
NACJ...........	National Association of Costume Jewelers [*Defunct*] (EA)
NACJP........	National Association of Criminal Justice Planners [*Defunct*] (EA)
NACK.........	National Advisory Committee on Kangaroos (BUAC)
NACK.........	Negative Acknowledgment [*Telecommunications*]
NACK.........	Nonacknowledgment Character [*Computer science*]
NACL.........	National Advisory Commission on Libraries
NACL.........	National Association for Community Leadership (EA)
NACL.........	Navy/ARPA [*Advanced Research Projects Agency*] Chemical LASER (MCD)
NACL.........	Nippon Aviatronics Corp. Ltd. [*Japan*]
NaCl...........	Sodium Chloride [*Salt*] [*Chemistry*] (DAVI)
NACLA	National Cooperation for Laboratory Accreditation (SAUS)
NACLA	North American Congress on Latin America (EA)
NACLC........	National Association of Community Legal Centers [*Australia*]
NACLE	National Association of Chimney Lining Engineers [*British*] (DBA)
NACLEO	National Association of Coin Laundry Equipment Operators (EA)
NACLIS	National Commission on Libraries and Information Science [*Washington, DC*]
NACLM	North African Claims Section [*World War II*]
NACLO	National Association of Canoe Liveries and Outfitters (EA)
NACLO	National Association of Community Leadership Organizations [*Later, National Association for Community Leadership*] (EA)
NACLP	North American Conference on Logic Programming (SAUS)
NACLS	National Association of Commission Lumber Salesmen
NACLS	North Alabama Cooperative Library System [*Library network*]
NACLS	North American Canon Law Society (NTPA)
NACLSO.......	National Assembly of Chief Livestock Sanitary Officials [*Later, United States Animal Health Association*] (EA)
NACM	National Association for Court Management (EA)
NACM	National Association of Chain Manufacturers (EA)
NACM	National Association of Charcoal Manufacturers [*British*] (DBA)
NACM	National Association of Cider Makers [*British*] (BI)
NACM	National Association of Colliery Managers [*British*] (DBA)
NACM	National Association of Cotton Manufacturers (BUAC)
NACM	National Association of Credit Management
NACM	Networks and Communications Marketing (SAUS)
NACMA	National Armored Cable Manufacturers Association (EA)
NACMA	National Association of Collegiate Marketing Administrators
NACMA	NATO ACCS Management Agency (SAUS)
NACMB	National Association of Certified Mortgage Bankers [*Later, NSREF*] (EA)
NACMC	National Association for Church Management Consultants (EA)
NACMC	National Association of Christian Marriage Counselors [*Defunct*] (EA)
NACMCF	National Advisory Committee on Microbiological Criteria for Foods
NACME	National Action Council for Minorities in Engineering (EA)
NACMEMS ...	National Association of Continuing Medical Education Meetings and Seminars [*Defunct*] (EA)
NACMHD	National Association of County Mental Health Directors (NTPA)
NACMIS	Navy Automated Civilian Management Information System
NACMO	National Association of Cigarette Machine Operators [*British*] (DBA)
NACMO	National Association of Competitive Mounted Orienteering (EA)
NACMO	NATO ACCS Management Organisation (SAUS)
NACMW	North American Council for Muslim Women (EA)
NACN	Newspaper Advertising Co-Op Network (EA)
NACN	North American Cellular Network (CGWS)
NAC (N & T)...	Decisions of the Native Appeal and Divorce Court (Transvaal and Natal) [*South Africa*] [*A publication*] (ILCA)
NAC (NE)......	Decisions of the Native Appeal Court (North Eastern Division) [*South Africa*] [*A publication*] (ILCA)
NACNE	National Advisory Council on Nutrition Education [*British*]
NACNEMS....	North American Cooperative Network of Enhanced Measurement Sites (SAUS)
NACNS	National Association of Clinical Nurse Specialists (NTPA)
NACO	Name Authority Co-Operative (NITA)
NACO	National Advisory Committee on Oceanography [*Marine science*] (MSC)
NACO	National Agricultural Co. [*St. Christopher and Nevis*] (BUAC)
NACO	National Agricultural Credit Office [*Vietnam*] (BUAC)
NACO	National Association of Charterboat Operators (EA)
NACO	National Association of Condominium Owners
NACO	National Association of Consumer Organizations
NACO	National Association of Cooperative Officials [*A union*] [*British*] (DCTA)
NACo	National Association of Counties (EA)
NACO	National Coordinated Cataloging Operations [*Library science*]
NACO	Navy Acquisition-Contracting Officer (MCD)
NACO	Navy Coolant [*Gunpowder*]
NACO	Night Alarm Cut-Off (SAUS)
NACO	Noise Abatement and Control Office (SAUS)
NACOA........	If Not Available Your Command, Obtain Accounting Data from Administrative Command [*Army*] (AABC)
NACOA........	National Advisory Committee on Oceans and Atmosphere [*Marine science*] (MSC)
NACOA........	National Association for Children of Alcholics (BUAC)
NACoA........	National Association for Children of Alcoholics (EA)
NACOA........	National Association for Children of Alcoholism and Other Addictions (EA)
NACOA........	National Association of Cruise Oriented Agents (TVEL)
NACODS	National Association of Colliery Overmen, Deputies, and Shotfirers [*A union*] [*British*] (DCTA)
NACOEJ	North American Conference on Ethiopian Jewry (EAIO)
NACOI	National Association of Canadians of Origins in India
NACOL........	National Advisory Commission on Libraries
NACOLADS...	National Council on Libraries, Archives and Documentation Services [*Jamaica*] (BUAC)
NACOM	National Communications [*System*]
NACOM	Northern Area Command
NACOMEX....	National Computer Exchange
NACON........	Newspaper Advertising Co-Op Network (EA)
NACOP	National Association of Chiefs of Police (NTPA)
NACOPRW ...	National Conference of Puerto Rican Women (EA)
NACOR........	National Advisory Committee on Radiation
NaCOR........	National Center on Occupational Readjustment [*Defunct*] (EA)
NACORE.......	National Association of Corporate Real Estate Executives (EA)
NACORF.......	National Association of Counties Research Foundation
NACOS........	National Communications Schedule
NACOS........	NATO Courier Service (NATG)
NACOS........	North African Chief of Staff [*World War II*]
NACOSH	National Advisory Committee on Occupational Safety and Health
NACOSH	National Advisory Committee on Scouting for the Handicapped (EA)
NACOSS	National Approval Council for Security Systems (BUAC)
NACP	National Academy of Cable Programming (NTCM)
NACP	National Accounts Capability Programme [*United Nations*] (EY)
NACP	National Association of Chiefs of Police (AD)
NACP	National Association of County Planners (EA)
NACP	Navy Acoustical Communication Program (MCD)
NACP	Network Against Coercive Psychiatry (EA)
NACP	North Atlantic Consultive Process (OSI)
NACPA	National Association of Church Personnel Administrators (EA)

NACPA......... National Association of County and Prosecuting Attorneys [*Later, NDAA*]
NACPA......... North American Concert Promoters Association (NTPA)
NACPAC....... North American Chronic Pain Association of Canada (SAUS)
NACPC........ North American Christian Peace Conference (EA)
NACPCC...... National Advisory Committee for Pig Carcase Competitions (BUAC)
NACPD........ National Association of County Planning Directors [*Later, NACP*] (EA)
NACPDCG .... National Association of Catholic Publishers and Dealers in Church Goods (EA)
NACPDE...... National Advice Centre for Postgraduate Dental Education (BUAC)
NACPR........ National Association of Corporate and Professional Recruiters (EA)
NACPRO ...... National Association of County Park and Recreation Officials (EA)
NACPU........ National Amalgamated Coal Porters' Union [*British*]
NACPUISCW... National Amalgamated Coal Porters' Union of Inland and Seaborne Coal Workers [*British*]
NACR.......... National Advisory Committee on Radiation
NACRC........ National Association of Community Relations Council (BUAC)
NACRC........ National Association of County Recorders and Clerks (EA)
NACRCD ...... National Advisory Council on Rural Civil Defense
NAC Re....... NAC RE Corp. [*Associated Press*] (SAG)
NACRE........ North American Coalition on Religion and Ecology (EA)
NACRF........ National Association of Counties Research Foundation (OICC)
NACRMR...... National Advisory Committee on Rhesus Monkey Requirements
NACRO........ National Association for the Care and Resettlement of Offenders [*British*]
nacro .... Night-Alarm Cutoff (AD)
NACRS........ National Asbestos-Contractor Registration System (COE)
NACRS........ North African Censorship Section, US [*World War II*]
NACR (SR)... Native Appeal Court Reports (Southern Rhodesia) [*A publication*] (ILCA)
NACRT........ National Association of Canadian Race Tracks
NACRU........ North American Committee for Reconciliation in Ulster (EA)
NACS .... National Advisory Committee on Semiconductors
NACS .... National Association for Check Safekeeping [*Washington, DC*] (EA)
NACS .... National Association for Chicano Studies (EA)
NACS .... National Association of Carpet Specialists [*Defunct*]
NACS .... National Association of Chimney Sweeps [*British*] (DBA)
NACS .... National Association of Christian Schools [*Defunct*] (EA)
NACS .... National Association of Christian Singles (EA)
NACS .... National Association of Civic Secretaries (EA)
NACS .... National Association of Collection Sites (EA)
NACS .... National Association of College Stores (EA)
NACS .... National Association of Computer Stores [*Later, IVCI*] [*Defunct*] (EA)
NACS .... National Association of Concession Services (EA)
NACS .... National Association of Consumer Shows (NTPA)
NACS .... National Association of Convenience Stores (EA)
NACS .... National Association of Cosmetology Schools (EA)
NACS .... National Association of County Surveyors (NTPA)
NACS .... Natural Areas of Canadian Significance [*NPPAC*]
NACS .... NetWare Asynchronous Communication Service [*Novell, Inc.*]
NACS .... Network Assisted Coordinated Science (ACAE)
NACS .... Neurologic and Adaptive Capacity Scoring [*System*]
NACS .... Nonlinear Automatic Control System (SAUS)
NACS .... Nordic Association for Clinical Sexology (BUAC)
NACS .... North American Catalysis Society (NTPA)
NACS .... North American Communications Corp. (SAUS)
NACS .... North Atlantic Current System [*Oceanography*]
NACS .... Northern Area Communications System (MCD)
NACS .... Nucleic Acid Chromatography System
NAC (S) .... Selected Decisions of the Native Appeal Court (Southern Division) [*South Africa*] [*A publication*] (ILCA)
NACSA......... National Advisory Committee on Safety in Agriculture
NACSA......... National Association for Corporate Speaker Activities (EA)
NACSA......... National Association of Casualty and Surety Agents [*Bethesda, MD*] (EA)
NACSA......... North American Computer Service Association (EA)
NACSAA...... National Advisory Council for South Asian Affairs (EA)
NACSAP...... National Alliance Concerned with School-Age Parents [*Defunct*] (EA)
NACSARS .... National Association of Companion Sitter Agencies and Referral Services [*Later, PCA*] (EA)
NACSB .... Naval Aviation Cadet Selection Board
NACSC........ National Association of Cold Storage Contractors (EA)
NACSCAOM... National Accreditation Commission for Schools and Colleges of Acupuncture and Oriental Medicine (EA)
NACSCC...... National Association of Community Schools, Colleges, and Centres [*British*] (DBA)
NACSCS...... National Advisory Council on Supplementary Centers and Services
NACSDA...... National Association of Commissioners, Secretaries, and Directors of Agriculture[*Later, NASDA*] (EA)
NACSDC...... North American Conference of Separated and Divorced Catholics (EA)
NACSE........ National Association of Casualty and Surety Executives [*New York, NY*] (EA)
NACSE .... National Association of Civil Service Employees (EA)
NACSE .... Non-Avionics Common Support Equipment (MCD)
NACSI .... National Communications Security Instruction (COE)
NACSI......... National COMSEC Information (SAUS)
NACSIC....... National Association of Cold Storage Insulation Contractors (EA)
NACSIM....... NATO Communications Security Information (NATG)
NACSIS....... National Academic Center for Science Information Systems (SAUS)
NACSIS....... National Center for Science Information Systems [*Japan*]
NACSM....... National Association of Catalog Showroom Merchandisers (EA)
NACSN......... North American Commission on Stratigraphic Nomenclature (SAUS)

NACSPMR.... National Association of Coordinators of State Programs for the Mentally Retarded[*Later, National Association of State Mental Retardation Program Directors*] (EA)
NACSS .... National Approved Council for Security Systems (WDAA)
NACSS .... National Association of Clerical and Supervisory Staffs (BUAC)
NACST .... National Association of Catholic School Teachers (EA)
NACSW........ National Action Committee on the Status of Women [*Canada*] (AD)
NACSW .... North American Association of Christians in Social Work (EA)
NACT .... NASA Activities [*A publication*]
NACT .... National Alliance of Cardiovascular Technologists (EA)
NACT .... National Association of Careers Teachers (AD)
NACT .... National Association of Chapter 13 Trustees (MHDB)
NACT .... National Association of Clinical Tutors [*British*] (DBA)
NACT .... National Association of Consumers and Travelers (EA)
NACT .... National Association of Corporate Treasurers [*Washington, DC*] (EA)
NACT .... National Association of Craftsman Tailors [*British*] (BI)
NACT .... National Association of Cycle Traders [*British*] (BI)
NACT .... National Association of Cycle Trades (AD)
NACT .... National Automatic Controller for Testing (MUGU)
NACTA .... National Association of Colleges and Teachers of Agriculture (EA)
NACTA .... National Association of Commissioned Travel Agents (TVEL)
NACTAC ...... Navy Antenna Computer Tracking and Command
NAC (T & N)... Reports of the Decisions of the Native Appeal Courts (Transvaal and Natal) [*South Africa*] [*A publication*] (ILCA)
NACTEFL...... National Advisory Council on the Teaching of English as a Foreign Language (EA)
NACTEP ...... National Association of County Training and Employment Professionals [*Washington, DC*] (EA)
NACTFO ...... National Association of County Treasurers and Finance Officers (EA)
NACTP .... National Association of Computerized Tax Processors (EA)
NACTST .... National Advisory Council on the Training and Supply of Teachers (AD)
NACTU .... National Affiliation of Carpet Trade Unions (BUAC)
NACTU .... National Council of Trade Unions [*South Africa*] (BUAC)
NACTU .... Night Attack Combat Training Unit [*Navy*]
NACU .... National Association of Colleges and Universities
NACUA........ National Association of College and University Administrators [*Superseded by NEA Higher Education Council*] (EA)
NACUA........ National Association of College and University Attorneys (EA)
NACUBO ..... National Association of College and University Business Office Associations (AD)
NACUBO ...... National Association of College and University Business Officers [*Washington, DC*] (EA)
NACUC........ National Association of College and University Chaplains and Directors of Religious Life (EA)
NACUC........ National Association of Credit Union Chairmen (NTPA)
NACUFS....... National Association of College and University Food Services (EA)
NACUP........ National Association of Credit Union Presidents (EA)
NACUSA...... National Association of Composers, USA (EA)
NACUSIP...... National Congress of Union in the Sugar Industry of the Philippines (BUAC)
NACUSO ...... National Association of Credit Union Service Organizations (NTPA)
NACUSS....... National Association of College and University Summer Sessions [*Later, NAASS*]
NACUTCD .... National Advisory Committee on Uniform Traffic Control Devices [*Terminated, 1979*] [*Department of Transportation*] (EGAO)
NACUTSO .... National Association of College and University Traffic and Security Officers (EA)
NACV .... National Association of Concerned Veterans (EA)
NACVA........ National Association of Certified Valuation Analysts (NTPA)
NACVCB....... National Association of Crime Victim Compensation Boards (EA)
NACVE .... National Advisory Council on Vocational Education
NA-CVR....... National Association for Crime Victims Rights (EA)
NACVS .... National Association of Councils for Voluntary Service (BUAC)
NACW .... National Advisory Committee on Women (AD)
NACW .... National Association of College Women [*Later, NAUW*] (EA)
NACW .... National Association of Commissions for Women (EA)
NACWAA...... National Association of Collegiate Women Athletic Administrators (NTPA)
NACWC....... National Association of Colored Women's Clubs (EA)
NACWD........ National Association of County Welfare Directors [*Later, NACHSA*] (EA)
NACWEP...... National Advisory Council on Women's Educational Programs (OICC)
NACWIS ...... Navy Controlled Waste Information System
NACWPI....... National Association of College Wind and Percussion Instructors (EA)
NACWPI....... National Association of College Wind and Percussion Instruments (AD)
NACWRR ..... National Advisory Committee on Water Resources Research [*Canada*]
NACWS....... Naval Aircraft Collision Warning System (SAUS)
NACWS........ North African Chemical Warfare Section [*World War II*]
NACX .... Northern Air Cargo, Inc. [*Air carrier designation symbol*]
NACYS .... National Advisory Council for Youth Services (AIE)
NAd............. Addison Public Library, Addison, NY [*Library symbol*] [*Library of Congress*] (LCLS)
nad .... Nadir (AD)
NAD .... Nadir (WDAA)
NAD .... Nansen Arctic Drilling program (SAUS)
NAD .... Nansen Arctic Drilling Project (SAUS)
NAD .... Naphthaleneacetamide [*Herbicide*]
NAD .... National Academy of Design (EA)
NAD .... National Advertising Division [*of the Council of Better Business Bureaus*]
NAD .... National Alliance for Democracy [*Political party*] (AD)

NAD	National Armaments Director (NATG)
NAD	National Association of the Deaf (EA)
NAD	National Audience Demographics Report [*Nielsen Television Index*] (NTCM)
NAD	NATO Air Doctrine (NATG)
NAd	Naval Adviser [*British*]
NAD	Naval Air Defense (NATG)
NAD	Naval Air Depot
NAD	Naval Air Detachment (MCD)
NAD	Naval Air Detail
NAD	Naval Air Development Center, Warminster, PA [*OCLC symbol*] (OCLC)
NAD	Naval Air Division [*British*]
NAD	Naval Ammunition Depot [*Charleston, SC*]
NAD	Naval Armament Depot [*British*]
NAD	Naval Aviation Depot (AAGC)
Nad	Nedezhda (AD)
NAD	Network Access Device
nad	Networking Addressing Device [*Computer science*] (AD)
NAD	New Antigenic Determinant [*Immunochemistry*]
NAD	Nicotene-Adenine Dinucleotide (SAUS)
NAD	Nicotinamide-Adenine Dinucleotide [*Preferred form, but also see ARPPRN, DPN, NADH*] [*Biochemistry*]
NAD	Nicotinamide Adenine Dinucleotide Oxidized (EDCT)
NAD	Nicotinic Acid Dehydrogenase [*An enzyme*] (AAMN)
NAD	Nielson Audience Demographic Report [*A publication*] (DOAD)
NAD	Night Air Defence [*British*] [*World War II*]
NAD	Nitric Acid Dihydrate [*Inorganic chemistry*]
Nad	Nitrosamide [*Biochemistry*]
NAD	No Abnormal Discovery [*Medicine*] (DB)
NAD	No Abnormality Demonstrable (SAUS)
NAD	No Abnormality Detected [*Medicine*]
NAD	No-Acid Descaling (IEEE)
NAD	No Active Disease (DAVI)
NAD	No Acute Distress [*Medicine*]
nad	No Apparent Defect (AD)
NAD	No Apparent Defect [*Shipping*]
NAD	No Apparent Distress [*Medicine*]
nad	No Appreciable Difference (AD)
nad	No Appreciable Disease (AD)
NAD	No Appreciable Disease [*Medicine*]
NAD	Nobelair [*Turkey*] [*ICAO designator*] (FAAC)
NAD	Node Administration (NITA)
NAD	Noise Amplitude Distribution
NAD	Nordiska Namden for Alkohol- och Drogforskning [*Nordic Council for Alcohol and Drug Research - NCADR*] (EAIO)
NAD	Normal Axis Deviation [*Medicine*]
NAD	North American Aero Dynasty [*Vancouver Stock Exchange symbol*]
NAD	North American Datum
NAD	North Atlantic Division [*Army Engineers*]
nad	Nothing Abnormal Detected (AD)
NAD	Nothing Abnormal Detected [*or Discovered*] [*Medicine*]
NAD	Nothing Abnormal Discovered (SAUS)
nad	Not on Active Duty [*Military*] (AD)
NAD	Not on Active Duty
NAD	Nuclear Accident Dosimeter (SAUS)
NAD	Nuclear Accident Dosimetry
NAD 27	North American Datum of 1927 (CARB)
NAD83	North American Datum of 1983 (USDC)
NADA	N-Acetyldopamine [*Biochemistry*]
NADA	National Art Dealers Association [*Later, ADA*] (EA)
NADA	National Association for Disabled Athletes (EA)
NADA	National Association of Dealers in Antiques (EA)
NADA	National Association of Dental Assistants (EA)
NADA	National Association of Drama Advisers [*British*]
NADA	National Association of Drug Addiction (AD)
NADA	National Automobile Dealers Association [*McLean, VA*] (EA)
NADA	National Democratic Alliance [*Zambia*] [*Political party*] (EY)
NADA	Navajo Army Depot Activity [*Arizona*] [*Army*]
NADA	New Animal Drug Application [*Food and Drug Administration*]
NADA	Numerical Analysis and Computing Science (SAUS)
NADABA	N-Adenosyldiaminobutyric Acid [*Biochemistry*] (DB)
NADABB	National Alzheimer's Disease Autopsy and Brain Bank (AD)
NADAC	National Air Duct Cleaners Association
NADAC	National Anti-Drug Abuse Campaign (AD)
NADAC	National Damage Assessment Center
NADAC	Naval ASW [*Antisubmarine Warfare*] Data Center (NVT)
NADAC	Navigation Data Assimilation Computer (IAA)
NADAC	Pacific Command, North Vietnam Air Defense Analysis and Coordinating Group (CINC)
NADACS	National Air Defense and Airspace Control System (ACAE)
NADAF	National Association of Decorative Architectural Finishes (EA)
NADAG	National Association of Diocesan Altar Guilds of the Protestant Episcopal Church (EA)
NADAP	National Association on Drug Abuse Problems (EA)
NADAPI	National Alcoholism and Drug Abuse Program Inventory [*Department of Health and Human Services*] (GFGA)
NADAR	No After Duty Action Required [*Military*]
NADAR	North American Data Airborne Recorder
NADase	Nicotinamide Adenine Dinucleosidase (SAUS)
NADase	Nicotinamide-Adenine Dinucleotide Glycohydrolase [*Also, DPNase*] [*An enzyme*]
NADASO	National Association Drug and Allied Sales Organizations [*Wyncote, PA*] (EA)
NADASO	National Association of Design and Art Service Organizations (EA)
NADB	National Aerometric Data Bank [*Office of Air and Radiation*] (COE)
NADB	National Air Data Branch [*Environmental Protection Agency*] [*Information service or system*] (IID)
NADB	National Atmospheric Data Bank (GNE)
NADB	National Audience Data Bank [*Newspaper Marketing Bureau*] [*Information service or system*] (CRD)
NADB	North American Development Bank
NADB	US EPA National Air Data Branch (SAUS)
NADBR	National Association for the Deaf, Blind, and Rubella [*British*]
NADBRH	National Association for Deaf-Blind and Rubella Handicapped (BUAC)
NADC	National Advisory Drug Committee [*HEW*]
NADC	National Animal Data Centre (BUAC)
NADC	National Animal Disease Center [*Ames, IA*] [*Department of Agriculture*] [*Research center*] (GRD)
NADC	National Anti-Drug Coalition [*Defunct*] (EA)
NADC	National Anti-Dumping Committee (EA)
NADC	National Arctic and Antarctic Data Centres (SAUS)
NADC	National Arts and Disability Center (SAUS)
NADC	National Association of Demolition Contractors (EA)
NADC	National Association of Demonstration Companies (NTPA)
NADC	National Association of Dredging Contractors (EA)
NADC	NATO Air Defense Committee
NADC	NATO Defense College [*Also, NADEFCOL, NDC*]
NADC	Naval Aide-de-Camp [*British military*] (DMA)
NADC	Naval Air Development Center [*Also, NADEVCEN, NAVAIRDEVCEN*] [*Warminster, PA*]
NADC	Naval Ammunition Depot, Concord [*California*]
NADC	North American Digital Cellular (CGWS)
NADC	North American Digital Cellular system (SAUS)
NADC	Northern Agricultural Development Corp. (AD)
NADC	Northern Region Agricultural Development Centre [*Thailand*] (BUAC)
NADC	Nothern Alberta Development Council (SAUS)
NADC	Nuclear Affairs Defence Council (SAUS)
NADCA	National Air Duct Cleaners Association
NADCA	National Animal Damage Control Association (EA)
NADCA	North American Die Casting Association (SAUS)
NADCA	North American Draft Cross Association (EA)
NADC-AC	Naval Air Development Center - Aerospace Crew Equipment Department
NADC-ACL	Naval Air Development Center - Aeronautical Computer Laboratory (DNAB)
NADC-AE	Naval Air Development Center - Aero-Electronic Technology Department
NADC-AI	Naval Air Development Center - Aeronautical Instruments Laboratory
NADC-AM	Naval Air Development Center - Aero-Mechanics Department
NADC-AML	Naval Air Development Center - Aeronautical Materials Laboratory (DNAB)
NADCAP	National Aerospace and Defense Contractors Accreditation Procedures (SAUS)
NADCAP	National Aerospace and Defense Contractors Accreditation Program [*DoD*]
NADC-AP	Naval Air Development Center - Aeronautical Photographic Experimental Laboratory
NADC-AR	Naval Air Development Center - Aviation Armament Laboratory
NADC-ASL	Naval Air Development Center - Aeronautical Structures Laboratory (DNAB)
NADC-ASW	Naval Air Development Center - Antisubmarine Warfare Laboratory
NADC-AW	Naval Air Development Center - Air Warfare Research Department
NADC-AWG	Naval Air Development Center - Acoustical Working Group
NADC-CS	Naval Air Development Center - Crew Systems Department
NADC-ED	Naval Air Development Center - Engineering Development Laboratory
NADC-EL	Naval Air Development Center - Aeronautical Electronic and Electrical Laboratory
NADCI	North American Die Casting Institute (SAUS)
NADC-LS	Naval Air Development Center - Life Sciences and Bio-Equipment Group
NADC-ML	Naval Air Development Center - Aviation Medical Acceleration Laboratory
NADC-MR	Naval Air Development Center - Aerospace Medical Research Department
NADCO	National Agricultural Development Co. [*Saudi Arabia*] (BUAC)
NADCO	National Association of Development Companies (EA)
NAD-CO	Naval Ammunition Depot, Concord [*California*]
NADCORP	National Development Corp. [*Ireland*] (BUAC)
NAD-CR	Naval Ammunition Depot, Crane [*Indiana*]
NADCRC	National Advisory Dental & Craniofacial Research Council (SAUS)
NADCs	National Antarctic Data Centres (SAUS)
NADC-SD	Naval Air Development Center - Systems Analysis and Engineering Department
NADC-ST	Naval Air Development Center - Aero Structures Department
NADC-SY	Naval Air Development Center - Systems Project Department
NADC-WR	Naval Air Development Center - Air Warfare Research Department
NADD	National Association for the Dually Diagnosed (PAZ)
NADD	National Association of Deputising Doctors [*British*] (DBA)
NADD	National Association of Diemakers and Diecutters [*Formerly, DDA*] (EA)
NADD	National Association of Disco Disc Jockeys [*Defunct*] (EA)
NADD	National Association of Distributors and Dealers of Structural Clay Products [*Later, NABD*] (EA)
NADD	NNational Association of Diaconante Directors (NTPA)
NADDC	National Association of Developmental Disabilities Councils (EA)
NADDIS	Narcotics and Dangerous Drugs Intelligence File (AD)
NADDM	National Association of Daytime Dress Manufacturers [*Defunct*]

NADDMI/MR...	National Association for the Dually Diagnosed Mental Illness/Mental Retardation (NTPA)
NADDRG......	North American Deep Drawing Research Group [*Automotive metal stampings*]
NADE..........	National Association for Design Education [*British*]
NADE..........	National Association for Developmental Education
NADE..........	National Association for Drama in Education [*Australia*]
NADE..........	National Association of Disability Examiners (EA)
NADE..........	National Association of Document Examiners (EA)
NADEC........	National Agricultural Development Co. [*Saudi Arabia*] (BUAC)
NADEC........	National Association of Development Education Centres [*British*] (DBA)
NADEC........	Navy Decision Center
NADEC........	Navy Development Center (CAAL)
NaDEC........	Sodium Diethyl Dithiocarbamate (SAUS)
NADECO......	National Development Co. [*Ghana*] (BUAC)
NADECT......	National Association for Drama in Education and Children's Theatre (BUAC)
NADEE........	National Association of Divisional Executives for Education [*British*]
NADEEC......	NATO Air Defense Electronic Environment Committee
NADeFA......	North American Deer Farmers Association (NTPA)
NaDefCo......	NATO [*North Atlantic Treaty Organization*] Defense College (AD)
NADEFCOL...	NATO Defense College [*Also, NADC, NDC*] [*Rome, Italy*]
NADEM........	National Association of Dairy Equipment Manufacturers [*Later, DFISA*] (EA)
NADEO........	National Association of Diocesan Ecumenical Officers (EA)
NADEP........	National Association of Disability Evaluating Professionals (NTPA)
NADEP........	Naval Aviation Depot (MCD)
NADEPA......	National Democratic Party [*Solomon Islands*] [*Political party*] (PPW)
NADET........	National Association of Distributive Education Teachers
NADE(V)......	National Association for Drama in Education (Victoria) [*Australia*]
NaDevCen....	Naval Air Development Center (AD)
NADEVCEN..	Naval Air Development Center [*Also, NADC, NAVAIRDEVCEN*]
NADEX........	NATO Data Exchange (NATG)
NADF..........	National Addison's Disease Foundation (EA)
NADF..........	National Adrenal Diseases Foundation (EA)
NADF..........	National Alzheimer's Disease Foundation (AD)
NADF..........	National Arbor Day Foundation (EA)
NADF..........	North American Directory Forum
NADFA........	North American Deer Farmers Association (EA)
NADFAS......	[*The*] National Association of Decorative and Fine Arts Societies [*British*]
NADFAS......	National Association of Design and Fine Art Societies (AD)
NADFD........	National Association of Decorative Fabric Distributors (EA)
NADFPM......	National Association of Domestic and Farm Pump Manufacturers [*Later, WSC*]
NADFS........	National Association of Drop Forgers and Stampers (AD)
NADG..........	Nicotinamide Adenine Dinucleotide Glycohydrolase [*An enzyme*] (DMAA)
NADGE........	NATO Air Defense Ground Environment
NADGE........	NATO Air Defense Ground Equipment
NADGECO....	NATO Air Defense Ground Environment Consortium
NADGEMO...	NADGE [*NATO Air Defense Ground Environment*] Management Office [*Belgium*]
NADGEMO...	NATO Air Defense Ground Environment Management Organization (NATG)
NADH..........	Dihydronicotinamide Adenine Dinucleotide (AD)
NADH..........	Naval Ammunition Depot, Hawaii
NADH..........	Nicotinamide-Adenine Dinucleotide (Reduced) [*See also NAD*] [*Biochemistry*]
NADHCI.......	North American District Heating and Cooling Institute [*Defunct*] (EA)
NADHPRS....	Naval Ammunition Depot Hawthorne Police Records System (DNAB)
NADI..........	National Association of Display Industries [*New York, NY*] (EA)
NADI..........	Naval Ammunition Depot, Indiana
NADIB........	North American Defense Industrial Base
NADIBO......	North American Defense Industrial Base Organization
NADIDE.......	Nicotinamide Adenine Dinucleotide (SAUS)
NADIN........	National Airspace Data Interchange Network [*FAA*] (TAG)
NADIN II......	National Airspace Data Interchange Network II [*National digital message switching network for aeronautical data*] (GAVI)
NADIP.........	Navy Display Improvement Program
NADIS.........	National Aerometric Data Information System [*Environmental Protection Agency*]
NADJ.........	National Association of Disk Jockeys (BUAC)
NADL........	National Animal Disease Laboratory [*Iowa*]
NADL........	National Association of Dental Laboratories (EA)
NADL........	Navy Authorized Data List (NG)
NADL........	Navy Avionics Development Laboratory (SAUS)
NADLCC......	National Association of Defense Lawyers in Criminal Cases [*Later, NACDL*] (EA)
NAD-LLL......	Naval Ammunition Depot - Lwlualei [*Hawaii*] (DNAB)
NADM........	National Association of Discount Merchants [*Defunct*] (EA)
NADM........	National Association of Doll Manufacturers [*Later, NADSTM*] (EA)
NADM........	Naval Administration
NADMAP......	Naval Architecture Design & Material Assistance Programme (SAUS)
NADMC.......	Naval Air Development and Material Center
NaDMC.......	Sodium Dimethyl Dithiocarbamate (SAUS)
NADME.......	Noise Amplitude Distribution Measuring Equipment (PDAA)
NADMR.......	National Association of Diversified Manufacturers Representatives [*Later, NAGMR*]
NADMW......	National Association of Direct Mail Writers
NAD/NADH...	Nicotinamide Adenine Dinucleotide (AD)
NADO.........	National Association of Development Organizations (EA)
NADO.........	Navy Accounts Disbursing Office
NADO.........	New Airport Development Office (SAUS)
NADO.........	New Airport Development Organization (SAUS)
NADOA.......	National Association of Division Order Analysts (EA)
NADOC.......	Naval Aviation Depot Operations Center (DOMA)
NADOI........	National Association of Dog Obedience Instructors (EA)
NADONA/LTC...	National Association of Directors of Nursing Administration in Long Term Care (EA)
NADOP.......	North American Defense Operational Plan (SAUS)
NADOP.......	North American Defense Operation Plan [*NORAD*]
NADOR.......	Notification of Accidents and Dangerous Occurrences Regulations 1980 (HEAS)
NADORF......	National Association of Development Organization Research Fund
NADORF......	National Association of Development Organizations Research Foundation (EA)
NADOT.......	North Atlantic Deepwater Oil Terminal (PDAA)
NADOW......	National Association for Training the Disabled in Office Work (AD)
NADP.........	National Acid Deposition Program [*Air pollution*]
NADP.........	National Association of Deafened People (BUAC)
NADP.........	National Association of Dental Plans (NTPA)
NADP.........	National Association of Desktop Publishers (EA)
NADP.........	National Association of Doctors in Practice [*British*] (DI)
NADP.........	National Atmospheric Deposition Program [*Department of Agriculture*]
NADP.........	NAVAIR Advanced Development Plan (MCD)
nadp.........	Nicotinamide Adenine Dinucleotide Phosphate (AD)
NADP.........	Nicotinamide-Adenine Dinucleotide Phosphate [*Preferred form, but see also TPN*] [*Biochemistry*]
NADP.........	Northern Alberta Dairy Pool (SAUS)
NADPAS......	National Association of Discharged Prisoners' Aid Societies [*British*] (DI)
NADPB.......	North Atlantic Defense Production Board (NATG)
NADPH.......	Dihydronicotinamide Adenine Dinucleotide Phosphate (AD)
nadph.......	Dihydronicotinamide Adenine Dinucleotide Phosphate (AD)
NADPH.......	Nicotinamide-Adenine Dinucleotide Phosphate (Reduced) [*Preferred form, but see also TPNH*] [*Biochemistry*]
NADR.........	Normalized Aggregate Data Rate (SAUS)
NADREG......	National Alliance for Democratic Restoration in Equatorial Guinea [*Switzerland*] (EAIO)
NADREPS....	National Armaments Directors Representatives
NADS........	National Advanced Driver Simulator [*NHTSA*] (TAG)
NADS........	National Armament Directors [*NATO*]
NADS........	National Association Diaper Services (EA)
NADS........	National Association for Down Syndrome (EA)
NADS........	National Automobile Driving Simulator
NADS........	Naval Air Development Station
NADS........	Nevada Automated Diagnostics System (SAUS)
NADS........	North American Data Systems (SAUS)
NADS........	North American Dostoevsky Society (EA)
NADS........	North Atlantic Defense System
NADSA.......	National Agricultural Diversification and Settlement Authority [*Sri Lanka*] (BUAC)
NADSA.......	National Association of Dramatic and Speech Arts (EA)
NADSA.......	North American Dairy Sheep Association (NTPA)
NADSC.......	National Association of Direct Selling Companies [*Later, DSA*] (EA)
NADSP.......	National Association of Dental Service Plans [*Insurance*] (DHSM)
NADSTM.....	National Association of Doll and Stuffed Toy Manufacturers (EA)
NADT........	National Association for Drama Therapy (EA)
NADTC.......	North Atlantic Air Defense Technical Center (SAUS)
NADTCA.....	North American Diecast Toy Collectors Association (EA)
NADTP.......	National Association of Desktop Publishers (NTPA)
NADU........	Naval Aircraft Delivery Unit
NADU........	Naval Air Development Unit (MUGU)
NADUC.......	Nimbus/Ats Data Utilization Center (SAUS)
NADUG.......	North American Datamanager Users Group (EA)
NADUS.......	National Association of Doctors in the United States (EA)
NADUSM.....	National Association of Deputy United States Marshals (EA)
NADVH.......	National Association of Drama with the Visually Handicapped (BUAC)
NADW........	National Association of Disabled Writers (BUAC)
NADW........	North Atlantic Deep Water [*Oceanography*]
NADWAGNS...	National Association of Deans of Women and Advisors to Girls in Negro Schools [*Defunct*] (EA)
NADWARN...	National Disaster Warning System (AD)
NADWARN...	Natural Disaster Warning
NADWARN...	Natural Disaster Warning System (IAA)
NADWAS.....	Natural Disaster Warning Survey (NOAA)
NADWAS.....	North American Dr. Who Appreciation Society (EA)
NADX........	National Dentex Corp. [*NASDAQ symbol*] (SAG)
NADX........	Natl Dentex [*NASDAQ symbol*] (TTSB)
Nae..........	Exchangeable Body Sodium (MAE)
NAE..........	N-Acylethanolamine [*Organic chemistry*]
NAE..........	Nake [*Tuamotu Archipelago*] [*Seismograph station code, US Geological Survey*] (SEIS)
NAE..........	National Academy of Education
NAE..........	National Academy of Engineering [*Washington, DC*] (GRD)
nae..........	National Administrative Expenses (AD)
NAE..........	National Administrative Expenses (NATG)
NAE..........	National Adoption Exchange (EA)
NAE..........	National Aeronautical Establishment [*Research center*] [*Canada*] (IRC)
NAE..........	National Association of Entrepreneurs
NAE..........	National Association of Evangelicals (EA)
NAE..........	Nations Air Express, Inc. [*FAA designator*] (FAAC)
NAE..........	Naval Aeronautical Establishment [*Canada*] (AD)
NAE..........	Naval Aircraft Establishment (AD)
NAE..........	Navy Acquisition Executive (MCD)
NAE..........	Net Acid Excretion (DMAA)
NAE..........	Netware Application Engine [*Networth, Inc.*]

NAE	New Age Encyclopedia [*A publication*]
nAe	No American Equivalent (AD)
NAE	No American Equivalent [*Language*]
NAE	Noise Acoustic Emitter [*Military*] (CAAL)
NAE	Noram Energy Corp. [*Formerly, Arkla, Inc.*] [*NYSE symbol*] (SAG)
NAE	Noram Financing I [*NYSE symbol*] (SAG)
NAE	North American Environmental, Inc. (SAUS)
NAE	Not Above or Equal (SAUS)
nae	Not Always Excused (AD)
NAE	Nursery Association Executives [*Later, NAENA*] (EA)
NAE4-HA	National Association of Extension 4-H Agents (EA)
NAEA	National Aerospace Education Association [*Formerly, NAEC*] [*Defunct*]
NAEA	National Art Education Archive (AIE)
NAEA	National Art Education Association (EA)
NAEA	National Artists Equity Association (EA)
NAEA	National Association of Enrolled Agents (EA)
NAEA	National Association of Estate Agents [*British*] (EAIO)
NAEA	National Association of Extension 4-H Agents (EA)
NAEA	Newspaper Advertising Executives Association [*Later, INAME*] (EA)
NAEA	Newspaper Advertising Executives Association of Canada (BUAC)
NAEA News	Newspaper Advertising Executives Association News (SAUS)
NAE-ASEB	National Academy of Engineering Aeronautics and Space Engineering Board
NAEB	National Association of Educational Broadcasters [*Formerly, Association of Collegeand University Broadcasting Stations (1934)*] (EA)
NAEB	National Association of Educational Buyers [*Woodbury, NY*] (EA)
NAEB	Naval Aviation Evaluation Board
NAEB	North African Economic Board [*World War II*]
NAEBM	National Association of Engine and Boat Manufacturers [*Later, NMMA*] (EA)
NAEC	Hungarys National Atomic Energy Commission (SAUS)
NAEC	National Aboriginal Education Committee (BUAC)
NAEC	National Advisory Eye Council
NAEC	National Aeronautical Establishment, Canada (BUAC)
NAEC	National Aerospace Education Council [*Later, NAEA*] (EA)
NAEC	National Agricultural Engineering Corp. [*China*] (BUAC)
NAEC	National Association Executives Club (EA)
NAEC	National Association for Educational Computing (EA)
NAEC	National Association of Electric Companies [*Later, EEI*] (EA)
NAEC	National Association of Elevator Contractors (EA)
NAEC	National Association of Engineering Companies (EA)
NAEC	National Association of Exhibition Contractors [*British*] (BI)
NAEC	National Atomic Energy Commission (SAUS)
NAEC	National Aviation Education Council [*Later, National Aerospace Education Council*] (AEBS)
NAEC	Naval Air Engineering Center [*Closed*]
NAEC	Northern Agricultural Energy Center
NAEC	Novell Authorized Education Center (SAUS)
NAECA	National Appliance Energy Conservation Act [*1987*]
NAEC-ACEL	Naval Air Engineering Center Aerospace Crew Equipment Laboratory [*Lakehurst, NJ*]
NAEC-AEL	Naval Air Engineering Center Aeronautical Engine Laboratory [*Lakehurst, NJ*]
NAEC-AML	Naval Air Engineering Center Aeronautical Materials Laboratory [*Lakehurst, NJ*]
NAEC-ASL	Naval Air Engineering Center Aeronautical Structures Laboratory [*Lakehurst, NJ*]
NAEC-ENG	Naval Air Engineering Center Engineering Department [*Lakehurst, NJ*]
NAECFO	Naval Air Engineering Center Field Office (DNAB)
NAEC-GSED	Naval Air Engineering Center Ground Support Equipment Department [*Lakehurst, NJ*]
NAECOE	National Academy of Engineering Committee on Ocean Engineering
NAECON	National Aerospace Electronics Conference [*IEEE*] (MCD)
NAEd	National Academy of Education (EA)
NAED	National Association of Electrical Distributors (EA)
NAED	National Association of Engravers and Diestampers (BUAC)
NAEDA	National American Eskimo Dog Association (EA)
NAEDA	North American Equipment Dealers Association (EA)
NAEDS	National Association of Educational Data Systems (IAA)
NAEDS	National Association of Engravers and Die-Stampers [*British*] (BI)
NAEDS	Nonaqueous Equipment Decontamination System (ACAE)
NAEE	National Association of Environmental Education [*British*] (DBA)
NAEE	North American Association for Environmental Education (EA)
NAEE	North American Association of Environmental Education (SAUS)
NAEEO	National Association for Equal Educational Opportunities (EA)
NAEF	Naval Air Engineering Facility (MCD)
NAEF	North American Environmental Fund (SAUS)
NAEFA	North American Economics and Finance Association (EA)
NAEF-ENG	Naval Air Engineering Facility Ship Installations Engineering Department [*Philadelphia, PA*]
NAEFR	North American English Ford Registry (EA)
NAEFTA	National Association of Enrolled Federal Tax Accountants (EA)
NAEG	Nevada Applied Ecology Group (SAUS)
NAEGA	North American Export Grain Association (EA)
NAEGS	National Association of Educational Guidance Services for Adults [*British*] (DBA)
NAEH	National Alliance to End Homelessness (EA)
NAEHCA	National Association of Employers on Health Care Action
NAEHCA	National Association of Employers on Health Care Alternatives (EA)
NAEHE	National Association of Extension Home Economists (EA)
NAEHMO	National Association of Employers on Health Maintenance Organizations [*Later, NAEHCA*] (EA)

NAEIAC	National Association of Educational Inspectors, Advisers, and Consultants (AIE)
NAEIC	Nevada Applied Ecology Information Center [*Department of Energy*] (IID)
NAEIR	National Association for the Exchange of Industrial Resources (EA)
NAEKM	National Association of Electronic Keyboard Manufacturers (EA)
NAEL	Naval Air Engineering Laboratory (MCD)
NAEL	No-Adverse-Effect Level [*Toxicology*] (LDT)
NAELA	National Academy of Elder Law Attorneys (EA)
NAELB	National Association of Equipment Leasing Brokers (NTPA)
NAELC	National Architect-Engineer Liaison Commission [*Defunct*] (EA)
NAEL-ENG	Naval Air Engineering Laboratory Ship Installations Engineering Department [*Philadelphia, PA*]
NAELSI	Naval Air Electronics Shipboard Installation
NAEM	National Association for Environmental Management
NAEM	National Association of Exposition Managers (EA)
NAEM	Naval Air Effect Model (PDAA)
NAEMB	National Academy of Engineering Marine Board
NAEMSP	National Association of Emergency Medical Service Physicians (EA)
NAEMSPA	National EMS Pilots Association (SAUS)
NAEMT	National Association of Emergency Medical Technicians (EA)
NAEN	National Association of Educational Negotiators (EA)
NAENA	Nursery Association Executives of North America (EA)
NAE-NEPP	National Academy of Engineering Navy Environmental Protection Program Study Group
NAENG	North African Engineer Section [*World War II*]
NAEO	National Activity Education Organization (EA)
NAEO	National Association of Extradition Officials (EA)
NAEOM	National Association of Electronic Organ Manufacturers
NAEOP	National Association of Educational Office Personnel (EA)
NAEP	National Assessment of Educational Progress (AD)
NAEP	National Assessment of Educational Progress, The Nation's Report Card (EA)
NAEP	National Association of Educational Programs [*Carnegie Foundation*] (AD)
NAEP	National Association of Environmental Professionals (EA)
NAEP	National Asthma Education Program (DMAA)
NAEPC	National Association of Estate Planning Councils (EA)
NAEPDC	National Adult Education Professional Development Consortium (NTPA)
NAEPIRS	National Assessment of Educational Progress Information Retrieval System [*National Institute of Education*] [*Database*]
NAEPIS	North America Engineering Parts Inquiry System
NAEPrA	Noram Energy $3 Cv Ex A Pfd [*NYSE symbol*] (TTSB)
NAEPS	National Academy of Economics and Political Science (EA)
NAER	National Association of Executive Recruiters (EA)
NAERC	North American Electric Reliability Council (EA)
NAERG	North American Emergency Response Guidebook (SAUS)
NAERIC	North American Equine Ranching Information Council (GVA)
NaEry	Sodium Erythorbate (SAUS)
NAES	National Association for Ethnic Studies (EA)
NAES	National Association of Ecumenical Staff (EA)
NAES	National Association of Educational Secretaries [*Later, NAEOP*] (EA)
NAES	National Association of Episcopal Schools (EA)
NAES	National Association of Executive Secretaries (EA)
NAES	Native American Educational Service [*Later, NAESC*] (EA)
NAES	Naval Air Experimental Station
NAES	Nevada Agricultural Experiment Station [*University of Nevada - Reno*] [*Research center*] (RCD)
NAES	North African Army Exchange Service [*World War II*]
NAES	North American Electronic Systems (SAUS)
NAESA	National Association of Elevator Safety Authorities (EA)
NAESA	North American Economic Studies Association (EA)
NAESC	National Association of Energy Service Companies (EA)
NAESC	Native American Educational Services College (EA)
NAESCO	National Association of Energy Service Companies (EA)
NAESP	National Association of Elementary School Principals (EA)
NAEST	National Archives for Electrical Science and Technology (PDAA)
NAESU	Naval Aviation Electronic Service Unit (MCD)
NAESU	Naval Aviation Engineering Service Unit [*Philadelphia, PA*]
NAESUDET	Naval Aviation Engineering Service Unit Detachment (DNAB)
NAET	National Association for Educational Television (NTCM)
NAET	National Association of Educational Technicians [*British*]
NAETS	Naval Air Emission-Tracking System
NAETV	National Association for Educational Television [*Defunct*]
NAEUSA	National Academy of Engineering of the United States of America (NTPA)
NAEW	NATO Airborne Early Warning
NAEWS	NATO Airborne Early Warning System
NAEWTF	NATO Aircrew Electronic Warfare Tactics Facility (NATG)
NAEYC	National Association for the Education of Young Children (EA)
NAF	Guilder [*Florin*] [*Monetary unit*] [*Netherlands Antilles*]
NAF	Nafimidone [*Biochemistry*]
NAF	Name and Address File [*IRS*]
NAF	National Abortion Federation (EA)
NAF	National Abortion Foundation (AD)
NAF	National Aging Foundation (EA)
NAF	National Amputation Foundation (EA)
NAF	National Analytical Facility [*National Oceanic and Atmospheric Administration*]
NAF	National Angling Federation [*British*]
NAF	National Anxiety Foundation (NRGU)
NAF	National Arts Foundation (EA)
NAF	National Ataxia Foundation (EA)
NAF	National Aviation Forum

NAF.............	Naval Aircraft Factory
NAF.............	Naval Air Facility
NAF.............	Naval Airfield (PIPO)
NAF.............	Naval Air Force
NAF.............	Naval Avionics Facility [Later, NAC] [Indianapolis, IN]
NAF.............	Nernst Approximation Formula [Physics]
NAF.............	Net Acid Flux [Medicine] (DMAA)
NAF.............	Netherland-America Foundation [Later, Netherlands-America Community Association] (EA)
NAF.............	Network Access Facility
NAF.............	New Age Federation (EA)
NAF.............	New Age Media Fund [NYSE symbol] (SPSG)
NAF.............	No Abnormal Findings [Medicine]
NAF.............	Nonadjacent Form (SAUS)
NAF.............	Nonappropriated Fund [or Funds]
naf.............	Nonappropriated Funds (AD)
NAF.............	Non-urea Adducting Fatty Acid [Food science]
NAF.............	Nordisk Anaestesiologisk Forening [Scandinavian Society of Anaesthesiologists - SSA] (EA)
NAF.............	Norges Automobil Fornund [Norway Automobile Association] (AD)
NAF.............	North American Federation of Third Order Franciscans (EA)
NAF.............	North American Fire [Vancouver Stock Exchange symbol]
NAF.............	North Anatolian Fault (SAUS)
NAF.............	Northern Africa (CARB)
NAF.............	Northern Africa Region (SAUS)
NAF.............	Northern Attack Force [Navy]
NAF.............	North West Atlantic Fisheries, Memorial University [UTLAS symbol]
NAF.............	Notice of Adverse Finding [Food and Drug Administration]
NAF.............	Nouvelle Action Francaise [New French Action] [Political party] (PPE)
NAF.............	Numbered Air Force (AFM)
NAF.............	Royal Netherlands Air Force [ICAO designator] (FAAC)
NaF.............	Sodium Fluoride [Chemistry] (DAVI)
NAFA	National Academy of Foreign Affairs (AD)
NAFA	National Aerobic Fitness Award (AD)
NAFA	National Aircraft Finance Association (EA)
NAFA	National Air Filtration Association (EA)
NAFA	National American Farmers Association [Defunct] (EA)
NAFA	National Association of Fine Arts [Defunct] (EA)
NAFA	National Association of Fleet Administrators [Iselin, NJ] (EA)
NAFA	National Association of Furniture Agents [Australia]
NAFA	National Association to Aid Fat Americans [Bellrose, NY]
NAFA	Net Acquisition of Financial Assets (ADA)
NAFA	Nonappropriated Fund Activity (CINC)
NAFA	North American Falconers Association (EA)
NAFA	North American Farm Alliance (EA)
NAFA	Northwest Atlantic Fisheries Act of 1950
NAFAC	National Association for Ambulatory Care [Formerly, NAFEC] (EA)
NAFAD	National Association of Fashion and Accessory Designers (EA)
NAFAG	NATO Air Force Advisory Group (NATG)
NAFAG	NATO Air Force Armaments Group
NAFAPAC	National Association for Association Political Action Committees (EA)
NAFARE	National Association for Families and Addiction Research and Education (PAZ)
NAFAS	National Association of Flower Arrangement Societies (AD)
NAFAS	National Association of Flower Arrangement Societies of Great Britain (BI)
NAFAS	Nonappropriated Fund Accounting System [Military] (DNAB)
NAFAX	National Facsimile Network [National Weather Service]
NAFB	National Association of Farm Broadcasters (EA)
NAFB	National Association of Franchised Businessmen [Defunct] (EA)
NAFB	Norton Air Force Base [California]
NAFB & AE...	National Association of Farriers, Blacksmiths, and Agricultural Engineers [British] (DBA)
NAFBO	National Association for Business Organizations [Baltimore, MD] (EA)
NAFBRAT	National Association for Better Radio and Television [Later, NABB] (EA)
NAFC	Nash Finch Co. [NASDAQ symbol] (TTSB)
NAFC	National Accounting and Finance Council [Alexandria, VA] (EA)
NAFC	National Anthropological Film Center [Smithsonian Institution] (GRD)
NAFC	National Anti-Fluoridation Campaign [British] (DBA)
NAFC	National Association of Fan Clubs (EA)
NAFC	National Association of Financial Consultants (EA)
NAFC	National Association of Food Chains (NADA)
NAFC	National Association of Formwork Contractors [British] (DBA)
NAFC	National Association of Friendship Centres [Canada]
NAFC	National Average Fuel Consumption
NAFC	Naval Air Ferry Command [World War II]
NAFC	Navy Accounting and Finance Center
NAFC	North American Fishing Club (EA)
NAFC	North American Forestry Commission [UN Food and Agriculture Organization]
NAFC	North American Forum on the Catechumenate (EA)
NAFC	Northern Attack Force Commander [Navy]
NAFC	Northwest Atlantic Fisheries Center (SAUS)
NAFCA	North American Family Campers Association (EA)
NAFCA	North American Poultry Cooperative Association (SAUS)
NAFCC	National Association for Family Child Care (NTPA)
NAFCD	National Association of Floor Covering Distributors (EA)
NAFCE	National Association of Federal Career Employees [Defunct] (EA)
NAFCI	National Association of Floor Covering Installers [Later, AIDS International] (EA)
NAFCM	National Association for Community Mediation (NTPA)
NAFCO	National Association of Franchise Companies (EA)
NAFCO	National Floor Products Co., Inc.
NAFCO	North Atlantic Fisheries Consultative Committee (SAUS)
NAFCO	Northwest Atlantic Fishery Consultative Organization (SAUS)
NAFCOM	Northern Africa Committee (SAUS)
NAFCOM	Northern Africa Regional Committee for START (SAUS)
NAFCR	National Association of Foster Care Reviewers (EA)
NAFCU	National Association of Federal Credit Unions (EA)
NAFD	National Air Forwarding Division [Institute of Freight Forwarders] (AD)
NAFD	National Association of Farm Directors (NTCM)
NAFD	National Association of Flour Distributors (EA)
NAFD	National Association of Funeral Directors [British] (BI)
NAFD	New America Fund (SAUS)
NAFDC	National Association for Family Day Care (EA)
NAFDI	National Foundation for Depressive Illness (EA)
NAFE	National Association for Female Executives [New York, NY] (EA)
NAFE	National Association for Film in Education [British]
NAFE	National Association for Free Enterprise [Defunct] (EA)
NAFE	National Association of Forensic Economists (EA)
NAFE	Non-Advanced Further Education [British]
NAFEA	National Association for the Education and Advancement of Cambodian, Laotian, and Vietnamese Americans
NAFEC	National Association of Farmer Elected Committeemen (EA)
NAFEC	National Association of Freestanding Emergency Centers [Later, NAAC] (EA)
NAFEC	National Aviation Facilities Experimental Center [of FAA] [Atlantic City, NJ]
NAFEC	North American Fund for Environmental Cooperation (SAUS)
NAFED	National Association of Fire Equipment Distributors (EA)
NAFEM........	National Association of Food Equipment Manufacturers (EA)
NAFEMS	National Agency for Finite Element Methods and Standards [British] (IRUK)
NAFEO	National Association for Equal Opportunity in Higher Education (EA)
NAFEPA	National Association of Federal Education Program Administrators (NTPA)
NAFEX	North American Fruit Explorers (EA)
NAFF	National Association for Freedom [British]
nAff.............	Need for Affection
naff.............	Need for Affiliation (AD)
N Aff	Need for Affiliation (DIPS)
NAFF	Need for Affiliation (MHDB)
NAFFP	National Association of Frozen Food Packers [Later, AFFI] (EA)
NAFFP	National Association of Frozen Food Producers (AD)
NAFFS	National Association of Fruits, Flavors, and Syrups (EA)
NAFFW	National Association of Full Figured Women (EA)
NAFGDA.......	National Auto and Flat Glass Dealers Association [Later, NGA]
NAFGPD.......	National Association of Foster Grandparent Program Directors (EA)
NAFI	National Association of Fire Investigators (EA)
NAFI	National Association of Flight Instructors (EA)
NAFI	Naval Air Fighting Instructions
NAFI	Naval Avionics Facility, Indianapolis [Later, NAC]
NAFI	Nonappropriated Fund Instrumentalities [DoD] (MCD)
NAFI	Northern Air Freight, Inc. (SAUS)
NAFIC	National Association of Fraternal Insurance Counsellors [Sheboygan, WI] (EA)
NAFIN	North African Finance Section [World War II]
NAFINSA......	Nacional Financiera [National Finance Coro.] [Spanish] (AD)
NAFIP	National Foreign Intelligence Program [DoD] (MCD)
NAFIPS	North American Fuzzy Information Processing Society (EA)
NAFIS	National Association of Federally Impacted Schools (EA)
NAFIS	National Automated Fingerprint Identification System
NAFIS	Naval Forces Intelligence Study (MCD)
NAFIS	Navigational Aid Flight Inspection System (AFM)
NAFISS	Nonappropriated Funds Information Standard System [Army]
NAFL	National Alliance for Family Life [Later, NACFT] (EA)
NAFLAC	Navy Department Fuel and Lubricants Advisory Committee [Ministry of Defense] [British] (PDAA)
NAFLANT	Naval Air Facilities, Atlantic
NAFLFD	National Association of Federally Licensed Firearms Dealers (EA)
NAFLI..........	Natural Flight Indication (MCD)
NAFLI..........	Natural Flight Instrument System
NAFLIR	Navigation Forward Looking Infrared (ACAE)
NAFM	National Armed Forces Museum (AD)
NAFM	National Association of Fan Manufacturers [Later, AMCA]
NAFM	National Association of Farmers' Markets (GVA)
NAFM	National Association of Flag Manufacturers
NAFM	National Association of Furniture Manufacturers [Later, AFMA] (EA)
NAFMA	NATO European Fighter Management Agency
NAFMAB	National Armed Forces Museum Advisory Board [Smithsonian Institution]
NAFMB	National Association of FM [Frequency Modulation] Broadcasters [Later, NRBA] (EA)
NAFMC	Nonappropriated Funds, Marine Corps (DNAB)
NAFMDA......	North American Folk Music and Dance Alliance (NTPA)
NAFMG	National Association of Foreign Medical Graduates [Later, ACIP]
NAFMIS	Nonappropriated Funds Management Information System
NAFMOW	National Action Forum for Midlife and Older Women (EA)
NAFMW	National Action for Former Military Wives (EA)
NAFN	Norton Administrator for Networks [Symantec Corp.] [Telecommunications] (PCM)
NAFO	National Association of Farmworker Organizations [Defunct] (EA)
NAFO	National Association of Fire Officers [British] (DI)
NAFO	Northwest Atlantic Fisheries Organization (EA)
NAFO	Organizaci"n de Pesca del Atl ntico Noroeste (SAUS)
NAFOW........	National Action Forum for Midlife and Older Women (EA)

NAFOW	National Action Forum for Older Women [*Later, NAFMOW*] (EA)
NAFP	National Association of Factoring Professionals (NTPA)
NAFP	National Association of Food Processors (ECON)
NAFP	Naval Air Force, Pacific Fleet (DNAB)
NAFP	New Armed Forces of the Philippines (AD)
NAFPA	National Alcohol Fuels Producers Association [*Defunct*] (EA)
NAFPA	National Association of Federal Education Program Administrators (EA)
NAFPAC	Naval Air Facilities, Pacific
NAFPB	National Association of Freight Payment Banks [*Pittsburgh, PA*] (EA)
NAFPC	National Academy for Fire Prevention and Control [*of FEMA*]
NAFPD	National Association of Family Planning Doctors [*British*] (DBA)
NAFPP	National Accelerated Food Production Project [*Agency for International Development*]
NAFPP	National Association of Fresh Produce Processors (EA)
NAFPU	North American Friends of Palestinian Universities [*Defunct*] (EA)
NAFR	National Association of First Responders (NTPA)
N Afr	North Africa
NAFRC	National Association of Fiscally Responsible Cities [*Defunct*] (EA)
NAFRC	North Atlantic Fisheries Research Center (PDAA)
NAFRD	National Association of Fleet Resale Dealers [*Los Angeles, CA*] (EA)
NAFRF	Navy Alternate Fuel Reference File [*Battelle Memorial Institute*] [*Information service or system*] [*Defunct*] (IID)
NAFRLG	National Alliance of Financially-Responsible Local Governments (AD)
NAFRTM	National Association of Farm and Ranch Trailer Manufacturers [*Defunct*] (EA)
NAFS	National Association of Fastener Stockholders [*British*] (DBA)
NAFS	National Association of Foot Specialists (AD)
NAFS	National Association of Forensic Sciences (AD)
NAFS	Naval Air Fighter School
NA/FS	Naval Aviator/Flight Surgeon (MCD)
NAFS	Newark Air Force Station [*Ohio*]
NAFSA	National Association for Foreign Student Affairs (EA)
NAFSA	National Association of Fire Science and Administration [*Defunct*] (EA)
NAFSA	National Association of Foreign Student Advisors (AD)
NAFSA	No American Flag Shipping Available
NAFSC	North American Farm Show Council (NTPA)
NAFSLAC	National Association of Federations of Syrian and Lebanese American Clubs (EA)
NAFSMA	National Association of Flood and Stormwater Management Agencies (NTPA)
NAFSO	National Association of Field Studies Officers [*British*] (DBA)
NAFSONW	Nonappropriated Fund Statement of Operations and Net Worth
NAFSWMA	National Association of Flood and Storm Water Management Agencies (EA)
NAFT	National Alternative Fuel Test (AD)
NAFT	Natural Adjuvant Factor Toxoid [*Medicine*]
NAFT	Network for Analysis of Fireball Trajectories (EA)
NAFT	No Accounting for Taste (GOBB)
NAFTA	National Amalgamated Furnishing Trades Association [*A union*] [*British*]
NAFTA	National Association of Futures Trading Advisors [*Defunct*] (EA)
NAFTA	National Association of Future Teachers of America [*Later, Student National Education Association*] (AEBS)
NAFTA	New Zealand-Australia Free Trade Agreement (AD)
NAFTA	North America Free Trade Agreement (SAUS)
NAFTA	North American Free Trade Agreement [*Passed in 1993*]
NAFTA	North American Free-Trade Area (ECON)
NAFTA	North Atlantic Free Trade Area
NAFTAT	National Association for the Advancement of Time (EA)
NAFTC	National Association of Freight Transportation Consultants (EA)
NAFTC	North American Forging Technology Conference (SAUS)
NAFTCO	National Ford Tool Collectors [*Automotive hobby group*]
NAFTF	National Association of Finishers of Textile Fabrics [*Later, ATMI*] (EA)
NAFTM	National Association of Fund Raising Ticket Manufacturers (NTPA)
NAFTOC	NORAD Automated Forward Tell Output to Canada (MCD)
NAFTRAC	National Foreign Trade Council (EA)
NAFTZ	National Association of Foreign-Trade Zones [*Washington, DC*] (EA)
NAFV	National Association of Federal Veterinarians (EA)
NAFW	National Association of Future Women [*Later, NAFWIC*] (EA)
NAFWA	North American Flowerbulb Wholesalers Association (EA)
NAFWIC	National Association for Women in Careers (EA)
NAFWR	National Association of Furniture Warehousemen and Removers (AD)
Nag	All India Reporter, Nagpur [*A publication*] (DLA)
NAG	Goddard Space Flight Center, Greenbelt, MD [*OCLC symbol*] (OCLC)
Nag	Indian Law Reports, Nagpur Series [*A publication*] (DLA)
Nag	Indian Rulings, Nagpur Series [*A publication*] (DLA)
NAG	N-Acetylglucosamine [*Biochemistry*]
NAG	N-Acetylglucosaminidase [*An enzyme*]
NAG	Nachrichten der Akademie der Wissenschaften in Goettingen. Philologisch-Historische Klasse [*A publication*] (BJA)
Nag	Nagasaki [*Japan*] (AD)
Nag	Nagoya [*Japan*] (AD)
NAG	Nagoya [*Japan*] [*Seismograph station code, US Geological Survey*] (SEIS)
NAG	Nagpur [*India*] [*Airport symbol*] (OAG)
NAG	Narrow Angle Glaucoma [*Medicine*]
NAG	National Academy of Geosciences (EA)
NAG	National Acquisitions Group [*Libraries*] [*British*]
NAG	National Action Group [*Antibusing organization*]
NAG	National Advisory Group, Convenience Stores/Petroleum Companies (EA)
NAG	National Air-Racing Group (EA)
NAG	National Assessment Group (SAUS)
NAG	National Association of Gagwriters (EA)
NAG	National Association of Gardeners [*Later, PGMS*] (EA)
NAG	National Association of Goldsmiths [*British*] (DI)
NAG	National Association of Grooms [*British*] (DI)
NAG	National Association of Groundsmen [*British*] (DI)
NAG	Natural Assessments Group (SAUS)
NAG	Naval Advisory Group
NAG	Naval Analysis Group (MCD)
NAG	Naval Applications Group
NAG	Navy Astronautics Group (MUGU)
NAG	Negro Actors Guild (NADA)
NAG	Negro Actors Guild of America (EA)
NAG	Neighborhood Action Group (AD)
NAG	NERVA [*Nuclear Engine for Rocket Vehicle Application*] Advisory Group [*NASA*] (KSC)
nag	Net Annual Gain (AD)
NAG	Net Annual Gain [*Business term*] (PDAA)
NAG	Netherlands Aerospace Group (SAUS)
NAG	Networking Advisory Group [*Library of Congress*]
N-Ag	Neutralization Antigenic Site [*Immunogenetics*]
Nag	No-Acronym Sort of Guy [*Term coined by William F. Doescher, publisher of "D & B Reports"*] [*Lifestyle classification*]
NAG	Nonagglutinable [*or Nonagglutinating*] [*Immunochemistry*]
NAG	Nonagglutinable (or Nonagglutinating) (SAUS)
NAG	Nor-Acme Gold Mines Ltd. [*Toronto Stock Exchange symbol*]
NAG	Northern Army Group (NATG)
NAG	Nova Scotia Agricultural College Library [*UTLAS symbol*]
NAG	Numerical Algorithms Group (CIST)
NAG	Nystagmus Action Group [*British*] (DBA)
NAGA	National Advertising Golf Association (EA)
NAGA	National Amputee Golf Association (EA)
NAGA	North American Gamebird Association (EA)
NAGA	North American Ginseng Association [*Defunct*] (EA)
NAGAP	National Association of Gay Alcoholism Professionals [*Later, NALGAP*] (EA)
NAGAP	National Association of Graduate Admissions Professionals (NTPA)
NAGARA	National Association of Government Archives and Records Administrators (EA)
NAGARD	NATO Advisory Group for Aeronautical Research and Development
Nagas	Nagasaki [*Japan*] (AD)
NAGASA	North American Graphic Arts Suppliers Association (NTPA)
NAGB	National Assessment Governing Board
NAGB & SPA	North American Game Breeders and Shooting Preserve Association [*Later, NAGA*] (EA)
NAGBM	National Association of Golf Ball Manufacturers (EA)
NAGC	National Association for Gifted Children (EA)
NAGC	National Association of Girls Clubs (EA)
NAGC	National Association of Government Communicators (EA)
NAGC	National Gaming Corp. [*NASDAQ symbol*] (SAG)
NAGC	Naval Armed Guard Center
NAGC	Navy Astronautics Group Conference [*Navy*]
NAGC	North American Gladiolus Council (EA)
NAGCD	National Association of Glass Container Distributors [*Later, NACD*] (EA)
NAGCM	National Association of Golf Club Manufacturers (EA)
NAGCO	Naval Air Ground Center
NAGCP	National Association of Greeting Card Publishers [*Later, GCA*] (EA)
NAGCR	North American Guild of Change Ringers (EA)
NAGDCA	National Association of Government Deferred Compensation Administrators (EA)
NAGDM	National Association of Garage Door Manufacturers (EA)
NAGE	National Association of Government Employees (EA)
NAGE	NATO Air Defense Group Environment (AABC)
N-age	Nuclear Age (AD)
NAGGL	National Association of Government Guaranteed Lenders (NTPA)
NagHammSt	Nag Hammadi Studies [*A publication*] (BJA)
NAGHSR	National Association of Governors' Highway Safety Representatives (EA)
NAGI	National Association of Government Inspectors [*Later, National Association of Government Inspectors and Quality Assurance Personnel*] (EA)
NAGI	Not A Good Idea (SAUS)
NAGIM	North American Gunnery Instruction Monitor
NAGI/QAP	National Association of Government Inspectors and Quality Assurance Personnel (EA)
Nag LJ	Nagpur Law Journal [*India*] [*A publication*] (DLA)
Nag LN	Nagpur Law Notes [*India*] [*A publication*] (DLA)
NAGLO	National Association of Governmental Labor Officials (EA)
Nag LR	Nagpur Law Reports [*India*] [*A publication*] (DLA)
NAGM	National Association of Glove Manufacturers (EA)
NAGM	National Association of Glue Manufacturers [*Defunct*] (EA)
NAGM	National Association of Governors and Managers [*British*] (DBA)
NAGMC	North Atlantic Council and Military Committee (SAUS)
NAGMR	National Association of General Merchandise Representatives [*Chicago, IL*] (EA)
NAGO	National Association of Greyhound Owners (GVA)
Nagp	Nagpur, India (AD)
NAGPFS	National Association of Governors' Councils on Physical Fitness and Sports (NTPA)

NAGPIPM..... National Association of Graphic and Product Identification Manufacturers (NTPA)
NAGPM........ National Association of Grained Plate Makers (AD)
NAGP/NCP North American Great Plains/North China Plain Project [Agriculture]
NAGPRA...... Native American Graves Protection and Repatriation Act [Enacted 1990]
NAGPTDU ... National Action Group for the Prevention and Treatment of Decubitus Ulcers (EA)
NAGRA........ National Association of Gambling Regulatory Agencies (EA)
NAGRA........ Nationalen Genossenschaft fuer die Lagerung Radioaktiver Abfaelle [National Cooperative Society for the Storage of Radioactive Wastes] [Germany] (AD)
NAGRA........ Nation Association of Govenment Archives and Records Administration (TELE)
NAGRP........ National Animal Genome Research Program (SAUS)
NAGS.......... National Allotments and Gardens Society Ltd. [British] (BI)
NAGS.......... National Association of Government Secretaries [Defunct]
NAGS.......... Naval Air Gunners School
NAGSC........ National Association of Government Service Contractors [Defunct] (EA)
NAGSCT...... National Association of Guidance Supervisors and Counselor Trainers
NAGT.......... National Association of Geology Teachers (EA)
NAGT.......... National Association of Geoscience Teachers (NTPA)
NAGTADD ... National Association of Government Training and Development Directors (NTPA)
NAGTC........ North American Gasoline Tax Conference (EA)
NAGUA........ Numerical Algorithms Group Users Association (SAUS)
Nag UCL Mag... Nagpur University. College of Law. Magazine [1933-34] [India] [A publication] (DLA)
NAGVG........ National Association Greenhouse Vegetable Growers (EA)
NAGWS........ National Association for Girls and Women in Sport (EA)
NAH .... Autism Services Center [Formerly, National Autism Hotline] (EA)
NAH .... Naha [Ryukyu Islands] [Airport symbol] (OAG)
NAH .... Nahanni Air Services Ltd. [Canada] [ICAO designator] (FAAC)
nah .... Nahuatlan [MARC language code] [Library of Congress] (LCCP)
Nah.............. Nahum [Old Testament book]
NAH .... National Association of Homebuilders (AD)
NAH .... National Autism Hotline (EA)
NAH .... Night Adoration in the Home (EA)
NAH .... No-Antihalation Film
NAH .... Nordic Association for Hydrology (EA)
NAH .... Nordic Association for the Handicapped (EA)
NAH .... Nordic Association of Hairdressers [Sweden] (EAIO)
NAH .... Not at Home
NAH .... Nutrition Action Health Letter (SAUS)
NAHA.......... National Association for Holistic Aromatherapy (NTPA)
NAHA.......... National Association of Handwriting Analysts
NAHA.......... National Association of Health Authorities [British] (EAIO)
NAHA.......... National Association of Health Authorities in England and Wales (AIE)
NAHA.......... National Association of Hotel Accountants [Later, International Association of Hospitality Accountants] (EA)
NAHA.......... North American Highway Association
NAHA.......... Norwegian-American Historical Association (EA)
NAHAD........ National Association of Hose and Accessories Distributors (EA)
Nahal.......... Na'or Halutsi Lohem [Fighting Pioneer Youth] [Israel] (AD)
NAHAL........ Noar Halutzi Lohem [Pioneering Fighting Youth] [Israel]
NAHAM...... National Association of Healthcare Access Management (EA)
NAHAM...... National Association of Hospital Admitting Managers (EA)
NAHAT........ National Association of Health Authorities and Trusts [British] (EAIO)
NAHAWA..... North American Heating and Airconditioning Wholesalers Association
NAHB .... National Alliance of Homebased Businesswomen [Defunct] (EA)
NAHB .... National Association of Home Builders (NADA)
NAHB .... National Association of Home Builders of the United States (EA)
NAHB .... National Association of Homes for Boys [Later, NFCCE]
NAHBB........ National Association of Home Based Businesses [Baltimore, MD]
NAHBE........ Naval Academy Heat Balanced Engine [Pronounced "knobby"]
NAHBO........ National Association of Hospital Broadcasting Organizations [British] (DBA)
NAHB/RC.... NAHB Remodelers Council (EA)
NAHC.......... National Advisory Health Council
NAHC.......... National Anti-Hunger Coalition (EA)
NAHC.......... National Association for Home Care (EA)
NAHC.......... National Association of Holiday Centres [British] (DBA)
NAHC.......... National Association of Homes for Children (EA)
NAHC.......... National Association of Housing Cooperatives (EA)
NAHC.......... North American Hunting Club (EA)
NAHCAC...... National Ad Hoc Committee Against Censorship (AD)
NAHCO........ National Association of Hispanic County Officials (NTPA)
NAHCR........ National Association of Healthcare Recruitment (EA)
NAHCS........ National Association of Health Career Schools (EA)
NAHCS........ National Association of Health Center Schools (DMAA)
NAHCSP...... National Association of Hospital Central Service Personnel [Later, IAHCSM] (EA)
NAHD.......... National Association for Hospital Development (EA)
NAHD.......... National Association for Human Development (EA)
NAHD.......... National Association of Hillel Directors [Later, IAHD] (EA)
NAHDDM .... National Association of House and Daytime Dress Manufacturers (EA)
NAHDO....... National Association of Health Data Organizations (EA)
NAHDSA...... National Association of Hebrew Day School Administrators (EA)
NAHE.......... National Alliance for Hydroelectric Energy (EA)
NAHE.......... National Association for Holocaust Education (EA)

NAHE.......... National Association for Humanities Education (EA)
NAHEE........ National Association for Humane and Environmental Education (EA)
NAHEM........ National Association of Health Estates Managers [British] (DBA)
NAHEMA...... NATO Helicopter Management Agency (SAUS)
NAHES........ National Association of Home Economics Supervisors [Later, NASSVHE] (EA)
NAHFAGIF.... National Archives and Historical Foundation of the American GI Forum
NAHFE........ National Association of Hispanic Federal Executives (EA)
NAHFO........ National Association of Hospital Fire Officers [British] (DBA)
NAHG.......... National Association of Homoeopathic Groups [British] (DBA)
NAHG.......... National Association of Humanistic Gerontology (EA)
NAHGT........ National Aboriginal Health Goals and Targets [Australia]
NAHHA........ National Association of Home Health Agencies [Later, NAHC] (EA)
NAHHH........ National Association of Hospital Hospitality Houses (EA)
NAHHIC....... National Association of House to House Installment Companies [Later, NAIC] (EA)
NAHI .... National Association of Home Inspectors (NTPA)
NAHI .... National Athletic Health Institute (EA)
NAHICUS ..... Nuclear Attack Hazards in the Continental United States
NAHIM........ National Association of Housing Information Managers (NTPA)
NAHIS......... National Arts and Handicapped Information Service (EA)
NAHJ........... National Association of Hispanic Journalists (EA)
NAHL........... North American Hockey League
NAHL........... North American Holding Corp. (SAUS)
NAHLS......... National Association of Hispanic and Latino Studies (NTPA)
NAHM .... National Association of Home Manufacturers [Later, HMC] (EA)
NAHM .... National Association of Hosiery Manufacturers (EA)
NAHM .... Norwegian-American Historical Museum (SAUS)
NAHMA........ National Affordable Housing Management Association (NTPA)
NAHMA........ National Assisted Housing Management Association (NTPA)
NAHMA........ National Association of Hotel and Motel Accountants [Later, International Association of Hospitality Accountants]
NAHMOR ..... National Association of HMO [Health Maintenance Organization] Regulators
NAHMS....... National Animal Health Monitoring System (SAUS)
NAHN.......... National Association of Hispanic Nurses (EA)
NAHNS........ National Association of the Holy Name Society (EA)
NAHO.......... National Association of Hearing Officials (NTPA)
NAHO.......... National Association of Homeowners [British] (DBA)
NAHOD .... N-Acetylhexosamine Oxidase (DB)
NAHP.......... National Association of Hispanic Publications (EA)
NAHP.......... National Association of Horseradish Packers [Defunct] (EA)
NAHP.......... National Association of Hypnotists and Psychotherapists [British] (DBA)
NAHPA........ National Association of Hospital Purchasing Agents [Later, NAHPMM] (EA)
NAHPM....... National Association of Hospital Purchasing Management [Later, NAHP MM] (EA)
NAHPMM..... National Association of Hospital Purchasing Materials Management (EA)
NAHPS......... North American Habitat Preservation Society (EA)
NAHQ.......... National Association for Healthcare Quality (EA)
NAHRMP...... National Association of Hotel and Restaurant Meat Purveyors [Later, NAMP] (EA)
NAHRO .... National Association of Housing and Redevelopment Officials (EA)
NAHRW....... National Association of Human Rights Workers (EA)
NAHS.......... National Aboriginal Health Strategy [Australia]
NAHS.......... National Association of Health Stores [British] (DBA)
NAHS.......... National Association of Horological Schools (EA)
NAHS.......... New American High Schools [Initiative]
NAHS.......... North American Heather Society (EA)
NAHS.......... North American Hernia Society (NTPA)
NAHS.......... North American Hyperthermia Society (SAUS)
NAHSA........ National Association for Hearing and Speech Action (EA)
NAHSA........ National Association of Hearing and Speech Agencies (AEBS)
NAHSA........ North American Horticultural Supply Association (EA)
NAHSC........ National Association of Homes and Services for Children (EA)
NAHSC........ National Automated Highway System Consortium
NAHSE........ National Association of Health Services Executives (EA)
NAHSL........ North Atlantic Health Sciences Libraries
NAHSO........ National Association of Hospital Supplies Officers [British] (BI)
NAHSPO...... National Association of Health Service Personnel Officers [British] (DBA)
NAHSQCD... National Association of Human Service Quality Control Directors (NTPA)
NAHSSO ..... National Association of Health Service Security Officers [British] (DBA)
NAHST........ National Association of Human Services Technologies [Defunct] (EA)
NAHSTA...... National Hiking and Ski Touring Association (AD)
NAHSWP..... National Aboriginal Health Strategy Working Party [Australia]
NAHT.......... National Association of Head Teachers [British]
NAHU.......... NAHU, an Association of Bull Users [Formerly, North American Honeywell Users Association]
NAHU.......... National Association of Health Underwriters [Washington, DC] (EA)
NAHU.......... North American Honeywell Users Association (SAUS)
NAHUC........ National Association of Health Unit Clerks-Coordinators (EA)
NAHUC........ National Association of Health Unit Coordinators [Formerly, National Association of Health Unit Clerks-Coordinators] (EA)
NAHW......... National Association of Hardwood Wholesalers [Defunct]
NAHWMUMC... National Association of Health and Welfare Ministries of the United Methodist Church [Later, United Methodist Association of Health and Welfare Ministries - UMA] (EA)
NAHWW....... National Association of Home and Workshop Writers (EA)
NAI.............. Annai [Guyana] [Airport symbol] (OAG)

NAI .... N-Acetylimidazole [*Organic chemistry*]
NAI .... Nairobi [*Kenya*] [*Seismograph station code, US Geological Survey*] (SEIS)
NAI .... Named Areas of Interest [*Army intelligence matrix*] (INF)
NAI .... Nanjing Aeronautical Institute [*China*] (BUAC)
NAI .... National Agricultural Institute [*Later, ACA*] (EA)
NAI .... National Apple Institute [*Later, IAI*] (EA)
NAI .... National Association of Independent Insurance Auditors and Engineers (NTPA)
NAI .... National Association of Instructors (BUAC)
NAI .... National Association of Interpretation (EA)
NAI .... Natural Alternatives International [*AMEX symbol*] (SPSG)
NAI .... Negro Airmen International (EA)
NAI .... Net Acid Input [*Medicine*] (DB)
NAI .... Net Annual Inflow [*Pensions*]
NAI .... Netherlands Arbitration Institute (ILCA)
NAI .... Network Associates, Inc. [*Computer science*]
NAI .... New Acronyms and Initialisms [*Later, NAIA*] [*A publication*]
NAI .... New Alchemy Institute [*Defunct*] (EA)
NAI .... No Accidental Injury (DMAA)
nai .... No Action Indicated (AD)
NAI .... No Action Indicated
NAI .... No Acute Infection (SAUS)
NAI .... No Acute Inflammation [*Medicine*] (DMAA)
nai .... No Address Instruction (AD)
NAI .... No-Address Instruction (AAG)
NAI .... No Airborne Intercept [*Fighter aircraft lacking airborne intercept RADAR*]
NAI .... Nonaccidental Injury
NAI .... Nonadherence Index (DMAA)
nai .... North American Indian [*MARC language code*] [*Library of Congress*] (LCCP)
NAI .... North American Internet Co.
NAI .... Northern Alberta Institute of Technology [*UTLAS symbol*]
NAI .... Northrop Aeronautical Institute [*Later, Northrop University*]
NAI .... Northrop Aircraft, Inc. (MCD)
NAI .... N'shei Agudath Israel (BJA)
NAI .... Nurse Attitudes Inventory (TES)
NAI .... Sodium Iodide (SAUS)
NAIA .... National Agricultural and Industrial Association [*Australia*]
NAIA .... National Association of Industrial Artists [*Later, IG*]
NAIA .... National Association of Insurance Agents [*Later, IIAA*] (EA)
NAIA .... National Association of Intercollegiate Athletics (EA)
NAIA .... New Acronyms, Initialisms, and Abbreviations [*Formerly, NAI*] [*A publication*]
NAIA .... North American Indian Association (EA)
NAIAD .... Nerve Agent Immobilised Enzyme Alarm and Detector (PDAA)
NAIB .... National Association of Independent Business [*Defunct*]
NAIB .... National Association of Insurance Brokers [*Washington, DC*] (EA)
NAIBD .... National Association of Industries for the Blind and Disabled [*British*] (DBA)
NAIC .... National Adoption Information Clearinghouse (EA)
NAIC .... National Advice and Information Centre for Outdoor Education [*Doncaster Metropolitan Institute of Higher Education*] [*British*] (CB)
NAIC .... National AIDS [*Acquired Immune Deficiency Syndrome*] Information Clearinghouse [*Information service or system*] (IID)
NAIC .... National Air Intelligence Center
NAIC .... National Art Industry Council [*Australia*]
NAIC .... National Association of Installment Companies [*New York, NY*] (EA)
NAIC .... National Association of Insurance Commissioners [*Kansas City, MO*] (EA)
NAIC .... National Association of Intercollegiate Commissioners (EA)
NAIC .... National Association of Investment Clubs [*British*] (DBA)
NAIC .... National Association of Investment Companies
NAIC .... National Association of Investors Corp. (EA)
NAIC .... National Astronomy and Ionosphere Center [*Ithaca, NY*] [*National Science Foundation*]
NAIC .... NATO Intelligence Centre (SAUS)
NAIC .... Naval Aircraft Investigation Center (AD)
NAIC .... Network Applications and Information Center
NAIC .... Newly Agro-Industrialized Country (SAUS)
NAIC .... Nigerian Army Intelligence Corps (SAUS)
NAIC .... Nuclear Accident and Incident Control [*Army*] (AABC)
NAICA .... National American Indian Cattlemen's Association (EA)
NAICC .... National Alliance of Independent Crop Consultants (EA)
NAICC .... National Association of Independent Computer Companies
NAICC .... Navigation-Aided Intelligent Cruise Control [*Automotive engineering*]
NAICC .... Nuclear Accident and Incident Control Center [*Army*] (AABC)
NAICCA .... National American Indian Court Clerks Association (EA)
NAICJA .... National American Indian Court Judges Association (EA)
NAICO .... Nuclear Accident and Incident Control Officer [*Army*] (AABC)
NAICOM/MIS... Navy Integrated Command Management Information System
NAICP .... Nuclear Accident and Incident Control Plan [*Army*]
NAICPS .... National Association of Independent Colleges and Private Schools (EA)
NAICS .... North American Industry Classification System (AAGC)
NAICU .... National Association of Independent Colleges and Universities (EA)
NAICV .... National Association of Ice Cream Vendors [*Defunct*] (EA)
NAID .... National Associations for Improved Depressives [*Defunct*] (EA)
NAID .... National Association of Industrial Distributors [*British*] (DBA)
NAID .... National Association of Installation Developers (EA)
NAID .... National Association of Interior Designers [*Defunct*] (EA)
NAIDA .... National Agricultural and Industrial Development Association [*Republic of Ireland*] (BI)

NAIDM .... National Association of Insecticide and Disinfectant Manufacturers (BUAC)
NAIDS .... North Atlantic Institute for Defense Studies (or Study) (SAUS)
NAIDST .... National AIDS Trust [*British*]
NAIEA .... National Association of Inspectors and Educational Advisers [*British*]
NAIEC .... National Association for Industry-Education Cooperation [*Buffalo, NY*] (EA)
NAIEHS .... National Association of Importers and Exporters of Hides and Skins [*Later, USHSLA*] (EA)
NAIEM .... National Association of Insect Electrocutor Manufacturers (EA)
NAIEO .... National Association of Inspectors of Schools and Educational Organisers [*British*] (BI)
NAIES .... National Adoption Information Exchange System [*Formerly, ARENA*] (EA)
NAIES .... National Association of Interdisciplinary Ethnic Studies (EA)
NAIF .... National Association for Irish Freedom (EA)
NAIF .... Navigation Ancillary Information Facility (ACAE)
NAIF .... Navigation and Ancillary Information Facility (RALS)
NAIF .... Nordiska Akademiska Idrottsforbund [*Scandinavian Federation for University Sport*] (EA)
NAIFA .... National Association of Independent Fee Appraisers (EA)
NAIFR .... National Association of Independent Food Retailers [*Defunct*] (EA)
NAIG .... National Insurance Group [*NASDAQ symbol*] (NQ)
NAIG .... Natl Insurance Group [*NASDAQ symbol*] (TTSB)
NAIG .... Nippon Atomic Industry Group [*Japan*]
NAIHC .... National American Indian Housing Council (EA)
NAII .... National Association of Ice Industries [*Later, PIA*]
NAII .... National Association of Independent Insurers [*Des Plaines, IL*] (EA)
NAII .... Natural Alternatives International [*NASDAQ symbol*] (SAG)
NAIIA .... National Association of Independent Insurance Adjusters [*Chicago, IL*] (EA)
NAIIU .... Not Authorized If Issued Under [*Army*]
NAIJ .... National Association for Irish Justice [*Superseded by National Association for Irish Freedom*] (EA)
NAIL .... National Argo Industries Ltd. [*Seychelles*] (BUAC)
NAIL .... National Association for Independent Living (EA)
NAIL .... National Association of Independent Lubes (EA)
NAIL .... National Association of Independent Lumbermen [*Defunct*] (EA)
NAIL .... Naval Aircraft Inventory Log (AD)
NAIL .... Neurotics Anonymous International Liaison (EA)
NAIL .... New African Investments, Ltd (SAUS)
NAIL .... North American Indian Landmarks [*A publication*]
NAILBA .... National Association of Independent Life Brokerage Agencies [*Washington, DC*] (EA)
NAILD .... National Association of Independent Lighting Distributors (EA)
NAILDD .... North American Interlibrary Loan and Document Delivery [*Project*] (TELE)
NAILG .... National Awards for Innovation in Local Government [*Australia*]
NAILM .... National Association of Institutional Laundry Managers [*Later, National Association of Institutional Linen Management*] (EA)
NAILM .... National Association of Institutional Linen Management (EA)
NAILS .... Albany Law School (SAUS)
NAILS .... National Airspace Integrated Logistics Support [*FAA*] (TAG)
NAILS .... National Automated Immigration Lookout System [*Immigration and Naturalization Service*]
NAILS .... Naval Aviation Integrated Logistic Support Task Force (NG)
NAILSC .... Naval Aviation Integrated Logistic Support Center (MCD)
NAILTE .... National Association of Instructional Leaders in Technical Education (EA)
NAIM .... NAIM [*North American Indian Mission*] Ministries (EA)
NAIM .... Number Allocation and Inspection Module (PDAA)
NAIMA .... North American Indian Museums Association (EA)
NAIMA .... North American Insulation Manufacturers Association (NTPA)
NAIMD .... National Association of Independent Music Dealers [*Defunct*] (EA)
NAIME .... National Association of Independent Maritime Educators (EA)
NAIMIS .... NAVAIRSYSCOM [*Naval Air Systems Command*] Integrated Management InformationSystem (DNAB)
NAIMS .... National Airspace Information System [*BTS*] (TAG)
NAIMSAL .... National Anti-Imperialist Movement in Solidarity with African Liberation (EA)
NAION .... Nonarteritic Anterior Ischemic Optic Neuropathy
NAIOP .... National Association of Industrial and Office Parks (EA)
NAIOP .... Navigational Aid Inoperative for Parts
naiop .... Navigational Aids Inoperative for Parts (AD)
NAIP .... National Assault on Illiteracy Program (EA)
NAIP .... National Association of Independent Publishers (EA)
NAIP .... National Association of Industrial Parks [*Later, NAIOP*]
NAIP .... National Association of Insured Persons [*Defunct*] (EA)
NAIP .... Neuronal Apoptosis Inhibitory Protein [*Genetics*]
NAIP .... Neuronal Apoptposos Inhibitory Protein [*Cytology*]
NAIPFA .... National Association of Independent Public Finance Advisors
NAIPR .... National Association of Independent Publishers Representatives (NTPA)
NAIPRC .... Netherlands Automated Information Processing Research Centre (NITA)
NAIPTS .... National Amalgamated Iron Plate Trade Society [*A union*] [*British*]
NAIR .... Narrow Absorption Infrared
NAIR .... National Arrangements for Incidents Involving Radioactivity [*Nuclear energy*] (NUCP)
NAIR .... National Association of Independent Resurfacers (EA)
NAIR .... National Association of Independent Retailers [*Ireland*] (BUAC)
NAIR .... Naval Air Systems Command Headquarters (ACAE)
NAIR .... Network Action Item Report (MCD)
NAIR .... Nonadrenergic Inhibitory Response (DB)
NAIRA .... Northamerican Industrial Representatives Association (NTPA)

NAIRD	National Association of Independent Record Distributors and Manufacturers (EA)
NAIRDM	National Association of Independent Record Distributors and Manufacturers (EA)
NAIRE	National Association of Internal Revenue Employees [*Later, NTEU*] (EA)
NAIREC	Nimbus Arctic Ice Reconnaissance [*Canadian project*]
Nairns	Nairnshire, Scotland (AD)
NAIRO	National Association of Intergroup Relations Officials [*Later, NAHRW*] (EA)
NAIRS	National Athletic Injury/Illness Reporting System [*Pennsylvania State University*] [*Defunct*]
NAIRS	Navy Aircraft and Readiness System
NAIRU	Naval Air Intelligence Reserve Units
NAIRU	Non-Accelerating-Inflation Rate of Unemployment
NAIS	National Administrative Information System [*Computer science*] (IID)
NAIS	National Aquaculture Information System (NOAA)
NAIS	National Association for Information Services (EA)
NAIS	National Association of Independent Schools (EA)
NAIS	National Association of Investigative Specialists (EA)
NAIS	Navy Attitudinal Information System (NVT)
NAIS	Neutral Administrative Inspection Scheme (COE)
NAIS	Neutral Administrative Inspection System (SAUS)
NAIS	Night Attack Interdiction System
NAISC	National American Indian Safety Council (EA)
NAISEO	National Association of Inspectors of Schools and Educational Organisers [*British*]
NAISS	National Association of Iron and Steel Stockholders (AD)
NAIT	National Alliance for Infusion Therapy [*An association*]
NAIT	National Association of Industrial Technologists
NAIT	National Association of Industrial Technology (EA)
NAIT	Naval Air Intermediate Training
NAIT	North American Islamic Trust (EA)
NAIT	Northern Alberta Institute of Technology [*Edmonton, AB*]
NAITA	National Association of Independent Travel Agents (BUAC)
NAI Tc	NAI Technologies [*Associated Press*] (SAG)
NAIT(C)	Naval Air Intermediate Training (Command)
NAITE	National Association of Industrial Teacher Educators [*Later, NAITTE*] (EA)
NAI Tech	NAI Technologies [*Associated Press*] (SAG)
NAITF	Naval Air Intercept Training Facility (MUGU)
NAITP	National Association of Income Tax Preparers [*Defunct*] (EA)
NAITPD	National Association of Independent Television Producers and Distributors [*Defunct*] (EA)
NAITTE	National Association of Industrial and Technical Teacher Educators (EA)
NAIVPP	National Association of Independent Veterinary Practices and Practitioners (GVA)
NAIW	National Association of Insurance Women (International) [*Tulsa, OK*] (EA)
NAIWA	North American Indian Women's Association (EA)
NAIWC	National Association of Inland Water Carriers [*British*] (BI)
NAIWC	National Association of Inland Waterway Carriers [*British*] (DBA)
NaIX	Sodium Isopropyl Xanthogenate (SAUS)
NAIY	National Association of Indian Youth (BUAC)
NAJ	Napierville Junction Railway Co. [*Later, NJ*] [*AAR code*]
NAJ	National Academy of Jazz (EA)
NAJ	National Aeronautics and Space Administration, Johnson Space Center, Houston, TX [*OCLC symbol*] (OCLC)
NAJ	National Association for Justice
NAJA	National Association of Jewelry Appraisers (EA)
NAJA	National Association of Junior Auxiliaries (EA)
NAJA	North American Judges Association [*Later, AJA*]
NAJAE	National Association of Jai Alai Frontons (NTPA)
NAJAFRA	National Jazz Fraternity
NAJAG	North African Judge Advocate General's Section [*World War II*]
NAJAKS	Nordic Association for Japanese and Korean Studies (BUAC)
NAJAS	National Association of Japan-America Societies
NAJC	National Assessment of Juvenile Correction [*University of Michigan*] (AD)
NAJC	Northern Australia Jockey Club (AD)
NAJC	Northwest Alabama Junior College (AD)
NAJCA	National Association of Juvenile Correctional Agencies (EA)
NAJCW	National Association of Jewish Center Workers [*Later, AJCW*] (EA)
NAJD	National Association of Journalism Directors [*Later, JEA*] (EA)
NAJD/MBAP	National Association of JD/MBA [*Juris Doctor/Master of Business Administration*] Professionals [*Defunct*] (EA)
NAJE	National Association of Jazz Education (AD)
NAJE	National Association of Jazz Educators [*Later, IAJE*] (EA)
NAJEM	North African Joint Economic Mission [*World War II*]
NAJF	National Association of Jai Alai Frontons (EA)
NAJFCHP	National Association of Jewish Family, Children's, and Health Professionals (EA)
NAJHA	National Association of Jewish Homes for the Aged [*Later, NAAJHHA*] (EA)
NAJHHA	North American Association of Jewish Homes and Housing for the Aging (EA)
NAJIT	National Association of Judiciary Interpreters and Translators (NTPA)
NAJLA	North American Junior Limousin Association (EA)
NAJRC	North African Joint Rearmament Committee [*World War II*]
NAJSA	North American Jewish Students Appeal (EA)
NAJSN	North American Jewish Students' Network (EA)
NAJU	Nordic Association of Journalists' Unions (EA)
NAJVS	National Association of Jewish Vocational Services (EA)
NAJYC	North American Jewish Youth Council [*Defunct*] (EA)

NAK	Nakhichevan [*Former USSR*] [*Seismograph station code, US Geological Survey*] [*Closed*] (SEIS)
NAK	National Auto Credit, Inc. [*NYSE symbol*] (SAG)
NAK	Negative Acknowledge [*or Acknowledgment*] [*Data communication*]
nak	Negative Acknowledge Character [*Computer science*] (AD)
NAK	Negative Acknowledge Character (ECII)
nak	Negative Knowledge (AD)
NAK	Network Acknowledgment
NAK	No Acknowledgement (SAUS)
NAK	Non-Acknowledge (SAUS)
NAK	Non-Acknowledgment (SAUS)
NAK	Not Acknowledged (SAUS)
nak	Nothing Adverse Known (AD)
NAK	Nothing Adverse Known (ADA)
NaK	Sodium-Potassium (SAUS)
NaK	Sodium-Potassium Alloy (SAUS)
Na K-ATPase	Adenosine Triphosphatase (Na, K-Activated) [*An enzyme*]
NAKBA	National Association to Keep and Bear Arms (EA)
nakl	Naklad [*Edition*] [*Polish*] (AD)
nakl	Nakladatel [*Edition*] [*Czech*] (AD)
NAKMAS	National Association of Karate & Martial Arts Schools (BUAC)
NAKN	National Anti-Klan Network (EA)
NAKOSTA	Natural Convection in the Stationary Condition [*Computer program*]
NAKS	North American Kant Society (EA)
NAl	Albany Public Library, Albany, NY [*Library symbol*] [*Library of Congress*] (LCLS)
NAL	N-Acetyllactopamine [*Biochemistry*]
NAL	Naloxone [*A drug*]
NAL	Name, Address, and Legal File [*Real estate*]
NAL	National Accelerator Laboratory [*AEC*]
NAL	National Acoustics Laboratory [*Australia*] (ECON)
NAL	National Aeronautical Laboratory (MCD)
NAL	National Aerospace Laboratory
NAL	National Agricultural Library [*Department of Agriculture*] [*Beltsville, MD*]
NAL	National Airlines (AD)
NAL	National Assistance League (EA)
NAL	National Association of Laity (EA)
NAL	National Association of Landowners (EA)
NAL	National Astronomical League
NAL	Naval Aeronautical Laboratory
NAL	Negro American League [*Baseball*] (NDBD)
NAL	NetWare Application Launcher [*Computer science*] (VLIE)
NAL	New Aalesund [*Norway*] [*Geomagnetic observatory code*]
NAL	Newalta Corp. [*Toronto Stock Exchange symbol*]
NAL	New American Library [*Publisher*]
NAL	New Assembly Language
NAL	Nigeria America Line (AD)
NAL	Niue Airways Ltd. (EY)
NAL	No Activity Log (MCD)
NAL	Noise Abatement League (SAUS)
NAL	Nonadherent Leukocyte (DB)
NAL	Non-Associated Labor (WDAA)
NAL	North American Library (SAUS)
NAL	North American Lighting [*Automotive industry supplier*]
NAL	Northway Aviation Ltd. [*Canada*] [*ICAO designator*] (FAAC)
NAL	Northwest Air Lines (SAUS)
NAL	Norwegian America Line
NAL	Novell Application Launcher [*Computer science*]
NAL	Numerical Analysis Laboratory (MCD)
nal	Sodium Iodide [*Pharmacology*] (DAVI)
NAlA	Albany Medical College, Albany, NY [*Library symbol*] [*Library of Congress*] (LCLS)
NALA	National Academy of Literary Arts (EA)
NALA	National Adult Literacy Agency [*Ireland*] (BUAC)
NALA	National Affiliation for Literacy Advance (EA)
NALA	National Agricultural Limestone Association [*Later, National Limestone Institute*]
NALA	National Association of Language Advisers [*British*]
NALA	National Association of Legal Assistants (EA)
NALAA	National Assembly of Local Arts Agencies (EA)
NALAC	National Association of Local Arts Councils (BUAC)
NALAM	National Association of Livestock Auction Markets
NAlb	Shelter Rock Public Library, Albertson, NY [*Library symbol*] [*Library of Congress*] (LCLS)
NALBA	North American Log Builders Association (EA)
NAlBC	Albany Business College, Albany, NY [*Library symbol*] [*Library of Congress*] (LCLS)
NAlbH	Human Resources Center, Albertson, NY [*Library symbol*] [*Library of Congress*] (LCLS)
NAlbHM	Herricks Middle School, Albertson, NY [*Library symbol*] [*Library of Congress*] (LCLS)
NAlbi	Swan Library, Albion, NY [*Library symbol*] [*Library of Congress*] (LCLS)
NAlbiH	Arnold Gregory Memorial Hospital, Albion, NY [*Library symbol*] [*Library of Congress*] (LCLS)
NAlbME	Meadow Drive Elementary School, Albertson, NY [*Library symbol*] [*Library of Congress*]
NALBOH	National Association of Local Boards of Health
NAlbSE	Searington Elementary School, Albertson, NY [*Library symbol*] [*Library of Congress*] (LCLS)
NALC	National Afro-American Labor Council (EA)
NALC	National Association of Ladies Circles of Great Britain and Ireland (BUAC)
NALC	National Association of Laryngectomee Clubs [*British*] (DBA)

NALC .... National Association of Lawyers for Children (BUAC)
NALC .... National Association of Letter Carriers of the USA (EA)
NALC .... National Association of Life Companies [*Washington, DC*] (EA)
NALC .... National Association of Litho Clubs (EA)
NALC .... National Association of Local Councils [*British*]
NALC .... National Association of Louisiana Catahoulas (EA)
NALC .... Natl Lodging [*NASDAQ symbol*] (TTSB)
NALC .... Naval Aviation Logistics Center (NVT)
NALC .... Navy Ammunition Logistics Code
NALC .... New Age Learning Center [*Defunct*] (EA)
NALC .... North American Landscape Characterization (SAUS)
NALCC .... National Automatic Laundry and Cleaning Council (EA)
NALCD .... National Agricultural Library and Centre for Documentation [*Hungary*] (BUAC)
NALCDVE..... National Association of Large City Directors of Vocational Education (EA)
NAICI .... Center for International Studies, Albany, NY [*Library symbol*] [*Library of Congress*] (LCLS)
NAICJ.......... New York State Division of Criminal Justice Services, Albany, NY [*Library symbol*] [*Library of Congress*] (LCLS)
NALCM .... National Association of Lace Curtain Manufacturers [*Defunct*]
Nalco.......... Nalco Chemical Co. [*Associated Press*] (SAG)
NALCO .... Naval Air Logistics Control Office
NALCO .... Newfoundland & Labrador Corp.
NALCOEASTPAC... Naval Air Logistics Control Office Eastern Pacific (DNAB)
NALCOEURREP... Naval Air Logistics Control Office European Representative
NALCOLANT... Naval Air Logistics Control Office Atlantic
NALCOM...... Naval Logistics Command (SAUS)
NALCOMIS... Naval Aviation Logistics Command Management Information System (MCD)
NALCOMIS-OS... Naval Air Logistics Command Management Information System for Operating and Support (DNAB)
NALCON....... Navy Laboratory Computer Network
NALCOPAC... Naval Air Logistics Control Office Pacific
NALCOPACREP... Naval Air Logistics Control Office Pacific Representative
NALCOREP... Naval Air Logistics Control Office Representative
NALCOWESTPAC... Naval Air Logistics Control Office Western Pacific (DNAB)
NALCOWESTPACREP... Naval Air Logistics Control Office Western Pacific Representative (DNAB)
NAICSR........ College of Saint Rose, Albany, NY [*Library symbol*] [*Library of Congress*] (LCLS)
NAID .... Dudley Observatory, Albany, NY [*Library symbol*] [*Library of Congress*] (LCLS)
NALD .... National Association of Limbless and Disabled [*British*] (DBA)
NALD .... National Association of Limbless Disabled (BUAC)
NALD .... Nonattainment Areas Lacking Demonstrations [*Environmental science*] (COE)
NALDA.......... Naval Aviation Logistics Data Analysis (NVT)
NaLDAP........ National Learning Disabilities Assistance Project
NALDEF........ Native American Legal Defense and Education Foundation (EA)
NAIDH.......... New York State Department of Health, Division of Laboratories and Research, Albany, NY [*Library symbol*] [*Library of Congress*] (LCLS)
NAIDS.......... New York State Department of State, Community Affairs Library, Albany, NY [*Library symbol*] [*Library of Congress*] (LCLS)
NALEAO....... National Association of Latino Elected and Appointed Officials (AD)
NALECOM.... National Law Enforcement Telecommunications System
NALED .... National Association of Limited Edition Dealers (EA)
NAleNH........ E. J. Noble Hospital, Medical Library, Alexandria Bay, NY [*Library symbol*] [*Library of Congress*] (LCLS)
NALEO .... National Association of Latino Elected and Appointed Officials (EA)
NAlf .... Alfred University, Alfred, NY [*Library symbol*] [*Library of Congress*] (LCLS)
NALF............ NAL Financial Group, Inc. [*NASDAQ symbol*] (SAG)
NALF............ National Agricultural Legal Fund [*Defunct*] (EA)
NALF............ Naval Auxiliary Landing Field (NG)
NALF............ Negro American Literature Forum [*A publication*] (ANEX)
NALF............ North American Limousin Foundation (EA)
NALF............ North American Loon Fund (EA)
NAlfC .... State University of New York, College of Ceramics at Alfred University, Alfred, NY [*Library symbol*] [*Library of Congress*] (LCLS)
NALFMA ...... National Association of Law Firm Marketing Administrators (EA)
NAL Fn .... NAL Financial Group, Inc. [*Associated Press*] (SAG)
NAlf-ST........ Alfred University, School of Theology, Alfred, NY [*Library symbol*] [*Library of Congress*] [*Obsolete*] (LCLS)
NAlfUA......... State University of New York, Agricultural and Technical College at Alfred, Alfred, NY [*Library symbol*] [*Library of Congress*] (LCLS)
NALG .... National Association for Loss and Grief [*Australia*]
NALG .... National Association of Left-Handed Golfers (EA)
NALGA......... National Association of Local Government Auditors (NTPA)
NALGAP........ National Association of Lesbian/Gay Alcoholism Professionals (EA)
NALGG......... National Association for Lesbian and Gay Gerontology (AD)
NALGHW...... National Association of Local Governments on Hazardous Wastes (EA)
NALGM .... National Association of Lawn and Garden Manufacturers [*Defunct*] (EA)
NALGM .... National Association of Leather Glove Manufacturers [*Later, NAGM*]
NALGO......... National and Local Government Officers' Association [*British*]
NALGO......... National Association of Local Government Officers (AIE)
NAIGS.......... United States Geological Survey, Water Resources Services, New York District, Albany, NY [*Library symbol*] [*Library of Congress*] (LCLS)
NALGWC...... National Association of Local Government Women's Committees (BUAC)
NAIH .... Hospital Educational and Research Fund, Inc., Albany, NY [*Library symbol*] [*Library of Congress*] (LCLS)
NALHC......... National Acoustic Laboratories Hearing Center [*Australia*]
NALHC......... North American Log Homes Council (EA)
NALHF .... National Association of Leagues of Hospital Friends [*British*] (DI)
NALHI .... National Authority for the Ladies Handbag Industry (EA)
NALHM .... National Association of Licensed House Managers [*Pronounced "nalem"*] [*A union*] [*British*] (DCTA)
NAII .... Albany Institute of History of Art, Albany, NY [*Library symbol*] [*Library of Congress*] (LCLS)
NALI............. National Agricultural Limestone Institute [*Later, National Limestone Institute*]
NALI............. National Association of Legal Investigators (EA)
NALI............. National Association of the Launderette Industry [*British*] (DBA)
NALI............. North Atlantic Lobster Institute (EA)
NALIC .... National Association of Loft Insulation Contractors [*British*] (DI)
NALIN .... National Library Information Network (TELE)
NALIS .... Nevada Academic Libraries Information System (SAUS)
NAIJ............. Junior College of Albany, Albany, NY [*Library symbol*] [*Library of Congress*] (LCLS)
NALJS.......... Nordic Atomic Libraries Joint Secretariat [*Information service or system*] (IID)
NALLA .... National Long-Lines Agency (NATG)
NALLADS..... Norway Army Low Level Air Defense System (ACAE)
NALLADS..... Norwegian Army Low Level Air Defence System (SAUS)
NALLD .... National Association of Learning Laboratory Directors [*Later, IALL*]
NAILL........... New York State Department of Law Library, Albany, NY [*Library symbol*] [*Library of Congress*] (LCLS)
NALLO .... National Association of License Law Officials [*Later, NARELLO*] (EA)
NAILS .... Albany Law School, Albany, NY [*Library symbol*] [*Library of Congress*] (LCLS)
NALLS .... National Aboriginal Literacy and Language Strategy [*Australia*]
NAIM .... Maria College, Albany, NY [*Library symbol*] [*Library of Congress*] (LCLS)
NALM........... National Association for Lay Ministry (EA)
NALM........... National Association of Lift Makers [*British*] (BI)
NALMA .... North American Land Mammal Age [*Geological epoch*]
NALMC .... National Association of Labor-Management Committees (EA)
NALMCO...... International Association of Lighting Management Companies (EA)
NALMCO...... National Association of Lighting Maintenance Contractors (EA)
NAIMem ...... Memorial Hospital, Medical Library, Albany, NY [*Library symbol*] [*Library of Congress*] (LCLS)
NAIMH......... New York State Department of Mental Hygiene, Mental Hygiene Research Library, Albany, NY [*Library symbol*] [*Library of Congress*] (LCLS)
NALMS .... North American Lake Management Society (EA)
NAIMV .... New York State Department of Motor Vehicles, Research Library, Albany, NY [*Library symbol*] [*Library of Congress*] (LCLS)
NALN .... National Agricultural Libraries Network [*National Agricultural Library*]
NALN .... Native Authority Legal Notice [*Northern Nigeria*] [*A publication*] (DLA)
NALN .... North African Liaison Section [*World War II*]
NALNET .... NASA Library Network [*NASA*] [*Washington, DC*] [*Library network*] (MCD)
NALO .... National Association of Launderette Owners (BUAC)
NALO .... National Association of Launderette Owners Ltd. [*British*] (BI)
NALO .... Naval Air Liaison Officer
NALO .... Naval Air Logistics Office (DOMA)
NALO .... Nitride Assisted Lift-Off (TIMI)
NALOG......... Natural Logarithm (IAA)
NALOH......... National Association Legions of Honor (EA)
NALOP.......... NATO Letter of Promulgation
NALOPKT..... Not a lot of people know that (SAUS)
NALOXONE... N-Allylnoroxymorphone [*Narcotic antagonist*]
NAIP .... Albany College of Pharmacy, Albany, NY [*Library symbol*] [*Library of Congress*] (LCLS)
NALP .... National Association for Law Placement (EA)
NALPA .... National American Legion Press Association (EA)
NALPM .... National Association of Lithographic Plate Manufacturers [*Defunct*] (EA)
NALPN .... National Association of Licensed Practical Nurses (EA)
NALR .... National Acid Lakes Registry [*Environmental Protection Agency*]
NALR .... National Association of Lighting Representatives (EA)
NALR .... North American Liturgy Resources (BUAC)
NALRET .... National Association for Learning Resources Educational Technology (BUAC)
NALS .... National Advisory Logistics Staff (NATG)
NALS .... National Association of Laboratory Suppliers [*Defunct*] (EA)
NALS .... National Association of Labor Students [*British*] (DI)
NALS .... National Association of Legal Secretaries (International) [*Tulsa, OK*] (EA)
NALS .... National Association of Lumber Salesmen (EA)
NALS .... Neonatal Advanced Life Support (NUJO)
NALS .... North American Lily Society (EA)
NAIS .... Saint Peter's Hospital, Albany, NY [*Library symbol*] [*Library of Congress*] (LCLS)
NALSA .... Native American Law Students Association (EA)
NALSA .... North American Land Sailing Association (AD)
NALSAP .... National Association of Leadership for Student Assistance Programs (NTPA)
NALSAS .... National Association for Legal Support of Alternative Schools (EA)
NALSAT .... National Association of Land Settlement Association Tenants (AD)
NALSC .... National Association of Legal Search Consultants (NTPA)
NALSF .... National ALS [*Amyotrophic Lateral Sclerosis*] Foundation (EA)
NALSI .... National Association of Life Science Industries [*Defunct*] (EA)
NALSO .... National Association of Labour Student Organisations [*British*] (BI)

NAISS.......... New York State Department of Social Sciences, Social Services and Statistics Library, Albany, NY [Library symbol] [Library of Congress] (LCLS)

Nal St P....... Nalton's Collection of State Papers [A publication] (DLA)

NAISU.......... State University of New York, Union List of Serials, Albany, NY [Library symbol] [Library of Congress] (LCLS)

NALSVHE.... National Association of Local Supervisors of Vocational Home Economics (EA)

NALT............ Naltrexone [A drug]

NALT............ National Association of the Legitimate Theatre [Defunct] (EA)

Nal (TI)....... Thallium-Activated Sodium Iodide [Scintillation detector] [Medicine] (MEDA)

NAItL .... La Salette Seminary, Altamont, NY [Library symbol] [Library of Congress] (LCLS)

NALTOACS... Navy Laboratory Technical Office for ADP and Communication Systems (GFGA)

NALTS .... National Advertising Lead Tracking System [Navy] (NVT)

NALU .... National Association of Life Underwriters [Washington, DC] (EA)

NAIU .... State University of New York at Albany, Albany, NY [Library symbol] [Library of Congress] (LCLS)

NALUAS....... North American Life Union Assurance Society (EA)

NAIU-F .... State University of New York at Albany, Filmdex, Albany, NY [Library symbol] [Library of Congress] (LCLS)

NAIUHL....... Upper Hudson Library Federation, Albany, NY [Library symbol] [Library of Congress] (LCLS)

NAIU-L .... State University of New York at Albany Library School, Albany, NY [Library symbol] [Library of Congress] (LCLS)

NAIULS....... New York State Union List of Serials, Albany, NY [Library symbol] [Library of Congress] (LCLS)

NAIU-PA ..... State University of New York at Albany, Graduate School of Public Affairs, Albany, NY [Library symbol] [Library of Congress] (LCLS)

NALUS .... National Association of Leagues, Umpires, and Scorers (EA)

NALV .... National Association of Legal Vendors (NTPA)

NAIVA .... United States Veterans Administration Hospital, Albany, NY [Library symbol] [Library of Congress] (LCLS)

NALW .... Not an A-List Writer [Screenwriter's lexicon]

NAM............ N-Acetylmethionine [Organic chemistry]

NAM............ N-(Acridinyl)maleimide [Organic chemistry]

NAM............ Namangan [Former USSR] [Seismograph station code, US Geological Survey] [Closed] (SEIS)

NAM............ NAM Corp. [Associated Press] (SAG)

NAM............ Name and Address Module [Computer science] (VLIE)

NAM............ Named

NAM............ Namibia [ANSI three-letter standard code] (CNC)

NAM............ Namlea [Indonesia] [Airport symbol] (OAG)

NAM............ NASA Access Mechanism (ITCA)

NAM............ National Account Management [Bell System]

NAM............ National Aero Manufacturing (AD)

NAM............ National Air Museum [of the Smithsonian Institution] [Later, NASM]

NAM............ National Apple Month (EA)

NAM............ National Arbitration & Mediation

NAM............ National Army Museum [British military] (DMA)

NAM............ National Association of Manufacturers (NTCM)

NAM............ National Average Maintenance (VLIE)

NAM............ Natural Actomyosins [Biochemistry]

NAM............ Nautical Air Miles

NAM............ Naval Aircraft Modification

NAM............ Naval Air Material (SAA)

NAM............ Naval Air Mechanic [British military] (DMA)

NAM............ Naval Aviation Museum [Pensacola, FL]

NAM............ Navy Achievement Medal [Military decoration]

NAM............ Nederlandsche Aluminium Maatschappij [Netherlands Aluminum Co.] (AD)

nam .... Network Access Machine [Computer science] (AD)

NAM............ Network Access Machine [National Institute of Standards and Technology] [Computer science]

NAM............ Network Access Method [Control Data Corp.] [Telecommunications] (TEL)

NAM............ Network Analysis Model

NAM............ New Account Memorandum

NAM............ New America Movement (EA)

NAM............ New American Man [Lifestyle classification coined by Robert Bly] (ECON)

NAM............ New Architectural Movement [British] (DI)

NAM............ Newspaper Association Managers (EA)

NAM............ Nicotinamide (SAUS)

NAM............ NOAA [National Oceanic and Atmospheric Administration] Accounting Manual (NOAA)

NAM............ Node Address Memory (SAUS)

NAM............ Nonadditive Mixing (DICI)

NAM............ Non-Addressable Memory (SAUS)

nam .... Non-Aligned Movement (AD)

NAM............ Nonaligned Movement

NAM............ Non-Alignment Movement (SAUS)

NAM............ Normal Adult Male (MELL)

N Am .... North America (AD)

NAM............ North America

NAM............ North American Metals Corp. [Vancouver Stock Exchange symbol]

NAM............ North American Movement (AD)

NAM............ North American Museum Corp. (SAUS)

NAM............ North American Region [USTTA] (TAG)

NAM............ Nortland Air Manitoba [Canada] [ICAO designator] (FAAC)

NAM............ Norwegian American Museum Corp. (EA)

NAM............ Number Assignment Module (VLIE)

NAM............ Numerical Assignment Number [Computer science]

NAM............ Nurses Against Misrepresentation (EA)

NAM............ State University of New York at Albany, Albany, NY [OCLC symbol] (OCLC)

Nam............ Vietnam

NAma........... Amagansett Free Library, Amagansett, NY [Library symbol] [Library of Congress] (LCLS)

NAMA.......... National Account Marketing Association (EA)

NAMA.......... National Agenda for a Multicultural Australia

NAMA.......... National Agri-Marketing Association (EA)

NAMA.......... National Air-Monitoring Audit [Environmental Protection Agency] (GFGA)

NAMA.......... National Assistance Management Association [Washington, DC] (EA)

NAMA.......... National Association of Master Appraisers (EA)

NAMA.......... National Association of Mathematics Advisers [British] (DBA)

NAMA.......... National Automatic Merchandising Association [Chicago, IL] (EA)

NAMA.......... National Automotive Muffler Association [Defunct] (EA)

NAMA.......... Naval Aeronautical Material Area (NG)

NAMA.......... New Amsterdam Musical Association (AD)

NAMA.......... North American Manx Association (EA)

NAMA.......... North American Maritime Agencies (AD)

NAMA.......... North American Mycological Association (EA)

NAMA.......... Northern Air Material Area (SAUS)

NAMAB .... National Air Museum Advisory Board (MUGU)

NAMAC........ National Alliance for Media Arts and Culture (NTPA)

NAMAC........ National Alliance of Media Arts Centers (EA)

NAMAC........ National Amateur Missile Analysis Center

NAMAC........ National Association of Men's Apparel Clubs [Later, NAMBAC, Bureau of WholesaleSales Representatives]

NAMAC........ National Association of Merger and Acquisition Consultants (EA)

NAMAD........ National Association of Minority Automobile Dealers [Detroit, MI] (EA)

NAMAE........ Northern Air Material (or Materiel) Area, Europe (SAUS)

NAMAE........ Northern Air Materiel Area, Europe [Army]

NAmaHi....... Amagansett Historical Association, Amagansett, NY [Library symbol] [Library of Congress] (LCLS)

NAMAINTRADET... Naval Air Maintenance Training Detachment (DNAB)

NAMAINTRAGRU... Naval Air Maintenance Training Group (DNAB)

NAMAP........ Northern Air Material (or Materiel) Area, Pacific (SAUS)

NAMAP........ Northern Air Materiel Area, Pacific [Army]

NAMAPUS.... Naval Assistant to the Military Aide to the President of the United States

NAMAR........ North American Mustang Association and Registry (EA)

NAMARA...... Navy and Marine Corps Appellate Review Activity (DNAB)

NAMARCO ... National Marketing Corp [Philippines] (BUAC)

NAMAS .... National Accreditation of Measurement and Sampling (SAUS)

NAMAS .... National Measurement Accreditation Service [Research center] [British] (IRC)

NAMAST ...... System of National Accounts and System of Material Product Balances [United Nations Statistical Office] [Information service or system] (CRD)

NAMAT .... Normal Material (SAUS)

NAMATCEN... Naval Air Material Center [Also, NAMC, NAVAIRMATCEN]

NAMATE .... Naval Air Material Command

NAMB .... National Agricultural Marketing Board [Canada] (BUAC)

NAMB .... National Association of Master Bakers [British] (DI)

NAMB .... National Association of Master Bakers, Confectioners, and Caterers [British] (DBA)

NAMB .... National Association of Media Brokers (EA)

NAMB .... National Association of Minority Businesses (AAGC)

NAMB .... National Association of Mortgage Brokers [Washington, DC] (EA)

NAMB .... Naval Academy Midshipmen Branch

NAMB .... Naval Amphibious Base

NAMBAC...... National Association of Men's and Boys' Apparel Clubs [Later, Bureau of Wholesale Sales Representatives] (EA)

NAMBC .... National Association of Milk Bottle Collectors (EA)

NAMBLA ...... North American Man-Boy Love Association

NAMBLA ...... North American Men-Boy Love Association (BUAC)

NAMBO .... National Association of Motor Bus Operators (AD)

NAMBO .... National Association of Motor Bus Owners [Later, ABA] (EA)

NaMBT........ Sodium-2-Mercaptobenzothiazole (SAUS)

NAMC .... NAM Corp. [NASDAQ symbol] (SAG)

NAMC .... Nanchang Aircraft Manufacturing Co. (SAUS)

NAMC .... National Air Material Center (KSC)

NAMC .... National Association of Management Consultants (EA)

NAMC .... National Association of Minority Contractors (EA)

NAMC .... National Association of Mothers' Centers (EA)

NAMC .... Naval Aerospace Medical Center

NAMC .... Naval Air Material Center [Also, NAMATCEN, NAVAIRMATCEN]

NAMC .... Naval Air Materiel Command

NAMC .... Nihon Aeroplane Manufacturing Co. (AD)

NAMC .... North American National Corp. (SAUS)

NAMC .... North Atlantic Military Committee

NAMC .... Northern Association of Management Consultants (COBU)

NAMCA .... National Association for Middle Class Americans (EA)

NAMC-AEL ... Naval Air Material Center - Aeronautical Engine Laboratory

NAMC-AIL ... Naval Air Material Center - Aeronautical Instruments Laboratory [Philadelphia, PA]

NAMC-AML... Naval Air Material Center - Aeronautical Materials Laboratory

NAMC-APEL... Naval Air Material Center - Aeronautical Photographic Experimental Laboratory

NAMCAR ...... North America/Caribbean

NAMC-ARRL... Naval Air Material Center - Aeronautical Radio and RADAR Laboratory

NAMC-ASL ... Naval Air Material Center - Aeronautical Structures Laboratory

NAMCC .... National Association of Mutual Casualty Companies (EA)

NAM-CDH .... Non Absorbing Mirror Constricted Double Heterostructure (NITA)
NAMCF .... National Association of Minority CPA [*Certified Public Accounting*] Firms
NAMCO .... Air-Cushion Vehicle built by Nakamura Seisakusho [*Usually used in com bination with numerals*] [*Japan*]
NAMCO .... Naval and Mechanical Co. (AD)
NAMCO .... North American Management Council (BUAC)
NAMCO .... North Atlantic Marine Cooperative Commission (BUAC)
NAM Cp ...... NAM Corp. [*Associated Press*] (SAG)
NAMCP .... National Association of Managed Care Physicians (EA)
NAMCPAF .... National Association of Minority Certified Public Accounting Firms (EA)
NAMCS .... National Ambulatory Medical Care Survey [*National Center for Health Statistics*]
NAMCU .... National Association of Minority Consultants and Urbanologists [*Defunct*] (EA)
NAMCW .... National Association of Maternal and Child Welfare [*British*]
NAMD .... National Association for Membership Development (NTPA)
NAMD .... National Association of Marble Dealers [*Later, MIA*] (EA)
NAMD .... National Association of Marine Dealers
NAMD .... National Association of Market Developers [*New York, NY*] (EA)
NAMD .... National Association of Membership Directors of Chambers of Commerce [*Defunct*] (EA)
NAMD .... Naval Ammunition Depot [*Charleston, SC*]
NAMD .... Newsletter of the Army Medical Department
NAMDA .... North American Medical/Dental Association (EA)
NAMDAR ...... North American Data Airborne Recorder (IAA)
NAMDB .... National Association of Medical-Dental Bureaus [*Later, MDHBA*]
NAMDDU ..... Naval Air Mine Defense Development Unit (MUGU)
NAMDEX ..... Name Index
NAMDI .... National Marine Data Inventory
NAMDRA ...... National American Motors Drivers and Racers Association (EA)
NAMDRC ...... National Association for Medical Direction of Respiratory Care (NTPA)
NAMDRC ...... National Association of Medical Directors for Respiratory Care (EA)
NAMDRP ...... Naval Aviation Maintenance Discrepancy Reporting Program (DNAB)
NAMDT .... National Association of Milliners, Dressmakers, and Tailors (EA)
NAME .... National Anti-Racist Movement in Education [*British*] (DBA)
NAME .... National Association for Mediation in Education (EA)
NAME .... National Association for Minority Education
NAME .... National Association for Multiracial Education [*British*]
NAME .... National Association of Management/Marketing Educators [*Defunct*] (EA)
NAME .... National Association of Marine Enginebuilders [*British*] (BI)
NAME .... National Association of Marine Engineers (AD)
NAME .... National Association of Marine Engineers of Canada (BUAC)
NAME .... National Association of Maritime Educators (NTPA)
NAME .... National Association of Media Educators (EA)
NAME .... National Association of Medical Examiners (EA)
NAME .... National Association of Metal Name Plate Manufacturers (AD)
NAME .... National Association of Miniature Enthusiasts (EA)
NAME .... National Association of Minority Entrepreneurs (EA)
NAME .... National Association of Modeling and Entertainment (EA)
NAME .... National Association of Name Plate Manufacturers, Inc.
NAME .... Nevi, Atrial Myxoma, Myxoid Neurofibroma, and Ephilides [*Syndrome*] [*Medicine*] (MELL)
NAME .... New American Music in Europe [*An association*] (BUAC)
NAME .... Nitroarginine Methyl Ester [*Organic chemistry*]
NAME .... North American Monogrammers and Embroiderers [*Defunct*] (EA)
NAME .... Nuclear Accident Modelling Exercise (SAUS)
NAMEB .... National Association of Marine Engine Builders (AD)
NAMEC .... National Association of Marine Engineers of Canada
NAMED .... North African Medical Section [*World War II*]
NAMEDCEN... Naval Aviation Medical Center (DNAB)
NAMEPA ...... National Association of Minority Engineering Program Administrators (EA)
NAMES .... National Association of Medical Equipment Suppliers (EA)
NAMES .... NAVDAC [*Naval Data Automation Command*] Assembly, Monitor, Executive System (PDAA)
NAMESAKES... Naval Aviators Must Energetically Sell Aviation to Keep Effective Strength
NAMESU ...... National Association of Music Executives in State Universities (EA)
NAMET .... Naval Mathematics and English Test [*British military*] (DMA)
NAMF .... National Association of Metal Finishers (EA)
NAMF .... Naval Aviation Museum Foundation (DNAB)
NAMF .... North American Multi-Frequency (SAUS)
NAMFAX ...... National and Aviation Meteorological Facsimile Network [*National Weather Service*]
NAMFC .... North Atlantic Mediterranean Freight Conference (EA)
NAMFI .... NATO Missile Firing Installation
NAMFREL .... National Citizens' Movement for Free Elections [*Philippines*] [*Political party*]
NAMFSM ..... National Association of Meat and Food Seasoning Manufacturers [*Later, NSMA*] (EA)
NAMG .... Narrow-Angle Mars Gate [*NASA*]
NAMG .... National Association of Mining Groups (EA)
NAMG .... National Association of Multiple Grocers [*British*] (BI)
NAMG .... North American Group Ltd. (SAUS)
NAMGAR...... North American MGA [*Morris Garage Automobile*] Register (EA)
NAMH .... National Association for Mental Health (EA)
NAMHA .... North American Morab Horse Association (EA)
NAMHH........ National Association of Methodist Hospitals and Homes
NAMHI .... National Association for the Mentally Handicapped of Ireland (EAIO)
NAMHO........ National Association of Mining History Organisations [*British*] (DBA)

NAmi .... Amityville Public Library, Amityville, NY [*Library symbol*] [*Library of Congress*] (LCLS)
NAMI .... National Alliance for the Mentally Ill (EA)
NAMI .... National Association of Malleable Ironfounders [*British*] (BI)
NAMI .... Naval Aerospace Medical Institute
NAMIA .... National Association of Mutual Insurance Agents [*Later, PIA*] (EA)
Namib .... Namibia (AD)
NAMIC .... National Association of Mutual Insurance Companies [*Indianapolis, IN*] (EA)
NAMID .... National Moving Image Database [*American Film Institute*] [*Information service or system*] (IID)
NAMIEP .... National AIDS Minority Information and Education Program (SAUS)
NAmiGH....... Brunswick General Hospital, Amityville, NY [*Library symbol*] [*Library of Congress*] (LCLS)
NAmiHS....... Amityville Memorial High School, Amityville, NY [*Library symbol*] [*Library of Congress*] (LCLS)
NAmiJH .... Amityville Junior High School, Amityville, NY [*Library symbol*] [*Library of Congress*] (LCLS)
NAMiiCom .... North Atlantic Military Committee (AD)
NAMILCOM... North Atlantic Military Committee
NAMILPO ..... NATO Military Posture (AABC)
NAMIM .... National Association of Musical Instrument Mechanics (EA)
NAMIS .... Nitride-Barrier Avalanche Injection Missile (MCD)
NAmiSH....... South Oaks Hospital, Amityville, NY [*Library symbol*] [*Library of Congress*] (LCLS)
NAMISTESTCEN... Naval Air Missile Test Center
naml .... Namligen [*Namely*] [*Swedish*] (AD)
NAML.......... National Applied Mathematics Laboratory [*National Institute of Standards and Technology*] (MCD)
NAML.......... National Association of Marine Laboratories (BUAC)
NAML.......... Naval Aircraft Materials Laboratory (MCD)
NAML Dig .... National Association of Manufacturers Law Digest [*A publication*] (DLA)
NAMLM........ National Association for Multi-Level Marketing (EA)
NAMLNC...... National Association of Medical Legal Nurse Consultants (EA)
NAMM .... National Association of Margarine Manufacturers (EA)
NAMM .... National Association of Mass Merchandisers (EA)
NAMM .... National Association of Master Masons [*British*] (DBA)
NAMM .... National Association of Mirror Manufacturers (EA)
NAMM .... National Association of Music Merchandisers (AD)
NAMM .... National Association of Music Merchants (EA)
NAMM .... North African Military Mission [*World War II*]
NAMM .... North American Music Merchants (SAUS)
NAMMA .... NATO Multi-Role Combat Aircraft Development and Production Management Agency
NAMMA .... North American Maritime Ministry Association (EA)
NAMMC ...... Natural Asphalt Mineowners' and Manufacturers' Council (AD)
NAMMC ...... North Atlantic Marine Mammal Commission (BUAC)
NAMMD ...... National Association of Marinas and Marine Dealers (EA)
NAMME .... National Association of Medical Minority Educators (EA)
NAMME .... National Association of Minority Media Executives (NTPA)
NAMMIS ...... Navy Aviation Maintenance and Material Support System (NG)
NAMMM ...... National Association of Musical Merchandise Manufacturers [*Later, GAMA*] (EA)
NAMMO ...... NATO Multi-Role Combat Aircraft Management Organization (PDAA)
NAMMO ...... North Atlantic Treaty Organization [*NATO*] Multi-Role Combat Aircraft Development and Production Management Organization (AAGC)
NAMMO Development a... NATO [*North Atlantic Treaty Organization*] Multi-Role Combat Aircraft Development a (AD)
NAMMOS .... Navy Manpower Mobilization System
NAMMR .... National Association for Milk Marketing Reform [*Later, NIDA*] (EA)
NAMMR .... North American Mini Moke Registry (EA)
NAMMS .... Navy Aviation Maintenance and Material Support System
NAMMW ...... National Association of Musical Merchandise Wholesalers [*Later, MDA*] (EA)
NAMN .... Nicotinic Acid Mononucleotide (DMAA)
NAMNPM..... National Association of Metal Name Plate Manufacturers
NAMO .... National Agricultural Marketing Officials [*Richmond, VA*] (EA)
NAMO .... National Association of Manufacturing Opticians (EA)
NAMO .... National Association of Multifamily Owners
NAMO .... Naval Aircraft Maintenance Orders
NAMOA .... National Association of Miscellaneous Ornamental and Architectural Products Contractors (EA)
NAMOC .... Northwest Atlantic Mid-Ocean Canyon (SAUS)
NAMORB..... North Atlantic Mid-Ocean-Ridge Basalt [*Geology*]
NAMOS .... National Art Museum of Sport (EA)
NAMP .... National Alliance of Mental Patients [*Later, NAPS*] (EA)
NAMP .... National Antibiotic Minimization Program [*Australia*]
NAMP .... National Association of Magazine Publishers [*Later, Magazine Publishers Association*]
NAMP .... National Association of Marble Producers (EA)
NAMP .... National Association of Married Priests (AD)
NAMP .... National Association of Mature People (EA)
NAMP .... National Association of Meal Programs (EA)
NAMP .... National Association of Meat Purveyors (EA)
NAMP .... National Association of Midwifery Practitioners [*Defunct*] (EA)
NAMP .... NATO Annual Manpower Plan (NATG)
NAMP .... Naval Aviation Maintenance Program (MCD)
NAMP .... Nonaccounting Majors Program
NAMP .... North American Meat Processors Association (NTPA)
NAMPA .... NATO Maritime Patrol Aircraft Agency (NATG)
NAMPBG....... National Association of Manufacturers of Pressed and Blown Glassware [*Defunct*] (EA)
nampg .... Nautical Air Miles per Gallon (AD)
NAMPI .... National Association of Missing Persons Investigators [*Defunct*] (EA)

NAMPMW.... Vietnam Prisoners of War [*An association*] (AD)
NAMPPF...... Nautical Air Miles per Pound of Fuel (AAG)
namppf........ Nautical Air Miles per Pound of Fuel (AD)
NAMPS........ Narrow Advanced Mobile Phone Service
NAMPS........ Narrowband Advanced Mobile Phone Service (CGWS)
NAMPS........ Narrow-Band Analog Mobile Phone Service [*Computer science*] (VLIE)
NAMPS........ National Association of Marine Products and Services (EA)
NAMPS........ Navy Manpower Planning System (NVT)
NAMPUS..... National Association of Master-Plumbers of the United States (BUAC)
NAMPW...... National Association of Meat Processors and Wholesalers (EA)
NAMPW...... National Association of Minority Political Women (EA)
NAMRA....... North American Mini-Champ Racing Association (EA)
NAMRAD..... Non-Atomic Military Research and Development [*Subcommittee*]
NAMRC...... North American Marten Rabbit Club (EA)
NAMRI....... Naval Aerospace Medical Research Institute (DNAB)
NAMRI........ North American Manufacturing Research Institute (SAUS)
NAMRI/SME... North American Manufacturing Research Institution of SME [*Society of Manufacturing Engineers*] (EA)
NAMRL....... Naval Aerospace Medical Research Laboratory
NAMRP....... National Apostolate with Mentally Retarded Persons (EA)
NAMRU....... Navy Medical Research Unit [*World War II*]
NAMRU....... Navy Medical Reserve Unit (DAVI)
NAms........... Amsterdam Free Library, Amsterdam, NY [*Library symbol*] [*Library of Congress*] (LCLS)
NAMS........... National Account Management Society (NTPA)
NAMS........... National Air Monitoring Station [*Environmental Protection Agency*] (ERG)
NAMS.......... National Air Monitoring System (EEVL)
NAMS.......... National Ambient Air Monitoring Station [*or System*] [*Environmental Protection Agency*]
NAMS.......... National Association of Marine Services (EA)
NAMS.......... National Association of Marine Surveyors (EA)
NAMS.......... National Association of Military Spouses (EA)
NAMS.......... National Association of Municipal Securities Dealers
NAMS.......... Network Analysis and Management System [*Computer science*] (VLIE)
NAMS.......... North American Membrane Society (EA)
NAMS.......... North American Menopause Society (EA)
NAMS.......... North American Micropaleontology Section (SAUS)
NAMS.......... Nurses and Army Medical Specialists
NAMSA....... NATO Maintenance and Supply Agency
NAMSA....... North American Multihull Sailing Association (EA)
NAMSB....... National Association of Men's Sportswear Buyers (EA)
NAMSB....... National Association of Mutual Savings Banks (EA)
NAMSC....... North American Maple Syrup Council (EA)
NAMSCO..... National Association of MDS [*Multipoint Distribution System*] Service Companies [*Later, MDSIA*] (EA)
NAMSDIC.... National Arthritis and Musculoskeletal and Skin Diseases Information Clearinghouse [*Later, NAMSIC*] (EA)
NAMSE........ National Association of Minority Students and Educators in Higher Education (EA)
NAMSIC....... National Arthritis and Musculoskeletal and Skin Diseases Information Clearinghouse
NAmsM........ Mohasco Corp., Corporate Planning Library, Amsterdam, NY [*Library symbol*] [*Library of Congress*] (LCLS)
NAMSO........ NATO Maintenance and Supply Organization [*Formerly, NATO Maintenance Supply Service Agency*] [*Luxembourg*]
NAMSO........ Navy Maintenance Support Office
NAMSOINST.. Navy Maintenance Support Office Instruction (MCD)
NAMSP........ National Association of Mail Service Pharmacies [*Later, AMCPA*] (EA)
NAMSR....... National Association of Multiple Shoe Repairers [*British*] (DBA)
NAMSRC...... National AM Stereophonic Radio Committee
NAMSS........ National Association Medical Staff Services (EA)
NAmSv......... North American Savings Bank [*Associated Press*] (SAG)
NAMT.......... National Association for Music Therapy (EA)
NAMT.......... Naval Aircraft Mobile Trainer
NAMT.......... Naval Air Maintenance Trainer (MUGU)
NAMT.......... Norwegian Association of Microbiological Technologists (BUAC)
NAMTA .... National Art Materials Trade Association (EA)
NAMTAC...... National Association of Management and Technical Assistance Centers [*Washington, DC*] (EA)
NamTai........ Nam Tai Electronics, Inc. [*Associated Press*] (SAG)
NAMTC .... Naval Air Missile Test Center
NAmTch....... North American Technologies Corp. [*Associated Press*] (SAG)
NAMTD .... Naval Air Maintenance Training Detachment
NAMTD .... Naval Air Maintenance Training Devices
NAMTG .... Naval Air Maintenance Training Group (MCD)
NAMTGD...... Naval Air Maintenance Training Group Detachment (DNAB)
NAMtge........ North American Mortgage Co. [*Associated Press*] (SAG)
NAMTM........ Naval Air Mobile Training Maintenance
NAMTRA....... Naval Air Maintenance Training
NAMTRADET... Naval Air Maintenance Training Detachment (MCD)
NAMTRAGRU... Naval Air Maintenance Training Group (MCD)
NAMTRAGRUDET... Naval Air Maintenance Training Group Detachment (DNAB)
NAMTRAGRUP... Naval Air Maintenance Training Group (SAA)
NAMTRATCLOFLT... Naval Air Maintenance Training Type Commander Liaison Office, Fleet (DNAB)
NAMTRATCLOLANT... Naval Air Maintenance Training Type Commander Liaison Officer, Atlantic (DNAB)
NAMTRATCLOPAC... Naval Air Maintenance Training Type Commander Liaison Office, Pacific (DNAB)
NAMTS .... Nippon Automatic Mobile Telephone System (SAUS)
NAMU .... Naval Aircraft Material Utility

NAMU .... Naval Aircraft Modification Unit
NAMV .... Narcissus Mosaic Virus [*Plant pathology*]
NAMW .... National Association of Media Women (EA)
NAMW .... National Association of Military Widows (EA)
NAMW .... National Association of Ministers' Wives [*Later, NAMWMW*] (EA)
NAMWB ...... National Association of Minority Women in Business [*Kansas City, MO*] (EA)
NAMWMW... National Association of Ministers' Wives and Ministers' Widows (EA)
NAMZ........... Neue Allgemeine Missions-Zeitschrift [*A publication*] (BJA)
NAN .... N-Acetylneuraminic Acid [*Also, AcNeu, NANA*] [*Biochemistry*]
NAN .... Nadi [*Fiji*] [*Airport symbol*] (OAG)
Nan .... Nancy (AD)
Nan .... Nanette (AD)
Nan .... Nanking [*China*] (AD)
NAN .... Nanking [*Republic of China*] [*Seismograph station code, US Geological Survey*] (SEIS)
NAN .... Nantucket Industries, Inc. [*AMEX symbol*] (SPSG)
NAN .... National Academy of Needlearts (EA)
NAN .... National Academy of Neuropsychology (EA)
NAN .... National AIDS [*Acquired Immune Deficiency Syndrome*] Network [*Defunct*] (EA)
NAN .... National Airlines, Inc. [*ICAO designator*] (FAAC)
NAN .... National Area Network [*Computer science*] (VLIE)
NAN .... National Association of Neighborhoods (EA)
NAN .... Network Application Node
NAN .... Neuraminidase (SAUS)
NAN .... News Agency of Nigeria (EY)
nan .... Nisi Aliter Notetur [*Unless Otherwise Noted*] [*Latin*]
nan .... Nisi Aliter Notetur [*Unless It is Otherwise Noted*] [*Latin*] (AD)
Nan .... Nitrosamine [*Biochemistry*]
NAN .... No Action Necessary [*Military*] (CINC)
NAN .... Non-Ammonia-Nitrogen (PDAA)
NAN .... North American Nippon Technologies Corp. [*Vancouver Stock Exchange symbol*]
NAN .... North Atlantic Network (EA)
NAN .... Norton Administrator for Networks [*Computer software*] [*Symantec Corp.*] (PCM)
NaN .... Not a Number [*Computer programming*] (BYTE)
nana .... N-Acetylneuraminic Acid (AD)
nana .... N-Acetylneuraminic Acid [*Also, AcNeu, NAN*] [*Biochemistry*]
NANA .... National Advertising News Association (AD)
NANA .... National Advertising Newspaper Association [*Later, SNA*] (EA)
NANA .... National Association of Nail Artists [*Later, NANAA*] (EA)
NANA .... Newsagents' Association of New South Wales and the Australian Capital Territory, Inc.
NANA .... North American Newspaper Alliance
NANA .... North American Normande Association (EA)
NANA .... Northwest Alaska Native Association [*Later, MA*]
NANAA......... National Aesthetician and Nail Artist Association [*Formerly, NANA*] [*WINBA*] [*Absorbed by*] (EA)
NANAC......... National Aircraft Noise Abatement Council [*Defunct*] (EA)
NANAC......... National Aviation Noise Abatement Council (AD)
NANACA...... National Association for Native American Children of Alcoholics (EA)
NANACOA...... National Association for Native American Children of Alcoholics (EA)
NANAI......... Dutch Actiongroup for Indians of North America
NANAP......... Non-Aligned News Agency Pool (BUAC)
NANASP......... National Association of Nutrition and Aging Services Programs (EA)
NANAWO......... Namibia National Women's Organzation (BUAC)
NAnB .... Bard College, Annandale-On-Hudson, NY [*Library symbol*] [*Library of Congress*] (LCLS)
NANB .... Non-A, Non-B [*Virology*]
NANB .... Nurses Association of New Brunswick (SAUS)
NANBH......... Non-A, Non-B Hepatitis [*Medicine*]
NANBPWC ... National Association of Negro Business and Professional Women's Clubs [*Washington, DC*] (EA)
NANBV......... Non-A, Non-B Hepatic Virus
NANC .... National Association of New Careerists (EA)
NANC .... Non-Adrenergic, Non-Cholinergic [*Neurology*]
NANC .... North American Numbering Council (CGWS)
NANCA......... North American Natural Casing Association (EA)
NANCB......... National Association of Negotiated Commissioned Brokers [*Defunct*] (EA)
NANCF......... North Atlantic Naval Coastal Frontier
NANCI......... New Aeronautical and Nautical Chart Investigations (NOAA)
NANCO......... National Association of Noise Control Officials (EA)
NANCRFUG... North American NCR [*National Cash Register Co.*] Financial Users Group (EA)
NAND.......... Inverted And Gate, Not And (SAUS)
NAND.......... Naval Ammunition and Net Depot
NAND.......... NOT-AND (SAUS)
NAND.......... Not And [*Logical operator*] [*Computer science*]
NAND.......... 'Not' and 'And' (NITA)
N & A.......... Nautical & Aviation Publishing Co.
N & A.......... Nipple and Areola [*Medicine*] (MELL)
NANDA......... North American Nursing Diagnosis Association (EA)
N&A.......... Notes and Application (SAUS)
N&CR......... [*The*] Nash and Cibinic Report [*A publication*] (AAGC)
N&D......... Nodular and Diffuse [*Medicine*] (MELL)
N & D......... Nodular and Diffuse Lymphoma [*Oncology*]
N&D......... Noise and Distortion (SAUS)
N&G......... Navigation and Guidance
NAND Gate... NOT-AND Gate (SAUS)
N & GS....... Navigation and Guidance Subsystem [*NASA*] (KSC)
N & H......... Nott and Hopkins' Reports [*United States Court of Claims*] [*A publication*] (DLA)

N & H.......... Nott and Huntington's Reports [*1-7 United States Court of Claims*] [*A publication*] (DLA)

N & Hop...... Nott and Hopkins' Reports [*United States Court of Claims*] [*A publication*] (DLA)

N & Hunt..... Nott and Huntington's Reports [*1-7 United States Court of Claims*] [*A publication*] (DLA)

N&M.......... Nerves and Muscles (DMAA)

N & M .... Nevile and Manning's English King's Bench Reports [*A publication*] (DLA)

N&M.......... Night and Morning (DMAA)

N & M .... November and May [*Denotes semiannual payments of interest or dividends in these months*] [*Business term*]

N & Macn.... Neville and Macnamara's Railway and Canal Cases [*1855-1950*] [*A publication*] (DLA)

N & MC....... Navy and Marine Corps [*Medal*]

N & Mc........ Nott and McCord's South Carolina Reports [*A publication*] (DLA)

N & McC...... Nott and McCord's South Carolina Reports [*A publication*] (DLA)

N & MCM .... Navy and Marine Corps Medal [*Military decoration*]

N & McN ..... Neville and Macnamara's Railway and Canal Cases [*1855-1950*] [*A publication*] (DLA)

N & M Mag... Nevile and Manning's English Magistrates' Cases [*A publication*] (DLA)

N & MMC .... Nevile and Manning's English Magistrates' Cases [*A publication*] (DLA)

N & P .... Nevile and Perry's English King's Bench Reports [*1836-38*] [*A publication*] (DLA)

N & P Mag... Nevile and Perry's English Magistrates' Cases [*1836-37*] [*A publication*] (DLA)

N & PMC .... Nevile and Perry's English Magistrates' Cases [*1836-37*] [*A publication*] (DLA)

N&PNWR.... Ninepipe and Pablo National Wildlife Refuge (SAUS)

N&Q........... Notes and Queries [*A publication*] (ANEX)

N&R Indication... Normal and Reverse Indication (SAUS)

N & S .... Nicholls and Stops' Reports [*1897-1904*] [*Tasmania*] [*A publication*] [*A publication*] (DLA)

N & SDCP.... Neurological and Sensory Disease Control Program

N & SE .... Nacogdoches & Southeastern Railroad (IIA)

N & T........... Navigation and Timing

N&T............. Nicotine and Tobacco (MELL)

N & T........... Nose and Throat [*Medicine*]

N & V .... Nausea and Vomiting

N & W .... Norfolk & Western Railway Co.

NANE .... National Association for Nursery Education [*Later, NAEYC*] (EA)

NANEAP....... North Africa, Near East, Asia, and Pacific Region [*Program of ACTION, an independent government agency*]

NANEP........ Navy Air Navigation Electronic Project

NANEWS..... Naval Aviation News

NANFA........ North American Native Fishes Association (EA)

NANFAC...... Naval Air Navigation Facility Advisory Committee

NANFM........ National Association of Non-Ferrous Scrap Metal Merchants (BUAC)

NANFORMS... Naval Aviator/Naval Flight Officer Reporting Management System (DNAB)

NANFPT ...... National Association of Natural Family Planning Teachers (BUAC)

NAng........... Angelica Free Library, Angelica, NY [*Library symbol*] [*Library of Congress*] (LCLS)

NANHC........ National Association of Neighborhood Health Centers [*Later, NACHC*] (EA)

NANHPH ..... National Association of Nursing Homes and Private Hospitals [*Australia*]

NANI .... National Academy of Nannies, Inc. (EA)

NANIME ...... Norfolk and Norwich Institute for Medical Education (SAUS)

NA/NLP....... National Association of Neuro-Linguistic Programming (EA)

NANM .... N-Allylnormetazocine [*Biochemistry*]

NANM .... N-Allylnormorphine [*Narcotic antagonist*]

NANM .... National Association of Negro Musicians (EA)

NANMT .... National Association of Nurse Massage Therapists

NANMV .... Nandina Mosaic Virus [*Plant pathology*]

NANN .... National Association of Neonatal Nurses (EA)

NANN .... National Association of Nursery Nurses (BUAC)

NANNP......... Nordic Association of Non-Commercial Phonogram Producers (EA)

nano-.......... Billionth (IDOE)

NANO.......... Nanometrics, Inc. [*NASDAQ symbol*] (NQ)

NANO.......... Non-linear AND, Non-linear OR (SAUS)

nano .... One billionth [*From the Latin nanus*] (WDMC)

NANOG........ North American Network Operators Group (SAUS)

NanomtR ..... Nanometrics, Inc. [*Associated Press*] (SAG)

NANOSAT .... Nanosatellite

nanova........ Non-Orthogonal Analysis of Variance (AD)

NANP .... National Alliance of Nurse Practitioners (EA)

NANP .... National Association of Naturopathic Physicians [*Defunct*] (EA)

NANP .... North American Numbering Plan [*A set of rules for the assignment of telephone area codes and the method by which calls are routed*] (DCDG)

NANPA........ North American Nature Photography Association

NANPE........ National Association of Newspaper Purchasing Executives [*Later, NPMA*] (EA)

NANPMA..... North American Nutrition and Preventive Medicine Association (EA)

NANPRH ..... National Association of Nurse Practitioners in Reproductive Health (EA)

NANR.......... National Association of Nurse Recruiters [*Later, NAHCR*] (EA)

NANS .... National Association for Neighborhood Schools (EA)

NANS .... National Association of Nigerian Students (BUAC)

NANS .... National Association of Non-Smokers (EA)

NANS .... National Catholic News Service (EA)

NANS .... Naval Air Navigation School

NANs .... Negative Axillary Node [*Medicine*] (MELL)

NANS .... Nevada Academy of Natural Sciences (SAUS)

NANS .... Night Attack Navigation System (ACAE)

NANS .... North American Nietzsche Society (EA)

NANS .... North Atlantic and Neighboring Seas

NANSI .... Nordic Automated Network of Shell Installation (SAUS)

NANSIM....... Nonlinear Active Network Simulation (SAUS)

NANT .... National Association of Nephrology Technologists (EA)

NANT .... National Associaton of Nephrology Technicians/Technologists (EA)

Nantck .... Nantucket Industries, Inc. [*Associated Press*] (SAG)

NANTDDDC.. National Association of Negro Tailors, Designers, Dressmakers, and Dry Cleaners (EA)

NANTIS .... Nottignham and Nottinghamshire Technical Information Service [*British*] (AD)

NANTS .... National Association of Naval Technical Supervisors (EA)

NANU .... National Association of NIDS [*National Investor Data Service*] Users (EA)

NANU .... National Association of Non-Unionists (BUAC)

NANU.......... Notice Advisory to NAVSTAR User (SAUS)

NANVH&SWO... National Assembly of National Voluntary Health and Social Welfare Organizations (AD)

NANWEP...... Navy Numerical Weather Prediction [*Computer system*] [*Control Data Corp.*]

NANWEP...... Navy Numerical Weather Problems [*Group*]

NANWR....... North American Network of Women Runners (EA)

NAO .... Charleston, SC [*Location identifier*] [*FAA*] (FAAL)

NAO .... Her Majesty's Nautical Almanac Office [*British*] (PDAA)

NAO .... National Academy of Opticianry (EA)

NAO .... National Accordion Organisation of the United Kingdom (BUAC)

NAO .... National Accordion Organization [*British*] (DBA)

NAO .... National Adhering Organization

NAO .... National Association of Outfitters (AD)

NAO .... National Astronomical Observatory [*Japan*]

NAO .... National Audit Office [*British*] (ECON)

NAO .... Nautical Almanac Office (BUAC)

NAO .... Naval Audit Office (DNAB)

NAO .... Naval Aviation Observer [*Obsolete*]

NAO .... NOAA [*National Oceanic and Atmospheric Administration*] Administrative Order (USDC)

NAO .... Noise Abatement Office (AD)

NAO .... Non-Asbestos Organic [*Friction materials*]

NAO .... Norsar Array Site 01A00 [*Norway*] [*Seismograph station code, US Geological Survey*] (SEIS)

NAO .... North American Airlines, Inc. [*ICAO designator*] (FAAC)

NAO .... North American Operations [*Automotive industry*]

NAO .... North Atlantic Oscillation [*Climatology*]

NAO .... Nurse Aide/Orderly (OICC)

NAOA .... National Apartment Owners Association [*Later, NAA*] (EA)

NAOA .... National Association of Older Americans [*Later, Heartline/National Association of Older Americans*] (EA)

NAOA .... Naval Aviation Observer Aerology (SAA)

NAOA .... Navy Officers Accounts Office (AD)

NAOAG......... North American Official Airline Guide (TRID)

NAOB .... Naval Aviation Observer Bombardier (MUGU)

NAOBMISB.. National Association of Operative Boiler Makers and Iron Ship Builders [*A union*] [*British*]

NAOC .... National Antique Oldsmobile Club (EA)

NAOC .... Naval Aviation Observer Controller (MUGU)

NAOC .... Naval Aviation Officer Candidate

NAOC .... Nigerian Agip Oil Co. (AD)

NAOC .... North Absheron Operating Co.

NAOCJ .... National Association of Operative Carpenters and Joiners [*A union*] [*British*]

NAOCP........ Novice Amateur Operator's Certificate of Proficiency [*Radio*]

NAOE .... National Association for Outdoor Education [*British*]

NAOEJ .... National Association of Oil Equipment Jobbers [*Later, PEI*] (EA)

NAOFD .... National Association of Office Furniture Dealers (NTPA)

NAOGE .... National Association of Government Engineers [*Defunct*] (EA)

NAOGTC...... North American Opel GT [*Gran Turismo*] Club (EA)

NAOH .... National Alliance for Oral Health (NTPA)

NaOH .... Sodium Hydroxide

NAOHSM...... National Association of Oil Heating Service Managers (EA)

NAOI .... Naval Aviation Observer Intercept (MUGU)

NAOIG......... North African Inspector General's Section [*World War II*]

NAOJ .... National Astronomical Observatory of Japan

NAOL .... National Association of Orchestra Leaders (EA)

NAOMI .... National Association of Ovulation Method Instructors [*British*] (DBA)

NAON .... National Association of Orthopaedic Nurses (EA)

NAON .... Naval Aviation Observer Navigator (MUGU)

NAOO .... National Association of Optometrists and Opticians (EA)

NAOO .... National Oceanic and Atmospheric Administration (SAUS)

NAOODA ..... North American Offshore One-Design Association (EA)

NAOP .... National Alliance for Optional Parenthood (DAVI)

NAOP .... National Association for Olmsted Parks (EA)

NAOP .... National Association of Operative Plasterers

NAOP .... National Association of Operative Plumbers [*A union*] [*British*]

NAOP .... Nonadditive Operational Project [*Military*]

NAOPL .... National Association of Operative Plasterers' Labourers [*A union*] [*British*]

NAOPS .... North Atlantic Ocean Prediction Systems (SAUS)

NAOR .... Naval Aviation Observer RADAR (MUGU)

NAORD .... North African Ordnance Section [*World War II*]

NAORPB ...... North Atlantic Ocean Regional Planning Board [*NATO*]

NAORPG....... North Atlantic Ocean Regional Planning Group [*NATO*] (NATG)

NAORTS....... Naval Aviation Ordnance Test Station

NAOS .... NASA Aircrew Oxygen System
NAOS .... North American Atmospheric Observing System (SAUS)
NAOS .... North Atlantic Ocean Station [WMO]
NAOSH .... Naitonal Authority for Occupational Safety and Health [Ireland] (BUAC)
NAOSMM ..... National Association of Scientific Material Managers (EA)
NAOSOF .... National Association of Soap Opera Fans
NAOSW .... National Association of Oncology Social Workers (EA)
NAOT .... National Association of Organ Teachers [Later, IAOT]
NAOT .... National Association of Orthopaedic Technologists (EA)
NAOT .... Naval Air Operational Training
NAOT .... Naval Aviation Observer Tactical (SAA)
NAOTB .... National Association of Off-Track Betting (EA)
NAOTC .... National Association of OTC [Over-the-Counter] Companies [Later, APTC] (EA)
NAOTC .... National Association of Timetable Collectors (EA)
NAOTC .... Naval Air Operational Training Command
NAOTD .... National Alliance of the Disabled (SAUS)
NAOTS .... Naval Aviation Ordnance Test Station
NAOWES ..... National Association of Older Worker Employment Services [Washington, DC] (EA)
NAP .... Armed Proletarian Nuclei [Italy]
NAP .... Bangladesh National Awami Party [Political party] (PPW)
nap .... Knapsack (AD)
nap .... Napalm (AD)
NAP .... Napa Resources, Inc. [Vancouver Stock Exchange symbol]
NAP .... Napay [Former USSR] [Seismograph station code, US Geological Survey] [Closed] (SEIS)
nap .... Naphtha (AD)
NAP .... Napier Air Service, Inc. [ICAO designator] (FAAC)
Nap .... Naples (AD)
NAP .... Naples [Italy] [Airport symbol] (OAG)
Nap .... Napoleon (AD)
NAP .... Napoleon [or Napoleonic]
NAP .... Napoleonic Age Philatelists (EA)
NAP .... [The] Narragansett Pier Railroad Co., Inc. [AAR code]
NAP .... Nasion Pogonion [Anatomy] (MAE)
NAP .... National Academies of Practice (NTPA)
NAP .... National Action Party [Sierra Leone] [Political party] (EY)
NAP .... National Action Party [Turkey] [Political party] (PD)
NAP .... National Advertising Program
NAP .... National Aerospace Plane (AD)
NAP .... National Afforestation Program (BUAC)
NAP .... National Agency for Privatisation [Romania] (BUAC)
NAP .... National Alliance Party [Sierra Leone] [Political party] (BUAC)
NAP .... National Apprenticeship Program [Bureau of Apprenticeship and Training] [Department of Labor]
NAP .... National Archives Publication
NAP .... National Association for the Paralysed (AD)
NAP .... National Association of Parliamentarians (EA)
NAP .... National Association of Planners [Defunct] (EA)
NAP .... National Association of Postmasters (NADA)
NAP .... National Association of Postmasters of the United States
NAP .... National Association of Publishers [Defunct] (EA)
NAP .... National Association of the Professions (EA)
NAP .... National Audit Plan
NAP .... National Awami Party [Pakistan] [Political party] (PD)
NAP .... National Awami Party-Bashani [Bangladesh] [Political party] (FEA)
NAP .... National Awareness Partner (TELE)
NAP .... National Processing, Inc. [NYSE symbol] (SAG)
NAP .... Native American Program (OICC)
NAP .... Native Americans in Philanthropy
NAP .... Naval Academy Prepatory Student (DNAB)
NAP .... Naval Air Plan (CAAL)
NAP .... Naval Airplane Pusher [Slang] (DNAB)
NAP .... Naval Air Priorities
NAP .... Naval Auxiliary Patrol [British military] (DMA)
nap .... Naval Aviation Pilot (AD)
NAP .... Naval Aviation Pilot
NAP :........... Naval Aviation Plan (NVT)
NAP .... Navigation Analysis Program [NASA] (NASA)
NAP .... Neighborhood Action Program [New York City] (EA)
NAP .... Neighborhood Awareness Program (AD)
NAP .... Nerve Action Potential [Medicine] (MELL)
NAP .... Network Access Point [Telecommunications]
NAP .... Network Access Pricing [Telecommunications] (TEL)
NAP .... Network Access Program [Computer science] (CIST)
NAP .... Network Access Protocol
NAP .... Network Applications Platform [Computer science] (CIST)
NAP .... Neutrophil Activating Protein
NAP .... Neutrophil Alkaline Phosphatase [An enzyme]
NAP .... New Age Patriot [An association] (EA)
NAP .... New Aspiration Party [Thailand]
NAP .... New Associations and Projects [Formerly, NA] [A publication]
NAP .... Niger Agricultural Project [Nigeria] (BUAC)
NAP .... Night Attack Program [Military]
NAP .... Nitroaminophenol [Organic chemistry]
NAP .... Noise Abatement Procedure (AAG)
NAP .... Nomina Anatomica Parisiensia [Medicine]
NA-P .... Nonabrasive-Polishing
NAP .... Nonacquisition Project [Military] (CAAL)
NAP .... Nonadvertising Promotion [Public relations] (WDMC)
nap .... Non-Agency Purchase (AD)
NAP .... Nonagency Purchase
NAP .... Nonaggression Pact

NAP .... Non-Arboreal Pollen [Palynology] (QUAC)
NAP .... Nonarborescent Pollen (SAUS)
NAP .... Nonnuclear Armament Plan (MCD)
NAP .... Normal Administrative Practice
NAP .... Normalized Abundance Pattern [Geochemistry]
NAP .... North American Philips Corp. (IAA)
NAP .... North Atlantic Pact (SAUS)
NAP .... North Australia Program
NAP .... Northern Agricultural Producers (BUAC)
NAP .... Not Applicable (SAUS)
NAP .... Not a Priori
nap .... Not at Present (AD)
NAP .... Not at Present
NAP .... Not Authorized POMCUS (SAUS)
NAP .... Nuclear Action Project (EA)
NAP .... Nuclear-Active Particles [Astrophysics]
NAP .... Nuclear Auxiliary Power
NAP .... Nuclei Armati Proletari [Armed Proletarian Nuclei] [Italian] (PD)
NAP .... Nucleic Acid Phosphate (or Phosphorus) (SAUS)
NAP .... Nucleic Acid Phosphorus [Biochemistry]
NAP .... Nucleoacidic Protein [Cytochemistry]
NAP .... Null Amsterdam Pegel (SAUS)
NAPA .... N-Acetyl-p-aminophenol [Organic chemistry]
NAPA .... N-Acetylprocainamide [Cardiac depressant]
NAPA .... National Academy of Public Administration (EA)
NAPA .... National Agricultural Plastics Association [Later, ASP] (EA)
NAPA .... National Agricultural Press Association (EA)
NAPA .... National Alcohol Producers' (BUAC)
NAPA .... National Amateur Press Association (EA)
NAPA .... National Asphalt Pavement Association (EA)
NAPA .... National Association for Photographic Art [Canada] (EAIO)
NAPA .... National Association for the Practice of Anthropology (EA)
NAPA .... National Association of Park Administrators [British] (BI)
NAPA .... National Association of Performing Artists
NAPA .... National Association of Polish Americans
NAPA .... National Association of Press Agencies (BUAC)
NAPA .... National Association of Pro America (EA)
NAPA .... National Association of Purchasing Agents [Later, NAPM] (EA)
NAPA .... National Association of the Partners of the Alliance [Later, Partners of the Americas] (EA)
NAPA .... National Automotive Parts Association (EA)
NAPA .... National Police Officers Association of America
NAPA .... Native American Press Association (EA)
NAPA .... Network Against Psychiatric Assault (EA)
NAPA .... North American Photonics Association [Defunct] (EA)
NAPA .... North American Pizza Association [Defunct]
NAPA .... North Atlantic Ports Association (EA)
NAPAA .... National Association for Promotional and Advertising Allowances, Inc. (NTPA)
NAPAAW ..... National Association of Professional Asian-American Women (EA)
NAPAC .... National Arson Prevention and Action Coalition (EA)
NAPAC .... National Association for Professional Associations and Corporations (EA)
NAPAC .... National Association of Paper and Advertising Collectors (EA)
NAPAC .... National Program for Acquisitions and Cataloging [Library of Congress]
NAPAEO ...... National Association of Principal Agricultural Education Officers [British]
NAPAF .... National Association of Private Art Foundations [Defunct] (EA)
NAPAG .... National Academies Policy Advisory Group
NAPall .... North American Palladium [Associated Press] (SAG)
napalm .... Naphthene Palmitate (AD)
NAPALM ...... Naphthenic and Palmitic Acids [Major constituents of flame thrower]
NAPALM ...... National ADP [Automatic Data Processing] Program for AMC Logistics Management [Army Materiel Command]
NAPALM ...... National Automatic Data Processing Program for Army Material Command Logistics Management (IAA)
NAPALSA .... National Asian Pacific American Law Student Association (EA)
NAPAMA .... National Association of Performing Arts Managers and Agents (EA)
NAPAMS .... Navy Automated Pilot Aptitude Measurement System
NAPAN .... National Association for the Prevention of Addiction to Narcotics [Later, NADAP]
NAPAP .... National Acidic Precipitation Assessment Program (BUAC)
NAPAP .... National Acid Precipitation Assessment Program [Council on Environmental Quality] [Washington, DC]
NAPAP .... National Atmospheric and Precipitation Assessment Program
NAPAP .... Noyaux Armes pour l'Autonomie Populaire [Armed Cells for Popular Autonomy] [France] (PD)
NAPARE ...... National Association for Perinatal Addiction Research and Education (EA)
NAPAS .... National Association of Protection and Advocacy Systems (EA)
NAPATMO .... NATO Patriot Management Office
NAPAVHEE... National Association of Postsecondary and Adult Vocational Home Economics Educators (EA)
NAPAW .... North American Process Algebra Workshop (SAUS)
NAPB .... National Agricultural Products Boards [Tanzania] (BUAC)
NAPB .... National Association for the Preservation of Baseball (EA)
NAPB .... National Association of Professional Bureaucrats [Later, INATAPROBU]
NAPBC .... National Action Plan on Breast Cancer
NAPBC .... Native American Public Broadcasting Consortium (EA)
NAPBFC ...... National Association of Pat Boone Fan Clubs (EA)
NAPBIRT ...... National Association of Professional Band Instrument Repair Technicians (EA)
NAPBL .... National Association of Professional Baseball Leagues (EA)

NAPBN......... National Air Pollution Background Network [*Environmental Protection Agency*] (GFGA)
NAPBTA........ National American Pit Bull Terrier Association (EA)
NAPC .... National Air Pollution Control (KSC)
NAPC .... National Alliance of Preservation Commissions (EA)
NAPC .... National Assault Prevention Center (EA)
NAPC .... National Association of Parish Councils [*British*] (BI)
NAPC .... National Association of Pastoral Counselors [*Defunct*] (EA)
NAPC .... National Association of Personnel Consultants [*Defunct*] (EA)
NAPC .... National Association of Pet Cemeteries [*Later, IAPC*]
NAPC .... National Association of Plumbing Contractors [*Later, NAPHCC*]
NAPC .... National Association of Precancel Collectors (EA)
NAPC .... Naval Air Photographic Center (DNAB)
NAPC .... Naval Air Priorities Center (DNAB)
NAPC .... Naval Air Project Coordinator (ACAE)
NAPC .... Naval Air Projects Co-ordination office (SAUS)
NAPC .... Naval Air Propulsion Center [*Trenton, NJ*]
NAPC .... Non-Adherent Peritoneal Cell (PDAA)
napc............ Non-Adherent Peritoneal Cells (AD)
NAPC .... North American Paleontological Convention
NAPC .... North American Paleontology Convention (SAUS)
NAPC .... North American Philips Corp. (SAUS)
NAPCA........ National Air Pollution Control Administration (AAGC)
NAPCA........ National Asian Pacific Center on Aging (EA)
NAPCA........ National Association of Pension Consultants and Administrators [*Atlanta, GA*] (EA)
NAPCA........ National Association of Pipe Coating Applicators (EA)
NAPCA........ National Association of Professional Contracts Administrators (AAGC)
NAPCA........ National Automatic Pistol Collectors Association (EA)
NAPCA........ North American Poultry Cooperative Association [*Defunct*] (EA)
NAPCAE....... National Association for Public Continuing and Adult Education (EA)
NAPCE .... National Association of Pastoral Care in Education [*British*] (DBA)
NAPCE .... National Association of Professors of Christian Education (EA)
NAPCMM-ELCA... Native American Program Commission for Multicultural Ministries of ELCA [*Evangelical Lutheran Church in America*] (EA)
NAPC/MS... Naval Air Propulsion Center Measurement and Information Systems Department [*Trenton, NJ*]
Napco .... Napco Security Systems, Inc. [*Associated Press*] (SAG)
NAPCOR....... National Association for Plastic Container Recovery (EA)
NAPC-PE...... Naval Air Propulsion Center Propulsion Engineering Department [*Trenton, NJ*]
NAPCR........ National Association for Puerto Rican Civil Rights
NAPCRG .... North American Primary Care Research Group (EA)
NAPCRO .... National Association of Police Community Relations Officers (EA)
NAPCS........ National Association of Postpartum Care Services (PAZ)
NAPCTAC..... National Air Pollution Control Techniques Advisory Committee [*Environmental Protection Agency*] (GFGA)
NAPCU......... Northwest Association of Private Colleges and Universities [*Library network*] (EA)
NAPCWA...... National Association of Public Child Welfare Administrators (EA)
NAPD .... National Association of Pharmaceutical Distributors [*British*] (BI)
NAPD .... National Association of Plastics Distributors (EA)
NAPD .... National Association of Police Driving (AD)
NAPD .... National Association of Precollege Directors (EA)
NAPD .... North American Pollen Database (QUAC)
NAPDA........ North American Professional Driver's Association [*Defunct*] (EA)
NAPDD........ Non-Acquisition Program Definition Document [*Navy*] (DOMA)
NAPDEA....... North American Professional Driver Education Association (EA)
NAPDP........ National Association of Prepaid Dental Plans (DMAA)
NAPE .... Naphthenic-Palmitic Acid [*Mixture used in flame-throwing weapons and bombs*] [*Also, NAPALM*] (VNW)
NAPE .... National Alliance of Postal Employees [*Later, NAPFE*]
NAPE .... National Association for Pseudoxanthoma Elasticum (NRGU)
NAPE .... National Association of Partners in Education
NAPE .... National Association of Physicians for the Environment (EA)
NAPE .... National Association of Port Employers [*British*]
NAPE .... National Association of Power Engineers (EA)
NAPE .... National Association of Primary Education [*British*] (DBA)
NAPE .... National Association of Private Enterprise [*Fort Worth, TX*] (EA)
NAPE .... National Association of Professional Educators (EA)
NAPE .... National Association of Professional Engravers (EA)
NAPE .... Nuclear Attack Preparedness Evaluation
NAPEC .... National Association of Professional Environmental Communicators (NTPA)
NAPEC .... Naval Ammunition Production Engineering Center
NAPECW...... National Association for Physical Education of College Women [*Later, NAPEHE*] (EA)
NAPEDNC ... National Association of Political Ex-Deportees of the Nazi Camps [*Italy*] [*Political party*] (EAIO)
NAPEGG....... Association of Professional Engineers, Geologists & Geophysicists of the Northwest Territories (AC)
NAPEHE...... National Association for Physical Education in Higher Education (EA)
NAPEM .... National Association of Public Exposition Managers [*Later, HGSEI*] (EA)
NAPENA...... National Association of Public Employer Negotiators and Administrators [*Later, NAPPENA*] (EA)
Na Pent .... Sodium Pentothal [*Thiopental Sodium*] [*A brand name*] [*Pharmacology*] (DAVI)
NAPEO .... National Association of Professional Employer Organizations (NTPA)
NAPEP .... National Association of Planners, Estimators, and Progressmen (EA)
NAPET .... National Association of Photo Equipment Technicians (EA)
NAPEX .... National Philatelic Exhibition
NAPF .... National Association of Pension Funds [*British*] (DI)
NAPF .... National Association of Petroleum Funds [*British*]
NAPF .... National Association of Plastic Fabricators (EA)

NAPF .... Naval Aviation Publication Facility
NAPF .... Nonappropriated Funds (DNAB)
NAPF .... North Atlantic Polar Front (SAUS)
NAPF .... Nuclear Age Peace Foundation (EA)
NAPFA .... National Association of Personal Financial Advisors (EA)
NAPFE .... National Alliance of Postal and Federal Employees (EA)
NAPFM .... National Association of Packaged Fuel Manufacturers [*Defunct*] (EA)
NAPFR .... National Association of Professional Fund Raisers (EA)
NAPFSC ...... National Association of Professional Forestry Schools and Colleges (WPI)
NAPG .... National Association of Professional Gardeners [*Later, PGMS*]
NAP(G) .... Naval Aviation Pilot (Glider)
NAPG .... News America Publishing Group
NaPG .... Sodium Pregnanediol Glucuronide [*Medicine*] (DMAA)
NAPGC .... National Association of Public Golf Courses [*British*] (BI)
NAPGCM ...... National Association of Private Geriatric Care Managers (EA)
NAPGCW...... National Association of Plasters, Granolithic, and Cement Workers [*A union*] [*British*]
naph .... Naphtha (AD)
NAPH .... Naphtha (ADA)
naph .... Naphthyl (AD)
NAPH .... Naphthyl [*Organic chemistry*] (MAE)
NAPH .... National Association of Professors of Hebrew (EA)
NAPH .... National Association of Public Hospitals (EA)
NAPH .... National Association of the Physically Handicapped (EA)
NAPH .... Nicotinamide Adenine Dinucleotide Phosphate [*An enzyme*] (DMAA)
NAPHA .... National Amusement Park Historical Association (EA)
NAPhA .... North American Photonics Association (EA)
NAPH & MSC... National Association of Plumbing, Heating, and Mechanical Service Contractors [*British*] (DBA)
NAPHC........ National Association of Plumbing/Heating/Cooling Contractors (AD)
NAPHCC...... National Association of Plumbing-Heating-Cooling Contractors [*Formerly, NAPC*]
NAPHS .... National Association of Psychiatric Health Systems (NTPA)
NAPHSIS..... National Association for Public Health Statistics and Information Systems (SAUS)
NAPHT .... National Association of Patients on Hemodialysis and Transplantation [*Later, AAKP*] (EA)
NAPI .... National Appaloosa Pony (EA)
NAPI .... National Association of Property Inspectors (NTPA)
NAPI .... National Association of the Pet Industry [*Defunct*] (EA)
NAPI .... Naval Aeronautical Publications Index (DNAB)
NAPI .... Neurobehavioral Assessment of the Preterm Infant [*Test*] (TMMY)
NAPI .... Numbering and Addressing Plan Identifier (SAUS)
NAPIA .... National Affiliate of Printing Industries of America (AD)
NAPIA .... National Association of Public Insurance Adjusters [*Baltimore, MD*] (EA)
NAPIAP .... National Agricultural Pesticide Impact Assessment Program [*Department of Agriculture*]
NAPIC .... National Association of Private Industry Councils [*Washington, DC*] (EA)
NAPIL .... National Association for Public Interest Law (EA)
NAPIM .... National Association of Printing Ink Manufacturers (EA)
NAPIS .... National Agricultural Pest Information System (AUEG)
NAPJPO ...... National Aerospace Plane Joint Programs Office
NAPL .... National Air Photo Library [*Canada*] (PDAA)
NAPL .... National Association of Photolithographers (IAA)
NAPL .... National Association of Police Laboratories (EA)
NAPL .... National Association of Printers and Lithographers (EA)
NAPL .... Nonaqueous Phase Liquid [*Chemistry*]
NAPLIB .... National Association Aerial of Photographic Libraries [*British*] (DBA)
NAPLO .... National Association of Power Loom Overlookers [*British*] (DBA)
NAPLP .... National Association of Para-Legal Personnel (AD)
NAP-LP .... National Association of Para-Legals Personnel (EA)
NAPLPS ...... North American Presentation Layer Protocol Suite (SAUS)
NAPLPS ...... North American Presentation Level Protocol Standard (DOM)
NAPLPS ...... North American Presentation Level Protocol Syntax [*Computer display system*] [*Pronounced "naplips"*]
NAPLS .... North American Presentation Level Protocol Syntax (ELAL)
NAPM .... National Association of Paper Merchants [*British*]
NAPM .... National Association of Pastoral Musicians (BUAC)
NAPM .... National Association of Pattern Manufacturers [*LA PPTBA*] (EA)
NAPM .... National Association of Perry Makers [*British*] (DBA)
NAPM .... National Association of Pharmaceutical Manufacturers (EA)
NAPM .... National Association of Photographic Manufacturers (EA)
NAPM .... National Association of Punch Manufacturers (EA)
NAPM .... National Association of Purchasing Management (EA)
NAP-M .... National Awami Party-Muzaffar [*Bangladesh*] [*Political party*] (FEA)
NAPMA .... NATO AEWC [*Airborne Early Warning and Control*] Program Management Agency
NAPMA .... North American Punch Manufacturers Association (NTPA)
NAPMDAC... National Air Pollution Manpower Development Advisory Committee [*Terminate d, 1976*] [*HEW*] (EGAO)
NAPMECA.... National Association of Postgraduate Medical Education Centre Administrators (BUAC)
NAPMG........ North African Provost Marshal General [*World War II*]
NAPMM .... National Association of Produce Market Managers [*Hartford, CT*] (EA)
NAPMO........ NATO Airborne Early Warning and Control Programme Management Organization [*Brunssum, Netherlands*]
NAPMR........ National Apostolate with People with Mental Retardation (EA)
NAPMW........ National Association of Professional Mortgage Women
NAPN .... National Association of Physician Nurses (EA)
NAPN .... Native American Policy Network
NAPN .... Native Authority Public Notice [*Nigeria*] [*A publication*] (ILCA)

NAPN .... North American Poetry Network (EA)
NAPNAP .... National Association of Pediatric Nurse Associates and Practitioners (EA)
NAPNE .... National Association for Practical Nurse Education (DAVI)
NAPNES .... National Association for Practical Nurse Education and Service (EA)
NAPNM .... National Association of Pipe Nipple Manufacturers [Defunct] (EA)
NAPNOC .... Neighborhood Arts Program National Organizing Committee (EA)
NAPNSC .... National Association of Private, Nontraditional Schools and Colleges (EA)
NAPNW .... Nurses Alliance for the Prevention of Nuclear War [Defunct] (EA)
NAPO .... NASA Pasadena Office
NAPO .... National Association of Performing Artists (AD)
NAPO .... National Association of Pizza Operators [Commercial firm] (EA)
NAPO .... National Association of Police Organizations (EA)
NAPO .... National Association of Pool Owners
NAPO .... National Association of Prison Officers [British] (DI)
NAPO .... National Association of Probation Officers [British] (DI)
NAPO .... National Association of Professional Organizers (EA)
NAPO .... National Association of Property Owners (EA)
NAPO .... National Association of Purchasing Agents (AD)
NAPO .... NATO Airborne Early Warning Program Office (NATG)
NAPO .... Naval Air Priorities Office
NAPO .... New Afrikan People's Organization (EA)
NAPO .... United National Association of Post Office Craftsmen [Later, APWU]
NAPOG .... Naval Airborne Project Press Operations Group [Hickam AFB, HI]
NAPOL .... North Atlantic Policy Working Group (SAUS)
NAPOLI .... National Politics [Behavioral science game]
NAPOMHWMGL... National Association of Post Office Mail Handlers, Watchmen, Messengers, and Group Leaders [Later, NPOMHWMGL] (EA)
NAPOTS .... National Aboriginal Project Officer Training Scheme [Australia]
NAPP .... National Association for the Protection of Punters (BUAC)
NAPP .... National Association of Paralegal Personnel (NTPA)
NAPP .... National Association of Patient Participation [British] (DBA)
NAPP .... National Association of Play Publishers
NAPP .... National Association of Poultry Packers Ltd. [British] (BI)
NAPP .... National Association of Priest Pilots (EA)
NAPP .... National Association of Printing Purchasers [Defunct] (EA)
NAPP .... National Association of Private Process Servers (EA)
NAPP .... Native American Publishing Program [of Harper & Row, Publishers, Inc.]
NAPP .... Naval Aviation Preparatory Program
NAPP .... Neighborhood Adult Participation Project
NAPP .... Net Aerial Primary Productivity [Forestry]
NAPP .... Non-Agricultural Pesticides Panel (HEAS)
NAPP .... Nonattainment Plan Provision [Environmental Protection Agency]
NAPPA .... National Association of Physical Plant Administrators of Universities and Colleges [Later, Association of Physical Plant Administrators of Universities and Colleges] (EA)
NAPPA .... National Association of Prevention Professionals and Advocates (NTPA)
NAPPA .... National Association of Pupil Personnel Administrators [Later, NAPSA] (EA)
NAPPB .... National Association of Professional Print Buyers (EA)
NAPPC .... National Association of Party Plan Companies [Defunct] (EA)
NAPPC .... North American Plant Preservation Council (NTPA)
NAPPENA ...... National Association of Public and Private Employer Negotiators and Administrators (EA)
NAPPF .... North American Power Petroleums, Inc. (SAUS)
NAPPH .... National Association of Private Psychiatric Hospitals (EA)
Nappie .... Neuilly, Auteil, and Passy [Elegant Paris neighborhoods; the term, Nappie, is used as a nickname for French Yuppies]
Nappies ...... New Age Professional People in Esoteric Studies [Lifestyle classification]
NAPPO .... National Association of Plant Patent Owners (EA)
NAPPO .... North American Plant Protection Organization [Canada] (BUAC)
Nap Pres ..... Napier. Prescription [A publication] (ILCA)
NAPPS .... National Association for the Preservation and Perpetuation of Storytelling (EA)
NAPPS .... National Association of Private Placement Syndicators [Later, California Investment Real Estate Forum] (EA)
NAPPS .... National Association of Private Process Servers (NTPA)
NAPPS .... National Association of Professional Pet Sitters (NTPA)
NAPPS .... National Association of Professional Process Servers (EA)
NAPPS .... North American Pediatric Pseudo-Obstruction Society (EA)
na pr .... Na Priklad [For Example] [Czech] (AD)
NAPR .... NASA Procurement Regulation
NAPR .... National Association for Pastoral Renewal [Defunct] (EA)
NAPR .... National Association of Park Rangers (EA)
NAPR .... National Association of Physician Recruiters (EA)
NAPR .... National Association of Pram Retailers (BUAC)
NAPR .... National Association of Publishers' Representatives (EA)
NAPR .... NATO Armaments Planning Review (NATG)
NAPRA .... National Association of Progressive Radio Announcers (EA)
NAPRA .... New Age Publishing and Retailing Alliance (EA)
NAPRA Int'l... New Age Publishing and Retailing Alliance International (NTPA)
NAPRALERT... Natural Products Alert [University of Illinois at Chicago] [Information service or system] (IID)
NAPRC .... National Association for the Prevention of Rape by Castration (AD)
NAPRCR ...... National Association for Puerto Rican Civil Rights (EA)
NAPRE .... National Association Practical Refrigerating Engineers [Later, RETA] (EA)
NAPRECA .... Natural Products Research Network for Eastern and Central Africa [UNESCO] [Ethiopia] (BUAC)
NAPRFMR.... National Association of Private Residential Facilities for the Mentally Retarded (EA)

NAPRI .... National Animal Production Research Institute [Nigeria] (BUAC)
NAPRI .... North American Pollutant Release Inventory (SAUS)
NaPro .... NaPro BioTherapeutics, Inc. [Associated Press] (SAG)
NaProBio .... NaPro BioTherapeutics, Inc. [Associated Press] (SAG)
NAPRS .... National Airspace Performance Reporting System [Aviation] (FAAC)
NAPRW .... Northwest African Photographic Reconnaissance Wing [World War II]
NAPS .... National Air Pollution Surveillance (EPAT)
NAPS .... National Alliance of Postal Supervisors (AD)
NAPS .... National Association for Premenstrual Syndrome (BUAC)
NAPS .... National Association for Professional Saleswomen (EA)
NAPS .... National Association of Personal Secretaries (BUAC)
NAPS .... National Association of Personnel Services (NTPA)
NAPS .... National Association of Pet Sitters (EA)
NAPS .... National Association of Postal Supervisors (EA)
NAPS .... National Association of Premenstrual Syndrome [British] (DBA)
NAPS .... National Association of Presbyterian Scouters (EA)
NAPS .... National Association of Private Secretaries [British] (BI)
NAPS .... National Association of Psychiatric Survivors (EA)
NAPS .... National Auricula and Primula Society (BUAC)
NAPS .... National Auxiliary Publications Service [American Society for Information Science]
NAPS .... Nationwide Association of Preserving Specialists [British] (DBA)
NAPS .... Naval Academy Preparatory School
NAPS .... Navy Acquisition Procedures Supplement [A publication] (AAGC)
NAPS .... Navy Automated Publications System (ACAE)
NAPS .... Nerve Agent Pre-Treatment Set [A cholinergic drug] [Used for protective immunization by the military]
NAPS .... Nerve Agent Pre-treatment Tablets (SAUS)
NAPS .... New Abstracts and Papers in Sleep (SAUS)
NAPS .... Night Aerial Photographic System
NAPS .... Nimbus Automatic Programming System (IEEE)
NAPS .... Nissan Air Pollution System (AD)
NAPS .... Nonspecific Air Pollution Syndrome
NAPS .... North American Patristic Society (EA)
NAPS .... North American Precis Syndicate
NAPS .... North American Pro Series [Auto racing]
NAPS .... North Anna Power Station [Virginia] [Nuclear energy] (NRCH)
NAPSA .... National Appliance Parts Suppliers Association (EA)
NAPSA .... National Association of Pretrial Service Agencies (AD)
NAPSA .... National Association of Public Service Advertisers [British] (DBA)
NAPSA .... National Association of Pupil Services Administrators (EA)
NAPSA .... North American Pediatric Subspecialty Association (SAUS)
NAPSAA ...... National Association of Public School Adult Administrators [Later, NAPSAE]
NAPSAC ...... International Association of Parents and Professionals for Safe Alternatives in Childbirth [Association retains acronym of its former name] (EA)
NAPSAC ...... National Association for the Protection from Sexual Abuse of Adults and Children with Learning Disabilities (BUAC)
NAPSAC ...... Naval Atomic Planning, Support, and Capabilities Report (NG)
NAPSAE ...... National Association for Public School Adult Educators [Later, NAPCAE] (EA)
NAPSAP ...... Naval Airship Program for Sizing and Performance (MCD)
Nap's bones... Napier's Bones [First slide rule] (AD)
NAPSEC ...... National Association of Private Schools for Exceptional Children (EA)
NAPSEO ...... National Association of Public Sector Equal Opportunity Officers
NAPSG .... National Association of Principals of Schools for Girls (EA)
NAPSIC .... North American Power Systems Interconnection Committee [US and Canada] [Electric power]
NAPSIS .... Navy Air Pollution Source Information System
NAPSLO .... National Association of Professional Surplus Lines Offices (EA)
NAPSOE ...... National Association of Public Service Organization Executives (EA)
NAPSS .... National Association of Professional Secretarial Services [Later, PASS] (EA)
NAPSS .... Numerical Analysis Problem Solving System
NAPSV .... National Association of Private Security Vaults (EA)
Napt .... Napton's Reports [4 Missouri] [A publication] (DLA)
NAPT .... National Association for Poetry Therapy (EA)
NAPT .... National Association for Proton Therapy (NTPA)
NAPT .... National Association for Pupil Transportation (EA)
NAPT .... National Association for the Prevention of Tuberculosis [British] (DI)
NAPT .... National Association of Percussion Teachers (BUAC)
NAPT .... National Association of Physical Therapists (EA)
NAPT .... Native American Public Telecommunications, Inc. (SAUS)
NAPT .... Naval Air Primary Training
NAPT .... Nordic Association of Plumbers and Tinsmiths (EAIO)
NAPTC .... Naval Air Primary Training Command
NAPTC .... Naval Air Propulsion Test Center [Later, NAPC]
NAPTCA ...... National Alliance for the Prevention and Treatment of Child Abuse (EA)
NAPTC-AED... Naval Air Propulsion Test Center - Aeronautical Engine Department
NAPTC-ATD... Naval Air Propulsion Test Center - Aeronautical Turbine Department
NAPTCC .... National Association of Psychiatric Treatment Centers for Children (EA)
NAPTC-OP ... Naval Air Propulsion Test Center - Operations and Plant Engineering Department
NAPTC-PE ... Naval Air Propulsion Test Center - Propulsion Technology and Project EngineeringDepartment
NAPTCRO .... Naval Air Primary Training Command Regional Office
NAPTDC .... National Association of Professional Truck Driving Champions (EA)
NAPTE .... National Association of Part-Time and Temporary Employees
NaPTEC .... National Primary Teacher Education Conference (AIE)
NAPTIC .... National Air Pollution Technical Information Center [of National Air Pollution Control Administration] [Also, APTIC] (DIT)
Napton .... Napton's Reports [4 Missouri] [A publication] (DLA)

NAPTR.......	National Association of Property Tax Representatives [*Defunct*] (EA)
NAPTS.......	National Association of Public Television Stations [*Later, APB*] (EA)
NAPTW.......	National Association of Pet Trade Wholesalers (BUAC)
NAPU.........	National Association of Professional Upholsterers [*Defunct*] (EA)
NAPU.........	Nuclear Auxiliary Power Unit
NAPUBFAC..	Naval Air Publication Facility (MCD)
NAPUS.......	National Association of Postmasters of the United States (EA)
NAPUS.......	Nuclear Auxiliary Power Unit System
NAPV.........	National Association of Prison Visitors [*British*] (BI)
NAPVD.......	National Association for the Prevention of Venereal Disease (AD)
NAPVI........	National Association for Parents of the Visually Impaired (EA)
NAPVO.......	National Association of Passenger Vessel Owners (EA)
NAPW........	National Association of Personnel Workers (EA)
NAPWA.......	National Association of People with AIDS (EA)
NAPWDA....	North American Police Work Dog Association (EA)
NAPWPT.....	National Association of Professional Word Processing Technicians [*Philadelphia, PA*] (EA)
NAQ..........	Narssarssuaq [*Denmark*] [*Geomagnetic observatory code*]
NAQ..........	Never Answered Questions (SAUS)
NAQ..........	Nursing Administration Quarterly (SAUS)
NAQAP.......	National Association of Quality Assurance Professionals (EA)
NAQDC.......	National Air Quality Data Center [*Australia*]
NAQI.........	National Air Quality Index (AD)
NAQMC......	North African Quartermaster Section [*World War II*]
NAQP........	National Association of Quick Printers (EA)
NAQUADAT...	National Water Quality Data Bank [*Environment Canada*] [*Information service or system*] (IID)
NAR..........	Air Continental, Inc. [*ICAO designator*] (FAAC)
NAR..........	Nagase Analbuminemia Rat
NAR..........	Nara [*Japan*] [*Seismograph station code, US Geological Survey*] (SEIS)
NAR..........	Narcotic (ROG)
NAR..........	Nare [*Colombia*] [*Airport symbol*] (OAG)
Nar..........	Narragansett (AD)
NAR..........	Narration [*Films, television, etc.*]
nar..........	Narrator (GROV)
NAR..........	Narrow (AAG)
nar..........	Narrow (AD)
NAR..........	Nasal Airway Resistance [*Medicine*]
NAR..........	National Archives and Records Service, Washington, DC [*OCLC symbol*] (OCLC)
NAR..........	National Asbestos Registry [*Environmental Protection Agency*] (GFGA)
NAR..........	National Association for the Retarded (DMAA)
NAR..........	National Association of Realtors (EA)
NAR..........	National Association of Rocketry (EA)
NAR..........	Naval Air Reserve
NAR..........	Naval Auxiliary Reserve
NAR..........	Naval Research and Development
NAR..........	Navy Ammunition Reclassification
NAR..........	Nelson Aldrich Rockefeller
NAR..........	Neo Aristero Revma [*Greece*] [*Political party*] (ECED)
NAR..........	Net Advertising Revenue [*Television*] [*British*]
nar..........	Net Assimilation Rate (AD)
NAR..........	Net Assimilation Rate [*Botany*]
NAR..........	New American Review (SAUS)
NAR..........	New Arrival Information [*Travel industry*] (TRID)
NAR..........	No Action [*or Answer*] Required (NVT)
NAR..........	No Adverse Reaction [*Medicine*] (MELL)
NAR..........	No Answer Required (SAUS)
nar..........	No Apparent Rate (AD)
NAR..........	No Apparent Reason (SAUS)
NAR..........	Noise-Adding Radiometer
NAR..........	Nominal Acceleration Radar (SAUS)
NAR..........	Non-Addressable Register (SAUS)
NAR..........	Non-Advocacy Review (ACAE)
NAR..........	Non-Advocate Review (SAUS)
NAR..........	Nordic Association for Rehabilitation [*Denmark*] (EAIO)
NAR..........	Nordiska Akademiker Radet [*Nordic Academic Council - NAC*] [*Defunct*] (EA)
NAR..........	North American Review [*A publication*] (BRI)
NAR..........	North American Rockwell Corp. [*Later, Rockwell International Corp.*] (MCD)
NAR..........	North American Route [*Aviation*]
NAR..........	North American Royalties (AD)
NAR..........	North Australia Railway
NAR..........	Northern Alberta Railways Co. [*AAR code*]
NAR..........	Nose Alone Reference [*Aviation*] (MCD)
NAR..........	Not According to Routine
NAR..........	Not at Risk (MELL)
NAR..........	Notice of Ammunition Reclassification [*Navy*] (NG)
NAR..........	Notification of Ammunition Reclassification [*Military*]
NAR..........	Nuclear Acoustic Resonance
NAR..........	Nuclear Androgen Receptor [*Endocrinology*]
NAR..........	Nuclear Assessment Routine (MCD)
NAR..........	Nuclei Armati Rivoluzionari [*Armed Revolutionary Nuclei*] [*Italian*] (PD)
NAR..........	Nucleic Acids Research [*A publication*]
NAR..........	Numerical Analysis Research (MCD)
NARA........	N3N Restorers Association (EA)
NARA........	Narcotics Addict Rehabilitation Act [*1966*]
NARA........	National Agrichemical Retailers Association (EPAT)
NARA........	National Air Resources Act (GFGA)
NARA........	National Alliance for Rural Action (EA)

NARA.........	National Aquatic Resources Agency [*Sri Lanka*] [*Marine science*] (OSRA)
NARA.........	National Archives and Records Administration [*Independent government agency*] [*Formerly, NARS*]
NARA.........	National Association for the Rescue of Animals [*British*] (DI)
NARA.........	National Association of Recovered Alcoholics [*Defunct*] (EA)
NARA.........	National Association of Rehabilitation Agencies (EA)
NARA.........	National Association of Republican Attorneys (EA)
NARA.........	National Association of Review Appraisers (EA)
NARA.........	Naval Aircraft Restorers Association (EA)
NARA.........	Navy Appellate Review Activity (ACAE)
NARA.........	Nippon Australian Relations Agreement (AD)
NARA.........	North American Radio Archives (EA)
NARA.........	North American Radon Association [*Defunct*] (EA)
NARA.........	North American Regional Alliance of IATA [*International Amateur Theatre Association*] (EA)
NARA.........	North American Rhea Association (NTPA)
NARA.........	Northern Auto Racing Association [*Sanctioning organization*]
NARAA.......	National Association of Recruitment Advertising Agencies [*Defunct*] (EA)
NARACC.....	National Association for Research and Action in Community Care [*British*] (DI)
NARACS.....	National Radio Communications System [*FAA*] (TAG)
NARAD.......	Naval Air Research and Development (MUGU)
NARAD.......	Navy Research and Development (AD)
NARADCOM..	Natick Research and Development Command [*Army*]
NARAG.......	National Association of Ratepayers' Action Groups [*British*] (DI)
NARAL.......	National Abortion and Reproductive Rights Acion League
NARAL.......	National Abortion Rights Action League (AD)
NARAL.......	National Association for the Repeal of Abortion Laws
NARAL.......	Net Advertising Revenue after Levy [*Television*] [*British*]
NARAL PAC..	National Abortion and Reproductive Rights Action League-Political Action Committee
NARAMU.....	National Association of Review Appraisers and Mortgage Underwriters (NTPA)
NARANEXOS...	Name, Rate, Service Number, and Expiration of Obligated Service [*Navy*]
NARANO.....	Name, Rate, and Service Number [*Navy*]
NarAnon.....	Narcotics Anonymous (MELL)
NARAS.......	National Academy of Recording Arts and Sciences (EA)
NARASO.....	Nevada Association Race and Sports Book Operators (EA)
NARASPO....	Navy Regional Airspace Officer (MUGU)
NARAT.......	NATO Request for Air Transport Support [*Military*]
NARATE......	Navy Advanced Radar Automatic Test Equipment (SAUS)
NARATE......	Navy Automatic RADAR Test Equipment (KSC)
NARATE......	Northrop Automatic RADAR Test System (SAA)
NARAVA......	National Archives and Records Administration Volunteer Association (EA)
NARB........	Narcotic Addict Rehabilitation Branch [*National Institute of Mental Health*]
NARB........	National Advertising Review Board [*New York, NY*] (EA)
NARB........	National Assembly of Religious Brothers (EA)
NARB........	National Assocation of Radio Broadcasters (NTCM)
NARB........	National Association for Regional Ballet [*Later, RDA*]
NARB........	National Association of Referees in Bankruptcy [*Later, National Conference of Bankruptcy Judges*] (EA)
NARB........	National Association of Retired Bankers [*Later, RBA*] (EA)
NARB........	Navy Art Review Board (DNAB)
NARB........	Nonazeotropic Refrigerant Blend
NARBA.......	North American Rare Bird Alert (SAUS)
NARBA.......	North American Regional Broadcasting Agreement [*To minimize interference between AM stations*]
NARBC.......	National Angora Rabbit Breeders Club (EA)
NARBEC.....	North American Regional Broadcasting Engineering Committee (SAUS)
NARBL.......	Net Advertising Revenue before Levy [*Television*] [*British*]
NARBS.......	Night/Day Angle Rate Bombing System (ACAE)
NARBW......	National Association of Railway Business Women (EA)
narc.........	Narcotic (AD)
NARC........	Narcotics [*FBI standardized term*]
narc.........	Narcotics Agent (AD)
NARC........	Narcotism [*Chemical dependency*] (DAVI)
NARC........	National Agricultural Research Center
NARC........	National Amateur Retriever Club (EA)
NARC........	National Archives and Records Service (AD)
NARC........	National Army Revolutionary Committee [*or Council*] [*Laos*]
NARC........	National Association for Retarded Citizens [*Later, ARC*] (EA)
NARC........	National Association of Regional Councils (EA)
NARC........	National Association of Retired Catholics (AD)
NARC........	Naval Air Research Center (DNAB)
NARC........	Naval Air Reserve Center (DNAB)
NARC........	Naval Alcohol Rehabilitation Center (DNAB)
NARC........	Ninth Area Radio Club (SAUS)
NARC........	Nonautomatic Relay Center (AABC)
NARC........	North American Riders Club (EA)
NARC........	North American Rockwell Corp. [*Later, Rockwell International Corp.*] (MCD)
NARC........	North Atlantic Route Chart (PIPO)
NARC........	Northern Automobile Racing Club [*Sanctioning organization*]
NARC........	Nuclear Age Resource Center (EA)
NARC........	Nucleus Arcuatus (DMAA)
NARCA.......	National Antidrug Reorganization and Coordination Act
NARCA.......	National Association of Retail Collection Attorneys (NTPA)
NARCE.......	National Association of Retired Civil Employees [*Later, NARFE*] (EA)
NARCF.......	National Association of Residential Care Facilities (NTPA)

NARCF......... National Association of Retail Clothiers and Furnishers [*Later, MRA*] (EA)
NARCINT...... Narcotics Intelligence [*Military*] (ADDR)
NARCL......... Nuclear Accident Response Capability Listing (MCD)
narco.......... Narcolepsy [*Neurology*] (DAVI)
narco.......... Narcotic (AD)
NARCO......... Narcotics Commission [*United Nations*] (AD)
narco.......... Narcotics Hospital (DAVI)
narco.......... Narcotics Officer (AD)
narco.......... Narcotics Treatment Center (DAVI)
NARCO......... National Aeronautical Corp. (MCD)
narcocard..... Narcotic-Addict Registration Card (AD)
narcodollars... Narcotic Traffic Dollars (AD)
NARCOG........ Narcotics Coordination Group [*CIA*]
NARCOM...... Narration, Commentary [*Motion pictures*]
NARCOM...... North Atlantic Relay Communication (SAUS)
NARCOM...... North Atlantic Relay Communication Satellite
NARCOM Satellite... North Atlantic Relay Communication Satellite (SAUS)
NARCOM System... North Atlantic Relay Communication System (SAUS)
Narconon...... Narcotics Anonymous [*An association*] (AD)
Nar Conv...... Nares' Penal Convictions [*1815*] [*A publication*] (DLA)
NAR CORP..... North American Rockwell Corp. [*Later, Rockwell International Corp.*]
narcos.......... Narcotics (AD)
narcos.......... Narcotics Police Officers (AD)
narcot.......... Narcotic (AD)
narcotest....... Narcotics Test (AD)
Narcotics L Bull... Narcotics Law Bulletin [*A publication*] (DLA)
narco-traf..... Narcotics Traffick (AD)
narcs.......... Narcotics (AD)
Narcs.......... Narcotics (MILB)
narcs.......... Narcotics Agents (AD)
narcs.......... Narcotics Hospital (AD)
narcs.......... Narcotics Officers (AD)
narcs.......... Narcotics Treatment Centers (AD)
NARCU......... National Association of Railroad and Utility Commissioners (NTCM)
NARCUP........ National Association for Retired Credit Union People (EA)
NArd.......... Ardmore Industrial Air Park (SAUS)
NArd.......... Ardsley Public Library, Ardsley, NY [*Library symbol*] [*Library of Congress*] (LCLS)
NARD.......... National Association of Regimental Drummers (AD)
NARD.......... National Association of Retail Druggists (EA)
NARD.......... National Association of Rudimental Drummers [*Defunct*]
NARD.......... Navy Alcohol Rehabilitation Drydock (DNAB)
NARD.......... Nonarticular Rheumatic Disorder [*Medicine*] (MELL)
nard.......... Spikenard (AD)
NARDA......... National Appliance and Radio TV Dealers Association (IAA)
NARDA......... National Association of Retail Dealers of America (EA)
NARDA......... Naval Air Research and Development Activities (SAA)
NARDAC....... Navy Regional Data Automation Center
NARDACWASHDC... Navy Regional Data Automation Center, Washington, DC (DNAB)
NArdCG......... CIBA-GEIGY Corp., Corporate Library, Ardsley, NY [*Library symbol*] [*Library of Congress*] (LCLS)
NARDELOG... Navy Rapid Delivery Logistics (AFIT)
NARDET........ Naval Air Reserve Detachment (DNAB)
NARDIC........ Navy Research and Development Information Center
NARDIS........ Navy Automated Research and Development Information System [*Later, NAVWUIS*]
Nar Div........ Narodni Divadlo [*National Theater*] [*Czechoslavakia*] (AD)
NARDIV........ Naval Air Reserve Divisions
NARDIV(FA)... Naval Air Reserve Division (Fleet Air) (DNAB)
NARDV......... National Association Rainbow Division Veterans (EA)
NARE.......... National Association for Remedial Education [*British*]
NARE.......... North Atlantic Regional Experiment [*Ozone measurement*]
NAREA......... National Association of Real Estate Appraisers (EA)
Na_{reab}.......... Sodium Reabsorption Rate [*Biochemistry*] (DAVI)
NAREB......... National Association of Real Estate Boards [*Later, National Association of Realtors*] (EA)
NAREB......... National Association of Real Estate Brokers
NAREBB....... National Association of Real Estate Buyer Brokers (EA)
NAREC........ National Association of Real Estate Companies (EA)
narec.......... Naval Research Electronic Computer (AD)
NAREC........ Naval Research Electronic Computer
NAREE......... National Association of Real Estate Editors (EA)
NAREFA....... North Atlantic Reference Fares (SAUS)
NaREIA........ National Real Estate Investors Association (NTPA)
NAREIF........ National Association of Real Estate Investment Funds [*Later, NAREIT*] (EA)
NAREIM....... National Association of Real Estate Investment Managers (NTPA)
NAREIT........ National Association of Real Estate Investment Trusts (EA)
NARELLO..... National Association of Real Estate License Law Officials (EA)
NAREMCO.... National Records Management Council (EA)
NAREP......... National Association of Real Estate Professionals (NTPA)
NARESU....... Naval Air Reserve Unit (DNAB)
NARETPA..... National Agricultural Research, Extension, and Teaching Policy Act of 1977
NARETU....... Naval Air Reserve Electronics Training Unit (DNAB)
NARF.......... American Rehabilitation Association [*Formerly, National Association of Rehabilitation Facilities*] (EA)
NARF.......... National Association of Rehabilitation Facilities (EA)
NARF.......... National Association of Retail Furnishers (AD)
NARF.......... Native American Rights Fund (EA)
NARF.......... Natural Axial Resonant Frequency (PDAA)
narf.......... Natural Axial-Resonant Frequency (AD)
NARF.......... Naval Aerospace Recovery Facility (SAUS)

NARF.......... Naval Aerospace Research Facility
NARF.......... Naval Air Reserve Force
NARF.......... Naval Air Rework Facility
NARF.......... Navy Arctic Research Facility
NARF.......... Nuclear Aerospace Research Facility (IEEE)
NARF.......... Nuclear Aircraft Research Facility (AD)
NARFE......... National Association of Retired Federal Employees (EA)
NARFFO....... Naval Air Rework Facility Field Office (DNAB)
NARFS......... Naval Air Reserve Force Squadron (DNAB)
NARGA......... National Association of Retail Grocers of Australia (AD)
NARGOM...... North American Research Group on Management (PDAA)
NARGS......... North American Rock Garden Society (EA)
NARGUS..... National Association of Retail Grocers of the United States [*Later, NGA*] (EA)
NARHA......... North American Riding for the Handicapped Association (EA)
NARHC........ National Association of River and Harbor Contractors [*Later, NADC*] (EA)
NARHS......... National Auto Racing Historical Society (EA)
NARI.......... National Ageing Research Institute (SAUS)
NARI.......... National Agriculture Research Institute (WDAA)
NARI.......... National AIDS Research Institute [*India*]
NARI.......... National Alliance for Reduction of Imprisonment [*Defunct*] (EA)
NARI.......... National Association of Recycling Industries [*Later, ISRI*] (EA)
NARI.......... National Association of Rehabilitation Instructors (EA)
NARI.......... National Association of Residents and Interns (EA)
NARI.......... National Association of the Remodeling Industry (EA)
NARI.......... National Atmospheric Research Institute (AD)
NARI.......... Native American Research Institute (EA)
NARI.......... Nuclear Aerospace Research Institute [*Air Force*]
NARIC......... National Academic Recognition Information Centre (AIE)
NARIC......... National Rehabilitation Information Center (EA)
NARICM....... National Association of Retail Ice Cream Manufacturers [*Later, NICYRA*] (EA)
Nar Inv........ Narcotics Investigation (AD)
NARISCO..... North American Rockwell Information Systems Co.
NARIST........ Naristillae [*Nasal Drops*] [*Pharmacy*]
narist.......... Naristillae [*Nasal Drops*] [*Latin*] (AD)
NARK.......... Nikolai Andreyvich Rimsky-Korsakov (AD)
Narkomvneshtorg... Narodny Komissariat Vneshney Torgovli [*People's Commissariat of Foreign Trade*] [*Russian*] (AD)
NARKOMVNUDEL... Narodnyi Komissariat Vnutrennikh Del [*People's Commissariat of Internal Affairs (1917-1946)*] [*Also known as NKVD*] [*Soviet secret police organization*]
NARL.......... National Aero Research Laboratory [*Canada*] (PDAA)
NARL.......... National Air and Radiation Laboratory (AUEG)
NARL.......... Naval Arctic Research Laboratory
NARL.......... No Adverse Response Level [*Medicine*] (HCT)
NARM.......... National Association of Recording Merchandisers (EA)
NARM.......... National Association of Relay Manufacturers (EA)
NARM.......... National Association of Restaurant Managers [*Scottsdale, AZ*] (EA)
NARM.......... National Association of Retail Merchants (EA)
NARM.......... Naturally Occurring or Accelerator-Produced Radioactive Material
NARM.......... Naval Resource Model (MCD)
NARM.......... Nuclear Accelerator-generated Radioactive Material (SAUS)
N-arm.......... Nuclear Armament (AD)
NARMC........ National Association of Regional Media Centers (EA)
NARMC........ National Association of Resident Management Corporations (NTPA)
NARMC........ Naval Aerospace and Regional Medical Center [*Bureau of Medicine*]
NARMC........ North Atlantic Regional Medical Center (SAUS)
NARMCO..... National Research and Manufacturing Co. (AD)
NARM-DPG... North Atlantic Rifted Margins Detailed Planning Group (SAUS)
N-armed....... Nuclear-Armed (AD)
NARMFD....... National Association of Retail Meat and Food Dealers
NARMH........ National Association for Rural Mental Health (EA)
NARMIC....... National Action/Research on the Military Industrial Complex (EA)
NArmN......... North Castle Library, Armonk, NY [*Library symbol*] [*Library of Congress*] (LCLS)
NARMP........ National Antibacterial Residue Minimization Program [*Australia*]
NARMPU....... Naval Air Reserve Mobile Photographic Unit (DNAB)
N-Arms Control... Nuclear Arms Control (SAUS)
N-Arms Race... Nuclear Arms Race (SAUS)
NARMU........ Naval Air Reserve Maintenance Units
NARN.......... National Association of Registered Nurses (EA)
NARND........ National Association of Radio News Directors (IAA)
NARO.......... National Agricultural Research Organization [*Netherlands*] (ECON)
NARO.......... National Association of Reimbursement Officers [*Washington, DC*] (EA)
NARO.......... National Association of Royalty Owners (EA)
NARO.......... Naval Aircraft Repair Organisation (SAUS)
NARO.......... North American Regional Office (AD)
NAROCTESTSTA... Naval Air Rocket Test Station
NARP.......... National Administrative Rehabilitation Programme [*United Nations program*]
NARP.......... National Association for Registered Plans (EA)
NARP.......... National Association of Railroad Passengers (EA)
NARP.......... National Association of Reunion Managers (NTPA)
NARP.......... Neurogenic Muscle Weakness, Ataxia, and Retinitis Pigmentosa [*Medicine*]
NARP.......... Neuropathy, Ataxia, Retinitis Pigmentosa (SAUS)
NARP.......... New Australian Republican Party [*Political party*]
NARP.......... Nonaqueous Reversed Phase [*Chromatography*]
NARP.......... Non-Broadcast Multiple Access Address Resolution Protocol (SAUS)
NARP.......... Nuclear Weapons Accident Report Procedures (AD)
NARPA......... National Air Rifle and Pistol Association [*British*]
NARPA......... National Association for Rights Protection and Advocacy (EA)

NARPD......... National Association for the Relief of Paget's Disease [*British*]
NARPM....... National Association of Residential Property Managers (NTPA)
NARPO....... National Association of Retired Police Officers [*British*] (DBA)
NARPPS....... National Association of Rehabilitation Professionals in the Private Sector (EA)
NARPS......... Northampton Air Raid Precautions Standard (SAUS)
NARPTR....... National Association of Railroad Property Tax Representatives (NTPA)
NARPV......... National Association for Remotely Piloted Vehicles (MCD)
NARR.......... Narrator [*or Narration*]
NARRD........ National Association of Record Retailer Dealers [*Defunct*] (EA)
Nar Rep Bul... Narodna Republika Bulgaria [*Bulgarian People's Republic*] [*Political party*] (AD)
Narr Mod..... Narrationes Modernae [*Style's English King's Bench Reports*] [*1646-55*] [*A publication*] (DLA)
NARRP......... National Association of Recreation Resource Planners (NTPA)
NARRS......... National Association of Radio Reading Services (EA)
NARS.......... Narrative Accomplishment Reporting System [*Department of Agriculture*] [*Information service or system*] (IID)
NARS.......... National Acupuncture Research Society (EA)
NARS.......... National Agricultural Research Systems (ECON)
NARS.......... National Annual Report Service [*NYSE*]
NARS.......... National Archives and Records Service [*of GSA*] [*Washington, DC*] [*Later, NARA*]
NARS.......... National Association of Radiation Survivors (EA)
NARS.......... National Association of Radiator Specialists [*British*] (DBA)
NARS.......... National Association of Radiotelephone Systems [*Later, Telocator Network of America*] (EA)
NARS.......... National Association of Rail Shippers (EA)
NARS.......... National Association of Refunders and Shoppers [*Defunct*] (EA)
NARS.......... National Association of Rehabilitation Secretaries (EA)
NARS.......... Naval Air Rescue Service (MUGU)
NARS.......... New Atlantean Research Society [*Defunct*] (EA)
NARS.......... Non-Affiliated Reserve Section (SAUS)
NARS.......... Northampton Activity Rating Scale [*Psychology*]
NARS.......... North Atlantic Radio System
NARSA......... National Automotive Radiator Service Association (EA)
NARS-A1...... National Archive and Record Service-Automation 1 (NITA)
NARSAB....... National Association of Rail Shippers Advisory Boards (EA)
NARSAD ...... National Alliance for Research on Schizophrenia and the Depressions (EA)
NARSAP....... National Advanced Remote Sensing Application Program
NARSC........ National Association of Reinforcing Steel Contractors (EA)
NARSID....... Non-Avalanche-Related Snow-Immersion Death
NARSIS........ National Association for Road Safety Instruction in Schools (AD)
NARSLL .... National Association to Reform State Liquor Laws [*Later, National Association to Reform State Drinking Ages*] [*Defunct*] (EA)
NARSNDF .... North Atlantic Regional Study Narrative Data File (SAUS)
NARST......... National Association for Research in Science Teaching (EA)
NARSTC....... Naval Air Rescue Training Command
NARSTO....... North American Research Strategy for Tropospheric Ozone
NARSUP ...... Navy Acquisition Regulations Supplement
NARSVA....... National Archives and Record Service Volunteer Association [*Later, NARAVA*] (EA)
NARSVPD .... National Association of Retired Senior Volunteer Program Directors (EA)
NART.......... National Association for Remedial Teaching (AEBS)
NART.......... National Association of Recreation Therapists [*Later, NTRS*] (EA)
NART.......... New Adult Reading Test
NART.......... North American Racing Team [*Auto racing*]
NARTA......... North American Restaurant and Tavern Alliance (EA)
NARTB......... National Association of Radio and Television Broadcasters [*Later, NAB*]
NARTC........ National Association of Railroad Trial Counsel (EA)
NARTC........ Naval Air Research Training Command
NARTC........ Naval Air Rocket Test Center (MUGU)
NARTC........ North American Regional Test Center (SAUS)
NARTC........ North America Regional Test Center (NATG)
NARTCE....... National Association for Released Time Christian Education (EA)
NARTE .... National Association of Radio and Telecommunications Engineers (EA)
NARTH........ National Association of Research and Therapy of Homosexuality (EA)
NARTM .... National Association of Rope and Twine Merchants (AD)
NARTRANS... North American Rockwell Training and Services [*Obsolete*]
NARTS......... National Association of Radio Telephone Systems [*Later, Telocator Network of America*] (IAA)
NARTS......... National Association of Reporter Training Schools [*Defunct*] (EA)
NARTS......... National Association of Resale and Thrift Shops (EA)
NARTS......... Naval Aeronautics Test Station
NARTS......... Naval Air Rocket Test Station
NARTU........ Naval Air Reserve Training Unit
NARU.......... Natural Rate of Unemployment [*Economics*]
NARU.......... Naval Air Reserve Unit (NVT)
NARU.......... North Australian Research Unit (AD)
NARUC........ National Association of Regulatory Utility Commissioners (EA)
NARUCE....... National Association of Regulatory Utility Commission Engineers (IAA)
NARUS......... Navy Aircraft Resources Utilization Study
NARVRE....... National Association of Retired and Veteran Railroad Employees (EA)
NARW.......... National Assembly of Religious Women (EA)
NARW.......... National Association of Refrigerated Warehouses [*Later, IARW*] (EA)
NARWA........ Nordic Agricultural Research Workers Association (EA)
NARWACL.... North American Regional World Anti-Communist League (AD)

NAS .... N-Acetylserotonin [*Biochemistry*]
NAS .... Narcotics Affairs Section [*Foreign service*]
NAS .... Narrow-Angle Sensor
nas............. Nasal (AD)
NAS .... Nasal
NAS .... Nasangga [*Fiji*] [*Seismograph station code, US Geological Survey*] (SEIS)
NAS .... Nassau [*Bahamas*] [*Airport symbol*] (OAG)
NAS .... National Academy of Sciences [*Washington, DC*]
NAS .... National Academy of Songwriters (EA)
NAS .... National Academy of Sports (EA)
NAS .... National Accreditation Service (SAUS)
NAS .... National Adoption Society (WDAA)
NAS .... National Advanced Systems (HGAA)
NAS .... National Advocates Society
NAS .... National Aerospace Standards Industrial Association (AAGC)
NAS .... National Agricultural Society (NADA)
NAS .... National Aircraft Standard (SAUS)
NAS .... National Aircraft Standards
NAS .... National Airspace System [*NASA*]
NAS .... National Alliance for Salvation [*Sudan*] [*Political party*] (MENA)
NAS .... National Aquarium Society (EA)
NAS .... National Aquatic School [*Red Cross*]
NAS .... National Association of Sanitarians [*Later, NEHA*] (EA)
NAS .... National Association of Scholars (EA)
NAS .... National Association of Schoolmasters [*British*]
NAS .... National Association of Shopfitters [*British*] (BI)
NAS .... National Association of Shopkeepers [*British*] (DBA)
NAS .... National Association of Specialized Carriers, Marietta GA [*STAC*]
NAS .... National Association of Stevedores (EA)
NAS .... National Association of Supervisors [*Later, Federal Managers Association*] (EA)
NAS .... National Astrological Society [*Defunct*] (EA)
NAS .... National Audubon Society (EA)
NAS .... National Autistic Society [*British*]
NAS .... National Aviation System [*FAA*]
NAS .... National Avionics Society (EA)
NAS .... National Seastar [*Vancouver Stock Exchange symbol*]
NAS .... Native American Studies (AD)
NAS .... Naval Air Service
NAS .... Naval Air Squadron (SAUS)
NAS .... Naval Air Station
NAS .... Naval Air Systems Command, Washington, DC [*OCLC symbol*] (OCLC)
NAS .... Naval Audit Service (DOMA)
NAS .... Navigation Avoidance System (KSC)
NAS .... Navy Advisory Section [*Vietnam*] (VNW)
NAS .... Neonatal Abstinence Syndrome (DAVI)
NAS .... Neonatal Airleak Syndrome [*Medicine*] (DMAA)
NAS .... NetWare Access Server [*Computer science*]
NAS .... Network Access Switch [*Telecommunications*] (MCD)
NAS .... Network Administration Station (ELAL)
NAS .... Network Analyzer Software
NAS .... Network Application Support [*Computer science*] (BTTJ)
NAS .... Network-Attached Storage [*Computer science*]
NAS .... Neuroallergic Syndrome [*Medicine*] (DMAA)
NAS .... New Attack Submarine [*Navy*] (MUSM)
NAS .... Newport Aeronautical Sales (SAUS)
NAS .... Newsreel Access Systems, Inc. [*Also, an information service or system*] (IID)
NAS .... No Abnormality Seen [*Medicine*] (MELL)
n-a-s............ No Added Salt (AD)
NAS .... No Added Salt [*Medicine*]
NAS .... Nocturnal Adoration Society (EA)
NAS .... Noise Abatement Society [*British*]
NAS .... Nominal Aggregate Signal (SAUS)
NAS .... Non-Assessable Stock [*Investment term*] (MHDW)
NAS .... Nonavailability Statement [*Military*]
NAS .... Non-Indigenous Aquatic Species [*Marine science*] (OSRA)
NAS .... Nonlinear Aerial System (SAUS)
NAS .... Nonlinear Antenna System
NAS .... Nord Amerikanischer Sangerbund (EA)
NAS .... Normalized Alignment Score
NAS .... North American Shale [*Geology*]
NAS .... North American Supply [*World War II*]
NAS .... North Arabian Sea (SAUS)
NAS .... Northeast Aviation Services Ltd. [*British*] [*ICAO designator*] (FAAC)
NAS .... Nozzle Actuating System [*Aerospace*] (MCD)
NAS .... Numecial Analysis Subroutines (SAUS)
NAS .... Numerical Aerodynamic Simulation [*NASA supercomputer system*]
NAS .... Numerical Aerodynamics Simulator (SAUS)
NAS .... Numerical Analysis Subroutines [*Computer science*] (BUR)
NAS .... Numerical and Atmospheric Sciences Network [*NASA*]
NAS .... Nursery Association Secretaries [*Later, Nursery Association Executives*] (EA)
NAS .... Nursing Auxiliary Service [*British*]
NASA .... National Acoustical Suppliers Association [*Defunct*] (EA)
NASA .... National Advertising Sales Association (EA)
NASA .... National Aeronautics and Space Act of 1958
NASA .... National Aeronautics and Space Administration [*Washington, DC*]
NASA .... National Aerospace Services Association [*Defunct*] (MCD)
NASA .... National Appliance Service Association (EA)
NASA .... National Association of School Affiliates (EA)
NASA .... National Association of Schools of Art (EA)
NASA .... National Association of Securities Administrators

NASA .... National Association of Shippers' Agents [*Washington, DC*] (EA)
NASA .... National Association of State Archeologists (EA)
NASA .... National Association of Student Anthropologists (SAUS)
NASA .... National Association of Synagogue Administrators (EA)
NASA .... National Automobile Salesmen's Association
NASA .... National Auto Sport Association
NASA .... Naval Aircraft Safety Activity (SAA)
NASA .... Newspaper Advertising Sales Association (EA)
NASA .... Nitrogen Atmosphere Sampling Analysis (SAUS)
NASA .... North American Sailing Association (AD)
NASA .... North American Savings Association (SAUS)
NASA .... North American Saxophone Alliance (EA)
NASA .... North American Securities Administrators Association [*Also, NASAA*] (EA)
NASA .... North American Shippers Association (EA)
NASA .... North American Singers Association (EA)
NASA .... North American Swiss Alliance (EA)
NASA .... North Atlantic Seafood Association [*Defunct*] (EA)
NASA .... North Atlantic Shippers Association (DS)
NASAA .... National Aeronautics and Space Administration Act (AD)
NASAA .... National Assembly of State Arts Agencies (EA)
NASAA .... National Association of State Approval Agencies (EA)
NASAA .... National Association of Student Activity Advisers (EA)
NASAA .... North American Securities Administrators Association [*Topeka, KS*] (EA)
NASA-AEC ... National Aeronautics and Space Administration and Atomic Energy Commission (SAA)
NASAB .... National Association of Shippers Advisory Boards (EA)
NASABCA .... National Aeronautics and Space Administration Board of Contract Appeals
NASABF ...... North America Statistical Areas Boundary File (SAUS)
NASA-CF Florida... National Aeronautics and Space Administration - Cocoa Beach, Florida (AD)
NASA-CO ..... National Aeronautics and Space Administration - Cleveland, Ohio (AD)
NASACOM.... NASA Communications System (SAUS)
NASACRE..... National Association for Standing Advisory Councils for Religious Education (AIE)
NASACT ...... National Association of State Auditors, Comptrollers, and Treasurers (EA)
NASACU...... National Association of State Approved Colleges and Universities (EA)
NASAD........ National Association of Schools of Art and Design (EA)
NASAD........ National Association of Sport Aircraft Designers (EA)
NASADAD .... National Association of State Alcohol and Drug Abuse Directors (EA)
NASAE .... National Association of Supervisors of Agricultural Education (EA)
NASA-EC California... National Aeronautics and Space Administration - Edwards, California (AD)
NASAEN ...... National Association for State-Enrolled Assistant Nurses (AD)
NASAERC..... NASA Electronic Research Center (IAA)
NASAF........ Northwest African Strategic Air Force [*British military*] (DMA)
NASA FAR Supp... National Aeronautics and Space Administration FAR Supplement [*A publication*] (AAGC)
NASAGA....... North American Simulation and Gaming Association (EA)
NASA-GM Maryland... National Aeronautics and Space Administration - Greenbelt, Maryland (AD)
NASA-HA Alabama... National Aeronautics and Space Administration - Huntsville, Alabama (AD)
NASAHOE .... National Association of Supervisors and Administrators of Health Occupations Education (EA)
NASA-HT...... National Aeronautics and Space Administration - Houston, Texas (AD)
NASAKOM.... Nasional, Agama, Kommunist [*Indonesian President Sukarno's policy of unity among National, Religious, and Communist forces*]
Nasakom ..... Nationalist-Communist (AD)
NASA-KSC ... National Aeronautics and Space Administration - Kennedy Space Center
NASAL .... National Association of Single Adult Leaders (EA)
NASAL .... Network of Single Adult Leaders (EA)
NASA LST Telescope... National Aeronautics and Space Administration Large Space Telescope (AD)
NASA-LV Virginia... National Aeronautics and Space Administration - Langley Field, Virginia (AD)
NASA-MC California... National Aeronautics and Space Administration - Moffett Field, California (AD)
NASAMECU... Natura Sanat, Medicus Curat [*Nature Heals, the Doctor Cures*] [*Title of collected talks by Dr. Georg Groddeck, published in 1913*]
NASAMS...... Norwegian Advanced Surface to Air Missile System (ACAE)
NASAMS...... Norwegian Advanced Surface-to-Air Missile System (SAUS)
NASA-MSC... National Aeronautics and Space Administration - Manned Spacecraft Center
NAS & FCA... National Automatic Sprinkler and Fire Control Association (AD)
NASANX...... Naval Air Station Annex (DNAB)
NASAO........ National Association of State Aeronautics and Organizations (SAUS)
NASAO........ National Association of State Aviation Officials (EA)
NASAOCARE... National Association of State Aviation Officials Center for Aviation Research and Education (EA)
NASAP .... National Association of Student Affairs Professionals (NTPA)
NASAP .... Navy Alcohol Safety Action Program (DNAB)
NASAP .... Network Analysis for Systems Applications Program [*Computer program*] [*NASA*]
NASAP .... Nonproliferation Alternative Systems Assessment Program [*Nuclear energy*] (NRCH)
NASAP .... North American Society of Adlerian Psychology (EA)
NASAP .... Nuclear Alternative System Assessment Program

NASAP .... Nuclear Alternative Systems Assessment Program (SAUS)
NASAPOFF... Navy Alcohol Safety Action Program Office (DNAB)
NASAPR...... National Aeronautics and Space Administration Procurement Regulations
NASAPRD.... National Aeronautics and Space Administration Procurement Regulations Directive
NASAR .... National Association for Search and Rescue (EA)
NASA/RECON... National Aeronautics and Space Administration Remote Console
NASARR ...... North American Search and Range RADAR [*Military*]
NASA-SC California... National Aeronautics and Space Administration - Santa Monica, California (AD)
NASASP...... National Association State Agencies for Surplus Property (EA)
NASASPS.... National Association of State Administrators and Supervisors of Private Schools (EA)
NASA-STAR... NASA Scientific and Technical Reports (NITA)
NASA/STIF... National Aeronautics and Space Administration/Scientific and Technical Information Facility
NASATE .... National Association of Substance Abuse Trainers and Educators (EA)
NASA-TR...... NASA Tank Reactor
NASB .... Nancy Ann Story Book [*Doll collecting*]
NASB .... National Association of School Boards (OICC)
NASB .... National Association of Spanish Broadcasters (EA)
NASB .... National Association of State Boards of Accountancy (AAGC)
NASB .... Navigational Aid Support Base
NASB .... New American Standard Bible [*A publication*] (BJA)
NASB .... North American Savings Bank FSB [*NASDAQ symbol*] (SAG)
NASB .... North Amer Svgs Bk [*NASDAQ symbol*] (TTSB)
NASBA .... National Association of State Boards of Accountancy [*New York, NY*] (EA)
NASBA .... National Automobile Safety Belt Association [*British*]
NASBA .... Nucleic Acid Sequence-Based Amplification [*Biochemistry*]
NASBCO....... National Association of School Bus Contract Operators [*Later, NSTA*] (EA)
NASBE .... National Association of State Boards of Education (EA)
NASBE .... National Association of Supervisors of Business Education [*Fort Lauderdale, FL*] (EA)
NASBERM... Naval Air Station, Bermuda
NASBHC...... National Assembly on School-Based Health Care (SAUS)
NASBIC........ National Association of Small Business Investment Companies [*Washington, DC*] (EA)
NASBITE ...... National Association of Small Business International Trade Educators (NTPA)
NASBLA .... National Association of State Boating Law Administrators (EA)
NASBO........ National Association of State Budget Officers (EA)
NASBO........ North African Shipping Board [*World War II*]
NASBOE....... National Association of Supervisors of Business and Office Education [*Later, NASBE*]
NASBOSA .... National Academy of Sciences Board on Ocean Science Affairs (PDAA)
NASBP........ National Association of Surety Bond Producers [*Bethesda, MD*] (EA)
NASBS .... North American Skull Base Society (EA)
NASC .... National Aeronautics and Space Council [*Terminated, 1973*]
NASC .... National Aircraft Standards Committee
NASC .... National Alliance for Safer Cities (EA)
NASC .... National Alliance of Senior Citizens (EA)
NASC .... Nuclear Aloe Science Council [*Later, IASC*]
NASC .... National Amalgamated Society of Coopers [*A union*] [*British*]
NASC .... National Aquatic Sports Camps
NASC .... National Association of Scaffolding Contractors [*British*] (DBA)
NASC .... National Association of School Counselors [*Defunct*] (EA)
NASC .... National Association of Service Contractors [*Defunct*] (EA)
NASC .... National Association of Solar Contractors (EA)
NASC .... National Association of Specialized Carriers [*Defunct*] (EA)
NASC .... National Association of Student Councils (EA)
NASC .... National Athletic Steering Committee (EA)
NASC .... NATO Supply Center
NASC .... Naval Aircraft Standards Committee (AFIT)
NASC .... Naval Air Systems Command
NASC .... Navy Aviation Safety Center (MUGU)
NASC .... Network Access Solutions [*NASDAQ symbol*] (SG)
NASC .... North American Shale Composite [*Geology*]
NASC .... North American Sporting Clays [*An association*]
NASC .... North American Sports Camps
NASC .... North American Stratigraphic Code (SAUS)
NASC .... North American Supply Council (SAUS)
NASC .... North America Supply Council
NASC .... North Atlantic Salmon Convention [*Marine science*] (OSRA)
NASC .... Northwest Association of Schools and Colleges (EA)
NASCA .... National Association for Corporate Speaker Activities [*Reston, VA*] (WDMC)
NASCA .... National Association of State Cable Agencies (EA)
NASCA .... National Association of State Conservation Agencies [*Washington, DC*]
NASCA .... North American Swing Club Association (EA)
NASCAD ...... NASA Computer Aided Design (SAUS)
NASCAP...... NASA Charging Analyzer Program (MCD)
NASCAR...... National Association for Stock Car Advancement and Research (AD)
NASCAR...... National Association for Stock Car Auto Racing (EA)
NASCAR...... National Association of Sports Car Racing (AD)
NASCAS ...... NAS Committee on Atmospheric Sciences (SAUS)
NASCAS ...... National Academy of Sciences Committee on Atmospheric Science
NASCAT ...... National Association of Securities and Commercial Law Attorneys (EA)
NASCC........ National Association of Service and Conservation Corps (EA)

NASCCD...... National Association of State Catholic Conference Directors (EA)
NASCCEN..... Naval Air Systems Command Representative, Central
NAS-CD...... National Academy of Sciences - Chemistry Division
NASCD........ National Association for Sickle Cell Disease (EA)
NASCD........ National Association of Soil Conservation Districts [Later, National Association of Conservation Districts]
NASCDC...... National Association for Sick Child Daycare Centers (PAZ)
NASCDD...... National Association of State Civil Defense Directors [Later, NEMA] (EA)
NASCH......... National Association of Swimming Clubs for the Handicapped [British] (DBA)
NASCI......... North American Society for Cardiac Imaging (SAUS)
NASCIS....... National Acute Spinal Cord Injury Study
NASCL........ North American Student Cooperative League
NASCLANT.... Naval Air Systems Command Representative, Atlantic
NASCMVE.... National Academy of Sciences Committee on Motor Vehicle Emissions (PDAA)
NASCO......... National Academy of Sciences Committee on Oceanography
NASCO......... National Association of Security Companies (NTPA)
NASCO......... National Association of Smaller Communities (EA)
NASCO......... National Association of State Charity Officials (EA)
NASCO......... National Automotive Service Co. (AD)
NASCO......... National Scientific Committee on Oceanography [Marine science] (MSC)
NASCO......... North American Students of Cooperation (EA)
NASCO......... North Atlantic Salmon Commission (SAUS)
NASCO......... North Atlantic Salmon Conservation Organization [Edinburgh, Scotland] (EAIO)
NASCOE....... National Association of ASCS [Agricultural Stabilization and Conservation Service] County Office Employees (EA)
Nascom....... NASA Communications
NASCOM..... NASA Communications Network
NASCOM..... NASA Worldwide Communications Network (MCD)
NASCOM...... National Aeronautics and Space Administration Tracking Network (AD)
NASCOM..... National Airspace Communications System
NASCom...... Naval Air Systems Command (AD)
NASCOM...... Naval Air Systems Command (MCD)
NASCOMIS.. Naval Air Station/Command Management Information System (MCD)
NASCOP....... NASA Communications Operating Procedures (MCD)
NAS/COW .... National Academy of Sciences/Committee on Water [Marine science] (MSC)
NASCP......... National Association of Sports for Cerebral Palsy [Later, USCPAA] (EA)
NASCP......... North American Society for Corporate Planning [Later, PF] (EA)
NASCPA....... North American Study Center for Polish Affairs (EA)
NASCPAC..... Naval Air Systems Command Representative, Pacific
NASCPD....... National Association of Senior Companion Project Directors (EA)
NASCPNCLA... Naval Air Systems Command Representative, Naval Air Training Command, Pensacola [Florida]
NASCRIST.... Naval Air Station Corpus Christi
NASCRL....... Naval Air Systems Command Representative, Atlantic
NASCRP....... Naval Air Systems Command Representative-Pacific (MCD)
NASCS........ National Association of Shoe Chain Stores [Later, FDRA] (EA)
NASCSP....... National Association for State Community Service Programs (EA)
NASCUMC.... National Association of Schools and Colleges of the United Methodist Church (EA)
NASCUS...... National Association of State Credit Union Supervisors (EA)
NASD.......... National Amalgamated Stevedores and Dockers (AD)
NASD.......... National Association for Staff Development [British] (DET)
NASD.......... National Association of Schools of Dance (EA)
NASD.......... National Association of Schools of Design [Later, NASA]
NASD.......... National Association of Securities Dealers [Washington, DC] (EA)
NASD.......... National Association of Selective Distributors [Defunct] (EA)
NASD.......... National Association of Service Dealers (EA)
NASD.......... Naval Air [or Aviation] Supply Depot
NASD.......... Naval Aviation Supply Depot (AD)
NASDA........ National Association of Sign and Display Advertisers [Defunct]
NASDA........ National Association of State Departments of Agriculture (EA)
NASDA........ National Association of State Development Agencies (EA)
NASDA........ National Space Development Agency [Japan]
NASDA........ North American South Devon Association (EA)
NASDAC...... National Aviation Safety Data Analysis Center [FAA] (TAG)
NASDAD...... National Association of Seventh-Day Adventist Dentists (EA)
NASDAGS .... National Association of State Directors of Administration and General Service (EA)
NASDAPC .... National Association of State Drug Abuse Program Coordinators [Later, NASADAD] (EA)
Nasdaq........ National Association of Securities Dealers Automated Quotations [The full name is the Nasdaq Stock Market] [Washington, DC] (WDMC)
NASDAQ ...... National Association of Securities Dealers Automated Quotations [Over-the-counter stock quotations] [Bunker Ramo Corp.] [Trumbell, CT] [Information service or system]
NASDAQS .... National Association of Security Dealers Automated Quotation System (AD)
NASDCD...... National Association of State Directors of Child Development
NASDDDS.... National Association of State Directors of Developmental Disability Services (NTPA)
NASDDP ...... National Association of State Directors for Disaster Preparedness [Later, NEMA] (EA)
NASDI......... National Association of Selective Distributors (EA)
NASDIEGO... Naval Air Station San Diego
NASDIM....... National Association of Securities Dealers and Investment Managers [Securities and Investment Board] [British]

NASDLET..... National Association of State Directors of Law Enforcement Training
NASDM........ National Association of Special Delivery Messengers [Later, APWU] [AFL-CIO] (EA)
NASDME...... National Association of State Directors of Migrant Education (EA)
NASDQ........ National Association of Securities Dealers Automated Quotations (SAUS)
NASDS......... National Amalgamated Stevedores' and Dockers' Society [A union] [British]
NASDS......... National Association of Scuba Diving Schools [Later, CA] [Commercial firm] (EA)
NASDS........ Naval Aviation Supply Distribution System (AFIT)
NASDS......... North American Sheep Dog Society (EA)
NASDSE...... National Association of State Directors of Special Education [Database producer] (EA)
NASDSSE.... National Association of State Directors and Supervisors of Secondary Education [Later, NASSDSE] (EA)
NASDT........ Naval Aviators' Speech Discrimination Test
NASDT........ North American Society for Dialysis and Transplantation (EA)
NASDTEC..... National Association of State Directors of Teacher Education and Certification (EA)
NASDU........ National Amalgamated Stevedores and Dockers Union [British] (BI)
NASDVA...... National Association of State Directors of Veterans Affairs (EA)
NASDVE...... National Association of State Directors of Vocational Education (EA)
NASDVTEC... National Association of State Directors of Vocational-Technical Education (NTPA)
NASE.......... National Academy of School Executives [of American Association of School Administrators]
NASE .... National Academy of Stationary Engineers [British] (DAS)
NASE .... National Association for the Self-Employed [Fort Worth, TX] (EA)
NASE .... National Association for the Study of Epilepsy (DAVI)
NASE .... National Association of Stationary Engineers (AD)
NASE .... National Association of Steel Exporters [Defunct] (EA)
nase........... Neutral Atom Space Engine (AD)
NASE .... Nonacoustic Submarine Effects (NVT)
NASEA .... National Association of Student Employment Administrators (EA)
NASEA .... Native American Science Education Association [Defunct] (EA)
NASEAB ...... Naval Air Systems Effectiveness Advisory Board
NASEAN...... National Association for State Enrolled Assistant Nurses
NASECODE... Numerical Analysis of Semiconductor Devices and Integrated Circuits [Computer science]
NASEDIO...... National Association of State Education Department Information Officers (EA)
NASEES ...... National Association for Soviet and East European Studies [British]
NASEM .... National Association of Satellite Equipment Manufacturers [Defunct] (EA)
NASEMP ..... National Association of State Educational Media Professionals (EA)
NASEMSD.... National Association of State EMS Directors (EA)
NASEN........ National Association for Special Educational Needs (AIE)
NASEN........ National Association of State Enrolled Nurses [British] (BI)
NASEO........ National Association of State Energy Officials (NTPA)
NASEPA ...... National Association of State Environmental Programs Agencies [Marine science] (MSC)
n-ASER .... Neutron-Accelerated Soft-Error Rate (SAUS)
NAS/ESB ..... National Academy of Sciences/Environmental Studies Board [Marine science] (MSC)
NASF .... National Aboriginal Sports Foundation (AD)
NASF .... National American Studies Faculty [Defunct] (EA)
NASF .... National Arts Stabilization Fund [Defunct] (EA)
NASF .... National Association of State Foresters (EA)
NASF .... Native American Scholarship Fund [An association] (EA)
NASF .... Navigation & Attack Systems Flight (SAUS)
NASF .... NIC [Naval Intelligence Center] Analyst Support Facility
NASF .... North American Soccer Foundation [Defunct] (EA)
NASF .... Numerical Aerodynamic Simulation Facility
NASFA .... National Association of State Facilities Administrators (EA)
NASFAA ...... National Association of Student Financial Aid Administrators (EA)
NASFCA ...... National Automatic Sprinkler and Fire Control Association (EA)
NASFCB ...... National Association of Specialty Food and Confection Brokers (EA)
NASFM .... National Association of State Fire Marshals (NTPA)
NASFM .... National Association of Store Fixture Manufacturers (EA)
NASFO .... National Asset Seizure and Forfeiture Office (AD)
NASFT .... National Association for the Specialty Food Trade (EA)
NASFW .... National Association of Solid Fuel Wholesalers [British] (DBA)
NASG .... National Alliance for Spiritual Growth (EA)
NASG .... New-Age Sensitive Guy (SAUS)
NASGA .... North American Strawberry Growers Association (EA)
NAS-GB....... Noise Abatement Society of Great Britain (AD)
NASGC .... National Association of Small Government Contractors (EA)
NaSGIM ...... National Study of Graduate Education in Internal Medicine (SAUS)
NAS/GRB .... National Academy of Sciences/Geophysical Research Board [Marine science] (MSC)
NASGS........ North African Secretary General Staff [World War II]
NASGTMO... Naval Air Station Guantanamo
NASGW ...... National Association of Sporting Goods Wholesalers (EA)
NASH .... Nahariya to Ashkelon [Proposed name for possible "super-city" formed by the urban sprawl between these two] [Israel]
Nash........... Nashville [Tennessee] (AD)
NASH .... National Association of Safety at Home [British] (DBA)
NASH .... National Association of Specimen Hunters (AD)
NASHA .... National Association for Speech and Hearing Action (EA)
NASHA .... North American Survival and Homesteading Association (AD)
NASHAC...... National Association for Safety and Health in the Arts and Crafts (EA)
NASHAW..... National Association for Statewide Health and Welfare (EA)
NASHC......... National All States Hobby Club [Defunct] (EA)

NashCtr........ Nashville Country Club [*Associated Press*] (SAG)
NashF.......... Nash Finch Co. [*Associated Press*] (SAG)
NASHOC....... North American Student Humanist Organizing Committee [*Defunct*] (EA)
Nash Pl........ Nash's Ohio Pleading and Practice [*A publication*] (DLA)
NASHRD ...... National Association of State Human Resource Directors (EA)
Nashua .... Nashua Corp. [*Associated Press*] (SAG)
Nashvl .... Nashville (BEE)
NASI .... National A (CDE)
NASI .... NetWare Asynchronous Services Interface [*Computer science*] (PCM)
NASI .... Nigerian Army School of Infantry
NASI .... Novell Asynchronous Services Interface
NASIB .... Naval Air Station, Imperial Beach (DNAB)
NASIC .... Northeast Academic Science Information Center
NASID .... National Association of the Sixth Infantry Division (EA)
NASIG .... North African Signal Section [*World War II*]
NASIG .... North American Serials Group (EA)
NASIG .... North American Serials Interest Group
NASILP .... National Association of Self-Instructional Language Programs (EA)
NASIMD .... National Association of the Sixth Infantry/Motorized Division [*Later, NASID*] (EA)
Nas Inst....... Nasmith's Institutes of English Private Law [*1873*] [*A publication*] (DLA)
Nas Inst Priv... Nasmith's Institutes of English Private Law [*1873*] [*A publication*] (DLA)
Nas Inst Pub... Nasmith's Institutes of English Public Law [*1873*] [*A publication*] (DLA)
NASIP .... National Aviation Safety Inspection Program [*RSPA*] (TAG)
NASIP .... NATO AEW System Improvement Programme (SAUS)
NASIR .... Nuclear Amplification by Stimulated Isomer Radiation (SAA)
NASIRC .... NASA Automated Systems Incident Response Capability
NASIRE........ National Association of State Information Resource Executives (AAGC)
NASIS .... NASA Aerospace Safety Information System
NASIS .... National Association for State Information Systems (EA)
NASIS .... NATO Subject Indicator System (NATG)
NASIS .... Nevada Statewide Information Service (SAUS)
NASIS .... Northeast Australian Satellite Imagery System (SAUS)
NASISS .... National Association of Sailing Instructors and Sailing Schools (EA)
NASJA .... North American Ski Journalists Association (EA)
NASJAX .... Naval Air Station Jacksonville
NASJE......... National Association of State Judicial Educators
NASL .... Nasal (DAVI)
NASL .... National Association of State Lotteries (EA)
NASL .... Naval Applied Science Laboratory
NASL .... North American Soccer League [*Defunct*] (EA)
NASLAKE .... Naval Air Station Lakehurst
NASLAT .... National Association of Securities and Commercial Law Attorneys (NTPA)
NASLI .... National Association for Senior Living Industries (EA)
NASLPA....... North American Soccer League Players Association [*Defunct*] (EA)
NASLR .... National Association of State Land Reclamationists (EA)
NASLS .... National Association of Small Loan Supervisors (EA)
NASM .... National Air and Space [*Warfare*] Model [*Air Force*]
NASM .... National Air and Space Museum [*Smithsonian Institution*] [*Formerly, NAM*]
NASM .... National Association for School Magazines [*British*] (BI)
NASM .... National Association of Sandwich Manufacturers [*Defunct*] (EA)
NASM .... National Association of Schools of Music (EA)
NASM .... National Association of Service Managers (EA)
NASM .... National Association of Service Merchandising (EA)
NASM .... National Association of State Militia
NASM .... National Association of Surrogate Mothers (EA)
NASM .... Naval Aviation School of Medicine
NASMA........ Parti Nasionalis Malaysia [*Political party*] (FEA)
NASMAC ...... Naval Air Software Management Advisory Committee (MCD)
NASMAP ...... NAS Management Automation Program [*FAA*] (TAG)
NASMAR...... National Association of Sack Merchants and Reclaimers [*British*] (BI)
NASMBCM ... National Association of Sanitary Milk Bottle Closure Manufacturers [*Defunct*] (EA)
NASMD........ National Association of Medicaid Directors (EA)
NASMD........ National Association of School Music Dealers (EA)
NASMD........ National Association of Sewing Machine Dealers [*Defunct*] (EA)
NASMD........ National Association of Sewing Machine Distributors [*Defunct*] (EA)
NASMD........ National Association of Sheet Music Dealers [*Later, NAMM*] (EA)
NASMD........ Northamerican Association of Sheet Metal Distributors [*Later, division of NHAW*] (EA)
NASMHPD .... National Association of State Mental Health Program Directors (EA)
NASMI .... National Association of Secondary Material Industries [*Later, NARI*] (EA)
NAS(MISC)... North American Supply Committee, Miscellaneous [*World War II*]
NASML .... National Air and Space Museum Library [*Smithsonian Institute*] (AD)
NASMO .... National Association of School Meals Organisers [*British*] (DBA)
NASMO .... NATO Starfighter Management Office
NASMP .... National Association of Sales and Marketing Professionals [*Defunct*] (EA)
NASMV .... National Association on Standard Medical Vocabulary (EA)
NASN.......... National Air Sampling Network [*Public Health Service*]
NASN.......... National Air Surveillance Network [*Environmental Protection Agency*]
NASN.......... National Association of School Nurses (EA)
NAS/NAE...... National Academy of Sciences/National Academy of Engineering [*Marine science*] (MSC)

NAS/NAE-SECAN... NAS/NAE [*National Academy of Sciences/National Academy of Engineering*] Science and Engineering Committee Advisory to NOAA [*National Oceanic and Atmospheric Administration*] [*Defunct*] (USDC)
NAS/NAE-SECAN... National Academy of Sciences/National Academy of Sciences Engineering Science and Engineering Committee Advisory to NOAA[*National Oceanic and Atmospheric Administration*] [*Marine science*] (OSRA)
NASNI .... Naval Air Station North Island
NAS-NRC .... National Academy of Sciences - National Research Council (EA)
NASNSA....... National Association of Special Needs State Administrators (EA)
NASO .... Natchez & Southern Railway Co. [*AAR code*] [*Terminated*]
NASO .... National Adult School Organisation [*British*]
NASO .... National Association of Sports Officials (EA)
NASO .... National Astrological Society [*Defunct*] (EA)
NASO .... National Astronomical Space Observatory
NASO .... Naval Aviation Supply Office
NASO .... Nonacoustic Sensor Operator [*Military*] (CAAL)
NASO .... North American Space Operations (SAUS)
NAS/OAB...... National Academy of Sciences/Ocean Affairs Board [*Marine science*] (MSC)
NASOC........ North American Singer Owners Club (EA)
NASOH........ North American Society for Oceanic History (EA)
NASOH........ North America Society for Oceanic History (SAUS)
NASOPT....... Network Analysis System with Optimization Facility [*NASA*] (IAA)
NA So Rhod... Southern Rhodesia Native Appeal Court Reports [*A publication*] (DLA)
NASORLO .... National Association of State Outdoor Recreation Liaison Officers (EA)
NAS/OSB...... National Academy of Sciences/Ocean Sciences Board [*Marine science*] (MSC)
NASP .... National Achievement Scholarship Program [*National Merit Scholarship Corp.*] (AEBS)
NASP .... National Aerospace Plane (AAGC)
NASP .... National Aerospace Plane Program [*NASA, DoD*]
NASP .... National Airport System Plans [*Department of Transportation*]
NASP .... National Airspace System Plan [*FAA*] (TAG)
NASP .... National Alternative Schools Program
NASP .... National Association for the Southern Poor (EA)
NASP .... National Association of School Psychologists (EA)
NASP .... National Association of Schools and Publishers (EA)
NASP .... National Association of Securities Professionals (EA)
NASP .... National Association of Single Persons (EA)
NASP .... National Atmospheric Sciences Program
NASP .... National Aviation System Plan [*A publication*]
NASP .... Naval Air Survivability Program (MCD)
NASP .... Navy Advanced SATCOM [*Satellite Communications*] Program (ANA)
NASP .... Navy Airship Program (SAUS)
NASP .... Negro, Anglo-Saxon Protestant
NA-SP .... Nonabrasive-Slightly Polishing (SAUS)
NASP .... North Atlantic Seaboard Program (QUAC)
NASP .... North Atlantic Seaboard Programme (SAUS)
NASPA........ National Association for Public Accountants (HGAA)
NASPA........ National Association of Student Personnel Administrators (EA)
NASPA........ National Society of Public Accountants (MCD)
NaSPA........ National Systems Programmers Association (EA)
NASPA........ North American Soccer Players Association [*Later, NASLPA*] (EA)
NASPAA....... National Association of Schools of Public Affairs and Administration (EA)
NASPAC....... National Airspace System Performance Analysis Capability [*FAA*] (TAG)
NASPALS..... Nas Precision Approach and Landing System [*FAA*] (TAG)
Nas Par ...... Nasionale Party [*National Party*] [*Political party*] (AD)
NASPCS....... National Advisory Service for Parents of Children with a Stoma (NRGU)
NASPD........ National Association of Plumbing Specialty Distributors (NTPA)
NASPD........ National Association of State Park Directors (EA)
NASPD........ National Association of Steel Pipe Distributors (EA)
NASPE .... National Association for Sport and Physical Education (EA)
NASPE .... National Association of State Personnel Executives (EA)
NASPE .... North American Society of Pacing and Electrophysiology (EA)
NASPENSA... Naval Air Station Pensacola
Nas Pers...... Nasionale Pers [*National Press*] [*South Africa*] (AD)
NASPG........ North American Society for Pediatric Gastroenterology [*Later, NASPGN*] (EA)
NASPGN ...... North American Society for Pediatric Gastroenterology and Nutrition (EA)
NASPHV...... National Association of State Public Health Veterinarians (EA)
NASP JPO..... NASP Joint Program Office (SAUS)
NASPL .... North American Association of State and Provincial Lotteries (NTPA)
NASPM .... National Association of Seed Potato Merchants [*British*] (BI)
NASPM .... National Association of Slipper and Playshoe Manufacturers (EA)
NASPO .... National Airspace System Program Office [*FAA*] (MCD)
NASPO .... National Alliance of Statewide Preservation Organizations (EA)
NASPO .... National Association of State Purchasing Officials (EA)
NASPO .... NATO Starfighter Production Organization
NASPO .... Naval Air System Program Office (SAUS)
NASPPR....... National Association of Service Providers in Private Rehabilitation (NTPA)
NASPR........ NASA Procurement Regulation (KSC)
NASPRFMR... National Association of Superintendents of Public Residential Facilities for theMentally Retarded
NASPSM...... National Association of Shirt, Pajama, and Sportswear Manufacturers [*Later, AAMA*]

NASPSPA.... North American Society for the Psychology of Sport and Physical Activity (EA)

Na-Spt .... Sodium Spot [Urine Test] [Biochemistry] (DAVI)

NASQAN ...... National Stream Quality Accounting Network [Department of the Interior]

NASQUON.... Naval Air Station Quonset Point

NASR .... National Annual Symposium on Reliability [IEEE] (MCD)

NASR .... National Association of Sitter Registries [Defunct] (EA)

NASR .... National Association of Solvent Recyclers (EA)

NASR .... National Association of Swine Records (EA)

NASR .... Naval & Air Staff Requirement (SAUS)

NASRA .... National Association of State Retirement Administrators (EA)

NASRC .... National Association of State Racing Commissioners [Later, ARCI] (EA)

NASRC .... North American Salmon Research Center [Later, Atlantic Salmon Research Institute] [Canada] [Research center] (RCD)

NASRC .... North Atlantic Salmon Research Center [Marine science] (MSC)

NASRN .... National Association of State Radio Networks (EA)

NASRO .... National Association of Shooting Range Owners (EA)

NASRP .... National Association of Special and Reserve Police [Defunct]

NASRP .... National Association of State Recreation Planners (EA)

NASRPM ...... National Association of State River Program Managers (EA)

NASRR .... North American Search and Range RADAR [Military]

NASRS .... Non-Available Status Reporting System (SAUS)

NASRS .... Not Available Status Report System [DoD]

NASRU .... Naval Air Systems Command Reserve Unit (MCD)

NASRWCBL.. National Amalgamated Society of Railway Wagon and Carriage Builders and Lifters [A union] [British]

NASS .... Narrow Angle Sun Sensor (SAA)

NASS .... Nassau (ROG)

Nass .... Nassau, Bahamas (AD)

NASS .... National Accident Sampling System [National Highway Traffic Safety Administration] [Washington, DC]

NASS .... National Agricultural Statistics Service [Department of Agriculture] [Information service or system] (IID)

NASS .... National Aids Support System [Military] (SAA)

NASS .... National Alliance for Safe Schools (EA)

NASS .... National Alliance of Supermarket Shoppers (EA)

NASS .... National Ankylosing Spondylitis Society [British] (DBA)

NASS .... National Association for Small Schools [British] (DI)

NASS .... National Association of Saw Shops (EA)

NASS .... National Association of School Superintendents (AD)

NASS .... National Association of Secretarial Services [St. Petersburg, FL] (EA)

NASS .... National Association of Secretaries of State (EA)

NASS .... National Association of Specialized Schools [Defunct] (EA)

NASS .... National Association of Steel Stockholders (MHDB)

NASS .... National Association of Suggestion Systems (EA)

NASS .... National Association of Summer Sessions [Later, NAASS]

NASS .... National Automotive Sampling System

NASS .... Naval Air Signal School

NASS .... Naval Anti-Submarine School (SAUS)

NASS .... Naval Armaments Stores System (PDAA)

NASS .... Navigation Satellite System (PDAA)

NASS .... Navy Advent Ship Station (SAA)

NASS .... Network Access Switching Subsystem [Telecommunications] (MCD)

NASS .... North African Special Service Section [World War II]

NASS .... North American Shagya-Arabian Society (EA)

NASS .... North American Spine Society (EA)

NASS .... North American Super Sports [Defunct] (EA)

NAS(S)...... North American Supply Committee, Scientific Subcommittee [World War II]

NASSA .... National Aerospace Services Association [Defunct] (EA)

NASSA .... National Art School Students' Association [Australia]

NASSA .... North American State Securities Administrators

NASSAM ..... National Association for the Self-Supporting Active Ministry (EA)

NASS & LS... National Association of State Savings and Loan Supervisors [Later, ACSSS] (EA)

NASSB .... National Association of Supervisors of State Banks [Later, CSBS] (EA)

NASSC .... National Alliance on Shaping Safer Cities [Later, NASC] (EA)

NASSCO ...... National Association of Sewer Service Companies (EA)

NASSCO ...... National Steel & Shipbuilding Co.

NASSCOM ... National Association of Software and Service Companies

NASSD .... National Association of School Security Directors (EA)

NASSD .... National Association of Sign Supply Distributors (NTPA)

NASSD .... North American Society of Scaffold Professionals (NTPA)

NASSDC...... National Social Science Documentation Centre [Information service or system] (IID)

NASSDE...... National Association of State Supervisors of Distributive Education (EA)

NASSDOC ... National Social Science Documentation Centre [Information service or system] (IID)

NASSDSE.... National Association of State Supervisors and Directors of Secondary Education (EA)

NAS/SEC .... National Academy of Sciences' Site Evaluation Committee

NASSH .... North American Society for Sport History (EA)

NASSHE...... National Association of State Supervisors of Home Economics [Later, NASSVHE]

NASSL .... National Association of Spanish Speaking Libirarians (EA)

NASSLEO.... National Association of School Safety and Law Enforcement Officers (NTPA)

NASSM .... National Association of Scissors and Shears Manufacturers (EA)

NASSM .... National Association of State Supervisors of Music (EA)

NASSM .... North American Society for Sport Management (EA)

NASSO .... National Association of Socialist Students' Organizations [Political party] (AD)

NASSP .... National Association of Secondary School Principals (EA)

NASSP .... North American Society for Social Philosophy (EA)

NASSP-B.... National Association of Secondary School Principals. Bulletin [A publication] (BRI)

NASSPE .... National Alliance of Spanish-Speaking People for Equality (EA)

NASSR .... Nahichevan Autonomous Soviet Socialist Republic (AD)

NASSS .... National Association of Support for Small Schools [British] (DBA)

NASSS .... North American Society for the Sociology of Sport (EA)

NASSSA .... National Association of State Social Security Administrators [Later, NCSSSA] (EA)

NASSTA ...... National Association of Secretaries of State Teachers Associations [Later, NCSEA] (EA)

NASSTIE ..... National Association of State Supervisors of Trade and Industrial Education (EA)

NASSTRAC... National Small Shipments Traffic Conference [Acronym now used as official name of association] (EA)

NASSTRAC... National Small Shipments Traffic Council

NASSVHE.... National Association of State Supervisors of Vocational Home Economics (EA)

NAST .... National Association of Schools of Theatre (EA)

NAST .... National Association of State Treasurers (EA)

NAST .... Naval & Air Staff Target (SAUS)

NAST .... Navigation/Attack Systems Trainer (PDAA)

NAST .... Navy Advent Ship Terminal (SAA)

NAST .... Nuclear Accident Support Team [Canada]

NASTA .... National Association of State Text Book Administrators (EA)

NASTAD...... National Alliance of State and Territorial AIDS [Acquired Immune-Deficiency Syndrome] Directors (NTPA)

NASTAD...... Naval Acoustic Sensor Training Aids Department (DNAB)

NASTAR...... National Standard Race [Skiing]

NASTART.... Normal After Start (SAUS)

NASTAT .... North American Society of Teachers of the Alexander Technique (EA)

NASTBD...... National Association of State Text Book Directors [Later, NASTA] (EA)

Nastc .... Nastech Pharmaceutical Co., Inc. [Associated Press] (SAG)

NASTC .... Naval Air Station Twin Cities (DNAB)

NASTD .... National Association of State and Territorial Apprenticeship Directors [Bureau of Apprenticeship and Training] [Department of Labor]

NASTD .... National Association of State Telecommunications Directors (EA)

Nastech ...... Nastech Pharmaceutical Co., Inc. [Associated Press] (SAG)

NASTEMP .... National Association of State Educational Media Professionals (EA)

NASTI .... Naval Air Station, Terminal Island (AD)

NASTI .... Next Assembly Support Table Index [Aerospace] (MCD)

NASTI .... North American Society for Trenchless Technology (SAUS)

NASTL .... National Anti-Steel-Trap League (AD)

NASTOCK..... North American Stock Market [I. P. Sharp Associates] [Canada] [Information service or system]

NASTPHV... National Association of State and Territorial Public Health Veterinarians [Later, NASPHV] (EA)

NASTRAN ... NASA Structural Analysis [Computer program]

NAS/TRB...... National Academy of Sciences/Transportation Board [Marine science] (MSC)

NASTS .... National Association for Science, Technology, and Society (EA)

NASTT .... North American Society for Trenchless Technology (EA)

NASTX .... Phoenix Equity Opportunities CI.A [Mutual fund ticker symbol] (SG)

NASU .... National Adult School Union [British] (DAS)

NASU .... National Association of State Universities [Later, NASULGC]

NASU .... National Association of System 3 Users (IAA)

NASU .... Navy Air Support Unit

NASU .... Navy Underwater Sound Laboratory (MUGU)

NASU .... North American Singers Union (EA)

NASUA .... National Association of State Units on Aging (EA)

NASUCA...... National Association of State Utility Consumer Advocates (EA)

NASULGC.... National Association of State Universities and Land-Grant Colleges (EA)

NASUP .... National Association on Service to Unmarried Parents (EA)

NAS-UWT .... National Association of Schoolmasters - Union of Women Teachers [British]

NASV .... International Academy of Sports Vision [Formerly, National Academy of Sports Vision] (EAIO)

NASV .... National Academy of Sports Vision (EA)

NASVG .... Nordic Association for Study and Vocational Guidance [See also NRSY] (EAIO)

NASVH .... National Association of State Veterans Homes (EA)

NASVO .... National Association of State Vocal Organizations (EA)

NASW .... National Association of Science Writers (EA)

NASW .... National Association of Social Workers (EA)

NASW .... National Association of Social Workers National Committee on Lesbian and Gay Issues (EA)

NASW .... North American Slope Water [Oceanography] (MSC)

NASWA .... North American Shortwave Association (EA)

NASWDU ...... Naval Air/Sea Warfare Development Unit (SAUS)

NASWF .... Naval Air Special Weapons Facility

NASWHP...... National Association of Sheltered Workshops and Homebound Programs [Later, NARF] (EA)

NASWM .... National Association of Scottish Woollen Manufacturers [British] (BI)

NASWS .... National Aeronautics and Space Administration White Sands [Proving ground]

NASWS .... Naval Anti Submarine Warfare Systems (ACAE)

NASWSC...... North American Society for Water and Soil Conservation

NASWSO...... National Association of Soft Water Service Operators [Later, WQA]

NAT............. Information Content Natural Unit [Information theory]

NAT	N-Acetyltransferase [*An enzyme*]	
NAT	N-Acetyltryptophan [*Biochemistry*]	
NAT	NASA Apollo Trajectory (KSC)	
NAT	NASA STI [*Scientific and Technical Information*] Facility, BWI Airport, MD [*Baltimore-Washington International*] [*OCLC symbol*] (OCLC)	
NAT	Natal [*Brazil*] [*Airport symbol*] (OAG)	
Nat	Natalia (AD)	
Nat	Natalie (AD)	
Nat	Natasha (AD)	
Nat	Nathalie (AD)	
Nat	Nathan (AD)	
Nat	Nathaniel (AD)	
nat	Nation (AD)	
Nat	Nation [*A publication*] (BRI)	
NAT	Nation	
Nat	National (AD)	
nat	National (AD)	
NAT	National	
NAT	National Academy of Teaching (EA)	
NAT	National Agency for Tourism	
NAT	National AIDS Trust (SAUS)	
NAT	National Air Transport (SAA)	
NAT	National Arbitration Tribunal [*British*]	
NAT	National Association of Toolmakers [*A union*] [*British*]	
NAT	National Drug Co. [*Research code symbol*]	
Nat	Nationalist (ODBW)	
NAT	Nationalist (WDAA)	
NAT	Nationality (AAG)	
Nat	National Party [*Australia*] [*Political party*]	
NAT	National Transport, Inc.	
NAT	Native (AAG)	
nat	Native (AD)	
NAT	Nativity [*Church calendars*] (ROG)	
NAT	Natrolite [*A zeolite*]	
NAT	Natural (AAG)	
nat	Natural (AD)	
Nat	Natural (ODBW)	
nat	Naturalist (AD)	
nat	Naturalization (AD)	
Nat	Naturalized [*Botany*]	
NAT	Natural Unit (IAA)	
nat	Nature (AD)	
Nat	Nature [*or Naturalist*]	
NAT	Naturist (WDAA)	
NAT	Natus [*Birth*] [*Latin*]	
nat	Natuurkunde [*Natural Science*] [*Dutch*] (AD)	
NAT	Naval Air Technical Services Facility (MUGU)	
NAT	Naval Air Terminal	
NAT	Naval Air Training	
NAT	Naval Anthropomorphic Teleoperater (DNAB)	
NAT	Navigational Aids Technician (DNAB)	
NAT	Nearly Airborne Truck (PDAA)	
NAT	Network Address Transaction [*Computer science*] (AGLO)	
NAT	Network Address Translation [*Computer science*]	
NAT	Network Analysis Team	
NAT	Network Analysis Technique (IAA)	
NAT	New Age Thinking	
NAT	New Attainment Target (AIE)	
NAT	Nitric Acid Trihydrate [*Inorganic chemistry*]	
NAT	Nitrosoanatabine [*Also, NAtB*] [*Organic chemistry*]	
NAT	No Action Taken	
NAT	Node Attached Table (SAUS)	
NAT	Non-Verbal Ability Tests [*Intelligence test*]	
NAT	Nordic American Tanker Shipping Ltd. [*AMEX symbol*] (SAG)	
nat	Normal Allowed Time (AD)	
NAT	Normal Allowed Time (IEEE)	
NAT	North African Theater [*World War II*]	
NAT	North Atlantic Air, Inc. [*ICAO designator*] (FAAC)	
NAT	North Atlantic Region [*USTTA*] (TAG)	
NAT	North Atlantic Regional Area [*Aviation*]	
NAT	North Atlantic Tracks (HLLA)	
NAT	North Atlantic Traffic (PIPO)	
NAT	North Atlantic Treaty	
NAT	Northern Airborne Technology Ltd. (SAUS)	
NAT	Not Air Transportable (ACAE)	
NAT	Not Attending Training	
NATA	N-Acetyl-Tryptophan-Amide [*Organic chemistry*]	
NATA	N-Acetyltyramine [*Biochemistry*]	
NATA	Narcotic Addict Treatment Act of 1974	
NATA	National Airfreight Trucking Alliance (EA)	
NATA	National Air Transportation Association (EA)	
NATA	National Association of Tax Accountants [*Defunct*] (EA)	
NATA	National Association of Tax Administrators (EA)	
NATA	National Association of Teachers' Agencies (EA)	
NATA	National Association of Teachers of Agriculture [*Australia*]	
NATA	National Association of Temple Administrators (EA)	
NATA	National Association of Testing Authorities (IAA)	
NATA	National Association of Transportation Advertising [*Later, Transit Advertising Association*]	
NATA	National Athletic Trainers Association (EA)	
NATA	National Automated Transportation Association (AD)	
NATA	National Automobile Transporters Association [*Detroit, MI*] (EA)	
NATA	National Automotive Trade Association	
NATA	National Aviation Trades Association	
NATA	North American Tasar Association (EA)	
NATA	North American Telecommunications Association (EA)	
NATA	North American Telephone Association (EA)	
NATA	North American Trakehner Association (EA)	
NATA	North American Travel Association [*Defunct*] (EA)	
NATA	North Atlantic Treaty Alliance	
NATA	Northern Air Transport Association (SAUS)	
NATA	Numerical Analysis Thermal Application (VLIE)	
Nat Absten	National Abstentionalist (AD)	
NATAC	North Atlantic Chemistry Experiment (QUAC)	
NATACMS	Navy Tactical Missile System (SAUS)	
NATAD	National Association of Textile and Apparel Distributors [*Defunct*] (EA)	
NATAF	Northwest African Tactical Air Force [*World War II*]	
Natal LJ	Natal Law Journal [*South Africa*] [*A publication*] (DLA)	
Natal LM	Natal Law Magazine [*South Africa*] [*A publication*] (DLA)	
Natal LQ	Natal Law Quarterly [*South Africa*] [*A publication*] (DLA)	
Natal LR	Natal Law Reports [*South Africa*] [*A publication*] (DLA)	
NatAlt	Natural Alternatives International [*Associated Press*] (SAG)	
NA T & N	Selected Decisions of the Native Appeal Court, Transvaal and Natal [*A publication*] (DLA)	
NATAPROBU	National Association of Professional Bureaucrats [*Later, INATAPROBU*]	
Nat Arc	National Archives (AD)	
NATARI	National Association of Traffic Accident Reconstructionists and Investigators (EA)	
NATAS	National Academy of Television Arts and Sciences (EA)	
NATAS	National Appropriate Technology Assistance Service [*Butte, MT*] [*Department of Energy*] (GRD)	
NATAS	NOAA AVHRR Transcription and Archive System (SAUS)	
NATAS	North American Thermal Analysis Society (EA)	
Nat Assn	National Association (AD)	
natat	Natation (AD)	
NATaT	National Association of Towns and Townships (EA)	
NatAutoC	National Auto Credit, Inc. Holding [*Associated Press*] (SAG)	
NATAW	National Association of Textile and Apparel Wholesalers [*Later, NATAD*] (EA)	
NATB	National Automobile Theft Bureau (EA)	
NATB	Naval Air Training Base	
NATB	Naval Training Bulletin	
NAtB	Nitrosoanatabine [*Organic chemistry*]	
NATB	Nonreading Aptitude Test Battery [*US Employment Service*] [*Department of Labor*]	
Nat Bank Reg	National Bankruptcy Register Reports [*United States*] [*A publication*] (DLA)	
Nat Bankr Law	National Bankruptcy Law [*A publication*] (DLA)	
Nat Bankr N & R	National Bankruptcy News and Reports [*A publication*] (DLA)	
Nat Bankr R	National Bankruptcy Register [*United States*] [*A publication*] (DLA)	
Nat Bankr Reg	National Bankruptcy Register [*United States*] [*A publication*] (DLA)	
Nat Bankr Rep	National Bankruptcy Register Reports [*United States*] [*A publication*] (DLA)	
Nat Bar J	National Bar Journal [*A publication*] (DLA)	
NATBASES	Naval Air Training Bases	
Nat BC	National Bank Cases [*United States*] [*A publication*] (DLA)	
NatBev	National Beverage Corp. [*Associated Press*] (SAG)	
NATBF	Northwest African Tactical Bomber Force [*World War II*]	
Nat BJ	National Bar Journal [*A publication*] (DLA)	
NATBM	Navy Anti-Tactical Ballistic Missile (SAUS)	
Nat BR	National Bankruptcy Register [*United States*] [*A publication*] (DLA)	
Nat Brev	Fitzherbert's Natura Brevium [*A publication*] (DLA)	
Nat Bur Econ Res	National Bureau of Economic Research (AD)	
NAT BUR ECON RES	National Bureau of Economic Research (WDAA)	
Nat Bur Stand Circ	National Bureau of Standards Circular [*A publication*] (AD)	
NAtC	Columbia-Greene Community College, Athens, NY [*Library symbol*] [*Library of Congress*] (LCLS)	
NATC	National Air Taxi Conference (SAA)	
NATC	National Air Traffic Controllers (AD)	
NATC	National Air Transportation Conferences [*Later, NATA*]	
NATC	National Alcohol Tax Coalition (EA)	
NATC	National Association of Taurine Clubs	
NATC	National Association of Tax Consultants (EA)	
NATC	National Association of Telemarketing Consultants [*Defunct*] (EA)	
NATC	Naval Air Technical Training Center (ACAE)	
NATC	Naval Air Test Center	
NATC	Naval Air Training Center	
NATC	Naval Air Training Command (CAAL)	
NATC	Nevada Automotive Test Center (SAUS)	
NATC	Nordic Amateur Theatre Council (EAIO)	
NATC	Nordic Automobile Technical Committee [*Defunct*] [*Denmark*] (EAIO)	
NATC	North Atlantic Treaty Council (NATG)	
NATC	Northwest African Training Command [*World War II*]	
NATC	Noval Air Test Center (IAA)	
NATCA	National Air Traffic Control Administration (SAUS)	
NATCA	National Air Traffic Controllers Association (EA)	
NATCA	National Association of Trial Court Administrators (EA)	
NATCA	North American Trap Collector Association (EA)	
NATCC	North American Touring Car Championship [*Automobile racing*]	
NATCC	Northwest African Troop Camer Command (SAUS)	
NATCC	Northwest African Troop Carrier Command [*World War II*]	
NATCD	National Association of Tobacco & Confectionery Distributors (AC)	
NATCEM	National Cemetery	
NATCENTATHLIT	National Centre for Athletic Literature (NITA)	
NATCG	National Association of Training Corps for Girls [*British*] (BI)	
Natch	Natchez (AD)	
natch	Naturally (AD)	

NATCO .... National Association of Transit Consumer Organizations (EA)
NATCO .... National Automatic Tool Co.
NATCO .... National Coordinator [Marine science] (MSC)
NATCO .... National Tank Co. (AD)
NATCO .... Navy Air Traffic Coordinating Officer
NATCO .... North American Transplant Coordinators Organization (EA)
NATCO .... Northern Advanced Technologies Corp. [Research center] (RCD)
NATCO .... Nuclear Auditing and Testing Co.
natcol .... Natural Color (AD)
NATCOL .... Natural Food Colours Association [Basel, Switzerland] (EAIO)
natcom .... National Communications (AD)
NATCOM ..... National Communications Symposium [IEEE]
NATCOM ..... National Conference on Communications (MCD)
NATCOM ..... NATO Communication (NATG)
Nat Con .... Nature Conservancy (BARN)
NatConv .... National Convenience Stores [Associated Press] (SAG)
NATCS .... National Air Traffic Control Service (IEEE)
NATCS .... National Air Traffic Control System (NATG)
Nat D .... De Natura Deorum [of Cicero] [Classical studies] (OCD)
NATD .... National Association of Teachers of Dancing [British] (DBA)
NATD .... National Association of Telecommunications Dealers (EA)
NATD .... National Association of Test Directors (EA)
NATD .... National Association of Tobacco Distributors (EA)
NATD .... National Association of Tool Dealers [British] (BI)
NATD .... National Diagnostics, Inc. [NASDAQ symbol] (SAG)
NATD .... Nuclear and Advanced Technology Division (SAUS)
NATDEC .... Naval Air Training Division Engineering Command (DNAB)
NATDEFSM ..... National Defense Service Medal [Military decoration]
Nat Dem .... National Democrats [Political party] (AD)
NatDiag .... National Diagnostics, Inc. [Associated Press] (SAG)
NATDP .... National Agricultural Text-Digitizing Project [National Agricultural Library]
NATDS .... National Association of Truck Driving Schools (EA)
NATDS .... Naval Air Tactical Data System (MCD)
NATDS .... Navy Automated Transportation Data System (DNAB)
NATDW .... National Diagnostics Wrrt [NASDAQ symbol] (TTSB)
NATE .... National Association for Teachers of Electronics [Defunct] (EA)
NATE .... National Association for the Teaching of English (AD)
NATE .... National Association of Teachers of English
NATE .... National Association of Temple Educators (EA)
NATE .... National Association of Trade Exchanges
NATE .... Native American Teacher Education (AD)
NATE .... Neutral Atmosphere Temperature Experiment
NATEBE .... National Association of Teacher Educators for Business Education [DeKalb, IL] (EA)
NATEBOE ..... National Association of Teacher Educators for Business and Office Education [Later, NATEBE] (EA)
NATEC .... Naval Air Technical Evaluation Center (IAA)
NATEC .... Naval Air Training and Experimental Command
NATECHTRA ... Naval Air Technical Training (DNAB)
NATECHTRACEN ... Naval Air Technical Training Center
NATECHTRAU ... Naval Air Technical Training Unit
NATECOM ..... Naval Airship Training and Experimentation Command
NatEdu .... National Education Corp. [Associated Press] (SAG)
NATEF .... National Automotive Technicians Education Foundation (EA)
NATEFACS ... National Association of Teacher Educators for Family and Consumer Sciences (NTPA)
NATEL .... Nortronics Automatic Test Equipment Language [Computer science]
NATELCA ..... National Association for Teaching English and other Community Languages to Adults [Formerly, NATELSA] (AIE)
NATELO .... NATO maritime air Telecommunications Organization (SAUS)
NatEng .... National Energy Group [Associated Press] (SAG)
NATES .... National Analysis of Trends in Emergency Systems [Canada] (MSC)
NATESA .... National Alliance of Television and Electronics Services Associations (IAA)
NATESA .... National Association of Television and Electronic Servicers of America [N ESSDA] [Absorbed by] (EA)
NATESLA ..... National Association for Teaching English as a Secondary Language to Adults [British] (DI)
NATESOL ..... National Association of Teachers of English for Speakers of Other Languages [England]
NATESTCEN ... Naval Air Test Center
NATEVHE ..... National Association of Teacher Educators for Vocational Home Economics (EA)
NATEX .... National Stock Exchange [Dissolved, 1975]
NATF .... National Automobile Theft Bureau
NATF .... Naval Advanced Tactical Fighter (SAUS)
NATF .... Naval Air Test Facility
NATF .... Navy Advanced Tactical Fighter (MCD)
NATF .... New Arrivals Task Force (MCD)
NATFACS ..... National Association of Teachers of Family and Consumer Sciences (NTPA)
NATFB .... National Archives Trust Fund Board
NATFC .... North American Toyah Fan Club (EA)
Nat Fed .... National Federation (AD)
NatFGs .... National Fuel Gas Co. [Associated Press] (SAG)
NATFHE .... National Association of Teachers in Further and Higher Education [British]
Nat For .... National Forum [A publication] (BRI)
NATFREQU ..... Natural Frequency (IAA)
NATF-SI .... Naval Air Test Facility - Ship Installations
NATG .... National Association of Training Groups [British] (DBA)
NATGA .... National Amateur Tobacco Growers' Association [British] (BI)
Nat Gal .... National Gallery (AD)
NAT GAL .... National Gallery [London] (WDAA)

NatGam .... National Gaming Corp. [Associated Press] (SAG)
Nat Geog Mag ... National Geographic Magazine [A publication] (AD)
Nat Geogr Mag ... National Geographic Magazine (SAUS)
NatGolf .... National Golf Properties [Associated Press] (SAG)
NatGsO .... National Gas & Oil Co. [Associated Press] (SAG)
NATH .... Nathan's Famous [NASDAQ symbol] (TTSB)
NATH .... Nathan's Famous, Inc. [NASDAQ symbol] (NQ)
Nathan .... Nathan's Common Law of South Africa [A publication] (DLA)
Nathans .... Nathan's Famous, Inc. [Associated Press] (SAG)
Nath B .... Nathaniel Bowditch
NATHE .... National Associations of Teachers of Home Economics [British]
NATHHAN .... National Challenged Homeschoolers Associated Network (PAZ)
nat hist .... Natural History (AD)
Nathl .... Nathaniel (AD)
NatHlth .... Natural Health Trends Corp. [Associated Press] (SAG)
NatHme .... National Home Centers [Commercial firm] [Associated Press] (SAG)
NatHP .... Nationwide Health Properties, Inc. [Associated Press] (SAG)
NATI .... National Instrument Corp. [NASDAQ symbol] (SAG)
NATIBO .... North American Technology and Industrial Base Organization
NATICH .... National Air Toxics Information Clearinghouse [Environmental Protection Agency] (GFGA)
NATIDC .... Netherlands-Australia Trade and Industrial Development Council (AD)
NATIE .... National Association for Trade and Industrial Education (EA)
NATII .... National Association of Trade and Industrial Instructors (EA)
NATINADS ... NATO Integrated Air Defense System (NATG)
Nat Inc Tax Mag ... National Income Tax Magazine [A publication] (DLA)
Nat Inf .... Nature Information (SAUS)
NatInst .... National Instrument Corp. [Associated Press] (SAG)
nation .... Nationality (AD)
National ADDA ... National Attention-Deficit Disorder Association (EA)
National PTA ... National Congress of Parents and Teachers (PAZ)
NATIP .... NATO Information & Press office (SAUS)
NATIP .... Navy Technical Information Program
NATIS .... National Information Systems [Later, GIP] [UNESCO]
NATIS .... Naval Air Training Information System
NATIS .... North Atlantic Treaty Information Service (NATG)
Nativ .... Nativity (AD)
NATIV .... Nativity
NATIV .... North American Test Instrument Vehicle [Air Force test rocket]
NATIVE .... North American Test Instrument Vehicle [Air force test rocket] (IAA)
Nat J Leg Ed ... National Journal of Legal Education [A publication] (DLA)
NATK .... North American Technologies Corp. [NASDAQ symbol] (SAG)
NATK .... North Amer Technologies Group [NASDAQ symbol] (TTSB)
NATKE .... National Association of Theatrical and Kine Employees (AD)
NATKE .... National Association of Theatrical and Kinema Employees [British] (DI)
NATL .... NAI Technologies [NASDAQ symbol] (SAG)
NATL .... National (AAG)
natl .... National (AD)
Natl .... National (AL)
NATL .... National Agricultural Transportation League [Defunct] (EA)
NATI .... Natl Instruments [NASDAQ symbol] (TTSB)
NATL .... Naval Aeronautical Turbine Laboratory
N Atl .... North Atlantic (AD)
N Atlantic Reg Bus L Rev ... North Atlantic Regional Business Law Review [A publication]
NATLAS .... National Testing Laboratory Accreditation Scheme [Military] [British]
Nat Law Guild Q ... National Lawyers Guild Quarterly [A publication] (DLA)
NatlBev .... National Beverage Corp. [Associated Press] (SAG)
NatlCity .... National City Corp. [Associated Press] (SAG)
Natl Civ Rev ... National Civic Review [A publication] (ILCA)
N Atl Cur ..... North Atlantic Current (AD)
Nat L Guild Q ... National Lawyers Guild Quarterly [A publication] (DLA)
Nat Lib .... National Liberal (AD)
NatLib .... National Liberal Party [Australia] [Political party]
Nat Lib .... National Library of Canada (AD)
NATLIBCAN ... National Library of Canada (AD)
NATLIBNZ ... National Library of New Zealand (AD)
Nat'l Income Tax Mag ... National Income Tax Magazine [A publication] (DLA)
Nat LJ .... Natal Law Journal [South Africa] [A publication] (DLA)
Nat'l Legal Mag ... National Legal Magazine [A publication] (DLA)
Nat LM .... Natal Law Magazine [South Africa] [A publication] (DLA)
Natlm .... Naturalism (VRA)
Natl Meas Lab Tech Pap CSIRO Anst ... Australia. Commonwealth Scientific and Industrial Research Organisation. National Measurement Laboratory. Technical Pape (SAUS)
Nat Louis U ... National-Louis University (GAGS)
Nat'l Pub Empl Rep ... National Public Employment Reporter [A publication] (DLA)
Nat LQ .... Natal Law Quarterly [South Africa] [A publication] (DLA)
Nat LR .... Natal Law Reports [South Africa] [A publication] (ILCA)
Nat L Rec ... National Law Record [A publication] (DLA)
NatlReg .... National Registry [Associated Press] (SAG)
Nat L Rep ... National Law Reporter [A publication] (DLA)
Natl Rep Sys ... National Reporter System (DLA)
Nat L Rev ... National Law Review [A publication] (DLA)
NatlRV .... National R.V. Holdings, Inc. [Associated Press] (SAG)
Nat'l School L Rptr ... National School Law Reporter [A publication] (DLA)
NATLSEMICON ... National Semiconductor Corp. (IAA)
Natl Stand Lab Tech Pap CSIRO Aust ... Australia Commonwealth Scientific and Industrial Research Organisation. National Standards Laboratory. Technical Paper (SAUS)
NatlStl .... National Steel Corp. [Associated Press] (SAG)
NATM .... National Association of Trailer Manufacturers (NTPA)
NATM .... New Austrian Tunneling Method (SAUS)

NATM.......... New Austrian Tunnel Method [*Civil engineering*]
NATMA .... National Award and Trophy Manufacturers Association (EA)
NATMAC ...... National Air Traffic Management Advisory Committee [*British*]
NATMAP ...... Division of National Mapping (SAUS)
NATMAP ..... National Mapping (AD)
NATMATMUS... National Automotive and Truck Model and Toy Museum of the United States
NATMC .... National Advanced Technology Management Conference
NatMFS........ National Medical Financial Services Corp. [*Associated Press*] (SAG)
NATMH .... National Association of Teachers of the Mentally Handicapped [*British*]
NatMicr........ Natural Microsystems Corp. [*Associated Press*] (SAG)
NATMILCOMSYS... National Military Command System
Nat Mon ..... National Monument (AD)
NAT MON ..... National Monument (WDAA)
NATMSACT... Naval Air Training Support Facility (AAGC)
Nat Mus....... Natal Museum (AD)
NATMUS ..... National Automobile and Truck Museum of the United States
NATMUS ..... National Automotive and Truck Museum of United States (EA)
Nat Mus....... National Museum (AD)
NATN .... National Association of Theatre Nurses [*British*] (BI)
NATN .... National Association of Traveling Nurses
NATNAV....... North Atlantic Navigation
NATNAVDENCEN... National Naval Dental Center (DNAB)
NATNAVMEDCEN... National Naval Medical Center [*Bethesda, MD*]
NATNAVRESMASTCONRADSTA... National Naval Reserve Master Control Radio Station (DNAB)
Natn Bank Mon Sum... National Bank. Monthly Summary [*A publication*]
Natn Bank Mon Sum Aust Cond... National Bank of Australasia. Monthly Summary of Australian Conditions [*A publication*]
Natnet.......... National Network [*Telecommunications*] [*British*]
Natn Farmer... National Farmer [*A publication*]
NatnGv03..... Nations Government Income Term 2003 [*Associated Press*] (SAG)
NatnGv04..... Nations Government Income Term 2004 [*Associated Press*] (SAG)
Natn Hosp ... National Hospital [*A publication*]
Natn Parks J... National Parks Journal [*A publication*]
Natn Rehab Digest... National Rehabilitation Digest [*A publication*]
NatnsBal...... Nations Balanced Target Maturity Fund [*Associated Press*] (SAG)
NatnsBk ...... NationsBank Corp. [*Associated Press*] (SAG)
Natn Times Mag... National Times Magazine [*A publication*]
NATO .... Narrow-Angle Target of Opportunity [*Photography*] [*NASA*]
NATO .... National Association of Taxicab Owners [*Later, ITA*] (EA)
NATO .... National Association of Telephone Operators [*A union*] [*British*]
NATO .... National Association of Theatre Owners (EA)
NATO .... National Association of Trailer Owners (EA)
NATO .... National Association of Travel Organizations [*Later, TIA*] (EA)
NATO .... No Action, Talk Only (DICI)
NATO .... North African Theater of Operations [*World War II*]
NATO .... North Atlantic Treaty Organization [*Facetious translation: "No Action, Talk Only"*] [*Brussels, Belgium*]
NATOA......... National Association of Telecommunications Officers and Advisors (EA)
NATO AEW... North Atlantic Treaty Organization Airborne Early Warning Program
NATO-AGARD... North Atlantic Treaty Organization - Advisory Group for Aeronautical Research and Development
NATO-ARW... NATO Advanced Research Workshop (SAUS)
Nat Obs ...... National Observer [*A publication*] (AD)
NATODC....... North Atlantic Treaty Organization Defense College (DNAB)
NATODEFCOL... North Atlantic Treaty Organization Defense College (DNAB)
NATOELLA ... North Atlantic Treaty Organization - European Long Lines Agency
NatOilwll ..... National Oilwell, Inc. [*Associated Press*] (SAG)
NAT-OJT ...... National On-the-Job Training Program [*Department of Labor*]
NATO Letter... North Atlantic Treaty Organization Letter (SAUS)
NATO-LRSS... North Atlantic Treaty Organization - Long-Range Scientific Studies
NATO MC ..... North Atlantic Treaty Organization Military Committee
NATOMILOCGRP... North Atlantic Treaty Organization - Military Oceanography Group (NATG)
NATOPS....... Naval Air Training and Operating Procedures Standardization (MCD)
NATOPS....... Naval Air Training Operating Practices (SAUS)
Nat Ord........ Natural Order [*Botany*] (BARN)
NATO-RDPP... North Atlantic Treaty Organization - Multilateral Research and Development Production Program
NATO-RDPP... North Atlantic Treaty Organization-Research and Development Production Program (SAUS)
NATOSAT..... North Atlantic Treaty Organization Satellite
NATO-SC ..... North Atlantic Treaty Organization - Science Committee
NATOUSA ..... North African Theater of Operations, United States Army [*World War II*]
NATP .... National Association of Tax Practitioners (EA)
NATP .... Natl Power plc [*LO, exchange symbol*] (TTSB)
NATPA .... North America Taiwanese Professors' Association (EA)
NAT PAC...... National PAC [*Political Action Committee*] (EA)
NATPE .... National Association of Television Program Executives (NTCM)
NATPE .... NATPE [*National Association of Television Program Executives*] International (EA)
Nat Peop ..... Native Peoples [*A publication*] (BRI)
nat phil........ Natural Philosophy (AD)
Nat Phil........ Natural Philosophy (BARN)
Nat Pk .... National Park (BARN)
NATPN........ North African Transportation Section [*World War II*]
NatProc....... National Processing, Inc. [*Associated Press*] (SAG)
NatProp .... National Propane Partners LP [*Associated Press*] (SAG)
NATPS .... National Association of Trade Protection Societies [*British*] (DBA)
NATR .... Natchez Trace Parkway [*National Park Service designation*]
NATR .... National Association of Tenants and Residents [*British*] (BI)

NATR .... National Association of Toy Retailers [*British*] (BI)
NATR .... National Representative [*Red Cross*]
Nat R .... National Review [*A publication*] (BRI)
NATR .... Natrium [*Sodium*] [*Pharmacy*]
natr.......... Natrium [*Sodium*] [*Latin*] (AD)
NATR .... Natural Resources
NATR .... Nature's Sunshine Prod [*NASDAQ symbol*] (TTSB)
NATR .... Nature's Sunshine Products, Inc. [*NASDAQ symbol*] (NQ)
NATR .... No Additional Traffic Reported [*Aviation*]
NATR .... Nordischer Amator Theater Rat [*Nordic Amateur Theatre Council - NATC*] (EAIO)
NATRA .... National Association of Television and Radio Announcers (NTCM)
NATRA .... National Association of Television and Radio Artists [*Inactive*]
NATRA .... Naval Air Training Command (AFIT)
NATRACOM... Naval Air Training Command (DNAB)
NATRADIVENGCOM... Naval Air Training Division Engineering Command (DNAB)
NATRAP....... Narrow-Band Transmission of RADAR Pictures (MCD)
NATRC........ North American Trail Ride Conference (EA)
NatRe .... National Re Corp. [*Associated Press*] (SAG)
NATRE .... North Atlantic Tracer Release Experiment (SAUS)
NatRecd....... National Record Mart, Inc. [*Associated Press*] (SAG)
Nat Reg .... National Register, Edited by Mead [*1816*] [*A publication*] (DLA)
Nat Rept Syst... National Reporter System (DLA)
Nat Resources... Nature and Resources (SAUS)
NATRFD .... National Association of Television-Radio Farm Directors [*Later, NAFB*] (EA)
NATRI .... National Association of Treasurers of Religious Institutes (EA)
NATRI .... Navy Training Requirements Information
NATRIP .... National Association of Tax Reducing Income Plans (NTPA)
NatrlHlth....... Natural Health Trends Corp. [*Associated Press*] (SAG)
NATRON ...... National Cash Register Electronic Data Processing System (MCD)
NAT-RPG ...... North Atlantic Treaty Regional Planning Group (NATG)
NatrSun ...... Natures Sunshine Products [*Associated Press*] (SAG)
NATS .... National Activity to Test Software
NATS .... National Air Toxics Strategy [*Environmental Protection Agency*] (GFGA)
NATS .... National Air Traffic Services [*British*]
NATS .... National Association of Teachers of Singing (EA)
NATS .... National Association of Temporary Services [*Alexandria, VA*] (EA)
NATS .... National Association of Textile Supervisors (EA)
Nats .... Nationalists (AD)
NATS .... National Securities Corp. [*NASDAQ symbol*] (NQ)
Nats .... Natsionalnyii [*National*] [*Russian*] (AD)
NATS .... Naval Air Test Station (AD)
NATS .... Naval Air Transport Service
NATS .... NCAR Airborne Telemetry System (SAUS)
NATS .... NCAR Aircraft Telemetry System (SAUS)
NATS .... Needlework and Accessories Trade Show (ITD)
NATS .... Negative Authorization Terminal System [*Computer science*] (MHDB)
NATS .... New Aircraft Tool System [*Army*]
NATS .... Noise Abatement Test System (FAAC)
NATS .... Nordisk Avisteknisk Samarbetsnamnd [*Nordic Joint Technical Press Board*] [*Sweden*] (EAIO)
NATS .... North American Truffling Society (EA)
NATS .... North Atlantic Track System (SAUS)
NATSA .... National Associated Truck Stops and Associates (EA)
NATSAA .... NATO Air Traffic Service Advisory Agency (NATG)
NATSC .... National Association of Training School Chaplains (EA)
NATSC .... National Association of Trap and Skeet Clubs (EA)
NAT SC ...... Natural Sciences (WDAA)
Nat ScD ...... Doctor of Natural Science (AD)
NAT SC D .... Doctor of Natural Science (WDAA)
Nat Sci Fdn... National Science Foundation (AD)
NATSECM ... National Security Medal
Nat Sec Soc... National Secular Society (AD)
Nat Semi ..... National Semiconductor Corp.
NATSEMI ..... National Semiconductor Inc. (AD)
NATSF........ Naval Air Technical Services Facility (MCD)
NATSFERRY... Naval Air Transport Service, Ferry Command [*World War II*]
NATSFQADIVLANT... Naval Air Technical Services Facility, Quality Assurance Division, Atlantic (DNAB)
NATSFQADIVPAC... Naval Air Technical Services Facility, Quality Assurance Division, Pacific (DNAB)
NATSIEP ...... National Aboriginal and Torres Strait Islander Education Policy [*Australia*]
NATSJA........ National Association of Training School and Juvenile Agencies [*Later, NAJCA*] (EA)
NATSLANT... Naval Air Transport Service, Atlantic Wing [*World War II*]
NATSO .... National Association of Truck Stop Operators (EA)
NATSOPA..... National Society of Operative Printers and Assistants [*British*]
NAT sound... Natural Sound [*Broadcasting*] (WDMC)
NATSPAC..... Naval Air Transport Service, Pacific Wing [*World War II*]
NATSPG...... North Atlantic Systems Planning Group [*Military*] (WDAA)
NATSRA....... North American Thermal Soil Recycling Association (NTPA)
NATSS .... National Association of Temporary and Staffing Services (NTPA)
NAT-STD...... NATO STANAG International Standards
NATSU .... Naval Air Technical Services Unit (NVT)
NATSU .... Nominated Air Traffic Service Unit (DA)
Nat Sup ...... National Superannuation (AD)
NatSurg....... National Surgery Centers, Inc. [*Associated Press*] (SAG)
NATSYN....... Natural and Synthetic [*Type of long-wearing rubber, which is actually wholly synthetic*]
NATT.......... National Association of Teachers of Travellers [*British*] (DBA)
NATT.......... National Association of Towns and Township Officials (EA)
NATT.......... Naval Air Technical Training

N Att	Naval Attache (AD)
N ATT	Naval Attache (WDAA)
NATT	North Atlantic Technology, Inc. (SAUS)
NATT	Northern Australian Tropical Transect (QUAC)
NATT	Northern Australia Tropical Transect (SAUS)
NAtt	Stevens Memorial Library, Attica, NY [Library symbol] [Library of Congress] (LCLS)
NATTA	Network of Alternative Technology and Technology Assessment (EAIO)
NATTA	North American Trackless Trolley Association (EA)
N-attack	Nuclear Attack (AD)
Nat Tax Mag	National Tax Magazine [A publication] (DLA)
NATTC	National Tank Truck Carriers (AD)
NATTC	Naval Air Technical Training Center
NATTCDET	Naval Air Technical Training Center Detachment (DNAB)
NATTCL	Naval Air Technical Training Center, Lakehurst (DNAB)
NAT/TFG	North Atlantic Traffic Forecasting Group (SAUS)
NATTFU	National Transsexual-Transvestite Feminization Union (EA)
NATTKE	National Association of Theatrical, Television, and Kine Employees [A union] [British] (DCTA)
NATTS	National Association of Trade and Technical Schools (EA)
NATTS	Naval Air Turbine Test Station
NATTS	North American Transvestite/Transsexual Society [Defunct] (EA)
NATTS-ATL	Naval Air Turbine Test Station - Aeronautical Turbine Laboratory
NATTU	Naval Air Technical Training Unit
Nat U	Nations Unies [United Nations] [French] (AD)
NATU	Naval Aircraft Torpedo Unit
Nat UL Rev	National University. Law Review [1921-31] [A publication] (DLA)
Nat Uni	National University (AD)
natur	Naturalist (AD)
NATUR	Naturalist (WDAA)
NATURBTESTSTA	Naval Air Turbine Test Station
Nature Struct Biol	Nature Structural Biology (MEC)
NaturlAlt	Natural Alternatives International [Associated Press] (SAG)
NATUS	Naturalized United States Citizen
NATUS	US message dealing with NATO subject matter (SAUS)
NATUSA	North African Theater of Operations (AD)
NATUSA	North African Theater, United States Army [World War II]
NATVA	National All Terrain Vehicle Association (AD)
NATVAS	National Academy of Television Arts and Sciences (EA)
NatVisn	National Vision Associates [Associated Press] (SAG)
NATW	National Association of Texaco Wholesalers (EA)
NATW	National Association of Town Watch (EA)
NATW	Natural Wonders [NASDAQ symbol] (TTSB)
NATW	Natural Wonders, Inc. [NASDAQ symbol] (SAG)
NATWA	National Auto and Truck Wreckers Association [Later, ADRA] (EA)
NATwA	North American Tiddlywinks Association (EA)
NATWARCOL	National War College [Later, UND] [DoD] (DNAB)
NATWC	National War College [Later, UND] [DoD]
NatWest	National Westminster [Bank]
NATWF	North American Tug of War Federation (EA)
NATWJ	National Alliance of Third World Journalists (EA)
NatWndr	Natural Wonders, Inc. [Associated Press] (SAG)
NATWP	Naval Air Transport Wing, Pacific
NAT WS	Nordic Amer Tanker Ship Wrrt [AMEX symbol] (TTSB)
naty	Naturally (AD)
NaTY	Sodium Hydrogen Phosphate-Tryptone-Yeast Extract [Growth medium] [Microbiology]
Natzd	Naturalized [Biology] (BARN)
NAU	Confederation Nordique des Cadres, Techniciens, et Autres Responsables [Nordic Confederation of Supervisors, Technicians, and Other Managers] (EAIO)
NAU	Nalcus Resources [Vancouver Stock Exchange symbol]
NAU	Napuka [Marquesas Islands] [Airport symbol] (OAG)
NAU	Narcotics Assistance Unit [Department of State]
Nau	Nauruan (AD)
Nau	Nauru Island (AD)
nau	Nautica [Nautical] [Spanish] (AD)
NAU	Naval Administrative Unit
NAU	Network Access Unit [Telecommunications]
NAU	Network Address [or Addressable] Unit [Computer science] (BUR)
NAU	Network Administration Utilities [Honeywell] (NITA)
NAU	Noise Augmentation Unit [Military] (CAAL)
NAU	Nordic Confederation of Supervisors, Technicians, and Other Managers [Formerly, Nordic Union of Foremen] (EA)
NAU	North Arizona University (AD)
NAU	Northern Arizona University (SAUS)
NAu	Seymour Library, Auburn, NY [Library symbol] [Library of Congress] (LCLS)
NAUA	National Aircraft Underwriters' Association (AD)
NAUA	National Automobile Underwriters Association [Later, ISO] (EA)
NAUB	National Association of Urban Bankers (EA)
NAuC	Cayuga County Community College, Auburn, NY [Library symbol] [Library of Congress] (LCLS)
NAUE	New and Unused Equipment (MCD)
NAUF	Name and Address Update File [IRS]
NAUFMA	National Association of Urban Flood Management Agencies [Later, NAFSWMA] (EA)
NAUFOF	North American UFO Federation [Defunct] (EA)
NAUFRED	National Association of Used Fitness and Rehabilitation Equipment Dealers (NTPA)
NAUFWP	National Association of University Fisheries and Wildlife Programs (NTPA)
NAUG	National AppleWorks Users Group (EA)
nauga	Naugahide (AD)

NAUHF	Northern Area Ultrahigh Frequency Radio System [Green Pine] (MCD)
NAuHi	Cayuga County Historical Society, Auburn, NY [Library symbol] [Library of Congress] (LCLS)
NAUI	National Association of Underwater Instructors (EA)
NAUL	Netherland-America University League [Defunct] (EA)
NAULAS	North American Union Life Assurance Society [Chicago, IL] (EA)
NAUM	National Association of Uniform Manufacturers [Later, NAUMD] (EA)
NAUMD	National Association of Uniform Manufacturers and Distributors (EA)
NAuMH	Auburn Memorial Hospital, Learning Resources Center, Auburn, NY [Library symbol] [Library of Congress] (LCLS)
NAUN	Nearest Active Upstream Neighbor [Computer science]
NAUN	Nearest Available Upstream Neighbor (MLOA)
NAU-OLC	North American Union of Sisters of Our Lady of Charity (TOCD)
NAUP	National Association of Unemployed Persons [Defunct] (EA)
NAUPA	National Amalgamated Union of Shop Assistants [A union] [British]
NAUPA	National Association of Unclaimed Property Administrators (EA)
NAURI	Nonaccelerating-Unemployment Rate of Inflation [Economics]
NAurW	Wells College, Aurora, NY [Library symbol] [Library of Congress] (LCLS)
NAUS	National Aerospace Utilization System (NOAA)
NAUS	National Association for Uniformed Services (EA)
NAuS	Seward House, Auburn, NY [Library symbol] [Library of Congress] (LCLS)
NAUSAWC	National Amalgamated Union of Shop Assistants, Warehousemen, and Clerks [A union] [British]
NAUS/SMW	National Association for Uniformed Services and Society of Military Widows (NTPA)
NAuT	Auburn Theological Seminary, Auburn, NY [Library symbol] [Library of Congress] [Obsolete] (LCLS)
NAUT	Nautica Enterprises [NASDAQ symbol] (TTSB)
NAUT	Nautica Enterprises, Inc. [NASDAQ symbol] (SAG)
NAUT	Nautical (AAG)
naut	Nautical (AD)
Naut	Nautical (DIAR)
NAUTEL	Nautical Electronic Laboratories Ltd. (SAUS)
NAUTIC	Naval Autonomous Intelligent Console (PDAA)
Nautica	Nautica Enterprises, Inc. [Associated Press] (SAG)
NAUTIS	Naval Autonomous Information System (AAG)
NAUTIS-F	Naval Autonomous Information System-Frigate (DOMA)
NAUTO	Nautophone
NAUTS	Nautical Miles (ROG)
NAUTT	National Association of Unions in the Textile Trade [British] (DCTA)
NAUW	National Association of University Women (EA)
NAUWS	Naval Advanced Undersea Weapons School
n aux b	New Auxiliary Boiler (AD)
NAV	Narrows [Virginia] [Seismograph station code, US Geological Survey] (SEIS)
NAVC	National American Veterans
NAV	National Association of Videographers [Defunct] (EA)
NAV	Natividade [Brazil] [Airport symbol] (AD)
Nav	Navaho (AD)
nav	Navajo [MARC language code] [Library of Congress] (LCCP)
Nav	Naval (AD)
nav	Naval (AD)
NAV	Naval (MSA)
NAV	Naval Artillery Volunteers [British] (ROG)
Nav	Navarra (AD)
Nav	Navarre (AD)
Nav	Navassa Island (AD)
NAV	Nav Flight Planning [Czech Republic] [FAA designator] (FAAC)
nav	Navigable (AD)
NAV	Navigate (AAG)
nav	Navigation (AD)
NAV	Navigation (GAVI)
NAV	Navigator (DSUE)
NAV	Navistar International Corp. [NYSE symbol] (SPSG)
NAV	Navy (AAG)
NAV	Net Annual Value [Business term] (ADA)
NAV	Net Asset Value
NAV	Next Generation Advanced Vehicle [Nippon Steel Corp.]
NAV	Nonalcoholic Volunteers
NAV	Non-Aqueous Volatiles (SAUS)
NAV	North American Ventures, Inc. [Vancouver Stock Exchange symbol]
NAV	Norton Anti-Virus [Computer science] (VLIE)
NAV	Nurserymens Association of Victoria (SAUS)
NAV	Visual Navigation (MCD)
NAVA	National Association for Variable Annuities
NAVA	National Association for Veterinary Acupuncture (EA)
NAVA	National Association of Veterinary Assistants [Defunct] (EA)
NAVA	National Audio-Visual Association [Later, ICIA] (EA)
NAVA	Navajo National Monument
NAVA	Net Asset Value (VLIE)
NAVA	Non-Added Value Activity (VLIE)
NAVA	North American Vexillological Association (EA)
NAVABSCOLLU	Navy Absentee Collection Unit (DNAB)
NAVAC	National Audiovisual Aids Centre [British]
NAVAC	North American Vaccine, Inc. (SAUS)
NAVACAD	Naval Academy
NA Vacc	North American Vaccine, Inc. [Associated Press] (SAG)
NAVACCTGFINCEN	Navy Accounting and Finance Center (DNAB)
NAVACD	Naval Academy (DNAB)
navaco	Navigation Action Cutout (AD)
NAVACO	Navigation Action Cutout Switchboard
NAVACT	All Navy Activities [A dispatch to all activities in an area]

NAVACTDET...   Naval Activities Detachment (DNAB)
NAVAD.........   Naval Administrator At [*Place*]
NAVADCOM...   Naval Administrative Command
NAVADGP ....   Naval Advisory Group
NAVADGRU...   Naval Advisory Group (CINC)
NAVADGRU...   Navy Administrative Group
NAV-ADMIN...   Navigation-Administration [*Inquiry program*] (AFIT)
NAVADMINCOM...   Naval Administrative Command (DNAB)
NAVADMINO...   Navy Administrative Office [*or Officer*]
NAVADMINU...   Naval Administration Unit (MUGU)
NAVADMINUANX...   Naval Administrative Unit Annex (DNAB)
NAVADS......   Navy Automated Transport Documentation System (DNAB)
NAVADUNIT...   Naval Administrative Unit
NAVADUNSEAWPNSCOL...   Naval Advanced Undersea Weapons School (DNAB)
NAVADVUSEAWPNSCOL...   Naval Advanced Undersea Weapons School (MUGU)
NAVAE.........   National Association for Vietnamese American Education (EA)
NAVAER.......   Navy Aeronautics
NAVAERAUDOFC...   Navy Area Audit Office [*London*] (DNAB)
NAVAEROMEDCEN...   Naval Aeronautical Medical Center
NAVAERORECOV...   Naval Aerospace Recovery Facility
NAVAERORECOVF...   Naval Aerospace Recovery Facility (AD)
NAVAERORECOVFAC...   Naval Aerospace Recovery Facility
NAVAEROSPMEDINST...   Naval Aerospace Medical Institute
NAVAEROSPMEDRSCHINST...   Naval Aerospace Medical Research Institute (DNAB)
NAVAERO(SP)OMEDRSCHLAB...   Naval Aerospace Medical Research Laboratory (DNAB)
NAVAERO(SP)RECFAC...   Naval Aerospace Recovery Facility (DNAB)
NAVAERO(SP)REGMEDCEN...   Naval Aerospace Medical Center (DNAB)
NAVAGLOBE...   Long-Distance Navigation System, Global [*Air Force*]
NAVAID........   Air Navigation Facilities (or Facility) (SAUS)
NAVAID........   Navigation Aid
NAVAID........   Navigational Aid (DNAB)
NAVAIDE......   Naval Aide
NavAide......   Naval Aide
NAVAIDS......   Navigation Aids (VLIE)
NAVAIDSUPPUNIT...   Navigational Aids Support Unit (DNAB)
NAVAIR........   Naval Air Systems Command
NAVAIR........   Naval Air Systems Command Headquarters (USDC)
NAVAIRANDACT...   Naval Air Research and Development Activities (MUGU)
NAVAIRDEVCEN...   Naval Air Development Center [*Also, NADC, NADEVCEN*] (MUGU)
NAVAIRDEVU...   Naval Air Development Unit (MUGU)
NAVAIRECONTECHSUPCEN...   Naval Air Reconnaissance Technical Support Center
NAVAIRENGCEN...   Naval Air Engineering Center [*Closed*]
NAVAIRENGCENFO...   Naval Air Engineering Center Field Office (DNAB)
NAVAIRENGLAB...   Naval Air Engineering Laboratory (DNAB)
NAVAIRENGRCEN...   Naval Air Engineering Center [*Closed*]
NAVAIRENGRFAC...   Naval Air Engineering Facility (MUGU)
NAVAIRESCEN...   Naval Air Reserve Center (DNAB)
NAVAIRESFORRON...   Naval Air Reserve Force Squadron (DNAB)
NAVAIRESMOPIXU...   Naval Air Reserve Mobile Photographic Unit (DNAB)
NAVAIRESU...   Naval Air Reserve Unit (DNAB)
NAVAIREWORKF...   Naval Air Rework Facility
NAVAIREWORKFAC...   Naval Air Rework Facility
NAVAIRFAC...   Naval Air Facility
NAVAIRINST...   Naval Air Systems Command Instruction
NavAirInstr...   Naval Air Command Instruction (AAGC)
NAVAIRINTO...   Naval Air Intelligence Office (MUGU)
NAVAIRLANT...   Naval Air Force, Atlantic Fleet
NAVAIRLOGOFF...   Naval Air Logistics Office (DNAB)
NAVAIRLOGTASKFORREP...   Naval Air Logistics Task Force Representative (DNAB)
NAVAIRMAINTRAGRU...   Naval Air Maintenance Training Group (DNAB)
NAVAIRMATCEN...   Naval Air Material Center [*Also, NAMATCEN, NAMC*] (MUGU)
NAVAIRMINDEFDEVU...   Naval Air Mine Defense Development Unit (MUGU)
NAVAIRNEWS...   Naval Aviation News [*A publication*] (DNAB)
NAVAIRPAC...   Naval Air Force, Pacific Fleet
NAVAIRPROPCEN...   Naval Air Propulsion Center (GRD)
NAVAIRPROPTESTCEN...   Naval Air Propeller Test Center
NAVAIRRES...   Naval Air Reserve
NAVAIRREWORKF...   Naval Air Rework Facility (AD)
NAVAIRSTA...   Naval Air Station (DNAB)
NAVAIRSUPPU...   Naval Air Support Unit
NAVAIRSYSCO...   Naval Air Systems Command (MCD)
NAVAIR SYSCOM...   Naval Air System Command (DOMA)
NAVAIRSYSCOM...   Naval Air Systems Command
NAVAIRSYSCOMFLEREADREP...   Naval Air Systems Command Fleet Readiness Representative (DNAB)
NAVAIRSYSCOMFLESUPREPCEN...   Naval Air Systems Command Fleet Supply Representative Center (DNAB)
NAVAIRSYSCOMHQ...   Naval Air Systems Command Headquarters
NAVAIRSYSCOMMETSYSDIV...   Naval Air Systems Command, Meteorological Systems Division (DNAB)
NAVAIRSYSCOMREP...   Naval Air Systems Command Representative
NAVAIRSYSCOMREPAC...   Naval Air Systems Command Representative, Pacific
NAVAIRSYSCOMREPCENT...   Naval Air Systems Command Representative, Central
NAVAIRSYSCOMREPLANT...   Naval Air Systems Command Representative, Atlantic
NAVAIRSYSCOMREP PNCLA...   Naval Air Systems Command Representative, Naval Air Training Command, Pensacola [*Florida*]
NAVAIRSYSCOMTARANDSYSDIV...   Naval Air Systems Command Target and Range Systems Command (DNAB)
NAVAIRTECHREP...   Naval Air Systems Command Technical Representative (DNAB)
NAVAIRTECHSERVFAC...   Naval Air Technical Services Facility (MUGU)
NAVAIRTERM...   Naval Air Terminal (DNAB)
NAVAIRTESTCEN...   Naval Air Test Center (MUGU)
NAVAIRTESTCENT...   Naval Air Test Center (GRD)

NAVAIRTESTFAC...   Naval Air Test Facility (MUGU)
NAVAIRTESTFACSHIPINSTAL...   Naval Air Test Facility - Ship Installations (DNAB)
NAVAIRTORPU...   Naval Aircraft Torpedo Unit (MUGU)
NAVAIRTRACEN...   Naval Air Training Center
NAVAIRTU ...   Naval Air Training Unit (DNAB)
NAVAIRTURBTESTSTA...   Naval Air Turbine Test Station (MUGU)
NAVAL.........   National Audio Visual Aids Library (AIE)
Naval E........   Naval Engineer (PGP)
NAVALOT.....   Allotment Division [*Navy*]
NAVALREHCEN...   Naval Alcohol Rehabilitation Center (DNAB)
NAVALREHDRYDOCK...   Navy Alcohol Rehabilitation Drydock (DNAB)
NAVALT.......   Navy Alterations
NAVAMDEP...   Naval Ammunition Depot [*Charleston, SC*]
NAVAMPROENGCEN...   Naval Ammunition Production Engineering Center (DNAB)
NAVANTRA...   Naval Air Advanced Training Center
NAVANTRACOM...   Naval Air Advanced Training Command
NAVAP........   National Association of VA [*Veterans Administration*] Physicians (EA)
NAVAPD.......   National Association of VA [*Veterans' Administration*] Physicians and Dentists (NTPA)
NAVAPI........   North American Voltage and Phase Indicator (IEEE)
NAVAPSCIENCLAB...   Naval Applied Science Laboratory (DNAB)
NAVAR........   Combined Navigation and Radar system (SAUS)
NAVAR........   Navigation Air RADAR (IAA)
NAVAR........   Navigation and Ranging (IAA)
NAVAR........   Navigation RADAR
NAVAR........   Radar Air Navigation and Control System (SAUS)
NAVARA......   Navy Appellate Review Activity
Nav Arch......   Naval Architect [*Academic degree*]
NAVAREAAUDSVC...   Naval Area Audit Service
NAVAREP.....   Natural Variability, Resilience and Buffer Capacity of the Bodden Ecosystem (SAUS)
NAVARHO...   Navigation and Radio Homing [*Aviation*]
NAVARMDEP...   Naval Armament Depot
Navarre........   Navarre Corp. [*Associated Press*] (SAG)
NAVASCOPE...   Airborne RADARscope Used in NAVAR (SAUS)
NAVASCOPE...   Navigation Airborne RADAR Scope [*Air Force*]
NAVASCREEN...   Navigation RADAR Screen [*Air Force*]
NAVASTROGRU...   Navy Astronautics Group (MUGU)
NAVASTROGRUHQTRINJFAC...   Navy Astronautics Group Headquarters, Tracking and Injection Facility (DNAB)
NAVASTROGRUP...   Navy Astronautics Group (SAA)
NAVASWDATACEN...   Navy Antisubmarine Warfare Data Center
NAVASWDATCEN...   Navy Antisubmarine Warfare Data Center (DNAB)
NAVATAC.....   Navy Antiterrorism Analysis Center (COE)
NAVATR......   Naval Air Systems [*Command Headquarters*] [*Marine science*] (OSRA)
NAVAUD ....   Navy Auditor
NAVAUDO ....   Navy Audit Office (DNAB)
NAVAUDSVC...   Director, Naval Audit Service
NAVAUDSVCAP...   Naval Audit Service, Capital Area (DNAB)
NAVAUDSVCHQ...   Naval Audit Service Headquarters (DNAB)
NAVAUDSVCNE...   Naval Audit Service, Northeast Area (DNAB)
NAVAUDSVCSE...   Naval Audit Service, Southeast Area (DNAB)
NAVAUDSVCWEST...   Naval Audit Service, Western Area (DNAB)
NavAus......   Navigation in Australian Waters (AD)
NAVAUTH ....   Naval Authority
NAVAUTODINSCEN...   Navy Automatic Digital Network Switching Center (DNAB)
NAVAVCEN...   Naval Audio-Visual Center (DNAB)
NAVAVENGSERVU...   Naval Aviation Engineering Services Unit [*Philadelphia, PA*] (DNAB)
NAVAVENGSERVUDET...   Naval Aviation Engineering Service Unit Detachment (DNAB)
NAVAVIONICFAC...   Naval Avionics Facility [*Later, NAC*] (MUGU)
NAVAVIONICSCEN...   Naval Avionics Center (DNAB)
NAVAVMEDCEN...   Naval Aviation Medical Center (DNAB)
NAVAVMUSEUM...   Naval Aviation Museum [*Pensacola, FL*] (DNAB)
NAVAVNENGRSERVU...   Naval Aviation Engineering Service Unit [*Philadelphia, PA*] (DNAB)
NAVAVNLOGCEN...   Naval Aviation Logistics Center (NVT)
NAVAVNLOGCENDET...   Naval Aviation Logistics Center Detachment (DNAB)
NAVAVNLOGCENFSO...   Naval Aviation Logistics Center Field Service Office (DNAB)
NAVAVNLOGCENMETALABOPS...   Naval Aviation Logistics Center Meteorology Calibration Laboratory Operations (DNAB)
NAVAVNMEDCEN...   Naval Aviation Medical Center (DNAB)
NAVAVNSAFECEN...   Naval Aviation Safety Center
NAVAVNSCOLCOM...   Naval Aviation School Command
NAVAVNWEPSFAC...   Naval Aviation Weapons Facilities
NAVAVNWPNSFAC...   Naval Aviation Weapons Facilities (DNAB)
NAVAVNWPNSFACDET...   Naval Aviation Weapons Facility Detachment (DNAB)
NAVB.........   National Association of Volunteer Bureaus [*British*] (EAIO)
NAVBALTAP...   Allied Naval Forces, Baltic Approaches [*NATO*] (NATG)
NAVBALTAP...   Naval Forces Baltic Approaches [*NATO*] (AD)
NAVBASE.....   Naval Base
NAVBASELANT...   Naval Bases Atlantic
NAVBASEPAC...   Naval Bases Pacific
NAVBCHGRU...   Naval Beach Group (DNAB)
NAVBCHPHIBREFTRAGRU...   Navy Beach Amphibious Refresher Training Group (DNAB)
NAVBCSTSVCDET...   Navy Broadcasting Service Detachment (DNAB)
NAVBCSTSVCDETTASA...   Navy Broadcasting Service Detachment Television Audio Support Activity (DNAB)
NAVBCSTSVCWASHDC...   Navy Broadcasting Service, Washington, DC (DNAB)
NAVBE ....   National Association for Vocational Business Education (AEBS)
NAVBEACHGRU...   Naval Beach Group (CINC)
NAVBIODYNLAB...   Naval Biodynamics Laboratory (DNAB)

NAVBIOLAB...   Naval Biological Laboratory (MUGU)
NAVBIOSCILAB...   Naval Biosciences Research Laboratory (DNAB)
NAVBIT.......   Naval Basic Instrument Trainer (PDAA)
navbm ....   Naval Ballistic Missile (AD)
NAVBM.......   Navy Ballistic Missile
NAVBMC.......   Navy Ballistic Missile Committee
NAVBOILAB...   Navy Boiler Laboratory
nav brz ....   Naval Bronze (AD)
Nav Bs ....   Naval Base (AD)
NAVC ....   Naval Audio Visual Center (ACAE)
NAVC ....   Naval Aviation Cadet
NAVC ....   North American Voyageur Council (EA)
NAVCA ....   North American Veterinary College Administrators (GVA)
NAVCAD ......   Naval Aviation Cadet
NavCad.......   Naval Cadet (AD)
NAVCALAB...   Navy Calibration Laboratory (DNAB)
NAVCALABANX...   Navy Calibration Laboratory Annex (DNAB)
NAVCALABMSG...   Navy Calibration Laboratory Meteorology Support Group (DNAB)
NAVCALABOPS...   Navy Calibration Laboratory Operations (DNAB)
NAVCALS....   Naval Communication Area Local Station (NVT)
NAVCAMS....   Naval Communication Area Master Station (NVT)
NAVCAMSEASTPAC...   Naval Communication Area Master Station, Eastern Pacific (DNAB)
NAVCAMSLANT...   Naval Communication Area Master Station, Atlantic (DNAB)
NAVCAMSMED...   Naval Communication Area Master Station, Mediterranean (DNAB)
NAVCAMSOAM...   Naval Communication Area Master Station, South America (DNAB)
NAVCAMSSPECCOMDIVLANT...   Naval Communication Area Master Station, Special Communications Division, Atlantic (DNAB)
NAVCARGOHANBN...   Naval Cargo Handling Battalion
NAVCAT ......   Naval Career Appraisal Team (MUGU)
NAVCAT ....   Naval Construction Action Team [Vietnam] (VNW)
NAVCBCEN...   Naval Construction Battalion Center
NAVCC ....   Naval Communications Center (MCD)
NAVCENFRACO...   Navy Central Freight Control Office
NAVCENT.....   Allied Naval Forces, Central Europe [NATO]
NAVCENT.....   Naval Forces [US] Central [Command] (DOMA)
NAVCENT.....   Navy, Central Command (SAUS)
NAVCG........   Coast Guard Publication [Formerly, NCG]
NAVCHAPGRU...   Navy Cargo Handling and Port Group (NVT)
NAVCHAPGRUDET...   Navy Cargo Handling and Port Group Detachment (DNAB)
NAVCINSUPPACT...   Navy Counterintelligence Support Activity (DNAB)
NAVCINSUPPCEN...   Navy Counterintelligence Support Center (DNAB)
NAVCINSUPPGRU...   Navy Counterintelligence Support Unit (DNAB)
NAVCIVENGLAB...   Navy Civil Engineering Laboratory (DNAB)
NAVCIVENGRLAB...   Naval Civil Engineering Laboratory
NAVCJ ....   National Association on Volunteers in Criminal Justice [Later, IAJV] (EA)
NAVCLODEP...   Naval Clothing Depot
NAVCLOTEXTOFC...   Navy Clothing and Textile Office (DNAB)
NAVCLOTEXTRSCHFAC...   Navy Clothing and Textile Research Facility [Natick, MA] (DNAB)
NAVCLOTEXTRSCHU...   Navy Clothing and Textile Research Unit
NAVCLOTHTEXOFC...   Navy Clothing and Textile Office (DNAB)
NAVCM........   Navigation Countermeasure (IAA)
NavCm........   Navigation Countermeasures and Deception (AD)
NAVCM........   Navigation Countermeasures and Deception
NAVCMD......   Navigation Command (MCD)
NAVCOASTSYSCEN...   Naval Coastal Systems Center [Panama City, FL] (DNAB)
NAVCOM......   Naval Communications [System]
navcom........   Navigation Communication (AD)
NAVCOM......   Navigator/Communications operator (SAUS)
NAVCOMCOM...   Naval Communications Command
NAVCOMM......   Naval Communications [System]
NAVCOMMAREA...   Naval Communications Area (NVT)
NAVCOMMCOM...   Naval Communications Command
NAVCOMMDET...   Naval Communication Station Detachment (DNAB)
NAVCOMMDETSPECCOMMDIV...   Naval Communication Station Detachment, Special Communications Division (DNAB)
NAVCOMMFAC...   Naval Communications Facility (NVT)
NAVCOMMHQ...   Naval Communications Headquarters (DNAB)
NAVCOMMIS...   Naval Communications Command Management Information System (MCD)
NAVCOMMOPNET...   Naval Communications Operation Network (DNAB)
NAVCOMMSTA...   Naval Communication Station
NAVCOMMSTASPECCOMMDIV...   Naval Communication Station, Special Communications Division (DNAB)
NAVCOMMSYS...   Naval Communication System (MUGU)
NAVCOMMSYSSUPPACT...   Naval Communications System Support Activity (DNAB)
NAVCOMMTRACEN...   Naval Communications Training Center (MUGU)
NAVCOMMU...   Naval Communication Unit
NAVCOMMUNR...   Naval Communications Unit, Naval Reserve (IAA)
NAVCOMPARS...   Naval Communications Processing and Routing System (MCD)
NAVCOMPT...   Office of the Comptroller of the Navy
NAVCOMPTINST...   Office of the Comptroller of the Navy Instruction
NAVCOMPTMAN...   Naval Comptroller Manual
NAVCOMSAT...   Naval Communications Satellite (VLIE)
NAVCOMSTA...   Naval Communications Station (CCCA)
NAVCOMSYSSUPPACT...   Naval Command Systems Support Activity (DNAB)
NAVCOMSYSSUPPCEN...   Naval Command Systems Support Center (DNAB)
NAVCOMSYSTO...   Navy Commissary Store (DNAB)
NAVCOMSYSTORE...   Navy Commissary Store
NAVCOMU ...   Naval Communications Unit
NAVCON ....   Naval Countermeasures (CINC)

NAVCON ......   Navigation Control Systems (RDA)
Nav Const...   Naval Constructor [Academic degree]
NAVCONSTRACEN...   Naval Construction Training Center (DNAB)
NAVCONSTRAU...   Naval Construction Training Unit (DNAB)
NAVCONSTREGT...   Naval Construction Regiment (DNAB)
NAVCONTDEP...   Navy Contracting Department (DNAB)
NAVCONTRACEN...   Naval Construction Training Center
NAVCONVHOSP...   Naval Convalescent Hospital
NAVCORCOURSECEN...   Naval Correspondence Course Center (DNAB)
NAVCORRCUSUNIT...   Navy Correctional Custody Unit (DNAB)
NAVCOSSACT...   Naval Command Systems Support Activity
NAVCOSSCEN...   Naval Command Systems Support Center (DNAB)
NAVCRUITAREA...   Navy Recruiting Area
NAVCRUITBRSTA...   Navy Recruiting Branch Station (DNAB)
NAVCRUITCOM...   Navy Recruiting Command (DNAB)
NAVCRUITCOMORIENTUNIT...   Navy Recruiting Command Orientation Unit (DNAB)
NAVCRUITCOMSAT...   Navy Recruiting Command Standardization and Audit Team (DNAB)
NAVCRUITCOMYPFLDREP...   Navy Recruiting Command Youth Programs Field Representative (DNAB)
NAVCRUITDIST...   Navy Recruiting District (DNAB)
NAVCRUITEXHIBCEN...   Navy Recruiting Exhibit Center (DNAB)
NAVCRUITEXHIBCENCAT...   Navy Recruiting Exhibit Center Catalog (DNAB)
NAVCRUITRACOM...   Navy Recruit Training Command (DNAB)
NAVCRUITSTA...   Navy Recruiting Station
NAVCSG......,   National Archives Volunteers Constitution Study Group [Defunct] (EA)
NAVCURRSUPPGRULANTFLT...   Naval Current Support Group, Atlantic Fleet (DNAB)
NAVCURRSUPPGRUNAVEUR...   Naval Current Support Group, Naval Forces, Europe (DNAB)
NAVCURRSUPPGRUPACFLT...   Naval Current Support Group, Pacific Fleet (DNAB)
NAVCURSERV...   Naval Courier Service
NAVCURSERVDET...   Naval Courier Service Detachment (DNAB)
NAVCURSERVHQ...   Naval Courier Service Headquarters
NAVD ....   National Association of Video Distributors (EA)
NAVD ....   North American Vertical Datum [National Oceanic and Atmospheric Administration]
NAVD88.......   North American Vertical Datum of 1988 (USDC)
NAVDAB.......   Navy Ocean Experimental Acoustic Data Bank (MSC)
NAVDAC.......   Naval Data Automation Command (MCD)
NAVDAC.......   Navigation Data Assimilation Center (AD)
navdac.......   Navigation Data Assimilation Computer (AD)
NAVDAC.......   Navigation Data Assimilation Computer
NAVDAD ......   Navigationally-Derived Air Data (MCD)
NAVDAF ......   Navy Data Automation Center (DNAB)
NAVDAMCONTRACEN...   Navy Damage Control Training Center
NAVDAR ......   Naval Defense Acquisition Regulations (MCD)
NAVDATACEN...   Naval Data Center (DNAB)
NAVDEFEASTPAC...   Naval Defense Forces, Eastern Pacific (DNAB)
NAVDEGSTA...   Navy Degaussing Station (DNAB)
NAVDEGSTALANT/PAC...   Naval Degaussing Station, Atlantic/Pacific
NAVDENCEN...   Naval Dental Center
NAVDENCLINIC...   Naval Dental Clinic
NAVDENSCOL...   Naval Dental School
NAVDENTECHSCOL...   Naval Dental Technicians School
Nav Dep ......   Naval Deputy [NATO] (AD)
NAVDEP......   Naval Deputy [NATO] (NATG)
NAVDEPCENT...   Naval Deputy to Commander-in-Chief, Allied Forces, Central Europe [NATO] (NATG)
NAVDEPNOAA...   Naval Deputy National Oceanic and Atmospheric Administration (DNAB)
NAVDEPT.....   Navy Department
NAVDES .....   Navy Design Selection List
NAVDESCOL...   Naval Destroyer School (NVT)
NAVDESSCOL...   Naval Destroyer School
NAVDET......   Naval Detachment
NAVDEVTRACEN...   Navy Development Training Center
NAVDI........   National Association for Ventilator Dependent Individuals (EA)
NAVDIS.......   Naval District
NAVDISBAR...   Navy Disciplinary Barracks (DNAB)
NAVDISCBAR...   Naval Disciplinary Barracks
NAVDISCOM...   Navy Disciplinary Command
NAVDISEAVECTORCONCEN...   Navy Disease Vector Control Center
NAVDISP......   Naval Dispensary
NAVDIST......   Naval District
NAVDISVECTTECOLCONCEN...   Navy Disease Vector Ecology and Control Center (DNAB)
NAVDIVSALVTRACEN...   Naval Diving and Salvage Training Center (DNAB)
NAVDOC ......   Navy Department Orientation Course (NG)
NAVDOCKS...   Bureau of Yards and Docks Publications [Obsolete] [Navy]
NAVDOCSP...   Bureau of Yards and Docks Publications [Obsolete] [Navy]
NAVDRUGREHCEN...   Naval Drug Rehabilitation Center (DNAB)
NAVE ....   National Assessment of Vocational Education [Department of Education] (GFGA)
Nav E..........   Naval Engineer [Academic degree]
NAVEA ....   National Adult Vocational Education Association (EA)
NAVEAMS....   Navigational Warning East Atlantic and Mediterranean [Navy] (PDAA)
NavEams....   Navigation in the Eastern Atlantic and the Mediterranean (AD)
NAVEARB....   Navy Employee Appeals Review Board (DNAB)
NavEast ......   Navigation along the East Coast of Asia (AD)
NAVEASTOCEANCEN...   Naval Eastern Oceanography Center (DNAB)
NAVED ....   National Association of Visual Education Dealers [Later, National Audio-Visual Association] (AEBS)
NAVEDTRA...   Naval Education and Training Command (MCD)

NAVEDTRA... Naval Education and Training Program Development Center [*Pensacola, FL*]
NAVEDTRACOM... Naval Education and Training Center [*or Command*] (DNAB)
NAVEDTRAPRODEVCEN... Naval Education and Training Program Development Center [*Pensacola, FL*] (DNAB)
NAVEDTRAPRODEVCENCODIV... Naval Education and Training Program Development Center Coordination Division (DNAB)
NAVEDTRAPRODEVCENDET... Naval Education and Training Program Development Center Detachment (DNAB)
NAVEDTRASUPPCEN... Naval Education and Training Support Center (DNAB)
NAVEDTRASUPPCENLANT... Naval Education and Training Support Center, Atlantic (DNAB)
NAVEDTRASUPPCENPAC... Naval Education and Training Support Center, Pacific (DNAB)
NAVEDTRASUPPCENPACNCFA... Naval Education and Training Support Center, Pacific, Navy Campus for Achievement (DNAB)
NAVEL .... Naloxone, Atropine, Valium, Epinephrine, Lidocaine [*Medicine*] (DMAA)
NAVELEC ..... Naval Electronics System Command (IAA)
NAVELECS .. Naval Electronic Systems Command (SAA)
NAVELECSYSCOM... Naval Electronics Systems Command
NAVELECSYSCOMCENLANTDIV... Naval Electronics Systems Command, Central Atlantic Division
NAVELECSYSCOMHQ... Naval Electronics Systems Command Headquarters
NAVELECSYSCOMNEDIV... Naval Electronics Systems Command, Northeast Division
NAVELECSYSCOMSEDIV... Naval Electronics Systems Command, Southeast Division
NAVELECSYSCOMWESTDIV... Naval Electronics Systems Command, Western Division
NAVELEM .... Navy Element (DNAB)
NAVELEX ..... Naval Electronics Systems Command
NAVELEX ..... Naval Electronic Systems Command Headquarters (USDC)
NAVELEXACTS... Naval Electronic Systems Command Activities (DNAB)
NAVELEXDET... Naval Electronic Systems Command Detachment (DNAB)
NAVELEXENGOFF... Naval Electronics Engineering Office (DNAB)
NAVELEXINST... Naval Electronics Systems Command Instruction
NAVELEXSITEREP... Naval Electronic Systems Command, Site Representative (DNAB)
NAVELEXSYSCOMCENDET... Naval Electronic Systems Command Center Detachment (DNAB)
NAVELEXSYSCOMDIV... Naval Electronic Systems Command Division (DNAB)
NAVELEXSYSCOMMIDWESTDIV... Naval Electronic Systems Command, Midwest Division (DNAB)
NAVELEXSYSCOMSEDIV... Naval Electronic Systems Command, Southeast Division (DNAB)
NAVELEXSYSTRAPUBMO... Naval Electronic Systems Command Training and Publications Management Office (DNAB)
NAVELEXTECHREP... Naval Electronic Systems Command Technical Representative (DNAB)
NAVELXSYSCOMTECHLREP... Naval Electronic Systems Command Technician Liaison Representative (DNAB)
NAVEMSCEN... Navy Electromagnetic Spectrum Center (DNAB)
NAVENENVSA... Navy Energy and Environmental Support Activity (DNAB)
NAVENGRXSTA... Naval Engineering Experiment Station
NAVENPVNTMEDU... Navy Environmental and Preventive Medicine Unit (DNAB)
NAVENVPREDRSCHFAC... Naval Environmental Prediction Research Facility (MCD)
NAVENVRHLTHCEN... Navy Environmental Health Center (DNAB)
NAVENVSUPPCEN... Navy Environmental Support Center (DNAB)
NAVENVSUPPO... Navy Environmental Support Office [*Obsolete*] (DNAB)
NAVEODFAC... Naval Explosive Ordnance Disposal Facility
NAVEODTECHCE... Naval Explosive Ordnance Disposal Technology Center [*Indian Head, MD*]
NAVEODTECHCEN... Naval Explosive Ordnance Disposal Technology Center [*Indian Head, MD*] (DNAB)
NAVEONIC ... Nautical Auto Vessel Environmental Ocean Naval Information Communications System (ACAE)
NAVESNP..... National Association of Vocational Education Special Needs Personnel (EA)
NAVETC .... Navy Educational Tape Catalog (DNAB)
NAVEUR....... Naval Forces, Europe (CCCA)
NAVEURWWMCCS DP... Naval Forces, Europe, Worldwide Military Command Control System, Data Processing (DNAB)
NAVEURWWMCCS EMSKD... Naval Forces, Europe, Worldwide Military Command Control System, Employment Schedule (DNAB)
NAVEURWWMCCS MOVREP... Naval Forces, Europe, Worldwide Military Command Control System, Movement Reports (DNAB)
NAVEURWWMCCS NAVFORSTA... Naval Forces, Europe, Worldwide Military Command Control System, Naval Forces Status (DNAB)
navex............ Navigation Exercise (AD)
NAVEX .... Navigation Exercise [*Navy*] (NVT)
NAVEX .... Norton AntiVirus Extension
NAVEXAM ... Naval Examining Board
NAVEXAMBD... Naval Examining Board (DNAB)
NAVEXAMCEN... Navy Examination Center
NAVEXAMCENADVAUTHLIST... Naval Examining Center Advancement Authorization List (DNAB)
NAVEXENGLANDCOM... Navy Exchange, England Complex (DNAB)
NAVEXHIBCEN... Naval Exhibit Center
NAVEXOS..... Executive Office of the Secretary [*Navy*]
NAVF .... Naval Avionics Facility [*Later, NAC*] (AFIT)
NAVF .... Norges Allmennvitenskapelige Forskningsrad [*Norwegian Research Council for Science and the Humanities*] [*Information service or system*] (IID)
NAVF .... Norwegian Natural Science Research Council (SAUS)

NAVFAC........ Naval Facilities Engineering Command [*Formerly, Bureau of Yards and Docks*]
NAVFAC........ Naval Facilities Engineering Command Headquarters (USDC)
NAVFAC........ Naval Facility
NAVFAC....... Navy Faces (NITA)
NAVFACCHESDIV... Naval Facilities Engineering Command, Chesapeake Division (DNAB)
NAVFACDM... Naval Facilities Engineering Command Design Manuals
NAVFACENG... Naval Facilities Engineering Command (CAAL)
NAVFACENGCOM... Naval Facilities Engineering Command [*Formerly, Bureau of Yards and Docks*]
NAVFACENGCOMCHESDIV... Naval Facilities Engineering Command, Chesapeake Division (DNAB)
NAVFACENGCOMCONTR... Naval Facilities Engineering Command Contractor
NAVFACENGCOMHQ... Naval Facilities Engineering Command Headquarters
NAVFACENGCOMLANTDIV... Naval Facilities Engineering Command, Atlantic Division (DNAB)
NAVFACENGCOMNORDIV... Naval Facilities Engineering Command, Northern Division (DNAB)
NAVFACENGCOMPACDIV... Naval Facilities Engineering Command, Pacific Division (DNAB)
NAVFACENGCOMSODIV... Naval Facilities Engineering Command, Southern Division (DNAB)
NAVFACENGCOMWESDIV... Naval Facilities Engineering Command, Western Division (DNAB)
NAVFACENSYSCOM... Naval Facilities Engineering Systems Command
NAVFACINST... Naval Facilities Engineering Command Instructions
NAVFACLANTDIV... Naval Facilities Engineering Command, Atlantic Division (DNAB)
NAVFACLANT/PAC... Naval Facilities Atlantic/Pacific
NAVFACNORDIV... Naval Facilities Engineering Command, Northern Division (DNAB)
NAVFACOC... Naval Facility Operational Center (DNAB)
NAVFACP... Naval Facilities Engineering Command Publications
NAVFAC P-68... Naval Facilities Engineering Command Contracting Manual [*A publication*] (AAGC)
NAVFACSODIV... Naval Facilities Engineering Comamnd, Southern Division (DNAB)
NAVFAC-TP-AD... Naval Facilities Engineering Command Technical Publications - Administration
NAVFAC-TP-MO... Naval Facilities Engineering Command Technical Publications - Maintenance Operation
NAVFAC-TP-PL... Naval Facilities Engineering Command Technical Publications - Planning
NAVFAC-TP-PU... Naval Facilities Engineering Command Technical Publications - Public Utilities
NAVFACWESDIV... Naval Facilities Engineering Command, Western Division (DNAB)
NAVFAMALWACT... Navy Family Allowance Activity
NAVFE .... Naval Forces Far East (AD)
NAVFEC ...... Naval Facilites (AD)
NAVFEC .... Naval Facilities Engineering Command [*Formerly, Bureau of Yards and Docks*]
NAVFECENGCOM... Naval Facilities Engineering Command (AD)
NAVFECO..... Naval Facilities Engineering Command (PDAA)
NAVFINCEN... Navy Finance Center
NAVFINCEN-CLEVE... Navy Finance Center - Cleveland [*Ohio*] (DNAB)
NAVFINCEN-WASH... Navy Finance Center - Washington, DC (DNAB)
NAVFINOFF... Navy Finance Office
NAVFITWEPSCOL... Navy Fighter Weapons School (DNAB)
NAVFLDINTO... Navy Field Intelligence Office (DNAB)
NAVFLDOPINTO... Naval Field Operational Intelligence Office
NAVFLDOPSUPPGRU... Naval Field Operations Support Group
NAVFLIGHTPREPSCOL... Naval Flight Preparatory School
NAVFLIR...... Navigational Forward Looking Infrared (ACAE)
NAVFLITHTDEMORON... Navy Flight Demonstration Squadron (DNAB)
NAVFOODMGTM... Navy Food Management Team (DNAB)
NAVFOR....... Naval Forces (AD)
NAVFORJAP... Naval Air Forces, Japan (AD)
NAVFORKOR... Naval Air Forces, Korea (AD)
NAVFORSTAT... Naval Force Status Report (NVT)
NAVFRCOORD... Navy Frequency Coordinator (DNAB)
NAVFROF...... Navy Freight Office
NAVFSSO..... Navy Food Services Office (DNAB)
NAVFSSO..... Navy Food Service Systems Office
NAVFUELDEP... Naval Fuel Depot
NAVFUELSUPO... Naval Fuel Supply Office
NAVFW .... Norton AntiVirus for Firewalls [*Symantec*] [*Computer science*]
NAVG .... Navigators Group [*NASDAQ symbol*]
NAVG .... [*The*] Navigators Group, Inc. [*NASDAQ symbol*] (NQ)
NAVGDENSCOL... Naval Graduate Dental School (DNAB)
NAVGEN....... Navy General Publications
NavgGp....... [*The*] Navigators Group, Inc. [*Associated Press*] (SAG)
NAVGMSCHOL... Navy Guided Missile School
NAVGMU...... Navy Guided Missile Unit
NAVGP......... Naval Advisory Group
NAVGRU...... Naval Group
NAVGSUP...... Navigational Guidance Support (NVT)
NAVGUN ...... Naval Gun Factory [*Later, NWF*]
NAVH .... National Aid to Visually Handicapped (AD)
NAVH .... National Association for Visually Handicapped (EA)
NAVH .... National Association of Voluntary Hostels [*British*] (DBA)
NAVHARS ... Navigation Heading and Altitude Reference System [*Aviation*] (PDAA)
NAVHET...... National Association of Vocational Home Economics Teachers (EA)
NAVHISTCEN... Naval History Center (DNAB)

NAVHISTDISPLAYCEN...   Navy Historical Display Center
NAVHLTHRSCHC...   Naval Health Research Center
NAVHLTHRSCHCEN...   Naval Health Research Center (DNAB)
NAVHO.........   National Association of Voluntary Help Organisers [British] (DBA)
NAVHOME....   Naval Home [Philadelphia, PA]
NAVHOME....   Naval Home Command (SAUS)
NAVHOMERESINFOSYS...   Naval Home Resident Information System (DNAB)
NAVHOSINGACT...   Naval Housing Activity (DNAB)
NAVHOSP.........   Naval Hospital
NAVHOSPCORPSCOL...   Naval Hospital Corps School
NAVHOUSINGACT...   Naval Housing Activity
NAVHT.........   National Association of Vocational Homemakers Teachers [Later, National Association of Vocational Home Economics Teachers] (EA)
Nav I...........   Navassa Island (AD)
NAVI ....   North American Ventures, Inc. (SAUS)
NAVI ....   Norton AntiVirus
NAVIC ....   Navy Information Center (MCD)
navicert ......   Naval Inspection Certificate (AD)
NAVICERT....   Navigation Certificate [Paper issued by British government to merchant vessel, certifying that cargo was non-contraband, that is, not consigned to Germany] [World War II]
NAVID..........   Navigation Aid (NASA)
NAVIG..........   Navigation
NAVIGA........   Welt Organisation fur Schiffsmodellbau und Schiffsmodellsport [World Organization for Modelship Building and Modelship Sport] [Austria] (EAIO)
NAVILCO......   Navy International Logistics Control Office (MCD)
NAVIMAC.....   Naval Immediate Area Coordinator (DNAB)
NavInd.........   Navigation in the Indian Ocean (AD)
NAVINFO......   Navy Information Office (DNAB)
NAVINRELACT...   Navy Internal Relations Activity (DNAB)
NAVINSGEN...   Naval Inspector General
NAVINTCOM...   Naval Intelligence Command
NAVINTCOMINST...   Naval Intelligence Command Instructions
NAVINTCOMM...   Naval Intelligence Command
NAVINTEL....   Naval Intelligence
NAVINTSUPPCEN...   Naval Intelligence Support Center (DNAB)
NAVINVSERV...   Naval Investigative Service (DNAB)
NAVINVSERVHQ...   Naval Investigative Service Headquarters (NVT)
NAVINVSERVO...   Naval Investigative Service Office
NAVINVSERVOREP...   Naval Investigative Service Office Representative (DNAB)
NAVINVSERVRA...   Naval Investigative Service Resident Agent (DNAB)
NAVION........   North American Aviation, Inc. [Later, Rockwell International Corp.] [Acronym also used to refer to light aircraft of World War II]
NAVISLO......   Naval Interservice Liaison Office (DNAB)
NAVISTAR....   formerly International Harvester (SAUS)
Navistar.......   Navistar International Corp. [Associated Press] (SAG)
NAVJAC......   North American Vane Jump Angle Computer
NAVJAG........   Judge Advocate General's Office Publications [Navy]
NAVJIT.........   Naval Jet Instrument Trainer
NAVJNTSERVACT...   Naval Joint Services Activity (DNAB)
NAVJUSTSCOL...   Naval Justice School
NAVL ....   National Anti-Vaccination League [British] (BI)
NAVL ....   Navigation Light (IAA)
NAVLEGSERVOFF...   Naval Legal Service Office (DNAB)
NAVLEGSERVOFFDET...   Naval Legal Service Office Detachment (DNAB)
NAVLIAGRU...   Naval Liaison Group (DNAB)
NAVLINKSTA...   Naval Link Station (DNAB)
NAVLIS ....   Navy Logistics Information System
NAVLO ....   Naval Liaison Officer
NAVLOGENGRU...   Naval Logistics Engineering Group (DNAB)
NAVLOGSIP...   Navy Logistic Support Improvement Plan (NG)
NAVLOS........   Navy Liaison Officer for Scouting (DNAB)
NAVMAA ......   Naval Mutual Aid Association (DNAB)
NAVMAC......   Navy Manpower and Material Analysis Center (DNAB)
NAVMACPAC...   Navy Manpower and Material Analysis Center, Pacific (DNAB)
NAVMACS.....   Naval Modular Automated Communications System (NVT)
NAVMAIRCOMCON...   Naval and Maritime Air Communications-Electronics Conference [NATO]
NAVMAP ......   Navy Missile Analysis Program (MCD)
NAVMAR ......   Naval Forces, Marianas (AD)
NAVMARCORESTRACEN...   Navy and Marine Corps Reserve Training Center
NAVMAREXHIBCEN...   Navy-Marine Corps Exhibit Center (DNAB)
NAVMARJUDACT...   Navy-Marine Corps Judiciary Activity
NAVMARTRIJUDCIR...   Navy-Marine Corps Trial Judiciary Court (DNAB)
NAVMARTRIJUDCIRBROFF...   Navy-Marine Corps Trial Judiciary Court Branch Office (DNAB)
NAVMARTRIJUDIC...   Navy-Marine Corps Trial Judiciary (DNAB)
NAVMASSO...   Navy Maintenance and Supply Systems Office (DNAB)
NAVMASSO...   Navy Management Systems Support Office (AAGC)
NAVMASSODET...   Navy Maintenance and Supply Systems Office Detachment (DNAB)
NAVMASSODETPAC...   Navy Maintenance and Supply Systems Office Detachment, Pacific (DNAB)
NAVMAT ......   Naval Material Command [Formerly, NMSE] (MCD)
NAVMAT ......   Office of Naval Materiel (SAUS)
NAVMATCOM...   Naval Material Command [Formerly, NMSE]
NAVMATCOMSUPPACT...   Naval Material Command Support Activity
NAVMAT COOPLAN...   Naval Material Command Contingency/Emergency Planning (DNAB)
NAVMATDATASYSGRU...   Naval Material Data Systems Group (DNAB)
NAVMATDET...   Naval Material Command Detachment (DNAB)
NAVMATEVALU...   Naval Material Evaluation Unit (DNAB)
NAVMATINST...   Naval Material Command Instruction

NAVMATMOCON...   Navy Material Movement Control Plan
NAVMATRANSOFC...   Naval Material Transportation Office (DNAB)
NAVMC ......   Navy-Marine Corps
NAVMEC ......   Naval Manpower Engineering Center (MCD)
NAVMED ......   Naval Aerospace Medical Institute (MCD)
NAVMED ......   Navy Medicine
NAVMEDADMINU...   Navy Medical Administrative Unit (DNAB)
NAVMEDATASERVCEN...   Naval Medical Data Service Center
NAVMEDCEN...   Navy Medical Center (DNAB)
NAVMEDCOM...   Naval Medical Command (ANA)
NAVMEDFLDRSCHLAB...   Navy Medical Field Research Laboratory (DNAB)
NAVMEDIS ...   Navy Medical Information System
NAVMEDLAB...   Naval Medical Laboratory (DNAB)
NAVMEDLABDET...   Naval Medical Laboratory Detachment (DNAB)
NAVMEDMATSUPPCOM...   Naval Medical Materiel Support Command (DNAB)
NAVMEDNPRSCHU...   Navy Medical Neuropsychiatric Research Unit (DNAB)
NAVMEDRSCHDEVCOM...   Naval Medical Research and Development Command (DNAB)
NAVMEDRSCHINST...   Naval Medical Research Institute
NAVMEDRSCHINSTDET...   Navy Medical Research Institute Detachment (DNAB)
NAVMEDRSCHU...   Naval Medical Research Unit
NAVMEDRSCHUDET...   Naval Medical Research Unit Detachment (DNAB)
NAVMEDRSHCHLAB...   Navy Medical Research Laboratory (DNAB)
NAVMEDSCOL...   Naval Medical School
NAVMEDSUPPU...   Navy Medical Support Unit (DNAB)
NAVMGTSYSCEN...   Naval Management Systems Center (MCD)
NAVMIC ....   Naval Maritime Intelligence Center [Formerly, NISC and then NTIC] (DOMA)
NAVMILPERSCOM...   Naval Military Personnel Command (MCD)
NAVMINCOMEASTA...   Navy Mine Countermeasures Station
NAVMINDEFLAB...   Navy Mine Defense Laboratory [Later, NCSC]
NAVMINDEP...   Navy Mine Depot
NAVMINENGRFAC...   Naval Mine Engineering Facility
NAVMINWARTRACEN...   Naval Mine Warfare Training Center
NAVMIRO ....   Naval Material Industrial Resources Office
NAVMIS ....   Naval Mission
NAVMIS ....   Navy Management Information System (MCD)
NavMisCen...   Naval Missile Center (AD)
NAVMISCEN...   Naval Missile Center [Point Mugu, CA] (MCD)
NAVMISFAC...   Naval Missile Facility [Also, NMF] (MUGU)
NAVMMAC ...   Navy Manpower and Material Analysis Center (NVT)
NAVMMACLANT...   Navy Manpower and Material Analysis Center, Atlantic
NAVMMACPAC...   Navy Manpower and Material Analysis Center, Pacific
NAVMOBCONSTBN...   Navy Mobile Construction Battalion
NAVMORTOFF...   Naval Mortuary Office (DNAB)
NAVMOVE....   Navigational Movements (SAUS)
NAVMTO ......   Navy Material Transportation Office
NAVMTO ......   Navy Movement and Transportation Office
NAVMTONORVA...   Naval Military Transportation Office, Norfolk, Virginia (DNAB)
NAVMTOREP...   Naval Military Transportation Office Representative (DNAB)
NAVMUTAID...   Navy Mutual Aid
NAVN ....   Naval Aviation News
NAVNET ....   Naval Network (VLIE)
NAVNET ....   Navigation Network (NVT)
NAVNET ....   Navy Network (DOMA)
NAVNETDEP...   Naval Net Depot
NAVNON ......   Allied Naval Forces, North Norway [NATO] (NATG)
NAVNON ......   Naval Forces, Northern Norway [NATO] (AD)
NavNoPac...   Navigation in the North Pacific (AD)
NavNorlant...   Navigation in the North Atlantic (AD)
NAVNORTH...   Allied Naval Forces, Northern Europe [NATO]
NAVNUPWRSCOL...   Navy Nuclear Power School (DNAB)
NAVNUPWRTRAU...   Naval Nuclear Power Training Unit (MCD)
NAVNUPWRU...   Naval Nuclear Power Unit
NAVO ....   National Association of Volvo Owners [Defunct] (EA)
NAVO ....   Naval Oceanographic Office (USDC)
NAVOBS.....   Naval Observatory (MUGU)
NAVOBSY ...   Naval Observatory [Navy]
NAVOBSYFLAGSTAFFSTA...   Naval Observatory Flagstaff [Arizona] Station
NAVOBSYSTA...   Naval Observatory Station (DNAB)
NAVOCEANCOM...   Naval Oceanography Command Support System (GFGA)
NAVOCEANCOMCEN...   Naval Oceanography Command Center (DNAB)
NAVOCEANCOMDET...   Naval Oceanography Command Detachment (MCD)
NAVOCEANCOMFAC...   Naval Oceanography Command Facility (DNAB)
NAVOCEANCOMMDET...   Naval Oceanography Communications Detachment (DNAB)
NAVOCEANDISTO...   Naval Oceanographic District Office
NAVOCEANO...   Naval Oceanographic Office [Also known as NOO; formerly, HO, NHO, USNHO] [Bay St. Louis, MS]
NavOceanO...   Naval Oceanographic Officer (AD)
NAVOCEANOAIRSUPPGRU...   Naval Oceanographic Office Aircraft Support Squadron (DNAB)
NAVOCEANODET...   Naval Oceanographic Office Detachment (DNAB)
NAVOCEANOFC...   Naval Oceanographic Office (DNAB)
NAVOCEANPROFAC...   Naval Ocean Processing Facility (DNAB)
NAVOCEANSURVINFOCEN...   Naval Ocean Surveillance Information Center (DNAB)
NAVOCEANSYSCEN...   Naval Ocean Systems Center [Formerly, NELC] (DNAB)
NAVOCEANSYSCENLAB...   Naval Ocean Systems Center Laboratory (DNAB)
NAVOCEANSYSCENLABDET...   Naval Ocean Systems Center Laboratory Detachment (DNAB)
NAVOCFORMED...   Naval On-Call Force, Mediterranean [NATO] (NATG)
NAVOCS.......   Naval Officer Candidate School
NAVOLF ....   Navy Outlying Landing Field (DNAB)
NAVOPFAC...   Naval Operating Facility

NAVOPHTHALSUPPTRACT... Naval Ophthalmic Support and Training Activity (DNAB)

NAVOPNET... Naval Operations Network (CINC)

NAVOPSUPPGRU... Naval Operations Support Group (DNAB)

NAVOPSUPPGRULANT... Naval Operations Support Group, Atlantic

NAVOPSUPPGRUPAC... Naval Operations Support Group, Pacific

NAVOPTINCEN... Naval Operations Intelligence Center (ACAE)

NAVORD ...... Naval Ordnance (MUGU)

NAVORD ...... Naval Ordnance Systems Command [*Later, Naval Sea Systems Command*]

NAVORD ...... Naval Ordnance Systems Command Headquarters (USDC)

NAVORDCH... Naval Ordnance Chart (MCD)

NAVORDENGFAC... Naval Ordnance Engineering Facility (DNAB)

NAVORDFAC... Naval Ordnance Facility

NAVORD ILS/MIS... Naval Ordnance Systems Command, Integrated Logistics Support / Management Information System (DNAB)

NAVORDINST... Naval Ordnance Systems Command Instruction

NAVORDLABFIELDIV... Naval Ordnance Laboratory Field Division (DNAB)

NAVORDLIST... Navy Ordnance List (DNAB)

NAVORDMISTESTFAC... Naval Ordnance Missile Test Facility

NAVORDSTA... Naval Ordnance Station

NAVORDSTADET... Naval Ordnance Station Detachment (DNAB)

NAVORD-SWOP... Naval Ordnance Systems Command, Special Weapons Ordnance Publication

NAVORDSYSCO... Naval Ordnance Systems Command [*Later, Naval Sea Systems Command*] (MCD)

NAVORDSYSCOM... Naval Ordnance Systems Command [*Later, Naval Sea Systems Command*]

NAVORDSYSCOMHQ... Naval Ordnance Systems Command Headquarters

NAVORDSYSSUPPO... Naval Ordnance Systems Support Office

NAVORDSYSUPPO... Naval Ordnance Systems Support Office (DNAB)

NAVORDSYSUPPOLANT... Naval Ordnance Systems Support Office, Atlantic (DNAB)

NAVORDSYSUPPOPAC... Naval Ordnance Systems Support Office, Pacific (DNAB)

NAVORDTECHREP... Naval Ordnance Technical Representative (MCD)

NAVORDTESTU... Naval Ordnance Test Unit

NAVORDU.... Naval Ordnance Unit

NAVORECSUPPACT... Naval Officer Record Support Activity (DNAB)

NAVOROUS... Naval Order of the United States [*Later, NOUS*] [*An association*] (EA)

NAVOSH ...... Navy Occupational Safety and Health (MCD)

NAVOSH DAP/MIS... Navy Occupational Safety and Deficiency Abatement/ Management Information System

NAVOSTAT... Navigation by Visual Observation of Satellites (DNAB)

NAVP .... National Association of Vision Professionals (EA)

NAVPA .... National Association of Veterans Program Administrators (EA)

NAVPAC... Navigation Package (DNAB)

NAVPACEN... Navy Public Affairs Center (DNAB)

NAVPAOEASCO... Naval Public Affairs Office, East Coast

NAVPAOMWEST... Naval Public Affairs Office, Midwest

NAVPAOWESCO... Naval Public Affairs Office, West Coast

NAVPBRO .... Naval Plant Branch Representative Officer (DNAB)

NAVPC .... National Association of Vision Program Consultants [*Later, NAVP*] (EA)

NAVPECO..... Naval Production Equipment Control Office

NAVPECOS... Navy Pentagon Computer Services Division (DNAB)

NAVPEP .... Navy Program Evaluation Procedures

NAVPERS..... Bureau of Naval Personnel [*Also, BNP, BUPERS*]

NAVPERS..... Naval Personnel (AD)

NAVPERSCEN... Naval Personnel Center

NAVPERSINST... Bureau of Naval Personnel Instruction

NAVPERS-PRD... Bureau of Naval Personnel - Personnel Research Division

NAVPERSPROGSUPPACT... Naval Personnel Program Support Activity

NAVPERSRANDCEN... Naval Personnel Research and Development Center

NAVPERSRANDCENWB... Naval Personnel Research and Development Center, Washington [*DC*] Branch (DNAB)

NAVPERSRANDLAB... Navy Personnel Research and Development Laboratory (DNAB)

NAVPERSREACT... Naval Personnel Research Activity

NAVPERSRSCHACT... Naval Personnel Research Activity

NAVPETOFF... Navy Petroleum Office

NAVPETRAU... Naval Petroleum Training Unit (DNAB)

NAVPETRES... Naval Petroleum Reserves

NAVPETRESO... Naval Petroleum Reserves Office

NAVPGCOL... Navy Postgraduate College

NAVPGSCOL... Naval Postgraduate School

NAVPHIBASE... Naval Amphibious Base (MUGU)

NAVPHIBASELANT... Naval Amphibious Base Atlantic

NAVPHIBSCOL... Naval Amphibious School (NVT)

NAVPHIL... Naval Forces - Philippines (AD)

NAVPHOTOCEN... Naval Photographic Center

NAVPLANTDEVU... Naval Plant Development Unit (DNAB)

NAVPLANTREP... Naval Plant Representative Office [*or Officer*] (MCD)

NAVPLANTREPO... Naval Plant Representative Office [*or Officer*]

NAVPLANTTECHREP... Naval Plant Technical Representative (DNAB)

NAVPO .... National Association of Van Pool Operators [*Later, Association of Commuter Transportation*] (EA)

NAVPOLAROCEANCEN... Naval Polar Oceanography Center (DNAB)

NAVPOOL .... Navigation Parameter Common Pool (NASA)

NAVPOOL .... Navigation [*Parameter Common*] Pool

NAVPORCO... Naval Port Control Office [*or Officer*]

NAVPORCOF... Naval Port Control Office [*or Officer*]

NAVPORTCO... Naval Port Control Office [*Or officer*] (DNAB)

NAVPOSTGRADSCOL... Naval Postgraduate School

NAVPOWFAC... Naval Powder Factory

NAVPrD........ Navistar Intl Cv Jr D Pref [*NYSE symbol*] (TTSB)

NAVPREFLIGHTSCOL... Naval Preflight School

NAVPrG........ Navistar Intl $6 cm Cv Pfd [*NYSE symbol*] (TTSB)

NAVPRIMSTDEPT... Navy Primary Standards Department (DNAB)

NAVPRIS... Naval Prison

NAVPRO ...... Naval Plant Representative Office [*or Officer*]

NAVPRO ...... Naval Procurement Office (SAUS)

NAVPROPLT... Naval Propellant Plant (DNAB)

NAVPROV... Naval Proving Ground [*Dahlgren, VA*]

NAVPTO....... Navy Passenger Transportation Office (DNAB)

NAVPUB...... Naval Publications (AD)

NAVPUB...... Navy Publications and Printing Service

NAVPUBFORMCEN... Naval Publications and Forms Center (MCD)

NAVPUBINST... Navy Publications and Printing Service Instruction

NAVPUBPRINTO... Navy Publications and Printing Office

NAVPUBPRINTSERV... Naval Publications and Printing Service (DNAB)

NAVPUBPRINTSERVO... Navy Publications and Printing Service Office

NAVPUBSCONBD... Navy Department Publications Control Board

NAVPUBWKSCEN... Navy Public Works Center

NAVPUBWKSDEPT... Navy Public Works Department (DNAB)

NAVPUR ...... Navy Purchasing Office

NAVPURDEP... Navy Purchasing Department (DNAB)

NAVPURO...... Navy Purchasing Office

NAVPVNTMEDU... Navy Preventive Medicine Unit

NAVR .... Navarre Corp. [*NASDAQ symbol*] (SAG)

NAVR .... Navigator (WGA)

NAVRA......... National Association of Volunteer Referral Agencies [*Australia*]

NAVRADCO... Naval Regional Active Duty Cryptologic Officer (DNAB)

NAVRADCON... Naval Radiological Control

NAVRADLDEFLAB... Navy Radiological Defense Laboratory

NAVRADRECFAC... Naval Radio Receiving Facility (DNAB)

NAVRADSTA... Naval Radio Station

NAVRADTRANSFAC... Naval Radio Transmitting Facility (DNAB)

NAVRDSATCOMMGRU... Naval Research and Development Satellite Communications Group (MUGU)

NAVRECCEN... Naval Recreation Center (DNAB)

NAVRECONTACSUPPCENLANT... Naval Reconnaissance and Tactical Support Center, Atlantic (DNAB)

NAVRECONTECHSUPPCEN... Naval Reconnaissance and Technical Support Center

NAVRECONTECHSUPPCENLANT... Naval Reconnaissance and Technical Support Center, Atlantic (DNAB)

NAVRECONTECHSUPPCENPAC... Naval Reconnaissance and Technical Support Center, Pacific (DNAB)

NAVRECSTA... Naval Receiving Station (NVT)

NAVREF .... National Association of Veterans' Research and Education Foundations (NTPA)

NAVREGAIRCARCONO... Navy Regional Air Cargo Central [*or Control*] Office (DNAB)

NAVREGCONTO... Navy Regional Contracting Office (DNAB)

NAVREGCONTODET... Navy Regional Contracting Office Detachment (DNAB)

NAVREGDENCEN... Navy Regional Dental Center (DNAB)

NAVREGDENCENBRFAC... Navy Regional Dental Center Branch Facility (DNAB)

NAVREGDENCLIN... Navy Regional Dental Clinic (DNAB)

NAVREGFINCEN... Navy Regional Finance Center

NAVREGFINCENBRKLN... Navy Regional Finance Center, Brooklyn [*New York*]

NAVREGFINCENGLAKES... Navy Regional Finance Center, Great Lakes (DNAB)

NAVREGFINCENNORVA... Navy Regional Finance Center, Norfolk, Virginia (DNAB)

NAVREGFINCENPEARL... Navy Regional Finance Center, Pearl Harbor [*Hawaii*] (DNAB)

NAVREGFINCENSDIEGO... Navy Regional Finance Center, San Diego [*California*] (DNAB)

NAVREGFINCENSFRAN... Navy Regional Finance Center, San Francisco [*California*] (DNAB)

NAVREGFINOFC... Navy Regional Finance Office (DNAB)

NAVREGMEDCEN... Naval Regional Medical Center (DNAB)

NAVREGMEDCENBRCLINIC... Naval Regional Medical Center Branch Clinic (DNAB)

NAVREGMEDCENBRHOSP... Naval Regional Medical Center Branch Hospital (DNAB)

NAVREGMEDCENCLINIC... Naval Regional Medical Center Clinic (DNAB)

NAVREGMEDCENDET... Naval Regional Medical Center Detachment (DNAB)

NAVREGPEO... Naval Regional Plant Equipment Office [*or Officer*] (DNAB)

NAVREGPROCO... Navy Regional Procurement Office (DNAB)

NAVREGS... Navy Regulations

NAVREL...... Navy Relief Society

NAVREPFAC... Naval Repair Facility (MCD)

NAVRES... Naval Reserve

NAVRESCEN... Naval Research Center (DNAB)

NAVRESCEN... Naval Reserve Center (DNAB)

NAVRESCOMICEDEFOR... Naval Reserve Commander, Iceland Defense Force (DNAB)

NAVRESFOR... Naval Reserve Force (DNAB)

NAVRESLAB... Naval Research Laboratory [*ONR*]

NAVRESMANPOWERCEN... Naval Reserve Manpower Center

NAVRESMANPWRCEN... Naval Reserve Manpower Center (DNAB)

NAVRESMIDSCOL... Naval Reserve Midshipmen's School

NAVRESO... Navy Resale System Office (PDAA)

NAVRESO... Navy Resale Systems Office

NAVRESOFSO... Navy Resale Systems Field Support Office (DNAB)

NAVRESOREACT... Naval Reserve Officer Recording Activity (DNAB)

NAVRESOREP... Navy Resale Systems Office Representative (DNAB)

NAVRESREDCOM... Naval Reserve Readiness Command (DNAB)

NAVRESREDCOMREG... Naval Reserve Readiness Command Region (DNAB)

NAVRESSECGRP... Naval Reserve Security Group (DNAB)

NAVRESSO... Navy Resale and Services Support Office

NAVRESSOFO... Navy Resale and Services Support Office, Field Office (DNAB)

NAVRESTRA... Naval Reserve Training (DNAB)
NAVRESTRACEN... Naval Reserve Training Center
NAVRESTRACOM... Naval Reserve Training Command
NAVRESTRAFAC... Naval Reserve Training Facility
NAVRESUBDET... Naval Reserve Submarine Detachment (DNAB)
NAVRESUPPOFC... Naval Reserve Support Office (DNAB)
NAVRESUPPOFCDET... Naval Reserve Support Office Detachment (DNAB)
NAVRETRAINCOM... Naval Retraining Command
NAVROM...... Romanian Merchant Marine (AD)
NAVROUTE... Navy Routing Office
NAVRSCHLAB... Naval Research Laboratory [ONR]
NAVS .... National Anti-Vivisection Society (EA)
NAVS .... National Association of Variety Stores [Defunct] (EA)
NAVS .... Navigation System
NAVS .... North American Vegetarian Society (EA)
NAVSAFECEN... Naval Safety Center
NAVSANDA... Bureau of Supplies and Accounts [Later, NSUPSC] [Navy]
navsat...... Navigational Satellite (AD)
NAVSAT... Navigational Satellite [NASA]
NavSat......... Navigation in the South Atlantic (AD)
NAVSATCOMMDET... Navy Satellite Communications Detachment (DNAB)
NAVSATCOMMFAC... Navy Satellite Communications Facility (DNAB)
NAVSATCOMMNET... Navy Satellite Communications Network (DNAB)
NAVSCAP..... Allied Naval Forces, Scandinavian Approaches [NATO] (NATG)
NAVSCAP..... Naval Forces, Scandinavian Approaches [NATO] (AD)
NAVSCIADV... Naval Science Advisor (DNAB)
NAVSCIENTECHINTCEN... Naval Scientific and Technical Intelligence Center
NAVSCITECHGRUFE... Naval Scientific and Technical Group, Far East (DNAB)
NAVSCOLCEOFF... Naval Civil Engineer Corps Officers School (DNAB)
NAVSCOLCOM... Naval Schools Command
NAVSCOLCOM NORVA... Naval Schools Command, Norfolk, Virginia
NAVSCOLCONST... Naval Schools Construction
NAVSCOLCRYPTOREP... Naval School of Cryptographic Repair (DNAB)
NAVSCOLCYROGENICS... Naval School of Cryogenics (DNAB)
NAVSCOLDEEPSEADIVER... Navy School for Deep Sea Divers (DNAB)
NAVSCOLEOD... Naval School of Explosive Ordnance Disposal (DNAB)
NAVSCOLHOSPADMIN... Naval School of Hospital Administration (DNAB)
NAVSCOLMINWAR... Naval School of Mine War (DNAB)
NAVSCOLMINWARFARE... Naval Mine Warfare School
NAVSCOLPHYDISTMGT... Naval School of Physical Distribution Management (DNAB)
NAVSCOLTRANSMGT... Naval School of Transportation Management (DNAB)
NAVSCSCOL... Naval Supply Corps School
NAVSCSCOLDET... Naval Supply Corps School Detachment (DNAB)
NAVSEA....... Naval Avionics Support Equipment Appraisal (NG)
NAVSEA....... Naval Sea [formerly, Ship] Systems Command (MCD)
NAVSEAADSO... Naval Sea Systems Command Automated Data Systems Office (DNAB)
NAVSEAADSODET... Naval Sea Systems Command Automated Data Systems Office Detachment (DNAB)
NAVSEACARCOORD... Naval Sea Cargo Coordinator (DNAB)
NAVSEACARCOR... Navy Sea Cargo Coordinator (NVT)
NAVSEACEN... Naval Sea Support Center (DNAB)
NAVSEACENFSO... Naval Sea Support Center, Fleet Support Office (DNAB)
NAVSEACENHAWLAB... Naval Sea Support Center, Hawaii Laboratory (DNAB)
NAVSEACENLANT... Naval Sea Support Center, Atlantic (MCD)
NAVSEACENLANTDET... Naval Sea Support Center, Atlantic Detachment (DNAB)
NAVSEACENPACDET... Naval Sea Support Center, Pacific Detachment (DNAB)
NAVSEACENREP... Naval Sea Support Center Representative (DNAB)
NAVSEACENTLANT... Naval Sea Support Center - Atlantic (AD)
NAVSEACENTPAC... Naval Sea Support Center - Pacific (AD)
NAVSEACOHREP... Naval Sea Systems Command Complex Overhaul Representative (DNAB)
NAVSEADET... Naval Sea Systems Command Detachment (DNAB)
NAVSEAMATREP... Naval Sea Systems Command Material Representative (DNAB)
NAVSEAMQAO... Naval Sea Systems Command Material Quality Assessment Office (DNAB)
NAVSEASYSCOM... Naval Sea [Formerly, Ship] Systems Command (DNAB)
NAVSEASYSCOMGTOWESTPAC... Naval Sea Systems Command Management Office, Western Pacific (DNAB)
NAVSEASYSCOMHQ... Naval Sea Systems Command Headquarters (DNAB)
NAVSEATECHREP... Naval Sea Systems Command Technical Representative (DNAB)
NAVSEC .... Naval Ship Engineering Center
NAVSECENGRFAC... Naval Security Engineering Facility
NAVSECGRU... Naval Security Group
NAVSECGRUACT... Navy Security Group Activity
NAVSECGRUACTFO... Naval Security Group Activity Field Office (DNAB)
NAVSECGRUACTSPECOMMDIV... Naval Security Group Activity, Special Communications Division (DNAB)
NAVSECGRUCOM... Naval Security Group Command (MCD)
NAVSECGRUDET... Naval Security Group Detachment
NAVSECGRUHQ... Navy Security Group Headquarters
NAVSECGRUMGDAT... Naval Security Group Command Management Data (DNAB)
NAVSECGRU MIS... Naval Security Group Management Information System (DNAB)
NAVSECINST... Naval Ship Engineering Center Instruction
NAVSECMECHSDIV... Naval Ship Engineering Center, Mechanicsburg [Pennsylvania] Division (DNAB)
NAVSECNORDIV... Naval Ship Engineering Center, Norfolk Division
NAVSECPHILA... Naval Ship Engineering Center, Philadelphia Division
NAVSECPHILAD... Naval Ship Engineering Center Philadelphia Division
NAVSECPHILADIV... Naval Ship Engineering Center, Philadelphia Division
NAVSECSDIEGODIV... Naval Ship Engineering Center, San Diego [California] Division (DNAB)

NAVSECSTA... Naval Security Station
NAVSEEACT... Naval Shore Electronics Engineering Activity
NAVSEEC... Naval Electronics Systems Command Headquarters
NAVSEG... Navigation Satellite Executive Steering Group
NAVSERVSCOLCOM... Naval Service School Command
NAVSEX... Naval Standing Exercises (NATG)
NAVSHIP... Naval Ship Systems Command [Later, NAVSEA, NSSC]
NAVSHIPCOM... Naval Ship Systems Command (AD)
NAVSHIPENGCEN... Naval Ship Engineering Center
NAVSHIPENGSUPPACT... Naval Ship Engineering Support Activity
NAVSHIPLO... Navy Shipbuilding Office
NAVSHIPMISENGSYS... Naval Ships Missile Systems Engineering System (DNAB)
NAVSHIPMISYSENGSTA... Naval Ship Missile System Engineering Station
NAVSHIPREPFAC... Naval Ship Repair Facility
NAVSHIPREPO... Naval Ship Repair Officer (DNAB)
NAVSHIPRSCHDEVCEN... Naval Ship Research and Development Center [Also, DTNSRDC] (DNAB)
NAVSHIPRSCHDEVCENANNA... Naval Ship Research and Development Center, Annapolis [Maryland] Division (DNAB)
NAVSHIPS ... Naval Ship Systems Command [Later, NAVSEA, NSSC]
NAVSHIPS ... Naval Ship Systems Command Headquarters [Formerly, BuShips] (USDC)
NAVSHIPSA... Navy Shipbuilding Scheduling Activity
NAVSHIPSINST... Naval Ship Systems Command Instruction
NAVSHIPSO... Navy Shipbuilding Scheduling Office
NAVSHIPSTO... Navy Ships' Store Office (DNAB)
NAVSHIPSYSCOM... Naval Ship Systems Command [Later, NAVSEA, NSSC]
NAVSHIPSYSCOMHQ... Naval Ship Systems Command Headquarters
NAVSHIPTECHSMAN... Navy Ship Technical Manual (DNAB)
NAVSHIPWPNSYSENGSTA... Naval Ship Weapon Systems Engineering Station [Port Hueneme, CA] (DNAB)
NAVSHIPWPNSYSENGSTADET... Naval Ship Weapon Systems Engineering Station Detachment (DNAB)
NAVSHIPWPNSYSENGSTAREP... Naval Ship Weapon Sytems Engineering Station Representative (DNAB)
NAVSHIPY ... Naval Shipyard (SAA)
NavShipyd ... Naval Shipyard (AD)
NAVSHIPYD... Naval Shipyard
NAVSIT... Navy Scholarship Information Team (DNAB)
NAVSITSUM... Naval Situation Summary (SAUS)
NAVSMO..... Navigation Satellite Management Office
NAVSO......... Naval Supply Office
NAVSO......... Navy, Secretary's Office
NAVSO......... Navy Staff Offices
NAVSONOR... Allied Naval Forces, South Norway (SAUS)
NavSoPac... Navigation of the South Pacific (AD)
NAVSOUTH... Allied Naval Forces, Southern Europe [NATO] (NATG)
NAVSOUTH... Naval Forces, Southern Europe (AD)
NAVSPACCOM... Naval Space Command (DOMA)
NAVSPASUR... Naval Space Surveillance [Center or System]
NAVSPASYSAC... Naval Space Systems Activity (DNAB)
NAVSPEC... Navy Specification (AAGC)
NAVSPECWAR... Naval Special Warfare (MUSM)
NAVSPECWARCOM... Navy Special Warfare Command (SAUS)
NAVSPECWARGP... Naval Special Warfare Group (AABC)
NAVSPECWARGRAUDET... Naval Special Warfare Group Detachment (DNAB)
NAVSPECWARGRU... Naval Special Warfare Group (NVT)
NAVSPECWARU... Naval Special Warfare Unit (DNAB)
NAVSPECWARUDET... Naval Special Warfare Unit Detachment (DNAB)
NAVSPOC .... Naval Space Operations Center (ACAE)
NAVSSES... Naval Ship Systems Engineering Station
NAVSSESDET... Naval Ship Systems Engineering Station Detachment (DNAB)
NAVSSI........ Navigation Sensor System Interface
NAVSTA........ Naval Station
NAVSTAG... Naval Standardization Agreement [NATO]
NAVSTALANT... Naval Stations Atlantic
NAVSTAPAC... Naval Stations Pacific
NAVSTAR... Navigational Star (SAUS)
NAVSTAR..... Navigation Satellite Tracking and Ranging [Later, GPS] [Air Force]
NAVSTAR..... Navigation System Using Time and Ranging (AD)
NAVSTAR..... Navy Study of Transport Aircraft Requirements
NAVSTARCODE... Naval Staff Target and Requirement Code (SAUS)
NAVSTAR-GPS... Navigation Satellite Tracking and Ranging Global Positioning System [Air Force] (MCD)
NAVSTD...... Navy Standard (AAGC)
NAVSTIC...... Naval Scientific and Technical Intelligence Center
NAVSTKWARCEN... Naval Strike Warfare Center (DOMA)
NAVSTRIP.... Navy Standard Requisitioning and Issuing Procedure
NAVSUBBASE... Naval Submarine Base
NAVSUBINSURV... Naval Sub-Board of Inspection and Survey (DNAB)
NAVSUBMEDCEN... Naval Submarine Medical Center
NAVSUBMEDRSCHLAB... Naval Submarine Medical Research Laboratory (DNAB)
NAVSUBSCOL... Naval Submarine School
NAVSUBSUPPBASE... Naval Submarine Support Base (DNAB)
NAVSUBSUPPBASEDET... Naval Submarine Support Base Detachment (DNAB)
NAVSUBSUPPFAC... Navy Submarine Support Facility (DNAB)
NAVSUBTRACENPAC... Naval Submarine Training Center, Pacific (DNAB)
NAVSUP....... Naval Supplies
NAVSUP....... Naval Supply Systems Command [Formerly, Bureau of Supplies and Accounts] (MCD)
NAVSUPACT... Naval Support Activity (NVT)
NAVSUPCEN... Naval Supply Center
NAVSUPDEP... Naval Supply Depot (DNAB)
NAVSUPDEPT... Naval Supply Department (DNAB)
NAVSUPFORANT... Naval Support Forces, Antarctica

NAVSUPGRU...   Naval Support Group   (NVT)
NAVSUPINST...   Naval Supply Systems Command Instruction
NAVSUPMIS...   Navy Supply Management Information System
NAVSUPO ....   Navy Supply Office   (DNAB)
NAVSUPOANX...   Navy Supply Office Annex   (DNAB)
NAVSUPORANT...   Naval Support Forces, Antarctica   (AD)
NAVSUPPACT...   Naval Supply [*or Support*] Activity
NAVSUPPACTDET...   Naval Support Activity Detachment   (DNAB)
NAVSUPPFOR...   Naval Support Force
NAVSUPPFORANTARCTIC...   Naval Support Forces, Antarctic
NAVSUPRANDDFAC...   Navy Supply Research and Development Facility   (DNAB)
NAVSUPRANDFA...   Naval Supply Research and Development Facility
NAVSUPSYSCOM...   Naval Supply Systems Command [*Formerly, Bureau of Supplies and Accounts*]
NAVSUPSYSCOMHQ...   Naval Supply System Command Headquarters
NAVSURFAC...   Naval Surface Force, Pacific
NAVSURFLANT...   Naval Surface Force, Atlantic   (DNAB)
NAVSURFLANTREADSUPPGRU...   Naval Surface Force, Atlantic Readiness Support Group   (DNAB)
NAVSURFPACDAT...   Naval Surface Force, Pacific Dependents' Assistance Team   (DNAB)
NAVSURFWPNCEN...   Naval Surface Weapons Center   (PDAA)
NAVSURMISYS...   Naval Surface Missile Systems   (MCD)
NAVSWC......   Naval Surface Warfare Center [*Silver Spring, MD*]
NAVSWC......   Naval Surface Weapons Center [*Later, NSWC*]   (CAAL)
NAVSWCFAC...   Naval Surface Weapons Center Facility   (DNAB)
NAVSWCREP...   Naval Surface Weapons Center Representative   (DNAB)
NAVSWOP ..   Naval Special Weapons Ordnance Publication
NAVSYD......   Naval Shipyard
NAVTA ....   National Automatic Vendors' Trade Association   (EA)
NAVTA ....   North American Veterinary Technician Association   (GVA)
NAVTAC ....   Navigation Tactical   (AD)
navtac.......   Navigation Tactical   (AD)
NAVTAC ....   Tactical Navigation System
NAVTACDATASYSDEVSITE...   Naval Tactical Data Systems Development and Evaluation Site   (DNAB)
NAVTACDOCACT...   Navy Tactical Doctrine Activity
NAVTACDOCDEVPRODACT...   Navy Tactical Doctrine Development and Production Activity   (DNAB)
NAVTACINTEROPSUPPACT...   Navy Tactical Interoperability Support Activity   (DNAB)
NAVTACINTEROPSUPPACTDET...   Navy Tactical Interoperability Support Activity Detachment   (DNAB)
NAVTACSAT...   Naval Tactical Satellite   (DNAB)
NAVTACSTANS...   Naval Tactical Standards   (MCD)
NAVTACSUPPACT...   Navy Tactical Support Activity   (NVT)
NAVTAG ....   Naval Tactical Game
NAVTAG ....   Navy Tactical Action Game
NAVTAS ....   Navigation and Target Acquisition System   (ACAE)
NAVTASC.....   Naval Telecommunications Automation Support Center   (DNAB)
NAVTASCDETLANT...   Naval Telecommunications Automation Support Center, Atlantic   (DNAB)
NAVTASCDETPAC...   Naval Telecommunications Automation Support Center, Pacific   (DNAB)
NAVTEC ....   National Association of Vocational-Technical Education Communicators   (EA)
NAVTECHJAP...   Naval Technical Mission to Japan
NAVTECHMISJAP...   Naval Technical Mission to Japan   (DNAB)
NAVTECHREP...   Naval Technical Representative
NAVTECHTRACEN...   Naval Air Technical Training Center
NAVTECHTRACENDET...   Naval Technical Training Center Detachment   (DNAB)
NAVTECMISEU...   Naval Technical Mission in Europe
NAVTELCOM...   Naval Telecommunications Command
NAVTELSYSIC...   Naval Telcommunications System Integration Center   (DNAB)
NAVTEX ....   Navigational and meteorological warning broadcast service   (SAUS)
NAVTIS ....   National Vessel Traffic Information System   (AD)
NAVTIS ....   Naval Training Information System   (MCD)
NAVTIS ADS...   Naval Training Information System with Automated Data Systems   (DNAB)
NAVTNG.......   Navigator Training [*Air Force*]
NAVTNGSq...   Navigator Training Squadron [*Air Force*]
NAVTORPSTA...   Naval Torpedo Station
NAVTP ....   National Association of Vertical Transportation Professionals
NAVTRA ....   Naval Training Command
NAVTRACEN...   Naval Training Center   (DNAB)
NAVTRACOM...   Naval Training Command
NAVTRADEV...   Naval Training Device Center
NAVTRADEVCEN...   Naval Training Device Center
NAVTRADEVSUPCEN...   Naval Training Devices Supply Center   (DNAB)
NAVTRADISTCEN...   Naval Training and Distribution Center
NAVTRAEQUIPC...   Naval Training Equipment Center
NAVTRAEQUIPCEN...   Naval Training Equipment Center
NAVTRAEQUIPCENFEO...   Naval Training Equipment Center Field Office   (DNAB)
NAVTRAEQUIPCENREPCEN...   Naval Training Equipment Center, Representative for the Center   (DNAB)
NAVTRAEQUIPCENREPLANT...   Naval Training Equipment Center Representative, Atlantic   (DNAB)
NAVTRAEQUIPCENREPPAC...   Naval Training Equipment Center Representative, Pacific   (DNAB)
NAVTRAFSAT...   Navigational/Traffic-Control Satellite   (MCD)
NAVTRAIDSCEN...   Naval Training Aids Center
NAVTRAINST...   Naval Training Support Command Instruction   (MCD)
NAVTRANSCO...   Naval Transportation Coordinating Office
NAVTRAPUBCEN...   Naval Training Publications Center   (MCD)
NAVTRASAT...   Navigation/Traffic Control Satellite   (MCD)
NAVTRASCOL...   Naval Training School

NAVTRASTA...   Naval Training Station
NAVTRASYSCEN...   Naval Training Systems Center [*Orlando, FL*]
NAVUSEARANDCEN...   Naval Undersea Research and Development Center   (MCD)
NAVUSEARESDEVCEN...   Naval Undersea Research and Development Center
NAVUSEAWARCEN...   Naval Undersea Warfare Center
NAVUWSEC...   Naval Underwater Weapons Systems Engineering Center   (AD)
NAVUWSES...   Naval Underwater Systems Engineering Center
NAVUWSOUNDLAB...   Naval Underwater Sound Laboratory [*Later, NUSC*]
NAVVF ....   National Association of the Van Valkenburg Family   (EA)
NAVWAG.......   Naval Warfare Analysis Group
NAVWARCOL...   Naval War College
Nav War C Rev...   Naval War College. Review [*A publication*]   (DLA)
NAVWASS....   Navigation and Weapon-Aiming Subsystem   (MCD)
NAVWEARSCHFA...   Navy Weather Research Facility
NAVWEASERV...   Naval Weather Service Command
NAVWEPEVALFAC...   Naval Weapons Evaluation Facility [*Kirtland Air Force Base, NM*]   (DNAB)
NAVWEPS...   Bureau of Naval Weapons [*Obsolete*]
NAVWESA...   Naval Weapons Engineering Support Activity
NAVWESS....   National Aviation Weather System Study   (NOAA)
NAVWESTOCEANCEN...   Naval Western Oceanographic Center   (DNAB)
NAVWPNCEN...   Naval Weapons Center   (MCD)
NAVWPNENGSUPPACT...   Naval Weapons Engineering Support Activity   (DNAB)
NAVWPNEVALFAC...   Naval Weapons Evaluation Facility [*Kirtland Air Force Base, NM*]
NAVWPNLAB...   Naval Weapons Laboratory [*Later, NSWC*]
NAVWPNQAO...   Naval Weapons Quality Assurance Office [*Washington, DC*]
NAVWPNQUALASSURO...   Naval Weapons Quality Assurance Office [*Washington, DC*]
NAVWPNSCEN...   Naval Weapons Center
NAVWPNSERVO...   Naval Weapons Services Office [*Also, NWSO, WEPSO*]
NAVWPNSTA...   Naval Weapons Station   (MCD)
NAVWPNSTRACEN...   Naval Weapons Training Center   (DNAB)
NAVWPNSUPPACT...   Naval Weapons Support Activity   (DNAB)
NAVWPNSUPPCEN...   Naval Weapons Support Center   (DNAB)
NAVWPNSYSANALO...   Naval Weapons Systems Analysis Office
NAVWUIS ....   Navy Work Unit Information Service   (IID)
NAVXDIVINGU...   Navy Experimental Diving Unit
NAVY ....   Never Again Volunteer Yourself   (SAUS)
NAVYCAB...   Navy Contract Adjustment Board   (AAGC)
NAVYEO......   Navigator's Yeoman [*British military*]   (DMA)
NAW ....   Narathiwat [*Thailand*] [*Airport symbol*]   (OAG)
NAW ....   National Agricultural Workers Union
NAW ....   National Association for Women   (NADA)
NAW ....   National Association of Wholesaler-Distributors [*Washington, DC*]   (EA)
NAW ....   National Association of Wholesalers   (NADA)
NAW ....   National Association of Widows [*British*]   (DI)
NAW ....   Negative Afterwave [*Microelectrode recording*]
NAW ....   Newair [*Denmark*] [*ICAO designator*]   (FAAC)
N/AW ....   Night/Adverse Weather   (SAUS)
N/AW ....   Night/Adverse Weather Evaluator   (IEEE)
N/AW ....   Night/All-Weather   (SAUS)
NAW ....   Non Acid Washed   (SAUS)
NAW ....   Non-All-Weather   (CINC)
NAW ....   North African Waters
NAW ....   Northwest African Waters
NAWA ....   National Academy of Western Art   (EA)
NAWA ....   National Apple Week Association [*Later, NAM*]   (EA)
NAWA ....   National Association of Women Artists   (EA)
NAWA ....   North American Warmblood Association   (EA)
NAWAC........   National Aviation Weather Advisory Committee [*Marine science*]   (OSRA)
NAWAC........   National Weather Analysis Center [*Air Force, Navy*]
NAWAF........   Navy with Air Force
NAWAPA......   North American Water and Power Alliance
NAWAR.......   Navy with Army
NAWARCOL...   Naval War College   (MUGU)
NAWAS........   National Attack Warning System [*Military*]   (IAA)
NAWAS........   National Warning System [*Civil Defense*]
NAWatch.....   North American Watch Corp. [*Associated Press*]   (SAG)
NAWAU.......   National Aviation Weather Advisory Unit [*Federal Aviation Administration*]   (USDC)
NAWB ....   National Association of Wine and Beer Makers [*British*]   (DBA)
NAWB ....   National Association of Wine Bottlers [*Later, NWA*]   (EA)
NAWBM ......   National Association of Window Blind Manufacturers [*British*]   (BI)
NAWBO........   National Association of Women Business Owners [*Chicago, IL*]   (EA)
NAWC ....   National Art Workers Community [*Later, FCA*]   (EA)
NAWC ....   National Association for Women in Careers [*Later, NAFWIC*]   (EA)
NAWC ....   National Association of Water Companies   (EA)
NAWC ....   National Association of Waterproofing Contractors   (NTPA)
NAWC ....   National Association of Women's Centers [*Defunct*]   (EA)
NAWC ....   National Association of Women's Clubs [*British*]   (DBA)
NAWC ....   Naval Air Warfare Center   (DOMA)
NAWC ....   Naval War College
NAWC ....   North American Watch Corp. [*NASDAQ symbol*]   (SAG)
NAWC ....   North American Watch Consultants   (SAUS)
NAWC ....   North Atlantic Women's Conference   (PSS)
NAWC ....   Number of Additional Words Coming   (CGWS)
NAWCAS......   National Association of Women's and Children's Apparel Salesmen [*Later, Bureau of Wholesale Sales Representatives*]   (EA)
NAWCC........   National Association of Watch and Clock Collectors   (EA)
NAWCC........   National Association of Women in Chambers of Commerce   (EA)
NAWCC........   North American Wetlands Conservation Council   (COE)
NAWCH........   National Association for the Welfare of Children in Hospital [*British*]

NAWCJ .... National Association of Women in Criminal Justice (EA)
NAWCM .... National Association of Wiping Cloth Manufacturers [*Later, IAWCM*] (EA)
NAWCWD .... Naval Air Warfare Center Weapons Divison
NAWCWPNS... Naval Air Warfare Center Weapons Division
NAWD .... Notice of Award
NAWDA .... North American Working Dog Association (EA)
NAWDAC ...... National Association for Women Deans, Administrators, and Counselors (EA)
NAWDC........ National Association of Waste Disposal Contractors [*British*] (DCTA)
NAWDC........ National Association of Women Deans and Counselors [*Later, NAWDAC*] (EA)
NAWDEX...... National Water Data Exchange [*United States Geological Survey*] [*Reston, VA*] [*Information service or system*]
NAWDEX...... National Weather Data Exchange (ACAE)
NAWDP........ National Association of Workforce Development Professionals (NTPA)
NAWE .... National Association for Women in Education (NTPA)
NAWE .... National Association of Waterfront Employers (NTPA)
NAWESA...... Naval Weapons Engineering Support Activity (PDAA)
NAWF .... National Aborigine Welfare Fund [*Australia*] (NADA)
NAWF .... Nodes Above White Flower [*Botany*]
NAWF .... North American Waterfowl Federation
NAWF .... North American Wildlife Foundation (EA)
NAWF .... North American Wolf Society (EA)
NAWFA .... North Atlantic Westbound Freight Association (DS)
NAWFC .... National Association of Wholesale Fur Cleaners
NAWFC .... National Association of Women Federal Contractors [*Later, NAWGC*] (EA)
NAWFMP ..... North American Waterfowl Management Plan of 1986 (COE)
NAWG .... National Association of Wheat Growers (EA)
NAWGA .... National-American Wholesale Grocers' Association (EA)
NAWGC........ National Association of Women Government Contractors [*Defunct*] (EA)
NAWGF .... National Association of Wheat Growers Foundation (EA)
NAWGP .... National Agenda for Women's Grants Program [*Australia*]
NAWH .... National Association of Women in Horticulture [*Defunct*] (EA)
NAWH.......... Norwegian-American Historical Museum (AD)
NAWHP .... National Association of Women's Health Professionals (NTPA)
NAWHSL...... National Association of Women Highway Safety Leaders (EA)
NAWiC .... National Association for Women in Careers [*Later, NAFWIC*] (EA)
NAWIC .... National Association of Women in Construction (EA)
NAWID .... National Association of Water Institute Directors (EA)
NAWID .... National Association of Writing Instrument Distributors (EA)
NAWJ .... National Association of Women Judges (EA)
NAWK .... National Association of Warehouse Keepers [*British*] (DBA)
NAWL .... National Association of Women Lawyers (EA)
NAWL .... North American Iterative Weighted Least Squares (SAA)
NAWLA .... North American Wholesale Lumber Association (EA)
NAWLT .... Nitric Acid Weight Loss Test (SAUS)
NAWM .... National Association of Wool Manufacturers [*Later, American Textile Manufacturers Institute*] (EA)
NAWM .... Naval Air Weapons Meet (MUGU)
NAWMD ...... National Association of Waste Material Dealers [*Later, NARI*]
NAWME .... National Average Weekly Male Earning
NAWMP .... National Association of Waste Material Producers [*Defunct*] (EA)
NAWMP .... Naval Aviation Weapons Maintenance Program (MCD)
NAWMP .... North American Waterfowl Management Plan (SAUS)
NAWND........ National Association of Wholesale Newspaper Distributors (DGA)
NAWP .... National Anti-Waste Programme [*British*] (DCTA)
NAWP .... National Association for Widowed People [*Later, IAWP*] (EA)
NAWP .... National Association of Women Pharmacists [*British*] (DBA)
NAWP .... North American Woodperson (SAUS)
NAWPA .... North American Water and Power Alliance
NAWPB .... National Association of Wholesale Pie Bakers (EA)
NAWPB .... National Association of Wine Producers and Bottlers [*Later, NWA*] (EA)
NAWPC........ National Aircraft War Production Council [*World War II*]
NAWPF .... National Aviation Weather Processing Facility [*FAA*] (TAG)
NAWPF .... North American Wildlife Park Foundation (EA)
NAWPM .... National Association of Wholesale Paint Merchants [*British*] (BI)
NAWPS........ National Association of Word Processing Specialists [*Later, WPS*] (EA)
NAWPU .... National Association of Water Power Users [*British*] (DBA)
NAWQC....... National Ambient Water Quality Criteria (WPI)
NAWR .... National Assembly of Women Religious (EA)
NAWRSRF ... New Age World Religious and Scientific Research Foundation (EA)
NAWS .... National Agricultural Workers Survey
NAWS .... National Aviation Weather System
NAWS .... Naval Air Weapons Station
NAWS .... North African War Shipping [*World War II*]
NAWS .... North American Wolf Society (EA)
NAWSS .... North American Wilderness Survival School
NAWST .... Night Attack Weapon Systems Trainer (SAUS)
NAWT .... National Animal Welfare Trust (WDAA)
NAWT .... National Association of Waste Transporters (NTPA)
NAWTPD...... Naval All Weather Testing Program Detachment
NAWTS .... National Association of World Trade Secretaries [*Later, AWTCE*] (EA)
NAWU .... National Agricultural Workers Union (EA)
NAWU.......... National Asphalt Workers' Union [*A union*] [*British*]
NAWU.......... Ovambo Namibia Workers Union (SAUS)
NAWW .... National Association of Wheat Weavers (EA)
NAWW, Inc.... National Association of Wheat Weavers

NAWWO....... National Association of Woolen and Worsted Overseers [*Later, NATS*] (EA)
NAX .... Ewa, HI [*Location identifier*] [*FAA*] (FAAL)
NAX .... New Arcadia Explorations [*Vancouver Stock Exchange symbol*]
NAX .... Norwegian Air Shuttle, AS [*FAA designator*] (FAAC)
NAXSTA ...... Naval Air Experimental Station
NAY .... Navegacion y Servicios Aereos Canarios SA [*Spain*] [*ICAO designator*] (FAAC)
NAY .... New Alster Energy [*Vancouver Stock Exchange symbol*]
NAY .... Not Available Yet [*Numismatic term*]
NAYA .... North American Yngling Association (EA)
NAYC .... National Association of Youth Clubs [*British*] (DI)
NAYCEO ...... National Association of Youth and Community Education Officers [*British*] (DI)
NAYGTA ...... North American Youth Glider Training Association
NAYO .... National Association of Youth Orchestras (EAIO)
NAYPCAS.... National Association of Young People's Counselling and Advisory Services [*British*] (DI)
NAYPIC .... National Association of Young People in Care [*British*]
NAYRE .... National Association for Year-Round Education (EA)
NAYRU .... North American Yacht Racing Union (EA)
NAYSI .... North American Youth Sport Institute (EA)
NAYT .... National Association of Youth Theatres [*British*] (DBA)
NAYTA .... National Association of Youth Training Agencies (AIE)
NAYW .... National Association for Young Writers [*Defunct*] (EA)
NAZ............. Nazarene
Naz .... Nazir (BJA)
NAZ............. Normal Analytical Zone [*Chemistry*]
NAZ............. Nuveen Arizona Premium Income [*NYSE symbol*] (SAG)
NAZ............. Nuveen AZ Prem Inc. Muni Fd [*NYSE symbol*] (TTSB)
NAZ............. Servicios Aereos del Nazas SA de CV [*Mexico*] [*ICAO designator*] (FAAC)
NAZI............ Nationalsozialistische Deutsche Arbeiterpartei [*National Socialist German Workers' Party, 1919-45*] [*Political party*]
NB................ Brooklyn Public Library, Brooklyn, NY [*Library symbol*] [*Library of Congress*] (LCLS)
NB................ Nabonidus and Belshazzar (BJA)
NB................ Nail Bed (DMAA)
NB................ Nanobarn [*Unit of Measure*]
nb .... Narrowband (IDOE)
NB................ Narrowband
NB................ Narrow Beam (NATG)
NB................ National Battlefield (BARN)
NB................ National Board
NB................ NationsBank Corp. [*NYSE symbol*] (SPSG)
NB................ Naval Base
NB................ Navigation Base (NASA)
NB................ Navy Band
NB................ Neath and Brecon Railway [*Wales*]
NB................ Nebraska (IAA)
Nb................ Nebraska State Library, Lincoln, NE [*Library symbol*] [*Library of Congress*] (LCLS)
NB................ Needle Biopsy [*Surgical procedure*] (DAVI)
NB................ Negative Binomial Distribution [*Statistics*]
NB................ Negri Body (AAMN)
NB................ Nemzeti Bank [*National Bank*] [*Hungarian*]
NB................ Neo-Babylonian [*or New Babylonian*] (BJA)
NB................ Nephroblastoma [*Medicine*] (MELL)
NB................ Nerve Block [*Medicine*] (MELL)
NB................ Network Booter [*Computer science*] (BYTE)
NB................ Neuro-Behccet [*Syndrome*] [*Medicine*] (DMAA)
NB................ Neuroblast [*Cytology*]
NB................ Neuroblastoma [*Medicine*] (DMAA)
NB................ Neurometric Battery (DMAA)
NB................ Neurometric Test Battery [*Neurometrics*]
NB................ Neutral Beam (ACAE)
NB................ Neutral Buoyancy [*Navy*] (SSD)
NB................ Neutron Beam (SAUS)
NB................ New Benloe's Reports, English King's Bench [*1531-1628*] [*A publication*] (DLA)
NB................ New Boiler
NB................ Newborn
NB................ New Bottom [*On ships*]
NB................ New Brunswick [*Canadian province*] [*Postal code*]
NB................ New Brunswick Reports [*A publication*] (DLA)
NB................ New Business
NB................ New Haven Airways [*ICAO designator*] (AD)
NB................ Next Brochure
NB................ Nigerian Bonny [*Crude oil*]
NB................ Night Blindness (MELL)
NB................ Night Bomber (or Bombing) (SAUS)
NB................ Nimbus [*Cloud*] [*Meteorology*]
Nb................ Niobium [*See Cb*] [*Chemical element*]
NB................ Nitrobenzene [*Organic chemistry*]
NB................ Nitrogen Base (NASA)
NB................ Nitrous Oxide-Barbiturate [*Organic chemistry*] (MAE)
NB................ No Ball [*Cricket*]
NB................ No Bias [*Relay*] [*Electronics*]
NB................ No Bid [*or Bidders*]
NB................ No Bowel Movement [*Gastroenterology*] (DAVI)
NB................ No Box
N/B............... No Brands (SAUS)
NB................ Noise Blanker
NB................ Noise Block (ELAL)
N/B............... Noise Power/Bandwidth

NB.............. Nomenclature Board [*Tasmania, Australia*]
NB.............. Nominal Bone (SAUS)
NB.............. Nominal Bore [*Tubing*]
NB.............. Nonbargaining (SAUS)
NB.............. Nonbattle [*Army*] (AABC)
NB.............. Nonbusiness [*IRS*]
NB.............. Nopol Benzyl (SAUS)
NB.............. Nordiska Batradet [*Nordic Boat Council*] [*Sweden*] (EAIO)
NB.............. Nordlands Bank [*Norway*]
NB.............. Normal Bowel Movement [*Gastroenterology*] (DAVI)
NB.............. Normal Bus (SAUS)
NB.............. Normoblast [*Hematology*] (AAMN)
NB.............. Northampton & Bath Railroad Co. [*AAR code*]
NB.............. Northbound
NB.............. North Britain [*i.e., Scotland*]
NB.............. Nosebleed (MELL)
NB.............. Not a Bean [*Penniless*] [*Facetious translation of NB, Nota Bene (Note Well)*] (DSUE)
nb.............. Nota Bene [*Note Well*] [*Latin*] (WDMC)
NB.............. Nota Bene [*Note Well*] [*Latin*]
NB.............. Not Bent [*Freight*]
NB.............. Not Blind [*Experimental conditions*]
NB.............. Notch Bend (SAUS)
NB.............. Notch-Bend (PDAA)
NB.............. Nuclear Blank (NRCH)
NB.............. Nuclear Boiler (NRCH)
NB.............. Nucleus Basalis [*Brain anatomy*]
NB.............. Nulla Bona [*No Goods*] [*Latin*] [*Legal term*] (DLA)
Nb.............. Number (SAUS)
Nb.............. Numbered (SAUS)
NB.............. Number of Bits (SAUS)
NB.............. Number of Bytes (SAUS)
Nb.............. Numbers [*Old Testament book*] (BJA)
NB.............. Nursing Building (SAUS)
NB.............. Nutrient Broth (MELL)
NB2............ Norsar Array Site 02B00 [*Norway*] [*Seismograph station code, US Geological Survey*] (SEIS)
NB 2d........ New Brunswick Reports, Second Series [*A publication*] (DLA)
NB3............ Norsar Array Site 03B00 [*Norway*] [*Seismograph station code, US Geological Survey*] (SEIS)
NB4............ Norsar Array Site 04B00 [*Norway*] [*Seismograph station code, US Geological Survey*] (SEIS)
NB5............ Norsar Array Site 05B00 [*Norway*] [*Seismograph station code, US Geological Survey*] (SEIS)
NBA .... Amateur Astronomers Association, Brooklyn, NY [*Library symbol*] [*Library of Congress*] (LCLS)
NBa............. Davenport Library, Bath, NY [*Library symbol*] [*Library of Congress*] (LCLS)
Nba............ Nambia (MILB)
NBA .... Narrowband Allocation
NBA .... Narrowband Analyzer
NBA .... Narrow-Beam Adapter
NBA .... National Ballet of America
NBA .... National Band Association (EA)
NBA .... National Bank Act of 1863
NBA .... National Bankers Association [*Washington, DC*] (EA)
NBA .... National Bankruptcy Act [*1898*]
NBA .... National Bar Association (EA)
NBA .... National Basketball Association (EA)
NBA .... National Beef Association (GVA)
NBA .... National Beefmaster Association (EA)
NBA .... National Benevolent Association of the Christian Church [*Disciples of Christ*] (EA)
NBA .... National Benzole and Allied Products Association [*British*] (BI)
NBA .... National Biographical Association (EA)
NBA .... National Bison Association (NTPA)
NBA .... National Boat Association (EA)
NBA .... National Book Awards [*Discontinued*]
NBA .... National Bowling Association (EA)
NBA .... National Boxing Association of America [*Later, WBA*]
NBA .... National Braille Association (EA)
NBA .... National Brassfoundry Association [*British*] (BI)
NBA .... National Broadcasting Authority [*Bangladesh*] (EY)
NBA .... National Broiler Association [*Later, NBC*]
NBA .... National Buffalo Association (EA)
NBA .... National Building Agency [*British*]
NBA .... National Business Association (EA)
NBA .... National Butterfly Association (EA)
NBA .... National Button Association
NBA .... N-Bromoacetamide [*Organic chemistry*]
NBA .... N-Butylamine [*Organic chemistry*]
NBA .... Net Book Agreement [*British*]
NBA .... Net Building Area (ADA)
NBA .... Neuromuscular Blocking Agent (SAUS)
NBA .... New Brunswick Area (SAA)
NBA .... Nickel-Base Alloy
NBA .... Non-Weight-Bearing Ambulation [*Orthopedics*] (DAVI)
NBA .... Normal Butyl Alcohol (SAUS)
NBA .... North British Academy
NBA .... North East Bolivian Airways [*ICAO designator*] (FAAC)
NBAA .... Amateur Astronomers Association, Brooklyn, NY [*Library symbol*] [*Library of Congress*] (LCLS)
NBAA .... National Business Aircraft Association (EA)
NBab............ Babylon Public Library, Babylon, NY [*Library symbol*] [*Library of Congress*] (LCLS)

NBAB .... Biological Station, Fisheries and Oceans Canada [*Station de Biologie, Peches et Oceans Canada*] St. Andrews, New Brunswick [*Library symbol*] [*National Library of Canada*] (NLC)
NBab........... Neo-Babylonian [*or New Babylonian*] (BJA)
NBAC .... National Bioethics Advisory Commission
NBAC .... National Bioethics Advisory Committee
NBAC .... National Biotechnology Advisory Committee [*Canada*]
NBAC .... National Black Alcoholism Council (EA)
NBACA .... National Broadcast Association for Community Affairs (NTPA)
NBACCH....... Charlotte County Historical Society, Inc., St. Andrews, New Brunswick [*Library symbol*] [*National Library of Canada*] (NLC)
NBACSTT ..... New Brunswick Association of Certified Survey Technicians and Technologists (SAUS)
NBAD .... National Bank of Abu Dhabi
NBAD .... Naval Bases Air Defense
NBAD .... N-beta-Alanyldopamine [*Biochemistry*]
NBADA .... National Barrel and Drum Association [*Later, NABADA - The Association of Container Reconditioners*] (EA)
NBAE .... National Basketball Association Entertainment
NBAE .... New Business Acquisition Expenditures (ACAE)
NBAF .... National Blonde d'Aquitaine Foundation
NBAGLE .... National Black Alliance for Graduate Level Education [*Defunct*] (EA)
NBAJ .... National Buffalo Association Juniors [*Defunct*] (EA)
NBAK .... National Bancorp of Alaska, Inc. [*NASDAQ symbol*] (NQ)
NBAK .... Natl Bancorp(AK) [*NASDAQ symbol*] (TTSB)
N balance .... Nitrogen Balance [*Medicine*] (WDAA)
NBald .... Baldwin Public Library, Baldwin (SAUS)
NBald .... Baldwin Public Library, Baldwin, NY [*Library symbol*] [*Library of Congress*] (LCLS)
NBaldBE ...... Brookside Elementary School, Baldwin, NY [*Library symbol*] [*Library of Congress*] (LCLS)
NBaldCE ...... Collidge Elementary School, Baldwin, NY [*Library symbol*] [*Library of Congress*] (LCLS)
NBaldGE ...... Grand Avenue Elementary School, Baldwin, NY [*Library symbol*] [*Library of Congress*] (LCLS)
NBaldHE ...... Harbor Elementary School, Baldwin, NY [*Library symbol*] [*Library of Congress*] (LCLS)
NBaldHJ ...... Harbor Junior High School, Baldwin, NY [*Library symbol*] [*Library of Congress*] (LCLS)
NBaldLE ...... Lenox Elementary School, Baldwin, NY [*Library symbol*] [*Library of Congress*] (LCLS)
NBaldME ...... Meadow Elementary School, Baldwin, NY [*Library symbol*] [*Library of Congress*] (LCLS)
NBaldMiE ... Milburn Elementary School, Baldwin, NY [*Library symbol*] [*Library of Congress*] (LCLS)
NBaldPE....... Plaza Elementary School, Baldwin, NY [*Library symbol*] [*Library of Congress*] (LCLS)
NBaldPrE ..... Prospect Elementary School, Baldwin, NY [*Library symbol*] [*Library of Congress*] (LCLS)
NBaldSE ...... Shubert Elementary School, Baldwin, NY [*Library symbol*] [*Library of Congress*] (LCLS)
NBaldSH ...... Baldwin Senior High School, Baldwin, NY [*Library symbol*] [*Library of Congress*] (LCLS)
NBaldStE ..... Steele Elementary School, Baldwin, NY [*Library symbol*] [*Library of Congress*] (LCLS)
NB Alsk........ National Bancorp of Alaska, Inc. [*Associated Press*] (SAG)
NB & BA .... National Bed-and-Breakfast Association (EA)
NB & C .... Norfolk, Baltimore & Carolina Line [*Steamship*] (MHDB)
NBAO .... New Brunswick Area Office [*Later, NBL*] [*AEC*]
NBAPA .... National Black American Paralegal Association (NTPA)
NBar .... Barker Free Library, Barker, NY [*Library symbol*] [*Library of Congress*] (LCLS)
nbar .... Nanobar [*One billionth of a bar*]
NBAR .... Non-Binding Allocation of Responsibility (COE)
NBAR .... Nonbinding Preliminary Allocation of Responsibility [*Environmental Protection Agency*] (FFDE)
NBARN........ New Brunswick Association of Registered Nurses (SAUS)
NBaryU........ Unified Theological Seminary, Barrytown, NY [*Library symbol*] [*Library of Congress*] (LCLS)
NBAs............ National Bioindustries Associations (SAUS)
NBAS .... Neonatal Behavioural Assessment Scale [*Developed by Brazelton*]
NBAS-K........ Neonatal Behavioral Assessment Scale-Kansas Revision (EDAC)
NBASLH....... National Black Association for Speech, Language and Hearing (EA)
NBat............ Richmond Memorial Library, Batavia, NY [*Library symbol*] [*Library of Congress*] (LCLS)
NBatC .... Genesee Community College, Batavia, NY [*Library symbol*] [*Library of Congress*] (LCLS)
NBatGB........ Genesse-Wyoming Board of Cooperative Education Services, Batavia, NY [*Library symbol*] [*Library of Congress*] (LCLS)
NBatGH........ Genesee Memorial Hospital, Batavia, NY [*Library symbol*] [*Library of Congress*] (LCLS)
NBatHHi....... Holland Purchase Historical Society, Batavia, NY [*Library symbol*] [*Library of Congress*] (LCLS)
NBatStJ........ Saint Jerome Hospital, Medical Library, Batavia, NY [*Library symbol*] [*Library of Congress*] (LCLS)
NBatV .... United States Veterans Administration Hospital, Library Service, Batavia, NY [*Library symbol*] [*Library of Congress*] (LCLS)
NBAU .... No Business as Usual (EA)
NBaVA .... United States Veterans Administration Hospital, Bath, NY [*Library symbol*] [*Library of Congress*] (LCLS)
NBAW .... Notable Black American Women [*A publication*]
NBAWADU ... National Black Anti-War Anti-Draft Union (EA)
NBayr.......... Bayville Free Library (SAUS)
NBayv .... Bayville Free Library, Bayville, NY [*Library symbol*] [*Library of Congress*] (LCLS)

NBayvE....... Bayville Elementary School, Bayville, NY [Library symbol] [Library of Congress] (LCLS)

NBayvI........ Bayville Intermediate School, Bayville, NY [Library symbol] [Library of Congress] (LCLS)

NBayvP....... Bayville Primary School, Bayville, NY [Library symbol] [Library of Congress] (LCLS)

NbB............ Beatrice Public Library, Beatrice, NE [Library symbol] [Library of Congress] (LCLS)

NBB .... Brooklyn Museum, Brooklyn, NY [Library symbol] [Library of Congress] (LCLS)

NBB .... Narrowband Beam [Physics]

NBB .... National Bank of Bahrain (EY)

NBB .... National Bank of Brunei

NBB .... New Bedford Institution for Savings (SAUS)

NBB .... New Business Beat (ACAE)

NBB .... Nike/Black Brant (SAUS)

NBB .... Number of Bytes of Binary (SAUS)

NBBA .... National Bed and Breakfast Association (NTPA)

NBBA .... National Beep Baseball Association (EA)

NBBA .... National Black Business Alliance (EA)

NBB & L ..... National Bath, Bed, and Linen Show (ITD)

NBBB .... National Better Business Bureau (NADA)

NBBC .... Bibliotheque Medicale, Hopital Regional Chaleur [Medical Library, Chaleur Regional Hospital] Bathurst, New Brunswick [Library symbol] [National Library of Canada] (NLC)

NBBC .... National Black Business Council

NBBCC .... College Communautaire du New Brunswick, Bathurst, New Brunswick [Library symbol] [National Library of Canada] (NLC)

NBBCN .... New Brunswick Breast Cancer Network (SAUS)

NBBDA .... National Burlap Bag Dealers Association [Later, Textile Bag and Packaging Association] (EA)

NbBe.......... Bellevue Public Library, Bellevue, NE [Library symbol] [Library of Congress] (LCLS)

NBB-E .... Brooklyn Museum, Wilbour Library of Egyptology, Brooklyn, NY [Library symbol] [Library of Congress] (LCLS)

NBBE .... National Board for Bakery Education [British] (BI)

NbBea........ Beatrice Public Library, Beatrice, NE [Library symbol] [Library of Congress] (LCLS)

NbBeL........ Bellevue Public Library, Bellevue, NE [Library symbol] [Library of Congress] (LCLS)

NBBI .... National Blue Books, Inc. [Canoga Park, CA] [Publisher]

NBBI .... National Board of Boiler and Pressure Vessel Inspectors (NTPA)

NBBI .... Nederlands Bureau voor Bibliotheekwezen en Informatieverzorging [Netherlands Organization for Libraries and Information Services] [Information service or system] (IID)

NBBL .... National Bath, Bed, and Linen Association (EA)

NbBla......... Blair Public Library, Blair, NE [Library symbol] [Library of Congress] (LCLS)

NBBLA .... National Bath, Bed, and Linen Association [Later, NBBL] (EA)

NbBlaD....... Dana College, Blair, NE [Library symbol] [Library of Congress] (LCLS)

NBBLC .... National Black on Black Love Campaign (EA)

NBBMA ...... National Beauty and Barber Manufacturers Association [Later, ABA] (EA)

NBBMK ...... Mussee de Kent, Bouctouche, New Brunswick [Library symbol] [National Library of Canada] (NLC)

NBBN .... Nepisiguit Centennial Public Library, Bathurst, New Brunswick [Library symbol] [National Library of Canada] (NLC)

NBBP .... National Board of Boiler & Pressure Vessel Inspectors

Nb-BPH...... Nebraska Library Commission, Library for Blind and Physically Handicapped, Lincoln, NE [Library symbol] [Library of Congress] (LCLS)

NBBPVI ...... National Board of Boiler and Pressure Vessel Inspectors (EA)

NBBQA .... National Barbecue Association

NbBro .... Broken Bow Carnegie Library, Broken Bow, NE [Library symbol] [Library of Congress] (LCLS)

NBBS .... New British Broadcasting Station (NADA)

NBBU .... New Brunswick Board of Underwriters (SAUS)

NBBWM ...... Central New Brunswick Woodmen's Museum, Boiestown, New Brunswick [Library symbol] [National Library of Canada] (NLC)

NBC .... Beaufort, SC [Location identifier] [FAA] (FAAL)

NBC .... Brooklyn College, Brooklyn, NY [Library symbol] [Library of Congress] (LCLS)

NBC .... Concordia College, Seward, NE [OCLC symbol] (OCLC)

NBC .... Cook [N. B.] Corp. Ltd. [Toronto Stock Exchange symbol] [Vancouver Stock Exchange symbol]

NBC .... Narrowband Conducted (IEEE)

NBC .... Nasobiliary Catheter [Medicine] (MELL)

NBC .... National Baseball Congress (EA)

NBC .... National Basketball Congress (NADA)

NBC .... National Battlefields Commission [See also CCBN]

NBC .... National Beagle Club (EA)

NBC .... National Beef Congress

NBC .... National Bibliographic Control

NBC .... National Biscuit Co. (EFIS)

NBC .... National Board for Certification in Dental Laboratory Technology (EA)

NBC .... National Book Committee [Defunct]

NBC .... National Book Council [Later, NBL] [United Kingdom]

NBC .... National Bowling Council (EA)

NBC .... National Boxing Council [British]

NBC .... National Boys' Club (WDAA)

NBC .... National Braille Club [Later, NBA] (EA)

NBC .... National Broadcasters' Club (NTCM)

NBC .... National Broadcasting Co., Inc. [New York, NY]

NBC .... National Broadcasting Commission (NADA)

NBC .... National Broiler Council (EA)

NBC .... National Broom Council [Later, NBMC] (EA)

NBC .... National Building Code

NBC .... National Building Code of Canada (HGAA)

NBC .... National Bus Co. [British]

NBC .... Natural Background Clutter

NBC .... Natural Birth Control

NBC .... Navy Beach Commando

NBC .... Navy Branch Clinic (ACAE)

NBC .... Neumann Boundary Conditions

NBC .... Newfoundland Base Command [Army] [World War II]

NBC .... Nies Babylonian Collection [Yale University] (BJA)

NBC .... Nigeria Broadcasting Corp. (SAUS)

NBC .... Nigerian Broadcasting Corp.

NBC .... No Back Cover

NBC .... Noise Balancing Circuit (DEN)

NBC .... Noise Balancing Control (IAA)

NBC .... Nonbattle Casualty (NVT)

NBC .... Nonbleeding Cable (SAUS)

NBC .... Nordic Boat Council (EA)

NBC .... Norwegian Bulk Carrier (SAUS)

NBC .... Nostalgia Book Club

NBC .... Not Backward-Compatible (SAUS)

NBC .... Nothing but Chaos (SAUS)

NBC .... Nuclear, Biological, and Chemical [Warfare]

NBC .... Number Base Conversion

NBC .... Nursing Bottle Caries [Medicine] (MELL)

NBCA .... Campbellton Centennial Public Library, New Brunswick [Library symbol] [National Library of Canada] (NLC)

NBCA .... National Band Council of Australia

NBCA .... National Bareboat Charter Association (NTPA)

NBCA .... National Baseball Congress of America (NADA)

NBCA .... National Beagle Club of America (EA)

NBCA .... National Bituminous Concrete Association [Later, NAPA] (EA)

NBCA .... National Business Circulation Association (EA)

NBCA .... Navy Department Board of Contract Appeals [1944-50] (AAGC)

NBCAA .... National Bible College Athletic Association (PSS)

NBCAC .... Chaleur Library Region, Campbellton, New Brunswick [Library symbol] [National Library of Canada] (NLC)

NBCAM ...... Campobello Public Library, New Brunswick [Library symbol] [National Library of Canada] (BIB)

NBCAP .... National Beacon Code Allocation Plan (FAAC)

NBCBP .... Bibliotheque Publique Mgr. Paquet, Caraquet, New Brunswick [Library symbol] [National Library of Canada] (NLC)

NBCC .... National Baby Care Council [Defunct] (EA)

NBCC .... National Beauty Career Center (EA)

NBCC .... National Bidders Control Center

NBCC .... National Bituminous Coal Commission [Functions transferred to Department of the Interior, 1939]

NBCC .... National Black Chamber of Commerce (EA)

NBCC .... National Board for Certified Counselors (EA)

NBCC .... National Book Critics Circle (EA)

NBCC .... National Breast Cancer Centre (SAUS)

NBCC .... National Breast Cancer Coalition

NBCC .... National Budget and Consultation Committee [Defunct] (EA)

NBCC .... National Building Code of Canada

NBCC .... National Bureau for Co-Operation in Child Care [British]

NBCC .... National Business Career Center (EA)

NBCC .... Netherlands British Chamber of Commerce (DS)

NBCC .... Nevoid Basal-Cell Carcinoma [Oncology]

NBCC .... New Brunswick Community College (SAUS)

NBCC .... Nigerian British Chamber of Commerce [London] (DCTA)

NBCC .... Nuclear, Biological, and Chemical Center

NBCC .... Nuclear, Biological, and Chemical Contamination (DOMA)

NBCC .... Nuclear, Biological, Chemical, Conventional [Warfare]

NBCCA .... National Business Council for Consumer Affairs [Terminated, 1974] [Department of Commerce] (EGAO)

NBCCA .... Northern British Columbia Construction Association (SAUS)

NBCCC .... Miramichi Campus, New Brunswick Community College [Campus Miramichi, College Communautaire du Nouveau-Brunswick], Chatham, New Brunswick [Library symbol] [National Library of Canada] (NLC)

NBCCC .... National Black Catholic Clergy Caucus (EA)

NBCCC .... National Bureau for Co-Operation in Child Care [British] (BI)

NBC-CDTP ... National Board for Certification - Certified Dental Technician Program (EA)

NBCCEDP..... National Breast and Cervical Cancer Early Detection Program (SAUS)

NBCCH....... National Board for Certified Clinical Hypnotherapists (NTPA)

NBCCS .... Nevoid Basal Cell Carcinoma Syndrome [Oncology] (DMAA)

NBCCW....... Nuclear, Biological, Chemical, Conventional Warfare (SAUS)

NBCD .... Natural Binary-Coded Decimal

NBCD .... Negate BCD [Binary-Coded Decimal] Number [Computer science]

NBCD .... Normal Binary Coded Decimal (SAUS)

NBCD .... Nuclear, Biological, and Chemical Defense (NATG)

NBCDC3 ..... NBCD Command, Control & Communications (SAUS)

NBCDC3T..... NBC defence & Damage C3 Trainer (SAUS)

NBCDCE...... Nuclear, Biological, and Chemical Defense Control Element [Military]

NBCDCODING... Normal Binary Coded Decimal Coding (SAUS)

NBC defense... Nuclear defense, Biological defense and Chemical defense (SAUS)

NBCDI........ National Black Child Development Institute (EA)

NBCDL........ National Board for Certification of Dental Laboratories [Later, CDL] (EA)

NBCDX .... Nuclear, Biological, and Chemical Defense Exercise [NATO] (NATG)

NBCE .... Nuclear, Biological, and Chemical Element

NbCen .... Hards Memorial Library, Central City, NE [*Library symbol*] [*Library of Congress*] (LCLS)
NbCenC .... Nebraska Central College, Central City, NE [*Library symbol*] [*Library of Congress*] [*Obsolete*] (LCLS)
NBCF .... Nuclear, Biological, Chemical & Fire (SAUS)
NBCFAE ...... National Black Coalition of Federal Aviation Employees (EA)
NBCFD .... Naval Base Consolidated Fire Department (DNAB)
NBCG .... National Bulk Commodities Group [*Australia*]
NBCGT .... National Business Consortium for the Gifted and Talented [*Defunct*] (EA)
NbCh .... Chadron Public Library, Chadron, NE [*Library symbol*] [*Library of Congress*] (LCLS)
NBCH .... Historical Society Nicolas Denys, Societe Historique Nicolas Denys, Caraquet, New Brunswick [*Library symbol*] [*National Library of Canada*] (NLC)
NBCHD .... Chatham, Hotel-Dieu Hospital, New Brunswick (SAUS)
NBCHD .... Health Sciences Library, Hotel-Dieu Hospital, Chatham, New Brunswick [*Library symbol*] [*National Library of Canada*] (BIB)
NBCHR .... Bibliotheque de la Sante, Centre Hospitalier Restigouche, Campbellton, New Brunswick [*Library symbol*] [*National Library of Canada*] (BIB)
NbChS .... Chadron State College, Chadron, NE [*Library symbol*] [*Library of Congress*] (LCLS)
NBCI .... NBC Internet
NBCi .... NBC Internet Inc.
NBCI .... Nigerian Bank for Commerce and Industry
NBCIA .... National Blue Crab Industry Association (EA)
NBCL .... National Beauty Culturists' League (EA)
NBCL .... National Birth Control League
NBCLEO .... National Black Caucus of Local Elected Officials (NTPA)
NBCM .... Miramichi Natural History Society, Chatham, New Brunswick [*Library symbol*] [*National Library of Canada*] (NLC)
NBCMA .... Mussee Acadien, Caraquet, New Brunswick [*Library symbol*] [*National Library of Canada*] (NLC)
NBC/MMT .... Nuclear Biological Contamination/Manufacturing Methods Technology (ACAE)
NBCMu .... Brooklyn Children's Museum, Brooklyn, NY [*Library symbol*] [*Library of Congress*] (LCLS)
NbCo .... Columbus Public Library, Columbus, NE [*Library symbol*] [*Library of Congress*] (LCLS)
NbCoC .... Platte Technical Community College, Columbus, NE [*Library symbol*] [*Library of Congress*] (LCLS)
NBCOT .... National Board for Certification of Orthopaedic Technologists (EA)
NBCP .... Brooklyn College of Pharmacy, Brooklyn, NY [*Library symbol*] [*Library of Congress*] (LCLS)
NBCP .... National Bladder Cancer Project [*National Cancer Institute*]
NBCPC .... National Board for Cardiovascular and Pulmonary Credentialing [*Later, Cardiovascular Credentialing International - CCI*] (EA)
NBCPC .... Nuclear, Biological & Chemical Protective Cover (SAUS)
NbCr .... Crete Public Library, Crete, NE [*Library symbol*] [*Library of Congress*] (LCLS)
NbCrD .... Doane College, Crete, NE [*Library symbol*] [*Library of Congress*] (LCLS)
NBCRS .... Nuclear-Biological-Chemical Reconnaissance System [*Military*]
NBCS .... National Black Communicators Society (EA)
NBCS .... St. Thomas University, Fredericton, New Brunswick [*Library symbol*] [*National Library of Canada*] (NLC)
NBCSA .... National Black Catholic Seminarians Association (EA)
NBCSDA .... National Broom Corn and Supply Dealers Association (EA)
NBCSH .... La Societe Historique de Clair, Inc., New Brunswick [*Library symbol*] [*National Library of Canada*] (NLC)
NBCSI .... National Board of the Coat and Suit Industry [*Defunct*] (EA)
NBCSL .... National Black Caucus of State Legislators (EA)
NBCSS .... Nuclear, Biological & Chemical Shelter System (SAUS)
NBcs TX ...... National Bancshares Corp. of Texas [*Associated Press*] (SAG)
NBCU .... National Bureau of Casualty Underwriters [*Later, ISO*] (EA)
NBC USA ..... National Baptist Convention, USA (EA)
NBCV .... Narrowband Coherent Video (IEEE)
NBCVHA .... Le Village Historique Acadien, Caraquet, New Brunswick [*Library symbol*] [*National Library of Canada*] (NLC)
NBCW .... National Bird Cage Week
NBCW .... National Board of Catholic Women [*British*]
NBCWARN .. Nuclear, Biological, and Chemical Warning
NBCWRS ..... Nuclear, Biological, and Chemical Warning and Reporting System
NBD .... Doane College, Crete, NE [*OCLC symbol*] (OCLC)
NBD .... Narrowband Detector
NBD .... National Bank of Dubai
NBD .... National Detroit Corp. [*EFIS*]
NBD .... NBD Bancorp, Inc. [*NYSE symbol*] (SPSG)
NBD .... Negative Binomial Distribution [*Statistics*]
NBD .... Neurogenic Bladder Dysfunction [*Medicine*]
NBD .... Neurologic Bladder Dysfunction [*Medicine*] (DB)
NBD .... Neutral Beam Divider
NBD .... Nitrobenzoxadiazole [*Organic chemistry*]
nbd .... No Big Deal [*Internet language*] [*Computer science*]
NBD .... No Brain Damage (MELL)
NBD .... Nondirectional Beacon
NBD .... Norbornadiene [*Organic chemistry*]
NBD .... Nucleotide Binding Domain [*Biochemistry*]
NBDA .... National Barrel and Drum Association
NBDA .... National Bicycle Dealers Association (EA)
NBDA .... National Black Deaf Advocates (EA)
NBDC .... National Blood Data Center [*American Blood Commission*] [*Information service or system*] (IID)
NBDC .... National Bomb Data Center

NBDC .... New Brunswick Development Corp. (SAUS)
NBDCA .... National Baptist Deacons Convention of America (EA)
NBDE .... National Bureau of Document Examiners (EA)
NBDEA .... National Beverage Dispensing Equipment Association (EA)
NB Dep Nat Resour Repr... New Brunswick Department of Natural Resources. Reprint (SAUS)
NBDF .... Narrow Band Device - Fix
NBDF .... Narrowband Dicke-Fix [*Electronics*] (CET)
NBDFB .... Nitrobenzenediazonium Tetrafluoroborate [*Organic chemistry*]
NBDFX .... Narrowband Dicke-Fix [*Electronics*] (MSA)
NBDKH .... Keillor House Museum, Dorchester, New Brunswick [*Library symbol*] [*National Library of Canada*] (NLC)
NBDL .... Narrowband Data Line
NBDL .... Narrowband Data Link (IAA)
NBDL .... Naval Biodynamics Laboratory (GRD)
NBDM .... Miramichi Salmon Museum, Inc., Doaktown, New Brunswick [*Library symbol*] [*National Library of Canada*] (NLC)
NBDMO .... N-Bromo(dimethyl)oxazolidinone [*Organic chemistry*]
NBDN .... Nuclear Blast Detector Network (SAUS)
NB-DNJ .... N-Butyldeoxynojirimycin [*Biochemistry*]
NBDP .... Narrow-Band Direct Printing (OTD)
NBD-PS .... Nitrobenzoxadiazole Phosphatidylserine [*Biochemistry*]
NBDRRM ...... Restigouche Regional Museum, Dalhousie, New Brunswick [*Library symbol*] [*National Library of Canada*] (NLC)
NBDS .... Nuclear Burst Detection Systems (MCD)
NBDVS .... Narrow Band Digital Voice System [*Telecommunications*] (LAIN)
NBE .... Dallas, TX [*Location identifier*] [*FAA*] (FAAL)
NbE .... Exeter Public Library, Exeter, NE [*Library symbol*] [*Library of Congress*] (LCLS)
NBE .... Near Band Edge (AAEL)
NBE .... Neutron Binding Energy
NBE .... Newburyport Birders' Exchange (EA)
NBE .... Nominal Band Edge
NBE .... Normal Binocular Experience [*Ophthalmology*]
NbE .... North by East
NBE .... Not Below or Equal (SAUS)
NBE .... Nova Beaucage Mines Ltd. [*Toronto Stock Exchange symbol*]
NBE .... Nuclear Binding Energy
NBEA .... National Ballroom and Entertainment Association (EA)
NBEA .... National Black Evangelical Association (EA)
NBEA .... National Broadcast Editorial Association (EA)
NBEA .... National Business Education Association [*Reston, VA*] (EA)
NBEBR .... Bibliotheque Regionale du Haut Saint-Jean, Edmundston, New Brunswick [*Library symbol*] [*National Library of Canada*] (NLC)
NBEC .... National Business and Education Council (OICC)
NBECC .... New Brunswick Community College, Edmundston, New Brunswick [*Library symbol*] [*National Library of Canada*] (NLC)
NBECN .... New Brunswick Education Computer Network (SAUS)
NBECS .... Nonresidential Building Energy Comsumption Survey [*Department of Energy*] (GFGA)
NBed .... Bedford Free Library, Bedford, NY [*Library symbol*] [*Library of Congress*] (LCLS)
NBEDC .... National Black Economic Development Conference
NBedh .... Bedford Hills Free Library, Bedford Hills, NY [*Library symbol*] [*Library of Congress*] (LCLS)
NBEF .... National Bowhunter Education Foundation (EA)
NBEI-Syndr... Non Butanol Extractable Iodine-Syndrome (SAUS)
NBel .... Bellport Memorial Library, Bellport, NY [*Library symbol*] [*Library of Congress*] (LCLS)
NBelf .... Belfast Public Library, Belfast, NY [*Library symbol*] [*Library of Congress*] (LCLS)
NBelL .... Long Island Library Resources Council, Inc., Bellport, NY [*Library symbol*] [*Library of Congress*] (LCLS)
NBellm .... Bellmore Memorial Library, Bellmore, NY [*Library symbol*] [*Library of Congress*] (LCLS)
NBellmCM ... Wellington C. Mepham High School, Bellmore, NY [*Library symbol*] [*Library of Congress*] (LCLS)
NBellmGJ .... Grand Avenue Junior High School, Bellmore, NY [*Library symbol*] [*Library of Congress*] (LCLS)
NBellmKH ... John F. Kennedy High School, Bellmore, NY [*Library symbol*] [*Library of Congress*] (LCLS)
NBellmR ...... C.H. Reinhard School, Bellmore, NY [*Library symbol*] [*Library of Congress*] (LCLS)
NBellmSE ... Shore Road Elementary School, Bellmore, NY [*Library symbol*] [*Library of Congress*] (LCLS)
NBellmWE ... Winthrop Avenue Elementary School, Bellmore, NY [*Library symbol*] [*Library of Congress*] (LCLS)
NBelS .... Suffolk Cooperative Library System, Bellport, NY [*Library symbol*] [*Library of Congress*] (LCLS)
NBEMM .... Musee de Madawaska, Edmundston, New Brunswick [*Library symbol*] [*National Library of Canada*] (NLC)
N Ben .... New Benloe's Reports, English King's Bench [*1531-1628*] [*A publication*] (DLA)
N Benl .... New Benloe's Reports, English King's Bench [*1531-1628*] [*A publication*] (DLA)
NBEO .... National Board of Examiners in Optometry (EA)
NBEOPS .... National Board of Examiners for Osteopathic Physicians and Surgeons [*Later, NBOME*] (EA)
NBEPC .... New Brunswick Electric Power Commission (SAUS)
NB Eq .... New Brunswick Equity Reports [*A publication*] (DLA)
NB Eq Ca .... New Brunswick Equity Cases [*A publication*] (DLA)
NB Eq R ...... New Brunswick Equity Reports [*A publication*] (DLA)
NB Eq Rep... New Brunswick Equity Reports [*A publication*] (DLA)
NBER .... National Bureau of Economic Research (EA)
NBER .... National Bureau of Engineering Registration

NBERA .... National Bicentennial Ethnic-Racial Alliance
NBerG .... Gillam-Grant Community Center Library, Bergen, NY [*Library symbol*] [*Library of Congress*] (LCLS)
NBernN .... Bernardsville News, Bernardsville, NJ [*Library symbol*] [*Library of Congress*] (LCLS)
NBerR .... Bergen Reading Center, Bergen, NY [*Library symbol*] [*Library of Congress*] (LCLS)
NBES .... National Business Equipment Survey [*British*]
NBES .... Near-Bottom Echo Sounder (SAUS)
NBESLM ...... Centre Universitaire Saint-Louis Maillet, Edmundston, New Brunswick [*Library symbol*] [*National Library of Canada*] (NLC)
NBet .... Bethpage Public Library, Bethpage, NY [*Library symbol*] [*Library of Congress*] (LCLS)
NBET .... National Business Entrance Test [*Education*] (AEBS)
NBetCaE ...... Campagne Elementary School, Bethpage, NY [*Library symbol*] [*Library of Congress*] (LCLS)
NBetCE .... Central Elementary School, Bethpage, NY [*Library symbol*] [*Library of Congress*] (LCLS)
NBETF .... Neutral-Beam Engineering Test Facility [*Lawrence Berkeley Laboratory*] [*Terminated*] [*Department of Energy*] (GRD)
NBetG .... Grumman Aerospace Corp., Bethpage, NY [*Library symbol*] [*Library of Congress*] (LCLS)
NBetH .... Mid-Island Hospital, Bethpage, NY [*Library symbol*] [*Library of Congress*] (LCLS)
NBethKJ ...... John F. Kennedy Junior High School, Bethpage, NY [*Library symbol*] [*Library of Congress*] (LCLS)
NBethSH ...... Bethpage Senior High School, Bethpage, NY [*Library symbol*] [*Library of Congress*] (LCLS)
NBetKE .... Kramer Elementary School, Bethpage, NY [*Library symbol*] [*Library of Congress*] (LCLS)
NBetKJ .... John F. Kennedy Junior High School, Bethpage, NY [*Library symbol*] [*Library of Congress*] (LCLS)
NBetSH .... Bethpage Senior High School, Bethpage, NY [*Library symbol*] [*Library of Congress*] (LCLS)
NBetWE .... John H. West Elementary School, Bethpage, NY [*Library symbol*] [*Library of Congress*] (LCLS)
NBF .... Brooklyn Friends School, New York, NY [*Library symbol*] [*Library of Congress*] (LCLS)
NBF .... Narrowband Filter
NBF .... National Bed Federation [*British*] (DBA)
NBF .... National Birman Fanciers (EA)
NBF .... National Boating Federation (EA)
NBF .... National Burn Federation (EA)
NBF .... Netbios Frame (SAUS)
NBF .... Neutral Buoyancy Facility [*Navy*] (MCD)
NBF .... New Biotechnology Firm
NBF .... New Business Funds (MCD)
NBF .... Nordisk Barnkirurgisk Forening [*Scandinavian Association of Paediatric Surgeons - SAPS*] [*Denmark*] (EAIO)
NBF .... Northbay Financial Corp. [*AMEX symbol*] (SPSG)
NBF .... North Bergen Federation of Public Libraries [*Library network*]
NBF .... Northwest AHEC [*Area Health Education Center*] - Bowman Gray School of Medicine, Taylorsville, NC [*OCLC symbol*] (OCLC)
NBF .... Not Breast Fed (MELL)
NBF .... Nucleotide Binding Fold [*Genetics*]
NBFA .... National Baseball Fan Association (EA)
NBFA .... National Business Forms Association [*Alexandria, VA*] (EA)
NBFA .... New Business Fund Authorization (MCD)
NBFA .... Provincial Archives of New-Brunswick Fredericton (SAUS)
NBFA .... Provincial Archives of New-Brunswick [*Archives Provinciales du Nouveau-Brunswick*] Fredericton, New Brunswick [*Library symbol*] [*National Library of Canada*] (NLC)
NBFAA .... National Burglar and Fire Alarm Association (EA)
NBFAFA .... Archives, Diocese of Fredericton, Anglican Church of Canada, New Brunswick [*Library symbol*] [*National Library of Canada*] (NLC)
NBFAG .... Research Station, Agriculture Canada [*Station de Recherches, Agriculture Canada*] Fredericton, New Brunswick [*Library symbol*] [*National Library of Canada*] (NLC)
NBFB .... Beaverbrook Collection, New Brunswick Archives, Fredericton, New Brunswick [*Library symbol*] [*National Library of Canada*] (NLC)
NbFb .... Fairbury Public Library, Fairbury, NE [*Library symbol*] [*Library of Congress*] (LCLS)
NbFbC .... Southeast Community College, Fairbury, NE [*Library symbol*] [*Library of Congress*] (LCLS)
NBFBS .... New Brunswick Barristers Society, Fredericton, New Brunswick [*Library symbol*] [*National Library of Canada*] (NLC)
NbFC .... Central Lutheran Theological Seminary, Fremont, NE [*Library symbol*] [*Library of Congress*] (LCLS)
NBFC .... New Brunswick Library Service, Fredericton, New Brunswick (SAUS)
NbFc .... Woods Memorial Library, Falls City, NE [*Library symbol*] [*Library of Congress*] (LCLS)
NBFCE .... NETBIOS Frames Control Program (SAUS)
NbFcP .... Woods Memorial Library, Falls City, NE [*Library symbol*] [*Library of Congress*] (LCLS)
NBFDEC ...... Dr. Everett Chalmers Hospital, Fredericton, New Brunswick [*Library symbol*] [*National Library of Canada*] (NLC)
NBFE .... Maritimes Forest Research Centre, Environment Canada [*Centre de Recherches Forestieres des Maritimes, Environnement Canada*] Fredericton, New Brunswick [*Library symbol*] [*National Library of Canada*] (NLC)
NBFED .... New Brunswick Department of Education, Fredericton, New Brunswick [*Library symbol*] [*National Library of Canada*] (NLC)
NBFFO .... National Board of Fur Farm Organizations (EA)

NBFHR .... New Brunswick Department of Historical Resources, Fredericton, New Brunswick [*Library symbol*] [*National Library of Canada*] (NLC)
NBFI .... Non-Bank Financial Institution (SAUS)
NBFI .... Non-Bank Financial Institutions [*Ghana*]
NBFI .... Non-Bank Financial Intermediary (ADA)
NBFJS .... Sunbury West Historical Society, Fredericton Junction, New Brunswick [*Library symbol*] [*National Library of Canada*] (NLC)
NBFJWO ...... National Bureau of Federated Jewish Women's Organizations (EA)
NBFKL .... Kings Landing Historical Settlement, Fredericton, New Brunswick [*Library symbol*] [*National Library of Canada*] (NLC)
NBFL .... Legislative Library [*Bibliotheque Legislative*] Fredericton, New Brunswick [*Library symbol*] [*National Library of Canada*] (NLC)
NBFL .... New Brunswick Federation of Labour
NBFLM .... Photogrammetry Branch, New Brunswick Department of Lands and Mines, Fredericton, New Brunswick [*Library symbol*] [*National Library of Canada*] (NLC)
NBFM .... Narrowband Frequency Modulation [*Radio*]
NBFMM .... Medley Memorial Library, Christ Church Cathedral, Fredericton, New Brunswick [*Library symbol*] [*National Library of Canada*] (NLC)
NBFNR .... New Brunswick Department of Natural Resources and Energy, Fredericton, New Brunswick [*Library symbol*] [*National Library of Canada*] (NLC)
NBFO .... National Black Feminist Organization
NBFP .... New Brunswick Power, Fredericton, New Brunswick [*Library symbol*] [*National Library of Canada*] (NLC)
NBFPO .... Premier's Office, Province of New Brunswick, Fredericton, New Brunswick [*Library symbol*] [*National Library of Canada*] (NLC)
NbFr .... Fremont Public Library, Fremont, NE [*Library symbol*] [*Library of Congress*] (LCLS)
NBFR .... Neutral Balance Force Reductions (SAUS)
NBFR .... Not Before [*ICAO designator*] (FAAC)
NbFrM .... Midland Lutheran College, Fremont, NE [*Library symbol*] [*Library of Congress*] (LCLS)
NBFRP .... New Brunswick Research and Productivity Council, Fredericton, New Brunswick [*Library symbol*] [*National Library of Canada*] (NLC)
NBFS .... National Bird-Feeding Society (EA)
NBFS .... New Balanced File Organization Scheme (MHDB)
NBFS .... Societe d'Histoire de la Riviere Saint Jean, Fredericton, New Brunswick [*Library symbol*] [*National Library of Canada*] (BIB)
NBFSS .... New Brunswick Department of Social Services, Fredericton, New Brunswick [*Library symbol*] [*National Library of Canada*] (NLC)
NBFT .... Bureau de Traduction, Gouvernement du Nouveau-Brunswick [*Translation Bureau, Governement of New Brunswick*] Fredericton, New Brunswick [*Library symbol*] [*National Library of Canada*] (NLC)
NBFTR .... New Brunswick Department of Transportation, Fredericton, New Brunswick [*Library symbol*] [*National Library of Canada*] (NLC)
NBFU .... National Board of Fire Underwriters [*Later, AIA*] (EA)
NBFU .... Newfoundland Board of Fire Underwriters (SAUS)
NBFU .... University of New Brunswick, Fredericton, New Brunswick [*Library symbol*] [*National Library of Canada*] (NLC)
NBFUA .... Archives and Special Collections Department, University of New Brunswick, Fredericton, New Brunswick [*Library symbol*] [*National Library of Canada*] (NLC)
NBFUE .... Engineering Library, University of New Brunswick, Fredericton [*Library symbol*] [*National Library of Canada*] (BIB)
NBFUL .... Law Library, University of New Brunswick, Fredericton, New Brunswick [*Library symbol*] [*National Library of Canada*] (NLC)
NBFUM .... Map Room, Government Documents Department, University of New Brunswick, Fredericton, New Brunswick [*Library symbol*] [*National Library of Canada*] (NLC)
NBFY .... York-Sunbury Historical Society, Fredericton, New Brunswick [*Library symbol*] [*National Library of Canada*] (NLC)
NBFYR .... York Regional Library, Fredericton, New Brunswick [*Library symbol*] [*National Library of Canada*] (NLC)
NBFYRC ...... New Brunswick Department of Youth, Recreation and Cultural Resources, Fredericton, New Brunswick [*Library symbol*] [*National Library of Canada*] (NLC)
NBG .... Bowman Gray School of Medicine, Winston-Salem, NC [*OCLC symbol*] (OCLC)
NBG .... Brooklyn Botanic Garden, Brooklyn, NY [*Library symbol*] [*Library of Congress*] (LCLS)
NbG .... Grand Island Public Library, Grand Island, NE [*Library symbol*] [*Library of Congress*] (LCLS)
NBG .... National Bank of Greece
NBG .... Naval Beach Group (NVT)
NBG .... Networking Business Group (SAUS)
NBG .... New Burlington Gallery (SAUS)
NBG .... New Orleans, LA [*Location identifier*] [*FAA*] (FAAL)
NBG .... Niederohmig Begrabenes Gebiet (SAUS)
NBG .... Nieuwe Vertaling Nederlands Bijbelgenootschap [*A publication*] (BJA)
NBG .... No Blasted Good [*Slang*]
NBG .... No Bloody Good [*British slang*]
NBGA .... National Bingo Game Association [*British*] (DBA)
NBGACF ...... Canadian Forces Base, Gagetown, New Brunswick [*Library symbol*] [*National Library of Canada*] (NLC)
NBGFCC ...... New Brunswick Community College, Grand Falls, New Brunswick [*Library symbol*] [*National Library of Canada*] (NLC)
NBGFH .... Grand Falls Historical Society, New Brunswick [*Library symbol*] [*National Library of Canada*] (NLC)
NBGG .... Grand Manan Historical Society, Grand Harbour, Grand Manan Island, New Brunswick [*Library symbol*] [*National Library of Canada*] (NLC)

NbGi .... Grand Island Public Library, Grand Island, NE [*Library symbol*] [*Library of Congress*] (LCLS)

NBGMM .... Grand Manan Museum, Grand Harbour, Grand Manan Island, New Brunswick, [*Library symbol*] [*National Library of Canada*] (NLC)

NBGQA .... National Building Granite Quarries Association (EA)

NBGRN .... Narrow Band Gaussian Random Noise (PDAA)

NBGS .... New Bedford Glass Society [*Defunct*] (EA)

NBH .... Hastings College, Hastings, NE [*OCLC symbol*] (OCLC)

NbH .... Hastings Public Library (SAUS)

NbH .... Hastings Public Library, Hastings, NE [*Library symbol*] [*Library of Congress*] (LCLS)

NBH .... National Bank of Hungary

NBH .... National Bellas Hess [*Inc.*] [*Commercial firm*]

NBH .... Network Busy Hour [*Telecommunications*] (TEL)

NBH .... North Bay [*Hawaii*] [*Seismograph station code, US Geological Survey*] [*Closed*] (SEIS)

NBHA .... National Barrel House Association

NBHA .... National Bicentennial Hospitality Alliance [*American Revolution Bicentennial Administration*]

NBHA .... National Builders' Hardware Association [*Later, DHI*] (EA)

NbHC .... Hastings College, Hastings, NE [*Library symbol*] [*Library of Congress*] (LCLS)

NBHCA .... Albert County Historical Society, Inc., Hopewell Cape, New Brunswick [*Library symbol*] [*National Library of Canada*] (NLC)

NBHCA .... National Belgian Hare Club of America [*Defunct*] (EA)

NbHCC .... Central Technical Community College, Hastings, NE [*Library symbol*] [*Library of Congress*] (LCLS)

NbHCro .... Crosier Fathers' Library, Hastings, NE [*Library symbol*] [*Library of Congress*] (LCLS)

NBHF .... Narrowband High Frequency Communications System (ACAE)

NbHi .... Nebraska State Historical Society, Lincoln, NE [*Library symbol*] [*Library of Congress*] (LCLS)

NbHo .... Holdrege-Phelps County Library, Holdrege, NE [*Library symbol*] [*Library of Congress*] (LCLS)

NBHPA .... National Black Health Planners Association (EA)

NBHS .... National Bureau for Handicapped Students [*British*] (CB)

NBHU .... Nitrogen Blower Heater Unit (SAUS)

NBi .... Binghamton Public Library, Binghamton, NY [*Library symbol*] [*Library of Congress*] (LCLS)

NBI .... Nabisco Brands, Inc. [*Toronto Stock Exchange symbol*]

NBI .... Nathaniel Branden Institute

NBI .... National BankAmericard, Inc. [*Later, Visa USA, Inc.*]

NBI .... National Bridge Inventory [*FHWA*] (TAG)

NBI .... Neutral Beam Injection (MCD)

NBI .... Nielsen Broadcast Index [*A. C. Nielsen Co.*] (NTCM)

NBI .... No Bone Injury [*Medicine*]

NBI .... Nonbattle Injuries

NBI .... Non-Battle-Injury (SAUS)

NBI .... Northern Business Information, Inc. [*New York, NY*] [*Information service or system*] (TSSD)

NBI .... Nothing but Initials [*Initialism is name of commercial word processor firm*]

NBI .... Nuclear Burst Indicator (NATG)

NBIA .... National Business Incubation Association

NBIAP .... National Biological Impact Assessment Program [*Computer science*] (IID)

NBiBT .... Broome Technical Community College, Binghamton, NY [*Library symbol*] [*Library of Congress*] (LCLS)

NBIC .... National Business Information Center [*Dun & Bradstreet*]

NBIC .... Northeast Bancorp, Inc. (SAUS)

NBICU .... Newborn Intensive Care Unit (MELL)

NBIE .... National Burn Information Exchange [*Information service or system*] (CRD)

NBiF .... Four County Library System, Binghamton, NY [*Library symbol*] [*Library of Congress*] (LCLS)

NBIF .... National Biotechnology Information Facility (SAUS)

NBII .... National Biological Information Infrastructure

NBiL .... Our Lady of Lourdes Hospital, Binghamton, NY [*Library symbol*] [*Library of Congress*] (LCLS)

NBIO .... North American Biologicals, Inc. [*NASDAQ symbol*] (NQ)

NBIP .... National Biomonitoring Inventory Program [*Department of Energy*] (MSC)

NBIRF .... National Brain Injury Research Foundation (EA)

NBiRM .... Roberson Museum and Science Center, Binghamton, NY [*Library symbol*] [*Library of Congress*] (LCLS)

NBIS .... National Bridge Inspection Standards [*FHWA*] (TAG)

NBIS .... Neutral Beam Injection System (SAUS)

NBIS .... New Brunswick Information Service (SAUS)

NBIS .... New Brunswick Land Surveyors (SAUS)

NBIS .... Northern Biosphere Information System (EOSA)

NBiSC .... New York State Supreme Court Law Library, Binghamton, NY [*Library symbol*] [*Library of Congress*] (LCLS)

NBiSEG .... New York State Electric & Gas Corp., Binghamton, NY [*Library symbol*] [*Library of Congress*] (LCLS)

NBiSL .... Singer Co., Link Division, Binghamton, NY [*Library symbol*] [*Library of Congress*] (LCLS)

NBiSU .... State University of New York at Binghamton, Binghamton, NY [*Library symbol*] [*Library of Congress*] (LCLS)

NBIT .... New Bedford Institute of Technology [*Massachusetts*]

NBIT .... New Brunswick Institute of Technology (SAUS)

NBIX .... Neurocrine Biosciences [*NASDAQ symbol*] (TTSB)

NBIX .... Neurocrine Biosciences, Inc. [*NASDAQ symbol*] (SAG)

NBJ .... Kingsbrook Jewish Medical Center, Brooklyn, NY [*Library symbol*] [*Library of Congress*] (LCLS)

NBJ .... National Bar Journal [*A publication*] (DLA)

NbK .... Kearney Public Library, Kearney, NE [*Library symbol*] [*Library of Congress*] (LCLS)

NBK .... Kingsborough Community College of the City University of New York, Brooklyn, NY [*Library symbol*] [*Library of Congress*] (LCLS)

NBK .... Nabu Network Corp. [*Toronto Stock Exchange symbol*]

NBK .... National Bank of Kuwait

NBK .... Natural Born Killers [*Movie title*]

NBK .... Nebelkerze [*Smoke-Candle*] [*German military - World War II*]

NBK .... Nordisk Bilteknisk Kommitte [*Nordic Automobile Technical Committee - NATC*] [*Defunct*] [*Denmark*] (EAIO)

NBKC .... Kingsborough Community College of the City University of New York, Brooklyn, NY [*Library symbol*] [*Library of Congress*] (LCLS)

NBKC .... New England Bancorp, Inc. (SAUS)

NBkCmce ..... Northern Bank of Commerce [*Associated Press*] (SAG)

NBkCmce ..... Northwest Bank of Commerce [*Oregon*] [*Associated Press*] (SAG)

NbKi .... Kimball Public Library, Kimball, NE [*Library symbol*] [*Library of Congress*] (LCLS)

NBKI .... Neutral Buffered Potassium Iodide (SAUS)

N Bkpt R ...... National Bankruptcy Register Reports [*United States*] [*A publication*] (DLA)

N Bkpt Reg... National Bankruptcy Register Reports [*United States*] [*A publication*] (DLA)

N Bk R .... National Bankruptcy Register Reports [*United States*] [*A publication*] (DLA)

NbKS .... Kearney State College, Kearney, NE [*Library symbol*] [*Library of Congress*] (LCLS)

NBL .... Brooklyn Law School, Brooklyn, NY [*Library symbol*] [*Library of Congress*] (LCLS)

NbL .... Lincoln City Libraries, Lincoln, NE [*Library symbol*] [*Library of Congress*] (LCLS)

NBL .... National Basketball League (NADA)

NBL .... National Bicycle League (EA)

NBL .... National Book League [*Formerly, NBC*]

NBL .... National Business League [*Washington, DC*] (EA)

NBL .... Naval Biological Laboratory (TIMI)

NBL .... Naval Biosciences Laboratory [*Research center*]

NBL .... Navy Basic Logistic [*Plan*]

NBL .... Nebraska Library Commission, Lincoln, NE [*OCLC symbol*] (OCLC)

NBL .... Neutral Beam Line (SAUS)

NBL .... Neutral Buoyancy Laboratory [*NASA*] (SPST)

NBL .... New Brunswick Laboratory [*Formerly, NBAO*] [*Argonne, IL*] [*Department of Energy*]

NBL .... Night Bombardment - Long Distance [*Air Force*]

NBL .... No Berth List [*Shipping*] (DS)

NBL .... Noble Affiliates, Inc. [*NYSE symbol*] (SPSG)

NBL .... Nocturnal Boundary Layer (SAUS)

NBL .... Norbaska Mines Ltd. [*Toronto Stock Exchange symbol*]

nbl .... Normoblast [*Hematology*]

NBL .... Not Bloody Likely [*British slang*]

NBL .... Nuclear Bomb Line (CINC)

NBla .... Blauvelt Free Library, Blauvelt, NY [*Library symbol*] [*Library of Congress*] (LCLS)

NBLA .... National Businesswomen's Leadership Association [*Defunct*] (EA)

NBlaD .... Dominican College, Blauvelt, NY [*Library symbol*] [*Library of Congress*] (LCLS)

NBLB .... Nebraska Law Bulletin [*A publication*] (DLA)

NBLC .... National Business Law Council [*Formerly, NABLT*] (EA)

Nb-LC .... Nebraska Public Library Commission, Lincoln, NE [*Library symbol*] [*Library of Congress*] (LCLS)

NBLCC .... National Black Lay Catholic Caucus (EA)

NBLD .... Narrowband Linear Detector (MCD)

NblD .... Noble Drilling Corp. [*Associated Press*] (SAG)

NBLE .... Nearly Best Linear Estimator [*Statistics*]

NbleDr .... Noble Drilling Corp. [*Associated Press*] (SAG)

NBLiCH .... Long Island College Hospital, Brooklyn, NY [*Library symbol*] [*Library of Congress*] (LCLS)

NBLiHi .... Long Island Historical Society, Brooklyn, NY [*Library symbol*] [*Library of Congress*] (LCLS)

NBLiU .... Long Island University, Brooklyn, NY [*Library symbol*] [*Library of Congress*] (LCLS)

NbLL .... Lincoln City Libraries, Lincoln, NE [*Library symbol*] [*Library of Congress*] (LCLS)

NbLNP .... United States Department of the Interior, National Park Service, Midwest Archaeological Center, Lincoln, NE [*Library symbol*] [*Library of Congress*] (LCLS)

NbLo .... Loup City Township Library, Loup City, NE [*Library symbol*] [*Library of Congress*] (LCLS)

NBLP .... National Bureau for Lathing and Plastering [*Later, International Institute for Lath and Plaster*] (EA)

NBLR .... National Black Leadership Roundtable (EA)

Nb-LR .... Nebraska Legislative Council, Reference Library, Lincoln, NE [*Library symbol*] [*Library of Congress*] (LCLS)

NBLR .... North Borneo Law Reports [*A publication*] (DLA)

NBLSA .... National/Black Law Student Association (EA)

NbLSc .... Southeast Community College, Lincoln, NE [*Library symbol*] [*Library of Congress*] (LCLS)

NbLU .... Union College, Lincoln, NE [*Library symbol*] [*Library of Congress*] (LCLS)

NbLVA .... United States Veterans Administration Hospital, Lincoln, NE [*Library symbol*] [*Library of Congress*] (LCLS)

NbLW .... Nebraska Wesleyan University, Lincoln, NE [*Library symbol*] [*Library of Congress*] (LCLS)

NBm .... Briarcliff Manor Public Library, Briarcliff Manor, NY [*Library symbol*] [*Library of Congress*] (LCLS)

NbM............ McCook Public Library, McCook, NE [*Library symbol*] [*Library of Congress*] (LCLS)
NBM........... Medical Research Library of Brooklyn, Brooklyn, NY [*Library symbol*] [*Library of Congress*] (LCLS)
NBM........... National Book Month
NBM........... National Building Museum (EA)
NBM........... National Bureau of Metrology
NBM........... Nation's Balanced Target Maturity Fund [*NYSE symbol*] (SAG)
NBM........... Navy Basic Modernization [*Plan*]
NBM........... New Brunswick Museum (SAUS)
NBM........... Nitro-Form Bind Medium [*Analytical biochemistry*]
NBM........... No Bowel Movement [*Medicine*] (DMAA)
NBM........... Normal Bone Marrow [*Medicine*] (DMAA)
NBM........... Normal Bowel Movement [*Medicine*] (DMAA)
NBM........... Nothing by Mouth
NBM........... Nuclear Ballistic Missile
NBM........... Nucleus Basalis Magnocellularis [*Cytology*]
nbM........... Nucleus Basalis of Meynert [*Brain anatomy*]
NBMA......... Non-Broadcast Multiple Access (VLIE)
NBMAIA...... National Broom Manufacturers and Allied Industries Association [*Later, NBMC*] (EA)
NBmB......... Briarcliff College, Briarcliff Manor, NY [*Library symbol*] [*Library of Congress*] (LCLS)
NBMB......... National Bus Military Bureau (EA)
NBMB......... N Binary Digits-M Binary Digits (NITA)
NBMBAA...... National Black MBA [*Master of Business Administration*] Association [*Chicago, IL*] (EA)
NbMC.......... McCook Community College, McCook, NE [*Library symbol*] [*Library of Congress*] (LCLS)
NBMC......... National Bar Mitzvah Club [*Later, AZYF*] (EA)
NBMC......... National Black Media Coalition (EA)
NBMC......... National Black Music Caucus - of the Music Educators National Conference (EA)
NBMC......... National Broom and Mop Council [*Defunct*]
NBMC......... National Businessmen's Council [*Defunct*] (EA)
NBMCM....... Minto Coal Museum, New Brunswick [*Library symbol*] [*National Library of Canada*] (NLC)
NBMCR........ Non-Book Materials Cataloguing Rules (NITA)
NBMDA....... National Building Material Distributors Association (EA)
NBMDR....... National Bone Marrow Donor Registry (EA)
NBME.......... Medgar Evers College of the City University of New York, Brooklyn, NY [*Library symbol*] [*Library of Congress*] (LCLS)
NBME.......... National Board of Medical Examiners (EA)
NBMG......... Navigational Bombing and Missile Guidance (MCD)
NBMGS........ Navigational Bombing and Missile Guidance System (AAG)
NBMHD........ Hopital Docteur Georges - L. Dumont [*Docteur Georges - L. Dumont Hospital*]Moncton, New Brunswick [*Library symbol*] [*National Library of Canada*] (NLC)
NbMi........... Milford Public Library, Milford, NE [*Library symbol*] [*Library of Congress*] (LCLS)
NB Miner Resour Branch Inf Circ... New Brunswick. Mineral Resources Branch Information Circular (SAUS)
NbMiS .... Southeast Community College, Milford, NE [*Library symbol*] [*Library of Congress*] (LCLS)
NBmK .... King's College, Briarcliff Manor, NY [*Library symbol*] [*Library of Congress*] (LCLS)
NbML.......... McCook Public Library, McCook, NE [*Library symbol*] [*Library of Congress*] (LCLS)
NBmIA .... Adirondack Historical Association Museum Library, Blue Mountain Lake, NY [*Library symbol*] [*Library of Congress*] (LCLS)
NBMMH .... Health Sciences Library, The Moncton Hospital, New Brunswick [*Library symbol*] [*National Library of Canada*] (NLC)
NBMO .... Nonbonding Molecular Orbital [*Physical chemistry*]
NBMOA....... National Black McDonald's Operators Association (EA)
NBMOAL...... Atlantic Lottery Corp. [*Societe des Loteries de l'Atlantique*], Moncton, New Brunswick [*Library symbol*] [*National Library of Canada*] (NLC)
NBMOCC..... New Brunswick Community College, Moncton, New Brunswick [*Library symbol*] [*National Library of Canada*] (NLC)
NBMOF .... Fisheries and Oceans Canada [*Peches et Oceans Canada*] Moncton, New Brunswick [*Library symbol*] [*National Library of Canada*] (NLC)
NBMOLM ..... Lutz Mountain Heritage Foundation, Inc., Moncton, New Brunswick [*Library symbol*] [*National Library of Canada*] (NLC)
NBMOM .... Moncton Museum, New Brunswick [*Library symbol*] [*National Library of Canada*] (NLC)
NBMORE...... Canada Department of Regional Industrial Expansion [*Ministere de l'Expansion Industrielle Regionale*] Moncton, New Brunswick [*Library symbol*] [*National Library of Canada*] (NLC)
NBMOTA...... Airworthiness Library, Atlantic Region, Transport Canada [*Bibliotheque de la Navigabilite Aerienne, Region de l'Atlantique, Transports Canada*] Moncton, New Brunswick [*Library symbol*] [*National Library of Canada*] (NLC)
NBMOTAR.... Atlantic Regional Library, Transport Canada [*Bibliotheque Regionale de l'Atlantique, Transports Canada*], Moncton, New Brunswick [*Library symbol*] [*National Library of Canada*] (NLC)
NBMOU....... Universite de Moncton, New Brunswick [*Library symbol*] [*National Library of Canada*] (NLC)
NBMOUA...... Archives Acadiennes, Universite de Moncton, New Brunswick [*Library symbol*] [*National Library of Canada*] (NLC)
NBMOUD...... Bibliotheque de Droit, Universite de Moncton, New Brunswick [*Library symbol*] [*National Library of Canada*] (NLC)
NBMOW...... Albert-Westmorland-Kent Regional Library, Moncton, New Brunswick [*Library symbol*] [*National Library of Canada*] (NLC)
NBMR .... NATO Basic Military Requirements (AABC)

NBMR .... Northern Bengal Mounted Rifles [*British military*] (DMA)
NBMS .... National Bulk Mail System [*Postal Service*]
NBMT .... NATO Basic Military Techniques (NATG)
NBmtT .... Bear Mountain Trailside Museum, Bear Mountain, NY [*Library symbol*] [*Library of Congress*] (LCLS)
NBMUX .... Neub. & Berman Munic. Secs. Trust [*Mutual fund ticker symbol*] (SG)
NBMV&NSL... New Bedford, Marthas Vineyard and Nantucket Steamship Line (SAUS)
Nbn............. Nabonidus (BJA)
NBN .... Narrow Band Nerve [*Neurology*] (DAVI)
NBN .... Narrowband Network
NBN .... Narrowband Noise
NBN .... National Bank of Nigeria Ltd.
NBN .... National Bibliography Number
NBN .... National Black Network [*A radio network*]
NBN .... National Book Number [*British*]
NBN .... Nationality Broadcasting Network [*Cable-television system*]
NBN .... Network for Better Nutrition (EA)
NBN .... Neubabylonisches Namenbuch zu den Geschaeftsurkunden [*A publication*] (BJA)
NBN .... New Bad News (SAUS)
NBN .... New Biological Nomenclature (SAUS)
NBN .... Newborn Nursery [*Medicine*]
NBN .... Newcastle Broadcasting Network [*Australian company broadcasting in Papua New Guinea*] (FEA)
NBN .... Nixdorf Broadband Network [*Communications*] [*British*]
NBN .... North British Airlines Ltd. [*ICAO designator*] (FAAC)
NBN .... Old Manse Library, Newcastle, New Brunswick [*Library symbol*] [*National Library of Canada*] (NLC)
NBNA .... National Bank of North America [*New York*]
NBNA .... National Black Nurses Association (EA)
NBNAM .... Archives of the Miramichi Historical Society, Newcastle, New Brunswick [*Library symbol*] [*National Library of Canada*] (NLC)
NbNb .... Neubabylonisches Namenbuch zu den Geschaeftsurkunden [*A publication*] (BJA)
NbNc .... Nebraska City Public Library, Nebraska City, NE [*Library symbol*] [*Library of Congress*] (LCLS)
NBNC .... New York City Community College of the City University of New York, Brooklyn, NY [*Library symbol*] [*Library of Congress*] (LCLS)
NBNC .... Noted but Not Corrected (MCD)
NbNcM .... Morton-James Public Library, Nebraska City, NE [*Library symbol*] [*Library of Congress*] (LCLS)
NBND .... Northbound (SAUS)
NBNDH .... New Denmark Historical Museum, New Brunswick [*Library symbol*] [*National Library of Canada*] (NLC)
NbNf .... Norfolk Public Library, Norfolk, NE [*Library symbol*] [*Library of Congress*] (LCLS)
NbNfN .... Northeast Technical Community College, Norfork, NE [*Library symbol*] [*Library of Congress*] (LCLS)
NBNM .... Health Sciences Library, Miramichi Hospital, Newcastle, New Brunswick [*Library symbol*] [*National Library of Canada*] (NLC)
NbNp .... North Platte Public Library, North Platte, NE [*Library symbol*] [*Library of Congress*] (LCLS)
NbNpM .... Mid-Plains Community College, North Platte, NE [*Library symbol*] [*Library of Congress*] (LCLS)
NBNR .... National Bankruptcy News and Reports [*A publication*] (DLA)
NBN Rep..... National Bankruptcy News and Reports [*A publication*] (DLA)
NBNS .... NetBIOS Name Service (SAUS)
NBo............. Bolivar Free Library, Bolivar, NY [*Library symbol*] [*Library of Congress*] (LCLS)
NBO .... Nairobi [*Kenya*] [*Airport symbol*] (OAG)
NBO .... National Bank of Oman Ltd. SAO (EY)
NBO .... Navy Bureau of Ordnance [*Obsolete*]
NBO .... Nebo Air Co. Ltd. [*Former USSR*] [*FAA designator*] (FAAC)
NBO .... Network Buildout (IEEE)
NBO .... Network Business Opportunity (VLIE)
NBO .... Network Byte Order (SAUS)
NBO .... New Business Opportunity (TIMI)
NBO .... Nonbed Occupancy (AAMN)
NBO .... Nonbonding Orbital (SAUS)
NBO .... Nonbridging Oxygen [*Materials science*]
NBO .... Nordiska Kooperativa och Allmannyttiga Bostadsforetags Organisation [*Organization of Cooperative and Non-Profit Making Housing Enterprises in the Nordic Countries*] (EAIO)
NBO .... Normal-Branch Oscillation [*Astronomy*]
NBO .... Norsar Array Site 01B00 [*Norway*] [*Seismograph station code, US Geological Survey*] (SEIS)
NbO .... Omaha Public Library, Omaha, NE [*Library symbol*] [*Library of Congress*] (LCLS)
NBO .... Omaha Public Library, Omaha, NE [*OCLC symbol*] (OCLC)
NBO .... Oromocto Public Library, New Brunswick [*Library symbol*] [*National Library of Canada*] (NLC)
NBOA .... National Ballroom Operators Association [*Later, National Ballroom and Entertainment Association*]
NBOA .... National Business Owners Association (EA)
NbOB .... Boys Town Center for the Study of Youth Development, Omaha, NE [*Library symbol*] [*Library of Congress*] (LCLS)
NbOC .... Creighton University, Omaha, NE [*Library symbol*] [*Library of Congress*] (LCLS)
NBOC .... Network Building Out Capacitor [*Telecommunications*] (TEL)
NBOC .... Newman Communications Corp. (SAUS)
NBOC .... Northern Bank of Commerce [*NASDAQ symbol*] (SAG)
NBOC .... Northern Bk Comm Ore [*NASDAQ symbol*] (TTSB)
NBOC .... Northwest Bank of Commerce [*Oregon*] [*NASDAQ symbol*] (SAG)

NbOC-A .... Creighton University, Alumni Library, Omaha, NE [*Library symbol*] [*Library of Congress*] (LCLS)

NbOC-D .... Creighton University, School of Dentistry, Omaha, NE [*Library symbol*] [*Library of Congress*] (LCLS)

NbOC-H .... Creighton University, Health Sciences Library, Omaha, NE [*Library symbol*] [*Library of Congress*] (LCLS)

NbOC-L .... Creighton University, School of Law, Omaha, NE [*Library symbol*] [*Library of Congress*] (LCLS)

NbOC-M .... Creighton University, School of Medicine and School of Pharmacy, Omaha, NE [*Library symbol*] [*Library of Congress*] (LCLS)

NbOD .... Duchesne College, Omaha, NE [*Library symbol*] [*Library of Congress*] (LCLS)

NbOg .... Goodall City Library, Ogallala, NE [*Library symbol*] [*Library of Congress*] (LCLS)

NbOGS .... Church of Jesus Christ of Latter-Day Saints, Genealogical Society Library, OmahaBranch, Omaha, NE [*Library symbol*] [*Library of Congress*] (LCLS)

NBoh .... Connetquot Public Library, Bohemia, NY [*Library symbol*] [*Library of Congress*] (LCLS)

NBohCH ...... Connetquot High School, Bohemia, NY [*Library symbol*] [*Library of Congress*] (LCLS)

NbOJ .... Joslyn Art Museum, Omaha, NE [*Library symbol*] [*Library of Congress*] (LCLS)

NBoL .... Bolivar Free Library, Bolivar, NY [*Library symbol*] [*Library of Congress*] (LCLS)

NBolS .... Marcella Sembrich Memorial Studio, Bolton Landing, NY [*Library symbol*] [*Library of Congress*] (LCLS)

N-BOMB ...... Neutron Bomb (GOBB)

N (Bomb) .... Neutron Bomb

N-Bomb ...... Nuclear Bomb (SAUS)

NbOMC .... Metropolitan Technical Community College, Omaha, NE [*Library symbol*] [*Library of Congress*] (LCLS)

NBOME .... National Board of Osteopathic Medical Examiners (EA)

NbONPS ...... United States National Park Service, Midwest Regional Office, Omaha, NE [*Library symbol*] [*Library of Congress*] (LCLS)

NbOP .... Presbyterian Theological Seminary, Omaha, NE [*Library symbol*] [*Library of Congress*] (LCLS)

NBOR .... Network Building Out Resistor [*Telecommunications*] (TEL)

NBOR .... Nucleus of Basal Optic Root [*Neuroanatomy*]

NbOsc .... Osceola Public Library, Osceola, NE [*Library symbol*] [*Library of Congress*] (LCLS)

NBOT .... National Board of Orthopaedic Technologists [*British*] (DAVI)

NbOU .... University of Nebraska at Omaha, Omaha, NE [*Library symbol*] [*Library of Congress*] (LCLS)

NBoU-E .... State University of New York at Buffalo, Educational Opportunity Center (SAUS)

NBoU-RP .... State University of New York at Buffalo, Roswell Park Memorial Institute (SAUS)

NbOV .... United States Veterans Administration Hospital, Omaha, NE [*Library symbol*] [*Library of Congress*] (LCLS)

NbOW .... Westside Community Schools, Omaha, NE [*Library symbol*] [*Library of Congress*] (LCLS)

NBp .... Bayport-Blue Point Public Library, Blue Point, NY [*Library symbol*] [*Library of Congress*] (LCLS)

NBP .... Name Binding Protocol [*Computer science*]

NBP .... National Battlefield Park (BARN)

NBP .... National Booster Program (AAG)

NBP .... National Braille Press (EA)

NBP .... National Business Publications [*Later, ABP*] (EA)

NBP .... Needle Biopsy of Prostate [*Medicine*] (MELL)

NBP .... Needs-Based Payment [*Job Training and Partnership Act*] (OICC)

NBP .... Net Biome Production (SAUS)

NBP .... Neutral Bitter Principle [*Pharmacy*]

NBP .... New Birth Party [*Cyprus*] [*Political party*]

NBP .... New Brooklyn Philharmonic (SAUS)

NBP .... (Nitrobenzyl)pyridine [*Organic chemistry*]

NBP .... No Baseband Processing (ACAE)

NBP .... NonBacterial Prostatis [*Medicine*]

NBP .... Non-invasive Blood Pressure (SAUS)

NBP .... Normal Boiling Point

NBP .... Northern Border Partners Ltd. [*NYSE symbol*] (SPSG)

NBP .... Nucleic Acid Binding Protein [*Biochemistry*]

NBP .... Nude Beach Pest (SAUS)

NBP .... Peru State College Library, Peru, NE [*OCLC symbol*] (OCLC)

NBP .... Pratt Institute, Brooklyn, NY [*Library symbol*] [*Library of Congress*] (LCLS)

NBPA .... National Back Pain Association (EAIO)

NBPA .... National Bark Producers Association (EA)

NBPA .... National Basketball Players Association (EA)

NBPA .... National Beverage Packaging Association (EA)

NBPA .... National Black People's Assembly (EA)

NBPA .... National Black Police Association (EA)

NBPA .... National Building Products Association [*Defunct*] (EA)

NBPA .... Navy Board for Production Awards

NBPA .... New Brunswick Potato Agency (SAUS)

NBPA .... Northeastern Bancorp (SAUS)

NBPASV ...... Southern Victoria Historical Society, Perth-Andover, New Brunswick [*Library symbol*] [*National Library of Canada*] (NLC)

NBPB .... National Biotechnology Policy Board

NBPC .... National Black Political Convention [*1972*]

NBPC .... National Black Programming Consortium (EA)

NBPC .... National Border Patrol Council (EA)

NBPC .... Neutral Beam Power Conversion (SAUS)

NBPDW .... National Brotherhood of Packinghouse and Dairy Workers [*Formerly, NBPW*] (EA)

NBPE .... National Board of Podiatry Examiners

NBPE .... National Board of Polygraph Examiners [*Later, APA*] (EA)

NBPerS .... Peru State College, Peru, NE [*Library symbol*] [*Library of Congress*] (LCLS)

NBPHA .... N-Benzoyl(phenyl)hydroxylamine [*Organic chemistry*]

NBPI .... National Board for Prices and Incomes [*British*]

NBPI .... Newspaper Benevolent and Provident Institution [*British*] (DGA)

NBPIW .... National Brotherhood of Packinghouse and Industrial Workers (EA)

NbPl .... Plattsmouth Public Library, Plattsmouth, NE [*Library symbol*] [*Library of Congress*] (LCLS)

NBPM .... Narrowband Phase Modulation (MCD)

NBPM .... Network-Based Project Management (PDAA)

NBPMC .... National Bureau of Professional Management Consultants (NTPA)

NBPME .... National Board of Podiatric Medical Examiners (EA)

NBPNPA .... National Board of Pediatric Nurse Practitioners and Associates [*Later, NCBPNP/N*] (EA)

NBPO .... NATO Bullpup Production Organization [*Missiles*] (NATG)

NBPol .... Polytechnic Institute of New York, Brooklyn, NY [*Library symbol*] [*Library of Congress*] (LCLS)

NBPol-G ...... Polytechnic Institute of New York, Long Island Graduate Center, Farmingdale, NY [*Library symbol*] [*Library of Congress*] (LCLS)

NBpP .... Bayport-Blue Point Public Library, Blue Point, NY [*Library symbol*] [*Library of Congress*] (LCLS)

NBPP .... National Black Political Party

NBPRP .... National Board for the Promotion of Rifle Practice (EA)

NBPRS .... National Black Public Relations Society (NTPA)

NBPS .... National Backgammon Players Society [*British*] (DBA)

NBPS .... Neutral Beam Power Systems (SAUS)

NBPTE .... National Board of Physical Therapy Examiners (EA)

NBPTS .... National Board for Professional Teaching Standards (EA)

NBPu .... Brooklyn Public Library, Brooklyn, NY [*Library symbol*] [*Library of Congress*] (LCLS)

NBPW .... National Brotherhood of Packinghouse Workers [*Later, NBPDW*]

NBQ .... Nitro(benzothiazolo)quinolinium Perchlorate [*Antineoplastic drug*]

NBQ .... No Broken Quantities (SAUS)

NBR .... Nabors Industries, Inc. [*AMEX symbol*] (SPSG)

NBR .... Narrowband Radiated (IEEE)

NBR .... National Bankruptcy Register Reports [*United States*] [*A publication*] (DLA)

NBR .... National Board of Review of Motion Pictures

NBR .... National Buildings Record [*British*]

NBR .... Neighborhood Business Revitalization [*Program*]

NBR .... Net Borrowing Requirement [*Banking*] (MHDW)

NBR .... New Beginnings Resources [*Vancouver Stock Exchange symbol*]

NBR .... New Brunswick Reports [*Maritime Law Book Co. Ltd.*] [*Canada*] [*Information service or system*] [*A publication*] (CRD)

NBR .... [*The*] Nightly Business Reports [*Television program*]

NBR .... Nitrile Based Rubber (SAUS)

NBR .... Nitrile Butadiene-Acrylonitrile Rubber (AAEL)

NBR .... Nitrile Butadiene Rubber (SAUS)

NBR .... Nonborrowed Reserve [*Banking*]

NBR .... Nonbreathing

NBR .... North British Railway

NBR .... Nuclear Boiler Rated (NRCH)

NBR .... Null Balance Recorder

nbr .... Number (ELAL)

NBR .... Number (KSC)

NBR .... Number of Bids Received [*DoD*]

NBR .... Nursing Boards Review [*Course*] [*American Journal of Nursing*]

NBR 2d .... New Brunswick Reports, Second Series [*A publication*] (DLA)

NBRA .... National Barrel Racing Association

NBRA .... National Basketball Referees Association (NTPA)

NBRA .... National Brain Research Association (EA)

NbRal .... Ralston Public Library, Ralston, NE [*Library symbol*] [*Library of Congress*] (LCLS)

NBR All .... Allen's New Brunswick Reports [*Canada*] [*A publication*] (DLA)

NBR Ber ...... Berton's New Brunswick Reports [*A publication*] (DLA)

NBRC .... National Black Republican Council (EA)

NBRC .... National Board for Respiratory Care (EA)

NBRCA .... Atlantic Institution, Correctional Service Canada [*Etablissement Atlantique, Service Correctionnel Canada*], Renous, New Brunswick [*Library symbol*] [*National Library of Canada*] (BIB)

NBR Carl .... Carleton's New Brunswick Reports [*A publication*] (DLA)

NBR Chip .... Chipman's New Brunswick Reports [*1825-35*] [*A publication*] (DLA)

NbRcW .... Willa Cather Pioneer Memorial, Red Cloud, NE [*Library symbol*] [*Library of Congress*] (LCLS)

NBre .... Brewster Public Library, Brewster, NY [*Library symbol*] [*Library of Congress*] (LCLS)

NBREH .... L'Eglise Historique St-Henri-De-Barachois, Robichaud, New Brunswick [*Library symbol*] [*National Library of Canada*] (NLC)

NBren .... Brentwood Public Library, Brentwood, NY [*Library symbol*] [*Library of Congress*] (LCLS)

NBrenEJ ...... East Junior High School, Brentwood, NY [*Library symbol*] [*Library of Congress*] (LCLS)

NBrenIMC .... District Instructional Media Center, Brentwood, NY [*Library symbol*] [*Library of Congress*] (LCLS)

NBrenSJ ...... Saint Joseph's College, Brentwood, NY [*Library symbol*] [*Library of Congress*] (LCLS)

NBrenST ...... Saint Josephs College, Brentwood (SAUS)

NB Rep .... New Brunswick Reports [*A publication*] (DLA)

NB Rev Stat... New Brunswick Revised Statutes [*Canada*] [*A publication*] (DLA)

NBRF .... National Biomedical Research Foundation [*Georgetown University*] [*Research center*]

NBRG .... National Basic Reference Graphic (MCD)

NBR Han...... Hannay's New Brunswick Reports [*12, 13 New Brunswick*] [*A publication*] (DLA)

NBri .... Bay Shore-Brightwaters Public Library, Brightwaters, NY [*Library symbol*] [*Library of Congress*] (LCLS)

NBrih .... Hampton Library, Bridgehampton, NY [*Library symbol*] [*Library of Congress*] (LCLS)

NBR Kerr.... Kerr's New Brunswick Reports [*A publication*] (DLA)

NBRL .... Naval Biomedical Research Laboratory

NBRL .... Naval Blood Research Laboratory [*Bureau of Medicine*]

NBRMP .... National Board of Review of Motion Pictures (EA)

NBRN.......... Nestart Library, Richibucto, New Brunswick [*Library symbol*] [*National Library of Canada*] (NLC)

NBrockU ...... State University of New York, College at Brockport, Brockport, NY [*Library symbol*] [*Library of Congress*] (LCLS)

NBron .... Bronxville Public Library, Bronxville, NY [*Library symbol*] [*Library of Congress*] (LCLS)

NBronC .... Concordia College, Bronxville, NY [*Library symbol*] [*Library of Congress*] (LCLS)

NBronSL ...... Sarah Lawrence College, Bronxville, NY [*Library symbol*] [*Library of Congress*] (LCLS)

NBroo .... Brookhaven Free Library, Brookhaven, NY [*Library symbol*] [*Library of Congress*] (LCLS)

NBrooHS..... Bellport Senior High School, Brookhaven, NY [*Library symbol*] [*Library of Congress*] (LCLS)

NBRP & B.... Pugsley and Burbridge's New Brunswick Reports [*A publication*] (DLA)

NBRP & T.... Pugsley and Trueman's New Brunswick Reports [*A publication*] (DLA)

NBRPC........ New Brunswick Research and Productivity Council

NBR Pug...... Pugsley's New Brunswick Reports [*A publication*] (DLA)

NBR Pugs... Pugsley's New Brunswick Reports [*1876-93*] [*Canada*] [*A publication*] (DLA)

NBRS .... Next Basic Records System [*Computer science*] (VLIE)

NBRSA........ National Bench Rest Shooters Association (EA)

NBRT .... National Board for Respiratory Therapy [*Formerly, ARIT*] [*Later, NBRC*] (EA)

NBR Tru...... Trueman's New Brunswick Reports [*A publication*] (DLA)

N Bruns ...... New Brunswick Reports [*A publication*] (DLA)

NBrunS .... New Brunswick Scientific Co., Inc. [*Associated Press*] (SAG)

NbRVt.......... Neubabylonische Rechts- und Verwaltungstexte [*A publication*] (BJA)

NbRVu......... Neubabylonische Rechts- und Verwaltungsurkunden Uebersetzt und Erlaeutert [*A publication*] (BJA)

NBS .... Bureau of Ships Publications [*Obsolete*] [*Navy*]

NBS .... Kekaha, Kauai, HI [*Location identifier*] [*FAA*] (FAAL)

NBS .... Narrowband Search (MCD)

NBS .... Narrowband Socket (SAUS)

NBS .... Narrow Beam Sounder (SAUS)

NBS .... National Australia Bank. Monthly Summary [*A publication*] (ADA)

NBS .... National Bakery School [*British*] (BI)

NBS .... National Battlefield Site (BARN)

NBS .... National Biological Survey [*Department of the Interior*]

NBS .... National Bird-Feeding Society (EA)

NBS .... National Blood Service (WDAA)

NBS .... National Board for Nursing, midwifery and health visiting (SAUS)

NBS .... National Bookkeepers' Society (EA)

NBS .... National Book Sale [*British*]

NBS .... National Bridal Service (EA)

NBS .... National Broadcasting Service [*Trinidad and Tobago*] (EY)

NBS .... National Broadcasting Service [*New Zealand*]

NBS .... National Broadcasting System

NBS .... National Brotherhood of Skiers (EA)

NBS .... National Bureau of Standards [*Department of Commerce*] [*Later, NIST*]

NBS .... National Bureau of Standards, Gaithersburg, MD [*OCLC symbol*] (OCLC)

NBS .... National Business Systems, Inc. [*Toronto Stock Exchange symbol*]

NBS .... National Button Society (EA)

NBS .... Natural Black Slate (MSA)

NBS .... Navigational Bombing System [*British military*] (DMA)

NBS .... Navy Broadcasting Service (ACAE)

NBS .... N-Bromosuccinimide [*Organic chemistry*]

NBS .... Needs-Based Staffing (ADA)

NBS .... Neighborhood Bible Studies (EA)

NBS .... Netherland Benevolent Society of New York [*Later, Netherlands-America CommunityAssociation*] (EA)

NBS .... Neurobehavioral Scale

NBS .... Neutral Buoyancy Simulator [*Navy*] (MCD)

NBS .... Nevoid Basal Cell Carcinoma Syndrome [*Oncology*] (DMAA)

NBS .... New British Standard [*Imperial wire gauge*]

NBS .... New Brunswick Scientific Co., Inc.

NBS .... Newcastle Business School [*British*] (ODBW)

NBS .... Nickel-Bonded Steel (SAUS)

NBS .... Night Bombardment - Short Distance [*Air Force*]

NBS .... Nijmegen Breakage Syndrome [*Medicine*] (DMAA)

NBS .... Nile Blue Sulfate (SAUS)

NBS .... Nimbus Aviation [*British*] [*ICAO designator*] (FAAC)

NBS .... No Bacteria Seen [*Clinical microbiology*]

NBS .... Nonbaseline Software Library (MCD)

NBS .... Nordiska Byggforskningsorgans Samarbetsgrupp [*Nordic Building Research Cooperation Group*] [*Iceland*] (EAIO)

NBS .... Normal Blood Serum (MAE)

NBS .... Normal Bowel Sounds [*Gastroenterology*] (DAVI)

NBS .... Normal Breath Sounds (SAUS)

NBS .... Normal Burm Serum (SAUS)

NBS .... Normal Burro Serum [*Biochemistry*] (DAVI)

NBS .... Normandy Base Section [*World War II*]

NBS .... Nothing Before Something [*Library cataloguing*] (DGA)

NBS .... Nuclear Backscattering Spectroscopy (EDCT)

NBS .... Nucleotide Binding Site [*Genetics*]

NBS .... Numeric Backspace (SAUS)

NBS .... Numeric Backspace Character [*Computer science*]

NBS .... Numismatic Bibliomania Society (EA)

NBS .... Saint John Regional Library, New Brunswick [*Library symbol*] [*National Library of Canada*] (NLC)

NbS............. Scottsbluff Public Library, Scottsbluff, NE [*Library symbol*] [*Library of Congress*] (LCLS)

NBSA .... National Bakery Suppliers Association (EA)

NBS-A .... National Bureau of Standards - Atomic (SAA)

NBSA .... Normalized Body Surface Area (SAUS)

NBSA .... Nurses' Board of South Australia

NBSAB .... Fort Beausejour Museum, Sackville, New Brunswick [*Library symbol*] [*National Library of Canada*] (NLC)

NBSAC .... National Boating Safety Advisory Council [*Department of Transportation*] [*Washington, DC*] (EGAO)

NBSACW...... Canadian Wildlife Service, Environment Canada [*Service Canadien de la Faune, Environnement Canada*] Sackville, New Brunswick [*Library symbol*] [*National Library of Canada*] (NLC)

NBSAE .... Norwegian-British-Swedish Antarctic Expedition [*1949-52*]

NBSAM .... Mount Allison University, Sackville, New Brunswick [*Library symbol*] [*National Library of Canada*] (NLC)

NBSAP .... National Biodiversity Strategy and Action Plan (SAUS)

NBSARM ...... Ross Memorial Library, St. Andrews, New Brunswick [*Library symbol*] [*National Library of Canada*] (BIB)

NBSBL .... National Bureau of Standards Boulder Laboratories

NBSC .... Health Sciences Library, Centracare Saint John, Inc., New Brunswick [*Library symbol*] [*National Library of Canada*] (NLC)

NBSC .... National Bank of South Carolina (EFIS)

NBSC .... National Black Sisters' Conference (EA)

NBSC .... New Brunswick Safety Council (SAUS)

NBSC .... New Brunswick Scientific Co., Inc. [*NASDAQ symbol*] (NQ)

NBSC .... Nitrobenzenesulfenyl Chloride [*Organic chemistry*]

NBSCA .... National Beauty Salon Chain Association [*Later, ICSA*] (EA)

NBSCCST .... National Bureau of Standards Center for Computer Sciences and Technology (DIT)

NBSCETT .... New Brunswick Society of Certified Engineering Technicians and Technologists (SAUS)

NBSCM .... Centre Marin, Shippagan, New Brunswick [*Library symbol*] [*National Library of Canada*] (NLC)

NBSCU......... Centre Universitaire de Shippagan, New Brunswick [*Library symbol*] [*National Library of Canada*] (NLC)

NBSD .... Night Bombardment - Short Distance [*Air Force*] (IEEE)

NBSDI.......... National Brands Soft Drinks Institute (EA)

NBsdQ .... Queensborough Community College of the City University of New York, Bayside, NY [*Library symbol*] [*Library of Congress*] (LCLS)

NbSe.......... Seward Public Library, Seward, NE [*Library symbol*] [*Library of Congress*] (LCLS)

NbSeT.......... Concordia Teachers College, Seward, NE [*Library symbol*] [*Library of Congress*] (LCLS)

NBSF .... Nitrobenzenesulfonyl Fluoride [*Organic chemistry*]

NBSFS .... National Bureau of Standards Frequency Standard (IEEE)

NBSG .... National Biotherapy Study Group (EA)

NbSHS......... Hiram Scott College, Scottsbluff, NE [*Library symbol*] [*Library of Congress*] [*Obsolete*] (LCLS)

NBSI .... North Bancshares, Inc. [*NASDAQ symbol*] (SAG)

NbSi.......... Sidney Public Library, Sidney, NE [*Library symbol*] [*Library of Congress*] (LCLS)

NBSIR.......... National Bureau of Standards Interagency Reports

NBSL .... New York City School Library System, Brooklyn, NY [*Library symbol*] [*Library of Congress*] (LCLS)

NBSLD .... National Bureau of Standards Load Determination [*Computer program*]

NBSM .... New Brunswick Museum, Saint John, New Brunswick [*Library symbol*] [*National Library of Canada*] (NLC)

NBSMA .... National Boot and Shoe Manufacturers' Association [*Later, FIA*]

NbSN.......... Nebraska Western College, Scottsbluff, NE [*Library symbol*] [*Library of Congress*] (LCLS)

NBSP .... Non-Breaking Space (VLIE)

NBSPA .... National Bark and Soil Producers Association (NTPA)

NBSQH......... Quaco Historical and Library Society, St. Martins, New Brunswick [*Library symbol*] [*National Library of Canada*] (NLC)

NBSR .... National Bureau of Standards Reactor

NBSRH........ Health Sciences Library, Saint John Regional Hospital [*Bibliotheque des Sciences de la Sante, Hopital Regional de Saint-Jean*], New Brunswick [*Library symbol*] [*National Library of Canada*] (NLC)

NBSS .... Narrowband Switching System (SAUS)

NBSS .... National Bank Surveillance System

NBSS .... National British Softbill Society (BI)

NBSS .... Naval Beach Signal Section

NBsSH .... Southside Hospital, Bay Shore, NY [*Library symbol*] [*Library of Congress*] (LCLS)

NBS-SIS ...... NBS-Standard Information Services (NITA)

NBSSSC....... St. Croix Public Library, St. Stephen, New Brunswick [*Library symbol*] [*National Library of Canada*] (NLC)

NBSSX........ Neub. & Berman Focus Fund [*Mutual fund ticker symbol*] (SG)

NBST .... Narrow Band Secure Terminal (ACAE)

NBST .... Narrowband Subscriber Terminal (CET)

NBST .... National Board for Science and Technology [*Ireland*] (PDAA)

NBST .... [*The*] New Braunfels & Servtex Railroad, Inc. [*AAR code*]

NbSt.......... Nimbostratus [*Cloud*] [*Meteorology*] (AIA)

NBSTAC...... St. Andrews Campus, New Brunswick Community College [*Library symbol*] [*National Library of Canada*] (BIB)
NBS/TAD...... National Bureau of Standards/Technical Analysis Division (NOAA)
NB Stat New Brunswick Statutes [*Canada*] [*A publication*] (DLA)
NBStF.......... Saint Francis College, Brooklyn, NY [*Library symbol*] [*Library of Congress*] (LCLS)
NBSTIM....... Le Musee de St-Isidore, Inc., New Brunswick [*Library symbol*] [*National Library of Canada*] (NLC)
NBStJC....... Saint Joseph's College, Brooklyn, NY [*Library symbol*] [*Library of Congress*] (LCLS)
NBS TN........ United States Department of Commerce. National Bureau of Standards. Technial Notes (SAUS)
NbSu........... Superior Carnegie Library, Superior, NE [*Library symbol*] [*Library of Congress*] (LCLS)
NBSU.......... University of New Brunswick, Saint John, New Brunswick [*Library symbol*] [*National Library of Canada*] (NLC)
NBSUH........ Kings County Historical Society, Sussex, New Brunswick [*Library symbol*] [*National Library of Canada*] (NLC)
NBSU-M....... State University of New York at Brooklyn, Medical Research Library, Brooklyn, NY [*Library symbol*] [*Library of Congress*] (LCLS)
NBSUS........ Sussex Public Library, New Brunswick [*Library symbol*] [*National Library of Canada*] (NLC)
NBSV .... Narrowband Secure Voice System [*Army*] (CAAL)
NBSVS........ Narrowband Secure Voice System [*Army*] (MCD)
NBSVS........ Saint John Vocational School, New Brunswick [*Library symbol*] [*National Library of Canada*] (NLC)
NBT............. Brunswick, ME [*Location identifier*] [*FAA*] (FAAL)
NBT............. Nagoya Bumpy Torus [*Military*]
NBT............. Narrow-Beam Transducer [*National Ocean Survey*]
NBT............. National Bancshares Corp. of Texas [*AMEX symbol*] (SAG)
NBT............. Navigator Bombardier Training [*Air Force*] (AFM)
NBT............. Negative Balance Test (IAA)
NBT............. Netherlands Board of Tourism (EA)
NBT............. Networks for Biotechnology
NBT............. Neurobiotin [*Biochemical labelling compound*]
NBT............. Neutral Buoyancy Trainer [*Navy*] (MCD)
NBT............. New Brunswick Telephone Co. Ltd. [*Toronto Stock Exchange symbol*]
NBT............. Nimbus Beacon Transmitter
NBT............. Nitro Blue Tetrazolium (SAUS)
NBT............. Nitroblue Tetrazolium [*A stain*] [*Hematology*]
NBT............. Non-Selective Bottom-to-Top (SAUS)
NBT............. Normal Breast Tissue [*Medicine*] (DB)
NBT............. Northern Ballet Theatre [*England*]
NBT............. Null-Balance Transmissometer (IEEE)
NBTA .... National Basketball Trainers Association (EA)
NBTA .... National Baton Twirling Association (EA)
NBTA .... National Board of Trial Advocacy (EA)
NBTA .... National Business Teachers Association (NADA)
NBTA .... National Business Travel Association (EA)
NBTA .... National Bus Traffic Association (EA)
NBTB .... NBT Bancorp. [*NASDAQ symbol*] (SAG)
NBT Bcp ...... NBT Bancorp [*Associated Press*] (SAG)
NBTC .... New Brands and Their Companies [*Formerly, NTN*] [*A publication*]
NBTC .... New Brunswick Teachers College
NBTD .... Nothing Better To Do (SAUS)
NBT-DF .... Nitroblue Tetrazolium Diformazan [*A stain*] [*Hematology*]
NBTDR........ Narrowband Time Domain Reflectometry (MCD)
NBTE.......... Nonbacterial Thrombotic Endocarditis [*Cardiology*]
NbTe.......... Tekamah Carnegie Public Library, Tekamah, NE [*Library symbol*] [*Library of Congress*] (LCLS)
NBTF.......... National Brain Tumor Foundation (EA)
NBTF.......... National Building Trades Federation [*A union*] [*British*]
NBTF.......... Neutral Beam Test Facility (SAUS)
NBTH .... Bibliotheque Medicale, Hotel-Dieu Saint-Joseph-De-Tracadie, New Brunswick [*Library symbol*] [*National Library of Canada*] (BIB)
NbTi........... Niobium Titanium (SAUS)
NBTI........... Nitrobenzylthioinosine [*Organic chemistry*]
NBTL.......... National Battery Test Laboratory [*Department of Energy*]
NBTL.......... Naval Boiler and Turbine Laboratory
NBTM.......... Le Musee Historique de Tracadie, New Brunswick [*Library symbol*] [*National Library of Canada*] (NLC)
NBT Meter... Null-Balance Transmission Meter (SAUS)
NBTNF........ Newborn, Term, Normal, Female [*Obstetrics*]
NBTNM........ Newborn, Term, Normal, Male [*Obstetrics*]
NBTPI .... National Book Trade Provident Institution [*British*] (DGA)
NBTPS......... National Book Trade Provident Society [*British*] (DI)
NBTR .... Narrowband Tape Recorder
NBTS .... National Blood Transfusion Service
NBTS .... Neutral Beam Test Stand (SAUS)
NBTS .... New Boston Tracking Station (SAA)
NBTS .... New Brunswick Theological Seminary [*New Jersey*]
NBTS .... Northern Baptist Theological Seminary [*Lombard, IL*]
NBTT........... Net Barter Terms of Trade
NBTY .... NBTY, Inc. [*NASDAQ symbol*] (SAG)
NBu............ Buffalo and Erie County Public Library, Buffalo, NY [*Library symbol*] [*Library of Congress*] (LCLS)
NBU .... Glenview, IL [*Location identifier*] [*FAA*] (FAAL)
NBU .... Natural Business Unit (VLIE)
NBU .... NBU Mines Ltd. [*Toronto Stock Exchange symbol*]
nbu .... Nebraska [*MARC country of publication code*] [*Library of Congress*] (LCCP)
NBU .... Net Built Units (TIMI)
NBU .... New Better than Used [*Statistics*]

NBU .... Nordiska Bankmannaunionen [*Confederation of Nordic Bank Employees' Unions*] (EA)
NBU .... University of Nebraska at Omaha, Omaha, NE [*OCLC symbol*] (OCLC)
NbU .... University of Nebraska, Lincoln, NE [*Library symbol*] [*Library of Congress*] (LCLS)
NBuA .... Allied Corp., Specialty Chemicals Division, Buffalo, NY [*Library symbol*] [*Library of Congress*] (LCLS)
NbU-A .... University of Nebraska, Agriculture Library, Lincoln, NE [*Library symbol*] [*Library of Congress*] (LCLS)
NBuAA .... Acres American, Inc., Buffalo, NY [*Library symbol*] [*Library of Congress*] (LCLS)
NBuACE .... United States Army, Corps of Engineers, Buffalo, NY [*Library symbol*] [*Library of Congress*] (LCLS)
NBuAK .... Albright-Knox Art Gallery Library, Buffalo Fine Arts Academy, Buffalo, NY [*Library symbol*] [*Library of Congress*] (LCLS)
NBuAn .... Andco, Inc., Buffalo, NY [*Library symbol*] [*Library of Congress*] (LCLS)
NBuB .... Buffalo Society of Natural Sciences, Buffalo Museum of Science, Buffalo, NY [*Library symbol*] [*Library of Congress*] (LCLS)
NBuBA .... Bell Aerosystems Co., Buffalo, NY [*Library symbol*] [*Library of Congress*] (LCLS)
NBuBE .... Buffalo and Erie County Public Library, Buffalo, NY [*Library symbol*] [*Library of Congress*] (LCLS)
NBuBLH ...... Bry-Lin Hospital, Buffalo, NY [*Library symbol*] [*Library of Congress*] (LCLS)
NBuBM .... Brystol-Myers Pharmaceuticals R & D, Buffalo, NY [*Library symbol*] [*Library of Congress*] (LCLS)
NBuBO .... Buffalo Organization for Social and Technological Innovation, Inc. (BOSTI), Buffalo, NY [*Library symbol*] [*Library of Congress*] (LCLS)
NBuBR .... Biblial Research Institute, Inc., Buffalo, NY [*Library symbol*] [*Library of Congress*] (LCLS)
NBuC .... State University of New York, College at Buffalo, Buffalo, NY [*Library symbol*] [*Library of Congress*] (LCLS)
NBuCA .... Cornell Aeronautical Laboratory, Buffalo, NY [*Library symbol*] [*Library of Congress*] (LCLS)
NBuCBL ...... Christel, Bean & Linihan, Buffalo, NY [*Library symbol*] [*Library of Congress*] (LCLS)
NBuCC .... Canisius College, Buffalo, NY [*Library symbol*] [*Library of Congress*] (LCLS)
NBuCEC ...... CECOS International, Buffalo, NY [*Library symbol*] [*Library of Congress*] (LCLS)
NBuCH .... Children's Hospital, Buffalo, NY [*Library symbol*] [*Library of Congress*] (LCLS)
NBuCo .... Buffalo Color Corp., Buffalo, NY [*Library symbol*] [*Library of Congress*] (LCLS)
NBuCoH .... Buffalo Columbus Hospital, Buffalo, NY [*Library symbol*] [*Library of Congress*] (LCLS)
NBuD .... D'Youville College, Buffalo, NY [*Library symbol*] [*Library of Congress*] (LCLS)
NBuDa .... Daemen College, Buffalo, NY [*Library symbol*] [*Library of Congress*] (LCLS)
NBuDD .... DeLancey Divinity School, Buffalo, NY [*Library symbol*] [*Library of Congress*] [*Obsolete*] (LCLS)
NBuDY .... E. I. Du Pont de Nemours & Co., Yerkes Research Laboratory, Buffalo, NY [*Library symbol*] [*Library of Congress*] (LCLS)
NBUE .... New Better than Used in Expectation [*Statistics*]
NBuEC .... Erie Community College-North, Buffalo, NY [*Library symbol*] [*Library of Congress*] (LCLS)
NBuEC-C ...... Erie Community College-North, City Campus, Buffalo, NY [*Library symbol*] [*Library of Congress*] (LCLS)
NBuEC-U ...... Erie Community College-North, Urban Center, Buffalo, NY [*Library symbol*] [*Library of Congress*] (LCLS)
NBuEE .... Ecology and Environment, Inc., Buffalo, NY [*Library symbol*] [*Library of Congress*] (LCLS)
NBuEMH ...... Edward J. Meyer Memorial Hospital Medical Library, Buffalo, NY [*Library symbol*] [*Library of Congress*] (LCLS)
NBuF .... Falcon Research & Development, Inc., Buffalo, NY [*Library symbol*] [*Library of Congress*] (LCLS)
NBUF .... National Black United Front (EA)
NBUF .... National Black United Fund (EA)
NBuG .... Grosvenor Reference Division, Buffalo and Erie County Public Library, Buffalo, NY [*Library symbol*] [*Library of Congress*] (LCLS)
NBuGC .... Graphic Controls Corp., Buffalo, NY [*Library symbol*] [*Library of Congress*] (LCLS)
NBuGD .... Goldome FSB, Bufflo, NY [*Library symbol*] [*Library of Congress*] (LCLS)
NBuGH........ Buffalo General Hospital, Buffalo, NY [*Library symbol*] [*Library of Congress*] (LCLS)
NBuGH-N ...... Buffalo General Hospital, School of Nursing, Buffalo, NY [*Library symbol*] [*Library of Congress*] (LCLS)
NBuHi .... Buffalo and Erie County Historical Society, Buffalo, NY [*Library symbol*] [*Library of Congress*] (LCLS)
NBuHSA .... Health Systems Agency of Western New York, Inc., Buffalo, NY [*Library symbol*] [*Library of Congress*] (LCLS)
NBuKMH ...... Kenmore Mercy Hospital, Medical Library, Buffalo, NY [*Library symbol*] [*Library of Congress*] (LCLS)
NbU-L .... University of Nebraska, College of Law, Lincoln, NE [*Library symbol*] [*Library of Congress*] (LCLS)
NBuLH .... Lafayette General Hospital, Buffalo, NY [*Library symbol*] [*Library of Congress*] (LCLS)
NBuLTV........ LTV Aerospace & Defense Co., Buffalo, NY [*Library symbol*] [*Library of Congress*] (LCLS)

NBuM............	Medaille College, Buffalo, NY [*Library symbol*] [*Library of Congress*] (LCLS)
NbU-M.........	University of Nebraska, College of Medicine, Omaha, NE [*Library symbol*] [*Library of Congress*] (LCLS)
NBuMM........	Marine Midland Services Corp., Technical Information Center, Buffalo, NY [*Library symbol*] [*Library of Congress*] (LCLS)
NBuNCE.......	National Center for Earthquake Engineering, Research Information Services, State, Buffalo, NY [*Library symbol*] [*Library of Congress*] (LCLS)
NBuPC.........	Buffalo Psychiatric Center, Buffalo, NY [*Library symbol*] [*Library of Congress*] (LCLS)
NBuPL	Pennwalt Corp., Lucidol Division, Buffalo, NY [*Library symbol*] [*Library of Congress*] (LCLS)
NBuRH	Rosary Hill College, Buffalo, NY [*Library symbol*] [*Library of Congress*] [*Obsolete*] (LCLS)
NBuRSI........	Reichert Scientific Instruments, Buffalo, NY [*Library symbol*] [*Library of Congress*] (LCLS)
NBUSA........	United States Army, Fort Hamilton Post Library, Fort Hamilton, Brooklyn, NY [*Library symbol*] [*Library of Congress*] (LCLS)
NBuSCA.......	SCA Chemical Services, Inc., Buffalo, NY [*Library symbol*] [*Library of Congress*] (LCLS)
NBuSCH.......	Sisters of Charity Hospital, Buffalo, NY [*Library symbol*] [*Library of Congress*] (LCLS)
NBuSD	Buffalo City School District, Buffalo, NY [*Library symbol*] [*Library of Congress*] (LCLS)
NBuSFH	St. Francis Hospital of Buffalo, Buffalo, NY [*Library symbol*] [*Library of Congress*] (LCLS)
NBuSK	Spencer Kellogg Division, Textron, Inc., Buffalo, NY [*Library symbol*] [*Library of Congress*] (LCLS)
NBuSMH.......	Sheehan Memorial Emergency Hospital, Buffalo, NY [*Library symbol*] [*Library of Congress*] (LCLS)
NBuSR	Sierra Research Corp., Buffalo, NY [*Library symbol*] [*Library of Congress*] (LCLS)
NBuStM	Saint Mary's School for the Deaf, Buffalo, NY [*Library symbol*] [*Library of Congress*] (LCLS)
NBuTC	Trocaire College, Buffalo, NY [*Library symbol*] [*Library of Congress*] (LCLS)
NBuU	State University of New York at Buffalo, Buffalo, NY [*Library symbol*] [*Library of Congress*] (LCLS)
NBuU-A........	State University of New York at Buffalo, Art Library, Buffalo, NY [*Library symbol*] [*Library of Congress*] (LCLS)
NBuU-AR	State University of New York at Buffalo, Archives, Buffalo, NY [*Library symbol*] [*Library of Congress*] (LCLS)
NBuU-BA......	State University of New York at Buffalo, Bell Annex, Buffalo, NY [*Library symbol*] [*Library of Congress*] (LCLS)
NBuU-BS......	State University of New York at Buffalo, Bell Science Library, Buffalo, NY [*Library symbol*] [*Library of Congress*] (LCLS)
NBuU-C.......	State University of New York at Buffalo, Chemistry Library, Buffalo, NY [*Library symbol*] [*Library of Congress*] (LCLS)
NBuU-CT......	University of Buffalo Foundation, Inc., Center for Tomorrow, State University of New York at Buffalo, Amherst, NY [*Library symbol*] [*Library of Congress*] (LCLS)
NBuU-D........	State University of New York at Buffalo, Documents Library, Buffalo, NY [*Library symbol*] [*Library of Congress*] (LCLS)
NBuU-E........	State University of New York at Buffalo, Educational Opportunity Center, Buffalo, NY [*Library symbol*] [*Library of Congress*] (LCLS)
NBuU-H........	State University of New York at Buffalo, Health Sciences Library, Buffalo, NY [*Library symbol*] [*Library of Congress*] (LCLS)
NBuU-HA	State University of New York at Buffalo, Harriman Library, Buffalo, NY [*Library symbol*] [*Library of Congress*] (LCLS)
NBuU-L........	State University of New York at Buffalo, Law Library, Buffalo, NY [*Library symbol*] [*Library of Congress*] (LCLS)
NBuU-LL......	State University of New York at Buffalo, Library Literature Library, Buffalo, NY [*Library symbol*] [*Library of Congress*] (LCLS)
NBuU-LS......	State University of New York at Buffalo, Library Science Library, Buffalo, NY [*Library symbol*] [*Library of Congress*] (LCLS)
NBuU-Mu.....	State University of New York at Buffalo, Music Library, Buffalo, NY [*Library symbol*] [*Library of Congress*] (LCLS)
NBuU-P........	State University of New York at Buffalo, Physics Library, Buffalo, NY [*Library symbol*] [*Library of Congress*] (LCLS)
NBuU-PO	State University of New York at Buffalo, Poetry Library, Buffalo, NY [*Library symbol*] [*Library of Congress*] (LCLS)
NBuU-R........	State University of New York at Buffalo, Reference, Buffalo, NY [*Library symbol*] [*Library of Congress*] (LCLS)
NBuU-RL......	State University of New York at Buffalo, Ridge Lea, Buffalo, NY [*Library symbol*] [*Library of Congress*] (LCLS)
NBuU-RP	State University of New York at Buffalo, Roswell Park Memorial Institute, Buffalo, NY [*Library symbol*] [*Library of Congress*] (LCLS)
NBuU-SE......	State University of New York at Buffalo, Science and Engineering Library, Buffalo, NY [*Library symbol*] [*Library of Congress*] (LCLS)
NBuVA.........	United States Veterans Administration Hospital, Buffalo, NY [*Library symbol*] [*Library of Congress*] (LCLS)
NBuVM	Villa Maria College of Buffalo, Buffalo, NY [*Library symbol*] [*Library of Congress*] (LCLS)
NBuVNA.......	Visiting Nursing Association of Buffalo, Buffalo, NY [*Library symbol*] [*Library of Congress*] (LCLS)
NBuW	Worthington Compressor & Engine International, Buffalo, NY [*Library symbol*] [*Library of Congress*] (LCLS)
NBuWeP......	Westwood Pharmaceuticals, Inc., Buffalo, NY [*Library symbol*] [*Library of Congress*] (LCLS)
NBUWH........	Carleton County Historical Society, Upper Woodstock, New Brunswick [*Library symbol*] [*National Library of Canada*] (NLC)
NBuWNED....	WNED-TV, Buffalo, NY [*Library symbol*] [*Library of Congress*] (LCLS)
NBuX	XACO, Inc., Buffalo, NY [*Library symbol*] [*Library of Congress*] (LCLS)
NBV	Net Book Value (TEL)
NbV..............	Valentine Public Library, Valentine, NE [*Library symbol*] [*Library of Congress*] (LCLS)
NBVA	National Bulk Vendors Association (EA)
NBVA	United States Veterans Administration Hospital, Brooklyn, NY [*Library symbol*] [*Library of Congress*] (LCLS)
NBV Ad	New Brunswick Vice Admiralty Reports [*A publication*] (DLA)
NBVA-O.......	United States Veterans Administration Hospital, Outpatient Clinic, Brooklyn, NY [*Library symbol*] [*Library of Congress*] (LCLS)
NBVCXO.......	Narrowband Voltage-Controlled Crystal Oscillator
NBVF	National Burn Victim Foundation (EA)
NBVM	Narrow-Band Voice Modulation (VLIE)
NBVO...........	National Black Veterans Organization [*Defunct*] (EA)
NBVS...........	Neutral Beam Vacuum System (SAUS)
NBW	L. P. Fisher Public Library, Woodstock, New Brunswick [*Library symbol*] [*National Library of Canada*] (NLC)
NBW	National Barristers' Wives [*Later, NABBS*] (EA)
NBW	National Book Week (NTCM)
NBW	Natural Bandwidths [*Spectroscopy*]
NBW	Nebraska Wesleyan University, Lincoln, NE [*OCLC symbol*] (OCLC)
nbw.............	Noise Bandwidth (IDOE)
NBW	Noise Bandwidth
NBW	Normal Birth Weight
NbW.............	North by West
NBWA	National Beer Wholesalers' Association (EA)
NBWA	National Blacksmiths and Welders Association (EA)
NBWA	National Buddhist Women's Associations (EA)
NbWayS.......	Wayne State College, Wayne, NE [*Library symbol*] [*Library of Congress*] (LCLS)
NBWH	Carleton Memorial Hospital, Woodstock, New Brunswick [*Library symbol*] [*National Library of Canada*] (BIB)
NBWHP........	National Black Women's Health Project (EA)
NbWi...........	Dvoracek Memorial Library, Wilber, NE [*Library symbol*] [*Library of Congress*] (LCLS)
NBWPLC.....	National Black Women's Political Leadership Caucus (EA)
NBWROP.....	Naval Bureau of Weapons Reserve Ordnance Plant
NBWTAU.....	National British Women's Total Abstinence Union (EAIO)
NBWV	Victoria-Carleton Courthouse, Woodstock, New Brunswick [*Library symbol*] [*National Library of Canada*] (NLC)
NBWY	York Regional Library, Headquarters No. 2, Woodstock, New Brunswick [*Library symbol*] [*National Library of Canada*] (NLC)
NBX	Jeffersn-Pilot 7.25% 'ACES' [*NYSE symbol*] (TTSB)
NBX	Jefferson Pilot [*NYSE symbol*] (SAG)
NBX	Nabire [*Indonesia*] [*Airport symbol*] (OAG)
NBY	NBC Capital [*AMEX symbol*] (SG)
NBY	Nearest Besselian Year
NBY	Nutrient Broth Yeast [*Microbiology*]
NbY.............	York Public Library, York, NE [*Library symbol*] [*Library of Congress*] (LCLS)
NbYC	York College, York, NE [*Library symbol*] [*Library of Congress*] (LCLS)
NBYLC	National Black Youth Leadership Council (EA)
NBysSH.......	Bay Shore Senior High School, Bay Shore, NY [*Library symbol*] [*Library of Congress*] (LCLS)
nc---...........	Central America [*MARC geographic area code*] [*Library of Congress*] (LCCP)
NC..............	Chloropicrin Stannic Chloride [*Inorganic chemistry*]
NC..............	La Nouvelle Clio [*Brussels*] [*A publication*] (BJA)
NC..............	NACCO Indus Inc. Cl'A' [*NYSE symbol*] (TTSB)
NC..............	Name Control [*IRS*]
NC..............	Nanocomposite [*Plastics*]
NC..............	Nano Crystal (AAEL)
NC..............	Nanocrystal (SAUS)
nc	Nanocurie [*Pne billionth of a curie*]
NC..............	Narrowband Communicative Services [*Telecommunications*]
NC..............	Narrow Coverage
NC..............	Nasal Cannula [*Medicine*] (MEDA)
NC..............	Nasal Catheter [*Medicine*] (MELL)
NC..............	Nashville, Chattanooga & St. Louis [*Louisville & Nashville Railroad Co.*] [*AAR code*]
NC..............	Natal Carabiniers [*British military*] (DMA)
NC..............	National Catholic News Service
NC..............	National Cemetery (IIA)
NC..............	National Center (IAA)
NC..............	National Certificate (WDAA)
NC..............	National Churches [*A publication*]
NC..............	National Coarse [*Thread*]
NC..............	National Colonialist Party [*Australia*] [*Political party*]
NC..............	National Cooperatives [*Later, UNICO*] [*An association*]
NC..............	National Course (SAUS)
NC..............	National Curriculum [*Education*] (AIE)
NC..............	Native Cavalry [*British military*] (DMA)
NC..............	NATO Center (NATG)
NC..............	NATO Confidential (NATG)
NC..............	Natural Cytotoxic [*Cells*] [*Immunochemistry*]
NC..............	Nature Conservancy [*NERC*] [*British*]
NC..............	Naval Cadet [*British*] (ROG)
NC..............	Naval Correspondence
NC..............	Navigation Computer
NC..............	Navigation Console
NC..............	Navy Component
NC..............	Navy Cross

NC	Neanderthal Conservative [Slang]
NC	Nearly Commensurate Model [Physics]
NC	Necrosis
Nc	Negative Wave in Children [Neurophysiology]
NC	Neighborhood Coalition (EA)
NC	Nerve Center [An association] (EA)
NC	Nerve Conduction
NC	Net Capital [Business term]
NC	Net Charter [Business term] (DS)
NC	Net Control (MCD)
NC	Net Cost
NC	Netilmicin-Clindamycin [Antibiotic combination]
NC	Network Card [British Rail]
NC	Network Channel [Broadcasting] (NTCM)
NC	Network Computer (PCM)
NC	Network Computing
NC	Network Congestion [Telecommunications] (TEL)
NC	Network Connect
NC	Network Connection [Computer science] (VLIE)
NC	Network Control (IAA)
NC	Network Controller
NC	Network Countdown
NC	Neural Crest [Anatomy]
NC	Neurocirculatory [Medicine] (DAVI)
NC	Neurologic Check [Medicine]
NC	Neutral Current [Physics]
NC	Neutralization Capacitor (IAA)
NC	Neutralizing Capacitance [or Coil] (DEN)
NC	Neutralizing Capacitance (or Capacitor) (SAUS)
NC	Neutron Content (SAUS)
NC	Neutron Contrast (SAUS)
NC	Neutron Controller [Nuclear energy] (NRCH)
N/C	New Account (ROG)
NC	Newair [ICAO designator] (AD)
NC	Newark College (SAUS)
NC	New Caledonia [ANSI two-letter standard code] (CNC)
NC	New Canada Press
NC	New Cases (Bingham's New Cases) in Common Pleas [1834-40] [A publication] (DLA)
NC	Newcastle Connection (SAUS)
NC	New Cavendish Books [Publisher] [British]
N/C	New Charter [Navigation]
NC	New Church (ROG)
NC	New College (SAUS)
NC	Newcomb College (SAUS)
NC	New Construction [Navy]
NC	New Consultants [A publication]
NC	New Crop
NC	Newnham College (SAUS)
NC	Neylan Conference (EA)
NC	Nichols College (SAUS)
NC	Nickel Cadmium (IAA)
NC	Nickel Clad
NC	Nickel-clad Copper (SAUS)
NC	Nickel Copper (SAUS)
NC	Night Coach [Airline designation]
N-C	Nightingale-Conant [Audio publisher]
NC	Nippon Club (EA)
NC	Nitrocellulose [Organic chemistry]
NC	Nitrocompound (SAUS)
NC	Nixdorf Computer (IAA)
NC	NOAA [National Oceanic and Atmospheric Administration] Corps (USDC)
NC	No Card (SAUS)
NC	No Carry (SAUS)
NC	No Casualty (MAE)
NC	No Change
NC	No Charge
NC	No Coil (MSA)
NC	No Collaterals [Medicine]
NC	No Comment (NASA)
NC	No Complaint (SAUS)
N/C	No Complaints [Medicine]
nc	No Connection (IDOE)
NC	No Connection [Valve pins] [Radio] [Technical drawings]
NC	No Contact
NC	No Contest [Sports]
NC	No Correction (SAUS)
NC	No Cost (AAG)
NC	No Credit (WGA)
NC	Node Centre (SAUS)
NC	Node Consistency (SAUS)
NC	Noise Correlation (MSA)
NC	Noise Criteria (or Criterion) (SAUS)
NC	Noiseless Camera (NTCM)
NC	Nominal Correction
NC	Nominating Committee [American Occupational Therapy Association]
NC	Noncallable (EBF)
NC	Noncallable Bond [Investment term]
NC	Noncarcinogen (SAUS)
NC	Noncoin (IAA)
NC	Noncollectable
NC	Non-Collectible (SAUS)
NC	Non-Color Sensitized Emulsion [Also called color-blind emulsion] (WDMC)
NC	Noncommercial [Rate] [Value of the English pound]
NC	Noncommissioned
NC	Noncomplex (MCD)
NC	Noncompliance [Noncompliant] (DAVI)
N/C	Non-Concur (SAUS)
NC	Non-Condensing (SAUS)
NC	Nonconforming
NC	Nonconformist [Indicating religious preference] [Military] [British]
NC	Non-Contact
NC	Non-Continuous Liner [Shipping] (DS)
NC	Noncontributory (DAVI)
NC	Non Conversational (SAUS)
NC	Nonconversational (IAA)
NC	Noncorrodible (SAUS)
NC	Non-Crystalline (OA)
NC	Non-Curling [Photographic film] (ROG)
NC	Nonlinear Capacitance
NC	Nonrecurring Costs (AAGC)
NC	Nordic Council
NC	NORDLEK Council (EAIO)
NC	Norfolk College (SAUS)
NC	Normal Children
NC	Normal Control
NC	Normal Cooling (SAUS)
NC	Normal Copy [Oncology]
NC	Normal Corrective Maneuver (SAUS)
NC	Normally Closed [Switch]
NC	Norman College (SAUS)
NC	Norman Conquest [of England, 1066]
NC	Normocephalic [On physical examination] [Medicine] (DAVI)
NC	North Carolina [Postal code]
NC	North Carolina Railroad
NC	North Carolina Reports [A publication] (DLA)
Nc	North Carolina State Library, Raleigh, NC [Library symbol] [Library of Congress] (LCLS)
NC	North Carolina Supreme Court Reports [A publication] (DLA)
NC1	North Central Airlines, Inc. [ICAO designator] (OAG)
NC	North Coast (ADA)
NC	Northcor Resources Ltd. [Vancouver Stock Exchange symbol]
NC	North Country (ROG)
NC	Northern Cascades (SAUS)
NC	Northern Command
NC	Northern Consolidated Airlines, Inc.
NC	Northern Counties (SAUS)
NC	Northern County (SAUS)
NC	Northland College (SAUS)
NC	Northrop Corp. (KSC)
NC	Northwestern College (SAUS)
NC	Norton Commander (SAUS)
NC	Norwegian Club (EA)
NC	Nose Clip (MELL)
NC	Nose Cone [Aviation] (AFM)
N/C	Nose Cone [Aerospace] (NAKS)
NC	Not Calculated (SAUS)
NC	Not Carried
NC	Not Coded (MCD)
NC	Not Competitive [Rejected research proposals] [National Institutes of Health]
NC	Not Complete (SAUS)
NC	Not Completed [Medicine] (DMAA)
NC	Not Connected [Electronics] (DEN)
NC	Not Controlled [Experimental conditions]
N/C	Not Critical (NASA)
NC	Not Cultured (MAE)
NC	Notes of Cases at Madras (Strange) [A publication] (DLA)
NC	Notes of Cases, English Ecclesiastical and Maritime Courts [1841-50] [A publication] (DLA)
NC	Novo Cruzado [Brazilian currency]
NC	Nuclear Capability
NC	Nuclear Congress
NC	Nuclear-Cytoplasmic [Ratio] [Cytology] (MAE)
NC	Nucleocapsid (DB)
NC	Nucleus of Ciliated Cell
NC	Nuestra Cuenta [Our Account] [Business term] [Spanish]
NC	"Nuff Ced" [Enough Said] [Slang]
NC	Nuffield College (SAUS)
NC	Number Cruncher (SAUS)
NC	Number Crusher (SAUS)
NC	Numbering Counter [Computer science] (OA)
NC	Number of unallocated channels at node (SAUS)
NC	Numerical Code (SAUS)
NC	Numerical Coding (SAUS)
NC	Numerical Control [Computer science]
NC	Numeric Coding (SAUS)
NC	Numeric Control (SAUS)
NC	Nurse Corps [Military]
NC	Sagrada Biblia [1944] [Eloino Nacar Fuster and Alberto Colunga] (BJA)
NC	Sandoz Pharmaceuticals [Research code symbol]
nc	Sodium Carbonate [CIPW classification] [Geology]
NC	Warner-Lambert Pharmaceutical Co. [Research code symbol]
NC1	Navy Counselor First Class (DNAB)
NC1	Nominal Correction 1 [Phasing Maneuver] [NASA] (NAKS)
NC3	Norsar Array Site 03C00 [Norway] [Seismograph station code, US Geological Survey] (SEIS)

NC³A .... Nuclear Command, Control, and Communications Assessment (COE)
NC³D .... National Coordinating Center for Curriculum Development
NC5 .... Norsar Array Site 05C00 [Norway] [Seismograph station code, US Geological Survey] (SEIS)
NC-17 .... No Children under 17 Admitted [Movie rating]
NCa .... Canton Free Library, Canton, NY [Library symbol] [Library of Congress] (LCLS)
NCA .... College of New Caledonia Library [UTLAS symbol]
NCA .... Jacksonville, NC [Location identifier] [FAA] (FAAL)
NCA .... National Campaign for the Arts [British] (DBA)
NCA .... National Camp Association (EA)
NCA .... National Camping Association (EA)
NCA .... National Candle Association (EA)
NCA .... National Canners Association [Later, NFPA] (EA)
NCA .... National Capital Award
NCA .... National Carousel Association (EA)
NCA .... National Cashmere Association [Defunct] (EA)
NCA .... National Caterers Association [Later, ICA] (EA)
NCA .... National Catfishing Association (EA)
NCA .... National Cathedral Association (EA)
NCA .... National Cattlemens Association (EA)
NCA .... National Caves Association (EA)
NCA .... National Caving Association [British] (DBA)
NCA .... National Cemetery Administration
NCA .... National Ceramic Association [Later, ICA] (EA)
NCA .... National Certificate of Agriculture [British]
NCA .... National Certification Agency (DMAA)
NCA .... National Certification Agency for Medical Laboratory Personnel (EA)
NCA .... National Chaplain's Association (EA)
NCA .... National Charcoal Association
NCA .... National Chastity Association (EA)
NCA .... National Cheerleaders Association (EA)
NCA .... National Childminding Association [British] (EAIO)
NCA .... National Chiropractic Association [Universal Chiropratic Association and American Chiropratic Association] [Later, American Chiropractic Association] [Formed by a merger of]
NCA .... National Christian Association
NCA .... National Civic Association
NCA .... National Climate Archive (QUAC)
NCA .... National Club Association (EA)
NCA .... National Coal Association (EA)
NCA .... National Coal Authority [Australia]
NCA .... National Coffee Association of the United States of America (EA)
NCA .... National Color-Bred Association (EA)
NCA .... National Command Authorities
NCA .... National Commission on Accrediting [Later, COPA] (EA)
NCA .... National Communication Agencies (NATG)
NCA .... National Communications Association (EA)
NCA .... National Composition Association [Later, NCPA] (EA)
NCA .... National Computer Association (EA)
NCA .... National Concilio of America (EA)
NCA .... National Confectioners Association of the United States (EA)
NCA .... National Conference of Artists (EA)
NCA .... National Congressional Analysis Corp. (IID)
NCA .... National Constables Association (EA)
NCA .... National Constructors Association (EA)
NCA .... National Contesters Association (EA)
NCA .... National Contingency Account (OICC)
NCA .... National Control Authority (SAUS)
NCA .... National Cosmetology Association (EA)
NCA .... National Costumers Association (EA)
NCA .... National Council for Aviculture [British] (DBA)
NCA .... National Council on Alcoholism [Later, NCADD] (EA)
NCA .... National Council on the Aging [Washington, DC]
NCA .... National Council on the Arts [of NFAH]
NCA .... National Coursing Association [Later, NGA] (EA)
NCA .... National Cranberry Association
NCA .... National Creameries Association [Later, NMPF] (EA)
NCA .... National Credit Association (NADA)
NCA .... National Cricket Association [British]
NCA .... National Crop Acreage Program [Department of Agriculture]
NCA .... Naval Center for Cost Analysis
NCA .... Naval Command Assistant
NCA .... Naval Communications Annex
NCA .... Navy Contract Administrator
NCA .... NCA Minerals [Vancouver Stock Exchange symbol]
NCA .... N-Carboxy Anhydride [Organic chemistry]
NCA .... N-Chloroacetamide [Organic chemistry]
NCA .... N-Chloroethylnorapomorphine [Organic chemistry, biochemistry]
NCA .... Netherlands Centre Alternatives to Animal Use (GVA)
NCA .... Network Career Advancement Institute [Telecommunications service] (TSSD)
NCA .... Network Communications Adapter [Computer science] (VLIE)
NCA .... Network Computer Architecture [Computer science] (VLIE)
NCA .... Network Computing Architecture [Computer science] (TNIG)
NCA .... Network for Community Activities
NCA .... Neurocirculatory Asthenia [Medicine]
NCA .... Neutralized Current Acid (ABAC)
NCA .... Neutrophil Chemotactic Activity [Clinical chemistry]
NCA .... Nevada Correctional Association
NCA .... New Communities Administration [HUD]
NCA .... Newfoundland Club of America (EA)
NCA .... News & Current Affairs (WDAA)
NC5 .... Ngorongoro Conservation Area (SAUS)
NCA .... Nickel-Copper Alloy (MSA)

NCA .... Nippon Cargo Airlines Co. Ltd. [Japan] [ICAO designator] (FAAC)
NCA .... No Congenital Abnormalities [Medicine] (MELL)
NCA .... No Copies Available (ADA)
NCA .... No Coupons Attached (DLA)
NCA .... Nodulocystic Acne [Medicine] (DMAA)
NCA .... Noise Control Act (EG)
NCA .... Noise Control Association (EA)
NCA .... Noncombat Aircraft [Military] (MCD)
NCA .... Noncommutative Algebra (SAUS)
NCA .... Non-Continuous Action (CCCA)
NCA .... Noncontractile Area (DB)
NCA .... Noncontractual Authorization
NCA .... Noncorrodible Aluminum (SAUS)
NCA .... Nonorganic Ceramic Adhesive
NCA .... Nonspecific Cross-Reacting Antigen [Immunology]
NCA .... Nor-Cal Aviation, Inc. (SAUS)
NCA .... Normal Coordinate Analysis
NCA .... North Caicos [British West Indies] [Airport symbol] (OAG)
NCA .... North Carolina Court of Appeals Reports [A publication] (DLA)
NCA .... North Central Airlines (SAUS)
NCA .... North Central Association (SAUS)
NCA .... North Central Association of Colleges and Secondary Schools [Later, NCACS]
NCA .... North Central Bible College, Minneapolis, MN [OCLC symbol] (OCLC)
NCA .... North Coast Airlines [Australia]
NCA .... Northern Communications Area [Military]
NCA .... Northern Consolidated Airlines, Inc.
NCA .... Northern Consultancy Association (COBU)
NCA .... Northwest Computing Association
NCA .... Norwegian Council for Africa
NCA .... Novell Certification Alliance (SAUS)
NCA .... Nuclear and Chemical Agency [Army]
NCA .... Nuclear Cerebral Angiogram [Medicine] (DMAA)
NCA .... Nurse Consultants Association (EA)
NCA .... Nuveen California Municipal Fund [NYSE symbol] (SPSG)
NcA .... Pack Memorial Public Library, Asheville, NC [Library symbol] [Library of Congress] (LCLS)
NCAA .... National Center for Audio Tapes Archive (EA)
NCAA .... National Center on Arts and the Aging (EA)
NCAA .... National Change of Address Association [Commercial firm] [New York, NY] (EA)
NCAA .... National Collegiate Athletic Association (EA)
NCAA .... National Command Authority Aircraft-747 [MTMC] (TAG)
NCAA .... National Credit Adjustment Association [New York, NY] (EA)
NCAA .... NATO Civil Air Augmentation (DOMA)
NCAA .... Naval Civilian Administrators Association [Later, NCMA] (EA)
NCAA .... Non-Nuclear Consumable Annual Analysis System (SAUS)
NCAAA .... National Center of Afro-American Artists
NCAAA .... National Council of Affiliated Advertising Agencies [Later, First Network of Affiliated Advertising Agencies] (EA)
NcAAB .... Asheville-Buncombe Technical Institute, Asheville, NC [Library symbol] [Library of Congress] (LCLS)
NCaaC .... Community College of the Finger Lakes, Canandaigua (SAUS)
NCAAC .... Northern California Athletic Conference (PSS)
NCAADA ...... National Community Action Agency Directors Association [Formerly, NCAAEDA] [Later, NACAA] (EA)
NCAADACCB... National Commission on Accreditation of Alcoholism and Drug Abuse Counselor Credentialing Bodies (EA)
NCAAE .... National Council of Administrators of Adult Education (EA)
NCAAEDA .... National Community Action Agency Executive Directors Association (EA)
NcAAH .... Appalachian Hall Medical Library, Asheville, NC [Library symbol] [Library of Congress] (LCLS)
NCAAL .... National Conference of African American Librarians
NcAAP .... Amcel Propulsion Co., Asheville, NC [Library symbol] [Library of Congress] (LCLS)
NCAAP .... National Coalition for Adequate Alcoholism Programs [Defunct] (EA)
NC-AAPSO ... Nigerian Committee of the Afro-Asian Peoples Solidarity Organization (SAUS)
NCAB .... National Association of Citizen Advice Bureaux [British]
NCAB .... National Cancer Advisory Board
NCAB .... National Collegiate Athletic Bureau [Later, NCSS] (EA)
NCAB .... National Committee for Amateur Baseball [Later, USBF]
NCAB .... Navy Contract Adjustment Board
NCABC .... National Catholic Association for Broadcasters/Communicators (EA)
NCABC .... National Citizens' Advice Bureaux Committee [British] (BI)
NcAbd .... Page Memorial Library, Aberdeen, NC [Library symbol] [Library of Congress] (LCLS)
NCABHP .... National Center for the Advancement of Blacks in the Health Professions (EA)
NcAbMR ...... North Carolina Marine Resources Center, Bogue Banks Library, Atlantic Beach, NC [Library symbol] [Library of Congress] (LCLS)
NcAC .... Cecils Junior College, Asheville, NC [Library symbol] [Library of Congress] (LCLS)
NCAC .... National Cancer Advisory Committee [Australia]
NCAC .... National Catholic Action Coalition [Defunct] (EA)
NCAC .... National Christian Action Coalition [Defunct] (EA)
NCAC .... National Civil Aviation Council [British] (BI)
NCAC .... National Clean Air Coalition [Defunct] (EA)
NCAC .... National Coalition Against Censorship (EA)
NCAC .... National Consumer Advisory Council
NCAC .... National Copyright Advisory Committee (NADA)
NCAC .... National Council Against Conscription [World War I] [British]
NCAC .... National Council of Acoustical Consultants (EA)

NCAC .... Navy Combat Art Collection (DNAB)
NCAC .... Nordic Customs Administrative Council (EA)
NCAC .... North Carolina Administrative Code [*A publication*] (AAGC)
NCAC .... North Coast Athletic Conference (PSS)
NCAC .... Northern Combat Area Command [*Myanmar*]
NCACC .... National Collection of Animal Cell Cultures (DB)
NCACC .... National Conference of Appellate Court Clerks (EA)
NCACE .... National Capital Association for Cooperative Education (MCD)
NC/AC-EC..... Narrow Coverage/Area Coverage to Earth Coverage (SAUS)
NCACME ...... National Center for Adult, Continuing, and Manpower Education [*Office of Education*]
NC/AC-NC/AC... Narrow Coverage/Area Coverage to Narrow Coverage/Area Coverage (SAUS)
NCACP .... National Campaign for the Abolition of Capital Punishment [*Founded in 1955*] [*British*]
NCACPS .... National Coalition to Abolish Corporal Punishment in Schools (EA)
NCACS .... National Coalition of Alternative Community Schools (EA)
NCACS .... North Central Association of Colleges and Schools (EA)
NCAD .... New Cumberland Army Depot [*Pennsylvania*] (AABC)
NCAD .... Northrop Computer Aided Design (ACAE)
NCAD .... Notice of Cancellation at Anniversary Date [*Insurance*] (DCTA)
NCADD .... National Commission Against Drunk Driving (EA)
NCADD .... National Council on Alcoholism and Drug Dependence (EA)
NCADH .... National Committee Against Discrimination in Housing [*Defunct*] (EA)
NCADI .... National Clearinghouse for Alcohol and Drug Abuse Information (PAZ)
NCADI .... National Clearinghouse for Alcohol and Drug Information [*US Public Health Service*] [*Information service or system*] (IID)
NC Admin Code... North Carolina Administrative Code [*A publication*] (DLA)
NCADP .... National Coalition Against the Death Penalty (EA)
NCADP .... National Coalition to Abolish the Death Penalty (EA)
NCADS .... Numerical Control Advisory and Demonstration Service (SAUS)
NCADV .... National Coalition Against Domestic Violence (EA)
NC Adv Legis Serv... North Carolina Advance Legislative Service (SAUS)
NC Adv Legis Serv... North Carolina Advance Legislative Service (Michie) [*A publication*] (DLA)
NCAE .... National Center for Alcohol Education [*National Institutes of Health*]
NCAE .... National Center for Audio Experimentation [*Defunct*] (EA)
NCAE .... National College of Agricultural Engineering [*British*] (ARC)
NCAE .... National Conference on Airborne Electronics (MCD)
NCAE .... National Council for Alcohol Education (DMAA)
NCAE .... National Council of Agricultural Employers (EA)
NCAE .... North Carolina Association of Educators (SAUS)
NCAEE .... National Committee on Art Education for the Elderly [*Defunct*] (EA)
NCAEF .... National Ceramic Association Educational Foundation (EA)
NCAEG .... National Confederation of American Ethnic Groups (EA)
NCAEI .... National Conference on the Application of Electrical Insulation
NCAES .... National Center for Analysis of Energy Systems (HGAA)
NCAF .... National Clean Air Fund (GFGA)
NCAF .... National Committee Against Fluoridation [*National Health Federation - NHF*] [*Absorbed by*] (EA)
NCAF .... National Community Action Foundation (EA)
NCAF .... Nationalist Chinese Air Force (SAUS)
NCAFB .... Normal Crop Acreage Farm Base
NCAFP .... National Committee on American Foreign Policy (EA)
NCAG .... National Council on the Arts and Government (EA)
NcAh .... Ahoskie Public Library, Ahoskie, NC [*Library symbol*] [*Library of Congress*] (LCLS)
NCAH .... National Child Abuse Hotline (MELL)
NCAH .... National Committee, Arts for the Handicapped [*Later, VSA*] (EA)
NCAHCP....... National Council on Alternative Health Care Policy (EA)
NcAHE .... Mountain Area Health Education Center, Health Sciences Library, Asheville, NC [*Library symbol*] [*Library of Congress*] (LCLS)
NCAHE .... National Commission on Allied Health Education [*American Occupational Therapy Association*]
NCAHF .... National Council Against Health Fraud (EA)
NcAHH .... Highland Hospital, Medical Library, Asheville, NC [*Library symbol*] [*Library of Congress*] (LCLS)
NcAhRC .... Roanoke-Chowan Technical Institute, Ahoskie, NC [*Library symbol*] [*Library of Congress*] (LCLS)
NCAHRN ...... National Central American Health Rights Network (EA)
NCAHUAC .... National Committee to Abolish the House Un-American Activities Committee [*Later, NCARL*] (EA)
NCAI .... Aitutaki [*Cook Islands*] [*ICAO location identifier*] (ICLI)
NCAI .... National Clearinghouse for Alcohol Information [*Rockville, MD*] [*National Institutes of Health*]
NCAI .... National Coalition for Adult Immunization
NCAI .... National Congress of American Indians (EA)
NCAI .... National Council of American Importers [*Later, AAEI*] (EA)
NCAI .... National Council on Alcoholism, Inc. (NADA)
NCA-I .... Neighborhood Cleaners Association-International (NTPA)
NCAIAE .... National Center for American Indian Alternative Education (EA)
NCAIANMHR... National Center for American Indian and Alaska Native Mental Health Research (EA)
NCAIC .... Nuclear Chemical Accident Incident Control (MCD)
NCAICU .... North Carolina Association of Independent Colleges and Universities (SAUS)
NCAIE .... National Center for American Indian Education [*Later, NCAIAE*] (EA)
NCAIE .... National Council of the Arts in Education [*Later, ACAE*] (EA)
NCAIED .... National Center for American Indian Enterprise Development (EA)
NCAIL .... National Council Against Illegal Liquor [*Defunct*] (EA)
NCAIP .... National Consumer Affairs Internship Program [*Defunct*] (EA)
NCAIR .... National Center for Automated Information Retrieval (IID)
NCAIR .... North Carolina Association for Institutional Research (EDAC)
NCAJ .... National Center for Administrative Justice [*Formerly, CAJ*] (EA)
NCA/JCS ...... National Command Authorities and Joint Chiefs of Staff
NCAJL......... National Council on Art in Jewish Life (EA)
NCaL........... Canton Free Library, Canton, NY [*Library symbol*] [*Library of Congress*] (LCLS)
NCAL .... National Centre for Athletics Literature (AIE)
NCAL .... National Committee for Adult Literacy [*British*] (DI)
N Cal .... New Caledonia
NcAlb.......... Albemarle-Stanly County Public Library, Albemarle, NC [*Library symbol*] [*Library of Congress*] (LCLS)
NcAlbS......... Stanly Technical Institute, Albemarle, NC [*Library symbol*] [*Library of Congress*] (LCLS)
NCALHBCU... National Consortium of Arts and Letters for Historically Black Colleges and Universities (EA)
NCALI .... National Clearinghouse for Alcohol Information [*National Institutes of Health*] (IID)
NCALL .... National Council on Agricultural Life and Labor Research Fund (EA)
NcAlP.......... Pamlico Technical Institute, Alliance, NC [*Library symbol*] [*Library of Congress*] (LCLS)
NCalv.......... Baiting Hollow Free Library, Calverton, NY [*Library symbol*] [*Library of Congress*] (LCLS)
NCAM .... National Center for Accessible Media (SAUS)
NCAM .... National Center for Advanced Materials [*Later, Berkeley Center for A dvanced Materials*]
NCAM .... Network Communication Access Method
N-CAM .... Neural Cell Adhesion Molecule [*Biochemistry*]
NCAM .... Neurall Cell Adhesion Molecule (SAUS)
NCAMI .... National Committee Against Mental Illness [*Defunct*] (EA)
NCAMLP ...... National Certification Agency for Medical Laboratory Personnel (MAE)
NCAMP........ National Coalition Against the Misuses of Pesticides (EA)
NCAMR........ Nordic Council for Arctic Medical Research (EA)
NCAN.......... Incan Superior Ltd. [*AAR code*]
NCAN.......... National Catholic AIDS Network (EA)
NCAN.......... National Citizens Action Network (EA)
NCAN.......... National Coalition of American Nuns (EA)
NCAN.......... National Committee for Amnesty Now (EA)
NCaN .... North Country Reference and Research Resources Council, Canton, NY [*Library symbol*] [*Library of Congress*] (LCLS)
NCAN.......... Number of Canisters [*Automotive emissions*]
NcAnA......... Anson Technical Institute, Ansonville, NC [*Library symbol*] [*Library of Congress*] (LCLS)
NCanC .... Community College of the Finger Lakes, Canandaigua, NY [*Library symbol*] [*Library of Congress*] (LCLS)
NcANCC .... United States National Oceanic and Atmospheric Administration, National ClimaticCenter, Ashville, NC [*Library symbol*] [*Library of Congress*] (LCLS)
NcAnd......... Andrews Carnegie Library, Andrews, NC [*Library symbol*] [*Library of Congress*] (LCLS)
NC & B........ Naval Courts and Boards
NC&C.......... Normal Coitus and Climax (MELL)
NC & CS...... Navigation Command and Control System
NC & SL...... Nashville, Chattanooga & St. Louis Railway (IIA)
NC & ST L.... Nashville, Chattanooga & St. Louis Railway
NCANH........ National Council for the Accreditation of Nursing Homes (NADA)
NCanHi .... Ontario County Historical Society, Canandaigua, NY [*Library symbol*] [*Library of Congress*] (LCLS)
NCaNNH ...... Northern New York Health Information Cooperative, Canton, NY [*Library symbol*] [*Library of Congress*] (LCLS)
NCanV .... United States Veterans Administration Hospital, Canandaigua, NY [*Library symbol*] [*Library of Congress*] (LCLS)
NCAO .... National Commission on Air Quality [*Environmental Protection Agency*] (ERG)
NCAO .... Naval Civil Affairs Officer [*World War II*]
NCAP .... Nansen Centennial Arctic Program (SAUS)
NCAP .... Nasal Continuous Airway Pressure [*Medicine*] (MELL)
N-CAP .... National Coalition Against Pornography (EA)
NCAP .... National Coalition of Abortion Providers (NTPA)
NCAP .... Naval Combat Air Patrol (DNAB)
NCAP .... Neighborhood Community Action Program
NCAP .... Nematic Curvilinear Aligned Phase [*Emulsion film used in windows*] [*Taliq Corp.*]
NCAP .... New Car Assessment Program [*Automobile testing*]
NCAP .... Night Combat Air Patrol [*Military*]
NCAP .... Nordic Council for Animal Protection (EA)
NCAP .... Northwest Coalition for Alternatives to Pesticides (GNE)
NCAP .... Nucleotide Column Affinity for Purification [*Biochemical analysis*]
N-CAP .... Nurses Coalition for Action in Politics
NCAPC .... National Center for Air Pollution Control [*Public Health Service*] [*Obsolete*]
NCAPC .... NATO Conventional Armaments Planning Committee (SAUS)
NCAPI .... Nuveen California Premium Income Municipal Fund [*Associated Press*] (SAG)
NCAPO .... National Council of Adoptive Parents Organizations [*NACAC*] [*Absorbed by*]
NC App .... North Carolina Appellate Reports [*A publication*] (AAGC)
NC App .... North Carolina Court of Appeals Reports [*A publication*] (DLA)
NCAPS .... Naval Control and Protection of Shipping (NVT)
NCapV .... United States Veterans Administration Hospital, Medical Library, Castle Point, NY [*Library symbol*] [*Library of Congress*] (LCLS)
NCAQ .... National Commission on Air Quality (GNE)
NCAR .... National Center for Association Resources (EA)
NCAR .... National Center for Atmospheric Research [*Boulder, CO*] [*National Science Foundation*] (GRD)
NCAR .... National Conference on the Advancement of Research (EA)
NCAR .... Navy Center for Acquisition Research [*Monterey, CA*]

NCAR .... Nonconformance and Corrective Action Reporting System [NASA] (KSC)
N Car .... North Carolina (DLA)
N Car .... North Carolina Reports [A publication] (DLA)
Nc-Ar .... North Carolina State Department of Archives and History, Raleigh (SAUS)
Nc-Ar .... North Carolina State Department of Archives and History, Raleigh, NC [Library symbol] [Library of Congress] (LCLS)
NcAr .... Sallie H. Jenkins Memorial Public Library, Aulander, NC [Library symbol] [Library of Congress] (LCLS)
NCARAI .... Navy Center for Applied Research in Artificial Intelligence [Washington, DC] (GRD)
NCARB .... National Council of Architectural Registration Boards (EA)
NCARC .... NATO Conventional Armament Review Committee (SAUS)
NCaRC .... North Country Reference and Research Resources Council, Canton, NY [Library symbol] [Library of Congress] [Obsolete] (LCLS)
NCARF .... National Committee for Amish Religious Freedom (EA)
NCARL .... National Committee Against Repressive Legislation (EA)
N Car Law Rep ... Carolina Law Repository (Reprint) [North Carolina] [A publication] (DLA)
NCARMD ...... National Commission on Arthritis and Related Musculoskeletal Disease
NCarNG .... North Carolina Natural Gas Corp. [Associated Press] (SAG)
NCarol Dent Gaz ... North Carolina Dental Gazette (SAUS)
N Carolina Cases ... North Carolina Reports [A publication] (DLA)
NCARP .... Collegiate Association for Research of Principle (EA)
N Car Rep ... North Carolina Reports [A publication] (DLA)
NCARRV ...... North Carolinians Against Racist and Religious Violence (SAUS)
NCAR System ... Non-conformance and Corrective Action Reporting System (SAUS)
NCAS .... National Coalition Against Surrogacy (EA)
NCAS .... National Coalition of Advocates for Students (EA)
NCAS .... National Collegiate Association for Secretaries [Defunct] (EA)
NCAS .... Neocarzinostatin [Zinostatin] [Antineoplastic drug]
NCas .... North Cascades (SAUS)
NcA-S .... Pack Memorial Public Library, Sondley Reference Library, Asheville, NC [Library symbol] [Library of Congress] (LCLS)
NCaS .... Saint Lawrence University, Canton, NY [Library symbol] [Library of Congress] (LCLS)
NCASA .... National Campaign Against Solvent Abuse [British] (DBA)
NCASA .... National Coalition Against Sexual Assault (EA)
NCASA .... Naval Civil Affairs Staging Area
NCASAA ...... National Court Appointed Special Advocates Association (EA)
NcAsbC .... Randolph Public Library, Asheboro, NC [Library symbol] [Library of Congress] (LCLS)
NcAsbH .... Randolph Hospital, Inc., Asheboro, NC [Library symbol] [Library of Congress] (LCLS)
NcAsbR .... Randolph Technical Institute, Asheboro, NC [Library symbol] [Library of Congress] (LCLS)
NCASC .... National Capital Administrative Support Center [Marine science] (OSRA)
NCASC .... National Council of Acupuncture Schools and Colleges (EA)
NCASC .... Nordic Council for Adult Studies in Church [See also NKS] (EAIO)
NCASEPS .... North Central Alaskan Seasonal Earned Premium Scale [Aviation] (AIA)
NCASF .... National Council of American-Soviet Friendship (EA)
NCASI .... National Council of the Paper Industry for Air and Stream Improvement (EA)
NCAT .... Atiu [Cook Islands] [ICAO location identifier] (ICLI)
NCAT .... National Catalog (AEPA)
NCAT .... National Center for Advanced Technology [Vienna, VA]
NCAT .... National Center for Appropriate Technology (EA)
NCAT .... National Center for Audiotape [Later, NCATA] (EA)
NCAT .... National Centre for Alternative Technology [British]
NCAT .... National Council of Athletic Training (NTPA)
NCAT .... National Program for Clear Air Turbulence [Air Force]
NCAT .... Naval College Aptitude Test (NVT)
NC/AT .... Normal Cephalic Atraumatic [Medicine] (DMAA)
NCAT .... Northampton College of Advanced Technology (SAUS)
NCATA .... National Cable Antenna Television Association of Canada (NTCM)
NCATA .... National Center for Audiotape Archive [Defunct] (EA)
NCATA .... National Coalition of Arts Therapy Associations (EA)
NCATB .... National Congress of Animal Trainers and Breeders (EA)
NCATE .... National Council for Accreditation of Teacher Education (EA)
NCATH .... National Campaign Against Toxic Hazards (EA)
NcATH .... Thoms Rehabilitation Hospital, Medical Library, Asheville, NC [Library symbol] [Library of Congress] (LCLS)
NcAu .... Sallie H. Jenkins Memorial Public Library, Aulander, NC [Library symbol] [Library of Congress] (LCLS)
NcAU .... University of North Carolina at Asheville, Asheville, NC [Library symbol] [Library of Congress] (LCLS)
NCaUA .... State University of New York, Agricultural and Technical College, Canton, NY [Library symbol] [Library of Congress] (LCLS)
NCAV .... National Coursing Association of Victoria [Australia]
NcAV .... United States Veterans Administration, Hospital Library Service, Asheville, NC [Library symbol] [Library of Congress] (LCLS)
NCAVAE ...... National Committee for Audio-Visual Aids in Education [British]
NCAVC .... National Center for the Analysis of Violent Crime [Quantico, VA] [Department of Justice] (GRD)
NCAW .... National Council for Animal Welfare (NADA)
NCAW .... Neutralized Current Acid Waste (ABAC)
NCAWA .... National Coinamatic Auto Wash Association [Later, ICA/NCC]
NCAWE .... National Council of Administrative Women in Education (EA)
NCAWP .... National Council for Alternative Work Patterns (EA)
NCAWRR ...... National Committee Against War, Racism, and Repression
NCAYR .... National Chaplains Association for Youth Rehabilitation [Defunct]

NCazC .... Cazenovia College, Cazenovia, NY [Library symbol] [Library of Congress] (LCLS)
NCB .... Barber-Scotia College, Concord, NC [OCLC symbol] (OCLC)
NCB .... Name Continuation Block (TIMI)
NCB .... Nanyang Commercial Bank [China]
NCB .... National Cargo Bureau (EA)
NCB .... National Central Bureau [INTERPOL term]
NCB .... National Children's Bureau [British]
NCB .... National Classification Board [American Trucking Association]
NCB .... National Coal Board [British]
NCB .... National Codification Bureau [NATO] (NATG)
NCB .... National Collection of Industrial Bacteria [British]
NCB .... National College of Business (IAA)
NCB .... National Commercial Bank [Saudi Arabia]
NCB .... National Commercial Bank [Jamaica]
NCB .... National Compliance Board [New Deal]
NCB .... National Conservation Bureau [Defunct]
NCB .... National Cooperative Bank (USGC)
NCB .... NATO Codification Bureau (SAUS)
NCB .... Naval Communications Board
NCB .... Naval Construction Battalion
NCB .... Navy Comptroller Budget (NG)
NCB .... Nederlandse Credietbank NV [Financial institution] [Netherlands] (EY)
NCB .... NetBIOS [Network Basic Input/Output System] Control Block [Computer science]
NCB .... Net Change of Biomass (CARB)
NCB .... Net Clearing Balance [Finance]
NCB .... Net Conservation Benefit (SAUS)
NCB .... Netherlands Convention Bureau (EA)
NCB .... Network Connect Block [Computer science] (CIST)
NCB .... Network Control Block
NCB .... Nevrite Cervico-Brachial (SAUS)
NCB .... New Century Bible [A publication] (BJA)
NC-B .... New Crime Buffer
NCB .... Nickel-Cadmium Battery
NCB .... Nippon Credit Bank [Japan]
NCB .... Nippon Cultural Broadcasting (SAUS)
NCB .... No Claim Bonus [Insurance] (ADA)
NCB .... No Code Blue [For terminal cases] [Medicine] (DAVI)
NCB .... Noncallable Bond [Investment term]
NCB .... North Caribou Flying Service Ltd. [Canada] [ICAO designator] (FAAC)
NCB .... Northwest Cherry Briners (SAUS)
NCB .... Northwest Cherry Briners Association (EA)
NCB .... Nuclear Contingency Branch (SAUS)
NcBa .... Mitchell County Library, Bakersville, NC [Library symbol] [Library of Congress] (LCLS)
NCBA .... National Candy Brokers Association (EA)
NCBA .... National Catholic Band Association (NTPA)
NCBA .... National Catholic Bandmasters' Association (EA)
NCBA .... National Cattle Breeders Association [British] (DBA)
NCBA .... National Cattlemen's Beef Association (GVA)
NCBA .... National Caucus and Center on Black Aged (EA)
NCBA .... National Chinchilla Breeders of America [Later, ECBC] (EA)
NCBA .... National Color-Bred Association (EA)
NCBA .... National Commodity and Barter Association (EA)
NCBA .... National Cooperative Business Association (EA)
NCBA .... National Council on Black Aging (EA)
NCBA .... Northern California Booksellers Association (SAUS)
NCBAE .... No-Claim Bonus as Earned [Insurance] (ODBW)
NcBaneL ...... Lees-McRae College, Banner Elk, NC [Library symbol] [Library of Congress] (LCLS)
NCBBC .... National Council of Bible Believing Churches [Later, CBBC] (EA)
NcBc .... Marianna Black Library, Bryson City, NC [Library symbol] [Library of Congress] (LCLS)
NCBC .... National Commerce Bancorp [NASDAQ symbol] (NQ)
NCBC .... National Committee for the Berne Convention [Defunct] (EA)
NCBC .... Natl Commerce Bancorp [NASDAQ symbol] (TTSB)
NCBC .... Naval Construction Battalion Center
NCBC .... New Century Bible Commentary [A publication]
NCBC .... North Carolina Biotechnology Center [Research center] (RCD)
NcBcF .... Fontana Regional Library, Bryson City, NC [Library symbol] [Library of Congress] (LCLS)
NCBCS .... National Conference of States on Building Codes and Standards (OICC)
NCBDE .... National Certification Board for Diabetes Educators (SAUS)
NcBe ..,........ Belmont Abbey College, Belmont, NC [Library symbol] [Library of Congress] (LCLS)
NCBE .... National City Bancshares [NASDAQ symbol] (SAG)
NCBE .... National Clearinghouse for Bilingual Education [Wheaton, MD]
NCBE .... National Conference of Bar Executives [Later, NABE] (EA)
NCBE .... National Council for Better Education (EA)
NCBE .... North County Business Exchange
NcBea .... Cateret County Public Library, Beaufort, NC [Library symbol] [Library of Congress] (LCLS)
NCBEA .... National Catholic Business Education Association [Emporia, KS] (EA)
NCBEA .... North Central Business Education Association (AEBS)
NcBeaAE ...... United States Marine Fisheries Service, Southeast Fisheries Center, Beaufort Laboratory, Beaufort, NC [Library symbol] [Library of Congress] (LCLS)
NCBEC .... National Center for Business and Economic Communication [American University] [Research center] (RCD)

NCBEE .... National Council of State Boards of Engineering Examiners [*Later,* NCEE] (IAA)
NCBEL .... [*The*] New Cambridge Bibliography of English Literature [*A publication*]
NCBES .... National Council of Black Engineers and Scientists (NTPA)
NcBeSH .... Sacred Heart College, McCarthy Library, Belmont, NC [*Library symbol*] [*Library of Congress*] (LCLS)
NcBesL .... Lithium Corp. of America, Ellestad Research Library, Bessemer City, NC [*Library symbol*] [*Library of Congress*] (LCLS)
NCBF .... National Conference of Bar Foundations (EA)
NCBF .... Non-Conventional Brake Fluid [*Automotive engineering*]
NCBFAA .... National Customs Brokers and Forwarders Association of America [*New York, NY*] (EA)
NCBFE .... National Center for a Barrier Free Environment (EA)
NCBG .... National Coalition of Black Gays (EA)
ncbh- .... British Honduras [*MARC geographic area code*] [*Library of Congress*] (LCCP)
NCBH .... National Coalition to Ban Handguns [*Later, CSGV*] (EA)
NCBHC .... National Committee on Black and Hispanic Concerns (EA)
NCBI .... National Center for Biotechnology Information (IID)
NCBI .... National Cotton Batting Institute (EA)
NCBIAE .... National Council of BIA [*Bureau of Indian Affairs*] Educators (EA)
NCBJ .... National Conference of Bankruptcy Judges (EA)
NCBJS .... National Council of Beth Jacob Schools [*Later, FCBJS*] (EA)
NcBl .... Bridger Memorial Public Library, Bladenboro, NC [*Library symbol*] [*Library of Congress*] (LCLS)
NCBL .... National Conference of Black Lawyers (EA)
NCBL .... Natural Convection Boiling Loops
NCBLG .... National Coalition of Black Lesbians and Gays (EA)
NcBlm .... Black Mountain Public Library, Black Mountain, NC [*Library symbol*] [*Library of Congress*] (LCLS)
NCBLRDC .... National Coalition of Black Lung and Respiratory Disease Clinics (EA)
NcBlv .... Phillip Leff Memorial Library, Beulaville, NC [*Library symbol*] [*Library of Congress*] (LCLS)
NCBM .... National City Bancorp [*NASDAQ symbol*] (NQ)
NCBM .... National Conference of Black Mayors (EA)
NCBM .... National Council on Business Mail (EA)
NCBM .... Natl City Bancorp'n [*NASDAQ symbol*] (TTSB)
NCBMP .... National Coalition of Black Meeting Planners (EA)
NCBMP .... National Council of Building Material Producers [*A union*] [*British*]
NcBo .... Watauga County Library, Boone, NC [*Library symbol*] [*Library of Congress*] (LCLS)
NcBoA .... Appalachian State University, Boone, NC [*Library symbol*] [*Library of Congress*] (LCLS)
NcBoHE .... Northwest Area Health Education Center, Boone, NC [*Library symbol*] [*Library of Congress*] (LCLS)
NcBoNM ..... New River Area Mental Health, Boone, NC [*Library symbol*] [*Library of Congress*] (LCLS)
NCBOR .... No Claim Bonus on Renewal [*Insurance*] (AIA)
NCBP .... National Conference of Bar Presidents (EA)
NCBPD .... National Consortium for Black Professional Development (EA)
Nc-BPH .... North Carolina Library for the Blind and Physically Handicapped, Raleigh, NC [*Library symbol*] [*Library of Congress*] (LCLS)
NCBPNP/N ... National Certification Board of Pediatric Nurse Practitioners and Nurses (EA)
NCBR .... National Center for Bilingual Research [*National Institute of Education*] [*Research center*] (RCD)
NCBR .... Near Commercial Breeder Reactor [*Also, PLBR*]
NCBR .... Nitride Cooled Breeder Reactor (SAUS)
NCBR .... Nordic Committee on Building Regulations (SAUS)
NcBre .... Transylvania County Library, Brevard, NC [*Library symbol*] [*Library of Congress*] (LCLS)
NcBreC .... Brevard College, Brevard, NC [*Library symbol*] [*Library of Congress*] (LCLS)
NCBS .... National Cage Bird Show (EA)
NCBS .... National Consumer Board for Stuttering (EA)
NCBS .... National Council for Black Studies (EA)
NCBSA .... National Candy Brokers and Salesmen's Association [*Later, NCBA*] (EA)
NcBsG .... Gardner-Webb College, Boiling Springs, NC [*Library symbol*] [*Library of Congress*] (LCLS)
NCBTA .... Nordic Cooperative of Brick and Tilemakers Associations (SAUS)
NcBuC .... Campbell College, Buies Creek, NC [*Library symbol*] [*Library of Congress*] (LCLS)
NcBuC-L ...... Campbell University, Law Library, Buies Creek, NC [*Library symbol*] [*Library of Congress*] (LCLS)
NcBur .... Central North Carolina Regional Library, Burlington, NC [*Library symbol*] [*Library of Congress*] (LCLS)
NcBurAT ...... AT&T Technologies Inc., Technical Library, Burlington, NC [*Library symbol*] [*Library of Congress*] (LCLS)
NcBurgP ...... Pender County Library, Burgaw, NC [*Library symbol*] [*Library of Congress*] (LCLS)
NcBurgP-H.. Pender County Library, Hampstead Branch Library, Hampstead, NC [*Library symbol*] [*Library of Congress*] (LCLS)
NcBurT .... Technical Institute of Alamance, Burlington, NC [*Library symbol*] [*Library of Congress*] (LCLS)
NcBurWE ..... Western Electric Co., Technical Library, Burlington, NC [*Library symbol*] [*Library of Congress*] (LCLS)
NcButM .... Murdoch Center, School Library, Butner, NC [*Library symbol*] [*Library of Congress*] (LCLS)
NcBv .... Yancey County Public Library, Burnsville, NC [*Library symbol*] [*Library of Congress*] (LCLS)
NCBVA .... National Concrete Burial Vault Association (EA)
NCBVP .... National Coalition on Black Voter Participation (EA)

NCBW .... National Cage Bird Week Association [*Defunct*] (EA)
NCBW .... National Coalition of 100 Black Women (EA)
NCBWA .... National Collegiate Baseball Writers Association (EA)
NcBy .... Palmico County Library, Bayboro, NC [*Library symbol*] [*Library of Congress*] (LCLS)
NCC .... Chadron State College, Chadron, NE [*OCLC symbol*] (OCLC)
NCC .... Dutch national computer catalogue (SAUS)
NCC .... NAACOG [*Nurses Association of the American College of Obstetricians and Gynecologists*] Certification Corp. (EA)
NCC .... NASA Class Code (NASA)
NCC .... NASA Communications Control (SAUS)
NCC .... National Cadet Corps (NADA)
NCC .... National Cambridge Collectors (EA)
NCC .... National Cancer Center (EA)
NCC .... National Can Corp. (EFIS)
NCC .... National Capital Commission [*Canada*]
NCC .... National Capon Council [*Defunct*] (EA)
NCC .... National Caravan Council Ltd. [*British*] (BI)
NCC .... National Carbon Co. (MCD)
NCC .... National Career Center (EA)
NCC .... National Carwash Council [*Later, ICA*] (EA)
NCC .... National Castings Council [*Defunct*] (EA)
NCC .... National Certification Commission (NTPA)
NCC .... National Certification Corporation for the Obstetric, Gynecologic and Neonatal Nursing Specialties (EA)
NCC .... National Certified Counselor (DHP)
NCC .... National Chile Center [*Formerly, NCCSC*] (EA)
NCC .... National Citizens Coalition [*Canada*]
NCC .... National Citizens Committee. Bulletin [*A publication*]
NCC .... National City Corp. [*NYSE symbol*] (CTT)
NCC .... National Clearing Corp. [*National Association of Securities Dealers*]
NCC .... National Clients Council (EA)
NCC .... National Climatic Center [*National Oceanic and Atmospheric Administration*]
NCC .... National Coaches Council [*Later, ANCC*] (EA)
NCC .... National Coal Council [*Department of Energy*] [*Arlington, VA*] (EGAO)
NCC .... National Command Center (ACAE)
NCC .... National Communications Club (EA)
NCC .... National Communications Command [*Army*] (RDA)
NCC .... National Communications Commission [*Uganda*] (ECON)
NCC .... National Company of Crossbowmen [*Defunct*] (EA)
NCC .... National Computer Center [*IRS*]
NCC .... National Computer Conference
NCC .... National Computer Council (NADA)
NCC .... National Computing Centre [*Manchester, England*]
NCC .... National Conference on Citizenship (EA)
NCC .... National Congressional Club (EA)
NCC .... National Consumer Council [*British*] (ILCA)
NCC .... National Consumers Congress [*Later, NCL*]
NCC .... National Container Committee [*Later, Uniform Classification Committee*] (EA)
NCC .... National Control Center (ELAL)
NCC .... National Coordinating Committee (USGC)
NCC .... National Coordinating Committee for the Promotion of History (EA)
NCC .... National Coordinating Committee to End the War [*Organization formed in 1965*] (VNW)
NCC .... National Coordinating Council on Drug Abuse Education and Information [*Later, NCCDE*] (EA)
NCC .... National Coordination Committee [*Responsible for administering the Work Incentive Program*]
NCC .... National Cotton Council of America (EA)
NCC .... National Council Against Conscription [*World War I*] [*British*]
NCC .... National Council of Churches (SHCU)
NCC .... National Council of Churches of Christ in the USA (EA)
NCC .... National Counselor Certification [*Psychology*]
NCC .... National Crime Commission
NCC .... National Cryptologic Command [*National Security Agency*]
NCC .... National Cultural Center [*Later, John F. Kennedy Center for the Performing Art s*]
NCC .... National Curriculum Council [*British*] (ECON)
NCC .... Native Council of Canada
NCC .... Natural Circulation Cooldown [*Nuclear energy*] (NUCP)
NCC .... Naturally Commutated Cycloconverter [*Electronics*] (EECA)
NCC .... Nature Conservancy Council [*British*]
NCC .... Navajo Community College [*Chinle, AZ*]
NCC .... Naval Command College (DOMA)
NCC .... Naval Component Command (CINC)
NCC .... Navigation Computer Control
NCC .... Navigation Control Console
NCC .... Navy Command Center (MCD)
NCC .... Navy Cost Center
NCC .... NetWare Console Commander [*Frye Computer Systems*] [*Telecommunications*] (PCM)
NCC .... NetWare Control Center [*Novell, Inc.*] [*Computer science*] (PCM)
NCC .... Network Communications Corp.
NCC .... Network Computer Center. (OA)
NCC .... Network Control Center [*Telecommunications*]
NCC .... Network Control Computer (HGAA)
NCC .... Network Coordination Center [*NASA*]
NCC .... Network of Concerned Correspondents (EA)
NCC .... Neural Crest Cell [*Cytology*]
NCC .... Neuronal Correlate of Consciousness
NCC .... New Chancery Cases (Younge and Collyer) [*1841-43*] [*England*] [*A publication*] (DLA)

NCC .... New Chemical Compound [*Food science*]
NCC .... New Common Carriers
NCC .... New Computer Center [*Social Security Administration*]
NCC .... New Construction and Conversion [*Navy*] (AFIT)
NCC .... New Consultants and Consulting Organizations Directory [*A publication*]
NCC .... Newfoundland Capital Corp. Ltd. [*Toronto Stock Exchange symbol*]
NCC .... Newhouse Communications Center (SAUS)
NCC .... Newspaper Comics Council [*Later, NFC*] (EA)
NCC .... Niagara County Community College [*UTLAS symbol*]
NCC .... Nitrogen Carbon Cycle (SAUS)
NCC .... Nitrogen Charging Console
NCC .... Noise Control Committee
NCC .... Nominal Corrective Combination (MCD)
NCC .... Noncarbohydrate Craver [*Nutrition*]
NCC .... Noncombatant Corps [*British*]
NCC .... NORAD Control Center [*Military*]
NCC .... Nordic Choral Committee (EAIO)
NCC .... Normal-Control Children [*Psychology*]
NCC .... Normal Corrective Combination (SAUS)
NCC .... Normally Closed Contact [*Switch*] (IAA)
NCC .... North Calotte Committee [*See also NKK*] [*Nordic Council of Ministers*] [*Finland*] (EAIO)
NCC .... North Central College [*Naperville, IL*]
NCC .... North Central Conference (PSS)
NCC .... North Coast Air Services Ltd. [*Canada*] [*ICAO designator*] (FAAC)
NCC .... Northwest Christian College [*Oregon*]
NCC .... Northwest Community College (SAUS)
NCC .... Northwood Control Centre (SAUS)
NCC .... Notre Cause Commune [*Benin*] [*Political party*] (EY)
NCC .... Numerical Control Code
NCC .... Nursing Clerical Coordinator
NcC .... Public Library of Charlotte and Mecklenburg County, Charlotte, NC [*Library symbol*] [*Library of Congress*] (LCLS)
NcCA .... Arthur Andersen & Co., Carolinas Central Library, Charlotte, NC [*Library symbol*] [*Library of Congress*] (LCLS)
NCCA .... Nash Car Club of America (EA)
NCCA .... National Carpet Cleaners Association [*British*] (EAIO)
NCCA .... National Catholic Camping Association [*Defunct*] (EA)
NCCA .... National Catholic Council on Alcoholism and Related Drug Problems (EA)
NCCA .... National Cedar Chest Association [*Defunct*] (EA)
NCCA .... National Center for Child Advocacy
NCCA .... National Center for Community Action (EA)
NCCA .... National Centre for Clinical Audit (SAUS)
NCCA .... National Chemical Credit Association (EA)
NCCA .... National Child Care Association (NTPA)
NCCA .... National Clergy Council on Alcoholism and Related Drug Problems (EA)
NCCA .... National Club Cricket Association [*British*] (BI)
NCCA .... National Coil Coaters Association (EA)
NCCA .... National Collegiate Conference Association (EA)
NCCA .... National Columbia Challenger Association (EA)
NCCA .... National Commission for Certifying Agencies (SAUS)
NCCA .... National Commission for the Certification of Acupuncture (EA)
NCCA .... National Commission for the Certification of Acupuncturists (EA)
NCCA .... National Committee on Central America (EA)
NCCA .... National Concrete Contractors Association [*Later, ASCC*] (EA)
NCCA .... National Cotton Council of America [*Memphis, TN*]
NCCA .... National Council for Critical Analysis [*Defunct*] (EA)
NCCA .... National Council for Culture and Art (EA)
NCCA .... National Court Clubs Association [*Later, IRSA*] (EA)
NCCA .... Naval Center for Cost Analysis
NCCA .... Negligence and Compensation Cases, Annotated [*A publication*] (DLA)
NCCA .... Nordic Committee for Central Africa [*Defunct*] (EA)
NCCA .... North Carolina Classical Association (SAUS)
NCCA .... North Carolina Correctional Association (SAUS)
NCCA 3d ..... Negligence and Compensation Cases, Annotated, Third Series [*A publication*] (DLA)
NCCAA .... National Christian College Athletic Association (EA)
NCCAC .... National Catholic Conference of Airport Chaplains (EA)
NCCACS .... National Council of Columbia Associations in Civil Service (EA)
NCCAE .... National Conference of Catholic Art Educators (AEBS)
NCCAE .... National Council of County Association Executives (EA)
NCCAFV .... National Council on Child Abuse and Family Violence (EA)
NcCaLM ...... United States Naval Medical Field Research Laboratory, Camp Lejeune, NC [*Library symbol*] [*Library of Congress*] (LCLS)
NcCaLMC ... United States Marine Corps, Marine Corps Base General Library, Camp Lejeune, NC [*Library symbol*] [*Library of Congress*] (LCLS)
NcCaLNM ... United States Navy, Naval Regional Medical Center, Library, Camp Lejeune, NC [*Library symbol*] [*Library of Congress*] (LCLS)
NCCAM .... National Center for Complementary and Alternative Medicine
NCCAN .... National Center on Child Abuse and Neglect [*Department of Health and Human Services*] [*Washington, DC*]
NCCAN .... National Clearinghouse on Child Abuse and Neglect Information (PAZ)
NCCA NS .... Negligence and Compensation Cases, Annotated, New Series [*A publication*] (DLA)
NCCAP .... National Certification Council for Activity Professionals (NTPA)
NcCar .... Moore County Library, Carthage, NC [*Library symbol*] [*Library of Congress*] (LCLS)
NCCAS .... National Center of Communication Arts and Sciences (EA)
NCCAS .... National Council for Clean Air and Streams
NCCAT .... National Committee for Clear Air Turbulence (KSC)

NCCB .... National Carpenters Craft Board [*Defunct*] (EA)
NCCB .... National Citizens Committee for Broadcasting (EA)
NCCB .... National Conference of Catholic Bishops (EA)
NCCB .... National Consumer Cooperative Bank
NCCB .... National Council to Combat Blindness [*Also known as Fight for Sight - FS*] (EA)
NCCB .... Netherlands Culture Collection of Bacteria (SAUS)
NCCBA .... National Caucus and Center on Black Aged (EA)
NCCBH .... National Council for Community Behavioral Healthcare (SAUS)
NCCBI .... National Coordinating Committee of the Beverage Industry
NCCBMI ...... National Consortium for Computer Based Music Instruction [*University of Delaware*] [*Research clearinghouse*] (EA)
NCCBN .... National Council of Churches Broadcasting Network (NTCM)
NCCC .... National Cambodia Crisis Committee [*Defunct*] (EA)
NCCC .... National Cancer Cytology Center [*Later, NCC*] (EA)
NCCC .... National Catholic Cemetery Conference (EA)
NCCC .... National Certified Career Counselor (DHP)
NCCC .... National Cervical Cancer Coalition (NRGU)
NCCC .... National Civilian Community Corps
NCCC .... National Conference of Catholic Charities (EA)
NCCC .... National Conservative Congressional Committee (EA)
NCCC .... National Consumer Credit Consultants (EA)
NCCC .... National Council of Churches of Christ in the USA [*Later, NCC*] (EA)
NCCC .... National Council of Community Churches [*Later, ICCC*] (EA)
NCCC .... National Council of Corvette Clubs (EA)
NCCC .... Niagara County Community College (SAUS)
NCCC .... Norris Cotton Cancer Center [*Dartmouth-Hitchcock Medical Center*] [*Research center*] (RCD)
NCCCC .... National Coalition for Campus Child Care (EA)
NCCCC .... National Council for Credentialing Career Counselors (DHP)
NCCCC .... Naval Command, Control Communications Center (IAA)
NCCCC .... North Central Community College Conference (PSS)
NCCCCA ...... National Collegiate Cross Country Coaches Association [*Later, USCCCA*] (EA)
NCCCD .... National Center Confraternity of Christian Doctrine (EA)
NCCCD .... National Center for Computer Crime Data (EA)
NcCCed .... Cedalion Systems, Inc., Information Resources, Charlotte, NC [*Library symbol*] [*Library of Congress*] (LCLS)
NcCCel .... Celanese Fibers Co., Technical Information Center, Charlotte (SAUS)
NcCCel .... Celanese Fibers Co., Technical Information Center, Charlotte, NC [*Library symbol*] [*Library of Congress*] (LCLS)
NCCCHE ...... National Certification Commission in Chemistry and Chemical Engineering (IAA)
NCCCLC ...... Naval Command Control Communications Laboratory Center
NcCCP .... Central Piedmont Community College, Charlotte, NC [*Library symbol*] [*Library of Congress*] (LCLS)
NCCCP .... National Center for Community Crime Prevention (EA)
NCCCR .... National Citizens Committee for Community Relations [*Defunct*]
NCCCTC ...... Non-Corrosive Cyclic Corrosion Test Chamber
NCCCWA ...... National Cotton Compress and Cotton Warehouse Association [*Later, CWAA*] (EA)
NcCD .... Duke Power Co., Information Systems Library, Charlotte, NC [*Library symbol*] [*Library of Congress*] (LCLS)
NCCD .... National Center for Chronic Disease Control [*Public Health Service*]
NCCD .... National College for Criminal Defense (EA)
NCCD .... National Council for Community Development (EA)
NCCD .... National Council for Criminal Defense (EA)
NCCD .... National Council on Crime and Delinquency (EA)
NCCDC .... National Center for Chronic Disease Control (DAVI)
NcCDD .... Duke Power Co., David Nabow Library, Charlotte, NC [*Library symbol*] [*Library of Congress*] (LCLS)
NCCDE .... National Coordinating Council on Drug Education [*Formerly, NCC*]
NCCDL .... National College of Criminal Defense Lawyers and Public Defenders (DLA)
NCCDN .... National Consortium of Chemical Dependency Nurses (EA)
NCCDPC ...... NATO Command, Control, and Information Systems and Automatic Data Processing Committee (NATG)
NCCDPHP .... National Center for Chronic Disease Prevention and Health Promotion
NCCD-R & I... National Council on Crime and Delinquency, Research and Information Division [*Research center*] (RCD)
NCCDS .... National Cooperative Crohn's Disease Study
NCCDS .... Network Control Center Data System (SSD)
NCCE .... National Center for Community Education (EA)
NCCE .... National Coalition for Consumer Education (EA)
NCCE .... National Commission for Cooperative Education (EA)
NCCE .... National Committee for Citizens in Education (EA)
NCCE .... Nordic Committee for Commercial Education [*See also NKH*] [*Odense, Denmark*] (EAIO)
NCCEA .... Neurosensory Center Comprehensive Examination for Aphasia (DAVI)
NCCED .... National Congress for Community Economic Development (EA)
NCCEM .... National Coordinating Council on Emergency Management (EA)
NCCEM .... National Council of Catholic Employers and Managers (EA)
NCCEWV ...... National Coordinating Committee to End the War in Vietnam [*Defunct*]
NCCF .... National Cancer Care Foundation (EA)
NCCF .... National Childhood Cancer Foundation (NRGU)
NCCF .... National Commission on Consumer Finance [*Terminated*]
NCCF .... National Council on Community Foundations [*Later, CF*] (EA)
NCCF .... Network Communications Control Facility [*IBM program product*]
NCCFL .... National Catholic Conference on Family Life (EA)
NCCG .... National Council on Compulsive Gambling [*Later, NAPG*] (EA)
NCCG .... Navy Central Clearance Group (DNAB)

NCCGDP ...... National Council of Chairmen of Graduate Departments of Psychology
NcCGS .... Church of Jesus Christ of Latter-Day Saints, Genealogical Society Library, Charlotte North Carolina Branch, Charlotte, NC [*Library symbol*] [*Library of Congress*] (LCLS)
NcCh .... Chapel Hill Public Library, Chapel Hill, NC [*Library symbol*] [*Library of Congress*] (LCLS)
NCCH .... National Council of Community Hospitals (EA)
NCCH .... National Council to Control Handguns [*Later, HCI*] (EA)
NCCH .... Nurses' Central Clearing House (AIE)
NCCHB .... National Committee on Concerns of Hispanics and Blacks [*Defunct*] (EA)
NCCHC .... National Commission on Correctional Health Care (EA)
NCCHE .... National Chicano Council for Higher Education [*Defunct*] (EA)
NCCHI .... National Cap and Cloth Hat Institute (EA)
NcCHM .... Helms, Mullis & Johnston Law Library, Charlotte, NC [*Library symbol*] [*Library of Congress*] (LCLS)
NCCHR .... National Commission on Confidentiality of Health Records [*Defunct*] (EA)
NCCHS .... National Commission on Community Public Health Services
NCCHS .... Nonirradiated Core Component Handling System (SAUS)
NCCHTA ...... National Coordinating Centre for Health Technology Assessment (SAUS)
NcCI .... IBM Corp., Library/15C, Charlotte, NC [*Library symbol*] [*Library of Congress*] (LCLS)
NCCI .... Nashville Country Club [*NASDAQ symbol*] (SAG)
NCCI .... National Commission on Coping with Interdependence (EA)
NCCI .... National Council on Compensation Insurance [*New York, NY*] (EA)
NCCI .... North Central Computer Institute [*Research center*] (RCD)
NCCIA .... North Carolina Crop Improvement Association (SAUS)
NCC/IBL ...... Nederlandse Centrale Catalogus/Interbibliothecair Leenverkeer System [*Netherlands Central Catalogue/Interlibrary Loan System*] [*Consortium of the Royal Library and University Libraries*] [*Information service or system*] (IID)
NCCIC .... National Child Care Information Center (SAUS)
NCCIDSA ...... North Central Chapter Infectious Diseases Society of America (SAUS)
NCCIHE .... North Carolina Center for Independent Higher Education (SAUS)
NCCIJ .... National Catholic Conference for Interracial Justice (EA)
NCCIP .... National Center for Clinical Infant Programs (EA)
NCCIP .... Nordic Cooperation Committee for International Politics, Including Conflict and Peace Research (EA)
NCCIR .... National Catholic Commission for Industrial Relations [*Australia*]
NCCIS .... NATO Command, Control, and Information System (NATG)
NCCIW .... Nashville Country Club Wrrt [*NASDAQ symbol*] (TTSB)
NcCJ .... Johnson C. Smith University, Charlotte, NC [*Library symbol*] [*Library of Congress*] (LCLS)
NCCJ .... National Conference of Christians and Jews (EA)
NCCJP & A... National Clearinghouse for Criminal Justice Planning and Architecture [*Defunct*] (EA)
NCCK .... Noncoherent Carrier Keying (IAA)
NCCL .... National Citizen Communication Lobby (EA)
NCCL .... National Conference of Catechetical Leadership (NTPA)
NCCL .... National Council for Civil Liberties [*British*]
NCCL .... National Council of Canadian Labour
NCCL .... National Council of Catholic Laity [*Defunct*] (EA)
NCCL .... National Council of Coal Lessors (EA)
NcCla .... Hocutt-Ellington Memorial Library, Clayton, NC [*Library symbol*] [*Library of Congress*] (LCLS)
NCC-LAW..... North Carolina Center for Laws Affecting Women, Inc. [*Research center*] (RCD)
NcCIH .... Haywood Technical Institute, Clyde, NC [*Library symbol*] [*Library of Congress*] (LCLS)
NcCli........... Sampson-Clinton Public Library, Clinton, NC [*Library symbol*] [*Library of Congress*] (LCLS)
NcCliS .... Sampson Technical Institute, Clinton, NC [*Library symbol*] [*Library of Congress*] (LCLS)
NCCLS .... National Committee for Clinical Laboratory Science
NCCLS .... National Committee for Clinical Laboratory Standards (EA)
NCCLS .... National Consumer Center for Legal Services [*Later, NRCCLS*] (EA)
NCCLS .... Nevada Center for Cooperative Library Services (SAUS)
NCCLVP ...... National Coordinating Committee on Large Volume Parenterals (BABM)
NCCM .... Master Chief Navy Counselor [*Navy rating*] (DNAB)
NcCM.......... Mecklenburg County Medical Society, Charlotte, NC [*Library symbol*] [*Library of Congress*] (LCLS)
NCCM .... National Council of Catholic Men (EA)
NCCMA .... National Corporate Cash Management Association (EA)
NCCMC .... Navy Civilian Career Management Center (ACAE)
NCCMCU ..... National Committee to Commemorate the Millenium of Christianity in the Ukraine (EA)
NCCMGI...... National Clearinghouse for Corporate Matching Gift Information (EA)
NCCMHC ..... National Council of Community Mental Health Centers (EA)
NCCMHS..... National Consortium for Child Mental Health Services (EA)
NCCMIRS..... Navy Civilian Career Management Inventory and Referral System (DNAB)
NcCML......... Medical Library of Mecklenburg County, Inc., Charlotte, NC [*Library symbol*] [*Library of Congress*] (LCLS)
NCCML .... National Committee for Careers in the Medical Laboratory [*Defunct*] (EA)
NCCMP .... National Coordinating Committee for Multiemployer Plans (EA)
NCCMP .... Navy Civilian Career Management Program (DNAB)
NCCMT .... National Committee for Careers in Medical Technology [*Later, NCCML*] (EA)
NCCN .... National Comprehensive Cancer Network [*Medical*]

NCCN .... National Council of Catholic Nurses [*Defunct*] (EA)
NCCN .... New Century Cyclopedia of Names [*A publication*]
NCCNA .... National Clearinghouse on Child Neglect and Abuse [*HEW*]
NC/CNC .... Numerical Control/Computer Numerical Control (SAUS)
NCCNHR ...... National Citizens Coalition for Nursing Home Reform (EA)
NcCo .... Concord Public Library, Concord, NC [*Library symbol*] [*Library of Congress*] (LCLS)
NCCO .... Enseco, Inc. (SAUS)
NCCO .... Neodymium, Cerium, Copper, Oxide [*Inorganic chemistry*]
NcCoB......... Barber-Scotia College, Concord, NC [*Library symbol*] [*Library of Congress*] (LCLS)
NcCoC......... Cabarrus County Library, Concord, NC [*Library symbol*] [*Library of Congress*] (LCLS)
NcCoCH .... Cabarrus County Health Department, Concord, NC [*Library symbol*] [*Library of Congress*] (LCLS)
NcCoi.......... Currituck County Public Library, Coinjock, NC [*Library symbol*] [*Library of Congress*] (LCLS)
NcCol.......... Polk County Public Library, Columbus (SAUS)
NcCol.......... Polk County Public Library, Columbus, NC [*Library symbol*] [*Library of Congress*] (LCLS)
NcCola........ Tyrrell County Public Library, Columbia, NC [*Library symbol*] [*Library of Congress*] (LCLS)
NC Computer... Numerical Control Computer (SAUS)
NcConC....... Concordia College, Conover, NC [*Library symbol*] [*Library of Congress*] [*Obsolete*] (LCLS)
NC Conf ...... North Carolina Conference Reports [*A publication*] (DLA)
NC Conf Rep... North Carolina Conference Reports [*A publication*] (DLA)
NCCOP........ National Corporation for the Care of Old People [*British*] (BI)
NCCOP........ North Carolina Computer Orientation Project
NcCorD .... Duke Power Co., Information Resource Center, Cornelius, NC [*Library symbol*] [*Library of Congress*] (LCLS)
NCCOS........ National Committee for Certificates in Office Studies [*British*]
NCCOSC....... Naval Command, Control, and Ocean Surveillance Center [*Formerly, NOSC and other activities*] (DOMA)
NCCP .... National Center for Children in Poverty (EA)
NCCP .... National Chinese Curriculum Project [*Australia*]
NCCP .... National Clearinghouse for Commuter Programs (EA)
NCCP .... National Coordinated Cataloging Program [*Library science*]
NCCP .... National Council on City Planning
NCCP .... NATO Commanders Communications Publication (NATG)
NCCP .... Navigation Control Console Panel
NCCP .... Northern California Cancer Program [*Research center*] (RCD)
NCCPA .... National Cinder Concrete Products Association (EA)
NCCPA .... National Commission on Certification of Physician's Assistants (EA)
NCCPA .... National Council of College Publications Advisers (EA)
NCCPAP ...... National Conference of CPA [*Certified Public Accountant*] Practitioners [*New York, NY*] (EA)
NCCPB .... National Council of Commercial Plant Breeders (EA)
NCCPC .... NATO Civil Communications Planning Committee (NATG)
NCCPG .... National Council for the Conservation of Plants and Gardens (PDAA)
NCCPL .... National Community Crime Prevention League (EA)
NcCpM........ United States Marine Corps, Air Station, Cherry Point, NC [*Library symbol*] [*Library of Congress*] (LCLS)
NCCPS .... National Citizens Commission for the Public Schools (AEBS)
NCCPT .... National Congress of Colored Parents and Teachers (AEBS)
NCCPV .... National Commission on the Causes and Prevention of Violence (EA)
NcCQ .... Queens College, Charlotte, NC [*Library symbol*] [*Library of Congress*] (LCLS)
nccr- .... Costa Rica [*MARC geographic area code*] [*Library of Congress*] (LCCP)
NCCR .... National Coalition for Cancer Research (EA)
NCCR .... National Committee for Cultural Resources
NCCR .... National Council for Children's Rights (EA)
NCCR .... National Council for Community Relations [*Later, NCMPR*] (EA)
NCCR .... National Council of Chain Restaurants (NTPA)
NCCR .... Network Control Center Representative (SSD)
NCCR .... New Construction/Conversion Requirements System [*Navy*]
NCCRE .... National Consumers Committee for Research and Education [*Later, NCL*] (EA)
NCCRI .... National Catholic Coalition for Responsible Investment (EA)
NCCR System... New Construction/Conversion Requirements System (SAUS)
NcCS.......... Charlotte-Mecklenburg Schools, Staff Development Center, Charlotte, NC [*Library symbol*] [*Library of Congress*] (LCLS)
NCCS .... NASA Center for Computational Sciences (SAUS)
NCCS .... National Carriers Contract Services [*National Freight Consortium*] [*British*]
NCCS .... National Catholic Committee on Scouting (EA)
NCCS .... National Catholic Community Service [*Defunct*] (EA)
NCCS .... National Catholic Conference for Seafarers (EA)
NCCS .... National Center for Charitable Statistics (EA)
NCCS .... National Center for Constitutional Studies (EA)
NCCS .... National Christ Child Society (EA)
NCCS .... National Climbing Classification System
NCCS .... National Coalition for Cancer Survivorship (EA)
NCCS .... National Command and Control System
NCCS .... National Council for Community Services to International Visitors [*Later, NCIV*]
NCCS .... Navigation/Command & Control System (SAUS)
NCCS .... Navy Camera Control System
NCCS .... Navy Command and Control System (NVT)
NCCS .... Nordic Church Council for Seamen [*Denmark*] (EAIO)
NCCS .... Nordic Council for Church Studies (EA)
NCCS .... Nuclear Command and Control System (SAUS)
NCCS .... Numerical Control Computer Sciences (SAUS)

NCCSA......... National Council for the Church and Social Action (EA)
NCCSA........ Nature Conservation Council of South Australia
NCCS-A...... Navy Command and Control System-Ashore (SAUS)
NCCSC........ National Coordinating Center in Solidarity with Chile [*Later, NCC*] (EA)
NCCSC........ Northern California Collegiate Ski Conference (PSS)
NcCSC .... Sandoz Chemical, Charlotte, NC [*Library symbol*] [*Library of Congress*] (LCLS)
NCCSCE....... National Council on Community Services and Continuing Education (EA)
NcCSH .... Sun-Health, Inc., Charlotte, NC [*Library symbol*] [*Library of Congress*] (LCLS)
NcCSI........... SIM International Resource Center, Charlotte, NC [*Library symbol*] [*Library of Congress*] (LCLS)
NCCSL .... National Center for Cross-Cultural Studies in Law [*Monash University*] [*Australia*]
NCCSS........ North Central Conference on Summer Schools (EA)
NCCT .... National Council for Civic Theatres Ltd. [*British*] (BI)
NCCTA........ National Council of Chemical Technician Affiliates
NCCTS .... National Catholic Conference for Total Stewardship (EA)
NCCU .... National Conference of Canadian Universities
NCCU .... Neurosurgical Critical Care Unit (NUJO)
NCCU .... Newborn Convalescent Care Unit [*Medicine*]
NCCU .... North Carolina Central University [*Durham*]
NcCU .... University of North Carolina at Charlotte, Charlotte, NC [*Library symbol*] [*Library of Congress*] (LCLS)
NC Curves ... Noise Criterion Curves (SAUS)
NCC/USA...... National Council of Churches of Christ in the USA (NTCM)
NCCUSL....... National Commission for Creation of Uniform State Laws
NCCUSL....... National Conference of Commissioners on Uniform State Laws (EA)
NcCuW........ Western Carolina University, Cullowhee, NC [*Library symbol*] [*Library of Congress*] (LCLS)
NCCV .... National Center for Church Vocations [*Later, NCVC*] (EA)
NCCV .... New Construction and Conversion [*Navy*]
NCCVL .... Northern California Collegiate Volleyball League (PSS)
NCCW .... National Chamber of Commerce for Women [*New York, NY*] (EA)
NCCW .... National Council of Career Women (EA)
NCCW .... National Council of Catholic Women (EA)
NCCWAO..... National Council of Community World Affairs Organizations (EA)
NCCWHO ..... National Citizens Committee for the World Health Organization [*Later, AAWH*] (EA)
NCCWS....... Nuclear Component Cooling Water System (SAUS)
NCCY .... National Committee for Children and Youth [*Later, NCOCY*] (EA)
NCCY .... National Council of Catholic Youth [*Defunct*] (EA)
NcCyL .... Lord Corp. Research and Development Library, Cary, NC [*Library symbol*] [*Library of Congress*] (LCLS)
NcCyS .... SAS Institute, Inc., Cary, NC [*Library symbol*] [*Library of Congress*] (LCLS)
NCCYSA ...... National Conference of Catholics in Youth Serving Agencies [*Defunct*] (EA)
nccz-............ Canal Zone [*MARC geographic area code*] [*Library of Congress*] (LCCP)
NCD .... AT&T Capital 8.25% 'PINES' [*NYSE symbol*] (SG)
NcD.............. Duke University, Durham, NC [*Library symbol*] [*Library of Congress*] (LCLS)
NCD .... National Center for the Diaconate [*Later, NAAND*] (EA)
NCD .... National Commission for Democracy [*Ghana*] [*Political party*]
NCD .... National Commission on Diabetes
NCD .... National Compliance Database [*Environmental Protection Agency*] (AEPA)
NCD .... National Control Data
NCD .... National Council on Disability (SAUS)
NCD .... National Council on Drugs [*Defunct*] (EA)
NCD .... Natural Circular Dichroism [*Optics*]
NCD .... Navy Cargo Document (DNAB)
NCD .... Navy Contracting Directives (MCD)
NCD .... Negotiable Certificate of Deposit (ADA)
NCD .... Negotiated Critical Dates [*Telecommunications*] (TEL)
NCD .... Nemine Contradicente [*No One Contradicting*] [*Latin*] [*Legal term*] (DLA)
NCD .... Network Computing Device (DCDG)
NCD .... Network Cryptographic Device
NCD .... Neurocirculatory Dystonia [*Medicine*] (DMAA)
NCD .... New Chemicals Database (SAUS)
NCD .... New Collegiate Dictionary (SAUS)
NCD .... New Component Design (IAA)
NCD .... Nicotinamide Cytosine Dinucleotide [*Biochemistry*]
NCD .... Nitrogen Clearance Delay (DMAA)
NCD .... No Can Do [*From pidgin English*]
NCD .... No Claim Discount [*Insurance*] (AIA)
NCD .... No Computed Data (HLLA)
NCD .... Noncallable Deposit [*Investment term*]
NCD .... Non Coasting Drive
NCD .... Non-Communicable Disease
NCD .... Non-Cumulative Dividend [*Business term*] (MHDW)
NCD .... Nonlinear Circular Dichroism
NCD .... Nonlinear Control Design [*Computer science*]
NCD .... Nordic Committee on Disability (EAIO)
NCD .... Nordic Council for the Deaf [*See also DNR*] (EAIO)
NCD .... Normal Childhood Diseases (DAVI)
NCD .... Normal Childhood Disorders [*Medicine*]
NCD .... Normalized Cumulative Deviation
NCD .... North Central Dairy Forwarders Tariff Bureau, Minneapolis MN [*STAC*]
NCD .... North Central Division [*Army Engineers*]

NCD .... Norton Change Directory [*Computer science*]
NCD .... Not Considered Disabling [*Medicine*] (MAE)
NCD .... Not Considered Disqualifying
NCD .... Notice of Credit Due
NCD .... Nova Scotia College of Art and Design Library [*UTLAS symbol*]
NCD .... Nuclear Commission Date (DNAB)
NCD .... Numerically Controlled Drafting (MCD)
NCDA .... National Career Development Association (EA)
NCDA .... National Center for Drug Analysis [*St. Louis*] [*FDA*]
NCDA .... National Ceramic Dealers Association (EA)
NCDA .... National College of District Attorneys
NCDA .... National Community Development Association (EA)
NCDA .... National Council on Drug Abuse [*Defunct*] (EA)
NCDA .... North Carolina Department of Agriculture (ROAS)
NCDAC .... National Civil Defense Advisory Council (EA)
NcDaD .... Davidson College, Davidson, NC [*Library symbol*] [*Library of Congress*] (LCLS)
NCDAD........ National Council for Diplomats in Art and Design [*British*] (BI)
NCDAI......... National Clearinghouse for Drug Abuse Information [*Public Health Service*] [*Rockville, MD*]
NcDalG .... Gaston College, Dallas, NC [*Library symbol*] [*Library of Congress*] (LCLS)
NcDan.......... Stokes County Public Library, Danbury, NC [*Library symbol*] [*Library of Congress*] (LCLS)
NCDAPA....... National Curtain, Drapery, and Allied Products Association [*Later, HFPA*]
NcD-B .... Duke University, Fuqua School of Business, Durham, NC [*Library symbol*] [*Library of Congress*] (LCLS)
NCDB .... National Center for Drugs and Biologics [*FDA*]
NCDB .... National Commercial and Development Bank [*Dominica*]
NCDB .... National Compliance Database [*Environmental Protection Agency*] (AEPA)
NCDBC........ National Center for the Development of Bilingual Curriculum (EA)
NCDC .... National Catholic Development Conference (EA)
NCDC .... National Center for Disease Control [*Public Health Service*]
NCDC .... National Climatic Data Center [*National Oceanic and Atmospheric Administration*] [*Information service or system*] (IID)
NCDC .... National Coalition for a Democratic Constitution [*Political group*] [*South Korea*]
NCDC .... National Committee for the Day Care of Children [*Later, DCCA*]
NCDC .... National Communicable Disease Center (MCD)
NCDC .... National Criminal Defense College
NCDC .... Naval Contract Distribution Center
NCDC .... New Community Development Corp. [*HUD*]
NCDC .... Nitro(carboxyphenyl)diphenylcarbamate [*Biochemistry*]
NCDC .... Norchenodeoxycholic Acid [*Biochemistry*]
NCDCA........ National Child Day Care Association (EA)
NCDCF .... National Civil Defense Computer Facility
NCDCR........ North Carolina Department of Cultural Resources
NCDCV........ Neonatal Calf Diarrhea Coronavirus
NcD-D.......... Duke University, Divinity School, Durham, NC [*Library symbol*] [*Library of Congress*] (LCLS)
NCDD.......... No Change in the Due Date (AFM)
NCDD-CCD... National Conference of Diocesan Directors of Religious Education (EA)
NCDDR........ National Center for the Dissemination of Disability Research (SAUS)
NCDDRE-CCD... National Conference of Diocesan Directors of Religious Education - CCD [*Continuing Christian Development*] (EA)
NcDe............ Denton Public Library, Denton, NC [*Library symbol*] [*Library of Congress*] (LCLS)
NCDE .... National Coalition for Democracy in Education [*Defunct*] (EA)
NCDF .... National Computer Dealer Forum (EA)
NCDF .... New Crop Development Fund (SAUS)
NCDF .... Non-Coded Digital Facsmile (SAUS)
NCDH .... National Committee Against Discrimination in Housing (EA)
NCDHM........ National Children's Dental Health Month [*American Dental Association*]
NCDI .... Network Computing Devices, Inc. [*NASDAQ symbol*] (SAG)
NCDIE .... Network Computing Devices [*NASDAQ symbol*] (TTSB)
NC Dir Ground Water Ground Water Circ... North Carolina. Division of Ground Water. Ground Water Circular (SAUS)
NC Dir Miner Resour Inf Circ... North Carolina. Division of Mineral Resources. Information Circular (SAUS)
NC Div Resour Plann Eval Miner Resour Sect Bull... North Carolina. Division of Resource Planning and Evaluation. Mineral Resources Section. Bulletin (SAUS)
NC Div Resour Plann Eval Miner Resour Sect Educ Ser... North Carolina. Division of Resource Planning and Evaluation. Mineral Resources Section. Educational Series (SAUS)
NC Div Resour Plann Eval Miner Resour Sect Reg Geol Ser... North Carolina. Division of Resource Planning and Evaluation. Mineral Resources Section. Regional Geology Series (SAUS)
NcD-L .... Duke University, School of Law, Durham, NC [*Library symbol*] [*Library of Congress*] (LCLS)
NCDL .... National Canine Defence League [*British*] (DI)
NCDM .... Numerical Control Drafting Machine (SAUS)
NCDM .... Numerically Controlled Drafting Machine (MCD)
NcD-MC .... Duke University, Medical Center, Durham, NC [*Library symbol*] [*Library of Congress*] (LCLS)
NcDnrUC...... Union Carbide Agricultural Products Co., Inc., Research Triangle Park, Durham (SAUS)
NCDO .... Navy Central Disbursing Office
NcDo........... Surry County-Dobson Library, Dobson, NC [*Library symbol*] [*Library of Congress*] (LCLS)

NcDoS .... Surry Community College, Dobson, NC [*Library symbol*] [*Library of Congress*] (LCLS)
NCDP .... Namibie Christelike Demokratiese Party [*Namibian Christian Democratic Party*] [*Political party*] (PPW)
NCDP .... Navigation Control/Display Panel (MCD)
NCDPEH ...... National Coalition for Disease Prevention and Environmental Health
NCDRC .... National Catholic Disaster Relief Committee (EA)
NCDRE .... National Conference of Directors of Religious Education (NTPA)
NCDS .... National Center for Disability Services (EA)
NCDS .... National Center for Dispute Settlement [*American Arbitration Association*] [*Later, CDS*]
NCDS .... National Child Development Study [*British*]
NCDS .... National Council for the Divorced and Separated [*British*] (DBA)
NCDS .... Naval Combat Data System
NCDS .... Navy Combat Direction System (MCD)
NCDS .... North Carolina Dental Society (SAUS)
NCDS .... Numerical Control Distribution System [*Computer science*] (MHDI)
NCDT .... National Council for Drama Training [*British*]
NCDT .... Noble-Collip Drum Trauma [*Physiology*]
NCDT .... Non-Chargeable Downtime
NCDT .... North Carolina Dance Theater
NCDT & E .... Naval Combat Demolition Training and Experimental Base [*Maui, HI*] (KSC)
NCDT & EBASE... Naval Combat Demolition Training and Experimental Base [*Maui, HI*]
NCDTO .... National Council of Dance Teacher Organizations [*Later, NDCA*] (EA)
NcDu .... Dunn Public Library, Dunn, NC [*Library symbol*] [*Library of Congress*] (LCLS)
NCDU .... Naval Combat Demolition Unit
NCDU .... Navigational Control & Display Unit (SAUS)
NcDubB .... Bladen Technical College, Dublin, NC [*Library symbol*] [*Library of Congress*] (LCLS)
NcDur .... Durham City-County Public Library, Durham, NC [*Library symbol*] [*Library of Congress*] (LCLS)
NcDurBC ..... Blue Cross & Blue Shield of North Carolina, Durham, NC [*Library symbol*] [*Library of Congress*] (LCLS)
NcDurBD ..... Becton, Dickinson & Co., Research Center Library, Research Triangle Park, Durham, NC [*Library symbol*] [*Library of Congress*] (LCLS)
NcDurC .... North Carolina Central University, Durham, NC [*Library symbol*] [*Library of Congress*] (LCLS)
NcDurCG ..... Ciba-Geigy Corp., Biotechnology Library, Durham, NC [*Library symbol*] [*Library of Congress*] (LCLS)
NcDurCL ..... North Carolina Central University, School of Library Science, Durham, NC [*Library symbol*] [*Library of Congress*] (LCLS)
NcDurCR ..... Chemstrand Research Center, Inc., Durham, NC [*Library symbol*] [*Library of Congress*] (LCLS)
NcDurEP ..... United States Environmental Protection Agency, Office of Administration, LibraryServices Branch, Park, Durham, NC [*Library symbol*] [*Library of Congress*] (LCLS)
NcDurF .... Forest History Society, Inc., Durham, NC [*Library symbol*] [*Library of Congress*] (LCLS)
NcDurG .... Glaxo, Inc., Durham, NC [*Library symbol*] [*Library of Congress*] (LCLS)
NcDurGH ..... Durham County General Hospital, Medical Library, Durham, NC [*Library symbol*] [*Library of Congress*] (LCLS)
NcDurHS ..... United States National Environmental Health Sciences Center, Durham, NC [*Library symbol*] [*Library of Congress*] (LCLS)
NcDurIBM ... International Business Machines Corp., IBM CPD Library, Durham, NC [*Library symbol*] [*Library of Congress*] (LCLS)
NcDurIF ...... International Fertility Research Program, Durham, NC [*Library symbol*] [*Library of Congress*] (LCLS)
NcDurIT ...... Chemical Industry institute of Toxicology, Durham, NC [*Library symbol*] [*Library of Congress*] (LCLS)
NcDurL .... Liggett & Myers, Inc. [*Later, Liggett Group, Inc.*], Durham, NC [*Library symbol*] [*Library of Congress*] (LCLS)
NcDurM ...... Monsanto Triangle Park Development Center, Durham, NC [*Library symbol*] [*Library of Congress*] (LCLS)
NcDurMi ..... Microelectronics Center Library, Durham, NC [*Library symbol*] [*Library of Congress*] (LCLS)
NcDurNH ..... National Humanities Center, Durham, NC [*Library symbol*] [*Library of Congress*] (LCLS)
NcDurRa ..... Radian Corp. Library, Durham, NC [*Library symbol*] [*Library of Congress*] (LCLS)
NcDurRT ..... Research Triangle Institute, Technical Library, Durham, NC [*Library symbol*] [*Library of Congress*] (LCLS)
NcDurSci .... North Carolina School of Science and Mathematics, Durham, NC [*Library symbol*] [*Library of Congress*] (LCLS)
NcDurST ..... North Carolina Science and Technology Research Center, Durham, NC [*Library symbol*] [*Library of Congress*] (LCLS)
NcDurT .... Durham Technical Institute, Durham, NC [*Library symbol*] [*Library of Congress*] (LCLS)
NcDurUC ..... Union Carbide Agricultural Products Co., Inc., Research Triangle Park, Durham, NC [*Library symbol*] [*Library of Congress*] (LCLS)
NcDurV .... United States Veterans Administration Hospital, Durham, NC [*Library symbol*] [*Library of Congress*] (LCLS)
NcDurW ...... Wellcome Research Laboratories, Durham, NC [*Library symbol*] [*Library of Congress*] (LCLS)
NcDurW-Gv... Burroughs Wellcome & Co., Greenville, NC [*Library symbol*] [*Library of Congress*] (LCLS)
NCDV .... Nebraska Calf Diarrhea Virus
NCDVD .... National Conference of Diocesan Vocation Directors (EA)
NcD-W .... Duke University, Woman's College, Durham, NC [*Library symbol*] [*Library of Congress*] (LCLS)

NcE .... Bladen County Public Library, Elizabethtown, NC [*Library symbol*] [*Library of Congress*] (LCLS)
NCe .... Middle Country Public Library, Centereach, NY [*Library symbol*] [*Library of Congress*] (LCLS)
NCE .... Nasa Cotopaxi [*Ecuador*] [*Seismograph station code, US Geological Survey*] (SEIS)
NCE .... National College of Education [*Illinois*]
NCE .... National Commission for Education (AIE)
NCE .... National Committee on the Emeriti (EA)
NCE .... National Council of Exchangors (EA)
NCE .... National Counselor Examination for Licensure & Certification (SAUS)
NCE .... Naughton Cardiac Exercise (MELL)
NCE .... Navigation & Command Equipment (SAUS)
NCE .... Navy Calibration Equipment List
NCE .... Navy Civil Engineer [*A publication*]
NCE .... Negative Contrast Echocardiography [*Medicine*] (DB)
NCE .... Network Communications Engineer (ACAE)
NCE .... Network Connection Element
NCE .... Network Control Elements (MCD)
NCE .... Network Control Engine [*Synoptics Communications, Inc.*]
NCE .... Neuritis of the Cauda Equina [*Medicine*]
NCE .... Neurologic Clinical Examination [*Medicine*] (MELL)
NCE .... Newark College of Engineering [*New Jersey*]
NCE .... New Catholic Edition [*Bible*]
NCE .... New Catholic Encyclopedia [*A publication*]
NCE .... New Century Energies [*NYSE symbol*] (SG)
NCE .... New Chemical Entity
NCE .... Nice [*France*] [*Airport symbol*] (OAG)
NCE .... No Change in Estimates
NCE .... Nomadic Computing Environment
NCE .... Noncommercial Education [*FCC*] (NTCM)
NCE .... Nonconvulsive Epilepsy [*Medicine*]
NCE .... Normal Calomel Electrode [*Electrochemistry*]
NCE .... Normal Chick Embryo
NCE .... Normal Curve Equivalent [*Testing*] (EDAC)
NCE .... Northcoast Executive Airlines [*ICAO designator*] (FAAC)
NCE .... NTID [*National Technical Institute for the Deaf*] Center on Employment (PAZ)
NCE .... Nuclear Capability Evaluation
NCE .... Nuclear Capability Exercise [*Army*] (AABC)
NCE .... Nuclear/Chemical Environment [*Battlefield condition*] (RDA)
NCEA .... National Catholic Educational Association (EA)
NCEA .... National Center for Economic Alternatives (EA)
NCEA .... National Center for Environmental Assessment (AEPA)
NCEA .... National Christian Education Association (EA)
NCEA .... National College Education and Admissions Foundation (EA)
NCEA .... National Community Education Association (EA)
NCEA .... National Consortium for Education Access (EA)
NCEA .... National Council for Educational Awards [*Ireland*]
NCEA .... N-(Carboxyethyl)alanine [*Biochemistry*]
NCEA .... North Carolina Education Association (SAUS)
NCEA .... North Central Electric Association (SAUS)
NCEarc .... National Conference of Executives of the Arc (NTPA)
NCEAS .... National Center for Ecological Analysis and Synthesis
NcEB .... Bladen Technical Institute, Elizabethtown, NC [*Library symbol*] [*Library of Congress*] (LCLS)
NcEb .... East Bend Public Library, East Bend, NC [*Library symbol*] [*Library of Congress*] (LCLS)
NCEB .... National Center for Educational Brokering [*Defunct*] (EA)
NCEB .... National Council for Environmental Balance (EA)
NCEB .... NATO Communications Electronics Board
NCEB .... North Coast Energy [*NASDAQ symbol*] (TTSB)
NCEBP .... North Coast Energy Cv'B'Pfd [*NASDAQ symbol*] (TTSB)
NCEBVS ...... National Chronic Epstein-Barr Virus Syndrome Association (EA)
NCEBW .... North Coast Energy Wrrt [*NASDAQ symbol*] (TTSB)
NC EB Welder... Numerically Controlled Electron Beam Welder (SAUS)
NCEC .... National Center for Educational Communication [*Office of Education*]
NCEC .... National Chemical Emergency Centre [*Atomic Energy Authority*] [*Didcot, Oxon., England*]
NCEC .... National Christian Education Council [*Church of England*]
NCEC .... National Commission for Electrologist Certification (EA)
NCEC .... National Committee for an Effective Congress (EA)
NCEC .... National Construction Employers Council [*Defunct*] (EA)
NCEC .... North Coast Environment Centre (SAUS)
NCEC .... North Coast Export Co. [*An association*] [*Defunct*] (EA)
NCECA .... National Council on Education for the Ceramic Arts (EA)
NC Ecc .... Notes of Cases, English Ecclesiastical and Maritime Courts [*1841-50*] [*A publication*] (DLA)
NCECD .... National Commission for Economic Conversion and Disarmament (EA)
NCECE .... National Council of Elected County Executives (EA)
NCECF .... National Children's Eye Care Foundation (EA)
NCECG .... National Coalition to Expand Charitable Giving [*Defunct*] (EA)
NCECS .... North Carolina Educational Computing Services (NITA)
NCECS .... North Carolina Educational Computing System (SAUS)
NCECW .... National Center for the Early Childhood Work Force (EA)
NcEd .... Eden Public Library, Eden, NC [*Library symbol*] [*Library of Congress*] (LCLS)
NCED .... National Center on Employment of the Deaf (EA)
NCEDC .... Northern California Earthquake Data Center
NCedHS .... Lawrence High School, Cedarhurst, NY [*Library symbol*] [*Library of Congress*] (LCLS)
NCEDL .... National Committee for Effective Design Legislation (EA)
NcEdR .... Rockingham County Public Library, Eden, NC [*Library symbol*] [*Library of Congress*] (LCLS)

NcEdR-M ..... Mayodan Public Library, Mayodan, NC [*Library symbol*] [*Library of Congress*] (LCLS)

NcEdR-R ...... Rockingham County Public Library, Reidsville Branch Library, Reidsville, NC [*Library symbol*] [*Library of Congress*] (LCLS)

NcEdR-S ...... Stoneville Public Library, Stoneville, NC [*Library symbol*] [*Library of Congress*] (LCLS)

NcEdt .... Shepard-Pruden Memorial Library, Edenton, NC [*Library symbol*] [*Library of Congress*] (LCLS)

NCEE .... National Catholic Educational Exhibitors (EA)

NCEE .... National Center on Education and Employment [*New York, NY*] [*Department of Education*] (GRD)

NCEE .... National Center on Education and the Economy

NCEE .... National Congress for Educational Excellence (EA)

NCEE .... National Council of Engineering Examiners (EA)

NCEE .... Northeast Consortium for Engineering Education (SAUS)

NCEEC .... Nested Cone Extendable Exit Cone (MCD)

NCEEER .... National Council for Eurasian and East European Research

NCEEF .... National Committee for Electrical Engineering Films

NCEER .... National Center for Earthquake Engineering Research [*Buffalo, NY*] (GRD)

NCEES .... National Council of Examiners for Engineering and Surveying (NTPA)

NCEET .... National Consortium for Environmental Education Training

NCEF .... National Calling and Emergency Frequencies (CET)

NCEF .... National Commission on Electronic Funds Transfers (MHDW)

NCEF .... Nomads' Charitable and Educational Foundation [*Australia*]

NCEF .... Non-Circumcision Educational Foundation (EA)

NCEFF .... National Committee for Education in Family Finance (EA)

NCE-FM .... Noncommercial Educational FM [*Frequency Modulation*] [*Telecommunications*] (OTD)

NCEFR .... National Council of Erectors, Fabricators, and Riggers (EA)

NCEFT .... National Commission on Electronic Fund Transfers

NCEG .... Numerical C Extensions Group (SAUS)

NCEHAI .... National Committee on Ethics of the Hearing Aid Industry [*Defunct*] (EA)

NCEHELP ..... National Conference of Executives of Higher Education Loan Plans [*Later, NCHELP*] (EA)

NCEHP .... National Center for the Exploration of Human Potential (EA)

NCEHPHP .... National Council on the Education of Health Professionals in Health Promotion (DAVI)

NCEHS .... National Center for Environmental Health Strategies (EA)

NcEl .... Kemp Memorial Library, Ellerbe, NC [*Library symbol*] [*Library of Congress*] (LCLS)

NCEL .... Naval Civil Engineering Laboratory

NCEL .... Navy Contractor Experience List

NCEL .... Nuclear Certified Equipment List (DNAB)

NcElc .... East Albemarle Regional Library, Elizabeth City, NC [*Library symbol*] [*Library of Congress*] (LCLS)

NcElcA .... College of the Albemarle, Elizabeth City, NC [*Library symbol*] [*Library of Congress*] (LCLS)

NcElcE .... Elizabeth City State University, Elizabeth City, NC [*Library symbol*] [*Library of Congress*] (LCLS)

NcElcP .... Pasquotank-Camden Library, Elizabeth City, NC [*Library symbol*] [*Library of Congress*] (LCLS)

NcElcR .... Roanoke Bible College, Mary E. Griffith Memorial Library, Elizabeth City, NC [*Library symbol*] [*Library of Congress*] (LCLS)

NcElk .... Elkin Public Library, Elkin, NC [*Library symbol*] [*Library of Congress*] (LCLS)

NcElon .... Elon College, Elon College, NC [*Library symbol*] [*Library of Congress*] (LCLS)

NcElonCH ... Historical Society of the Southern Convention, Congregation of Christian Churches, Elon College (SAUS)

NcElonCH ... Historical Society of the Southern Convention, Congregation of Christian Churches, Elon College, NC [*Library symbol*] [*Library of Congress*] (LCLS)

NcElonP ...... Primitive Baptist Library, Elon College, NC [*Library symbol*] [*Library of Congress*] (LCLS)

NCEM .... National Center for Electron Microscopy [*Berkeley, CA*] [*Lawrence Berkeley Laboratory*] [*Department of Energy*]

NCEMC .... National Committee on the Education of Migrant Children [*of the National Child Labor Committee*] (EA)

NCEMCH ..... National Center for Education in Maternal and Child Health (EA)

NCEMMH ..... National Center, Educational Media and Materials for the Handicapped [*Defunct*] (EA)

NCEMP .... National Center for Energy Management and Power

NCEMSF ...... National Collegiate Emergency Medical Services Foundation (SAUS)

NCEMT .... National Center for Excellence in Metalworking Technology [*Navy*]

NcEn .... Lilly Pike Sullivan Municipal Library, Enfield, NC [*Library symbol*] [*Library of Congress*] (LCLS)

NCEN .... National Commission on Egg Nutrition

NCEN .... Network Compatibility Engineer (ACAE)

NCEN .... New Century Financial

NCEN .... North Central

NC ENA .... North Carolina Emergency Nurses Association (SAUS)

NCen Assn Q.. North Central Association. Quarterly (SAUS)

NcEnk .... American Enka Corp., Enka, NC [*Library symbol*] [*Library of Congress*] (LCLS)

NCent .... Nineteenth Century (SAUS)

NCentBsh .... North Central Bancshares, Inc. [*Associated Press*] (SAG)

N Cent School L Rev... North Central School Law Review [*A publication*] (DLA)

NCEO .... National Center for Employee Ownership (EA)

NCEO .... National Center for Exploitation of the Oceans

NCEO .... Non-Conforming End Office (CCCA)

NCEOA .... National Council of Educational Opportunity Associations (EA)

NCEP .... National Center for Education in Politics [*Defunct*] (EA)

NCEP .... National Centers for Environmental Prediction [*Marine science*] (OSRA)

NCEP .... National Cholesterol Education Program

NCEP .... National Cholesterol Education Program Coordinating Committee [*National Institutes of Health*] (EGAO)

NCEP .... National Council for the Encouragement of Patriotism (EA)

NCEP .... National Council on Employment Policy (EA)

NCEPI .... National Center for Environmental Publications and Information (AEPA)

NcEr .... Erwin Public Library, Erwin, NC [*Library symbol*] [*Library of Congress*] (LCLS)

NCER .... National Center for Earthquake Research [*US Geological Survey*]

NCER .... National Conference on Electromagnetic Relays

NCER .... National Council on Educational Research [*Later, NCERI*] [*Department of Education*] [*Washington, DC*]

NCERACCS... National Coalition to End Racism in America's Child Care System (EA)

NCERD .... National Center for Educational Research and Development [*HEW*]

NCERT .... National Council for Educational Research and Training (WDAA)

nces- .... El Salvador [*MARC geographic area code*] [*Library of Congress*] (LCCP)

NCES .... National Center for Education Standards

NCES .... National Center for Education Statistics [*Office of Education*] [*Later, CES*]

NCES .... National Council for Educational Standards (AIE)

NCES .... New Careers in Employment Security (OICC)

NCES .... Normal Curve Equivalent Scores [*Testing*] (EDAC)

NCES .... North Central Experiment Station [*University of Minnesota*] [*Research center*] (RCD)

NCES .... North Country Educational Services [*Library network*]

NCESA .... National Class E Scow Association (EA)

NCESGR ...... National Committee for Employer Support of the Guard and Reserve (EA)

NCET .... National Center for Educational Technology [*Office of Education*]

NCET .... National Coastal Ecosystems Team [*Office of Biological Services, United States Fish and Wildlife Service*] (MSC)

NCET .... National Conference of English Teachers (BARN)

NCET .... National Council for Educational Technology [*British*]

NCETA .... National Center for Education and Training in Addictions [*Australia*]

NCEUS .... National Commission on Employment and Unemployment Statistics [*Bureau of Labor Statistics*] (GFGA)

NCEW .... National Conference of Editorial Writers (EA)

NCEY .... National Committee on Employment of Youth [*National Child Labor Committee*] (EA)

NCEZ .... National Coalition for Enterprise Zones [*San Diego, CA*] (EA)

NCF .... AT&T Capital 8.125% 'PINES' [*NYSE symbol*] (SG)

NCF .... Narramore Christian Foundation (EA)

NCF .... National Cancer Foundation

NCF .... National Chamber Foundation (EA)

NCF .... National Civics Federation

NCF .... National Clayware Federation [*British*] (DBA)

NCF .... National Commission on a Free and Responsible Media (EA)

NCF .... National Communications Forum [*National Engineering Consortium, Inc.*] [*Chicago, IL*] [*Telecommunications*] (TSSD)

NCF .... National Conservative Foundation (EA)

NCF .... National Consumer Federation (NADA)

NCF .... National Control Facility [*FAA*] (TAG)

NCF .... National Craniofacial Foundation [*Later, ICF*] (EA)

NCF .... National Cristina Foundation (EA)

NCF .... NATO Composite Force

NCF .... Naval Communications Facility (MUGU)

NCF .... Naval Construction Force (NVT)

NCF .... Naval Contingency Force (SAUS)

NCF .... Nerve Cell Food

NCF .... Net Cash Flow

NCF .... NetWare Command File [*Computer science*] (VLIE)

NCF .... NetWare Configuration File [*Computer science*]

NCF .... Network Control Facility (COE)

NCF .... Neutrophil Chemotactic Factor [*Hematology*]

NCF .... Neutrophil Cytosol Factor [*Cytology*]

NCF .... Newton-Cotes Formula [*Mathematics*]

NCF .... Nineteenth-Century Fiction [*A publication*] (ANEX)

NCF .... No Clean Flux (SAUS)

NCF .... No Clean Flux Process [*Computer manufacturing*] (PCM)

NCF .... No Conscription Fellowship [*England, World War I*]

NCF .... No Containment Failure [*Environmental science*] (COE)

NCF .... Nominal Characteristics File (IEEE)

NCF .... Noncold Front [*Meteorology*]

NCF .... Non-Crimp Fabric [*Plastics*]

NCF .... Nonflammable Cellulosic Foam

NCF .... Nuclear Capable Forces (MCD)

NCF .... Nucleonia Calibration Facility (SAUS)

NCF .... Nucleonics Calibration Facility (RDA)

NCF .... Nugget Coombs Foundation for Indigenous Studies [*Australia*]

NCF .... Nurses Christian Fellowship (EA)

NCFA .... Narcolepsy and Cataplexy Foundation of America (EA)

NCFA .... National Cat Fanciers' Association [*Defunct*] (EA)

NCFA ....:. National Collection of Fine Arts [*Later, National Mus eum of American Art*]

NCFA .... National Collegiate Football Association (EA)

NCFA .... National Commercial Finance Association (EA)

NCFA .... National Commission of Fine Arts (NADA)

NCFA .... National Committee for Adoption (EA)

NCFA .... National Consumer Finance Association (EA)

NCFA .... National Council for Adoption [*Formerly National Committee for Adoption*] (PAZ)
NCFA .... Naval Campus for Achievement (NVT)
NCFA .... North Carolina Forestry Association (WPI)
NCFA .... North Central Field Area
NCFA .... Nurses' Christian Fellowship of Australia
NCFAE .... National Council of Forestry Association Executives (EA)
NCFAP .... Naval Campus for Achievement Program (MCD)
NcFayC .... Cumberland County Public Library, Fayetteville, NC [*Library symbol*] [*Library of Congress*] (LCLS)
NcFayC-F ..... Cumberland County Public Library, North Carolina Foreign Language Center, Fayetteville, NC [*Library symbol*] [*Library of Congress*] (LCLS)
NcFayCFH ... Cape Fear Valley Hospital, Medical Library, Fayetteville, NC [*Library symbol*] [*Library of Congress*] (LCLS)
NcFayH .... Fayetteville Area Health Education Foundation, Inc., Fayetteville, NC [*Library symbol*] [*Library of Congress*] (LCLS)
NcFayM .... Methodist College, Fayetteville, NC [*Library symbol*] [*Library of Congress*] (LCLS)
NcFayR .... Rutledge College, Fayetteville, NC [*Library symbol*] [*Library of Congress*] (LCLS)
NcFayS .... Fayetteville State University, Fayetteville, NC [*Library symbol*] [*Library of Congress*] (LCLS)
NcFayT .... Fayetteville Technical Institute, Fayetteville, NC [*Library symbol*] [*Library of Congress*] (LCLS)
NcFayV .... United States Veterans Administration Medical Center, Fayetteville, NC [*Library symbol*] [*Library of Congress*] (LCLS)
NCFB .... National Collection of Food Bacteria (MELL)
NcFb .... United States Army, Special Services Library System, Fort Bragg, NC [*Library symbol*] [*Library of Congress*] (LCLS)
NcFbH .... United States Army, Womack Army Hospital, Fort Bragg, NC [*Library symbol*] [*Library of Congress*] (LCLS)
NcFbIM .... United States Army, Institute for Military Assistance, Marquat Memorial Library, Fort Bragg, NC [*Library symbol*] [*Library of Congress*] (LCLS)
NcFc .... Mooneyham Public Library, Forest City, NC [*Library symbol*] [*Library of Congress*] (LCLS)
NCFC .... National Coalition for a Free Cuba (EA)
NCFC .... National Commercial Finance Conference [*Later, NCFA*] (EA)
NCFC .... National Congress for Men and Children [*An association*] (PAZ)
NCFC .... National Council of Farmer Cooperatives (EA)
NCFCA .... National Congress of Floor Covering Associations [*Defunct*] (EA)
NCFD .... National Corporate Fund for Dance (EA)
NCFD .... New Computer Family D (SAA)
NCFDA .... National Council on Federal Disaster Assistance
NCFDAL ...... National Committee for Fair Divorce and Alimony Laws (EA)
NCFDITFS ... National Committee for the Full Development of Instructional Television Fixed Services [*ITFS regulation*] (NTCM)
NCFE .... National Campaign for Freedom of Expression
NCFE .... National Center for Financial Education (EA)
NCFE .... National Committee for Full Employment [*Defunct*] (EA)
NCFE .... National Commodity Futures Examination
NCFEA .... North Carolina Federation of Electronic Associations (SAUS)
NCFEAD .... National Council for Foundation Education in Art and Design (AIE)
NCFEPS .... National Commission for Full Employment Policy Studies (OICC)
NCFES .... North Central Forest Experiment Station [*St. Paul, MN*] [*Department of Agriculture*] (GRD)
NCFFR .... National Commission on Fraudulent Financial Reporting [*Defunct*] (EA)
NCFI .... National Cold Fusion Institute [*Closed June 30, 1991*]
NCFI .... North Carolina Alliance of Community (TBD)
NCFI .... North Carolina Foam Insulation (SAUS)
NCFIRB .... North Carolina Fire Insurance Rating Bureau (SAUS)
NCFIS .... National Center for Freedom of Information Studies (EA)
NCFJE .... National Committee for the Furtherance of Jewish Education (EA)
NCFL .... National Catholic Forensic League (EA)
NCFL .... National Center for Family Literacy (PAZ)
NCFLIS .... National Council on Foreign Language and International Studies (EA)
NCFM .... National Coalition of Free Men (EA)
NCFM .... National Commission on Food Marketing
NCFMF .... National Committee for Fluid Mechanics Films
NCFMS .... Naval Comptroller Financial Management Service
NCFNP .... National Committee for a Freedom Now Party [*Defunct*] (EA)
NCFO .... National Conference of Firemen and Oilers (NTPA)
NCFP .... National Conference on Fluid Power (EA)
NCFPC .... National Center for Fish Protein Concentrate [*Fish and Wildlife Service*]
NCFPC .... National Commission on Fire Prevention and Control
NCFPI .... National Clearinghouse for Family Planning Information [*Database*]
NCFPO .... Northern California Field Procurement Office (ACAE)
NCFPS .... National Center for Family Planning Services [*Health Services and Mental Health Administration, HEW*]
NCFPV .... Non-Continuous Flow Primer Valve (SAUS)
NcFr .... Macon County Public Library, Franklin, NC [*Library symbol*] [*Library of Congress*] (LCLS)
NCFR .... National Campaign for Firework Reform [*British*] (DBA)
NCFR .... National Council for Family Reconciliation (EA)
NCFR .... National Council on Family Relations (EA)
NCF Receiver... Non-Frequency-Conversion Receiver (SAUS)
NCFRF .... National Cystic Fibrosis Research Foundation [*Later, Cystic Fibrosis Foundation*] (EA)
NcFrt .... Franklinton Public Library, Franklinton, NC [*Library symbol*] [*Library of Congress*] (LCLS)
NCFS .... National College of Foot Surgeons (EA)
NCFS .... National Committee on Films for Safety [*Defunct*] (EA)

NCFS .... National Conference of Friendly Societies [*British*] (DBA)
NCFS .... Near Constant Force Suspension
NCFS .... Noncontingent Footshock
NCFS .... North Country Educational Services (SAUS)
NCFSA .... National Chronic Fatigue Syndrome Association (EA)
NCFSD .... NORAD Cost Factors and System Data [*Military*] (MCD)
NCFSFA .... National Chronic Fatigue Syndrome and Fibromyalgia Association [*Formerly, National Chronic Fatigue Syndrome Association*] (EA)
NCFSK .... Noncoherent Frequency Shift Keying
NCFSU .... Naval Construction Force Support Unit (NVT)
NCFT .... National Council for Families and Television (EA)
NCFTF .... National Consumer Fraud Task Force (EA)
NCFTJ .... National Conference on Federal Trial Judges (EA)
NcFv .... Farmville Public Library, Farmville, NC [*Library symbol*] [*Library of Congress*] (LCLS)
NCFVP .... National Center for Film and Video Preservation (EA)
NCFVSI .... National Council for Fishing Vessel Safety and Insurance (EA)
NCG .... Coast Guard Publication [*Later, NAVCG*]
NcG .... Greensboro Public Library, Greensboro, NC [*Library symbol*] [*Library of Congress*] (LCLS)
NCG .... Nanochannel Glass
NCG .... National Contractors Group [*British*] (DBA)
NCG .... National Council for the Gifted (EA)
NCG .... Network Control Group [*Manned Space Flight Network*]
NCG .... New College Graduate (BARN)
NCG .... Nickel-Coated Graphite [*Materials technology*]
NCG .... Nicotine Chewing Gum (PDAA)
NCG .... Non-Condensable Gas (SAUS)
NCG .... Noncondensible Gases
NCG .... North Carolina Nat Gas [*NYSE symbol*] (TTSB)
NCG .... Nova-Cogesco Resources, Inc. [*Toronto Stock Exchange symbol*]
NCG .... Nuclear Cratering Group [*Later, EERA*] [*Army*]
NCG .... Nueva Casas Grandes [*Mexico*] [*Airport symbol*] (AD)
NCG .... Null Command Generator
NCG .... Numerical Control Graphics (MCD)
NcGa .... Gaston-Lincoln Regional Library, Gastonia, NC [*Library symbol*] [*Library of Congress*] (LCLS)
NCGA .... National Church Goods Association (EA)
NCGA .... National Collegiate Gymnastics Association (PSS)
NCGA .... National Computer Graphics Association (EA)
NCGA .... National Corn Growers Association (EA)
NCGA .... National Cotton Ginners' Association (EA)
NCGA .... National Council on Governmental Accounting (EA)
NcGA .... North Carolina Agricultural and Technical State University, Greensboro, NC [*Library symbol*] [*Library of Congress*] (LCLS)
NcGaH .... Gaston Memorial Hospital, Inc., Medical Library, Gastonia (SAUS)
NcGaH .... Gaston Memorial Hospital, Inc., Medical Library, Gastonia, NC [*Library symbol*] [*Library of Congress*] (LCLS)
NcGaL.......... Gaston-Lincoln Regional Library, Gastonia, NC [*Library symbol*] [*Library of Congress*] (LCLS)
NcGAT .... AT&T Technologies Inc., Legal Library, Greensboro, NC [*Library symbol*] [*Library of Congress*] (LCLS)
NcGatr .... Gates County Library, Gatesville (SAUS)
NcGav .... Gates County Library, Gatesville, NC [*Library symbol*] [*Library of Congress*] (LCLS)
NcGB .... Bennett College, Greensboro, NC [*Library symbol*] [*Library of Congress*] (LCLS)
NcGBI .... Burlington Industries, Inc., Information Services Library, Greensboro, NC [*Library symbol*] [*Library of Congress*] (LCLS)
NcGBur .... Burlington Industries, Inc., Information Services Library, Greensboro (SAUS)
NcGBur .... Burlington Industries, Inc., Information Services Library, Greensboro, NC [*Library symbol*] [*Library of Congress*] (LCLS)
NcGC .... Greensboro College, Greensboro, NC [*Library symbol*] [*Library of Congress*] (LCLS)
NCGC .... National Catholic Guidance Conference [*Later, ARVIC*] (EA)
NCGCC .... National Convention of Gospel Choirs and Choruses (EA)
NcGCG .... Ciba-Geigy Corp., Technical Information Service, Greensboro, NC [*Library symbol*] [*Library of Congress*] (LCLS)
NcGCH .... Wesley Long Community Hospital, Inc., Greensboro, NC [*Library symbol*] [*Library of Congress*] (LCLS)
NcGCL .... Center for Creative Leadership, Greensboro, NC [*Library symbol*] [*Library of Congress*] (LCLS)
NcGCM .... Cone Mills Corp., Greensboro, NC [*Library symbol*] [*Library of Congress*] (LCLS)
NCGE .... National Council for Geographic Education (EA)
NCGE/J .... Journal of Geography. National Council of Geographic Education (journ.) (SAUS)
NC Gen Stat... General Statutes of North Carolina [*A publication*] (DLA)
NCGEP .... National Council on Graduate Education in Psychology
NcGf .... Granite Falls Public Library, Granite Falls, NC [*Library symbol*] [*Library of Congress*] (LCLS)
NCGF .... Nickel-Coated Graphite Fiber (SAUS)
NcGG .... Guilford College, Greensboro, NC [*Library symbol*] [*Library of Congress*] (LCLS)
NCGG .... National Committee for Geodesy and Geophysics (MCD)
NcGGil .... Gilbarco Corp. Library, Greensboro, NC [*Library symbol*] [*Library of Congress*] (LCLS)
NcGGT .... Guilford Technical Community College, Learning Resource Center, Greensboro, NC [*Library symbol*] [*Library of Congress*] (LCLS)
NcGH .... Moses H. Cone Memorial Hospital, Medical Library, Greensboro, NC [*Library symbol*] [*Library of Congress*] (LCLS)
NCGIC .... National Cartographic and Geographic Information Center [*Geological Survey*] [*Reston, VA*] [*Database*]
NCGIF .... National Cherry Growers and Industries Foundation (EA)

NCGIS.......... National Council of Guilds for Infant Survival (EA)
NcGL............ Lorillard Research Center, Greensboro, NC [*Library symbol*] [*Library of Congress*] (LCLS)
NCGLC........ National Caucus of Gay and Lesbian Counselors (EA)
NCGMCTC.... National Chevy/GMC Truckin' Club [*Defunct*] (EA)
NCGNP........ National Conference of Gerontological Nurse Practitioners (SAUS)
NcGo............ Wayne County Public Library, Goldsboro, NC [*Library symbol*] [*Library of Congress*] (LCLS)
NcGoCH....... Cherry Hospital, Learning Resource Center, Goldsboro, NC [*Library symbol*] [*Library of Congress*] (LCLS)
NcGoO......... O'Berry Center, Professional Library, Goldsboro, NC [*Library symbol*] [*Library of Congress*] (LCLS)
NcGoW........ Wayne Community College, Goldsboro, NC [*Library symbol*] [*Library of Congress*] (LCLS)
NcGPS......... Greensboro Public Schools, Greensboro, NC [*Library symbol*] [*Library of Congress*] (LCLS)
NCGR........... National Center for Genome Resources
NCGR........... National Clonal Germplasm Repository [*Corvallis, OR*] [*Agricultural Research Service*] [*Department of Agriculture*] (GRD)
NCGR........... National Council for GeoCosmic Research (EA)
NCGR........... National Council on Gene Resources (EA)
NcGrE........... East Carolina University, Greenville, NC [*Library symbol*] [*Library of Congress*] (LCLS)
NcGrE-H........ East Carolina University, Health Sciences Library, Greenville, NC [*Library symbol*] [*Library of Congress*] (LCLS)
NcGrP........... Pitt Technical Institute, Greenville, NC [*Library symbol*] [*Library of Congress*] (LCLS)
NcGrS .... Sheppard Memorial Library, Greenville, NC [*Library symbol*] [*Library of Congress*] (LCLS)
NCGS........... National Coalition of Girls Schools (NTPA)
NCGS........... National Cooperative Gallstone Study
NCGS........... New Century Gilders Society [*A union*] [*British*]
NCGS........... Nuclear Criteria Group Secretariat [*Air Force Weapons Laboratory*] [*Kirtland Air Force Base, NM*]
NCGS........... Nuclear Criteria Group Secretary (NAKS)
NCGSTDS .... National Coalition of Gay Sexually Transmitted Disease Services [*Defunct*] (EA)
ncgt-............ Guatemala [*MARC geographic area code*] [*Library of Congress*] (LCCP)
NCGT .... Nitrogen-cooled Closed-cycle Gas Turbine (SAUS)
NcGU .... University of North Carolina at Greensboro, Greensboro, NC [*Library symbol*] [*Library of Congress*] (LCLS)
NcGWE .... Western Electric Co., Legal Library, Greensboro, NC [*Library symbol*] [*Library of Congress*] (LCLS)
NCGWR........ National Center for Ground Water Research [*Stillwater, OK*] [*Environmental Protection Agency*] (GRD)
NCH .... Hamilton & Kirkland Colleges, Clinton, NY [*Library symbol*] [*Library of Congress*] (LCLS)
NCH .... Nachingwea [*Tanzania*] [*Airport symbol*] (OAG)
NCH .... National Center for Homeopathy (EA)
NCH .... National Center on Educational Media and Materials for the Handicapped, Columbus, OH [*Inactive*] [*OCLC symbol*] (OCLC)
NCH .... National Children's Home [*British*]
NCH .... National Clearinghouse [*Public Health Service*]
NCH .... National Coalition for the Homeless (EA)
NCH .... National Cocaine Hotline
NCH .... National Committee on Housing
NCH .... National Council on the Humanities [*Washington, DC*]
NCH .... NCH Corp. [*Formerly, National Chemsearch Corp.*] [*NYSE symbol*] (SPSG)
NCH .... Negative Channel [*Computer science*] (IAA)
NCH .... Network Connection Handler
NCH .... Nielson Clearing House [*A.C. Nielson Co.*] (DOAD)
NCH .... Notched
NCH .... Number [*or Name*] Changed [*Telephone Listing*] (BARN)
NCH .... Nylon Clay Hydride [*Plastics*]
NCha............ Chatham Public Library, Chatham, NY [*Library symbol*] [*Library of Congress*] (LCLS)
NcHa............ Hamlet Public Library, Hamlet, NC [*Library symbol*] [*Library of Congress*] (LCLS)
NCHA........... National Campers and Hikers Association (EA)
NCHA........... National Capital Housing Authority
NCHA........... National Crossbow Hunters Association (EA)
NCHA........... National Cutting Horse Association (EA)
NCHA........... Northern Collegiate Hockey Association (PSS)
NCHAA......... National Cutting Horse Association of Australia
NChaL........... Chatham Public Library, Chatman, NY [*Library symbol*] [*Library of Congress*] (LCLS)
NcHal........... Halifax County Library, Halifax, NC [*Library symbol*] [*Library of Congress*] (LCLS)
NChap.......... Chappaqua Library, Chappaqua, NY [*Library symbol*] [*Library of Congress*] (LCLS)
NcHaR .... Richmond Technical Institute, Hamlet, NC [*Library symbol*] [*Library of Congress*] (LCLS)
NcHav.......... Havelock-Craven County Public Library, Havelock, NC [*Library symbol*] [*Library of Congress*] (LCLS)
NcHavCr ...... Craven Community College, Havelock Learning Center, Havelock, NC [*Library symbol*] [*Library of Congress*] (LCLS)
NcHay.......... Moss Memorial Library, Hayesville, NC [*Library symbol*] [*Library of Congress*] (LCLS)
NCHC .... National Clogging and Hoedown Council (EA)
NCHC .... National Collegiate Honors Council (EA)
NCHC .... National Council of Health Centers [*Formerly, NCHCS*] [*Later, AHCA*] (EA)
NCHCA......... National Commission for Health Certifying Agencies (EA)

NCHCS........ National Council of Health Care Services (EA)
NCHCT .... National Center for Health Care Technology [*US Congress agency*]
NCHDI.......... National Center for Hearing Dog Information [*Later, HDRC*] (EA)
NcHe............ H. Leslie Perry Memorial Library, Henderson, NC [*Library symbol*] [*Library of Congress*] (LCLS)
NCHE .... National Center for Health Education (EA)
NCHE .... National Committee on Household Employment
NCHE .... National Council for History Education (EA)
NCheH .... Saint Joseph Intercommunity Hospital, Cheektowaga, NY [*Library symbol*] [*Library of Congress*] (LCLS)
NCHELP ...... National Council of Higher Education Loan Programs (EA)
NCHEML ...... National Chemical Laboratory (MCD)
NCHEMS ...... National Center for Higher Education Management Systems (EA)
NCHER......... National Center for Homecare Education and Research [*Defunct*] (EA)
NCHES .... National Child Health and Education Study [*University of Bristol*] [*British*]
NcHeV.......... Vance County Technical Institute, Henderson, NC [*Library symbol*] [*Library of Congress*] (LCLS)
NCHF .... Navy Cargo Handling Force (COE)
NCHF .... Northern California Hemophilia Foundation (SAUS)
NcHf............ Perquimans County Library, Hertford, NC [*Library symbol*] [*Library of Congress*] (LCLS)
NCHFCI........ National Committee to Honor the Fourteenth Centennial of Islam (EA)
NCHFFA .... National Council of Health Facilities Finance Authorities (NTPA)
N CHG .... Normal Charge (MHDB)
NCHGD .... National Clearinghouse for Human Genetic Diseases [*Later, NCEMCH*] [*Public Health Service*] [*Information service or system*] (IID)
NCHGR .... National Center for Human Genome Research
NCHHA .... National Council of Homemakers and Home Health Aides
NCHHHSO.... National Coalition of Hispanic Health and Human Services Organizations (EA)
NCHI .... National Council of the Housing Industry (EA)
NcHil .... Confederate Memorial Library, Hillsboro, NC [*Library symbol*] [*Library of Congress*] (LCLS)
NCHLA......... National Committee for a Human Life Amendment (EA)
NCHLRR ...... National Commission on Human Life, Reproduction, and Rhythm (EA)
NCHLS .... National Council on Health Laboratory Services (EA)
NCHM .... National Center for Housing Management (EA)
NCHMHHSO... National Coalition of Hispanic Mental Health and Human Services Organizations [*Later, NCHHHSO*]
NCHMI......... National Centers for Health and Medical Information, Inc. [*Research center*] (RCD)
NCHMOS...... Negative Channel Metal-Oxide Semiconductor (IAA)
NCHMT .... National Capital Historical Museum of Transportation (EA)
ncho-........... Honduras [*MARC geographic area code*] [*Library of Congress*] (LCCP)
NCHO .... National Chicano Health Organization (EA)
NcHp............ High Point Public Library, High Point, NC [*Library symbol*] [*Library of Congress*] (LCLS)
NCHP .... National Corp. for Housing Partnerships
NCHP .... National Council of Hospice Professionals (SAUS)
NCHP .... Nickel-Chromium Honeycomb Panel
NCHPA......... National Center for Health Promotion and Aging (EA)
NcHpC .... High Point College, High Point, NC [*Library symbol*] [*Library of Congress*] (LCLS)
NCHPC......... National Consortium for High Performance Computing (DDC)
NCHPD......... National Council on Health Planning and Development
NcHpH .... High Point Regional Hospital Medical Library, High Point, NC [*Library symbol*] [*Library of Congress*] (LCLS)
NCHR .... National Coalition for Haitian Refugees (EA)
NCHR .... National Coalition for Haitian Rights (EA)
N Ch R .... Nelson's English Chancery Reports [*A publication*] (DLA)
Nchr............ Numismatic Chronicle (SAUS)
NCHRP......... National Cooperative Highway Research Program
NCHRTM....... National Clearing House of Rehabilitation Training Materials [*Oklahoma State University*] [*Information service or system*] (IID)
NcHs............ Hudson Library, Highlands, NC [*Library symbol*] [*Library of Congress*] (LCLS)
NCHS .... National Center for Health Statistics [*Public Health Service*] [*Hyattsville, MD*] [*Originator and database*]
NCHS .... National Committee on Homemaker Service [*Superseded by NHC*] (EA)
NCHSR......... Australian National Centre in HIV Social Research (SAUS)
NCHSR......... National Center for Health Services Research
NCHSR......... National Center for Health Services Research and Health Care Technology Assessment [*Rockville, MD*] [*Public Health Service*] (GRD)
NCHSR & D... National Center for Health Services Research and Development [*Later, NCHSR*] [*HEW*]
NCHSRD ...... National Center for Health Services Research and Development [*Later, NCHSR*] [*HEW*]
NcHu............ Hudson Public Library, Hudson, NC [*Library symbol*] [*Library of Congress*] (LCLS)
NcHv............ Henderson County Public Library, Hendersonville, NC [*Library symbol*] [*Library of Congress*] (LCLS)
NcHvH .... Blue Ridge Technical Institute, Hendersonville, NC [*Library symbol*] [*Library of Congress*] (LCLS)
NcHvME....... Mother Earth News, Hendersonville, NC [*Library symbol*] [*Library of Congress*] (LCLS)
NCHVR......... National Center for HIV [*Human Immunodeficiency Virus*] Virology Research [*Australia*]

NCHVRFE..... National College for Heating, Ventilating, Refrigeration, and Fan Engineering (MCD)
NCHW......... National Council of Hispanic Women (EA)
NCHWPPTA... National Conference of Health, Welfare, and Pension Plans, Trustees and Administrators [*Later, International Foundation of Employee Benefit Plans*] (EA)
NcHy........... Elbert Ivey Memorial Library, Hickory, NC [*Library symbol*] [*Library of Congress*] (LCLS)
NcHyC......... Catawba Valley Technical Institute, Hickory, NC [*Library symbol*] [*Library of Congress*] (LCLS)
NcHyCH .... Catawba Memorial Hospital, Northwest AHEC Library at Hickory, Hickory, NC [*Library symbol*] [*Library of Congress*] (LCLS)
NcHyCM...... Catawba Area Mental Health Center, Hickory, NC [*Library symbol*] [*Library of Congress*] (LCLS)
NcHyFH....... Glenn R. Frye Memorial Hospital, Hickory, NC [*Library symbol*] [*Library of Congress*] (LCLS)
NcHyL......... Lenoir Rhyne College, Hickory, NC [*Library symbol*] [*Library of Congress*] (LCLS)
NcHyMH ...... Hickory Memorial Hospital Library, Hickory, NC [*Library symbol*] [*Library of Congress*] (LCLS)
NcHyS......... Siecor Corp., Technical Information Center, Hickory, NC [*Library symbol*] [*Library of Congress*] (LCLS)
NCI............. Camden County Library, Voorhees (SAUS)
NCi............. Central Islip Public Library, Central Islip, NY [*Library symbol*] [*Library of Congress*] (LCLS)
nCi............. Nanocurie [*One billionth of a curie*]
NCI............. Naphthalene Creosote, Iodoform [*Powder for lice*]
NCI............. National Cancer Institute [*Database producer*] [*Bethesda, MD*] [*National Institutes of Health*] [*Department of Health and Human Services*]
NCI............. National Captioning Institute (EA)
NCI............. National Cheese Institute (EA)
NCI............. National Components, Inc. (EFIS)
NCI............. National Computer Index [*National Computing Centre Ltd.*] [*British*] [*Information service or system*] (CRD)
NCI............. National Computer Institute (MCD)
NCI............. National Computing Industries (NITA)
NCI............. National Council for Inordinacy (EA)
NCI............. National Critics Institute (EA)
NCI............. Natural Casing Institute [*Later, International Natural Sausage Casing Institute*] (EA)
NCI............. Naval Cost Inspector
NCI............. Navigant Consulting [*NYSE symbol*] (SG)
NCI............. Navigation Control Indicator (MCD)
NCI............. Necocli [*Colombia*] [*Airport symbol*] (OAG)
NCI............. Negative Chemical Ionization [*Spectrometry*]
NCI............. Network Channel Interface (SAUS)
NCI............. Network Communications International [*Telecommunications service*] (TSSD)
NCI............. Network Computer, Inc. (IGQR)
NCI............. Neutral Countries Intelligence [*of Ministry of Economic Warfare*] [*British*] [*World War II*]
NCI............. New Community Instrument [*European Community*] (MHDB)
NCI............. New Concepts Initiative (ACAE)
NCI............. New Creation Institute (EA)
NCI............. No Common Interest
NCI............. No-Cost Item (AAG)
NCI............. Nodular Cast Iron (SAUS)
NCI............. Nomenclature Control Index (MCD)
NCI............. Nominal Correction I [*Phasing maneuver*] (MCD)
NCI............. Noncoded Information [*Computer science*] (IBMDP)
NCI............. Noncoherent Integration
NCI............. Noncriterion Ischemic (DMAA)
NCI............. North Conway Institute (EA)
NCI............. Northeast Computer Institute (HGAA)
NCI............. Notice of Change Inception (MCD)
NCI............. Notice of Change Incorporation (MCD)
NCI............. Nuclear Capability Inspection (CINC)
NCI............. Nuclear Contour Index [*Cytology*]
NCI............. Nuclear Control Institute (EA)
NCI............. Numerical Coded Instruction (SAUS)
NCI............. Nurse Competency Inventory
NCI............. Nursing Care Integration [*Medicine*] (DMAA)
NCI............. Nursing Citation Index
NCI............. Office of New Concepts and Initiatives [*Air Force*] (TEL)
NCI............. Southwest New Jersey Consortium for Health Information Service, Voorhees, NJ [*OCLC symbol*] (OCLC)
NCIA .... National Cavity Installation Association [*British*]
NCIA .... National Center on Institutions and Alternatives (EA)
NCIA .... National Crop Insurance Association [*Shawnee Mission, KS*] (EA)
NCIAC......... National Construction Industry Arbitration Committee (EA)
NCIAC......... North Central Intercollegiate Athletic Conference (PSS)
NCIAED .... National Center for Information and Advice on Educational Disadvantage
NCIB .... National Charities Information Bureau (EA)
NCIB .... National Collection of Industrial Bacteria [*British*]
NCI Bldg...... NCI Building Systems [*Associated Press*] (SAG)
NCIBRD........ National Center for Integrated Bioremediation Research & Development [*Initiated in Michigan with government funding, 1994*]
NCIC .... National Cancer Institute of Canada
NCIC .... National Career Information Center [*Defunct*] (EA)
NCIC .... National Cartographic Information Center [*United States Geological Survey*] [*Reston, VA*]
NCIC .... National Commission on the Indian Canadian

NCIC .... National Congress of Italian Canadians
NCIC .... National Construction Industry Council (EA)
NCIC .... National Crime Information Center [*FBI*] [*Washington, DC*]
NCIC .... National Crime Information Computer (SAUS)
NCIC .... National Crop Insurance Council [*Inactive*] (EA)
NCIC .... Network Communications Interface, Common (MCD)
NCIC .... Network Control Interface Channel [*Computer science*] (VLIE)
NCIC .... Non-Circumcision Information Center (EA)
NCIC .... Nonconfidential Information Center (AEPA)
NCIC .... Northwest Coastal Information Center [*Marine science*] (MSC)
NCIC .... Northwest Conference of Independent Colleges (PSS)
NCICA .... National Counter Intelligence Corps Association (EA)
NCIC Ops ...... North Carolina Industrial Commission Advance Sheets [*A publication*] (DLA)
NCICU .... National Council of Independent Colleges and Universities [*Later, NAICU*]
NCID .... National Council for Industrial Defense (EA)
NCID .... Non-Cooperative Identification (ACAE)
NCIDQ........ National Council for Interior Design Qualification (EA)
NCIE........... National Coalition for Indian Education (EA)
NCIES .... National Center for the Improvement of Educational Systems [*Office of Education*]
NCIES .... National Committee for International Education through Satellites (EA)
NCIESD......... National Conference on International Economic and Social Development [*Later, IDC*]
NCIH .... National Conference on Industrial Hydraulics
NCIH .... National Council for International Health (EA)
NCIHC......... National Council for Interior Horticultural Certification (EA)
NCII .... National Council for Industrial Innovation (EA)
NCII .... National Council of Individual Investors
NCIJC......... National Council of Independent Junior Colleges [*Defunct*]
nCi/L......... Nanocuries per Liter (EEVL)
NCIL........... National Council on Independent Living (EA)
NCILT........... National Centre for Industrial Language Training [*British*] (DI)
NCIM........... National Commission on Infant Mortality (MELL)
NCIMA .... National Cellulose Insulation Manufacturers Association
NCIMC......... National Council of Industrial Management Clubs [*Later, IMC*] (EA)
NCIMS......... National Conference on Interstate Milk Shipments
NCIMS......... Negative Chemical Ionization Mass Spectra
NCIMS .... Numerical Control Information Management System (MCD)
NCIN .... National Credit Information Network
NCIN .... North Carolina Information Network [*Library network*]
NCINAS....... National Council of Industrial Naval Air Stations (EA)
NCINASEO ... National Council of Industrial Naval Air Stations Employee Organizations [*Formerly, NCNASEO*] (EA)
NCIO .... National Congress of Inventors Organizations (EA)
NCIO .... National Council on Indian Opportunity (EA)
NCIP .... National Center to Improve Practice (SAUS)
NCIP .... National Council for Industrial Peace [*Defunct*] (EA)
NCIP .... No Change in Price (MCD)
NCIP .... Non-Contributory Invalid Pension [*British*] (DI)
NCIP .... North American Collections Inventory Project [*Established 1982*] [*Library science*]
NCIP .... Northeast Corridor Improvement Program (SAUS)
NCIP .... Novell Certified Internet Professional (SAUS)
NCIPA .... National Committee for Independent Political Action (EA)
NCIPLA .... National Council of Intellectual Property Law Associations (EA)
NCIR .... National Center for Immigrants' Rights [*Later, NILC*] (EA)
NCIR .... National Center for Initiative Review (EA)
NCIR .... National Conference on Industrial Research
NCIRF......... National Center for Initiative Review Foundation [*Defunct*] (EA)
NCIRLS........ North Central Regional Library System [*Library network*]
NCIS .... Nadir Climate Interferometer Spectrometer (MCD)
NCIS .... National Chemical Information System (DIT)
NCIS .... National Coalition of Independent Scholars
NCIS .... National Council of Independent Schools [*Later, National Association of Independent Schools*] (AEBS)
NCIS .... National Credit Information Service [*TRW, Inc.*] [*Long Beach, CA*] [*Credit-information databank*]
NCIS .... National Criminal Intelligence Service (WA)
NCIS .... National Criminal Investigation Service (WDAA)
NCIS .... National Crop Insurance Services (EA)
NCIS .... Naval Criminal Investigative Service
NCIS .... Navy Cost Information System
NCIS .... Nuclear Criticality Information System [*Lawrence Livermore National Laboratory*] [*Information service or system*] (IID)
NCISC......... Naval Counterintelligence Support Center
NCISD......... National Coalition on Immune System Disorders (EA)
NCISE......... National Center for Improving Science Education (EA)
NCiSH......... Central Islip State Hospital, Central Islip, NY [*Library symbol*] [*Library of Congress*] (LCLS)
NCISS .... National Council of Investigation and Security Services (EA)
NCIT........... National Committee for Insurance Taxation (EA)
NCIT........... National Council of Independent Truckers [*Defunct*] (EA)
NCIT........... National Council of Inland Transport [*British*] (DBA)
NCIT........... Numerical Control Inspection Tape (MCD)
NCITC......... National Clothing Industry Training Committee [*Australia*]
NCITD......... National Committee on International Trade Documentation [*MARAD*] (TAG)
NCITD......... National Council on International Trade Documentation [*In association name: NCITD - The International Trade Facilitation Council*] (EA)
NCITR......... National Center for Intermedia Transport Research [*Los Angeles, CA*] (GRD)

NCITS .... National Committee for Information Technology Standards [*Washington, DC*] (DDC)
NCITT .... National Committee for the In-Service Training of Teachers [*Scotland*] (AIE)
NCIU .... Network Common Interface Unit
NCIU .... Network Common Interference Unit (MCD)
NCIU .... Network Communications Interface, Unique
NCIV .... National Council for International Visitors (EA)
NcJ .... Jamestown Public Library, Jamestown, NC [*Library symbol*] [*Library of Congress*] (LCLS)
NCJ .... Johnson C. Smith University, James B. Duke Memorial Library, Charlotte, NC [*OCLC symbol*] (OCLC)
NCJ .... Needle Catheter Jejunostomy [*Medicine*] (DMAA)
NCJA .... National Criminal Justice Association (EA)
NcJa .... Onslow County Public Library, Jacksonville, NC [*Library symbol*] [*Library of Congress*] (LCLS)
NcJaC .... Coastal Carolina Community College, Jacksonville, NC [*Library symbol*] [*Library of Congress*] (LCLS)
NcJac .... Northampton County Memorial Library, Jackson, NC [*Library symbol*] [*Library of Congress*] (LCLS)
NcJacL .... Northampton County Memorial Library, Jackson, NC [*Library symbol*] [*Library of Congress*] (LCLS)
NcJaMC .... United States Marine Corps, Marine Corps Air Station, Special Services for Station Library, New River Base, Jacksonville, NC [*Library symbol*] [*Library of Congress*] (LCLS)
NCJAR .... National Council for Japanese American Redress [*Defunct*] (EA)
NCJAVM ...... National Council on Jewish Audio-Visual Materials (EA)
NCJC .... National Conference of Judicial Councils [*Defunct*] (EA)
NCJCC .... National Council of Jewish Correctional Chaplains [*Later, AJCCA*] (EA)
NCJCJ .... National Council of Juvenile Court Judges [*Later, NCJFCJ*] (EA)
NCJCS .... National Conference of Jewish Communal Service [*Later, CJCS*] (EA)
NCJD .... National Coalition for a Just Draft (EA)
NCJD .... National Congress of Jewish Deaf (EA)
NCJE .... National Council for Jewish Education [*Later, CJE*] (EA)
NCJF .... National Center for Jewish Film (EA)
NCJFCJ .... National Council of Juvenile and Family Court Judges (EA)
NcJG .... Guilford Technical Institute, Jamestown, NC [*Library symbol*] [*Library of Congress*] (LCLS)
NCJISN .... National Council of Jewish Invalids Survivors of Nazism [*Later, CHSD*] (EA)
NCJISS .... National Criminal Justice Information and Statistics Service
NCJJ .... National Center for Jobs and Justice (EA)
NCJJ .... National Center for Juvenile Justice (EA)
NCJMS .... National Center for Job Market Studies [*Commercial firm*] [*Washington, DC*] (EA)
NcJo .... Jonesville-Arlington Public Library, Jonesville, NC [*Library symbol*] [*Library of Congress*] (LCLS)
NCJO .... National Council of Junior Outdoorsmen (EA)
NCJ of L ...... North Carolina Journal of Law [*A publication*] (DLA)
NCJPS .... National Center for Jewish Policy Studies
NCJR .... National Coalition for Jail Reform [*Defunct*] (EA)
NCJRS .... National Criminal Justice Reference Service [*Department of Justice*] [*Information service or system*]
NcJRS .... Ragsdale Senior High School, Jamestown, NC [*Library symbol*] [*Library of Congress*] (LCLS)
NCJSB .... National Commission on Jobs and Small Business [*Defunct*] (EA)
NCJSC .... National Criminal Justice Statistics Center
NCJT .... Nordic Committee of Journalism Teachers (EA)
NCJW .... National Council of Jewish Women (EA)
NCJWA .... National Council of Jewish Women of Australia
NCK .... Camden County College, Voorhees, NJ [*OCLC symbol*] (OCLC)
NcK .... Kinston-Lenoir County Public Library, Kinston, NC [*Library symbol*] [*Library of Congress*] (LCLS)
NCK .... Nagycenk [*Hungary*] [*Geomagnetic observatory code*]
NCK .... Neck
NCK .... Nickelodeon Industries Corp. [*Vancouver Stock Exchange symbol*]
NCK .... Norman, Craig & Kummel [*Advertising agency*]
NcKa .... Cannon Memorial YMCA Public Library, Kannapolis, NC [*Library symbol*] [*Library of Congress*] (LCLS)
NCKA .... National Catholic Kindergarten Association (AEBS)
NcKbMR ...... North Carolina Marine Resources Center, Fort Fisher, Kure Beach, NC [*Library symbol*] [*Library of Congress*] (LCLS)
NcKC .... Kinston-Lenoir County Public Library, Caswell Center Library, Kinston, NC [*Library symbol*] [*Library of Congress*] (LCLS)
NcKeD .... Duplin County, Dorothy Wightman Library, Kenansville, NC [*Library symbol*] [*Library of Congress*] (LCLS)
NcKeS .... James Sprunt Technical Institute, Kenansville, NC [*Library symbol*] [*Library of Congress*] (LCLS)
NcKg .... King Public Library, King, NC [*Library symbol*] [*Library of Congress*] (LCLS)
NcKiK .... Kittrell College, Kittrell, NC [*Library symbol*] [*Library of Congress*] (LCLS)
NcKL .... Lenoir Community College, Kinston, NC [*Library symbol*] [*Library of Congress*] (LCLS)
NCKL .... North Central Kansas Libraries System [*Library network*]
NcKm .... Jacob S. Mauney Memorial Library, Kings Mountain, NC [*Library symbol*] [*Library of Congress*] (LCLS)
NcKn .... Kenly Public Library, Kenly, NC [*Library symbol*] [*Library of Congress*] (LCLS)
NCKWM .... National Committee for the Korean War Memorial [*Later, KWVM*] (EA)
NCL .... Camden County Library, Voorhees, NJ [*OCLC symbol*] (OCLC)
NCL .... Financial

NCL .... National Carriers Ltd. [*British*] (DCTA)
NCL .... National Center for the Laity (EA)
NCL .... National Central Library [*United Kingdom*]
NCL .... National Character Laboratory (EA)
NCL .... National Chemical Laboratory
NCL .... National Civic League (EA)
NCL .... National Coalition for Literacy (EA)
NCL .... National Commuter Airways [*British*] [*ICAO designator*] (FAAC)
NCL .... National Consumers League (EA)
NCL .... National Council of Labour [*British*] (DCTA)
NCL .... National Cycle League (EA)
NCL .... Navy Calibration Laboratory
NCL .... Navy Code Logistic [*Plan*]
NCL .... Network Control Language
NCL .... Neuronal Ceroid Lipofuscinosis [*Medicine*]
NCL .... New Caledonia [*ANSI three-letter standard code*] (CNC)
NCL .... Newcastle [*England*] [*Airport symbol*] (OAG)
NCL .... Node Compatibility List [*Telecommunications*] (TEL)
NCL .... Node Control Logic [*Computer science*] (VLIE)
NCL .... Noise Control Laboratory [*Pennsylvania State University*] [*Research center*] (RCD)
NCL .... Norfolk, VA [*Location identifier*] [*FAA*] (FAAL)
NCL .... Normal Card Listing (SAUS)
NCL .... Norwegian Caribbean Lines
NCL .... Norwegian Cruise Line (TVEL)
NCL .... Norwegian Cruise Lines (TRID)
NCL .... Nucleolin (DMAA)
NCL .... Null Convention Logic (SAUS)
NCL .... Numerical Control Language [*Computer science*] (VLIE)
NCL .... Numerically Controlled Lathe
NCL .... NuVeen Ins CA Prem Inc Muni 2 [*NYSE symbol*] (TTSB)
NCL .... Nuveen Insured California Premium Income Municipal II [*NYSE symbol*] (SPSG)
NcL .... Scotland County Memorial Library, Laurinburg, NC [*Library symbol*] [*Library of Congress*] (LCLS)
NCLA .... National C-Lark Association (EA)
NCLA .... National Council of Local Administrators of Vocational Education and Practical Arts (EA)
NCLA .... North Carolina Library Association (SAUS)
NCLAB .... National Center for Laboratory Animal Sciences (SAUS)
NCLAN .... National Crop Loss Assessment Network
NCL & SW ... National Conference of Lawyers and Social Workers
NC Law Repos... North Carolina Law Repository [*A publication*] (DLA)
NC Law Repository... North Carolina Law Repository (Reprint) [*A publication*] (DLA)
NCLB .... North Central Laboratories, Inc. (SAUS)
NCLC .... National Catholic Liturgical Conference (EA)
NCLC .... National Caucus of Labor Committees
NCLC .... National Chamber Litigation Center (EA)
NCLC .... National Child Labor Committee (EA)
NCLC .... National Christian Life Community of the United States of America (EA)
NCLC .... National Consumer Law Center (EA)
NCLC .... National Council of Labour Colleges
NCLC .... National Council on Legal Clinics [*Later, CLEPR*]
NCLC .... Nineteenth Century Literary Criticism [*A publication*]
NCLC .... Noncombatant Labour Corps [*British*]
NCLCH .... National Civil Liberties Clearing House [*Defunct*] (EA)
NCLCI .... National Christian Leadership Conference for Israel (EA)
NCLD .... National Center for Law and Deafness [*Formerly, National Center for Law and the Deaf*] (EA)
NCLD .... National Center for Law and the Deaf (EA)
NCLD .... National Center for Learning Disabilities (EA)
NCLD .... Williamsport District Library Center [*Library network*]
NCLE .... National Contact Lens Examiners (EA)
NcLeC .... Caldwell County Public Library, Lenoir, NC [*Library symbol*] [*Library of Congress*] (LCLS)
NcLeCT .... Caldwell Community College and Technical Institute, Lenoir, NC [*Library symbol*] [*Library of Congress*] (LCLS)
NCLEHA .... National Conference of Local Environmental Health Administrators (EA)
NCLER .... National Clearinghouse on Licensure, Enforcement, and Regulation (EA)
NCLEX .... National Council Licensure Examination
NCLEX-RN ... National Council Licensure Examination for Registered Nurses
NCLF .... National Coalition to Legalize Freedom (EA)
NCLG .... National Committee for Latin and Greek (EA)
NCLG .... National Conference of Lieutenant Governors (EA)
NCLH .... National Center for Law and the Handicapped [*Defunct*] (EA)
NCLHA .... National Conference of Law Historians of America (EA)
NCLI .... National Committee for Labor Israel [*Later, NCLIIHC*] (EA)
NCLIIHC ...... National Committee for Labor Israel-Israel Histadrut Campaign (EA)
NcLil .... Harnett County Public Library, Lillington, NC [*Library symbol*] [*Library of Congress*] (LCLS)
NcLiL .... Lincoln County Memorial Library, Lincolnton, NC [*Library symbol*] [*Library of Congress*] (LCLS)
NClinc .... Clinton Corners Reading Center, Clinton Corners, NY [*Library symbol*] [*Library of Congress*] (LCLS)
NCLIP .... North Coast Life Ins Cv'A'Pfd [*NASDAQ symbol*] (TTSB)
NCLIP .... North Coast Life Insurance Co. [*NASDAQ symbol*] (SAG)
NCLIS .... National Commission on Libraries and Information Science [*Washington, DC*]
NCLIS .... National Council for Languages and International Studies (EA)
NcLit .... Littleton Public Library, Littleton, NC [*Library symbol*] [*Library of Congress*] (LCLS)

NCLJ	North Carolina Law Journal [*A publication*] (DLA)
NcLjUM	United Methodist Church, Commission on Archives and History, Lake Junaluska, NC [*Library symbol*] [*Library of Congress*] (LCLS)
NcLk	Rockingham County Library, Leakesville, NC [*Library symbol*] [*Library of Congress*] (LCLS)
NCLLF	National Civil Liberties Legal Foundation [*Inactive*] (EA)
NcLo	Franklin County Library, Louisburg, NC [*Library symbol*] [*Library of Congress*] (LCLS)
NCLO	Naval Communication Liaison Officer (IAA)
NcLo-B	Franklin County Library, Bunn Branch Library, Bunn, NC [*Library symbol*] [*Library of Congress*] (LCLS)
NcLoC	Louisburg College, Louisburg, NC [*Library symbol*] [*Library of Congress*] (LCLS)
NCLP	National Conference on Law and Poverty
NCLP	National Contract Laboratory Program (COE)
NCLP	Numerically Controlled Line Plotter
NCLPWA	National Council of Local Public Welfare Administrators (EA)
NCLR	National Center for Legislative Research [*Defunct*] (EA)
NCLR	National Center for Lesbian Rights (EA)
NCLR	National Coalition for Land Reform (EA)
NCLR	National Council for Labor Reform (EA)
NCLR	National Council of La Raza (EA)
NCL Rep	North Carolina Law Repository [*A publication*] (DLA)
NCL Reps	North Carolina Law Repository (Reprint) [*A publication*] (DLA)
NCLS	National Clearinghouse for Legal Services [*Legal Services Corp.*] [*Information service or system*] (IID)
NCLS	National Committee for Liberation of Slovakia (EA)
NCLS	National Conference of Lawyers and Scientists [*Joint project of the American Association for the Advancement of Science and the American Bar Association*]
NCLS	National Conference of State Legislatures [*Australia*]
NCLS	North Country Library System [*Library network*]
NcLS	Saint Andrews Presbyterian College, Laurinburg, NC [*Library symbol*] [*Library of Congress*] (LCLS)
NCLT	Night Carrier Landing Trainer [*Navy*]
NCLTA	National Cigar Leaf Tobacco Association [*Defunct*] (EA)
NcLu	Robeson County Public Library, Lumberton, NC [*Library symbol*] [*Library of Congress*] (LCLS)
NcLuH	Southeastern General Hospital, Medical Library, Lumberton, NC [*Library symbol*] [*Library of Congress*] (LCLS)
NcLuR	Robeson Technical Institute, Lumbarton, NC [*Library symbol*] [*Library of Congress*] (LCLS)
NcLxD	Davidson County Public Library, Lexington, NC [*Library symbol*] [*Library of Congress*] (LCLS)
NcLxDC	Davidson County Community College, Lexington, NC [*Library symbol*] [*Library of Congress*] (LCLS)
NCm	Center Moriches Free Public Library, Center Moriches, NY [*Library symbol*] [*Library of Congress*] (LCLS)
NCM	Court Martial Reports, Navy Cases [*A publication*] (DLA)
NCM	Mars Hill College, Mars Hill, NC [*OCLC symbol*] (OCLC)
NCM	Nailfold Capillary Microscope (DAVI)
NCM	National Center for Men (EA)
NCM	National Coal Model [*Department of Energy*] (GFGA)
NCM	National Coastal Monitoring (USDC)
NCM	National College of Music [*British*] (DI)
NCM	National Congress for Men (EA)
NCM	National Corvette Museum
NCM	National Cursillo Movement (EA)
NCM	Natural Clay Mosaic (DICI)
NcM	Navy Commendation Medal
NCM	Navy Correspondence Manual
NCM	Net Control Master (MCD)
NCM	Network Connection Management [*Computer science*] (VLIE)
NCM	Network Control Module
NCM	Newcastle Conservatorium of Music [*Australia*]
NCM	New Moon [*Queensland*] [*Airport symbol*] (AD)
NCM	Nicaraguan Campaign Medal
NCM	Nippon Calculating Machine Co. [*Japan*] (PDAA)
NCM	Nitrocellulose Membrane
NCM	No Compromise Majority [*An association*] (EA)
NCM	Node Controller Module (SAUS)
NCM	Noise Canceling Microphone
NCM	Noise Cancelling Microphone (SAUS)
NCM	Non Compos Mentis [*Not of Sound Mind*] [*Latin*] (LWAP)
NCM	Noncorrosive Metal
NCM	Noncrew Member
NCM	Nordic Council of Ministers (EAIO)
NCM	Nordic Council on Medicines [*See also NLN*] (EAIO)
NCM	Normal Human Colon Mucosal [*Cells*]
NCM	North Carolina Motor Carriers Association [*STAC*]
NCM	Northern Conservatory of Music [*Maine*]
NCM	Northern Cruise Master (SAA)
NCM	Notice of Commencement of Manufacture [*Toxic Substances Control Act*] [*Environmental Protection Agency*] (EPA)
NCM	Numerical Controlled Machine
NCM	Nurse Case Manager (DMAA)
NCM	Nuveen California Municipal Income [*NYSE symbol*] (SPSG)
NCMA	National Campus Ministry Association (EA)
NCMA	National Catalog Managers Association (EA)
NCMA	National Ceramic Manufacturers Association
NCMA	National Childminding Association [*British*] (DBA)
NCMA	National Concrete Masonry Association (EA)
NCMA	National Contract Management Association (EA)
NCMA	National Corporate Medical Associates [*An association*]
NCMA	National Council of Millinery Associations (EA)
NCMA	National Council of Moving Associations (EA)
NCMA	Naval Civilian Manager's Association (EA)
NCMA	Newspaper Credit Managers' Association (EA)
NCMA	North Carolina Museum of Art (SAUS)
NcMad	Madison Public Library, Madison, NC [*Library symbol*] [*Library of Congress*] (LCLS)
NCMAF	National Conference on Ministry to the Armed Forces (EA)
NCMAG	National Computer Center Management Advisory Group (COE)
NcMaM	McDowell Technical Institute, Marion, NC [*Library symbol*] [*Library of Congress*] (LCLS)
NcMaMC	McDowell County Public Library, Marion, NC [*Library symbol*] [*Library of Congress*] (LCLS)
NcMan	Dare County Library, Manteo, NC [*Library symbol*] [*Library of Congress*] (LCLS)
NcManA	College of the Albemarle, Dare County Center Library, Manteo, NC [*Library symbol*] [*Library of Congress*] (LCLS)
NcManMR	North Carolina Marine Resources Center, Roanoke Island Resource Library, Manteo, NC [*Library symbol*] [*Library of Congress*] (LCLS)
NcMarM	Madison County Public Library, Marshall, NC [*Library symbol*] [*Library of Congress*] (LCLS)
NcMauDC	North Carolina Department of Corrections, Eastern Correctional Center Library, Maury, NC [*Library symbol*] [*Library of Congress*] (LCLS)
NcMax	Gilbert Patterson Memorial Public Library, Maxton, NC [*Library symbol*] [*Library of Congress*] (LCLS)
NCMC	National Capital Management Corp. [*NASDAQ symbol*] (NQ)
NCMC	National Center on Missing Children (NADA)
NCMC	National Coalition for Marine Conservation (EA)
NCMC	National Conference of Metropolitan Courts
NCMC	Natl Capital Mgmt [*NASDAQ symbol*] (TTSB)
NCMC	Natural Cell-Mediated Cytotoxicity [*Immunochemistry*]
NCMC	N-Carboxymethylchitosan [*Biochemistry*]
NCMC	Non-Classical Mesoscale Circulations (SAUS)
NCMC	NORAD Cheyenne Mountain Complex [*Military*] (AABC)
NCMC	Nordic Council for Music Conservatories (EA)
NCMC	Numerically-Controlled Machine Center (IAA)
NCMC	Numeric Control Machining Center (SAUS)
NcMcC	Carteret Technical Institute, Morehead City (SAUS)
NcMcC	Carteret Technical Institute, Morehead City, NC [*Library symbol*] [*Library of Congress*] (LCLS)
NcMccH	McCain Hospital, Medical Library, McCain, NC [*Library symbol*] [*Library of Congress*] (LCLS)
NcMccS	Sandhills Youth Center, McCain, NC [*Library symbol*] [*Library of Congress*] (LCLS)
NCMCE	National Council of Minority Consulting Engineers (IAA)
NCMCG	National Construction Machinery Credit Group [*Park Ridge, IL*] (EA)
NCM Company	Nippon Calculating Machine Co. (SAUS)
NCMD	National Center for Municipal Development (EA)
NCMDA	National Coin Machine Distributors Association (EA)
NCMDA	National Commission on Marijuana and Drug Abuse [*Presidential advisory committee, terminated 1973*]
NCMDLRJO	National Council of Marriage and Divorce Law Reform and Justice Organizations (EA)
NCME	National Center for Mediation Education (EA)
NCME	National Council on Measurement in Education (EA)
NCME	Network for Continuing Medical Education (EA)
NCME	Northern Counties Motor & Engineering Co. Ltd. [*British*] (DCTA)
NCME	Numerically Controlled Machine Equipment
NCMEA	National Catholic Music Educators Association [*Later, NPM*] (EA)
NCMEC	National Center for Missing and Exploited Children (EA)
NCMES	Numerically Controlled Measuring and Evaluating System (SAUS)
NCMESD	National Coalition for More Effective School Discipline (EA)
NCMET	Nonclosed Shell Many Electron Theory [*Physics*]
NcMf	Murfreesboro Public Library, Murfreesboro, NC [*Library symbol*] [*Library of Congress*] (LCLS)
NCMF	National Carvers Museum Foundation [*Defunct*] (EA)
NCMF	National Church Music Fellowship [*Defunct*]
NcMfC	Chowan College, Murfreesboro, NC [*Library symbol*] [*Library of Congress*] (LCLS)
NCMFST	National Committee for Motor Fleet Supervisor Training (EA)
NcMG	Graham Evangelistic Association, Montreat, NC [*Library symbol*] [*Library of Congress*] (LCLS)
NCMG	Mangaia [*Cook Islands*] [*ICAO location identifier*] (ICLI)
NCMH	National Clearinghouse for Mental Health Information (NITA)
NCMH	National Committee for Mental Health (DAVI)
NCMH	National Committee for Mental Hygiene (DAVI)
NCMH	National Committee on Maternal Health (EA)
NCMH	National Council for Monday Holidays
NCMHA	North Carolina Mobile Home Association
NcMhC	Mars Hill College, Mars Hill, NC [*Library symbol*] [*Library of Congress*] (LCLS)
NCMHC	National Community Mental Healthcare Council (NTPA)
NCMHC	National Community Mental Heathcare Council (EA)
NCMHCE	National Clinical Mental Health Counseling Examination (SAUS)
NcMHi	Historical Foundation of the Presbyterian and Reformed Churches, Montreat, NC [*Library symbol*] [*Library of Congress*] (LCLS)
NCMHI	National Clearinghouse for Mental Health Information [*Public Health Service*] [*Rockville, MD*] [*Database*] (HEW)
NCMHS	National Conference on Mental Health Statistics [*Department of Health and Human Services*] (GFGA)
NCMI	National Coin Machine Institute (EA)
NCMI	National Committee Against Mental Illness (EA)
NCMI	National Council of Music Importers [*Later, NCMIE*]
NCMI	National Country Maintenance Index (IAA)

NCMIE	....	National Council of Music Importers and Exporters (EA)
NcMiP	....	Pfeiffer College, Misenheimer, NC [Library symbol] [Library of Congress] (LCLS)
NCMJ	....	National Contract Management Journal [A publication] (AAGC)
NCMK	....	Mauke [Cook Islands] [ICAO location identifier] (ICLI)
NCMLB	....	National Council of Mailing List Brokers [Later, MLBPA] (EA)
NcMM	....	Montreat-Anderson College, Montreat, NC [Library symbol] [Library of Congress] (LCLS)
NCmM	....	Museum Manor of Saint George, Center Moriches, NY [Library symbol] [Library of Congress] (LCLS)
NCMM	....	Nuveen California Municipal Market Opportunity Fund [Associated Press] (SAG)
NCmMM	.....	Museum Manor of Saint George, Center Moriches, NY [Library symbol] [Library of Congress] (LCLS)
NCMN	....	Manuae [Cook Islands] [ICAO location identifier] (ICLI)
NCMO	....	National Case Mix Office (SAUS)
NCMO	....	Navigational Aids/Communications Management Office [Air Force] (CET)
NcMoBH	......	Broughton Hospital, Staff Library, Morganton, NC [Library symbol] [Library of Congress] (LCLS)
NcMoc	....	Davie County Public Library, Mocksville, NC [Library symbol] [Library of Congress] (LCLS)
NcMoFM	......	Foothills Area Mental Health, North Carolina School for the Deaf, Morganton, NC [Library symbol] [Library of Congress] (LCLS)
NcMoGH	......	Grace Hospital, Medical Library, Morganton, NC [Library symbol] [Library of Congress] (LCLS)
NcMoM	....	Morganton-Burke Library, Inc., Morganton, NC [Library symbol] [Library of Congress] (LCLS)
NcMon	....	Union County Public Library, Monroe, NC [Library symbol] [Library of Congress] (LCLS)
NcMorB	....	Bell Northern Research, Inc., Learning Resources Center, Morrisville, NC [Library symbol] [Library of Congress] (LCLS)
NcMoW	....	Western Piedmont Community College, Morganton, NC [Library symbol] [Library of Congress] (LCLS)
NcMoWC	.....	Western Carolina Center, Staff Library, Morganton, NC [Library symbol] [Library of Congress] (LCLS)
NcMoWCC	...	Western Correctional Center, Morganton, NC [Library symbol] [Library of Congress] (LCLS)
NCMP	....	National Commission for Manpower Policy [Department of Labor]
NCMP	....	National Commission on Materials Policy
NCMP	....	Navy Capabilities and Mobilization Plan (DOMA)
NCMPA	....	National Corrugated Metal Pipe Association [Later, NCSPA] (EA)
NCMPR	....	National Council for Marketing and Public Relations (EA)
NCMR	....	Matiaro [Cook Islands] [ICAO location identifier] (ICLI)
NCMR	....	National Centre for Marine Research (SAUS)
NCMR	....	National Committee for Monetary Reform (EA)
NCMR	....	Nonconforming Material Report
NCMR	....	North Canterbury Mounted Rifles [British military] (DMA)
NCMRED	......	National Council on Marine Resources and Engineering Development [Later, ICMSE]
NCMRWF	.....	National Centre for Medium Range Weather Forecasting [New Delhi, India]
NCMS	....	National Center for Manufacturing Sciences [Research center]
NCMS	....	National Classification Management Society (EA)
NCMS	....	National Council of Marine Sciences
NCMS	....	Numerically-Controlled Machine System (IAA)
NCMS	....	Numerically Controlled Machining System (SAUS)
NCMS	....	Numerically-Controlled Manufacture System (IAA)
NCMS	....	Numerically Controlled Manufacturing System (SAUS)
NCMT	....	Numerical Controlled Machine Tool (SAUS)
NCMT	....	Numerical Control of Machine Tools (SAUS)
NCMT	....	Numerically Controlled Machine Tool
NcMta	....	Mount Airy Public Library, Mount Airy, NC [Library symbol] [Library of Congress] (LCLS)
NCMTA	....	National Council of Marine Trade Associations
NcMtaC	....	Crossroads Center, Mount Airy, NC [Library symbol] [Library of Congress] (LCLS)
NcMtC	....	Mount Olive College, Mount Olive, NC [Library symbol] [Library of Congress] (LCLS)
NCMTE	....	National Council on Medical Technology Education [Defunct]
NCMTI	....	Noncoherent Moving Target Indicator (MCD)
NCMTT	....	National Council for Mother Tongue Teaching (AIE)
NcMu	....	Murphy Public Library, Murphy, NC [Library symbol] [Library of Congress] (LCLS)
NCMUE	....	National Council on Measurements Used in Education [Later, National Council on Measurement in Education] (AEBS)
NcMuN	....	Nantahala Regional Library, Murphy, NC [Library symbol] [Library of Congress] (LCLS)
NcMuT	....	Tri-County Technical Institute, Murphy, NC [Library symbol] [Library of Congress] (LCLS)
NcMv	....	Mooresville Public Library, Mooresville, NC [Library symbol] [Library of Congress] (LCLS)
NCMV	....	Northern Cereal Mosaic Virus [Plant pathology]
N/cmy	....	Newton per Square Centimeter (SAUS)
n-cn-	....	Canada [MARC geographic area code] [Library of Congress] (LCCP)
NCN	....	Nasociliary Nerve [Medicine]
NCN	....	National Airlines (Chile), SA [FAA designator] (FAAC)
NCN	....	National Cardiovascular Network
NCN	....	National Christian Network [Cable-television system]
NCN	....	National Computer Network Corp. [Information service or system] (IID)
NCN	....	National Council of Nurses [British] (DI)
NCN	....	Navy Control Number (MCD)
NCN	....	Network Control Node
NCN	....	New Caledonian Nickel (SAUS)
NCN	....	New Century Network (SAUS)
NCN	....	Nitrocarbonitrate (EEVL)
NCN	....	Nixdorf Communications Network [Nixdorf] [Germany]
NCN	....	Non-Casein Nitrogen (OA)
NCNA	....	National Council of Nonprofit Associations
NCNA	....	National Council on Noise Abatement (EA)
NCNA	....	New China News Agency
NCNA	....	North Carolina Nurses Association (SAUS)
n-cn-ab	....	Alberta [MARC geographic area code] [Library of Congress] (LCCP)
NCNASEO	....	National Council of Naval Air Stations Employee Organizations [Later, NCINASEO] (EA)
NCNB	....	National Center for Nonprofit Boards (EA)
NCNB	....	North Carolina National Bank (EFIS)
n-cn-bc	....	British Columbia [MARC geographic area code] [Library of Congress] (LCCP)
NcNbC	....	Craven Technical Institute, New Bern, NC [Library symbol] [Library of Congress] (LCLS)
NcNbCP	....	Craven-Pamlico-Carteret Regional Library, New Bern, NC [Library symbol] [Library of Congress] (LCLS)
NCNC	....	National Captive Nations Committee (EA)
NCNC	....	National Council of Nigeria and the Cameroons [Political party]
NCNC	....	Normochromic Normocytic [Medicine] (MEDA)
NCNC	....	Normochromic, Normocytic Anemia [Hematology] (DAVI)
NCNCA	....	Normochromic, Normocytic Anemia [Hematology] (DAVI)
NCND	....	Neither Confirm nor Deny
NCNE	....	National Campaign for Nursery Education [British]
NCNE	....	National Center for Neighborhood Enterprise (EA)
NcNep	....	Newport Public Library, Newport, NC [Library symbol] [Library of Congress] (LCLS)
NCNEVAW	....	National Communications Network for the Elimination of Violence Against Women [NCADV] [Absorbed by] (EA)
NcNew	....	Avery-Morrison Public Library, Newland, NC [Library symbol] [Library of Congress] (LCLS)
NCNG	....	North Carolina Natural Gas Corp. (SAUS)
NCNGD	....	Not Crushed or Not Ground
n-cnh-	....	Hudson Bay [MARC geographic area code] [Library of Congress] (LCCP)
NCNIA	....	Northern California Nursing Informatics Association (SAUS)
n-cnm-	....	Maritime Provinces [MARC geographic area code] [Library of Congress] (LCCP)
n-cn-mb	....	Manitoba [MARC geographic area code] [Library of Congress] (LCCP)
NCNMLG	......	Northern California and Nevada Medical Group (SAUS)
n-cn-nf	....	Newfoundland [MARC geographic area code] [Library of Congress] (LCCP)
n-cn-nk	....	New Brunswick [MARC geographic area code] [Library of Congress] (LCCP)
n-cn-ns	....	Nova Scotia [MARC geographic area code] [Library of Congress] (LCCP)
n-cn-nt	....	Northwest Territories [MARC geographic area code] [Library of Congress] (LCCP)
N/CNO	....	Navy/Chief of Naval Operations (AAG)
n-cn-on	....	Ontario [MARC geographic area code] [Library of Congress] (LCCP)
NCNP	....	National Child Nutrition Project (EA)
NCNP	....	National Conference for New Politics [Organization formed in 1966 to support peace candidates] (VNW)
NCNP	....	North Cascades National Park (SAUS)
n-cnp-	....	Prairie Provinces [MARC geographic area code] [Library of Congress] (LCCP)
n-cn-pi	....	Prince Edward Island [Canada] [MARC geographic area code] [Library of Congress] (LCCP)
NCNPSA	......	National Conference of Non-Profit Shipping Associations (EA)
ncnq-	....	Nicaragua [MARC geographic area code] [Library of Congress] (LCCP)
n-cn-qu	....	Quebec [MARC geographic area code] [Library of Congress] (LCCP)
NCNR	....	National Center for Nursing Research [Bethesda, MD] [Department of Health and Human Services] (GRD)
NCNS	....	Nassau [Cook Islands] [ICAO location identifier] (ICLI)
NCNS	....	National Catholic News Service (EA)
NCNS	....	No Complications, No Sequelae (SAUS)
NCNS	....	North Central Name Society (EA)
n-cn-sn	....	Saskatchewan [MARC geographic area code] [Library of Congress] (LCCP)
NcNt	....	Catawba County Library, Newton, NC [Library symbol] [Library of Congress] (LCLS)
NCNT	....	Netcentives
NCNTUCW	......	National Commission on New Technological Uses of Copyrighted Works [Terminated, 1978] [Library of Congress]
NcNv	....	Harold D. Cooley Library, Nashville, NC [Library symbol] [Library of Congress] (LCLS)
NCNW	....	National Congress of Neighborhood Women (EA)
NCNW	....	National Council of Negro Women (EA)
NCNW	....	Nearly Certain New Work (MCD)
NcNw	....	Wilkes County Public Library, North Wilkesboro, NC [Library symbol] [Library of Congress] (LCLS)
NcNwA	....	Appalachian Regional Library, North Wilkesboro, NC [Library symbol] [Library of Congress] (LCLS)
NCNY	....	Netherland Club of New York (EA)
NCNY	....	Newswomen's Club of New York (EA)
n-cn-yk	....	Yukon Territory [MARC geographic area code] [Library of Congress] (LCCP)
NCo	....	Commack Public Library, Commack, NY [Library symbol] [Library of Congress] (LCLS)
NCO	....	National Commission for Information and Conscientization on Development Cooperation [Netherlands]

NCO	National Council of Obesity (EA)
NCO	Nationalist Chams Organization (EA)
NCO	Negotiated Consent Order [*Environmental Protection Agency*] (ERG)
NCO	Net Control (CAAL)
NCO	Net Control Operator (CCCA)
NCO	Net Control Outstation [*Military*] (DOMA)
NCO	Network Control Office [*Telecommunications*] (TEL)
NCO	New Consultants [*A publication*]
NCO	No Complaints Offered (SAUS)
NCO	No-Cost Option (SAUS)
NCO	No Crossing Over (SAUS)
NCO	Noncombatant Evacuation Order [*Navy*] (CINC)
NCO	Noncombat Operations [*Military*] (CAAL)
NCO	Noncommissioned Officer [*Military*]
NCO	Non Compliance Order [*Environmental Protection Agency*]
NCO	Norsar Array Site 01C00 [*Norway*] [*Seismograph station code, US Geological Survey*] (SEIS)
NCO	North Canadian Oils Ltd. [*Toronto Stock Exchange symbol*]
NCO	North Carolina Department of Transportation, Raleigh, NC [*OCLC symbol*] (OCLC)
NCO	Nuclear Control Order [*Military*] (MUSM)
NCO	Number-Controlled Oscillator
NCO	Numerically Controlled Oscillator (SAUS)
NCO	Nuveen California Municipal Market Opportunities [*NYSE symbol*] (SPSG)
NCO	Nuveen CA Muni Mkt Oppt [*NYSE symbol*] (TTSB)
NCOA	National Campground Owners Association (EA)
NCOA	National Change of Address Service [*US Postal Service*]
NCOA	National Chevelle Owners Association (EA)
NCOA	National Condominium Owners Association [*Defunct*]
NCOA	National Corvette Owners' Association (EA)
NCOA	National Council on the Aging (EA)
NCOA	Noncommissioned Officer Academy [*Military*] (AABC)
NCOA	Non-Commissioned Officers Association of the United States of America (EA)
NCOAUSA	Non-Commissioned Officers Association of the United States of America (SAUS)
NCOB	No Cargo On Board (SAUS)
NCoBJ	Burr Junior High School, Commack, NY [*Library symbol*] [*Library of Congress*] (LCLS)
NCOBPS	National Conference of Black Political Scientists (EA)
NCOBQ	Noncommissioned Officer Bachelor Quarters [*Military*] (AFM)
N'COBRA	National Coalition of Blacks for Reparations in America (ECON)
NCobUA	State University of New York, Agricultural and Technical College at Cobleskill, Cobleskill, NY [*Library symbol*] [*Library of Congress*] (LCLS)
NCOC	National Commission on Organized Crime (NADA)
NCOC	National Council on Organized Crime (EA)
NCOC	Noncommissioned Officer Course (VNW)
NCoCE	Cedar Road Elementary School, Commack, NY [*Library symbol*] [*Library of Congress*] (LCLS)
NCOCY	National Council of Organizations for Children and Youth (EA)
NCOD	National Catholic Office for the Deaf (EA)
NCOD	National Coming Out Day [*An association*] (EA)
NCOD	National Coming Out Day Campaign (EA)
NCOD	National Commission on Orphan Diseases [*Department of Health and Human Services*] (GFGA)
NCODE	National Clearinghouse on Development Education [*Information service or system*] (IID)
NCODP	Noncommissioned Officer Development Program [*Army*] (INF)
NCOER	Noncommissioned Officer Evaluation Report [*Army*]
NCO-ER	Noncommissioned Officer Evaluation Reporting [*Army*] (INF)
NCOES	Noncommissioned Officer Education System [*Military*] (AABC)
NC of A	Newfoundland Club of America (EA)
NCOG	NCO Group, Inc. [*NASDAQ symbol*] (SAG)
NcOG	Richard H. Thornton Memorial Library, Oxford, NC [*Library symbol*] [*Library of Congress*] (LCLS)
NCOGD	National Council for the Observance of Grandparent's Day (EA)
NCO Grp	NCO Group, Inc. [*Associated Press*]
NCOHC	Northern California Occupational Health Center [*University of California*] [*Research center*] (RCD)
NCO/HPCC	National Coordination Office for High Performance Computing and Communications
NCoHS-N	North High School, Commack, NY [*Library symbol*] [*Library of Congress*] (LCLS)
NCoHS-S	South High School, Commack, NY [*Library symbol*] [*Library of Congress*] (LCLS)
NCOI	National Council for the Omnibus Industry [*British*]
NCOIC	Noncommissioned Officer-in-Charge [*Military*]
NCoIE	Indian Hollow Elementary School, Commack, NY [*Library symbol*] [*Library of Congress*] (LCLS)
NCOIL	National Conference of Insurance Legislators (EA)
NCOL	National Council on Occupational Licensing [*Formerly, COL*] [*Defunct*] (EA)
NCol	New Colophon (SAUS)
NCO Lamp	Non-Cut-Off Lamp (SAUS)
NCOLANT	Net Control Officer, Atlantic [*Navy*] (DNAB)
NCOLG	National Coordinating Office for Latin and Greek [*Later, NCLG*] (EA)
NColnA	Albany Area Board of Cooperative Education Services, Colonie, NY [*Library symbol*] [*Library of Congress*] (LCLS)
NCOLP	Noncommissioned Officer Logistics Program [*Army*] (AABC)
NCOLS	Noncommissioned Officers' Leadership School [*Air Force*] (AFM)
NCOLUG	North Carolina Online User Group (NITA)
NCOM	NEC Computerised Operation and Maintenance System (NITA)
NCOM	News Communications [*NASDAQ symbol*] (TTSB)
NCOM	News Communications, Inc. [*NASDAQ symbol*] (SAG)
NCOMBL	Noncombustible (MSA)
NCOMD	National Committee on the Observance of Mothers' Day [*Later, MDC*] (EA)
NCOMDR	National Clearinghouse on Marital and Date Rape (EA)
NCOMED	Net Control Officer, Mediterranean [*Navy*] (DNAB)
NCOMM	Naval Communications Command
NCOMP	National Catholic Office for Motion Pictures [*Later, Office for Film and Broadcasting*]
NCOMR	National Clearinghouse on Marital Rape [*Later, NCOMDR*] (EA)
NCON	Encon Systems [*NASDAQ symbol*] (SAG)
NCoNE	North Ridge Elementary School, Commack, NY [*Library symbol*] [*Library of Congress*] (LCLS)
NConL	Notes on Contemporary Literature [*A publication*] (ANEX)
NCoOE	Old Farms Elementary School, Commack, NY [*Library symbol*] [*Library of Congress*] (LCLS)
NCooHi	New York State Historical Association, Cooperstown, NY [*Library symbol*] [*Library of Congress*] (LCLS)
NCOOM	Noncommissioned Officers' Open Mess [*Military*] (AFM)
NCop	Copiague Memorial Public Library, Copiague, NY [*Library symbol*] [*Library of Congress*] (LCLS)
NCOP	National Council on Philanthropy [*Later, IS*] (EA)
NCOP	New Choreographers On Point
NCOPA	National Conference of Police Associations (EA)
NCOPAC	Net Control Officer, Pacific [*Navy*] (DNAB)
NCOPD	National Catholic Office for Persons with Disabilities (EA)
NCOPDP	Noncommissioned Officer Professional Development Program [*Army*] (INF)
NCOPDR	NCO [*Noncommissioned Officer*] Professional Development Ribbon [*Military decoration*] (GFGA)
NCOPE	National Council of Preservation Executives (EA)
NCOPF	National Council for One Parent Families [*British*]
NCopH	Lakeside Hospital, Copiague, NY [*Library symbol*] [*Library of Congress*] (LCLS)
NCopHS	Copiague High School, Copiague, NY [*Library symbol*] [*Library of Congress*] (LCLS)
NCOQ	Non-Cost of Quality (SAUS)
NCoRE	Rolling Hills Elementary School, Commack, NY [*Library symbol*] [*Library of Congress*] (LCLS)
NCorf	Corfu Free Library, Corfu, NY [*Library symbol*] [*Library of Congress*] (LCLS)
NCorn	Cornwall Public Library, Cornwall, NY [*Library symbol*] [*Library of Congress*] (LCLS)
NCornB	Harvard Black Rock Forest, Cornwall, NY [*Library symbol*] [*Library of Congress*] (LCLS)
NCorni	Corning Public Library, Corning, NY [*Library symbol*] [*Library of Congress*] (LCLS)
NCorniC	Corning Glass Works, Corning, NY [*Library symbol*] [*Library of Congress*] (LCLS)
NCorniCC	Corning Community College, Corning, NY [*Library symbol*] [*Library of Congress*] (LCLS)
NCorniFL	College Center of the Finger Lakes, Corning, NY [*Library symbol*] [*Library of Congress*] (LCLS)
NCorniM	Corning Museum of Glass, Corning, NY [*Library symbol*] [*Library of Congress*] (LCLS)
NCorniS	Southern Tier Library System, Corning, NY [*Library symbol*] [*Library of Congress*] (LCLS)
NCort	Cortland Free Library (SAUS)
NCort	Cortland Free Library, Cortland, NY [*Library symbol*] [*Library of Congress*] (LCLS)
NCORT	National Catholic Office for Radio and Television [*Later, Office for Film and Broadcasting*]
NCortHi	Cortland County Historical Society, Cortland, NY [*Library symbol*] [*Library of Congress*] (LCLS)
NCortSC	Smith-Corona Laboratory, Cortland, NY [*Library symbol*] [*Library of Congress*] (LCLS)
NCortU	State University of New York, College at Cortland, Cortland, NY [*Library symbol*] [*Library of Congress*] (LCLS)
NCOS	Comite de Liaison des Organisations Non-Gouvernementales de Developpement aupres des Communautes Europeennes [*Liaison Committee of Development Non-Governmental Organizations to the European Communities*] (EAIO)
NCOS	National Centre for Orchestral Studies [*Goldsmiths' College*] [*British*] (CB)
NCOS	National Commission on Space [*Terminated, 1986*] (EGAO)
NCOS	National Commission on Superconductivity [*Presidential advisory commission*] (EGAO)
NCOS	National Council on Stuttering (EA)
NCOS	Non-Concurrent Operating System [*Sperry UNIVAC*]
NCOSCC	National Central Office for the Suppression of Counterfeit Currency [*British*]
NCoSJ	Saw Mill Junior High School, Commack, NY [*Library symbol*] [*Library of Congress*] (LCLS)
NCOSTA	National Council of Officers of State Teachers Associations (EA)
NcOtV	United States Veterans Administration Hospital, Oteen, NC [*Library symbol*] [*Library of Congress*] (LCLS)
NCoWE	Wood Park Elementary School, Commack, NY [*Library symbol*] [*Library of Congress*] (LCLS)
NCOWFL	National Center on Women and Family Law (EA)
NCoxHi	Greene County Historical Society, Inc., Coxsakie, NY [*Library symbol*] [*Library of Congress*] (LCLS)
NcP	Given Memorial Library, Pinehurst, NC [*Library symbol*] [*Library of Congress*] (LCLS)
NCP	National Cancer Program [*National Institutes of Health*]
NCP	National Caries Program [*Public Health Service*] (GRD)

NCP .... National Car Parks [*British*]
NCP .... National Choreography Project
NCP .... National Circus Project (EA)
NCP .... National Climate Program [*Rockville, MD*] [*National Oceanic and Atmospheric Administration*]
NCP .... National Collegiate Players (EA)
NCP .... National Command Post (ACAE)
NCP .... National Commission on Population (SAUS)
NCP .... National Commission on Productivity [*Later, National Productivity Council*]
NCP .... National Commodity-Processing Program [*Department of Agriculture*] (GFGA)
NCP .... National Contingency Plan [*Hazardous wastes*] [*Environmental Protection Agency*]
NCP .... National Convention Party [*Gambia*] [*Political party*] (PPW)
NCP .... National Council of Psychotherapists and Hypnotherapy Register [*British*] (DBA)
NCP .... National Council on Philanthropy [*Later, IS*]
NCP .... National Curriculum Project
NCP .... National Cycling Proficiency (BARN)
NCP .... National Inventory Control Point [*Military*]
NCP .... National Oil and Hazardous Substances Contingency Plan
NCP .... Natural Clay Pavers (DICI)
NCP .... Naval Capabilities Plan
NCP .... N-Chlorothiophosphoramide [*Organic chemistry*]
NCP .... N-Cholorpiperidine [*Organic chemistry*]
NCP .... Nepali Congress Party [*Political party*] (EY)
NCP .... Net Combat Power
NCP .... Net Community Productivity (FFDE)
NCP .... Net Control Procedure
NCP .... Netherlands and Colonial Philately
NCP .... NetWare Core Protocol [*Computer science*]
NCP .... Network Communications Program (TIMI)
NCP .... Network Control Point [*Telecommunications*]
NCP .... Network Control Processor [*Telecommunications*] (TSSD)
NCP .... Network Control Program [*IBM Corp.*] [*Telecommunications*] (BUR)
NCP .... Network Control Protocol [*Telecommunications*]
NCP .... New Call to Peacemaking (EA)
NCP .... New Communities Program [*Defunct*] (EA)
NCP .... New Community Projects [*A publication*]
NCP .... Nickel-Chromium Panel
NCP .... Nitrogen Charge Panel [*Later, MRAC*] (AAG)
NCP .... No Caffeine [*or*] Pepper (DAVI)
NCP .... No-Copy Paper
NCP .... Noctilucent Cloud Particles
NCP .... Noise Control Plan (SAUS)
NCP .... Non Carbon Paper (SAUS)
NCP .... Noncarbon Paper (IAA)
NCP .... Noncollagen Protein
NCP .... Noncompliance Penalties (EEVL)
NCP .... Noncompliance Penalty [*Environmental Protection Agency*] (EPA)
NCP .... Non-Conformance Penalties [*Automotive emissions standards*]
NCP .... Nonconformance Penalty (EEVL)
NCP .... Nonconformance Pickup (SAUS)
NCP .... Non-Consultative Party (SAUS)
NCP .... Non-Custodial Parent
NCP .... Non-United States Coalition Partner (DOMA)
NCP .... Normal Circular Pitch (MSA)
NCP .... North Celestial Pole [*Astronomy*]
NCP .... North Central Pacific (TVEL)
NCP .... Not Copy Protected [*Computer science*] (IGQR)
NCP .... Nuclear Contingency Plan (MCD)
NCP .... Number of Channel Programs (SAUS)
NCP .... Numerically-Controlled Peripheral (IAA)
NCP .... Nursing Care Plan
NCP .... Nutation Control Processor (ACAE)
NCP .... Nutrition Center of the Philippines (SAUS)
NCP .... Nutrition in Clinical Practice (SAUS)
NCP .... Nuveen California Performance Plus Municipal [*NYSE symbol*] (SPSG)
NCP .... Nuveen CA Perf Plus Muni [*NYSE symbol*] (TTSB)
NCPA .... National Center for Policy Alternatives [*Later, CPA*] (EA)
NCPA .... National Coalition of Patriotic Americans (EA)
NCPA .... National Committee for the Prevention of Alcoholism and Drug Dependency [*Later, NCPADD*] (EA)
NCPA .... National Composition and Prepress Association (EA)
NCPA .... National Conservation Policy Act [*1979*]
NCPA .... National Cottonseed Products Association (EA)
NCPA .... National Crime Prevention Association [*Defunct*] (EA)
NCPAC .... National Conservative Political Action Committee (EA)
NCPAD .... National Council on Psychological Aspects of Disability (EA)
NCPADD ...... National Committee for the Prevention of Alcoholism and Drug Dependency (EA)
NCPAG .... National CPA [*Certified Public Accountant*] Group [*Later, BKR International*] (EA)
NCPAMA ...... Noise Control Product and Materials Association [*Later, NCA*] (IAA)
NCPAMT ...... National Coalition of Psychiatrists Against Motorcoach Therapy (EA)
N-CPAP .... Nasal Continuous Positive Airway Pressure [*Medicine*] (DMAA)
NCPAS .... National Computer Program Abstract Service, Inc. (IID)
NC/PAT .... National Council for the Public Assessment of Technology [*Defunct*]
NCPB .... National Cancer Policy Board
NCPB .... Navy Council of Personnel Boards (ACAE)
NcPb .... Pinebluff Public Library, Pinebluff, NC [*Library symbol*] [*Library of Congress*] (LCLS)
NCPC .... National Cancer Pain Coalition

NCPC .... National Capital Planning Commission [*Formerly, NCPPC*]
NCPC .... National Chrysler Products Club (EA)
NCPC .... National Citizens Participation Council (EA)
NCPC .... National Coal Policy Conference [*Defunct*] (EA)
NCPC .... National Collegiate Poultry Club
NCPC .... National Crime Prevention Council (EA)
NCPC .... Naval Civilian Personnel Command (ACAE)
NCPC .... Northern Canada Power Commission (SAUS)
NCPC .... Nose Cone Protective Covering [*Aviation*]
NCPCA .... National Center for the Prosecution of Child Abuse (EA)
NCPCA .... National Committee for Peace in Central America [*Defunct*] (EA)
NCPCA .... National Committee for Prevention of Child Abuse (EA)
NCPCA .... National Committee to Prevent Child Abuse (EA)
NCPCC .... National Clearinghouse for Poison Control Centers (EA)
NCpCE .... Cherry Lane Elementary School, Carle Place, NY [*Library symbol*] [*Library of Congress*] (LCLS)
NCPCF .... National Coalition for the Protection of Children and Families (EA)
NCPCINST... Naval Civilian Personnel Command Instructions (MCD)
NCPCO .... National Climate Program Coordinating Office
NCPCR .... National Center for Prevention and Control of Rape [*National Institutes of Health*]
NCPCU .... National Council of Postal Credit Unions (NTPA)
NCPD .... National Catholic Office for Persons with Disabilities (EA)
NCPD .... Navy Current Procurement Directive
NCPDI .... National Coastal Pollutant Discharge Inventory (CARB)
NCPDM .... National Council of Physical Distribution Management
NCPDP .... National Council for Prescription Drug Programs (EA)
NCPDS .... Navy Civilian Personnel Data System
NCPE .... National Committee on Pay Equity (EA)
NCPE .... National Council for Preservation Education
NCPE .... Netware Core Protocol Extension (SAUS)
NCPE .... Noncardiac Pulmonary Edema [*Medicine*]
NCPEA .... National College Physical Education Association [*Later, NCPEAM*] (EA)
NCPEA .... National Conference of Professors of Educational Administration [*Later, NAPEHE*] (EA)
NCPEAM ...... National College Physical Education Association for Men [*Later, NAPEHE*]
NCPEARL .... National Coalition for Public Education and Religious Liberty (EA)
NCPEG .... Navy Contractor Performance Evaluation Group
NCPEP .... New Century Policies Educational Programs (EA)
NCPERL ...... National Coalition for Public Education and Religious Liberty (EA)
NCPERS ...... National Conference on Public Employee Retirement Systems (EA)
NcPeS .... Pembroke State University, Pembroke, NC [*Library symbol*] [*Library of Congress*] (LCLS)
NCPF .... National Council on Private Forests (EA)
NcPfO .... Olin Corp., Ecusta-Film Technical Library, Pisgah Forest, NC [*Library symbol*] [*Library of Congress*] (LCLS)
NCPG .... National Catholic Pharmacists Guild of the United States (EA)
NCPG .... National Committee on Planned Giving (NFD)
NCPG .... National Council on Problem Gambling (EA)
NCPG .... Nozzleless Center-Perforated Grain (MCD)
NCPGA .... North Carolina Personnel and Guidance Association (SAUS)
NCPGG .... National Center for Petroleum Geology and Geophysics [*Australia*]
NCPH .... National Council on Public History [*Database producer*]
NCpHS .... Carle Place High School, Carle Place, NY [*Library symbol*] [*Library of Congress*] (LCLS)
NCPHU .... North Coast Public Health Unit (SAUS)
NCPI .... National Clay Pipe Institute (EA)
NCPI .... National Committee on Property Insurance [*Boston, MA*] (EA)
NCPI .... National Computer Program Index (IAA)
NCPI .... National Conference on Parent Involvement (EA)
NCPI .... National Crime Prevention Institute (EA)
NCPI .... Navy Civilian Personnel Instructions
NCPIE .... National Coalition for Parent Involvement in Education
NCPIE .... National Conference on Prescription Medicine Information and Education
NCPIE .... National Council of Patient Information and Education (EA)
NCPIM .... National Commission to Prevent Infant Mortality
NCPISA .... National Collaborative Project for Indicators of Sustainable Development (SAUS)
NCPL .... Kirkland Town Library, Clinton, NY [*Library symbol*] [*Library of Congress*] (LCLS)
NCPL .... National Center for Preservation Law (EA)
NCPL .... National Collegiate Parachuting League (EA)
NCPLA .... National Council of Patent Law Associations [*Later, NCIPLA*] (EA)
NCPLD .... Noncoupled
NCPLF .... National Congenital Pulmonary Lymphangiectasis Foundation (NRGU)
NcPly .... Washington County Library, Plymouth, NC [*Library symbol*] [*Library of Congress*] (LCLS)
NcPlyP .... Pettigrew Regional Library, Plymouth, NC [*Library symbol*] [*Library of Congress*] (LCLS)
NcPm .... Charles H. Stone Memorial Library, Pilot Mountain, NC [*Library symbol*] [*Library of Congress*] (LCLS)
NCPM .... National Centre for Popular Music [*England*] (WDAA)
NCPM .... National Clay Pot Manufacturers (EA)
NCPM .... National Conference of Personal Managers (EA)
NCPM .... Noncritical Phase Matching (IAA)
NCPMA .... National Clay Pot Manufacturers Association (NTPA)
NCPMA .... Noise Control Products and Materials Association [*Later, NCA*] (EA)
ncpn- .... Panama [*MARC geographic area code*] [*Library of Congress*] (LCCP)
NCPNFUNW... National Coalition for a Policy of No-First-Use of Nuclear Weapons (EA)
NCPO .... National Chronic Pain Outreach Association (EA)

NCPO .... National Climate Program Office [*National Oceanic and Atmospheric Administration*]
NCPO .... National Climate Project Office (SAUS)
NCPO .... Nordic Council for Physical Oceanography (EA)
NcPo .... United States Air Force, Pope Air Force Base, Base Library, Pope AFB, NC [*Library symbol*] [*Library of Congress*] (LCLS)
NCPOA .... National Chief Petty Officers' Association (EA)
NCPOA .... National Chronic Pain Outreach Association, Inc. (PAZ)
NcPoIA .... Anson Technical College, Learning Resources Center, Polk Campus, Polkton (SAUS)
NcPoIA .... Anson Technical College, Learning Resources Center, Polk Campus, Polkton, NC [*Library symbol*] [*Library of Congress*] (LCLS)
NCPP .... National Coal Policy Project
NCPP .... National Council on Public Policy (EA)
NCPP .... National Council on Public Polls (EA)
NCPPA .... National Coalition for Promoting Physical Activity (MELL)
NCPPB .... National Collection of Plant Pathogenic Bacteria (DMAA)
NCPPC .... National Capital Park and Planning Commission [*Later, NCPC*]
NCPPL .... Numerical Control Parts Programming Language (SAUS)
NCPPP .... National Council for Public-Private Partnerships (EA)
NCPPR .... National Center for Public Policy Research (EA)
NCPQWL ..... National Center for Productivity and Quality of Working Life [*Later, National Productivity Council*]
NCPR .... National Center for Patient's Rights (MELL)
NCPR .... National Championship Poker Run [*American Motorcyclists Association*]
NCPR .... National Congress of Petroleum Retailers [*Later, SSDA*] (EA)
NCPR .... No Cardiopulmonary Resuscitation [*For terminal patients*] (DAVI)
NCpRE .... Rushmore Elementary School, Carle Place, NY [*Library symbol*] [*Library of Congress*] (LCLS)
NCPRP .... National Coastal Pollution Research Program [*Environmental Protection Agency*] (MSC)
NCPRR .... National Congress for Puerto Rican Rights (EA)
NCPRV .... National Congress of Puerto Rican Veterans (EA)
NCPRV .... National Council of Puerto Rican Volunteers [*Defunct*] (EA)
NCPS .... National Cat Protection Society (EA)
NCPS .... National Circus Preservation Society (EA)
NCPS .... National Coalition to Prevent Shoplifting (EA)
NCPS .... National Commission on Product Safety
NCPS .... National Commission on the Public Service [*Defunct*] (EA)
NCPS .... Netware Cross-Platform Services (SAUS)
NCPS .... Nigerian College of Petroleum Studies [*Kaduna, Northern Nigeria*]
NCPS .... Non-Contributory Pension Scheme (DLA)
NCPS .... Nuclear Contingency Planning System (MCD)
NCPSA .... National Child Passenger Safety Association [*Later, NPSA*] (EA)
NCPSC .... National Committee on Paper Stock Conservation
NCPSD .... Normalized Cross-Power Spectral Density
NCPSF .... National Council of Professional Services Firms [*Later, PSC*] (EA)
NCPSIDS ..... National Center for the Prevention of Sudden Infant Death Syndrome (EA)
NCPSSM ...... National Committee to Preserve Social Security and Medicare (EA)
NCPT .... National Conference on Power Transmission (EA)
NCPT .... National Congress of Parents and Teachers [*Later, National PTA*] (EA)
NCPT .... Nationally-Certified Psychiatric Technician
NCPT .... Navy Central Planning Team [*NATO*] (NATG)
NCPTA .... National Confederation of Parent Teacher Associations [*British*]
NCPTCAN .... National Center for the Prevention and Treatment of Child Abuse and Neglect (EA)
NCPTF .... National Campaign for a Peace Tax Fund (EA)
NCPTO .... National China Painting Teachers Organization [*Later, IPAT*] (EA)
NCPTT .... National Center for Preservation Technology and Training (SAUS)
NCPTWA ...... National Clearinghouse for Periodical Title Word Abbreviations [*ANSI*]
NCPUA .... National Committee on Pesticide Use in Agriculture [*Canada*]
NCP/VS .... NCP Virtual Storage (NITA)
NCPVS .... Network Control Program Virtual Storage [*Telecommunications*] (IAA)
NCPW .... National Country Party of Western Australia [*Political party*]
NCPWB .... National Certified Pipe Welding Bureau (EA)
NCPWSF ..... National Congenital Port Wine Stain Foundation (EA)
NCPY .... Penrhyn [*Cook Islands*] [*ICAO location identifier*] (ICLI)
NCPYA .... National Conference of Public Youth Agencies [*Defunct*] (EA)
NCQ .... Marietta, GA [*Location identifier*] [*FAA*] (FAAL)
NCQA .... National Committee for Quality Assurance (EA)
NCQHC .... National Committee for Quality Health Care (EA)
NCQIE .... National Coalition for Quality Integrated Education (EA)
NCQR .... National Council for Quality and Reliabiltiy [*British*] (BI)
NCR .... Air Sur [*Spain*] [*ICAO designator*] (FAAC)
NCR .... National Capital Region
NCR .... National Cash Register [*Computer science*] (NADA)
NCR .... National Cash Register Co. [*Later, NCR Corp.*] [*Computer manufacturer*]
NCR .... National Civic Review [*A publication*] (BRI)
NCR .... National Coalition for Research in Neurological and Communicative Disorders (EA)
NCR .... National Coalition for Research in Neurological Disorders (EA)
NCR .... National Council of Resistance for Liberty and Independence [*Iran*] (PD)
NCR .... Naval Construction Regiment (NVT)
NCR .... Navy Code Room
NCR .... NCR Corp. [*NYSE symbol*] (SG)
NCR .... Network Change Request [*NASA*] (KSC)
NCR .... Network Control Room [*Television*]
NCR .... Neutrophil Complement Rosettes [*Hematology*]
NCR .... New Christian Right (SAUS)

NCR .... New Cinema Review [*A publication*]
N Cr .... New York Criminal Reports [*A publication*] (DLA)
NCR .... Nickerson, C. R., San Francisco CA [*STAC*]
NCR .... Nicorandil [*Biochemistry*]
NCR .... Nippon Cataloguing Rules (SAUS)
NCR .... Nitrile-Chloroprene Rubber
NCR .... No Calibration Required (MCD)
NCR .... No Canadian Rights
NCR .... No Carbon Required (NG)
NCR .... No Circuit Request (SAUS)
NCR .... Noncoding Region [*Genetics*]
NCR .... Non-Combat Ready [*Military*] (SAA)
NCR .... Non-Combustible Residue [*Automotive engineering*]
NCR .... Non-Communist Resistance (EA)
NCR .... Noncompliance Report [*Environmental Protection Agency*] (EPA)
NCR .... Non-Compliance request (SAUS)
NCR .... Nonconformance Record [*NASA*] (KSC)
NCR .... Nonconformance Report [*Nuclear energy*] (NRCH)
NCR .... Non-Conforming Reports (SAUS)
NCR .... Nonconserved Region [*Genetics*]
NCR .... Non-Selective Catalyst Reduction [*Diesel engine emissions*]
NCR .... Normotensive Control (DB)
NCR .... North Carolina Register [*A publication*] (AAGC)
NCR .... Northern Capital Region (SAUS)
NCR .... Northern Central Railway [*British*] (ROG)
NCR .... Not Combat Ready (SAUS)
NCR .... Notification of Change Report (NRCH)
NCR .... Nucal Resources Ltd. [*Vancouver Stock Exchange symbol*]
NCR .... Nuclear (AAG)
NCR .... Nuclear Cytoplasmic Ratio [*Cytology*]
NCR .... Number of Collisions Register (SAUS)
NCR .... Ontario Library Service - Voyageur [*UTLAS symbol*]
NcR .... Wake County Public Libraries, Raleigh, NC [*Library symbol*] [*Library of Congress*] (LCLS)
NcRa .... Hoke County Public Library, Raeford, NC [*Library symbol*] [*Library of Congress*] (LCLS)
NCRA .... National Cancer Registrar's Association (NTPA)
NCRA .... National Cellular Resellers' Association (EA)
NCRA .... National Center on Rural Aging (EA)
NCRA .... National Championship Racing Association [*Auto racing*]
NCRA .... National Coalition of Redevelopment Agencies (EA)
NCRA .... National Coal Resource Assessment
NCRA .... National Cooperative Refinery Association [*Commercial firm*] (EA)
NCRA .... National Cooperative Research Act [*1984*]
NCRA .... National Correctional Recreational Association (EA)
NCRA .... National Council of Research Administrators
NCRA .... National Court Reporters Association
NCRA .... National Crew and Rowing Association (PSS)
NCRAC .... National Community Relations Advisory Council [*Later, NJCRAC*] (EA)
NCRB .... North Campus Recreation Building (SAUS)
NCRC .... National Catholic Resettlement Council (EA)
NCRC .... National Cave Rescue Commission
NCRC .... National Climate Research Committee (QUAC)
NCRC .... National Committee for a Representative Congress (EA)
NCRC .... National Community Reinvestment Coalition
NCRC .... Nickel-Cadmium Rechargeable Cell
NCRC .... Non-Child-Resistant Container (MELL)
NcR-C .... Wake County Public Libraries, Cameron Village Regional Library, Raleigh, NC [*Library symbol*] [*Library of Congress*] (LCLS)
NCRC/AODA... National Certification Reciprocity Consortium/Alcoholism and Other Drug Abuse (EA)
NCRCH .... Nordic Committee of the Research Councils for the Humanities (EA)
NcRCPL .... Carolina Power & Light Co., Technical Library, Raleigh, NC [*Library symbol*] [*Library of Congress*] (LCLS)
NCRCRD ...... North Central Regional Center for Rural Development [*Iowa State University*] [*Research center*] (RCD)
NCRD .... National Council on Resource Development (EA)
NCRD .... National Council to Repeal the Draft [*Defunct*] (EA)
NCRDA .... National Center for Research into Drug Abuse [*Australia*]
NCRDC .... National Capital Region, District of Columbia (MCD)
NcRDC .... North Carolina Department of Corrections, Central Prison School, Raleigh, NC [*Library symbol*] [*Library of Congress*] (LCLS)
NCRDC .... Northern Colorado Research-Demonstration Center [*Colorado State University*] [*Research center*] (RCD)
NcRDD .... North Carolina Department of Human Resources, Dorothea Dix Hospital, F. T. Fuller Staff Library, Raleigh, NC [*Library symbol*] [*Library of Congress*] (LCLS)
NCRDL .... Nautical Charting Research and Development Laboratory [*National Oceanic and Atmospheric Administration*]
NCRDP .... Nimba County Rural Development Plan (SAUS)
NCRDS .... National Coal Resources Data System [*Geological Survey*] [*Databank*] [*Information service or system*] (IID)
NCRDTA .... National Council of Refuse Disposal Trade Associations
NCRE .... National Conference on Research in English (EA)
NCRE .... National Council on Rehabilitation Education (EA)
NCRE .... Naval Construction Research Establishment [*British*] (AAG)
NC Reg .... North Carolina Register [*A publication*] (AAGC)
NcReH .... Annie Penn Hospital, Medical Library, Reidsville, NC [*Library symbol*] [*Library of Congress*] (LCLS)
NCREIF .... National Council of Real Estate Investment Fiduciaries (EA)
NCREL .... North Central Regional Educational Laboratory [*Elmhurst, IL*] [*Department of Education*] (GRD)
NC Rep .... North Carolina Reports [*A publication*] (DLA)
NC Rep Appendix... North Carolina Reports, Appendix [*A publication*] (DLA)

NC Reports... North Carolina Reports [*A publication*] (DLA)

NcRf............ Eden Public Library, Eden, NC [*Library symbol*] [*Library of Congress*] (LCLS)

NCRF.......... National Court Reporters Foundation

NcR-F.......... Wake County Public Libraries, Fuquay-Varina Public Library, Fuquay-Varina, NC [*Library symbol*] [*Library of Congress*] (LCLS)

NCRFCL....... National Commission on Reform of Federal Criminal Laws

NCRFP........ National Council for a Responsible Firearms Policy [*Defunct*] (EA)

NCRFRA...... National Committee to Repeal the Federal Reserve Act (EA)

NCRFSCU .... National Commission on the Role and Future of State Colleges and Universities [*Defunct*] (EA)

NCRG.......... Avarua/Rarotonga International [*Cook Islands*] [*ICAO location identifier*] (ICLI)

NcRGM .... North Carolina Department of Human Resources, The Governor Morehead School, Raleigh, NC [*Library symbol*] [*Library of Congress*] (LCLS)

NcRGP......... State of North Carolina, Governor's Press Office State Capital Building, Raleigh, NC [*Library symbol*] [*Library of Congress*] (LCLS)

NcRGS........ Church of Jesus Christ of Latter-Day Saints, Genealogical Society Library, Raleigh Branch, Raleigh, NC [*Library symbol*] [*Library of Congress*] (LCLS)

NCRH.......... National Center for Radiological Health [*Public Health Service*]

NCRH.......... North Coast Railroad Historical Society (EA)

NcRH.......... W. W. Holding Technical Institute, Raleigh, NC [*Library symbol*] [*Library of Congress*] (LCLS)

NCRHI......... National Council for Reliable Health Information (SAUS)

NcRHR........ North Carolina Department of Human Resources, Public Health Library, Raleigh, NC [*Library symbol*] [*Library of Congress*] (LCLS)

NCRI .... National Center for Resource Innovations

NCRI .... National Coastal Resources Research and Development Institute [*Newport, OR*] [*Department of Commerce*] (GRD)

NCRI .... National Consumer Research Institute (EA)

NCRIB........ Naval Communications Improvement Review Board (DNAB)

NCRIC........ National Chemical Response and Information Center [*Established by the Chemical Manufacturers Association to provide information and advice during emergencies*]

NCRICT....... Northern China Research Institute of Computer Technology (SAUS)

NCRIPTAL.... National Center for Research to Improve Postsecondary Teaching and Learning [*Ann Arbor, MI*] [*Department of Education*] (GRD)

NCRIS......... National Committee to Restore Internal Security (EA)

NcRJP.......... Jaakko Poyry, Inc., Raleigh, NC [*Library symbol*] [*Library of Congress*] (LCLS)

NCRK.......... Rakahanga [*Cook Islands*] [*ICAO location identifier*] (ICLI)

NCRL .... National Canners Association Research Laboratory

NCRL .... National Citizens Radio League (IAA)

NCRLC .... National Catholic Rural Life Conference (EA)

NCRLC .... National Committee on Regional Library Cooperation

NCRLL .... National Conference on Research in Language and Literacy (NTPA)

NCRLS .... National Committee for Russian Language Study [*American Association for the Advancement of Slavic Studies*] (EDAC)

NCRLS .... National Committee of Religious Leaders of Safety (EA)

NcRM.......... Meredith College, Raleigh, NC [*Library symbol*] [*Library of Congress*] (LCLS)

NCRM .... National Conference on Radiation Measurements

NCRM .... Nordic Council for Railway Music (EA)

NcRm.......... Thomas Hackney Braswell Memorial Library, Rocky Mount, NC [*Library symbol*] [*Library of Congress*] (LCLS)

NcRMA .... North Carolina Museum of Art in Raleigh, Raleigh, NC [*Library symbol*] [*Library of Congress*] (LCLS)

NcRMC .... Meredith College, Raleigh, NC [*Library symbol*] [*Library of Congress*] (LCLS)

NCRMD........ National Capital Region, Maryland (MCD)

NcRmE........ Edgecombe Technical College, Learning Resources Center, Rocky Mount, NC [*Library symbol*] [*Library of Congress*] (LCLS)

NcRMG .... Measurements Group, Inc., Raleigh, NC [*Library symbol*] [*Library of Congress*] (LCLS)

NcRmHE ...... Area L AHEC Library, Rocky Mount, NC [*Library symbol*] [*Library of Congress*] (LCLS)

NcRmN .... Nash Technical Institute, Rocky Mount, NC [*Library symbol*] [*Library of Congress*] (LCLS)

NcRMNH...... North Carolina State Museum of Natural History, Raleigh, NC [*Library symbol*] [*Library of Congress*] (LCLS)

NcRMNH-B... North Carolina State Museum of Natural History, H. H. Brimley Memorial Library, Raleigh, NC [*Library symbol*] [*Library of Congress*] (LCLS)

NcRmW .... North Carolina Wesleyan College, Rocky Mount, NC [*Library symbol*] [*Library of Congress*] (LCLS)

NCRND .... National Committee for Research in Neurological Disorders [*Later, NCR*] (EA)

NcRNO......... News and Observer Publishing Co., Raleigh, NC [*Library symbol*] [*Library of Congress*] (LCLS)

NcRNR......... North Carolina Department of Natural Resources and Community Development, Raleigh, NC [*Library symbol*] [*Library of Congress*] (LCLS)

NCRNT......... National Committee for Rescue from NAZI Terror [*British*]

NcRo.......... Rockingham-Richmond County Library, Rockingham, NC [*Library symbol*] [*Library of Congress*] (LCLS)

NcRob.......... Bemis Memorial Library, Robbinsville, NC [*Library symbol*] [*Library of Congress*] (LCLS)

NCROBOT .... Numerically Controlled Robot (SAUS)

NcRobS........ Snowbird Community Library, Robbinsville, NC [*Library symbol*] [*Library of Congress*] (LCLS)

NCroh .... Croton Free Library, Croton-On-Hudson, NY [*Library symbol*] [*Library of Congress*] (LCLS)

NCrohH .... Hudson Institute, Croton-On-Hudson, NY [*Library symbol*] [*Library of Congress*] (LCLS)

NcRop.......... Roper Community Library and Resource Center, Inc., Roper, NC [*Library symbol*] [*Library of Congress*] (LCLS)

NCROPA ...... National Campaign for the Reform of the Obscene Publications Acts [*British*] (DBA)

NcRoS .... Sandhills Regional Library, Rockingham, NC [*Library symbol*] [*Library of Congress*] (LCLS)

NcRov.......... Robersonville Public Library, Robersonville, NC [*Library symbol*] [*Library of Congress*] (LCLS)

NcRox.......... Person County Public Library, Roxboro, NC [*Library symbol*] [*Library of Congress*] (LCLS)

NcRoxP........ Person Technical Institute, Roxboro, NC [*Library symbol*] [*Library of Congress*] (LCLS)

NCRP .... National Climatic Research Program

NCRP .... National Commission on Radiological Protection

NCRP .... National Committee for Responsible Patriotism (EA)

NCRP .... National Committee for Responsive Philanthropy (EA)

NCRP .... National Council for Research and Planning (EA)

NCRP .... National Council on Radiation Protection and Measurements [*Later, NCRPM*]

NCRP .... Non-Compulsory Reporting Point (PIPO)

NCRP .... Non-Residential Conditional Purchase (SAUS)

NcRP .... Peace College, Raleigh, NC [*Library symbol*] [*Library of Congress*] (LCLS)

NCR paper... No Carbon Required Paper

NCRPC........ National Capital Regional Planning Council [*Terminated, 1966*]

NCRPCV...... National Council of Returned Peace Corps Volunteers (EA)

NCRPDA ...... National Centre for Research into the Prevention of Drug Abuse (SAUS)

NCRPE .... National Council on Religion and Public Education (EA)

NcRPI .... North Carolina Department of Public Instruction, Education Information Services, Raleigh, NC [*Library symbol*] [*Library of Congress*] (LCLS)

NCRPM........ National Council on Radiation Protection and Measurements (EA)

NcRPS .... Pointer & Spruill Library, Raleigh, NC [*Library symbol*] [*Library of Congress*] (LCLS)

NCRR .... National Center for Research Resources [*National Institutes of Health*]

NCRR .... National Center for Resource Recovery [*Defunct*]

NCRR .... National Credit Union Administration Rules and Regulations

NCRR .... Nordic Council of Reindeer Research (EAIO)

NcRr .... Roanoke Rapids Public Library, Roanoke Rapids, NC [*Library symbol*] [*Library of Congress*] (LCLS)

NCRRC........ National Committee to Reopen the Rosenberg Case (EA)

NCRRF........ Norris Communications Corp. [*NASDAQ symbol*] (SAG)

NcRRH........ Rex Hospital Library, Raleigh, NC [*Library symbol*] [*Library of Congress*] (LCLS)

NCRRHA ...... National Confederation of Registered Rest Home Associations [*British*] (DBA)

NCRRRC...... North Country Reference and Research Resources Council [*Information service or system*] (IID)

NCRS .... National Clearinghouse on Revenue Sharing [*Defunct*]

NCRS .... National Committee for Rural Schools [*Defunct*] (EA)

NCRS .... National Corvette Restorers Society (EA)

NcRS .... North Carolina State University at Raleigh, Raleigh, NC [*Library symbol*] [*Library of Congress*] (LCLS)

NCRSA .... National Commercial Refrigeration Sales Association (EA)

NcRSA .... Saint Augustine's College, Raleigh, NC [*Library symbol*] [*Library of Congress*] (LCLS)

NcRSh .... Shaw University, Raleigh, NC [*Library symbol*] [*Library of Congress*] (LCLS)

NcRSM .... Saint Mary's Junior College, Raleigh, NC [*Library symbol*] [*Library of Congress*] (LCLS)

NcRS-P........ North Carolina State University at Raleigh, Photocopy Services, Raleigh, NC [*Library symbol*] [*Library of Congress*] (LCLS)

NCRSR........ National Congenital Rubella Syndrome Registry [*Centers for Disease Control*]

NcRS-V........ North Carolina State University, School of Veterinary Medicine, Raleigh, NC [*Library symbol*] [*Library of Congress*] (LCLS)

NCRT .... National College of Rubber Technology (PDAA)

NCRTE .... National Center for Research on Teacher Education [*East Lansing, MI*] [*Department of Education*] (GRD)

NCR/TSI....... NCR Telecommunication Services, Inc. (TSSD)

NcRu.......... Norris Public Library, Rutherfordton, NC [*Library symbol*] [*Library of Congress*] (LCLS)

NCRUCE....... National Conference of Regulatory Utility Commission Engineers (EA)

NcRuR .... Rutherford County Library, Inc., Rutherfordton, NC [*Library symbol*] [*Library of Congress*] (LCLS)

NCRV .... National Committee for Radiation Victims (EA)

NCRVA........ National Capital Region, Virginia (MCD)

NCRVD........ National Conference of Religious Vocation Directors [*Later, NRVC*] (EA)

NCRVDM..... National Conference of Religious Vocation Directors of Men [*Later, NCRVD*] (EA)

NCRVE .... National Center for Research in Vocational Education (EA)

NCRW .... National Council for Research on Women (EA)

NCRW......... Neutralized Cladding Removal Waste (ABAC)

NCRW......... Nuclear Cladding Removal Waste (SAUS)

NcRWCM ..... Wake County Hospital System, Wake County Medical Center, Raleigh, NC [*Library symbol*] [*Library of Congress*] (LCLS)

NcRWHD...... Wake County Health Department, Raleigh, NC [*Library symbol*] [*Library of Congress*] (LCLS)
NCRWS....... National Campaign for Radioactive Waste Safety (EA)
NCRY........... National Commission on Resources for Youth
NCS .... INMARSAT Network Coordination Station (SAUS)
NCS .... National Cartoonists Society (EA)
NCS .... National Cemetery System
NCS .... National Center for Stuttering (EA)
NCS .... National Chrysanthemum Society (EA)
NCS .... National Cockatiel Society (EA)
NCS .... National Commemorative Society [*Defunct*]
NCS .... National Committee on Safety
NCS .... National Communications System [*DoD*]
NCS .... National Compliance Strategy (GNE)
NCS .... National Computer Systems, Inc.
NCS .... National Conference of States on Building Codes and Standards, Inc.
NCS .... National Conference on Solicitations (EA)
NCS .... National Consensus Standards (MCD)
NCS .... National Conservation Strategy (GNE)
NCS .... National Convenience Stores, Inc. [*NYSE symbol*] (SPSG)
NCS .... National Corrosion Service [*British*] (IRUK)
NCS .... National Council of Stutterers [*Later, NCOS*] (EA)
NCS .... National Crime Squad (WDAA)
NCS .... National Crime Stoppers [*Later, ACF*] (EA)
NCS .... National Crime Survey [*University of Michigan*] [*Database*]
NCS .... National Cryptologic School [*National Security Agency*]
NCS .... Nationwide Cellular Service, Inc. (EFIS)
NCS .... NATO Codification System (SAUS)
NCS .... Naval Canteen Service [*British military*] (DMA)
NCS .... Naval Combat System (SAUS)
NCS .... Naval Communications Station [*or System*]
NCS .... Naval Compass Stabilizer (PDAA)
NCS .... Naval Control of Shipping [*NATO*] (NATG)
NCS .... Navigational Computer Set (MCD)
NCS .... Navigation Control Simulator
NCS .... N-Chlorosuccinimide [*Organic chemistry*]
NCS .... NCI Building Systems [*NYSE symbol*] (SG)
NCS .... NCR [*NCR Corp.*] Century Software
NCS .... Nearest Cross Street (ADA)
NCS .... Needlework and Craft Showcase (ITD)
NCS .... Neocarzinostatin [*Zinostatin*] [*Antineoplastic drug*]
NCS .... NERC Computing Service (SAUS)
NCS .... Nerve Conduction Studies [*Neurology*] (DAVI)
NCS .... Net Control Station [*Communications*] [*Amateur radio*]
NCS .... Network Clock Signal (CCCA)
NCS .... Network Communications Server [*J & L Information Systems*]
NCS .... Network Communication Standard (AAEL)
NCS .... Network Communication System (IAA)
NCS .... Network Computer System (ACAE)
NCS .... Network Computing System [*Computer science*] (AGLO)
NCS .... Network Control Station (IAA)
NCS .... Network Control System
NCS .... Network Coordination Station
NCS .... Network Co-ordination System (NITA)
NCS .... Newborn Calf Serum [*Immunology*]
NCS .... Newcastle [*South Africa*] [*Airport symbol*] (OAG)
NCS .... Nielsen Coverage Service [*A.C. Nielson Co.*] (DOAD)
NCS .... Nineteenth Century Series [*A publication*]
NCS .... NMIC [*National Military Intelligence Center*] Control Subsystem
NCS .... No Checking Signal [*Telecommunications*] (TEL)
NCS .... No Concentrated Sweets [*Medicine*] (DMAA)
NCS .... Node Centre Switch (SAUS)
NCS .... Noncallable Security [*Investment term*]
NCS .... Noncircumferential Stenosis [*Medicine*] (DMAA)
NCS .... Non-Collimated Source (PDAA)
NCS .... Non-Conventional System [*Post coordinate indexing*] (NITA)
NCS .... Noncoronary Sinus [*Cardiology*] (AAMN)
NCS .... Noncritical Sensitive [*DoD*]
NCS .... Noncrystalline Solid [*Physics*]
NCS .... Noncrystallographic Symmetry [*Chemistry*]
NCS .... Nonwater Cooling System
NCS .... North Carolina State (SAUS)
NCS .... North Carolina State Library, Raleigh, NC [*OCLC symbol*] (OCLC)
NCS .... Northern Cross Society (EA)
NCS .... Northwest Communication System (SAUS)
NCS .... Norwegian Certification System (SAUS)
NCS .... Norwegian Continental Shelf (RIMS)
NCS .... Nuclear-Chicago Solubilizer
NCS .... Nuclear Components Spare (IAA)
NCS .... Nuclear Components Spares (SAUS)
NCS .... Nuclear Criticality Safety (NRCH)
NCS .... Nuclear-Powered Container Ship (PDAA)
NCS .... Nucleolar Channel System
NCS .... Nucleus Support Crew [*Navy*] (DNAB)
NCS .... Nueva Concepcion [*El Salvador*] [*Seismograph station code, US Geological Survey*] [*Closed*] (SEIS)
NCS .... Numerical Category Scaling
NCS .... Numerical Control Society [*Later, NCS/AIMTECH*] (EA)
NCS .... Numerical Control System (IAA)
NCS .... Nutation Control System (MCD)
NCS .... Simpson Air Ltd. [*Canada*] [*ICAO designator*] (FAAC)
NCSA .... National Capital Speakers Association (EA)
NCSA .... National Carl Schurz Association [*Defunct*] (EA)
NCSA .... National Center for Statistics and Analysis [*National Highway Traffic Safety Administration*] [*Washington, DC*] (GRD)

NCSA .... National Center for Supercomputer Applications (NITA)
NCSA .... National Center for Supercomputing Applications [*University of Illinois*] [*National Science Foundation*] [*Research center*] (RCD)
NCSA .... National Church Secretaries Association [*Defunct*] (EA)
NCSA .... National Club Sports Association (EA)
NCSA .... National Coffee Service Association [*Vienna, VA*] (EA)
NCSA .... National Collegiate Ski Association (EA)
NCSA .... National Committee for Senior Americans (EA)
NCSA .... National Committee of State Associations
NCSA .... National Computational Science Alliance [*Supercomputing center*]
NCSA .... National Computer Security Association [*Computer science*] (PCM)
NCSA .... National Confectionery Salesmen's Association of America (EA)
NCSA .... National Construction Software Association (EA)
NCSA .... National Contract Sweepers Association [*Later, NCSI*] (EA)
NCSA .... National Council of Seamen's Agencies [*Later, ICOSA*] (EA)
NCSA .... National Crushed Stone Association [*Later, NSA*] (EA)
NCSA .... National Cued Speech Association (EA)
NCSA .... National Customer Service Association (SAUS)
NCSA .... National Customs Service Association [*Later, NTEU*] (EA)
NCSA .... National Strength and Conditioning Association
NCSA .... Newsagency Council of South Australia
NCSA .... Newspaper Collectors Society of America (EA)
NCSA .... No Charge Storage Agreement (AAGC)
NCSA .... Non-Chemical Shift Anisotropy [*Physical chemistry*]
NCSA .... Noncommercial Spot Announcement [*Public service announcement*] (NTCM)
NCSA .... North Carolina School of the Arts (SAUS)
NCSA .... North Coast of South America (SAUS)
NCSAB........ National Council of State Agencies for the Blind (EA)
NCSABMT.... National Campaign to Save the ABM [*Antiballistic missile*] Treaty [*Defunct*] (EA)
NcSaC.......... Central Carolina Technical Institute, Sanford, NC [*Library symbol*] [*Library of Congress*] (LCLS)
NCSAC........ National Catholic Social Action Conference [*Defunct*] (EA)
NCSAC........ National Child Support Advocacy Coalition (EA)
NCSAC........ Nuclear Cross Sections Advisory Committee
NcSaCi........ Cilco, Sanford, NC [*Library symbol*] [*Library of Congress*] (LCLS)
NCSAG........ Nuclear Cross Section Advisory Group (NRCH)
NCS/AIMTECH... Numerical Control Society/AIMTECH [*Association for Integrated Manufacturing Technology*] (EA)
NcSaL.......... Lee County Library, Sanford, NC [*Library symbol*] [*Library of Congress*] (LCLS)
NcSaI.......... Rowan Public Library, Salisbury, NC [*Library symbol*] [*Library of Congress*] (LCLS)
NcSaIC........ Catawba College, Salisbury, NC [*Library symbol*] [*Library of Congress*] (LCLS)
NcSaLCL..... Lee County Library, Sanford, NC [*Library symbol*] [*Library of Congress*] (LCLS)
NcSaI-E....... Rowan Public Library East Branch, Rockwell, NC [*Library symbol*] [*Library of Congress*] (LCLS)
NcSaIL........ Livingstone College, Salisbury, NC [*Library symbol*] [*Library of Congress*] (LCLS)
NcSaIR .... Rowan Technical Institute, Salisbury, NC [*Library symbol*] [*Library of Congress*] (LCLS)
NcSaIRH..... Rowan Memorial Hospital Area, Health Education Center, Salisbury, NC [*Library symbol*] [*Library of Congress*] (LCLS)
NcSaI-S ...... Rowan Public Library, South Rowan Branch, Landis, NC [*Library symbol*] [*Library of Congress*] (LCLS)
NcSaITM..... Tri-County Mental Health Center, Salisbury, NC [*Library symbol*] [*Library of Congress*] (LCLS)
NcSaIVA ..... United States Veterans Administration Center, Medical Library, Salisbury, NC [*Library symbol*] [*Library of Congress*] (LCLS)
NCSAnet ..... [*The*] National Center for Supercomputing Applications Network [*Computer science*] (TNIG)
NCSAP........ National Council for Single Adoptive Parents (EA)
NCSASR...... National Center for Small-Angle Scattering Research [*Oak Ridge, TN*] [*Department of Energy*] (GRD)
NCSAW....... National Catholic Society for Animal Welfare [*Later, ISAR*] (EA)
NCSB .... National Centre for School Biotechnology (AIE)
NCSBA........ North Carolina School Boards Association (SAUS)
NCSBCS...... National Conference of States on Building Codes and Standards (EA)
NCSBEE...... National Council of State Boards of Engineering Examiners [*Later, NCEE*] (EA)
NCSBI .... National Council for Small Business Innovation
NcSbJ .... North Carolina Justice Academy, Salemburg, NC [*Library symbol*] [*Library of Congress*] (LCLS)
NCSBMD..... National Council for Small Business Management Development [*Later, ICSB*] (EA)
NCSBN....... National Council of State Boards of Nursing (EA)
NCSBN....... National Council of State Boards of Nursing, Inc.
NcSbP......... Southwood College, Salemburg, NC [*Library symbol*] [*Library of Congress*] (LCLS)
NCSC .... National Catholic Stewardship Council (EA)
NCSC .... National Center for State Courts (EA)
NCSC .... National Child Safety Council (EA)
NCSC .... National Communications Security Committee (ACAE)
NCSC .... National Communication System Circulars
NCSC .... National Computer Security Center (IGQR)
NCSC .... National Computer Security Council
NCSC .... National Council of Senior Citizens (EA)
NCSC .... National Council on Schoolhouse Construction [*Later, CEFP*] (EA)
NCSC .... Naval Coastal Systems Center [*Panama City, FL*]
NCSC .... Navy Command Support Center (MCD)
NCSC .... Neighborhood Community Service Centers

NCSC .... Neural Crest Stem Cell
NCSC .... North Carolina State College
Nc-SC .... North Carolina State Supreme Court, Raleigh, NC [*Library symbol*] [*Library of Congress*] (LCLS)
NCSC .... North Carolina Supercomputing Center (SAUS)
NCSC .... Nuclear Criticality Safety Committee (SAUS)
NCSCBHEP... National Center for the Study of Collective Bargaining in Higher Education and the Professions (EA)
NCSCC .... National Championship Stock Car Racing [*Later, NASCAR*]
NCSCCY .... National Council of State Committees for Children and Youth (EA)
NCSCEE .... National Council of State Consultants in Elementary Education [*Defunct*] (EA)
NCSCI .... National Center for Standards and Certification Information [*Gaithersburg, MD*] [*Database*] [*National Institute of Standards and Technology*]
NCSCJ .... National Conference of Special Court Judges (EA)
NCSCJPA ..... National Conference of State Criminal Justice Planning Administrators [*Later, NCJA*] (EA)
NCSCL .... National Committee for Sexual Civil Liberties (EA)
NcScn .... Scotland Neck Memorial Library, Scotland Neck, NC [*Library symbol*] [*Library of Congress*] (LCLS)
NCSCPAS..... National Center for the Study of Corporal Punishment and Alternatives in the Schools (EA)
NCSCR.......... North Carolina State College Reactor
NCSCT .... National Center for School and College Television
NCSD .... National Child Safety Development [*British*]
NCSD .... National Council on Student Development (EA)
NCSDCJC..... National Council of State Directors of Community Junior Colleges (NTPA)
NCSDR.......... National Commission on Sleep Disorders Research
NCSE .... National Center for Science Education (EA)
NCSE .... National Commission on Safety Education [*Defunct*] (EA)
NCSE .... National Committee on Secondary Education [*of NASSP*]
NCSE .... National Council for Special Education [*British*]
NCSE .... Nonconvulsive Status Epilepticus [*Medicine*] (MELL)
NCSE .... North Carolina Society of Engineers (SAUS)
NcSe.......... Selma Public Library, Selma, NC [*Library symbol*] [*Library of Congress*] (LCLS)
NCSEA .... National Child Support Enforcement Association (EA)
NCSEA .... National Community School Education Association [*Later, NCEA*] (EA)
NCSEA .... National Council of State Education Associations (EA)
NcSEA.......... North Carolina Society of Enrolled Agents (SAUS)
NCSEE .... National Coalition for Sex Equity in Education (EA)
NCSEER .... National Council for Soviet and East European Research (EA)
NCSEES .... Nordic Committee for Soviet and East European Studies (EA)
NCSEMSTC... National Council of State Emergency Medical Services Training Coordinators (EA)
NC Sess Laws... Session Laws of North Carolina [*A publication*] (DLA)
NCSEX .... Naval Control of Shipping Exercises
NCSF .... National Catholic Society of Foresters (EA)
NCSF .... National Cold Storage Federation [*British*] (DBA)
NCSF .... National College Student Foundation [*Defunct*] (EA)
NCSFA .... National Conference of State Fleet Administrators (EA)
NCSFI .... National Coalition to Stop Food Irradiation (EA)
NCSFP .... National Council on Synthetic Fuels Production [*Later, CSF*] (EA)
NCSFWI .... National Coalition to Stop Food and Water Irradiation (EA)
NCSG .... National Carcinoid Support Group, Inc. (NRGU)
NCSG .... National Chimney Sweep Guild (EA)
NCSGC .... National Council of State Garden Clubs (EA)
NCSGSO .... National Conference of State General Service Officers [*Later, NASDAGS*] (EA)
NcSh .... Cleveland County Memorial Library, Shelby, NC [*Library symbol*] [*Library of Congress*] (LCLS)
NCsh .... Cold Spring Harbor Public Library, Cold Spring Harbor, NY [*Library symbol*] [*Library of Congress*] (LCLS)
NCSH .... National Clearinghouse for Smoking and Health [*Public Health Service*]
NCSH .... Newton College of the Sacred Heart [*Later, Newton College*] [*Massachusetts*]
NCSHA.......... National Council of State Housing Agencies (NTPA)
NCSHA.......... Naval Communications System Headquarters Activity (SAA)
NCshB.......... Cold Spring Harbor Biological Laboratory, Cold Spring Harbor, NY [*Library symbol*] [*Library of Congress*] (LCLS)
NcShC.......... Cleveland County Technical Institute, Shelby, NC [*Library symbol*] [*Library of Congress*] (LCLS)
NCshL.......... Cold Spring Harbor Public Library, Cold Spring Harbor, NY [*Library symbol*] [*Library of Congress*] (LCLS)
NCS Hlt.......... NCS Healthcare, Inc. [*Associated Press*] (SAG)
NCSHPO .... National Conference of State Historic Preservation Officers (EA)
NCSHSA....... National Council of State Human Service Administrators (EA)
NCshWM....... Whaling Museum Society, Inc., Cold Spring Harbor, NY [*Library symbol*] [*Library of Congress*] (LCLS)
NCSI .... National Communication System Instructions
NCSI .... National Contract Sweepers Institute (EA)
NCSI .... National Convenience Stores, Inc. [*NASDAQ symbol*] (SAG)
NCSI .... National Council for Stream Improvement (EA)
NCSI .... National Council of Savings Institutions (EMRF)
NCSI .... National Council of Self-Insurers [*Chicago, IL*] (EA)
NCSI .... National Curriculum Study Institute [*Associaton for Supervision and Curriculum Development*] (EDAC)
NCSI .... Network Communications Services Interface [*Computer science*] (PCM)
NCSIT .... National Coalition to Support Indian Treaties (EA)
NCSITSG...... National Community Services Industry Training Steering Group [*Australia*]
NCSJ.......... National College of the State Judiciary (DLA)
NCSJ.......... National Conference on Soviet Jewry (EA)
NCSJ.......... Naval Communication Station, Japan
NcSj.......... United States Air Force, Seymour Johnson Air Force Base, Base Library, Seymour Johnson AFB, NC [*Library symbol*] [*Library of Congress*] (LCLS)
NCSL .... National Center for Service-Learning [*Defunct*] (EA)
NCSL .... National Civil Service League [*Defunct*] (EA)
NCSL .... National Computer Systems Laboratory (VLIE)
NCSL .... National Conference of Standards Laboratories (EA)
NCSL .... National Conference of State Legislatures (EA)
NCSL .... National Council of State Legislatures (WPI)
NCSL .... Naval Coastal Systems Laboratory [*Later, NCSC*]
NCSL .... Naval Code and Signal Laboratory
NCSL .... Near-Coincident Site Lattice [*Crystallography*]
NCSLA .... National Conference of State Liquor Administrators (EA)
NCSLL .... National Conference of State Legislative Leaders [*Later, NCSL*] (EA)
NCSLO .... Naval Control of Shipping Liaison Officer
NCSM .... National Communication System Memoranda
NCSM .... National Council of Supervisors of Mathematics (EA)
NCSMA .... Nonadaptive Carrier Sensing Multiple Access (SAUS)
NCSMA .... Nonpersistent Carrier Sensing Multiple Access (SAUS)
NCSMHC....... National Council for the Single Mother and Her Child [*Australia*]
NcSmJ .... Johnston County Technical Institute, Smithfield (SAUS)
NCSMX.......... National Campaign to Stop the MX [*Defunct*] (EA)
NcSn.......... Greene County Public Library, Snow Hill (SAUS)
NCSN.......... National Computer Service Network (EA)
NCSN.......... National Council for School Nurses [*of AAHPER*]
NCSNE.......... Naval Control of Shipping in Northern European Command Area [*NATO*] (NATG)
NCSO .... National Council of Salesmen's Organizations [*New York, NY*] (EA)
NCSO .... Naval Control of Shipping Officer
NCSO .... Naval Control of Shipping Operations
NCSO .... Naval Control Service Office [*World War II British Routing Service*]
NCSO .... North Carolina Symphony Orchestra (SAUS)
NCSOICC...... North Carolina State Occupational Information Coordinating Committee (EDAC)
NcSopS-L .... Southport-Brunswick County Library, Leland Branch Library, Leland, NC [*Library symbol*] [*Library of Congress*] (LCLS)
NcSopS-W ... Southport-Brunswick County Library, West Brunswick Branch Library, Shallotte, NC [*Library symbol*] [*Library of Congress*] (LCLS)
NCSORG ...... Naval Control of Shipping Organization
NCSP .... National Center for Surrogate Parenting [*Later, IAI*] [*Commercial firm*] (EA)
NCSP .... National Conference on State Parks [*Later, NRPA*] (EA)
NCSP .... National Crime Stop Program (EA)
NCSP .... Naval Communication Station, Philippines (DNAB)
NCSP .... NOMESKO Classification of Surgical Procedure (SAUS)
NCSP .... Nordic Committee on Salaries and Personnel [*Nordic Council of Ministers*] [*Copenhagen, Denmark*] (EAIO)
NCSP .... Northern Cod Science Program (SAUS)
NcSp.......... Southern Pines Public Library, Southern Pines, NC [*Library symbol*] [*Library of Congress*] (LCLS)
NcSpa.......... Alleghany County Public Library, Sparta, NC [*Library symbol*] [*Library of Congress*] (LCLS)
NCSPA .... National Corrugated Steel Pipe Association (EA)
NCSPA .... North Carolina State Ports Authority
NCSPAA....... National Council of School Press and Advisers Association
NCSPAE .... National Council of State Pharmaceutical Association Executives (EA)
NCSPAE .... National Council of State Pharmacy Association Executives (NTPA)
NCSPAS .... National Conference of State Pharmaceutical Association Secretaries [*Later, NCSPAE*]
NcSph .... Spring Hope Public Library, Spring Hope, NC [*Library symbol*] [*Library of Congress*] (LCLS)
NcSpi.......... Spindale Public Library, Spindale, NC [*Library symbol*] [*Library of Congress*] (LCLS)
NcSpiI.......... Isothermal Community College, Spindale, NC [*Library symbol*] [*Library of Congress*] (LCLS)
NcSpiR .... Rutherford County Library, Inc., Spindale, NC [*Library symbol*] [*Library of Congress*] (LCLS)
NCSPP .... National Center for Social Policy and Practice (EA)
NcSppA.......... Avery-Mitchell-Yancey Regional Library, Spruce Pine, NC [*Library symbol*] [*Library of Congress*] (LCLS)
NcSppM .... Mayland Technical Institute, Spruce Pine, NC [*Library symbol*] [*Library of Congress*] (LCLS)
NcSpr.......... Spray Public Library, Spray, NC [*Library symbol*] [*Library of Congress*] (LCLS)
NCSPS .... National Committee for Support of the Public Schools [*Later, NCCE*] (EA)
NcSpS.......... Sandhills Community College, Southern Pines, NC [*Library symbol*] [*Library of Congress*] (LCLS)
NCSPWA...... National Council of State Public Welfare Administrators [*Later, NCSHSA*] (EA)
NCSR .... National Centre for Systems Reliability [*Research center*] [*British*] (CB)
NCSRA.......... National Conference of State Retail Associations (EA)
NCSRLL....... North Carolina Studies in Romance Languages and Literatur (SAUS)
NCSRP.......... North Central Soybean Research Program (SAUS)
NCSS .... National Cactus and Succulent Society [*British*] (BI)
NCSS .... National Center for Social Statistics [*HEW*]
NCSS .... National Collegiate Sports Services (EA)
NCSS .... National Commission on Supplies and Shortages [*Terminated, 1977*]

NCSS .... National Computer Security System (ACAE)
NCSS .... National Conference of Shomrim Societies (EA)
NCSS .... National Conference of State Societies (EA)
NCSS .... National Conference on Student Services (EA)
NCSs .... National Conservation Strategies (SAUS)
NCSS .... National Conversational Software Systems, Inc.
NCSS .... National Cooperative Soil Survey
NCSS .... National Council for the Social Studies (EA)
NCSS .... National Council of Social Service [British]
NCSS .... National Crash Severity Study [National Highway Traffic Safety Administration]
NCSS .... Navy Command Support System (MCD)
NCSS .... NCS Healthcare, Inc. [NASDAQ symbol] (SAG)
NCSS .... NCS HealthCare 'A' [NASDAQ symbol] (TTSB)
NCSS .... NGT Command and Status System (SAUS)
NCSS .... Non Commentary Sources Statements (SAUS)
NCSS .... Non-Contact Smart Sensor
NCSS .... Nordic Council of Ski Schools (EAIO)
NCSS .... Number Cruncher Statistical System [Computer software] (PCM)
NCSS .... Number Crunching Statistical System (SAUS)
NCSSA .... Naval Command Systems Support Activity
NCSSAD ...... National Council of Secondary School Athletic Directors (EA)
NCSSB .... National Coalition for Seat Belts on School Buses (EA)
NCSSC .... Naval Command Systems Support Center
NCSSE .... National Coalition to Support Sexuality Education [Fact sheet published by the Sexuality Information and Education Coalition of the United States (SIECUS)] (PAZ)
NCSSFL .... National Council of State Supervisors of Foreign Languages (EA)
NCSSIA .... National Council of State Self-Insurers Associations [Later, NCSI] (EA)
NCSSM .... National Council of State Supervisors of Music (EA)
NCSSM .... North Carolina School of Science and Mathematics [Free, residential public high school for gifted students]
NCSSMA ..... National Council of Social Security Management Associations (EA)
NCSSSA ...... National Conference of State Social Security Administrators (EA)
NCSSW .... Nordic Committee of Schools of Social Work (EAIO)
NcSt .... Iredell Public Library, Statesville, NC [Library symbol] [Library of Congress] (LCLS)
NCST .... National Center for Software Technology [India] (DDC)
NCST .... National Certification Skills Test [Psychiatry]
NCST .... National Coalition for Science and Technology [Defunct] (EA)
NCSTAR ...... National Committee of Shatnez Testers and Researchers (EA)
NCSTAS ...... National Council of Scientific and Technical Art Societies [Later, IG] (EA)
NC State Univ Sch Agric Life Sci Annu Rep... North Carolina State University. School of Agriculture and Life Sciences. Annual. Report (SAUS)
NCSTD .... National Council of State Travel Directors (EA)
NcStH .... Iredell Memorial Hospital, Statesville, NC [Library symbol] [Library of Congress] (LCLS)
NCstLf .... North Coast Life Insurance Co. [Associated Press] (SAG)
NcStMC....... Mitchell College, Statesville, NC [Library symbol] [Library of Congress] (LCLS)
NcStpR .... Robeson Technical Institute, St. Pauls, NC [Library symbol] [Library of Congress] [Obsolete] (LCLS)
NCSTR .... NATO Communication System Technical Recommendation (NATG)
NC Str......... Strange's Notes of Cases, Madras [1798-1816] [A publication] (DLA)
NC/STRC..... North Carolina Science and Technology Research Center [North Carolina Department of Commerce] [Research center] (RCD)
NCSTRL ...... Networked Computer Science Technical Reference Library
NCSTS .... National Conference of State Transportation Specialists (EA)
NCSTSR ...... National Council of Superintendents of Training Schools and Reformatories [Later, International Conference of Administrators Residential Centers for Youth -ICA] (EA)
NCSU .... Network Channel Service Unit [Computer science] (TNIG)
NCSU .... North Carolina State University [Raleigh]
NC SU CAPPS... North Carolina State University Center for Aseptic Processing and Packaging Studies (SAUS)
NcSupB........ Brunswick Technical College, Supply, NC [Library symbol] [Library of Congress] (LCLS)
NCSW .... National Conference of Social Workers
NCSW .... National Conference on Social Welfare [Defunct] (EA)
NCSW .... National Council for the Single Woman and Her Dependants Ltd. [British] (BI)
NcSw .... Swannanoa Public Library, Swannanoa, NC [Library symbol] [Library of Congress] (LCLS)
NcSwC .... Chemtronics, Inc., Swannanoa, NC [Library symbol] [Library of Congress] (LCLS)
NCSWCL...... National [Presidential] Commission on State Workmen's Compensation Laws
NCSWD........ National Center for Solid Waste Disposal [Later, National Center for Resource Recovery] (EA)
NCSWD........ National Center for the Study of Wilson's Disease (EA)
NCSWD........ National Council for the Single Woman and Her Dependants (EA)
NCSWDI....... National Combination Storm Window and Door Institute [Defunct] (EA)
NCSW-ECO... Naval Warfare Center, East Coast Operations (SAUS)
NC Switch.... Normally Closed Switch (SAUS)
NcSwW .... Warren Wilson College, Swannanoa, NC [Library symbol] [Library of Congress] (LCLS)
NCSX .... Shipping Control Exercise [NATO exercises] (NATG)
NcSy .... Jackson County Public Library, Sylva, NC [Library symbol] [Library of Congress] (LCLS)
NCSY .... National Conference of Synagogue Youth (EA)
NcSyS......... Southwestern Technical Institute, Sylva, NC [Library symbol] [Library of Congress] (LCLS)

NCT............. Name Changed To
NCT............. National Centre of Tribology [Risley Nuclear Laboratories] [British] (CB)
NCT............. National Chamber of Trade [British] (BI)
NCT............. National Childbirth Trust [British]
NCT............. National College Television [Cable-television system] (WDMC)
N Ct .... Native Court [Ghana] [A publication] (DLA)
NCT............. NATO Comparative Testing (RDA)
NCT............. NATO Comparative Test programme (SAUS)
NCT............. Neoclassical Radiation Theory
NCT............. Nerve Conduction Tests [Neurology] (DAVI)
NCT............. Nerve Conduction Time [neurology] (DAVI)
NCT............. Net Cost of Transport
NCT............. Network Computing Tools (TIMI)
NCT............. Network Control Terminal (MCD)
NCT............. Neural Crest Tumor [Oncology]
NCT............. Neutral Contour Technology [Automotive engineering]
NCT............. Newcourt Credit Group [NYSE symbol] (SG)
NCT............. New Curing Technology
NCT............. Nicoya [Costa Rica] [Airport symbol] (AD)
NCT............. Night Closing Trunks [Telecommunications] (TEL)
NCT............. Nitrocellulose Tubular (SAUS)
nct............. No Charge for Terms (SAUS)
nct............. No Civil Twilight (SAUS)
NCT............. Noise Cancellation Technology (PS)
NCT............. Non-Chargeable Time (DGA)
NCT............. Non-Competitive Tenders [Business term] (MHDW)
NCT............. Non-Contact Time (AIE)
NCT............. Noncontact Tonometer (SAUS)
NCT............. Noncontact Tonometry (MELL)
NCT............. Non-Co-operative Target (SAUS)
NCT............. Nordic Cooperation on Telecommunications (EAIO)
NCT............. North Coast Industries Ltd. [Vancouver Stock Exchange symbol]
NCT............. Northern Cultural Trust [South Australia]
NCT............. Number Connection Test
NCT............. Nursing Care Technician (MELL)
NcTA........... Edgecombe County Memorial Library, Tarboro (SAUS)
NcTA........... Edgecombe County Memorial Library, Tarboro, NC [Library symbol] [Library of Congress] (LCLS)
NCTA........... National Cable Television Association, Inc.
NCTA........... National Capital Transportation Agency [Functions transferred to Washington Metropolitan Area Transit Authority]
NCTA........... National Cattle Theft Act
NCTA........... National Ceramic Teachers Association (EA)
NCTA........... National Child Transport Association (NTPA)
NCTA........... National Christmas Tree Association (EA)
NCTA........... National Council for Technological Awards [British]
NCTA........... National Council for the Traditional Arts (EA)
NCTA........... Navajo Code Talkers Association (EA)
NCTA........... North Country Trail Association (EA)
NcTaE .... Edgecombe County Technical Institute, Tarboro, NC [Library symbol] [Library of Congress] (LCLS)
NCTAF .... Nuclear Communications Task Force (SAUS)
NcTaH......... Edgecomb General Hospital Library, Tarboro, NC [Library symbol] [Library of Congress] (LCLS)
NCTAM .... National Committee for Theoretical and Applied Mechanics [British]
NCTAMS ..... Naval Computer and Telecommunications Area Master Station (DOMA)
NcTa-P........ Edgecombe County Memorial Library, Pinetops Branch, Pinetops, NC [Library symbol] [Library of Congress] (LCLS)
NcTayA .... Alexander County Public Library, Taylorsville, NC [Library symbol] [Library of Congress] (LCLS)
NCTC .... National Cancer Institute Tissue Culture [Medium]
NCTC .... National Catholic Theatre Conference (EA)
NCTC .... National Collection of Type Cultures [British]
NCTC .... Naval Communications Training Center
NCTC .... Naval Computer and Telecommunications Command (DOMA)
NCTC .... Naval Construction Training Center
NCTCA .... National Collegiate Track Coaches Association (EA)
NCTCA .... National Council of Teachers for Critical Analysis (AEBS)
NCTCP .... National Coalition of Title I/Chapter I Parents (EA)
NCTD .... National College of Teachers of the Deaf [British]
NCTE .... National Council for Textile Education (EA)
NCTE .... National Council for Torah Education (EA)
NCTE .... National Council of Teachers of English
NCTE .... Network Channel Terminating Equipment [Telecommunications]
NCTE .... No-Cost Time Extension (MCD)
NCTE .... North Central Turfgrass Exposition [Illinois Turfgrass Foundation] (TSPED)
NCTEC .... Northern Counties Technical Examinations Council (SAUS)
NC Telephone... Non-Coin Telephone (SAUS)
NCTEPS ...... National Commission on Teacher Education and Professional Standards [Defunct] (EA)
NC Term R... North Carolina Term Reports [A publication] (DLA)
NC Term Rep... North Carolina Term Reports [A publication] (DLA)
NCTET .... National Coalition for Technology Education and Training
NCTF .... National Check Traders Federation [British] (BI)
NCTF .... National Corporate Theatre Fund (EA)
NCTFC .... North Central Texas Film Cooperative [Library network]
NCTGA .... National Christmas Tree Growers Association [Later, National Christmas Tree Association] (EA)
NcTh .... Thomasville Public Library, Thomasville, NC [Library symbol] [Library of Congress] (LCLS)
NcThCH....... Community General Hospital Library, Thomasville, NC [Library symbol] [Library of Congress] (LCLS)

NcThDM.......	Davidson Area Mental Health Center, Thomasville, NC [*Library symbol*] [*Library of Congress*] (LCLS)
NCTI............	National Cable Television Institute (EA)
NCTI............	National Consumer Testing Institute (BARN)
NCTI............	Noise Cancellation Tech [*NASDAQ symbol*] (TTSB)
NCTI............	Noise Cancellation Technologies, Inc. [*NASDAQ symbol*] (SAG)
NCTI............	Non-Co-operative Target Identification (SAUS)
NCTIP........	National Coalition of ESEA [*Elementary and Secondary Education Act*] Title I Parents (EA)
NCTIP........	National Committee on the Treatment of Intractable Pain (EA)
NCTI/R........	Non-Cooperative Target Identification/ Recognition (SAUS)
NCTJ..........	National Council for the Training of Journalists [*British*]
NCTL..........	National Commercial Temperance League [*British*] (BI)
NCTL..........	National Computer and Telecommunications Laboratory (VLIE)
NCTM..........	National Council of Teachers of Mathematics (EA)
NCTM..........	Non-Contact Temperature Measurements (SAUS)
NCTO	Naval Central Torpedo Office
NCTO	Navy Clothing and Textile Supply Office
NCTOG	North Central Texas Council of Governments
NCTP	National Cryptologic Training Plan (MCD)
NCTPD........	National Council for Teacher-Centred Professional Development [*British*] (DBA)
NCTPI	Nuveen Connecticut Premium Income Municipal Fund [*Associated Press*] (SAG)
NcTr............	Montgomery County Public Library, Troy, NC [*Library symbol*] [*Library of Congress*] (LCLS)
NCTR	National Center for Telephone Research [*Louis Harris and Associates*] [*Commercial firm*] (EA)
NCTR	National Center for Therapeutic Riding (EA)
NCTR	National Center for Toxicological Research [*Department of Health and Human Services*] [*Jefferson, AR*]
NCTR	National Council on Teacher Retirement (EA)
NCTR	Naval Commercial Traffic Regulations
NCTR	Noncooperative Target Recognition (MCD)
NCTR	Nordic Council for Tax Research (EA)
NCTR	Taylor's North Carolina Term Reports [*A publication*] (DLA)
NCTRC	National Council for Therapeutic Recreation Certification (EA)
NcTrDC	North Carolina Department of Corrections, Troy, NC [*Library symbol*] [*Library of Congress*] (LCLS)
NCT Rep	North Carolina Term Reports [*A publication*] (DLA)
NCTRF	Navy Clothing and Textile Research Facility [*Natick, MA*]
NCTRH........	National Council for Therapy and Rehabilitation through Horticulture (EA)
NcTrM..........	Montgomery Technical Institute, Troy, NC [*Library symbol*] [*Library of Congress*] (LCLS)
NCTRP	National Cooperative Transit Research and Development Program [*TRB*] (TAG)
NCTRU........	Navy Clothing and Textile Research Unit (MCD)
NCTS	National Center for Tourism Studies [*Australia*]
NCTS	National Council of Technical Schools (EA)
NCTS	Naval Computer & Telecommunications Station (SAUS)
NCTS	Navy Civilian Technical Specialist (MCD)
NCTS	Non-Contacting Test System (VLIE)
NCTS	Northeast Corridor Transportation System [*Boston to Washington high-speed transportation*]
NCTSI	National Council of Technical Service Industries [*Later, Contract Services Association of America - CSA*]
NCTT..........	National Committee on Tunneling Technology
NCTT..........	Norwegian Council for Technical Terminology (SAUS)
NCTT..........	Nuclear Certification Test Team (MCD)
NCTTA	National Competitiveness Technology Transfer Act [*1989*] [*Department of Energy*]
NCTTF........	Northern Counties Textile Trades' Federation [*British*] (DCTA)
NCTU..........	Northern Carpet Trades Union [*British*] (DCTA)
NCTV	National Coalition on Television Violence (EA)
NCTV	National College Television [*Cable-television system*]
NCTW	National Conference of Tuberculosis Workers [*Later, CLAS*] (EA)
NCTWU........	National Cigar and Tobacco Workers' Union [*British*]
NCTWX	Nicholas II Fund [*Mutual fund ticker symbol*] (SG)
NcTy	Lanier Library Association, Inc., Tryon, NC [*Library symbol*] [*Library of Congress*] (LCLS)
NCtyB..........	National City Bancorp [*Associated Press*] (SAG)
NCtyBn........	National City Bancshares [*Associated Press*] (SAG)
NcTyI	Isothermal Community College, Polk Campus, Tryon, NC [*Library symbol*] [*Library of Congress*] (LCLS)
NcTyl	Isothermal Community College, Polk Campus, Tryon (SAUS)
NCTYL	National College for the Training of Youth Leaders [*British*] (BI)
NCu..............	Cuba Library, Cuba, NY [*Library symbol*] [*Library of Congress*] (LCLS)
NCU	National Communications Union [*British*]
NCU	National Conference for Unification [*South Korea*] [*Political party*] (PPW)
NCU	National Cutlery Union [*British*]
NCU	National Cyclists' Union [*British*]
NCU	Naval Communications Unit (IAA)
NCU	Navigation Computer Unit
NCU	Navigation Control and Display Unit (MCD)
NCU	Network Configuration Utility [*Telecommunications*]
NCU	Network Control Unit [*Computer science*]
NCU	New Cinch Uranium [*Vancouver Stock Exchange symbol*]
NCU	Nitrogen Control Unit (AAG)
NCU	Nonconforming Use (ADA)
ncu...............	North Carolina [*MARC country of publication code*] [*Library of Congress*] (LCCP)
NCU	North Carolina University (SAUS)
NCU	Nozzle Control Unit [*NASA*]
NCU	Number Crunching Unit (MHDB)
NCU	Numerical Control Unit (SAUS)
NCU	Nuveen California Premium Income Municipal Fund [*AMEX symbol*] (SAG)
NCU	Nuveen CA Prem Inc. Muni [*AMEX symbol*] (TTSB)
NCU	Union College, Lincoln, NE [*OCLC symbol*] (OCLC)
NcU	University of North Carolina, Chapel Hill, NC [*Library symbol*] [*Library of Congress*] (LCLS)
NCU	University of North Carolina, Mathematics-Physics Library (SAUS)
NCUA	National Credit Union Administration
NCUA	National Credit Union Association (NADA)
NCUAAE.......	National Council of Urban Administrators of Adult Education (OICC)
NCUAS........	Northwest College and University Association for Science (SAUS)
NcU-BPR......	University of North Carolina, Bureau of Public Records, Collection and Research,Chapel Hill, NC [*Library symbol*] [*Library of Congress*] (LCLS)
NCUC..........	National Commission on Unemployment Compensation (NADA)
NCUC..........	North Carolina Utilities Commission Reports [*A publication*] (DLA)
NCUC..........	Nuclear Chemistry Users Committee
NCUCIF........	National Credit Union Share Insurance Fund (EBF)
NCU(E)........	National Communications Union, Engineering Group [*British*]
NCUEA........	National Center for Urban Ethnic Affairs (EA)
NCUEA........	National Council of Urban Education Associations (EA)
NCUES	National Center for Urban Environmental Studies [*Defunct*] (EA)
NCUF	National Computer Users Forum [*National Computing Center*] (PDAA)
NCUG..........	National Centrex Users Group (CIST)
NCUG..........	Nevada COBOL [*Common Business-Oriented Language*] Users Group [*Defunct*] (EA)
NCUGAE.......	National Computer User Group in Agricultural Education (NITA)
NcU-H..........	University of North Carolina, Division of Health Affairs, Chapel Hill, NC [*Library symbol*] [*Library of Congress*] (LCLS)
NCUI	National Center for Urban and Industrial Health [*Public Health Service*]
NcU-IG........	University of North Carolina, Institute of Government Library, Chapel Hill, NC [*Library symbol*] [*Library of Congress*] (LCLS)
NCuL............	Cuba Library, Cuba, NY [*Library symbol*] [*Library of Congress*] (LCLS)
NcU-L	University of North Carolina, Law Library, Chapel Hill, NC [*Library symbol*] [*Library of Congress*] (LCLS)
NcU-LS	University of North Carolina at Chapel Hill, Library School, Chapel Hill, NC [*Library symbol*] [*Library of Congress*] (LCLS)
NCUMA........	National Credit Union Management Association (EA)
NCUMC........	National Council for the Unmarried Mother and Her Child [*British*] (ILCA)
NcU-MS	University of North Carolina, Institute of Marine Sciences, Morehead City, NC [*Library symbol*] [*Library of Congress*] (LCLS)
NCUP	National Conference of University Professors (AIE)
NCUP	No Commission until Paid
NCUPI..........	National Coalition for Universities in the Public Interest [*Defunct*] (EA)
NCUPM........	National Council of United Presbyterian Men (EA)
NcU-Pop	University of North Carolina, Carolina Population Center, Technical Information Service, Chapel Hill, NC [*Library symbol*] [*Library of Congress*] (LCLS)
NCUPRSE	National Consortium of Universities Preparing Rural Special Educators [*Defunct*] (EA)
NCUR	National Committee for Utilities Radio (MCD)
NCUR	National Conferences on Undergraduate Research [*An association*]
NCURA........	National Council of University Research Administrators (EA)
NCURSRV....	Naval Courier Service (ACAE)
NCUSA........	Navy Club of the United States of America (EA)
NCUSAA.......	Navy Club of the United States of America Auxiliary (EA)
NCUSAR	National Council on US-Arab Relations (EA)
NCUSCR	National Committee on United States-China Relations (EA)
NCUSCT.......	National Council for US-China Trade [*Later, USCBC*] (EA)
NCUSIF	National Credit Union Share Insurance Fund
NCUSIOGT ...	National Council of the United States, International Organization of Good Templars (EA)
NCUTLO.......	National Committee on Uniform Traffic Laws and Ordinances (EA)
NCUUA.......	National Council for Universal and Unconditional Amnesty [*For Vietnam-War resisters*] [*Defunct*] (EA)
NCV	Navigation Computer Unit
NCV	Nerve Conduction Velocity [*Electrophysiology*]
NCV	Net Calorific Value (PDAA)
NCV	New Concept Van
NCV	No Commercial Value [*Business term*]
NCV	No Cone Value (SAUS)
NCV	No Core Value [*Business term*]
NCV	No Customs Value (DS)
NCV	Non-Cholera Vibrios [*Microbiology*]
NCV	Normalized Critical View
NCV	Noze Control Vehicle (SAUS)
NCVA	National Center for Voluntary Action [*Later, NVC*]
NcVal..........	Valdese Public Library, Valdese, NC [*Library symbol*] [*Library of Congress*] (LCLS)
NcValH	Valdese General Hospital, Valdese, NC [*Library symbol*] [*Library of Congress*] (LCLS)
NCVC	National Catholic Vocation Council [*Defunct*] (EA)
NCVC	National Congress on Volunteerism and Citizenship [*Bicentennial event, 1976*]
NCVE	National Council on Vocational Education [*Department of Education*] [*Washington, DC*] (EGAO)

NCVECS .... National Center for Vehicle Emissions Control and Safety [*Colorado State University*]

NCVG .... National Council for Vocational Qualifications (COBU)

NCVHS .... National Committee on Vital and Health Statistics [*Department of Health and Human Services*] (GFGA)

NCVL .... Northeast College Volleyball League (PSS)

NCVMA .... North Carolina Veterinary Medical Association (GVA)

NCVO .... National Council for Voluntary Organisations [*British*] (ILCA)

NCVOTE .... National Center for Vocational, Occupational, and Technical Education [*Office of Education*]

NCVP .... Natural Circulation Verification Program [*Nuclear energy*] (NRCH)

NCVP .... Noncapsid Viral Protein [*Biochemistry*]

NCVQ .... National Council for Vocational Qualifications [*British*]

NCVR .... National Conference of Vicars for Religious (EA)

NCVS .... National Credential Verification Service (MCD)

NCVS .... National Crime Victimization Survey [*Department of Justice*] (ECON)

NCVS .... Nerve Conduction Velocity Studies [*Medicine*] (MEDA)

NCW .... National Council of Women of Great Britain (BI)

NCW .... National Council of Women of the United States (EA)

NCW .... Newberry College, Newberry, SC [*OCLC symbol*] (OCLC)

NCW .... No Change in Weather (SAUS)

NCW .... Non-Code Word (SAUS)

NCW .... North Central Washington (SAUS)

NCW .... North City West (SAUS)

NCW .... Nose Cone Warhead [*Aviation*] (NATG)

NCW .... Not Complied With [*Military*]

NcW .... Wilmington Public Library, Wilmington, NC [*Library symbol*] [*Library of Congress*] (LCLS)

NcWa .... George H. and Laura E. Brown Library, Washington, NC [*Library symbol*] [*Library of Congress*] (LCLS)

NCWA .... National Candy Wholesalers Association (EA)

NCWA .... National Children's Wear Association [*British*] (EAIO)

NCWA .... NATO Civil Wartime Agency (NATG)

NCWA .... Newsagency Council of Western Australia

NCWA .... Northeast College Wrestling Association (PSS)

NcWaB .... Beaufort County Technical Institute, Washington, NC [*Library symbol*] [*Library of Congress*] (LCLS)

NcWaBHM ... Beaufort, Hyde, Martin Regional Library, Washington, NC [*Library symbol*] [*Library of Congress*] (LCLS)

NcWad .... Anson County Library, Wadesboro, NC [*Library symbol*] [*Library of Congress*] (LCLS)

NcWadAS .... Anson County Senior High School, Medial Center, Wadesboro, NC [*Library symbol*] [*Library of Congress*] (LCLS)

NcWal .... Thelma Dingus Bryant Library, Wallace, NC [*Library symbol*] [*Library of Congress*] (LCLS)

NCWAO .... National Council of World Affairs Organizations (EA)

NcWarW .... Warren County Memorial Library, Warrenton, NC [*Library symbol*] [*Library of Congress*] (LCLS)

NCWAS .... National Coal Workers Autopsy Study

NcWaw .... Warsaw Public Library, Warsaw, NC [*Library symbol*] [*Library of Congress*] (LCLS)

NcWayH .... Haywood County Public Library, Waynesville, NC [*Library symbol*] [*Library of Congress*] (LCLS)

NcWayH-C ... Haywood County Public Library, Canton Branch, Canton, NC [*Library symbol*] [*Library of Congress*] (LCLS)

NCWBA .... National Conference of Women's Bar Associations (EA)

NCWC .... National Carwash Council

NCWC .... National Catholic Welfare Conference [*Later, USCC*] (EA)

NCWC .... National Catholic Welfare Conference News Service (NTCM)

NCWC .... National Council of Women Chiropractors (EA)

NCWC .... National Council of Women of Canada

NcWc .... Walnut Cove Public Library, Walnut Cove, NC [*Library symbol*] [*Library of Congress*] (LCLS)

NcW-C .... Wilmington Public Library, College Square Branch, Wilmington (SAUS)

NcWC .... Wilmington Public Library, College Square Branch, Wilmington, NC [*Library symbol*] [*Library of Congress*] (LCLS)

NCWCC .... North Central Weed Control Committee (SAUS)

NcWCF........ Cape Fear Technical Institute, Wilmington, NC [*Library symbol*] [*Library of Congress*] (LCLS)

NcWcL .... Walnut Cove Public Library, Walnut Cove, NC [*Library symbol*] [*Library of Congress*] (LCLS)

NCWD .... National Coalition for Women in Defense (EA)

NcWea .... Bess Tilson Sprinkle Memorial Library, Weaverville, NC [*Library symbol*] [*Library of Congress*] (LCLS)

NcWek .... North Davidson Public Library, Welcome (SAUS)

NcWel.......... Weldon Memorial Library, Weldon, NC [*Library symbol*] [*Library of Congress*] (LCLS)

NcWelc .... North Davidson Public Library, Welcome, NC [*Library symbol*] [*Library of Congress*] (LCLS)

NcWelH .... Halifax County Technical Institute, Weldon, NC [*Library symbol*] [*Library of Congress*] (LCLS)

NcWeR .... Rockingham Community College, Wentworth, NC [*Library symbol*] [*Library of Congress*] (LCLS)

NCWF .... Northern California Womens Facility (SAUS)

NCWFC .... National Council of Women of Free Czechoslovakia (EA)

NCWFD .... National Committee for World Food Day [*Later, USNCWFD*] (EA)

NcWfSB .... Southeastern Baptist Theological Seminary, Wake Forest, NC [*Library symbol*] [*Library of Congress*] (LCLS)

NCWGA........ Natural Colored Wool Growers Association (EA)

NCWGB .... National Council of Women of Great Britain (DI)

NcWGE .... General Electric Co., WMD Technical Library, Wilmington (SAUS)

NCWGE .... National Coalition for Women and Girls in Education (EA)

NcWhC......... Columbus County Public Library, Whiteville, NC [*Library symbol*] [*Library of Congress*] (LCLS)

NcWHE .... Wilmington Area Health Education Center Medical Library, Wilmington, NC [*Library symbol*] [*Library of Congress*] (LCLS)

NcWhS......... Southeastern Community College, Whiteville, NC [*Library symbol*] [*Library of Congress*] (LCLS)

NcWil.......... Wilson County Public Library, Wilson, NC [*Library symbol*] [*Library of Congress*] (LCLS)

NcWilA .... Atlantic Christian College, Wilson, NC [*Library symbol*] [*Library of Congress*] (LCLS)

NcWilB .... Beddingfield High School Library, Wilson, NC [*Library symbol*] [*Library of Congress*] (LCLS)

NcWilC .... Carolina Disciplina Library, Wilson, NC [*Library symbol*] [*Library of Congress*] (LCLS)

NcWilE........ North Carolina Department of Human Resources, Eastern North Carolina School for the Deaf, Wilson (SAUS)

NcWilE........ North Carolina Department of Human Resources, Eastern North Carolina School for the Deaf, Wilson, NC [*Library symbol*] [*Library of Congress*] (LCLS)

NcWilF .... Fike High School Library, Wilson, NC [*Library symbol*] [*Library of Congress*] (LCLS)

NcWilH .... Wilson Memorial Hospital, Wilson, NC [*Library symbol*] [*Library of Congress*] (LCLS)

NcWilHS ...... Hunt High School Library, Wilson, NC [*Library symbol*] [*Library of Congress*] (LCLS)

NcWill .... Martin Memorial Library, Williamston, NC [*Library symbol*] [*Library of Congress*] (LCLS)

NcWillM .... Martin Technical Institute, Williamston, NC [*Library symbol*] [*Library of Congress*] (LCLS)

NcWilW .... Wilson County Technical Institute, Wilson, NC [*Library symbol*] [*Library of Congress*] (LCLS)

NcWin.......... Wingate College, Wingate, NC [*Library symbol*] [*Library of Congress*] (LCLS)

NcWind........ Lawrence Memorial Library, Windsor, NC [*Library symbol*] [*Library of Congress*] (LCLS)

NcWintA .... Albermarle Regional Library, Winton, NC [*Library symbol*] [*Library of Congress*] (LCLS)

NCWIS .... New Computerized World Information Service [*Information service or system*] (IID)

NcWiW .... Wilkes Community College, Wilkesboro, NC [*Library symbol*] [*Library of Congress*] (LCLS)

NcWj........... Ashe County Public Library, West Jefferson, NC [*Library symbol*] [*Library of Congress*] (LCLS)

NCWM .... National Conference on Weights and Measures (EA)

NCWM .... National Congress of Women in Music (EA)

NcWMM...... Miller-Motte Business College, Wilmington, NC [*Library symbol*] [*Library of Congress*] (LCLS)

NcWN .... New Hanover County Public Library, Wilmington, NC [*Library symbol*]

NcWN-C....... New Hanover County Public Library, Carolina Beach Branch Library (SAUS)

NcWNC .... New Hanover County Public Library, Carolina Beach Branch Library, Carolina Beach, NC [*Library symbol*] [*Library of Congress*] (LCLS)

NCWNSW .... National Council of Women of New South Wales [*Australia*]

NCWP .... National Communications Working Party [*Australia*] [*Political party*]

NCWP .... Near Coastal Waters Program (WPI)

NCWPA........ National Committee for Women in Public Administration (EA)

NCWPA........ National Council for the Welfare of Prisoners Abroad [*British*] (DI)

NCWPTF ..... National Council for a World Peace Tax Fund (EA)

NCWQ .... National Commission on Water Quality [*National Academy of Sciences*]

NCWQ .... National Council of Women of Queensland [*Australia*]

NCWR......... Nordic Council for Wildlife Research (EAIO)

NCWRU....... North Central Watershed Research Unit [*Department of Agriculture*] (GRD)

NcWs.......... Forsyth County Public Library System, Winston-Salem, NC [*Library symbol*] [*Library of Congress*] (LCLS)

NCWS .... Non-Community Water System [*Environmental Protection Agency*]

NCWSA........ National Collegiate Water Ski Association (EA)

NcWsA......... North-West AHEC Library at Winston-Salem, Bowman-Gray School of Medicine, Winston-Salem, NC [*Library symbol*] [*Library of Congress*] (LCLS)

NcWsAT....... AT & Technologies, Inc., Winston-Salem, NC [*Library symbol*] [*Library of Congress*] (LCLS)

NcWsAT-R ... AT & T Technologies, Inc., Winston-Salem, NC [*Library symbol*] [*Library of Congress*] (LCLS)

NCWSBA..... National Council of Wool Selling Brokers of Australia

NcWs-C....... Forsyth County Public Library, Clemmons Branch Library, Clemmons, NC [*Library symbol*] [*Library of Congress*] (LCLS)

NcWs-E....... Forsyth County Public Library, East Winston Branch, Winston-Salem, NC [*Library symbol*] [*Library of Congress*] (LCLS)

NcWsF........ Forsyth Technical Institute, Winston-Salem, NC [*Library symbol*] [*Library of Congress*] (LCLS)

NcWsFM..... Forsyth-Stokes Area Mental Health Center, Winston-Salem, NC [*Library symbol*] [*Library of Congress*] (LCLS)

NcWs-K....... Forsyth County Public Library, Kernersville Branch Library, Kernersville, NC [*Library symbol*] [*Library of Congress*] (LCLS)

NcWsM........ Moravian Archives, Winston-Salem, NC [*Library symbol*] [*Library of Congress*] (LCLS)

NcWsMES.... Museum of Early Southern Decorative Arts, MESDA Library, Winston-Salem, NC [*Library symbol*] [*Library of Congress*] (LCLS)

NcWsMM..... Moravian Music Foundation, Winston-Salem, NC [*Library symbol*] [*Library of Congress*] (LCLS)

NcWsN......... North Carolina School of the Arts, Winston-Salem, NC [*Library symbol*] [*Library of Congress*] (LCLS)

NcWs-R ...... Forsyth County Public Library, Reynolda Manor Branch, Winston-Salem, NC [*Library symbol*] [*Library of Congress*] (LCLS)
NcWsR .... Reynolds Tobacco Co., Winston-Salem, NC [*Library symbol*] [*Library of Congress*] (LCLS)
NcWsRI .... Reynolds Industries, Corporate Library, Winston-Salem, NC [*Library symbol*] [*Library of Congress*] (LCLS)
NcWsR-M .... Reynolds Tobacco Co., Marketing Development Intelligence Center, Winston-Salem, NC [*Library symbol*] [*Library of Congress*] (LCLS)
NcWsR-R ..... Reynolds Tobacco Co., Research and Development Technical Information Services, Winston-Salem, NC [*Library symbol*] [*Library of Congress*] (LCLS)
NcWs-RS ..... Forsyth County Public Library, Rural Hall/Stanleyville Branch Library, Rural Hall, NC [*Library symbol*] [*Library of Congress*] (LCLS)
NcWs-S .... Forsyth County Public Library, Southside Branch, Winston-Salem, NC [*Library symbol*] [*Library of Congress*] (LCLS)
NCWSS .... North Central Weed Science Society (SAUS)
NcWsS .... Salem College, Winston-Salem, NC [*Library symbol*] [*Library of Congress*] (LCLS)
NcWs-T .... Forsyth County Public Library, Thruway Branch, Winston-Salem, NC [*Library symbol*] [*Library of Congress*] (LCLS)
NcWsU .... Winston-Salem State University, Winston-Salem, NC [*Library symbol*] [*Library of Congress*] (LCLS)
NcWsW .... Wake Forest University, Winston-Salem, NC [*Library symbol*] [*Library of Congress*] (LCLS)
NcWsW-B .... Wake Forest University, Babcock Graduate School of Management, Winston-Salem, NC [*Library symbol*] [*Library of Congress*] (LCLS)
NcWsWE ...... Western Electric Co., Lexington Road Technical Library, Winston-Salem, NC [*Library symbol*] [*Library of Congress*] (LCLS)
NcWsWE-R... Western Electric Co., Reynolda Road Technical Library, Winston-Salem, NC [*Library symbol*] [*Library of Congress*] (LCLS)
NcWsW-L ..... Wake Forest University, Law Library, Winston-Salem, NC [*Library symbol*] [*Library of Congress*] (LCLS)
NcWsW-M ... Wake Forest University, Bowman Gray School of Medicine, Wake Forest, NC [*Library symbol*] [*Library of Congress*] (LCLS)
NCWT .... National Council of Women of Tasmania [*Australia*]
NCWTF .... Naval Commander Western Task Force
NCWTM .... National Council on Wholistic Therapeutics and Medicine [*Defunct*] (EA)
NCW Trf Cy... New Control Word Transfer Cycle (SAUS)
NCWU .... National Catholic Women's Union (EA)
NcWU .... University of North Carolina at Wilmington, Wilmington, NC [*Library symbol*] [*Library of Congress*] (LCLS)
NCWUS .... National Council of Women of the United States (WDAA)
NCWUSA...... National Council of Women of the United States of America (DI)
NCWV .... National Council of Women of Victoria [*Australia*]
NCWW .... National Commission on Working Women (EA)
NCWWA ...... National Council of Women of Western Australia
NCX .... Corpus Christi, TX [*Location identifier*] [*FAA*] (FAAL)
NCX .... NCN Exploration & Development [*Vancouver Stock Exchange symbol*]
NCX .... North Carolina Central University, Durham, NC [*OCLC symbol*] (OCLC)
NCX .... NOVA Chemicals [*NYSE symbol*] (SG)
NCY .... Annecy [*France*] [*Airport symbol*] (OAG)
NcY .... Hyconeechee Regional Library, Yanceyville, NC [*Library symbol*] [*Library of Congress*] (LCLS)
NCY .... Nancy Aviation [*France*] [*ICAO designator*] (FAAC)
NCY .... National Collaboration for Youth (EA)
N-CY .... Natural-Colored Yellow [*Diamonds*]
NCY .... New Century Resources [*Vancouver Stock Exchange symbol*]
NCY .... North Central Yiddish (BJA)
NCY .... Yorktown, VA [*Location identifier*] [*FAA*] (FAAL)
NCYA .... National Catholic Youth Association [*British*] (BI)
NcYad.......... Yadkin County Public Library, Yadkinville, NC [*Library symbol*] [*Library of Congress*] (LCLS)
NCYC .... National Catholic Youth Council
NCYC .... National Collection of Yeast Cultures [*AFRC Institute of Food Research*] [*British*] [*Information service or system*] (IID)
NCYC .... National Council of Yacht Clubs (EA)
N CYC BN .... Northern Cyclist Battalion [*British military*] (DMA)
NCYC CAT.... National Collection of Yeast Cultures Catalogue [*Norwich Laboratory*] [*Norfolk, England*] [*Information service or system*] [*A publication*] (IID)
NCYD .... National Center for Youth with Disabilities (EA)
NCYF .... National Crusaders Youth Federation (EA)
NCYFS .... National Children and Youth Fitness Study [*HHS*]
NcYG .... Gunn Memorial Public Library, Yanceyville, NC [*Library symbol*] [*Library of Congress*] (LCLS)
NCYI .... National Council of Young Israel (EA)
NCYL .... National Center for Youth Law (EA)
NCYL .... Number of Cylinders [*Automotive emissions*]
NcYo............ Youngsville Public Library, Youngsville, NC [*Library symbol*] [*Library of Congress*] (LCLS)
NCYOF .... National CYO [*Catholic Youth Organizations*] Federation (EA)
NCYP .... National Conference of Yeshiva Principals (EA)
NCYRE .... National Council for Year-Round Education [*Later, NAYRE*] (EA)
NCYSI .... National Clearinghouse on Youth Sports Information [*Operated by the National Alliance for Youth Sports*] (PAZ)
NCYSP........ National Committee on Youth Suicide Prevention (EA)
NCYWA....... Nordic Child and Youth Welfare Alliance (EA)
NCz............. New Cruzado [*Monetary unit*] [*Brazil*] (BARN)
NcZG........... Glaxo, Inc., Zebulon, NC [*Library symbol*] [*Library of Congress*] (LCLS)

ND .... Aerospatiale [*Societe Nationale Industrielle Aerospatiale*] [*France*] [*ICAO aircraft manufacturer identifier*] (ICAO)
ND .... Diploma in Naturopathy [*British*]
ND .... Doctor of Naturopathic Medicine (PGP)
ND .... Doctor of Naturopathy
ND .... Doctor of Nursing (PGP)
ND .... Environment Near Death (SAUS)
ND .... Named (ROG)
ND .... Narrowband Distributive Services [*Telecommunications*]
ND .... NASA [*National Aeronautics and Space Administration*] Document
ND .... Nasal Deformity (DAVI)
ND .... National Debt
ND .... National Diploma [*Academic degree*] (AIE)
ND .... Native Defect (AAEL)
ND .... Natural Death [*Medicine*]
ND .... Natural Draught
ND .... Naval Dispensary
ND .... Naval Distillate Fuel (NVT)
ND .... Naval District
ND .... Naval Draftsman (ROG)
ND .... Navigation Display (MCD)
ND .... Navy Department
N-D .... N-Dimensional (MCD)
ND .... Nea Demokratia [*New Democracy*] [*Greece*] [*Political party*] (PPE)
N/D .... Need Date (MCD)
ND .... Negative Declaration (NRCH)
ND .... Negatives and Deposition (DGA)
Nd .... Neodymium [*Chemical element*]
ND .... Neonatal Death [*Medicine*] (MAE)
ND .... Neoplastic Disease [*Medicine*]
ND .... Nervous Debility [*Medicine*]
ND .... Net Debt
ND .... Network Development [*Computer science*] (VLIE)
ND .... Network Directorate (SSD)
ND .... Neurologic Deficit [*Medicine*]
ND .... Neuropathic Doctor (BARN)
ND .... Neurotic Depression [*Psychiatry*]
ND .... Neutral Density [*Photography*]
ND .... Neutral Density Filter (WDMC)
ND .... Neutral-Drive [*Automotive engineering*]
ND .... Neutron Density
ND .... Neutron Detector (SAUS)
ND .... Neutron Diffraction (MCD)
ND .... Newcastle Disease [*Virus*] [*Also, NDV*]
ND .... New Dawn [*An association*] (EA)
ND .... New Deal (DAS)
ND .... New Deck [*On ships*]
ND .... New Democracy [*European political movement*] (ECON)
ND .... New Developments Research Branch [*Bureau of Naval Personnel*] [*Washington, DC*]
ND .... New Directions [*Later, Democratic Alternatives - DA*] (EA)
ND .... New Donor (AAEL)
ND .... New Dramatists (EA)
ND .... New Drug
ND .... New Drugs [*A publication*]
Nd .... Newfoundland Reports [*A publication*] (DLA)
ND .... News Director (NTCM)
ND .... Newsletters Directory [*Later, NIP*] [*A publication*]
ND .... Next Day [*Stock exchange term*] (SPSG)
ND .... Next Day's Delivery
ND .... Nhan Dan Newspaper [*A publication*]
ND .... Nickajack Dam [*TVA*]
ND .... Nippondenso Co. [*Toyota Motor Corp.*]
ND .... No Data
nd .... No Date (VRA)
ND .... No Date [*of publication*]
ND .... No Decision [*Sports*]
ND .... Node Dissection [*Medicine*]
ND .... No Deed (SAUS)
N/D .... No Defects
ND .... No Degree Objective (SAUS)
ND .... No Delay (SAUS)
ND .... No Delivery (SAUS)
ND .... No Detect
ND .... No Discharge (SAUS)
ND .... No Discount [*Business term*] (DS)
ND .... No Disease [*Medicine*]
ND .... No Drawing [*Engineering*]
ND .... No Drinking (SAUS)
ND .... No Drugs (SAUS)
ND .... Nondelay [*Military*]
ND .... Nondelivery [*Shipping*]
nd .... non-delivery (SAUS)
ND .... Non-Denominational
ND .... Non-Descript (WDMC)
N/D .... Non-Destructive (SAUS)
ND .... Nondestructive Count (ACAE)
ND .... Nondetect (SAUS)
ND .... Nondetectable [*Medicine*] (DB)
ND .... Nondeterministic (IAA)
ND .... Nondiabetic [*Medicine*]
ND .... Nondirectional (IAA)
ND .... Nondirectional Antenna
ND .... Nondirectional Microphone (WDMC)
ND .... Nondirector (IAA)

ND	Nondisabling [*Medicine*]
ND	Non Disponible [*Not Available*] [*French*]
ND	Non-Distended (SAUS)
N/D	Non-Drinker [*Medicine*]
ND	Nonduty [*Military*]
ND	Nordair [*ICAO designator*] (AD)
ND	Nordair Ltd. [*Canada*] [*ICAO designator*] (OAG)
ND	Normal Delivery [*Obstetrics*]
ND	Normal Deployability Posture (SAUS)
ND	Normal Detail (ELAL)
ND	Normal Development [*Pediatrics*] (DAVI)
ND	Normal Direction (SAUS)
ND	Normal Distribution (SAUS)
ND	Normal Duty (SAUS)
ND	Normalized Difference (SAUS)
ND	North Dakota [*Postal code*]
Nd	North Dakota State Library, Bismarck, ND [*Library symbol*] [*Library of Congress*] (LCLS)
ND	North Dakota Supreme Court Reports [*1890-1953*] [*A publication*] (DLA)
ND	Northern District (DLA)
ND	Nose Down [*Aviation*]
ND	Nose Drops [*Pharmacy*] (DAVI)
ND	Nostra Domina [*Our Lady*] [*Latin*]
nd	Not Dated (EBF)
ND	Not Dated [*Banking, bibliography*]
ND	Not Deeded (SAUS)
ND	Not Desirable (ELAL)
ND	Not Detected [*or Detectable*] [*Medicine*]
ND	Not Determinable (SAUS)
ND	Not Determined [*Medicine*]
ND	Not Diagnosed [*Medicine*]
ND	Not Directly (DGA)
ND	Not Done
ND	Not Drawn (SAUS)
ND	Nothing Doing [*Amateur radio slang*]
ND	Notre Dame (NTIO)
ND	Notre Dame Sisters (TOCD)
ND	Nouvelle Droite [*New Right*] [*France*] [*Political party*] (WDAA)
ND	Nuclear Data Corp. (SAUS)
ND	Nuclear Detonation (SAUS)
ND	Nuclear Device (AAG)
ND	Nucleotidase (SAUS)
ND	Number Detector (SAUS)
Nd	Number of Dissimilar Matches
ND	Number of Document [*Online database field identifier*]
ND	Numerical Data (SAUS)
ND	Numerical Display (SAUS)
ND	Nursing Doctorale (SAUS)
ND	Nursing Doctorate
ND	Nutritionally Deprived (MELL)
ND	Nutrition Disorder (MELL)
ND	Ny Demokrati [*New Democracy*] [*Sweden*] [*Political party*] (EY)
ND	Romania [*License plate code assigned to foreign diplomats in the US*]
ND	University of Notre Dame [*Indiana*]
nd	Updated (VRA)
Nd2	Nord-Aviation 262 [*Airplane code*]
NDA	Bandanaira [*Indonesia*] [*Airport symbol*] (OAG)
NDA	Naphthalenedicarboxaldehyde [*Organic chemistry*]
NDA	National Dairy Association (NADA)
NDA	National Dairymen's Association, Inc. [*British*] (BI)
NDA	National Dance Association (EA)
NDA	National Defense Act
NDA	National Defense Area (AABC)
NDA	National Democratic Alliance [*Sierra Leone*] [*Political party*] (EY)
NDA	National Democratic Alliance [*Sudan*] [*Political party*]
NDA	National Dental Association (EA)
NDA	National Denturist Association (EA)
NDA	National Diploma in Agriculture [*British*]
NDA	National Dome Association [*Later, NDC*] (EA)
NDA	National Door Association [*Defunct*]
NDA	National Drilling Association (NTPA)
NDA	NAUI [*National Association of Underwater Instructors*] Diving Association (EA)
NDA	Naval Discipline Act [*British military*] (DMA)
NDA	Network Delivery Access (SAUS)
NDA	Neutral Detector Assembly
NDA	Nevada (ROG)
NDA	New Desk Accessories [*Utility program*] [*Apple Computers, Inc.*] [*Computer science*]
NDA	New Drug Application [*FDA*]
NDA	New Drug Approval (MELL)
NDA	Newspaper Design Award (DGA)
NDA	Nigerian Defense Academy (SAUS)
NDA	Night Driving Aid (ACAE)
NDA	Ninos de las Americas [*Children of the Americas*] (EAIO)
NDA	No Data Available [*Computer science*]
NDA	No Demonstrable Antibody [*Medicine*] (MAE)
NDA	No Detectable Activity
NDA	No Diagnosis of Anything
NDA	Nonadecanoic Acid [*Organic chemistry*]
NDA	Non-Destructive Addition (SAUS)
NDA	Nondestructive Analysis (SAUS)
NDA	Nondestructive Assay

NDA	Nondimensional Analysis
NDA	Non Disclosure Agreement (SAUS)
NDA	Non-Disclosure Agreement (WDMC)
NDA	Nonresonant Deflection Amplifier
NDA	Nordair Ltd. [*Toronto Stock Exchange symbol*]
NDA	Northern Airways, Inc. [*ICAO designator*] (FAAC)
NDA	Not Diagnosed with Anything
NDA	Nuclear Development Associates, Inc. (SAUS)
NDA	Nuclear Device Association (AAG)
NDA	[*The*] Nuzi Dialect of Akkadian [*A publication*] (BJA)
NDAA	National Dental Assistants Association (EA)
NDAA	National District Attorneys Association (EA)
NDAA	Non-Developmental Airlift Aircraft [*Military*]
NDAA	Not Dated At All (SAUS)
NDAAC	Navy Drug and Alcohol Advisory Council (DNAB)
NDA & LB	Naval District Affairs and Logistics Branch
NDAB	Numerical Data Advisory Board [*National Academy of Sciences*] [*Information service or system*] (IID)
NDAC	National Defense Advisory Commission [*World War II*]
NDAC	National Defense Advisory Committee (NADA)
NDAC	National Defense Advisory Council (SAUS)
NDAC	NATO Data-Buoy System [*National Oceanic and Atmospheric Administration*]
NDAC	Naval Data Automation Command (ACAE)
NDAC	No Data Accepted [*Computer science*] (IAA)
NDAC	Normalized Differential Absorption Cross-section (SAUS)
NDAC	North Dakota Administrative Code [*A publication*] (AAGC)
NDAC	North Dakota Agricultural College
NDAC	Not Data Accepted (SAUS)
NDACP	Nuclear Defense Affairs Committee [*NATO*]
NDACP	Navy Drug Abuse Control Program (DNAB)
NDACS	Navy Drug Abuse Counselor School (DNAB)
NDACS	Network Diagnostic and Control Systems (ADA)
NDACSS	Navy Department Advisory Committee on Structural Steel
NdAD	Nicotinamide Deoxyadenosine Dinucleotide (SAUS)
ND Admin Code...	North Dakota Administrative Code [*A publication*] (DLA)
NDADS	NSSDC Data Archive and Distribution System (SAUS)
NDAFA	National Directory of Accounting Firms and Accountants [*A publication*]
ND Agr E	National Diploma in Agricultural Engineering [*British*]
NDAIS	Nondestructive assay isotopic system (SAUS)
N DAK	North Dakota (AAG)
N Dak	North Dakota (NTIO)
N Dak	North Dakota Reports [*A publication*] (DLA)
ND Ala	United States District Court for the Northern District of Alabama (DLA)
ND ALV	Nondefective Avian Leucosis Virus (SAUS)
NDAM	New Disk Access Method [*Computer science*] (MHDI)
NDANG	North Dakota Air National Guard (MUSM)
NDAP	Nationalsozialistische Deutsche Arbeiterpartei [*National Socialist German Workers' Party, 1919-45*] [*Political party*] (PPW)
NDAPTA	National Drivers Association for the Prevention of Traffic Accidents [*Defunct*] (EA)
NDARC	National Drug and Alcohol Research Center [*University of New South Wales*] [*Australia*]
NDASSP	North Dakota Association of Secondary School Principals (SAUS)
ND ASV	Nondefective Avian Sarcoma Virus (SAUS)
NDAT	Nondestructible Aiming Target
NDAT	Non-Destructive Assay Technique [*Military*] (PDAA)
NData	National Data Corp. [*Associated Press*] (SAG)
NDATUS	National Drug and Alcohol Treatment Utilization Survey [*Department of Health and Human Services*] (GFGA)
NDB	Name Definition Block (TIMI)
NDB	National Discount Brokers Group [*NYSE symbol*] [*Formerly, Sherwood Group*] (SG)
NDB	Nautical Directional Beacon (IAA)
NDB	Naval Disciplinary Barracks
NDB	Navy Department Bulletin [*A publication*]
NDB	Net Debit Balance
NDB	Net Decision Benefit (NUCP)
NDB	New Domestic Boiler (SAUS)
NDB	New Donkey Boiler (SAUS)
NDB	Niger Delta Congress (SAUS)
NDB	Niue Development Board (SAUS)
NDB	Non Directional Beacon (SAUS)
NDB	Nondirectional Beacon (AFM)
NDB	Non-Directional Radio Beacon (PIPO)
NDB	Nouadhibou [*Mauritania*] [*Airport symbol*] (OAG)
NDB	Nuclear Depth Bomb (NVT)
NDB	Numeric Data Base [*INPADOC*] [*Computer science*]
NDBA	National Data Base on Aging (EDAC)
NDBA	National Deaf Bowling Association (EA)
NDBA	New Directions in Biblical Archaeology [*A publication*] (BJA)
NDBA	Nitrosodibutylamine [*Organic chemistry*]
NDB-ADF	Non-Directional Beacon-Automatic Direction Finder (SAUS)
NDBB	North Dakota Bar Brief [*A publication*] (DLA)
NdBC	Bismarck Junior College, Bismarck, ND [*Library symbol*] [*Library of Congress*] (LCLS)
NDBC	National Data Buoy Center [*National Oceanic and Atmospheric Administration*] [*Also, an information service or system*] (IID)
NDBC	National Day of Bread Committee [*Defunct*] (EA)
NDBC	National Dry Bean Council (EA)
NDBC	National Duckpin Bowling Congress (EA)
NDBC	NOAA Data Buoy Center (SAUS)
NDBCA	Navy Department Board of Contract Appeals

NDBDM......... Navy Department Board of Decorations and Medals (DNAB)
NDBDP......... National Data Buoy Development Project [*Later, NDBO*] [*Coast Guard*] (MSC)
NdBH .... Bismarck Hospital, School of Nursing Library, Bismarck, ND [*Library symbol*] [*Library of Congress*] (LCLS)
NdBHD......... North Dakota State Health Department, Bismarck, ND [*Library symbol*] [*Library of Congress*] (LCLS)
NdBHwy....... North Dakota State Highway Department, Bismarck, ND [*Library symbol*] [*Library of Congress*] (LCLS)
NDBI .... National Dairymen's Benevolent Institution, Inc. [*British*] (BI)
NDBL .... National Deaf-Blind League [*British*] (EAIO)
NDB/L.......... Nondireetional Beacon/Locator (SAUS)
NDBLO......... Not to Descend Below [*Aviation*] (FAAC)
NdBM .... Mary College, Bismarck, ND [*Library symbol*] [*Library of Congress*] (LCLS)
NDBMS........ Network Database Management System
NDBMS........ Nonstandard Database Management System (SAUS)
NDBO.......... National Data Buoy Office [*Marine science*] (OSRA)
NdBoU .... North Dakota State University, Bottineau Branch, Bottineau, ND [*Library symbol*] [*Library of Congress*] (LCLS)
NDBP .... National Data Buoy Program [*National Oceanic and Atmospheric Administration*] (GFGA)
NdBPI .... North Dakota State Department of Public Instruction, Bismarck, ND [*Library symbol*] [*Library of Congress*] (LCLS)
NDBPSA...... Non-Denominational Bible Prophecy Study Association (EA)
NdBPW .... North Dakota State Public Welfare Board, Bismarck, ND [*Library symbol*] [*Library of Congress*] (LCLS)
NdBQ .... Quain and Ramstad Clinic, Bismarck, ND [*Library symbol*] [*Library of Congress*] (LCLS)
Nd-BR .... Butadiene Rubber Based on Neodymium Catalyst (SAUS)
NDBS .... National Data Buoy System
NDBS .... Naval Despatch Boat Service
NDBS .... Non-standard Database System (SAUS)
NDBULCUMED... Navy Department Bulletins, Cumulative Editions [*A publication*]
NdBV .... Bismarck [*Veterans Memorial*] Public Library, Bismarck, ND [*Library symbol*] [*Library of Congress*] (LCLS)
NDC .... Air Nordic SWE Aviation, AB [*Sweden*] [*FAA designator*] (FAAC)
NDC .... Naphthalene Dicarboxylate [*Organic chemistry*]
NDC .... Natick Development Center [*Massachusetts*] [*Army*]
NDC .... National Dairy Council (EA)
NDC .... National Data Communication
NDC .... National Data Corp. [*NYSE symbol*] (SPSG)
NDC .... National Debt Commission [*Australia*]
NDC .... National Defence College [*British*]
NDC .... National Defence Committee [*Ghana*] [*Political party*] (PPW)
NDC .... National Defence Company [*British military*] (DMA)
NDC .... National Defence Contribution [*British*]
NDC .... National Defence Corps [*British*]
NDC .... National Defense College [*Australia*]
NDC .... National Defense Council (KSC)
NDC .... National Democratic Club (EA)
NDC .... National Democratic Congress [*Ghana*] [*Political party*] (ECON)
NDC .... National Democratic Congress [*Grenada*] [*Political party*] (EY)
NDC .... National Design Council [*Canada*]
NDC .... National DeSoto Club (EA)
NDC .... National Development Corp. [*Dominica*] (EY)
NDC .... National Development Council (EA)
NDC .... National Directory of Churches, Synagogues, and Other Houses of Worship [*A publication*]
NDC .... National Disaster Coalition
NDC .... National Distributing Co., Inc. (EFIS)
NDC .... National Distribution Circuit (ACAE)
NDC .... National Diving Council
NDC .... National Dome Council (EA)
NDC .... National Drug Code [*FDA*]
NDC .... National Duckling Council [*Defunct*] (EA)
NDC .... Natl Data [*NYSE symbol*] (TTSB)
NDC .... NATO Defense College [*Also, NADC, NADEFCOL*] (NATG)
NDC .... Natural Distribution Certificate (WDAA)
NDC .... Naval Data Center
NDC .... Naval Dental Clinic
NDC .... Naval Doctrine Command (COE)
NDC .... Navigation Display and Computer (MCD)
NDC .... Negative Differential Conductivity (OA)
NDC .... Network Data Collection (SAUS)
NDC .... Network Data Control (MCD)
NDC .... Network Diagnostic Control
NDC .... Neurologic Disease Control
NDC .... New Democratic Coalition
NDC .... New Die Cast [*Honda Motor Co. Ltd.*]
NDC .... New Directions in Creativity Program (EDAC)
NDC .... New Dramatists Committee [*Later, ND*] (EA)
NDC .... Newport Design Center (ACAE)
NDC .... Nippon Decimal Classification [*Library science*]
NDC .... No Date Club [*Brooklyn girls - no dates for the duration*] [*World War II*]
NDC .... Node Data Controller (SAUS)
NDC .... No Direct Charge
NDC .... Noise Dose Count (IAA)
NDC .... Nondairy Cattle (CARB)
NDC .... Nondestructive Characterization (SAUS)
NDC .... Non-Destructive Cleaning (SAUS)
NDC .... Non-Destructive Cursor (SAUS)
NDC .... Nondifferentiated Cell [*Medicine*] (DMAA)
NDC .... Non-Double-Couple [*Seismology*]

NDC .... NORAD Direction Center [*Military*]
NDC .... Normalized Device Coordinates [*Computer science*]
NDC .... Northern Development Co. [*British*] (ECON)
NDC .... Northwest Drama Conference (EA)
NDC .... Notice of Drawing Change [*Navy*] (DNAB)
NDC .... Notre Dame College [*Missouri, New Hampshire, Ohio*]
NDC .... Notre Dame College, Manchester, NH [*Inactive*] [*OCLC symbol*] (OCLC)
NDC .... Noyes Data Corp.
NDC .... Nuclear Data Committee (NRCH)
NDC .... Nuclear Design and Construction [*British*]
NDC .... Nuclear Design Calculations [*Program*]
NDC .... Nuclear Detector Circuit (SAUS)
NDC .... Nuclear Development Corp. (SAUS)
NDCA .... Naphthalenedicarboxylic Acid [*Organic chemistry*]
NDCA .... National Dance Council of America (EA)
NDCA .... National Deaf Children's Association [*British*]
NDCA .... National Drilling Contractors Association (EA)
NDCA .... Nuclear Development Corp. of America
NDCAC........ North Dakota College Athletic Conference (PSS)
ND Cal .... United States District Court for the Northern District of California (DLA)
NdCan.......... Cando Public Library, Cando, ND [*Library symbol*] [*Library of Congress*] (LCLS)
NDCC .... National Defense Cadet Corps
NDCC .... Navy Department Corrosion Committee
NDCC .... Nondirectional Cross-Country (MCD)
NDCC .... North Dakota Century Code [*A publication*]
NDCCC........ National Defense Communications Control Center (MCD)
NDCD .... National Drug Code Directory [*FDA*] [*A publication*]
NDCDAR ..... National Defense Committee of the Daughters of the American Revolution (EA)
NDCEE .... National Defense Center for Environmental Excellence [*DoD*] (RDA)
ND Cent Code... North Dakota Century Code [*A publication*] (DLA)
NDCF .... National Defense Council Foundation (EA)
NDCG .... Nursing Development Conference Group (DMAA)
NDCMP........ North Dakota Cloud Modification Project (SAUS)
NdCo........... Cooperstown Public Library, Cooperstown, ND [*Library symbol*] [*Library of Congress*] (LCLS)
NDCO .... Noble Drilling Corp. (SAUS)
NDColl .... National Defence College [*British*]
NDCP .... Navy Decision Coordinating Paper
NDCP .... Navy Development Concept Paper (CAAL)
NDC Program... Nuclear Design Calculations Program (SAUS)
NDC-PS....... No Drawing Change Project Slip
NdCr .... Divide County Library, Crosby, ND [*Library symbol*] [*Library of Congress*] (LCLS)
NDCR.......... Noise Distortion Clearance Range (SAUS)
NDCS .... National Deaf Children's Society [*British*] (BI)
NDCT .... Natural Draft Cooling Tower [*Nuclear energy*] (NRCH)
NDCT .... Non-Secure Data Communication Terminal (DWSG)
NDD .... Duke University Library, Durham, NC [*OCLC symbol*] (OCLC)
NDd .... Dundee Library, Dundee, NY [*Library symbol*] [*Library of Congress*] (LCLS)
NDD .... National Diploma in Dairying [*British*]
NDD .... National Diploma in Design [*British*]
NDD .... NATO Deducible Directory (SAUS)
NDD .... Navigation and Direction Division [*British military*] (DMA)
NDD .... Negotiation Decision Document [*Environmental Protection Agency*] (EPA)
NDD .... Net Defence Department [*Navy*] [*British*]
NDD .... Neutron Density Distribution (SAUS)
NDD .... New Democratic Dimensions (EA)
NDD .... Nitro(dimethyl)dihydrobenzofuran [*Organic chemistry*]
NDD .... No Dialysis Days [*Nephrology*] (DAVI)
NDD .... Nondeferred Development (MCD)
NDD .... Norton Disk Doctor [*Computer science*]
NDD .... Novo Redondo [*Angola*] [*Airport symbol*] (AD)
NDD .... Nuclear Detection Device (MCD)
NDD .... Sumbe [*Angola*] [*Airport symbol*] (OAG)
NDd .... Woman's Study Club & Library, Dundee, NY [*Library symbol*] [*Library of Congress*] (LCLS)
NDDA .... National Demolition Derby Association (EA)
NDD & RF ... Naval Dry Dock and Repair Facility
NDDC .... National Defeat Dukakis Campaign (EA)
NDDC .... Navy Department Duty Chaplain (DNAB)
NDDC .... NORAD Division Direction Center [*Military*] (AABC)
NdDe .... Devils Lake Carnegie Library, Devils Lake, ND [*Library symbol*] [*Library of Congress*] (LCLS)
NdDeH .... Mercy Hospital, Devils Lake, ND [*Library symbol*] [*Library of Congress*] (LCLS)
NDDEIC........ National Digestive Diseases Education and Information Clearinghouse [*Public Health Service*] [*Later, NDDIC*] (IID)
NdDeL .... Lake Region Junior College, Devils Lake, ND [*Library symbol*] [*Library of Congress*] (LCLS)
NDDG .... National Diabetes Data Group [*British*]
NdDi .... Dickinson Public Library, Dickinson, ND [*Library symbol*] [*Library of Congress*] (LCLS)
NDDIC .... National Digestive Diseases Information Clearinghouse (EA)
NdDiS .... Dickinson State College, Dickinson, ND [*Library symbol*] [*Library of Congress*] (LCLS)
NdDiStJ .... Saint Joseph Hospital, Dickinson, ND [*Library symbol*] [*Library of Congress*] (LCLS)
NDDL .... Neutral Data Definition Language [*Computer science*] (VLIE)
NDDN.......... National Dry Deposition Network (GNE)

NDDN............ Norwegian Defence Digital Network (SAUS)
NDDO............ Neglect of Diatomic Differential Overlap [*Quantum mechanics*]
NDDP............ NATO Defense Data Program (AABC)
NDDS............ National Disability Data System [*Social Security Administration*] (GFGA)
NDDS............ Nuclear Detonation Detection System (DOMA)
NDE .... IndyMac Mortgage Holdings [*NYSE symbol*] [*Formerly, INMC Mortgage Holdings*]
NDE .... Mandera [*Kenya*] [*Airport symbol*] (OAG)
NDE .... National Defense Education
NDE .... National Defense Emergency [*Headquarters*] (MCD)
NDE .... National Dinghy Exhibition [*British*]
NDE .... Navy Department Establishments [*British*]
NDE .... N-Demethylencainide [*Organic chemistry*]
NDE .... Near-Death Experience
NDE .... Nevada Desert Experience (EA)
NDE .... News Development Environment (SAUS)
NDE .... No Date Established
NDE .... No Delay Expected
NDE .... Nondestructive Evaluation
NDE .... Nondestructive Examination [*Nuclear energy*] (NRCH)
NDE .... Nondiabetic Extremity [*Medicine*] (DMAA)
NDE .... Notodden [*Norway*] [*Airport symbol*] (AD)
NDEA .... National Defense Education Act [*1958*]
NDEA .... National Defense Emergency Authorization
NDEA .... National Display Equipment Association [*British*] (BI)
NDEA .... Nitrosodiethylamine [*Organic chemistry*]
nDEA .... No Deviation of Electrical Axis [*On electrocardiogram*] [*Cardiology*] (DAVI)
N de Aqi ..... Nicholas de Aquila [*Flourished, 1197-1217*] [*Authority cited in pre-1607 legal work*] (DSA)
NDEC .... NDE Environmental Corp. [*NASDAQ symbol*] (NQ)
NDEC .... Nursing Diagnosis and Extension Classification (SAUS)
NDEF .... Not Defined (SAUS)
NDEF .... Not to be Defined (VLIE)
N-Defense ... Nuclear Defense (SAUS)
NDEI .... National Defense Education Institute
NDEITA .... National Dance-Exercise Instructor's Training Association (EA)
NDEL .... Non-Destructive Evaluation Laboratory [*NASA*]
NDELA .... Nitrosodiethanolamine [*Also, NDEOL*] [*Organic chemistry*]
NdEIN .... State Normal and Industrial School, Ellendale, ND [*Library symbol*] [*Library of Congress*] [*Obsolete*] (LCLS)
NdEIT .... Trinity Bible Institute, Ellendale, ND [*Library symbol*] [*Library of Congress*] (LCLS)
NDemP .... National Democratic Party [*British*]
NDEO .... Naval Disability Evaluation Office (ACAE)
NDEOL .... Nitrosodiethanolamine [*Also, NDELA*] [*Organic chemistry*]
NDEP .... Nevada Division of Environmental Protection
NDER .... National Defense Executive Reserve
NDERR......... National Defense Executive Reserve Roster [*of the CSC*]
NDERWF..... Navy Department Employees Recreation and Welfare Fund (MCD)
NDES .... Normal Digital Echo Suppressor [*Telecommunications*] (TEL)
NDETP .... National Drug Education Training Program [*HEW*]
NDeUA........ State University of New York, Agricultural and Technical College at Delhi, Delhi, NY [*Library symbol*] [*Library of Congress*] (LCLS)
NDEW .... Nuclear-Driven Directed-Energy Weapon
NDEWT .... Nuclear Directed Energy Weapon Technology programme (SAUS)
NDex........... Dexter Free Library, Dexter, NY [*Library symbol*] [*Library of Congress*] (LCLS)
NDEX .... Newspaper Index [*Bell & Howell Co.*] [*Database*]
NDf .... Dobbs Ferry Public Library, Dobbs Ferry, NY [*Library symbol*] [*Library of Congress*] (LCLS)
NdF.............. Fargo Public Library, Fargo, ND [*Library symbol*] [*Library of Congress*] (LCLS)
NDF.............. Nacelle Drag Efficiency [*Factor*] [*Aerospace*]
NDF.............. Nandi [*Fiji*] [*Seismograph station code, US Geological Survey*] (SEIS)
NDF.............. Narrative Data File (CARB)
NDF.............. National Democratic Front [*Guyana*] [*Political party*] (EY)
NDF.............. National Democratic Front [*Myanmar*] [*Political party*] (FEA)
NDF.............. National Democratic Front [*Pakistan*] [*Political party*] (FEA)
NDF.............. National Democratic Front [*Philippines*] [*Political party*] (FEA)
NDF.............. National Democratic Front [*Yemen*] [*Political party*] (PD)
NDF.............. National Democratic Front [*Iran*] [*Political party*] (PD)
NDF.............. National Diploma in Forestry [*British*]
NDF.............. National Dividend Foundation (EA)
NDF.............. National Drilling Federation [*Later, IDF*] (EA)
NDF.............. Naval Dairy Farm
NDF.............. Naval Defence Force [*British military*] (DMA)
NDF.............. Navy Distillate Fuel (DNAB)
NDF.............. Neutral Density Factor (SAUS)
NDF.............. Neutral Density Filter
NDF.............. Neutral Detergent Fiber [*Food analysis*]
NDF.............. New Democratic Forum (EA)
NDF.............. New Dimensions Foundation (EA)
NDF.............. New Dosage Form [*Medicine*] (MAE)
NDF.............. Nicolas-Durand-Favre [*Disease*] [*Medicine*] (DB)
NDF.............. Night Defense Fire (DNAB)
NDF.............. No Diagnostic Findings [*Medicine*] (DMAA)
NDF.............. No Disease Found (DAVI)
NDF.............. Non-Deterministic Fortran [*Computer science*] (VLIE)
NDF.............. Nondipole Field [*Electromagnetism*]
NDDO............ Non-linear Discriminant Function (SAUS)
NDF.............. Nonlinear Distortion Factor [*Telecommunications*] (OA)
NDF.............. Nonrecursive Digital Filter [*Navy*] (IAA)

NDF .... Number of Discontinuity Functions (SAUS)
NDFA .... National Dietary Foods Association [*Later, NNFA*] (EA)
NDFA .... National Drama Festivals Association [*British*] (BI)
NdFA .... North Dakota State University, Fargo, ND [*Library symbol*] [*Library of Congress*] (LCLS)
NdFC .... Cass County Court House, Fargo (SAUS)
NDFC .... National Days Fan Club (EA)
NDF/CAD ...... Nondestructive Evaluation/Computer-Aided Design (SAUS)
NdFD .... Dakota Clinic, Fargo, ND [*Library symbol*] [*Library of Congress*] (LCLS)
NDFEA .... Northwest Dried Fruit Export Association [*Defunct*] (EA)
nd filter .... Neutral-Density Filter [*Photography*] (WDMC)
NDfL .... Dobbs Ferry Public Library, Dobbs Ferry, NY [*Library symbol*] [*Library of Congress*] (LCLS)
NDFL .... National Defense Foreign Language [*Fellowship*]
ND Fla .... United States District Court for the Northern District of Florida (DLA)
NdFM .... Masonic Grand Lodge Library, Fargo, ND [*Library symbol*] [*Library of Congress*] (LCLS)
NDfM .... Mercy College, Dobbs Ferry, NY [*Library symbol*] [*Library of Congress*] (LCLS)
NdFMG .... Masonic Grand Lodge, Fargo, ND [*Library symbol*] [*Library of Congress*] (LCLS)
NdFN .... Neuropsychiatric Hospital, Fargo, ND [*Library symbol*] [*Library of Congress*] (LCLS)
NDFS .... Non-Dwelling Floor Space (SAA)
NDfS .... Stauffer Chemical Co., Eastern Research Center, Dobbs Ferry, NY [*Library symbol*] [*Library of Congress*] (LCLS)
NdFStJ......... Saint John's Hospital, Fargo, ND [*Library symbol*] [*Library of Congress*] (LCLS)
NdFStL......... Saint Luke's Hospital, Fargo, ND [*Library symbol*] [*Library of Congress*] (LCLS)
NdFStLN ...... Saint Luke's School of Nursing, Fargo, ND [*Library symbol*] [*Library of Congress*] (LCLS)
NDFTA .... National Dried Fruit Trade Association [*British*] (DBA)
NdFVA .... United States Veterans Administration Hospital, Fargo, ND [*Library symbol*] [*Library of Congress*] (LCLS)
NDFYP .... Navy Department Five Year Plan
NdG .... Grand Forks Public Library, Grand Forks, ND [*Library symbol*] [*Library of Congress*] (LCLS)
NDG .... National Dance Guild [*Later, ADG*]
NDG .... National Distribution Guide [*Mailing technique*]
NDG .... No Date Given (AFM)
NDGA .... National Depression Glass Association (EA)
NDGA .... National Dog Groomers Association (EA)
NDGA .... Nordihydroguaiaretic Acid [*Antioxidant, food additive*]
ND GA .... United States District Court for the Northern District of Georgia (DLA)
NDGAA .... National Dog Groomers Association of America (EA)
NDGC.......... National Design Graphics Competition (VLIE)
NDGE .... NATO Air Defense Ground Environment
NdGIT .... United States Air Force Institute of Technology, Grand Forks AFB, ND [*Library symbol*] [*Library of Congress*] (LCLS)
NDGL........... Neodymium-Doped Glass LASER
NDGO.......... Navy Department General Order
NDGP.......... Nepean Division of General Practice (SAUS)
NdGrC......... Carnegie Bookmobile Library, Grafton, ND [*Library symbol*] [*Library of Congress*] (LCLS)
NDGS.......... National Defense General Staff (NATG)
NDGS.......... National Duncan Glass Society (EA)
NdGUH........ Grand Forks United Hospital, Grand Forks, ND [*Library symbol*] [*Library of Congress*] (LCLS)
NDGW.......... Native Daughters of the Golden West (EA)
NDH .... Delhi [*India*] [*Airport symbol*] (AD)
NDH .... National Defense Headquarters [*Canada*]
NDH .... National Diploma in Horticulture [*British*]
NDH .... Natural Disaster Hospitals [*Public Health Service*]
NDH .... New Departure Hyatt Division [*General Motors Corp.*]
NDH .... No Damage History [*Aviation*] (PIPO)
NDH .... Royal North Devonshire Yeomanry Hussars [*British military*] (DMA)
NdHa .... Harvey Public Library, Harvey, ND [*Library symbol*] [*Library of Congress*] (LCLS)
NDHA .... National Dental Hygienists' Association (EA)
NDHA .... National District Heating Association [*Later, IDHCA*] (EA)
NDHECN ...... North Dakota Higher Education Computer Network (VLIE)
NDHFP .... New Developments Human Factors Program [*Navy*]
NdHi .... State Historical Society of North Dakota, Bismarck, ND [*Library symbol*] [*Library of Congress*] (LCLS)
NDHIA .... National Dairy Herd Improvement Association (GVA)
NDHQ.......... National Defence Headquarters [*Canada*]
NDHS.......... New Drop High School (SAUS)
NDHS.......... Nimbus Data Handling System
NDHX.......... Natural Draft Heat Exchanger [*Nuclear energy*] (NRCH)
NDI .... Dickinson State College, Dickinson, ND [*OCLC symbol*] (OCLC)
NDI .... KS Nordic Air, Denmark [*ICAO designator*] (FAAC)
NDI .... Namudi [*Papua New Guinea*] [*Airport symbol*] (OAG)
NDI .... National Dance Institute (EA)
NDI .... National Death Index [*Department of Health and Human Services*] (GFGA)
NDI .... National Democratic Institute for International Affairs
NDI .... National Design, Inc. (PCM)
NDI .... Nephrogenic Diabetes Insipidus [*Endocrinology*]
NDI .... Network Development and Implementation Group [*National Research Council of Canada*]
NDI .... Network Distributed ISDN (SAUS)
NDI .... New Delhi [*India*] [*Seismograph station code, US Geological Survey*] (SEIS)

NDI	Nielsen Drug Index [*Marketing*] (DOAD)
NDI	Nissan Design International
NDI	No-Dig International [*A publication*]
NDI	Noise Depreciation Index
NDI	Non-Combat Development Item
NDI	Nondestructive Inspection (AFM)
NDI	Non-Developmental Item [*Military*] (INF)
NDI	Non-Developmental Items (SAUS)
NDI	Non-Development [*or Developmental*] Issue [*or Item*]
NDI	Nuclear Data, Inc. (SAUS)
NDI	Numerical Designation Index (IEEE)
NDI	Numerical Design Index (SAUS)
NDIA	National Defense Industrial Association
NDIA	New Denver International Airport (COE)
NDiag	National Diagnostics, Inc. [*Associated Press*] (SAG)
NDIAG	Norton Diagnostics (SAUS)
NDIC	National Defence Industries Council (SAUS)
NDIC	National Diabetes Information Clearinghouse [*Public Health Service*] (IID)
NDIC	NATO Defense Information Complex (NATG)
NDIC	Nuclear Data Information Center [*ORNL*]
NDIC	Nuclear Desalination Information Center
NDICE	Non-Developmental Items Candidate Evaluation
NDICF	North Dakota Independent College Fund (SAUS)
n Dicke	des n-ten Farbfilters
NDIIA	National Democratic Institute for International Affairs (EA)
NDIL	Non-Destructive Inspection Laboratory (SAUS)
ND III	United States District Court for the Northern District of Illinois (DLA)
NDIMC	NATO Defense Information Management Committee (NATG)
ND Ind	United States District Court for the Northern District of Indiana (DLA)
ND Iowa	United States District Court for the Northern District of Iowa (DLA)
NDIR	Nondispersive Infrared [*Analyzer*]
NDIR	Nondispersive Infrared Analysis (EEVL)
NDIR	Non-Dispersive Infrared Radiation (SAUS)
NDIR	Non-Dispersive Infrared Spectroscopy (AAEL)
NDIRA	Nondispersive Infrared Analysis (COE)
NDIR Analyzer	Nondispersive Infrared Analyzer (SAUS)
NDIRS	North Dakota Institute for Regional Studies (SAUS)
NDIS	National Document and Information Service [*Australia*]
NDIS	Network Driver Interface Specification [*Computer science*] (PCM)
NDIS	Nissan Direct Ignition System [*Automotive engineering*]
NDIS	North Dakota State Industrial School
NDIU	National Drugs Intelligence Unit [*Metropolitan Police*] [*British*]
NDIY	North Devon Imperial Yeomanry [*British military*] (DMA)
NdJ	Alfred Dickey Free Library, Jamestown, ND [*Library symbol*] [*Library of Congress*] (LCLS)
NDJ	Jamestown College, Jamestown, ND [*OCLC symbol*] (OCLC)
NDJ	N'Djamena [*Chad*] [*Airport symbol*] (OAG)
NdJC	Jamestown College, Jamestown, ND [*Library symbol*] [*Library of Congress*] (LCLS)
NDJCC	North Dakota Junior College Conference (PSS)
NdJF	North Dakota Farmers Union Resource Library, Jamestown, ND [*Library symbol*] [*Library of Congress*] (LCLS)
NdJN	Northern Prairie Wildlife Research Center, Jamestown, ND [*Library symbol*] [*Library of Congress*] (LCLS)
NdJSH	State Hospital, Jamestown, ND [*Library symbol*] [*Library of Congress*] (LCLS)
NDK	Nachrichtendienstkonzept (SAUS)
NDK	Namorik [*Marshall Islands*] [*Airport symbol*] (OAG)
NDK	Network Developer's Kit [*Computer science*] (AGLO)
NDK	Network Development Kit [*Computer science*] (VLIE)
NDK	Nucleoside Diphosphate Kinase [*An enzyme*]
NDKSBX	South Weymouth, MA [*Location identifier*] [*FAA*] (FAAL)
	Journal. Agricultural Laboratory (journ.) (SAUS)
NDL	Duke University, Law Library, Durham, NC [*OCLC symbol*] (OCLC)
NDL	National Defence Headquarters Library [*UTLAS symbol*]
NDL	National Democratic League [*Early British political party*]
NDL	National Demographics & Lifestyles, Inc.
NDL	National Diet Library [*Japan*]
NDL	National Digital Library (TELE)
NDL	Natural Daylight
NDL	Needle (MSA)
NDL	Neon Discharge Lighting [*Automotive lighting*]
NDL	Network Database Language [*Telecommunications*] (OSI)
NDL	Network Definition Language [*Burroughs Corp.*]
NDL	Ni-Cal Developments Ltd. [*Vancouver Stock Exchange symbol*]
NDL	No Decompression Limit
NDL	Nonconductive Data Link (SAUS)
NDL	Norddeutscher Lloyd [*German steamship company*]
Nd-L	North Dakota State Law Library, Bismarck (SAUS)
Nd-L	North Dakota State Law Library, Bismarck, ND [*Library symbol*] [*Library of Congress*] (LCLS)
NDL	Nuclear Data Link System [*Nuclear Regulatory Commission*]
NDL	Nuclear Defense Laboratory [*Army*]
NDL	Nuclear Diagnostic Laboratories, Inc. (EFIS)
NDL	Numerical Drawing List
NDLA	North Dakota Library Association
NDLB	National Dock Labour Board [*British*]
NDLC	Network Data Link Control
ND Lens	Night & Day Lens (SAUS)
NdLibC	North Dakota State Library Commission, Bismarck, ND [*Library symbol*] [*Library of Congress*] (LCLS)
NDLM	Nondestructive Laser Mapping (SAUS)
NDLOA	National Disabled Law Officers Association (EA)
NDLT	N-Channel Depletion-Load Triode Inverter
NDLTD	Networked Digital Library of Theses and Dissertations
NDLUP	Nonduplicate (SAUS)
ndlwk	Needlework (VRA)
NDM	Ferrocarriles Nacionales de Mexico [*AAR code*]
NDM	Mary College, Library, Bismarck, ND [*OCLC symbol*] (OCLC)
NDM	Nadym Airlines [*Russian Federation*] [*ICAO designator*] (FAAC)
NDM	National Data Manager (SAUS)
NDM	National Dried (Milk) [*Brand name for the British government's dried milk for babies - manufacturer undisclosed*]
NDM	N-Desmethyl-Methsuximide [*Biochemistry*] (AAMN)
NDM	Negative Differential Mobility (IEEE)
NDM	Network Database Management [*Computer science*] (VLIE)
NDM	Neutron Dose Monitor
NDM	New Democratic Movement (EA)
NDM	New Dimensions in Medicine
NDM	Newspaper Designated Market (WDMC)
NDM	Nigerian Democratic Movement (SAUS)
NDM	Nomad Energy & Resources [*Vancouver Stock Exchange symbol*]
NDM	Normal Data Mode (SAUS)
NDM	Normal Disconnected Mode (SAUS)
NDM	Normal Disconnect Mode (SAUS)
NDM	North Durham Militia [*British military*] (DMA)
NDMA	National Dimension Manufacturers Association (EA)
NDMA	National Door Manufacturers Association [*Later, NWWDA*]
NDMA	National Dress Manufacturers Association [*Later, AMA*] (EA)
NDMA	Nitrosodimethylaniline [*Chemistry*] (DAVI)
NDMA	N-Nitrosodimethylamine [*Also, DMN, DMNA*] [*Organic chemistry*]
NDMA	Nonprescription Drug Manufacturers Association (EA)
NDMAC	Nonprescription Drug Manufacturers Association of Canada (SAUS)
NdMan	Mandan Public Library, Mandan, ND [*Library symbol*] [*Library of Congress*] (LCLS)
NdManMH	North Dakota Memorial Mental Health and Retardation Center, Mandan, ND [*Library symbol*] [*Library of Congress*] (LCLS)
NdManN	North Dakota Industrial School, Mandan, ND [*Library symbol*] [*Library of Congress*] (LCLS)
NdManNG	United States Northern Great Plains Research Center, Mandan, ND [*Library symbol*] [*Library of Congress*] (LCLS)
NdMayS	Mayville State College, Mayville, ND [*Library symbol*] [*Library of Congress*] (LCLS)
NDMB	National Defense Mediation Board [*World War II*]
NDMC	National Drought Mitigation Center
NDMC	NATO Defense Manpower Committee (NATG)
NDMC	N-Desmethylclobazam [*Biochemistry*]
NDMDA	National Depressive and Manic Depressive Association (EA)
NdMin	Minot Public Library, Minot, ND [*Library symbol*] [*Library of Congress*] (LCLS)
NdMinAF	United States Air Force, Base Library, Minot AFB, ND [*Library symbol*] [*Library of Congress*] (LCLS)
NdMinIT	United States Air Force Institute of Technology, Minot AFB, ND [*Library symbol*] [*Library of Congress*] (LCLS)
NdMinN	Northwest Bible College, Minot, ND [*Library symbol*] [*Library of Congress*] (LCLS)
NdMinS	Minot State College, Minot, ND [*Library symbol*] [*Library of Congress*] (LCLS)
NdMinT-M	Trinity Medical Center, August Cameron Medical Library, Minot, ND [*Library symbol*] [*Library of Congress*] (LCLS)
NdMinT-N	Trinity Medical Center, School of Nursing, Minot, ND [*Library symbol*] [*Library of Congress*] (LCLS)
ND Miss	United States District Court for the Northern District of Mississippi (DLA)
NDML	Neutral Data Manipulation Language [*Computer science*]
NDML	Never During My Lifetime (SAUS)
NdMo	Mott Public Library, Mott, ND [*Library symbol*] [*Library of Congress*] (LCLS)
NDMP	Network Data Management Protocol (SAUS)
NDMPI	Nitrosodimethylpiperazinium Iodide [*Organic chemistry*]
NDMS	National Debt Management System [*Social Security Administration*] (GFGA)
NDMS	National Disaster Medical System
NDMS	Navigation Data Management System (SAUS)
NDMS	Netware Distributed Management Services [*Novell, Inc.*] (PCM)
NDMS	Network Design and Management System
NDMS	Noise Deficiency Management System
NDMS	Non-Directional Mud-and-Snow (PDAA)
NDMSP	Navy Department Mobilization Security Plan (NG)
NDMTB	Nondeployment Mobilization Troop Basis (AABC)
NDMTP	National Defense Manufacturing Technology Plan
NDMWC	National Domestic Meatworks Wholesalers Council [*Australia*]
NDN	National Diffusion Network [*Department of Education*] [*Information service or system*] (IID)
NDN	National Directory of Newsletters and Reporting Services [*A publication*]
NDN	Naval Digital Network (SAUS)
NDN	New Data Network (IAA)
NDN	Ninety-Nine Cent Only Stores [*NYSE symbol*] (SAG)
NDN	Nodal Data Network (SAUS)
NDN	Non-Delivery Notice (SAUS)
NDN	Non-Delivery Notification (SAUS)
NDN	Nonsynaptic Diffusion Neurotransmission [*Neurology*]
NDN	Nordic Data Network (SAUS)
NDN	Nu-Dawn Resources, Inc. [*Vancouver Stock Exchange symbol*]
nDNA	Deoxyribonucleic Acid, Nuclear [*Biochemistry, genetics*]
NDNHI	North Dakota Natural Heritage Inventory [*North Dakota State Department of Natural Resources*] [*Bismarck*] [*Information service or system*] (IID)

NDNO............ National Directory of Nonprofit Organizations [*A publication*]
NDNR............ Normalized Differences of Nadir Reflectivity (SAUS)
NDNT............ Not Dressed nor Tanned
NDNY............ United States District Court for the Northern District of New York (DLA)
NDO............ National Debt Office [*British*]
NDO............ National Diving Officer (SAUS)
NDO............ Navy Disbursing Office
NDO............ Negotiate Downward Only (MCD)
NDO............ Netherlands Development Organization (SAUS)
NDO............ Network Development Office [*Library of Congress*]
NDOA............ National Dog Owners' Association [*British*] (BI)
NDOC............ National Defense Operations Center (ACAE)
NDOC............ Neurological Dysfunctions of Children [*Test*]
NDOC............ Non Departmental Output Class (SAUS)
ND Ohio...... United States District Court for the Northern District of Ohio (DLA)
ND Okla...... United States District Court for the Northern District of Oklahoma (DLA)
NDOP............ Navy Designated Overhaul Point (CAAL)
NDOS............ National Defense Operations Section [*FCC*]
NDOS............ New Disc Operating System (NITA)
NDOW............ Nevada Division of Wildlife (SAUS)
NDp............ Deer Park Public Library (SAUS)
NDp............ Deer Park Public Library, Deer Park, NY [*Library symbol*] [*Library of Congress*] (LCLS)
NDP............ National Democracy Party [*Thailand*] [*Political party*] (PPW)
NDP............ National Democratic Party [*Iraq*] [*Political party*] (BJA)
NDP............ National Democratic Party [*Sierra Leone*] [*Political party*] (EY)
NDP............ National Democratic Party [*Pakistan*] [*Political party*] (PD)
NDP............ National Democratic Party [*Solomon Islands*] [*Political party*] (PPW)
NDP............ National Democratic Party [*Namibia*] [*Political party*] (PPW)
NDP............ National Democratic Party [*Egypt*] [*Political party*] (PPW)
NDP............ National Democratic Party [*India*] [*Political party*] (PPW)
NDP............ National Democratic Party [*Morocco*] [*Political party*] (PPW)
NDP............ National Democratic Party [*Grenada*] [*Political party*] (PPW)
NDP............ National Democratic Party [*Rhodesia and Nyasaland*] [*Political party*]
NDP............ Nationaldemokratische Partei [*National Democratic Party*] [*Austria*] [*Political party*] (PPW)
NDP............ National Determination Party (EA)
NDP............ National Development Party [*Montserrat*] [*Political party*] (EY)
NDP............ National Diocesan Press [*Later, Episcopal Communicators*] (EA)
NDP............ National Diploma in Poultry Husbandry [*British*]
NDP............ National Disclosure Policy [*Military*] (MCD)
NDP............ Nationalist Democracy Party [*Turkey*] [*Political party*] (PPW)
NDP............ Nationwide Demonstration Program
NDP............ Naval Doctrine Publication (DOMA)
NDP............ Navy Department Personnel
NDP............ Neighborhood Development Program [*Urban renewal*]
NDP............ Net Dietary Protein (MAE)
NDP............ Net Domestic Product [*Business term*] (PDAA)
NDP............ Neurological Disorders Program [*National Institute of Neurological and Communicative Disorders and Stroke*]
NDP............ Neutron Depth Profiling [*Analytical chemistry*]
NDP............ New Democratic Party [*Seychelles*] [*Political party*] (EY)
NDP............ New Democratic Party [*South Korea*] [*Political party*] (PPW)
NDP............ New Democratic Party [*St. Vincent*] [*Political party*] (PPW)
NDP............ New Democratic Party [*Facetious translations: "Never Dies Politically," "No Dreams of Prosperity"*] [*Canada*] [*Political party*] (PPW)
NDP............ Night Defensive Position [*Military*]
NDP............ Normal Diametral Pitch (MSA)
NDP............ Normal Diametric Pitch (SAUS)
NDP............ Nuclear Desalination Plant
NDP............ Nuclear Disarmament Party [*Australia*] [*Political party*]
NDP............ Nucleoside Diphosphatase (SAUS)
NDP............ Nucleoside Diphosphate [*Biochemistry*]
NDP............ Numerical Data Processing (SAUS)
NDP............ Numerical Data Processor (SAUS)
NDP............ Numeric Data Package (SAUS)
NDP............ Numeric Data Processor
NDP............ Pensacola, FL [*Location identifier*] [*FAA*] (FAAL)
NDPA............ National Decorated Packaging Association
NDPA............ National Decorating Products Association (EA)
NDPA............ National Directory Publishing Association (NTPA)
NDPA............ Network Problem Determination Application (SAUS)
NDPA............ Nitrosodipropylamine [*Also, DPN, DPNA*] [*Organic chemistry*]
NDPB............ National Drug Policy Board [*Department of Justice*] (GFGA)
NDPB............ Non-Departmental Public Body [*British*]
NDPBC............ National Duck Pin Bowling Congress [*Later, NDBC*] (EA)
NDPC............ National Democratic Policy Committee (EA)
NDPC............ National [*Military Information*] Disclosure Policy Committee
NDPC............ National Dropout Prevention Center (EA)
NDPC............ National Drowning Prevention Coalition (EA)
NDPC............ Network Data Processing Center (TIMI)
NDpCal........ Net Dietary Protein Energy Ratio (WDAA)
NDPD............ National Data Processing Division [*Environmental Protection Agency*] (GFGA)
NDPD............ Nationaldemokratische Partei Deutschlands [*German National Democratic Party*] [*Political party*]
NDPF............ NASA Data Processing Facility (MCD)
NDPGA............ North Dakota Personnel and Guidance Association (SAUS)
NDPhA............ N-Nitrosodiphenylamine [*Organic chemistry*]
NDpHS......... Deer Park High School, Deer Park, NY [*Library symbol*] [*Library of Congress*] (LCLS)
NDPIC............ Navy Department Program Information Center

NDPK............ Nucleoside Diphosphate Kinase (SAUS)
NDPK............ Nucleoside Diphosphokinase [*An enzyme*]
NDPK............ Nucleotide Diphosphate Kinase [*An enzyme*]
NDPL............ National Democratic Party of Liberia [*Political party*] (EY)
NDPN............ National Dropout Prevention Network (EA)
NDPO............ National Defence Programme Outline (SAUS)
NDPP............ (Nitrobenzyl)(Diethylaminophenylazo)-pyridinium Bromide [*Reagent*]
NDPR............ NATO Defense Planning Review (NATG)
NDPR............ Nuclear Duty Position Roster (MCD)
NDPRP............ National Defense Project Rating Plan
NDPS............ National Data Processing Service [*British*] (DCTA)
NDPS............ Non-Disruptive Path Switching (SAUS)
NDPS............ Novell Distributed Print Services [*Computer science*]
NDQ............ NASA Delta Quotation (MCD)
ND(Q)............ Nominal Defendant (Queensland) [*Australia*]
NDQ............ North Dakota Quarterly [*A publication*] (ANEX)
NDR............ Andrea Airlines SA [*Peru*] [*ICAO designator*] (FAAC)
NDR............ Nador [*Morocco*] [*Airport symbol*] (AD)
NDR............ National Derby Rallies (EA)
NDR............ National Dog Registry (EA)
NDR............ National Driver Register
NDR............ National Drug Co. [*Research code symbol*]
NDR............ Negative Differential Resistance [*Electronics*]
NDR............ Neonatal Death Rate [*Medicine*] (DMAA)
NDR............ Net Difference Report (IAA)
NDR............ Network Data Reduction
NDR............ Network Data Representation [*Computer science*]
NDR............ Neutral Detergent Residue [*Food analysis*]
NDR............ New Dimensions Radio (EA)
NDR............ New Document Reference (SAUS)
NDR............ Non-Delivery Report (SAUS)
NDR............ Nondestructive Read [*Computer science*]
NDR............ Non-Destructive Readout (SAUS)
NDR............ Norddeutscher Rundfunk [*Radio network*] [*Germany*]
NDR............ Normal Daily Requirement [*Military*]
NDR............ Normal Detrusor Reflex (DMAA)
NDR............ Normotensive Donor Rat
NDR............ Nuclear Double Resonance [*Analytical chemistry*]
NDRA............ National Deafblind & Rubella Association (WDAA)
NDRA............ Nostalgia Drag Race Association (EA)
NDRB............ New Developments Research Branch [*Navy*] (MCD)
NDRC............ National Defense Research Committee [*of Office of Scientific Research and Development*] [*World War II*]
NDRC............ Non Destructive Read Character [*Computer science*] (ELAL)
NDRC............ Nutrient Data Research Center (SAUS)
NDRE............ Norwegian Defense Research Establishment
ND Res Found Bull... North Dakota Research Foundation Bulletin [*A publication*]
NDRF............ National Debt Repayment Foundation (EA)
NDRF............ National Defense Reserve Fleet [*Maritime Administration, Department of Commerce*]
NDRG............ NATO Defense Research Group (NATG)
NDRI............ National Diabetes Research Interchange [*Research center*] (RCD)
NDRI............ Naval Dental Research Institute
NDRL............ Notre Dame Radiation Laboratory [*University of Notre Dame*] [*Research center*] (RCD)
NDRM............ Neesby Delayed Release Mechanism [*Medicine*]
NDRM............ Non-Destructive Readout Memory (SAUS)
NDRO............ Nondestructive Read Only [*Computer science*] (IAA)
NDRO............ Nondestructive Readout [*Computer science*]
NDROS........ Non-Destructive Read-Only Storage (SAUS)
NDRP............ New Democratic Republican Party [*South Korea*] [*Political party*] (EY)
NDRS............ National Driver Register Service [*Department of Transportation*]
NDRS............ Nuclear Definition and Reporting System (AAG)
NDRSWG............ NATO Data Requirements and Standards Working Group (NATG)
NDRT............ Nelson-Denny Reading Test (EDAC)
NDRW............ Non-Destructive Read and Write (SAUS)
NDRW............ Nondestructive Read/Write [*Computer science*]
NDryT............ Tompkins-Cortland Community College, Division of Instructional and Learning Resources, Dryden, NY [*Library symbol*] [*Library of Congress*] (LCLS)
NDS............ Congregation of Notre Dame de Sion [*Roman Catholic women's religious order*]
NDS............ Name Definition Segment (TIMI)
NDS............ National Dahlia Society [*British*] (DBA)
NDS............ National Decision Systems [*Information service or system*] (IID)
NDS............ National Defense Stockpile [*Collection of materials essential to the defense industry*]
NDS............ National Design Specification [*For wood construction*] (WPI)
NDS............ National Dioxin Study [*Environmental Protection Agency*] (GFGA)
NDS............ National Disposal Site [*Environmental Protection Agency*] (GFGA)
NDS............ Naval Dental School
NDS............ Navigation Data Systems Inc. (SAUS)
NDS............ Navigation Development Satellite (MCD)
NDS............ Navigation Display System
NDS............ Navy Data System
NDS............ Navy Directive System (NVT)
NDS............ Navy Display System
NDS............ Needs [*Automotive advertising*]
NDS............ NetWare Directory Services [*Novell, Inc.*] [*Computer science*] (PCM)
NDS............ Network Data Series (MHDI)
NDS............ Network Data System (SAUS)
NDS............ Network Development System (IAA)
NDS............ Neurologic Disability Score
NDS............ Neutral-Drive Switch [*Automotive engineering*]

NDS	Neutron Doped Silicon (IAA)
NDS	New Drug Submission [*Medicine*] (DB)
NDS	Newport Design System (ACAE)
NDS	Nicholas Data [*Vancouver Stock Exchange symbol*]
NDS	Nominal Detectable Signal (IAA)
NDS	Noncommunications Detection System (MCD)
NDS	Non-Developmental Software
N-DS	Non-Dust Storm (SAUS)
NDS	Nonparametric Detection Scheme [*Communication signal*]
NDS	Non-selective Direct Substitution (SAUS)
NDS	Nordic Demographic Society (EA)
NDS	Nordstress (Australia) Pt Ltd. [*FAA designator*] (FAAC)
NDS	Normal Dog Serum [*Medicine*] (DMAA)
NDS	North Dakota State (SAUS)
NDS	North Dakota State Library Commission, Bismarck, ND [*OCLC symbol*] (OCLC)
NDS	Novell Directory Service [*Computer Networking*] (PCM)
NDS	Nuclear Data Sheets [*National Academy of Sciences*]
NDS	Nuclear Detection Satellite
NDS	Nuclear Detection System (MCD)
NDS	Nuclear Detonation Detection System
NDS	Nuclear Detonation System (SAUS)
NDSA	National Disposal Services Association (EA)
NDSB	Narcotic Drugs Supervisory Body [*UN*]
NDSB	Navy Dependents School Branch
ND/SB	Nuclear Depth/Strike Bomb (DOMA)
NDSBA	North Dakota School Boards Association (SAUS)
NDSC	National Down Syndrome Congress (EA)
NDSC	Network for the Detection of Stratospheric Change [*New Zealand*] (USDC)
NDSCS	National Duck Stamp Collectors Society
NDSE	Nondeliverable Support Equipment
NdSEA	North Dakota Society of Enrolled Agents (SAUS)
NDSEG	National Defense Science and Engineering
NDSEG	National Defense Science and Engineering Graduate
ND Sess Laws	Laws of North Dakota [*A publication*] (DLA)
NDSF	National Defense Sealift Fund (DOMA)
NDSF	North Dakota School of Forestry
NDSHS	North Dakota State Horticultural Society (SAUS)
NDSL	National Direct [*formerly, Defense*] Student Loan [*later, Perkins Loan*] [*Department of Education*]
NDSL	Non Domestic Substances List [*Canada*]
NDSM	National Defense Service Medal [*Military decoration*]
NDSM	Nondeterministic State Machine (SAUS)
NDSN	National Drug Strategy Network (EA)
NDSN	Nobody Don't Say Nothing
NDSN	Nordson Corp. [*NASDAQ symbol*] (NQ)
NDSOS	Navy Deep Sea Oceanographic System
NDSPE	North Dakota Society of Professional Engineers (SAUS)
NDSS	National Down Syndrome Society (EA)
NDSS	National DS Society
NDSs	Nuclear Delivery Systems (SAUS)
NDSSS	North Dakota State School of Science (SAUS)
NDST	Nondimensional Special Tooling (SAUS)
NDSTC	National Defence Science & Technology Commission (SAUS)
NDSTC	Naval Dive and Salvage Training Center (SAUS)
NDSTC	Naval Diving and Salvage Training Center (DNAB)
NDSTIC	National Defence Science Technology & Industry Commission (SAUS)
NDSU	North Dakota State University
NDT	Ferrocarril Nacional de Tehuantepec [*AAR code*]
NDT	National Diploma in the Science and Practice of Turfculture and Sports Ground Management [*British*]
NDT	Nephrology Dialysis Transplantation (SAUS)
NDT	Net Data Throughout
NDT	Network Description Table (MHDI)
NDT	Network Design Tool (ACAE)
NDT	Neuro-Developmental Treatment [*Physical therapy*]
NDT	Nevada Dance Theatre
NDT	New Dictionary of Thoughts [*A publication*]
NDT	New Dimensions [*Vancouver Stock Exchange symbol*]
NDT	Newfoundland Daylight Time (SAUS)
NDT	Nil-Ductility Temperature [*Metallurgy*]
NDT	Nil-Ductility Transition [*Metallurgy*] (IEEE)
NDT	No Dial Tone [*Of a telephone*] (WDMC)
NDT	Noise Detection Threshold (DMAA)
NDT	Nondestructive Test (DMAA)
NDT	Nondestructive Testing
NDT	Non-Distributive Trade (SAUS)
NDT	Non-Lethal Disabling Technology
NDT	Normal Device Termination (SAUS)
NDT	Nuclear Detection Test (IAA)
NDTA	National Defense Transportation Association (EA)
NDTA	National Dental Technicians Association [*Defunct*] (EA)
NDTA	Neurodevelopmental Treatment Association (EA)
NDTA	Night Driving Training Aid [*Army*]
NDTA	Non Destructive Testing Association (SAUS)
NDTA	Nondestructive Testing Association (SAUS)
NDTA	Non-Destructive Testing Association of Australia
NDT & E	Nondestructive Testing and Evaluation Programs [*Pennsylvania State University*] [*Research center*] (RCD)
NDTC	National Drug Trade Conference (EA)
NDTC	Naval Device Training Center
NDTC	Nondestructive Testing Center (IEEE)
NDTC	Nottingham and District Technical College (SAUS)
NDTE	Nondestructive Testing Equipment (SAUS)
NDTE	North Dakota Tracer Experiment (USDC)
ND Tex	United States District Court for the Northern District of Texas (DLA)
NDTF	Nondestructive Test Facility (MCD)
Ndthl	Neanderthal (VRA)
NDTI	Nondestructive Testing and Inspection
NDTIAC	Non-Destructive Testing Information Center [*Army Materials and Mechanics Research Center*] (PDAA)
NDTIB	Nondestructive Testing and Inspection Building
NDTL	Nondestructive Test Laboratory (MCD)
NDTMA	National Drain Tile Manufacturers Association [*Defunct*] (EA)
NDTMA	Non Destructive Testing Management Association (NTPA)
NDTP	Network Development Test Plan (ACAE)
NDTP	North Dakota Thunderstorm Project (SAUS)
NDTP	Nuclear Data Tape Program
NDTRAN	Notre Dame Translator [*Programming language*] [*1977*] [*Computer science*] (CSR)
NDTS	Nonlinear Dynamics Time Series (SAUS)
NDTT	Nil-Ductility Transition Temperature [*Metallurgy*]
NDU	National Defense University, Washington, DC [*OCLC symbol*] (OCLC)
NDU	National Democratic Union [*Zimbabwe*] [*Political party*] (PPW)
NDU	Navigation Display Unit [*Military*]
NDU	NDU Resources [*Vancouver Stock Exchange symbol*]
NDU	Nederlandse Dagbladunie
NDU	Network Device Utility (SAUS)
N/D/U	None Done Up [*Bookselling*]
ndu	North Dakota [*MARC country of publication code*] [*Library of Congress*] (LCCP)
NDU	Notre Dame University (SAUS)
NDU	Nuclear Data Unit [*International Atomic Energy Agency*] (DIT)
NDU	Rundu [*Namibia*] [*Airport symbol*] (OAG)
NdU	University of North Dakota, Grand Forks, ND [*Library symbol*] [*Library of Congress*] (LCLS)
NDUC	Nimbus Data Utilization Center
NdU-El	University of North Dakota, Ellendale Branch, Ellendale, ND [*Library symbol*] [*Library of Congress*] [*Obsolete*] (LCLS)
NDUF	National Democratic United Front [*Later, FNDF*] [*Myanmar*] [*Political party*] (PD)
NdU-L	University of North Dakota, Law Library, Grand Forks, ND [*Library symbol*] [*Library of Congress*] (LCLS)
NdU-M	University of North Dakota, Medical Library, Grand Forks, ND [*Library symbol*] [*Library of Congress*] (LCLS)
NDunBH	Brooks Memorial Hospital Medical Center, Dunkirk, NY [*Library symbol*] [*Library of Congress*] (LCLS)
NDUP	Nonduplicate
NDUP	Nonduplication (SAUS)
NDUSTA	New Duty Station [*Navy*]
NDUV	Nondispersion Ultraviolet (EEVL)
NDUV	Nondispersive Ultraviolet
NDUV	Non-Dispersive Ultraviolet Spectroscopy (AAEL)
NDV	Newcastle Disease Virus [*Also, ND*]
NDV	Not to Delay Delivery
NDV	Not to Delay Vessel
NDV	Nuclear Delivery Vehicle
NDV	Valley City State College, Valley City, ND [*OCLC symbol*] (OCLC)
NDV	Washington, DC [*Location identifier*] [*FAA*] (FAAL)
NdVc	Valley City Public Library, Valley City, ND [*Library symbol*] [*Library of Congress*] (LCLS)
NdVcT	Valley City State College, Valley City, ND [*Library symbol*] [*Library of Congress*] (LCLS)
NDVI	Normalized Difference Vegetation Index [*Plant biota*]
NDW	Naval District Washington
NDW	North Dakota State School of Science, Mildred Johnson Library, Wahpeton, ND [*OCLC symbol*] (OCLC)
NDW	Norton Desktop for Windows [*Symantec Corp.*] [*Computer science*] (PCM)
NDWAC	National Drinking Water Advisory Council [*Environmental Protection Agency*]
NdWah	Leach Public Library, Wahpeton, ND [*Library symbol*] [*Library of Congress*] (LCLS)
NdWahS	North Dakota State School of Science, Wahpeton, ND [*Library symbol*] [*Library of Congress*] (LCLS)
NDWB	North Devon Water Board (SAUS)
NDWBA	National Deaf Women's Bowling Association (EA)
NdWi	James Memorial Library, Williston, ND [*Library symbol*] [*Library of Congress*] (LCLS)
NdWiU	University of North Dakota, Williston Branch, Williston, ND [*Library symbol*] [*Library of Congress*] (LCLS)
NdWiW	West Plains Rural Library, Williston, ND [*Library symbol*] [*Library of Congress*] (LCLS)
NDWP	National Demonstration Water Project (EA)
NDWRRI	North Dakota Water Resources Research Institute [*Fargo, ND*] [*Department of the Interior*] (GRD)
NDWU	National Domestic Workers Union (EA)
NDX	Northern Dynasty Explorations Ltd. [*Toronto Stock Exchange symbol*] [*Vancouver Stock Exchange symbol*]
NDxhBJ	Burr's Lane Junior High School, Dix Hills, NY [*Library symbol*] [*Library of Congress*] (LCLS)
NDxhFE	Forest Park Elementary School, Dix Hills, NY [*Library symbol*] [*Library of Congress*] (LCLS)
NDxhH	Half Hollow Hills Community Public Library, Dix Hills, NY [*Library symbol*] [*Library of Congress*] (LCLS)
NDxhHH-E	Half Hollow Hills High School East, Dix Hills, NY [*Library symbol*] [*Library of Congress*] (LCLS)

NDxHH-W...	Half Hollow Hills High School West, Dix Hills, NY [*Library symbol*] [*Library of Congress*] (LCLS)
NDxhHT	Half Hollow Hills District Teacher's Center, Dix Hills, NY [*Library symbol*] [*Library of Congress*] (LCLS)
NDY	Dahlgren, VA [*Location identifier*] [*FAA*] (FAAL)
NDY	Neodymium-Doped Yttralox [*Ceramic*]
NDY	Nonresonant Deflection Yoke
NDY	Not Diagnosed Yet (SAUS)
NDY	Sanday [*Scotland*] [*Airport symbol*] (OAG)
Nd:YAG	Neodymium-Doped: Yttrium Aluminum Garnet [*LASER technology*]
NDYL	Neodymium-Doped YAG [*Yttrium Aluminum Garnet*] LASER
NDZ	Milton, FL [*Location identifier*] [*FAA*] (FAAL)
NE	Air New England [*ICAO designator*] (AD)
Ne	Algemeen Rijksarchief te s'Gravenhage (Central State Archives), The Hague, Netherlands [*Library symbol*] [*Library of Congress*] (LCLS)
NE	Left Nationalists [*Spain*] [*Political party*] (PPW)
NE	Narcotics Education [*An association*] (EA)
NE	National Emergency
NE	National Estate
NE	National Exchequer [*British*]
NE	National Executive (ADA)
NE	National Exhibition [*British*]
NE	Naval Engineer [*Academic degree*]
NE	Navy Evaluation
NE	Near East (BJA)
NE	Near Effect (DIPS)
NE	Nebraska [*Postal code*]
NE	Necrotic Enteritis [*Medicine*] (MELL)
NE	Negative Expectancy [*Psychometrics*]
NE	Negatives and Etching (DGA)
NE	Negotiated Exit [*Telecommunications*] (OSI)
Ne	Nehemiah [*Old Testament book*] (BJA)
NE	Neiva [*Sociedade Construtora Aeronautica Neiva Ltda.*] [*Brazil*] [*ICAO aircraft manufacturer identifier*] (ICAO)
NE	Neomycin [*Antibacterial compound*]
Ne	Neon [*Chemical element*] (ODBW)
ne	Neon (VRA)
NE	Neon [*Chemical element*]
ne	Nephelite [*CIPW classification*] [*Geology*]
NE	Nephropathia Epidemica [*Medicine*]
NE)	Nerve Ending (MAE)
NE	Nerve Excitability [*Test*]
NE	Nervous Exhaustion (MELL)
NE	Net Earnings
ne	Netherlands [*MARC country of publication code*] [*Library of Congress*] (LCCP)
NE	Netherlands
NE	Network Element (MLOA)
NE	Neumann-Electroporation [*Gene technology*]
NE	Neural Excitation [*neurology*] (DAVI)
NE	Neurologic Examination [*Medicine*]
NE	Neutral Endopeptidase [*An enzyme*]
NE	Neutral Excitation
NE	New Edition
NE	New Editions [*Record label*]
NE	New Engine [*On ships*]
NE	New England
NE	New England Patriots [*National Football League*] [*1971-present*] (NFLA)
NE	[*The*] New English Bible [*1961*] [*A publication*] (BJA)
NE	New Executable [*Computer science*] (PCM)
NE	News Editor (ADA)
NE	Niacin Equivalent
NE	Nickel Equivalent [*Coinage*]
NE	Niger [*ANSI two-letter standard code*] (CNC)
NE	Night Experimental [*British military*] (DMA)
NE	Noble Drilling Corp. [*NYSE symbol*] (SG)
NE	Nodal Exchange (MCD)
NE	No Earthly Chance (DSUE)
NE	No Ectopy [*Medicine*] (MEDA)
NE	No Effects
NE	No Equal (ELAL)
NE	Noise-Equivalent (IAA)
NE	Non-Effective (SAUS)
NE	Nonelastic [*Medicine*] (MAE)
NE	Nonelastic Elongation (SAUS)
NE	Non-English Speaker [*Airline notation*]
NE	Nonessential
NE	Non Exempt (SAUS)
NE	Nonexempt (TIMI)
NE	Norepinephrine [*Also known as NA: Noradrenaline*] [*Biochemistry*]
NE	Normal Excitability [*Medicine*]
NE	Normally Energized (NRCH)
NE	North East (SAUS)
NE	Northeast
NE	Northeast Airlines, Inc. [*Obsolete*]
NE	North Eastern (SAUS)
NE	North Eastern Reporter [*A publication*] (DLA)
NE	Northern Electric (SAUS)
NE	Not Editable (SAUS)
NE-HH-W...	Not Elevated [*Laboratory science*] (DAVI)
NE	Not Employed
NE	Not Engaged
NE	Not Enlarged [*Medicine*]
NE	Not Entered (MARI)
NE	Not Entitled [*British military*] (DMA)
NE	Not Equal [*Relational operator*]
NE	Not Equal To (NITA)
NE	Not Essential (SAUS)
NE	Not Evaluated (INF)
NE	Not Examined [*Medicine*]
ne	Not Exceeding (MARI)
N/E	Not Exceeding
NE	Not Explosive
NE	Notice of Exception (MCD)
N/E	Not to Exceed (SAUS)
NE	Nuclear Electric (WDAA)
NE	Nuclear Energy (COE)
NE	Nuclear Engineer
NE	Nuclear Envelope [*Cytology*]
NE	Nuclear Equipment (SAUS)
NE	Nuclear Explosive
NE	Nuclear Extract [*Cytology*]
NE	Numeric Editing (SAUS)
NE	Nursing Educator (AAMN)
NE	Office of Nuclear Energy (SAUS)
NE 2d	North Eastern Reporter, Second Series [*West*] [*A publication*] (AAGC)
ne/4 mos	new edition expected in four months (SAUS)
ne/6m	new edition in preparation, expected in 6 months (SAUS)
ne/6 mos	new edition expected in six months (SAUS)
NE-10	Northeast-10 Conference (PSS)
NEa	Eastchester Public Library, Eastchester, NY [*Library symbol*] [*Library of Congress*] (LCLS)
NEA	Nashville Entertainment Association (EA)
NEA	National Economic Association (EA)
NEA	National Editorial Association [*Later, NNA*] (EA)
NEA	National Education Association (EA)
NEA	National Electronic Associations [*Later, NESSDA*]
NEA	National Employment Association [*Later, NAPC*] (EA)
NEA	National Endowment for the Arts
NEA	National Energy Accounts [*Department of Commerce*] [*Information service or system*] (IID)
NEA	National Energy Act (GFGA)
NEA	National Erectors Association (EA)
NEA	Natural Energy Association [*British*]
NEA	Nearctic Resources, Inc. [*Toronto Stock Exchange symbol*]
NEA	Near-Earth Asteroid [*Astronomy*]
NEA	Near Eastern Affairs [*Department of State*]
NEA	Neath [*Welsh depot code*]
NEA	Negative Electron Affinity [*Photocathode*]
NEA	Nelson & Albemarle Railway [*AAR code*]
NEA	Nenana [*Alaska*] [*Seismograph station code, US Geological Survey*] (SEIS)
NEA	Neoplasm Embryonic Antigen (DB)
NEA	Network Equivalent Analysis
NE-a	Neuroepithelioma (SAUS)
NEA	New England Airlines, Inc. [*ICAO designator*] (FAAC)
NEA	New England Aquarium (SAUS)
NEA	New Entitlement Authority
NEA	Newsletter Editors' Association [*Australia*]
NEA	Newspaper Enterprise Association [*A syndicate*]
NEA	Nitrogen Enriched Air (ACAE)
NEA	No Evidence of Abnormality [*Medicine*] (DMAA)
NEA	Noise-Equivalent Angle (MCD)
NEA	Northeast Airlines, Inc. [*Obsolete*]
NEA	Northeast Asia (CINC)
NEA	Northern Electric Authority (SAUS)
NEA	Northern Examining Association [*British*]
NEA	Nuclear Energy Agency [*See also AEN*] [*Organization for Economic Cooperation and Development*] (EAIO)
NEA	Nuclear Engineering Associates (SAUS)
NEA	Null Error Amplifier
NEA	Nurse Education Act
NEA	Nutrition Education Association (EA)
NeAA	Gemeente Archief van Amsterdam, Amsterdam, Netherlands [*Library symbol*] [*Library of Congress*] (LCLS)
NEAA	National Employment Assistance Act (OICC)
NEAA	Non-Essential Amino Acid (SAUS)
NEAA	Northeastern Anthropological Association (SAUS)
NEAA	Norwegian Elkhound Association of America (EA)
NEAAN	Non-Essential Amino Acid N [*Biochemistry*] (PDAA)
NEAATS	Northeast Asia Association of Theological Schools
NEAB	Northern Examinations and Assessment Board (AIE)
NEABFGP	New England Advisory Board for Fish and Game Problems [*Defunct*]
NEabG	Genesee County Landmark Society, East Bethany (SAUS)
NEabG	Genesee County Landmark Society, East Bethany, NY [*Library symbol*] [*Library of Congress*] (LCLS)
NEAC	New English Art Club [*British*]
NEAC	Nippon Electric Automatic Computer (IEEE)
NEAC	Northeast Air Command
NEACDS	Naval Emergency Air Cargo Delivery System (CAAL)
NEACH	New England Automated Clearing House Association
NEACP	National Emergency Airborne Command Post [*Pronounced "kneecap"*] [*Modified Boeing 747 jet to be used as a military control center by the President or Vice President during a nuclear war or other crisis*]
NEACRP	Nuclear Energy Agency Committee on Reactor Physics [*OECD*] (EY)

NEACSS	New England Association of Colleges and Secondary Schools [*Later, NEASC*] (EA)
NEA-DB	NEA [*Nuclear Energy Agency*] Data Bank [*OECD*] [*Information service or system*] (IID)
NEADS	National Educational Association of Disabled Students (SAUS)
NEADS	National Education for Assistance Dog Services [*Formerly, New England Assistance Dog Service*] (PAZ)
NEADS	Near East and African Development Service
NEADS	Network Engineering Administrative Data System [*AT & T*]
NEADS	Northeast Air Defense Sector (SAUS)
NEADS	North East Atlantic Dynamics Studies (SAUS)
NEADS	Northeast Atlantic Dynamics Studies [*Marine science*] (MSC)
NEADW	Northeast Atlantic Deep Water [*Oceanography*]
NEAF	Near East Air Force [*British*]
NEAF	New Era Aboriginal Fellowship (SAUS)
NEAFC	North-East Atlantic Fisheries Commission [*British*] (EAIO)
NEAFC	North East Atlantic Fisheries Convention (SAUS)
NEAFCS	National Extension Association of Family & Consumer Sciences (NTPA)
NEAG	Nevada Environmental Advisory (SAUS)
NEAG	Nevada Environmental Advisory Group (SAUS)
NEAG	New English Art Gallery (SAUS)
NEAGC	National Early American Glass Club (EA)
NEAHI	Near East Animal Health Institute
NEAIS	National Elder Abuse Incidence Study (SAUS)
NEAM	Nonvolatile Electrically Alterable Memory
NEAN	National Execution Alert Network (EA)
NEAN	North European ADS-B Network (SAUS)
NE&B	New Engines and Boilers (SAUS)
NEANDC	Nuclear Energy Agency Nuclear Data Committee [*OECD*] (EY)
NEANMCC	Navy Element Alternate National Military Command Center (MCD)
NEanpHE	Harley Avenue Elementary School, East Northport, NY [*Library symbol*] [*Library of Congress*] (LCLS)
NeAO	Rijksinstituut voor Orlogsdocumentatie, Amsterdam, Netherlands [*Library symbol*] [*Library of Congress*] (LCLS)
NEAP	National Energy Audit Program [*Canada*]
NEAP	Near Earth Asteroid Prospector (SAUS)
NEAP	Novell Education Academic Partner (VLIE)
NEAPACC	North East Atlantic Palaeoceanography and Climate Change (SAUS)
NEAPD	Northeastern Air Procurement District
NEAPs	National Environmental Action Plans (SAUS)
NEAQ	Northern Electricity Authority of Queensland [*Australia*]
NEAR	National Electronic Accounting and Reporting System (VLIE)
NEAR	National Emergency Alarm Repeater [*Civil defense warning system for homes*]
NEAR	Nationwide/Worldwide Emergency Ambulance Return
NEAR	Near-Earth Asteroid Rendezvous (MCD)
NEAR	New England Action Research Project
NEAR	Nielsen Engineering & Research, Inc.
NEARA	New England Antiquities Research Association (EA)
NEARA	New England Archeological Research Association (SAUS)
NEARELF	Near East Land Forces [*British military*] (DMA)
NEARGOOS	North East Asian Regional GOOS (SAUS)
NEARNAVDIST	Nearest Naval District
NEARnet	[*The*] New England Academic and Research Network [*Computer science*] (TNIG)
NEARO	New England Albanian Relief Organization
NEARP	New England Appalachian Research Project [*University of Maine at Orono*] [*Research center*] (RCD)
NEARS	Navy Evaluation of Advanced Reconnaissance Systems
NEARS	Near Earth Asteroid Returned Samples [*NASA, proposed*]
NEARSS	Northeast Area Remote Sensing System Association (SAUS)
NEARTIP	Near-Term Improvement Program [*For torpedos*] (MCD)
NEARYP	National Employers Association of Rayon Yarn Producers [*British*] (BI)
NEAS	National Engineering Aptitude Search
NEAS	National European American Society (EA)
NEAS	Near East Archaeological Society (EA)
NEAS	Newsletter of Engineering Analysis Software [*A publication*] (MCD)
NEASA	Near Eastern, African, and South Asian Affairs [*Department of State*]
NEASC	New England Association of Schools and Colleges (EA)
NEA/SCEC	NEA/Salleri-Chialsa Electricity Co. (SAUS)
NEASCUS	New England Association of School, College and University Staffing (SAUS)
NE Asiat J Th	Northeast Asia Journal of Theology (SAUS)
NEASIM	Network Analytical Simulator (PDAA)
NEASP	Navy Enlisted Advanced School Program
NEaspHS	Eastport High School, Eastport, NY [*Library symbol*] [*Library of Congress*] (LCLS)
NeAT	Koninklijk Instituut voor de Tropen, Amsterdam, Netherlands [*Library symbol*] [*Library of Congress*] (LCLS)
NEAT	National Cash Register Electronic Autocoding Technique [*Computer science*] (IAA)
NEAT	National Electronic Autocoding Technique (MHDB)
NEAT	Navy Electronics Application Trainer
NEAT	Navy Embarked Advisory Team
NEAT	NCR [*NCR Corp.*] Electronic Autocoding Technique [*Computer science*]
NEAT	Near-Earth Asteroid Tracking
NEAT	New Eindhoven Architectural Toolbox (VLIE)
NEAT	New Enhanced Advanced Technology (CIST)
NEAT	New Enhanced Technology
NEAT	New Equipment Advisory Team (ACAE)
NEAT	Next Advanced Technology (SAUS)
NEAT	Nonexercise activity thermogenesis
NEAT	Novell Easy Administration Tool (SAUS)
NEATE	New England Association of Teachers of English (AEBS)
NEATICC	Northeast Asia Tactical Information Communications Center (DNAB)
NEATO	North East Asian Treaty Organization (NATG)
NeAU	University of Amsterdam, Amsterdam, Netherlands [*Library symbol*] [*Library of Congress*] (LCLS)
NEAuC	Christ the King Seminary, East Aurora, NY [*Library symbol*] [*Library of Congress*] (LCLS)
NEAuF	Fisher-Price Toys, East Aurora, NY [*Library symbol*] [*Library of Congress*] (LCLS)
NEAuH	Elbert Hubbard Library Museum, East Aurora, NY [*Library symbol*] [*Library of Congress*] (LCLS)
NEAuS	Saint John Vianney Seminary, East Aurora, NY [*Library symbol*] [*Library of Congress*] (LCLS)
NEawNE	North Side Elementary School, East Williston, NY [*Library symbol*] [*Library of Congress*] (LCLS)
NEB	Department of Aeronautics State of Nebraska [*FAA designator*] (FAAC)
NEB	National Energy Board [*Canada*]
NEB	National Enterprise Board [*Later, BTG*] [*British*]
NEB	Nebelwerfer [*German six-barrelled mortar*] (DSUE)
Neb	Nebraska (ODBW)
NEB	Nebraska
Neb	Nebraska Supreme Court Reports [*A publication*] (DLA)
NEB	Nebula [*Spray*] [*Pharmacy*]
NEB	Neuroepithelial Bodies [*Anatomy*]
NEB	New England Business Services [*NYSE symbol*] (SAG)
NEB	New England Bus Svc [*NYSE symbol*] (TTSB)
NEB	New England Motor Rate Bureau Inc., Burlington MA [*STAC*]
NEB	New England Review and Bread Loaf Quarterly (SAUS)
NEB	[*The*] New English Bible [*1961*] [*A publication*]
NEB	Nissim Ezra Benjamin [*Shanghai*] (BJA)
NEB	Noise-Equivalent Bandwidth
NEB	Nonenzymatic Maillard Browning [*Food technology*]
NEB	Nonisothermal Energy Balance (SAUS)
NEB	North-Eastbound [*Aviation*] (FAAC)
NEB	North Equatorial Belt [*Planet Jupiter*]
NEB	Nuclear, Electronic, Biological (SAUS)
NEB	Nuclear Energy Board [*Republic of Ireland*] (NUCP)
NEB	Nuclear Envelope Breakdown [*Also, NEBD*] [*Cytology*]
NEB	Nuclear Exoatmospheric Burst (SAUS)
Neb	United States District Court for the District of Nebraska (DLA)
NEBA	NASA Employee Benefit Association (SAUS)
NEBA	North East Bolivian Airways [*ICAO designator*] (FAAC)
Neb Admin R	Nebraska Administrative Rules and Regulations [*A publication*] (DLA)
NEBB	National Environmental Balancing Bureau (EA)
NEBBA	Northeastern Bird-Banding Association [*Later, AFO*] (EA)
NEBBS	Naval Environmental Bulletin Board System
Nebby	Negative-Equity Baby Boomer [*Lifestyle classification*]
nEbC	no-European-before-Columbus (SAUS)
NEBD	Nuclear Envelope Breakdown [*Also, NEB*] [*Cytology*]
NEbE	Northeast by East
NEBHE	New England Board of Higher Education [*Information service or system*]
NEBI	National Employee Benefits Institute [*Washington, DC*] (EA)
NEBIC	New England Bibliographic Instruction Collection
NEBIS	North of England Biotechnology Information Service [*University of Newcastle-Upon-Tyne Medical School*] [*England*] [*Information service or system*] (IID)
NEBIT	New and Expanding Business and Industry Training (OICC)
NEBK	National Enterprise Bank [*Washington, DC*] (NQ)
Neb LB	Nebraska Law Bulletin [*A publication*] (DLA)
Neb Leg N	Nebraska Legal News [*A publication*] (DLA)
NEBM	No Eating between Meals
NEBMA	Neben-Munitionsanstalt [*Branch ammunition depot*] [*German military - World War II*]
NEbN	Northeast by North
NEBOSH	National Examination Board in Occupational Safety and Health (PDAA)
NEBP	Nicaraguan Exile Relocation Program (SAUS)
NEBR	Nebraska (AAG)
Nebr	Nebraska (ODBW)
Nebr	Nebraska Reports [*A publication*] (DLA)
Neb RC	Nebraska Railway Commission Reports [*A publication*] (DLA)
Neb Rev Stat	Revised Statutes of Nebraska [*A publication*] (DLA)
Nebr LB	Nebraska Law Bulletin [*A publication*] (DLA)
NEBS	Network Equipment Building Specifications (TIMI)
NEBS	Network Equipment-Building System
NEBS	New England Business Service, Inc. [*NASDAQ symbol*] (NQ)
NEBS	New Equipment Building System (SAUS)
NEBS	New Exporters to Border States (SAUS)
NEBSS	National Examinations Board in Supervisory Studies [*British*]
Neb Sup Ct J	Nebraska Supreme Court Journal [*A publication*] (DLA)
NEBUL	Nebula [*Spray*] [*Pharmacy*]
NEBULA	Natural Electronic Business User's Language [*International Computers Ltd.*]
Neb (Unof)	Nebraska Unofficial Reports [*A publication*] (DLA)
Neb Unoff	Nebraska Unofficial Reports [*A publication*] (DLA)
NE Bus	New England Business Services [*Associated Press*] (SAG)
NEBW	Nonvacuum Electron Beam Welding
Neb WCC	Nebraska Workmen's Compensation Court. Bulletin [*A publication*] (DLA)
NEC	National Economic Council [*Defunct*] (EA)

NEC............. National Economists Club (EA)
NEC............. National Ecumenical Coalition (EA)
NEC............. National Education Center for Paraprofessionals in Mental Health (EA)
NEC............. National Education Corp. [NYSE symbol] (SPSG)
NEC............. National Egg Council [Later, PEIA] (EA)
NEC............. National Electoral Commission [Nigeria] (ECON)
NEC............. National Electrical Code
NEC............. National Electronics Conference (AEBS)
NEC............. National Electronics Council (NITA)
NEC............. National Emblem Club (EA)
NEC............. National Emergency Council [Abolished, 1939]
NEC............. National Employers' Committee
NEC............. National Empowerment Consortium [Investment group] [South Africa]
NEC............. National Engineering Consortium (EA)
NEC............. National Entertainment Conference [Later, NECAA] (EA)
NEC............. National Exchange Club (EA)
NEC............. National Executive Committee [British] (DCTA)
NEC............. National Executive Council (WDAA)
NEC............. National Exhibition Centre [British]
NEC............. National Extension College [England]
NEC............. Natl Education [NYSE symbol] (TTSB)
NEC............. Naval Examining Center
NEC............. Naval Exercise Coordinator (CINC)
NEC............. Naval Exhibit Center
NEC............. Navy Enlisted Classification (NG)
NEC............. Navy Enlisted Code
NEC............. Nebraska State Railway Commission [STAC]
NEC............. NEC Corp. [Associated Press] (SAG)
NEC............. Necessary (AABC)
NEC............. Necessity
NEC............. Necochea [Argentina] [Airport symbol] (OAG)
NEC............. Necrotizing Enterocolitis [Medicine]
NEC............. Negro Ensemble Company [A theatre group]
NEC............. Netherlands Electrotechnical Committee
NEC............. Nett Explosives Content (HEAS)
NEC............. Network Emergency Co-Ordinator (HEAS)
NEC............. Neuroendocrine Cell [Cytology]
NEC............. Neuroendocrine Convertase (DMAA)
NEC............. Never Ending Conflict (VLIE)
NEC............. New England College, Henniker, NH [OCLC symbol] (OCLC)
NEC............. New England Commuter, Inc. (SAUS)
NEC............. New England Conservatory of Music (BARN)
NEC............. New England Council (EA)
NEC............. Newspaper Editor's Course [Defense Information School] (DNAB)
NEC............. Nippon Electric Co. [Japan]
NEC............. Nippon Electronic Corp. (SAUS)
NEC............. No-Error Check (IAA)
NEC............. No Essential Changes (DMAA)
NEC............. No Eye Contact [Psychology]
NEC............. Noise-Equivalent Charge (PDAA)
NEC............. Nonengineering Change (DNAB)
NEC............. Non-Error Check (VLIE)
NEC............. Nonesterified Cholesterol (DMAA)
NEC............. Northeast Coast (SAUS)
NEC............. Northeast Conference (PSS)
NEC............. Northeast Conference on the Teaching of Foreign Languages (EA)
NEC............. North East Corner [Freemasonry]
NEC............. Northeast Corridor [Railroad line] (EGAO)
NEC............. North Equatorial Current [Oceanography] (MSC)
NEC............. Northern European Command [NATO] (NATG)
NEC............. Northern European Countries
NEC............. Northern Europe Committee [NATO] (NATG)
NEC............. Not Else Classified (DMAA)
nec............. Not Elsewhere Classified (ODBW)
NEC............. Not Elsewhere Classified
NEC............. Notes of English Ecclesiastical Cases [A publication] (DLA)
NEC............. Nuclear Energy Center (NRCH)
NEC............. Nuclear Energy Commission (USDC)
NEC............. Nuclear Equipment Corp. (SAUS)
NEC............. Nucleus of Epidermal Cell
NEC............. Nursing Ethics Committee (DMAA)
NECA .... National Electrical Contractors Association (EA)
NECA .... National Employment Counseling Association (EA)
NECA .... National Employment Counselors Association (EA)
NECA .... National Episcopal Coalition on Alcohol [Later, NECAD] (EA)
NECA .... National Exchange Carrier Association (EA)
NECA .... National Explorers and Collectors Association (EA)
NECA .... Near East College Association (EA)
NECA .... N-Ethylcarboxamide Adenosine [Biochemistry]
NECA .... Numismatic Error Collectors of America (EA)
NECAA .... National Entertainment and Campus Activities Association [Formerly, NEC] (EA)
NECAC .... New England College Athletic Conference (PSS)
NECAD .... National Episcopal Coalition on Alcohol and Drugs (EA)
NECAF .... National Electromagnetic Compatibility Analysis Facility [Department of Commerce] (PDAA)
NECA Newsletter... Numismatic Error Collectors of America Newsletter (SAUS)
NECAP .... NASA Energy-Cost Analysis Program
NECAP .... Navigation Equipment Capability Analysis (KSC)
NECAP .... Nutmeg Electric Companies Atomic Project
NECAR .... National Engineers Commission on Air Resources (PDAA)
NECAR .... New Electric Car [Automotive engineering]
NECB .... New England Coastal Basins (SAUS)
NECB .... New England Comm Bancorp'A' [NASDAQ symbol] (TTSB)

NECB .... New England Community Bancorp, Inc. [NASDAQ symbol] (SAG)
NE CBcp .... New England Community Bancorp, Inc. [Associated Press] (SAG)
NECC .... National Education Computer Center
NECC .... National Emergency Coordination Center (BARN)
NECC .... New England Collegiate Conference (PSS)
NECC .... New England Congressional Caucus [Defunct] (EA)
NECC .... Northeast Computer Center [Military] (AABC)
NECC .... North Equatorial Countercurrent [Oceanography]
NECC .... Northern Essex Community College [Haverhill, MA]
NECCAC .... Northeast Community College Athletic Conference (PSS)
NECCB .... National Education Council of the Christian Brothers [Later, RECCB] (EA)
NECCC .... New England Correctional Coordinating Council (SAUS)
NEC CCIS .... Northern European Command, Command & Control System (SAUS)
NECCO .... New England Confectionery Co.
NECCO .... Northern Essex Community College [Haverhill, MA]
NECCR .... North of England Children's Cancer Research Unit
NECCTA .... National Educational Closed-Circuit Television Association [British]
NECCWA ...... New England College Conference Wrestling Associaton (PSS)
NECDC .... New England Consumer Development Council
NECEA .... National Engineering Construction Employers Association [British] (DBA)
NECEC .... New England Catholic Education Center (AEBS)
NECEL .... New England Coalition of Educational Leaders (SAUS)
NECF .... National Exchange Club Foundation for the Prevention of Child Abuse (EA)
NECG .... National Engineering Council for Guidance (EA)
NECH .... National Employment Clearing House [American Chemical Society]
NECH .... National Event Clearinghouse Database [National Event Clearinghouse, Inc.] [Information service or system] (CRD)
NECHE .... Northeastern Colorado Hail Experiment
NECHI .... Northeastern Consortium for Health Information [Library network]
NECI .... Noise Exposure Computer Integrator (PDAA)
NECIEB .... Northeast Coast Institution of Engineers and Shipbuilders (SAUS)
NECIES .... North East Coast Institution of Engineers and Shipbuilders (EAIO)
NECIP .... Northeast Corridor Improvement Project [Department of Transportation]
NECIS .... Naval Environmental Compliance Information System
NECIS .... NEC Information Systems, Inc. [Boxborough, MA]
NECIS .... Nippon Electric Company Information Systems, Inc. (SAUS)
NECJ .... New England Classical Journal (SAUS)
NECK .... Neck [Commonly used] (OPSA)
NECL .... Nonepitheliotropic Cutaneous Lymphosarcomas (SAUS)
NECLC .... National Emergency Civil Liberties Committee (EA)
NECM .... New England Conference Management [Australia]
NECM .... New England Conservatory of Music [Boston, MA]
NECMA .... New England County Metropolitan Areas
NECMD .... Newark Contract Management District (SAA)
NECMG .... Northeast Computer Measurement Group (SAUS)
NECNVA ...... New England Committee for Nonviolent Action [Later, CNVA] (EA)
NECO .... Nippon Electric Co. (IAA)
NECO .... Nuclear Engineering Co., Inc.
NECO .... Nuclear Engineering Company, Inc. (SAUS)
NECOE .... New England Center for Organizational Effectiveness (EA)
NECON .... Northeastern Conference (SAUS)
NECOP .... Nutrient-Enhanced Coastal Ocean Productivity [Marine science] (OSRA)
NECOR .... North East Consortium (SAUS)
NECOS .... Communication Net Control Station [Navy] (NVT)
NECOS .... Nepal Community Support Group (SAUS)
NECOS .... Northern European Chiefs of Staff [NATO] (NATG)
NECOS .... Northern Europe Chiefs of Staff (SAUS)
NECP .... National Eye Care Project [Foundation of the American Academy of Ophthalmology] (EA)
NECP .... New England College of Pharmacy
NECP .... Nonengineering Change Proposal
NECPA .... National Emergency Command Post Afloat
NECPA .... National Energy Conservation Policy Act [1978]
NECPL .... NATO Exploratory Conference on Production Logistics (NATG)
NECPR .... New External Cardiopulmonary Resuscitation
NECPUC .... New England Conference of Public Utility Commissioners (SAUS)
NECPWA ...... Northeast Club for Pre-War Austins [British] (EAIO)
NECQ .... National Electronics Component Qualification System (AAEL)
NEC Research... Nippon Electric Company Research (SAUS)
NECRMP ...... Northeast Corridor Regional Modeling Project [Environmental Protection Agency] (GFGA)
Necro .... Necrofile [A publication]
NECROL .... Necrology (WDAA)
necrp .... Necropolis (VRA)
NECS .... National Electrical Code Standards
NECS .... National Elephant Collectors Society (EA)
NECS .... Nationwide Educational Computer Service (IEEE)
NECS .... Navy Embedded Computer System (ACAE)
NECS .... New England Collectors Society (SAUS)
NECS .... Normal Environmental Control System (SAUS)
NECSA .... Navigational Electronic Chart System Association (SAUS)
NECSS .... Nuclear Energy Center Site Survey (NRCH)
NECT .... North East China Transect (SAUS)
NECTA .... National Electric Comfort Trade Association [Defunct] (EA)
NECTA .... Naval Environmental Command Tactical Aid (SAUS)
NECTAR .... Network of European CNS [Central Nervous System] Transplantation and Restoration
NECTAR .... Network of European Communications and Transport Activities Research (SAUS)

NECTEC........ National Electronics and Computer Technology Center [*Thailand*] (DDC)
NECTP......... North East Corridor Transportation Project (SAUS)
NECTP......... Northeast Corridor Transportation Project
NECWA........ New England College Wrestling Association (PSS)
NECY........... Necessary
NECY........... Necessity (WDAA)
NED............. Naphthylethylenediamine Dihydrochloride [*Organic chemistry*]
NED............. National Endowment for Democracy (EA)
NED............. Naval Equipment Department [*British military*] (DMA)
NED............. Navigation Error Data (MUGU)
Ned............. Nedarim (BJA)
NED............. Network Engineering Division (ACAE)
NED............. NeverEnding Disk [*Computer software*] [*Sytron Corp.*] (PCM)
NED............. Newark [*Delaware*] [*Seismograph station code, US Geological Survey*] (SEIS)
N Ed........... New Edition (SAUS)
NED............. New Editor [*Computer program*] [*Air Force*] (MCD)
NED............. New England Division [*Army Engineers*]
NED............. New English Dictionary [*i.e., the Oxford English Dictionary*]
NED............. No-Effect Dose [*Medicine*] (LDT)
NED............. No Evidence of Disease
NED............. No Expiration Date
NED............. Noise Emitting Diode (SAUS)
NED............. Nonenzymatic Glycosylation [*Biochemistry*] (DAVI)
NED............. Normal Equivalent Deviate (or Deviation) (SAUS)
NED............. North, East, and Down
NED............. Northeastern University, Boston, MA [*OCLC symbol*] (OCLC)
NED............. Northrop Electronics Division (ACAE)
NED............. Nuclear Energy Division [*General Electric Co.*]
NED............. Nuclear Engineering Directorate [*Army*]
NEDA.......... National Economic Development Association
NEDA.......... National Electronic Distributors Association (EA)
NEDA.......... National Emergency Defense Airlift
NEDA.......... National Environmental Development Association (EA)
NEDA.......... National Equipment Distributors Association [*Defunct*] (EA)
NEDA.......... National Exhaust Distributors Association [*Later, NEDA/USA*] (EA)
Neda........... Nedarim (BJA)
NEDA/CAAP... National Environmental Development Association/Clean Air Act Project [*Defunct*] (EA)
NEDA/GRND... National Environmental Development Association/Ground Water Project (EA)
NEDAM........ Nuclear Effects Damage Assessment Methodologies (SAUS)
NEDA/USA ... National Exhaust Distributors Association/Undercar Specialists Association [*Defunct*] (EA)
NEDAX......... Nippon Electric Data Exchange (SAUS)
NEDB.......... National Exposure Data Base (HEAS)
NEDC.......... National Economic Development Council [*Nickname: Neddie*] [*British*]
NEDC.......... National Engineering Design Challenge (VLIE)
NeDC.......... New England Document Conservation Center, Andover, MA [*Library symbol*] [*Library of Congress*] (LCLS)
NEDC.......... New European Driving Cycle [*Automotive emissions*]
NEDCC........ New England Document Conservation Center [*Information service or system*] (IID)
NEDCC........ Northeast Document Conservation Center
NEDCO........ Non-Electronic Part Data Collection (PDAA)
NEDCO........ Northeast Dairy Cooperative Federation [*Defunct*] (EA)
NEDD.......... NATO & European Defence Directorate (SAUS)
NEDECO....... Netherlands Engineering Consultants
NEDED........ Naval Explosive Development Engineering Department (DNAB)
NEDEL......... No Epidemiologically Detectable Exposure Level [*Medicine*] (HCT)
NEDELA....... Network Definition Language [*Computer science*] (PDAA)
NEDEP........ Navy Enlisted Dietetic Education Program
NEDEPA....... Nea Demokratiki Parataxi [*Cyprus*] [*Political party*] (PPE)
NeDF........... New England Data Film, Inc., Milford, CT [*Library symbol*] [*Library of Congress*] (LCLS)
NEDGP........ New England Division of General Practice (SAUS)
NEDI........... Nobel Education Dynamics, Inc. [*NASDAQ symbol*] (SAG)
NEDIPA....... Nea Demokratiki Parataxi [*Cyprus*] [*Political party*] (PPW)
NEDIPS........ NEC Dataflow Image Processing System (NITA)
NEDIS.......... National Environmental Data and Information Service [*Marine science*] (MSC)
NEDL.......... New England Deposit Library
NEDI........... Nobel Ed Dynamics [*NASDAQ symbol*] (TTSB)
NEDLC........ National Economic Development and Law Center [*Berkeley, CA*] [*Research center*] (EA)
NEDLIB........ Networked European Deposit Library (TELE)
NEDN......... Naval Environmental Data Network
NEDN.......... Naval Worldwide Environmental Data Network (MCD)
NEDO......... National Eating Disorders Organization (EA)
NEDO......... National Economic Development Office [*British*]
NEDO......... New Energy and Industrial Technology Development Organization
NEDPS......... Nacken Electronic Data Processing System (SAUS)
NEDR......... Noise Equivalent Delta Reflectivity (SAUS)
NEDRES....... National Environmental Data Referral Service [*Online database*] [*National Oceanic and Atmospheric Administration*] [*Washington, DC*]
NEDS.......... National Emissions Data System [*Environmental Protection Agency*] [*Information service or system*]
NEDS.......... Naval Environmental Data System (CAAL)
NEDS.......... Naval Environmental Display Station (CAAL)
NEDS.......... New Enlisted Distribution System (NVT)
NEDS.......... Nonviolent Explosive Destructive System (MCD)
NEDSA........ Non-Erasing Determination (or Deterministic) Stack Automation (SAUS)

NEDSA........ Nonerasing Deterministic Stack Automation [*Computer science*] (IAA)
NEDT.......... National Educational Development Test
NEDT.......... Noise-Equivalent Differential Temperature
NeDTH........ Technische Hogeschool Delft, Delft, Netherlands [*Library symbol*] [*Library of Congress*] (LCLS)
NEDTRA...... Naval Education and Training Command (MCD)
NEDU......... Naval Experimental Diving Unit (SAUS)
NEDU......... Navy Experimental Diving Unit [*Panama City, FL*]
NEDWSA...... Non-Erasing Deterministic Writing Stack Acceptor (SAUS)
NEE........... National Electrical Effect
NEE........... National Electrology Educators (EA)
NEE........... Needle Electrode Examination [*Medicine*] (DMAA)
NEE........... Net Ecosystem Exchange [*Biology*]
NEE........... New England Express [*Steamship*] (MHDW)
NEE........... Noise-Equivalent Energy (MCD)
NEE........... Noise Equivalent Exposure [*Photonics*]
NEE........... Norethindrone/Ethinyl Estradiol [*Oral contraceptive*]
NEE........... Normalized Error Energy (SAUS)
NEE........... Northeast Airlines [*FAA designator*] (FAAC)
NEE........... Northeast Express Regional Airlines, Inc. [*ICAO designator*] (FAAC)
NEE........... North Enter Earth (ACAE)
NEESA........ North-East Electricity Authority (SAUS)
NEEB.......... North East Engineering Bureau (SAUS)
NEEB.......... North Eastern Electricity Board [*British*]
NEEB.......... Northeastern Electricity Board (SAUS)
NEEC.......... National Environmental Enforcement Council [*National Association of Attorneys General*] (EPA)
NEEC.......... National Export Expansion Council [*Terminated, 1973*] [*Department of Commerce*]
NEEC.......... Not Entailing Excessive Cost [*Environmental technology*]
NEEC.......... Nuclear Explosion Effects Center
NEED.......... National Energy Education Development Project (EA)
NEED.......... National Environmental Education Development [*Program of National Park Service*] [*Defunct*]
NEED.......... Native Employment and Educational Development [*Canada*]
NEED.......... Near East Emergency Donations
Need.......... Needham's Annual Summary of Tax Cases [*England*] [*A publication*] (DLA)
NEED.......... Need, Inc. [*An association*] (EA)
NEED.......... Negro Education Emergency Drive
NEED.......... New Employment Expansion and Development [*Canada*]
NEEDHA...... National Electrical Engineering Department Heads Association (EA)
NEEDIS........ National Enterprise Education Development and Information Service (AIE)
NEEDS........ NASA End-to-End Data Systems
NEEDS........ National Emergency Equipment Data System (NITA)
NEEDS........ Navy Education and Employment Development System (MCD)
NEEDS........ Neighborhood Environmental Evaluation and Decision System [*Health Services and Mental Health Administration*]
NEEDS........ New England Electronic Data System (SAUS)
NEEDS........ Nikkei Economic Electronic Databank System (SAUS)
NEEDS-IR..... NIKKEI Economic Electronic Databank Service - Information Retrieval [*Information service or system*] [*Japan*] (IID)
NEEDS-TS.... NIKKEI Economic Electronic Databank Service - Time Sharing [*Information service or system*] [*Japan*] (IID)
NEEE........... Near East Equine Encephalomyelitis [*Medicine*] (DMAA)
NeEinP........ Philips Research Laboratories, Eindhoven, Netherlands [*Library symbol*] [*Library of Congress*] (LCLS)
NeEinT........ Technische Hogeschool te Eindhoven, Eindhoven, Netherlands, [*Library symbol*] [*Library of Congress*] (LCLS)
NEEITC........ National Electrical and Electronic Industry Training Committee [*Australia*]
NEEJ........... National Environmental Enforcement Journal [*National Association of Attorneys General*] [*A publication*] (EPA)
NEEL........... National Environmental Education Landmarks [*Department of the Interior*]
NEELS......... National Emergency Equipment Locator System [*Environment Canada*] [*Information service or system*] (CRD)
NEEMA........ New England Educational Media Association
NEEMIS....... New England Energy Management Information System
NEEP.......... Negative End Expiratory Pressure [*Medicine*]
NEEP.......... New England Economic Project (NITA)
NEEP.......... Nuclear Dectronics Effects Program (SAUS)
NE'ER......... Never (ROG)
NEERI........ National Environmental Engineering Research Institute
NEERS........ National Earthquake Early Reporting System (NOAA)
NEERS........ New England Estuarine Research Society (SAUS)
NEES.......... Naval Engineering Experiment Station
NEES.......... New England Electric Service (SAUS)
NEES.......... New England Electric System
NEESA........ Naval Energy and Environmental Support Activity
NEESAB....... National Energy Extension Service Advisory Board [*Department of Energy*] [*Washington, DC*] (EGAO)
NEET.......... Navy Extended Electrode Technique (PDAA)
NEET.......... Nonlinear Estimation for Exoatmospheric Trajectories (ACAE)
NEETF......... National Environmental Education and Training Foundation [*An association*] (PS)
NEETS........ Naval Electronics Environmental Training System (MCD)
NEETU........ National Engineering and Electrical Trade Union [*Republic of Ireland*] (BI)
NEEWSSOP... NATO Europe Early Warning System Standard Operating Procedures (NATG)
NEF........... National Educators Fellowship [*Later, CEAI*]
NEF........... National Energy Foundation (EA)
NEF........... National Extra Fine [*Thread*]

NEF............. Naval Emergency Fund [*A budget category*]
NEF............. Near East Foundation (EA)
NEF............. Negative-Regulatory Factor [*Genetics*]
NeF............. Nephritic Factor [*Clinical medicine*]
NEF............. Network Element Function [*Computer science*] (VLIE)
NEF............. New Education Fellowship [*Later, WEF*]
NEF............. No Further Clearance Required [*Aviation*] (FAAC)
NEF............. Noise Equivalent Flux (SAUS)
NEF............. Noise-Equivalent Flux
NEF............. Noise Exposure Forecast [*Aircraft*]
NEF............. Nordiska Ekonomiska Forskningsradet [*Nordic Economic Research Council - NERC*] (EAIO)
NEF............. Northern Elders Forum (SAUS)
NEF............. Nurses Educational Funds (EA)
NEF............. Scudder New Europe Fund [*NYSE symbol*] (SPSG)
NEFA........... Narcotic Educational Foundation of America (EA)
NEFA........... New European Fighter Aircraft (PS)
NEFA........... Nonesterified Fatty Acid [*Biochemistry*]
NEFA........... North East Forest Alliance (SAUS)
NEFA........... Northeast Frontier Agency (SAUS)
NEFARS ...... Nuclear Effects from Analysis of Residual Signatures
NEFBRACS.. Nearfield Bearing and Range Accuracy Calibration System (PDAA)
NEFC.......... NATO Electronic Warfare Fusion Cell (SAUS)
NEFC.......... Near East Forestry Commission
NEFC.......... New England Football Conference (PSS)
NEFC.......... Northeast Fisheries Center [*Department of Commerce*] [*Woods Hole, MA*]
NEFCCO ...... New England Fish Co. (SAUS)
NEFCO .... New England Fish Co.
NEFCO .... Nordic Environment Finance Corp. (SAUS)
NEFD .... Noise-Equivalent Flux Density
NEFDA .... New England Fisheries Development Association (EA)
NEFDF .... New England Fisheries Development Foundation [*Later, NEFDA*] (EA)
NEFE........... New England Fish Exchange (EA)
NEFEC......... Northeast Fisheries Center [*National Marine Fisheries Service*] (USDC)
NEFES......... Northeastern Forest Experiment Station [*Department of Agriculture*] [*Broomall, PA*] (GRD)
NEFFS......... Northeastern Forest Experiment Station (SAUS)
NEFGX .... New England Growth [*Mutual fund ticker symbol*] (SG)
NEFI........... New England Fuel Institute
NEFIRA .... New England Fire Insurance Rating Association (SAUS)
NEFMA .... NATO EFA Management Agency (SAUS)
NEFMC .... New England Fisheries Management Council
NEFMO .... NATO European Fighter Management Organization (MCD)
NEFO .... National Electronics Facilities Organization
NEFOS .... New Emerging Forces
NEFP .... New England Free Press [*Publisher*]
NEFPO .... New England Field Procurement Office (ACAE)
NEFPS .... National Enginemen and Firemen's Protection Society [*A union*] [*British*]
NEFS........... Network Extensible File System [*Computer science*] (VLIE)
NEFSA .... National Education Field Service Association [*Defunct*] (EA)
NEFSG .... Northeastern Forest Soils Group (SAUS)
NEFTIC........ Northeastern Forest Tree Improvement Conference (SAUS)
NEG........... Energy East [*NYSE symbol*] [*Formerly, New York State E&G*]
NEG........... National Environmental Group (EFIS)
Neg........... Nega'im (BJA)
NEG .... Negate a Binary Number [*Computer science*]
NEG .... Negation (WDAA)
NEG .... Negative (AAG)
neg .... Negative (VRA)
NEG .... Neglect [*FBI standardized term*]
NEG .... Negligible (AAG)
NEG .... Negotiable (ADA)
NEG .... Negril [*Jamaica*] [*Airport symbol*] (OAG)
NEG .... Negro
NEG .... Nitrogen Efficiency for Growth (SAUS)
NEG .... Nonevaporable Getter (SAUS)
NEG .... Numerical Experimentation Group [*Marine science*] (OSRA)
NEGA .... National Ex-Offender Grant Alliance [*Defunct*] (EA)
NEGA .... New England Gerontological Association (EA)
Negb.......... Negotiable
NEGB .... Northeastern Gas Board (SAUS)
Neg C .... Negligence Cases [*Commerce Clearing House*] [*A publication*] (DLA)
Neg Cas....... Bloomfield's Manumission (or Negro) Cases [*New Jersey*] [*A publication*] (DLA)
NEGD.......... Negotiated (ROG)
NEGDEF .... Navy Enlisted Ground Defense Emergency Force
NEGF .... Neurite Growth-Promoting Factor (DMAA)
NEGI .... National Federation of Engineering and General Ironfounders [*British*] (BI)
Neg Inst....... Negotiable Instrument [*Legal term*] (DLA)
NEGISTOR ... Negative Resistor (PDAA)
NEGIT .... Negative Impedance Transistor [*Electronics*] (IAA)
Negl........... Negligence
Negl & Comp Cas Ann... Negligence and Compensation Cases, Annotated [*A publication*] (DLA)
Negl & Comp Cas Ann 3d... Negligence and Compensation Cases, Annotated, Third Series [*A publication*] (DLA)
Negl & Comp Cas Ann (NS)... Negligence and Compensation Cases, Annotated, New Series [*A publication*] (DLA)
Negl Cas...... Negligence Cases [*Commerce Clearing House*] [*A publication*] (DLA)

Negl Cas 2d... Negligence Cases, Second Series [*Commerce Clearing House*] [*A publication*] (DLA)
NEGN .... Negotiation (ROG)
NEGOA .... Northeast Gulf of Alaska [*Marine science*] (MSC)
NEGOT .... Negotiable [*Legal shorthand*] (LWAP)
NEGPED....... Negotiator's Planned Execution Date (MCD)
NEGPR........ Negative Print
NEGPT........ Negative Print (VRA)
NEGRO........ National Economic Growth and Reconstruction Organization [*Black entrepreneurial organization*]
NEGRO........ New England Grass Roots Organization
Negro Cas ... Bloomfield's Manumission (or Negro) Cases [*New Jersey*] [*A publication*] (DLA)
NEGRS .... Negative Report Submitted [*Army*] (AABC)
NEGRSBM.... Negative Report Submitted [*Army*] (AABC)
negs........... Negatives [*Film*] (WDMC)
NEGTAX ...... Negative Tax (MHDW)
NEGX .... National Energy Group [*NASDAQ symbol*] (SAG)
NEGX .... Natl Energy Group'A' [*NASDAQ symbol*] (TTSB)
NEGX .... Negate a Binary Number with Extend [*Computer science*]
NEGY .... Neutral-Equivalent Gasoline Yield [*Petroleum chemistry*]
NEH............ East Carolina University, Health Sciences Library, Greenville, NC [*OCLC symbol*] (OCLC)
NEh............ East Hampton Free Library, East Hampton, NY [*Library symbol*] [*Library of Congress*] (LCLS)
NEH............ National Endowment for the Humanities
Neh............ Nehemiah [*Old Testament book*]
NEH............ Nuclear Effects Handbook
NEHA .... National Environmental Health Association (EA)
NEHA .... National Executive Housekeepers Association (EA)
NeHB .... Bureau voor de Industriele Eigendom, Bibliotheek Octrooiraad, The Hague, Netherlands [*Library symbol*] [*Library of Congress*] (LCLS)
NEHC .... National Extension Homemakers Council (EA)
NEHE .... Nurses for Environmental Health Education (DAVI)
NEHEP .... National Eye Health Education Program [*Information service or system*] (IID)
NEHF .... National Eye and Health Foundation (EA)
NEHGS........ New England Historic Genealogical Society (EA)
NEHI .... Northwest Educators of the Hearing Impaired (EDAC)
NeHKB .... Koninklijke Bibliotheek [*Royal Library*], The Hague, Netherlands [*Library symbol*] [*Library of Congress*] (LCLS)
NEHRC........ New England History Resources Center [*University of New England*] [*Australia*]
NEHRP........ National Earthquake Hazards Reduction Program [*Federal Emergency Management Agency*] [*Washington, DC*] (EGAO)
NeHSU........ Staatsuitgeverij Christoffel Plantijnstaat (State Printing Office), The Hague, Netherlands [*Library symbol*] [*Library of Congress*] (LCLS)
NEi............. East Islip Public Library, East Islip, NY [*Library symbol*] [*Library of Congress*] (LCLS)
NEI............. Narcotics Education, Inc. (EA)
NEI............. National Elevator Industry (NTPA)
NEI............. National Enterprises (EFIS)
NEI............. National Estuarine Inventory
NEI............. National Eye Institute [*Formerly, NINDB*] [*Department of Health and Human Services*] [*Bethesda, MD*] [*National Institutes of Health*]
NEI............. Nature Expeditions International (GNE)
NEI............. Neipperg [*Federal Republic of Germany*] [*Seismograph station code, US Geological Survey*] (SEIS)
NEI............. Netherlands East Indies
NEI............. New England Institute (SAUS)
NEI............. New England Instrument (SAUS)
NEI............. New Enterprise Institute [*University of Southern Maine*] [*Research center*] (RCD)
NEI............. New Equipment Introduction [*Army*] (AABC)
NEI............. Noise Equivalent Input (SAUS)
NEI............. Noise-Equivalent Input
NEI............. Noise Equivalent Intensity (SAUS)
NEI............. Noise-Equivalent Intensity
NEI............. Noise Equivalent Irradiance (CIST)
NEI............. Noise Exposure Index (SAUS)
NEI............. Non Est Inventus [*It Has Not Been Found or Discovered*] [*Latin*]
NEI............. Non Explosive Initiator (ACAE)
NEI............. Nordic Energy Index [*Database*] [*Nordic Atomic Libraries Joint Secretariat*] [*Information service or system*] (IID)
NEI............. Northern Electric Industries [*British*]
NEI............. Northern Engineering Industries [*Commercial firm*] [*British*]
NEI............. Not Elsewhere Included (SAUS)
nei .... Not Elsewhere Included or Indicated (EBF)
NEI............. Not Elsewhere Indicated
NEI............. Nouvelles Equipes Internationales [*Later, European Christian Democratic Union*]
NEI............. Nuclear Energy Institute (NTPA)
NEI............. US National Eye Institute (SAUS)
NEIAL......... North East Iowa Academic Libraries [*Library network*]
NEIB........... Northeast Indiana Banc [*NASDAQ symbol*] (TTSB)
NEIB........... Northeast Indiana Bancorp, Inc. [*NASDAQ symbol*] (SAG)
NEIC........... National Earthquake Information Center [*US Geological Survey*]
NEIC........... National Electronic Information Corp. [*Information service or system*] (IID)
NEIC........... National Energy Information Center [*Department of Energy*] [*Washington, DC*]
NEIC........... National Enforcement Investigations Center [*Environmental Protection Agency*] (EG)

NEIC	National Equivalence Information Centre (AIE)
NEIC	NATO Equipment Interpretation Course (MCD)
NEIC	New England Information Center [Information service or system]
NEIC	Northeast Independent Conference (PSS)
NEIC	North East Insurance [NASDAQ symbol] (TTSB)
NEIC	North East Insurance Co. [NASDAQ symbol] (NQ)
NEICA	National Energy Information Center Affiliate [University of New Mexico] (IID)
NEICE	North of England Institute for Christian Education
NEIDA	Network of Educational Innovation for Development in Africa (EAIO)
NEIDS	North East Interim Data System (WDAA)
NEIED	National Educational Institute for Economic Development (EA)
NEIETC	New England Interstate Environmental Training Center
NEIF	Near-Earth Instrumentation Facility [NASA] (KSC)
NEII	National Elevator Industry, Inc. (EA)
NEII	National Engineering Information Initiative (SAUS)
NEIL	Neon Indicating Light
NEIL	Nordic Energy Index, Literature [Database] [Nordic Atomic Libraries Joint Secretariat] [Information service or system] (CRD)
NEILC	New England Interstate Library Compact (SAUS)
NeimM	Neiman-Marcus Group [Associated Press] (SAG)
NEIMME	North of England Institute of Mining and Mechanical Engineers (SAUS)
NeINBc	Northeast Indiana Bancorp, Inc. [Associated Press] (SAG)
NE Ins	North East Insurance Co. [Associated Press] (SAG)
NEIP	National Environmental Indicators Programme (SAUS)
NEIPG	National Electronic Industries Procurement Group
NEIR	Narrative End Item Report [NASA] (KSC)
NEIR	Neither (ROG)
NEIRIS	Northeast Regional Library System (SAUS)
NEIRLS	Northeast Regional Library System [Library network]
NEIS	National Earthquake Information Service [United States Geological Survey] (IID)
NEIS	National Emissions Inventory System [Database] [Environment Canada] [Information service or system] (CRD)
NEIS	National Engineering Information System (BUR)
NEIS	National Environmental Information Symposium
NEIS	Nuclear Energy Information Service [An association] (EA)
NEISA	New England Intercollegiate Sailing Association
NEISS	National Electronic Injury Surveillance System [Consumer Product Safety Commission] [Washington, DC] [Databank]
NEIT	New Equipment Introductory Team [Army] (AABC)
NEITA	National Excellence in Teaching Award [Australia]
NEIULS	Northeast Iowa Union List of Serials
NEIWPCC	New England Interstate Water Pollution Control Commission
NEIX	Nordic Energy Index [Database] [Nordic Atomic Libraries Joint Secretariat] [Information service or system] (CRD)
NEJ	Seattle, WA [Location identifier] [FAA] (FAAL)
NEJA	National Entertainment Journalists Association [Defunct] (EA)
NEJM	New England Journal of Medicine [A publication]
NEJS	Near Eastern and Judaistic Studies (BJA)
NEK	Naval Equerry to the King
NEKASA	New England Knitwear and Sportswear Association (EA)
NEKDA	New England Kiln Drying Association (EA)
NEKL	Northeast Kansas Library System [Library network]
NEKOA	New England Knitted Outerwear Association [Later, NEKASA] (EA)
NEL	East Carolina University, Department of Library Science, Greenville, NC [OCLC symbol] (OCLC)
NEl	Greenburgh Public Library, Elmsford, NY [Library symbol] [Library of Congress] (LCLS)
NEL	Lakehurst, NJ [Location identifier] [FAA] (FAAL)
NEL	National Electronics Laboratory (IDOE)
NEL	National Emancipation League [Nigeria]
NEL	National Engineering Laboratory [Scotland]
NEL	National Engineering Laboratory [Superseded IAT] [Gaithersburg, MD] [National Institute of Standards and Technology]
NEL	National Epilepsy League [Later, EFA] (EA)
NEL	Naval Command Control Communications Laboratory Center
NEL	Naval Electronics Laboratory
NEL	Naval Explosive Laboratory
NEL	Navy Electronics Laboratory [San Diego, CA]
NEL	Nelson [Nevada] [Seismograph station code, US Geological Survey] (SEIS)
Nel	Nelson's English Chancery Reports [A publication] (DLA)
NEL	Neon Light (IAA)
NEL	New England Mutual Life Insurance Co. (EFIS)
NEL	New English Library [Publishers] [British]
NEL	NewTel Enterprises Ltd. [Toronto Stock Exchange symbol]
NEL	No Effect Level (ADA)
NEL	Noise Exposure Level (SAUS)
NEL	Non-English Language
NEL	Nonspecific Excitability Level [Animal behavior]
NEL	Northern Extratropical Land [Geography]
NEL	Nuclear Electronics Laboratory (SAUS)
NEL	Nuclear Energy Laboratory [Research center] (RCD)
NEL	Nuclear Engineering Laboratory [University of Utah] [Research center] (RCD)
NELA	National Electric Light Association
NELA	National Employment Lawyers Association (EA)
NELA	New England Library Association
NELA	Northeastern Loggers Association (EA)
NELAC	National Environment Laboratory Accreditation Conference [Environmental Protection Agency]
NELAT	Navy Electronics Laboratory Assembly Tester
NELATS	Naval Electronics Laboratory Automatic Tester System (DNAB)
NELB	New England Library Board [Library network]
NELC	Naval Electronics Center (TIMI)
NELC	Naval Electronics Laboratory Center [Later, NOSC]
NELCON	New-Zealand Electronics Convention (SAUS)
NELCON NZ	National Electronics Conference, New Zealand [IEEE]
Nel CR	Nelson's English Chancery Reports [A publication] (DLA)
NEld	Sunshine Hall Free Library, Eldred, NY [Library symbol] [Library of Congress] (LCLS)
NELDIC	Nippon Electric Layout Design for Integrated Circuits (SAUS)
NELEC	Nonelectric
NELEX	Naval Electronics Systems Command Headquarters
NeLH	National Electronic Library for Health (SAUS)
NELIA	Nuclear Energy Liability Insurance Association [Later, ANI] (EA)
NELIAC	Naval Electronics Laboratory International ALGOL Compilers
NELINET	New England Library Information Network
NELIS	Noncommunications Emitter Location and Identification System (MCD)
NELIS-A	Noncommunications Emitter Location and Identification System - Airborne
NELL	Nellcor, Inc. [NASDAQ symbol] (NQ)
NELL	Nellcor Puritan Bennett [NASDAQ symbol] (TTSB)
Nell	Nell's Reports [1845-55] [Ceylon] [A publication] (DLA)
NELL	North East Lancashire Libraries (SAUS)
NELLCO	New England Law Library Consortium, Inc. [Harvard Law School] [Information service or system] (IID)
Nellcor	Nellcor, Inc. [Associated Press] (SAG)
NElle	Ellenville Public Library, Ellenville, NY [Library symbol] [Library of Congress] (LCLS)
NELM	Northeastern Lumber Manufacturers Association
NEIm	Steele Memorial Library of Elmira and Chemung County, Elmira, NY [Library symbol] [Library of Congress] (LCLS)
NELMA	Northeastern Lumber Manufacturers Association (EA)
NEImC	Elmira College, Elmira, NY [Library symbol] [Library of Congress] (LCLS)
NEImhC	City Hospital at Elmhurst, Elmhurst, NY [Library symbol] [Library of Congress] (LCLS)
NEImHi	Chemung County Historical Society, Elmira, NY [Library symbol] [Library of Congress] (LCLS)
NEImM	Mount Saviour Monastery, Elmira, NY [Library symbol] [Library of Congress] (LCLS)
NEImo	Elmont Public Library, Elmont, NY [Library symbol] [Library of Congress] (LCLS)
NEImoAE	Alden Terrace Elementary School, Elmont, NY [Library symbol] [Library of Congress] (LCLS)
NEImoCCE	Clara H. Carlson Elementary School, Elmont, NY [Library symbol] [Library of Congress] (LCLS)
NEImoCE	Covert Elementary School, Elmont, NY [Library symbol] [Library of Congress] (LCLS)
NEImoDE	Dutch Broadway Elementary School, Elmont, NY [Library symbol] [Library of Congress] (LCLS)
NEImoGE	Gotham Avenue Elementary School, Elmont, NY [Library symbol] [Library of Congress] (LCLS)
NEImoMH	Elmont Memorial High School, Elmont, NY [Library symbol] [Library of Congress] (LCLS)
NEImoSE	Stewart Elementary School, Elmont, NY [Library symbol] [Library of Congress] (LCLS)
NEImP	Elmira Psychiatric Center, Elmira, NY [Library symbol] [Library of Congress] (LCLS)
NEImsAr	Weschester County Archives, Elmsford, NY [Library symbol] [Library of Congress] (LCLS)
NEImSC	Supreme Court Law Library-Elmira, Elmira, NY [Library symbol] [Library of Congress] (LCLS)
NEImsSW	Southern Westchester BOCES School, Elmsford, NY [Library symbol] [Library of Congress] (LCLS)
NELOS	Navy Electronics Laboratory Operating System
NELP	National Employment Law Project [New York, NY] (EA)
NELP	Navy Environmental Leadership Program
NELP	North East London Polytechnic [School] [England]
NELPA	Northwest Electric Light and Power Association (SAUS)
NELPAC	National Engineering Laboratory's Thermophysical Properties Package [British] [Information service or system] (IID)
NELPIA	Nuclear Energy Liability Property Insurance Association [Later, ANI]
NeLR	Rijksuniversiteit Leiden, Leiden, Netherlands [Library symbol] [Library of Congress] (LCLS)
NELRC	National Epilepsy Library and Resource Center [Epilepsy Foundation of America] [Information service or system] (IID)
NELS	National Educational Longitudinal Survey
NELS	National Environmental Laboratories [Proposed]
Nels	Nelson's English Chancery Reports [A publication] (DLA)
NELS	Northwest Europe Loran Steering Committee (SAUS)
NELS	Nuclear Effects Link Simulator (SAUS)
Nels 8vo	Nelson's English Chancery Reports [A publication] (DLA)
NELS:88	National Education Longitudinal Study of 1988 [Department of Education] (GFGA)
NELSA	Northeast Library Service Area [Library network]
Nels Abr	Nelson's Abridgment of the Common Law [A publication] (DLA)
Nels Cler	Nelson's Rights of the Clergy [A publication] (DLA)
Nels F	Finch's English Chancery Reports, by Nelson [1673-81] [A publication] (DLA)
Nels Fol	Finch's English Chancery Reports, by Nelson [1673-81] [A publication] (DLA)
Nels Lex Man	Nelson's Lex Maneriorum [A publication] (DLA)
NelsnB	Nelson [Thomas], Inc. [Associated Press] (SAG)
NelsnT	Nelson [Thomas], Inc. [Associated Press] (SAG)
NELSON	News Editing and Layout System of Newspapers (DGA)

Nelson (Eng)... Nelson's English Chancery Reports [*A publication*] (DLA)
Nelson's Rep... Nelson Tempore Finch [*1673-81*] [*A publication*] (DLA)
NELTAS......... North East Lancashire Technical Advisory Services (SAUS)
NELTS......... Number of Elements Loaded [*Army*]
NeLV........... Koninklijk Instituut voor Taal-, Land-, en Volkenkunde, Leiden, Netherlands [*Library symbol*] [*Library of Congress*] (LCLS)
NELV........... Nerine Latent Virus [*Plant pathology*]
NELWA .... New England Lumber Women's Association [*Defunct*] (EA)
NEm............ East Meadow Public Library, East Meadow, NY [*Library symbol*] [*Library of Congress*] (LCLS)
NEM........... Metropolitan Technical Community College, Omaha, NE [*OCLC symbol*] (OCLC)
nem .... Nahrungs Einheit Milch [*Nahrungsteinheit Milch*] [*Nutritional milk unit*] [*Dietetics*] (DAVI)
Nem........... Nemean [*of Pindar*] [*Classical studies*] (OCD)
NEM........... Nemuro [*Japan*] [*Seismograph station code, US Geological Survey*] (SEIS)
NEM........... N-Ethylmaleimide [*Also, NEMI*] [*Organic chemistry*]
NEM........... N-Ethylmorpholine [*Organic chemistry*]
nEM........... NetworkMCI Enterprise Management
NEM........... New Electronic Media (NTCM)
NeM........... New England Micrographics, Inc., Waltham, MA [*Library symbol*] [*Library of Congress*] (LCLS)
NEM........... Newmont Mining [*NYSE symbol*] (TTSB)
NEM........... Newmont Mining Corp. [*NYSE symbol*] (SPSG)
NEM........... Nickel Electroformed Mold
NEM........... Nitrogen Ethylmorpholine (SAUS)
NEM........... No Evidence of Malignancy [*Medicine*] (MELL)
NEM........... Noise Equivalent to Man (SAUS)
NEM........... Nonelectronic Maintenance
NEM........... Non-Erasable Memory (SAUS)
NEM........... Noram Environment [*Vancouver Stock Exchange symbol*]
nem .... Not Elsewhere Mentioned (EBF)
NEM........... Not Elsewhere Mentioned
NEM........... Nothing Else Matters (SAUS)
NEM........... Numbered Error Message (SAUS)
NEM........... Numerical Exerciser for Memory (TIMI)
NEMA........ National Early Music Association [*British*] (DBA)
NEMA........ National Eclectic Medical Association [*Defunct*] (EA)
NEMA........ National Educational Management Association (EA)
NEMA........ National Electrical Manufacturers Association (EA)
NEMA........ National Electricity Manufacturers' Association (NITA)
NEMA........ National Emergency Management Association (EA)
NEMA........ National Emergency Medicine Association (EA)
NEMA........ Nematode [*Threadworm*]
NEMA........ Nematron Corp. [*NASDAQ symbol*] (SAG)
NEMAC ...... National Energy Management Advisory Committee [*British*]
NEMAC ...... Normal Error Model Analysis Chart
NEMAG ...... Negative Effective Mass Amplifiers and Generators
NEM Area ... Northeastern Mediterranean Area (SAUS)
NEMAS ...... New England Marine Advisory Service
NEMAS ...... Nursing Education Module Authoring System
NEMATOL .... Nematology
NEmBGE ..... Bowling Green Elementary School, East Meadow, NY [*Library symbol*] [*Library of Congress*] (LCLS)
NEmBWE .... Barnum Woods Elementary School, East Meadow, NY [*Library symbol*] [*Library of Congress*] (LCLS)
NEMC........ National Export Meatworks Council [*Australia*]
NEMC........ New England Medical Center [*Boston, MA*]
NEMCA ...... NATO Electromagnetic Compatibility Agency (NATG)
NEMCA ...... Non-Faradaic Electrochemical Modification of Catalytic Activity [*Chemistry*]
NEMCC ...... Nonessential Motor Control Center (AAG)
NEMCH ...... New England Medical Center Hospitals
NEmCJS...... W. T. Clarke Junior-Senior High School, East Meadow, NY [*Library symbol*] [*Library of Congress*] (LCLS)
nem con ..... Nemine Contradicente [*No One Contradicting*] [*Latin*] (WA)
NEM CON.... Nemine Contradicente [*No One Contradicting*] [*Latin*] [*Legal term*]
NEMD .... Nonequilibrium Molecular Dynamics [*Chemical property simulation technique*]
NEMD .... Nonspecific Esophageal Motility Disorder [*Gastroenterology*] (DAVI)
NEMD .... Nonspecific Esophageal Motor Dysfunction [*Medicine*]
NEMDA ...... Northeastern Minnesota Development Association
NEMDGP..... Northeast Melbourne Division of General Practice (SAUS)
NEM DISS.... Nemine Dissentiente [*No One Dissenting*] [*Latin*]
NEMEA ...... New England Media Evaluators Association
NEMEDRI..... North European and Mediterranean Routing Information [*Naval Oceanographic Office*]
NEMEX...... National Energy Management Exhibition and Conference (ITD)
NEMFB ...... New England Motor Freight Bureau (SAUS)
NEMG .... New England Medical Gazette (SAUS)
NEMG T RL... New England MG "T" Register Ltd. (EA)
NEmH .... Meadowbrook Hospital, East Meadow, NY [*Library symbol*] [*Library of Congress*] (LCLS)
NEMI.......... National Elevator Manufacturing Industry [*Later, NEII*] (EA)
NEMI.......... N-Ethylmaleimide [*Also, NEM*] [*Organic chemistry*]
NEMI.......... North European Management Institute (SAUS)
NEMI.......... Nuclear Electromagnetic Interference (SAUS)
NEMIC .... New England Materials-Instruction Center
NEMISYS .... New Mexico Information System [*Library network*]
NEmL.......... East Meadow Public Library, East Meadow, NY [*Library symbol*] [*Library of Congress*] (LCLS)
NEMLA....... New England Modern Language Association (AEBS)
NEmMC....... Nassau County Medical Center, East Meadow, NY [*Library symbol*] [*Library of Congress*] (LCLS)

NEmMcE ..... McVey Elementary School, East Meadow, NY [*Library symbol*] [*Library of Congress*] (LCLS)
NEMMCO ..... National Electricity Market Management Company, Ltd. [*Australia*] [*Commercial firm*]
NEmME....... Meadowbrook Elementary School, East Meadow, NY [*Library symbol*] [*Library of Congress*] (LCLS)
NEmMH....... East Meadow High School, East Meadow, NY [*Library symbol*] [*Library of Congress*] (LCLS)
NEmNHi...... Nassau County Historical Museum, East Meadow, NY [*Library symbol*] [*Library of Congress*] (LCLS)
NEMO .... Naval Experimental Manned Observatory
NEMO .... Navy EarthMap Explorer
NEMO .... Never Ever Mention Outside [*Secret computer toy project of Axlon, Inc.*]
NeMO .... New Millennium Observatory
NEMO .... Nonempirical Molecular Orbitals [*Atomic physics*]
NEMO .... Not Emanating from Main Office (SAUS)
NEMO .... Not Emanating Main Office [*Remote broadcast*] (NTCM)
NEMO .... Nuclear Exchange Model
NEMOS .... Network Management Operations Support [*Computer science*] (AGLO)
NEMP......... Nuclear Electromagnetic Propagation
NEMP......... Nuclear Electromagnetic Pulse (AABC)
NEMPA .... North-Eastern Master Printers Alliance (SAUS)
NEMPAC ..... National Emergency Medicine Political Action Committee (SAUS)
NEmPE .... Parkway Elementary School, East Meadow, NY [*Library symbol*] [*Library of Congress*] (LCLS)
NEMPET...... Northeast Microbial Physiologists, Ecologists and Taxonomists (SAUS)
NEMPS .... National Environmental Monitoring and Prediction System (MCD)
NEMPs .... National Environment Management Plans (SAUS)
NEMQO....... Non Est Mortale Quod Opto [*It Is No Mortal Thing I Desire*] [*Motto of Friedrich III, Duke of Schleswig-Holstein-Gottorp (1597-1659)*] [*Latin*]
NEMR .... National E [*Electronic*]-Mail Registry [*Information service or system*] (TSSD)
NEMRA .... National Electrical Manufacturers Representatives Association (EA)
NEMRB .... New England Motor Rate Bureau
NEMRIP....... New England Marine Resources Information Program [*University of Rhode Island*] [*Later, NEMAS*]
NEMRL .... New England Marine Research Laboratory (ABAC)
NEMS .... National Aeronautics and Space Administration [*NASA*] Equipment Management System (AAGC)
NEMS........ National Emergency Management System (ACAE)
NEMS........ National Exchange Market System
NEMS........ Navigation and Environmental Monitoring System (ACAE)
NEMS........ Near-Earth Magnetospheric Satellite
NEMS........ Nimbus E Microwave Spectrometer [*Meteorology*]
NEMS........ Non-External-Moving Surface (SAUS)
NEMSPA ..... National EMS [*Emergency Medical Service*] Pilots Association (EA)
NEMT........ Naval Emergency Monitoring Teams (PDAA)
NEMTA....... New England Men's Track Association (PSS)
NEMVAC ..... Noncombatant Emergency and Evacuation Plan (NVT)
NE-MWCC ... Northeast-Midwest Congressional Coalition (EA)
NEmWJ....... Woodland Junior High School, East Meadow, NY [*Library symbol*] [*Library of Congress*] (LCLS)
NEN .... New England Nuclear Corp. (SAUS)
NEN .... New Eyes for the Needy (EA)
nen .... Noise and Exposure Number (SAUS)
NEN .... North-East Airlines Ltd. [*Nigeria*] [*FAA designator*] (FAAC)
NEN .... Northstar Energy Corp. [*Toronto Stock Exchange symbol*]
NEN .... Nursing Ethics Network (SAUS)
NEN .... Whitehouse, FL [*Location identifier*] [*FAA*] (FAAL)
NENA .... National Emergency Number Association (CGWS)
NENA .... National Emergency Nurses Affiliation (SAUS)
NENB .... Nevada National Bancorporation (SAUS)
NENCL .... Nonenclosed (SAUS)
NENCL .... Nonenclosure
ne/nd .... new edition in preparation-no date can be given (SAUS)
NE/ND .... New Edition / No Date [*of Publication*] (DGA)
NENEP .... Navy Enlisted Nursing Education Program
N-Energy...... Nuclear Energy (SAUS)
NENG .... New England
NEngEI....... New England Electric System [*Associated Press*] (SAG)
NEngInv....... New England Investment Companies Ltd. [*Associated Press*] (SAG)
N Eng J Med... New England Journal of Medicine (MEC)
N Eng J Prison L... New England Journal on Prison Law [*A publication*] (DLA)
N Engl Fruit Meet Proc Annu Meet Mass Fruit Grow Assoc... New England Fruit Meetings. Proceedings. Annual Meeting. Massachusetts Fruit Growers Association (SAUS)
N Eng M Gaz... New England Medical Gazette (SAUS)
N Eng Rep... New England Reporter [*A publication*] (DLA)
N EnI .... International Business Machines Corp., Systems Development Library, Endicott (SAUS)
NEnI .... International Business Machines Corp., Systems Development Library, Endicott, NY [*Library symbol*] [*Library of Congress*] (LCLS)
N ENMLD .... Not Enameled [*Freight*]
NENOA8...... Japanese Journal of Tropical Agriculture (journ.) (SAUS)
NEnoVM...... James Vernon Middle School, East Norwich, NY [*Library symbol*] [*Library of Congress*] (LCLS)
NENP .... New England National Park (SAUS)
NEO .... National Electrolysis Organization [*Later, SCME*] (EA)
NEO .... National Energy Office [*Executive Office of the President*]
NEO .... Near-Earth Object [*Astronomy*]

NEO	Near-Earth Orbit
NEO	Neoarsphenamine [or Neosalvarsan] [Medicine]
NEO	Neocomian [Paleontology]
NEO	Neomycin [Antibiotic compound]
NEO	Neonatal [Medicine]
NEO	Neonatology [Medicine] (MELL)
NEO	Neopharm, Inc. [AMEX symbol] (SAG)
neo	neovascularization (SAUS)
NEO	New Employee Orientation (TIMI)
NEO	Noncombatant Evacuation Operation [Army] (INF)
NEO	Noncombatant Evacuation Order [Army] (AABC)
NEO	Northeastern Operations Office [NASA]
NEO	Northeast Oklahoma R. R. [AAR code]
NEO	Pensacola, FL [Location identifier] [FAA] (FAAL)
NEOB	New Executive Office Building [Washington, DC]
NEOC	National Earth Observations Center [National Oceanic and Atmospheric Administration]
NEOCOMP	New Computational Formulas
NEOCON	National Exposition of Contract Interior Furnishings
NEOCON	Neoconservative
NEOCON	Neomycin, Colistin, Nystatin [Antineoplastic drug regimen]
NEOCS	Navy Enlisted Occupational Classification System (NVT)
NEODA	National Edible Oil Distributors Association [British] (DBA)
NEODA	Naval Explosive Ordnance Disposal Association
NEODF	Naval Explosive Ordnance Disposal Facility
NEO-DHC	Neohesperidin Dihydrochalcone [Also, NHDC] [Sweetening agent]
NEODTC	Naval Explosive Ordnance Disposal Technology Center [Indian Head, MD] (DNAB)
NEOF	Neoforma.com, Inc. [NASDAQ symbol] (SG)
NEOF	No Evidence of Failure (MCD)
NEOF	Nordic Engineer Officers' Federation (EA)
NEOG	Neogen Corp. [NASDAQ symbol] (NQ)
Neogen	Neogen Corp. [Associated Press] (SAG)
NEOL	Neolens, Inc. [NASDAQ symbol] (NQ)
Neol	Neolithic (VRA)
NEOL	Neologism
NEOM	NeoMedia Technologies, Inc. [NASDAQ symbol] (SAG)
NEOM	No Evidence of Malignancy [Medicine] (MELL)
NEOMAL	Northeastern Ohio Major Academic Libraries [The College of Wooster] [Wooster, OH] [Later, NEOMARL] [Library network]
NEOMARL	Northeast Ohio Major Academic and Research Libraries [Library network] [Information service or system] (IID)
NeoMd	NeoMedia Technologies, Inc. [Associated Press] (SAG)
NeoMdia	NeoMedia Technologies, Inc. [Associated Press] (SAG)
NEOME	New Electroactive Organic Materials for Electronics [Esprit]
NEON	New Era of Networks [NASDAQ symbol] (SG)
NEOP	Neoprobe Corp. [NASDAQ symbol] (SAG)
NEOP	New Earth Observation Projects
NEOP	New Employees Orientation Program (SAUS)
NEOP	New England Order of Protection [Later, Woodmen of the World Life Insurance Society] (EA)
NeoPath	NeoPath, Inc. [Associated Press] (SAG)
Neophrm	Neopharm, Inc. [Associated Press] (SAG)
NEO-PI	NEO [Neuroticism, Extraversion, Openness to Experience] Personality Inventory [Personality development test] [Psychology]
Neopr	Neoprobe Corp. [Associated Press] (SAG)
Neoprobe	Neoprobe Corp. [Associated Press] (SAG)
NEOPW	Neoprobe Corp. Wrrt'E' [NASDAQ symbol] (TTSB)
NEORMP	Northeastern Ohio Regional Medical Program (SAUS)
NeoRx	NeoRx Corp. [Associated Press] (SAG)
NEOS	National Earth Orientation Service (ACAE)
NEOS	NeoStar Retail Group [NASDAQ symbol] (SAG)
NEOS	New Employee Orientation Seminars (TIMI)
NeoStar	NeoStar Retail Group [Associated Press] (SAG)
NEO SULF	Neomycin Sulfate (SAUS)
NEOT	NeoTherapeutics, Inc. [NASDAQ symbol] (SAG)
NeoTher	NeoTherapeutics, Inc. [Associated Press] (SAG)
NeoThr	NeoTherapeutics, Inc. [Associated Press] (SAG)
NEOU	Navigators' and Engineering Officers' Union [British]
Neoz	Neozyme Corp. [Associated Press] (SAG)
N/EP	Name on End-Paper [Antiquarian book trade]
NEP	National Education Program (EA)
NEP	National Emphasis Program [Occupational Safety and Health Administration]
NEP	National Energy Plan (COE)
NEP	National Energy Program [or Plan] [Canada]
NEP	National Estuary Program [Federal government]
NEP	Natural Effects Processor
NEP	Near-Earth Phase [NASA]
NEP	Nearest Equivalent Product
NEP	Needle Exchange Program
NEP	Negative Equally Probable
NEP	Negative Expiratory Pressure [Medicine]
NEP	Nemzeti Egyseg Partja [Party of National Unity] [Hungary] [Political party] (PPE)
Nep	Nepal (VRA)
nep	Nepali [MARC language code] [Library of Congress] (LCCP)
NEP	NEPC Airlines [India] [FAA designator] (FAAC)
NEP	Nepean Public Library [UTLAS symbol]
NEP	Nephrology [Medical specialty] (DHSM)
Nep	Nepos [First century BC] [Classical studies] (OCD)
NEP	Neptune (ROG)
NEP	Nerve-Ending Particle (OA)
NEP	Net Earned Premiums [Insurance] (MARI)

NEP	Net Ecosystem Production [Biology]
NEP	N-Ethylpyrrolidinone [Organic chemistry]
NEP	Network Entry Point (AAGC)
NEP	Neutral Endopeptidase [An enzyme]
N-Ep	Neutralizing Epitope [Immunogenetics]
NEP	Neverending Program (IAA)
NEP	New Ecological Paradigm (SAUS)
NEP	New Economic Plan (SAUS)
NEP	New Economic Policy [Program of former USSR, 1921-28; also US wage/price freeze and controls of Nixon Administration, 1971]
NEP	New Edition Pending [Publishing]
NEP	New England Pathology (SAUS)
NEP	New England Plant (NRCH)
NEP	New Equipment Practice
NEP	Newton Extrapolation Polynominal (SAUS)
NEP	Nixon Economic Policy (SAUS)
NEP	No Evidence of Pathology [Medicine] (DMAA)
NEP	Noise-Equivalent Power
NEP	Nominal Entry Point [Aerospace] (NAKS)
NEP	Nonelectronic Part
NEP	Nonelutable Polar Compounds [Analytical chemistry]
NEP	Non-Employee Pass (ACAE)
NEP	Non-English-Proficient
NEP	Normal Entry Point (MCD)
NEP	Northeast Pennsylvania Finl. [AMEX symbol] (SG)
NEP	Not Elsewhere Provided (SAUS)
NEP	Nuclear Earth Penetration programme (SAUS)
NEP	Nuclear Electric Propulsion [System]
NEP	Nuclear Environment Protection (SAUS)
NEP	Nude-Encounter Parlor (SAUS)
NEP	Numerical Experimentation Panel (SAUS)
NEP	Nu Pacific Resources Ltd. [Vancouver Stock Exchange symbol]
NEPA	National Enginemen's Protection Association [A union] [British]
NEPA	National Environmental Policy Act (EG)
NEPA	National Environmental Policy Act of 1969
NEPA	National Environmental Protection Agency [China]
NEPA	National Euchre Players Association (EA)
NEPA	Northeast Pacific Area
NEPA	Nuclear Energy for Propulsion of Aircraft
NEPA	Nuclear Energy Powered Aircraft (SAUS)
NEPA	Nuclear Energy Propulsion of Aircraft (SAUS)
NEPA	Nuclear Environmental Protection Agency (SAUS)
NEPAL	National Egg Packers' Association Ltd. [British] (BI)
NEP & P	New England Printer and Publisher [A publication] (DGA)
NEPB	National Energy Protection Board
NEPBC	Northeastern Pennsylvania Bibliographic Center [King's College] [Wilkes-Barre, PA] [Library network]
NEPC	New England Power Co.
NEPCC	North East Pacific Culture Collection [of marine organisms] [University of British Columbia]
NEPCO	New England Provision Co.
NEPCON	National Electronic Packaging and Production Conference
NEPD	No Evidence of Pulmonary Disease (DAVI)
NEPD	Noise-Equivalent Power Density
NEPDB	Navy Environmental Protection Data Base [Obsolete]
NEPE	National Emergency Planning Establishment [Canada]
NEPE	Nez Perce National Historical Park
NEPE	Nitrate Ester Plasticized Polyethylene (PDAA)
NEPEA	New England Project on Education of the Aging [Defunct] (EA)
NEPEC	Curran Memorial Library, Port Au Port East, Newfoundland (SAUS)
NEPEC	National Earthquake Prediction Evaluation Council [US Geological Survey]
NEPEX	New England Power Exchange
NEPH	Nephelometer (SAUS)
neph	Nephew (GEAB)
neph	Nephrite (VRA)
NEPH	Nephrology
NEPHAT	Northeastern Pacific Hurricane Analog Tracker
NEPHGE	Nonequilibrium pH Gradient Gel Electrophoresis
NEPHIS	Nested Phrase Indexing System [Automated indexing system] [University of Western Ontario]
NEPI	National Environmental Policy Institute [Washington, D.C.]
NEPIA	Nuclear Energy Property Insurance Association [Later, ANI] (EA)
NEPIRC	Northeastern Pennsylvania Industrial Resource Center
NEPIS	N-Ethyl(phenylisoxazolium)sulfonate [Organic chemistry]
NEPL	National Endowment for the Preservation of Liberty [Foundation created by Carl Channell to collect funds for Nicaraguan CONTRAs]
NEPMA	National Engine Parts Manufacturers Association (EA)
NEPMU	Navy Environmental and Preventive Medicine Unit (NVT)
NEPN	Near-Earth Phase Network [NASA] (KSC)
NEPO	NATO Equipment Policy Objective (NATG)
NEPO	New Entrant Prison Officer (WDAA)
NEPOOL	New England Power Pool
NEPP	National Energy Policy Plan
NEPP	Nuclear Effects Post Processor (ACAE)
NEPPCO	Northeastern Poultry Producers Council [Later, PEIA] (EA)
NEPPS	National Environmental Performance Partnership System
NEPR	NATO Electronic Parts Recommendations (AABC)
NEPr	Noble Drilling $1.50 Cv Pfd [NYSE symbol] (TTSB)
NEPR	Nuclear Explosion Pulse Reaction (AAG)
NEPRA	National Electric Power Regulatory Authority [Pakistan]
NEPRAC	National Electron Probe Resource for Analysis of Cells [Harvard University] [Research center] (RCD)
NEPRF	Naval Environmental Prediction Research Facility

NEPRS .... New Equipment Personnel Requirements Summary [*Army*]

NEPS .... National Economic Projections Series [*NPA Data Services, Inc.*] [*Information service or system*] (CRD)

NEPS .... National Estuarine Pollution Study [*Federal Water Quality Administration*] (MSC)

NEPSS .... Navy Environmental Protection Support Service

NEPSWL ...... New England Plant, Soil, and Water Laboratory [*Department of Agriculture*] [*Research center*] (RCD)

NEP System... Nuclear Electric Propulsion System (SAUS)

NEPT .... Neptune (WDAA)

NEPT .... No Evidence of Pulmonary Tuberculosis [*Medicine*]

NEPTUNE ...... North-Eastern Electronic Peak Tracing Unit and Numerical Evaluator (IEEE)

NEPU .... Northern Elements Progression Union [*Nigeria*] [*Political party*]

NEQ .... New England Quarterly [*A publication*] (BRI)

NEQ .... Non-Equivalence (SAUS)

NEQ .... Northeast Quadrant (SAUS)

NEQ .... Not Equal (EECA)

NER .... Air Newark, Inc. [*ICAO designator*] (FAAC)

NEr .... East Rockaway Public Library, East Rockaway, NY [*Library symbol*] [*Library of Congress*] (LCLS)

NER .... National Educational Radio

NER .... National Emissions Report [*Environmental Protection Agency*] (GFGA)

NER .... National Engineers Register (IAA)

NER .... Near East Report [*A publication*] (BJA)

Ner. .... Neriglissar (BJA)

Ner. .... Nero [*of Suetonius*] [*Classical studies*] (OCD)

NER .... Nervine [*Medicine*] (ROG)

NER .... Network for Economic Rights [*Defunct*] (EA)

NER .... Neutral External Rotation [*Sports medicine*]

NER .... Never-Exceed Redline [*Aerospace*] (AAG)

NER .... New Employee Registry (SAUS)

NER .... New England Reporter [*A publication*] (DLA)

NER .... New English Review (SAUS)

NER .... Niger [*ANSI three-letter standard code*] (CNC)

NER .... No Evidence of Recurrence [*Medicine*] (MAE)

NER .... Noise-Equivalent Radiance

NER .... Nonconformance Event Record [*NASA*] (KSC)

NER .... Nondestructive Examination Report (SAUS)

NER .... Nonionizing Electromagnetic Radiation

NER .... North Eastern Railway [*British*]

NER .... Northeastern Regional Library, Cimarron, NM [*OCLC symbol*] (OCLC)

NER .... North Eastern Reporter [*Commonly cited NE*] [*A publication*] (DLA)

NER .... Not Economically Repairable

NER .... Nuclear Electric Resonance (PDAA)

NER .... Nucleotide-Excision Repair

NERA .... National Economic Research Associates

NERA .... National Emergency Relief Administration

NERA .... Naval Enlisted Reserve Association (EA)

Nera. .... Nera & Musica [*Record label*] [*Norway*]

NERA .... New England Reading Association (AEBS)

NeraAS .... Nera AS [*Associated Press*] (SAG)

NERAC .... New England Research Application Center [*University of Connecticut*]

NERAIC .... Northern European Region Air Information Center (SAUS)

NERAIC .... North European Region Air Information Center (NATG)

NERAM .... Network Reliability Assessment Model (PDAA)

NERAy .... Nera-AS [*NASDAQ symbol*] (SAG)

NERAY .... Nera AS ADS [*NASDAQ symbol*] (TTSB)

NERB .... North East Regional Board of Dental Examiners (SAUS)

NERBA .... New England Road Builders Association (SAUS)

NERBC .... New England River Basin Commission

NERBS .... National Electric Rate Book by States [*A publication*]

NERC .... National Electronic Reliability Council (NTCM)

NERC .... National Electronics Research Council

NERC .... National English Rabbit Club [*British*] (BI)

NERC .... National Environmental Research Center [*Later, CERL*] [*Environmental Protection Agency*]

NERC .... National Environmental Research Council (NITA)

NERC .... National Environment Resource Council [*British*] (NRCH)

NERC .... National Equal Rights Council (EA)

NERC .... Natural Environment Research Council [*Research center*] [*British*] (IRC)

NERC .... New England Regional Commission [*Terminated, 1981*] [*Department of Commerce*]

NERC .... New England Research Center (SAUS)

NERC .... New En-Route Center (SAUS)

NERC .... Newton-Evans Research Co., Inc. [*Ellicott City, MD*] [*Information service or system*] (TSSD)

NERC .... Nordic Economic Research Council (EA)

NERC .... North American Electric Reliability Council (EA)

NERC .... Nuclear Energy Research Center [*Also, CEEN, SCK*] [*Belgium*]

NERC .... Regional Conference for the Near East [*UN Food and Agriculture Organization*]

NErCE .... Centre Elementary School, East Rockaway, NY [*Library symbol*] [*Library of Congress*] (LCLS)

NERCIC .... Northeast Regional Coastal Information Center [*Marine science*] (MSC)

NERCOE ...... New England Resource Center for Occupational Education

NERCOM ...... New England Regional Commission [*Department of Commerce*] [*Terminated, 1981*] (EGAO)

NERCOMM... New England Regional Commission [*Terminated, 1981*] [*Department of Commerce*] (NOAA)

NERComP ... New England Regional Computing Program, Inc. [*Boston, MA*]

NERCP .... Naval European Research Contract Program (NG)

NERD .... National Establishment for Real Dorks (SAUS)

NERD .... Neuro-Evolutionary Rostral Developer (ACAE)

NERD .... Newman's Electronic Rhyming Dictionary [*Computer software*] (PCM)

NERD .... No Evidence of Recurrent Disease [*Medicine*] (MAE)

NERDA .... New England Rural Development Association

NERDAS ...... NASA Earth Resources Data Annotation System (MCD)

NERDC .... Northeast Regional Data Center [*University of Florida*] [*Research center*] (RCD)

NEREIS .... European deep-sea drilling program ship (SAUS)

NEREIS .... Novel European Research Ship (SAUS)

NEREM .... Northeast Electronics Research and Engineering Meeting

NEREN .... Nebraska Research and Education Network (SAUS)

NE Rep .... New England Reporter [*A publication*] (DLA)

NE Rep .... North Eastern Reporter [*Commonly cited NE*] [*A publication*] (DLA)

NEREP .... Nuclear Execution and Reporting (SAUS)

NEREP .... Nuclear Execution and Reporting Plan (COE)

NE Reporter... North Eastern Reporter [*Commonly cited NE*] [*A publication*] (DLA)

NE Repr .... North Eastern Reporter [*Commonly cited NE*] [*A publication*] (DLA)

NERF .... National Eye Research Foundation [*Later, NEHF*] (EA)

NERFC .... North East River Forecast Center (SAUS)

NERGG .... New England Regional Genetics Group (NRGU)

NERHL .... Northeastern Radiological Health Laboratory [*Massachusetts*]

NErHS .... East Rockaway High School, East Rockaway, NY [*Library symbol*] [*Library of Congress*] (LCLS)

NERI .... National Electronics Research Initiative [*British*]

NERICOMP... Northeast Rhode Island Computer Project (SAUS)

NERIS .... National Educational Resources Information Service [*British*]

NERIS .... National Energy Referal Information System (NITA)

NERIT .... Northeast Regional Implementation Team [*Army Corps of Engineers*]

NERL .... National Ecological Research Laboratory [*Environmental Protection Agency*]

NERL .... Northeast Research Libraries

NERL .... Nuclear Engineering Research Laboratory (SAUS)

NE Rlty .... New England Realty Associates Ltd. [*Associated Press*] (SAG)

NERMLS ...... New England Regional Medical Library Service (EA)

NERN .... National Educational Radio Network [*Defunct*] (NTCM)

NERO .... National Energy Resources Organization (EA)

NERO .... Near-Earth Rescue and Operations [*NASA*]

NERO .... Noninvasive Evaluation of Radiation Output [*Medicine*] (DMAA)

NERO .... Nuclear Effects Rocket Operations

NERO .... Nutrition Education Research Organization (SAUS)

NERO .... Sodium [*Na*] Experimental Reactor of Zero Power [*British*] (DEN)

NEROC .... Northeast Radio Observatory Corp.

NEROS .... ASRL-RTP Northeast Regional Oxidant Study (SAUS)

NEROS .... Northeast Regional Oxidant Study [*Environmental Protection Agency*] (GFGA)

NERP .... National Environmental Research Park [*Marine science*] (MSC)

NERP .... Nicaraguan Exile Relocation Program [*CIA*]

NERPG .... Northern European Regional Planning Group [*NATO*] (NATG)

NERPRC ...... New England Regional Primate Research Center [*Harvard University*] [*Research center*] (RCD)

NERRA .... New England Roentgen Ray Association (SAUS)

NERRA .... New Equipment Resources Requirements Analysis [*Army*] (AABC)

NErRE .... Rhame Elementary School, East Rockaway, NY [*Library symbol*] [*Library of Congress*] (LCLS)

NERRS .... National Estuarine Research Reserve System (USDC)

NERRS .... New England Roentgen Ray Society (SAUS)

NERRT .... Nuclear Energy Reactor Review Team (SAUS)

NERS .... Neurotic/Endogenous Rating Scale (DB)

NERSA .... Centrale Nucleaire Europeenne a Neutrons Rapides SA [*France*] (PDAA)

NERSA .... European Fast Reactor Power Station (SAUS)

NERSA .... Northeast Rail Service Act [*1981*] [*Also, NRSA*]

NERSC .... Nansen Environmental and Remote Sensing Center (SAUS)

NERSC .... National Energy Research Scientific Computing Center

NERSE .... Nutrition, Exercise, Relaxation, Sleep, and Enjoyment

NERSICA ...... National Established Repair, Service, and Improvement Contractors Association [*Later, National Remodelers Association*]

NERSP .... Navy Environmental Remote Sensing Program

NERU .... Nursing Education Research Unit

NERV .... Nervous [*Medicine*]

NERV .... Nuclear Emergency Recovery Vehicle (NUCP)

NERV .... Nuclear Emulsion Recovery Vehicle (MUGU)

NERV .... Nuclear Energy Research Vehicle

NERV .... Nuclear Engine Recovery Vehicle (SAUS)

NERVA .... Nuclear Engine for Rocket Vehicle Application [*NASA*]

NErWE .... Waverly Park Elementary School, East Rockaway, NY [*Library symbol*] [*Library of Congress*] (LCLS)

NERX .... NeoRx Corp. [*NASDAQ symbol*] (NQ)

NE-Rx .... Northeast Regional Exchange (SAUS)

NERXP .... NeoRx $2.4375 Cv Exch Pfd [*NASDAQ symbol*] (TTSB)

NERXW .... Neorx Corp. Wrrt [*NASDAQ symbol*] (TTSB)

NES .... National Eczema Society [*British*]

NES .... National Election Studies [*Conducts national surveys of the American electorate*]

NES .... National Energy Software [*Department of Energy*] [*Information service or system*] (CRD)

NES .... National Energy Strategy [*Department of Energy*] (ECON)

NES .... National Enuresis Society (EA)

NES .... National Estimating Society [*Later, SCEA*] (EA)

NES .... National European American Society

NES .... National Eutrophication Survey [*Environmental Protection Agency*]

NES .... Naval Engineering Standard (SAUS)

NES .... Naval Examination Service [*British military*] (DMA)
NES .... Naval Experimenting Station
NES .... Near Eastern Society (EA)
NES .... Near Eastern Studies [*A publication*] (BJA)
NES .... Near-End Suppressor (IAA)
NES .... Nesmont Industry [*Vancouver Stock Exchange symbol*]
NES .... Net Encryption System (SAUS)
NES .... Netherlands' Ecological Society [*Multinational association*] (EAIO)
NES .... N-Ethylsuccinimide [*Organic chemistry*]
NES .... Network Environmental Systems, Inc. (EFIS)
NES .... Neurobehavioral Evaluation System
NES .... New Earnings Survey [*British*]
NES .... New England Electric System [*NYSE symbol*] (SPSG)
NES .... New England El Sys [*NYSE symbol*] (TTSB)
NES .... New Enlisted System [*Navy*] (DNAB)
NES .... News Election Service [*Vote-counting consortium of the major TV networks and two wire services*]
NES .... News Electronic Service (SAUS)
NES .... Night Effects Simulator (SAUS)
NES .... Nintendo Entertainment System [*Video game*]
NES .... Noise-Equivalent Signal (IEEE)
NES .... Non-English-Speaking (ADA)
NES .... Nonerasable Storage [*Computer science*]
NES .... Nordeste, Linhas Aereas Regionais SA [*Brazil*] [*ICAO designator*] (FAAC)
NES .... Nordiska Ergonomisallskapet [*Nordic Ergonomic Society*] (EAIO)
NES .... Northeast Environmental Services, Inc. (EFIS)
NES .... Northern Eurasia Study (SAUS)
NES .... North of 60. Environmental Studies (SAUS)
NES .... Not Elsewhere Specified
NES .... Not Elsewhere Stated (SAUS)
NES .... Nowhere Else Specified (SAUS)
NES .... Nowhere Else Stated (SAUS)
NES .... Nuclear Energy System (SAUS)
NES .... Nuclear Estate with Small holdings (SAUS)
NES .... Nuclear Export Signal [*Biochemistry*]
NES .... Nucleus Estate and Smallholders (SAUS)
NES .... Numerical Engineering Society [*British*] (DBA)
NESA .... John H. Nelson Environmental Study Area [*University of Kansas*] [*Research center*] (RCD)
NESA .... National Eagle Scout Association (EA)
NESA .... National Electric Sign Association (EA)
NESA .... National Emission Standards Act [*1967*]
NESA .... National Employment Service Act [*1933*]
NESA .... National Energy Services Association (NTPA)
NESA .... National Energy Specialist Association (EA)
NESA .... National Environmental Specialist Association (EA)
NESA .... National Environmental Study Areas Program [*National Park Service*] [*Defunct*]
NESA .... Near East and South Asia [*Department of State*]
NE/SA .... Near East/South Asia Council of Overseas Schools (EA)
NESA .... New England School of Art
NESAC .... National Environmental Services Administration Committee [*Marine science*] (MSC)
NES&L .... Nuclear Engineering, Safety & Licensing (SAUS)
NESB .... National Environmental Specimen Bank [*Energy Research and Development Administration*]
NESB .... Non-English-Speaking Background (ADA)
NESB .... Number of Equally Strong Beams [*Military*] (CAAL)
NESB1 .... First Generation Non-English-Speaking Background
NESB2 .... Second Generation Non-English-Speaking Background
NESBA .... National Earth Shelter Builders Association [*Defunct*] (EA)
NESBA .... National Executive of Small Business Agencies [*Australia*]
NESBAC .... Northeast Shetland Basin Area Communications (SAUS)
NESBU .... Nuclear Energy Systems Business Unit Westinghouse (SAUS)
NESC .... National Electrical Safety Code [*Also, NEC*] (NTCM)
NESC .... National Electric Safety Code (SAA)
NESC .... National Energy Software Center [*Department of Energy*] [*Information service or system*] (IID)
NESC .... National Enquiry into Scholarly Communication
NESC .... National Environmental Satellite Center [*Formerly, National Weather Satellite Center*] [*Later, National Environmental Satellite Service*]
NESC .... National Environmental Supercomputing Center (AEPA)
NESC .... National Environmental Svc. [*NASDAQ symbol*] (TTSB)
NESC .... National Executive Service Corps [*New York, NY*] (EA)
NESC .... Naval Electronics Systems Command
NESC .... Navy Electromagnetic Spectrum Center (DNAB)
NESC .... Neuroepithelial Stem Cells [*Medicine*]
NESC .... Newcastle Electric Supply Co. (SAUS)
NESC .... New England Science Center (SAUS)
NESC .... Non-English-Speaking Country
NESC .... Nuclear and Environmental Safety Council (SAUS)
NESC .... Nuclear Engineering and Science Conference (SAUS)
NESC .... Nuclear Engineering and Scientific Congress (MCD)
NESCA .... National Environmental Systems Contractors Association [*Later, ACCA*] (EA)
NESCAC .... New England Small College Athletic Conference
NESCAUM .... North East States for Coordinated Air Use Management
NESCH .... New England Society of Clinical Hypnosis (SAUS)
NESCNSC .... Net Evaluation Subcommittee, National Security Council (AABC)
NESCO .... National Energy Supply Corp. [*Proposed*]
NESCO .... National Engineering Science Co.
NESCO .... Naval Environmental Support Office [*Marine science*] (MSC)
NESCO .... Nigerian Electricity Supply Corp. African Workers' Union
NesCom .... IEEE-SA Standards Board New Standards Committee (SAUS)
NESCOM .... New Standards Projects Committee (SAUS)
NESCTM .... National Environmental Satellite Center Technical Memoranda (NOAA)
NESCWS .... Nonessential Services Chilled Water System [*Nuclear energy*] (NRCH)
NESDA .... National Electronic Service Dealers Association [*Later, NESSDA*] (EA)
NESDA .... National Equipment Servicing Dealers Association (EA)
NESDA .... Network for Environment and Sustainable Development for Africa (SAUS)
NESDA .... Northeast Scotland Development Authority (SAUS)
NESDEC .... New England School Development Council (EA)
NESDIS .... National Earth Satellite Data and Information System (SAUS)
NESDIS .... National Environmental Satellite, Data, and Information Service [*Washington, DC*] [*National Oceanic and Atmospheric Administration*] (GRD)
NESDRES .... National Environmental Data Referral Service [*Marine science*] (OSRA)
NESE .... Neue Ephemeris fuer Semitische Epigraphik [*Wiesbaden*] [*A publication*] (BJA)
NESEA .... Naval Electronic Systems Engineering Activity
NESEA .... Northeast Sustainable Energy Association (SAUS)
NESEC .... Naval Electronics Systems Engineering Center (MCD)
NESEP .... Navy Enlisted Scientific Education Program
NESF .... Normal Engineered Safety Features [*Nuclear energy*] (NRCH)
NESFD .... Noise Equivalent Spectral Flux Density (SAUS)
NESHAP .... National Emission Standards for Hazardous Air Pollutants [*Environmental Protection Agency*]
NESHAPS .... National Emission Standard for Hazard Air Pollutants [*Environmental science*] (COE)
NESHAPS .... National Emission Standards for Hazardous Air Pollutants (WPI)
NESIP .... Naval Explosive Safety Improvement Program
NESIP/POA & M ... Naval Explosive Safety Improvement Program / Plan of Action and Milestones (DNAB)
NESL .... Northeast Shipbuilders Ltd. [*Commercial firm*] [*British*]
NESLA .... New England Shoe and Leather Association (EA)
NESLI .... National Electronic Site License Initiative
NESLS .... North East of Scotland Library Service (SAUS)
NEsM .... Mount Saint Alphonsus Seminary, Esopus, NY [*Library symbol*] [*Library of Congress*] (LCLS)
NESMRA .... New England Super-Modified Racing Association
NESN .... NATO English-Speaking Nations
NESN .... New England Sports Network [*Cable-television system*]
NESNE .... New England Society of Newspaper Editors (SAUS)
NESO .... Naval Air Engineering Support Office [*Norfolk, VA*]
NESO .... Naval Electronic Sensor Operator [*Canadian Navy*]
NESO .... Naval Engineering Service Office (MCD)
NESO .... Navy Environmental Support Office [*Obsolete*]
NESO .... New Employee Safety Orientation (SAUS)
NESO .... Northeastern Society of Orthodontists (DMAA)
NESOSC .... New England Society of Open Salts Collectors (EA)
NESP .... National Environmental Studies Project [*Defunct*] (EA)
NESP .... Navy EHF [*Extremely High Frequency*] Satellite Program (DOMA)
NESP .... Northeastern Society of Periodontists (SAUS)
NESP .... Nurse Education Support Program
NESR .... Natural Environment Support Room (MCD)
NESR .... Noise-Equivalent Spectral Radiance [*Physics*]
NESRA .... National Employee Services and Recreation Association (EA)
NESRF .... Northern Environmental Studies Revolving Fund (SAUS)
NESS .... NASA Expert Simulation System (NITA)
NESS .... National Easter Seal Society (EA)
NESS .... National Emergency Steel Specification [*World War II*]
NESS .... National Environmental Satellite Service [*National Oceanic and Atmospheric Administration*] [*Telecommunications*] (TEL)
NESS .... Naval Engineering Support System (SAUS)
NESS .... Network and Evaluation Simulation System (NITA)
NESS .... Northeast Satellite Systems [*Avoca, PA*] [*Telecommunications*] (TSSD)
NESS .... Nuclear Effects Simulation Study
NESSDA .... National Electronic Sales and Service Dealers Association (EA)
NEssDS .... Dunlap Society, Essex, NY [*Library symbol*] [*Library of Congress*] (LCLS)
NESSEC .... Naval Electronics Systems Security Engineering Center (MCD)
NESSUS .... Nonlinear Evaluation of Stochastic Structures Under Stress (ACAE)
NEST .... National Emergency Survivable Troop System (AABC)
NEST .... Naval Experimental Satellite Terminal (IEEE)
NEST .... New and Emerging Sciences and Technologies
NEST .... New El Salvador Today (EA)
NEST .... New Expanding Shelter Technology [*Residential construction*]
NEST .... Node Execution Selection Table (SAUS)
NEST .... Nonelectric Stimulus Transfer
NEST .... Non-surgical Embryonic Selective Thinning (SAUS)
NEST .... Novell Embedded Systems Technology [*Novell, Inc.*] [*Computer science*]
NEST .... Nuclear Effects Support Team
NEST .... Nuclear Emergency Search Team [*Department of Energy*]
NEST .... Nuclear Energy Search Team (SAUS)
NEST .... Nuclear Explosive Simulation Technique
NESTA .... National Earth Science Teachers Association (EA)
NESTED .... Naval Electronic Systems Test and Evaluation Detachment
NESTEF .... Naval Electronic Systems Test and Evaluation Facility
NESTEV .... Naval Electronics Systems Test and Evaluation (IAA)
NESTOR .... Netherlands Educational and Scientific Titles for Online Retrieval (TELE)
NESTOR .... Neutron Source Thermal Reactor [*British*] (DEN)

NESTOR......	Newsagent Project under eLib (SAUS)
NESTOR......	Nuclear Reactor Winfrith (SAUS)
NESTS	Nonelectric Stimulus Transfer System
NestU........	Northeast Utilities [*Associated Press*] (SAG)
NESW	Non-Essential Service Water
NESW	Nonessential Service Water Relay Pump [*Nuclear energy*] (IAA)
NET............	Centre for Agricultural Publications and Documents, Wageningen, Netherlands [*OCLC symbol*] (OCLC)
Net............	Internet (DCDG)
NET............	NASA Employee Team (SAUS)
NET............	Nasoendotracheal Tube [*Medicine*]
NET............	National Educational Television [*Later, EBC*]
NET............	National Empowerment Television
NET............	National Environmental Testing, Inc. (EFIS)
NET............	National Estate Tasmania [*Australia*]
NETC.........	National Evangelization Teams (EA)
NET............	Negative Entropy Trap
NET............	Nerve Excitability Test [*Medicine*] (DMAA)
NET............	Net Energy Thrust
NET............	Net Equivalent Temperature
NET............	Net.Explosive Weight (MSA)
NET............	NETI Technologies, Inc. [*Vancouver Stock Exchange symbol*]
NET............	Netto [*Lowest*]
NET............	Network [*Telecommunications*] (AAG)
net............	Network (WDMC)
NET............	Network Aviation Services (NIG) Ltd. [*FAA designator*] (FAAC)
NET............	Network-Entity Title [*Computer science*] (VLIE)
NET............	Network Equipment Technologies [*Computer science*] (VLIE)
NET............	Neuroectodermal Tumor [*Medicine*] (DMAA)
NET............	Neuroelectric Therapy [*Substance detoxification*]
NET............	Neuroendocrine Transducer [*Medicine*] (MELL)
NET............	Neuroendocrine Tumor [*Medicine*] (DMAA)
NET............	New England Telephone (SAUS)
NET............	New Equipment Training [*Army*] (AABC)
NET............	New Era Technologies, Inc. [*Washington, DC*] [*Telecommunications*] (TSSD)
NET............	Newton Emission Theory [*Physics*]
NET............	Next European Torus [*Formerly, Joint European Torus (JET)*]
NET............	Nimbus Experiment Team [*NASA*]
NET............	Nippon Educational Television Co. Ltd. (SAUS)
NET............	Nitrigin Eireann Teoranta [*Nationalized industry*] [*Ireland*] (EY)
NET............	No Earlier Than (SAUS)
NET............	No Electronic Theft [*Act*]
NET............	No Evidence of Tumor [*Medicine*]
NET............	Noise Enforcement Team (SAUS)
NET............	Noise Equivalent Target (CCCA)
NET............	Noise Equivalent Temperature (SAUS)
NET............	Noise-Equivalent Temperature
NET............	Noise Evaluation Test (IAA)
NET............	Nonlethal Entanglement Technology
NET............	Nonradiative Energy Transfer [*Physics*]
NET............	Norepinephrine Transporter [*Medicine*] (DMAA)
NET............	Norethisterone [*Oral contraceptive ingredient*]
NET............	Normal Environmental Temperature (SAUS)
NET............	Norme Europeene de Telecommunications [*Telecommunications*] (OSI)
NET............	North European Oil Royalty Trust [*NYSE symbol*] (SPSG)
NET............	North Europn Oil Rty Tr [*NYSE symbol*] (TTSB)
NET............	Not Earlier Than
NET............	Nuclear Effects Test
NET............	Nuclear Electronic Transistor (SAUS)
NET............	Nuclear Emergency Teams [*DASA*]
NET............	Nuclear Energy Team
NET............	Nuclear Engineer Trainee
NET............	Number of Element Types
NET............	Nutrition Education Training (SAUS)
NETA.........	International Electrical Testing Association (EA)
NETA.........	National Educational Telecommunications Association (AGLO)
NETA.........	National Employment and Training Association [*Upland, CA*] (EA)
NETA.........	National Environmental Training Association (EA)
NETA.........	Network Associates [*NASDAQ symbol*] [*Formerly, McAfee Associates*] (SG)
NETA.........	New England Telecommunications Association (CIST)
NETA.........	Northeast Test Area [*Military*] (MCD)
NETA.........	Northwest Electronic Technical Association (SAUS)
NETAC........	Nuclear Energy Trade Associations' Conference
NETANAL....	Network Analysis (PDAA)
NETAPPS	Net Ad-Produced Purchases [*Advertising*]
NetBEUI.......	NetBIOS [*Network Basic Input/Output System*] Extended User Interface [*Microsoft Corp.*] (PCM)
NetBIOS.......	Network Basic Input/Output System [*Computer science*] (DOM)
NETBIOS	Network Basic Input/Output System [*Computer software*]
NETBLT........	Network Block Transfer [*Computer science*] (VLIE)
NETC..........	National Emergency Training Center
NETC..........	National Emergency Transportation Center
NETC..........	Naval Education and Training Center [*or Command*] (NVT)
NETC..........	NETCM On-Line Comm Svcs [*NASDAQ symbol*] (TTSB)
NETC..........	Netcom On-Line Communications Services, Inc. [*NASDAQ symbol*] (SAG)
NETC..........	New England Theatre Conference (EA)
NETC..........	New England Trail Conference (EA)
NETC..........	No Explosion of the Total Contents [*Business term*] (DCTA)
NETC..........	Northeast Transportation Coalition
NET CDF	Network Common Data Format [*Computer science*]

NETCHE	Nebraska Educational Television Council for Higher Education, Inc. [*Library network*]
NETCO	North Western Employes Transportation Corp. [*Successor to Chicago & North Western Railway*]
Netcom	Netcom On-Line Communictions Services, Inc. [*Associated Press*] (SAG)
NETCOM	Network Communications
NETCOM	Network Control Communications [*Deep Space Instrumentation Facility, NASA*]
NETCON	Network Control [*Computer science*] (MHDB)
NETCONSTA...	Net Control Station [*Computer science*] (VLIE)
NETD	Noise Equivalent Temperature Difference (SAUS)
NETD	Noise-Equivalent Temperature Difference [*Thermography*]
NETD	Noneffective Transit Depot (SAUS)
NETDA	Network Design and Analysis [*Computer science*] (VLIE)
NETDC	New England Trophoblastic Disease Center
NetDDE	Network Dynamic Data Exchange [*Computer science*] (VLIE)
NETDP	National Environmental Technology Demonstration Program (BCP)
NETDS	Near-Earth Tracking and Data System
NETE	Naval Engineering Test Establishment [*Canadian Armed Forces*] (PDAA)
NETE	Network of European Teacher Education (AIE)
NETEP	Northern European Terrestrial Ecosystem Profile (SAUS)
NETF	Netframe Systems [*NASDAQ symbol*] (SAG)
NETF	Nuclear Energy Test Facility (AFM)
NETF	Nuclear Engineering Test Facility (AAG)
NETFIPCBR...	Naval Education and Training Financial Information Processing Branch (DNAB)
NETFMS......	Naval Education and Training Financial Management System (DNAB)
Netframe	Netframe Systems [*Associated Press*] (SAG)
NETFS.........	National Educational Television/Film Service (WGA)
NETG	National Education Training Group (EFIS)
NETG	NetGravity, Inc. [*NASDAQ symbol*] (SG)
NETG	Network General [*NASDAQ symbol*] (TTSB)
NETG	Network General Corp. [*NASDAQ symbol*] (CTT)
NetGALA......	Network of Gay and Lesbian Alumni Associations (EA)
NETGEN	Network Generation [*Computer science*] (MHDB)
NETH	National Employ the Handicapped Week
Neth..........	Netherlands (ODBW)
NETH	Netherlands
Neth Ant	Netherlands Antilles
Netherl Intl L Rev...	Netherlands Yearbook of International Law [*The Hague, Netherlands*] [*A publication*] (DLA)
Neth Int'l L Rev...	Netherlands International Law Review [*A publication*] (DLA)
Nethl..........	Netherlands (VRA)
Neth P	Netherlands Pharmacopoeia [*A publication*]
NETHW	National Employ the Handicapped Week (OICC)
Neth YB Int'l Law...	Netherlands Yearbook of International Law [*A publication*] (DLA)
NETI..........	Network Technologies International, Inc. [*Ann Arbor, MI*] [*Telecommunications*] (TSSD)
NETIC.........	Nonretentive Nonshocksensitive (SAUS)
Netiquette.....	Internet Etiquette [*Computer science*]
NETISA	Naval Education and Training Information Systems Activity (DNAB)
NET IVHU....	Next European Torus/In-Vessel Handling Unit (SAUS)
NETK.........	Network Express [*NASDAQ symbol*] (TTSB)
NETK.........	Network Express, Inc. [*NASDAQ symbol*] (SAG)
NETL.........	National Energy Technology Laboratory
NETL.........	National Export Traffic League [*New York, NY*] (EA)
NETL.........	NetLive Communications, Inc. [*NASDAQ symbol*] (SAG)
NETL.........	Nuclear Engineering Teaching Laboratory [*University of Texas at Austin*] [*Research center*] (RCD)
NetLive	NetLive Communications, Inc. [*Associated Press*] (SAG)
NETLS.........	Northeast Texas Library System [*Library network*]
NETLS/DPL...	Northeast Texas Library System/Dallas Public Library Film Service [*Library network*]
NETLSS........	Northeast Texas Library System (SAUS)
NET Ltd.......	Nigerian External Telecommunications Ltd. [*Lagos*]
NETM.........	NetManage, Inc. [*NASDAQ symbol*] (SAG)
n et m	Nocte et Mane [*Night and Morning*] [*Latin*] [*Pharmacy*] (DAVI)
N et M	Nocte et Mane [*Night and Morning*] [*Pharmacy*]
NETMA........	Nobody Ever Tells Me Anything [*Executive complaint*]
Netmed........	Netmed, Inc. [*Associated Press*] (SAG)
NETMIS........	Naval Education and Training Management Information System (MCD)
Netmng........	NetManage, Inc. [*Associated Press*] (SAG)
NETMUX	Network Multiplexer (NITA)
NETN.........	Networks North [*NASDAQ symbol*] (SG)
NET/NLT	No Earlier Than/No Later Than (MCD)
NETO.........	NetObjects, Inc. [*NASDAQ symbol*] (SG)
NETOP........	Network Operator Process [*Computer science*] (MHDB)
NETOPS.......	Nuclear Emergency Team Operations (AFM)
NETP.........	Net Perceptions [*NASDAQ symbol*] (SG)
NETP.........	New Equipment Training Plan (SAUS)
NETP.........	New Equipment Training Program [*Army*] (AABC)
NETPARS......	Network Performing Analysis Reporting System (SAUS)
NetPC	Network Personal Computer (IGQR)
NETPDC.......	Naval Education and Training Program Development Center [*Pensacola, FL*] (DNAB)
NETR	NATO Electronic Technical Recommendation (PDAA)
NETR	No Essential Traffic Reported [*Aviation*]
NETR	Nuclear Engineering Test Reactor [*Air Force*]
NETRA	New England Trail Rider Association (EA)
NETRAS........	Nuclear Electric Transfer Stage (SAUS)
NETRB	New England Territory Railroad Bureau

NETRC	National Educational Television and Radio Center [*Later, EBC*] (EA)
NETREM	Net Requirementes Estimation Model (PDAA)
NETR-FTC	New England Territory Railroads Freight Traffic Committee
Netrix	Netrix Corp. [*Associated Press*] (SAG)
NETRJE	Network Remote Job Entry [*Telecommunications*] (OSI)
NE TR S NUM...	Ne Tradas sine Nummo [*Cash on Delivery*] [*Latin*]
nets	Communication Networks (SAUS)
NETS	National Education Technology Standards
NETS	National Electronics Teachers' Service [*Defunct*]
NETS	National Emergency Telecommunications System (CCCA)
NETS	Nationwide Emergency Telecommunications System [*DoD*]
NETS	Navy Engineering Technical Services (NG)
NETS	Nebraska Electronic Transfer System
NETS	Network Electrical Technique System (IAA)
NETS	Network Event Theatre, Inc. [*NASDAQ symbol*] (SAG)
NETS	Network for Electronic Transfers System
NETS	Network of Employees for Traffic Safety [*NHTSA*] (TAG)
NETS	Network Techniques
NETS	Network Testing Section [*Social Security Administration*]
NETS	Neurodysfunction Eye Test System [*Medical*]
NETS	New Examiner Training School [*Federal Home Loan Bank Board*]
NETS	New Threats Simulator (ACAE)
NETSC	Naval Education and Training Support Center (DNAB)
NETSCL	Naval Education and Training Support Center, Atlantic (DNAB)
NETSCP	Naval Education and Training Support Center, Pacific (DNAB)
Netscpe	Netscape Communications Corp. [*Associated Press*] (SAG)
NETSET	Network Synthesis and Evaluation Technique [*Computer science*]
NETSET	Network Systems and Evaluation Technique (NITA)
NETSIM	[*Traffic*] Network Simulation [*TXDOT*] (TAG)
NETSL	New England Technical Services Librarians
Netsmrt	Netsmart Technologies, Inc. [*Associated Press*] (SAG)
NETSO	Northern European Transhipment Organization [*NATO*] (NATG)
NETSO	Northern European Transshipment Organization (SAUS)
NETSP	New Equipment Training Support Package
NetSrce	NetSource Communications, Inc. [*Associated Press*] (SAG)
NETSS	National Electronic Telecommunications System for Surveillance [*Center for Disease Control*]
NETSS	National Electronic Telecommunication Surveillance System (SAUS)
NetStar	NetStar, Inc. [*Associated Press*] (SAG)
NETSW	Network Event Theater Wrrt [*NASDAQ symbol*] (TTSB)
NETSYO	Network Security Officer (SAUS)
NETT	National Emphysema Treatment Trial (SAUS)
NETT	Netter Digital Entertainment, Inc. [*NASDAQ symbol*] (SAG)
NETT	Net Tons [*Shipping*]
NETT	Network Environmental Technology Transfer [*Europe*] [*An association*]
NETT	New Employment, Transition, and Training [*Department of Labor*] (OICC)
NETT	New Equipment Training Team [*Army*]
NETT	Notes on Elementary Tactical Training (SAUS)
NETTEL	Network Telecommunications, Inc. [*Denver, CO*] [*Telecommunications*] (TSSD)
Netter	Netter Digital Entertainment, Inc. [*Associated Press*] (SAG)
NetterD	Netter Digital Entertainment, Inc. [*Associated Press*] (SAG)
NETTING	Emission trading used to avoid PSD/NSR permit review requirements (SAUS)
NETTO	Network Training Officer (SAUS)
NETTSP	New Equipment Training Test Support Package (MCD)
NETTW	Netter Digital Entm't Wrrt [*NASDAQ symbol*] (TTSB)
NETV	Nebraska ETV [*Educational Television*] Network [*Lincoln, NE*] [*Telecommunications*] (TSSD)
NetV	NetVantage, Inc. [*Associated Press*] (SAG)
NETVA	NetVantage, Inc. [*NASDAQ symbol*] (SAG)
NETVA	NetVantage Inc.'A' [*NASDAQ symbol*] (TTSB)
NetVant	NetVantage, Inc. [*Associated Press*] (SAG)
NETVU	NetVantage Inc. Unit [*NASDAQ symbol*] (TTSB)
NETVW	NetVantage Inc. Wrrt'A' [*NASDAQ symbol*] (TTSB)
NETVZ	NetVantage Inc. Wrrt'B' [*NASDAQ symbol*] (TTSB)
NetwkAp	Network Appliance Corp. [*Associated Press*] (SAG)
NetwkE	Network Event Theatre, Inc. [*Associated Press*] (SAG)
Networth	Networth, Inc. [*Associated Press*] (SAG)
netwrkg	Networking (BARN)
NETX	Network Equipment Technologies, Inc. (MHDW)
NEU	(Naphthyl)ethyl Urea [*Organic chemistry*]
NEU	Neuchatel [*Switzerland*] [*Seismograph station code, US Geological Survey*] [*Closed*] (SEIS)
Neu	Neuraminic Acid [*Biochemistry*]
neu	Neurilemma [*Neurology*] (DAVI)
NEU	Neuroscience (SAUS)
Neu	Neutrality (SAUS)
NEU	Transportes Aereos Neuquinos Sociedad de Estado [*Argentina*] [*ICAO designator*] (FAAC)
NeuAc	N-Acetylneuraminic Acid
NEUC	National Engine Use Council [*Defunct*] (EA)
NEUCC	Northern European Universities Computer Centre [*Denmark*] (PDAA)
NEUCC	Northern Europe University Computing Centre (SAUS)
NEUCC	Northern Europe University Computing Complex (SAUS)
Neucrine	Neurocrine Biosciences, Inc. [*Associated Press*] (SAG)
NEUDATA	Neutron Data Under Direct Access (NITA)
Neu-Epi-a	Neuroepithelioma (SAUS)
NEUFCH	Neufchatel [*Imprint*] (ROG)
NEUG	National Epson Users Group (EA)
NEUIC	National Employee Union Information Center (EA)
NEUM	Non-European Unrity Movement [*South Africa*] (PD)
Neumed	Neuromedical Systems, Inc. [*Associated Press*] (SAG)

Neur	Neuralgia (SAUS)
Neur	Neurasthenia (SAUS)
Neur	Neuritis (SAUS)
neur	Neurology [*Medicine*] (MAE)
NeUR	Rijksuniversiteit te Utrecht, Utrecht, Netherlands [*Library symbol*] [*Library of Congress*] (LCLS)
NEUR-A	Neurogenic Battery Acute (DAVI)
Neural Netw...	Neural Networks (SAUS)
Neurex	Neurex Corp. [*Associated Press*] (SAG)
Neurgn	Neurogen Corp. [*Associated Press*] (SAG)
Neuro	Neurologic [*Medicine*] (AMHC)
NEURO	Neurology [*or Neurological*]
neuro	neurotic (SAUS)
NEurO	North European Oil Royalty Trust [*Associated Press*] (SAG)
neurobio	neurobiological (SAUS)
Neurobio	neurobiologist (SAUS)
Neurobio	Neurobiology (SAUS)
NEUROBIOL...	Neurobiology
Neurobiol Biochem Morphol...	Neurobiology, Biochemistry and Morphology (SAUS)
Neurol	Neurologist (SAUS)
NEUROL	Neurology
NEUROLGST...	Neurobiologist
Neurol India...	Neurology India (SAUS)
Neuropath	Neuropathology [*or Neuropathologist*] (DAVI)
neurophys....	neurophysiological (SAUS)
Neuropsychiat...	Neuropsychiatry (SAUS)
neuropsycho...	neuropsychological (SAUS)
NEURO SC ...	Neuroscience Building (SAUS)
neurosci	neuroscientist (SAUS)
Neurosci Res...	Neuroscience Research (SAUS)
Neurospora Newrsl...	Neurospora Newsletter (SAUS)
Neuro-Surg...	Neurosurgeon (BABM)
Neuro-Surg...	Neurosurgery [*or Neurosurgeon*] (DAVI)
NeuroTc	Neurobiological Technologies, Inc. [*Associated Press*] (SAG)
NEURS	Navy Energy Usage Reporting System (DNAB)
neurs	neurosis (SAUS)
NEUS	New Extensions for Utilizing Scientists, Inc.
NEUS	Northeastern United States
NEUS	Nuclear Electric Unmanned Spacecraft (SAUS)
NEUS	Nuclear-Electric Unmanned Spacecraft
NEUSSN	Northeastern United States Seismic Network (NRCH)
neut	Neuter (BEE)
NEUT	Neuter
NEUT	Neutral (AAG)
neut	Neutral (SHCU)
neut	neutralize (SAUS)
NEUT	Neutralizer (SAUS)
NEUT	Neutralizing (SAUS)
neut	Neutrophil [*Hematology*]
neut equiv ...	Neutralization Equivalent [*Chemistry*]
NEUTN	Neutralization [*Electronics*] (ECII)
Neutr	Neutralization (SAUS)
Neutron	Neutral Ion (SAUS)
NEV	Nederlandse Ecologen Vereniging [*Netherlands Ecological Society*] [*Multinational association*] (EAIO)
NEV	Negative Expected Value
NEV	Neighborhood Electric Vehicle
NEV	Net Economic Value
NEV	Neutral-to-Earth Voltage [*Electrical power transmission*]
NEV	Nevada (AAG)
Nev	Nevada (ODBW)
NEV	Nevada Airlines, Inc. (SAUS)
Nev	Nevada Supreme Court Reports [*A publication*] (DLA)
NEV	Nevis [*Leeward Islands*] [*Airport symbol*] (OAG)
NEV	Nieghborhood Electric Vehicle
NEV	Non-Equivalent (SAUS)
NEV	Nuevo Energy Co. [*NYSE symbol*] (SPSG)
NEV	Nuevo Financing I [*NYSE symbol*] (SAG)
NEVA	Nevada Resources
NEVA	North Eastern Vecturists Association
NEVA	North of England Veterinary Association (GVA)
NEVADA	Net Energy Verification and Determination Analyzer (ACAE)
Nevada Rep...	Nevada Reports [*A publication*] (DLA)
Nevada Repts...	Nevada Reports [*A publication*] (DLA)
Nev Admin Code...	Nevada Administrative Code [*A publication*] (DLA)
Nev & M......	Nevile and Manning's English King's Bench Reports [*A publication*] (ILCA)
Nev & Mac...	Neville and Macnamara's Railway Cases [*1855-1950*] [*A publication*] (DLA)
Nev & MacN...	Neville and Macnamara's Railway and Canal Cases [*1855-1950*] [*A publication*] (DLA)
Nev & Man...	Nevile and Manning's English King's Bench Reports [*A publication*] (DLA)
Nev & Man Mag Cas...	Nevile and Manning's English Magistrates' Cases [*A publication*] (DLA)
Nev & Mcn...	Neville and Macnamara's Railway Cases [*England*] [*A publication*] (DLA)
Nev & M (Eng)...	Nevile and Manning's English King's Bench Reports [*A publication*] (DLA)
Nev & MKB...	Nevile and Manning's English King's Bench Reports [*A publication*] (DLA)
Nev & MMC...	Nevile and Manning's English Magistrates' Cases [*A publication*] (DLA)
Nev & P......	Nevile and Perry's English King's Bench Reports [*1836-38*] [*A publication*] (DLA)

Nev & P....... Nevile and Perry's English Magistrates' Cases [1836-37] [A publication] (DLA)

Nev & PKB... Nevile and Perry's English King's Bench Reports [1836-38] [A publication] (DLA)

Nev & P Mag Cas... Nevile and Perry's English Magistrates' Cases [1836-37] [A publication] (DLA)

Nev & PMC... Nevile and Perry's English Magistrates' Cases [1836-37] [A publication] (DLA)

NEVATV ...... Nebraska VA Television Network [Telecommunications service] (TSSD)

NEVDGP....... North East Valley Division of General Practice (SAUS)

NEVE........... Nonempirical Valence-Electron [Physics]

NevEngy ...... Nevada Energy Co., Inc. [Associated Press] (SAG)

NEVLESS ...... Nevertheless (ROG)

Nev Nurses Assoc Q Newslett... Nevada Nurses Association. Quarterly Newsletter (SAUS)

NEVOT .... Network Voice Terminal [Telecommunications]

Nev PSC Op... Nevada Public Service Commission Opinions [A publication] (DLA)

NevPw .... Nevada Power Co. [Associated Press] (SAG)

Nev Rev Stat... Nevada Revised Statutes [A publication] (DLA)

NEVRLS .... Nevertheless

Nev SBJ....... Nevada State Bar Journal [A publication] (DLA)

Nev Stats..... Statutes of Nevada [A publication] (DLA)

Nev St Bar J... Nevada State Bar Journal [A publication] (DLA)

Nev Univ Dp G M B... Nevada University. Department of Geology and Mining Bulletin (SAUS)

NEVX .... Nerine Virus X [Plant pathology]

NEW........... Hawarden BAE [British] [ICAO designator] (FAAC)

NEW........... National Electronics Week

NEW........... National Energy Watch [Edison Electric Institute]

NEW........... Native Egg White

NEW........... Navy Early Warning

NEW........... Net Economic Welfare [Economic indicator]

NEW........... Net Explosive Weight (AFM)

new........... Newari [MARC language code] [Library of Congress] (LCCP)

NEW........... Newark [Diocesan abbreviation] [New Jersey] (TOCD)

NEW........... New College of California, San Francisco, CA [OCLC symbol] (OCLC)

New .... New College, Oxford (SAUS)

New .... Newell's Illinois Appeal Reports [A publication] (DLA)

NEW........... New England Air Express, Inc. [ICAO designator] (FAAC)

NEW........... New England Inv Cos. L.P. [NYSE symbol] (TTSB)

NEW........... New England Investment Companies [Formerly, Reich & Tang Ltd.] [NYSE symbol] (SPSG)

NEW........... New Experimental Wagon [Automotive engineering]

NEW........... New Information (SAUS)

NEW........... New Orleans, LA [Location identifier] [FAA] (FAAL)

NEW........... Newport [Washington] [Seismograph station code, US Geological Survey] (SEIS)

NEW........... Newport [Quebec] [Geomagnetic observatory code]

NEW........... Newtec Industries Ltd. [Vancouver Stock Exchange symbol]

NEW........... Newton

NEW........... Non-Traditional Employment for Women

NEW........... Northeast Water (SAUS)

NEW........... Nuclear Energy Women [Defunct] (EA)

NEW........... Nursery Education Week (AEBS)

NEW........... Nvest L.P. [NYSE symbol] [Formerly, New England Investment Companies]

NEw........... Thomas E. Ryan Public Library, East Williston, NY [Library symbol] [Library of Congress] (LCLS)

NEW8C .... New England Women's 8 Conference (PSS)

NEWA .... National Electrical Wholesalers Association

NEWA .... Nuclear Energy Writers Association [Defunct]

NEWAC....... NATO Electronic Warfare Advisory Committee (NATG)

NEWAC....... New England Women's Athletic Conference (PSS)

New ACP ..... New American and Canadian Poetry (SAUS)

New Ad....... New Advocate [A publication] (BRI)

NewAD........ Newspaper Archive Developments Ltd., New Haven, CT [Library symbol] [Library of Congress] (LCLS)

New Age...... New Age Journal [A publication] (BRI)

NewAge .... New Age Media Fund [Associated Press] (SAG)

NEW AM....... Berlin, VT [AM radio station call letters] (BROA)

NEW AM....... Madisonville, TX [AM radio station call letters] (BROA)

NewAm........ New America High Income Fund [Associated Press] (SAG)

New Am Cyc... New American Cyclopaedia [A publication] (ROG)

New Am Lib... New American Library (SAUS)

New Ann Reg... New Annual Register [London] [A publication] (DLA)

Newark L Rev... University of Newark. Law Review [A publication] (DLA)

New Asian Post... New Australasian Post (SAUS)

NEWB .... Newberry Bancorp [NASDAQ symbol] (TTSB)

NEWB .... Newberry Bancorp, Inc. [NASDAQ symbol] (SAG)

Newb .... Newberry's United States District Court, Admiralty Reports [A publication] (DLA)

NEWB .... Newbury [Municipal borough in England]

Newb Adm... Newberry's United States District Court, Admiralty Reports [A publication] (DLA)

New Benl..... New Benloe's Reports, English King's Bench [1531-1628] [A publication] (DLA)

New B Eq Ca... New Brunswick Equity Cases [A publication] (DLA)

New B Eq Rep... New Brunswick Equity Reports [A publication] (DLA)

Newberry..... Newberry's United States District Court, Admiralty Reports [A publication] (DLA)

Newberry Adm (F)... Newberry's United States District Court, Admiralty Reports [A publication] (DLA)

Newberry's Ad Rep... Newberry's United States District Court, Admiralty Reports [A publication] (DLA)

New Biol...... New Biologist (SAUS)

NewbNk ...... Newbridge Networks, Inc. [Associated Press] (SAG)

Newbon .... Newbon's Private Bills Reports [1895-99] [England] [A publication] (DLA)

New Br .... New Brunswick Reports [A publication] (DLA)

New Br Eq (Can)... New Brunswick Equity Reports [Canada] [A publication] (DLA)

New Br Eq Cas (Can)... New Brunswick Equity Cases [Canada] [A publication] (DLA)

New Br R..... New Brunswick Reports [A publication] (DLA)

Newbyth ...... Newbyth's Manuscript Decisions, Scotch Session Cases [A publication] (DLA)

NEWC .... Newcastle [Name of two cities in England]

NEWC .... Newcor, Inc. [NASDAQ symbol] (SAG)

NewCare..... New Care Health Corp. [Associated Press] (SAG)

New Cas ...... New Cases (SAUS)

New Cas...... New Cases (Bingham's New Cases) [A publication] (DLA)

New Cas Eq... New Cases in Equity [8, 9 Modern Reports] [1721-55] [A publication] (DLA)

Newcastle Inst Ed J... Institutes of Education of the Universities of Newcastle Upon Tyne and Durham. Journal (journ.) (SAUS)

New Cath World... New Catholic World (SAUS)

NEWCC .... Northeastern Weed Control Conference [Later, NEWSS] (EA)

NEWC L .... Newcastle-Under-Lyme [City in England] (ROG)

NEWCN....... New Construction [Navy]

New Col...... New Columbia (SAUS)

Newcor........ Newcor, Inc. [Associated Press] (SAG)

NewDay....... New Day Beverage, Inc. [Associated Press] (SAG)

NEWE.......... Newport Electronics, Inc. (SAUS)

New Ed Rev and Enl... New Edition, Revised and Enlarged (SAUS)

Newell .... Newell Co. [Associated Press] (SAG)

Newell .... Newell's Appeals Reports [48-90 Illinois] [A publication] (DLA)

Newell Defam... Newell on Defamation, Slander, and Libel [A publication] (DLA)

Newell Eject... Newell's Treatise on the Action of Ejectment [A publication] (DLA)

Newell Mal Pros... Newell's Treatise on Malicious Prosecution [A publication] (DLA)

Newell Sland & L... Newell on Slander and Libel [A publication] (DLA)

New Eng...... New England Reporter [A publication] (DLA)

New Eng Cons Music... New England Conservatory of Music (GAGS)

NEWENGGRU... New England Group (DNAB)

New Eng J Crim&Civil Confinement... New England Journal on Criminal and Civil Confinement (SAUS)

New Engl Univ Bull... New England University. Bulletin [A publication]

New Eng R... New England Reporter [A publication] (DLA)

New Eng Rep... New England Reporter [A publication] (DLA)

New Eng Sch Law... New England School of Law (GAGS)

New ER........ New England Review [A publication] (BRI)

Newf........... Newfoundland (SHCU)

NEWF.......... Newfoundland [with Labrador, a Canadian province]

NewfEx .... Newfield Exploration [Associated Press] (SAG)

NEWFLD ...... Newfoundland [with Labrador, a Canadian province]

Newfld LR ... Newfoundland Law Reports [A publication] (DLA)

Newf LR ...... Newfoundland Law Reports [A publication] (DLA)

NEW FM ...... Alberta, VA [FM radio station call letters] (BROA)

NEW FM ...... Pukatawagan, Manitoba [FM radio station call letters] (BROA)

NEWFO........ Newfoundland [with Labrador, a Canadian province]

New For....... New Forests (SAUS)

Newfoundland and Labrador Mineral Resources Div Bull... Newfoundland and Labrador. Department of Mines, Agriculture and Resources. Mineral Resources Division. Bulletin (SAUS)

Newfoundland Geol Survey Inf Circ Rept... Newfoundland Geological Survey. Information Circular. Report (SAUS)

Newfoundl LR... Newfoundland Law Reports [A publication] (DLA)

Newfoundl R... Newfoundland Reports [A publication] (DLA)

Newfoundl Sel Cas... Newfoundland Select Cases [A publication] (DLA)

NEWFPS ...... New England Wild Flower Preservation Society (SAUS)

NEWFS .... New England Wild Flower Society (EA)

Newf S Ct.... Newfoundland Supreme Court Decisions [A publication] (DLA)

Newf Sel Cas... Newfoundland Select Cases [A publication] (DLA)

New Gener Comput... New Generation Computing

New Grove... New Grove Dictionary of Music and Musicians [A publication]

New Guinea Austral Pacific SE Asia... New Guinea and Australia, the Pacific and South East Asia (SAUS)

NEWH .... New Horizons Worldwide, Inc. [NASDAQ symbol] (SAG)

Newhal .... Newhall Land & Farming Co. [Associated Press] (SAG)

New Hamp... New Hampshire Reports [A publication] (DLA)

New Hamp Profiles... New Hampshire Profiles (SAUS)

New Hamp R... New Hampshire Reports [A publication] (DLA)

New Hamp Rep... New Hampshire Reports [A publication] (DLA)

New Hampshire Rep... New Hampshire Reports [A publication] (DLA)

New Heb Con... New Hebrides Condominium (SAUS)

New Hebr ... New Hebrides (NTIO)

NewHrz........ New Horizons Savings & Loan Association [Associated Press] (SAG)

NEWI .... New West Eyeworks [NASDAQ symbol] (TTSB)

NEWI .... New West Eyeworks, Inc. [NASDAQ symbol] (SAG)

NEWIL .... Northeast Wisconsin Intertype Libraries [Library network]

New Ind....... New International Review (SAUS)

New Ir Jur... New Irish Jurist and Local Government Review [1900-05] [A publication] (DLA)

NEWISA .... New England Women's Intercollegiate Sailing Association

New J Chem... New Journal of Chemistry (MEC)

New Jersey... New Jersey Law Reports [A publication] (DLA)

New Jersey Eq... New Jersey Equity Reports [A publication] (DLA)

New Jersey Equity... New Jersey Equity Reports [A publication] (DLA)

New Jersey Leg Rec... New Jersey Legal Record [*A publication*] (DLA)

New Jersey L Rev... New Jersey Law Review [*A publication*] (DLA)

New Jersey SBA Qu... New Jersey State Bar Association. Quarterly [*A publication*] (DLA)

New Journ... New Journalist [*A publication*]

New J Stat&Oper Res... New Journal of Statistics and Operational Research (SAUS)

NEWLAND.... Northeast Water Polynya Project, land based (SAUS)

NEWLC....... NATO Electronic Warfare Liaison Committee

Newl Ch PR... Newland's Chancery Practice [*A publication*] (DLA)

Newl Ch Prac... Newland's Chancery Practice [*A publication*] (DLA)

Newl Cont.... Newland on Contracts [*1806*] [*A publication*] (DLA)

NEWLNE....... New Line Cinema Corp. (SAUS)

NEWLON...... New London, Connecticut [*Navy*]

NEWM........ New England and World Missions (EA)

NEW M....... New Mexico (ROG)

New Mag Cas... New Magistrates' Cases (Bittleston, Wise, and Parnell) [*1844-51*] [*A publication*] (DLA)

NEWMAST... National Education Workshop for Math and Science Teachers (SAUS)

New Mat World... New Materials World (SAUS)

Newm Conv... Newman on Conveyancing [*A publication*] (DLA)

New Mex BA... New Mexico State Bar Association, Minutes [*A publication*] (DLA)

New Mexico Bur Mines and Mineral Resources Bull... New Mexico. Bureau of Mines and Mineral Resources. Bulletin (SAUS)

New Mexico Bur Mines and Mineral Resources Circ... New Mexico. Bureau of Mines and Mineral Resources. Circular (SAUS)

New Mexico Bur Mines and Mineral Resources Geol Map... New Mexico. Bureau of Mines and Mineral Resources. Geologic Map (SAUS)

New Mexico Bur Mines and Mineral Resources Mem... New Mexico. Bureau of Mines and Mineral Resources. Memoir (SAUS)

New Mex Magazine... New Mexico Magazine (SAUS)

New Mex SBA... New Mexico State Bar Association, Report of Proceedings [*A publication*] (DLA)

NEWMOA..... Northeast Waste Management Officials Association

NEW MOONS... NASA Evaluation with Models of Optimized Nuclear Spacecraft

NewmtM...... Newmont Mining [*Associated Press*] (SAG)

Newn .... Newnham College, Oxford (SAUS)

New Nat Brev... New Natura Brevium [*A publication*] (DLA)

New NB ...... New Natura Brevium [*A publication*] (DSA)

NEwNE........ North Side Elementary School, East Williston, NY [*Library symbol*] [*Library of Congress*] (LCLS)

NEWOT .... Naval Electronic Warfare Operator Trainer (MCD)

NewOv........ Newscorp Overseas Ltd. [*Associated Press*] (SAG)

NEWP .... Newport [*England*]

NEWP .... Newport Corp. [*NASDAQ symbol*] (NQ)

New Par ...... New Paragraph (SAUS)

NEWPEX...... Northeast Wood Products Expo [*In company name, NEWPEX, Inc.*] (TSPED)

New Phil Orch... New Philharmonia Orchestra (SAUS)

NEWPIL .... NADGE [*NATO Air Defense Ground Environment*] Early Warning Program Information Leaflet (NATG)

NEWPIN....... New Parent-Infant Network (AIE)

NEWPOSITREP... New [*Corrected*] Position Report (NVT)

New Pract Case... New Practice Cases [*1844-48*] [*A publication*] (DLA)

New Pr Cases... New Practice Cases [*1844-48*] [*A publication*] (DLA)

Newpt.......... Newport Corp. [*Associated Press*] (SAG)

NEWQ .... Newquay [*Urban district in England*]

NEWR .... New England Realty Associates Ltd. [*NASDAQ symbol*] (NQ)

New R .... New Republic [*A publication*] (BRI)

NEWRAD...... New Radiometry

NEWRADS..... Nuclear Explosion Warning and Radiological Data System

New Rep...... Bosanquet and Puller's New Reports, English Common Pleas [*1804-07*] [*A publication*] (DLA)

New Rep..... New Reports [*1862-65*] [*England*] [*A publication*] (DLA)

NEWRIT .... Northeast Water Resources Information Terminal (IID)

NEWRZ........ New Englad Rlty Assoc L.P. [*NASDAQ symbol*] (TTSB)

NEWS .... National Extreme Weather Systems (SAUS)

NEWS .... Naval Electronic Warfare Simulator

NEWS .... Navy Electronic Warfare Simulator (SAUS)

NEWS .... Neighborhood Environmental Workshops (EA)

NEWS .... NetWare Early-Warning System [*Frye Computer Systems, Inc.*] [*Computer science*] (PCM)

NEWS .... Network Extensible Window System [*Computer science*]

NEWS .... New England Wild Flower Society (EA)

NEWS .... New European Wide Warranty System [*General Motors Corp.*]

NEWS .... New Product Early Warning System

NEWS .... Newspaper/Microcopy Library (SAUS)

NEWS .... Novell Electronic Webcasting Service (SAUS)

NewSAfr ...... New South Africa Fund [*Associated Press*] (SAG)

NEWSAR...... Nuclear Energy Waste Space Transportation and Removal (GFGA)

New Sci....... New Scientist [*A publication*] (BRI)

NewsCm ...... News Communictions, Inc. [*Associated Press*] (SAG)

NewsCorp ...... News Corp Ltd. [*Associated Press*] (SAG)

NewsCp .... [*The*] News Corp. Ltd. [*Associated Press*] (SAG)

New Series... Martin's Louisiana Reports, New Series [*A publication*] (DLA)

New Sess Cas... New Session Cases (Carrow, Hamerton, and Allen) [*1844-51*] [*A publication*] (DLA)

News For Hist... News of Forest History (SAUS)

NEWSL .... Newsletter

Newsl Aust Coll Ed Qd... Australian College of Education. Queensland Chapter. Newsletter [*A publication*]

Newsl Aust Natn Ass Ment Hlth... Australian National Association for Mental Health. Newsletter [*A publication*]

Newsl Commonw Sci Counc Earth Sci Programme... Newsletter. Commonwealth Science Council. Earth Sciences Programme (SAUS)

News Lepid Soc... News. Lepidopterists Society (SAUS)

Newslett ...... Newsletter (DIAR)

Newslett Environ Mutagen Soc... Newsletter of the Environmental Mutagen Society (SAUS)

Newsl Inst Foresters Aust... Institute of Foresters of Australia. Newsletter (journ.) (SAUS)

Newsl Leg Act... Newsletter on Legislative Activities [*Council of Europe*] [*A publication*] (DLA)

Newsl R&D Uranium Explor Tech... Newsletter. R and D in Uranium Exploration Techniques (SAUS)

Newsl Statist Soc Aust... Statistical Society of Australia. Newsletter [*A publication*]

NEWSLTR .... Newsletter

News Nisshin Steel... News from Nisshin Steel (SAUS)

New South Wales Univ Sch Civ Eng UNICIV Rep... University of New South Wales. School of Civil Engineering UNICIV Report (SAUS)

Newsp .... Newspaper (SAUS)

News Physiol Sci... News in Physiological Sciences (SAUS)

News Rohde Schwarz... News from Rohde and Schwarz (SAUS)

NEWSS .... Northeastern Weed Science Society [*Formerly, NEWCC*] (EA)

NEWSTAR.... Nuclear Energy Waste Space Transportation and Removal (GOBB)

NewSvg....... Newnan Savings Bank [*Associated Press*] (SAG)

NEW T .... Newcastle-Upon-Tyne [*City in England*] (ROG)

NEWT.......... News Terminal

NEWT.......... Newton [*England*]

NEWT.......... Not Environmentally Worse Than (WDAA)

New TB .... New Technical Books [*A publication*] (BRI)

New Technol Jpn... New Technology Japan (SAUS)

New Term Rep... Dowling and Ryland's English King's Bench Reports [*A publication*] (DLA)

New Term Rep... New Term Reports [*A publication*] (DLA)

New Test ..... New Testament (NTIO)

NEWTS .... Naval Electronic Warfare Training System

NEWW .... New World Computer (SAUS)

NewWA .... New England Water Works Association (SAUS)

NewWrld..... New World Communictions Corp. [*Associated Press*] (SAG)

New York... New York Magazine [*A publication*] (BRI)

New York Acad of Sci Annals... New York Academy of Sciences, Annals (SAUS)

New York Att'y Gen Annual Rep... New York Attorney General Reports [*A publication*] (DLA)

New York City BA Bul... Bulletin. Association of the Bar of the City of New York [*A publication*] (DLA)

New York R... New York Court of Appeals Reports [*A publication*] (DLA)

New York Rep... New York Court of Appeals Reports [*A publication*] (DLA)

New York Supp... New York Supplement [*A publication*] (DLA)

New Yugo L... New Yugoslav Law [*A publication*] (DLA)

NEWZAD...... New Zealand Army Detachment (CINC)

New Zealand... Dominion of New Zealand (SAUS)

New Zealand Archit... New Zealand Architect (SAUS)

New Zeal Jur R... New Zealand Jurist Reports [*A publication*] (DLA)

New Zeal L... New Zealand Law Reports [*A publication*] (DLA)

New Zeal LR... New Zealand Law Reports [*A publication*] (DLA)

NEX............. National Exchange, Inc. [*McLean, VA*] [*Telecommunications*] (TSSD)

NEX............. Non-Cyclic Executive Lover Level Computer Software Component (SAUS)

NEX............. Nonepoxide Xanthophyll [*Organic chemistry*]

NEX............. Nonexempt (TIMI)

NEX............. Nonfueled experiment (SAUS)

NEX............. Northern Executive Aviation Ltd. [*British*] [*ICAO designator*] (FAAC)

NEX............. Nose to Ear to Xiphoid [*Medicine*]

N EX .... Not Exceeding [*Freight*]

NEXAFS....... Near-Edge X-Ray Absorption Fine Structure [*For study of surfaces*]

NEXAIR....... Next Generation Upper Air System [*National Weather Service*]

NEXAIR System... Next-generation upper Air System (SAUS)

NEXCO........ National Association of Export Companies [*New York, NY*] (EA)

NEXCOM...... Navy Exchange Service Command

NexGen....... NexGen, Inc. [*Associated Press*] (SAG)

NexGen........ Next Generation (SAUS)

N-Exports...... Nuclear Exports (SAUS)

NEXRAD...... Next Generation Weather RADAR [*National Weather Service*]

Nexstar........ NeXstar Pharmaceuticals [*Associated Press*] (SAG)

NEXT.......... Hooker Enterprises, Inc. (SAUS)

NEXT.......... Nationwide Evaluation of X-Ray Trends

NEXT.......... NATO Experimental Tactics (NATG)

NEXT.......... Near-End Crosstalk [*Bell System*]

NExt.......... New Experiences in Teaching [*Mathematics*]

NEXT.......... New/Experimental Techniques (MCD)

NEXT.......... New Extended Technology (SAUS)

NEXT.......... NextHealth, Inc. [*NASDAQ symbol*] (SAG)

NexT........... Nexus Telecommunication Systems Ltd. [*Associated Press*] (SAG)

NextelCm...... Nextel Communications [*Commercial firm*] [*Associated Press*] (SAG)

NextHlth....... NextHealth, Inc. [*Associated Press*] (SAG)

NEXUS .... NASA Engineering Extendible United Software system (SAUS)

NEXUS .... Nature and Earth United with Science [*Brand of hair products*]

NEXUS .... Nucleus Expert User System (NITA)

NEXUS .... Numerical Examination of Urban Smog (IAA)

NexusTel ...... Nexus Telecommunication Systems Ltd. [*Associated Press*] (SAG)

NEY............. Neomycin Egg Yolk [*Agar*] [*Microbiology*]

NEY............. Neyland [*British depot code*]

NEY............. Northeastern Yiddish [*Language, etc.*] (BJA)

NEYAL .... North East and Yorkshire Academic Libraries Consortium (SAUS)

NEYO .... New York City National Park Service Group

NEZ............. Northern Economic Zone (SAUS)

NEZC.......... New England Zoological Club (SAUS)

NEZP..........	Net Euphotic Zone Production [Oceanography]
NEZP..........	Nezperce Railroad Co. [AAR code]
NEZs..........	New Economic Zones (SAUS)
NF..............	Air Vanuatu [Airline code] [Australia]
NF..............	Eaton Laboratories, Inc. [Research code symbol]
NF..............	EJA/Newport [ICAO designator] (AD)
NF..............	Fujisawa Pharmaceutical Co. [Japan] [Research code symbol]
NF..............	Nafcillin [An antibiotic]
nF..............	Nanofarad [One billionth of a farad]
nF..............	Nanofiltration
NF..............	Narodni Fronta [National Front] [Former Czechoslovakia] [Political party] (PPE)
NF..............	National Federation of Nonpublic School State Accrediting Associations (NTPA)
NF..............	National Fine [Thread]
NF..............	National Forest (IIA)
NF..............	National Formulary [A publication listing standard drugs]
NF..............	National Foundation
NF..............	National Front [British] [Political party] (CDAI)
NF..............	Natural Flat
NF..............	Natural Flood (MCD)
NF..............	Natural Food (MCD)
NF..............	Near Face [Technical drawings]
NF..............	Nebramycin Factor [An antibacterial compound]
NF..............	Necrotising Fasciitis [Medicine] (WDAA)
NF..............	Negro Female
NF..............	Neighborhood Final Fade
NF..............	Nephritic Factor [Clinical medicine]
NF..............	Nested or Flat [Freight]
NF..............	Neue Folge [New Series] [Bibliography] [German]
NF..............	Neurofibromatosis [Medicine]
NF..............	Neurofibromatosis, Inc. [An association] (EA)
NF..............	Neurofilament [Neurophysiology]
NF..............	Neutral Filter (SAUS)
NF..............	Neutral Fraction
NF..............	Neutron Filter (SAUS)
NF..............	Neutron Flux [Nuclear energy] (NRCH)
N/F..............	Neutrons per Fission
NF..............	Nevrofibromatosis (SAUS)
NF..............	New Face [Collectibles]
NF..............	Newfoundland [with Labrador, a Canadian province] [Postal code]
NF..............	Newfoundland Reports [A publication] (DLA)
NF..............	New French [Language, etc.] (ROG)
NF..............	Newspaper Fund (EA)
NF..............	Nichibei Fujinkai [An association] (EA)
NF..............	Nickel Faced (DGA)
NF..............	Niederfrequenz [Audio Frequency] [German military - World War II]
NF..............	Nieman Foundation (EA)
NF..............	Nieuw Front [New Front] [Suriname] [Political party] (EY)
NF..............	Night Fighter (SAUS)
NF..............	Night Fighter Aircraft
NF..............	Night Frequency [Aviation] (IAA)
NF..............	Nitrofluoranthene [Organic chemistry]
NF..............	Nobel Foundation (EA)
NF..............	No Flash [Phototypesetting] (DGA)
NF..............	No Fly [Shrewd tradesman] [Slang] [British] (DSUE)
NF..............	No Fool
NF..............	No Form (AAG)
NF..............	No Fracture (SAUS)
n/f..............	No Funds (WDMC)
n/f..............	No Funds [Banking]
NF..............	Noise Factor
NF..............	Noise Figure
NF..............	Noise Frequency (MSA)
NF..............	Noise Fuse (MCD)
NF..............	None Found [Medicine]
NF..............	Nonferrous
NF..............	Nonfiction (NTCM)
NF..............	Nonfiler [IRS]
NF..............	Nonfiltered
N-F..............	Nonfordable (SAUS)
NF..............	Non-Fragments (NITA)
NF..............	Nonfunction (AAMN)
NF..............	Nonfundable
NF..............	Nonne-Froin [Syndrome] [Medicine] (DB)
NF..............	Nonwhite Female
NF..............	Noranda Forest, Inc. [Toronto Stock Exchange symbol] [Vancouver Stock Exchange symbol]
NF..............	Nordiska Fabriksarbetarefederationen [Nordic Federation of Factory Workers Unions - NFFWU] (EAIO)
NF..............	Nordmanns-Forbunder [Norsemen's Federation] (EA)
NF..............	Norfolk [Virginia] [Navy Yard]
NF..............	Norfolk Island [ANSI two-letter standard code] (CNC)
NF..............	Normal Flow [Medicine]
NF..............	Normal Form [Database design rule] [Computer science] (PCM)
NF..............	Normal Format (SAUS)
NF..............	Normal Formula
NF..............	Normal Frequency [Telecommunications] (NTCM)
NF..............	Norman French [Language, etc.]
NF..............	Norsk Front [Norwegian Front] (PD)
NF..............	Northern Foundation [Canada] (EAIO)
NF..............	Northern French [Language, etc.] (ROG)
NF..............	North Following [Astronomy]
NFs..............	Northumberland Fusiliers [British military] (DMA)
NF..............	Nose Fairing [Missiles]
NF..............	Nose Fuse [Aviation]
NF..............	Nose Fuse (or Fuze) (SAUS)
NF..............	Not Fertilized
NF..............	Not Fordable [Maps and charts]
NF..............	Not Forgeable (SAUS)
NF..............	Not Found [Telephone listing] [Telecommunications] (TEL)
NF..............	Not Releasable to Foreign Nationals (SAUS)
NF..............	Nouveau Franc [New Franc] [Monetary unit] [Introduced in 1960] [France]
NF..............	Nozzle Flow (SAUS)
NF..............	Nuclear Factor [Cytology]
NF..............	Nuclear Fission (SAUS)
NF..............	Nuclear Red Fast [A dye]
NF..............	Number Format (SAUS)
NF..............	Nutrition Foundation [Later, ILSI-NF]
NF..............	Royal Northumberland Fusiliers [Military unit] [British]
NF1..............	Neurofibromatosis Type 1 [Medicine]
NFA..............	Cast Metals Association (EA)
NFA..............	Naga Federal Army [India]
NFA..............	Name Field Address (SAUS)
NFA..............	Natal Field Artillery [British military] (DMA)
NFA..............	National Faculty Association (NADA)
NFA..............	National Faculty Association of Community and Junior Colleges [Later, NEA Higher Education Council]
NFA..............	National Families in Action (EA)
NFA..............	National Farmers' Association [Republic of Ireland] (BI)
NFA..............	National Federation of Anglers [British] (BI)
NFA..............	National Film Archive [British Film Institute]
NFA..............	National Film, Television, and Sound Archives [Ottawa] [UTLAS symbol]
NFA..............	National Finance Adjusters (NTPA)
NFA..............	National Fire Academy (COE)
NFA..............	National Firearms Act
NFA..............	National Firearms Association [Canada]
NFA..............	National Fishermen's Association [Australia]
NFA..............	National Fitness Association [Later, NHCA] (EA)
NFA..............	National Florist Association (EA)
NFA..............	National Flute Association (EA)
NFA..............	National Food Administration
NFA..............	National Foremen's Association [A union] [British]
NFA..............	National Forensic Association (EA)
NFA..............	National Foundation for Asthma (EA)
NFA..............	National Foundry Association (EA)
NFA..............	National Franchisee Association (EA)
NFA..............	National Freedom Academy (EA)
NFA..............	National Front of Ahvaz [Iran]
NFA..............	National Frumps of America (EA)
NFA..............	National Futures Association (EA)
NFA..............	Natural Food Associates (EA)
NFA..............	Naval Fuel Annex
NFA..............	Net Financial Assets (BARN)
NFA..............	Net Fixed Assets (TIMI)
NFA..............	New Farmers of America [Later, FFA] (EA)
NFA..............	New Fighter Aircraft (MCD)
NFA..............	News and Feature Assistant (WDMC)
nfa..............	News and Feature Assistant [An employee of a TV network] (WDMC)
NFA..............	New South Wales Farmers Association (SAUS)
NFA..............	Night Fighter Association
NFA..............	Nitrogen Filling Assembly
NFA..............	Nixon Family Association (EA)
NFA..............	No Fire Area [Military] (INF)
NFA..............	No Fixed Abode
NFA..............	No Flow Assemblies (COE)
NFA..............	No Further Action
NFA..............	Nondeterministic Finite Automaton
NFA..............	Non-Financial Agreement (OICC)
NFA..............	Non-Food Agricultural [Commodity Price Index] (ECON)
NFA..............	Nonhydroxylated Fatty Acid [Organic chemistry]
NFA..............	Northern Forum Academy (SAUS)
NFA..............	North Flying AS [Denmark] [ICAO designator] (FAAC)
NFA..............	Northwest Festivals Association (EA)
NFA..............	Northwest Fisheries Association (EA)
NFA..............	Northwest Forestry Association (EA)
NFA..............	Not for Attribution [Military]
NFA..............	Not Forgotten Association [British] (DBA)
NFA..............	Nuclear Free America (EA)
NFA..............	Nutritional Foods Association [Australia]
NFAA..............	National Fashion Accessories Association (NTPA)
NFAA..............	National Federation of Advertising Agencies [Later, IFAA] (EA)
NFAA..............	National Field Archery Association (EA)
NFAA..............	National Forum for the Advancement of Aquatics (EA)
NFAA..............	National Foundation for Advancement in the Arts (EA)
NFAA..............	Neuro-Fibromatosis Association of Australia
NFAA..............	Nordic Forwarding Agents Association [Defunct] (EA)
NFAA..............	Northern Federation of Advertisers Associations [Stockholm, Sweden] (EAIO)
NFAA..............	Nuclear Fuel Assurance Act
NFAARr..........	Nuclear Flash Absorber Arrester Resister reflector (SAUS)
NFAAUM........	National Federation of Asian American United Methodists (EA)
NFAC..........	Arnolds Cove Public Library, Newfoundland [Library symbol] [National Library of Canada] (NLC)
NFAC..........	National Food and Agricultural Council (NADA)
NFAC..........	National Foreign Assessment Center [CIA]
NFAC..........	National Foundation for Asthmatic Children at Tucson [Later, NFA] (EA)

NFAC	National Franchise Association Coalition (EA)
NFAC	National Full-Scale Aerodynamics Complex [*Ames Research Center, CA*] [*NASA*]
NFAC	Naval Facilities Engineering Command Headquarters
NFAC	NFA Corp. (SAUS)
NFACJC	National Faculty Association of Community and Junior Colleges [*Later, NEA Higher Education Council*]
NFADB	National Family Association for Deaf-Blind [*Sponsored by the Helen Keller National Center for Deaf-Blind Youths and Adults (HKNC)*] (PAZ)
NFAF	Naval Fleet Auxiliary Force
NFAH	National Federation of American Hungarians (EA)
NFAH	National Federation of Hungarian-Americans
NFAH	National Foundation on the Arts and Humanities
NFAHA	National Foundation on the Arts and Humanities Act [*1965*]
NFAHS	National Foundation for Affordable Housing Solutions (EA)
NFaiB	Board of Cooperative Educational Services - Monroe I, Fairport, NY [*Library symbol*] [*Library of Congress*] (LCLS)
NFAIO	National Federation of Asian Indian Organizations in America [*Later, NFIAA*] .(EA)
NFAIS	National Federation of Abstracting and Indexing Services (NITA)
NFAIS	National Federation of Abstracting and Information Services (EA)
NFAIS	National Federation of American Information Services [*International Council of Scientific Unions*]
NFAL	National Foundation of Arts and Letters (WDAA)
N-Fallout	Nuclear Fallout (SAUS)
NFAM	National Foundation for the Australian Musical
NFAM	Network File Access Method
NFAN	National Filter Analysis Network [*Environmental Protection Agency*] (GFGA)
NFANA	Norwegian Fjord Association of North America (EA)
NF & F	Natural Food and Farming [*A publication*]
NF&M	Nuclear Fuels & Materials Department (SAUS)
NFAP	Nerve Fiber Action Potentials [*Neurophysiology*]
NFAP	Network File Access Protocol
NFAP	Nuclear Free Australia Party [*Political party*]
NFAPC	National Fisheries Adjustment Program Committee [*Australia*]
NFar	Farmingdale Public Library, Farmingdale, NY [*Library symbol*] [*Library of Congress*] (LCLS)
NFAR	No Further Action Required (DAVI)
NFarB	BioResearch, Inc., Farmingdale, NY [*Library symbol*] [*Library of Congress*] (LCLS)
NFarEE	East Memorial Elementary School, Farmingdale, NY [*Library symbol*] [*Library of Congress*] (LCLS)
NFarF	Fairchild-Hiller Corp. [*Later, Fairchild Industries, Inc.*], Republic Aviati on Division, Farmingdale, NY [*Library symbol*] [*Library of Congress*] (LCLS)
NFarHS	Howitt School, Farmingdale, NY [*Library symbol*] [*Library of Congress*] (LCLS)
NFarNE	Northside Elementary School, Farmingdale, NY [*Library symbol*] [*Library of Congress*] (LCLS)
NFarSH	Farmingdale Senior High School, Farmingdale, NY [*Library symbol*] [*Library of Congress*] (LCLS)
NFarUA	State University of New York, Agricultural and Technical College at Farmingdale,Farmingdale, NY [*Library symbol*] [*Library of Congress*] (LCLS)
NFarWP	Woodward Parkway School, Farmingdale, NY [*Library symbol*] [*Library of Congress*] (LCLS)
NFAS	National Field Archery Society [*British*] (DBA)
NFAS	Non Facilities-Associated Signaling (SAUS)
NFASG	National Fashion Accessories Salesmen's Guild (EA)
NFAT	Nuclear Factor of Activated T-Cells [*Genetics*]
NFAWSR	North Fork American Wild and Scenic River (COE)
NFay	Fayetteville Free Library, Fayetteville (SAUS)
NFay	Fayetteville Free Library, Fayetteville, NY [*Library symbol*] [*Library of Congress*] (LCLS)
NFB	Booth Memorial Hospital, Flushing, NY [*Library symbol*] [*Library of Congress*] (LCLS)
NFB	Mount Clemens, MI [*Location identifier*] [*FAA*] (FAAL)
NFB	National Federation of the Blind (EA)
NFB	National Film Board [*Canada*] (WDMC)
NFB	National Film Board of Canada [*UTLAS symbol*]
NFB	National Foundation for the Blind (DMAA)
NFB	Naval Frontier Base
NFB	Negative Feedback (DEN)
NFB	New Fibers International [*Vancouver Stock Exchange symbol*]
NFB	Niagara Frontier Tariff Bureau, Inc., Buffalo NY [*STAC*]
NFB	Node of First-Fruiting Branch [*Botany*] (OA)
NFB	No Feed Back (AEBS)
NFB	Nonfermenting Bacteria
NFB	North Fork Bancorp [*NYSE symbol*] (SPSG)
NFBA	National Family Business Association [*Tarzana, CA*] (EA)
NFBA	National Farm Borrowers Association (EA)
NFBA	National Food Brokers Association (EA)
NFBA	National Frame Builders Association (EA)
NFBC	National Family Business Council [*Northbrook, IL*] (EA)
NFBC	National Film Board of Canada
NFBC	Newfoundland Base Command [*Army*] [*World War II*]
NFBC	North Fork Bancorp (MHDW)
NFBCA	National Federation of Blind Citizens of Australia
NFBF	Bishops Falls Public Library, Newfoundland [*Library symbol*] [*National Library of Canada*] (NLC)
NFBF	National Farm Bureau Federation
NFBF	Noninverting Feedback Bridging Fault (SAUS)
NFBG	National Federation of Badger Groups [*British*] (DBA)

NFBI	Bell Island Public Library, Newfoundland [*Library symbol*] [*National Library of Canada*] (NLC)
NFBI	Netherlands Flower-Bulb Institute [*Defunct*] (EA)
NFBI	Nonresidential Fixed Business Investment (MCD)
NFBN	National Food Bank Network (EA)
NFBO	Bonavista Public Library, Newfoundland [*Library symbol*] [*National Library of Canada*] (NLC)
NfBoo	Holmes Library, Boonton (SAUS)
NFBOT	Botwood Public Library, Newfoundland [*Library symbol*] [*National Library of Canada*] (NLC)
NFBPA	National Forum for Black Public Administrators (EA)
NFBPM	National Federation of Builders' and Plumbers' Merchants [*British*] (BI)
NFBPT	National Federation for Biblio/Poetry Therapy (EA)
NFBPW	National Federation of Business and Professional Women's Clubs (WGA)
NFBPWC	National Federation of Business and Professional Women's Clubs (EA)
NFBQ	Rural District Memorial Library, Badgers Quay, Newfoundland [*Library symbol*] [*National Library of Canada*] (NLC)
NFBR	Bay Roberts Public Library, Newfoundland [*Library symbol*] [*National Library of Canada*] (NLC)
NFBR	National Foundation for Biomedical Research [*An association*]
NFBR	National Foundation for Brain Research (EA)
NFBRI	Brigus Public Library, Newfoundland [*Library symbol*] [*National Library of Canada*] (NLC)
NFBS	National Freehold Building Society [*British*]
NFBSS	National Federation of Bakery Students' Societies [*British*] (BI)
NFBTE	National Federation of Building Trades Employers [*British*] (DCTA)
NFBTO	National Federation of Building Trades Operatives [*British*]
NFBU	Buchans Public Library, Newfoundland [*Library symbol*] [*National Library of Canada*] (NLC)
NFBU	National Federation of Bus Users [*British*]
NFBU	National Fire Brigades Union (ROG)
NFBUK	National Federation for the Blind [*British*] (DBA)
NFBUR	Burgeo Public Library, Newfoundland [*Library symbol*] [*National Library of Canada*] (NLC)
NFBURI	Burin Public Library, Newfoundland [*Library symbol*] [*National Library of Canada*] (NLC)
NFBV	Baie Verte Public Library, Newfoundland [*Library symbol*] [*National Library of Canada*] (NLC)
NFBWA	National Federation of Buddhist Women's Associations [*Later, BCAFBWA*] (EA)
NFBWW	Nordic Federation of Building and Wood Workers (EA)
NFC	Carbonear Public Library, Newfoundland [*Library symbol*] [*National Library of Canada*] (NLC)
NFC	Name Formula Card
NFC	National Farm Coalition [*Defunct*] (EA)
NFC	National Federated Craft (EA)
NFC	National Fenestration Council [*Later, PGMC*] (EA)
NFC	National Fertility Center (DAVI)
NFC	National Field Communication (TIMI)
NFC	National Film Carriers (EA)
NFC	National Finance Center (USDC)
NFC	National Firebird Club (EA)
NFC	National Fire Code
NFC	National Food Conference Association (EA)
NFC	National Football Conference [*of NFL*]
NFC	National Forensic Center (EA)
NFC	National Fraternal Congress [*Later, NFCA*]
NFC	National Freight Consortium (WDAA)
NFC	National Freight Corp. [*British*]
NFC	National Fructose Center (EA)
NFC	National Fund Chairman [*or Co-chairman*] [*Red Cross*]
NFC	Native Forest Council (EA)
NFC	Navy Federal Credit Union
NFC	Navy Finance Center
NFC	Near-Frictionless Carbon
NFC	Negative Factor Counting
NFC	Negative Feedback Circuit
nfc	Newfoundland [*MARC country of publication code*] [*Library of Congress*] (LCCP)
NFC	News for Farmer Cooperatives [*A publication*]
NFC	Newsline Fan Club (EA)
NFC	Newsline II Fan Club (EA)
NFC	Newspaper Features Council (EA)
NFC	NFC Ltd. [*Associated Press*] (SAG)
NFC	NFC PLC [*AMEX symbol*] (SPSG)
NFC	NFC plc ADS [*AMEX symbol*] (TTSB)
NFC	Nighttime Fatal Crash
NFC	No Frequency Conversion (SAUS)
NFC	No Front Cover
NFC	No Further Clearance Required (KSC)
NFC	No Further Consequences (NRCH)
NFC	Nonfavorably Considered (DAVI)
NFC	Nordisk Forening for Cellforskning [*Nordic Society for Cell Biology - NSCB*] (EAIO)
NFC	Nose Fairing Container [*Missiles*]
NFC	Nuclear Fuel Cycle (NUCP)
NFC	Numbered Fleet Commander (DOMA)
NFCA	Carmanville Public Library, Newfoundland [*Library symbol*] [*National Library of Canada*] (NLC)
NFCA	National Family Caregivers Association (NTPA)
NFCA	National Federation of Community Associations [*British*] (DI)
NFCA	National Floor Covering Association [*Canada*] (EAIO)

NFCA .... National Foster Care Association [*British*] (EAIO)
NFCA .... National Fraternal Congress of America [*Naperville, IL*] (EA)
NFCA .... National Fuel Credit Association [*Defunct*]
NFCA .... Near-Field Calibration Array (PDAA)
NFCA .... Nonfuel Core Array [*Nuclear energy*] (NRCH)
NFCA .... Northern Fishing Companies Association (SAUS)
NFCAA .... National Fencing Coaches Association of America (EA)
NFCADA ...... National Family Council Against Drug Abuse [*Formerly, NFCDA*] (EA)
NFC(ALLOT)... Navy Finance Center (Allotments Division) (DNAB)
NFCARW ...... National Federation of Cuban-American Republican Women (EA)
NFCAT .... Joseph E. Clouter Memorial Library, Catalina, Newfoundland [*Library symbol*] [*National Library of Canada*] (NLC)
NFCB .... Corner Brook City Public Library, Newfoundland [*Library symbol*] [*National Library of Canada*] (NLC)
NFCB .... National Federation of Community Broadcasters (EA)
NFCBF .... Newfoundland Department of Forest Resources and Lands, Corner Brook, New Foundland [*Library symbol*] [*National Library of Canada*] (NLC)
NFCBFT....... Fisher Institute of Applied Arts and Technology, Corner Brook, Newfoundland [*Library symbol*] [*National Library of Canada*] (NLC)
NFCBM .... Sir Wilfred Grenfell College, Memorial University, Corner Brook, Newfoundland [*Library symbol*] [*National Library of Canada*] (NLC)
NFCBR .... Regional Library, Corner Brook, Newfoundland [*Library symbol*] [*National Library of Canada*] (NLC)
NFCBRO....... National Federation of Citizen Band Radio Operators (EA)
NFCBW .... Western Memorial Hospital, Corner Brook, Newfoundland [*Library symbol*] [*National Library of Canada*] (NLC)
NFCC .... National Family Conciliation Council [*British*] (DI)
NFCC .... National Farm-City Council (EA)
NFCC .... National Foundation for Consumer Credit [*Silver Spring, MD*] (EA)
NFCC .... National Free Clinic Council [*Superseded by NCAHCP*]
NFCC .... Navy Finance Center, Cleveland (ACAE)
NFCC .... Neighborhood Family-Care Center (MEDA)
NFC(CAD) .... Navy Finance Center (Central Accounts Division) (DNAB)
NFCCE .... National Fellowship of Child Care Executives (EA)
NFC-CLEVE... Navy Finance Center - Cleveland [*Ohio*] (DNAB)
NFCCS .... National Federation of Catholic College Students [*Defunct*] (EA)
NFCDA .... National Family Council on Drug Addiction [*Later, NFCADA*] (EA)
NFCDCU....... National Federation of Community Development Credit Unions [*New York, NY*] (EA)
NFCDS .... National Federation of Clubs for Divorced and Separated [*British*] (BI)
NFCE.......... Centreville Public Library, Newfoundland [*Library symbol*] [*National Library of Canada*] (NLC)
NFCEO .... National Foundation for Conservation and Environmental Officers [*Defunct*] (EA)
NFCF.......... Churchill Falls Public Library, Newfoundland [*Library symbol*] [*National Library of Canada*] (NLC)
NFCF.......... National Federation of City Farms [*British*] (EAIO)
NFCG .... National Federation of Consumer Groups [*British*] (ILCA)
NFCGA .... National Federation of Constructional Glass Associations [*British*] (BI)
NFCGC .... National Federation of Coffee Growers of Colombia [*See also FNCC*] (EA)
NFCGH .... Carbonear General Hospital, Newfoundland [*Library symbol*] [*National Library of Canada*] (NLC)
NFCH .... Corner Brook City Public Library, Newfoundland (SAUS)
NFCH .... Cow Head Public Library, Newfoundland [*Library symbol*] [*National Library of Canada*] (NLC)
NFCH .... National Foundation for the Chemically Hypersensitive (EA)
NFCI.......... Change Islands Public Library, Newfoundland [*Library symbol*] [*National Library of Canada*] (NLC)
NFCI.......... National Federation of Clay Industries [*British*] (BI)
NFCIS .... Nuclear Fuel Cycle Information System [*Database*] [*International Atomic Energy Agency*] [*United Nations*] (DUND)
NFCJ.......... National Forum on Criminal Justice [*Formerly, NICD*] [*Inactive*] (EA)
NFCL.......... Clarenville Public Library, Newfoundland [*Library symbol*] [*National Library of Canada*] (NLC)
NFC-L .... National Fisheries Center - Leetown [*Department of the Interior*] (GRD)
NFCM.......... National Front Constitutional Movement [*British*]
NFCO .... Cormack Public Library, Newfoundland [*Library symbol*] [*National Library of Canada*] (NLC)
NFCO .... National Federation of Community Organizations [*British*] (EAIO)
NFCP .... Channel/Port Aux Basques Public Library, Newfoundland [*Library symbol*] [*National Library of Canada*] (NLC)
NFCP .... Nuclear Fuel Cycle and Production Division (SAUS)
NFCPG .... National Federation of Catholic Physicians' Guilds (EA)
NFCPO .... National Forum of Catholic Parent Organizations [*Defunct*] (EA)
NFCR .... Narrow Cold-Frontal Rainbands (SAUS)
NFCR .... National Foundation for Cancer Research (EA)
NFCRC .... National Fisheries Contaminant Research Center (EA)
NFC Receiver... No-Frequency-Conversion Receiver (SAUS)
NFCS .... National Federation of Catholic Seminarians [*Defunct*] (EA)
NFCS .... National Federation of Construction Supervisors [*British*] (BI)
NFCs .... National Focal Centres (SAUS)
NFCS .... Naval Field Contracting System (AAGC)
NFCS .... Night-Fire [*Rifle*] Control Sight [*Army*]
NFCS .... Nuclear Forces Communications Satellite
NFCSG .... Cape St. George Public Library, Newfoundland [*Library symbol*] [*National Library of Canada*] (NLC)
NFCSIT .... National Federation of Cold Storage and Ice Trades [*British*] (BI)

NFCT.......... National Federation of Class Teachers (AIE)
NFCT.......... Nonfederal Control Tower [*For chart use only*]
NFCTA .... National Federation of Continuative Teachers' Associations [*British*]
NFCTA .... National Federation of Corn Trade Associations [*British*] (BI)
NFCTA .... National Fibre Can and Tube Association [*Later, CCTI*] (EA)
NFCU .... Navy Federal Credit Union
NFCUS .... National Federation of Canadian University Students
NFCW .... Cartwright Public Library, Newfoundland [*Library symbol*] [*National Library of Canada*] (BIB)
NFC-WASH... Navy Finance Center - Washington, DC (DNAB)
NFCYM .... National Federation for Catholic Youth Ministry (EA)
NFD .... Dover Public Library, Newfoundland [*Library symbol*] [*National Library of Canada*] (BIB)
NFD .... Eurowings (NFD & RFG Luftverhehrs AG) [*Germany*] [*ICAO designator*] (FAAC)
NFD .... National Faculty Directory [*A publication*]
NFD .... National Fax Directory [*A publication*]
NFD .... National Federation for Decency (EA)
NFD .... National Federation of Drapers and Allied Traders Ltd. [*Republic of Ireland*] (BI)
NFD .... Naval Fuel Depot
NFD .... Network Flow Diagrams (CTAS)
NFD .... Neurofibrillary Degeneration [*Medicine*]
NFD .... Neutron Flux Density [*Nuclear energy*]
NFD .... Newfoundland [*with Labrador, a Canadian province*]
NFD .... Newfoundland Tracking Station
NFD .... No Family Doctor (MELL)
NFD .... No Fixed Date
NFD .... No Foreign Dissemination [*Intelligence classification*] (MCD)
NFD .... No Further Description (SAUS)
NFD .... No Further Details (GOBB)
NFD .... Noise-Free Device (SAUS)
NFD .... Non-Familial Disease (MELL)
NFD .... Non-Fatal Defect (VLIE)
NFD .... Nonfat Dry (SAUS)
NFD .... Norfolk, Franklin & Danville Railway Co. [*AAR code*]
NFD .... Northern Frontier District [*Kenya*]
NFD .... Nuclear Energy and Surplus Facilities DOE-RL Management Division (SAUS)
NFD .... Nuclear Fuels Division (SAUS)
NFD .... Nueva Fuerza Democratica [*New Democratic Force*] [*Colombia*] [*Political party*] (EY)
NFDA .... National Fastener Distributors Association (EA)
NFDA .... National Food Distributors Association (EA)
NFDA .... National Funeral Directors Association (EA)
NFDC .... Dark Cove Public Library, Newfoundland [*Library symbol*] [*National Library of Canada*] (NLC)
NFDC .... National Father's Day Committee (EA)
NFDC .... National Federation of Demolition Contractors [*British*] (EAIO)
NFDC .... National Fertilizer Development Center [*Tennessee Valley Authority*] [*Muscle Shoals, AL*]
NFDC .... National Flight Data Center [*FAA*]
NFDCAMD.... National Food, Drug, and Cosmetic Association of Manufacturers and Distributors [*Defunct*] (EA)
NFDD .... National Flight Data Digest [*FAA*] (TAG)
NFDF .... National Flag Day Foundation (EA)
NFDH .... Daniels Harbour Public Library, Newfoundland [*Library symbol*] [*National Library of Canada*] (NLC)
NFDH .... National Foundation of Dentistry for the Handicapped (EA)
NFDL .... Deer Lake Public Library, Newfoundland [*Library symbol*] [*National Library of Canada*] (NLC)
NFDLF .... Northern Frontier District Liberation Front (SAUS)
NFDM .... Nonfat Dry Milk
NFDMA .... National Funeral Directors and Morticians Association (EA)
NFDPM .... National Federation of Data Processing Manufacturing (NITA)
NFDPS .... National Flight Data Processing System [*ICAO*] (DA)
NFDR .... Neurofacial-Digitorenal Syndrome [*Medicine*] (DMAA)
NFDRS........ National Fire Danger Rating System [*US Forest Service*]
NFDW .... National Federation of Democratic Women (EA)
NFE............ Fentress, VA [*Location identifier*] [*FAA*] (FAAL)
NFE............ National Faculty Exchange (EA)
NFE............ Naval Facilities Engineering Command, Alexandria, VA [*OCLC symbol*] (OCLC)
NFE............ Near Free Electron (AAEL)
NFE............ Nearly Free Electron [*Physics*] (OA)
NFE............ Network Front End
NFE............ Neutron Flux Experiment (SAUS)
NFE............ News from Ethiopia [*A publication*]
NFE............ Nitride Forming Element [*Metal treating*]
NFE............ Nitrogen-Free Extract [*Analytical chemistry*]
NFE............ No First Error (VLIE)
NFE............ Nonferrous Extract (DMAA)
NFE............ Nonformal Education
NFE............ Northwest Fruit Exporters (NTPA)
NFE............ Nose Fairing Exit [*Missiles*]
NFE............ Not Fully Equipped [*of aircraft*] [*Air Force*]
NFE............ Nuclear Faraday Effect (SAUS)
NFEA .... National Federated Electrical Association (MHDB)
NFEA .... National Federation of Export Associations [*New York, NY*] (EA)
NFEA .... Newspaper Farm Editors of America (EA)
NFEA .... Non-Fleet Experienced Aviator (NVT)
NFEAC .... National Foundation for Education in American Citizenship (EA)
NF-EBM .... Noise Forced Energy Balance Model (SAUS)
NFEC.......... National Food and Energy Council (EA)
NFEC.......... National Foundation for Environmental Control (EA)

NFEC............ Naval Facilities Engineering Command [*Formerly, Bureau of Yards and Docks*] (IEEE)
NFEC............ Newspaper Food Editors Conference (EA)
NFECC .... National Fusion Energy Computer Center [*Lawrence Livermore National Laboratory*] (MCD)
NFED .... National Foundation for Ectodermal Dysplasias (EA)
NFEF .... National Free Enterprise Foundation [*Australia*]
NFEJ .... Nepal Forum of Environmental Journalists (SAUS)
NFER .... National Foundation for Educational Research [*British*] (DET)
NFER .... National Foundation for Educational Research in England and Wales (IID)
NFER .... National Foundation for Eye Research (EA)
NFER .... Nonferrous
NFERC .... National Fertilizer and Environmental Research Center (CARB)
NFERF .... National Fisheries Education and Research Foundation (EA)
NFERO .... Non Ferrous (VLIE)
NFES............ No Fire, Empty Seat [*Automotive safety, air bags*]
NFESC .... Naval Facilities Engineering Service Center (BCP)
NFET .... N-Channel Junction Field-Effect Transistor (IDOE)
NFETA.......... National Foundry and Engineering Training Association [*British*]
NFETM .... National Federation of Engineers' Tools Manufacturers (MHDB)
NFEW .... National Forum for Executive Women [*Washington, DC*] (EA)
NFEWA .... Newspaper Food Editors and Writers Association (EA)
NFF.............. Fogo Public Library, Newfoundland [*Library symbol*] [*National Library of Canada*] (NLC)
NFF.............. Jacksonville, FL [*Location identifier*] [*FAA*] (FAAL)
NFF.............. Natal Field Force [*British military*] (DMA)
NFF.............. National Fatherland Front [*Afghanistan*] [*Political party*] (FEA)
NFF.............. National Federation of Fishermen [*Inactive*] (EA)
NFF.............. National Federation of Fishmongers [*British*] (DBA)
NFF.............. National Fitness Foundation (EA)
NFF.............. National Flag Foundation (EA)
NFF.............. National Flood Frequency Program [*Computer science*]
NFF.............. National Football Foundation and Hall of Fame (EA)
NFF.............. National Forum Foundation (EA)
NFF.............. National Froebel Foundation [*British*] (BI)
NFF.............. Naval Fuel Facility
NFF.............. Neff Corp'A' [*NYSE symbol*] (SG)
NFF.............. Negation as Finite Failure (RALS)
NFF.............. Nemzeti Fueggetlensegi Front [*National Independence Front*] [*Hungary*] [*Political party*] (PPE)
NFF.............. Neutral File Format [*Computer science*] (VLIE)
NFF.............. New Forests Fund (EA)
NFF.............. No Failures Found (SAUS)
NFF.............. No Fault Found (MCD)
NFF.............. No Form Feed (VLIE)
NFF.............. No Frills Fund
Nff.............. Nordisk Forening for Folkendansforskning [*Nordic Association for Folk Dance Research*] [*Sweden*] (EAIO)
NFF.............. Normal Freezing Furnace (SAUS)
NFF.............. Nuclear Freeze Foundation [*Defunct*] (EA)
NFF.............. Numbered Fleet Flagship [*Navy*]
NFFA............ Ba [*Fiji*] [*ICAO location identifier*] (ICLI)
NFFA............ National Flying Farmers Association [*Later, International Flying Farmers*]
NFFA............ National Folk Festival Association [*Later, National Council for the TraditionalArts*]
NFFA............ National Frozen Food Association (EA)
NFFAO .... National FFA [*Future Farmers of America*] Organization (EA)
NFFAW .... Newfoundland Fishermen, Food and Allied Workers Union (SAUS)
NFFC............ Nancy Fisher Fan Club (EA)
NFFC............ National Family Farm Coalition (EA)
NFFC............ National Fantasy Fan Club for Disneyana Enthusiasts
NFFC............ National Film Finance Corp. [*British*] (BI)
NFFDA .... National Frozen Food Distributors Association [*Later, NFFA*]
NFFDF .... National Fraternal Flag Day Foundation [*Defunct*] (EA)
NFFE .... National Federation of Federal Employees (EA)
NFFF .... Nandi [*Fiji*] [*ICAO location identifier*] (ICLI)
NFFF .... National Fantasy Fan Federation
NFFF .... National Federation of Fish Friers [*British*] (BI)
NFFGB .... National Federation of Flemish Giant Breeders [*Later, NFFGRB*]
NFFGRB ...... National Federation of Flemish Giant Rabbit Breeders (EA)
NFFH .... Fox Harbour Public Library, Newfoundland [*Library symbol*] [*National Library of Canada*] (NLC)
NFFI............ Not Fit for Issue [*Navy*]
NFFL............ Northern Forest Fire Laboratory [*Later, Intermountain Fire Sciences Laboratory*] [*Research center*] (RCD)
NFFN............ Nandi/International [*Fiji*] [*ICAO location identifier*] (ICLI)
NFFO .... Fortune Public Library, Newfoundland [*Library symbol*] [*National Library of Canada*] (NLC)
NFFO .... Malolo Lailai [*Fiji*] [*ICAO location identifier*] (ICLI)
NFFO .... National Federation of Fishermen's Organisations (EAIO)
NFFO .... Non-Fossil Fuel Obligation [*Pronounced "Noffo"*] [*Nuclear power*]
NFFPT.......... National Federation of Fruit and Potato Trades [*British*] (BI)
NFFQO .... National Federation of Freestone Quarry Owners [*British*] (BI)
NFFR............ Freshwater Public Library, Newfoundland [*Library symbol*] [*National Library of Canada*] (NLC)
NFFR............ National Foundation for Facial Reconstruction (EA)
NFFR............ Rabi [*Fiji*] [*ICAO location identifier*] (ICLI)
NFFS............ National Foundation of Funeral Service (EA)
NFFS............ Nonfederal Financial Support (SAUS)
NFFS............ Non-Ferrous Founders Society (EA)
NFFTU .... National Federation of Furniture Trade Unions [*British*] (BI)
NFFWU .... Nordic Federation of Factory Workers Unions (EA)

NFG .... Gander Public Library, Newfoundland [*Library symbol*] [*National Library of Canada*] (NLC)
NFG .... Nagaland Federal Government [*India*]
NFG .... National Freight Group
NFG .... National Fuel Gas Co. [*NYSE symbol*] (SPSG)
NFG .... Natl Fuel Gas [*NYSE symbol*] (TTSB)
NFG .... Network Flow Graph [*Computer science*] (VLIE)
NFG .... No Flux Gate (SAUS)
NFG .... Northwest Fruit Growers (EA)
NFG .... Not Functioning Good (SAUS)
NFG .... Oceanside, CA [*Location identifier*] [*FAA*] (FAAL)
NFGA .... Garnish Public Library, Newfoundland [*Library symbol*] [*National Library of Canada*] (NLC)
NFGAU .... Gaultois Public Library, Newfoundland [*Library symbol*] [*National Library of Canada*] (BIB)
NFGB .... Grand Bank Public Library, Newfoundland [*Library symbol*] [*National Library of Canada*] (NLC)
NFGBM .... Medical Library, Melville Hospital, Goose-Bay, Newfoundland [*Library symbol*] [*National Library of Canada*] (BIB)
NFGBM .... National Fellowship of Grace Brethren Ministers (EA)
NFGC .... National Federation of Grain Cooperatives [*Later, NCFC*] (EA)
NFGCA .... National Federation of Grandmother Clubs of America (EA)
NFGF .... Regional Library, Grand Falls, Newfoundland [*Library symbol*] [*National Library of Canada*] (NLC)
NFGFC .... Central Region Libraries, Grand Falls, Newfoundland [*Library symbol*] [*National Library of Canada*] (NLC)
NFGFH .... Central Newfoundland Hospital, Grand Falls, Newfoundland [*Library symbol*] [*National Library of Canada*] (NLC)
NFGFHA .... Harmsworth Public Library, Grand Falls, Newfoundland [*Library symbol*] [*National Library of Canada*] (NLC)
NFGJPH .... James Paton Memorial Hospital, Gander, Newfoundland [*Library symbol*] [*National Library of Canada*] (NLC)
NFGL .... Glenwood Public Library, Newfoundland [*Library symbol*] [*National Library of Canada*] (NLC)
NFGLO .... Glovertown Public Library, Newfoundland [*Library symbol*] [*National Library of Canada*] (NLC)
NFGMIC .... National Federation of Grange Mutual Insurance Companies [*Glastonbury, CT*] (EA)
NFGND......... National Foundation for Genetics and Neuromuscular Disease [*Later, NGF*]
NFGNE .... National Fund for Graduate Nursing Education [*Defunct*]
NFGO .... Goulds Public Library, Newfoundland [*Library symbol*] [*National Library of Canada*] (BIB)
NFGOCM ...... National Forum of Greek Orthodox Church Musicians (EA)
NFGOPC...... National Federation of the Grand Order of Pachyderm Clubs (EA)
NFGR .... Greenspond Public Library, Newfoundland [*Library symbol*] [*National Library of Canada*] (NLC)
NFGS .... National Federation of Gramophone Societies (EAIO)
NFGS .... National Fenton Glass Society (EA)
NFH .... Holyrood Public Library, Newfoundland [*Library symbol*] [*National Library of Canada*] (BIB)
NFH .... National Federation of Hairdressers (WDAA)
NFH .... National Fish Hatchery
NFH .... Native Field Hospital [*British military*] (DMA)
NFH .... Nonfamilial Hematuria [*Medicine*] (DMAA)
NFHA .... National Federation of Housing Associations [*British*] (DBA)
NFHA .... National Fox Hunters Association (EA)
NFHANA....... Norwegian Fjord Horse Association of North America [*Later, NFANA*] (EA)
NFHAS .... National Faculty of Humanities, Arts, and Sciences (EA)
NFHB .... Harbour Breton Public Library, Newfoundland [*Library symbol*] [*National Library of Canada*] (NLC)
NFHBA .... Hare Bay Public Library, Newfoundland [*Library symbol*] [*National Library of Canada*] (NLC)
NFHC .... National Federation of Hispanics in Communication (EA)
NFHC .... National Federation of Housing Coops [*British*] (DBA)
NFHC .... National Federation of Housing Counselors (EA)
NFHC .... National Foot Health Council [*Defunct*] (EA)
NFHC .... National Foundation for History of Chemistry (EA)
NFHCF .... National Flotation Health Care Foundation (EA)
NFHD .... National Foundation for the Handicapped and Disabled [*Defunct*] (EA)
NFHE .... Hermitage Public Library, Newfoundland [*Library symbol*] [*National Library of Canada*] (NLC)
NFHE .... Non-Irradiated Fuel Handling Equipment [*Nuclear energy*] (NRCH)
NFHEA .... National Farm Home Editors Association [*Defunct*] (EA)
NFHG .... Harbour Grace Public Library, Newfoundland [*Library symbol*] [*National Library of Canada*] (NLC)
NFHH .... Harrys Harbour Public Library, Newfoundland [*Library symbol*] [*National Library of Canada*] (NLC)
NFhM .... Medical Society of the County of Queens, Forest Hills, NY [*Library symbol*] [*Library of Congress*] (LCLS)
NFHO .... Caaf Ho Nandi [*Fiji*] [*ICAO location identifier*] (ICLI)
NFHO .... National Federation of Housestaff Organizations (EA)
NFHON........ National Federation of Hispanic Owned Newspapers (NTPA)
NFHPER....... National Foundation for Health, Physical Education, and Recreation [*Defunct*]
NFHRL .... National Fish Health Research Laboratory [*Department of the Interior*] [*Kearneysville, WV*] (GRD)
NFHTP .... National Federation of Hebrew Teachers and Principals [*Defunct*] (EA)
NFHV .... Happy Valley Public Library, Newfoundland [*Library symbol*] [*National Library of Canada*] (NLC)
NFI.............. Narrow Fabrics Institute (EA)
NFI.............. National Fisheries Center [*Marine science*] (OSRA)

NFI...............	National Fisheries Institute (EA)
NFI...............	Natural Food Institute [*Defunct*] (EA)
NFI...............	Naturfreunde-Internationale [*International Friends of Nature - IFN*] (EAIO)
NFI...............	Net Fundable Issues (DNAB)
NFI...............	News Features of India [*Press agency*]
NFI...............	New Signet Resources [*Vancouver Stock Exchange symbol*]
NFI...............	Nielsen Food Index [*Marketing*] (DOAD)
NFI...............	Noise Figure Indicator
NFI...............	Not Further Identified (MCD)
NFI...............	NovaStar Financial [*NYSE symbol*] (SG)
NFI...............	Nutrition Foundation of India (SAUS)
NFIA...........	National Families in Action [*An association*] (EA)
NFIA...........	National Feed Ingredients Association (EA)
NFIA...........	National Flood Insurance Act of 1968 (COE)
NFIA...........	National Flood Insurers Association [*Defunct*] (EA)
NFIA...........	National Forest Industries Association [*Australia*]
NFIA...........	Nonappropriated Fund Instrumentalities Act
NFIAA.........	National Federation of Indian American Associations (EA)
NFIB...........	National Federation of Independent Business [*San Mateo, CA*] (EA)
NFIB...........	National Foreign Intelligence Board [*Formerly, USIB*] [*Military*]
NFIC...........	National Foundation for Ileitis and Colitis (EA)
NFIC...........	National Fraud Information Center
NFICA.........	National Federation Interscholastic Coaches Association (EA)
NFICA.........	National Forest Industries Campaign Association [*Australia*]
NFICSC.......	National Foundation for Ileitis and Colitis Sports Council (EA)
NFID...........	National Foundation for Infectious Diseases (EA)
NFIE...........	National Foundation for the Improvement of Education (EA)
NFIEC.........	Niagara Frontier Industry Education Council (SAUS)
NFIL...........	Nuclear Factor Interleukin [*Genetics*]
NFIMA........	National Federation Interscholastic Music Association (EA)
NFIMA........	Nonferrous Ingot Metal Institute (SAUS)
NFIOA.........	National Federation Interscholastic Officials Association (EA)
NFIP...........	National Flood Insurance Program [*Federal Emergency Management Agency*]
NFIP...........	National Foreign Intelligence Program [*DoD*]
NFIP...........	National Foreign Intelligence Programme (SAUS)
NFIP...........	National Foundation for Infantile Paralysis [*Later, MDBDF*]
NFIPA.........	National Fire Protection Association (WPI)
NFIPS.........	National Flood Insurance Program System [*Federal Emergency Management Agency*] (GFGA)
NFIR...........	National Federation of Indian Railwaymen
NFIRF.........	Nature Farming International Research Foundation (EAIO)
NFIRS.........	National Fire Incident Reporting System [*Federal Emergency Management Agency*] (GFGA)
NFIS...........	Naval Fighting Instruction School
NFIS...........	Nicolet Federated Library System (SAUS)
NFIS...........	Non-Formatted Information System [*Computer science*] (VLIE)
NFISDA.......	National Federation Interscholastic Speech and Debate Association (EA)
NFisi.........	Fishers Island Library Association, Fishers Island, NY [*Library symbol*] [*Library of Congress*] (LCLS)
NFisk.........	Blodgett Memorial Library, Fishkill, NY [*Library symbol*] [*Library of Congress*] (LCLS)
NFISM........	National Federation of Iron and Steel Merchants [*British*] (BI)
NFISYD.......	National Federation of Independent Scrap Yard Dealers (EA)
NFITC.........	National Forest Industries Training Council [*Australia*]
NFIU...........	National Federation of Independent Unions
NFJ...........	Milton, FL [*Location identifier*] [*FAA*] (FAAL)
NFJC...........	National Foundation for Jewish Culture (EA)
NFJGD........	National Foundation for Jewish Genetic Diseases (EA)
NFJM........	National Foundation for Junior Museums [*Later, NSYF*]
NFJMC.......	National Federation of Jewish Men's Clubs (EA)
NFJU........	Nordic Federation of Journalists Unions (SAUS)
NFK...........	Neuer Fundamentalkatalog (SAUS)
NFK...........	Niederfrequenz-Koppelfeld (SAUS)
NFK...........	Norfolk Island [*ANSI three-letter standard code*] (CNC)
NFK...........	Nuclear Factor Kappa (DMAA)
NFKK.........	Nordisk Forening for Klinisk Kemi [*Scandinavian Society for Clinical Chemistry - SSCC*] [*Finland*] (EAIO)
NFKP.........	Kings Point Public Library, Newfoundland [*Library symbol*] [*National Library of Canada*] (NLC)
NFKPA.......	National Federation of Kidney Patients Association [*British*] (DI)
NFL...........	Fallon, NV [*Location identifier*] [*FAA*] (FAAL)
NFL...........	Labrador City Public Library, Newfoundland [*Library symbol*] [*National Library of Canada*] (NLC)
NFL...........	National Federation of Laymen (EA)
NFL...........	National Film Library (NADA)
NFL...........	National Football League (EA)
NFL...........	National Forensic League (EA)
NFL...........	National Foresters League (NADA)
NFL...........	National Fund Leadership [*Group*] [*Red Cross*]
NFL...........	Naval Standard Flange (MSA)
NFL...........	Nerve Fiber Layer [*Neurology*] (DAVI)
NFL...........	Neurofilament Protein, Light Polypeptide (DMAA)
NFL...........	New Foreign Launch (ACAE)
NFL...........	Newfoundland and Prince Edward Island Reports [*Maritime Law Book Co. Ltd.*] [*Canada*] [*Information service or system*] (CRD)
NFL...........	Newfoundland Federation of Labour (SAUS)
NFL...........	Newfoundland Light & Power Co. Ltd. [*Toronto Stock Exchange symbol*]
NFL...........	Newlands Field Laboratory [*University of Nevada - Reno*] [*Research center*] (RCD)
NFL...........	No Field Lubrication (PDAA)
NFL...........	No Fire Line [*Military*]
NFL...........	No Phone Listed [*Cablegram marking*] [*British*]
NFL...........	Normal Female Liver [*Hepatology*]
NFL...........	Northaire Freight Lines Ltd. [*ICAO designator*] (FAAC)
NFL...........	Nurses for Laughter
NFL...........	Nuveen Ins FL Prem Inc. Muni [*NYSE symbol*] (TTSB)
NFL...........	Nuveen Insured Florida Premium Income Municipal [*NYSE symbol*] (SPSG)
NFLA.........	L'Anse Au Loup Public Library, Newfoundland [*Library symbol*] [*National Library of Canada*] (NLC)
NFLA.........	National Football League Alumni (EA)
NFLA.........	National Front for the Liberation of Angola (EA)
NFLA.........	Nuclear-Free Local Authorities (WDAA)
NFL Alumni...	National Football League Alumni [*An association*] (EA)
NFLC.........	National Federation of Land Councils [*Australia*]
NFLC.........	Northern Forest Lands Council (WPI)
NFLCC........	National Fishing Lure Collectors Club (EA)
NFLCP........	National Federation of Local Cable Programmers (EA)
NFLD.........	Nerve Fiber Layer Defect [*Medicine*] (DMAA)
Nfld.........	Newfoundland [*Canada*] (DD)
NFLD.........	Newfoundland [*with Labrador, a Canadian province*]
Nfld.........	Newfoundland Supreme Court Decisions [*Canada*] [*A publication*] (DLA)
NFLD.........	Northfield Laboratories [*NASDAQ symbol*] (TTSB)
NFLD.........	Northfield Laboratories, Inc. [*NASDAQ symbol*] (SAG)
Nfld LR.......	Newfoundland Law Reports [*A publication*] (DLA)
Nfld R.......	Newfoundland Reports [*A publication*] (DLA)
Nfld Rev Stat...	Newfoundland Revised Statutes [*Canada*] [*A publication*] (DLA)
NFLDS........	National Fire Loss Data System [*Military*] (PDAA)
Nfld Sel Cas...	Newfoundland Select Cases [*A publication*] (DLA)
Nfld Stat.....	Newfoundland Statutes [*Canada*] [*A publication*] (DLA)
NFLE.........	Lewisporte Public Library, Newfoundland [*Library symbol*] [*National Library of Canada*] (NLC)
NFLF.........	National Family Life Foundation (EA)
NFLF.........	Nylon Full-Line Filter
NFLHB........	Blow Me Down School/Public Library, Lark Harbour, Newfoundland [*Library symbol*] [*National Library of Canada*] (NLC)
NFLI.........	Northern Fraternal Life Insurance (EA)
NFLI.........	Nutrition For Life International, Inc. [*NASDAQ symbol*] (SAG)
NFLI.........	Nutrition For Life Intl. [*NASDAQ symbol*] (TTSB)
NFLIO........	Training Department, Iron Ore Co. of Canada, Labrador City, Newfoundland [*Library symbol*] [*National Library of Canada*] (NLC)
NFLIW........	Nutrition For Life Intl. Wrrt [*NASDAQ symbol*] (TTSB)
NflkSo........	Norfolk Southern Corp. [*Associated Press*] (SAG)
NFLO.........	Lourdes Public Library, Newfoundland [*Library symbol*] [*National Library of Canada*] (NLC)
NFlp.........	Floral Park Public Library, Floral Park (SAUS)
NFlp.........	Floral Park Public Library, Floral Park, NY [*Library symbol*] [*Library of Congress*] (LCLS)
NFLPA........	National Football League Players Association (EA)
NFLPA........	National Free Lance Photographers Association (EA)
NFlpBE........	Floral Park-Bellerose Elementary School, Floral Park, NY [*Library symbol*] [*Library of Congress*] (LCLS)
NFlpCE........	John Lewis Childs Elementary School, Floral Park, NY [*Library symbol*] [*Library of Congress*] (LCLS)
NFlpMH........	Floral Park Memeorial High School, Floral Park, NY [*Library symbol*] [*Library of Congress*] (LCLS)
NFLPN........	National Federation of Licensed Practical Nurses (EA)
NFlpSH........	Sewanhaka High School, Floral Park, NY [*Library symbol*] [*Library of Congress*] (LCLS)
NFLQI.........	Nuveen Florida Quality Income Municipal Fund [*Associated Press*] (SAG)
NFLS.........	La Scie Public Library, Newfoundland [*Library symbol*] [*National Library of Canada*] (NLC)
NFLS.........	Nicolet Federated Library System [*Library network*]
NFLSV........	National Front for the Liberation of South Vietnam
NFLTHC........	National Foundation for Long Term Health Care [*Defunct*] (EA)
NFLU.........	Lumsden Public Library, Newfoundland [*Library symbol*] [*National Library of Canada*] (NLC)
NFM.........	Conception Bay South Public Library, Manuels, Newfoundland [*Library symbol*] [*National Library of Canada*] (NLC)
NFM.........	Midland Lutheran College, Fremont, NE [*OCLC symbol*] (OCLC)
NFM.........	Narrowband Frequency Modulation [*Radio*]
NFM.........	Network File Manager [*Computer science*] (VLIE)
NFM.........	Neurofilament Protein, Medium Polypeptide (DMAA)
NFM.........	New Frontiers of Medicine [*An association*] (EA)
NFM.........	Next Full Moon [*Freemasonry*] (ROG)
NFM.........	Noise Figure Meter
NFM.........	Nonfat Milk (OA)
NFM.........	Nonferromagnetic (SAUS)
NFM.........	Nonferrous Metal
NFM.........	Normal Fundamental Mode (SAUS)
NFM.........	Northern Fowl Mite [*Immunology*]
NFM.........	North-Finding Module (RDA)
NFM.........	Nuclear Ferromagnetism (SAUS)
NFMA.........	Marystown Public Library, Newfoundland [*Library symbol*] [*National Library of Canada*] (NLC)
NFMA.........	National Federation of Municipal Analysts (NTPA)
NFMA.........	National Fireplace Makers Association [*British*] (BI)
NFMA.........	National Footwear Manufacturers Association [*Later, FIA*]
NFMA.........	National Forest Management Act (GFGA)
NFMA.........	Needleroom Felt Manufacturers Association [*British*] (DBA)
NFMA.........	Northwest Farm Managers Association (EA)
NFMA.........	Norwegian Furniture Manufacturers Association (SAUS)

NFMA............	November, February, May, and August [*Denotes quarterly payments of interest or dividends in these months*] [*Business term*]
NFMAA	National Federation Music Adjudicator Association (EA)
NFMC............	National Federation of Music Clubs (EA)
NFMC............	National Film Music Council [*Defunct*]
NFMC............	Not Fully Mission Capable (ACAE)
NFMC............	Nutritious Food Management Committee (SAUS)
NFMCS	Not Fully Mission Capable Supply (SAUS)
NFMD	National Foundation for Muscular Dystrophy
NFMD	National Foundation for the March of Dimes (NADA)
NFME	National Fund for Medical Education (EA)
NFME	Nordic Federation for Medical Education [*Denmark*] (EAIO)
NFMHA	National Federation of Milk Hauler Associations (EA)
NFMHJ..........	John B. Wheeler Memorial Library, Musgrave Harbour, Newfoundland [*Library symbol*] [*National Library of Canada*] (NLC)
NFMHO.........	National Foundation Manufactured Home Owners (EA)
NFMLTA.......	National Federation of Modern Language Teachers Associations (EA)
NFMM..........	National Fellowship of Methodist Musicians (EA)
NFMN	National Fallout Monitoring Network
NFMOA	National Fish Meal and Oil Association (EA)
NFMP...........	Mount Pearl Public Library, Newfoundland [*Library symbol*] [*National Library of Canada*] (NLC)
NFMP...........	National Federation of Master Painters and Decorators of England and Wales (BI)
NFMP...........	Nonferrous Metal Powder
NFMPC	Non-Ferrous Metals Producers Committee (EA)
NFMR	National Foundation for Metabolic Research [*Defunct*] (EA)
NFMR	Non-Linear Ferromagnetic Resonance (PDAA)
NFMR	Nordisk Forening for Medisinsk Radiologi [*Scandinavian Radiological Society - SRS*] (EAIO)
NFMRAD......	Null Filter Mobile RADAR (PDAA)
NFMS...........	National Federation of Music Societies [*British*]
NFMS...........	National Fetal Mortality Survey [*Department of Health and Human Services*] (GFGA)
NFMS...........	Navy Fleet Material Support (MCD)
NFMS...........	Nitrogen Flow Measuring System
NFMS...........	Noise Figure Meter System
NFMS...........	Nonfat Milk Solids (OA)
NFMSAEG	Naval Fleet Missile System Analysis and Evaluation Group
NFMSAEGA...	Naval Fleet Missile System Analysis and Evaluation Group Annex (MCD)
NFMSO	Navy Fleet Material Support Office (DNAB)
NFMT...........	National Federation of Meat Traders [*British*] (BI)
NFMT...........	Navy Food Management Team (DNAB)
NFMWC	National Federation of Master Window Cleaners [*British*] (DBA)
NFMY	National Festival of Music for Youth (AIE)
NFN	National Fathers' Network [*An association*] (PAZ)
NFN	National Federation of Non-Profits (NTPA)
NFN	Newly Founded Nest [*Ornithology*]
NFN	No Form Necessary
NFN	No Further Need (MUGU)
NFn	Not for Resuscitation [*Medicine*] (WDAA)
NFn	Nouvelle Front NAZI [*New NAZI Front*] [*French*] (PD)
NFNA	National Flight Nurses Association (EA)
NFNA	Nausori/International [*Fiji*] [*ICAO location identifier*] (ICLI)
NFNA	Norris Arm Public Library, Newfoundland [*Library symbol*] [*National Library of Canada*] (NLC)
NFNB	Bureta [*Fiji*] [*ICAO location identifier*] (ICLI)
NFND	Deumba [*Fiji*] [*ICAO location identifier*] (ICLI)
NFND	National Foundation for Neuromuscular Diseases [*Later, NGF*] (EA)
NFNG	Ngau [*Fiji*] [*ICAO location identifier*] (ICLI)
NFNH	Lauthala Islands [*Fiji*] [*ICAO location identifier*] (ICLI)
NFNID..........	National Foundation for Non-Invasive Diagnostics (EA)
NFNK	Lakemba [*Fiji*] [*ICAO location identifier*] (ICLI)
NFNL	Lambasa [*Fiji*] [*ICAO location identifier*] (ICLI)
NFNLI	Labrador Inuit Association, Nain, Newfoundland [*Library symbol*] [*National Library of Canada*] (NLC)
NFNLI	Labrador Unit Association, Nain, Newfoundland [*Library symbol*] [*National Library of Canada*] (NLC)
NFNM	Matei [*Fiji*] [*ICAO location identifier*] (ICLI)
NFNN	Vanuabalavu [*Fiji*] [*ICAO location identifier*] (ICLI)
NFNO	Koro [*Fiji*] [*ICAO location identifier*] (ICLI)
NFNP	National Food and Nutrition Policy [*Australia*]
NFNP	Norris Point Public Library, Newfoundland [*Library symbol*] [*National Library of Canada*] (NLC)
NFNR	Rotuma [*Fiji*] [*ICAO location identifier*] (ICLI)
NFNS	Neurofibromatosis-Noonan Syndrome [*Medicine*] (DMAA)
NFNS	Savusavu [*Fiji*] [*ICAO location identifier*] (ICLI)
N FNSHD......	Not Finished [*Freight*]
NFNT	New Font Numbering Table (SAUS)
NFNTU.........	National Federation of Furniture Trade Union [*British*]
NFNU	Bua [*Fiji*] [*ICAO location identifier*] (ICLI)
NFNU	National Federation of Nurses' Unions [*See also FNSII*]
NFNV	Vatukoula [*Fiji*] [*ICAO location identifier*] (ICLI)
NFNW	Wakaya [*Fiji*] [*ICAO location identifier*] (ICLI)
NFNWF........	Navy Fleet Numerical Weather Facility [*Marine science*] (MSC)
NFO	National Family Opinion
NFO	National Farmers Organization (EA)
NFO	Naval Flight Officer
NFO	Navy Finance Office
NFO	News from the Ukraine [*A publication*]
NFO	NFO Worldwide [*NYSE symbol*] (SG)
NFO	Non-Fluid Oil (SAUS)
NFO	Non Free Out (SAUS)

NFO	Normal Fuel Oil (DNAB)
NFO	Norvell Family Organization (EA)
NFO	Not Fully Open (MCD)
NFOAPA.......	National Federation of Old Age Pensioners' Associations [*British*] (BI)
NFO(B).........	Naval Flight Officer (Bombardier) (DNAB)
NFOBA	National Fats and Oils Brokers Association [*Defunct*] (EA)
NFOC	Naval Facility Operational Center (DNAB)
NFOC	Naval Flight Officer Candidate (DNAB)
NFO(C)........	Naval Flight Officer (Controller) (DNAB)
NFOF	Fiji [*Fiji*] [*ICAO location identifier*] (ICLI)
NFOFL	National Federation of Officers for Life (EA)
NFOHA	National Federation of Off-Licence Holders Associations of England and Wales (BI)
NFO(I).........	Naval Flight Officer (RADAR Intercept) (DNAB)
NFOIO	Naval Field Operational Intelligence Office (NVT)
NFOIODET....	Naval Field Operational Intelligence Office Detachment (DNAB)
NFOM	Near Field Optical Microscopy (AAEL)
NFO(N)	Naval Flight Officer (Navigator) (DNAB)
NFOO	Naval Forward Observing Officer [*British military*] (DMA)
NFOP	National Fraternal Order of Police (NTPA)
NFOP	Old Perlican Public Library, Newfoundland [*Library symbol*] [*National Library of Canada*] (NLC)
NFoPA	National Forest Products Association [*Washington, DC*]
NFOR	National Forest Products Association
NFOR	NFO Research [*NASDAQ symbol*] (TTSB)
NFOR	NFO Research, Inc. [*NASDAQ symbol*] (SAG)
NFO Rs	NFO Research, Inc. [*Associated Press*] (SAG)
NFOSG........	Naval Field Operations Support Group
NFOU	Number of Fourier Coefficients (SAUS)
NFOV	Narrow Field of View
NFP	Marietta, GA [*Location identifier*] [*FAA*] (FAAL)
NFP	Nandrolone Furylpropionate [*Pharmacology*]
NFP	National Family Partnership [*An association*] (EA)
NFP	National Federation of Parents for Drug-Free Youth (EA)
NFP	National Federation Party [*Fiji*] [*Political party*] (PPW)
NFP	National Fire Academy Library, Emmitsburg, MD [*OCLC symbol*] (OCLC)
NFP	National Focal Points (DCTA)
NFP	Nationalist Front for Progress [*Solomon Islands*] [*Political party*] (FEA)
NFP	Natural Family Planning
NFP	Neighborhood Facilities Program (OICC)
NFP	Network Facilities Package [*Computer science*] (ELAL)
NFP	Network for Fitness Professionals [*Australia*]
NFP	Neurofilament Protein [*Neurophysiology*]
NFP	New Federalist Party (EA)
NFP	New Forests Project (EA)
NFP	New Frontier Party [*Japan*] [*Political party*]
NFP	New Frontier Petroleum Corp. (SAUS)
NFP	N-Formylmethionylphenylalanine [*Biochemistry*]
NFP	No File Protect [*Computer science*] (VLIE)
NFP	Nonflare Proton
NFP	Norfolk Petroleum Ltd. [*Vancouver Stock Exchange symbol*]
NFP	Normal Failure Period
NFP	Northern Frontier Province [*Kenya*]
NFP	Not for Profit (ADA)
NFP	Not for Publication (ADA)
NFP	Nuclear Fire Plan (SAUS)
NFP	Nuclear Fuel Processing (SAUS)
NFP	Placentia Public Library, Newfoundland [*Library symbol*] [*National Library of Canada*] (NLC)
NFPA	National Federation of Paralegal Associations (EA)
NFPA	National Fire Protection Association (EA)
NFPA	National Flaxseed Processors Association (EA)
NFPA	National Flexible Packaging Association [*Later, FPA*] (EA)
NFPA	National Flight Paramedics Association (EA)
NFPA	National Fluid Power Association (EA)
NFPA	National Food Processors Association (EA)
NFPA	National Forest Products Association (EA)
NFPA	National Foster Parent Association (EA)
NFPA	Natural Family Planning Association of Connecticut (EA)
NFPA	Niagara Frontier Port Authority (SAUS)
NFPA	Pasadena Public Library, Newfoundland [*Library symbol*] [*National Library of Canada*] (NLC)
NFPB	National Friends of Public Broadcasting (EA)
NFPC	National Federation of Plastering Contractors [*British*] (BI)
NFPC	National Federation of Priests' Councils (EA)
NFPC	National Forest Planning Committee (WPI)
NFPC	Niagara Falls Power Co. (SAUS)
NFPC	Pouch Cove Public Library, Newfoundland [*Library symbol*] [*National Library of Canada*] (NLC)
NFPCA	National Fire Prevention and Control Administration [*Later, United States Fire Administration*] [*Department of Commerce*]
NFPDC........	National Federation of Painting and Decorating Contractors [*British*] (DBA)
NFPDHE......	National Federation of Plumbers and Domestic Heating Engineers [*British*] (BI)
NFPE	NATO Force Planning Exercise (NATG)
NFPE	Non-Financial Public Enterprise [*British*]
NFPEC	Curran Memorial Library, Port Au Port East, Newfoundland [*Library symbol*] [*National Library of Canada*] (NLC)
NFPEDA.......	National Farm and Power Equipment Dealers Association [*Later, NAEDA*] (EA)
NF/PFOG......	National Federation of Parents and Friends of Gays (EA)

NFPHC......... National Federation of Permanent Holiday Camps Ltd. [*British*] (BI)
NFPI............. National Frozen Pizza Institute (EA)
NFPL............. Point Leamington Public Library, Newfoundland [*Library symbol*] [*National Library of Canada*] (NLC)
NFPLA .... National Foundation for Professional Legal Assistants (EA)
NFPM........... Nuclear Flight Propulsion Module (KSC)
NFPMA .... National Feeder Pig Marketing Association (EA)
NFPMA .... National Foundation for Peroneal Muscular Atrophy (EA)
NFPMC .... National Farm Products Marketing Council [*Canada*]
NFPNS......... Natural Family Planning National Secretariat [*Australia*]
NFPO .... National Federation of Professional Organizations (EA)
NFPO .... National Federation of Property Owners [*British*] (BI)
NFPOC......... National Federation of Post Office Clerks [*Later, APWU*]
NFPOD......... National Foundation for the Prevention of Oral Disease [*Defunct*] (EA)
NFPPE .... Nuclear Force Policy, Planning and Execution (SAUS)
NFPR .... National Fund for Research into Poliomyelitis and Other Crippling Diseases [*British*] (BI)
NFPRHA ...... National Family Planning and Reproductive Health Association (EA)
NFPs............ National Focal Points (SAUS)
NFPS .... Naval Flight Preparatory School
NFPS .... Naval Future Policy Staff [*British*]
NFPS .... Navy Field Purchase Systems (NG)
NFPS .... Nuclear Flight Propulsion System (AAG)
NFPS .... Port Saunders Public Library, Newfoundland [*Library symbol*] [*National Library of Canada*] (NLC)
NFPTC .... National Federation of Postal and Telegraph Clerks [*A union*] [*British*]
NFPW .... National Federation of Press Women (EA)
NFPW .... National Federation of Professional Workers [*British*] (DI)
NFPW .... Port Au Port West School/Public Library, Newfoundland [*Library symbol*] [*National Library of Canada*] (NLC)
NFQ .... Night Frequency (FAAC)
NFQC .... Queens College, Flushing, NY [*Library symbol*] [*Library of Congress*] (LCLS)
NFR .... National Field Research [*British*]
NFR .... National Film Board Reference Library [*UTLAS symbol*]
NFR .... National Finals Rodeo
NFR .... National Fire Rating (SARE)
NFR .... NATO Frigate Replacement (SAUS)
NFR .... Naturvetenskapliga forskningsradet [*Swedish Natural Science Research Council*]
NFR .... Near-Field Recording [*Computer science*] (PCM)
NFR .... Negative Flux Rate (IEEE)
NFR .... Nephron Filtration Rate [*Physiology*]
NFR .... Net Financing Requirement
NFR .... Net Flux Radiometer [*Instrumentation*]
NFR .... New Frontier Petroleum Corp. [*Vancouver Stock Exchange symbol*]
nfr .... no further record found (SAUS)
NFR .... Nordisk Forening for Rehabilitering [*Nordic Association for Rehabilitation*] (EAIO)
NFR .... Northeast Frontier Railway (SAUS)
N FR............. Northern French [*Language, etc.*] (ROG)
NFR .... Norwegian Research Council (SAUS)
NFR .... Not a Functional Requirement (SAUS)
NFR .... Not for Report (SAUS)
NFR .... Not for Resuscitation [*Hospital patient classification*]
NFR .... Nothing Further to Report (SAUS)
NFR .... Nuclear Fission Reactor
NFR .... Nuclear Fuel Reprocessing (SAUS)
NFR .... Nursing Field Representative [*Red Cross*]
NFR-90 .... NATO Frigate for the 1990s
NFRA .... National Forest Recreation Association (EA)
NFRA .... Robert's Arm Public Library, Newfoundland [*Library symbol*] [*National Library of Canada*] (BIB)
NFRAP......... No Further Remedial Action Planned (EEVL)
NFRAP......... No Further Response Action Planned (BCP)
NFRC .... National Federation of Roofing Contractors [*British*] (EAIO)
NFRC .... National Fenestration Rating Council (EA)
NFRC .... National Finals Rodeo Committee (EA)
NFRC .... National Forest Research Council (WPI)
NFRC .... National Forest Reservation Commission [*Terminated, 1976; functions transferred to Department of Agriculture*]
NFRC .... Northeast Financial Resources Corp. (SAUS)
NFRC .... Northwest First Regional Consultants (SAUS)
NFRCD......... National Fund for Research into Crippling Diseases [*British*] (DI)
NFred........... Darwin R. Barker Library Association, Fredonia, NY [*Library symbol*] [*Library of Congress*] (LCLS)
NFredCB ...... Chautauqua County Board of Cooperative Educational Services, Fredonia, NY [*Library symbol*] [*Library of Congress*] (LCLS)
NFredU .... State University of New York, College at Fredonia, Fredonia, NY [*Library symbol*] [*Library of Congress*] (LCLS)
NFree........... Freeport Memorial Library, Freeport, NY [*Library symbol*] [*Library of Congress*] (LCLS)
NFreeAE ...... Archer Elementary School, Freeport, NY [*Library symbol*] [*Library of Congress*] (LCLS)
NFreeAtE ..... Caroline G. Atkinson Elementary School, Freeport, NY [*Library symbol*] [*Library of Congress*] (LCLS)
NFreeBE ...... Bayview Avenue Elementary School, Freeport, NY [*Library symbol*] [*Library of Congress*] (LCLS)
NFreeCE ...... Columbus Elementary School, Freeport, NY [*Library symbol*] [*Library of Congress*] (LCLS)
NFreeDH...... Doctors Hospital, Freeport, NY [*Library symbol*] [*Library of Congress*] (LCLS)

NFreeDJ ...... Dodd Junior High School, Freeport, NY [*Library symbol*] [*Library of Congress*] (LCLS)
NFreeEC ...... Early Childhood Center, Freeport, NY [*Library symbol*] [*Library of Congress*] (LCLS)
NFreeGE ...... Leo F. Giblyn Elementary School, Freeport, NY [*Library symbol*] [*Library of Congress*] (LCLS)
NFreeH .... Freeport Hospital, Freeport, NY [*Library symbol*] [*Library of Congress*] (LCLS)
NFreeHS...... Freeport High School, Freeport, NY [*Library symbol*] [*Library of Congress*] (LCLS)
NFRH .... Rocky Harbour Public School, Newfoundland [*Library symbol*] [*National Library of Canada*] (NLC)
NFRM .... National Foundation for Research in Medicine (EA)
NFRMC .... National Foundation for Rural Medical Care [*Defunct*] (EA)
NFRN .... National Federation of Retail Newsagents [*British*]
NFRP .... Marie S. Penney Memorial Library, Ramea, Newfoundland [*Library symbol*] [*National Library of Canada*] (NLC)
NFRRC......... Nuclear Fuel Recovery and Receiving Center (NRCH)
NFRS .... National Fancy Rat Society [*British*] (DBA)
NFRW .... National Federation of Republican Women (EA)
NFS .... Fayetteville State University, Fayetteville, NC [*OCLC symbol*] (OCLC)
NFs .... Franklin Square Public Library, Franklin Square, NY [*Library symbol*] [*Library of Congress*] (LCLS)
NFS .... National Aeronautics and Space Administration FAR Supplement [*A publication*] (AAGC)
NFS .... National Federation of Settlements [*Later, UNCA*]
NFS .... National Fertility Study
NFS............. National Field Service Corp. [*Suffern, NY*] [*Telecommunications*] (TSSD)
NFS .... National Film Society [*Defunct*] (EA)
NFS .... National Fire Service [*British*]
NFS .... National Flying Service [*British*]
NFS .... National Food Situation [*Series*] [*A publication*]
NFS .... National Food Survey [*British*]
NFS .... National Forest Service (COE)
NFS .... National Forest System (GNE)
NFS .... National Fuchsia Society (EA)
NFS .... Nationwide Finl Svcs'A' [*NYSE symbol*] (SG)
NFS .... Naval Flying Station [*British*]
NFS .... Navy Facilities System
NFS .... Navy Field Service
NFS .... Network Facilities Services (SAUS)
NFS .... Network File System
NFS .... Neutron Flux Spectra [*Nuclear energy*]
NFS .... Neutron Flux Spectrum (SAUS)
NFS .... New Fighter Squadron (SAUS)
NFS .... New Financial Status (SAUS)
NFS .... Nitrofuraldehyde Semicarbazone [*Germicide*]
NFS .... Nitrogen Flow System
NFS .... No Fracture Seen [*Medicine*] (DMAA)
NFS .... Noise Frequency Spectrum
NFS .... Nonfriendly Submarines (MCD)
NFS .... Non Functional Status (SAUS)
NFS .... Nordiska Forbundet for Statskunskap [*Nordic Political Science Association - NPSA*] [*Norway*] (EAIO)
NFS .... Not for Sale
NFS .... Not Fully Successful (SAUS)
NFS .... Not on Flying Status
NFS .... Nozzle Flow Sensor (MCD)
NFS .... Nuclear Facility Safety (SAUS)
NFS .... Nuclear Fuel Services, Erwin, Tennessee (SAUS)
NFS .... Nuclear Fuel Services Fuel Fabrication Plant
NFS .... Nuclear Fuel Services Plant (NRCH)
NFS............. Number Field Sieve (SAUS)
NFS .... NWFS Capital Financing Trust [*NYSE symbol*] (SAG)
NFSA .... National Federation of Sea Anglers [*British*]
NFSA .... National Fertilizer Solutions Association (EA)
NFSA .... National Field Selling Association (NTPA)
NFSA .... National Fire Sprinkler Association (EA)
NFSA .... National Food Service Association (EA)
NFSA .... National Food Standards Agreement [*Australia*]
NFSA .... Navy Field Safety Association (EA)
NFSA .... New Fuel Storage Area (NRCH)
NFSA .... News from Saudi Arabia [*A publication*] (BJA)
NFSA .... Provincial Archives of Newfoundland and Labrador, St. John's, Newfoundland [*Library symbol*] [*National Library of Canada*] (NLC)
NFSAG .... Research Station, Agriculture Canada [*Station de Recherches, Agriculture Canada*] St. John's, Newfoundland [*Library symbol*] [*National Library of Canada*] (NLC)
NFSAIC........ Charles Curtis Memorial Hospital, International Grenfell Association, St. Anthony, Newfoundland [*Library symbol*] [*National Library of Canada*] (NLC)
NFSAIS .... National Federation of Science Abstracting and Indexing Services [*Later, NFAIS*] (EA)
NFSAL .... St. Alban's Public Library, Newfoundland [*Library symbol*] [*National Library of Canada*] (NLC)
NFSAN .... St. Anthony Public Library, Newfoundland [*Library symbol*] [*National Library of Canada*] (NLC)
NFS & NC .... National Federation of Settlements and Neighborhood Centers [*Later, UNCA*] (EA)
NFSANS....... Naskapi School/Public Library, Sops Arm, Newfoundland [*Library symbol*] [*National Library of Canada*] (NLC)
NFSB .... Spaniards Bay Public Library, Newfoundland [*Library symbol*] [*National Library of Canada*] (NLC)

NFSBC .... Boys' Club, St. John's, Newfoundland [*Library symbol*] [*National Library of Canada*] (NLC)

NFSBCS .... Cape Shore Public Library, St. Brides, Newfoundland [*Library symbol*] [*National Library of Canada*] (NLC)

NFSBS .... Bay St. George Community College, Stephenville, Newfoundland [*Library symbol*] [*National Library of Canada*] (NLC)

NFSC .... National Federation of Stamp Clubs (EA)

NFSC .... Nuclear Fuel Services Corporation (ABAC)

NFSC .... Seal Cove Public Library, Newfoundland [*Library symbol*] [*National Library of Canada*] (NLC)

NFSCA .... Children's and Adults' Library, St. John's, Newfoundland [*Library symbol*] [*National Library of Canada*] (NLC)

NFSCAEE ..... Environment Division, Newfoundland Department of Consumer Affairs and Environment, St. John's, Newfoundland [*Library symbol*] [*National Library of Canada*] (NLC)

NFSCCU .... National Federation of Savings and Cooperative Credit Unions [*British*] (DBA)

NFSCF .... Newfoundland and Labrador Institute of Fisheries and Marine Technology (Marine Institute), St. John's, New Foundland [*Library symbol*] [*National Library of Canada*] (NLC)

NFsCH .... H. Frank Carey High School, Franklin Square, NY [*Library symbol*] [*Library of Congress*] (LCLS)

NFSCJ .... Dr. Charles A. Janeway Child Health Centre, St. John's, Newfoundland [*Library symbol*] [*National Library of Canada*] (NLC)

NFSCR .... Children's Rehabilitation Centre, St. John's, Newfoundland [*Library symbol*] [*National Library of Canada*] (NLC)

NFSCSW .... National Federation of Societies for Clinical Social Work (EA)

NFSCT .... Cabot Institute of Applied Arts and Technology, St. John's, Newfoundland [*Library symbol*] [*National Library of Canada*] (NLC)

NFSCTM ...... Topsail Campus Resource Centre, Cabot Institute of Applied Arts and Technology, St. John's, Newfoundland [*Library symbol*] [*National Library of Canada*] (NLC)

NFSD .... National Aeronautics and Space Administration FAR Supplement Directive (AAGC)

NFSD .... National Federation of Spiritual Directors (EA)

NFSD .... National Food Safety Database (SAUS)

NFSD .... National Fraternal Society of the Deaf [*Mount Prospect, IL*] (EA)

NFSD .... Nonfused (MSA)

NFSE .... National Federation for the Self-Employed and Small Businesses [*British*] (DBA)

NFSE .... National Federation of Sales Executives [*Later, Sales and Marketing Executives International*]

NFSE .... National Federation of Self Employed [*British*]

NFSEC .... Newfoundland Forest Research Centre, Environment Canada [*Centre de RecherchesForestieres de Terre-Neuve, Environnement Canada*] St. John's, Newfoundland [*Library symbol*] [*National Library of Canada*] (NLC)

NFSEEP .... National Foundation for the Study of Equal Employment [*Washington, DC*] (EA)

NFSF .... National Freedom Shrine Foundation (EA)

NFSF .... NFS Financial Corp. [*NASDAQ symbol*] (NQ)

NFSF .... North-West Atlantic Fisheries Centre, Fisheries and Oceans Canada [*Centre de Pecheries de l'Atlantique du Nord-Ouest, Peches et Oceans Canada*] St. John's,Newfoundland [*Library symbol*] [*National Library of Canada*] (NLC)

NFSFJG .... St. Judes Central High School Public Library/Bay St. George South Public LibraryLibrary, St. Fintans, Newfoundland [*Library symbol*] [*National Library of Canada*] (NLC)

NFSFS .... Newfoundland Forest Service, St. John's, Newfoundland [*Library symbol*] [*National Library of Canada*] (NLC)

NFSG .... National Federation of Students of German (EA)

NFSG .... Newfoundland Public Library Services, St. Johns, Newfoundland (SAUS)

NFSG .... Provinical Reference and Resource Library, Newfoundland Public Library Services,St. John's, New Foundland [*Library symbol*] [*National Library of Canada*] (NLC)

NFSGE .... St. Georges Public Library, Newfoundland [*Library symbol*] [*National Library of Canada*] (NLC)

NFSGGH ...... C. A Pippy Jr. Medical Library, Grace General Hospital, St. John's, Newfoundland [*Library symbol*] [*National Library of Canada*] (NLC)

NFSGGHN .... School of Nursing, Grace General Hospital, St. John's, Newfoundland [*Library symbol*] [*National Library of Canada*] (NLC)

NFSGH .... General Hospital Corp., St. John's, Newfoundland [*Library symbol*] [*National Library of Canada*] (NLC)

NFSGHN ...... Nursing Education, General Hospital Corp., St. John's, Newfoundland [*Library symbol*] [*National Library of Canada*] (NLC)

NFSGO .... Gosling Library, St. John's, Newfoundland [*Library symbol*] [*National Library of Canada*] (NLC)

NFSH .... National Federation of Spiritual Healers (EA)

NFSH .... National Federation of State High School Associations

NFSH .... Southern Harbour Public Library, Newfoundland [*Library symbol*] [*National Library of Canada*] (NLC)

NFSHC .... National Federation of State Humanities Councils (EA)

NFSHE .... Health Education Division, Newfoundland Department of Health, St. John's, Newfoundland [*Library symbol*] [*National Library of Canada*] (NLC)

NFSHPH .... Public Health Nursing Division, Newfoundland Department of Health, St. John's, Newfoundland [*Library symbol*] [*National Library of Canada*] (NLC)

NFSHSA .... National Federation of State High School Associations (EA)

NFSHSAA ..... National Federation of State High School Athletic Associations [*Later, NFSHSA*] (EA)

NFSICA .... Institute of Chartered Accountants of Newfoundland, St. John's, Newfoundland [*Library symbol*] [*National Library of Canada*] (NLC)

NFsJE .... John Street Elementary School, Franklin Square, NY [*Library symbol*] [*Library of Congress*] (LCLS)

NFSJL .... Law Library, Newfoundland Department of Justice, St. John's, Newfoundland [*Library symbol*] [*National Library of Canada*] (NLC)

NFSK .... Kindale Public Library, Stephenville, Newfoundland [*Library symbol*] [*National Library of Canada*] (NLC)

NFSK .... Narrowband Frequency Shift Keying (MCD)

NFSL .... Legislative Library, St. John's, Newfoundland [*Library symbol*] [*National Library of Canada*] (NLC)

NFSL .... Newnan Savings Bank [*NASDAQ symbol*] (NQ)

NFSL .... Newnan Svgs Bank FSB [*NASDAQ symbol*] (TTSB)

NFSL .... No Fighter Suitably Located (SAA)

NFSL .... Nucleus Fleet Sealift

NFSLA .... St. Lawrence Public Library, Newfoundland [*Library symbol*] [*National Library of Canada*] (NLC)

NFSLG .... St. Lunaire-Griquet Public Library, St. Lunaire, Newfoundland [*Library symbol*] [*National Library of Canada*] (NLC)

NFSLP .... Central Records Library, Newfoundland Light and Power Co. Ltd., St. John's, Newfoundland [*Library symbol*] [*National Library of Canada*] (NLC)

NFSLS .... Law Society of Newfoundland, St. John's, Newfoundland [*Library symbol*] [*National Library of Canada*] (NLC)

NFSM .... Memorial University, St. John's, Newfoundland [*Library symbol*] [*National Library of Canada*] (NLC)

NFSM .... National Fraternity of Student Musicians (EA)

NFSM .... Queen Elizabeth II Library, Memorial University of Newfoundland, St. John's, Newfoundland [*Library symbol*] [*National Library of Canada*] (NLC)

NFSMA .... National Fruit and Syrup Manufacturers Association (EA)

NFSMA .... Provincial Planning Office, Newfoundland Department of Municipal Affairs, St. John's, Newfoundland [*Library symbol*] [*National Library of Canada*] (NLC)

NFSME .... Newfoundland Department of Mines and Energy, St. John's, Newfoundland [*Library symbol*] [*National Library of Canada*] (NLC)

NFSMEC .... Curriculum Materials Centre, Education Library, Memorial University, St. John's,Newfoundland [*Library symbol*] [*National Library of Canada*] (NLC)

NFSMED ...... Education Library, Memorial University, St. John's, Newfoundland [*Library symbol*] [*National Library of Canada*] (NLC)

NFSMEM ...... Publications and Information Section, Mineral Development Division Library, Newfoundland Department of Mines and Energy, St. John's, Newfoundland [*Library symbol*] [*National Library of Canada*] (NLC)

NFSMG .... Department of Geography, Memorial University, St. John's, Newfoundland [*Library symbol*] [*National Library of Canada*] (NLC)

NFSMLS ...... Library Studies Program, Memorial University of Newfoundland, St. John's, Newfoundland [*Library symbol*] [*National Library of Canada*] (BIB)

NFSMM .... Health Sciences Library, Memorial University, St. John's, Newfoundland [*Library symbol*] [*National Library of Canada*] (NLC)

NFSMMH ..... Maritime History Archive, Memorial University, St. John's, Newfoundland [*Library symbol*] [*National Library of Canada*] (BIB)

NFSMO .... Ocean Engineering Centre, Memorial University, St. John's, Newfoundland [*Library symbol*] [*National Library of Canada*] (NLC)

NFSN .... NATO French-Speaking Nations

NFsNH .... North Junior-Senior High School, Franklin Square, NY [*Library symbol*] [*Library of Congress*] (LCLS)

NFSNI .... National Research Council IRAP [*Industrial Research Assistance Program*], St. John's, Newfoundland [*Library symbol*] [*National Library of Canada*] (NLC)

NFSNL .... Newfoundland and Labrador Hydro, St. John's, Newfoundland [*Library symbol*] [*National Library of Canada*] (NLC)

NFSNLD .... Newfoundland and Labrador Development Corp., St. John's, Newfoundland [*Library symbol*] [*National Library of Canada*] (NLC)

NFSNO .... National Federation for Specialty Nursing Organizations (EA)

NFSO .... Navy Fuel Supply Office

NFSP .... National Federation of Sub-Postmasters [*British*] (DBA)

NFSP .... Netware File Service Protocol (SAUS)

NFSP .... Non-Flight Switch Panel

NFSP .... Nuclear Fuel Services Plant (SAUS)

NFSP .... Springdale Public Library, Newfoundland [*Library symbol*] [*National Library of Canada*] (NLC)

NFsPE .... Polk Street Elementary School, Franklin Square, NY [*Library symbol*] [*Library of Congress*] (LCLS)

NFSPR .... Provincial Reference Library, St. John's, Newfoundland [*Library symbol*] [*National Library of Canada*] (NLC)

NFSPS .... National Federation of State Poetry Societies (EA)

NFSQ .... Queen's College, St. John's, Newfoundland [*Library symbol*] [*National Library of Canada*] (NLC)

NFSR .... National Finals Steer Roping

NFSRA .... National Fitness Southern Recreation Association [*Australia*]

NFSRD .... Newfoundland Department of Rural Development, St. John's, Newfoundland [*Library symbol*] [*National Library of Canada*] (NLC)

NFSREX .... Canada Department of Regional Industrial Expansion [*Ministere de l'Expansion Industrielle Regionale*] St. John's, Newfoundland [*Library symbol*] [*National Library of Canada*] (NLC)
NFSS .... National Fallout Shelter Survey [*Civil Defense*]
NFSS .... National Federation of Sailing Schools [*British*]
NFSS .... National Finch and Softbill Society (EA)
NFSS .... New Font Selection Scheme (SAUS)
NFSS .... Nucleus Fleet Scientific Support
NFSSC .... St. Clare's Mercy Hospital, St. John's, Newfoundland [*Library symbol*] [*National Library of Canada*] (NLC)
NFSSCN .... School of Nursing, St. Clare's Mercy Hospital, St. John's, Newfoundland [*Library symbol*] [*National Library of Canada*] (NLC)
NFSSO .... Navy Food Service System Office (ACAE)
NFSSW .... Newfoundland Status of Women Council, St. John's, Newfoundland [*Library symbol*] [*National Library of Canada*] (NLC)
NFST .... Newfoundland Department of Tourism, St. John's, Newfoundland [*Library symbol*] [*National Library of Canada*] (NLC)
NFST .... Nuclear Effects Support Team (SAUS)
NFSTA .... Newfoundland Teachers' Association, St. John's, Newfoundland [*Library symbol*] [*National Library of Canada*] (NLC)
NFSTC .... Stephenville Crossing Public Library, Newfoundland [*Library symbol*] [*National Library of Canada*] (NLC)
NFSTCG .... Canadian Coast Guard [*Garde Cotiere Canadienne*] St. John's, Newfoundland [*Library symbol*] [*Obsolete*] [*National Library of Canada*] (NLC)
NFSTPG .... National Foundation for the Study and Treatment of Pathological Gambling [*Defunct*] (EA)
NFSTR .... Medical Library, Sir Thomas Roddick Hospital, Stephenville, Newfoundland [*Library symbol*] [*National Library of Canada*] (NLC)
NFSU .... Nonflying Support Unit
NFSU .... Summerford Public Library, Newfoundland [*Library symbol*] [*National Library of Canada*] (NLC)
NFSU .... Suva/Nausori [*Fiji*] [*ICAO location identifier*] (ICLI)
NFSVP .... National Forest Service Volunteers Program (EA)
NFsWE .... Washington Street Elementary School, Franklin Square, NY [*Library symbol*] [*Library of Congress*] (LCLS)
NFSWH .... Health Services, Waterford Hospital, St. John's, Newfoundland [*Library symbol*] [*National Library of Canada*] (NLC)
NFSWMM .... National Federation of Scale and Weighing Machine Manufacturers [*British*] (DBA)
NFsWS .... Willow Road School, Franklin Square, NY [*Library symbol*] [*Library of Congress*] (LCLS)
NFT .... National Film and Television Sound Archives [*National Film Board of Canada*] [*UTLAS symbol*]
NFT .... National Film Theatre [*British*]
NFT .... National Foundation for Transplants [*Established in 1983 as the Liver Organ Transplant Fund*] (NRGU)
NFT .... Navigation Flight Test [*Aviation*] (DA)
NFT .... Navy Flight Test (MCD)
NFT .... Nefteyugansk Aviation Division [*Russian Federation*] [*ICAO designator*] (FAAC)
NFT .... Networks File Transfer
NFT .... Neurofibrillary Tangle [*Brain anatomy*]
NFT .... Newfoundland Telephone Co. Ltd. [*Toronto Stock Exchange symbol*]
NFT .... Newfoundland Time (SAUS)
NFT .... New Frontiers in Theology [*A publication*] (BJA)
NFT .... N-Formimidoylthienamycin [*Biochemistry*]
NFT .... No Filing Time [*Aviation*]
NFT .... No Fixed Time (SAUS)
NFT .... No Forwarding Time (SAUS)
NFT .... No Further Treatment [*Medicine*] (MELL)
NFT .... Non-Firing Test [*Military*]
NFT .... Non-Functional Test (SAA)
NFT .... Normal Fuel-Oil Tank (MSA)
NFT .... Nutrient Film Technique
nft3 .... normal cubic feet (SAUS)
NFTA .... National Federation of Taxicab Associations [*British*] (DBA)
NFTA .... National Feminist Therapist Association (EA)
NFTA .... National Fillings Trades Association [*British*] (DBA)
NFTA .... National Freight Transportation Association [*Rocky River, OH*] (EA)
NFTA .... New Feminist Talent Associates (EA)
NFTA .... Niagara Frontier Transportation Authority (SAUS)
NFTA .... Night-Fire [*Rifle*] Training Aid [*Army*] (INF)
NFTA .... Nitrogen Fixing Tree Association [*University of Hawaii*] [*Research center*] (RCD)
NFTB .... National Federation of Temple Brotherhoods (EA)
NFTB .... Naval Fleet Training Base
NFTB .... Niagara Frontier Tariff Bureau
NFTB .... Nuclear Flight Test Base
NFTC .... National Foreign Trade Council [*New York, NY*] (EA)
NFTC .... National Furniture Traffic Conference (EA)
NFTD .... Normal, Full Term Delivery [*Obstetrics*]
NFTE .... Eua [*Tonga*] [*ICAO location identifier*] (ICLI)
NFTF .... Night Fighting Training Facility [*Army*] (INF)
NFTF .... Tongatapu/Fua'Amotu International [*Tonga*] [*ICAO location identifier*] (ICLI)
NFTI .... Naval Firefighters Thermal Imager (ACAE)
NFTL .... Ha'Apai Lifuka [*Tonga*] [*ICAO location identifier*] (ICLI)
NFTMS........ National Federation of Terrazzo-Mosaic Specialists [*British*] (BI)
NFTN .... Nuku'Alofa [*Tonga*] [*ICAO location identifier*] (ICLI)
NFTO .... Niuafo'Ou [*Tonga*] [*ICAO location identifier*] (ICLI)
NFTO .... Torbay Public Library, Newfoundland [*Library symbol*] [*National Library of Canada*] (NLC)

NFTP .... Niuatoputapu [*Tonga*] [*ICAO location identifier*] (ICLI)
NFTR .... Trepassey Public Library, Newfoundland [*Library symbol*] [*National Library of Canada*] (NLC)
NFTS .... National Federation of Temple Sisterhoods (EA)
NFTS .... National Film and Television School [*British*]
NFTS .... Naval Fixed Telecommunications System (SAUS)
NFTS .... Naval Flight Training School
NFTS .... Women of Reform Judaism, the Federation of Temple Sisterhoods (EA)
NFTSA .... National Film, Television, and Sound Archives [*Canada*]
NFTSD .... Normal Full-Term Spontaneous Delivery [*Obstetrics*] (DAVI)
NFtT .... Fort Ticonderoga Association Museum and Library, Fort Ticonderoga, NY [*Library symbol*] [*Library of Congress*] (LCLS)
NFTT .... Nonorganic Failure to Thrive [*Neonatology*] [*Pediatrics*] (DAVI)
NFT UK .... Norsk Forsvarsteknologi A/S (SAUS)
NFTV .... Vava'u [*Tonga*] [*ICAO location identifier*] (ICLI)
NFTW .... National Federation of Telephone Workers [*Later, CWA*]
NFTW .... National Federation of Tobacco Workers [*A union*] [*British*]
NFTW .... Twillingate Public Library, Newfoundland [*Library symbol*] [*National Library of Canada*] (NLC)
NFTY .... North American Federation of Temple Youth (EA)
NFTZ .... Non Free Trade Zone (DS)
NFU .... National Farmers' Union [*British*]
NFU .... National Film Unit (BARN)
NFU .... Niho Fukushi University [*UTLAS symbol*]
NFU .... Non First Use (SAUS)
NFU .... Not for Us [*Communications*]
NFUCWC..... National Foundation for Unemployment Compensation and Workers Compensation (EA)
N-Fuel .... Nuclear Fuel (SAUS)
NFUF .... Codroy Valley Public Library, Upper Ferry, Newfoundland [*Library symbol*] [*National Library of Canada*] (NLC)
NFUI .... Upper Island Cove Public Library, Newfoundland [*Library symbol*] [*National Library of Canada*] (NLC)
NFV .... National Field Volunteer [*Red Cross*]
NFV .... Naval Forces Vietnam (VNW)
NFV .... No Further Visits [*Medicine*]
NFV .... Nordischer Friseurverband [*Nordic Association of Hairdressers*] [*Sweden*] (EAIO)
NFV .... Point Barrow, AK [*Location identifier*] [*FAA*] (FAAL)
NFV .... Victoria Public Library, Newfoundland [*Library symbol*] [*National Library of Canada*] (NLC)
NFVA .... Net Free Vent Area [*Roofing*]
NFVC .... National Frozen Vegetable Council [*Later, FVC*] (EA)
NFVLS .... National Federation of Voluntary Literacy Schemes [*British*]
NFVOA........ Northern Fishing Vessel Owners Association [*Defunct*] (EA)
NFVP .... National Film and Video Productions [*Australia*]
NFVT .... National Federation of Vehicle Trades [*British*] (BI)
NFW .... Lakehurst, NJ [*Location identifier*] [*FAA*] (FAAL)
NFW .... New Field Wildcat (SAUS)
NFW .... Non-Fuel-Wasting (MCD)
NFW .... Nursed Fairly Well [*Medicine*] (DMAA)
NFWA .... National Farm Workers of America
NFWA .... National Furniture Warehousemen's Association [*Later, NMSA*] (EA)
NFWA .... Neuromuscular Foundation of Western Australia
NFWA .... Wabush Public Library, Newfoundland [*Library symbol*] [*National Library of Canada*] (NLC)
NFWBO .... National Foundation for Women Business Owners
NFWC .... National Fire Waste Council
NFWD .... New Field Wildcat Drilling [*Petroleum technology*]
NFWE........... Edgar L. M. Roberts Memorial Library, Woodypoint, Newfoundland [*Library symbol*] [*National Library of Canada*] (NLC)
NFWE........... National Federation of Woman's Exchanges (EA)
NFWF .... National Fish and Wildlife Foundation (EPA)
NFWG .... National Federation of Wholesale Grocers and Provision Merchants [*British*] (BI)
NFWH .... National Foundation for Wholistic Medicine [*Defunct*] (EA)
NFWH .... Whitbourne Public Library, Newfoundland [*Library symbol*] [*National Library of Canada*] (NLC)
NFWHF .... National Fresh Water Fishing Hall of Fame
NFWI .... National Federation of Women's Institutes [*British*]
NFWI .... Windsor Memorial Public Library, Newfoundland [*Library symbol*] [*National Library of Canada*] (NLC)
NFWIN .... Winterton Public Library, Newfoundland [*Library symbol*] [*National Library of Canada*] (NLC)
NFWM .... National Farm Worker Ministry (EA)
NFWPM .... National Federation of Wholesalers and Poultry Merchants [*British*] (DBA)
NFWS .... Navy Fighter Weapons School (DNAB)
NFWT .... National Foundation of Wheelchair Tennis (EA)
NFWV .... Wesleyville Public Library, Newfoundland [*Library symbol*] [*National Library of Canada*] (NLC)
NFWW .... National Federation of Women Workers [*British*]
NFWY .... Wesleyville Public Library, Newfoundland (SAUS)
NFX .... Newfield Exploration [*NYSE symbol*] (TTSB)
NFX .... Newfield Exploration Co. [*NYSE symbol*] (SPSG)
NFX .... Nuclear Factor X (DMAA)
NFXD .... National Fax Directory [*A publication*]
NFXF .... National Fragile X Foundation (EA)
NFY .... Notify [*Telecommunications*] (TEL)
NFYD .... Notified [*Telecommunications*] (TEL)
NFYFC .... National Federation of Young Farmers' Clubs (EAIO)
NFYG .... Notifying (SAUS)
NFZ .... National Front of Zimbabwe (PPW)
NFZ .... (Nitro)furfuralsemicarbazone [*Organic chemistry*]

NFZ............	No Fire Zone [*Military*]
NFZ............	Nuclear Free Zone (AFM)
NFZ............	Nuclear Weapons Free Zone (SAUS)
NFZR..........	Nuclear Free Zone Registry [*Defunct*] (EA)
NG	Gill Aviation Ltd. (SAUS)
NG	Green Hills Aviation [*ICAO designator*] (AD)
ng	Nanogram [*One billionth of a gram*]
NG	Narrow Gage (NAKS)
NG	Narrow Gauge
NG	Nasogastric [*Medicine*]
NG	National Gallery [*London*]
NG	National Gathering [*Jordan*] [*A publication*] (BJA)
NG	National Grange (EA)
NG	National Grid [*British Ordnance Survey maps*]
NG	National Guard [*or Guardsman*]
NG	Natural Gas
NG	Natural Gas Shutoff [*NFPA pre-fire planning symbol*] (NFPA)
NG	Natural, Grazed [*Agriculture*]
NG	Naval Gunfire (SAA)
NG	Navy General [*MCD files*]
NG	NAZI Government (BJA)
NG	Negative Glow (IDOE)
NG	Neopentyl Glycol [*Organic chemistry*]
NG	Nephridial Gland
NG	New Genus
NG	New Gnostics Special Interest Group (EA)
NG	New Granada
NG	New Group
NG	New Growth [*Medicine*]
NG	New Guinea
NG	Newly Generated
NG	Newsgroup (SAUS)
NG	Next Generation (SAUS)
ng	Niger [*MARC country of publication code*] [*Library of Congress*] (LCCP)
NG	Nigeria [*ANSI two-letter standard code*] (CNC)
NG	Nitrogen Gauge (MCD)
NG	Nitroglycerin [*Also, GTN, NTG*] [*Explosive, vasodilator*]
N-G	Nitro-Glycerine (SAUS)
NG	Nitroguanidine [*Organic chemistry*]
NG	Noble Gases [*Nuclear energy*] (NRCH)
NG	Noble Grand
NG	Noble Guard [*Freemasonry*] (ROG)
NG	Nodose Ganglion [*Medicine*] (DB)
NG	Nodular Goiter [*Medicine*] (MELL)
NG	No Go [*i.e., an unacceptable arrangement*]
NG	No Good [*Similar to IC - Inspected and Condemned*]
NG	No Gum [*Philately*]
NG	Non-Government (OTD)
NG	Nongraduate
NG	Normal Graduate
NG	Normoglycemia [*Medicine*] (MELL)
NG	Normotensive Group [*Cardiology*]
NG	Norwegian
NG	Norwegium [*Chemistry*] (ROG)
NG	Nose Gear [*Aviation*] (MCD)
NG	Nose Guard (SAUS)
NG	Not Given (ADA)
NG	Not Good
NG	Not Greater (SAUS)
NG	Not Ground (SAUS)
NG	Not Guilty
NG	Nottingham [*Postcode*] (ODBW)
NG	No Window Glazing
NG	Nuclear Galaxy (BARN)
NG	Nut Grounds (SAUS)
NG	Royal North Gloucestershire Militia [*British military*] (DMA)
NGA	Associated Natural Gas Corp. (SAUS)
NGA	National Gallery of Art [*Washington, DC*]
NGA	National Gallery of Art, Washington, DC [*OCLC symbol*] (OCLC)
NGA	National Gallery of Australia
NGA	National Gallery of Canada Library [*UTLAS symbol*]
NGA	National Gardening Association (EA)
NGA	National Glass Association (EA)
NGA	National Gliding Association [*Later, SSA*]
NGA	National Governors' Association (EA)
NGA	National Grant Agency
NGA	National Graphical Association [*British printers' union*]
NGA	National Greyhound Association (EA)
NGA	National Grocers Association (EA)
NGA	National Guardianship Association (NTPA)
NGA	NATO Guidelines Area (NATG)
NGA	Natural Gas Association (EPA)
NGA	Naval Gunfire Assistant
NGA	Needlework Guild of America [*Later, NGAI*] (EA)
NGA	Never Go Away (SAUS)
NGA	New Generation Alliance (SAUS)
NGA	Next Generation Accounting (TIMI)
NGA	Nigeria [*ANSI three-letter standard code*] (CNC)
Nga	Nigeria (MILB)
NGA	Nutrient Gelatin Agar [*Microbiology*]
NGA	WAAC (Nigeria) Ltd. Nigeria Airways [*ICAO designator*] (FAAC)
NGA	Young [*Australia*] [*Airport symbol*] (OAG)
NGAA	National Girls Athletic Association [*Defunct*]
NGAA	Natural Gasoline Association of America [*Later, GPA*]
NGAB	Abaiang [*Kiribati*] [*ICAO location identifier*] (ICLI)
NGaC	Capuchin Theological Seminary, Garrison, NY [*Library symbol*] [*Library of Congress*] (LCLS)
NGAC	National Greenhouse Advisory Committee [*Australia*]
NGAC	National Guard Air Corps (WDAA)
NGAD	Nobody Gives a Damn
NGAD	Notice Given Arrival Date (MARI)
NGADA	National Graphic Arts Dealers Association (EA)
NGAI	NGA [*Needlework Guild of America*], Inc. (EA)
NGAL	Chestatee Regional Library [*Library network*]
NGAM	Noble Gas Activity Monitor (IEEE)
NG & A	National Gift and Art Association (EA)
NGAO	New Governmental Advisory Organizations [*A publication*]
NGAPI	Nuveen Georgia Premium Income Municipal Fund [*Associated Press*] (SAG)
NGARP	National Guard and Army Reserve Policy
NGAS	Naval Gunfire Air Spotting
NGAS	Needs-Based Goal Attainment Scale (EDAC)
NGAS	North General Area Services (SAUS)
NGASR	Navy, Army & Air Staff Requirement (SAUS)
NGAST	Navy, Army & Air Staff Target (SAUS)
NGATM	New Generation Air Traffic Manager (GAVI)
NGAUS	National Guard Association of the United States (EA)
NGAYA	National Gay Alliance for Young Adults (EA)
NGAZ	NATO Gazetteer (MCD)
NGB	Army National Guard Bureau (BCP)
NGB	National Garden Bureau (EA)
NGB	National Governing Body [*United States Olympic Committee*]
NGB	National Guard Base
NGB	National Guard Bureau [*Army*]
ngb	Natural Gum Blend [*Philately*]
NGB	Neues Goettinger Bibelwerk [*A publication*] (BJA)
NGB	Neurogenic Bladder [*Medicine*] (MELL)
NGB	Nordic Gene Bank (CARB)
NGB	Northern Gas Board (SAUS)
NGBR	Beru [*Kiribati*] [*ICAO location identifier*] (ICLI)
NGBRI	Not Guilty by Reason of Insanity
NGc	Garden City Public Library, Garden City, NY [*Library symbol*] [*Library of Congress*] (LCLS)
NGC	Gloucester County College, Voorhees, NJ [*OCLC symbol*] (OCLC)
NGC	National Gallery of Canada
NGC	National Gambling Commission (NADA)
NGC	National Gasohol Commission [*Defunct*] (EA)
NGC	National General Corp. (EFIS)
NGC	National Giro Centre [*British*] (DCTA)
NGC	National Glass Clubs (EA)
NGC	National Gloster Club (EA)
NGC	National Goose Council (NTPA)
NGC	National Governors Conference [*Later, NGA*]
NGC	National Guideline Clearinghouse (SAUS)
NGC	National Guild of Churchmen (EA)
NGC	National Guinea Club
NGC	National Gypsy Council [*British*] (DBA)
NGC	Natural Gas Clearinghouse
ngc	Natural Gum Crease [*Philately*]
NGC	Naval Gunfire Control (SAUS)
NGC	Near Galactic Catalog
NGC	New General Catalogue [*Astronomy*]
NGC	New Generation Computer (SAUS)
NGC	Newmont Gold Co. [*NYSE symbol*] (SPSG)
NGC	Next Generation Controller (TIMI)
NGC	Next Group Clause (SAUS)
NGC	Noise Generator Card
NGC	Nordic Geodetic Commission (EA)
NGC	North Georgia College [*Dahlonaga*]
NGC	Nozzle Gap Control [*Aerospace*] (AAG)
NGC	Nucleus Gigantocellularis (SAUS)
NGC	Nucleus Reticularis Gigantocellularis [*Brain anatomy*]
NGC	Numismatic Guarantee Corp. (SAUS)
NGcA	Adelphi University, Garden City, NY [*Library symbol*] [*Library of Congress*] (LCLS)
NGCAA	National Golf Clubs Advisory Association [*British*] (DBA)
NGCADMM	Next Generation Computer-Aided Design (SAUS)
Ng-CAM	Neuralglial Cell Adhesion Model [*Biochemistry*]
NgCAM	Neural-Glial Cell Adhesion Molecule (SAUS)
NGCC	National Guard Computer Center
NGCC	North German Coal Control [*Post-World War II*]
NGcCC	Nassau Community College, Garden City, NY [*Library symbol*] [*Library of Congress*] (LCLS)
NGC Cp	NGC Corp. [*Associated Press*] (SAG)
NGCDO	North German Coal Distribution Organization [*Post-World War II*]
NGcE	Endo Laboratories, Inc., Garden City, NY [*Library symbol*] [*Library of Congress*] (LCLS)
NGcG	George Mercer, Jr., School of Theology, Garden City, NY [*Library symbol*] [*Library of Congress*] (LCLS)
NGcHE	Homestead Elementary School, Garden City, NY [*Library symbol*] [*Library of Congress*] (LCLS)
NGCIC	Natural Gas Consumers Information Center (EA)
NGcJ	Garden City Junior High School, Garden City, NY [*Library symbol*] [*Library of Congress*] (LCLS)
NGcLE	Locust Elementary School, Garden City, NY [*Library symbol*] [*Library of Congress*] (LCLS)
NGCM	Navy Good Conduct Medal
NGCMA	National Golf Car Manufacturers Association (NTPA)

NGcMH .... Mineola High School, Garden City Park, NY [*Library symbol*] [*Library of Congress*] (LCLS)
NGCMS .... National Guild of Community Music Schools [*Later, NGCSA*] (EA)
NGcN .... Nassau Academy of Medicine, Garden City, NY [*Library symbol*] [*Library of Congress*] (LCLS)
NGcNe .... Newsday, Garden City, NY [*Library symbol*] [*Library of Congress*] (LCLS)
NGcNLS ...... Nassau Library System, Garden City, NY [*Library symbol*] [*Library of Congress*] (LCLS)
NGCOW .... National Gypsum Wrrt [*NASDAQ symbol*] (TTSB)
NGCP .... National Guild of Catholic Psychiatrists (EA)
NGcpMH ...... Mineola High School, Garden City Park, NY [*Library symbol*] [*Library of Congress*] (LCLS)
NGcR .... Nassau County Research Library, Garden City, NY [*Library symbol*] [*Library of Congress*] (LCLS)
NGCR .... Next Generation Computer Resources (DWSG)
NGCSA .... National Guild of Community Schools of the Arts (EA)
NGcSAE ...... Stratford Avenue Elementary School, Garden City, NY [*Library symbol*] [*Library of Congress*] (LCLS)
NGcSE .... Stewart Avenue Elementary School, Garden City, NY [*Library symbol*] [*Library of Congress*] (LCLS)
NGcSH .... Garden City Senior High School, Garden City, NY [*Library symbol*] [*Library of Congress*] (LCLS)
NGcSS .... Scully, Scott, Murphy, and Presser, Garden City, NY [*Library symbol*] [*Library of Congress*] (LCLS)
NGcStP .... Saint Paul's School, Garden City, NY [*Library symbol*] [*Library of Congress*] (LCLS)
NGCT .... Navy General Classification Test (DNAB)
NGD .... National Grassland Demonstration [*British*]
NGD .... National Guild of Decoupeurs (EA)
NGD .... New Geographical Dictionary (SAUS)
NGD .... New Golden Sceptre Minerals Ltd. [*Toronto Stock Exchange symbol*] [*Vancouver Stock Exchange symbol*]
NGD .... Nicotinamide Guanine Dinucleotide (SAUS)
Ngd .... Nitrosoguanidine [*Biochemistry*]
NGDA .... National Glass Dealers Association [*Later, NGA*] (EA)
NGDA .... New Generation Design Automation (SAUS)
NGDA .... Non-Grounded Disc and Annulus (SAUS)
NGDA .... Nordihydroguaiaretic Acid (ACAE)
NGDA Arrangement... Non-Grounded Disc and Annulus Arrangement (SAUS)
NGDB .... National Geochemical Data Bank [*Natural Environment Research Council*] [*Information service or system*] (IID)
NGDBFC ...... Nitty Gritty Dirt Band Fan Club (EA)
NGDC .... National Geophysical Data Center [*Later, NGSDC*] [*Boulder, CO*] [*National Oceanic and Atmospheric Administration*] (MCD)
NGDD .... New Generation Desktop Design (SAUS)
NGDF .... National Grave's Disease Foundation (EA)
NGDI .... National Geo Data Information (SAUS)
NGDM&M ... New Grove Dictionary of Music and Musicians (SAUS)
NGDS .... Naval Graduate Dental School
NGE .... National Grain Exchange [*Australia*]
NGE .... Navigation Guidance Equipment (MCD)
NGE .... New York State Electric & Gas Corp. [*NYSE symbol*] (SPSG)
NGE .... N'Gaoundere [*Cameroon*] [*Airport symbol*] (OAG)
NGE .... Noise Generation Equipment (ACAE)
NGE .... Not Greater or Equal (SAUS)
NGEC .... National Gypsy Education Council [*British*]
NGEDA .... National Guard Executive Directors Association (NTPA)
NG-EGDN .... Nitroglycerine Ethylene Glycol Dinitrate (SAUS)
NGEN .... New Generation Foods, Inc. (SAUS)
n gen .... New Genus [*Biology*] (BARN)
NGEN .... Noise Generator (MSA)
NGeno .... Wadsworth Library, Geneseo, NY [*Library symbol*] [*Library of Congress*] (LCLS)
NGenoA .... Livingston County Archives, Geneseo, NY [*Library symbol*] [*Library of Congress*] (LCLS)
NGenoLS ..... Livingston-Steuben-Wyoming Educational Communication Center (BOCES), Geneseo, NY [*Library symbol*] [*Library of Congress*] (LCLS)
NGenoU .... State University of New York, College at Geneseo, Geneseo, NY [*Library symbol*] [*Library of Congress*] (LCLS)
NGEPr .... N.Y. State E&G, 3.75% Pfd [*NYSE symbol*] (TTSB)
NGEPrD .... N.Y. State E&G Adj Rt B Pfd [*NYSE symbol*] (TTSB)
NGEPrE .... N.Y. State E&G 7.40% Pfd [*NYSE symbol*] (TTSB)
NGEPSSC .... Navy Graduate Education Program Select Study Committee [*Terminated, 1975*] (EGAO)
NGF .... Kaneohe, HI [*Location identifier*] [*FAA*] (FAAL)
NGF .... National Gaucher Foundation (EA)
NGF .... National Genetics Foundation [*Defunct*] (EA)
NGF .... National Golf Foundation (EA)
NGF .... Nations Government Income Term Trust 2004 [*NYSE symbol*] (SAG)
NGF .... Nations Gvt Inc. Term Tr 2004 [*NYSE symbol*] (TTSB)
NGF .... Natural Guard Fund [*Defunct*] (EA)
NGF .... Naval Gun Factory [*Later, NWF*]
NGF .... Naval Gunfire
NGF .... Nerve Growth Factor [*A protein*] [*Biochemistry*]
NGF .... Nevada Goldfields Corp. [*Toronto Stock Exchange symbol*]
NGF .... New Games Foundation [*Defunct*] (EA)
NGF .... New Guinea Force [*Army*] [*World War II*]
NGF .... Nordic Gunners Federation
NGF .... Normalized Gain Function (SAUS)
NGF .... Northern Group of Forces [*Commonwealth of Independent States*] (NATG)
NGFA .... National Grain and Feed Association (EA)
NGFCF .... Nevada Goldfields Corp. (MHDW)

NGFEX .... Naval Gunfire Exercise (NVT)
NGFF .... Funafuti [*Tuvalu*] [*ICAO location identifier*] (ICLI)
NGFLO .... Naval Gunfire Liaison Officer
NGFLT .... Naval Gunfire Liaison Team
NGFO .... Nanumea [*Tuvalu*] [*ICAO location identifier*] (ICLI)
NGFO .... Naval Gunfire Officer
NGFP .... National Graduate Fellowship Program [*Department of Education*] (GFGA)
NGFR .... Nerve Growth Factor Receptor [*Neurobiology*]
NGFS .... National Grigsby Family Society (EA)
NGFS .... Naval Gunfire Support (NVT)
NGFT .... National Guard on Field Training Exercises
NGFT .... Naval Gunfire Liaison Team (MUGU)
NGFU .... Funafuti/International [*Tuvalu*] [*ICAO location identifier*] (ICLI)
NGG .... Air Trans NG Group Moldova [*FAA designator*] (FAAC)
NGG .... Negative Grid Generator
NGG .... Network Group Germany (SAUS)
NGGA .... National Greentown Glass Association (EA)
NGGC .... National Grape Growers Cooperative (NTPA)
NGGR .... Nonglucogenic/Glucogenic Ratio (DB)
NGH .... Hobart and William Smith Colleges, Geneva, NY [*Library symbol*] [*Library of Congress*] (LCLS)
NGH .... Nabisco Group Holdings [*NYSE symbol*] (SG)
NGH .... NASA Grant Handbook
NGH .... National Guard [*Hawaii*] [*Seismograph station code, US Geological Survey*] (SEIS)
NGH .... National Guild of Hypnotists (EA)
NGHA .... 91st General Hospital Association (EA)
NGHBRHD... Neighborhood
NGHEF .... National Gay Health Education Foundation (EA)
NGI .... Nasogastric Intubation [*Medicine*] (MELL)
NGI .... National Garden Institute
NGI .... National Genomics Institute (SAUS)
NGI .... Nations Government Income Term Trust [*NYSE symbol*] (SPSG)
NGI .... Nations Gvt Inc. Term Tr 2003 [*NYSE symbol*] (TTSB)
NGI .... Natural Gas Industry [*Australia*]
NGI .... Next Generation Internet [*Computer science*]
NGI .... Ngau [*Fiji*] [*Airport symbol*] (OAG)
NGI .... Non-Government Institution (SAUS)
NGI .... Not Guilty by Reason of Insanity
NGI .... Not Guilty, Insanity (SAUS)
NGI .... Nuclear Globulin Inclusions (DMAA)
NGI .... Nurses' Global Impressions (DB)
NGI .... N-W Group, Inc. [*Toronto Stock Exchange symbol*]
NGIB .... National Geodetic Information Branch [*National Oceanic and Atmospheric Administration*]
NGIC .... National Geodetic Information Center [*National Oceanic and Atmospheric Administration*] (IID)
NGIC .... National Guard Intelligence Center [*USA*]
NGIFF .... Next Generation IFF (SAUS)
NGiG .... Gibco/Invenex, Grand Island (SAUS)
NGiG .... Gibco/Invenex, Grand Island, NY [*Library symbol*] [*Library of Congress*] (LCLS)
NGiHC .... Hooker Chemicals & Plastics Corp., Corporate Technical and Services Center Research Library, Grand Island, NY [*Library symbol*] [*Library of Congress*] (LCLS)
NGIO .... Next Generation Input Output (SAUS)
NGIPSCA ..... National GI Pipe Smokers Club of America (EA)
NGIS .... Next Generation Information System (SAUS)
NGISC .... National Gambling Impact Study Commission
NgIU .... University of Ibadan, Ibadan, Nigeria [*Library symbol*] [*Library of Congress*] (LCLS)
n giv .... Not Given (DAVI)
NGJ .... Beaufort, SC [*Location identifier*] [*FAA*] (FAAL)
NGJ .... Nigerian Geographical Journal [*A publication*]
NGJA .... National Gymnastics Judges Association (EA)
NGJC .... North Greenville Junior College [*South Carolina*]
NGK .... New Greek [*Language, etc.*]
NGK .... Niemegk [*German Democratic Republic*] [*Geomagnetic observatory code*]
n-gl- .... Greenland [*MARC geographic area code*] [*Library of Congress*] (LCCP)
NGl .... Harborfields Public Library, Greenlawn, NY [*Library symbol*] [*Library of Congress*] (LCLS)
NGL .... Natural Gas Liquids
NGL .... Natural Ground Level
NGL .... Neodymium Glass LASER
NGL .... Neon Glow Lamp
NGL .... NGC Corp. [*NYSE symbol*] (TTSB)
NGL .... No Gimbal Lock
NGL .... No Greater Love (EA)
NGL .... Normalair-Garrett Ltd. [*British*] (IRUK)
NGL .... North Gasline [*Alaska*] [*Seismograph station code, US Geological Survey*] (SEIS)
NGL .... North German Lloyd Line (SAUS)
NGL .... Nose Gear Launch (MCD)
NGL .... Trident NGL Holdings, Inc. [*NYSE symbol*] (SPSG)
NGlc .... Glen Cove Public Library, Glen Cove, NY [*Library symbol*] [*Library of Congress*] (LCLS)
NGLC .... Next Generation Level Control (SAUS)
NGlcC .... Community Hospital at Glen Cove, Glen Cove, NY [*Library symbol*] [*Library of Congress*] (LCLS)
NGlcCE .... Coles Elementary School, Glen Cove, NY [*Library symbol*] [*Library of Congress*] (LCLS)

NGIcCoE	Connolly Elementary School, Glen Cove, NY [*Library symbol*] [*Library of Congress*] (LCLS)
NGIcDE	Deasy Elementary School, Glen Cove, NY [*Library symbol*] [*Library of Congress*] (LCLS)
NGIcF-L	Friends Academy, Lower School, Glen Cove, NY [*Library symbol*] [*Library of Congress*] (LCLS)
NGIcF-U	Friends Academy, Upper School, Glen Cove, NY [*Library symbol*] [*Library of Congress*] (LCLS)
NGIcGE	Gribbin Elementary School, Glen Cove, NY [*Library symbol*] [*Library of Congress*] (LCLS)
NGIcHS	Glen Cove High School, Glen Cove, NY [*Library symbol*] [*Library of Congress*] (LCLS)
NGIcLE........	Landing Elementary School, Glen Cove, NY [*Library symbol*] [*Library of Congress*] (LCLS)
NGIcM	Garvie's Point Museum, Glen Cove, NY [*Library symbol*] [*Library of Congress*] (LCLS)
NGIcMS	Glen Cove Middle School, Glen Cove, NY [*Library symbol*] [*Library of Congress*] (LCLS)
NGIcP	Pall Corp., Glen Cove, NY [*Library symbol*] [*Library of Congress*] (LCLS)
NGIcW	Webb Institute of Naval Architecture, Glen Cove, NY [*Library symbol*] [*Library of Congress*] (LCLS)
NGIf	Crandall Library, Glens Falls, NY [*Library symbol*] [*Library of Congress*] (LCLS)
NGIfAC........	Adirondack Community College, Glens Falls, NY [*Library symbol*] [*Library of Congress*] (LCLS)
NGIH............	Hazeltine Corp., Greenlawn, NY [*Library symbol*] [*Library of Congress*] (LCLS)
NGIhC	New York Chiropractic College, Glen Head, NY [*Library symbol*] [*Library of Congress*] (LCLS)
NGIhES	Glen Head Elementary School, Glen Head, NY [*Library symbol*] [*Library of Congress*] (LCLS)
NGIhGE........	Glenwood Landing Elementary School, Glen Head, NY [*Library symbol*] [*Library of Congress*] (LCLS)
NGIhNH........	North Shore High School, Glen Head, NY [*Library symbol*] [*Library of Congress*] (LCLS)
NGIhNJ........	North Shore Junior High School, Glen Head, NY [*Library symbol*] [*Library of Congress*] (LCLS)
NGIHS..........	Harborfields High School, Greenlawn, NY [*Library symbol*] [*Library of Congress*] (LCLS)
NGLIOGT......	National Grand Lodge, International Order of Good Templars [*Later, NCUSIOGT*] (EA)
NGIo	Gloversville Free Library, Gloversville, NY [*Library symbol*] [*Library of Congress*] (LCLS)
NGLO	Naval Gunfire Liaison Officer
NGLR	Neodymium Glass LASER Rod
NGLS	Non-Governmental Liaison Service [*World Resources Institute*]
NGLTF.........	National Gay and Lesbian Task Force (EA)
NGIwES.......	Glenwood Landing Elementary School, Glenwood Landing, NY [*Library symbol*] [*Library of Congress*] (LCLS)
N GLZD........	Not Glazed [*Freight*]
NGM	Agana Naval Air Station [*FAA*] (TAG)
ngm	Nanogram [*Measurement*] (DAVI)
NGM	Naval General Message (SAUS)
NGM	Nested Grid Model [*Marine science*] (OSRA)
NGM	NetWare Global Messaging [*Computer science*] (CDE)
NGM	Neutron-Gamma Monte Carlo [*Computer science*]
NGM	New Ridge Resources [*Vancouver Stock Exchange symbol*]
NGM	Nitrogen Generation Module (NASA)
NGM	Noise Generation Mechanism
NGMA	Maiana [*Kiribati*] [*ICAO location identifier*] (ICLI)
NGMA	National Gadget Manufacturers Association
NGMA	National Gas Measurement Association (EA)
NGMA	National Geoscience Mapping Accord [*Australia*]
NGMA	National Gospel Music Association (EA)
NGMA	National Grants Management Association (AAGC)
NGMA	National Greenhouse Manufacturers Association (EA)
N Gmc	North Germanic (SAUS)
NGMEX.........	Northern Gulf of Mexico (SAUS)
NGMH	New Generation Military Hospital (SAUS)
NGMK	Marakei [*Kiribati*] [*ICAO location identifier*] (ICLI)
NGMN..........	Makin [*Kiribati*] [*ICAO location identifier*] (ICLI)
NGMP..........	New Guinea Marine Products (SAUS)
NGMRD........	New Generation Mark Reader (or Reading) (SAUS)
NGN	Nagano [*Japan*] [*Seismograph station code, US Geological Survey*] (SEIS)
NGN	Nargana [*Panama*] [*Airport symbol*] (OAG)
NGN	National Geographic Names Data Base [*Geological Survey*] [*Database*]
NGN	News Group Newspapers [*British*]
NGN	NRG Resources Ltd. [*Vancouver Stock Exchange symbol*]
NGNA..........	National Gerontological Nursing Association (NTPA)
NGNA..........	Neutrogena Corp. (SAUS)
NGNC	Non-Government Non-Catholic [*School*]
NGNF..........	National Guard Not in Federal Service
NGNF..........	Next Generation Navy Fighter (ACAE)
NG/NS.........	Next Generation/Notional System [*Army*]
NGNU..........	Nikunau [*Kiribati*] [*ICAO location identifier*] (ICLI)
NGO	Nago [*Ryukyu Islands*] [*Seismograph station code, US Geological Survey*] (SEIS)
NGO	Nagoya [*Japan*] [*Airport symbol*] (OAG)
NGO	National Gas Outlet [*Thread*]
NGO	Naval Gunfire Officer
NGO	Navy Guidance Official [*British*]
NGO............	Neuro-Genetic Optimizer (PCM)
NGO............	Nitroglycerin Ointment [*Pharmacy*] (CPH)
NGO............	Non-Gazetted Officer [*India*] (WDAA)
NGO............	Nongovernmental Observer
NGO............	Nongovernmental Organization [*Generic term*]
NGOC..........	Naval Gunfire Operations Center
NGOC..........	North German Oil Control [*Post-World War II*]
NGOCD	Non-Governmental Organization Committee on Disarmament (EA)
NGO Committee...	Non-Governmental Organizations Committee on UNICEF (EA)
NGOCS.........	National Guard Officer Candidate School
NGO/GO	Non Governmental Organisation/ Governmental Organisation (SAUS)
NGoH	Hillside Hospital, Glen Oaks, NY [*Library symbol*] [*Library of Congress*] (LCLS)
NGON	Onotoa [*Kiribati*] [*ICAO location identifier*] (ICLI)
NGos...........	Goshen Library and Historical Society, Goshen, NY [*Library symbol*] [*Library of Congress*] (LCLS)
NGOS	Non-Governmental Organisations
NGosA	Arden Hill Hospital Medical Library, Goshen, NY [*Library symbol*] [*Library of Congress*] (LCLS)
NGou	Reading Room Association Library, Gouverneur, NY [*Library symbol*] [*Library of Congress*] (LCLS)
NGowH	Tri-County Memorial Hospital, Gowanda, NY [*Library symbol*] [*Library of Congress*] (LCLS)
NGP............	Corpus Christi, TX [*Location identifier*] [*FAA*] (FAAL)
NGP............	Greensboro Public Library, Greensboro, NC [*OCLC symbol*] (OCLC)
NGP............	Nano Glass Pellet
NGP............	Natural Gas Pressure
NGP............	Navigation Processor (IGSL)
NGP............	Nearest Grid Point (PDAA)
NGP............	Network Graphics Protocol
NGP............	Neue Grosse Partei [*New Great Party*] [*Germany*] [*Political party*] (PPW)
NGP............	New Gatineau Pulp [*Pulp and paper technology*]
NGP............	Next Generation Processor (ACAE)
NGP............	N-Glycidylpyrrolidone [*Organic chemistry*]
Ngp............	Nominal Group [*Linguistics*]
NGP............	Northern Galactic Pole
NGP............	North Galactic Pole
NGPA..........	National Gas Policy Act (GFGA)
NGPA..........	National Guard Personnel, Army
NGPA..........	Natural Gas Policy Act [*1978*]
NGPA..........	Natural Gas Processors Association [*Later, GPA*] (EA)
NGPE..........	Neurogenic Pulmonary Edema [*Medicine*] (MELL)
NGPEC........	National Guard Professional Education Center [*North Little Rock, AR*]
NGPF..........	North General Purpose Facilities (SAUS)
NGPL..........	Natural Gas Plant Liquids [*DOE*] (TAG)
NGPP..........	National Guild of Professional Paperhangers (EA)
NGPRP........	Northern Great Plains Resource Program [*Dept. of the Interior, Dept. of Agriculture and Environmental Protection Agency*] (PDAA)
NGPRS........	Northern Great Plains Research Center [*Department of Agriculture*] [*Research center*] (RCD)
NGPS	Navstar Global Positioning System (SAUS)
NGPSA........	Natural Gas Pipeline Safety Act [*1968*]
NGPSA........	Natural Gas Processors Suppliers Association [*Later, GPSA*] (EA)
NGPT	National Guild of Piano Teachers (EA)
NGQ............	Nongovernment Quarters (AFM)
NGR............	Narrow Gauge Railways Ltd. [*Wales*]
NGR............	Narrow Gauze Roll [*Medicine*]
NGR............	Nasogastric Replacement [*Medicine*] (DMAA)
NGR............	National Guard Register
NGR............	National Guard Regulations
NGR............	Neutral Grounding Resistor (SAUS)
NGR............	Newbold General Refractories (SAUS)
N GR............	New Greek [*Language, etc.*] (ROG)
N-GR...........	New York State Library, General Reference Library, Albany, NY [*Library symbol*] [*Library of Congress*] (LCLS)
Ngr.............	Niger (MILB)
NGR............	Nigerum [*Papua New Guinea*] [*Airport symbol*] (OAG)
NGR............	Night-Goggle Readable (SAUS)
ngr.............	Non-Geared (SAUS)
NGR............	Non-Grain-Raising [*Coating technology*]
NGR............	Nongrain-Raising Stain (SAUS)
NGR............	Nongrain Rating (SAUS)
NGR............	Norgold Resources [*Vancouver Stock Exchange symbol*]
NGR............	Nuclear Gamma-ray Resonance (SAUS)
NGR............	Nuclear Gamma Ray Spectroscopy (EDCT)
NGR............	Nuclear Gamma Resonance (SAUS)
NGRA..........	National Gay Rights Advocates [*Defunct*] (EA)
NGRC..........	National Government of the Republic of China
NGRC..........	National Greyhound Racing Club [*British*] (DI)
NGRE..........	Negative Glucocorticoid Response Element [*Biochemistry*]
NGRF..........	National Ghost Ranch Foundation (EA)
NGRI..........	Not Guilty by Reason of Insanity
NGrl............	Greenwood Lake Public Library, Greenwood, NY [*Library symbol*] [*Library of Congress*] (LCLS)
NGrlHS	Harborfields High School, Greenlawn, NY [*Library symbol*] [*Library of Congress*] (LCLS)
NGrn	Great Neck Library, Great Neck, NY [*Library symbol*] [*Library of Congress*] (LCLS)
NGrnBE........	Baker Elementary School, Great Neck, NY [*Library symbol*] [*Library of Congress*] (LCLS)
NGrnKE........	Kennedy Elementary School, Great Neck, NY [*Library symbol*] [*Library of Congress*] (LCLS)
NGrnKJE........	Kensington-Johnson Elementary School, Great Neck, NY [*Library symbol*] [*Library of Congress*] (LCLS)

NGrnLE .... Lakeville Elementary School, Great Neck, NY [*Library symbol*] [*Library of Congress*] (LCLS)
NGrnMiS ...... John L. Miller-Great Neck North High School, Great Neck, NY [*Library symbol*] [*Library of Congress*] (LCLS)
NGrnMS .... Great Neck South Middle School, Great Neck, NY [*Library symbol*] [*Library of Congress*] (LCLS)
NGrnNA .... Network Analysis Corp., Great Neck, NY [*Library symbol*] [*Library of Congress*] (LCLS)
NGrnNM .... Great Neck North Middle School, Great Neck, NY [*Library symbol*] [*Library of Congress*] (LCLS)
NGrnPE .... Parkville Elementary School, Great Neck, NY [*Library symbol*] [*Library of Congress*] (LCLS)
NGrnS .... Sperry Rand Corp., Sperry Gyroscope Division, Great Neck, NY [*Library symbol*] [*Library of Congress*] (LCLS)
NGrnSH .... Great Neck South Senior High School, Great Neck, NY [*Library symbol*] [*Library of Congress*] (LCLS)
NGrnSRE ..... Saddle Rock Elementary School, Great Neck, NY [*Library symbol*] [*Library of Congress*] (LCLS)
NGroT .... Tompkins-Cortland Community College, Groton, NY [*Library symbol*] [*Library of Congress*] [*Obsolete*] (LCLS)
NGrpAg .... United States Department of Agriculture, Plum Island Animal Disease Laboratory Library, Greenport, NY [*Library symbol*] [*Library of Congress*] (LCLS)
NGrpEH .... Eastern Long Island Hospital, Greenport, NY [*Library symbol*] [*Library of Congress*] (LCLS)
NGRS .... Narrow Gauge Railway Society [*British*]
NGRS .... National Geodetic Reference System [*National Oceanic and Atmospheric Administration*]
NGRS .... National Goals Research Staff
NGS .... General Air Services Ltd. [*Nigeria*] [*ICAO designator*] (FAAC)
NGS .... Nagasaki [*Japan*] [*Airport symbol*] (OAG)
NGS .... National Gardens Scheme Charitable Trust (EAIO)
NGS .... National Gas Straight [*Thread*]
NGS .... National Genealogical Society (EA)
NGS .... National Geodetic Survey [*National Oceanic and Atmospheric Administration*]
NGS .... National Geodetic System (OTD)
NGS .... National Geographic Service
NGS .... National Geographic Society (EA)
NGS .... National Geriatrics Society (EA)
NGS .... National Gladiolus Society (EA)
NGS .... National Goldfish Society
NGS .... National Graniteware Society (EA)
NGS .... Natural Ground Surface
NGS .... Naval Gunfire Support
NGS .... Naval Gun Support (SAUS)
NGS .... Neutral Gear Switch [*Automotive engineering*]
NGS .... Neutral Grain Spirits
NGS .... New Generation System (SAUS)
NGS .... New Guidance System (SAUS)
NGS .... No Gallstones [*Medicine*]
NGS .... Nominal Guidance Scheme (OA)
NGS .... Non-Immune [*or Normal*] Goat Serum
NGS .... Normal Goat Serum (DMAA)
NGS .... Nuclear Generating Site (SAUS)
NGS .... Nuclear Generating Station (BARN)
NGS .... Nucleonic Gauging System
NGS .... Numerical Geometry System (SAUS)
NGSA .... National Golf Salesmen Association [*Defunct*] (EA)
NGSA .... Natural Gas Supply Association (EA)
NGSA .... Nerve Growth Stimulating Activity [*Biochemistry*]
NGSB .... Non-Government Standards Bodies (SAUS)
NGSC .... National Gay Student Center [*Defunct*] (EA)
NGSC .... National Gender Selection Center (EA)
NGSCO .... National Geodetic Survey Operations Center [*National Oceanic and Atmospheric Administration*]
NGSDC .... National Geophysical and Solar-Terrestrial Data Center [*National Oceanic and Atmospheric Administration*] (IID)
NGSEF .... National Geographic Society Education Foundation (EA)
NGSF .... Noble Gas Storage Facility (NRCH)
NGSFO .... Naval Gunfire Support Forward Observer [*British*]
NGSIC .... National Geodetic Survey Information Center [*National Oceanic and Atmospheric Administration*] (IID)
NGSLO .... Naval Gunfire Support Forward Observer (SAUS)
NGSLO .... Naval Gunfire Support Liaison Officer
NGSM .... National Gold Star Mothers [*Defunct*] (EA)
NGSMA .... Natural Gasoline Supply Men's Association [*Later, GPSA*]
NGSNY .... National Guard State of New York (HGAA)
NGSP .... National Geodetic Satellite Program [*NASA*]
NGSP .... National Glycohemoglobin Standardization Program (SAUS)
NGSP .... National Grain Sorghum Producers (NTPA)
NGSP .... National Guilds of St. Paul (EA)
NGSP .... Next Generation Signal Processor (SAUS)
NGSP .... Nonglycosylated Serum Protein
NGSQ .... National Genealogical Society Quarterly [*A publication*] (BRI)
NGSR .... Nizams Guaranteed State Railway (SAUS)
NGSS .... Next Generation Sky Survey (SAUS)
NGSS .... Non-Government Schools' Secretariat [*South Australia*]
NGSSLO .... Naval Gunfire Support Senior Liaison Officer (SAUS)
NGSSO .... Naval Gunfire Support Staff Officer
NGST .... Next Generation Space Telescope [*NASA*]
NGSTDC .... National Geophysical and Solar-Terrestrial Data Center [*National Oceanic and Atmospheric Administration*]
NGT .... Berclair, TX [*Location identifier*] [*FAA*] (FAAL)
NGT .... Eastern American Natural Gas Trust [*NYSE symbol*] (SAG)

NGT .... Eastern AmerNatlGasTr'SPERs' [*NYSE symbol*] (TTSB)
NGT .... Nagatsuro [*Irozaki*] [*Japan*] [*Seismograph station code, US Geological Survey*] (SEIS)
NGT .... NASA Ground Terminal (MCD)
NGT .... Nasogastric Tube [*Medicine*] (CPH)
NGT .... National Gas Taper [*Thread*]
NGT .... National Guard Technician (MCD)
NGT .... National Guild of Telephonists [*British*] (BI)
NGT .... Natural Gas Temperature
NGT .... Neon Globe Tube
NGT .... New Generation Technology (SAUS)
NGT .... New Generation Trainer (SAUS)
NGT .... New Generation Truck [*Concept vehicle*]
NGT .... Next Generation Technology (SAUS)
NGT .... Next Generation Trainer [*Air Force*]
NGT .... Night
NGT .... Noise Generator Tube
NGT .... Nominal Grouping Technique
NGT .... Nonsymmetrical Growth Theory (SAUS)
NGT .... Nonsymmetric Gravitational Theory
NGT .... Northern General Transport Co. [*British*] (DCTA)
NGT .... North German Traders (SAUS)
NGT .... Not Greater Than
NGTA .... National Gas Transportation Association (NTPA)
NGTA .... Next Generation Trainer Aircraft (MCD)
NGTA .... Nonguaranteed Trade Arrears (IMH)
NGTA .... Tarawa/Bonriki International [*Kiribati*] [*ICAO location identifier*] (ICLI)
NGTB .... Abemama [*Kiribati*] [*ICAO location identifier*] (ICLI)
NGTC .... National Grain Trade Council (EA)
NGTE .... National Gas Turbine Establishment [*British*]
NGTE .... Tabiteuea (North) [*Kiribati*] [*ICAO location identifier*] (ICLI)
NGTF .... National Gay Task Force [*Later, NGLTF*] (EA)
NGTG .... NCAR [*National Center for Atmospheric Research*] GARP Task Group [*Global Atmospheric Research Program*]
NGTM .... Tamana [*Kiribati*] [*ICAO location identifier*] (ICLI)
NGTO .... Nonouti [*Kiribati*] [*ICAO location identifier*] (ICLI)
NGTOW .... Normal Gross Take-Off Weight (SAUS)
NGTP .... Natural Gas Tank Pressure
NGTR .... Arorae [*Kiribati*] [*ICAO location identifier*] (ICLI)
NGTS .... Tabiteuea (South) [*Kiribati*] [*ICAO location identifier*] (ICLI)
NGTT .... Natural Gas Tank Temperature
NGTT .... Tarawa/Betio [*Kiribati*] [*ICAO location identifier*] (ICLI)
NGTU .... Butaritari [*Kiribati*] [*ICAO location identifier*] (ICLI)
NGU .... Geological Survey of Norway (SAUS)
NGU .... Nachalnik Glavnoyo Upravlenia [*Chief of Main Directorate*] [*Soviet military rank*]
nGU .... Nano-Goldblatt Units [*Clinical chemistry*]
NGU .... Nongonococcal Urethritis [*Medicine*]
NGU .... Norfolk, VA [*Location identifier*] [*FAA*] (FAAL)
NGU .... University of North Carolina, Greensboro, Greensboro, NC [*OCLC symbol*] (OCLC)
NGUAX .... Neub. & Berman Guardian Fund [*Mutual fund ticker symbol*] (SG)
NGUI .... New-Generation Electronic Unit Injector [*Automotive fuel systems*]
N GUI .... New Guinea Territory (WDAA)
N Guin .... New Guinea
NGUK .... Aranuka [*Kiribati*] [*ICAO location identifier*] (ICLI)
NGuNA .... New York State Nurses Association, Guilderland, NY [*Library symbol*] [*Library of Congress*] (LCLS)
NGUS .... National Guard of the United States
NGUT .... National Group of Unit Trusts [*British*] (DI)
NGV .... Angoavia Angola [*FAA designator*] (FAAC)
NGV .... Natural Gas for Vehicles
NGV .... Natural Gas Vehicle
NGV .... New Goldcore Ventures [*Vancouver Stock Exchange symbol*]
NGV .... Nongonococcal Vulvovaginitis (SAUS)
NGV .... Nozzle Guide Vanes [*Aviation*] (AIA)
NGVC .... National Guard Volunteer Corps [*British military*] (DMA)
NGVC .... Natural Gas Vehicle Coalition (NTPA)
NGVD .... National Geodetic Vertical Datum [*National Oceanic and Atmospheric Administration*]
NGvHI .... Harbor Hill Intermediate School, Greenvale, NY [*Library symbol*] [*Library of Congress*] (LCLS)
NGVIA .... Natural Gas Vehicle Industry Alliance
NGvP .... Long Island University, C. W. Post Center, Greenvale, NY [*Library symbol*] [*Library of Congress*] (LCLS)
NGVP .... Natural Gas Vehicle Partnership
NGVR .... New Guinea Volunteer Reserve
NGVTP .... Natural Gas Vehicle Technology Partnership [*Automotive industry cooperative research*]
NGW .... Corpus Christi, TX [*Location identifier*] [*FAA*] (FAAL)
NGW .... Gardner-Webb College, Boiling Springs, NC [*OCLC symbol*] (OCLC)
NGW .... National Gallery of Art, Washington, DC
NGW .... Newly Generated Waste (SAUS)
NGW .... No Gift Wrap [*Mail-order catalogs*]
NGW .... Nuclear Gravity Weapon (SAUS)
NGWA .... National Ground Water Association (NTPA)
NGWASOREP ... Ngwane Socialist Revolutionary Party (SAUS)
NGWIC .... National Ground Water Information Center [*National Water Well Association*] [*Information service or system*] (IID)
NGWLM .... Next Generation Water Level Measurement system (SAUS)
NGWS .... Next Generation Windows Services [*Computer science*] (VLIE)
NGX .... Northgate Explor [*NYSE symbol*] (TTSB)
NGX .... Northgate Exploration Ltd. [*NYSE symbol*] [*Toronto Stock Exchange symbol*] (SPSG)
NGYN .... National Gay Youth Network (EA)

NGZ	Alameda, CA [*Location identifier*] [*FAA*]　(FAAL)
NH	All Nippon [*ICAO designator*]　(AD)
NH	All Nippon Airways Co. Ltd.　(SAUS)
NH	Editions Nouveaux Horizons [*US government imprint*]
NH	Hamilton Public Library, Hamilton, NY [*Library symbol*] [*Library of Congress*]　(LCLS)
NH	Hydrazine　(SAUS)
NH	Nahum [*Bible*]
nH	Nanohenry [*One billionth of a henry*]　(IEEE)
NH	Nash-Healey [*Model of automobile, now out of production*]
NH	National Heritage [*British*] [*An association*]　(DBA)
NH	National Highway
NH	National Hunt [*British*]
NH	NATO Helicopter [*NH-90*]　(DOMA)
NH	Natriuretic Hormone　(DB)
NH	Natural Health　(SAUS)
NH	Natural History [*A publication*]　(BRI)
NH	Naval Home [*Philadelphia, PA*]
NH	Naval Hospital
NH	Neo-Hebrew　(BJA)
NH	Neonatal Hepatitis [*Medicine*]　(DB)
NH	Neonatal Hypothyroidism [*Cretinism*] [*Medicine*]
NH	Neurohormone [*Medicine*]　(MELL)
NH	Neurologic History　(SAUS)
NH	Never Hinged [*Philately*]
NH	New Hampshire [*Postal code*]
Nh	New Hampshire State Library, Concord, NH [*Library symbol*] [*Library of Congress*]　(LCLS)
NH	New Hampshire Supreme Court Reports [*A publication*]　(DLA)
NH	New Haven [*Connecticut*]
NH	New Haven Elm City　(SAUS)
NH	New Head [*Also, NL*] [*News stories*]　(NTCM)
NH	New High [*Investment term*]
NH	New Holland N.V. [*NYSE symbol*]　(SG)
NH	New York, New Haven & Hartford R. R. [*AAR code*]
N/H	Next Higher Assembly [*Engineering*]
NH	Nike Hercules [*Surface-to-air missile system*]　(MCD)
NH	Nippon Airways　(SAUS)
NH	Nodal-His [*Medicine*]　(MEDA)
NH	Nodular Histiocytic [*Lymphoma*] [*Oncology*]　(DAVI)
NH	No Hurry　(SAUS)
NH	Nominal Height　(MCD)
NH	Non-Busy Hour　(VLIE)
NH	Nonhandicapped
NH	Nonhuman　(MAE)
NH	Nonhygroscopic
NH	Norfolk Howard [*Refers to a bed-bug*] [*Slang*]　(DSUE)
NH	Northern Canada Mines Ltd. [*Toronto Stock Exchange symbol*]
NH	Northern Hemisphere
Nh	Northern Hogsucker [*Ichthyology*]
N H	North Hall　(SAUS)
NH	Northumberland Hussars [*British military*]　(DMA)
NH	Not Held
NH	Novikoff Hepatoma [*Medicine*]　(DB)
NH	Nursing Home
NH₃	Ammonia　(GNE)
NH4 ClO4	Ammonium Perchlorate　(SAUS)
NHA	American Foundation for Management Research, Hamilton, NY [*Library symbol*] [*Library of Congress*]　(LCLS)
NHA	Nahanni Mines Ltd. [*Toronto Stock Exchange symbol*]
NHA	National Fashion Accessories Association　(EA)
NHA	National Hairdressers' Association [*British*]　(BI)
NHA	National Handbag Association　(EA)
NHA	National Hay Association　(EA)
NHA	National Health Agencies　(EA)
NHA	National Health Association
NHA	National Hearing Association　(EA)
NHA	National Hemophilia Association　(DAVI)
NHA	National Heritage Act [*Protects national treasures from sale out of the country*] [*British*]
NHA	National Hide Association [*Later, USHSLA*]　(EA)
NHA	National Hobo Association　(EA)
NHA	National Hockey Association [*to 1917*]
NHA	National Holiness Association [*Later, CHA*]　(EA)
NHA	National Homeowners Association　(EA)
NHA	National Homeschool Association　(EA)
NHA	National Housewives Association [*British*]　(DBA)
NHA	National Housing Act [*1934, 1954*]
NHA	National Housing Administration
NHA	National Housing Agency [*Superseded by HHFA, 1947; then by HUD, 1965*]
NHA	National Humanities Alliance　(EA)
NHA	National Hunters Association　(EA)
NHA	National Hydrogen Association　(NTPA)
NHA	National Hydropower Association　(EA)
NHA	National Hypertension Association　(EA)
NHA	National Hypoglycemia Association　(EA)
NHA	Nationwide Hotel Association
NHA	Never Has Anything　(SAUS)
NHA	New Homemakers of America [*Later, FHA*]　(EA)
NHA	New Humanity Alliance　(EA)
NHA	Next Higher Assembly [*Engineering*]
NHA	Next Higher Authority　(MUGU)
NHA	Nhatrang [*Vietnam*] [*Seismograph station code, US Geological Survey*] [*Closed*]　(SEIS)
NHA	Nigerian Housing Administration　(SAUS)
NHA	Nitrohippuric Acid [*Organic chemistry*]
NHA	Nonhydrogen Atom [*Chemistry*]
NHA	Nonspecific Hepatocellular Abnormality [*Medicine*]　(MAE)
NHA	Northwest Hardwood Association [*Later, WHA*]　(EA)
NHA	Nursing Home Administration　(SAUS)
NHA	Nutritional Health Alliance
NHAAP	National Heart Attack Alert Program
NHAC	National Health Awareness Center [*Later, NHSAC*]　(EA)
NHACE	National Hispanic Association of Construction Enterprises　(EA)
NHACES	New Hampshire Association for Computer Education Statewide　(EDAC)
NHACFC	National Health Agencies for the Combined Federal Campaign [*Formerly, FSCNHA*] [*Later, NVHA*]　(EA)
NH Act	National Housing Act [*1934, 1954*]　(DLA)
NH Admin Code...	New Hampshire Code of Administrative Rules [*A publication*]　(DLA)
NH Admin Rules Ann...	New Hampshire Code of Administrative Rules Annotated [*A publication*]　(AAGC)
NHAES	New Hampshire Agricultural Experiment Station [*University of New Hampshire*] [*Research center*]　(RCD)
NHaHS	Harborfields High School, Harborfields, NY [*Library symbol*] [*Library of Congress*]　(LCLS)
NHAIAC	National Highway Accident and Injury Analysis Center
NHAM	National Hose Assemblies Manufacturers Association [*Defunct*]
NHamB	Hampton Bays Public Library, Hampton Bays, NY [*Library symbol*] [*Library of Congress*] [*Obsolete*]　(LCLS)
NHamH	Hilbert College, Hamburg, NY [*Library symbol*] [*Library of Congress*]　(LCLS)
N Hamp	New Hampshire Reports [*A publication*]　(DLA)
NHampB	Hampton Bays Public Library, Hampton Bays, NY [*Library symbol*] [*Library of Congress*]　(LCLS)
N Hamp Rep...	New Hampshire Reports [*A publication*]　(DLA)
N Hampshire Rep...	New Hampshire Reports [*A publication*]　(DLA)
NH & C	Railway and Canal Cases [*1835-55*] [*England*] [*A publication*]　(DLA)
NH&RA	National Housing & Rehabilitation Association　(NTPA)
NH & S	Needham, Harper & Steers [*Advertising agency*]
NH & S	Nuclear Hardening and Survivability
NH&S	Nuclear Hardness and Survivability　(SAUS)
NHANES	National Health and Nutritional Examination Survey
NHANG	New Hampshire Air National Guard　(MUSM)
NHaOM	Oldfield Middle School, Harborfield, NY [*Library symbol*] [*Library of Congress*]　(LCLS)
NHAP	National High-Altitude Photography Program　(CARB)
NHapS	Suffolk County Department of Health Service, Hauppauge, NY [*Library symbol*] [*Library of Congress*]　(LCLS)
NHapSA	Suffolk Academy of Medicine, Hauppauge, NY [*Library symbol*] [*Library of Congress*]　(LCLS)
Nh-Ar	New Hampshire Department of Administration and Control, Division of Archives and Records Management, Concord, NH [*Library symbol*] [*Library of Congress*]　(LCLS)
NHAR	Next Higher Assembly Removal Frequency [*Engineering*]　(MCD)
NHarC	Harriman College, Harriman, NY [*Library symbol*] [*Library of Congress*]　(LCLS)
NHARC	Nursing Home Advisory and Research Council　(EA)
NHarn	Harrison Public Library, Harrison, NY [*Library symbol*] [*Library of Congress*]　(LCLS)
NHarnC	Westchester County Courthouse, Harrison, NY [*Library symbol*] [*Library of Congress*]　(LCLS)
NHas	Hastings-On-Hudson Public Library, Hastings-On-Hudson, NY [*Library symbol*] [*Library of Congress*]　(LCLS)
NHAS	National Healthcare Antifraud Association [*Address unknown*]　(EA)
NHAS	National Hearing Aid Society　(EA)
NHASA	National Handbag and Accessories Salesmen's Association　(EA)
NHasI	Institute of Society, Ethics, and Life Sciences, The Hastings Center, Hastings-On-Hudson, NY [*Library symbol*] [*Library of Congress*]　(LCLS)
NHAT	Neutron Hardness Assurance Test
NHauS	Suffolk County Department of Health Service, Hauppauge, NY [*Library symbol*] [*Library of Congress*]　(LCLS)
NHAW	Northamerican Heating and Airconditioning Wholesalers Association　(EA)
NHAW	Notable Hispanic American Women [*A publication*]
NHB	Kodiak [*Alaska*] [*Airport symbol*]　(AD)
NHB	NASA Handbook　(KSC)
NHB	National Harbours Board [*Canada*]
NHB	National Health Board
NHB	National Naval Medical Center [*Maryland*] [*Seismograph station code, US Geological Survey*] [*Closed*]　(SEIS)
NH-B	Naval Hospital-Bethesda　(ACAE)
NHB	New Hibernian [*Vancouver Stock Exchange symbol*]
NHB	Nitro(hydroxy)benzoic Acid [*Organic chemistry*]
NHB	Northland Harbour Board　(SAUS)
NHBC	National House Building Council [*British*]
NHBE	Normal Human Bronchial Epithelial [*Cells*]
NHBIA	New Hampshire Brain Injury Association　(SAUS)
NHBPCC	National High Blood Pressure Coordinating Committee
NHBPEP	National High Blood Pressure Education Program
NHBPM	National Housebuilders' and Plumbers' Merchants [*British*]　(DI)
NHBRA	National Housebuilders' Registration Association [*British*]　(DI)
NHBRC	National House-Builders Registration Council [*British*]　(ILCA)
NHBS	Natural History Book Service Ltd.
NHBS	Navy Headquarters Budgeting System　(GFGA)
NHBS/NHPS...	Navy Headquarters Budgeting System/Navy Headquarters Programming System　(GFGA)

NHBU.......... New Hampshire Board of Underwriters (SAUS)
NHBW.......... National Hook-Up of Black Women (EA)
NHC .... Colgate University, Hamilton, NY [*Library symbol*] [*Library of Congress*] (LCLS)
NHC .... National Havurah Committee (EA)
NHC .... National Healthcare Ltd. [*AMEX symbol*] (SPSG)
NHC .... National Health Council (EA)
NHC .... National Heart Council (EA)
NHC .... National Homecaring Council [*Later, FHH*] (EA)
NHC .... National Horse Carriers Association, Inc., Frankfort KY [*STAC*]
NHC .... National Housing Center (EA)
NHC .... National Housing Conference (EA)
NHC .... National Housing Council [*of the HHFA*] [*Abolished, 1965*]
NHC .... National Humanities Center (EA)
NHC .... National Hunt Committee [*British*] (DI)
NHC .... National Hunt Cup [*British*] (ROG)
NHC .... National Hurricane Center [*National Weather Service*]
NHC .... Native High Court Reports [*South Africa*] [*A publication*] (DLA)
NHC .... Natl Healthcare L.P. [*AMEX symbol*] (TTSB)
NHC .... Natural Hydrocarbon [*Organic chemistry*]
NHC .... Navy Department Library, Naval Historical Center, Washington, DC [*OCLC symbol*] (OCLC)
NHC .... Neighborhood Health Center [*Generic term*] (DHSM)
NHC .... Neohemocyte [*An artificial red blood cell*]
NHC .... Neonatal Hypocalcemia [*Medicine*] (DB)
NHC .... New Hall College (SAUS)
NHC .... New Haven [*Connecticut*] [*Seismograph station code, US Geological Survey*] [*Closed*] (SEIS)
NHC .... New Zealand National Health Committee (SAUS)
NHC .... Next Hop Client (SAUS)
NHC .... N-Hexylcarborane [*Rocket fuel*] (RDA)
NHC .... Nicaraguan Humanitarian Coalition (SAUS)
NHC .... Nonhistone Chromosomal Protein [*Genetics*] (MAE)
NHC .... Normal-Hexylcarbane (MCD)
NHC .... Northwest Horticultural Council (EA)
NHC .... Northwest Hydraulic Consultants (SAUS)
NHC .... Numatec Hanford Corp. (SAUS)
NHC .... Nursing Home Care (MELL)
NHC .... United States National Hurricane Center (SAUS)
NHCA.......... National Hairdressers and Cosmetologists Association (EA)
NHCA.......... National Health Club Association (EA)
NHCA.......... National Hearing Conservation Association (EA)
NHCA.......... National Hispanic Congress on Alcoholism [*Defunct*] (EA)
NHCA.......... National Hispanic Council on Aging (EA)
NHCAA........ National Health Care Anti-Fraud Association (EA)
NHCAP........ Native Hawaiian Culture and Arts Program [*An association*] (EA)
NHCBS........ New Hampshire Council for Better Schools (SAUS)
NHCC.......... NASA Headquarters Computer Center
N-HCC........ Nash-Healey Car Club (EA)
NHCC.......... National Havurah Coordinating Committee (EA)
NHCC.......... National Health Care Campaign [*Defunct*] (EA)
NHCC.......... National Hebrew Culture Council (EA)
NHCC.......... National Hispanic Corporate Council (EA)
NHCCOEP ... National Hispanic Colorectal Cancer Outreach and Education Project (SAUS)
NHCE.......... Non-Highly Compensated Employee
NHCES........ National Health Care Expenditures Study (DHSM)
NHCFD........ National Health Care Foundation for the Deaf [*Later, Deaf-REACH*] (EA)
NHCI.......... National Home Centers [*NASDAQ symbol*] (SAG)
NhCla.......... Fiske Free Library, Claremont, NH [*Library symbol*] [*Library of Congress*] (LCLS)
NHCoA........ National Hispanic Council on Aging (EA)
NHCP.......... National HUMINT Collection Plan (MCD)
NHCP.......... Nonhistone Chromosomal Protein [*Genetics*]
NHCS.......... National Health Care Survey [*Department of Health and Human Services*] (GFGA)
NHCS.......... National Home Center Show (ITD)
NHCSA........ National Historic Communal Societies Association [*Later, CSA*] (EA)
NhCSp .... Saint Paul's School, Concord, NH [*Library symbol*] [*Library of Congress*] (LCLS)
NhCT........... New Hampshire Technical Institute, Concord, NH [*Library symbol*] [*Library of Congress*] (LCLS)
NHCU.......... Nursing Home Care Unit [*Veterans Administration*]
NHCUC........ New Hampshire College and University Council, Library Policy Committee [*Library network*]
NhD .... Dartmouth College, Hanover (SAUS)
NhD .... Dartmouth College, Hanover, NH [*Library symbol*] [*Library of Congress*] (LCLS)
NHD............ Doctor of Natural History (WDAA)
NHD............ National History Day (EA)
NHD............ Nevada Highway Department (SAUS)
NHD............ New Harding Group, Inc. [*Toronto Stock Exchange symbol*]
NHD............ Normal Hair Distribution [*Medicine*] (DAVI)
NHD............ Not Heard [*Communications*]
NHDA.......... National Huntington's Disease Association [*Later, HDSA*] (EA)
NHDAA........ National Home Demonstration Agents' Association [*Later, NAEHE*] (EA)
NhD-BE .... Dartmouth College, Business Administration and Engineering Library, Hanover, NH [*Library symbol*] [*Library of Congress*] (LCLS)
NHDC.......... National Hansen's Disease Center (DMAA)
NHDC.......... National Home Demonstration Council [*Later, NEHC*] (EA)
NHDC.......... NATO HAWK Documentation Center [*Missiles*] (NATG)
NHDC.......... Naval Historical Display Center

NHDC.......... Neohesperidin Dihydrochalcone [*Also, NEO-DHC*] [*Sweetening agent*]
NhD-D .... Dartmouth College, Dana Biomedical Library, Hanover, NH [*Library symbol*] [*Library of Congress*] (LCLS)
NHDF .... Normal Human Diploid Fibroblast [*Medicine*] (DMAA)
NhD-H .... Dartmouth College, Hood Museum, Hanover, NH [*Library symbol*] [*Library of Congress*] (LCLS)
NHDI........... Notch Die [*Tool*] (AAG)
NhD-K .... Dartmouth College, Kresge Physical Sciences Library, Hanover, NH [*Library symbol*] [*Library of Congress*] (LCLS)
NHDL.......... Nonhigh Density Lipoprotein [*Medicine*] (DMAA)
NHDNA .... Nucleohistone Deoxyribonucleic Acid
NhDo .... Dover Public Library, Dover, NH [*Library symbol*] [*Library of Congress*] (LCLS)
NhD-P .... Dartmouth College, Paddock Music Library, Hanover, NH [*Library symbol*] [*Library of Congress*] (LCLS)
NHDS .... National Health Data System (DMAA)
NHDS .... National Hospital Discharge Survey
NHDS .... Nonhazardous Dry Solid [*Shipping classification*]
NHDSC .... National Hot Dog and Sausage Council (EA)
NHE .... National Housing Endowment (EA)
NHE .... Nitrogen Heat Exchange
NHE .... Normal Hydrogen Electrode
NHE .... North Hennepin Community College Library, Brooklyn Park, MN [*OCLC symbol*] (OCLC)
NHE .... Nuclease-Hypersensitive Element [*Biochemistry*]
NHEA .... National Higher Education Association (EA)
NHEA .... New Hampshire Education Association (SAUS)
NHEB .... National Home Enlargement Bureau [*British*] (DI)
N HEB.......... New Hebrew [*Language, etc.*] (ROG)
N HEB.......... New Hebrides (ROG)
N Heb.......... New Hebrides (SHCU)
NHEC .... Northern Hemisphere Exchange Center (SAUS)
NHEC Station... North Hemispheric Central Station (SAUS)
NHEDLP....... National Housing and Economic Development Law Project
NHEF .... National Health Education Foundation
NHEIAP....... New Hampshire Educational Improvement and Assessment Program
NHEIAY....... Japanese Journal of Smooth Muscle Research (journ.) (SAUS)
NHEK .... Normal Human Epidermal Keratinocyte
NHeLP .... National Health Law Program (EA)
NHELP .... New Hitachi Effective Library for Programming (NITA)
NHELTR....... National High Energy Laser Test Range (ACAE)
NHem .... Hempstead Public Library, Hempstead, NY [*Library symbol*] [*Library of Congress*] (LCLS)
NHEM .... Normal Human Epidermal Melanocyte [*Cytology*]
NHemB .... Burns & Roe, Inc., Branch Library, Hempstead, NY [*Library symbol*] [*Library of Congress*] (LCLS)
NHemCE ...... William S. Covert School, Hempstead, NY [*Library symbol*] [*Library of Congress*] (LCLS)
NHemFE ...... Franklin School, Hempstead, NY [*Library symbol*] [*Library of Congress*] (LCLS)
NHemFuE .... Fulton School, Hempstead, NY [*Library symbol*] [*Library of Congress*] (LCLS)
NHemGH...... Hempstead General Hospital, Medical Center, Hempstead, NY [*Library symbol*] [*Library of Congress*] (LCLS)
NHemH........ Hofstra University, Hempstead, NY [*Library symbol*] [*Library of Congress*] (LCLS)
NHemJE ...... Jackson Elementary School, Hempstead, NY [*Library symbol*] [*Library of Congress*] (LCLS)
NHEML .... National Hurricane and Experimental Meteorology Laboratory [*Marine science*] (MSC)
NHEML .... United States National Hurricane Experimental Meteorological Laboratory (SAUS)
NHemLE ...... Ludlum School, Hempstead, NY [*Library symbol*] [*Library of Congress*] (LCLS)
NHemLJ....... Lawrence Road Junior High School, Hempstead, NY [*Library symbol*] [*Library of Congress*] (LCLS)
NHemME ...... Marshall School, Hempstead, NY [*Library symbol*] [*Library of Congress*] (LCLS)
NHemMS ..... Hempstead Middle School, Hempstead, NY [*Library symbol*] [*Library of Congress*] (LCLS)
NHemNH...... Nassau County Department of Health, Hempstead, NY [*Library symbol*] [*Library of Congress*] (LCLS)
NHemNHR ... Nassau County Department of Health, Division of Laboratories and Research, Hempstead, NY [*Library symbol*] [*Library of Congress*] (LCLS)
NHemPE ...... Prospect School, Hempstead, NY [*Library symbol*] [*Library of Congress*] (LCLS)
NHemSH ...... Hempstead Senior High School, Hempstead, NY [*Library symbol*] [*Library of Congress*] (LCLS)
NHemWE ..... Washington School, Hempstead, NY [*Library symbol*] [*Library of Congress*] (LCLS)
NHen .... Henderson Free Library, Henderson, NY [*Library symbol*] [*Library of Congress*] (LCLS)
NHEN .... National Holistic Education Network (EA)
NHENMA...... National Hand Embroidery and Novelty Manufacturers Association [*Defunct*] (EA)
NHEP .... Nicaragua-Honduras Education Project (EA)
NHEP .... Nuclear Hardness Evaluation Procedures Program (ACAE)
NHEPLC ...... Nepal Hydro and Electric Production Limited Company (SAUS)
NHERI......... National Home Education Research Institute (EA)
NHerkCHi.... Herkimer County Historical Society, Herkimer, NY [*Library symbol*] [*Library of Congress*]
NHerrSH ..... Herricks Senior High School, Herricks, NY [*Library symbol*] [*Library of Congress*] (LCLS)

NHES .... National Health Enhancement Systems, Inc. [*NASDAQ symbol*] (NQ)
NHES .... National Health Examination Survey [*Department of Health and Human Services*] (GFGA)
NHES .... National Humane Education Society (EA)
NHES .... Natl Health Enhancement Sys [*NASDAQ symbol*] (TTSB)
NHESA .... National Higher Education Staff Association [*Defunct*] (EA)
NHESP .... Natural Heritage and Endangered Species Program [*Massachusetts State Division of Fisheries and Wildlife*] [*Also, an information service or system*] (IID)
NHew .... Hewlett-Woodmere Public Library, Hewlett, NY [*Library symbol*] [*Library of Congress*] (LCLS)
NHewE .... Hewlett Elementary School, Hewlett, NY [*Library symbol*] [*Library of Congress*] (LCLS)
NHewFC .... Franlin Early Childhood Center, Hewlett, NY [*Library symbol*] [*Library of Congress*] (LCLS)
NHewFE .... Franklin Elementary School, Hewlett, NY [*Library symbol*] [*Library of Congress*] (LCLS)
NHewLD ...... Lawrence Country Day School, Hewlett, NY [*Library symbol*] [*Library of Congress*] (LCLS)
NHewOE ...... Ogden Elementary School, Hewlett, NY [*Library symbol*] [*Library of Congress*] (LCLS)
NHewSH ...... G. W. Hewlett Senior High School, Hewlett, NY [*Library symbol*] [*Library of Congress*] (LCLS)
NHewWM ... Woodmere Middle School, Hewlett, NY [*Library symbol*] [*Library of Congress*] (LCLS)
NhExP .... Phillips Exeter Academy, Exeter, NH [*Library symbol*] [*Library of Congress*] (LCLS)
NHF .... National Hairdressers' Federation [*British*] (BI)
NHF .... National Handicapped Foundation (EA)
NHF .... National Headache Foundation (EA)
NHF .... National Health Federation (EA)
NHF .... National Health Foundation (NADA)
NHF .... National Heart Foundation (NADA)
NHF .... National Hemophilia Foundation (EA)
NHF .... National Humanities Faculty [*Later, NFHAS*] (EA)
NHF .... National Hunting and Fishing [*In "NHF" Day*] [*National Rifle Association*]
NHF .... National Hydrocephalus Foundation (EA)
NHF .... Natural Heritage Fund (SAUS)
NHF .... Nausori Highlands [*Fiji*] [*Seismograph station code, US Geological Survey*] (SEIS)
NHF .... Naval Historical Foundation (EA)
NHF .... New Halfa [*Sudan*] [*Airport symbol*] (OAG)
NHF .... Nonimmune Hydrops Fetalis [*Medicine*] (DMAA)
NHF .... Nordic Hydrological Association (SAUS)
NHF .... Nordiska Handikappforbundet [*Nordic Association for the Handicapped - NAH*] (EAIO)
NHF .... Nordisk Herpetologisk Forening [*Scandinavian Herpetological Society - SHS*] (EAIO)
NHF .... Nordisk Hydrologisk Forening [*Nordic Association for Hydrology - NAH*] [*Denmark*] (EAIO)
NHFA .... National Home Furnishings Association (EA)
NHFF .... National Historical Fire Foundation (EA)
NHFL .... National Home Fashions League (EA)
NHFP .... New Hebrides Federal Party [*Political party*] (PPW)
NHFPL .... New Haven Free Public Library (SAUS)
NhFr .... Franklin Public Library, Franklin, NH [*Library symbol*] [*Library of Congress*] (LCLS)
NHFRA .... National Hay Fever Relief Association [*Defunct*] (EA)
NHG .... Newhawk Gold Mines Ltd. [*Toronto Stock Exchange symbol*] [*Vancouver Stock Exchange symbol*]
NHG .... New High German [*Language, etc.*]
NHG .... Normal Human Globulin [*or anticancer substance derived from NHG*] [*Biochemistry*]
NHG .... Northern Hemisphere Glaciation
NHGJ .... Normal Human Gastric Juice [*Medicine*] (DMAA)
NHGRI .... National Human Genome Research Institute (HGEN)
NHGS .... Non-Hydrogenous Gas Delivery System (SAUS)
NHH .... Neither Help nor Hinder
NHH .... Neurohypophyseal Hormone (DB)
NhHaCR .... United States Army, Cold Regions Research and Engineering Laboratory, Hanover, NH [*Library symbol*] [*Library of Congress*] (LCLS)
NHHC .... National Home Health Care Corp. [*NASDAQ symbol*] (SPSG)
NHHC .... Natl Home Health Care [*NASDAQ symbol*] (TTSB)
NhHen .... Tucker Free Library, Henniker, NH [*Library symbol*] [*Library of Congress*] (LCLS)
NhHenN ...... New England College, Henniker, NH [*Library symbol*] [*Library of Congress*] (LCLS)
NhHi .... New Hampshire Historical Society, Concord, NH [*Library symbol*] [*Library of Congress*] (LCLS)
NH His S .... New Hampshire Historical Society. Prroceedings (SAUS)
NhHopA .... New Hampshire Antiquarian Society, Hopkinton, NH [*Library symbol*] [*Library of Congress*] (LCLS)
NHHRA .... National Hereford Hog Record Association (EA)
NHHS .... New Hampshire Historical Society (SAUS)
NHHS .... Non-Household Sources (SAUS)
NH-HY .... Harvard University, Harvard-Yenching Institute [*Chinese-Japanese Library*], Cambridge, MA [*Library symbol*] [*Library of Congress*] (LCLS)
NHI .... Jacksonville, FL [*Location identifier*] [*FAA*] (FAAL)
NHI .... Naphtali Herz Imber (BJA)
NHI .... Nathan Hale Institute (EA)
NHI .... National Health Insurance [*British*]
NHI .... National Health Investors [*NYSE symbol*] (SPSG)

NHI .... National Heart Institute [*Later, NHLI, NHLBI*] [*National Institutes of Health*]
NHI .... National Highway Institute
NHI .... National Hobby Institute [*Defunct*]
NHI .... National Housing Institute (EA)
NHI .... National Humanities Institute (EA)
NHI .... NATO Helicopter Industries (SAUS)
NHI .... Nelson Holdings International Ltd. [*Toronto Stock Exchange symbol*] [*Vancouver Stock Exchange symbol*]
NHi .... New York Historical Society, New York, NY [*Library symbol*] [*Library of Congress*] (LCLS)
NHI .... Nielsen Home Video Index [*A. C. Nielsen Co.*] (NTCM)
NHI .... No Humans Involved (SAUS)
NHIA .... National Holography and Imaging Association (EA)
NHIC .... NASA Hazards Identification Committee (KSC)
NHIC .... National Health Information Clearinghouse [*Public Health Service*] [*Later, ODPHP Health Information Center*] (IID)
NHIC .... National Heritage Insurance Co.
NHIC .... National Home Improvement Council [*Later, NARI*] (EA)
NHIC .... Nichols-Homeshield, Inc. (SAUS)
NHick .... Hicksville Free Public Library, Hicksville, NY [*Library symbol*] [*Library of Congress*] (LCLS)
NHickAd ...... Hicksville Administration, Hicksville, NY [*Library symbol*] [*Library of Congress*] (LCLS)
NHickBE ...... Burns Elementary School, Hicksville, NY [*Library symbol*] [*Library of Congress*] (LCLS)
NHickCE ...... Old Country Elementary School, Hicksville, NY [*Library symbol*] [*Library of Congress*] (LCLS)
NHickDLE .... Dutch Lane Elementary School, Hicksville, NY [*Library symbol*] [*Library of Congress*] (LCLS)
NHickEE ...... East Elementary School, Hicksville, NY [*Library symbol*] [*Library of Congress*] (LCLS)
NHickFE ...... Fork Elementary School, Hicksville, NY [*Library symbol*] [*Library of Congress*] (LCLS)
NHickHT ...... Holy Trinity Diocesan High School, Hicksville, NY [*Library symbol*] [*Library of Congress*] (LCLS)
NHickL .... Long Island Lighting Co., Hicksville, NY [*Library symbol*] [*Library of Congress*] (LCLS)
NHickLE ...... Lee Elementary School, Hicksville, NY [*Library symbol*] [*Library of Congress*] (LCLS)
NHickOL ...... Our Lady of Mercy School, Hicksville, NY [*Library symbol*] [*Library of Congress*] (LCLS)
NHickSH ...... Hicksville Senior High School, Hicksville, NY [*Library symbol*] [*Library of Congress*] (LCLS)
NHickWE ..... Willet Elementary School, Hicksville, NY [*Library symbol*] [*Library of Congress*] (LCLS)
NHickWoE... Woodland Avenue Elementary School, Hicksville, NY [*Library symbol*] [*Library of Congress*] (LCLS)
NHIDA.......... No-Hands-in-the-Die-Area (SAUS)
NHIF .... Brain Injury Association [*Formerly, National Head Injury Foundation*] (EA)
NHIF .... National Head Injury Foundation (EA)
NHig .... Highland Free Library, Highland, NY [*Library symbol*] [*Library of Congress*] (LCLS)
NHigfL .... Ladycliff College, Highland Falls, NY [*Library symbol*] [*Library of Congress*] (LCLS)
NHigm .... Rushmore Memorial Library, Highland Mills, NY [*Library symbol*] [*Library of Congress*] (LCLS)
NHIP .... Natl Hlth Inv 8.50%Cv Pfd [*NYSE symbol*] (TTSB)
NHIP .... Nursing Home Improvement Program [*National Institute of Mental Health*]
NHIR .... Natural History Information Retrieval System [*Smithsonian Institution*]
NHIR .... New Hope & Ivyland Railroad Co. [*AAR code*]
NHIS .... National Health Interview Survey [*Department of Health and Human Services*] (GFGA)
NHIS .... Navy Hazardous Materials Information System (DNAB)
NHIS .... New Hampshire International Speedway [*Loudon*]
NHIS .... Nuclear Hardening Interceptor Structure
NHIS .... Nursing Home Information Service (EA)
NHISCH........ National Health Interview Survey of Child Health [*Department of Health and Human Services*]
NHIY .... Northumberland Hussars Imperial Yeomanry [*British military*] (DMA)
NHJ............. Nathaniel Hawthorne Journal [*A publication*] (ANEX)
NHJA .... National Hunter and Jumper Association (EA)
NHjl .... International Business Machines Corp., Components Division Library, Hopewell Junction, NY [*Library symbol*] [*Library of Congress*] (LCLS)
NHK .... Frank Aviation, Inc. (SAUS)
NHK .... Nippon Hoso Kyokai [*Japanese national broadcasting system*] (NTCM)
NHK .... Normal Human Kidney [*Medicine*] (DMAA)
NHK .... Patuxent River, MD [*Location identifier*] [*FAA*] (FAAL)
NhKe............ Keene Public Library, Keene, NH [*Library symbol*] [*Library of Congress*] (LCLS)
NhKeHi .... Historical Society of Cheshire County, Keene (SAUS)
NhKeHi .... Historical Society of Cheshire County, Keene, NH [*Library symbol*] [*Library of Congress*] (LCLS)
NhKeK .... Keene State College, Keene, NH [*Library symbol*] [*Library of Congress*] (LCLS)
NHKidQ........ New Horizon Kids Quest, Inc. [*Associated Press*] (SAG)
NHK Lab Note... NHK Laboratories Note (SAUS)
NHK Tech J... NHK Technical Journal (SAUS)
NHKYA........ National Hand Knitting Yarn Association [*Later, NHKYC*] (EA)
NHKYC......... National Hand Knitting Yarn Committee [*Defunct*] (EA)

NHL	Hamilton Public Library, Hamilton, NY [*Library symbol*] [*Library of Congress*] (LCLS)
NHL	National Historic Landmark
NHL	National Hockey League (EA)
NHL	Negro Heritage Library
NHL	Newhall Land & Farming Co. [*NYSE symbol*] (SPSG)
NHL	Nodular Histiocytic Lymphoma [*Oncology*]
NHL	Noise Interference Level (MELL)
NHL	Non-Hodgkin's Lymphoma [*Oncology*]
NHL	Nordic Federation of Heart and Lung Associations (EA)
NHL	Normal Hearing Level (MELL)
NHL	Normal Hormone Level (MELL)
NHL	Normal Human Lymphocyte
NHL	Northcal Resources [*Vancouver Stock Exchange symbol*]
NHL	Notes from Hume's Lectures [*A publication*] (DLA)
NHLA	National Hardwood Lumber Association (EA)
NHLA	National Health Lawyers Association (EA)
NHLA	National Hispanic Leadership Agenda (EA)
NHLA	National Housewives' League of America (EA)
NHLA	National Housewives League of America for Economic Security (EA)
NHLA	Norwegian Heart and Lung Association (SAUS)
NHLBAC	National Heart, Lung, and Blood Advisory Council [*National Institutes of Health*]
NHLBCA	National Hockey League Booster Clubs Association (EA)
NHLBI	National Heart, Lung, and Blood Institute [*Bethesda, MD*] [*National Institutes of Health*]
NHLBIC	National Heart, Lung, and Blood Information Center (PAZ)
NHLBI OEI	NHLBI Obesity Education Initiative (SAUS)
NHLC	National Hispanic Leadership Conference (EA)
NHLC	National Home Loans Corp. [*British*]
NhLe	Lebanon Public Library, Lebanon, NH [*Library symbol*] [*Library of Congress*] (LCLS)
NhLeHi	Lebanon Historical Society, Lebanon, NH [*Library symbol*] [*Library of Congress*] (LCLS)
NHLF	National Heritage Lottery Fund [*British*] (WDAA)
NHLI	National Heart and Lung Institute [*Later, NHLBI*] [*National Institutes of Health*]
NHLP	National Housing Law Project (EA)
NHLPA	National Hockey League Player's Association (EA)
NHL Rep	New Hampshire Law Reporter [*A publication*] (DLA)
NHltCre	National Healthcare Ltd. [*Associated Press*] (SAG)
NhM	Manchester City Library, Manchester, NH [*Library symbol*] [*Library of Congress*] (LCLS)
NHM	Natural History Museum [*British*]
NHM	Niihama [*Japan*] [*Seismograph station code, US Geological Survey*] [*Closed*] (SEIS)
NHM	Nitrosohexamethyleneimine [*Organic chemistry*]
NHM	No Hot Metal [*Photocomposition*]
NHM	Nonhostile Missing [*Military*] (CINC)
NHM	Normal Human Milk
NHM	Nozzle Hinge Moment
NHM	Nuclear Hyperfine Magnetic [*Rare-earth alloy*]
NHM	University of New Hampshire, Durham, NH [*OCLC symbol*] (OCLC)
NHMA	National Handle Manufacturers Association [*Defunct*] (EA)
NHMA	National Hispanic Medical Association (SAUS)
NHMA	National Housewares Manufacturers Association (EA)
NHMA	New Hampshire Medical Association (SAUS)
NHMC	National Hispanic Media Coalition (EA)
NHMC	National Hispanic Media Conference (EA)
NHMC	National Hotline for Missing Children (MELL)
NHMC	Normal Human Mammary Cell
NHMEL	National High Magnetic Field Laboratory
NHMF	National Heritage Memoiral Fund (WDAA)
NHMF	National Heritage Memorial Fund (AIE)
NHMFL	National High Magnetic Field Laboratory [*Florida State University*]
NHMIE	National Hazardous Materials Information Exchange (EEVL)
NHMILCOM	NATO HAWK Military Committee [*Missiles*] (AABC)
NHML	Non-Hodgkin's Malignant Lymphoma [*Oncology*] (DMAA)
NhMND	Notre Dame College, Manchester, NH [*Library symbol*] [*Library of Congress*] (LCLS)
NHMO	NATO HAWK Management Office [*Missiles*] (NATG)
NHmpTh	New Hampshire Thrift Bancshares, Inc. [*Associated Press*] (SAG)
NHMRC	National Health and Medical Research Council (DAVI)
NHMRC	National Hotel & Motel Reservations Corp.
NHMS	New Hampshire Medical Society (SAUS)
NhMSA	Saint Anselm's College, Manchester, NH [*Library symbol*] [*Library of Congress*] (LCLS)
NHMT	Nuclear-Hardened Mosaic Technology (SAUS)
NhMV	United States Veterans Administration Hospital, Manchester, NH [*Library symbol*] [*Library of Congress*] (LCLS)
NHN	National Homes Network [*British*] (DI)
NHN	Natural Heritage Network (SAUS)
NHN	Nebraska HealthNetwork [*Information service or system*] (IID)
NHN	Northern Horizon [*Vancouver Stock Exchange symbol*]
NhNa	Nashua Public Library, Nashua, NH [*Library symbol*] [*Library of Congress*] (LCLS)
NHNA	New Hampshire Nurses Association (SAUS)
NhNaR	Rivier College, Nashua, NH [*Library symbol*] [*Library of Congress*] (LCLS)
NhNaS	Sanders Associates, Inc., Technical Library, Nashua, NH [*Library symbol*] [*Library of Congress*] (LCLS)
NhNelC	Colby Junior College for Women [*Later, CSC*], New London, NH [*Library symbol*] [*Library of Congress*] (LCLS)
NHNP	New Hebrides National Party [*Political party*] (FEA)
NHNR	National Highway Needs Report [*Department of Transportation*]
NHO	M/I Schottenstein Homes [*NYSE symbol*] (TTSB)
NHO	National Hospice and Palliative Care Organization (NRGU)
NHO	National Hospice Organization (EA)
NHO	Navy Hydrographic Office [*Later, NOO*]
NHO	Northern Hemisphere Observatory [*Canary Islands*] (PDAA)
NHOA	National Hemi Owners Association (EA)
NHOH	Never Heard of Him (or Her) (SAUS)
NHolbHS	Sachem High School North, Holbrook (SAUS)
NHolb	Sachem Public Library, Holbrook, NY [*Library symbol*] [*Library of Congress*] (LCLS)
NHolbHS	Sachem High School North, Holbrook, NY [*Library symbol*] [*Library of Congress*] (LCLS)
NHolbSJ	Seneca Junior High School, Holbrook, NY [*Library symbol*] [*Library of Congress*] (LCLS)
NHoll	Community Free Library, Holley, NY [*Library symbol*] [*Library of Congress*] (LCLS)
NHOP	National Hurricane Operations Plan (DNAB)
NHorizn	New Horizon Kids Quest, Inc. [*Associated Press*] (SAG)
NHorW	Westinghouse Electric Corp., Engineering Library, Horseheads, NY [*Library symbol*] [*Library of Congress*] (LCLS)
NHOS	Naval Hospital
NHOS	Nuclear Hardened Optical Sensor (ACAE)
NHOYOA	National Home of Your Own Alliance (NRGU)
NHP	National Hamiltonian Party (EA)
NHP	National Historic Park (BARN)
NHP	National Housing Partnership [*HUD*]
NHP	National Humanitarian Party [*Political party*] [*Australia*]
NHP	Nationwide Health Prop [*NYSE symbol*] (TTSB)
NHP	Nationwide Health Properties, Inc. [*NYSE symbol*] (SPSG)
NHP	Natural History Press (DGA)
NHP	Neighborhood Health Program [*Generic term*]
NHP	Net Horsepower [*Engineering*]
NHP	Network Host Protocol
NHP	New Haven Free Public Library, New Haven, CT [*OCLC symbol*] (OCLC)
NHP	New Health Practitioners [*Nurse practitioners and physician assistants*]
NHP	New Hebrides Protectorate (SAUS)
NHP	NHP, Inc. [*Associated Press*] (SAG)
NHP	Nitrogen High Pressure
NHP	Nodular Hyperplasia of Prostate [*Medicine*] (MELL)
NHP	Nominal Horsepower
NHP	Nonhemoglobin Protein [*Medicine*] (MELL)
NHP	Nonhistone Protein (DB)
NHP	Nonhuman Primate
NHP	Noninverted Hand Position [*Neuropsychology*]
NHP	Normal Hearing Peer [*of the hearing-impaired*]
NHP	Normal Human-Pooled Plasma
NHP	Nuclear Heart Pacer
NHP	Numeric Hand-Printing (SAUS)
NHP	Nursing Home Placement (DAVI)
NHPA	National Hispanic Psychological Association [*Defunct*] (EA)
NHPA	National Historic Preservation Act (GNE)
NHPA	National Historic Preservation Act of 1966
NHPA	National Horseshoe Pitchers Association of America (EA)
NH-PA	Nurse Healers - Professional Associates (NTPA)
NHPA	Nurse Healers - Professional Associates (EA)
NHPAA	National Historic Preservation Act Amendments of 1980 (COE)
NHPAA	National Horseshoe Pitchers Association of America (EA)
NHPC	National Health Planning Council (DMAA)
NHPC	National Historical Publications Commission [*Later, NHPRC*]
NHPDA	National Honey Packers and Dealers Association (EA)
NHPDPA	National Health Promotion and Disease Prevention Act of 1976 (COE)
NHPE	Nuclear Hardening Evaluation Procedures (SAUS)
NHPF	National Health Policy Forum (EA)
NHPGA	New Hampshire Personnel and Guidance Association (SAUS)
NhPHi	Peterborough Historical Society, Peterborough, NH [*Library symbol*] [*Library of Congress*] (LCLS)
NHPI	NHP, Inc. [*NASDAQ symbol*] (SAG)
NHPIC	National Health Planning Information Center [*Public Health Service*] [*Database*] (IID)
NHpJR	James Roosevelt Library, Hyde Park, NY [*Library symbol*] [*Library of Congress*] [*Obsolete*] (LCLS)
NHPL	New Hampshire Public Library (SAUS)
NHPL	New Haven Public Library (SAUS)
NHPL Bul	New Hampshire Public Library Bulletin (SAUS)
NHPLO	NATO HAWK Production and Logistics Organization [*France*] (NATG)
NhPIS	Plymouth State College of the University of New Hampshire, Plymouth, NH [*Library symbol*] [*Library of Congress*] (LCLS)
NHPMA	Northern Hardwood and Pine Manufacturers Association [*Defunct*] (EA)
NHPN	National Highway Planning Network [*FHWA*] (TAG)
NHPO	NATO HAWK Production Organization [*Missiles*]
NhPoA	Portsmouth Athenaeum, Portsmouth, NH [*Library symbol*] [*Library of Congress*] (LCLS)
NhPoS	Strawbery Banke, Portsmouth, NH [*Library symbol*] [*Library of Congress*] (LCLS)
NHPP	National Health Professions Placement Network
NHPP	National Hormone and Pituitary Program (EA)
NHPP	Non-Homogeneous Poisson Process (SAUS)
NHpR	Franklin D. Roosevelt Library, Hyde Park, NY [*Library symbol*] [*Library of Congress*] [*Obsolete*] (LCLS)
NHPRC	National Historical Publications and Records Commission [*Formerly, NHPC*] [*Washington, DC*]

NHPRO .... National Historical Publications and Records Commission
NHPRO .... Nitrosohydroxyproline [*Organic chemistry*]
NHPS .... New Hampshire Pharmaceutica Association (SAUS)
NHPSCR .... New Hampshire Public Service Commission Reports [*A publication*] (DLA)
NHPYR .... Nitrosohydroxypyrrolidine [*Organic chemistry*]
NHQ .... NASA Headquarters
NHQ .... National Headquarters
NHQ .... Naval Headquarters (SAUS)
NHQ .... Nuclear Hyperfine Quadrupolar [*Rare-earth alloy*]
NHQC .... National Hispanic Quincentennial Commission (EA)
NHQRA .... Nursing Home Quality Reform Act
NHR .... National Handwriting Recognition (VLIE)
NHR .... National Heritage (EFIS)
NHR .... National Housewives Register [*British*]
NHR .... National Hunt Rules [*British*]
NHR .... Natl Health Realty [*AMEX symbol*] (SG)
NHR .... Naval High Refresh display system (SAUS)
NHR .... Net Histocompatibility Ratio
NHR .... New Hampshire Reports [*A publication*] (DLA)
NHR .... Non Hierarchial Routing (SAUS)
NHR .... Non-Hierarchical Routing (VLIE)
NHR .... North Hart Resources [*Vancouver Stock Exchange symbol*]
NHR .... Nova/Husky Research Corp. (SAUS)
NHR .... Nova/Husky Research Corp. Ltd. [*UTLAS symbol*]
NHRA .... National Hot Rod Association (EA)
NHRA .... National Housing and Rehabilitation Association (EA)
NHRA .... National Human Resources Association (NTPA)
NHRA .... Next Higher Recoverable Assembly (SAUS)
NHRA .... Next Higher Repairable Assembly (MCD)
NHRAC .... National Health Resources Advisory Committee [*Terminated, 1978*] [*General Services Administration*] (EGAO)
NHRAIC .... Natural Hazards Research and Applications Information Center [*University of Colorado - Boulder*] [*Research center*] (RCD)
NHRAW .... Northamerican Heating, Refrigeration, and Airconditioning Wholesalers Association (NTPA)
NHRB .... National Health Review Board [*Proposed medical-care price regulator*] (ECON)
NHRC .... National Health Research Center (DAVI)
NHRC .... National Human Rights Committee (EA)
NHRC .... National Human Rights Congress [*Australia*]
NHRC .... National Hydrology Research Centre (CARB)
NHRC .... Naval Health Research Center (GRD)
NHRC .... Nigerian Human Rights Community (SAUS)
NHRCPPUS... National Human Rights Campaign for Political Prisoners in the US (EA)
NHRD .... National Health Planning and Resource Development Act [*1974*] (DHSM)
NHRDP .... National Health Research and Development Program [*Canada*]
NHRE .... National Hail Research Experiment
NHRE .... United States National Hail Research Experiment (SAUS)
NH Rep .... New Hampshire Reports [*A publication*] (DLA)
NH Rev Stat... New Hampshire Revised Statutes [*A publication*] (AAGC)
NH Rev Stat Ann... New Hampshire Revised Statutes, Annotated [*A publication*] (DLA)
NHRI .... National Health Research Institutes [*Taiwan*]
NHRI .... National Hydrology Research Institute [*Canada*]
NHRL .... National Hurricane Research Laboratory [*Later, AOML*]
NHRL .... Northern Hemisphere Reference Line [*Geology*]
NHRP .... National Heart Research Project (EA)
NHRP .... National Hurricane Research Project
NHRP .... Next Hop Resolution Protocol [*Computer science*]
NHRP .... Next Hop Routing Protocol (SAUS)
NHRR .... New Haven Railroad
NHRRC .... National Hybrid Rice Research Center [*China*]
NHRS .... New Hampshire Revised Statutes [*A publication*] (DLA)
NHrzWrld .... New Horizons Worldwide, Inc. [*Associated Press*] (SAG)
NHS .... Das Nordhebraeische Sagenbuch [*A publication*] (BJA)
NHS .... International Society for the Prevention and Mitigation of Natural Hazards (SAUS)
NhS .... Kelley Memorial Library, Salem, NH [*Library symbol*] [*Library of Congress*] (LCLS)
NHS .... Nag Hammadi Studies [*A publication*] (BJA)
NHS .... Nathaniel Hawthorne Society (EA)
NHS .... National Handcraft Society [*Commercial firm*] (EA)
NHS .... National Handicapped Sports (EA)
NHS .... National Health Service [*British*]
NHS .... National Health Survey
NHS .... National Helicopter Services (SAUS)
NHS .... National Highway System
NHS .... National Historical Society [*Commercial firm*] (EA)
NHS .... National Historic Site (BARN)
NHS .... National Honor Society (EA)
NHS .... National Huguenot Society (EA)
NHS .... Native Human Serum Pooled [*Hematology*] (DAVI)
NHS .... Natural Human Serum
NHS .... Naval Honor Schools (AFIT)
NHS .... Neighborhood Housing Services [*Generic term*]
NHS .... New Hampshire Tracking Station
NHS .... New Hampshire State Library, Concord, NH [*OCLC symbol*] (OCLC)
NHS .... New Hampshire Tracking Station
NHS .... Newport Historical Society (SAUS)
NHS .... Next Hop Server (SAUS)
NHS .... N-Hydroxysuccinimide [*Organic chemistry*]
NHS .... Nikon Historical Society (EA)

NHS .... Normal Horse Serum
NHS .... Normal Human Sera (or Serum) (SAUS)
NHS .... Normal Human Serum
NHS .... North Hampton [*South Carolina*] [*Seismograph station code, US Geological Survey*] [*Closed*] (SEIS)
NHSA .... National Handicapped Skiers Association [*British*] (DBA)
NHSA .... National Head Start Association (EA)
NHSA .... National Heart Savers Association (EA)
NHSA .... National Highway Safety Administration [*Formerly, NHSB; later, NHTSA*] [*Department of Transportation*]
NHSA .... National Home Service Association [*Defunct*] (EA)
NHSA .... National Horse Show Association of America (EA)
NHSA .... Natural History Society of Australia
NHSA .... Naval Historical Society of Australia
NHSA .... Negro Historical Society of America
NHSA .... Neighborhood Housing Services of America (EA)
NHSAA .... National Horse Show Association of America (EA)
NHSAA .... New Hampshire School Administrators Association (SAUS)
NHSAC .... National Health and Safety Awareness Center [*Defunct*] (EA)
NHSAC .... National Highway Safety Advisory Committee
NHSACA .... National High School Athletic Coaches Association (EA)
NHSAS .... National Health Service Audit Staff [*Department of Health and Social Security*] [*British*]
NHSB .... National High School Band Institute (EA)
NHSB .... National Highway Safety Bureau [*Later, NHSA, NHTSA*] [*Department of Transportation*]
NHSB .... New Hampshire Savings Bank Corp. (SAUS)
NHSBA .... New Hampshire School Boards Association (SAUS)
NHsBE .... Birchwood Elementary School, Huntington Station, NY [*Library symbol*] [*Library of Congress*] (LCLS)
NHSBVA .... National High School Boys Volleyball Association (EA)
NHSC .... National Health Service Corps [*Department of Health and Human Services*]
NHSC .... National Highway Safety Council (NADA)
NHSC .... National Home Study Council (EA)
NHSC .... National Horse Show Commission (EA)
NHsCE .... Countrywood Elementary School, Huntington Station, NY [*Library symbol*] [*Library of Congress*] (LCLS)
NHSCP .... National Household Survey Capability Program [*United Nations*]
NHSCVO .... National Health Screening Council for Volunteer Organizations (EA)
NHSD .... National Health Survey Division [*of OSG*]
NHSD .... NATO HAWK Support Department [*Missiles*] (NATG)
NhSEA .... New Hampshire Society of Enrolled Agents (SAUS)
NHSF .... National Hispanic Scholarship Fund (EA)
NHSF .... National Horse Show Foundation (EA)
NHsH .... Half Hollow Hills Community Public Library, Huntington Station, NY [*Library symbol*] [*Library of Congress*] (LCLS)
NHsK .... KLD Associates, Inc., Huntington Station, NY [*Library symbol*] [*Library of Congress*] (LCLS)
NHSL .... New Hampshire State Library (SAUS)
NHSL .... New Horizons Savings & Loan Association [*NASDAQ symbol*] (SPSG)
NHSL .... NHS Financial [*NASDAQ symbol*] (TTSB)
NHSM .... No Hepatosplenomegaly [*On physical examination*] [*Gastroenterology*] (DAVI)
NHsME .... Maplewood Elementary School, Huntington Station, NY [*Library symbol*] [*Library of Congress*] (LCLS)
NHsMJ .... Memorial Junior High School, Huntington Station, NY [*Library symbol*] [*Library of Congress*] (LCLS)
NHsOE .... Oakwood Elementary School, Huntington Station, NY [*Library symbol*] [*Library of Congress*] (LCLS)
NHSP .... N-Hydroxysuccinimidyl Palmitate [*Organic chemistry*]
NHSR .... National Hospital Service Reserve [*British*]
NHSRA .... National Handicapped Sports and Recreation Association [*Later, NHS*] (EA)
NHSRA .... National High School Rodeo Association (EA)
NHSRP .... National Hail Suppression Research Program (SAUS)
NHSS .... National Herb Study Society (EA)
NHsS .... South Huntington Public Library, Huntington Station, NY [*Library symbol*] [*Library of Congress*] (LCLS)
NHsSAHS .... Saint Anthony's High School, Huntington Station, NY [*Library symbol*] [*Library of Congress*] (LCLS)
NHsSE .... Silaswood Elementary School, Huntington Station, NY [*Library symbol*] [*Library of Congress*] (LCLS)
NHsSJH .... Henry L. Stinson Junior High School, Huntington Station, NY [*Library symbol*] [*Library of Congress*] (LCLS)
NHST .... Null Hypothesis Significance Testing (DIPS)
NHSV .... Normal Hourly Space Velocity [*Emission control*]
NHsW .... Walt Whitman Birthplace Association, Huntington Station, NY [*Library symbol*] [*Library of Congress*] (LCLS)
NHsWH .... Walt Whitman High School, Huntington Station, NY [*Library symbol*] [*Library of Congress*] (LCLS)
NHT .... Corpus Christi, TX [*Location identifier*] [*FAA*] (FAAL)
NHT .... Nationwide Housing Trust [*British*]
NHT .... Natural Heritage Trust (SAUS)
NHT .... Nernst Heat Theorem [*Physics*]
NHT .... Nonpenetrating Head Trauma [*Medicine*] (DMAA)
NHT .... Now Hear This (EFIS)
NHT .... Nursing Home Type (ADA)
NHTAC .... Natural Heritage Trust Advisory Committee (SAUS)
NHTB .... New Hampshire Thrift [*NASDAQ symbol*] (TTSB)
NHTB .... New Hampshire Thrift Bancshares, Inc. [*NASDAQ symbol*] (NQ)
NHTC .... Natural Health Trends Corp. [*NASDAQ symbol*] (SAG)
NHTCW .... Natural Health Trends Wrrt'A' [*NASDAQ symbol*] (TTSB)
NHTCZ .... Natural Health Trends Wrrt'B' [*NASDAQ symbol*] (TTSB)

NHTD .... NASA Headquarters Telephone Directory
NHTI .... New Hampshire Technical Institute (SAUS)
NHTP .... Nursing Home-Type Patient
NHTPC .... National Housing and Town Planning Council [*British*]
NHTS .... New Hampshire Tracking Station (SAA)
NHTSA .... National Highway Traffic Safety Act (EEVL)
NHTSA .... National Highway Traffic Safety Administration [*Formerly, NHSB, NHSA*] [*Department of Transportation*]
NHTSA .... National Highway Transportation Safety Administration (EBF)
NHTU .... Naval Hovercraft Trials Unit
NH Turn ...... New Hampshire Turnpike (SAUS)
NHu .... Huntington Public Library, Huntington, NY [*Library symbol*] [*Library of Congress*] (LCLS)
nhu .... New Hampshire [*MARC country of publication code*] [*Library of Congress*] (LCCP)
NhU .... University of New Hampshire, Durham, NH [*Library symbol*] [*Library of Congress*] (LCLS)
NHUBW .... National Hook-Up of Black Women (EA)
NHUC .... National Highway Users Conference [*Later, HUF*]
NHuCE .... Cuba Hill Elementary School, Huntington, NY [*Library symbol*] [*Library of Congress*] (LCLS)
NHudC .... Columbia-Greene Community College, Hudson, NY [*Library symbol*] [*Library of Congress*] (LCLS)
NHudDAR .... Daughters of the American Revolution, Hendrick Hudson Chapter, Hudson, NY [*Library symbol*] [*Library of Congress*] (LCLS)
NHudHi .... Columbia County, New York Official Historian, Hudson, NY [*Library symbol*] [*Library of Congress*] (LCLS)
NhudO .... Olana State Historic Site, Hudson, NY [*Library symbol*] [*Library of Congress*] (LCLS)
NHuEJ .... Elwood Junior High School, Huntington, NY [*Library symbol*] [*Library of Congress*] (LCLS)
NHuFE .... Flower Hill Elementary School, Huntington, NY [*Library symbol*] [*Library of Congress*] (LCLS)
NHuFJ .... Finley Junior High School, Huntington, NY [*Library symbol*] [*Library of Congress*] (LCLS)
NHuGH .... John H. Glenn High School, Huntington, NY [*Library symbol*] [*Library of Congress*] (LCLS)
NHuH .... Huntington Hospital, Huntington, NY [*Library symbol*] [*Library of Congress*] (LCLS)
NHuHAE ...... Harley Avenue Elementary School, Huntington, NY [*Library symbol*] [*Library of Congress*] (LCLS)
NHuHE .... Huntington Elementary School, Huntington, NY [*Library symbol*] [*Library of Congress*] (LCLS)
NHuHi .... Huntington Historical Society, Huntington, NY [*Library symbol*] [*Library of Congress*] (LCLS)
NHuHS .... Huntington High School, Huntington, NY [*Library symbol*] [*Library of Congress*] (LCLS)
NHuI .... Immaculate Conception Seminary, Huntington, NY [*Library symbol*] [*Library of Congress*] (LCLS)
NHuJE .... Jefferson Elementary School, Huntington, NY [*Library symbol*] [*Library of Congress*] (LCLS)
NHuL .... Huntington Public Library, Huntington, NY [*Library symbol*] [*Library of Congress*] (LCLS)
NHuMHS ...... Madonna Heights High School, Huntington, NY [*Library symbol*] [*Library of Congress*] (LCLS)
NhuSE .... Southdown Elementary School, Huntington, NY [*Library symbol*] [*Library of Congress*] (LCLS)
NHusk .... KLD Associates, Inc., Huntington Station, NY [*Library symbol*] [*Library of Congress*] (LCLS)
NHusMJ .... Memorial Junior High School, Huntington Station, NY [*Library symbol*] [*Library of Congress*] (LCLS)
NHusWH ...... Walt Whitman High School, Huntington Station, NY [*Library symbol*] [*Library of Congress*] (LCLS)
NHuTJ .... R. K. Toaz Junior High School, Huntington, NY [*Library symbol*] [*Library of Congress*] (LCLS)
NHV .... New Haven Clock and Watch (SAUS)
NHV .... Nuku Hiva [*French Polynesia*] [*Airport symbol*] (OAG)
NHvL............ Long Island Lighting Co., Hicksville, NY [*Library symbol*] [*Library of Congress*] (LCLS)
NHW .... National Health and Welfare Mutual Life Insurance Association [*Formerly, NHWRA*] (EA)
NHW .... Neuhebraeisches Woerterbuch [*A publication*] (BJA)
NHW .... New Hospital for Women [*1904*] [*British*] (ROG)
NHW .... Night Hawk Resources Ltd. [*Vancouver Stock Exchange symbol*]
NhWalHi ...... Walpole Historical Society, Walpole, NH [*Library symbol*] [*Library of Congress*] (LCLS)
NHWK .... Harris Computer Systems [*NASDAQ symbol*] (TTSB)
NHWK .... Harris Computer Systems Corp. [*NASDAQ symbol*] (SAG)
NHWM .... Normal Human White Matter (DB)
NHWP .... Northeast Hazardous Waste Project [*Environmental Protection Agency*] (GFGA)
NHWRA........ National Health and Welfare Retirement Association [*Later, NHW*] (EA)
NHWRDDC... NW Hazardous Waste Research, Development & Demonstration Center (SAUS)
NHWS .... National Hurricane Warning Service [*National Weather Service*]
NHWU .... Non-Heatset Web Unit (EA)
NHWZSP....... National Highway Work Zone Safety Program
NHX .... Albany, GA [*Location identifier*] [*FAA*] (FAAL)
nhx............. Narthex (VRA)
NHY .... NIPSCO Industries [*NYSE symbol*] (TTSB)
NHY .... Norsk Hydro AS [*NYSE symbol*] (SPSG)
NHY .... Northumberland Hussars Yeomanry [*British military*] (DMA)

NHyF............ General Services Administration, National Archives and Record Service, Franklin D. Roosevelt Library, Hyde Park, NY [*Library symbol*] [*Library of Congress*] (LCLS)
NHZ .... Brunswick, ME [*Location identifier*] [*FAA*] (FAAL)
nhz............... Nanohertz (ELAL)
NHZ .... Nominal Hazard Zone [*Environmental science*] (COE)
NI................ [*First*] Cranial Nerve [*Second cranial nerve is NII, etc., through NVIII*] [*Medicine*] (DAVI)
NI................ Das Neue Israel [*A publication*] (BJA)
NI................ Inversion of the Note series (SAUS)
NI................ NAMBA [*North American Model Boating Association*] International (EA)
NI................ National Income
NI................ National Insurance [*British*]
NI................ National Interest
NI................ National Intervenors [*Defunct*] (EA)
NI................ Nation Institute (EA)
NI................ Nation of Ishmael [*An association*] (EA)
NI................ Native Infantry [*Indian Armed Forces regiment*]
NI................ Natural Intelligence (VLIE)
NI................ Nautical Institute [*British*] (EAIO)
NI................ Naval Infantry (SAUS)
NI................ Naval Instructor [*British*]
NI................ Naval Intelligence
NI................ Near Instantaneous (VLIE)
NI................ Need International [*An association*] (EA)
NI................ Negotiable Instrument
NI................ Neighbourhood Interchangeability (SAUS)
NI................ Netherlands Indies [*Later, Republic of Indonesia*]
NI................ Net Income
NI................ Net Interest
NI................ Network Identification [*Broadcasting*] (NTCM)
NI................ Network Interface [*Computer science*] (VLIE)
NI................ Network International (EA)
NI................ Neuraminidase Inhibition [*Medicine*] (DMAA)
NI................ Neurointermediate Lobe [*Of the pituitary*]
NI................ Neurological Impairment
NI................ Neurological Institute
NI................ Neurologically Intact [*Medicine*]
NI................ Neutralization Index [*Medicine*] (DMAA)
NI................ Neutraminidase Inhibition (PDAA)
NI................ New Impression [*Publishing*]
NI................ New Initiatives
NI................ New Internationalist [*Australia*] [*A publication*]
NI................ New Ireland
NI................ New Issue [*Publishing*]
NI................ News International [*An association*] (EA)
NI................ Niagara Institute (EA)
NI................ Nicaragua [*ANSI two-letter standard code*] (CNC)
NI................ Nicaraguan Airways (SAUS)
NI................ Nickel (SHCU)
ni................ Nickel (VRA)
NI................ Nickel [*Chemical element*]
NI................ Nicolaus de Tudeschis [*Deceased, 1445*] [*Authority cited in pre-1607 legal work*] (DSA)
Ni................ Nicolaus Furiosus [*Flourished, 12th century*] [*Authority cited in pre-1607 legal work*] (DSA)
NI................ Night (AABC)
Ni................ Nike (SAUS)
NI................ NIPSCO Industries [*NYSE symbol*] (SPSG)
NI................ NiSource, Inc. [*NYSE symbol*] (SG)
NI................ Nitrogen [*Chemical element*]
NI................ No Imprint (ADA)
NI................ No Information
NI................ No Interaction [*Medicine*]
NI................ Noise Index
N/I.............. Noise to Interference (SAUS)
N/I.............. Noise to Interference Ratio [*Telecommunications*] (TEL)
NI................ No Issue
NI................ Non-Aligned [*Political group*] [*EC*] (ECED)
NI................ Non Indicate (VLIE)
NI................ Non-Indicate (SAUS)
NI................ Noninductive (DEN)
NI................ Noninhibit (SAUS)
NI................ Non-Inhibitable Interrupt (MHDB)
NI................ Non-Interlaced (CDE)
N/I.............. Non-Interlaced (VLIE)
NI................ Nonintervention
NI................ Noninvasive Index [*Medicine*]
NI................ Non-inverting Input (SAUS)
NI................ Nonviolence International (EA)
NI................ Normal Impurity [*Metals*]
NI................ Normal Inferior
NI................ Northern Indiana Public Service Co. [*NYSE symbol*] (SAG)
NI................ Northern Indiana Railway
NI................ Northern Ireland Law Reports [*A publication*] (DLA)
NI................ Northern Island (SAUS)
NI................ North Indiana Public Service Co. [*AMEX symbol*] (SAG)
NI................ North Island [*New Zealand*] (BARN)
NI................ Notice of Information [*Computer science*]
NI................ Not Identified
NIyF............ Notifiable Installation (HEAS)
NI................ Not Illustrated [*Publishing*]
NI................ Not In
NI................ Not Indicated [*Laboratory science*] (DAVI)

NI	Not Informed
NI	Not Inoculated
NI	Not Interested
NI	Not Isolated
NI	Not Issued (AAG)
NI	Nuclear Instrumentation (NRCH)
NI	Nuclear Island (NRCH)
NI	Numerical Index (BUR)
NI	Numeric Information (SAUS)
NI	Numeric Item (SAUS)
NI	Numismatics International (EA)
NI	Tompkins County Public Library, Ithaca, NY [Library symbol] [Library of Congress] (LCLS)
NIA	National Ice Association [Later, PIA] (EA)
NIA	National Iceboat Authority
NIA	National Impala Association (EA)
NIA	National Income Accounts
NIA	National Inholders Association [Database producer] (EA)
NIA	National Institute on Aging [Bethesda, MD] [National Institutes of Health]
NIA	National Insulation Association (NTPA)
NIA	National Insulator Association (EA)
NIA	National Insurance Association [Chicago, IL] (EA)
NIA	National Intelligence Authority [1946-1947]
NIA	National International Academy
NIA	National Involvement Association (EA)
NIA	National Irrigation Administration (NADA)
NIA	Naval Intelligence Activity (DOMA)
NIA	Navy Industrial Association [Later, NSIA]
NIA	Neighborhood Improvement Association (BARN)
NIA	Neighborhoods-in-Action [An association] (EA)
NIA	Nephelometric Immunoassay [Analytical chemistry]
NIA	Nephelometric Inhibition Assay [Analytical chemistry] (MAE)
NIA	Net Internal Area
NIA	Network Information Access (SAUS)
NIA	Network Interface Adapter [Computer science] (AGLO)
NIA	Neuromuscular Integrative Action
NIA	Newspaper Institute of America (EA)
NIA	Next Instruction Address (SAUS)
nia	Niacin (MELL)
NIA	Nickel-Iron Alloy
NIA	Nitroisatoic Anhydride [Organic chemistry]
NIA	No Information Available
NIA	No Input Acknowledge [Computer science]
NIA	Noise Impact Area (SAUS)
NIA	Norfolk Island [Australia] [Seismograph station code, US Geological Survey] [Closed] (SEIS)
NIA	Norfolk Island Airlines [Australia] [ICAO designator] (FAAC)
NIA	Not in Action (SAUS)
NIA	NOVA Interface Adapter (SAUS)
NIA	Nutrition Institute of America [Inactive] (EA)
NIAA	National Independent Agents' Association [Australia]
NIAA	National Indian Athletic Association (EA)
NIAA	National Industrial Advertisers Association [Later, B/PAA]
NIAA	National Institute of Animal Agriculture [Defunct] (EA)
NIAA	National Institute on Alcohol Abuse and Alcoholism (SAUS)
NIAA	No Idea At All (SAUS)
NIAA	Northern Iowa Athletic Association (PSS)
NIAA	Nuclear Industries Association of America (SAUS)
NIAAA	National Institute on Alcohol Abuse and Alcoholism [Rockville, MD] [Public Health Service] [Department of Health and Human Services]
NIAAA	National Interscholastic Athletic Administrators Association (EA)
NIAA-DTF	National Industry Associations Anti-Dumping Task Force [Australia]
NIAAP	Indian Army Ammunition Plant (SAUS)
NIAB	National Institute of Agricultural Botany (WDAA)
NIAB	Naval Intelligence Advisory Board (DNAB)
NIABS	National Institute for Applied Behavioral Science
NIABY	Not in Anyone's Back Yard (PA)
NIAC	NASA Industrial Application Center [University of Southern California] [Los Angeles] [Information service or system] (IID)
NIAC	NASA Industrial Applications Center [University of Pittsburgh] [Pittsburgh, PA]
NIAC	National Industry Advisory Committee [Terminated, 1986] [FCC]
NIAC	National Information and Analysis Center
NIAC	National Insulation and Abatement Contractors Association (EA)
NIAC	National Insurance Advisory Committee [British] (DCTA)
NIAC	Nebraska-Iowa Athletic Conference (PSS)
NIAC	Nissho-Iwai American Corp. (SAUS)
NIAC	Northern Ireland Automation Centre [Queen's University of Belfast] (CB)
NIAC	Nuclear Insurance Association of Canada
NIAC	Nutritional Information and Analysis Center [Illinois Institute of Technology and Institute of Food Technologists] (IID)
NIACA	National Indirect Air Carrier Association [Defunct] (EA)
NIACE	National Institute for the Advancement of Career Education [Defunct] (EA)
NIACE	National Institute of Adult Continuing Education [British]
NIACRO	Northern Ireland Association for the Care and Resettlement of Offenders (DI)
NIACT	Night Action [American diplomat's jargon]
NIAD	National Institute on Adult Daycare
NIADA	National Independent Automobile Dealers Association (EA)
NIADA	National Institute of American Doll Artists (EA)

NIADDK	National Institute of Arthritis, Diabetes, and Digestive and Kidney Diseases [National Institutes of Health] (EA)
NIAE	National Institute for Architectural Education (EA)
NIAE	National Institute of Agricultural Engineering [Research center] [British] (IRC)
NIAF	National Italian American Foundation (EA)
NIAG	NATO Industrial Advisory Group (MCD)
NIAG	Niagara (ROG)
NIAG	Niagara Corp. [NASDAQ symbol] (SAG)
Niag	Niagara Corp. [Associated Press] (SAG)
NI AG	Nickel Silver (SAUS)
Niagara	Fort Niagara, Niagara Falls, Niagara-on-the-Lake, Niagara River, Niagara University (SAUS)
Niagara U	Niagara University (GAGS)
NiagCp	Niagara Corp. [Associated Press] (SAG)
NIAGRC	National Institute on Aging's Gerontology Research Center (MELL)
NIAGW	Niagar Corp. Wrrt [NASDAQ symbol] (TTSB)
NIAH	National Indian AIDS Hotline
NIAID	National Institute of Allergy and Infectious Diseases [of National Institutes of Health] [Department of Health and Human Services] [Bethesda, MD]
NIAISA	Northwest Indiana Area Library Services Authority (SAUS)
NIAJ	Niagara Junction Railway Co. [Absorbed into Consolidated Rail Corp.] [AAR code]
NIAL	National Institute of Arts and Letters [Later, AAIAL] (EA)
NIAL	Network for Informal Adult Learning (AIE)
NIAL	Not In Active Labor [Obstetrics] (DAVI)
NIALSA	Northwest Indiana Area Library Services Authority [Library network]
NIAM	National Institute of Advertising Management
NiaM	Niagara Mohawk Power Corp. [Associated Press] (SAG)
NIAMDD	National Institute of Arthritis, Metabolism, and Digestive Diseases [Formerly, NIAMD] [Later, NIADDK] [National Institutes of Health]
NiaMP	Niagara Mohawk Power Corp. [Associated Press] (SAG)
NIAMS	National Institute of Arthritis and Musculoskeletal and Skin Diseases [Bethesda, MD] [Department of Health and Human Services] (GRD)
NIAMSD	National Institute of Arthritis and Musculoskeletal and Skin Diseases [Department of Health and Human Services] (GFGA)
NIAMSK	National Institute of Arthritis and Musculoskeletal and Skin Diseases
NI&C	Hippon Information and Communication (SAUS)
NI & C	Nippon Information and Communication [Joint venture of IBM Corp. Japan and Nippon Telegraph and Telephone]
NI&C	Nippon Information & Communication Corp. (SAUS)
NI & RT	Numerical Index and Requirement Table (MCD)
NIANSW	Nursery Industry Association of New South Wales [Australia]
NIAP	National Income and Products [Economics]
NIAP	National Information Assurance Partnership
NIAP	Noninverting Amplifier Pair
NIAR	National Institute of Agrobiological Resources [Japan]
NIAR	National Institute of Atmospheric Research
NIAR	Neutron-Induced Autoradiography
NIAS	National Institute for Advanced Studies (EA)
NIAS	National Institute of Aeronautical Sciences
NIAS	National Institute of Airworthiness Surveyors [Australia]
NIAS	Netware Internet Access Server
NIASA	National Insurance Actuarial and Statistical Association [Later, ISO]
NIASE	National Institute for Automotive Service Excellence
NIAT	Non-Indexable Address Tag (SAA)
NIAT	Nursery Industry Association of Tasmania [Australia]
NIAWA	Nursery Industry Association of Western Australia [Australia]
NIAWR	National Institute on Aging, Work, and Retirement [Washington, DC] (EA)
NIB	National Identification Bureau [British]
NIB	National Industries for the Blind (EA)
NIB	National Information Bureau [Information service or system] (EA)
NIB	National Institute for the Blind (EA)
NIB	National Investment Bank [Ghana] (EY)
NIB	Navigation Information Bulletin
NIB	Negative Impedance Booster [Electronics]
NIB	Negative Ion Beam
NIB	Negative Ion Blemish
NIB	Network Interface Board
NIB	New Iberia Bancorp [AMEX symbol] (TTSB)
NIB	New Iberia Bancorp, Inc. [AMEX symbol] (SAG)
NIB	New in Box [Watch collecting]
NIB	Nigeria International Bank Ltd.
NIB	Node Initialization Block [Computer science] (IBMDP)
NIB	Noise Investigation Bureau (SAUS)
NIB	Noninterference Basis
NIB	Nordic Investment Bank (GNE)
NIB	North Ingalls Building (SAUS)
NIB	Not to Interface Base
NIBA	National Industrial Belting Association (EA)
NIBA	National Insurance Buyers Association
NIBA	Nebraska Independent Bankers Association (TBD)
NIBAA	National Insurance Brokers' Association of Australia
NIBC	Northern Ireland Base Command [World War II]
NIBCA	National Intercollegiate Boxing Coaches Association (EA)
NIberia	New Iberia Bancorp, Inc. [Associated Press] (SAG)
NIberiaB	New Iberia Bancorp [Associated Press] (SAG)
NIBESA	National Independent Bank Equipment and Systems Association [Park Ridge, IL] (EA)
NIBGE	National Institute of Biotechnology and Genetic Engineering [Pakistan]
NIBID	National Investment Bank for Industrial Development [Greece]

NIBJL........... National Information Bureau for Jewish Life (EA)
NIBL............ National Industrial Basic Language (MHDB)
NIBL............ National Industrial Basketball League (EA)
NIBM............ National Institute for Burn Medicine (EA)
NIBMAR....... No Independence before Majority African Rule [*British policy in regard to Rhodesia*]
NIBOR.......... New York Interbank Official Rate
NIBP............ Noninvasive Blood Pressure [*Medicine*] (DMAA)
Ni-BR........... Butadiene Rubber Based on Nickel Catalyst (SAUS)
NIBRA.......... National Independent Bicycle Rep Association [*Defunct*] (EA)
NIBS............ National Institute of Building Sciences (EA)
NIBS............ National Interim Bankruptcy System (AAGC)
NIBS............ Neural, Informational, and Behavioral Science
NIBS............ Neutral Industry Booking System (AAGC)
NIBS............ Nippon Institute of Biological Sciences (DAVI)
NIBS............ Nuffield Interactive Book System [*British*] (TELE)
NIBS Bulletin... Nippon Institute for Biological Science Bulletin (SAUS)
NIBSC.......... National Institute for Biological Standards and Control [*British*]
NIBTN.......... Nitroisobutametriol Trinitrate [*An explosive*]
NIC.............. Cornell University, Ithaca, NY [*Library symbol*] [*Library of Congress*] (LCLS)
NIC.............. Naphthylisocyanate [*Organic chemistry*]
NIC.............. National Impeachment Coalition [*Defunct*] (EA)
NIC.............. National Incomes Commission [*Nickname: Nicky*] [*British*]
NIC.............. National Indications Center [*Disbanded*] [*DoD*]
NIC.............. National Industrial Council (EA)
NIC.............. National Informatics Center [*India*] [*Information service or system*]
NIC.............. National Information Clearinghouse [*for Infants with Disabilities and Life-Threatening Conditions*] (PAZ)
NIC.............. National Information Clearinghouse for Infants with Disabilities and Life-Threatening Conditions
NIC.............. National Institute of Corrections [*Department of Justice*]
NIC.............. National Institute of Creativity [*Defunct*] (EA)
NIC.............. National Institute of Credit [*New York, NY*] (EA)
NIC.............. National Insurance Certificate [*British*]
NIC.............. National Insurance Contribution [*British*] (ECON)
NIC.............. National Insurance Contributions [*British*]
NIC.............. National Integrated Services Digital Network Council
NIC.............. National Intelligence Committee
NIC.............. National Interagency Council on Smoking and Health [*New York, NY*]
NIC.............. National Interfraternity Conference (EA)
NIC.............. National Interrogation Center [*Military*]
NIC.............. National Interstate Council of State Boards of Cosmetology (EA)
NIC.............. National Inventors Council [*Terminated, 1974*] [*National Institute of Standards and Technology*]
NIC.............. Natural Image Computer (PDAA)
NIC.............. Nauru Island Council [*Australia*]
NIC.............. Naval Intelligence Code [*World War II*] [*British*]
NIC.............. Naval Intelligence Command
NIC.............. Navigation Information Center
NIC.............. Navy Information Center
NIC.............. Nearly Instantaneous Compounding (MCD)
NIC.............. Neck Injury Criteria [*Automotive safety testing*]
NIC.............. Negative Immittance Converter [*Electronics*]
NIC.............. Negative Impedance Converter [*Electronics*]
NIC.............. Negative Ion Chamber
NIC.............. Neighborhood Info Centers Project (EA)
NIC.............. Neonatal Inclusion Conjunctivitis [*Medicine*] (MELL)
NIC.............. Neonatal Intensive Care
NIC.............. Netherlands Information Combine [*Delft*] [*Information service or system*] (IID)
NIC.............. Net Interest Cost [*Investment term*]
NIC.............. Network Information Center [*Advanced Research Projects Agency*] [*DoD*]
NIC.............. Network Interface Card [*Computer science*]
NIC.............. Network Interface Control
NIC.............. Neurogenic Intermittent Claudication [*Medicine*] (DMAA)
NIC.............. New Community Instrument for Borrowing & Lending (WDAA)
NIC.............. New Initial Commissions [*Business term*]
NIC.............. New International Commentary on the New Testament [*A publication*] (BJA)
NIC.............. Newly Industrialised (or Industralized, or Industrializing) Coutries (or Country) (SAUS)
NIC.............. Newly Industrializing Country (ECON)
NIC.............. Newspaper Indexing Center [*Flint, MI*]
NIC.............. Newsprint Information Committee [*Defunct*] (EA)
NIC.............. Niagara International Center (or Centre) (SAUS)
Nic............... Nicander [*Second century BC*] [*Classical studies*] (OCD)
NIC.............. Nicaragua [*ANSI three-letter standard code*] (CNC)
Nic............... Nicaragua (VRA)
NIC.............. Nicaraguan Information Center (EA)
NIC.............. Nickling Resources, Inc. [*Vancouver Stock Exchange symbol*]
Nic............... Nicolaus de Tudeschis [*Deceased, 1445*] [*Authority cited in pre-1607 legal work*] (DSA)
NIC.............. Nicolet Instrument Corp. (SAUS)
NIC.............. Nicosia [*Cyprus*] [*Airport symbol*] (AD)
Nic............... Nicotinyl (SAUS)
Nic............... Nicotinyl Alcohol [*Biochemistry*] (MAE)
nic............... Niger-Congo [*MARC language code*] [*Library of Congress*] (LCCP)
NIC.............. Nineteen-Hundred Indexing and Cataloging (DIT)
NIC.............. Nippon International Containers (SAUS)
NIC.............. NIPSCO Capital Markets [*NYSE symbol*] (SAG)
NIC.............. NIPSCO Cap Mkt 7.75% Debt Sec [*NYSE symbol*] (TTSB)
NIC.............. Noise Isolation Class (PDAA)
NIC.............. Nomarski Interference Contrast (SAUS)
NIC.............. Nominal Index Card (WDAA)
NIC.............. Non-Intel [*Corp.*]-Compatible Chips [*Computer science*]
NIC.............. Non-Intervention in Chile [*An association*] (EA)
NIC.............. Noninvasive Carotid [*Study*] [*Cardiology*] (DAVI)
NIC.............. Nonisothermal Calorimeter (SAUS)
NIC.............. Northern Illinois Commuter [*ICAO designator*] (FAAC)
NIC.............. Northern Intercollegiate Conference (PSS)
NIC.............. Not in Contact [*Electronics*] (DEN)
NIC.............. Not in Contract [*Technical drawings*]
NIC.............. Nudist Information Center [*Defunct*] (EA)
NIC.............. Numeric Intensive Computing (SAUS)
N i C........... Nurse in Charge (SAUS)
NIC.............. Nursing Interim Care (MELL)
NIC.............. Nursing Interventions Classification (SAUS)
NIC.............. US National Ice Centre (SAUS)
NICA............ National Ice Carving Association (EA)
NICA............ National Indian Counselors Association (EA)
NICA............ National Institute of Conveyancing Agents [*British*] (DBA)
NICA............ National Insulation Contractors Association [*Later, NIAC*] (EA)
NICA............ National Interfaith Coalition on Aging (EA)
NICA............ Netherlands Indies Civil Affairs Organization [*World War II*]
NICA............ Nicaragua Interfaith Committee for Action (EA)
NICA............ Nicaraguense de Aviacion SA [*Nicaragua*] [*ICAO designator*] (FAAC)
NICA............ Non-Interactive Computer Applications (SAUS)
NICAC.......... Nebraska Intercollegiate Athletic Conference (PSS)
NICAD.......... Nickel Cadmium (NG)
NiCad........... Nickel-Cadmium
NiCad Battery... Nickel Cadmium Battery (SAUS)
Ni-cad Cell... Nickel Cadmium Cell (SAUS)
Nic Adult Bast... Nicolas' Adulterine Bastardy [*1836*] [*A publication*] (DLA)
NICAM.......... Near-Instantaneous Companded Audio Multiplex (WDAA)
NICAM.......... Near-Instantaneous Companding Audio Multiplex (WDAA)
NICAM.......... Near Instantaneously Companded Audio Multiplex
Nic & Fl Reg... Nicoll and Flaxman on Registration [*A publication*] (DLA)
NICAP.......... National Investigations Committee on Aerial Phenomena
NICAP.......... Nuveen Insured California Premium Income Municipal [*Associated Press*] (SAG)
NICAP2........ Nuveen Insured California Premium Income Municipal Fund 2 [*Associated Press*] (SAG)
NICAR.......... Nicaragua
NICARD........ Navy/Industry Cooperative Research and Development Program (MCD)
NICAS.......... Nuveen Insured California Select Tax Free [*Associated Press*] (SAG)
NICATELSAT... Nicaraguan Telecommunication by Satellite [*Commercial firm*]
NICB............ National Industrial Conference Board [*Later, TCB*] (EA)
NICB............ National Insurance Crime Bureau (NTPA)
Nic Bel......... Nicolaus Bellonus [*Flourished, 1542-47*] [*Authority cited in pre-1607 legal work*] (DSA)
Nic Boe........ Nicolaus Boerius [*Authority cited in pre-1607 legal work*] (DSA)
NICC............ National Industrial Conservation Conference
NICC............ National Inventory Control Center (MCD)
NICC............ Nationalized Industries Computer Committee (NITA)
NICC............ Neonatal Intensive Care Center (DAVI)
NICC............ Nevis Island Cultural Center of the US (EA)
NICCF.......... National Ice Core Curatorial Facility (SAUS)
NICCW.......... Nuclear Island Closed Cooling Water (SAUS)
NICCWS........ Nuclear Island Closed Cooling Water System (SAUS)
NICCYH........ National Information Center for Children and Youth with Handicaps (EA)
NICD............ National Information Center on Deafness (EA)
NICD............ National Institute on Crime and Delinquency [*Later, NFCJ*] (EA)
NICD............ Nickel Cadmium (MCD)
Ni-Cd........... Nickel-Cadmium
NICDA.......... National Imported Car Dealers Association (EA)
Nice............. Eunice (SAUS)
NICE............ National Information Conference and Exposition [*Associated Information Managers*]
NICE............ National Institute for Clinical Excellence
NICE............ National Institute for Computers in Engineering [*Defunct*] (EA)
NICE............ National Institute for Consumer Education
NICE............ National Institute of Ceramic Engineers (EA)
NICE............ National Institute of Clinical Excellence
NICE............ Nationally-Integrated Caring Employees [*Union*] [*British*] (DI)
NICE............ National Society of Fund Raisers Institute of Continuing Education [*Former name of the National Society of Fund Raising Executives Foundation*] (NFD)
NICE............ Network Information and Control Exchange [*Computer science*] (CIST)
NICE............ NICE-Systems ADR [*NASDAQ symbol*] (SG)
NICE............ Noninvasive Carotid Examination [*Cardiology*] (DAVI)
NICE............ Noninvasive Cerebrovascular Examination [*Cardiology*] (DAVI)
NICE............ Nonlinear, Iterative Constrained Estimator (MCD)
NICE............ Nonprofit International Consortium for Eiffel (EA)
NICE............ Normal Input-Output Control Executive [*Computer science*]
NICE............ Northern Indiana Consortium for Education [*Library network*]
NICE............ Nosocomial Infection Control in Europe (SAUS)
NICE^3.......... National Industrial Competitiveness through Efficiency: Energy, Environment, andEconomics [*Environmental Protection Agency*]
NICEC.......... National Institute for Careers Education and Counselling [*Research center*] [*British*] (IRC)
NICEDD........ National Institute for Continuing Education in Developmental Disabilities (EA)
NICEIC.......... National Inspection Council for Electrical Installation Contracting [*British*]
NICEL........... National Institute for Citizen Education in the Law (EA)

Nic Elec......	Nicolsons Dections in Scotland (SAUS)	NICRA.........	National Ice Cream Retailers Association [*Later, NICYRA*] (EA)
Nic Elec......	Nicolson's Elections in Scotland [*A publication*] (DLA)	NICRA.........	Northern Ireland Civil Rights Association
NICEM........	National Information Center for Educational Materials (NITA)	NICRAD.......	Navy/Industry Cooperative Research and Development
NICEM........	National Information Center for Educational Media [*Later, AV Online*] (EA)	Nicralloy......	Nickel-Chrome Alloy (SAUS)
		NICRISP......	Navy Integrated Comprehensible Repairable Item Scheduling Program
NICER.........	Northern Ireland Council for Educational Research (AIE)	NICRO.........	National Institute for Crime Prevention and Rehabilitation of Offenders
NICET.........	National Institute for Certification in Engineering Technologies (EA)		
NICEY........	NICE-Systems ADR [*NASDAQ symbol*] (TTSB)	Ni-Cr S	Nickel-Chromium Steel (SAUS)
NICF..........	National Institute of Carpet Fitters [*British*] (DBA)	NICS	NAS Interfacility Communications System [*FAA*] (TAG)
NICF..........	Northern Ireland Cycling Federation (SAUS)	NICS	National Airspace System Interfacility Communications System (FAAC)
NICG	National Interagency Coordination Group [*National Atmospheric Electricity Hazards Program*] (MCD)	NICS	National Instant Check System
		NICS	National Institute for Chemical Studies (EA)
NICH	National Information Center for the Handicapped (EA)	NICS	National Insurance Contributions System [*Department of Health and Social Security*] [*British*]
NICH	Nitches, Inc. [*NASDAQ symbol*] (SAG)		
NICH	Non-Intervention in Chile [*An association*] (EA)	NICS	NATO Integrated Communications System (NATG)
NICHA........	Northern Ireland Chest and Heat Association (SAUS)	NICS	Network Integrity Control System
Nic Ha C	Nicholl, Hare, and Carrow's Railway and Canal Cases [*1835-55*] [*A publication*] (DLA)	NICS	Newly Industrialized Countries (DFIT)
		NICS	Nissan's Induction Control System [*Automotive engineering*]
Nich Adult Bast...	Nicholas on Adulterine Bastardy [*A publication*] (DLA)	NICSA	National Investment Company Service Association (NTPA)
Nic H & C	Nicholl, Hare, and Carrow's Railway and Canal Cases [*1835-55*] [*A publication*] (ILCA)	NICSBC	National Interstate Council of State Boards of Cosmetology (NTPA)
		NICS COA	NICS Control Operating Authority (SAUS)
NICHCY.......	National Information Center for Children and Youth with Disabilities (PAZ)	NICSE	National Institute for Child Support Enforcement [*Commercial firm*] (EA)
NICHD........	National Institute of Child Health and Human Development [*Bethesda, MD*] [*National Institutes of Health*] (GRD)		
		NICSEM	National Information Center for Special Education Materials [*University of Southern California*] [*Los Angeles, CA*]
Nich H & C..	Nicholl, Hare, and Carrow's Railway and Canal Cases [*1835-55*] [*A publication*] (DLA)	NICSEM/NIMIS...	National Information Center for Special Education Material/National Instructional Material Information System (EDAC)
NICHHD	National Institute of Child Health and Human Development [*National Institutes of Health*]		
		NICSH.........	National Interagency Council on Smoking and Health [*Defunct*] (EA)
NICHINS	Nichols Institute (SAUS)	Nic Sic Do ...	Nicolaus (Siculus Doctor) de Tudeschis [*Deceased, 1445*] [*Authority cited in pre-1607 legal work*] (DSA)
Nicholl H & C..	Nicholl, Hare, and Carrow [*1835-55*] [*A publication*] (DLA)		
Nichols-Cahill...	Nichols-Cahill's Annotated New York Civil Practice Acts [*A publication*] (DLA)	NICSMA	NATO Integrated Communications System Management Agency (NATG)
Nicholson	Nicholson's Manuscript Decisions, Scotch Session Cases [*A publication*] (DLA)	NICSO	NATO Integrated Communications System Organization [*Brussels, Belgium*] (NATG)
NICHROME..	Nickel Chromium [*Alloy*] [*Trade name*]	NICSOI.......	NICS Operating Instruction (SAUS)
NichRs........	Nichols Research Corp. [*Associated Press*] (SAG)	NICSS	Nellis Integrated Communications Switching System (ACAE)
NICI	National Insulation Certification Institute (EA)	NICSS	Northern Ireland Council of Social Science
NICI	National Interagency Counterdrug Institute [*Camp San Luis Obispo, CA*] (DOMA)	NICSX	Nicholas Fund [*Mutual fund ticker symbol*] (SG)
		NICT..........	National Incident Coordination Team [*Environmental science*] (EPAT)
NICI	Negative Ion Chemical Ionization [*Spectrometry*]	NIC-TRANS...	Naval Intelligence Command - Translation Division
NICIA	Northern Ireland Coal Importers Association (SAUS)	NICU	Neonatal [*or Newborn*] Intensive Care Unit
NICIMS	Negative Ion Chemical Ionization Mass Spectroscopy	NICU	Neurological Intensive Care Unit [*Medicine*]
NICIS	Nikon Intracellular Calcium Ion System	NICU	Neurosurgical Intensive Care Unit [*Medicine*] (DMAA)
NICJ...........	National Institute for Consumer Justice	NICU	Newborn Intensive Care Unit [*Medicine*] (DB)
NICK	Name Information Correlation Key	NICU	Nippon International Container Unit (SAUS)
NICK	Nature's Initial Cosmic Kickstart	NICU	Nonimmunologic Contact Urticaria [*Medicine*] (DMAA)
NICK	Nickelodeon [*Cable television channel*]	NI-CU Alloy...	Nickel-Copper Alloy (SAUS)
nick............	Nickname	NICUFO.......	National Investigations Committee on Unidentified Flying Objects (EA)
NICKA........	Codeword, Nickname and Exercise Term System (SAUS)		
NICKA3.......	Japanese Journal of Zootechnical Science (journ.) (SAUS)	NIC US........	National Ice Centre (SAUS)
NICL..........	National Ice Core Laboratory (SAUS)	NICWM	National Information Center on Women and the Military [*Later, WMP*] (EA)
NICL..........	Nickel Resoures Development Corp. (SAUS)		
NICLC	National Institute on Community-Based Long-Term Care (EA)	NICYRA.......	National Ice Cream and Yogurt Retailers Association (EA)
NICLF.........	Ni-Cal Developments Ltd. (MHDW)	NID	Inyokern, CA [*Location identifier*] [*FAA*] (FAAL)
NICLOG.......	National Information Center for Local Government Records [*Canada*]	NID	Namespace Identifier
		NID	National Institute for the Deaf (WDAA)
NICM	National Institute for Campus Ministries (EA)	NID	National Institute of Drycleaning [*Later, IFI*] (EA)
NICM	National Institute of Comparative Medicine (DAVI)	NID	National Institute of Dyslexia [*Defunct*] (EA)
NICM	Nuffield Institute of Comparative Medicine (SAUS)	NID	National Intelligence Daily [*CIA*] [*A publication*] (MUSM)
NICMA	National Ice Cream Mix Association (EA)	NID	Naval Intelligence Database (DOMA)
NICMA	National Industrial Cafeteria Managers Association [*Later, SFM*] (EA)	NID	Naval Intelligence Division [*British*]
		NID	Negligible Individual Dose [*Environmental Protection Agency*]
NICMC	National Institute of Certified Moving Consultants (NTPA)	NID	Network In-Dial [*Automatic Voice Network*] (CET)
NICMOS.......	Near-Infrared Camera and Multiobject Spectrograph [*Astronomy*]	NID	Network Interface Device [*Telecommunications*]
NICMOS.......	Near-Infrared Camera and Multiobject Spectrometer	NID	New Interactive Display [*NEC*] [*Computer science*] (PCM)
NICN	Navy Item Control Number (MCD)	NID	New International Dictionary [*Webster's*] [*A publication*]
NICNT	New International Commentary on the New Testament [*A publication*] (BJA)	NID	Next ID (SAUS)
		Nid............	Niddah (BJA)
NICO	National Insurance Consumer Organization (EA)	NID............	Nonequilibrium Ionospheric Disturbance [*Geophysics*]
NICO	Navy Indochina Clearing Office (DNAB)	NID	Non Illusion Direction (SAUS)
NICO	Navy Inventory Control Office	NID	Nonillusion Direction [*Ophthalmology*]
Nico	Nicolaus de Tudeschis [*Deceased, 1445*] [*Authority cited in pre-1607 legal work*] (DSA)	NID	Non-Immunologic Disease [*Medicine*] (MELL)
		NID	Noninsulin-Dependent [*Diabetes*] [*Endocrinology*] (DAVI)
NICOA.........	National Independent Coal Operators Association [*Defunct*] (EA)	NID	Non-Interactive Display (CCCA)
NICOA.........	National Indian Council on Aging (EA)	NID	Non-Internal Development [*DoD*]
Nico Alex....	Nicolaus de Alexandria [*Authority cited in pre-1607 legal work*] (DSA)	NID	Northern Ireland District
NICOL........	National Insurance Corp. of Liberia (EY)	NID	Not in Distress [*Medicine*] (MELL)
NICOL........	Network Information Center On-Line (SAUS)	NID	Nuclear Instruments and Detectors [*IEEE*] (MCD)
NICOL.........	New Integrated Computer Language	NIDA	99th Infantry Division Association (EA)
NICOL.........	New International Commercial Language (SAUS)	NIDA	National Independent Dairy-Food Association (EA)
NICOL.........	Nineteen-Hundred Commercial Language	NIDA	National Industrial Distributors Association [*Philadelphia, PA*] (EA)
Nicolas	Proceedings and Ordinances of the Privy Council, Edited by Sir Harry Nicolas [*A publication*] (DLA)	NIDA	National Institute on Drug Abuse [*Department of Health and Human Services*] [*Rockville, MD*]
Nicollet.......	Nicollet Process Engineering, Inc. [*Associated Press*] (SAG)		
NICOP.........	Navy Industry Cooperation Plan	NIDA	National Insurance Development Act of 1975
NICOP.........	Nickel Copper	NIDA	Northeastern Industrial Developers (or Development) Association (SAUS)
NICOR........	NICOR, Inc. [*Formerly, Northern Illinois Gas Co.*] [*Associated Press*] (SAG)		
		NIDA	Northern Ireland Development Agency (SAUS)
NICORD	Navy/Industry Cooperative Research and Development Program	NIDA	Numerically Integrated Differential Analyzer [*Computer science*]
NICOS	Newfoundland Institute for Cold Ocean Science [*Memorial University of Newfoundland*] [*Canada*] [*Research center*] (RCD)	NIDA	Numerically Integrating Differential Analyzer (SAUS)
		NIDA Res Mono..	National Institute on Drug Abuse Research Monographs (MEC)
NICOV.........	National Information Center on Volunteerism [*Later, NVC*] (EA)	NIDA Res Monogr...	NIDA Research Monograph (SAUS)
NICP	National Inventory Control Point [*Military*]	NIDAS.........	Nixdorf Integrated Data Accounting System (SAUS)
NICP	Nuclear Incident Control Plan		
Nic R	Nicolaus Rufulus [*Flourished, 13th century*] [*Authority cited in pre-1607 legal work*] (DSA)		

NIDC .... National Insurance Development Corp. [*Government-sponsored organization*]
NIDC .... Newly Industrialized Developing Country
NIDC .... Northern Ireland Development Council (SAUS)
NIDCC .... National Internal Defense Coordination Center [*Army*] (AABC)
NIDCD .... National Institute on Deafness and Other Communication Disorders [*National Institutes of Health*] (EGAO)
NIDCR .... National Institute of Dental and Craniofacial Research
NIDCR .... National Institute of Dental Craniofacial Research
NIDD .... Non-Insulin-Dependent Diabetes [*Medicine*]
NIDDK .... National Institute of Diabetes and Digestive and Kidney Diseases [*Public Health Service*] [*Also, an information service or system*] (IID)
NIDDKD .... National Institute of Diabetes and Digestive and Kidney Diseases [*Department of Health and Human Services*] (GFGA)
NIDDM .... Non-Insulin-Dependent Diabetes Mellitus [*Medicine*]
NIDDY .... Non-Insulin-Dependent Diabetes in the Young [*Medicine*] (DMAA)
NIDE .... Numerical Integration of Differential Equation (VLIE)
NIDE .... Numerical Integration of Differential Equations (SAUS)
NIDI .... Nickel Development Institute (EAIO)
NIDIR .... Nike Digital Instrumentation Radar (SAUS)
NIDL .... Network Interface Definition Language [*Computer science*]
NIDLR .... Office of the Director of Law Reform, Northern Ireland (DLA)
NIDM .... National Institute for Disaster Mobilization
NIDM .... Noninsulin-Dependent Diabetes Mellitus [*Endocrinology*] (DAVI)
NIDN .... Navy Intelligence Data Network (MCD)
NIDOC .... National Information and Documentation Center
NIDOCD .... National Institute on Deafness and Other Communication Disorders [*NIH*]
NIDR .... National Institute for Dispute Resolution (EA)
NIDR .... National Institute of Dental Research [*Public Health Service*] [*Bethesda, MD*]
NIDR .... Networked Information Discovery and Retrieval (TELE)
NIDRR .... National Institute on Disability and Rehabilitation Research [*Washington, DC*] [*Department of Education*] (GRD)
NIDS .... National Institute for Defense Studies (SAUS)
NIDS .... National Institute of Diaper Services [*Defunct*] (EA)
NIDS .... National Institutional Delivery System
NIDS .... National Intelligence Display System (ACAE)
NIDS .... National Inventory of Documentary Sources [*British*]
NIDS .... National Investor Data Service (EA)
NIDS .... Navigation Instrument Development Unit
NIDS .... Network Interface Data System [*NASA*]
NIDS .... NEXRAD Information Dissemination Service (SAUS)
NIDS .... Nonionic Detergent Soluble (DMAA)
NIDS .... Nuclear Integrated Data System
NIDX .... Network Intrusion Detection Expert system (SAUS)
NIE .... NASA Interface Equipment (MCD)
NIE .... National Index of Ecosystems [*Australia*]
NIE .... National Institute for the Environment [*Proposed government agency*]
NIE .... National Institute of Education [*Department of Education*] [*Washington, DC*]
NIE .... National Institute of Education, Washington, DC [*OCLC symbol*] (OCLC)
NIE .... National Intelligence Estimate
NIE .... Natural and Induced Environment (SPST)
NIE .... Negative Ion Erosion
NIE .... Netherlands Institute of Ecology
NIE .... Neutron Ionization Effect
NIE .... Newly-Industrialized Economy
NIE .... Newspaper in Education (SAUS)
NIE .... Newspaper in Education Program
NIE .... Newton Internet Enabler (SAUS)
NIE .... Niedzica [*Poland*] [*Seismograph station code, US Geological Survey*] (SEIS)
NIE .... Non-Interference Experiment (SAUS)
NIE .... Not Included Elsewhere
NIEA .... National Indian Education Association (EA)
NIEAC .... National Indian Education Advisory Committee [*Terminated, 1974*] [*Department of the Interior*] (EGAO)
NIECC .... National Industrial Energy Conservation Council (MCD)
NIEF .... National Ironfounding Employers Association [*British*] (BI)
NIEHS .... National Institute of Environmental Health Sciences [*Research Triangle Park, NC*] [*National Institutes of Health*]
NIEHS .... National Institute of Environmental Health Service [*Marine science*] (OSRA)
NIEI .... National Indoor Environmental Institute (EPA)
NIEI .... National Institute of Electromedical Information (EA)
niel .... Niello (VRA)
NIEL .... Non-Ionizing Energy Loss (SAUS)
NIEM .... National Industrial Engineering Mission (AABC)
NIEM .... Northern Institute for Environmental and Minority Law (SAUS)
NIEMR .... Non-Ionizing Electro-Magnetic Radiation (VLIE)
Nient Cul ..... Nient Culpable [*Not Guilty*] [*Latin*] [*Legal term*] (DLA)
NIEO .... New International Economic Order
NIEO .... Non-Incorporated Engineering Order (SAUS)
NIEP .... National Independent Energy Producers (NTPA)
NIEP .... Natural and Induced Environments Panel (SPST)
NIER .... National Industrial Equipment Reserve [*of DMS*]
NIER .... National Institute for Educational Research (NITA)
NIERC .... Northern Ireland Economic Research Centre
NIES .... National Institute for Environmental Studies (CARB)
NIES .... National Intelligence Estimates [*Summaries of foreign policy information and advice prepared for the president*] [*Known informally as "knees"*]

NIESO .... Non-materiel Individual Enhancement for the SOF Operator (SAUS)
NIESR .... National Institute of Economic and Social Research [*British*]
NIETB .... National Imagery Exploitation Target Base (MCD)
NIETS .... National Imagery Exploitation Tasking Study
NIETU .... National Independent Enginemen's Trade Union [*British*]
NIEU .... Negro Industrial and Economic Union
NIEWS .... NTCS-A Imagery Exploitation Workstation (SAUS)
NIEX .... Niagara Exchange Corp. (SAUS)
NIF .... National Ichthyosis Foundation (EA)
NIF .... National Ignition Facility [*Lawrence Livermore National Laboratory*] [*Department of Energy*] (PS)
NIF .... National Income Forecasting (ADA)
NIF .... National Innovation Fund [*South Africa*]
NIF .... National Institute for the Family (EA)
NIF .... National Interfraternity Foundation (EA)
NIF .... National Inventors Foundation (EA)
NIF .... National Investment Fund [*Poland*] [*Finance*]
NIF .... National Iranian Front [*Political party*]
NIF .... National Islamic Front [*Sudan*] [*Political party*]
NIF .... National Issues Forums (EA)
NIF .... Navy Industrial Fund
NIF .... Negative Inspiratory Force [*Medicine*]
NIF .... Network Information Files [*Burroughs Corp.*]
NIF .... Network Information Frame (SAUS)
NIF .... Network Interface Function (SPST)
NIF .... Neutrophil Immobilizing Factor (DMAA)
NIF .... Neutrophil Migration Inhibition Factor
NIF .... New Israel Fund (EA)
NIF .... Nickel-Iron Film
NIF .... Nifedipine [*Pharmacology*]
nif .... Nitrogen-Fixing [*Biology*] (BARN)
NIF .... Noise Improvement Factor (IEEE)
NIF .... Nonintestinal Fibroblast [*Medicine*] (DMAA)
NIF .... Note-Issuance Facility [*Banking*]
NIF .... Notice of Intent to Fine (SAUS)
NIF .... Not Industrially Funded [*Military*]
NIF .... Not in File
NIF .... Nuclear Information File (AFM)
NIF .... Nuveen Prem Insured Muni Inc. [*NYSE symbol*] (TTSB)
NIF .... Nuveen Premium Insured Municipal Income [*NYSE symbol*] (SPSG)
NIFA .... National Intercollegiate Flying Association (EA)
NIFAC .... Night Forward Air Controller [*Aircraft*]
NIFADCS ...... National Institute of Furnace and Air Duct Cleaning Specialists (EA)
NIFAST .... National Industrial Fire and Safety Centre (ACII)
NIFB .... National Institute of Farm Brokers [*Later, NIFLB*] (EA)
NIFC .... National Interagency Firefighting Center
NIFDA .... National Independent Flag Dealers Association (NTPA)
NIFDA .... National Institutional Food Distributor Associates (EA)
NIFE .... Nomenclature-in-Federal Employment
NIFEGS .... Northern Ireland Further Education Guidance Service (AIE)
NIFER .... National Institute for Full Employment Research [*Department of Labor*] (OICC)
NIFES .... National Industrial Fuel Efficiency Service [*British*]
NIFF .... Nordiska Ickekommersielles Fonogramproducenters Forening [*Nordic Association of Non-Commercial Phonogram Producers - NANPP*] (EAIO)
NIFF .... Notation Interchange File Format [*Computer science*] (VLIE)
NIFFTE .... Noncooperative Identification Friend or Foe Technology Evaluation (RDA)
NIFI .... National Institute for the Foodservice Industry (EA)
NIFL .... Finger Lakes Library System, Ithaca, NY [*Library symbol*] [*Library of Congress*] (LCLS)
NIFLB .... National Institute of Farm and Land Brokers [*Later, FLI*] (EA)
NIFLP .... Nuveen Insured Florida Premium Income Municipal Fund [*Associated Press*] (SAG)
NIFM .... Northwest Independent Forest Manufacturers (WPI)
NIFMA .... Nigerian Furniture Manufacturers Association (SAUS)
NIFMS .... NAVAIR [*Naval Air Systems Command*] Industrial Finance Management System (MCD)
NIFO .... Next In, First Out [*Queuing technique*]
NIFOB .... Non-Injurious Free-on-Board
NIFP .... National Institute for Federal Procurement (AAGC)
NIFP .... National Institute of Fresh Produce [*British*] (DBA)
NIFRS .... Navy Industrial Fund-Reporting System (MCD)
NIFS .... National Institute for Farm Safety (EA)
NIFS .... NT [*New Technology*] File System [*Microsoft Corp.*]
NIFTE .... Neon Indicator Functional Test Equipment
NIFTI .... Near-Isotropic Flux Turbulence Instrument [*Oceanography*]
NIFTP .... File transfer network in the United Kingdom (SAUS)
NIFTP .... Network Independent File Transfer Program (HGAA)
NIFTP .... Network Independent File Transfer Protocol (PDAA)
NIFTS .... Naval Integrated Flight Training System (MCD)
NI/FWM .... New, Incorporated/Fourth World Movement (EA)
NIG .... Aero Contractors Company of Nigeria Ltd. [*ICAO designator*] (FAAC)
NIG .... National Institute of Genetics [*Japan*]
NIG .... National Interest Group (HEAS)
NIG .... Nationwide Investigations Group [*British*]
NIG .... Naval Inspector General
NIG .... Negative Ion Generator (ADA)
Nig. .... Niger [*African nation*] (NTIO)
NIG .... Niger [*Black*] [*Pharmacy*]
NIG .... Nigeria
Nig. .... Nigerian (SAUS)
NIG .... Nikunau [*Kiribati*] [*Airport symbol*] (OAG)
NIG .... Nonimmunoglobulin [*Medicine*] (DB)

NIG .... Non Isolated Gate (SAUS)
NIG .... Nordic Industrial Group (SAUS)
NIG .... Nude Ionization Gauge
NIGA .... National Indian Gaming Association (NTPA)
NIGA .... Neutron-Induced Gamma Activity (AABC)
NIGA .... Nuclear Indirect Gamma Activity (SAUS)
NIGA .... Nuclear-Induced Ground Radioactivity (NATG)
NIGAB .... Annual Report. National Institute of Genetics (journ.) (SAUS)
NIG&P .... Nanjing Institute of Geology and Paleontology [*China*]
Nig Ann Int'l L... Nigerian Annual of International Law [*A publication*] (DLA)
Nig Bar J.... Nigerian Bar Journal [*A publication*] (DLA)
Nig BJ .... Nigerian Bar Journal [*A publication*] (DLA)
NIGC .... National Indian Gaming Commission (AGLO)
NIGCS .... National Imperial Glass Collectors Society (EA)
NIGDA .... National Industrial Glove Distributors Association (EA)
NIGEC .... National Institute for Global Environmental Change [*University of Southern California and Department of Energy*]
Niger .... Nigerian (DIAR)
Nigeria .... Federal Republic of Nigeria (SAUS)
Nigeria Bar J... Nigerian Bar Journal. Annual Journal of the Nigeria Bar Association [*Lagos, Nigeria*] [*A publication*] (DLA)
Nigeria Fed Dep For Res Annu Rep... Nigeria Federal Department of Forest Research Annual Report (SAUS)
Nigeria LR... Nigeria Law Reports [*A publication*] (DLA)
Nigerian Ann Int'l L... Nigerian Annual of International Law [*A publication*] (DLA)
Nigerian LJ... Nigerian Law Journal [*A publication*] (DLA)
NIGFET .... Non-Insulated-Gate Field-Effect Transistor (SAUS)
NIGHTCAP ... Night Combat Air Patrol [*Military*] (NVT)
NIGL .... NERC Isotope Geosciences Laboratory (SAUS)
Nig Lawy Q... Nigeria Lawyer's Quarterly [*A publication*] (DLA)
Nig LJ .... Nigerian Law Journal [*A publication*] (DLA)
Nig LQ .... Nigeria Lawyer's Quarterly [*A publication*] (ILCA)
Nig LQR .... Nigerian Law Quarterly Review [*A publication*] (DLA)
Nig LR .... Nigeria Law Reports [*A publication*] (DLA)
NIGMS .... National Institute of General Medical Sciences [*National Institutes of Health*] [*Bethesda, MD*]
NIGP .... Nanjing Institute of Geology and Paleontology [*China*]
NIGP .... National Institute of Governmental Purchasing (EA)
Nigr .... Nigeria (VRA)
Nigr .... Nigrinus [*of Lucian*] [*Classical studies*] (OCD)
NIGRO .... Northern Ireland General Register Office (SAUS)
NIGS .... Non-Inertial Guidance Set (SAA)
NIH .... Hoffmann-La Roche, Inc. [*Research code symbol*]
NIH .... National Institute for the Humanities [*Yale University*] [*National Endowment for the Humanities*]
NIH .... National Institute of Hardware [*British*] (BI)
NIH .... National Institute of Housecraft [*British*] (BI)
NIH .... National Institute on the Holocaust [*Later, AFIP*] (EA)
NIH .... National Institutes of Health [*Public Health Service*] [*Bethesda, MD*]
NIH .... New Inn Hall [*British*] (ROG)
NIH .... Nonimmune Hydrops [*Medicine*]
NIH .... Nonirradiated Handling (SAUS)
NIH .... North Irish Horse [*Military unit*] [*British*]
NIH .... Not Invented Here (NITA)
NIH .... Not Invented Here Syndrome [*Business Management*]
NIHB .... National Indian Health Board (EA)
NIHBC .... Northern Ireland House Building Council (SAUS)
NIHC .... Northern Ireland House of Commons
NIHCA .... Northern Ireland Hotels and Caterers Association (ODBW)
NIHD .... Noise-Induced Hearing Damage [*Medicine*] (MEDA)
NIHE .... National Institute for Higher Education [*Defunct*] (ACII)
NIHE .... Northern Ireland Housing Executive (SAUS)
NIHEC .... Northern Ireland Higher Education Council (SAUS)
NIHERST .... National Institute of Higher Education (Research, Science, and Technology) [*Spain*]
NIHF .... Nonimmune Hydrops Fetalis [*Medicine*]
NIHGR .... National Institute for Human Genome Research [*National Institutes of Health*] (BARN)
NIHHD .... National Institute of Health and Human Development
NIHHS .... Notification of Installations Handling Hazardous Substances Regulations 1982 (HEAS)
NIHi .... DeWitt Historical Society of Tompkins County, Ithaca, NY [*Library symbol*] [*Library of Congress*] (LCLS)
NIHL .... Noise-Induced Hearing Loss
NIHOE .... Nitrogen, Helium, and Oxygen Experiment (DNAB)
NIHQ .... Nautical Institute Headquarters (SAUS)
NIHR .... National Institute of Handicapped Research [*Department of Health and Human Services*] [*Later, NIDRR*] [*Washington, DC*]
NIHS .... National Institute of Health Sciences (SAUS)
NIHS .... National Institute of Hypertension Studies - Institute of Hypertension School ofResearch (EA)
NIHS .... NAVEUR Intelligence Highlights Summary (MCD)
NIHSA .... Newfoundland Industrial Health and Safety Association (SAUS)
NIHT .... Northern Ireland Housing Trust (SAUS)
NIHTA .... Northern Ireland Head Teachers' Association
NIHYSOB .... Now I Have You, Son of a Bitch [*Term coined by Kenneth Blanchard, author of "The One-Minute Manager"*]
NII .... National Industries, Inc. (EFIS)
NII .... National Information Infrastructure [*Proposed 1992*] [*Telecommunications*]
NII .... National Intergroup (EFIS)
NII .... NATO Item Identification (NATG)
NII .... Negative Immittance Inverter (PDAA)
NII .... Neruonal Intranuclear Inclusion [*Neurophysiology*]
NII .... Net Interest Income (TDOB)
NII .... Niigata [*Japan*] [*Seismograph station code, US Geological Survey*] (SEIS)
NII .... Nuclear Installations Inspectorate [*British*]
NIIA .... Nonisotropic Immunoassay
NIIC .... Ithaca College, Ithaca, NY [*Library symbol*] [*Library of Congress*] (LCLS)
NIIC .... National Injury Information Clearinghouse [*Consumer Product Safety Commission*]
NIIC .... NORAD Intelligence Indications Center (MCD)
NIIC .... Northern Illinois Intercollegiate Conference (PSS)
NIICP .... No Increase in Contract Price
NIICU .... National Institute of Independent Colleges and Universities (EA)
NIID .... Netherlands Defense Manufacturers Association (SAUS)
NIIG .... NATO Item Identification Guide (NATG)
NIIIP .... National Industrial Information Infrastructure Protocol [*Computer science*] (VLIE)
NIIN .... National Item Identification Number (MCD)
NII Nor .... NII Norsat International, Inc. [*Associated Press*] (SAG)
NIIO .... New International Information Order (NITA)
NIIP .... National Institute of Industrial Psychology (PDAA)
NIIP .... Net International Investment Position
NIIR .... Non-Imaging Infrared Sensor (SAUS)
NIIRS .... National Image Interpretability Rating Scale
NIIRS .... National Imagery Interpretation Rating Scale (MCD)
NIIS .... National Institute of Infant Services [*Later, NADS*]
NIIS .... New Image Industries [*NASDAQ symbol*] (TTSB)
NIIS .... New Image Industries, Inc. [*NASDAQ symbol*] (NQ)
NIIS .... New Item Introductory Schedule (AAGC)
NIIS .... Niagara Institute for International Studies [*Canada*]
NIIS .... Nigeria Institute for International Studies (SAUS)
NIIS .... Nuclear Issues Information Service (IID)
NIIT .... National Information Infrastructure Testbed [*Telecommunications*] (PCM)
NIIU .... Neozyme Corp. [*NASDAQ symbol*] (SAG)
NIJ .... National Institute of Justice (USGC)
NIJ .... New Irish Jurist [*A publication*] (DLA)
NIJC .... North Idaho Junior College (SAUS)
NIJD .... National Institute of Judicial Dynamics [*Defunct*] (EA)
NIJH .... National Institute for Jewish Hospice (EA)
NIJJDP .... National Institute for Juvenile Justice and Delinquency Prevention
NIJR .... New Irish Jurist [*A publication*] (DLA)
NIK .... Boston, MA [*Location identifier*] [*FAA*] (FAAL)
NIK .... Nickel [*Watchmaking*] (ROG)
NIK .... Nickel Rim Mines Ltd. [*Toronto Stock Exchange symbol*]
NIK .... Nikolski [*Alaska*] [*Seismograph station code, US Geological Survey*] [*Closed*] (SEIS)
nik .... Northern Ireland [*MARC country of publication code*] [*Library of Congress*] (LCCP)
NIK .... Novye Inostrannyye Knigi [*New Foreign Books*] [*A publication*]
NIKA .... Northern Ireland Korfball Association (EAIO)
NikeB .... Nike, Inc. [*Associated Press*] (SAG)
NIKKEI .... Nihon Keizai Shimbun, Inc. [*Tokyo, Japan*] (IID)
Nikkei Electron... Nikkei Electronics (SAUS)
NIKO .... Nigerian Korean Co. (SAUS)
NIKOS .... New Internet Knowledge Systems [*Computer science*] (DDC)
NIKT .... Neue Informations- und Kommunikationstechnologien (SAUS)
NIKU .... Niku Corp. [*NASDAQ symbol*] (SG)
NIL .... Negotiable Instruments Law (DLA)
NIL .... Network Interface Layer [*Computer science*] (VLIE)
NIL .... Neurointermediate Lobe [*Neuroanatomy*]
NIL .... Nilore [*Pakistan*] [*Seismograph station code, US Geological Survey*] (SEIS)
NIL .... Nitrogen Inerting Line (IEEE)
NIL .... Noise Immission Level (SAUS)
NIL .... Noise Immunity Level (SAUS)
NIL .... No Limit (NASA)
NIL .... Nothing in Light Disease [*Nephrotic Syndrome*] (DAVI)
NIL .... Nothing in Light Microscopy (MELL)
NIL .... Nothing to Send [*Amateur radio shorthand*] (WDAA)
NIL .... Not in Labor [*Medicine*]
NIL .... Nuclear-Induced Lightning
NILA .... National Industrial Leather Association [*Later, NIBA*] (EA)
NILab .... Northern Ireland Labour Party [*Political party*] [*Defunct*]
NILB .... National Indian Lutheran Board (EA)
NILC .... National Immigration Law Center (EA)
NILE .... National Institute of Labor Education [*Defunct*] (EA)
NILE .... NATO Improved Link 11 (SAUS)
NILE .... Naval Inflatable Liferaft Equipment (SAUS)
NILE .... Naval Inflatable Life-Saving Equipment [*British military*] (DMA)
NILE .... Number of Inverters Along Any Loop is Even (MHDI)
NILE & CJ .... National Institute of Law Enforcement and Criminal Justice [*Law Enforcement Assistance Administration*]
NILECJ .... National Institute of Law Enforcement and Criminal Justice [*Law Enforcement Assistance Administration*]
Niles Reg .... Niles' Weekly Register [*A publication*] (DLA)
NILF .... Not in Labor Force (GFGA)
NILFP .... National Institute of Locker and Freezer Provisioners [*Later, AAMP*] (EA)
NILGOSC .... Northern Ireland Local Government Officers Superannuation Committee
NIIH .... Herkimer County Community College, Ilion, NY [*Library symbol*] [*Library of Congress*] (LCLS)
NILI .... Netsah Israel Lo Yeshakker (BJA)
NILI .... Newark Island Layered Intrusion [*Geology*] [*Canada*]
NILI .... Northern Interior Lumber Industries (SAUS)

NILIC	Northern Illinois Iowa Conference (PSS)
NILKY	No Income, Lots of Kids [*Lifestyle classification*]
N III U Pr	Northern Illinois University Press (SAUS)
NILN	Nylon Insert Lock Nut
NILO	Naval Intelligence Liaison Officer (NVT)
NILP	Northern Ireland Labour Party [*Political party*] [*Defunct*] (PPW)
NILPT	National Institute for Low Power Television [*Defunct*] (EA)
NILR	Northern Ireland Law Reports [*A publication*] (DLA)
NILRC	Northern Illinois Learning Resources Cooperative [*Library network*]
Nil Reg	Niles' Weekly Register [*A publication*] (DLA)
NILS	Naval Intelligence Locating Summary (MCD)
NILS	Newsletter of International Labour Studies [*Netherlands*]
NILS	Northern Illinois Library System [*Library network*]
NILS	Nuclear Instrument Landing System
NILT	National Institute for Lay Training [*Defunct*] (EA)
NILT	Nursing Intervention Lexicon and Taxonomy (SAUS)
NILTC	National Industrial Language Training Centre (AIE)
NILU	National Intelligence Liaison Unit (SAUS)
NILU	Norwegian Institute for Air Research (SAUS)
NILU	Norwegian Institute for/of Air Research (SAUS)
NILUG	National Independent Lynx User Group (NITA)
NIM	National Impact Model [*Environmental Protection Agency*] (ERG)
NIM	National Islamic Movement (SAUS)
NIM	Naval Inspector of Machinery
NIM	Net Interest Margin [*Banking*]
NIM	Networked Interactive Multimedia
NIM	Network Injection Molding
NIM	Network Installation Manager [*Computer science*] (VLIE)
NIM	Network Interface Machine [*Datapac*]
NIM	Network Interface Module [*Telecommunications*] (TSSD)
NIM	Network Interface Monitor
NIM	Neurological Impress Method (EDAC)
NIM	Newspapers in Microform (NITA)
NIM	Niamey [*Niger*] [*Airport symbol*] (OAG)
NIM	Night Intruder Mission [*Air Force*]
NIM	No Immediate Miracles [*Acronym and facetious translation derived from turning President Gerald Ford's anti-inflation WIN buttons upside down*] [*See WIN entry*]
NIM	Noninterrupt Mode
NIM	NORAD Intelligence Memorandum (MCD)
NIM	Normal-Incidence Monochromator
NIM	Normal Integration Mode
NIM	North Irish Militia [*Military unit*] [*British*]
NIM	Nothing in Mind [*Acronym and facetious translation derived from turning President Gerald Ford's anti-inflation WIN buttons upside down*] [*See WIN entry*]
NIM	Nuclear Instrumentation Module
NIM	Nuclear Instrument Module (SAUS)
NIM	Nuveen Select Maturities Municipal [*NYSE symbol*] (SPSG)
NIM	Nylon Insulation Material
NIM	University of North Carolina at Asheville, Asheville, NC [*OCLC symbol*] (OCLC)
NIM	US Neutron Interactive Materials Program (SAUS)
NIMA	National Imagery and Mapping Agency [*Military*]
NIMA	National Institute on Mental Health
NIMA	National Insulation Manufacturers Association [*Later, Thermal Insulation Manufacturers Association*] (EA)
NIMA	Noninherited Maternal Antigen [*Genetics*] [*Immunology*]
NIMA	Northern Ireland Ministry of Agriculture (SAUS)
NIMAB	National Indian Manpower Advisory Board
NIMAC	National Interscholastic Music Activities Commission [*Defunct*] (EA)
NIMAT	Newfoundland Institute for Management Advancement and Training (SAUS)
NIMBAS	[*The*] Netherlands Insitute for MBA Studies
NIMBIN	Nuclear Instrumentation Modular Bin
NIMBUS	Network Information Management Client-Based User Service [*Marine science*] (OSRA)
Nimbus	Nimbus CD International, Inc. [*Associated Press*] (SAG)
NIMBUS	United States Meteorological Satellite (SAUS)
NIMBUS-7	NOAA [*National Oceanic and Atmospheric Administration*] Satellite (USDC)
NIMBY	Not in My Back Yard [*i.e., garbage incinerators, prisons, roads, etc.*]
NIMC	National Institute of Management Counsellors (EA)
NIMC	National Institute of Materials and Chemical Research [*Japan*]
NIMC	National Institute of Municipal Clerks [*Later, IIMC*]
NIMC	Nodding Image Motion Compensation [*Instrumentation*]
NIMC	Noninventoriable Manufacturing Cost (TIMI)
NIMCGA	Northern Indiana Muck Crop Growers Association [*Defunct*] (EA)
NIMCP	NATO Information Management Control Point (NATG)
NIMCSSC	National Military Command Systems Support Center (SAUS)
NIMD	Not in My District (SAUS)
NIME	National Institute for Multicultural Education [*Defunct*] (EA)
NIMEX	Nomenclature for Imports and Exports [*European Community*] (PDAA)
NIMEY	Not in My Election Year [*Slang*]
NIMFR	National Institutes of Marriage and Family Relations (EA)
NIMFR	Normal Incidence Multifilter Radiometer (SAUS)
NIMFY	Not in My Front Yard [*i.e., Garbage incinerators, landfills, etc.*]
NIMH	National Institute of Medical Herbalists [*British*]
NIMH	National Institute of Mental Health [*Rockville, MD*] [*Department of Health and Human Services*]
NiMH	Nickel-Metal Hydride [*Organic chemistry*] (PS)
NIMIC	NATO [*North Atlantic Treaty Organization*] Insensitive Munitions Information Center
NIMIC	NATO Insensitive Munitions Information Centre (SAUS)
NIMIC	Not in My Insurance Company [*Insurance slang*]
NIMIS	National Instructional Materials Information System
NIMIT	Nimbus Integration and Test [*NASA*] (KSC)
NIMJ	Near Infrared Miniaturized Jammer
NIML	National Independence Movement of Latvia [*Political party*]
NIMLO	National Institute of Municipal Law Officers (EA)
NIMLO Mun L Rev	National Institute of Municipal Law Officers. Municipal Law Review [*A publication*] (DLA)
NIMM	Nuclear-Induced Missile Malfunction (SAUS)
NIMMA	Northern Ireland Mixed Marriage Association
NIMMP	National Institute of Marine Medicine and Pharmacology [*Proposed*] [*National Institutes of Health*]
NIMMS	New Integrated Modular Management System (SAUS)
NIMMS	Nineteen-Hundred Integrated Modular Management System
NIMN	Not in My Neighborhood (SAUS)
NIMO	Numerical Indicator Multiple Oscilloscope (SAUS)
NiMoV	Nickel-Molybdenum-Vanadium
NIMP	National Intern Matching Program [*Later, NRMP*] (EA)
NIMP	NATO Interoperability Management Plan
NIMP	New and Improved Materials and Processes (PDAA)
N IMP	New Impression [*Publishing*] (DGA)
NIMPA	National Independent Meat Packers Association [*Later, NMA*] (EA)
NIMPA	Newly Installed Machine Performance Analysis (SAUS)
NIMPH	Network Interface Message Processing Host [*NERComP*]
NIMPHE	Nuclear Isotope Monopropellant Hydrazine Engine
NIMQ	Not in My Queue (WDAA)
NIMR	National Institute for Medical Research [*British*]
NIMR	Navy Industrial Management Reviews (NG)
NIMROD	National Institute for Medical Research Online Database (PDAA)
NIMROD	Nineteen-Hundred [*Computer*] Management and Recovery of Documentation (PDAA)
NIMROD	Northern Illinois Meteorological Research on Downbursts [*National Center for Atmospheric Research*]
NIMRS	Navy Integrated Message Reporting System (MCD)
NIMS	Fairhaven International Ltd. (SAUS)
NIMS	National Infant Mortality Survey [*Department of Health and Human Services*] (GFGA)
NIMS	National Information Management System
NIMS	National Ingredient Marketing Specialists (EA)
NIMS	Nationwide Improved Mail Service [*Postal Service*]
NIMS	Near Infrared Mapping Spectrometer [*Instrument on Galileo spacecraft*] [*NASA*]
NIMS	Nevada Information Management System (SAUS)
NIMS	Noiseless Integral Magnetic Scanners (ACAE)
NIMS	Nuclear Instrumentation Modular System (MCD)
NIMSC	Nonconsumable Item Materiel Support Code [*Military*] (AFIT)
NIMSCO	NODC [*National Oceanographic Data Center*] Index to Instrument Measures Subsurface Current Observations [*Marine science*] (MSC)
NIMSDP	Non-Innovator Multiple Source Drug Product
NIMSR	Nonconsumable Item Materiel Support Request [*Military*] (AFIT)
NIMT	National Institute for Management Technology (SAUS)
NIMT	National Institute for Music Theater [*Defunct*] (EA)
NIMTECH	New and Improved Technology [*British*]
NIMTOF	Not in My Term of Office [*Government slang*]
NIMTOO	Not in My Term of Office (PA)
NIMU	Non-Invasive Monitoring Systems, Inc. (SAUS)
NIMU	North Island Mutual Insurance (SAUS)
NIN	National Information Network [*ASTIA*]
NIN	National Inservice Network
NIN	Neighbors in Need [*An association*]
NIN	Nine Inch Nails [*Rock music group*]
NIN	Nine West Group [*NYSE symbol*] (TTSB)
NIN	Nine West Group, Inc. [*NYSE symbol*] (SPSG)
NIN	Ninhydrine [*Chemical agent used in espionage*]
NIN	Ninilchik [*Alaska*] [*Seismograph station code, US Geological Survey*] [*Closed*] (SEIS)
NIN	Ninilchik, AK [*Location identifier*] [*FAA*] (FAAL)
NIN	Norsat International, Inc. [*Vancouver Stock Exchange symbol*]
NINA	National Institute Northern Accelerator (PDAA)
NINA	Neutron Instruments for Nuclear Analysis (PDAA)
NINA	No Irish Need Apply [*Classified advertising*]
NINA	Norwegian Institute for Nature Research (SAUS)
NINB	National Institute of Neurology and Blindness (WDAA)
NINCDS	National Institute of Neurological and Communicative Disorders and Stroke [*Formerly, NINDS*] [*Public Health Service*] [*Bethesda, MD*]
NINDB	National Institute of Neurological Diseases and Blindness [*Later, NEI, NINDS*] [*National Institutes of Health*]
NINDC	Northern Independence Conference (PSS)
NInDE	Elementary School No. 2, Inwood, NY [*Library symbol*] [*Library of Congress*] (LCLS)
NINDS	National Institute of Neurological Diseases and Stroke [*Formerly, NINDB*] [*Later, NINCDS*] [*National Institutes of Health*]
NINDS	National Institute of Neurological Disorders and Stroke
NIndTP	National Independent Teenage Party [*British*]
NINE	National Infertility Network Exchange [*An association*] (EA)
NINE	Ninth-Plate (VRA)
NINE	Number Nine Visual Tech [*NASDAQ symbol*] (TTSB)
NINE	Number Nine Visual Technology, Inc. [*NASDAQ symbol*] (SAG)
Nine-C Lit	Nineteenth-Century Literature [*A publication*] (BRI)
NINES	Norfolk Information Exchange Scheme (NITA)
NineWest	Nine West Group, Inc. [*Associated Press*] (SAG)
NINFRA	National Independent Nursery Furniture Retailers Association (EA)
NINIA	Nephelometric Inhibition Immunoassay [*Analytical chemistry*]

Nink	No Income, No Kids [*Lifestyle classification*]
NINO	No Input, No Output (SAUS)
NINO	No Inspector, No Operator (ODBW)
NINO	Nothing In Nothing Out (SAUS)
NINOW	Non-Interest-Bearing Negotiable Order of Withdrawal [*Banking*]
NINR	National Institute for Nursing Research
NINS	Northern Ireland News Service [*Information service or system*] (IID)
NINST	Non-Instrument Runway [*Aviation*] (DA)
NINST	Nose Instantaneous [*Aerospace*]
N Instr Meth	Nuclear Instruments and Methods (SAUS)
NINVS	Noninvasive Neurovascular Study [*Medicine*] (DAVI)
NInWE	Elementary School No. 4, Inwood, NY [*Library symbol*] [*Library of Congress*] (LCLS)
NINYP	Nuveen Insured New York Premium Income Municipal [*Associated Press*] (SAG)
NINYS	Nuveen Insured New York Select Tax Free Income [*Associated Press*] (SAG)
NIO	National Institute of Oceanography [*British*] (IID)
NIO	National Intelligence Officer (MCD)
NIO	Naval Inspector of Ordnance
NIO	Navigational Information Office
NIO	Navy Institute of Oceanography
NIO	Network Input-Output (TIMI)
NIO	Nieuwe Internationale Orde [*Netherlands*]
NIO	Niobium [*See Cb*] [*Chemical element*] (ROG)
NIO	Nioki [*Zaire*] [*Airport symbol*] (OAG)
NIO	Northern Ireland Office
NIO	Nuveen Ins Muni Oppt Fd [*NYSE symbol*] (TTSB)
NIO	Nuveen Insurance Municipal Opportunity Fund (SAUS)
NIO	Nuveen Insured Municipal Opportunity Fund [*NYSE symbol*] (SPSG)
NIOBE	Numerical Integration of the Boltzmann Transport Equation
NIOD	Network In-Out Dial [*Automatic Voice Network*] (CET)
NIOF	National Institute of Oceanography and Fisheries [*Egypt*] [*Marine science*] (OSRA)
NIOG	Nationalized Industries Overseas Group [*British*] (DCTA)
NIOK	National Institute for Overseas Koreans (EA)
NIOK	Nederlands Instituut voor Onderzoek in de Katalyse [*Netherlands Institute for Catalysis Research*]
NIOP	National Institute of Oilseed Products (EA)
NIOPSWL	New Input/Output Program Status Word Location [*Computer science*] (MHDI)
NIOS	Nixdorf Integrated Office System (HGAA)
NIOS	Northern Ireland Orchid Society (EAIO)
NIOSH	National Institute for Occupational Safety and Health [*Public Health Service*] [*Cincinnati, OH*] [*Database producer*]
NIOSHTIC	National Institute for Occupational Safety and Health Technical Information Center [*Database*] [*NIOSH*] [*Information service or system*] (CRD)
NIOTC	Naval Inshore Operations Training Center (NVT)
NIOZ	Institute of Marine Scientific Research (SAUS)
NIOZ	Netherlands Institute for Sea Research [*Marine science*] (OSRA)
NIp	Island Park Public Library, Island Park, NY [*Library symbol*] [*Library of Congress*] (LCLS)
NIP	Jacksonville, FL [*Location identifier*] [*FAA*] (FAAL)
NIP	Mononitroiodophenyl [*Organic chemistry*] (DAVI)
NIP	NADGE [*NATO Air Defense Ground Environment*] Improvement Plan (NATG)
NIP	Namibia Independence Party [*Political party*] (PPW)
NIP	National and International Program (SAUS)
NIP	National Identification Program for the Advancement of Women in Higher EducationAdministration (EA)
NIP	National Impatient Profile (MEDA)
NIP	National Implementation Plan (SAUS)
NIP	National Independence Party [*Namibia*] [*Political party*] (PPW)
NIP	National Industrial Partner
NIP	National Inspection Plan [*RSPA*] (TAG)
NIP	National Institute of Polarology [*Research center*] [*British*] (IRUK)
NIP	National Integration Party [*Liberia*] [*Political party*] (EY)
NIP	National Intelligence Priorities (MCD)
NIP	National Inventory Programme [*National Museums of Canada*] [*Later, CHIN*]
NIP	Naval Institute Press [*Publisher*]
NIP	Naval Intelligence Professionals (EA)
NIP	Navy Interceptor Program
NIP	Negative Inspiratory Pressure [*Medicine*] (DAVI)
NIP	Neighbourhood Improvement Program [*Canada*]
NIP	Network Input Processor [*Computer science*] (MCD)
NIP	Network Interface Processor (MCD)
NIP	Neuroleptic-Induced Parkinsonism (SAUS)
NIP	Newhall Investment Properties (SAUS)
NIP	New Impact Resources, Inc. [*Vancouver Stock Exchange symbol*]
NIP	New Incentive Package (ADA)
NIP	Newsletters in Print [*Formerly, ND*] [*A publication*]
NIP	Nipple (AAG)
Nip	Nippon (SAUS)
NIP	Nipponese
NIP	No Infection Present [*Medicine*] (DMAA)
NIP	No Inflammation Present (SAUS)
NIP	Nonimpact Printer
NIP	Non-Indexing Part (SAUS)
NIP	Normal Impact Point
NIP	Normal Incidence Pyrheliometer (PDAA)
NIP	Normal Investment Practice
NIP	Northern Ireland Parliament (SAUS)
NIP	Notice of Intelligence Potential [*Military*] (AFM)

NIP	Notice of Intent to Purchase [*DoD*]
NIP	Not in Possession (SAUS)
NIP	Not in Practice (CMD)
NIP	Nucleus Initialization Procedure (SAUS)
NIP	Nucleus Initialization Program [*Computer science*]
NIP	Numeric Indicator Performance
NIP	Numero d'Identification Personnel [*Personal Identification Number - PIN*]
NIP	Numismatic Indexes Project (SAUS)
NIPA	National Income and Product Accounts [*The WEFA Group*] [*Information service*] [*Information service or system*] (CRD)
NIPA	National Institute of Pension Administrators [*Santa Ana, CA*] (EA)
NIPA	National Institute of Public Affairs
NIPA	N-Isopropylacrylamide [*Organic chemistry*]
NIPA	Noninherited Paternal Antigen [*Genetics*] [*Immunology*]
NIPA	Noninterference Performance Assessment
NIPA	Non-local Independent Pixel Approximation (SAUS)
NIPA	Nordens Institut pa Aland [*Nordic Institute in Aland - NIA*] [*Finland*] (EAIO)
NIPA	Northern Ireland Ploughing Association (EAIO)
NIPA	Northern Ireland Police Authority
NIPA	Notice of Initiation of Procurement Action (NRCH)
NIPAGRAM	National Income and Product Account Data by Mailgram [*NTIS*]
NIPALS	Noniterative Partial Least Squares [*Algorithm*]
NIPALS	Nonlinear Iterative Partial Least Squares (SAUS)
NIP & TB	Northern Ireland Postal and Telecommunications Board
NIPAW	National Inhalants & Poisons Awareness Week (SAUS)
NIPC	National Infrastructure Protection Center
NIPC	N-Isopropylcarbazole [*Organic chemistry*]
NIPCC	National Industrial Pollution Control Council [*Terminated, 1973*] [*Department of Commerce*]
NIPD	Nightly Intermittent Peritoneal Dialysis (SAUS)
NIPD	Not in the Public Domain
NIPDE	National Initiative for Product Data Exchange
NIPDWR	National Interim Primary Drinking Water Regulations [*Environmental Protection Agency*]
NIPDWS	National Interim Primary Drinking Water Standards [*Environmental Protection Agency*]
NIPE	Noninvasive Peripheral Vascular Examination [*or Evaluation*] (DAVI)
NIPER	National Institute for Petroleum and Energy Research [*Formerly, BETC*] [*Department of Energy*] [*Bartlesville, OK*]
NIPERA	Nickel Producers Environmental Research Association
NIPF	Nonindustrial Private Forest Owners (WPI)
NIPF	Northern Ireland Peace Forum
NIPFDA	National Independent Poultry and Food Distributors Association (EA)
NIPGM	National Institute on Park and Grounds Management (EA)
NIPH	National Institute of Poultry Husbandry [*British*] (BI)
NIPH	National Institute of Public Health
NIpHE	Francis X. Hegarty Elementary School, Island Park, NY [*Library symbol*] [*Library of Congress*] (LCLS)
NIPHL	Noise-Induced Permanent Hearing Loss (PDAA)
NIPHLE	National Institute of Packaging, Handling, and Logistic Engineers (EA)
NIPHYS	Nitrogen Physiology of Forest Plants and Soils (SAUS)
NIPILS	New Irish Professionals in London [*Lifestyle classification*]
NIPIM2	Nuveen Insured Premium Income Municipal Fund 2 [*Associated Press*] (SAG)
NIPIMn	Nuveen Insured Premium Income Municipal Fund [*Associated Press*] (SAG)
NIPIMS	NAVMAT Instructional Procurement Inventory Monitoring System (MCD)
NIPIR	Nuclear Immediate Photo Interpretation Report (MCD)
NIpL	Lincoln Orens School, Island Park, NY [*Library symbol*] [*Library of Congress*] (LCLS)
NIPM	National Institute of Public Management (EA)
NIPN	NEC Corp. [*NASDAQ symbol*] (SAG)
NIP/NLG	National Immigration Project of the National Lawyers Guild (EA)
NIPNY	NEC Corp. ADR [*NASDAQ symbol*] (TTSB)
NIPO	Navy International Program Office (SAUS)
NIPO	Negative Input, Positive Output
NIPOLOS	Nonimpact Off-Line Operating System [*Computer science*]
NIPP	National Institute for Public Policy (EA)
NIPP	National Intelligence Projection for Planning (AFM)
NIPP	Net Income per Partner [*Business term*]
NIPP	Nonimpact Printing Process (MCD)
NIPPE	National Income per Person Employed
NIPPI	Japan Aircraft Manufacturing Co. Ltd. (SAUS)
NIPPING	Nonimpact Printing (DGA)
NippnTT	Nippon Telegraph & Telephone Co. [*Associated Press*] (SAG)
Nippon Kokan Tech Rep	Nippon Kokan Technical Report (SAUS)
Nippon Stainless Tech Rep	Nippon Stainless Technical Report (SAUS)
Nippon Steel Tech Rep	Nippon Steel Technical Report (SAUS)
Nippon Tungsten Rev	Nippon Tungsten Review (SAUS)
NIPR	National Industrial Plant Reserve
NIPR	Naval Intelligence Publication Register (NVT)
ni pr	Nisi Prius [*Unless Before*] [*Legal term*] [*Latin*] (WGA)
NIPr	North'n Ind Pub Sv.4 1/4%cmPfd [*AMEX symbol*] (TTSB)
NIPrA	North'n Ind Pub Sv Adj RtA Pfd [*NYSE symbol*] (TTSB)
NI PRI	Nisi Prius [*Unless Before*] [*Legal term*] [*Latin*]
NIPS	National Information Processing System [*Military*]
NIPS	National Institute for Public Services
NIPS	National Inventory of Pollution Sources [*Database*] [*Environment Canada*] [*Information service or system*] (CRD)
NIPS	Nationwide Integrated Postal Service [*Postal Service*]
NIPS	Naval Intelligence Processing System

NIPS	Navy Information Policy Summaries (NG)
NIPS	New Inventory Pricing Systems (MCD)
NIPS	Nippon Information Processing System [*Nippon Shuppan Hanbai, Inc.*] [*Database*]
NIPS	NIPSCO Capital Markets [*Associated Press*] (SAG)
NIPS	Nixdorf Inventory and Production-control System (SAUS)
NIPS	Northern Indiana Public Service Co. [*Associated Press*] (SAG)
NIPS	Not in Profile Students (SAUS)
NIPS	Nottingham Image Processing System (SAUS)
NIPS	NTCS-A Intelligence Processing System (SAUS)
NIPSA	Northern Ireland Public Service Alliance (EAIO)
NIPSCO	NIPSCO Industries [*Associated Press*] (SAG)
NIPSSA	Naval Intelligence Processing System Support Activity
NIPT	New Information Processing Technologies
NIPT	New Information Processing Technology Project [*Japan*] (ECON)
NIPTS	Noise-Induced Permanent Threshold Shift [*Hearing*]
NIR	Acrylonitrile-Isoprene Rubber (SAUS)
NIR	Beeville, TX [*Location identifier*] [*FAA*] (FAAL)
NIr	Irvington Public Library, Irvington, NY [*Library symbol*] [*Library of Congress*] (LCLS)
NIR	National Inventory Record [*DoD*]
NIR	Near Infrared (ECII)
NIR	Near-Infrared Reflectance (DB)
NIR	Near Infrared Region
NIR	Nerve Impulse Recorder
NIR	Networked Information Resource (TELE)
NIR	Network Information Registry [*Computer science*] (VLIE)
NIR	Network Information Retrieval
NIR	New Ireland Review [*A publication*] (ROG)
NIR	Next Inferior Rank
NIR	Next Instruction Register (NITA)
NIR	Nickel-Iron Refinery (SAUS)
NIR	Nighttime Infrared
NIR	Nitrile Isoprene Rubber (SAUS)
NIR	Nitrite Reductase [*An enzyme*]
NIR	No Individual Requirement (MSA)
NIR	Noninductive Resistor
NIR	Non-Insulin-Requiring [*Medicine*]
NIR	Non-Ionizing Radiant (SAUS)
NIR	Non-Ionizing Radiation (SAUS)
NIR	Norskair [*Norway*] [*ICAO designator*] (FAAC)
N Ir	Northern Ireland Law Reports [*A publication*] (DLA)
NIR	Northern Ireland Railways Co. Ltd.
NIR	Nose Impact Rocket (NATG)
NIRA	Designer of SUPERPHENIX with Novatome (SAUS)
NIRA	Italian Fast Nuclear Reactor Co Genova (SAUS)
NIRA	National Industrial Recovery Act [*1933*]
NIRA	National Industrial Recovery Administration (WDAA)
NIRA	National Industrial Recreation Association [*Later, NESRA*] (EA)
NIRA	National Industrial Reserve Act of 1948
NIRA	National Intercollegiate Rodeo Association (EA)
NIRA	National Iridology Research Association (NTPA)
NIRA	Navy Industrial Relations Activity (DNAB)
NIRA	Navy Internal Relations Activity (DNAB)
NIRA	Near Infrared Reflectance Analysis
NIRA	Newspaper Industries Research Association (SAUS)
NIRA	Niravoice, Inc. (SAUS)
NIRA	Nitrite Reductase (DB)
NIRAP	Naval Industrial Reserve Aircraft Plant (MUGU)
NIRAS	National Institute of Research and Advanced Studies [*Proposed*]
NIRB	National Industrial Recovery Board [*Terminated, 1935*]
NIRB	Nuclear Insurance Rating Bureau
NIRC	National Industrial Relations Court [*British*]
NIRC	National Information Retrieval Colloquium [*Later, Benjamin Franklin Colloquium on Information Science*]
NIRC	National Institute of Rug Cleaning [*Superseded by AIDS International*] (EA)
NIRC	Negative Ion Recombination Chamber
NIRCF	National Immigration, Refugee and Citizenship Forum (EA)
NIRD	National Institute for Research in Dairying [*British*]
NIRD	Nonimmune Renal Disease [*Medicine*] (DMAA)
NIRDR	Nonintegrated Radar (SAUS)
NIRE	National Institute for Rehabilitation Engineering (EA)
N Ire	Northern Ireland (NTIO)
N IRE	Northern Ireland
N Ire	North Ireland (SHCU)
NIREB	National Institute of Real Estate Brokers [*Later, Realtors National Marketing Institute*] (EA)
NIREX	Nuclear Industry Radioactive Waste Executive [*British*] (ECON)
NIRFOODPS	Nonscanning Infrared Focal Plan Options Study (ACAE)
NIRI	National Information Research Institute
NIRI	National Investor Relations Institute [*Washington, DC*] (EA)
NIRL	Negligible Individual Risk Level (GNE)
N Ir LR	Northern Ireland Law Reports [*A publication*] (DLA)
NIRM	Network for Information Retrieval in Mammology
NIRMA	Nuclear Information and Records Management Association (EA)
NIRMP	National Intern and Resident Matching Program (DAVI)
NIRMS	Noble Gas-Ion Reflection Mass Spectroscopy (SAUS)
NIRNS	National Institute for Research in Nuclear Science [*British*]
NIRO	Nike-Iroquois [*Rockets*]
NIROC	National Institute of Red Orange Canaries and All Other Cage Birds (EA)
NIROP	Naval Industrial Reserve Ordnance Plant (MCD)
NIRO Rocket	Nike-Iroquois Rocket (SAUS)
NIROS	Near Infrared Oxygen Sufficiency Scope [*Monitors oxygen delivery to brain during surgery*] (DAVI)
NIROS	Nixdorf Real-Time Operating System (NITA)
NIRPL	Navy Industrial Readiness Planning List (NG)
N Ir Pub Gen Acts	Northern Ireland Public General Acts [*A publication*] (DLA)
NIRRL	Northern Ireland Regional Research Laboratory (SAUS)
NIRS	National Information Research Institute (ELAL)
NIRS	National Inorganic and Radionuclides Survey [*Environmental Protection Agency*]
NIRS	National Institute for Radiological Science [*Japan*]
NIRS	Near Infrared Reflectance Spectroscopy [*Britton Chance*]
NIRS	Nuclear Information and Resource Service (EA)
NIRSA	National Intramural-Recreational Sports Association (EA)
N Ir Stat	Northern Ireland Statutes [*A publication*] (DLA)
NIRTS	National Income Realty Trust [*NASDAQ symbol*] (NQ)
NIRTS	Natl Inc. Rlty Tr SBI [*NASDAQ symbol*] (TTSB)
NIRTS	New Integrated Range Timing System
NIrvH	Lake Shore Hospital, Irving, NY [*Library symbol*] [*Library of Congress*] (LCLS)
NIs	Islip Public Library, Islip, NY [*Library symbol*] [*Library of Congress*] (LCLS)
NIS	Names Information Socket (VLIE)
NIS	NASA Interface System (MCD)
NIS	National Immunisation Strategy (SAUS)
NIS	National Income Statistics [*British*]
NIS	National Information Systems [*Later, GIP*] [*UNESCO*] (BUR)
NIS	National Information Systems, Inc. [*Information service or system*] (IID)
NIS	National Institute of Science (EA)
NIS	National Insurance Surcharge [*A separately accounted tax on employment*] [*British*]
NIS	National Intelligence Scale (DIPS)
NIS	National Intelligence Service (NADA)
NIS	National Intelligence Summary (MCD)
NIS	National Intelligence Survey
NIS	National Interdepartmental Seminar [*Military*]
NIS	National Inventory System [*Department of Agriculture*] (GFGA)
NIS	NATO Identification System
NIS	NATO International Staff (SAUS)
NIS	Naval Intelligence School
NIS	Naval Investigative Service
NIS	Navy Inspection Service
NIS	Negative Ion Source
NIS	Negotiation Information System
NIS	Neighborhood Information Service
NIS	Net Identification Sign (SAUS)
NIS	Network Information Service
NIS	Network Information System [*AT & T*]
NIS	Network Interface System
NIS	Neutron Inelastic Scattering
NIS	Neutron Instrumentation System (IEEE)
NIS	New Independent States of the former Soviet Union (SAUS)
NIS	Newly-Independent States [*Of former Soviet Union*]
NIS	News and Information Service [*National Broadcasting Co.*]
NIS	Nicaraguense de Aviacion SA [*Nicaragua*] [*ICAO designator*] (FAAC)
NIS	Nickel-Iron System
NIS	Night Illumination System
NIS	N-Iodosuccinimide [*Organic chemistry*]
NIS	Nippon Information System (SAUS)
NIS	No Inflammatory signs [*Medicine*] (MELL)
NIS	No Intermediate Storage [*Industrial engineering*]
NIS	Noise Information System [*Environmental Protection Agency*] (IID)
NIS	Nonconsumable Item Subgroup [*Military*] (AFIT)
NIS	Nonimmune Sheep Serum (DB)
NIS	Normal Incidence Spectrometer (PDAA)
NIS	Norton Internet Security [*Symantec Corp.*]
NIS	Norwegian International Shipsregister (RIMS)
NIS	Not in Scope (SAUS)
NIS	Not in Stock
NIS	Not in System (SAUS)
NIS	NOVA Corp. [*NYSE symbol*] (TTSB)
NIS	Nova Corp. (Georgia) [*NYSE symbol*] (SAG)
NIS	Nuclear Instrumentation System (NRCH)
NIS	Number Indicating System (SAUS)
NIS	Numerical Information Storage (SAUS)
NIS	Shekel (ODBW)
NISA	National Inconvenienced Sportsmen's Association [*Later, NHSRA*] (EA)
NISA	National Industrial Sand Association (EA)
NISA	National Industrial Service Association [*Later, EASA*]
NISA	National Industrial Stores Association (EA)
NISA	National Institute of Supply Associations
NISA	New Information Services Architecture (SAUS)
NISA	Northeast Intercollegiate Sailing Association (PSS)
NISA	Numerically Integrated Elements for System Analysis (MCD)
NISARC	National Information Storage and Retrieval Center
NISBCO	National Interreligious Service Board for Conscientious Objectors (EA)
Nisbet	Nisbet of Dirleton's Scotch Session Cases [*1665-77*] [*A publication*] (DLA)
NISBS	National Institute of Social and Behavioral Science (EA)
NISC	National Independent Study Center [*Civil Service Commission*]
NISC	National Industrial Space Committee
NISC	National Industry Safety Committee (NADA)
NISC	National Information Services Corp. (IID)

NISC	National Institute of Senior Centers (EA)
NISC	National Intelligence Study Center (EA)
NISC	National Inter Seminary Council
NISC	National Intramural Sports Council
NISC	Naval Intelligence Support Center (TIMI)
NISC	Network Information and Support Center [Computer science] (VLIE)
NISC	Network Information Systems Center (AGLO)
NISCA	National Interscholastic Swimming Coaches Association of America (EA)
N I S C N E	Nursing Information Systems Council of New England (SAUS)
NISCO	Nuclear Installation Services Co. (NRCH)
NISCON	National Industrial Safety Conference (PDAA)
NISCR	South Central Research Library Council, Ithaca, NY [Library symbol] [Library of Congress] (LCLS)
NISC-TRANS	Naval Intelligence Support Center Translation Division
NISCUE	National Institute for State Credit Union Examination [McLean, VA] (EA)
NISD	National Institute of Steel Detailing (EA)
NISDA	Northeast Intercollegiate Swimming and Diving Association (PSS)
N-ISDN	National ISDN [Integrated Services Digital Network] [Telecommunications]
NISE	Naval In-Service Engineering (IGSL)
NISE	NCCOSC In-Service Engineering (SAUS)
NISE	Neighborhood Information Sharing Exchange [Defunct] (EA)
NISE	Normalized Integral Squared Error
NISEC	National Institute for the Study of Educational Change
NISEC	Northern Ireland Schools Examination Council (AIE)
NISEE	National Information Service for Earthquake Engineering (EA)
NISG	National Institute of Student Governments [Defunct] (EA)
NISG	Navy Installation Survey Group
NISGAZ	National Intelligence Survey Gazetteer
NISGUA	Network in Solidarity with the People of Guatemala (EA)
NISH	National Industries for the Severely Handicapped (EA)
NISH	National Information Sources on the Handicapped [Clearinghouse on the Handicapped] [Database]
NISH	National Institute of Senior Housing (EA)
NISH	Naval Intelligence Support Headquarters (CCCA)
NISH	Nonisotopic In Situ Hybridization [Analytical biochemistry]
NISHQ	Naval Investigative Service Headquarters
NISI	Network Information Services Infrastructure (SAUS)
NISI	Northwest Instrument Systems, Inc. (SAUS)
NI-SIL	Nickel-Silver
Nisi Prius & Gen T Rep	Nisi Prius and General Term Reports [Ohio] [A publication] (DLA)
Nisi Prius Rep	Ohio Nisi Prius Reports [A publication] (DLA)
NISL	National Indoor Soccer League [Australia]
NISL	National Intercollegiate Swimming League (PSS)
NISLAPP	National Institute for Science, Law, and Public Policy (EA)
NISM	Non-Deterministic Incomplete Sequential Machine (PDAA)
NISMART	National Incidence Studies of Missing, Abducted, Runaway, and Thrownaway Children
NISMF	Naval Inactive Ship Maintenance Facility
NISMO	Nissan Motorsports
NISO	National Individual Standing Offer (ACAE)
NISO	National Information Standards Organization
NISO	National Information Standards Organization - Z39 (EA)
NISO	Naval Investigative Service Office (NVT)
NISOA	National Intercollegiate Soccer Officials Association (EA)
NISOD	National Institute for Staff and Organizational Development (OICC)
NISOR	Naval Investigative Service Office Representative (DNAB)
NISORS	Nigerian Society of Remote Sensing (SAUS)
NISP	National Industrial Security Program [A publication] (AAGC)
NISP	National Information System for Psychology
NISP	Navy Integrated Space Program (NG)
NISP	Networked Information Services Project [Computer science] (VLIE)
NISP	Nuclear Weapons Intelligence Support Plan (COE)
NISP	Number of Identified Specimens (SAUS)
NISP	NUWEP [Nuclear Weapon] Intelligence Support Plan [Military]
NISPA	National Information System for Physics and Astronomy (NITA)
NISPOM	National Industrial Security Program Manual [A publication] (AAGC)
NISR	National Intelligence Situation Report (MCD)
NISR	Navy Initial Support Requirement (AFIT)
NISRA	National Industrial Salvage and Recovery Association [British] (BI)
NISRA	National Intercollegiate Squash Racquets Association (EA)
NISRA	Naval Investigative Service Resident Agent (NVT)
NISREGFORENSICLAB	Naval Investigative Service Regional Forensic Laboratory (DNAB)
NISS	National Information of Software and Services (AIE)
NISS	National Institute of Social Sciences (EA)
NISS	National ITV Satellite Schedule (SAUS)
NISS	Navigation Interface Subsystem
NISS	New Information Systems and Services [A publication]
NISS	Nosocomial Infection Surveillance System [Medicine] (MELL)
Nissan	Nissan Motor Co. Ltd. [Associated Press] (SAG)
NISSM	Navy Interim Surface Ship Model (CAAL)
NISSOL	NAVAIR [Naval Air Systems Command] Initial Supply Support Outfitting List (MCD)
NISSPAC	NISS Public Access Collections (SAUS)
NISSPO	NATO Identification System Special Project Office
NISSU	Naval Investigative Service Satellite Unit (DNAB)
NIST	National Information System for Science and Technology (NITA)
NIST	National Institute for Standardisation Technology (SAUS)
NIST	National Institute for Standards and Technology
NIST	National Institute for Standards and Testing (EEVL)
NIST	National Institute of Science and Technology (NADA)
NIST	National Institute of Standards and Technology [Formerly, NBS] [Gaithersburg, MD] [Department of Commerce]
NIST	National Intelligence Support Team (COE)
NIST	Naval Institute of Standards & Technology (SAUS)
NIST	Non-Interchangeable Screw Thread (SAUS)
NIST	North-American Institute for Standards and Telecommunications (SAUS)
NIST-7	National Institute of Standards and Technology, Seventh Generation (MED)
N/ISTA	National/International Safe Transit Association (NTPA)
NISTA	Northern Independent Steel Training Association (AIE)
NISTARS	Naval Integrated Storage Tracking and Retrieval System
NISTAV	Niederschlags-Verzeichnis der Niederschlagsstationen (SAUS)
NIST Connection	Non-Interchangeable Screw Threaded Connection (SAUS)
NIST-EEEL	National Institute of Standards & Technology - Electronics and EE Lab
NISTF	National Information Systems Task Force [Society of American Archivists] [Information service or system] (IID)
NISTIR	National Institute of Standards and Technology Interagency Report
NISU	National Injury Surveillance Unit [Australia]
NISUCO	Nigerian Sugar Co. (SAUS)
NISUS	Neutron Intermediate Standard Uranium Source (PDAA)
NISW	National Institute for Social Work (SAUS)
NISW	National Institute of Social Work [British]
NISW	Naval In-Shore Warfare (PDAA)
NISWA	National Indian Social Workers Association (EA)
NIT	Midwest Aviation Corp. [ICAO designator] (FAAC)
NIT	National Institute of Technology
NIT	National Instructional Television [Superseded by AIT] (EA)
NIT	National Intelligence Test [Psychology]
NIT	National Intelligence Topic (MCD)
NIT	National Invitation Tournament [Basketball]
NIT	Native Interface Tester [Computer science] (VLIE)
NIT	Nearly Intelligent Terminal [Computer science] (ELAL)
NIT	Negative Income Tax
NIT	Network Information Technology
NIT	Network Interface Task [Computer science] (CIST)
NIT	Nevada Institute of Technology (SAUS)
NIT	New Industrial Technology (SAUS)
NIT	New Information Technologies (or Technology) (SAUS)
NIT	New Information Technology
NIT	New Investment Technology
NIT	New Technology, Incorporated (ACAE)
NIT	Nippon Institute of Technology (SAUS)
NIT	Nitrate (SAUS)
NIT	Nitrum [Chemistry] (ROG)
NIT	None in Town [Bookselling]
NIT	Non-Intelligent Terminal (NITA)
NIT	Nonlinear Inertialess Three-Pole [Telecommunications] (OA)
NIT	Norfolk International Terminal
NIT	Normal Incidence Technique [Structural testing]
NIT	Northrop Institute of Technology (SAUS)
NIT	Northrop International Terminals (SAUS)
NIT	Norwegian Institute of Technology (SAUS)
NIT	Not In Therapy (SAUS)
NIT	Nuclear Irradiation Test
NIT	Numerical Indicator Tube (SAUS)
NIT	Nurses in Transition (EA)
NITA	National Indoor Tennis Association [Formerly, ITA] [Later, NTA] (EA)
NITA	National Industrial Television Association [Later, ITVA] (EA)
NITA	National Institute for Trial Advocacy (EA)
NITA	National Instructional Television Association (NTCM)
NITA	National Intravenous Therapy Association [Later, INS] (EA)
NITAT	Northern Ireland Training & Advisory Team (SAUS)
NITB	Northern Ireland Tourist Board
NITB	Tompkins-Seneca-Tioga Board of Cooperative Educational Services, Ithaca, NY [Library symbol] [Library of Congress] (LCLS)
NITC	National Information Technology Committee [Thailand] (DDC)
NITC	National Information Transfer Centre (NITA)
NITC	National Instructional Television Center (NTCM)
NITC	National Intelligence Tasking Center [CIA]
NITCCU	Northern Information Technology Centre Consultancy Unit (NITA)
Nitches	Nitches, Inc. [Associated Press] (SAG)
NITD	Noninsulin-Treated Disease [Medicine] (MELL)
NITE	National Institute of Technology & Evaluation (SAUS)
NITE	Navy Integrated Terminal Evaluation
NITE	Night Imaging Thermal Equipment [Army] (INF)
NITEC	National Information Technology in Education Centre (ACII)
NITEDEVRON	Night Development Squadron
NITEOP	Night Imaging Through Electro-Optic Package [Military] [British]
NITE-OP	Night Imaging Trough Electro-Optics (SAUS)
NITEP	National Incinerator Testing and Evaluation Program [Environmental Protection Agency] (GFGA)
NITES	NTCS-A/Navy Integrated Tactical Environmental (SAUS)
NITEWOG	Naval Integrated Test and Evaluation Working Group (MCD)
NITF	National Imagery Transmission Format (DOMA)
NITF	National Interreligious Task Force (EA)
NITF	Nuclear Instrument Test Facilities
NITFSJ	National Interreligious Task Force on Soviet Jewry (EA)
NITHC	Northern Ireland Transport Holding Co. (SAUS)
NITINOL	Nickel Titanium Naval Ordnance Laboratory [An alloy named by William Buehler of the NOL] (KSC)
Nitinol	Nitinol Medical Technologies, Inc. [Associated Press] (SAG)
NITL	National Industrial Traffic League (EA)
NITL	National Industrial Transportation League (EA)

NITM........... National Income Tax Magazine [*A publication*] (DLA)
NIT-MCS ..... Nippon Telephone and Telegraph-Mobile Cellular System (CGWS)
NITMDA....... National Indoor Track Meet Directors Association (EA)
NITOL .... Norway-net with IT for Open Learning (SAUS)
NITO/W........ National Intelligence Tasking Office, Warning and Crisis Management (ACAE)
NIT OX......... Nitmus Oxide (SAUS)
NIT OX........ Nitrous Oxide [*Laughing gas*] (AAMN)
NITP........... National Industrial Training Program [*Canada*]
NITP........... National Institutional Training Program [*Canada*]
NITP........... Nibbling Template
NITPA .... National Institutional Teacher Placement Association [*Later, ASCUS*]
NITPICKERS... National Institute of Technical Processors, Information Consultants, Keyword Experts, and Retrieval Specialists [*Fictitious organization*]
NITR .... Nitrite (SAUS)
NITR .... Nonimmune Transfusion Reaction [*Medicine*] (MELL)
NITRAS....... Navy Integrated Training Resources and Administration System (NVT)
NITRC........ National Indian Training and Research Center (EA)
NITREX....... Nitrogen Saturation Experiments (SAUS)
NITRO........ National Independent Textiles Retailers Organizations (NTPA)
NITRO........ Nitrocellulose (WDAA)
NITRO........ Nitrogen [*Chemical element*]
nitro.......... Nitroglycerin [*Pharmacy*]
Nitro .... Nitroglycerine (SAUS)
NITRO........ Sodium Nitroprusside [*Pharmacology*] (DAVI)
NITROS....... Nitrostarch (AAG)
NITSTL........ Nitride Steel
NITTS.......... Noise Induced Temporary Threshold Shift (SAUS)
NITU.......... Notice of Interim Trail Use [*Interstate Commerce Commission*]
NITUC......... National Independent Truckers Unity Council [*Defunct*] (EA)
NITV.......... National Iranian Television (NADA)
NITV.......... Network for Instructional Television (SAUS)
NIU .... NATO Interface Unit (MCD)
NIU .... Naval Intelligence Unit
NIU .... Navigation Interface Unit [*Navy*] (CAAL)
NIU .... Network Interface Unit [*Computer science*]
NIU .... Niue [*ANSI three-letter standard code*] (CNC)
NIU .... Niumate [*Tonga*] [*Seismograph station code, US Geological Survey*] [*Closed*] (SEIS)
NIU .... North american ISDN Users (SAUS)
NIU .... Northern Illinois University [*Dekalb, IL*]
NIU .... Northern Interparliamentary Union (SAUS)
NIU .... University of Northern Iowa, Cedar Falls, IA [*OCLC symbol*] (OCLC)
NIUC .... National Independent Union Council [*Later, NFIU*]
NIUE .... Alofi/Niue International [*Niue Island*] [*ICAO location identifier*] (ICLI)
NIUF .... National Inshore Union of Fishermen [*British*]
NIUF .... North American ISDN Users Forum (SAUS)
NIULPE ...... National Institute for Uniform Licensing of Power Engineers'
NIUSR........ National Institute for Urban Search and Rescue (SAUS)
NIUW .... National Institute for Urban Wildlife (EA)
NIV.......... National Institute for Virology [*South Africa*]
NIV.......... National Institute of Victimology (EA)
NIV.......... Negative Ion Vacancy
NIV.......... Neutron-Induced Voltagwe (NUCP)
NIV.......... Newbury International Ventures, Inc. [*Vancouver Stock Exchange symbol*]
NIV.......... New International Version [*of the Bible*] [*A publication*]
NIV.......... Nivalenol [*A mycotoxin*]
NIV.......... Nodule-Inducing Virus
NIV.......... Non-Immigrant Visa (SAUS)
NIV.......... Non-Invasive Ventilation (SAUS)
NIVA .... National Independent Vendors Association [*Defunct*] (EA)
NIVA .... North of Ireland Veterinary Association (GVA)
NIVA .... Norwegian Institute for Water Research (SAUS)
NIVC .... National Interactive Video Centre [*British*]
NIVEA .... Night Vision Equipment for Armor
NIVR .... Netherlands Agency for Aerospace Programs
NIW .... National Industrial Workers Union
NIW .... Naval Inshore Warfare Project
NIW .... Night in Weather (ACAE)
NIW .... Nonlethal Incapacitating Weapon
NIWA .... New Zealand National Institue for Water and Atmospheric Research (SAUS)
NIWAR........ National Institute of Water and Atmospheric Research (SAUS)
NIWC .... National Institute for Women of Color (EA)
NIWC .... Naval Inshore Warfare Command (NVT)
NIWC .... Northern Ireland Womens Coalition (SAUS)
NIWF .... Network Interworking Function (MLOA)
NIWFA .... National Intercollegiate Women's Fencing Association (EA)
NIWG .... National Institute for the Word of God (EA)
NIWKC .... National Institute of Wood Kitchen Cabinets [*Later, KCMA*]
NIWL .... National Institute for Work and Learning (EA)
NIWR .... National Institutes for Water Resources (NTPA)
NIWS .... National Institute on Workshop Standards [*Defunct*] (EA)
NIWS .... National Integrated Wage Structure (ADA)
NIWS .... News Information Weekly Service
NIWTU .... Naval Inshore Warfare Task Unit (MCD)
NIWU .... National Industrial Workers Union (EA)
NIX........... Nioro [*Mali*] [*Airport symbol*] (OAG)
Nix........... Nixa [*Record label*] [*Great Britain, etc.; including Vanguard label re-issues*]
NIX........... Nix-O-Tine Pharmaceuticals Ltd. [*Vancouver Stock Exchange symbol*]

NIX........... Nix-o-Tine Pharmacy (SAUS)
NIX........... Pacific Beach, WA [*Location identifier*] [*FAA*] (FAAL)
Nix Dig ...... Nixon's Digest of Laws [*New Jersey*] [*A publication*] (DLA)
Nix F.......... Nixon's Forms [*A publication*] (DLA)
NIXSW .... Normal Incidence X-ray Standing Wave (SAUS)
NIXT.......... Normal Incidence X-Ray Telescope
NIXX.......... Nix-O-Tine Pharmaceuticals Ltd. (SAUS)
NIY........... Norfolk, VA [*Location identifier*] [*FAA*] (FAAL)
NIY........... Northamptonshire Imperial Yeomanry [*British military*] (DMA)
NIY........... Northumberland Imperial Yeomanry [*British military*] (DMA)
NIYC.......... National Indian Youth Council (EA)
NIZ........... Nizhne-Angarsk [*Former USSR*] [*Seismograph station code, US Geological Survey*] (SEIS)
NIZC.......... National Industrial Zoning Committee (EA)
NJ........... Namakwaland Lugdiens [*ICAO designator*] (AD)
NJ........... Namakwaland Lugdiens Bpk [*South Africa*] [*ICAO designator*] (ICDA)
nJ .... Nanojoule [*One billionth of a joule*]
NJ........... Napierville Junction Railway Co. [*AAR code*]
NJ........... Nasojejunal [*Medicine*]
NJ........... Network Junction [*Telecommunications*] (OA)
NJ........... Neue Justiz. Zeitschrift fuer Recht und Rechtswissenschaft [*Berlin, German Democratic Republic*] [*A publication*] (DLA)
NJ........... New Jaguar [*Jaguar PLC*]
NJ........... New Japan Aircraft Maintenance Co. Ltd. [*Japan*] [*ICAO aircraft manufacturer identifier*] (ICAO)
NJ........... New Jason [*Charter-party clause*] [*Business term*] (DS)
NJ........... New Jersey [*Postal code*]
Nj........... New Jersey State Library, Trenton, NJ [*Library symbol*] [*Library of Congress*] (LCLS)
NJ........... New Jersey Supreme Court Reports [*A publication*] (DLA)
NJ........... New Journalism [*Refers to specific style, as that of writer Tom Wolfe*]
NJ........... Non Justifying [*Typography*] (DGA)
NJ........... Non-Juxtaposed (SAUS)
NJ........... Notice of Judgment (Official) [*Legal term*] (DLA)
NJ........... Nylon Jacket
NJA.......... National Jail Association [*Later, AJA*] (EA)
NJA.......... National Jewellers' Association [*British*] (BI)
NJA.......... National Jogging Association [*Later, ARFA*] (EA)
NJA.......... National Jousting Association (EA)
NJA.......... National Judges Association (EA)
NJA.......... New Jewish Agenda (EA)
NJA.......... Nozzle Jetevator Assembly
NJA.......... Sky Air Cargo Services (UK) Ltd. [*British*] [*ICAO designator*] (FAAC)
NJAA......... National Junior Angus Association (EA)
NjAc......... Atlantic City Free Public Library, Atlantic City, NJ [*Library symbol*] [*Library of Congress*] (LCLS)
NJAC......... National Joint Advisory Council [*on labor-management relations*] [*British*]
NJAC......... New Jersey Administrative Code [*A publication*]
NJAC......... New Jersey Athletic Conference (PSS)
NjAcCoC .... Atlantic County Clerk, Atlantic City, NJ [*Library symbol*] [*Library of Congress*] (LCLS)
NjAcFA....... United States Federal Aviation Administration, National Aviation Facilities Experimental Center, Atlantic City, NJ [*Library symbol*] [*Library of Congress*] (LCLS)
NjAcJ .... Jewish Record, Atlantic City, NJ [*Library symbol*] [*Library of Congress*] (LCLS)
NjAcP......... Press Publishing Co., Atlantic City, NJ [*Library symbol*] [*Library of Congress*] (LCLS)
NjAcPI .... Popolo Italiano, Atlantic City, NJ [*Library symbol*] [*Library of Congress*] (LCLS)
NjAcR .... Atlantic City Reporter, Atlantic City, NJ [*Library symbol*] [*Library of Congress*] (LCLS)
NJACU .... New Jersey Association of Colleges and Universities (SAUS)
NJAD .... Nozzle Joint Assembly Demonstration
NJ Admin Code... New Jersey Administrative Code [*A publication*] (DLA)
NJAG .... National Jewish Artisans Guild [*Defunct*] (EA)
NJAIC......... New Jersey Asparagus Industry Council (EA)
NJAIS......... New Jersey Association of Independent Schools (SAUS)
NjAI .... Allentown Public Library, Allentown, NJ [*Library symbol*] [*Library of Congress*] (LCLS)
NjAIA .... Allentown Printing Service, Allentown, NJ [*Library symbol*] [*Library of Congress*] (LCLS)
NjAIB .... Allentown Borough Hall, Allentown, NJ [*Library symbol*] [*Library of Congress*] (LCLS)
NjAlHi......... Allentown Historical Society, Allentown, NJ [*Library symbol*] [*Library of Congress*] (LCLS)
NJam .... James Prendergast Free Library, Jamestown, NY [*Library symbol*] [*Library of Congress*] (LCLS)
NJamC........ Chautauqua-Cattaraugus Library System, Jamestown, NY [*Library symbol*] [*Library of Congress*] (LCLS)
NJamCC....... Jamestown Community College, Jamestown, NY [*Library symbol*] [*Library of Congress*] (LCLS)
NJamH........ Jamestown General Hospital, Jamestown, NY [*Library symbol*] [*Library of Congress*] (LCLS)
NJamW........ Woman's Christian Association Hospital, Jamestown, NY [*Library symbol*] [*Library of Congress*] (LCLS)
NJANG .... New Jersey Air National Guard (MUSM)
NJAR .... New Jersey Administrative Reports [*A publication*]
NjAs.......... Asbury Park Free Public Library, Asbury Park, NJ [*Library symbol*] [*Library of Congress*] (LCLS)
NJASBO ...... New Jersey Association of School Business Officials (SAUS)
NjAsP.......... Asbury Park Press, Asbury Park, NJ [*Library symbol*] [*Library of Congress*] (LCLS)

NjAsS........... Spotlight Magazine, Asbury Park, NJ [*Library symbol*] [*Library of Congress*] (LCLS)

NJASSPS..... New Jersey Association of Secondary School Principals and Supervisors (SAUS)

NjAt .... Atlantic Highlands Public Library Association, Atlantic Highlands, NJ [*Library symbol*] [*Library of Congress*] (LCLS)

NjAuV .... Weekly Visitor, Audubon, NJ [*Library symbol*] [*Library of Congress*] (LCLS)

NjAveT......... Tabloid Lithographers, Inc., Avenel, NJ [*Library symbol*] [*Library of Congress*] (LCLS)

NjAvH .... Herald, Avalon, NJ [*Library symbol*] [*Library of Congress*] (LCLS)

NJB.............. Appalachian State University, Boone, NC [*OCLC symbol*] (OCLC)

NjB.............. Bridgeton Free Public Library, Bridgeton, NJ [*Library symbol*] [*Library of Congress*] (LCLS)

NJB.............. New Jerusalem Bible [*1985*] [*A publication*] (ODCC)

NjBa............ Bayonne Free Public Library, Bayonne, NJ [*Library symbol*] [*Library of Congress*] (LCLS)

NjBaF........... Facts of Bayonne Publishing Co., Bayonne, NJ [*Library symbol*] [*Library of Congress*] (LCLS)

NjBaFAR..... Federal Archives and Records Center, General Services Administration, Bayonne, NJ [*Library symbol*] [*Library of Congress*] (LCLS)

NjBaNSRF.... United States Naval Supply Research and Development Facility, Bayonne, NJ [*Library symbol*] [*Library of Congress*] (LCLS)

NjBAP .... Cumberland County Advertiser-Press, Inc., Bridgeton, NJ [*Library symbol*] [*Library of Congress*] (LCLS)

NjBarHi........ Barrington Historical Society (SAUS)

NjBarHi........ Barrington Historical Society, Barrington, NJ [*Library symbol*] [*Library of Congress*] (LCLS)

NjBas........... Bernards Township Library, Inc., Basking Ridge, NJ [*Library symbol*] [*Library of Congress*] (LCLS)

NjBb............. Bound Brook Memorial Library, Bound Brook, NJ [*Library symbol*] [*Library of Congress*] (LCLS)

NjBbA .... American Cyanamid Co., Organic Chemicals Division, Bound Brook, NJ [*Library symbol*] [*Library of Congress*] (LCLS)

NjBbC .... Bound Brook Chronicle, Bound Brook, NJ [*Library symbol*] [*Library of Congress*] (LCLS)

NJBBF.......... National Judo Black Belt Federation of the USA (EA)

NjBbU........... Union Carbide Plastics Co., Bound Brook, NJ [*Library symbol*] [*Library of Congress*] (LCLS)

NjBCoC .... Cumberland County Clerk, Bridgeton, NJ [*Library symbol*] [*Library of Congress*] (LCLS)

NjBe............. Belleville Free Public Library, Belleville, NJ [*Library symbol*] [*Library of Congress*] (LCLS)

NjBeA .... Ad-Print, Belleville, NJ [*Library symbol*] [*Library of Congress*] (LCLS)

NjBeacO ...... Daily Observer, Beachwood, NJ [*Library symbol*] [*Library of Congress*] (LCLS)

NjBel .... Belmar Public Library, Belmar, NJ [*Library symbol*] [*Library of Congress*] (LCLS)

NjBelvCoC ... Warren County Clerk, Belvidere, NJ [*Library symbol*] [*Library of Congress*] (LCLS)

NjBelvW .... Warren County Library, Belvidere, NJ [*Library symbol*] [*Library of Congress*] (LCLS)

NjBer .... Bergenfield Free Public Library, Bergenfield, NJ [*Library symbol*] [*Library of Congress*] (LCLS)

NjBerl .... Marie Fleche Memorial Library, Berlin, NJ [*Library symbol*] [*Library of Congress*] (LCLS)

NjBern .... Bernardsville Library Association, Bernardsville, NJ [*Library symbol*] [*Library of Congress*] (LCLS)

NjBernN....... Bernardsville News, Bernardsville, NJ [*Library symbol*] [*Library of Congress*] (LCLS)

NjBeT........... Belleville Telegram, Belleville, NJ [*Library symbol*] [*Library of Congress*] (LCLS)

NjBh............. Berkley Heights Public Library, Berkley Heights, NJ [*Library symbol*] [*Library of Congress*] (LCLS)

NjBl .... Bloomfield Public Library, Bloomfield, NJ [*Library symbol*] [*Library of Congress*] (LCLS)

NjBla .... Gloucester Township [*Blackwood*] Library, Blackwood, NJ [*Library symbol*] [*Library of Congress*] (LCLS)

NjBlaC .... Camden County College, Blackwood, NJ [*Library symbol*] [*Library of Congress*] (LCLS)

NjBlaCG .... Camden-Gloucester Newspapers, Blackwood, NJ [*Library symbol*] [*Library of Congress*] (LCLS)

NjBlaiP .... Blairstown Press, Blairstown, NJ [*Library symbol*] [*Library of Congress*] (LCLS)

NjBlC .... Bloomfield College, Bloomfield, NJ [*Library symbol*] [*Library of Congress*] (LCLS)

NjBlHi.......... Historical Society of Bloomfield, Bloomfield, NJ [*Library symbol*] [*Library of Congress*] (LCLS)

NjBlI .... Independent Press, Bloomfield, NJ [*Library symbol*] [*Library of Congress*] (LCLS)

NjBlM .... Academy of Medicine of New Jersey, Bloomfield, NJ [*Library symbol*] [*Library of Congress*] (LCLS)

NjBlS .... Shering Corp., Bloomfield, NJ [*Library symbol*] [*Library of Congress*] (LCLS)

NjBlW .... Westinghouse Electric Corp., Lamp Division, Bloomfield, NJ [*Library symbol*] [*Library of Congress*] (LCLS)

NjBN .... Bridgeton Evening News, Bridgeton, NJ [*Library symbol*] [*Library of Congress*] (LCLS)

NjBo............. Bogota Public Library, Bogota, NJ [*Library symbol*] [*Library of Congress*] (LCLS)

NjBoo........... Holmes Library, Boonton, NJ [*Library symbol*] [*Library of Congress*] (LCLS)

NjBooT......... Times-Bulletin, Boonton, NJ [*Library symbol*] [*Library of Congress*] (LCLS)

NjBorHi........ Bordentown Historical Society, Bordentown, NJ [*Library symbol*] [*Library of Congress*] (LCLS)

NjBorL .... Lorraine Publishing, Inc., Bordentown, NJ [*Library symbol*] [*Library of Congress*] (LCLS)

NjBriCN........ Plainfield Courier-News, Bridgewater, NJ [*Library symbol*] [*Library of Congress*] (LCLS)

NjBrigT .... Brigantine Times, Brigantine, NJ [*Library symbol*] [*Library of Congress*] (LCLS)

NjBro .... Mendham Township Library, Brookside, NJ [*Library symbol*] [*Library of Congress*] (LCLS)

NjBrS .... Seacoast Newspapers, Brick Town, NJ [*Library symbol*] [*Library of Congress*] (LCLS)

NjBu............. Library Co. of Burlington, Burlington, NJ [*Library symbol*] [*Library of Congress*] (LCLS)

NjBuHi .... Burlington County Historical Society, Burlington, NJ [*Library symbol*] [*Library of Congress*] (LCLS)

NjButA .... Argus Printing & Publishing Co., Butler, NJ [*Library symbol*] [*Library of Congress*] (LCLS)

NjC.............. Chatham Public Library, Chatham, NJ [*Library symbol*] [*Library of Congress*] (LCLS)

NJC.............. Natchez Junior College [*Mississippi*]

NJC.............. National Jewish Center [*Australia*]

NJC.............. National Jewish Coalition (EA)

NJC.............. National Joint Council (AIE)

NJC.............. National Judicial College (EA)

NJC.............. National Security Caucus Institute (EA)

NJC.............. Navarro Junior College [*Texas*]

NJC.............. Navy Job Classification Manual

NJC.............. New Jersey Central Railroad

NJC.............. Newton Junior College [*Massachusetts*]

NJC.............. Nordic Journal of Computing (SAUS)

NJC.............. Norfolk Junior College [*Nebraska*]

NJCa............ Not Just Cows (SAUS)

NjCa............ Camden Free Public Library, Camden, NJ [*Library symbol*] [*Library of Congress*] (LCLS)

NJCAA .... National Job Corps Alumni Association [*Washington, DC*] (EA)

NJCAA .... National Junior College Athletic Association (EA)

NjCaC .... Cooper Medical Center, Camden, NJ [*Library symbol*] [*Library of Congress*] (LCLS)

NjCaHi......... Camden County Historical Society, Camden, NJ [*Library symbol*] [*Library of Congress*] (LCLS)

NjCal .... Caldwell Free Public Library, Caldwell, NJ [*Library symbol*] [*Library of Congress*] (LCLS)

NjCalC .... Caldwell College, Caldwell, NJ [*Library symbol*] [*Library of Congress*] (LCLS)

NjCalP .... Caldwell Progress, Caldwell, NJ [*Library symbol*] [*Library of Congress*] (LCLS)

NjCaN .... Camden News, Camden, NJ [*Library symbol*] [*Library of Congress*] (LCLS)

NjCapS .... Star and Wave, Cape May, NJ [*Library symbol*] [*Library of Congress*] (LCLS)

NJCAPT & C... National Joint Council for Administrative, Professional, Technical, and ClericalStaff [*British*]

NjCaRD........ Radio Corp. of America, Communications Systems Division, Camden, NJ [*Library symbol*] [*Library of Congress*] (LCLS)

NjCarpD....... E. I. Du Pont de Nemours & Co., Carney's Point Development Laboratory, Carney's Point, NJ [*Library symbol*] [*Library of Congress*] (LCLS)

NjCaSH........ Catholic Star Herald, Camden, NJ [*Library symbol*] [*Library of Congress*] (LCLS)

NjCaUR........ Union Reporter, Camden, NJ [*Library symbol*] [*Library of Congress*] (LCLS)

NJCBI.......... National Joint Council for the Building Industry [*British*] (DCTA)

NJCBSPT ...... New Jersey College Basic Skills Placement Test (EDAC)

NjCC............ Chatham Courier, Chatham, NJ [*Library symbol*] [*Library of Congress*] (LCLS)

NJCC............ National Joint Computer Committee [*of ACM, AIEE, IRE*] [*Superseded by AFIPS*]

NJCC............ Northeastern Junior College of Colorado [*Sterling*]

NJCCA .... National Japanese Canadian Citizens' Association

NJCCOE .... Nordic Joint Committee of Commercial and Office Executives (EA)

NJCDE .... Nordic Joint Committee for Domestic Education (EA)

NjCE............ Chatham Township Echoes, Chatham, NJ [*Library symbol*] [*Library of Congress*] (LCLS)

NJCEC.......... NATO Joint Communications-Electronics Committee (NATG)

NJCF............ National Juvenile Court Foundation (EA)

NJCF............ New Jersey Conservation Foundation (SAUS)

NjCg............ Cedar Grove Public Library, Cedar Grove, NJ [*Library symbol*] [*Library of Congress*] (LCLS)

NjCh............ Cherry Hill Free Public Library, Cherry Hill, NJ [*Library symbol*] [*Library of Congress*] (LCLS)

NJ Ch........... New Jersey Equity Reports [*A publication*] (DLA)

NJCHC .... National Joint Council for Handicapped Children [*British*]

NjChCP .... Courier Post, Cherry Hill, NJ [*Library symbol*] [*Library of Congress*] (LCLS)

NjChe........... Chester Free Public Library, Chester, NJ [*Library symbol*] [*Library of Congress*] (LCLS)

NjChJ........... Jewish Federation of Camden County, Cherry Hill, NJ [*Library symbol*] [*Library of Congress*] (LCLS)

NjChM .... Cherry Hill Medical Center, Cherry Hill, NJ [*Library symbol*] [*Library of Congress*] (LCLS)

NjChSG .... Shoppers Guide, Cherry Hill, NJ [*Library symbol*] [*Library of Congress*] (LCLS)

NjChSN .... Suburban Newspaper Group, Cherry Hill, NJ [*Library symbol*] [*Library of Congress*] (LCLS)

NjCiL............ Cinnaminson Little Paper, Cinnaminson, NJ [*Library symbol*] [*Library of Congress*] (LCLS)

NjCl .... Clark Free Public Library, Clark, NJ [*Library symbol*] [*Library of Congress*] (LCLS)

NJCL............. Network Job Control Language [*Computer science*]

NJCLAFB...... National Joint Council for Local Authority Fire Brigades [*British*]

NJCLD........... National Joint Committee for Learning Disabilities

NJCLE.......... Institute for Continuing Legal Education, New Jersey (DLA)

NjClif .... Clifton Public Library, Clifton, NJ [*Library symbol*] [*Library of Congress*] (LCLS)

NjClifB .... New Jersey Business Review, Clifton, NJ [*Library symbol*] [*Library of Congress*] (LCLS)

NjClifI .... Clifton Independent Prospector, Clifton, NJ [*Library symbol*] [*Library of Congress*] (LCLS)

NjClifL .... Clifton Leader, Clifton, NJ [*Library symbol*] [*Library of Congress*] (LCLS)

NjClifP .... Clifton Publishing Co., Clifton, NJ [*Library symbol*] [*Library of Congress*] (LCLS)

NjClifPE .... Post Eagle Publishing Co., Clifton, NJ [*Library symbol*] [*Library of Congress*] (LCLS)

NjClifW .... Woodward-Clyde Consultants, Clifton, NJ [*Library symbol*] [*Library of Congress*] (LCLS)

NjClinH........ Hunterdon Review, Clinton, NJ [*Library symbol*] [*Library of Congress*] (LCLS)

NjClp .... Cliffside Park Public Library, Cliffside Park, NJ [*Library symbol*] [*Library of Congress*] (LCLS)

NjClpP .... Palisades Printing Corp., Cliffside Park, NJ [*Library symbol*] [*Library of Congress*] (LCLS)

NjCmCo .... Cape May County Library, Cape May Court House, NJ [*Library symbol*] [*Library of Congress*] (LCLS)

NjCmCoC ..... Cape May County Clerk, Cape May Court House, NJ [*Library symbol*] [*Library of Congress*] (LCLS)

NjCmG .... Cape May County Gazette, Cape May Court House, NJ [*Library symbol*] [*Library of Congress*] (LCLS)

NJCMS......... New Jersey Chamber Music Society (SAUS)

NjCo............. Collingswood Free Public Library, Collingswood, NJ [*Library symbol*] [*Library of Congress*] (LCLS)

NjCoB .... Christian Beacon, Collingswood, NJ [*Library symbol*] [*Library of Congress*] (LCLS)

NjCoC .... Collingswood Publishing Co., Collingswood, NJ [*Library symbol*] [*Library of Congress*] (LCLS)

NjColS .... South Jersey Ad-Visor, Cologne, NJ [*Library symbol*] [*Library of Congress*] (LCLS)

NjConC .... College of Saint Elizabeth, Convent Station, NJ [*Library symbol*] [*Library of Congress*] (LCLS)

NJCOS .... National Jewish Committee on Scouting (EA)

NjCoT........... Camden County Times, Collingswood, NJ [*Library symbol*] [*Library of Congress*] (LCLS)

NjCr.............. Cranford Public Library, Cranford, NJ [*Library symbol*] [*Library of Congress*] (LCLS)

NJCRAC .... National Jewish Community Relations Advisory Council (EA)

NjCrbP.......... Cranbury Press, Cranbury, NJ [*Library symbol*] [*Library of Congress*] (LCLS)

NjCrC .... Cranford Citizen & Chronicle, Cranford, NJ [*Library symbol*] [*Library of Congress*] (LCLS)

NjCrHi .... Cranford Historical Society, Cranford, NJ [*Library symbol*] [*Library of Congress*] (LCLS)

NjCrU .... Union College, Cranford, NJ [*Library symbol*] [*Library of Congress*] (LCLS)

NJCS............ National Jewish Committee on Scouting (EA)

NJCSA .... National Juvenile Court Services Association (EA)

NJCSE.......... National Jewish Civil Service Employees (EA)

NjD .... Dover Public Library, Dover, NJ [*Library symbol*] [*Library of Congress*] (LCLS)

NjDA .... Daily Advance, Dover, NJ [*Library symbol*] [*Library of Congress*] (LCLS)

NJDA .... National Juvenile Detention Association (EA)

NJDA .... New Jersey Dental Association (SAUS)

NjDC .... County College of Morris, Dover, NJ [*Library symbol*] [*Library of Congress*] (LCLS)

NJDDC.......... New Jersey Development Disabilities Council (EDAC)

NjDe .... Denville Free Public Library, Denville, NJ [*Library symbol*] [*Library of Congress*] (LCLS)

NjDeC........... Citizen of Morris County, Denville, NJ [*Library symbol*] [*Library of Congress*] (LCLS)

NJDEP .... New Jersey Department of Environmental Protection

NJDEPE........ New Jersey Department of Environmental Protection and Energy (SAUS)

NJDFC.......... New Jersey Devils Fan Club (EA)

NJDOT .... New Jersey Department of Transport (SAUS)

NjDPA........... United States Army, Armament Research and Development Command, Science and Technical Library, Dover Site Dover (SAUS)

NjDPA........... United States Army, Armament Research and Development Command, Science and Technical Library, Dover Site, Dover, NJ [*Library symbol*] [*Library of Congress*] (LCLS)

NJE .... Network Job Entry

NJE .... New Jersey Equity Reports [*A publication*] (DLA)

NJE .... New Jersey Experiment (SAUS)

Nj-E .... New Jersey State Library, Department of Education, Trenton, NJ [*Library symbol*] [*Library of Congress*] (LCLS)

NJE .... Office of Cancer and Toxic Substances Research, Trenton, NJ [*OCLC symbol*] (OCLC)

NjEa............. Eatontown Public Library, Eatontown, NJ [*Library symbol*] [*Library of Congress*] (LCLS)

NjEb............. East Brunswick Public Library, East Brunswick, NJ [*Library symbol*] [*Library of Congress*] (LCLS)

NjEbGS .... Church of Jesus Christ of Latter-Day Saints, Genealogical Society Library, East Brunswick Stake Branch, East Brunswick, NJ [*Library symbol*] [*Library of Congress*] (LCLS)

NjEbS........... Sentinel Publishing Co., East Brunswick, NJ [*Library symbol*] [*Library of Congress*] (LCLS)

NjEdE........... Engelhard Minerals & Chemicals Corp. [*Later, Engelhard Corp.*], Research Library, Edison, NJ [*Library symbol*] [*Library of Congress*] (LCLS)

NjEdM.......... Middlesex County College, Edison, NJ [*Library symbol*] [*Library of Congress*] (LCLS)

NjEgN .... Egg Harbor News, Egg Harbor City, NJ [*Library symbol*] [*Library of Congress*] (LCLS)

NjEh............. East Hanover Public Library, East Hanover, NJ [*Library symbol*] [*Library of Congress*] (LCLS)

NjEli............. Elizabeth Free Public Library, Elizabeth, NJ [*Library symbol*] [*Library of Congress*] (LCLS)

NjEliCoC....... Union County Clerk, Elizabeth, NJ [*Library symbol*] [*Library of Congress*] (LCLS)

NjEliJ .... Daily Journal, Elizabeth, NJ [*Library symbol*] [*Library of Congress*] (LCLS)

NjEIT .... Elmer Times, Elmer, NJ [*Library symbol*] [*Library of Congress*] (LCLS)

NjEn............. Englewood Library, Englewood, NJ [*Library symbol*] [*Library of Congress*] (LCLS)

NjEncL .... Thomas J. Lipton, Inc., Englewood Cliffs, NJ [*Library symbol*] [*Library of Congress*] (LCLS)

NjEncStP...... Saint Peter's College, Englewood Cliffs, NJ [*Library symbol*] [*Library of Congress*] (LCLS)

NJE/NJI........ Network Job Entry, Including Network Job Interface

NjEnP........... Englewood Press, Englewood, NJ [*Library symbol*] [*Library of Congress*] (LCLS)

NjEnPa......... Palisades Newspapers, Englewood, NJ [*Library symbol*] [*Library of Congress*] (LCLS)

NjEnS........... North Jersey Suburbanite, Englewood, NJ [*Library symbol*] [*Library of Congress*] (LCLS)

NjEo............. East Orange Free Public Library, East Orange, NJ [*Library symbol*] [*Library of Congress*] (LCLS)

NjEoA........... Advocate, East Orange, NJ [*Library symbol*] [*Library of Congress*] (LCLS)

NjEoS........... Sokol USA, East Orange, NJ [*Library symbol*] [*Library of Congress*] (LCLS)

NjEoU .... Upsala College, East Orange, NJ [*Library symbol*] [*Library of Congress*] (LCLS)

NjEoV........... United States Veterans Administration Hospital, East Orange, NJ [*Library symbol*] [*Library of Congress*] (LCLS)

NJ Eq........... New Jersey Equity Reports [*A publication*] (DLA)

NJ Eq R........ New Jersey Equity Reports [*A publication*] (DLA)

NJ Equity..... New Jersey Equity Reports [*A publication*] (DLA)

NJer............. Jericho Public Library, Jericho, NY [*Library symbol*] [*Library of Congress*] (LCLS)

NJerC........... Long Island Association of Commerce and Industry, Jericho, NY [*Library symbol*] [*Library of Congress*] (LCLS)

NJerCE........ Cantiague Elementary School, Jericho, NY [*Library symbol*] [*Library of Congress*] (LCLS)

NJerHS .... Jericho Senior High School, Jericho, NY [*Library symbol*] [*Library of Congress*] (LCLS)

NJerJE......... George Jackson Elementary School, Jericho, NY [*Library symbol*] [*Library of Congress*] (LCLS)

NJerS........... Staff Supermarket Associates, Inc., Jericho, NY [*Library symbol*] [*Library of Congress*] (LCLS)

N Jersey R.... New Jersey Law Reports [*A publication*] (DLA)

NJES............ Nozzle Joint Environmental Simulators (SAUS)

NJESS.......... Nigerian Journal of Economic and Social Studies [*A publication*]

NjEwB.......... Bergen Citizen, Edgewater, NJ [*Library symbol*] [*Library of Congress*] (LCLS)

NjEwJJ......... Johnson & Johnson Dental Product Co., East Windsor, NJ [*Library symbol*] [*Library of Congress*] (LCLS)

NJF .... Cherry Point, NC [*Location identifier*] [*FAA*] (FAAL)

NjF............... Fair Lawn Free Public Library, Fair Lawn, NJ [*Library symbol*] [*Library of Congress*] (LCLS)

NJF .... Nordiska Journalistforbundet [*Nordic Association of Journalists Unions - NAJU*] (EAIO)

NJF .... Nordiske Jordbrugsforskeres Forening [*Nordic Agricultural Research Workers Association - NARWA*] (EAIO)

NJF .... Scandinavian Agricultural Research Workers' Association

NJFA............ National Justice Foundation of America (EA)

NJFAA.......... Federal Aviation Administration, Eastern Region Library, Jamaica, NY [*Library symbol*] [*Library of Congress*] (LCLS)

NJFC............ Norma Jean Fan Club (EA)

NJFD............ Notices of Judgment, United States Food and Drug Administration [*A publication*] (DLA)

NjFdA........... United States Army, Special Services Post Library, Fort Dix, NJ [*Library symbol*] [*Library of Congress*] (LCLS)

NjFf............. Fairfield Free Public Library, Fairfield, NJ [*Library symbol*] [*Library of Congress*] (LCLS)

NjFhUGA...... United States Golf Association, Far Hills, NJ [*Library symbol*] [*Library of Congress*] (LCLS)

NjFlCoC........ Hunterdon County Clerk, Flemington, NJ [*Library symbol*] [*Library of Congress*] (LCLS)

NjFlD .... Hunterdon County Democrat, Flemington, NJ [*Library symbol*] [*Library of Congress*] (LCLS)

NjFlH .... Hunterdon County Library, Flemington, NJ [*Library symbol*] [*Library of Congress*] (LCLS)

NjFlHi .... Hunterdon County Historical Society, Flemington, NJ [*Library symbol*] [*Library of Congress*] (LCLS)

NjFlM .... Hunterdon Medical Center, Flemington, NJ [*Library symbol*] [*Library of Congress*] (LCLS)

NjFmE-TD .... United States Army, Electronics Command, Technical Documents Branch, Fort Monmouth, NJ [*Library symbol*] [*Library of Congress*] (LCLS)

NjFmS .... United States Army, Signal School, Fort Monmouth (SAUS)

NjFmS .... United States Army, Signal School, Fort Monmouth, NJ [*Library symbol*] [*Library of Congress*] (LCLS)

NjFNB .... Shopper-News Beacon, Fair Lawn, NJ [*Library symbol*] [*Library of Congress*] (LCLS)

NjFp .... Florham Park Public Library, Florham Park, NJ [*Library symbol*] [*Library of Congress*] (LCLS)

NjFpEx .... Exxon Research & Engineering Co., Engineering Information Center, Florham Park, NJ [*Library symbol*] [*Library of Congress*] (LCLS)

NjFpN .... Florham Park Community News, Florham Park, NJ [*Library symbol*] [*Library of Congress*] (LCLS)

NjFr .... Freehold Public Library, Freehold, NJ [*Library symbol*] [*Library of Congress*] (LCLS)

NJFR .... National Joint Fiction Reserve

NjFraS .... Suburban News, Franklin Lakes, NJ [*Library symbol*] [*Library of Congress*] (LCLS)

NjFrCoC ...... Clerk of Monmouth County, Freehold, NJ [*Library symbol*] [*Library of Congress*] (LCLS)

NjFrHi .... Monmouth County Historical Association, Freehold, NJ [*Library symbol*] [*Library of Congress*] (LCLS)

NjFrM .... Monmouth County Library, Freehold, NJ [*Library symbol*] [*Library of Congress*] (LCLS)

NjFrS .... Schreiber Publishing Co., Freehold, NJ [*Library symbol*] [*Library of Congress*] (LCLS)

NjFrtD .... Delaware Valley News, Frenchtown, NJ [*Library symbol*] [*Library of Congress*] (LCLS)

NjFrvA .... Advertiser, Franklinville, NJ [*Library symbol*] [*Library of Congress*] (LCLS)

NjFvW .... West New Yorker, Inc., Fairview, NJ [*Library symbol*] [*Library of Congress*] (LCLS)

NJG .... Glassboro State College, Glassboro, NJ [*OCLC symbol*] (OCLC)

NJG .... Nachtjagugeschwader [*Night Fighter*] [*German*]

NJG .... Nice Jewish Girl [*Slang*]

NjGaB .... Bergen Gazette, Inc., Garfield, NJ [*Library symbol*] [*Library of Congress*] (LCLS)

NjGaG .... Garfield Guardian, Garfield, NJ [*Library symbol*] [*Library of Congress*] (LCLS)

NjGaS .... Glassboro State College, Glassboro (SAUS)

NjGb .... Glassboro Public Library, Glassboro, NJ [*Library symbol*] [*Library of Congress*] (LCLS)

NjGbS .... Glassboro State College, Glassboro, NJ [*Library symbol*] [*Library of Congress*] (LCLS)

NJGFE .... Nordic Joint Group for Forest Entomology (EA)

NjGiD .... E. I. Du Pont de Nemours & Co., Eastern Laboratory Library, Gibbstown, NJ [*Library symbol*] [*Library of Congress*] (LCLS)

NjGl .... Gloucester City Library, Gloucester City, NJ [*Library symbol*] [*Library of Congress*] (LCLS)

NjGlN .... Gloucester City News, Gloucester City, NJ [*Library symbol*] [*Library of Congress*] (LCLS)

NjGlri .... Glen Ridge Free Public Library, Glen Ridge, NJ [*Library symbol*] [*Library of Congress*] (LCLS)

NjGlriA .... Associated Technical Services, Inc., Glen Ridge, NJ [*Library symbol*] [*Library of Congress*] (LCLS)

NjGrbR .... Raritan Valley Hospital, Greenbrook, NJ [*Library symbol*] [*Library of Congress*] (LCLS)

NjGrHi .... Cumberland County Historical Society, Greenwich, NJ [*Library symbol*] [*Library of Congress*] (LCLS)

NJGSC .... National Jewish Girl Scout Committee (EA)

NjH .... Haddonfield Public Library, Haddonfield, NJ [*Library symbol*] [*Library of Congress*] (LCLS)

NJHA .... National Junior Horticultural Association (EA)

NJHA .... New Jersey Hospital Association (SAUS)

NjHaC .... Centenary College for Women, Hackettstown, NJ [*Library symbol*] [*Library of Congress*] (LCLS)

NjHack .... Johnson Free Public Library, Hackensack, NJ [*Library symbol*] [*Library of Congress*] (LCLS)

NjHackR .... Bergen Record, Hackensack, NJ [*Library symbol*] [*Library of Congress*] (LCLS)

NjHam .... Hammonton Public Library, Hammonton, NJ [*Library symbol*] [*Library of Congress*] (LCLS)

NjHamN .... News Publishing Co., Hammonton, NJ [*Library symbol*] [*Library of Congress*] (LCLS)

NjHanS .... Sandoz, Inc., Hanover, NJ [*Library symbol*] [*Library of Congress*] (LCLS)

NjHarN .... Diamond Shamrock Corp., Harrison, NJ [*Library symbol*] [*Library of Congress*] (LCLS)

NjHarR .... Radio Corp. of America, Electronics Division, Harrison, NJ [*Library symbol*] [*Library of Congress*] (LCLS)

NjHas .... Hasbrouck Heights Free Public Library, Hasbrouck Heights, NJ [*Library symbol*] [*Library of Congress*] (LCLS)

NjHaS .... Star Gazette, Hackettstown, NJ [*Library symbol*] [*Library of Congress*] (LCLS)

NjHaSG .... Star Gazette, Hackettstown, NJ [*Library symbol*] [*Library of Congress*] (LCLS)

NjHasO .... Observer, Hasbrouck Heights, NJ [*Library symbol*] [*Library of Congress*] (LCLS)

NjHawD .... Dodds Publishing Co., Hawthorne, NJ [*Library symbol*] [*Library of Congress*] (LCLS)

NjHawP .... Hawthorne Press, Inc., Hawthorne, NJ [*Library symbol*] [*Library of Congress*] (LCLS)

NjHb .... Hillsborough Public Library, Hillsborough, NJ [*Library symbol*] [*Library of Congress*] (LCLS)

NJHC .... National Jewish Hospitality Committee (EA)

NjHh .... Haddon Heights Public Library, Haddon Heights, NJ [*Library symbol*] [*Library of Congress*] (LCLS)

NJHHCC .... National Joint Heavy and Highway Construction Committee (EA)

NjHHi .... Historical Society of Haddonfield, Haddonfield, NJ [*Library symbol*] [*Library of Congress*] (LCLS)

NjHi .... New Jersey Historical Society, Newark, NJ [*Library symbol*] [*Library of Congress*] (LCLS)

NjHibP .... High Bridge Painting Co., High Bridge, NJ [*Library symbol*] [*Library of Congress*] (LCLS)

NjHig .... Hightstown Memorial Library, Hightstown, NJ [*Library symbol*] [*Library of Congress*] (LCLS)

NjHigG .... Hightstown Gazette, Hightstown, NJ [*Library symbol*] [*Library of Congress*] (LCLS)

NjHigN .... NL Industries, Inc., Hightstown, NJ [*Library symbol*] [*Library of Congress*] (LCLS)

NjHigP .... Peddie School, Hightstown, NJ [*Library symbol*] [*Library of Congress*] (LCLS)

NjHil .... Hillside Free Public Library, Hillside, NJ [*Library symbol*] [*Library of Congress*] (LCLS)

NjHilT .... Hillside Times, Hillside, NJ [*Library symbol*] [*Library of Congress*] (LCLS)

NJ Hist Soc... New Jersey Historical Society (SAUS)

NJHMFA .... New Jersey Housing & Mortgage Finance Agency

NJH/NAC ...... National Jewish Hospital/National Asthma Center [*Later, National Jewish Center for Immunology and Respiratory Medicine*] (EA)

NjHo .... Hoboken Free Public Library, Hoboken, NJ [*Library symbol*] [*Library of Congress*] (LCLS)

NjHoGF .... General Foods Corp., Hoboken, NJ [*Library symbol*] [*Library of Congress*] (LCLS)

NjHolB .... Bell Telephone Laboratories, Inc., Technical Information Library, Holmdel, NJ [*Library symbol*] [*Library of Congress*] (LCLS)

NjHop .... Hopewell Public Library, Hopewell, NJ [*Library symbol*] [*Library of Congress*] (LCLS)

NjHopM .... Hopewell Museum, Hopewell, NJ [*Library symbol*] [*Library of Congress*] (LCLS)

NjHopN .... Hopewell Valley News, Hopewell, NJ [*Library symbol*] [*Library of Congress*] (LCLS)

NjHoS .... Stevens Institute of Technology, Hoboken, NJ [*Library symbol*] [*Library of Congress*] (LCLS)

NjHowB .... Booster Press, Howell, NJ [*Library symbol*] [*Library of Congress*] (LCLS)

NJHS .... New Jersey Historical Society (SAUS)

NjI .... Free Public Library of Irvington, Irvington, NJ [*Library symbol*] [*Library of Congress*] (LCLS)

NJI .... Network Job Interface

NJI .... New Jersey Institute of Technology, Newark, NJ [*OCLC symbol*] (OCLC)

NJIC .... National Joint Industrial Council [*Pharmacology*] [*British*]

NJIFR .... Notices of Judgment, Federal Insecticide, Fungicide, and Rodenticide Act [*A publication*] (DLA)

NJII .... New Jersey, Indiana & Illinois Railroad Co. [*AAR code*]

NJIS .... National Jewish Information Service (for the Propagation of Judaism) [*Defunct*] (EA)

NJIT .... New Jersey Institute of Technology (GAGS)

NjJ .... Jersey City Free Public Library, Jersey City, NJ [*Library symbol*] [*Library of Congress*] (LCLS)

NJJ .... Jersey City State College, Jersey City, NJ [*OCLC symbol*] (OCLC)

NJJ .... Niijima [*Japan*] [*Seismograph station code, US Geological Survey*] [*Closed*] (SEIS)

NjJa .... Library at Jamesburg, Jamesburg, NJ [*Library symbol*] [*Library of Congress*] (LCLS)

NjJacN .... Jackson News, Jackson, NJ [*Library symbol*] [*Library of Congress*] (LCLS)

NjJacP .... Jackson Township Publishing Co., Jackson, NJ [*Library symbol*] [*Library of Congress*] (LCLS)

NjJJ .... Jewish Standard, Jersey City, NJ [*Library symbol*] [*Library of Congress*] (LCLS)

NjJJJ .... Jersey Journal, Jersey City, NJ [*Library symbol*] [*Library of Congress*] (LCLS)

NjJS .... Jersey City State College, Jersey City, NJ [*Library symbol*] [*Library of Congress*] (LCLS)

NjJStP .... Saint Peter's College, Jersey City, NJ [*Library symbol*] [*Library of Congress*] (LCLS)

NjJUB .... Urner-Barry Publications, Jersey City, NJ [*Library symbol*] [*Library of Congress*] (LCLS)

NJK .... El Centro, CA [*Location identifier*] [*FAA*] (FAAL)

NJK .... Kean College of New Jersey, Union, NJ [*OCLC symbol*] (OCLC)

NjK .... Kearny Public Library, Kearny, NJ [*Library symbol*] [*Library of Congress*] (LCLS)

NJK .... Not Just Kidding (SAUS)

NjKeHS .... Keansburg High School, Keansburg, NJ [*Library symbol*] [*Library of Congress*] (LCLS)

NjKey .... Keyport Free Public Library, Keyport, NJ [*Library symbol*] [*Library of Congress*] (LCLS)

NjKO .... Kearny Observer, Kearny, NJ [*Library symbol*] [*Library of Congress*] (LCLS)

NjKWT .... Western Electric Co., Kearny, NJ [*Library symbol*] [*Library of Congress*] (LCLS)

NjL .... Lodi Memorial Library, Lodi, NJ [*Library symbol*] [*Library of Congress*] (LCLS)

NJL .... New Jersey Law Reports [*A publication*] (DLA)
NJL .... New Jersey State Library, Trenton, NJ [*OCLC symbol*] (OCLC)
NJLA .... New Jersey Library Association
NjLaHi .... Lake Hopatcong Historical Society, Lake Hopatcong, NJ [*Library symbol*] [*Library of Congress*] (LCLS)
NjLak .... Lakewood Public Library, Lakewood, NJ [*Library symbol*] [*Library of Congress*] (LCLS)
NjLakC .... Ocean County Citizen, Lakewood, NJ [*Library symbol*] [*Library of Congress*] (LCLS)
NjLakG .... Georgian Court College, Lakewood, NJ [*Library symbol*] [*Library of Congress*] (LCLS)
NjLakhM ...... Manchester Publishing Co., Lakehurst, NJ [*Library symbol*] [*Library of Congress*] (LCLS)
NjLakT .... Ocean County Daily Times, Lakewood, NJ [*Library symbol*] [*Library of Congress*] (LCLS)
NjLamB .... Lambertville Beacon, Lambertville, NJ [*Library symbol*] [*Library of Congress*] (LCLS)
NJ Law .... New Jersey Law Reports [*A publication*] (DLA)
NJ Law N .... New Jersey Law News [*A publication*] (DLA)
NjLawR .... Rider College, Lawrenceville, NJ [*Library symbol*] [*Library of Congress*] (LCLS)
NJ Law Rep .. New Jersey Law Reports [*A publication*] (DLA)
NJLC .... National Juvenile Law Center [*Later, NCYL*] (EA)
NjLe .... Leonia Public Library, Leonia, NJ [*Library symbol*] [*Library of Congress*] (LCLS)
NjLedW .... West Morris Star Journal, Ledgewood, NJ [*Library symbol*] [*Library of Congress*] (LCLS)
NJ Leg Rec ... New Jersey Legal Record [*A publication*] (DLA)
NjLF .... Felician College, Lodi, NJ [*Library symbol*] [*Library of Congress*] (LCLS)
NjLf .... Little Falls Free Public Library, Little Falls, NJ [*Library symbol*] [*Library of Congress*] (LCLS)
NJLFC .... New Jersey Film Circuit [*Library network*]
NjLh .... Lake Hiawatha Public Library, Lake Hiawatha, NJ [*Library symbol*] [*Library of Congress*] (LCLS)
NjLhP .... Pennysaver Publishing Co., Lake Hiawatha, NJ [*Library symbol*] [*Library of Congress*] (LCLS)
NjLi .... Free Public Library of Livingston, Livingston, NJ [*Library symbol*] [*Library of Congress*] (LCLS)
NjLin .... Linden Free Public Library, Linden, NJ [*Library symbol*] [*Library of Congress*] (LCLS)
NjLincB .... Brookdale Community College, Lincroft, NJ [*Library symbol*] [*Library of Congress*] (LCLS)
NjLinEx .... Exxon Research & Engineering Co., Company and Literature Information Center Library, Linden, NJ [*Library symbol*] [*Library of Congress*] (LCLS)
NjLinEx-M .... Exxon Research & Engineering Co., Medical Research Library, Linden, NJ [*Library symbol*] [*Library of Congress*] (LCLS)
NjLivStB ...... Saint Barnabas Medical Center, Staff Library, Livingston, NJ [*Library symbol*] [*Library of Congress*] (LCLS)
NjLiW .... West Essex Tribune, Livingston, NJ [*Library symbol*] [*Library of Congress*] (LCLS)
NjLob .... Long Branch Public Library, Long Branch, NJ [*Library symbol*] [*Library of Congress*] (LCLS)
NjLp .... Lincoln Park Public Library, Lincoln Park, NJ [*Library symbol*] [*Library of Congress*] (LCLS)
NjLP .... Paci Press, Lodi, NJ [*Library symbol*] [*Library of Congress*] (LCLS)
NjLpBHi .... Beavertown Historical Society, Lincoln Park, NJ [*Library symbol*] [*Library of Congress*] (LCLS)
NjLpH .... Lincoln Herald, Lincoln Park, NJ [*Library symbol*] [*Library of Congress*] (LCLS)
NjLPP .... Paci Press, Lodi, NJ [*Library symbol*] [*Library of Congress*] (LCLS)
NJL Rep ...... New Jersey Law Reports [*A publication*] (DLA)
NJL Rev ...... New Jersey Law Review [*A publication*] (DLA)
NjLwR .... Record Breeze, Lindenwold, NJ [*Library symbol*] [*Library of Congress*] (LCLS)
NjLy .... Lyndhurst Public Library, Lyndhurst, NJ [*Library symbol*] [*Library of Congress*] (LCLS)
NjLyL .... Leader Publications, Lyndhurst, NJ [*Library symbol*] [*Library of Congress*] (LCLS)
NjLyoV .... United States Veterans Administration Hospital, Lyons, NJ [*Library symbol*] [*Library of Congress*] (LCLS)
NjM .... Free Public Library of the Borough of Madison, Madison, NJ [*Library symbol*] [*Library of Congress*] (LCLS)
NJM .... Montclair State College, Upper Montclair, NJ [*OCLC symbol*] (OCLC)
NJM .... New Jersey Miscellaneous Reports [*A publication*] (DLA)
NJM .... New JEWEL Movement (SAUS)
NJM .... Swansboro, NC [*Location identifier*] [*FAA*] (FAAL)
NJMA .... National Jail Managers Association [*Later, AJA*] (EA)
NjMah .... Free Public Library of the Township of Mahwah, Mahwah, NJ [*Library symbol*] [*Library of Congress*] (LCLS)
NjMahR .... Ramapo College of New Jersey, Mahwah, NJ [*Library symbol*] [*Library of Congress*] (LCLS)
NjMal .... Franklin Township Public Library, Malaga, NJ [*Library symbol*] [*Library of Congress*] (LCLS)
NjMan .... Manasquan Public Library, Manasquan, NJ [*Library symbol*] [*Library of Congress*] (LCLS)
NjManhT ...... Times Beacon Co., Manahawkin, NJ [*Library symbol*] [*Library of Congress*] (LCLS)
NjManS .... Coast Star, Manasquan, NJ [*Library symbol*] [*Library of Congress*] (LCLS)
NjMap .... Maplewood Memorial Library, Maplewood, NJ [*Library symbol*] [*Library of Congress*] (LCLS)
NjMapW ...... Worrall Publishing Co., Maplewood, NJ [*Library symbol*] [*Library of Congress*] (LCLS)

NjMat .... Matawan Joint Free Public Library, Matawan, NJ [*Library symbol*] [*Library of Congress*] (LCLS)
NjMatB .... Bayshore Independent, Matawan, NJ [*Library symbol*] [*Library of Congress*] (LCLS)
NjMatHi .... Madison Township Historical Society, Matawan, NJ [*Library symbol*] [*Library of Congress*] (LCLS)
NjMayO .... Our Town, Maywood, NJ [*Library symbol*] [*Library of Congress*] (LCLS)
NJMC .... National Jewish Music Council [*Later, Jewish Welfare Board Jewish Music Council*] (EA)
NjMcUSAF ... United States Air Force, Base Library, McGuire Air Force Base, NJ [*Library symbol*] [*Library of Congress*] (LCLS)
NjMD .... Drew University, Madison, NJ [*Library symbol*] [*Library of Congress*] (LCLS)
NJMDC .... NORAD Joint Manual Direction Center [*Military*]
NjMD-T .... Drew University, Theological School, Madison, NJ [*Library symbol*] [*Library of Congress*] (LCLS)
NjMe .... Free Public Library, Metuchen, NJ [*Library symbol*] [*Library of Congress*] (LCLS)
NjME .... Madison Eagle, Madison, NJ [*Library symbol*] [*Library of Congress*] (LCLS)
NjMedR .... Central Record, Medford, NJ [*Library symbol*] [*Library of Congress*] (LCLS)
NjMen .... Mendham Public Library, Mendham, NJ [*Library symbol*] [*Library of Congress*] (LCLS)
NjMenO .... Observer-Tribune, Mendham, NJ [*Library symbol*] [*Library of Congress*] (LCLS)
NjMF .... Fairleigh Dickinson University, Madison, NJ [*Library symbol*] [*Library of Congress*] (LCLS)
NjMhB .... Burlington County Area Reference Library, Mount Holly, NJ [*Library symbol*] [*Library of Congress*] (LCLS)
NjMhCoC .... Burlington County Clerk, Mount Holly, NJ [*Library symbol*] [*Library of Congress*] (LCLS)
NjMhH .... Burlington County Herald, Mount Holly, NJ [*Library symbol*] [*Library of Congress*] (LCLS)
NjMHi .... Madison Historical Society, Madison, NJ [*Library symbol*] [*Library of Congress*] (LCLS)
NjMhL .... Burlington County Lyceum [*Mount Holly Public Library*], Mount Holly, NJ [*Library symbol*] [*Library of Congress*] (LCLS)
NjMhPM .... Burlington County Prison Museum, Mount Holly, NJ [*Library symbol*] [*Library of Congress*] (LCLS)
NJMI .... Catholic Medical Center of Brooklyn & Queens, Inc., Jamaica, NY [*Library symbol*] [*Library of Congress*] (LCLS)
NJMI .... Mary Immaculate Hospital, School of Nursing, Jamaica, NY [*Library symbol*] [*Library of Congress*] (LCLS)
NjMi .... Middletown Township Free Public Library, Middletown, NJ [*Library symbol*] [*Library of Congress*] (LCLS)
NJMI .... New Junior Maudsley Inventory [*Psychology*]
NjMiA .... Advisor, Middletown, NJ [*Library symbol*] [*Library of Congress*] (LCLS)
NjMiC .... Courier, Middletown, NJ [*Library symbol*] [*Library of Congress*] (LCLS)
NjMid .... Middlesex Public Library, Middlesex, NJ [*Library symbol*] [*Library of Congress*] (LCLS)
NjMil .... Millburn Free Public Library, Millburn, NJ [*Library symbol*] [*Library of Congress*] (LCLS)
NjMilt .... Milltown Public Library, Milltown, NJ [*Library symbol*] [*Library of Congress*] (LCLS)
NjMilv .... Millville Public Library, Millville, NJ [*Library symbol*] [*Library of Congress*] (LCLS)
NjMilvHi ...... Wheaton Historical Association, Millville, NJ [*Library symbol*] [*Library of Congress*] (LCLS)
NjMilvM .... Millville Daily, Millville, NJ [*Library symbol*] [*Library of Congress*] (LCLS)
NjMiP .... Middletown Township Public Library, Middletown, NJ [*Library symbol*] [*Library of Congress*] (LCLS)
NJ Mis .... New Jersey Miscellaneous Reports [*A publication*] (DLA)
NJ Misc .... New Jersey Miscellaneous Reports [*A publication*] (DLA)
NJ Mis R ..... New Jersey Miscellaneous Reports [*A publication*] (DLA)
NjMj .... South Brunswick Free Public Library, Monmouth Junction, NJ [*Library symbol*] [*Library of Congress*] (LCLS)
NjMlA .... Atlantic County Library, Mays Landing, NJ [*Library symbol*] [*Library of Congress*] (LCLS)
NjMlAC .... Atlantic Community College, Mays Landing, NJ [*Library symbol*] [*Library of Congress*] (LCLS)
NjMlCoC ...... Atlantic County Clerk, Mays Landing, NJ [*Library symbol*] [*Library of Congress*] (LCLS)
NjMlR .... Atlantic County Record, Mays Landing, NJ [*Library symbol*] [*Library of Congress*] (LCLS)
NjMo .... Joint Free Public Library of Morristown and Morris Township, Morristown, NJ [*Library symbol*] [*Library of Congress*] (LCLS)
NjMoAT .... American Telephone & Telegraph Co., Morristown Corporate Marketing Library, Morristown, NJ [*Library symbol*] [*Library of Congress*] (LCLS)
NjMoCoC ..... Morris County Clerk, Morristown, NJ [*Library symbol*] [*Library of Congress*] (LCLS)
NjMoH .... Morristown Memorial Hospital, Morristown, NJ [*Library symbol*] [*Library of Congress*] (LCLS)
NjMoHP .... Morristown National Historical Park, Morristown, NJ [*Library symbol*] [*Library of Congress*] (LCLS)
NjMon .... Montclair Free Public Library, Montclair, NJ [*Library symbol*] [*Library of Congress*] (LCLS)
NjMonM .... Montclair Times, Montclair, NJ [*Library symbol*] [*Library of Congress*] (LCLS)
NJ Monthly ... New Jersey Monthly (SAUS)

NjMor	Moorestown Free Library, Moorestown, NJ [*Library symbol*] [*Library of Congress*] (LCLS)
NjMorR	Radio Corp. of America, Missile and Surface Radar Division, Moorestown, NJ [*Library symbol*] [*Library of Congress*] (LCLS)
NjMou	Mountain Lakes Public Library, Mountain Lakes, NJ [*Library symbol*] [*Library of Congress*] (LCLS)
NjMouHi	Mountain Lakes Historical Society, Mountain Lakes, NJ [*Library symbol*] [*Library of Congress*] (LCLS)
NjMov	Montvale Free Public Library, Montvale, NJ [*Library symbol*] [*Library of Congress*] (LCLS)
NjMovL	Lehn & Fink Products Co., Montvale, NJ [*Library symbol*] [*Library of Congress*] (LCLS)
NjMp	Morris Plains Public Library, Morris Plains, NJ [*Library symbol*] [*Library of Congress*] (LCLS)
NJMP	New Jersey Marine Police (SAUS)
NJMP	New Jewish Media Project [*JMS*] [*Absorbed by*] (EA)
NjMpN	Morris News-Bee, Morris Plains, NJ [*Library symbol*] [*Library of Congress*] (LCLS)
NjMpW	Warner-Lambert Research Institute, Morris Plains, NJ [*Library symbol*] [*Library of Congress*] (LCLS)
NJMR	Nordisk Verbane Musik Rad [*Nordic Council for Railway Music - NCRM*] (EAIO)
NjMs	Maple Shade Public Library, Maple Shade, NJ [*Library symbol*] [*Library of Congress*] (LCLS)
NJMS	New Jersey Medical School [*Newark*]
NjMsP	Maple Shade Progress Press, Maple Shade, NJ [*Library symbol*] [*Library of Congress*] (LCLS)
NjMuA	Air Reduction Co., Inc., Central Research Department Library, Murray Hill, NJ [*Library symbol*] [*Library of Congress*] (LCLS)
NjMuB	Bell Telephone Laboratories, Inc., Murray Hill, NJ [*Library symbol*] [*Library of Congress*] (LCLS)
NjMuhHi	Harrison Township Historical Society, Mullica Hill, NJ [*Library symbol*] [*Library of Congress*] (LCLS)
NJN	College of Medicine and Dentistry of New Jersey, Newark, NJ [*OCLC symbol*] (OCLC)
NjN	Newark Public Library, Newark, NJ [*Library symbol*] [*Library of Congress*] (LCLS)
NJN	New Jersey Network [*Trenton*] [*Telecommunications service*] (TSSD)
NjNA	United States Attorney's Office, Law Library, Newark, NJ [*Library symbol*] [*Library of Congress*] (LCLS)
NjNAA	New Jersey Afro-American, Newark, NJ [*Library symbol*] [*Library of Congress*] (LCLS)
NjNb	New Brunswick Free Public Library, New Brunswick, NJ [*Library symbol*] [*Library of Congress*] (LCLS)
NjNbH	Home News, New Brunswick, NJ [*Library symbol*] [*Library of Congress*] (LCLS)
NjNbJJ	Johnson & Johnson, Research Center, New Brunswick, NJ [*Library symbol*] [*Library of Congress*] (LCLS)
NjNbM	Middlesex General Hospital, New Brunswick, NJ [*Library symbol*] [*Library of Congress*] (LCLS)
NjNbS	New Brunswick Theological Seminary, New Brunswick, NJ [*Library symbol*] [*Library of Congress*] (LCLS)
NjNbSI	Squibb-Beechnut, Inc., New Brunswick, NJ [*Library symbol*] [*Library of Congress*] (LCLS)
NjNbSp	New Brunswick Spokesman, New Brunswick, NJ [*Library symbol*] [*Library of Congress*] (LCLS)
NjNbStP	Saint Peter's Medical Center, New Brunswick, NJ [*Library symbol*] [*Library of Congress*] (LCLS)
NjNC	New Jersey Institute of Technology, Newark, NJ [*Library symbol*] [*Library of Congress*] (LCLS)
NjNCM	New Jersey College of Medicine and Dentistry, Newark, NJ [*Library symbol*] [*Library of Congress*] (LCLS)
NjNE	Essex County College, Newark, NJ [*Library symbol*] [*Library of Congress*] (LCLS)
NjNeP	New Egypt Press, New Egypt, NJ [*Library symbol*] [*Library of Congress*] (LCLS)
NjNet	Dennis Memorial Library, Newton, NJ [*Library symbol*] [*Library of Congress*] (LCLS)
NjNetcN	News Leader, Netcong, NJ [*Library symbol*] [*Library of Congress*] (LCLS)
NjNetCoC	Sussex County Clerk, Newton, NJ [*Library symbol*] [*Library of Congress*] (LCLS)
NjNetDB	Don Bosco College, Newton, NJ [*Library symbol*] [*Library of Congress*] (LCLS)
NjNetH	New Jersey Herald, Newton, NJ [*Library symbol*] [*Library of Congress*] (LCLS)
NjNetS	Sussex County Library, Newton, NJ [*Library symbol*] [*Library of Congress*] (LCLS)
NjNetSHi	Sussex County Historical Society, Newton, NJ [*Library symbol*] [*Library of Congress*] (LCLS)
NjNhBHi	Bergen County Historical Society, North Hackensack, NJ [*Library symbol*] [*Library of Congress*] (LCLS)
NjNI	Ironbound Crier, Newark, NJ [*Library symbol*] [*Library of Congress*] (LCLS)
NjNIJS	Institute of Jazz Studies, Rutgers, the State University, Newark, NJ [*Library symbol*] [*Library of Congress*] (LCLS)
NjNIM	International Musician, Newark, NJ [*Library symbol*] [*Library of Congress*] (LCLS)
NjNIT	Italian Tribune, Newark, NJ [*Library symbol*] [*Library of Congress*] (LCLS)
NjNJL	Jewish Ledger, Newark, NJ [*Library symbol*] [*Library of Congress*] (LCLS)
NjNJN	Jewish News, Newark, NJ [*Library symbol*] [*Library of Congress*] (LCLS)
NjNL	Luso-Americano, Newark, NJ [*Library symbol*] [*Library of Congress*] (LCLS)
NjNLH	New Jersey Labor Herald, Newark, NJ [*Library symbol*] [*Library of Congress*] (LCLS)
NjNN	Nite-Lite, Newark, NJ [*Library symbol*] [*Library of Congress*] (LCLS)
NjNoA	Atlantic County Advertiser, Northfield, NJ [*Library symbol*] [*Library of Congress*] (LCLS)
NjNoa	North Arlington Free Public Library, North Arlington, NJ [*Library symbol*] [*Library of Congress*] (LCLS)
NjNoaP	North Arlington Free Public Library, North Arlington, NJ [*Library symbol*] [*Library of Congress*] (LCLS)
NjNor	Norwood Public Library, Norwood, NJ [*Library symbol*] [*Library of Congress*] (LCLS)
NjNp	New Providence Memorial Library, New Providence, NJ [*Library symbol*] [*Library of Congress*] (LCLS)
NjNpD	Dispatch, New Providence, NJ [*Library symbol*] [*Library of Congress*] (LCLS)
NjNpHi	New Providence Historical Society, New Providence, NJ [*Library symbol*] [*Library of Congress*] (LCLS)
NjNpI	Independent Press, New Providence, NJ [*Library symbol*] [*Library of Congress*] (LCLS)
NjNPSE	Public Service Electric & Gas Co., Newark, NJ [*Library symbol*] [*Library of Congress*] (LCLS)
NjNT	Tribuna di North Jersey, Newark, NJ [*Library symbol*] [*Library of Congress*] (LCLS)
NjNu	Nutley Free Public Library, Nutley, NJ [*Library symbol*] [*Library of Congress*] (LCLS)
NjNuH	Hoffmann-La Roche, Inc., Scientific Library, Nutley, NJ [*Library symbol*] [*Library of Congress*] (LCLS)
NjNuHi	Nutley Historical Society, Nutley, NJ [*Library symbol*] [*Library of Congress*] (LCLS)
NjNuS	Sun-Bank Newspapers, Nutley, NJ [*Library symbol*] [*Library of Congress*] (LCLS)
NJNY	New Jersey & New York R. R. [*AAR code*]
NjO	Free Public Library of the City of Orange, Orange, NJ [*Library symbol*] [*Library of Congress*] (LCLS)
NjOak	Oakland Public Library, Oakland, NJ [*Library symbol*] [*Library of Congress*] (LCLS)
NjOaS	Shore Publishers, Inc., Oakhurst, NJ [*Library symbol*] [*Library of Congress*] (LCLS)
NjOcM	Ocean City Historical Museum, Ocean City, NJ [*Library symbol*] [*Library of Congress*] (LCLS)
NjOcS	Sentinel Ledger, Ocean City, NJ [*Library symbol*] [*Library of Congress*] (LCLS)
NjOgT	Ocean Grove Times, Ocean Grove, NJ [*Library symbol*] [*Library of Congress*] (LCLS)
NjOrd	Oradell Public Library, Oradell, NJ [*Library symbol*] [*Library of Congress*] (LCLS)
NjOrdB	Burns & Roe, Inc., Oradell, NJ [*Library symbol*] [*Library of Congress*] (LCLS)
NJosnU	United Health Services, Wilson Hospital, Johnson City, NY [*Library symbol*] [*Library of Congress*] (LCLS)
NJostF	Fulton-Montgomery Community College, Johnstown, NY [*Library symbol*] [*Library of Congress*] (LCLS)
NjOtR	Fleming H. Revell Co., Old Tappan, NJ [*Library symbol*] [*Library of Congress*] (LCLS)
NjOW	Worrall Publications, Inc., Orange, NJ [*Library symbol*] [*Library of Congress*] (LCLS)
NJP	National Jury Project (EA)
NJP	Network Job Processing
NJP	Nonjudicial Punishment [*Military*]
NjP	Princeton University, Princeton, NJ [*Library symbol*] [*Library of Congress*] (LCLS)
NJP	Warminster, PA [*Location identifier*] [*FAA*] (FAAL)
NJP	William Patterson College of New Jersey, Wayne, NJ [*OCLC symbol*] (OCLC)
NjPA	American Cyanamid Co., Agricultural Division, Princeton, NJ [*Library symbol*] [*Library of Congress*] (LCLS)
NjP-A	Art Museum of Princeton University, Princeton, NJ [*Library symbol*] [*Library of Congress*] (LCLS)
NJPA	National Juice Products Association (EA)
NjPalN	Bergen News, Palisades Park, NJ [*Library symbol*] [*Library of Congress*] (LCLS)
NjPar	Paramus Public Library, Paramus, NJ [*Library symbol*] [*Library of Congress*] (LCLS)
NjParB	Bergen Community College, Paramus, NJ [*Library symbol*] [*Library of Congress*] (LCLS)
NjParkHi	Pascack Historical Society and Museum, Park Ridge, NJ [*Library symbol*] [*Library of Congress*] (LCLS)
NjParkP	Pascack Publications Corp., Park Ridge, NJ [*Library symbol*] [*Library of Congress*] (LCLS)
NjParR	Ridgewood Newspapers, Paramus, NJ [*Library symbol*] [*Library of Congress*] (LCLS)
NjParT	Town News, Paramus, NJ [*Library symbol*] [*Library of Congress*] (LCLS)
NjPas	Passaic Public Library, Passaic, NJ [*Library symbol*] [*Library of Congress*] (LCLS)
NjPasC	Passaic Citizen, Passaic, NJ [*Library symbol*] [*Library of Congress*] (LCLS)
NjPasCS	Catholic Sokol Printing Co., Passaic, NJ [*Library symbol*] [*Library of Congress*] (LCLS)
NjPasE	Eastern Catholic Life, Passaic, NJ [*Library symbol*] [*Library of Congress*] (LCLS)
NjPasH	Herald News, Passaic, NJ [*Library symbol*] [*Library of Congress*] (LCLS)

NjPat .... Paterson Free Public Library, Paterson, NJ [*Library symbol*] [*Library of Congress*] (LCLS)

NjPatCoC ..... Passaic County Clerk, Paterson, NJ [*Library symbol*] [*Library of Congress*] (LCLS)

NjPatNe .... News, Paterson, NJ [*Library symbol*] [*Library of Congress*] (LCLS)

NjPatPHi ...... Passaic County Historical Society, Paterson, NJ [*Library symbol*] [*Library of Congress*] (LCLS)

NjPatSA .... Saint Anthony's Guild, Franciscan Monastery, Paterson, NJ [*Library symbol*] [*Library of Congress*] (LCLS)

NjPatV .... Voce Italiana, Paterson, NJ [*Library symbol*] [*Library of Congress*] (LCLS)

NjPauR .... Record, Paulsboro, NJ [*Library symbol*] [*Library of Congress*] (LCLS)

NjPauS .... Mobil Research & Development Corp., Paulsboro, NJ [*Library symbol*] [*Library of Congress*] (LCLS)

NJPBA .... New Jersey Public Broadcasting Authority (SAUS)

NJPC .... National Joint Practice Commission (DMAA)

NjPD .... Daily Princetonian, Princeton, NJ [*Library symbol*] [*Library of Congress*] (LCLS)

NJPDDATC... National Joint Painting, Decorating, and Drywall Apprenticeship and Training Committee (EA)

NjPE .... Educational Testing Service, Princeton, NJ [*Library symbol*] [*Library of Congress*] (LCLS)

NjPeB .... Burlington County College, Pemberton, NJ [*Library symbol*] [*Library of Congress*] (LCLS)

NjPegR .... Penns Grove Record, Penns Grove, NJ [*Library symbol*] [*Library of Congress*] (LCLS)

NjPenP .... Pennsauken Resume, Pennsauken, NJ [*Library symbol*] [*Library of Congress*] (LCLS)

NjPeqB .... Beacon, Pequannock, NJ [*Library symbol*] [*Library of Congress*] (LCLS)

NjPera .... Perth Amboy Free Public Library, Perth Amboy, NJ [*Library symbol*] [*Library of Congress*] (LCLS)

NjPeraSo ..... Universum Sokol Publishers, Perth Amboy, NJ [*Library symbol*] [*Library of Congress*] (LCLS)

NjPERS .... E. R. Squibb & Sons, Princeton, NJ [*Library symbol*] [*Library of Congress*] (LCLS)

NjPeT .... Times Advertising Printing Co., Pemberton, NJ [*Library symbol*] [*Library of Congress*] (LCLS)

NjPF .... FMC Corp., Princeton (SAUS)

NjP-G .... Princeton University, Gest Library, Princeton, NJ [*Library symbol*] [*Library of Congress*] (LCLS)

NJPGA .... New Jersey Personnel and Guidance Association (SAUS)

NjPh .... Phillipsburg Free Public Library, Phillipsburg, NJ [*Library symbol*] [*Library of Congress*] (LCLS)

NJPHA .... National Junior Polled Hereford Association (EA)

NJPHC .... National Junior Polled Hereford Council [*Later, NJPHA*] (EA)

NjPHi .... Historical Society of Princeton, Princeton, NJ [*Library symbol*] [*Library of Congress*] (LCLS)

NjPhP .... Free Press, Phillipsburg, NJ [*Library symbol*] [*Library of Congress*] (LCLS)

NjPI .... Institute for Advanced Study, Princeton, NJ [*Library symbol*] [*Library of Congress*] (LCLS)

NjPi .... McCowan Memorial Library, Pitman, NJ [*Library symbol*] [*Library of Congress*] (LCLS)

NjPiM .... McCowan Memorial Library, Pitman, NJ [*Library symbol*] [*Library of Congress*] (LCLS)

NjPJ .... Robert Wood Johnson Foundation Library, Princeton, NJ [*Library symbol*] [*Library of Congress*] (LCLS)

NjPl .... Emanuel Einstein Free Public Library, Pompton Lakes (SAUS)

NjPl .... Emanuel Einstein Free Public Library, Pompton Lakes, NJ [*Library symbol*] [*Library of Congress*] (LCLS)

NjPla .... Plainfield Public Library, Plainfield, NJ [*Library symbol*] [*Library of Congress*] (LCLS)

NjPlaM .... Muhlenberg Hospital, Plainfield, NJ [*Library symbol*] [*Library of Congress*] (LCLS)

NjPlaSDB.... Seventh Day Baptist Historical Society, Plainfield, NJ [*Library symbol*] [*Library of Congress*] (LCLS)

NjPlaT .... Plainfield Times, Plainfield, NJ [*Library symbol*] [*Library of Congress*] (LCLS)

NjPlaV .... Voice, Plainfield, NJ [*Library symbol*] [*Library of Congress*] (LCLS)

NjPleM .... Mainland Journal, Pleasantville, NJ [*Library symbol*] [*Library of Congress*] (LCLS)

NjPM .... Mobil Research & Development Corp., Central Research Division Library, Princeton, NJ [*Library symbol*] [*Library of Congress*] (LCLS)

NJPMB .... Navy Jet-Propelled-Missile Board

NjPMC .... Medical Center at Princeton, Princeton, NJ [*Library symbol*] [*Library of Congress*] (LCLS)

NjPoiO .... Ocean County Leader, Point Pleasant Beach, NJ [*Library symbol*] [*Library of Congress*] (LCLS)

NjPoR .... Richard Stockton State College, Pomona, NJ [*Library symbol*] [*Library of Congress*] (LCLS)

NjPP .... Princeton Packet, Inc., Princeton, NJ [*Library symbol*] [*Library of Congress*] (LCLS)

NjPpE .... Eastern Historical Commission, Prospect Park, NJ [*Library symbol*] [*Library of Congress*] (LCLS)

NjP-Pop .... Princeton University, Office of Population Research, Princeton, NJ [*Library symbol*] [*Library of Congress*] (LCLS)

NjPPP .... Princeton Public Library, Princeton, NJ [*Library symbol*] [*Library of Congress*] (LCLS)

NjPRCA........ Radio Corp. of America, Laboratories Division, Princeton, NJ [*Library symbol*] [*Library of Congress*] (LCLS)

NjPS .... Princeton Shopping News, Princeton, NJ [*Library symbol*] [*Library of Congress*] (LCLS)

NjP-SC........ Princeton University, Princeton Special Collection, Princeton, NJ [*Library symbol*] [*Library of Congress*] (LCLS)

NjPStJ .... Saint Joseph's College, Princeton, NJ [*Library symbol*] [*Library of Congress*] (LCLS)

NjPT............ Princeton Theological Seminary, Princeton, NJ [*Library symbol*] [*Library of Congress*] (LCLS)

NjPTe.......... Textile Research Institute, Princeton, NJ [*Library symbol*] [*Library of Congress*] (LCLS)

NjPTT.......... Town Topics, Inc., Princeton, NJ [*Library symbol*] [*Library of Congress*] (LCLS)

NjPW .... Western Electric Co., Inc., Engineering Research Center, Princeton, NJ [*Library symbol*] [*Library of Congress*] (LCLS)

NjPwAT....... American Telephone & Telegraph Co. Resource Center, Piscataway, NJ [*Library symbol*] [*Library of Congress*] (LCLS)

NjPwC.......... Colgate-Palmolive Co., Technical Information Center, Piscataway, NJ [*Library symbol*] [*Library of Congress*] (LCLS)

NjPwIE......... Institute of Electrical and Electronics Engineers, Piscataway, NJ [*Library symbol*] [*Library of Congress*] (LCLS)

NJQ............ Queens Borough Public Library, Jamaica, NY [*Library symbol*] [*Library of Congress*] (LCLS)

NJQH .... Queens Hospital Center, Jamaica, NY [*Library symbol*] [*Library of Congress*] (LCLS)

NJR............. New Jersey Register [*A publication*] (DLA)

NJR............. New Jersey Resources [*NYSE symbol*] (TTSB)

NJR............. New Jersey Resources Corp. [*NYSE symbol*] (SPSG)

NJR............. New JEWEL Regime [*Grenada*]

NJR............. Noise-to-Jammer Ratio (SAUS)

NJR............. Nonjob Routed [*Military*] (AFIT)

NjR............. Rutgers-[*The*] State University, New Brunswick, NJ [*Library symbol*] [*Library of Congress*] (LCLS)

NJRA .... National Juvenile Restitution Association [*Later, ARA*] (EA)

NjRah .... Rahway Public Library, Rahway, NJ [*Library symbol*] [*Library of Congress*] (LCLS)

NjRahB .... Bauer Publishing & Printing Ltd., Rahway, NJ [*Library symbol*] [*Library of Congress*] (LCLS)

NjRahM .... Merck, Sharp & Dohme [*Later, Merck & Co., Inc.*] Research Laboratory, Research Library, Rahway, NJ [*Library symbol*] [*Library of Congress*] (LCLS)

NjRam .... Ramsey Free Public Library, Ramsey, NJ [*Library symbol*] [*Library of Congress*] (LCLS)

NjRamH....... Home and Store News, Ramsey, NJ [*Library symbol*] [*Library of Congress*] (LCLS)

NjRamI .... Immaculate Conception Theological Seminary, Ramsey, NJ [*Library symbol*] [*Library of Congress*] (LCLS)

NjRarO......... Ortho Pharmaceutical Corp., Raritan, NJ [*Library symbol*] [*Library of Congress*] (LCLS)

NjRarOD ...... Ortho Diagnostics, Raritan, NJ [*Library symbol*] [*Library of Congress*] (LCLS)

NjRb .... Red Bank Public Library, Red Bank, NJ [*Library symbol*] [*Library of Congress*] (LCLS)

NjRbR .... Daily Register, Red Bank, NJ [*Library symbol*] [*Library of Congress*] (LCLS)

NJRC .... National Jewish Resource Center (EA)

NJRC .... New Jersey Board of Railroad Commissioners Annual Reports [*A publication*] (DLA)

NjRdR.......... Riverdale Publishing Co., Riverdale, NJ [*Library symbol*] [*Library of Congress*] (LCLS)

NJ Rep .... New Jersey Law Reports [*A publication*] (DLA)

NJ Re Tit N... New Jersey Realty Title News [*A publication*] (DLA)

NJ Rev Stat... New Jersey Revised Statutes [*A publication*] (DLA)

NjRf............ Ridgefield Public Library, Ridgefield, NJ [*Library symbol*] [*Library of Congress*] (LCLS)

NjRh .... Rocky Hill Public Library, Rocky Hill, NJ [*Library symbol*] [*Library of Congress*] (LCLS)

NjRiv .... Riverside Public Library, Riverside, NJ [*Library symbol*] [*Library of Congress*] (LCLS)

NjRive .... River Edge Free Public Library, River Edge, NJ [*Library symbol*] [*Library of Congress*] (LCLS)

NjR-L .... Rutgers-[*The*] State University, Rutgers-Camden School of Law, Camden, NJ [*Library symbol*] [*Library of Congress*] (LCLS)

NjR-NL........ Rutgers, The State University, Law School Library-Newark, Newark, NJ [*Library symbol*] [*Library of Congress*] (LCLS)

NjRo .... Roseland Public Library, Roseland, NJ [*Library symbol*] [*Library of Congress*] (LCLS)

NjRocM....... Morris County News, Rockaway, NJ [*Library symbol*] [*Library of Congress*] (LCLS)

NjRos.......... Roselle Free Public Library, Roselle, NJ [*Library symbol*] [*Library of Congress*] (LCLS)

NJROTC .... Naval Junior Reserve Officer Training Corps

NjRp .... Ridgefield Park Free Public Library, Ridgefield Park, NJ [*Library symbol*] [*Library of Congress*] (LCLS)

NjRpS .... Sun Bulletin, Ridgefield Park, NJ [*Library symbol*] [*Library of Congress*] (LCLS)

NjR-S .... Rutgers-[*The*] State University, College of South Jersey, Camden, NJ [*Library symbol*] [*Library of Congress*] (LCLS)

NJRsc .... New Jersey Resources [*Associated Press*] (SAG)

NjRu .... Rutherford Free Public Library, Rutherford, NJ [*Library symbol*] [*Library of Congress*] (LCLS)

NjRuB .... Becton, Dickinson & Co., Rutherford, NJ [*Library symbol*] [*Library of Congress*] (LCLS)

NjRuF .... Fairleigh Dickinson University, Rutherford, NJ [*Library symbol*] [*Library of Congress*] (LCLS)

NjRw........... Ridgewood Library, Ridgewood, NJ [*Library symbol*] [*Library of Congress*] (LCLS)

NjRwN .... Ridgewood News, Ridgewood, NJ [*Library symbol*] [*Library of Congress*] (LCLS)

NjRwPHi ...... Paramus Historical and Preservation Society, Ridgewood, NJ [*Library symbol*] [*Library of Congress*] (LCLS)

NJS .... New Jersey Superior Court Reports [*A publication*] (DLA)

NJS .... Noise Jammer Simulator [*Telecommunications*] (TEL)

NJS .... Stockton State College, Pomona, NJ [*OCLC symbol*] (OCLC)

NjS .... Summit Free Public Library, Summit, NJ [*Library symbol*] [*Library of Congress*] (LCLS)

NJSA .... New Jersey Statutes, Annotated [*A publication*]

NjSabN .... News Dispatch, Saddle Brook, NJ [*Library symbol*] [*Library of Congress*] (LCLS)

NjSalCoC ..... Salem County Clerk, Salem, NJ [*Library symbol*] [*Library of Congress*] (LCLS)

NjSalHi .... Salem County Historical Society, Salem, NJ [*Library symbol*] [*Library of Congress*] (LCLS)

NjSalS .... Sunbeam Publishing Co., Salem, NJ [*Library symbol*] [*Library of Congress*] (LCLS)

NJSBA .... New Jersey School Boards Association (SAUS)

NJSBAQ .... New Jersey State Bar Association. Quarterly [*A publication*] (DLA)

NjSbB .... Beachcomber, Ship Bottom, NJ [*Library symbol*] [*Library of Congress*] (LCLS)

NjSbbU .... Saint Sophia Ukrainian Orthodox Seminary, South Bound Brook, NJ [*Library symbol*] [*Library of Congress*] (LCLS)

NJSBJ .... New Jersey State Bar Journal [*A publication*] (DLA)

NJSBTA Ops... New Jersey State Board of Tax Appeals, Opinions [*A publication*] (DLA)

NjSC .... Ciba Pharmaceutical Co., Research Library, Summit, NJ [*Library symbol*] [*Library of Congress*] (LCLS)

NjSCC .... Summit City Clerk, Summit, NJ [*Library symbol*] [*Library of Congress*] (LCLS)

NjScp .... Scotch Plains Public Library, Scotch Plains, NJ [*Library symbol*] [*Library of Congress*] (LCLS)

NjScpT .... Times, Scotch Plains, NJ [*Library symbol*] [*Library of Congress*] (LCLS)

NJSD .... National Joint Service Delegations (NATG)

NJSDC .... New Jersey State Data Center [*New Jersey State Department of Labor*] [*Trenton*] [*Information service or system*] (IID)

NjSe .... Secaucus Free Public Library, Secaucus, NJ [*Library symbol*] [*Library of Congress*] (LCLS)

NjSEA .... New Jersey Society of Enrolled Agents (SAUS)

NjSeH .... Secaucus Home News, Secaucus, NJ [*Library symbol*] [*Library of Congress*] (LCLS)

NJ Sess Law Serv... New Jersey Session Law Service [*A publication*] (DLA)

NjSewG .... Gloucester County College, Sewell, NJ [*Library symbol*] [*Library of Congress*] (LCLS)

NjSewHi ...... Washington Township Historical Society, Sewell, NJ [*Library symbol*] [*Library of Congress*] (LCLS)

NJSGA .... National Junior Santa Gertrudis Association (EA)

NjSGS .... Church of Jesus Christ of Latter-Day Saints, Genealogical Society Library, Caldwell Branch, Summit, NJ [*Library symbol*] [*Library of Congress*] (LCLS)

NjSH .... Summit Herald, Summit, NJ [*Library symbol*] [*Library of Congress*] (LCLS)

NjShO .... Ocean County Review, Seaside Heights, NJ [*Library symbol*] [*Library of Congress*] (LCLS)

NJSHS .... National Junior Science and Humanities Symposium

NJSHS .... New Jersey State Horticultural Society (SAUS)

NjSicTR .... Cape May County Times and Seven Mile Beach Reporter, Sea Isle City, NJ [*Library symbol*] [*Library of Congress*] (LCLS)

NJSN .... National Job Sharing Network (EA)

NJSNA .... New Jersey State Nurses Associaton (SAUS)

NJSO .... National Jazz Service Organization (EA)

NjSo .... Somerville Free Public Library, Somerville, NJ [*Library symbol*] [*Library of Congress*] (LCLS)

NjSoa .... South Amboy Public Library, South Amboy, NJ [*Library symbol*] [*Library of Congress*] (LCLS)

NjSoaP .... South Amboy Publishing Co., South Amboy, NJ [*Library symbol*] [*Library of Congress*] (LCLS)

NjSobC .... Central Post, South Brunswick, NJ [*Library symbol*] [*Library of Congress*] (LCLS)

NjSoCo .... Somerset County Library, Somerville, NJ [*Library symbol*] [*Library of Congress*] (LCLS)

NjSoCoC ...... Somerset County Clerk, Somerville, NJ [*Library symbol*] [*Library of Congress*] (LCLS)

NjSoE .... Ethicon, Inc., Somerville (SAUS)

NjSoH .... Somerset Hospital, Somerville, NJ [*Library symbol*] [*Library of Congress*] (LCLS)

NjSoHR .... Hoechst-Roussel Pharmaceuticals, Inc., Somerville, NJ [*Library symbol*] [*Library of Congress*] (LCLS)

NjSoM .... Somerset Messenger-Gazette, Somerville, NJ [*Library symbol*] [*Library of Congress*] (LCLS)

NjSoo .... South Orange Public Library, South Orange, NJ [*Library symbol*] [*Library of Congress*] (LCLS)

NjSooS .... Seton Hall University, South Orange, NJ [*Library symbol*] [*Library of Congress*] (LCLS)

NjSooS-L ...... Seton Hall University, Law Library, Newark, NJ [*Library symbol*] [*Library of Congress*] (LCLS)

NjSop .... South Plainfield Free Public Library, South Plainfield, NJ [*Library symbol*] [*Library of Congress*] (LCLS)

NjSopA .... American Smelting & Refining Co., Research Department Library, South Plainfield,NJ [*Library symbol*] [*Library of Congress*] (LCLS)

NjSopP .... PAMCAM, Inc., South Plainfield, NJ [*Library symbol*] [*Library of Congress*] (LCLS)

NjSoS .... Somerset County College, Somerville, NJ [*Library symbol*] [*Library of Congress*] (LCLS)

NjSosS .... Somerset Spectator, Somerset, NJ [*Library symbol*] [*Library of Congress*] (LCLS)

NjSoVA .... United States Veterans Administration Supply Depot, Somerville, NJ [*Library symbol*] [*Library of Congress*] (LCLS)

NJSP .... New Jersey State Police (SAUS)

NjSp .... Springfield Free Public Library, Springfield, NJ [*Library symbol*] [*Library of Congress*] (LCLS)

NJSPE .... New Jersey Society of Professional Engineers (SAUS)

NjSpl .... Spring Lake Public Library, Spring Lake, NJ [*Library symbol*] [*Library of Congress*] (LCLS)

NjSpW .... Western Electric Co., Springfield, NJ [*Library symbol*] [*Library of Congress*] (LCLS)

NJST .... New Jersey Steel [*NASDAQ symbol*] (TTSB)

NJST .... New Jersey Steel Corp. [*NASDAQ symbol*] (NQ)

NjSt .... Passaic Township Public Library, Stirling, NJ [*Library symbol*] [*Library of Congress*] (LCLS)

NJ Stat Ann (West)... New Jersey Statutes, Annotated (West) [*A publication*] (DLA)

NJ St BJ ...... New Jersey State Bar Journal [*A publication*] (DLA)

NJ Stl .... New Jersey Steel Corp. [*Associated Press*] (SAG)

NjStR .... Recorder Publishing Co., Stirling, NJ [*Library symbol*] [*Library of Congress*] (LCLS)

NjStrK .... John F. Kennedy Memorial Hospital, Stratford, NJ [*Library symbol*] [*Library of Congress*] (LCLS)

NjSu .... Roxbury Public Library, Succasunna, NJ [*Library symbol*] [*Library of Congress*] (LCLS)

NJ Sup .... New Jersey Superior Court Reports [*A publication*] (DLA)

NJ Super ..... New Jersey Superior Court Reports [*A publication*] (DLA)

NjSw .... Swedesboro Free Public Library, Swedesboro, NJ [*Library symbol*] [*Library of Congress*] (LCLS)

NjSwN .... Swedesboro News, Swedesboro, NJ [*Library symbol*] [*Library of Congress*] (LCLS)

NJT .... National Jewish Television [*Cable-television system*]

NJT .... Societe Novajet [*France*] [*ICAO designator*] (FAAC)

NjT .... Trenton Free Public Library, Trenton, NJ [*Library symbol*] [*Library of Congress*] (LCLS)

NJT .... Trenton State College, Trenton, NJ [*OCLC symbol*] (OCLC)

NjTCP .... Commercial Printing Co., Trenton, NJ [*Library symbol*] [*Library of Congress*] (LCLS)

NjTea .... Teaneck Public Library, Teaneck, NJ [*Library symbol*] [*Library of Congress*] (LCLS)

NjTeaF .... Fairleigh Dickinson University, Teaneck, NJ [*Library symbol*] [*Library of Congress*] (LCLS)

NjTeaL .... Luther College, Teaneck, NJ [*Library symbol*] [*Library of Congress*] (LCLS)

NjTen .... Tenafly Public Library, Tenafly, NJ [*Library symbol*] [*Library of Congress*] (LCLS)

NJTL .... National Junior Tennis League (EA)

NJTL Bulletin... New Jersey Tuberculosis League Bulletin (SAUS)

NjTM .... Monitor, Trenton, NJ [*Library symbol*] [*Library of Congress*] (LCLS)

NjTMC .... Mercer County Community College, Trenton, NJ [*Library symbol*] [*Library of Congress*] (LCLS)

NjTPP .... Planned Parenthood of Mercer Area, Trenton, NJ [*Library symbol*] [*Library of Congress*] (LCLS)

NjTR .... Rider College, Trenton, NJ [*Library symbol*] [*Library of Congress*] (LCLS)

NjTrCo .... Ocean County Public Library, Toms River, NJ [*Library symbol*] [*Library of Congress*] (LCLS)

NjTrCoC ...... Ocean County Clerk, Toms River, NJ [*Library symbol*] [*Library of Congress*] (LCLS)

NjTrO .... Ocean County College, Toms River, NJ [*Library symbol*] [*Library of Congress*] (LCLS)

NjTrR .... Reporter, Toms River, NJ [*Library symbol*] [*Library of Congress*] (LCLS)

NjTS .... Trenton State College, Trenton, NJ [*Library symbol*] [*Library of Congress*] (LCLS)

NjTSch .... Schweats, Inc., Trenton, NJ [*Library symbol*] [*Library of Congress*] (LCLS)

NjTStF .... Saint Francis Medical Center, Health Science Library, Trenton, NJ [*Library symbol*] [*Library of Congress*] (LCLS)

NjTTr .... Trentonian, Trenton, NJ [*Library symbol*] [*Library of Congress*] (LCLS)

NjTTT .... Trenton Times Newspapers, Trenton, NJ [*Library symbol*] [*Library of Congress*] (LCLS)

NJ Turn .... New Jersey Turnpike (SAUS)

nju .... New Jersey [*MARC country of publication code*] [*Library of Congress*] (LCCP)

NJU .... Nordic Judo Union (EAIO)

NJU .... Northern Jiaotong Univeristy [*China*]

NjU .... Union Township Public Library, Union, NJ [*Library symbol*] [*Library of Congress*] (LCLS)

NjUbl .... International Flavors & Fragrances, Inc., Union Beach, NJ [*Library symbol*] [*Library of Congress*] (LCLS)

NjUc .... Union City Free Public Library, Union City, NJ [*Library symbol*] [*Library of Congress*] (LCLS)

NjUcD .... Dispatch, Union City, NJ [*Library symbol*] [*Library of Congress*] (LCLS)

NjUcS .... Shield, Union City, NJ [*Library symbol*] [*Library of Congress*] (LCLS)

NjUcSM .... Saint Michael's Passionist Monastery, Union City, NJ [*Library symbol*] [*Library of Congress*] (LCLS)

NjUJ .... Jewish Community News, Union, NJ [*Library symbol*] [*Library of Congress*] (LCLS)

NjUN .... Kean College of New Jersey, Union, NJ [*Library symbol*] [*Library of Congress*] (LCLS)

NjUpM .... Montclair State College, Upper Montclair, NJ [*Library symbol*] [*Library of Congress*] (LCLS)

NjUpM-C ...... China Institute of New Jersey, Montclair State College, Upper Montclair, NJ [*Library symbol*] [*Library of Congress*] (LCLS)

NJUS .... Netherlands Jurisprudence (NITA)

NjUS .... Suburban Publishing Co., Union, NJ [*Library symbol*] [*Library of Congress*] (LCLS)

NjUsrHi .... Upper Saddle River Historical Committee, Upper Saddle River, NJ [*Library symbol*] [*Library of Congress*] (LCLS)

NJUZA9 .... Japanese Journal of Veterinary Science (journ.) (SAUS)

NJV .... Nederlandse Juristenvereniging [*Netherlands Lawyers Association*] (ILCA)

NjV .... Vineland Free Public Library, Vineland, NJ [*Library symbol*] [*Library of Congress*] (LCLS)

NjVC .... Cumberland County College, Vineland, NJ [*Library symbol*] [*Library of Congress*] (LCLS)

NjVcP .... Ventnor City Public Library, Ventnor City, NJ [*Library symbol*] [*Library of Congress*] (LCLS)

NJVGA .... National Junior Vegetable Growers Association [*Later, NJHA*] (EA)

NjVHi .... Vineland Historical and Antiquarian Society, Vineland, NJ [*Library symbol*] [*Library of Congress*] (LCLS)

NjVT .... Times Journal, Vineland, NJ [*Library symbol*] [*Library of Congress*] (LCLS)

NJW .... Norris Junction [*Wyoming*] [*Seismograph station code, US Geological Survey*] (SEIS)

NjW .... Wayne Public Library, Wayne, NJ [*Library symbol*] [*Library of Congress*] (LCLS)

NjWa .... Warren Township Public Library, Warren, NJ [*Library symbol*] [*Library of Congress*] (LCLS)

NjWas .... Washington Free Public Library, Washington, NJ [*Library symbol*] [*Library of Congress*] (LCLS)

NjWasW .... Washington Star, Washington, NJ [*Library symbol*] [*Library of Congress*] (LCLS)

NJWB .... National Jewish Welfare Board [*Later, JWB*]

NjWdHi .... Gloucester County Historical Society, Woodbury, NJ [*Library symbol*] [*Library of Congress*] (LCLS)

NjWdT .... Woodbury Daily Times, Woodbury, NJ [*Library symbol*] [*Library of Congress*] (LCLS)

NjWef .... Westfield Memorial Library, Westfield, NJ [*Library symbol*] [*Library of Congress*] (LCLS)

NjWefW .... Wyckoff Printing Co., Westfield, NJ [*Library symbol*] [*Library of Congress*] (LCLS)

NjWem .... Haddon Township Free Library, Westmont, NJ [*Library symbol*] [*Library of Congress*] (LCLS)

NjWemT ...... Camden County Times, Westmont, NJ [*Library symbol*] [*Library of Congress*] (LCLS)

NjWesny ...... West New York Public Library, West New York, NJ [*Library symbol*] [*Library of Congress*] (LCLS)

NjWew .... Westwood Free Public Library, Westwood, NJ [*Library symbol*] [*Library of Congress*] (LCLS)

NjWewP .... Pascack Valley Community Life, Westwood, NJ [*Library symbol*] [*Library of Congress*] (LCLS)

NjWewW .... Westwood Publications, Westwood, NJ [*Library symbol*] [*Library of Congress*] (LCLS)

NjWF .... Fairleigh Dickinson University, Wayne, NJ [*Library symbol*] [*Library of Congress*] (LCLS)

NjWhi .... Whippanong Public Library, Whippany, NJ [*Library symbol*] [*Library of Congress*] (LCLS)

NjWhiB .... Bell Telephone Laboratories, Inc., Technical Information Library, Whippany, NJ [*Library symbol*] [*Library of Congress*] (LCLS)

NjWhiM .... Morris County Free Library, Whippany, NJ [*Library symbol*] [*Library of Congress*] (LCLS)

NjWhiR .... Regional Weekly News, Whippany, NJ [*Library symbol*] [*Library of Congress*] (LCLS)

NjWhsH .... Hunterdon Review, Whitehouse Station, NJ [*Library symbol*] [*Library of Congress*] (LCLS)

NjWi .... Willingboro Public Library, Willingboro, NJ [*Library symbol*] [*Library of Congress*] (LCLS)

NjWilH .... Williamstown High School, Williamstown, NJ [*Library symbol*] [*Library of Congress*] (LCLS)

NjWiT .... Burlington County Times, Willingboro, NJ [*Library symbol*] [*Library of Congress*] (LCLS)

NjWlM .... Monmouth College, West Long Beach, NJ [*Library symbol*] [*Library of Congress*] (LCLS)

NjWMN .... Matzner Suburban Newspapers, Wayne, NJ [*Library symbol*] [*Library of Congress*] (LCLS)

NjWo .... West Orange Free Public Library, West Orange, NJ [*Library symbol*] [*Library of Congress*] (LCLS)

NjWoE .... Edison National Historic Site, West Orange, NJ [*Library symbol*] [*Library of Congress*] (LCLS)

NjWolA .... Alphonsus College, Woodcliff Lake, NJ [*Library symbol*] [*Library of Congress*] (LCLS)

NjWoo .... Free Public Library of Woodbridge, Woodbridge, NJ [*Library symbol*] [*Library of Congress*] (LCLS)

NjWooN .... News-Tribune, Woodbridge, NJ [*Library symbol*] [*Library of Congress*] (LCLS)

NjWor .... Wood Ridge Memorial Library, Wood Ridge, NJ [*Library symbol*] [*Library of Congress*] (LCLS)

NjWP .... William Paterson College of New Jersey, Wayne, NJ [*Library symbol*] [*Library of Congress*] (LCLS)

NJWPC .... National Jobs with Peace Campaign (EA)

NjWw .... Wildwood Crest Public Library, Wildwood, NJ [*Library symbol*] [*Library of Congress*] (LCLS)

NjWwHi .... Wildwood Historical Commission, Wildwood, NJ [*Library symbol*] [*Library of Congress*] (LCLS)

NjWwL .... Wildwood Leader, Wildwood, NJ [*Library symbol*] [*Library of Congress*] (LCLS)

NjWwP .... National Association of Precancel Collectors, Wildwood, NJ [*Library symbol*] [*Library of Congress*] (LCLS)

NjWy .... Wyckoff Free Public Library, Wyckoff, NJ [*Library symbol*] [*Library of Congress*] (LCLS)

NjWyN .... Wyckoff News, Wyckoff, NJ [*Library symbol*] [*Library of Congress*] (LCLS)

NJY .... Newjay Resources Ltd. [*Vancouver Stock Exchange symbol*]

NJY .... York College of the City University of New York, Jamaica, NY [*Library symbol*] [*Library of Congress*] (LCLS)

NJZ .... New Jersey Zinc (SAUS)

NjZaA .... Alma White College, Zarephath, NJ [*Library symbol*] [*Library of Congress*] (LCLS)

Nk .... Naik [*British military*] (DMA)

NK .... Natural Killer [*Cell*] [*Immunochemistry*]

NK .... Neck (AAG)

NK .... Neon Komma [*New Party*] [*Greek*] [*Political party*] (PPE)

NK .... Neurokinin [*Biochemistry*]

NK .... New Kingdom [*Egyptology*] (ROG)

NK .... Next of Kin

NK .... Nielsen-Kellerman

NK .... Nippon Kaiji Kyokai [*Japanese ship classification society*] (DS)

NK .... No Ketones [*Organic chemistry*] (DAVI)

NK .... No Kidding [*An association*] [*Canada*] (EAIO)

NK .... Nomemklatur Kommission [*Commission on Nomenclature*] [*Germany*] (DAVI)

NK .... Nordiska Kemistradet [*Chemical Societies of the Nordic Countries*] (EAIO)

NK .... Normalized Kinetic (SAUS)

NK .... Normal Keratinocyte (DB)

n/k .... Not Known (DMAA)

NK .... Not Known

NK .... Nuclear Kill

NKa .... Katonah Village Library, Katonah, NY [*Library symbol*] [*Library of Congress*] (LCLS)

NKA .... National Kindergarten Association [*Defunct*] (EA)

NKA .... Neurokinin A [*Biochemistry*]

NKA .... Nikiskha [*Alaska*] [*Seismograph station code, US Geological Survey*] (SEIS)

NKA .... No Known Allergies [*Medicine*]

NKA .... Norcanair [*Canada*] [*ICAO designator*] (FAAC)

NKA .... Nordic Liaison Committee for Atomic Energy (SAUS)

NKA .... Nordisk Kontaktorgan for Atomenergisporgsmal [*Nordic Liaison Committee for Atomic Energy*] (EAIO)

NKA .... North Korean Army

NKA .... Now Known As (DLA)

NKABEA .... National Korean American Bilingual Educators Association [*Defunct*] (EA)

NKAF .... Natural Killer-Cell Activating Factor [*Immunology*]

NKAF .... North Korean Air Force

NKAO .... Nagorno-Karabakh Autonomous Oblast

NKB .... Bear Stearns Companies, Inc. [*AMEX symbol*] (SAG)

NKB .... Neurokinin B [*Biochemistry*]

NKB .... No Known Basis (MELL)

NKB .... Nordiska Kommitten for Byggbestammelser [*Nordic Committee on Building Regulations - NCBR*] [*Finland*] (EAIO)

NKB .... Norges Kommunalbank [*Bank*] [*Norway*]

NKBA .... National Kitchen and Bath Association (EA)

NKC .... Merrill Lynch & Co. [*AMEX symbol*] (SAG)

NKC .... National Kidney Centre [*British*] (CB)

NKC .... Natural Killer Cells [*Microbiology*] (DAVI)

nkc .... New Brunswick [*MARC country of publication code*] [*Library of Congress*] (LCCP)

NKC .... Newtek Capital [*AMEX symbol*]

NKC .... Nonketotic Coma [*Medicine*] (DMAA)

NKC .... Nouakchott [*Mauritania*] [*Airport symbol*] (OAG)

NKCA .... National Kidney Cancer Association

NKCA .... National Kitchen Cabinet Association [*Later, KCMA*] (EA)

NKCA .... National Knife Collectors Association (EA)

NKCA .... Natural Killer Cell Activity [*Medicine*] (DMAA)

NKCF .... National Keratoconus Foundation (NRGU)

NKCF .... Natural Killer (Cell) Cytotoxic Factor [*Immunochemistry*]

NKCP .... North Kalimantan Communist Party [*Malaysia*] [*Political party*] (PD)

NKD .... No Known Disease (SAUS)

NKDA .... No Known Drug Allergies [*Medicine*]

NKDC .... Nonketotic Diabetic Coma [*Medicine*] (CPH)

NKDF .... National Kidney Disease Foundation [*Later, NKF*] (EA)

NKDS .... Navy Key Distribution System (CAAL)

NKE .... Nake [*Ryukyu Islands*] [*Seismograph station code, US Geological Survey*] [*Closed*] (SEIS)

NKE .... Nike, Inc. Class B [*NYSE symbol*] (SPSG)

NKE .... NIKE, Inc. Cl'B' [*NYSE symbol*] (TTSB)

NKE .... Nortek Capital Corp. [*Formerly, Nortek Energy Corp.*] [*Vancouver Stock Exchange symbol*]

NKendOHi .... Orleans County Historical Society, Kendall, NY [*Library symbol*] [*Library of Congress*] (LCLS)

NKEW .... Nuclear Kinetic Energy Weapon (SAUS)

NKEWA .... New Kuban Education and Welfare Association (EA)

NKEZA4 .... Japanese Journal of Public Health (journ.) (SAUS)

NKF .... National Kidney Foundation (EA)

NKF .... Nordiske Kvinners Fredsnettverk [*Nordic Women's Peace Network*] [*Denmark, Finland, Norway, and Sweden*] (EAIO)

NKF .... Nordisk Konstforbund [*Nordic Art Association*] [*Norway*] (EAIO)

NKFA .... No Known Food Allergies [*Medicine*] (DMAA)

NKF-DOQI.... National Kidney Foundation-Dialysis Outcomes Quality Initiative (SAUS)
NKFO .... Nordisk Kollegium for Fysisk Oceanografi [*Nordic Council for Physical Oceanography - NCPO*] (EAIO)
NKFTA .... National Kosher Food Trade Association [*Defunct*] (EA)
NKG .... Nanjing [*China*] [*Airport symbol*] (OAG)
NkG .... Newton K. Gregg, Novato, CA [*Library symbol*] [*Library of Congress*] (LCLS)
NKGB .... Peoples Commissariat for State Security (SAUS)
NKGB-NKVD... Narodnyi Komissariat Gosudarstvennoe Bezopasnosti-Narodnyi Komissariat Vnutrennikh Del [*Later, KGB*]
NKH .... Kaneohe Bay, HI [*Location identifier*] [*FAA*] (FAAL)
NKH .... Nonketotic Hyperglycemia [*Endocrinology*] (DAVI)
NKH .... Nonketotic Hyperosmotic [*Medicine*] (MAE)
NKH .... Nordisk Komite for Handelsundervisning [*Nordic Committee for Commercial Education - NCCE*] [*Odense, Denmark*] (EAIO)
NKHA .... National Kerosene Heater Association (EA)
NKHA .... Nonketotic Hyperosmolar Acidosis [*Medicine*]
NKHHC........ Nonketotic Hyperosmolar Hyperglycemis Coma [*Also, HHNK*] [*Medicine*]
NKHS .... Nonketotic Hyperosmolar Syndrome [*Biochemistry*] (DAVI)
NKHS .... Normal Krebs-Henseleit Solution (DB)
NKI .... Nash-Kelvinator International [*Automobile manufacturer, now out of production*]
NKI .... Nikolski [*Alaska*] [*Seismograph station code, US Geological Survey*] (SEIS)
NKiB .... Benedictine Hospital, Medical Library, Kingston, NY [*Library symbol*] [*Library of Congress*] (LCLS)
NKiC .... Children's Home of Kingston, Kingston, NY [*Library symbol*] [*Library of Congress*] (LCLS)
NKID .... Narodnyi Komissariat Inostrannykh Del [*People's Commissariat of Foreign Affairs*] [*Former USSR*] (LAIN)
NKID .... Noodle Kidoodle [*NASDAQ symbol*] (TTSB)
NKID .... Noodle Kidoodle, Inc. [*NASDAQ symbol*] (SAG)
NKiHL .... Kingston Hospital Libraries, Kingston, NY [*Library symbol*] [*Library of Congress*] (LCLS)
NKiI .... International Business Machines Corp., Kingston, NY [*Library symbol*] [*Library of Congress*] (LCLS)
NKipM .... United States Merchant Marine Academy, Kings Point, NY [*Library symbol*] [*Library of Congress*] (LCLS)
NKJV........... New King James Version of the Bible [*A publication*]
NKK .... Nordkalottkommitten [*North Calotte Committee - NCC*] [*Finland*] (EAIO)
NKK .... North Calotte Committee (SAUS)
NKK .... Novo-Kazalinsk [*Former USSR*] [*Geomagnetic observatory code*]
NKKGAB....... Japanese Poultry Science (journ.) (SAUS)
NKK Tech Rep... NKK Technical Report (SAUS)
NKK Tech Rev... NKK Technical Review (SAUS)
NKL............. Nemeth-Kellner Leukemia
NKL............. New Keel [*On ships*]
NKL............. New Kelore Mines Ltd. [*Toronto Stock Exchange symbol*]
NKL............. Nickel
NKL............. Nkolo [*Zaire*] [*Airport symbol*] (AD)
NKL C .... Nickel Copper [*Freight*]
NKL FCD...... Nickel Faced (DGA)
NKM............ Nakhla [*Morocco*] [*Seismograph station code, US Geological Survey*] (SEIS)
NKM............ New Park Mining (SAUS)
NKM............ University of North Carolina at Charlotte, Charlotte, NC [*OCLC symbol*] (OCLC)
NKMA .... National Knitwear Manufacturers Association (EA)
NKMA .... No Known Medication Allergies (DAVI)
NKMB .... Nordisk Kollegium for Marinbiologi [*Nordic Council for Marine Biology - NCMB*] [*Italy*] (EAIO)
NKMU .... National Kangaroo Monitoring Unit [*Australia*]
NKN............. Neurokinin (DMAA)
NKN............. North Korean Navy
NKO .... Narodnyi Komissariat Oborony [*People's Commissariat of Defense*] [*Existed until 1946*] [*Former USSR*]
NKO .... Need to Know Only [*Espionage*]
NKOA .... National Knitted Outerwear Association [*Later, NKSA*] (EA)
NKOT .... Nu-kote Holding 'A' [*NASDAQ symbol*] (TTSB)
NKOT .... Nu-Kote Holding, Inc. [*NASDAQ symbol*] (SAG)
NKOTB .... New Kids on the Block [*Music group*]
NKP .... Nakorn Phanom [*Air base northeast of Bangkok*]
NKP .... Nasionale Konserwatiewe Party [*National Conservative Party*] [*South Africa*] [*Political party*] (PPW)
NKP .... New Kensington [*Pennsylvania*] [*Seismograph station code, US Geological Survey*] [*Closed*] (SEIS)
NKP .... New Korea Party [*South Korea*]
NKP .... Nickel Plate Railroad (SAUS)
NKP .... Norges Kommunistiske Parti [*Norwegian Communist Party*] [*Political party*] (PPE)
NKPA .... National Kraut Packers Association (EA)
NKPA .... North Korean Peoples Army (SAUS)
NKpaH .... Kings Park State Hospital, Kings Park, NY [*Library symbol*] [*Library of Congress*] (LCLS)
NKpK .... Keuka College, Keuka Park, NY [*Library symbol*] [*Library of Congress*] (LCLS)
NKPR .... Innkeepers USA Trust [*NASDAQ symbol*] (SAG)
NKP RTAB ... Nakhon Phanom Royal Thai Air Base [*Leased by USAF during the Vietnam War*] (VNW)
NKR .... Nakanohara [*Japan*] [*Seismograph station code, US Geological Survey*] (SEIS)
NKR .... New Kenrell Resources [*Vancouver Stock Exchange symbol*]

NKR .... Nordisk Konservatorierad [*Nordic Council for Music Conservatories - NCMC*] (EAIO)
NKR .... Normal Rat Kidney (DB)
N KR............ Norwegian Krone [*Monetary unit*]
NKRC .... No Known Relatives or Concerned
NKS .... Needle-Knife Sphincterotomy [*Medicine*] (MELL)
NKS .... Network of Kindred Spirits (EA)
NKS .... Nordic Nuclear Safety Project (SAUS)
NKS .... Nordisk Kirkelig Studierad [*Nordic Council for Adult Studies in Chruch - NCASC*] (EAIO)
NKSA .... National Knitwear and Sportswear Association (EA)
NKSC .... National Korean Studies Center [*Australia*]
NKSF .... Natural Killer-Cell Stimulatory Factor [*Immunology*]
NKSR .... Non-Kernel Security Related (SAUS)
NKSRS .... Non-Kernel Security Related Software (ACAE)
NKT............. Cherry Point, NC [*Location identifier*] [*FAA*] (FAAL)
NKT............. Nankipoo [*Tennessee*] [*Seismograph station code, US Geological Survey*] (SEIS)
NKT............. National Kakapo Team (SAUS)
NKT............. Nihon Kai Telecasting (SAUS)
NKT............. None Kept in Town
NKTAD .... Journal. Gyeongsang National University. Natural Sciences (journ.) (SAUS)
NKU .... Nakusp Resources Ltd. [*Vancouver Stock Exchange symbol*]
NKU .... Nkaus [*Lesotho*] [*Airport symbol*] (OAG)
NKUDIC....... National Kidney and Urologic Diseases Information Clearinghouse (EA)
NKUSA........ Neturei Karta of USA (EA)
NKVD .... Narodnyi Kommissariat Vnutrennikh Del [*People's Commissariat for Internal Affairs*] [*Former USSR*] (NADA)
NKVMF .... Narodnyy Kommissariat Voyenno-Morskogo Flota [*People's Commissariat of the Navy*] [*Former USSR*] (LAIN)
NKX .... San Diego, CA [*Location identifier*] [*FAA*] (FAAL)
N Ky St LF... Northern Kentucky State Law Forum [*A publication*] (DLA)
NKYu .... Narodnyy Kommissariat Yustitsii [*People's Commissariat of Justice*] [*Former USSR*] (LAIN)
NKYZA2 .... Jaganese Journal of Thoracic Diseases (SAUS)
NKz............. Kwanza (ODBW)
NKZ............. Nuclear Killing Zone [*Military*] [*British*]
NL .... Air Liberia [*ICAO designator*] (AD)
nl--- .... Great Lakes [*MARC geographic area code*] [*Library of Congress*] (LCCP)
NL .... Lima Public Library, Lima, NY [*Library symbol*] [*Library of Congress*] (LCLS)
NL .... Nailable [*Technical drawings*]
nl .... Nanoliter [*One billionth of a liter*] (MAE)
NL .... Nasolacrimal [*Medicine*] (DAVI)
NL .... Natick Laboratories [*Army*] (MCD)
NL .... National Lakeshore (BARN)
NL .... National Lead (EFIS)
NL .... National League (NTIO)
NL .... National League of Professional Baseball Clubs (EA)
NL .... National Liberal [*British politics*]
NL .... National Library [*Canada*]
NL .... Native Language (BARN)
NL .... Naturalist's Library [*A publication*]
NL .... Natural Language [*Computer software*]
NL .... Natural Log [*or Logarithm*] (WDAA)
NL .... Naval Lighter
NL .... Navigating Lieutenant [*Navy*] [*British*] (ROG)
N/L............. Navigation/Localizer (IEEE)
NL .... Navy League of the United States
NL .... Navy Library (WDAA)
NL .... Navy List [*British military*] (DMA)
NL .... Nebenlager [*Branch Camp*] [*German military - World War II*]
NL .... Nelson's Lutwyche, English Common Pleas Reports [*A publication*] (DLA)
NL .... Neon Lamp (KSC)
NL .... Netherlands [*ANSI two-letter standard code*] (CNC)
NI .... Netherlands (MILB)
NL .... Net Loss
NL .... Neurilemmona [*Oncology*]
NL .... Neuroleptic (SAUS)
NL .... Neutral Lipid (DB)
NL .... Neutron Log (SAUS)
nl .... New Caledonia [*MARC country of publication code*] [*Library of Congress*] (LCCP)
NL .... New Latin [*Language, etc.*]
NL .... New Lead [*Also, NH*] [*News stories*] (NTCM)
NL .... New Leader [*A publication*] (BRI)
nl .... New Line (WDMC)
NL .... New Line [*Computer science*]
NL .... New London, Connecticut [*Navy*]
NL .... Newsletter (WDMC)
N-L............. New York State Library, Law Library, Albany, NY [*Library symbol*] [*Library of Congress*] (LCLS)
NL .... Night Letter
NL .... NL Industries, Inc. [*Formerly, National Lead Co.*] [*NYSE symbol*] (SPSG)
NL .... Nodular Lymphoma [*Oncology*] (DAVI)
NL .... Noiseless (SAUS)
NL .... Noise Level (SAUS)
NL .... No Label (SAUS)
NL .... No Layers (SAUS)
N/L............. No Ledger (SAA)

NL..............	No Liability (ADA)
NL..............	No License [Traffic offense charge]
NL..............	No Limit (NASA)
NL..............	No Liner (DS)
NL..............	No Load
NL..............	Non-Labeled [Tape] [Computer science]
NL..............	Non Licet [It Is Not Permitted] [Latin]
NL..............	Nonlinear
NL..............	Non Liquet [It Is Not Clear] [Latin]
NL..............	Non-Loaded (NITA)
NL..............	Nonlocking
NL..............	Non Longe [Not Far] [Latin]
NL..............	Non-Lubricant (SAUS)
NL..............	Nonprogrammer Language [Computer science] (PDAA)
n/l..............	Normal Limits
NL..............	Normal Lungs
NL..............	North Latitude
NL..............	North Library (SAUS)
NL..............	Nose Left [Aviation] (MCD)
NL..............	Notless (SAUS)
NL..............	Not Licensed (SAUS)
NL..............	Not Listed (AFM)
NL..............	Not Located
NL..............	Nulead [Journalism] [Slang] (WDMC)
NL..............	Number Language (SAUS)
NL..............	Number Lines (SAUS)
NL..............	Number of unallocated channels on link (SAUS)
NL..............	Nurses for Laughter [Defunct] (EA)
NL..............	Nyhan-Lesch [Syndrome] [Medicine] (DB)
NL/1..............	Non-programmer Language 1 (SAUS)
NLA..............	Children's Leukemia Research Association [Formerly, National Leukemia Association] (EA)
NLA..............	National Laboratory Accreditation Service (SAUS)
NLA..............	National Landscape Association (EA)
NLA..............	National Leather Association (EA)
NLA..............	National Leukemia Association (EA)
NLA..............	National Liberation Army [Bolivia]
NLA..............	National Librarians Association (EA)
NLA..............	National Libraries Authority
NLA..............	National Library Act
NLA..............	National Library of Australia (NITA)
NLA..............	National Library of Canada, Cataloguing Branch [UTLAS symbol]
NLA..............	National Lime Association (EA)
NLA..............	National Limousine Association (EA)
NLA..............	National Locksmiths Association (EA)
NLA..............	NATO Lot Acceptance (MCD)
NLA..............	Navy League of Australia
NLA..............	Ndola [Zambia] [Airport symbol] (OAG)
NLA..............	Neiltown Air Ltd. [Canada] [ICAO designator] (FAAC)
NLA..............	Net Lettable Area
NLA..............	Neuroleptanalgesia [Altered state of awareness] [Medicine] (AAMN)
NLA..............	Neuroleptic Anesthesia
NLA..............	Neuroleptoanesthesia [Medicine] (DMAA)
NLA..............	Nevada Library Association (SAUS)
NLA..............	Newfoundland Library Association (SAUS)
NLA..............	New Large Airplane
NLA..............	New Larger Aeroplanes (SAUS)
NLA..............	New Libertarian Alliance (EA)
NLA..............	New Libertian Alliance (SAUS)
NLA..............	Next Lower Assembly (MCD)
NLA..............	Nine Lives Associates (EA)
NLA..............	Nonlinear Amplifier
NLA..............	Nonlinear Analysis (SAUS)
NLA..............	Nonuniform Linear Array
NLA..............	Normalized Load Access (NITA)
NLA..............	Normalized Local Address [Computer science] (CIST)
NLA..............	Normal Lactase Activity [Medicine] (DMAA)
NLA..............	Norris-LaGuardia Act (MHDB)
NLA	Not Long Ago (SAUS)
NLAA	National Legal Aid Association
NLAAM	N-Desmethyl-levo-alpha-Acetylmethadol [Opiate]
NLAB	National Laboratory Accreditation Bureau (SAUS)
NLABS	Natick Laboratories [Army] (AABC)
NLAC	National Listen America Club (EA)
NLacOH	Our Lady of Victory Hospital, Lackawanna, NY [Library symbol] [Library of Congress] (LCLS)
NLADA	National Legal Aid and Defender Association (EA)
NLADA Brief...	National Legal Aid and Defender Association Briefcase [A publication] (DLA)
NLAES	National Longitudinal Alcohol Epidemiologic Survey (SAUS)
NLakrHS	Sachem High School South, Lake Ronkonkoma, NY [Library symbol] [Library of Congress] (LCLS)
NLAL..........	Nodule-Like Alveolar Lesion [Medicine] (DB)
NLanEB.......	Erie No. 1 Board of Coopertive Educational Services, Lancaster, NY [Library symbol] [Library of Congress] (LCLS)
NLANR..........	National Laboratory for Applied Network Research (DDC)
NLanS..........	Scott Aviation, Lancaster, NY [Library symbol] [Library of Congress] (LCLS)
NLAP	National Lab Audit Program (COE)
NLAPW	National League of American Pen Women (EA)
NLar..........	Larchmont Public Library, Larchmont, NY [Library symbol] [Library of Congress] (LCLS)
NLAS	National Laboratory Accreditation Service (SAUS)
NLAS	National Lum and Abner Society (EA)

NLaw	Peninsula Public Library, Lawrence, NY [Library symbol] [Library of Congress] (LCLS)
NLawBS.......	Brandeis School, Lawrence, NY [Library symbol] [Library of Congress] (LCLS)
NLawCE.......	Central Elementary School, Lawrence, NY [Library symbol] [Library of Congress] (LCLS)
NLawChE.......	Cedarhurst Elementary School, Lawrence, NY [Library symbol] [Library of Congress] (LCLS)
NLawDE.......	Donahue Elementary School, Lawrence, NY [Library symbol] [Library of Congress] (LCLS)
NLawJH	Lawrence Junior High School, Lawrence, NY [Library symbol] [Library of Congress] (LCLS)
NLawPE.......	Peninsula Elementary School, Lawrence, NY [Library symbol] [Library of Congress] (LCLS)
NLawrPE.......	Peninsula Elementary School, Lawrence (SAUS)
NLawSH.......	Lawrence Senior High School, Lawrence, NY [Library symbol] [Library of Congress] (LCLS)
NLawWE.......	Wansee Elementary School, Lawrence, NY [Library symbol] [Library of Congress] (LCLS)
NLB..............	National Labor Board (WDAA)
NLB..............	National Library for the Blind
NLB..............	National Library of Canada, Locations Division [UTLAS symbol]
NLB..............	National Lighting Bureau (EA)
NLB..............	Needle Liver Biopsy [Medicine] (DMAA)
NLB..............	Network Load Balancing
NLB..............	No Lunch Break
NLB..............	Nonlinear Buckling (SAUS)
NLB..............	Northern Lighthouse Board (SAUS)
NLB..............	Nuclear Light Bulb
NLB..............	Number of Lines of Binary (SAUS)
NLBA..............	National Lead Burning Association (EA)
NLBA..............	National Licensed Beverage Association (EA)
NLBA..............	Nonlinear Buckling Analysis (SAUS)
NLB & D.....	National League for the Blind and Disabled [British] (DBA)
NLBC..............	National Livestock Brand Conference [Later, International Livestock Brand Conference]
NLBD..............	National League of the Blind and Disabled [A union] [British] (DCTA)
NLBI..............	National League of the Blind of Ireland (EAIO)
NLBMDA......	National Lumber and Building Material Dealers Association (EA)
NLBRA..............	National Little Britches Rodeo Association (EA)
NLC..............	Lemoore, CA [Location identifier] [FAA] (FAAL)
NLC..............	NADGE [NATO Air Defense Ground Environment] Logistics Committee (NATG)
NLC..............	Nalco Chemical [NYSE symbol] (TTSB)
NLC..............	Nalco Chemical Co. [NYSE symbol] (SPSG)
NLC..............	National Laboratory Center [Bureau of Alcohol, Tobacco, and Firearms] [Rockville, MD] (GRD)
NLC..............	National Labour Congress [Nigeria] (ECON)
NLC..............	National Lawyers Club (EA)
NLC..............	National Leadership Committee [Military]
NLC..............	National Leadership Council [Defunct] (EA)
NLC..............	National League of Cities (EA)
NLC..............	National Legislative Conference [Later, NCSL] (EA)
NLC..............	National Legislative Council [Later, NCSL]
NLC..............	National Liberal Club [British]
NLC..............	National Liberation Committee [South Africa]
NLC..............	National Liberty Committee (EA)
NLC..............	National Library of Canada
NLC..............	National Library of Canada, Ottawa, ON, Canada [OCLC symbol] (OCLC)
NLC..............	National Library of China
NLC..............	National Lifeguard Championships (EA)
NLC..............	National Liturgical Commission [Catholic Church] [Australia]
NLC..............	National Location Code [Civil Defense]
NLC..............	National Logistical Command (MCD)
NLC..............	National Lutheran Council [Later, LC/USA] (EA)
NLC..............	Natural Language Command [Computer science]
NLC..............	Navy Law Center (DNAB)
NLC..............	Negro Labor Committee [Defunct] (EA)
NLC..............	Nematic Liquid Crystal [Physical chemistry]
NLC..............	Network Language Center (MHDB)
NLC..............	New Liberal Club [Shin Jiyu Club] [Japan] (PPW)
NLC..............	New Line Character [Keyboard] [Computer science] (MDG)
NLC..............	New Location Code [Military]
NLC..............	New Orleans & Lower Coast Railroad Co. [AAR code]
NLC..............	News and Letters Committee (EA)
NLC..............	Next Linear Collider [Proposed]
NLC..............	Nocturnal Leg Cramps [Medicine] (MELL)
NLC..............	Node Location Code (PDAA)
NLC..............	Noise-Level Cable
NLC..............	Non-Linear Capacitor (SAUS)
NLC..............	Non-Linear Condenser (SAUS)
NLC..............	Nonlinear Control (SAUS)
NLC..............	Nordic Literature Committee [Copenhagen, Denmark] (EAIO)
NLC..............	Northern Libraries Colloquy (EA)
NLC..............	Northland Library System [Library network]
NLCA..............	Norlaudanosolinecarboxylic Acid [Biochemistry]
NLCA..............	Norlithocholic Acid [Biochemistry]
NLCA..............	Norwegian Lutheran Church of America (IIA)
NLCAA..............	National Little College Athletic Association [Later, NSCAA] (EA)
NLCAB..............	National Library of Canada Advisory Board
NLCACBC......	National League of Cuban American Community-Based Centers (EA)
NLC&C..........	Normal Libido, Coitus and Climax [Medicine] (MELL)
NLCC..........	National Latino Communications Center (SAUS)
NLCC	Navy League Cadet Corps (EA)

NLCC .... NORTHAG Logistics Command Center (SAUS)
NLCD .... National Liberation Council Decree [1966-69] [Ghana] [A publication] (DLA)
NLCEA .... Naval Laboratory Centers' Employee Association (DNAB)
NLCH .... National Legislative Council for the Handicapped (EA)
NLCIF........... National Light Castings Ironfounders' Federation [British] (BI)
NLCM .... National Lutheran Campus Ministry (EA)
NLCM........... Non-Lethal Countermeasures (SAUS)
NLCMDD...... National Legal Center for the Medically Dependent and Disabled (EA)
NLCOA .... National Leadership Coalition on AIDS [Acquired Immune Deficiency Syndrome] (EA)
NLCP .... Navy Logistics Capabilities Plan
NLCP-FY...... Navy Logistics Capabilities Plan - Fiscal Year (DNAB)
NLCPI .... National Legal Center for the Public Interest (EA)
NLCR .... New Line, Carriage Return (SAUS)
NLCS .... National Computer Systems, Inc. [NASDAQ symbol] (NQ)
NLCS .... National League Championship Series [Baseball]
NLCS .... National Lutheran Commission on Scouting [Defunct] (EA)
NLCS .... Natl Computer Sys [NASDAQ symbol] (TTSB)
NLCS .... Nordic Leather Chemists Society [Formerly, IVLIC Scandinavian Section] (EA)
NLCS .... North London Collegiate School (SAUS)
NLCSDHRES... National Labor Committee in Support of Democracy and Human Rights in El Salvador (EA)
NLCSE .... Non-Linear Charge Storage Element (PDAA)
NLCSJ.......... National Lawyers Committee for Soviet Jewry (EA)
NLCWC .... National Lincoln-Civil War Council (EA)
NLD .... Namakwaland Lugdiens (EDMS) BPK [South Africa] [ICAO designator] (FAAC)
NLD .... NASA Launch Director
NLD .... Nasolabial Distance [Medicine] (MELL)
NLD .... Nasolacrimal Duct [Medicine] (DAVI)
NLD .... National League for Democracy [Myanmar] [Political party] (EY)
NLD .... National Legal Databases (IID)
NLD .... National Legion of Decency [Later, National Catholic Office for Motion Pictures] (EA)
NLD .... Naval Electrical Department [British military] (DMA)
NLD .... Naval Lighter [Pontoon] Dock
NLD .... Necrobiosis Lipoidica Diabeticorum [Medicine]
NLD .... Netherlands [ANSI three-letter standard code] (CNC)
NLD .... No Load (MSA)
NLD .... Nonlinear Distortion (SAUS)
NLD .... Nonverbal Learning Disability
NLD .... Northland Bank [Toronto Stock Exchange symbol] [Vancouver Stock Exchange symbol]
NLD .... Not in Line of Duty [as of an injury] [Military]
NLD .... Nuevo Laredo [Mexico] [Airport symbol] (OAG)
NLDA .... National Livestock Dealers Association [Later, Livestock Marketing Association] (EA)
NLDA .... National Luggage Dealers Association (EA)
NLDB .... Natural Language Data Base
NLDC .... National Legal Data Center [Defunct] (EA)
NLDC .... Newfoundland and Labrador Development Corp. (SAUS)
NLDDE .... Non-Linear Differential-Difference Equation (SAUS)
NLDF .... National Leigh's Disease Foundation (EA)
NLDF .... Naval Local Defense Forces
NLDGP .... Non-Linear Discrete Goal Programming (SAUS)
NLDI .... Nasolacrimal Duct Impatency [Medicine] (MELL)
NLDM .... Network Logical Data Manager (NITA)
NLDN .... National Lightning Detection Network
NLDO .... Nasolacrimal Duct Obstruction [Medicine] (MELL)
NLDS .... National Lightning Detection System (SAUS)
NLDTS .... Nonlinear Discrete-Time System (SAUS)
NLDV .... National League of Disabled Voters (EA)
NLE .... National Library of Education
NLE .... National Livestock Exchange [Defunct] (EA)
NLE .... Neonatal Lupus Erythematosus [Medicine] (MELL)
NLE .... Nonlinear Editing (SAUS)
NLE .... Nonlinear Element
NLE .... Nonlinear Equation (SAUS)
NLE .... Nonlinear Estimation (SAUS)
Nle .... Norleucine [A nonessential amino acid] [Biochemistry]
Nle .... Norleucyl (SAUS)
NLE .... Northern Commuter Airlines [New Zealand] [ICAO designator] (FAAC)
NLE .... North Leave Earth (ACAE)
NLE .... Not Less or Equal (SAUS)
NLEA .... National Lumber Exporters Association [Later, AHEC] (EA)
NLEA .... National Lupus Erythematosus Association (MELL)
NLEA .... Nutrition Labeling Act (SAUS)
NLEA .... Nutrition Labeling and Education Act [1990] [Food and Drug Administration]
NLEACH ...... Northleach [England]
NLEC............ National Law Enforcement Council (EA)
NLEC............ National Lutheran Educational Conference [Later, LECNA] (EA)
NLEEF .... National Law Enforcement Emergency Frequency (LAIN)
NLEF .... National Legislative Education Foundation (EA)
NLEF .... National Lupus Erythematosus Foundation [Defunct] (EA)
NLEF .... Nonlinear Electric Field (SAUS)
NLEFM......... Nonlinear Elastic Fracture Mechanics (SAUS)
NLEMA......... National Lutheran Editors and Managers Association [Defunct] (EA)
NLEOMF ...... National Law Enforcement Officers Memorial Fund (EA)
NLer............. Woodward Memorial Library, LeRoy, NY [Library symbol] [Library of Congress] (LCLS)

NLerHi......... LeRoy Historical Society, LeRoy, NY [Library symbol] [Library of Congress] (LCLS)
NLETS......... National Law Enforcement Telecommunications System
NLETS......... National Law Enforcement Teletype System (COE)
Nleu............. Norleucine (DB)
NLev............ Levittown Public Library, Levittown, NY [Library symbol] [Library of Congress] (LCLS)
NLEV........... National Low-Emission Vehicles
NLevAE........ Abbey Lane Elementary School, Levittown, NY [Library symbol] [Library of Congress] (LCLS)
NLevDH........ Division Avenue High School, Levittown, NY [Library symbol] [Library of Congress] (LCLS)
NLevEC........ Levittown Memorial Education Center, Levittown, NY [Library symbol] [Library of Congress] (LCLS)
NLevGE........ Gardiners Avenue Elementary School, Levittown, NY [Library symbol] [Library of Congress] (LCLS)
NLevGGE ..... Geneva N. Gallow Elementary School, Levittown, NY [Library symbol] [Library of Congress] (LCLS)
NLevI .... Island Trees Public Library, Levittown, NY [Library symbol] [Library of Congress] (LCLS)
NLevIH........ Island Trees High School, Levittown, NY [Library symbol] [Library of Congress] (LCLS)
NLevIJ .... Island Trees Memorial Junior High School, Levittown, NY [Library symbol] [Library of Congress] (LCLS)
NLevJSE ...... J. Fred Sparke Elementary School, Levittown, NY [Library symbol] [Library of Congress] (LCLS)
NLevLE........ Lee Road Elementary School, Levittown, NY [Library symbol] [Library of Congress] (LCLS)
NLevMH....... General Douglas McArthur High School, Levittown, NY [Library symbol] [Library of Congress] (LCLS)
NLevMSE...... Michael F. Stokes Elementary School, Levittown, NY [Library symbol] [Library of Congress] (LCLS)
NLevNE........ Northside Elementary School, Levittown, NY [Library symbol] [Library of Congress] (LCLS)
NLevSJ .... Jonas E. Salk Junior High School, Levittown, NY [Library symbol] [Library of Congress] (LCLS)
NLevSLE...... Summit Lane Elementary School, Levittown, NY [Library symbol] [Library of Congress] (LCLS)
NLevSNE...... Seaman Neck Elementary School, Levittown, NY [Library symbol] [Library of Congress] (LCLS)
NLevWM...... Wisdom Middle School, Levittown, NY [Library symbol] [Library of Congress] (LCLS)
NLew .... Lewiston Public Library, Lewiston, NY [Library symbol] [Library of Congress] (LCLS)
NLewStM..... Mount Saint Mary's Hospital, Lewiston, NY [Library symbol] [Library of Congress] (LCLS)
NLf............... Little Falls Public Library, Little Falls, NY [Library symbol] [Library of Congress] (LCLS)
NLF............... Nasolabial Fold [Medicine] (DAVI)
NLF............... National Fuelcorp Ltd. [Vancouver Stock Exchange symbol]
NLF............... National Laser Facility
NLF............... National League of Families of Prisoners and Missing in Southeast Asia
NLF............... National Legal Foundation (EA)
NLF............... National Liberal Federation [British]
NLF............... National Liberation Front [South Africa] [Political party] (PD)
NLF............... National Liberation Front [Myanmar] [Political party] (PD)
NLF............... National Liberation Front [Aden] [Political party]
NLF............... National Liberation Front [Vietnam] [Political party]
NLF............... Navigation Light Flasher
NLF............... Nearest Landing Field
NLF............... Neonatal Lung Fibroblast [Medicine] (DMAA)
NLF............... Neutral Lipid Fraction [Biochemistry]
NLF............... New Leadership Fund (EA)
NLF............... No-Load Field (SAUS)
NLF............... No-Load Funds
NLF............... Nonlactose Fermenting [Organism] [Medicine] (DB)
NLF............... Non-Linear Filter (SAUS)
NLF............... North Luzon Force [Army] [World War II]
NLF............... Westair Aviation, Inc. [Canada] [ICAO designator] (FAAC)
NLFA........... National Lamb Feeders Association (EA)
NLFA........... National Livestock Feeders Association [Later, NCA] (EA)
NLFED .... Naval Landing Force Equipment Depot
NLFM.......... Noise-Level Frequency Monitor
NLFMA........ National Law Firm Marketing Association (EA)
NLFPA .... National Liberation Front Party Apparatus [Algeria]
NLFS........... Nucleus Landing Force Staff (DNAB)
NLFSV .... National Liberation Front of South Vietnam [Political party]
NLFT........... No-Load Frame Time
NLG............. National Gas & Oil Corp. [AMEX symbol] (SPSG)
NLG............. National Lawyers Guild (EA)
NLG............. Natl Gas & Oil [AMEX symbol] (TTSB)
NLG............. Nelson Lagoon [Alaska] [Airport symbol] (OAG)
NLG............. No-Load Governed [Equipment design]
NLG............. North Louisiana & Gulf Railroad Co. [AAR code]
NLG............. Nose Landing Gear [Aviation]
NLG............. Null Line Gap
NLG............. Numismatic Literary Guild (EA)
NLGA........... National Lumber Grading Agency [Canada]
NLGAWVA.... National Legion of Greek-American War Veterans in America (EA)
NLGC.......... Nauru Local Government Council [Australia]
NLGC.......... Noise-Level Gain Control (MCD)
NLGDA........ National Lawn and Garden Distributors Association (EA)
NLGHA........ National Lesbian and Gay Health Association (EA)
NLGHF........ National Lesbian and Gay Health Foundation (EA)

NLGI .... National Lubricating Grease Institute (EA)
NLGLA .... National Lesbian and Gay Lawyers Association (NTPA)
NLGLP .... National Laboratory Gene Library Project (HGEN)
NLGPDC ...... National Lawyer's Guild Peace and Disarmament Committee [*Later, NLGPDS*] (EA)
NLGPDS ...... National Lawyer's Guild Peace and Disarmament Society (EA)
NLGPDS ...... National Lawyer's Guild Peace and Disarmament Subcommittee (EA)
NLGQ .... National Lawyers Guild Quarterly [*A publication*] (DLA)
NLH .... New Lao Hak [*Lao Patriotic Front*] [*Vietnam*] [*Political party*]
NLH .... New Life Hamlet [*See also NLHS, NLHZ*] [*Vietnam*] [*Military*]
NLH .... New Literary History: A Journal of Theory and Interpretation [*A publication*] (ANEX)
NLH .... Non-Locating Head [*Engineering*] (OA)
NLHA .... National Leased Housing Association [*Washington, DC*] (EA)
NLHO .... National Latina Health Organization (EAIO)
NLHP .... National Literacy and Health Program (SAUS)
NLHRSA ...... National Left-Handers Racquet Sports Association (EA)
NLHS .... New Lao Hak Sat [*New Life Hamlet*] [*See also NLH*] [*Vietnam*] [*Military*]
NLHZ .... New Lao Hak Zat [*New Life Hamlet*] [*See also NLH, NLHS*] [*Vietnam*] [*Military*]
NLI .... National Landscape Institute
NLI .... National Language Interface (NITA)
NLI .... National Leadership Institute [*Defunct*] (EA)
NLI .... National Library of Ireland (AIE)
NLI .... National Limestone Institute [*Later, NSA*] (EA)
NLI .... Neodymium LASER Illuminator
NLI .... New Learning Initiative (AIE)
NLI .... Noise Limit Indicator
NLI .... Nonlinear Interpolating (IEEE)
NLI .... Non-Linear Interpolator (SAUS)
NLI .... Northern Lights College Library [*UTLAS symbol*]
NLI .... Not Logged In (SAUS)
NLI .... NovaNET Learning
NLI .... NTL, Inc. [*NYSE symbol*]
NLI .... Nursing Literature Index (SAUS)
NLIA .... National Languages Institute of Australia
NLib .... Liberty Public Library, Liberty, NY [*Library symbol*] [*Library of Congress*] (LCLS)
NLIC .... National Landslide Information Center [*US Geological Survey*]
NLIC .... National Lead Information Center (AEPA)
NLicL .... LaGuardia Community College of the City University of New York, Long Island Cit y, NY [*Library symbol*] [*Library of Congress*] (LCLS)
NLicP .... PepsiCo, Inc., Research Library, Long Island, NY [*Library symbol*] [*Library of Congress*] (LCLS)
NLIF .... Nonlinear Interference Filter [*Electronics*]
NLIHC .... National Low Income Housing Coalition (EA)
NLIMT .... Newfoundland and Labrador Institute of Marine Technology (SAUS)
NLin .... Lindenhurst Memorial Library, Lindenhurst, NY [*Library symbol*] [*Library of Congress*] (LCLS)
NLIN .... NOAA [*National Oceanic and Atmospheric Administration*] Library and Information Network [*Marine science*] (OSRA)
NLin .... Nonlinear
NL Ind .... NL Industries, Inc. [*Formerly, National Lead Co.*] [*Associated Press*] (SAG)
NLinHS .... Lindenhurst High School, Lindenhurst, NY [*Library symbol*] [*Library of Congress*] (LCLS)
NLinJS .... Lindenhurst Junior High School, Lindenhurst, NY [*Library symbol*] [*Library of Congress*] (LCLS)
NLIS .... National Lesbian Information Service
NLIS .... Navy Logistics Information System
NLISA .... National League of Insured Savings Associations [*Later, NSLL*] (EA)
NLJ .... Nagpur Law Journal [*India*] [*A publication*] (DLA)
NLJ .... New Law Journal [*A publication*] (ILCA)
NLK .... Neuroleukin [*Biochemistry*]
NLK .... Norfolk Island [*Airport symbol*] (OAG)
NLK .... Norlink Air Ltd. [*British*] [*ICAO designator*] (FAAC)
NLKF .... Nonlinear Kalman Filter
NLL .... National Aeronautical Research Institute [*Netherlands*] (SAA)
NLL .... National Lacrosse League [*Disbanded*]
NLL .... National Lending Library for Science and Technology [*Later, BLLD*] [*British Library*]
NLL .... National Liberal League [*Later, NLSCS*] (EA)
NLL .... Negative Logic Level
NLL .... New England School of Law Library, Boston, MA [*OCLC symbol*] (OCLC)
NLL .... New Library of Law [*Harrisburg, PA*] [*A publication*] (DLA)
NLL .... New Library of Law and Equity [*England*] [*A publication*] (DLA)
NLL .... New Life League (EA)
NLL .... New London [*Connecticut*] Laboratory [*Navy*] (DNAB)
NLL .... Night Low Level (SAUS)
NLL .... Normal Liquid Level [*Engineering*]
NLL .... Northern Limit Line [*Korea*]
NLL .... Nullagine [*Australia*] [*Airport symbol*] (OAG)
NLLAP .... National Lead Laboratory Accreditation Program
NLLC .... National Labor Law Center (EA)
NLLC .... National Languages and Literacy Council [*Australia*]
NLLS .... Nonlinear Least Square [*Mathematics*]
NLLSQ .... Nonlinear Least Squares [*Computer program*]
NLLST .... National Lending Library for Science and Technology [*Later, BLL*] [*British*]
NL LT .... Net Laying Light (SAA)
NLLTF .... Night Low-Level Terrain-Following (SAUS)
NLM .... National Language Mediator

NLM .... National Library of Medicine [*Public Health Service*] [*Bethesda, MD*] [*Database producer*]
NLM .... National Library of Medicine, Bethesda, MD [*OCLC symbol*] (OCLC)
NLM .... Natural Language Mode [*Computer science*]
NLM .... Naval Ordnance Lab [*Maryland*] [*Seismograph station code, US Geological Survey*] [*Closed*] (SEIS)
NLM .... Nederlands Luchtvaart Maatschappij [*Airline*] [*Netherlands*]
NLM .... NetWare Loadable Module [*Computer science*] (DDC)
NLM .... Network Loadable Module (GAVI)
NLM .... New Library of Music [*A publication*]
NLM .... Noise Level Monitor (DMAA)
NLM .... Nonlinear Mapping (MCD)
NLM .... Nuclear Level Mixing [*Physics*]
NLMA .... National Lumber Manufacturers Association [*Later, NFPA*] (EA)
NLMA .... Northeastern Lumber Manufacturers Association
NLMBX .... Neub. & Berman Ltd. Maturity Bond Fund [*Mutual fund ticker symbol*] (SG)
NLMC .... National Latino Media Coalition [*Citizen's group*] (NTCM)
NLMC .... National League of Masonic Clubs (EA)
NLMC .... Nocturnal Leg Muscle Cramp [*Medicine*] (MELL)
NLMC .... Nordic Labor Market Committee (SAUS)
NLMC .... Nordic Labour Market Committee (EAIO)
NLMC .... North Lilly Mining Co. [*NASDAQ symbol*] (NQ)
NLMC .... North Lily Mining [*NASDAQ symbol*] (TTSB)
NLME .... Non-Linear Material Effect (PDAA)
NLMF .... National Labor-Management Foundation (EA)
NLMF .... Nonlinear Magnetic Field (SAUS)
NLMF .... Nucleus of Longitudinal Muscle Fiber
NLMFA .... No-Load Mutual Fund Association (EA)
NLMI .... Newfoundland and Labrador Marine Institute (SAUS)
NLMS .... Navigational Lane Marking System [*Navy*] (DOMA)
NLMS .... Navy Logistics Management School
NLMS .... Numerical Largeness of More Significant [*Statistics*]
NLMWT .... National Liberation Movement of Western Togoland
NLN .... National League for Nursing (EA)
NLN .... National Library Network
NLN .... National Lymphedema Network (SAUS)
NLN .... Navy Learning Network
NLN .... New Line Cinema (EFIS)
NLN .... New Lintex Minerals [*Vancouver Stock Exchange symbol*]
NLN .... No Longer Needed (AABC)
NLN .... Nordiska Lakemedelsnamnden [*Nordic Council on Medicines - NCM*] (EAIO)
NLN .... Northwest Missouri Library Network [*Library network*]
NLNA .... National Landscape Nurserymen's Association [*Later, NLA*] (EA)
NLNE .... National League for Nursing Education (DAVI)
NLnet .... [*The*] Newfoundland and Labrador Network [*Canada*] [*Computer science*] (TNIG)
NLNGNE ...... National League of Nursing Graduate Nursing Examination (GAGS)
NLNP .... National Library Network Program (AEPA)
NLNR .... Nonlinear (MSA)
NLNS .... New Lightweight Night Sight (INF)
NLO .... Nasolacrimal Occlusion [*Medicine*]
NLO .... Naval Liaison Officer
NLO .... No-Limit Order
NLO .... Non-Linear Operator (CCCA)
NLO .... Nonlinear Optics (IEEE)
NLO .... Non-Linear Optimizer (SAUS)
NLO .... Nonlocalized Orbital (SAUS)
NLob .... Long Beach Public Library, Long Beach, NY [*Library symbol*] [*Library of Congress*] (LCLS)
NLobBK .... Blackhealth Kindergarten School, Long Beach, NY [*Library symbol*] [*Library of Congress*] (LCLS)
NLobES .... East School, Long Beach, NY [*Library symbol*] [*Library of Congress*] (LCLS)
NLobH .... Long Beach Memorial Hospital, Long Beach, NY [*Library symbol*] [*Library of Congress*] (LCLS)
NLobJH .... Long Beach Junior High School, Long Beach, NY [*Library symbol*] [*Library of Congress*] (LCLS)
NLobLE .... Lido Elementary School, Long Beach, NY [*Library symbol*] [*Library of Congress*] (LCLS)
NLobLS .... Lindell Boulevard School, Long Beach, NY [*Library symbol*] [*Library of Congress*] (LCLS)
NLobM .... Long Beach Middle School, Long Beach, NY [*Library symbol*] [*Library of Congress*] (LCLS)
NLobMS ...... Magnolia School, Long Beach, NY [*Library symbol*] [*Library of Congress*] (LCLS)
NLobSH .... Long Beach Senior High School, Long Beach, NY [*Library symbol*] [*Library of Congress*] (LCLS)
NLobWE ...... West Elementary School, Long Beach, NY [*Library symbol*] [*Library of Congress*] (LCLS)
NLock .... Lockport Public Library, Lockport, NY [*Library symbol*] [*Library of Congress*] (LCLS)
NLockH .... Lockport Memorial Hospital, Doctor's Library, Lockport, NY [*Library symbol*] [*Library of Congress*] (LCLS)
NLockMt ...... Mount View Health Facility, Lockport, NY [*Library symbol*] [*Library of Congress*] (LCLS)
NLockNHi .... Niagara County Historical Society, Lockport, NY [*Library symbol*] [*Library of Congress*] (LCLS)
NLOGM .... Navy Liaison Office for Guided Missiles (MCD)
NLOMA .... National Lutheran Outdoors Ministry Association (EA)
NLOMTF ...... Non-Linear Optical Monomer Thin Films (SAUS)
NLON .... New London, Inc. (SAUS)
NLONTEVDET... New London Test and Evaluation Detachment [*Navy*]
NLOOC .... Non-Linear Optical Organic Crystals (SAUS)

NLOP	Nonlinear Optical Polymer
NLOrLanyard	Netherlands Orange Lanyard [*Military decoration*]
NLOS	Natural Language Operating System
NLOS	Nonline of Sight
NLOS-AT/AD	Nonline-of-Sight Antitank/Air Defense Vehicle [*Army*]
NLOS-CA	Non-Line-of-Sight-Combined Arms System [*INF*]
NLOS/IOE	Nonline-of-Sight / Internal Operator Equipment (DWSG)
NLOS-R	Non-Line-of-Sight-Rear [*Army*] (DOMA)
NLouvGS	Church of Jesus Christ of Latter-Day Saints, Genealogical Society Library, Albany New York Stake Branch, Loudonville, NY [*Library symbol*] [*Library of Congress*] (LCLS)
NLouvS	Siena College, Loudonville, NY [*Library symbol*] [*Library of Congress*] (LCLS)
NLowLH	Lewis County General Hospital, Medical Library, Lowville, NY [*Library symbol*] [*Library of Congress*] (LCLS)
NLp	Lake Placid Public Library, Lake Placid, NY [*Library symbol*] [*Library of Congress*] (LCLS)
NLP	Narodnoliberalna Partiia [*National Liberal Party*] [*Bulgaria*] [*Political party*] (PPE)
NLP	National Labour Party [*Sierra Leone*] [*Political party*] (EY)
NLP	National Land for People [*An association*] (EA)
NLP	National League of Postmasters of the United States
NLP	National Liberal Party [*Bermuda*] [*Political party*] (EY)
NLP	National Liberation Party [*Gambia*] [*Political party*] (PPW)
NLP	National Realty Ltd. [*AMEX symbol*] (SPSG)
NLP	Natl Realty L.P. [*AMEX symbol*] (TTSB)
NLP	Natural Language Parsing (IDAI)
NLP	Natural Language Processing [*Computer science*]
NLP	Natural Law Party [*Australia*] [*Political party*]
NLP	Neglected Language Program
NLP	Neighborhood Loan Program
NLP	Nelspruit [*South Africa*] [*Airport symbol*] (OAG)
NLP	Net Level Premium [*Insurance*]
nlp	Neuro-Linguistic Programmers (SAUS)
NLP	Neurolinguistic Programming
NLP	New Left Party [*Political party*] [*Australia*]
NLP	Nodular Liquifying Panniculitis [*Dermatology*] (DAVI)
NLP	No Light Perception [*Ophthalmology*]
NLP	Non-Linear Programming [*Computer science*] (VLIE)
NLP	Normal Light Perception [*Physiology*] (MAH)
NLP	Normal Link Pulse (SAUS)
NLPC	n-Laurylpyridinium Chloride [*Detergent*]
NLPCA	Nonlinear Principal Components Analysis (IDAI)
NLPGA	National LP-Gas Association (EA)
NLPID	Network Layer Protocol Identifier [*Computer science*] (VLIE)
NLPM	National League of Postmasters of the United States (EA)
NLPM	Newspaper Lines per Minute (DGA)
NLPNEF	National Licensed Practical Nurses Educational Foundation [*Defunct*] (EA)
NLPQ	Natural Language Processing System for Queuing Problems [*Computer science*] (PDAA)
NLPR	National Laboratory of Psychical Research [*British*]
NLPS	Natural Language Processing Segment [*Computer science*]
NLpSA	Lake Placid School of Art, Fine Arts Library, Lake Placid, NY [*Library symbol*] [*Library of Congress*] (LCLS)
NLpT	Tissue Culture Association, Lake Placid, NY [*Library symbol*] [*Library of Congress*] (LCLS)
NLPTL	National Lutheran Parent-Teacher League (EA)
NLQ	Natural Language Query [*Software*] [*Battelle Software Products Center*]
NLQ	Near Letter Quality [*Computer printer*]
NLQ	Nigeria Lawyer's Quarterly [*A publication*] (DLA)
NLQ	Nonlinear Quantization [*Telecommunications*] (NTCM)
NLQ	Not Letter Quality (NITA)
NLQP	Natural Language Query Processor (ACAE)
NLQR	Nigeria Law Quarterly Review [*A publication*] (DLA)
NLR	Nagpur Law Reports [*India*] [*A publication*] (DLA)
NLR	Natal Law Reports [*India*] [*A publication*] (DLA)
NLR	National Liquid Reserves Money Market Fund
NLR	National Research Laboratory [*Netherlands*] (GAVI)
NLR	NATO Liaison Representative (MCD)
NLp	Nearest Living Relative (SAUS)
NLR	Neodymium LASER Range-Finder
NLR	Net Liquidity Ratio (PDAA)
NLR	Newfoundland Law Reports [*A publication*] (DLA)
NLR	New Law Reports [*Ceylon*] [*A publication*] (DLA)
N-LR	New York State Library, Legislative Reference Library, Albany, NY [*Library symbol*] [*Library of Congress*] (LCLS)
NLR	Nigeria Law Reports [*A publication*] (DLA)
NLR	Noise Load Ratio
NLR	Nolan Resources Ltd. [*Vancouver Stock Exchange symbol*]
NLR	No Load Ratio (VLIE)
NLR	No-Load Ratio (SAUS)
NLR	Non-Linear Refraction
NLR	Nonlinear Regression [*Mathematics*]
NLR	Nonlinear Resistance (IDOE)
NLR	Nonlinear Resistive
NLR	Nonlinear Resistor [*Electronics*] (ECII)
NLR	North London Railway [*British*]
NLR	Nyasaland Law Reports [*A publication*] (DLA)
NLR	South African Law Reports, Natal Province Division [*1910-46*] [*A publication*] (DLA)
NLRA	National Labor Relations Act [*1935*]
NLRA	National Lakes and Rivers Association [*Defunct*] (EA)
NLRB	National Labor Relations Board [*Department of Labor*] [*Washington, DC*]
NLRB	National Labor Relations Board Decisions and Orders [*A publication*] (DLA)
NLRB Ann Rep	National Labor Relations Board Annual Report [*A publication*] (DLA)
NLRB Dec	National Labor Relations Board Decisions [*A publication*] (DLA)
NLRBP	National Labor Relations Board Professional Association
NLRBPA	National Labor Relations Board Professional Association (EA)
NLRBU	National Labor Relations Board Union (EA)
NLRCA	National Lilac Rabbit Club of America (EA)
NLRCCAP	National Legal Resource Center for Child Advocacy and Protection [*Later, ABACCL*] (EA)
NLREG	Non-Linear Regression (SAUS)
NI Res Men Health&Behav Sc	Newsletter for Research in Mental Health and Behavioral Sciences (SAUS)
NL Rev	Northeastern Law Review [*A publication*] (DLA)
NLRG	Narrow-Line Radio Galaxy
NLRG	Navy Long-Range Guidance
NLRI	Network Layer Reachability Information [*Computer science*] (VLIE)
NLRO	North Liberty Radio Observatory (SAUS)
NLROG	Navy Long-Range Objectives Group (DNAB)
NLR (OS)	Natal Law Reports, Old Series [*1867-72*] [*South Africa*] [*A publication*] (DLA)
NLRSS	Navy Long-Range Strategic Study
NLRU	Nordens Liberale og Radikale Ungdom [*Nordic Liberal and Radical Youth*] (EAIO)
NLS	Holland Schreiner International Air Training (SAUS)
NLS	Nassau Library System [*Library network*]
NLS	National Language Support [*Computer science*] (PCM)
NLS	National Launch System (ECON)
NLS	National Library of Scotland (NITA)
NLS	National Library Service for the Blind and Physically Handicapped [*Also, NLS /BPH*] [*Library of Congress*]
NLS	National Longitudinal Survey [*Statistics*]
NLS	National Longitudinal Surveys of Labor Market Experience [*Ohio State University*] [*Columbus*] [*Information service or system*] (IID)
NLS	Native Language System (VLIE)
NLS	Natural Law Society (EA)
NLS	Navigating Light System
NLS	Negative Lens Systems
NLS	Neodymium LASER System
NLS	Network Library System
NLS	Network License System [*Computer science*] (CIST)
NLS	New Launch System (SAUS)
NLS	New Least Square (PDAA)
NLS	New Least Squares (SAUS)
NLs	New Leftists (SAUS)
NLS	Node Logic Shelf (VLIE)
NLS	Noise Line State (SAUS)
NLS	No-Load Speed
NLS	No-Load Start
NLS	Non-Linear Least Squares [*Statistics*]
NLS	Nonlinear Smoothing
NLS	Non-Linear Systems (SAUS)
NLS	Nordic Language Secretariat [*See also SLN*] [*Norway*] (EAIO)
NLS	Nordiske Laererorganisationers Samrad [*Council of Nordic Teachers' Association*] [*Sweden*] (EAIO)
NLS	Normal Lymphocyte Supernatant (DB)
NLS	North Carolina Central University, School of Library Science, Durham, NC [*OCLC symbol*] (OCLC)
NLS	Nuclear Localization Signal [*Biochemistry*]
NLS	Nuclear Location Sequence [*Cytology*]
NLS	On-Line System [*Stanford Research Institute*] [*Computer science*]
NLSA	National Liquor Stores Association (EA)
NLSA	National Lithuanian Society of America (EA)
NLSA	National Locksmith Suppliers Association (EA)
NLSBA	National Lincoln Sheep Breeders' Association (EA)
NLS/BPH	National Library Service for the Blind and Physically Handicapped [*Also, NLS*] [*Library of Congress*] [*Computer science*] (IID)
NLSC	National Language Services Center (VLIE)
NLSC	National Logistics Supply Center [*Marine science*] (OSRA)
NLSC	Navy Lockheed Service Center
NLSC	Non-Locking Shift Character [*Computer science*] (VLIE)
NLSC	Northeastern Louisiana State College
NLSCS	National League for Separation of Church and State (EA)
NLSDAP	Non-Linear System Data Presentation [*Computer science*] (VLIE)
NLSF	National Life Share Foundation (EA)
NLSF	Navy Logistics Support Force (DOMA)
NLsH	Frederic R. Harris, Inc., Lake Success, NY [*Library symbol*] [*Library of Congress*] (LCLS)
NLSI	National Library of Science and Invention [*British*] (DIT)
NLS Inc	Non-Linear Systems, Inc. (SAUS)
NLSL	North Land Savings & Loan Association (SAUS)
NLSLS	National Library of Scotland Lending Services (NITA)
NLsM	Medical Society of the State of New York, Lake Success, NY [*Library symbol*] [*Library of Congress*] (LCLS)
NLSMA	National Lamp and Shade Manufacturers' Association (IAA)
NLSMA	National Longitudinal Study of Mathematical Abilities
NLSMB	National Live Stock and Meat Board (EA)
NLSO	Naval Legal Service Office (ACAE)
NLSP	Neighborhood Legal Services Program
NLSP	NetWare Link Services Protocol [*Novell, Inc.*] (PCM)
NLSPA	National Live Stock Producers Association (EA)

NLSPN.........	National List of Scientific Plant Names [*Department of Agriculture*] (IID)
NLSS	Navy Logistics Systems School
NLSS	New London Submarine School [*Navy*] (MCD)
NLSSA........	National Litigation Support Services Association (NTPA)
NLSST	Nonlinear Sea Surface Temperature (USDC)
NLSSTUF	Non-Linear System Statistical Utility Feature (SAUS)
NLST...........	Nonlisted Name [*Telecommunications*] (TEL)
NLSU	National League for Social Understanding (EA)
NLSY	National Longitudinal Study of Youth
NLSY	National Longitudinal Survey of Youth
NLT.............	Negative Line Transmission [*Noise limiter*] (IAA)
NLT.............	Net Long Ton
NLT.............	Newfoundland Labrador Air Transport Ltd. [*Canada*] [*ICAO designator*] (FAAC)
NLT.............	New Logic Technology (SAUS)
NLT.............	New London Training Unit [*Navy*]
NLT.............	Night Letter [*Telegraphic communications*]
NLT.............	Noise Limiter (IAA)
NLT.............	No Later Than (SAUS)
NLT.............	No Left Turn (SAUS)
NLT.............	Non Light-Tight (SAUS)
NLT.............	Non-Linear Time Sequence (ABAC)
NLT.............	Normal Lube-Oil Tank (MSA)
NLT.............	Normal Lymphocyte Transfer [*Immunochemistry*]
NLT.............	Not Later Than
NLT.............	Not Less Than
NLT.............	Not Lower Than (SAUS)
NLT.............	Nucleus Lateralis Tuberis (DMAA)
NLT.............	Nucleus Load Table (SAUS)
NLTA..........	National Lawn Tennis Association (WDAA)
NLTA..........	National League of Teachers' Associations [*Defunct*] (EA)
NLTC..........	National Livestock Tax Committee [*Later, NCA*] (EA)
NLTCDP	National Long-Term Care Channeling Demonstration Program [*Department of Health and Human Services*] (GFGA)
NLTE..........	Nonlocal Thermodynamic Equilibrium
NLTF...........	National Leather Trades Federation [*A union*] [*British*]
NLT-HP	New Logic Technology-High Performance (SAUS)
NLTI...........	Non-Linear Time-Invariant (SAUS)
NLTNIF	National Low-Temperature Neutron Irradiation Facility [*Oak Ridge, TN*] [*Department of Energy*] (GRD)
NLTRA........	National Land Title Reclamation Association (EA)
NLT Reaction...	Normal Lymphocyte Transfer Reaction (SAUS)
NLTS..........	Near Launch Tracking System
NLT-S	New Logic Technology-Slow (SAUS)
NLTU	New London Training Unit (SAUS)
NLTV..........	Non-Linear Time-Varying (SAUS)
NLU	Naval Field Liaison Unit (DNAB)
NLU	Normal Latch Up (COE)
NLUC	National Land Use Classification (PDAA)
NLUF	National LASER Users Facility [*Rochester, NY*] [*Department of Energy*] (GRD)
NLUPP	Northern Land Use Planning Program (SAUS)
NLUS	Navy League of the United States (EA)
NLUTS	National Labourers' Union Trade Society [*British*]
NLv	Locust Valley Public Library, Locust Valley, NY [*Library symbol*] [*Library of Congress*] (LCLS)
NLV.............	Narcissus Latent Virus
NLVA	National Licensed Victuallers Association [*British*] (DBA)
NLvBI..........	Bayville Intermediate School, Locust Valley, NY [*Library symbol*] [*Library of Congress*] (LCLS)
NLVF...........	North Las Vegas Facility (SAUS)
NLVF...........	Norway Agricultural Research Council (SAUS)
NLvHS	Locust Valley High School, Locust Valley, NY [*Library symbol*] [*Library of Congress*] (LCLS)
NLvI............	Locust Valley Intermediate School, Locust Valley, NY [*Library symbol*] [*Library of Congress*] (LCLS)
NLvMP........	A.M. MacArthur Primary School, Locust Valley, NY [*Library symbol*] [*Library of Congress*] (LCLS)
NLVP	NASA Launch Vehicle Planning Project (MCD)
NLVR	Nonlinear Vacuum Regulator Valve [*Automotive engineering*]
NLW............	National Lawyers Wives (EA)
NLW............	National Library of Wales (WDAA)
NLW............	National Library Week
NLW............	Nominal Line Width
NLW............	Nonlinear Wave (SAUS)
NLWF..........	Futuna/Pointe Vele [*Wallis and Futuna Islands*] [*ICAO location identifier*] (ICLI)
NLWM	Non-Linear Wave Mixing (SAUS)
NLWRA.......	National Land and Water Resources Audit (SAUS)
NLWRAAC....	National Land and Water Resources Audit Advisory Committee (SAUS)
NLWW	Wallis/Hihifo [*Wallis and Futuna Islands*] [*ICAO location identifier*] (ICLI)
NLX.............	NLX Resources, Inc. [*Toronto Stock Exchange symbol*]
NLY.............	Annaly Mortgage Mgmt [*NYSE symbol*] (SG)
NLY.............	Northerly
NLynAE........	Atlantic Avenue School, Lynbrook, NY [*Library symbol*] [*Library of Congress*] (LCLS)
NLynd	Yates Community Library, Lyndonville, NY [*Library symbol*] [*Library of Congress*] (LCLS)
NLynDE........	Davidson Avenue Elementary School, Lynbrook, NY [*Library symbol*] [*Library of Congress*] (LCLS)
NLyndHi......	Lyndonville Historical Society, Lyndonville, NY [*Library symbol*] [*Library of Congress*] (LCLS)
NLynHS........	Lynbrook High School, Lynbrook NY [*Library symbol*] [*Library of Congress*] (LCLS)
NLynME.......	Marion Street Elementary School, Lynbrook, NY [*Library symbol*] [*Library of Congress*] (LCLS)
NLynNM.......	North Middle School, Lynbrook, NY [*Library symbol*] [*Library of Congress*] (LCLS)
NLynSM.......	Lynbrook South Middle School, Lynbrook, NY [*Library symbol*] [*Library of Congress*] (LCLS)
NLynWPE....	Waverly Park Elementary School, Lynbrook, NY [*Library symbol*] [*Library of Congress*] (LCLS)
nm---	Gulf of Mexico [*MARC geographic area code*] [*Library of Congress*] (LCCP)
NM.............	Mt. Cook Airlines [*ICAO designator*] (AD)
NM.............	Nachmittag [*Afternoon*] [*German*]
NM.............	Nanomemory (IAA)
NM.............	Nano Meter (ACAE)
NM.............	Nanometer (DIPS)
nm.............	Nanometer [*One billionth of a meter*]
nM.............	Nanomole [*One billionth of a mole*]
NM.............	Narrow Market [*Investment term*]
NM.............	Nationalist Movement (EA)
NM.............	National Magazine Co. Ltd. [*Publisher*] [*British*]
NM.............	National Match
NM.............	National Media Corp. [*NYSE symbol*] (SPSG)
NM.............	National Monument (GNE)
NM.............	National Motor Volunteers [*British military*] (DMA)
NM.............	Nations Ministries (EA)
NM.............	Natl Media Corp. [*NYSE symbol*] (TTSB)
NM.............	Natriuretic Material [*Physiology*]
NM.............	Naturally Occurring Mutants
nm.............	Nautical Mile (MILB)
NM.............	Nautical Mile [*6,080 feet*]
NM.............	Naval Mission (AFIT)
NM.............	Navigation Multiplexer [*Navy*] (CAAL)
NM.............	Navy Mines (MCD)
NM.............	Near Match (MCD)
nm.............	Near-Metacentric [*Botany*]
NM.............	Near Mint [*Condition*] [*Numismatics, deltiology, etc.*]
NM.............	Negro Male
NM.............	Neiman-Marcus
NM.............	Neomycin [*Medicine*] (MELL)
NM.............	Neonatal Meningitis [*Medicine*] (MELL)
NM.............	Netherlands Museum [*Later, HHT*] (EA)
NM.............	Net Imports [*Economics*]
NM.............	Network Management (MLOA)
NM.............	Network Manager (MCD)
NM.............	Neuromotor [*Neurology*] (DAVI)
NM.............	Neuromuscular
NM.............	Nevermind (SAUS)
NM.............	Newly Molded
NM.............	New Material [*FAR clauses*] (AAGC)
NM.............	New Measurement
NM.............	New Mexico [*Postal code*]
Nm.............	New Mexico State Library, Santa Fe, NM [*Library symbol*] [*Library of Congress*] (LCLS)
NM.............	New Mexico Supreme Court Reports [*A publication*] (DLA)
NM.............	New Mexico Territorial Court (DLA)
NM.............	New Moon [*Moon phase*]
Nm.............	Newton-Meter (SAUS)
N/m.............	Newton per Meter (or Metre) (SAUS)
N-M.............	New York State Library, Medical Library, Albany, NY [*Library symbol*] [*Library of Congress*] (LCLS)
NM.............	Nickeloid Metals (SAUS)
Nm.............	Nicotiana mesophilia [*Tobacco*]
NM.............	Nictitating Membrane [*Animal anatomy*]
NM.............	Nigeria Museum (SAUS)
NM.............	Night and morning (DAVI)
NM.............	Night Message
NM.............	Nilsson Model (SAUS)
NM.............	Nitrogen Mustard [*Also, HN, M, MBA*] [*Antineoplastic drug, war-gas base*]
NM.............	Nitromethane [*Organic chemistry*]
NM.............	Noble Metal (SAUS)
NM.............	Nocte et Mane [*Night and Morning*] [*Pharmacy*]
NM.............	Nocturnal Myoclonus [*Medicine*] (MELL)
NM.............	Nodular Melanoma [*Oncology*]
NM.............	Nodular Mixed Lymphoma [*Oncology*] (DAVI)
NM.............	Noise Margin (SAUS)
NM.............	Noise Meter (MSA)
N/m.............	No Mark (EBF)
NM.............	No Mark
NM.............	No Match (SAUS)
NM.............	No Measurement (SAUS)
NM.............	Nomenclature (SAUS)
NM.............	Nomen Masculinam [*Masculine Name*] [*Latin*] (ROG)
NM.............	No Message
NM.............	None Minted [*Numismatic term*]
NM.............	Nonmagnetic (IAA)
NM.............	Nonmalignant [*Medicine*] (MELL)
NM.............	Nonmember (SAUS)
NM.............	Nonmetal (SAUS)
NM.............	Nonmetallic
NM.............	Nonmotile [*Microbiology*]
NM.............	Nonwhite Male

NM...............	Nordiska Metallarbetaresekretariatet [*Nordic Metalworkers Secretariat - NMS*] (EAIO)
NM...............	Normal Mode (SAUS)
NM...............	Normetadrenaline [*Biochemistry*] (DAVI)
NM...............	Northeastern Mortgage Co., Inc. (SAUS)
NM...............	Notice to Mariner
N/M.............	Not Marked [*Business term*]
NM...............	Not Married
NM...............	Not Meaningful
NM...............	Not Measurable [*or Measured*]
NM...............	Not Measured (SAUS)
NM...............	Not Mentioned (SAUS)
n/m.............	Not Mentioned [*Medicine*]
NM...............	Noun Modifier [*Linguistics*]
NM...............	Nuclear Magnetic
NM...............	Nuclear Magnetism (SAUS)
nm...............	Nuclear Magneton (ABAC)
NM...............	Nuclear Magnetron (MSA)
NM...............	Nuclear Materials (SAUS)
NM...............	Nuclear Measurement (IAA)
NM...............	Nuclear Medicine
NM...............	Nuclear Membrane (DB)
NM...............	Nuclear Model (SAUS)
NM...............	Null Matrix (SAUS)
NM...............	Numbering Machine (SAUS)
NM...............	Number Module (SAUS)
NM...............	Number of Matrices (SAUS)
Nm...............	Numbers [*Old Testament book*]
NM...............	Numerical Machining (SAUS)
NM...............	Numeric Move (SAUS)
NM...............	Nutmeg (ADA)
NM...............	Nutrient Medium (SAUS)
NM...............	Nux Moschata [*Nutmeg*] [*Pharmacology*] (ROG)
N/m²	Newtons per Square Meter [*Pascals*] (IDOE)
NmA.............	Albuquerque Public Library, Albuquerque, NM [*Library symbol*] [*Library of Congress*] (LCLS)
NMA.............	Miami, FL [*Location identifier*] [*FAA*] (FAAL)
NMA.............	Minute Men of America (NADA)
NMA.............	Naphthalenemethylamine [*Reagent*] [*Organic chemistry*]
NMA.............	Nashville Music Association [*Later, NEA*] (EA)
NMA.............	National Malaria Association (DAVI)
NMA.............	National Management Association [*Dayton, OH*] (EA)
NMA.............	National Management Award [*GAMC*]
NMA.............	National Marina Association [*Defunct*] (EA)
NMA.............	National Maritime Alliance (NTPA)
NMA.............	National Maritime Authority [*Australia*]
NMA.............	National Meat Association [*Formerly, NIMPA*] (EA)
NMA.............	National Medical Association (EA)
NMA.............	National Microfilm Association [*Later, National Micrographics Association, now AIIM*] [*Trade association*]
NMA.............	National Microform Association (NITA)
NMA.............	National Micrographics Association [*Later, AIIM*] [*Trade association*] (EA)
NMA.............	National Midwives Association (EA)
NMA.............	National Military Authority (NATG)
NMA.............	National Mime Association [*Later, NMTA*] (EA)
NMA.............	National Mining Association (NTPA)
NMA.............	National Motorists Association (EA)
NMA.............	National Museum of Antiquities in Scotland
NMA.............	National Music Academy [*Australia*]
NMA.............	National Mustang Association (EA)
NMA.............	NATO Military Authorities (NATG)
NMA.............	Natural Marketing Association [*Woodland Hills, CA*] (EA)
NMA.............	Navy Mutual Aid Association (EA)
NMA.............	Needle Makers Association [*British*] (BI)
NMA.............	Negligee Manufacturers Association [*Later, IAMA*]
NMA.............	Netherlands Military Administration [*World War II*]
NMA.............	Neue Mozart-Ausgabe [*A publication*]
NMA.............	Neurogenic Muscular Atrophy [*Medicine*]
NMA.............	New Music Articles [*A publication*]
NMA.............	Nicaragua Medical Aid (EA)
NMA.............	N-Methylaspartate [*Organic chemistry*]
NMA.............	N-Methylaspartic Acid [*An amino acid*]
NMA.............	N-Methylolacrylamide [*Organic chemistry*]
NMA.............	Nobeyama Millimeter Array (SAUS)
NMA.............	Noma Industries Ltd. [*Toronto Stock Exchange symbol*]
NMA.............	Non-Marine Association [*Lloyd's Underwriters*] (AIA)
NMA.............	Nonmass Analysed (SAUS)
NMA.............	Nonmass Analyzed [*Photovoltaic energy systems*]
NMA.............	Nonmedical Attendant (AABC)
NMA.............	Nonprofit Management Association (EA)
NMA.............	Nonresonant Magnetic Amplifier
NMA.............	Normal Method of Acquisition (MCD)
NMA.............	Northwest Mining Association (EA)
NMA.............	Nuclear Materials Accountability (SAUS)
NMA.............	Nuveen Muni Advantage Fd [*NYSE symbol*] (TTSB)
NMA.............	Nuveen Municipal Advantage Fund [*NYSE symbol*] (SPSG)
NMA.............	University of Albuquerque, Albuquerque, NM [*OCLC symbol*] (OCLC)
NMa.............	Wead Library, Malone, NY [*Library symbol*] [*Library of Congress*] (LCLS)
NMAA..........	National Machine Accountants Association [*Later, DPMA*]
NMAA..........	National Metal Awning Association [*Defunct*] (EA)
NMAA..........	National Mobilization Against AIDS [*Acquired Immune Deficiency Syndrome*] (EA)
NMAA..........	National Multimedia Association of America (DDC)
NMAA..........	National Museum of African Art [*Smithsonian Institution*]
NMAA..........	Navy Mutual Aid Association
NMAA..........	Nursing Mothers' Association of Australia
NmAAc........	Albuquerque Academy, Albuquerque, NM [*Library symbol*] [*Library of Congress*] (LCLS)
NmAACF.....	ACF Industries, Inc., Albuquerque, NM [*Library symbol*] [*Library of Congress*] (LCLS)
NmAAF.......	United States Air Force, Weapons Laboratory, Kirtland Air Force Base, Albuquerque, NM [*Library symbol*] [*Library of Congress*] (LCLS)
NmAAM......	United States Army, Medical Library, Sandia Base, Albuquerque, NM [*Library symbol*] [*Library of Congress*] (LCLS)
NMAA Newsletter...	Nursing Mothers Association of Australia. Newsletter (SAUS)
NMAB	National Market Advisory Board [*SEC*]
NMAB	National Materials Advisory Board (EA)
N-MAb	Neutralizing Monoclonal Antibody [*Immunology*]
NMAB	N-Monochloro(amino)butyric Acid [*Organic chemistry*]
NmABD........	BDM Corp., Albuquerque, NM [*Library symbol*] [*Library of Congress*] (LCLS)
NMAC	National Medical Audiovisual Center [*of the National Library of Medicine*] [*LHNCBC*] [*Absorbed by*] (EA)
NMAC	National Minority AIDS [*Acquired Immune Deficiency Syndrome*] Council (EA)
NMAC	Naval Missile and Astronautics Center
NMAC	Near Midair Collision
NMAC	Nissan Motor Acceptance Corp.
NMAC	Nuclear Materials Accounting and Control
NMACS	Nuclear Materials Accounting Cost System (SAUS)
NMACT	Nuclear Materials Accounting Control Team [*British*] (NUCP)
NmADAS	United States Defense Atomic Support Agency, Sandia Base, Albuquerque, NM [*Library symbol*] [*Library of Congress*] (LCLS)
NmA-EP	Albuquerque Public Library, Ernie Pyle Memorial Branch, Albuquerque, NM [*Library symbol*] [*Library of Congress*] (LCLS)
NMAF..........	National Medical Association Foundation [*Defunct*] (EA)
NMAFA	National Museum of African Art [*Smithsonian Institution*] (GFGA)
NMAG	Nonmagnetic (MSA)
N Mag Ca ...	New Magistrates' Cases [*England*] [*A publication*] (DLA)
NmAGen	New Mexico Genealogical Society, Inc., Albuquerque, NM [*Library symbol*] [*Library of Congress*] (LCLS)
NM Ag Exp...	New Mexico. Agricultural Experiment Station. Publications (SAUS)
NmAGS	Church of Jesus Christ of Latter-Day Saints, Genealogical Society Library, Albuquerque Branch, Albuquerque, NM [*Library symbol*] [*Library of Congress*] (LCLS)
NMah	Mahopac Library Association, Mahopac, NY [*Library symbol*] [*Library of Congress*] (LCLS)
NmAHS	Honeywell Sperry Inc., Defense System Division, Albuquerque, NM [*Library symbol*] [*Library of Congress*] (LCLS)
NMAHSTC....	National Museum of American History, Science, Technology, and Culture [*Smithsonian Institution*]
NmAI	Alamogordo Public Library, Alamogordo, NM [*Library symbol*] [*Library of Congress*] (LCLS)
NmAL..........	Lovelace Foundation for Medical Education and Research, Albuquerque, NM [*Library symbol*] [*Library of Congress*] (LCLS)
NMAL..........	Northeast Marine Animal Lifeline
NmA-LG......	Albuquerque Public Library, Los Griegos Branch, Albuquerque, NM [*Library symbol*] [*Library of Congress*] (LCLS)
NMalv	Malverne Public Library, Malverne, NY [*Library symbol*] [*Library of Congress*] (LCLS)
NMalvDE.....	Davison Elementary School, Malverne, NY [*Library symbol*] [*Library of Congress*] (LCLS)
NMalvHM	Howard T. Herber Middle School, Malverne, NY [*Library symbol*] [*Library of Congress*] (LCLS)
NMalvLE......	Lindner Elementary School, Malverne, NY [*Library symbol*] [*Library of Congress*] (LCLS)
NMalvSH	Malverne Senior High School, Malverne, NY [*Library symbol*] [*Library of Congress*] (LCLS)
NMam..........	Mamaroneck Free Library, Mamaroneck, NY [*Library symbol*] [*Library of Congress*] (LCLS)
NmAM	Montessori School, Albuquerque, NM [*Library symbol*] [*Library of Congress*] (LCLS)
NMamL........	Mamaroneck Free Library, Mamaroneck, NY [*Library symbol*] [*Library of Congress*] (LCLS)
NM & S	Bureau of Medicine and Surgery Publications [*Navy*]
NM&SA........	National Moving & Storage Association [*MTMC*] (TAG)
NManh........	Manhasset Public Library, Manhasset, NY [*Library symbol*] [*Library of Congress*] (LCLS)
NManhH	North Shore Hospital, Manhasset, NY [*Library symbol*] [*Library of Congress*] (LCLS)
NManhJH....	Manhasset Junior High School, Manhasset, NY [*Library symbol*] [*Library of Congress*] (LCLS)
NManhJSH...	Manhasset Junior-Senior High School, Manhasset, NY [*Library symbol*] [*Library of Congress*] (LCLS)
NManhM.....	Manhasset Medical Center Hospital, Manhasset, NY [*Library symbol*] [*Library of Congress*] (LCLS)
NManhME....	Munsey Park Elementary School, Manhasset, NY [*Library symbol*] [*Library of Congress*] (LCLS)
NManhSE....	Shelter Rock Elementary School, Manhasset, NY [*Library symbol*] [*Library of Congress*] (LCLS)
NManhSH ...	Manhasset Senior High School, Manhasset, NY [*Library symbol*] [*Library of Congress*] (LCLS)
NManhSM....	Saint Mary's Boys High School, Manhasset, NY [*Library symbol*] [*Library of Congress*] (LCLS)
NMANX	Neub. & Berman Manhattan Fund [*Mutual fund ticker symbol*] (SG)
NMAP	Navy Military Assistance Programs

NmA-PP....... Albuquerque Public Library, Prospect Park Branch, Albuquerque, NM [*Library symbol*] [*Library of Congress*] (LCLS)

NM App .... New Mexico Court of Appeals (DLA)

NMAQCR...... New Mexico Air Quality Control Region (SAUS)

NMAQD........ New Mexico Air Quality District (SAUS)

NmAr .... Artesia Public Library, Artesia, NM [*Library symbol*] [*Library of Congress*] (LCLS)

NMar .... Marcellus Free Library, Marcellus, NY [*Library symbol*] [*Library of Congress*] (LCLS)

Nm-Ar .... New Mexico State Records Center and Archives, Santa Fe, NM [*Library symbol*] [*Library of Congress*] (LCLS)

NMARC .... Navy and Marine Corps Acquisition Review Committee [*Terminated, 1975*] (MCD)

NMarcP....... Marcy Psychiatric Center, Marcy, NY [*Library symbol*] [*Library of Congress*] (LCLS)

NmArP....... Artesia Public Library, Artesia, NM [*Library symbol*] [*Library of Congress*] (LCLS)

NMas.......... Henry H. Warren Memorial Library, Massena (SAUS)

NMAS .... National Map Accuracy Standards (PDAA)

NMAS .... National Marine Advisory Service [*National Oceanic and Atmospheric Administration*] (MSC)

NMAS .... Norwegian Metrology and Accreditation Service (SAUS)

NmAS .... Sandia Corp., Albuquerque, NM [*Library symbol*] [*Library of Congress*] (LCLS)

NMasL......... Massena Public Library, Massena, NY [*Library symbol*] [*Library of Congress*] (LCLS)

NMasMH...... Massena Memorial Hospital, Massena, NY [*Library symbol*] [*Library of Congress*] (LCLS)

NMass .... Massapequa Public Library, Massapequa, NY [*Library symbol*] [*Library of Congress*] (LCLS)

NMassAJ ..... J. Lewis Ames Junior High School, Massapequa, NY [*Library symbol*] [*Library of Congress*] (LCLS)

NMassBE..... Birch Elementary School, Massapequa, NY [*Library symbol*] [*Library of Congress*] (LCLS)

NMassBH..... Berner High School, Massapequa, NY [*Library symbol*] [*Library of Congress*] (LCLS)

NMassELE ... East Lake Elementary School, Massapequa, NY [*Library symbol*] [*Library of Congress*] (LCLS)

NMassFE ..... Fairfield Elementary School, Massapequa, NY [*Library symbol*] [*Library of Congress*] (LCLS)

NMassHE..... Hawthorn Elementary School, Massapequa, NY [*Library symbol*] [*Library of Congress*] (LCLS)

NMassHS.... Masspequa High School, Massapequa, NY [*Library symbol*] [*Library of Congress*] (LCLS)

NMassLE ..... Lockhart Elementary School, Massapequa, NY [*Library symbol*] [*Library of Congress*] (LCLS)

NmassMJ..... J.P. McKenna Junior High School, Massapequa, NY [*Library symbol*] [*Library of Congress*] (LCLS)

NMassSE..... Charles E. Schwarting Elementary School, Massapequa, NY [*Library symbol*] [*Library of Congress*] (LCLS)

NMassUE..... Unqua Elementary School, Massapequa, NY [*Library symbol*] [*Library of Congress*] (LCLS)

NMat.......... Mattituck Free Library, Mattituck, NY [*Library symbol*] [*Library of Congress*] (LCLS)

NMAT.......... Night-Time Marine Air Temperature

N-Materials... Nuclear Materials (SAUS)

NMATP .... Navy Military Assistance Training Program (NG)

Nmatrn .... Nematron Corp. [*Associated Press*] (SAG)

NMAU .... Naval Medical Administration Unit (DNAB)

NmAU .... University of Albuquerque, Albuquerque, NM [*Library symbol*] [*Library of Congress*] (LCLS)

NmAVA .... United States Veterans Administration Hospital, Albuquerque, NM [*Library symbol*] [*Library of Congress*] (LCLS)

NMAX .... Nonwireline Multiple-Access Communications Exchange System (PDAA)

NMb............. Mastics-Moriches-Shirley Community Library, Mastic Beach, NY [*Library symbol*] [*Library of Congress*] (LCLS)

NMB............. Namib Air (Pty) Ltd. [*Namibia*] [*ICAO designator*] (FAAC)

NMB............. National Marine Board [*British*] [*World War II*]

NMB............. National Maritime Board

NMB............. National Meat Brokers [*Australia*]

NMB............. National Mediation Board [*Department of Labor*]

NMB............. National Metric Board

NMB............. National Motel Brokers (EA)

NMB............. National Mutual Benefit [*Madison, WI*] (EA)

NMB............. Naval Meteorological Branch [*British*]

NMB............. Naval Minecraft Base

NMB............. Naval Model Basin

NMB............. Neuromuscular Blockade [*Medicine*]

NMB............. New Methylene Blue [*Organic chemistry*]

NMB............. Nippon Miniature Bearing (SAUS)

NMB............. Nippon Miniature Bearing Corp. (EFIS)

NMB............. Noise, Measurement Buoy

NMB............. No Military Branch

NMB............. Non-Maturing Balance

NMB............. Not Member of a Branch

nmb .... Number Book

NMBA .... National Marine Bankers Association [*Chicago, IL*] (EA)

NMBA .... Neuromuscular Blocking Agent

NMBA .... (Nitrosomethylamino) Butyric Acid [*Organic chemistry*]

NMBC .... National Minority Business Campaign [*Later, NMBD*] (EA)

NMBC .... National Minority Business Council [*New York, NY*] (EA)

NMbCH .... Bayview Community Hospital, Mastic Beach, NY [*Library symbol*] [*Library of Congress*] (LCLS)

NMBD .... National Minority Business Directories [*Minneapolis, MN*] (EA)

NmBeN .... Northwestern Regional Library, Belen, NM [*Library symbol*] [*Library of Congress*] (LCLS)

NMBF........... National Manufacturers of Beverage Flavors [*Defunct*] (EA)

NMBHF .... Naismith Memorial Basketball Hall of Fame (EA)

NMB Journal... Nigerian Marketing Board Journal (SAUS)

NMBMMR .... New Mexico Bureau of Mines and Mineral Resources [*New Mexico Institute of Mining and Technology*] [*Research center*] (RCD)

NMbr .... Millbrook Library, Millbrook, NY [*Library symbol*] [*Library of Congress*] (LCLS)

NMBR .... NATO Military Basic Requirement (MCD)

NMbrB .... Bennett College, Millbrook, NY [*Library symbol*] [*Library of Congress*] (LCLS)

NMBS .... Nationale Maatschappij der Belgische Spoorwegen [*Railway*] [*Belgium*] (EY)

NMBS .... Nimbus CD International, Inc. [*NASDAQ symbol*] (SAG)

NMBS .... Nimbus CD Intl. [*NASDAQ symbol*] (TTSB)

NMBT........... New Main Battle Tank [*Military*] (RDA)

NMBT........... New Milford Bank & Trust Co. [*NASDAQ symbol*] (CTT)

NMBT........... New Milford BK & Tr Conn [*NASDAQ symbol*] (TTSB)

NM Bur Mines Miner Resour Hydrol Rep... New Mexico. Bureau of Mines and Mineral Resources Hydrologic Report (SAUS)

NM Bur Mines Miner Resour Prog Rep... New Mexico. Bureau of Mines and Mineral Resources Report (SAUS)

NmC............ Carlsbad Public Library, Carlsbad, NM [*Library symbol*] [*Library of Congress*] (LCLS)

NMC............ Marine Corps Publications [*Later, NAVMC*]

NMC............ Meredith College, Raleigh, NC [*OCLC symbol*] (OCLC)

NMC............ Nail Manufacturers Council (EA)

NMC............ Natal Medical Corps [*British military*] (DMA)

NMC............ National Magazine Co.

NMC............ National Mail Centers, Inc. [*Telecommunications service*] (TSSD)

NMC............ National Manpower Council

NMC............ National Marine Center (USDC)

NMC............ National Maritime Council [*Defunct*] (EA)

NMC............ National Mastitis Council

NMC............ National Medical Care

NMC............ National Memorials Committee [*Australia*]

NMC............ National Message Center [*Overland Park, KS*] (TSSD)

NMC............ National Meteorological Center [*National Oceanic and Atmospheric Administration*] [*Information service or system*] (IID)

NMC............ National Migrant Clearinghouse (OICC)

NMC............ National Military Council [*Surinam*] (PD)

NMC............ National Missionary Council [*Australia*]

NMC............ National Motorsports Committee (EA)

NMC............ National Mouse Club [*British*] (BI)

NMC............ National Museum of Canada

NMC............ National Music Camp [*Interlochen, MI*]

NMC............ National Music Council (EA)

NMC............ NATO Manual on Codification (NATG)

NMC............ Naval Material Command [*Formerly, NMSE*]

NMC............ Naval Medical Center [*Bethesda, MD*]

NMC............ Naval Memorandum Correction (NVT)

NMC............ Naval Missile Center [*Point Mugu, CA*]

NMC............ Naval Mission Center (KSC)

NMC............ NAVA [*National Audio-Visual Association*] Materials Council (EA)

NMC............ Navigation Map Computer

NMC............ Navy Mail Clerk

NMC............ Navy Memorandum Correction

NMC............ Nebraska Motor Carriers Association, Petroleum Carriers' Conference, Inc., OmahaNE [*STAC*]

NMC............ Net Matchable Cost

NMC............ Network Management Center [*Computer science*]

NMC............ Network Management Computer (SAUS)

NMC............ Network Management Console [*Industrial Networking, Inc.*]

NMC............ Network Measurement Center

NMC............ Neuromuscular Control [*Medicine*] (DMAA)

NMC............ New Muon Collaboration (SAUS)

NMC............ Nine Mile Canyon [*California*] [*Seismograph station code, US Geological Survey*] (SEIS)

NMC............ Noble Metal Catalyst [*Automotive engineering*]

NMC............ No More Credit [*Business term*] (ADA)

NMC............ Non-Marginal Check (SAUS)

NMC............ Nonmetallic Cable (SAUS)

NMC............ Non-Metropolitan Counties [*British*]

NMC............ Non-Mission Capable [*Military*] (INF)

NMC............ Nonmotor Condition [*Medicine*] (DMAA)

NMC............ Northern Mining Corp. (SAUS)

NMC............ Northern Montana College [*Havre*]

NMC............ Northwestern Michigan College [*Traverse City*]

NMC............ Not Mission Capable (MCD)

NMC............ NSSDC Master Catalog (SAUS)

NMC............ Nuclear Material Control (SAUS)

NMC............ Nuclear Material Convention (SAUS)

NMC............ Nuclear Metal Conference

NMC............ Nucleus Reticularis Magnocellularis [*Medicine*] (DMAA)

NMC............ Numac Energy [*AMEX symbol*] (SPSG)

NMC............ Numac Oil & Gas Ltd. (SAUS)

NMC............ Numeric (SAUS)

NMC............ Numerical Modelling Center (SAUS)

NMC............ Nurse Managed Center (MEDA)

NMC............ Nursery Marketing Council (EA)

NMC............ Nursing Mothers Counsel [*An association*] (EA)

NMC............ Public Archives of Canada, National Map Collection [*UTLAS symbol*]

NMC............ San Francisco, CA [*Location identifier*] [*FAA*] (FAAL)

NMCA .... National Marble Club of America (EA)

NMCA	National Meat Canners Association (EA)
NMCA	National Military Command Authority (NVT)
NMCA	National Mossberg Collectors Association (EA)
NMCA	National Motorcycle Commuter Association [Defunct] (EA)
NMCA	National Musclecar Association (EA)
NMCA	Navy Mothers' Clubs of America (EA)
N-McAb..........	Neutralizing Monoclonal Antibody [Immunology]
NMCAC	National Motor Carrier Advisory Committee [MTMC] (TAG)
NM CAMP....	University Division, National Music Camp, Interlochen (SAUS)
NMC&A	Nuclear Material Control and Accountability (SAUS)
NMCB	National Metric Conversion Board (NADA)
NMCB	National Munitions Control Board [World War II]
NMCB	National Museum of Canada Bulletin [A publication]
NMCB	Navy Mobile Construction Battalion (CINC)
NMCC	National Management Career Curriculum [Office of Personnel Management] (GFGA)
NMCC	National Manpower Coordinating Committee [Department of Labor]
NMCC	National Military Command Center [DoD]
NMCC	Navy-Marine Corps Council [Defunct] (EA)
NMCC	Network Management Control Center [Telecommunications]
NMCC	Nonmyeloid Cell Content (DB)
NMCC	Northeast-Midwest Congressional Coalition (EA)
NMCCDDA ...	National Model Cities Community Development Directors Association [Later, NCDA] (EA)
NMCCIS	NATO Military Command and Control and Information System (NATG)
NMCC/MC....	NMCC/Message Center (SAUS)
NMCCS	Nuclear Materials Control Computer System (SAUS)
NMCDA	National Model Cities Directors Association [Later, NCDA] (EA)
NMCEC	Navy-Marine Corps Exhibit Center
NMCES	National Medical Care Expenditures Survey [Department of Health and Human Services] (GFGA)
NMCGB	National Music Council of Great Britain (EAIO)
NMCGRF......	Navy-Marine Corps-Coast Guard Residence Foundation
NMCHC..........	National Maternal and Child Health Clearinghouse (EA)
NMCI	National Multicultural Institute (EA)
NmCiN	Northeastern Regional Library, Cimarron, NM [Library symbol] [Library of Congress] (LCLS)
NMCIRD........	Naval Material Command Industrial Resources Detachment (DNAB)
NMCJS	Naval Member, Canadian Joint Staff
NmCl	Clovis-Carver Public Library, Clovis, NM [Library symbol] [Library of Congress] (LCLS)
NMCL..........	Navy Missile Center Laboratory (KSC)
NmCla	Albert W. Thompson Memorial Library, Clayton, NM [Library symbol] [Library of Congress] (LCLS)
NMCLA	Bethesda Military Librarians Group [Library network]
NmClA	United States Air Force, Cannon Air Force Base, Clovis, NM [Library symbol] [Library of Congress] (LCLS)
NmClaP	Albert W. Thompson Memorial Library, Clayton, NM [Library symbol] [Library of Congress] (LCLS)
NMCLK	Navy Mail Clerk
NMCM	Navy and Marine Corps Medal [Military decoration]
NMCM	Noble Metals Compatibility Melters (SAUS)
NMCM	Not Mission Capable, Maintenance (NVT)
NMCMS	Not Mission Capable Maintenance Scheduled (SAUS)
NMCMU	Not Mission Capable Maintenance Unscheduled (SAUS)
NMCNCR......	Naval Medical Command National Capital Region (ACAE)
NMCO	Navy Material Cataloging Office
NMCOM.......	Naval Material Command [Formerly, NMSE] (MCD)
NmCP	United States Potash Co., Carlsbad, NM [Library symbol] [Library of Congress] (LCLS)
NMCPP	New Mexico Center for Particle Physics (SAUS)
NMCRB........	Navy Military Construction Review Board
NMCRC	Navy-Marine Corps Reserve Center (NVT)
NMCRS	Navy-Marine Corps Relief Society
NMCRTC	Navy and Marine Corps Reserve Training Center
NMCS	National Medic-Card [Commercial firm] (EA)
NMCS	National Medicinal Chemistry Symposium
NMCS	National Military Command System
NMCS	Navy Mine Countermeasures Station (MUGU)
NMCS	Nickel Manganese Chromium Steel (SAUS)
NMCS	Not Mission Capable, Supply (MCD)
NMCS	Nuclear Materials Control System (IEEE)
NMCSA	Navy Material Command Support Activity
NMC SEB	New Media Center, School of Education Building (SAUS)
NMCSHA	National Morgan Cutting and Stock Horse Association (EA)
NMCSS	National Military Command System Standards (AFM)
NMCSSC......	National Military Command System Support Center (AABC)
NMCUES	National Medical Care Utilization and Expenditure Survey [Department of Health and Human Services] [A publication] (DHSM)
NmD	Deming Public Library, Deming, NM [Library symbol] [Library of Congress] (LCLS)
NMD	NASA Management Delegations (MCD)
NMD	National Mapping Division (SAUS)
NMD	National Missile Defense [DoD]
NMD	National Museum of Dentistry (SAUS)
NMD	Naval Mine Depot
NMD	Navy Marine Diesel Fuel
NMD	Neosynephrine/Mydriacil Dilation [Medicine] (MELL)
NMD	Netmed, Inc. [AMEX symbol] (SAG)
NMD	NeuroMotor Disease (SAUS)
NMD	Neuromuscular Disease [Medicine] (MELL)
NMD	Neuromyodysplasia [Medicine] (MELL)
NMD	Nonmonetary Determination [Unemployment insurance] (OICC)
NMD	Normal Muscle Development (DAVI)
NMD	Norwegian Maritime Directorate (RIMS)
NMD	Nuclear Medicine Department (SAUS)
NMD	Nu-Media Industry International [Vancouver Stock Exchange symbol]
NMD	Nutritional Muscular Dystrophy (SAUS)
NMD	Nutrition Monitoring Division [Department of Agriculture] (GFGA)
NMDA	National Marine Distributors Association (EA)
NMDA	National Medical and Dental Association (EA)
NMDA	National Metal Decorators Association (EA)
NMDA	National Midas Dealers Association (EA)
NMDA	National Motorcycle Dealers Association [Later, NMRA] (EA)
NMDA	National Motorcycle Dismantelers Association (EA)
NMDA	National Motor Drivers' Association [A union] [British]
NMDA	N-Methyl-D-Aspartate [Medicine] (MELL)
NMDA	N-Methyl-D-Aspartic Acid [An amino acid]
NMDA	Nonresonant Magnetic Deflection Amplifier
NMDAR	N-Methyl-D-Aspartic Acid Receptor [Neurochemistry]
nMDC..........	Native Macrophage-Derived Chemokine [Immunology]
NMDC..........	Nonmagnetic Drill Collar [Well drilling technology]
NMDCEF	National Medico-Dental Conference for the Evaluation of Fluoridation [Later, Medical-Dental Committee on Evaluation of Fluoridation] (EA)
NM Dep Game Fish Bull...	New Mexico. Department of Game and Fish Bulletin (SAUS)
NMDF	Navy Management Data File (DNAB)
NMDG..........	N-Methyl-D-Glucamine [Biochemistry]
NMD/GBR	National Missile Defense-Ground Based RADAR [Army] (RDA)
NMDIS	National Marine Data and Information Service [China] [Marine science] (OSRA)
NMDIS	National Music and Disability Information Service [British]
NMDL	Naval Mine Defense Laboratory [Naval Facilities Engineering Command] [Panama City, FL]
NMDL	Navy Management Data List (NG)
NMDL	Navy Material Data List
NMDP	National Marrow Donor Program [Department of Health and Human Services]
NMDP	Neomenthyldiphenylphosphine [Organic chemistry]
NMDPI	Nuveen Maryland Premium Income Municipal Fund [Associated Press] (SAG)
NMDR	Nuclear Magnetic Double Resonance
NMDRP.......	National Military Discharge Review Project (EA)
NMDS	Naval Mine Disposal School
NMDS	Network Management Directory Services (NITA)
NMDS	New Music Distribution Service (EA)
NMDS	Nonmetric Multidimensional Scaling [Statistics]
NMDS	Nursing Minimum Data Set (SAUS)
NMDSC	Naval Medical Data Service Center (DNAB)
NMDSG.......	Naval Material Data Systems Group (DNAB)
NMDU	Newspaper and Mail Deliverers Union of New York and Vicinity (EA)
NMDY	Nonresonant Magnetic Deflection Yoke
NMDY	Normandy Oil & Gas Co. (SAUS)
NMDZ	NATO Maritime Defense Zone (NATG)
NmE	Espanola Public Library, Espanola, NM [Library symbol] [Library of Congress] (LCLS)
NME	National Marriage Encounter (EA)
NME	National Military Establishment [Designated Department of Defense, 1949]
NME	Naval Material Establishment (DOMA)
NME	Necrolytic Migratory Erythema [Dermatology]
NME	Network Management Entity (MLOA)
NME	Newly Maturing Economy [Business term]
NME	New Molecular Entity [Chemistry]
NME	New Musical Express [A publication] (WDAA)
NME	Nightmute [Alaska] [Airport symbol] (OAG)
NME	Nissan Motorsports Europe
NME	Noise-Measuring Equipment
NME	Nonlinear Mesoscopic Elastic
NME	Non-Market Economy (JAGO)
NME	Nonsupervisory Manufacturing Engineer
NME	Norton Mobile Essentials [Symantec]
NMEA	National Marine Educators Association (EA)
NMEA	National Marine Electronics Association (EA)
NMEBA	National Marine Engineers' Beneficial Association (EA)
NMEC..........	National Metric Education Center [Western Michigan University]
NMEC..........	Nuclear Material Control Center (NUCP)
NMED	Inmed Corp. (SAUS)
NMed..........	Lee-Whedon Memorial Library, Medina, NY [Library symbol] [Library of Congress] (LCLS)
NMED	New Mexico Environmental Department
NMEDA	National Mobility Equipment Dealers Association (NTPA)
NMedH	Medina Memorial Hospital, Medina, NY [Library symbol] [Library of Congress] (LCLS)
NMedia........	National Media Corp. [Associated Press] (SAG)
N-Medicine...	Nuclear Medicine (SAUS)
N-Med Tech...	Nuclear-Medicine Technician (SAUS)
NMEF..........	Naval Mine Engineering Facility
NMEFC.......	National Marine Environmental Forecasting Center [China] [Marine science] (OSRA)
NMEG..........	Nisei Mass Evacuation Group
NMEIA	National Machine Embellishment Instructors and Artists (NTPA)
NMEIA	National Machine Embroidery Instructors Association (EA)
NMEIAA	National Machine Embroidery Instructors Association of America (EA)
NMEIB	New Mexico Environmental Improvement Board (EA)
NMEL..........	Navy Marine Engineering Laboratory [Later, David W. Taylor Naval Ship Research and Development Center] (KSC)

NMEL	Nuclear Mechano-Electronic Laboratory (SAUS)
NMeIA	Airborne Institute Laboratories, Melville, NY [Library symbol] [Library of Congress] (LCLS)
NMeIH	Holzmacher, McLendon & Murrell, Inc., Melville, NY [Library symbol] [Library of Congress] (LCLS)
NMeIL	Litcom Library, Melville, NY [Library symbol] [Library of Congress] (LCLS)
NMeIS	Suffolk State School, Melville, NY [Library symbol] [Library of Congress] (LCLS)
NMeISC	Sagamore Children's Center, Melville, NY [Library symbol] [Library of Congress] (LCLS)
NmEN	Northern Regional Library, Espanola, NM [Library symbol] [Library of Congress] (LCLS)
NMERI	New Mexico Engineering Research Institute [University of New Mexico] [Research center] (RCD)
NMerk	Merrick Public Library, Merrick, NY [Library symbol] [Library of Congress] (LCLS)
NMerkBE	Birch Elementary School, Merrick, NY [Library symbol] [Library of Congress] (LCLS)
NMerk CE	Chatterton Elementary School, Merrick, NY [Library symbol] [Library of Congress] (LCLS)
NMerkCH	Sanford H. Calhoun High School, Merrick, NY [Library symbol] [Library of Congress] (LCLS)
NMerkF	Five Towns College, Merrick, NY [Library symbol] [Library of Congress] (LCLS)
NMerkLE	Lakeside Elementary School, Merrick, NY [Library symbol] [Library of Congress] (LCLS)
NMerkMJ	Merrick Avenue Junior High School, Merrick, NY [Library symbol] [Library of Congress] (LCLS)
NMES	National Medical Expenditure Survey [Department of Health and Human Services] (GFGA)
NMES	Naval Marine Engineering Station
NMET	Naval Mobile Environmental Team (COE)
NMEU	Naval Material Evaluation Unit (DNAB)
N Mex	New Mexico (SHCU)
NMEX	New Mexico
N Mex Highlands U	New Mexico Highlands University (GAGS)
N Mex Inst M&T	New Mexico Institute of Mining and Technology (GAGS)
NMexMilDist	New Mexico Military District (SAUS)
N Mex State Engineer Office Tech Rept	New Mexico State Engineer Office. Technical Report (SAUS)
N Mex St U	New Mexico State University (GAGS)
NMF	Boston, MA [Location identifier] [FAA] (FAAL)
NmF	Farmington Public Library, Farmington, NM [Library symbol] [Library of Congress] (LCLS)
NMF	National Marfan Foundation (EA)
NMF	National Medical Fellowships (EA)
NMF	National Migraine Foundation [Later, National Headache Foundation - NHF] (EA)
NMF	National Motor Freight Traffic Association Inc., Agent, Washington DC [STAC]
NMF	National Myoclonus Foundation [Defunct] (EA)
NMF	Naval Missile Facility [Also, NAVMISFAC]
NMF	Navy Management Fund
NMF	Network Management Forum [Computer science] (VLIE)
NMF	Neutron Multiplier Facility (SAUS)
NMF	New Master File
NMF	N-Methylformamide [Antineoplastic compound]
NMF	N-Methyl Fucosamine [Organic chemistry]
NMF	Nonmaster File [Computer science]
NMF	Nonmember Firm [of NYSE]
NMF	Nonmigrating Fraction [of spermatozoa] [Medicine]
NMF	Non-Negative Matrix Factorization
NMF	Nonprofit Mailers Federation (EA)
NMF	Nonuniform Magnetic Field
NMF	Nordiska Maskinbefalsfederationen [Nordic Engineer Officers' Federation - NEOF] (EAIO)
NMF	Normal Mode Functions (SAUS)
NMFA	National Military Family Association (EA)
NMFC	National Magazine and Film Carriers (NTPA)
NMFC	National Magazine, Book, and Film Carriers Conference (NTPA)
NMFC	National Motor Freight Classification
NMFCR	National Motor Freight Classification Rules
NMFEC	National Medical Foundation for Eye Care [Later, AAO] (EA)
NMFECC	National Magnetic Fusion Energy Computer Center [Department of Energy] (MCD)
NmFGS	Church of Jesus Christ of Latter-Day Saints, Genealogical Society Library, Farmington Branch, Farmington, NM [Library symbol] [Library of Congress] (LCLS)
NMFHAWAREA	Naval Missile Facility, Hawaiian Area (MUGU)
NMFHG	National Master Farm Homemakers Guild (EA)
NMFI	National Master Facility Inventory [Department of Health and Human Services] (GFGA)
NmfL	National Microfilms Ltd., Dublin, Ireland [Library symbol] [Library of Congress] (LCLS)
NMFMA	National Mutual Fund Managers Association [Defunct] (EA)
NMFP	Nuclear Mean Free Path (SAUS)
NMFPA	Naval Missile Facility, Point Arguello
NMFPM	Naval Missile Facility, Point Mugu [California] (SAA)
NMFR	NAPALM [National ADP Program for AMC Logistics Management] Master File Record
NMFRL	Naval Medical Field Research Laboratory [Camp Lejeune, NC]
NmFs	Fort Sumner Public Library, Fort Sumner, NM [Library symbol] [Library of Congress] (LCLS)

NMFS	National Marine Fisheries Service [Formerly, Bureau of Commercial Fisheries] [National Oceanic and Atmospheric Administration] [Washington, DC]
NMFS	National Medical Financial Services Corp. [NASDAQ symbol] (SAG)
NMFS	National Mortality Followback Survey [National Center for Health Statistics]
NMFS	Natl Medical Finl Svcs [NASDAQ symbol] (TTSB)
NMFS	Night Missile Flash Simulator (MCD)
NMFS	Nuclear Materials Faclities Stabilization (SAUS)
NMFT	New Material Flight Tests
NMFTA	National Motor Freight Traffic Association [Alexandria, VA] (EA)
NMFWA	National Military Fish and Wildlife Association (EA)
NMFWA	Neuromuscular Foundation of Western Australia
NmG	Gallup Public Library, Gallup, NM [Library symbol] [Library of Congress] (LCLS)
NMG	Navy Metrication Group (DNAB)
NMG	Navy Military Government
NMG	Neiman-Marcus Group [NYSE symbol] (SPSG)
NM (G)	New Mexico Reports (Gildersleeve) [1852-89] [A publication] (DLA)
NMG	New Orleans, LA [Location identifier] [FAA] (FAAL)
NMG	Numerical Master Geometry [System]
NMG	San Miguel [Panama] [Airport symbol] (OAG)
NMGA	National Military Guidance Association (EA)
NMGC	National Marriage Guidance Council [British] (ILCA)
NMGC	NeoMagic Corp. [NASDAQ symbol] (SG)
NMGCS	National Milk Glass Collectors Society
NM Geol Soc Field Conf Guideb	New Mexico Geological Society. Feld Conference Guidebook (SAUS)
NmGr	Mother Whiteside Memorial Library, Grants, NM [Library symbol] [Library of Congress] (LCLS)
NMGRA	National Museum and Gallery Registration Association (EA)
NMG System	Numerical Master Geometry System (SAUS)
NMh	Library of Poultney Bigelow, Malden-On-Hudson, NY [Library symbol] [Library of Congress] (LCLS)
NMH	Nautical Miles per Hour
NMH	New Mexico Highlands [New Mexico] [Seismograph station code, US Geological Survey] (SEIS)
NMH	New Mexico Highlands University, Las Vegas, NM [OCLC symbol] (OCLC)
NMH	N-Methylhydroxylamine [Organic chemistry]
NMH	No-Mar Hammer (SAUS)
NMH	Northwestern Memorial Hospital (SAUS)
NmHa	Hatch Public Library, Hatch, NM [Library symbol] [Library of Congress] (LCLS)
NMHA	National Mental Health Association (EA)
NMHA	National Minority Health Association (EA)
NMHA	National Mobile Home Association (EA)
NmHARL	Aeromedical Library, 6571st Aeromedical Research Laboratory, Holloman AFB, NM [Library symbol] [Library of Congress] (LCLS)
NMHC	National Materials Handling Centre [Cranfield Institute of Technology] [British] (CB)
NMHC	National Multi Housing Council (EA)
NMHC	Nonmethane Hydrocarbons [Organic chemistry]
NMHCA	National Mental Health Consumers' Association (EA)
NMHCC	National Managed Health Care Congress (HGEN)
NMHCE	Non-Methane Hydrocarbon Equivalent (EEVL)
NMHCSHC	National Mental Health Consumer Self-Help Clearinghouse (EA)
NMHF	National Manufactured Housing Federation (EA)
NMHFA	National Manufactured Housing Finance Association [Defunct] (EA)
NmHi	Historical Society of New Mexico, Santa Fe (SAUS)
NmHi	Historical Society of New Mexico, Santa Fe, NM [Library symbol] [Library of Congress] (LCLS)
NMHID	National Mental Health Institute on Deafness (SAUS)
NmHo	Hobbs Public Library, Hobbs, NM [Library symbol] [Library of Congress] (LCLS)
NmHoC	New Mexico Junior College, Hobbs, NM [Library symbol] [Library of Congress] (LCLS)
NmHORA	United States Air Force, Office of Research Analyses, Technical Library, Holloman AFB, Albuquerque, NM [Library symbol] [Library of Congress] (LCLS)
NmHoSW	College of the Southwest, Hobbs, NM [Library symbol] [Library of Congress] (LCLS)
NM/HR	Nautical Mile/Hour (MCD)
NMHS	National Maritime Historical Society (EA)
NMHS	National Mental Health Strategy (SAUS)
NMHS	National Meteorological and Hydrological Service (SAUS)
NMHS	Not-Made-Here Syndrome (VLIE)
NMHSPE	New Mexico High School Proficiency Examination (EDAC)
NMHT	National Museum of History and Technology [Later, National Museum of American History] (GRD)
NMHU	New Mexico Highlands University [Las Vegas, NM]
NMHWMS	New Mexico Hazardous Waste Management Society (SAUS)
NMI	Minot State College, Minot, ND [OCLC symbol] (OCLC)
NMI	NASA Management Instruction (KSC)
NMI	NASA Management Issuance (MCD)
NMI	National Macaroni Institute (EA)
NMI	National Maglev Initiative [Department of Transportation]
NMI	National Maintenance Index (IAA)
NMI	National Manpower Institute [Later, NIWL] (EA)
NMI	National Maritime Institute [British]
NMI	Native Method Invocation (VLIE)
nmi	Nautical Mile (NAKS)
NMI	Nautical Mile
NMI	New Material Introductory [Team] [Military]
NMI	New Millennium Interferometer (SAUS)

NMI............	New Model Introduction (VLIE)
NMI............	Nissan Motorsports International [*Automotive competition*]
NMI............	No Meaningful Improvement (MELL)
nmi............	No Middle Initial (SHCU)
NMI............	No Middle Initial
NMI............	Nonmajor Item (MCD)
NMI............	Non Maskable Interrupt (SAUS)
NMI............	Nonmasking [*or Nonmaskable*] Interrupt
NMI............	Northeast-Midwest Institute (EA)
NMI............	Northwest Microfilm, Inc. [*Information service or system*] (IID)
NMI............	Nuclear Magnetic Imaging
NMI............	Nuclear Materials Information (SAUS)
NMI............	Nuclear Metals, Inc.
NMI............	Nuveen Municipal Income Fund [*NYSE symbol*] (SPSG)
NMi............	Thrall Library, Middletown, NY [*Library symbol*] [*Library of Congress*] (LCLS)
NMIA..........	National Military Intelligence Association (EA)
NMIAPO......	New Montreal International Airport Project [*Canada*]
NMIB	New Material Introductory Briefing [*Military*] (MCD)
NMIBT........	New Material Introductory Briefing Team [*Military*] (MCD)
NMIC	National Maritime Intelligence Center [*Created in 1992 from intelligence activities in the Washington, D.C., area*] [*Navy*] (DOMA)
NMIC	National Meat Industry Council (EA)
NMIC	National Military Information Center
NMIC	National Military Intelligence Center (CCCA)
NMIC	National Missile Industry Conference (AAG)
NMIC	Not Made in Canada [*Business term*]
NMICA	New Mexico Independent College Association (SAUS)
NMICC	National Military Intelligence Collection Center (SAUS)
NMICSS......	NMIC [*National Military Information Center*] Support System (MCD)
NMIDA	N-Methyliminodiacetic Acid [*Organic chemistry*]
NMidp........	Middleport Free Library, Middleport, NY [*Library symbol*] [*Library of Congress*] (LCLS)
NMidpF.......	FMC Corp., Niagara Chemical Division, R and D Library, Middleport, NY [*Library symbol*] [*Library of Congress*] (LCLS)
NMIHS........	National Maternal and Infant Health Survey [*Department of Health and Human Services*] (GFGA)
NMil..........	Millerton Free Library, Millerton, NY [*Library symbol*] [*Library of Congress*] (LCLS)
NMIL..........	New Materiel Introductory Letter [*Army*] (AABC)
NMILA	NASA Merritt Island Launch Area (SAA)
NMilBc.......	New Milford Savings Bank [*Associated Press*] (SAG)
NMilt	Sarah Hull Hallock Free Library, Milton, NY [*Library symbol*] [*Library of Congress*] (LCLS)
NMIMT........	New Mexico Institute of Mining and Technology [*Socorro*]
NMin..........	Mineola Memorial Library, Mineola, NY [*Library symbol*] [*Library of Congress*] (LCLS)
NMinH	Nassau Hospital, Mineola, NY [*Library symbol*] [*Library of Congress*] (LCLS)
NMinHe	Hampton Elementary School, Mineola, NY [*Library symbol*] [*Library of Congress*] (LCLS)
NMinJE.......	Jackson Avenue Elementary School, Mineola, NY [*Library symbol*] [*Library of Congress*] (LCLS)
NMinME......	Meadow Elementary School, Mineola, NY [*Library symbol*] [*Library of Congress*] (LCLS)
NMinMJ......	Mineola Junior High School, Mineola, NY [*Library symbol*] [*Library of Congress*] (LCLS)
NMinMS	Mineola Middle School, Mineola, NY [*Library symbol*] [*Library of Congress*] (LCLS)
NMinNCL	Nassau County Law Library, Mineola, NY [*Library symbol*] [*Library of Congress*] (LCLS)
NMiOC........	Orange County Community College, Middletown, NY [*Library symbol*] [*Library of Congress*] (LCLS)
NMIP	New Major Investment Program [*Australia*]
NMIPC........	National Military Intelligence Production Center (SAUS)
NMIQI........	Nuveen Michigan Quality Income Municipal Fund [*Associated Press*] (SAG)
NMiR	Ramapo Catskill Library System, Middletown, NY [*Library symbol*] [*Library of Congress*] (LCLS)
NMIRO........	Naval Material Industrial Resources Office
NMIS	National Military Indications System (MCD)
NMIS	Naval Manpower Information System
NMIS	Newspapers Mutual Insurance Society Ltd. [*British*] (BI)
NMIS	Nuclear Materials Information System
NMIS	Nuclear Materials Inventory System (NRCH)
NMIS	Nursing Management Information System (DMAA)
NMISC........	National Military Intelligence Support Center (SAUS)
NMISMAN....	Navy Manpower Information System Manual (DNAB)
NMIST	National Military Intelligence Support Team [*Defense Intelligence Agency*] (DOMA)
NMIT..........	New Materiel Introductory Team [*Army*] (AABC)
NMIT..........	Nuclear Material Item Transfer (SAUS)
NMITC	Navy and Marine Corps Intelligence Training Center (DOMA)
NMIU	Nordic Meat Industry Union (EA)
NMIW	Northwest Marine Iron Works (AAGC)
NmJ...........	Jal Public Library, Jal, NM [*Library symbol*] [*Library of Congress*] (LCLS)
NMJ...........	Neuromuscular injection (SAUS)
NMJ...........	Neuromuscular Junction [*Anatomy*]
NM (J)	New Mexico Reports (Johnson) [*A publication*] (DLA)
NMJ...........	Northern Masonic Jurisdiction (SAUS)
NMJC..........	National Men's Judo Championships [*British*]
NMJC..........	Northeastern Mississippi Junior College [*Senatobia*]
NMJC..........	Northwest Mississippi Junior College
NMJL..........	National Mah Jongg League (EA)
NMK..........	Cape May, NJ [*Location identifier*] [*FAA*] (FAAL)
NMK..........	Niagara Mohawk Power Corp. [*NYSE symbol*] (SPSG)
NMK..........	Niagara Mohawk Pwr [*NYSE symbol*] (TTSB)
NMKL.........	Nordisk Metodikkommitte for Livsmedel [*Nordic Committee on Food Analysis*] (EAIO)
NMKPr........	Niagara Moh Pwr Adj Rt A Pfd [*NYSE symbol*] (TTSB)
NMKPrA......	Niag Moh Pwr 3.40% Pfd [*NYSE symbol*] (TTSB)
NMKPrB......	Niag Moh Pwr 3.60% Pfd [*NYSE symbol*] (TTSB)
NMKPrC......	Niag Moh Pwr 3.90% Pfd [*NYSE symbol*] (TTSB)
NMKPrD......	Niag Moh Pwr 4.10% Pfd [*NYSE symbol*] (TTSB)
NMKPrE......	Niag Moh Pwr 4.85% Pfd [*NYSE symbol*] (TTSB)
NMKPrG......	Niag Moh Pwr 5.25% Pfd [*NYSE symbol*] (TTSB)
NMKPrI.......	Niag Moh Pwr 7.72% Pfd [*NYSE symbol*] (TTSB)
NMKPrK......	Niagara Mohawk Pwr Adj C Pfd [*NYSE symbol*] (TTSB)
NMKPrM.....	Niagara Moh Pwr 9.50% Pfd [*NYSE symbol*] (TTSB)
NML..........	Narragansett Marine Laboratory [*University of Rhode Island*]
NML..........	National Magnet Laboratory
NML..........	National Measurement Laboratory [*Gaithersburg, MD*] [*National Institute of Standards and Technology*] (GRD)
NML..........	National Media Laboratory (SAUS)
NML..........	National Medical Library (DAVI)
NML..........	National Metrology Laboratory (ACII)
NML..........	National Municipal League
NML..........	National Music League (EA)
NML..........	Native Machine Language [*Computer science*]
NML..........	Nautical Mile
NML..........	Naval Materials Management (SAA)
NML..........	Naval Multiple Launcher (SAUS)
NML..........	Navy Management List (AFIT)
NML..........	Network Management Layer [*Computer science*] (VLIE)
NML..........	New Mathematical Library [*School Mathematics Study Group*]
Nm-L	New Mexico Supreme Court Law Library, Santa Fe, NM [*Library symbol*] [*Library of Congress*] (LCLS)
NML..........	Nodular Mixed Lymphoma [*Oncology*] (DAVI)
NML..........	No Mail Label
NML..........	No Man's Land [*Medical slang, cardiology*]
NML..........	Nonocclusive Mesenteric Infarction [*Medicine*] (MELL)
NML..........	Normal
NML..........	Normal Male Infant (MELL)
NML..........	Northwestern Mutual Life (SAUS)
NML..........	Nuclear Magnetic Logging (IAA)
NML..........	Nuclear Magnetism Log (PDAA)
NML..........	University of New Mexico, School of Law, Albuquerque, NM [*OCLC symbol*] (OCLC)
NmLa.........	Mesa Public Library, Los Alamos, NM [*Library symbol*] [*Library of Congress*] (LCLS)
NMLA.........	New Mexico Library Association (SAUS)
NmLaS.......	Los Alamos Scientific Laboratory, Los Alamos, NM [*Library symbol*] [*Library of Congress*] (LCLS)
NmLaS-M	Los Alamos Scientific Laboratory, Medical Library, Los Alamos, NM [*Library symbol*] [*Library of Congress*] (LCLS)
NmLaU	University of New Mexico, Los Alamos, NM [*Library symbol*] [*Library of Congress*] (LCLS)
NMLC.........	Normalized Mass Loss Coefficient [*Nuclear energy*] (NUCP)
NmLc.........	Thomas Branigan Memorial Library, Las Cruces, NM [*Library symbol*] [*Library of Congress*] (LCLS)
NMLCF.......	Nuclear Measurements & Logging Calibration (SAUS)
NmLcU.......	New Mexico State University, Las Cruces, NM [*Library symbol*] [*Library of Congress*] (LCLS)
NMLO	National Media Liaison Officer
NmLor	Lordsburg-Hidalgo Public Library, Lordsburg, NM [*Library symbol*] [*Library of Congress*] (LCLS)
NmLov........	Lovington Public Library, Lovington, NM [*Library symbol*] [*Library of Congress*] (LCLS)
NmLovS.......	Southeastern Regional Library Center, Lovington, NM [*Library symbol*] [*Library of Congress*] (LCLS)
NMLR	Nigerian Monthly Law Reports [*1964-65*] [*A publication*] (DLA)
NMLRA	National Muzzle Loading Rifle Association (EA)
NMLS.........	National Microwave Landing System (MCD)
NMLT.........	New Material Laboratory Tests
NmLv.........	Las Vegas Carnegie Library, Las Vegas, NM [*Library symbol*] [*Library of Congress*] (LCLS)
NmLvH.......	New Mexico Highlands University, Las Vegas, NM [*Library symbol*] [*Library of Congress*] (LCLS)
NmLvSH	New Mexico State Hospital, Las Vegas, NM [*Library symbol*] [*Library of Congress*] (LCLS)
NMLZMMAX...	Normalize by Matrix Maximum (SAUS)
NMM..........	Meridian, MS [*Location identifier*] [*FAA*] (FAAL)
NMM..........	NASA Management Manual
NMM..........	National Maritime Museum [*British*]
NMM..........	NetWare Management Map [*Computer science*] (VLIE)
NMM..........	Network Measurement Machine [*Computer Network*] (IAA)
NMM..........	Neutron Magnetic Moment
NMM..........	New Madrid [*Missouri*] [*Seismograph station code, US Geological Survey*] [*Closed*] (SEIS)
NMM..........	New Mexico Military Institute, Roswell, NM [*OCLC symbol*] (OCLC)
N-mm.........	Newton-Millimeter (SAUS)
NMM..........	N-Methylmorpholine [*Organic chemistry*]
NMM..........	Nodular Malignant Melanoma [*Medicine*] (DB)
NMM..........	Noisemont Mining (SAUS)
NMM..........	Nonmetal Material (SAUS)
NMM..........	Nonne-Milroy-Meige [*Syndrome*] [*Medicine*] (DB)
NMM..........	Norsemont Mining [*Vancouver Stock Exchange symbol*]
NMM..........	Nuclear Magnetic Moment (SAUS)

NMM............ Nuclear Materials Management
NMMA .... National Macaroni Manufacturers Association [*Later, NPA*] (EA)
NMMA .... National Maintenance Management Association [*Defunct*] (EA)
NMMA .... National Marine Manufacturers Association (EA)
NMMC .... National Adult Education Clearinghouse (NAEC)/National Multimedia Center for Adult Education [*Information service or system*] [*Defunct*] (IID)
NMMC .... National Marina Manufacturers Consortium [*Defunct*] (EA)
NMMD .... Nuclear Materials Management Department (SAUS)
NmMeB........ Bent-Mescalero School Library, Mescalero, NM [*Library symbol*] [*Library of Congress*] (LCLS)
NMMFO .... Navy Maintenance Management Field Office
NMMFO(W)... Navy Maintenance Management Field Office (West) (DNAB)
NMMHMO.... Network and Mixed Model Health Maintenance Organization [*Insurance*] (WYGK)
NMMHOF..... National Mobile/Manufactured Home Owners Foundation [*Later, NFMHO*] (EA)
NMMI.......... New Mexico Military Institute [*Roswell*] (MCD)
NMML.......... National Marine Mammal Laboratory [*National Marine Fisheries Service*]
NMMLC .... New Moon Matchbox and Label Club (EA)
NMMM........ Navy Maintenance and Material Management System [*Also known as MMM, NMMMS, 3M*]
NMMMS ..... Navy Maintenance and Material Management System [*Also known as MMM, NMMM, 3M*]
NMMPS ...... National Military Message Processor System (CCCA)
NmMS .... Montezuma Seminary, Montezuma, NM [*Library symbol*] [*Library of Congress*] (LCLS)
NMMS .... Navy Mast Mounted Sight (SAUS)
NMMSA .... NASA Microgravity Materials Science Assessment Task Force (SAUS)
NMMSB .... Non-Nuclear Munitions Safety Board
NMMSN .... National Marine Mammal Stranding Network (EA)
NMMSS .... Nuclear Materials Management and Safeguards System (NRCH)
NMMW .... Near Millimeter Wave System [*Telecommunications*] (TEL)
N/mmy .... Newton per Square Millimeter (SAUS)
NMN .... Nicotinamide-Mononucleotide [*Biochemistry*]
NMN .... No Middle Name
NMN .... Normetanephrine [*Also, Methylnorepinephrine*] [*Biochemistry*]
NMN .... NRD Mining Ltd. [*Vancouver Stock Exchange symbol*]
NMNA .... National Male Nurse Association [*Later, AAMN*] (EA)
NMNA .... New Mexico Nurses Association (SAUS)
NMNase ...... Nicotinamidenucleotide Phosphoribohydrolase [*An enzyme*]
NMND .... Naval Magazine and Net Depot
NMNFO .... Navy Maintenance Field Office (NVT)
NMNH .... National Museum of National History
NMNH .... National Museum of Natural History [*Smithsonian Institution*]
NMNH .... Nicotinamide Mononucleotide, Reduced Form (SAUS)
NMNRU .... National Medical Neuropsychiatric Research Unit (DMAA)
NMNRU .... Naval Medical Neuropsychiatric Research Unit
NMNS .... National Museum of Natural Sciences [*National Museums of Canada*] [*Research center*] (RCD)
NMO .... Long Beach, CA [*Location identifier*] [*FAA*] (FAAL)
NMO .... National Medical Organisation (ACII)
NMO .... National Military Objectives (SAUS)
NMO .... National Mobility Office [*British*]
NMO .... Navy Management Office
NMO .... Nitroso-Morpholin (SAUS)
NMO .... N-Methylmorpholine N-Oxide [*Organic chemistry*]
NMO .... Noble Mines & Oils Ltd. [*Toronto Stock Exchange symbol*]
NMO .... Normal Manual Operation (KSC)
NMO .... Normal Mode Operation
NMO .... Normal Move-Out (SAUS)
NMO .... Norman [*Oklahoma*] [*Seismograph station code, US Geological Survey*] [*Closed*] (SEIS)
NMO .... Number of Critical Micro-Operations [*Computer science*] (MHDI)
NMO .... Nuveen Municipal Market Opportunities [*NYSE symbol*] (SPSG)
NMO .... Nuveen Muni Mkt Oppt [*NYSE symbol*] (TTSB)
NMOA .... National Mail Order Association [*Los Angeles, CA*] (EA)
NMOC .... New Man On Campus (SAUS)
NMOC .... Non-Methane Organic Compound [*Environmental chemistry*]
NMOCOD ..... [*The*] Nonmateriel Objectives Coordinating Document [*Army*] (RDA)
NMOG .... Non-Methane Organic Gas [*Organic chemistry*]
nmol .... Nanomole [*One billionth of a mole*] (MAE)
NMoN .... New York Ocean Science Laboratory, Montauk, NY [*Library symbol*] [*Library of Congress*] (LCLS)
NMONA....... National Mail Order Nurserymen's Association [*Later, MAN*] (EA)
NMontr .... Hendrick Hudson Free Library, Montrose, NY [*Library symbol*] [*Library of Congress*] (LCLS)
NMontrVA .... United States Veterans Administration Hospital, Montrose, NY [*Library symbol*] [*Library of Congress*] (LCLS)
NMOP .... National Mission Operating Procedures (AAG)
NMOPI .... Nuveen Missouri Premium Income Municipal Fund [*Associated Press*] (SAG)
NMOR .... Nitrosomorpholine [*Also, NNM*] [*Organic chemistry*]
NMOS .... Negative Channel Metal-Oxide Semiconductor
NMOS .... Network Mission and Operations Support
NMOS .... Nonvolatile Metal-Oxide Semiconductor (MCD)
NMOSAW..... Naval and Military Order of the Spanish-American War (EA)
NMOS/SOS... Nitrite Metal Oxide Silicon/Silicon on Sapphire (SAUS)
NMOST .... Nitrite Metal Oxide Silicon Transistor (SAUS)
NMP............ National Maintenance Point [*Military*] (AABC)
NMP............ National Meter Programming (NRCH)
NMP............ National Military Command System Master Plan (SAUS)
NMP............ National Military Park

NMP............ National Municipal Policy [*Environmental Protection Agency*] (EPA)
NMP............ Naval Management Program
NMP............ Naval Medical Publication
NMP............ Naval Message Processing (MCD)
NMP............ Navigational Microfilm Projector
NMP............ Navy Manning Plan (NVT)
NMP............ Nederlands Middenstands Partij [*Netherlands Middle Class Party*] [*Political party*] (PPE)
NMP............ Net Material Product [*Economics*]
NMP............ Network Management Protocol [*Computer science*] (TNIG)
NMP............ Network Modem Program (SAUS)
NM/P........... New Material/Process (MCD)
NMP............ New Millenium Program (SAUS)
NMP............ N-Methylphenazium [*Organic chemistry*]
NMP............ N-Methylphthalimide [*Organic chemistry*]
NMP............ N-Methylpyrrolidone [*Organic chemistry*]
NMP............ Normal Menstrual Period [*Gynecology*] (MAE)
NMP............ Not Machine Pressed
NMP............ Nucleoside Monophosphate [*Biochemistry*]
NMP............ Nuveen Michigan Premium Income Municipal [*NYSE symbol*] (SPSG)
NMP............ Nuveen MI Prem Inc. Muni [*NYSE symbol*] (TTSB)
NmP........... Portales Public Library, Portales, NM [*Library symbol*] [*Library of Congress*] (LCLS)
NMPA .... National Motorsports Press Association (EA)
NMPA .... National Music Publishers' Association (EA)
NMPA .... NATO Maritime Patrol Aircraft (NATG)
NMPA .... New Mexico Philatelic Association (EA)
NMPA .... (Nitrosomethylamino) Propionic Acid [*Organic chemistry*]
NMPA .... Nitrosomethylpropylamine [*Organic chemistry*]
NMPAP .... Noise Minimization Pad Assignment Problem (VLIE)
NMPASC ..... NATO Maritime Patrol Aircraft Steering Committee (NATG)
NMPATA ..... National Music Printers and Allied Trades Association (EA)
NMPB .... National Millinery Planning Board [*Defunct*] (EA)
NMPC .... National Maintenance Publications Center [*Army*] (AABC)
NMPC .... National Milk Publicity Council [*British*] (BI)
NMPC .... National Minority Purchasing Council [*Later, NMSDC*] (EA)
NMPC .... National Moratorium on Prison Construction [*Defunct*] (EA)
NMPC .... Naval Military Personnel Command (ANA)
NMPC .... Niagara Mohawk Power Co. (SAUS)
NMPC .... NutraMax Products, Inc. [*NASDAQ symbol*] (SAG)
NMPCRECSREDIVREGOFF... Naval Military Personnel Command, Recreational Services Division, Regional Office (DNAB)
NMPD .... Nitromethylpropanediol [*Organic chemistry*]
NMPDN....... National Materials Property Data Network (EA)
NmPE.......... Eastern New Mexico University, Portales, NM [*Library symbol*] [*Library of Congress*] (LCLS)
NMPF .... National Milk Producers Federation (EA)
NMPF .... Network Management Productivity Facility [*Computer science*] (VLIE)
NMPF .... Normal Magnitude Probability Function
NMPFT .... National Museum of Photography, Film & Television (WDAA)
NMPG .... New Mexico Proving Ground [*Army*]
NMPGA....... New Mexico Personnel and Guidance Association (SAUS)
NMPIS .... National Marine Pollution Information System [*Marine science*] (OSRA)
NMPIS .... National Marine Pollution Information Systems (USDC)
NMPK .... Nucleoside Monophosphate Kinase (SAUS)
NMPL......... Netscape/Mozilla Public License (SAUS)
NMPL......... New Material Planning Letter (MCD)
NMPNC....... Naval Medical Program for Nuclear Casualties
NMPNS ...... Nine Mile Point Nuclear Station (NRCH)
NMPO .... Navy Motion Picture Office
NMPO .... Nordic Master Painters' Organization (EA)
NMPP .... Nautical Miles per Pound (MCD)
NMPP .... Nouvelles Messageries de la Presse Parisienne [*Paris press distribution agency*]
NMPPO........ National Marine Pollution Program Office [*Marine science*] (OSRA)
NMPS .... Matritech, Inc. [*NASDAQ symbol*] (SAG)
NMPS .... Nautical Miles per Second
NMPS .... Naval Military Pay System (ACAE)
NMPS .... Navy Motion Picture Service
NMPSMOPIXDISTOFF... Navy Motion Picture Service, Motion Picture Distribution Office (DNAB)
NMPTP .... N-Methyl(phenyl)tetrahydropyridine [*Biochemistry*]
NMPX .... Navy Motion Picture Exchange
NMQAAC...... National Mammography Quality Assurance Advisory Committee [*U.S. Food and Drug Administration*]
NMQR .... New Music Quarterly Review [*Record label*]
NMQUE .... Nocte Maneque [*Night and Morning*] [*Pharmacy*]
NMR .... Centre for Nuclear Magnetic Resonance [*University of Warwick*] [*British*] (CB)
NMR .... Nappamerrie [*Queensland*] [*Airport symbol*] (AD)
NMR .... Natal Mounted Rifles [*British military*] (DMA)
NMR .... National Military Representatives with SHAPE [*NATO*]
NMR .... National Milk Record [*British*] (BI)
NMR .... National Missile Range (KSC)
NMR .... National Museum of Racing (EA)
NMR .... National Museum of Racing and Hall of Fame (EA)
NMR .... Natural Magnetic Remanence [*Geophysics*]
NMR .... Naval Medical Research Institute, Washington, DC [*OCLC symbol*] (OCLC)
NMR .... Naval Missile Range
NMR .... Navy Management Review [*A publication*]
NMR .... Neomar Resources Ltd. [*Toronto Stock Exchange symbol*]
NMR .... Neonatal Mortality Rate [*Medicine*] (DMAA)
NMR .... Neonatal Mortality Risk [*Medicine*]

NMR .... New Material Release (MCD)
NMR .... New Mexico Regulations (SAUS)
NMR .... New Mobile Radar (SAUS)
NMR .... News Media Representative (COE)
NMR .... Nictitating Membrane Response [*Neurophysiology*]
NMR .... Nielsen Media Research [*NYSE symbol*] [*Formerly, Cognizant Corp.*]
NMR .... N. M. De Rothschild & Co. [*Merchant bank*] [*British*]
NMR .... N-Modular Redundancy (RALS)
NMR .... NMR of America, Inc. [*Associated Press*] (SAG)
NMR .... No Maintenance Required (SAUS)
NMR .... No Maintenance Requirement (NVT)
NMR .... No Master Record [*Military*] (AFIT)
NMR .... Nonconforming Material Report (MCD)
NMR .... Nordic Council of Ministers (SAUS)
NMR .... Normal Mode Rejection
NMR .... Nuclear Magnetic Relaxation
nmr .... Nuclear Magnetic Resonance (HGEN)
NMR .... Nuclear Magnetic Resonance [*Also, NUMAR*] [*Atomic physics*]
NmR .... Roswell Carnegie Library, Roswell, NM [*Library symbol*] [*Library of Congress*] (LCLS)
NMR .... San Juan, PR [*Location identifier*] [*FAA*] (FAAL)
NmRa .... Arthur Johnson Memorial Library, Raton, NM [*Library symbol*] [*Library of Congress*] (LCLS)
NMRA .... National Marine Representatives Association (EA)
NMRA .... National Mine Rescue Association
NMRA .... National Mobile Radio Association [*Defunct*] (EA)
NMRA .... National Model Railroad Association (EA)
NMRA .... National Motorcycle Racing Association (EA)
NMRA .... National Motorcycle Retailers Association [*Defunct*] (EA)
NMRA .... National Mud Racing Association
NMRA .... Not Mission Ready and Available (SAUS)
NMR & DA... Navy Material Redistribution and Disposition Administration
NMR & DO... Navy Material Redistribution and Disposal Office [*or Officer*]
NMRAS .... Nuclear Material Report and Analysis System [*Energy Research and Development Administration*]
NMRAS .... Nuclear Materials Report and Analysis System (SAUS)
NMRB .... National Mutual Royal Bank [*Australia*] (ADA)
NMRC .... National Maritime Research Center [*Maritime Administration*] [*Also, an information service or system*] (IID)
NMRC .... National Meat Retail Council [*Australia*]
NMRC .... National Men's Resource Center (EA)
NMRC .... National Microelectronics Research Centre (NITA)
NMRC .... Navy Material Redistribution Center
NMRC .... Neuromuscular Research Center [*Boston University*]
NMR-CT ...... Nuclear Magnetic Resonance Computer Tomography (SAUS)
NMRD .... Nuclear Magnetic Relaxation Dispension [*Physics*]
NMRDC .... Naval Medical Research and Development Command (MCD)
NmRE .... Eastern New Mexico University, Roswell Campus, Roswell, NM [*Library symbol*] [*Library of Congress*] (LCLS)
NMREC .... National Maritime Resource Center [*MARAD*] (TAG)
NM Reg .... New Mexico Register [*A publication*] (AAGC)
NMRF .... Navy-Marine Corps Residence Foundation (DNAB)
NMRG .... Navy Mid-Range Guidance
NMRI .... National Mass Retailing Institute [*New York, NY*] (EA)
NMRI .... National Medical Research Institute (MAE)
NMRI .... Naval Medical Research Institute
NMRI .... Nuclear Magnetic Resonance Imaging
NMRL .... Naval Medical Research Laboratory
NMRLIT ...... Nuclear Magnetic Resonance Literature System [*Chemical Information Systems, Inc.*] [*Information service or system*]
NmRM .... New Mexico Military Institute, Roswell (SAUS)
NmRM .... New Mexico Military Institute, Roswell, NM [*Library symbol*] [*Library of Congress*] (LCLS)
NMRN .... National Meteorological Rocket Network
NMRO .... Navy Mid-Range Objectives
NMR-ON ...... Nuclear Magnetic Resonance-Oriented Nuclei (SAUS)
NMRP .... National Migrant Resource Program (EA)
NMRP .... New Mexico Research Park (SAUS)
NMRP .... Nuclear Magnetic Resonance Program
NMRR .... NMR of America [*NASDAQ symbol*] (TTSB)
NMRR .... NMR of America, Inc. [*NASDAQ symbol*] (NQ)
NMRR .... Normal-Mode Rejection Ratio [*Electronics*] (BARN)
NMRS .... National Mobile Radio System [*Later, Telocator Network of America*] (EA)
NMRS .... Navy Manpower Requirements System (NVT)
NMRS .... Nuclear Magnetic Resonance Spectroscopy (DMAA)
NMRS .... Numerous (FAAC)
NMR Spectroscopy... Nuclear Magnetic Resonance Spectroscopy (SAUS)
NMR Spectrum... Nuclear Magnetic Resonance Spectrum (SAUS)
NMRT .... New Members Round Table [*American Library Association*]
NMRT .... Nimbus Meteorological Radiation Tape [*NASA*]
NMRTC .... Navy and Marine Corps Reserve Training Center
NMRTC .... New Mexico Research and Treatment Center (SAUS)
NMRU .... Naval Medical Research Unit
NmRu .... Ruidoso Public Library (SAUS)
NmRu .... Ruidoso Public Library, Ruidoso, NM [*Library symbol*] [*Library of Congress*] (LCLS)
NMRX .... Numerex Corp. [*NASDAQ symbol*] (SAG)
NMS .... Ancient Egyptian Arabic Order Nobles of the Mystic Shrine (EA)
NMS .... Namsang [*Myanmar*] [*Airport symbol*] (OAG)
NMS .... National Management Systems [*Information service or system*] (IID)
NMS .... National Marine Service, Inc. (EFIS)
NMS .... National Maritime System [*MARAD*] (TAG)
NMS .... National Market System

NMS .... National Master Specification [*Construction Specifications Canada*] [*Information service or system*] (IID)
NMS .... National Measurement Service (SAUS)
NMS .... National Measurement System [*National Institute of Standards and Technology*]
NMS .... National Medicine Society [*British*]
NMS .... National Military Strategy (DOMA)
NMS .... National Mobility Scheme [*British*]
NMS .... Natural Matrix Standard
NMS .... Natural Mortality Schedule [*Biology*]
NMS .... Naval Medical School (MCD)
NMS .... Naval Meteorological Service
NMS .... Navigation and Mayday System [*Automotive engineering*]
NMS .... Navigation Management System (PDAA)
NMS .... Navy Mid-Range Study
NMS .... NetWare Management System [*Novell, Inc.*] (PCM)
NMS .... Network Management Services [*Ohio Bell Communications, Inc.*] [*Cleveland, OH*] [*Telecommunications*] (TSSD)
NMS .... Network Management Signal [*Telecommunications*] (TEL)
NMS .... Network Management Station (MLOA)
NMS .... Network Management System (DA)
NMS .... Network Measurement System [*Computer network*]
NMS .... Network Monitoring Station (SAUS)
NMS .... Neuroleptic Malignant Syndrome
NMS .... Neuromuscular Stimulator [*Neurology*] (DAVI)
NMS .... Neuro-Musculo-Skeletal [*Medicine*]
NMS .... Neutral Mass Spectrometer [*Instrumentation*]
NMS .... Neutral Meson Spectrometer (SAUS)
NMS .... Neutron Monitoring System [*Nuclear energy*] (NRCH)
NMS .... New Management Strategy (SAUS)
NMS .... New Management System (SAUS)
NMS .... New Manning System [*Army*] (MCD)
NMS .... New Mexico State Library, Santa Fe, NM [*OCLC symbol*] (OCLC)
NMS .... New Mexico Statutes [*A publication*] (DLA)
NMS .... New Music Seminar
NMS .... New Music Society [*Australia*]
NMS .... Nitrogen Measuring System
NMS .... Nobles of the Mystic Shrine (SAUS)
NMS .... Noise Measuring Set [*Telecommunications*] (TEL)
NMS .... Noise Monitoring System (ACAE)
NMS .... Nonmajor System (MCD)
NMS .... Nonmedical Science Category (DAVI)
NMS .... Non-Member State (SAUS)
NMS .... Non-Metric Multidimensional Scaling (PDAA)
NMS .... Nonprofit Management Strategies [*A publication*]
NMS .... Nordic Metalworkers Secretariat (EA)
NMS .... Normal Market Size Transaction
NMS .... Normal Mouse Serum
NMS .... Nuclear Materials Safeguards
NMS .... Nuclear Medical Science (SAUS)
NMS .... Nuclear-Powered Merchant Ship (PDAA)
NmS .... Santa Fe City and County Public Library, Santa Fe, NM [*Library symbol*] [*Library of Congress*] (LCLS)
NMSA .... National Metal Spinners Association (EA)
NMSA .... National Middle School Association (EA)
NMSA .... National Moving and Storage Association (EA)
NMSA .... New Mexico Statutes Annotated [*A publication*] (AAGC)
NMSA .... Nonnuclear Munitions Storage Area [*Air Force*] (DOMA)
NMSA .... Nonstandard Metropolitan Statistical Area
NMSA .... North Atlantic Treaty Organization [*NATO*] Mutual Support Act (AAGC)
NMSB .... Navy Manpower Survey Board
NMSB .... NewMil Bancorp [*NASDAQ symbol*] (TTSB)
NMSB .... New Milford Savings Bank [*NASDAQ symbol*] (NQ)
NmSC .... College of Santa Fe, Santa Fe, NM [*Library symbol*] [*Library of Congress*] (LCLS)
NMSC .... National Main Street Center (EA)
NMSC .... National Maple Syrup Council [*Later, NAMSC*]
NMSC .... National Merit Scholarship Corp. (EA)
NMSC .... Naval Medical Supply Unit (DNAB)
NMSC .... Navy Management Systems Center (PDAA)
NMSC .... Nerve and Muscle Stimulating Current
NMSC .... Nonferrous Metals Society of China (SAUS)
NMSC .... Nonmartensitic Structural Component (SAUS)
NMSC .... Nonmelanoma Skin Cancer [*Medicine*]
NMSC .... Non-Military Supplies Committee [*Combined Production and Resources Board*] [*British*] [*World War II*]
NMSC .... Northeast-Midwest Senate Coalition (EA)
NMSC .... Northwest Missouri State College [*Later, Northwest Missouri State University*]
NMSC .... Nutrition Management [*NASDAQ symbol*] (SAG)
NmSc .... Silver City Public Library, Silver City, NM [*Library symbol*] [*Library of Congress*] (LCLS)
NMSCA .... Navy Material Command Support Activity (PDAA)
NMSCA .... Nutrition Mgmt Svcs'A' [*NASDAQ symbol*] (TTSB)
NmSCS .... College of Santa Fe, Santa Fe, NM [*Library symbol*] [*Library of Congress*] (LCLS)
NmScSW ...... Southwestern Regional Library, Silver City, NM [*Library symbol*] [*Library of Congress*] (LCLS)
NMSCW ...... Nutrition Mgmt Svcs Wrrt [*NASDAQ symbol*] (TTSB)
NmScW .... Western New Mexico University, Silver City, NM [*Library symbol*] [*Library of Congress*] (LCLS)
NMSD .... National Match Support Detachment [*Ammunition supplier*]
NMSD .... National Military Strategy Document (DOMA)
NMSD .... Naval Medical Supply Depot

NMSD	Next Most Significant Digit [*Computer science*]
NMSDC	National Minority Supplier Development Council (EA)
NMSE	Naval Material Support Establishment [*After 1966, NAVMAT, NMCOM, NMC*]
NMSE	Normalized Mean Square Error (SAUS)
NMSE	Normalized Minimum Square Error (SAUS)
NmSEA	New Mexico Society of Enrolled Agents (SAUS)
NMSF	Normalized Mean Square Error (DMAA)
NMSHC	Bureau of Medicine and Surgery Hospital Corps Publication [*Later, NAVMED*] [*Navy*]
NMSI	National Mini-Storage Institute [*Defunct*] (EA)
NMSI	National Museum of Science & Industry (WDAA)
NMSIDS	Near-Miss Sudden Infant Death Syndrome [*Medicine*] (DMAA)
NMSK	Namesake (ABBR)
NMSL	National Maximum Speed Limit [*NHTSA*] (TAG)
NmSM	Museum of New Mexico, Santa Fe, NM [*Library symbol*] [*Library of Congress*] (LCLS)
NMSM	New Mexico School of Mines (AAG)
NmSM-A	Museum of New Mexico, Laboratory of Anthropology, Santa Fe, NM [*Library symbol*] [*Library of Congress*] (LCLS)
NMSMK	Numismatic (ABBR)
NMSMTST ...	Numismaticist (ABBR)
NMSO	NATO Maintenance and Support Operation (AFM)
NMSO	Naval Manpower Survey Office (NVT)
NMSO	N-Methylnitroanisole [*Organic chemistry*]
NMSO	Nuclear Missile Safety Office [*or Officer*] (AFM)
NmSo	Socorro Public Library (SAUS)
NmSo	Socorro Public Library, Socorro, NM [*Library symbol*] [*Library of Congress*] (LCLS)
NmSoI	New Mexico Institute of Mining and Technology, Socorro, NM [*Library symbol*] [*Library of Congress*] (LCLS)
NmSP	New Mexico State Penitentiary Library, Santa Fe, NM [*Library symbol*] [*Library of Congress*] (LCLS)
NMSP	New Mon State Party [*Myanmar*] [*Political party*]
NMSP	N-Methylspiperone [*Biochemistry*]
NmSp	Springer Public Library, Springer, NM [*Library symbol*] [*Library of Congress*] (LCLS)
NmSpP	Springer Public Library, Springer, NM [*Library symbol*] [*Library of Congress*] (LCLS)
NMSQT	National Merit Scholarship Qualifying Test
NmSr	Moise Memorial Library, Santa Rosa, NM [*Library symbol*] [*Library of Congress*] (LCLS)
NMSR	New Mexico State Road (SAUS)
NMSRA	National Master Shoe Rebuilders Association (EA)
NMSRC	National Middle School Resource Center (EA)
NMSS	NASCOM [*Naval Air Systems Command*] Manual Scheduling System
NMSS	National Meteorological Satellite System (IAA)
NMSS	National Multiple Sclerosis Society (EA)
NMSS	National Multipurpose Space Station
NMSS	Natural Microsystems [*NASDAQ symbol*] (TTSB)
NMSS	Natural Microsystems Corp. [*NASDAQ symbol*] (SAG)
NMSS	Nemesis (ABBR)
NMSS	Nuclear Materials Safety and Safeguards (SAUS)
NMSS	Office of Nuclear Materials Safety and Safeguards [*Nuclear Regulatory Commission*]
NMSSA	National Multiple Sclerosis Society of Australia
NMSSA	NATO Maintenance Supply Service Agency [*Later, NAMSO*]
NMSSO	Navy Maintenance and Supply Systems Office (DNAB)
NMSSS	NATO Maintenance Supply Service System
NMSST	Naval Manpower Shore Survey Team (NVT)
NmSStJ	Saint Johns College in Santa Fe (SAUS)
NMST	Materials System Test (SAUS)
NMST	New Materials System Test [*Obsolete*] [*Nuclear energy*]
NM Stat Ann...	New Mexico Statutes, Annotated [*A publication*] (DLA)
NM State Eng Off Tech Rep...	New Mexico State Engineer Office. Technical Report (SAUS)
NM State Univ Agric Exp Stn Res Rep...	New Mexico State University. Agricultural Experiment Station. Research Report (SAUS)
NMSU	Naval Motion Study Unit [*British*]
NMSU	New Mexico State University
NmSuAF	United States Air Force, Sacramento Peak Observatory, Sunspot, NM [*Library symbol*] [*Library of Congress*] (LCLS)
NMSVA	Navy Mail Service Veterans Association (EA)
NMSZ	New Madrid Seismic Zone [*Geology*]
NMT	Barrow, AK [*Location identifier*] [*FAA*] (FAAL)
NMT	National Museum of Transport [*Later, TMA*] (EA)
NMT	Neuromuscular Tension [*Medicine*]
NMT	Neuromuscular Transmission [*Physiology*]
NMT	New Mexico Institute of Mining and Technology, Socorro, NM [*OCLC symbol*] (OCLC)
NMT	N-Methyltransferase (DB)
NMT	N-Monomethyltryptamine [*Organic chemistry*]
NMT	N-Myristoyl Acyltransferase [*An enzyme*]
NMT	Noble-Metal-Coated Titanium [*Anode*]
NMT	Noise Measurement Technique (SAUS)
NMT	No More Than [*Pharmacy*] (DAVI)
NMT	No More Trouble [*Coates' brand of cotton thread*] (ROG)
NMT	Nonmetalic [*Technical drawings*]
NMT	Nordic Mobile Telephone [*Radio-telephone system for car users*] [*Denmark, Finland, Norway, Sweden*]
NMT	Nordic Mobile Telephone Network (NITA)
NMT	Nordic Mobile Telephone System (SAUS)
NMT	Norepinephrine N-Methyl-Transferase (SAUS)
NMT	Nor More Than (SAUS)
NMT	Northwest Marine Trade Association (EA)
NMT	Norwegian Method of Tunnelling [*Civil engineering*]
NMT	Notification of Master Tool (NASA)
NMT	Not More Than
NMT	Nuclear Medicine Technologist (MELL)
NMT	Nuclear Medicine Technology
NMT	Number of Module Types
NMT	Nuveen MA Prem Inc. Muni Fd [*NYSE symbol*] (TTSB)
NMT	Nuveen Massachusetts Premium Income Municipal Fund [*NYSE symbol*] (SPSG)
NMTA	National Manpower Training Association [*Later, NETA*] (EA)
NMTA	National Metal Trades Association [*Later, AAIM*] (EA)
NMTA	National Movement Theatre Association (EA)
NMTBA	National Machine Tool Builders' Association [*Later, AMT*] (EA)
NMTBD	No More to Be Done [*Medicine*]
NMTC	Naval Mine Testing Center (MCD)
NMTC	Naval Missile Testing Center
NMTC	North Metropolitan Tramways Co. [*British*] (ROG)
NMTC	Nucleon-Meson Transport Code
NMTC	Numerical Technologies [*NASDAQ symbol*] (SG)
NMTCB	Nuclear Medicine Technology Certification Board (EA)
NMTD	Nonmetastatic Trophoblastic Disease [*Medicine*] (DMAA)
NMTD	Nuclear Materials Transfer Document
NMTF	National Market Traders Federation [*British*] (DBA)
NMTF	National Metal Trades Federation [*British*] (DBA)
NMTF	Naval Mine Test Facility
NMTFA	National Master Tile Fixers Association [*British*] (DBA)
NMTHC	Nonmethane Total Hydrocarbons [*Organic chemistry*]
NmTHF	Harwood Foundation, Taos, NM [*Library symbol*] [*Library of Congress*] (LCLS)
NMTI	Neuromedical Technologies, Inc. (SAUS)
NMTI	Nitinol Medical Technologies, Inc. [*NASDAQ symbol*] (SAG)
NMTI	NMT Medical [*NASDAQ symbol*] (SG)
NMtK	Mount Kisco Public Library, Mount Kisco, NY [*Library symbol*] [*Library of Congress*] (LCLS)
NmTKC	Kit Carson Memorial Foundation, Inc., Taos, NM [*Library symbol*] [*Library of Congress*] (LCLS)
NMTLK	Nonmetallic (ABBR)
NMTLM	Nuclear Materials Transportation Logistics Model (SAUS)
NMTN	National Music Theater Network (EA)
NMTO	Navy Material Transportation Office
NMTP	National Means Test Proposal
NMTR	Nuclear Materials Transfer Report
NmTr	Truth Or Consequences Public Library, Truth Or Consequences, NM [*Library symbol*] [*Library of Congress*] (LCLS)
NMTS	National Milk Testing Service
NMTS	Navy Military Technical Specialist (MCD)
NMTS	Neuromuscular Tension State [*Medicine*] (DMAA)
NMTS	Noise Measurement Test Set
NmTu	Tucumcari Public Library, Tucumcari, NM [*Library symbol*] [*Library of Congress*] (LCLS)
NmTuE	Eastern Plains Regional Library, Tucumcari, NM [*Library symbol*] [*Library of Congress*] (LCLS)
NMtv	Mount Vernon Public Library, Mount Vernon, NY [*Library symbol*] [*Library of Congress*] (LCLS)
NMTX	Novametrics Medical Systems [*NASDAQ symbol*] (SAG)
NMTX	Novametrix Medical Systems, Inc. [*NASDAQ symbol*] (NQ)
NMTX	Novametrix Med Sys [*NASDAQ symbol*] (TTSB)
NMTXW	Novametrix Med Sys Wrt'A' [*NASDAQ symbol*] (TTSB)
NMTXZ	Novametrix Med Sys Wrrt'B' [*NASDAQ symbol*] (TTSB)
NMU	Brunswick, ME [*Location identifier*] [*FAA*] (FAAL)
NMU	National Maritime Union (USDC)
NMU	National Maritime Union of America (EA)
NMU	National Museums of Canada Library [*UTLAS symbol*]
NMU	Navigation Management Unit (HLLA)
NMU	Network Monitor Unit [*Telecommunications*] (TSSD)
NMU	Neuromuscular Unit [*Medicine*]
nmu	New Mexico [*MARC country of publication code*] [*Library of Congress*] (LCCP)
NMU	Nitrosomethylurea [*Also, MNU*] [*Organic chemistry*]
NMU	Nitrosomethylurethane (SAUS)
NMU	Nordic Musicians' Union (EA)
NMU	Northern Michigan University [*Marquette*]
NmU	University of New Mexico, Albuquerque, NM [*Library symbol*] [*Library of Congress*] (LCLS)
NMUC	National Medical Utilization Committee [*HEW*]
NmU-L	University of New Mexico, Law Library, Albuquerque, NM [*Library symbol*] [*Library of Congress*] (LCLS)
NmU-M	University of New Mexico, Library of the Medical Sciences, School of Medicine and Bernalillo County Medical Society, Albuquerque, NM [*Library symbol*] [*Library of Congress*] (LCLS)
NMuP	Muttontown Preserve, Muttontown, NY [*Library symbol*] [*Library of Congress*] (LCLS)
NMusic R	New Music Review (SAUS)
NMV	National Museum of Victoria (SAUS)
NMV	Nitrogen Manual Valve (MCD)
NMV	Normal Mode Voltage (SAUS)
NMVCA	National Military Vehicle Collectors Association [*Defunct*]
NMVD	Null Multi-Valued Dependency (SAUS)
NMVMA	New Mexico Veterinary Medical Association (GVA)
NMVO	Navy Manpower Validation Office (DNAB)
NMVOC	Nonmethane Volatile Organic Carbon [*Environmental chemistry*]
NMVOC	Non-Methane Volatile Organic Chemicals (SAUS)
NMVOC	Non-Methane Volatile Organic Compounds (SAUS)
NMVOLANT...	Navy Manpower Validation Office, Atlantic (DNAB)
NMVOPAC...	Navy Manpower Validation Office, Pacific (DNAB)

NMVP	Navy Manpower Validation Program (NG)
NMVSA	Navy Manpower Validation Support Activity
NMVSAC	National Motor Vehicle Safety Advisory Council (EA)
NMVT	Network Management Vector Command (SAUS)
NMVTA	National Motor Vehicle Theft Act
NMvUA	State University of New York, Agricultural and Technical College at Morrisville, Morrisville, NY [*Library symbol*] [*Library of Congress*] (LCLS)
NMW	Astoria, OR [*Location identifier*] [*FAA*] (FAAL)
NMW	Naval Mine Warfare (DOMA)
NMW	Normal Molecular Weight
NMW	Notes on Mississippi Writers [*A publication*] (ANEX)
NMW	Western Carolina University, Cullowhee, NC [*OCLC symbol*] (OCLC)
NMWA	National Military Wives Association [*Later, NMFA*] (EA)
NMWA	National Mineral Wool Association [*Later, MIMA*]
NMWC	National Migrant Workers Council [*Farmington Hills, MI*] (EA)
NMWC	Nelson, Marlborough, and West Coast Regiment [*British military*] (DMA)
NMWC	New Mexico Western College
NMWIA	National Mineral Wool Insulation Association [*Formerly, NMWA*] [*Later, MIMA*] (EA)
NMWL	Normal Molecular Weight, Low in Extractables
NmWM	White Sands Missile Range Library, White Sands Missile Range, NM [*Library symbol*] [*Library of Congress*] (LCLS)
NMWP	National Migrant Worker Program [*Department of Labor*]
NMWP	National Mixed Waste Program (ABAC)
NMWQL	National Marine Water Quality Laboratory [*Environmental Protection Agency*] (MSC)
NMWS	Naval Meroka Weapon System (SAUS)
NMWS	Naval Mine Warfare School
NMWTC	Naval Mine Warfare Training Center
NMWTS	Naval Mine Warfare Test Station
NMWTS	Naval Mine Warfare Training School
n-mx-	Mexico [*MARC geographic area code*] [*Library of Congress*] (LCCP)
NMX	Not Multiplexed (ACAE)
NMxAr	New Mexico & Arizona Land Co. [*Associated Press*] (SAG)
NMxB	Board of Cooperative Educational Services, Regional Resource Center, Mexico, NY [*Library symbol*] [*Library of Congress*] (LCLS)
NMY	Mayville State College, Mayville, ND [*OCLC symbol*] (OCLC)
N/my	Newton per Square Meter (or Metre) (SAUS)
NMY	Nonresonant Magnetic Yoke
NMY	Nuveen Maryland Premium Income Municipal Fund [*NYSE symbol*] (SPSG)
NMY	Nuveen MD Prem Inc. Muni Fd [*NYSE symbol*] (TTSB)
NMyM	Maryknoll Fathers Seminary, Maryknoll, NY [*Library symbol*] [*Library of Congress*] (LCLS)
NMZ	Norman Resources Ltd. [*Vancouver Stock Exchange symbol*]
NMZ	Willow Grove, PA [*Location identifier*] [*FAA*] (FAAL)
NN	Air Trails [*ICAO designator*] (AD)
N:N	Azo Group [*Chemical group with two nitrogen atoms*] (MEDA)
nn	Footnotes (DLA)
NN	Names (ABBR)
NN	NASA Notice
NN	National Neighbors (EA)
NN	National Networker [*An association*] (EA)
NN	Natural, Nongrazed [*Agriculture*]
NN	Nearest Neighbor [*Mathematics*] [*Computer search term*]
NN	Necessary Nuisance [*i.e., a husband*] [*Slang*]
NN	Neonatal (DAVI)
NN	Nerves
nn	Nervi Nerves [*Neurology*] [*Latin*] (DAVI)
NN	Neurotics Nomine [*British*]
NN	Neutral and Nonaligned [*Nations*]
NN	Neutralization Number (SAUS)
N-N	Neutron-Neutron Logging (SAUS)
NN	Nevada Northern Railway Co. [*AAR code*]
NN	Nevocellular Nevus (MELL)
NN	Nevus Network (NRGU)
NN	Newbridge Networks [*NYSE symbol*] (TTSB)
NN	Newbridge Networks, Inc. [*NYSE symbol*] (SAG)
nn	New Hebrides [*MARC country of publication code*] [*Library of Congress*] (LCCP)
NN	New Nationals [*Political party*] [*Australia*]
NN	Newspaper News [*A publication*]
NN	New York Public Library (SAUS)
NN	Next Node (SAUS)
NN	Nicaragua Network (EA)
NN	Nicaragua Network Education Fund (EA)
NN	Nigerian Navy
NN	Nightmare Networker (SAUS)
NN	Night-Night (SAUS)
NN	noch nicht besetzt (SAUS)
NN	Noise Network (WDAA)
N/N	Noise-to-Noise (SAUS)
nn	Nomen Nescio [*Unknown*] [*Latin*] (GPO)
nn	Nomen Novum [*New Name*] [*Latin*] (DAVI)
NN	Nomina [*Names*] [*Latin*]
NN	No Name
NN	No News (SAUS)
N/N	Non-Negotiable (SAUS)
NN	Nonnuclear (ACAE)
NN	Non-Nuclear Lance (MCD)
N/N	No Noting (SAUS)
NN	Non-Participating National (OTD)

N/N	No Number (SAUS)
NN	Noon
NN	Normalnull [*Mean Sea Level*] [*German*]
NN	Normal Nutrition (MELL)
N/N	Normocytic/Normochromic Anemia (DAVI)
NN	Northampton [*Postcode*] (ODBW)
N/N	Northrop/Nortronics (SAUS)
NN	Northwestern National (EFIS)
NN	Notes [*Finance*]
NN	Not Nested [*Freight*]
NN	Not Normal
n N	Not North Of (RIMS)
N/N	Not North Of
N/N	Not to Be Noted [*Business term*]
NN	Nouns
NN	Nuclear Network (EA)
NN	Nucleon-Nucleon
NN	Nurse Notes (SAUS)
N/N	Nurses' Notes (MAE)
NN	Nurturing Network [*An association*] (EA)
NN	Office of Nonproliferation and National Security (SAUS)
NNA	American Geographical Society, New York, NY [*Library symbol*] [*Library of Congress*] (LCLS)
NNA	Nana [*Peru*] [*Seismograph station code, US Geological Survey*] (SEIS)
nna	Nanoampere (ELAL)
NNA	National Neckwear Association (EA)
NNA	National Needlework Association (EA)
NNA	National Newman Apostolate
NNA	National News Agency [*Lebanon*]
NNA	National Newspaper Association (EA)
NNA	National Notary Association (EA)
NNA	National Notion Association [*Later, AHSA*] (EA)
NNA	National Numismatic Association (EA)
NNA	Neonatal Nurses Association (SAUS)
NNA	Neutral/Nonaligned [*Countries*]
NNA	Neutral Non-Allied (ACAE)
NNA	Nevada Nurses Association (SAUS)
NNA	New Nadina Explorations [*Vancouver Stock Exchange symbol*]
NNA	New Network Architecture
NNA	N-Nitrosamine [*Organic chemistry*]
NNA	Nonhistone Nucleoprotein Antibodies [*Immunochemistry*]
NNA	Nonnarcotic Analgesics [*Medicine*] (MELL)
NNA	Normochromic, Normocytic Anemia (DAVI)
NNAA	Augusta Warshaw Advertising Library, New York, NY [*Library symbol*] [*Library of Congress*] (LCLS)
NNAA	National Newman Alumni Association [*Defunct*] (EA)
NNAA	Native North American Almanac [*A publication*]
NNAAI	American Alpine Club, New York, NY [*Library symbol*] [*Library of Congress*] (LCLS)
NNAAr	American Arbitration Association, New York, NY [*Library symbol*] [*Library of Congress*] (LCLS)
NNAB	American Bible Society, New York, NY [*Library symbol*] [*Library of Congress*] (LCLS)
NNABA	American Bankers Association, New York, NY [*Library symbol*] [*Library of Congress*] (LCLS)
NNA-Ber	NNA-Berichte (SAUS)
NNAC	National Native American Cooperative (EA)
NNAC	National Noise Abatement Council [*Defunct*]
NNACC	National Native American Chamber of Commerce [*Defunct*] (EA)
NNACS	American Cancer Society, New York, NY [*Library symbol*] [*Library of Congress*] (LCLS)
NNAD	Anti-Defamation League of B'nai B'rith, New York, NY [*Library symbol*] [*Library of Congress*] (LCLS)
NNADAP	National Native Alcohol and Drug Abuse Program [*Canada*]
NNAdv	American Association of Advertising Agencies, New York, NY [*Library symbol*] [*Library of Congress*] (LCLS)
NNAF	American Foundation for the Blind, New York, NY [*Library symbol*] [*Library of Congress*] (LCLS)
NNAFS	National Newman Association of Faculty and Staff [*Defunct*] (EA)
NNAG	American Gas Association, New York, NY [*Library symbol*] [*Library of Congress*] (LCLS)
NNAG	NATO Naval Advisory Group (NATG)
NNAG	NATO Naval Armaments Group (NATG)
NNAI	American Irish Historical Society, New York, NY [*Library symbol*] [*Library of Congress*] (LCLS)
NNAIA	American Institute of Certified Public Accountants, New York, NY [*Library symbol*] [*Library of Congress*] (LCLS)
NNAIAA	American Institute of Aeronautics and Astronautics, Technical Information Service, New York, NY [*Library symbol*] [*Library of Congress*] (LCLS)
NNAIL	Austrain Institute Library, New York, NY [*Library symbol*] [*Library of Congress*] (LCLS)
NNAIP	American Institute of Physics, New York, NY [*Library symbol*] [*Library of Congress*] (LCLS)
NNAJ	American Jewish Committee, New York, NY [*Library symbol*] [*Library of Congress*] (LCLS)
NNAJN	American Journal of Nursing Co., New York, NY [*Library symbol*] [*Library of Congress*] (LCLS)
NNAKC	American Kennel Club, New York, NY [*Library symbol*] [*Library of Congress*] (LCLS)
NNAL	American Academy of Arts and Letters, New York, NY [*Library symbol*] [*Library of Congress*] (LCLS)
NNAMA	American Management Associations, New York, NY [*Library symbol*] [*Library of Congress*] (LCLS)

NNAMM .... American Merchant Marine Library Association, New York, NY [*Library symbol*] [*Library of Congress*] (LCLS)

NNAN .... American Numismatic Society, New York, NY [*Library symbol*] [*Library of Congress*] (LCLS)

NNAn .... Anthology Film Archives, New York, NY [*Library symbol*] [*Library of Congress*] (LCLS)

NNan .... Nanuet Public Library, Nanuet, NY [*Library symbol*] [*Library of Congress*] (LCLS)

NNAnF .... Anthology Film Archives, New York, NY [*Library symbol*] [*Library of Congress*] (LCLS)

NNanL .... Nanuet Public Library, Nanuet, NY [*Library symbol*] [*Library of Congress*] (LCLS)

NNAP .... NAVAIR [*Naval Air Systems Command*] Naval Aviation Plan (MCD)

NNAPS .... Night Navigation and Pilotage System

NNAPW .... National Network of Asian and Pacific Women (EA)

NNAS .... Neonatal Narcotic Abstinence Syndrome [*Medicine*] (DMAA)

NNASA .... American National Standards Institute, New York, NY [*Library symbol*] [*Library of Congress*] (LCLS)

NNASF .... American-Scandinavian Foundation, New York, NY [*Library symbol*] [*Library of Congress*] (LCLS)

NNASovM .... American-Soviet Medical Society, New York, NY [*Library symbol*] [*Library of Congress*] [*Obsolete*] (LCLS)

NNASP .... American Society for Psychical Research, New York, NY [*Library symbol*] [*Library of Congress*] (LCLS)

NNAT .... American Telephone & Telegraph Co., Corporate Research Library, New York, NY [*Library symbol*] [*Library of Congress*] (LCLS)

NNAT .... Naglieri Nonverbal Ability Test (DIPS)

NNAUR .... Australian Consulate-General, Australian Reference Library, New York, NY [*Library symbol*] [*Library of Congress*] (LCLS)

NNAuS .... National Audubon Society, New York, NY [*Library symbol*] [*Library of Congress*] (LCLS)

N/NAVEXOS... Navy/Executive Offices (AAG)

NNAVS .... Association for Voluntary Sterilization, Inc., International Project, New York, NY [*Library symbol*] [*Library of Congress*] (LCLS)

NNAW .... Native North American Writers [*A publication*]

NNAy .... American Home Products Corp., Ayerst Medical Library, New York, NY [*Library symbol*] [*Library of Congress*] (LCLS)

NNB .... Association of the Bar of the City of New York, New York, NY [*Library symbol*] [*Library of Congress*] (LCLS)

NNB .... National Needlecraft Bureau (EA)

NNB .... National News Bureau [*Commercial firm*] (EA)

NNB .... New Natura Brevium [*A publication*] (DSA)

NN-B .... New York Public Library, Albert A. and Henry W. Berg Collection, New York, NY [*Library symbol*] [*Library of Congress*] (LCLS)

NNb .... North Babylon Public Library, North Babylon, NY [*Library symbol*] [*Library of Congress*] (LCLS)

NNB .... Northumberland and Newcastle Board of Education [*UTLAS symbol*]

NNBa .... Barnard College, Columbia University, New York, NY [*Library symbol*] [*Library of Congress*] (LCLS)

NNBA .... National Nurses in Business Association (EA)

NN Ball .... NN Ball & Roller, Inc. [*Associated Press*] (SAG)

NNBBC .... Bernard M. Baruch College of the City University of New York, New York, NY [*Library symbol*] [*Library of Congress*] (LCLS)

NNbBE .... Belmont Elementary School, North Babylon, NY [*Library symbol*] [*Library of Congress*] (LCLS)

NNBC .... Bronx Community College, New York (SAUS)

NNBC .... Bronx Community College, New York, NY [*Library symbol*] [*Library of Congress*] (LCLS)

NNBC .... National Network of Bilingual Centers (EA)

NNBC .... Node-Negative Breast Cancer (MELL)

NNBCLA .... Negative Negabinary Carry-Look-Ahead Adder [*Computer science*] (MHDI)

NNbe .... North Bellmore Public Library, North Bellmore, NY [*Library symbol*] [*Library of Congress*] (LCLS)

NNbeDE .... Dinkelmeyer Elementary School, North Bellmore, NY [*Library symbol*] [*Library of Congress*] (LCLS)

NNbeGE .... Gunther Elementary School, North Bellmore, NY [*Library symbol*] [*Library of Congress*] (LCLS)

NNbeJJ .... Jerusalem Avenue Junior High School, North Bellmore, NY [*Library symbol*] [*Library of Congress*] (LCLS)

NNbeNE .... Newbridge Road Elementary School, North Bellmore, NY [*Library symbol*] [*Library of Congress*] (LCLS)

NNbePE .... Park Elementary School, North Bellmore, NY [*Library symbol*] [*Library of Congress*] (LCLS)

NNBeS .... Bentley School, New York, NY [*Library symbol*] [*Library of Congress*] (LCLS)

NNbeSME .... Saw Mill Elementary School, North Bellmore, NY [*Library symbol*] [*Library of Congress*] (LCLS)

NNBG .... New York Botanical Garden, Bronx, NY [*Library symbol*] [*Library of Congress*] (LCLS)

NNbHS .... North Babylon High School, North Babylon, NY [*Library symbol*] [*Library of Congress*] (LCLS)

NNBI .... Beth Israel Medical Center, New York, NY [*Library symbol*] [*Library of Congress*] (LCLS)

NNBIS .... National Narcotics Border Interdiction System

NNBL .... National Negro Business League [*Later, National Business League*]

NNbL .... North Babylon Public Library, North Babylon, NY [*Library symbol*] [*Library of Congress*] (LCLS)

NNbLE .... William E. De Luca Jr. Elementary School, North Babylon, NY [*Library symbol*] [*Library of Congress*] (LCLS)

NNBLI .... British Information Services, New York, NY [*Library symbol*] [*Library of Congress*] (LCLS)

NNBMC .... Borough of Manhattan Community College, New York, NY [*Library symbol*] [*Library of Congress*] (LCLS)

NNbMJ .... Robert Moses Junior High School, North Babylon, NY [*Library symbol*] [*Library of Congress*] (LCLS)

NNbPE .... Parliment Place Elementary School, North Babylon, NY [*Library symbol*] [*Library of Congress*] (LCLS)

NN-Br .... New York Public Library, Branch Library System, New York, NY [*Library symbol*] [*Library of Congress*] (LCLS)

NNBR .... NN Ball & Roller [*NASDAQ symbol*] (TTSB)

NNBR .... NN Ball & Roller, Inc. [*NASDAQ symbol*] (SAG)

NNBS .... Biblical Seminary in New York, New York, NY [*Library symbol*] [*Library of Congress*] (LCLS)

NNBSC .... Bank Street College of Education, New York, NY [*Library symbol*] [*Library of Congress*] (LCLS)

NNbWE .... Woods Road Elementary School, North Babylon, NY [*Library symbol*] [*Library of Congress*] (LCLS)

NNC .... Columbia University, New York (SAUS)

NNC .... Columbia University, New York, NY [*Library symbol*] [*Library of Congress*] (LCLS)

NNC .... Naga National Council [*India*] (PD)

NNC .... Natal Native Contingent [*British military*] (DMA)

NNC .... National Namibia Concerns (EA)

NNC .... National Neighborhood Coalition (EA)

NNC .... National Network Congestion Signal (NITA)

NNC .... National News Council (EA)

NNC .... National Nomad Club [*Defunct*] (EA)

NNC .... National Nuclear Corp. [*British*]

NNC .... National Nudist Council [*Defunct*] (EA)

NNC .... National Nutrition Consortium [*Defunct*] (EA)

NNC .... Navy Nurse Corps

NNC .... Neutral Nations Committee [*CINCPAC*] (CINC)

NN/C .... Night Noise Group C [*Aircraft*]

NNC .... Nolan, Norton & Co., Inc., Lexington, MA [*OCLC symbol*] (OCLC)

NNC .... Non-Noise Certificated Aircraft (DA)

NNC .... Non-Noise Certified Aircraft (SAUS)

NNC .... Northern Navigation Co. Ltd. [*AAR code*]

NNC .... Northwest Nazarene College [*Nampa, ID*]

NNC .... Notice of Noncompliance (EPA)

NNC .... Nuance (ABBR)

NNC .... Nudist National Committee (EA)

NNC .... Nuveen NC Prem Inc. Muni [*NYSE symbol*] (TTSB)

NNC .... Nuveen North Carolina Premium Income Municipal Fund [*NYSE symbol*] (SPSG)

NNC-A .... Columbia University, Avery Library of Architecture, New York, NY [*Library symbol*] [*Library of Congress*] (LCLS)

NNCA .... National Newman Chaplains Association [*Later, CCMA*] (EA)

NNCA .... Navy Nurse Corps Association (SAUS)

NNCAA .... National Negro County Agents Association (EA)

NNCAM .... Cravath, Swaine & Moore, New York, NY [*Library symbol*] [*Library of Congress*] (LCLS)

NNCar .... Carnegie Corp. of New York, New York, NY [*Library symbol*] [*Library of Congress*] (LCLS)

NNCB .... [*The*] College Board, New York, NY [*Library symbol*] [*Library of Congress*] (LCLS)

NNC-B .... Columbia University, Biological Sciences Library, New York, NY [*Library symbol*] [*Library of Congress*] (LCLS)

NNC-BE .... Columbia University, Business-Economic Library, New York, NY [*Library symbol*] [*Library of Congress*] (LCLS)

NNCBN .... City Bank, North America, New York, NY [*Library symbol*] [*Library of Congress*] (LCLS)

NNCBS .... Columbia Broadcasting System, Inc., New York, NY [*Library symbol*] [*Library of Congress*] (LCLS)

NNCC .... Chemists' Club, New York, NY [*Library symbol*] [*Library of Congress*] (LCLS)

NNCC .... National Network Control Centre [*Communications*] [*British*]

NNCC .... National Nursing Consultative Committee [*Australia*]

NNCC .... Navy Nurse Corps Candidate (DNAB)

NNCCA .... Canadian Centre for Architecture, New York, NY [*Library symbol*] [*Library of Congress*] (LCLS)

NNCCG .... Canadian Consulate General Library, New York, NY [*Library symbol*] [*Library of Congress*] (LCLS)

NNCCVTE ..... National Network for Curriculum Coordination in Vocational and Technical Education (OICC)

NNCE .... Carnegie Endowment for International Peace, New York, NY [*Library symbol*] [*Library of Congress*] (LCLS)

NNC-EA .... Columbia University, East Asiatic Library, New York, NY [*Library symbol*] [*Library of Congress*] (LCLS)

NNCEF .... Child Education Foundation, New York, NY [*Library symbol*] [*Library of Congress*] [*Obsolete*] (LCLS)

NNCenC .... Century Association, New York, NY [*Library symbol*] [*Library of Congress*] (LCLS)

NNCEP .... Centro de Estudios Puertorriquenos, New York, NY [*Library symbol*] [*Library of Congress*] (LCLS)

NNCF .... Commonwealth Fund, New York, NY [*Library symbol*] [*Library of Congress*] (LCLS)

NNCF .... National Newman Club Federation [*Defunct*] (EA)

NNCFo .... Council on Foundations, New York, NY [*Library symbol*] [*Library of Congress*] (LCLS)

NNCFR .... Council on Foreign Relations, New York, NY [*Library symbol*] [*Library of Congress*] (LCLS)

NNC-G .... Columbia University, Lamont-Doherty Geological Observatory, Palisades, NY [*Library symbol*] [*Library of Congress*] (LCLS)

NNCG .... Norwegian Consulate General, New York, NY [*Library symbol*] [*Library of Congress*] (LCLS)

NNCh .... Chadbourne & Parke, New York, NY [*Library symbol*] [*Library of Congress*] (LCLS)

NNCI .... College of Insurance, New York, NY [*Library symbol*] [*Library of Congress*] (LCLS)

NNCit .... Cities Service Co., Corporate Library, New York, NY [*Library symbol*] [*Library of Congress*] (LCLS)

NNC-L .... Columbia University, Law Library, New York, NY [*Library symbol*] [*Library of Congress*] (LCLS)

NNC-M .... Columbia University, Medical Library, New York, NY [*Library symbol*] [*Library of Congress*] (LCLS)

NNCN .... Northern Nigeria Case Notes [*A publication*] (DLA)

NNCo .... Collectors Club, New York, NY [*Library symbol*] [*Library of Congress*] (LCLS)

NNcoM .... Moore-Cottrell Subscription Agencies, Inc., North Cohocton, NY [*Library symbol*] [*Library of Congress*] (LCLS)

NNConE .... Consolidated Edison Co., Inc., New York, NY [*Library symbol*] [*Library of Congress*] (LCLS)

NNCoo .... Cooper Union for the Advancement of Science and Art, New York, NY [*Library symbol*] [*Library of Congress*] (LCLS)

NNCorI .... Cornell University, New York State School of Industrial and Labor Relations, Sanford V. Lenz Library, New York, NY [*Library symbol*] [*Library of Congress*] (LCLS)

NNCorM .... Cornell University, Medical College, New York, NY [*Library symbol*] [*Library of Congress*] (LCLS)

NNCorM-A ... New York Hospital-Cornell Medical Center Archives, New York, NY [*Library symbol*] [*Library of Congress*] (LCLS)

NNCorM-D ... Cornell University, Medical College, Oskar Diethelm Historical Library, New York, NY [*Library symbol*] [*Library of Congress*] (LCLS)

NNC-P .... Columbia University, College of Pharmacy, New York, NY [*Library symbol*] [*Library of Congress*] (LCLS)

NNCP .... Pfizer, Inc., New York, NY [*Library symbol*] [*Library of Congress*] (LCLS)

NNCPI .... Nuveen North Carolina Premium Income Municipal Fund [*Associated Press*] (SAG)

NNCPL .... College of Police Science, New York, NY [*Library symbol*] [*Library of Congress*] (LCLS)

NNCPM .... New York College of Podiatric Medicine, New York, NY [*Library symbol*] [*Library of Congress*] (LCLS)

NNC-Pop ...... Columbia University, International Institute for the Study of Human Reproduction, Center for Population and Family Health, New York, NY [*Library symbol*] [*Library of Congress*] (LCLS)

NNC-Ps .... Columbia University, Psychology Library, New York, NY [*Library symbol*] [*Library of Congress*] (LCLS)

NNCR .... North Norfolk Coast Reserves (SAUS)

NNcR .... Roberts Wesleyan College, North Chili, NY [*Library symbol*] [*Library of Congress*] (LCLS)

NNCre .... Creedmoor Psychiatric Center, Queens Village, New York, NY [*Library symbol*] [*Library of Congress*] (LCLS)

NNCREW ...... National Network of Commercial Real Estate Women (NTPA)

NNCS .... Child Study Association of America, New York, NY [*Library symbol*] [*Library of Congress*] (LCLS)

NNCS .... NICS Network Control System (SAUS)

NNCSC .... National Neutron Cross Section Center [*AEC*] (MCD)

NNC-T .... Columbia University, Teachers College, New York, NY [*Library symbol*] [*Library of Congress*] (LCLS)

NNC-Typ ...... Columbia University, American Typefounders' Library, New York, NY [*Library symbol*] [*Library of Congress*] (LCLS)

NNCU-C .... City University of New York, Central Office, New York, NY [*Library symbol*] [*Library of Congress*] (LCLS)

NNCU-G .... City University of New York, Graduate Center, New York, NY [*Library symbol*] [*Library of Congress*] (LCLS)

NNCU-L .... City University of New York, Law School, Flushing, NY [*Library symbol*] [*Library of Congress*] (LCLS)

NNCU-T .... City University of New York, Division of Teacher Education, New York, NY [*Library symbol*] [*Library of Congress*] (LCLS)

NNCX .... Newbridge Networks Corp. (SAUS)

NND .... Dover Publications, New York, NY [*Library symbol*] [*Library of Congress*] (LCLS)

NND .... National Network Dialing [*Telecommunications*] (TEL)

NND .... National Number Dialing [*Telecommunications*] (DCTA)

NND .... Naval Net Depot

NND .... Neo-Natal Death [*Medicine*]

NND .... New and Nonofficial Drugs [*AMA*]

NND .... Nonspecific Nonerosive Duodenitis [*Medicine*] (DMAA)

NNDC .... National Naval Dental Center

NNDC .... National New Democratic Coalition (EA)

NNDC .... National Nuclear Data Center [*Department of Energy*] [*Database producer*] (IID)

NNDCG .... Danish Consultate General, Reference Library, New York, NY [*Library symbol*] [*Library of Congress*] (LCLS)

NNDE .... Nearest-Neighbor Distance Error [*Algorithm*]

NNDP .... Debevoise & Plimpton, New York, NY [*Library symbol*] [*Library of Congress*] (LCLS)

NNDP .... Naga National Democratic Party [*India*] [*Political party*] (PPW)

NNDPA .... N-Nitrosodiphenylamine [*Organic chemistry*]

NNDPW .... Davis, Polk & Wardwell, Law Library, New York, NY [*Library symbol*] [*Library of Congress*] (LCLS)

NNDR .... National Non-Domestic Rate [*British*]

NNDSS .... National Notification Disease Surveillance System [*Centers for Disease Control*]

NNDTC .... National Nondestructive Testing Centre [*Atomic Energy Authority*] [*Information service or system*] (IID)

NNE .... Engineering Societies Library, New York, NY [*Library symbol*] [*Library of Congress*] (LCLS)

NNE .... Neonatal Necrotizing Enterocolitis [*Medicine*] (AAMN)

NNE .... Noise and Number Exposure (PDAA)

NNE .... Nonneuronal Enolase [*Medicine*] (DMAA)

NNE .... Nonneuron-Specific Enolase [*An enzyme*]

NNE .... Nonstandard Negro English

NNE .... North by North East (SAUS)

NNE .... North-Northeast

NNEA .... National Negro Evangelical Association [*Later, NBEA*]

NNEB .... National Nursery Examination Board

NNebg .... Newburgh Free Library, Newburgh, NY [*Library symbol*] [*Library of Congress*] (LCLS)

NNebgE .... Epiphany Apostolic College, Newburgh, NY [*Library symbol*] [*Library of Congress*] (LCLS)

NNebgL .... Ninth Judicial District Law Library, Newburgh, NY [*Library symbol*] [*Library of Congress*] (LCLS)

NNebgM .... Mount Saint Mary College, Newburgh, NY [*Library symbol*] [*Library of Congress*] (LCLS)

NNebgWM ... Washington's Headquarters Museum, Newburgh, NY [*Library symbol*] [*Library of Congress*] (LCLS)

NNebpHH .... Herricks High School, New Hyde Park (SAUS)

NNEC .... Explorers Club, New York, NY [*Library symbol*] [*Library of Congress*] (LCLS)

NNec .... New City Free Library, New City, NY [*Library symbol*] [*Library of Congress*] (LCLS)

NNECA .... National Network of Episcopal Clergy Associations (EA)

NNECH .... National Nutrition Education Clearing House [*Society for Nutrition Education*] (IID)

NNecL .... New City Free Library, New City, NY [*Library symbol*] [*Library of Congress*] (LCLS)

NNEEDD ...... NOAA N-ROSS/ERS-1 Environmental Data Development (SAUS)

NNEF .... Educational Film Library Association, New York, NY [*Library symbol*] [*Library of Congress*] (LCLS)

NNef .... Newfane Public Library, Newfane, NY [*Library symbol*] [*Library of Congress*] (LCLS)

NNefH .... Inter-Community Memorial Hospital, Newfane, NY [*Library symbol*] [*Library of Congress*] (LCLS)

NNefL .... Newfane Free Library, Newfane, NY [*Library symbol*] [*Library of Congress*] (LCLS)

NNegbM .... Mount St. Mary College, Newburgh, NY [*Library symbol*] [*Library of Congress*] (LCLS)

NNegbWM ... Washington's Headquarters Museum, Newburgh, NY [*Library symbol*] [*Library of Congress*] (LCLS)

NNehpHH .... Herricks High School, New Hyde Park, NY [*Library symbol*] [*Library of Congress*] (LCLS)

NNEL .... Equitable Life Assurance Society of the United States, Medical Library, New York, NY [*Library symbol*] [*Library of Congress*] (LCLS)

NNEL-M .... Equitable Life Assurance Society of the United States, Medical Library, New York, NY [*Library symbol*] [*Library of Congress*] (LCLS)

NNepa .... Elting Memorial Library, New Paltz, NY [*Library symbol*] [*Library of Congress*] (LCLS)

NNepaSU .... State University of New York, College at New Paltz, New Paltz, NY [*Library symbol*] [*Library of Congress*] (LCLS)

NNer .... New Rochelle Public Library, New Rochelle, NY [*Library symbol*] [*Library of Congress*] (LCLS)

NNerAIS .... United States Army, Information School, Fort Slocum, New Rochelle, NY [*Library symbol*] [*Library of Congress*] (LCLS)

NNerC .... College of New Rochelle, New Rochelle, NY [*Library symbol*] [*Library of Congress*] (LCLS)

NNerI .... Iona College, New Rochelle (SAUS)

NNerI .... Iona College, New Rochelle, NY [*Library symbol*] [*Library of Congress*] (LCLS)

NNERN .... North-Northeastern (SAUS)

NNES .... National Nuclear Energy Series [*of AEC-sponsored books*]

NNESCC ...... Northern New England Small College Conference (PSS)

NNEU .... Naval Nuclear Evaluation Unit

NNEW .... Ernst & Whinney, Audit Management Services, New York, NY [*Library symbol*] [*Library of Congress*] (LCLS)

NNEWD .... North-Northeastward (FAAC)

NNEXF .... Newscope Resources Ltd. [*NASDAQ symbol*] (SAG)

NNF .... Fordham University, New York, NY [*Library symbol*] [*Library of Congress*] (LCLS)

NNF .... Namibia National Front [*Political party*] (PPW)

NNF .... National Nephrosis Foundation [*Later, NKF*]

NNF .... National Neurofibromatosis Foundation (PAZ)

NNF .... National Newman Foundation [*Defunct*] (EA)

NNF .... National Newspaper Foundation (EA)

NNF .... National Nothing Foundation [*Defunct*] (EA)

NNF .... Negation Normal Form (IDAI)

NNF .... Nordisk Neurokirurgisk Forening [*Scandinavian Neurosurgical Society - SNS*] (EAIO)

NNF .... Nordisk Neurologisk Forening [*Scandinavian Neurological Association - SNA*] (EAIO)

NNF .... Northern Nurses Federation [*Norway*]

NNF .... Nuveen Ins. NY Prem Inc. Muni [*NYSE symbol*] (TTSB)

NNF .... Nuveen Insured New York Premium Income Municipal [*NYSE symbol*] (SPSG)

NNFA .... National Nutritional Foods Association (EA)

NNFB .... Ford, Bacon & Davis, Inc., New York, NY [*Library symbol*] [*Library of Congress*] (LCLS)

NNFBC .... First Boston Corporation, New York, NY [*Library symbol*] [*Library of Congress*] (LCLS)

NNFC .... Finch College, New York, NY [*Library symbol*] [*Library of Congress*] (LCLS)

NNFE .... Free Europe Committee, New York, NY [*Library symbol*] [*Library of Congress*] (LCLS)

NNFF .... Ford Foundation, New York, NY [*Library symbol*] [*Library of Congress*] (LCLS)
NNFF .... National Neurofibromatosis Foundation (EA)
NNFF .... Not Nested or Folded Flat [*Freight*]
NNFF-FL ...... Ford Foundation, Ford Foundation Library, New York, NY [*Library symbol*] [*Library of Congress*] (LCLS)
NNFFu .... Franklin Furnance Archives, New York, NY [*Library symbol*] [*Library of Congress*] (LCLS)
NNFI .... French Institute/Alliance Francaise, New York, NY [*Library symbol*] [*Library of Congress*] (LCLS)
NNFIT .... Fashion Institute of Technology, New York, NY [*Library symbol*] [*Library of Congress*] (LCLS)
NNF-L .... Fordham University, Law Library, New York, NY [*Library symbol*] [*Library of Congress*] (LCLS)
NNFL .... Religious Society of Friends [*Quakers*], New York, NY [*Library symbol*] [*Library of Congress*] (LCLS)
NNF-LC .... Fordham University, Library at Lincoln Center, New York (SAUS)
NNF-LC .... Fordham University, Library at Lincoln Center, New York, NY [*Library symbol*] [*Library of Congress*] (LCLS)
NNFM .... Grand Lodge of New York, F & AM Library and Museum, New York, NY [*Library symbol*] [*Library of Congress*] (LCLS)
NNFoC .... Foundation Center Library, New York, NY [*Library symbol*] [*Library of Congress*] (LCLS)
NNFoM .... Forbes Magazine, Inc., New York, NY [*Library symbol*] [*Library of Congress*] (LCLS)
NNFP .... Nuclear Nitrogen Fixation Plant
NNFr .... Frick Art Reference Library, New York, NY [*Library symbol*] [*Library of Congress*] (LCLS)
NNF-RS .... Fordham University, Institute of Contemporary Russian Studies, New York, NY [*Library symbol*] [*Library of Congress*] (LCLS)
NNFS .... Nordic Narrow/16mm Film Society (EA)
NNFT .... National Federation of Textiles, New York, NY [*Library symbol*] [*Library of Congress*] (LCLS)
NNFU .... Nuclear Nonfirst Use
NNG .... General Theological Seminary of the Protestant Episcopal Church, New York, NY [*Library symbol*] [*Library of Congress*] (LCLS)
NNG .... Nanning [*China*] [*Airport symbol*] (OAG)
NNG .... National Network of Grantmakers (EA)
NNG .... National Number Group (NITA)
NNG .... Nonspecific Nonerosive Gastritis [*Medicine*] (DMAA)
NNG .... Northern Natural Gas (SAUS)
NNGA .... Northern Nut Growers Association (EA)
NNGBSW ..... National Network of Graduate Business School Women [*Knoxville, TN*] (EA)
NNGI .... National Aeronautics and Space Administration, Goddard Institute for Space Studies, New York, NY [*Library symbol*] [*Library of Congress*] (LCLS)
NNGoe .... Goethe House, German Cultural Institute, New York, NY [*Library symbol*] [*Library of Congress*] (LCLS)
NNGr .... Grolier Club, New York, NY [*Library symbol*] [*Library of Congress*] (LCLS)
NNGS .... Church of Jesus Christ of Latter-Day Saints, Genealogical Society Library, New York Branch, New York, NY [*Library symbol*] [*Library of Congress*] (LCLS)
NNGu .... Solomon R. Guggenheim Museum, New York, NY [*Library symbol*] [*Library of Congress*] (LCLS)
NNH .... Hispanic Society of America, New York, NY [*Library symbol*] [*Library of Congress*] (LCLS)
NNH .... Natal Native Horse [*British military*] (DMA)
NNH .... National Humanities Center, Research Triangle Park, NC [*OCLC symbol*] (OCLC)
NNH .... Nordiska Namnden for Handikappfragor [*Nordic Committee on Disability - NCD*] [*Sweden*] (EAIO)
NNHA .... National Novice Hockey Association [*Later, HNA*] (EA)
NNHC .... Hostos Community College, New York, NY [*Library symbol*] [*Library of Congress*] (LCLS)
NNHC .... Natal Native High Court Reports [*1899-1915*] [*South Africa*] [*A publication*] (DLA)
NNHCF-C ..... Holy Cross Friary, Juniper Carol Library, New York, NY [*Library symbol*] [*Library of Congress*] (LCLS)
NNHE .... New York City Board of Higher Education, New York, NY [*Library symbol*] [*Library of Congress*] (LCLS)
NNHeb .... Hebrew Union College - Jewish Institute of Religion, New York, NY [*Library symbol*] [*Library of Congress*] (LCLS)
NNHH .... Harlem Hospital Center, Medical Library, New York, NY [*Library symbol*] [*Library of Congress*] (LCLS)
NNHHR .... Hughes, Hubbard & Reed, New York, NY [*Library symbol*] [*Library of Congress*] (LCLS)
NNHL .... National Novice Hockey League [*Later, NNHA*] (EA)
NNHol .... Holland Society of New York, New York, NY [*Library symbol*] [*Library of Congress*] (LCLS)
NNHor .... Horticultural Society of New York, Inc., New York, NY [*Library symbol*] [*Library of Congress*] (LCLS)
NNhp .... New Hyde Park Public Library, New Hyde Park, NY [*Library symbol*] [*Library of Congress*] (LCLS)
NNhpDE .... Denton Avenue Elementary School, New Hyde Park, NY [*Library symbol*] [*Library of Congress*] (LCLS)
NNhpGE .... Garden City Park School, New Hyde Park, NY [*Library symbol*] [*Library of Congress*] (LCLS)
NNhpH .... Hillside Public Library, New Hyde Park, NY [*Library symbol*] [*Library of Congress*] (LCLS)
NNhpHE .... Hillside Grade School, New Hyde Park, NY [*Library symbol*] [*Library of Congress*] (LCLS)
NNhpHH .... Herricks High School, New Hyde Park, NY [*Library symbol*] [*Library of Congress*] (LCLS)

NNhpJ .... Long Island Jewish Hospital, New Hyde Park, NY [*Library symbol*] [*Library of Congress*] (LCLS)
NNhpME ...... Manor-Oaks-William R. Bowie School, New Hyde Park, NY [*Library symbol*] [*Library of Congress*] (LCLS)
NNhpMH ...... New Hyde Park Memorial High School, New Hyde Park, NY [*Library symbol*] [*Library of Congress*] (LCLS)
NNhpNE .... New Hyde Park Road School, New Hyde Park, NY [*Library symbol*] [*Library of Congress*] (LCLS)
NNHR .... New York City Human Resources Administration, New York, NY [*Library symbol*] [*Library of Congress*] (LCLS)
NNHS .... Hospital for Special Surgery, New York, NY [*Library symbol*] [*Library of Congress*] (LCLS)
NNHS .... National Nursing Home Survey [*Department of Health and Human Services*] (GFGA)
NNhS .... Special Metals Corp., New Hartford, NY [*Library symbol*] [*Library of Congress*] (LCLS)
NNHuC .... Hunter College of the City University of New York, New York, NY [*Library symbol*] [*Library of Congress*] (LCLS)
NNHWW ...... H.W. Wilson Co., Bronx, NY [*Library symbol*] [*Library of Congress*] (LCLS)
NNI .... National Newspaper Index [*Information Access Co.*] [*Bibliographic database*] [*Information service or system*] (IID)
NNI .... Net National Income [*Economics*]
NNI .... Net-Net Income [*Business term*]
NNI .... Network-Network Interface (RALS)
NNI .... Network Node Interface [*Computer science*]
NNI .... New Nickerie [*Surinam*] [*Airport symbol*] (AD)
NNI .... Next Node Index (SAUS)
NNI .... Next Node Indicator (SAUS)
NNI .... Noise and Nuisance Index (SAUS)
NNI .... Noise and Number Index
NNI .... Noise Nuisance Index (PDAA)
NNI .... Nonnuclear Instrumentation (NRCH)
NNI .... Non-Numeric Information (SAUS)
NNI .... Norwegian Nobel Institute (SAUS)
NNI .... Nucleon-Nucleon Interaction
NNI .... Office of Naval Intelligence Publications
NNIA .... American Institute of Aeronautics and Astronautics, New York, NY [*Library symbol*] [*Library of Congress*] (LCLS)
NNia .... Niagara Falls Public Library, Niagara Falls, NY [*Library symbol*] [*Library of Congress*] (LCLS)
NNiaA .... Airco Speer Research & Development Laboratories, Niagara Falls, NY [*Library symbol*] [*Library of Congress*] (LCLS)
NNiaB .... Bell Aerospace Textron, Technical Library, Niagara Falls, NY [*Library symbol*] [*Library of Congress*] (LCLS)
NNiaC .... Niagara County Community College, Niagara Falls, NY [*Library symbol*] [*Library of Congress*] (LCLS)
NNiaCa .... Carborundum Co., Niagara Falls, NY [*Library symbol*] [*Library of Congress*] (LCLS)
NNiaD .... E. I. Du Pont de Nemours & Co., Electrochemical Department, Niagara Falls, NY [*Library symbol*] [*Library of Congress*] (LCLS)
NNiaEM .... Elkem Metals Co., Niagara Falls, NY [*Library symbol*] [*Library of Congress*] (LCLS)
NNiaH .... Hooker Chemical Corp. [*Later, Hooker Chemicals & Plastics Corp.*], Niagara Falls, NY [*Library symbol*] [*Library of Congress*] (LCLS)
NNiaHC .... Hooker Chemicals & Plastics Corp., Business Library, Niagara Falls, NY [*Library symbol*] [*Library of Congress*] (LCLS)
NNiaM .... Moore Business Forms, Niagara Falls, NY [*Library symbol*] [*Library of Congress*] (LCLS)
NNiaMed .... Niagara Falls Memorial Medical Center, Medical Library, Niagara Falls, NY [*Library symbol*] [*Library of Congress*] (LCLS)
NNiaN .... National Lead Co., Research Library, Niagara Falls, NY [*Library symbol*] [*Library of Congress*] (LCLS)
NNiaNC .... NIACET Corporation, Niagara Falls, NY [*Library symbol*] [*Library of Congress*] (LCLS)
NNiaNL .... Nioga Library System, Niagara Falls, NY [*Library symbol*] [*Library of Congress*] (LCLS)
NNiaO .... Occidental Chemical Corp., Technical Information Center, Niagra Falls, NY [*Library symbol*] [*Library of Congress*] (LCLS)
NNiaSE .... Sohio Engineered Materials Co., Research and Development Library, Niagara Falls, NY [*Library symbol*] [*Library of Congress*] (LCLS)
NNiaTC .... TAM Ceramics, Inc., Niagara Falls, NY [*Library symbol*] [*Library of Congress*] (LCLS)
NNiaTV .... Trott Vocational High School, Niagara Falls, NY [*Library symbol*] [*Library of Congress*] (LCLS)
NNiaU .... Niagara University, Niagara University, NY [*Library symbol*] [*Library of Congress*] (LCLS)
NNiaUC .... Union Carbide Corp., Niagara Falls, NY [*Library symbol*] [*Library of Congress*] (LCLS)
NNIC .... Normalized Noise Isolation Class (SAUS)
NNICC .... National Narcotics Intelligence Consumers Committee [*Drug Enforcement Administration*] [*Washington, DC*] (EGAO)
NNIG .... Netherlands Naval Industries Group (SAUS)
NNI-I .... NASA Standard Initiator-Type I (SAUS)
NNIIC .... Istituto Italiano Di Cultura Biblioteca, New York, NY [*Library symbol*] [*Library of Congress*] (LCLS)
NNIIE .... Institute of International Education, New York, NY [*Library symbol*] [*Library of Congress*] (LCLS)
NNIMD .... Institute for Muscle Disease, New York, NY [*Library symbol*] [*Library of Congress*] [*Obsolete*] (LCLS)
NNIND .... International Nickel Co., Technical Library, New York, NY [*Library symbol*] [*Library of Congress*] (LCLS)
NNInS .... Insurance Society of New York, New York, NY [*Library symbol*] [*Library of Congress*] (LCLS)

NNIP .... Institute of Public Administration, New York, NY [*Library symbol*] [*Library of Congress*] (LCLS)

NNIPF .... International Planned Parenthood Federation, Documentation and Publications Center, New York, NY [*Library symbol*] [*Library of Congress*] (LCLS)

NNIR .... Industrial Relations Counselors, New York, NY [*Library symbol*] [*Library of Congress*] (LCLS)

NNIRR .... National Network for Immigrant and Refugee Rights (EA)

NNIS .... Library for Intercultural Studies, Inc., New York, NY [*Library symbol*] [*Library of Congress*] (LCLS)

NNIS .... National Nosocomial Infections Study [*Medicine*] (DMAA)

NNIS .... National Nosocomial Infections Surveillance [*Medicine*]

NNIS .... Nonnuclear Instrumentation System (NRCH)

NNISS .... Nosocomial Infections Surveillance System [*Center for Disease Control*]

NNJ .... Jewish Theological Seminary of America, New York, NY [*Library symbol*] [*Library of Congress*] (LCLS)

NNJ .... Nakano [*Japan*] [*Seismograph station code, US Geological Survey*] (SEIS)

NNJ .... Nuveen New Jersey Premium Income Municipal [*NYSE symbol*] (SPSG)

NNJ .... Nuveen NJ Prem Inc. Muni [*NYSE symbol*] (TTSB)

NNJa .... Juilliard School of Music, New York (SAUS)

NNJef .... Jefferson School of Social Science, New York, NY [*Library symbol*] [*Library of Congress*] [*Obsolete*] (LCLS)

NNJH .... Joint Health Library, New York, NY [*Library symbol*] [*Library of Congress*] [*Obsolete*] (LCLS)

NNJHK .... Jenny Hunter's Kindergarten and Primary Training School, New York, NY [*Library symbol*] [*Library of Congress*] [*Obsolete*] (LCLS)

NNJJ .... John Jay College of Criminal Justice, New York, NY [*Library symbol*] [*Library of Congress*] (LCLS)

NNJS .... Japan Society Library, New York, NY [*Library symbol*] [*Library of Congress*] (LCLS)

NNJu .... Juilliard School of Music, New York, NY [*Library symbol*] [*Library of Congress*] (LCLS)

NNK .... Naknek [*Alaska*] [*Airport symbol*] (OAG)

NNK .... Nic-Nik Resources [*Vancouver Stock Exchange symbol*]

NNK .... Nicotine-Derived Nitrosaminoketone

NNK .... Nonnuclear Kill

NNK .... Notify Next of Kind (SAUS)

NNKKAA ...... Journal. Agricultural Chemical Society of Japan (journ.) (SAUS)

NNKRAS ..... Non-Nuclear Kill Requirements and Applications Study [*Military*]

NNL .... Beeville, TX [*Location identifier*] (FAA) (FAAL)

NNL .... Herbert H. Lehman College of the City University of New York, New York, NY [*Library symbol*] [*Library of Congress*] (LCLS)

NNL .... Negro National League [*Baseball*] (NDBD)

NN-L .... New York Public Library, Research Library for the Performing Arts at Lincoln Center, New York, NY [*Library symbol*] [*Library of Congress*] (LCLS)

NNL .... Nigerian National Line (SAUS)

NNL .... Ninilchik [*Alaska*] [*Seismograph station code, US Geological Survey*] (SEIS)

NNL .... Nondalton [*Alaska*] [*Airport symbol*] (OAG)

NNL .... No Net Loss

NNL .... No New Laboratory (MELL)

NNL .... Non-Newtonian Liquid (SAUS)

NNL .... Non-Nuclear Lance Missile (PDAA)

NNLBI .... Leo Baeck Institute, New York, NY [*Library symbol*] [*Library of Congress*] (LCLS)

NNLC .... Lutheran Council in the USA, New York, NY [*Library symbol*] [*Library of Congress*] (LCLS)

NNLC .... Ngwane National Liberatory Congress [*Swaziland*]

NNLDA .... National Network of Learning Disabled Adults (EA)

NNLehman... Lehman Corp., New York, NY [*Library symbol*] [*Library of Congress*] (LCLS)

NNLH .... Lenox Hill Hospital, Medical Library, New York, NY [*Library symbol*] [*Library of Congress*] (LCLS)

NNLI .... New York Law Institute, New York, NY [*Library symbol*] [*Library of Congress*] (LCLS)

NNLM .... National Network of Libraries of Medicine

NNLN .... Northern Nigeria Legal Notes [*A publication*] (DLA)

NNLP .... National Natural Landmarks Program (WPI)

NNLR .... Law Reprints, New York, NY [*Library symbol*] [*Library of Congress*] (LCLS)

NNLR .... Northern Nigeria Law Reports [*A publication*] (DLA)

NNLS .... New York Law School Library, New York, NY [*Library symbol*] [*Library of Congress*] (LCLS)

NNLS .... Non-Negative Least Squares (ARMP)

NNM .... American Museum of Natural History, New York, NY [*Library symbol*] [*Library of Congress*] (LCLS)

NNM .... Davidson College, Davidson, NC [*OCLC symbol*] (OCLC)

NNM .... Nasdaq National Market (SG)

NNM .... Neonatal Mortality [*Medicine*] (DMAA)

NNM .... Network Node Manager (SAUS)

NN-M .... New York Public Library, Municipal Reference Library, New York, NY [*Library symbol*] [*Library of Congress*] (LCLS)

NNM .... Next New Moon (SAUS)

NNM .... Next (or Nearest) New Moon [*Freemasonry*] (ROG)

NNM .... Nicolle-Novy-MacNeal [*Medium*] [*Microbiology*] (DAVI)

NNM .... N-Nitrosomorpholine [*Also, NMOR*] [*Organic chemistry*]

NNM .... Node-to-Node Message (SAUS)

NNM .... No Neutral Mode

NNm .... North Merrick Public Library, North Merrick, NY [*Library symbol*] [*Library of Congress*] (LCLS)

NNM .... Nuveen New York Municipal Income [*AMEX symbol*] (SPSG)

NNMa .... Marymount Manhattan College, New York, NY [*Library symbol*] [*Library of Congress*] (LCLS)

NNMAI .... Museum of the American Indian, New York, NY [*Library symbol*] [*Library of Congress*] (LCLS)

NNMan .... Manhattan College, New York, NY [*Library symbol*] [*Library of Congress*] (LCLS)

NNMB .... Methodist Board of Missions, New York, NY [*Library symbol*] [*Library of Congress*] (LCLS)

NNMB .... National Nutrition Monitoring Bureau (SAUS)

NNmBJ .... Brookside Junior High School, North Merrick, NY [*Library symbol*] [*Library of Congress*] (LCLS)

NNMC .... Mannes College of Music, New York, NY [*Library symbol*] [*Library of Congress*] (LCLS)

NNMC .... National Naval Medical Center [*Bethesda, MD*]

NNmCE .... Camp Avenue Elementary School, North Merrick, NY [*Library symbol*] [*Library of Congress*] (LCLS)

NNMcGraw... McGraw-Hill, Inc., New York, NY [*Library symbol*] [*Library of Congress*] (LCLS)

NNME .... Mid-European Studies Center, New York, NY [*Library symbol*] [*Library of Congress*] (LCLS)

NNMec........ General Society of Mechanics and Tradesmen, New York, NY [*Library symbol*] [*Library of Congress*] (LCLS)

NNMel .... Andrew W. Mellon Foundation, New York, NY [*Library symbol*] [*Library of Congress*] (LCLS)

NN-Mel .... New York Public Library, Mellon Microfilm Collection, New York, NY [*Library symbol*] [*Library of Congress*] (LCLS)

NNMer......... Mercantile Library Association, New York, NY [*Library symbol*] [*Library of Congress*] (LCLS)

NNMF .... Markle Foundation, New York, NY [*Library symbol*] [*Library of Congress*] (LCLS)

NNmFE .... Harold D. Fayette Elementary School, North Merrick, NY [*Library symbol*] [*Library of Congress*] (LCLS)

NNMH .... Montefiore Hospital, New York, NY [*Library symbol*] [*Library of Congress*] (LCLS)

NNMi .... Millenium Film Workshop, New York, NY [*Library symbol*] [*Library of Congress*] (LCLS)

NNMI .... Nonlinear Normal Mode Initialization (SAUS)

NNML .... Metropolitan Life Insurance Co., New York, NY [*Library symbol*] [*Library of Congress*] (LCLS)

NNMLC .... Medical Library Center of New York, New York, NY [*Library symbol*] [*Library of Congress*] (LCLS)

NNMM .... Metropolitan Museum of Art, New York, NY [*Library symbol*] [*Library of Congress*] (LCLS)

NNMMA ...... Museum of Modern Art, New York, NY [*Library symbol*] [*Library of Congress*] (LCLS)

NNMMA-F... Museum of Modern Art, Film Study Center, New York, NY [*Library symbol*] [*Library of Congress*] (LCLS)

NNMMA-U ... Metropolitian Museum of Art, Uris Library and Resources Center, New York, NY [*Library symbol*] [*Library of Congress*] (LCLS)

NNMM-C...... Metropolitan Museum of Art, The Cloisters Library, New York, NY [*Library symbol*] [*Library of Congress*] (LCLS)

NNMM-CI.... Metropolitan Museum of Art, Costume Institute, New York, NY [*Library symbol*] [*Library of Congress*] (LCLS)

NNmN......... North Merrick Public Library, North Merrick, NY [*Library symbol*] [*Library of Congress*] (LCLS)

NNMO......... Mobil Oil Corp., Secretariat Library, New York, NY [*Library symbol*] [*Library of Congress*] (LCLS)

NnmOE .... Old Mill Road Elementary School, North Merrick, NY [*Library symbol*] [*Library of Congress*] (LCLS)

NNMoMA .... Museum of Modern Art, New York, NY [*Library symbol*] [*Library of Congress*] (LCLS)

NNMP......... Motion Picture Association of America, Inc., Research Department Library, New York, NY [*Library symbol*] [*Library of Congress*] (LCLS)

NNMPA........ Museum of Primitive Art, New York, NY [*Library symbol*] [*Library of Congress*] (LCLS)

NNmPE .... Park Avenue Elementary School, North Merrick, NY [*Library symbol*] [*Library of Congress*] (LCLS)

NN-MPH ...... New York Public Library, Public Health Division, New York, NY [*Library symbol*] [*Library of Congress*] (LCLS)

NNMR......... Missionary Research Library, New York, NY [*Library symbol*] [*Library of Congress*] (LCLS)

NNMRR....... New York Metropolitan Reference and Research Library Agency, Inc., New York, NY [*Library symbol*] [*Library of Congress*] (LCLS)

NNMS .... Manhattan State Hospital, New York, NY [*Library symbol*] [*Library of Congress*] (LCLS)

NNMS .... National Nutrition-Monitoring System [*Department of Agriculture*] (GFGA)

NNMS .... Nazareth National Motor Speedway [*Pennsylvania*]

NNMSB .... Nonnuclear Munitions Safety Board [*Military*]

NNMSCP...... Nonnuclear Munitions Safety Control Program [*Military*]

NNMSE .... Network Node Manager Special Edition

NNMSG .... Nonnuclear Munitions Safety Group [*Air Force*] (AFM)

NNMSGP...... Nonnuclear Munitions Safety Group [*Air Force*]

NNMSK........ Memorial Sloan-Kettering Cancer Center, New York, NY [*Library symbol*] [*Library of Congress*] (LCLS)

NNMSM .... Manhattan School of Music, New York, NY [*Library symbol*] [*Library of Congress*] (LCLS)

NNMT .... Newport News Marine Terminal

NNMtS .... Mount Sinai Hospital, New York, NY [*Library symbol*] [*Library of Congress*] (LCLS)

NNMtSM...... Mount Sinai School of Medicine of the City University of New York, New York, NY [*Library symbol*] [*Library of Congress*] (LCLS)

NNMtSV....... College of Mount Saint Vincent, New York, NY [*Library symbol*] [*Library of Congress*] (LCLS)

NNMus......... Museum of the City of New York, New York, NY [*Library symbol*] [*Library of Congress*] (LCLS)
NNN .... Commercial Net Lease Realty, Inc. [*NYSE symbol*] (SAG)
NNN .... Commercial Net Lease Rlty [*NYSE symbol*] (TTSB)
NNN .... Nannies Need Nannies Association [*British*] (DBA)
NNN .... National Navy Notice
NNN .... National Nostalgic Nova (EA)
NNN .... Next Nearest Neighbor [*Chemical physics*]
NNN .... Nicolle-Novy-MacNeal [*Medium*] [*Medicine*] (MEDA)
NNN .... Nihon News Network (SAUS)
NNN .... Nitrosonornicotine [*Organic chemistry*]
NNN .... N-Nitrosonornicotine [*Organic chemistry*]
NNN .... No National Name
NNN .... No Native Named (SAUS)
NNN .... Non-Normalized Number (SAUS)
NNN .... No No Nanette [*Broadway musical*]
NNN .... Noramco Mining Corp. [*Toronto Stock Exchange symbol*] [*Vancouver Stock Exchange symbol*]
NNN .... Novy, MacNeal, and Nicolle's Medium [*Medicine*] (MAE)
NNNA .... No Name, No Address
NNNA .... Non-Native Network Attachment (SAUS)
NNNAM........ New York Academy of Medicine, New York, NY [*Library symbol*] [*Library of Congress*] (LCLS)
NNNASA ...... National Aeronautical and Space Administration, Institute for Space Studies, NewYork, NY [*Library symbol*] [*Library of Congress*] (LCLS)
NNNBC........ National Broadcasting Co., Inc., General Library, New York, NY [*Library symbol*] [*Library of Congress*] (LCLS)
NNNBC-I ...... National Broadcasting Co., Inc., Information Unit, Research Department, New York, NY [*Library symbol*] [*Library of Congress*] (LCLS)
NNNC.......... New York Chamber of Commerce, New York, NY [*Library symbol*] [*Library of Congress*] (LCLS)
NNNCC-Ar.... New York County Clerk Archives, Division of Old Records, New York, NY [*Library symbol*] [*Library of Congress*] (LCLS)
NNNCL......... New York County Lawyers Association, New York, NY [*Library symbol*] [*Library of Congress*] (LCLS)
NNNCR .... National Council for Resources on Women, New York, NY [*Library symbol*] [*Library of Congress*] (LCLS)
NNNDO .... Neglect of Non-Neighbor Differential Overlap [*Physics*]
NNNDR .... Narcotic and Drug Research, Inc., New York, NY [*Library symbol*] [*Library of Congress*] (LCLS)
NNNel.......... Netherlands Information Service, New York, NY [*Library symbol*] [*Library of Congress*] (LCLS)
NNNGB .... New York Genealogical and Biographical Society, New York, NY [*Library symbol*] [*Library of Congress*] (LCLS)
NNNH.......... National Health Agencies Library, New York, NY [*Library symbol*] [*Library of Congress*] [*Obsolete*] (LCLS)
NNNHi .... Naval History Society, New York, NY [*Library symbol*] [*Library of Congress*] [*Obsolete*] (LCLS)
NNNM .... New York Medical College, Flower and Fifth Avenue Hospitals, New York, NY [*Library symbol*] [*Library of Congress*] (LCLS)
NNNMCA...... New Museum of Contemporary Art, New York, NY [*Library symbol*] [*Library of Congress*] (LCLS)
NNNN.......... End of Message (SAUS)
NNNPsan .... New York Psychoanalytic Institute, New York, NY [*Library symbol*] [*Library of Congress*] (LCLS)
NNNPSC ..... National No-Nukes Prison Support Collective (EA)
NNNPsI....... New York State Department of Mental Hygiene, Psychiatric Institute, New York, NY [*Library symbol*] [*Library of Congress*] (LCLS)
NNNR.......... Noss National Nature Reserve (SAUS)
NNNS.......... New School for Social Research, New York, NY [*Library symbol*] [*Library of Congress*] (LCLS)
NNNSB........ National Society for the Prevention of Blindness, New York, NY [*Library symbol*] [*Library of Congress*] (LCLS)
NNNT .... New York Theological Seminary, New York, NY [*Library symbol*] [*Library of Congress*] (LCLS)
NNNTSH ...... Naukove Tovarystvo Imeni Shevchenka (Shevchenko Scientific Society, Inc.), New York, NY [*Library symbol*] [*Library of Congress*] (LCLS)
NNNWA....... N. W. Ayer & Son, New York, NY [*Library symbol*] [*Library of Congress*] (LCLS)
NNO .... Naga Nationalist Organization [*India*]
N-NO........... New York-New Orleans (SAUS)
NNO .... No New Orders [*Medical Records*] (DAVI)
NNO .... Nord-Nord-Ouest [*North-Northwest*] [*French*]
NNO .... Northern Orion Explorations [*Vancouver Stock Exchange symbol*]
NNO .... Nuveen N.Y. Muni Market Opportunity (EFIS)
NNOA.......... National Naval Officers Association (EA)
NNOC.......... National Network Operations Center [*Ottawa, ON*] [*Telecommunications*] (TSSD)
NNOC.......... Nigerian National Oil Co. (SAUS)
NNomAE ...... Albany Avenue Elementary School, North Massapequa, NY [*Library symbol*] [*Library of Congress*] (LCLS)
NNomEE ...... Eastplain Elementary School, North Massapequa, NY [*Library symbol*] [*Library of Congress*] (LCLS)
NNomPH...... Plainedge High School, North Massapequa, NY [*Library symbol*] [*Library of Congress*] (LCLS)
NNomPJ ...... Sylvia Packard Junior High School, North Massapequa, NY [*Library symbol*] [*Library of Congress*] (LCLS)
NNOPE........ Naturists and Nudists Opposing Pornographic Exploitation (EA)
NNopo .... Northport Public Library (SAUS)
NNopo .... Northport Public Library, Northport, NY [*Library symbol*] [*Library of Congress*] (LCLS)

NNopo-E ...... Northport Public Library, East Northport Branch, East Northport, NY [*Library symbol*] [*Library of Congress*] (LCLS)
NNopoHS..... Northport High School, Northport, NY [*Library symbol*] [*Library of Congress*] (LCLS)
NNopoJH..... Northport Junior High School, Northport, NY [*Library symbol*] [*Library of Congress*] (LCLS)
NNopoVA..... United States Veterans Administration Hospital, Northport, NY [*Library symbol*] [*Library of Congress*] (LCLS)
NNOR.......... Nonnuclear Ordnance Requirement (MCD)
NNorP .... Norwich Pharmacal Co., Norwich, NY [*Library symbol*] [*Library of Congress*] (LCLS)
nNOS .... Neuronal Nitric Oxide Synthase [*An enzyme*]
NNosCE....... Sea Cliff Elementary School, North Shore, NY [*Library symbol*] [*Library of Congress*] (LCLS)
NnosJH....... North Shore Junior High School, North Shore, NY [*Library symbol*] [*Library of Congress*] (LCLS)
NNosSH .... North Shore Senior High School, North Shore, NY [*Library symbol*] [*Library of Congress*] (LCLS)
NNOt........... New York Orthopaedic Hospital, New York, NY [*Library symbol*] [*Library of Congress*] (LCLS)
NNot........... North Tonawanda Public Library, North Tonawanda, NY [*Library symbol*] [*Library of Congress*] (LCLS)
NNOT.......... Not Necessarily on Topic (SAUS)
NNotD .... DeGraff Memorial Hospital, North Tonawanda, NY [*Library symbol*] [*Library of Congress*] (LCLS)
NNotHC........ Hooker Chemicals & Plastics Corp., Durez Division Library, North Tonawanda, NY [*Library symbol*] [*Library of Congress*] (LCLS)
NNotL .... Lawless Container Corp., North Tonawanda, NY [*Library symbol*] [*Library of Congress*] (LCLS)
NNotP .... North Tonawanda Public Library, North Tonawanda, NY [*Library symbol*] [*Library of Congress*] (LCLS)
N NOV .... Nomen Novum [*New Name*] [*Latin*] (BABM)
n nov .... Nomen Novum [*New Name*] [*Latin*] [*Pharmacy*] (DAVI)
NNP .... Needle-Nosed Probe
NNP .... Negative Node Point
NNP .... Neonatal Nurse Practitioner (DAVI)
NNP .... Nerve Net Pulse [*Neurobiology*]
NNP .... Net National Product [*Economics*]
NNP .... Ngezi National Park (SAUS)
NNP .... Nimule National Park (SAUS)
NNP .... Non-Negation Property (SAUS)
NNP .... Nuveen New York Performance Plus Municipal [*NYSE symbol*] (SPSG)
NNP .... Nuveen NY Perform Plus Muni [*NYSE symbol*] (TTSB)
NNPA.......... National Negro Press Association [*Defunct*] (EA)
NNPA.......... National Newspaper Promotion Association [*Later, INPA*] (EA)
NNPA.......... National Newspaper Publishers Association (EA)
NNPA.......... Nuclear Nonproliferation Act [*1975*]
NNPA.......... Port Authority of New York and New Jersey, New York, NY [*Library symbol*] [*Library of Congress*] (LCLS)
NNParS........ Parsons School of Design, New York, NY [*Library symbol*] [*Library of Congress*] (LCLS)
NNPaul .... Paul, Weiss, Rifkind, Wharton & Garrison, Law Library, New York, NY [*Library symbol*] [*Library of Congress*] (LCLS)
NNPaW....... Payne Whitney Clinic, New York, NY [*Library symbol*] [*Library of Congress*] (LCLS)
NNPBD........ National Network to Prevent Birth Defects (MELL)
NNPC.......... Nigerian National Petroleum Corp. (ECON)
NNPC.......... Pace College, New York, NY [*Library symbol*] [*Library of Congress*] (LCLS)
NNPCC........ National Nutrition Policy Coordination Committee (SAUS)
NNPC-L....... Pace University, Law Library, White Plains, NY [*Library symbol*] [*Library of Congress*] (LCLS)
NNPE-NC ..... National Council of the Protestant Episcopal Church, New York, NY [*Library symbol*] [*Library of Congress*] (LCLS)
NNPennie..... Pennie, Edmonds, Morton, Taylor & Adams, New York, NY [*Library symbol*] [*Library of Congress*] (LCLS)
NNPf .... Carl H. Pforzheimer Library, New York, NY [*Library symbol*] [*Library of Congress*] (LCLS)
NNPH-O .... Institute of Ophthalmology, Presbyterian Hospital, New York, NY [*Library symbol*] [*Library of Congress*] (LCLS)
NNPHR .... New York City Public Health Research Laboratory, New York, NY [*Library symbol*] [*Library of Congress*] (LCLS)
NNPHW........ National New Professional Health Workers [*Later, NPSAPHA*] (EA)
NNPI .... Naval Nuclear Propulsion Information (MCD)
NNPIA.......... Polish Institute of Art and Sciences in America, Inc., Research Library, New York, NY [*Library symbol*] [*Library of Congress*] (LCLS)
n-n p-i-f........ never-never pay-infull (SAUS)
NNPlan........ Planning Assistance, Inc., New York, NY [*Library symbol*] [*Library of Congress*] (LCLS)
NNPM .... Pierpont Morgan Library, New York, NY [*Library symbol*] [*Library of Congress*] (LCLS)
NNPopC....... Population Council, New York, NY [*Library symbol*] [*Library of Congress*] (LCLS)
NNPPFA........ Planned Parenthood Federation of America, Inc., Katharine Dexter McCormick Library, New York, NY [*Library symbol*] [*Library of Congress*] (LCLS)
NNPPNYC .... Planned Parenthood of New York City, Inc., Abraham Stone Memorial Library, Margaret Sanger Center, New York, NY [*Library symbol*] [*Library of Congress*] (LCLS)
NNPRM........ United Presbyterian Mission Library of the United Presbyterian Church in the USA, New York, NY [*Library symbol*] [*Library of Congress*] (LCLS)
NNPS........... Navy Nuclear Power School (DNAB)

NNPS .... Norco Nuclear Power Station (NRCH)

NNPSPP ...... National Non-Point Source Pollution Program (GNE)

NNPTU .... Naval Nuclear Power Training Unit (DNAB)

NNPU .... Naval Nuclear Power Unit [Obsolete]

NNR .... City College of City University of New York, New York, NY [Library symbol] [Library of Congress] (LCLS)

NNR .... National Narcolepsy Registry [Founded in 1996] (NRGU)

NNR .... National Nature Reserve [British]

NNR .... National Number Routed [Telecommunications] (TEL)

NNR .... Nearest-Neighbor Rule [Mathematics]

NNR .... Nevada North Resources [Vancouver Stock Exchange symbol]

NNR .... New and Nonofficial Remedies [A publication]

NNR .... Nordiska Nykterhetsradet [Nordic Temperance Council - NTC] (EAIO)

NNR .... Normalized Noise Reduction (SAUS)

NNR .... Northern NORAD [North American Air Defense] Region (SAA)

NNR .... Not Necessary to Return (SAUS)

NNR .... Novell Network Registry (SAUS)

NNRA .... National Negro Republican Assembly [Defunct]

NNRB .... National Neurological Research Bank [Veterans Administration Medical Center] [Research center] (RCD)

NNRB .... Recording for the Blind, Inc., New York, NY [Library symbol] [Library of Congress] (LCLS)

NNRC .... Neutral Nations Repatriation Commission (SAUS)

NNRDC .... National Nuclear Rocket Development Center [Also known as NRDS]

NNRDF .... National Nuclear Rocket Development Facility (AAG)

NNRecA .... National Recreation Association [Later, NRPA], New York, NY [Library symbol] [Library of Congress] (LCLS)

NNreP .... Regional Plan Association, Inc., Library, New York, NY [Library symbol] [Library of Congress] (LCLS)

NNRF .... National Neurological Research Foundation (EA)

NNRG .... Nevada Energy Co., Inc. [NASDAQ symbol] (SAG)

NNRGA .... Nevada Energy [NASDAQ symbol] (TTSB)

NNRH .... Roosevelt Hospital, Medical Library, New York, NY [Library symbol] [Library of Congress] (LCLS)

NNRIS .... Nebraska Natural Resources Information System [Nebraska State Natural Resources Commission] [Lincoln] [Information service or system] (IID)

NNRo .... Theodore Roosevelt Association, New York, NY [Library symbol] [Library of Congress] (LCLS)

NNRocF .... Rockefeller Foundation, New York, NY [Library symbol] [Library of Congress] (LCLS)

NNRocFA .... Rockefeller Family & Associates, Inc., Office Library, New York, NY [Library symbol] [Library of Congress] (LCLS)

NNRoI .... Rochdale Institute, New York, NY [Library symbol] [Library of Congress] (LCLS)

NNRom .... Romanian Library, New York, NY [Library symbol] [Library of Congress] (LCLS)

NNRRB .... R. R. Bowker Co., New York, NY [Library symbol] [Library of Congress] (LCLS)

NNRT .... Non-Nucleoside Reverse Transcriptase [Biochemistry]

NNRT .... Racquet and Tennis Club, New York, NY [Library symbol] [Library of Congress] (LCLS)

NNRTC .... Northwest Natural Resource Technologies Consortium

NNRTI .... Non-Nucleoside Reverse Transcriptase Inhibitor [Biochemistry]

NNRU .... Rockefeller University, New York, NY [Library symbol] [Library of Congress] (LCLS)

NNRU-P .... Rockefeller University, Population Council, Bio-Medical Library, New York, NY [Library symbol] [Library of Congress] (LCLS)

NNRY .... Nunnery (ABBR)

NNRYS .... National Network of Runaway and Youth Services (EA)

NNS .... National Narrowcast Service [Public Broadcasting Service] [Arlington, VA] [Telecommunications service] (TSSD)

NNS .... National Natality Survey

NNS .... National Network Services (NITA)

NNS .... National Newspaper Syndicate

NNS .... Navy Navigation Satellite

NNS .... Navy News Service (DOMA)

NNS .... Near Net Shape (ACAE)

NNS .... Neonatal Society [British] (DBA)

NNS .... Neural Network Simulator

NNS .... Newhouse News Service (WDMC)

NNS .... Newport News Shipbuilding (DOMA)

NNS .... New York Society Library, New York, NY [Library symbol] [Library of Congress] (LCLS)

NNS .... Non-Native Speakers (EDAC)

NNS .... Nonnuclear Safety (NRCH)

NNS .... Nonnutritive Sweetener

NNS .... Norfolk Naval Shipyard [Portsmouth, VA] (MCD)

NNs .... North Salem Free Library, North Salem, NY [Library symbol] [Library of Congress] (LCLS)

NNS .... Nucleon-Nucleon Scattering

NNSA .... National Nurses Society on Addictions (EA)

NNSaB .... Salomon Brothers, New York, NY [Library symbol] [Library of Congress] (LCLS)

NNSAE .... Society of Automotive Engineers, New York, NY [Library symbol] [Library of Congress] (LCLS)

NNS&DDC .... Newport News Shipbuilding and Dry Dock Co. (SAUS)

NNSAR .... Sons of the American Revolution, Empire State Society Library, New York, NY [Library symbol] [Library of Congress] (LCLS)

NNSAS .... Skadden, Arps, Slate, Meagher & Flom, New York, NY [Library symbol] [Library of Congress] (LCLS)

NNSB .... Simmons-Boardman Publishing Corp., New York, NY [Library symbol] [Library of Congress] [Obsolete] (LCLS)

NNSB & DDCO .... Newport News Shipbuilding & Dry Dock Co. (DNAB)

NNSC .... Neutral Nations Supervisory Commission

NN-Sc .... New York Public Library, Schomburg Collection, New York, NY [Library symbol] [Library of Congress] (LCLS)

NNSC .... Non-Nuclear Strategic Capabilities (SAUS)

NNSC .... NSF [National Science] Network Service Center [Internet] (TNIG)

NNSC .... Smithsonian Institution, Cooper-Hewitt Museum of Decorative Arts and Design, New York, NY [Library symbol] [Library of Congress] (LCLS)

NNSDO .... National Nursing Staff Development Organization (NTPA)

NNSeag .... Joseph E. Seagram & Sons, Inc., New York, NY [Library symbol] [Library of Congress] (LCLS)

NNSF .... National Natural Science Foundation

NNSG .... NASCOM [NASA Communications Network] Network Scheduling Group

NNShA .... Shubert Archive, New York, NY [Library symbol] [Library of Congress] (LCLS)

NNSIHi .... Staten Island Historical Society, New York, NY [Library symbol] [Library of Congress] (LCLS)

NNSII .... Staten Island Institute of Arts and Sciences, New York, NY [Library symbol] [Library of Congress] (LCLS)

NNSIS .... Swedish Information Service, New York, NY [Library symbol] [Library of Congress] (LCLS)

NNSJD .... Cathedral of Saint John the Divine, New York, NY [Library symbol] [Library of Congress] (LCLS)

NNSL .... Newport News Savings Bank (SAUS)

NNSL .... Nigerian National Shipping Line (SAUS)

NNSN .... No National Stock Number (AABC)

NNSNP .... National Network in Solidarity with the Nicaraguan People (EA)

NNSPG .... National Network in Solidarity with the People of Guatemala (EA)

NNSPo .... Standard & Poor's Corp., New York, NY [Library symbol] [Library of Congress] (LCLS)

NNSR .... Sons of the Revolution in the State of New York, New York, NY [Library symbol] [Library of Congress] (LCLS)

NNSS .... Navy Navigational Satellite System

NNSS .... Shearman & Sterling Library, New York, NY [Library symbol] [Library of Congress] (LCLS)

NNSSS .... South Street Seaport Museum, New York, NY [Library symbol] [Library of Congress] (LCLS)

NNSTB .... Simpson, Thacher & Bartlett, Law Library, New York, NY [Library symbol] [Library of Congress] (LCLS)

NNStJ .... St. John's University, Jamaica, NY [Library symbol] [Library of Congress] (LCLS)

NNStL .... Saint Luke's Hospital, Richard Walker Bolling Memorial Medical Library, New York, NY [Library symbol] [Library of Congress] (LCLS)

NNStOD .... Standard Oil Co. (New Jersey), New York, NY [Library symbol] [Library of Congress] (LCLS)

NNSTWG ...... Nonnuclear Survivability Technology Working Group (AFIT)

NNSU-MC .... State University of New York, Maritime College, Fort Schuyler, Bronx, NY [Library symbol] [Library of Congress] (LCLS)

NNSU-Op ..... State University of New York, College of Optometry, New York, NY [Library symbol] [Library of Congress] (LCLS)

NNS/VPP ...... Non-Nuclear Survivability/ Vulnerability Program Plan (SAUS)

NNSW .... Nonnuclear Strategic Warfare

NNSWM .... National Network for Social Work Managers (EA)

NNSY .... Norfolk Naval Shipyard [Portsmouth, VA]

NNT .... Nan [Thailand] [Airport symbol] (OAG)

NNT .... Nanotec Canada, Inc. [Vancouver Stock Exchange symbol]

NNT .... Nearest Neighbor Tool [Mathematical technique] (USDC)

NNT .... New York Times, New York, NY [Library symbol] [Library of Congress] (LCLS)

NNT .... Notice Number Tracking (MCD)

NNT .... Number Needed to Treat

NNTAICH ...... Technical Assistance Information Clearing House, New York, NY [Library symbol] [Library of Congress] (LCLS)

NNTAPS .... National Nuclear Targeting Policy (CCCA)

NNTax .... Tax Foundation, Inc., New York, NY [Library symbol] [Library of Congress] (LCLS)

NNTC .... National Nondestructive Testing Centre [Atomic Energy Authority] [Information service or system] (IID)

NNTC .... Norwich and Norfolk Terrier Club (EA)

NNTC .... Teachers College, New York, NY [Library symbol] [Library of Congress] (LCLS)

NNTEP .... Northern Nigeria Teacher Education Project [University of Wisconsin] (AEBS)

NNTF .... Traphagen School of Fashion, New York, NY [Library symbol] [Library of Congress] (LCLS)

NNTIA .... Teachers Insurance and Annuity Association of America, New York, NY [Library symbol] [Library of Congress] (LCLS)

NNTM .... Tobacco Merchants Association of the United States, New York, NY [Library symbol] [Library of Congress] (LCLS)

NNTN .... Not Necessarily the News [Cable television comedy program]

NNTO .... Norwegian National Travel Office (SAUS)

NNTP .... National Nuclear Test Plan [Later, NNTRP]

NNTP .... Network News Transfer Protocol (TELE)

NNTP .... Network News Transport Protocol [Telecommunications]

NNTRP .... National Nuclear Test Readiness Program [Formerly, NNTP]

NNTT .... National New Technology Telescope [Proposed] [National Science Foundation]

NNttR .... Rockefeller Archive Center, Rockefeller University, North Tarrytown, NY [Library symbol] [Library of Congress] (LCLS)

NNU .... Nanuque [Brazil] [Airport symbol] (AD)

NNU .... Neonatal Unit [Medicine] (DMAA)

NNU .... Net Nitrogen Utilization [Medicine] (DAVI)

NNU .... New York University, New York, NY [Library symbol] [Library of Congress] (LCLS)

NNU	Nordic Numismatic Union (EAIO)
NNU-B	New York University, Graduate School of Business Administration, New York, NY [*Library symbol*] [*Library of Congress*] (LCLS)
NNU-C	New York University, School of Commerce, New York, NY [*Library symbol*] [*Library of Congress*] (LCLS)
NNU-D	New York University, College of Dentistry, New York, NY [*Library symbol*] [*Library of Congress*] (LCLS)
NNU-ES	New York University, Engineering and Science Library, New York, NY [*Library symbol*] [*Library of Congress*] (LCLS)
NNU-F	New York University, Fales Collection, New York, NY [*Library symbol*] [*Library of Congress*] (LCLS)
NNU-FA	New York University, Institute of Fine Arts, New York, NY [*Library symbol*] [*Library of Congress*] (LCLS)
NNU-G	New York University, Wall Street Library, New York, NY [*Library symbol*] [*Library of Congress*] (LCLS)
NNU-H	New York University, University Heights Library, Bronn, NY [*Library symbol*] [*Library of Congress*] (LCLS)
NNUH	United Hospital Fund of New York, New York, NY [*Library symbol*] [*Library of Congress*] (LCLS)
NNU-IEM	New York University, Institute of Environmental Medicine, Tuxedo Park, NY [*Library symbol*] [*Library of Congress*] (LCLS)
NNU-L	New York University, School of Law, New York, NY [*Library symbol*] [*Library of Congress*] (LCLS)
NNU-LA	New York University, Fobert F. Wagner Labor Archives, New York Labor Records Survey, New York,NY [*Library symbol*] [*Library of Congress*] (LCLS)
NNU-M	New York University, Medical Center, New York, NY [*Library symbol*] [*Library of Congress*] (LCLS)
NNUN	United Nations Library, New York, NY [*Library symbol*] [*Library of Congress*] (LCLS)
NNUnC	University Club, New York, NY [*Library symbol*] [*Library of Congress*] (LCLS)
NNUN-CF	United Nations Childrens Fund, New York, NY [*Library symbol*] [*Library of Congress*] (LCLS)
NNUni	Unipub, Inc., New York, NY [*Library symbol*] [*Library of Congress*] (LCLS)
NNUnionC	Union Club, New York, NY [*Library symbol*] [*Library of Congress*] (LCLS)
NNUnionL	Union League Club, New York, NY [*Library symbol*] [*Library of Congress*] (LCLS)
NNUN-PA	United Nations Fund for Population Activities, New York, NY [*Library symbol*] [*Library of Congress*] (LCLS)
NNUN-W	United Nations, Woodrow Wilson Memorial Library, New York, NY [*Library symbol*] [*Library of Congress*] (LCLS)
NNU-T	New York University, Tamiment Library, New York, NY [*Library symbol*] [*Library of Congress*] (LCLS)
NNUT	Union Theological Seminary, New York, NY [*Library symbol*] [*Library of Congress*] (LCLS)
NNUT-Mc	Union Theological Seminary, McAlpin Collection, New York, NY [*Library symbol*] [*Library of Congress*] (LCLS)
NNUVAN	Ukrainian Academy of Arts and Sciences in the United States, New York, NY [*Library symbol*] [*Library of Congress*] (LCLS)
NNUVE	Nonnegative Unbiased Variance Estimator [*Statistics*]
NNU-W	New York University, Washington Square Library, New York, NY [*Library symbol*] [*Library of Congress*] (LCLS)
NNU-We	New York University, Joe Weinstein Residence Halls Library, New York, NY [*Library symbol*] [*Library of Congress*] (LCLS)
NNV	National Naval Volunteers
NNVAB	United States Veterans Administration Hospital, Bronx, NY [*Library symbol*] [*Library of Congress*] (LCLS)
NNVAM	United States Veterans Administration Hospital (Manhattan), New York, NY [*Library symbol*] [*Library of Congress*] (LCLS)
NNW	North by North West (SAUS)
NNW	North-Northwest
NNWB	Navy Nuclear Weapons Bulletin [*A publication*]
NNWB	Net National Well Being
NNWC	Nonnuclear Weapons Country
NNWF	National Network of Women's Funds (EA)
NNWFG	Wilkie, Farr & Gallagher, New York, NY [*Library symbol*] [*Library of Congress*] (LCLS)
NNWG	Wenner-Gren Foundation for Anthropological Research, New York, NY [*Library symbol*] [*Library of Congress*] (LCLS)
NNWH	Nonnormal Working Hours
NNWH	Walter Hampden Memorial Library, New York, NY [*Library symbol*] [*Library of Congress*] (LCLS)
NNWhit	Whitney Museum of American Art, New York, NY [*Library symbol*] [*Library of Congress*] (LCLS)
NNWI	Neonatal Narcotic Withdrawal Index [*Medicine*] (DMAA)
NNWM	William Douglas McAdams, Inc., Medical Library, New York, NY [*Library symbol*] [*Library of Congress*] (LCLS)
NNWML	Wagner College, Staten Island, NY [*Library symbol*] [*Library of Congress*] (LCLS)
NNWO	Navy Nuclear Weapons Officer (DNAB)
NNWP	National Network of Women Philanthropists (NFD)
NNWR	Noxubee National Wildlife Refuge (SAUS)
NNWRN	North-Northwestern (SAUS)
NNWS	National Network of Women in Sales [*Defunct*] (EA)
NNWS	Nonnuclear Weapons State
NNWSI	Nevada Nuclear Waste Storage Investigations
NNWWD	North-Northwestward (SAUS)
NNWWD	North-Westward (FAAC)
NNY	Nanyang [*China*] [*Airport symbol*] (OAG)
NNY	Nuveen New York Municipal Fund [*NYSE symbol*] (SPSG)
NNY	Nuveen NY Muni Val Fd [*NYSE symbol*] (TTSB)
NNy	Nyack Library, Nyack, NY [*Library symbol*] [*Library of Congress*] (LCLS)
NNYAB	National Network of Youth Advisory Boards (EA)
NNYC	Yale Club, New York, NY [*Library symbol*] [*Library of Congress*] (LCLS)
NNYD	Norfolk Navy Yard [*Virginia*] [*Later, Norfolk Naval Shipyard*]
NNYI	YIVO Institute for Jewish Research, New York, NY [*Library symbol*] [*Library of Congress*] (LCLS)
NNYIQ	Nuveen New York Investment Quality Municipal Fund [*Associated Press*] (SAG)
NNYM	Nuveen New York Municipal Income Fund (SAUS)
NNyM	Nyack Missionary College, Nyack, NY [*Library symbol*] [*Library of Congress*] (LCLS)
NNYMCA	Young Men's Christian Association, National Council Historical Library, New York, NY [*Library symbol*] [*Library of Congress*] (LCLS)
NNYMCA-GC	Young Men's Christian Association, Grand Central Branch Library, New York, NY [*Library symbol*] [*Library of Congress*] (LCLS)
NNYMCA-NC	Young Men's Christian Association, National Council Historical Library, New York, NY [*Library symbol*] [*Library of Congress*] (LCLS)
NNYMI	Nuveen New York Municipal Income Fund [*Associated Press*] (SAG)
NNYMV	Nuveen New York Municipal Value Fund [*Associated Press*] (SAG)
NNYSQ	Nuveen New York Select Quality Municipal Fund [*Associated Press*] (SAG)
NNYU	Yeshiva University, New York, NY [*Library symbol*] [*Library of Congress*] (LCLS)
NNYU-HJ	Yeshiva University, Mendel Gottesman Library of Hebraica Judaica, New York, NY [*Library symbol*] [*Library of Congress*] (LCLS)
NNYU-M	Yeshiva University, Albert Einstein College of Medicine, Bronx, NY [*Library symbol*] [*Library of Congress*] (LCLS)
NNYU-S	Yeshiva University, Stern College, New York, NY [*Library symbol*] [*Library of Congress*] (LCLS)
NNZ	New York Zoological Society, New York, NY [*Library symbol*] [*Library of Congress*] (LCLS)
NNZ	Point Sur, CA [*Location identifier*] [*FAA*] (FAAL)
NNZCG	New Zealand Consulate General, Library, New York, NY [*Library symbol*] [*Library of Congress*] (LCLS)
NNZi	Zionist Archives and Library, New York, NY [*Library symbol*] [*Library of Congress*] (LCLS)
NO	Air North [*ICAO designator*] (AD)
N/O	In the Name of (SAUS)
NO	Lifts Not Operating [*Skiing*]
NO	Nachalnik Otdelenia [*Chief of Department*] [*Soviet military rank*]
NO	Narcotics Officer
NO	National Office
NO	National Office, Office of Federal Contract Compliance Programs (AAGC)
NO	National Outlook: an Australian Christian Monthly [*A publication*] (APTA)
NO	Native Officer [*British military*] (DMA)
NO	Natural Orbital [*Physical chemistry*]
NO	Natural Order [*Botany*]
NO	Naval Observatory [*Navy*]
NO	Naval Officer
NO	Navigation Officer
NO	Negative [*British naval signaling*]
NO	Neuromyelitis Optica (SAUS)
NO	Neutral Officer (SAUS)
NO	Neutral Oil
NO	New Options (EA)
NO	New Order [*Defunct*] (EA)
NO	New Orleans [*Louisiana*]
NO	New Orleans Saints [*National Football League*] [*1967-present*] (NFLA)
NO	Night Observation (SAUS)
NO	Nitric Oxide
NO	Nitrogen Dioxide (SAUS)
NO	Nitrogen Monoxide
NO	Nitrogen Oxide [*Emission control*] [*Automotive engineering*]
NO	Noah (ABBR)
No	Nobelium [*Chemical element*]
No	Nocturia [*Urology*] (DAVI)
n/o	None Obtained [*Medicine*]
NO	Nonobese [*Medicine*] (DMAA)
NO	Nonofficial
NO	Nonoriginal
NO	No Operational (SAUS)
N/O	No Orders [*Business term*]
NO	No Palpable Nodes [*Oncology*]
NO	Nord-Ouest [*Northwest*] [*French*]
NO	Normally Open [*Switch*]
NO	Normal Operation (SAUS)
no	North (SHCU)
NO	North
NO	North Central Airlines, Inc.
NO	Northern (ABBR)
N/O	North Of [*In outdoor advertising*] (WDMC)
NO	Norway [*ANSI two-letter standard code*] (CNC)
no	Norway [*MARC country of publication code*] [*Library of Congress*] (LCCP)
No	Norway (MILB)
NO	Nose [*Horse racing*]
NO	Notes [*Online database field identifier*]
NO	Not for Off [*Kennedy Space Center Distribution*] (NAKS)

NO	Not Operational (SAUS)	
NO	Not Or [Logical operator] [Computer science]	
N/O	Not Otherwise	
NO	Not Our Publication	
NO	Not Ours (SAUS)	
N/O	Not Out [Bookselling]	
NO	November (ADA)	
NO	Nuestra Orden [Our Order] [Spanish] [Business term]	
NO	Nuffield Observatory (SAUS)	
No.	Number (EBF)	
NO	Number (EY)	
no	Number (WDMC)	
NO	Numero [In Number] [Pharmacy] (ROG)	
NO	Nurse's Office (DMAA)	
NO	Nursing Officer [British]	
NO	Oneida Library (SAUS)	
NO	Oneida Library, Oneida, NY [Library symbol] [Library of Congress] (LCLS)	
NO	Stickstoffmonoxid (SAUS)	
No 1	first (SAUS)	
No 1	first person (SAUS)	
No 1	first quality (SAUS)	
No 1	first rate (SAUS)	
NO2	Nitrogen Dioxide	
NO₃	Nitrate (GNE)	
No9Vis	Number Nine Visual Technology, Inc. [Associated Press] (SAG)	
NOA	National Oceanographic Association	
NOA	National Officers Association (EA)	
NOA	National Onion Association (EA)	
NOA	National Opera Association (EA)	
NOA	National Optical Association [Later, NAOO]	
NOA	National Optometric Association (EA)	
NOA	National Orchestral Association (EA)	
NOA	National Outboard Association [Defunct] (EA)	
NOA	National Outdoorsmen's Association [Defunct] (EA)	
NOA	NATO Oil Authority (NATG)	
NOA	Natural Optical Activity	
NOA	Natural Orange Aroma	
NOA	Nature of Action [Military] (AFM)	
NOA	Nearest Onshore Area (EEVL)	
NOA	Net on Air (SAUS)	
NOA	Network-Oriented Analysis and Transformation Unit [Computer science] (MHDB)	
NOA	New London, CT [Location identifier] [FAA] (FAAL)	
NOA	New Obligational Authority	
NOA	Non-Operational Aircraft (SAUS)	
NOA	Norontair [Canada] [ICAO designator] (FAAC)	
NOA	Northwest Orient Airlines, Inc.	
NOA	Notice of Arrival (EEVL)	
NOA	Notice of Availability (MCD)	
NOA	Not Operationally Assigned	
N-O-A	Not-Or-And [Computer science]	
NOA	Not Otherwise Authorized	
NOA	NSWC Office Automation (SAUS)	
NOA	Nueva Organizacion Antiterrorista [New Anti-Terrorist Organization] [Guatemala] (PD)	
NOA	University of North Carolina, Chapel Hill Library School, Chapel Hill, NC [OCLC symbol] (OCLC)	
NOAA	National Oceanic and Atmospheric Administration [Rockville, MD] [Pronounced "Noah"]	
NOAA	Nonoperating Aircraft Authorization	
NOAA	US National Oceanic and Atmospheric Administration (SAUS)	
NOAADN	National Organization for Advancement of Associate Degree Nursing (EA)	
NOAA-FSL	NOAA [National Oceanic and Atmospheric Administration]-Forecast Systems Lab	
NOAA-JTRE	National Oceanic and Atmospheric Administration Joint Tsunami Research Effort	
NOAAnet	NOAA network (SAUS)	
NOAA-NOS	National Oceanic and Atmospheric Administration - National Ocean Service (DNAB)	
NOAA-NWS	National Oceanic and Atmospheric Administration - National Weather Service (DNAB)	
NOAA-PMEL	National Oceanic and Atmospheric Administration Pacific Marine Environmental Laboratory	
NOAAport	NOAA data-delivery system (SAUS)	
NOAA-TR-NMFS-Circ	National Oceanic and Atmospheric Administration Technical Report-National MarineFisheries Service-Circular [A publication] (PDAA)	
NOAA-TR-NMFS-SSRF	National Oceanic and Atmospheric Administration-Technical Report-National MarineFisheries Service-Special Scientific Report Fisheries (PDAA)	
NOAB	National Outdoor Advertising Bureau [Defunct] (EA)	
NO-AB	New Orleans-Algiers Bridge (SAUS)	
NOAB	North American Bancorporation, Inc. (SAUS)	
NOAC	National Operations and Automation Conference (HGAA)	
NOAC	Nature of Action Code [Environmental science] (EPAT)	
No a/c	No Account (EBF)	
NOAC	Nordic Accelerator-Based-Research Committee (SAUS)	
NOAC	Nuclear Operations Analysis Center [Department of Energy] [Information service or system] (IID)	
NOACT	Naval Overseas Air Cargo Terminal	
NOACT	No Action (MUGU)	
NOACTLANT	Naval Ordnance Activities, Atlantic	
NOACTPAC	Naval Ordnance Activities, Pacific	

NOaD	Dowling College, Oakdale, NY [Library symbol] [Library of Congress] (LCLS)	
NOAD	National Organization for Apraxia and Dyspraxia (EA)	
No Adams St C	North Adams State College (GAGS)	
NOADN	National Oceanic and Atmospheric Data Network	
NOADN	National Organization for Associate Degree Nursing (EA)	
NOADS	Newspapers Opposed to Advertising Death by Smoking (SAUS)	
No Adv	No Advice (EBF)	
NOAEL	No Observed Adverse Effect Level [Toxicology] (EG)	
NOaf	Oakfield Public Library (Haxton Memorial), Oakfield, NY [Library symbol] [Library of Congress] (LCLS)	
NOAFIRM	Affirmative Replies Neither Required nor Desired (MUGU)	
NOAG	Naval Objectives Analysis Group	
NOAH	Narrow-Band Optimiziation of the Alignment of Highways (PDAA)	
NOAH	National Ocean Agency Headquarters	
NOAH	National Organization for Albinism and Hypopigmentation (EA)	
NOAH	New Opportunities for Animal Health scientists (SAUS)	
NOAH	New York Online Access to Health	
NOAH	New York Online Access to Health Home Page [Database]	
NOAH	Nitrous Oxide and Halocarbons Division (SAUS)	
NOAH	Noarko Resources, Inc. (SAUS)	
NOAH	Norwegian Adapted HAWK [Hughes Aircraft Co.]	
NOAHS	New Opportunities in Animal Health Sciences	
Noahs Ark Toy Libr Handicapped Child Newsletter	Noahs Ark Toy Library for Handicapped Children. Newsletter (SAUS)	
NOaJH	Oakdale-Bohemia Junior High School (SAUS)	
NOaJH	Oakdale-Bohemia Junior High School, Oakdale, NY [Library symbol] [Library of Congress] (LCLS)	
NOALA	Noise-Operated Automatic Level Adjuster (or Adjustment) (SAUS)	
NOAM	Noan Mizrachi [American Zionist organization]	
NOAM	Nuclear Ordnance Air Force Materiel [Military] (AFIT)	
NOAMTRAC	North America Trail Complex (EA)	
NO & LC	New Orleans & Lower Coast Railroad Co. (IIA)	
NOAO	National Optical Astronomical Observatories	
NOAO	National Optical Astronomy Observatories [Tucson, AZ] [National Science Foundation]	
NOAO	Navy Officers, Accounts Office (MUGU)	
NOAP	National Ocean Access Project (EA)	
NOAP	Naval Overseas Air Cargo Terminal, Pearl (MUGU)	
NOAP	Navy Oil Analysis Program (NG)	
NOAPP	National Organization of Adolescent Pregnancy and Parenting (EA)	
NOAPP	National Organization on Adolescent Pregnancy, Parenting, and Prevention (PAZ)	
NOAPS	National Oil and Acrylic Painters Society	
NOARB	National Organization for an American Revolution (EA)	
NOARB	New Orleans Army Base (SAA)	
No Ariz U	Northern Arizona University (GAGS)	
NOARL	National Oceanographic and Atmospheric Research Laboratory (USDC)	
NOARL	Naval Ocean and Atmosphere Research Laboratory [USA] [Marine science] (OSRA)	
NOART	New Orleans Army Terminal	
NOASSR	North Ossetian Autonomous Soviet Socialist Republic (SAUS)	
NOB	National Oil Board (NATG)	
NOB	Naval Operating Base	
NOB	Naval Order of Battle	
NOB	Naval Ordnance Bulletin [A publication]	
NOB	Nobeoka [Japan] [Seismograph station code, US Geological Survey] (SEIS)	
NOB	Nobile [Nobly] [Music] (ROG)	
NOB	Nobility (ABBR)	
NOB	Nobis [With Us] [Latin] (ROG)	
NOB	Noble (ABBR)	
NOB	Non-Biased Optical Bistable [Device] (AAEL)	
NOB	Nonobese [A diabetic mouse strain]	
NOB	No Open Burning (SAUS)	
NOB	North Bay Cooperative Library System, Santa Rosa (SAUS)	
NOB	North Bay Cooperative Library System, Santa Rosa, CA [OCLC symbol] (OCLC)	
NOB	North Outpatient Building (SAUS)	
NOB	Norwest Corp. [NYSE symbol] (SPSG)	
NOB	Notes over Bonds [Finance] (NUMA)	
NOB	Not on Board (SAUS)	
NOB	Not on Bonus	
NOB	Nuclear Order of Battle (AFM)	
NOB	Number of Bursts	
NOB	San Francisco, CA [Location identifier] [FAA] (FAAL)	
NOBA	Nitrosobenzamide [Organic chemistry]	
NOBA	Norwegian Zero Power Reactor Assembly (SAUS)	
NOBAR	National Organization for Birthfathers and Adoption Reform (EA)	
NOBC	National Office for Black Catholics (EA)	
NOBC	National Order of Battlefield Commissions (EA)	
NOBC	National Organization of Bar Counsel (EA)	
NOBC	Naval Officer Billet Classifications [or Code]	
NOBCA	National Organization of Black College Alumni (EA)	
NOBCCE	National Organization of Black Chemists and Chemical Engineers [Later, NOPABCCE] (EA)	
NOBCChE	National Organization for Professional Advancement of Black Chemists and Chemical Engineers	
NOBCO	National Organization of Black County Officials (EA)	
NOBDUCHAR	Naval Operating Base, Dutch Harbor, Aleutians	
NOBE	Nordstrom, Inc. [NASDAQ symbol] (NQ)	
NoBeFi	Fiskeridirektoratet [Directorate of Fisheries], Bergen-Nordens, Norway [Library symbol] [Library of Congress] (LCLS)	
Nobel	Nobel Insurance Ltd. [Associated Press] (SAG)	

NobelEd....... Nobel Education Dynamics, Inc. [*Associated Press*] (SAG)
NOBELS...... New Office and Business Education Learning System
NoBeU ... Universitetet i Bergen [*University of Bergen*], Bergen, Norway [*Library symbol*] [*Library of Congress*] (LCLS)
NOBFRAN ... Naval Operating Base, San Francisco, California
NOBH........... Nobility Homes [*NASDAQ symbol*] (TTSB)
NOBH........... Nobility Homes, Inc. [*NASDAQ symbol*] (NQ)
NobiltyH ..... Nobility Homes, Inc. [*Associated Press*] (SAG)
NOBIN.......... Stichting Nederlands Orgaan voor de Bevordering van de Informatieverzorging [*Netherlands Organization for Information Policy*] [*Information service or system*] [*Defunct*] (IID)
No Biz.......... No Business (SAUS)
NOBL .... Nobel Insurance Ltd. [*NASDAQ symbol*] (NQ)
NOBL .... Noble International [*NASDAQ symbol*] (SG)
NoblAf .... Noble Affiliates, Inc. [*Associated Press*] (SAG)
NOBLE .... National Organization of Black Law Enforcement Executives (EA)
Noble........... Noble's Current Court Decisions [*New York*] [*A publication*] (DLA)
NOBLE......... North of Boston Library Exchange
NobleR .... Noble Roman's, Inc. [*Associated Press*] (SAG)
NOBLF .... Nobel Insurance [*NASDAQ symbol*] (TTSB)
NOB LIB ...... North Outpatient Building Library (SAUS)
NobltyH....... Nobility Homes [*Associated Press*] (SAG)
NOBMN........ Nobleman (ABBR)
NoBncshs..... North Bancshares, Inc. [*Associated Press*] (SAG)
NOBNEWT.... Naval Operating Base, Newport, Rhode Island
NOBO........... Nonobjecting Beneficial Owner (SAUS)
NoBordr....... Northern Border Partners Ltd. [*Associated Press*] (SAG)
NOBP........... Nitrosobenzopyrone [*Organic chemistry*]
NOBR........... Nobler (ABBR)
NOBS........... Naval Observatory [*Navy*]
NOBS........... Naval Operating Base Supplies (DNAB)
N Obs........... Nihil Obstat [*Official Approval*] [*Latin*]
NOBS........... Nonanoyloxybenzene (EDCT)
NOBS........... Nonanoyloxybenzene Sulfonate [*Laundry bleach activator*]
NOBS........... Nursing Observation of Behaviour Syndromes (DB)
NOBSOLO .... Naval Operating Base, Coco Solo, Canal Zone
NOBST........ Noblest (ABBR)
NOBSY......... Naval Observatory [*Navy*]
NOBT........... New Orleans Board of Trade (EA)
NOBT........... Nobility (ABBR)
NOBT........... Nonoperative Biopsy Technique [*Medicine*] (MELL)
NOBTRIN...... Naval Operating Base, Trinidad
NOBTS .... Naval Order of Battle Textual Summary (MCD)
NOBWN....... Noblewomen (ABBR)
NOBY........... Nobly (ABBR)
NOC .... Ascor Flyservice AS [*Norway*] [*ICAO designator*] (FAAC)
NOC .... National Oceanographic Center [*Marine science*] (MSC)
NOC .... National Oceanographic Council (NADA)
NOC .... National Offshore Council (EA)
NOC .... National Olympic Committee (NADA)
NOC .... National Online Circuit [*Defunct*] (EA)
NOC .... National Opportunity Camps for the Pre-Teen Child (EA)
NOC .... Natural Organic Carbon
NOC .... Naval Oceanographic Command (SAUS)
NOC .... Naval Operations Center (NVT)
NOC .... Navy Officer's Classification
NOC .... Network Operation Center [*Bell System*]
NOC .... Network Operations Control [*NASA*] (KSC)
NOC .... New Orleans Consortium [*Library network*]
noc.............. Noctis [*Night*] [*Medicine*]
NOC .... Nominal Operating Cell [*Photovoltaic energy systems*]
NOC .... Nonionic Organic Compound [*Organic chemistry*]
NOC .... Non-Ionic Organic Contaminant [*Environmental chemistry*]
NOC .... Normally Open Contact [*Switch*] (IAA)
NOC .... Norris Communications Corp. [*Vancouver Stock Exchange symbol*]
NOC .... Northrop Corp. [*NYSE symbol*] (SPSG)
NOC .... Northrop Grumman [*NYSE symbol*] (TTSB)
NOC .... Northrop Grumman Corp. [*NYSE symbol*] (SAG)
NOC .... Northwest Ohio Consortium [*Library network*]
NOC .... Norwegian Government Office of Culture [*Record label*]
NOC .... Notation of Content [*Aerospace*]
NOC .... Not-Carry (SAUS)
NOC .... Notice of Cancellation (AAGC)
NOC .... Notice of Change (MCD)
NOC .... Notice of Commencement (EPA)
NOC .... Notice of Construction (EEVL)
NOC .... Notice of Contents [*Indexing*]
NOC .... Not Otherwise Classified
NOC .... Not Otherwise Coded (GFGA)
NOC .... Nuclear Operations Center (MCD)
NOC .... Nuclear Ordnance Commission [*Military*] (AFIT)
NOC .... Number of Children (SAUS)
NOC .... Numerical Optimisation Centre [*British*]
NOC .... Nursing Outcomes Classification (SAUS)
NOC .... Nuttall Ornithological Club (EA)
NOc............. Oceanside Free Library, Oceanside, NY [*Library symbol*] [*Library of Congress*] (LCLS)
NOC .... University of North Carolina, Chapel Hill, Chapel Hill, NC [*OCLC symbol*] (OCLC)
NOCA........... National Organization for Competency Assurance (EA)
NOCA........... Nitrosooxazolidinecarboxylic Acid [*Organic chemistry*]
NOCA........... North Cascades National Park
No Ca Ecc & Mar... Notes of Cases, English Ecclesiastical and Maritime Courts [*1841-50*] [*A publication*] (DLA)
NOCAP........ National Oral Cancer Awareness Program (SAUS)

No Car Ag & Tech... North Carolina Agricultural & Technical State University (GAGS)
No Car Cent U... North Carolina Central University (GAGS)
No Car St U (Raleigh)... North Carolina State University (Raleigh) (GAGS)
NOcaS .... Shaker Museum Foundation, Inc., Old Catham, NY [*Library symbol*] [*Library of Congress*] (LCLS)
No Cas LJ..... Notes of Cases, Law Journal [*A publication*] (DLA)
NOCB........... New Orleans City Ballet
NocBE.......... Walter S. Boardman Elementary School, Oceanside, NY [*Library symbol*] [*Library of Congress*] (LCLS)
NOCC........... National Ovarian Cancer Coalition, Inc. (NRGU)
NOCC........... NATO Oil Crisis Contingent (NATG)
NOCC........... Navigation Operational Checkout Computer
NOCC........... Navigation Operator's Control Console
NOCC........... Network Operations Control Center [*Manned Space Flight Network, NASA*]
NOCC........... New Orleans Crime Commission (SAUS)
NOCC........... North Peralta Community College (SAUS)
NOCCC........ No Control Circuit Contacts (MSA)
NOCCE......... No Clubbing, Cyanosis or Edema (SAUS)
NOCC/JTWC... Naval Oceanography Command Center/Joint Typhoon Warning Center
NOCD........... Not Our Class, Dear [*Slang*]
NOCE........... New Orleans Commodity Exchange (EA)
NOCEM........ National Organization for Civic Education & Election Monitoring [*Lira, Uganda*]
NOCERCC ... National Organization for Continuing Education of Roman Catholic Clergy (EA)
NOCF .... National Office Computer Facility [*IRS*]
NOCF .... Naval Oceanography Command Facility (DNAB)
NocFE.......... Elementary School #3, Oceanside, NY [*Library symbol*] [*Library of Congress*] (LCLS)
NOcH .... South Nassau Communities Hospital, Oceanside, NY [*Library symbol*] [*Library of Congress*] (LCLS)
NOCHA........ National Off-Campus Housing Association [*Defunct*] (EA)
NOCI .... Nederlandse Organisatie voor Chemische Informatie (NITA)
NOCI .... Non Orthogonal Configuration Interaction (AAEL)
NOCIG......... Night Only Calligraphic Image Generator
NOC II......... Nuclear Operations Concept II [*Military*]
NO-CIRC ...... National Organization of Circumcision Information Resource Centers (EA)
NOCIRC........ National Organization of Circumcision Information Resource Centers (PAZ)
No-Clo Z....... No-Clone Zone (SAUS)
NOCM .... National Organization for Changing Men (EA)
NOCM .... Nuclear Ordnance Commodity Manager (AFM)
NocME......... Elementary School #8, Oceanside, NY [*Library symbol*] [*Library of Congress*] (LCLS)
NOCMIS....... NOC Management Information System (SAUS)
NocMS......... Oceanside Middle School, Oceanside, NY [*Library symbol*] [*Library of Congress*] (LCLS)
NOCN .... National Ocean Communications Network (USDC)
NOCN .... National Open College Network (AIE)
NOCN .... No Connection [*Travel industry*] (TRID)
NocNE.......... Elementary School #5, Oceanside, NY [*Library symbol*] [*Library of Congress*] (LCLS)
NOCO .... Noise Correlation
No Co .... Northern Counties (SAUS)
No Co .... Northern Countries (SAUS)
NOCO .... Norwegian Oil Consortium (SAUS)
NOCO .... Nuclear Ordnance Cataloging Officer [*Military*]
NOCO .... Nuclear Ordnance Catalog Office [*DoD*]
No Code ...... do not resuscitate (SAUS)
NOCOL......... No Collision (SAUS)
NOCONIT...... No Continuing Interest (NG)
NOCONTRACT... Not Releasable to Contractors (MCD)
NOCOPOR.... Nordic Cooperation in Polar Research (SAUS)
NOCOR........ Neglect of Core Orbitals [*Physical chemistry*]
NOCP........... Network Operator Control Program
No-CPR........ No Cardiopulmonary Resuscitation [*Medicine*] (MELL)
NOCR........... Network Operations Control Room
NOCSA......... National Olympic Committee of South Africa (ECON)
NOCSAE....... National Operating Committee on Standards for Athletic Equipment (EA)
NOcSE .... Florence A. Smith School, Oceanside, NY [*Library symbol*] [*Library of Congress*] (LCLS)
NocSH .... Oceanside Senior High School, Oceanside, NY [*Library symbol*] [*Library of Congress*] (LCLS)
NOCT .... Navy Overseas Cargo Terminals
NOCT .... Nocte [*At Night*] [*Pharmacy*] (ROG)
noct .... Nocturnal (CPH)
NOCT .... Nominal [*or Normal*] Operating Cell Temperature [*Photovoltaic energy systems*]
NOCT MANEQ... Nocte Maneque [*Night and Morning*] [*Pharmacy*]
NOCUS......... Nord Computer Users Society (SAUS)
NOCUS......... North Continental US (SAUS)
NOD .... National Organization on Disability (EA)
NOD .... Naval Ordnance Department [*British*]
NOD .... Naval Ordnance Depot
NOD .... Navy Operational Deception (MCD)
NOD .... Network Operations Directive [*NASA*] (KSC)
NOD .... Network Operations Division
NOD .... Network Out-Dial [*Automatic Voice Network*] (CET)
NOD .... New Offshore Dischargement (NATG)
NOD .... New-Onset Diabetes [*Medicine*] (MELL)

NOD............ Night Observation Device
NOD III......... Nitrogenous Oxidation (SAUS)
NOD............ Noise Output Device
NOD............ Nondefinitive Pattern [Laboratory science] (DAVI)
NOD............ Nonobese Diabetic [Mouse strain]
NOD............ Non-Offensive Defence (SAUS)
NOD............ Norris Dam [TVA]
NOD............ Notice of Decision (COE)
NOD............ Notice of Deficiency (EPA)
NOD............ Notify of Death (DAVI)
NOD............ Not Otherwise Defined (SAUS)
NOD............ Not Otherwise Diagnosed
NODA.......... National Operatic and Dramatic Association (EAIO)
NODA.......... National Orientation Directors Association (EA)
NODA.......... National Outdoor Drama Association [Defunct] (EA)
NODA.......... Night Operatic and Dramatic Association (SAUS)
NODA.......... Normal-Octyl & -Deyl Adipate [Organic chemistry]
NODAC....... Naval Ordnance Data Automation Center
NODAC....... Navy Occupational Development and Analysis Center (DNAB)
No Dak St U... North Dakota State University (GAGS)
NODAL........ Network-Oriented Data Acquisition Language
NODAN........ Noise-Operated Device for Antinoise [Telecommunications] (TEL)
NODAP........ Nonlinear Distortion Analysis Program [Bell System]
NODAS........ Network-Oriented Data Acquisition System (MHDI)
NODC.......... National Oceanographic Data Center [Databank originator] [Washington, DC] [National Oceanic and Atmospheric Administration]
NODC.......... Naval Oceanographic Distribution Center
NODC.......... Naval Operating Development Center
NODC.......... Non-Oil Developing Countries (SAUS)
NODC.......... Non-OPEC Developing Country (NUCP)
NODCAB ...... National Oceanographic Data Center Advisory Board [National Oceanic and Atmospheric Administration] (NOAA)
NODCC........ Noble Order, Descendants of the Conqueror and His Companions (EA)
NODD.......... Nord Orphan Drug Designation Database (SAUS)
NODDS .... Naval Oceanographic Data Distribution System
NODDY .... Notions, Oddities, Doodads & Delights of Yesterday
NODE.......... National Organization of Downsized Employees
NODE.......... Noise Diode [Electronics] (IAA)
NODEL........ Not to Delay
NODESTA..... Will Not Depart This Station [Army] (AABC)
NODI........... Notice of Delayed [or Delinquent] Item
NODI........... Notice of Delayed Items (SAUS)
NODI........... Notice of Delinquent Item (SAUS)
NODIS......... No Distribution [Military security classification] (AFM)
NODIS......... Northern Ohio Data and Information Service [Cleveland State University] [Information service or system] (IID)
NODIS......... NSSDC Online Data and Information System (SAUS)
NODL.......... National Office for Decent Literature [Defunct]
NODL.......... Not on Drawing List (MCD)
NODLR........ Night Observation Device, LASAR Ranging (TIMI)
NODLR........ Night Observation Device, Long-Range [Army] (RDA)
NODM......... Ferrocarril Nor-Oeste de Mexico [Mexico North Western Railroad] [AAR code]
NODM......... National Organization of Dance and Mime [British] (DBA)
NODMR....... Night Observation Device, Medium-Range [Army]
NODO......... NASA Orbital Debris Observatory (SAUS)
NODOZ....... Nuclear Offense/Defense Operational Zone (ACAE)
NODRA........ National One Design Racing Association (EA)
NODS.......... NASA Ocean Data System (EOSA)
NODS.......... National Oversight Database (AEPA)
NODS.......... Navy Overseas Dependents School
NODS.......... Near-Object Detection Sensor [Automotive electronics]
NODS.......... Near Obstacle Detection System [General Motors-Delco Co.]
NODS.......... Night Observation & Detection System (SAUS)
NOE .... Nap of the Earth [Night helicopter flight] [Army]
NOE .... No Ophthalmologic Examination [Medicine]
NOE .... No Other Entry (ADA)
NOE .... NORAD Operational Evaluation (MCD)
NOE .... Norden-Norddeich [Germany] [Airport symbol]
NOE .... Notice of Exception
NOE .... Notice of Exception Oceanographic Foundation (SAUS)
NOE .... Notice of Execution
NOE .... Not Otherwise Enumerated
NOE .... Nuclear Overhauser Effect
NOE .... Nuclear Overhauser Enhancement (DB)
NOE .... Number of Employees (SAUS)
NOE .... Number of Errors (SAUS)
NOEA .... National Outdoor Events Association [British] (DBA)
No East Rep... Northeastern Reporter [Commonly cited NE] [A publication] (DLA)
NOEB .... NATO Oil Executive Board (NATG)
NOEB-E....... NATO Oil Executive Board - East
NOEB-W...... NATO Oil Executive Board - West
NOEC .... No Effects Concentration [British environmental standard]
NOEC .... No Observed Effect Concentration [Toxicology]
NOECC .... Northeast College Conference (PSS)
NOECOMM... Nap-of-the-Earth Communications [Night helicopter flight]
NOED .... New Oxford English Dictionary [Proposed]
NOEDS .... Nuclear Overhauser Enhancement Difference Spectrometry
NOEF .... Naval Ordnance Engineering Facility (DNAB)
NOEHI.......... No One Else Has It [Lexicography]
No E III U ..... Northeastern Illinois University (GAGS)
NOEL .... National Organization of Episcopalians for Life (EA)
NOEL .... National Ornament and Electric Lights Christmas Association (EA)

NOEL .... Naval Ordnance Electronics Laboratory
NOEL .... Noel Group [NASDAQ symbol] (TTSB)
NOEL .... Noel Group, Inc. [NASDAQ symbol] (SAG)
NOEL .... Nonobservable Effect Level (SAUS)
NOEL .... No Observed Effect Level [Toxicology]
NOEL .... Number of Errors Left (SAUS)
No E La U ..... Northeast Louisiana University (GAGS)
NoelGp .... Noel Group, Inc. [Associated Press] (SAG)
No E Mo St U... Northeast Missouri State University (GAGS)
No E Ohio U... Northeastern Ohio University (GAGS)
NOEP .... Neue Oekonomische Politik [New Economic Policy] [Germany]
NOES .... National Operational Environmental Satellite Service (MCD)
NOESS .... National Operational Environmental Satellite System
No E St U ..... Northeastern State University (GAGS)
NoestUt....... Northeast Utilities [Associated Press] (SAG)
NOESY........ Nuclear Overhauser Effect Spectroscopy
NOESY........ Nuclear Overhauser enhancement and Exchange Spectroscopy (SAUS)
No et Vet Test... Novi et Veteris Testamenti (DSA)
NOEU .... Naval Ordnance Experimental Unit
No E U .... Northeastern University (GAGS)
NOF .... Fonnafly AS [Norway] [ICAO designator] (FAAC)
NOF .... National Oceanographic Facility [Marine science] (OSRA)
NOF .... National Optical Font [Typography]
NOF .... National Osteopathic Foundation (EA)
NOF .... National Osteoporosis Foundation (EA)
NOF .... Naval Operating Facility
NOF .... Naval Ordnance Facility
NOF .... NCR [NCR Corp.] Optical Font (MCD)
NOF .... Network Operations and Facilities
NOF .... Network Operations Forum [Exchange Carriers Standards Association] [Telecommunications]
NOF .... Neurite Outgrowth Factor [Biochemistry]
NOF .... Nickel Offsets Ltd. [Toronto Stock Exchange symbol]
NOF .... Nitrogen-Oxygen-Fluorine (SAUS)
NOF .... Nitrosyl Fluoride (SAA)
NOF .... Node Operator Facility (SAUS)
NOF .... Notice of Findings (SAUS)
NOF .... Not on File (SAUS)
NOF .... St. Petersburg, FL [Location identifier] [FAA] (FAAL)
NOFA .... National Office Furniture Association [Later, NOPA] (EA)
NOFA .... Natural Organic Farmers Association (EA)
NOFA .... Notice of Funding Availability [Department of Housing and Urban Development] (GFGA)
NOFAD .... Naval Ocean Floor Analysis Division (DNAB)
NOFAS .... National Organization on Fetal Alcohol Syndrome (MELL)
NOFBF .... Noninverting Output Bridging Fault (SAUS)
N of Cas ...... Notes of Cases at Madras (Strange) [A publication] (DLA)
N of Cas ...... Notes of Cases, English Ecclesiastical and Maritime Courts [1841-50] [A publication] (DLA)
N of Eng ...... North of England (SAUS)
NOFI .... National Oil Fuel Institute [Later, NOJC] (EA)
NOFIN .... No Further Information
NoFkBc .... North Fork Bancorp [Associated Press] (SAG)
NOFMA .... National Oak Flooring Manufacturers Association (EA)
NOFOA .... Naval Office for Occupied Areas [World War II]
NOFODIS ..... No Foreign Dissemination [Intelligence classification]
NOFORN ...... No Foreign Nationals (SAUS)
NOFORN ...... Not Releasable to Foreign Nationals [Military security classification]
NOFRC........ Northern Forest Research Centre [Canadian Forestry Service of Agriculture Canada] [Research center] (RCD)
NOFS .... National Option and Futures Society [Defunct] (EA)
NOFT .... Naval Overseas Freight Terminal
NOFT .... Nonorganic Failure-to-Thrive [Medicine] (DMAA)
NOFT .... Notification of Foreign Travel (AFM)
NOFTT .... Nonorganic Failure-to-Thrive [Medicine] (MEDA)
NOG .... Arizona-Nogales [Mexico] [Airport symbol] (AD)
nog .... noggin (SAUS)
NOG .... North Carolina Natural Gas [NYSE symbol] (SAG)
NOG .... NSAPAC Operations Group
NOG .... Nuclear Oncogenes [Medicine] (MELL)
NOG .... Nuclear Ordnance Group [Air Force] (MCD)
NOG .... Numbering
NOg .... Ogdensburg Public Library, Ogdensburg, NY [Library symbol] [Library of Congress] (LCLS)
NOGA .... National Osteopathic Guild Association (EA)
NOGAD .... Noise-Operated Gain-Adjusting Device
Nogal.......... Nogales, Sonora, Mexico (SAUS)
NOGAP........ Northern Oil and Gas Action Plan (SAUS)
NOGAP........ Northern Oil and Gas Action Program (SAUS)
NOGAPS ...... National Oceanographic Global Atmospheric Prediction System (WEAT)
NOGAPS ...... Navy Operational Global Atmospheric Prediction System
NOGC .... Nicklos Oil & Gas (SAUS)
NOGGA .... National Ornamental Goldfish Growers Association (EA)
NOgH .... A. Barton Hepburn Hospital, Ogdensburg, NY [Library symbol] [Library of Congress] (LCLS)
NOGIC......... Night-Only Computer Image Generation (SAUS)
NOGKAV ...... Agricultural Research (journ.) (SAUS)
NOGL .... Naval Ordnance Gauge Laboratory
NOGL .... Nizam's Own Golgonda Lancers [British military] (DMA)
NOGLSTP..... National Organization of Gay and Lesbian Scientists and Technical Professionals (EA)
NOgM .... Mater Dei College, Ogdensburg, NY [Library symbol] [Library of Congress] (LCLS)

NOGM.......... No Gammopathy Detected [*Biochemistry*] (DAVI)
NOgRM........ Remington Art Memorial Museum, Ogdensburg, NY [*Library symbol*] [*Library of Congress*] (LCLS)
NOGS.......... Night Observation Gunship (MCD)
NOGS.......... Night Observation Gunship System (SAUS)
NOgSH........ Saint Lawrence State Hospital, Ogdensburg, NY [*Library symbol*] [*Library of Congress*] (LCLS)
NOgW .... Wadhams Hall Seminary College, Ogdensburg, NY [*Library symbol*] [*Library of Congress*] (LCLS)
NOH .... Chicago, IL [*Location identifier*] [*FAA*] (FAAL)
NOH .... Night Observation Helicopter (MCD)
NOH .... Nitric Oxide ferro-Hemochrome (SAUS)
NOH .... University of North Carolina, Health Science Library, Chapel Hill, NC [*OCLC symbol*] (OCLC)
NOHA......... Nutrition for Optimal Health Association (EA)
NOHALICE... Nitrous Oxide and Halocarbon Intercalibration Experiment (SAUS)
NOHARMM... National Organization to Halt the Abuse and Routine Mutilation of Males (EA)
NOHb .... Nitric Oxide Hemoglobin (SAUS)
NOHD.......... Nominal Ocular Hazard Distance (SAUS)
NOHIC .... National Oral Health Information Clearinghouse (PAZ)
NOHIMS...... Navy Occupational Health Information Management System
NOHL .... North Hills Electronics, Inc. (SAUS)
NoHo .... North of Houston Street [*Artists' colony in New York City*] [*See also SoHo, SoSo, TriBeCa*]
NOHOL........ Not Holding [*a given course or altitude*] [*Aviation*]
NOHP.......... Not Otherwise Herein Provided
NOHQI......... Nuveen Ohio Quality Income Municipal Fund [*Associated Press*] (SAG)
NOHS.......... National Oceanographic Hazard Survey (NITA)
NOHS.......... National Organization of Human Services [*Defunct*] (EA)
NOHSCP ..... National Oil and Hazardous Substances Contingency Plan [*Environmental Protection Agency*] (ERG)
NOHSE........ National Organization of Human Service Education (EA)
NOHSM........ National Occupational Health Survey of Mining [*Department of Health and Human Services*] (GFGA)
NOHSN .... National Organization of Hospital Schools of Nursing [*Defunct*] (EA)
NOI .... Detroit, MI [*Location identifier*] [*FAA*] (FAAL)
NOI .... National Oilwell, Inc. [*NYSE symbol*] (SAG)
NOI .... National Opera Institute (EA)
NOI .... Nation of Islam [*Religion*]
NOI .... NAVWEPS ORDALT Instruction (MCD)
NOI .... Netherlands Offset Industry
NOI .... Net Operating Income
NOI .... Nevus Outreach, Inc. (NRGU)
NOI .... Node Operator Interface (NITA)
NOI .... Noise Com, Inc. (SPSG)
NOI .... Nonoperational Intelligence
NOI .... No-Operation Instruction (SAUS)
NOI .... Notice of Inquiry (IEEE)
NOI .... Notice of Intent (MCD)
NOI .... Notice of Intention
NOI .... Notice of Interest (DEMM)
NOI .... Not Otherwise Identified (NG)
NOI .... Not Otherwise Indexed
NOIA .... National Ocean Industries Association (EA)
NOIA .... Newfoundland Ocean Industries Association (SAUS)
NOIAN........ National Operations Intelligence Analysis Net (CCCA)
NOIAW........ National Organization of Italian-American Women (EA)
NOIBN......... Not Otherwise Identified [*or Indicated*] by Name [*Military*] (AABC)
NOIBN......... Not Otherwise Indexed by Name [*Tariffs*]
NOIBN......... Not Otherwise Indicated by Number (SAUS)
NOIC .... National Oceanographic Instrumentation Center [*National Oceanic and Atmospheric Administration*]
NOIC .... National Osteopathic Interfraternity Council (EA)
NOIC .... Naval Ocean Intelligence Center (DOMA)
NOIC .... Naval Officer-in-Charge
NOIC .... Navy Operational Intelligence Center [*Now Naval Maritime Intelligence Center (NAVMIC)*] (DOMA)
NOIC .... Notice of Intent to Cancel [*Environmental Protection Agency*] (EPAT)
NOICC .... National Occupational Information Coordinating Committee [*Washington, DC*]
NOIE .... Naval Ordnance Inspection Establishment [*Ministry of Defence*] [*British*] (PDAA)
NOIFN .... No Information Available (SAUS)
NOII .... Non-Occlusive Intestinal Ischemia [*Medicine*] (DMAA)
NOIL .... Norris Oil Co. (SAUS)
No III U ...... Northern Illinois University (GAGS)
NOIM .... Nuclear Ordnance Inventory Manager (SAUS)
NOIO.......... Naval Ordnance Inspecting Officer
NOIS .... National Occupational Information Service
NOIS .... Notice of Intent to Suspend [*Environmental Protection Agency*] (EPAT)
NOISE......... National Organisation of Initiatives for Social Education [*British*] (DBA)
NOISE......... National Organization for Improving School Environments [*Defunct*] (EA)
NOISE......... National Organization to Insure a Sound-Controlled Environment (EA)
NOISE......... National Organization to Insure Survival Economics (EA)
NOISE......... Netscape, Oracle, IBM, Sun-and Everybody Else
NOISE......... Noise Information Service
NoiseCT....... Noise Cancellation Technologies, Inc. [*Associated Press*] (SAG)
Noise Reg Rep... Noise Regulation Reporter [*Bureau of National Affairs*] [*A publication*] (DLA)

Noise Reg Rep BNA... Noise Regulation Reporter. Bureau of National Affair (SAUS)
NOITSDSL.... Not Included in Technical Service Demand Stockage Lists (SAUS)
NOITU .... National Organization of Industrial Trade Unions (EA)
NOIWON...... National Operations and Intelligence Watch Officers Network (MCD)
NOIZ .... Micronetics, Inc. [*NASDAQ symbol*] (NQ)
NOIZ .... Micronetics Wireless [*NASDAQ symbol*] (TTSB)
NOJ............. Kodiak, AK [*Location identifier*] [*FAA*] (FAAL)
NOJ............. New Orleans Jassband (WDAA)
NOJC .... National Oil Jobbers Council [*Later, PMAA*] (EA)
NOJC .... New Orleans Jazz Club (EA)
NOJC .... Northern Oklahoma Junior College
NOJSM .... National Office of Jesuit Social Ministries (EA)
NOK .... Next of Kin
NOK .... Nokia Corp. [*NYSE symbol*] (SAG)
NOK .... Noril'sk [*Former USSR*] [*Geomagnetic observatory code*]
NOKD.......... Not Our Kind, Dear [*Slang*]
No Kent U .... Northern Kentucky University (GAGS)
Nokia .... Nokia Corp. [*Associated Press*] (SAG)
NOKL .... Northwestern Oklahoma Railroad Co. [*AAR code*]
Nok Mort .... Nokes' Mortgages and Receiverships [*3rd ed.*] [*1951*] [*A publication*] (DLA)
NOKW......... NAZI Oberkommando der Wehrmacht [*NAZI Armed Forces High Command*] [*World War II*] [*German*] (BJA)
NOL .... National Old Lacers [*Later, IOL*] (EA)
NOL .... National Ordnance Laboratory
NOL .... National Overseas Airline Co. [*Egypt*] [*ICAO designator*] (FAAC)
NOL .... Naval Ordnance Laboratory [*Later, NSWC*]
NOL .... Net Operating Loss
NOL .... New Orleans - Loyola [*Louisiana*] [*Seismograph station code, US Geological Survey*] (SEIS)
NOL .... Noel Industries, Inc. (SAUS)
Nol............. Nolan's English Magistrates' Cases [*A publication*] (DLA)
Nol............. Nolan's English Settlement Cases [*A publication*] (DLA)
NOL .... Normal Operational Loss [*Nuclear energy*]
NOL .... Norse Oriental Lines (MHDW)
NOL .... Northland Oils Ltd. [*Toronto Stock Exchange symbol*]
NOI .... Olean Public Library, Olean, NY [*Library symbol*] [*Library of Congress*] (LCLS)
NOLA .... National Association for Outlaw and Lawman History (EA)
NOLA .... Northeastern Ohio Library Association [*Library network*]
NOLAC .... National Organization of Liaison for Allocation of Circuit (NATG)
Nolan.......... Nolan on the Poor Laws [*A publication*] (DLA)
Nolan.......... Nolan's English Magistrates' Cases [*A publication*] (DLA)
Noland........ Noland Co. [*Associated Press*] (SAG)
NOLAP .... Non-Linear Analysis Program (PDAA)
NOLB .... Novaferon Laboratories, Inc. (SAUS)
NOLC .... National Obscenity Law Center (IID)
NOLC .... National One-Liners Club (EA)
NOLC .... Naval Ordnance Laboratory Corona
nol con .... Nolo Contendere [*I Do Not Wish to Contend*] [*Legal term*] [*Latin*] (BARN)
NOID........... Dresser Industries, Inc., Dresser Clark Division, Olean, NY [*Library symbol*] [*Library of Congress*] (LCLS)
NOLD.......... Noland Co. [*NASDAQ symbol*] (NQ)
NOLDAR ...... Noludar [*A hypnotic*] [*Roche laboratories*] (DAVI)
NOLDC........ Non-Oil Less-Developed Country
NOLDS........ Naval Ordnance Laboratory Data Service (ACAE)
NOLEO........ Notice to Law Enforcement Officials
NOLF .... Nursing Organization Liaison Forum (SAUS)
NOIH .... Olean General Hospital, Olean, NY [*Library symbol*] [*Library of Congress*] (LCLS)
NOLHGA ...... National Organization of Life and Health Guaranty Associations [*An association*]
NOLM .... Nonlinear Optical Loop Mirror [*Optical computing*]
Nol Mag ..... Nolan's English Magistrates' Cases [*A publication*] (DLA)
NOL-MDI..... Naval Ordnance Laboratory Miss Distance Indicator
NOLO .... No Live Operator (NG)
NOLO .... No Local Operator (SAUS)
NOLOC........ No Location (AABC)
NOLOG........ No Logging (SAUS)
NOLPE .... National Organization on Legal Problems of Education (EA)
NOLPE Sch LJ... NOLPE [*National Organization on Legal Problems of Education*] School Law Journal [*A publication*] (DLA)
NOLPE School LJ... NOLPE [*National Organization on Legal Problems of Education*] School Law Journal [*A publication*] (DLA)
Nol PL .... Nolan on the Poor Laws [*A publication*] (DLA)
NOL PROS... Nolle Prosequi [*Unwilling to Prosecute*] [*Legal term*] [*Latin*]
nol-pros...... nol-prossed (SAUS)
nol-pros....... nol prossing (SAUS)
NO-LQ......... No Living Quarters (SAUS)
NOLS .... National Oceanographic Laboratory System
NOLS .... National Organization for Legal Services (EA)
NOLS .... National Outdoor Leadership School
NOLS .... Nuclear Ordnance Logistics Systems (SAUS)
NOISFH........ Saint Francis Hospital, Olean, NY [*Library symbol*] [*Library of Congress*] (LCLS)
NoISL.......... Cattaraugus-Allegany School Library System, Olean, NY [*Library symbol*] [*Library of Congress*] (LCLS)
NOLSS........ Nuclear Ordnance Logistics Support System (SAUS)
NOLSW........ National Organization Legal Services Workers (NTPA)
NOLTESTFAC... Naval Ordnance Laboratory Test Facility (SAA)
NOLTF .... Naval Ordnance Laboratory Test Facility
NOL/WO...... Naval Ordnance Laboratory, White Oak [*Maryland*]
NOM .... National Online Meeting [*Conference*] (IT)

NOM	National Organization for Men (EA)
NOM	National Organization for Men Legal Defense and Education Fund
NOM	Natural Organic Matter
NOM	Network Operations Manager [Manned Space Flight Network, NASA]
NOM	Network Output Multiplexer [Telecommunications] (MCD)
NOM	Newspapers on Microfilm
NOM	Ninth October Movement (SAUS)
NOM	Nomad River [Papua New Guinea] [Airport symbol] (OAG)
NOM	Noman [Italy] [FAA designator] (FAAC)
NOM	Nome [Alaska] [Seismograph station code, US Geological Survey] [Closed] (SEIS)
NOM	Nomenclature (AAG)
NOM	Nominal (AAG)
NOM	Nominate (AFM)
Nom	Nominating (AL)
nom-Nominative	(SHCU)
NOM	Nominative
NOM	No Offense Meant (SAUS)
NOM	Norbeau Mines, Inc. [Toronto Stock Exchange symbol]
NOM	Normal Extraocular Movements [Ophthalmology] (DAVI)
NOM	Number of Open Microphones
NOM	Nuveen Missouri Premium Income Municipal Fund [AMEX symbol] (SPSG)
NOM	Nuveen MO Prem, Inc. Muni [AMEX symbol] (TTSB)
NOM	Opa Locka, FL [Location identifier] [FAA] (FAAL)
NOMA	National Office Management Association [Later, AMS]
NOMA	National Oil Marketers Association [Defunct] (EA)
NOMA	National Organization of Minority Architects (EA)
NOMAC	Noise Modulation and Correlation (SAUS)
NOMAD	National Organisational Management Database
NOMAD	National Organization of Miniaturists and Dollers (EA)
NOMAD	Naval Operations & Maintenance Aviation Deck (SAUS)
NOMAD	Navy Oceanographic Meteorological Association (USDC)
NOMAD	Navy Oceanographic Meteorological Automatic Device
NOMAD	Navy Operation and Maintenance Aviation Deck (MCD)
NOMAD	Neutrino Oscillation Magnetic Detector
NOMAD	Nominal Michigan Algorithmic Decoder (SAUS)
NOMAD	Nozzle Materials Application and Design (MCD)
NOMAG	Nonmagnetic (IAA)
NOMb	Nitric Oxide Myoglobin [Food technology]
NOMBOS	Nonmine Bottom Objects [Navy] (NVT)
NOMC	National Organization for Migrant Children [Later, NCEMC] (EA)
Nom Cap	Nominal Capital (SAUS)
nom cons	Nomen Conservandum [Retained Name] [Latin]
NOMD	Nominated (ABBR)
NOMDA	National Office Machine Dealers Association (EA)
Nom Dam	Nominal Damages (SAUS)
nom dub	Nomen Dubium [Doubtful Name] [Latin]
NOME	National Origin Minority Education [New Hampshire Department of Education] (EDAC)
NOMEE	Nominee [Legal shorthand] (LWAP)
NOMEN	Nomenclature (AFM)
NOMES	New England Offshore Mining Experiment Study (NOAA)
NOMESKO	Nordic Medico-Statistical Committee (SAUS)
NOMFS	New England Offshore Mining Experiment Study (SAUS)
NOMG	Nominating (ABBR)
NOMHICE	Non-Methane Hydrocarbon Intercomparison Experiment (SAUS)
NOMI	Nonocclusive Mesenteric Infarction [Medicine] (AAMN)
NOMI	Nonocclusive Mesenteric Ischemia [Medicine]
No Mich U	Northern Michigan University (GAGS)
nom illeg	Nomen Illegitimum [Illegitimate Name] [Latin]
NOMIN	Nominative (WDAA)
nom inval	Nomen Invalidum [Name Not Valid] [Latin]
NOMIS	National Online Manpower Information System [Manpower Services Commission] [Information service or system] (IID)
NOMIS	Naval Ordnance Management Information System
NOMIS	Nuclear Operations and Maintenance Information Service (IID)
NOML	Nominal (ROG)
NOMLM	Nominalism (ABBR)
NOMLT	Nominalist (ABBR)
NOMLY	Nominally (ABBR)
NOMMA	National Ornamental and Miscellaneous Metals Association (EA)
NOM MUD	Nomen Nudum [A Name without Designation] [Latin] (BABM)
NOMN	Nomination
nom nov	Nomen Novum [New Name] [Latin]
nom nud	Nomen Nudum [Invalid Name] [Biology, taxonomy] [Latin]
NOMOP	No Record of Mustering-Out Payment (DNAB)
NOMOTC	National Organization of Mothers of Twins Clubs (EA)
NOMP	Navy Ocean Modeling and Prediction Program (SAUS)
nom prov	Nomen Provisiorum [Provisional Name] [Latin]
NOMR	Nominator (ABBR)
nom rej	Nomen Rejiciendum [Rejected Name] [Latin]
NOMRP	Normal Return Point (MCD)
NOMS	Network Operations Management System [Computer science]
NOMS	Nuclear Operations Monitoring System (MCD)
NOMSA	National Office Machine Service Association [Paramount, CA] (EA)
NOMSS	National Operational Meteorological Satellite System
NOMSS	Navy Oceanographic and Meteorological Support System (MCD)
Nom Std	Nominal Standard (SAUS)
nom superfl	Nomen Superfluum [Superfluous Name] [Latin]
NOMTF	Naval Ordnance Missile Test Facility
NOMTS	Naval Ordnance Missile Test Station [White Sands Missile Range, NM] (GRD)
NOMUS	Nordisk Musikkomite [Nordic Music Committee] (EAIO)
NOMV	Nominative (ABBR)

NOMW	National Organizational of Mall Walkers
NOMW	National Organization of Mall Walkers (EA)
NON	National Organization for Non-Parents [Later, NAOP]
Non	Nonoc (SAUS)
NON	Nonouti [Kiribati] [Airport symbol] (OAG)
NON	Normine Resources Ltd. [Vancouver Stock Exchange symbol]
NON	North Norway (NATG)
NON	Notice of Noncompliance (EPA)
No N	Novae Narrationes [New Counts] [1516] [A publication] (DLA)
NONA	Notice of Nonavailability
Non Acpc	Non-Acceptance (SAUS)
Nonacq	Nonacquiescence by Commissioner in a Tax Court or Board of Tax Appeals Decision [United States] [Legal term] (DLA)
NONADD	Nonadditivity [Statistics]
NON AL OCC	Non Alibi Occurrit [It Occurs in No Other Place] [Latin] (ROG)
non-Annex I	Parties Countries without a quantified CO_2 commitment (SAUS)
Nonappr	Nonappropriated (SAUS)
non arrl	non-arrival (SAUS)
NON-BUS	Nonbusiness [IRS]
NONCAN	Noncancellable [Insurance]
Non-Chk	Non Check (SAUS)
NonChk	Noncheck (SAUS)
NONCIT	Noncitizen (AABC)
noncm	Non-Cumulative (SG)
NON-CM	Noncumulative (ABBR)
NONCNST	Nonconsent
NONCOHO	Noncoherent Oscillator (MCD)
Non-Coll	Non Collegiate (SAUS)
noncoll	Noncollinear (MHDI)
NONCOM	Noncommissioned Officer [Military]
NON COM	Non Compos Mentis [Not in Sound Mind] [Latin] (ROG)
NONCOMECM	Noncommunications Electronics Countermeasures [Military] (AABC)
NONCOMJAM	Noncommunications Jamming [Military] (AABC)
NONCON	Nonconformist
NON COND	Non-Condensing (SAUS)
NON CUL	Non Culpabilis [Not Guilty] [Latin] (ROG)
NON-CUM	Non-Cumulative [Business term]
Non-cum	Noncumulative (EBF)
NOND	Non Detected [Laboratory science] (DAVI)
nondely	non-delivery (SAUS)
Nondestr Test	Nondestructive Testing (SAUS)
Nondestr Test Commun	Nondestructive Testing Communications (SAUS)
NONE	National Organization for Non-Enumeration (EA)
NONE	New Orleans & Northeastern R. R. [AAR code]
None	Nonesuch (SAUS)
NONE	Not One (SAUS)
NONEG	Negative Replies Neither Required nor Desired
NONEL	Non-Electric (SAUS)
NOneoC	Hartwick College, Oneonta, NY [Library symbol] [Library of Congress] (LCLS)
NOneoU	State University of New York, College at Oneonta, Oneonta, NY [Library symbol] [Library of Congress] (LCLS)
NONF	Nonfasting [Laboratory science] (DAVI)
Non Ferr Met World	Non Ferrous Metal World (SAUS)
Nonferrous Met	Nonferrous Metals (SAUS)
non flam	non-flammable (SAUS)
NONFLMB	Nonflammable
NON-FRAG	Non-Fragmentation [Bomb]
NONGAP	Nonlinear Grain Analysis Program (MCD)
N/ONI	Navy/Office of Naval Intelligence (AAG)
Non-Ind	Nonindicate (SAUS)
Non Ind	Non-Indication (SAUS)
NONLIN	Nonlinear (IAA)
Nonlinear Anal Theory Appl Proc Int Summer Sch	Nonlinear Analysis. Theory and Applications. Proceedings. International Summer School (SAUS)
Nonlinear Sci Today	Nonlinear Science Today (SAUS)
NONMAGCI	Nonmagnetic Cast Iron (IAA)
NON-MSA	Non-Standard Metropolitan Statistical Area (OICC)
NON-MTI	Non-Moving Target Indicator (SAUS)
Non Negl	Non-Negotiable (SAUS)
NON/NOV	Notices of Noncompliance/Notices of Violation [Navy]
NON-NSN	Not Assigned a National Stock Number
NON OBS	Non Obstante [Notwithstanding] [Latin]
NON OBST	Non Obstante [Notwithstanding] [Latin] (ROG)
Non Op	Non-Operational (SAUS)
NONP	Nonpackaged
NONP	Nonpareil (ADA)
NONP	Non-Precision Approach Runway [Aviation] (DA)
NONPAR	Nonparticipating [Insurance]
Non-Par	Non-Participating Provider
Non-par	Non-Participating Provider
NONPAYT	Nonpayment (ROG)
NONPERF	Nonperforated (ABBR)
NONPF	National Organization of Nurse Practitioner Faculties (NTPA)
nonpoly	Nonpolychrome (VRA)
Nonpr	Nonprofit (PROS)
NONPROF	Nonprofessional
NON PROS	Non Prosequitur [Does Not Prosecute] [Latin]
non pyt	non-payment (SAUS)
N/ONR	Navy/Office of Naval Research (AAG)
Non-REM	Nonrapid Eye Movement [Type of sleep] (MAE)
NON REP	Non Repetatur [Do Not Repeat] [Pharmacy]
Non Repetat	Non Repetatur [Do Not Repeat] [Pharmacy]

NON RES	Nonresident (WDAA)
NONRET.......	Nonreturnable (SAUS)
Non-Rev	Non-Reversible (SAUS)
Non-Rev PL..	Non-Reversible Plug (SAUS)
Non-Rev Skt..	Non-Reversible Socket (SAUS)
NONRSNT....	Nonresonant (IAA)
Non Rtnl	Non-Returnable (SAUS)
NONS..........	Nonspecific [Laboratory science] (DAVI)
NONSAP	Nonlinear Structural Analysis Program [Computer science]
non segs......	Nonsegmented Neutrophils [Medicine] (CPH)
NON SEQ	Non Sequitur [It Does Not Follow] [Latin]
NONSKED	Nonscheduled (ABBR)
NON-SLIP	Non-Speech Language Initiation Program
NON-SLKG ...	Nonslaking (SAUS)
nonstand.....	Nonstandard (BEE)
NONSTAND...	Nonstandard (WDAA)
NON STD	Non Standard (SAUS)
NONSTD	Nonstandard
NONStY........	Non-Standard Yiddish (BJA)
NONSUB	Nonsubmarine [Navy] (NVT)
NONSYN	Nonsynchronous
NONTAX	Nontaxable (SAUS)
NONTSDSL...	Not Included in Technical Service Demand Stockage Lists [Army] (AABC)
NONTT	Nonentity (ABBR)
Non-U	Not Upper Class (SAUS)
NONUM.......	Notional Number (NVT)
non-vis	Nonvisualization (DAVI)
NON-VON.....	Non-Von Neumann [Experimental computer, not based on the principles of Von Neumann computer design, under construction at Columbia University]
nonvtg	Non-Voting (SG)
NON-VTG	Non-Voting [Business term]
Non-vtg.......	Nonvoting (EBF)
Nonwovens Ind...	Nonwovens Industry (SAUS)
Nonwovens Rep Int...	Nonwovens Report International (SAUS)
NOO	Naoro [Papua New Guinea] [Airport symbol] (OAG)
NOO	National Organization Order (USDC)
NOO	Naval Oceanographic Office [Also known as NAVOCEANO; formerly, HO, NHO, USNHO]
NOO	Naval Oceanographic Office, Washington, DC [Inactive] [OCLC symbol] (OCLC)
NOO	Nevada Operations Office [Department of Energy]
NOO	Notice of Obligation [Military] (AFM)
NOOA..........	New Orleans Opera Association (SAUS)
NOOB..........	Not Out of Bed [Medicine] (DAVI)
NOOD..........	National Offshore One-Design [Boating regatta]
NOOD..........	Nitrix Oxide Optical Detector (SAUS)
NoodKid......	Noodle Kidoodle, Inc. [Associated Press] (SAG)
No of Cas Madras...	Notes of Cases at Madras (Strange) [A publication] (DLA)
NOOIAC........	National Offshore Operations Industry Advisory Committee [Coast Guard]
Nooney	Nooney Realty Trust, Inc. [Associated Press] (SAG)
NOOOA........	NORAD Office of Operational Analysis (IAA)
NO-OP	Flight Not Operating [Travel industry]
NOOP..........	No Operation [Computer science]
no-op	No Operator [Telemarketing] (WDMC)
NOOP..........	No Opinion [Computer science]
NO OP Instruction...	No-Operation Instruction (SAUS)
NOOS..........	Navy Oceanographic Observations from Space (SAUS)
NOOS..........	Nuclear Orbit-to-Orbit Shuttle [NASA]
NOO-SP	Naval Oceanographic Office Special Publication
NOOU..........	Not One of Us [Slang]
NoOU	Universitetet i Oslo [University of Oslo], Oslo, Norway [Library symbol] [Library of Congress] (LCLS)
NoOU-M.......	Universitetet i Oslo, Matematisk-Naturvitenskapelige Fakultet [University of Oslo, Department of Mathematics and Natural Sciences], Oslo, Norway [Library symbol] [Library of Congress] (LCLS)
NOP	Brooklyn, NY [Location identifier] [FAA] (FAAL)
NOP	National Onderzoek Persmedia [Database] [Stichting Nationaal Onderzoek Persmedia] [Netherlands] [Information service or system] (CRD)
NOP	National Opinion Poll
NOP	National Oracy Project (AIE)
NOP	National Outpatient Profile [Medicine] (MEDA)
NOP	Naval Oceanographic Publication
NOP	Naval Officer Procurement
NOP	Naval Ordnance Plant
NOP	Navigation Operating Procedure
NOP	Navy Objectives Plan
NOP	Near Object Probe (SAA)
NOP	Net Orders Processed [Business term] (DOAD)
NOP	Network Operations Procedure [Manned Space Flight Network, NASA]
NOP	Newscorp Overseas Ltd. [NYSE symbol] (SPSG)
NOP	Noncoherent Optical Processor
NOP	Nonoperating (KSC)
NOP	No Ocular Pain (SAUS)
NOP	No Operation [Computer science]
NOP	Normal Operating Procedure (NRCH)
NOP	Normed Programming (SAUS)
NOP	North Oscura Peak [White Sands Missile Range] [Army]
NOP	Notice of Procurement [Navy] (NG)
NOP	Not on Production
NOP	Not Operative (SAUS)
nop	Not Otherwise Provided (EBF)
NOP	Not Otherwise Provided
NOP	Not Our Publication
NOP	Novair-Aviacao Geral SA [Portugal] [ICAO designator] (FAAC)
NOP	Nuclear Operating Plan (SAUS)
NOP	Nuclear Operations (COE)
NOP	Nuclear Operations Plan (MCD)
NOP	Nuclear Ordnance Platoon [Marine Corps] (NVT)
NOP	Null Operation [Computer science]
NOP	Number of Openings [Technical drawings]
NOP	Number of Passes (MSA)
NOP	Numerical Oceanographic Prediction (PDAA)
NOP	Office of the Chief of Navy Operations (SAUS)
NOPA..........	National Office Products Association (EA)
NOPA..........	National Oilseed Processors Association (EA)
NOPA..........	Network Operations Performance Analysis [Manned Space Flight Network, NASA]
NOPAA........	National Office Products Association of Australia
NOPABCCE..	National Organization for Professional Advancement of Black Chemists and Chemical Engineers (EA)
NOPAC........	North Pacific [Aviation] (FAAC)
NOPAR........	Do Not Pass to Air Defense RADAR [Air Traffic Control] (FAAC)
No Par........	No Paragraph (SAUS)
NOPAT	Net Operating Profit after Tax
NOPB	New Orleans Public Belt Railroad [AAR code]
NOPC	Naval Oceanographic Processing Center (DOMA)
NOPCL........	Naval Officer Personnel Circular Letter
NOPCO........	National Oil Products Co. [Later, NOPCO Chemical Co.]
NOPD..........	New Orleans Police Department [Initialism also used as title of TV series]
NOPE	National Organization of Poll-Ettes (EA)
NOPE	Naturists and Nudists Opposing Pornographic Exploitation (EA)
NOPE	New Orleans Port of Embarkation
NOPE	No Promotion [Refers to lack of publicity in the record business]
NOPE	Not on Planet Earth [Waste management slang]
NOPEC........	Non-members of OPEC (SAUS)
NOPEC........	Non-OPEC [Oil producing countries which are not members of OPEC]
NOPECO.......	Northern Transvaal Peoples Congress (SAUS)
NOPEOL.......	National Organization to Promote English as the Official Language (EA)
NOPES	Non-Occupational Pesticide Exposure Study [Environmental Protection Agency] (GFGA)
NOPEX	Northern Hemisphere Climate Processes Experiment (SAUS)
NOPEX	Northern Hemisphere Climate Process Land-Surface Experiment (SAUS)
NOPF	National Oceanographic Processing Facility (DOMA)
NOPF	Naval Oceanographic Processing Facility (ANA)
NOPF	Naval Ordnance Plant, Forest Park [Illinois]
nopf	Not Otherwise Provided For (EBF)
N O Phil	New Orleans Philharmonic (SAUS)
NOPHN........	National Organization for Public Health Nursing (HGAA)
NOPHYSRET...	Not Required to Take New Physical Provided No Material Change since Recent Retirement Physical [Military]
NOPI	Naval Ordnance Plant Institute (MCD)
NOPL	Naval Ordnance Plant, Louisville [Kentucky]
NOPL	New Orleans Public Library (SAUS)
NOPLAN.......	No Operational Plan Published (SAUS)
NOPMS........	Network-Oriented Project Management System (PDAA)
NOP-N	Nordiska Publiceringsnamnden for Naturvetenskap [Nordic Publishing Board in Science] (EAIO)
NOPN..........	Normally Open [Switch]
NOPO	New Orleans Philharmonic Orchestra (SAUS)
NOPO	Nuclear Operations Planning Office (COE)
NOPOL........	No Pollution
NOPPA........	National Ocean Pollution Planning Act of 1978
NOPPA........	Nitroso(oxopropyl)propylamine [Organic chemistry]
NOPPO........	National Ocean Pollution Program Office (GNE)
NOPPrA.......	Newscp Pverseas Ltd Pref [NYSE symbol] (TTSB)
NOPPrB.......	Newscp Overseas Ltd Adj Pref [NYSE symbol] (TTSB)
NOPR	Notice of Proposed Rule Making [Federal agencies]
NOP Region...	North Pacific Region (SAUS)
NOPRI.........	National Orthotic and Prosthetic Research Institute (EA)
NOPROCAN...	If Not Already Processed, Orders Cancelled [Military]
NOPS	National Ocean Policy Study [US Senate]
NOPS	Network Order Processing System (TIMI)
NOPS	New Orleans Public Service (SAUS)
NOPS	Nike Operator Proficiency Scale [Army]
NOPS	Nimbus Observation Processing System (ACAE)
NOPS	Nimbus Observations Processing System (SAUS)
NOPS	Noncoherent Optical Processing System
NOPT	Naval Organisation Project Team (SAUS)
NOPT	Neon Communications [NASDAQ symbol]
NOPT	No Procedure Turn (SAUS)
NOPT	No Procedure Turn Required [Aviation]
NOPUS........	National Occupant Protection Use Survey [NHTSA] (TAG)
NoPVDM.......	N'Oubliez Pas Vos Decorations Maconniques [Do Not Forget Your Masonic Regalia] [Freemasonry] [French]
NOPWC.......	National Old People's Welfare Council (NADA)
NO-PYR	N-Nitrosopyrrolidine [Also, NYPR] [Biochemistry, organic chemistry]
NOQUIS	Nucleonic Oil Quantity Indication System [Air Force]
NOR	AS Norving [Norway] [ICAO designator] (FAAC)
NOR	Logic circuit usable as either AND or OR (SAUS)
NOR	National Organization for Rehabilitation [British]

NOR	Network Operations Representative (ACAE)
nor	Nitrogen ohne Radikal [*Chemical prefix*]
NOR	Nitrogen Oxide Reduction [*Research in automotive air pollution*]
NOR	Nonoperational Ready (NVT)
NOR	Non-Ordinary Resident [*British*]
NOR	Non-Relay (SAUS)
NOR	Noradrenaline [*or Norepinephrine*] [*Endocrinology*] (DAVI)
NOR	Noranda, Inc. [*Toronto Stock Exchange symbol*] [*Vancouver Stock Exchange symbol*]
NOR	Norbornadiene [*Also, NBD*] [*Organic chemistry*]
NOR	Nord [*Greenland*] [*Seismograph station code, US Geological Survey*] [*Closed*] (SEIS)
NOR	Nordfjordur [*Iceland*] [*Airport symbol*] (OAG)
NOR	Nordic Organisation for Reindeer Research (SAUS)
NOR	Nordisk Organ for Reinforskning [*Nordic Council of Reindeer Research*] [*Norway*] (EAIO)
NOR	Norepinephrine (SAUS)
NOR	NORfluoxetine (SAUS)
NOR	Norhtwestern Corp. [*NYSE symbol*] [*Formerly, Northwestern Pub. Svc.*]
Nor	Norma [*Constellation*]
NOR	Normal (KSC)
Nor	Norman (SHCU)
NOR	Norman
NOR	Normandale Community College, Bloomington, MN [*OCLC symbol*] (OCLC)
nor	North (SHCU)
NOR	North
NOR	North Central Airlines, Inc.
NOR	Northern (SAUS)
NOR	Northrup Flight Strip (SAUS)
NOR	NorthWestern Corp. [*NYSE symbol*] (SG)
NOR	Norway [*ANSI three-letter standard code*] (CNC)
Nor	Norway (VRA)
nor	Norwegian [*MARC language code*] [*Library of Congress*] (LCCP)
NOR	Norwich [*City in England*] (ROG)
NOR	Norwich [*Diocesan abbreviation*] [*Connecticut*] (TOCD)
NOR	Not and Or (SAUS)
NOR	Notice of Readiness [*Shipping*]
NOR	Notice of Revision
NOR	Notices of Revision (SAUS)
NOR	Not Operationally Ready [*Military*] (AFM)
NOR	Not Or [*Logical operator*] [*Computer science*]
NOR	Not Otherwiese Rated (SAUS)
NOR	Nucleolar Organizer Region [*in chromosomes*]
NOR	Nucleolus Organizer Region [*Genetics*] (DOG)
NOR	Number of Rounds [*Military*] (CINC)
NOR	San Diego, CA [*Location identifier*] [*FAA*] (FAAL)
NORA	National Oil Recyclers Association (GNE)
NORA	National Online Regulatory Access [*Data Development, Inc.*] [*Information service or system*] (CRD)
NORA	Norwegian Zero Power Reactor Assembly
NORA	Notice of Recruitment Activity (SAUS)
NORAC	No Radio Contact [*Aviation*]
NORAD	North American Aerospace Defense (SAUS)
NORAD	North American Aerospace Defense Command [*FAA*] (TAG)
NORAD	North American Air Defense [*Integrated United States-Canada command*]
NORAD	North American Air Defense Command (AAGC)
NORAD	North American Defense Command (SAUS)
NORAD	North Atlantic Aerospace Defense Command (SAUS)
NORAD	Norwegian Agency for Development Cooperation (SAUS)
NORAD	Norwegian Agency for International Development
NORADCOC	North American Air Defense Combat Operations Center [*Military*] (AFM)
NORAD CPX	North American Air Defense Command Post Exercise (SAA)
NORADCRU	North American Air Defense Orientation Cruise (NVT)
Noradr	Noradrenaline [*Norepinephrine*] [*Endocrinology*] (DAVI)
NorAE	Norwegian Antarctic Expedition [*1956-*]
NORAG	Northern Army Group (SAUS)
NORAGRIC	Norwegian Centre for International Agricultural Development (SAUS)
NORAID	Irish Northern Aid Committee (EA)
NORAID	Northern Aid (SAUS)
NORAID	Norwegian Agency for International Development
NORAIL	Northrop Overhead Rail Assembly and Installation Line (SAA)
NORAIM	Not Operationally Ready, Aircraft Intermediate Maintenance [*Military*] (DNAB)
Noram	Noram Energy Corp. [*Associated Press*] (SAG)
Noram	Noram Financing I [*Associated Press*] (SAG)
NoramE	Noram Energy Corp. [*Formerly, Arkla, Inc.*] [*Associated Press*] (SAG)
Norand	Norand Corp. [*Associated Press*] (SAG)
Nor Ant	Norwegian Antarctic (SAUS)
Nor Ant	Norwegian Antarctica (SAUS)
NORAP	Northwestern Alumni Players
NORAPS	Navy Operational Regional Atmospheric Prediction System (MCD)
Nor Arc	Norwegian Arctic (SAUS)
NORASDEFLANT	North American Antisubmarine Defense Force, Atlantic (NATG)
NORATS	Navy Operational Radio and Telephone Switchboard (NVT)
NOrb	Orangeburg Public Library, Orangeburg, NY [*Library symbol*] [*Library of Congress*] (LCLS)
NORBA	National Off-Road Bicycle Association [*Later, USCF*] (EA)
NORBAT	Nordic Battalion (SAUS)
NOrbR	Rockland State Hospital, Medical Library, Orangeburg, NY [*Library symbol*] [*Library of Congress*] (LCLS)
NORBS	Northern Base Section [*Corsica*]
NORC	National Oceanographic Records Center
NORC	National Opinion Research Center [*University of Chicago*]
NORC	Naturally Occurring Retirement Community
NORC	Naval Ordnance Research Computer (RALS)
NORC	Naval Ordnance Research Calculator [*or Computer*] [*Naval Ordnance Proving Ground*]
NORC	Nippon Ocean Racing Club (SAUS)
Norc	Norcross' Reports [*23-24 Nevada*] [*A publication*] (DLA)
NORC	Normal Curve [*Laboratory science*] (DAVI)
Norc	Normally Occurring Retirement Community
NORC	Nuclear Ordnance Record Card (NVT)
NOrc	Orchard Park Public Library, Orchard Park, NY [*Library symbol*] [*Library of Congress*] (LCLS)
NorCACHA	North Carolina Automated Clearing House Association (TBD)
NORCAISEC	Northern California Section, Western Sea Frontier (SAUS)
NORCALSEC	Northern California Section, Western Sea Frontier
NORCANUKUS	Norway, Canada, United Kingdom, United States (DOMA)
NORCAP	National Organisation of Counselling Adoptees and Their Parents [*British*] (DBA)
NORCCIS	Norwegian Command Control Information System (ACAE)
NOrcE	Erie Community College-South, Orchard Park, NY [*Library symbol*] [*Library of Congress*] (LCLS)
NorcEB	Erie-Cattaraugus Board of Cooperative Educational Services, Orchard Park, NY [*Library symbol*] [*Library of Congress*] (LCLS)
NORCEN	Norcen Energy Resources Ltd. (SAUS)
NORCO	National Oil Recovery Corp.
Nor Co	Northern Command (SAUS)
NORCOM	Nonrecurring Cost Model (SAUS)
NORCOM	Northern Command (SAUS)
NorCran	Northland Cranberries [*Associated Press*] (SAG)
NORCSEX	Norwegian Continental Shelf Experiment (SAUS)
Nor Cur	Norwegian Current (SAUS)
NORCUS	Northwest College and University Association for Science [*Richland, WA*] [*Department of Energy*] (GRD)
NORD	Bureau of Ordnance Publication [*Later, NAVORD*] [*Navy*]
NORD	National Organization for Rare Disorders (EA)
NORD	National Organization for Rare Disorders, Inc.
NORD	Naval Ordnance
Nord	Nordic (DIAR)
NORD	Norsk Data (NITA)
NORD	Not Ordered, This Part of Package (DAVI)
NORD	Nursing Orderly (SAUS)
NORDA	Naval Oceanographic Research and Development Administration [*USA*] [*Marine science*] (OSRA)
NORDA	Naval Ocean Research and Development Activity [*Bay St. Louis, MS*]
NORDDOK	Nordic Committee on Information and Documentation (SAUS)
NordDRG	Nordic DRG (SAUS)
NORDEC	Nordic Economic Union (SAUS)
NORDEK	Nordic Customs Union (EBF)
NORDEK	Nordic Economic Community (SAUS)
NORDEK	Norway, Denmark, Finland, Sweden [*Nordic Economic Community*] [*Trade bloc*]
NORDEL	Nordic Electricity Union (SAUS)
NORDEL	Organization for Nordic Electrical Cooperation (EA)
NORDIATRANS	Association for Nordic Transplant and Dialysis Personnel (EAIO)
Nordic	Nordic American Tanker Shipping Ltd. [*Associated Press*] (SAG)
NORDICOM	Nordic Documentation Center for Mass Communication Research [*Database ori ginator*] [*Finland*] [*Information service or system*] (IID)
Nordic Pulp Paper Res J	Nordic Pulp and Paper Research Journal (SAUS)
NORDIHS	Nordic Integrated Hydrographic System (SAUS)
NORDINFO	Nordic Council for Scientific Information and Research Libraries (SAUS)
NORDINFO	Nordiska Samarbetsorganet for Vetenskaplig Information [*Nordic Council for Scientific Information and Research Libraries*] [*Finland*] (EAIO)
NORDITA	Nordic Institute for Theoretic Atomic Physics [*Later, NIIP*] (EY)
NORDMAP	European Nordic Pollen Data Mapping Project (SAUS)
NORDMAP	Nordic Pollen Data Mapping Project (SAUS)
NORDO	No Radio
Nord P	Nordic Pharmacopoeia [*A publication*]
NordPac	Nord Pacific Ltd. [*Associated Press*] (SAG)
NordPc	Nord Pacific Ltd. [*Associated Press*] (SAG)
NORDPOST	Nordic Postal Union Conference (SAUS)
NORDQUA	Nordic Association for Quaternary Research (SAUS)
NordRs	Nord Resources Corp. [*Associated Press*] (SAG)
NORDSAT	Scandinavian Countries Broadcast Satellite (MCD)
Nordser	Nordisk Samkatalog foer Seriella Medicinska Publikationer [*Karolinska Institutets Bibliotek och Informationscentral*] [*Sweden*] [*Information service or system*] (CRD)
Nordsn	Nordson Corp. [*Associated Press*] (SAG)
Nordst	Nordstrom, Inc. [*Associated Press*] (SAG)
NORDTEL	Nordiskt Samarbete Inom Telekommunikation [*Nordic Cooperation on Telecommunications*] [*Finland*] (EAIO)
NORDTEST	Organisation for testing in the Nordic countries (SAUS)
NORDUNet	Nordic Countries Network
NORDUnet	[*The*] Nordic University Network (TNIG)
NORE	Northeast
NOREA	Nordic Radio Evangelic Association (SAUS)
NOREASTNAVFACENGCOM	Northeast Division Naval Facilities Engineering Command
NOREC	No Record
NOREC	Northern Environmental Council [*Defunct*] (EA)
NORECHAN	Northeast Subarea Channel (NATG)

NOREF......... No Reference
Norelco Rep... Norelco Report (SAUS)
NOREP.......... No Reply (SAUS)
NOREP.......... No Reply Received
NOREP......... No Report Prepared (SAUS)
NOREP.......... Not Reportable
NORESS......... Norwegian Regional Seismic Array
Norex.......... Norex America, Inc. [*Associated Press*] (SAG)
NOREX......... Nuclear Operational Readiness Exercise (NVT)
NORF.......... National Offense Reserve Fleet (ACAE)
Norf.......... Norfolk [*County in England*] (ODBW)
NORF.......... Norfolk [*County in England*]
NORFISH ..... North Pacific Fisheries Project (NOAA)
NORFLK....... Norfolk [*County in England*]
NORFORM..... Not Releasable to Foreign Nationals
Nor Fr.......... Norman French [*Language, etc.*] (DLA)
Nor Fr.......... Norman-French (SAUS)
Norf S.......... Norfolk Southern, Norfolk & Western, Southern Railway (SAUS)
NOR Gate .... NOT OR Gate (SAUS)
NORGD .... National Organization for the Rights of Guide Dogs (EA)
NORGLAC ..... Northern Great Lakes Area Council
NORGRAIN..... North American Grain Charter (SAUS)
NORGRAPH... Northeast Graphics Conference and Printing Show [*Printing Industry Association of Connecticut and Western Massachusetts*] (TSPED)
NORI.......... National Office for the Rights of the Indigent [*Later, LDF*]
NORIANE....... Normes et Reglements Informations Automatisees Accessibles en Ligne [*Automated Standards and Regulations Information Online*] [*Database*] [*French Association for Standardization*] [*Information service or system*] (IID)
NORIF.......... Natural Oocyte Retrieval Intravaginal Fertilization [*Alternative to traditional in-vitro fertilization (IVF)*] (PAZ)
NORIF.......... Non-stimulated Oocyte Retrieval In Fertilization (SAUS)
NORIMB...... Norimberge [*Nuremberg*] [*Imprint*] (ROG)
NORIP.......... NORAD Intelligence Plan [*Military*] (AABC)
NORIS.......... North Island (MUGU)
NORIV.......... No Arrival Report [*Aviation*] (FAAC)
NORK.......... [*The*] New Orleans Rhythm Kings [*Jazz band*]
NORKZ........ Norsk-Data AS (MHDW)
NORL.......... Nordic Limited, Inc.
Norland....... Norland Medical Systems, Inc. [*Associated Press*] (SAG)
NORLANT .... North Atlantic Area (MUGU)
NORLANT .... Northern Sub-Area Eastern Atlantic Command (SAUS)
NORLANTAACS... North Atlantic Airways and Air Communications Service (SAA)
NORLANTEX... North Atlantic - Training Exercise (MCD)
NorldCr........ Northland Cranberries, Inc. [*Associated Press*] (SAG)
norleu.......... Norleucine [*Biochemistry*] (DAVI)
NORLEU........ Norleucine [*A nonessential amino acid*] [*Biochemistry*]
N Orl N&S J... New Orleans Medical and Surgical Journal (SAUS)
NOR-LUCS... Northern Software Consultants-Library Updating and Compiling System (SAUS)
NORLUCS .... Nother Software Consultants Library Updating and Compiling System (SAUS)
NORM.......... National Office Resources Management [*IRS*]
NORM.......... National Organization for Raw Materials (EA)
NORM.......... National Organization of Restoring Men (SAUS)
NORM.......... Naturally Occurring Radioactive Material (FFDE)
Norm .... Norma [*Constellation*]
NORM .... Normal [*or Normalize*] (AAG)
Norm .... Normal (DIAR)
NORM.......... Normal (ELAL)
norm.......... Normal (NTIO)
Norm .... Normalized (SAUS)
NORM.......... Norman [*or Normandy*]
Norm .... Normative Analysis (SAUS)
NORM.......... Normative Operating Reporting Method
NORM.......... Normetal [*AAR code*]
NORM.......... Not Operationally Ready Maintenance [*Military*] (NG)
NORM.......... Not Operational Ready Materiel [*Military*] (AFIT)
NORM.......... Nuclear Operational Readiness Maneuver (NVT)
NORM.......... Nuclear Ordnance Readiness Manpower
NORMA......... No Remote Memory Access (RALS)
NORMAGS .... Northern Magnetic and Gravity Survey (SAUS)
NORMAL........ Nova Realtime Macro Language (SAUS)
NORMARSEN... Norwegian Maritime Remote Sensing (SAUS)
NORMATERM... Normalisation, Automatisation de la Terminologie [*Standardization and Automation of Terminology*] [*Databank*] [*France*] [*Information service or system*] (IID)
NORMCLSD... Normally Closed [*Switch*] [*Electronics*] (IAA)
NORMEDS ... Northern Meteorological Data System (ACAE)
NORMET....... Normetanephrine [*Also, Methylnorepinephrine*] [*Biochemistry*] (AAMN)
NORM(F) ..... Not Operationally Ready Maintenance - Flyable [*Military*] (MCD)
NORM(G)...... Not Operationally Ready Maintenance - Grounded [*Military*] (MCD)
NORML........ National Organization for the Reform of Marijuana Laws (EA)
NORML........ National Organization for the Reinforcement of Marijuana Laws (NADA)
NORML........ National Organization for the Repeal of Marijuana Laws (NADA)
NORML........ Normal (DAVI)
NORM/MAG.... Normal/Magnified (SAUS)
NORMOPN.... Normally Open [*Switch*] [*Electronics*] (IAA)
NORM OPN SW... Normally Open Switch (SAUS)
NORMSHOR... Normal Tour of Shore Duty
NORM-UK.... National Organization of Restoring Men-UK (SAUS)
NORO.......... Not Operationally Ready Other [*Military*] (AFM)
NOROEC ...... NORAD Operational Employment Concept [*Military*] (AABC)

Noroil .... Norwegian Oil (SAUS)
NORONTAIR... Northern Ontario Airways (SAUS)
NORP.......... New Oil Reference Price (or Pricing) (SAUS)
NORP.......... Nord Pacific Ltd. [*NASDAQ symbol*] (SAG)
NORP.......... NORPAC Explorations Services (SAUS)
NORPAC...... Naval Overhaul and Repair Pacific (MUGU)
Nor Pac ...... Northern Pacific (SAUS)
NORPAC...... Northern Pacific Railway Co.
NORPAC ..... North Pacific [*Military*]
NORPAC Project... North Pacific Project (SAUS)
Nor Pat....... Norman. Letters Patent [*1853*] [*A publication*] (DLA)
NORPAT....... Northern Patrol (SAUS)
NORPAX...... North Pacific Expedition (SAUS)
NORPAX...... North Pacific Experiment [*National Science Foundation*]
NORPI.......... No Pilot Balloon Observation Will Be Filed Next Collection Unless Weather Changes Siginificantly [*NWS*] (FAAC)
NOrpOHi ..... Oyster Pond Historical Society, Orient Point, NY [*Library symbol*] [*Library of Congress*] (LCLS)
Nor Pro Pr... North's Probate Practice [*Illinois*] [*A publication*] (DLA)
NORPY........ Nord Pacific Ltd ADR [*NASDAQ symbol*] (TTSB)
NORQR .... NORAD Qualitative Requirement [*Military*] (AABC)
NORR.......... No Reply Received (FAAC)
Norr .... Norris' Reports [*82-96 Pennsylvania*] [*A publication*] (DLA)
NORRA .... National Off-Road Racing Association
NORRD .... No Reply Received (NOAA)
Norrell........ Norrell Corp. [*Associated Press*] (SAG)
NORRF........ Norris Communications [*NASDAQ symbol*] (TTSB)
Norris .... Norris' Reports [*82-96 Pennsylvania*] [*A publication*] (DLA)
Norris & L Perpetuities... Norris and Leach on Rule Against Perpetuities [*A publication*] (DLA)
NorrisC .... Norris Communications Corp. [*Associated Press*] (SAG)
Norris Seamen... Norris' Law of Seamen [*A publication*] (DLA)
Norr Peake... Norris' Edition of Peake's Law of Evidence [*A publication*] (DLA)
NORRS .... Naval Operational Readiness Reporting Systems
NORS .... National Organization for Rivers (SAUS)
NORS .... National Organization for River Sports (EA)
NORS.......... New Old Replacement Stock [*Automotive parts*]
NORS.......... North Atlantic Regional Research (SAUS)
NORS .... Not Operationally Ready for Service [*Military*] (VNW)
NORS .... Not Operationally Ready, Spare parts (SAUS)
NORS .... Not Operationally Ready Supply [*Military*]
NORS .... Not Operationally Ready System [*Military*]
NORSAIR.... Not Operationally Ready Supply Aeronautical Items Report (SAUS)
NORSAIR.... Not Operationally Ready Supply Aviation Items Report [*Military*]
NORSAR ...... Norwegian Seismic Array [*Royal Norwegian Council for Scientific and Industrial Research*]
NORSAT....... Norwegian Satellite System
NORSAT....... Norwegian Domestic Satellite (SAUS)
NORSE........ Norsul Oil & Mining (SAUS)
NORSE........ Nuclear Optical & Radar Signature Estimation (SAUS)
NORSE........ Nuclear Optical and Radar System Effects (SAUS)
NORSEACENT... North Sea Subarea (NATG)
NORSEC....... Northern Security Exhibition [*British*] (ITD)
NORSEX....... Norwegian Remote Sensing Experiment [*in marginal ice zone*]
NORSF........ Not Operationally Ready Supply Flyable [*Military*] (MCD)
NORS-G....... Not Operationally Ready for Service - Grounded (VNW)
NORSG........ Not Operationally Ready Supply Grounded [*Military*] (NG)
NORS Group... Northern Offshore Resources Study Group (SAUS)
NORSHIPCO... Norfolk Shipbuilding & Drydock Corp. (SAUS)
NORSIB........ NORAD Space Intelligence Bulletin [*DoD*]
Norsk.......... Norsk Hydro [*Associated Press*] (SAG)
Norskie........ Norwegian-American (SAUS)
NORSMAP ... Norwegian Remote Sensing Spectroscopy for Mapping and Monitoring of Algal Blooms and Pollution (SAUS)
NORSN........ Not Operationally Ready Supply Nongrounded [*Military*] (NG)
NORSNET .... National Oceanographic Reference Station Network (NOAA)
NORSOLS .... Northern Solomons Area
NORSPEC .... North Sea Spectrum (SAUS)
NORST........ No Restrictions (FAAC)
Norstan........ Norstan, Inc. [*Associated Press*] (SAG)
NORSTAR .... Norden Search Terrain Avoidance RADAR (SAA)
NorSys........ Nortech Systems, Inc. [*Associated Press*] (SAG)
NORT.......... Nuclear Ordnance Readiness Test (NVT)
NORTAM...... Northrop Terminal Attrition Model (SAA)
NORTEB...... Norwegian Telecommunications Users Group
Nortek........ Nortek, Inc. [*Associated Press*] (SAG)
NORTEL....... Northern Telecom
Nortel .... Northern Telecom [*Canada*]
NorTel......... Northern Telecom Ltd. [*Associated Press*] (SAG)
Nortel100..... Nortel Inversora SA [*Associated Press*] (SAG)
NORTEP....... Northern Teacher Education Program (SAUS)
North .... Northampton County Reporter [*Pennsylvania*] [*A publication*] (DLA)
NORTH........ Northerly (ABBR)
NORTH........ Northern (ABBR)
NORTH........ Northern Operations of Rail Transportation and Highways [*Alaska*]
North .... Reports Tempore Northington [*Eden. English Chancery Reports*] [*1757-67*] [*A publication*] (DLA)
North Africa... Africa north of the Tropic of Cancer (SAUS)
North Africa... Algeria, Egypt, Libya, Morocco, Tunisia (SAUS)
NORTHAG.... North [*European*] Army Group [*NATO*]
NORTHAG.... Northern Army Group, Central Europe (SAUS)
NORTHAG.... North European Army Group (SAUS)
Northam...... Northampton Law Reporter [*Pennsylvania*] [*A publication*] (DLA)
Northam Law Rep... Northampton County Law Reporter [*Pennsylvania*] [*A publication*] (DLA)

Northam L Rep... Northampton Law Reporter [*Pennsylvania*] [*A publication*] (DLA)

Northamp Co Repr... Northampton County Reporter [*Pennsylvania*] [*A publication*] (DLA)

Northampton Co Rep... Northampton County Reporter [*Pennsylvania*] [*A publication*] (DLA)

North & G.... North and Guthrie's Appeals Reports [*68-80 Missouri*] [*A publication*] (DLA)

Northants..... Northamptonshire (DIAR)

NORTHANTS... Northamptonshire [*County in England*]

Northbay...... Northbay Financial Corp. [*Associated Press*] (SAG)

North BH...... North Broken Hill (SAUS)

North Car J Int'l L & Comm... North Carolina Journal of International Law and Commercial Regulation [*A publication*] (DLA)

North Carolina College LJ... North Carolina College Law Journal [*A publication*] (DLA)

North Carolina Div Mineral Resources Geol Map Ser... North Carolina. Department of Conservation and Development. Division of Mineral Resources. Geologic Map Series (SAUS)

North Carolina Div Mineral Resources Inf Circ... North Carolina. Department of Conservation and Development. Division of Mineral Resources. Information Circular (SAUS)

North Carolina Div Mineral Resources Spec Pub... North Carolina. Department of Conservation and Development. Division of Mineral Resources. Special Publication (SAUS)

North Co...... Northampton County Reporter [*Pennsylvania*] [*A publication*] (DLA)

North Co Rep... Northampton County Reporter [*Pennsylvania*] [*A publication*] (DLA)

North Co R (PA)... Northampton County Reporter [*Pennsylvania*] [*A publication*] (DLA)

NORTHD...... Northumberland [*County in England*] (ROG)

Northeast Golf Sci... Northeast Gulf Science (SAUS)

Northern Institute... Northern Region Correction Institute at Fairbanks, Alaska (SAUS)

Northern J Appl Forestry... Northern Journal of Applied Forestry (SAUS)

Northerns..... Burlington, Great Northern and Northern Pacific railroads (SAUS)

North Irel Gov Minist Commer Mem Geol Surv... Northern Ireland. Government. Ministry of Commerce. Memoirs. Geological Survey (SAUS)

North Jersey Coast... Atlantic City to the Atlantic Highlands (SAUS)

North Ken'y SL Rev... Northern Kentucky State Law Review [*A publication*] (DLA)

North Log Timber... Northern Logger and Timber Processor (SAUS)

NORTHM...... Northumberland (ABBR)

NORTH'N..... Northampton [*City in England*] (ROG)

Northop U.... Northop University (GAGS)

North Pole... discovered by American explorers Frederick A Cook and Robert E Peary in 1909 (SAUS)

North Pr...... North's Probate Practice [*Illinois*] [*A publication*] (DLA)

Northrim...... Northrim Bank [*Associated Press*] (SAG)

Northrop ULJ... Northrop University. Law Journal of Aerospace, Energy, and the Environment [*A publication*] (DLA)

Northrop ULT Aero Energy and Envt... Northrop University. Law Journal of Aerospace, Energy and the Environment (SAUS)

North Scod Coll Agric Bull... North of Scotland College of Agriculture. Bulletin (SAUS)

North St L.... North. Study of the Laws [*1824*] [*A publication*] (DLA)

NORTHUM... Northumberland [*County in England*]

Northum...... Northumberland County Legal News [*Pennsylvania*] [*A publication*] (DLA)

Northumb.... Northumberland [*County in England*] (ODBW)

NORTHUMB... Northumberland [*County in England*] (ROG)

Northumb Co... Northumberland County Legal News [*Pennsylvania*] [*A publication*] (DLA)

Northumberland Co Leg Jour... Northumberland Legal Journal [*Pennsylvania*] [*A publication*] (DLA)

Northumberland LJ... Northumberland Legal Journal [*Pennsylvania*] [*A publication*] (DLA)

Northumb Legal J... Northumberland Legal Journal [*Pennsylvania*] [*A publication*] (DLA)

Northumb LJ... Northumberland Legal Journal News [*Pennsylvania*] [*A publication*] (DLA)

Northumb LN... Northumberland Legal Journal [*Pennsylvania*] [*A publication*] (DLA)

Northum Co Leg N... Northumberland County Legal News [*Pennsylvania*] [*A publication*] (ILCA)

Northum Leg J... Northumberland Legal Journal [*Pennsylvania*] [*A publication*] (DLA)

Northum Leg J (PA)... Northumberland Legal Journal [*Pennsylvania*] [*A publication*] (DLA)

Northum Leg N (PA)... Northumberland County Legal News [*Pennsylvania*] [*A publication*] (DLA)

North-West Dent... North-West Dentistry (SAUS)

Northwestern U... Northwestern University (GAGS)

NorthWest Miller... Northwestern Miller (SAUS)

North WLJ... Northwestern Law Journal [*A publication*] (DLA)

Northw Rep... Northwestern Reporter [*Commonly cited NW*] [*A publication*] (DLA)

NORTIC...... NORAD [*North American Aerospace Defense Command*] Technical Intelligence Center (DOMA)

NORTLANT... North Atlantic

Nort LC... Norton's Leading Cases on Inheritance [*India*] [*A publication*] (DLA)

NortMc......... Norton McNaughton, Inc. [*Associated Press*] (SAG)

NORTNK...... Nortankers, Inc. (SAUS)

Norton... Norton's Cases on Hindu Law of Inheritance [*1870-71*] [*India*] [*A publication*] (DLA)

NORTR........ Nortronics Corp.

Nortraship .. Norwegian Trade and Shipping Mission (SAUS)

NortrpG........ Northrop Grumman Corp. [*Formerly, Northrup Corp.*] [*Associated Press*] (SAG)

NorTrst......... Northern Trust Corp. [*Associated Press*] (SAG)

NorTst......... Northern Trust Corp. [*Associated Press*] (SAG)

NORVA......... Norfolk, Virginia [*Navy*]

NORVAGRP... Norfolk, Virginia Group [*Navy*]

NORVAL......... Norvaline [*Biochemistry*]

NORVIC......... Norvicensis [*Norwich*] [*Imprint*] (ROG)

NORVIPS ..... Northrup Voice Interruption Priority System (MUGU)

NORW........... Norway [*or Norwegian*]

Norw........... Norwegian (BEE)

NORW........... Norwich [*City in England*] (ROG)

Norw Canners Export J... Norwegian Canners Export Journal (SAUS)

NORWEB...... Northwestern Electricity Board (NADA)

Norweb........ NORWEB PLC [*Associated Press*] (SAG)

NORWELD ... Northwest Library District [*Library network*]

NORWESSEAFRON... Northwestern Sea Frontier

NORWESSEC... Northwestern Sector, Western Sea Frontier

Norwest....... Norwest Corp. [*Associated Press*] (SAG)

NORWESTLANT... Northwest Atlantic [*Military*]

NORWESTNAVFACENGCOM... Northwest Division Naval Facilities Engineering Command

NorwFn........ Norwich Financial Corp. [*Associated Press*] (SAG)

NORWICH..... Knickers Off Ready When I Come Home [*Correspondence*] (DSUE)

NorwlkSv .... Norwalk Savings Society [*Associated Press*] (SAG)

Norwood...... Norwood Promotional Products [*Associated Press*] (SAG)

Norw P .... Norwegian Patent (SAUS)

Norwt......... Norwest Corp. [*Associated Press*] (SAG)

NORWY....... NORWEB PLC [*NASDAQ symbol*] (SAG)

NOS .... National Ocean Service [*Formerly, Coast and Geodetic Survey*] [*Washington, DC*] [*National Oceanic and Atmospheric Administration*]

NOS .... National Ocean Survey (NOAA)

NOS .... National Office Staff [*American Occupational Therapy Association*]

NOS .... National Operational Satellite

NOS .... National Oratorio Society [*Defunct*] (EA)

NOS .... National Osteoporosis Society [*British*]

NOS .... NATO Office of Security (NATG)

NOS .... Naval Ordnance Station

NOS .... Nederlandse Omroep Stichting [*Radio and television network*] [*Netherlands*]

NOS .... Network Operating System

NOS .... Network Queueing System [*Computer science*] (CIST)

NOS .... New Old Stock [*Automotive parts*]

NOS .... Night Observation Sight [*Air Force*]

NOS .... Night Observation Surveillance (SAUS)

NOS .... Night Observation System [*Navy*] (CAAL)

NOS .... Night Operation Sight (SAUS)

NOS .... Night Operation System [*Aviation*]

NOS .... Nimbus Operational System

NOS .... Nine O'Clock Service (WDAA)

NOS .... Nirtous Oxide Systems (SAUS)

NOS .... Nitric Oxide Synthase [*An enzyme*]

NOS .... Nodal Operating System (SAUS)

NOS .... Nonobese Subject (MELL)

NOS .... Non-Ocular Source [*Physiology*]

NOS .... Nonoriented Satellite

NOS .... No Organisms Seen (MELL)

NOS .... Nopaline Synthase [*An enzyme*]

NOS .... Northern State College Library, Aberdeen, SD [*OCLC symbol*] (OCLC)

NOS .... Northern Tropospheric Oxidants Study (SAUS)

NOS .... Northstar Resources Ltd. [*Toronto Stock Exchange symbol*]

NOS .... Norway Airlines [*ICAO designator*] (FAAC)

NOS .... Nosing (ABBR)

NOS .... Nossi-Be [*Madagascar*] [*Airport symbol*] (OAG)

NOS .... Nostalgia [*A radio station format*] (WDMC)

NOS .... Not Off Sanctions (WDAA)

NOS .... Not of Specific Origin (SAUS)

NOS .... Not on Shelf (ADA)

NOS .... Not Otherwise Specified (AFM)

nos............ Not Otherwise Stated (EBF)

NOS .... Not Otherwise Stated

NOS .... Nought Output Signal (SAUS)

NOS .... Nouvel Ordre Social [*New Social Order*] [*Switzerland*] (PD)

NOS .... Number of Stops (IAA)

NOS .... Numbers (AAG)

nos............ Numbers (WDMC)

NOs............ Oswego City Library, Oswego, NY [*Library symbol*] [*Library of Congress*] (LCLS)

NOSA .... National Occupational Safety Association (NADA)

NOSA .... National Outerwear and Sportswear Association (EA)

NOSAC........ National Offshore Safety Advisory Committee [*Coast Guard*]

NOSAD........ National Organization for Seasonal Affective Disorder (EA)

NOSALF .... Nordiska Samfundet for Latinamerika Forskning [*Nordic Association for Research on Latin America*] [*Sweden*] (EAIO)

NOSAMS...... National Ocean Sciences AMS Facility (SAUS)

NOSAP........ National Ocean Survey Analytical Plotter [*NOAA*] (PDAA)

NOSAR........ No Search and Rescue required (SAUS)

NOSB .... National Organic Standards Board

NOSBE........ Network Operating System/Batch Environment

NOSC.......... Naval Oceanographic Systems Command (CCCA)

NOSC.......... Naval Ocean Systems Center [*Formerly, NELC*]

NOSC.......... Naval Ordnance Systems Command [*Later, Naval Sea Systems Command*]

NOSC.......... Nonoscillating

NOsC .... Oswego County Library System, Oswego, NY [*Library symbol*] [*Library of Congress*] (LCLS)
NOSCAF ...... New Orleans Sickle Cell Anemia Foundation (SAUS)
NOSCL .... Naval Ocean Systems Center Laboratory (DNAB)
NosCom .... IEEE-SA Standards Board New Opportunities in Standards Committee (SAUS)
NOSCP .... National Ocean Sediment Coring Program (NOAA)
NOSD .... Nosed (ABBR)
NoSdeSv ...... North Side Savings Bank [*Associated Press*] (SAG)
NOSE .... National Odd Shoe Exchange (EA)
NOSE .... Neighbors Opposing Smelly Emissions [*Student legal action organization*]
NOSE .... Neotronics Olfactory Sensing Equipment [*Neotronics Scientific*] (PS)
NOSECS .... NAMMA Order Supply EDP Computer System (SAUS)
NOSG .... Nosing (ABBR)
NOSGLANT... Naval Operations Support Group, Atlantic
NOSGPAC ... Naval Operations Support Group, Pacific
NOSH .... Hain Food Group [*NASDAQ symbol*] (TTSB)
NOSH .... Hain Food Group, Inc. [*NASDAQ symbol*] (SAG)
NOS-H .... Nordiska Samarbetsnamnden for Humanistisk Forskning [*Nordic Committee of the Research Councils for the Humanities - NCRCH*] (EA)
NOSH .... No Show [*Travel industry*] (TRID)
NOsH .... Oswego Hospital, Oswego, NY [*Library symbol*] [*Library of Congress*] (LCLS)
NOsHi .... Oswego County Historical Society, Oswego, NY [*Library symbol*] [*Library of Congress*] (LCLS)
NOsI .... International Business Machines Corp., Oswego, NY [*Library symbol*] [*Library of Congress*] (LCLS)
NOSI .... Nitric Oxide Synthase Inhibitor [*Medicine*] (MELL)
NOSI .... Now Simultaneous (SAUS)
NOSIC .... Naval Ocean Surveillance Information Center
NOSIC .... Naval Ocean Surveillance Intelligence Command (CCCA)
NOSIC .... Naval Operations Support Information Center [*Navy*]
NOSIC .... Neurologic Outcome Scale for Infants and Children [*Medicine*] (DMAA)
NOSIE .... Nurses Observation Scale for Inpatient Evaluation [*Psychiatry*]
NO SIG .... No Signature (SAUS)
NOSIG .... No Significant (SAUS)
NOSIG .... No Significant Change [*Used to qualify weather phenomena*]
NOSIGCHNG... No Significant Change (SAUS)
NOSIH .... Naval Ordnance Station, Indian Head (MCD)
NOSINS .... Nosiness (ABBR)
NOSL .... Naval Ordnance Station, Louisville [*Kentucky*]
NOSL .... Night-Day Optical Survey of Lightning [*NASA*]
NOSL .... Night/Day Optical Survey of Thunderstorm Lightning (NAKS)
NOSL .... Night-time Optical Survey of Lightning (SAUS)
NOSLA .... National Oil Scouts and Landmen's Association [*Later, IOSA*]
NOSL-QA ..... Naval Ordnance Station, Louisville Quality Assurance Department [*Kentucky*]
NOS-LSCR ... National Ocean Survey Lake Survey Center [*National Oceanic and Atmospheric Administration*]
NOSM .... Navy Occupation Service Medal
NOSM .... Noise Diotic, Signal Monaural (PDAA)
NOSMO .... Norden Optics Setting, Mechanized Operation [*Air Force bombsight*]
NOSMO .... No Smoking (SAUS)
No Smoke/Drugs... No Smoking or Drugs (SAUS)
NOS-N .... Samarbetsnamnden for de Nordiska Naturvetenskapliga Forskningraden [*Joint Committee of the Nordic Natural Science Research Councils - JCNNSRC*] (EA)
NOSO .... Naval Ordnance Supply Office (MUGU)
NOSO .... Not of Specific Origin
NOSOPEX .... Northern Sumatra Offshore Petroleum Exploration (SAUS)
NOSORD ...... Not in Sequential Order (SAUS)
NOSP .... National Ophthalmic Speakers Programme [*Canada*]
NOSP .... Naval Ordnance Special Projects
NOSP .... Network Operations Support Plan [*NASA*] (KSC)
NOSP .... Network Operation Support Program [*Computer science*]
NOSPI .... Newsletter on Serials Pricing Issues (SAUS)
NOSPL .... No Special Observation Taken [*NWS*] (FAAC)
NOSR .... National Office for Social Responsibility (EA)
NOSS .... National Oceanic Satellite System (MCD)
NOSS .... National Oceanic Survey Satellite (NAKS)
NOSS .... National Ocean Survey System [*Cooperative program of governmental agencies*]
NOSS .... National Office Support System (NITA)
NOSS .... National Orbiting Space Station
NOSS .... Navy Ocean Surveillance System
NOSS .... Network Operating Software System [*Computer science*] (AGLO)
NOSS .... Network Operations Support Specialist (ACAE)
NOSS .... Nimbus Operational Satellite System [*GSFC/USWB*]
NOss .... Ossining Public Library, Ossining, NY [*Library symbol*] [*Library of Congress*] (LCLS)
NOSSA .... New Orleans Steamship Association (EA)
NOSSCR ...... National Organization of Social Security Claimants' Representatives (EA)
NOSSO .... Naval Ordnance Systems Support Office (MCD)
NOSSOLANT.. Naval Ordnance Systems Support Office, Atlantic
NOSSOPAC... Naval Ordnance Systems Support Office, Pacific
NOSSOREP... Naval Ordnance Systems Support Office Representative (DNAB)
NOST .... Knights of the Square Table (EA)
NOST .... Near-term Optical Sensor Technology (SAUS)
NOST .... Nuclear Operational Systems Test
NOSTA .... National Ocean Science and Technology Agency
NOSTA .... Naval Ophthalmic Support and Training Activity

No St C .... Northern State College (South Dakota) (GAGS)
NoStPw .... Northern States Power Co. [*Associated Press*] (SAG)
NOSTS .... National Ocean Survey Tide Station [*Marine science*] (MSC)
NOsU .... State University of New York, College at Oswego, Oswego, NY [*Library symbol*] [*Library of Congress*] (LCLS)
NOSUB........ Not Subject to load (SAUS)
NOSUM........ Notice to Airmen Summary (SAUS)
NOS/VE .... Network Operating System / Virtual Environment (HGAA)
NO Switch ... Normally Open Switch (SAUS)
NOT .... New Organization Training
NOT .... New Orleans Terminal [*AAR code*]
NOT .... Nocturnal Oxygen Therapy [*Medicine*] (DMAA)
NOT .... Nordic Optical Telescope
NOT .... Noront Resources Ltd. [*Vancouver Stock Exchange symbol*]
NOT .... Notary (WDAA)
NOT .... Notation (ROG)
NOT .... Noted
NOT .... Notice (ROG)
NOT .... Notion
NOT .... Not Oiltight (SAUS)
NOT .... Not Our Title [*Publishing*] (WDMC)
NOT .... Nucleus of the Optic Tract [*Eye anatomy*]
NOT .... Number of Turns (IAA)
NOTA .... National Organ Transplant Act [*1984*]
NOTA .... None of the Above [*Politics*]
NOTACGENSEA... Nontactical Generator, Southeast Asia
NOTACK....... No Attack Area [*Military*] (NVT)
NOTAD........ Notice to Airmen Address
NOTAEI .... National Old Timers' Association of the Energy Industry (EA)
NOTAL .... Not at All
NOTAL .... Not Sent to All Addresses (SAUS)
NOTAL .... Not to, nor Needed by, All
Notam .... Notices to Airmen (PIAV)
NOTAM .... Notice to Airmen
NOTAM .... Notice to Mariners (DOMA)
NOTAMS ...... Notice to Airmen and Sailors (SAUS)
NOTAP .... Navy Occupational Task Analysis Program (NVT)
NOTAR........ No-Tail Rotor [*Helicopters*]
NOTARC....... National Old Timers Auto Racing Club (EA)
NOTAS .... Notice to Airmen Summary
NOTB .... National Ophthalmic Treatment Board [*British*]
NOTBA .... National Ophthalmic Treatment Board Association [*British*]
NOTC .... Naval Ordnance Test Center (KSC)
Not Cas .... Notes of Cases at Madras (Strange) [*A publication*] (DLA)
Not Cas........ Notes of Cases, English Ecclesiastical and Maritime Courts [*1841-50*] [*A publication*] (DLA)
Not Cas Ecc & M... Notes of Cases, English Ecclesiastical and Maritime Courts [*1841-50*] [*A publication*] (DLA)
Not Cas Madras... Notes of Cases at Madras (Strange) [*A publication*] (DLA)
NOTCOMM... Not Commissioned [*Military*]
Notc on Fac... Notcutt on Factories and Workshops [*2nd ed.*] [*1879*] [*A publication*] (DLA)
Not Dec .... Notes of Decisions [*Martin's North Carolina Reports*] [*A publication*] (DLA)
Not Dig .... Boddam and Greenwood's Notanda Digest [*A publication*] (DLA)
Not Dign ...... Notitia Dignitatum [*Classical studies*] (OCD)
note .... Footnote in Cross-Reference (DLA)
NOTEF .... National Organ Transplant Education Foundation (EA)
NOTEMPS .... Nontemporary Storage of Household Goods System (SAUS)
NOTEMPS ... Nontemporary Storage System (MCD)
NOTES .... National Organization of Telecommunications Engineers and Scientists [*Washington, DC*] [*Telecommunications*] (TSSD)
Notes .... Notes (Music Library Association) [*A publication*] (BRI)
Notes Higher Ed... Notes on Higher Education [*A publication*]
Notes of Ca... Notes of Cases [*England*] [*A publication*] (DLA)
Notes of Cas... Notes of Cases, English Ecclesiastical and Maritime Courts [*1841-50*] [*A publication*] (DLA)
Notes of Cases... Notes of Cases, English Ecclesiastical and Maritime Courts [*1841-50*] [*A publication*] (DLA)
Notes on US... Notes on United States Reports [*A publication*] (DLA)
Notes Read... Notes and Queries for Readers and Writers, Collectors and Librarians (SAUS)
NotesRec R... Notes and Records. Royal Society of London (SAUS)
No Test........ Novum Testamentum (DSA)
NO-TFA....... National Old-Time Fiddlers' Association (EA)
notg .... nothing (SAUS)
NOTIF .... Notification
NO-TILL....... No Tillage (SAUS)
NOTIN......... Notification (ROG)
NOTIP .... Night Observation Television in a Pod
NOTIP .... Northern-Tier Integration Project [*Military*] (DNAB)
NOTIS .... Network Operations Trouble Information System [*Telecommunications*] (TEL)
NOTIS .... Northwestern Online Total Integrated System [*Northwestern University Library*] [*Library automation project*] [*Information service or system*] (IID)
Not J........... Notaries Journal [*A publication*] (DLA)
N-O-T-L....... Niagara-On-The-Lake [*Ontario*]
NOTL .... Notarial (ROG)
NOTM .... National Organization of Tutoring and Mentoring Centers (EA)
NOTM .... New Orleans, Texas & Mexico [*AAR code*]
NOTMAR..... Notice to Mariner (NVT)
NoTN .... Norges Tekniske Vitenskapsakademi [*Norwegian Academy for Technical Sciences*], Trondheim, Norway [*Library symbol*] [*Library of Congress*] (LCLS)

NOTN	Notion (ABBR)
NoTNG	Norges Geologiske Undersoeklse Biblioteket [*Geological Survey of Norway*], Trondheim, Norway [*Library symbol*] [*Library of Congress*] (LCLS)
NOTNO	Notional Number (NVT)
NOTO	Non-Official Trade Organisation [*British*]
NOTO	Numbering Tool (AAG)
NOTOF	Notice to Airmen Office
Not Op	Wilmot's Notes of Opinions and Judgments [*A publication*] (DLA)
NOTOPM	No-Touch Ocular Pulse Measurement (SAUS)
notox	non toxic (SAUS)
NOTOX	No Toxic Incinerator Group [*Political party*]
NOTOX	Not to Exceed (NOAA)
Not prat	Notice pour le praticien (SAUS)
Not Pub	Notary Public (EBF)
NOTR	National Order of Trench Rats (EA)
NOTR	No Traffic Rights [*Travel industry*] (TRID)
Notrad	No Traditions [*Internet*]
Notre Dame Est Plan Inst...	Notre Dame Estate Planning Institute. Proceedings [*A publication*] (DLA)
Notre Dame J Leg...	Notre Dame Journal of Legislation [*A publication*] (DLA)
NOTRTR	National Organization of Test, Research, and Training Reactors [*Later, TRTR*] (EA)
NOTS	Naval Ocean Transport Service [*Changed to MSTS in 1949 now MSC*] (DOMA)
NOTS	Naval Ordnance Test Station
NOTS	Naval Overseas Transport Service
NOTS	New Era Dianetics for OTs (SAUS)
NOTS	NOAA [*National Oceanic and Atmospheric Administration*] Operational Telecommunications System (NOAA)
NOTS	Nuclear Orbit Transfer Stage (PDAA)
NOT SAFE	National Organization Taunting Safety and Fairness Everywhere (EA)
NoTT	Nordic Theatre Technicians (SAUS)
Nott & Hop...	Nott and Hopkins' Reports [*United States Court of Claims*] [*A publication*] (DLA)
Nott & Hunt...	Nott and Huntington's Reports [*1-7 United States Court of Claims*] [*A publication*] (DLA)
Nott & McC...	Nott and McCord's South Carolina Reports [*A publication*] (DLA)
Nott & M'C (SC)...	Nott and M'Cord's South Carolina Reports [*A publication*] (DLA)
NOTTM	Nottingham [*County in England*]
Nott Mech L...	Non on the Mechanics Lien Law (SAUS)
Nott Mech L...	Nott on the Mechanics' Lien Law [*A publication*] (DLA)
Notts	Nottinghamshire [*County in England*] (ODBW)
NOTTS	Nottinghamshire [*County in England*]
NOTU	Naval Operational Training Unit
NOTU	Naval Ordnance Test Unit
NoTU	Universitetet i Trondheim [*University of Trondheim*], Trondheim, Norway [*Library symbol*] [*Library of Congress*] (LCLS)
NOTUN	Notice of Unreliability
NoTU-T	Universitetet i Trondheim, Norges Tekniske Hogskole [*University of Trondheim, Norwegian Institute of Technology*], Trondheim-NTH, Norway [*Library symbol*] [*Library of Congress*] (LCLS)
NoTU-V	Universitetet i Trondheim, Kongelige Norske Videnskabers Selskabs [*University of Trondheim, Royal Norwegian Society of Sciences and Letters*], Trondheim, N orway [*Library symbol*] [*Library of Congress*] (LCLS)
NOTWG	Notwithstanding
NOTWSTG	Notwithstanding
NOTWT	Do Not Transmit by Radio (NATG)
NOTY	Notary (ROG)
NOU	Naval Ordnance Unit
NOU	Noumea [*New Caledonia*] [*Airport symbol*] (OAG)
NOU	Nouvelles (NITA)
NOU	Sitka, AK [*Location identifier*] [*FAA*] (FAAL)
NOUE	Notification of Unusual Event (GOBB)
nough	enough (SAUS)
NOUR	Nourish (ABBR)
NOURD	Nourished (ABBR)
NOURG	Nourishing (ABBR)
NOURT	Nourishment (ABBR)
NOUS	Naval Order of the United States (EA)
Nouv Rev	Nouvelle Revue de Droit Francais [*Paris*] [*A publication*] (DLA)
NOV	Avianova SpA [*Italy*] [*ICAO designator*] (FAAC)
NOV	Huambo [*Angola*] [*Airport symbol*] (OAG)
NOV	Night Only Visual (ACAE)
NOV	Nodamura Virus
NOV	Non Obstante Veredicto [*Judgment Notwithstanding*] [*Latin*] [*Legal term*] (DLA)
NOV	Nonoccluded Virus
NOV	Notice of Violation [*Nuclear energy*] (NRCH)
NOV	NovaCare [*NYSE symbol*] (SPSG)
NOV	Nova Lisboa [*Angola*] [*Airport symbol*] (AD)
NOV	Novamin, Inc. [*Toronto Stock Exchange symbol*]
NOV	Novara [*Sicily*] [*Seismograph station code, US Geological Survey*] (SEIS)
NOV	Novation [*Legal term*] (DLA)
NOV	Novel (ROG)
NOV	Novelist (ABBR)
Nov	Novellae [*Classical studies*] (OCD)
NOV	Novello & Co. [*Publisher*]
NOV	November (AAG)
Nov	November (ODBW)
nov	Novembre [*November*] [*French*] (ASC)
NOV	Novitiate (ROG)
nov	Novum [*New*] [*Latin*] (MAE)
NOVA	National Organization for Victim Assistance (EA)
NOVA	National Outdoor Volleyball Association [*Defunct*] (EA)
NOVA	National Overhead Evaluation Assessment [*Term for the restructuring process begun at E. F. Hutton after the October 1987 stock market collapse*]
NOVA	Network Organization via Advanced Architecture [*Marubeni Corp.*]
NOVA	Northern Ohio Valley Area (SAUS)
NOVA	Northern Valley Private Industry Council [*Sunnyvale, CA*] (ECON)
Nova	Nova Corp. [*Associated Press*] (SAG)
NOVA	Nova Med Eyecare [*NASDAQ symbol*]
NOVA	Nova Natural Resources Corp. (SAUS)
NOVA	Nova Omega Ventura Apollo [*General Motors automobiles*]
NOVA	Nurses Organization of Veterans Affairs (EA)
NOVA	Nutritional Oncology Vascular Access
NovaCre	NovaCare [*Associated Press*] (SAG)
Novadig	Novadigm, Inc. [*Associated Press*] (SAG)
NOVAM	Navy Oceanographic Vertical Aerosol Model (SAUS)
Novatk	Novatek International, Inc. [*Associated Press*] (SAG)
NOVATOR	Novye Torit [*Newly Flattened*] [*KGB term for newly recruited agent abroad*]
Nova U	Nova University (GAGS)
Novavx	Novavax, Inc. [*Associated Press*] (SAG)
NOVC	Novice (ABBR)
NOVCAM	Nonvolatile Charge-Addressed Memory [*Computer science*] (PDAA)
NOV/CD	Notice of Violation / Compliance Demand (EPA)
Nov Com Fragm...	Novae Comoediae Fragmenta in Papyris Reperta Exceptis Menandreis [*A publication*] (OCD)
Novdec	November and December (SAUS)
NOVE	NOMOS Verlagskatalog [*NOMOS Datapool*] [*Information service or system*] (IID)
NOVEL	Narrative Output Vocabulary Editing Language [*Psychiatric test*]
NOVEL	New York Online Virtual Electronic Library
Novell	Novell, Inc. [*Associated Press*] (SAG)
Noven	Noven Pharmaceuticals, Inc. [*Associated Press*] (SAG)
NOVI	Novitron International, Inc. [*NASDAQ symbol*] (SAG)
NOVICE	Night Operational Vision and the Individual Combat Engineer (MCD)
Novitrn	Novitron International, Inc. [*Associated Press*] (SAG)
NOVL	Novell, Inc. [*NASDAQ symbol*] (NQ)
NOVLT	Novelty
Novlus	Novellus Systems, Inc. [*Associated Press*] (SAG)
NOVM	No Obvious Value Mail [*Postal service*]
Novmtx	Novametrics Medical Systems [*Associated Press*] (SAG)
Novmtx	Novametrix Medical Systems, Inc. [*Associated Press*] (SAG)
NOVN	Noven Pharmaceuticals [*NASDAQ symbol*] (TTSB)
NOVN	Noven Pharmaceuticals, Inc. [*NASDAQ symbol*] (NQ)
NOV N	Novum Nomen [*New Name*] [*Latin*] (BABM)
nov n	Novum Nomen [*New Name*] [*Latin*] (DAVI)
NovoNdk	Novo Nordisk AS [*Associated Press*] (SAG)
Novoste	Novoste Corp. [*Associated Press*] (SAG)
NOVP	Novantrone, Oncovin, Vinblastine, Prednisone [*Antineoplastic drug*] (CDI)
NOVR	Novar Electronics Corp. (SAUS)
NOVRAM	Non-Volatile Random Access Memory [*Computer science*]
NOVRAM	Nonvolotile Static RAM (NITA)
NOVS	National Office of Vital Statistics [*Public Health Service*] [*Obsolete*]
Nov Sc Dec...	Nova Scotia Decisions [*A publication*] (DLA)
Nov Sc LR...	Nova Scotia Law Reports [*A publication*] (DLA)
NOV SP	Novum Species [*New Species*] [*Latin*] (BABM)
nov sp	Novum Species [*New species*] [*Latin*] (DAVI)
NOVST	Novelist (ABBR)
NOVT	Novelty (ABBR)
NOVT	Novoste Corp [*NASDAQ symbol*] (TTSB)
NOVX	Nova Pharmaceutical Corp. (SAUS)
NOW	MAI Systems [*AMEX symbol*] (TTSB)
NOW	MAI Systems Corp. [*AMEX symbol*] (SAG)
NOW	National Organization for Women (EA)
NOW	National Organizations of the World [*A publication*]
NOW	National Overhaul Warranty [*Automotive engineering*]
NOW	Negotiable Order of Withdrawal [*Banking*]
NOW	Neighbors of Woodcraft [*Portland, OR*] (EA)
NOW	Network of Workstations (RALS)
NOW	Network Order Wire [*Military*] (CAAL)
NOW	New Opportunities for Women (SAUS)
NOW	News of the World [*A publication*] (DGA)
NOW	Nonhazardous Oil Field Waste [*Environmental Protection Agency*] (FFDE)
NOW	North Water (SAUS)
NOW	Northway Explorations Ltd. [*Toronto Stock Exchange symbol*]
NOW	Nurture-Outreach-Witness [*Religion*]
NOW	Nutrition on the Web [*Internet site for teens*]
NOW	Port Angeles, WA [*Location identifier*] [*FAA*] (FAAL)
NOW	Royal Norwegian Air Force [*ICAO designator*] (FAAC)
NOW account...	Negotiable Order of Withdrawal Account (EBF)
NOWAI	Neshei Ubenos Agudath Israel [*Antwerp*] (BJA)
NOWAPA	North American Water and Power Alliance (NADA)
NOWD	Northward (ABBR)
NOWESP	North-West European Shelf Programme (SAUS)
No West Rep...	Northwestern Reporter [*Commonly cited NW*] [*A publication*] (DLA)
NOweWJ	Wheatley Junior-Senior High School, Old Westbury, NY [*Library symbol*] [*Library of Congress*] (LCLS)
NOwHC-U	Old Westbury School of the Holy Child, Upper School, Old Westbury, NY [*Library symbol*] [*Library of Congress*] (LCLS)
NOWIS	National Older Workers Information System [*American Association of Retired Persons*] [*Information service or system*] [*Defunct*] (IID)
NOWL	National Order of Women Legislators (EA)

NOW LDEF... NOW [*National Organization for Women*] Legal Defense and Education Fund (EA)
NOWL/NFWL... National Order of Women Legislators/National Foundation for Women Legislators (NTPA)
NOWME....... National Organisation for Women's Management Education [*British*] (DI)
No W Mo St U... Nortwest Missouri State University (GAGS)
NOwNC........ New York College of Osteopathic Medicine, Old Westbury, NY [*Library symbol*] [*Library of Congress*] (LCLS)
NOwNI......... New York Institute of Technology, Old Westbury, NY [*Library symbol*] [*Library of Congress*] (LCLS)
NOwNI-C...... New York Institute of Technology, Commack Center Library, Commack, NY [*Library symbol*] [*Library of Congress*] (LCLS)
NOwNI-CI.... New York Institute of Technical, Central Islip, NY [*Library symbol*] [*Library of Congress*] (LCLS)
NOwNI-N...... New York Institute of Technology, New York, NY [*Library symbol*] [*Library of Congress*] (LCLS)
No W Okla St U... Northwestern Oklahoma State University (GAGS)
NOWPA....... National Osteopathic Women Physician's Association (EA)
NOWPAP..... North-West Pacific Action Plan (SAUS)
NOWP-OM ... National Older Workers Programs - Operation Mainstream [*Department of Labor*]
NOWR.......... Nuclear Ordnance War Reserve [*Military*] (AFIT)
NOWRA........ National Onsite Waste Water Recycling Association (AEPA)
NOWS.......... NVG Operations Weather Software (SAUS)
NOWSA........ National One-Write Systems Association (EA)
Nowsc......... Nowsco Well Services Ltd. [*Associated Press*] (SAG)
No W St U La... Northwestern State University of Louisiana (GAGS)
NOWT......... North-West Telecommunications, Inc. (SAUS)
NOwU .... State University of New York, College at Old Westbury, Oyster Bay, NY [*Library symbol*] [*Library of Congress*] (LCLS)
NOWUS........ Normal Operation with Unscram [*Nuclear energy*] (NRCH)
NOwWJ........ Wheatley Junior-Senior High School, Old Westbury, NY [*Library symbol*] [*Library of Congress*] (LCLS)
NOWWN ...... National Organization of World War Nurses (EA)
NOX .... Air Nordic in Vasteras AB [*Sweden*] [*ICAO designator*] (FAAC)
NOx............. generic oxides of nitrogen (SAUS)
NOX............. Nitrogen Oxide (COE)
NOX............. Nitrogen-Oxygen (SAUS)
NOX............. Nitrous Oxide [*Laughing gas*]
NOX............. Novavax, Inc. [*AMEX symbol*] (SAG)
NOX............. Noxious (ABBR)
NOx............. Oxford Memorial Library, Oxford, NY [*Library symbol*] [*Library of Congress*] (LCLS)
NOx............. Oxide of Nitrogen (SAUS)
NOX............. Stickstoffoxide (SAUS)
NOXA........... Naphth-2yl-Oxyacetic Acid (LDT)
NOXA........... Naphthoxyacetic Acid [*Organic chemistry*]
NOXL........... Noxell Corp. (SAUS)
NOXO........... Noxso Corp. [*NASDAQ symbol*] (NQ)
Noxso........... Noxso Corp. [*Associated Press*] (SAG)
NOXY.......... Noxiously (ABBR)
NOXZEMA.... Knocks Eczema [*Acronym, brand name for skin cream, said to be taken from this phrase*]
NOY .... Not Online Yet (BEE)
NOY .... Not Out Yet
Noy............. Noy's English King's Bench Reports [*1559-1649*] [*A publication*] (DLA)
NOy............. Oyster Bay-East Norwich Public Library, Oyster Bay, NY [*Library symbol*] [*Library of Congress*] (LCLS)
NOy............. total active Nitrogen (SAUS)
Noy Ch U..... Noyes on Charitable Uses [*A publication*] (DLA)
Noye........... Grounds and Maxims of English Law, by William Noye (journ.) (SAUS)
Noy (Eng) .... Noy's English King's Bench Reports [*1559-1649*] [*A publication*] (DLA)
Noye's Max... Maxims of the Laws of England, by William Noye [*A publication*] (DLA)
NOyHS......... Oyster Bay High School, Oyster Bay, NY [*Library symbol*] [*Library of Congress*] (LCLS)
Noy Max...... Noy's Maxims [*A publication*] (DLA)
NOyRE .... Theodore Roosevelt Elementary School, Oyster Bay, NY [*Library symbol*] [*Library of Congress*] (LCLS)
NOYS.......... National Organization for Youth Safety [*NHTSA*] (TAG)
NOyStD........ Saint Dominic High School, Oyster Bay, NY [*Library symbol*] [*Library of Congress*] (LCLS)
NOZ .... Elizabeth City, NC [*Location identifier*] [*FAA*] (FAAL)
NOZ .... New Process Co. (SAUS)
NOZ .... No Operating Zone (DA)
NOZ .... Normal Operating Zone (SAUS)
NOZ .... Nozzle (AAG)
NOZE .... US National Ozone Expedition [*1986*] [*McMurdo Station, Antarctica*]
NOZE-1 ...... National Ozone Expedition (SAUS)
NP.............. Adriance Memorial Library, Poughkeepsie, NY [*Library symbol*] [*Library of Congress*] (LCLS)
NP.............. Desert Pacific [*ICAO designator*] (AD)
np--- .... Great Plains [*MARC geographic area code*] [*Library of Congress*] (LCCP)
NP.............. Heavylift Cargo Airlines (SAUS)
NP.............. Nacionalista Party [*Philippines*]
NP.............. Nairobi Protocol (JAGO)
NP.............. Name of Publisher (NITA)
NP.............. Nameplate
NP.............. NAPALM [*Naphthenic and Palmitic Acids*] (NATG)
NP.............. [*The*] Narragansett Pier Railroad Co. Inc. (IIA)

NP.............. Nasal Prongs [*For administration of oxygen*] (DAVI)
NP.............. Nasionale Party van Suid-Afrika [*National Party of South Africa*] [*Political party*] (PPW)
NP.............. Nasionale Party van Suidwesafrika [*National Party of South West Africa*] [*Namibia*] [*Political party*] (PPW)
NP.............. Nasopharyngeal [*or Nasopharynx*] [*Medicine*]
NP.............. Nationalist Parnellite [*British*] (ROG)
NP.............. Nationalist Party [*Malta*] [*Political party*] (PPE)
NP.............. Nationalist Party [*Philippines*] [*Political party*] (PPW)
NP.............. National Parks [*A publication*] (BRI)
NP.............. National Party [*Papua New Guinea*] [*Political party*] (PPW)
NP.............. National Pipe [*Thread*]
NP.............. National Police (CINC)
NP.............. National Porkettes (EA)
NP.............. National Power PLC [*NYSE symbol*] (SAG)
NP.............. National Primary (OTD)
NP.............. National Publishing Co. [*Philadelphia*]
NP.............. Nation Party [*Turkey*] [*Political party*] (PPW)
NP.............. Natural Passivation [*Metallurgy*]
NP.............. Naval Party [*British military*] (DMA)
NP.............. Naval Patrol [*British military*] (DMA)
NP.............. Naval Pattern [*British military*] (DMA)
NP.............. Naval Pension [*British*] (ROG)
NP.............. Naval Police [*British*] (ROG)
NP.............. Naval Prison
NP.............. Naval Publication (IEEE)
NP.............. Navy Publications & printing service (SAUS)
NP.............. Neap Tide
NP.............. Near Point
NP.............. Needle Position [*on dial*]
NP.............. Negative Prescreening [*Marketing*]
NP.............. Negative Pressure (NRCH)
NP.............. Neo-Punic (BJA)
NP.............. Nepal [*ANSI two-letter standard code*] (CNC)
np .... Nepal [*MARC country of publication code*] [*Library of Congress*] (LCCP)
Np .... Neper [*A unit on a natural logarithmic scale*]
NP.............. Neptunium (NAKS)
Np .... Neptunium [*Chemical element*]
NP.............. Net Position [*Business term*]
NP.............. Net Price [*Business term*] (MHDW)
NP.............. Net Proceeds
NP.............. Net Profit
NP.............. Network Planning [*Computer science*]
NP.............. Network Program (NASA)
NP.............. Network Project [*An association*] (EA)
NP.............. Neuritic Plaque [*Pathology*]
NP.............. Neuropathology [*Medicine*]
NP.............. Neuropeptide (SAUS)
NP.............. Neurophysin [*Biochemistry*]
NP.............. Neurophysiological
NP.............. Neuropsychiatric
N/P............. Neuro-Psychiatry [*Medical Officer designation*] [*British*]
NP.............. Neutrino Patents (SAUS)
NP.............. Neutron Porosity (CARB)
NP.............. Newly Presented (DMAA)
NP.............. New Page (SAUS)
np .... New Paragraph (WDMC)
NP.............. New Paragraph
NP.............. New Party (EA)
NP.............. New Patient
NP.............. New Pattern [*British military*] (DMA)
np .... New Pence [*Monetary unit in Great Britain since 1971*]
NP.............. New Permutations
NP.............. New Perspectives (SAUS)
NP.............. New Point [*Used in correcting manuscripts, etc.*]
NP.............. New Police (SAUS)
NP.............. Newport [*Rhode Island*]
NP.............. New Position
NP.............. New Providence
N/P............. Newspaper
NP.............. Next Page (SAUS)
NP.............. Next Position (SAUS)
NP.............. Nickel Plated [*Guns*]
NP.............. Niemann-Pick [*Disease*] [*Medicine*] (DB)
NP.............. Nifurpipone
NP.............. Nippon Investment Corp. [*Vancouver Stock Exchange symbol*]
NP.............. Nisi Prius [*Unless Before*] [*Legal term*] [*Latin*]
NP.............. Nitrogen-Phosphorus [*Chemistry*] (MAE)
NP.............. Nitrophenide [*Pharmacology*]
NP.............. Nitrophenoacetylamino Caproate
np .... nitroproof (SAUS)
NP.............. Nitropropane [*Organic chemistry*]
NP.............. Nitro Proved [*Rifle mark*] (DICI)
NP.............. Nitroprusside [*A vasodilator*]
NP.............. Nitropyrene [*Organic chemistry*]
NP.............. Nitrosopiperidine [*Organic chemistry*]
NP.............. Nobel Prize
NP.............. Nodal Point (SAUS)
NP.............. Noise Parameter (SAUS)
NP.............. Noise Power (SAUS)
NP.............. Nomen Proprium [*Proper Name*] [*Latin*]
NP.............. Nominal Horsepower (IAA)
NP.............. Nominal Phrase (SAUS)
NP.............. Nominal Pressure (SAUS)

NP	Non-deterministic-Polynomial (SAUS)
NP	Nondeterministic Polynomial [Mathematics]
NP	Nonpapillate [Type of seed] [Botany]
NP	Nonparental (SAUS)
NP	Nonparticipating [Insurance or finance]
N-P	Non-Partisan (SAUS)
NP	Non-Patents (NITA)
N/P	Nonpayment (ROG)
NP	Nonpermanent (SAUS)
NP	Nonperson
NP	Non-Plastic (SAUS)
NP	Nonpolarized [Computer science]
NP	Nonpolice (BARN)
NP	Nonpractising Member [Chiropody] [British]
NP	Nonprint [Computer science] (IAA)
NP	Nonprinting (SAUS)
NP	Nonprocurable
NP	Nonproducer (SAUS)
NP	Nonprofit (BARN)
NP	Nonpropelled (AAG)
NP	Nonpurgeable (SAUS)
NP	Nonylphenol [Organic chemistry]
NP	No Pagination (SAUS)
NP	No Paging
NP	No Parity
NP	No Parking (SAUS)
NP	No Party with the Name of the Recipient of the Message [International telex abbreviation] (WDMC)
NP	No Payment (SAUS)
NP	No Pin [Electronics] (OA)
np	No Place (WDMC)
NP	No Place [of publication] [Bibliography]
np	No Place of Publication (WDAA)
NP	No Predators [Ecology]
NP	No Print [Telecommunications] (TEL)
NP	No Printer Listed (NTCM)
NP	No Problem (SAUS)
NP	No Prospect [In sports]
NP	No Protest [Banking]
NP	No Publisher Listed (NTCM)
NP	Normal Phase [Chromatography]
NP	Normal Pitch (ADA)
NP	Normal Plasma [Medicine] (MAE)
NP	Normal Pregnancy [Medicine]
NP	Normal Pressure
NP	Normal Profit [Business term] (MHDW)
NP	Northern Pacific (SAUS)
NP	Northern Pacific Railway Co. (MHDW)
NP	Northern Pine [Utility pole] [Telecommunications] (TEL)
NP	North Park (SAUS)
NP	North Pole [Also, PN]
NP	Norwegian Patent (SAUS)
NP	Norwegian Polar Institute (SAUS)
NP	Nose Plug (SAUS)
Np	Notary Public (WDAA)
np	Notary Public (WDAA)
NP	Notary Public
NP	Note Payable (SAUS)
N/P	Notes Payable [Finance] (DFIT)
NP	Not Paginated (SAUS)
NP	Not Palpable (SAUS)
NP	Not Perceptible [Medicine]
NP	Not Performed
NP	Not Planned
NP	Not Practiced [Medicine]
NP	Not Preferred
NP	Not Present (DAVI)
NP	Not Pressed or Glazed [Paper] (DGA)
NP	Not Printed (ILCA)
NP	Not Provably (SAUS)
N/P	Not Provided (KSC)
NP	Not Published (SAUS)
NP	Noun Phrase [Linguistics]
NP	Nuclear Pile (SAUS)
NP	Nuclear Polarization (SAUS)
NP	Nuclear Power (GOBB)
NP	Nuclear Preparation (SAUS)
NP	Nuclear Propulsion (SAUS)
NP	Nucleophasmic (SAUS)
NP	Nucleoplasmic [Index] [Cytology]
NP	Nucleoprotein [Biochemistry]
NP	Nucleoside Phosphorylase [An enzyme]
np	Nucleotide Pair [Genetics] (DOG)
NP	Nucleotide Phosphorylase (DB)
NP	Nucleus Pulposus [Medicine] (DAVI)
NP	Null Parameter (SAUS)
NP	Number of Pitches [Baseball term] (NDBD)
NP	Number of Primary Turns (IAA)
N_p	Number of Primary Turns (IDOE)
NP	Number of Steps, Polynomial Time [Mathematics]
NP	Nursed Poorly [Medicine] (DMAA)
NP	Nurse Practitioner
NP	Nurse Prescriber (NUJO)
NP	Nursing Procedure
NP	Nurturing Parent [Psychology] (DHP)
NP	Ohio Nisi Prius Reports [A publication] (DLA)
NP.PP	Natl Power PLC Interim ADS [NYSE symbol] (TTSB)
NP0	Negative-Positive-Zero
NPA	Committee for a National Peace Academy [Later, N-PAC] (EA)
NPA	Napan [West Irian, Indonesia] [Airport symbol] (AD)
NPA	Naphthylphthalamic Acid [Organic chemistry]
NPA	Naptalam (EDCT)
NPA	National Paddleball Association (EA)
NPA	National Panel of Arbitrators
NPA	National Paperboard Association [Later, API]
NPA	National Paralegal Association (EA)
NPA	National Parenthood Association (NADA)
NPA	National Parents Association
NPA	National Parking Association (EA)
NPA	National Parks Act (SAUS)
NPA	National Parks and Access to the Countryside Act [Town planning] [British]
NPA	National Parks Association [Later, NPCA] (EA)
NPA	National Particleboard Association (EA)
NPA	National Pasta Association (EA)
NPA	National Patrolmen's Association
NPA	National Pawnbrokers Association (EA)
NPA	National Payphone Association (EA)
NPA	National Peace Academy
NPA	National Pediculosis Association (EA)
NPA	National People's Action (EA)
NPA	National Perinatal Association (EA)
NPA	National Peripheral Association (EA)
NPA	National Personnel Associates
NPA	National Pet Association [Defunct] (EA)
NPA	National Petroleum Association [Later, NPRA]
NPA	National Pharmaceutical Alliance (NTPA)
NPA	National Pharmaceutical Association [Washington, DC]
NPA	National Phlebotomy Association (EA)
NPA	National Pigeon Association [Defunct] (EA)
NPA	National Pilots Association [Defunct] (EA)
NPA	National Pistol Association [British] (DI)
NPA	National Pituitary Agency [Later, NHPP]
NPA	National Planning Association (EA)
NPA	National Plastercraft Association (EA)
NPA	National Platelet Association (NRGU)
NPA	National Playbus Association [British] (DBA)
NPA	National Podiatry Association [Later, NPMA] (EA)
NPA	National Poker Association (EA)
NPA	National Portage Association [British] (DBA)
NPA	National Ports Authority [British]
NPA	National Postmasters Auxiliary (EA)
NPA	National Poultry Association [Australia]
NPA	National Prescription Audit
NPA	National Preservers Association [Later, International Jelly and Preserve Association] (EA)
NPA	National Priority Area [Military]
NPA	National Proctologic Association (EA)
NPA	National Production Authority [Functions merged into BDSA, 1953]
NPA	National Productivity Authority (MHDB)
NPA	National Prohibition Act
NPA	National Psychological Association [Defunct] (EA)
NPA	Naval Procurement Account
NPA	Navy Postal Affairs Section Publication
NPA	Navy Purchasing Activity (AFIT)
NPA	Near Point Accommodation [Ophthalmology]
NPA	Neighborhood Publication Area Report [Bureau of the Census] (GFGA)
NPA	Network Performance Analyzer [Computer science] (ITCA)
NPA	Network Professional Association (SAUS)
NPA	Network Program Analysis by ADI [Area of Dominant Influence] [Arbitron Ratings Co.] [Information service or system] (CRD)
NPA	Neutrons per Absorption (DEN)
NPA	New People's Army [Philippines] (PD)
NPA	New Populist Action [Defunct] (EA)
NPA	New Product Announcements [Predicasts, Inc.] [Cleveland, OH] [Information service or system] (IID)
NPA	Newsletter Publishers Association (NTPA)
NPA	Newspaper Publishers' Association [British] (DCTA)
NPA	Nigel Press Association Ltd. (SAUS)
NPA	Nigerian Ports Authority (SAUS)
NPA	Nine Pin Association [Schauenburg, Federal Republic of Germany] (EAIO)
NPA	Nonbuffered Pyrophosphatase Activity
NPA	Non-Parallel Application (SAUS)
NPA	Non-Par Approved
NPA	Non-Principal Axis
NPA	No Power Alarm (SAUS)
NPA	No Previous Admission [Medicine] (MEDA)
NPA	No Price Available [Business term] (ADA)
NPA	Normal Pressure Angle
NPA	Northern Pipeline Agency [Ottawa, ON]
NPA	North Pacific Airlines (SAUS)
NPA	North Plains Area (SARE)
NPA	Notice of Proposed Amendment (DA)
NPA	Novel Plasminogen Activator [Anticlotting agent]
NPA	N-Propylamine [Organic chemistry]
NPA.PP	Nuclear Plant Analyzer (NRCH)
NPA	Numbering Plan Area [Bell System] [Telecommunications]
NPA	Number Plan Area (SAUS)

NPA	Numerical Production Analysis (IEEE)
NPA	Nurse Practice Act (SAUS)
NPA	Pensacola, FL [Location identifier] [FAA] (FAAL)
NPA	PTS [Predicasts, Inc.] New Product Announcements/Plus [Information service or system] (IID)
NPAA	National Park Academy of the Arts (EA)
NPAA	National Photographic Art Archive [Victoria and Albert Museum] [British]
NPAA	National Postal Arts Association (EA)
NPAA	Noise Pollution and Abatement Act (GFGA)
NPAACT	National Parks Association of the Australian Capital Territory
NPAB	Navy Price Adjustment Board
NPAB	Nuclear Power Advisory Board (PDAA)
NPABC	National Public Affairs Center for Television (NADA)
NPAC	National Parks Advisory Council [Australia]
N-PAC	National Peace Academy Campaign [Formerly, NPA] (EA)
NPAC	National Peace Action Coalition
NPAC	National Plantation Advisory Committee
NPAC	National Political Action Committee (EA)
NPAC	National Program for Acquisitions and Cataloging [Library of Congress]
NPAC	National Project in Agricutural Communication (PDAA)
NPAC	Navy Procurement Assignment Committee
NPAC	Nonconducted Premature Atrial Contractions [Medicine] (MELL)
NPAC	Northeast Parallel Architectures Center [Syracuse University] [Research center] (RCD)
NPAC	Northern Pipeline Agency Canada [See also APNC]
NPACC	Nominated Primary Alternate Command Centre (SAUS)
N Pac Cur	North Pacific Current (SAUS)
NPACE	Nurse Practitioner Association for Continuing Education (SAUS)
NPACI	National Partnership for Advanced Computational Infrastructure [Supercomputing Center]
NPACI	National Production Advisory Council on Industry [British]
NPACOE	National Panhellenic Association of Central Office Executives (EA)
NPACSE	National Political Action Committee for Scientists and Engineers
NPACT	National Public Affairs Center for Television [Defunct]
NPAED	National Progress Association for Economic Development (EA)
NPAF	National Peace Academy Foundation (EA)
NPAF	National Picture & Frame Co. [NASDAQ symbol] (SAG)
NPAF	National Pledge of Allegiance Foundation (EA)
NPAFC	North Pacific Anadromous Fish Commission (SAUS)
NPA(G)R	National Parks and Access to the Countryside (Grants) Regulations [Town planning] [British]
NPAH	Nitrated Polycyclic Aromatic Hydrocarbons [Automotive emissions] [Organic chemistry]
NPAI	Network Protocol Addressing Information [Telecommunications] (OSI)
NPAI	Nevada Public Affairs Institute [University of Nevada - Reno] [Research center] (RCD)
NPals	Palisades Free Library, Palisades, NY [Library symbol] [Library of Congress] (LCLS)
NPAM	Navy Priorities and Allocations Manual (DNAB)
NPAM	Nonpermanent Active Militia
NPAN	National Plan for Australian Newspapers
NPAN	Newspapers Proprietors Association of Nigeria (SAUS)
NP & GT Rep	Nisi Prius and General Term Reports [Ohio] [A publication] (DLA)
NP & OSR	Naval Petroleum and Oil Shale Reserve
NP & PA	National Paperbox and Packaging Association (EA)
NPANX	Naval Potomac Annex
NPAP	National Psychological Association for Psychoanalysis (EA)
NPAP	Navy Public Affairs Plan (DNAB)
NPAP	Niue People's Action Party [Political party] (EY)
NPAR	Negative-Positive Acknowledgment and Retransmission [Telecommunications] (IAA)
NPAR	Nonstandard Part Approval Request (MCD)
NPAR	Nuclear Plant Aging Research Program (COE)
NP/ARCA	National Pacific/Asian Resource Center on Aging (EA)
NPAS	National Policy Assistance Standards (AAGC)
NPAS	National Public Awareness Strategy (SAUS)
NPAS	New Products Analysis System (SAUS)
NPAS	Normalized Photoacoustic Signal [Instrumentation]
NPASO	National Postsecondary Agriculture Student Organization (EA)
NPAT	National Political Awareness Test [Sent to all candidates in presidential, congressional, gubernatorial, and most state legislative races]
NPat	Patchogue Library, Patchogue, NY [Library symbol] [Library of Congress] (LCLS)
NPatB	Brookhaven Town Hall, Historical Collection, Patchogue, NY [Library symbol] [Library of Congress] (LCLS)
NPatBH	Brookhaven Memorial Hospital, Patchogue, NY [Library symbol] [Library of Congress] (LCLS)
NPatSJ	Saint Joseph's College, Patchogue, NY [Library symbol] [Library of Congress] (LCLS)
NPAV	National Parks Association of Victoria [Australia]
NPAWT	National Plan of Action for Women in TAFE [Technical and Further Education] [Australia]
NPB	NADGE [NATO Air Defense Ground Environment] Policy Board (NATG)
NPB	National Park Board (NADA)
NPB	National Parole Board [Canada]
NPB	National Planning Board [Terminated, 1944; superseded by National Resources Board]
NPB	National Plant Board (EA)
NPB	National Plumbing Bureau (NTPA)
NPB	National Prayer Breakfast (EA)
NPB	National Productivity Board (NADA)

NPB	Neutral Particle Beam (MCD)
NPB	Neutron Particle Beam (SAUS)
NPB	Newspaper Bag (ROG)
NPB	Nodal Premature Beat [Cardiology]
NPB	Nonplasminogen Binding [Hematology]
NPB	Nonprimate Biosatellite
NPB	Non-Protein Bound [Medicine] (DMAA)
NPB	Norfolk & Portsmouth Belt Line Railroad Co. [AAR code]
NPB	North Pacific Bank (SAUS)
NPB	Nuclear Powered Bomber (SAUS)
NPBA	National Palomino Breeders Association [Inactive]
NPBA	National Paper Box Association [Formerly, NPBMA; later NP & PA] (EA)
NPBA	National Perinatal Bereavement Association [Defunct] (EA)
NPBA	National Pig Breeders' Association [British] (BI)
NPBA	National Pocket Billiards Association (EA)
NPBA	National Police Bloodhound Association (EA)
NPBA	National Poro Beautician Association [Defunct] (EA)
NPBA	Natural Product Broker Association [St. Augustine, FL] (EA)
NPBC	National Penn Bancshares, Inc. [NASDAQ symbol] (NQ)
NPBC	National Progressive Broadcast Coalition [Defunct] (EA)
NPBC	Natl Penn Bancshares [NASDAQ symbol] (TTSB)
NPBC	Newer Predominantly Black College (SAUS)
NPBE	National Political Button Exchange [An association] [Defunct] (EA)
NPBE	Nitrophenyl Butyl Ether [Organic chemistry]
NPBE	Nonlinear Poisson-Boltzmann Equation [Physical chemistry]
NPBEA	National Poultry, Butter, and Egg Association [Defunct] (EA)
NPBFC	National Pat Boone Fan Club (EA)
NPBI	National Pretzel Bakers Institute [Defunct] (EA)
NPBIE	Nuetral Particle Beam Integration Experiment (SAUS)
NPBMA	National Paper Box Manufacturers Association (EA)
NPBOA	National Party Boat Owners Alliance (EA)
NPBRO	Naval Plant Branch Representative Office
NPBS	Navy Personnel Billeting System (DNAB)
NPBSA	National Paper Box Supplies Association [Defunct] (EA)
NPBSV	Neutral Particle Beam Space Vehicle (SAUS)
NPBW	Neutral Particle Beam Weapon [Military] (MUSM)
NPC	Nasal Point of Conversion [Medicine] (MELL)
NPC	NASA Procurement Circular
NPC	NASA Publication Control (KSC)
NPC	Nasopancreatic Catheter [Medicine] (MELL)
NPC	Nasopharyngeal Carcinoma [Medicine]
NPC	National Packaging Confederation [British] (DBA)
NPC	National Panhellenic Conference (EA)
NPC	National Patent Council (EA)
NPC	National Peace Council [British]
NPC	National Peach Council (EA)
NPC	National Peanut Council (EA)
NPC	National People's Congress [China] [Political party] (PPW)
NPC	National People's Congress [Nigeria] [Political party]
NPC	National Periodicals Center
NPC	National Personnel Consultants [Later, NAPC] [Defunct] (EA)
NPC	National Petroleum Council [Department of Energy] (EA)
NPC	National Pharmaceutical Council (EA)
NPC	National Philatelic Center [Australia]
NPC	National Philatelic Collections [Smithsonian Institution]
NPC	Neutral Pizza Co. (EFIS)
NPC	National Playwrights Conference (EA)
NPC	National Plumbing Code
NPC	National Poetry Circle [Cambridge] [British]
NPC	National Ports Council [British]
NPC	National Potato Council (EA)
NPC	National Press Club (EA)
NPC	National Prime Contractor (NATG)
NPC	National Processing Centre [Marine science] (MSC)
NPC	National Productivity Council [Inactive]
NPC	National Publicity Council for Health and Welfare Services [Later, NPRC]
NPC	Native Preacher Co. [An association] (EA)
NPC	NATO Parliamentarians' Conference
NPC	NATO Pipeline Committee
NPC	NATO Programming Center (NATG)
NPC	Nauru Phosphate Commission [Australia]
NPC	Naval Personnel Committee [British military] (DMA)
NPC	Naval Photographic Center
NPC	Navy Policy Council
NPC	Navy Procurement Circular
NPC	Near Point of Convergence [Ophthalmology]
NPC	Needle Punch Card
NPC	Neplanocin A [Biochemistry]
NPC	Network Parameter Control (SAUS)
NPC	Neuropsychiatry Clerical Procedure [Navy]
NPC	Neuropsychiatry Clerical Technician [Navy]
NPC	New Peoples Center (SAUS)
NPC	New Practice Cases [Legal] [British]
NPC	New Practice Cases. Bail Court [1844-48] [A publication] (DLA)
npc	New Process Companys trademark (SAUS)
NPC	News and Periodicals Corp. (SAUS)
NPC	Niagara Parks Commission (SAUS)
NP-C	Niemann-Pick Type C [Disease] [Medicine]
NPC	Nigerian Population Commission (SAUS)
NPC	Ninety Pound Charge
NPC	Nippon PetroChemicals (SAUS)
NPC	Nisi Prius Cases [England] [A publication] (DLA)
NPC	Nitrogen Purge Control

NPC	Nodal Premature Contraction [*Cardiology*] (MAE)
NPC	Nominal Protection Coefficient [*Business term*]
NPC	Nonparenchymal Cell (DB)
NPC	Non Participating Countries (SAUS)
NPC	Nonphased Color [*Television signals*] (NTCM)
NPC	Non Player Character (SAUS)
NPC	Nonplayer Characters [*Computer science*]
NPC	Nonprinting Character [*Computer science*]
NPC	Nonproductive Cough [*Medicine*] (DAVI)
NPC	No Previous Carrier [*Insurance*]
NPC	No Previous Complaint [*Medicine*] (DAVI)
NPC	Normal Phase Chromatography
NPC	Normal Plane Change Maneuver (SAUS)
NPC	Northern Pacific Conference (PSS)
NPC	Northern Peoples Congress (SAUS)
NPC	North Pacific Coast Freight Bureau, Seattle WA [*STAC*]
NPC	North Pacific Industry [*Vancouver Stock Exchange symbol*]
NPC	North Polar Cap [*A filamentary mark on Mars*]
NPC	NPC International, Inc. [*Associated Press*] (SAG)
NPC	Nuclear Pore Complex [*Protein*]
NPC	Nuclear Power Co. (NRCH)
NPC	Nuclear Propulsion Committee (SAUS)
NPC	Nucleonic Products Co. (SAUS)
NPC	Numerical Positioning Control (SAUS)
NPC	Numerical Print Control (SAUS)
NPC	Nursing and Personal Care
NPC	Nuveen Ins CA Prem Inc. Muni [*NYSE symbol*] (TTSB)
NPC	Nuveen Insured California Premium Income Municipal [*NYSE symbol*] (SPSG)
NPC	Public Library of Charlotte and Mecklenburg County, Charlotte, NC [*OCLC symbol*] (OCLC)
NPCa	Nasopharyngeal Carcinoma [*Medicine*] (MAE)
NPCA	National Paint and Coatings Association (EA)
NPCA	National Parks and Conservation Association (EA)
NPCA	National Peace Corps Association (EA)
NPCA	National Peer Counseling Association (DHP)
NPCA	National Pest Control Association (EA)
NPCA	National Pig Carvers Association (EA)
NPCA	National Plastercraft Association (EA)
NPCA	National Precast Concrete Association (EA)
NPCA	National Progressive Consumers Alliance (EA)
NPCBW	National Political Congress of Black Women (EA)
NPCC	National Poison Control Center (DAVI)
NPCC	National Pop Can Collectors (EA)
NPCC	National Possum Co-ordinating Committee (SAUS)
NPCC	National Prostate Cancer Coalition (SAUS)
NPCC	Northeast Power Coordinating Council [*Regional power council*]
NPCC	North Peralta Community College [*California*]
NPC/CBS	National Planning Commission/Central Bureau of Statistics (SAUS)
NPCCI	Notification Procedures for Confidential Commercial Information (COE)
NPC/COES	National Panhellenic Conference of Central Office Executives (EA)
NPCD	National Association of Parish Coordinators/Directors of Religious Education (EA)
NPCDN	National Private Circuit Digital Network (PDAA)
NP Cells	Nonproducer Cells (SAUS)
NPCF	National Pollution Control Foundation
NPCFB	North Pacific Coast Freight Bureau
NPCI	National Potato Chip Institute [*Later, SFA*]
NPCI	NPC International, Inc. [*NASDAQ symbol*] (SAG)
NPCI	NPC Intl. [*NASDAQ symbol*] (TTSB)
NPCIL	Nuclear Power Corp. of India Ltd.
NPC Intl	NPC International, Inc. [*Associated Press*] (SAG)
NPCL	North Pacific Coast Line (MHDB)
N-PCL	Not-for-Profit Corp. Law [*New York, NY*] [*A publication*]
NP-CLT	Neuropsychiatry Clerical Procedure Technician [*Navy*]
NPCMW	North Pacific Central Mode Water [*Marine science*] (OSRA)
NPCN	National Poison Center Network (EA)
NPC/NCC	National Planning Commission/National Computer Centre (SAUS)
NPCNU	Neopentyl(chloroethyl)nitrosourea [*Biochemistry*]
NPCO	Negative Patient-Care Outcome [*Medicine*] (WDAA)
NP Code	Non-Print Code (SAUS)
N-P, Complete	Nondeterministic Polynomial Complete Problem [*Mathematics*]
NPCP	Nairobi Peoples' Convention Party
NPCP	National Prostatic Cancer Project
NPCPL	Normal Process Complementary Pass transistor Logic (SAUS)
NPCR	No Periodic Calibration Required (MCD)
NPCR	No Programmed Calibration Required (MCD)
NPCR	Normalized Protein Catabolic Rate (SAUS)
NPCS	National Population Control Secretariat [*Australia*]
NPCSD	North Pacific Co-operative Security Dialog (SAUS)
NP-CT	Naval Personnel Conversion Tables
NP Cult	Nasopharyngeal Culture [*Bacteriology*] (CPH)
NPCW	National Pork Council Women (EA)
NPD	Napped (ABBR)
NPD	Narcissistic Personality Disorder [*Medicine*] (DMAA)
NPD	NASA Policy Directive
NPD	NASA Program Director (SSD)
NPD	Nationaldemokratische Partei Deutschlands [*National Democratic Party of Germany*] [*Political party*] (PPE)
NPD	National Niemann Pick Disease Foundation (EA)
NPD	National Paint Distributors (EA)
NPD	National Party for Democracy [*Zambia*] [*Political party*] (EY)
NPD	National Patent Development Corp. [*AMEX symbol*] (SPSG)
NPD	National Philanthropy Day (NFD)

NPD	National Policy Debate [*Nuclear energy*] (NRCH)
NPD	National Power Demonstration (IEEE)
NPD	National Program Director
NPD	National Program for Dermatology
NPD	Natl Patent Devel [*AMEX symbol*] (TTSB)
NPD	Natriuretic Plasma Dialysate [*Medicine*] (MAE)
NPD	Navy Procurement Directives
NPD	Nees Politikes Dynameis [*New Political Forces*] [*Greek*] [*Political party*] (PPE)
NPD	Negative Pressure Device [*Medicine*] (DMAA)
NPD	Neimann-Pick Disease (CPH)
NPD	Network Protection Device [*Telecommunications*] (TEL)
NPD	Network Protective Device (NITA)
NPD	Neutron Powder Diffractometer (SAUS)
NPD	New Product Development [*Business term*]
NPD	New Products Digest (SAUS)
NPD	New Providence Development Co. Ltd. [*Toronto Stock Exchange symbol*]
NPD	Newspaper Press Directory [*A publication*] (DGA)
NPD	Niemann-Pick Disease [*Medicine*]
NPD	Night Perimeter Defense
NPD	Nitrogen-Phosphorus Detector [*Analytical instrumentation*]
NPD	Nitrogen, Phosphorus Gas Chromatographic Detector [*Spectroscopy*]
NPD	Nocturnal Paroxysmal Dystonia [*Medicine*] (MELL)
NPD	Nominal Percent Defective
NPD	Nonparental Ditype [*Genetics*]
NPD	Non-Planar Dipole (SAUS)
NPD	Nonprescription Drug (MELL)
NPD	No Pay Due [*Military*] (ADDR)
NPD	No Payroll Division
NPD	North Pacific Division [*Army*] [*World War II*]
NPD	North Pacific Drift [*Oceanography*]
NPD	North Polar Distance
NPD	Nouveau Parti Democratique [*New Democratic Party*] [*Canada*] [*Political party*] (EAIO)
NPD	N-Player Prisoneris Dilemma
NPD	Nuclear Physics Division (SAUS)
NPD	Nuclear Power Demonstration [*of a reactor*]
NPD	Nuclear Power Development (SAUS)
NPD	Nuclear Power Division (SAA)
NPD	Nuclei Postero Dorsalis (SAUS)
NPD	South African Law Reports, Natal Province Division [*A publication*] (DLA)
NPDA	National Pharmaceutical Distributors' Association [*Australia*]
NPDA	National Plywood Distributors Association (EA)
NPDA	National Privy Diggers Association (EA)
NPDA	National Pyrotechnic Distributors Association [*APA*] [*Absorbed by*] (EA)
NPDA	Network Problem Determination Aid (NITA)
NPDA	Network Problem Determination Application [*Computer science*]
NPDAA	National Pharmaceutical Direct Advertising Association [*Defunct*] (EA)
NPDB	National Practitioner Data Bank [*Information service or system*] (IID)
NPDB	Nuclear Plant Databank (NRCH)
NPDBA	National Pet Dealers and Breeders Association [*Defunct*] (EA)
NPDC	Dutchess Community College, Poughkeepsie, NY [*Library symbol*] [*Library of Congress*] (LCLS)
NPDC	National Patent Development Corp.
NPDC	National Peace Day Celebration (EA)
NPDC	National Planning Data Corp. [*Information service or system*] (IID)
NPDC	National Poetry Day Committee (EA)
NPDC	Neurofibromatosis-Pheochromocytoma-Duodenal Carcinoid [*Syndrome*] [*Medicine*] (DMAA)
NPDCM	Dutchess County Mental Health Center, Poughkeepsie, NY [*Library symbol*] [*Library of Congress*] (LCLS)
NPDDE	Nitrophenyl Dodecyl Ether [*Organic chemistry*]
NPDE	Nonlinear Partial Differential Equation
NPDEA	National Professional Driver Education Association (AEBS)
NPDES	National Pollutant Discharge Elimination System [*Environmental Protection Agency*]
NPDES	Nuclear Pollution Discharge Elimination Specification (SAUS)
NPDES	Nuclear Pollution Discharge Elimination System (SAUS)
NPDF	Normal Probability Distribution Function
NPDI	Nonperformance of Duty because Imprisoned [*Navy*]
NPDL	Nodular Poorly Differentiated Lymphocyte
NPDM	Navy Program Decision Meeting (DOMA)
NPDN	Nordic Public Data Network [*Denmark, Finland, Iceland, Norway and Sweden*] (PDAA)
NPDNA	Nucleoprotamine Deoxyribonucleic Acid
NPDO	Nacelle Product Development Organization (MCD)
NPDO	Non-Profit Distributing Organization (PDAA)
NPDR	NCO Professional Development Ribbon [*Military decoration*]
NPDR	Nonproliferative Diabetic Retinopathy [*Medicine*] (MAE)
NPD Reactor	Nuclear Power Demonstration Reactor (SAUS)
NPDS	National Pollutant Discharge Elimination System [*Environmental Protection Agency*] (ERG)
NPDS	NMCC Processing and Display System (SAUS)
NPDS	Nuclear Particle Detection Subsystem (SAUS)
NPDS	Nuclear Particle Detection System (KSC)
NPDSA	National Public Domain Software Archive (AIE)
NPDU	Naval Plant Development Unit (DNAB)
NPDU	Network Protocol Data Unit [*Telecommunications*] (OSI)
NPDW	North Pacific Deep Water [*Oceanography*]
NPDWG	Networking Project for Disabled Women and Girls (EA)

NPDWR..........	National Primary Drinking Water Regulations [*Environmental Protection Agency*]
NPD'............	No Pathologic Diagnosis [*Medicine*] (BARN)
NPE.............	Elizabeth City State University, Elizabeth City, NC [*OCLC symbol*] (OCLC)
NPE.............	Napier [*New Zealand*] [*Airport symbol*] (OAG)
NPE.............	Nasal Physical Examination
NPE.............	National Plastic Exposition
NPE.............	National Population Enquiry
NPE.............	Natural Parity Exchange [*Physics*] (OA)
NPE.............	Naval Pilot Evaluation (MUGU)
NPE.............	Navy Preliminary Evaluation
NPE.............	Network Processing Element (NITA)
NPE.............	New Preliminary Evaluation (MCD)
NPE.............	New Product Engineering (SAUS)
NPE.............	Nonpolluting Engine [*Rocketdyne/Commonwealth Edison Co.*]
NPE.............	Nonpotential Energy [*of molecules*]
NPE.............	Nonylphenol Ethoxylate [*Organic chemistry*]
NPE.............	Nuclear Photographic Emulsion
NPE.............	Nuclear Planning and Execution (SAUS)
NPE.............	Nuclear Planning and Execution System (MCD)
NPE.............	Nuclear Power Engineering (IAA)
NPE.............	Nuveen Ins Prem Inc. Muni [*NYSE symbol*] (TTSB)
NPE.............	Nuveen Insured Premium Income Municipal [*NYSE symbol*] (SPSG)
NPEA...........	National Patio Enclosure Association (EA)
NPEA...........	National Printing Equipment Association [*Later, NPES*] (EA)
N-Peace......	Nuclear Peace (SAUS)
NPEB..........	Nonparametric Empirical Bayes [*Statistics*]
NPEC..........	National Panhellenic Editors Conference (EA)
NPEC..........	Native Plants Extracts Cooperative [*Australia*]
NPEC..........	Nuclear Power Engineering Committee [*Nuclear Regulatory Commission*] (NRCH)
NPECCD......	National Public Education Campaign on Clinical Depression
NPED..........	Nuclear-Powered Energy Depot
NPee...........	Field Library, Inc., Peekskill, NY [*Library symbol*] [*Library of Congress*] (LCLS)
NPEE...........	NP Energy Corp. (SAUS)
NPEF...........	New Product Evaluation Form
NPEGE.........	Nonyl Phenyl Eicosa-Ethylene Glycol Ether (SAUS)
NPel...........	Pelham Public Library, Pelham, NY [*Library symbol*] [*Library of Congress*] (LCLS)
NPELRA......	National Public Employer Labor Relations Association (EA)
NPEO..........	Nonylphenol Polyethoxylate [*Organic chemistry*]
NPE/PES......	Nuclear Power Engineering/Power Engineering Society (SAUS)
NPER..........	National Public Employment Reporter Database [*Information service or system*] (IID)
NPerbA........	J. N. Adam Developmental Center, Perrysburg, NY [*Library symbol*] [*Library of Congress*] (LCLS)
NPES..........	Association for Suppliers of Printing and Publishing Technologies (SAUS)
NPES..........	National Printing Equipment and Supply Association (EA)
NPES..........	National Printing Equipment Show
NPE(S)........	Nuclear Planning and Execution (Service) (DOMA)
NPES..........	Nuclear Planning and Execution System (COE)
NPESA........	National Printing Equipment & Supply Association, Inc.
NPESO........	NAVSHIPS [*Naval Ship Systems Command*] Plant Equipment Support Office
NPET..........	Newport Petroleums (SAUS)
NPET..........	Nicollet Process Engineering, Inc. [*NASDAQ symbol*] (SAG)
NPET..........	Nicollet Process Engr [*NASDAQ symbol*] (TTSB)
NPET..........	Nonpetroleum
NPEV..........	Nonpolio Enterovirus [*Infectious Diseases*] (DAVI)
NPEX..........	Normal Priority Exit (IAA)
NPF............	Names Project Foundation (EA)
NPF............	National Paraplegia Foundation (EA)
NPF............	National Park Foundation (EA)
NPF............	National Parkinson Foundation (EA)
NPF............	National Pharmaceutical Foundation (EA)
NPF............	National Piano Foundation (EA)
NPF............	National Pig Fair [*British*] (ITD)
NPF............	National Poetry Foundation (EA)
NPF............	National Police Force [*South Vietnam*] (VNW)
NPF............	National Policy Forum
NPF............	National Press Foundation (EA)
NPF............	National Progressive Front [*Iraq*] [*Political party*] (PPW)
NPF............	National Psoriasis Foundation (EA)
NPF............	Naval Parachute Facility (MCD)
NPF............	Naval Powder Factory
NPF............	Naval Procurement Fund [*Budget appropriation title*]
NPF............	NAVSTAR [*Navigation Satellite Tracking and Ranging*] Processing Facility (MCD)
NPF............	Net Propulsion Force (MCD)
NPF............	Network Pulse Forming
NPF............	Neutrons per Fission (DEN)
NPF............	Newspaper Press Fund (DGA)
NPF............	Newsprint Pulp Flat (SAUS)
NPF............	Newtonian Potential Function [*Mathematics*]
NPF............	Nicaragua Peace Fleet [*Defunct*] (EA)
NPF............	Nonpublic Funds [*Canadian Forces*]
NPF............	No Private Facilities (SAUS)
NPF............	No Problem Found (SAUS)
NPF............	Nordisk Plastikkirurgisk Forening [*Scandinavian Association of Plastic Surgeons - SAPS*] (EAIO)
NPF............	North Pyrenean Fault [*Geology*]
npf.............	Not Provided For (ODBW)
NPF............	Not Provided For
NPF............	Nuclear Power Facility (NRCH)
NPF............	Nuclear Problems Forum (SAUS)
NPF............	Nucleopore Filter
NPF............	Nuveen Premium Municipal Income [*NYSE symbol*] (SPSG)
NPF............	Nuveen Prem Muni Income [*NYSE symbol*] (TTSB)
NPFA...........	National Peanut Festival Association
NPFA...........	National Playing Fields Association [*British*]
NPFA...........	National Prepared Food Association (NTPA)
NPF & PP......	Naval Prison Farms and Prison Personnel [*Budget appropriation title*]
NPFC..........	National Pro-Family Coalition (EA)
NPFC..........	Naval Publications and Forms Center
NPFC..........	North Pacific Fisheries Commission (NOAA)
NPFC..........	North Pacific Fur Seal Commission [*Defunct*]
NPFC..........	Northwest Pacific Fisheries Center (SAUS)
NPFDA........	National Poultry and Food Distributors Association (NTPA)
NPFF..........	National Police Field Force [*Military*]
NPFF..........	Normal Probability Frequency Function
NPFFA........	National Prepared Frozen Food Association (EA)
NPFFG........	National Plant, Flower, and Fruit Guild (EA)
NPFFPA......	National Prepared Frozen Food Processors Association [*Later, NPFFA*] (EA)
NPFI..........	National Plant Food Institute [*Later, TFI*] (EA)
NPFID.........	Nitrogen-Phosphorus-Flame Ionization Detector [*Instrumentation*]
NPFL..........	National Patriotic Front of Liberia [*Political party*] (EY)
NPFM..........	Neural Pulse Frequency Modulation (PDAA)
NPFMC........	Northern Prawn Fishery Management Committee [*Australia*]
NPFMC........	North Pacific Fishery Management Council [*National Oceanic and Atmospheric Administration*] (GFGA)
NPFO..........	Nuclear Power Field Office (IEEE)
N-PFPS........	Navy Portable Flight Planning Software
NPFR..........	Normalized Peak Filling Rate [*Cardiology*]
NPFRC........	North Pacific Fisheries Research Center [*National Oceanic and Atmospheric Administration*]
NPFS..........	Naval Preflight School
NPFS..........	No Prior or Current Federal Service (AABC)
NPFSC........	North Pacific Fur Seal Commission [*Defunct*]
NPFT..........	Neurotic Personality Factor Test [*Psychology*]
NPFTA........	National Personal Fitness Trainers Association (EA)
NPFVAS......	Northern Prawn Fishery Voluntary Assistance Scheme (SAUS)
NPFZ..........	North Pyrenean Fault Zone [*Geology*]
NPG...........	Napping (ABBR)
NPG...........	National Peace Garden (EA)
NPG...........	National Portrait Gallery [*Smithsonian Institution*]
NPG...........	NATO Planning Group (NATG)
NPG...........	Naval Proving Ground [*Dahlgren, VA*]
NPG...........	Negative Population Growth (EA)
NPG...........	Neopentylglycol [*Organic chemistry*]
NPG...........	Nevada Proving Ground (BARN)
NPG...........	New Performance Gallery [*San Francisco*]
NPG...........	New Power Generation (SAUS)
NPG...........	New Product Group (SAUS)
NPG...........	Non-Aqueous Propylene Glycol [*Automotive coolant*]
NPG...........	Nonpregnant (MELL)
NPG...........	Nonprocessor Grant (IAA)
NPG...........	Nonunit Personnel Generator (DOMA)
NPG...........	Normalized Electron-Peak to Gamma-Peak [*Electronics*] (OA)
NPG...........	Normalized Programming Generator (IAA)
NPG...........	Not Paged [*Publishing*]
NPG...........	N-Phenylglycine [*Organic chemistry*]
NPG...........	Nuclear Planning Group [*NATO*]
NPG...........	Nuclear Power Group [*British*] [*Defunct*] (NUCP)
NPG...........	Nuveen GA Prem Inc. Muni [*AMEX symbol*] (TTSB)
NPG...........	Nuveen Georgia Premium Income Municipal Fund [*AMEX symbol*] (SPSG)
NPG...........	Ontario Library Service Nipigon/Thunder Bay Public Library [*UTLAS symbol*]
NPGA..........	National Propane Gas Association (NTPA)
NPGA..........	National Pygmy Goat Association (EA)
NPGA..........	Nevada Personnel and Guidance Association (SAUS)
NPGB..........	(Nitrophenyl)guanidinobenzoate [*Organic chemistry*]
NPGC..........	National Pell Grant Coalition (EA)
NPG-GMA ...	N-Phenylglycine Glycidyl Methacrylate [*Organic chemistry*]
NPGLINAC ...	Naval Postgraduate School Linear Accelerator
NPGPA........	Non-Powder Gun Products Association (EA)
NPGS..........	National Plant Germplasm System [*Department of Agriculture*]
NPGS..........	Naval Postgraduate School
NPGS..........	Nuclear Power Generating Station (NRCH)
NPGTC........	National Prairie Grouse Technical Council (EA)
NPH...........	Association of Nordic Paper Historians [*See also FNPH*] [*Sweden*] (EAIO)
NPH...........	Nalcap Holdings, Inc. [*Vancouver Stock Exchange symbol*]
NPH...........	Natural Period in Heave
NPH...........	Natural Protamine Hagadorn [*Insulin*]
NPH...........	Natural Protein Hagedorn (DB)
NPH...........	Nephi [*Utah*] [*Airport symbol*] (OAG)
NPH...........	Neurophysin [*Biochemistry*]
NPH...........	Neutral Protamine Hagadorn [*Insulin suspension*]
NPH...........	Non Processed Header (SAUS)
NPH...........	No Parse Headers (SAUS)
NPH...........	No Previous History [*Medicine*] (DAVI)
NPH...........	No Profit Here [*Business term*]
NPH...........	Normal Paraffin Hydrocarbon
NPH...........	Normal Pressure Hydrocephalus [*Medicine*]
NPh...........	Northern Phoenician (BJA)

NPH	North Pit [Hawaii] [Seismograph station code, US Geological Survey] (SEIS)
NPHA	Nanga Parbat/Haramosh Axis [Himalayan geology]
NPHA	National Park Hospitality Association (NTPA)
NPHA	National Peer Helpers Association (EA)
NPhA	National Pharmaceutical Association (EA)
NPHA	National Plott Hound Association (EA)
NPHA	National Prison Hospice Association (NTPA)
NPHAP	National Pesticide Hazard Assessment Program (EPAT)
NPHB	Nonphotochemical Hole Burning [Spectrometry]
NPhD	Doctor of Natural Philosophy
NPHE	Nitrophenyl Hexyl Ether [Organic chemistry]
NPHOE	Nitrophenyl Hydroxyoctyl Ether [Organic chemistry]
NPHP	National Public Health Partnership (SAUS)
NPHPRS	National Public Health Program Reporting System [Department of Health and Human Services]
NPHR	National Foreign Intelligence Plan for Human Resources (MCD)
NPhR	Neue Philologische Rundschau [A publication] (BJA)
NPHR	Notice Papers-House of Representatives (SAUS)
NPHRC	National Pediatric HIV Resource Center (PAZ)
NPHS	Northwick Park Heart Study (DAVI)
NPHWA	National Presbyterian Health and Welfare Association [Later, PHEWA]
NPhx	Nasopharynx [Anatomy] (DAVI)
NPI	International Business Machines Corp., Systems Development Division, Poughkeepsie (SAUS)
NPI	International Business Machines Corp., Systems Development Division, Poughkeepsie, NY [Library symbol] [Library of Congress] (LCLS)
NPI	Narcissistic Personality Inventory [Psychology] (EDAC)
NPI	Nasopharyngeal Intubation [Medicine] (MELL)
NPI	National Paralegal Institute (EA)
NPI	National Parkinson Institute
NPI	National Pollutant Inventory
NPI	National Presto Industries, Inc. (EFIS)
NPI	National Provident Institution [Wales]
NPI	National Provider Identifier (SAUS)
NPI	National Purchasing Institute (EA)
NPI	Neighbourhood Partial Interchangeability (SAUS)
NPI	Net Premium Income [Insurance] (AIA)
NPI	NeuroPsychiatric Institute [UCLA]
NPI	New Partnership Initiative (SAUS)
NPI	New Product Introduction (SAUS)
NPI	NEXRAD [Next Generation Weather Radar] Product Interface [Marine science] (OSRA)
NPI	Nippon Pulp Industry (SAUS)
NPI	Nonprecision Instrument (SAUS)
NPI	Nonprocedural Interface [Computer science]
NPI	No Present Illness
NPI	No Previous Information [to tip off a US Customs Service seizure]
NPI	Nordic Productivity Institute (SAUS)
NPI	Normick Perron, Inc. [Toronto Stock Exchange symbol]
NPI	Northampton Polytechnic Institute (SAUS)
NPI	North Pocatello Valley [Idaho] [Seismograph station code, US Geological Survey] (SEIS)
NPI	Nuclear Propulsion Initiative (ABAC)
NPI	Nucleoplasmic Index [Medicine] (DMAA)
NPI	Numbering Plan Identification (SAUS)
NPI	Numbering Plan Indicator [Computer science] (TNIG)
NPI	Number Planning Area (SAUS)
NPI	Nuveen Prem Income Muni [NYSE symbol] (TTSB)
NPI	Nuveen Premium Income Municipal Fund, Inc. [NYSE symbol] (SPSG)
NPIA	Nanny Pop-Ins Association [Defunct] (EA)
NPIA	National Pet Insurance Association (GVA)
NPIA	National Photography Instructors Association (EA)
NPIA	Norfolk Port and Industrial Authority (SAUS)
NPIAS	National Plan of Integrated Airport Systems [BTS] [FAA] (TAG)
NPIC	National Pesticide Information Clearinghouse [Later, NPTN] (EA)
NPIC	National Pharmacy Insurance Council [Defunct] (EA)
NPIC	National Photographic Intelligence Center (MUSM)
NPIC	National Photographic Interpretation Center [CIA]
NPIC	Naval Photographic Interpretation Center
NPIC	Neurogenic Peripheral Intermittent Claudication [Medicine] (DMAA)
NPIC	Nitrosopipecolic Acid [Organic chemistry]
NPie	Piermont Public Library, Piermont, NY [Library symbol] [Library of Congress] (LCLS)
NPIF	National Peace Institute Foundation (EA)
NPIG	Nuclear Power Information Group [British] (NUCP)
NPIL	Nepal Paper Industries Ltd.
NPIN	National Parent Education Network
NPIN	National Parent Information Network
NPIN	National Prevention Information Network [Internet resource]
NPIN	Negative-Positive-Intrinsic-Negative [Electron device] (MSA)
NPIP	National Poultry Improvement Plan (EA)
NPIP	Nitrosopiperidine [Also, NP] [Organic chemistry]
NPIPF	Newspaper and Printing Industries Pension Fund [British] (BI)
NPiPNA	N-Paraffins, iso-Paraffins, Naphthenes and Aromatics [Gasoline analysis]
NPIR	No Periodic Inspection Required [Military] (AFIT)
NPIRG	National Public Interest Research Group (EA)
NPIRI	National Printing Ink Research Institute (EA)
NPIRS	National Pesticide Information Retrieval System [Purdue University] [West Lafayette, IN] [Database]
NPIS	National Physics Information System [American Institute of Physics] [New York, NY] (DIT)
NP/IS	National Premium Incentive Show (ITD)
NPIS	New Product Information Service [Department of Commerce]
NPIS	Nuclear Plant Island Structure (NRCH)
NPITI	National Project for the Improvement of Televised Instruction [National Association of Educational Broadcasters]
NPIU	Network Processing and Interface Unit (NITA)
NPIU	Numerical Processing and Interface Unit [Computer science] (MHDB)
NPIW	North Pacific Intermediate Water [Marine science] (OSRA)
NPIX	Network Peripherals [NASDAQ symbol] (TTSB)
NPIX	Network Peripherals, Inc. [NASDAQ symbol] (SAG)
NPJ	Corpus Christi, TX [Location identifier] [FAA] (FAAL)
NPJ	Night Photo Jet (SAUS)
NPJ	Number of Projects in the RTD-projects (SAUS)
NPj	Port Jefferson Free Library, Port Jefferson, NY [Library symbol] [Library of Congress] (LCLS)
NPjES	Port Jefferson Elementary School, Port Jefferson, NY [Library symbol] [Library of Congress] (LCLS)
NPjMH	John T. Mather Memorial Hospital, Port Jefferson, NY [Library symbol] [Library of Congress] (LCLS)
NPJPA	National Prune Juice Packers Association (EA)
NPjs	Port Jefferson Station-Terryville Public Library, Port Jefferson Station, NY [Library symbol] [Library of Congress] (LCLS)
NPjSCH	Saint Charles Hospital, Port Jefferson, NY [Library symbol] [Library of Congress] (LCLS)
NPJT	Nonparoxysmal Atrioventricular Junction Tachycardia [Cardiology]
NPjVH	Earl L. Vandermeulen High School, Port Jefferson, NY [Library symbol] [Library of Congress] (LCLS)
NPK	Nationale Partij Kombinatie [National Party Alliance] [Surinam] [Political party] (PPW)
NPK	National Presto Industries, Inc. [NYSE symbol] (SPSG)
NPK	Natl Presto Indus. [NYSE symbol] (SG)
NPK	Natrium, Phosphorus, Kalium (SAUS)
N-P-K	Nitrogen-Phosphate-Potash (SAUS)
NPK	Nitrogen, Phosphorus, Potassium [Fertilizer components]
NPK	Noble Peak Resources Ltd. [Vancouver Stock Exchange symbol]
NPK	Nodal Point Keying
NPK	Non-Printing Key (SAUS)
NPKA	National Paving and Kerb Association [British] (DBA)
NPL	Free Public Library of Newark, Newark, NJ [OCLC symbol] (OCLC)
NPL	Nameplate (MSA)
NPL	Naples [Italy] [Seismograph station code, US Geological Survey] [Closed] (SEIS)
NPL	National Physical Laboratory [Research center] [British] (IRC)
NPL	National Physics Laboratory (KSC)
NPL	National Priorities List [Hazardous wastes] [Environmental Protection Agency]
NPL	National Priority List (AUEG)
NPL	National Propane Partners LP [NYSE symbol] (SAG)
NPL	National Puzzlers' League (EA)
NPL	Natural Processing Language [Computer science] (HGAA)
NPL	Neon Pilot Light
NPL	Neoproteolipid [Hematology]
NPL	Nepal [ANSI three-letter standard code] (CNC)
NPL	Nepheline Resources Ltd. [Vancouver Stock Exchange symbol]
NPL	Netscape Public License
NPL	Newark Public Library (SAUS)
NPL	Newfoundland Public Library Services [UTLAS symbol]
NPL	New Plymouth [New Zealand] [Airport symbol] (OAG)
NPL	New Product Line
NPL	New Program Language (SAUS)
NPL	New Programming Language [1974] [Later, PL/1] [Computer science]
NPL	Nippon Peripherals Ltd. (SAUS)
NPL	NOAAPORT Liaison (SAUS)
NPL	Nodular Poorly Differentiated Lymphoma [Oncology] (DAVI)
NPL	Noise Pollution Level
NPL	Nonparametric Multipoint Linkage [Mathematics]
NPL	Nonpartisan League [Political party in North Dakota opposed by the IVA]
NPL	Nonpersonal Liability
NPL	Non Procedural Language (SAUS)
NPL	Nonprocedural Language (TIMI)
NPL	Nonprogramming Language (IAA)
NPL	Nonstandard Parts List (MCD)
NPL	No Perception of Light [Ophthalmology] (CPH)
NPL	No Phonon Line (SAUS)
NPL	Norfolk Public Library (SAUS)
NPL	Normal Power Level (KSC)
NPL	Northwest Pipeline Corp. (SAUS)
npl	Noun, Plural [Grammar] (CDAI)
NPL	Numerical Parts List (MCD)
NPL	Numerical Preference List [Military] (AFIT)
NPl	Plainview-Old Bethpage Public Library, Plainview, NY [Library symbol] [Library of Congress] (LCLS)
NPL	Zero Phonon Line
NPLA	National Perishable Logistics Association (NTPA)
NPLA	New Product Line Audit
NPla	Plattsburgh Public Library, Plattsburgh, NY [Library symbol] [Library of Congress] (LCLS)
NPlaB	Bellarmine College, Plattsburgh, NY [Library symbol] [Library of Congress] (LCLS)
NPlaC	Champlain College, Plattsburgh, NY [Library symbol] [Library of Congress] [Obsolete] (LCLS)

NPLAC .... National People Living with AIDS [*Acquired Immune Deficiency Syndrome*] Coalition [*Australia*]
NPlaCC .... Clinton Community College, Plattsburgh, NY [*Library symbol*] [*Library of Congress*] (LCLS)
NPlaCEF ...... Clinton-Essex-Franklin Library System, Plattsburgh, NY [*Library symbol*] [*Library of Congress*] (LCLS)
NPlaCN .... Champlain Valley School of Nursing, Plattsburgh, NY [*Library symbol*] [*Library of Congress*] (LCLS)
NPL-AERO ... National Physical Laboratory, Aerodynamics Division [*British*]
NPLAN .... National Plan for Australian Newspapers
NPlaP .... Champlain Valley Physicians Hospital, Plattsburgh, NY [*Library symbol*] [*Library of Congress*] (LCLS)
NPlaU .... State University of New York, College at Plattsburgh, Plattsburgh, NY [*Library symbol*] [*Library of Congress*] (LCLS)
NPlBE .... Old Bethpage Elementary School, Plainview, NY [*Library symbol*] [*Library of Congress*] (LCLS)
NPlBM .... Plainview-Old Bethpage Middle School, Plainview, NY [*Library symbol*] [*Library of Congress*] (LCLS)
NPLC .... National Pedigree Livestock Council (EA)
NPLC .... National Product Liability Council (EA)
NPLC .... Normal Phase Liquid Chromatography
NPlCH .... Central General Hospital, Plainview, NY [*Library symbol*] [*Library of Congress*] (LCLS)
NPLD .... National Pro-Life Democrats (EA)
NPle .... Mount Pleasant Public Library, Pleasantville, NY [*Library symbol*] [*Library of Congress*] (LCLS)
NPLEI.......... National Police Law Enforcement Institute (EA)
NPleP .... Pace University Westchester, Pleasantville, NY [*Library symbol*] [*Library of Congress*] (LCLS)
NPLF........... National Preservation Loan Fund [*National Trust for Historic Preservation*]
NPLG .... Navy Program Language Group
NPLG .... Night Plane Guard Station (NVT)
NPLG .... Night Plane Landing Guard (NVT)
NPlGS......... Church of Jesus Christ of Latter-Day Saints, Genealogical Society Library, Plainview Branch, Plainview, NY [*Library symbol*] [*Library of Congress*] (LCLS)
NPLGS .... Night Plane Guard Station (SAUS)
NPLI........... Netpliance, Inc. [*NASDAQ symbol*] (SG)
NPlJE .... Jamaica Elementary School, Plainview, NY [*Library symbol*] [*Library of Congress*] (LCLS)
NPlKH......... John F. Kennedy High School, Plainview, NY [*Library symbol*] [*Library of Congress*] (LCLS)
NPlMC .... Nassau County Medical Center, Plainview Division, Plainview, NY [*Library symbol*] [*Library of Congress*] (LCLS)
NPlMM .... H.B. Mattlin Middle School, Plainview, NY [*Library symbol*] [*Library of Congress*] (LCLS)
NPlnRI........ New Plan Realty Trust [*Associated Press*] (SAG)
NPLO .... NATO Production and Logistics Organization (NATG)
NP-L PAC..... National Pro-Life Political Action Committee [*Defunct*] (EA)
NPlPE .... Pasadena Elementary School, Plainview, NY [*Library symbol*] [*Library of Congress*] (LCLS)
NPlPwE........ Parkway Elementary School, Plainview, NY [*Library symbol*] [*Library of Congress*] (LCLS)
NPLR .... Nyasaland Protectorate Law Reports [*A publication*] (ILCA)
NPLS .... Network Plus [*NASDAQ symbol*] (SG)
NPLS .... Nonplus (ABBR)
NPLSD .... Nonplused (ABBR)
NPlSH......... Plainview-Old Bethpage Senior High School, Plainview, NY [*Library symbol*] [*Library of Congress*] (LCLS)
N/PLT......... Name Plate [*Automotive engineering*]
NPLT.......... North Platte Basin (SAUS)
NPLTC .... National Public Law Training Center (EA)
NPLU .... Not People Like Us (SAUS)
N PLUR .... Neuter Plural [*Grammar*] (OCD)
NPM........... Counts per Minute (IDOE)
NPM........... Marist College, Poughkeepsie, NY [*Library symbol*] [*Library of Congress*] (LCLS)
NPM........... Narrowband Phase Modulation (DEN)
NPM........... National Association of Pastoral Musicians (EA)
NPM........... National Program Manager [*Environmental Protection Agency*] (GFGA)
NPM........... Natural Particulate Matter [*Oceanography*]
NPM........... Naval Provost Marshal (SAUS)
NPM........... Naval Provost Martial [*British*]
NPM........... Navy Programming Manual
NPM........... Neonatal-Perinatal Medicine [*Medical specialty*] (DHSM)
Np/m.......... Neper per Meter
NPM........... Network Performance Monitor (NITA)
NPM........... New Privateer Mines [*Vancouver Stock Exchange symbol*]
NPM........... Noise Power Meter (SAUS)
NPM........... Non-Print Media [*Advertising*]
NPM........... North Pahute Mesa [*Nevada*] [*Seismograph station code, US Geological Survey*] (SEIS)
NPM........... Nothing per Mouth [*Medicine*] (DMAA)
NPM........... Nuclear Paramagnetism (SAUS)
npm........... number of points in the point-matching method (SAUS)
NPM........... Nuveen Prem Income Muni 2 [*NYSE symbol*] (TTSB)
NPM........... Nuveen Premium Income Municipal 2 [*NYSE symbol*] (SPSG)
NPMA .... National Piano Manufacturers Association of America [*Later, PMAI*] (EA)
NPMA .... National Podiatric Medical Association (EA)
NPMA .... National Property Management Association (EA)
NPMA .... Navy Personnel Management Academy (DNAB)
NPMA .... Newspaper Purchasing Management Association (EA)

NPMC .... National Pecan Marketing Council (EA)
NPMCA .... National Paper Marketing Council of Australia
NPMG .... NATO Patriot Management Group (MCD)
NPMH .... Mid-Hudson Libraries, Poughkeepsie, NY [*Library symbol*] [*Library of Congress*] (LCLS)
NPMHU........ National Postal Mail Handlers Union (EA)
NPMI .... Nordic Pool for Marine Insurance [*Helsinki, Finland*] (EA)
NPMP .... National Pesticide Monitoring Program [*Later, National Contaminant Biomonitoring Program*] [*US Fish and Wildlife Service*]
NPMR .... National Premium Manufacturers Representatives [*Later, IMRA*] (EA)
NPMTC .... Navy Pacific Missile Test Center (MCD)
NPMTC .... Nuclear Propulsion Mobile Training Team (SAUS)
NPMTT .... Nuclear Propulsion Mobile Training Team [*Military*] (CAAL)
NPN .... NASA Part Number (MCD)
NPN .... National Particulate Network [*Environmental Protection Agency*] (GFGA)
NPN .... National Party of Nigeria [*Political party*] (PPW)
NPN .... National Performance Network (EA)
NPN .... National Prevention Network (EA)
NPN .... National Prices Network
N-P-N......... Negative-Positive-Negative [*Transistor*] (CET)
NPN .... Negative-Positive-Negative
NPN .... New Product Network [*Television*]
NPN .... New Pseudonyms and Nicknames [*A publication*]
NPN .... Non-Par Not Approved
NPN .... Non-Physician Practitioner (SAUS)
NPN .... Nonprotein Nitrogen [*Analytical chemistry*]
NPN .... Normal Propyl Nitrate (MCD)
NPN .... Notes Public Network (SAUS)
NPNA .... No Protest Nonacceptance [*Banking*]
NPNA .... Normalized Protein equivalent of total Nitrogen Appearance (SAUS)
NPNCA .... National Parks and Nature Conservation Authority [*Australia*]
NPNCF........ Nicene and Post-Nicene Christian Fathers [*A publication*] (ODCC)
NPN Compound... Nonprotein Nitrogenous Compound (SAUS)
NP/ND......... Not Published/No Date (SAUS)
NPNP .... Negative-Positive-Negative-Positive [*Transistor*]
NPNR.......... Network for Psychiatric Nursing Research (SAUS)
NP NS......... Ohio Nisi Prius Reports, New Series [*A publication*] (DLA)
NPNT.......... NorthPoint Communic Grp. [*NASDAQ symbol*] (SG)
NPO .... Design & manufacturing facility (SAUS)
NPO .... Naphthylphenyloxazole [*Biochemical analysis*]
NPO .... NASA Pasadena Office (MCD)
NPO .... National [*or New*] Post Office Building
NPO .... National Project Office
NPO .... Naval Port Officer
NPO .... Navy Post Office
NPO .... Navy Program Objectives (NG)
NPO .... Navy Purchasing Office
NPO .... Negative-Positive O Temperature Coefficient (AEBE)
NPO .... Negative Positive Zero (IAA)
NPO .... Neighborhood Patrol Office [*or Officer*]
NPO .... New Personnel Orientation (MCD)
NPO .... New Philharmonic Orchestra [*British*]
NPO .... Nil per Os [*Nothing by Mouth*] [*Medicine*]
NPO .... Nonpenetrating Orbit (SAUS)
NPO .... Non Per Os [*Nothing by Mouth*] [*Latin*] (BABM)
NPO .... Non-Profit Organization (SAUS)
NPO .... No Part on Order (MCD)
NPO .... Norpet Resources Ltd. [*Toronto Stock Exchange symbol*]
NPO .... Nothing per Os (SAUS)
NPO .... Not Pickled Ordinary [*Metal industry*]
NPO .... Nuclear Plant Operator (NRCH)
NPO .... Nuclear Power Operator (SAUS)
NPO .... Nuclear Propulsion Office
NPO .... Nucleus Preopticus (DMAA)
NPO .... Preoptic Nucleus (DB)
NPO .... Strategic Systems Project Office, Washington, DC [*OCLC symbol*] (OCLC)
NPOAA........ National Police Officers Association of America (EA)
NPOC .... National Point of Contact (PDAA)
NPOC .... Navy Polar Oceanographic Center (DNAB)
NPOC .... Nonpurgeable Organic Carbon
NPODS........ Navy Publishing on Demand System (AAGC)
NPOE .... Nitrophenyl Octyl Ether [*Organic chemistry*]
NPOEV .... Nuclear-Powered Ocean Engineering Vehicle [*Minisub*]
NP Ohio ...... Ohio Nisi Prius Reports [*A publication*] (DLA)
NPO/HS....... Nulla per Os Hora Somni [*Nothing by Mouth at Bedtime*] [*Latin*] [*Pharmacy*] (MAH)
NPOI.......... Navy Prototype Optical Interferometer
NPOL.......... Nuclear Pollution [*Environmental science*] (COE)
NPOLA........ Navy Purchasing Office, Los Angeles
NPOLE .... North-seeking Pole (SAUS)
N-Pollution.. Nuclear Pollution (SAUS)
NPOMHWMGL... National Post Office Mail Handlers, Watchmen, Messengers, and Group Leaders [*Later, NPMHU*] (EA)
NPO-NIA ...... Nonprofit Organizations National Insurance Alliance (SAUS)
NPOP .... NASA Polar Orbiting Platform (EOSA)
NPOPR........ Not Paid on Prior Rolls
NPoq.......... Beekman Community Library Reading Center, Poughquag, NY [*Library symbol*] [*Library of Congress*] (LCLS)
NP or D ...... No Place or Date
NP or DP ..... No Place or Date of Publication (SAUS)
NPOS .... Nitrite Positive [*Organic chemistry*] (DAVI)
NPOS .... Nurses Professional Orientation Scale (DMAA)
NPOST........ Nonperturbative Open-Shell Theory [*Physics*]

NPot............	Potsdam Public Library, Potsdam, NY [*Library symbol*] [*Library of Congress*] (LCLS)
NPotC	Clarkson College of Technology, Potsdam, NY [*Library symbol*] [*Library of Congress*] (LCLS)
NPotU	State University of New York, College at Potsdam, Potsdam, NY [*Library symbol*] [*Library of Congress*] (LCLS)
NPour	Hiram Halley Memorial Library, Pound Ridge, NY [*Library symbol*] [*Library of Congress*] (LCLS)
N-Power	Nuclear Power (SAUS)
NPP	National Patriotic Party [*Liberia*] [*Political party*] (EY)
NPP	National Peach Partners [*Defunct*] (EA)
NPP	National People's Party [*Pakistan*] [*Political party*] (FEA)
NPP	National Periodicals Publications, Inc.
NPP	National Policy Paper [*Army*] (AABC)
NPP	National Pretreatment Program [*Metal finishing technology*]
NPP	National Priority Pool (SAUS)
NPP	National Priority Program [*NHTSA*] (TAG)
NPP	National Prison Project (EA)
NPP	National Procurement Point [*Military*] (RDA)
NPP	National Progressive Party [*Iraq*] [*Political party*] (BJA)
NPP	National Prohibition Party (EA)
NPP	Naval Propellant Plant
NPP	Navy Propellant Plant (DNAB)
NPP	Negative Picture Phase
NPP	Nemzeti Paraszt Part [*National Peasant Party*] [*Hungary*] [*Political party*] (PPE)
NPP	Neodymium Pentaphosphate [*Inorganic chemistry*]
NPP	Net Primary Production
NPP	Net Primary Productivity
NPP	Network Power Processor [*Acme Electric Corp.*] [*Computer science*] (PCM)
NPP	Network Protocol Processor
NPP	Neuropathic Pain [*Medicine*] (MELL)
NPP	Neuroperfusion Pump [*Medicine*] (MELL)
NPP	New Patriotic Party [*Ghana*] [*Political party*] (ECON)
NPP	New People's Party [*North Korea*] [*Political party*] (FEA)
NPP	New Physics Project (AIE)
NPP	New Policy Proposal (SAUS)
NPP	New Product Planning (IAA)
NPP	New Progressive Party [*Puerto Rico*] [*Political party*]
NPP	Nigerian People's Party [*Political party*] (PPW)
NPP	Nitrogen, Phosphorus, Potassium (SAUS)
NPP	Nitrophenyl Phosphate [*Biochemical analysis*]
NPP	Nitrophenylprolinol [*Organic chemistry*]
NPP	Nitropropenyl Pivalate [*Organic chemistry*]
NPP	Non-Penetrating Periscope [*DARPA*]
NPP	No Passed Proof
NPP	Normal Pool Plasma [*Clinical chemistry*]
NPP	Normal Postpartum [*Medicine*] (MELL)
NPP	North American Power [*Vancouver Stock Exchange symbol*]
NPP	Notice of Proposed Procurement (SAUS)
NPP	Nozzleless Performance Program Module (MCD)
NPP	N-Pentylpalmitamide [*Organic chemistry*]
NPP	Nuclear Power Plant (IEEE)
NPP	Nurse Practitioner Project
NPP	Nuveen Performance Plus Municipal [*NYSE symbol*] (SPSG)
NPP	Nuveen Perform Plus Muni [*NYSE symbol*] (TTSB)
NPPA	National Parks and Primitive Areas
NPPA	National Pickle Packers Association [*Later, PPI*]
NPPA	National Pizza and Pasta Association (EA)
NPPA	National Press Photographers Association (EA)
NPPA	National Probation and Parole Association [*Later, NCCD*]
NPPA	Northwest Pulp and Paper Association (SAUS)
NPPAC	National and Provincial Parks Association of Canada
NPPAG	National Program Production and Aquisition Grant [*Corporation for Public Broadcasting*] [*Radio*] (NTCM)
NPPase........	Nitrophenylphosphatase (DB)
NPPB	National Poisons and Pesticides Board [*Sweden*]
NPPB	National Potato Promotion Board (EA)
NPPB	Nitro(Phenylpropylamino) Benzoate [*Organic chemistry*]
NPPC	National Pork Producers Council (EA)
NPPC	National Power Policy Committee [*World War II*]
NPPC	Navy Programming Planning Council
NPPC	Northwest Power Planning Council (SAUS)
NPPC	Nuclear Power Plant Co. Ltd.
NPPC	Nuclear Power Plant Consultant (IDAI)
NPPC	Numeric Parts Preference Code [*Military*] (AFIT)
NPPC	Nursing Professional Practice Council (DMAA)
NPPD	(Nitrophenyl)pentadienal [*Tracer chemical*] [*Organic chemistry*]
NPPD	Nitrophenylpentadiene Aldehyde (SAUS)
NPPE	Negative Pressure Pulmonary Edema [*Medicine*] (DMAA)
NPPE	Nitrophenyl Pentyl Ether [*Organic chemistry*]
NPPE	Nuclear Power Propulsion Evaluation (NG)
NPPF	National Poultry Producers Federation [*Defunct*] (EA)
NPPI	Navy Program Progress Item (CAAL)
NPPI	Negative Pressure Patient Isolator [*Medicine*] (WDAA)
NPPI	Norwood Promotional Prd [*NASDAQ symbol*] (TTSB)
NPPI	Norwood Promotional Products [*NASDAQ symbol*] (SAG)
NPPL	National Parks and Public Lands [*Victoria, Australia*]
NPPL	National Private Pilots License (SAUS)
NPPL	Neuropsychopharmacology Laboratory [*Wayne State University*] [*Research center*]
NPPN	Nitroxyperoxypropyl Nitrate [*Environmental chemistry*]
NPPN	NUDO [*Namibia United Democratic Organization*] Progressive Party of Namibia [*Political party*] (PPW)
NPPO	Navy Program Planning Office
NPPO	Navy Publications and Printing Office
NPP/QAS......	Naval Propellant Plant Quality Assurance Department [*Indian Head, MD*]
NPPR	Nationalist Party of Puerto Rico (NADA)
NPPR	Navy Program Progress Report
NPPR	Nonproductive Procurement Directive
NPPRE	Nitrophenyl Propyl Ether [*Organic chemistry*]
NPPS	Navy Planning and Programming System
NPPS	Navy Publications and Printing Service
NPPSA	Naval Personnel Program Support Activity (ACAE)
NPPSBO.......	Navy Publications and Printing Service Branch Office
NPPSIS	National Parent to Parent Support & Information Systems, Inc.
NPPSMO......	Navy Publications and Printing Service Management Office
NPPSO........	Navy Publications and Printing Service Office
NPPSSOEASTDIV...	Navy Publications and Printing Service, Southeastern Division (DNAB)
NPPSWESTDIV...	Navy Publications and Printing Service, Western Division (DNAB)
NPPTA	National Public Parks Tennis Association (EA)
NPPTS	Nuclear Power Plant Training Simulator (PDAA)
NPPU	Net Postprandial Protein Utilization
NPPW	National Poison Prevention Week
NPQ	Not Physically Qualified (MELL)
NPQAA	Natural Products Quality Assurance Alliance
NPR	Napier [*New Zealand*] [*Seismograph station code, US Geological Survey*] [*Closed*] (SEIS)
NPR	Napper (ABBR)
NPR	Narodowa Partia Robotnicza [*National Workers Party*] [*Poland*] [*Political party*] (PPE)
NPR	National Aeronautics and Space Administration Procurement Regulation [*A publication*] (AAGC)
NPR	National Parks and Access to the Countryside Regulations [*Town planning*] [*British*]
NPR	National Partnership for Reinventing Government
NPR	National Performance Review [*A publication*]
NPR	National Public Radio [*Washington, DC*] [*Telecommunications*] (TSSD)
NPR	Naval Petroleum Reserves
NPR	Naval Plant Representative
NPR	Navy Payroll (DNAB)
NPR	Navy Preliminary Revision (DNAB)
NPR	Navy Procurement Regulation
NPR	Negro Puerto Rican
NPR	Neoricans in Puerto Rico (EA)
NPR	Neptune Resources Corp. [*Toronto Stock Exchange symbol*]
NPR	Net Pool Return
NPR	Net Protein Ratio [*Nutrition*]
NPR	Network Process Engineering (SAUS)
NPR	New Plan Realty Trust SBI [*NYSE symbol*] (SPSG)
NPR	New Plan Rlty Tr SBI [*NYSE symbol*] (TTSB)
NPR	New Production Reactor [*Department of Energy*]
NPR	Night Press Rate [*of newspapers*]
NPR	Nisi Prius Reports [*A publication*] (DLA)
NPR	Noise Pollution Ratio (SAUS)
NPR	Noise Power Ratio
NPR	Noise Prediction and Reduction
NPR	Noise Preferential Route [*Aviation*] (DA)
NPR	Nonperiodic Review (TIMI)
NPR	Non Persistant Reference (SAUS)
NPR	Non-Procedural Reference (SAUS)
NPR	Nonprocessor Request (IAA)
NPR	Nonproduction Release (MCD)
NPR	No Power Recovery (SAUS)
NPR	Normal Pulse Rate [*Medicine*] (DMAA)
NPR	North Polar Region
NPR	Notice of Program Reimbursement (MEDA)
NPR	Notice of Proposed Rule Making [*Federal agencies*] (GFGA)
NPR	Nozzle Pressure Ratio [*Aviation*]
NPR	Nuclear Paramagnetic Resonance (MCD)
NPR	Nuclear Posture Review [*DoD*]
NPR	Nuclear Power Reactor
NPR	Nuclear Pulse Rocket [*NASA*]
NPR	Nucleoside Phosphoribosyl (DMAA)
NPR	Numerical Position Readout (IAA)
NPR	Numeric Position Readout (SAUS)
NPR	Office of New Production Reactors (SAUS)
NPr	Pearl River Public Library, Pearl River, NY [*Library symbol*] [*Library of Congress*] (LCLS)
NPrA	American Cyanamid Co., Lederle Laboratories, Pearl River, NY [*Library symbol*] [*Library of Congress*] (LCLS)
NPRA	National Parks and Recreation Act of 1978 (COE)
NPRA	National Parks and Recreation Association (NADA)
NPRA	National Personal Robot Association [*Later, NSRA*] (EA)
NPRA	National Petroleum Refiners Association (EA)
NPRA	National Petroleum Reserve-Alaska
NPRA	Naval Personnel Research Activity
NPRA	Newspaper Personnel Relations Association (EA)
NPR&D	Navy Property Redistribution and Disposal (AAGC)
N/P Ratio......	Nitrogen/Phosphorus Ratio (SAUS)
NPRC	National Personnel Records Center [*National Archives and Records Service*]
NPRC	National Polystyrene Recycling Co.
NPRC	National Project on Resource Coordination for Justice Statistics and Information [*Canada*]

NPRC	National Public Relations Council of Health and Welfare Services [*Formerly, NPC*]
NPRC	National Puerto Rican Coalition (EA)
NPRC	Newspaper Production and Research Center
NPRC	Nonproliferation Program Review Committee [*US, multiagency*]
NPRC	Nuclear Power Range Channel (IEEE)
NPRC (CPR)	National Personnel Records Center (Civilian Personnel Records) [*National Archives and Records Service*] (AFM)
NPRCG	Nuclear Public Relations Contact Group
NPRC (MPR)	National Personnel Records Center (Military Personnel Records) [*National Archives and Records Service*] (AFM)
NPRD	NASA Procurement Regulation Directive
NPRD	Nonelectronic Parts Reliability Data (MCD)
NPRD	Nuclear Plant Reliability Data
NPRDA	National Precure Retread Dealers Association [*Defunct*] (EA)
NPRDC	National Public Resources Defense Council (NUCP)
NPRDC	Navy Personnel Research and Development Center (GRD)
NPRDL	Naval Personnel Research and Development Laboratory
NPRDS	Nuclear Plant Reliability Data System (NRCH)
NPres	National Preserve
NPRF	National Priority Reserve Fund [*Australia*]
NPRF	National Puerto Rican Forum (EA)
NPRF	Noise Power Ratio Floor (SAUS)
NPRF	Northrop Pulse Radiation Facility
NPRFT	Nonprofit (ABBR)
NPRH	Nurse Practitioners in Reproductive Health (SAUS)
NPRI	Nasopharyngeal Radium Irradiation [*Medicine*] (MELL)
NPRI	National Psychiatric Reform Institute
NPRIS	Nuclear Planning & Resource Information System (SAUS)
NPRL	Navy Prosthetics Research Laboratory
NPRL	Nonprocedural Referencing Language
NPRL	No Parallel Traffic (SAUS)
NPRM	Neopharm Inc. [*NASDAQ symbol*] (TTSB)
NPRM	Notice of Proposed Rule Making [*Federal agencies*]
NPRMW	Neopharm Inc. Wrrt [*NASDAQ symbol*] (TTSB)
NPRN	Neoprene [*Synthetic rubber*]
NPRN	North American Public Relations Network (NTPA)
NPRO	NaPro BioTherapeutics, Inc. [*NASDAQ symbol*] (SAG)
NPRO	Naval Petroleum Reserves Office
NPRO	Naval Representative Offices (ACAE)
NPRO	Navy Plant Representative Office
NPRO	N-Nitrosoproline [*Organic chemistry*]
NPRO	Non-Process Run-Out (SAUS)
NPROA	Nitrosoprolylalanine [*Organic chemistry*]
N Process	Normal Process (SAUS)
NPROCL	Non-Procedural Language (VLIE)
NPROG	Nitrosoprolylglycine [*Organic chemistry*]
N-Project	Nuclear-power Project (SAUS)
N-Proliferation	Nuclear Proliferation (SAUS)
N-Propulsion	Nuclear Propulsion (SAUS)
NPROW	Napro Biotheraputics Wrrts [*NASDAQ symbol*] (TTSB)
NPRP	Northern Pecan Research Program (SAUS)
NPRPA	Naval Petroleum Reserves Production Act (AAGC)
NPRR	National Public Relations Roundtable [*Defunct*]
NPRR	Net Pool Return Rule
NPRS	NASA Procurement Regulation Supplement
NPRS	Negative Poll Response State (IAA)
NPRS	Newpark Resources, Inc. [*NASDAQ symbol*] (SAG)
NPRS	Nonpersistent (FAAC)
NPRTSN	Nonpartisan (ABBR)
NPRTSNSP	Nonpartisanship (ABBR)
NPRTX	Neub. & Berman Partners Fund [*Mutual fund ticker symbol*] (SG)
NPRTZ	Nonpolarized Return-to-Zero Recording (SAUS)
NPRV	Nitrogen Pressure Relief Valve
NPRWC	National Puerto Rican Women's Caucus [*Defunct*] (EA)
NPRZ	Non-Polarized Return-to-Zero Recording (VLIE)
NPS	Counts per Second (IDOE)
NPS	Honolulu, HI [*Location identifier*] [*FAA*] (FAAL)
NPS	Narcotics Prevention Service (NADA)
NPS	NASA Planning Studies (KSC)
NPS	Nationale Partij Suriname [*Surinam National Party*] [*Political party*] (PPW)
NPS	National Park Service [*Department of the Interior*]
NPS	National Parole Service [*Canada*]
NPS	National Periodicals System
NPS	National Permit Strategy [*Environmental Protection Agency*] (GFGA)
NPS	National Pesticide Survey [*Environmental Protection Agency*] (GFGA)
NPS	National Philatelic Society [*Defunct*] (EA)
NPS	National Phone Services, Inc.
NPS	National Poetry Secretariat [*British*] [*An association*] (DBA)
NPS	National Poetry Series
NPS	National Pony Society [*British*] (DI)
NPS	National Prisoner Statistics [*An association*]
NPS	Naval Postgraduate School
NPS	Navy Personnel Survey
NPS	Navy Primary Standards (MSA)
NPS	Neapolis [*Greece*] [*Seismograph station code, US Geological Survey*] (SEIS)
NPS	Negative Potential Shifts [*Neurophysiology*]
NPS	Network Photo System (SAUS)
NPS	Network Processing Supervisor [*Honeywell, Inc.*]
NPS	Network Processor System (NITA)
NPS	Network Product Support [*Computer science*] (VLIE)
NPS	Neutral Pressure Switch
NPS	New Products Support (VLIE)
NPS	Newspaper Pagination System [*Typography*] (DGA)
NPS	Night Photographic System
NPS	Night Pilotage System (ACAE)
NPS	Ninhydrin-Positive-Substance (SAUS)
NPS	Nitrided Pressureless Sintering (SAUS)
NPS	Nitrophenyl Sulfenyl [*Organic chemistry*]
Nps	Nitrophenylthio(nitrophenylsulfonyl) [*Biochemistry*]
NPS	Noise Power Spectra [*Spectrometry*]
NPS	Nominal Pipe Size (SAA)
NPS	Noncumulative Preferred Stock [*Investment term*] (MHDW)
NPS	Non-Parallel Share (SAUS)
NPS	Nonperishable Subsistence
NPS	Non-Pneumatic Spare [*Automotive engineering*]
NPS	Nonpoint Source [*Environmental Protection Agency*] (AEPA)
NPS	Nonpoint Source Pollution [*Agricultural engineering*]
NPS	Non-Prior Service (MCD)
NPS	Non-Professorial Staff (SAUS)
NPS	No-Par Stock [*Investment term*] (MHDW)
NPS	No Prior Service [*Military*]
NPS	Normalized Plateau Slope
NPS	Normal Pipe Size
NPS	North Polar Sequence
NPS	Northwestern Public Service Co. [*NYSE symbol*] (SPSG)
NPS	Northwestern Pub Svc [*NYSE symbol*] (TTSB)
NPs	Notaries Public (SAUS)
NPS	Notice Papers-Senate (SAUS)
NPS	Novell Productivity Specialist [*Computer science*] (VLIE)
NPS	Nuclear and Plasma Sciences (MCD)
NPS	Nuclear Planning System (COE)
NPS	Nuclear Power Source
NPS	Nuclear Power Station (SAUS)
NPS	Nuclear Power System
NPS	Numerical Plotting System (VLIE)
NPS	NWPS Capital Financing Tr PERCS [*NYSE symbol*] (SAG)
NPS	US National Park Service (SAUS)
NPSA	National Passenger Safety Association [*Defunct*] (EA)
NPSA	National Pecan Shellers Association (EA)
NPSA	National Pegboard Systems Association (EA)
NPSA	National Psychic Science Association (EA)
NPSA	New Program Status Area (IEEE)
NPSA	Novitiate of Saint Andrew-On-Hudson, Poughkeepsie, NY [*Library symbol*] [*Library of Congress*] (LCLS)
NPSAPHA	New Professionals Section of the American Public Health Association (SAUS)
NPSAS	National Postsecondary Student Aid Study [*Department of Education*] (GFGA)
NPSB	National Prisoner Statistics Bulletin [*Department of Justice*]
NPSB	News Print Service Bureau
NPS BBS	Nonpoint Source Electronic Bulletin Board System [*Environmental Protection Agency*] (AEPA)
NPSC	Naval Personnel Separation Center
NPSC	New Paradigm Software [*NASDAQ symbol*] (SAG)
NPSC	Nursing Policy Studies Centre [*University of Warwick*] [*British*] (CB)
NPS-CL	Nitrophenyl Sulfenyl Chloride
NPS/CPSU/UW	National Park Service Cooperative Park Studies Unit, University of Washington [*Research center*] (RCD)
NPSCW	New Paradigm Software Wrrt [*NASDAQ symbol*] (TTSB)
NPSD	Naval Photographic Services Depot
NPSD	Neutron Power Spectral Density (OA)
NPSD	Noise Power Spectre Density
NPSD	Noise Power Spectrum Density (SAUS)
NPSD	Normalized Power Spectral Density (SAUS)
NPSDN	Nordic Packet Switched Data Network (NITA)
NPSE	National Premium Sales Executives (EA)
NPSE	Navy Peridontal Screening Examination (DNAB)
NPSF	National Pipe Straight Fine [*Mechanical engineering*]
NPSF	National Straight Pipe Threads for Dry Seal Pressure Tight Joints
NPSFR	Net Public Sector Financing Requirement [*Business term*]
NPSG	NPS Technologies Group, Inc. (SAUS)
NPSH	National Straight Pipe Threads for Hose Couplings and Nipples
NPSH	Net Positive Suction Head [*Pumps*]
NPSH	Niagara Parks School of Horticulture (SAUS)
NPSH	Nonprotein Sulfhydryl [*Biochemistry*]
NPSH	Not Positive Suction Head (COE)
NPSHA	Net Positive Suction Head Available [*Pumps*] (PDAA)
NPSHR	Net Positive Suction Head Required [*Chemical or food processing*]
NPSI	National Pipe Straight Intermediate [*Mechanical engineering*]
NPSI	Network Control Program Packet Switching Interface [*Computer science*] (HGAA)
NPSI	Network Packet Switch Interface [*Computer science*] (VLIE)
NPSI	Network Protocol Service Interface [*Computer science*] (VLIE)
NPSI	Nursing Performance Simulation Instrument
NPSL	National Professional Soccer League [*Later, NASL*]
NPSL	National Straight Pipe Threads for Locknuts and Locknut Pipe Threads
NPSM	Non-Productive Standard Minute (PDAA)
NPSMS	Nonpoint Source Management System (WPI)
NPSNL	South Eastern New York Library Resources Council, Poughkeepsie, NY [*Library symbol*] [*Library of Congress*] (LCLS)
NPSO	Nonpaired Spatial Orbitals [*Atomic physics*]
NPSP	National People's Salvation Party [*Zambia*] [*Political party*] (EY)
NPSP	Net Positive Static Pressure (NASA)
NPSP	Net Positive Suction Pressure [*Cryogenics*]
NPSP	N-Phenylselenenylphthalimide [*Organic chemistry*]
NPSP	NPS Pharmaceuticals [*NASDAQ symbol*] (TTSB)

NPsP............	Paul Smiths College, Paul Smiths, NY [*Library symbol*] [*Library of Congress*] (LCLS)
NPSPA	National Pecan Shellers and Processors Association (EA)
NPS Phm.....	NPS Pharmaceutical, Inc. [*Associated Press*] (SAG)
NPSPrA.........	NWPS Cap Fin 8.125% Tr Sec 1 [*NYSE symbol*] (TTSB)
NPSR...........	No Primary Staff Responsibility [*Army*] (AABC)
NPSRA.........	National Professional Squash Racquets Association (EA)
NPSRC.........	National Professional Standards Review Council [*Terminated, 1982*] [*HEW*] (EGAO)
NPSRI	National Public Services Research Institute
NPSS	IEEE Nuclear and Plasma Sciences Society (EA)
NPSS	NASA Packet Switch System (SAUS)
NPSS	National Police and Security Service [*Republic of Vietnam*]
NPSS	National Proficiency Survey Series [*Scannell*] (TES)
NPSS	Noms Propres Sud-Semitiques [*A publication*] (BJA)
NPSS	Non-Public School Section [*American Association of School Librarians*]
NPSS	Nordic Post Security Service
NPSS	Nuclear and Plasma Sciences Society (SAUS)
NPSST	Nuclear and Plasma Science Symposium (MCD)
NPST	Native Pituitary-Derived Somatotropin [*Endocrinology*]
NPST	Native Porcine Somatotropin [*Endocrinology*]
NPSTN	National Public Switched Telecommunications Network (MHDI)
NPSU	Nuclear Plant Safety Unit (SAUS)
NPSWL	New Program Status Word Location
NPSWU	Newpark Resources Uts (SAUS)
NPT	Executive Aviation Services (SAUS)
NPT	Nasal Provocation Test [*Immunology*]
NPT	National Periodic Test [*Telecommunications*] (OTD)
NPT	National Petroleum Corp. Ltd. [*Toronto Stock Exchange symbol*]
NPT	National Pipe Taper [*Mechanical engineering*]
NPT	National Pipe Thread (GOBB)
NPT	National Taper Pipe [*Thread*]
NPT	Navy Pointer Tracker (MCD)
NPT	Neomycin Phosphotransferase [*An enzyme*]
NPT	Neoprecipitin Test [*Oncology*]
NPT	Neopyrithiamine Hydrochloride [*Chemistry*] (DAVI)
NPT	Network Planning Technique [*Computer science*] (IEEE)
NPT	Neuroectodermal Pigmented Tumor [*Medicine*] (MELL)
NPT	Neuropsychiatry
NPT	Neuropsychiatry Technician [*Navy*]
NPT	New Periodical Titles [*of British Union Catalogue of Periodicals*]
NPT	Newport [*Rhode Island*] [*Airport symbol*] (OAG)
NPT	Newport Ebbw Junction [*British depot code*]
NPT	New Product Tiers [*Telecommunications*] (OTD)
NPT	Nocturnal Penile Tumescence [*Psychiatry*]
NPT	Noise Protection Transformer (SAUS)
NPT	Non-Packet-making Terminal (SAUS)
NPT	Non-Packet Mode Terminal (MHDB)
NPT	Non-Packet-mode Terminal (SAUS)
NPT	Nonprogrammable Terminal (SAUS)
NPT	Non-Proliferation Treaty (MUSM)
NPT	Non-Punch Through (AAEL)
NPT	Nonpyramidal Tract
NPT	Normal Pressure and Temperature
NPT	Nuclear Non-Proliferation Treaty [*United Nations*] (ECON)
NPT	Nuclear Proliferation Treaty (SAUS)
NPT	Nucleoside Phosphotransferase (DB)
NPT	Nuveen Prem Income Muni 4 [*NYSE symbol*] (TTSB)
NPT	Nuveen Premium Income Municipal Fund IV [*NYSE symbol*] (SPSG)
NPT	Portland Terminal R. R. Co. [*Formerly, Northern Pacific Terminal R. R.*] [*AAR code*]
NPTA	National Paper Trade Association (EA)
NPTA	National Passenger Traffic Association [*Later, NBTA*] (EA)
NPTA	National Perishable Transportation Association (EA)
NPTA	National Piano Travelers Association (EA)
NPTA	National Postal Transport Association [*Later, APWU*]
NPTA	Nevada Parent Teacher Association (SAUS)
NPTA	New Periodical Title Abbreviations [*A publication*]
NPTA	Nordstrom Personal Touch America [*E-mail shopping service*]
NPTC	National Postal and Travelers Censorship [*Army*] (AABC)
NPTC	National Private Truck Council (NTPA)
NPTC	National Proficiency Test Council (AIE)
NPtc............	Port Chester Public Library, Port Chester, NY [*Library symbol*] [*Library of Congress*] (LCLS)
NPTCO	National Postal and Travelers Censorship Organization [*Army*] (AABC)
NPTcU	United Hospital, Port Chester, NY [*Library symbol*] [*Library of Congress*] (LCLS)
NPTD	Nitrogen Phosphorus Thermionic Detector [*Instrumentation*]
NPT/E...........	Navy Parachute Team / East Coast (DNAB)
NPte............	Port Ewen Free Library, Port Ewen, NY [*Library symbol*] [*Library of Congress*] (LCLS)
NPTF...........	National Pipe Thread Fine (SARE)
NPTF...........	National Taper Pipe Threads for Dry Seal Pressure Tight Joints
NPTF...........	Nuclear Power Task Force
NPTF...........	Nuclear Proof Test Facility [*Proposed, but never built*] (NRCH)
NPTFB	National Park Trust Fund Board [*Later, NPF*]
NPTG	Nuclear Power Task Group [*Navy*] (MCD)
NPTH	NeoPath, Inc. [*NASDAQ symbol*] (SAG)
NPTI...........	Nissan Performance Technology, Inc.
NPtjer	Port Jervis Free Public Library, Port Jervis, NY [*Library symbol*] [*Library of Congress*] (LCLS)
NPTL...........	National Police Testing Laboratories (EA)
NPTL...........	Nuptial (ABBR)

NPTN	National Pesticide Telecommunication Network (EA)
NPTN	National Public Telecomputing Network (TNIG)
NPTO	National Petroleum Technology Office
NPTR	National Parachute Test Range (MCD)
NPTR	National Taper Pipe Threads for Railing Fixtures
NPTRE	Nuclear-Powered Turbo-Reciprocating Engine
NPTRL	Naval Personnel and Training Research Laboratory [*Formerly, Personnel Research Activity*]
NPTS	Nationwide Personal Transportation Study [*Department of Transportation*] (GFGA)
NPTS	Nationwide Personal Transportation Survey [*BTS*] [*FHWA*] (TAG)
NPTS	Noise Parameter Test System (SAUS)
NPTSM	Nepotism (ABBR)
NPTST	Nepotist (ABBR)
NPTT	Nocturnal Penile Tumescence Test [*Medicine*] (MELL)
NPTU	Naval Petroleum Training Unit (DNAB)
NPT/W	Navy Parachute Team / West Coast (DNAB)
NPtw	Port Washington Public Library, Port Washington, NY [*Library symbol*] [*Library of Congress*] (LCLS)
NptwDE........	Daly Elementary School, Port Washington, NY [*Library symbol*] [*Library of Congress*] (LCLS)
NPtwGE........	Guggenheim Elementary School, Port Washington, NY [*Library symbol*] [*Library of Congress*] (LCLS)
NPtwJSE.......	John Philip Sousa Elementary School, Port Washington, NY [*Library symbol*] [*Library of Congress*] (LCLS)
NptwME........	Manorhaven Elementary School, Port Washington, NY [*Library symbol*] [*Library of Congress*] (LCLS)
NPtwMSE......	Main Street Elementary School, Port Washington, NY [*Library symbol*] [*Library of Congress*] (LCLS)
NPtwSH	Paul D. Schreiber High School, Port Washington, NY [*Library symbol*] [*Library of Congress*] (LCLS)
NPtwSSE......	South Salem Elementary School, Port Washington, NY [*Library symbol*] [*Library of Congress*] (LCLS)
NPtwWJ.......	Carrie Palmer Weber Junior High School, Port Washington, NY [*Library symbol*] [*Library of Congress*] (LCLS)
NPTWZI	North Pacific Trade Winds Zone Investigation (NOAA)
NPTZ	North Pacific Transition Zone [*Marine science*] (OSRA)
NPU	National Pharmaceutical Union (PDAA)
NPU	National Postal Union [*Later, APWU*]
NPU	Naval Parachute Unit
NPU	Navigation Processor Unit (MCD)
NPU	Ne Plus Ultra [*No Further; i.e., the pinnacle of attainment*] [*French*]
NPU	Net Protein Utilization [*Nutrition*]
NPU	Network Processing Unit
NPU	Newspaper Press Union (DGA)
NPU	Nitrogen Pressure Unit (MCD)
NPU	Nitrogen Purge Unit (MCD)
NPU	Nordic Postal Union (EA)
NPU	Not Passed Urine [*Medicine*]
npubl	no publisher (SAUS)
NPUD...........	National Party for Unity and Democracy [*Mauritania*] [*Political party*] (EY)
NPUG	National Prime User Group (GNE)
NPUI	Nursing Process Utilization Inventory (DMAA)
NPUP	National Progressive Unionist Party [*Egypt*] [*Political party*] (PPW)
NPur	Purchase Free Library, Purchase, NY [*Library symbol*] [*Library of Congress*] (LCLS)
NPurMC	Manhattanville College, Purchase, NY [*Library symbol*] [*Library of Congress*] (LCLS)
NPurU	State University of New York, College at Purchase, Purchase, NY [*Library symbol*] [*Library of Congress*] (LCLS)
NPurW	Westchester Academy of Medicine, Purchase, NY [*Library symbol*] [*Library of Congress*] (LCLS)
NPV	National Present Volume Method [*Management*]
NPV	Naturpolitische Volkspartei [*People's Party for Nature Policy*] [*Germany*] [*Political party*] (PPW)
NPV	Negative Predictive Value [*Experimentation*]
NPV	Negative Pressure Ventilation [*Medicine*] (MELL)
NPV	Net Present Value [*Accounting*]
NPV	New Plymouth Ventures, Inc. [*Vancouver Stock Exchange symbol*]
NPV	Nitrogen Pressure Valve (KSC)
NPV	Nonpropulsive Vent (KSC)
NPV	No Par Value [*Stock exchange term*]
NPV	Nuclear Polyhedrosis Virus
NPV	Nuveen VA Prem Inc. Muni Fd [*NYSE symbol*] (TTSB)
NPV	Nuveen Virginia Premium Income Municipal Fund [*NYSE symbol*] (SPSG)
NPV	Vassar College, Poughkeepsie, NY [*Library symbol*] [*Library of Congress*] (LCLS)
NPVCE.........	Net Present Value for Current Expendable Launch Vehicles [*NASA*] (KSC)
NPVH	Net Present Value at the Horizon (PDAA)
NPVLA	National Paint, Varnish, and Lacquer Association [*Later, NPCA*] (EA)
NPV-Mu	Vassar College, George Sherman Dickerson Music Library, Poughkeepsie, NY [*Library symbol*] [*Library of Congress*] (LCLS)
NPVNE........	Net Present Value for New Expendable Launch Vehicles [*NASA*] (KSC)
NPVS	No-Par-Value Stock [*Stock exchange term*]
NPVSH	Net Present Value for Space Shuttle [*NASA*] (KSC)
NPW	International Union of Allied Novelty and Production Workers
NPW	National Party of Western Australia [*Political party*]
NPW	Network for Professional Women [*Hartford, CT*] (EA)
npw.............	New-Pool Wildcat (SAUS)
NPW	Nissan Production Way [*Automotive manufacturing*]
NPW	No Peace Without Justice [*An association*]

NPW .... Nuveen WA Prem Inc. Muni Fd [*AMEX symbol*] (TTSB)
NPW .... Nuveen Washington Premium Income Municipal Fund [*AMEX symbol*] (SPSG)
NPWA .... National Pure Water Association [*British*]
NPWAC .... National Parks and Wildlife Advisory Council [*Tasmania, Australia*]
NPwADS ...... National Power PLC [*Associated Press*] (SAG)
NPWC .... National Parks and Wildlife Conservation Act (SAUS)
NPWC .... National Press Women's Club (NTCM)
NPWC .... Navy Public Works Center
NPWD .... Navy Public Works Department
NPWFNSW... National Parks and Wildlife Foundation of New South Wales [*Australia*]
NPWIC .... National Prisoner of War Information Center (DOMA)
NPWOA .... National Piggly Wiggly Operators Association (EA)
NPWRC .... Northern Prairie Wildlife Research Center [*Jamestown, ND*] [*Department of the Interior*] (GRD)
NPWS .... NATO Planning Workshop (NATG)
NPX .... New Pioneer Exploration [*Vancouver Stock Exchange symbol*]
NPX .... Norpropoxyphene (DB)
NPX .... Numeric Processor Extension (SAUS)
NPX .... Nuveen Ins Prem Inc. Muni 2 [*NYSE symbol*] (TTSB)
NPX .... Nuveen Insured Premium Income Municipal Fund [*NYSE symbol*] (SPSG)
NPY .... Neuropeptide Y [*Biochemistry*]
NPY .... Nuveen PA Prem Inc. Muni 2 [*NYSE symbol*] (TTSB)
NPY .... Nuveen Pennsylvania Premium Income Municipal [*NYSE symbol*] (SPSG)
NPy .... Penn Yan Public Library, Penn Yan, NY [*Library symbol*] [*Library of Congress*] (LCLS)
NPYLI .... Neuropeptide Y-Like Immunoreactivity [*Medicine*] (DB)
NPYR .... Nitrosopyrrolidine [*Also, NYPYR*] [*Organic chemistry*]
NPYRR .... N-Nitrosopyrrolidine [*Organic chemistry*]
NPZ .... New Plymouth [*New Zealand*] [*Seismograph station code, US Geological Survey*] [*Closed*] (SEIS)
NPZ .... North Pyrenean Zone [*Geology*]
NQ .... Cumberland Airlines [*ICAO designator*] (AD)
NQ .... Net Quick Assets
NQ .... Neural Quantum [*Theory*] [*Sensory discrimination*]
NQ .... Neurological Quotient (SAUS)
nq .... Nicaragua [*MARC country of publication code*] [*Library of Congress*] (LCCP)
NQ .... No Quotations (SAUS)
NQ .... No Quote (SAUS)
NQ .... Northwest Territorial Airlines (SAUS)
NQ .... Quoque Library, Quoque, NY [*Library symbol*] [*Library of Congress*] (LCLS)
NQA .... Memphis, TN [*Location identifier*] [*FAA*] (FAAL)
NQA .... National Quality Award [*LIMRA, NALU*]
NQA .... National Quilting Association (EA)
NQA .... Net Quick Assets
NQA .... No Questions Asked (SAUS)
NQA .... North Carolina Agricultural and Technical State University, Greensboro (SAUS)
NQA .... North Carolina Agricultural and Technical State University, Greensboro, NC [*OCLC symbol*] (OCLC)
NQA .... Nursing Quality Assurance (DMAA)
NQAA .... Nuclear Quality Assurance Agency
NQAPO .... Nuclear Quality Assurance Program Office (SAUS)
NQB .... National Quotation Bureau [*Stock market*]
NQB .... No Qualified Bidders [*Investment term*] (DFIT)
NQC .... NASA Quality Control (KSC)
NQC .... National Quotations Committee [*of the National Association of Securities Dealers*]
NQC .... Nuclear Quality Control (DNAB)
NQC .... Nuveen CA Inv Qual Muni [*NYSE symbol*] (TTSB)
NQC .... Nuveen California Investment Quality Municipal Fund [*NYSE symbol*] (SPSG)
NQCC .... Nuclear Quadrupole Coupling Constant [*Physics*]
NQCRRP ...... North Queensland Community Rainforest Reforestation Program (SAUS)
NQD .... Nonquaded [*Telecommunications*] (TEL)
NQD .... Notice of Quality Discrepancy
NQE .... Nuclear Quality Engineering (DNAB)
NQF .... Nuveen FL Inv Qua Muni [*NYSE symbol*] (TTSB)
NQF .... Nuveen Florida Investment Quality Municipal [*NYSE symbol*] (SPSG)
NQHR .... National Quarter Horse Registry (EA)
NQI .... Kingsville, TX [*Location identifier*] [*FAA*] (FAAL)
NQI .... Nuveen Ins Qual Muni [*NYSE symbol*] (TTSB)
NQI .... Nuveen Insured Quality Municipal [*NYSE symbol*] (SPSG)
NQIC .... National Quality Information Centre [*Institute of Quality Assurance*] [*Information service or system*] (IID)
NQJ .... Nuveen New Jersey Investment Quality Municipal [*NYSE symbol*] (SPSG)
NQJ .... Nuveen NJ Inv Qua Muni [*NYSE symbol*] (TTSB)
NQKA .... Northwest Quoin Key Association [*Defunct*] (EA)
NQL .... National Quick Lube Ltd. [*Vancouver Stock Exchange symbol*]
NQL .... North Queensland Libraries: A Directory [*Australia*] [*A publication*]
NQL .... Nouveau Quartier Latin [*Paris bookstore*]
NQL .... Nuclear Quadrupole Interaction [*Physics*]
NQLA .... North Queensland Logging Association [*Australia*]
NQM .... Midway/Henderson Naval Station, HI [*Location identifier*] [*FAA*] (FAAL)
NQM .... Navy Quality Management
NQM .... Nuveen Investment Quality Municipal [*NYSE symbol*] (SPSG)
NQM .... Nuveen Inv Quality Muni [*NYSE symbol*] (TTSB)

NQMFP .... North Queensland Multifunction Polis [*Australia*]
NQN .... Neuquen [*Argentina*] [*Airport symbol*] (OAG)
NQN .... Nuveen New York Investment Quality Municipal Fund [*NYSE symbol*] (SPSG)
NQN .... Nuveen NY Inv Qual Muni [*NYSE symbol*] (TTSB)
NQN .... Transportes Aereos Neuquen [*Argentina*] [*ICAO designator*] (FAAC)
NQNS .... Notes & Queries, New Series (SAUS)
NQO .... Nitroquinoline Oxide [*Organic chemistry*]
NQOKD .... Not Quite Our Kind, Dear (SAUS)
NQOS .... Not Quite Our Sort (IIA)
NQOT .... Not Quite Our Type (SAUS)
NQP .... Nuveen PA Inv Qua Muni [*NYSE symbol*] (TTSB)
NQP .... Nuveen Pennsylvania Investment Quality Municipal [*NYSE symbol*] (SPSG)
NQPA .... National Quarter Pony Association (EA)
NQPC .... National Quartz Producers Council (EA)
NQPP .... National Quarantine Publicity Program [*Australia*]
NQR .... New Quebec Raglan Mines Ltd. [*Toronto Stock Exchange symbol*]
NQR .... Non-Quadratic Residues (MHDB)
NQR .... Nuclear Quadruple Resonance (SAUS)
NQR .... Nuclear Quadrupole Resonance [*Frequencies*]
NQRC .... National Quadraphonic Radio Committee
NQR Frequency... Nuclear Quadrupole Resonance Frequency (SAUS)
NQRL .... Nor-Quest Resources Ltd. (SAUS)
NQRR .... Nuclear Quadrupole Resonance Response
NQRS .... Nuclear Quadrupole Resonance Spectroscopy (SAUS)
NQS .... Nuveen Select Quality Municipal [*NYSE symbol*] (SPSG)
NQS .... Nuveen Select Qual Muni [*NYSE symbol*] (TTSB)
NQSO .... Nonqualified Stock Options (WYGK)
NQSQ .... Nonqualified Stock Option (SAUS)
NQT .... Network Quality Tester (NITA)
NQT .... Newly Qualified to Teach (GFGA)
NQT .... Nonlanguage Qualification Test
NQT .... Nor-Quest Resources Ltd. [*Vancouver Stock Exchange symbol*]
NQTGCA....... North Queensland Tobacco Growers Cooperative Association [*Australia*]
NQ Theory ... Neural Quantum Theory (SAUS)
NQTV .... North Queensland Television [*Australia*]
NQU .... Not Quite Us [*Lower in social status*] [*Slang*] [*British*]
NQU .... Nuqui [*Colombia*] [*Airport symbol*] (OAG)
NQU .... Nuveen Qual Income Muni Fd [*NYSE symbol*] (TTSB)
NQU .... Nuveen Quality Income Municipal Fund [*NYSE symbol*] (SPSG)
NQWMI........ Non-Q-Wave Myocardial Infarction [*Cardiology*] (CPH)
NQX .... Key West, FL [*Location identifier*] [*FAA*] (FAAL)
NQY .... Newquay [*England*] [*Airport symbol*] (OAG)
NR .... Bosanquet and Puller's New Reports, English Common Pleas [*1804-07*] [*A publication*] (DLA)
NR .... CSE Aviation Ltd. (SAUS)
NR .... Nachrichtenregiment [*Signal Regiment*] [*German military - World War II*]
NR .... Narrow Resonance [*Nuclear energy*] (NRCH)
NR .... Natal Reports [*South Africa*] [*A publication*] (DLA)
NR .... National Range
NR .... National Recovery Act
NR .... National Recovery Administration [*Voided by Supreme Court, 1935*]
NR .... National Register (COE)
NR .... National Report (OICC)
NR .... National Reporter [*Maritime Law Book Co. Ltd.*] [*Canada*] [*Information service or system*] (CRD)
NR .... National Reserve [*British military*] (DMA)
NR .... NATO Restricted (NATG)
NR .... Natural Resources
NR .... Natural Rubber
NR .... Nauru [*ANSI two-letter standard code*] (CNC)
NR .... Naval Rating
NR .... Naval Reactors (GAAI)
NR .... Naval Reserve
NR .... Navigational RADAR
NR .... Navy Regulations
NR .... Near (EY)
nr .... Near (VRA)
NR .... Negative Resistance [*Electronics*]
NR .... Negligible Risk (MELL)
NR .... Nerve Root (MELL)
NR .... Net Register [*Shipping*]
NR .... Neural Retina [*Ophthalmology*]
NR .... Neutral Red [*An indicator*]
NR .... Neutral-Reverse [*Automotive engineering*]
NR .... Neutron Radiography (SAUS)
NR .... Newhall Resources (SAUS)
NR .... Newpark Resources [*NYSE symbol*] (TTSB)
NR .... New Range (IAA)
NR .... New Reports [*1862-65*] [*England*] [*A publication*] (DLA)
NR .... New Republic (SAUS)
NR .... Next Renewal
NR .... Next to Reading Matter [*Also, NRM*] [*Advertising*] (NTCM)
NR .... Nicaraguan Resistance [*An association*] (EA)
NR .... Nicolaus Rufulus [*Flourished, 13th century*] [*Authority cited in pre-1607 legal work*] (DSA)
NR .... Nicotinamide Riboside (SAUS)
nr .... Nigeria [*MARC country of publication code*] [*Library of Congress*] (LCCP)
NR .... Nigeria Regiment [*British military*] (DMA)
NR .... Nitrate Reductase [*An enzyme*]
NR .... Nitrile Resin (SAUS)

NR	Nitrile Rubber [*Organic chemistry*]
NR	Nodal Rhythm [*Cardiology*] (DAVI)
NR	No-Good Recording (SAUS)
NR	Noise Rating (NASA)
NR	Noise Ratio
NR	Noise Ration
NR	Noise Reduction (IAA)
NR	Noise-Reduction (SAUS)
NR	Nonconformance Report [*Nuclear energy*] (NRCH)
NR	Nonlinear Resistance (IAA)
NR	Nonradiative (SAUS)
NR	Nonradioactive (SAUS)
NR	Nonrated
NR	Nonreactive [*Relay*]
NR	Nonrebreathing [*Medicine*] (AAMN)
nr	Non Recorded [*Genealogy*] (GEAB)
NR	Nonrecoverable (IEEE)
NR	Non-Recurring (ACAE)
NR	Nonreduced (SAUS)
NR	Nonredundancy (SAUS)
NR	Nonrefundable [*Airline fare code*]
NR	Nonregistered (AABC)
NR	Nonreimbursement (SAUS)
NR	Non Repetatur [*Do Not Repeat*] [*Pharmacy*]
NR	Nonresident [*British*]
NR	Nonresponder [*Strain of mice*]
NR	Non-Response (WDMC)
NR	Nonreturnable [*Beverage bottles*]
NR	Nonreversing (IAA)
NR	Nonspecific Gene Resistance [*Genetics*]
NR	No Radiation (MAE)
NR	NORAD Region (IAA)
NR	No Rate [*Travel industry*] (TVEL)
N/R	No Record (AAG)
NR	No Recurrence (SAUS)
NR	No Refill [*Pharmacy*]
NR	No Release (AAG)
NR	No Remittance
NR	No Report [*Medicine*]
NR	No Requirement
NR	No Residency Requirement [*Voter registration*]
NR	No Respiration (MELL)
NR	No Response [*Medicine*]
NR	No Return (SAUS)
NR	Norfolk Rangers [*British military*] (DMA)
NR	Norgold Russet Potato
NR	No Risk [*Business term*]
NR	Normal (MAE)
NR	Normal Range
N-R	Normal-Rebroadcast (SAUS)
NR	Normal Record [*Medicine*] (DAVI)
NR	Normal Responder
NR	Normotensive Rat [*Medicine*] (DMAA)
nr	norm-referenced (SAUS)
NR	Northern Range [*Navigation*]
NR	Northern Rhodesia [*Later, Zambia*]
NR	North Riding [*England*] (ROG)
NR	North River [*New York, New Jersey*]
NR	Northward Aviation Ltd. (MHDW)
NR	Nose Right [*Aviation*] (MCD)
N/R	Notes Receivable
NR	Notice of Rating Required [*Civil Service*]
N/R	Notice of Readiness [*Shipping*]
NR	Not Ranked (SAUS)
NR	Not Rated
NR	Not Readable
NR	Not Recommended (SAUS)
NR	Not Recorded
N/R	Not Remarkable [*Medicine*]
NR	Not Repeat (SAUS)
NR	Not Reported
NR	Not Required
NR	Not Resolved (MAE)
N/R	Not Responsible For
NR	Nuchal Rigidity [*Medicine*]
NR	Nuclear Radiation
NR	Nuclear Radiology [*Medical specialty*] (DHSM)
NR	Nuclear Reaction (SAUS)
NR	Nuclear Reactor
NR	Nuclear Reporting (SAUS)
NR	Nuclear Research Submarine (MCD)
NR	Nuestra Remesa [*Our Remittance*] [*Spanish*] [*Business term*]
NR	Nufort Resources, Inc. [*Toronto Stock Exchange symbol*]
NR	Number (AAG)
NR	Number of Report (SAUS)
NR	Number of Runs
NR	Nurse
NR	Nursing Representative [*Red Cross*]
NR	Nursing Services (HCT)
NR	Nutritive Ratio
NR	Nystagmus Recorder
NR	Reynold's Number [*Viscosity*] (MAE)
NR	Rochester Public Library, Rochester, NY [*Library symbol*] [*Library of Congress*] (LCLS)
nr---	Rocky Mountain Region [*MARC geographic area code*] [*Library of Congress*] (LCCP)
NR	Submersible Research Vehicle (Nuclear Propulsion) [*Navy ship symbol*]
NRA	Coupeville, WA [*Location identifier*] [*FAA*] (FAAL)
NRA	Narrandera [*Australia*] [*Airport symbol*] (OAG)
NRA	NASA Research Announcement
NRA	National Racing Authority (NADA)
NRA	National Reclamation Association [*Later, National Water Resources Association*] (EA)
NRA	National Record of Achievement [*British*] (DET)
NRA	National Recovery Act
NRA	National Recovery Administration [*Voided by Supreme Court, 1935*]
NRA	National Recreation Area [*National Park Service*] (GFGA)
NRA	National Recreation Association [*Later, NRPA*] (EA)
NRA	National Reform Association (EA)
NRA	National Register of Archives [*Historical Manuscripts Commission*] [*British*]
NRA	National Rehabilitation Association (EA)
NRA	National Remodelers Association [*Later, NARI*]
NRA	National Renderers Association (EA)
NRA	National Republican Alliance [*Australia*]
NRA	National Resistance Army [*Uganda*] (PD)
NRA	National Restaurant Association (EA)
NRA	National Retirement Association [*Australia*]
NRA	National Rifle Association (NADA)
NRA	National Rifle Association of America (EA)
NRA	National Rivers Authority [*British*]
NRA	National Roads Authority [*1997*] [*Malawi*]
NRA	National Roommate Association [*Later, ASRS*] (EA)
NRA	National Rounders Association [*British*] (BI)
NRA	NATO Refugees Agency (NATG)
NRA	Naval Radio Activity
NRA	Naval Reserve Association (EA)
NRA	Navy Recruiting Area (DNAB)
NRA	Negative Resistance Amplifier (PDAA)
NRA	Net Rentable Area (ADA)
NRA	Network Resolution Area
NRA	Never Refuse Anything (SAUS)
NRA	New Era Development Ltd. [*Vancouver Stock Exchange symbol*]
NRA	New Regional Airliner
NRA	Nitra Air [*Slovakia*] [*FAA designator*] (FAAC)
NRA	Nitrate Reductase (DB)
NRA	Non-Recurrrence Action (SAA)
NRA	Nonredundant Array
NRA	Nonregistered Accountable [*Military*]
NRA	Nonresident Alien
NRA	No Repair Action [*Military*]
NRA	Normal Retirement Age
NRA	North River [*Alaska*] [*Seismograph station code, US Geological Survey*] (SEIS)
NRA	Northrop Radio Service, Inc. (SAUS)
NRA	Nothing Recorded Against [*Security investigation result*] [*British*]
NRA	Nuclear Radiation Absorber
NRA	Nuclear Radiation Absorber (or Adsorber) (SAUS)
NRA	Nuclear Reaction Analysis
NRA	Nuclear Regulatory Agency
NRA	Nuclear Reserved Area (SAUS)
NRA	Nucleus Raphe Alatus [*Neurology*]
NRA	Nucleus Retroambigualis [*Neurology*] (DAVI)
NRA	St. Augustines College, Raleigh (SAUS)
NRA	St. Augustine's College, Raleigh, NC [*OCLC symbol*] (OCLC)
NRAA	National Railway Appliances Association [*Later, REMSA*] (EA)
NRAA	National Rehabilitation Administration Association (NTPA)
NRAA	National Renal Administrators Association (EA)
NRAA	National Rifle Association of America
NRAB	American Baptist Historical Society, Rochester, NY [*Library symbol*] [*Library of Congress*] (LCLS)
NRAB	National Railroad Adjustment Board
NRAB	National Railroad Adjustment Board Awards [*A publication*] (DLA)
NRAB	Naval Reserve Aviation Base
NRAB (1st D)	United States National Railroad Adjustment Board Awards, First Division [*A publication*] (DLA)
NRAB (2d D)	United States National Railroad Adjustment Board Awards, Second Division [*A publication*] (DLA)
NRAB (3d D)	United States National Railroad Adjustment Board Awards, Third Division [*A publication*] (DLA)
NRAB (4th D)	United States National Railroad Adjustment Board Awards, Fourth Division [*A publication*] (DLA)
NRAC	National Resources Analysis Center
NRAC	National Rural Advisory Council (NADA)
NRAC	Natural Resources Audit Council
NRAC	Naval Research Advisory Committee
NRACCO	Navy Regional Air Cargo Central [*or Control*] Office
NRAD	National Racquetball Association of the Deaf (EA)
NRaD	Naval Research and Development (SAUS)
NRAD	No Risk After Discharge [*Shipping*]
NRADUSA	National Racquetball Association of the Deaf of the USA [*Later, NRAD*] (EA)
NRAF	Naval Reserve Auxiliary Field
NRAF	Navy Recruiting Aids Facility (DNAB)
NRAF	Nonrheumatic Atrial Fibrillation [*Medicine*] (MELL)
NRAF	Not Running at Finish [*Automobile racing*]
NRAG	Naval Research Advisory Group (KSC)
NRAI	National Residential Appraisers Institute (EA)

NRAL .... New York State Appellate Division, Law Library, Rochester, NY [Library symbol] [Library of Congress] (LCLS)
NRAL .... No Risk after Landing (MARI)
NRALCC .... Northern Region Airlift Control Center (SAUS)
NRALD .... Northern Region Airlift Division (SAUS)
NRAM .... Non-Volatile Random Access Memory [Computer science]
NRAMEG ...... National Restaurant Association Marketing Executives Group [Defunct] (EA)
NRAMRG ..... National Restaurant Association Market Research Group [Defunct] (EA)
NR & HC ...... National Rivers and Harbors Congress [Later, WRC]
NRans .... Ransomville Free Library, Ransomville, NY [Library symbol] [Library of Congress] (LCLS)
NRAO .... National Radio Astronomy Observatory [Charlottesville, VA] [National Science Foundation] (GRD)
NRAO .... Navy Regional Accounts Office
NRAP .... Naturally Radioactive Product (NRCH)
NRAS .... National Radio Astronomy Observatory [Charlottesville, VA] [National Science Foundation] (GRD)
NRAS .... Navy Readiness Analysis System
nras .... No Risk after Shipment (MARI)
NRAS .... Nuclear Release Authentication System [Seventh Army] (AABC)
NRASF .... National Registry of Ambulatory Surgical Facilities (EA)
NRAT .... Nonrationed (AABC)
NRB .... Mayport, FL [Location identifier] [FAA] (FAAL)
NRB .... National Religious Broadcasters (EA)
NRB .... National Research Bureau [Commercial firm] (EA)
NRB .... National Resources Board [Terminated, 1935; functions transferred to National Resources Committee]
NRB .... National Roads Board (NADA)
NRB .... Natural Rubber Bureau [Later, MRB] (EA)
NRB .... Naval Reactor Branch (MUGU)
NRB .... Naval Repair Base
NRB .... Navy Recruiting Bureau
NRB .... Navy Reservation Bureau
NRB .... Nerve Root Block (MELL)
NRB .... New Redundancy Benefit [To reduce unemployment] [British]
NRB .... Nonconformance Review Board [Nuclear Regulatory Commission] (NRCH)
NRB .... Nonrejoining Break [Medicine] (DMAA)
NRB .... Non-Reportable Birth [Medicine] (MEDA)
NRB .... Normalized Relative Backscatter (ARMP)
NRB .... Northern Research Basins (SAUS)
NRB .... Nuclear Reactors Branch [AEC]
NRB .... Nuclear Resonance Broadening (SAUS)
NRB1CL .... Nuclear Reactor Operator, First-Class Badge [Military decoration] (GFGA)
NRB2CL .... Nuclear Reactor Operator, Second-Class Badge [Military decoration] (GFGA)
NRBA .... National Radio Broadcasters Association [NAB] [Absorbed by] (EA)
NRBA .... National Registered Builders Association [British] (DBA)
NRBBAS ...... Nuclear Reactor Operator, Basic Badge [Military decoration] (GFGA)
NRBC .... National Rare Blood Club [Later, NRBC/NYBC] (EA)
NRBC .... Normal Red Blood Cell [Medicine] (DMAA)
NRBC .... Nucleated Red Blood Cell
NRBC/NYBC... National Rare Blood Club/New York Blood Center (EA)
NRBE .... Native Races of the British Empire [A publication]
NRBF .... Normalized Radial Basis Function (IDAI)
NRBF .... Number of Rounds between Failures [Quality control] (MCD)
NRBL .... Bausch & Lomb, Inc., Rochester, NY [Library symbol] [Library of Congress] (LCLS)
NRBL-S .... Bausch & Lomb, Inc., SOFLENS Division, Technical Information Center, Rochester, NY [Library symbol] [Library of Congress] (LCLS)
NRBP .... Natural Resource-Based Product
NRBP .... New Reports of Bosanquet and Puller [A publication] (DLA)
NRBQ .... New Rhythm and Blues Quartet [Rock music group]
NRBQ .... Nurses' Registration Board of Queensland [Australia]
NRBS .... Navy Recruiting Branch Station (DNAB)
NRBS .... Nonrebreathing System [Medicine] (DAVI)
NRBSUPV .... Nuclear Reactor Operator, Shift Supervisor Badge [Military decoration] (GFGA)
NRC .... Crows Landing, CA [Location identifier] [FAA] (FAAL)
NRC .... NAC RE Corp. [NYSE symbol] (SAG)
NRC .... National Racquetball Club (EA)
NRC .... National Radio Club [Defunct] (EA)
NRC .... National Radio Conference [Broadcast regulations] (NTCM)
NRC .... National Railroad Construction and Maintenance Association, Inc. (EA)
NRC .... National Ramah Commission (EA)
NRC .... National Reading Conference (EA)
NRC .... National Realty Club [New York, NY] (EA)
NRC .... National Realty Committee [Washington, DC] (EA)
NRC .... National Reconditioning Order [National Weather Service] (USDC)
NRC .... National Records Center
NRC .... National Recycling Coalition (EA)
NRC .... National Recycling Corp. (EFIS)
NRC .... National Redemption Council [Ghana]
NRC .... National Referral Center [Defunct] (EA)
NRC .... National Register Criteria (COE)
NRC .... National Rehabilitation Center (MELL)
NRC .... National Remodelers Council [Later, NAHB/RC] (EA)
NRC .... National Replacement Character (AGLO)
NRC .... National Reprographic Centre for Documentation [British]
NRC .... National Republican Club (EA)

NRC .... National Republican Convention [Nigeria] [Political party]
NRC .... National Research Center (NATG)
NRC .... National Research Corp.
NRC .... National Research Council [National Academy of Sciences] [Washington, DC]
NRC .... National Research Council, Canada [Research center] (IRC)
NRC .... National Resistance Committee (EA)
NRC .... National Resource Center for Paraprofessionals in Special Education and Related Human Services (EA)
NRC .... National Resources Committee [Functions transferred to National Resources Planning Board]
NRC .... National Response Center [Environmental Protection Agency]
NRC .... National Retreat Centre [British] (CB)
NRC .... National Riding Committee [Later, ANRC] (EA)
NRC .... National Rocket Club [Later, NSC]
NRC .... National Rural Center (EA)
NRC .... Natural Resources Center [University of Alabama] [Research center] (RCD)
NRC .... Natural Resources Council of America (EA)
NRC .... Natural Rights Center (EA)
NRC .... Naval Radio Compass (IAA)
NRC .... Naval Radiological Control (DNAB)
NRC .... Naval Records Club [Later, INRO]
NRC .... Naval Recreation Center (DNAB)
NRC .... Naval Research Co. - Reserves
NRC .... Naval Retraining Command
NRC .... Navy Reconnaissance Center (MCD)
NRC .... Navy Recruiting Command (DNAB)
NRC .... Navy Reserve Centers (NVT)
NRC .... Negative Resistance Characteristic [Electrophysiology]
NRC .... Nerve Root Canal (MELL)
NRC .... Nerve Root Compression (MELL)
NRC .... Netherlands Red Cross
NRC .... Net Replacement Cost [Accounting]
NRC .... Networking Routing Center (MHDB)
NRC .... Network Reliability Coordinator
NRC .... Neutron Radiation Capture
NRC .... Newfoundland Safety Council (SAUS)
NRC .... Newport Research Corp. (SAUS)
NRC .... New Research Centers [A publication]
NRC .... New Right Coalition (EA)
NRC .... Newspaper Research Council (EA)
NRC .... Nichols Research Corporation (ACAE)
NRC .... Nigerian Railway Corp. (SAUS)
NRC .... Nitrogen Consumption Rate (DB)
NRC .... Noise-Rating Curve (OA)
NRC .... Noise Reduction Circuitry (SAUS)
NRC .... Noise Reduction Coefficient [of insulation]
NRC .... Nonrecurring Change (SAUS)
NRC .... Nonrecurring Charge (SAUS)
NRC .... Non-Recurring Charges (SAUS)
NRC .... Nonrecurring Connection (SAUS)
NRC .... Nonrecurring Costs [Accounting] (KSC)
NRC .... Nonrecurring Recoupment Charge (ACAE)
NRC .... Nonreusable Container (SAUS)
NRC .... Non-Reusable Containers (GNE)
NRC .... Non-unit-Related Cargo (DOMA)
NRC .... Noranda Research Center (SAUS)
NRC .... Norco Resources [Vancouver Stock Exchange symbol]
NRC .... No Record [Travel industry] (TVEL)
NRC .... Normal Rated Current (SAUS)
NRC .... Normal Retinal Correspondence
NRC .... North Carolina State University, Raleigh, NC [OCLC symbol] (OCLC)
NRC .... Norwegian Refugee Council
NRC .... Norwegian Research Council (SAUS)
NRC .... Notch Root Contraction (OA)
NRC .... Not Recommended for Children (ADA)
NRC .... Not Routine Care [Medicine]
NRC .... Nuclear Radiation Center [Washington State University] [Research center] (RCD)
NRC .... Nuclear Reactor Control (SAUS)
NRC .... Nuclear Recycling Consultants (EA)
NRC .... Nuclear Regulatory Commission [Washington, DC]
NRC .... Nuclear Reporting Cell (SAUS)
NRC .... Nuclear Research Council
NRC .... Nurses for the Rights of the Child (SAUS)
NRC .... Nutrition-Related Complications [Medicine]
NRC .... US National Research Council (SAUS)
NRCA .... National Reamer Collectors Association (EA)
NRCA .... National Rebel Class Association (EA)
NRCA .... National Recovery and Collection Association (EA)
NRCA .... National Redbone Coonhound Association (EA)
NRCA .... National Refrigeration Contractors Association (NTPA)
NRCA .... National Rehabilitation Counseling Association (EA)
NRCA .... National Resources Council of America
NRCA .... National Retail Credit Association [Later, ICA]
NRCA .... National Roofing Contractors Association (EA)
NRCA .... Nonconformance Reporting and Corrective Action (SAUS)
NRC-ACAC ... National Research Council Army Countermine Advisory Committee
NRCAR .... Nuclear Regulatory Commission Acquisition Regulation (AAGC)
NRCC .... National Registry in Clinical Chemistry (EA)
NRCC .... National Registry of Clinical Chemists (SARE)
NRCC .... National Republican Coalition for Choice (EA)
NRCC .... National Republican Congressional Committee (EA)
NRCC .... National Research Council of Canada

NRCC .... National Resource for Computation in Chemistry [*Lawrence Berkeley Laboratory*] [*Terminated, 1981*]
NRCC .... Naval Regional Contracting Center (AAGC)
NRCC .... NORAD Region Combat Center [*Military*]
NRCCL .... Norwegian Research Center for Computers and Law (NITA)
NRCCLS .... National Resource Center for Consumers of Legal Services (EA)
NRCCS .... National Research Council Committee on Salmonella (EA)
NRCD .... National Redemption Council Decree [*Ghana*] [*A publication*] (DLA)
NRCd .... National Reprographic Centre for Documentation [*Hatfield Polytechnic Institute*] [*Hertfordshire, England*] [*Evaluation and information group*] [*Information service or system*]
NRCd .... National Reprographic Centre for Documentation Study (NITA)
NRCDA .... North Region Cooperative Development Agency [*British*]
NRCDES .... National Research Council Division of Earth Sciences [*Marine science*] (OSRA)
NRC/DME ..... National Research Council of Canada, Division of Mechanical Engineering [*Research center*] (RCD)
NRCF .... Not Reconfirmed [*Travel industry*] (TVEL)
NRCHB .... Naval Reserve Cargo-Handling Battalion
NRCHMI........ National Resource Center on Homelessness and Mental Illness (EA)
NRCHTB .... Naval Reserve Cargo-Handling Training Battalion
NRCI .... National Radio Co., Inc. (IAA)
NRCI .... National Rainbow Coalition, Inc. (EA)
NRCI .... National Red Cherry Institute (EA)
NRCI .... Nuclear Regulatory Commission Issuances [*A publication*] (DLA)
NRCL .... National Research Council Library (DIT)
NRCL .... Nonrenal Clearance [*Medicine*] (DMAA)
NRCLS .... National Resource Center for Consumers of Legal Services (DLA)
NRCLSE .... National Resource for Computers in Life Science Education (SAUS)
NRC-MAC .... National Research Council - Mine Advisory Committee
NRC/MAI ...... National Railroad Construction and Maintenance Association, Inc. (EA)
NRCMC .... National Resource Center for Minority Contractors (EA)
NRCMCA....... National Radiator Core Manufacturing Credit Association [*Later, NRMCA*] (EA)
NRCMF .... NRC Master File (NITA)
NRC-NAS .... National Research Council - National Academy of Sciences (AAG)
NRCP .... National Research Council for the Philippines (CARB)
NRCP .... Nonreinforced Concrete Pipe [*Technical drawings*]
NRCP .... Norcap Financial Corp. (SAUS)
NRCPR......... Nuclear Regulatory Commission Procurement Regulation (AAGC)
NRCPS .... National Research Council on Peace Strategy (EA)
NRCR .... Colgate-Rochester Divinity School, Rochester, NY [*Library symbol*] [*Library of Congress*] (LCLS)
NRCR .... Northern Railway of Costa Rica (SAUS)
NR Crit .... Nuclear Rocket Critical (SAUS)
NRC RRC ..... NRC Report Review Committee (SAUS)
NRCS .... National Resources Conservation Service (PA)
NRCS .... National Roller Canary Society [*British*] (BI)
NRCS .... Natural Resources Conservation Service
NRCS .... Normalized RADAR Cross Section
NRCS .... Normalized Radar Cross-Section (SAUS)
NRCS .... Nuclear Reactor Control System (SAUS)
NRCS .... United States Natural Resources Conservation Service
NRCSA......... National Registration Center for Study Abroad (EA)
NRCSA......... Neurological Resources Center of South Australia
NRCSL .... National Research Center on Student Learning [*University of Pittsburgh*] [*Research center*] (RCD)
NRCSM .... Narcissism (ABBR)
NRCST .... Narcissist (ABBR)
NRCST .... National Referral Center for Science and Technology (MCD)
NRCT .... National Registry of Childhood Tumors [*British*]
NRCT .... National Research Council of Thailand (CARB)
NRCTK .... Narcotic (ABBR)
NRC-TOX .... National Research Council - Committee on Toxicology
NRCV .... Consolidated Vacuum Corp., Rochester, NY [*Library symbol*] [*Library of Congress*] (LCLS)
NRCWA .... National Resource Center on Women and AIDS [*Acquired Immune Deficiency Syndrome*] (EA)
NRCX .... New Retail Concepts, Inc. (SAUS)
NRCX .... Nuclear Regulary Commission (EBF)
NRCY .... Not Received Yet (SAUS)
NRCYS .... National Resource Center for Youth Services (EA)
NRD .... Aeronardi SpA [*Italy*] [*ICAO designator*] (FAAC)
NRD .... National Range Division [*Air Force*]
NRD .... National Range Documentation (MUGU)
NRD .... National Registered Designer [*British*]
NRD .... Natural Resource Damage [*Environmental science*]
NRD .... Natural Resources Division [*An association*] (EAIO)
NRD .... Naval Radio Direction Finder (IAA)
NRD .... Naval Recruiting Department [*British military*] (DMA)
NRD .... Naval Research and Development (KSC)
NRD .... Navy Recruiting District (DNAB)
NRD .... Negative Resistance Diode
NRD .... Nerve Root Damage (MELL)
NRD .... Nominal Rim Diameter [*Automotive engineering*]
NRD .... Nonradiative Dielectric (SAUS)
NRD .... Nonrenal Death (MAE)
NRD .... Nonreplenishable Demand
NRD .... Norderney [*Germany*] [*Airport symbol*] (OAG)
NRD .... Nordlingen [*Federal Republic of Germany*] [*Seismograph station code, US Geological Survey*] [*Closed*] (SEIS)
NRD .... Nord Resources [*NYSE symbol*] (TTSB)
NRD .... Nord Resources Corp. [*NYSE symbol*] (SPSG)
NRD .... No Record of Destination [*Aviation*]

NRD .... Normal Retirement Date
NR/D .... Not Required, but Desired
NRD .... Nuclear Radiation Detector
NRD .... Nucleus Raphe Dorsalis [*Neuroanatomy*]
NRD .... Office of Naval Research and Development
NRDA .... Nevada Research and Development Area (SAUS)
NRDB .... National Residue Database
NRDB .... Nonreversing, Dynamic Braking (IAA)
NRDC .... N-Arginine Dibasic Convertase [*An enzyme*]
NRDC .... Natick Research and Development Center [*Army*] (INF)
NRDC .... National Research & Development Corp. [*Later, BTG*] [*British*]
NRDC .... National Resources Defence Council (ECON)
NRDC .... National Respiratory Disease Conference (DAVI)
NRDC .... National Retail Distribution Certificate [*British*]
NRDC .... National Running Data Center, Inc. [*Defunct*] (EA)
NRDC .... Natural Resources Defense Council (EA)
NRDC .... Navy Relief Society, Washington, DC, Auxiliary
NRDC .... Navy Research and Development Committee
NRDCA......... National Roof Deck Contractors Association (EA)
NRDEC .... Natick Research Development and Engineering Center [*Army*] (INF)
NRDF .... Non-Recursive Digital File (NITA)
NRDF .... Nonrecursive Digital Filter [*Navy*]
NRDFS .... Naval Radio Direction Finder Service
NRDI .... National Rural Development Institute (EA)
NRDL .... Naval Radiological Defense Laboratory
NRDL .... Navy Radiological Defense Laboratory (DNAB)
NRDLS .... National Rural Development Leaders School (OICC)
NRDM .... NRD Mining Ltd. (SAUS)
NRDM .... Nuclear Weapons Reconnaissance Data Manual (COE)
NRDO .... National Research and Development Organization (WDAA)
NRDO .... Navy Radio (NOAA)
NRDP .... National Rural Development Partnership
NRDR .... Consolidated NRD Resources Ltd. (SAUS)
NRDR .... Non-Resetting Data Reconstruction (PDAA)
NRDR-CF .... Non-Resetting Data Reconstruction with Continuous Feedback (PDAA)
NRDR-CF .... Non-Resetting Data Reconstructor with Continuous Feedback (SAUS)
NRDR-DF .... Non-Resetting Data Reconstruction with Digital Feedback (SAUS)
NRDR-DF .... Non-Resetting Data Reconstruction with Discrete Feedback (PDAA)
NRDR-DF .... Non-Resetting Data Reconstructor with Digital Feedback (SAUS)
NRDS .... Neonatal Respiratory Distress Syndrome [*Medicine*] (MELL)
NRDS .... Nuclear Rocket Detection System [*NASA*]
NRDS .... Nuclear Rocket Development Station
NRDSCG ...... Naval Research and Development Satellite Communications Group (SAA)
NRDU-V ...... Navy Research and Development Unit - Vietnam (MCD)
NRE .... Aviones Are, SA de CV [*Mexico*] [*FAA designator*] (FAAC)
NRE .... Eastman Kodak Co., Rochester, NY [*Library symbol*] [*Library of Congress*] (LCLS)
NRE .... National Real Estate Corp. [*NYSE symbol*] (SPSG)
NRE .... National Resource Explorations Ltd. [*Toronto Stock Exchange symbol*] [*Vancouver Stock Exchange symbol*]
NRE .... Natl Re Corp. [*NYSE symbol*] (TTSB)
NRE .... Naval Research Establishment
NRE .... Negative Regulatory Element [*Genetics*]
NRE .... Negative Resistance Effect
NRE .... Negative Resistance Element [*Electronics*] (IAA)
NRE .... New and Renewable Energy (PDAA)
NRE .... New York Revised Laws [*A publication*] (DLA)
NRE .... Nonrecurring Engineering (AAEL)
NRE .... Nonrecurring Engineering Expense
NRE .... Non Recurring Expense (ACAE)
NRE .... Nonrotating Earth (NATG)
NRE .... Not Receiving Additional Irrigation [*Agriculture*]
NRE .... Nuclear Receptor Element [*Biochemistry*]
NRE .... Nuclear Rocket Engine (AAG)
NRe .... [*Reynolds*] Number [*Aerodynamics*] (BARN)
NRE .... Point Mugu, CA [*Location identifier*] [*FAA*] (FAAL)
NRE-A .... Eastman Kodak Co., Apparatus Division, Rochester, NY [*Library symbol*] [*Library of Congress*] (LCLS)
NREA .... National Rural Education Association (EA)
NREAN......... Northern Rivers Energy Action Network [*Australia*]
NRE-B .... Kodak (Near East) Ltd., Beirut, Lebanon [*Library symbol*] [*Library of Congress*] (LCLS)
NREB .... Naval Reserve Evaluation Board (DNAB)
NREBX .... Mgn. Stanley D. Witter Natural Resources Cl.B [*Mutual fund ticker symbol*] (SG)
NREC .... National Reconnaissance Executive Committee (LAIN)
NREC .... National Resources Evaluation Center [*of OEP*] [*Nuclear effects*]
NREC .... Natural Resources and Environment Committee [*Victoria, Australia*]
NREC .... Navy Recruiting Exhibit Center (ACAE)
NRECA......... National Rural Electric Cooperative Association (EA)
NREd .... Eastman Dental Center, Basil G. Bibby Library, Rochester, NY [*Library symbol*] [*Library of Congress*] (LCLS)
NRed .... Red Hook Public Library, Red Hook, NY [*Library symbol*] [*Library of Congress*] (LCLS)
NREDC .... National Rocket Engine Development Complex (SAUS)
NRedL .... Red Hook Public Library, Red Hook, NY [*Library symbol*] [*Library of Congress*] (LCLS)
NRE-E .... Eastman Kodak Co., Engineering Division, Rochester, NY [*Library symbol*] [*Library of Congress*] (LCLS)
NREEC .... Natural Resources and Environmental Education Center [*Oklahoma State University*] [*Research center*] (RCD)
NREF .... North Russia Expeditionary Force [*World War I*] [*Canada*]

NREFA .... National Real Estate Fliers Association [*Later, Real Estate Aviation Chapter*] (EA)
NREH .... Normal Renin Essential Hypertension [*Medicine*] (DMAA)
NREH .... Nuclear Radiation Effects Handbook (SAA)
NREL .... CSIRO News Releases (SAUS)
NRE-L .... Kodak Ltd., Recordak Division, London, United Kingdom [*Library symbol*] [*Library of Congress*] (LCLS)
NREL .... National Renewable Energy Laboratory [*Department of Energy*]
NRE-M .... Eastman Kodak Co., Health and Safety Laboratory, Rochester, NY [*Library symbol*] [*Library of Congress*] (LCLS)
nREM .... Nonrapid Eye Movement (DIPS)
NREM .... Nonrapid Eye Movement [*Type of sleep*]
NREMS .... Nonrapid Eye Movement Sleep [*Neurology*]
NREMT .... National Registry of Emergency Medical Technicians (EA)
NREMT-P ..... National Registry of Emergency Medical Technicians - Paramedics (DAVI)
NREN .... National Research and Education Network [*Federal government*]
NRenSA .... Saint Anthony-On-Hudson Theological Seminary, Rensselaer, NY [*Library symbol*] [*Library of Congress*] (LCLS)
NRenSW ...... Sterling-Winthrop Research Institute, Rensselaer, NY [*Library symbol*] [*Library of Congress*] (LCLS)
NRE-P .... Eastman Kodak Co., Photographic Technology Library, Rochester, NY [*Library symbol*] [*Library of Congress*] (LCLS)
NREP .... Name Removed from End-Paper [*Antiquarian book trade*]
NREP .... National Registry of Environmental Professionals (EA)
NREP .... National Reliability Evaluation Program [*Nuclear Regulatory Commission*]
NREP .... Neutron Resonance Escape Probability [*Nuclear energy*] (NRCH)
NRE-R .... Eastman Kodak Co., Research Laboratories, Rochester, NY [*Library symbol*] [*Library of Congress*] (LCLS)
NRER .... Non-Rejected Earth Radiance (SAUS)
NRERC .... National Rural Education Research Consortium [*Defunct*] (EA)
NRES .... Natural Resources, Energy, and Environment [*Office of Management and Budget*]
NRES .... Naval Receiving Station
NRES .... Nichols Research [*NASDAQ symbol*] (TTSB)
NRES .... Nichols Research Corp. [*NASDAQ symbol*] (NQ)
NRETN .... Nonreturn
NREVSS .... National Respiratory and Enteric Virus Surveillance System
NRF .... National Republican Foundation (EA)
NRF .... National Research Foundation [*Research center*] (RCD)
NRF .... National Retail Federation (EA)
NRF .... National Roofing Foundation (EA)
NRF .... National Rowing Foundation (EA)
NRF .... National Rural Fellows (EA)
NRF .... Naval Reactor Facility
NRF .... ·Naval Repair Facility
NRF .... Naval Reserve Fleet [*or Force*]
NRF .... Neurite Retraction Factor [*Biochemistry*]
NRF .... Neurosciences Research Foundation (DAVI)
NRF .... Never Removed from Box [*Doll collecting*]
NRF .... Newport Restoration Foundation (EA)
NRF .... Nitrogen Rejection Facility [*Process engineering*]
NRF .... No Redeeming Features
NRF .... No Reflight
NRF .... No Reinforcement [*Psychology*]
NRF .... Normal Renal Function [*Medicine*] (DMAA)
NRF .... Not Running at the Finish [*Automobile racing term*]
NRF .... Nuclear Reactor Fuel (SAUS)
NRF .... Nuclear Resonance Fluorescence (IAA)
NRF .... Nutrition Research Foundation [*Australia*]
NRF .... R. T. French Co., Rochester, NY [*Library symbol*] [*Library of Congress*] (LCLS)
NRFA .... National Retail Florists Association [*Defunct*]
NRFA .... National Retail Furniture Association [*Later, NHFA*] (EA)
NRFA .... National Rural Fire Authority (SAUS)
NRFB .... Never Removed from Box [*Doll collecting*]
NRFBS .... National Research Foundation for Business Statistics (EA)
NRFC .... National Railroad Freight Committee (EA)
NRFC .... Navy Regional Finance Center
NRFC-B .... Navy Regional Finance Center, Brooklyn [*New York*] (DNAB)
NRFC-GL ..... Navy Regional Finance Center, Great Lakes (DNAB)
NRFC-N .... Navy Regional Finance Center, Norfolk [*Virginia*] (DNAB)
NRFC-PH .... Navy Regional Finance Center, Pearl Harbor [*Hawaii*] (DNAB)
NRFC-SD ..... Navy Regional Finance Center, San Diego [*California*] (DNAB)
NRFC-SF ...... Navy Regional Finance Center, San Francisco [*California*] (DNAB)
NRFD .... Not Ready for Data
NRFEA .... National Retail Farm Equipment Association [*Later, NFPEDA*]
NRFF .... National Research Foundation for Fertility [*Inactive*] (EA)
NRFI .... National Rail Freight Initiative [*Australia*]
NRFI .... Nonrecurring Finished Intelligence (MCD)
NRFI .... Not Ready for Issue
NRFL .... National Rugby Football League (NADA)
NRFMAU ..... Naval Reserve Fleet Management Assistance Unit (DNAB)
NRFO .... Navy Regional Finance Office
NRFO .... Nonrecovergent Fan-Out (SAUS)
NRFS .... Naval Reserve Force Study Group (DNAB)
NRFS .... Nichols Research Corp. (SAUS)
NRFSA .... Navy Radio Frequency Spectrum Activity
NRFSEA .... National Reciprocal and Family Support Enforcement Association [*Later, NCSEA*] (EA)
NRFU .... Nonresponse Follow-Up [*Bureau of the Census*] (GFGA)
NRG .... Energy (ABBR)
NRG .... Nautical Research Guild (EA)
NRG .... Naval Research Group

NRG .... Northern Rhodesia Gazette [*A publication*] (DLA)
NRG .... Ross Aviation, Inc. [*ICAO designator*] (FAAC)
NRG .... Tri-Lite, Inc. [*AMEX symbol*] (SPSG)
NRGA .... National Rice Growers Association [*Defunct*] (EA)
NRGas .... Rochester Gas & Electric Corp., Technical Information Center, Rochester, NY [*Library symbol*] [*Library of Congress*] (LCLS)
NRGC .... Nucleus Reticularis Gigantocellularis [*Neuroanatomy*]
NRGD-SC ..... Stromberg-Carlson Corp., Rochester, NY [*Library symbol*] [*Library of Congress*] (LCLS)
NRGE .... George Eastman House, Rochester, NY [*Library symbol*] [*Library of Congress*] (LCLS)
NRGI .... National Energy Group [*NASDAQ symbol*] (SAG)
NRGM .... National Responsibility Group Minute (HEAS)
NRGN .... Neurogen Corp. [*NASDAQ symbol*] (NQ)
NRGR .... General Railway Signal Co., Rochester, NY [*Library symbol*] [*Library of Congress*] (LCLS)
NRGS .... Church of Jesus Christ of Latter-Day Saints, Genealogical Society Library, Rochester Branch, Rochester, NY [*Library symbol*] [*Library of Congress*] (LCLS)
NRH .... Natural Rate Hypothesis [*Economics*]
NRH .... Nodular Regenerative Hyperplasia [*of liver*] [*Medicine*]
NRH .... Nonready Hours
NRH .... No Reply Heard [*ICAO designator*] (FAAC)
NRHA .... National Radio Heritage Association (EA)
NRHA .... National Reining Horse Association (EA)
NRHA .... National Retail Hardware Association (EA)
NRHA .... National Roller Hockey Association of Great Britain (BI)
NRHA .... National Rural Health Association (EA)
NRHA .... Northern Rivers Hydrophonic Association [*Australia*]
NRhbA .... Astor Home for Children, Rhinebeck, NY [*Library symbol*] [*Library of Congress*] (LCLS)
NRHC .... National Rental Housing Council [*Later, NMHC*] (EA)
NRHC .... National Rivers and Harbors Congress [*Later, WRC*]
NRHC .... National Rural Housing Coalition (EA)
NRHCA .... National Rural Health Care Association [*Formerly, NRPCA*] (EA)
NRhDH .... Long Island Doctors' Hospital, Roslyn Heights, NY [*Library symbol*] [*Library of Congress*] (LCLS)
NRHE .... Nonregenerative Heat Exchanger [*Nuclear energy*] (NRCH)
NRHGC .... National Republican Heritage Groups (Nationalities) Council (EA)
NRHi .... Rochester Historical Society, Rochester, NY [*Library symbol*] [*Library of Congress*] (LCLS)
NRHN .... National Rural Health Network (SAUS)
NRHP .... National Register of Historic Places [*A publication*]
NRHP .... National Register of Hypnotherapists and Psychotherapists [*British*] (DBA)
NRHP .... National River Health Program (SAUS)
NRHQ .... Northern Region Headquarters (SAUS)
NRHS .... National Railway Historical Society (EA)
NRHS .... New Royal Horticultural Society [*British*]
NRHSA .... National Retail Hobby Store Association (NTPA)
NRHU .... National Rural Health Unit [*Australia*]
NRHX .... Nonregenerative Heat Exchanger [*Nuclear energy*] (NRCH)
NRI .... National Radio Institute
NRI .... National Research Initiative
NRI .... National Research Institute [*Audience research organization*] (NTCM)
NRI .... National Research Inventory (SAUS)
NRI .... National Resource Inventory [*US database on erosion*]
NRI .... National Rivers Inventory (GNE)
NRI .... Nationsrent, Inc. [*NYSE symbol*] (SG)
NRI .... Natural Resources Institute [*University of Greenwich*] [*British*]
NRI .... Natural Resources International
NRI .... Nerve Root Involvement (SAUS)
NRI .... Nerve Root Irritation (SAUS)
NRI .... Net Radio Interface [*Telecommunications*] (TEL)
NRI .... Neurological and Related Intervention [*Medicine*]
NRI .... Neutral Regular Insulin
NRI .... New Records, Inc. [*Record label*]
NRI .... New Ring Index [*of chemical compounds*] [*A publication*]
NRI .... Nomura Research Institute (NITA)
NRI .... Nonrecurring Installation Charge [*Telecommunications*] (TEL)
NRI .... Nonrecurring Investment (NASA)
NRI .... Nonrepairable Item (MCD)
NRI .... Nonresident Instruction (MCD)
NRI .... Non-Respiratory Infection [*Medicine*] (DMAA)
NRI .... Non-Roster Invitee [*Baseball term*] (NDBD)
NRI .... Noril'sk [*Former USSR*] [*Seismograph station code, US Geological Survey*] (SEIS)
NRI .... Novagold Resources, Inc. [*Toronto Stock Exchange symbol*]
NRI .... Number of Records Ignored (SAA)
NRIA .... Narrow Resonance Infinite Absorber (PDAA)
NRIA .... National Railroad Intermodal Association [*Defunct*] (EA)
NRIAD .... National Register of Industrial Art Designers [*British*] (DAS)
NRIC .... National Rehabilitation Information Center [*Catholic University of America*] [*Bibliographic Database*] [*Washington, DC*]
NRIC .... Negative Return in Cartridge [*Advanced photo system*]
NRIC .... Non-Reciprocal Impedance Converter (PDAA)
NRIC .... Nuclear Research Information Center [*American Nuclear Center*] [*Information service or system*] (IID)
NRICGP .... National Research Initiative Competitive Grants Program (SAUS)
NRICH .... National Resource Institute on Children and Youth with Handicaps [*Defunct*] (EA)
NRID .... National Registry [*NASDAQ symbol*] (SAG)
NRID .... National Registry of Interpreters for the Deaf (SAUS)
NRiding Sch Libr Guild Bull... North Riding School Library. Guild Bulletin (SAUS)
NRIFSD .... Non-Recoverable In-Flight Shut-Down (ACAE)

NRIIA	National Republican Institute for International Affairs (EA)
NRIM	Narrow Resonance Infinite Mass [*Nuclear energy*] (NRCH)
NRIM	Northrim Bank [*NASDAQ symbol*] (SAG)
NRIMS	National Research Institute for Mathematical Sciences [*South Africa*]
NRIP	Navy Reserve Intelligence Program (MCD)
NRIP	Number of Rejected Initial Pickups
NRIPMVLIC	Nonresident Interprovince Motor Vehicle Liability Insurance Card [*For travel in Canada*]
NRIS	Natural Resource Information System [*Department of the Interior*]
NRIS	New Mexico Natural Resources Information System [*New Mexico State Department of Natural Resources*] [*Santa Fe*] (IID)
NRIS	Nursing Research Initiative for Scotland (SAUS)
NRITL	Northeastern Regional Instructional Television Library (SAUS)
NRITL	Northeastern Regional Instructional Television Library, Cambridge (SAUS)
NRIUW	Naval Reserve Inshore Undersea Warfare (DNAB)
NRJ	Natural Resources Journal [*A publication*] (BRI)
NRJ	Non-Reciprocal Junction (PDAA)
NRK	Newark (ABBR)
NRK	Normal Rat Kidney
NRK	Normotensive Rat Kidney
NRK	Norrkoping [*Sweden*] [*Airport symbol*] (OAG)
NRK	Norsk Rikskringkasting [*Norwegian Broadcasting Corporation*]
NRK	Nurek [*Former USSR*] [*Seismograph station code, US Geological Survey*] [*Closed*] (SEIS)
NRKF	Normal Rat Kidney Fibroblast [*Cytology*]
NRkpJH	Rocky Point Junior-Senior High School, Rocky Point, NY [*Library symbol*] [*Library of Congress*] (LCLS)
NRL	Naneco Resources Ltd. [*Vancouver Stock Exchange symbol*]
NRL	National Reference Library [*British*] (NUCP)
NRL	National Registry for Librarians (EA)
NRL	National Research Laboratory
NRL	National Research Library [*Canada*] (DIT)
NRL	National Resources Library
NRL	Naval Research Laboratory [*Washington, DC*] [*Seismograph station code, US Geological Survey*] [*Closed*] (SEIS)
NRL	Naval Research Laboratory, Washington, DC [*OCLC symbol*] (OCLC)
NRL	Network Restructuring Language
NRL	New York Revised Laws [*A publication*] (DLA)
NRL	Night Ration Locker (MSA)
NRL	Normal Rated Load
NRL	Normal Response Level
NRL	Normal Running Load (SAUS)
NRL	Norrell Corp. [*NYSE symbol*] (SAG)
NRL	Norske Reindriftsamers Lansforbund [*Norway*]
NRL	North Ronaldsay [*Scotland*] [*Airport symbol*] (OAG)
NRL	Nuclear Reactor Laboratory [*Massachusetts Institute of Technology*] [*Research center*] (RCD)
NRL	Nuclear Referral List (SAUS)
NRL	Nuclear Weapons Reconnaissance List (COE)
NRL	Nucleus Reticularis Lateralis (DB)
NRL	Nutrition Research Laboratory (SAUS)
NRLA	Network Repair Level Analysis
NRLA	Northeastern Retail Lumbermen's Association (EA)
NRLC	National Railway Labor Conference (EA)
NRLC	National Right to Life Committee (EA)
NRLCA	National Rural Letter Carriers' Association (EA)
NRLCHESBAYDET	Naval Research Laboratory, Chesapeake Bay Detachment (DNAB)
NRLD	Norland Medical Systems [*NASDAQ symbol*] (TTSB)
NRLD	Norland Medical Systems, Inc. [*NASDAQ symbol*] (SAG)
NRLDA	National Retail Lumber Dealers Association [*Later, NLBMDA*]
NRL/EOTPO	Naval Research Laboratory Electro-Optical Technology Program Office [*Washington, DC*]
NRLETF	National Right to Life Educational Trust Fund (EA)
NRLF	Lincoln First Bank of Rochester, Rochester, NY [*Library symbol*] [*Library of Congress*] (LCLS)
NRLFLTSUPPDET	Naval Research Laboratory, Flight Support Detachment (DNAB)
NRLGY	Neurology
NRLM	National Research Lab of Metrology [*Japan*]
NRLN	Northern Regional Legal Notice [*1954-61*] [*Nigeria*] [*A publication*] (DLA)
NRLP	National Railway Labor Panel [*World War II*]
NRLR	Northern Rhodesia Law Reports [*A publication*] (DLA)
NRLREP	Naval Research Laboratory Representative (DNAB)
NRLSI	National Reference Library of Science and Invention [*of the British Museum*]
NRLSITEDET	Naval Research Laboratory, Field Site Detachment (DNAB)
NRLSPECPROJDET	Naval Research Laboratory, Special Projects Detachment (DNAB)
NRL/SVIC	Naval Research Laboratory Shock and Vibration Information Center [*ONR*]
NRLUWSREFDET	Naval Research Laboratory, Underwater Sound Reference Detachment (DNAB)
NRM	Nara [*Mali*] [*Airport symbol*] (OAG)
NRM	National Railway Museum (WDAA)
NRM	National Registry of Microbiologists (DAVI)
NRM	National Resistance Movement [*Uganda*] (PD)
NRM	National Revolutionary Movement [*France*]
NRM	Natural Remanent Magnetism [*or Magnetization*]
NRM	Natural Remanent Magnetization (SAUS)
NRM	Natural Resource Management
NRM	Naval Reserve Medal
NRM	Next to Reading Matter [*Advertising*] (WDMC)

NRM	Nonrecurring Maintenance [*NASA*] (KSC)
NRM	Non-Routine Maintenance (SAUS)
NRM	Normalize (DEN)
NRM	Normal Range of Motion (MELL)
NRM	Normal Response Mode
NRM	Normal Retinal Movement (SAUS)
NRM	Norm-Referenced Measurement [*Education*]
NRM	Northair Mines Ltd. [*Toronto Stock Exchange symbol*] [*Vancouver Stock Exchange symbol*]
NRM	Northern Rocky Mountains
NRM	Northern Roller Mills (SAUS)
NRM	North Rainier Mesa [*Nevada*] [*Seismograph station code, US Geological Survey*] (SEIS)
NRM	NRM Energy Co. Ltd.
NRM	Nuclear Radiation Monitor (SAUS)
NRM	Nucleus Reticularis Magnocellularis (DB)
NRM	Numeral Reading Machine
NRM	Rochester Museum and Science Center, Rochester, NY [*Library symbol*] [*Library of Congress*] (LCLS)
NRMA	National Reloading Manufacturers Association (EA)
NRMA	National Retail Merchants Association [*New York, NY*] (EA)
NRMA	Nuclear Records Management Association (EA)
NRMADI	Non Recedet Malum a Domo Ingrati [*Evil Shall Not Depart from the House of theUngrateful*] [(*After Prov., XVII. 13*) *Motto of Julius, Duke of Braunschweig-Wolfenbuttel (1529-89)*] [*Latin*]
NRMC	Monroe Community College, Rochester, NY [*Library symbol*] [*Library of Congress*] (LCLS)
NRMC	National Records Management Council (EA)
NRMC	National Resources Management Corp.
NRMC	Naval Records Management Center
NRMC	Naval Regional Medical Center (NVT)
NRMC	Naval Reserve Manpower Center
NRMC	Northeast Rat and Mouse Club (EA)
NRMCA	National Radiator Manufacturing Credit Association (EA)
NRMCA	National Ready Mixed Concrete Association (EA)
NRMCEN	Naval Records Management Center
NRMCI	Northeast Rat and Mouse Club (EA)
NRME	Notched, Returned, and Mitred Ends [*Construction*]
NRMEC	North American Rockwell Microelectronics Co. [*Obsolete*]
NRMF	New Road Map Foundation (EA)
NRMI	National Record Mart, Inc. [*NASDAQ symbol*] (SAG)
NRMI	National Registry of Myocardial Infarction
NRMI	Natl Record Mart [*NASDAQ symbol*] (TTSB)
NRMI	Naval Medical Research Unit (SAUS)
NRMIUW	Naval Reserve Mobile Inshore Undersea Warfare (DNAB)
NRML	Monroe County Library System, Rochester, NY [*Library symbol*] [*Library of Congress*] (LCLS)
NRML	Normal (WGA)
NRMLC	Normalcy (ABBR)
NRMLT	Normality (ABBR)
NRMLY	Normally (ABBR)
NRMLZ	Normalize (ABBR)
NRMLZD	Normalized (ABBR)
NRMLZG	Normalizing (ABBR)
NRMLZN	Normalization (ABBR)
NRMLZR	Normalizer (ABBR)
NRMM	National Register of Microform Masters [*Library of Congress*]
NRMM	NATO Reference Mobility Model
NRMOMAGU	Naval Reserve Mobile Mine Assembly Group (DNAB)
NRMP	National Records Management Program (AEPA)
NRMP	National Resident Matching Program (EA)
NRMRL	National Risk Management Research Laboratory [*Environmental Protection Agency*] (AEPA)
NRMS	National Registry of Medical Secretaries (EA)
NRMS	Natural Resource Management System [*Army Corps of Engineers*] [*Database*]
NRMS	Naval Reserve Midshipmen's School
NRMS	Neutralization-Reionization Mass Spectrometry
NRMS	Nominal Root Mean Square (IAA)
NRMS	Norman Rockwell Memorial Society (EA)
NRMS Value	Nominal Root Mean Square Value (SAUS)
NRMT	Northern Rocky Mountain Trench [*Geology*]
NRMT	Nuclear Resonance Magnetometer Tool (SAUS)
NRMTC	Nordoff-Robbins Music Therapy Centre Ltd. [*British*] (CB)
NRMU	Natural Resources Management [*Organization of Eastern Caribbean States*]
NRMU	Northern Rhodesia European Mineworkers' Union
NRMV	Normative (ABBR)
NRMVY	Normatively (ABBR)
NRMW	Margaret Woodbury Strong Museum, Rochester, NY [*Library symbol*] [*Library of Congress*] (LCLS)
NRM Wind Scale	Northern Rocky Mountains Wind Scale (SAUS)
NRMWRP	Northern Rocky Mountain Wolf Recovery Plan
NRN	Naryn [*Former USSR*] [*Seismograph station code, US Geological Survey*] (SEIS)
NRN	National Research Network (SAUS)
NRN	National Resource Network [*Commercial firm*] (EA)
NRN	Natural Radioactive Nuclides
NRN	Negative Run Number [*Computer science*] (OA)
NRN	Noise Rating Number (SAUS)
NRN	No Reply Necessary (SAUS)
NRN	Northern
NRN	Novell Remote Network (SAUS)
NRN	Royal Netherlands Navy [*ICAO designator*] (FAAC)
nRNA	Ribonucleic Acid, Nuclear [*Biochemistry, genetics*]

NRNC.......... Nazareth College of Rochester, Rochester, NY [*Library symbol*] [*Library of Congress*] (LCLS)
NRND.......... Norand Corp. [*NASDAQ symbol*] (SAG)
NRNFC........ National Rick Nelson Fan Club (EA)
NRNHD........ Nixon, Hargrave, Devans & Doyle, Rochester, NY [*Library symbol*] [*Library of Congress*] (LCLS)
NRNLR........ Northern Region of Nigeria Law Reports [*A publication*] (DLA)
NRNP.......... Nuclear Ribonucleoprotein [*Medicine*] (DMAA)
NRNR.......... National Rotorcraft Noise Reduction [*Program to reduce noise of helicopters*]
NRNS.......... Nearness (ABBR)
NRO............ National Range Operations (RDA)
NRO............ National Reconnaissance Office [*Air Force/CIA*]
NRO............ National Reconnaissance Organization [*CIA*]
NRO............ Naval Research Objectives
NRO............ Navy Retail Office (AFIT)
NRO............ Negative Resistance Oscillator [*Electronics*]
NRO............ Nobeyama Radio Observatory
NRO............ Nonresident-Owned Funds [*Investment term*]
NRO............ Non-Returnable Outer (SAUS)
NRO............ No Results Observed (SAUS)
NRock......... Rockville Centre Public Library, Rockville Centre, NY [*Library symbol*] [*Library of Congress*] (LCLS)
NRockH....... Mercy Hospital, Rockville Centre, NY [*Library symbol*] [*Library of Congress*] (LCLS)
NRockHE..... Hewett Elementary School, Rockville Centre, NY [*Library symbol*] [*Library of Congress*] (LCLS)
NRockL....... Lakeview Public Library, Rockville Centre, NY [*Library symbol*] [*Library of Congress*] (LCLS)
NRockM...... Molloy College, Rockville Centre, NY [*Library symbol*] [*Library of Congress*] (LCLS)
NRockRE..... Riverside School, Rockville Centre, NY [*Library symbol*] [*Library of Congress*] (LCLS)
NRockSMS... South Side Middle School, Rockville Centre, NY [*Library symbol*] [*Library of Congress*] (LCLS)
NRockSSH ... South Side Senior High School, Rockville Centre, NY [*Library symbol*] [*Library of Congress*] (LCLS)
NRockWE..... Wilson Elementary School, Rockville Centre, NY [*Library symbol*] [*Library of Congress*] (LCLS)
NRockWR..... Woodfield Road School, Rockville Centre, NY [*Library symbol*] [*Library of Congress*] (LCLS)
NRockWS.... Floyd B. Watson School, Rockville Centre, NY [*Library symbol*] [*Library of Congress*] (LCLS)
NROE.......... Naval Reactor Organic Experiment
NROFF........ New Run-OFF (SAUS)
nroff.......... Nontypesetting Runoff [*Computer science*] (CDE)
NROK.......... Northern Rockies Intermontane Basins (SAUS)
NRom .... Jervis Library Association, Rome, NY [*Library symbol*] [*Library of Congress*] (LCLS)
NROM.......... Noble Romns [*NASDAQ symbol*] (TTSB)
NROM.......... Normal Range of Motion (SAUS)
NRomA........ Rome Air Development Center, Rome, NY [*Library symbol*] [*Library of Congress*] (LCLS)
NRomAF...... United States Air Force, Base Library, Griffiss Air Force Base, Rome, NY [*Library symbol*] [*Library of Congress*] (LCLS)
NRomAF-R... United States Air Force, Rome Air Development Center, Griffiss, NY [*Library symbol*] [*Library of Congress*] (LCLS)
NROMM........ Netherlands Register of Microform Masters (TELE)
NROO.......... Naval Reactors Operations Office
NRoos......... Roosevelt Community Library, Roosevelt, NY [*Library symbol*] [*Library of Congress*] (LCLS)
NRoosCE..... Centennial Elementary School, Roosevelt, NY [*Library symbol*] [*Library of Congress*] (LCLS)
NRoosDP .... Daniels Primary Center, Roosevelt, NY [*Library symbol*] [*Library of Congress*] (LCLS)
NRoosJH..... Roosevelt Junior-Senior High School, Roosevelt, NY [*Library symbol*] [*Library of Congress*] (LCLS)
NRoosPK..... Prekindergarten School, Roosevelt, NY [*Library symbol*] [*Library of Congress*] (LCLS)
NRoosRE .... Theadore Roosevelt Elementary School, Roosevelt, NY [*Library symbol*] [*Library of Congress*] (LCLS)
NRoosWE.... Washington-Rose Elementary School, Roosevelt, NY [*Library symbol*] [*Library of Congress*] (LCLS)
NROPS........ New Riders of the Purple Sage [*Rock music group*]
NROS.......... Naval Reserve Officer School
NRosl......... Bryant Library, Roslyn, NY [*Library symbol*] [*Library of Congress*] (LCLS)
NRoslH....... Saint Francis Hospital, Roslyn, NY [*Library symbol*] [*Library of Congress*] (LCLS)
NRoslhEI..... East Hills Intermediate School, Roslyn Heights, NY [*Library symbol*] [*Library of Congress*] (LCLS)
NRoslhHP.... Heights Primary School, Roslyn Heights, NY [*Library symbol*] [*Library of Congress*] (LCLS)
NRoslhHS ... Roslyn High School, Roslyn Heights, NY [*Library symbol*] [*Library of Congress*] (LCLS)
NRoslhJH.... Roslyn Junior High School, Roslyn Heights, NY [*Library symbol*] [*Library of Congress*] (LCLS)
NRoslHS ..... Roslyn High School, Roslyn, NY [*Library symbol*] [*Library of Congress*] (LCLS)
NRoslhWI .... Willets Road Intermediate School, Roslyn Heights, NY [*Library symbol*] [*Library of Congress*] (LCLS)
NRoslJH ..... Roslyn Junior High School, Roslyn, NY [*Library symbol*] [*Library of Congress*] (LCLS)
N-ROSS....... Naval Remote Ocean Sensing System (SAUS)
N-ROSS .... Naval Research Oceanographic Satellite System (SAUS)

NROSS.......... Navy Remote Ocean Sensing System [*Proposed*]
NROTC........ Naval Reserve Officers' Training Corps
NROTCBA .... National Reserve Officers' Training Corps Band Association (AEBS)
NROTCU .... Naval Reserve Officers' Training Corps Unit (DNAB)
NROTCUNAVADMINU... Naval Reserve Officers' Training Corps Unit and Administrative Unit (DNAB)
NROVA........ National Record of Vocational Achievement (AIE)
NRP............ National Religious Party [*Hamiflaga Hadatit Leumit*] [*Israel*] [*Political party*] (PPW)
NRP............ National Reporting Program [*National Institute of Mental Health*] [*Department of Health and Human Services*] (GFGA)
NRP............ National Republican Party [*Guyana*] [*Political party*] (EY)
NRP............ National Resistance Party [*Political party*] (BJA)
NRP............ National Review Panel [*Work Incentive Program*] [*Department of Labor*]
NRP............ National Route Program (GAVI)
N/RP.......... Neoclassical/Rational Planning
NRP............ Net Rating Point [*Advertising*] (DOAD)
NRP............ Net Rating Points [*Media ratings*] (NTCM)
NRP............ Network Resource Planning [*Computer science*] (CIST)
NRP............ Neurosciences Research Program [*Massachusetts Institute of Technology*]
NRP............ Nevis Reformation Party [*Political party*]
NRP............ New Republic Party [*South Africa*] [*Political party*] (PPW)
NRP............ New Rhodesia Party [*Political party*]
NRP............ Noise Review Program [*Navy*] (DNAB)
NRP............ Nonregistered Publication
NRP............ Nonreportable Property [*Military*]
NRP............ Non-Revenue Passenger [*Travel industry*] (TRID)
NRP............ Nonstationary Random Process
NRP............ Non-unit Related Personnel [*Military*] (DOMA)
NRP............ No Replacement Part (SAUS)
NRP............ Normal Rated Power
NRP............ Notice of Research Project
NRP............ NRP, Inc. [*Associated Press*] (SAG)
NRP............ Nuclear Reform Project (EA)
NRP............ Nucleus Reticularis Parvocellularis (DB)
NRP............ Null Reading Position (SAUS)
NRP............ Nuwe Republiekparty [*New Republic Party*] [*Political party*] [*Afrikaans*]
NRP............ People's Republican Party [*Turkey*] [*Political party*]
NRP............ Pfaudler Technical Library, Rochester, NY [*Library symbol*] [*Library of Congress*] (LCLS)
NRpA .... Ayerst Science Laboratory, Rouses Point, NY [*Library symbol*] [*Library of Congress*] (LCLS)
NRPA.......... National Recreation and Park Association (EA)
NRPA.......... Non-Redundant Pinhole Array (PDAA)
NRPAC........ Naval Reserve Public Affairs Co.
NRPAI........ National Rifle and Pistol Association of Ireland (EAIO)
NRPAIN....... National Register of Prominent Americans and International Notables (EA)
NRPB.......... National Radiological Protection Board [*British*]
NRPB.......... National Research Planning Board
NRPB.......... National Resources Planning Board [*Abolished, 1943*]
NRPB.......... Naval Research Planning Board (DNAB)
NRPB.......... Naval Reserve Policy Board (DNAB)
NRPB.......... Nickerson RPB Ltd. [*British*] (IRUK)
NRPC.......... National Railroad Passenger Corp. [*Government rail transportation*]
NRPC.......... National Register Publishing Co. [*Information service or system*] (IID)
NRPC.......... Naval Reserve Personnel Center (DNAB)
NRPC.......... Nucleus Reticularis Pontis Caudalis (DB)
NRPCA........ National Rural Primary Care Association [*Later, NRHCA*] (EA)
NRPD.......... National Radiological Protection Board [*British*]
NRPEO........ Naval Regional Plant Equipment Office [*or Officer*] (DNAB)
NRPF.......... National Railroad Pension Forum [*Defunct*] (EA)
NRPF.......... National Retinitis Pigmentosa Foundation [*Later, RPFFB*] (EA)
NRPG.......... National Retinoblastoma Parents Group (EA)
NRPG.......... Nucleus Reticularis Paragigantocellularis (DB)
NRPH.......... Park Ridge Hospital, Medical Library, Rochester, NY [*Library symbol*] [*Library of Congress*] (LCLS)
NRPIO.......... Naval Registered Publications Issuing Office
NRPJ .... Nezavisna Radnicka Partija Jugoslavije [*Independent Labor Party of Yugoslavia*] [*Political party*]
N-R PL........ Non-Reversible Plug (SAUS)
NRPlanP...... Planned Parenthood of Rochester and Monroe County, Rochester, NY [*Library symbol*] [*Library of Congress*] (LCLS)
NRPM.......... Nonregistered Publications Memoranda
NRPM.......... Nuclear Weapons Reconnaissance Planning Manual (COE)
NRPO.......... Naval Regional Procurement Office
NRPP.......... Pennwalt Corp., Pharmaceutical Division Research Library, Rochester, NY [*Library symbol*] [*Library of Congress*] (LCLS)
NRPRA........ Natural Rubber Producers' Research Association [*British*] (BI)
NRPS.......... Naval Radiological Protection Service (PDAA)
NRPS.......... New Riders of the Purple Sage [*Rock music group*]
NRPS.......... Non-Ribosomal Peptide Synthetase [*An enzyme*]
NRPSA........ National Retail Pet Supply Association [*Defunct*] (EA)
NRPSGA...... National Retail Pet Store and Groomers Association (EA)
NRPTC........ National Register of Potentially Toxic Chemicals (GNE)
NRR............ National Research Register (SAUS)
NRR............ Naval Research Reactor
NRR............ Naval Research Requirement
NRR............ Naval Reserve Requirement (MCD)
NRR............ Negative Radial Rake (IAA)
NRR............ Negative Resistance Repeater [*Electronics*] (IAA)
NRR............ Net Reproduction Rate [*Medicine*] (DMAA)

NRR	Net Reproductive Rate
NRR	Net Retail Requirements
NRR	Noise Reduction Rating [*Audio technology*] (EG)
NRR	Nonreactive Resistor (SAUS)
NRR	No Response Required
NRR	No Resume Required
NRR	Northern Rhodesia Regiment
NRR	North Reno [*Nevada*] [*Seismograph station code, US Geological Survey*] (SEIS)
NRR	Note, Record, Report [*Medical records and nursing*] (DAVI)
NRR	Nuclear Reactor Regulation (ABAC)
NRR	Nuclear Reactor Research (SAUS)
NRR	Nuclear Rocket Reactor
NRR	Office of Nuclear Reactor Regulation [*Nuclear Regulatory Commission*]
NRR	Roosevelt Roads, PR [*Location identifier*] [*FAA*] (FAAL)
NRRA	National Rail Regulatory Authority [*Australia*]
NRRA	National Resource Recovery Association (EA)
NRRA	National Risk Retention Association (EA)
NRRA	National Romany Rights Association (WDAA)
NRRAD	Narrated (ABBR)
NRRAG	Narrating (ABBR)
NRRAN	Narration (ABBR)
NRR & C	Russell and Chesley's Nova Scotia Reports [*A publication*] (DLA)
NRRAR	Narrator (ABBR)
NRRAS	Navy Readiness Reporting and Analysis System (MCD)
NRRAV	Narrative (ABBR)
NRRB	National Recovery Review Board [*Terminated, 1934*]
NRRC	National Rex Rabbit Club (EA)
NRRC	Naval Research Reserve Co.
NRRC	Naval Reserve Readiness Command (ACAE)
NRRC	Northern Regional Research Center [*Formerly, NRRL*] [*Peoria, IL*] [*Department of Agriculture*]
NRRC	Nuclear Risk Reduction Center (DOMA)
NRRD	Norstan, Inc. [*NASDAQ symbol*] (NQ)
NR Relay	Non-Reactive Relay (SAUS)
NRRF	Naval Radio Receiving Facility (DNAB)
NRRF	Naval Reserve Readiness Facility (DNAB)
NRRFSS	National Research and Resource Facility for Submicron Structures [*Cornell University*] [*Research center*] (RCD)
NRRI	National Regulatory Research Institute [*Ohio State University*] [*Research center*] (RCD)
NRRI	Natural Resources Research Institute [*Research center*] (RCD)
NRRI	Rochester Institute of Technology, Rochester, NY [*Library symbol*] [*Library of Congress*] (LCLS)
NRRI-C	Rochester Institute of Technology, Melbert B. Cary, Jr. Graphic Arts Collection,Rochester, NY [*Library symbol*] [*Library of Congress*] (LCLS)
NRRL	Northern Regional Research Laboratory [*Later, NRRC*] [*Department of Agriculture*]
NRRO	Naval Radio Research Observatory (IAA)
NRRO	Nuclear Radiation-Resistant Oils (NRCH)
NRRP	National Reservoir Research Program [*Department of the Interior*] (GRD)
NRRP	Sybron Corp., Rochester, NY [*Library symbol*] [*Library of Congress*] (LCLS)
NRRPC	National Rural and Resources Press Club [*Australia*]
NRRR	Rochester Reference Research and Resources Council, Rochester, NY [*Library symbol*] [*Library of Congress*] (LCLS)
NRRS	Naval Radio Research Station
NRRS	Nebraska Reading Retrieval System (EDAC)
NRRS	No Remaining Radiation Service [*Unit*] [*Military*]
NRS	Atlantic Richfield Co. [*ICAO designator*] (FAAC)
NRS	Imperial Beach, CA [*Location identifier*] [*FAA*] (FAAL)
NRS	Name Registration Scheme [*Telecommunications*] (OSI)
NRS	National Radio Station (IAA)
NRS	National Readership Survey [*British*]
NRS	National Real Estate Service [*Canada*]
NRS	National Reemployment Service
NRS	National Reporter System [*Database*] [*Maritime Law Book Co. Ltd.*] [*Information service or system*] (CRD)
NRS	National Reserves System (SAUS)
NRS	National Runaway Switchboard (EA)
NRS	Nationwide Refrigeration Supplies [*British*]
NRS	Naval Radio Station
NRS	Naval Receiving Station
NRS	Naval Recruiting Service [*British military*] (DMA)
NRS	Naval Recruiting Station
NRS	Naval Research Section [*Library of Congress*] (MCD)
NRS	Naval Rocket Society (IAA)
NRS	Navy Records Society [*British*] (DBA)
NRS	Navy Relief Society (EA)
NRS	Network Resource Server [*J & L Information Systems*]
NRS	Neurobehavioral Rating Scale [*Medicine*] (DMAA)
NRS	Nevada Revised Statutes [*A publication*]
NRS	Newborn Rights Society (EA)
NRS	New Reading System (SAUS)
NRS	New Rural Society [*HUD project*]
NRS	Night Reconnaissance System
NRS	Nitrogen Recharge Station
NRS	Noise-Reduction System (SAUS)
NRS	Nonconformance Reporting System (NASA)
NRS	Nonconforming Reporting System
NRS	Non-Rising Stem [*Valve*] (DICI)
NRS	No Rate Specified [*Travel industry*] (TRID)

NRS	Normal Rabbit Serum [*Culture medium*]
NRS	Normal Rake System (SAUS)
NRS	Normal Rat Serum [*Hematology*]
NRS	Normal Reference Serum (MAE)
NRS	North-Holland Research Series In Early Detection and Prevention of Behaviour Disorders (SAUS)
NRS	Novell Replication Services (SAUS)
NRS	Nuclear Radiation Shield
NRS	Nuclear Reaction Spectrometry (BARN)
NRS	Nuclear Rocket Shuttle (KSC)
NRS	Numerical Rating Scale (DMAA)
NRS	Numerical Rating System [*Insurance*]
NRS	Nurse (ABBR)
NRSA	National Remote Sensing Agency [*India*]
NRSA	National Rental Service Association (EA)
NRSA	National Research Service Awards [*Department of Health and Human Services*]
NRSA	National Rose Society of Australia
NRSA	Natural Rubber Shippers Association (EA)
NRSA	Northeast Rail Service Act [*1981*] [*Also, NERSA*]
NRSB	Saint Bernard's Seminary and College, Rochester, NY [*Library symbol*] [*Library of Congress*] (LCLS)
NRSC	National Radio Systems Committee
NRSC	National Remote Sensing Centre [*Royal Aircraft Establishment Space Department*] [*British*] (CB)
NRSC	National Republican Senatorial Committee (EA)
NRSC	Naval Reserve Supply Company (DNAB)
NRSC	Nordic Road Safety Council [*See also NTR*] [*Helsinki, Finland*] (EAIO)
NRSCC	National Reference System in Clinical Chemistry (DAVI)
NRSCC	National Registry System for Chemical Compounds (DIT)
NRSCO	Navy Recruiting Station Commanding Officer
NRSD	Nursed (ABBR)
NRSDNC	Nonresidence (ABBR)
NRSDNT	Nonresident (ABBR)
NRSE	Neuron-Restrictive Silencer Element [*Neurogenesis*]
NRSE	Nurse (ABBR)
NRSe	Sear-Brown Associates, PC, Rochester, NY [*Library symbol*] [*Library of Congress*] (LCLS)
NRSED	Nursed (ABBR)
NRSEG	Nursing (ABBR)
NRSEMD	Nursemaid (ABBR)
NRSEP	National Roster of Scientific and Engineering Personnel (IAA)
NRSF	National Rehabilitation and Service Foundation (EA)
NRSF	National Reye's Syndrome Foundation (EA)
NRSF	Neuron-Restrictive Silencer Factor [*Neurogenesis*]
NRSFPS	National Reporting System for Family Planning Services [*National Institutes of Health*]
NRSG	Naval Reserve Security Group (DNAB)
NRSG	Nursing
NRSH	Nourish (ABBR)
NRSHD	Nourished (ABBR)
NRSHG	Nourishing (ABBR)
NRSHNT	Nourishment (ABBR)
NRSI	National Reading Styles Institute
NRSITD	Near-Sighted (ABBR)
NRSITNS	Near-Sightedness (ABBR)
NRSJ	Saint John Fisher College, Rochester, NY [*Library symbol*] [*Library of Congress*] (LCLS)
N-R Skt	Non-Reversible Socket (SAUS)
NRSL	Navy Radio and Sound Laboratory (IAA)
NRSO	Navy Resale Systems Office
NRSP	National Remote Sensing Program [*Marine science*] (OSRA)
NRSP	National Remote Sensing Programme (USDC)
NRSP	Nonrestorative Sleep Pattern (MELL)
NrSph	Spring Hope Public Library (SAUS)
NRS(R)	Naval Radio Station (Receiving) (DNAB)
nrsry	Nursery
NRS(S)	Naval Radio Station (Sending) (DNAB)
NRSSC	National Rural and Small Schools Consortium (EA)
NRSSFR Laser	Nonresonant Superradiant Spin-Flip Raman Laser (SAUS)
NRSSG	Nuclear Reactor Systems Safety Group [*Air Force*]
NRSSGP	Nuclear Reactor Systems Safety Group [*Air Force*]
NRSSO	Navy Resale and Services Support Office (DNAB)
NRST	Nonreactive Solute Transport (SAUS)
NRSTCTV	Nonrestrictive (ABBR)
NRSTK	Narcisistic (ABBR)
NRSTP	National Register of Scientific and Technical Personnel (IAA)
NRSV	Necrotic Ringspot Virus [*of prunes*]
NRSV	New Revised Standard Version [*1989*] [*A publication*] (ODCC)
NRSW	Nuclear River Service Water (IEEE)
NRSY	Nordiska Forbundet for Studie- och Yrkesvagledning [*Nordic Association for Study and Vocational Guidance - NASVG*] (EAIO)
NRSY	Nursery
NRT	Burroughs Wellcome & Co., Research Triangle Park, NC [*OCLC symbol*] (OCLC)
nrt	Narrator [*MARC relator code*] [*Library of Congress*] (LCCP)
NRT	National Rally Terminology [*Automotive competition*]
NRT	National Recreation Trail (COE)
NRT	National Repertory Theatre Foundation [*Defunct*] (EA)
NRT	National Resource Trustee (BCP)
NRT	National Response Team [*RSPA*] (TAG)
NRT	National Response Team for Oil and Hazardous Materials Spills [*Environmental Protection Agency*] [*Washington, DC*] (EGAO)
NRT	National Responsibility Team (HEAS)

NRT .... Naval Revolutionary Technology Initiative (ACAE)
NRT .... Navy Reserve Training
NRT .... Near-Real Time
NRT .... Neighbours of the Roundtable (EA)
NRT .... Net Registered Tonnage
NRT .... Net Register Tons [Shipping]
NRT .... Network Readiness Test (KSC)
NRT .... Neuromuscular Re-Education Techniques (DAVI)
NRT .... Neutron Radiographic Testing (SAUS)
NRT .... Nicotine-Replacement Therapy [Medicine]
NRT .... Noise-Riding Threshold (SAUS)
NRT .... Nonradiating Target
NRT .... Nonreal Time
NRT .... Non-Requesting Terminal (SAUS)
NRT .... Nonrequestor Terminal (IAA)
NRT .... No Right Turn (SAUS)
NRT .... Normal Rated Thrust (AAG)
NRT .... Norm-Referenced Testing [Education]
NRT .... Nortel Inversora 10%'MEDS' [NYSE symbol] (TTSB)
NRT .... Nortel Inversora SA [NYSE symbol] (SAG)
NRT .... Northern Airlines, Inc. (SAUS)
NRT .... Northfield [Vermont] [Seismograph station code, US Geological Survey] [Closed] (SEIS)
NRT .... Norton Co. (SAUS)
NRT .... Notion Round Table (EA)
NRT .... Nucleus Reticularis Thalami [Neuroanatomy]
NRT .... Taylor Instrument Cos., Rochester (SAUS)
NRT .... Taylor Instrument Cos., Rochester, NY [Library symbol] [Library of Congress] (LCLS)
NRT .... Tokyo-Narita [Japan] [Airport symbol] (OAG)
NRTA .... National Retired Teachers Association, Division of AARP (EA)
NRTAC .... National Recreation Trails Advisory Committee (COE)
NRTAC .... National Road Trauma Advisory Council [Australia]
NRT & CMA... National Retail Tea and Coffee Merchants Association
NRTB .... Naval Reserve Training Branch
nrtb .... No Risk until on Board (MARI)
NRTC .... National Retail Trade Centre (EAIO)
NRTC .... National Rotorcraft Technology Center
NRTC .... Naval Reserve Training Center
NRTC .... Nonreal-Time Conversion Subsystem [Space Flight Operations Facility, NASA]
NRTC .... Normalized Re-instrumented Terrain Computer (SAUS)
NRTC .... Northrop Research and Technology Center (ACAE)
NRTCOMD ... Naval Reserve Training Command
NRTC Subsystem... Non Real Time Conversion Subsystem (SAUS)
NRT DAS ..... Non-Real Time Data Automation System (SAUS)
NRTDAS ...... Nonreal-Time Data Automation System [NASA] (IAA)
NRTEC .... National Rural Teacher Education Consortium [National Rural Development Institute] [Later, NRSSC] (EA)
NRTEM .... Near Real Time Exploitation Module (ACAE)
NRTF .... National Recreation Trails Fund (COE)
NRTF .... Naval Radio Transmitting Facility (DNAB)
NRTH .... North (ABBR)
NrthFce .... North Face, Inc. (The) [Associated Press] (SAG)
NRTHSD ...... Northside
NRTHUM ...... Northumberland [County in England] (ROG)
NRTI .... National Rehabilitation Training Institute [Defunct] (EA)
NRTI .... Nooney Realty Trust [NASDAQ symbol] (TTSB)
NRTI .... Nooney Realty Trust, Inc. [NASDAQ symbol] (NQ)
NRTI .... Nucleoside Revenue Transcript Inhibitor [Biochemistry]
NRTIPT .... Naval Reserve Training in Port (NVT)
NRTK .... Nonreceptor Tyrosine Kinase [An enzyme]
NRTL .... Nationally Recognized Testing Laboratory (COE)
NRTL .... Nonlinear Resistor Transistor Logic (SAUS)
NRTL .... Non-Random Two-Liquid [Equation of state]
NRTL Eq ...... Non-Random Two-Liquid Equation (SAUS)
NRTM .... Near Real Time Module (ACAE)
NRTN .... Norton Enterprises, Inc. (SAUS)
NRTO .... National Remotivation Therapy Organization (EA)
NRTOB .... No Risk Till on Board (SAUS)
NRTOI .... National Range Technical Operating Instructions [NASA] (KSC)
NRTOR........ No Risk Till On Rail (SAUS)
NRTOR........ No Risk to Attach till on Rail (MARI)
nrtor............ No Risk until Waterborne (MARI)
NRTP .... Nucleus Reticularis Tegmenti Pontis [Neuroanatomy]
NRTR .... Near-Real-Time Reconnaissance (MCD)
NRTR .... Nurture (ABBR)
NRTRD .... Nurtured (ABBR)
NRTRG........ Nurturing (ABBR)
NRTS .... National Reactor Test Station [INEL] (NRCH)
NRTS .... Not Repairable This Ship [Navy] (AFIT)
NRTS .... Not Reparable This Station
NRTS .... Nuclear Reactor Testing Station (SAUS)
NRTSC .... Naval Reconnaissance and Technical Support Center
NRTSCPAC... Naval Reconnaissance and Technical Support Center, Pacific (DNAB)
NRT-VBR ..... Non Real-Time Variable Bit Rate (SAUS)
NRTWB .... No Risk Till Water Borne (SAUS)
NRTWB .... No Risk to Attach till Waterborne (MARI)
NRTWC .... National Right to Work Committee (EA)
NRTWG....... Nutrient Reduction Targets Working Group (SAUS)
NRTWLDEF... National Right to Work Legal Defense and Education Foundation [Also, NRWLDF] (EA)
NRTY .... Norton McNaughton [NASDAQ symbol] (TTSB)
NRTY .... Norton McNaughton, Inc. [NASDAQ symbol] (SAG)

NRU .... National Reactor Universal
NRU .... National Research Universal [Nuclear reactor] [Canada]
NRU .... National Rural Utilities Cooperative Finance Corp. [NYSE symbol] (SAG)
NRU .... Natural Resource Unit [Environmental unit]
NRU .... Nauru [ANSI three-letter standard code] (CNC)
NRU .... Network Resource Unit (MHDB)
NRU .... Neuropsychiatric Research Unit [Navy]
NRU .... Neutral Red Uptake (DMAA)
N Ru .... Nicolaus Rufulus [Flourished, 13th century] [Authority cited in pre-1607 legal work] (DSA)
NRU .... Nitrogen Rejection Unit [Process engineering]
NRU .... Nonreplaceable Unit (IAA)
NRU .... North Reference Unit (SAUS)
NRU .... Not Recently Used [Replacement algorithm] [Computer science] (BYTE)
NRU .... Nuclear Reactor Universal (SAUS)
NRU .... University of Rochester, Rochester, NY [Library symbol] [Library of Congress] (LCLS)
NRU-A .... University of Rochester, Memorial Art Gallery, Rochester, NY [Library symbol] [Library of Congress] (LCLS)
NRUCFC...... National Rural Utilities Cooperative Finance Corp. (EA)
NRU-M........ University of Rochester, School of Medicine and Dentistry, Rochester, NY [Library symbol] [Library of Congress] (LCLS)
NRU-Mus..... University of Rochester, Eastman School of Music, Rochester, NY [Library symbol] [Library of Congress] (LCLS)
NRurU45...... National Rural Utilities Cooperative Finance Corp. [Associated Press] (SAG)
NRUS.......... Neighbors Are Us (PA)
NRUS.......... Nonlinear Resonant Ultrasound Spectroscopy
NRU-W........ University of Rochester, Women's College, Rochester, NY [Library symbol] [Library of Congress] (LCLS)
NRV .... Navarre Resources [Vancouver Stock Exchange symbol]
NRV .... Nerve (ABBR)
NRV .... Net Realizable Value
NRV .... Neubabylonische Rechts- und Verwaltungsurkunden [A publication] (BJA)
NRV .... Nodal Route Vector (SAUS)
NRV .... Non-Return Valve (SAUS)
NRV .... Nonrevenue [Passengers or cargo] [Transportation]
NRV .... Northamptonshire Rifle Volunteer Corps [British military] (DMA)
NRV .... North Carolina State University, School of Veterinary Medicine, Raleigh, NC [OCLC symbol] (OCLC)
NRV .... North Vancouver Airlines Ltd. [Canada] [FAA designator] (FAAC)
NRV .... Nucleus Reticularis Ventralis (DB)
NRVA.......... Net Realizable Value Accounting (ADA)
NRVC.......... National Religious Vocation Conference (EA)
NRvCH........ Central Suffolk Hospital, Riverhead, NY [Library symbol] [Library of Congress] (LCLS)
NRVD.......... Nerved (ABBR)
NRVG.......... Nerving (ABBR)
NRVH.......... National RV Holdings, Inc. [NASDAQ symbol] (SAG)
NRVH.......... Natl R.V.Holding [NASDAQ symbol] (TTSB)
NRVI........... Nervy (ABBR)
NRVLS........ Nerveless (ABBR)
NRVMA....... National Roadside Vegetation Management Association (EA)
NRVOC....... National RV [Recreational Vehicle] Owners Club (EA)
NRvS .... Suffolk County Historical Society, Riverhead, NY [Library symbol] [Library of Congress] (LCLS)
NRVSBL...... Nonreversible
NRvSL .... Supreme Court Law Library, Tenth Judicial District, Riverhead, NY [Library symbol] [Library of Congress] (LCLS)
NRVU.......... Nervous (ABBR)
NRVUNS...... Nervousness (ABBR)
NRVUS........ Nervous (ABBR)
NRVUSNS.... Nervousness (ABBR)
NRVUSY...... Nervously (ABBR)
NRVUY........ Nervously (ABBR)
NRVWRKG... Nerve-Wracking (ABBR)
NRW .... NCL Holdings ADS [NYSE symbol] (SG)
NRW .... New Right Watch [An association] (EA)
NRW .... Nonradioactive Waste [Nuclear energy] (NRCH)
NRW .... Non-Reversed Word (SAUS)
NRW .... Norwegian (ABBR)
NRW .... Nuclear RADWASTE (IEEE)
NRW .... Number of Remaining Words
NR/WA........ National Rep/Wholesaler Association (EA)
NRWA........ National Rural Water Association (EA)
NRWC........ National Right to Work Committee (EA)
NRWD........ Narrowed (ABBR)
NRWG........ Narrowing (ABBR)
NRWG........ Neutron Radiography Working Group [EURATOM]
NRW-KA...... National Registry of Willys-Knight Automobiles [Later, W-O-KR]
NRWLDEF.... National Right to Work Legal Defense and Education Foundation [Later, NRWLDF] (EA)
NRWLDF..... National Right to Work Legal Defense Foundation (EA)
NRWMDD .... Narrow-Minded (ABBR)
NRWMDDNS... Narrow-Mindedness (ABBR)
NRWO......... Nuclear RADWASTE [Radioactive Waste] Operator (IAA)
NRWT......... Non-Resident Withholding Tax (SAUS)
NRWV......... Nonradioactive Waste Vent [Nuclear energy] (NRCH)
NRX .... National Research Experiment [Canadian reactor]
NRX .... NERVA [Nuclear Engine for Rocket Vehicle Application] Reactor Experiment
NRX .... Nuclear Engine Reactor Experiment (NRCH)

NRX	Nuclear Reactor Experiment (SAUS)
NRX	Nuclear Reactor, Experimental
NRX	Xerox Corp., Rochester, NY [*Library symbol*] [*Library of Congress*] (LCLS)
NRX(C)	Nonreturn-to-Zero (Change) Recording
NRX-CX	Nuclear Engine Reactor Critical Assembly (SAA)
NRX-EST	NERVA [*Nuclear Engine for Rocket Vehicle Applications*] Reactor Experiment-EngineSystem Test (SAA)
NRY	Nearly (ABBR)
Nry	Newry (SAUS)
NRy	Rye Free Reading Room, Rye, NY [*Library symbol*] [*Library of Congress*] (LCLS)
NRyHi	Rye Historical Society, Rye, NY [*Library symbol*] [*Library of Congress*] (LCLS)
NRyS	Sloan-Kettering Institute for Cancer Research, Rye, NY [*Library symbol*] [*Library of Congress*] (LCLS)
NRZ	Nonreturn to Zero [*Data transmission*]
NRZ	Not Return to Zero (SAUS)
NRZ	Null Reception Zone
NRZ1	Nonreturn to Zero Change on One (BUR)
NRZ1	Non-Return-to-Zero-One (SAUS)
NRZC	Nonreturn to Zero Change
NRZC Code	Nonreturn-to-Zero Change Recording (SAUS)
NRZ Code	Non-Returning-to-Zero Code (SAUS)
NRZ Code	Non-Return-to-Zero Code (SAUS)
NRZI	Non-Return to Zero Indicates (SAUS)
NRZI	Nonreturn-to-Zero Indicator (SAUS)
NRZI	Non-Return-to-Zero Indiscrete (SAUS)
NRZI	Nonreturn to Zero Inverted [*Recording method*]
NRZI	Nonreturn-to-Zero Inverted (SAUS)
NRZI	NRZ Indicator (NITA)
NRZ-L	Non Return to Zero Level (ACAE)
NRZL	Nonreturn to Zero Level
NRZL	Nonreturn to Zero Logic (MCD)
NRZL	Nonreturn-to-Zero Logic (SAUS)
NRZM	Nonreturn to Zero Mark
NRZR	Non-Return-to-Zero Recording (SAUS)
NRZ-S	Non-Return to Zero-Space (MCD)
N S	Edward Henry Kraus Natural Science Building (SAUS)
NS	Graduate of the Royal Naval Staff College, Greenwich [*British*]
NS	Nachalnik Sektora [*Chief of Sector*] [*Soviet military rank*]
NS	Name Server
NS	Nano Second (AGLO)
ns	Nanosecond [*One billionth of a second*] [*Also, nsec*]
NS	Naram-Sin (BJA)
NS	Narodna Stranka [*People's Party*] [*Montenegro*] [*Political party*] (EY)
NS	Narodnye Sotsialisty [*Popular Socialists*] [*Former USSR*] [*Political party*] (PPE)
N-S	Nassi-Schneiderman [*Computer science*]
NS	National Savings [*British*]
NS	National Scientific [*Vancouver Stock Exchange symbol*]
NS	National Seashore (BARN)
NS	National Service [*in the armed forces*] [*British*]
NS	National Society
NS	National Sojourners (EA)
NS	National Special [*Thread*]
NS	National Standard (IEEE)
NS	National Steel [*NYSE symbol*] (SPSG)
NS	National Strategy
NS	National Samling [*National Union*] [*Norway*] (PD)
NS	Natl Steel 'B' [*NYSE symbol*] (TTSB)
NS	NATO Secret (NATG)
NS	NATO Surveillance (NATG)
NS	Natural Sciences
NS	Natural Stupidness (SAUS)
NS	[*The*] Naturist Society (EA)
NS	Naval School (MCD)
NS	Naval Shipyard
NS	Naval Station
NS	Naval Stores [*British*]
NS	Navigation Subsystem (OA)
NS	NAVSHIPS [*Naval Ship Systems Command*] Publication
NS	Near Side [*Technical drawings*]
NS	Near Space
NS	Nederlandse Spoorwegen [*Netherlands Railways*]
NS	Neoplasm Staging [*Medicine*] (MELL)
NS	Neo Sumerian (BJA)
N/S	Neosynephrine (SAUS)
NS	Nephrosclerosis [*Medicine*]
NS	Nephrotic Syndrome [*Medicine*] (DAVI)
NS	Nerine Society [*Defunct*] (EA)
NS	Nerves (SAUS)
NS	Nervous System
NS	Net Sales (MHDW)
NS	Net Surplus
NS	Networked Systems [*Automotive engineering*]
NS	Network Service [*Computer science*] (TNIG)
NS	Neue Sachlichkeit [*New Objectivity*] [*Pre-World War II group of German artists*]
NS	Neuroelectric Society [*Defunct*] (EA)
NS	Neurologic Signs [*Medicine*] (CPH)
NS	Neurologic Survey [*Medicine*] (MAE)
ns	neuropsychiatric (SAUS)
NS	Neurosecretory
NS	Neurosurgery [*Medicine*]

NS	Neuro-Syphilis [*Medicine*]
NS	Neurotic Score [*Psychology*]
NS	Neutron Spectrometer (SAUS)
N/S	Neutrons per Second
NS	Neutron Star (SAUS)
NS	Newport Steel Corp. (EFIS)
NS	News [*A radio station format*] (WDMC)
NS	New School
ns	New Series (RION)
NS	New Series [*Bibliography*]
NS	New Side
NS	New Signal (ELAL)
NS	Newspaper Society [*British*]
n/s	Newsstand [*Also N/S*] (WDMC)
NS	New Statesman [*A publication*] (BRI)
NS	New Style
NS	New Synchonization (SAUS)
NS	New System [*Computer science*]
NS	Next State (SAUS)
NS	Next System [*Computer science*]
NS	Nickel Silver [*Used in minting coins*]
NS	Nickel Steel
NS	Niederschlagstaub (SAUS)
Ns	Nielsbohrium [*Proposed name and symbol for recently-discovered element*]
NS	Nietzsche Society (EA)
NS	Night Switch (SAUS)
NS	Nimbostratus [*Cloud*] [*Meteorology*]
Ns	Nimbostratus Cloud (WEAT)
NS	Nitrogen Supply
NS	Nitrogen System
NS	Nobelstiftelsen [*Nobel Foundation - NF*] (EAIO)
NS	Nockian Society (EA)
NS	Nodularia Spumigena (SAUS)
NS	Nodular Sclerosis [*Medicine*] (AAMN)
NS	Noise Sensitivity (IAA)
NS	Noise Suppressor (SAUS)
NS	Noise Supressor [*Radio*] (NTCM)
NS	Nonscheduled
NS	Nonschizophrenic [*Psychology*]
NS	Nonsequenced (IAA)
NS	Nonserviceable (MSA)
NS	Nonshorting (IAA)
NS	Nonskew (IAA)
NS	Nonslip (ABBR)
NS	Nonsmutted [*Plant pathology*]
NS	Nonspecific (SAUS)
NS	Nonspecified
NS	Non-Staining (SAUS)
NS	Nonstandard (AABC)
NS	Nonstatus Candidates May Apply [*Civil Service*]
NS	Nonstimulation
NS	Nonstop [*Aviation*]
NS	Non-Stored (SAUS)
NS	Nonstructural [*Protein*] (DB)
NS	Non Structure
NS	Nonsymptomatic [*Medicine*] (MAE)
NS	Noonans Syndrome (SAUS)
NS	Nordisk Speditorforbund [*Nordic Forwarding Agents Association - NFAA*] [*Defunct*] (EAIO)
NS	Nordisk Svommeforbund [*Nordic Swimming Federations Association - NSFA*] (EAIO)
NS	Norfolk Southern Railway Co. [*AAR code*]
NS	Normally Shut (NRCH)
N/S	Normal Saline [*Medicine*] (AMHC)
NS	Normal Segment
NS	Normal Serum
NS	Normal Sodium (DB)
NS	Normal State (SAUS)
NS	North Sea (SAUS)
NS	North Sea - Nonrigid Airship [*Royal Naval Air Service*] [*British*]
N/S	North Side [*In outdoor advertising*] (WDMC)
NS	North Somerset Imperial Yeomanry [*British military*] (DMA)
NS	North-South
NS	No Sample (MAE)
NS	No Scramble (IAA)
NS	Nose [*Horse racing*]
ns	No Sequelae [*Aftereffects*] [*Medicine*] (MAE)
N/S	No Service (SAUS)
NS	No Show (SAUS)
NS	No Signal (SAUS)
NS	No Sound [*Script notation*] (NTCM)
NS	No Sparring (DS)
NS	No Specimen [*Medicine*]
N/S	No Stamp [*Deltiology*]
NS	No Standard (SAUS)
NS	No Stimulation [*Neurophysiology*]
NS	No Stock (SAUS)
NS	Nostro Signore [*Our Lord*]
NS	No Surgery Performed
NS	Notch Strength (SAUS)
NS	Note Series (SAUS)
NS	Note Statement (SAUS)
N/S	Not in Stock (SAUS)
NS	Notre Seigneur [*Our Lord*] [*French*]

N/S............ Not Scheduled (SAUS)
NS.............. Not Seen
NS.............. Not Signed (SAUS)
NS.............. Not Significant
ns .... Not Specified (EBF)
NS.............. Not Specified
NS.............. Not Sprinklered [Insurance]
NS.............. Not Stated
NS.............. Not Stocked
NS.............. Not Stung
n/s .... Not Sufficient (WDMC)
NS.............. Not Sufficient
NS.............. Not Suitable
NS.............. Not Suppressed
NS.............. Not Switchable (MCD)
NS.............. Nougth State (SAUS)
NS.............. Noun Substantive [Grammar] (ROG)
NS.............. Nourishing Stout [Brewing] (ROG)
NS.............. Nova Scotia [Canadian province] [Postal code]
NS.............. Noxious Stimuli
NS.............. Noxious Substances (COE)
NS.............. Nuclear Safety (COE)
NS.............. Nuclear Science
NS.............. Nuclear Sclerosis [Ophthalmology]
NS.............. Nuclear Ship
NS.............. Nuclear Shuffle (SAUS)
NS.............. Nuclear Shuttle (NASA)
NS.............. Nuclear Spectroscopy (SAUS)
NS.............. Nuclear Submarine
NS.............. Nuclear Systems
NS.............. Nuernberger [ICAO designator] (AD)
NS.............. Null Statement (SAUS)
NS.............. Number of Secondary Turns (IAA)
N_s .... Number of Secondary Turns (IDOE)
NS.............. Number Series (SAUS)
NS.............. Number System (SAUS)
NS.............. Numerical Signal (SAUS)
NS.............. Numismatic Society
NS.............. Nursing Services
NS.............. Nursing Sister [Navy] [British]
NS.............. Nutation Synchronous (ACAE)
NS.............. Nutrition Society [British] (EAIO)
NS.............. Nylon Suture [Medicine]
NS.............. Nzingha Society (EA)
ns .... Sodium Metasilicate [CIPW classification] [Geology]
Ns .... Surface Refractivity (CET)
NS4........... Nuclear Steam Supply Shutoff System (SAUS)
NSa............ Bancroft Public Library, Salem, NY [Library symbol] [Library of Congress] (LCLS)
NSA .... Naphthalene Sulfonic Acid [Organic chemistry]
NSA .... Napoleonic Society of America (EA)
NSA .... National Safety Association (NADA)
NSA .... National Sawmilling Association [British] (BI)
NSA .... National Scrabble Association (EA)
NSA .... National Secretaries Association (International) [Later, PSI] (EA)
NSA .... National Security Act (AAG)
NSA .... National Security Agency [Acronym is facetiously translated as No Such Agency or Never Say Anything because of staffers' reluctance to give interviews] [DoD]
NSA .... National Security Agency, Fort George G. Meade, MD [OCLC symbol] (OCLC)
NSA .... National Security Archive
NSA .... National Security Area (COE)
NSA .... National Seniors' Association [Australia]
NSA .... National Service Acts [British]
NSA .... National Sheep Association [British] (DBA)
NSA .... National Shellfisheries Association (EA)
NSA .... National Sheriffs' Association (EA)
NSA .... National Shipping Authority [Department of Commerce]
NSA .... National Showmen's Association (EA)
NSA .... National Shuffleboard Association (EA)
NSA .... National Silo Association [Later, ISA] (EA)
NSA .... National Skating Association of Great Britain
NSA .... National Ski Association of America [Later, United States Ski Association]
NSA .... National Slag Association (EA)
NSA .... National Slate Association (EA)
NSA .... National Smokers Alliance
NSA .... National Snurfing Association (EA)
NSA .... National Society of Accountants (NTPA)
NSA .... National Society of Andersonville (EA)
NSA .... National Society of Artists (EA)
NSA .... National Society of Auctioneers [Later, National Auctioneers Association]
NSA .... National Softball Association (EA)
NSA .... National Sound Archive [British Library]
NSA .... National Speakers Association (EA)
NSA .... National Spiritual Alliance of the USA (EA)
NSA .... National Sports Association (EA)
NSA .... National Sprint Association [British] (DBA)
NSA .... National Sprouting Association (EA)
NSA .... National Standards Association (NADA)
NSA .... National Standards Association, Inc. [Bethesda, MD]
NSA .... National Steeplechase Association (EA)
NSA .... National Stereoscopic Association (EA)

NSA .... National Stone Association (EA)
NSA .... National Stroke Association (EA)
NSA .... National Student Association [Later, USSA]
NSA .... National Students Association (NADA)
NSA .... National Sunflower Association (EA)
NSA .... National System Architecture
NSA .... Nausea (KSC)
NSA .... Naval Stock Account
NSA .... Naval Supply Account
NSA .... Naval Support Activity [Vietnam]
NSA .... Navy Supply Annex (AFIT)
NSA .... Neighborhood Strategy Area [Program] [HUD]
NSA .... Nepal Studies Association (EA)
NSA .... Network Software Associates, Inc.
NSA .... Neurological Society of America (DAVI)
NSA .... Neurological Society of Australasia
NSA .... Neurosurgical Society of America (EA)
NSA .... New Sabina Resources Ltd. [Vancouver Stock Exchange symbol]
NSA .... New Shipborne Aircraft [Canada]
NSA .... New South Africa Fund [NYSE symbol] (SAG)
NSA .... Next Station Addressing (SAUS)
NSA .... Nichiren Shoshu Soka Gakkai of America [Buddhist organization] (EA)
NSA .... Nile Safaris Aviation [Sudan] [ICAO designator] (FAAC)
NSA .... Nitrosylsulfuric Acid [Inorganic chemistry]
NSA .... Node Switching Assembly (SSD)
NSA .... Noise Suppressor Assembly
NSA .... Nominal Stress Approach (PDAA)
NSA .... Nonenyl Succinic Anhydride (SAUS)
NSA .... Non-Self-Averaging (SAUS)
NSA .... Non-Sequenced Acknowledgement (SAUS)
NSA .... Nonsequenced Acknowledgment (IAA)
NSA .... Non-Sterling Area (PDAA)
NSA .... Non-surgical Sperm Aspiration (SAUS)
NSA .... Nonylsuccinic Acid [Organic chemistry]
NSA .... Noosa [Australia] [Airport symbol] (OAG)
NSA .... Normalised Site Attenuation (SAUS)
NSA .... Normal Serum Albumin [Clinical chemistry]
NSA .... Northeastern Saengerbund of America (EA)
NSA .... Northern Slope of Alaska (CARB)
NSA .... North Sea Assets [Investment firm] [British]
NSA .... North-South Acceleration
NSA .... Norwegian Seamen's Association (EA)
nsa............ No Salt Added (DMAA)
NSA .... No Salt Added
NSA .... No Serious Abnormality (DAVI)
NSA .... No Significant Abnormalities [Medicine]
NSA .... No Significant Anomaly [Medicine] (DMAA)
NSA .... No Suitable Applicant (SAUS)
NSA .... Not Seasonally Adjusted [US Census terminology]
NSA .... Nuclear Science Abstracts (ABAC)
NSA .... Nuclear Science Association (NADA)
NSA .... Nuclear Stock Association [British] (DBA)
NSA .... Nuclear Suppliers Association (EA)
NSA .... Nuclear Systems Analysis
NSA .... Number of Signals Averaged (DMAA)
NSA .... Nursery School Association [British] (BARN)
NSA .... Nurses Supply Association (SAUS)
NSAA .... National Sales Achievement Award [NALU]
NSAA .... National Ski Areas Association (EA)
NSAA .... National Space and Aeronautics Agency (MCD)
NSAA .... National Sulphuric Acid Association [British] (DBA)
NSAA .... National Supply Association of America [Later, NSDA] (EA)
NSAA .... National Surgical Assistant Association (NTPA)
NSAA .... Norwegian Singers Association of America (EA)
NSAA .... Nova Scotia Association of Architecture (SAUS)
NSA/AAO...... North Slope of Alaska and Adjacent Arctic Ocean (SAUS)
NSA/AAO...... NSA/Adjacent Arctic Ocean (SAUS)
NSAAB........ National Security Agency Advisory Board [Fort George G. Meade, MD] (EGAO)
NSAAC........ Atlantic Co-Operator, Antigonish, Nova Scotia [Library symbol] [National Library of Canada] (NLC)
NSABA........ National Spiritual Assembly of Baha'is of Australia
NSABP........ National Surgical Adjuvant Breast and Bowel Project (DAVI)
NSABP........ National Surgical Adjuvant Breast Project
NSAC .... National Society for Autistic Children [British]
NSAC .... National Society of Accountants for Cooperatives (EA)
NSAC .... National Space Activities Council (ACAE)
NSAC .... National Spiritualist Association of Churches (EA)
NSAC .... National Sport Aviation Council [Defunct] (EA)
NSAC .... National Student Action Center (EA)
NSAC .... National Student Aid Coalition [Defunct] (EA)
NSAC .... Norwegian Society of Automatic Control (SAUS)
NSAC .... Nova Scotia Agricultural College
NSAC .... NSAC, the National Society for Children and Adults with Autism (EA)
NSAC .... Nuclear Safety Advisory Committee (NUCP)
NSAC .... Nuclear Safety Analysis Center [Electric Power Research Institute] (NRCH)
NSACG........ Nuclear Strike Alternate Control Group (NATG)
NSACS........ National Society for the Abolition of Cruel Sports [British] (BI)
NSACS........ Naval Ships Advanced Communications System (SAA)
NSACSS....... National Security Agency/Central Security Service (AABC)
NSAD .... National Society of Art Directors (EA)
NSAD .... Naval Support Activity, Da Nang [Vietnam] (VNW)
NSAD .... Naval Support Activity Detachment (DNAB)

NSAD .... No Sign of Acute Disease (MELL)
NSAD .... No Sign of Significant Disease (SAUS)
NSAD .... Nuclear Safety Analysis Document (KSC)
NSADN......... Daily News, Amherst, Nova Scotia [Library symbol] [National Library of Canada] (NLC)
NSAE .... National Society for Art Education [British]
NSAE .... National Society of Architectural Engineers (EA)
NSAF .... National Sanitation Foundation (IAA)
NSAF .... Naval Supply Account Fund
NSAFC .... National Service Armed Forces Act [British]
NSAFF .... National Society Against Factory Farming [British] (DBA)
NSAG .... Negative Channel Self-Aligned Gate (IAA)
NSAGT......... New South African Group Test [Intelligence test]
NSAH .... Heritage Association of Antigonish, Nova Scotia [Library symbol] [National Library of Canada] (NLC)
NSAI .... Nashville Songwriters Association, International (EA)
NSAI .... National Standards Authority of Ireland [Irish Science and Technology Agency] (IRC)
NSAI .... Need Satisfaction of Activity Interview
NSAI .... Neutropenia Support Association, Inc. (NRGU)
NSAI .... Nonsteroidal Anti-Inflammatory [Pharmacochemistry]
NSAI .... NSA International [NASDAQ symbol] (TTSB)
NSAI .... NSA International, Inc. [NASDAQ symbol] (SAG)
NSAIA .... Nonsteroidal Anti-Inflammatory Agent
NSAIDS .... Non-Steroidal Anti-Inflammatory Drugs (SAUS)
NSAIN.......... Indian and Northern Affairs Canada [Affaires Indiennes et du Nord Canada],Amherst, Nova Scotia [Library symbol] [National Library of Canada] (BIB)
NSAIN.......... Indian and Northern Affairs Canada, Amherst, Nova Scotia (SAUS)
NSA Int........ NSA International, Inc. [Associated Press] (SAG)
NSAJ........... National Secretariat Australia Jaycees
NSAL .... National Society of Arts and Letters (EA)
NSALC .... Nonsmoking Attributable Lung Cancer
NSalDH........ Salamanca District Hospital, Salamanca, NY [Library symbol] [Library of Congress] (LCLS)
NSALO .... National Security Agency Liaison Officer
NSAM .... National Security Agency Memorandum
NSAM .... Naval School of Aviation Medicine
NSAM .... Norwegian Advanced Surface to Air Missile System
NSAMC .... Cumberland Regional Library, Amherst, Nova Scotia [Library symbol] [National Library of Canada] (NLC)
NS Am Law Register... American Law Register (SAUS)
NS Am Law Register... American Law Register (Reprint) [Ohio] [A publication] (DLA)
NSAMRMS... Maritime Resource Management Service [Service d'Amenagement des Ressources des Maritimes] Amherst, Nova Scotia [Library symbol] [National Library of Canada] (NLC)
NSAN........... Nissan Motor Co. Ltd. [NASDAQ symbol] (NQ)
NSan........... Sanborn-Pekin Free Library, Sanborn, NY [Library symbol] [Library of Congress] (LCLS)
NS & E .... New Systems and Enhancements (MCD)
NS & L .... NS & L Bancorp, Inc. [Associated Press] (SAG)
NS & S .... New Statesman & Society [A publication] (BRI)
NS & SO...... Nervous System and Sense Organs
NS & T .... National Status and Trends (GNE)
NS & T .... Naval Science and Tactics
NSanF.......... National Sanitation Foundation
NSANL .... Non-Sectarian Anti-NAZI League (EA)
NSanO .... Orleans-Niagara Board of Cooperative Educational Services, Associates Special Educational Instruction Materials Center, Sanborn, NY [Library symbol] [Library of Congress] (LCLS)
NSanO-C...... Orleans-Niagara Board of Cooperative Educational Services, Educational Communications Center, Sanborn, NY [Library symbol] [Library of Congress] (LCLS)
NSanO-S...... Orleans-Niagara Board of Cooperative Educational Services, Sanborn, NY [Library symbol] [Library of Congress] (LCLS)
NSANY......... Nissan Motor Co. ADR [NASDAQ symbol] (TTSB)
NSAP .... Apia [Western Samoa] [ICAO location identifier] (ICLI)
NSAP .... National Socialist Action Party [British]
NSAP .... National Society for Animal Protection (EA)
NSAP .... National Strategic Acquisition Plan (SAUS)
NSAP .... Navy Science Assistance Program (CAAL)
NSAP .... Network Service Access Point [Telecommunications] (OSI)
NSAPAC .... National Security Agency Pacific (CINC)
NSAPEA .... Nordic Society Against Painful Experiments on Animals (EA)
NSAPI.......... Netscape Server API [All-Purpose Interface] [Computer science]
NSA Publication... Nursery School Association Publication (SAUS)
NSAR .... Annapolis Valley Regional Library, Annapolis Royal, NS [Library symbol] [National Library of Canada] (NLC)
NSAR .... Nitrososarcosine [Organic chemistry]
NSARC......... Navy Systems Acquisition Review Council
NSARF .... Fort Anne Museum, Annapolis Royal, Nova Scotia [Library symbol] [National Library of Canada] (NLC)
NSAS .... National Society of Appraiser Specialists (NTPA)
NSAS .... Naval Support Activity, Saigon [Vietnam] (VNW)
NSAS .... Near Infrared Spectral Analysis Software
NSAS .... Nonscheduled Air Services (AAG)
NSAS .... Nonsystemic Antacid Suspension [Medicine] (MELL)
NSAS .... Nuclear Sealed Authentication System (AABC)
NSAS .... St. Francis Xavier University, Antigonish, Nova Scotia [Library symbol] [National Library of Canada] (NLC)
NSASAB........ National Security Agency Scientific Advisory Board [Ft. George G. Meade, MD] (EGAO)
NSASC .... Chemistry Department, St. Francis Xavier University, Antigonish, Nova Scotia [Library symbol] [National Library of Canada] (NLC)

NSAT .... NATO Small Arms Test (MCD)
NSAT .... NAVMAT [Navy Material Command] Special Assistance Team (DNAB)
NSAT .... NII Norsat International, Inc. [NASDAQ symbol] (SAG)
NSATE .... NII Norsat Intl. [NASDAQ symbol] (TTSB)
NSATS .... NAVMAT [Navy Material Command] Selected Acquisitions Tracking System (DNAB)
NSAU .... Asau [Western Samoa] [ICAO location identifier] (ICLI)
NSau........... Saugerties Public Library, Saugerties, NY [Library symbol] [Library of Congress] (LCLS)
NSauF.......... Ferroxcube Corp., Suagerties, NY [Library symbol] [Library of Congress] (LCLS)
NSA-US........ National Spiritual Assembly of the Baha'is of the US (EA)
NSAW .... National Society of Asphalt Workers [A union] [British]
NSAWI .... National Substance Abuse Web Index (SAUS)
NSay........... Sayville Library, Sayville, NY [Library symbol] [Library of Congress] (LCLS)
NSB .... Bimini-North [Bahamas] [Airport symbol] (OAG)
NSB .... Natal Shark Board (SAUS)
NSB .... Nationaal-Socialistische Beweging [National Socialist Movement] [Netherlands] [Political party] (PPE)
NSB .... National Savings Bank [British]
NSB .... National Science Board [National Science Foundation]
NSB .... National Small Business Association [Later, NSBU]
NSB .... National Socialist Board [Dutch National Socialist Party of 1931; later, Dutch NAZI Party] [Political party]
NSB .... NATO Security Board (NATG)
NSB .... Naval Standardization Board
NSB .... Naval Studies Board [National Academy of Sciences] (DOMA)
NSB .... Naval Submarine Base
NSB .... Near Surface Burst (MCD)
NSB .... Network of Small Businesses [Lyndhurst, OH] (EA)
NSB .... Newsprint Service Bureau [Later, API] (EA)
NSB .... Nippon Short-wave Broadcasting (SAUS)
NSB .... Nonspecific Binder
NSB .... Non-Statutory Body
NSB .... Nonsustained Breakdown (IAA)
NSB .... Nordisk Sammanslutning for Barnavard [Nordic Child and Youth Welfare Alliance - NCYWA] (EA)
NSB .... Nord-Sud [Benin] [ICAO designator] (FAAC)
NSB .... Norges Statsbaner [Norwegian State Railways]
NSB .... Northeast Federal (SAUS)
NSB .... Northern Soviet Boundary
NSB .... North Slope Borough (ARMP)
NSB .... Not Separately Billed
NSB .... Nuclear Standards Board (SAUS)
NSBA .... National Saanen Breeders Association (EA)
NSBA .... National Safe Boating Association (EA)
NSBA .... National School Band Association [British] (DBA)
NSBA .... National School Boards Association (EA)
NSBA .... National Semi-Professional Baseball Association (EA)
NSBA .... National Sheep Breeders' Association [British] (BI)
NSBA .... National Shrimp Breeders Association (EA)
NSBA .... National Small Business Association [Later, NSBU]
NSBA .... National Snaffle Bit Association (EA)
NSBA .... National Sugar Brokers Association (EA)
NSBB .... National Society for Business Budgeting [Later, PEI]
NSBBA .... National Small Business Benefits Association (EA)
NSBC .... National Safe Boating Council (EA)
NSBC .... National Safety Belt Coalition [NHTSA] (TAG)
NSBC .... National Shoeboard Conference (EA)
NSBC .... National Student Book Club
NSBC Bcp ..... Natural Science Book Club
NS Bcp .... NS Bancorp, Inc. [Associated Press] (SAG)
NSBCSH....... Cape Sable Historical Society, Barrington, Nova Scotia [Library symbol] [National Library of Canada] (NLC)
NSBD .... Narrow Spectral Band Detection
NSBD .... National Society of Bank Directors [Formerly, NABD] [Later, ASBD] (EA)
NSBD .... New Services Business Development (TIMI)
NSBDM........ DesBrisay Museum and National Exhibit Centre, Bridgewater, Nova Scotia [Library symbol] [National Library of Canada] (NLC)
NSBE .... National Society of Black Engineers (EA)
NSBEO .... National Sonic Boom Evaluation Office [Air Force] (MCD)
NSBET .... National Society of Biomedical Equipment Technicians (EA)
NSBF .... National Scientific Balloon Facility [Palestine, TX] [NASA]
NSBGCA....... National Small Business Government Contractors Association [Defunct] (EA)
NSBGW........ National Society of Brushmakers and General Workers [A union] [British] (DCTA)
NS/BH .... Neutron-Star/Black-Hole
NSBI .... NS Bancorp, Inc. [NASDAQ symbol] (SAG)
NSbIA .... Institute of Advanced Studies of World Religions, Stony Brook, NY [Library symbol] [Library of Congress] (LCLS)
NSBISS .... NATO Security Bureau Industrial Security Section (NATG)
NSBIU .... Nova Scotia Board of Insurance Underwriters (SAUS)
NSBJH .... James House, Bridgetown, Nova Scotia [Library symbol] [National Library of Canada] (NLC)
NSBK .... North Side Savings Bank [NASDAQ symbol] (NQ)
NSBL .... Lighthouse Publishing Ltd., Bridgewater, Nova Scotia [Library symbol] [National Library of Canada] (NLC)
NSBLE .... Leader, Berwick, Nova Scotia [Library symbol] [National Library of Canada] (NLC)
NSBM .... Monitor, Bridgetown, Nova Scotia [Library symbol] [National Library of Canada] (NLC)

NSBMA	National Small Business Men's Association [Later, NSBU]
NSBNL	Naval Submarine Base - New London (MCD)
NSBP	National Society of Black Physicists (EA)
NSBPA	National Shrimp Breaders and Processors Association (EA)
NSBPH	National Library Service for the Blind and Physically Handicapped [Library of Congress] [Washington, DC] [Library network]
NSBR	Register, Berwick, Nova Scotia [Library symbol] [National Library of Canada] (NLC)
NSBRH	Bear River Historical Society, Nova Scotia [Library symbol] [National Library of Canada] (NLC)
NSBRI	National Space Biomedical Research Institute (SAUS)
NSBRO	National Service Board for Religious Objectors [Later, NISBCO] (EA)
NSBS	South Shore Regional Library, Bridgewater, Nova Scotia [Library symbol] [National Library of Canada] (NLC)
NSbSM	Suffolk Museum at Stony Brook, Stony Brook, NY [Library symbol] [Library of Congress] (LCLS)
NSBSSA	National Strict Baptist Sunday School Association [British]
NSBSSN	South Shore News, Bridgewater, Nova Scotia [Library symbol] [National Library of Canada] (NLC)
NSbSU	State University of New York at Stony Brook, Stony Brook, NY [Library symbol] [Library of Congress] (LCLS)
NSbSU-H	State University of New York at Stony Brook, Health Sciences Library, Stony Brook, NY [Library symbol] [Library of Congress] (LCLS)
NSBT	National Swiss Battle Tank (MCD)
NSBT	Not Series by Title (MCD)
NSBU	National Small Business United [Washington, DC] (EA)
NSBVCA	Victoria County Archives and Museum, Baddeck, Nova Scotia [Library symbol] [National Library of Canada] (NLC)
NSBWC	National Safe Boating Week Committee [Later, NSBC]
NSBWK	Western King's Memorial Hospital, Berwick, Nova Scotia [Library symbol] [National Library of Canada] (NLC)
NSC	Arthur D. Little, Inc. [Research code symbol]
NSC	Bristol-Myers Co. [Research code symbol]
NSC	Hoffmann-La Roche, Inc. [Research code symbol]
NSC	NASCAR [National Association for Stock Car Auto Racing] Street Classics [Later, WW] (EA)
NSC	Nasdaq Small Cap (SG)
NSC	National Cancer Institute [Research code symbol]
NSC	National Safety Corp.
NSC	National Safety Council (NADA)
NSC	National Safflower Council [Defunct] (EA)
NSC	National Savings Certificates [British] (DAS)
NSC	National Savings Committee [British]
NSC	National Science Council [Irish] (MSC)
NSC	National Security Council
NSC	National Semiconductor Corp.
NSC	National Service Center
NSC	National Shrimp Congress (EA)
NSC	National Simulation Capability (SAUS)
NSC	National Simulation Council (SAA)
NSC	National Slavic Convention (EA)
NSC	National Smallgoods Council [Australia]
NSC	National Snorkellers Club [British] (DBA)
NSC	National Society of Chauffeurs [A union] [British]
NSC	National Society of Computer/Genealogists [Defunct] (EA)
NSC	National Society of Cwens
NSC	National Space Club (EA)
NSC	National Space Council
NSC	National Spiritualist Church [British]
NSC	National Staff Committee [Nurses and midwives] [British]
NSC	National Standards Commission (NADA)
NSC	National Stinson Club (EA)
NSC	National Stinson Club - 108 Series (EA)
NSC	National Supercomputer Center (CIST)
NSC	National Supply Class [Military] (AFIT)
NSC	National Surface Cleaning, Inc. (EFIS)
NSC	National Survey of Children
NSC	National Synthetics Collection [Smithsonian Institution]
NSC	NATO [North Atlantic Treaty Organization] Science Committee (EAIO)
NSC	NATO Steering Committee (NATG)
NSC	NATO Supply Center (NATG)
NSC	NATO Supply Classification
NSC	Naval Coastal Systems Center [Florida]
NSC	Naval Safety Center (MCD)
NSC	Naval School Command
NSC	Naval Sea Cadets
NSC	Naval Space Command (MCD)
NSC	Naval Staff College (DOMA)
NSC	Naval Supply Center
NSC	Navigation and Sensor Computer
NSC	Navigation Star Catalogue
NSC	Navy Service Center
NSC	Net Sale Certificate (DGA)
NSC	Network Service Center [Telecommunications]
NSC	Network Support Committee (ACAE)
NSC	Network Switching Center [Telecommunications] (TEL)
NSC	Network Systems Corp. [Brooklyn Park, MN] [Telecommunications] (TSSD)
NSC	Neuroscience Center (SAUS)
NSC	Neurosecretory Cells
NSC	Newark State College (SAUS)
NSC	Newscope Resources Ltd. [Toronto Stock Exchange symbol]
NSC	New Session Cases [Scotland] [A publication] (DLA)
NSC	Newtex SS [Steamship company] [AAR code]
NSC	Nicaragua Solidarity Campaign (EAIO)
NSC	Nippon Steel Corp. [Japan]
NSC	Nodal Switching Center
NSC	Nodal Switching Center (or Centre) (SAUS)
NSC	Noise Suppression Circuit (DEN)
NSC	Nomenclature Sequence Code [Navy] (AFIT)
NSC	Nominal Single Dose [Pharmacology] (DAVI)
NSC	Non-Sequential Computer (VLIE)
NSC	Non-Service-Connected
NSC	Nordic Saami Council (SAUS)
NSC	Norfolk Southern [NYSE symbol] (TTSB)
NSC	Norfolk Southern Railway [NYSE symbol] (SPSG)
NSC	Northeastern State College [Oklahoma]
NSC	North Sea Conference (SAUS)
NSC	North Star Congress (PSS)
NSC	North Stonington [Connecticut] [Seismograph station code, US Geological Survey] (SEIS)
NSC	Norwegian Space Center (or Centre) (SAUS)
NSC	No Significant Change [Medicine]
NSC	No Significant Cloud [Meteorology] (FAAC)
NSC	Nothing So Called [Bookselling]
NSC	Notice of Schedule Change (SAUS)
NSC	Not Service-Connected [Medicine] (MEDA)
nsc	Nova Scotia [MARC country of publication code] [Library of Congress] (LCCP)
NSC	NSC Corp. [Associated Press] (SAG)
NSC	Nuclear Safety Concern (SAUS)
NSC	Nuclear Safety Convention (SAUS)
NSC	Nuclear Science Center [Louisiana State University] [Research center] (RCD)
NSC	Nuclear Services Corporation (ABAC)
NSC	Numerical Sequence Code
NSC	Nursing Sentence Completions [Nursing school test]
NSC	Nutrition Society of Canada (SAUS)
NSC	Salem College, Winston-Salem, NC [OCLC symbol] (OCLC)
NSCA	NASCOM [NASA Communications Network] Assembly
NSCA	National institute for Supercomputing Applications (SAUS)
NSCA	National Satellite Cable Association [Defunct] (EA)
NSCA	National Scrip Collectors Association (EA)
NSCA	National Senior Citizens Association [Commercial firm] (EA)
NSCA	National Shrimp Canners Association
NSCA	National Ski Credit Association (EA)
NSCA	National Soccer Coaches Association of America (EA)
NSCA	National Society for Clean Air [British] (DCTA)
NSCA	National Society of Commercial Agents [Australia]
NSCA	National Sound and Communications Association (EA)
NSCA	National Spinal Cord Association (DHP)
NSCA	National Sporting Clays Association
NSCA	National Strength and Conditioning Association (EA)
NSCA	National Subacute Care Association (EA)
NSCA	National Systems Contractors Association (NTPA)
NSCA	Natural Sausage Casings Association [British] (DBA)
NSCA	Nevada State Council on the Arts (SAUS)
NSCA	Northwest Salmon Canners Association (EA)
NSCA	Nova Scotia College of Art
NSCA	Nutrient Starch Cycloheximide Agar [Microbiology]
NSca	Scarsdale Public Library, Scarsdale, NY [Library symbol] [Library of Congress] (LCLS)
NSCAA	National Small College Athletic Association (EA)
NSCAA	National Soccer Coaches Association of America (NTPA)
NSCAA	[The] National Society for Children and Adults with Autism 2 [Formerly, NSAC] (EA)
NSCAA	Nutrient Starch Cycloheximide Antibiotic Agar [Microbiology]
NSCAD	Nova Scotia College of Art and Design (SAUS)
NSCAE	National Standards Council of American Embroiderers [Later, CAE] (EA)
NSCAEU	National Service Conference of the American Ethical Union (EA)
NSCAH	National Student Campaign Against Hunger [Later, NSCAHH] (EA)
NSCAHH	National Student Campaign Against Hunger and Homelessness (EA)
NSCAMP	National Stock Control and Maintenance Point [Army] (AFIT)
NSC & MP	National Stock Control and Maintenance Point [Army] (AABC)
NSCAR	National Society of the Children of the American Revolution (EA)
NSCAS	Archelaus Smith Museum, Centreville (Shelburne Co.), Nova Scotia [Library symbol] [National Library of Canada] (NLC)
NSCAT	NASA [or NROSS] Scatterometer [Instrumentation]
NSCAT	NROSS Scatterometer (SAUS)
N-SCATT	Navy Scatterometer (MCD)
NSCAV	National Safety Council of Australia, Victoria Division
NSCB	NBSC Corp. [NASDAQ symbol] (NQ)
NSCB	Nordic Society for Cell Biology (EA)
NSCC	National Securities Clearing Corp.
NSCC	National Service Coordinating Committee [Ministry of Labour and National Service] [British] [World War II]
NSCC	National Siamese Cat Club (EA)
NSCC	National Social Conditioning Camps [Later, NOC] (EA)
NSCC	National Society for Crippled Children (DAVI)
NSCC	Naval Sea Cadet Corps (NVT)
NSCC	Navy Sea Cargo Coordinator (DNAB)
NSCC	New Sudan Council of Churches
NSCC	North Shore Community College [Beverly, MA]
NSCC	NSC Corp. [NASDAQ symbol] (SAG)
NSCC	Nuclear Services Closed Cooling (IEEE)
NSCCA	National Society for Crippled Children and Adults [Later, NESS] (EA)
NSCCA	National Sports Car Club of America

NSCCA .... Nuclear Safety Cross-Check Analysis (DOMA)
NSCCF .... Canadian Forces Base, Cornwallis, Nova Scotia [*Library symbol*] [*National Library of Canada*] (NLC)
NSCCFE .... Ensign, Canadian Forces Base, Cornwallis, Nova Scotia [*Library symbol*] [*National Library of Canada*] (NLC)
NSCCLO ...... Naval Sea Cadet Corps Liaison Officer (DNAB)
NSCCM .... Cumberland County Museum, Amherst, Nova Scotia [*Library symbol*] [*National Library of Canada*] (NLC)
NSCD .... National School Development Council (AEE)
NSCD .... Nonservice-Connected Disability (MAE)
NSCD .... Nuclear Service Control Date (DNAB)
NSCDA .... National Society of Colonial Dames of America (EA)
N Sc Dec ..... Nova Scotia Decisions [*A publication*] (DLA)
NSCDET .... Naval Supply Center Detachment (DNAB)
NSCDP .... Non-Sexist Child Development Project (EA)
NSCDRF .... National Sickle Cell Disease Research Foundation [*Defunct*] (EA)
NSCE .... NetSource Communications, Inc. [*NASDAQ symbol*] (SAG)
NSCEC .... National School Curriculum Center for Educational Computing [*Defunct*] (EA)
NSCEE .... National Schools Committee for Economic Education (EA)
NSCEO .... National Society of Chief Executive Officers [*Defunct*] (EA)
NSCF .... National Skin Cancer Foundation [*Later, SCF*] (EA)
NSCF .... National Student Christian Federation [*Later, UCM*] (EA)
NSCF .... Naval Small Craft Facilities
NSCF .... Northstar Computer Forms [*NASDAQ symbol*] (TTSB)
NSCF .... Northstar Computer Forms, Inc. [*NASDAQ symbol*] (SAG)
NSCFA .... National Support Center for Families of the Aging [*Defunct*] (EA)
NSCG .... Northeastern Spoon Collectors Guild (EA)
NSCH .... Canso Historical Society, Nova Scotia [*Library symbol*] [*National Library of Canada*] (NLC)
NSch .... Schenectady County Public Library, Schenectady, NY [*Library symbol*] [*Library of Congress*] (LCLS)
NSchC .... Schenectady County Community College, Schenectady, NY [*Library symbol*] [*Library of Congress*] (LCLS)
NSchE .... Ellis Hospital, Schenectady, NY [*Library symbol*] [*Library of Congress*] (LCLS)
NSCHE .... Non-Specific Cholinesterase (SAUS)
NSCHF .... National Sprint Car Hall of Fame [*Iowa*]
NSchGEKA .. General Electric Co., Knolls Atomic Laboratory, Technical Library, Schenectady, NY [*Library symbol*] [*Library of Congress*] (LCLS)
NSchGEM .... General Electric Co., Main Library, Schenectady (SAUS)
NSchGEM .... General Electric Co., Main Library, Schenectady, NY [*Library symbol*] [*Library of Congress*] (LCLS)
NSchGER ..... General Electric Co., Research Laboratory, Schenectady, NY [*Library symbol*] [*Library of Congress*] (LCLS)
NSchGERB ... General Electric Co., R and D Center, Branch Library, Schenectady, NY [*Library symbol*] [*Library of Congress*] (LCLS)
NScHLC .... Capital District Library Council, Schenectady, NY [*Library symbol*] [*Library of Congress*] (LCLS)
NSchM .... Mohawk Valley Library Association, Schenectady, NY [*Library symbol*] [*Library of Congress*] (LCLS)
NSchoCHi .... Schoharie County Historical Society, Schoharie, NY [*Library symbol*] [*Library of Congress*] (LCLS)
NSchSC .... Schenectady Chemicals, Inc., Schenectady, NY [*Library symbol*] [*Library of Congress*] (LCLS)
N Sch Social Research... [*The*] New School for Social Research (GAGS)
NSchStC ...... Saint Clare's Hospital, Physicians' Library, Schenectady, NY [*Library symbol*] [*Library of Congress*] (LCLS)
NSchU .... Union College, Schenectady, NY [*Library symbol*] [*Library of Congress*] (LCLS)
NSCI .... NASCOM System Control Interface [*NASA*] (MCD)
NSCI .... National Surgery Centers, Inc. [*NASDAQ symbol*] (SAG)
NSCI .... Natl Surgery Centers [*NASDAQ symbol*] (TTSB)
NSCIA .... National Spinal Cord Injury Association
NSCIA .... National Supervisory Council for Intruder Alarms [*British*] (DBA)
NSCIC .... National Security Council Intelligence Committee [*Inactive*]
NSCIC .... National Soybean Crop Improvement Council
NSCID .... National Security Council Intelligence Directive [*Pronounced "nee-sid"*] (AFM)
NSCIF .... National Spinal Cord Injury Foundation [*Formerly, NPF*] [*Later, NSCIA*] (EA)
NSCIG .... National Security Council Interdepartmental Group (MCD)
NSCISC .... National Spinal Cord Injury Statistical Center Database [*University of Alabama in Birmingham*] [*Information service or system*] (CRD)
NSCL .... National Superconducting Cyclotron Laboratory [*Michigan State University*] [*National Science Foundation*] [*Research center*] (RCD)
NSCLC .... National Senior Citizens Law Center (EA)
NSCLC .... Non-Small-Cell Lung Cancer [*Oncology*]
NSCLS .... North State Cooperative Library System [*Library network*]
NSCM .... National Society of Cycle Makers [*A union*] [*British*]
NSCM .... NATO Supply Code for Manufacturing (MCD)
NSCM .... Non-Stockpile Chemical Materiel [*Military*] (RDA)
NSCMP .... Non-Stockpile Chemical Material Program [*Army*]
NSCN .... National Socialist Council of Nagaland [*India*] (PD)
NSCNC .... Nascence (ABBR)
NSCNQH ...... North Queens Heritage Society, Caledonia, Nova Scotia [*Library symbol*] [*National Library of Canada*] (NLC)
NSCNT .... Nascent (ABBR)
NSCO .... National Scientific Committee on Oceanography
NSCO .... Naval Sea Cargo Coordinator (DNAB)
NSCO .... Naval Shipping Control Officer (SAUS)
NSCORT .... NASA Specialized Center for Research and Training
NSCP .... National Scalable Cluster Project [*Computer science*] (ITCA)
NSCP .... National Society of Compliance Professionals (EA)

NSCP .... National Soil Conservation Program [*Canada*]
NSCP .... Naval Stores Conservation Program
NSCP .... Navy Staffing Criteria Program
NSCP .... Netscape Communications [*NASDAQ symbol*] (TTSB)
NSCP .... Netscape Communications Corp. [*NASDAQ symbol*] (SAG)
NSCPA .... National Society of Certified Public Accountants (EA)
NSCPC .... National Student Consumer Protection Council (EA)
NSCPS .... Naval Supply Center, Puget Sound [*Bremerton, WA*] (DNAB)
NSCPT .... National Society for Cardiovascular and Pulmonary Technology (EA)
NSCR .... National Society for Cancer Relief [*British*]
NSCR .... National Sport Custom Registry (EA)
NSCR .... Non-Selective Catalytic Reduction [*Chemistry*]
NSCR .... Nuclear Science Center Reactor
NSCRC .... National Stock Car Racing Commission
NSCRDFO ... National Study Commission on Records and Documents of Federal Officials
NSCS .... National Scouting Collectors Society (EA)
NSCS .... National Security Council System (COE)
NSCS .... National Sisters Communications Service [*Later, CCM*] (EA)
NSCS .... National Small Craft School [*Red Cross*]
NSCS .... Naval Strategic Communications Simulator (MCD)
NSCS .... Navy Supply Corps School
NSCS .... Network Service Center System [*Computer science*] (VLIE)
NSCS .... Night Shift Call System (DMAA)
NSCS .... North Star Computer Society (EA)
NSCS .... Universite Sainte-Anne, Church Point, Nova Scotia [*Library symbol*] [*National Library of Canada*] (NLC)
NSCSA .... Centre Acadien, Universite Sainte-Anne, Church Point, Nova Scotia [*Library symbol*] [*National Library of Canada*] (BIB)
NSCSC .... National School Calendar Study Committee
NSCSCC ...... National Standard for Common System Component Characteristics (MCD)
NSCSL .... National Center for Service Learning (EBF)
NSCSS .... National Society of Consulting Soil Scientists
NSCSWD ...... No Small Craft or Storm Warnings are Being Displayed [*Weather*]
NSCT .... National Students Center for Thailand
NSCT .... Niagara, St. Catharines & Toronto [*AAR code*]
NSCT .... North Staffordshire College of Technology (SAUS)
NSCTE .... National Society of College Teachers of Education [*Later, SPE*] (EA)
NSCTI .... National Society for Cardiopulmonary Technology, Inc. (DAVI)
NSCTRN ...... Nonsectarian (ABBR)
NSCUFA .... Nova Scotia Council of University Faculty Associations (SAUS)
NSCVPT .... National Society for Cardiovascular and Pulmonary Technology (EA)
NSCVR .... National Student Campaign for Voter Registration (EA)
NSCW .... National Society of Cycle Workers [*A union*] [*British*]
NSCWS .... Nuclear Services Cooling Water System (SAUS)
NSD .... Dartmouth Regional Library, Dartmouth, Nova Scotia [*Library symbol*] [*National Library of Canada*] (NLC)
NSD .... Ferrosan [*Denmark*] [*Research code symbol*]
NSD .... Geldert and Oxley's Nova Scotia Decisions [*7-9 Nova Scotia Reports*] [*1866-75*] [*Canada*] [*A publication*] (DLA)
NSD .... Nairobi Sheep Disease [*Medicine*] (DMAA)
NSD .... NASA Standard Detonator (SAUS)
NSD .... National Aeronautics and Space Administration Standard Detonator (NAKS)
NSD .... National Security and Defense (ABAC)
NSD .... National Security Directive (SAUS)
NSD .... National Security Division (ACAE)
NSD .... National Silage Demonstration [*British*]
NSD .... National Smooth Dancers (DICI)
NSD .... National Standard Co. [*NYSE symbol*] (SAG)
NSD .... Naval Stores Department [*British military*] (DMA)
NSD .... Naval Supply Depot
NSD .... Navy Support Date (NG)
NSD .... Neonatal Staphylococcal Disease [*Medicine*] (DB)
NSD .... Network Security Device (SAUS)
NSD .... Network Status Display
NSD .... New Spirit Research [*Vancouver Stock Exchange symbol*]
NSD .... Next Most Significant Digit [*Computer science*]
NSD .... Night Sleep Deprivation [*Medicine*] (DMAA)
NSD .... Noise Suppression Device
NSD .... Nominal Single Dose [*Medicine*] (DB)
NSD .... Nominal Standard Dose [*Medicine*]
NSD .... Nonlinear Sampled Data [*Computer science*] (VLIE)
NSD .... Non-Self-Destroying
NSD .... Non-Sequential Disc (or Disk) (SAUS)
NSD .... Nonsequential Disk [*Computer science*] (IAA)
NSD .... Nonsoapy Detergent (SAUS)
NSD .... Non-Stored and Delayed (SAUS)
NSD .... Normal, Spontaneous Delivery [*Obstetrics*]
NSD .... Normal Standard Dose [*Oncology radiation*]
NSD .... Norsk Samfunnsvitenskapelig Datatjeneste [*Norwegian Social Science Data Services*] [*Information service or system*] (IID)
NSD .... Northside Aviation Ltd. [*British*] [*ICAO designator*] (FAAC)
NSD .... No Significant Defect (SAUS)
NSD .... No Significant Defects [*or Deficiency*] [*Medicine*]
NSD .... No Significant Deficiency (SAUS)
NSD .... No Significant Deterioration (SAUS)
NSD .... No Significant Deviation [*Medicine*]
NSD .... No Significant Difference [*Medicine*]
NSD .... No Significant Disease [*Medicine*]
NSD .... No Structure Detected (EEVL)
NSD .... United States Library of Congress, Washington, DC [*OCLC symbol*] (OCLC)
NSDA .... National Soft Drink Association (EA)

NSDA .... National Spasmodic Dysphonia Association (EA)
NSDA .... National Sprayer and Duster Association (EA)
NSDA .... National Supply Distributors Association [*Dayton, OH*] (EA)
NSDA .... National Surplus Dealers Association (EA)
NSDA .... Naval Supply Depot Annex
NSDA .... Nissan Safety Device Advisor [*Driver information system*]
NSDA .... Non-Self Deployment Aircraft (SAUS)
NSDA .... Non-Self Destruct Alternative [*Army*]
NSDA .... Nonsteroid Dependent Asthmatic [*Medicine*] (DAVI)
NSDAB .... Non-Self-Deployable Aircraft and Boats (MCD)
NSDAP .... Nationalsozialistische Deutsche Arbeiterpartei [*National Socialist German Workers' Party, 1919-45*] [*Political party*]
NSDAP-AO ... NSDAP Auslands- und Aufbauorganisation (EA)
NSDAR .... National Society, Daughters of the American Revolution (EA)
NSDAT .... Naval School of Dental Assisting and Technology (DNAB)
NSDAVNDEPT... Naval Supply Depot Aviation Department (DNAB)
NSDB .... Bedford Institute of Oceanography [*Institut Oceanographique de Bedford*] Dartmouth, Nova Scotia [*Library symbol*] [*National Library of Canada*] (NLC)
NSDB .... National Science Development Board
NSDB .... National Soil Database (SAUS)
NSDB .... NSD Bancorp [*NASDAQ symbol*] (SAG)
NSD Bc .... NSD Bancorp [*Associated Press*] (SAG)
NSDBE .... National Society, Daughters of the British Empire (EA)
NSDBR .... National Society, Daughters of the Barons of Runnemede (EA)
NSDC .... Courier, Digby, Nova Scotia [*Library symbol*] [*National Library of Canada*] (NLC)
NSDC .... National School Development Council (EA)
NSDC .... National Serials Data Centre [*British Library*] (PDAA)
NSDC .... National Space Development Center (ACAE)
NSDC .... National Square Dance Convention (EA)
NSDC .... National Staff Development Committee [*Australia*]
NSDC .... National Staff Development Council (EA)
NSDC .... Naval Special Devices Center (SAA)
NSDC .... Nonsuppurative Destructive Cholangitis [*Medicine*]
NSDC .... NORAD Sector Direction Center [*Military*]
NSDC .... Northern Shipowners' Defence Club [*See also NORDISK*] (EAIO)
NSDC .... Northern Shipowners Defense Council (SAUS)
NSDC .... Nova Scotia Design Craftsmen (SAUS)
NSDCM .... NORAD Sector Direction Center Manual [*Military*]
NSDD .... National Security Decision Directive
NSDDET .... Naval Supply Depot Detachment (DNAB)
NSDDS .... Dartmouth District School Board, Nova Scotia [*Library symbol*] [*National Library of Canada*] (NLC)
NSDE .... Environment Canada [*Environnement Canada*] Dartmouth, Nova Scotia [*Library symbol*] [*National Library of Canada*] (NLC)
NSDEA .... National Soda Dispensing Equipment Association (EA)
NS Dec .... Nova Scotia Decisions [*A publication*] (DLA)
NSDEQ .... National Society, Descendants of Early Quakers (EA)
NSDF .... National Student Drama Festival [*British*]
NSDF .... Navy Standard Distillate Fuel (NVT)
NSDG .... Digby General Hospital, Nova Scotia [*Library symbol*] [*National Library of Canada*] (NLC)
NSDGH .... Dartmouth General Hospital, Nova Scotia [*Library symbol*] [*National Library of Canada*] (NLC)
NSDGP .... Northern Sydey Division of General Practice (SAUS)
NSDH .... Hermes Electronics Ltd., Dartmouth, Novia Scotia [*Library symbol*] [*National Library of Canada*] (NLC)
NSDI .... National Sales Development Institute
NSDI .... National Spatial Data Infrastructure [*BTS*] (TAG)
NSDJA .... National Sash and Door Jobbers Association (EA)
NSDL .... National Soil Dynamics Laboratory [*Auburn, AL*] [*Department of Agriculture*] (GRD)
NSDL .... Navy Standard Distribution List (MCD)
NSDLANT/PAC... Naval Supply Depots, Atlantic/Pacific
NSDLMM ..... National Society of Descendants of Lords of the Maryland Manors (EA)
NSDM .... Mirror, Digby, Nova Scotia [*Library symbol*] [*National Library of Canada*] (NLC)
NSDM .... National Security Decision Memorandum [*Air Force*]
NSDM .... New School for Democratic Management [*Inactive*] (EA)
NSDM .... Nuclear Sediment Density Meter (PDAA)
NSDMM .... MacLaren Plansearch Ltd., Dartmouth, Nova Scotia [*Library symbol*] [*National Library of Canada*] (NLC)
NSDNHM ..... North Highlands Museum, Dingwall, Nova Scotia [*Library symbol*] [*National Library of Canada*] (NLC)
NSDNSH ...... Nova Scotia Hospital, Dartmouth, Nova Scotia [*Library symbol*] [*National Library of Canada*] (NLC)
NSDO .... National Seed and Development Organisation [*British*]
NSDP .... NASCOM System Development Plan
NSDP .... National Serials Data Program [*Library of Congress*] (EA)
NSDP .... National Society of Denture Prosthetists [*Later, ADP*]
NSDP .... Norfolk Sample Drug Program
NSDR .... National Ships Destination Room (NATG)
NSDR .... National Silver Dollar Roundtable (EA)
NSDR .... No-son Dependency Ratio [*Demographics*]
NSDRC .... National Standard Reference Data Center (VLIE)
NSDRV .... Dartmouth Regional Vocational School, Dartmouth, Nova Scotia [*Library symbol*] [*National Library of Canada*] (NLC)
NSDS .... Navy School, Diving and Salvage (NVT)
NSDS .... Neutron Spectrometer Digital System
NSDSA .... Naval Sea Data Support Activity (NVT)
NSDTA .... National Staff Development and Training Association (EA)
NSDU .... Network Service Data Unit [*Telecommunications*] (OSI)
NSDUP .... National Society, Daughters of Utah Pioneers (EA)

NSDV .... Netted Secure Digital Voice (MCD)
NSDWR .... National Secondary Drinking Water Regualtions (GNE)
NSE .... Milton, FL [*Location identifier*] [*FAA*] (FAAL)
NSE .... Nagoya Stock Exchange [*Japan*] (NUMA)
NSE .... National Sales Executives
NSE .... National Seafood Educators (EA)
NSE .... National Society for Epilepsy [*British*]
NSE .... National Stock Exchange [*Dissolved, 1975*]
NSE .... National Student Exchange (EA)
NSE .... National Support Elements [*British military*] (DMA)
NSE .... Natural Space Environment
NSE .... Naval Shore Establishment
NSE .... Naval Support Element (DOMA)
NSE .... Navier-Stokes Equation
NSE .... Navigation Support Equipment
NSE .... Net Sales Entered (TIMI)
NSE .... Network Service Element [*Telecommunications*] (OSI)
NSE .... Network Software Environment [*Computer science*] (VLIE)
NSE .... Network SouthEast [*British Rail*] (ECON)
NSE .... Network Support Encyclopedia (VLIE)
NSE .... Network Systems Engineer (SSD)
NSE .... Neuron-Specific Enolase [*Formerly, NSP*] [*An enzyme*]
NSE .... Neuropsychological Status Examination [*Psychology*]
NSE .... Neutral Stream Etch (AAEL)
NSE .... New York Stock Exchange (EBF)
NSE .... NiSource, Inc. [*NYSE symbol*]
NSE .... Nitroguanidine Support Element (MCD)
NSE .... Noise (ABBR)
NSE .... Nonsecurity Exemption [*Military*]
NSE .... Nonspecific Esterase [*An enzyme*]
NSE .... Normal Saline Enema [*Medicine*] (MELL)
NSE .... North Steaming Error (SAA)
NSE .... Northwest Sports Enterprises Ltd. [*Vancouver Stock Exchange symbol*]
NSE .... Nottingham Society of Engineers (SAUS)
NSE .... Nuclear Science and Engineering [*A publication*]
NSE .... Nuclear Statistical Equilibrium [*Physics*]
NSE .... Nuclear Support Equipment
NSE .... Nuclear Systems Engineering
NSE .... Number of Simultaneous Engagements [*Military*]
NSE .... Satena Servicios de Aeronavegacion A Territorios Nac [*Colombia*] [*ICAO designator*] (FAAC)
NSEA .... National Standards Educators Association (EA)
NSEA .... Naval Sea systems command headquarters (SAUS)
NSea .... Seaford Public Library, Seaford, NY [*Library symbol*] [*Library of Congress*] (LCLS)
NSeacES ...... Sea Cliff Elementary School, Sea Cliff, NY [*Library symbol*] [*Library of Congress*] (LCLS)
NSEAD .... National Society for Education in Art and Design (EAIO)
NSeaHE .... Seaford Harbor Elementary School, Seaford, NY [*Library symbol*] [*Library of Congress*] (LCLS)
NSeaME ...... Seaford Manor Elementary School, Seaford, NY [*Library symbol*] [*Library of Congress*] (LCLS)
NSeaMH ...... Massapequa General Hospital, Seaford, NY [*Library symbol*] [*Library of Congress*] (LCLS)
NSeaMS ...... Seaford Middle School, Seaford, NY [*Library symbol*] [*Library of Congress*] (LCLS)
NSeaP .... Plainedge Public Library, Seaford, NY [*Library symbol*] [*Library of Congress*] (LCLS)
NSeaSH .... Seaford Senior High School, Seaford, NY [*Library symbol*] [*Library of Congress*] (LCLS)
NSeaTM ...... Tackapausha Museum, Seaford, NY [*Library symbol*] [*Library of Congress*] (LCLS)
nsec .... Nanosecond [*One billionth of a second*] [*Also, ns*]
NSEC .... National Security Group, Inc. [*NASDAQ symbol*] (SAG)
NSEC .... National Service Entertainments Council [*British*]
NSEC .... National Society of Environmental Consultants (EA)
NSEC .... National System for Emergency Coordination (EPAT)
NSEC .... Natl Security Group [*NASDAQ symbol*] (TTSB)
NSEC .... Naval Ship Engineering Center (MCD)
NSEC .... Nuclear Science and Engineering Corp. (SAUS)
NSecIn .... National Security Group, Inc. [*Associated Press*] (SAG)
NSECINST... Naval Ship Engineering Center Instruction
NSEDP .... National Sex Equity Demonstration Project (EDAC)
NSEE .... National Society for Experiential Education (NTPA)
NSEEC .... Naval Shore Electronics Engineering Center [*Terminated, 1966*] (MCD)
NSEF .... National SANE Education Fund (EA)
NSEF .... National Student Educational Fund (EA)
NSEF .... Navy Security Engineering Facility
NSEF .... New Society Educational Foundation (EA)
NSEH .... Neutron Scattering Experimental Hall (SAUS)
NSEI .... Norwegian Society for Electronic Information (SAUS)
NSEIP .... Norwegian Society for Electronic Information Processing (SAUS)
NSel .... Middle Country Public Library, Selden Branch, Selden, NY [*Library symbol*] [*Library of Congress*] (LCLS)
NSELA .... National Science Education Leadership Association (NTPA)
NSelC .... Suffolk County Community College, Selden, NY [*Library symbol*] [*Library of Congress*] (LCLS)
NSelC-E ...... Suffolk County Community College, Eastern Campus, Riverhead, NY [*Library symbol*] [*Library of Congress*] (LCLS)
NSelC-W ..... Suffolk County Community College, Western Campus, Brentwood, NY [*Library symbol*] [*Library of Congress*] (LCLS)
NSELH .... East Lake Ainslie Historical Society, Nova Scotia [*Library symbol*] [*National Library of Canada*] (BIB)

NSELS	Noiseless (ABBR)
NSem...........	National Semiconductor Corp. [Associated Press] (SAG)
NSEM...........	Nederlandsche Standard Electric Maatschappij (NITA)
NSEMA	National Spray Equipment Manufacturers Association (EA)
NSEN	Network Simulations Engineer (SSD)
NSENS	Noisiness (ABBR)
NSEP	National Security and Emergency Preparedness
NSEP	National Security Education Program [The Academy for Educational Development]
NSEP	National System for Emergency Preparedness (EPAT)
NS/EQ	New Source and Environmental Questionnaire [Environmental Protection Agency] (EG)
NSERC	Natural Sciences and Engineering Research Council of Canada [Research center] (IRC)
NSERI	National Solar Energy Research Institute [Energy Research and Development Administration]
NSES	National Security Electronic Surveillance
NSES	National Society of Electrotypers and Stereotypers [British] (BI)
NSESG	North Sea Environmental Study Group (SAUS)
NSetSP	Society for the Preservation of Long Island Antiquities, Setauket, NY [Library symbol] [Library of Congress] (LCLS)
NSewCH	H.F. Carey High School, Sewanhaka, NY [Library symbol] [Library of Congress] (LCLS)
NSewEH.......	Elmont Memorial High School, Sewanhaka, NY [Library symbol] [Library of Congress] (LCLS)
NSewNH	New Hyde Park Memorial High School, Sewanhaka, NY [Library symbol] [Library of Congress] (LCLS)
NSewSJ.......	Stanforth Junior High School, Sewanhaka, NY [Library symbol] [Library of Congress] (LCLS)
NSF.............	Camp Springs, MD [Location identifier] [FAA] (FAAL)
NSF.............	National Salvation Front [Romania] [Political party]
NSF.............	National Sanitation Foundation (EA)
NSF.............	National Schizophrenia Fellowship [British]
NSF.............	National Science Foundation (EA)
NSF.............	National Science Foundation, Washington, DC [OCLC symbol] (OCLC)
NSF.............	National Scoliosis Foundation (EA)
NSF.............	National Sex Forum [Later, ET] (EA)
NSF.............	National Sharecroppers Fund (EA)
NSF.............	National Ski Federation (BARN)
NSF.............	National Sleep Foundation (MELL)
NSF.............	National Soaring Foundation (EA)
NSF.............	National Squash Federation [British] (DBA)
NSF.............	National Stockbrokers Forum [Later, CFC] (EA)
NSF.............	National Strike Force [Marine science] (MSC)
NSF.............	National Support Facility (ACAE)
NSF.............	Naval Stock Fund
NSF.............	Naval Supersonic Facility
NSF.............	Naval Supply Force
NSF.............	Naval Support Force (MCD)
NSF.............	Navy Security Force
NSF.............	Navy Special Fuel
NSF.............	Navy Stock Fund (DOMA)
NSF.............	Negotiated Search Facility [Information retrieval]
NSF.............	NEM [N-Ethylmaleimide]-Sensitive Fusion [Biochemistry]
NSF.............	N-Ethylmaleimide-Sensitive Fusion (protein) [Organic chemistry]
NSF.............	Net Square Feet (MCD)
NSem...........	Neutron Scattering Facility [Oak Ridge, TN] [Oak Ridge National Laboratory] [Department of Energy] (GRD)
NSF.............	Nightstick Fracture [Medicine] (MELL)
NSF.............	Nitrogen Supply Flask
NSF.............	Nodular Subepidermal Fibrosis [Dermatology] (DAVI)
NSF.............	Noncancerous Skin Fibroblast [Medicine]
NSF.............	Nonsaponifiable (SAUS)
NSF.............	Non-Spin-Flip [Solid state physics]
NSF.............	Non-Standard Facilities (SAUS)
NSF.............	Non Standard Format (SAUS)
NSF.............	Nonsterile Field Soil [Agronomy]
NSF.............	Nonstock Fund
NSF.............	Non-Sufficient Funds (SAUS)
NSF.............	Nordiska Skattevetenskapliga Forskningradet [Nordic Council for Tax Research - NCTR] (EAIO)
NSF.............	No Significant Findings (SAUS)
NSF.............	Notes Storage File (SAUS)
nsf	Not Sufficient Funds [Banking] (ODBW)
NSF.............	Not Sufficient Funds [Banking]
NSF.............	Nuclear Safety Facility
NSF.............	Nuclear Science Foundation (IAA)
NSF.............	Nuclear Structure Facility [British]
NSFA	Faleolo/International [Western Samoa] [ICAO location identifier] (ICLI)
NSFA	National Science Foundation Act [1950]
NSFA	Naval Support Force, Antarctica (DNAB)
NSFA	Nondeterministic Finite State Automaton (SAUS)
NSFA	Nordic Swimming Federations Association (EA)
NSFAC	National Student Financial Aid Council [Later, NASFAA] (EA)
NSFAR	National Science Foundation Acquisition Regulation [A publication] (AAGC)
NSFB	New School of Family Birthing (EA)
NSFC	Nancy Sinatra Fan Club (EA)
NSFC	National Small Flows Clearinghouse [Environmental Protection Agency] (AEPA)
NSFC	National Society of Film Critics
NSFC	Nat Stuckey Fan Club [Defunct] (EA)
NSFC	Natural Science Foudation of China
NSFC	Natural Science Foundation of China
NSFC	Northern States Financial Corp. [NASDAQ symbol] (SAG)
NSFC	Northern States Finl [NASDAQ symbol] (TTSB)
NSFCC	National Strike Force Co-ordination Center (SAUS)
NSFCCDLR...	National Society of Fathers for Child Custody and Divorce Law Reform [Later, FER] (EA)
NSFD	Notice of Structural and/or Functional Deficiency (SAUS)
NSFFC	National Save the Family Farm Coalition (EA)
NSFG	National Survey of Family Growth
NSFGA	Nova Scotia Fruit Growers Association (SAUS)
NSFH	North-South Fine, Hundreds
NSFI	Fagali'I [Western Samoa] [ICAO location identifier] (ICLI)
NSF-I	National Science Fair - International
NSF/IDOE....	National Science Foundation Office for the International Decade of Ocean Exploration
NSfK	Nordiska Samarbetsradet for Kriminologi [Scandinavian Research Council for Criminology - SRCC] [Finland] (EAIO)
NSFL	National Sanitation Foundation Laboratory
NSFL	New Strip File (SAUS)
NSFL	Nova Scotia Federation of Labour (SAUS)
NSFNET	National Science Foundation Network
NSFNet	National Science Foundation Network
NSFNet	NSF Network (SAUS)
NSFO	Navy Special [or Standard] Fuel Oil
NSFORT.......	Non-Standard FORTRAN [Computer science] (PDAA)
NSFP	Natural Suppressor Factor Protein (DB)
NSFP	Non-Sodium Fire Protection [Nuclear energy] (NRCH)
NSFPA	National Suppliers to Food Processors Association (EA)
NSFPR	National Science Foundation Procurement Regulation [A publication] (AAGC)
NSFR	National Society of Fund Raisers [Later, NSFRE] (EA)
NSFR	Nitroxide Stable Free Radical [For tissue NMR]
NSFRC	National Silver Fox Rabbit Club (EA)
NSFRE	National Society of Fund Raising Executives (EA)
NSFRE Foundation...	National Society of Fund Raising Executives Foundation [Formerly the National Society of Fund Raisers Institute of Continuing Education and the National Society of Fund Raising Executives] (NFD)
NSFRE Institute...	Former name of the National Society of Fund Rainsing Executives Foundation (NFD)
NSFS	National Society for Shut-Ins (EA)
NSFS	Net Section Fracture Strength (PDAA)
NSfSC	Sullivan County Community College, South Fallsburg, NY [Library symbol] [Library of Congress] (LCLS)
NSF/STAH....	National Science Foundation Program for Science and Technology Aid to the Handicapped
NSFT...........	North-South Fine, Tens
NSFTD	Normal, Spontaneous, Full Term Delivery [Obstetrics]
NSFTL.........	National Sanitation Foundation Testing Laboratory, Inc. (MSA)
NSFU	Needle Stampers' and Filers' Union [British]
NSFU	North-South Fine, Units
NSF Univ	Federal Support to Universities, Colleges and Nonprofit Institutions (SAUS)
NSG	Aircompany Liana JSA [Ukraine] [FAA designator] (FAAC)
NSG	National Society for Graphology (EA)
NSG	National Steering Group (AIE)
NSG	National Supply Group [Military] (AFIT)
NSG	Natural Systems Group (SAUS)
NSG	Naval Security Group
NSG	Network Services Group (SAUS)
NSG	Network Support Group (NITA)
NSG	Neurosecretory Granules
NSG	Newspaper Systems Group (EA)
NSG	Noise Signal Generator (SAUS)
NSG	Non-Statutory Guidance [British] (DET)
NSG	Non-Statutory Guidelines (WDAA)
NSG	North Seeking Gyro
NSG	Not So Good
NSG	Nuclear Suppliers' Group [Australia] (ECON)
Nsg	Nursing (AMHC)
NSG	Nursing
NSGA	National Sand and Gravel Association [Later, NAA] (EA)
NSGA	National Sporting Goods Association (EA)
NSGA	Naval Security Group Activity
NSGC	National Self Government Committee (EA)
NSGC	National Society of Genetic Counselors (EA)
NSGC	National Swine Growers Council [Later, NPPC] (EA)
NSGC	Naval Security Group Command (DNAB)
NSGCC	Coastal Courier, Glace Bay, Nova Scotia [Library symbol] [National Library of Canada] (NLC)
NSGCFA.......	Aurora, Canadian Forces Base, Greenwood, Nova Scotia [Library symbol] [National Library of Canada] (NLC)
NSGCH........	Naval Security Group Command Headquarters
NSGCHQ.....	Naval Security Group Command Headquarters (SAUS)
NSGCT.......	Nonsiminomatous Germ Cell Turmors [Medicine] (MEDA)
NSGCTT.......	Nonseminomatous Germ Cell Tumors of the Testes
NSGD	National Sea Grant Depository [National Oceanic and Atmospheric Administration] [Information service or system] (IID)
NSGD	National Support Group for Dermatomyositis (EA)
NSGD	National Support Group for PM/DM [Formerly, National Support Group for Dermatomyositis] (EA)
NS-GFW.......	Noise Substest of the Goldman-Fristoe-Woodcock Auditory Skills Test Battery (EDAC)
NSGIB	NAVSHIPS [Naval Ship Systems Command] General Information Book

NSGLS .... Nordisk Sekretariat for Gartneri- Land-, og Skovarbejderforbund [*Nordic Secretariat for Agricultural and Horticultural Workers - NSAHW*] [*Denmark*] [*Defunct*] (EAIO)

NSGN .... Noise Generator (CET)

NSGOC .... Naval Security Group Orientation Course (DNAB)

NSGOC .... Old Court House Museum, Guysborough, Nova Scotia [*Library symbol*] [*National Library of Canada*] (NLC)

NS Grp .... NS Group, Inc. [*Associated Press*] (SAG)

Nsg Sta .... Nursing Station (DAVI)

NSGT .... National Aeronautics and Space Administration Ground Terminal (NAKS)

NSGT .... Non-Self-Governing Territories [*United Nations*]

NSGTMEM ... National Society of General Tool Makers, Engineers, and Machinists [*A union*] [*British*]

NSGTP .... Naval Security Group Training Publication (DNAB)

NSGW .... National Society of Glass Workers [*A union*] [*British*]

NSGW .... Native Sons of the Golden West (EA)

NSH .... Halifax City Regional Library, Nova Scotia [*Library symbol*] [*National Library of Canada*] (NLC)

NSh .... John Jermain Memorial Public Library, Sag Harbor, NY [*Library symbol*] [*Library of Congress*] (LCLS)

NSH .... Nashua Corp. [*NYSE symbol*] (SPSG)

NSH .... Nashville [*Diocesan abbreviation*] [*Tennessee*] (TOCD)

NSH .... National Society for Histotechnology (EA)

NSH .... National Society of Hypnotherapists (EA)

NSH .... Naval School of Health Sciences, Bethesda, MD [*OCLC symbol*] (OCLC)

NSH .... New Search & rescue Helicopter (SAUS)

NSH .... Nordisk Samarbeidskomite for Husstellundervisning [*Nordic Joint Committee for Domestic Education - NJCDE*] (EAIO)

NSH .... Northern-Southern Hybrid [*Hemoglobin phenotype of Rana pipiens*]

NSH .... Northville State Hospital (SAUS)

NSH .... No Stock on Hand (SAUS)

NSH .... Not So Hot [*Slang*]

NSH .... Nutritional Secondary Hyperparathyroidism (SAUS)

NSHA .... National Steeplechase and Hunt Association (EA)

NSHA .... National Stock Horse Association (EA)

NSHAC-FP ... National Self-Help Action Center - Food Program (EA)

NSHAG .... Art Gallery of Nova Scotia, Halifax, Nova Scotia [*Library symbol*] [*National Library of Canada*] (NLC)

NSHANSS .... Synod Office, Diocese of Nova Scotia, Anglican Church of Canada, Halifax, Nova Scotia [*Library symbol*] [*National Library of Canada*] (NLC)

NSHAR .... Algas Resources Ltd., Halifax, Nova Scotia [*Library symbol*] [*National Library of Canada*] (NLC)

NSHAVI .... [*The*] Atlantic Provinces Resource Centre for the Visually-Impaired, Halifax, Nova Scotia [*Library symbol*] [*National Library of Canada*] (NLC)

NSHAVI .... Atlantic Provinces Resource Centre for the Visually Impaired, Halifax, Nova Scotia (SAUS)

NSHBS .... Nova Scotia Barristers Society, Halifax, Nova Scotia [*Library symbol*] [*National Library of Canada*] (NLC)

NSHC .... Cambridge Military Library, Halifax, Nova Scotia [*Library symbol*] [*National Library of Canada*] (NLC)

NSHC .... National Self-Help Clearinghouse (EA)

NSHC .... National Silver-Haired Congress (EA)

NSHC .... National Syrian Hamster Council [*British*] (DBA)

NSHC .... North Sea Hydrographic Commission [*of the International Hydrographic Organization*] [*Belgium*]

NSHC .... North Sea Hyperbaric Centre (SAUS)

NSHCA .... Nova Scotia College of Art and Design, Halifax, Nova Scotia [*Library symbol*] [*National Library of Canada*] (NLC)

NSHCB .... Music and Record Library, Canadian Broadcasting Corp. [*Musicotheque et Discotheque, Societe Radio-Canada*] Halifax, Nova Scotia [*Library symbol*] [*National Library of Canada*] (NLC)

NSHCBC ...... Canadian British Consultants Ltd., Halifax, Nova Scotia [*Library symbol*] [*National Library of Canada*] (NLC)

NSHCBF ...... Film Library, CBHT-TV, Halifax, Nova Scotia [*Library symbol*] [*National Library of Canada*] (NLC)

NSHCD .... Law Library, Cox, Downie & Co., Halifax, Nova Scotia [*Library symbol*] [*National Library of Canada*] (NLC)

NSHCDD ...... Nova Scotia Commission on Drug Dependency, Halifax, Nova Scotia [*Library symbol*] [*National Library of Canada*] (NLC)

NSHCFM ..... Maritime Command Museum, Canadian Forces Base, Halifax, Nova Scotia [*Library symbol*] [*National Library of Canada*] (BIB)

NSHCH .... Camp Hill Hospital, Halifax, Nova Scotia [*Library symbol*] [*National Library of Canada*] (NLC)

NSHCIC .... National Solar Heating and Cooling Information Center [*Later, CAREIRS*]

NSHCIC .... Nova Scotia Communications and Information Centre, Halifax, Nova Scotia [*Library symbol*] [*National Library of Canada*] (NLC)

NSHD .... Dalhousie University, Halifax, Nova Scotia [*Library symbol*] [*National Library of Canada*] (NLC)

NSHD .... Nodular Sclerosing Hodgkin's Disease [*Medicine*] (DMAA)

NSHDA .... Archives, Dalhousie University, Halifax, Nova Scotia [*Library symbol*] [*National Library of Canada*] (BIB)

NSHDAG ...... Nova Scotia Department of the Attorney-General, Halifax, Nova Scotia [*Library symbol*] [*National Library of Canada*] (NLC)

NSHDCA ...... Nova Scotia Department of Consumer Affairs, Halifax, Nova Scotia [*Library symbol*] [*National Library of Canada*] (NLC)

NSHDD .... Nova Scotia Department of Industry, Trade, and Technology, Halifax, Nova Scotia [*Library symbol*] [*National Library of Canada*] (NLC)

NSHDE .... Nova Scotia Department of the Environment, Halifax, Nova Scotia [*Library symbol*] [*National Library of Canada*] (NLC)

NSHDEA ...... Resource Centre, Ecology Action Centre, Dalhousie University, Halifax, Nova Scotia [*Library symbol*] [*National Library of Canada*] (NLC)

NSHDF .... Nova Scotia Department of Fisheries, Halifax, Nova Scotia [*Library symbol*] [*National Library of Canada*] (NLC)

NSHDH .... Nova Scotia Department of Transportation, Halifax, Nova Scotia [*Library symbol*] [*National Library of Canada*] (NLC)

NSHDIP .... Institute of Public Affairs, Dalhousie University, Halifax, Nova Scotia, [*Library symbol*] [*National Library of Canada*] (NLC)

NSHDIR .... School of Resources and Environmental Studies, Dalhousie University, Halifax, Nova Scotia [*Library symbol*] [*National Library of Canada*] (NLC)

NSHDL .... Law School, Dalhousie University, Halifax, Nova Scotia [*Library symbol*] [*National Library of Canada*] (NLC)

NSHDLS .... School of Library Service, Dalhousie University, Halifax, Nova Scotia [*Library symbol*] [*National Library of Canada*] (NLC)

NSHDM .... W. K. Kellogg Health Sciences Library, Dalhousie University, Halifax, Nova Scotia [*Library symbol*] [*National Library of Canada*] (NLC)

NSHDMA ...... Map Library, Dalhousie University, Halifax, Nova Scotia [*Library symbol*] [*National Library of Canada*] (NLC)

NSHDOL ...... Nova Scotia Department of Labour and Manpower, Halifax, Nova Scotia [*Library symbol*] [*National Library of Canada*] (NLC)

NSHDOM .... Nova Scotia Department of Mines, Halifax, Nova Scotia [*Library symbol*] [*National Library of Canada*] (NLC)

NSHDOS ...... Dalhousie Ocean Studies Programme, Dalhousie University, Halifax, Nova Scotia [*Library symbol*] [*National Library of Canada*] (NLC)

NSHDR .... Cultural Affairs Library, Nova Scotia Department of Tourism and Culture, Halifa x, Nova Scotia [*Library symbol*] [*National Library of Canada*] (NLC)

NSHDS .... MacDonald Science Library, Dalhousie University, Halifax, Nova Scotia [*Library symbol*] [*National Library of Canada*] (NLC)

NSHDS .... National Society for Hebrew Day Schools (NTPA)

NSHE .... [*The*] New Schaff-Herzog Encyclopaedia of Religious Knowledge [*A publication*] (BJA)

NSHEB .... North of Scotland Hydro-Electric Board (ECON)

NShei .... Shelter Island Public Library Society, Shelter Island, NY [*Library symbol*] [*Library of Congress*] (LCLS)

NSherb .... Sherburne Public Library, Sherburne, NY [*Library symbol*] [*Library of Congress*] (LCLS)

NSHF .... Fisheries and Oceans Canada [*Peches et Oceans Canada*] Halifax, Nova Scotia [*Library symbol*] [*National Library of Canada*] (NLC)

NSHF .... Scotia-Fundy Regional Library, Fisheries and Oceans Canada [*Bibliotheque de la Region Scotia-Fundy, Peches et Oceans Canada*], Halifax, Nova Scotia [*Library symbol*] [*National Library of Canada*] (NLC)

NSHFIF .... Federal-Provincial Taxation and Fiscal Relations Library, Nova Scotia Departmentof Finance, Halifax, Nova Scotia [*Library symbol*] [*National Library of Canada*] (NLC)

NSHH .... Nova Scotia Department of Health, Halifax, Nova Scotia [*Library symbol*] [*National Library of Canada*] (NLC)

NSHHC .... Halifax County Regional Library, Lower Sackville, Nova Scotia [*Library symbol*] [*National Library of Canada*] (NLC)

NSHHE .... Halifax Herald Ltd., Nova Scotia [*Library symbol*] [*National Library of Canada*] (NLC)

NSHHI .... Health Services Library, Halifax Infirmary, Nova Scotia [*Library symbol*] [*National Library of Canada*] (NLC)

NSHHR .... Nova Scotia Human Rights Commission, Halifax, Nova Scotia [*Library symbol*] [*National Library of Canada*] (NLC)

NSHHS .... Hantsport and Area Historical Society, Nova Scotia [*Library symbol*] [*National Library of Canada*] (NLC)

NSHIAP .... Atlantic Regional Library, Parks Canada [*Bibliotheque Regionale de l'Atlantique, Parcs Canada*] Halifax, Nova Scotia [*Library symbol*] [*National Library of Canada*] (NLC)

NSHIC .... International Centre for Ocean Development, Halifax, Nova Scotia [*Library symbol*] [*National Library of Canada*] (BIB)

NSHJ .... Canada Department of Justice [*Ministere de la Justice*] Halifax, Nova Scotia [*Library symbol*] [*National Library of Canada*] (NLC)

NSHK .... University of King's College, Halifax, Nova Scotia [*Library symbol*] [*National Library of Canada*] (NLC)

NSHKH .... Izaak Walton Killam Hospital for Children, Halifax, Nova Scotia [*Library symbol*] [*National Library of Canada*] (NLC)

NSHKJ .... School of Journalism, University of King's College, Halifax, Nova Scotia [*Library symbol*] [*National Library of Canada*] (NLC)

NSHKMGM ... Kitz, Matheson, Green & MacIsaac Law Firm, Halifax, Nova Scotia [*Library symbol*] [*National Library of Canada*] (NLC)

NSHL .... Legislative Library, Halifax, Nova Scotia [*Library symbol*] [*National Library of Canada*] (NLC)

NSHLA .... Nova Scotia Legal Aid, Halifax, Nova Scotia [*Library symbol*] [*National Library of Canada*] (BIB)

NSHLP .... Liberal Party of Nova Scotia, Halifax [*Library symbol*] [*National Library of Canada*] (BIB)

NSHM .... Atlantic Regional Laboratory, National Research Council [*Laboratoire Regionalde l'Atlantique, Conseil National de Recherches du Canada*] Halifax, Nova Sco tia [*Library symbol*] [*National Library of Canada*] (NLC)

NSHMA .... Nova Scotia Department of Municipal Affairs, Halifax, Nova Scotia [*Library symbol*] [*National Library of Canada*] (NLC)

NSHMBA ...... National Society of Hispanic MBAs (EA)

NSHMC .... Maritime Conservatory of Music, Halifax, Nova Scotia [*Library symbol*] [*National Library of Canada*] (NLC)

NSHMCA ...... Archives, Maritime Conference, United Church of Canada Halifax, Nova Scotia [*Library symbol*] [*National Conference of Commissioners on Uniform State Laws*] (BIB)

NSHMCR ...... Law Library, McInnes, Cooper & Robertson, Halifax, Nova Scotia [*Library symbol*] [*National Library of Canada*] (NLC)

NSHML	Martec Ltd., Halifax, Nova Scotia [*Library symbol*] [*National Library of Canada*] (NLC)
NSHMM	Maritime Museum of the Atlantic, Halifax, Nova Scotia [*Library symbol*] [*National Library of Canada*] (NLC)
NSHMO	Mobil Oil Canada Ltd., Halifax, Nova Scotia [*Library symbol*] [*National Library of Canada*] (NLC)
NSHMS	Nova Scotia Museum, Halifax, Nova Scotia [*Library symbol*] [*National Library of Canada*] (NLC)
NSHMT	Regional Library, Canadian Coast Guard [*Bibliotheque Regionale, Garde CotiereCanadienne*] Dartmouth, Nova Scotia [*Library symbol*] [*National Library of Canada*] (NLC)
NSHMTT	Information Resource Centre, Maritime Tel & Tel, Halifax, Nova Scotia [*Library symbol*] [*National Library of Canada*] (NLC)
NSHN	Defence Research Establishment Atlantic, Canada Department of National Defence [*Centre de Recherches pour la Defense Atlantique, Ministere de la Defense Nationale*] Dartmouth, Nova Scotia [*Library symbol*] [*National Library of Canada*] (NLC)
NSHND	Reference and Recreational Library (Stadacona), Canada Department of National Defence [*Bibliotheque de Consultation et de Lecture (Stadacona), Ministere de la Defense Nationale*] Halifax, Nova Scotia [*Library symbol*] [*National Library of Canada*] (NLC)
NSHNF	National Film Board [*Office National du Film*], Halifax, Nova Scotia [*Library symbol*] [*National Library of Canada*] (NLC)
NSHNI	Nova Scotia Nautical Institute, Halifax, Nova Scotia [*Library symbol*] [*National Library of Canada*] (NLC)
NSHNP	Nova Scotia Newspaper Project, Halifax [*Library symbol*] [*National Library of Canada*] (BIB)
NSHNS	Ships Recreational Library, Canadian Forces Base Halifax [*Bibliotheque Recreative, Base des Forces Canadiennes Halifax*], Nova Scotia [*Library symbol*] [*National Library of Canada*] (BIB)
NSHO	Naval Service Headquarters, Ottawa (DNAB)
NShor	Shoreham-Wading River Public Library, Shoreham, NY [*Library symbol*] [*Library of Congress*] (LCLS)
NShorHS	Shoreham-Wading River High School, Shoreham, NY [*Library symbol*] [*Library of Congress*] (LCLS)
NSHP	Nova Scotia Public Archives, Halifax, Nova Scotia [*Library symbol*] [*National Library of Canada*] (NLC)
NSHPC	Corporate Research and Information Centre, Nova Scotia Power Corp., Halifax, Nova Scotia [*Library symbol*] [*National Library of Canada*] (NLC)
NSHPH	Atlantic School of Theology, Halifax, Nova Scotia [*Library symbol*] [*National Library of Canada*] (NLC)
NSHPI	Planning Information Office, City of Halifax, Nova Scotia [*Library symbol*] [*National Library of Canada*] (NLC)
NSHPL	Nova Scotia Union Catalogue, Nova Scotia Provincial Library, Halifax, Nova Scotia [*Library symbol*] [*National Library of Canada*] (NLC)
NSHPLX	Reference Services, Nova Scotia Provinical Library, Halifax, Nova Scotia [*Library symbol*] [*National Library of Canada*] (NLC)
NSHPT	Neonatal Severe Hyperparathyroidism [*Medicine*] (DMAA)
NSHPW	Atlantic Regional Library, Public Works Canada [*Bibliotheque Regionale de l'Atlantique, Travaux Publics Canada*] Halifax, Nova Scotia [*Library symbol*] [*National Library of Canada*] (NLC)
NSHQ	Naval Service Headquarters [*Canada*]
NSHQ	Naval Staff Headquarters [*British military*] (DMA)
NShr	John C. Hart Memorial Library, Shrub Oak, NY [*Library symbol*] [*Library of Congress*] (LCLS)
NSHR	National Show Horse Registry (EA)
NSHR	Nova Scotia Research Foundation, Dartmouth, Nova Scotia [*Library symbol*] [*National Library of Canada*] (NLC)
NSHRC	National Self-Help Resource Center [*Defunct*] (EA)
NSHRC	National Shared Housing Resource Center (EA)
NSHRC	Nova Scotia Rehabilitation Centre, Halifax, Nova Scotia [*Library symbol*] [*National Library of Canada*] (NLC)
NSHRCA	Roman Catholic Archdiocesan Archives, Halifax, Nova Scotia [*Library symbol*] [*National Library of Canada*] (BIB)
NSHRL	Nova Scotia Regional Libraries, Halifax, Nova Scotia [*Library symbol*] [*National Library of Canada*] (NLC)
NSHRP	Photogrammetry Division, Nova Scotia Research Foundation, Halifax, Nova Scotia [*Library symbol*] [*Obsolete*] [*National Library of Canada*] (NLC)
NSHS	National Slavic Honor Society (EA)
NSHS	Naval School of Health Sciences [*Bethesda, MD*]
NSHS	St. Mary's University, Halifax, Nova Scotia [*Library symbol*] [*National Library of Canada*] (NLC)
NSHSDET	Naval School of Health Sciences Detachment (DNAB)
NSHSG	Sable Gas Systems Ltd., Halifax, Nova Scotia [*Library symbol*] [*National Library of Canada*] (NLC)
NSHSMC	Stewart, MacKeen & Covert Law Firm, Halifax, Nova Scotia [*Library symbol*] [*National Library of Canada*] (NLC)
NSHSP	Social Development Division Library, Social Planning Department, City of Halifax, Nova Scotia [*Library symbol*] [*National Library of Canada*] (NLC)
NSHSPT	Ferguson Library for Print Handicapped Students, Patrick Power Library, St. Mary's University, Halifax, Nova Scotia [*Library symbol*] [*National Library of Canada*] (NLC)
NSHSS	Nova Scotia Department of Community Services, Halifax, Nova Scotia [*Library symbol*] [*National Library of Canada*] (NLC)
NSHSW	Maritime School of Social Work, Halifax, Nova Scotia [*Library symbol*] [*National Library of Canada*] (NLC)
NSHT	Technical University of Nova Scotia, Halifax, Nova Scotia [*Library symbol*] [*National Library of Canada*] (NLC)
NSHTI	Nova Scotia Institute of Technology, Halifax, Nova Scotia [*Library symbol*] [*National Library of Canada*] (NLC)
NSHTU	Nova Scotia Teachers Union, Halifax, Nova Scotia [*Library symbol*] [*National Library of Canada*] (NLC)
NSHV	Mount Saint Vincent University, Halifax, Nova Scotia [*Library symbol*] [*National Library of Canada*] (NLC)
NSHVA	Art Gallery, Mount Saint Vincent University, Halifax, Nova Scotia [*Library symbol*] [*National Library of Canada*] (NLC)
NSHVGH	Health Sciences Library, Victoria General Hospital, Halifax, Nova Scotia [*Library symbol*] [*National Library of Canada*] (NLC)
NSHVH	Halifax Regional Vocational School, Nova Scotia [*Library symbol*] [*National Library of Canada*] (NLC)
NSHVTT	Nova Scotia Department of Advanced Education and Job Training, Halifax, Nova S cotia [*Library symbol*] [*National Library of Canada*] (NLC)
NSHW	Atlantic Region, Atmospheric Environment Service, Environment Canada [*Bureau Regional de l'Atlantique, Service de l'Environnement Atmospherique, Environnement Canada*] Halifax, Nova Scotia [*Library symbol*] [*National Library of Canada*] (NLC)
NShW	Sag Harbor Whaling and Historical Museum, Sag Harbor, NY [*Library symbol*] [*Library of Congress*] (LCLS)
NSI	Handbook of North-Semitic Inscriptions [*A publication*] (BJA)
NSI	Name Service Independent (SAUS)
NSI	NASA Science Internet
NSI	NASA [*National Aeronautical and Space Administration*] Standard Indicator
NSI	NASA Standard Initiator (NASA)
NSI	National environmental Satellite data and Information service (SAUS)
NSI	National Security Index of the American Security Council [*A publication*] (DLA)
NSI	National Security Information (NRCH)
NSI	National Service Industries, Inc. [*NYSE symbol*] (SPSG)
NSI	National Service [*Life*] Insurance
NSI	National Shipbuilding Initiative [*MARAD*] (TAG)
NSI	National Shoe Institute (EA)
NSI	National Space Institute [*Later, NSS*] (EA)
NSI	National Supervisory Inspectorate [*British*] (EECA)
NSI	Natl Service Indus [*NYSE symbol*] (TTSB)
NSI	Naval Science Instructor (DNAB)
NSI	Negative Self-Image [*Psychology*]
NSI	Network Solutions
NSI	Network Solutions, Inc.
NSI	Network Strategies, Inc. [*Fairfax, VA*] [*Telecommunications*] (TSSD)
NSI	Network Support, Inc.
NSI	Neurosciences Institute (DAVI)
NSI	Next Sequential Instruction
NSI	Nielsen Station Index [*Nielsen Media Research*] [*Information service or system*]
NSI	Nitrogen Solubility Index [*Analytical chemistry*]
NSI	Noise Source Instrumentation
NSI	Nonsatellite Identification
NSI	Nonsequenced Information (IAA)
NSI	Non-SNA Interconnect (SAUS)
NSI	Non-Specific Illness (WDAA)
NSI	Nonspecific Infection [*Medicine*] (MELL)
NSI	Nonspecific Sexually Transmitted Infection [*Medicine*]
NSI	Nonstandard Item
NSI	Nonstocked Item
NSI	Nonstreptococcal Infection [*Medicine*] (MELL)
NSI	Non-Syncytium-Inducing [*Cytology*]
NSI	Norsk Senter for Informatikk [*Norwegian Center for Informatics*] [*Information service or system*] (IID)
NSI	North-South Institute [*Canada*] (EAIO)
NSI	Norton Simon, Inc. (EFIS)
NSI	No Sign of Infection (SAUS)
NSI	No Sign of Inflammation (SAUS)
NSI	No Signs of Infection [*Medicine*] (DMAA)
NSI	Not Seriously Injured [*Environmental science*] (COE)
NSI	Nuclear Safety Inspection (NVT)
NSI	Nuclear Safety Institute
NSI	Nuclear Services International
NSI	Nuclear Status Indicator (DNAB)
NSI	Nuclear Surety Inspection
NSI	Numetic Signal Insignia (SAUS)
NSI	San Nicolas Island, CA [*Location identifier*] [*FAA*] (FAAL)
NSI-1	NASA [*National Aeronautics and Space Administration*] Standard Initiator -Type 1 [*Formerly, SMSI*] (NASA)
NSIA	National Security and International Affairs [*Office of Management and Budget*]
NSIA	National Security Industrial Association (EA)
NSIAC	National Student Involvement Assistance Center [*Boston University*] [*Defunct*]
NSIAC	Northern Sun Intercollegiate Athletic Conference (PSS)
NSIAD	National Security and International Affairs Division (AAGC)
NSIC	National Spinal Injuries Centre [*Stoke Mandeville Hospital*] [*British*] (CB)
NSIC	National Storage Industry Consortium
NSIC	National Strategy Information Center (EA)
NSIC	Naval Security and Investigative Command
NSIC	Next Senior in Command [*Navy*]
NSIC	Northern Sun Intercollegiate Conference (PSS)
NSIC	Noster Salvator Iesus Christus [*Our Savior, Jesus Christ*] [*Latin*]
NSIC	Nuclear Safety Information Center
NSIC	Nuclear Strike Information Center
NSiC	Staten Island Community College, Staten Island, NY [*Library symbol*] [*Library of Congress*] [*Obsolete*] (LCLS)

NSiCS .... College of Staten Island, St. George Campus, Staten Island, NY [Library symbol] [Library of Congress] (LCLS)
NSICU .... Neurosurgical Intensive Care Unit [Medicine] (DMAA)
NSID .... National Society of Interior Designers [Later, ASID]
NSIDC .... National Snow and Ice Data Center [National Oceanic and Atmospheric Administration] (GFGA)
NSIDH .... National System of Interstate and Defense Highways (AFIT)
NSidHi .... Sidney New York Historical Society, Sidney, NY [Library symbol] [Library of Congress] (LCLS)
NSidS .... Bendix Corp., Electrical Components Division, Engineering Library, Sidney, NY [Library symbol] [Library of Congress] (LCLS)
NSIDS .... National Shut-In Day Society (EA)
NSIDSC .... National Sudden Infant Death Syndrome Clearinghouse (EA)
NSIDSF .... National Sudden Infant Death Syndrome Foundation (EA)
NSIDSF .... SIDS Alliance (EA)
NSIEE .... National Society for Internships and Experiential Education (EA)
NSIF .... National Swine Improvement Federation (EA)
NSIF .... Near Space Instrumentation Facility [NASA] (KSC)
NSIG .... North Sea Island Group (SAUS)
NSI-I .... NASA Standard Initiator-Type I (SAUS)
NSiIR .... New York State Department of Mental Hygiene, Institute for Basic Research in Mental Retardation, Staten Island, NY [Library symbol] [Library of Congress] (LCLS)
NSIL .... National Seafood Inspection Laboratory [Pascagoula, MS] [Department of Commerce] (GRD)
NSIL .... Nonsaturating Inverter Logic (IAA)
NSILA .... Nonsuppressible Insulin-Like Activity [Cytochemistry]
NSiIStC .... Saint Columban's Seminary, Silver Creek, NY [Library symbol] [Library of Congress] [Obsolete] (LCLS)
NSIME .... North Staffordshire Institute of Mining Engineers (SAUS)
NSiND .... Notre Dame College of Staten Island, Staten Island, NY [Library symbol] [Library of Congress] (LCLS)
N Sing .... Noun Singular (SAUS)
NSIO .... Nova Scotia Information Office (SAUS)
NSIP .... Nonlinear Signal and Image Processing (SAUS)
NSIPA .... National Society of Insurance Premium Auditors (EA)
NSIPS .... NRL [Naval Research Laboratory] Satellite Image Processing System [Marine science] (OSRA)
NSIR .... Nosier (ABBR)
NSiRC .... Richmond College, Staten Island, NY [Library symbol] [Library of Congress] [Obsolete] (LCLS)
NSIS .... NASA Software Information System (SSD)
NSIS .... National Shut-In Society (EA)
NSIS .... National Survey of Instructional Staff [Department of Education] (GFGA)
NSIS .... New Submarine Intercept Sonar (SAUS)
NSISL .... New South Intercollegiate Swimming League (PSS)
NSiSV .... Saint Vincent's Medical Center of Richmond, Staten Island, NY [Library symbol] [Library of Congress] (LCLS)
NSIT .... Insight Enterprises, Inc. [NASDAQ symbol] (SAG)
NSIT .... Insiht Enterprises [NASDAQ symbol] (TTSB)
NSIT .... Not Safe in Taxis
NSIT .... Nova Scotia Institute of Technology (SAUS)
NSIT .... Trudeau Institute, Saranac Lake (SAUS)
N-SITE .... Near-Term System Integration Test and Evaluation (ACAE)
NSITF .... National Ship Installations Test Facility
NSIX .... Neuromedical Systems [NASDAQ symbol] (TTSB)
NSIX .... Neuromedical Systems, Inc. [NASDAQ symbol] (SAG)
NSIY .... North Somerset Imperial Yeomanry [British military] (DMA)
NSJ .... Nuclear Society of Japan (SAUS)
NSJ .... Nuestro Senor Jesucristo [Our Lord, Jesus Christ] [Spanish]
NSJC .... National Society of Journeymen Curriers [A union] [British]
NSJC .... Noster Salvator Jesus Christus [Our Savior, Jesus Christ] [Latin]
NSJC .... Notre Seigneur Jesus Christ [Our Lord, Jesus Christ] [French]
NSK .... New Skies Satellites ADS [NYSE symbol]
NSK .... Nippon Seiko Kabushiki Kaisha [Japan]
NSK .... Not Specified by Kind (MHDI)
NSKC .... National Safe Kids Campaign (EA)
NSKER .... Efamol Research Institute, Kentville, Nova Scotia [Library symbol] [National Library of Canada] (NLC)
NSKIP .... Nordiska Samarbetskommitten for Internationell Politik [Nordic Cooperation Committee for International Politics, Including Conflict and Peace Research] (EAIO)
NSKKR .... Kings Regional Vocational School, Kentville, Nova Scotia [Library symbol] [National Library of Canada] (NLC)
NSKL .... Wildlife Division, Nova Scotia Department of Lands and Forests, Kentville, Nova Scotia [Library symbol] [National Library of Canada] (NLC)
NSKOK .... Old Kings Courthouse Heritage Museum, Kentville, Nova Scotia [Library symbol] [National Library of Canada] (NLC)
NSKR .... Research Station, Agriculture Canada [Station de Recherches, Agriculture Canada] Kentville, Nova Scotia [Library symbol] [National Library of Canada] (NLC)
NSKVH .... Valley Health Services Association, Kentville, Nova Scotia [Library symbol] [National Library of Canada] (NLC)
NSKY .... New Sky Communications, Inc. (SAUS)
NSL .... Nasal (ABBR)
NSL .... Nasion-Sella Line [Brain anatomy]
NSL .... National Science Laboratories (KSC)
NSL .... National Science Library [Later, Canada Institute for Scientific and Technical Information] (DIT)
NSL .... National Service League [British military] (DMA)
NSL .... National Soccer League (EA)
NSL .... National Standards Laboratory [Formerly, IBS, IMR] [National Institute of Standards and Technology]

NSL .... National Story League (EA)
NSL .... Naval Submarine League (EA)
NSL .... Naval Supersonic Laboratory
NSL .... Navigating Sub-Lieutenant [Navy] [British] (ROG)
NSL .... Navy Standards Laboratory
NSL .... Navy Stock List
NSL .... Net Switching Loss [Telecommunications] (TEL)
NSL .... New Simulation Language (SAUS)
NSL .... New Special Libraries [A publication]
NSL .... Next State List (SAUS)
NSL .... Nonstandard Label [Computer science]
NSL .... Nonstockage List
NSL .... North Air Lines (SAUS)
NSL .... Northern Scientific Laboratory (SAUS)
NSL .... Northrup Space Laboratories (KSC)
NSL .... Norwood & St. Lawrence Railroad Co. [AAR code]
NSL .... Not Stock Listed
NSL .... Nuclear Safety Line
NSL .... Numidian Support League (SAUS)
NSi .... Saranac Lake Free Library, Saranac Lake, NY [Library symbol] [Library of Congress] (LCLS)
NSLA .... Louisbourg Archives, Nova Scotia [Library symbol] [National Library of Canada] (NLC)
NSLA .... National Society of Literature and the Arts (EA)
NSLA .... National Staff Leasing Association (EA)
NSLA .... Nova Scotia Library Association
NSLAL .... Nova Scotia Land Survey Institute, Lawrencetown, Nova Scotia [Library symbol] [National Library of Canada] (NLC)
NSLB .... NS&L Bancorp [NASDAQ symbol] (TTSB)
NSLB .... NS & L Bancorp, Inc. [NASDAQ symbol] (SAG)
NSLC .... Naval Sea Logistics Center
NSLC .... Nuclear Safety and Licensing Commission
NSLF .... Fortress of Louisbourg, Canada National Historic Park [Forteresse de Louisbourg, Parc Historique National] Nova Scotia [Library symbol] [National Library of Canada] (NLC)
NSLF .... National Socialist Liberation Front (NADA)
NSLF .... Nonself
NSLFM .... Fisheries Museum of the Atlantic, Lunenburg, Nova Scotia [Library symbol] [National Library of Canada] (NLC)
NSLFP .... Fort Point Museum, La Have, Nova Scotia [Library symbol] [National Library of Canada] (NLC)
NSIH .... General Hospital of Saranac Lake, Saranac Lake, NY [Library symbol] [Library of Congress] (LCLS)
NSLHS .... Lunenburg Heritage Society, Nova Scotia [Library symbol] [National Library of Canada] (NLC)
NSLI .... National Service Life Insurance
NSLI .... National Street Law Institute (EA)
NSLIN .... Nonstandard Line Item Number [Army] (AABC)
NSLL .... National Save-a-Life League [Defunct] (EA)
NSLL .... National Savings and Loan League [Formerly, NLISA] (EA)
NSLLS .... Lockeport Little School Museum, Nova Scotia [Library symbol] [National Library of Canada] (NLC)
NSINC .... North Country Community College, Saranac Lake, NY [Library symbol] [Library of Congress] (LCLS)
NSLP .... National School Lunch Program [Department of Agriculture]
NSLPE .... Progress-Enterprise, Lunenburg, Nova Scotia [Library symbol] [National Library of Canada] (NLC)
NSLQCM .... Queens County Museum, Liverpool, Nova Scotia [Library symbol] [National Library of Canada] (NLC)
NSLR .... Nova Scotia Law Reports [A publication] (DLA)
NSLRB .... National Steel Labor Relations Board [New Deal]
NSLRB .... Nova Scotia Labour Relations Board (SAUS)
NSLRS .... National School Labor Relations Service [Later, LMRS] (EA)
NSLS .... National Synchrotron Light Source [Brookhaven National Laboratory]
NSLS .... North Suburban Library System, Wheeling, IL [Library network]
NSLSA .... National Surf Life Saving Association of America [Later, USLA] (EA)
NSLSI .... Nova Scotia Land Survey Institute (SAUS)
NSLSRA .... National Society of Live Stock Record Associations (EA)
NSIT .... Trudeau Institute, Saranac Lake, NY [Library symbol] [Library of Congress] (LCLS)
N/S-LTI-G/T .... National/State Leadership Training Institute on Gifted and Talented (EA)
NSIW .... Will Rogers Memorial Fund, Saranac Lake, NY [Library symbol] [Library of Congress] (LCLS)
NSLY .... Nasally (ABBR)
NSLY .... Noisily (ABBR)
NSM .... Narrow Band Sensor Monitor (ACAE)
NSM .... National Search and Rescue Manual (COE)
NSM .... National Security Management [Military]
NSM .... National Security Medal [Military decoration]
NSM .... National Selected Morticians (EA)
NSM .... National Semiconductor Corp. [NYSE symbol] (SPSG)
NSM .... National Serviceman [British military] (DMA)
NSM .... National Soaring Museum (DICI)
NSM .... National Socialist Movement (EA)
NSM .... National Student Marketing
NSM .... Natl Semiconductor [NYSE symbol] (TTSB)
NSM .... Naval School of Music
NSM .... Net-Shared Memory
NSM .... Network Security Module
NSM .... Network Space Monitor (SAA)
NSM .... Network Station Manager
NSM .... Network Status Monitor [NASA] (KSC)
NSM .... Network Support Manager (ACAE)
NSM .... Network/Systems Management (SAUS)

NSM............	Neurosecretory Material (MAE)
NSM............	Neurosecretory Motoneurons
NSM............	Nevada State Museum (SAUS)
NSM............	New Schools Movement [Defunct] (EA)
NSM............	New Smoking Material [A wood cellulose-based tobacco substitute]
NSM............	Nice Safe Man [Slang]
NSM............	Nitsanim [Israel] [Later, AMT] [Geomagnetic observatory code]
NSM............	Noise Source Meter
NSM............	Nonantigenic Specific Mediator (DB)
NSM............	Nondeterministic Sequential Machine (IAA)
NSM............	Norseman [Australia] [Airport symbol] (OAG)
NSM............	Northern Student Movement [Defunct] (EA)
NSM............	North-South Map [Via orbiter]
NSM............	Nova Scotia Museum
NSM............	Nuclear Shell Modell (SAUS)
Nsm............	Number of similar matches (SAUS)
NSM............	Number System Matrix (SAUS)
NSM............	Nutrient Sporulation Medium [Medicine] (DMAA)
NSm............	Smithtown Public Library, Smithtown, NY [Library symbol] [Library of Congress] (LCLS)
N-S/M²	Newton Second per Square Meter (WDAA)
NSMA	Maota [Western Samoa] [ICAO location identifier] (ICLI)
NSMA	National Scale Men's Association (EA)
NSMA	National Seasoning Manufacturers Association (EA)
NSMA	National Second Mortgage Association [Center Square, PA] (EA)
NSMA	National Shoe Manufacturers Association [Later, FIA] (EA)
NSMA	National Soup Mix Association [Defunct] (EA)
NSMAPMAWOL...	Not So Much a Programme, More a Way of Life [British television program]
NSMATCC	NATO Small Arms Test Control Commission (MCD)
NSMB	Nuclear Standards Management Board (SAUS)
NSMC	National Security Management Course [National Defense University] (GFGA)
NSMC	National Student Marketing Corp.
NSMC	Naval Submarine Medical Center
NSMCA	National Spirit, Metropolitan Club of America (EA)
NSMCM	Naval Supplement, Manual for Courts-Martial [United States] [A publication] (DLA)
NSMDO.......	Naval Systems Management & Development Office (SAUS)
NSME.........	Eastern Counties Regional Library, Mulgrave, Nova Scotia [Library symbol] [National Library of Canada] (NLC)
NSME.........	Night Sight Maintenance Facility (TIMI)
NSME.........	Nonstandard Measuring Equipment (SAUS)
NSMEX	Examiner, Middleton, Nova Scotia [Library symbol] [National Library of Canada] (NLC)
NSMFA	North Sea Mine Force Association (EA)
NSMG	Naval School of Military Government
NSMG & A..	Naval School of Military Government and Administration
NSmGH.......	Smithtown General Hospital, Smithtown, NY [Library symbol] [Library of Congress] (LCLS)
NSMH	Nuclear Systems Material Handbook (NRCH)
NSMHC......	National Society for Mentally Handicapped Children [British] (BI)
NSmHSE.....	Smithtown High School East, Smithtown, NY [Library symbol] [Library of Congress] (LCLS)
NSmHSW....	Smithtown High School West, Smithtown, NY [Library symbol] [Library of Congress] (LCLS)
NSMI	National Sports Medicine Institute (SAUS)
NSML	Low-Sodium Meal [Airline notation] (ADA)
NSMM	Macdonald Museum, Middleton, Nova Scotia [Library symbol] [National Library of Canada] (NLC)
NSMM	National Society of Metal Mechanics [A union] [British] (DCTA)
NSMM	National Sustainment Maintenance Management [Army]
NSMO	NASTRAN [NASA Structural Analysis] Systems Management Office
NSMP	National Society of Master Patternmakers [British] (BI)
NSMP	National Society of Mural Painters (EA)
NSMP	Navy Support and Mobilization Plan (NVT)
NSMPA	National Screw Machine Products Association (EA)
NSMR	National Society for Medical Research (EA)
NSMR	Non-Store Marketing Report [A publication]
NSMRL	Naval Submarine Medical Research Laboratory
NSMRSE.....	National Study of Mathematics Requirements for Scientists and Engineers
NSMRTS.....	Nuclear Submarine Maneuvering Room Training Simulator (PDAA)
NSMS	National Safety Management Society (EA)
NSMS	National Sheet Music Society (EA)
NSMS	Network Server Management System [Tylink Corp.]
NSMS²	Soldiers Memorial Hospital, Middleton, Nova Scotia [Library symbol] [National Library of Canada] (NLC)
NSMSES	Naval Ship Missile System Engineering Station
NSMSESDETLANT...	Naval Ship Missile System Engineering Station Detachment, Atlantic (MUGU)
NSmSJH	Saint John's Smithtown Hospital, Smithtown, NY [Library symbol] [Library of Congress] (LCLS)
NSMT.........	National Society of Master Thatchers [British] (DBA)
NSMT.........	National Society of Medical Technologists
NSMTD	Northwest Suburban Mass Transit District (SAUS)
NSMV	Valley Mirror, Middleton, Nova Scotia [Library symbol] [National Library of Canada] (NLC)
NSMW	Naval Schools Mine Warfare
Ns/my	Newton Second per Square Meter (SAUS)
NSN	Military Sealift Command, Washington, DC [OCLC symbol] (OCLC)
NSN	National Sleep Network (SAUS)
NSN	National Stock Number (MCD)
NSN	NATO Stock Number (NATG)
NSN	Nelson [New Zealand] [Airport symbol] (OAG)

NSN	Nephrotoxic Serum Nephritis [Medicine] (DMAA)
NSN	New Substances Notification (SARE)
NSN	Nicotine-Stimulated Neurophysin [Biochemistry]
NSN	Northern Science Network (SAUS)
NSN	North Star Network [Defunct] (EA)
NSN	No Stock Number
Nsn	Number of Similar Negative Matches
NSN	Nurses Support Network [Later, NIT] (EA)
NSNA........	National Socialist Nederlandse Arbeiders Partij [Netherlands group favoring integration of the Netherlands into the German reich] [World War II]
NSNA........	National Student Nurses' Association (EA)
NSNA........	Newcomen Society in North America (EA)
NSNA........	No Stock Number Assigned
NSNC........	National Society of Newspaper Columnists (NTPA)
NSNC........	Nova Scotia Normal College
NSNCE.......	Nuisance (ABBR)
NSNCL.......	Nonsensical (ABBR)
NSND........	Nonsymptomatic, Nondisabling (MAE)
NSND........	Normal Saline Nose Drops [Pharmacology] (DAVI)
NSNE........	Nappan Experimental Farm, Nova Scotia [Library symbol] [National Library of Canada] (NLC)
NSNEW	National Society of New England Women (EA)
NSNF	Nonstrategic Nuclear Forces (MCD)
NSnfG	GTE Sylvania, Inc., Electronic Components Group, Seneca Falls, NY [Library symbol] [Library of Congress] (LCLS)
NSNGA.......	Aberdeen Hospital, New Glasgow, Nova Scotia [Library symbol] [National Library of Canada] (NLC)
NSNGE	Evening News, New Glasgow, Nova Scotia [Library symbol] [National Library of Canada] (NLC)
NSNGH	New Glasgow Senior High School, Nova Scotia [Library symbol] [National Library of Canada] (BIB)
NSNGP	Pictou-Antigonish Regional Library, New Glasgow, Nova Scotia [Library symbol] [National Library of Canada] (NLC)
NSNHC.......	Cabot Archives, Neil's Harbour, Nova Scotia [Library symbol] [National Library of Canada] (NLC)
NSNMDR	National Stock Number Master Data Records (MCD)
NSNMK......	Kentville Publishing, New Minas, Nova Scotia [Library symbol] [National Library of Canada] (NLC)
NSNN	Northern Science News Newsletter (SAUS)
NSNP	No Space, No Print [Computer science] (MHDI)
NSNRP.......	Nonstock Numbered Repair Parts
NSNS	Nonsense (ABBR)
NSNSCLY....	Nonsensically (ABBR)
NSO	NASA Support Operation (KSC)
NSO	National Security Office [or Officer] (GFGA)
NSO	National Service Officer [Ministry of Labour and National Service] [British] [World War II]
NSO	National Solar Observatory [Tucson, AZ] [National Science Foundation] (GRD)
NSO	National Standardization Office [US Army Materiel Command]
NSO	National Symphony Orchestra
NSO	Naval Staff Officer
NSO	Naval Store Officer [British]
NSO	Navigation/Systems Operator (SAUS)
NSO	Navy Staff Offices (ACAE)
NSO	Navy Subsistence Office (DNAB)
NSO	Neighborhood Service Organization
NSO	Neosporin Ointment [Medicine] (CPH)
NSO	Network Support Office [NASA]
NSO	New American Shoe Co., Inc. (SAUS)
NSO	Next Standing Order
NSO	Nitrogen, Sulfur, and Oxygen [In chemical compounds]
NSO	Nitrogen, Sulfur, Oxygen (SAUS)
NSO	Noise Suppression Oscillator (MCD)
NSO	Nonferrous Smelter Order [Environmental Protection Agency]
NSO	Norfolk Symphony Orchestra (SAUS)
NSO	Northern Sinfonia Orchestra (SAUS)
nso...........	Northern Sotho [MARC language code] [Library of Congress] (LCCP)
NSO	North State Cooperative Library System, Willows, CA [OCLC symbol] (OCLC)
NSO	No Spares Ordered (AAG)
NSO	nSTOR Technologies [AMEX symbol] (SG)
NSO	Nuclear Safety Office [or Officer] [Air Force] (AFM)
NSO	Nucleus Supraopticus (DMAA)
NSO	Numeric Stockage Objective [Items] [DoD]
NSO	Scone [Australia] [Airport symbol] (OAG)
NSo...........	Somers Library, Somers, NY [Library symbol] [Library of Congress] (LCLS)
NSOA	National School Orchestra Association (EA)
NSOA	National Symphony Orchestra Association (EA)
NSOA	Nuclear Safety Operational Analysis (NRCH)
NSoa	Rogers Memorial Library, Southampton, NY [Library symbol] [Library of Congress] (LCLS)
NSoaH	Southampton Hospital, Southampton, NY [Library symbol] [Library of Congress] (LCLS)
NSoaS	Long Island University, Southampton College, Southampton, NY [Library symbol] [Library of Congress] (LCLS)
NSOB	New Senate Office Building
NSOC	National SIGINT [Signal Intelligence] Operations Center (MCD)
NSOC	Navy Satellite Operations Center (NVT)
NSOC	New South Conference (PSS)
NSOC	Norbornene Spiroorthocarbonate [Organic chemistry]
NSOD	Naval School of Ordnance Disposal
NSODCC	North Sumatra Oil Development Corporation Co. (SAUS)

NSOEA......... National Stationery and Office Equipment Association [*Later, NOPA*] (EA)
NSOF........... Naval Status of Forces (MCD)
NSOF........... Navy Special Operations Force (AABC)
NSOG........... Navy Special Operations Group [*SEALS that operated in Vietnam*] (VNW)
NSOGA........ National Seniors' Open Golf Association (EA)
NSoHi.......... Somers Historical Society, Somers, NY [*Library symbol*] [*Library of Congress*] (LCLS)
NSOHSC ...... National Survey of Oral Health in School Children [*Department of Health and Human Services*] (GFGA)
NSOJ .... Journal, Oxford, Nova Scotia [*Library symbol*] [*National Library of Canada*] (NLC)
NSOL........... Network Solutions [*NASDAQ symbol*] (SG)
NSOM.......... Near Field Scanning Optical Microscopy
NSoo........... Southold Free Library, Southold, NY [*Library symbol*] [*Library of Congress*] (LCLS)
NSOP........... National Second Opinion Program (EA)
NSOPCD ...... National Society of Old Plymouth Colony Descendants (EA)
NSOPF......... National Survey of Postsecondary Faculty [*Department of Education*] (GFGA)
NSOR.......... No Shop Order Required
NSos........... South Salem Library, South Salem, NY [*Library symbol*] [*Library of Congress*] (LCLS)
NSOSG........ North Sea Oceanographical Study Group [*British*]
NSOW.......... Naval Statement of Work (ACAE)
NSOW.......... Norwegian Sea Overflow Water (SAUS)
NSP .... NASA Support Plan (KSC)
NSP .... National Salvation Party [*Milli Selamet Partisi*] [*Turkey*] [*Political party*] (PPW)
NSP .... National Sea Products Ltd. [*Toronto Stock Exchange symbol*]
NSP .... National Search and Rescue Plan (COE)
NSP .... National Seoposengwe Party [*Bophuthatswana*] [*Political party*] (PPW)
NSP .... National Services Program (SAUS)
NSP .... National Ski Patrol System (EA)
NSP .... National Socialist Party [*New Zealand*] [*Political party*] (PD)
NSP .... National Society of Painters [*A union*] [*British*]
NSP .... National Society of Professors [*Later, NEA Higher Education Council*] (EA)
NSP .... National Space Program (AAG)
NSP .... National Stolen Property
NSP .... National Stuttering Project (EA)
NSP .... Native Signal Processing [*Computer science*] (PCM)
NSP .... Naval Special Projects (ACAE)
NSP .... Navigational Satellite Program [*NASA*] (IAA)
NSP .... Navy Safety Program (DNAB)
NSP .... Navy Space Project
NSP .... Navy Special Projects office (SAUS)
NSP .... Navy Standard Part
NSP .... Navy Support Plan
NSP .... Neighborhood Statistics Program [*Bureau of the Census*] (GFGA)
NSP .... Net Social Profitability
NSP .... Network Service Point (SAUS)
NSP .... Network Service Provider [*Telecommunications*]
NSP .... Network Services Protocol [*Digital Equipment Corp.*] [*Telecommunications*] (TEL)
NSP .... Network Signal Processor (NASA)
NSP .... Network Support Plan [*NASA*] (KSC)
NSP .... Network Support Processor (NITA)
NSP .... Neurological Shellfish Poisoning (USDC)
NSP .... Neuron-Specific Protein [*Later, NSE*] [*Biochemistry*]
NSP .... Neurotoxic Shellfish Poisoning [*Medicine*]
NSP .... Neutral Steer Point (SAUS)
NSP .... New Species
NSP .... Nominal Stagnation Point
NSP .... Non-Self-Propelled
NSP .... Nonseries Parallel (IAA)
NSP .... Nonspecific Prostatitis [*Medicine*] (ADA)
NSP .... Nonstandard Holding Pattern (SAUS)
NSP .... Nonstandard Part
NSP .... Nonstorage Protein [*Food technology*]
NSP .... Nonstructural Protein (DMAA)
NSP .... Non-Swelling and Paintable (SAUS)
NSP .... Non-volatile, Serially Programmable (SAUS)
NSP .... Nordiska Sjoforsakringspoolen [*Nordic Pool for Marine Insurance - NPMI*] (EA)
NSP .... Normal Serum Pool
NSP .... Normal Stage Punching (SAUS)
NSP .... Normal Superphosphate [*Fertilizer*]
NSP .... Northern States Power Co. [*NYSE symbol*] (SPSG)
NSP .... Northern States Pwr [*NYSE symbol*] (TTSB)
NSP .... North Solomons Province (SAUS)
NSP .... No Separate Billing Price (MCD)
NSP .... Nose Shipping Plug
NSP .... Not Separately Priced (NG)
NSP .... N-Succinylperimycin (DB)
NSP .... Nuclear Strike Plan [*Army*] (AABC)
Nsp............. Number of Similar Positive Matches
NSP .... Numeric Space (SAUS)
NSP .... Numeric Space Character [*Computer science*]
NSP .... Numeric Subroutine Package [*Computer science*] (CIST)
NSP .... Nutritional Support Panel [*Dietetics*] (DAVI)
nsp............... Species Nova [*New Species*] [*Latin*] (EES)

NSP .... St. Andrews Presbyterian College, Laurinburg, NC [*OCLC symbol*] (OCLC)
NSPA .... Advocate, Pictou, Nova Scotia [*Library symbol*] [*National Library of Canada*] (NLC)
NSPA .... National Scholastic Press Association (EA)
NSPA .... National Shrimp Processors Association (EA)
NSPA .... National Socialist Party of America (EA)
NSPA .... National Society of Public Accountants [*Alexandria, VA*] (EA)
NSPA .... National Soybean Processors Association [*Later, NOPA*] (EA)
NSPA .... National Split Pea Association [*Defunct*]
NSPA .... National Standard Parts Association [*Later, ASIA*]
NSPA .... National State Printing Association (EA)
NSPA .... National Stolen Property Act
NSPA .... Navy Shore Patrol Administration (WDAA)
NSPA .... Nova Scotia Pharmaceutical Association (SAUS)
NSPA .... Pictou Advocate, Nova Scotia [*Library symbol*] [*National Library of Canada*] (NLC)
NSPAC .... National Security Political Action Committee [*Defunct*] (EA)
NSPAR .... Nonstandard Part Approval Request
NSpaT......... Saint Thomas Aquinas College, Sparkill, NY [*Library symbol*] [*Library of Congress*] (LCLS)
NSPB .... National Society to Prevent Blindness (EA)
NSPB .... Prevent Blindness America [*Formerly, National Society to Prevent Blindness*] (EA)
NSPBB .... Burning Bush Museum, Pictou, Nova Scotia [*Library symbol*] [*National Library of Canada*] (BIB)
NSPB/PBA.... National Society to Prevent Blindness/Prevent Blindness America (NTPA)
NSPC .... National Security Planning Commission
NSPC .... National Society of Painters in Casein (EA)
NSPC .... National Sound-Program Center [*Telecommunications*] (TEL)
NSPC .... National Standard Plumbing Code Committee (EA)
NSPC .... National Straight Pipe Threads in Pipe Couplings
NSPC .... Nova Scotia Power Corp. (SAUS)
NSPCA .... National Society for the Prevention of Cruelty to Animals
NSPCA .... National Society of Painters in Casein and Acrylic (EA)
NSPCB .... National Society for the Preservation of Covered Bridges (EA)
NSPCC .... National Society for the Prevention of Cruelty to Children
NSPCC .... Naval Ships Parts Control Center (MCD)
NSPCM .... National Society for Prevention of Cruelty to Mushrooms (EA)
NSPD .... Naval Shore Patrol Detachment
NSPE .... National Society of Professional Engineers (EA)
NSPE .... Navy Senior Procurement Executive (AAGC)
NSPE .... Network Services Procedure Error (ELAL)
NSPE .... Nuclear Superheat Performance Evaluation (SAUS)
NSPE .... Specimen Unobtainable [*Laboratory science*] (DAVI)
NSpeB .... Board of Cooperative Educational Services (BOCES), Spencerport, NY [*Library symbol*] [*Library of Congress*] (LCLS)
N-SPECS...... Navy Specifications (AAGC)
NSPF .... National Swimming Pool Foundation (EA)
nspf .... Not Specially Provided For (EBF)
NSPF .... Not Specifically Provided For
NSPFEA .... National Spray Painting and Finishing Equipment Association [*Later, NSEMA*] (EA)
NSPG .... National Security Planning Group
NSPH .... Neonatal Severe Hyperparathyroidism [*Medicine*] (DMAA)
NSPHM........ Port Hastings Museum and Archives, Nova Scotia [*Library symbol*] [*National Library of Canada*] (NLC)
NSPI .... National Society for Performance and Instruction (EA)
NSPI .... National Society for Programmed Instruction (IAA)
NSPI .... National Spa and Pool Institute (EA)
NSPI .... National Spatial Data Infrastructure [*BTS*] (TAG)
NSPI .... Nonstorage Protein Isolate [*Food technology*]
NSPIAE .... National Society of Professional Insurance Agency Executives (NTPA)
NSPIE .... National Society for the Promotion of Industrial Education [*Later, AVA*]
NSPK .... NetSpeak Corp. [*NASDAQ symbol*] (SG)
NSPKU......... National Society for Phenylketonuria and Allied Disorders [*British*] (DBA)
NSPL .... NASA Standard Parts List (SAUS)
NSPLO .... NATO Sidewinder Production and Logistics Organization [*Missiles*] (NATG)
NSPMH........ McCulloch House, Pictou, Nova Scotia [*Library symbol*] [*National Library of Canada*] (NLC)
NSPNC .... North Cumberland Historical Society, Pugwash, Nova Scotia [*Library symbol*] [*National Library of Canada*] (NLC)
NSPO .... NATO Sea Sparrow Project Office (MCD)
NSPO .... NATO Sidewinder Production Organization [*Missiles*] (NATG)
NSPO .... NATO Sidewinder Program Office [*Missiles*] (NATG)
NSPO .... Naval Ship Production Overseer [*British*]
NSPO .... Naval Space Projects Office
NSPO .... Navy Special Projects Office
NSPO .... Nuclear Systems Project Office [*Air Research and Development Command*] [*Air Force*] (AAG)
NS-POG .... NAVSHIPS [*Naval Ship Systems Command*] Propulsion Operating Guides
NSPOL......... Non-Scheduled Operations Policy (SAUS)
NSPP .... National Serials Pilot Project
NSPP .... Nuclear Safety Pilot Plant [*ORNL*]
NSPPrA .... Non'n St Pwr Minn,$3.60 Pfd [*NYSE symbol*] (TTSB)
NSPPrB .... No'n St Pwr Minn,$4.08 Pfd [*NYSE symbol*] (TTSB)
NSPPrC .... No'n Pwr Minn,$4.10 Pfd [*NYSE symbol*] (TTSB)
NSPPrE .... No's St Pwr Minn.$4.16 Pfd [*NYSE symbol*] (TTSB)
NSPPrG........ No'n St Pwr Minn.$4.56 Pfd [*NYSE symbol*] (TTSB)

NSPPrH........	No'n St Pwr Minn,$6.80 Pfd [*NYSE symbol*] (TTSB)
NSPPrI.........	No'n St Pwr Minn,$7.00 Pfd [*NYSE symbol*] (TTSB)
NSPR	INSpire Insurance Solutions [*NASDAQ symbol*] (SG)
NSPR	National Society for Park Resources (EA)
NSPR	National Society of Patient Representatives of the American Hospital Association (EA)
NSPR	National Society of Pershing Rifles (EA)
NSPR	Netscape Portable Runtime (SAUS)
NSPR	Nonstandard Part Approval Request
NSPR	Record, Parrsboro, Nova Scotia [*Library symbol*] [*National Library of Canada*] (NLC)
NSPRA........	National School Public Relations Association (EA)
NSPRCA.......	National Society for Patient Representation and Consumer Affairs (NTPA)
NSPRCA.......	National Society of Patient Representation and Consumer Affairs of the American Hospital Association (EA)
NSPrD..........	No'n St Pwr Minn,$4.11 Pfd [*NYSE symbol*] (TTSB)
NSPRDS	New Systems Personnel Requirements Data System [*Navy*]
NSPRI	Nigeria Store Product Research Institute (SAUS)
NSPRM........	National Society of Professional Resident Managers (EA)
NSPRS	Nigerian Society for Photogrammetry and Remote Sensing (SAUS)
NSPRT	Nonsupport (ABBR)
NSPRV	Pictou Regional Vocational School, Nova Scotia [*Library symbol*] [*National Library of Canada*] (NLC)
NSprvCH......	Bertrand Chaffee Hospital, Springville, NY [*Library symbol*] [*Library of Congress*] (LCLS)
NSPS	National Ski Patrol System (EA)
NSPS	National Society of Professional Sanitarians (EA)
NSPS	National Society of Professional Surveyors (EA)
NSPS	National Standards of Performance for Stationary Sources (ACII)
NSPS	National Stockpile Purchase Specification [*for metals*]
NSPS	National Sweet Pea Society [*British*] (BI)
NSPS	New Source Performance Standards [*Environmental Protection Agency*] (AEPA)
NSPS	Nonsynchronous Pulse Suppression (MCD)
NSPS	Nuclear Safety Protection System (NRCH)
NSPS	Nuclear Strike Planning System (MCD)
NSPSE	National Society of Painters, Sculptors, and Engravers [*British*] (DI)
NSPSH.........	Parrsboro Shore Historical Society, Parrsboro, Nova Scotia [*Library symbol*] [*National Library of Canada*] (BIB)
NSPSR........	New Source Performance Standard Review (SAUS)
NSPSS	Scotia Sun, Port Hawkesbury, Nova Scotia [*Library symbol*] [*National Library of Canada*] (NLC)
NSPST	National Society of Pharmaceutical Sales Trainers (EA)
NSPV	Nandina Stem-Pitting Virus [*Plant pathology*]
NSPV	Number of Scans per Vehicle (OA)
NSPVT	Nonsustained Polymorphic Ventricular Tachycardia [*Cardiology*] (DAVI)
NSPw	Northern States Power Co. [*Associated Press*] (SAG)
NSPWA	National Society Patriotic Women of America
NSQ	Neuroticism Scale Questionnaire [*Psychology*]
NSQ	Not Sufficient Quantity [*Clinical chemistry*]
NSQ	Nurse Satisfaction Questionnaire
NSQC	National Society of Quality Circles [*British*] (DBA)
NSR	Mount Vernon, WA [*Location identifier*] [*FAA*] (FAAL)
NSR	Nasoseptal Reconstruction [*Otorhinolaryngology*] (DAVI)
NSR	Natinal Securities & Research Corp. (EFIS)
NSR	National Air Charter PT [*Indonesia*] [*ICAO designator*] (FAAC)
NSR	National Scenic Riverway
NSR	National Scientific Register
NSR	National Security Review (AAGC)
NSR	National Shipping Report [*NATO*]
NSR	National Shipping Representative (NATG)
NSR	National Shorthand Reporter [*A publication*]
NSR	National Singles Registry (EA)
NSR	National Slow Rate (NASA)
NSR	National Swine Registry (NTPA)
NSR	NATO Staff Requirements (MCD)
NSR	Naval Staff Requirement (SAUS)
NSR	Naval Supply Requirement (DNAB)
NSR	Net Survival Rate
NSR	Neutron Source Reactor
NSR	New Source Review [*A publication*] (EPA)
NSR	Night Sky Radiation
NSR	Nitrile Silicone Rubber [*Organic chemistry*]
NSR	Noise-to-Signal Ratio (IAA)
NSR	Nominal Slow Rate [*NASA*] (KSC)
NSR	Non Sequential Recording (SAUS)
NSR	Non-Shared Resources (SAUS)
NSR	Non Significant Result [*Medicine*]
NSR	Non Slug Return (SAUS)
NSR	Non-Source Routed (SAUS)
NSR	Nonspecific Reaction [*Medicine*] (DMAA)
NSR	Non-Storage Resources (SAUS)
NSR	Norair Science Report (SAA)
NSR	Nordic Shooting Region (EAIO)
NSR	Nordiska Skidskolans Rad [*Nordic Council of Ski Schools - NCSS*] [*Finland*] (EAIO)
NSR	Nordiska Skogsarbetsstudiernas Rad [*Nordic Research Council on Forest Operations*] [*Sweden*] (EAIO)
NSR	Nordisk Skuespillerrad [*Nordic Actors' Council - NAC*] [*Sweden*] (EAIO)
NSR	Norfolk Southern Railway Co. [*NYSE symbol*] (SAG)
NSR	Normal Service Request (ELAL)
NSR	Normal Sinus Rhythm [*Medicine*] (DMAA)
NSR	Normal Slow Rate Maneuver (NASA)
NSR	Norske Samers Riksforbund [*Norway*]
NSR	Northern Sea Route (NATG)
NSR	North Staffordshire Railway [*British*] (ROG)
NSR	No Sign of Recurrence [*Medicine*] (DMAA)
NSR	No Slot Release (ELAL)
NSR	No Staff Responsibility [*Army*] (AABC)
NSR	Notch Strength Ratio (SAUS)
NSR	Notch Stress Rupture (SAUS)
NSR	Not Seen Regularly [*Medicine*] (DAVI)
NSR	Nova Scotia Provincial Library [*UTLAS symbol*]
NSR	Nova Scotia Regiment [*Canada*] (DMA)
NSR	NSR Resources, Inc. [*Toronto Stock Exchange symbol*]
NSR	Nuclear Spin Relaxation [*Physics*]
NSR	Nuclear Structure References [*Brookhaven National Laboratory*] [*Information service or system*]
NSR	Nutrient Supply Rate [*Oceanography*]
NSR2	Second Coelliptic Maneuver (SAUS)
NSRA	National Scooter Riders Association [*British*] (DBA)
NSRA	National Service Robot Association (EA)
NSRA	National Shoe Retailers Association (EA)
NSRA	National Shorthand Reporters Association (EA)
NSRA	National Ski Retailers Association (EA)
NSRA	National Smallbore Rifle Association [*British*]
NSRA	National Society for Research into Allergy [*British*]
NSRA	National Street Rod Association
NSRA	National Swim and Recreation Association (EA)
NSRA	North-South Reconstruction Advisors (SAUS)
NSRA	Nuclear Safety Research Association [*See also GAKK*] [*Japan*] (NRCH)
NSRB	National Security Resources Board [*Functions transferred to ODM, 1953*]
NSRB	Nuclear Safety Review Board (NRCH)
NSRBD........	National Security Resources Board [*Functions transferred to ODM, 1953*] (GFGA)
NSRC	National SIDS Resource Center (EA)
NSRC	National Silver Rabbit Club (EA)
NSRC	National Stereophonic Radio Committee
NSRC	National Sudden Infant Death Syndrome Resource Center (NRGU)
NSRC	NeoSynthesis Research Centre [*Sri Lanka*] (EAIO)
NSRC	North Stratford Railroad Corp. [*AAR code*]
NSR Coch	Cochran's Nova Scotia Reports [*1859*] [*A publication*] (DLA)
NSR Coh.....	Cohen's Nova Scotia Reports [*A publication*] (DLA)
NSRD	National Security Resources Development
NSRD	National Software Reuse Directory (SAUS)
NSRDB........	National SIGINT [*Signal Intelligence*] Requirements Database (MCD)
NSRDB........	National Solar Radiation Data Base (SAUS)
NSRDB........	Nova Scotia Resources Development Board (SAUS)
NSRDC........	National Standards Reference Data Center
NSRDC........	[*David W. Taylor*] Naval Ship Research and Development Center (AAGC)
NSRDC/A	Naval Ship Research and Development Center, Annapolis [*Maryland*] Division (DNAB)
NSRDC(AD)...	Naval Ship Research and Development Center (Annapolis Division)
NSRDCANNADIV..	Naval Ship Research and Development Center, Annapolis [*Maryland*] Division (DNAB)
NSRDF........	Naval Supply Research and Development Facility
NSRDL........	Naval Ship Research and Development Laboratory (MCD)
NSRDL/A......	Naval Ship Research and Development Laboratory, Annapolis [*Maryland*]
NSRDL/PC ...	Naval Ship Research and Development Laboratory, Panama City [*Florida*] [*Later, NCSC*]
NSRDS........	National Standard Reference Data System [*Gaithersburg, MD*] [*National Institute of Standards and Technology*]
NSREA........	National Society of Real Estate Appraisers (NTPA)
NSREC........	National Society's Religious Education Centre (AIE)
NSREF.........	National Society for Real Estate Finance [*Washington, DC*] (EA)
NS Rev Stat...	Nova Scotia Revised Statutes [*Canada*] [*A publication*] (DLA)
NSRF	National Stroke Recovery Foundation (EA)
NSRF	Naval Ship Repair Facility (MCD)
NSRF	Naval Strategic Reserve Fleet
NSRF	Nova Scotia Research Foundation (SAUS)
NSRFC.........	Nova Scotia Research Foundation Corp. [*Crown Corp.*] [*Canada*] (IRC)
NSRG..........	Northern Science Research Group (SAUS)
NSRG & O ...	Nova Scotia Reports, by Geldert and Oxley [*A publication*] (DLA)
NSRG & R ...	Nova Scotia Reports, by Geldert and Russell [*A publication*] (DLA)
NSRJ	Nova Scotia Reports (James) [*A publication*] (DLA)
NSR (James)...	Nova Scotia Reports (James) [*Canada*] [*A publication*] (DLA)
NSRL	National SIGINT [*Signal Intelligence*] Requirements List (MCD)
NSRL	Nuclear Structure Research Laboratory (NRCH)
NSRM..........	National Strategy for Rangeland Management [*Australia*]
NSRMCA......	National Star Route Mail Contractors Association (EA)
NSRMP........	Net Survival Rate for Monocyclic Process
NSRN..........	National School Resource Network [*Defunct*] (EA)
NSRO..........	Navy Resale System Office (PDAA)
NSR Old	Oldright's Nova Scotia Reports [*A publication*] (DLA)
NSRP	National Search and Rescue Plan
NSRP	National States Rights Party (EA)
NSRP	Neutral Seat Reference Point (MCD)
NSRP	Nonstandard Part Request
NSRP	Nontechnical Support Real Property
NSRP	Nordic Society for Radiation Protection [*See also NSFS*] [*Helsinki, Finland*] (EAIO)
NSRPIE........	Non-technical Support Real Property Installed Equipment (SAUS)

NSRPr.......... NorfolkSo'nRy$2.60cmPfd [*NYSE symbol*] (TTSB)

NSR/PSD ...... New Source Review and Prevention of Significant Deterioration Permitting (SAUS)

NSR PSU ..... Non Self-Representing Primary Sampling Unit [*Bureau of the Census*] (GFGA)

NSRQCE....... National Symposium on Reliability and Quality Control in Electronics (MCD)

NSRR.......... Normal Sinus Rate and Rhythm [*Cardiology*] (DAVI)

NSRR........... Nuclear Safety Research Reactors (NRCH)

NSRR & C ... Russell and Chesley's Nova Scotia Reports [*10-12 Nova Scotia Reports*] [*1875-79*] [*A publication*] (DLA)

NSRR & G ... Russell and Geldert's Nova Scotia Reports [*A publication*] (DLA)

NSRS........... NASA Safety Reporting System (SAUS)

NSRS........... National Scholarship Research Service [*Information service or system*] (IID)

NSRS........... National Shoreline Refuse Survey [*British*]

NSRS........... National Spatial Reference System [*Marine science*] (OSRA)

NSRS........... National Supply Radio Station (MCD)

NSRS........... Naval Supply Radio Station

NSRT........... Near-Surface Radiation Thermometer

NSRT........... Near Surface Reference Temperature [*Oceanography*]

NSRT........... North South Roundtable (EAIO)

NSR Thom ... Thomson's Nova Scotia Reports [*A publication*] (DLA)

NSRU........... North Star Universal [*NASDAQ symbol*] (TTSB)

NSRU........... North Star Universal, Inc. [*NASDAQ symbol*] (NQ)

NSrU........... Ulster County Community College, Stone Ridge, NY [*Library symbol*] [*Library of Congress*] (LCLS)

NSRW.......... Nuclear Service Raw Water (IEEE)

NSR Wall.... Wallace's Nova Scotia Reports [*6 Nova Scotia Reports*] [*1884-1907*] [*A publication*] (DLA)

NSRWP........ Nuclear Service Raw Water Pump [*Electronics*] (IAA)

NSRy .... Norfolk Southern Railway Co. [*Associated Press*] (SAG)

NSS .... Namespace Specific String (SAUS)

NSS .... Name Switch Service (SAUS)

NSS .... National Sample Survey (PDAA)

NSS .... National Sculpture Society (EA)

NSS .... National Search and Rescue Secretariat [*Canada*] (DA)

NSS .... National Secular Society [*British*] (DBA)

NSS .... National Seismic Stations

NSS .... National Serigraph Society [*Defunct*]

NSS .... National Service Secretariat (EA)

NSS .... National Slovak Society of the USA

NSS .... National Snapdragon Society (EA)

NSS .... National Space Society (EA)

NSS .... National Space Station [*NASA*] (IAA)

NSS .... National Speleological Society (EA)

NSS .... National Staff Side [*British*]

NSS .... National Stockpile Site

NSS .... National Study Service [*Defunct*] (EA)

NSS .... National Supply System (MCD)

NSS .... National Surveillance Scheme (WDAA)

NS/S .... Native Seeds/SEARCH [*Southwestern Endangered Arid-Land Resource Clearing House*] (EA)

NSS .... Naval Sea Systems Command, Washington, DC [*OCLC symbol*] (OCLC)

NSS .... Naval Security Station (NVT)

NSS .... Naval Simulation System [*DoD*]

NSS .... Naval Strategic Study

NSS .... Navigation Subsystem Switchboard

NSS .... Navy Secondary Standards (MSA)

NSS .... Navy Shore Station (IAA)

NSS .... Navy Standard Score (DNAB)

NSS .... Navy Strategic Study

NSS .... Navy Supply System

NSS .... Near-Source Simulation (SAUS)

NSS .... Network Supervisor System

NSS .... Network Support System [*Computer science*]

NSS .... Network Synchronization Subsystem [*Telecommunications*] (TEL)

NSS .... Network System Simulator (ACAE)

NSS .... Neurological Soft Signs [*Occupational therapy*]

NSS .... Neuropathy Symptom Score

NSS .... Neutral Safety Switch [*Automotive engineering*]

NSS .... Neutral Speed Stability (PDAA)

NSS .... Neutron Scattering Society

NSS .... Neutron Spectrometer System

NSS .... [*The*] Newburgh & South Shore Railway Co. [*AAR code*]

NSS .... New Shakespeare Society (SAUS)

NSS .... New Simulation System (SAUS)

NSS .... New Statesman and Society [*A publication*]

NSS .... New Suppliers Service (SAUS)

NSS .... New System Simulator (SAUS)

NSS .... Nitrogen Supply Subsystem

NSS .... Nitrogen Supply System [*or Subsystem*] (AAG)

NSS .... NMIC [*National Military Information Center*] Support System (MCD)

NSS .... Nodal Switching Subsystem (SAUS)

NSS .... Nodding Subdish System

NSS .... Noise Suppressor System (MCD)

NSS .... Non-Salt Sensitive

NSS .... Non-Sea Salt

nss .... Non-Sea-Salt (CARB)

NSS .... Non-Seasalt Sulphate (QUAC)

NSSPr .... Non-Self-Sustaining [*Container ship*] (MCD)

NSS .... Nonspatial Statistics (SAUS)

NSS .... Nonstandard Facilities Setup [*Computer science*]

NSS .... Non Subscriber Site (ACAE)

NSS .... Nordic Statistical Secretariat (SAUS)

NSS .... Nordiska Kommitten for Samordning av Elektriska Sakerhetsfragor [*Nordic Committee for Coordination of Electrical Safety Matters*] (EAIO)

NSS .... Nordiska Statistiska Sekretariatet [*Nordic Statistical Secretariat*] (EAIO)

NSS .... Normal Saline Solution

NSS .... Normal Size and Shape (SAUS)

NSS .... Northstar Aviation, Inc. [*ICAO designator*] (FAAC)

NSS .... Northwest Steam Society (EA)

NSS .... Nortronics System Support

NSS .... No Study Section (SAUS)

NSS .... Not Statistically Significant (MAE)

NSS .... NS Group [*NYSE symbol*] (SPSG)

NSS .... Nuclear Science Symposium (PDAA)

NSS .... Nuclear Steam System (NRCH)

NSSA .... National Sanitary Supply Association [*Later, ISSA*] (EA)

NSSA .... National Scholastic Surfing Association (EA)

NSSA .... National Science Supervisors Association (EA)

NSSA .... National Senior Sports Association (EA)

NSSA .... National Sjogren's Syndrome Association (EA)

NSSA .... National Skeet Shooting Association (EA)

NSSA .... National Sportscasters and Sportswriters Association (EA)

NSSA .... National Suffolk Sheep Association (EA)

NSSA .... National Sunday School Association [*Defunct*] (EA)

NSSA .... National Swim School Association (EA)

NSSA .... Navy Space Systems Activity [*Los Angeles, CA*] (MCD)

NSSA .... Nematological Society of Southern Africa (EAIO)

NSSA .... New York Skirt and Sportswear Association (EA)

N-SSA.......... North-South Skirmish Association (EA)

NSSA .... Nova Scotia Salmon Association (SAUS)

NSSA .... Nova Scotia Society of Artists [*1922-72*] [*Canada*] (NGC)

NSSAB .... National Selective Service Appeal Board [*of SSS*] [*Inactive since 1975*]

NSSAC .... National Society, Sons of the American Colonists [*Defunct*] (EA)

NSS&FFA.... National Soft Serve and Fast Food Association (NTPA)

NSSAR .... National Society, Sons of the American Revolution (EA)

NSSB .... National Society of Scabbard and Blade (EA)

NSSB .... Norwich Financial [*NASDAQ symbol*] (TTSB)

NSSB .... Norwich Financial Corp. [*NASDAQ symbol*] (NQ)

NSSC .... Cape Breton Regional Library, Sydney, Nova Scotia [*Library symbol*] [*National Library of Canada*] (NLC)

NSSC .... Napco Security Sys [*NASDAQ symbol*] (TTSB)

NSSC .... Napco Security Systems, Inc. [*NASDAQ symbol*] (NQ)

NSSC .... NASA Safety Standards Committee

NSSC .... National School Safety Center

NSSC .... National Science Strategy Committee (SAUS)

NSSC .... National Society for the Study of Communication [*Later, ICA*] (EA)

NSSC .... National Soil Survey Committee [*Canada*]

NSSC .... National Space Science Center [*British*]

NSSC .... Naval Sea [*formerly, Ship*] Systems Command

NSSC .... Neutral Sulfite Semichemical [*Pulp*]

NSSC .... Neutral Sulfite Semimechanical Process (EDCT)

NSSC .... Nordic Symposium on Super Conductivity (SAUS)

NSSC .... Normal Size, Shape, and Consistency [*Medicine*] (MELL)

NSSC .... Nova Scotia Safety Council (SAUS)

NSSCB .... Cape Breton Post, Sydney, Nova Scotia [*Library symbol*] [*National Library of Canada*] (NLC)

NSSCBD....... Cape Breton Development Corp., Sydney, Nova Scotia [*Library symbol*] [*National Library of Canada*] (NLC)

NSSCBH....... Cape Breton Hospital, Sydney, Nova Scotia [*Library symbol*] [*National Library of Canada*] (NLC)

NSSCC .... National Space Surveillance Control Center

NSSCDS....... Naval Small Ship Combat Data System (SAA)

NSSCG .... Canadian Coast Guard College [*College de la Garde Cotiere Canadienne*] Sydney, Nova Scotia [*Library symbol*] [*National Library of Canada*] (NLC)

NSSCM .... Shelburne County Museum, Nova Scotia [*Library symbol*] [*National Library of Canada*] (NLC)

NSSCO......... Coast Guard, Shelburne, Nova Scotia [*Library symbol*] [*National Library of Canada*] (NLC)

NSS Co .... Northern Steam Ship Co. (SAUS)

NSSCS .... Non-Self-Sustaining Containership [*Environmental science*] (COE)

NSSD .... National Security Study Directive (ACAE)

NSSD .... National Strategy for Sustainable Development [*Australia*]

NSSD .... North Shore Sanitary District, Lake County (SAUS)

NSSDC........ National Space Science Data Center [*Greenbelt, MD*] [*NASA*] (MCD)

NSSDP........ National Society of Sons and Daughters of the Pilgrims (EA)

NSSDU........ Normal Data Session Service Data Unit (SAUS)

NSsE........... Empire State College, Saratoga Springs, NY [*Library symbol*] [*Library of Congress*] (LCLS)

NSSE .... National Society for the Study of Education (EA)

NSSE .... National Study of School Evaluation (EA)

NSSE .... Nordic Subarctic-Subalpine Ecology (SAUS)

NSSEA .... National School Supply and Equipment Association (EA)

NSSEB .... Non-Social Security Equivalent Benefit

NSSET .... National Symposium on Space Electronics and Telemetry [*IEEE*] (MCD)

NSSF .... National Shooting Sports Foundation (EA)

NSSF .... National Social Science Foundation [*Proposed in 1966*]

NSSF .... Near Surface Storage Facility (ABAC)

N/SSF .... Novice, Society of St. Francis

NSSFA .... Nationala Single Service Food Association (EA)

NSSFC .... National Severe Storms Forecast Center [*National Oceanic and Atmospheric Administration*]

NSSFC	National Society of Student Film Critics [Defunct] (EA)
NSSFFA	National Soft Serve and Fast Food Association (EA)
NSSFNS......	National Scholarship Service and Fund for Negro Students (EA)
NSSG	National Ski Study Group [Defunct]
NSSGA........	Nicherin Shoshu Soka Gakkai Academy (SAUS)
NSSHA	National Spotted Saddle Horse Association (EA)
NSSHA	National Student Speech and Hearing Association [Later, NSSLHA] (EA)
NSSHCF	Canadian Forces Base Barrington, Stone Horse, Nova Scotia [Library symbol] [National Library of Canada] (NLC)
NSSHDC	National Spanish Speaking Housing Development Corp.
NSSHET	Newcomen Society for the Study of the History of Engineering and Technology [British] (EAIO)
NSSI	Nuclear Support Services, Inc. [NASDAQ symbol] (NQ)
NS-SIB	NAVSHIPS [Naval Ship Systems Command] Ship Information Booklets
NSSIC	National Student Strike Information Center [Brandeis University]
NSSJD	Community of the Nursing Sisters of St. John the Divine [Anglican religious community]
NSSK	National Society of Student Keyboardists (EA)
NSSK	North-South Station-Keeping (PDAA)
NSSL	National Seed Storage Laboratory [Department of Agriculture] [Fort Collins, CO] (GRD)
NSSL	National Service Star Legion (EA)
NSSL	National Severe Storms Laboratory [National Oceanic and Atmospheric Administration] [Research center]
NSSL	National Society of State Legislators [Later, NCSL]
NSSL	National Survey of State Laws [A publication]
NSSLC	National Social Science and Law Center (EA)
NSSLHA	National Student Speech Language Hearing Association (EA)
NSSLP	National Social Science and Law Project (EA)
NSSM	National Security Study Memorandum [Obsolete]
NSSM	Navy Spread Spectrum MODEM (MCD)
NSSMM	Memorial High School, Sydney Mines, Nova Scotia [Library symbol] [National Library of Canada] (NLC)
NSSMS	NATO Sea Sparrow Missile System
NSSN	National Speed Sport News [A publication]
NSSN	National Standard Shipping Note (DS)
NSSN	National Standards Systems Network
NSSNF	Naval Strategic Systems Navigation Facility
NSSO	National Second Surgical Opinion Program (MELL)
NSSO	National Society of Student Organists [Later, NSSK] (EA)
NSSO	National Solar Space Observatory [NASA]
NSSO	Navy Ships' Store Office [PX]
NSSP	National Severe Storms Project [National Oceanic and Atmospheric Administration]
NSSP	National Shellfish Sanitation Program [Food and Drug Administration] (GFGA)
NSSP	National Syrian Socialist Party [Lebanon] [Political party]
NSSP	Nava Sama Samaja Party [New Equal Society Party] [Sri Lanka] [Political party] (PPW)
NSSP	Neutralization Self-Solidification Process (PDAA)
NSSP	Nonreporting Secondary Stock Point (AFIT)
NSSP	Normal Size, Shape, and Position [On examination] [Anatomy] (DAVI)
NSSPAVAF...	Normal Size, Shape, and Position Anteverted, and Anteflexed [Uterus] [On examination] [Gynecology] (DAVI)
NSSPO........	Navy Strategic Systems Projects Office (ACAE)
NSSPS	New Space Signals Processing Stations (ACAE)
NSSR	National Spotted Swine Record (EA)
NSSR	New School for Social Research [New York, NY]
NSSR	Nordic Cooperation for Sami and Reindeer Questions (SAUS)
NSSR	Nordic Society of Space Research
NSSR	Nuclear Science Series Report (SAUS)
NSSR	Record, Springhill, Nova Scotia [Library symbol] [National Library of Canada] (NLC)
NSSRA	National Ski & Snowboard Retailers Association (NTPA)
NSSRI.........	Nervous System Sports-Related Injury [Medicine]
NSSRM	Soluth Rawdon Museum, Nova Scotia [Library symbol] [National Library of Canada] (NLC)
NSSS	National Sewage Sludge Survey [Environmental Protection Agency]
NSSS	National Space Surveillance System
NSSS	Nuclear Steam Supply System [Vendor] (NRCH)
NSSS	Nuclear Steam System Supply (SAUS)
NSsS	Skidmore College, Saratoga Springs, NY [Library symbol] [Library of Congress] (LCLS)
NSsSA	Southern Adirondack Library System, Saratoga Springs, NY [Library symbol] [Library of Congress] (LCLS)
NSsSC	Supreme Court Library at Saratoga Springs, Saratoga Springs, NY [Library symbol] [Library of Congress] (LCLS)
NSSSE	National Study of Secondary School Evaluation [Later, NSSE] (EA)
NSSSRH	St. Rita's Hospital, Sydney, Nova Scotia [Library symbol] [National Library of Canada] (NLC)
NSSSS	Nuclear Steam Supply Shutoff System (NRCH)
NSST	Non-Smoking Seat [Travel industry] (TRID)
NSST	Nonspecific ST Segment Changes [On electroencephalogram] [Cardiology] (DAVI)
NSST	Northwestern Syntax Screening Test [Education]
NSST	No Smoking Seat [Travel industry] (TVEL)
NSSTA	National Structured Settlements Trade Association (EA)
NS Stat........	Nova Scotia Statutes [Canada] [A publication] (DLA)
NSSTC	National Small Shipments Traffic Conference (EA)
NSSTE	National Society of Sales Training Executives [Orlando, FL] (EA)
NSS Test	Neutral Salt Spray Test (SAUS)

NSSTT	Nonspecific ST and T [Wave on electrocardiogram] [Cardiology] (DAVI)
NSSU	National Steam Service Union [British]
NSSU	National Sunday School Union [British]
NSSUP........	National Society of the Sons of Utah Pioneers (EA)
NSSX	National Sanitary Supply Co. [NASDAQ symbol] (NQ)
NSSX	Natl Sanitary Supply [NASDAQ symbol] (TTSB)
NSSX	University College of Cape Breton, Sydney, Nova Scotia [Library symbol] [National Library of Canada] (NLC)
NSSXA	Archives and General Library, College of Cape Breton, Sydney, Nova Scotia [Library symbol] [National Library of Canada] (NLC)
NSSY	Norwalk Savings Society [NASDAQ symbol] (SAG)
NSSYA	National Small Sailing Yacht Association (EA)
NST	Aviacion Ejecutiva del Noroeste SA de CV [Mexico] [ICAO designator] (FAAC)
NST............	Nasty (ABBR)
NST............	National Scenic Trail
NST............	National Security Technology (ABAC)
NST............	National Skills Training
NST............	National Standard Taper (IAA)
NST............	National Symposium on Telemetering (MCD)
NST............	Navy Shipboard Terminal
NST............	Navy Standard Teleprinter (DOMA)
NST............	Nest (ABBR)
NST............	Nesting Module (MCD)
NST............	Network Support Team [NASA] (KSC)
NST............	Newfoundland Standard Time [Aviation] (AIA)
NST............	New Serial Titles [A publication of Library of Congress]
NST............	New Serial Titles, Library of Congress, Washington, DC [OCLC symbol] (OCLC)
NST............	New York Air (SAUS)
NST............	Nigata Sogo Television (SAUS)
NST............	Node Systems Trainer (SAUS)
NST............	Noise Source Tube
NST............	Noise, Spikes, and Transients (PDAA)
NST............	Nonshivering Thermogenesis [Physiology]
NST............	Nonslip Tread [Technical drawings]
NST............	Non Standard Transmission (SAUS)
NST............	Nonstress Test [Gynecology]
NST............	Normal Sphincter Tone [Gastroenterology] (DAVI)
NST............	North Solomon Trench [Geoscience]
NST............	North Sumatra Time (SAUS)
NST............	No Sales Tax (SAUS)
NST............	Not Sooner Than
NST............	Nuclear and Space Talks (DOMA)
NST............	Nuclear Spin Tomography (DB)
NST............	Numerical Surface Techniques (SAUS)
NST............	Numerical Surveying Technique (PDAA)
NST............	Nutritional Support Team [Dietetics] (DAVI)
NSTA	Anesta Corp. [NASDAQ symbol] (SAG)
NSTA	National Safe Transit Association (EA)
NSTA	National School Transportation Association (EA)
NSTA	National Science Teachers Association (EA)
NSTA	National Security Traders Association [Later, STA] (EA)
NSTA	National Shoe Traveler's Association (EA)
NSTA	National Spasmodic Torticollis Association (EA)
NSTA	National Squash Tennis Association (EA)
NSTA	Nova Scotia Agricultural College, Truro, Nova Scotia [Library symbol] [National Library of Canada] (NLC)
NS-TAB	NAVSHIPS [Naval Ship Systems Command] Training Aid Bulletins
NSTAC	National Security Telecommunications Advisory Committee (NITA)
NSTAF	National Solar Technical Audience File [Solar Energy Research Institute] [Database]
N Staff........	North Staffordshire (SAUS)
NSTAG	National Science and Technology Advisory Group [Australia]
NStand........	National Standard Co. [Associated Press] (SAG)
NSTAP	National Strategic Acquisition Plan (SAUS)
NSTAP	National Strategic Targeting and Attack Policy (CINC)
NSTARS	Navy Standard Tracking and Retrieval System (MCD)
NStarU........	North Star Universal, Inc. [Associated Press] (SAG)
NSTB	Biblio-Tech Ltd., Three Fathom Harbor, Nova Scotia [Library symbol] [National Library of Canada] (NLC)
NSTB	National Science and Technology Board [Singapore]
NStBU.........	St. Bonaventure University, St. Bonaventure, NY [Library symbol] [Library of Congress] (LCLS)
NSTC	Colchester - East Hants Regional Library, Truro, Nova Scotia [Library symbol] [National Library of Canada] (NLC)
NSTC	National Science and Technology Council [Formerly, FCCSET]
NSTC	National Security Training Commission [Expired, 1957]
NSTC	National Shade Tree Conference [Later, ISA]
NSTC	National Spiritualist Teachers Club (EA)
NSTC	Nineteenth Century Short Title Catalogue [Avero Publications Ltd.] [Information service or system] [British] (CRD)
NSTC	Nonsmokers' Travel Club [Defunct] (EA)
NSTC	Norwegian Save the Children (SAUS)
NSTC	Not Subject to Call (MHDB)
NSTC	Nova Scotia Teachers College [Canada]
NSTC	Nova Scotia Technical College
NSTCH	Colchester Historical Society, Truro, Nova Scotia [Library symbol] [National Library of Canada] (BIB)
NST-D	Navy Standard Transmission [Dension hydraulics] (CAAL)
NSTD	Nested [Packaging]
NSTD	Non-System Training Devices [USA]
NSTDB.........	National Strategic Target Data Base (CINC)
NSTDH........	National STD [Sexually Transmitted Disease] Hotline (EA)

NSTDN......... Daily News, Truro, Nova Scotia [*Library symbol*] [*National Library of Canada*] (NLC)
NSTDP......... National Society of Tole and Decorative Painters (EA)
N-STDS......... Navy Standards (AAGC)
NSTE......... National Society of Telephone Employees [*A union*] [*British*]
NSTEP......... National Spit Tobacco Education Program [*An initiative of Oral Health America*]
NSTEP......... Naval Scientist Training and Exchange Program (DNAB)
NSTF......... Fraser Culture Centre, Tatamagouche, Nova Scotia [*Library symbol*] [*National Library of Canada*] (NLC)
NSTF......... National Scholarship Trust Fund [*An affiliate of the Graphic Arts Technical Foundation*]
NSTF......... Near Surface Test Facility [*Nuclear energy*] (NUCP)
NSTF......... Neutron Sensor Testing Facility (IAA)
NSTF......... North Sea Task Force (SAUS)
NSTF......... Nuclear Science and Technology Facility [*State University of New York at Buffalo*] [*Research center*] (RCD)
NSTFI......... Nuveen Select Tax Free Income Portfolio [*Associated Press*] (SAG)
NSTFI2......... Nuveen Select Tax Free Income Portfolio 2 [*Associated Press*] (SAG)
NSTFI3......... Nuveen Select Tax Free Income Portfolio 3 [*Associated Press*] (SAG)
NSTG......... Nesting (ABBR)
NSTG......... Nuclear Strike Target Graphic (MCD)
NSTI......... NASCOM [*NASA Communications Network*] Simulation Traffic Interface (SSD)
NSTI......... Norwalk State Technical Institute (SAUS)
NSTIC......... Naval Science and Technology Information Centre (NITA)
NSTIC......... Naval Scientific and Technical Information Centre [*Later, DRIC*] [*British*] (MCD)
NSTIC......... Navy Scientific and Technical Intelligence Center (IEEE)
NSTICLANT... Naval Scientific and Technical Intelligence Center, Atlantic (DNAB)
NSTICPAC... Naval Scientific and Technical Intelligence Center, Pacific (DNAB)
NSTIM......... Islands Museum and Tourist Bureau, Tiverton, Nova Scotia [*Library symbol*] [*National Library of Canada*] (NLC)
NStj......... Margaret Reaney Memorial Library, St. Johnsville, NY [*Library symbol*] [*Library of Congress*] (LCLS)
NSTK......... Nastech Pharmaceutical [*NASDAQ symbol*] (TTSB)
NSTK......... Nastech Pharmaceuticals [*NASDAQ symbol*] (SAG)
NSTKW......... Nastech Pharmaceutical Wrrt [*NASDAQ symbol*] (TTSB)
NSTL......... National Software-Testing Laboratories [*Computer science*]
NSTL......... National Space Technology Laboratories [*Formerly, MTF*] [*Mississippi*] [*NASA*]
NSTL......... National Strategic Target Line [*or List*] (AFM)
NSTL......... Nestled (ABBR)
NSTL......... Nuclear Services and Training Laboratory [*Ohio State University*] [*Research center*] (RCD)
NSTLG......... Nestling (ABBR)
NSTLG......... Nostalgia (ABBR)
NSTLGC......... Nostalgic (ABBR)
NSTM......... Naval School Transportation Management
NSTM......... Navy Ship Technical Manual (CAAL)
NSTM......... Navy Standard Test Model (CAAL)
NSTM......... Nordiska Skeppstekniska Mote [*Joint Committee of Nordic Marine Technology - JCNMT*] (EAIO)
NS-TMI......... NAVSHIPS [*Naval Ship Systems Command*] Technical Manual Index
NSTN......... Naval Shore Telecommunications Network (SAUS)
NSTN......... Nonstandard Telephone Number [*Telecommunications*] (TEL)
NSTN......... [*The*] Nova Scotia Technology Network [*Canada*] [*Computer science*] (TNIG)
NSTNS......... Nastiness (ABBR)
NSTO......... New System Training Office [*Army*]
NSTO......... Non Statutory Training Organisation [*British*]
NSTOA......... National Ski Touring Operators' Association (EA)
NSTP......... National Society of TV Producers (NTCM)
NSTP......... National Solar Terrestrial Program (SAUS)
NSTP......... Non-Stop (SAUS)
NSTP......... Northern Science Training Program (SAUS)
NSTP......... Nuffield Science Teaching Project (SAUS)
NSTP......... Nuffield Service Teaching Project
NSTPC......... Nova Scotia Tidal Power Corp. (SAUS)
NSTPS......... Law Library, Patterson, Smith, Mathews & Grant, Truro, Nova Scotia [*Library symbol*] [*National Library of Canada*] (NLC)
NSTR......... Naval Sea Systems Command Technical Representative
NSTR......... Northstar Health Services, Inc. [*NASDAQ symbol*] (SAG)
NSTR......... Northstar Minerals (SAUS)
NSTR......... Record, Truro, Nova Scotia [*Library symbol*] [*National Library of Canada*] (NLC)
NSTRE......... Northstar Health Svcs [*NASDAQ symbol*] (TTSB)
NSTRTU......... National Strategy to Reduce Tobacco Use (SAUS)
NSTS......... National Sea Training Schools [*British*]
NSTS......... National Secure Telephone System (SAUS)
NSTS......... National Securities Trading System
NSTS......... National Space Transportation System
NSTS......... National Student Traffic Safety Program [*National Commission on Safety Education*] [*Washington, DC*] (AEBS)
NST-S......... National Support Team-Sarajevo [*Military*]
NSTS......... Navy Stockpile to Target Sequence
NSTS......... NCC [*Navy Command Center*] Security Test System
NSTS......... Northwestern States Portland Cement Co. (SAUS)
NSTSPO......... National Space Transportation System Program Office (SSD)
NSTT......... National Sea Training Trusts [*British*] (DS)
NSTT......... Naval Strategy Think Tank (DOMA)
NSTT......... Nonseminomatous Testicular Tumor [*Medicine*] (DMAA)

NSTT......... Nova Scotia Teachers' College, Truro, Nova Scotia [*Library symbol*] [*National Library of Canada*] (NLC)
NSTTF......... National Solar Thermal Test Facility [*Sandia National Laboratories*]
NSTU......... Pago Pago/International, Tutuila Island [*American Samoa*] [*ICAO location identifier*] (ICLI)
NST-V......... Navy Standard Transmission [*Vickers hydraulics*] (CAAL)
NSTW......... National Science and Technology Week [*An annual outreach program begun in 1985 by the National Science Foundation*]
NSTX......... National Spherical Torus Experiment [*Plasma physics*]
NSTY......... Nastily (ABBR)
NSU......... Naval Scout Unit
NSU......... Neckarsulm [*Location in Wuerttemberg, Germany, of NSU Werke, automobile manufacturer; initialism used as name of its cars*]
NSU......... Neighborhood Stabilization Unit (LAIN)
NSU......... Network Service Unit (NITA)
NSU......... Neurosurgical Unit [*Medicine*] (DMAA)
NSU......... Nitrogen Supply Unit (AAG)
NSU......... Nonspecific Urethritis [*Medicine*]
NSU......... Non-Switching Unit (SAUS)
NSU......... Norfolk State University (SAUS)
NSU......... North Stansbury [*Utah*] [*Seismograph station code, US Geological Survey*] (SEIS)
NSU......... Nuova Sinistra Unita [*New United Left*] [*Italy*] [*Political party*] (PPE)
NSUA......... Nigerian Students Union in the Americas (EA)
NSUB......... Neighbourhood Substitutability (SAUS)
NSUC......... North Staffordshire University College (SAUS)
NSuf......... Suffern Free Library, Suffern, NY [*Library symbol*] [*Library of Congress*] (LCLS)
NSufA......... Avon Products, Inc., Suffern, NY [*Library symbol*] [*Library of Congress*] (LCLS)
NSufR......... Rockland Community College, Suffern, NY [*Library symbol*] [*Library of Congress*] (LCLS)
NSUG......... Nihon Sun Users Group (SAUS)
NSUK......... Nichiren Shoshu of the UK [*Buddhist organization*] (DI)
N/Sun Sent... News/Sun-Sentinel (SAUS)
NSUP......... Naval Supply Systems Command Headquarters
N-Super......... Nuclear-powered Supercarner (SAUS)
NSUPSC......... Naval Supply Systems Command [*Formerly, Bureau of Supplies and Accounts*] (MCD)
NSURG......... Neurosurgery [*Medicine*]
NSUS......... Newcomen Society of the United States (EA)
NSv......... Finkelstein Memorial Library, Spring Valley, NY [*Library symbol*] [*Library of Congress*] (LCLS)
NSV......... National Socialist Vanguard (EA)
NSV......... Natl Equipment Svcs. [*NYSE symbol*] (SG)
NSV......... Negative Supply Voltage
NSV......... Net Sales Value (BUR)
NSV......... Netted Secure Voice [*Military*] (CAAL)
NSV......... Neurosecretory Vesicle [*Neuroanatomy*]
NSV......... Noise, Shock, and Vibration (PDAA)
NSV......... Nonautomatic Self-Verification [*Computer science*] (MDG)
NSV......... Nonspecific Vaginitis [*Medicine*]
NSV......... Nonspinning Vehicle
NSV......... Nova Scotia Savings & Loans Co. [*Toronto Stock Exchange symbol*]
NSV......... Nuclear Service Vessel
NSVA......... Navy Seabee Veterans of America (EA)
NSVA......... New South Wales Vigoro Association [*Australia*]
NSVC......... National Sisters Vocation Conference [*Later, NRVC*] (EA)
NSVD......... Normal Spontaneous Vaginal Delivery [*Obstetrics*] (DMAA)
NSVEA......... Natural-Source Vitamin E Association (EA)
NSVP......... National School Volunteer Program (EA)
NSVP......... National Student Volunteer Program [*Later, NCSL*] (EA)
NS/VPP......... Nuclear Survivability/ Vulnerability Program Plan (SAUS)
N/SVQ......... National/Scottish Vocational Qualification (WDAA)
NSVRA......... National Stenomask Verbatim Reporters Association (NTPA)
NSVT......... Nonsustained Ventricular Tachycardia [*Medicine*] (CPH)
NSW......... Ansett Airlines of New South Wales [*Australia*] [*ICAO designator*] (FAAC)
NSW......... Herbarium of New South Wales (SAUS)
NSW......... National Software Works
NSW......... Naval Special Warfare (NVT)
NSW......... Neutron Spin Wave (SAUS)
NSW......... New South Wales (WA)
NSW......... Northwestern Steel & Wire Co. (SAUS)
NSW......... NSP [*National Aeronautical and Space Administration Support Plan*] Status Word
NSWA......... Acadia University, Wolfville, Nova Scotia [*Library symbol*] [*National Library of Canada*] (NLC)
NSWA......... National Social Welfare Assembly [*Later, National Assembly of National Voluntary Health and Social Welfare Organizations*] (EA)
NSWA......... National Soft Wheat Association [*Later, MNF*] (EA)
NSWA......... National Stripper Well Association (EA)
NSWA......... North Shore Writers Alliance (EA)
NSW Adm... New South Wales Reports, Admiralty [*A publication*] (DLA)
NSWAEM.... New South Wales Assemblies' Evangelic Mission [*Australia*]
NSWAG......... Department of Geography, Acadia University, Wolfville, Nova Scotia [*Library symbol*] [*Obsolete*] [*National Library of Canada*] (NLC)
NSWAGTC... New South Wales Association of Gifted and Talented Children [*Australia*]
NSWAHP..... New South Wales Association of Health Professions [*Australia*]
NSWAIP......... Australian Institute of Physics, NSW Branch (SAUS)
NSWALC..... New South Wales Adult Literacy Council [*Australia*]
NS Wales L... New South Wales Law [*A publication*] (DLA)
NS Wales LR Eq... New South Wales Law Reports, Equity [*A publication*] (DLA)

NSWAMH..... New South Waks Association for Mental Health (SAUS)
NSWAP........ National Socialist White American Party [Political party]
NSWAPA...... New South Wales Amateur Pistol Association [Australia]
NSWAR....... New South Wales Arbitration Reports [A publication] (DLA)
NSWAS....... New South Wales Association of Sephardim [Australia]
NSWAWL..... New South Wales Animal Welfare League [Australia]
NSWAWPA.. New South Wales Amateur Water Polo Association [Australia]
NSWB......... New South Wales Bushmen [British military] (DMA)
NSWBA....... New South Wales Bar Association [Australia]
NSWBA....... New South Wales Basketball Association [Australia]
NSWBA....... New South Wales Bridge Association [Australia]
NSWBAC...... New South Wales Buying Advisory Center [Australia]
NSWBACE.... New South Wales Board of Adult and Community Education [Australia]
NSWBBA...... New South Wales Bloodhorse Breeders' Association [Australia]
NSWBC....... Black Cultural Centre for Nova Scotia, Westphal [Library symbol] [National Library of Canada] (BIB)
NSWBCS...... New South Wales Bookmakers' Cooperative Society [Australia]
NSWBGA...... New South Wales Bowling Greenkeepers' Association [Australia]
NSWBIC....... New South Wales Banana Industry Committee [Australia]
NSWBJE ...... New South Wales Board of Jewish Education [Australia]
NSW Bktcy Cas... New South Wales Reports, Bankruptcy Cases [A publication] (DLA)
NSWBL....... New South Wales Basketball League [Australia]
NSWBS....... New South Wales Board of Surveyors [Australia]
NSWBSA...... New South Wales Board Sailing Association [Australia]
NSWC......... Naval Surface Warfare [or Weapons] Center [Dahlgren, VA]
NSWC......... New South Wales Centre (SAUS)
NSWCA....... New South Wales Canoe Association [Australia]
NSWCA....... New South Wales Coal Association [Australia]
NSWCA....... New South Wales Council on the Aging [Australia]
NSW CAC Report... New South Wales Corporate Affairs Commission. Report [Australia] [A publication]
NSWCAF...... Naval Surface Weapons Center Acoustic Facility (GRD)
NSW Carpenters J... New South Wales Carpenters Journal (SAUS)
NSWCC....... New South Wales Canine Council [Australia]
NSWCC....... New South Wales Council of Churches [Australia]
NSWCCFT.... New South Wales Council for Children's Films and Television [Australia]
NSWCCU...... New South Wales Churches Cricket Union [Australia]
NSWC/DL.... Naval Surface Weapons Center, Dahlgren Laboratory
NSWC Eq..... New South Wales Law Reports, Equity [A publication] (DLA)
NSWCF....... New South Wales Cycling Federation [Australia]
NSWCFA...... New South Wales Canning Fruitgrowers' Association [Australia]
NSWCFVI..... New South Wales Chamber of Fruit and Vegetable Industries [Australia]
NSWCGA...... New South Wales Cane Growers' Association [Australia]
NSWCGA...... New South Wales Cherry Growers' Association [Australia]
NSWCGA...... New South Wales Chicken Growers' Association [Australia]
NSWCGC...... New South Wales Citrus Growers' Council [Australia]
NSWCHS...... New South Wales Cooperative Housing Society [Australia]
NSWCM...... New South Wales State Conservatorium of Music (SAUS)
NSWCMACA... New South Wales Chinese Martial Arts and Cultural Association [Australia]
NSWCMC..... New South Wales Chicken Meat Council [Australia]
NSWCMOA... New South Wales Coal Mine Owners' Association [Australia]
NSWCOA...... New South Wales Colliery Officials' Association [Australia]
NSWCOHO... New South Wales Council of Heritage Organizations [Australia]
NSWCOTA.... New South Wales Council on the Aging [Australia]
NSWCPA...... New South Wales Coal Proprietors' Association [Australia]
NSWCPC..... New South Wales Child Protection Council [Australia]
NSWCRL...... New South Wales Law Reports, Supreme Court [A publication] (DLA)
NSWCSA...... New South Wales Churches Soccer Association [Australia]
NSWCSA...... New South Wales Cold Storage Association [Australia]
NSWCTA...... New South Wales Council of Tourist Associations [Australia]
NSWCUA...... New South Wales Credit Unit Association [Australia]
NSWCUA...... New South Wales Cricket Umpires' Association [Australia]
NSWCUEA.... New South Wales Credit Union Employers' Association [Australia]
NSWC/WOL... Naval Surface Weapons Center, White Oak Laboratory
NSWCYMCA... New South Wales Council of the Young Men's Christian Associations [Australia]
NSWDAA...... New South Wales Domestic Abattoirs Association [Australia]
NSWDAA...... New South Wales Drug and Alcohol Authority [Australia]
NSWDAHAC... National Society Women Descendants of the Ancient and Honorable Artillery Company (EA)
NSWDBA...... New South Wales Deer Breeders' Association [Australia]
NSW Dep Agric Dir Sci Serv Entomol Branch Insect Pest Leafl... New South Wales. Department of Agriculture. Division of Science Services. Entomology Branch. Insect Pest Leaflet (SAUS)
NSW Dep Mines Tech Rep... New South Wales. Department of Mines. Coalfields Branch. Technical Report (SAUS)
NSW Dept Forestry Bull... New South Wales. Department of Forestry. Bulletin [Australia] [A publication]
NSWDFA...... New South Wales Dairy Farmers' Association [Australia]
NSWDFA...... New South Wales Deer Farmers' Association [Australia]
NSWDFB...... New South Wales Dried Fruits Board [Australia]
NSWDIC...... New South Wales Dairy Industry Conference [Australia]
NSWDPA...... New South Wales Dairy Products Association [Australia]
NSWDSC...... New South Wales Dam Safety Committee [Australia]
NSWDU...... New South Wales Debating Union [Australia]
NSWEEU...... New South Wales Education Exports Unit [Australia]
NSWEK....... Eastern King's Memorial Hospital, Wolfville, Nova Scotia [Library symbol] [National Library of Canada] (NLC)
NSWEPA...... New South Wales Environment Protection Authority (SAUS)
NSWEPC...... New South Wales Egg Producers' Cooperative [Australia]

NSWEPOWA... New South Wales Ex-Prisoners of War Association [Australia]
NSW Eq Rep... New South Wales Law Reports, Equity [A publication] (DLA)
NSWETF...... New South Wales Education and Training Foundation [Australia]
NSWFA...... New South Wales Farmers' Association [Australia]
NSWFB....... New South Wales Fire Brigades [Australia]
NSWFBEU.... New South Wales Fire Brigade Employee's Union [Australia]
NSWFC....... New South Wales Fitness Council [Australia]
NSWFC....... New South Wales Forestry Commission (SAUS)
NSWFCHA... New South Wales Farm and Country Holiday Association [Australia]
NSWFF....... New South Wales Folk Federation [Australia]
NSWFG....... New South Wales Furniture Guild [Australia]
NSWFGA...... New South Wales Flower Growers' Association [Australia]
NSWFGHC ... New South Wales Free Growers' Horticultural Council [Australia]
NSWFHU...... New South Wales Friends of the Hebrew University [Australia]
NSWFIA...... New South Wales Farmers' Industrial Association [Australia]
NSWFIC...... New South Wales Fishing Industry Council [Australia]
NSWFITC..... New South Wales Food Industry Training Council [Australia]
NSWFITC..... New South Wales Furniture Industry Training Council [Australia]
NSWFMC..... New South Wales Flour Millers' Council [Australia]
NSWFPA...... New South Wales Forest Products Association [Australia]
NSWFPCA... New South Wales Federation of Parents and Citizens' Associations [Australia]
NSWFS...... New South Wales Fabian Society [Australia]
NSWFTO..... New South Wales Film and Television Office [Australia]
NSWG......... Naval Special Warfare Group (NVT)
NSWG......... New South Wales Government (SAUS)
NSWG......... North Sea Working Group [Advisory Committee on Pollution of the Sea]
NSWG......... Nuclear Safety Working Group (CINC)
NSWGA...... New South Wales Golf Association [Australia]
NSWGB....... New South Wales Grains Board [Australia]
NSWGBOTA... New South Wales Greyhound Breeders, Owners and Trainers Association [Australia]
NSWGC...... New South Wales Gun Club [Australia]
NSWGCB..... New South Wales Guild of Craft Bookbinders [Australia]
NSWGCHS .. New South Wales Group of Cooperative Housing Societies [Australia]
NSWGCSUA... New South Wales Glass and Ceramic Silica Users' Association [Australia]
NSW Geol Surv 1:250000 Geol Ser... New South Wales. Geological Survey. 1:250,000 Geological Series (SAUS)
NSW Geol Survey Mineral Resour... New South Wales. Geological Survey. Mineral Resources [Australia] [A publication]
NSWGFL...... New South Wales Gridiron Football League [Australia]
NSWGFM..... New South Wales Guild of Furniture Manufacturers [Australia]
NSWGIS...... New South Wales Government Information Service [Australia]
NSWGMA..... New South Wales Girls' Marching Association [Australia]
NSWGMA..... New South Wales Glass Merchants' Association [Australia]
NSWGR....... New South Wales Government Railways (SAUS)
NSWGTB..... New South Wales Government Tourist Bureau (SAUS)
NSWGTC..... New South Wales Government Travel Center [Australia]
NSWH....... Wolfville Historical Museum, Nova Scotia [Library symbol] [National Library of Canada] (NLC)
NSWHA....... New South Wales Hockey Association [Australia]
NSWHC....... New South Wales Health Commission (SAUS)
NSWHCA..... New South Wales Homeless Children's Association [Australia]
NSWHEA..... New South Wales Horticultural Exporters' Association [Australia]
NSWHGA..... New South Wales Hospital Group Apprentices Scheme [Australia]
NSWHJ...... Hants Journal, Windsor, Nova Scotia [Library symbol] [National Library of Canada] (NLC)
NSWHPAC ... New South Wales Hospitals Planning Advisory Center [Australia]
NSWHRA..... New South Wales Hot Rod Association [Australia]
NSWHS...... New South Wales Humanist Society [Australia]
NSWHTA...... New South Wales Hardcourt Tennis Association [Australia]
NSWI......... National Safe Workplace Institute (EA)
NSWICCA... New South Wales Indo-China Chinese Association
NSWID........ New South Wales Institute of Dieticians [Australia]
NSWIG........ New South Wales Industrial Gazette [Australia] [A publication]
NSW Inc Acts... New South Wales Incorporated Acts [A publication] (DLA)
NSW Ind Arbtn... New South Wales Industrial Arbitration Cases [A publication] (DLA)
NSW Ind Arbtn Cas... New South Wales Industrial Arbitration Cases [A publication] (DLA)
NSW Indus Arb R... New South Wales Industrial Arbitration Reports [A publication] (DLA)
NSWIP........ New South Wales Institute of Physiotherapy [Australia]
NSWIP........ New South Wales Institute of Psychotherapy [Australia]
NSWJB....... New South Wales Judgements Bulletin [Australia] [A publication]
NSWJBD...... New South Wales Jewish Board of Deputies [Australia]
NSWJCU...... New South Wales Junior Cricket Union [Australia]
NSWJHS...... New South Wales Jersey Herd Society [Australia]
NSWJT........ Materials Laboratory Library, Nova Scotia Department of Transportation, Windsor Junction, Nova Scotia [Library symbol] [National Library of Canada] (NLC)
NSWJWM ... New South Wales Jewish War Memorial [Australia]
NSWKE....... King's-Edgehill School, Windsor, Nova Scotia [Library symbol] [National Library of Canada] (NLC)
NSWL........ Naval Surface Warfare Laboratory
NSWL .... New South Wales Lotteries [Australia]
NSW Land App... New South Wales Land Appeal Court Cases [A publication] (DLA)
NSW Land App Cts... New South Wales Land Appeal Courts (DLA)
NSW Law Repts... New South Wales Law Reports [A publication]
NSWLC....... New South Wales Leagues Club [Australia]
NSWLHPB.... New South Wales Ladies Highland Pipe Band [Australia]

NSW Local Gov't R... New South Wales Local Government Reports [*A publication*] (DLA)
NSWLR........ New South Wales Letters of Registration (SAUS)
NSWLRC....... New South Wales Law Reform Commission [*Australia*] (ILCA)
NSWLSEA.... New South Wales Live Stock Exporters' Association [*Australia*]
NSWLVR...... New South Wales Land Valuation Reports (SAUS)
NSWMA....... National Soft Wheat Millers Association [*Later, MNF*] (EA)
NSWMA....... National Solid Wastes Management Association (EA)
NSWMA....... New South Wales Marching Association [*Australia*]
NSWMA....... New South Wales Midwives' Association [*Australia*]
NSWMB....... New South Wales Medical Board [*Australia*]
NSWMEA..... New South Wales Meat Exporters' Association [*Australia*]
NSWMEQB... New South Wales Migrant Employment and Qualifications Board [*Australia*]
NSWMH....... New South Wales Masonic Hospital [*Australia*]
NSWMIA...... New South Wales Meat Industry Authority [*Australia*]
NSWMSB..... New South Wales Maritime Services Board (SAUS)
NSWNA........ New South Wales Netball Association [*Australia*]
NSWNA........ New South Wales Nurses Association (SAUS)
NSWNCA...... New South Wales National Coursing Association [*Australia*]
NSWNGA..... New South Wales Nut Growers' Association [*Australia*]
NSWNPWS... New South Wales National Parks and Wildlife Service [*Australia*]
NSWNRB..... New South Wales Nurses' Registration Board [*Australia*]
NSWO.......... Nuclear Surface Warfare Officer [*Navy*] (DOMA)
NSWODA..... New South Wales Oyster Distributors' Association [*Australia*]
NSWOTA...... New South Wales Occupational Therapy Association [*Australia*]
NSWOTA...... New South Wales Operating Theatre Association [*Australia*]
NSWOTA...... New South Wales Organic Traders' Association [*Australia*]
NSWP.......... New South Wales Police (SAUS)
NSWP.......... Non-Soviet Warsaw Pact (NATG)
NSWPA........ New South Wales Poker Association [*Australia*]
NSWPA........ New South Wales Polo Association [*Australia*]
NSWPACC.... New South Wales Police Aero Club Company [*Australia*]
NSWPAG...... New South Wales Prisoners Action Group (SAUS)
NSWPBA...... New South Wales Pipe Band Association [*Australia*]
NSWPC........ New South Wales Parachute Council [*Australia*]
NSWPC........ New South Wales Parents' Council [*Australia*]
NSWPC........ New South Wales Prices Commission [*Australia*]
NSWPEA...... New South Wales Physical Education Association [*Australia*]
NSWPGA...... New South Wales Professional Golfers' Association [*Australia*]
NSWPL........ New South Wales Police Legacy [*Australia*]
NSWPMOA... New South Wales Public Medical Officers' Association [*Australia*]
NSWPOA...... New South Wales Property Owners' Association [*Australia*]
NSWPP........ National Socialist White People's Party [*Formerly, American NAZI Party*] (EA)
NSWPP........ New South Wales Parliamentary Papers [*A publication*]
NSWPR........ Newspaper
NSW Priv Com Papers... New South Wales Privacy Committee. Papers [*Australia*] [*A publication*]
NSWPSPOA... New South Wales Public Service Professional Officers' Association [*Australia*]
NSW Pub Acts... New South Wales Public Acts [*A publication*] (DLA)
NSW Pub Stat... New South Wales Public Statutes [*A publication*] (DLA)
NSWRA........ New South Wales Rifle Association [*Australia*]
NSWRA........ New South Wales Rowing Association [*Australia*]
NSWRAA...... New South Wales Rural Assistance Authority [*Australia*]
NSW Railway & Tramway Mag... New South Wales Railway and Tramway Magazine [*Australia*] [*A publication*]
NSWRCSA... New South Wales Registered Cereal Seedgrowers' Association [*Australia*]
NSWRDCU... New South Wales Rural Divisions Co-ordinating Unit (SAUS)
NSW Regs B&Ords... New South Wales Regulations, By-Laws and Ordinances (SAUS)
NSWRFAC.... New South Wales Recreational Fishing Advisory Council [*Australia*]
NSWRFL...... New South Wales Rugby Football League [*Australia*]
NSWRFS...... New South Wales Rod Fishers' Society [*Australia*]
NSWRITC.... New South Wales Rural Industry Training Committee [*Australia*]
NSWRLIFA... New South Wales Rugby League Insurance Finance Agency [*Australia*]
NSWRTA...... New South Wales Road Transport Association [*Australia*]
NSWRTEHF... New South Wales Railway and Transport Employees' Hospital Fund [*Australia*]
NSWRTLA.... New South Wales Right to Life Association [*Australia*]
NSWRTM..... New South Wales Rail Transport Museum [*Australia*]
NSWRTTC.... New South Wales Road Transport Training Council [*Australia*]
NSWS.......... National Surface Water Survey (GNE)
NSWS.......... Neutron Spin-Wave Scattering (SAUS)
NSWS.......... Nondegenerate Series of Weighted Sum (SAUS)
NSWS.......... Nuclear Service Water System (NRCH)
NSWSA........ New South Wales Ski Association [*Australia*]
NSWSA........ New South Wales Softball Association [*Australia*]
NSWSA........ New South Wales Swimming Association [*Australia*]
NSWSACW... New South Wales Standing Advisory Committee on Wheat [*Australia*]
NSWSBA...... New South Wales Sheepbreeders' Association [*Australia*]
NSWSCC...... New South Wales Society for Crippled Children [*Australia*]
NSWSCC...... New South Wales State Cancer Committee [*Australia*]
NSWSCR...... New South Wales Supreme Court Reports [*A publication*] (DLA)
NSW S Ct Cas... New South Wales Supreme Court Cases [*A publication*] (DLA)
NSW S Ct R... New South Wales Supreme Court Reports [*A publication*] (DLA)
NSWSDA...... New South Wales Soft Drink Association [*Australia*]
NSWSES...... Naval Ship Weapon Systems Engineering Station [*Port Hueneme, CA*]
NSWSF........ New South Wales Soccer Federation [*Australia*]
NSWSGA...... New South Wales Seed Growers' Association [*Australia*]
NSWSHS...... New South Wales School of Hypnotic Sciences [*Australia*]
NSWSJC...... New South Wales Show Jumping Council [*Australia*]
NSWSK........ New South Wales Shorinjiryu Karate-do Association [*Australia*]
NSWSMBA... New South Wales Stud Merino Breeders' Association [*Australia*]
NSWSO........ New South Wales Superannuation Office [*Australia*]
NSWSRCTG... New South Wales Sales Representatives and Commercial Travellers' Guild [*Australia*]
NSWSS........ New South Wales Supply Service [*Australia*]
NSWSTC...... New South Wales Science and Technology Council [*Australia*]
NSWSTM..... New South Wales School of Therapeutic Massage [*Australia*]
NSWTA........ National Senior Women's Tennis Association (EA)
NSWTA........ New South Wales Transport Association (SAUS)
NSWTAFEC... New South Wales Technical and Further Education Commission [*Australia*]
NSWTC........ New South Wales Taxi Council [*Australia*]
NSWTC........ New South Wales Tourism Commission [*Australia*]
NSWTC........ New South Wales Travel Center [*Australia*]
NSWTEU...... New South Wales Theatrical Employees' Union [*Australia*]
NSWTF........ New South Wales Teachers Federation (SAUS)
NSWTG........ Naval Special Warfare Task Group (CAAL)
NSWTITC..... New South Wales Timber Industry Training Council [*Australia*]
NSWTLMB... New South Wales Tobacco Leaf Marketing Board [*Australia*]
NSWU.......... Naval Special Warfare Unit (DOMA)
NSW Univ Sch Civ Eng UNICIV Rep Ser R... New South Wales University. School of Civil Engineering. UNICIV Report. Series R (SAUS)
NSW Univ UNICIV Rep... University of New South Wales. School of Civil Engineering UNICIV Report (SAUS)
NSWUT........ New South Wales University of Technology (SAUS)
NSWVRA...... New South Wales Video Retailers' Association [*Australia*]
NSWWA....... New South Wales Wrestling Association [*Australia*]
NSWWA....... North Shore Women Writers Alliance [*Later, NSWA*] (EA)
NSWWAC..... New South Wales Women's Advisory Council [*Australia*]
NSW Watt Conserv Irrig Comm Surv Thirty NSW River Valleys Re... New South Wales. Water Conservation and Irrigation Commission. Survey of Thirty New South Wales River Valleys. Report (SAUS)
NSWWH....... West Hants Historical Society Museum, Windsor, Nova Scotia [*Library symbol*] [*National Library of Canada*] (NLC)
NSWWJA..... New South Wales Women Justices' Association [*Australia*]
NSW Worker's Comp R... New South Wales Worker's Compensation Reports [*A publication*] (DLA)
NSWWP....... New South Wales Water Polo [*Australia*] [*An association*]
NSWWSA..... New South Wales Water Ski Association [*Australia*]
NSWWSBA... New South Wales Wool Selling Brokers' Association [*Australia*]
NSX............ Neurosurgical Examination (MELL)
NSXB.......... Neutron Star X-Ray Binary [*Astrophysics*]
NSY............ Naval Shipyard
NSY............ New Scotland Yard
NSY............ Noisy (ABBR)
NSY............ North Salopian Yeomanry [*British military*] (DMA)
NSY............ North Somerset Yeomanry [*British military*] (DMA)
NSY............ Nursery (DAVI)
NSy............ Onondaga County Public Library, Syracuse, NY [*Library symbol*] [*Library of Congress*] (LCLS)
NSY............ Western Counties Regional Library, Yarmouth, Nova Scotia [*Library symbol*] [*National Library of Canada*] (NLC)
NSyA.......... Allied Corp., Solvay Process Division, Syracuse, NY [*Library symbol*] [*Library of Congress*] (LCLS)
NSYA.......... National School Yearbook Association [*Later, NSY/NA*]
NSyAF......... United States Air Force, Hancock Air Base Library, Syracuse, NY [*Library symbol*] [*Library of Congress*] (LCLS)
NSyAg......... Agway, Inc., Syracuse, NY [*Library symbol*] [*Library of Congress*] (LCLS)
NSyBL......... Bristol Laboratories, Syracuse, NY [*Library symbol*] [*Library of Congress*] (LCLS)
NSyC.......... Carrier Corp., Syracuse, NY [*Library symbol*] [*Library of Congress*] (LCLS)
NSYC.......... Courrier de la Nouvelle-Ecosse, Yarmouth, Nova Scotia [*Library symbol*] [*National Library of Canada*] (NLC)
NSyCA........ United States Court of Appeals, Syracuse, NY [*Library symbol*] [*Library of Congress*] (LCLS)
NSYCDA...... Archives, Diocese of Yarmouth, Catholic Church, Nova Scotia [*Library symbol*] [*National Library of Canada*] (NLC)
NSyCH........ Crouse-Irving Hospital, Syracuse, NY [*Library symbol*] [*Library of Congress*] (LCLS)
NSYD.......... Naval Shipyard
NSYDCN...... Diocese of Central New York, Syracuse, NY [*Library symbol*] [*Library of Congress*] (LCLS)
NSyEd......... Educational Opportunity Center, Syracuse, NY [*Library symbol*] [*Library of Congress*] (LCLS)
NSYF.......... Natural Science for Youth Foundation (EA)
NSYFG........ Fundy Group Publications, Yarmouth, Nova Scotia [*Library symbol*] [*National Library of Canada*] (NLC)
NSyGE........ General Electric Co., Syracuse, NY [*Library symbol*] [*Library of Congress*] (LCLS)
NSyGH........ Community-General Hospital, Syracuse, NY [*Library symbol*] [*Library of Congress*] (LCLS)
NSYHM....... Research Library, Yarmouth County Historical Society, Yarmouth, Nova Scotia [*Library symbol*] [*National Library of Canada*] (NLC)
NSyL.......... LeMoyne College, Syracuse, NY [*Library symbol*] [*Library of Congress*] (LCLS)
NSyLG........ Loretto Geriatric Center, Educational Resource Center, Syracuse, NY [*Library symbol*] [*Library of Congress*] (LCLS)
NSyMR........ Maria Regina College, Syracuse, NY [*Library symbol*] [*Library of Congress*] (LCLS)
NSyN.......... City Normal School, Syracuse, NY [*Library symbol*] [*Library of Congress*] [*Obsolete*] (LCLS)

NSY/NA....... National School Yearbook/Newspaper Association [Defunct] (EA)
NSyo........... Syosset Public Library, Syosset, NY [Library symbol] [Library of Congress] (LCLS)
NSyOB....... Onondaga-Courtland-Madison Board of Cooperative Education Service, Syracuse, NY [Library symbol] [Library of Congress] (LCLS)
NSyoBaE...... Baylis Elementary School, Syosset, NY [Library symbol] [Library of Congress] (LCLS)
NSyoBE....... Berry Hill Elementary School, Syosset, NY [Library symbol] [Library of Congress] (LCLS)
NSyOC......... Onondaga Community College, Syracuse, NY [Library symbol] [Library of Congress] (LCLS)
NSyoF......... Fairchild Space and Defense System, Syosset, NY [Library symbol] [Library of Congress] (LCLS)
NSyoG........ United States Geological Survey, Water Resources Division, Syosset, NY [Library symbol] [Library of Congress] (LCLS)
NSyoH........ Syosset Hospital, Syosset, NY [Library symbol] [Library of Congress] (LCLS)
NSyOHi....... Onondaga Historical Association, Syracuse, NY [Library symbol] [Library of Congress] (LCLS)
NSyOL......... Onondaga Library System, Syracuse, NY [Library symbol] [Library of Congress] (LCLS)
NSyoOL....... Our Lady of Mercy Academy, Syosset, NY [Library symbol] [Library of Congress] (LCLS)
NSyoP......... PRD Electronics, Inc., Information Center Library, Syosset, NY [Library symbol] [Library of Congress] (LCLS)
NSyoRE....... Robbins Elementary School, Syosset, NY [Library symbol] [Library of Congress] (LCLS)
NSyoSGE..... South Grove Elementary School, Syosset, NY [Library symbol] [Library of Congress] (LCLS)
NSyoSH....... Syosset Senior High School, Syosset, NY [Library symbol] [Library of Congress] (LCLS)
NSyoSRE..... Split Rock Elementary School, Syosset, NY [Library symbol] [Library of Congress] (LCLS)
NSyoSwJ..... South Woods Junior High School, Syosset, NY [Library symbol] [Library of Congress] (LCLS)
NSyoTJ....... Harry B. Thompson Junior High School, Syosset, NY [Library symbol] [Library of Congress] (LCLS)
NSyoVE....... Village Elementary School, Syosset, NY [Library symbol] [Library of Congress] (LCLS)
NSyoWE....... Willits Elementary School, Syosset, NY [Library symbol] [Library of Congress] (LCLS)
NSyoWhE.... Whitman Elementary School, Syosset, NY [Library symbol] [Library of Congress] (LCLS)
NSYR.......... Medical Library, Yarmouth Regional Hospital, Nova Scotia [Library symbol] [National Library of Canada] (BIB)
NSyR .... Syracuse Research Corp., Syracuse, NY [Library symbol] [Library of Congress] (LCLS)
NSYS .... Nortech Systems [NASDAQ symbol] (TTSB)
NSYS .... Nortech Systems, Inc. [NASDAQ symbol] (SAG)
NSySC .... New York State Supreme Court Law Library, Syracuse, NY [Library symbol] [Library of Congress] (LCLS)
NSySJ......... Saint Joseph's Hospital, School of Nursing and Medical Library, Syracuse, NY [Library symbol] [Library of Congress] (LCLS)
NSYSP........ National Summer Youth Sports Program
NSySU-F..... State University of New York, College of Environmental Sciences and Forestry at Syracuse University, Syracuse, NY [Library symbol] [Library of Congress] (LCLS)
NSySU-M .... State University of New York, Upstate Medical Center, Syracuse, NY [Library symbol] [Library of Congress] (LCLS)
NSyT........... Technology Club of Syracuse, Syracuse, NY [Library symbol] [Library of Congress] (LCLS)
NSyU .... Syracuse University, Syracuse, NY [Library symbol] [Library of Congress] (LCLS)
NSyU-CE...... Syracuse University, Library of Continuing Education at Syracuse, Syracuse, NY [Library symbol] [Library of Congress] (LCLS)
NSyU-G........ Syracuse University, Educational Resources Center of the All-University Gerontology Center, Syracuse, NY [Library symbol] [Library of Congress] (LCLS)
NSyVA .... United States Veterans Administration Hospital, Syracuse, NY [Library symbol] [Library of Congress] (LCLS)
NSZP .... Nemzeti Szabadelvu Part [National Liberal Party] [Hungary] [Political party] (PPE)
NT............... Iraq-Saudi Arabia Neutral Zone [ANSI two-letter standard code] (CNC)
NT............... Lake State Airways [ICAO designator] (AD)
N-T.............. Nal-Tel [Race of maize]
nT............... Nanotesla
NT............... Narrower Term [Indexing]
NT............... Naso-Tracheal [Medicine]
NT............... National Taranesc [National Peasant Party] [Romania] [Political party] (PPE)
NT............... National Team
NT............... National Theatre [Great Britain]
NT............... National Trust (WDAA)
NT............... National Trust for Historic Preservation
NT............... Natty (ABBR)
NT............... Naturalization Test
NT............... Naval Training
NT............... Navy Type (MSA)
NT............... Neap Tide
NT............... Near Term
NT............... Neat [Plain] [Bookbinding] (ROG)
NT............... Neonatal Tetanus
NT............... Neotetrazolium

NT............. Nephrostomy Tube [Nephrology] (DAVI)
NT............. Nerve Treatment (SAUS)
NT............. Nested-Task [Computer science] (BYTE)
NT............. Net (WDAA)
NT............. Netilmicin-Ticarcillin [Antibiotic combination]
NT............. Nett [Net] [British] (ROG)
NT............. Net Tax [IRS]
N/t............. Net Terms [Business term] (DS)
NT............. Net Tons [Shipping]
NT............. Network Terminal (MCD)
NT............. Network Termination [Telecommunications]
NT............. Network Terminator (SAUS)
NT............. Neural Tube [Anatomy]
NT............. Neurologically Typical [Psychology]
NT............. Neurotensin [Biochemistry]
NT............. Neurotoxin [Biochemistry]
NT............. Neurotransmitter (SAUS)
NT............. Neurotrophin [Neurobiology]
NT............. Neuter (WGA)
NT............. Neutralization Test [Chemistry]
NT............. Neutralizing (MAE)
NT............. Neutral Zone [Internet country code]
NT............. Neutron Transmitter [Nuclear energy] (NRCH)
NT............. Nevada Territory [Prior to statehood]
NT............. Newfoundland Time (SAUS)
NT............. News/Talk [Radio programming format] (WDMC)
NT............. New Taiwan
NT............. New Technology [Microsoft operating system] [Computer science] (PCM)
N/T............. New Terms [Business term]
NT............. New Territories [Hong Kong]
NT............. New Testament (WDAA)
NT............. New Thailand Dollar [Monetary unit]
nt............. Newton (NASA)
NT............. Newton
NT............. Newtonian Telescope (SAUS)
NT............. New Towns [British]
NT............. New Translation
NT............. New Trouble (SAUS)
Nt............. Nicotiana tabacum [Tobacco]
NT............. Night (ROG)
NT............. Night Telegram
NT............. Night Tracer (SAUS)
NT............. Night Trunk [Business term] (DCTA)
nt............. Nit [Unit of luminance]
NT............. Niton (ABBR)
Nt............. Nitron (SAUS)
NT............. Node Tracker [Frye Computer Systems] [Telecommunications] (PCM)
NT............. Node Type (SAUS)
NT............. Noise Temperature (ACAE)
NT............. Noise Thermometer (SAUS)
NT............. Nome Time (SAUS)
N/T............. None in Town [Bookselling]
N/T............. Nonmeasured Time
NT............. Non-T Cell [Cytology]
NT............. Nontender (DAVI)
NT............. Nontight (AAG)
NT............. Nontronite (SAUS)
NT............. Nontryptophan [Protein-bound fluorescence]
NT............. Nontumorous [Medicine] (DB)
NT............. Nontypeable (MAE)
NT............. Nordiska Transportarbetarefederationen [Nordic Transportworkers' Federation - NTF] (EAIO)
NT............. Nordisk Traebeskyttelsesrad [Nordic Wood Preservation Council - NWPC] (EAIO)
NT............. Normalized and Tempered (MCD)
NT............. Normal Temperature (ADA)
NT............. Normal Threat (SAUS)
NT............. Normal Tour
NT............. Nortel Networks [NYSE symbol] (SG)
NT............. Northern Air Taxis Ltd. (SAUS)
NT............. Northern Tablelands (SAUS)
NT............. Northern Telecom (SAUS)
NT............. Northern Territory (ACAE)
NT............. Northern Territory Herbarium International Acronym (SAUS)
NT............. Northwest Territories [Postal code] [Canada]
NT............. Nortriptyline [Antidepressant drug]
NT............. Nose Tackle (SAUS)
NT............. Note [Online database field identifier]
N/T............. No Terms [Shipping]
NT............. No Test
NT............. No Tested (SAUS)
NT............. No Tillage [Agriculture]
NT............. No Tone (SAUS)
NT............. No Tool (SAA)
NT............. No Trace [Counterintelligence]
NT............. No Transmission [Telecommunications]
NT............. No Trump [in game of bridge]
NT............. Not Technical (SAUS)
NT............. Not Tender (DAVI)
NT............. Not Tested
NT............. Not Titled [Accounting]
NT............. Not Typical
NT............. Novum Testamentum [New Testament] [of the Bible]

NT...............	Nuclear Transfer
NT...............	Nucleotidase [*An enzyme*] (DAVI)
nt...............	Nucleotide [*Genetics*] (DOG)
NT...............	Nuisance Tax (MHDW)
NT...............	Numbering Transmitter
NT...............	Number of Teams (SAUS)
NT...............	Number of Teeth (SAUS)
NT...............	Number of Tracks (SAUS)
NT...............	Number Theory (SAUS)
NT...............	Numerical Table (SAUS)
NT...............	Nurse Technician
NT...............	Thermal Necrosis [*Roentgenology*]
NT...............	Troy Public Library, Troy, NY [*Library symbol*] [*Library of Congress*] (LCLS)
NT-1............	Network Terminator Type 1 (PCM)
NT-3............	Neurotrophin-3 (SAUS)
NTA.............	Fujisawa Pharmaceutical Co. [*Japan*] [*Research code symbol*]
NTA.............	Naphthoyltrifluoroacetone [*Organic chemistry*]
NTA.............	Narcotics Treatment Administration [*Washington, DC*]
NTA.............	National Tabletop Association (EA)
NTA.............	National Tattoo Association (EA)
NTA.............	National Tax Association [*Later, NTA-TIA*] (EA)
NTA.............	National Tax Association-Tax Institute of America (NTPA)
NTA.............	National Taxidermists Association [*Defunct*] (EA)
NTA.............	National Taxpayers Alliance (EA)
NTA.............	National Teachers Association (AEE)
NTA.............	National Technical Association (EA)
NTA.............	National Telecommunications Agency
NTA.............	National Telefilm Associates, Inc. (NTCM)
NTA.............	National Tennis Academy [*Commercial firm*] (EA)
NTA.............	National Tennis Association [*Later, IRJA*] (EA)
NTA.............	National Threshers Association (EA)
NTA.............	National Tour Association (EA)
NTA.............	National Tourism Administration [*China*] (EY)
NTA.............	National Tourist Association (NADA)
NTA.............	National Translator Association (EA)
NTA.............	National Trappers Association (EA)
NTA.............	National Triton Association (EA)
NTA.............	National Trolleybus Association [*British*]
NTA.............	National Troubleshooting Association (NTPA)
NTA.............	National Tuberculosis Association [*Later, American Lung Association*] (EA)
NTA.............	National Tutoring Association (NTPA)
NTA.............	National Type Approval (PDAA)
NTA.............	Natural Thymocytotoxic Autoantibody (DB)
NTA.............	Naval Technical Assistants
NTA.............	Navy Technical Assessment (MCD)
NTA.............	Navy Technician Authorization (NG)
NTA.............	Near-Terminal Area [*Airports*]
NTA.............	Negotiated Testing Agreement (EEVL)
NTA.............	Neher Tetrode Amplifier
NTA.............	Net Tangible Assets [*Business term*] (ADA)
NTA.............	Net Technical Assessment (MCD)
NTA.............	Nevada Test Site Array [*Nevada*] [*Seismograph station code, US Geological Survey*] (SEIS)
NTA.............	New Territories Administration (SAUS)
NTA.............	New Testament Abstracts [*A publication*]
NTA.............	New Towns Act [*Town planning*] [*British*]
NTA.............	New Transatlantic Agenda
NTA.............	Nielsen Television Area (WDAA)
NTA.............	Nitrilotriacetate (SAUS)
nta.............	nitrilotriacetic (SAUS)
NTA.............	Nitrilotriacetic Acid [*Organic chemistry*]
NTA.............	Northern Textile Association (EA)
NTA.............	Northern Thunderbird Air Ltd. [*Canada*] [*ICAO designator*] (FAAC)
NTA.............	Northern Trade Association (SAUS)
NTA.............	Northwest Territory Alliance (EA)
NTA.............	Norwegian Telecommunications Administration [*or Agency*] [*Oslo*]
NTA.............	Not in Target Area (SAUS)
NTA.............	Nuclear Target Analysis (SAUS)
NTA.............	Nuclear Test Aircraft
NTA.............	Nurse Training Act
NTa.............	Warner Library, Tarrytown, NY [*Library symbol*] [*Library of Congress*] (LCLS)
NTAA	National Travelers Aid Association (EA)
NTAA	Tahiti/FAAA [*French Polynesia*] [*ICAO location identifier*] (ICLI)
NTAB	Nephrotoxic Antibody [*Medicine*] (MAE)
NTAB	Northern Territory Architects' Board [*Australia*]
NTAB	Notable (ABBR)
NTAB	Nuclear Technical Advisory Board [*American National Standards Institute*]
NTA Bul	Newfoundland Teachers Association. Bulletin (SAUS)
NTABY	Notably (ABBR)
NTAC	National Technical Assistance Center on Family Violence [*Defunct*] (EA)
NTAC	Naval Training Aids Center (DNAB)
NTAC	New Technology Access Centre (AIE)
NTACF	Northern Territory Anti-Cancer Foundation
NTACS	National Truck Activity & Commodity Survey (SAUS)
NTACS	Nationwide Truck Activity Survey [*BTS*] [*FHWA*] (TAG)
NTAF..........	Naval Training Aids Facility (DNAB)
NTAG	Network Technical Architecture Group [*Library of Congress*]
NTaGF	General Foods Technical Center Library, Tarrytown, NY [*Library symbol*] [*Library of Congress*] (LCLS)

NTaHi	Historical Society of the Tarrytowns, Tarrytown, NY [*Library symbol*] [*Library of Congress*] (LCLS)
NTAI	Nam Tai Electronics, Inc. [*NASDAQ symbol*] (NQ)
NTaI	Washington Irving Home, Sleepy Hollow Restorations, Tarrytown, NY [*Library symbol*] [*Library of Congress*] [*Obsolete*] (LCLS)
NTAIDSC......	Northern Territory AIDS [*Acquired Immune Deficiency Syndrome*] Council [*Australia*]
NTAIF	Nam Tai Electronics [*NASDAQ symbol*] (TTSB)
NTAJ..........	Newfoundland Teachers Association. Journal (SAUS)
NTaM	Marymount College, Tarrytown, NY [*Library symbol*] [*Library of Congress*] (LCLS)
NTAM	New Testament Archaeology Monographs [*A publication*] (BJA)
NTAMS	Northern Territory Aerial Medical Service (SAUS)
NTAN	Nitrilotriacetonitrile [*Organic chemistry*]
NT & SA	National Trust & Savings Association (MHDB)
NTAOCH......	Notice to Air Operator Certificate Holders (SAUS)
NTAP	National Targeting and Attack Policy (CINC)
NTAP	National Track Analysis Program [*Aviation*] (FAAC)
NTAP	Network Appliance [*NASDAQ symbol*] (TTSB)
NTAP	Network Appliance Corp. [*NASDAQ symbol*] (TTSB)
NTAP	Notices to Airmen Publication [*A publication*] (FAAC)
NTap	Tappan Free Library, Tappan, NY [*Library symbol*] [*Library of Congress*] (LCLS)
NTA Proceedings...	National Tax Association. Proceedings [*A publication*] (DLA)
NTAR	Nonviolent Techniques Against Rape [*An association*] (EA)
NTAR	Rurutu [*French Polynesia*] [*ICAO location identifier*] (ICLI)
NTARH	National Teen Age Republican Headquarters (EA)
NTARS	National Transportation Analysis Regions [*FHWA*] (TAG)
NTARY	Notary (ABBR)
NTAS	New Technology Advanced Server (SAUS)
NTAs	Nielsen Television Areas (SAUS)
NTAS	Northern Territory Archives Service [*Australia*]
NTAS	Norwegian Tracking Adjunct System (ACAE)
NTAS	NT Advamced Server (SAUS)
NTaS	Sleepy Hollow Restorations, Tarrytown, NY [*Library symbol*] [*Library of Congress*] (LCLS)
NTAS	Windows NT Advanced Server (SAUS)
NTAT..........	Near-Term ACME Technology (SAUS)
NTAT..........	Tubuai/Mataura [*French Polynesia*] [*ICAO location identifier*] (ICLI)
NTATB	Northwestern Truck Association and Tariff Bureau (SAUS)
NTATC	National Transportation Apprenticeship and Training Conference [*Bureau of Apprenticeship and Training*] [*Department of Labor*]
NTA-TIA	National Tax Association - Tax Institute of America (EA)
NTATN	Notation (ABBR)
NTATNL	Notational (ABBR)
NTaUC	Union Carbide Corp., Tarrytown Technical Center, Tarrytown, NY [*Library symbol*] [*Library of Congress*] (LCLS)
NtAust.........	National Australia Bank [*Associated Press*] (SAG)
NTAVL	Not Available (NOAA)
NTB.............	National Target Base (MCD)
NTB.............	National Test Bed [*Military*] (SDI)
N-t-B..........	Nitroso-tert-Butane (SAUS)
NTB.............	Non-selective Top-to-Bottom (SAUS)
NTB.............	Nontariff Barrier [*Kennedy Round*]
NTB.............	Nontumor-Bearing
NTB.............	Norsk Telegrambyra [*Norwegian News Agency*]
NTB.............	Northumbria Tourist Board [*British*] (DCTA)
NTB.............	Notable (ABBR)
NTB.............	No Talent Bum [*Slang*]
NTB.............	Not to Be (SAUS)
NTB.............	Nuclear Test Ban
NTBA	Name to be Advised [*Travel industry*] (TVEL)
NTBA	National Tour Brokers Association (EA)
NTBA	Network Terminator Basicrate Access (SAUS)
NTBA	Northern Territory Bowls Association [*Australia*]
NTBB	National Temporal Bone Banks Program of the DRF [*Deafness Research Foundation*] (EA)
N/TBC	Nontuberculous [*Medicine*] (DAVI)
NTBIC	National Test Bed Integration Contract (ACAE)
NTBIC	Northern Territory Buffalo Industry Council [*Australia*]
NTBJPO	National Test Bed Joint Program Office (ACAE)
NTBK	Net.Bank [*NASDAQ symbol*] (SG)
NTBK	Notebook (ABBR)
Ntbk	Notebook (DIAR)
NTBL..........	Nuffield Talking Book Library (SAUS)
NTBM..........	NU-Tech Bio-Med [*NASDAQ symbol*] (TTSB)
NTBM..........	Nu-Tech Bio Med, Inc. [*NASDAQ symbol*] (SAG)
NTBP	Normal Temperature and Blood Pressure (SAUS)
NTBPSC	Nepal, Tibet, and Bhutan Philatelic Study Circle (EA)
NTBR	National Temporal Bone Registry (EA)
NTBR	Not to Be Resuscitated
NTBRB	Northern Territory Building Referees' Board [*Australia*]
NTBS	Northern Territory Board of Studies [*Australia*]
NTBSIM	National Test Bed Simulation (ACAE)
NTBT..........	Nuclear Test Ban Treaty (CCCA)
NT BUR STNDS...	National Bureau of Standards [*Department of Commerce*] (WDAA)
NTBY	Notably (ABBR)
NTC.............	Gibson Aviation [*ICAO designator*] (FAAC)
NTC.............	National Tasking Center (MCD)
NTC.............	National Teachers Corps
NTC.............	National Team Championship [*Swimming*] [*British*] (ROG)
NTC.............	National Teen Challenge (EA)
NTC.............	National Telecommunications Conference [*IEEE*]
NTC.............	National Telemedia Council (EA)

NTC	National Television Center [*Telecommunications*] (TEL)
NTC	National Territorial Command (MCD)
NTC	National Test Center (NATG)
NTC	National Thanksgiving Commission (EA)
NTC	National Theatre Conference (EA)
NTC	National Thrift Committee [*Defunct*] (EA)
NTC	National Timesharing Council (EA)
NTC	National Traditionalist Caucus (EA)
NTC	National Trails Council (EA)
NTC	National Training Center [*Military*] (INF)
NTC	National Training Center [*Red Cross*] [*Charlottesville, VA*]
NTC	National Translations Center [*John Crerar Library*] [*Information service or system*]
NTC	National Transportation Center [*Large city situated at a key junction of rail, air, and highway transportation*] [*Postal Service*]
NTC	National Travel Club [*Commercial firm*] (EA)
NTC	National Treatment Consortium for Alcohol and Other Drugs (EA)
NTC	National Troopers Coalition (EA)
NTC	National Tuberculosis Center (SAUS)
NTC	Naturally Occurring Top Component [*Virology*]
NTC	Nautical Training Corps [*British military*] (DMA)
NTC	Naval Training Center
NTC	Naval Training Command
NTC	Navy Test Controller (DNAB)
NTC	Negative Temperature Coefficient
NTC	Negative Thermal Coefficient (IAA)
NTC	Neotetrazolium Chloride [*A dye*]
NTC	Network Transmission Committee [*Video Transmission Engineering Committee*] (NTCM)
NTC	Nigerian Tobacco Co. (SAUS)
NTC	Nissan Technical Center [*Automobile manufacturing*]
NTC	Nonthermal Continuum (SAUS)
NTC	Noranda Technology Center (SAUS)
NTC	Nordic Temperance Council (EA)
NTC	Nordic Theater Committee [*Later, NTDC*] (EAIO)
NTC	Normal Tour of Duty Completed
NTC	Northern Telecommunications (SAUS)
NTC	Northern Telecommunication Station (SAUS)
ntc	Northwest Territories [*MARC country of publication code*] [*Library of Congress*] (LCCP)
NTC	Norwegian Trade Council (EA)
NTC	Norwich Terrier Club [*Later, NNTC*] (EA)
NTC	Notice
NTC	No Traffic Reported [*Air Traffic Control*] (FAAC)
NTC	Nucleon Transport Code
NTC	Nu-Trans Cooperative (EA)
NTC	Nuveen Connecticut Premium Income Municipal Fund [*NYSE symbol*] (SPSG)
NTC	Nuveen CT Prem Inc. Muni [*NYSE symbol*] (TTSB)
NTCA	National Telephone Cooperative Association (EA)
NTCA	National Tile Contractors Association (EA)
NTCA	National Town Class Association (EA)
NTCA	National Tribal Chairman's Association [*Defunct*] (EA)
NTCA	N-Nitrosothioazolidine Carboxylic Acid [*Organic chemistry*]
NTCA	Non-Tutorial Computer Application (SAUS)
NTCA	Northern Territory Cattlemens Association (SAUS)
NTCA	Northern Territory Cricket Association [*Australia*]
NtCapit	National Capital Management Corp. [*Associated Press*] (SAG)
NTCAVAL	Notice of Availability
NTC/AW	National Training Center / Air Warrior System (DWSG)
NTCB	(Nitro)thiocyanatobenzoic Acid [*Organic chemistry*]
NTCB	Northern Territory Convention Bureau [*Australia*]
NTCB	Noticeable (ABBR)
NTCBY	Noticeably (ABBR)
NTCC	National Type Culture Collection (MELL)
NTCC	Naval Tactical Communications Center (MCD)
NTCC	Naval Telecommunications Center (DOMA)
NTCC	Neutron Transport Computer Code
NTCC	Nimbus Technical Control Center
NTCC	Northern Territory Conservation Commission [*Australia*]
NTCCDET	Naval Telecommunications Center Detachment (DNAB)
NTCCL	Northern Territory Council for Civil Liberties (SAUS)
NTCCS	Naval Tactical Command and Control System (PDAA)
NTCD	Newark Transportation Control Depot (SAUS)
NTCD	Nitro(thiocyano)benzoic Acid [*Organic chemistry*]
NTCD	Noticed (ABBR)
NTCDC	Northern Territory Counter Disaster Council [*Australia*]
NTCF	National Telemarketing Fulfillment Center
NTCF	National Toxic Campaign Fund [*An association*]
NTCFA	Northern Territory Commercial Fishermen's Association [*Australia*]
NTCFA	Northern Territory Crab Fishermen's Association [*Australia*]
NTCG	Noticing (ABBR)
NTCGA	Northern Territory Community Government Association [*Australia*]
Ntch	Notch (SAUS)
NTCHA	National Taxi and Car Hire Association [*British*] (BI)
NTCHBA	National Trust Closely Held Business Association (EA)
NTCI	National Training Center - Phase I (MCD)
NTCKR	Nutcracker (ABBR)
NTCL	Nautical
NTCLP	Northern Territory Country Liberal Party [*Australia*] [*Political party*]
NTCMA	National Traditional Country Music Association [*Later, NTMA*] (EA)
NtCmcBc	National Commerce Bancorp [*Associated Press*] (SAG)
NTCMP	Northern Territory Chamber of Mines and Petroleum [*Australia*]
NtCnv	National Convenience Stores, Inc. [*Associated Press*] (SAG)
NTCOSS	Northern Territory Council of Social Service [*Australia*]
NTCOTA	Northern Territory Council on the Aging [*Australia*]
NTCP	Near-Term Construction Permit [*Nuclear energy*] (NRCH)
NTCP	Nightcap (ABBR)
NTCP	Non-Traditional Casting Project (EA)
NtCptr	National Computer Systems, Inc. [*Associated Press*] (SAG)
NTCS	Nonverbal Test of Cognitive Skills [*Intelligence test*]
NTCS-A	Navy Tactical Command System Afloat (DOMA)
NTCSD	Naval Training Center, San Diego
NTCSOC	Naval Telecommunications Command Satellite Operations Center (MCD)
NTCSS	Navy Tactical Command and Support System (SAUS)
NTCT	National Tennis Center Trust [*Australia*]
NTCT	Naval Tactics & Command Trainer (SAUS)
NTCTA	Northern Territory Clay Target Association [*Australia*]
NTCU	Need to See You [*Online dialog*]
NTD	Das Neue Testament Deutsch. Neues Goettinger Bibelwerk [*A publication*] (BJA)
NTD	NASA Test Director (MCD)
NTD	National Tap Dance Co. of Canada
NTD	National Technology Databank [*Singapore*] (DDC)
NTD	National Theatre of the Deaf (EA)
NTD	National Transit Database [*FTA*] (TAG)
NTD	Naval Training Department [*British military*] (DMA)
NTD	Negative to Date [*Medicine*] (MELL)
NTD	Neural Tube (Closure) Defect [*Medicine*]
NTD	Neutron Transmutation Doped [*Silicon for semiconductor use*]
NTD	Neutron Transmutation Doping (AAEL)
NTD	New Tyee Resources [*Vancouver Stock Exchange symbol*]
NTD	Nissan Torque Demand [*Automotive engineering*]
NTD	Nitroblue Tetrazolium Dye [*Test*] [*Laboratory science*] (DAVI)
NTD	Noise Tone Difference (DMAA)
NTD	Nontight Door
NTD	Noted (SAUS)
NTD	N-Tone International Ltd. [*Vancouver Stock Exchange symbol*]
NTD	Nuclear Test Directorate [*Air Force*]
NTD	Nuclear Training Division (SAUS)
NTD	Port Hueneme, CA [*Location identifier*] [*FAA*] (FAAL)
NTDA	National Trade Development Association (WDAA)
NTDA	National Trailer Dealers Association (EA)
NTDA	National Tyre Distributors Association [*British*] (DBA)
NTDA	Navy Tactical Doctrine Activity (NVT)
NTDAAM	National Trust for the Development of African American Men (EA)
NTDAB	Northern Territory Drug and Alcohol Board [*Australia*]
NTDB	National Trade Data Bank (EGAO)
NTDB	National Trade Database (ACII)
NTDC	NanoTechnology Development Corp.
NTDC	Naval Training Devices Center [*Port Washington, LI*]
NTDC	Nordic Theatre and Dance Committee (EAIO)
NTDDPA	Navy Tactical Doctrine Development and Production Activity
NTDE	North Dakota Tracer Experiment [*Marine science*] (OSRA)
NtDentex	National Dentex Corp. [*Associated Press*] (SAG)
NTDG	National Teaching Development Grant [*Australia*]
NTDI	NATO Target Data Inventory (MCD)
NTDO	Navy Technical Data Office [*of the Office of Naval Material*]
NTDP	New Technology Demonstration Program (SAUS)
NTDPMA	National Tool, Die, and Precision Machining Association [*Later, NTMA*] (EA)
NTDRA	National Tire Dealers and Retreaders Association (EA)
NTDRP	Northern Territory Drought Releif Policy (SAUS)
NTDS	Naval Tactical-Display System (ACAE)
NTDS	Naval Technical Data System (IAA)
NTDS	Navy Tactical Data System
NTDS	Northern Telecom Data Systems (NITA)
NTDSC	Nondestructive Testing Data Support Center [*DoD*] (MCD)
NTDS/LBTS	Naval Tactical Data System / Land-Based Test Site (DNAB)
NTDT	Non-Time Dependent Target (ACAE)
NTE	Nantes [*France*] [*Airport symbol*] (OAG)
NTE	National Teacher Examination
NTE	National Transportation Exchange
NTE	National Treasury Employees Union
NTE	Navy Technical Evaluation (NG)
NTE	Navy Teletypewriter Exchange [*Later, NTX*]
NTE	Negative Thermal Expansion [*Physics*]
NTE	Network Terminating Equipment [*Telecommunications*] (IAA)
NTE	Neuropathy Target Esterase [*Medicine*] (DMAA)
NTE	Neurotoxic Esterase [*Medicine*] (DMAA)
NTE	Neutral Thermal Environment [*Medicine*] (MELL)
NTE	Neutron Transient Effect
NTE	Non-orthogonal Timing Error (SAUS)
NTE	Nontactical Equipment
NTE	Non-Traditional Exports (SAUS)
NTE	Northern Eagle Mines [*Vancouver Stock Exchange symbol*]
NTE	Not to Exceed [*Aviation*]
NTE	Nursing the Environment
NTEA	National Tax Equality Association (EA)
NTEA	National Telecommunications Electronics Administration
NTEA	National Time Equipment Association (EA)
NTEA	National Truck Equipment Association (EA)
NTeam	National TechTeam, Inc. [*Associated Press*] (SAG)
NTEC	National Telecommunications Education Committee [*North American Telecommunications Association*] [*Washington, DC*] [*Telecommunications service*] (TSSD)
NTEC	National Traction Engine Club [*British*] (DBA)
NTEC	Naval Training Equipment Center
NTEC	Neose Technologies [*NASDAQ symbol*] (TTSB)

N-Tec.......... Nuclear Technology (SAUS)
NTech.......... National Technical Systems, Inc. [*Associated Press*] (SAG)
NTECPE.......... Naval Training Equipment Center, Project Engineer
NTEF.......... National Tennis Educational Foundation [*Later, NTFHF*] (EA)
NTEG.......... Integ Inc. [*NASDAQ symbol*] (SAG)
NTEI.......... New Technical Education Initiative (AIE)
NTE/IOTE.......... Navy Technical Evaluation/Initial Operational Test and Evaluation (MCD)
NTEL.......... No-Toxic-Effect Level [*Toxicology*] (LDT)
NTelpd.......... Northwest Teleproductions, Inc. [*Associated Press*] (SAG)
NTEO.......... Northern Territory Electoral Office [*Australia*]
NTEP.......... National Type Evaluation Program [*Environmental Protection Agency*]
NTEP.......... New Technology Employment Program (SAUS)
NTEP.......... Norwegian Terrestrial Ecosystem Profile (SAUS)
NTEP.......... Not to Exceed Price (SAUS)
NTEPQ.......... Not to Exceed Price Quoted (SAUS)
NTER.......... Normalized Transmission Energy Requirement
N Terr.......... Northern Territory
N Terr Austl Ord... Northern Territorial Ordinances [*Australia*] [*A publication*] (DLA)
NTES.......... Northern Territory Emergency Service [*Australia*]
N-TEST.......... Nuclear Testing (WDAA)
NTET.......... National Traction Engine Trust [*British*] (DBA)
NTEU.......... National Treasury Employees Union (EA)
NTEXIS.......... North Texas Interconnected System (SAUS)
NTeZ.......... North Temperate Zone [*Planet Jupiter*]
NTF.......... National Tactical Force (NATG)
NTF.......... National Tennis Foundation [*Formerly, NTEF*] [*Later, NTFHF*] (EA)
NTF.......... National Test Facility [*Military*] (SDI)
NTF.......... National Theater File [*Theater Sources, Inc.*] [*Information service or system*] [*Defunct*] (IID)
NTF.......... National Tidal Facility [*Flinders University*] [*Australia*]
NTF.......... National Trainers Federation [*British*] (DBA)
NTF.......... National Transfer Format (VLIE)
NTF.......... National Transonic Facility [*NASA*]
NTF.......... National Transport Federation [*Australia*]
NTF.......... National Turkey Federation (EA)
NTF.......... Naval Task Force
NTF.......... Navy Technological Forecast
NTF.......... Network Transfer Function (ELAL)
NTF.......... Neurotrophic Factor [*Medicine*] (DMAA)
NTF.......... Neutral Transfer Format (SAUS)
NTF.......... New Tactical Fighter (ACAE)
NTF.......... Nigerian Trust Fund [*African Development Bank*]
NTF.......... Nigeria Trust Fund (SAUS)
NTF.......... Nitrofurantoin (SAUS)
NTF.......... Nordic Transportworkers' Federation [*See also NT*] (EAIO)
NTF.......... Nordisk Thoraxkirurgisk Forening [*Scandinavian Association for Thoracic and Cardiovascular Surgery - SATCS*] (EAIO)
NTF.......... Normal Throat Flora [*Medicine*] (DMAA)
NTF.......... Notify
NTF.......... No Trouble Found
NTF.......... No Trouble Fund (SAUS)
NTF.......... Nuclear Test Facility
NTF.......... Number Type Flag (SAUS)
NTFA.......... National Teaching-Family Association (EA)
NTFA.......... National Track and Field Association [*Superseded by ANG*] (EA)
NTFAO.......... National Task Force on Autocratic Options (EA)
NTFC.......... National Telemarketing Fulfillment Center
NTFC.......... National Television Film Council (EA)
NTFC.......... NATO Tactical Fighter Center
NTFC.......... Nonlinear Transient Fuel Film Compsensation [*Automotive fuel system*]
NTFDC.......... Non Theatrical Film Distributors Council (EA)
NTFEEG.......... National Task Force on Education for Economic Growth (EA)
NTFHF.......... National Tennis Foundation and Hall of Fame [*Later, ITHOF*] (EA)
NTFIC.......... Northern Territory Fishing Industry Council [*Australia*]
NTFITC.......... Northern Territory Fishing Industry Training Committee [*Australia*]
NTFL.......... National Touch Football Leagues (EA)
NTFNC.......... Northern Territory Field Naturalists' Club [*Australia*]
NTFND.......... No Trouble Found [*Aviation*] (FAAC)
NTFP.......... National Task Force on Prostitution (EA)
NTFS.......... Network of Tropical Fisheries Scientists [*Marine science*] (OSRA)
NTFS.......... New Technology File System [*Computer science*] (VLIE)
NTFS.......... Northern Territory Fire Service [*Australia*]
NTFS.......... NT File System [*Computer science*]
NTFTA.......... National Toy Fox Terrier Association (EA)
NTFWTC.......... NATO Tactical Fighter Weapons Training Center
NTFY.......... Notify (AFM)
NTG.......... Natco Group 'A' [*NYSE symbol*] (SG)
NTG.......... Nitroglycerin [*Also, GTN, NG*] [*Explosive, vasodilator*]
Ntg.......... Nitroglycerine [*Medicine*] (AMHC)
NTG.......... Nitrosoguanidine [*Organic chemistry*]
NTG.......... Nontactical Generator (RDA)
NTG.......... Non-Technical Generator [*Army*]
NTG.......... Nontoxic Goiter [*Medicine*]
NTG.......... Nontreatment Group [*Medical research*] (DAVI)
NTG.......... Normal Tension Glaucoma (SAUS)
NTG.......... Normal Triglyceridemic (DB)
NTG.......... Not Too Good (SAUS)
NTG.......... N-Tolylglycine [*Organic chemistry*]
NTG.......... Nuclear Test Gage [*Environmental science*] (COE)
NTGA.......... Anaa [*French Polynesia*] [*ICAO location identifier*] (ICLI)
NTGA.......... National Tabletop and Giftware Association (NTPA)
NTGA.......... National Traveler's Gasoline Advisory (DICI)
NTGB.......... Fangatau [*French Polynesia*] [*ICAO location identifier*] (ICLI)
NTGB.......... North Thames Gas Board (SAUS)
NTGC.......... Tikehau [*French Polynesia*] [*ICAO location identifier*] (ICLI)
NTGD.......... Apataki [*French Polynesia*] [*ICAO location identifier*] (ICLI)
NTGDS.......... Non-Tritium Gas Delivery System (SAUS)
NTGE.......... Reao [*French Polynesia*] [*ICAO location identifier*] (ICLI)
NTGF.......... Fakarava [*French Polynesia*] [*ICAO location identifier*] (ICLI)
NTGH.......... Hikueru [*French Polynesia*] [*ICAO location identifier*] (ICLI)
NTGI.......... Manihi [*French Polynesia*] [*ICAO location identifier*] (ICLI)
NTGIS.......... National Transit Geographic Information System [*FTA*] (TAG)
NTGJ.......... Totegegie [*French Polynesia*] [*ICAO location identifier*] (ICLI)
NTGK.......... Kaukura [*French Polynesia*] [*ICAO location identifier*] (ICLI)
NTGk.......... New Testament Greek (BARN)
NTGL.......... Fakahina [*French Polynesia*] [*ICAO location identifier*] (ICLI)
NTGM.......... Makemo [*French Polynesia*] [*ICAO location identifier*] (ICLI)
NTGMA.......... Northern Territory Girls' Marching Association [*Australia*]
NTGMB.......... Northern Territory Grain Marketing Board [*Australia*]
NTGN.......... Napuka [*French Polynesia*] [*ICAO location identifier*] (ICLI)
NTGO.......... Nitroglycerine Ointment [*Pharmacy*]
NTGO.......... Tatakoto [*French Polynesia*] [*ICAO location identifier*] (ICLI)
NTGP.......... Northern Territory Government Publications [*Australia*]
NTGP.......... Puka Puka [*French Polynesia*] [*ICAO location identifier*] (ICLI)
NTGPE.......... Northern Territory Government Pipeline Executive [*Australia*]
NTGPO.......... Northern Territory Government Printing Office [*Australia*]
NTGQ.......... Pukarua [*French Polynesia*] [*ICAO location identifier*] (ICLI)
NTGR.......... Aratica [*French Polynesia*] [*ICAO location identifier*] (ICLI)
NTGR.......... New Testament Greek (BJA)
NTGS.......... Northwest Territory Genealogical Society (EA)
NTG SL.......... Nitroglycerin Sublingual [*Pharmacology*] (DAVI)
NtGsO.......... National Gas & Oil Corp. [*Associated Press*] (SAG)
NTGT.......... Takapoto [*French Polynesia*] [*ICAO location identifier*] (ICLI)
NTGU.......... Arutua [*French Polynesia*] [*ICAO location identifier*] (ICLI)
NTGV.......... Mataiva [*French Polynesia*] [*ICAO location identifier*] (ICLI)
NTGW.......... Nukutavake [*French Polynesia*] [*ICAO location identifier*] (ICLI)
NTGX.......... net.Genesis Corp. [*NASDAQ symbol*] (SG)
NTGY.......... Tureia [*French Polynesia*] [*ICAO location identifier*] (ICLI)
NTH.......... Hudson Valley Community College, Troy, NY [*Library symbol*] [*Library of Congress*] (LCLS)
NtH.......... Natural Health Trends Corp. [*Associated Press*] (SAG)
NTH.......... New Testament Handbooks [*A publication*]
NTH.......... New Training Helicopter (SAUS)
NTH.......... Northern Platinum [*Vancouver Stock Exchange symbol*]
NTH.......... No Therapy Helpful (SAUS)
NTHA.......... National Temple Hill Association (EA)
NTHA.......... Northern Territory Hockey Association [*Australia*]
Nth BHH.......... North Broken Hill Holdings (SAUS)
NTHC.......... Northern Territory Housing Commission [*Australia*]
NTHCS.......... National Toothpick Holder Collector's Society (EA)
NthCsE.......... North Coast Energy [*Associated Press*] (SAG)
NthCst.......... North Coast Energy, Inc. [*Associated Press*] (SAG)
NthCstE.......... North Coast Energy [*Associated Press*] (SAG)
NTHEST.......... Northeast
NTHESTN.......... Northeastern
NTHEX.......... Northeast Investors Tr. [*Mutual fund ticker symbol*] (SG)
NthfldLb.......... Northfield Laboratories, Inc. [*Associated Press*] (SAG)
nthg.......... nothing (SAUS)
Nthgat.......... Northgate Exploration Ltd. [*Associated Press*] (SAG)
NtHHlt.......... National Home Health Care Corp. [*Associated Press*] (SAG)
NTHL.......... National Treasure Hunters League [*Defunct*] (EA)
NthLily.......... North Lilly Mining Co. [*Associated Press*] (SAG)
NtHlt.......... National Health Investors [*Associated Press*] (SAG)
NtHlthE.......... National Health Enhancement Systems, Inc. [*Associated Press*] (SAG)
NtHltI.......... National Health Investors [*Associated Press*] (SAG)
Nthmb.......... Northumberland [*County in England*] (WGA)
NTHMF.......... Northair Mines Ltd. (SAUS)
Nthn.......... Northern (TBD)
NTHN.......... Northern
NthnTch.......... Northern Technologies International [*Associated Press*] (SAG)
NTHP.......... National Trust for Historic Preservation (EA)
N-Threat.......... Nuclear Threat (SAUS)
NTHRN.......... Northern
NthStat.......... Northern States Financial Corp. [*Associated Press*] (SAG)
NthstCF.......... Northstar Computer Forms, Inc. [*Associated Press*] (SAG)
NthstrHl.......... Northstar Health Services, Inc. [*Associated Press*] (SAG)
NTHV.......... Near-Term Hybrid Vehicle (PDAA)
NTHWST.......... Northwest
NTHWSTN.......... Northwestern
NTHZ.......... N-Nitrosothiazolidine [*Organic chemistry*]
NTI.......... Bintuni [*Indonesia*] [*Airport symbol*] (OAG)
NTI.......... Nadic-Terminated Imide [*Polymer technology*]
NTI.......... National Tactical Interface (MCD)
NTI.......... National Technology Initiative [*Program introduced by President Bush in February 1992*]
NTI.......... National Theatre Institute (EA)
NTI.......... National Toxics Inventory [*Environmental science*] (EPAT)
NTI.......... National Trade Index
NTI.......... National Tune Index [*A publication*]
NTI.......... Naval Travel Instructions
NTI.......... Near Term Initiative (ACAE)
NTI.......... Need Ticketing Information [*Travel industry*] (TRID)
NTI.......... Nesbitt Thomson, Inc. [*Toronto Stock Exchange symbol*] [*Vancouver Stock Exchange symbol*]
NTI.......... NeuROM Technology, Inc.
NTI.......... Neuropsychiatric Interest Checklist

NTI............. Nielsen Television Index [*Nielsen Media Research*] [*Information service or system*]
NTI............. Noise Transmission Impairment [*Telecommunications*]
NTI............. Nonthyroidal Illness [*Medicine*]
NTI............. Nordman [*Idaho*] [*Seismograph station code, US Geological Survey*] [*Closed*] (SEIS)
NTI............. Northern Technology International [*AMEX symbol*] (SPSG)
NTI............. No Travel Involved [*Military*]
NTIA.......... National Telecommunications and Information Administration [*Department of Commerce*] [*Washington, DC*]
NTIA.......... Netia Holdings ADS [*NASDAQ symbol*] (SG)
NTIAC .... Nondestructive Testing Information Analysis Center [*Army Materials and Mechanics Research Center*] [*Watertown, MA*]
NTIB.......... National Technology and Industrial Base (AAGC)
NTIC.......... Immaculate Conception Seminary, College of Philosophy, Troy, NY [*Library symbol*] [*Library of Congress*] (LCLS)
NTIC.......... National Training and Information Center (EA)
NTIC.......... Naval Technical Intelligence Center [*Pronounced N-tech; Formerly, NISC, now NAVMIC*] (DOMA)
NTIC.......... Nondestructive Testing Information Center [*Battelle Memorial Institute*] [*Databank*] [*Information service or system*] (IID)
NTICED .... National Training Institute for Community Economic Development (EA)
NTICL .... National Technical Information Centre and Library (NITA)
NTID .... National Technical Institute for the Deaf [*Rochester Institute of Technology*] [*Research center*]
NTIES.......... National Treatment Improvement Evaluation Study [*Department of Health and Human Services*]
NTIF........... National Taxpayers' Investigative Fund (EA)
NTIF........... New Threat Intermediate Frequency (TIMI)
NTIG.......... Nontreated Immunoglobulin [*Medicine*] (DMAA)
NTIH.......... Normal Terminate Interrupt Handler (MCD)
NTII........... Neurobiological Technologies, Inc. [*NASDAQ symbol*] (SAG)
NTIK.......... Nontactical Instrumentation Kit [*Military*] (DWSG)
NTIM.......... Not That It Matters (SAUS)
NTIMM........ Not That It Matters Much (SAUS)
NTIMS .... Negative-Ion Thermal Ionization Mass Spectrometry
NTIOC........ No Travel Involved for Officer Concerned [*Military*]
N-TIP .... National Technology Investment Programme [*Canada*]
NTIP.......... National Turkey Improvement Plan
NTIPP .... Navy Technical Information Presentation Program (MCD)
NTIPS .... Navy Technical Information Presentation System (MCD)
NTIPS .... Navy Technical Information Processing System (ACAE)
NTIR .... Nederlands Tijdschrift voor Internationaal Recht [*Netherlands*] [*A publication*] (ILCA)
NTIR .... Nontechnical Intelligence Report
NTIRA .... National Trucking Industrial Relations Association (EA)
NTIS........... National Technical Information Service [*Department of Commerce*] [*Springfield, VA*] [*Database producer and database*]
NTIS........... Navy Thermal Imaging System (SAUS)
NTIS........... NEC [*Nippon Electric Company*]-Toshiba Information Systems, Inc. [*Japan*]
NTIS........... Nippon Technical Information Service (SAUS)
NTIS........... NMOS Technical Information Services (SAUS)
NTIS........... Nondestructive Testing Information System (SAA)
NTISSC .... National Telecommunications and Information System Security Committee (NITA)
NTITC.......... National Tourism Industry Training Council [*Australia*]
NTITS.......... Northern Territory Interpreter and Translator Service [*Australia*]
NTJ............ Nigeria Trade Journal [*A publication*]
NTJCAC....... Northern Texas Junior College Athletic Conference (PSS)
NTK .... Need to Know (MCD)
NTK .... Newton Tool Kit [*Computer science*]
NTK .... New York Air (SAUS)
NTK .... Nontactical Kit [*Military*] (DWSG)
NTK .... Nordisk Teaterkomite [*Nordic Theater Committee - NTC*] (EAIO)
NTK .... Nortek, Inc. [*NYSE symbol*] (SPSG)
NTK .... Nunatak [*Alaska*] [*Seismograph station code, US Geological Survey*] (SEIS)
NTK .... Tustin, CA [*Location identifier*] [*FAA*] (FAAL)
NTKK .... Net2000 Communications [*NASDAQ symbol*] (SG)
NTKR .... Takaroa [*French Polynesia*] [*ICAO location identifier*] (ICLI)
NTL .... Jacksonville, NC [*Location identifier*] [*FAA*] (FAAL)
ntL .... National (DD)
NTL .... National
NTL .... National Technology Ltd. (NITA)
NTL .... National Temperance League [*Later, ACAP*] (EA)
NTL .... National Tennis League
NTL .... National Testing Laboratories [*Australia*]
NTL .... National Training Laboratories [*Later, NTLI*] (EA)
NTL .... Natural Thermo Luminescence (IAA)
NTL .... Neon Test Light
NTL .... Nevertheless (SAUS)
NTL .... Newcastle [*Australia*] [*Airport symbol*] (OAG)
NTL .... Night Telegraph Letter
NTL .... Nonthreshold Logic (IAA)
NTL .... Nonuniform Transmission Line [*Computer science*] (IAA)
NTL .... Northair Aviation Ltd. [*British*] [*ICAO designator*] (FAAC)
NTL .... Northern Technol Intl. [*AMEX symbol*] (SPSG)
NTL .... Northern Telecom Ltd. [*Toronto Stock Exchange symbol*] [*Vancouver Stock Exchange symbol*]
NTL .... Northern Territory Library [*Australia*]
NTL .... No Time Lost [*Military*]
NTL .... NovAtel Communications Ltd. [*UTLAS symbol*]
NTL .... Novosti Tehniksoi Literatury (NITA)

NTL .... Nuclear Technology Laboratory [*Stanford University*] (MCD)
NTL .... Nuclear Thermionics Laboratory
NTL .... Nuclear Transport Ltd. [*British*] (IRUK)
NTLA.......... National Toy Libraries Association [*British*] (EAIO)
NTLA.......... Nebraska Test of Learning Aptitude [*Education*]
NTLAM........ New Technology Lunar Astronomy Mission (SAUS)
NTLAT......... Northern Territory Land Acquisition Tribunal [*Australia*]
NTLB.......... Northern Territory Land Board [*Australia*]
NTLC.......... National Tax-Limitation Committee (EA)
NTLC.......... National Trades and Labour Congress [*Canada*]
NTLC.......... National Traffic Law Center [*MHTSA*] (TAG)
NtlCity .... National City Corp. [*Associated Press*] (SAG)
NTLDO........ Navy Terminal Leave Disbursing Office
NTLEN .... Nutlet Length [*Botany*]
NTLF .... National Taxpayers Legal Fund (EA)
NTLF .... Northern Troops and Landing Force
NTLGA........ Northern Territory Local Government Association [*Australia*]
NTLGGC...... Northern Territory Local Government Grants Commission [*Australia*]
NTLI .... Neurotensin-Like Immunoreactivity
NTLI .... NTL, Inc. [*NASDAQ symbol*] (SG)
NTLI .... NTL Institute (EA)
NtlInco .... National Income Realty Trust [*Associated Press*] (SAG)
NtlIns.......... National Insurance Group [*Associated Press*] (SAG)
NTLIS......... Northern Territory Land Information System (SAUS)
NtlPict .... National Picture & Frame Co. [*Associated Press*] (SAG)
NTLPSS....... Non-real-time Launch Processing Software System (SAUS)
NtlRlty .... National Realty Ltd. [*Associated Press*] (SAG)
NTLS.......... National Truck Leasing System (EA)
NTLS.......... Non-Transposed Loop Sensor (PDAA)
NTLSEA....... Northern Territory Live Stock Exporters' Association [*Australia*]
NtlSecs........ National Securities Corp. [*Associated Press*] (SAG)
NtlWire........ National Wireless Holdings, Inc. [*Associated Press*] (SAG)
NtlWstA....... National Westminster Bank Ltd. [*Associated Press*] (SAG)
NTM .... Narrowband Trunk Module [*Telecommunications*]
NTM .... National Technical Means [*For monitoring compliance with the provisions of an agreement*]
NTM .... NAVAIR Test Manual (MCD)
NTM .... Nazarene Theological Seminary, Kansas City, MO [*OCLC symbol*] (OCLC)
NTM .... Net Ton Mile [*Shipping*]
NTM .... Network Test Manager (ACAE)
NTM .... Network Traffic Management [*Computer science*] (VLIE)
NTM .... New to Market (JAGO)
NTM .... New Tribes Mission (EA)
NTM .... Night Message (MSA)
NTM .... Nondeterministic Turing Machine (RALS)
NTM .... Nontariff Measures
NTM .... Non-Transition Metal (MCD)
NTM .... Non-Tuberculous Mycobacteria [*Microbiology*]
NTM .... Normal Transmitting Male [*Genetics*]
NTM .... North American Airlines, Inc. [*Canada*] [*ICAO designator*] (FAAC)
NTM .... Northern Territory Art Gallery and Museum, Darwin (SAUS)
NtM .... Norton Micro Images, Inc., Trenton, NJ [*Library symbol*] [*Library of Congress*] (LCLS)
NTM .... Notice to Mariners
NTM .... Notice to Move (SAUS)
NTM .... Not to My Knowledge
NTM .... Nutmeg Industries, Inc. (SAUS)
NTMA.......... National Tank Manufacturers Association [*Defunct*] (EA)
NTMA.......... National Terrazzo and Mosaic Association (EA)
NTMA.......... National Tooling and Machining Association (EA)
NTMA.......... National Traditional Music Association (EA)
NTMB.......... Nontuberculous Mycobacterium [*A bacterium*] (DAVI)
NTMD .... Nuku Hiva [*French Polynesia*] [*ICAO location identifier*] (ICLI)
NTME.......... Naval Technical Mission in Europe
NtMerc........ National Mercantile Bancorp [*Associated Press*] (SAG)
NTMG .... Nutmeg Federal Savings & Loan Association [*NASDAQ symbol*] (SAG)
NTMG .... Nutmeg Fedl Svgs & Loan [*NASDAQ symbol*] (TTSB)
NTMI .... Net Ton of Molten Iron
NTMI .... Nontransmural Myocardial Infarction [*Cardiology*] (CPH)
NTMICP....... National Topographic Map Inventory Control Point
NTMJ.......... Naval Technical Mission to Japan
NTML.......... National Tillage Machinery Laboratory [*Department of Agriculture*] [*Research center*] (GRD)
NTMN .... Hiva-Oa/Atuana [*French Polynesia*] [*ICAO location identifier*] (ICLI)
NTMN .... National Thrift and Mortgage News [*A publication*]
NTMNG........ Nontoxic, Multinodular Goiter [*Medicine*] (DAVI)
NTMP.......... Nike Target Measurements Program
NTMP.......... Nitrate Motion Picture (VRA)
NTMP.......... Nitrilo-Tris-Methylene Phosphoric Acid (SAUS)
NTMP.......... Ua Pou [*French Polynesia*] [*ICAO location identifier*] (ICLI)
NTMPA........ Northern Territory Marine and Ports Authority [*Australia*]
NTMS.......... Northern Territory Medical Service (SAUS)
NTMT.......... Navigation Tender Maintenance Training (DNAB)
NTMU......... Ua Huka [*French Polynesia*] [*ICAO location identifier*] (ICLI)
NTMVSA...... National Traffic and Motor Vehicle Safety Act
NTMWG .... Nuclear Test Monitoring Working Group [*Military*]
NTN .... National Airways Corp. (Pty) Ltd. [*South Africa*] [*ICAO designator*] (FAAC)
NTN .... National TeleAccess Network [*Database of physician opportunities*]
NTN .... National Telecommunications Network [*Rockville, MD*] (TSSD)
NTN .... National Towing News [*A publication*] (EAAP)
NTN .... National Trends Network (EPA)
NTN .... Nephrotoxic Nephritis [*Medicine*]

NTN .... Network Terminal Number [*Telecommunications*]
NTN .... Network Termination Number [*Computer science*] (TNIG)
NTN .... Neutralized Twisted Nematic (VLIE)
NTN .... Neutral Twisted Nematic [*Computer science*] (PCM)
NTN .... Neutron [*A nuclear particle*] (MSA)
NTN .... Newton [*Diocesan abbreviation*] [*Melkite United States*] (TOCD)
NTN .... Newton College, Newton, MA [*Inactive*] [*OCLC symbol*] (OCLC)
NTN .... New Trade Names [*Later, NBTC*] [*A publication*]
NTN .... Normanton [*Australia*] [*Airport symbol*] (OAG)
NTN .... Northern Territory News [*A publication*]
NTN .... Norton Co., Coated Abrasive Division, R and D Department, Troy, NY [*Library symbol*] [*Library of Congress*] (LCLS)
NTN .... NTN Canada, Inc. [*Associated Press*] (SAG)
NTN .... NTN Communications [*AMEX symbol*] (TTSB)
NTN .... NTN Communications, Inc. [*AMEX symbol*] (SPSG)
NTNA .... Northern Territory Nurserymen's Association [*Australia*]
NTNC .... Nippon Television Network Corp. (SAUS)
NTNC .... NTN Canada, Inc. [*NASDAQ symbol*] (SAG)
NTNC .... NTN Cda [*NASDAQ symbol*] (TTSB)
NTN Cda ...... NTN Canada, Inc. [*Associated Press*] (SAG)
NTNCom ...... NTN Communications, Inc. [*Associated Press*] (SAG)
NTNCW .... Non-Transient Non-Community Water System (EEVL)
NTNCWS ...... Non-Transient Non-Community Water System [*Environmental Protection Agency*]
NTNF .... Norges Teknisk-Naturvitenskapelige Forskningsraad [*Online database*]
NTNG .... Nitrate Negative (VRA)
NTNV .... Narcissus Tip Necrosis Virus [*Plant pathology*]
NTNX .... NTN Communications, Inc. (SAUS)
NTNYT .... Not the New York Times [*A publication*]
NTO .... Name To (AAG)
NTO .... National Tenants Organization [*Defunct*] (EA)
NTO .... National Tourist Office (TVEL)
NTO .... National Turnover [*Economics*]
NTO .... Natural Transition Orbitals [*Atomic physics*]
NTO .... Naval Technology Office [*Arlington, VA*] (GRD)
NTO .... Naval Transport Officer
NTO .... Network Terminal Operator
NTO .... Network Terminal Option [*Computer science*]
NTO .... New Technology Opportunities [*Program*] [*US government*]
NTO .... Nitrogen Tetroxide [*Inorganic chemistry*]
NTO .... Nonorthogonal Timing Error (IAA)
NTO .... Non-Target Organism (EES)
NTO .... Nontraditional Occupations
NTO .... No Try On [*Purchaser did not have a fitting*] [*Merchandising slang*]
NTO .... Not Taken Out [*Insurance*]
NTO .... Not Tried On (SAUS)
NTO .... Nuclear Technologies Office (SAUS)
NTO .... Santo Antao [*Cape Verde Islands*] [*Airport symbol*] (OAG)
NTOC .... Naval Telecommunications Operations Center (DNAB)
NTOC .... Number to Character (SAUS)
NTOCDET ...... Naval Telecommunications Operations Center Detachment (DNAB)
NTOF .... National Traumatic Occupational Fatalities [*Surveillance system run by National Institute for Occupational Safety and Health*]
NTOFMS ...... Neutral Time-of-Flight Mass Spectroscopy [*Aviation*]
NTOFMS ...... Neutral Time-of-Flight Spectroscopy (SAUS)
NTOL .... Near-Term Operating License [*Nuclear energy*] (NRCH)
NTOL .... Normal Takeoff and Landing [*Aviation*] (MCD)
NTOMC .... National Tung Oil Marketing Cooperative [*Defunct*] (EA)
NTonHi .... Historical Society of the Tonawandas, Tonawanda, NY [*Library symbol*] [*Library of Congress*] (LCLS)
NTonL .... Union Carbide Corp., Linde Division, Tonawanda, NY [*Library symbol*] [*Library of Congress*] (LCLS)
NTonS.......... Sheridan Park Hospital, Inc., Tonawanda, NY [*Library symbol*] [*Library of Congress*] (LCLS)
NTOP .... Net2Phone [*NASDAQ symbol*] (SG)
NTOP .... New Technology Opportunities Program [*US government*]
NTORS .... Naval Torpedo Station
NTOS .... Natural Therapeutic and Osteopathic Society and Register [*British*] (DBA)
NTOTC .... National Training and Operational Technology Center [*Environmental Protection Agency*] (IID)
NTP .... Nathian [*Pakistan*] [*Seismograph station code, US Geological Survey*] (SEIS)
NTP .... National Tasking Plan [*Military*]
NTP .... National Toxicology Program [*Department of Health and Human Services*] [*Research Triangle Park, NC*]
NTP .... National Transportation Policy
NTP .... Naval Tactical Publication (NVT)
NTP .... Naval Telecommunications Procedures (NVT)
NTP .... Naval Telecommunications Publication (NVT)
NTP .... Navy Technological Projections
NTP .... Navy Training Plan (NVT)
NTP .... Near Time Processing (IAA)
NTP .... Network Terminal Protocol
NTP .... Network Terminating Point [*Telecommunications*] (TEL)
NTP .... Network Termination Processor
NTP .... Network Test Panel [*NASA*] (KSC)
NTP .... Network Time Protocol
NTP .... Network Transaction Processing [*Computer science*] (VLIE)
NTP .... Neuronal Thread Protein [*Biology*]
NTP .... Nistransair [*Republic of Moldova*] [*FAA designator*] (FAAC)
NTP .... Nitrol Paste [*Pharmacology*] (DAVI)
NTP .... Nitroprusside [*A vasodilator*]
NTP .... Nontree Pollen (SAUS)

NTP............ Nonzero Temperature Plasma
NTP............ Normal Temperature and Pressure [*Medicine*]
NTP............ Normal Temperature and Progress (SAUS)
NTP............ Notice to Proceed (KSC)
NTP............ No Title Page [*Bibliography*]
NTP............ Nuclear Target Planning (SAUS)
NTP............ Nuclear Test Plant
NTP............ Nuclear Thermal Propulsion (COE)
NTP............ Nuclear Transportation Project (EA)
NTP............ Nucleoside Triphosphate [*Biochemistry*]
NTP............ Number of Theoretical Plates
NTP............ Numerical Tape Punch
NTP............ Sodium Nitroprusside [*An antihypertensive and reagent*] [*Pharmacology*] (DAVI)
NTPA .... National Tractor Pullers Association (EA)
NTPA .... National Trotting Pony Association [*Later, ITPA*]
NTPA .... Naval Technical Proficiency Assist (NVT)
NTPA .... Netopia, Inc. [*NASDAQ symbol*] (SG)
NTPA .... Northern Territory Planning Authority [*Australia*]
NTPA .... Northern Territory Police Association [*Australia*]
NTPAC .... Northern Territory Planning Appeals Committee [*Australia*]
NtPatnt .... National Patent Development Corp. [*Associated Press*] (SAG)
NTPAW .... National Transportation Public Affairs Workshop
NTPC .... National Technical Processing Center
NTPC .... National Temperance and Prohibition Council (EA)
NTPC .... Naval Training Publications Center
NTPC .... Navy Training Plan Conference
NTPCC .... Northern Transvaal Peoples Coordinating Committee (SAUS)
NTPD .... Network Time Protocol Daemon [*Computer science*] (VLIE)
NTPD .... Normal Temperature and Pressure Dry (ACAE)
NTPD .... Normal Temperature, Pressure Differential (MCD)
NTPDLB ...... Northern Territory Plumbers and Drainers Licensing Board [*Australia*]
NTPE .... Non-Tactical Peripheral Equipment [*Military*]
NtPenn........ National Penn Bancshares, Inc. [*Associated Press*] (SAG)
NTPF .... National Tile Promotion Federation [*Defunct*] (EA)
NTPF .... Near-Term Prepositioning Forces [*Navy*]
NTPF .... Number of Terminals per Failure [*Computer science*]
NTPG .... National Textile Processors Guild [*Defunct*] (EA)
NTPH .... Nucleosidetriphosphate Pyrophosphatase [*An enzyme*]
NTPHINB...... National Trust for Places of Historic Interest or Natural Beauty [*British*] (EAIO)
NTPI............ Navy Technical Proficiency Inspection (NG)
NTPI............ Nuclear Training Proficiency Inspection [*Navy*] (DOMA)
NTP/IDCSP.. Navy Test Plan for Initial Defense Communications Satellite Program (DNAB)
NTPL.......... Navy Technical Proficiency List
NTPL.......... Nut Plate (AAG)
NTPNC........ Northern Territory Place Names Committee [*Australia*]
NTPO .... National Transuranic Waste Program Office [*Department of Energy*] (GAAI)
NTPO .... Nitrilotrimethylenephosphonic Acid [*Organic chemistry*]
NTPOC........ Navy Technical Point of Contact (DOMA)
NTPP .... Normal through Patch Panel (MCD)
NTPR .... Nuclear Targeting Policy Review (MCD)
NTPR .... Nuclear Test Personnel Review Program (SAUS)
NtPrest .... National Presto Industries, Inc. [*Associated Press*] (SAG)
NTPS .... Naval Test Pilot School
NTPS .... Near-Term Prepositioned Ships
NTPWA ...... Northern Territory Power and Water Authority [*Australia*]
NtPwADS .... National Power PLC [*Associated Press*] (SAG)
NtPwIntr ...... National Power PLC [*Associated Press*] (SAG)
NTQ .... National Trust of Queensland [*Australia*]
NTQ .... Nebennieren, Thymus, Quotient [*Test*] [*Medicine*]
NTR .... National Tape Repository (EA)
NTR .... National Transcontinental Railway [*Canada*]
NTR .... Navigational Time Reference (AAG)
NTR .... Navy Technical Representative (MCD)
NTR .... Negative True Rake (IAA)
NTR .... Nernst-Thomson Rule [*Physics*]
NTR .... Net-of-Tax Rate (ECON)
NTR .... Net Total Requirement (VLIE)
NTR .... Neutron Test Reactors (KSC)
NTR .... New Technology Report
NTR .... Next Task Register
NTR .... Nine Thousand Remote (ELAL)
NTR .... Noise Temperature Ratio (AAG)
NTR .... Non Tactical Radio (SAUS)
NTR .... Nonthermal Radiation (SAUS)
NTR .... Nontranslated Region [*Genetics*]
NTR .... Non-Typing Reperforator (SAUS)
NTR .... Nordiska Trafiksakerhetsradet [*Nordic Road Safety Council - NRSC*] [*Finland*] (EAIO)
NTR .... Nordisk Tolladministrativt Rad [*Nordic Customs Administrative Council - NCAC*] (EAIO)
NTR .... Northern Test Range (SAUS)
NTR .... No Texts Required [*Education*]
NTR .... Nothing to Report
NTR .... No Traffic Reported [*Aviation*]
NTR .... No Treatment Required [*Medicine*] (WDAA)
NTR .... Nuclear Test Reactor [*Also known as GETR*]
NTR .... Nucledyne Training Reactor (SAUS)
NTR .... Nutrition
NTR .... Rensselaer Polytechnic Institute, Troy, NY [*Library symbol*] [*Library of Congress*] (LCLS)
NTRA .... National Television Rental Association [*British*]

NTRA	National Trailer Rental Association (EA)
NTRA	National Tumor Registrars Association (EA)
NTRA	National Tyre Recycling Association [British] (DBA)
NTRA	Northern Territory Rifle Association [Australia]
N Trans S Dec...	National Transportation Safety Board Decisions [A publication] (DLA)
NTRAS	NT Remote Access Services (SAUS)
NTRB	Northern Territory Reserve Board (SAUS)
NTRC	National Tourism Review Commission
NTRC	National Toxins Research Center (DMAA)
NTRC	Natural Toxins Research Center [Public Health Service] (GRD)
NTRC	Northern Territory Rural College [Australia]
NTRDA	National Tuberculosis and Respiratory Diseases Association [Later, American Lung Association]
NT Rep	New Term Reports, English Queen's Bench [A publication] (DLA)
NT Repts	New Term Reports, English Queen's Bench [A publication] (DLA)
NTRG	New Testament Reading Guide [Collegeville, MN] [A publication] (BJA)
NTRGLB	Northern Territory Racing, Gaming and Liquor Board [Australia]
NTRL	NASA Technology Readiness Level (SSD)
NTRL	Natural
NTRL	Naval Training Research Laboratory (WDAA)
NtrlH	Natural Health Trends Corp. [Associated Press] (SAG)
NTRLLy	Naturally
NTRM	Nitrogen-Tillage-Residue Management (GNE)
NTRMA	National Tile Roofing Manufacturing Association (EA)
NTRP	No Traffic Reported [Aviation] (FAAC)
NTRS	National Therapeutic Recreation Society (EA)
NTRS	Nationwide Trailer Rental System
NTRS	Navy Tactical Reconnaissance System (ACAE)
NTRS	Northern Trust [NASDAQ symbol] (TTSB)
NTRS	Northern Trust Corp. [NASDAQ symbol] (NQ)
NTRS	Russell Sage College, Troy, NY [Library symbol] [Library of Congress] (LCLS)
NTRU	Northern Territory Rugby Union [Australia]
NTRX	Netrix Corp. [NASDAQ symbol] (SAG)
NTrZ	North Tropical Zone [Planet Jupiter]
NTS	Cirrus Air, Inc. [ICAO designator] (FAAC)
NTS	Namens Trau- und Sterberegister der Judenschaft [A publication] (BJA)
NTS	Narodno Trudovoi Soyuz [People's Labor Union] [Frankfurt, Federal Republic of Germany] (PD)
NTS	NASA Test Support
NTS	Nasotracheal Suction [Medical procedure] (DAVI)
NTS	National Technical Systems
NTS	National Technical Systems Inc. [Commercial firm]
NTS	National Thespian Society [Later, ITS] (EA)
NTS	National Traffic System [Amateur radio]
NTS	National Transportation Statistics [or Survey] [Department of Transportation]
NTS	National Transportation System [BTS] (TAG)
NTS	National Travel Survey [Census Bureau]
NTS	National Trust for Scotland (DI)
NTS	National Tulip Society [Defunct] (EA)
NTS	Naval Target Subdivision [G-2, SHAEF]
NTS	Naval Telecommunications System (NVT)
NTS	Naval Torpedo Station
NTS	Naval Training School
NTS	Naval Training Station
NTS	Naval Transportation Service [Later, MSC]
NTS	Navigational Technology Satellite (MCD)
NTS	Navigation Technology Satellite (PDAA)
NTS	Navigation Technology System (IAA)
NTS	Navigator Training Squadron [Air Force]
NTS	Navy Technology Satellite
NTS	Near Term Schedule (MCD)
NTS	Negative Torque Signal (MSA)
NTS	Network/TDRSS [Tracking and Data Relay Satellite System] [NASA] (MCD)
NTS	Nevada Test Site [Department of Energy]
NTS	Nevada Test Site, Mercury, Nevada (SAUS)
NTS	New Tube Shelter [British]
NTS	New Typesetting System (SAUS)
NTS	Night Targeting System (SAUS)
NTS	Nitroglycerin Transdermal System [Pharmacy]
NTS	Nontariff Size
NTS	Nontemporary Storage [Personal property]
NTS	Non-Traffic Sensitive [Costs] [Telecommunications]
NTS	Nontranscribed Spacer [Genetics]
NTS	Nordiske Teleansattes Samarbeidsorgan [Nordic Telecommunications Association] (EAIO)
NTS	Notch Tensile Strength (OA)
Nts	Notes (EBF)
NTS	Notes [Finance]
NTS	Not to Scale [Drafting]
NTS	No Turn Signal (SAUS)
NTS	Nuclear Test Site (MCD)
NTS	Nuclear Test Stage (AAG)
NTS	Nucleus Tractus Solitarii [Brain anatomy]
NTS	Number of Theoretical Stages [Chemical engineering]
NTS	Nutrition Today Society [Defunct] (EA)
NTS	Samaritan Hospital, Troy, NY [Library symbol] [Library of Congress] (LCLS)
NTSA	National Tay-Sachs Association [Later, NTSAD] (EA)
NTSA	National Technical Services Association (EA)
NTSA	National Traffic Safety Agency [Federal Highway Administration]
NTSA	National Trails System Act (COE)
NTSA	National Training Systems Association (EA)
NTSA	National Transportation Safety Association [Defunct] (EA)
NTSA	National T-Shirt Association (EA)
NTSA	National Tuberous Sclerosis Association (EA)
NTSA	Naval Telecommunications System Architect (MCD)
NTSA	Navy Tactical Support Activity (DNAB)
NTSA	Northern Territory Softball Association [Australia]
NTSA	Norway Technical Science Academy
NTSAD	National Tay-Sachs and Allied Diseases Association (EA)
NTSAI	National Target Shooting Association of Ireland
NtSanit	National Sanitary Supply Co. [Associated Press] (SAG)
NTSB	National Traffic Safety Bureau
NTSB	National Transportation Safety Board [Independent government agency] [Washington, DC]
NTSB	Northern Territory Surveyor Board [Australia]
NTSC	National Science and Technology Council (DDC)
NTSC	National Tax Strike Coalition (EA)
NTSC	National Technical Systems, Inc. [NASDAQ symbol] (NQ)
NTSC	National Television Standard Code [Video equipment] (RDA)
NTSC	National Television Standards Committee
NTSC	National Television System Committee [Formed in 1936]
NTSC	Natl Technical Sys [NQS] (TTSB)
NTSC	Naval Training Systems Center [Orlando, FL]
NTSC	Never The Same Color (SAUS)
NTSC	Never Twice the Same Color (SAUS)
NTSC	Nonextrusion Texturized Soy Concentrate
NTSC	Northern Telecom Systems Corp. (SAUS)
NTSC	North Texas State College [Later, North Texas State University]
NTSCH	Naval Training School
NTSD	Normal Theory Sampling Distribution (SAUS)
NTSDS	Near-Term Swimmer Defense System
NTSE	Naval Telecommunications System Engineer (MCD)
NTSE	Nontactical Support Equipment (MCD)
NTSEA	National Trade Show Exhibitors Association [Later, IEA] (EA)
NTS EIS	Nevada Test Site Environmental Impact Statement
NtSemi	National Semiconductor Corp. [Associated Press] (SAG)
NTSF	National Technical Scholarship Foundation (AEBS)
NTSF	Nonextrusion Texturized Soy Flour
NTSH	Near-Term Scout Helicopter [Army]
NTSI	National Tire Svcs [NASDAQ symbol] (TTSB)
NTSI	National Tribunal of Second Instance [Catholic Church] [Australia]
NTSI	Nonextrusion Texturized Soy Isolate
NTSK	Nordiska Tele-Satelit Kommitton [Norway]
NTSL	Nonintegrated Two-Stage Liquid (ABAC)
NTSM	Saint Mary's Hospital, Troy, NY [Library symbol] [Library of Congress] (LCLS)
Ntsmrt	Netsmart Technologies, Inc. [Associated Press] (SAG)
NTSO	NASA Test Support Office (KSC)
NTSR	National Tunis Sheep Registry (EA)
NTSR	NetStar, Inc. [NASDAQ symbol] (SAG)
NTSRI	National Tunis Sheep Registry (NTPA)
NTSRP	Nontechnical Services Real Property
NTSRVA	Nevada Test Site Radiation Victim Association (EA)
NTSSC	Northern Territory School Sports Council [Australia]
NTSSO	Nevada Test Site Safety Office (SAUS)
NTST	Netsmart Technologies, Inc. [NASDAQ symbol] (SAG)
NTSTN	Naval Telecommunications System Test Node (CAAL)
NtSvIn	National Service Industries, Inc. [Associated Press] (SAG)
NTT	Nasotracheal Tube [Medicine] (DAVI)
NTT	National Training Team [Operated by the Helen Keller National Center for Deaf-Blind Youths and Adults (HKNC)] (PAZ)
NTT	National Tree Trust (WPI)
NTT	Nearly Total Thyroidectomy [Medicine] (DMAA)
NTT	New England Telephone and Telegraph Co. (SAUS)
NTT	New Technology Telescopes [Under development]
NTT	Nippon Tel & Tel ADS [NYSE symbol] (TTSB)
NTT	Nippon Telegraph & Telephone Co. [NYSE symbol] (SAG)
NTT	Nippon Telegraph & Telephone Corp. [Telecommunications and videotex company] [Japan]
NTT	Nippon Telephone and Telegraph (SAUS)
NTT	Non-Tactical Tape [Military]
NTT	Nuiatoputapu [Tonga] [Airport symbol] (OAG)
NTT	Numbered Test Trunk
NTT	Number Theoretic Transform (MHDI)
NTTA	National Tobacco Tax Association (EA)
NTTAB	Northern Territory Totalizator Agency Board [Australia]
NTTAWWT	Not That Theres Anything Wrong With That (SAUS)
NTTB	Bora Bora/Motu-Mute [French Polynesia] [ICAO location identifier] (ICLI)
NTTBR	Nineteen Thirty-Two Buick Registry (EA)
NTTC	National Tank Truck Carriers [Alexandria, VA] (EA)
NTTC	National Technology Transfer Center [NASA]
NTTC	Naval Technical Training Center
NTTC	NAVFAC [Naval Facilities Engineering Command] Technical Training Center
NTTCIW	National Technical Task Committee on Industrial Wastes
NTTE	Non-Tactical Training Equipment [Military]
NTTE	Tetiaroa [French Polynesia] [ICAO location identifier] (ICLI)
NTTF	Networking and Telecommunications Task Force [Computer science] (TNIG)
NTTF	Network Test and Training Facility [Goddard Space Flight Center]
NTTFX	Hancock(J) Global Technology [Mutual fund ticker symbol] (SG)
NTTG	Rangiroa [French Polynesia] [ICAO location identifier] (ICLI)

NTTH	Huahine/Fare [*French Polynesia*] [*ICAO location identifier*] (ICLI)
NTT-IT	Nippon Telegraph and Telephone-Intelligent Technology (SAUS)
NTTLC.........	Northern Territory Trades and Labor Council [*Australia*]
NTTM.........	Moorea/Temae [*French Polynesia*] [*ICAO location identifier*] (ICLI)
NTTO	Hao [*French Polynesia*] [*ICAO location identifier*] (ICLI)
NTTP..........	Maupiti [*French Polynesia*] [*ICAO location identifier*] (ICLI)
NTTPC	Nippon Telegraph & Telephone Public Corp. [*Telecommunications*] (IAA)
NTT Pupl Corp...	Nippon Telegraph and Telephone Public Corp. (SAUS)
NTTR	Naval Torpedo Testing Range
NTTR	Nontactical Telecommunications Requirement [*Army*] (AABC)
NTTR	Raiatea/Uturoa [*French Polynesia*] [*ICAO location identifier*] (ICLI)
NTTRL	National Tissue Typing Reference Laboratory (PDAA)
NTTS..........	National Technology Transfer Center
NTTS..........	Northern Territory Teaching Service (SAUS)
NTTT..........	Tahiti [*French Polynesia*] [*ICAO location identifier*] (ICLI)
NTTTTI........	National Truck Tank and Trailer Tank Institute [*Later, Tank Conference of the Truck Trailer Manufacturers Association*]
NTTX..........	Mururoa [*French Polynesia*] [*ICAO location identifier*] (ICLI)
NTU	National Taxpayers Union (EA)
NTU	National Technological University [*Fort Collins, CO*]
NTU	National Tenants Union [*Defunct*] (EA)
NTU	Naval Training Unit
NTU	Navigation Training Unit (SAUS)
NTU	Navy Toxicology Unit
NTU	Nephelometric Turbidity Unit [*Analytical chemistry*]
NTU	Network Terminating [*or Termination*] Unit
NTU	New Threat Upgrade [*Military*] (CAAL)
NTU	Nishi Tokyo University (SAUS)
NTU	Nonimmune Transfer Utensil [*i.e., spoon*] [*Slang*]
NTU	Nordisk Trafikskoleunion [*Nordic Union of Motor Schools Associations - NUMSA*] [*Finland*] (EAIO)
NTU	Normal Trading Unit
NTU	Not Taken Up
NTU	Nuclear Training Unit (MCD)
NTU	Number of Transfer Units
NTU	Oceana, VA [*Location identifier*] [*FAA*] (FAAL)
NTUC	National Trades Union Congress (NADA)
NTUC	National Trade Union Congress [*Singapore*]
NTUC	National Trade Union Council [*Hungary*]
NTUC	National Trade Union Council for Human Rights (EA)
NTUC	Nigerian Trade Union Congress
NTUC	Nyasaland Trade Union Congress
NTuc	Tuckahoe Public Library, Tuckahoe, NY [*Library symbol*] [*Library of Congress*] (LCLS)
NTucW.......	Westchester County Historical Society, Tuckahoe, NY [*Library symbol*] [*Library of Congress*] (LCLS)
NTULC	Negro Trade Union Leadership Council
NTuPSC	Sunmount Development Center, Staff Library, Tupper Lake, NY [*Library symbol*] [*Library of Congress*] (LCLS)
NTUV	Vahitahi [*French Polynesia*] [*ICAO location identifier*] (ICLI)
NTuxp	Tuxedo Park Library, Tuxedo Park, NY [*Library symbol*] [*Library of Congress*] (LCLS)
NTuxpI........	International Paper Co., Corporate Research and Development Division, Technical Information Center, Tuxedo Park, NY [*Library symbol*] [*Library of Congress*] (LCLS)
NTV............	Nerve Tissue Vaccine [*Medicine*] (DMAA)
NTV............	Nervous Tissue Vaccine (AAMN)
NTVC..........	Neurotransmitter Vesicle [*Medicine*] (MELL)
NTV............	Nippon Television Network Corp. [*Japan*]
NTV............	Nonlinear Thickness Variation (SAUS)
NTV............	Nontactical Vehicle [*Army*]
NTV............	NTV Oil Services Industries, Inc. [*Vancouver Stock Exchange symbol*]
NTVA	Nondeterministic Time Variant Automation [*Mathematics*] (IAA)
NTVEI.........	New Technical and Vocational Education Initiative (AIE)
NTVES	Northern Territory Voluntary Euthanasia Society (SAUS)
NTVLRO.......	National Television Licensing and Records Office [*British*]
NTVS	Navy Television System
NTVT..........	Non-Toxic Vinyl Tubing
NTVU	National Trust Volunteer Unit [*British*] (EAIO)
NTW	Navigator Training Wing [*Military*]
NTW	Navy Theater Wide
NTW...........	Non-Pressure Thermit Welding (PDAA)
NTW...........	Normal Tool Wear
NTW...........	Nose, Tail, Waist [*Aviation*]
NTW...........	Not to Worry (SAUS)
NTWA	National Trust of Western Australia
NTWA	National Turf Writers Association (EA)
NtwExp	Network Express, Inc. [*Associated Press*] (SAG)
NTWH	National Theatre Workshop of the Handicapped (EA)
NTWISTDG...	Notwithstanding (SAUS)
NTWK	Network (MSA)
NTWK	Network Long Distance [*NASDAQ symbol*] (TTSB)
NTWK	Network Long Distance, Inc. [*NASDAQ symbol*] (SAG)
NtwkC........	Network Connection, Inc. [*Associated Press*] (SAG)
NtwkCn.......	Network Connection, Inc. [*Associated Press*] (SAG)
NtwkEq.......	Network Equipment Technologies, Inc. [*Associated Press*] (SAG)
NtwkG........	Network General Corp. [*Associated Press*] (SAG)
NtwkLng......	Network Long Distance, Inc. [*Associated Press*] (SAG)
NtwkPeri.....	Network Periphrals, Inc. [*Associated Press*] (SAG)
NtwkSix	Network Six, Inc. [*Associated Press*] (SAG)
NtWnLf	National Western Life Insurance Co. [*Associated Press*] (SAG)
NTWR	New Threat Warning Receiver (ACAE)
NTWRK........	Network
NTWRKNG ...	Networking
NTWS	New Threat Warning System [*Military*]
NTWS	Nontrack while Scan
NtWst..........	National Westminster Bank Ltd. [*Associated Press*] (SAG)
NtWstmin	National Westminster Bank Ltd. [*Associated Press*] (SAG)
nt wt	Net Weight (WDAA)
NT WT	Net Weight
NTX	Naltrexone [*Medicine*] (MELL)
NTX	National Teletypewriter Exchange (IAA)
NTX	Naval Teletypewriter Exchange [*Formerly, NTE*]
NTX	Neonatal Thymectomy [*Medicine*]
NTX	Networking and Expansion [*Computer science*] (PCM)
NTX	Northern Air Service, Inc. [*ICAO designator*] (FAAC)
NTX	Nuveen Texas Quality Income [*NYSE symbol*] (SPSG)
NTX	Nuveen TX Qual Income Muni [*NYSE symbol*] (TTSB)
NTXQI........	Nuveen Texas Quality Income [*Associated Press*] (SAG)
NTY	Not This Year (SAUS)
NTY	Sun City [*South Africa*] [*Airport symbol*] (OAG)
N-type.........	Jungian intuitive type (SAUS)
NT YT	Not Yet (SAUS)
NTZ	Indstrie Natuzzi ADS [*NYSE symbol*] (TTSB)
NTZ	Industrie Natuzzi [*NYSE symbol*] (SPSG)
NTZ	Iraq-Saudi Arabia Neutral Zone [*ANSI three-letter standard code*] (CNC)
NTZ	Nitazoxanide [*Medicine*] (TAD)
NTZ	Normal Transformation Zone (DMAA)
NTZ	Northern Transgressive Zone [*Geology*]
NTZ	North Temperate Zone [*Planet Jupiter*]
NTZ	No Transgression Zone (SAUS)
NU	Astronomy Department Library, Nanjing University (SAUS)
NU	Lipnur [*Indonesia*] [*ICAO aircraft manufacturer identifier*] (ICAO)
NU	Nachalnik Uprovlenia [*Chief of Directorate*] [*Soviet military rank*]
NU	Name Unknown
nU	Nanounit [*One billionth of a standard unit*]
NU	National Union (EA)
NU	National Unity Party [*British*] [*Political party*]
NU	NATO Unclassified (NATG)
nu	Nauru [*MARC country of publication code*] [*Library of Congress*] (LCCP)
NU	Nebraska University (MCD)
NU	Nebraska Unofficial Reports [*A publication*] (DLA)
NU	Neurologically Unique
NU	Neurology (DAVI)
NU	New Ulm [*Diocesan abbreviation*] [*Minnesota*] (TOCD)
NU	New Uses [*Research test*] [*Psychology*]
Nu	Ngultrum [*Monetary unit*] [*Bhutan*] (BARN)
NU	Nihon University
NU	Niigata University (SAUS)
NU	Niue [*ANSI two-letter standard code*] (CNC)
NU	Nonuniform (SAUS)
NU	Northeast Utilities [*NYSE symbol*] (SPSG)
NU	Northern Union [*Rugby*] [*British*] (DAS)
NU	Northrop Unit [*Of hydrolytic enzyme activity*]
NU	North Up [*Automotive engineering*]
NU	Norwich Union (WDAA)
NU	Norwich University (SAUS)
NU	Nose Up [*Aviation*]
NU	Nothing Unsatisfactory (MHDB)
NU	Not Used
NU	No Umbra (SAUS)
Nu	Nucleolus [*Cytology*]
Nu	Nucleophile
nu	Nude [*Mouse*] [*Medicine*] (DMAA)
NU	Nu-Gro Corp. [*Toronto Stock Exchange symbol*]
NU	Nullified Unpostable [*Computer science*]
Nu	Numbers [*Old Testament book*] (BJA)
NU	Number Unobtainable [*Telecommunications*]
Nu.............	Nusselt Number [*IUPAC*]
NU	Southwest Airlines [*ICAO designator*] (AD)
NU0B	Numeric 0 Bit (SAUS)
NU1B	Numeric 1 Bit (SAUS)
NUA	Nations Unies des Animaux [*United Animal Nations - UAN*] (EA)
NUA	Net Unrealized Appreciation Tax
NUA	Network User Address
NUA	Network Users Association [*Defunct*] (EA)
NUA	Nonylundecyladipat (SAUS)
NUA	Not Under the Act
NUA	Nuclear Agency [*Army*]
NUA	Nuna Air AS [*Denmark*] [*ICAO designator*] (FAAC)
NUAA	NSW Users and AIDS Association (SAUS)
NUAAW.......	National Union of Agricultural and Allied Workers [*British*]
NUABA........	National United Affiliated Beverage Association (EA)
NUAC	National Urban Affairs Council
NUAD	Nucleus Average Optical Density [*Microscopy*]
NUADC........	National Underwater Accident Data Center
NUAF Material...	Non-Urea-Adduct-Forming Material (SAUS)
NUAH	Nutrition and Health
NUANS........	Newly Upgraded Automated Name Search (SAUS)
NUAT	Nordisk Union for Alkoholfri Trafikk [*Scandinavian Union for Non-Alcoholic Traffic - SUNAT*] (EA)
NUATFAC....	Nordiska Unionen for Arbetsledare, Tekniska Funktionarer och andra Chefer [*Nordic Confederation of Supervisors, Technicians and Other Managers*] (EAIO)
NUB	National Union of Busmen [*British*]
NUB	Navy Uniform Board (DNAB)

NUB	Net Units Billed (TIMI)
NUB	Northumberland Mines Ltd. [*Toronto Stock Exchange symbol*]
NUB	North University Building
Nub	Nubes [*Clouds*] [*of Aristophanes*] [*Classical studies*] (OCD)
nub	Nubian [*MARC language code*] [*Library of Congress*] (LCCP)
NUBA	National UHF [*Ultrahigh Frequency*] Broadcasters Association (EA)
NUBC	National Uniform-Billing Committee [*Insurance*] (DAVI)
NUBE	National Union of Bank Employees [*Later, Banking, Insurance, and Finance Union*] (DCTA)
NUBF	National Union of British Fishermen
NUBIC	Nuclear Bunkered Instrumentation Center (MCD)
NUBICWOPS	Nuclear, Biological, and Chemical Warfare Operations [*Military*]
NUBLU	New Basic Logic Unit [*Computer science*] (MHDI)
NUBOMCWKT	National Union of Blastfurnacemen, Ore Miners, Coke Workers, and Kindred Trades [*British*] (DCTA)
NUBS	National Unemployment Benefit System [*Department of Health and Social Security*] [*British*]
NUBSO	National Union of Boot and Shoe Operatives [*British*]
NUBTC	National Union of Boot Top Cutters [*British*]
NUC	National Underseas Research Center (CARB)
NUC	National Unification Council [*Philippines*] [*Political party*] (FEA)
NUC	National Union Catalog: Pre-1956 Imprints [*A publication*]
NUC	National Union of Carriers [*British*]
NUC	National University Consortium for Telecommunications in Teaching (EA)
NUC	National Urban Coalition (EA)
NUC	Naval Undersea Center [*Later, NOSC*] (MCD)
NUC	Naval Undersea Research and Development Center [*Marine science*] (OSRA)
NUC	Navy Unit Commendation [*Military decoration*]
NUC	Neutral Unit of Construction (TVEL)
NUC	New University Conference
NUC	Nipissing University College (SAUS)
NUC	Nonspecific Ulcerative Colitis [*Medicine*] (MELL)
NUC	Non-Uniformity Compensation (ACAE)
NUC	Non-Uniformity Correction
NUC	Not Under Command (SAUS)
NUC	Not Under Control (SAUS)
nuc	Nuclear (MILB)
NUC	Nuclear
NUC	Nucleated
Nuc	[*A*] Nucleoside [*Also, N*]
NUC	Nucleus (WDAA)
NUC	Nucorr Petroleums Ltd. [*Toronto Stock Exchange symbol*]
NUC	Nulliparous Uterine Cervix [*Medicine*] (MELL)
NUC	Nuveen California Quality Income Municipal [*NYSE symbol*] (SPSG)
NUC	Nuveen CA Qual Income Muni [*NYSE symbol*] (TTSB)
NUC	San Clemente Island, CA [*Location identifier*] [*FAA*] (FAAL)
NUCA	National Utility Contractors' Association (EA)
NUCAA	National United Church Association of America (EA)
NUCAL	National Union Catalog Author List
NUCAP	Nuclear Cannon Projectile [*Army*]
NUCAP	Nuclear Capabilities Data Base (SAUS)
NUCAP	Nuclear Capability [*Military*]
NUCAP	Nuclear Capability Report (CINC)
Nucaps	National Union of Civil and Public Servants [*British*] (DBA)
Nu-car Prep	New-car Preparation (SAUS)
NUCAS	Nuclear Authentication System
NUCAW	National Union of Clerks and Administrative Workers [*British*]
NUCBO	National Uniform Certification of Building Operators (EA)
NUCC	North Up Cursor Centered [*Automotive engineering*]
NUCD	Nuclear Deployment (SAUS)
NUCDEF	Nuclear Defense (AABC)
NUCDETS	Nuclear Detonation Detection and Reporting System (AABC)
NUCDSK	New Cell Disk (SAUS)
Nuc E	Nuclear Engineer
NUCEA	National University Continuing Education Association (EA)
NUCEWA	Nuclear Weapons Availability (SAUS)
NUCEX	Nuclear Exercise [*Also, NUKEX*] (NVT)
NUCFO	Nuclear Force Posture
NUCH	Nucha [*Nape of the Neck*] [*Latin*] (ROG)
NUCIA	National Union of Cooperative Insurance Agents [*British*]
NUCINT	Nuclear Intelligence (MCD)
Nuci Sci Technol	Nuclear Science and Technology (SAUS)
NUCISE	National Union of Cooperative Insurance Society Employees [*British*]
NUCL	Nuclear
NUCL	Nucleus
Nucl Austral Bull	Nuclear Australia Bulletin (SAUS)
Nuc L Bull	Nuclear Law Bulletin [*A publication*] (ILCA)
Nucl Data	Nuclear Data (SAUS)
NUCLE	Nuclear
Nuclear Reg Rep (CCH)	Nuclear Regulation Reports (Commerce Clearing House) [*A publication*] (DLA)
Nucl Engng&Des	Nuclear Engineering and Design (SAUS)
NUCLENOR	Controles Nucleares del Norte, SA [*Spain*]
Nucl Eur	Nuclear Europe (SAUS)
NUCLEX	International Nuclear Industrial Fair and Technical Meeting (SAUS)
NUCLEX	Nuclear Industries Exhibition
NUCLEX	Nuclear Loadout Exercise [*Military*] (NVT)
Nucl Fusion Plasma Phys	Nuclear Fusion and Plasma Physics (SAUS)
Nucl Instrum	Nuclear Instrumentation (SAUS)
Nucl Instrum Methods A	Nuclear Instruments and Methods A (SAUS)
Nucl Instrum Methods B	Nuclear Instruments and Methods B (SAUS)
Nucl Mater Manage	Nuclear Materials Management (SAUS)
Nucl News	Nuclear News (SAUS)
Nucl Phys	Nuclear Physics (MEC)
Nucl Prof	Nuclear Professional (SAUS)
Nucl Res Cent	Nuclear Research Center (SAUS)
Nucl Sci Appl B Phys Sci	Nuclear Science and Applications, Series B: Physical Sciences (SAUS)
Nucl Sci Appl Ser A	Nuclear Science and Applications. Series A. Biological Science (SAUS)
Nucl Tech	Nuclear Techniques (SAUS)
Nucl Tracks Methods Instrum and Appl	Nuclear Tracks. Methods, Instruments and Applications (SAUS)
NUCM	North Up Cursor Moving [*Automotive engineering*]
NUCM	Nuclear Metals [*NASDAQ symbol*] (TTSB)
NUCM	Nuclear Metals, Inc. [*NASDAQ symbol*] (NQ)
NUCMATTS	Nuclear Materials Transportation Tracking System (SAUS)
NUCMC	National Union Catalog of Manuscript Collections [*Library of Congress*]
NucMet	Nuclear Metals, Inc. [*Associated Press*] (SAG)
NUCMUN	Nuclear Munitions (RDA)
NUCO	National Union of Certified Officers [*British*]
NUCO	NuCo2 Inc. [*NASDAQ symbol*] (TTSB)
NUCO	Nucorp, Inc. (SAUS)
NUCO	Numerical Code (NATG)
NUCO	Numerical Coding (SAUS)
NuCo2	NuCo2, Inc. [*Associated Press*] (SAG)
NUCOINS	Nutrition Consumer Information System (SAUS)
NUCOL	Numerical Control Language [*Computer science*] (PDAA)
NUCOM	Nuclear Effects on Joint Force Communications (MCD)
NUCOM	Numerical Contouring Mechanism
NUCOR	Nuclear Corporation (SAUS)
NUCOR	Nuclear Development Corporation of South Africa (SAUS)
Nucor	Nucor Corp. [*Associated Press*] (SAG)
NUCP	National Union of Czechoslovak Protestants in America and Canada [*Defunct*] (EA)
NUCP	New Century Entertainment Corp. (SAUS)
NUC PHY	Nuclear Physics (WDAA)
NUCPS	National Union of Civil and Public Servants [*British*]
NUCPWR	Nuclear Powered (NVT)
NucReaOpBasBad	Nuclear Reactor Operator, Basic Badge [*Military decoration*] (AABC)
NucReaOpFCBad	Nuclear Reactor Operator, First-Class Badge [*Military decoration*] (AABC)
NucReaOpSCBad	Nuclear Reactor Operator, Second-Class Badge [*Military decoration*] (AABC)
NucReaOpSftSupvBad	Nuclear Reactor Operator, Shift Supervisor Badge [*Military decoration*] (AABC)
Nuc Reg Com	Nuclear Regulatory Commission (SAUS)
NUCREP	Nuclear Damage Report (AABC)
NUCS	National Union of Christian Schools [*Later, CSI*] (EA)
NUCS	National Union of Club Stewards [*British*] (DBA)
NUCSAM	Nuclear Surface-to-Air Missile (NVT)
NucSciAb	Nuclear Science Abstracts (SAUS)
NUCSE	National Union of Czechoslovak Students in Exile (EA)
NUCSEQ	Nucleotide Sequencing Search System [*NIH/EPA Chemical Information System*] [*Database*]
NUCSTAT	Nuclear Operational Status (SAUS)
NUCSTAT	Nuclear Operational Status Report (NATG)
NUCUAA	National United Church Ushers Association of America (EA)
NUCURES	Northeastern University Center for Urban and Regional Economic Studies [*Research center*] (RCD)
NUCWA	Nuclear Weapons Accounting (MCD)
NUCWAL	Nuclear Weapons Allocation Logistics (SAUS)
NUCWAR	Nuclear War
NUCWARN	Nuclear Warning Message [*Military*] (ADDR)
NUCWEP	Nuclear Weapons (SAUS)
NUCWPN	Nuclear Weapon (AABC)
NUCWPNSTRACEN	Nuclear Weapons Training Center
NUCY	New Century Bank Corp. (SAUS)
NUD	Adak, AK [*Location identifier*] [*FAA*] (FAAL)
NUD	En Nahud [*Sudan*] [*Airport symbol*] (AD)
NUD	National Union of the Deaf [*British*]
NUD	Naval Unit Disseminator (RDA)
NUD	Nebraska University Disease or N. Underdahl Disease [*A disease of swine named both for the place where it was originally identified and for the person who isolated the causative agent*]
NUD	Nonulcer Dyspepsia [*Gastroenterology*] (DAVI)
NUD	Non-Update (SAUS)
nud	nudism (SAUS)
nud	nudist (SAUS)
NUDA & GO	National Union of Domestic Appliances and General Operatives [*British*] (DBA)
NUDAC	Nuclear Data Center (IAA)
NUDAGMW	National Union of Domestic Appliance and General Metal-Workers [*British*] (DCTA)
NUDAGO	National Union of Domestic Appliances & General Operatives (WDAA)
NUDAP	Nuclear Detonating Data Points (MCD)
NUDAW	National Union of Shop Distributive and Allied Workers [*British*]
NUDBTW	National Union of Dyers, Bleachers, and Textile Workers [*British*] (DCTA)
NUDET	Nuclear Detection (MCD)
NUDET	Nuclear Detonation (COE)
NUDET	Nuclear Detonation Evaluation Technique (MCD)
NUDET Rpt	Nuclear Detonation Report (SAUS)
NUDETS	Nuclear Detection and Reporting System
NUDETS	Nuclear Detection System (SAUS)

NUDETS........ Nuclear Detonation Detection and Reporting System
NUDETS........ Nuclear Detonation Reporting System (SAUS)
NUDIA.......... Nutrio et Dieta. European Review of Nutrition and Dietetics (SAUS)
NUDO........... National United Democratic Organization [Namibia] [Political party] (PPW)
NUDOR........ Numerical Data Processor (SAUS)
NUDORE........ Nuclear Doctrine Organization and Equipment (MCD)
NUDWSS........ National Union of Docks, Wharves, and Shipping Staffs [British]
NUE............. Net Units Entered (TIMI)
NUE............. Nitrogen Utilization Efficiency [Ecology]
NUE............. Niue [Niue Island] [Seismograph station code, US Geological Survey] (SEIS)
NUE............. Nucor Corp. [NYSE symbol] (SPSG)
NUE............. Nuremberg [Germany] [Airport symbol] (OAG)
NUEA.......... National University Extension Association [Later, NUCEA] (EA)
NUERA......... Nuclear Extended Range Aircraft [Proposed] [Air Force]
NUESNA....... National Union of Eritrean Students - North America (EA)
NUET........... National Union of Elementary Teachers [British]
NuevEn........ Nuevo Energy Co. [Associated Press] (SAG)
NUEW.......... National Union of Eritrean Women - North America (EA)
NUEXCO........ Nuclear Exchange Corp. (SAUS)
NUF............. National Ulcer Foundation (EA)
NUF............. National Unifying Force [Zimbabwe] [Political party] (PPW)
NUF............. National Union of Firemen [British] (DAS)
NUF............. National Unity Front [Poland] [Political party] (PPW)
NUF............. National Urban Fellows (EA)
NUF............. Natural Uranium Fuel
NUF............. Noise Ulterior Flux (SAUS)
NUF............. Nonwoven Unidirectional-glass Fibre (SAUS)
NUF............. Nordisk Urologisk Forening [Scandinavian Association of Urology - SAU] (EAIO)
NUF............. Nuveen Florida Quality Income Municipal [NYSE symbol] (SPSG)
NUF............. Nuveen FL Qual Income Muni [NYSE symbol] (TTSB)
NUFAC......... Nuclear Weapons Planning Factors for Land Combat Forces (SAUS)
NUFAM........ Nuclear Fire Planning and Assessment Model (MCD)
NUFAS......... NATO UHF Frequency Assignment System (SAUS)
NUFCOR........ Nuclear Fuels Corp. (SAUS)
NUFCW........ National Union of Funeral and Cemetery Workers [British] (BI)
NUFD.......... Naval Unit, Fort Detrick [Maryland]
NUFDC........ Northgate Universal Floppy Drive Controller [Computer science]
NUFGW........ National Union of Flint Glassworkers [British] (DBA)
NUFI........... National Unfinished Furniture Institute [Defunct] (EA)
Nufi........... Nuffield College, Oxford (SAUS)
NUFLAT........ National Union of Footwear, Leather, and Allied Trades [British] (DCTA)
NUFLV......... National United Front for the Liberation of Vietnam (EA)
NUFO.......... New Focus [NASDAQ symbol]
NUFON......... Northern UFO Network [British]
NUFP.......... Not Used for Production (AAG)
NUFP.......... Number of Uncorrected Flight Plans (SAA)
NUFRONLIV... National United Front for the Liberation of Vietnam (EA)
NUFS.......... National United Front of Somalia [Political party] (EY)
NUFS.......... National Utility Financial Statement Model [Department of Energy] (GFGA)
NUFSO......... National Union of Funeral Service Operatives [British] (DI)
NUFTIC........ Nuclear Fuels Technology Information Center (DIT)
NUFTO......... National Union of Furniture Trade Operatives [British]
NUFUCO........ Nuclear Fuel Cost (PDAA)
NUG........... Federation of NCR [NCR Corp.] User Groups (EA)
NUG........... National Union of Glovers [British]
NUG........... Necrotizing Ulcerative Gingivitis [Dentistry]
NUG........... Nonutility Generator
nug........... nuggar (SAUS)
NUGMW....... National Union of General and Municipal Workers [British]
NUGO.......... Nugget Oil Corp. (SAUS)
NUGP.......... Nominal Unit Ground Pressure (SAUS)
NUGS.......... Nonutility Generating Source
NUGSAT....... National Union of Gold, Silver, and Allied Trades [British] (DCTA)
NUGT.......... Nugget Exploration, Inc. (SAUS)
NUH........... National Union for the Homeless (EA)
NUHADI....... Nuclear Helicopter Air Density Indicating [System] [Army]
NUHC......... Nu Horizons Electronics [NASDAQ symbol] (TTSB)
NUHC......... Nu-Horizons Electronics Corp. [NASDAQ symbol] (SAG)
NUHELI........ Nuclear Helicopter Lift Indicator (KSC)
NUHKW....... National Union of Hosiery and Knitwear Workers [British] (DCTA)
NuHoriz....... Nu-Horizons Electronics Corp. [Associated Press] (SAG)
NUHS.......... New Utrecht High School (SAUS)
NUI........... National University of Ireland
NUI........... NetWare Users International
NUI........... Networks Unlimited, Inc. [Defunct] (EA)
NUI........... Network User Identifier [or Identification] [Password]
NUI........... Norwegian Underwater Institute (SAUS)
NUI........... Notebook User Interface [Penpoint] [Computer science]
NUI........... NUI Corp. [NYSE symbol] (SPSG)
NUI........... Nuiqsut [Alaska] [Airport symbol] (OAG)
NUI........... Number User Identification (DMAA)
NUI........... Patuxent River, MD [Location identifier] [FAA] (FAAL)
NUIA.......... National United Italian Associations (EA)
NUIC.......... National Urban Indian Council (EA)
NUIR.......... National Union for Independence and Revolution [Chad] [Political party]
NUIS.......... National Union of Iraqi Students [British] (DI)
NUIS.......... Navy Unit Identification System (NVT)
NUIU.......... New University Industrial Unit [New University of Ulster] [Research center] [British]

NUIW.......... National Union of Insurance Workers [British] (DCTA)
NUJ........... National Union of Journalists [British]
NUJ........... Nuveen New Jersey Quality Income Municipal (SAUS)
NUJMB........ Northern Universities Joint Matriculation Board (AIE)
NUK........... Nukutavake [French Polynesia] [Airport symbol] (OAG)
NUKE.......... Nuclear
nuke leak.... nuclear radioactive leak (SAUS)
NUKES........ Nuclear Explosives (SAUS)
NUKEX........ Nuclear Exercise [Also, NUCEX] (NVT)
NUKFAT....... National Union of Knitwear, Footwear & Apparel Trades (WDAA)
NUKO......... Nuko Information Sys [NASDAQ symbol] (TTSB)
NUKO......... Nuko Information Systems, Inc. [NASDAQ symbol] (SAG)
NukoInfo...... Nuko Information Systems Inc. [Associated Press] (SAG)
NuKote........ Nu-Kote Holding, Inc. [Associated Press] (SAG)
NUL........... Dummy Device (SAUS)
NUL........... National and University Library [Israel] (BJA)
NUL........... National Union for Liberation [Philippines] [Political party] (PPW)
NUL........... National Urban League (EA)
NUL........... New Universal Library [A publication]
NUL........... New Upper Lateral [Botany]
NUL........... Nihon University [UTLAS symbol]
NUL........... No Device (SAUS)
NUL........... Non-GSE [Ground Support Equipment] Utilization List [NASA] (NASA)
NUL........... Northwestern University Library (SAUS)
NUL........... No Upper Limit (MHDW)
NUL........... Nu-Lady Gold Mines [Vancouver Stock Exchange symbol]
NUL........... Nulato [Alaska] [Airport symbol] (OAG)
NUL........... Null (OSI)
NUL........... Null Character [Keyboard] [Computer science]
NULAC........ Nuclear Liquid Air Cycle Engine
NULACE........ Nuclear Liquid Air Cycle Engine
NULBA........ National United Licensees Beverage Association [Later, NUABA] (EA)
NULC......... National Union of Liberal Clubs [British] (DBA)
NULCAIS..... Northwestern University Library Computer-Assisted Information Service (OLDSS)
NULCW....... National Union of Lift and Crane Workers [British]
NULEOA....... National United Law Enforcement Officers Association (EA)
NULF......... National United Liberation Front [Myanmar] [Political party] (FEA)
NULF......... Nullify (SAUS)
NULFG........ Nullifying (SAUS)
NULFN........ Nullification (SAUS)
nullies........ nullifiers (SAUS)
nullip......... Nullipara [obstetrics] (DAVI)
NULMW....... National Union of Lock and Metal Workers [British] (DCTA)
NULO......... NASA Unmanned Launch Operations (MCD)
NULO......... National Union of Labour Organisers [British] (DBA)
NULOR........ Neuron Location and Ranging
NULS......... National Underwater Laboratory System [Marine science] (MSC)
NULS......... Net Unit-Load Size (MHDB)
NULU......... New Library Utility
NUM........... Error in Use of Numbers [Used in correcting manuscripts, etc.]
NUM........... National Union of Mineworkers [South Africa]
NUM........... National Unity Movement [Sierra Leone] [Political party] (EY)
NUM........... New Ulster Movement (SAUS)
Num........... Numa [of Plutarch] [Classical studies] (OCD)
NUM........... Numadu [Japan] [Seismograph station code, US Geological Survey] [Closed] (SEIS)
NUM........... Number [or Numerator, or Numeric]
NUM........... Numbering (SAUS)
Num........... Numbers [Old Testament book]
num........... Numeral (ELAL)
NUM........... Numeral [or Numerical]
Num........... Numerator (SAUS)
NUM........... Numerics (SAUS)
NUM........... Numerologist (SAUS)
num........... numerology (SAUS)
NUM........... Nurse Unit Manager
NUM........... Nuveen Michigan Quality Income Municipal [NYSE symbol] (SPSG)
NUM........... Nuveen MI Qual Income Muni [NYSE symbol] (TTSB)
NUMA......... National Underwater and Marine Agency (MCD)
NUMA......... Nonuniform - Memory - Access [Computer science]
NUMA......... Non Uniform Memory Address (SAUS)
NUMA......... Non-Uniform Memory Architecture (SAUS)
NUMA......... Nuclear Mitotic Apparatus [Medicine] (DMAA)
NUMAC........ Northumbrian Universities Multiple Access Computer (NITA)
Numac........ Numac Energy [Associated Press] (SAG)
NUMAC........ Numac Oil & Gas Ltd. (SAUS)
Num Adj...... Numeral Adjective (SAUS)
NUMAR........ Nuclear Magnetic Resonance [Also, NMR]
Numar........ Numar Corp. [Associated Press] (SAG)
NUMARC........ Nuclear Management and Resources Council (EA)
NUMARCOM... Nuclear Power for Marine Purposes Committee (MCD)
NUMAS........ Numerical Multifactor Assessment System (ADA)
NUMAST....... National Union of Marine Aviation and Shipping Transport [British]
NUMB......... Numbered
Numb......... Numbers [Old Testament book]
NUMBR........ Number (DAVI)
NUMC......... Newcastle University Mountaineering Club [Australia]
NUMD......... Numed Home Health Care, Inc. [NASDAQ symbol] (SAG)
Numd......... Numed Home Health Care, Inc. [Associated Press] (SAG)
NUMD......... NuMED Home Hlth Care [NASDAQ symbol] (TTSB)
NUMDW....... NuMED Home Health Care Wrrt [NASDAQ symbol] (TTSB)
NUME......... Numerical Methods in Engineering (SAUS)

NUMEC .... Nuclear Materials & Equipment Corp.
NUMEC .... Nuclear Uranium Materials and Equipment Corp. (GAAI)
Numed .... Numed Home Health Care, Inc. [*Associated Press*] (SAG)
NumedH ...... Numed Home Health Care, Inc. [*Associated Press*] (SAG)
NUMEPS ..... Numeric Meta Language Processing System (PDAA)
Numer .... Numerative (SAUS)
NUMERALS... Numerical Analysis System (BUR)
Numerex...... Numerex Corp. [*Associated Press*] (SAG)
Numer Heat Transf A... Numerical Heat Transfer A (SAUS)
Numer Heat Transf B... Numerical Heat Transfer B (SAUS)
NUMERIS..... French ISDN Network (SAUS)
Numer Methods Partial Diff Equations... Numerical Methods for Partial Differential
       Equations (SAUS)
NUMETA ...... Numerical Methods in Engineering-Theory and Applications (SAUS)
NuMI............ Neutrinos at the Main Injector [*Fermilab*]
Numi............ Numismatic (DIAR)
Numid.......... Numidian
NUMIS .... Navy Uniform Management Information System
NUMIS .... Northwestern University Multislice and Imaging System (SAUS)
Numis.......... Numismatic (SAUS)
NUMIS .... Numismatics
NUMISM...... Numismatics
Num Lock .... Numeric Lock [*Computer science*]
NUMM .... National Union of Masters and Mates [*British*]
NUMMA .... Nuclear Materials Management (SAUS)
NUMMI .... New United Motor Manufacturing, Inc. [*Joint venture of Toyota Motor
       Corp . and General Motors Corp.*]
NUMPES ..... Numeric Meta-Language Processing System (SAUS)
NUMR .... Numar Corp. [*NASDAQ symbol*] (SAG)
NumR .... Numbers Rabbah
NUMRUL...... Commonwealth Statutory Rules: Numbered (SAUS)
NUMS .... Nuclear Materials Security (NRCH)
NUMS .... Nu-Med, Inc. (EFIS)
NUMS .... Numerous (ROG)
NUMSA........ National Union of Metalworkers of South Africa
NUMW .... National Unemployed Workers' Movement [*British*]
NUN .... Network User Name [*Telecommunications*] (OSI)
NUN .... Nunasi-Central Airlines Ltd. [*Canada*] [*ICAO designator*] (FAAC)
NUN .... Nuveen New York Quality Income Municipal [*NYSE symbol*] (SPSG)
NUN .... Nuveen NY Qual Income Muni [*NYSE symbol*] (TTSB)
NUN .... Pensacola, FL [*Location identifier*] [*FAA*] (FAAL)
NUn .... Uniondale Public Library, Uniondale, NY [*Library symbol*] [*Library of
       Congress*] (LCLS)
NUNA.......... Not Used on Next Assembly (AAG)
NUnCCE ...... Cornelius Court Elementary School, Uniondale, NY [*Library symbol*]
       [*Library of Congress*] (LCLS)
NUnCE .... California Elementary School, Uniondale, NY [*Library symbol*]
       [*Library of Congress*] (LCLS)
NUnH .... Uniondale High School, Uniondale, NY [*Library symbol*] [*Library of
       Congress*] (LCLS)
NUnLJ .... Lawrence Junior High School, Uniondale, NY [*Library symbol*]
       [*Library of Congress*] (LCLS)
NUnNE .... Northern Parkway Elementary School, Uniondale, NY [*Library
       symbol*] [*Library of Congress*] (LCLS)
NUnSE .... Smith Elementary School, Uniondale, NY [*Library symbol*] [*Library of
       Congress*] (LCLS)
NUnStA .... Saint Agnes Cathedral High School, Uniondale, NY [*Library symbol*]
       [*Library of Congress*] (LCLS)
NUnTHJ .... Turtle Hook Junior High School, Uniondale, NY [*Library symbol*]
       [*Library of Congress*] (LCLS)
NUnWE .... Walnut Elementary School, Uniondale, NY [*Library symbol*] [*Library
       of Congress*] (LCLS)
NUO .... Nugold Enterprises Corp. [*Vancouver Stock Exchange symbol*]
NUO .... Nuveen Ohio Quality Income Municipal [*NYSE symbol*] (SPSG)
NUO .... Nuveen OH Qual Incme Muni [*NYSE symbol*] (TTSB)
NUOL........... Naval Underwater Ordnance Laboratory (NOAA)
NUOM.......... Northern Union of Operative Masons [*British*]
NUOR........... Nuclear Ordnance (SAUS)
NUOS........... Naval Underwater Ordnance Station
NUP .... Nationalist Unionist Party [*Sudan*]
NUP .... National Umma Party [*Sudan*] [*Political party*]
NUP .... National Union of Protestants
NUP .... National United Party [*Vanuatu*] [*Political party*] (EY)
NUP .... National Unity Party [*British*] [*Political party*] (EA)
NUP .... Negro Universities Press (AEBS)
NUP .... New Union Party [*Later, IUP*] (EA)
NUP .... Nonylundecylphthalat (SAUS)
NUP .... Nunapitchuk [*Alaska*] [*Airport symbol*] (OAG)
NUP .... Nuveen Pennsylvania Quality Income Municipal (SAUS)
NUPAC........ Nuclear Packaging Inc (SAUS)
NUPAD........ Nuclear-Powered Active Detection System
NUPAD System... Nuclear-Powered Active Detection System (SAUS)
NUpB .... United States Brookhaven National Laboratory, Upton, NY [*Library
       symbol*] [*Library of Congress*] (LCLS)
NUPB & PW... National Union of Printing, Bookbinding, and Paperworkers
       [*British*] (DGA)
NUpB-MH .... United States Brookhaven National Laboratory, Medical Research
       Center Hospital, Upton, NY [*Library symbol*] [*Library of
       Congress*] (LCLS)
NUPBP........ National Union of Printing, Bookbinding, and Paperworkers [*British*]
NUPC.......... Nupec Resources (SAUS)
NUPD.......... Non-Uniform Punched Document (SAUS)
NUPDTU ..... National Union of Painters and Decorators Trade Union [*British*]
NUPE .... National Union of Public Employees [*British*]
NUPEC........ Nuclear Power Engineering Test Center (NRCH)

NUPGE........ National Union of Provincial Government Employees [*Canada*]
NUPI........... Norwegian Institute for International Affairs (SAUS)
NUPLEX...... Nuclear Complex
NUPOC....... Nuclear Propulsion Officer Candidate [*Navy*]
NUPOC-S .... Nuclear Propulsion Officer Candidate - Submarine (DNAB)
NUPPS .... Nonuniform Progressive Phase Shift (IAA)
NUPPSCO ... Nuclear Power Plant Standards Committee (SAUS)
NUPS .... Nordic Union of Private Schools (EA)
NUPT .... National Union of Press Telegraphists [*British*] (DGA)
NUPWR....... Nuclear Power [*or Powered*] (DNAB)
NUPWRU..... Nuclear Power Unit (DNAB)
NUQ .... Mountain View, CA [*Location identifier*] [*FAA*] (FAAL)
NUR .... Natchez, Urania & Ruston Railway Co. [*AAR code*]
NUR .... National Union of Railwaymen [*British*]
NUR .... Net Unduplicated Research
Nur............. Nitrosourea [*Biochemistry*]
NUR .... Nonuniformity Ratio
NUR .... Not Under Repair (MARI)
NUR .... Nurmijarvi [*Finland*] [*Seismograph station code, US Geological
       Survey*] (SEIS)
NUR .... Nurse (AABC)
NUR .... Nuspar Resources [*Vancouver Stock Exchange symbol*]
NURA.......... National Union of Rate-Payers' Associations [*British*] (BI)
NURADS ...... Netted Universal Radar System (ACAE)
NURAT......... Newcastle University Root Analogue Tunneller (SAUS)
NuraTL........ Nur Advanced Technologies Ltd. [*Associated Press*] (SAG)
NURB.......... National Uniform Business Rate [*British*]
NURB.......... Neville Upper Reservoir Buffer [*Medicine*] (DMAA)
NURBS........ Nonuniform Rational B-Spline [*A type of spline*] [*Computer science*]
NURBS........ Nonuniform Relational B-Spline [*Micro Cadam 3-D*] [*Computer
       science*]
NURC.......... National Undersea Research Center [*Virgin Islands*]
NURC.......... National Union of Railway Clerks [*British*]
NURC.......... National Union of Retail Confectioners [*British*] (BI)
NURDC........ Naval Undersea Research and Development Center
NURE .... National Uranium Resource Evaluation [*Program*] [*Energy Research
       and Development Administration*]
NUREC........ Nuclear Regulatory Commission (SAUS)
NURED........ Nuclear Requirements Determination [*Military*]
NUREG........ Criteria for Preparation and Evaluation of Radiological Regulations
       and Guides (SAUS)
NUREG........ Nuclear Regulatory Commission
NUREG........ U. S. Nuclear Regulatory Commission (SAUS)
NUREM........ Nuclear Requirements Methodology [*Military*]
NUREP........ New York University Resonance Escape Probability [*Code*] [*Nuclear
       energy*] (NRCH)
NUREP........ Nuclear Reporting (SAUS)
NUREQ........ Nuclear Requirements [*Military*]
NUREX........ Nuclear Requirements Extrapolation [*Model*] (MCD)
NU/RF......... National Urban/Rural Fellows (EA)
NURF .... National Utility Reference File [*Department of Energy*]
NURF .... Nucleosome Remodeling Factor [*Analytical biochemistry*]
NURIG .... Navy Utility Regulatory Intervention Group (DNAB)
NURO.......... Neurotech Corp. (SAUS)
NUROC........ Nuclear Rocket Project (SAA)
NURP.......... National Undersea Research Program [*Department of Commerce*]
       (GRD)
NURP.......... Nationwide Urban Runoff Program [*Water pollution*]
NURP.......... NOAA [*National Oceanic and Atmospheric Administration*] Undersea
       Research Program [*Marine science*] (OSRA)
NURS.......... International Nursing Services, Inc. [*NASDAQ symbol*] (SAG)
NURS.......... International Nursing Svcs [*NASDAQ symbol*] (TTSB)
NURS.......... Nursery
Nurs............ Nurses (AL)
Nurs............ Nursing (AL)
NURS.......... Nursing
NURsc......... New Jersey Resources [*Associated Press*] (SAG)
NURSE........ Nurses Underrepresented in Social Equality (BABM)
NURSE........ Nursing
NURSEDETS... Nurse Detachments [*Army*]
Nurs Mirror... Nursing Mirror and Midwives Journal (SAUS)
NURSW....... International Nursing Wrrt [*NASDAQ symbol*] (TTSB)
NURSW....... Nursing System-Wide
NURT .... National Union of Retail Tobacconists [*British*] (BI)
NURTE .... Nur Advanced Technologies Ltd. [*NASDAQ symbol*] (SAG)
NURX.......... Nuclear Pharmacy, Inc. (SAUS)
NUS .... National Union of Scalemakers [*British*] (DCTA)
NUS .... National Union of Seamen [*British*]
NUS .... National Union of Students [*British*]
NUS .... National University of Singapore
NUS .... National Utility Services [*British*]
NUS .... New Upper Stage [*NASA*] (KSC)
NUS .... Nominal Ultimate Strength (IAA)
NUS .... Nonuniformly Spaced (IAA)
NUS .... Norsup [*Vanuatu*] [*Airport symbol*] (OAG)
NUS .... No Upper Stage (IGSL)
NUS .... Nuclear Upper Stage (SAUS)
NUS .... Nuclear Utility Services
NUS .... NUS Corp. (GAAI)
NUS .... Nu Skin Enterprises [*NYSE symbol*] [*Formerly, Nu Skin Asia Pacific*]
NUS .... Nu Skin Enterprises 'A' [*NYSE symbol*] (SG)
NUS .... Nu-Start Resource Corp. [*Vancouver Stock Exchange symbol*]
n-us- .... United States [*MARC geographic area code*] [*Library of Congress*]
       (LCCP)

n-usa-.......... Appalachian Area [*MARC geographic area code*] [*Library of Congress*] (LCCP)

NUSA.......... National Union of Shop Assistants [*British*] (DAS)

N/USA.......... National/United Service Agencies

NUSA.......... Neighborhoods USA (EA)

NUSA.......... Ninth United States Army

NUSAC......... Nuclear Sciences Advisory Committee [*Department of Energy/National Science Foundation*]

NUSACC....... National United States-Arab Chamber of Commerce (EA)

n-us-ak........ Alaska [*MARC geographic area code*] [*Library of Congress*] (LCCP)

n-us-al......... Alabama [*MARC geographic area code*] [*Library of Congress*] (LCCP)

n-us-ar........ Arkansas [*MARC geographic area code*] [*Library of Congress*] (LCCP)

NUSAR........ Nuclear Sweep and RADAR (IAA)

NUSAS........ National Union of South African Students

NUSAS........ Navy Underwater Swimmer Assault System (SAA)

NUSAT........ Northern Utah Satellite

NUSAT........ Nuclear Saturn (SAUS)

n-us-az........ Arizona [*MARC geographic area code*] [*Library of Congress*] (LCCP)

NUSBA........ Nuclear Science and Applications, Series B: Physical Sciences (SAUS)

NUSC.......... Naval Undersea Systems Center (SAUS)

NUSC.......... Naval Underwater Systems Center/Command (USDC)

n-usc-.......... North Central States [*MARC geographic area code*] [*Library of Congress*] (LCCP)

n-us-ca........ California [*MARC geographic area code*] [*Library of Congress*] (LCCP)

NUSCAT...... New Airborne Scatterometer (MCD)

NUSCDET.... Naval Underwater Systems Center Detachment (DNAB)

NUSC/NL...... Naval Underwater Systems Center, New London [*Connecticut*]

NUSC/NPT.... Naval Underwater Systems Center, Newport [*Rhode Island*]

n-us-co........ Colorado [*MARC geographic area code*] [*Library of Congress*] (LCCP)

NUSCOT...... Nuclear Submarine Control Trainer (PDAA)

NUSCOT...... Nuclear Submarine Simulator Complex (SAUS)

n-us-ct......... Connecticut [*MARC geographic area code*] [*Library of Congress*] (LCCP)

NUSD.......... Nucleus Sum Optical Density [*Microscopy*]

n-us-dc........ District of Columbia [*MARC geographic area code*] [*Library of Congress*] (LCCP)

n-us-de........ Delaware [*MARC geographic area code*] [*Library of Congress*] (LCCP)

n-use-.......... Northeast (United States) [*MARC geographic area code*] [*Library of Congress*] (LCCP)

NUSEC......... Naval Underwater Systems Engineering Center (MUGU)

NUSFDB...... NUS [*National University of Singapore*] Financial Database [*Information service or system*] (IID)

n-us-fl......... Florida [*MARC geographic area code*] [*Library of Congress*] (LCCP)

n-us-ga........ Georgia [*MARC geographic area code*] [*Library of Congress*] (LCCP)

NUSGGMW... National Union of Stove Grate and General Metal Workers [*British*]

NUSGW....... National Union of Stove and Grate Workers [*British*]

NUSH.......... Nucleus Shape [*Microscopy*]

n-us-hi........ Hawaii [*MARC geographic area code*] [*Library of Congress*] (LCCP)

n-us-ia........ Iowa [*MARC geographic area code*] [*Library of Congress*] (LCCP)

n-us-id......... Idaho [*MARC geographic area code*] [*Library of Congress*] (LCCP)

n-us-il......... Illinois [*MARC geographic area code*] [*Library of Congress*] (LCCP)

n-us-in........ Indiana [*MARC geographic area code*] [*Library of Congress*] (LCCP)

n-us-ks........ Kansas [*MARC geographic area code*] [*Library of Congress*] (LCCP)

n-us-ky........ Kentucky [*MARC geographic area code*] [*Library of Congress*] (LCCP)

n-usl-.......... Middle Atlantic States [*MARC geographic area code*] [*Library of Congress*] (LCCP)

NUSL.......... Naval Underwater Sound Laboratory [*Later, NUSC*]

n-us-la........ Louisiana [*MARC geographic area code*] [*Library of Congress*] (LCCP)

NUSLUM...... Nuclear Detonation Summary (SAUS)

n-usm-......... Mississippi River and Basin [*MARC geographic area code*] [*Library of Congress*] (LCCP)

n-us-ma....... Massachusetts [*MARC geographic area code*] [*Library of Congress*] (LCCP)

n-us-md....... Maryland [*MARC geographic area code*] [*Library of Congress*] (LCCP)

n-us-me....... Maine [*MARC geographic area code*] [*Library of Congress*] (LCCP)

n-us-mi....... Michigan [*MARC geographic area code*] [*Library of Congress*] (LCCP)

n-us-mn....... Minnesota [*MARC geographic area code*] [*Library of Congress*] (LCCP)

n-us-mo....... Missouri [*MARC geographic area code*] [*Library of Congress*] (LCCP)

n-us-ms....... Mississippi [*MARC geographic area code*] [*Library of Congress*] (LCCP)

n-us-mt....... Montana [*MARC geographic area code*] [*Library of Congress*] (LCCP)

NUSMWCHDE... National Union of Sheet Metal Workers, Coppersmiths, Heating and Domestic Engineers [*British*] (DCTA)

n-usn-.......... New England [*MARC geographic area code*] [*Library of Congress*] (LCCP)

n-us-nb....... Nebraska [*MARC geographic area code*] [*Library of Congress*] (LCCP)

n-us-nc....... North Carolina [*MARC geographic area code*] [*Library of Congress*] (LCCP)

n-us-nd....... North Dakota [*MARC geographic area code*] [*Library of Congress*] (LCCP)

n-us-nh....... New Hampshire [*MARC geographic area code*] [*Library of Congress*] (LCCP)

n-us-nj........ New Jersey [*MARC geographic area code*] [*Library of Congress*] (LCCP)

n-us-nm....... New Mexico [*MARC geographic area code*] [*Library of Congress*] (LCCP)

n-us-nv....... Nevada [*MARC geographic area code*] [*Library of Congress*] (LCCP)

n-us-ny....... New York [*MARC geographic area code*] [*Library of Congress*] (LCCP)

n-uso-.......... Ohio River and Basin [*MARC geographic area code*] [*Library of Congress*] (LCCP)

n-us-oh....... Ohio [*MARC geographic area code*] [*Library of Congress*] (LCCP)

n-us-ok....... Oklahoma [*MARC geographic area code*] [*Library of Congress*] (LCCP)

n-us-or........ Oregon [*MARC geographic area code*] [*Library of Congress*] (LCCP)

NUSOS......... Nuclear Underwater Sound Source (NG)

n-usp-.......... Pacific and Mountain States [*MARC geographic area code*] [*Library of Congress*] (LCCP)

n-us-pa....... Pennsylvania [*MARC geographic area code*] [*Library of Congress*] (LCCP)

NUSPRAW.... National Union of Storeworkers, Packers, Rubber and Allied Workers [*Australia*]

n-us-ri........ Rhode Island [*MARC geographic area code*] [*Library of Congress*] (LCCP)

NUSRL........ Navy Underwater Sound Reference Laboratory

n-uss-.......... Missouri River and Basin [*MARC geographic area code*] [*Library of Congress*] (LCCP)

NUSS.......... National Union of School Students [*British*] (DI)

NUSS.......... Nuclear Safety Standard (PDAA)

n-us-sc....... South Carolina [*MARC geographic area code*] [*Library of Congress*] (LCCP)

n-us-sd....... South Dakota [*MARC geographic area code*] [*Library of Congress*] (LCCP)

NUSSE........ Nonuniform Simple Surface Evaporated Model (MCD)

n-ust-.......... Southwest (United States) [*MARC geographic area code*] [*Library of Congress*] (LCCP)

n-us-tn........ Tennessee [*MARC geographic area code*] [*Library of Congress*] (LCCP)

n-us-tx........ Texas [*MARC geographic area code*] [*Library of Congress*] (LCCP)

NUSU.......... Nuclear Superheating (SAA)

n-usu-.......... Southern States [*MARC geographic area code*] [*Library of Congress*] (LCCP)

NUSU-CX..... Nuclear Superheat Critical Experiment (SAA)

NUSUM....... Nuclear Detonation Summary (NVT)

NUSUM....... Numerical Summary (SAUS)

NUSUM....... Numerical Summary Message (SAUS)

NUSUM....... Numerical Summary Report [*Military*] (AFM)

n-us-ut........ Utah [*MARC geographic area code*] [*Library of Congress*] (LCCP)

n-us-va....... Virginia [*MARC geographic area code*] [*Library of Congress*] (LCCP)

n-us-vt........ Vermont [*MARC geographic area code*] [*Library of Congress*] (LCCP)

n-usw-......... Northwest (United States) [*MARC geographic area code*] [*Library of Congress*] (LCCP)

n-us-wa....... Washington [*MARC geographic area code*] [*Library of Congress*] (LCCP)

n-us-wi....... Wisconsin [*MARC geographic area code*] [*Library of Congress*] (LCCP)

n-us-wv....... West Virginia [*MARC geographic area code*] [*Library of Congress*] (LCCP)

n-us-wy....... Wyoming [*MARC geographic area code*] [*Library of Congress*] (LCCP)

NUSZ.......... Nucleus Size [*Microscopy*]

NUT .... Mauna Loa Macadamia 'A' [*NYSE symbol*] (TTSB)

NUT .... Mauna Loa Macadamia Partners LP [*NYSE symbol*] (SPSG)

NUT .... National Union of Teachers [*British*]

NUT .... Nautilus Resources Ltd. [*Vancouver Stock Exchange symbol*]

N-U-T.......... Newcastle-Upon-Tyne [*City in England*]

NUT .... Nonobstructive Urinary Tract [*Medicine*] (MELL)

NUT .... Northeast University of Technology (SAUS)

NUT .... Number Unobtainable Tone [*Telecommunications*] (TEL)

NUT .... Nutrient (SAUS)

NUt .... Utica Public Library, Utica, NY [*Library symbol*] [*Library of Congress*] (LCLS)

NUTA .... Nagoya University Tandem Accelerator centre (SAUS)

NUTA .... National Used Truck Association

NUtC .... Utica College of Syracuse University, Utica, NY [*Library symbol*] [*Library of Congress*] (LCLS)

NUTEC........ Norwegian Underwater Technology Center (SAUS)

NU-TEC....... Nuclear Detection [*Radiation monitoring device*] (WDAA)

Nu-Tech....... Nu-Tech Bio Med, Inc. [*Associated Press*] (SAG)

Nu-Tek........ National Board for Industrial and Technical Development (SAUS)

NUTEK........ Swedish National Board for Industrial and Technical Development (SAUS)

NuTeV......... Neutrinos at the Tevatron

NUTEX........ Nuclear Tactical Exercise

NUTG.......... National Union of Townswomen's Guilds [*British*]

NUtGE......... General Electric Co., Utica, NY [*Library symbol*] [*Library of Congress*] (LCLS)

NUTGW....... National Union of Tailors and Garments Workers [*British*]

NUthHi........ Oneida Historical Society, Utica, NY [*Library symbol*] [*Library of Congress*] (LCLS)

NUTI .... NASCOM User Traffic Interface [*NASA*] (MCD)

NUTI .... Northwestern University Traffic Institute (SAUS)

NUTIS......... Numerical and Textile Information System (PDAA)

NUTIS......... Numerical and Textual Information System (SAUS)

NUTK.......... Nu Tech Industries (SAUS)

NUTL .... Nonuniform Transmission Line (IAA)

NUtM	Munson-Williams-Proctor Institute, Utica, NY [*Library symbol*] [*Library of Congress*] (LCLS)
NUTM	Nutmeg Industries, Inc. (MHDW)
NUTMAQ	Nuclear Techniques in Mining and Quarrying (SAUS)
NutmgFd	Nutmeg Federal Savings & Loan Association [*Associated Press*] (SAG)
NUtMI	Utica Mutual Insurance Co., Utica, NY [*Library symbol*] [*Library of Congress*] (LCLS)
NUtMM	Masonic Medical Research Laboratory, Utica, NY [*Library symbol*] [*Library of Congress*] (LCLS)
NUtMV	Mohawk Valley Community College, Utica, NY [*Library symbol*] [*Library of Congress*] (LCLS)
NUtMVL	Mohawk Valley Learning Resource Center, Utica Psychiatric Center, Utica, NY [*Library symbol*] [*Library of Congress*] (LCLS)
NUtMY	Mid-York Library System, Utica, NY [*Library symbol*] [*Library of Congress*] (LCLS)
NUTN	National Union of Trained Nurses [*British*] (DI)
NUTN	National University Teleconference Network [*Stillwater, OK*] [*Telecommunications*] (TSSD)
NUTP	National Uranium Tailings Program [*Canada*]
NUtP	Utica Psychiatric Center, Utica, NY [*Library symbol*] [*Library of Congress*] (LCLS)
NUTPW	National Union of Tin Plate Workers [*British*]
NUTR	Nutrition (AABC)
NUTRAT	Nuclear Uses Technology Reaction Analysis Team
Nutr Dieta....	Nutrio et Dieta. European Review of Nutrition and Dietetics (SAUS)
NUTRI	Nutrition
NUTRL	Nutritional
NutrLf	Nutrition For Life International, Inc. [*Associated Press*] (SAG)
NutrLfe	Nutrition for Life International, Inc. [*Associated Press*] (SAG)
Nutrmax	NutraMax Products, Inc. [*Associated Press*] (SAG)
NutrMg	Nutrition Management [*Associated Press*] (SAG)
NutrMgt	Nutrition Management [*Associated Press*] (SAG)
NUTS	Newcastle University Teaching System (SAUS)
NUTS	New Universeal Terminology Subjects
NUTS	Nuclear-Utilization Theories (SAUS)
NUTS	Nutrition World, Inc. (SAUS)
NUtSC	New York State Supreme Court Law Library, Utica, NY [*Library symbol*] [*Library of Congress*] (LCLS)
NUtSU	State University of New York, College at Utica-Rome, Utica, NY [*Library symbol*] [*Library of Congress*] (LCLS)
NUTT	National Union of Tobacco Trades [*British*]
NUTTAB	Nutrient Data Table
NUTX	Nucleus Texture [*Microscopy*]
NUU	New Universal Union (EA)
NUU	New University of Ulster [*Ireland*] (DI)
NUUSFE	National Union of United States Forces Employees [*South Korea*]
NUUT	National Union of Uncertified Teachers [*British*]
NUV	Near Ultraviolet
NUV	Norges Unge Venstre [*Norway*]
NUV	Nuveen Municipal Value Fund, Inc. [*NYSE symbol*] (SPSG)
NUV	Nuveen Muni Value Fd [*NYSE symbol*] (TTSB)
NuvAZ	Nuveen Arizona Premium Income [*Associated Press*] (SAG)
NUVB	National Union of Vehicle Builders [*British*]
NuvCal	Nuveen California Municipal Value Fund [*Associated Press*] (SAG)
NUVI	NuVision, Inc. (SAUS)
NuvMu	Nuveen Municipal Value Fund, Inc. [*Associated Press*] (SAG)
NuvPI	Nuveen Premium Income Municipal Fund, Inc. [*Associated Press*] (SAG)
NuvPI2	Nuveen Premium Income Municipal Fund 2 [*Associated Press*] (SAG)
NuvPI4	Nuveen Premium Income Municipal Fund 4 [*Associated Press*] (SAG)
NuvPP	Nuveen Performance Plus Municipal Fund [*Associated Press*] (SAG)
NuvQInc	Nuveen Quality Income Municipal Fund [*Associated Press*] (SAG)
NuvSel	Nuveen Select Quality [*Associated Press*] (SAG)
NUVW	National Union of Vehicular Workers [*British*]
NuvWA	Nuveen Washington Premium Income Municipal Fund [*Associated Press*] (SAG)
NUW	National Universities Week [*Canada*]
NUW	Nu-West Group Ltd. [*Toronto Stock Exchange symbol*]
NUW	Whidbey Island, WA [*Location identifier*] [*FAA*] (FAAL)
NUWA	National Unemployed Workers Association (NADA)
NUWAR........	Nuclear Warfare (SAUS)
NUWATI.......	Nuclear Work Authorization Technical Instruction (DNAB)
NUWAX	Nuclear Weapons Accident Exercises
NUWC	Naval Undersea Warfare Center [*Later, NURDC*]
NUWDAT......	National Union of Wallcoverings, Decorative and Allied Trades [*British*] (DGA)
NUWEAMP...	Nuclear Weapons Employment and Acquisition Master Plan (ACAE)
NUWEDS......	Nuclear Weapons Deniel System (SAUS)
NUWEDS......	Nuclear Weapons Emergency Destruction System (SAUS)
NUWEDS......	Nuclear Weapons Emergency Destruct System [*Navy*] (ANA)
NUWEP	Nuclear Weapon Employment Policy (MCD)
NUWEP	Nuclear Weapons Effect Planning
NUWEP	Nuclear Weapons Employment Plan (SAUS)
NUWEP	Nuclear Weapons Employment Policy (SAUS)
NUWEP	Nuclear Weapons Employment Procedures (SAUS)
NUWES	Naval Undersea Warfare Engineering Station (MCD)
NUWES	Naval Underwater Weapons Evaluation Station
NUWMF	Naval Undersea Warfare Museum Foundation (PDAA)
NUWPNSTRACEN...	Nuclear Weapons Training Center (MCD)
NUWPNSUPANX...	Nuclear Weapons Supply Annex
NUWPNTRACEN...	Nuclear Weapons Training Center
NUWPNTRACENLANT...	Nuclear Weapons Training Center, Atlantic
NUWPNTRACENPAC...	Nuclear Weapons Training Center, Pacific
NUWRES......	Naval Underwater Weapons Research and Engineering Station
NUWS	Naval Underwater Weapons Station (MCD)
NUWSAMBS...	National United Women's Societies of the Adoration of the Most Blessed Sacrament (EA)
NUWSEC......	Naval Underwater Weapons Systems Engineering Center
NUWT	National Union of Women Teachers [*British*] (DAS)
NUWT	Northeast Utilities [*NASDAQ symbol*] (SAG)
NuWt	Nu-West Industries, Inc. [*Associated Press*] (SAG)
NUWTW.......	Northeast Utils Wrrt [*NASDAQ symbol*] (TTSB)
NUWW	National Union of Women Workers (MHDB)
NUYC	Nordic Union of Young Conservatives (EA)
NV	Naamloze Vennootschap [*Limited Company, Corporation*] [*Netherlands*] (GPO)
NV	Naked Vision
nV	Nanovolt [*One billionth of a volt*] (IEEE)
N./V............	Nausea and Vomiting [*Medicine*] (AMHC)
NV	Near Vertical [*Aerospace*]
NV	Near Vision (MELL)
NV	Needle Valve
NV	Negative Variation [*Medicine*] (MAE)
NV	Nerve and Vein [*Medicine*] (DAVI)
NV	Net Value
NV	Neurovascular [*Anatomy*]
NV	Neutralization Value (IAA)
NV	Nevada [*Postal code*]
Nv	Nevada State Library, Carson City, NV [*Library symbol*] [*Library of Congress*] (LCLS)
NV	New Version [*of the Bible*]
NV	Next Visit [*Medicine*]
NV	Night Vision (SAUS)
NV	Night Vision Device [*Optics*]
NV	Nominal Value (SAUS)
NV	Nonvaccinated
NV	Nonvenereal [*Medicine*]
NV	Nonveteran
nv	Non Vidi [*Not Seen*] [*Latin*]
NV	Nonvintage [*Wine*]
NV	Non-Virtual (AGLO)
nv	Nonvirulent [*Pathology*]
nv	Non Visus [*Not Seen*] [*Latin*] (EES)
NV	Nonvolatile
NV	Nonvoting [*Investment term*]
NVX	No Overflow (SAUS)
NV	Nord-Viscount (SAUS)
NV	Nord-Viscount Corp.
NV	Normalized in Vacuum (SAUS)
NV	Normalized Volume (SAUS)
NV	Normal Value [*Clinical chemistry*]
NV	Normal Vetting (SAUS)
NV	Norske Veritas [*Norwegian ship classification society*] (DS)
NV	North Anna [*Virginia*] [*Seismograph station code, US Geological Survey*] [*Closed*]
NV	Northern Executive Aviation Ltd. (SAUS)
N-V	Northrop-Ventura (SAA)
NV	Northwest Territorial Airways [*ICAO designator*] (AD)
NV	Norwalk Virus [*Medicine*] (MELL)
NV	Not Vaccinated [*Medicine*]
N/V............	No Value [*Legal term*] (DLA)
NV	Nozzle Vanes (AAG)
NV	Nozzle Velocity (SAUS)
NV	Nuclear Vessel (TVEL)
NV	Nuclear Vitrification (SAUS)
NV	Nuisance Value (MHDB)
N/V............	Number of Engine Revolutions per Minute per Vehicle Miles per Hour [*Automotive engineering*]
NV	Number of Variables (SAUS)
NVA	Nationale Volksarmee [*National Peoples' Army*] [*Germany*]
NVA	National Variety Artists [*Defunct*] (EA)
NVA	National Velthrow Association (EA)
NVA	National Veterans Association (EA)
NVA	National Viatical Association (ECON)
NVA	National Villa Association [*British*] (BI)
NVA	National Vista Alliance (EA)
NVA	National Vulvodynia Association [*Disseminate information about vulvar pain and establish support networks across the country*] [*Medicine*]
NVA	Native Vegetation Authority [*South Australia*]
NVA	Near Visual Acuity [*Medicine*]
NVA	Negative Vorticity Advection [*NWS*] (FAAC)
NVA	Neiva [*Colombia*] [*Airport symbol*] (OAG)
NVA	Nile Valley Aviation Co. [*Egypt*] [*ICAO designator*] (FAAC)
NVA	Non-Violent Alternatives [*An association*] (EA)
NvA	Normalized Volt-Ampere
NVA	North Vietnamese Army
Nva	Norvaline [*Biochemistry*]
Nva	Norvalyl (SAUS)
NVA	NOVA Corp.(Cda) [*NYSE symbol*] (TTSB)
NVA	Nova Corp. of Alberta [*Later, Nova Corp.*] [*NYSE symbol*] [*Toronto Stock Exchange symbol*] (SPSG)
NVA	No Voltage Amplification [*Electronics*] (IAA)
NVA	N-Vinylacetamide [*Organic chemistry*]
NVAC	Natal Voluntary Ambulance Corps [*British military*] (DMA)
NVAC	National Vaccine Advisory Committee [*Reports to Congress, Health and Human Services*]

NVAC .... North Vietnamese Army Captured
NVAC .... Sunny Von Bulow National Victim Advocacy Center [*Later, NVC*] (EA)
NVACP .... Neighborhoods, Voluntary Associations and Consumer Protection [*Environmental Protection Agency*] (ERG)
NVAF .... North Vietnamese Air Force
NVAFB .... North Vandenberg Air Force Base (NASA)
NVAL .... National Vision Associates [*NASDAQ symbol*] (SAG)
NVAL .... Natl Vision Associates [*NASDAQ symbol*] (TTSB)
Nval .... Norvaline (DB)
NVAL .... Not Available
NValHi .... Columbia County Historical Library, Valatie, NY [*Library symbol*] [*Library of Congress*] (LCLS)
NValhM .... Westchester Medical Center, Valhalla, NY [*Library symbol*] [*Library of Congress*] (LCLS)
NValhW .... Westchester Community College, Valhalla, NY [*Library symbol*] [*Library of Congress*] (LCLS)
NVAN .... Non-Violent Anarchist Network (EA)
NV & EOL .... Night Vision and Electro-Optics Laboratory [*Army*] (RDA)
NV & H .... Nuclear Survivability and Hardening
NVAPI .... Nuveen Virginia Premium Income Municipal Fund [*Associated Press*] (SAG)
Nv-Ar .... Nevada State Library, Division of State Archives, Carson City, NV [*Library symbol*] [*Library of Congress*] (LCLS)
NVAR .... Normalized Variance (PDAA)
NVAS .... Night Vision Attack System
NVAS .... North Vietnamese Army Suspect
NVASD .... Night Vision Aerial Surveillance Device
NVASS .... Night Vision Airborne Surveillance System
NVATA .... National Vocational Agricultural Teachers' Association (EA)
NVB .... Inco Ltd. [*NYSE symbol*] (SAG)
NVB .... Napa Valley Bancorp (EFIS)
NVB .... National Volunteer Brigade [*South African equivalent of the British Home Guard*]
NVB .... Navigational Base (KSC)
NVB .... Nederlandse Volksbeweging [*Dutch People's Movement*] [*Political party*] (PPE)
NVB .... Neurovascular Bundle [*Medicine*] (DB)
NVB .... Night Vision Binocular
NVB .... Noise & Vibration Bulletin (SAUS)
Nvb .... November (CDAI)
NVBA .... National Veteran Boxers Association (EA)
NvBc .... Boulder City Library, Boulder City, NV [*Library symbol*] [*Library of Congress*] (LCLS)
NvBcBM .... United States Bureau of Mines, Boulder City Metallurgy Research Laboratories, Boulder City, NV [*Library symbol*] [*Library of Congress*] (LCLS)
NvBcER .... United States Energy Research and Development Administration, Boulder City Metallurgy Research Laboratories, Boulder City, NV [*Library symbol*] [*Library of Congress*] (LCLS)
NVBF .... Nordic federation of Research Libraries (SAUS)
NVBF .... Nordisk Vetenskapliga Bibliotekarie-Forbundet [*Scandinavian Federation of Research Librarians*] (EA)
NvBL .... Lehman Caves National Monument, Baker, NV [*Library symbol*] [*Library of Congress*] (LCLS)
NVBR .... Nevada Basin and Range (SAUS)
NVB-SG .... Dutch Serials Group (SAUS)
NVC .... National Victim Center (EA)
NVC .... National Victims of Crime (EA)
NVCP .... National Video Clearinghouse [*Defunct*] (EA)
NVC .... National Video Corp.
NVC .... National Volunteer Center (EA)
NVC .... Nonverbal Communication (ADA)
NVCP .... Noverco, Inc. [*Toronto Stock Exchange symbol*]
NVC .... Nuriootpa Viticulture Center [*Australia*]
NVC .... Nuveen California Select Quality Municipal [*NYSE symbol*] (SPSG)
NVC .... Nuveen CA Select Qual Muni [*NYSE symbol*] (TTSB)
NvC .... Ormsby Public Library, Carson City, NV [*Library symbol*] [*Library of Congress*] (LCLS)
NVCA .... National Valentine Collectors' Association (EA)
NVCA .... National Van Conversion Association (EA)
NVCA .... National Vehicle Conversion Association
NVCA .... National Venture Capital Association [*Arlington, VA*] (EA)
NvCAQI .... Nuveen California Quality Income Municipal [*Associated Press*] (SAG)
NVCASE .... National Voluntary Conformity Assessment System (SAUS)
NVCC .... Northern Virginia Community College
NVCF .... National Victims of Crime Foundation (EA)
NVCH .... National Volunteer Clearinghouse for the Homeless [*Defunct*] (EA)
NvCIQ .... Nuveen California Investment Quality Municipal Fund [*Associated Press*] (SAG)
NV-CJD .... New Variant Creutzfeldt-Jakob Disease [*Medicine*]
NVCJD .... New Variant of Creutzfeldt-Jakob Disease (SAUS)
NvCMI .... Nuveen California Municipal Income Fund [*Associated Press*] (SAG)
NVCO .... Nodaway Valley Co. (SAUS)
NVCP .... Network Voice Conferencing Protocol (CCCA)
NVCPP .... Nuveen California Performance Plus Municipal Fund [*Associated Press*] (SAG)
NVCS .... Nissan Valve Control System [*Automotive engineering*]
NvCSQ .... Nuveen California Select Quality Municipal Fund [*Associated Press*] (SAG)
NVCT .... Nonverbal Classification Test
NVCZ .... N-Vinylcarbazole [*Organic chemistry*]
NVD .... Nausea, Vomiting, Diarrhea [*Medicine*]
NVD .... Neck Vein Distention [*Medicine*]

NVD .... Neovascularization of the Disc [*Ophthalmology*] (DAVI)
NVD .... Neurovesicle Dysfunction [*Medicine*] (DMAA)
NVD .... Nevada, MO [*Location identifier*] [*FAA*] (FAAL)
NVD .... Newcastle Virus Disease [*Veterinary medicine*] (MAE)
NVD .... Nickel Vapor Deposition [*Metal treatment*]
NVD .... Night Viewing Device (SAUS)
NVD .... Night Vision Device [*Optics*]
NVD .... Nonvalvular Disease [*Medicine*] (DMAA)
NVD .... Nonvalvular Heart Disease (MAE)
NVD .... Normal Vaginal Delivery [*Medicine*] (DMAA)
NVD .... North Vancouver District Public Library [*UTLAS symbol*]
NVD .... No Value Declared [*Business term*] (DCTA)
NVD .... No Venous Distention [*Medicine*] (MEDA)
NVD .... Number of Vessels Diseased [*Medicine*] (DB)
NVDA .... National Vitamin Distributors Association (EA)
N/V/D/C .... Nausea/Vomiting/Diarrhea/ Constipation (SAUS)
NV DISTRINAL... NV Distribution International (SAUS)
NVDM .... Network Virtual Data Manager [*Computer science*] (IAA)
NVDM .... Novadigm, Inc. [*NASDAQ symbol*] (SAG)
NVDML .... Network Virtual Data Management Language [*Telecommunications*] (OSI)
NVE .... Colvin Aviation, Inc. [*ICAO designator*] (FAAC)
NvE .... Elko County Library, Elko, NV [*Library symbol*] [*Library of Congress*] (LCLS)
NVE .... Native Valve Endocarditis [*Medicine*]
NVE .... Neovascular Edema [*Ophthalmology*] (DAVI)
NVE .... Neovascularization Elsewhere [*Cardiology*] (DAVI)
NVE .... New Vessels Elsewhere [*Medicine*] (AMHC)
NVE .... Night Vision Equipment (MCD)
NVE .... Nonvisual Eyepiece
NVe .... Vestal Public Library, Vestal, NY [*Library symbol*] [*Library of Congress*] (LCLS)
NVEB .... Non-Vacuum Electron Beam (SAUS)
NVEBW .... Non-Vacuum Electron Beam Welding (PDAA)
NVEC .... Night Vision Equipment Corp. (SAUS)
NVEE............ Non-Volatile Ether Extract (SAUS)
NVEF .... National Vocational Educational Foundation (EA)
NVeGS .... Church of Jesus Christ of Latter-Day Saints, Genealogical Society Library, Ithaca Branch, Vestal, NY [*Library symbol*] [*Library of Congress*] (LCLS)
NvEHi .... Northeastern Nevada Historical Society, Elko, NV [*Library symbol*] [*Library of Congress*] (LCLS)
NVEL .... Navel
NVeL .... Vestal Public Library, Vestal, NY [*Library symbol*] [*Library of Congress*] (LCLS)
NvEIGS .... Church of Jesus Christ of Latter-Day Saints, Genealogical Society Library, Ely Branch, Ely, NV [*Library symbol*] [*Library of Congress*] (LCLS)
NVEOC .... Night Vision and Electro-Optics Center [*Fort Belvoir, VA*] [*US Army Communications-Electronics Command*] (RDA)
NVEOD .... Night Vision and Electro Optics Directorate [*Army*] (RDA)
NVEOL .... Night Vision and Electro-Optics Laboratory [*Army*] (GRD)
NVEPDC .... National Vocational Educational Professional Development Consortium [*Later, NVEPDF*] (EA)
NVEPDF .... National Vocational Educational Professional Development Foundation [*Later, NVEF*] (EA)
NVESD .... Night Vision and Electronic Sensors Directorate [*Army*] (RDA)
NVETS .... National Vocational Education and Training System [*Australia*]
NVEX .... Nevex Gold Co., Inc. (SAUS)
NVF .... Nasal Visual Field (DB)
NVF .... National Vitamin Foundation (EA)
NVF .... National Vitiligo Foundation (EA)
NVF .... National Volunteer Force (WDAA)
NVF .... Nordisk Vejteknisk Forbund [*Nordic Association of Road and Traffic Engineering*] (EAIO)
NVFC .... National Volunteer Fire Council (EA)
NVFEL.......... National Vehicle and Fuel Emissions Laboratory
NVFET.......... Non-Volatile Field-Effect-Transistor [*Electronics*]
NvFGS .... Church of Jesus Christ of Latter-Day Saints, Genealogical Society Library, Fallon Branch, Fallon, NV [*Library symbol*] [*Library of Congress*] (LCLS)
NVFI .... National Vitiligo Foundation (PAZ)
NvFL .... Nuveen Florida Investment Quality Municipal Fund [*Associated Press*] (SAG)
NVFR .... Night VFR (SAUS)
NVFR .... Night Visual Flight Rating
NVG .... National Trust Co. [*Toronto Stock Exchange symbol*]
NVG .... Neovascular Glaucoma (DAVI)
NVG .... Neoviridogrisein [*Antibacterial*]
NVG .... Night Vision Goggles
NVG .... Night Vision Group
NVG .... Null Voltage Generator (SAUS)
NVGA .... National Vocational Guidance Association (EA)
NVGC .... Night Vision Goggle Compatibility (SAUS)
NVGGA......... Napa Valley Grape Growers Association (EA)
NVGI .... National Voluntary Groups Institute (EA)
NvGM .... Mormon Station State Park, Genoa, NV [*Library symbol*] [*Library of Congress*] (LCLS)
NVGS .... Night Vision Goggle Sensor (DWSG)
NVGTN .... Navigation
NvH .... Henderson District Public Library, Henderson, NV [*Library symbol*] [*Library of Congress*] (LCLS)
NVH .... National R.V. Holdings [*NYSE symbol*]
NVH .... Natl R.V.Holdings [*NYSE symbol*] (SG)
NVH .... Nitrogen Vent Header [*Nuclear energy*] (NRCH)

NVH .... Noise, Vibration, Harshness [*Automotive technology*]
NVHA .... National Voluntary Health Agencies (EA)
NvHi .... Nevada State Historical Society, Reno, NV [*Library symbol*] [*Library of Congress*] (LCLS)
NvHV-A .... United States Veterans Administration Hospital, Ambulatory Care Service, Henderson, NV [*Library symbol*] [*Library of Congress*] (LCLS)
NVI .... Near Vertical Incident (ACAE)
NVI .... Neovascularization of the Iris (SAUS)
NVI .... Night Vision Imaging (DWSG)
NVI .... Non-Value Indicator [*Type of postage stamp*] (ODBW)
NVI .... Nordic Volcanological Institute (SAUS)
NVI .... Normalized Vegetation Index [*Meteorology*]
NVI .... No Value Indicated [*Stamp collecting*]
NVIC .... National Vaccine Information Center
NVIC .... Navigational and Vessel Inspection Circular [*Coast Guard*] (GFGA)
NVIC .... N-Viro International [*NASDAQ symbol*] (TTSB)
NVIC .... N-Viro International Corp. [*NASDAQ symbol*] (SAG)
NVICP .... National Vaccine Injury Compensation Program (PAZ)
NVIEW .... NVIEW Corp. [*Associated Press*] (SAG)
NVII .... Navy Vocational Interest Inventory (NVT)
NvIMO .... Nuveen Insurance Municipal Opportunity Fund [*Associated Press*] (SAG)
NvInQI .... Nuveen Insured Quality Fund [*Associated Press*] (SAG)
NvIQI .... Nuveen Investment Quality Municipal Fund [*Associated Press*] (SAG)
N-ViroInt ...... N-Viro International [*Associated Press*] (SAG)
NVIS .... Nearly Vertical Incident Skywave [*Propagation model*] (MCD)
NVIS .... Night Vision Imaging System
nVision .... N-Vision, Inc. [*Associated Press*] (SAG)
NVK .... Milton, FL [*Location identifier*] [*FAA*] (FAAL)
NVK .... Narvik [*Norway*] [*Airport symbol*] (OAG)
NVL .... Hunting Aviation Services Ltd. [*British*] [*ICAO designator*] (FAAC)
NvL .... Las Vegas Public Library, Las Vegas, NV [*Library symbol*] [*Library of Congress*] (LCLS)
NVL .... Night Vision Laboratory [*Army*]
NVL .... No Visible Lesion [*Medicine*] (MELL)
NVL .... Novolazarevskaya [*Antarctica*] [*Seismograph station code, US Geological Survey*] (SEIS)
NVLA .... National Vehicle Leasing Association (EA)
NVLA .... National Viewers' and Listeners' Association [*British*]
NVLAP .... National Association of Voluntary laboratory Accreditation Practices
NVLAP .... National Voluntary Laboratory Accreditation Program [*Gaithersburg, MD*] [*National Institute of Standards and Technology*]
NvLBM .... Basic Magnesium, Inc., Las Vegas, NV [*Library symbol*] [*Library of Congress*] [*Obsolete*] (LCLS)
NvLC .... Clark County Library, Las Vegas, NV [*Library symbol*] [*Library of Congress*] (LCLS)
NVLC .... National Veterans Law Center [*Defunct*] (EA)
NVLD .... Natural Vacuum Leak Detection [*Automotive testing*]
NVLD .... Non-Verbal Learning Disability
NvLGS .... Church of Jesus Christ of Latter-Day Saints, Genealogical Society Library, Las Vegas Branch, Las Vegas, NV [*Library symbol*] [*Library of Congress*] (LCLS)
NvLN .... University of Nevada, Las Vegas, NV [*Library symbol*] [*Library of Congress*] (LCLS)
NVLS .... Novellus Systems [*NASDAQ symbol*] (TTSB)
NVLS .... Novellus Systems, Inc. [*NASDAQ symbol*] (CTT)
NVLSPM ...... Night Vision Laboratories Static Performance Model (SAUS)
NVM .... National Voter Mobilization [*Defunct*] (EA)
NVM .... Nativity of the Virgin Mary
NVM .... Nonvolatile Matter
NVM .... Nonvolatile Memory [*Computer science*] (HGAA)
NVM .... Non-Volatile Random Access Memory [*Computer science*]
NVM .... Non-Voltage Matter (SAUS)
NVM .... Nova Marketing Ltd. [*Vancouver Stock Exchange symbol*]
NVMA .... National Veterinary Medical Association (WDAA)
NVMA .... Nebraska Veterinary Medical Association (GVA)
NVMA .... Noise and Vibration Monitor Analyzer [*Military*] (CAAL)
NvMAd .... Nuveen Municipal Advantage Fund [*Associated Press*] (SAG)
NvMAP .... Nuveen Massachusetts Premium Income Municipal Fund [*Associated Press*] (SAG)
NvMcK .... Kinnear Public Library, McGill, NV [*Library symbol*] [*Library of Congress*] (LCLS)
NvMiD .... Douglas County Library, Minden, NV [*Library symbol*] [*Library of Congress*] (LCLS)
NvMIPI .... Nuveen Michigan Premium Income Municipal [*Associated Press*] (SAG)
NvMO .... Nuveen Municipal Opportunity Fund [*Associated Press*] (SAG)
NVMS .... Night Visibility Measuring Set
NVMS .... Noise and Vibration Monitoring System (SAUS)
Nvmt .... Novametrics Medical Systems [*Associated Press*] (SAG)
Nvmt .... Novametrix Medical Systems, Inc. [*Associated Press*] (SAG)
NvMul .... Nuveen Municipal Income Fund [*Associated Press*] (SAG)
NvMus .... Nevada State Museum, Capital Complex, Carson City, NV [*Library symbol*] [*Library of Congress*] (LCLS)
NVMV .... Nicotiana Velutina Mosaic Virus [*Plant pathology*]
NVN .... Nirvana Industries Ltd. [*Vancouver Stock Exchange symbol*]
NVN .... Non-Von Neumann
NVN .... North Vietnam (VNW)
NVN .... Noun-Verb-Noun [*Education of the hearing-impaired*]
NVN .... Nuveen New York Select Quality Municipal [*NYSE symbol*] (SPSG)
NVN .... Nuveen NY Selct Qual Muni [*NYSE symbol*] (TTSB)
NVNA .... Non-Volatile Nitrosamine [*Organic chemistry*]
NVNAF .... North Vietnamese Air Force

NvNJ .... Nuveen New Jersey Investment Quality Municipal Fund [*Associated Press*] (SAG)
NvNJPI .... Nuveen New Jersey Premium Income Municipal [*Associated Press*] (SAG)
NVNN .... North Vietnamese Navy
NvNoIC .... Clark County Community College, North Las Vegas, NV [*Library symbol*] [*Library of Congress*] (LCLS)
NVNTA .... Night Vision Net Technical Assessment (MCD)
NVNW .... Novo Networks [*NASDAQ symbol*]
NvNYP .... Nuveen New York Performance Plus Municipal Fund [*Associated Press*] (SAG)
NvNYQI .... Nuveen New York Quality Income Municipal [*Associated Press*] (SAG)
NVO .... Coalition of National Voluntary Organizations [*Also, National Voluntary Organizations*] (AC)
NVO .... Nevada Operations Office [*Department of Energy*] (MCD)
NVO .... New Vehicle Order
NVO .... Nonverbal Operation
NVO .... Nonvessel Operator [*Shipping*]
NVO .... Non-Visual User Object (SAUS)
NVO .... Nonvolatile Organic [*Residue of thermal processing*]
NVO .... Novo Nordisk A/S ADR [*NYSE symbol*] (SPSG)
NVOAD .... National Voluntary Organizations Active in Disaster (EA)
NVOC .... Nitroveratryloxycarbonyl [*Organic radical*]
NVOC .... Nonvessel-Owning Carrier [*Shipping*] (DS)
NVOCC .... New Version Ocean Container Control (SAUS)
NVOCC .... New Version Overseas Container Control (SAUS)
NVOCC .... Nonvessel Operating Common Carrier [*Shipping*]
NVOCC .... Nonvessel-Owning Common Carrier [*Shipping*] (DS)
NVOCC .... Non-Volatile Ocean Container Control (SAUS)
NVOD .... Near Video on Demand (WDAA)
NvoFn .... Nuevo Financing I [*Associated Press*] (SAG)
NVOI .... National Voice of Iran [*Clandestine, Soviet-backed radio station*]
NVOILA .... National Voluntary Organizations for Independent Living for the Aging (EA)
NVOL .... Nonvolative (SAUS)
NVOO .... Nevada Operations Office [*Department of Energy*]
NVOP .... National Veteran's Outreach Program (EA)
NVORDCH ... Naval Ordnance Chart
NVP .... National Vaccine Program [*National Institutes of Health*]
NVP .... Nausea and Vomiting in Pregnancy
NVP .... Network Voice Protocol (CCCA)
NVP .... Nevada Power Co. [*NYSE symbol*] (SPSG)
NVP .... Nevirpine [*Organic chemistry*]
NVP .... Night Visibility Plan (SAUS)
NVP .... Nominal Velocity of Propagation [*Electronics*] (PCM)
NVP .... N-Vinylpyrrolidone [*Organic chemistry*]
NVPA .... National Visual Presentation Association (EA)
NvPA .... Nuveen Pennsylvania Investment Quality Municipal Fund [*Associated Press*] (SAG)
NvPAP2 .... Nuveen Pennsylvania Premium Income Municipal Fund [*Associated Press*] (SAG)
NvPIM .... Nuveen Premier Insured Municipal Income Fund [*Associated Press*] (SAG)
NvPMI .... Nuveen Premium Municipal Income Fund [*Associated Press*] (SAG)
NVPO .... Nuclear Vehicle Projects Office [*NASA*]
NVPOWG ..... NASA/VAFB [*National Aeronautical and Space Administration/Vandenburg Air Force Base*] Payload Operations Working Group
NVPP .... National Vehicle Population Poll (COE)
NVPP .... National Vehicle Population Profile
NVPS .... Night Vision Pilotage Subsystem (SAUS)
NVPS .... Night Vision Pilotage System [*Military*]
NVP-U .... Nationale Volkspartij - Unie [*National United People's Party*] [*Netherlands Antilles*] [*Political party*] (PPW)
NVQ .... National Vocational Qualification (WDAA)
NVQ .... National Vocation Qualification [*British*]
NVR .... National Video Resources
NVR .... Naval Vessel Register (MCD)
NVR .... Nonvolatile Residue (NAKS)
NVR .... Norfolk Volunteer Regiment [*British military*] (DMA)
NVR .... No Verification Required [*NASA*]
NVR .... No Voltage Release [*Electronics*]
NVR .... NVA [*North Vietnam Army*] Regulars (VNW)
NVR .... NVR, Inc. [*AMEX symbol*] (SPSG)
NVR.WS .... NVR Inc. Wrrt [*AMEX symbol*] (TTSB)
NVRAM .... Nonvolatile Random-Access Memory [*Computer science*]
NVRC .... National Retirees Volunteer Coalition [*An association*]
NvREr .... United States Energy Research Development Administration, Reno, NV [*Library symbol*] [*Library of Congress*] (LCLS)
NvRFM .... Grand Lodge of the Free and Accepted Masons of the State of Nevada, Reno, NV [*Library symbol*] [*Library of Congress*] (LCLS)
NvRGS .... Church of Jesus Christ of Latter-Day Saints, Genealogical Society Library, Reno Branch, Reno, NV [*Library symbol*] [*Library of Congress*] (LCLS)
NvRH .... Harrah's Automobile Collection and Pony Express Museum, Reno, NV [*Library symbol*] [*Library of Congress*] (LCLS)
NVRIA .... National Vision Research Institute of Australia
NvRNC .... National College of the State Judiciary, Law Library, Reno, NV [*Library symbol*] [*Library of Congress*] (LCLS)
NVROM .... Non-Volatile Read-Only Memory (SAUS)
NVRS .... National Vegetable Research Station [*Research center*] [*British*] (IRC)
NVRS .... Night Vision Reconnaissance System
NVRS .... Numerical Value Rating System [*Navy*]

NvRW .... Washoe County Library, Reno, NV [*Library symbol*] [*Library of Congress*] (LCLS)

NvRWL .... Washoe County Law Library, Reno, NV [*Library symbol*] [*Library of Congress*] (LCLS)

NVs .... Henry Waldinger Memorial Library, Valley Stream, NY [*Library symbol*] [*Library of Congress*] (LCLS)

NVS .... Narrowband Voice Security

NVS .... National Vegetable Society [*British*] (DBA)

NVS .... Neurological Vital Signs [*Medicine*]

NVS .... Neutron Velocity Selector

NVS .... Night Vision Safety [*Automotive rear-view mirrors*]

NVS .... Night Vision Sight (ACAE)

NVS .... Night Vision System

NVS .... Nonvolatile Storage (SAUS)

NVS .... Nonvoting Stock [*Investment term*]

NVS .... Novosibirsk [*Former USSR*] [*Seismograph station code, US Geological Survey*] (SEIS)

NVS .... Number of Video Samples

NVS .... Southeastern Baptist Theological Seminary, Wake Forest, NC [*OCLC symbol*] (OCLC)

NVSA .... Ablow [*Vanuatu*] [*ICAO location identifier*] (ICLI)

NVSA .... Natuurbestuurvereniging van Suidelike Afrika [*Southern African Wildlife Management Association - SAWMA*] [*Pretoria, South Africa*] (EAIO)

NVSA .... Nematologiese Vereniging van Suidelike Afrika [*Nematological Society of Southern Africa*] (EAIO)

NVsAE .... Alden Terrace Elementary School, Valley Stream, NY [*Library symbol*] [*Library of Congress*] (LCLS)

NVsBAE .... Brooklyn Avenue School, Valley Stream, NY [*Library symbol*] [*Library of Congress*] (LCLS)

NVsBE .... William L. Buck School, Valley Stream, NY [*Library symbol*] [*Library of Congress*] (LCLS)

NVSC .... Sola [*Vanuatu*] [*ICAO location identifier*] (ICLI)

NVsCE .... Robert W. Carbonaro School, Valley Stream, NY [*Library symbol*] [*Library of Congress*] (LCLS)

NVsCSE .... Clear Stream Avenue Elementary School, Valley Stream, NY [*Library symbol*] [*Library of Congress*] (LCLS)

NVsCSH .... Central Senior High School, Valley Stream, NY [*Library symbol*] [*Library of Congress*] (LCLS)

NVSD .... Lo-Linua [*Vanuatu*] [*ICAO location identifier*] (ICLI)

NVSD .... National Vital Statistics Division [*National Center for Health Statistics*] [*Obsolete*]

NVSD .... Night Vision System Development [*Military*]

NVsDE .... Devet Elementary School, Valley Stream, NY [*Library symbol*] [*Library of Congress*] (LCLS)

NVSDS .... New Vehicle Satisfaction with Dealer Service [*Quality research*]

NVSE .... Emae [*Vanuatu*] [*ICAO location identifier*] (ICLI)

NVSF .... Graig Cove [*Vanuatu*] [*ICAO location identifier*] (ICLI)

NVsFE .... Forest Elementary School, Valley Stream, NY [*Library symbol*] [*Library of Congress*] (LCLS)

NVsFH .... Franklin General Hospital, Valley Stream, NY [*Library symbol*] [*Library of Congress*] (LCLS)

NVSG .... Longana [*Vanuatu*] [*ICAO location identifier*] (ICLI)

NVSH .... Nonvocal Severely Handicapped

NVSH .... Sara [*Vanuatu*] [*ICAO location identifier*] (ICLI)

NVsHE .... Howell Road School, Valley Stream, NY [*Library symbol*] [*Library of Congress*] (LCLS)

NVSIMM ..... Non-Volatile Single Inline Memory Module (SAUS)

NVSL .... Lamap [*Vanuatu*] [*ICAO location identifier*] (ICLI)

NVSL .... National Veterinary Services Laboratory [*Ames, IA*] [*Department of Agriculture*] (GRD)

NVSM .... Lamen-Bay [*Vanuatu*] [*ICAO location identifier*] (ICLI)

NVSM .... Nonvolatile Semiconductor Memory (MCD)

NVSMD .... Nonvolatile Semiconductor Memory Device (PDAA)

NVsMJH ...... Memorial Junior High School, Valley Stream, NY [*Library symbol*] [*Library of Congress*] (LCLS)

NvSMM .... Nuveen Select Maturities Municipal Fund [*Associated Press*] (SAG)

NVSN .... Maewo-Naone [*Vanuatu*] [*ICAO location identifier*] (ICLI)

NVSN .... N-Vision, Inc. [*NASDAQ symbol*] (SAG)

NVsNSH .... Valley Stream North High School, Valley Stream, NY [*Library symbol*] [*Library of Congress*] (LCLS)

NVSNW .... n-Vision Inc. Wrrt [*NASDAQ symbol*] (TTSB)

NVSO .... Lonorore [*Vanuatu*] [*ICAO location identifier*] (ICLI)

NVsOE .... Ogden Elementary School, Valley Stream, NY [*Library symbol*] [*Library of Congress*] (LCLS)

N-VSOS .... Non-Verbal Scale of Suffering [*Personality development test*] [*Psychology*]

NVSP .... Norsup [*Vanuatu*] [*ICAO location identifier*] (ICLI)

NVSR .... Redcliff [*Vanuatu*] [*ICAO location identifier*] (ICLI)

nvSRAM ...... Nonvolatile Static Random Access Memory (SAUS)

NVSS .... National Vital Statistics System [*Department of Health and Human Services*] (GFGA)

NVSS .... Nonvolatile Suspended Solids [*Environmental chemistry*]

NVSS .... Normal-Variant Short Stature [*Medicine*]

NVSS .... Santo/Pekoa [*Vanuatu*] [*ICAO location identifier*] (ICLI)

NVsSAE .... Shaw Avenue Elementary School, Valley Stream, NY [*Library symbol*] [*Library of Congress*] (LCLS)

NVsSSH .... South Senior High School, Valley Stream, NY [*Library symbol*] [*Library of Congress*] (LCLS)

NVST .... Tongoa [*Vanuatu*] [*ICAO location identifier*] (ICLI)

NVSU .... Ulei [*Vanuatu*] [*ICAO location identifier*] (ICLI)

NVSV .... Valesdir [*Vanuatu*] [*ICAO location identifier*] (ICLI)

NVSW .... Walaha [*Vanuatu*] [*ICAO location identifier*] (ICLI)

NVsWE .... Willow Elementary School, Valley Stream, NY [*Library symbol*] [*Library of Congress*] (LCLS)

NVsWhE .... Wheeler Elementary School, Valley Stream, NY [*Library symbol*] [*Library of Congress*] (LCLS)

NVSX .... South West Bay [*Vanuatu*] [*ICAO location identifier*] (ICLI)

NVSZ .... North West Santo [*Vanuatu*] [*ICAO location identifier*] (ICLI)

NVT .... Navegantes [*Brazil*] [*Airport symbol*] (OAG)

NVT .... Nelson Vending Technology Ltd. [*Toronto Stock Exchange symbol*]

NVT .... Nerve, Vein, and Tendon (DAVI)

NVT .... Network Validation Testing [*Telecommunications*] (CIST)

NVT .... Network Virtual Terminal

NVT .... Neuton Visiting Time (IAA)

NVT .... Norton Villiers Triumph [*Automobile manufacturer*] [*British*]

NVT .... Novell Virtual Terminal [*Novell, Inc.*] [*Computer science*] (PCM)

NVT .... Nuisance Valve Tactics

NVTA .... National Visiting Teachers Association (EA)

NVTCS .... Nissan Valve Timing Control System

NVTG .... Norton Villiers Triumph Group [*Automobile manufacturer*] [*British*]

NVTHLSS ..... Nevertheless (ROG)

NV-THS .... National Vocational-Technical Honor Society (EA)

NVTK .... Novatek International, Inc. [*NASDAQ symbol*] (SAG)

NVTOC .... Nonvolatile Total Organic Carbon [*Environmental chemistry*]

NVTS .... National Vocational Training Service

NVTS .... Null Voltage Test Set (MCD)

NVTWUGBI... National Vehicular Traffic Workers' Union of Great Britain and Ireland

nvu.............. Nevada [*MARC country of publication code*] [*Library of Congress*] (LCCP)

NvU.............. University of Nevada, Reno, NV [*Library symbol*] [*Library of Congress*] (LCLS)

NVUE .... NVIEW Corp. [*NASDAQ symbol*] (SAG)

NVVA .... Anatom [*Vanuatu*] [*ICAO location identifier*] (ICLI)

NVVA .... Napa Valley Vintners Association (EA)

NVVB .... Aniwa [*Vanuatu*] [*ICAO location identifier*] (ICLI)

NVVC .... National Vietnam Veterans Coalition (EA)

NV/VC .... North Vietnamese/Vietcong (SAUS)

NVVCCG ...... North Vietnamese and Viet Cong Collecting Group [*Defunct*] (EA)

NVVD .... Dillon's Bay [*Vanuatu*] [*ICAO location identifier*] (ICLI)

NVVF .... Futuna [*Vanuatu*] [*ICAO location identifier*] (ICLI)

NVVI .... Ipota [*Vanuatu*] [*ICAO location identifier*] (ICLI)

NVVJ........... Forari [*Vanuatu*] [*ICAO location identifier*] (ICLI)

NVVK .... Lenakel [*Vanuatu*] [*ICAO location identifier*] (ICLI)

NVVQ .... Quoin Hill [*Vanuatu*] [*ICAO location identifier*] (ICLI)

NVVRS .... National Vietnam Veterans Readjustment Study [*Veterans Administration*]

NVVV .... Port-Vila/Bauerfield [*Vanuatu*] [*ICAO location identifier*] (ICLI)

NVWA .... National Volkswagen Association (EA)

NV Wine ...... Nonvintage Wine (SAUS)

NVWLA .... Napa Valley Wine Library Association (EA)

NVWSC .... Nonvolatile Whole Smoke Condensate [*Environmental chemistry*] (AAMN)

NVX .... North American Vaccine [*AMEX symbol*] (TTSB)

NVX .... North American Vaccine, Inc. [*AMEX symbol*] (SAG)

NVY .... Royal Navy [*British*] [*ICAO designator*] (FAAC)

NW .... Chicago & North Western Railway (SAUS)

NW .... Naked Weight

NW .... Naked Wire (IAA)

nW .... Nanowatt [*One billionth of a watt*]

NW .... Narrow White [*Automotive tire design*]

NW .... Narrow Widths [*Construction*]

NW .... Nasal Wash [*Medicine*] (DMAA)

NW .... NASA Waiver (KSC)

NW .... National Westminster Bancorp, Inc. [*NYSE symbol*] (SPSG)

NW .... National Women's Conference Committee [*Formerly, CCNWC*] (EA)

NW .... Natl Westminster ADS [*NYSE symbol*] (TTSB)

NW .... Nat-War Alliance [*Defunct*] (EA)

NW .... Naval Air Systems Command

NW .... Net Weight

NW .... Network (NASA)

NW .... Network Cells [*Botany*]

NW .... Net Worth

NW .... Neville and Winther's Acid

NW .... Neville-Winter (SAUS)

NW .... New

NW .... Newsweek [*A publication*] (BRI)

NW .... New Wave [*Style of music*]

NW .... New World [*Translation of the Holy Scriptures*] [*A publication*] (BJA)

NW .... Nominal Width (NATG)

NW .... Non-Weathering (SAUS)

NW .... Norfolk & Western Railway Co. [*AAR code*]

NW .... Normal Waste [*Nuclear energy*] (NRCH)

NW .... Norman-Wood Disease [*Medicine*] (DB)

NW .... Northern Wings Ltd (SAUS)

NW .... North Wales

NW .... North West (SAUS)

NW .... Northwest

NW .... North-Western (SAUS)

NW.............. North-Western Provinces, High Court Reports [*India*] [*A publication*] (DLA)

NW.............. North Western Reporter [*National Reporter System*] [*A publication*] (DLA)

NW.............. Northwest Orient Airlines, Inc. [*ICAO designator*]

NW.............. Nor-Weberine [*Biochemistry*]

NW.............. Nose Wheel [*Aviation*] (MCD)

NW.............. Not Waiverable (COE)

NW.............. Now

NW.............. No Wait [*Industrial engineering*]

NW.............. No Wind [*Air*] Position [*Navigation*]

NW.............	Nuclear Warfare
NW.............	Nuclear Waste (SAUS)
NW.............	Nuclear Weapon (NG)
NW.............	Nucleonia Week (SAUS)
NW.............	Number of Weeks (SAUS)
nw---	West Indies [MARC geographic area code] [Library of Congress] (LCCP)
NW2.............	New River [California] [Seismograph station code, US Geological Survey] (SEIS)
NW 2d	North Western Reporter, Second Series [West] [A publication] (AAGC)
NWA	Moheli [Comoro Islands] [Airport symbol] (OAG)
NWA	Narrogin [Australia] [Seismograph station code, US Geological Survey] (SEIS)
NWA	National Water Alliance (EA)
NWA	National Waterfowl Alliance, Waterfowl USA [Later, WUSA] (EA)
NWA	National Watermelon Association (NTPA)
NWA	National Water Well Association, Worthington, OH [OCLC symbol] (OCLC)
NWA	National Weather Association (EA)
NWA	National Welders Association [A union] [British]
NWA	National Wellness Association (EA)
NWA	National Wine Association [Defunct] (EA)
NWA	National Wrestling Alliance (DAVI)
NWA	National Writers Association (NTPA)
NWA	Naval Warfare Analysis (MCD)
NWA	Naval Weapons Annex
NWA	Navy Wifeline Association (EA)
NWA	New Work Authorized (MCD)
NWA	New World Alliance [Defunct] (EA)
NWA	Northumbrian Water Authority [British] (DCTA)
NWA	North West Africa (SAUS)
NWA	Northwest Airlines, Inc. [ICAO designator] (FAAC)
NWA	Northwestern Australia (SAUS)
NWA	Northwest Orient Airlines, Inc. (MCD)
NWA	Nothin' Worth Askin' [Rap recording group]
NWA	Nuclear Weapon Accident (SAUS)
NWAA	National Wheelchair Athletic Association (EA)
NWAA	National Women's Automotive Association [Defunct] (EA)
NWAACC.....	Northwest Athletic Association of Community Colleges (PSS)
NWAAF	Northwest African Air Forces [World War II]
NWAB	Necks with Any Boy [Slang]
NWAC	National Weather Analysis Center [Air Force, Navy]
NWAC	National Wheelchair Athletic Committee
NWAC	National Women's Advisory Council (NADA)
NWAC	Native Women's Association of Canada
NWAC	Northeast Women's Athletic Conference (PSS)
NWAC	Northwest Airlines'A' [NASDAQ symbol] (TTSB)
NWAC	Northwest Airlines Corp. [NASDAQ symbol] (SAG)
NWAC	Northwestern Area Command (SAUS)
NWadd........	Hepburn Library, Waddington, NY [Library symbol] [Library of Congress] (LCLS)
NWAF	New World Archeological Foundation (SAUS)
NWAFC	Northwest and Alaska Fisheries Center [National Marine Fisheries Service] [Department of Commerce] [Research center] (RCD)
NWAG	Naval Warfare Analysis Group
NWAHACA ...	National Warm Air Heating and Air Conditioning Association [Later, ACCA] (EA)
NWAI	Nuclear Weapons Acceptance Inspection (NG)
NWAIB	Nuclear Weapon Accident Investigation Board (AABC)
NWald	Josephine-Louise Public Library, Walden, NY [Library symbol] [Library of Congress] (LCLS)
NWall	Wallkill Public Library, Wallkill, NY [Library symbol] [Library of Congress] (LCLS)
NWan...........	Wantagh Public Library, Wantagh, NY [Library symbol] [Library of Congress] (LCLS)
NWanE........	Wantagh Elementary School, Wantagh, NY [Library symbol] [Library of Congress] (LCLS)
NWanFLE....	Forest Lake Elementary School, Wantagh, NY [Library symbol] [Library of Congress] (LCLS)
NWanJH	Wantagh Junior High School, Wantagh, NY [Library symbol] [Library of Congress] (LCLS)
NWanJS......	Wantagh Junior-Senior High, Wantagh, NY [Library symbol] [Library of Congress] (LCLS)
NWanME.....	Mandalay Elementary School, Wantagh, NY [Library symbol] [Library of Congress] (LCLS)
NWanSH.....	Wantagh Senior High School, Wantagh, NY [Library symbol] [Library of Congress] (LCLS)
NWanSPE ...	Sunrise Park Elementary School, Wantagh, NY [Library symbol] [Library of Congress] (LCLS)
NWAO	Narrogin [Australia] [Seismograph station code, US Geological Survey] (SEIS)
NWAP	National White American Party (BJA)
NWapA	Mount Alvernia Seminary, Wappingers Falls, NY [Library symbol] [Library of Congress] (LCLS)
NWAPP	National Woman Abuse Prevention Project (EA)
nwaq-	Antigua [MARC geographic area code] [Library of Congress] (LCCP)
NWAR	New Air Flight, Inc. (SAUS)
N-War........	Nuclear Warfare (SAUS)
NWARC.......	Navy Weapons Assessment Research Centre (SAUS)
NWas...........	Moffat Library Association, Washingtonville, NY [Library symbol] [Library of Congress] (LCLS)
NWASC.......	Northwest Association of Schools and Colleges (DHP)
NWASI........	Northrop Worldwide Aircraft Services Inc. (SAUS)
N-Waste	Nuclear Waste (SAUS)

NWAT	Nuclear Weapon Assist Team (SAUS)
NWatfG........	General Electric Co., Silicone Products Department, Waterford, NY [Library symbol] [Library of Congress] (LCLS)
NWatt	Roswell P. Flower Memorial Public Library, Watertown, NY [Library symbol] [Library of Congress] (LCLS)
NWattJ........	Jefferson Community College, Watertown, NY [Library symbol] [Library of Congress] (LCLS)
NWattJHi	Jefferson County Historical Society, Watertown, NY [Library symbol] [Library of Congress] (LCLS)
NWattKH	Samaritan Keep Nursing Home, Medical Library, Watertown, NY [Library symbol] [Library of Congress] (LCLS)
NWattMH	Mercy Hospital of Watertown, Watertown, NY [Library symbol] [Library of Congress] (LCLS)
NWattN	North Country Library System, Watertown, NY [Library symbol] [Library of Congress] (LCLS)
NWatvlA	Watervliet Arsenal Library, Watervliet, NY [Library symbol] [Library of Congress] (LCLS)
NWAVL	Now Available (NOAA)
NWB	National Wiring Bureau [Defunct] (EA)
NWB	Naval Weapons Bulletin
NWB	Nederlandse Waterschapsbank NV [Waterschaps Bank of the Netherlands]
NWB	New War Department Building [Obsolete]
NWB	Next Working Block (SAUS)
NWB	Non-Weight-Bearing [Orthopedics and physical therapy] (DAVI)
NWB	Northwestbound [ICAO designator] (FAAC)
NWB	North Western Bell (HGAA)
NWB	Northwest Towboat Tariff Bureau, Inc., Seattle WA [STAC]
NWB	No Weight-Bearing [orthopedics] (DAVI)
NWBA	National Wheelchair Basketball Association (EA)
nwbb-	Barbados [MARC geographic area code] [Library of Congress] (LCCP)
NWBB	Noumea [New Caledonia] [ICAO location identifier] (ICLI)
NwbBc	Newberry Bancorp, Inc. [Associated Press] (SAG)
nwbc-	Barbuda [MARC geographic area code] [Library of Congress] (LCCP)
NWbC	Cardion Electronics, Woodbury, NY [Library symbol] [Library of Congress] (LCLS)
NWBC	National Women's Business Council
NWBC	National Wooden Box Council [Later, NWPCA] (EA)
nwbf-	Bahamas [MARC geographic area code] [Library of Congress] (LCCP)
NWBHI	Nuclear Weapon Burst Height Indicator
NWbN	Northwest by North
NWBW	National Women Bowling Writers Association (EA)
NWbW	Northwest by West
NWbW	Waldemar Medical Research Foundation, Woodbury, NY [Library symbol] [Library of Congress] (LCLS)
NWC	National Waco Club (EA)
NWC	National War College [Later, UND] [DoD]
NWC	National Warning Center [Civil Defense]
NWC	National Water Center (EA)
NWC	National Water Commission [Terminated, 1973]
NWC	National Water Council [British] (DCTA)
NWC	National Waterfowl Council (EA)
NWC	National Watershed Congress (EA)
NWC	National Waterways Conference (EA)
NWC	National Wildlife Centre (SAUS)
NWC	National Wiretap Commission [Department of Justice]
NWC	National Women's Coalition [Defunct] (EA)
NWC	National Woodie Club
NWC	National Writers Club (EA)
NWC	Nationwide Cellular Service, Inc. (EFIS)
NWC	Naval War College
NWC	Naval Weapons Center
NWC	Navy Widow's Certificate (GEAB)
NWC	Net Working Capital
NWC	Net Worth Certificate (EBF)
NWC	New ACS Ltd. [United Republic of Tanzania] [FAA designator] (FAAC)
NWC	New World Club (EA)
NWC	New World Coalition (EA)
NWC	Northwest Cape
NWC	Northwest College [Washington]
NWC	North West Community College Library [UTLAS symbol]
NWC	Nuclear War Capability (AAG)
NWC	Nuclear Weapons Center (SAUS)
NWC	Nuclear Weapons Complex (COE)
NWC	Nuclear Weapons Control
NWC	Nuclear Weapons Council (SAUS)
NWC	Wingate College, Wingate, NC [OCLC symbol] (OCLC)
NWCA	National Water Carriers Association
NWCA	National Woodcarvers Association (EA)
NWCA	National Wrestling Coaches Association (EA)
NWCA	National Writing Centers Association (NTPA)
NWCA	Navy Wives Clubs of America (EA)
NWCA	NewCare Health [NASDAQ symbol] (TTSB)
NWCA	New Care Health Corp. [NASDAQ symbol] (SAG)
NWCA	Northwest Cherry Briners Association
NWCAA	National War College Alumni Association
NWCAEU.....	National Women's Conference of the American Ethical Union (EA)
NWC/ARP ...	Naval War College Advanced Research Program [Newport, RI]
NWCC	National Water Co. Conference [Later, NAWC]
NWCC	National Women's Conference Committee (EA)
NWCC	Neutron Well Coincidence Counter [Nuclear energy] (NRCH)
NWCC	Northern Wyoming Community College (SAUS)

NWCC	Northwest Christian College [*Oregon*]
NWCC	Northwestern Weed Control Conference (SAUS)
NWCC	Noumea/La Tontouta [*New Caledonia*] [*ICAO location identifier*] (ICLI)
NWC/CA	Naval Weapons Center, Corona Annex [*California*]
NWC/CAR	Naval War College Center for Advanced Research [*Newport, RI*]
NWCCL	Naval Weapons Center, Corona Laboratories [*California*]
NWCCS	Naval Worldwide Command and Control System (MCD)
NWCDC	North West Cooperative Development Council [*British*]
NWCF	New Waste Calcining Facility [*Nuclear energy*] (NUCP)
NWCF	Northwest Citizens Forum (SAUS)
NWCG	New World Communic Grp'A' [*NASDAQ symbol*] (TTSB)
NWCG	New World Communictions Corp. [*NASDAQ symbol*] (SAG)
NWCG	Nuclear Weapons Coordinating Group
NWCHA	Northwest Clearing House Association (TBD)
NWCI	New World Coffee [*NASDAQ symbol*] (TTSB)
NWCI	New World Coffee, Inc. [*NASDAQ symbol*] (SAG)
NWCIEP	Nation-Wide Committee on Import-Export Policy [*Defunct*] (EA)
nwcj-	Cayman Islands [*MARC geographic area code*] [*Library of Congress*] (LCCP)
NwCm	News Communications, Inc. [*Associated Press*] (SAG)
NWCME	National Winter Convention on Military Electronics [*IEEE*] (MCD)
NWC/NW	Naval War College / Naval Warfare Course (DNAB)
nwco-	Curacao Group [*MARC geographic area code*] [*Library of Congress*] (LCCP)
NWCO	National Water Conservation Order (SAUS)
NWCP	National Wetlands Conservation Project [*Defunct*] (EA)
NWCP	Navy Weight-Control Program (DNAB)
NWCP	Noxious Weeds Control Program (SAUS)
NWCR	Naval War College Review [*A publication*]
NWCR	Nuclear Weapons Correction Report [*Army*] (AABC)
NWCRB	Navy War Contracts Relief Board
NWCS	NATO-Wide Communications System (NATG)
NWCS	Netware Workstation Compatible Service (SAUS)
NWCS	Nuclear Weapons Control System
NWCTU	National Woman's Christian Temperance Union (WDAA)
nwcu	Cuba [*MARC geographic area code*] [*Library of Congress*] (LCCP)
NWD	Naval Weapons Directory
NWD	Navigation Weapon Delivery (ACAE)
NWD	Network Wide Directory
NWD	New World Dictionary [*A publication*]
NWD	Normal Well Developed (MELL)
NWD	Northwest Air Services Ltd. [*Nigeria*] [*ICAO designator*] (FAAC)
NWD	Northwest Drug Co. Ltd. [*Toronto Stock Exchange symbol*]
NWD	Nuclear Weapon Disposal (SAUS)
NWD	Number of Words (MSA)
NWDA	National Wholesale Druggists' Association (EA)
NWDA	National Wine Distributors' Association (EA)
NwDay	New Day Beverage, Inc. [*Associated Press*] (SAG)
NWDC	National Wildlife Defence Council (USDC)
NWDC	National Wildlife Defense Council [*Marine science*] (OSRA)
NWDC	Navigation/Weapon Delivery Computer (PDAA)
NWDC	Northwest Drama Conference (EA)
NWDC/S	Navigation/Weapons Delivery Computer/System
NWDEN	Number of Words per Entry (MSA)
NWDGA	National Wholesale Dry Goods Association [*Later, NATAD*]
NWDL	Modular Well-Differentiated Lymphocytic Lymphoma [*Medicine*] (MELL)
NWdmA	Woodmere Academy, Woodmere, NY [*Library symbol*] [*Library of Congress*] (LCLS)
NWdmE	No. 6 Elementary School, Woodmere, NY [*Library symbol*] [*Library of Congress*] (LCLS)
NWDO	National Workforce Development Office (COE)
NWDP	Nuclear Weapons Development Project (SAUS)
nwdq-	Dominica [*MARC geographic area code*] [*Library of Congress*] (LCCP)
nwdr-	Dominican Republic [*MARC geographic area code*] [*Library of Congress*] (LCCP)
NWDS	National Water Data System [*US Geological Survey*] [*Reston, VA*]
NWDS	Navigation/Weapons Delivery System
NWDS	Network Wide Directory System (MHDI)
NWDS	Noah Worcester Dermatological Society (EA)
NWDS	Number of Words
NWDSEN	Number of Words per Entry
NWE	Narrow Width Effect (IAA)
NWE	Newline Resources Ltd. [*Vancouver Stock Exchange symbol*]
NWE	New World Entertainment Ltd. (SAUS)
NWE	Northwest Aero Associates, Inc. [*FAA designator*] (FAAC)
NWE	Nuclear Weapons Effects
NWe	Westbury Memorial Public Library, Westbury, NY [*Library symbol*] [*Library of Congress*] (LCLS)
NWEA	National Women's Economic Alliance [*Washington, DC*] (EA)
NWEA	National Wood Energy Association (EA)
NWEAF	National Women's Economic Alliance Foundation (NTPA)
NWEAMP	Nuclear Weapons Employment Acquisition Master Plan (CCCA)
NWEB	Northwestern Electricity Board [*British*]
NWeBE	Board of Cooperative Educational Services, Nassau Education Resource Center, Westbury, NY [*Library symbol*] [*Library of Congress*] (LCLS)
NWeBGE	Bowling Green Elementary School, Westbury, NY [*Library symbol*] [*Library of Congress*] (LCLS)
NWebPH	Pilgrim Hospital, West Brentwood, NY [*Library symbol*] [*Library of Congress*] (LCLS)
NWEC	Nuclear Weapons Effects Course (MCD)
NWEC	Nuclear Weapons Employment Course (SAUS)

NWeCJS	W. Tresper Clarke Junior-Senior High School, Westbury, NY [*Library symbol*] [*Library of Congress*] (LCLS)
NWED	Nuclear Weapon Effects Development
NWeDE	Drexel Elementary School, Westbury, NY [*Library symbol*] [*Library of Congress*] (LCLS)
NWEE	National Women's Employment and Education [*Defunct*] (EA)
NWEF	National Women's Education Fund (EA)
NWEF	Naval Weapons Evaluation Facility [*Kirtland Air Force Base, NM*]
NWEF	New World Education Fund (EA)
NWEF	North Western Expeditionary Force [*Norway*] [*World War II*]
NWEF	Nuclear Weapons Education Fund (EA)
NWef	Patterson Library, Westfield, NY [*Library symbol*] [*Library of Congress*] (LCLS)
NWefHi	Chautauqua County Historical Society, Westfield, NY [*Library symbol*] [*Library of Congress*] (LCLS)
NWefMH	Westfield Memorial Hospital, Inc., Westfield, NY [*Library symbol*] [*Library of Congress*] (LCLS)
NWehb	Westhampton Free Library, Westhampton Beach, NY [*Library symbol*] [*Library of Congress*] (LCLS)
NWehbJH	Westhampton Beach Junior High School, Westhampton Beach, NY [*Library symbol*] [*Library of Congress*] (LCLS)
NWeJH	Westbury Junior High School, Westbury, NY [*Library symbol*] [*Library of Congress*] (LCLS)
NWel	David A. Howe Public Library, Wellsville, NY [*Library symbol*] [*Library of Congress*] (LCLS)
NWEL	Nuclear Weapons Effects Laboratory
NWelH	Jones Memorial Hospital, Wellsville, NY [*Library symbol*] [*Library of Congress*] (LCLS)
NWeM	Metco, Inc., Westbury, NY [*Library symbol*] [*Library of Congress*] (LCLS)
NWEN	Northwest Engineering Co. (SAUS)
NWEO	Nuclear Weapon Effects Office [*DoD*] (RDA)
NWEO	Nuclear Weapon Employment Officer (AABC)
NWEP	Nuclear Weapons Effects Panel
NWePLE	Powell's Lane Elementary School, Westbury, NY [*Library symbol*] [*Library of Congress*] (LCLS)
NWePSE	Park School Early Childhood Center, Westbury, NY [*Library symbol*] [*Library of Congress*] (LCLS)
NWEQ	Northwest Equity Corp. [*NASDAQ symbol*] (TTSB)
NWER	Nuclear Weapons Effects Research [*Army*]
NWER/T	Nuclear Weapons Effects Research and Testing [*Army*] (RDA)
NWES	Naval Weapons Engineering Support activity office (SAUS)
NWES	New World Exploration Society (SAUS)
NWES	Nuclear Weapons Electronic Specialist (AABC)
NWes	Olive Free Library Association, West Shokan, NY [*Library symbol*] [*Library of Congress*] (LCLS)
NWESA	Naval Weapons Engineering Support Activity (MCD)
NWesbHS	West Bablyon High School, West Babylon, NY [*Library symbol*] [*Library of Congress*] (LCLS)
NWesbJH	West Babylon Junior High School, West Babylon, NY [*Library symbol*] [*Library of Congress*] (LCLS)
NWeSH	Westbury Senior High School, Westbury, NY [*Library symbol*] [*Library of Congress*] (LCLS)
NWesyM	Suffolk Marine Museum, West Sayville, NY [*Library symbol*] [*Library of Congress*] (LCLS)
NWET	Nuclear Weapon Effects Test
nweu-	Sint Eustatius [*MARC geographic area code*] [*Library of Congress*] (LCCP)
NWevNS	West Valley Nuclear Services Co., West Valley, NY [*Library symbol*] [*Library of Congress*] (LCLS)
NWF	International Women's Forum [*National Women's Forum*] [*Acronym is based on former name,*] (EA)
NWF	National War Formulary
NWF	National War Fund
NWF	National Welfare Fund (WDAA)
NWF	National Wildlife Federation (EA)
NWF	Naval Weapons Factory [*Formerly, NGF*]
NWF	Naval Working Fund [*Navy, Coast Guard*]
NWF	New Wilderness Foundation (EA)
NWF	New World Foundation (EA)
NWF	Nuclear Waste Fund (NUCP)
NWF	Numerical Weather Facility
NWFA	National Wholesale Furniture Association (EA)
NWFA	National Wood Flooring Association (EA)
NWFA	Northwest Farm Managers Association (EA)
NWFA	Northwest Fisheries Association (EA)
NWFAL	Nation-Wide Fallout (SAA)
NWFC	Nuclear Weapons Freeze Campaign (EA)
NWFF	North West Frontier Fellowship (EA)
NWFI	Non-Woven Fabrics Institute [*Defunct*] (EA)
NWFMA	Northwest Farm Managers Association
NWFN	Northwestern Financial (SAUS)
NWFP	North-West Frontier Province [*Pakistan*] (PD)
NWFP	Nuclear Weapons Fire Planning (MCD)
NWFP	Rocky Flats/Nuclear Weapons Facilities Project [*Organization with goal of nuclear disarmament*] [*Defunct*] (EA)
NWF Pak	North West Frontier, Pakistan (ILCA)
NWFS	NetWare File System [*Computer science*]
NWFS	NWS Capital Financing Trust [*Associated Press*] (SAG)
NWFSPCN	Nahanni National Park, Parks Canada [*Parc National Nahanni, Parcs Canada*] Fort Simpson, Northwest Territories [*Library symbol*] [*National Library of Canada*] (NLC)
NWFSPCW	Wood Buffalo National Park, Parks Canada [*Parc National Wood Buffalo, Parcs Canada*] Fort Smith, Northwest Territories [*Library symbol*] [*National Library of Canada*] (NLC)

NWFST	Thebacha College Library, Fort Smith, Northwest Territories [*Library symbol*] [*National Library of Canada*] (NLC)
NWFWA	Northwest Forest Workers Association [*Defunct*] (EA)
NWFZ	Nuclear Weapons-Free Zone
NWG	National Wire Gauge
NWG	New Goliath Minerals Ltd. [*Toronto Stock Exchange symbol*] [*Vancouver Stock Exchange symbol*]
NWG	North West Gold Corp. (SAUS)
nwga-	Greater Antilles [*MARC geographic area code*] [*Library of Congress*] (LCCP)
NWGA	National Wool Growers Association [*Later, ASIA*] (EA)
NWGA	Northwest Guides Association [*Defunct*]
NWGB	Northwestern Gas Board (SAUS)
nwgd	Grenada [*MARC geographic area code*] [*Library of Congress*] (LCCP)
NWGDE	Nordic Working Group on Development Education [*Nordic Council of Ministers*] [*Denmark*] (EAIO)
nwgp-	Guadeloupe [*MARC geographic area code*] [*Library of Congress*] (LCCP)
NWGP	Nuclear War Graphics Project [*Defunct*] (EA)
nwgs-	Grenadines [*MARC geographic area code*] [*Library of Congress*] (LCCP)
NWGS	Naval Warfare Gaming System
NWGS	North Wall of the Gulf Stream (QUAC)
NWGSFW	National Working Group on Screw Fly Worm [*Australia*]
NWGWU	National Warehouse and General Workers' Union [*British*]
NWH	Nawa Air Transport [*Hungary*] [*ICAO designator*] (FAAC)
NWH	New Hombre Resources [*Vancouver Stock Exchange symbol*]
NWH	Normal Working Hours
NWh	West Hempstead Public Library, West Hempstead, NY [*Library symbol*] [*Library of Congress*] (LCLS)
NWHA	National Wholesale Hardware Association (EA)
NWHC	National Women's Health Coalition [*Later, IWHC*]
NWHC	Naval Weapons Handling Center
NWhCE	Cornwell Avenue School, West Hempstead, NY [*Library symbol*] [*Library of Congress*] (LCLS)
NWHF	National Wildlife Health Foundation (EA)
NWHF	National Women's Hall of Fame (EA)
NWhh	Whitehall Free Library, Whitehall, NY [*Library symbol*] [*Library of Congress*] (LCLS)
NWhHS	West Hempstead High School, West Hempstead, NY [*Library symbol*] [*Library of Congress*] (LCLS)
nwhi-	Hispaniola [*MARC geographic area code*] [*Library of Congress*] (LCCP)
NWHI	Northwestern Hawaiian Islands
NWHL	National Wildlife Health Laboratory [*Department of the Interior*] (GRD)
NWHL	Naval Weapons Handling Laboratory
NWhMS	West Hempstead Middle School, West Hempstead, NY [*Library symbol*] [*Library of Congress*] (LCLS)
NWHN	National Women's Health Network (EA)
NWHP	National Women's History Project (EA)
NWhp	White Plains Public Library, White Plains, NY [*Library symbol*] [*Library of Congress*] (LCLS)
NWhpG	College of White Plains, White Plains, NY [*Library symbol*] [*Library of Congress*] (LCLS)
NWhpI	IBM Library Processing Center, White Plains, NY [*Library symbol*] [*Library of Congress*] (LCLS)
NWhpNC	Nynex Corp., White Plains, NY [*Library symbol*] [*Library of Congress*] (LCLS)
NWhpNH	New York Hospital, Westchester Division, White Plains, NY [*Library symbol*] [*Library of Congress*] (LCLS)
NWhpSC	New York State Supreme Court Law Library, White Plains, NY [*Library symbol*] [*Library of Congress*] (LCLS)
NWhpT	Texaco Inc., Corp. Library, White Plains, NY [*Library symbol*] [*Library of Congress*] (LCLS)
NWhpTI	Temple Israel Library, White Plains, NY [*Library symbol*] [*Library of Congress*] (LCLS)
NWhpW	Westchester Library System, White Plains, NY [*Library symbol*] [*Library of Congress*] (LCLS)
NWHRC	National Women's Health Resource Center (EA)
NWHRN	Northwest Territories Public Library Services, Hay River, Northwest Territories [*Library symbol*] [*National Library of Canada*] (NLC)
NWHSLC	Northern Wisconsin Health Science Library Cooperative [*Library network*]
nwht-	Haiti [*MARC geographic area code*] [*Library of Congress*] (LCCP)
NWhWE	George Washington School, West Hempstead, NY [*Library symbol*] [*Library of Congress*] (LCLS)
NWI	National Wetlands Inventory
NWI	Netherlands West Indies
NWI	Networking and World Information [*Electronic information and communications exchange service*]
NWI	New Work Item (RALS)
NWI	Northwest Industries Ltd. (SAUS)
NWI	Norwich [*England*] [*Airport symbol*] (OAG)
NWI	Nuclear Weapons Inventory (SSD)
NWI	Nuinsco Resources Ltd. [*Toronto Stock Exchange symbol*]
NWi	West Islip Public Library, West Islip, NY [*Library symbol*] [*Library of Congress*] (LCLS)
NWIAC	Arctic College, Iqualuit, Northwest Territories [*Library symbol*] [*National Library of Canada*] (BIB)
NWIB	National Westminster Investment Bank [*British*]
NWIB	Northwest Illinois Bancorp, Inc. (SAUS)
NWIC	National Water Information Clearinghouse [*Proposed*] [*US Geological Survey*]
NWIC	National Women's Insurance Center (EA)
NWIC	Northeast Women's Intercollegiate Association (PSS)
NWICO	New World Information and Communications Order [*UNESCO*]
NWIDA	North West Industrial Development Association (SAUS)
NWiH	Good Samaritan Hospital, West Islip, NY [*Library symbol*] [*Library of Congress*] (LCLS)
NWII	Inuvik Scientific Resource Centre, Indian and Northern Affairs Canada [*CentreScientifique de Ressources d'Inuvik, Affaires Indiennes et du Nord Canada*], Northwest Territories [*Library symbol*] [*National Library of Canada*] (NLC)
NWIIE	Eastern Arctic Research Laboratory, Indian and Northern Affairs Canada [*Laboratoire de Recherches Arctique de l'Est, Affaires Indiennes et du Nord Canada*], Igloolik, Northwest Territories [*Library symbol*] [*National Library of Canada*] (BIB)
NWiIP	Willard Psychiatric Center, Willard, NY [*Library symbol*] [*Library of Congress*] (LCLS)
NWiIs	Wilson Free Library, Wilson, NY [*Library symbol*] [*Library of Congress*] (LCLS)
NWiIsHi	Wilson Historical Society, Wilson, NY [*Library symbol*] [*Library of Congress*] (LCLS)
NwImag	New Image Industries, Inc. [*Associated Press*] (SAG)
NWin	Windham Public Library, Windham, NY [*Library symbol*] [*Library of Congress*] (LCLS)
NWIO	New World Information Order [*Term coined by the Nonaligned Countries at their Fifth Summit Meeting in 1976*]
NWIP	Naval Warfare Information Publication
NWIP	Naval Warfare Intercept Procedures (MCD)
NWIP	Netware Internet Protocol (SAUS)
NWIP	North Wales Independent Press
NWIR	National Wireless Holdings, Inc. [*NASDAQ symbol*] (SAG)
NWIR	Natl Wireless Hldgs [*NASDAQ symbol*] (TTSB)
NWIRP	Naval Weapons Industrial Reserve Plant (AFM)
NWIRP	Naval Weapons Integration Reserve Plant (TIMI)
NWIS	National Water Information System [*Department of the Interior*] (GFGA)
NWIS	Naval Weaponeering Information Sheet (MCD)
NWISO	Naval Weapons Industrial Support Office (DNAB)
NWIT	Nuclear Waste Isolation Technology (NUCP)
NWIYRA	North West Intercollegiate Yacht Racing Association
NWJA	National Wholesale Jewelers Association [*Later, AJDA*] (EA)
nwjm	Jamaica [*MARC geographic area code*] [*Library of Congress*] (LCCP)
NWK	Network Equipment Technologies, Inc. [*NYSE symbol*] (SPSG)
NWK	Network Equip Tech [*NYSE symbol*] (TTSB)
NWK	Norwalk Public Library, Norwalk, CT [*Inactive*] [*OCLC symbol*] (OCLC)
NwkCmp	Network Computing Devices, Inc. [*Associated Press*] (SAG)
NwkIm	Network Imaging Corp. [*Associated Press*] (SAG)
NwkImg	Network Imaging Corp. [*Associated Press*] (SAG)
NWKLS	Northwest Kansas Library System [*Library network*]
NWL	National Water Lift Co. (MCD)
NWL	National Women's League of the United Synagogue of America [*Later, AWL*] (EA)
NWL	Natural Wavelength
NWL	Naval Weapons Laboratory [*Later, NSWC*]
NWL	Newell Co. [*NYSE symbol*] (SPSG)
NWL	Newline Development [*Vancouver Stock Exchange symbol*]
NWL	Normal Water Leg [*Nuclear energy*] (NRCH)
NWL	Normal Water Level (IAA)
NWL	North Wright Air, Ltd. [*Canada*] [*FAA designator*] (FAAC)
nwla-	Lesser Antilles [*MARC geographic area code*] [*Library of Congress*] (LCCP)
NWLA	National Women and the Law Association (EA)
NWLA	Northern Woods Logging Association (EA)
NW Law Rev	Northwestern Law Review [*A publication*] (DLA)
NWLB	National War Labor Board [*World War II*]
NWLC	National Women's Law Center (EA)
NWL/D	Naval Weapons Laboratory / Dahlgren [*Virginia*] (DNAB)
NWldP	New World Power Corp. (The) [*Associated Press*] (SAG)
NWldPwr	[*The*] New World Power Corp. [*Associated Press*] (SAG)
NWLDYA	National Wholesale Lumber Distributing Yard Association (EA)
NWLE	Nuclear Weapons Logistical Element (SAUS)
NWLEE	Northwest Law Enforcement Equipment (SAUS)
NWLF	National Watermen and Lightermen's Federation [*A union*] [*British*]
NWLF	New World Liberation Front
nwli-	Leeward Islands [*MARC geographic area code*] [*Library of Congress*] (LCCP)
NWLI	National Western Life Insurance Co. [*NASDAQ symbol*] (NQ)
NWLIA	Natl Western Life Ins'A' [*NASDAQ symbol*] (TTSB)
NWLISN	Northwest Land Information System Network (CARB)
NWL Rev	North Western Law Review [*Chicago*] [*A publication*] (DLA)
NWLS	Northwest Wisconsin Library System [*Library network*]
NWLSD	Northwest London Subdistrict (SAUS)
NWly	Northwesterly (SAUS)
NWM	Morris County Free Library, Whippany, NJ [*OCLC symbol*] (OCLC)
NWM	Newfields Minerals Ltd. [*Toronto Stock Exchange symbol*]
NWM	New Ways Ministry (EA)
NWM	New World Monkey
NWM	Non-Woven Medium [*Automotive engineering*]
NWM	Northwest Monsoon
NWM	Nuclear Waste Management (SAUS)
NWM	Nuclear Waste Materials (SAUS)
NWM	United States Military Academy, West Point, NY [*Library symbol*] [*Library of Congress*] (LCLS)
NWMA	National Woodwork Manufacturers Association [*Formerly, NDMA*] [*Later, NWWDA*] (EA)

NWMA	Northwest Mining Association (EA)
NWMAF	National Women's Martial Arts Federation (EA)
NWMC	National Wool Marketing Corp. (EA)
NWMC	Northwest Michigan College
NWMCC	Nuclear Waste Materials Characterization Center (SAUS)
NWMF	National Women's Music Festival (EA)
NWMF	Nuclear Weapons Maintenance Foreman (AABC)
NWMI	Newfields Minerals, Inc. (SAUS)
NwMilfd	New Milford Bank & Trust Co. [Associated Press] (SAG)
nwmj-	Montserrat [MARC geographic area code] [Library of Congress] (LCCP)
NWMKT	Newmarket [Urban district in England]
NWML	National Women's Mailing List (EA)
N/Wmn	Night Watchman (SAUS)
NWMP	North-West Mounted Police [Later, RCMP] [Canada]
NWMP	Nuclear Weapons Master Plan (SAUS)
NWMPA	North Wales Master Printers Alliance (SAUS)
nwmq-	Martinique [MARC geographic area code] [Library of Congress] (LCCP)
NWMRS	National Waste Minimization and Recycling Strategy [Australia]
NWMS	Nazarene World Mission Society (EA)
NWMS	Northwest Medical Service (SAUS)
NWMS	Nuclear Weapons Maintenance Specialist (AABC)
NwmtG	Newmont Gold Co. [Associated Press] (SAG)
NWMTI	Northwest Medical Team International
NWN	National Wireless Network (SAUS)
NWN	National Workers Network [Defunct] (EA)
NWN	Newcan Minerals [Vancouver Stock Exchange symbol]
NWN	New Warrior Network [An association] (EA)
NWN	Nonwhite Noise
NWN	Northwestern
NWN	Northwinds Northern Ltd. [Canada] [ICAO designator] (FAAC)
NWN	Nuclear Waste News [Business Publishers, Inc.] [No longer available online] [Information service or system] (CRD)
nwna-	Netherlands Antilles [MARC geographic area code] [Library of Congress] (LCCP)
NWNet	Northwestern States Network [Computer science] (TNIG)
NWnet	North West Net (SAUS)
NWNG	Northwest Natural Gas [NASDAQ symbol] (TTSB)
NWNG	Northwest Natural Gas Co. [NASDAQ symbol] (NQ)
NWNSA	National Women's Neckwear and Scarf Association (EA)
NWNT	North Wales Naturalists Trust (SAUS)
NW-NW	No Work - No Woo [Slogan adopted by women war workers in Albina shipyards in Portland, Oregon, who agreed not to date men who were absent from work] [World War II]
NWO	Directory of National Women's Organizations [A publication]
NWO	NASA Washington Office (KSC)
NWO	Negation Weapons Officer (ACAE)
NWO	Netherlands Organization for Scientific Research
NWO	New Work Opportunities [A publication]
NWO	New World Order [Bush administration]
NWO	Nonwoven Oriented
NWO	No World Order (SAUS)
NWOA	National Woodland Owners Association (EA)
NWOA	Nuclear Weapons Orientation Advanced Course (SAUS)
NWOBHM	New Wave of British Heavy Metal [Rock music type, 1979-81]
NWOC	Naval Weather and Oceanographic Center (DOMA)
NWOC	New Way of Computing (SAUS)
NWOC	New Woman On Campus (SAUS)
NWOFC	Numerical Weather and Oceanographic Forecasting Center [Marine science] (MSC)
NWOO	NATO Wartime Oil Organization (NATG)
NWOR	Neworld Bancorp, Inc. [NASDAQ symbol] (NQ)
n-word	nonce word (SAUS)
NWORG	North Western Operational Research Group (SAUS)
NWP	National Water Project [Later, RCAP] (EA)
NWP	National Woman's Party (EA)
NWP	National Writing Project (EA)
NWP	Nationwide Outdoor Recreation Plan [Bureau of Outdoor Recreation]
NWP	NATO and Warsaw Pact [Projects] (NATG)
NWP	Naval Warfare Procedures (MCD)
NWP	Naval Warfare Publications
NWP	Naval Weapons Plant (AAG)
NWP	Naval Weapons Publications
NWP	Net Written Premiums [Insurance] (MARI)
NWP	Northwestern Pacific Railroad Co. [AAR code]
NWP	North-Western Provinces, High Court Reports [India] [A publication] (DLA)
NWP	Northwest Passage (ROG)
NWP	Northwest Plastics, Inc. (EFIS)
NWP	North West Provinces (SAUS)
NWP	Northwest Provinces
NWP	Nuclear Waste Project [Defunct] (EA)
NWP	Numerical Weather Prediction
NWP	NWP Resources [Vancouver Stock Exchange symbol]
NWp	Williston Park Public Library, Williston Park, NY [Library symbol] [Library of Congress] (LCLS)
NWPA	Nuclear Waste Policy Act (NRCH)
NWPA	Nuclear Waste Policy Act of 1982 (GAAI)
NWPAG	NATO Wartime Preliminary Analysis Group (NATG)
NwPar	New Paradigm Software [Associated Press] (SAG)
NWPB	National Watermelon Promotion Board
NWPC	National Women's Political Caucus (EA)
NWPC	[The] New World Power Corp. [NASDAQ symbol] (SAG)
NWPC	Northwest Provinces Code [India] [A publication] (DLA)

NWPCA	National Wooden Pallet and Container Association (EA)
NWPCB	Naval Warfare Planning Chart Bases (MCD)
NWPCE	New World Power [NASDAQ symbol] (TTSB)
NWPCP	National Wetlands Priority Conservation Plan (COE)
NWpCsE	Center Street Elementary School, Williston Park, NY [Library symbol] [Library of Congress] (LCLS)
NWPF	National Water Purification Foundation
NWPF	New Waste Processing Facility (SAUS)
NWPF	Nonwoven Polyester Fabric
NWPFC	Northwest Pacific Fisheries Commission (SAUS)
NWPH	Newport Pharmaceuticals International, Inc. (SAUS)
NWPHC	Northwest Provinces, High Court Reports [India] [A publication] (DLA)
NwpkRs	Newpark Resources, Inc. [Associated Press] (SAG)
NWPL	Naval Warfare Publications Library (NVT)
NWPM	Numerical Weather Prediction Model (CARB)
NWPMA	National Wooden Pallet Manufacturers Association [Later, NWPCA] (EA)
NWPN	Nordic Womens Peace Network (SAUS)
NWPO	Northwest Pacific Oceanographers [An association] (NOAA)
NWPOG	Numerical Weather Prediction Operational Grid (SAA)
NWPP	Nationwide Permit Program [Army Corps of Engineers] (GFGA)
NWPPCA	Auyuittuq National Park, Parks Canada [Parc National Auyuittuq, Parcs Canada] Pangnirtung, Northwest Territories [Library symbol] [National Library of Canada] (NLC)
nwpr-	Puerto Rico [MARC geographic area code] [Library of Congress] (LCCP)
NWPrA	Natl Westminister Pref'A'ADS [NYSE symbol] (TTSB)
NWPrB	Natl Westminister Pref'B'ADS [NYSE symbol] (TTSB)
Nwprt News	Newport News (SAUS)
NWPS	National Wilderness Preservation System
NWPS	Northwestern Public Service Co. [Associated Press] (SAG)
NWPS	NWPS Capital Financing Tr PERCS [Associated Press] (SAG)
NWPSC	Nationwide Postal-Strike Contingency Plan (DNAB)
NWPSC	Northwestern Public Service Co. (SAUS)
NWPU	Numerical Weather Prediction Unit (DNAB)
NWPW	Naval Weapons Plant, Washington, DC
NWPX	Northwest Pipe [NASDAQ symbol] (TTSB)
NWPYVO	National Working Party of Youth Volunteer Organisers (AIE)
NWQ	Northwest Digital Ltd. [Toronto Stock Exchange symbol]
NWQ	Northwest Quadrant (SAUS)
NWQI	National Water Quality Inventory [Environmental Protection Agency]
NWQL	National Water Quality Laboratory
NWQSS	National Water Quality Surveillance System [Dicontinued, 1981] [Environmental Protection Agency]
NWR	National Welfare Rights (WDAA)
NWR	National Wildlife Refuge (WDAA)
NWR	National Women's Register [British] (DBA)
NWR	Navy Weapons Requirement
NWR	News Relationships (SAUS)
NWR	Next Word Request
NWR	Niwot Ridge (SAUS)
NWR	Normotensive Wistar Rat (DB)
NWR	North Western Railway [India]
NWR	Northwestern Reporter [Commonly cited NW] [A publication] (DLA)
NWR	Nuclear Weapons Report [Army] (AABC)
NWRA	National Waterbed Retailers Association (EA)
NWRA	National Water Resources Association (EA)
NWRA	National Wheel and Rim Association (EA)
NWRA	National Wildlife Refuge Association (EA)
NWRA	National Wildlife Rehabilitators Association (EA)
NWRA	National Women's Rowing Association [Later, USRA] (EA)
NWRBBE	Basin Planning Report. New York State Water Resources Commission. Series ENB (journ.) (SAUS)
NWRC	National Weather Records Center [Later, National Climatic Center] [National Oceanic and Atmospheric Administration]
NWRC	National Wildflower Research Center (EA)
NWRC	Naval Warfare Research Center (MCD)
NWRC	Nebraska Water Resources Center [University of Nebraska - Lincoln] [Research center] (RCD)
NWRC	Northeast Watershed Research Center [University Park, PA] [Department of Agriculture] (GRD)
NWREL	Northwest Regional Educational Laboratory [Portland, OR] [Research center]
NW Rep	Northwestern Reporter [Commonly cited NW] [A publication] (DLA)
NWREP	Nuclear Weapons Report (COE)
NW Repr	North Western Reporter [A publication] (DLA)
NW Rev Ord	Northwest Territories Revised Ordinances [Canada] [A publication] (DLA)
NWRF	Naval Weather Research Facility
NWRHB	North West Regional Health Board [Tasmania, Australia]
NWRI	National Water Research Institute [Environment Canada] [Research center] (RCD)
NwrldCf	New World Coffee, Inc. [Associated Press] (SAG)
NWRLF	New World Radical Liberation Front (NADA)
NWRLS	North Western Regional Library System (SAUS)
NWRN	Northwestern (FAAC)
NWRO	National Welfare Rights Organization [Defunct]
NWRP	Nuclear Weapons Release Procedures (SAUS)
NWRS	National Wildlife Refuge System (WDAA)
NWRS	North-West Recording Society [Record label]
NWRS	Nuclear Weapons Requirements Study (CINC)
NwRSA	Northwest Region Spinners Association (EA)
NWRT	National Wildlife Rescue Team (EA)
NWRWA	North West Regional Water Authority [Tasmania, Australia]

NWS	National Watercolor Society (EA)
NWS	National Waterways Study [*Marine science*] (MSC)
NWS	National Weather Service [*Formerly, US Weather Bureau*] [*Silver Spring, MD*] [*National Oceanic and Atmospheric Administration*]
NWS	National Winter Sports [*Association*] [*Defunct*] (EA)
NWS	Naval Weapons Station
NWS	Navy Weather Service
NWS	[*The*] News Corp. Ltd. [*NYSE symbol*] (SPSG)
NWS	News Corp. Ltd ADS [*NYSE symbol*] (TTSB)
NWS	New Workers Scheme (AIE)
NWS	New World Society (EA)
NWS	New World Symphony (SAUS)
NWS	Nimbus Weather Satellite
NWS	Non-Heatset Web Section (NTPA)
NWS	Nonprogrammable Workstation (SAUS)
NWS	Normal Water Surface (ADA)
NWS	North Warning System (MCD)
NWS	North-West Semitic (BJA)
NWS	Northwest States (ROG)
NWS	Norway Station [*South Africa*] [*Later, SNA*] [*Geomagnetic observatory code*]
NWS	Nose Wheel Steering [*Aviation*]
NWS	Nosewheel Steering (SAUS)
NWS	Nowsco Well Service Ltd. [*Toronto Stock Exchange symbol*]
NWS	Nuclear Weapon Site (CCCA)
NWS	Nuclear Weapons State
NWS	Nuclear Weapons Storage (SAUS)
NWS	Nuclear Weapon Storage (ACAE)
NWS	Weather radar system (SAUS)
NWSA	National Water Slide Association (EA)
NWSA	National Welding Supply Association (EA)
NWSA	National Wheelchair Softball Association (EA)
NWSA	National Winter Sports Association
NWSA	National Women's Studies Association (EA)
NWSA	National Women's Suffrage Association (WDAA)
NWSA	Naval Weapons Support Activity
NWSA	Naval Weather Service Association (EA)
NWSA	Nose Wheel Steering Actuator (SAUS)
NWSA	Nose Wheel Steering Amplifier [*Aviation*] (MCD)
NWSA	Nuclear Weapons Supply Annex
NWSA Jnl	NWSA Journal [*A publication*] (BRI)
NWSAP	Naval Weapons Station Acceptance Program (MCD)
NWSB	National Wage Stabilization Board [*Superseded NWLB, 1945; terminated, 1947*]
NWSB	Northwest Savings Bank [*NASDAQ symbol*] (SAG)
NWSB	Nuclear Warfare Status Branch (CINC)
nwsb-	Saint-Barthelemy [*MARC geographic area code*] [*Library of Congress*] (LCCP)
NWSC	National Water Safety Congress (EA)
NWSC	National Weather Satellite Center [*Later, National Environmental Satellite Service*]
NWSC	National Weather Service Center (MCD)
NWSC	National Women's Student Coalition (EA)
NWSC	Naval Weapons Support Center (MCD)
NWSC	Naval Weather Service Command
NWSCA	National Water and Soil Conservation Agency (BARN)
NWSCC	Nuclear Weapons System Control Console (MCD)
NWSC/CR	Naval Weapons Support Center, Crane [*Indiana*]
Nwscop	Newscope Resources Ltd. [*Associated Press*] (SAG)
NWS-CR	National Weather Service-Central Region (PDAA)
NWSD	Naval Weather Service Detachment [*or Division*]
nwsd-	Saba [*MARC geographic area code*] [*Library of Congress*] (LCCP)
NWSDGP	North West Slopes Division of General Practice (SAUS)
NWSED	Naval Weather Service Environmental Detachment [*Navy*]
NWSEO	National Weather Service Employees Organization (EA)
NWS-ER	National Weather Service-Eastern Region (PDAA)
NWSF	Northwest Sea Frontier
NWSF	Nuclear Weapons Storage Facility [*Army*] (AABC)
NWSFO	NEXRAD Weather Service Forecast Office (SAUS)
NWSFO	NWS [*National Weather Service*] Forecast Office [*Marine science*] (OSRA)
NWSG	Nuclear War Study Group (EA)
NWSG	Nuclear Weapon Systems Surety Group [*Army*]
NWsH	Houghton College, Buffalo Campus, West Seneca, NY [*Library symbol*] [*Library of Congress*] (LCLS)
NWSH	National Weather Service Headquarters
NWsHeaC	Health Care Plan Medical Center, West Seneca, NY [*Library symbol*] [*Library of Congress*] (LCLS)
NWSI	New World Services, Inc.
NWSIA	National Water Supply Improvement Association [*Later, IDA*] (EA)
NWSLF	Nowsco WellService [*NASDAQ symbol*] (TTSB)
NWSLF	Nowsco Well Services [*NASDAQ symbol*] (SAG)
NWSM	Nuclear Weapons Stockpile Memorandum
NWSO	Naval Weapons Services Office [*Also known as NAVWPNSERVO, WEPSO*]
NWSO	Naval Weather Service Office
NWSP	Nuclear Weapon Stockpile Plan (SAUS)
nwspa	Newspaper (VRA)
NWSPr	News Corp. Ltd Pfd ADS [*NYSE symbol*] (TTSB)
NWSPR	Newsprint (SAUS)
NWSRFS	National Weather Service River Forecast System (NOAA)
NWSRS	National Wild and Scenic Rivers System
NWSS	National Weather Satellite System (KSC)
NWSS	National Women's Scuba Society (EA)
NWSS	National Wool Sorters' Society [*A union*] [*British*] (DCTA)
NWSS	Navy WWMCCS [*World-Wide Military Command and Control System*] Standardization Software
NWSS	Network Six, Inc. [*NASDAQ symbol*] (SAG)
NWSS	Nuclear Weapons Support Section [*Army*] (AABC)
NWsS	West Seneca State School, West Seneca, NY [*Library symbol*] [*Library of Congress*] (LCLS)
NWSSC	Nepal Water Supply and Sewerage Corp. (SAUS)
NWSSG	Nuclear Weapons System Safety Group
NWSSG	Nuclear Weapons System Satellite Group [*Military*] (IAA)
NWSSGP	Nuclear Weapons System Safety Group
NWS-SR	National Weather Service-Southern Region (PDAA)
NWST	NewStar Media [*NASDAQ symbol*] [*Formerly, Dove Entertainment*]
nwst-	St. Martin (Sint Maarten) [*MARC geographic area code*] [*Library of Congress*] (LCCP)
NwstAirl	Northwest Airlines Corp. [*Associated Press*] (SAG)
NWSTC	National Weather Service Telecommunications (SAUS)
NwstEqty	Northwest Equity Corp. [*Associated Press*] (SAG)
NWSTG	National Weather Service Telecommunications Gateway
NWSTG	NWS [*National Weather Service*] Telecommunications Gateway [*Marine science*] (OSRA)
NwStlWr	Northwestern Steel & Wire Co. [*Associated Press*] (SAG)
NwstSBk	Northwest Savings Bank [*Associated Press*] (SAG)
NWSTTC	National Weather Service Technical Training Center
nwsv-	Swan Islands [*MARC geographic area code*] [*Library of Congress*] (LCCP)
NWSW	Northwestern Steel & Wire Co. [*NASDAQ symbol*] (SAG)
NWSW	Nothwestern Steel & Wire [*NASDAQ symbol*] (TTSB)
NWS-WR	National Weather Service-Western Region (PDAA)
NWSY	Naval Weapons Station, Yorktown [*Virginia*]
N WT	Net Weight
NWT	New World Translation (of the Holy Scriptures) [*A publication*] (BJA)
NWT	Non-Waste Technology (SAUS)
NWT	Nonwatertight [*Packaging*] (AAG)
NWT	Northwestern Terminal R. R. [*AAR code*]
NWT	Northwestern Utilities Ltd. [*Toronto Stock Exchange symbol*]
NWT	Northwest Territorial Airways [*Canada*] [*ICAO designator*] (FAAC)
NWT	Northwest Territories [*Canada*]
NWT	Nowata [*Papua New Guinea*] [*Airport symbol*] (OAG)
NWT	Nylon Wire Tie
NWTA	National Waterways Transport Association [*British*]
NWTA	National Woman's Trucking Association [*Defunct*] (EA)
NWTA	National Wool Trade Association [*Defunct*] (EA)
NWTA	North West Territory Alliance (EA)
NWTB	New Water-Tube Boiler (SAUS)
NWTB	Northwestern Tariff Bureau
NWTB	North West Tourist Board [*British*] (DCTA)
NWTC	National Wetlands Technical Council (EA)
NWTC	Naval Weapon Test Center [*China Lake, California*] [*Navy*]
NWTC	Northern Warfare Training Center [*Army*] (MCD)
NWTC	Nuclear Weapons Training Center
nwtc-	Turks and Caicos Islands [*MARC geographic area code*] [*Library of Congress*] (LCCP)
NWTCL	Nuclear Weapons Training Center, Atlantic (DNAB)
NWTCP	Nuclear Weapons Training Center, Pacific (DNAB)
NWTD	Nonwatertight Door (ADA)
NWTDB	Naval Warfare Tactical Data Base (DOMA)
NWTDB	New Water-Tube Donkey Boiler (SAUS)
NWTEC	National Wool Textile Export Corp. [*British*] (BI)
NW Terr	Northwest Territories, Supreme Court Reports [*A publication*] (DLA)
NWTF	National Wild Turkey Federation (EA)
NWTFL	Northwest Territories Federation of Labour (SAUS)
NWTG	Nuclear Weapons Training Group (DNAB)
NWTGD	Northwest Gold Corp. (SAUS)
NWTGL	Nuclear Weapons Training Group, Atlantic (DNAB)
NWTGP	Nuclear Weapons Training Group, Pacific (DNAB)
NWTH	Networth, Inc. [*NASDAQ symbol*] (SAG)
NWTI	National Wood Tank Institute (EA)
NWTI	Nuclear Weapons Technical Inspections
NWTK	North West Token Kai [*An association*] (EA)
NWTL	Northwest Teleprod'ns [*NASDAQ symbol*] (TTSB)
NWTL	Northwest Teleproductions, Inc. [*NASDAQ symbol*] (NQ)
NWTLR	North West Territories Law Reports [*A publication*] (DLA)
NWTO	Network for Work Time Options [*San Francisco, CA*] (EA)
NWT Ord	Northwest Territories Ordinances [*Canada*] [*A publication*] (DLA)
NWTP	Naval Warfare Tactical Publication (DNAB)
NWTR	North West Territories Reports [*1885-1907*] [*Canada*] [*A publication*] (DLA)
nwtr-	Trinidad and Tobago [*MARC geographic area code*] [*Library of Congress*] (LCCP)
NWTRB	Nuclear Waste Technical Review Board [*Nuclear energy*] (EGAO)
NWTRCC	National War Tax Resistance Coordinating Committee (EA)
NWT Rev Ord	Northwest Territories Revised Ordinances [*Canada*] [*A publication*] (DLA)
NWTRNA	Northwest Territories Registered Nurses Association (SAUS)
NWTS	National Waste Terminal Storage [*For radioactive wastes*]
NWTS	National Wilms' Tumor Study [*Oncology*]
NWTS	Naval Weapons Test Station
NWT/S	Nuclear Weapons Technician/Specialist (AAG)
NWTSG	National Wilms' Tumor Study Group [*Oncology*]
NWTS-RSP	NWTS Repository Sealing Program (SAUS)
NWU	National Workers Union (NADA)
NWU	National Writers Union (EA)
NWU	Nebraska Wesleyan University
NWU	Northwestern University School of Law (DLA)
NWU	Nose Wheel Up [*Aviation*]

nwuc- .... United States Miscellaneous Caribbean Islands [*MARC geographic area code*] [*Library of Congress*] (LCCP)

NWUIS .... Navy Work Unit Information System (DNAB)

NWUS .... Northwestern United States

NWV .... Newcoast Silver Mines [*Vancouver Stock Exchange symbol*]

NWV .... Norfolk, VA [*Location identifier*] [*FAA*] (FAAL)

nwvb- .... Virgin Islands, British [*MARC geographic area code*] [*Library of Congress*] (LCCP)

NWvH .... Millard Fillmore Suburban Hospital, Williamsville, NY [*Library symbol*] [*Library of Congress*] (LCLS)

nwvi- .... Virgin Islands of the US [*MARC geographic area code*] [*Library of Congress*] (LCCP)

NWVIz .... New Visions Entertainment Corp. (SAUS)

nwvr- .... Virgin Islands [*MARC geographic area code*] [*Library of Congress*] (LCCP)

NWvS .... Sanders Associates, Inc., Williamsville, NY [*Library symbol*] [*Library of Congress*] (LCLS)

NWW .... Newgate Resources [*Vancouver Stock Exchange symbol*]

NWW .... New Ways to Work (EA)

NWW .... North West Airline [*Australia*] [*ICAO designator*] (FAAC)

NWW .... Nose Wheel Well [*Aviation*] (MCD)

NWWA .... National Water Well Association [*Database producer*] (EA)

NWWA .... North-West Water Authority [*British*] (DCTA)

NWWA .... Tiga, Iles Loyaute [*New Caledonia*] [*ICAO location identifier*] (ICLI)

NWWC .... Ile Art/Wala, Iles Belep [*New Caledonia*] [*ICAO location identifier*] (ICLI)

NWWC .... National White Wyandotte Club [*Defunct*] (EA)

NwWCof ...... New World Coffee, Inc. [*Associated Press*] (SAG)

NWWCSS .... Naval Worldwide Command Support System (MCD)

NWWD .... Kone [*New Caledonia*] [*ICAO location identifier*] (ICLI)

NWWDA .... National Wood Window and Door Association (EA)

NWWE .... Ile Des Pins/Moue [*New Caledonia*] [*ICAO location identifier*] (ICLI)

NwWEye ...... New West Eyeworks, Inc. [*Associated Press*] (SAG)

NWWF .... Voh [*New Caledonia*] [*ICAO location identifier*] (ICLI)

NWWH .... Houailou/Nesson [*New Caledonia*] [*ICAO location identifier*] (ICLI)

NWWI .... Hienghene/Henri Martinet [*New Caledonia*] [*ICAO location identifier*] (ICLI)

nwwi- .... Windward Islands [*MARC geographic area code*] [*Library of Congress*] (LCCP)

NWWIIGPA .. National World War II Glider Pilots Association (EA)

NWWJ .... Poum [*New Caledonia*] [*ICAO location identifier*] (ICLI)

NWWK .... Koumac [*New Caledonia*] [*ICAO location identifier*] (ICLI)

NWWL .... Lifou/Ouanaham, Iles Loyaute [*New Caledonia*] [*ICAO location identifier*] (ICLI)

NWWM .... Noumea/Magenta [*New Caledonia*] [*ICAO location identifier*] (ICLI)

NWWN .... Noumea [*New Caledonia*] [*ICAO location identifier*] (ICLI)

NWWO .... Ile Ouen/Edmond-Cane [*New Caledonia*] [*ICAO location identifier*] (ICLI)

NWWOX .... Phoenix Aberdeen Worldwide Opportunities [*Mutual fund ticker symbol*] (SG)

NWWQ .... Mueo/Nickel [*New Caledonia*] [*ICAO location identifier*] (ICLI)

NWWR .... Mare/La Roche, Iles Loyaute [*New Caledonia*] [*ICAO location identifier*] (ICLI)

NWWS .... NOAA [*National Oceanic and Atmospheric Administration*] Weather Wire Service (NOAA)

NWWS .... Plaine Des Lacs [*New Caledonia*] [*ICAO location identifier*] (ICLI)

NWWU .... Touho [*New Caledonia*] [*ICAO location identifier*] (ICLI)

NWWV .... Ouvea/Ouloup, Iles Loyaute [*New Caledonia*] [*ICAO location identifier*] (ICLI)

NWWW .... Noumea/La Tontouta [*New Caledonia*] [*ICAO location identifier*] (ICLI)

NWWY .... Ouaco/Paquiepe [*New Caledonia*] [*ICAO location identifier*] (ICLI)

NWX .... National Westminster Bank PLC [*NYSE symbol*] (SAG)

NWX .... New Minex Resources Ltd. [*Vancouver Stock Exchange symbol*]

nwxi- .... St. Christopher-Nevis-Anguilla [*MARC geographic area code*] [*Library of Congress*] (LCCP)

nwxk- .... St. Lucia [*MARC geographic area code*] [*Library of Congress*] (LCCP)

nwxm .... St. Vincent [*MARC geographic area code*] [*Library of Congress*] (LCCP)

NWXPrA ...... Natl Westminster Bk Ex Cap Sec [*NYSE symbol*] (TTSB)

nwy .... newly (SAUS)

NWY .... New Penn Energy [*Vancouver Stock Exchange symbol*]

NWy .... Wyoming Free Public Library, Wyoming, NY [*Library symbol*] [*Library of Congress*] (LCLS)

NWY .... Yellowknife Public Library, Northwest Territories [*Library symbol*] [*National Library of Canada*] (NLC)

NWya .... Wyandanch Public Library, Wyandanch, NY [*Library symbol*] [*Library of Congress*] (LCLS)

NWyaHEC .... LaFrancis Hardiman Early Childhood Center, Wyandanch, NY [*Library symbol*] [*Library of Congress*] (LCLS)

NwyaHS ...... Wyandanch Memorial High School, Wyandanch, NY [*Library symbol*] [*Library of Congress*] (LCLS)

NWyaKE ...... Martin Luther King Elementary School, Wyandanch, NY [*Library symbol*] [*Library of Congress*] (LCLS)

NWyaOMS ... Milton Olive Middle School, Wyandanch, NY [*Library symbol*] [*Library of Congress*] (LCLS)

NWyaSE ...... Straightpath Elementary School, Wyandanch, NY [*Library symbol*] [*Library of Congress*] (LCLS)

NWYC .... Court Library, Department of Justice, Yellowknife, Northwest Territories [*Library symbol*] [*National Library of Canada*] (BIB)

NWYC .... National Write Your Congressman [*An association*] (EA)

NWYCC .... National Write Your Congressman [*Also known as National Write Your Congressman Club*] (EA)

NWYCJ .... Cooper-Johnson, Yellowknife, Northwest Territories [*Library symbol*] [*National Library of Canada*] (BIB)

NWYD .... Dene Nation, Yellowknife, Northwest Territories [*Library symbol*] [*National Library of Canada*] (BIB)

NWYECW ...... Canadian Wildlife Service, Environment Canada [*Service Canadien de la Faune, Environnement Canada*] Yellowknife, Northwest Territories [*Library symbol*] [*National Library of Canada*] (NLC)

NWYEEP ...... Assessment and Coordination Branch, Environmental Protection Service, Environment Canada [*Direction de l'Evaluation et de la Coordination, Service de la Protection de l'Environnement, Environnement Canada*] Yellowknife, Northwest Territories [*Library symbol*] [*National Library of Canada*] (NLC)

NWYGI .... Government Library, Government of the Northwest Territories, Yellow kn ife, Northwest Territories [*Library symbol*] [*National Library of Canada*] (NLC)

NWYIN .... Indian and Northern Affairs Canada [*Affaires Indiennes et du Nord Canada*] Yellowknife, Northwest Territories [*Library symbol*] [*National Library of Canada*] (NLC)

NWYND .... Northern Region Information System (NORIS), Canada Department of National Defence [*Reseau d'Information de la Region du Nord (NORIS), Ministere de la DefenseNationale*] Yellowknife, Northwest Territories [*Library symbol*] [*National Library of Canada*] (NLC)

NWYOS .... Dr. Otto Schaefer Health Resource Centre, Yellowknife, Northwest Territories [*Library symbol*] [*National Library of Canada*] (NLC)

NWYPC .... Parks Canada [*Parcs Canada*] Yellowknife, Northwest Territories [*Library symbol*] [*National Library of Canada*] (NLC)

NWYPW .... Technical Resource Centre, Department of Public Works and Highways, Government of the Northwest Territories, Yellowknife, Northwest Territories [*Library symbol*] [*National Library of Canada*] (BIB)

NWYRR .... Renewable Resources Library, Government of the Northwest Territories, Yellowknife, Northwest Territories [*Library symbol*] [*National Library of Canada*] (NLC)

NWYWNH .... Prince of Wales Northern Heritage Centre, Government of the Northwest Territories, Yellowknife, Northwest Territories [*Library symbol*] [*National Library of Canada*] (NLC)

Nx .... Nephrectomy [*Medicine*] (MELL)

NX .... Net Exports

NX .... New Zealand Air Charter [*ICAO designator*] (AD)

NX .... Nonexpendable (SAUS)

nx .... Norfolk Island [*MARC country of publication code*] [*Library of Congress*] (LCCP)

NX .... Normal to X-Axis (MCD)

NX .... Nose to X-Axis (MCD)

NX .... Not Exceeding

NX .... Not Expendable (MUGU)

NX .... Notice to Marines (SAUS)

nx .... Nourishment [*Dietetics*] (DAVI)

NX .... Quanex Corp. [*NYSE symbol*] (SPSG)

NXA .... Nodal Exchange Area (MHDB)

NXA .... Nolisair International, Inc. [*Canada*] [*ICAO designator*] (FAAC)

NXA .... Norex America [*AMEX symbol*] (TTSB)

NXA .... Norex America, Inc. [*AMEX symbol*] (SPSG)

NXA .... Norex Industries [*AMEX symbol*] [*Formerly, Norex America*] (SG)

NXA .... Siem Industries [*AMEX symbol*] [*Formerly, Norex Industries*]

NXA .... Wake County Public Library, Raleigh, NC [*OCLC symbol*] (OCLC)

NXB .... Neurotoxin B

NXB .... Non-X-Ray Background

NX Button .... Entrance-Exit Button (SAUS)

NXC .... Nuveen Ins CA Sel Tax-Free Inc. [*NYSE symbol*] (TTSB)

NXC .... Nuveen Insured California Select Tax-Free Income [*NYSE symbol*] (SPSG)

NXCD .... NextCard, Inc. [*NASDAQ symbol*] (SG)

NXCI .... National Xeriscape Council, Inc. [*An association*] (EA)

NXCO .... Neurex Corp. [*NASDAQ symbol*] (SAG)

NX Console... Entrance-Exit Console (SAUS)

NXD .... Non-Executive Director (SAUS)

NXDO .... Nike-X Development Office [*Army*] (AABC)

NXGN .... NexGen, Inc. [*NASDAQ symbol*] (SAG)

NXI .... Oak Harbor, WA [*Location identifier*] [*FAA*] (FAAL)

NX Interlocking... Entrance-Exit Interlocking (SAUS)

NXL .... Napoleon Exploration [*Vancouver Stock Exchange symbol*]

NXL............. New Plan Excel Realty Trust [*Formerly, New Plan Excel Realty*] [*NYSE symbol*]

n-xl- .... St. Pierre and Miquelon [*MARC geographic area code*] [*Library of Congress*] (LCCP)

NXLK .... NEXTLINK Communications'A' [*NASDAQ symbol*] (SG)

NXM .... Non-Existent Memory (MHDB)

NXM .... Noramex Minerals [*Vancouver Stock Exchange symbol*]

NX Machine... Entrance-Exit Machine (SAUS)

NXMIS .... Nike-X Management Information System [*Army*]

NX MO .... Next Month (SAUS)

NXN .... Milton, FL [*Location identifier*] [*FAA*] (FAAL)

NXN .... No Christian Name

NXN .... Nuveen Ins NY Sel Tax-Free Inc. [*NYSE symbol*] (TTSB)

NXN .... Nuveen Insured New York Select Tax-Free Income [*NYSE symbol*] (SPSG)

NXP .... Norberts XML Parser (SAUS)

NXP .... Noxe Resources Corp. [*Vancouver Stock Exchange symbol*]

NXP .... Nuveen Select Tax-Free Inc. [*NYSE symbol*] (TTSB)

NXP .... Nuveen Select Tax-Free Income [*NYSE symbol*] (SPSG)

NXP .... Twentynine Palms, CA [*Location identifier*] [*FAA*] (FAAL)

NX Panel ..... Entrance-Exit Panel (SAUS)

NXPM .... Nike-X Project Manager [*Army*] (AABC)

NXPO	Nike-X Program [*or Project*] Office [*Army*]
NXPRG	Nike-X Program Review Group [*Army*] (AABC)
NXQ	Nuveen Selct Tax-Free Inc. 2 [*NYSE symbol*] (TTSB)
NXQ	Nuveen Select Tax-Free Income 2 [*NYSE symbol*] (SPSG)
NXR	Noncrossing Rule
NXR	Nuveen Selct Tax-Free Inc. 3 [*NYSE symbol*] (TTSB)
NXR	Nuveen Select Tax-Free Income 3 [*NYSE symbol*] (SPSG)
NXRA	Nextera Enterprises'A' [*NASDAQ symbol*] (SG)
NXS	Nexus Resources Corp. [*Vancouver Stock Exchange symbol*] [*Toronto Stock Exchange symbol*]
NXSM	Nike-X System Manager [*Army*] (AABC)
NXSMO	Nike-X System Manager's Office [*Army*]
NXSO	Nike-X Support Office [*Army*]
NXSPC	Nexus Telecommunication Systems Ltd. [*NASDAQ symbol*] (SAG)
NXSR	Non-Extraction Steam Rate (PDAA)
NX System	Entrance-Exit System (SAUS)
NXT	Next
NX Tower	Entrance-Exit Tower (SAUS)
NXTP	Nextel Partners 'A' [*NASDAQ symbol*] (SG)
NXTR	NeXstar Pharmaceutical [*NASDAQ symbol*] (SAG)
NXTR	NeXstar Pharmaceuticals [*NASDAQ symbol*] (TTSB)
NXT SSN	Next Season (SAUS)
NXUL	Nexus Telecommunication Systems Ltd. [*NASDAQ symbol*] (SAG)
NXULF	Nexus Telecomm Sys Wrrt [*NASDAQ symbol*] (TTSB)
NXUS	Nexus Telecommunication Systems Ltd. [*NASDAQ symbol*] (SAG)
NXUSF	Nexus Telecommns Sys Ltd [*NASDAQ symbol*] (TTSB)
NXUW	Nexus Telecommunication Systems Ltd. [*NASDAQ symbol*] (SAG)
NXUWF	Nexus Telecommuns Sys Wrrt'A' [*NASDAQ symbol*] (TTSB)
NXUZ	Nexus Telecommunication Systems Ltd. [*NASDAQ symbol*] (SAG)
NXUZF	Nexus Telecommuns Sys Wrrt'B' [*NASDAQ symbol*] (TTSB)
NXW	University of North Carolina, Wilmington, Wilmington, NC [*OCLC symbol*] (OCLC)
NX WK	Next Week (SAUS)
NXWPC	Nexus Telecommunication Systems Ltd. [*NASDAQ symbol*] (SAG)
NXX	End Office Code (CGWS)
NXX	Willow Grove, PA [*Location identifier*] [*FAA*] (FAAL)
NX YR	Next Year (SAUS)
NXZPC	Nexus Telecommunication Systems Ltd. [*NASDAQ symbol*] (SAG)
NY	John Dewey [*Final letters of his first and last name used as a pseudonym*] [*American author, 1859-1952*]
NY	Navy Yard
NY	Nelen Yubu [*A publication*] (APTA)
NY	Net Yield
NY	New Year
NY	New York [*City or state*] [*Postal code*]
NY	New York [*Naval Shipyard*]
NY	New York Airways, Inc. [*ICAO designator*]
NY	New York Court of Appeals Reports [*A publication*] (DLA)
NY	New Yorker [*A publication*] (BRI)
Ny	Niles (SAUS)
NY	Noorduyn Aviation Ltd. [*Canada*] [*ICAO aircraft manufacturer identifier*] (ICAO)
NY	Normal to Y-Axis (MCD)
NY	Northamptonshire Yeomanry [*British military*] (DMA)
NY	Northumberland Yeomanry [*British military*] (DMA)
NY	Nose to Y-Axis (NASA)
NY	Not Yield (ELAL)
NY	No Year [*of publication*] [*Bibliography*]
NY	Nuclear Yellow [*A fluorescent dye*]
NY	Nuclear Yield
NY	Nyasaland (ROG)
Ny	Nylan (SAUS)
NY	Nylon [*Tire design*]
NY	Yonkers Public Library, Yonkers, NY [*Library symbol*] [*Library of Congress*] (LCLS)
NY 2d	New York Court of Appeals Reports, Second Series [*A publication*] (DLA)
NYA	National Yogurt Association (EA)
NYA	National Youth Administration [*Terminated, 1943*]
NYA	National Youth Alliance (EA)
NYA	Neighborhood Youth Administration (OICC)
NYA	New York Airways, Inc. [*Air carrier designation symbol*]
NYA	New York Aquarium (SAUS)
NYA	Not Yet Answered
nya	Nyanja [*MARC language code*] [*Library of Congress*] (LCCP)
NYAB	National Youth Advisory Board [*Environmental Protection Agency*]
NYAB	New York Air Brake Co.
NYABIC	New York Association for Brain Injured Children
NY Acad Sci Ann	New York Academy of Sciences, Annals (SAUS)
NYACH	New York Automated Clearing House (TBD)
NYADC	New York Air Defense Center (SAUS)
NY Admin Code	Official Compilation of Codes, Rules, and Regulations of the State of New York [*A publication*] (DLA)
NYADS	New York Air Defense Sector (SAA)
NYAES-C	New York Agricultural Experiment Station (Cornell University) [*Research center*] (RCD)
NYAIC	New York Association of Industrial Communicators [*Later, NY/IABC*] (EA)
NYAL	National Yugoslav Army of Liberation [*World War II*]
NYAL	New York Airlines (SAUS)
NYALR	New Yorkers for Abortion Law Repeal (EA)
NYAM	New York Academy of Medicine
NYAM	New York Academy of Music
NYAMP	New York Advertising Media Planners [*Defunct*] (EA)
NYANA	New York Association for New Americans (EA)

NY & E	New York & Erie Railroad
NY & NE	New York & New England Railroad [*Nickname: Now You Are Nearing Eternity*]
NY & NH	New York & New Haven Railroad
NYANG	New York Air National Guard (MUSM)
NY Ann Ca	New York Annotated Cases [*A publication*] (DLA)
NY Ann Cas	New York Annotated Cases [*A publication*] (DLA)
NY Anno Cas	New York Annotated Cases [*A publication*] (DLA)
NY Anno Dig	New York Annotated Digest [*A publication*] (ILCA)
NY Annot Dig	New York Annotated Digest [*A publication*] (DLA)
NYAO	New York Assay Office (SAUS)
NYap	Middle Island Central Public Library, Yaphank, NY [*Library symbol*] [*Library of Congress*] (LCLS)
NYAP	New York Assembly Program [*Computer science*]
NYAP	New York Average Price per Share [*Stock market*]
NY App Dec	New York Court of Appeals Decisions [*A publication*] (DLA)
NY App Div	New York Supreme Court, Appellate Division Reports [*A publication*] (DLA)
NYARTCC	New York Air Route Traffic Control Center (SAUS)
NYAS	New York Academy of Sciences (EA)
NYAS	New York Asian Society (SAUS)
NYATI	New York Agricultural and Technical Institute (SAUS)
NYB	National Youth Bureau [*British*]
NYB	New York Bancorp [*NYSE symbol*] (SAG)
NYB	New York Bancorp Inc. [*AMEX symbol*] (SPSG)
NYB	New York Bight [*Oceanography*] (MSC)
NYB	North York Board of Education [*UTLAS symbol*]
NYBA	National Young Buddhist Association [*Defunct*] (EA)
NYBagel	New York Bagel Enterprises, Inc. [*Associated Press*] (SAG)
NYB & M	New York, Boston & Montreal Railroad
NY Bank Law	New York Banking Law [*A publication*] (DLA)
NYBC	National Yiddish Book Center (EA)
NYBC	New York Bancorp, Inc. (SAUS)
NYBC	New York Business Communicators [*Later, NY/IABC*] (EA)
NY Bcp	New York Bancorp [*Associated Press*] (SAG)
NY Bcp	New York Bancorp, Inc. [*Associated Press*] (SAG)
NYBE	National Yiddish Book Exchange (EA)
NYBFU	New York Board of Fire Underwriters (BARN)
NYBG	New York Botanical Garden
NYBID	New York interbank bid rate (SAUS)
NYBOR	New York interbank offered rate (SAUS)
NYBOS	Navy Yard, Boston, Massachusetts [*Obsolete*]
NYBOT	New York Board of Trade
NYBP	New York Bight Project (SAUS)
NYBPE	New York Business Press Editors [*New York, NY*] (EA)
NYBS	New York Bagel Enterprises, Inc. [*NASDAQ symbol*] (SAG)
NYBS	New York Browning Society (EA)
NYBSBC	New York Bureau of State Building Codes (BARN)
NYBT	Boyce Thompson Institute for Plant Research, Yonkers, NY [*Library symbol*] [*Library of Congress*] (LCLS)
NYBT	New York Board of Trade [*New York, NY*] (EA)
NYC	Charley [*Nevada*] [*Seismograph station code, US Geological Survey*] [*Closed*] (SEIS)
NYC	Neighborhood Youth Corps [*Department of Labor*] [*Terminated*]
NYC	New York Central R. R. [*Later, Penn Central*] [*AAR code*]
NYC	New York Circus (EA)
NYC	New York City
NYC	New York, Motor Carrier Conference [*STAC*]
NYC	New York [*New York*]/Newark [*New Jersey*] [*Airport symbol*] (OAG)
NYC	New York, NY [*Location identifier*] [*FAA*] (FAAL)
NYCA	New York City Affiliate (SAUS)
NYCA	New York Court of Appeals Reports [*A publication*] (DLA)
NYCAC	New York Collegiate Athletic Conference (PSS)
NYC & HR	New York Central & Hudson River Railroad
NYC & HRR	New York Central & Hudson River Railroad (ROG)
NYC & SL	New York, Chicago and St. Louis Railroad Co. (IIA)
NYC & STL	New York, Chicago & St. Louis Railroad Co.
NY Cas Err	Caines' New York Cases in Error [*A publication*] (DLA)
NY Cas in Error	Caines' New York Cases in Error [*A publication*] (DLA)
NYCATC	New York City Athletic Conference (PSS)
NYCB	New York City Ballet
NYCBA	New York City Bar Association. Bulletin [*A publication*] (DLA)
NYCBA Bull	Bulletin. Association of the Bar of the City of New York [*A publication*] (DLA)
NYCBAN	New York Center Beacon Alphanumerics [*FAA*]
NYCC	New York Candy Club (EA)
NYCC	New York City Commission for the United Nations, Consular Corps, and International Business (EA)
NYCC	New York Cultural Center (SAUS)
NYCCA	New York Cocoa Clearing Association (EA)
NYCCC	New York City Community College
NYCCD	New York Current Court Decisions [*A publication*] (DLA)
NYCCH	New York Advance Digest Service (Commerce Clearing House), Cited by Year [*A publication*] (DLA)
NYCCI	New York Corset Club (EA)
NYCCIW	New York City Correctional Institution for Women (SAUS)
NYCDC	New York City Department of Correction (SAUS)
NYCDC	New York Curtain and Drapery Club (EA)
NYCE	New York Cash Exchange [*Automated teller machine network*]
NYCE	New York Cocoa Exchange [*Later, CSCE*]
NYCE	New York College of Education (SAUS)
NYCE	New York, Commodities Exchange
NYCE	New York, Commodity Exchange (SAUS)
NYCE	New York Cotton Exchange (EA)
NYCE	New York Curb Exchange [*Later, AMEX*]

NYCER......... New York Conference on Electronic Reliability (MCD)
NYCERS....... New York City Employees Retirement System (SAUS)
NYCFMA...... New York Credit and Financial Management Association [*New York, NY*] (EA)
NY Ch.......... Chancery Sentinel [*New York*] [*A publication*] (DLA)
NYCH.......... National Youth Coalition on Housing [*Australia*]
NYCHA........ New York City Housing Authority (SAUS)
NYCHA........ New York Clearing House Association [*New York, NY*] (EA)
NYCHARL .... Navy Yard, Charleston, South Carolina
NY-CHI....... New York-Chicago
NY Ch Sent... New York Chancery Sentinel [*A publication*] (DLA)
NYCI .... New York City's First [*First beluga whale born at the New York Aquarium, 1981*] [*Pronounced "Nicky"*]
NY City Ct... New York City Court [*A publication*] (DLA)
NY City Ct Rep.. New York City Court Reports [*A publication*] (DLA)
NY City Ct Supp... New York City Court Reports, Supplement [*A publication*] (DLA)
NY City Hall Rec... New York City Hall Recorder [*A publication*] (ILCA)
NY City H Rec... New York City Hall Recorder [*A publication*] (DLA)
NY Civ Prac Law & R... New York Civil Practice Law and Rules [*A publication*] (DLA)
NY Civ Pro... New York Civil Procedure [*A publication*] (DLA)
NY Civ Proc... New York Civil Procedure [*A publication*] (ILCA)
NY Civ Proc (NS)... New York Civil Procedure, New Series [*A publication*] (DLA)
NY Civ Proc R... New York Civil Procedure Reports [*A publication*] (DLA)
NY Civ Proc Rep... Civil Procedure Reports [*New York*] [*A publication*] (DLA)
NY Civ Proc R NS... New York Civil Procedure Reports, New Series [*A publication*] (DLA)
NY Civ Pro R... New York Civil Procedure Reports [*A publication*] (ILCA)
NY Civ Pro R NS... New York Civil Procedure Reports, New Series [*A publication*] (ILCA)
NY Civ Pr Rep... New York Civil Procedure Reports [*A publication*] (ILCA)
NYCJG .... Nikka Yuko Centennial Japanese Garden (SAUS)
NYCM .... NYCOM Information Services, Inc. (SAUS)
NYCMA........ New York Clothing Manufacturers Association (EA)
NYCMD........ New York Contract Management District (SAA)
NYCME .... New York Clothing Manufacturers Exchange [*Later, NYCMA*] (EA)
NYCMSL...... New York County Medical Society Library (SAUS)
NYCN .... New York Connecting Railroad [*AAR code*]
NYCNHA ...... New York City Nursing Home Association (SAUS)
NYCO .... New York City Opera
NYCO .... NYCOR, Inc. [*NASDAQ symbol*] (NQ)
NYCOA .... NYCOR Inc.'A' [*NASDAQ symbol*] (TTSB)
NY Code R... New York Code Reporter [*A publication*] (DLA)
NY Code Rep... New York Code Reporter [*A publication*] (DLA)
NY Code Rep NS... New York Code Reports, New Series [*A publication*] (DLA)
NY Code Report... New York Code Reporter [*A publication*] (DLA)
NY Code Report NS... New York Code Reporter, New Series [*A publication*] (DLA)
NY Code Reports NS... New York Code Reporter, New Series [*A publication*] (DLA)
NY Code Reptr... New York Code Reporter [*A publication*] (DLA)
NY Code Reptr NS... New York Code Reporter, New Series [*A publication*] (DLA)
NY Code R NS... New York Code Reports, New Series [*A publication*] (DLA)
NY Cond ...... New York Condensed Reports [*1881-82*] [*A publication*] (DLA)
Nycor.......... NYCOR, Inc. [*Associated Press*] (SAG)
NY Co Rem... New York Code of Remedial Justice [*A publication*] (DLA)
NYCP .... Civil Procedure Reports [*New York*] [*A publication*] (DLA)
NYCPB .... New York Consumer Protection Board (SAUS)
NYCPD .... New York City Police Department (SAUS)
NYCPM .... New York City Police Museum (SAUS)
NY Cr .... New York Criminal Reports [*A publication*] (DLA)
NYCRC .... New York Civil Rights Coalition (SAUS)
NY Crim....... New York Criminal Reports [*A publication*] (DLA)
NY Crim R... New York Criminal Reports [*A publication*] (DLA)
NY Crim Rep... New York Criminal Reports [*A publication*] (DLA)
NYCRR........ New York Codes, Rules, and Regulations [*A publication*] (DLA)
NY Cr R .... New York Criminal Reports [*A publication*] (DLA)
NY Cr Rep ... New York Criminal Reports [*A publication*] (DLA)
NYCS .... New York Chamber Symphony (SAUS)
NYCS .... New York Choral Society (SAUS)
NYCS .... New York Cipher Society (EA)
NYCS .... New York City Shoes, Inc. (SAUS)
NYCSA .... New York Coat and Suit Association (EA)
NYCSA .... New York College Stores Association
NYCSCE ...... New York Coffee, Sugar, and Cocoa Exchange
NYCSE .... New York Coffee and Sugar Exchange [*Later, CSCE*] (EA)
NYCSG .... New York Constitution Study Group (EA)
NYCSLS .... New York C. S. Lewis Society (EA)
NYCSMA ...... National Young Christian Students' Movement of Australia
NYCT .... New York Community Trust (SAUS)
NYCTA .... New York Central Transit Authority (SAUS)
NYCTA .... New York City Transit Authority (SAUS)
NY Ct App... New York Court of Appeals (DLA)
NYCTC .... New York City Technical College
NYCTCG .... New York Cold Type Composition Group [*Later, TANY*] (EA)
NYCTN .... New York Cotton Exchange (EBF)
NYCTNCA..... New York Cotton Exchange, Citrus Associates
NYCUC .... New York City Urban Corps (EA)
NYCWRU .... New York Cooperative Wildlife Research Unit (SAUS)
NYCX .... New York Commodity Exchange (SAUS)
NYD .... Navy Yard
NYD .... New York Datum (NRCH)
NYD .... New York Dock Railway [*AAR code*]
NYD .... Not Yet Dead (SAUS)
NYD .... Not Yet Detected (SAUS)
NYD .... Not Yet Determined (SAUS)
NYD .... Not Yet Diagnosed [*Facetious translation: "Not Yet Dead"*] [*Medicine*]

NYD .... Not Yet Discovered (DMAA)
NYD .... Not Yet Dressed (SAUS)
NYD .... Nycomed ASA ADS [*NYSE symbol*] (TTSB)
NY Daily L Gaz... New York Daily Law Gazette [*A publication*] (DLA)
NY Daily L Reg... New York Daily Law Register [*A publication*] (DLA)
NY Daily Reg... New York Daily Register [*A publication*] (DLA)
NY Daily Tr... New York Daily Transcript, Old and New Series [*A publication*] (DLA)
NYDCC......... New York Drama Critics Circle (EA)
NY Dep't R... New York Department Records [*A publication*] (DLA)
NYDF.......... National Youth Development Foundation [*Defunct*] (EA)
NYDISS........ New York Disposal Surveillance System [*U.S. Army Corps of Engineers*]
NYDLWC Dec... New York State Department of Labor. Court Decisions of Workmen's Compensation [*A publication*] (DLA)
NYDMC........ New York Downstate Medical Center (SAUS)
NYDO .... National Youth Development Officer (AIE)
NYDP .... Neighborhood Youth Development Program
NYD Poultry... New York Dressed Poultry (SAUS)
NYDR.......... New York Department Reports [*A publication*] (DLA)
NYDR.......... New York Dock Railway (SAUS)
NYE .... Nycomed Amersham ADS [*NYSE symbol*] (SG)
Nye .... Nye's Reports [*18-21 Utah*] [*A publication*] (DLA)
NYEC .... National Youth Employment Coalition
NYEG .... New York State Electric & Gas Corp. [*Associated Press*] (SAG)
NY El Cas... New York Election Cases [*A publication*] (DLA)
NY Elec Cas... New York Election Cases [*A publication*] (DLA)
NY Elect Cas... New York Election Cases [*A publication*] (DLA)
NYER .... Nyer Med Group [*NASDAQ symbol*] (TTSB)
NYER .... Nyer Medical Group [*NASDAQ symbol*] (SAG)
NyerMd........ Nyer Medical Group [*Associated Press*] (SAG)
NYES .... Elizabeth Seton College, Yonkers, NY [*Library symbol*] [*Library of Congress*] (LCLS)
NYES .... New York Electrical Society (SAUS)
NYES .... New York Entomological Society (SAUS)
NYET LC ...... Not Yet in Library of Congress [*Suggested name for the Library of Congress computer system*]
NYETR .... New York Estate Tax Reports [*Prentice-Hall, Inc.*] [*A publication*] (DLA)
NYEWW ...... New York Exchange for Woman's Work [*New York, NY*] (EA)
NYF........... National Yeomen F [*Defunct*] (EA)
NYF........... National Youth Foundation [*Australia*]
NYF........... New York Foundation
NYF........... New York Futures Exchange
NY Farms&Markets Dept... New York State Department of Farms and Markets. Publications (DLA)
NYFBT .... New York Film Board of Trade [*Defunct*] (EA)
NYFBX .... Mgn. Stanley D. Witter N.Y. Tax Free Cl.B [*Mutual fund ticker symbol*] (SG)
NYFC .... New York Film Critics (EA)
NYFCC .... New York Film Critics Circle (SAUS)
NYFCC .... New York Futures Clearing Corp. [*New York Futures Exchange*]
NYFD .... New York Fashion Designers [*Later, NYFDF*] (EA)
NYFDF .... New York Fashion Designers and Foundation [*Defunct*] (EA)
NYFDM .... New York Fire Department Museum (SAUS)
NYFE .... New York Futures Exchange [*Pronounced "knife"*]
NYFEA .... National Young Farmer Educational Association (EA)
NYFFFBA ..... New York Foreign Freight Forwarders and Brokers Association [*New York, NY*] (EA)
NYFH .... New York Foundling Hospital (SAUS)
NYFIRO........ New York Fire Insurance Rating Organization (SAUS)
NY Food Life Sci Bull... New Yorks Food and Life Sciences Bulletin (SAUS)
NYFRF .... New York Fertility Research Foundation [*Later, FRF*] (EA)
NYFUO......... New York Federation of Urban Organizations
NYFW .... New York Film Works, Inc. (SAUS)
NYFWA........ New York Financial Writers' Association (EA)
NYG .... Geigy Pharmaceuticals, Yonkers, NY [*Library symbol*] [*Library of Congress*] (LCLS)
NYG .... New York Giants [*National Football League*] [*1925-present*] (NFLA)
NYG .... New York State Library, Albany, NY [*OCLC symbol*] (OCLC)
NYG .... Nyge Aero AB [*Sweden*] [*ICAO designator*] (FAAC)
NYG .... Quantico, VA [*Location identifier*] [*FAA*] (FAAL)
NYGB .... New York Genealogical and Biographical Society (SAUS)
NYGBR........ New York Genealogical and Biographical Society Record (SAUS)
NYGBS........ New York Genealogical and Biographical Society (EA)
NYGC .... New York Governor's Conference
NYGJB .... New York Guild for Jewish Blind [*Later, JGB*]
NYGS .... New York Graphic Society (SAUS)
NYH .... New York Helicopter Corp. [*ICAO designator*] (FAAC)
NYH .... New York Hospital
NYHA.......... National Yacht Harbour Association [*British*] (BI)
NYHA.......... New York Heart Association [*Classifications I, II, III, and IV*] [*Cardiology*] (DAVI)
NYHA.......... New York Heart Associaton (MEDA)
NYHC .... New York Health Care, Inc. [*NASDAQ symbol*] (SAG)
NYHD .... New York House of Detention (SAUS)
NYhl .... International Business Machines Corp., Thomas J. Watson Research Center, Yorktown Heights, NY [*Library symbol*] [*Library of Congress*] (LCLS)
NY Hist Soc... New York Historical Society (SAUS)
NYHlthC....... New York Health Care, Inc. [*Associated Press*] (SAG)
NYhP.......... Putnam North Westchester S.L.S., Yorktown Heights, NY [*Library symbol*] [*Library of Congress*] (LCLS)
NYHS .... New York Herpetological Society (SAUS)
NYHS .... New York Historical Society (SAUS)

NYHSL	New York Health and Safety Laboratory [*Energy Research and Development Administration*]
NYHT	New York Herald Tribune [*Defunct newspaper*]
NYHTB	New York Herald Tribune Books (SAUS)
NYHTBR	New York Herald Tribune. Book Review (SAUS)
NYI	New York Institute
NYI	Not Yet Impacted (SAUS)
NYI	NSF Young Investigator (SAUS)
NYI	Sunyani [*Ghana*] [*Airport symbol*] (OAG)
NYIA	New York International Airport (SAUS)
NY/IABC	New York/International Association of Business Communicators [*New York, NY*] (EA)
NYIAS	New York Institute of the Aerospace Sciences (SAUS)
NYIBC	New York International Ballet Competition
NYIBC	New York Islanders Booster Club (EA)
NYIBS	New York International Bible Society (EA)
NYIC	New York Iroquois Conference (EA)
NYICD	New York Institute for Child Development (EA)
NYID	Not-Yet-Invented Device (SAUS)
NYIDA	New York Importers and Distillers Association (EA)
NYIE	New York Insurance Exchange
NYIF	New York Index - Finance [*Stock market*]
NYIF	New York Institute of Finance (ECON)
NYIH	New York Institute for the Humanities (SAUS)
NYII	New York Index - Industrials [*Stock market*]
NYIL	Netherlands Yearbook of International Law [*A publication*] (DLA)
NYIT	New York Index - Transportation [*Stock market*]
NYIT	New York Institute of Technology
NYIU	New York Index - Utilities [*Stock market*]
NYJ	Joshua Tree [*Nevada*] [*Seismograph station code, US Geological Survey*] [*Closed*] (SEIS)
NYJ	National Young Judaea (EA)
NYJ	New York Jets [*National Football League*] [*1963-present*] (NFLA)
NYJM	New York Journal of Mathematics (SAUS)
NYJO	National Youth Jazz Orchestra [*British*]
NY Jud Rep	New York Judicial Repository [*A publication*] (DLA)
NY Jud Repos	New York Judicial Repository [*A publication*] (DLA)
NY Jur	New York Jurisprudence [*A publication*] (DLA)
NY Jur	New York Jurist [*A publication*] (DLA)
NYK	New York [*City*]
NYK	Nippon Yusen Kaisha Line (SAUS)
NYK	North York Public Library [*UTLAS symbol*]
NYKGRP	New York Group [*Navy*]
NYL	Neodymium YAG [*Yttrium Aluminum Garnet*] LASER
NYL	Nylon (MSA)
NYL	Yuma, AZ [*Location identifier*] [*FAA*] (FAAL)
NYLA	New York Library Association
NYLA Bulletin	New York Library Association Bulletin (SAUS)
NY Law Bul	New York Monthly Law Bulletin [*A publication*] (DLA)
NY Law Gaz	New York Law Gazette [*A publication*] (DLA)
NY Law (McKinney)	McKinney's Consolidated Laws of New York [*A publication*] (DLA)
NY Law Sch	New York Law School (GAGS)
NY-LAX	New York-Los Angeles (SAUS)
NYLB	[*The*] New York & Long Branch Railroad Co. [*Absorbed into Consolidated Rail Corp.*] [*AAR code*]
NYLC	National Young Life Campaign [*British*]
NYLC	National Youth Leadership Council (EA)
NYLC Ann	New York Leading Cases, Annotated [*A publication*] (DLA)
NYL Cas	New York Leading Cases [*A publication*] (DLA)
NYLE & W	New York, Lake Erie & Western Railroad [*Later, EL*] [*Nickname: Now You Lay Easy and Wait*]
NY Leg N	New York Legal News [*1880-82*] [*A publication*] (DLA)
NY Leg Obs	New York Legal Observer (Owen) [*A publication*] (DLA)
NY Leg Reg	New York Legal Register [*A publication*] (DLA)
NYLEX USA	New York Leather Exposition [*American European Trade and Exhibition Center*]
NYLFIN	Nylon Finish (SAUS)
NYLG	New York Law Group [*Later, BAHRGNY*] (EA)
NYL Gaz	New York Law Gazette [*A publication*] (DLA)
NY Lib Assn Bul	New York Library Association Bulletin (SAUS)
NYLIC	New York Library Instruction Clearinghouse (SAUS)
NY LIFE	New York Life (EFIS)
NYLO	New York Legal Observer [*A publication*] (DLA)
NYLR	Neodymium YAG [*Yttrium Aluminum Garnet*] LASER Range-Finder
Ny LR	Nyasaland Law Reports [*South Africa*] [*A publication*] (DLA)
NYLRB	New York State Labor Relations Board Decisions [*A publication*] (DLA)
NYLRB Dec	New York State Labor Relations Board Decisions and Orders [*A publication*] (DLA)
NYL Rec	New York Law Record [*A publication*] (DLA)
NYLS	New York Law School
NYLS	New York State Longitudinal Study (EDAC)
NYLSMA	New York Lamp and Shade Manufacturers Association (EA)
NYLS Stud L Rev	New York Law School. Student Law Review [*A publication*]
NYLTI	National Youth Leadership Training Institute
NYM	Anonymous (SAUS)
NYM	Climax Mine [*Nevada*] [*Seismograph station code, US Geological Survey*] [*Closed*] (SEIS)
NYM	New York Mercantile Exchange
NYM	New York Minute (SAUS)
NYM	New York Movers Tariff Bureau, Inc. (SAUS)
NYM	New York Movers Tariff Bureau, Inc., New York NY [*STAC*]
nym	Nyamwezi [*MARC language code*] [*Library of Congress*] (LCCP)
NYM	NYMAGIC, Inc. [*Formerly, New York Marine & General Insurance Co.*] [*NYSE symbol*] (SPSG)
NYMA	New York City Metropolitan Area
NYMA	New York Metropolitan Area (SAUS)
NYMA	New York Mounters Association [*New York, NY*] (EA)
NYMAGC	NYMAGIC, Inc. [*Formerly, New York Marine & General Insurance Co.*] [*Associated Press*] (SAG)
NYM&S Brief	New York Medical and Surgical Brief (SAUS)
NYMC	New York Maritime College (SAUS)
NYMC	New York Medical College [*Valhalla, NY*]
NYME	New York Mercantile Exchange (EA)
NY Med C	New York Medicine College (GAGS)
NYMEX	New York Mercantile Exchange (EA)
NYMI	Navy Yard, Mare Island, California
NY-MIA	New York-Miami (SAUS)
NY Misc	New York Miscellaneous Reports [*A publication*] (DLA)
NY Misc 2d	New York Miscellaneous Reports. Second Series [*A publication*] (DLA)
NYMM	New York Merchandise Mart
NYMNEX	New York Mercantile Exchange
NYMO	National Youth Ministry Organization (EA)
NY Mo Law Bul	New York Monthly Law Bulletin [*A publication*] (DLA)
NY Mo L Bul	New York Monthly Law Bulletin [*A publication*] (DLA)
NY Mo LR	New York Monthly Law Reports [*A publication*] (DLA)
NY Mo L Rec	New York Monthly Law Record [*A publication*] (DLA)
NY Month L Bul	New York Monthly Law Bulletin [*A publication*] (DLA)
NY Month LR	New York Monthly Law Reports [*A publication*] (DLA)
NY Month L Rep	New York Monthly Law Reports [*A publication*] (DLA)
NY Monthly Law Bul	New York Monthly Law Bulletin [*A publication*] (DLA)
NYMPH	Nymphomaniac (DSUE)
nymphm	Nymphaeum (VRA)
NYMPHO	Nymphomania (SAUS)
NYMPHO	Nymphomaniac (DSUE)
NYMPHO	Nymphomaniacal (SAUS)
NYMRRLA	New York Metropolitan Reference and Research Library Agency (SAUS)
NYMS	New York Microscopical Society (EA)
NY Mun Gaz	New York Municipal Gazette [*A publication*] (DLA)
NYN	Non-Von Neumann
NYN	NYNEX Corp. [*NYSE symbol*] (SPSG)
NYN	Nyngan [*Australia*] [*Airport symbol*] (OAG)
NYNASHIPYD	New York Naval Shipyard (SAUS)
NYNCY	NYNEX CableCommsGrpADS Unit [*NASDAQ symbol*] (TTSB)
NYNCY	Nynex Cable Communications Group PLC [*NASDAQ symbol*] (SAG)
NYNEX	New York New England Exchange [*Telecommunications*]
Nynex	NYNEX Corp. [*Associated Press*] (SAG)
NYNH & H	New York, New Haven & Hartford R. R.
NYNJDDA	New York and New Jersey Dry Dock Association [*Defunct*] (EA)
NYNMA	New York New Media Association (IGQR)
NYNOR	Navy Yard, Norfolk, Virginia
NYNP	Northern Yukon National Park (SAUS)
NYNR	New York National Review (SAUS)
NYNS	New York Naval Shipyards [*Obsolete*]
NYNS-ML	New York Naval Shipyard, Material Laboratory (MCD)
NynxCbl	Nynex Cable Communications Group PLC [*Associated Press*] (SAG)
NYNYD	New York Navy Yard (DNAB)
NYNYK	Navy Yard, New York, New York
NYO	National Youth Orchestra [*British*] (DI)
NYO	New York Oils Ltd. [*Toronto Stock Exchange symbol*]
NYO	New York Operations [*AEC*] (MCD)
NYO	New York Operations Office (SAUS)
NYO	Not Yet Operating (DA)
NYO	Not Yet Out (SAUS)
nyo	Nyoro [*MARC language code*] [*Library of Congress*] (LCCP)
NYo	Youngstown Free Library, Youngstown, NY [*Library symbol*] [*Library of Congress*] (LCLS)
NYO & W	New York, Ontario & Western Railway Co.
NYOC	New York Opera Co. (SAUS)
NYOD	New York Ordnance District [*Military*] (MUGU)
NY Off Dept R	New York Official Department Reports [*A publication*] (DLA)
NYOL	New York On-Line [*Information service or system*] (IID)
NYOL	New York Opera Library (SAUS)
NYoOF	Old Fort Niagara Association, Youngstown, NY [*Library symbol*] [*Library of Congress*] (LCLS)
NY Op Att Gen	Opinions of the Attorneys-General of New York [*A publication*] (DLA)
NY Ops Atty Gen	Opinions of the Attorney General of New York [*A publication*] (DLA)
NYork J Med	New York Journal of Medicine (SAUS)
NYORT	New York Opera Repertory Theatre (SAUS)
NYOSL	New York Ocean Science Laboratory
NYOTBC	New York Off-Track Betting Corp. (SAUS)
NYP	New York-Pennsylvania League [*Baseball*]
NYP	New York Port (SAUS)
NYP	New York Press (WDMC)
NYP	New York Public Library, Serials, New York, NY [*OCLC symbol*] (OCLC)
NYP	Not Yet Published
NYP	Not Your Problem (SAUS)
NYPA	New York Port Authority
NYPAA	National Yellow Pages Agency Association [*Tucson, AZ*] (EA)
NYP & B	New York, Providence & Boston Railroad
NYPC	New York Pigment Club (EA)
NYPC	New York Programming Center (SAUS)

NYPD .... New York Police Department [*Initialism also used as title of TV series*]
NYPDis .... New York Procurement District (SAUS)
NYPE .... New York Port of Embarkation [*Military*]
NYPE .... New York Produce Exchange [*Defunct*] (EA)
NYPF .... National Young Professionals Forum (EA)
NYPFO .... New York Air Force Procurement Field Office
NYPFO .... New York Procurement Field Office (SAUS)
NYPH .... Navy Yard, Pearl Harbor, Hawaii
NYPHIL .... Navy Yard, Philadelphia, Pennsylvania
NYPHR .... New York Physicians for Human Rights (SAUS)
NYPIRG .... New York Public Interest Research Group
NYPL .... New York Public Library [*New York, NY*]
NYPLA .... New York Patent Law Association (SAUS)
NYPLC .... National Youth Pro-Life Coalition (EA)
NYPLR .... New York Prime Loan Rate [*Finance*] (DS)
NYPM .... National Yellow Pages Monitor (EFIS)
NYPM .... National Yokefellow Prison Ministry [*Later, YPM*] (EA)
NYPM .... Navy Youth Program Manager (MCD)
NYPM .... New York Pro Musica (SAUS)
NYPMA .... New York Paper Merchants Association (EA)
NYPMA Bulletin... New York Personnel Management Association Bulletin (SAUS)
NYPO .... New York Philharmonic Orchestra (SAUS)
NYPO .... New York Publicity Outlet [*A publication*] (WDMC)
NYPOE .... New York Port of Embarkation [*Military*]
NYPORT .... Navy Yard, Portsmouth, New Hampshire
NYPP .... New York Power Pool (SAUS)
NYPR .... New York Practice Reports [*A publication*] (DLA)
NYPR .... N-Nitrosopyrrolidine [*Also, NO-PYR*] [*Biochemistry, organic chemistry*]
NYPRPG ...... New York Publishers Rights and Permissions Group (EA)
NY Pr Rep ... New York Practice Reports [*A publication*] (DLA)
NYPS .... National Yellow Pages Service
NYPS .... Navy Yard, Puget Sound [*Bremerton*], Washington
NYPS .... New York Paleontological Society (SAUS)
NYPS .... New York Psychiatric Society (SAUS)
NYPS .... New York Publishing Society (SAUS)
NYP-SA .... National Yellow Pages Service Association (WDMC)
NYPSC .... New York Public Service Commission (SAUS)
NYPSO .... New York Philharmonic Symphony Orchestra
NYPSS .... New York Philharmonic-Symphony Society (SAUS)
NYPYR .... Nitrosopyrrolidine [*Also, NPYR*] [*Organic chemistry*]
NYR .... National Young Republicans (NADA)
NYR .... Neodymium YAG [*Yttrium Aluminum Garnet*] Range-Finder
NYR .... New York Court of Appeals Reports [*A publication*] (DLA)
NYR .... Not Yet Reported [*Air Force*]
NYR .... Not Yet Required (MUGU)
NYR .... Not Yet Returned [*Military*]
NYR .... Nuclear Yield Requirement (NATG)
NYR .... Receiver Site [*Nevada*] [*Seismograph station code, US Geological Survey*] [*Closed*] (SEIS)
NYRA .... New York Racing Association (SAUS)
NYRA .... New York Racing Authority [*Cable-television system*]
NYRAPG ...... New York Rights and Permissions Group (EA)
NYRB .... New York Review of Books [*A publication*] (BRI)
NYRC .... New York Railroad Commission Reports [*A publication*] (DLA)
NY Rec .... New York Record [*A publication*] (DLA)
NY Reg .... New York Daily Register [*A publication*] (DLA)
NY Rep .... New York Court of Appeals Reports [*A publication*] (DLA)
NY Reps ..... New York Court of Appeals Reports [*A publication*] (DLA)
NY Reptr ..... New York Reporter [*A publication*] (ILCA)
NYRFC .... New York Rangers Fan Club (EA)
NYRG .... New York Rubber Group (SAUS)
NYRL .... New York Revised Laws [*A publication*] (DLA)
NYRM .... New York Reformatory for Men (SAUS)
NYRMA .... New York Raincoat Manufacturers Association (EA)
NYRRC .... New York Road Runners Club (EA)
NYRS .... New York Revised Statutes [*A publication*] (DLA)
NYRS .... New York Roentgen Society (SAUS)
NYRS .... New Youth Research Survey [*Religious education test*]
NYRW .... New York Reformatory for Women (SAUS)
NYS .... New York Shavians (EA)
NYS .... New York State
NYS .... New York State Electric & Gas Corp. [*Associated Press*] (SAG)
NYS .... New York State Reporter [*A publication*] (DLA)
NYS .... New York State Union List, Albany, NY [*OCLC symbol*] (OCLC)
NYS .... New York Supplement [*A publication*] (DLA)
NYS .... Not Yet Specified
NYS .... Syncline Ridge [*Nevada*] [*Seismograph station code, US Geological Survey*] [*Closed*] (SEIS)
NYS .... Yonkers School System, Yonkers, NY [*Library symbol*] [*Library of Congress*] (LCLS)
NYS 2d .... New York Supplement, Second Series [*A publication*] (DLA)
NYSA .... New York Shipping Association (EA)
NYSA .... New York State Assembly (SAUS)
NYSAA .... New York State Archeological Association (SAUS)
NYSAA .... New York State Aviation Association (SAUS)
NYSAC .... New York State Athletic Commission (BARN)
NYSAES ...... New York State Agricultural Experiment Station (SAUS)
NYSAIS .... New York State Association of Independent Schools (SAUS)
NYSAJC .... New York State Association of Junior Colleges (SAUS)
NY-SAN .... New York-San Diego (SAUS)
NYSASBO .... New York State Association of School Business Officials (SAUS)
NYSASDA .... New York State Atomic and Space Development Authority (SAUS)

NYSASS .... New York State Association of Service Stations [*Later, NYSASSRS*] (EA)
NYSASSRS... New York State Association of Service Stations and Repair Shops (EA)
NYSAVC ...... New York State Audio-Visual Council (SAUS)
NYSBA .... New York State Bar Association (SAUS)
NYSBA Bull... New York State Bar Association. Bulletin [*A publication*] (DLA)
NYSBB .... New York State Banking Board (SAUS)
NY S B BULL... New York State Bar Bulletin [*A publication*] (LWAP)
NYSBC .... New York State Barge Canal (SAUS)
NYSBJ .... New York State Bar Journal (SAUS)
NYSC .... New York Shipbuilding Corp.
NYSC .... Thompson and Cook's New York Supreme Court Reports [*A publication*] (DLA)
NYSCA .... National Youth Sports Coaches Association (EA)
NYSCAT ...... New York State Union Catalog of Film and Video [*Mid-Hudson Library System*] [*Information service or system*] (IID)
NYSCC .... New York State College of Ceramics (SAUS)
NYSCC .... New York State Crime Commission (SAUS)
NYSCCJ ...... New York State Co-alition for Criminal Justice (SAUS)
NY Sch Indus Rel... New York State School of Industrial Relations (SAUS)
NYSCS .... New York State Colonization Society [*Defunct*] (EA)
NYSCSDA .... New York State Council of School District Administrators (SAUS)
NYS Ct........ New York State Superior Court Reports [*A publication*] (DLA)
NYSD .... New York Society for the Deaf [*Formerly, JSD*] (EA)
NYSDA .... New York Security Dealers Association (EA)
NYSDCS ...... New York State Department of Correctional Services (SAUS)
NYSDEC ...... New York State Department of Environmental Conservation
NYSDH .... New York State Department of Health (SAUS)
NYSDR .... New York State Department Reports [*A publication*] (DLA)
NYSE .... New York Stock Exchange [*New York, NY*] (EA)
NYSE .... New York Stock Exchange Guide [*Commerce Clearing House*] [*A publication*] (DLA)
NySEA .... New York Society of Enrolled Agents (SAUS)
NY Sea Grant L and Poly J... New York Sea Grant Law and Policy Journal (SAUS)
NYSEG .... New York State Electric & Gas Corp. [*Associated Press*] (SAG)
NYSEM .... New York Society of Electron Microscopy (SAUS)
NY Sen J .... New York Senate Journal [*A publication*] (DLA)
NYSERDA .... New York State Energy Research and Development Authority
NYSERNET... New York State Educational and Research Network
NYSERNet.... New York State Education and Research Network, Inc. [*Telecommunications service*] (TSSD)
NYSES .... New York State Employment Service (SAUS)
NYSF .... National Youth Science Foundation
NYSF .... New York Shakespeare Festival (SAUS)
NY-SFO .... New York-San Francisco (SAUS)
NYSFTCA .... New York State Fruit Testing Cooperative Association (EA)
NYSGI .... New York Sea Grant Institute [*Albany, NY*] [*Department of Commerce*] (GRD)
NYSHESC .... New York State Higher Education Service (SAUS)
NYSIIS .... New York State Identification and Intelligence System
NYSILL .... New York State Interlibrary Loan [*Network*]
NYSILL .... New York State Inter-Library Loans System (NITA)
NYSILL Network... New York State Inter-Library Loan Network (SAUS)
NYSL .... New York Society Library (SAUS)
NYSL .... New York State Library (SAUS)
NYSM .... New York State Museum (SAUS)
NYSMM .... New York State Maritime Museum (SAUS)
NYSNA .... New York State Nurses Association (SAUS)
NYSNACC ... New York State Narcotic Addiction Control Commission (SAUS)
NYSNC .... New York State Narcotics Commission (SAUS)
NYSNI........ New York State Nutrition Institute (SAUS)
NYSNY .... New York Naval Shipyard (New York)
NYSO .... New York String Orchestra (SAUS)
NYSP .... New York School of Printing (DGA)
NYSP .... New York State Police (SAUS)
NYSPA .... New York State Pharmaceutical Association (SAUS)
NYSPA .... New York State Power Authority (SAUS)
NYSPCC ...... New York Society for the Prevention of Cruelty to Children
NY Spec Term R... Howard's New York Practice Reports [*A publication*] (DLA)
NY Spec Term Rep... Howard's New York Practice Reports [*A publication*] (DLA)
NYSPGA ...... New York State Personnel and Guidance Association (SAUS)
NYSPI .... New York State Psychiatric Institute [*New York State Office of Mental Hygiene*] [*Research center*] (RCD)
NYSPIN........ New York State Police Intelligence Network (SAUS)
NYSPIN........ New York Statewide Police Information Network (SAUS)
NYSR .... New York State Reporter [*A publication*] (DLA)
NYSRS .... New York State Radiological Society (SAUS)
NYSSA .... New York Society of Security Analysts [*New York, NY*] (EA)
NYSSA .... New York State Student Assembly (SAUS)
NYSSCPA .... NY State Society of CPAs (SAUS)
NYSSDA ...... New York State Safe Deposit Association [*New York, NY*] (EA)
NYSSF .... National Youth Sports Safety Foundation (EA)
NYSSILR...... New York State School of Industrial and Labor Relations (SAUS)
NYSSIM ...... New York State Society of Industrial Medicine (SAUS)
NYSSMA ...... New York State School Music Association (SAUS)
NYSSOS ...... New York State Society of Orthopaedic Surgeons (SAUS)
NYSSPE ...... New York State Society of Professional Engineers (SAUS)
NYSSTF ...... New York State Science and Technology Foundation (RDA)
NY St .... New York State Reporter [*A publication*] (DLA)
NYST .... Nystagmus [*Medicine*]
NYSTA .... New York State Teachers Association (SAUS)
NYSTA .... New York State Thruway Authority (SAUS)
NY State R... New York State Reporter [*A publication*] (DLA)
NY State Rep... New York State Reporter [*A publication*] (DLA)

NY St Ba A...   New York State Bar Association. Bulletin [*A publication*] (DLA)
NY St Bull ...   New York State Bulletin (AAGC)
NY St Dept Rep...   New York State Department Reports [*A publication*] (DLA)
NYSTDL.......   Agricultural Research. Seoul National University (journ.) (SAUS)
NYStJ.........   Saint Joseph's Seminary, Dunwoodie, Yonkers, NY [*Library symbol*]
    [*Library of Congress*] (LCLS)
NY St R ....   New York State Reporter [*A publication*] (DLA)
NY St Rep ...   New York State Reporter [*A publication*] (DLA)
NY St Repr...   New York State Reporter [*A publication*] (DLA)
NYSU ....   New York State University (SAUS)
NY Sup Ct...   New York Supreme Court Reports [*A publication*] (DLA)
NY Sup Ct Rep...   Thompson and Cook's New York Supreme Court Reports
    [*A publication*] (DLA)
NY Sup Ct (T & C)...   Thompson and Cook's New York Supreme Court Reports
    [*A publication*] (DLA)
NY Super.....   New York Superior Court Reports [*A publication*] (DLA)
NY Super Ct..   New York Superior Court Reports [*Various reporters*]
    [*A publication*] (DLA)
NY Super Ct R...   New York Superior Court Reports [*A publication*] (DLA)
NY Super Ct Rep...   New York Superior Court Reports [*A publication*] (DLA)
NY Supl ....   New York Supplement [*A publication*] (DLA)
NY Supp ......   New York Supplement [*A publication*] (DLA)
NY Supp 2d...   New York Supplement, Second Series [*A publication*] (DLA)
NY Suppl .....   New York Supplement [*A publication*] (DLA)
NY Supr.......   New York Superior Court Reports [*A publication*] (DLA)
NY Supr Ct..   New York Superior Court Reports [*A publication*] (DLA)
NY Supr Ct R...   New York Superior Court Reports [*A publication*] (DLA)
NY Supr Ct Rep...   New York Superior Court Reports [*A publication*] (DLA)
NY Supr Ct Repts (T & C)...   New York Supreme Court Reports, by Thompson and
    Cook [*A publication*] (DLA)
NY Suprm Ct...   New York Supreme Court Reports [*A publication*] (DLA)
NYSUT ....   New York State United Teachers (SAUS)
NYSV ....   Narcissus Yellow Stripe Virus [*Plant pathology*]
NYSW ....   New York, Susquehanna & Western Railroad Co. [*AAR code*]
NYSWAC......   New York State Women's Collegiate Athletic Conference (PSS)
NYSWGGI ...   New York State Wine Grape Growers, Inc. (EA)
NYT.............   National Youth Theatre [*British*]
NYT.............   New Yiddish Theater (BJA)
NYT.............   New York Testing Laboratories, Inc.
NYT.............   [*The*] New York Times Co. [*AMEX symbol*] (SPSG)
NYT.............   New York Titans [*National Football League*] [*1960-62*] (NFLA)
NYTA ....   New York Theatre Annual [*A publication*]
NYTA ....   New York Times Cl'A' [*AMEX symbol*] (TTSB)
NYTA ....   New York Transit Authority (SAUS)
NY Tax Cas...   New York Tax Cases [*Commerce Clearing House*] [*A publication*]
    (DLA)
NYTB ....   New York Theatre Ballet
NYTBIO........   [*The*] New York Times Biographical File [*The New York Times Co.*]
    [*Information service or system*] (CRD)
NYTBR ....   New York Times Book Review [*A publication*] (BRI)
NYTCL ....   New York Temperance Civic League [*Later, AYE*] (EA)
NYTEI.........   New York Tax Exempt Income Fund [*Associated Press*] (SAG)
Nytest ....   NYTEST Environmental, Inc. [*Associated Press*] (SAG)
NY Them ....   New York Themis [*New York City*] [*A publication*] (DLA)
NY Thru ......   New York Thruway (SAUS)
NYT/IB ....   New York Times Information Bank
NYTIC ....   New York Technical Institute, Cincinnati (SAUS)
NY Tim ....   [*The*] New York Times Co. [*Associated Press*] (SAG)
NYTIS ....   New York Times Information Service, Inc. [*Mead Data Central*]
    [*Database originator and host*] (IID)
NYTLa ....   New York Times (Late Edition) [*A publication*] (BRI)
NYTLC ....   New York Taxi & Limousine Commission (WDAA)
NYTNS ....   New York Times News Service
NY TOR.......   New York-Toronto (SAUS)
NYTR ....   New York Term Reports (Caines' Reports) [*A publication*] (DLA)
NY Trans .....   New York Transcript [*Numbers 1-11*] [*1861*] [*New York City*]
    [*A publication*] (DLA)
NY Trans App...   New York Transcript Appeals Reports [*A publication*] (DLA)
NY Trans NS...   New York Transcript, New Series [*New York City*] [*A publication*]
    (DLA)
NY Trans Rep...   New York Transcript Reports [*A publication*] (DLA)
NYT Rep......   Caines' Term Reports [*New York*] [*A publication*] (DLA)
NYTS ....   New York Theological Seminary
NYTS ....   Nytest Environmental [*NASDAQ symbol*] (TTSB)
NYTS ....   NYTEST Environmental, Inc. [*NASDAQ symbol*] (NQ)
NYTTS ....   New York Turtle and Tortoise Society (EA)
NYTU ....   New York Theological Union (SAUS)
nyu.............   New York [*MARC country of publication code*] [*Library of
    Congress*] (LCCP)
NYU ....   New York University
NYU ....   Nyaung-U [*Myanmar*] [*Airport symbol*] (OAG)
NYU Conf Charitable...   New York University. Conference on Charitable
    Foundations. Proceedings [*A publication*] (DLA)
NYU Conf Charitable Fdn...   New York University. Conference on Charitable
    Foundations. Proceedings [*A publication*] (DLA)
NYU Conf on Char Found Proc...   Conference on Charitable Foundations.
    Proceedings. New York University [*A publication*] (DLA)
NYU Conf on Char Found Proc...   Conference on Charitable Foundations.
    Proceedings. New York University (journ.) (SAUS)
NYUIMS.......   New York University Institute of Mathematical Sciences (SAUS)
NYUIMS.......   New York University-Institute of Mathematical Sciences (SAUS)
NYUL ....   New York University Library
NYUL Center Bull...   New York University. Law Center. Bulletin [*A publication*]
    (DLA)

NYULT ....   New York University School of Continuing Education, Continuing
    Education in Law and Taxation [*A publication*] (DLA)
NYUMC ....   New York University Medical Center (SAUS)
NYUMC ....   New York Upstate Medical Center (SAUS)
NY Unconsol laws...   New York Unconsolidated Laws (SAUS)
NY Unconsol Laws...   New York Unconsolidated Laws (McKinney) [*A publication*]
    (DLA)
NYUP ....   New York University Press (DGA)
NYU Rev L&Soc Change...   New York University. Review of Law and Social
    Change (SAUS)
NYU Rev Law & Soc...   New York University. Review of Law and Social Change
    [*A publication*] (DLA)
NYU Rev Law&Soc C...   New York University. Review of Law and Social Change
    (SAUS)
NYUSM ....   New York University School of Medicine (SAUS)
NYUTI ....   New York University Tax Institute (DLA)
NYU/Ultra....   New York Universitys Ultracomputer (SAUS)
NYV ....   Vern [*Nevada*] [*Seismograph station code, US Geological Survey*]
    [*Closed*] (SEIS)
NYVTX ....   Davis New York Venture Cl.A [*Mutual fund ticker symbol*] (SG)
NYWA ....   National Youth Work Alliance (EA)
NYWASH......   Navy Yard, Washington, DC [*Obsolete*]
NYWC ....   New York Wine Council (EA)
NYWCC ....   New York Water Color Club [*1890-1941*] (NGC)
NY Week Dig...   New York Weekly Digest [*A publication*] (DLA)
NY Weekly Dig...   New York Weekly Digest [*A publication*] (DLA)
NYWF ....   New York World's Fair
NYWGF ....   New York Wine/Grape Foundation (EA)
NY Wkly Dig...   New York Weekly Digest [*A publication*] (DLA)
NYY ....   New York Yanks [*National Football League*] [*1950-51*] (NFLA)
NYYP ....   New York Yellow Pages, Inc.
NYZP ....   New York Zoological Park
NYZS ....   New York Zoological Society
NYZZA3.......   Journal. Japan Pharmaceutical Association (journ.) (SAUS)
NZ.............   Air New Zealand Ltd. (Domestic Division) [*ICAO designator*] (ICDA)
Nz ....   National Library of New Zealand, Wellington, New Zealand [*Library
    symbol*] [*Library of Congress*] (LCLS)
NZ.............   Neutrality Zone
NZ.............   New Mexico & Arizona Land Co. [*AMEX symbol*] (SPSG)
NZ.............   New Mexico/Ariz Land [*AMEX symbol*] (TTSB)
NZ.............   New Zealand [*ANSI two-letter standard code*] (CNC)
nz.............   New Zealand [*MARC country of publication code*] [*Library of
    Congress*] (LCCP)
NZ.............   New Zealand National Airways Corp. [*ICAO designator*]
NZ.............   New Zealand Reports [*A publication*] (DLA)
N-Z.............   Nike-Zeus [*Missiles*] (AAG)
NZ.............   Non-Zero (VLIE)
NZ.............   Normal Acceleration
NZ.............   Normal load factor (SAUS)
NZ.............   Normal to Z-Axis (MCD)
NZ.............   Nose to Z-Axis (MCD)
NZ.............   Not Zero (SAUS)
NZ.............   No Zero (SAUS)
NZ.............   Nuclear Zone
NZA ....   Niobium Zinc Alloy
NZAA ....   Auckland/International [*New Zealand*] [*ICAO location identifier*] (ICLI)
NZAA ....   New Zealand Antique Arms Association (SAUS)
NZAA ....   New Zealand Auto Association (SAUS)
NZAB ....   New Zealand Association of Bacteriologists (SAUS)
NZABC ....   New Zealand Audit Bureau of Circulation (SAUS)
NZABM ....   New Zealand Anglican Board of Missions (SAUS)
NZAC ....   New Zealand Accommodation Council (SAUS)
NZAC ....   New Zealand Alpine Club (SAUS)
NZACE ....   New Zealand Association for Community Education (SAUS)
NZACT ....   New Zealand Association of Chemistry Teachers (SAUS)
NZACU ....   New Zealand Auto Cycle Union (SAUS)
NZADS ....   New Zealand Association for Disabled Skiers (SAUS)
NZAF ....   New Zealand Air Force (DAS)
NZAF ....   New Zealand Authors Fund (SAUS)
NZAF ....   New Zealand Aviation Federation (SAUS)
NZAFB ....   New Zealand Air Force Base (SAUS)
NzAGS ....   Church of Jesus Christ of Latter-Day Saints, Genealogical Society
    Library, Auckland Branch, Auckland, New Zealand [*Library
    symbol*] [*Library of Congress*] (LCLS)
NZAHBS......   New Zealand Arab Horse Breeders Society (SAUS)
NZAHPER....   New Zealand Association of Health, Physical Education and
    Recreation (SAUS)
NZAI ....   New Zealand Antarctic Institute (SAUS)
NZAK ....   Auckland [*New Zealand*] [*ICAO location identifier*] (ICLI)
NZALO ....   New Zealand Air Liaison Officer (SAUS)
NZALT.........   New Zealand Association of Language Teachers (SAUS)
NZANN........   New Zealand Association of Neonatal Nurses (SAUS)
NZAP ....   New Zealand Associated Press (BARN)
NZAP ....   Taupo [*New Zealand*] [*ICAO location identifier*] (ICLI)
NZAPA ....   New Zealand Airline Pilots Association (SAUS)
NZ App Rep...   New Zealand Appeal Reports [*A publication*] (DLA)
NZAPS ....   Nike-Zeus Automatic Programming System [*Missiles*]
NZAQ ....   Auckland [*New Zealand*] [*ICAO location identifier*] (ICLI)
NZAR ....   Ardmore [*New Zealand*] [*ICAO location identifier*] (ICLI)
NZARE ....   New Zealand Association for Research on Education (SAUS)
NZARP ....   New Zealand Antarctic Research Programme (SAUS)
NZART ....   New Zealand Amateur Radio Transmitters Association (SAUS)
NZAS ....   New Zealand Aluminium Smelters (SAUS)
NZAS ....   New Zealand Antarctic Society (SAUS)
NZAS ....   New Zealand Arthritis Society (SAUS)

NZASA .... New Zealand Asian Studies Association (SAUS)
NZASC .... New Zealand Administrative Staff College (SAUS)
NZASC .... New Zealand Association of Soil Conservators (SAUS)
NZASF .... New Zealand Association of Small Farmers (SAUS)
NZASW .... New Zealand Association of Social Workers (SAUS)
NZATD .... New Zealand Association of Training and Development (SAUS)
NzAU .... Auckland University, Auckland, New Zealand [*Library symbol*] [*Library of Congress*] (LCLS)
NZAWA .... New Zealand Air Womens Association (SAUS)
NZ Awards ... New Zealand Awards, Recommendations, Agreements, Etc. [*A publication*] (DLA)
NZB .... New Zealand Black [*Mice hybrids*]
NZB .... Nonzero Binary (NASA)
NZB .... Royal New Zealand Ballet
NZBA .... New Zealand Bankers Association (SAUS)
NZBA .... New Zealand Biotechnology Association (SAUS)
NZBA .... New Zealand Bowling Association (SAUS)
NZBC .... New Zealand Broadcasting Commission (WDAA)
NZBC .... New Zealand Broadcasting Corp.
NZBCSO .... New Zealand Broadcasting Corporation Symphony Orchestra (SAUS)
NZBIE .... New Zealand Bureau of Importers and Exporters (SAUS)
NZB Mice ..... New Zealand Black Mice (SAUS)
NZB Mouse ... New Zealand Black Mouse (SAUS)
NZBS .... New Zealand Broadcasting Service
NZBTO .... New Zealand Book Trade Organisation (SAUS)
NZC .... Jacksonville, FL [*Location identifier*] [*FAA*] (FAAL)
NZC .... New Zealand Certificate (SAUS)
NZC .... New Zealand Chocolate [*Mouse*] (DMAA)
NZC .... New Zealand Cross (DAS)
NZC .... North Carolina School of the Arts, Winston-Salem (SAUS)
NZCA .... Campbell Island [*New Zealand*] [*ICAO location identifier*] (ICLI)
NZCA .... New Zealand Conservation Authority (SAUS)
NZCAR .... New Zealand Civil Aviation Regulations (SAUS)
NZCAS .... New Zealand Clean Air Society (SAUS)
NZCAU .... New Zealand Conservation Authority Unit (SAUS)
NZCC .... New Zealand Chamber of Commerce (SAUS)
NZCC .... New Zealand Conservation Corps (SAUS)
NZCD .... New Zealand Certificate in Draughting (SAUS)
NZCDC .... New Zealand Cooperative Dairy Co. (SAUS)
NZCE .... New Zealand Certificate in Engineering (SAUS)
NZCEA .... New Zealand Combined Educational Associations (SAUS)
NZCER .... New Zealand Council for Educational Research (WDAA)
NZCF .... New Zealand Cycling Federation (SAUS)
NZCG .... New Zealand Chemists Guild (SAUS)
NZCGF .... New Zealand Coast Guard Federation (SAUS)
NZCGP .... New Zealand College of General Practitioners (SAUS)
NzCGS .... Church of Jesus Christ of Latter-Day Saints, Genealogical Society Library, Canterbury Branch, Christchurch, New Zealand [*Library symbol*] [*Library of Congress*] (LCLS)
NZCGS .... New Zealand Standard Classification of all Goods and Services (SAUS)
NZCH .... Christchurch/International [*New Zealand*] [*ICAO location identifier*] (ICLI)
NZCH .... New Zealand Cement Holdings (SAUS)
NZCI .... Chatham Island/Tuuta [*New Zealand*] [*ICAO location identifier*] (ICLI)
NZCLA .... New Zealand Childrens Literature Association (SAUS)
NZCLS .... New Zealand Certificate of Land Surveying (SAUS)
NZCM .... McMurdo Sound, Antarctica [*New Zealand*] [*ICAO location identifier*] (ICLI)
NZCMA .... New Zealand Cable Makers Association (SAUS)
NZCMA .... New Zealand Concrete Masonry Association (SAUS)
NZCMF .... New Zealand Coal Merchants Federation (SAUS)
NZCO .... Christchurch [*New Zealand*] [*ICAO location identifier*] (ICLI)
NZ Col LJ .... New Zealand Colonial Law Journal [*A publication*] (DLA)
NZCPS .... New Zealand Coastal Policy Statement (SAUS)
NZCRA .... New Zealand Coal Research Association (SAUS)
NZCRA .... New Zealand Concrete Research Association (SAUS)
NZCRS .... New Zealand Council for Recreation and Sports (SAUS)
NZCS .... New Zealand Certificate in Science (SAUS)
NZCS .... New Zealand Certificate in Statistics (SAUS)
NZCS .... New Zealand Computer Society (SAUS)
NzCSI-A .... New Zealand Department of Scientific and Industrial Research, Antarctic Division, Christchurch, New Zealand [*Library symbol*] [*Library of Congress*] (LCLS)
NZ Ct App .... New Zealand Court of Appeals (DLA)
NZ Ct Arb .... New Zealand Court of Arbitration (DLA)
NZCTF .... New Zealand Cycle Traders Federation (SAUS)
NZCTOA .... New Zealand Container Terminal Operators Association (SAUS)
NZCUL .... New Zealand Credit Union League (SAUS)
NZD .... New Zealand Division (SAUS)
NZD .... New Zealand Dollar (SAUS)
NZD .... New Zoo Developments (SAUS)
NZD .... Nonzero Digit (ECII)
NZDA .... New Zealand Dairy Association (SAUS)
NZDA .... New Zealand Deerstalkers Association (SAUS)
NZDA .... New Zealand Department of Agriculture (SAUS)
NZDA .... New Zealand Dietetic Association (SAUS)
NZDCMBA .... New Zealand Dairy Confectionary and Mixed Biscuits Association (SAUS)
NZDCS .... New Zealand Department of Census and Statistics (SAUS)
NZDE .... New Zealand Department of Education (SAUS)
NZDF .... Christchurch/International [*New Zealand*] [*ICAO location identifier*] (ICLI)
NZDF .... New Zealand Defence Force (SAUS)
NZDF .... New Zealand Drug Foundation (SAUS)
NZDFA .... New Zealand Deer Farmers Association (SAUS)
NZDLS .... New Zealand Department of Lands and Survey (SAUS)
NZDN .... Dunedin [*New Zealand*] [*ICAO location identifier*] (ICLI)
NZDRI .... New Zealand Dairy Research Institute (SAUS)
NZDS .... New Zealand Drama School (SAUS)
NZDT .... New Zealand Daylight Time (SAUS)
NZDVA .... New Zealand Dunkirk Veterans Association (SAUS)
NZDXRA .... New Zealand DX Radio Association (SAUS)
NZE .... Glenview, IL [*Location identifier*] [*FAA*] (FAAL)
NZE .... New Zealand Engineers (SAUS)
NZE .... New Zealand English (SAUS)
NZE .... North Zenith East
NZE .... Nzerekore [*Guinea*] [*Airport symbol*] (AD)
N Zea .... New Zealand (VRA)
NZEA .... New Zealand Esperanto Association (SAUS)
NZEAS .... New Zealand East Asia Service (SAUS)
NZEAS .... New Zealand Educational Administration Society (SAUS)
NZEB .... New Zealand Electricity Board (SAUS)
NZECF .... New Zealand Electrical Contractors Federation (SAUS)
NZEF .... New Zealand Employees Federation (SAUS)
NZEF .... New Zealand Employers' Federation (ODBW)
NZEF .... New Zealand Expeditionary Force (WDAA)
NZEFIP .... New Zealand Expeditionary Force in the Pacific (WDAA)
NZEI .... New Zealand Educational Institute (WDAA)
NZEI .... New Zealand Electronics Institute (SAUS)
NZERF .... New Zealand Engine Research Foundation (SAUS)
NZERF .... New Zealand Equine Research Foundation (SAUS)
NZES .... New Zealand Ecological Society (SAUS)
NZES .... New Zealand Employment Service (SAUS)
NZESA .... New Zealand Education Standards Association (SAUS)
NZESA .... New Zealand European Shipping Association (SAUS)
NZE System ... North-Zenith-East System (SAUS)
NZF .... Near Zero Field
NZFB .... New Zealand Foundation for the Blind (SAUS)
NZFCA .... New Zealand Farmers Cooperative Association (SAUS)
NZFCA .... New Zealand Freezing Companies Association (SAUS)
NZFCDC .... New Zealand Farmers Cooperative Distributing Co. (SAUS)
NZFCMA ..... New Zealand Ferro Cement Marine Association (SAUS)
NZFF .... New Zealand Farmers Fertiliser (SAUS)
NZFF .... New Zealand Federated Farmers (SAUS)
NZFF .... New Zealand Fruitgrowers Federation (SAUS)
NZFFA .... New Zealand Federation of Freshwater Anglers (SAUS)
NZFG .... New Zealand Psychic Gazette (SAUS)
NZFGC .... New Zealand Fish and Game Council (SAUS)
NZFHA .... New Zealand Finance Houses Association (SAUS)
NZFKTA .... New Zealand Free Kindergarten Teachers Association (SAUS)
NZFKU .... New Zealand Free Kindergarten Union (SAUS)
NZFL .... New Zealand Federation of Labor (ODBW)
NZFMA .... New Zealand Ferrocement Marine Association (SAUS)
NZFMC .... New Zealand Federation of Master Cleaners (SAUS)
NZFMRA ..... New Zealand Fertiliser (or Fertilizer) Manufacturers Research Association (SAUS)
NZFOE .... New Zealand Futures and Options Exchange (NUMA)
NZFP .... New Zealand Family Physician (SAUS)
NZFPA .... New Zealand Family Planning Association (SAUS)
NZFRI .... New Zealand Forest Research Institute (SAUS)
NZFS .... New Zealand Film Service (SAUS)
NZFUW .... New Zealand Federation of University Women (SAUS)
NZFWA .... New Zealand Farm Workers Association (SAUS)
NZG .... Near Zero Gravity
NZG .... New Zealand Government (SAUS)
NZG .... North Carolina School of the Arts, Winston-Salem, NC [*OCLC symbol*] (OCLC)
NZGA .... New Zealand Gliding Association (SAUS)
NZ Gaz LR ... New Zealand Gazette Law Reports [*A publication*] (DLA)
NZGBHTB .... New Zealand Game Bird Habitat Trust board (SAUS)
NZGenS .... New Zealand Genetical Society (SAUS)
NZGGA .... New Zealand Geographer (SAUS)
NZGLR .... New Zealand Gazette Law Reports [*A publication*] (DLA)
NZGR .... New Zealand Government Railways (SAUS)
NZGS .... Gisborne [*New Zealand*] [*ICAO location identifier*] (ICLI)
NZGS .... New Zealand Geological Survey (SAUS)
NZGTB .... New Zealand Government Tourist Bureau (SAUS)
NZGTC .... New Zealand Government Travel Commissioner (SAUS)
NZGTO .... New Zealand Government Tourist Office (SAUS)
NZH .... New Zealand Helicopters (SAUS)
NZHC .... New Zealand High Commission (SAUS)
NZHF .... New Zealand Heart Foundation (SAUS)
NZHGA .... New Zealand Hang Gliding Association (SAUS)
NZHI .... New Zealand Horological Institute (SAUS)
NZHK .... Hokitika [*New Zealand*] [*ICAO location identifier*] (ICLI)
NZHN .... Hamilton [*New Zealand*] [*ICAO location identifier*] (ICLI)
NZHO .... Wellington [*New Zealand*] [*ICAO location identifier*] (ICLI)
NZHPT .... New Zealand Historic Places Trust (SAUS)
NZHS .... New Zealand Horse Society (SAUS)
NZHTA .... New Zealand Health Technology Assessment (SAUS)
NZI .... New Zealand Insulators (SAUS)
NZI .... New Zealand Insurance (SAUS)
NZIA .... New Zealand Institute of Architects (SAUS)
NZIA .... New Zealand Institute of Architecture (SAUS)
NZIA .... New Zealand Irrigation Association (SAUS)
NZIA Journal ... New Zealand Institute of Architecture Journal (SAUS)
NZIAS .... New Zealand Institute of Agricultural Science (SAUS)
NZIC .... New Zealand Institute of Chemistry
NZIC .... New Zealand Intelligence Council (SAUS)

NZICFM........ New Zealand Institute of Credit and Financial Management (SAUS)
NZICM......... New Zealand Institute of Credit Management (SAUS)
NZID............ New Zealand Institute of Draughtsmen (SAUS)
NZIDA.......... New Zealand Invention Development Authority (SAUS)
NZIDC.......... New Zealand Industrial Design Council (SAUS)
NZIE............ New Zealand Institute of Engineers (SAUS)
NZIELEC....... New Zealand Institute of Electricians (SAUS)
NZIEPC........ New Zealand Indonesia Economic Promotion Council (SAUS)
NZIER.......... New Zealand Institute of Economic Research
NZIET........... New Zealand Institute of Engineering Technicians (SAUS)
NZIF............ New Zealand Institute of Foresters (SAUS)
NZIG............ New Zealand Institute of Gases (SAUS)
NZIH............ New Zealand Institute of Horticulture (SAUS)
NZIHVE........ New Zealand Institute of Heating and Ventilation Engineers (SAUS)
NZIIS........... New Zealand Institute of Industial Safety (SAUS)
NZILA........... New Zealand Institute of Landscape Architects (SAUS)
NZIM............ New Zealand Institute of Mining (SAUS)
NZIME........... New Zealand Institute of Mechanical Engineers (SAUS)
NZIMP.......... New Zealand Institute of Medical Photography (SAUS)
NZ Ind Arb... New Zealand Industrial Arbitration Awards [*A publication*] (DLA)
NZIP............. New Zealand Institute of Printing (SAUS)
NZIPA........... New Zealand Institute of Public Administration (SAUS)
NZIPE........... New Zealand Institution of Professional Engineers (SAUS)
NZIPM.......... New Zealand Institute of Personnel Management (SAUS)
NZIPRA........ New Zealand Institute of Parks and Recreation Administration (SAUS)
NZIPS........... New Zealand Institute of Purchasing and Supply (SAUS)
NZIRE........... New Zealand Institute of Refrigeration Engineers (SAUS)
NZIS............. New Zealand Information Service (SAUS)
NZIS............. New Zealand Institute of Surveyors (SAUS)
NZISM.......... New Zealand Institute of Safety Management (SAUS)
NZIT............. New Zealand Institute of Travel (SAUS)
NZIUW.......... New Zealand Industrial Union of Workers (SAUS)
NZJ.............. Naze [*Ryukyu Islands*] [*Seismograph station code, US Geological Survey*] (SEIS)
NZJ.............. Santa Ana, CA [*Location identifier*] [*FAA*] (FAAL)
NZJHPER..... New Zealand Journal of Health, Physical Education and Recreation (SAUS)
NZJP............ New Zealand Justice of the Peace [*1876-77*] [*A publication*] (DLA)
NZ J Phys Educ... New Zealand Journal of Health, Physical Education and Recreation (SAUS)
NZJU............ New Zealand Journalists Union (SAUS)
NZ Jur......... New Zealand Jurist [*1873-78*] [*A publication*] (DLA)
NZ Jur Mining Law... Jurist Reports, New Series, Cases in Mining Law [*New Zealand*] [*A publication*] (DLA)
NZ Jur NS.... New Zealand Jurist, New Series [*A publication*] (DLA)
NZKB........... Wellington/Kilbirnie [*New Zealand*] [*ICAO location identifier*] (ICLI)
NZKI............ Kaikoura [*New Zealand*] [*ICAO location identifier*] (ICLI)
NZKL............ Wellington/Kelburn [*New Zealand*] [*ICAO location identifier*] (ICLI)
NZKMB......... New Zealand Kiwifruit Marketing Board
NZKT............ Kaitaia [*New Zealand*] [*ICAO location identifier*] (ICLI)
NZKVA.......... New Zealand Korean Veterans Association (SAUS)
NZKX............ Kaitaia [*New Zealand*] [*ICAO location identifier*] (ICLI)
NZL.............. New Zealand [*ANSI three-letter standard code*] (CNC)
NZL.............. New Zealand Line (SAUS)
NZLA............ New Zealand Legal Association (SAUS)
NZLA............ New Zealand Loggers Association (SAUS)
NZ Law Soc N... New Zealand Law Society. Newsletter [*A publication*] (DLA)
NZLCC.......... New Zealand Litter Control Council (SAUS)
NZLF............ New Zealand Literary Fund (SAUS)
NZLGR.......... Local Government Reports [*New Zealand*] [*A publication*] (DLA)
NZLIRA......... New Zealand Logging Industry Research Association (SAUS)
NZLJMC....... New Zealand Law Journal, Magistrates' Court Decisions [*A publication*] (DLA)
NZLL............ New Zealand Light Leathers (SAUS)
NZLO............ New Zealand Liaison Officer
NZLP............ New Zealand Labour Party [*Political party*] (PPW)
NZLR............ New Zealand Law Reports [*A publication*] (DLA)
NZLRCA....... New Zealand Law Reports, Court of Appeal [*A publication*] (DLA)
NZLS............ New Zealand Law Society (SAUS)
NZLS............ New Zealand Library School (SAUS)
NZLS............ New Zealand Library Service (SAUS)
NZLS............ New Zealand Securities (SAUS)
NZLT............ New Zealand Land Care Trust (SAUS)
NZM............. Mount Cook Airlines [*New Zealand*] [*ICAO designator*] (FAAC)
NZMA........... New Zealand Medical Association (SAUS)
NZMA........... New Zealand Modelling Association (SAUS)
NZMA........... New Zealand Motel Association (SAUS)
NZMAF......... New Zealand Ministry of Agriculture and Fisheries (SAUS)
NZM&WB.... New Zealand Meat and Wool Board (SAUS)
NZMB........... New Zealand Meat Board (SAUS)
NZMBF......... New Zealand Master Builders Federation (SAUS)
NZMC........... New Zealand Maori Council (SAUS)
NZMCA......... New Zealand Motor Caravan Association (SAUS)
NZMEA......... New Zealand Mining and Exploration Association Inc. (SAUS)
NZMF........... Milford Sound [*New Zealand*] [*ICAO location identifier*] (ICLI)
NZMF........... New Zealand Manufacturers Federation (SAUS)
NZMF........... New Zealand Military Forces (SAUS)
NZMF........... New Zealand Motel Federation (SAUS)
NZMF........... New Zealand Music Federation (SAUS)
NZMFA......... New Zealand Master Floorcovering Association (SAUS)
NZMGA......... New Zealand Mountain Guides Association (SAUS)
NZMGC......... New Zealand Marriage Guidance Council (SAUS)
N-Z Missile... Nike-Zeus Missile (SAUS)
NZMN........... New Zealand Merchant Navy (DAS)
NZMOT......... New Zealand Ministry of Transport (SAUS)
NZMPH......... New Zealand Meat Packing House (SAUS)
NZMR........... New Zealand Mounted Rines (SAUS)
NZMRC......... New Zealand Medical Research Council (SAUS)
NZMS........... New Zealand Mapping Service (SAUS)
NZMS........... New Zealand Meteorological Service [*Marine science*] (OSRA)
NZMSC......... New Zealand Mountain Safety Council (SAUS)
NZMSS......... New Zealand Marine Sciences Society (SAUS)
NZMTCB...... New Zealand Motor Trade Certification Board (SAUS)
NZMTMA...... New Zealand Methods Time Measurement Association (SAUS)
NZ Mu Dep Fish Tech Rep... New Zealand Marine Department. Fisheries Technical Report (SAUS)
NZMWA........ New Zealand Maori Wardens Association (SAUS)
NZMWU........ New Zealand Meat Workers Union (SAUS)
NZN.............. Niedersachsischer Zeitschriftennachweis [*Deutsches Bibliotheksinstitut*] [*Germany*] [*Information service or system*] (CRD)
NZNA............ New Zealand Nurserymens Association (SAUS)
NZNA............ New Zealand Nurses Association (SAUS)
NZ Natl Radiat Lab Environ Radioact Annu Rep... New Zealand. National Radiation Laboratory. Environmental Radioactivity. Annual Report (SAUS)
NZNB............ New Zealand Naval Board [*Wellington*]
NZNCC.......... New Zealand Nature Conservation Council (SAUS)
NZNEDA........ New Zealand National Electronics Development Association (SAUS)
NZNF............ New Zealand Neurological Foundation (SAUS)
NZNFC.......... Norma Zimmer National Fan Club (EA)
NZNFU.......... New Zealand National Film Unit (SAUS)
NZNO............ New Zealand Nurses Orgainisation (SAUS)
NZNP............ New Plymouth [*New Zealand*] [*ICAO location identifier*] (ICLI)
NZNPA.......... New Zealand Newspaper Proprietors Association (SAUS)
NZNR............ Napier [*New Zealand*] [*ICAO location identifier*] (ICLI)
NZNRAC....... New Zealand National Research Advisory Council (SAUS)
NZNS............ Nelson [*New Zealand*] [*ICAO location identifier*] (ICLI)
NZNTA.......... New Zealand National Travel Association (SAUS)
NZNV............ Invercargill [*New Zealand*] [*ICAO location identifier*] (ICLI)
NZNZ............ Nonzero-Nonzero (SAUS)
NZO.............. New Zealand Obese [*Mouse*] [*Medicine*] (DMAA)
NZOA............ New Zealand Optometrical Association (SAUS)
NZOC............ New Zealand Opera Co. (SAUS)
NZOH............ Ohakea [*New Zealand*] [*ICAO location identifier*] (ICLI)
NZOI............. New Zealand Oceanographic Institute
NZ Ords........ Ordinances of the Legislative Council of New Zealand [*A publication*] (DLA)
NZOU............ Oamaru [*New Zealand*] [*ICAO location identifier*] (ICLI)
NZP.............. National Zoological Park [*Smithsonian Institution*]
NZP.............. New Zealand Pacific (SAUS)
NZP.............. New Zealand Players (SAUS)
NZP.............. New Zealand Police (SAUS)
NZPA............ New Zealand Police Association (SAUS)
NZPA............ New Zealand Press Association
NZP&TC....... New Zealand Post and Telegraph Corps (SAUS)
NZPARS........ New Zealand Prisoners Aid and Rehabilitation Society (SAUS)
NZPB............ New Zealand Pony Breeders (SAUS)
NZPB............ New Zealand Potato Board (SAUS)
NZPBA.......... New Zealand Power Boat Association (SAUS)
NZPBA.......... New Zealand Publishers Association (SAUS)
NZPBR.......... New Zealand Pony Breeders Register (SAUS)
NZPBS.......... New Zealand Pony Breeders Society (SAUS)
NZPC............ New Zealand Peace Council (SAUS)
NZPC............ New Zealand Petroleum Company Ltd. (SAUS)
NZPC............ New Zealand Planning Council (SAUS)
NZPC............ New Zealand Press Council (SAUS)
NZPC............ New Zealand Print Council (SAUS)
NZPCA.......... New Zealand Portland Cement Association (SAUS)
NZPCC.......... New Zealand Privy Council Cases [*A publication*] (DLA)
NZPC Cas.... New Zealand Privy Council Cases [*A publication*] (DLA)
NZPEA.......... New Zealand Port Employers Association (SAUS)
NZPECC....... New Zealand Committee of the Pacific Economic Cooperation Council
NZPGMF....... New Zealand Post Graduate Medical Federation (SAUS)
NZPM............ New Zealand Paper Mills (SAUS)
NZPM............ Palmerston North [*New Zealand*] [*ICAO location identifier*] (ICLI)
NZPMS.......... New Zealand Plumbers Merchants Society (SAUS)
NZPO............ New Zealand Post Office [*Telecommunications*]
NZPP............ Paraparaumu [*New Zealand*] [*ICAO location identifier*] (ICLI)
NZPPA.......... New Zealand Professional Photographers Association (SAUS)
NZPPTA........ New Zealand Post Primary Teachers Association (SAUS)
NZPS............ New Zealand Park Service (SAUS)
NZPS............ New Zealand Police Service (SAUS)
NZPSA.......... New Zealand Political Studies Association (SAUS)
NZPSA.......... New Zealand Public Service Association (SAUS)
NZPTA.......... New Zealand Parent Teachers Association (SAUS)
NZPTO.......... New Zealand Public Trust Office (SAUS)
NZQHA.......... New Zealand Quarter Horse Association (SAUS)
NZQN............ Queenstown [*New Zealand*] [*ICAO location identifier*] (ICLI)
NZR.............. New Zealand Red [*Rabbit*] [*Medicine*] (DMAA)
NZR.............. Non-Zero Result (SAUS)
NZRA............ New Zealand Recreation Association (SAUS)
NZRC............ New Zealand Red Cross (SAUS)
NZ Rep......... New Zealand Reports, Court of Appeals [*A publication*] (DLA)
NZ Repr Stat... Reprint of the Statutes of New Zealand [*A publication*] (DLA)
NZRFU.......... New Zealand Rugby Football Union
NZRLS.......... New Zealand Railway and Locomotive Society (SAUS)
NZRMA.......... New Zealand Ready Mix Concrete Association (SAUS)
NZRMTA....... New Zealand Retail Motor Trade Association (SAUS)

NZRN .... New Zealand Registered Nurse (SAUS)
NZRN .... Raoul Island [*New Zealand*] [*ICAO location identifier*] (ICLI)
NZRNC .... New Zealand Radio Navigation Chart (SAUS)
NZRO .... Rotorua [*New Zealand*] [*ICAO location identifier*] (ICLI)
NZRR .... New Zealand Rough Riders [*Military*] (ROG)
NZR Regs & B... Rules, Regulations, and By-Laws under New Zealand Statutes [*A publication*] (DLA)
NZRRS .... New Zealand Railways Road Services (SAUS)
NZRTA .... New Zealand Road Transport Association (SAUS)
NZS .... Near-Zero Stamping (VLIE)
NZS .... New Zealand Ship (SAUS)
NZS .... New Zealand Standard (SAUS)
NZS .... Nonzero Sum [*Genetics*]
NZSB .... New Zealand Soil Bureau (SAUS)
NZSB .... New Zealand Speech Board (SAUS)
NZSB .... New Zealand Survey Board (SAUS)
NZSBG .... New Zealand South British Group (SAUS)
NZSC .... New Zealand Sealers Club (SAUS)
NZSC .... New Zealand Securities Commission (SAUS)
NZSC .... New Zealand Squid Co. (SAUS)
NZSC .... New Zealand Standards Council (SAUS)
NZSC .... New Zealand Supreme Court [*A publication*] (DLA)
NZSCA .... New Zealand Sheep and Cattlemens Association (SAUS)
NZSCA .... New Zealand Society of Customs Agents (SAUS)
NZSCA .... New Zealand Soil Conservation Association (SAUS)
NZSCC .... New Zealand Standard Country Code (SAUS)
NZSCES .... New Zealand Society of Certified Executive Secretaries (SAUS)
NZSCHA .... New Zealand Society of Custom House Agents (SAUS)
NZSCI .... New Zealand Standard Classification of Imports (SAUS)
NZS Co .... New Zealand Shipping Co. (SAUS)
NZSCO .... New Zealand Standard Classification of Occupations (SAUS)
NZSCS .... New Zealand Senior Citizens Service (SAUS)
NZSDA .... New Zealand Sign and Display Association (SAUS)
NZSDA .... New Zealand Stamp Dealers Association (SAUS)
NZSE .... New Zealand Stock Exchange
NZSEAFRON... New Zealand Sea Frontier
NZSG .... Non-Zero-Sum Game (MHDW)
NZSI .... New Zealand Seismological Institute (SAUS)
NZSIA .... New Zealand Security Industry Association (SAUS)
NZSID .... New Zealand Society of Industrial Designers (SAUS)
NZSL .... New Zealand Shipping Line (SAUS)
NZSL .... New Zealand Steel Ltd. (SAUS)
NZSLO .... New Zealand Scientific Liaison Office (SAUS)
NZSNA .... New Zealand Society of National Accounts (SAUS)
NZ Soc Earthquake Eng Bull... New Zealand Society for Earhtquake Engineering. Bulletin (SAUS)
NZSS .... New Zealand Social Security (SAUS)
NZSS .... New Zealand Speleological Society (SAUS)
NZ Stat .... Statutes of New Zealand [*A publication*] (DLA)
NZ Stat Regs... New Zealand Statutory Regulations [*A publication*] (DLA)
NZSWWS ..... New Zealand Spinning, Weaving and Woolcrafts Society (SAUS)
NZT .... New Zealand Time (SAUS)
NZT .... Nonzero Test (IAA)
NZT .... Nonzero Transfer
NZT .... Telecom Corp. New Zealand [*NYSE symbol*] (SPSG)
NZT .... Telecom Corp. New Zealand ADS [*NYSE symbol*] (TTSB)
NZTB .... New Zealand Tourism Board (EA)
NZTBR .... New Zealand Taxation Board of Review Decisions [*A publication*] (DLA)
NZTC .... New Zealand Trade Commission (SAUS)
NZTCA .... New Zealand Teachers College Association (SAUS)
NZTCB .... New Zealand Trade Certification Board (SAUS)
NZTCI .... New Zealand Technical College Institute (SAUS)
NZTCI .... New Zealand Technical Correspondence Institute (SAUS)

NZTF .... New Zealand Theatre Federation (SAUS)
NZTG .... Tauranga [*New Zealand*] [*ICAO location identifier*] (ICLI)
NZTJWG ..... Nike-Zeus Target Joint Working Group [*Missiles*] (MUGU)
NZTO .... New Zealand Tourism Office (EA)
NZTP .... New Zealand Tourist and Publicity Office [*Later, NZTO*] (EA)
NZTPA .... New Zealand Japan Parliamentary Association (SAUS)
NZTS .... New Zealand Treaty Series [*A publication*] (DLA)
NZTU .... Timaru [*New Zealand*] [*ICAO location identifier*] (ICLI)
NZTV .... Nike-Zeus Target Vehicle [*Missiles*] (IAA)
NzTvGS .... Church of Jesus Christ of Latter-Day Saints, Genealogical Society Library, Temple View Branch, Temple View, New Zealand [*Library symbol*] [*Library of Congress*] (LCLS)
NZUA .... New Zealand Underwater Association (SAUS)
NZUA .... New Zealand Underwriters Association (SAUS)
NZUE .... New Zealand Unit Express (SAUS)
NZUKCC ...... New Zealand-United Kingdom Chamber of Commerce (SAUS)
NZUNINET .... New Zealand University Network
NZUSUGI ..... New Zealand Unix System User Group, Inc. (SAUS)
NZV .... New Zealand Victoria (SAUS)
NZVA .... New Zealand Veterinary Association (GVA)
NZW .... New Zealand White [*Mice hybrids*]
NZW .... South Weymouth, MA [*Location identifier*] [*FAA*] (FAAL)
NZWA .... Chatham Island/Waitangi [*New Zealand*] [*ICAO location identifier*] (ICLI)
NZWA .... New Zealand Woolbuyers Association (SAUS)
NZW&PCS ... New Zealand Weed and Pest Control Society (SAUS)
NZWB .... New Zealand Wool Board (SAUS)
NZWB .... Woodbourne [*New Zealand*] [*ICAO location identifier*] (ICLI)
NZWCC .... New Zealand Weed Control Conference (SAUS)
NZWEA .... New Zealand Workers Educational Association (SAUS)
NZWG .... Wigram [*New Zealand*] [*ICAO location identifier*] (ICLI)
NzWGAL ...... General Assembly Library, Wellington, New Zealand, [*Library symbol*] [*Library of Congress*] (LCLS)
NzWGS .... Church of Jesus Christ of Latter-Day Saints, Genealogical Society Library, Wellington Stake Branch, Wellington, New Zealand [*Library symbol*] [*Library of Congress*] (LCLS)
NZWK .... Whakatane [*New Zealand*] [*ICAO location identifier*] (ICLI)
NZW Mice ... New Zealand White Mice (SAUS)
NZW Mouse... New Zealand White Mouse (SAUS)
NzWMW .... New Zealand Ministry of Works and Development, Head Office Library, Wellington, New Zealand [*Library symbol*] [*Library of Congress*] (LCLS)
NZWN .... Wellington/International [*New Zealand*] [*ICAO location identifier*] (ICLI)
NzWNA .... National Archives, Wellington, New Zealand [*Library symbol*] [*Library of Congress*] (LCLS)
NZWP .... Whenuapai [*New Zealand*] [*ICAO location identifier*] (ICLI)
NZWQ .... Wellington [*New Zealand*] [*ICAO location identifier*] (ICLI)
NZWR .... Whangarei [*New Zealand*] [*ICAO location identifier*] (ICLI)
NZWRAC ...... New Zealand Womens Royal Army Corps (SAUS)
NZWS .... New Zealand Wildlife Service (SAUS)
NZWS .... Westport [*New Zealand*] [*ICAO location identifier*] (ICLI)
NZWSC .... New Zealand Water Safety Council (SAUS)
NZWTA .... New Zealand Wool Testing Authority (SAUS)
NZWU .... Wanganui [*New Zealand*] [*ICAO location identifier*] (ICLI)
NZWWC .... New Zealand Working Womens Council (SAUS)
NZWWF .... New Zealand Waterside Workers Federation (SAUS)
NZY .... San Diego, CA [*Location identifier*] [*FAA*] (FAAL)
NZYF .... New Zealand Yachting Federation (SAUS)
NZYHA .... New Zealand Youth Hostels Association (SAUS)
NZYM .... Synthetech, Inc. [*NASDAQ symbol*] (NQ)
NZZA .... Auckland [*New Zealand*] [*ICAO location identifier*] (ICLI)
NZZC .... Christchurch [*New Zealand*] [*ICAO location identifier*] (ICLI)
NZZO .... Auckland [*New Zealand*] [*ICAO location identifier*] (ICLI)
NZZW .... Wellington [*New Zealand*] [*ICAO location identifier*] (ICLI)

O

By Acronym

O .... Absence of Sex Chromosome (DAVI)
O .... Angel (SAUS)
O .... An Oige [The Irish Youth Hostels Association] [Founded in 1931]
O .... Center of the Earth (SAUS)
O .... Cleared to the Outer Marker (SAUS)
O .... Deamino [As substituent on nucleoside] [Biochemistry]
O .... for those innocent souls (SAUS)
O .... Horizontal Opposed [Aircraft engine]
O .... Law Opinions [A publication] (DLA)
O .... New Orleans [Louisiana] [Mint mark, when appearing on US coins]
                  [Obsolete]
O .... None (DAVI)
O .... Nonmotile [Laboratory science] (DAVI)
O .... Oasis
o .... Oath (GEAB)
O .... Oath
O .... Oberst [Colonel] [German military - World War II]
O .... Obiit [He, or She, Died] [Latin]
O .... Object
O .... Objective
O .... Oblast [Governmental subdivision in USSR corresponding to a
                  province or state]
O .... Oboe [Phonetic alphabet] [World War II] (DSUE)
O .... Observation Aircraft [Designation for all US military aircraft]
O .... Observer
O .... Obsolescent (AFIT)
O .... Obstetrics [Medicine] (MAE)
O .... Obvious (STED)
O .... Occasional [Concerning occurrence of species]
O .... Occidental
O .... Occipital (STED)
O .... Occiput [Medicine]
O .... Occlusal [Dentistry]
O .... Occupation (ADA)
O .... Occurrence
O .... Ocean [Maps and charts]
O .... Oceanic (SAUS)
O .... Oceanic Steamship Company (SAUS)
O .... Octal [Number system with a base of eight] [Computer science]
                  (BUR)
O .... Octarius [Pint] [Pharmacy]
O .... Octavo [Book from 20 to 25 centimeters in height] [Bibliography]
O .... October
O .... Octupole [Physics] (OA)
O .... Oculus [Eye] [Latin]
O .... Odericus [Flourished, 1166-1200] [Authority cited in pre-1607 legal
                  work] (DSA)
O .... Off
O .... Offered [Stock exchange term] (SPSG)
O .... Office [or Officer]
O .... Office of Operations [Coast Guard]
O .... Official [Rate] [Value of the English pound]
O .... Often (STED)
O .... Ohio
O .... Ohio Reports [A publication] (DLA)
O .... Ohio State Library, Columbus, OH [Library symbol] [Library of
                  Congress] (LCLS)
O .... Ohm [Electricity]
O .... Ohne [Antigen] [Immunology]
o .... Oil (VRA)
O .... Oil
O .... Oklahoma (DLA)
O .... Old
O .... Olivine Subgroup [Fayalite, forsterite] [CIPW classification] [Geology]
O .... Oman (MILB)
O .... Omicron [Fifteenth letter of the Greek alphabet] (NASA)
O .... Omnipol Foreign Trade Corp. [Former Czechoslovakia] [ICAO aircraft
                  manufacturer identifier] (ICAO)
O .... Omnivore
O .... Oncovin [Leurocristine, Vincristine] [Also, LCR, V, VC, VCR]
                  [Antineoplastic drug]
O .... Ongoing
O .... Only
O .... Ontario (DLA)
O .... Ontario Reports [A publication] (DLA)
O .... Ontario Securities Commission [Canada]

O .... Opacity (MCD)
O .... Open [Dancing position]
O .... Open-Air Places [Parks, pools, etc.] [Public-performance tariff class]
                  [British]
O .... Open Circuit
O .... Opening
O .... Operand [Computer science]
O .... Operating Room Attendant [Ranking title] [British Royal Navy]
O .... Operation
O .... Operator
O .... Operon [Genetics]
O .... Ophthalmology [Medical Officer designation] [British]
O .... Opium [Slang]
O .... Optimus [Best] [Latin]
O .... Optional Dishes [School meals] [British]
O .... Options [Computer science] [Telecommunications]
O .... Oral [Medicine]
O .... Orange [Color] [Medicine] (DMAA)
O .... Orange [Phonetic alphabet] [Royal Navy] [World War I] [Pre-World
                  War I] (DSUE)
O .... Orange [Maps and charts]
O .... Orbit [Medicine] (DAVI)
O .... Orchid Flowering [Horticulture]
O .... Ordained
O .... Order
O .... Orderly [Medicine] (DAVI)
O .... Orders Group [British military] (DMA)
O .... Ordinance
O .... Ordinary
O .... Ordinary Level [School graduating grade] [British]
O .... Ordinary Ray [Direction of]
O .... Ordinate [Mathematics] (MSA)
O .... Ordinis [By the Order Of] [Latin]
O .... Ordnance
O .... Ordonnanzoffizier [Special-Missions Staff Officer] [German military -
                  World War II]
O .... Oregon (ROG)
O .... Oregon Reports [A publication] (DLA)
o .... Organ
O .... Organ
O .... Organic [Soil]
O .... Organism [Psychology]
O .... Organization
O .... Organized Naval Reserve
O .... Orient [Freemasonry]
O .... Oriental
O .... Origin (IDOE)
O .... Origin
O .... Original
O .... Original Response (DIPS)
o .... Ortho [Chemistry]
O .... Orthodox [Judaism]
O .... Orthopedic (STED)
O .... Os [Bone] [Latin]
O .... Oscar [Phonetic alphabet] [International] (DSUE)
O .... Oscillation or Fluctuation in Behavior [Psychology]
O .... Oscillators [JETDS nomenclature] [Military] (CET)
O .... Osphradium [An organ in mollusks]
O .... Osten [East] [German]
O .... Osteocyte (MELL)
O .... Ostiole [Biology]
O .... Other
O .... Other Program (NTCM)
O .... Otto's United States Supreme Court Reports [91-107 United States]
                  [A publication] (DLA)
O .... Ouest [West] [French]
o .... Out (VLIE)
O .... Out
O .... Outboard (DS)
O .... Outfield [Baseball]
O .... Outlay (GFGA)
O .... Outlet
O .... Output (BUR)
o .... Output (IDOE)
O .... Outside Cylinders [Trains] [British]

O	Outside Edge [*Skating*]
O	Outstanding (ADWA)
O	Ovary
O	Ovation (WGA)
O	Oven
O	Over
O	Overall (IAA)
O	Overall Rating [*Broadcasting*]
O	Overcast
O	Overflow (VLIE)
o	Overruled [*Ruling in cited case expressly overruled*] [*Used in Shepard's Citations*] [*Legal term*] (DLA)
O	Overseer
O	Ovulation
O	Ovule [*Botany*]
O	Owner
O	Oxford [*County borough in England*]
O	Oxidative (STED)
O	Oxygen [*Chemical element*]
O	Oxygenium (SAUS)
O	Realty Income Corp. [*NYSE symbol*] (SAG)
O	Respirations [*on anesthesia chart*] (DAVI)
O	Shoulder Season [*Airline fare code*]
O	Solicitor's Opinion [*A publication*] (DLA)
O	South African Law Reports, Orange Free State Provincial Division [*1910-46*] [*A publication*] (DLA)
O	Without Film [*Bacteriology*] (DAVI)
O1	Ensign [*Navy*]
O1	Organized Naval Reserve Seagoing
O1	Second Lieutenant [*Air Force, Army, Marine Corps*]
O^2	Both Eyes [*Pharmacy*]
O2	First Lieutenant [*Air Force, Army, Marine Corps*]
O2	Lieutenant Junior Grade [*Navy*]
O2	molecular Oxygen (SAUS)
O2	Organized Naval Reserve Aviation
O$_2$	Oxygen (IDOE)
O-2A	Oligodendrocytes and Type 2 Astrocytes [*Neurology*]
O$_2$ Cap	Oxygen Capacity (MAE)
O2S	Oxygen Sensor [*Automotive engineering*]
O$_2$sat	Oxygen Saturation (MAE)
O$_2$V	Oxygen Ventilation Equivalent [*Laboratory science*] (DAVI)
O3	Captain [*Air Force, Army, Marine Corps*]
O3	Lieutenant [*Navy*]
O$_3$	Ozone (PS)
O4	Lieutenant Commander [*Navy*]
O4	Major [*Air Force, Army, Marine Corps*]
O4O	October 4th Organization (EA)
O5	Commander [*Navy*]
O5	Lieutenant Colonel [*Air Force, Army, Marine Corps*]
O-5-P	Orotidine-5-Phosphate
O6	Captain [*Navy*]
O6	Colonel [*Air Force, Army, Marine Corps*]
O7	Brigadier General [*Air Force, Army, Marine Corps*]
O7	Commodore [*Navy*]
O8	Major General [*Air Force, Army, Marine Corps*]
O8	Rear Admiral [*Navy*]
O9	Lieutenant General [*Air Force, Army, Marine Corps*]
O9	Vice Admiral [*Navy*]
O10	Admiral [*Navy*]
O10	General [*Air Force, Army, Marine Corps*]
OA	Almonte Public Library, Ontario [*Library symbol*] [*National Library of Canada*] (NLC)
OA	Object Adapter (SAUS)
O-A	Objective Analytic Batteries [*Personality development test*] [*Psychology*]
OA	Objective Aperture [*Microscopy*]
OA	Objective Area [*Military*]
OA	Oblate Sisters of the Assumption [*Roman Catholic religious order*]
OA	Obligation Authority [*Army*]
OA	Obstacle Avoidance (MCD)
OA	Obstructive Apnea [*Medicine*] (MELL)
OA	Occipital Artery [*Anatomy*]
OA	Occipito-Anterior (SAUS)
OA	Occiput Anterior [*Medicine*]
OA	Ocean Acre [*Marine science*] (MSC)
OA	Ocular Albinism [*Medicine*] (MELL)
OA	Odd Address (SAUS)
O/A	Offer Accepted (ADA)
OA	Office Address (WDAA)
OA	Office Assistant (SAUS)
OA	Office Audit [*IRS*]
OA	Office Automation
OA	Office for Accreditation [*American Library Association*]
OA	Office of Administration [*NASA*]
OA	Office of Applications [*NASA*]
OA	Office of Audits (COE)
OA	Office of Operations Analysis [*Arms Control and Disarmament Agency*] (GRD)
OA	Office of the Administrator
OA	Officers Association [*British military*] (DMA)
OA	Official Assignee (ROG)
OA	Ohio Appellate Reports [*A publication*] (DLA)
OA	Oil-Immened Self-Cooled (SAUS)
OA	Oil-immersed Air-cooled (SAUS)
OA	Oil-Immersed Self-Cooled [*Transformer*] (IEEE)

OA	Oil-to-Air (SAUS)
OA	Old Account [*Banking*]
OA	Old Age
OA	Old Assyrian (BJA)
OA	Oleic Acid [*Medicine*] (DMAA)
OA	Olymbiaki Aeroporia [*Olympic Airlines*]
OA	Olympic Airways [*Greece*] [*ICAO designator*] (OAG)
OA	Omniaerial (SAUS)
OA	Omniantenna
OA	Omnirange Antenna (IAA)
oa	On Acceptance (EBF)
OA	On Acceptance [*Business term*]
OA	On Account [*Business and trade*]
OA	On Account Of
O/A	On Application (NITA)
OA	On Arrival (ADA)
O/A	On or About (WDAA)
o/a	On or About (WDMC)
O/A	Open Access [*Library shelves*] (DGA)
OA	Open Access
OA	Open Account
OA	Open Agility
OA	Open Annealed [*Metal industry*]
OA	Open Architecture [*Telecommunications*] (IAA)
OA	Opera America [*An association*] (EA)
OA	Operand Address (NITA)
OA	Operand Address Register [*Computer science*]
OA	Operating Agency
OA	Operating Aircraft
OA	Operating Assemblies [*JETDS nomenclature*] [*Military*] (CET)
OA	Operating Authorization
OA	Operational Advice
OA	Operational Aft (MCD)
OA	Operational Amplifier [*Telecommunications*] (TEL)
OA	Operational [*or operations*] Analysis
OA	Operational Architecture (SAUS)
OA	Operational Area (SAUS)
OA	Operational Assessment (SAUS)
OA	Operationally Available (NATG)
OA	Operation Analysis [*or Analyst*] (WDAA)
OA	Operation Appreciation (EA)
O/A	Operations/Administration (SSD)
OA	Operations Advisor [*NASA*]
OA	Operations Analysis (SAUS)
OA	Operations Analyst (SAUS)
OA	Operations Area
OA	Operator Access (IAA)
OA	Operator Assistance [*Telecommunications*] (VLIE)
OA	Operator Availability (SAUS)
OA	Ophthalmic Artery (SAUS)
OA	Opiate Analgesia
OA	Opioid Analgesics [*Medicine*] (MELL)
OA	Optical Absorption (SAUS)
OA	Optical Adjunct
OA	Optical Augmentation (ACAE)
OA	Optic Atrophy (CPH)
OA	Optic Axis (SAUS)
OA	Optoacoustic [*Cell*]
OA	Oral Administration (MELL)
OA	Oral Alimentation [*Gastroenterology*] (DAVI)
OA	Oral Apparatus [*Zoology*]
OA	Orbital Assembly (MCD)
OA	Orbit Analysis
OA	Orbit Analyst (MCD)
O/A	Orbit/Attitude (ACAE)
OA	Orbiter Access Arm [*NASA*]
OA	Order Action (VLIE)
OA	Order Address (SAUS)
OA	Order Administration (SAUS)
O/A	Order Authority (MCD)
OA	Order of AHEPA [*Also known as American Hellenic Educational Progressive Association*] (EA)
OA	Order of Australia (WDAA)
OA	Order of the Alhambra (EA)
OA	Order of the Arrow (EA)
O/A	Ordnance Alteration (MCD)
OA	Ordnance Artificer [*Obsolete*] [*Navy*] [*British*]
OA	Organic Acid (AAEL)
OA	Organizational Analysis
OA	Organizational Assessment
O/A	Original-Abfuellung [*On estate-bottled German wine labels*]
OA	Original Address (SAUS)
OA	Originating Agency (SAA)
OA	Orlando Aerospace [*Martin Marietta*] (RDA)
OA	Oro Americano [*American Gold*] [*Spanish*] [*Business term*]
OA	Osborne Association (EA)
OA	Osteoarthritis [*Medicine*]
OA	Osteogenesis Imperfecta [*Brittle bone disease*]
OA	Other Appointments
OA	Other Articles
OA	Oudh Appeals [*India*] [*A publication*] (DLA)
O/A	Our Account [*Business term*]
O/A	Outer Anchorage [*Navigation*]
OA	Outgoing Access (SAUS)
OA	Output Acknowledge (SAUS)

OA	Output Amplifier (SAUS)	OAAT	Ortho-Aminoazotoluene [A dye] [Organic chemistry]
OA	Output Amplitude	OAATM	Office of the Assistant for Automation (SAUS)
OA	Output Available (SAUS)	OAAU	Organization of Afro-American Unity
OA	Output Axis	OAAU	Orthogonal Array Arithmetic Unit [Computer science]
OA	Outside Air (SAUS)	OAAV	Organization of African-American Veterans (EA)
OA	Ovalbumin [Also, OV, OVA, OVAL] [Biochemistry]	OAB	Attawapiskat Band Library, Ontario [Library symbol] [National Library of Canada] (BIB)
OA	Overachievers Anonymous (EA)		
OA	Overaction (SAUS)	OAB	Moab, UT [Location identifier] [FAA] (FAAL)
OA	Over Aged (RIMS)	OAB	Oakland [California] Army Base (VNW)
OA	Overaging (SAUS)	OAB	Ocean Affairs Board [National Academy of Sciences] (MSC)
OA	Overall [Technical drawings]	OAB	Old-Age Benefits
OA	Overall noise level (SAUS)	OAB	Olive Advisory Board [Defunct] (EA)
OA	Overeaters Anonymous (EA)	OAB	One-to-All Broadcast (SAUS)
OA	Overfire Airport [Combustion technology]	OAB	Ordnance Assembly Building (MUGU)
OA	Overflow Area (SAUS)	OAB	Organisation Africaine du Bois [African Timber Organization] (EAIO)
OA	Overhead Approach (SAUS)	OAB	Outer Air Battle [Navy] (ANA)
OA	Overtime Authorization (AAG)	OAB	Overseas Affairs Branch [Army]
OA	Oxalic Acid [Organic chemistry] (AAMN)	OAB	Overseas Appointments Bureau [Christian Education Movement] [British] (AEBS)
OA	Oxamic Acid (SAUS)		
OA	Oxygen Absorbed (SAUS)	OAB	Owners Abroad Aviation Ltd. [British] [ICAO designator] (FAAC)
OA	Services to the Aged under the Older Americans Act [Public human service program] (PHSD)	OAB	Oxford Annotated Bible [New York] [A publication] (BJA)
		OABA	Burleigh-Anstruther and Chandos Union Public Library, Apsley, Ontario [Library symbol] [National Library of Canada] (BIB)
OA 2d	Ohio Appellate Reports, Second Series [A publication] (DLA)		
OA-37B	Dragonfly (SAUS)	OABA	Outdoor Amusement Business Association (EA)
OAA	Argentine Accreditation Body (SAUS)	OABD	Behsood [Afghanistan] [ICAO location identifier] (ICLI)
OAA	Hereditary Order of Armigerous Augustans (EA)	OABETA	Office Appliance and Business Equipment Trades Association (HGAA)
OAA	Nora, AK [Location identifier] [FAA] (FAAL)		
OAA	o-Aminoacetanilide [Organic chemistry]	OABG	Baghlan [Afghanistan] [ICAO location identifier] (ICLI)
OAA	Obstetric Anaesthetists Association [British] (DBA)	OABK	Bandkamalkhan [Afghanistan] [ICAO location identifier] (ICLI)
OAA	Office of Academic Affairs	OABM	Outer Air Battle Missile (ACAE)
OAA	Office of Administrative Appeals [U.S. Department of Labor] (BARN)	OABN	Bamyan [Afghanistan] [ICAO location identifier] (ICLI)
OaA	Office of Aging (SAUS)	OABP	Organic Anion Binding Protein [Biochemistry]
OAA	Office of Air Accidents (SAUS)	OABR	Bamar [Afghanistan] [ICAO location identifier] (ICLI)
OAA	Office of Assessment and Assurance (SAUS)	OABS	Sarday [Afghanistan] [ICAO location identifier] (ICLI)
OAA	Office of Aviation Affairs [Army]	OABT	Bost [Afghanistan] [ICAO location identifier] (ICLI)
OAA	Oglethorpe Astronomical Association [Savannah, Georgia]	OABT	Ortho-Aminobenzenethiol [Organic chemistry]
OAA	Old-Age Assistance [Superseded by SSI] [HEW]	OAC	Acton Public Library, Ontario [Library symbol] [National Library of Canada] (NLC)
OAA	Older Americans Act [1965]		
OAA	Older Americans Almanac [A publication]	OAC	Cleveland Institute of Art, Cleveland, OH [OCLC symbol] (OCLC)
OAA	Ontario Association of Architects [1890] [Canada] (NGC)	OAC	Oceanic Affairs Committee (BUAC)
OAA	Open Agent Architecture (SAUS)	OAC	Oceanic Area Control [Aviation] (FAAC)
OAA	Open Arcade Architecture (SAUS)	OAC	Oceanographic Advisory Committee [Navy Oceanographer] (USDC)
OAA	Optical Acquisition Aid [Deep Space Instrumentation Facility, NASA]	OAC	Office of Academic Computing [Research center] (RCD)
OAA	Opticians Association of America (EA)	OAC	Office of Antiboycott Compliance
OAA	Orbiter Access Arm [NASA] (NASA)	OAC	Officer Advanced Course [Army] (INF)
OAA	Orbiter Alternate Airfield [NASA] (MCD)	OAC	Officers Advanced Course (SAUS)
OAA	Order of Australia Association	OAC	Official Acceptance of Construction (SAUS)
OAA	Organic Acidemia Association (EA)	OAC	Officials Antarctic Committee (SAUS)
OAA	Organisation des Nations Unies pour l'Alimentation et l'Agriculture [Food and Agriculture Organization of the United Nations]	OAC	Ohio Administrative Code [A publication] (AAGC)
		OAC	Ohio Athletic Conference (PSS)
OAA	Organization of Athletic Administrators [Defunct] (EA)	Oac	On Approval of Credit
OAA	Orient Airlines Association (EA)	OAC	On Approved Credit
OAA	Other Acronymic Agencies	OAC	One-Address Code (SAUS)
OAA	Outdoor Advertising Association (BARN)	OAC	One-Address Computer (SAUS)
OAA	Outdoor Advertising Association of Great Britain (BUAC)	OAC	Ontario Academic Course (SAUS)
OAA	Oxalacetic Acid (SAUS)	OAC	Ontario Agricultural College [Canada]
OAA	Oxaloacetate (SAUS)	OAC	Ontario Appeal Cases [Database] [Maritime Law Book Co. Ltd.] [Information service or system] (CRD)
OAA	Oxaloacetic [or Oxalacetic] Acid [Organic chemistry]		
OAA	Oxley Aviation [Australia] [ICAO designator] (FAAC)	OAC	Ontario Arts Council
OAAA	Oceania Amateur Athletic Association (EAIO)	OAC	Open Air Campaigners, US (EA)
OAAA	Order of Americans of Armorial Ancestry (EA)	OAC	Operating Agency Code (AFM)
OAAA	Outdoor Advertising Association of America [Washington, DC] (EA)	OAC	Operation Anti-Christ (EA)
OAAA	Outdoor Advertising Association of Australia, Inc. (BUAC)	OAC	Operation of Aircraft Costs (DNAB)
OAAB	Objective-Analytic Anxiety Battery [Psychology]	OAC	Operations Advisory Committee (SAUS)
OAAC	Ocean Affairs Advisory Committee [Department of State] (MSC)	OAC	Operations Analysis Center
OAAC	Older Americans Advocacy Commission [HEW]	OAC	Operations Analysis Chief [Air Force]
OAAC	Outdoor Advertising Association of Canada (BUAC)	OAC	Operator Access Console (SAUS)
OAAD	Amdar [Afghanistan] [ICAO location identifier] (ICLI)	OAC	Optical Absorption Coefficient (AAEL)
OAAD	Ovarian Ascorbic Acid Depletion [Test]	OAC	Optical Acceleration Cancellation [Vision]
OAADM	Ovarian Ascorbic Acid Depletion Material	OAC	Optical Area Correlator
OAAD Test	Ovarian Ascorbic Acid Depletion Test (SAUS)	OAC	Optimal Automatic Control
OAAD Test	Ovarian Ascorbic Acid Depletion Test (SAUS)	OAC	Optimally Adaptive Control (SAUS)
OAAI	Office of Air Accidents Investigation (SAUS)	OAC	Optimized Aftercooled [Truck engineering]
OAAIS	Office of Administrative Analysis, Information, and Statistics [Red Cross]	OAC	Optimum Approach Course [Navy] (NVT)
		OAC	Ordnance Ammunition Command [Merged with Munitions Command] [Army]
OAAK	Andkhoi [Afghanistan] [ICAO location identifier] (ICLI)		
OA & C	Ohio Circuit Court Decisions [A publication] (DLA)	OAC	Ordo ab Chao [Order Out of Chaos] [Freemasonry] [Latin]
OA&M	Operations Administration & Maintainance (SAUS)	OAC	Oregon Administrative Code [A publication] (AAGC)
OA & M	Operations, Administration, and Maintenance [Telecommunications]	OAC	Oregon Agriculture College (SAUS)
OA&M	Operations Administration & Management (SAUS)	OAC	Oriental Airlines Ltd. [Nigeria] [ICAO designator] (FAAC)
OA & MS	Office of Administration and Management Services [Employment and Training Administration] [Department of Labor]	OAC	Original Acquisition Cost (AAGC)
		OAC	Original Air Conditioning (IIA)
OA & S	Other Arms and Services [Military]	OAC	Orleans Area Command
OAAPS	Organization for Afro-Asian Peoples Solidarity	OAC	Outdoor Advertising Council (BUAC)
OAARD	Office of the Assistant Administrator for Research and Development [HEW]	OAC	Outer Approach Channel
		OAC	Overseas Automotive Club (EA)
OAAS	Asmar [Afghanistan] [ICAO location identifier] (ICLI)	OACA	Ontario Arms Collectors Association (SAUS)
OAA/S	Observer's Assessment of Alertness / Sedation Scale [Medicine]	OACB	Charburjak [Afghanistan] [ICAO location identifier] (ICLI)
OAAS	Office of the Administrative Assistant to the Secretary of the Army (SAUS)	OACB	Output Area Control Block (SAUS)
		OACC	Chakhcharan [Afghanistan] [ICAO location identifier] (ICLI)
OAAS	Omnibus Army Aircraft Survivability Study (SAUS)	OACC	Oceanic Area Control Centre
OAAS	Ontario Association of Agricultural Societies [Canada] (BUAC)	OACC	Older Americans Consumer Cooperative [Washington, DC] (EA)
OAASN	Office of the Administrative Assistant to the Secretary of the Army	OACD	Office of Agricultural and Chemical Development [of TVA]
OAASN	Office of the Administrative Assistant to the Secretary of the Navy (SAUS)	OACDT	Order Acknowledge Date (SAUS)
		OACDT	Outback Areas Community Developmnent Trust [Australia]

OA Cell........ Opto-Acoustic Cell (SAUS)
OACES......... Ocean-Atmosphere Carbon Exchange Study [*Marine science*] (OSRA)
OACETT........ Ontario Association of Certified Engineering Technicians and Technologists (SAUS)
OACG........... Office of the Assistant Comptroller General (AAGC)
OACH........... Acton High School, Ontario [*Library symbol*] [*National Library of Canada*] (NLC)
OACI............ Ontario Academic Courses Institute (SAUS)
OACI............ Optical Automatic Car Identification
OACI............ Organisation de l'Aviation Civile Internationale [*International Civil Aviation Organization*] [*French*] [*United Nations*]
OACI............ Organizacion de Aviacion Civil Internacional [*International Civil Aviation Organization*] [*Spanish*] [*United Nations*] (DUND)
OACII........... Operational Approved Configuration Identification Index (SAA)
OACIS........... Ocean-Atmospheric Climatic Interaction Studies
OACIS........... Oregon Advanced Computing Institute [*Research center*] (RCD)
OACJC.......... Oklahoma Association of Community and Junior Colleges (SAUS)
OACLD.......... Ontario Association for Children with Learning Disabilities (SAUS)
OACM........... Offensive Air Combat Manoeuvre (SAUS)
OACO........... Operation and Checkout [*NASA*] (IAA)
OAC of S...... Office of the Assistant Chief of Staff [*Military*]
OACP........... Canada Publishing Corp., Agincourt, Ontario [*Library symbol*] [*National Library of Canada*] (BIB)
OACP........... Operational Analysis Code Package (PDAA)
OACR........... Office of the Admiral Commanding Reserves [*Navy*] [*British*]
OACS........... Office of the Assistant Chief of Staff [*Military*] (AAG)
OACSA......... Office of the Assistant Chief of Staff for Automation and Communications [*Military*] (MCD)
OACSAC....... Office of the Assistant Chief of Staff for Automation and Communications [*Military*]
OACSC-E...... Office of the Assistant Chief of Staff for Communications-Electronics (AABC)
OACSEA....... Older American Community Service Employment Act [*1975*]
OACSFOR.... Office of the Assistant Chief of Staff for Force Development [*Army*]
OACSI.......... Office of the Assistant Chief of Staff for Intelligence [*Army*]
OACSIM....... Office of the Assistant Chief of Staff for Information Management [*Military*]
OACSU......... Off-Air Call Set-Up (SAUS)
OACT........... Office of Advanced Concepts and Technology (SAUS)
OACT........... Office of the Actuary [*Department of Health and Human Services*] (GFGA)
OACT........... Officer, Airman, Civilian, and Total (MCD)
OACT........... Ohio Association of Classroom Teachers (SAUS)
OACT........... Organisation Africaine de Cartographie et de Teledetection [*Algeria*] (EAIO)
OACT........... Ormone Adrenocorticotropina [*Italian*] [*Medicine*]
OACUL......... Ontario Association of College and University Libraries (SAUS)
OAD............. Adria Laboratories, Inc., Columbus, OH [*OCLC symbol*] (OCLC)
OAD............. Obstructive Airway Disease [*Medicine*]
OAD............. Obstructive Arterial Disease [*Medicine*] (MELL)
OAD............. Occlusive Arterial Disease (SAUS)
OAD............. Office of Administration
OAD............. Officers' Accounts Division [*Navy*]
OAD............. Officers' Assignment Division, The Adjutant General's Office [*Army*]
OAD............. Open Architecture Driver (SAUS)
OAD............. Opening of Anterior Digestive [*Gland*]
OAD............. Operational Active Data [*Navy*]
OAD............. Operational Analysis Division [*Air Force*]
OAD............. Operational Availability Data [*Military*]
OAD............. Operational Availability Data (or Date) (SAUS)
OAD............. Operational Availability Date [*Nuclear Regulatory Commission*] (GFGA)
OAD............. Operations Analysis Division (SAUS)
OAD............. Operator Aiding Demonstrator (SAUS)
OAD............. Optical Activity Detection
OAD............. Optoacoustic Device (SAUS)
OAD............. Orbiter Atmospheric Drag [*NASA*]
OAD............. Ordered, Adjudged, and Decreed (WDAA)
OAD............. Ordered to Active Duty (AABC)
OAD............. Ordering and Distributing (IAA)
OAD............. Oregon Association of the Deaf (SAUS)
OAD............. Organic Anionic Dye [*Medicine*] (DMAA)
OAD............. Organization Address (SAUS)
OAD............. Organizations and Agencies Directories Series [*A publication*]
OAD............. Original Air Date [*of program's first telecast*]
OAD............. Overall Absolute Deviation [*Mathematics*]
OAD............. Overall Density (SAUS)
OAD............. Overall Depth (WDAA)
OAD............. Overall Dimensions (IAA)
OAD............. Overlay Area Description (TIMI)
OAD............. Oxford American Dictionary [*A publication*]
OAD............. Special Audit Division (AAGC)
OADAB......... Office of the Assistant Director of the Army Budget
OADAP......... Office of Alcoholism and Drug Abuse Prevention [*Department of Health and Human Services*]
OADARS....... Optical Aids to Detection and Ranging Systems (SAUS)
OADC........... Oleate-Albumin-Dextrose-Catalase [*Medium*] (DMAA)
OADC........... Oleic Acid, Albumin, Dextrose, Catalase
OADCE......... Open Architecture Distribution Computing Environment (TIMI)
OADD........... Dawlatabad [*Afghanistan*] [*ICAO location identifier*] (ICLI)
OA/DDP........ Office Automation / Distributed Data Processing (MHDI)
OADEMQA.... Office of Acid Deposition, Environmental Monitoring, and Quality Assurance [*Environmental Protection Agency*] (GFGA)
OADF........... Darra-I-Soof [*Afghanistan*] [*ICAO location identifier*] (ICLI)
OA-DG.......... Occupational Area Defense Grouping (DNAB)
OADG........... Open Architecture Development Group [*IBM Corp.*] (CDE)
OAD Gland... Opening of Anterior Digestive Gland (SAUS)
OADH........... One-Arm Dove Hunt Association (EA)
OADH........... Organization of Advanced Disabled Hobbyists (EA)
OADMS......... Office of Automated Data Management Services [*General Services Administration*]
OADMT......... Oliphant Auditory Discrimination Memory Test [*Medicine*] (STED)
OAdN........... Ohio Northern University, Ada, OH [*Library symbol*] [*Library of Congress*] (LCLS)
OADP........... Organisation de l'Action Democratique et Populaire [*Morocco*]
OADPM......... Office of ADP Management (SAUS)
OADPS......... Office of Automatic Data Processing Services (AAGC)
OADR........... Office of Agricultural Defense Relations [*New Deal*]
OADR........... Originating Agency Determination Required (MCD)
OADS........... Omnidirectional Air Data System
OADSS......... Office Assignment Decision Support System (SAUS)
OADV........... Devar [*Afghanistan*] [*ICAO location identifier*] (ICLI)
OADW........... Wazakhwa [*Afghanistan*] [*ICAO location identifier*] (ICLI)
OADZ........... Darwaz [*Afghanistan*] [*ICAO location identifier*] (ICLI)
OAE............. NOAA [*National Oceanic and Atmospheric Administration*]-LISD Seattle Center, Seattle, WA [*OCLC symbol*] (OCLC)
OAE............. Occupational and Adult Education [*Office of Education*] (OICC)
OAE............. Oceanic Anoxic Event
OAE............. Office of Analysis and Evaluation [*Environmental Protection Agency*] (EPA)
OAE............. Officer of Arms Extraordinary [*College of Arms/Heralds' College*] [*British*]
OAE............. Old Antarctic Explorer
OAE............. Operational Analysis and Exercises (SAUS)
OAE............. Operational Area Evaluation [*Environmental science*] (COE)
OAE............. Optical Alignment Equipment
OAE............. Optima Energy Corp. [*Vancouver Stock Exchange symbol*]
OAE............. Orbiting Astronomical Explorer [*NASA*] (IIA)
OAE............. Orchestra of the Age of Enlightenment [*British*]
OAE............. Organization of Architectural Employees
OAE............. Orzeck Aphasia Evaluation [*Psychology*]
OAE............. Oscillating-Analyzer Ellipsometer (PDAA)
OAE............. Otoacoustic Emission [*Audiology*]
OAEAO......... Ontario Association of Education Administration Officials (SAUS)
OAEC........... Essa Centennial Library, Angus, Ontario [*Library symbol*] [*National Library of Canada*] (BIB)
OAEC........... Organization for Asian Economic Cooperation (SAUS)
OAEFI.......... Astorville Branch, East Ferris Township Public Library, Ontario (SAUS)
OAEFT.......... Astorville Branch, East Ferris Township Public Library, Ontario [*Library symbol*] [*National Library of Canada*] (NLC)
OAEK........... Keshm [*Afghanistan*] [*ICAO location identifier*] (ICLI)
OAEM........... Eshkashem [*Afghanistan*] [*ICAO location identifier*] (ICLI)
OAEM........... Ontario Approved Educational Microcomputers (SAUS)
OAEQ........... Islam Qala [*Afghanistan*] [*ICAO location identifier*] (ICLI)
OAES........... Ohio Agricultural Experimental Station (SAUS)
OAESA......... Ohio Association of Elementary School Administrators (SAUS)
OAET........... Elma Township Public Library, Atwood, Ontario [*Library symbol*] [*National Library of Canada*] (NLC)
OAET........... Office of Aeronautics, Exploration, and Technology (SAUS)
OAF............. Austrian Air Ambulance [*ICAO designator*] (FAAC)
OAF............. Occidentale Afrique Francaise [*French West Africa*]
OAF............. Office of Alcohol Fuels [*Department of Energy*]
OAF............. Officer Assignment Folder [*Military*] (AFM)
OAF............. Ontario Ministry of Agriculture and Food [*UTLAS symbol*]
OAF............. Open Air Factor
OAF............. Optimum Array Filter (SAUS)
OAF............. Options for Animals Foundation (EA)
OAF............. Orbital Antenna Farm (PDAA)
OAF............. Origin Address Field [*Computer science*] (IBMDP)
OAF............. Origination Address Field (SAUS)
OAF............. Orthodox and Anglican Fellowship (EA)
OAF............. Osteoclast Activating Factor [*Endocrinology*]
OAF............. Overhaul Attrition Factor (SAUS)
OAF............. Oxygen Alternate Fill
OA/FA.......... Oil-immersed Air-cooled/Forced-Air-cooled (SAUS)
OAFB........... Offutt Air Force Base [*Nebraska*] (AAG)
OAFC........... Arden Branch, Frontenac County Library, Ontario [*Library symbol*] [*National Library of Canada*] (BIB)
OAFC........... Occupational Analysis Field Center
OAFC........... Office of Air Force Chaplains
OAFC........... Official Aerrage Fan Club [*Defunct*] (EA)
OAFCCD....... Ontario Association for Families of Children with Communication Disorders (SAUS)
OAFD........... Orbiter Air Flight Deck [*NASA*] (MCD)
OAFG........... Khost-O-Fering [*Afghanistan*] [*ICAO location identifier*] (ICLI)
OA/FI........... Operational Assurance/Fault Isolation (MCD)
OAFIE.......... Office of Armed Forces Information and Education
OAFM........... On or After Full Moon [*Freemasonry*] (ROG)
OAFR........... Farah [*Afghanistan*] [*ICAO location identifier*] (ICLI)
OAFSC......... Other Air Force Speciality Code (SAUS)
OAFT........... Official Air Freight Tariffs
OAFTO......... Orbiter Atmospheric Flight Test Office [*NASA*] (NASA)
OAFU........... Observers Advanced Flying Unit (SAUS)
OAFZ........... Faizabad [*Afghanistan*] [*ICAO location identifier*] (ICLI)
OAG............. Oblique Anterior Gauche [*Left Anterior Oblique Position*] [*Medicine*]
OAG............. Office of the Adjutant General [*Military*] (MCD)
OAG............. Office of the Attorney-General
OAG............. Official Airline Guide, Inc. [*ICAO designator*] (FAAC)

OAG .... Official Airline Guides, Inc. [*Information service or system*] (IID)
OAG .... Oleoyl(acetyl)glycerol [*Organic chemistry*]
OAG .... Online Air Guide (SAUS)
OAG .... Online Airlines Guide [*A publication*]
OAG .... Open Angle Glaucoma [*Ophthalmology*]
OAG .... Open Application Group (SAUS)
OAG .... Open Applications Group [*An association*] (NTPA)
OAG .... Operand Address Generator (SAUS)
OAG .... Opinions of the Attorney General
OAG .... Optical Alignment Group
OAG .... Orange [*Australia*] [*Airport symbol*] (OAG)
OAG .... Ostriches Ambling Gracefully
OAGA .... Ghaziabad [*Afghanistan*] [*ICAO location identifier*] (ICLI)
OAGB .... Osteopathic Association of Great Britain
OAGCM .... Ocean-Atmosphere General Circulation Model [*Oceanography*]
OAGD .... Gader [*Afghanistan*] [*ICAO location identifier*] (ICLI)
OAG-EE .... Official Airline Guide-Electronic Edition [*Official Airline Guides, Inc.*] [*Database*]
OAGL .... Gage Educational Publishing Ltd., Agincourt, Ontario [*Library symbol*] [*National Library of Canada*] (NLC)
OAGL .... Gulistan [*Afghanistan*] [*ICAO location identifier*] (ICLI)
OAGM .... Ghelmeen [*Afghanistan*] [*ICAO location identifier*] (ICLI)
OAG Massachusetts... Massachusetts Attorney General Reports [*A publication*] (DLA)
OAGN .... Ghazni [*Afghanistan*] [*ICAO location identifier*] (ICLI)
OAGS .... Gasar [*Afghanistan*] [*ICAO location identifier*] (ICLI)
OAG West Virginia... West Virginia Attorney General Reports [*A publication*] (DLA)
OAGZ .... Gardez [*Afghanistan*] [*ICAO location identifier*] (ICLI)
OAH .... Ancaster High and Vocational School, Ontario [*Library symbol*] [*National Library of Canada*] (NLC)
OAH .... Office of Aboriginal Health [*Australia*]
OAH .... Office of Administrative Hearings (SAUS)
OAH .... Organization of American Historians (EA)
OAH .... Outstanding American Handgunner (GOBB)
OAH .... Ovarian Androgenic Hyperfunction [*Medicine*] (DMAA)
OAH .... Overall Height [*Automotive specifications*]
OAH .... Overhead Air Hoist
OAHE .... Hazrat Eman [*Afghanistan*] [*ICAO location identifier*] (ICLI)
OAHE .... Ohio Association for Higher Education (SAUS)
OAHJ .... Hajigak [*Afghanistan*] [*ICAO location identifier*] (ICLI)
OAHN .... Khwahan [*Afghanistan*] [*ICAO location identifier*] (ICLI)
OAHR .... Herat [*Afghanistan*] [*ICAO location identifier*] (ICLI)
OAHS .... O-Acetylhomoserine (thiol)-lyase [*An enzyme*]
OAI .... Office Appliance Institute
OAI .... Office of Aeronautical Intelligence (SAUS)
OAI .... Office of Analysis and Inspections [*Department of Health and Human Services*] (GFGA)
OAI .... Office of Audit and Inspection [*Energy Research and Development Administration*]
OAI .... Office of Audit and Investigation [*United States Geological Survey*]
OAI .... Ohio Aerospace Institute
OAI .... One-Address Instruction (SAUS)
OAI .... Open Application Interface
OAI .... Opera America, Inc. (SAUS)
OAI .... Optical Associates Inc. (NITA)
OAI .... OR Accumulators to Indicators (SAUS)
OAI .... Or-and-Invert (SAUS)
OAI .... Organization of African Immigrants (SAUS)
OAI .... Osborne Association, Inc. (SAUS)
OAI .... Outside Air Intake (NRCH)
OAIAC .... Operational Area Industry Advisory Committee [*Civil Defense*]
OAIB .... Old-Age Insurance Benefit (MHDB)
OAICU .... Oklahoma Association of Independent Colleges and Universities (SAUS)
OAID .... Older Americans Information Directory [*A publication*]
OAIDE .... Operational Assistance and Instructive Data Equipment
OAII .... Ocean-Atmosphere-Ice Interactions Program (SAUS)
OAIM .... Office of Aviation Information Management [*Department of Transportation*] [*Information service or system*] (IID)
OAINN .... Ohio Aerospace Institute Neural Networks (HGEN)
OAIP .... Ontario Assessment Instrument Pool [*Educational test*] [*Canada*]
OAIP .... Organic Ablative Insulative Plastic
OAIS .... Online Administrative Information System (SAUS)
OAIS .... Opinion, Attitude, and Interest Survey [*Psychology*]
OAISN .... OJCS Automated Information System Network (SAUS)
OAIT .... Office of American Indian Trust
OAIW .... International Waxes Ltd., Agincourt, Ontario [*Library symbol*] [*National Library of Canada*] (NLC)
OAJ .... Ajax Public Library, Ontario [*Library symbol*] [*National Library of Canada*] (NLC)
OAJ .... Jacksonville [*North Carolina*] [*Airport symbol*] (OAG)
OAJ .... Jacksonville, NC [*Location identifier*] [*FAA*] (FAAL)
OAJ .... Open Apophyseal Joint (DB)
OAJ .... Opening Altitude Judgement [*Parachuting*] (DICI)
OAJL .... Jalalabad [*Afghanistan*] [*ICAO location identifier*] (ICLI)
OAJS .... Jabul Saraj [*Afghanistan*] [*ICAO location identifier*] (ICLI)
OAJW .... Jawand [*Afghanistan*] [*ICAO location identifier*] (ICLI)
OAk .... Akron Public Library, Akron, OH [*Library symbol*] [*Library of Congress*] (LCLS)
OAK .... Oakfield [*New York*] [*Seismograph station code, US Geological Survey*] [*Closed*] (SEIS)
OAK .... Oak Industries, Inc. [*NYSE symbol*] (SPSG)
OAK .... Oakland [*California*] [*Airport symbol*]
OAK .... Oakland Operations Office (DOGT)
Oak .... Oakland Raiders [*National Football League*] [*1960-81*] (NFLA)

OAK .... Oakwood College, Huntsville, AL [*OCLC symbol*] (OCLC)
OAK .... Oakwood Petroleums Ltd. [*Toronto Stock Exchange symbol*]
OAK .... Object Application Kernel (SAUS)
OAK .... Oklahoma-Arkansas-Kansas League [*Old baseball league*]
OAK .... Older Americans Corps [*Proposed*]
OAK .... Optical Alignment Kit (MCD)
OAK .... Organization for the Advancement of Knowledge (EA)
OAK .... Overhaul Alignment Kit (MCD)
OAK .... San Francisco [*California*] Oakland [*Airport symbol*] (OAG)
OAKA .... Koban [*Afghanistan*] [*ICAO location identifier*] (ICLI)
OAKB .... Kabul Ad [*Afghanistan*] [*ICAO location identifier*] (ICLI)
OAKC .... Oakhurst Capital, Inc. [*NASDAQ symbol*] (SAG)
OAKC .... Oakhurst Co. [*NASDAQ symbol*] (TTSB)
OAKC .... Oakhurst Co., Inc. [*NASDAQ symbol*] (SAG)
OAkCh .... Akron Child Guidance Center, Akron, OH [*Library symbol*] [*Library of Congress*] (LCLS)
OAKD .... Kamdesh [*Afghanistan*] [*ICAO location identifier*] (ICLI)
OAKE .... Organization of American Kodaly Educators (EA)
OAkF .... Firestone Tire & Rubber Co., Akron, OH [*Library symbol*] [*Library of Congress*] (LCLS)
OAKF .... Oak Hill Financial, Inc. [*NASDAQ symbol*] (SAG)
OAKG .... Khojaghar [*Afghanistan*] [*ICAO location identifier*] (ICLI)
OAkGr .... B. F. Goodrich Co., Akron, OH [*Library symbol*] [*Library of Congress*] (LCLS)
OAkGy .... Goodyear Tire & Rubber Co., Akron, OH [*Library symbol*] [*Library of Congress*] (LCLS)
OakHill .... Oak Hill Financial, Inc. [*Associated Press*] (SAG)
OakHill .... Oak Hill Sportswear Corp. [*Associated Press*] (SAG)
OakHillF ...... Oak Hill Financial, Inc. [*Associated Press*] (SAG)
Oakhurst ..... Oakhurst Capital, Inc. [*Associated Press*] (SAG)
Oakhurst ..... Oakhurst Co., Inc. [*Associated Press*] (SAG)
OakInds .... Oak Industries, Inc. [*Associated Press*] (SAG)
OAKIX .... Oakmark International Fund [*Mutual fund ticker symbol*] (SG)
OAKJ .... Kajaki [*Afghanistan*] [*ICAO location identifier*] (ICLI)
OAkk .... Old Akkadian (BJA)
OAKL .... Konjak-I-Logar [*Afghanistan*] [*ICAO location identifier*] (ICLI)
Oakland U ... Oakland University (GAGS)
Oakly .... Oakly, Inc. [*Associated Press*] (SAG)
OAKM .... Kamar [*Afghanistan*] [*ICAO location identifier*] (ICLI)
OAKMX .... Oakmark Fund [*Mutual fund ticker symbol*] (SG)
OAKN .... Kandahar [*Afghanistan*] [*ICAO location identifier*] (ICLI)
OAKR .... Kaldar [*Afghanistan*] [*ICAO location identifier*] (ICLI)
OAKR .... Oakridge Energy, Inc. (SAUS)
Oak Ridge Natl Lab Met Ceram Tech Rep... Oak Ridge National Laboratory Metals and Ceramics Technical Report (SAUS)
OAKS .... Khost [*Afghanistan*] [*ICAO location identifier*] (ICLI)
OAKS .... River Oaks Furniture [*NASDAQ symbol*] (TTSB)
OAKS .... River Oaks Furniture, Inc. [*NASDAQ symbol*] (SAG)
Oak Sym ..... Oakland Symphony (SAUS)
OAKT .... Kalat [*Afghanistan*] [*ICAO location identifier*] (ICLI)
OAKT .... Oak Technology [*NASDAQ symbol*] (TTSB)
OAKT .... Oak Technology, Inc. [*NASDAQ symbol*] (SAG)
OakTch .... Oak Technology, Inc. [*Associated Press*] (SAG)
OAkU .... University of Akron, Akron, OH [*Library symbol*] [*Library of Congress*] (LCLS)
OAkU-L .... University of Akron, School of Law, Akron, Ohio [*Library symbol*] [*Library of Congress*] (LCLS)
Oakwood ..... Oakwood Homes Corp. [*Associated Press*] (SAG)
OAKX .... Kabul [*Afghanistan*] [*ICAO location identifier*] (ICLI)
OAKZ .... Karez-I-Mir [*Afghanistan*] [*ICAO location identifier*] (ICLI)
OAL .... Alliston Memorial Public Library, Ontario [*Library symbol*] [*National Library of Canada*] (BIB)
OAL .... Audit Liaison Division (AAGC)
OAL .... Coaldale, NV [*Location identifier*] [*FAA*] (FAAL)
OAL .... National Oceanic and Atmospheric Administration, Miami Branch, Miami, FL [*OCLC symbol*] (OCLC)
OAL .... Office of Administrative Law (SAUS)
OAL .... Office of Arts and Libraries [*British*]
OAL .... Olympic Airways SA [*Greece*] [*ICAO designator*] (FAAC)
OAL .... Operational Applications Laboratory [*Air Force*]
OAL .... Operations and Logistics (IAA)
OAL .... Order Action List [*Military*] (DNAB)
OAL .... Order of Ancient Lights
OAL .... Ordnance Aerophysics Laboratory
OAL .... Overall Length [*Automotive specifications*]
OAL .... Overall Level (NASA)
OALAC .... Amherstview Branch, Lennox and Addington County Public Library, Ontario [*Library symbol*] [*National Library of Canada*] (NLC)
OALAC .... Older Americans' Legal Action Center (DICI)
OAlB .... Babcock & Wilcox Co., Alliance, OH [*Library symbol*] [*Library of Congress*] (LCLS)
OALC .... Ogden Air Logistics Center (MCD)
OALDCE .... Oxford Advanced Learner's Dictionary of Current English
OALF .... Organic Acid Labile Fluoride [*Chemistry*] (AAMN)
OALF .... Oromo Abo Liberation Front [*Ethiopia*] [*Political party*] (EY)
OALG .... Logar [*Afghanistan*] [*ICAO location identifier*] (ICLI)
OALJ .... Office of Administrative Law Judges [*Department of Agriculture*] (GFGA)
OALL .... Allenford Branch, Bruce County Public Library, Ontario [*Library symbol*] [*National Library of Canada*] (NLC)
OALL .... Lal [*Afghanistan*] [*ICAO location identifier*] (ICLI)
OALL .... Ossification of Anterior Longitudinal Ligament [*Medicine*] (STED)
OAlM .... Mount Union College, Alliance, OH [*Library symbol*] [*Library of Congress*] (LCLS)
OALM .... Of a Like Mind [*An association*] (EA)

OALM..........	Optical Address Light Modulator [*Instrumentation*]
OALMA	Orthopedic Appliance and Limb Manufacturers Association [*Later, AOPA*]
OALN	Laghman [*Afghanistan*] [*ICAO location identifier*] (ICLI)
OALOS	Office for Ocean Affairs and the Law of the Sea [*United Nations*] (GNE)
OALS	Observer Air Lock System (OA)
OALS	Office of Arid Lands Studies [*University of Arizona*] [*Research center*] (RCD)
OALS	Orbiter Automatic Landing System (MCD)
OALT..........	Ontario Association of Library Technicians (SAUS)
OALT..........	Operational Acceptable Level of Traffic [*FAA*] (TAG)
O ALT HOR...	Omnibus Alternis Horis [*Every Other Hour*] [*Pharmacy*] (ROG)
OAM..........	Oamaru [*New Zealand*] [*Airport symbol*] (OAG)
OAM..........	Object Access Method (SAUS)
OAM..........	Oblique Abdominal Muscle [*Medicine*] (MELL)
OAM..........	Office Administration Manual (SAUS)
OAM..........	Office of Administration and Management [*Employment and Training Administration*] [*Department of Labor*]
OAM..........	Office of Aerospace Medicine [*NASA*] (MCD)
OAM..........	Office of Alternative Medicine [*National Institutes of Health*]
OAM..........	Office of Automation and Manpower [*Department of Labor*] [*See also OMAT*]
OAM..........	Office of Aviation Medicine [*FAA*]
OAM..........	One Australian Movement [*Political party*]
OAM..........	Ontario Agricultural Museum (SAUS)
OAM..........	Onze Alma Mater (BJA)
OAM..........	Open-Air Mission
OAM..........	Operand Addressing Mode (SAUS)
OAM..........	Operation, Administration, Maintenance (SAUS)
OAM..........	Operational, Administrative and Maintenance (SAUS)
OAM..........	Operation and Maintenance (SAUS)
OAM..........	Operations, Administration, and Maintenance (CIST)
OAM..........	Operations and Management (MCD)
OAM..........	Operator Assistance Menu (SAUS)
OAM..........	Optimum Artillery Mix (SAA)
OAM..........	Orbit Adjust Module (IGSL)
OAM..........	Orbital Assembly Module (MCD)
OAM..........	Order of Ancient Maccabees (BJA)
OAM..........	Order of Australia Medal (SAUS)
OAM..........	Organization and Methods [*Military*] (AFIT)
OAM..........	Orthopedic Appliance Mechanic [*Navy*]
OAM..........	Oscillator Activity Monitor [*Telecommunications*] (TEL)
OAM..........	Outer Acrosomal Membrane [*Medicine*] (DMAA)
OAMA	Office Automation Management Association (EA)
OAMA	Ogden Air Material Area [*AFLC*]
OAMA	Oil Appliance Manufacturers' Association [*British*] (BI)
OAMAC	Oceanic and Atmospheric Management Advisory Committee [*National Oceanic and Atmospheric Administration*] (EGAO)
OAM&P	Operations, Administration, Maintenance and Provisioning (SAUS)
OAMCE	Optical Alignment, Monitoring, and Calibration Equipment
OAMDG........	Omnia ad Majorem Dei Gloriam [*All to the Greater Glory of God*] [*Latin*]
OAMEX	Ocean-Atmosphere Exchange Processes [*Marine science*] (MSC)
OAMEX	Ocean-Atmosphere Materials Exchange (SAUS)
OAMF..........	Fort Malden National Historic Park, Amherstburg, Ontario [*Library symbol*] [*National Library of Canada*] (NLC)
OAMHS........	Ameliasburgh Historical Society, Ontario [*Library symbol*] [*National Library of Canada*] (BIB)
OAMK	Mukur [*Afghanistan*] [*ICAO location identifier*] (ICLI)
OAML..........	Oceanographic and Atmospheric Master Library (SAUS)
OAML..........	Ontario Association of Medical Laboratories (SAUS)
OAMN	Maimama [*Afghanistan*] [*ICAO location identifier*] (ICLI)
OAMN	Operations and Maintenance, Navy (AFIT)
OAMP	Optical Airborne Measurement Platform (SAUS)
OAMP	Optical Analog Matrix Processing
OAMRT........	Ontario Association of Medical Radiation Technologists (SAUS)
OAMS	Mazar-I-Sharif [*Afghanistan*] [*ICAO location identifier*] (ICLI)
OAMS	Office of Administrative and Management Systems [*Social Security Administration*]
OAMS	Optical Angular Motion Sensor
OAMS	Orbital Altitude and Maneuvering System (IAA)
OAMS	Orbital Attitude and Maneuvering System [*NASA*]
OAMS	Orbit Attitude and Maneuvering System (SAUS)
OAMS	Organic and Atmospheric Mass Spectrometer (KSC)
OAMT..........	Munta [*Afghanistan*] [*ICAO location identifier*] (ICLI)
OAN	Curriculum Resources Centre, Niagara South Board of Education, Allanburg, Ontario [*Library symbol*] [*National Library of Canada*] (BIB)
OAN	NMFS [*National Marine Fisheries Service*] Southeast Fisheries Center, Beaufort Laboratory, Beaufort, NC [*OCLC symbol*] (OCLC)
OAN	Ocean Aids to Navigation [*Coast Guard*]
OAN	Omega Arts Network (EA)
OAN	Optical Access Networking [*Computer science*] (VLIE)
OANA	Organisation of Asian News Agencies (BUAC)
OANA	Organization of Asia-Pacific News Agencies [*Malaysia*] (EY)
OANC	Orbiter Ancillary (SAUS)
OAND	Origin and Destination (NITA)
O & A	Observation and Assessment [*Medicine*]
O & A	October and April [*Denotes semiannual payments of interest or dividends in these months*] [*Business term*]
O&A	Odontectomy and Alveolectomy (SAUS)
O&A	Orbit and Attitude (ACAE)

O & A (Date)...	Oath and Acceptance Date [*Date from which a military officer's commissioned service runs*]
O & B	Opium and Belladonna [*Pharmacy*] (MAE)
o & c	Onset and Course [*Medicine*] (AD)
O&C	Onset and Course (SAUS)
O & C	Onset and Course [*of a disease*] [*Medicine*]
O & C	Operation and Checkout [*NASA*]
O&C	Operations and Checkout (SAUS)
O&C	Operations and Control (NAKS)
O & C	Oxford and Cambridge Schools Examination Board [*British*] (DCTA)
O & CC	Order and Change Control (AAG)
o & cc	Order and Change Control (AD)
O & CM	Organist and Choir Master (ROG)
O&CO..........	Operational and Checkout (SAUS)
O & C/O	Operation and Checkout [*O & C is preferred*] [*NASA*] (KSC)
O&D	Ordering and Distribution (SAUS)
O&D	Organization & Deployment (SAUS)
o & d	Origin and Destination (AD)
O & D	Origin and Destination [*Aviation*]
O & E..........	Observation and Evaluation [*Medicine*] (DAVI)
O & E..........	Observation and Examination [*Medicine*]
O&E..........	Officers and Employees (SAUS)
O and E	Officers and Employers (SAUS)
o & e	Operations and Engineering (AD)
O&E..........	Operations and Engineering (SAUS)
O & E..........	Operations and Engineering
O&EP	Occupational and Environmental Protection (SAUS)
O & F..........	Organizations and Functions (MCD)
O & FN	Ordnance and Facilities - Navy
O&FN..........	Ordnance and Facilities-Navy (SAUS)
O & FS	Operations and Flight Support [*NASA*] (NASA)
O&G..........	Obstetrics and Gynecology (DMAA)
O&G..........	Oil and Gas (EEVL)
O&G..........	Oil and Grease (EEVL)
O& G Jour ...	Oil and Gas Journal. Forecast/Review (SAUS)
O & G/PF......	Oil and Gas/Pipeline Facilities
O&H..........	Oxygen and Hydrogen (SAUS)
O & I	Operations and Intelligence [*Section*] [*Army*] (INF)
o & i	Organizational and Intermediate (AD)
O & I	Outline and Installation (MCD)
O&IA..........	Operations and Integration Agreement (SAUS)
O & IR	Operation and Inspection Record (KSC)
O & K	Orenstein & Koppel (AD)
O&L..........	Osteoporosis and Leukemia [*Medicine*] (MELL)
O & LS	Ocean and Lake Surveys [*Budget appropriation title*] [*Navy*]
O & M	Ogilvy & Mather [*Advertising agency*]
O & M	Ohio & Morenci Railroad (IIA)
O&M..........	Operating and Maintenance [*USCG*] (TAG)
O & M	Operation and Maintenance (DOMA)
O&M..........	Operations and Maintenance (CIST)
O & M	Operations and Management
O & M	Organization and Management
O & M	Organization and Methods (AABC)
O & M	Orientation and Mobility [*for the blind*]
O&M..........	Outline and Mounting (ACAE)
O&M..........	Region 4 O&M Municipal Inventory (SAUS)
O & MA	Operation and Maintenance Activities (AAG)
O&MA..........	Operation and Maintenance, Army (AAGC)
O and MA ...	Operations and Maintenance-Army (SAUS)
O & M-DA....	Operation and Maintenance, Defense Agencies [*DoD*]
O&M-DA....	Operation and Maintenanee, Defense Agencies (SAUS)
O & MF.......	Operation and Maintenance Facilities (MUGU)
O & MFH	Operation and Maintenance, Family Housing [*Army*] (AABC)
O & MMC	Operations and Maintenance, Marine Corps
O & MN	Operation and Maintenance, Navy
O&MN..........	Operations and Maintenance, Navy (SAUS)
O & MN	Overhaul and Maintenance, Navy (MCD)
O & MNR	Operation and Maintenance, Naval Reserve (NVT)
O&M Service...	Operation and Maintenance Service (SAUS)
O&N..........	Old and New (SAUS)
O & N	Oregon & Northwestern Railroad Co. (IIA)
O&O............	On and Off (DMAA)
O & O	One and Only (IIA)
o-and-o	one-and-only (SAUS)
O & O	Operational and Organizational (RDA)
O & O	Organization and Operation
O & O	Owned and Operated
O & OP	Organizational and Operational Plan [*Army*]
O & OS	Ordnance and Ordnance Stores [*Navy*]
OANDOS	Ordnance and Ordnance Stores [*Coast Guard*]
O&P..........	Objectives and Policies (TIMI)
O & P	Operations and Procedures (KSC)
O&P..........	Organization & Procedures (SAUS)
O & P	Ova and Parasites [*Medicine*]
O & PC	Owl and the Pussy Cat [*Poem by Edward Lear, 1871*]
o&r	Ocean and Rail (EBF)
O&R..........	Ocean and Rail (SAUS)
O & R	Ocean and Rail [*Shipping*]
OANDR	Operation and Regulation
O&R..........	Operations and Robotics (SPST)
O and R	Optimal and Right (SAUS)
O & R (Date).	Overhaul and Repair
O & S	Operation and Support Funds [*DoD*] (RDA)
O&S..........	Operation & Sustainment (SAUS)
O&S..........	Operations and Service (CCCA)

O & S	Operations and Support (MCD)
O&S	Operations and Sustainment
O & S	Optics and Sensors Program
O&S	Over and Short (SAUS)
O & S	Over and Short Account [Business term]
O & SCMIS	Operating and Support Costs Management Information System
O & S HA	Operating and Support Hazard Analysis
O & ST	Order and Shipping Time [Military] (MCD)
O & T	Operations and Training [Military]
O & T	Organization and Training [Military]
OANDT	Organization and Training Division [Supreme Headquarters Allied Powers Europe] (NATG)
O & T	Oyer and Terminer [Hear and Determine] [Legal term] (DLA)
O&U	Over and Under (SAUS)
O & W	Oldest and Wisest [Nickname for President Ronald Reagan]
O & W	Oneida & Western Railroad (IIA)
O & W	Ontario & Western Railroad [Nickname: Old and Weary]
O and W	Optimal and Wrong (SAUS)
O & W Dig.	Oldham and White's Digest of Laws [Texas] [A publication] (DLA)
O & Y	Olympia & York [Commercial firm] [Canada] (ECON)
OANFE	Operational Aircraft Not Fully Equipped (NG)
OANI	Office of the Administrator of Norfolk Island [Australia]
OANM	On or After New Moon [Freemasonry] (ROG)
OANR	Nawor [Afghanistan] [ICAO location identifier] (ICLI)
OANR	Office of Air, Noise, and Radiation [Environmental Protection Agency] (ERG)
OANS	Occupied Area News Service [Military] (IAA)
OANS	Salang-I-Shamali [Afghanistan] [ICAO location identifier] (ICLI)
OANT	Normanby Township Community and School Library, Ayton, Ontario [Library symbol] [National Library of Canada] (NLC)
OA/NWOB	Open Allotments/Navy-Wide Operating Budgets (MCD)
OAO	Arkhangelsk 2 Aviation Division [Former USSR] [FAA designator] (FAAC)
OAO	National Oceanic and Atmospheric Administration, Miami, Miami, FL [OCLC symbol] (OCLC)
OAO	Off and On (SAUS)
OAO	Office of Aircraft Operations [Miami, FL] [National Oceanic and Atmospheric Administration] (GRD)
OAO	One and Only [A favorite girl or boy friend]
OAO	Ontario Association of Orthodontists (SAUS)
OAO	Operational and Organizational (MCD)
OAO	Orbited Assembly Operation
OAO	Orbiting Astronomical Observatory [NASA]
OAO	Orthogonalized Atomic Orbital (OA)
OAO	Outdoor Adventure Online [America Online]
OAO	Over and Out (VLIE)
OAO 3	Orbiting Astronomical Observatory (SAUS)
OAOAF	Operations Analysis Office, Air Force (MCD)
OAOAFLC	Operations Analysis Office, Air Force Logistics Command (MCD)
OAOB	Obeh [Afghanistan] [ICAO location identifier] (ICLI)
OAOCR	Oxygen Adsorption, Outgassing and Chemical Reduction (SAUS)
OAOG	Urgoon [Afghanistan] [ICAO location identifier] (ICLI)
OAOI	On and Off Instruments [Aviation]
OAOO	Deshoo [Afghanistan] [ICAO location identifier] (ICLI)
OAOP	Older Adult Offender Project [of the Alston Wilkes Society] (EA)
OAOR	Oxygen Adsorption, Out-gassing, and Chemical Reduction (PDAA)
OAP	NMFS [National Marine Fisheries Service] Northeast Fisheries Center, WoodsHole, MA [OCLC symbol] (OCLC)
OAP	Observation Amphibian Plane [Coast Guard]
OAP	Occupational Ability Patterns [Psychologic test] (STED)
OAP	Occupational Aptitude Pattern [US Employment Service] [Department of Labor]
OAP	Oceanic Automation Program [FAA] (TAG)
OAP	Office of Adolescent Pregnancy [Medicine] (BABM)
OAP	Office of Aerial Phenomena [Air Force]
OAP	Office of Aircraft Production [World War II]
OAP	Office of Air Programs [Obsolete] [Environmental Protection Agency]
OAP	Office of Alien Property [World War II] (DLA)
OAP	Office of Antarctic Programs [National Science Foundation] [Later, Division of Polar Programs]
OAP	Office of Atomic Programs [DoD]
OAP	Office of the Assistant to the President (SAUS)
OAP	Office of the Director of Aerospace Programs [Air Force]
OAP	Offset Aiming Point (AFM)
OAP	Oil Analysis Program [Military] (AFIT)
OAP	Old-Age Pension [or Pensioner]
OAP	Old Age Pensioner (SAUS)
OAP	On-Axis Pointing (PDAA)
OAP	Oncovin [Vincristine], Ara-C, Prednisone [Antineoplastic drug regimen]
OAP	Ontario Apprenticeship Program (SAUS)
OAP	Operating and Assurance Program (SAUS)
OAP	Operation Angel Plane (EA)
OAP	Operations and Procedures (IAA)
OAP	Ophthalmic Arterial Pressure [Medicine]
OAP	Ophthalmic Artery Pressure [Medicine] (STED)
OAP	Optical Adjunct Program (ACAE)
OAP	Optical Augmentation Project
OAP	Optical Axial Plane (SAUS)
OAP	Optically Active Polymer
OAP	Ordinary Alterations Plan [Navy] (OAG)
OAP	Organic Ablative Plastic
OAP	Organizational Assessment Package (ACAE)
OAP	Ortho-Aminoacelophenone (SAUS)
OAP	Ortho-Aminoacetophenone [Organic chemistry]

OAP	Ortho-Amino-Phenols [Medicine] (MELL)
OAP	Orthogonal Array Processor [Computer]
OAP	Orthosorb Absorbable Pin [Medicine] (MELL)
OAP	Osteoarthropathy [Medicine] (MAE)
OAP	Outlet Absolute Pressure
OAP	Outline Acquisition Plan [Army]
OAP	Overall Average Percentage (DNAB)
OAP	Over Fire Air Port
OAP	Overlapping Atomic Potential (SAUS)
OAP	Oxygen at Atmospheric Pressure
OAPBC	Office for Advancement of Public Black Colleges [of the National Association of State Universities and Land Grant Colleges] (EA)
OAP-BLEO	Oncovin [Vincristine] ARA-C [Cytarabine or cytosine arabinoside] Prednisone, Bleomycin [Antineoplastic drug regimen] (DAVI)
OAPC	Office of Alien Property Custodian [World War II]
OAPC	Office of the Alien Property Custodian (SAUS)
OAPCA	Organotin Antifouling Paint Control Act (SAUS)
OAPCA	Organotin Antifouling Paint Control Act of 1988
OAPCB	Old-Age-Pensioner CBer [Experienced citizens band radio operator]
OAPEC	Organization of Arab Oil Exporting Countries (SAUS)
OAPEC	Organization of Arab Petroleum Exporting Countries [See also OPAEP] [OPEC] [Kuwait] [Absorbed by]
OAPEP	Organisation Arabe des Pays Exportateurs de Petrole [Organization of Arab Petroleum Exporting Countries]
OAPG	Paghman [Afghanistan] [ICAO location identifier] (ICLI)
OAPJ	Pan Jao [Afghanistan] [ICAO location identifier] (ICLI)
OAPM	Optimal Amplitude and Phase Modulation
OAPNA	Organization of Asian-Pacific News Agencies (BUAC)
OAPO	Eastern Pacific Tuna Fishing Organization [Marine science] (OSRA)
OAPP	Office of Adolescent Pregnancy Programs [HEW]
O App	Ohio Appellate Reports [A publication] (DLA)
O App 2d	Ohio Appellate Reports, Second Series [A publication] (DLA)
OAPQ	Office of Assistance Program Quality (SAUS)
OAPS	Orbit Adjust Propulsion Subsystem [NASA]
OAPU	Old Age Pension Union (SAUS)
OAPU	Overseas Air Preparation Unit [British military] (DMA)
OAPWL	Overall Power Watt Level (PDAA)
OAQ	National Climatic Center, Ashville, NC [OCLC symbol] (OCLC)
OAQ	Observatorio Astronomico de Quito [Ecuador] [Seismograph station code, US Geological Survey] (SEIS)
OAQ	Order of Architects of Quebec [1974, founded 1890 as PQAA] [Canada] (NGC)
OAQD	Qades [Afghanistan] [ICAO location identifier] (ICLI)
OAQK	Qala-I-Nyazkhan [Afghanistan] [ICAO location identifier] (ICLI)
OAQM	Kron Monjan [Afghanistan] [ICAO location identifier] (ICLI)
OAQN	Qala-I-Naw [Afghanistan] [ICAO location identifier] (ICLI)
OAQPS	Office of Air Quality Planning and Standards [Environmental Protection Agency]
OAQPS	US EPA Office of Air Quality Planning and Standards (SAUS)
OAQPSTTN	Office of Air Quality Planning and Standards Technology Transfer Network [Environmental Protection Agency] (AEPA)
OAQQ	Qarqin [Afghanistan] [ICAO location identifier] (ICLI)
OAQR	Qaisar [Afghanistan] [ICAO location identifier] (ICLI)
OAQS	Online Associative Query System (NITA)
OAR	Arnprior Public Library, Ontario [Library symbol] [National Library of Canada] (NLC)
OAR	Augustinian Recollect Sisters (TOCD)
OAR	Monterey/Fort Ord, CA [Location identifier] [FAA] (FAAL)
OaR	Oakland Raiders [National Football League] [1995-present] (NFLA)
OAR	Object Address Register (SAUS)
OAR	Oceanic and Atmospheric Research (SAUS)
OAR	Offender Aid and Restoration (EA)
OAR	Office of Aerospace Research [Air Force]
OAR	Office of AIDS Research [National Institute of Health]
OAR	Office of Air and Radiation [Environmental Protection Agency] (GFGA)
OAR	Office of Analysis and Review [Army, Navy]
OAR	Office of Atmospheric Research (SAUS)
OAR	Office of Oceanic and Atmospheric Research [National Oceanic and Atmospheric Administration]
OAR	Ohio Appellate Reports [A publication] (DLA)
OAR	Ohio Art [AMEX symbol] (TTSB)
OAR	[The] Ohio Art Co. [AMEX symbol] (SPSG)
O-Ar	Ohio State Archives, Columbus, OH [Library symbol] [Library of Congress] (LCLS)
O Ar	Old Arabic (SAUS)
OAR	Ontario Appeal Reports [A publication] (DLA)
OAR	Open Air Range
OAR	Open Architecture Receiver [Telecommunications]
OAR	Operand Address Register [Computer science] (IAA)
OAR	Operational Address Register [Computer science] (IAA)
OAR	Operational Analysis Research (SAUS)
OAR	Operational Availability and Reliability [Military]
OAR	Operation Assessment and Readiness [Environmental science] (COE)
OAR	Operations Activity Recorder (VLIE)
OAR	Operations Analysis Report
OAR	Operations and Regulations (IAA)
OAR	Operator Authorization Record [Computer science] (IBMDP)
OAR	Optical Angle Readout
OAR	Optical Automatic Ranging
OAR	Optional Address Register (VLIE)
OAR	ORDALT [Ordnance Alterations] Accomplishment Requirement (NG)
OAR	Ordering as Required (MHDB)

OAR	Order of the Augustinian Recollects [*Roman Catholic men's religious order*]
OAR	Ordnance Accomplishment Requirement (SAUS)
OAR	Ordnance Allowance Report [*Navy*]
OAR	Ordnance Alteration Reporting
OAR	Ordnance Alteration Requirement (NG)
OAR	Oregon Administrative Rules (SARE)
OAR	Organized Air Reserve
OAR	Orientation/Alertness Remediation (STED)
OAR	Original Action Record
OAR	Other Administrative Reasons [*Medicine*] (MAE)
OAR	Ottawa Ankle Rules
OAR	Over All Rate [*Real estate*] (DICI)
OAR	Overall Rate of Return [*Business term*]
OAR	Overhaul and Repair
OAR	Overtime Authorization Request (MCD)
OAR	Oxford Applied Research [*Software manufacturer*] [*British*]
OARAC	Office of Aerospace Research Automatic Computer (SAUS)
OARAC	Office of Air Research Automatic Computer
OARB	Azilda Branch, Rayside-Balfour Public Library, Ontario [*Library symbol*] [*National Library of Canada*] (NLC)
OARB	Oakland Army Base [*California*] (AABC)
OARBC	Boeing of Canada Ltd., Arnprior, Ontario [*Library symbol*] [*National Library of Canada*] (BIB)
OARC	Office of Air Research Automatic Calculator (SAUS)
OARC	Ordinary Administrative Radio Conference
OARD	Arthur District High School, Arthur, Ontario [*Library symbol*] [*National Library of Canada*] (NLC)
OARDC	Ohio Agricultural Research and Development Center [*Ohio State University*] [*Research center*] (RCD)
OARE	Orbital Acceleration Research Experiment (SAUS)
OARG	Uruzgan [*Afghanistan*] [*ICAO location identifier*] (ICLI)
OARM	Dilaram [*Afghanistan*] [*ICAO location identifier*] (ICLI)
OARM	Middlesex County Public Library, Arva, Ontario [*Library symbol*] [*National Library of Canada*] (NLC)
OARM	Office of Administration and Resources Management [*Environmental Protection Agency*] (GFGA)
OARMS	Armstrong Community Library, Ontario [*Library symbol*] [*National Library of Canada*] (NLC)
OAR-N	Office of Analysis and Review, Navy (MUGU)
OARnet	Ohio Academic Research Network
OARnet	[*The*] Ohio Academic Resources Network [*Computer science*] (TNIG)
OARP	Office of Advanced Research Programs [*Later, OART*] [*NASA*]
OARP	Old Age Revolving Pensions (SAUS)
OARP	Operator Accelerated Retraining Program [*Nuclear energy*] (NRCH)
OARP	Rimpa [*Afghanistan*] [*ICAO location identifier*] (ICLI)
OARS	Ocean Area Reconnaissance Satellite [*Antisubmarine warfare*]
OARS	Ocean Atmosphere Response Studies [*Marine science*] (MSC)
OARS	Ocean Reconnaissance Submarine [*NATO*] (LAIN)
OARS	Offenders Aid Rehabilitation Services (SAUS)
OARS	Office Automation Reporting Service (NITA)
OARS	On-Line Automated Reference Service [*Library science*]
OARS	Ontario Association for Remote Sensing (SAUS)
OARS	Opening Automated Report Service [*NYSE*]
OART	Oakland Army Terminal [*California*]
OART	Office of Advanced Research and Technology [*Later, OAST*] [*NASA*]
OARTS	Oceanic Air Route Tracking System (SAUS)
OAR/USA	Offender Aid and Restoration USA [*An association*] (EA)
OAS	O-Acetylserine (thiol)-lyase [*An enzyme*]
OAS	Oasis [*Board on Geographic Names*]
OAS	Oasis Residential [*NYSE symbol*] (SPSG)
OAS	Obstacle Assessment Surface [*Aviation*] (DA)
OAS	Occupational Aspiration Scale [*Education*]
OAS	Occupied Areas Section [*Military government*]
OAS	Offensive Air Support (MCD)
OAS	Offensive Attack System (DOMA)
OAS	Offensive Avionics System
OAS	Office Automation System (NASA)
OAS	Office for Advanced Studies (AAG)
OAS	Office of Administrative Systems [*Department of Agriculture*] (GFGA)
OAS	Office of Advanced Studies (SAUS)
OAS	Office of Airline Statistics [*U.S. Department of Transportation*] (BARN)
OAS	Office of Appalachian Studies (SAUS)
OAS	Office of Oceanic and Atmospheric Services [*National Oceanic and Atmospheric Administration*] (MSC)
OAS	Office of the Assistant for Study Support [*Air Force*]
OAS	Office of the Assistant Secretary [*Defense*] [*Navy*]
OAS	Ohio Academy of Science (PDAA)
OAS	Oklahoma Academy of Science (BUAC)
OAS	Old Age and Survivors' Insurance (IAA)
OAS	Old-Age Security
OAS	Olley Air Service Ltd.
OAS	Oman Aviation Services Co. [*ICAO designator*] (FAAC)
OAS	On Active Service
OAS	One-Address-System (SAUS)
OAS	One-to-All Scatter (VLIE)
OAS	Ontario Archaeological Association (SAUS)
OAS	Open-Health Acid Steel (SAUS)
OAS	Open-Hearth Acid Steel
OAS	Operational Announcing System (IAA)
OAS	Ophthalmic Anesthesia Society (SAUS)
OAS	Opiate Abstinence Syndrome [*Medicine*] (MELL)
OAS	Optical Alignment Sights [*NASA*]
OAS	Optical Array Spectrometer

OAS	Optical Augmentation System
OAS	Optics and Sensors [*Program*] (MCD)
OAS	Option Adjusted Spread
OAS	Optoacoustic Spectrometry [*Also, PAS*]
OAS	Optoacoustic Spectroscopy (SAUS)
OAS	Oracle Application Server [*Computer science*] (VLIE)
OAS	Oral Allergy Syndrome [*Medicine*] (DMAA)
OAS	Orbit Adjust Subsystem (SAUS)
OAS	Orbiter Aeroflight Simulator [*NASA*] (NASA)
OAS	Orbiter Atmospheric Simulator [*NASA*] (MCD)
OAS	Orbiter Avionia System (SAUS)
OAS	Orbiter Avionics System [*NASA*] (NASA)
OAS	Orbitor Avionics Simulator [*NASA*]
OAS	Order Allocation System (VLIE)
OAS	Order Automation System (TIMI)
OAS	Ordinary Ammunition Storage (SAUS)
OAS	Ordinary Ammunition Stowage (SAUS)
OAS	Organisation de l'Armee Secrete [*Secret Army Organization*] [*France*] (PD)
OAS	Organizational Accounting Structure (IAA)
OAS	Organization of American States (EA)
OAS	Organization of Arab Students in the USA and Canada (EA)
OAS	Oriental and African Studies
OAS	Origin-of-Assembly Sequence [*Genetics*]
OAS	Orthopedic Appliance Service
OAS	Osmotically Active Substance [*Medicine*] (DMAA)
OAS	Other Active Military Service (DNAB)
OAS	Other Approved Studies (ADA)
OAS	Output Amplitude Stability
OAS	Oxygen Activated Sludge (DICI)
OAS	Secret Army Organisation [*Algeria*] (BUAC)
OAS²	Officer Accession/Separation System (MCD)
OASAA	Other Arms NCOs Skill At Arms (SAUS)
OASAALT	Office of the Assistant Secretary of the Army for Acquisition, Logistics and Technology
OASAALT	Office of the Assistant Secretary of the Army for Acquisition, Logistics, and Technology
OASAF	Office of Assistant Secretary of Air Force
OASAF	Optical Active Surface Approach Fuze
OASA (FM) ..	Office of the Assistant Secretary of the Army (Financial Management) (MUGU)
OASA (I & L)...	Office of the Assistant Secretary of the Army (Installations and Logistics) (MUGU)
OASAM	Office of the Assistant Secretary for Administration and Management (SAUS)
OASA(M & RA)...	Office of the Assistant Secretary of the Army (Manpower and Reserve Affairs)
OASA (R & D)...	Office of the Assistant Secretary of the Army (Research and Development) (MUGU)
OASARDA	Office of the Assistant Secretary of the Army (Research, Development and Aquisition) (RDA)
OASAS	Office of Alcoholism and Substance Abuse Services [*U.S. Department of Health and Human Services*] (BARN)
OASB	Sarobi [*Afghanistan*] [*ICAO location identifier*] (ICLI)
OASBO	Office of Asbestos and Small Business Ombudsman [*Environmental Protection Agency*]
OASBO	Ohio Association of School Business Officials (SAUS)
OASBO	Oregon Association of School Business Officials (SAUS)
OAsC	Ashland College, Ashland, OH [*Library symbol*] [*Library of Congress*] (LCLS)
OASC	Office Automation Steering Committee (SAUS)
OASC	Office Automation Support Center
OASC	Office of Advanced Scientific Computing [*National Science Foundation*]
OASC	Officer & Aircrew Selection Center (or Centre) (SAUS)
OASCB	Orbiter Avionics Software Control Board [*NASA*] (NASA)
OASCMIS	Operating and Support Costs Management Information System (MCD)
OASD	Office of the Assistant Secretary of Defense
OASD	Shindand [*Afghanistan*] [*ICAO location identifier*] (ICLI)
OASD-AE	Office of the Assistant Secretary of Defense, Application in Engineering (SAUS)
OASD(AE)	Office of the Assistant Secretary of Defense (Applications Engineer) (MCD)
OASD-C	Office of the Assistant Secretary of Defense - Comptroller
OASDG	Alexandria Branch, Stormount, Dundas, and Glengarry County Public Library, Ontario [*Library symbol*] [*National Library of Canada*] (NLC)
OASD(HA)....	Office of the Assistant Secretary of Defense (Health Affairs) (DNAB)
OASDHI........	Old-Age, Survivors, Disability, and Health Insurance [*Program*] [*Social Security Administration*]
OASDI..........	Old-Age, Survivors, and Disability Insurance [*Program*] [*Social Security Administration*]
OASD/IL.......	Office of the Assistant Secretary of Defense/Installations and Logistics (SAUS)
OASDI Program...	Old-Age and Survivors Disability Insurance Program (SAUS)
OASD/ISA	Office of the Assistant Secretary of Defense/International Security Affairs (SAUS)
OASD/ISP	Office of the Assistant Secretary of Defense for International Security Policy (SAUS)
OASD(MRA)...	Office of the Assistant Secretary of Defense (Manpower and Reserve Affairs)
OASD (MRA & L)...	Office of Assistant Secretary of Defense (Manpower-Reserve Affairs and Logistics) (MCD)
OASD(PA)....	Office of the Assistant Secretary of Defense (Public Affairs) (NTCM)

OASD-R&D... Office Assistant Secretary of Defense, Research and Development (SAUS)

OASD(R & D)... Office of the Assistant Secretary of Defense (Research and Development) (MCD)

OASD(SA).... Office of the Assistant Secretary of Defense (Systems Analysis) (CINC)

OASD-S&L.... Office Assistant Secretary of Defense, Supply and Logistics (SAUS)

OASD(S & L)... Office of the Assistant Secretary of Defense (Supply and Logistics) [*Obsolete*] (MCD)

OASD(T) Office of the Assistant Secretary of Defense (Telecommunications)

OASE Offensive Aircraft Survivability Equipment

OASE Office Automation Services (SAUS)

OAS/EOM.... Organization of American States Electoral Observation Mission

OASES Open Access Satellite Education Services (EDAC)

OASES Organization for American-Soviet Exchanges (EA)

OASES Oxygen-Activated Sludge Environmental System (SAUS)

OASET Office of the Assistant Secretary for Employment and Training [*Department of Labor*]

OASF Office Automation System Facility (SAUS)

OASF Orbital Astronomy Support Facility (SAUS)

OASF Orbiting Astronomical Support Facility (MCD)

OASFP Old Alliance Society of French Polishers [*A union*] [*British*]

OASG Office Automation Specialist Group (NITA)

OASG Sheberghan [*Afghanistan*] [*ICAO location identifier*] (ICLI)

OASH Obstructive Asymmetrical Septal Hypertrophy [*Medicine*] (CPH)

OASH Office of the Assistant Secretary for Health [*Department of Health and Human Services*]

OASH Office of the Assistant Secretary for Housing (SAUS)

OASHA Operating and Support Hazard Analysis (MCD)

OASHDI... Old Age Survivors Health and Disability Program [*Health insurance*] (GHCT)

OASHDS Office of the Assistant Secretary for Human Development Services (SAUS)

OAsht Ashtabula County District Library, Ashtabula, OH [*Library symbol*] [*Library of Congress*] (LCLS)

OAshtK Kent State University, Ashtabula Regional Campus, Ashtabula, OH [*Library symbol*] [*Library of Congress*] (LCLS)

OASI Office Automation Society International (EA)

OASI Old-Age and Survivors Insurance [*Program*] [*Social Security Administration*]

OASI Old America Stores [*NASDAQ symbol*] (TTSB)

OASI Old Americia Stores, Inc. [*NASDAQ symbol*] (SAG)

OASIA Office of the Assistant Secretary for International Affairs [*Department of the Treasury*]

OASIS Observation, Analysis and Simulation of Interacting Systems (SAUS)

OASIS Observation at Several Interacting Scales (SAUS)

OASIS Observations At Several Interacting Scales (SAUS)

OASIS Obstetric Anesthesia Safety Improvement Study (SAUS)

OASIS Occupational Aptitude Survey and Interest Schedule

OASIS Ocean All-Source Information System

OASIS Ocean Atmospheric Surveillance and Information System (SAUS)

OASIS Oceanic and Atmospheric Satellite Imaging System (SAUS)

OASIS Oceanic and Atmospheric Scientific Information System [*National Oceanic and Atmospheric Administration*] (MCD)

OASIS Oceanic Area System Improvement Study (SAUS)

OASIS Oceanographic and Atmospheric Support and Information System (SAUS)

OASIS Office Administration Simulation Study

OASIS Office Automation Secure Information System (SAUS)

OASIS Office Automation Services and Information Systems (SAUS)

OASIS Office for Academic Support in Service (SAUS)

OASIS Office of Academic Support Instructional Services (SAUS)

OASIS Ohio of the American Society for Information Science (SAUS)

OASIS Older Adult Service and Information System (SAUS)

OASIS Older Adult Singles in Support (SAUS)

OASIS Onboard at Site Invoicing System [*IBM Computer Program*]

OASIS Online Administrative Information System [*Computer science*] (IAA)

OASIS Online Application System Interactive Software (SAUS)

OASIS On-line Asperger Syndrome Information and Support (SAUS)

OASIS Online Automotive Service Information System [*Ford Motor Co.*]

OASIS Open Access Same-Time Information Service [*Joint venture from IBM and TradeWave Corp.*]

OASIS Open and Secure Information Systems (SAUS)

OASIS Operational Analysis and System Interface System

OASIS Operational Analysis Strategic Interaction Simulator (SAUS)

OASIS Operational and Supportability Implementation System [*FAA*] (TAG)

OASIS Operational Applications of Special Intelligence System (MCD)

OASIS Operational Automated Ships Information System (SAUS)

OASIS Operational Automatic Scheduling Information System (MUGU)

OASIS Operation Analysis Strategic Interaction Simulator [*Nuclear war games*]

OASIS Optimized Air-to-Surface Infrared Seeker

OASIS Orbiter Experiments Program Autonomous Supporting Instrumentation System (SAUS)

OASIS Order, Accounting, Stock, Invoicing and Statistics (MHDB)

OASIS Order and Schedules Input System (MCD)

OASIS Organisation for Article Standards in Science (SAUS)

OASIS Organization for Applied Science in Society

OASIS Organization for the Advancement of Structured Information Standards (SAUS)

OASIS Organized Adoption Search Information Services (EA)

OASIS Outlook and Situation Information System [*Department of Agriculture*] [*Defunct*] (IID)

OASIS Outpatient Appointment Scheduling and Information System

OASIS Overseas Access Service for Information Systems (SAUS)

OASIS Over-the-Horizon Airborne Sensor Information System [*Navy*] (DOMA)

OASIS Overweight & Seeking Infertility Support (SAUS)

OASIS Ownership Accountability of Selected Secondary Items Stocked

OASIS OzonAction Strategic Information System

OASIS-AS Occupational Aptitude Survey and Interest Schedule - Aptitude Survey [*Vocational guidance test*]

OASIS-IS Occupational Aptitude Survey and Interest Schedule - Interest Schedule [*Vocational guidance test*]

OasisR Oasis Residential, Inc. [*Associated Press*] (SAG)

OasisRsd Oasis Residential, Inc. [*Associated Press*] (SAG)

OASK Serka [*Afghanistan*] [*ICAO location identifier*] (ICLI)

OASL Salam [*Afghanistan*] [*ICAO location identifier*] (ICLI)

OASM Office of Aerospace Medicine [*NASA*] (KSC)

OASM Ohm-Ampere-Second Meter [*System of units*]

OASM Samangan [*Afghanistan*] [*ICAO location identifier*] (ICLI)

OASMA Offensive Air Support Mission Analysis (MCD)

OASMS Ordnance Ammunition Surveillance and Maintenance School [*Army*]

OASN Office of the Assistant Secretary of the Navy

OASN Sheghnan [*Afghanistan*] [*ICAO location identifier*] (ICLI)

OASN(FM)... Office of the Assistant Secretary of the Navy for Financial Management

OASN(I & L)... Office of the Assistant Secretary of the Navy for Installations and Logistics

OASN(M/RA)... Office of the Assistant Secretary of the Navy (Manpower and Reserve Affairs)

OASN(M/RA/L)... Office of the Assistant Secretary of the Navy (Manpower, Reserve Affairs, and Logistics)

OASN(P & RF)... Office of the Assistant Secretary of the Navy for Personnel and Reserve Force

OASN(R & D)... Office of the Assistant Secretary of the Navy for Research and Development

OAS-OGN.... Organization of American States-Observer Group in Nicaragua

OASP Organic Acid Soluble Phosphorus

OASP Over-All Sound Pressure (PDAA)

OASP Sare Pul [*Afghanistan*] [*ICAO location identifier*] (ICLI)

OASPL Overall Sound Pressure Level

OASPrA Oasis Residential $2.25'A' Pfd [*NYSE symbol*] (TTSB)

OASR Office of Aeronautical and Space Research [*Later, OART*] [*NASA*]

OASR Sabar [*Afghanistan*] [*ICAO location identifier*] (ICLI)

OAss Old Assyrian (BJA)

OASS Salang-I-Junubi [*Afghanistan*] [*ICAO location identifier*] (ICLI)

OASSO Operational Applications of Satellite Snowcover Observations [*NASA*]

OAsT Ashland Theological Seminary, Ashland, OH [*Library symbol*] [*Library of Congress*] (LCLS)

OAST Office of Aeronautical and Space Technology [*Formerly, OART*] [*NASA*]

OAST Order and Shipping Time [*Military*] (AFIT)

OAST Overland Air Superiority Training [*Navy*] (DOMA)

OAST Shur Tepa [*Afghanistan*] [*ICAO location identifier*] (ICLI)

OASTP Office of the Assistant Secretary for Technology Policy [*U.S. Department of Commerce*] (BARN)

OASU Oceanographic Air Survey Unit

OASV Orbital Assembly Support Vehicle

OASW Office of the Assistant Secretary of War [*World War II*]

OASy Officer Accession/Separation System (SAUS)

OASYS Obstacle Avoidance System [*Army*] (RDA)

OASYS Office Automation System

OASYS Order Allocation System

OAT Atikokan Public Library, Ontario [*Library symbol*] [*National Library of Canada*] (NLC)

OAT Ocean Acoustic Tomography

OAT Office Automation Tools (TIMI)

OAT Office for Advanced Technology [*Air Force*]

OAT Office for the Advancement of Telehealth (SAUS)

OAT Office of Advanced Technology (SAUS)

OAT On-Air Test [*Telecommunications*] (DOAD)

OAT One at a Time

OAT Open-Air Theater

OAT Operating Acceptance Test (SAUS)

OAT Operating Ambient Temperature

OAT Operational Acceptance Test

OAT Operational Air Traffic (NATG)

OAT Optical Adaptive Technique

OAT Optional Application Tapes (SAUS)

OAT Optometry Admissions Test (GAGS)

OAT Organic Acid Technology [*Automotive cooling systems*]

OAT Ornithineaminotransferase [*An enzyme*]

OAT Ornithine keto-acid Aminotransferase (SAUS)

OAT Outer Atmospheric Temperature (IAA)

OAT Outside Air Temperature [*Aviation*]

OAT Overall Test

OAT Overseas Airways Transmission (SAUS)

OAT Oxide-Aligned Transistor [*Electronics*] (PDAA)

OAT Oxoacid Aminotransferase Inhibition (DB)

OAT Quaker Oats Co. [*NYSE symbol*] [*Toronto Stock Exchange symbol*] (SPSG)

OAT Sogervair/Transoceanic Aviation [*France*] [*ICAO designator*] (FAAC)

OATA Optical Acquisition and Tracking Aid Assembly

OATA Assembly... Optical Acquisition and Tracking Aid Assembly (SAUS)

OATC Oceanic Air Traffic Center

OATC Oceanic Air Traffic Control (SAUS)

OATC Officers Advanced Training Course (SAUS)

OATC Overseas Air Traffic Control

OATD Toorghondi [*Afghanistan*] [*ICAO location identifier*] (ICLI)

OATG .... Tashkurghan [*Afghanistan*] [*ICAO location identifier*] (ICLI)
OATH .... Atikokan High School, Ontario [*Library symbol*] [*National Library of Canada*] (NLC)
OATHS .... One-in-a-Thousand Society (EA)
OATK .... Kotal [*Afghanistan*] [*ICAO location identifier*] (ICLI)
OATM .... Atikokan Centennial Museum, Ontario [*Library symbol*] [*National Library of Canada*] (BIB)
OATM .... Operations Analysis Technical Memorandum (SAUS)
OATM .... Orbiter Antenna Test Model [*NASA*]
OATMEAL .... Optimum Allocation of Test and Equipment Manpower Against Logistics
OATN .... Tereen [*Afghanistan*] [*ICAO location identifier*] (ICLI)
OATP .... On-Aircraft Test Procedure (MCD)
OATP .... Operational Acceptance Test Procedure (NRCH)
OATQ .... Taluqan [*Afghanistan*] [*ICAO location identifier*] (ICLI)
OATRU .... Organic and Associated Terrain Research Unit (SAUS)
OATS .... Office Automation Technology Services [*AT&T*] (CIST)
OATS .... Office of Air Transportation Security [*FAA*]
OATS .... Old-Age Theatre Society (SAUS)
OATS .... On-Board Acoustic Tracking System [*Navy*] (CAAL)
OATS .... Open Architecture Test System (MCD)
OATS .... Operational Air Training School (SAUS)
OATS .... Optical Attitude Transfer System (SSD)
OATS .... Optical Augmentation Target Screen (ACAE)
OATS .... Optimum Aerial Target Sensor
OATS .... Orbit and Attitude Tracking (GAVI)
OATS .... Original Article Tear Sheets
OATS .... Original Article Tearsheet Service (NITA)
OATS .... Original Article Text Service
OATS .... Outdoor Advertising Total System (PDAA)
OATS .... Overall Test Set
OATS .... Over Armor Technology Synthesis (RDA)
OATS .... Oxford Air Training School [*British*] (PIAV)
OATS .... Wild Oats Markets, Inc. [*NASDAQ symbol*] (SAG)
OATT .... Officials at the Track [*Motorsports*]
OATUS .... On a Totally Unrelated Subject (ADWA)
OATUU .... Organisation of African Trade Union Unity [*Formerly, AATUF, ATUC*] [*See also OUSA*] [*Accra, Ghana*] (EAIO)
OATW .... Tewara [*Afghanistan*] [*ICAO location identifier*] (ICLI)
OATZ .... Tesak [*Afghanistan*] [*ICAO location identifier*] (ICLI)
OAU .... Aurora Public Library, Ontario [*Library symbol*] [*National Library of Canada*] (NLC)
OAU .... Ohio University, Athens, OH [*Library symbol*] [*Library of Congress*] (LCLS)
OAU .... Operator Assistance Unit (NITA)
OAU .... Optical Alignment Unit
OAU .... Organization for African Unity (NADA)
OAU .... Organization of African Unity
OAU .... Original Sixteen To One Mine [*PC, exchange symbol*] (TTSB)
OAU .... Oriol Avia [*Russian Federation*] [*ICAO designator*] (FAAC)
OAUH .... Aurora Historical Society, Ontario [*Library symbol*] [*National Library of Canada*] (NLC)
OAUHS .... PRECIS Project, Aurora High School, Ontario [*Library symbol*] [*National Library of Canada*] (NLC)
OAULC .... OAU [*Organization of African Unity*] Liberation Committee [*Addis Ababa, Ethiopia*] (EAIO)
OAUM .... Aurora Museum, Ontario [*Library symbol*] [*National Library of Canada*] (BIB)
OAUS .... On an Unrelated Subject (ADWA)
OAUS .... Sterling Drug Ltd., Aurora, Ontario [*Library symbol*] [*National Library of Canada*] (BIB)
OAU/STRC ... Organization of African Unity Scientific and Technical Research Commission [*Marine science*] (MSC)
OAUYCE ...... York County Board of Education, Aurora, Ontario [*Library symbol*] [*National Library of Canada*] (NLC)
OAUZ .... Kunduz [*Afghanistan*] [*ICAO location identifier*] (ICLI)
O-A-V .... Object-Attribute-Value
oav .... oculoauriculovertebral (SAUS)
OAV .... Oculoauriculovertebral Dysplasia [*Medicine*] (MAE)
OAV .... Omni-Aviacao e Tecnologia Lda. [*Portugal*] [*ICAO designator*] (FAAC)
OAV .... Operational Aerospace Vehicle
OAV .... Original Animation Video (SAUS)
OAVC of SA.. Office of the Assistant Vice Chief of Staff, Army [*Later, OAVCSA*] (AABC)
OAVCSA....... Office of the Assistant Vice Chief of Staff, Army [*Formerly, OAVC of SA*] (AABC)
OAVD .... Oculoauriculovertebral Dysplasia [*Medicine*] (MEDA)
OAVE .... Occupational, Adult, and Vocational Education (OICC)
OAvG .... B. F. Goodrich Chemical Co. [*of B. F. Goodrich Co.*], Development Center Library, Avon Lake, OH [*Library symbol*] [*Library of Congress*] (LCLS)
OAVP .... Older Americans Volunteer Program [*ACTION*]
OAVSDG ...... Avonmore Branch, Stormont, Dundas, and Glengarry County Public Library, Ontario [*Library symbol*] [*National Library of Canada*] (BIB)
OAVTME ...... Office of Adult, Vocational, Technical, and Manpower Education [*Office of Education*]
OAW .... Old Abandoned Well (WDAA)
OAW .... Optically Assisted Winchester [*Computer science*]
OAW .... Oral Airways (MELL)
OAW .... Overall Width
OAW .... Oxyacetylene Welding
OAWC .... Overseas Air Weapons Control (SAUS)
OAWCS .... Overseas Air Weapons Control System

OAWM .... Office of Air and Water Measurement [*National Institute of Standards and Technology*]
OAWO .... Opening Abductory Wedge Osteotomy [*Medicine*] (MELL)
OAWOP........ Ontario Police College, Aylmer West, Ontario [*Library symbol*] [*National Library of Canada*] (NLC)
OAWP .... Office of Air and Water Programs (OICC)
OAWP .... Operations Analysis Working Paper [*NASA*] (KSC)
OAWR .... Office of Agricultural War Relations [*World War II*]
OAWR .... Office of Atmospheric Water Resources [*Bureau of Reclamation*]
OAWRMR .... Other Acquisition War Reserve Material Requirements (MCD)
OAWU .... Wurtach [*Afghanistan*] [*ICAO location identifier*] (ICLI)
OAWZ .... Wazirabad [*Afghanistan*] [*ICAO location identifier*] (ICLI)
OAX .... Oaxaca [*Mexico*] [*Airport symbol*] (OAG)
OAX .... Oaxaca [*Mexico*] [*Seismograph station code, US Geological Survey*] (SEIS)
OAX .... Operational Aviation Services - Australia [*ICAO designator*] (FAAC)
OAXTC .... Ocean Atmosphere Exchange of Trace Compounds (SAUS)
OAY .... Moses Point, AK [*Location identifier*] [*FAA*] (FAAL)
OAY .... NOAA [*National Oceanic and Atmospheric Administration*] Geophysical Fluid Dynamics Laboratory, Princeton, NJ [*OCLC symbol*] (OCLC)
OAY .... Outstanding Airmen of the Year (SAUS)
OAYM .... Aylmer District Museum, Ontario [*Library symbol*] [*National Library of Canada*] (BIB)
OAYQ .... Yangi Qala [*Afghanistan*] [*ICAO location identifier*] (ICLI)
OAYR .... Outstanding Airman of the Year Ribbon [*Military decoration*] (AFM)
OAZB .... Zebak [*Afghanistan*] [*ICAO location identifier*] (ICLI)
OAZG .... Zaranj [*Afghanistan*] [*ICAO location identifier*] (ICLI)
OB............... Austrian Airtransport (SAUS)
OB............... Brockville Public Library, Ontario [*Library symbol*] [*National Library of Canada*] (NLC)
OB............... Brought Over (ROG)
Ob............... Obadiah [*Old Testament book*]
OB............... Oberlerchner [*Joseph Oberlerchner Holzindustrie*] [*Austria*] [*ICAO aircraft manufacturer identifier*] (ICAO)
ob............... Obese
OB............... Obeum [*Nickname for toilets at Cambridge University*] [*Slang*] [*British*] (DSUE)
OB............... Obidiah [*Old Testament*]
OB............... Obiit [*He, or She, Died*] [*Latin*]
ob............... Obiter [*Incidentally*] [*Latin*] (GPO)
OB............... Obituary Notice (DSUE)
OB............... Objection (ROG)
OB............... Objective [*Microscopy*]
OB............... Objective Benefit (MAE)
OB............... Obligation (ROG)
OB............... Obligation Bond
OB............... Obligatory
OB............... Obliteration
OB............... Obliterative Bronchiolitis [*Medicine*] (MELL)
ob............... Oblong [*Bookbinding*] (WDMC)
OB............... Oblong
ob............... Oboe (WDAA)
OB............... Oboe
OB............... Obolus [*Coin*] [*Latin*] (ADA)
OB............... O'Brien Energy & Resources Ltd. [*Toronto Stock Exchange symbol*]
OB............... Obscure (KSC)
OB............... Observation (WGA)
OB............... Observation Balloon (SAUS)
OB............... Observed Bearing [*Navigation*]
OB............... Obsolete (AABC)
OB............... Obstetrician
ob............... Obstetrics (SHCU)
OB............... Obstetrics [*Medicine*]
OB............... Obtuse Bisectrix [*Crystallography*]
ob............... Obvious (ADWA)
OB............... Occult Bleeding [*Medicine*]
OB + ... Occult Blood Positive [*Medicine*] (DAVI)
OB............... Occupational Behavior
OB............... Ocean Beach (SAUS)
OB............... Ocean Bottom
OB............... Octal-to-Binary [*Computer science*] (BUR)
OB............... Octave Band
O-B............. Oerlikon-Buehrle [*Switzerland*]
OB............... Off-Broadway (WGA)
OB............... Offensive Back [*Football*]
OB............... Official Board of Ballroom Dancing [*British*] (BI)
OB............... Official Bulletin (SAUS)
OB............... Official Bulletin. International Commission for Air Navigation [*A publication*] (DLA)
OB............... Official Business (ELAL)
OB............... Oil Base (SAUS)
OB............... Oil Bearing (DCTA)
OB............... Oil Bomb
OB............... Oil-Break (SAUS)
OB............... Old Babylonian (BJA)
OB............... [*The*] Old Bailey [*London court*]
OB............... Old Bonded [*Whiskey*] (ROG)
OB............... Old Boy [*Communications operators' colloquialism*]
OB............... Old Buildings [*British Admiralty*]
OB............... Olecranon Bursitis [*Medicine*] (MELL)
OB............... Oligoclonal Band [*Analytical biochemistry*]
OB............... Ombudsman for Business [*Department of Commerce*]
OB............... On Base [*Baseball*] (GOBB)
OB............... On Being: the Servant's Servant [*A publication*] (APTA)

OB	On Board
O/B	Onboard (NAKS)
OB	One-Bearing (SAUS)
OB	Opal Air [ICAO designator] (AD)
OB	Opening of Books
ob	Opera Buffa [Music] (GROV)
OB	Operating Base [Navy]
OB	Operating Budget (AFM)
OB	Operational Base [Navy]
OB	Operation Brotherhood
OB	Operations Branch (HEAS)
OB	Optical Bench (SAUS)
OB	Optometrists' Board [Australian Capital Territory]
OB	Or Better [Business term]
OB	Ordered Back
OB	Order of Battle [Military]
OB	Order of Burma [British military] (DMA)
OB	Order of the Bath
OB	Order of the Boer People (SAUS)
OB	Order of the Boer State (SAUS)
OB	Ordnance Battalion [Navy]
OB	Ordnance Board [Navy]
OB	Oregon Ballet
OB	Organization Blocks (SAUS)
OB	Organized Baseball (NDBD)
OB	Orgelbuechlein [Little Organ Book] [Bach] [Music]
OB	Orientalische Bibliographie [A publication] (BJA)
OB	Ortsbatterie [Local Battery] [German military - World War II]
OB	Outboard
ob	Outboard Buffer (SAUS)
OB	Outbound (WDAA)
OB	Out of Bounds [Sports] (GOBB)
OB	Out-of-Business (OICC)
OB	Output Block (SAUS)
OB	Output Buffer [Computer science]
OB	Output Bus [Computer science]
OB	Outside Broadcast (EY)
OB	Outside Bugs [Nonresident staff at a school] [British] (DSUE)
OB	Outward Bound (EA)
OB	Over Bath [Classified advertising] (ADA)
OB	Overboard (AAG)
OB	Over Bought (SAUS)
OB	Overburden (SAUS)
OB	Overseas Brats [Commercial firm] (EA)
OB	Overseas Broadcast [or Broadcasting] (IAA)
OB	Owena Bank [Nigeria]
OB	Own Brand (MHDB)
OB	Oxford Biographies [A publication]
OB	Peru [International civil aircraft marking] (ODBW)
OB1KB	Order of Battle Version 1 Knowledge Based (SAUS)
OBA	Barrie Public Library, Ontario [Library symbol] [National Library of Canada] (NLC)
OBA	Oasis Bungera [Antarctica] [Seismograph station code, US Geological Survey] [Closed] (SEIS)
OBA	Oberhasli Breeders of America (EA)
OBA	Object Behavior Analysis [Computer science]
OBA	Octave Band Analyzer
OBA	Off Boresight Angle (MCD)
OBA	Office of Business Administration [Later, Office of Administration] [NASA]
OBA	Office of Business Affairs [Northern Territory, Australia]
OBA	Office of Business Analysis [Information service or system] (IID)
OBA	Oil Burning Apparatus (SAUS)
OBA	On-Base Average [Baseball term] (NDBD)
OBA	Online Banking Association (SAUS)
OBA	Open Broadcasting Authority [Noncommercial TV channel] [British]
OBA	Operating Basis Accident [Environmental science] (COE)
OBA	Operating Budget Authority (MCD)
OBA	Optical Barrel Assembly (ACAE)
OBA	Optical Base Assembly (KSC)
OBA	Optical Bleaching Agent (SAUS)
OBA	Optical Brightening Agents
OBA	Ornithyl-Beta-Alanine [Biochemistry]
OBA	Outward Bound Australia
OBA	Over Burner Air
OBA	Oxygen Breathing Apparatus
OBAA	Oil Burning Apparatus Association (BUAC)
OBAALA	Organisation for Black Arts Advancement and Learning Activities [British]
OBAC	One Bit Adder Computer (SAUS)
Obad	Obadiah [Old Testament book]
OBAD	Object Average Optical Density [Microscopy]
OBAD	Operating Budget Authority Document [Military] (AFIT)
OBADRS	Octave Band Automatic Data Reduction System
OBAG	Georgian Bay Regional Library, Barrie, Ontario [Library symbol] [National Library of Canada] (NLC)
OBAGC	Georgian College of Applied Arts and Technology, Barrie, Ontario [Library symbol] [National Library of Canada] (NLC)
OBAL	Balmertown Public Library, Ontario [Library symbol] [National Library of Canada] (NLC)
OBAN	Bancroft Public Library, Ontario [Library symbol] [National Library of Canada] (NLC)
OBAN	Operating Budget Account Number [Air Force]
OBAN	United Public Library, Carlow, Dungannon and Mayo Townships, Bancroft, Ontario (SAUS)

OB & F	Ollivier, Bell, and Fitzgerald's Court of Appeal Reports [1878-80] [New Zealand] [A publication] (DLA)
OB & F (CA)	Ollivier, Bell, and Fitzgerald's Court of Appeal Reports [1878-80] [New Zealand] [A publication] (DLA)
OB & FNZ	Ollivier, Bell, and Fitzgerald's New Zealand Reports [A publication] (DLA)
OB & F (SC)	Ollivier, Bell, and Fitzgerald's Supreme Court Reports [New Zealand] [A publication] (DLA)
OB & PA	Office of Budget and Program Analysis [Department of Agriculture] (GFGA)
Ob&Sol	Objection and Solution (SAUS)
OBANU	United Public Library, Carlow, Dungannon, and Mayo Townships, Bancroft, Ontario [Library symbol] [National Library of Canada] (BIB)
OBAP	Organization of Black Airline Pilots (EA)
OBAR	Ohio Bar (NITA)
OBAR	Ohio Bar Automated Research (SAUS)
OBarb	Barberton Public Library, Barberton, OH [Library symbol] [Library of Congress] (LCLS)
OBarn	Barnesville Public Library, Barnesville, OH [Library symbol] [Library of Congress] (LCLS)
OBAS	Organ Builders' Amalgamated Society [A union] [British]
OBAS	Simcoe County Co-Op, Barrie, Ontario [Library symbol] [National Library of Canada] (NLC)
OBAT	Augusta Township Public Library, Brockville, Ontario [Library symbol] [National Library of Canada] (NLC)
OBat	Clermont County Public Library, Batavia, OH [Library symbol] [Library of Congress] (LCLS)
OBAT	Olympic International Bank & Trust Co. (SAUS)
OBATA	Ontario Biological Aeration Tillage Association (SAUS)
OBatC	Clermont General and Technical College, Batavia, OH [Library symbol] [Library of Congress] (LCLS)
OBatH	Clermont Mercy Hospital, Batavia, OH [Library symbol] [Library of Congress] (LCLS)
OBAWS	On-Board Aircraft Weighing System (MCD)
OBB	Barry's Bay Public Library, Ontario [Library symbol] [National Library of Canada] (NLC)
OBB	Obbligato [Essential] [Music]
OBB	Obsidian Butte [California] [Seismograph station code, US Geological Survey] (SEIS)
OBB	Oesterreichische Bundesbahnen [Austrian Federal Railways]
OBB	Old Battleship [Navy]
OBB	On-Board Buffer (CIST)
OBB	One Button Boy (SAUS)
OBB	Operation Better Block
OBB	Own Bed Bath [Medicine] (DMAA)
OBB	Oxybisbenzene [Organic chemistry]
OBBB	Bahrain [Bahrain] [ICAO location identifier] (ICLI)
OBBD	Official Board of Ballroom Dancing [British]
OBBFC	Official Betty Boop Fan Club (EA)
OBBI	Bahrain/International [Bahrain] [ICAO location identifier] (ICLI)
Obbl	Obbligato [Essential] [Music]
OBBM	Brant County Historical Museum, Brantford, Ontario [Library symbol] [National Library of Canada] (NLC)
Obbmo	Obbligatissimo [Your Obedient Servant] [Italian]
OBBMV	Madawaska Valley District High School, Barry's Bay, Ontario [Library symbol] [National Library of Canada] (NLC)
OBBO	Observation Balloon
OBC	Barwick Community Library, Ontario [Library symbol] [National Library of Canada] (BIB)
OBC	Obock [Djibouti] [Airport symbol] (OAG)
OBC	Oceania Basketball Confederation [Australia] (EA)
OBC	Off Boresight Correction [Military] (CAAL)
OBC	Officer Basic Course [Military]
OBC	Ohio Bell Communications, Inc. [Cleveland] [Telecommunications] (TSSD)
OBC	Old Bottle Club of Great Britain (BUAC)
OBC	Old Boys' Corps [Military] [British]
OBC	On-Board Checkout [Aircraft]
OBC	On-Board Computer (MCD)
OBC	On-Board Controller [Telecommunications]
OBC	One Big Computer [Proposed model for automation of the New York and American stock exchanges]
OBC	Optical Bar Camera [NASA] (LAIN)
OBC	Optical Bar Code (SAUS)
OBC	Optical Barrel Camera (SAUS)
OBC	Order of British Columbia [Canada] (DD)
OBC	Ore Bulk Carrier (SAUS)
OBC	Osaka Broadcasting Corporation (SAUS)
OBC	Ouachita Baptist College [Arkadelphia, AR] [Later, OBU]
OBC	Outboard Boating Club of America [Defunct] (EA)
OBC	Outer Back Cover (SAUS)
OBC	Outside Back Cover [Publishing] (WDMC)
OBC	Oversea Broadcasting (SAUS)
OBC	Overseas Bankers' Club [British]
OBC	Overseas Book Centre
OBC	Oxide-Coated Brush Cathode
OBCA	Office of Bank Customer Affairs [FDIC]
OBCAB	Albion-Bolton Branch, Town of Caledon Public Libraries, Bolton, Ontario [Library symbol] [National Library of Canada] (NLC)
OBCC	Olympic Broadcasting Corporation (SAUS)
OBCC	Ore Bulk Car Container (SAUS)
OBC Carrier	Ore Bulk Container Carrier (SAUS)
OBCC Carrier	Ore Bulk Car Container Carrier (SAUS)

OBCCL .... Canada Cement Lafarge Ltd., Belleville, Ontario [*Library symbol*] [*National Library of Canada*] (NLC)

OBCE .... On-Board Checkout Equipment (MCD)

OBCE .... Operational Baseline Cost Estimate [*Army*]

OBCGEH .... Housewares and Home Entertainment Department, Canada General Electric Co. Ltd., Barrie, Ontario [*Library symbol*] [*National Library of Canada*] (NLC)

OBCH .... Overseas Booksellers' Clearing House (DGA)

OBCI .... Ocean Bio-Chem [*NASDAQ symbol*] (TTSB)

OBCI .... Ocean Bio-Chem, Inc. [*NASDAQ symbol*] (NQ)

OBCI .... On-Board Controller Interface [*Telecommunications*]

OBCIEP .... Ontario Breast Cancer Information Exchange Partnership (SAUS)

OBCO .... On-Board Checkout [*NASA*] (KSC)

OBCOOP .... Observation Control Optimization (SAUS)

OB/CP .... Observation/Command Post (DNAB)

OBCP .... Ortho-Benzyl-para-chlorophenol [*Disinfectant*]

OBCR .... Optical Bar Code Reader (NITA)

OBCS .... Chromatographic Specialties Ltd., Brockville, Ontario [*Library symbol*] [*National Library of Canada*] (NLC)

OBCS .... On-Board Checkout Subsystem [*NASA*] (NASA)

OBCS .... On-Board Checkout [*Instrumentation*] System

Obd .... Obadiah [*Old Testament book*] (BJA)

OBD .... Odorant-Binding Protein (DB)

OBD .... Off Board Drone (ACAE)

OBD .... Office of Business Development [*Economic Development Administration*]

o/bd .... Oil on Board (VRA)

OBD .... Omnibearing Distance

OBD .... On-Board Diagnostics [*Chrysler Corp.'s computer system*]

OBD .... Online Bugs Database (SAUS)

OBD .... Open Blade Damper (OA)

OBD .... Operational Base Development (AAG)

OBD .... Operation Buckle Down [*NHTSA*] (TAG)

OBD .... Optical Beam Deflection

OBD .... Ordnance Base Depot (SAUS)

OBD .... Organic Brain Disease

OBD .... Organization for Black Designers

OBDB .... On-Board Data Bank (DNAB)

OBDC .... On-Board Diagnostics Class

OBDC .... Open Database Connectivity [*Computer science*]

OBDC .... Otago Business Development Centre (SAUS)

OBDD .... Ordered Bicontinuous Double Diamond [*Phase structure*]

OBDD .... Ordered Binary Decision Diagram [*Computer science*] (VLIE)

OBDE .... Dollman Electronics Canada Ltd., Brampton, Ontario [*Library symbol*] [*National Library of Canada*] (NLC)

OBDH .... On Board Data Handling (ACAE)

OBDH .... On-Board Data Handling (SAUS)

OBDICS .... Order Backlog Delivery and Installation Control System (VLIE)

OBDIF .... Order of Battle Data Interchange Format (SAUS)

OBDII .... On-oard Diagnostics-Second Generation

OB DK .... Observation Deck (WDAA)

OBDM .... On-Board Data Management (SAUS)

OBDO .... Oceanographic, Boarding, and Diving Officer [*Navy*] [*British*]

OBDT .... Obedient

OBDV .... Oat Blue Dwarf Virus [*Plant pathology*]

OBE .... Belleville Public Library, Ontario [*Library symbol*] [*National Library of Canada*] (NLC)

OBE .... Oberlin College, Oberlin, OH [*OCLC symbol*] (OCLC)

OBE .... Offboard Expendables (SAUS)

OBE .... Office of Biological Education (DAVI)

OBE .... Office of Business Economics [*Later, Office of Economic Analysis*] [*Department of Commerce*]

OBE .... Officer of the British Empire (SAUS)

OBE .... Officer of the Most Excellent Order of the British Empire (WDAA)

OBE .... Officer of the Order of the British Empire (NGC)

OBE .... Okeechobee, FL [*Location identifier*] [*FAA*] (FAAL)

OBE .... Onboard Electronics Operating Basis Earthquake (SAUS)

OBE .... On-Board Equipment

OBE .... One-Boson Exchange [*Physics*] (OA)

OBE .... Online Banking Excellence (SAUS)

OBE .... Open Both Ends (SAUS)

OBE .... Operating Basis Earthquake [*Nuclear reactor*] (NRCH)

OBE .... Operating Basis Event (IEEE)

OBE .... Order of the British Empire [*Facetious translations: Old Boiled Egg, Other Buggers' Efforts*]

OBE .... Other Buggers Efforts (SAUS)

OBE .... Ottawa Board of Education, Library Services Centre [*UTLAS symbol*]

OBE .... Outcome-Based Education [*School reform*]

OBE .... Outerback End

OBE .... Out-of-Body Experience [*Parapsychology*]

OBE .... Output Buffer Empty [*Computer science*] (VLIE)

OBE .... Overcome [*or Overtaken*] by Events

OBE .... Overtaken by Events (SAUS)

OBEA .... Ontario Business Education Association (SAUS)

OBEA .... Oregon Business Education Association (EDAC)

OBEAB .... Beaverton Branch, Brock Township Public Library, Ontario [*Library symbol*] [*National Library of Canada*] (BIB)

OBEAR .... Beardmore Public Library, Ontario [*Library symbol*] [*National Library of Canada*] (NLC)

OBEATE .... Beaverton-Thorah Eldon Historical Society, Inc., Ontario [*Library symbol*] [*National Library of Canada*] (NLC)

OBEC .... Organization for Economic Cooperation and Development (EBF)

OBECO .... Outboard Engine Cutoff [*NASA*] (KSC)

OBED .... Beamsville District Secondary School, Ontario [*Library symbol*] [*National Library of Canada*] (NLC)

OBed .... Bedford Public Library, Bedford, OH [*Library symbol*] [*Library of Congress*] (LCLS)

OBedF .... Ferro Corp., Chemical Library, Bedford, OH [*Library symbol*] [*Library of Congress*] (LCLS)

OBEDS .... Deloro Stellite Co., Belleville, Ontario [*Library symbol*] [*National Library of Canada*] (BIB)

OBEE .... Beeton Public Library, Ontario [*Library symbol*] [*National Library of Canada*] (BIB)

OBEGOSC .... Organizational Effectiveness General Officer Steering Committee (MCD)

OBEH .... Hastings County Historical Society, Belleville, Ontario [*Library symbol*] [*National Library of Canada*] (BIB)

OBEHP .... Hastings and Prince Edward County Health Unit, Belleville, Ontario [*Library symbol*] [*National Library of Canada*] (BIB)

OBEL .... Loyalist College of Applied Arts and Technology, Belleville, Ontario [*Library symbol*] [*National Library of Canada*] (NLC)

Obel .... Obelisk (SAUS)

OBELF .... Fleming Branch, Lincoln Public Library, Beamsville, Ontario [*Library symbol*] [*National Library of Canada*] (BIB)

OBEM .... Beachville Ye Olde Museum, Ontario [*Library symbol*] [*National Library of Canada*] (BIB)

OBEM .... Object-Based Equipment Model (AAEL)

OBEM .... One-Boson Exchange Model

OBEM .... Operational Battery Effectiveness Model (MCD)

OBEMLA ...... Office of Bilingual Education and Minority Language Affairs [*Department of Education*] (GFGA)

O Ben .... Old Benloe's Reports, English Common Pleas [*1486-1580*] [*A publication*] (DLA)

OBENFX .... Olive Branch Entry Fix (SAUS)

O Benl .... Old Benloe's Reports, English Common Pleas [*1486-1580*] [*A publication*] (DLA)

OBEP .... One-Boson Exchange Potential

OBEr .... OB [*Out-of-the-Body*] Experient [*Parapsychology*]

OBER .... Office of Biological and Environmental Research (HGEN)

OBerB .... Baldwin-Wallace College, Berea, OH [*Library symbol*] [*Library of Congress*] (LCLS)

OBERS .... Office of Business Economics Research Service (NRCH)

OBERST .... Oberstimme [*Upper Part*] [*Music*]

OBERW .... Oberwerk [*Upper Work*] [*Music*]

OBES .... Office of Basic Energy Sciences (COE)

OBES .... Office of Basic Energy Services [*Department of Energy*]

OBES .... Office of Basic Engineering Sciences (SAUS)

OBES .... Ohio Bureau of Employment Services (SAUS)

OBES .... Orthonormal Basis of an Error Space [*Statistics*]

OBESA .... Stephens-Adamson, Belleville, Ontario [*Library symbol*] [*National Library of Canada*] (NLC)

OBESG .... Office of Basic Energy Science/Geosciences [*Department of Energy*]

Obesity&Bariatric Med... Obesity and Bariatric Medicine (SAUS)

OBESSI .... Organizing Bureau of European School Student Unions (SAUS)

OBESSU ...... Organising Bureau of European School Student Unions (EAIO)

OBEV .... Oxford Book of English Verse (SAUS)

OBEWS .... On-Board Electronic Warfare Simulation [*Air Force*]

OBEX .... Object Exchange [*Computer science*] (PCM)

OBEXFX .... Olive Branch Exit Fix (SAUS)

OBF .... Octave Band Filter

OBF .... One-Bar Function (OA)

OBf .... Open Book Fracture [*Medicine*] (MELL)

OBF .... Operating Basis Flood (SAUS)

OBF .... Operational Base Facility

OBF .... Organ Blood Flow [*Physiology*]

OBF .... Ottawa Board of Education, Library Services Centre (Films) [*UTLAS symbol*]

OBF .... Output Buffer Full [*Computer science*] (IAA)

OBFAR .... Burks Falls, Armour, and Ryerson Union Library, Burks Falls, Ontario [*Library symbol*] [*National Library of Canada*] (NLC)

OBFC .... Barriefield Branch, Frontenac County Library, Ontario [*Library symbol*] [*National Library of Canada*] (BIB)

OBFC .... O'Leary Brothers Fan Club (EA)

OBFCS .... On Board Fire Control System (SAUS)

OBFM .... Offensive Basic Flight Manoeuvres (SAUS)

OBFM .... On or Before Full Moon [*Freemasonry*] (ROG)

OBFNO .... Northern Ontario Public School Principals' Association, Burks Falls, Ontario [*Library symbol*] [*National Library of Canada*] (NLC)

OBFS .... Octave Band Filter Set

OBFS .... Office of Basic Energy Services (SAUS)

OBFS .... Offshore Bulk Fuel System

OBFS .... Organization of Biological Field Stations (EA)

OBFS .... Overseas Base Facilities Summary [*Navy*]

OBFSSU ...... Organising Bureau of European School Student Unions (SAUS)

obfusc .... obfuscated (SAUS)

Ob G .... Obergericht [*Court of Appeal*] [*German*] (DLA)

OBG .... Oberg Industries Ltd. [*Vancouver Stock Exchange symbol*]

OBG .... Obigarm [*Former USSR*] [*Seismograph station code, US Geological Survey*] [*Closed*] (SEIS)

OBG .... Obstetrics-Gynecology [*Medicine*]

OBG .... Oldie but Goodie [*Music*]

OBGA .... Office of Block Grant Assistance (SAUS)

OBgCE .... Conneaut Elementary School, Bowling Green, OH [*Library symbol*] [*Library of Congress*] (LCLS)

OBgCrE .... Crim Elementary School, Bowling Green, OH [*Library symbol*] [*Library of Congress*] (LCLS)

ob gene ...... Obese Gene [*Medicine*] (MELL)

OBGI .... Orion Broadcasting Group, Inc. (SAUS)

OBgJH .... Bowling Green Junior High School, Bowling Green, OH [*Library symbol*] [*Library of Congress*] (LCLS)

OBgKE .... Kenwood Elementary School, Bowling Green, OH [*Library symbol*] [*Library of Congress*] (LCLS)

OBgRE .... Ridge Elementary School, Bowling Green, OH [*Library symbol*] [*Library of Congress*] (LCLS)

OBGS .... On-Board Gunnery Simulator (PDAA)

OBGS .... Orbital Bombardment Guidance System

OBgSH .... Bowling Green Senior High School, Bowling Green, OH [*Library symbol*] [*Library of Congress*] (LCLS)

OBgSME ...... South Main Elementary School, Bowling Green, OH [*Library symbol*] [*Library of Congress*] (LCLS)

OBGT .... Old Babylonian Grammatical Texts [*A publication*] (BJA)

OBgU .... Bowling Green State University, Bowling Green, OH [*Library symbol*] [*Library of Congress*] (LCLS)

OBgU-C ...... Bowling Green State University, Center for Archival Collections, Bowling Green, OH [*Library symbol*] [*Library of Congress*] (LCLS)

OB-GYN ...... Obstetrical-Gynecological (SAUS)

OB-GYN ...... Obstetrician-Gynecologist (PAZ)

OB-GYN ...... Obstetrics-Gynecology [*Medicine*]

ob-gyn .... Obstetrics/Gynecology (SHCU)

OBH .... Office Busy Hour [*Telecommunications*] (TEL)

OBH .... Oil Bath Heater

OBH .... Old Berkeley Hunt [*British*]

OBH .... Old Berkshire Hounds [*British*]

OBH .... Old Highland Blend [*Whisky*] (ROG)

OBH .... Operational Biomedical Harness

OBH .... Wolbach, NE [*Location identifier*] [*FAA*] (FAAL)

OBHFC .... Official Bobby Hart Fan Club (EA)

OBHT .... Tecumseh Township Public Library, Bond Head, Ontario [*Library symbol*] [*National Library of Canada*] (BIB)

OBI .... Obidos [*Brazil*] [*Airport symbol*] (AD)

obi .... obiectum (SAUS)

OBI .... Obihiro [*Japan*] [*Seismograph station code, US Geological Survey*] (SEIS)

OBI .... Obligated Involuntary Officer [*Military*]

OBI .... Obliterate (SAUS)

OBI .... Office du Baccalaureat International [*International Baccalaureate Office - IBO*] (EAIO)

OBI .... Office of Basic Instrumentation [*National Bureau of Standards*]

OBI .... Old Babylonian Inscriptions [*A publication*] (BJA)

OBI .... Omnibearing Indicator [*Radio*]

OBI .... Online Book Initiative [*Trademark name*] [*Internet*]

OBI .... Open-Back Inclinable

OBI .... Open-Back Inclinable Press [*Manufacturing term*]

OBI .... Open Buying on the Internet [*Computer science*]

OBI .... Operation Blessing International [*An association*]

OBI .... Optical-Beam-Induced (SAUS)

OBI .... Order of British India

OBI .... Organisation du Baccalaureate International [*International Baccalaureate Organisation - IBO*] (EAIO)

OBI .... Osaka Bioscience Institute [*Japan*]

OBIA .... Ontario Brain Injury Association (SAUS)

OBIC .... Optical Beam Induced Contrast (SAUS)

OBIC .... Optical Beam Induced Current [*Electronics*] (AAEL)

OBIC .... Optical-Beam-Induced Current (SAUS)

O BID .... Omni Bidus [*Every Two Days*] [*Pharmacy*] (ROG)

OBIE .... Obie Media Corp. [*NASDAQ symbol*] (SAG)

ObieMed ...... Obie Media Corp. [*Associated Press*] (SAG)

OBIFC .... Osmond Boys International Fan Club (EA)

OBIFCO .... On-Board In-Flight Checkout (MCD)

OBIG .... Oesterreichisches Bundesinstitut fuer Gesundheitswesen [*Austrian National Institute for Public Health*] [*Information service or system*] (IID)

OBIGGS .... On-Board Inert Gas Generator System [*Aviation*] (MCD)

O BIH .... Omni Bihora [*Every Two Hours*] [*Pharmacy*] (ROG)

OBINXTO ..... Obiit in Christo [*Died in Christ*] [*Latin*]

OBIP .... Ontario Business Incentive Program (SAUS)

OBI Press ..... Open Back Inclinable Press (SAUS)

OBIPS .... Optical Band Imager and Photometer System [*Aerospace*]

OBIRCH .... Optical-Beam-Induced Resistance Change (SAUS)

OBIS .... Optical Backplane Interconnect System programme (SAUS)

OBIS .... Optimum Burn-In Screening

OBIS .... Outdoor Biology Instructional Strategies [*National Science Foundation project*]

OBIT .... Obiit [*He, or She, Died*] [*Latin*]

Obit .... Obiter [*A publication*]

OBIT .... Obituary (GOBB)

obit .... Obituary [*Journalism*] [*Also, ob*] (WDMC)

OBIT .... Obituary Notice (DSUE)

OBIU .... On-Board Interface Unit (DWSG)

OBIWR .... Whitefish River Band Public Library, Birch Island, Ontario [*Library symbol*] [*National Library of Canada*] (NLC)

OBJ .... Intermediate Object Code File [*Computer science*]

OBJ .... Object (AAG)

obj .... Object (VRA)

OBJ .... Object File (SAUS)

OBJ .... Objection (WDAA)

obj .... Objection (WDAA)

Obj .... Objective (AMHC)

OBJ .... Oklahoma Bar Association. Journal [*A publication*] (DLA)

OBJ .... Operation Buster-Jangle [*Atomic weapons testing*]

OBJ .... Orthodox Black Jews (BJA)

OBJ .... Query Object Systems [*AMEX symbol*]

ObjDes .... Object Design, Inc. [*Associated Press*] (SAG)

OBJN .... Objection

ObjSoft .... ObjectSoft Corp. [*Associated Press*] (SAG)

ObjSys .... Objective Systems Integrators, Inc. [*Associated Press*] (SAG)

OBJV .... Objective (MSA)

OBK .... Northbrook, IL [*Location identifier*] [*FAA*] (FAAL)

OBK .... Open Breaker Keying (SAUS)

OBK .... Organisation pour l'Amenagement et le Developpement du Bassin de la Riviere Kagera [*Organization for the Management and Development of the Kagera River Basin - KBO*] (EAIO)

OBL .... League of Off-Broadway Theatres and Producers (EA)

OBL .... Object-Based Language (AAEL)

OBL .... Oblast [*Governmental subdivision in USSR corresponding to a province or state*]

OBL .... Obligation (ADA)

OBL .... Obligato [*Obbligato*] [*Music*] (ROG)

OBL .... Oblique (AABC)

obl .... Oblique (STED)

obl .... Oblong [*Bookbinding*] (WDMC)

OBL .... Oblong

obl .... obloquy (SAUS)

OBL .... Ocean Beach Library (SAUS)

OBL .... Oceanic Boundary Layer

OBL .... Office of Business Liaison

OBL .... Office of Business Loans [*Economic Development Administration*]

OBL .... Ohio Barge Line (SAUS)

OBL .... Older Bill of Lading (SAUS)

OBL .... One Block Look-Ahead [*Computer science*]

obl .... Opera-Ballet [*Music*] (GROV)

OBL .... Operational Base Launch [*Air Force*]

OBL .... Order Bill of Lading [*Shipping*]

OBL .... Order of the Brave Librarian (SAUS)

OBL .... Outlined Black Letters [*Tire design*]

OBL .... Outside of the Battery Limits [*Engineering economics*]

OBL .... Outstanding Balance List [*IRS*]

OBla .... Blanchester Public Library, Blanchester, OH [*Library symbol*] [*Library of Congress*] (LCLS)

OBLAC .... Bath Branch, Lennox and Addington County Public Library, Ontario [*Library symbol*] [*National Library of Canada*] (NLC)

OBLACS .... Sandburst Branch, Lennox and Addington County Public Library, Bath, Ontario [*Library symbol*] [*National Library of Canada*] (BIB)

OBLAT .... Oblatum [*Cachet*] [*Pharmacy*]

OBLAUTH..... Obligation Authority [*Army*] (AABC)

OBIC .... Bluffton College, Bluffton, OH [*Library symbol*] [*Library of Congress*] (LCLS)

OBIC-M .... Bluffton College, Mennonite Historical Library, Bluffton, OH [*Library symbol*] [*Library of Congress*] (LCLS)

OBLG .... Obligate (AABC)

OBLH .... Bloomfield-Hallowell Union Library, Bloomfield, Ontario [*Library symbol*] [*National Library of Canada*] (BIB)

OBLI .... Oxford and Bucks Light Infantry [*Military unit*] [*British*]

Oblig .... Obligation (TBD)

OBLIGN........ Obligation (ROG)

OBLISERV ..... Obligated Services of [*numbers of months indicated*] Required [*Navy*]

OBLISERVNATRA... Obligated to Serve Three and One-Half Years Following Date of Completion of Training within the Naval Air Training Command (SAUS)

OBLISERVONEASIX... Obligated to Serve on Active Duty One Year for Each Six Months Schooling or Fraction Thereof [*Navy*]

OBLISERVTHREETIME... Obligated to Serve on Active Duty a Period Three Times the Length of Period of Education [*Navy*]

OBLISERVTWOYR... Obligated to Serve on Active Duty a Period of Two Years [*Navy*]

OBLN .... Obligation (AFM)

OBLR .... Blind River Public Library, Ontario [*Library symbol*] [*National Library of Canada*] (NLC)

Obl Serv ..... Obligation Service (SAUS)

OBLu........... Old Babylonian Version of Lu [*A publication*] (BJA)

OBlv........... Bliss Memorial Public Library, Bloomville, OH [*Library symbol*] [*Library of Congress*] (LCLS)

OBM........... Aviaobshemash [*Former USSR*] [*FAA designator*] (FAAC)

OBM........... Morobe [*Papua New Guinea*] [*Airport symbol*] (OAG)

OBM........... Oberlin College, Conservatory of Music, Library, Oberlin, OH [*OCLC symbol*] (OCLC)

OBM........... Ocean Biogeochemical Model

OBM........... Ogilvy Benson & Mather Ltd. (EFIS)

OBM........... Oil-Base Mud (SAUS)

OBM........... Ontario Basic Mapping (SAUS)

OBM........... Optical Business Machines, Inc. (SAUS)

OBM........... Optimal Body Mass [*Ecology*]

OBM........... Ordnance Bench Mark (IAA)

OBM........... Oriental Boat Mission [*Later, International Missions*] (EA)

OBM........... Oxygen-Bottom Blown Maxhutte (SAUS)

OBM........... Ulan Bator [*Mongolia*] [*Seismograph station code, US Geological Survey*] [*Closed*] (SEIS)

OBMA .... Outboard Boat Manufacturers Association [*Later, NMMA*] (EA)

OBMC .... Officers' Basic Military Corps [*Air Force*]

OBMC .... Outbound Midcourse Correction [*NASA*] (KSC)

Ob MOK....... Oberbefehlshaber der Marine-Oberkommandos (SAUS)

OBMP .... Bruce Mines and Plummer Additional Union Public Library, Bruce Mines, Ontario [*Library symbol*] [*National Library of Canada*] (NLC)

OBMPH .... Observed Miles per Hour [*Automotive emissions*]

OBMS .... Objectives-Based Management System (ADA)

OBN .... Oban [*Scotland*] [*Airport symbol*] (OAG)

OBN .... Obninsk [*Former USSR*] [*Seismograph station code, US Geological Survey*] (SEIS)
OBN .... Occult Blood Negative [*Medicine*] (DAVI)
OBN .... Office Balancing Network [*Telecommunications*] (TEL)
OBN .... Office of Biochemical Nomenclature [*NAS-NRC*]
OBN .... On-Board Navigation
OBN .... Open Library Network (SAUS)
OBN .... Optical Broadband Network (SAUS)
OBN .... Out-of-Band Noise
OBNA .... Only But Not All (NITA)
OBNE .... Department 9911, Northern Telecom Ltd., Belleville, Ontario [*Library symbol*] [*National Library of Canada*] [*Obsolete*] (NLC)
OBNM .... On or Before New Moon [*Freemasonry*] (ROG)
OBNR .... Oil Burner Route (SAUS)
OBNR .... Olive Branch Route (SAUS)
OBNREN Point... Oil Burner Entry Point (SAUS)
OBNREX Point... Oil Burner Exit Point (SAUS)
OBNTC .... Old Boys Network Turtle Club (EA)
OBO .... Obihiro [*Japan*] [*Airport symbol*] (OAG)
OBO .... Obock [*Djibouti*] [*Seismograph station code, US Geological Survey*] (SEIS)
OBO .... Official Business Only (AFM)
OBO .... Oil/Bulk/On Carrier (SAUS)
OBO .... Oil/Bulk/Ore (SAUS)
OBO .... Oil/Bulk/Ore Carrier [*Multipurpose bulk carrier*] (DS)
obo .... Or Best Offer (SHCU)
OBO .... Or Best Offer [*Classified advertising*]
OBO .... Orbital Bomber (IAA)
OBO .... Order Book Official [*Investment term*]
OBO .... Order by Order
O/B/O .... Ore/Bulk/Oil [*Bulk carrier vessel*]
OBO .... Ore/Bulk/Oil carrier (SAUS)
OBO .... Organization of Bricklin Owners (EA)
OBO .... Output Back-Off (SAUS)
OBOA .... Ontario Building Officials Association [*Canada*] (AAGC)
OBOC .... Ore/Bulk/Oil Carrier (SAUS)
OBO Carrier... Oil/Bulk/Oil Carrier (SAUS)
OBO Carrier... Oil/Bulk/Ore Carrier (SAUS)
OB/OD .... Open Burning/Open Detonation [*Military*]
OBOE .... Observed Bombing of Enemy
OBOE .... Offensive Built Operational Environment (ACAE)
OBOE .... Offensive Burst Operating Environment
OBOE .... Offshore Buoy-Observing Equipment (PDAA)
OBOE .... Offshore Buoy Observing System (SAUS)
OBOE Radar... Observed Bombing of Enemy Radar (SAUS)
OBOF .... Old Buffer over Forty [*Elderly recruits*] [*World War I*] [*British*]
OBOG .... On-Board Oxygen-Generation [*For military aviation*]
OBOGS.......... On-Board Oxygen Generating System [*Navy*] (CAAL)
OBOLC .... Caledon Public Libraries, Bolton, Ontario [*Library symbol*] [*National Library of Canada*] (NLC)
OBOM .... Bowmanville Museum, Ontario [*Library symbol*] [*National Library of Canada*] (BIB)
OBON .... Newcastle Public Library Board, Bowmanville, Ontario [*Library symbol*] [*National Library of Canada*] (NLC)
OBONF.......... Bonfield Public Library, Ontario [*Library symbol*] [*National Library of Canada*] (NLC)
OBOS .... Ore/Bulk/Oil Ship (SAUS)
OBOS .... Our Bodies Ourselves [*A publication*]
OBP .... Occult Blood Positive [*Medicine*] (DAVI)
OBP .... Occupational Back Pain
OBP .... Octyl Benzyl Phthalate (EDCT)
OBP .... Odorant-Binding Protein [*Biochemistry*]
OBP .... Offensive Beating Posture (SAUS)
OBP .... Offshore Biological Programme (SAUS)
OBP .... Oil Breather Pressure
OBP .... On-Base Percentage [*Baseball*]
OBP .... On-Board Processing (SAUS)
OBP .... On-Board Processor
OBP .... On-Line Benefits Processing
OBP .... Open Break Position [*Dancing*]
OBP .... Ordinary Bulb Plate (SAUS)
OBP .... Osteoporosis and Back Pain [*Medicine*] (MELL)
OBP .... Outer (Edge of) Basal Piece
OBP .... Ova, Blood, and Parasites [*Medicine*] (MAE)
obp .... Oxygen at High Pressure (AD)
OBPA .... Outer Banks Protection Act (AAGC)
OBPA .... Oxybisphenoxarsine [*Organic chemistry*]
OBPC .... Optical Bar Panoramic Camera (SAUS)
OB PH .... Oblique Photography (WDAA)
OBPH .... People Helping People, Inc., Brantford, Ontario [*Library symbol*] [*National Library of Canada*] (NLC)
OBPI .... Otisville BioPharm, Inc. (SAUS)
OBQ .... Optometrists' Board of Queensland
OBR .... Bradford Public Library, Ontario [*Library symbol*] [*National Library of Canada*] (NLC)
OBR .... Office of Budget and Reports
OBR .... Ohio Board of Regents (SAUS)
OBR .... One-Button-Recording [*Video technology*]
OBR .... Optical Bar Code
OBR .... Optical Bar Code Reader (MHDB)
OBR .... Optical Bar Recognition [*Commonly known as a bar code*] (WDMC)
OBR .... Optical Beam Riding (SAUS)
OBR .... Origin of Bidirectional Replication [*Genetics*]
OBR .... Osteoporosis from Bed Rest [*Medicine*] (MELL)
OBR .... Outboard Recorder [*Computer science*] (BUR)

OBR .... Outboard Recording (SAUS)
OBR .... Owens, B. R., Montebello CA [*STAC*]
OBRA .... Brampton Public Library, Ontario [*Library symbol*] [*National Library of Canada*] (NLC)
OBRA .... Office of Business Research and Analysis [*Department of Commerce*]
OBRA .... Omnibus Budget Reconciliation Act [*1987*]
OBRA .... Omnibus Budget Reconciliation Act of 1990 (COE)
OBRA .... Overseas Broadcasting Representatives Association (IAA)
OBRAC.......... Bracebridge Public Library, Ontario [*Library symbol*] [*National Library of Canada*] (NLC)
OBRAD .... Oblate Radial (PDAA)
OBRAM .... Chinguacousy Township Public Library, Bramalea, Ontario [*Library symbol*] [*National Library of Canada*] (NLC)
OBRAMB ..... Bell Northern Research, Bramalea, Ontario [*Library symbol*] [*National Library of Canada*] (NLC)
OBRANT...... Northern Telecom, Brampton, Ontario [*Library symbol*] [*National Library of Canada*] (NLC)
OBRAPA ..... Archives, Region of Peel, Brampton, Ontario [*Library symbol*] [*National Library of Canada*] (BIB)
OBRASC...... Brampton Campus, Sheridan College, Brampton, Ontario [*Library symbol*] [*National Library of Canada*] (BIB)
OBRC .... Operating Budget Review Committee [*Military*]
OBRER .... Blind River Refinery, Eldorado Resources Ltd., Ontario [*Library symbol*] [*National Library of Canada*] (NLC)
OBRET .... Old Breton [*Language, etc.*]
OBrG .... B. F. Goodrich Co., Technical Library, Brecksville, OH [*Library symbol*] [*Library of Congress*] (LCLS)
OBRH .... Home Care Program, Brockville, Ontario [*Library symbol*] [*National Library of Canada*] (BIB)
OBRI .... Belle River Public Library, Ontario [*Library symbol*] [*National Library of Canada*] (NLC)
O Bridg ...... Orlando Bridgman's English Common Pleas Reports [*A publication*] (DLA)
O Bridg (Eng)... Orlando Bridgman's English Common Pleas Reports [*A publication*] (DLA)
O Bridgm ..... Orlando Bridgman's English Common Pleas Reports [*A publication*] (DLA)
O'Brien .... O'Brien's Upper Canada Reports [*A publication*] (DLA)
OBRIG.......... Brighton Public Library, Ontario [*Library symbol*] [*National Library of Canada*] (BIB)
O'Bri Lawy... O'Brien's Lawyer's Rule of Holy Life [*A publication*] (DLA)
O'Bri ML...... O'Brien's Military Law [*A publication*] (DLA)
OBRIS .... Smith Township Public Library, Bridgenorth, Ontario [*Library symbol*] [*National Library of Canada*] (BIB)
OBRIT .... Britt Area Community Library, Britt, Ontario [*Library symbol*] [*National Library of Canada*] (NLC)
OBRIT .... Old British [*Language, etc.*]
OBRM .... W. Ross MacDonald School, Brantford, Ontario [*Library symbol*] [*National Library of Canada*] (NLC)
OBRMR........ Mississauga Reserve Library, Blind River, Ontario [*Library symbol*] [*National Library of Canada*] (NLC)
OBRNR .... Oil Burner
OBRO .... Or Best Reasonable Offer
OBRO .... Oxford-On-Rideau Township Public Library, Burritt's Rapids, Ontario [*Library symbol*] [*National Library of Canada*] (BIB)
OBROW........ Ochotnicza Brygada Robotnicza Obrony Warszawy [*A publication*] (BJA)
OBRP .... On-Board Repair Parts [*Navy*]
OBRP .... Pauline Johnson College, Brantford, Ontario [*Library symbol*] [*National Library of Canada*] (NLC)
OBRPH........ Library Resources & Information Centre, Brockville Psychiatric Hospital, Ontario [*Library symbol*] [*National Library of Canada*] (NLC)
OBRR .... Obstetric Recovery Room (STED)
OBRT .... Brantford Public Library, Ontario [*Library symbol*] [*National Library of Canada*] (NLC)
OBrV .... United States Veterans Administration Hospital, Brecksville, OH [*Library symbol*] [*Library of Congress*] (LCLS)
OBRWI........ [*The*] Woodland Indian Cultural Educational Centre, Brantford, Ontario [*Library symbol*] [*National Library of Canada*] (NLC)
OBS .... Aubenas [*France*] [*Airport symbol*] (OAG)
OBS .... Obesity [*Medicine*] (DMAA)
OBS .... Obligations (ROG)
obs .... Obscene (SHCU)
Obs .... Obscene [*Legal term*]
obs .... Obscura (VRA)
OBS .... Obscurant
OBS .... Obscure (ADA)
obs .... Observation (MILB)
OBS .... Observation (ROG)
OBS .... Observation Balloon System (SAUS)
OBS .... Observatory
OBS .... Observe
Obs .... Observer (London) [*A publication*] (BRI)
OBS .... Obsolescence (SAUS)
OBS .... Obsolete (AAG)
obs .... Obsolete (STED)
OBS .... Obstacle (AABC)
Obs .... Obstacle Light [*Aviation*] (DA)
OBS .... Obstetrical Service [*Medicine*] (MAE)
OBS .... Obstetrics [*Medicine*]
obs .... Obstruction [*Baseball term*] (NDBD)
OBS .... Obstruction (WGA)

OBS .... Ocean Bottom Seismometer [*California*] [*Seismograph station code, US Geological Survey*] [*Closed*] (SEIS)
OBS .... Ocean Bottom Station
OBS .... Ocean Bottom Suspension (SAUS)
OBS .... Office of Biological Service [*Marine science*] (MSC)
OBS .... Office of Boating Safety [*Coast Guard*]
OBS .... Official Bulletin Station [*Amateur radio*]
OBS .... Oita Broadcasting Service (SAUS)
OBS .... Old Babylonian Sumerian (BJA)
OBS .... Old Bailey's Sessions Papers [*A publication*] (DLA)
OBS .... Omnibearing Selector [*Radio*]
OBS .... Onboard Shuttle (ACAE)
OBS .... On-Board Spares [*Army*]
OBS .... On-Board System [*Navy*] (CAAL)
OBS .... Online BookStore [*Commercial firm*]
OBS .... Online Business Systems (SAUS)
OBS .... On-Line Business Systems, Inc. [*Information service or system*] (IID)
OBS .... Open-Back Stationary Press [*Manufacturing term*]
OBS .... Open Bidding Service (SAUS)
OBS .... Open-Hearth Basic Steel
OBS .... Opera Ballet School (DICI)
OBS .... Operand Buffering System [*Computer science*] (IAA)
OBS .... Operational Bioinstrumentation System [*NASA*]
OBS .... Operational Biomedical Sensors (NASA)
OBS .... Operational Biomedical Systems (KSC)
OBS .... Optical Beam Scanner
OBS .... Optical Beam Steering
OBS .... Optimum Blending System (VLIE)
OBS .... Orange Badge Scheme [*Disabled parking permit*] [*British*]
OBS .... Orbital Bombardment System
OBS .... Organic Brain Syndrome [*Psychiatry*]
OBS .... Organizational Breakdown Structure (SAUS)
OBS .... Organization Breakdown Structure [*Computer science*] (PCM)
OBS .... Organized Behavioral System (WDMC)
OBS .... Oriental and Biblical Studies [*A publication*] (BJA)
OBS .... OSIS [*Ocean Surveillance Information System*] Baseline System [*Navy*]
OBS .... Ottawa Board of Education, Library Services Centre (Software) [*UTLAS symbol*]
OBS .... Outlined Black Letters on One Side [*Tire design*]
OBS .... Output Buffer Storage (SAUS)
OBS .... Output Buffer Store (SAUS)
OBS .... Oxford Bibliographical Society (DGA)
OBS .... Sidney Township Public Library, Batawa, Ontario [*Library symbol*] [*National Library of Canada*] (BIB)
OBSC .... Obscure
OBSC .... Obscured Light [*Navigation signal*]
OBSC .... Obscuring (SAUS)
obscen .... obscenity (SAUS)
OBSCIS .... Offender Based State Corrections Information System (OICC)
OBSD .... Object Sum Optical Density [*Microscopy*]
obsd .... Observed (STED)
OBSD .... Observed
OBSD .... Optical Beam Steering Device
OBSERV ...... Observatory
OBSET .... Observation Set (SAUS)
OBSH .... Object Shape [*Microscopy*]
OBSH .... Oxybis(benzenesulfonylhydrazine) [*Organic chemistry*]
Obs Handb Can... Observers Handbook. Royal Astronomical Society of Canada (SAUS)
OBSHT .... Obstacle Height
OBSL .... St. Lawrence College [*College Saint-Laurent*], Brockville, Ontario [*Library symbol*] [*National Library of Canada*] (NLC)
Obs Lt......... Observer Lieutenant [*British military*] (DMA)
Obs Mer Alt... Observed Meridian Altitude (SAUS)
OBSN .... Observation (AAG)
OBSN FL..... Observation Flash (SAUS)
OBSNFL....... Observation Flight (IAA)
OBSN L....... Observation Line (SAUS)
OBSOL .... Obsolescent
Obsoles ...... Obsolescent
OBSP .... Obiit sine Prole [*Died without Issue*] [*Latin*]
OBSP .... Old Bailey's Sessions Papers [*Legal term*] [*British*]
OBS PAT..... Observation Patrol (SAUS)
OBS PL....... Observation Plane (SAUS)
OBSPL .... Octave Band Sound Pressure Level
OBSPM .... Obiit sine Prole Masculus [*He, or She, Died without Male Issue*] [*Latin*]
OBSR .... Observation
OBSRON...... Observation Squadron
OBSRVTRY... Observatory
OBSS .... Ocean Bottom Scanning SONAR
OBSS .... Off Board Sensor Systems (ACAE)
OBSS .... Operations Briefing Support System (ACAE)
Obs Spot...... Observation Spot [*Control point*] [*Nautical charts*]
OBS Station... Ocean Bottom Seismographic Station (SAUS)
OBST .... Object Management System of STONE (SAUS)
OBST .... Obstacle (AFM)
OBST .... Obstetric
Obst............ Obstetrician (STED)
OBST .... Obstetrics [*Medicine*]
obst .... Obstipation (STED)
OBST .... Obstruction (AFM)
obst .... Obstruction (PIAV)
OBST CL...... Obstacle Clearing (SAUS)

obstet .... Obstetric (STED)
OBSTET....... Obstetrics [*Medicine*]
Obst Gynec... Obstetria and Gynecology (SAUS)
Obst J Gr Brit... Obstetrical Journal of Great Britain and Ireland (SAUS)
obstl .... Obstruction Light (AD)
OBSTN .... Obstruction (MSA)
OBSTR .... Obstruct (SAUS)
obstr .... Obstruction (AD)
Obstr........... Obstruction
OBSTRN ...... Obstetrician [*Medicine*]
OBSTRUCT... Obstructive (SAUS)
OBSUED...... Oberbefehlshaber Suedost [*Headquarters, Commander-in-Chief, South*] [*Southern Germany and several army groups on the Eastern Front*] [*German military - World War II*]
OBSUM .... Order of Battle Summary [*Military*] (MCD)
obsv........... Observation (AD)
OBSV .... Observation (IAA)
obsv........... Observatory (AD)
OBSV .... Observatory (IAA)
obsv........... Observer (AD)
OBSV .... Observer
OBSVE .... Observe (ROG)
OBSY .... Observatory (AABC)
ob syn .... Organic Brain Syndrome [*Medicine*] (AD)
OBSZ .... Object Size [*Microscopy*]
obt .... Obedient (AD)
OBT............ Obedient
OBT............ Obiit [*He, or She, Died*] [*Latin*]
obt .... Obiit [*He Died*] [*Latin*] (AD)
OBT............ Observer Training [*Army*]
obt .... Obtained (STED)
OBT............ Office of Building Technologies (SAUS)
OBT............ Officers Basic Training (ACAE)
OBT............ On-Board Trainer [*Navy*] (CAAL)
OBT............ One Billion Trees program (SAUS)
OBT............ Oriental Bank & Trust [*NYSE symbol*] (TTSB)
OBT............ Overseas Branch Transfer (AD)
OBT............ Sisters Oblates to the Blessed Trinity (TOCD)
OBTA .... Oak Bark Tanners' Association (AD)
OBTAINDORSETRANS... Obtain Endorsement to Transport (DNAB)
obtd .... Obtained (AD)
OBTD .... Obtained
OBTEX .... Offboard Targeting Experiments (GAVI)
OBTG .... Obtaining (ROG)
OBTN .... Obtain (ROG)
obts .... Offender-Based Transaction Statistics (AD)
OBTS .... Offender Base Transaction Statistical System [*Department of Justice*] [*Database*] [*Information service or system*] (IID)
OBTS .... On-Board Test Set (SAUS)
OBTS .... Organizational Behavior Teaching Society (EA)
OBTVR........ Office for Battlefield Technical Vulnerability Reduction [*Army*] (RDA)
OBTW .... Oh, By the Way [*Computer hacker terminology*] (NHD)
OBTX .... Object Texture [*Microscopy*]
OBU .... Burlington Public Library, Ontario [*Library symbol*] [*National Library of Canada*] (NLC)
OBU .... Kobuk [*Alaska*] [*Airport symbol*] (OAG)
OBU .... Kobuk, AK [*Location identifier*] [*FAA*] (FAAL)
OBU .... Ocean Information System Baseline Upgrade (SAUS)
OBU .... Offshore Banking Unit
OBU .... Oklahoma Baptist University
OBU .... One Big Union [*A reference to Canada*]
OBU .... Operational Base Unit [*British military*] (DMA)
OBU .... Operative Bootmakers Union (AD)
OBU .... Operative Builders' Union [*British*]
OBU .... OSIS [*Ocean Surveillance Information System*] Baseline Upgrade [*Navy*]
OBU .... Ouachita Baptist University [*Arkadelphia, AR*] [*Formerly, OBC*]
OBUA .... Operating in Built-Up-Areas (SAUS)
OBUC......... Canada Centre for Inland Waters [*Centre Canadien des Eaux Interieures*], Burlington, Ontario [*Library symbol*] [*National Library of Canada*] (NLC)
OBUCC........ Canadian Canners Ltd., Burlington, Ontario [*Library symbol*] [*National Library of Canada*] (NLC)
OBUFBL ...... Bayfield Laboratory, Ocean Science and Surveys, Fisheries and Oceans Canada [*Laboratoire Bayfield, Science et Leves Oceaniques, Peches et Oceans Canada*] Burlington, Ontario [*Library symbol*] [*National Library of Canada*] (NLC)
OBUJB .... Joseph Brant Memorial Hospital, Burlington, Ontario [*Library symbol*] [*National Library of Canada*] (BIB)
OBUL .... Lord Elgin High School, Burlington, Ontario [*Library symbol*] [*National Library of Canada*] (NLC)
O Bul .... Old Bulgarian (AD)
OBulg.......... Old Bulgarian [*Language*] (BARN)
OBUR.......... Burford Public Library, Ontario [*Library symbol*] [*National Library of Canada*] (BIB)
OBur .... Burton Public Library, Burton, OH [*Library symbol*] [*Library of Congress*] (LCLS)
o/bur .... Oil on Burlap (VRA)
OB-US......... Obstetrical Ultrasound (STED)
OBUS.......... Obstetric Ultrasound [*Microcomputer system dealing with results of obstetric ultrasound examinations*]
OBUTS........ Organ Builders' United Trade Society [*A union*] [*British*]
OBUV.......... Operative Bakers' Union of Victoria [*Australia*]
OBv............ Bellevue Public Library, Bellevue, OH [*Library symbol*] [*Library of Congress*] (LCLS)

OBV	Bobcaygeon Branch, Victoria County Public Library, Ontario [*Library symbol*] [*National Library of Canada*] (BIB)
OBV	Obligated Volunteer Officer [*Military*]
OBV	Observe (SAUS)
OBV	Obstacle Breaching Vehicle [*Military*]
obv	Obverse (AD)
OBV	Obverse
obv	Obvious (AD)
obv	Ocean Boarding Vessel (AD)
OBV	Ocean Boarding Vessel
obv	Octane Blending Value (AD)
OBV	Octane Blending Value (PDAA)
OBV	On-Balance Volume [*Measurement devised by stock market technician Joseph Granville*]
OBV	Operation Big Vote (EA)
OBV	Outside Broadcasting Van (SAUS)
OBV	Oxidizer Bleed Valve (NASA)
OBVACT	On-Board Visual Aimer Continuation Trainer (SAUS)
OBVP	Obiit Vita Patris [*He, or She, Died in the Lifetime of His, or Her, Father*] [*Latin*]
obvy	Obviously (AD)
OBW	Oberwerk [*Upper Work*] [*Music*]
Obw	Oberwerk [*Highest Organ Bank*] [*German*] (AD)
obw	Observation Window (AD)
OBW	Observation Window
OBW	Oxford Bible Warehouse [*British*] (ROG)
OBWC	Westinghouse Canada, Inc., Burlington, Ontario [*Library symbol*] [*National Library of Canada*] (NLC)
OBWO	O-Type Backward-Wave Oscillator (IDOE)
O-BWO	Type-O Backward Wave Oscillator (SAUS)
OBX	Oslo Stock Exchange [*Norway*] (NUMA)
OBy	Old Byblian (BJA)
OBZ	Outer Border Zone [*Geology*]
OC	Air California [*Air carrier designation symbol*] (AD)
OC	Cornwall Public Library, Ontario [*Library symbol*] [*National Library of Canada*] (NLC)
OC	Degrees Celsius
OC	Jersey. Ordres du Conseil [*A publication*] (DLA)
OC	Oakwood College (SAUS)
OC	Oberlin College (AD)
OC	Object Class [*Military*]
O/C	Object Classification (NG)
OC	Object Computer (SAUS)
OC	Objective Capability
OC	Oblate College (AD)
OC	Observation Car [*British*]
OC	Observer Computer (SAUS)
OC	Observer-Controller [*Army*] (INF)
OC	Observer Corps [*Became ROC, 1941*] [*British*]
OC	Obsessive Compulsive (PAZ)
OC	Obstacle Clearance (PDAA)
oc	Obstetrical Conjugate [*Medicine*] (AD)
OC	Obstetric Conjugate [*Pelvic measurement*] [*Gynecology*]
OC	Obstruction Chart
OC	Occidental
OC	Occidental College (AD)
OC	Occipital Cortex [*Brain anatomy*]
OC	Occlusocervical [*Dentistry*]
OC	Occulentum [*Medicine*] (CPH)
Oc	Occulting Light [*Navigation signal*]
OC	Occupied [*International telex abbreviation*] (WDMC)
OC	Occurs (MDG)
Oc	Ocean (AD)
Oc	Ocean
oc	Ocean (AD)
OC	Oceanographic Devices [*JETDS nomenclature*] [*Military*] (CET)
O/C	O'Clock (ROG)
Oc	Octahedral [*Molecular geometry*]
OC	Octal Code (SAUS)
OC	October (ADA)
Oc	Octyl [*Biochemistry*]
OC	Ocular [*Microscopy*]
OC	Oculentum [*Eye Ointment*] [*Pharmacy*]
OC	Odessa College (AD)
oc	Odor Control (AD)
OC	Odor Control
OC	Oedipus Coloneus [*of Sophocles*] [*Classical studies*] (OCD)
OC	Of Course
OC	Off-Camera [*Film*] (WDMC)
OC	Off Center (WGA)
OC	Off Cover (SAUS)
OC	Offensive Center [*Football*]
OC	Office Call [*Medicine*]
OC	Office Consultation (AD)
OC	Office Copy
OC	Office of Censorship [*Terminated, 1945*] [*Military*]
OC	Office of Compliance [*U.S. Food and Drug Administration*]
OC	Office of the Commissioner [*Office of Education*]
OC	Office of the Comptroller
O/C	Officer Cadet [*British military*] (DMA)
OC	Officer Candidate [*Military*]
OC	Officer Commanding [*Military*]
OC	Officer in Charge (AD)
OC	Officer, Order of Canada [*Decoration*] (CMD)
OC	Officers' Cook
OC	Official Circular [*Poor Law Board, etc.*] [*A publication*] (DLA)
OC	Official Classification
OC	Official Communication (SAUS)
OC	Off-Machine Coated [*Paper*] (DGA)
OC	Ohio College (AD)
OC	Oil Cooler
OC	Oiler Contact (SAUS)
o/c	Oil on Canvas (VRA)
OC	Okolona College (AD)
OC	Old Carthusian
OC	Old Category Code (NITA)
OC	Old Catholic
OC	Old Chap [*Amateur radio shorthand*] (WDAA)
O/C	Old Charter [*Business and trade*]
OC	Old Cheltonian [*British*] (ROG)
OC	Old Code [*Louisiana Code of 1808*] [*A publication*] (DLA)
OC	Old Crop
OC	Oleoresin Capsicum (BARN)
OC	Olivet College (AD)
OC	Olympic College (AD)
OC	On Call (BUR)
oc	On Camera (AD)
OC	On Camera (WDMC)
OC	On Cards
oc	On Center (AD)
OC	On Center [*Technical drawings*]
O/C	On Completion (SAUS)
oc	On-Condition (NAKS)
OC	On-Condition (NASA)
OC	On Consignment (MHDB)
OC	On Course [*Navigation*]
OC	Online Chronicle (NITA)
OC	Only Child
OC	Ope Consilio [*By Aid and Counsel*] [*Latin*] [*Legal term*] (DLA)
OC	Open Channel (SAUS)
oc	Open Charter (AD)
OC	Open Charter [*Business term*]
OC	Open Chock [*Shipfitting*]
oc	Open Circuit (NAKS)
OC	Open Circuit
OC	Open Circuited (SAUS)
OC	Open Circular [*Configuration of DNA*] [*Microbiology*]
O/C	Open/Closed [*Mouth*] [*Doll collecting*]
OC	Open Cockpit (SAUS)
OC	Open Coil (SAUS)
OC	Open Collector (IAA)
OC	Open College (AIE)
OC	Open Commitment (SAUS)
OC	Open Contract
OC	Open Control (SAUS)
o/c	Open Cover (AD)
O/C	Open Cover [*Shipping*]
OC	Open Crossing (HEAS)
oc	Open Cup (AD)
OC	Open Cup [*Electronics*]
oc	Opera Comique [*Music*] (GROV)
OC	Opera-Comique [*Comic Opera*] [*French*] (AD)
OC	Opera Company (AD)
OC	Operand Channel (SAUS)
OC	Operating Characteristic
OC	Operating Coil (IAA)
OC	Operating Company
OC	Operating Contractor (SAUS)
OC	Operating Control (SAUS)
OC	Operating Curve (NRCH)
OC	Operational Calculus (SAUS)
OC	Operational Capability (AAG)
OC	Operational Characteristic (SAUS)
OC	Operational Check (MCD)
OC	Operational Circular (HEAS)
OC	Operational Command (SAUS)
OC	Operational Computer (IEEE)
OC	Operational Concept (SAUS)
OC	Operational Condition (SAUS)
OC	Operational Control (SAUS)
OC	Operation Code (IAA)
OC	Operation CORK [*Joan B. Kroc Foundation*] [*CORK is derived from the foundation name*] [*Defunct*] (EA)
OC	Operation Crossroads [*Atomic weapons testing*]
OC	Operations Center [*Military*]
OC	Operations Chief [*Deep Space Network, NASA*]
OC	Operations Commence (SAUS)
OC	Operations Communications (SAUS)
OC	Operations Conductor (MUGU)
OC	Operations Contract (SAUS)
OC	Operations Control
OC	Operations Controller (SAUS)
OC	Operations Coordinator (SAUS)
O/C	Operations Critical (MCD)
OC	Operator Call (SAUS)
OC	Operator Centralization (VLIE)
OC	Operator Circuit [*Telecommunications*] (IAA)
OC	Operator Command (NITA)
OC	Opere Citato [*In the Work Cited*] [*Latin*] (WDAA)
OC	Opportunity Cost (MHDB)

OC..............	Optical Carrier
OC..............	Optical Cavity [*LASER technology*] (EECA)
OC..............	Optical Center (SAUS)
OC..............	Optical Channel (SAUS)
OC..............	Optical Communication (ELAL)
OC..............	Optical Computer (SAUS)
OC..............	Optical Coupler (SAUS)
OC..............	Optic Chiasm [*Anatomy*]
OC..............	Optimal Control (SAUS)
OC..............	Optimizing Control (SAUS)
OC..............	Optometric Corp. (AD)
OC..............	Oral Care [*Denistry*] (DAVI)
oc	Oral Contraceptive [*Medicine*] (AD)
OC..............	Oral Contraceptive [*Endocrinology*]
OC..............	Orbital Check (MCD)
oc	Orbital Check [*NASA*] (NAKS)
OC..............	Order Canceled
OC..............	Order Card
OC..............	Order Code (SAUS)
OC..............	Order Confirmation (SAUS)
OC..............	Order in Council [*A publication*] (DLA)
OC..............	Orderly Corporal [*British*]
OC..............	Order of Canada (SAUS)
OC..............	Order of Cistercians [*Roman Catholic religious order*]
OC..............	Ordinary Capital Account [*Inter-American Development Bank*]
OC..............	Ordinary Chondrite [*A type of meteorite*]
OC..............	Ordinary Colourless (SAUS)
OC..............	Ordnance Chart (MCD)
OC..............	Ordnance College [*Military*] [*British*] (ROG)
OC..............	Ordo Charitatis [*Fathers of the Order of Charity*] [*Roman Catholic religious order*]
OC..............	Organic Carbon
OC..............	Organic Chemistry (SAUS)
OC..............	Organizational Chart
o/c	Organized Crime (AD)
OC..............	Organochlorine [*Also, OCL*] [*Organic chemistry*]
OC..............	Organo Corale [*Choir Organ*] [*Latin*] (AD)
OC..............	Organ of Consultation
OC..............	Oriel College (AD)
OC..............	Oriens Christianus [*A publication*] (ODCC)
OC..............	Original Claim (MAE)
OC..............	Original Cosmopolitans [*Defunct*] (EA)
OC..............	Original Cover
OC..............	Orion Capital Corp. [*NYSE symbol*] (SPSG)
OC..............	Orlando College (AD)
OC..............	Orphans' Court (DLA)
OC..............	Oscillating Current (SAUS)
OC..............	Osteocalcin [*Biochemistry*]
OC..............	Osteochondritis (DB)
OC..............	Osteocyte (SAUS)
OC..............	Otero College (AD)
OC..............	Otter Controls Ltd. (SAUS)
OC..............	Oudh Cases [*India*] [*A publication*] (DLA)
OC..............	Out Cold [*Slang*]
OC..............	Outer Canthus (DB)
OC..............	Outflow Channels [*A filamentary mark on Mars*]
OC..............	Outing Club
OC..............	Outlet Contact
O/C	Out of Charge [*Customs*]
OC..............	Output Card (SAUS)
OC..............	Output Class (SAUS)
OC..............	Output Code (SAUS)
OC..............	Output Computer
OC..............	Output Controller (VLIE)
OC..............	Outside Circumference (MSA)
OC..............	Outsiders Club (EAIO)
OC..............	Over Center (SAUS)
o/c	Overcharge (AD)
O/C	Overcharge
O/C	Overcharging (SAUS)
OC..............	Over-Compounded (SAUS)
OC..............	Overcorrected (SAUS)
oc	Overcurrent (NAKS)
OC..............	Overcurrent
oc	Overdraft Charge [*Banking*] (AD)
OC..............	Overhaul Cycle (SAUS)
OC..............	Overseas Chinese (AD)
OC..............	Overseas Commands [*Air Force*]
O/C	Overseas Country (ODBW)
O/C	Over-the-Counter [*Also, OTC*] [*Stock exchange term*]
OC..............	Over-the-Horizon Compressed (MCD)
OC..............	Oxidation Catalyst [*Automotive engineering*]
OC..............	Oxide Cathode
OC..............	Oxygen Chemisorption (SAUS)
OC..............	Oxygen Consumed
OC..............	Oxygen Cutting [*Welding*]
OC..............	Public Library of Cincinnati and Hamilton County, Cincinnati, OH [*Library symbol*] [*Library of Congress*] (LCLS)
OC-5	Organizing Committee for a Fifth Estate (AD)
OCA	Aeroservicios Carabobo CA (ASERCA) [*Venzuela*] [*ICAO designator*] (FAAC)
OCA	Campbellford Branch, Northumberland County Public Library, Ontario [*Library symbol*] [*National Library of Canada*] (NLC)
OCA	Carmelite Vietnamese of Our Lady of Mt. Carmel (TOCD)

OCA	Cincinnati Art Museum, Cincinnati, OH [*Library symbol*] [*Library of Congress*] (LCLS)
OCA	Creighton University, Alumni Library, Omaha, NE [*OCLC symbol*] (OCLC)
OCA	Observatoire de la Cote d'Azur [*France*]
OCA	Obsessive-Compulsive Anonymous (EA)
OCA	Obstacle Clearance Altitude [*Aviation*] (DA)
oca..............	Ocarina (AD)
OCA	Ocean Control Authority
OCA	Oceanic Control Area [*ICAO*]
OCA	Ocean Reef Club [*Florida*] [*Airport symbol*] (OAG)
OCA	Oceans and Coastal Areas
OCA	Oculocutaneous Albinism [*Medicine*] (DAVI)
OCA	Offensive Counterair [*Army*] (ADDR)
OCA	Office, Comptroller of the Army
OCA	Office of Competitive Assessment [*Department of Commerce*]
OCA	Office of Computing Activities [*Later, DCR*] [*National Science Foundation*]
OCA	Office of Congressional Affairs [*Energy Research and Development Administration*]
OCA	Office of Consumer Advisor [*USDA*]
OCA	Office of Consumer Affairs [*US Postal Service ombudsman*]
OCA	Office of the City Attorney (AD)
OCA	Office of the Community Advocate [*Australian Capital Territory*]
OCA	Officers' Caterer [*Navy*] [*British*]
OCA	Ohio College Association (AD)
OCA	Ohio Courts of Appeals Reports [*A publication*] (DLA)
OCA	Oil Company of Australia (AD)
OCA	Old Comrades Association [*British military*] (DMA)
OCA	Oldsmobile Club of America (EA)
OCA	Olivopontocerebellar Atrophy [*Medicine*] (DMAA)
OCA	Olympic Council of Asia [*Hawalli, Kuwait*] (EAIO)
OCA	Oncovin [*Vincristine*] Cyclophosphamide, Adriamycin [*Doxorubicin*] [*Antineoplastic drug regimen*] (DAVI)
OCA	Ontario Chiropractic Association (SAUS)
OCA	Ontario College of Agriculture
OCA	Ontario College of Art
OCA	Opencast Coal Act [*Town planning*] [*British*]
OCA	Open College of Arts [*British*]
OCA	Open Communication Architecture (CIST)
OCA	Open Component Architecture (SAUS)
OCA	Operational Control Authority [*NATO*]
OCA	Operation Crossroads Africa (EA)
OCA	Operation of Combined Arms (SAUS)
OCA	Operations of Combined Arms (SAUS)
OCA	Oral Contraceptive Agent [*Endocrinology*]
OCA	Orbital Carrier Aircraft (IGSL)
OCA	Order of the Crown in America [*Later, TOCA*] (EA)
OCA	Oregon Corrections Association (AD)
OCA	Organisation Combat Anarchiste [*Anarchist Combat Organization*] [*France*] [*Political party*] (PPW)
OCA	Organizacion de las Cooperativas de America [*Organization of the Cooperatives of America - OCA*] (EAIO)
OCA	Organization of Chinese Americans (EA)
OCA	Organization of the Cooperatives of America (SAUS)
OCA	Original Classification Authority (SAUS)
OCA	[*The*] Orthodox Church of America
OCA	Osteopathic Cranial Association [*Later, CA*]
OCA	Other Competitive Action (SAUS)
OCA	Otterhound Club of America (EA)
OCA	Output Communications Adapter (SAUS)
OCA	Outstanding Claims Advance [*Insurance*] (AIA)
OCA	Owner Controlled Area (SAUS)
OCA	Oxychloride Cement Association [*Defunct*]
OCAA	Oklahoma City-Ada-Atoka Railway Co. [*AAR code*]
OCAA	Organization of Central American Armies (AD)
OCAAF	Order of the Chief of the Army Air Forces
OCAAR........	Occupational Accidents Analysis and Reporting
OCAB	Cannington Branch, Brock Township Public Library, Ontario [*Library symbol*] [*National Library of Canada*] (BIB)
OCAB	Overseas Correspondents Association Bangladesh (BUAC)
OCAC	Ocean Acre Project [*Marine science*] (MSC)
OCAC	Office of the Chief of Air Corps [*World War II*]
OCAC	Officer Commanding Administrative Centre [*World War I*] [*British*]
OCAC	Open-Circuit After-Charge [*Automotive engineering*]
OCAC	Operations, Control, and Analysis Center (DOMA)
OCACV	Open-Circuit After-Charge Voltage [*Automotive engineering*]
OCad	Cadiz Public Library, Cadiz, OH [*Library symbol*] [*Library of Congress*] (LCLS)
OCAD	Occlusive Cartoid Artery Disease [*Medicine*] (DMAA)
OCAD	Occupational and Career Analysis Development (SAUS)
OCAD	Optical Character and Detect (SAUS)
OCAD	Orcad, Inc. [*NASDAQ symbol*] (SAG)
OCADA	Office of the Chief, Air Defense Artillery
OCADS	Oklahoma City Air Defense Sector (SAA)
OCAE	United States Army Engineer Division, Ohio River, Technical Library, Cincinnati,OH [*Library symbol*] [*Library of Congress*] (LCLS)
OCAF	Office, Chief of Aerospace (SAA)
OCAF	Oklahomans for Children and Families
OCAFF	Office, Chief of Army Field Forces
OCAHO	Office of the Chief Administrative Hearing Officer (SAUS)
OCAI	Orthodontic Centers of Amer [*NASDAQ symbol*] (TTSB)
OCAI	Orthodontic Centers of America, Inc. [*NASDAQ symbol*] (SAG)
OCAJ...........	American Jewish Periodical Center, Cincinnati, OH [*Library symbol*] [*Library of Congress*] (LCLS)

OCAJA .... American Jewish Archives, Cincinnati, OH [*Library symbol*] [*Library of Congress*] (LCLS)

OCal............. Caldwell Public Library, Caldwell, OH [*Library symbol*] [*Library of Congress*] (LCLS)

OCAL .... Ocal, Inc. [*NASDAQ symbol*] (SAG)

Ocal............. Octo Archives, Inc., Laurel, MD [*Library symbol*] [*Library of Congress*] (LCLS)

ocal .... On-Line Cryptanalytic Aid Language [*Computer science*] (AD)

OCAL .... Online Cryptanalytic Aid Language [*Computer science*]

OCAL .... Organization of Communist Action in Lebanon (PD)

OCAL .... Overseas Containers Australia Ltd

OCAL .... Overseas Containers of Australia, Ltd. (AD)

OCAL .... [*The*] Oxford Companion to American Literature [*A publication*]

OCALA .... Open Common Annotation Language (SAUS)

OCALC .... Oklahoma City Air Logistic Center [*Formerly, OCAMA*] (MCD)

O'Callaghan New Neth... O'Callaghan's History of New Netherland [*A publication*] (DLA)

OCAM .... Afro-Malagasy Common Organization (SAUS)

OCAM .... Common Organization of African, Malagasy, and Mauritian States (EBF)

OCAM .... Office, Computing, and Accounting Machinery

OCAM .... Ontario Center for Advanced Manufacturing (SAUS)

OCAM .... Organisation Commune Africaine et Mauricienne [*African and Mauritian Common Organization*] [*Formerly, Organisation Commune Africaine et Malgache*]

OCAMA .... Oklahoma City Air Materiel Area [*Later, OCALC*]

OCAMA-SED... Oklahoma City Air Materiel Area [*later, OCALC*] Service Engineering Division

OCamd......... Preble County District Library, Camden Branch, Camden, OH [*Library symbol*] [*Library of Congress*] (LCLS)

OCAMM .... Organisation Commune Africaine, Malgache, et Mauricienne [*African, Malagasy, and Mauritian Common Organization*] [*Formerly, Organisation Commune Africaine et Malgache*] [*Later, OCAM*]

OCan........... Canton Public Library Association, Canton, OH [*Library symbol*] [*Library of Congress*] (LCLS)

OCAN .... Officer Candidate Airman

OC & E .... Oregon, California, and Eastern Railroad (AD)

OC & R .... Operations, Commitments, and Requirements [*Military*]

OC & S .... Ordnance Center and School [*Army*] (RDA)

OC&T........... Office of Certification and Training (AD)

OCanK .... Kent State University, Stark County Regional Campus, Canton, OH [*Library symbol*] [*Library of Congress*] (LCLS)

OCanM .... Malone College, Canton, OH [*Library symbol*] [*Library of Congress*] (LCLS)

OCanS .... Stark County District Library, Canton, OH [*Library symbol*] [*Library of Congress*] (LCLS)

OCanW .... Walsh College, Canton, OH [*Library symbol*] [*Library of Congress*] (LCLS)

OCAO .... Athenaeum of Ohio, Eugene H. Maly Library, Cincinnati, OH [*Library symbol*] [*Library of Congress*] (LCLS)

OCAP .... Capreol Public Library, Ontario [*Library symbol*] [*National Library of Canada*] (NLC)

OCAP .... Oceans and Coastal Areas Programme (SAUS)

OCAP .... Ontario Career Action Program (SAUS)

OCAP .... Open Channel Air Preheater [*Heat exchanger*]

OCAP .... Operating Criteria and Procedures (SAUS)

OCA/PAC...... Oceans and Coastal Areas Programme Activity Centre (SAUS)

OCAPO......... Office of Compliance Analysis and Program Operations [*Environmental Protection Agency*] (GFGA)

OCAPT .... Ontario Center for Automotive Parts Technology (SAUS)

OCAQ .... Ordre de Comptables Agrees du Quebec [*Canada*] (DD)

OCAR .... Cargill Branch, Bruce County Public Library, Ontario [*Library symbol*] [*National Library of Canada*] (NLC)

OCAR .... Office of the Chief, Army Reserve (AABC)

OCARD........ Cardinal Public Library, Ontario [*Library symbol*] [*National Library of Canada*] (BIB)

OCareyS ...... Our Lady of Carey Seminary, Carey, OH [*Library symbol*] [*Library of Congress*] (LCLS)

OCARINA ..... Ocean, Atmosphere, Research and Investigation with Acoustic Techniques (SAUS)

OCarm .... Calced Carmelites (TOCD)

OCarm .... Carmelite Fathers and Brothers (TOCD)

ocarm .... Carmelite Fathers and Brothers (TOCD)

OCarm .... Carmelite Nuns of the Ancient Observance (TOCD)

OCarm .... Carmelite Sisters (Corpus Christi) (TOCD)

OCarm .... Carmelite Sisters for Aged and Infirm (TOCD)

OCarm .... Congregation of Our Lady of Mount Carmel (TOCD)

OCarm .... Institute of the Sisters of Our Lady of Mt. Carmel (TOCD)

OCARM........ Order of Brothers of the Blessed Virgin Mary of Mount Carmel [*Rome, Italy*] (EAIO)

OCART .... Cartier Public Library, Ontario [*Library symbol*] [*National Library of Canada*] (NLC)

ocart .... Order of Carthusians (TOCD)

OCart .... Order of Carthusians [*Roman Catholic religious order*]

OCartSC....... Saint Charles Seminary, Carthagena, OH [*Library symbol*] [*Library of Congress*] (LCLS)

OCAS .... Office, Coordinator of Army Studies (AABC)

OCAS .... Office of Carrier Accounts and Statistics [*of CAB*]

OCAS .... Office of Civil Aviation Security (AD)

OCAS .... Office of the Chief of Air Service [*World War II*]

OCAS .... Officer-in-Charge of Armament Supply

OCAS .... Ohio Casualty Corp. [*NASDAQ symbol*] (NQ)

OCAS .... Ohio College of Applied Science

OCAS .... Online Cryptanalytic Aid System [*Computer science*] (IEEE)

OCAS .... Ordnance Configuration Accounting System [*Navy*]

OCAS .... Organization of Central American States [*See also ODECA*] [*San Salvador, El Salvador*] (EAIO)

OCAS .... Out of Controlled Airspace [*Aviation*] (FAAC)

OCASA .... Overseas Chinese Association of South Australia

OCASP .... Olivetti Complete Accounting and Stock Package (SAUS)

Ocass Pap Fla State Collect Arthropods... Occasional Papers. Florida State Collection of Arthropods (SAUS)

O Cat .... Old Catalan (AD)

OCAT .... Optometric College Aptitude Test (WDAA)

OCAT .... Optometry College Admissions Test (WDAA)

OCATE .... Oregon Center for Advanced Technology Education (SAUS)

OCATOUR .... Office National Centrafricain du Tourisme (EY)

OCAU .... Observation, Classification, and Allocation Unit (WDAA)

OCAW .... Oil, Chemical, and Atomic Workers International Union (EA)

OCAW .... Organization of Chinese American Women (EA)

OCB .... Cache Bay Public Library, Ontario [*Library symbol*] [*National Library of Canada*] (NLC)

OCB .... Cincinnati Bible Seminary, Cincinnati, OH [*Library symbol*] [*Library of Congress*] (LCLS)

OCB .... Obsessive-Compulsive Behavior (MELL)

OCB .... Ocean Crust Boundary (SAUS)

OCB .... Officer Career Brief [*Resume*] [*Military*]

OCB .... Officers' Cadet Battalion [*British*]

OCB .... Off-Machine Coated Board [*Paper*] (DGA)

OCB .... Offshore Certification Bureau [*British*] (CB)

OCB .... Oil [*Operated*] Circuit Breaker

ocb .... Oil Circuit Breaker (AD)

OCB .... Oil Collection Basin (NRCH)

OCB .... Oil Control Board [*British*]

OCB .... Oil-Cooled Disc Brake [*Automotive engineering*]

OCB .... Oil-operated Circuit Breaker (SAUS)

OCB .... Olivocochlear Bundle (SAUS)

OCB .... Operated Circuit Breaker (SAUS)

OCB .... Operations Center Building (SAUS)

OCB .... Operations Coordinating Board [*Terminated, 1961*] [*National Security Council*]

OCB .... Outer Core Barrel (SAUS)

OCB .... Outgoing Calls Barred [*Telecommunications*] (TEL)

OCB .... Output Current Booster

OCB .... Override Control BITS [*Binary Digits*] [*Computer science*]

OCB .... Over-the-Counter Batch [*Stock exchange term*] (MHDW)

OCBA .... Ortho-Chlorobenzoic Acid [*Organic chemistry*]

OCBB .... Operating Cost Board Budget (ACAE)

OCBC .... Ortho-Chlorobenzyl Chloride [*Organic chemistry*]

OCBC .... Overseas Chinese Banking Corp. (AD)

OCBF .... Outer Cortical Blood-Flow [*Medicine*] (DB)

OCBH .... Bethesda Base Hospital, Information Resource Center, Cincinnati, OH [*Library symbol*] [*Library of Congress*] (LCLS)

oc b/l .... Ocean Bill of Lading (AD)

OC/B/L .... Ocean Bill of Lading [*Shipping*]

OCBN .... Ortho-Chlorobenzonitrile [*Organic chemistry*]

OCBOA........ Other Comprehensive Bases of Accounting (ADA)

OCBP .... Output Control Block Pointer (SAUS)

OCBR .... Other than Cost Base Review [*DoD*]

OCBR .... Output Channel Buffer Register [*Computer science*] (IAA)

OCB(S)........ Oil Control Board, Supply [*British*]

OCBSD........ Officer Commanding, Base Supply Depot (SAUS)

OCC .... CARSTAB Corp., Research Library, Cincinnati, OH [*Library symbol*] [*Library of Congress*] (LCLS)

OCC .... Coca [*Ecuador*] [*Airport symbol*] (OAG)

OCC .... Object-Centered Coordinate (DMAA)

OCC .... Object Class Code [*Military*] (AFM)

OCC .... Obus a Charge Creuse (SAUS)

occ .... Occasional

occ............. Occasionally (AD)

OCC .... Occasionally

occ............. Occidental (SHCU)

occ............. Occipital [*or Occiput*] [*Anatomy*] (MAE)

OCC .... Occiput (SAUS)

OCC .... Occluded Corrosion Cell (PDAA)

OCC .... Occlusion

OCC .... Occultation [*Astronomy*]

Occ .... Occulting (AD)

OCC .... Occulting Light [*Navigation signal*]

occ............. Occupation (AD)

OCC .... Occupation (AFM)

OCC .... Occupied (IAA)

OCC .... Occupied Command Center [*Military*]

OCC .... Occurrence

Occ .... Occurs (ILCA)

OCC .... Ocean City College [*Maryland*]

OCC .... Ocean Coordinating Committee [*IEEE*] (MSC)

OCC .... Ocean Cruising Club [*British*] (DI)

OCC .... Oceanic Control Center (OA)

OCC .... OCLC [*Online Computer Library Center*] Library, Columbus, OH [*OCLC symbol*] (OCLC)

OCC .... Octagon Car Club [*Later, MOCC*] (EAIO)

OCC .... Octal Correction Cards [*Computer science*]

OCC .... Ocutech Canada [*Vancouver Stock Exchange symbol*]

OCC .... Office Communications Cabinet (SAUS)

OCC .... Office of Cancer Communications [*Department of Health and Human Services*] (GFGA)

OCC .... Office of Chemical Control (COE)

occ............. Office of Contract Compliance (NAKS)

OCC .... Office of Contract Compliance [*NASA*] (NASA)

OCC .... Office of the Chief Counsel [*U.S. Food and Drug Administration*]
OCC .... Office of the Comptroller of the Currency [*Department of the Treasury*]
OCC .... Office of the Director of Command, Control, and Communications [*Air Force*]
OCC .... Officer Candidate Class (SAUS)
OCC .... Officer Commanding, Camp (SAUS)
OCC .... Officers' Chief Cook
OCC .... Official Custodian of Charities [*British*]
OCC .... Offset Course Computer (SAUS)
OCC .... Offshore Construction Council (BUAC)
OCC .... Offshore Craft Conference (BUAC)
OCC .... Offsite Coordination Center [*Environmental science*] (COE)
OCC .... Ohio Circuit Reports [*or Decisions*] [*A publication*] (DLA)
OCC .... Ohio College of Chiropody
OCC .... Ohio Conservation Consortium [*Library network*]
OCC .... Oklahoma Crime Commission (AD)
OCC .... Old Corrugated Container [*Paper recycling*]
OCC .... Olney Communication College (AD)
OCC .... Olney Community College (SAUS)
OCC .... Olympic Committee Congress
OCC .... Omnibus Crime Control and Safe Streets Act [*1968*]
OCC .... Onondaga Community College (AD)
OCC .... Onsite Construction Contractor (SAUS)
OCC .... Open Channel Cooperative
OCC .... Open Circuit Characteristic (IAA)
OCC .... Open-Circuit Characteristic (SAUS)
OCC .... Open, Cooperative Computing (SAUS)
OCC .... Operating Characteristics Curve
OCC .... Operational Computer Complex (KSC)
OCC .... Operational Control Center (or Centre) (SAUS)
OCC .... Operations Command Center (ACAE)
OCC .... Operations Control Center [*or Console*] (AFM)
occ .... Operations Control Center (NAKS)
OCC .... Operations Control Console (SAUS)
OCC .... Operator Control Command (BUR)
OCC .... Operator Control Console [*Canadian Navy*]
OCC .... Operator's Computer Console
OCC .... Oppenheimer Capital Ltd. [*NYSE symbol*] (SPSG)
OCC .... Oppenheimer Cap L.P. [*NYSE symbol*] (TTSB)
OCC .... Opposition Coordinating Committee (SAUS)
OCC .... Optical Circuit and Component (NITA)
OCC .... Option Clearing Corp.
OCC .... Oral Cholecystography [*Medicine*] (DMAA)
OCC .... Oral Contraceptive Council [*Defunct*] (EA)
OCC .... Orange Carpet Crowd [*An association*]
OCC .... Orange Coast College [*Formerly, OCJC*] [*Costa Mesa, CA*]
OCC .... Order Control Card (VLIE)
OCC .... Order of Calced Carmelites [*Roman Catholic religious order*] (DICI)
OCC .... Ordnance Command Converter [*Military*] (IAA)
OCC .... Ordo Carmelitarum Calceatorum [*Carmelites*] [*Roman Catholic religious order*]
OCC .... Organic Carbon Cycle
OCC .... Organic Consultative Committee [*Victoria, Australia*]
OCC .... Organisation Combat Communiste [*Communist Combat Organization*] [*France*] [*Political party*] (PPW)
OCC .... Organization Chart and Charter (SAUS)
OCC .... Osborne Computer Corporation (NITA)
OCC .... Other Common Carrier [*Telecommunications*]
OCC .... Other Communications Company
OCC .... Outer Critics Circle (EA)
OCC .... Output Circuit Check [*Electronics*]
OCC .... Output Code Converter (SAUS)
OCC .... Output Control Character (SAUS)
OCC .... Owens Community College in Ohio (SAUS)
OCCA .... Ocean Cargo Clearance Authority (DOMA)
OCCA .... Office, Chief of Civil Affairs
OCCA .... Office of Compliance and Consumer Assistance (SAUS)
OCCA .... Officer-in-Charge of Civilian Affairs [*in newly occupied countries*] [*Army*] [*World War II*]
OCCA .... Oil and Colour Chemists' Association
OCCA .... Omnibus Crime Control Act of 1970 (OICC)
OCCA .... Open, Cooperative Computing Architecture (SAUS)
OCCA .... Organized Crime Control Act of 1970
OCCABA ...... Overseas Communications Cooperation Association (SAUS)
OCCABA ...... Open Circuit Compressed Air Breathing Apparatus (SAUS)
OCCAC .... Ohio Community College Athletic Conference (PSS)
OCCAM .... Ocean Circulation and Climate Advanced Modelling
occas .... Occasional (AD)
Occas .... Occasional (DIAR)
OCCAS .... Occasional
Occas .... Occasional Light [*Navigation signal*]
occas .... Occasionally (NTIO)
OCCASL ...... Occasional
Occas Pap Inst Min Metall... Occasional Papers Institution of Mining and Metallurgy (SAUS)
Occas Pap R Coll Gen Pract... Occasional Paper/Royal College of General Practitioners (SAUS)
Occas Pap San Diego Soc Nat Hist... Occasional Papers. San Diego Society of Natural History (SAUS)
OCCB .... Operational Configuration Control Board (AFM)
OCCB .... Organized Crime Control Bureau (LAIN)
OCC-BL .... Occult Blood [*Medicine*] (DAVI)
OCCBP .... Organization for Collectors of Covered Bridge Postcards (EA)
OCCC .... Obfuscated C Code Contest (SAUS)

OCCC .... Oil Control Coordination Committee (AD)
OCCC .... Oocyte-Corona-Cumulus Complex
OCCC .... Open Chest Cardiac Compression [*Cardiology*] (DAVI)
OCCC .... Orange County Community College (AD)
OCCC .... Organized Crime-Control Commission [*California*] (AD)
OCCCA .... Office of Congressional, Community, and Consumer Affairs
OCCCE .... Organization for Coordination and Cooperation in the Control of Major Endemic Diseases
OCCCF .... Operator Communication and Control Facility (SAUS)
Oc C Cm O... Office of the Chief Chemical Officer (AD)
OCCD .... Com Dev Ltd., Cambridge, Ontario [*Library symbol*] [*National Library of Canada*] (NLC)
occd .... Occupied (AD)
OCCDC .... Oregon Coastal Conservation and Development Commission (AD)
OCC-E .... Office of the Chief of Communications-Electronics [*Army*] (AABC)
OCCE .... Oklahoma Citizen's Commission on Education (EDAC)
OCCE .... Operational Clothing and Combat Equipment (SAUS)
OCCEDCA.... Organization for Co-Ordination in Control of Endemic Diseases in Central Africa (EA)
OCCF .... Oklahoma City Community Foundation (AD)
OCCF .... Operator Communication and Control Facility [*IBM Corp.*]
OCCF .... Optical Cable [*NASDAQ symbol*] (TTSB)
OCCF .... Optical Cable Corp. [*NASDAQ symbol*] (SAG)
OCCGE .... Organisation de Coordination et de Cooperation pour la Lutte Contre les Grandes Endemies [*Organization for Co-Ordination and Co-Operation in the Control of Major Endemic Diseases*] (EAIO)
OCCGERMDL... Army of Occupation of Germany Medal [*Military decoration*]
OCCH .... Childrens Hospital Research Foundation, Research Library, Cincinnati (SAUS)
OCCH .... Children's Hospital Research Foundation, Research Library, Cincinnati, OH [*Library symbol*] [*Library of Congress*] (LCLS)
OCCH .... Office, Chief of Chaplains [*Formerly, OC of Ch*] [*Army*] (AABC)
Occ Heal ANZ... Occupational Health Australia and New Zealand [*A publication*]
Occ Health&Sfty... Occupational Health and Safety (SAUS)
OCCI .... Optical Coincidence Coordinate Indexing (PDAA)
Occident ...... Occidental (DIAR)
Occidental C... Occidental College (GAGS)
OCCIM .... Christ Hospital Institute of Medical Research, Research Library, Cincinnati, OH [*Library symbol*] [*Library of Congress*] (LCLS)
OCCIN .... Process Technology Department, Inco Ltd., Copper Cliff, Ontario [*Library symbol*] [*National Library of Canada*] (BIB)
occip .... Occipital (AD)
OCCIP .... Occiput [*Anatomy*] (WDAA)
OcciPet .... Occidental Petroleum Corp. [*Associated Press*] (SAG)
OcciPt .... Occidental Petroleum Corp. [*Associated Press*] (SAG)
OCCIS .... Operational Command and Control Intelligence System [*Army*] (AABC)
OCCIS .... Operations Command and Control Information System [*Military*]
occl .... Occlude (AD)
OCCL .... Occluded (SAUS)
OCCL .... Occluding (SAUS)
OCCL .... Occlusal (SAUS)
OCCL .... Ontario Community College Librarians [*Canada*] (AD)
OCCM .... Ocean Carbon Cycle Model (SAUS)
OCCM .... Office of Commercial Communications Management (AFM)
OCCM .... Open Chest Cardiac Massage [*Cardiology*] (DAVI)
OCCM .... Optical Counter-Countermeasures
OCCMDL ..... Army of Occupation Medal [*Military decoration*]
OCCMDL ..... Occupation Medal (SAUS)
OCCMED ..... Occupational Medicine (AABC)
OCCMH .... Cambridge Memorial Hospital, Ontario [*Library symbol*] [*National Library of Canada*] (BIB)
OCCMLC ..... Office, Chief, Chemical Corps [*Army*]
OCCMLO ..... Office of the Chief Chemical Officer [*Military*]
OCCMS .... Occupational Measurement Squadron [*Air Force*]
OCCN .... Occasion
OCCN .... Occasionally (SAUS)
Occ N .... Occasional Notes, Canada Law Times [*A publication*] (DLA)
OCCN .... Occidental Nebraska Federal Savings Bank (SAUS)
Occ Newsl ... Occasional Newsletter [*American Bar Association, Committee on Environmental Law*] [*A publication*] (ILCA)
OCC/NIBS .... Ohio Consultive Council of the National Institute of Building Sciences (SAUS)
OCC NS .... Ohio Circuit Court Reports, New Series [*A publication*] (DLA)
OCCO .... Office Canadien de Commercialisation des Oeufs
OCCO .... Office of the Chief Chemical Officer [*Military*] (AAG)
OCCP .... Octachlorocyclopentene [*Organic chemistry*]
OCCP .... Outside Communications Cable Plant (CET)
Occ Pap Univ NSW... University of New South Wales. Occasional Papers [*A publication*]
OCCPR .... Open-Chest Cardiopulmonary Resuscitation
OCCR .... Cramahe Township Public Library, Castleton, Ontario [*Library symbol*] [*National Library of Canada*] (BIB)
OCCR .... Overseas Custody (Child Removal)
OCCS .... Oce Copy Control System (NITA)
OCCS .... Office of Combined Chiefs of Staff [*World War II*]
OCCS .... Office of Computer and Communication Systems (NITA)
OCCS .... Officer Career Counseling System [*Army*] (RDA)
OCCS .... Operational Command and Control System [*Army*] (AABC)
OCCS .... Optical Contrast Contour Seeker
OCCS .... Ordnance and Chemical Center and School [*Army*] (MCD)
OCCSA .... Ohio Correctional and Court Services Association (AD)
OCCSLY ...... Occasionally (SAUS)
OCCSPEC..... Occupational Specialities [*A publication*] (DNAB)

OCCT .... Collingwood Township Public Library, Clarksburg, Ontario [*Library symbol*] [*National Library of Canada*] (NLC)
OccTh .... Occupational Therapist (SAUS)
occ th .... Occupational Therapy (AD)
OccTh .... Occupational Therapy [*or Therapist*] (DAVI)
OccuHlt .... Occupational Health & Rehabilitation, Inc. [*Associated Press*] (SAG)
OCCULT ...... Optical Coven Communications Using Laser Transceivers (SAUS)
OCCULT ...... Optical Covert Communications Using LASER Transceivers (MCD)
OCCULT ...... Ordered Computer Collation of Unprepared Literary Texts
OCCULT ...... Orser Complete Conversational User-Language Translator (SAUS)
occup .... Occupation (AD)
OCCUP .... Occupational
OCCUPON .... Occupation (ROG)
OCCUPTN .... Occupation
OCCUPTNL ... Occupational
OccuSys .... OccuSystems, Inc. [*Associated Press*] (SAG)
OCCWC .... Office of Chief of Counsel, War Crimes [*Allied German Occupation Forces*]
OC Cycle ...... Open-Close Cycle (SAUS)
OCD .... Carmelitas del Sagrado Corazon (TOCD)
OCD .... Carmelite Sisters of the Most Sacred Heart of Los Angeles (TOCD)
OCD .... Central Office for General Defense (SAUS)
OCD .... Discalced Carmelite Fathers (TOCD)
ocd .... Discalced Carmelite Friars (TOCD)
OCD .... Discalced Carmelite Nuns (TOCD)
ocd .... Obsessive Compulsive Disorder [*Medicine*] (AD)
ocd .... Obsessive-Compulsive Disorder [*Psychology*]
OCD .... Occupation Centres for Defectives [*British*]
OCD .... Ocean Chemistry Division [*Atlantic Oceanographic and Meteorological Laboratory*] (USDC)
OCD .... Off Chip Driver (VLIE)
OCD .... Office of Child Development [*HEW*]
OCD .... Office of Civil Defense
OCD .... Office of Civilian Defense [*Within Office of Emergency Management*] [*World War II*]
OCD .... Office of Collection and Dissemination (SAUS)
OCD .... Office of Community Development [*HUD*]
OCD .... Office of the Center Director [*U.S. Food and Drug Admistration*]
OCD .... Offshore and Coastal Dispersion (GNE)
OCD .... Ohio Circuit Court Decisions [*A publication*] (DLA)
OCD .... Online Communications Drive [*or Driver*] [*Computer science*] (WDAA)
ocd .... On-Line Communications Driver [*Computer science*] (AD)
OCD .... Operational Capability Date (AAG)
ocd .... Operational Capability Date (AD)
OCD .... Operational Capability Demonstration (AAGC)
OCD .... Operational Capability Development
OCD .... Operational Concept Demonstration (SAUS)
OCD .... Operational Concept Document
OCD .... Operations Concept Document
ocd .... Optical Character Definition [*Computer science*] (AD)
OCD .... Orbis Computer Deutschland (SAUS)
OCD .... Ordnance Classification of Defects [*Navy*]
OCD .... Ordo Carmelitarum Discalceatorum [*Order of Discalced, or Barefoot, Carmelites*] [*Roman Catholic religious order*]
OCD .... Organ-Confined Disease [*Medicine*] (MELL)
OCD .... Osteochondritis Dissecans [*Medicine*]
OC/D .... Other Cargo Damage (SAUS)
OCD .... Other Checkable Deposits [*Federal Reserve system*] (GFGA)
OCD .... Outer Canthal Distance [*Medicine*] (MELL)
O/C/D .... Out of Collector's District [*Bookselling*] (ROG)
OCD .... Output-only Console Device (SAUS)
ocd .... Ovarian Cholesterol Depletion [*Medicine*] (AD)
OCD .... Ovarian Cholesterol Depletion [*Test*]
OCD .... Overhaul Consumption Data
OCD .... [*The*] Oxford Classical Dictionary [*A publication*] (ODCC)
OCD .... Oxygen Cost Diagram (DMAA)
OCDA .... Officer Commanding, Divisional Artillery (SAUS)
OCDA .... Ordnance Corps Detroit Arsenal (SAUS)
o/cdbd .... Oil on Cardboard (VRA)
OCDD .... Octachlorodibenzodioxin [*Organic chemistry*]
OCDD .... On-Line Call Detail Delivery [*AT&T*] (CIST)
OCDE .... Officer Commanding, Divisional Engineers (SAUS)
OCDE .... Organisation de Cooperation et de Developpement Economiques [*Organization for Economic Cooperation and Development - OECD*] [*France*] (EAIO)
OCDE .... Organizacion de Cooperacion y Desarrollo Economicos [*Organization for Economic Cooperation and Development - OECD*] [*Spain*] (MSC)
OCDETF .... Organized Crime Drug Enforcement Task Force
OCDF .... Operations Control and Display Facility [*Military*] (RDA)
OCDM .... Office of Civil and Defense Mobilization [*Merged with Office of Emergency Planning*]
OCDM .... Offshore and Coastal Dispersion Model [*Environmental science*] (COE)
OCDMS .... On-Board Checkout and Data Management System (MCD)
OCDN .... Order for Correction of Defect of Nonconformance
OCDP .... Officer Career Development Program
OCDQ .... Organizational Climate Description Questionnaire
OCDr .... Drackett Co., Research and Development Library, Cincinnati, OH [*Library symbol*] [*Library of Congress*] (LCLS)
OCDR .... Office of Collateral Development Responsibility (AFM)
OCDR .... Officer Control Distribution Report
OCDR .... Orbiter Critical Design Review [*NASA*] (NASA)
OCDRE .... Organic-Cooled Deuterium Reactor Experiment [*Nuclear energy*]
OCDS .... Officer Commanding, Divisional Signals (SAUS)

OCDS .... Offline Control Data Set (SAUS)
OCDS .... Output Command Data Set [*Computer science*] (ELAL)
OCDS .... Overseas College of Defence Studies [*British*]
OCDS .... Secular Order of Discalced Carmelites [*Rome, Italy*] (EAIO)
O/CDT .... Officer Cadet [*Military*] (WDAA)
O/Cdt .... Officer-Cadet (AD)
OCdt .... Officer-Commandant (SAUS)
OCD Test ...... Ovarian Cholestrol Depletion Test (SAUS)
OCDU .... Optics Coupling Data [*or Display*] Unit [*Guidance and navigation*] (KSC)
OCDU .... Optics Coupling Display Unit (SAUS)
OCDW .... Ocean Climate Data Workshop (SAUS)
OCE .... Edgecliff College, Cincinnati, OH [*Library symbol*] [*Library of Congress*] (LCLS)
OCE .... Helicocean [*France*] [*ICAO designator*] (FAAC)
OCE .... Ocean City [*Maryland*] [*Airport symbol*] (OAG)
OCE .... Ocean Color Experiment [*NASA*]
OCE .... Ocean Covered Earth (OA)
Oce .... Oceanic [*Record label*]
OCE .... Odessa Commodity Exchange [*Ukraine*] (EY)
OCE .... Office, Chief of Engineers [*Army*]
OCE .... Office of Career Education [*Office of Education*]
OCE .... Office of Coastal Environment [*National Oceanic and Atmospheric Administration*]
OCE .... Office of Criminal Enforcement [*Environmental Protection Agency*] (EPA)
OCE .... Office of Cultural Exchange [*Department of State*]
OCE .... Office of the Chief Economist (AAGC)
OCE .... Office of the Director of Civil Engineering [*Air Force*]
OCE .... Officer Commanding Exercises [*Military*]
OCE .... Officer Conducting the Exercise [*Navy, Coast Guard*] [*Military*]
OCE .... Officer Corps Engineers
OCE .... Omega Chi Epsilon [*Honor society*] (EA)
OCE .... OMGUS [*Office of Military Government, United States*] Civilian Employees Association [*Post-World War II, Germany*]
OCE .... Ontario College of Education
OCE .... Open Collaborative Environment [*Apple Computer, Inc.*]
oce .... Operational Control Equipment (AD)
OCE .... Optical Control Electronics (SAUS)
OCE .... Orbital Computations Engineer (ACAE)
OCE .... Oregon, California & Eastern Railway Co. [*AAR code*]
OCE .... Oregon College of Education
OCE .... Organizational Climate Exercise II [*Test*] (TMMY)
OCE .... Oscillating Current Element
OCE .... Other Common carrier channel Equipment (SAUS)
OCE .... Other Controllable Expenses (MEDA)
OCE .... Unesco Division of Marine Sciences (SAUS)
OCEA .... Outstanding Civil Engineering Achievement [*Award*] [*American Society of Civil Engineers*]
OCEA Award ... Outstanding Civil Engineering Achievement Award (SAUS)
OCEAC .... Organisation de Coordination pour la Lutte Contre les Endemies en Afrique Centrale [*Organization for Co-Ordination in Control of Endemic Diseases in Central Africa - OCCEDCA*] (EAIO)
OCEAN .... Ocean Color Environment Archive Network (SAUS)
OCEAN .... Ocean Colour European Archive Network (SAUS)
Ocean .... Oceania (DIAR)
OCEAN .... Oceanographic Coordination, Evaluation, and Analysis Network
Ocean .... Ocean Transport and Trading Ltd. (SAUS)
OCEAN .... Organisation de la Communaute Europeenne des Avitailleurs des Navires [*Ship Suppliers' Organization of the European Community - SSOEC*] [*Hague, Netherlands*] (EAIO)
Ocean&Shoreline Manage... Ocean and Shoreline Management (SAUS)
OCEANAV .... Naval Oceanography Command [*Marine science*] (MSC)
OCEANAV .... Oceanographer of the Navy
OCEANAVINST... Naval Oceanographic Office Instruction
OceanB .... Ocean Bio-Chem, Inc. [*Associated Press*] (SAG)
OCEANDEVRON... Oceanographic Development Squadron [*Navy*] (DNAB)
Ocean E .... Ocean Engineer (PGP)
Oceaner .... Oceaneering International, Inc. [*Associated Press*] (SAG)
OceanF .... Ocean Financial Corp. [*Associated Press*] (SAG)
OCEANIC ...... Ocean Information Center (SAUS)
OCEANIC ...... Ocean Network Information Center [*Information service or system*] (IID)
Ocean Inst ... Oceanografiska Institute [*Oceanographic Institute*] [*Goeteborg, Sweden*] (AD)
OCEANLANT... Ocean Subarea (Atlantic) [*NATO*] (NATG)
Ocean Man... Ocean Management [*A publication*] (ILCA)
OCEANO .... Oceanic Fluxes of NO and NOx (SAUS)
oceano .... Oceanologist (AD)
oceanog .... Oceanography (AD)
OCEANOG ..... Oceanography
OCEANOGR ... Oceanographer (SAUS)
OCEANOGR ... Oceanographic (SAUS)
Oceanogr Mar Biol Annu Rev... Oceanography and Marine Biology: Annual Review (SAUS)
Oceanogr Mar Biol Annu Rev... Oceanogrraphy and Marine Biology Annual Review (SAUS)
OceanOpt ...... Ocean Optique Distributors, Inc. [*Associated Press*] (SAG)
OCEAN-PC... Ocean Personal Computer Project (SAUS)
OCEANS .... Offshore and Civil Engineering Analysis System (SAUS)
OCEANS .... Omnibus Conference on Experimental Aspects of NMR [*Nuclear Magnetic Resonance*] Spectroscopy (MUGU)
OCEANSAT... Ocean Studies Satellite (SAUS)
OCEANSYSLANT... Ocean Systems, Atlantic
OCEANSYSPAC... Ocean Systems, Pacific

OCEC .... Officials Committee on Expenditure Control (SAUS)
OCED .... Office of Comprehensive Employment Development [*Department of Labor*]
OCED .... Organization for Economic Co-Operation and Development (WPI)
OCedC .... Cedarville College, Cedarville, OH [*Library symbol*] [*Library of Congress*] (LCLS)
OCEFT......... Corbeil Branch, East Ferris Township Public Library, Ontario [*Library symbol*] [*National Library of Canada*] (NLC)
OCEI............. Ocean Construction Equipment Inventory (DNAB)
OCel............. Dwyer-Mercer County District Library, Celina, OH [*Library symbol*] [*Library of Congress*] (LCLS)
OCEL............ Optical Coating Evaluation Laboratory (AD)
OCEL............ Oxford Companion to English Literature [*A publication*] (AD)
OCELAC ...... Camden East Branch, Lennox and Addington County Library, Ontario [*Library symbol*] [*National Library of Canada*] (NLC)
OCEleC .... Cincinnati Electronics Corporation, Cincinnati, OH [*Library symbol*] [*Library of Congress*] (LCLS)
O Celt .... Old Celtic (AD)
OCEM .... Office of Cooperative Environmental Management (SAUS)
OCEmI .... Emery Industries, Inc., Research Library, Cincinnati, OH [*Library symbol*] [*Library of Congress*] (LCLS)
OCEN .... Oce-Van der Grinten NV [*Netherlands*] [*NASDAQ symbol*]
OCENY .... Oce-van der Grinten ADR [*NASDAQ symbol*] (TTSB)
Oce-NY .... Oce-Van der Grinten NV [*Associated Press*] (SAG)
OCEO .... Office of the Commissioner for Equal Opportunity [*Australia*]
OCEO .... Open Change Engineering Orders (SAUS)
OCEP .... Office of Community Employment Programs [*Department of Labor*]
OCEP .... Officials Committee on Energy Policy (SAUS)
OCEPA .... Office of Communications, Education, and Public Affairs (AUEG)
OCEPA .... United States Environmental Protection Agency, Cincinnati, OH [*Library symbol*] [*Library of Congress*] (LCLS)
OCE Potential... Open Circuit Electrode Potential (SAUS)
OCESL .... Office of Criminal Enforcement and Special Litigation (COE)
OCf............... Chagrin Falls Public Library, Chagrin Falls, OH [*Library symbol*] [*Library of Congress*] (LCLS)
OCF............. Objects Components Framework (VLIE)
OCF............. Obsessive Compulsive Foundation (EA)
OCF............. Ocala [*Florida*] [*Airport symbol*] (OAG)
OCF............. Office of the Chief of Finance [*Military*]
OCF............. Officers' Christian Fellowship of the USA (EA)
OCF............. Officiating Chaplain to the Forces [*Military*] [*British*]
OCF............. On-Board Computational Facility [*NASA*] (NASA)
OCF............. Ontario Cancer Foundation (SAUS)
OCF............. Open Channel Flow
OCF............. Open Computing Facility
OCF............. Operational Control Facility (SAA)
OCF............. Operation Code Field (SAUS)
OCF............. Operator Console Facility [*Computer science*] (IBMDP)
OCF............. Orbiter Computational Facility [*NASA*] (NASA)
OCF............. Organic Crystal Growth Facility (SAUS)
OCF............. Orientation Correlation Function (SAUS)
ocf.............. Originally Cultured Formulation (AD)
OCF............. Ossining Correctional Facility [*Sing Sing*] (AD)
OCF............. Osteopathy in the Cranial Field (SAUS)
OCF............. Output Characteristic Function (SAUS)
OCF............. Owens-Corning Fiberglas Corp. [*NYSE symbol*] (SPSG)
OCF............. Owner Control File (TIMI)
OCF............. Ozenji Critical Facility [*Nuclear reactor*] [*Japan*]
OCFA .... Overseas Christian Fellowship Australia
OCF & A ...... Office, Chief of Finance and Accounting [*Army*] (AABC)
OCFC .... Cloyne Branch, Frontenac County Library, Ontario [*Library symbol*] [*National Library of Canada*] (BIB)
OCFC .... Ocean Financial Corp. [*NASDAQ symbol*] (SAG)
OCFC .... Overseas Combined Federal Campaign [*Red Cross*]
OCFDA........ United States Food and Drug Administration, Cincinnati, OH [*Library symbol*] [*Library of Congress*] (LCLS)
OCFMFP ...... Ontario Centre for Farm Machinery and Food Processing Technology, Chatham, Ontario [*Library symbol*] [*National Library of Canada*] (NLC)
OCFMFPT .... Ontario Center for Farm Machinery and Food Processing Technologies (SAUS)
OCF-ML .... Organisation Communiste de France - Marxiste-Leniniste [*Communist Organization of France - Marxist-Leninist*] (PPW)
OCFNT .... Occluded Front (SAUS)
OCFNT .... Occuluded Front [*NWS*] (FAAC)
OCFP .... Office of Commercial and Financial Policy [*Department of Commerce*]
OCFP .... Operator Command Function Processor [*Computer science*] (MHDI)
OCFR .... Oxford Committee for Family Relief [*British*] (AD)
OCFR .... Oxford Committee for Famine Relief [*British*] (DI)
OCFT .... Office of Curriculum Frameworks and Textbooks (AD)
OCG .... Cincinnati General Hospital, Medical Library, Cincinnati, OH [*Library symbol*] [*Library of Congress*] (LCLS)
OCG .... Occupational Changes in a Generation [*Socioeconomics*]
OCG .... OCG Technology, Inc. [*Associated Press*] (SAG)
OCG .... Oesterreichische Computer Gesellschaft [*Austrian Computer Society*] [*German*] (AD)
OCG .... Office of Challenge Grants [*National Endowment for the Humanities*] (BARN)
OCG .... Office of the Commanding General [*Army*]
OCG .... Office of the Comptroller General (AAGC)
OCG .... Official Cruise Guide (TVEL)
ocg.............. Omnicardiogram [*Medicine*] (AD)
OCG .... Omnicardiogram [*Medicine*] (DMAA)
OCG .... Operations Control Group (SAUS)

OCG .... Optimal Code Generation
OCG .... Oral Cholecystogram (SAUS)
OCG .... Oral Cholecystography [*or Cholecystogram*] [*Radiology*]
OCG .... Orbital Curve of Growth [*Mathematics*]
OCG .... Osborne & Chappel Goldfields US [*Toronto Stock Exchange symbol*]
OCG .... Overall Conflict Graph (VLIE)
OCG .... Oxygen Consumption Gauge
OCGA .... Official Code of Georgia, Annotated [*A publication*] (DLA)
OCGF .... Organic Crystal Growth Facility (SAUS)
OCGF .... Organic Crystal Growth Laboratory Facility (SAUS)
OCGH .... Cornwall General Hospital, Ontario [*Library symbol*] [*National Library of Canada*] (NLC)
OCGI .... Omni Capital Group (EFIS)
OCGM .... Office of Cabinet and Government Management [*Australia*]
OCGS .... Church of Jesus Christ of Latter-Day Saints, Genealogical Society Library, Cincinnati Branch, Cincinnati, OH [*Library symbol*] [*Library of Congress*] (LCLS)
OCGS .... Ontario Council on Graduate Studies (SAUS)
OCGSH........ Good Samaritan Hospital, Medical Library, Cincinnati, OH [*Library symbol*] [*Library of Congress*] (LCLS)
OCGT .... OCG Technology [*NASDAQ symbol*] (TTSB)
OCGT .... OCG Technology, Inc. [*NASDAQ symbol*] (NQ)
OCGT .... Open-Cycle Gas Turbine (PDAA)
OCH .... Chesley Branch, Bruce County Public Library, Ontario [*Library symbol*] [*National Library of Canada*] (NLC)
OCh.............. Chillicothe and Ross County Public Library, Chillicothe, OH [*Library symbol*] [*Library of Congress*] (LCLS)
OCH .... Hebrew Union College - Jewish Institute of Religion, Cincinnati, OH [*Library symbol*] [*Library of Congress*] (LCLS)
OCH .... Nacogdoches, TX [*Location identifier*] [*FAA*] (FAAL)
OCH .... Obedience Champion [*Dog show term*]
OCH .... Obstacle Clearance Height [*Aviation*] (FAAC)
och............... Ochre (AD)
OCH .... Ochre [*Philately*] (ROG)
OCH .... Office for Communication in the Humanities (NITA)
OCH .... Oral Contraceptive Hormone (DB)
OCH .... Orbiter Common Hardware [*NASA*] (NASA)
OCH .... Order of the Compassionate Heart (EA)
OCH .... Organ Clearing House (EA)
OCH .... Outpatient Clinic (Hospital) [*Veterans Administration*]
OCHA .... Chatham Public Library, Ontario [*Library symbol*] [*National Library of Canada*] (NLC)
OCHA .... Office for the Coordination of Humanitarian Affairs [*United Nations*]
OCHA .... Oregon Clearing House Association (TBD)
OChaG .... Geauga County Public Library, Chardon, OH [*Library symbol*] [*Library of Congress*] (LCLS)
OCHAH .... Chatham Public General Hospital, Ontario [*Library symbol*] [*National Library of Canada*] (NLC)
OCHAK........ Chatham-Kent Museum, Chatham, Ontario [*Library symbol*] [*National Library of Canada*] (NLC)
OCHAKC...... Kent County Public Library, Chatham, Ontario [*Library symbol*] [*National Library of Canada*] (NLC)
OCHAMPUS... Office for the Civilian Health and Medical Program of the Uniformed Services (AABC)
OCHAMPUS... Office of Civilian Health and Medical Program of the Uniformed Services (USGC)
OCHAMPUSEUR... Office of the Civilian Health and Medical Program of the Uniformed Services in Europe (DNAB)
OCHAP......... Chapleau Public Library, Ontario [*Library symbol*] [*National Library of Canada*] (NLC)
OCharlys...... OCharleys, Inc. [*Associated Press*] (SAG)
OCHAT........ Thames Arts Centre, Chatham, Ontario [*Library symbol*] [*National Library of Canada*] (NLC)
OCHC .... Operator Call Handling Center [*Telecommunications*] (TEL)
OCHCB........ Huron County Board of Education, Clinton, Ontario [*Library symbol*] [*National Library of Canada*] (NLC)
OCHDC........ Hilton Davis Chemical Co., Cincinnati, OH [*Library symbol*] [*Library of Congress*] (LCLS)
OCHERB........ Chelmsford Branch, Rayside-Balfour Public Library, Chelmsford, Ontario [*Library symbol*] [*National Library of Canada*] (NLC)
OCHIN.......... Norton Co. Electric, Chippewa, Ontario [*Library symbol*] [*National Library of Canada*] (NLC)
OC-HLTHLB... Occupational Health Labels [*Army*]
OCHM .... Haldimand County Museum Board, Cayuga, Ontario [*Library symbol*] [*National Library of Canada*] (NLC)
OCHP .... Cincinnati Historical Society, Cincinnati, OH [*Library symbol*] [*Library of Congress*] (LCLS)
OCHR .... Oil Catcher
OCHRE......... Optical Character Recognition Engine (PDAA)
OCHS .... Old Colony Historical Society (AD)
OCHSDG ...... Chesterville Branch, Stormont, Dundas, and Glengarry County Public Library, Ontario [*Library symbol*] [*National Library of Canada*] (BIB)
OChU .... Ohio University, Chillicothe Branch Campus, Chillicothe, OH [*Library symbol*] [*Library of Congress*] (LCLS)
OCHWL........ Wollaston and Limerick Public Library, Coe Hill, Ontario [*Library symbol*] [*National Library of Canada*] (BIB)
OCI.............. Integrated Revolutionary Organizations [*Cuba*] (PPW)
OCI.............. Object Code Insertion (SAUS)
OCI.............. Occlude (DA)
OCI.............. Ocean Color Imager [*Meteorology*] [*NASA*]
OCI.............. Ocean Industry (SAUS)
OCI.............. O.C. International [*Formerly, Orient Crusades Gospel Outreach*] (EA)
OCI.............. Office of Community Investment [*Federal Home Loan Bank Board*]

OCI .... Office of Computer Information [Department of Commerce] [Originator and database]
OCI .... Office of Corollary Interest [DoD]
OCI .... Office of Criminal Investigation [Environmental Protection Agency] (EPA)
OCI .... Office of Current Intelligence (MCD)
OCI .... Office of the Coordinator of Information (AD)
OCI .... Old Canada Investment Corp. Ltd. [Toronto Stock Exchange symbol]
OCI .... Olympic Council of Ireland (EAIO)
OCI .... Ontario Cancer Institute [UTLAS symbol]
OCI .... Open Circuit Inductance (IAA)
OCI .... Operational Checkout Instruction (AD)
OCI .... Operation Child Identification [Defunct] (EA)
OCI .... Operator Control Interface (OA)
OCI .... Optically-Coupled Insulator (IAA)
OCI .... Optically Coupled Isolator
OCI .... Organisation Communiste Internationaliste [Internationalist Communist Organization] [France] [Political party] (PPW)
OCI .... Organisation de la Conference Islamique [Organization of the Islamic Conference - OIC] [Jeddah, Saudi Arabia] (EAIO)
OCI .... Organizational Climate Index [Test]
OCI .... Organizational Conflict of Interest (AAGC)
OCI .... Organization City (SAUS)
oci .... Organization Conflict of Interest (AD)
OCI .... Organized Crime Intelligence Unit [Law Enforcement Assistance Administration]
OCI .... Oryzacystatins I [Biochemistry]
OCI .... Other Cooperating Institutions (SAUS)
OCI .... Out of City Indicator
OCI .... Outpatient Clinic (Independent) [Veterans Administration]
OCI .... Oxide Control and Indication (NRCH)
OCIA .... Organic Crop Improvement Association (EA)
OCIAA .... Office of Coordinator of Inter-American Affairs [World War II]
OCIB .... Beausoleil Indian Band Library, Christian Island, Ontario [Library symbol] [National Library of Canada] (BIB)
OCIB .... Organized Crime Intelligence Bureau (AD)
OCIC .... Officer Commanding in Charge [Facetious acronym] [Army] [British] (DSUE)
OCIC .... Organisation Catholique Internationale du Cinema et de l'Audiovisuel [International Catholic Organization for Cinema and Audiovisual] (EAIO)
OCID .... Dyke College, Cleveland (SAUS)
OCID .... Organized Crime Intelligence Division (SAUS)
OCIE .... Organizational Clothing and Individual Equipment [Military]
OCIEP .... Office of the Commissioners of Inquiry for Environment and Planning [Australia]
OCIF .... Out Card in File
OCII .... Oryzacystatins II [Biochemistry]
OCIL .... Ocilla Industries, Inc. (SAUS)
OCIL .... Office of Community and Intergovernmental Liaison [Environmental Protection Agency] (GFGA)
OCIMF .... Oil Companies International Marine Forum [British] (EAIO)
OCINFO .... Office of the Chief of Information [Military]
OCIR .... Office of Community and Intergovernmental Relations (COE)
OCIR .... Operational Capability Inprovement Request Out of Commission, In Reserve [Vesselstatus] (DNAB)
OCIR .... Out of Commission in Reserve (SAUS)
OCirP .... Pickaway County District Public Library, Circleville, OH [Library symbol] [Library of Congress] (LCLS)
OCIS .... Oacis Healthcare Holdings Corp. [NASDAQ symbol] (SAG)
OCIS .... Office for Church in Society (EA)
OCIS .... Office of Computing and Information Services [University of Georgia] [Research center] (RCD)
OCIS .... Oncology Center Information System (MELL)
OCIS .... On-line Chemical Information System (SAUS)
OCIS .... Operational Control Information System [Computer science] (VLIE)
OCIS .... Organized Crime Information System [Federal Bureau of Investigation] [Information service or system] (IID)
OCIS .... OSHA [Occupational Safety and Health Administration] Computerized Information System [Environmental science]
OCIS .... Oxford Centre for Islamic Studies [British]
OcisHlth ...... Oacis Healthcare Holdings Corp. [Associated Press] (SAG)
OCist .... Cistercian Fathers (TOCD)
ocist .... Cistercian Fathers (TOCD)
OCist .... Cisterdan Nuns (TOCD)
O CIST .... Ordinis Cisterciensis [Cistercian Order] (ROG)
OCITA .... Office of the Chemical Industry Trade Advisor
OCIU .... Optical Cable Interface Unit (MCD)
OCJ .... Ocho Rios [Jamaica] [Airport symbol] (OAG)
OCJ .... Optional Construction Joint
OCJA .... Oklahoma Criminal Justice Association (AD)
OCJC .... Orange Coast Junior College [California] [Later, OCC]
OCJCS .... Office of the Chairman, Joint Chiefs of Staff (MCD)
OCJH .... Jewish Hospital, Medical Library, Cincinnati, OH [Library symbol] [Library of Congress] (LCLS)
OCJH-N ...... Jewish Hospital, School of Nursing, Cincinnati, OH [Library symbol] [Library of Congress] (LCLS)
OCJP .... Office of Criminal Justice Planning (AD)
OCJP .... Office of Criminal Justice Program (OICC)
OCK .... Chalk River Public Library, Ontario [Library symbol] [National Library of Canada] (BIB)
OCK .... Kent State University, Stark County Regional Campus, Canton, OH [OCLC symbol] (OCLC)
OCK .... Operation Control Key [Computer science] (IAA)

OCKA .... Atomic Energy of Canada [L'Energie Atomique du Canada] Chalk River, Ontario [Library symbol] [National Library of Canada] (NLC)
OCKE .... Petawawa National Forestry Institute, Canadian Forestry Service, Environment Canada [Institut Forestier National Petawawa, Service Canadien des Forets, Environnement Canada] Chalk River, Ontario [Library symbol] [National Library of Canada] (NLC)
Ocl .... Cleveland Public Library (SAUS)
OCl .... Cleveland Public Library, Cleveland, OH [Library symbol] [Library of Congress] (LCLS)
OCL .... Object Constraint Language (VLIE)
OCL .... Obstacle Clearance Limit (SAUS)
OCL .... Obstruction Clearance Limit [Aviation] (PIPO)
OCL .... Ocean Cargo Line (AD)
OCL .... Ocellus
OCL .... Office of Congressional Liaison [Environmental Protection Agency] (GFGA)
OCL .... Offshore Commercial Loan
OCL .... Oil City Lubricants Ltd. [Vancouver Stock Exchange symbol]
OCL .... Old Light Cruiser [Navy symbol]
OCL .... Operating Control Language [Computer science] (VLIE)
OCL .... Operational Check List (MUGU)
OCL .... Operational Control Level
OCL .... Operation Control Language [Computer programming]
ocl .... Operator Control Language (AD)
OCL .... Operators Control Language [Computer science] (BUR)
ocl .... Optical Communications Linkage (AD)
OCL .... Ordnance Circular Letter
OCL .... Organochlorine [Also, OC] [Organic chemistry]
OCL .... Orthopedic Casting Laboratory (DAVI)
OCL .... OS/2 inside Class Library (SAUS)
OCL .... Outgoing Correspondence Log (AAG)
OCL .... Output Capacitorless (SAUS)
OCL .... Output Capacity Loading [Computer science] (ELAL)
OCL .... Overall Cartridge Length (SAUS)
OCL .... Overall Connection Loss [Telecommunications] (TEL)
OCL .... Overcorrected Lens (SAUS)
OCL .... Overhaul Cycle Limit
OCL .... Over-Night Cargo Ltd. [Nigeria] [ICAO designator] (FAAC)
OCL .... Overseas Container Line (AD)
OCL .... Overseas Containers Ltd. (AD)
OCL .... Overseas Currency Loan
OCIA .... Alcan Aluminum Co., Cleveland, OH [Library symbol] [Library of Congress] (LCLS)
OCLA .... Office of Congressional and Legislative Affairs [U.S. Department of Interior] (BARN)
OCLA .... Oregon Compiled Laws Annotated [A publication]
OCL/ACT ..... Overseas Container Lines and Associated Container Transport (AD)
OCLAE .... Organizacion Continental Latinoamericana de Estudiantes [Latin American Continental Students' Organization] (EAIO)
OCIAM .... Arthur G. McKee & Co., Cleveland, OH [Library symbol] [Library of Congress] (LCLS)
OCLaw .... Cincinnati Law Library Association, Cincinnati, OH [Library symbol] [Library of Congress] (LCLS)
OCLB .... Office Club, Inc. (SAUS)
OCIBE .... Board of Education, Cleveland, OH [Library symbol] [Library of Congress] (LCLS)
OCIBHS .... Benedictine High School, Cleveland, OH [Library symbol] [Library of Congress] (LCLS)
OCI-BPH ..... Ohio Regional Library, Braille and Talking Books Division, Cleveland Public Library, Cleveland, OH [Library symbol] [Library of Congress] (LCLS)
OCIBS .... Blessed Sacrament Seminary, Cleveland, OH [Library symbol] [Library of Congress] (LCLS)
OCIC .... Cleveland Clinic Educational Foundation, Cleveland, OH [Library symbol] [Library of Congress] (LCLS)
OCLC .... Ohio College Library Center (BARN)
OCLC .... Online Computer Library Center [Formerly, Ohio College Library Center. Initialism used in reference to cataloging system it developed] [Information service or system]
OCICC .... Cuyahoga Community College, Cleveland, OH [Library symbol] [Library of Congress] (LCLS)
OCICh .... Christian Science Reading Room, Cleveland, OH [Library symbol] [Library of Congress] (LCLS)
OCICIM .... Cleveland Institute of Music, Cleveland, OH [Library symbol] [Library of Congress] (LCLS)
OCICo .... Cuyahoga County Public Library, Cleveland, OH [Library symbol] [Library of Congress] (LCLS)
OCID .... Dyke College, Cleveland, OH [Library symbol] [Library of Congress] (LCLS)
OCLD .... Occlude (SAUS)
OCLD .... Oil-Cooled
OCIDe .... Deaconess Hospital, Medical Library, Cleveland, OH [Library symbol] [Library of Congress] (LCLS)
OCLDP-K..... Open Court Language Development Program: Kindergarten (EDAC)
OCLE .... Continuing Legal Education, University of Oklahoma Law Center (DLA)
OCIFRB .... Federal Reserve Bank of Cleveland, Cleveland, OH [Library symbol] [Library of Congress] (LCLS)
OCIG .... Glidden Co. Research Library, Cleveland, OH [Library symbol] [Library of Congress] (LCLS)
OCIGC .... Garden Center of Greater Cleveland, Cleveland, OH [Library symbol] [Library of Congress] (LCLS)

OCIGI .... Gould, Incorporated, Gould Information Center, Cleveland, OH [*Library symbol*] [*Library of Congress*] (LCLS)

OCIh .... Cleveland Heights-University Heights Public Library, Cleveland Heights, OH [*Library symbol*] [*Library of Congress*] (LCLS)

OCLI .... Curve Lake Indian Band Library, Ontario [*Library symbol*] [*National Library of Canada*] (BIB)

OCLI .... Optical Coating Lab [*NASDAQ symbol*] (TTSB)

OCLI .... Optical Coating Laboratories, Inc. (PCM)

OCLI .... Optical Coating Laboratory, Inc. [*NASDAQ symbol*] (NQ)

OCLIPS .... Operational Climate Prediction and Services [*Marine science*] (OSRA)

OCIJC .... John Carroll University, Cleveland, OH [*Library symbol*] [*Library of Congress*] (LCLS)

OCIL .... General Electric Co., Light Research Laboratory, Cleveland, OH [*Library symbol*] [*Library of Congress*] (LCLS)

OCLL .... Office, Chief of Legislative Liaison [*Military*]

OCILH .... Lakeside Hospital, Cleveland, OH [*Library symbol*] [*Library of Congress*] (LCLS)

OCLloyd .... Lloyd Library and Museum, Cincinnati, OH [*Library symbol*] [*Library of Congress*] (LCLS)

OCIMA .... Cleveland Museum of Art, Cleveland, OH [*Library symbol*] [*Library of Congress*] (LCLS)

OCIMGH .... Cleveland Metropolitan General Hospital, Cleveland, OH [*Library symbol*] [*Library of Congress*] (LCLS)

OCIMN .... Cleveland Museum of Natural History, Cleveland, OH [*Library symbol*] [*Library of Congress*] (LCLS)

OCIMt .... Mount Sinai Hospital, Cleveland, OH [*Library symbol*] [*Library of Congress*] (LCLS)

OCINASA ...... National Aeronautics and Space Administration, Lewis Research Center, Cleveland, OH [*Library symbol*] [*Library of Congress*] (LCLS)

OCIND .... Notre Dame College, Cleveland, OH [*Library symbol*] [*Library of Congress*] (LCLS)

OCLNR .... Oil Cleaner

OCIO .... Chlorine Dioxide (SAUS)

OCIP .... Park Synagogue, Cleveland, OH [*Library symbol*] [*Library of Congress*] (LCLS)

OCLR .... Oil Cooler

OCIRC .... Rowfant Club, Cleveland, OH [*Library symbol*] [*Library of Congress*] (LCLS)

OCISA .... Cleveland Institute of Art, Cleveland, OH [*Library symbol*] [*Library of Congress*] (LCLS)

OCISS .... Saint Stanislaus Seminary, Cleveland, OH [*Library symbol*] [*Library of Congress*] (LCLS)

OCIStJ .... Saint John College of Cleveland, Cleveland, OH [*Library symbol*] [*Library of Congress*] (LCLS)

OCIStM .... Saint Mary's Seminary, Cleveland, OH [*Library symbol*] [*Library of Congress*] (LCLS)

OCITem .... Temple Library, Tiffereth Israel Congregation, Cleveland, OH [*Library symbol*] [*Library of Congress*] (LCLS)

OCIU .... Cleveland State University, Cleveland, OH [*Library symbol*] [*Library of Congress*] (LCLS)

OCLU .... Overseas Container Line Unit (AD)

O CLUB .... Officers Club [*Military*] (GOBB)

OCIU-L .... Cleveland-Marshall College of Law, Cleveland State University, Cleveland, OH [*Library symbol*] [*Library of Congress*] (LCLS)

OCIUr .... Ursuline College, Pepper Pike, OH [*Library symbol*] [*Library of Congress*] (LCLS)

OCLUS .... Outside Continental Limits of United States [*Military*]

OCIV .... United States Veterans Administration Hospital, Cleveland, OH [*Library symbol*] [*Library of Congress*] (LCLS)

OCIW .... Case Western Reserve University, Cleveland, OH [*Library symbol*] [*Library of Congress*] (LCLS)

OCIW-H .... Case Western Reserve University, Cleveland Health Sciences Library, Cleveland, OH [*Library symbol*] [*Library of Congress*] (LCLS)

OCIWHi .... Western Reserve Historical Society, Cleveland, OH [*Library symbol*] [*Library of Congress*] (LCLS)

OCIWHi-AM... Western Reserve Historical Society, Frederick C. Crawford Auto-Aviation Museum, Cleveland, OH [*Library symbol*] [*Library of Congress*] (LCLS)

OCIW-L .... Case Western Reserve University, Law Library, Cleveland, OH [*Library symbol*] [*Library of Congress*] (LCLS)

OCIW-LS ..... Case Western Reserve University, School of Library Science, Cleveland, OH [*Library symbol*] [*Library of Congress*] (LCLS)

OCIW-S .... Case Western Reserve University, Sears Library, Cleveland, OH [*Library symbol*] [*Library of Congress*] (LCLS)

OCIW-SS ...... Case Western Reserve University, School of Applied Social Science, Cleveland, OH [*Library symbol*] [*Library of Congress*] (LCLS)

OCM .... Cincinnati Masonic Temple, Cincinnati, OH [*Library symbol*] [*Library of Congress*] (LCLS)

OCM .... Creighton University, Health Sciences Library, Omaha, NE [*OCLC symbol*] (OCLC)

OCM .... Matchedash Public Library, Coldwater, Ontario [*Library symbol*] [*National Library of Canada*] (BIB)

OCM .... Ocean Circulation Model (QUAC)

OCM .... Ocean Color Monitor (ACAE)

OCM .... Ocean Colour Monitor (SAUS)

OCM .... Ocular Connection Machine (VLIE)

OCM .... Office of Compliance Monitoring [*Environmental Protection Agency*] (GFGA)

OCM .... Office of Country Marketing [*Department of Commerce*] (IMH)

OCM .... Office of the Commission [*Nuclear energy*] (NRCH)

OCM .... Ohm Centimeter (IAA)

o-cm .... Ohm-Centimetre (SAUS)

ocm .... Oil Content Monitor (AD)

OCM .... Oil Content Monitor [*Navy*] (CAAL)

OCM .... On-Camera Meteorologist

OCM .... On-Condition Maintenance (AABC)

OCM .... One-Channel Map [*Computer science*] [*NASA*]

OCM .... One Chip Module (SAUS)

OCM .... Ontario Center for Microelectronics (SAUS)

OCM .... Operator Console Module (TIMI)

OCM .... Operator Console Monitor

OCM .... Operator's Control Module

OCM .... Optical Contour Maximization [*Chemistry*]

OCM .... Optical Countermeasures

OCM .... Ordnance Committee Meeting (AAG)

OCM .... Ordnance Committee Minutes [*Military*]

OCM .... Ordo Constantini Magni [*International Constantinian Order*] (EA)

ocm .... Organic Content Monitor (NAKS)

OCM .... Organic Content Monitor (NASA)

OCM .... Origin of Columellar Muscle

OCM .... Oscillator and Clock Module

OCM .... Outline of Cultural Materials [*Human Relations Area Files*] [*Information retrieval*]

OCM .... Oxford Companion to Music [*A publication*] (AD)

OCM .... Oxidative Coupling of Methane [*Chemistry*]

OCMA .... Oil Companies' Materials Association [*British*] (BI)

OCMCEN ...... Occupational Measurement Center [*Air Force*]

OCMCU .... One-Chip Microcomputer Unit (SAUS)

OCME .... Oceanographic Community Modeling Effort (SAUS)

OCMH .... Madonna House Library, Combermere, Ontario [*Library symbol*] [*National Library of Canada*] (NLC)

OCMH .... Office of the Chief of Military History [*Army*]

OCMI .... Officer-in-Charge, Marine Inspection Office [*Coast Guard*]

OCMii .... Cincinnati Milacron, Inc., Research Library, Cincinnati, OH [*Library symbol*] [*Library of Congress*] (LCLS)

OCMiiC .... Cincinnati Milacron, Inc., Corporate Information Center, Cincinnati, OH [*Library symbol*] [*Library of Congress*] (LCLS)

OCMii-T .... Cincinnati Milacron, Inc., Technical Information Center, Cincinnati, OH [*Library symbol*] [*Library of Congress*] (LCLS)

OCMIP .... Ocean Carbon-Cycle Model Intercomparison Project (SAUS)

OCM-LP .... Organizacao Comunista Marxista-Leninista Portuguesa [*Portuguese Communist Organization, Marxist-Leninist*] [*Political party*] (PPE)

OCMLR .... Organisation Communiste Marxiste-Leniniste de la Reunion [*Reunionese Communist Organization, Marxist-Leninist*] [*Political party*] (PPW)

OCMM .... Office of Civilian Manpower Management [*Later, Office of Civilian Personnel*] [*Navy*]

OCMMINST... Office of Civilian Manpower Management Instruction [*Navy*]

OCMM-N ...... Office of Civilian Manpower Management - Navy

OCMN .... Merrell-National Laboratories, Cincinnati, OH [*Library symbol*] [*Library of Congress*] (LCLS)

OCMODL ..... Operating Cost Model

OCMR .... On-Condition Maintenance Rate (MCD)

OCMR .... Ontario Centre for Materials Research [*Canada*] [*Research center*] (RCD)

OCMR .... Organic-Cooled and Moderated Reactor (SAUS)

OCMS .... Onboard and Checkout Monitoring System (SAUS)

OCMS .... On-Board Checkout and Monitoring System [*NASA*] (KSC)

OCMS .... On-Chip test and Maintenance System (SAUS)

OCMS .... Operative Crate Makers' Society [*A union*] [*British*]

OCMS .... Optional Calling Measured Service [*Telecommunications*] (TEL)

OCMS .... Ordnance Command Management System

OCMS .... Ordnance Committee Meeting Standards (AAG)

OCMSq .... Occupational Measurement Squadron [*Air Force*]

OCMTC .... Officer Commanding Motor Transport Company (SAUS)

OCMU .... Ocmulgee National Monument

OCN .... Canadian Park Service, Environment Canada [*Service Canadien des Parcs, Environnement Canada*], Cornwall, Ontario [*Library symbol*] [*National Library of Canada*] (NLC)

ocn .... Ocean (BEE)

OCN .... Ocean

OCN .... Oceanair-Transportes Aereos Regional SA [*Portugal*] [*ICAO designator*] (FAAC)

OCN .... Ocean Airways, Inc. (SAUS)

OCN .... Oceania (CARB)

OCN .... Oceanside, CA [*Location identifier*] [*FAA*] (FAAL)

OCN .... Oculomotor Nucleus [*Eye anatomy*]

OCN .... Office of the Commissioner of Namibia (BUAC)

OC-N .... Office of the Comptroller of the Navy

OCN .... Oncology Certified Nurse (NUJO)

OCN .... Open College Network (AIE)

OCN .... Operational Carrier Number (SAUS)

OCN .... Operation Completion Notice (AAG)

OC-n .... Optical Carrier-n (SAUS)

OCN .... Optimal Channel Network [*Physics*]

OCN .... Optimal Climate Normals [*Climatology*]

OCN .... Orcana Resources Ltd. [*Vancouver Stock Exchange symbol*]

OCN .... Order Control Number (NASA)

OCN .... Organization Change Notice

OCN .... Organized Crime Narcotics Program [*Department of Justice*]

OCN .... Over Castle Rock [*New York*] [*Seismograph station code, US Geological Survey*] (SEIS)

OCNAUD ...... Oficina del Coordinador de las Naciones Unidas para la Ayuda en los Desastres [*Office of the Coordinator of the United Nations for Help in Disasters*] [*Spanish*] (AD)

OCNAV .... Office of the Oceanographer of the Navy

Ocn Bch .... Ocean Beach (AD)

OCNC.......... Coniston Branch, Nickel Centre Public Library, Ontario [*Library symbol*] [*National Library of Canada*] (NLC)

OCNew......... New Church Library, Cincinnati, OH [*Library symbol*] [*Library of Congress*] [*Obsolete*] (LCLS)

OCnf............. Canal Fulton Public Library, Canal Fulton, OH [*Library symbol*] [*Library of Congress*] (LCLS)

OCNFT........ Ocean Front (TVEL)

OCNGA......... Officer-in-Charge of National Guard Affairs

OCNGH .... Garden Hill Branch, Northumberland County Public Library, Campbellcroft, Ontario [*Library symbol*] [*National Library of Canada*] (BIB)

OCNGS........ Oyster Creek Nuclear Generating Station (NRCH)

OCNHT......... North Himsworth Township Public Library, Callander, Ontario [*Library symbol*] [*National Library of Canada*] (NLC)

OCNI............ Optimal Communications, Navigation and Identification (ACAE)

OCNIOS........ National Institute for Occupational Safety and Health, Cincinnati, OH [*Library symbol*] [*Library of Congress*] (LCLS)

ocnl .... Occasional (AD)

OCNL .... Occasional

OCNLY .... Occasionally

OCNM .... Oregon Caves National Monument (AD)

OCNM ...... Organization of the Crimean Tatar National Movement (BUAC)

OCNMAP...... Ocean Map [*Marine science*] (OSRA)

OCNO .... Office of the Chief of Naval Operations

OCNPP......... Oyster Creek Nuclear Power Plant (NRCH)

OCNPR......... Operation and Conservation of Naval Petroleum Reserves [*Budget appropriation title*]

OCNR .... Office of the Chief of Naval Research (SAUS)

OCNS .... Oklahoma City NORAD [*North American Air Defense*] Sector (SAA)

OCNSW......... Outdoor Club of New South Wales [*Australia*]

OCNVW......... Ocean View (TRID)

OCNWU .... Organizing Committee for a National Writers Union (EA)

OCO .... Cobourg Public Library, Ontario [*Library symbol*] [*National Library of Canada*] (NLC)

Oco .... Columbus Public Library (SAUS)

OCo.,.......... Columbus Public Library, Columbus, OH [*Library symbol*] [*Library of Congress*] (LCLS)

OCO .... Object Code Only (HGAA)

OCO .... Office, Chief of Ordnance [*Army*]

OCO .... Office of Central Operations [*Bureau of Health Insurance*]

OCO .... Office of Civil Operations [*Coordinated US civilian pacification efforts in Vietnam*] (VNW)

OCO .... Off-Load Control Officer [*Navy*] (ANA)

OCO .... Oil/Coal/Ore (SAUS)

OCO .... Old Cornish [*Language, etc.*]

OCO .... OMS [*Orbital Maneuvering Subsystem*] Cutoff [*NASA*] (NASA)

OCO .... One-Cancels-the-Other Order [*Business term*]

OCO .... Ontario College of Ophthalmology [*Canada*] (AD)

oco............. Open-Close-Open (AD)

OCO .... Open-Close-Open [*Technical drawings*]

OCO .... Operating Capital Outlay (WPI)

OCO .... Operational Capabilities Objectives (SAUS)

OCO .... Operational Capability Objective [*Army*]

OCO .... Operational Checkout (AAG)

OCO .... Operations Console Operator (MUGU)

OCO .... Optically-Coupled Oscillator [*Instrumentation*]

OCO .... Ordnance Corps Order (AAG)

OCO .... Public Library of Columbus and Franklin County, Columbus, OH [*OCLC symbol*] (OCLC)

OCOA............ Art Gallery of Cobourg, Ontario [*Library symbol*] [*National Library of Canada*] (NLC)

OCoa............ Columbiana Public Library, Columbiana, OH [*Library symbol*] [*Library of Congress*] (LCLS)

OCOA .... Organismo Coordinador de Operaciones Antisubversivas [*Coordinating Organism of Antisubversive Operations*] [*Uruguay*] (AD)

OCoAC .... American Ceramic Society, Columbus, OH [*Library symbol*] [*Library of Congress*] (LCLS)

OCOAP......... Oscillating-Compensator Oscillating-Analyzer Polarimeter (PDAA)

OCoB .... Battelle-Columbus Laboratories, Columbus, OH [*Library symbol*] [*Library of Congress*] (LCLS)

OCOB .... Cobalt Public Library, Ontario [*Library symbol*] [*National Library of Canada*] (BIB)

OCOBD......... Cobden Public Library, Ontario [*Library symbol*] [*National Library of Canada*] (BIB)

OCoBex........ Bexley Public Library, Columbus, OH [*Library symbol*] [*Library of Congress*] (LCLS)

OCoC .... Capital University, Columbus, OH [*Library symbol*] [*Library of Congress*] (LCLS)

OCOC .... Cochrane Public Library, Ontario [*Library symbol*] [*National Library of Canada*] (NLC)

OCOCC........ Ontario CAD/CAM Centre, Cambridge, Ontario [*Library symbol*] [*National Library of Canada*] (NLC)

OCoC-L .... Capital University, School of Law, Columbus, OH [*Library symbol*] [*Library of Congress*] (LCLS)

OCoCT .... Columbus Technical Institute, Columbus, OH [*Library symbol*] [*Library of Congress*] (LCLS)

OCoCU .... Capital University, Columbus, OH [*Library symbol*] [*Library of Congress*] (LCLS)

OCO Cycle ... Open-Close-Open Cycle (SAUS)

OCoD .... Ohio Dominican College, Columbus, OH [*Library symbol*] [*Library of Congress*] (LCLS)

OCOD.......... Organization for Cooperation in Overseas Development [*Canada*] (EAIO)

OCoE .... Evangelical Lutheran Theological Seminary, Columbus, OH [*Library symbol*] [*Library of Congress*] (LCLS)

OCOE .... Office of the Chief of Engineers [*Army*] (RDA)

OCoF .... Franklin University, Columbus, OH [*Library symbol*] [*Library of Congress*] (LCLS)

OC of AC..... Office of the Chief of Air Corps [*World War II*]

OC of AS..... Office of the Chief of Air Staff [*World War II*]

OC of Ch..... Office, Chief of Chaplains [*Later, OCCH*] [*Army*] (AABC)

OC of F....... Office of the Chief of Finance [*Military*]

OC of ORD... Office, Chief of Ordnance [*Army*]

OC of SA..... Office, Chief of Staff, Army (AABC)

OC of SptS... Office of the Chief of Support Services [*Army*] (AABC)

OC of T....... Office, Chief of Transportation [*Army*]

OCoG .... Grandview Heights Library, Columbus, OH [*Library symbol*] [*Library of Congress*] (LCLS)

OCOGC........ Official Centennial Olympic Games Club (EA)

OCOGF......... General Foods Ltd., Cobourg, Ontario [*Library symbol*] [*National Library of Canada*] (NLC)

OCoGS......... Church of Jesus Christ of Latter-Day Saints, Genealogical Society Library, Columbus Branch, Columbus, OH [*Library symbol*] [*Library of Congress*] (LCLS)

OCOKA........ Observation and Fields of Fire, Cover, and Concealment, Obstacles and Movement, Key Terrain, and Avenues of Approach [*Military*]

OCOKA......... Observation and Fields of Fire, Cover and Concealment, Obstacles, Key Terrain, Avenues of Approach (MCD)

OCOKA......... Observation and Fire, Concealment and Cover, Obstacles, Key Terrain, Avenues of Approach [*Military*]

OCOL .... Collingwood Public Library, Ontario [*Library symbol*] [*National Library of Canada*] (NLC)

OCOLB .... Colborne Public Library, Ontario [*Library symbol*] [*National Library of Canada*] (BIB)

OCoLC .... OCLC Online Computer Library Center, Dublin, OH [*Library symbol*] [*Library of Congress*] (LCLS)

OCoLC .... Ohio College Library Center, Columbus, OH [*Library symbol*] [*Library of Congress*] (LCLS)

OCOLD .... Coldwater Memorial Public Library, Ontario [*Library symbol*] [*National Library of Canada*] (BIB)

OCOM .... Oficina Central de Organizacion y Metodos [*Central Office of Organization and Methods*] [*Spain*] (AD)

OCOM .... Outlet Communications, Inc. [*NASDAQ symbol*] (NQ)

OComS .... Office of Community Services (AD)

OCOMS........ Office of Community Services [*Military*]

OCON .... Northumberland and Newcastle Board of Education, Cobourg, Ontario [*Library symbol*] [*National Library of Canada*] (NLC)

OCON .... Orders for Correction of Nonconformance [*Navy*] (NG)

OCoNC......... National Center on Educational Media and Materials for the Handicapped, Columbus, OH [*Library symbol*] [*Library of Congress*] (LCLS)

OConCL....... Carnegie Public Library, Conneaut, OH [*Library symbol*] [*Library of Congress*] (LCLS)

OCONT........ Oil Control

OConUS....... Outside Continental Limits of the United States (AD)

OCONUS ...... Outside Continental United States [*Military*]

OCOO .... Cookstown Public Library, Ontario [*Library symbol*] [*National Library of Canada*] (BIB)

OCoO .... Ohioana Library, Columbus, OH [*Library symbol*] [*Library of Congress*] (LCLS)

OCOO .... Osteopathic College of Ophthalmology and Otorhinolaryngology (EA)

OCOO .... Osteopathic Colleges of Ophthalmology and Otolaryngology-Head and Neck Surgery (EA)

OC Ooutput... Open Collector Output (SAUS)

OCOP .... Outline Contingency Operation Plan (COE)

OCoR .... Riverside Methodist Hospital, Columbus, OH [*Library symbol*] [*Library of Congress*] (LCLS)

OCORD .... Office, Chief of Ordnance [*Army*]

O Corn .... Old Cornish (AD)

OCOS.......... Ocean Climate Observing System (SAUS)

OCoSH......... Columbus State Hospital, Columbus, OH [*Library symbol*] [*Library of Congress*] (LCLS)

OCOT .... Office, Chief of Transportation [*Army*]

OCoV .... Center for Vocational and Technical Education, Ohio State University, Columbus, OH [*Library symbol*] [*Library of Congress*] (LCLS)

OCoY .... Young Men's Christian Association, Columbus, OH [*Library symbol*] [*Library of Congress*] (LCLS)

OCP .... Carleton Place Public Library, Ontario [*Library symbol*] [*National Library of Canada*] (NLC)

OCP .... Obstacle [*or Obstruction*] Clearance Panel [*Aviation*] (OA)

OCP .... Occupational Cluster Program (OICC)

OCP .... Ocean Culture Product

OCP .... Ocean Surveillance Product (SAUS)

OCP .... Octacalcium Phosphate [*Inorganic chemistry*]

OCP .... Ocular Cicatricial Pemphigoid [*Ophthalmology*]

OCP .... Oerlikon-Contraves Pyrotec AG (SAUS)

OCP .... Office of Civilian Personnel [*Military*]

OCP .... Office of Commercial Programs [*NASA*]

OCP .... Office of Consumer Protection (AD)

OCP .... Office of Cultural Presentations (AD)

OCP .... Office of the Chief of Protocol [*US Department of State*] (AD)

OCP .... Officer Candidate Programme [*British military*] (DMA)

OCP .... Official Crude Prices [*Petroleum Intelligence Weekly*] [*Information service or system*] (CRD)

OCP .... Oficina Central de Personal [*Central Personnel Office*] [*Spain*] (AD)

OCP .... Olefin Co-Polymer [*Lubricants*]

OCP .... Onchocerciasis Chemotherapy Project [*WHO*]

OCP .... Onchocerciasis Control Program [*World Health Organization*] (BUAC)

OCP	One-Component Plasma
OCP	Ontario College of Pharmacy
OCP	Open Circuit Potential (PDAA)
OCP	Operating [or Operational] Control Procedure (MSA)
OCP	Operational Capability Plan [Army]
OCP	Operational Checkout Procedure [NASA] (KSC)
OCP	Operational Communications Plan (MCD)
OCP	Operational Computer Program (ACAE)
OCP	Operational Configuration Processing (COE)
OCP	Operational Control Panel
OCP	Operation Control Panel (SAUS)
OCP	Operations Control Plan (AAG)
OCP	Operator Command Processor (TIMI)
OCP	Operators Control Panel (SAUS)
OCP	Optical Character Printing
OCP	Oral Contraceptive Pill [Gynecology] [Pharmacology] (DAVI)
OCP	Orbital Combustion Process (PDAA)
OCP	Orbital Control Program (SAA)
OCP	Orbital Correction Program [NASA] (KSC)
OCP	Order Code Processor [International Computers Ltd.]
OCP	Organizational Competitiveness Program [Motivational program]
OCP	Organization of Czech Palynologists (SAUS)
OCP	Orientalia Christiana Periodica [A publication] (ODCC)
OCP	Ortho-Chlorophenol [Organic chemistry]
OCP	Ostacalcium Phosphate [A fertilizer]
OCP	Out of Commission for Parts (AFM)
OCP	Output Control Program
OCP	Output Control Pulse (NASA)
ocp............	Output Control Pulses (AD)
OCP	Ova, Cysts, Parasites [Gastroenterology] (DAVI)
OCP	Overcharge Protection (ACAE)
OCP	Overhead Control Panel [Automotive engineering]
OCP	Overland Common Point [Imported item] [Business term]
ocp............	Overland Common Points (AD)
OCP	Overload Control Process [Telecommunications] (TEL)
OCP	Overseas Common Point [Exported item] [Business term]
OCP	Overseas Communications Project (SAUS)
OCP	Owners and Contractors Protective [Insurance]
OCP	Oxford Concordance Project (NITA)
OCP	Public Library of Cincinnati and Hamilton County, Cincinnati, OH [OCLC symbol] (OCLC)
OCPA	O-Chlorophenylacetic Acid (SAUS)
OCPA	Office, Chief of Public Affairs [Army]
OCPA	Office of Congressional and Public Affairs [FCC] (TSSD)
OCPA	Office of Governmental and Public Affairs (SAUS)
OCPA	Ortho-Chlorophenoxyacetic Acid [Organic chemistry]
OCPA	Ortho-Chlorophenylacetic Acid [Organic chemistry]
OCPAC	Orange County Performing Arts Center, Segerstrom Hall, Costa Mesa (SAUS)
OCPCA	Oil and Chemical Plant Constructors' Association [British]
OCPCJR	Office of Crime Prevention and Criminal Justice Research (AD)
OCPCSB	Operational Computer Program Configuration Sub-Board (SAUS)
OCPD	Obsessive-Compulsive Personality Disorder (MELL)
OCPD	Occult Constrictive Pericardial Disease [Cardiology] (CPH)
OCPD	Officer Commanding Police Division (SAUS)
OCPD	Officer-in-Charge Police District (AD)
OCPDB	Organic Chemical Producers Data Base (NITA)
OCPED	Office de Commercialisation du Poisson d'Eau Douce [Freshwater Fish Marketing Corp. - FFMC]
OCPG	Goodwood Data Systems Ltd., Carleton Place, Ontario [Library symbol] [National Library of Canada] (NLC)
OCPG	Procter & Gamble Co., Cincinnati, OH [Library symbol] [Library of Congress] (LCLS)
OCPG-H	Procter and Gamble Co., Health and Beauty Library, Cincinnati, OH [Library symbol] [Library of Congress] (LCLS)
OCPG-I.........	Procter & Gamble Co., Ivorydale Technical Center, Cincinnati, OH [Library symbol] [Library of Congress] (LCLS)
OCPG-Mv	Procter & Gamble Co., Miami Valley Laboratories, Cincinnati, OH [Library symbol] [Library of Congress] (LCLS)
OCPG-Sw	Procter & Gamble Co., Sharon Woods Technical Center, Technical Library, Cincinnati, OH [Library symbol] [Library of Congress] (LCLS)
OCPG-Wh	Procter & Gamble Co., Winton Hill Technical Center, Cincinnati, OH [Library symbol] [Library of Congress] (LCLS)
OCPH	Providence Hospital, Medical Library, Cincinnati, OH [Library symbol] [Library of Congress] (LCLS)
OCPI	Ohio Cancer Pain Initiative (SAUS)
OCPI	Optical Communic. Prod 'A' [NASDAQ symbol]
OCPINST.......	Office of Civilian Personnel Instruction [Navy] (MCD)
OCPL	Leigh Instruments Ltd., Carleton Place, Ontario [Library symbol] [National Library of Canada] (NLC)
OCPL	Oklahoma City Public Library (AD)
OCPL	Onondaga Library System [Library network]
OCPL	Orange County Public Library [Florida]
OCPLACS	Ontario Cooperative Program in Latin American and Caribbean Studies [Research center] (RCD)
OCPM	Optically Connected Parallel Machines [Computer science]
OCPNA........	Ortho-Chloro-para-nitroaniline [Organic chemistry]
OCPO	Office of Civilian Personnel Operations [Air Force]
OCPO	Office of Computer Processing Operations [Social Security Administration]
OCPO	Operations Cargo Passenger Office (DNAB)
OCPP	Orbiter Cloud Photopolarimeter [NASA]
OCPP	(Ortho-Chlorophenoxy)propionic Acid [Organic chemistry]

OCPR..........	Office of Claims and Payments Requirements [Social Security Administration]
OCPR..........	Office of Collateral Policy Responsibility (AFM)
OCPR..........	Operation and Conversion of Naval Petroleum Reserves (DNAB)
OCPS..........	I. P. Sharp Associates Ltd., Carleton Place, Ontario [Library symbol] [National Library of Canada] (NLC)
OCPS..........	Office Canadien du Poisson Sale [Canadian Saltfish Corporation]
OCPS..........	Office of Census and Population Studies [British]
OCPS..........	Officer Candidate Preparatory School (DNAB)
OCPS..........	Orbiter Camera Payload System (SAUS)
OCPS..........	Oxygen Cabin Pressurization Section [NASA] (KSC)
OCPSF	Organic Chemical, Plastic, and Synthetic Fiber
OCPV	Open Circuit Photovoltage (SAUS)
OCPW	Office of Chief of Psychological Warfare (LAIN)
OCQ	Membre de l'Ordre des Chimistes du Quebec [Canada] (DD)
OCQ	Oconto, WI [Location identifier] [FAA] (FAAL)
OCQ	Oneida Ltd. [NYSE symbol] (SPSG)
OCQM	Office of Chief Quartermaster [Military]
OCR	Creemore Public Library, Ontario [Library symbol] [National Library of Canada] (BIB)
OCR	Norcross, GA [Location identifier] [FAA] (FAAL)
OCR	Occupational Safety and Health Control Report [Navy]
OCR	Occurrence (SAUS)
OCR	Ocean Colour Radiometer (SAUS)
OCR	O'Connell Ranch [California] [Seismograph station code, US Geological Survey] (SEIS)
OCR	Oculocardiac Reflex [Physiology]
OCR	Office for Civil Rights [Department of Education]
OCR	Office of Civilian Requirements [Division of War Production Board] [World War II]
OCR	Office of Civil Rights [Environmental Protection Agency] (GFGA)
OCR	Office of Coal Research [Energy Research and Development Administration]
OCR	Office of Collateral Responsibility (AFM)
OCR	Office of Community Relations (COE)
OCR	Office of Coordinating Responsibility [Air Force]
OCR	Office of Corollary Responsibility (ACAE)
OCR	Office of the County Recorder (AD)
OCR	Oil Circuit Recloser
OCR	Oil Control Ring [Automotive engineering]
O Cr	Oklahoma Criminal Reports [A publication] (DLA)
OCR	Omnicare, Inc. [NYSE symbol] (SPSG)
OCR	Operational Capability Release
OCR	Operational Capability Requirement (SAUS)
OCR	Operational Change Report [Military] (NVT)
OCR	Operational Concept Review (ACAE)
OCR	Operational Control Record [Nuclear energy] (NRCH)
OCR	Operations Capability Reference (SSD)
OCR	Operations Control Room [Military] (CAAL)
OCR	Optical Card Reader (SAUS)
ocr............	Optical Character Reader [Computer science] (AD)
OCR	Optical Character Reader [Computer science]
OCR	Optical Character Recognition [Computer science]
OCR	Optical Character Resolution [Ligature Co.] (PCM)
OCR	Optical Code Reader (or Reading) (SAUS)
OCR	Optical Curve Recognition (SAUS)
OCR	Opticat Character Recognition (SAUS)
OCR	Optimum Change Regulator (SAUS)
OCR	Optimum Charge Regulator
OCR	Optional Character Reader [Computer science] (DA)
OCR	Oracle Resources [Vancouver Stock Exchange symbol]
OCR	Order Change Record (SAUS)
OCR	Order Control Record (SAA)
OCR	Order of Corporate Reunion [British]
OCR	Order of the Crown of Rumania
OCR	Ordo Reformatorum Cisterciensium [Cistercians, Trappists] [Roman Catholic men's religious order]
OCR	Organic-Cooled Reactor [Nuclear energy] (OA)
OCR	Organisation for the Collaboration of Railways [See also OSShD] [Warsaw, Poland] (EAIO)
OCR	Organization Change Request
OCR	Organization of work Camps of the Revolution (SAUS)
OCR	Organized Crime and Racketeering Section [Department of Justice] (DLA)
OCR	Output Control Register
OCR	Over Consolidated Ratio [Nuclear energy] (NUCP)
OCR	Overcurrent Relay (MSA)
OCR	Overhaul Component Requirement [NASA] (KSC)
OCR	Overhead Component Requirement (IAA)
OCR	Oxidizable Carbon Ratio
OCRA	Office Communications Research Association (SAUS)
OCRA	Officer Commanding, Royal Artillery (SAUS)
OCRA	Optical Character Recognition - ANSI Standard (Font A) [Computer science]
OCR-A.........	Optical Character Recognition-Font A (SAUS)
OCR-A.........	Optical Character Recognition Type A (SAUS)
OCRA	Organisation Clandestine de la Revolution Algerienne [Secret Organization of the Algerian Revolution] [France] (AD)
OCRA	Overseas Company Registration Agents Ltd. (ECON)
OCRASC......	Officer Commanding, Royal Army Service Corps (SAUS)
OCRB	Optical Character Recognition - ANSI Standard (Font B) [Computer science]
OCRB	Optical Character Recognition Bar [Computer science] (IAA)
OCR-B.........	Optical Character Recognition-Font B (SAUS)
OCR-B.........	Optical Character Recognition Type B (SAUS)

OCRBI .... Organization for Cooperation in the Roller Bearings Industry [*Warsaw, Poland*] (EAIO)

OCRC .... Ocean Climate Research Committee (SAUS)

O Cr C .... Oudh Criminal Cases [*India*] [*A publication*] (DLA)

OCRCWA...... Outcare Civil Rehabilitation Council of Western Australia

OCRD .... Ocean Climate Research Division [*Pacific Marine Environmental Laboratory*] (USDC)

OCRD .... Oculocerebrorenal Disease [*Medicine*] (MELL)

OCRD .... Office, Chief of Research and Development [*Army*]

OCRD .... Office of Crystalline Repository Development (SAUS)

OCRE .... Office of Conservation and Renewable Energy (COE)

OCRE .... Officer Commanding, Royal Engineers (SAUS)

OCRE .... Optical Character Reader Equipment (CCCA)

OCRE .... Optical Character Recognition Equipment [*Computer science*] (AABC)

ocre .... Optical Character Recognition Equipment [*Computer science*] (AD)

OCRE .... Organizations Concerned about Rural Education (AD)

oCRF .... Ovine Corticotrophin Releasing Factor [*Endocrinology*]

OCRHA .... Overseas Command Records Holding Area [*Army*]

OCRI .... Office Canadien pour un Renouveau Industriel [*Canadian Office for Industrial Revival*]

OCRI .... Ottawa-Carleton Research Institute (SAUS)

OCRIT .... Office of Combat Indentification Technology [*Army*]

OCRIT .... Optical Character Recognizing Intelligent Terminal [*Computer science*] (IAA)

ocrit .... Optical Character-Recognizing Intelligent Terminal [*Computer science*] (AD)

OCRM .... Ocean and Coastal Resource Management (GNE)

OCRM .... Office of Coastal Resource Management (USDC)

OCRM .... Officer Commanding Royal Marines [*British military*] (DMA)

OCRM .... Orbiter Crash and Rescue Manuals [*NASA*]

OCRM .... Outer Core Restraint Module (SAUS)

OCRMI .... Officer Commanding Royal Marines (SAUS)

OCRO .... Office of Central Records Operations (SAUS)

OCRR .... Office of the Coordinator, Regulatory Reform [*Canada*]

OCRS .... Oculocerebrorenal Syndrome [*Medicine*] (DMAA)

OCRS .... Online Computing Reviews Service (RALS)

OCRS .... Ontario Centre for Remote Sensing [*Canada*]

OCRS .... Operational Change Reporting System (SAUS)

OCRS .... Optical Character Recognition System (NITA)

OCRS .... Organisation Commune des Regions Sahariennes [*Common Organization of the Saharan Regions*]

OCRS .... Organized Crime and Racketeering Section [*Department of Justice*]

OCRSDG ...... Crysler Branch, Stormont, Dundas, and Glengarry County Library, Ontario [*Library symbol*] [*National Library of Canada*] (BIB)

OCRSF .... Organized Crime and Racketeering Strike Force (AD)

OcrstLb .... Ocurest Laboratories, Inc. [*Associated Press*] (SAG)

OCRT .... Ontario Consultants on Religious Tolerance

OCRU .... Office of Communication and Research Utilization (AD)

OCRUA .... Optical Character Recognition Users Association [*Later, RTUA*] (EA)

OCRW .... Raymond Walters General and Technical College, Cincinnati, OH [*Library symbol*] [*Library of Congress*] (LCLS)

OCR WAND... Optical Character Reader Wand (SAUS)

OCRWM .... Office of Civilian Radioactive Waste Management [*Oak Ridge National Laboratory*]

OCRX .... OncoRx, Inc. [*NASDAQ symbol*] (SAG)

OCS .... Cities Service Co., Technical Center - Energy Resources Group, Research Library, Tulsa, OK [*OCLC symbol*] (OCLC)

OCS .... Object Compatibility Standard (AAG)

OCS .... Obsessive Compulsive Scale [*Psychology*] (EDAC)

ocs.......... Obstacle Clearance Surface (AD)

OCS .... Obstruction Clearance Surface (SAUS)

OCS .... O-Carbonyl Sulfide (SAUS)

OCS .... Occipital Condyle Syndrome [*Medicine*] (MELL)

OCS .... Occult Congenital Syphilis [*Medicine*] (MELL)

OCS .... Ocean Color Scanner (PDAA)

OCS .... Ocean Culture System

OCS .... Octachlorostyrene [*Organic chemistry*]

OCS .... Octopine Synthase [*An enzyme*]

OCS .... Office, Chief of Staff [*Army*]

OCS .... Office Cleaning Service [*Commercial firm*] [*British*]

OCS .... Office Communications System (SAUS)

OCS .... Office Computer System (IAA)

OCS .... Office for Consumer Services [*HEW*]

OCS .... Office of Civilian Supply [*Division of War Production Board*]

OCS .... Office of Commercial Services [*Department of Commerce*]

OCS .... Office of Commodity Standards (SAUS)

OCS .... Office of Communication Systems [*Air Force*]

OCS .... Office of Community Services [*Family Support Administration*] [*Department of Health and Human Services*] (GFGA)

OCS .... Office of Community Services [*Bureau of Indian Affairs*]

OCS .... Office of Computing Services [*Georgia Institute of Technology*] [*Research center*] (RCD)

OCS .... Office of Contact Settlement (SAUS)

OCS .... Office of Contract Settlement [*Functions transferred to GSA, 1949; now obsolete*]

OCS .... Office of the Chief Scientist

OCS .... Office of the Chief Surgeon [*Military*]

OCS .... Officer Cadet School (SAUS)

OCS .... Officer Candidate School [*Military*]

OCS .... Officers' Chief Steward [*Navy*]

OCS .... Officers Command School (SAUS)

OCS .... Oil Conditioning System [*Automotive lubricants*]

OCS .... Oklahoma Climatological Society (SAUS)

OCS .... Old Church Slavonic [*Language, etc.*]

OCS .... On-Board Checkout System [*NASA*]

ocs.......... Onboard Checkout System [*NASA*] (NAKS)

OCS .... On Call System (SAUS)

OCS .... On-Card Sequencer (VLIE)

ocs.......... On Company Service (AD)

OCS .... One-Control Switch (SAUS)

OCS .... Open Cabling System (SAUS)

OCS .... Open Canalicular System [*Hematology*]

OCS .... Open-Circuit-Stable

OCS .... Operating Control System [*Computer science*] (VLIE)

OCS .... Operational Call Sign (IAA)

OCS .... Operational Characteristics (NATG)

OCS .... Operational Computer Software (VLIE)

OCS .... Operational Control Segment (SSD)

OCS .... Operational Control System (SAUS)

OCS .... Operations Control System

OCS .... Operator Communications Software (SAUS)

OCS .... Operator Console Services (VLIE)

OCS .... Operator Control Station (SAUS)

OCS .... Operator's Connection Set (IAA)

OCS .... Optical Character Scanner [*Computer science*]

OCS .... Optical Communications System (SAUS)

OCS .... Optical Communication System (SAUS)

OCS .... Optical Communicator System (MCD)

OCS .... Optical Computer System (IAA)

OCS .... Optical Contact Sensor

OCS .... Optical Contrasting Seeker (MCD)

OCS .... Optimizing Control System (SAUS)

OCS .... Optimum Coordinated Shipboard [*or Shorebased*] Allowance List (DNAB)

OCS .... Oral Contraceptive Steroid [*Medicine*] (MELL)

OCS .... Orbit Computation System (MCD)

OCS .... Orbit Correction Subsystem (NOAA)

OCS .... Order Communications System (SAUS)

OCS .... Order Communications Systems (VLIE)

OCS .... Order Control System (SAUS)

OCS .... Order of the Cross Society (EA)

OCS .... Organe de Controle des Stupefiants [*Narcotic Drug Control Organization*] [*France*] (AD)

OCS .... Organocyclosiloxane (SAUS)

OCS .... Oriel Computer Services Ltd. (NITA)

OCS .... Oriental Ceramic Society (EA)

OCS .... Oriental Chair of Solomon [*Freemasonry*]

OCS .... Oriented Cellular Structure

OCS .... Orifice of Coronary Sinus [*Medicine*] (MELL)

OCS .... Original Combat System (SAUS)

OCS .... Ornithodoros Coriaceus Spirochete [*Entomology*]

OCS .... Outer Continental Shelf

ocs.......... Outler Continental Shelf (AD)

OCS .... Outpatient Clinic Substation [*Veterans Administration*]

OCS .... Output Control Subsystem

OCS .... Output Control System (SAUS)

OCS .... Outside Chip Storage (SAUS)

OCS .... Overload Control Subsystem [*Telecommunications*] (TEL)

OCS .... Overload Control System (SAUS)

OCS .... Overseas Civil Servants (AD)

OCS .... Overseas Communication Service [*India*] (BUAC)

OCS .... Overseas Courier Service (AD)

OCS .... Overspeed Control System (AAG)

OCS .... Saint Thomas Institute, Cincinnati, OH [*Library symbol*] [*Library of Congress*] (LCLS)

OCSA .... Office, Chief of Staff, Army

OCSA .... Ohio Collegiate Soccer Association (PSS)

OCSA .... Ontario Council of Safety Associations (SAUS)

OCSA .... Orchid Society of South Australia

OCSA .... Outstanding Civilian Service Award

OCSAA .... Official Committee on Service Attaches and Advisers [*British*]

OCSAB .... Office of Contract Settlement Appeal Board [*Abolished, 1952*]

OCSAB .... Outer Continental Shelf Advisory Board [*Marine science*] (MSC)

OCSAN .... Organisation pour la Conservation du Saumon de l'Atlantique Nord [*North Atlantic Salmon Conservation Organization*] [*Scotland*] (EAIO)

OCSAPB ...... Outer Continental Shelf Environmental Assessment Program. Arctic Project Bulletin (SAUS)

OCSAPSB.... Outer Continental Shelf Environmental Assessment Program. Arctic Project Special Bulletin (SAUS)

OCSB .... Outer Continental Shelf Environmental Assessment Program. Bering Sea-Gulf of Alaska Newsletter (SAUS)

OCSC .... Outer Continental Shelf Committee [*Congressional committee*] (MSC)

OCSD .... Obsessive Compulsive Spectrum Disorder [*Psychology*]

OCSD .... Oculocraniosomatic Disease [*Medicine*] (DMAA)

OCSDG .... Stormont, Dundas, and Glengarry County Public Library, Cornwall, Ontario [*Library symbol*] [*National Library of Canada*] (NLC)

OCSDGL ...... Stormont, Dundas, and Glengarry Law Association, Cornwall, Ontario [*Library symbol*] [*National Library of Canada*] (BIB)

OCSE .... Office of Child Support Enforcement [*Department of Health and Human Services*]

OCSEA .... Outer Continental Shelf Environmental Assessment [*Marine science*] (MSC)

OCSEAC ...... Outer Continental Shelf Environmental Studies Advisory Commission [*Department of the Interior*] (MSC)

OCSEAP .... Outer Continental Shelf Environmental Assessment Program [*Department of Commerce, Department of the Interior*]

OCSEF .... Outer Continental Shelf Events File [*Department of the Interior*] (MSC)

OCSEP	Outer Continental Shelf Energy Program [*Marine science*] (MSC)
ocsf	Office Contents Special Form [*Inventor*] (AD)
OCSF	Office Contents Special Form [*Insurance*]
OCSIGO	Office of the Chief Signal Officer
OCSL	Oriel Computer Services Limited (NITA)
OCSL	St. Lawrence College [*College Saint-Laurent*], Cornwall, Ontario [*Library symbol*] [*National Library of Canada*] (NLC)
OCSLA	Outer Continental Shelf Lands Act
OCSLAA	Outer Continental Shelf Lands Act Amendments of 1978 (COE)
OCSM	Organization of Canadian Symphony Musicians [*See also OMOSC*]
OCSM	Outer Continental Shelf Oil and Gas Supply Model [*Department of Energy*] (GFGA)
ocsn	Occasion (AD)
ocsnl	Occasional (AD)
ocsnly	Occasionally (AD)
ocso	[*The*] Cistercians Order of the Strict Observance, Trappists (TOCD)
OCSO	Office of the Chief Signal Officer
OCSO	Order of Cistercian Nuns of the Strict Observance [*Roman Catholic religious order*]
OCSO	Order of Cistercians of the Strict Observance [*Trappists*] [*Roman Catholic men's religious order*]
OCSOT	Overall Combat Systems Operability Test (NVT)
OCSP	Office of Cued Speech Programs [*Gallaudet College*] [*Research center*] (RCD)
OCSP	On-Line Certificate Status Protocol [*Computer science*] (VLIE)
OCSP	Out of Commission, Special [*Vessel status*] (DNAB)
OCSPC	Outer Continental Shelf Policy Committee [*California*] (AD)
OCSPWAR	Office of the Chief of Special Warfare [*Army*]
OCSR	Optical Cable Signal Repeater (MCD)
OCSR	Serpent River Band Public Library, Cutler, Ontario [*Library symbol*] [*National Library of Canada*] (NLC)
OCSS	Office of the Chief of Support Services [*Army*]
OCST	Office of Cable Signal Theft [*National Cable Television Association*] (NTCM)
OCST	Office of Commercial Space Transportation [*NASA*]
OCST	Overcast (AABC)
ocst	Overcast (AD)
OC Stage	Open Collector Stage (SAUS)
OCStFH	Saint Francis/Saint George Hospital, Cincinnati, OH [*Library symbol*] [*Library of Congress*] (LCLS)
OCStG	Saint Gregory Seminary, Cincinnati, OH [*Library symbol*] [*Library of Congress*] (LCLS)
OCSTL	On-Board Checkout System Test Language [*NASA*] (KSC)
OCSW	Objective Crew-Served Weapon
OCT	Cincinnati Technical College, Cincinnati, OH [*Library symbol*] [*Library of Congress*] [*OCLC symbol*] (LCLS)
OCT	Object Classification Test (DMAA)
OCT	Object Code Translator (SAUS)
OCT	O-Chlorotoluene (SAUS)
OCT	Octagon (AAG)
oct	Octagon (AD)
OCT	Octahedral [*Molecular geometry*] (IAA)
oct	Octal (AD)
OCT	Octal [*Number system with a base of eight*] [*Computer science*] (CET)
OCT	Octane (AAG)
oct	Octane (AD)
OCT	Octanol [*Organic chemistry*]
Oct	Octans [*Constellation*] (WDAA)
Oct	Octanus [*Constellation*]
OCT	Octarius [*Pint*] [*Pharmacy*]
oct	Octave (AD)
OCT	Octave (ADA)
Oct	Octavius (AD)
oct	Octavo (AD)
OCT	Octavo [*Book from 20 to 25 centimeters in height*] [*Bibliography*]
oct	Octet (AD)
OCT	Octet (GOBB)
Oct	October (AD)
OCT	October (EY)
oct	Octobre [*October*] [*French*] (ASC)
OCT	Octuple (MSA)
OCT	Office, Chief of Transportation [*Army*]
OCT	Office of Critical Tables [*NAS-NRC*]
OCT	Office of the Chief of Transportation (SAUS)
OCT	Officer Candidate Test [*Army*]
OCT	Officer Classification Test
OCT	Operational Climatic Testing (MCD)
OCT	Operational Cycle Time
OCT	Operations Control Team [*Deep Space Network, NASA*]
OCT	Operator Control Table (SAUS)
OCT	Optical Coherence Tomography [*Medicine*]
OCT	Optical Contract Seeker (MCD)
OCT	Optimal Control Theory
OCT	Optimal Cutting Temperature [*Material for tissue fixation*]
OCT	Optimized Compensation Transactions (SAUS)
OCT	Oral Contraceptive Therapy [*Endocrinology*] (AAMN)
OCT	Orbital Circularization Technique
OCT	Organisation Communiste des Travailleurs [*Communist Organization of Workers*] [*France*] [*Political party*] (PPW)
OCT	Ornithin-Carbonyl-Transferase
OCT	Ornithine Carbamoyltransferase [*Also, OTC*] [*An enzyme*]
OCT	Ortho-Chlorotoluene [*Organic chemistry*]
OCT	Orthotopic Cardiac Transplantation [*Medicine*] (DMAA)
OCT	Output Clock Trigger (IAA)
OCT	Overseas Container Transportation (SAUS)
OCT	Overseas Countries and Territories [*Common Market*]
OCT	Oxford Classical Texts [*A publication*] (OCD)
OCT	Oxytocin Challenge Test [*Medicine*]
OCTA	Oceanic Control Area [*Aviation*] (DA)
OCTA	Octanucleotide [*Biochemistry*]
OCTA	Octapentadiene [*Toxic chemical*]
OCTA	Office of the Chemical Industry Trade Advisor (SAUS)
OCTA	On-Line Corporation Tax Assessment [*British*]
OCTA	Oregon-California Trails Association (EA)
OCTA	Ortho-Cyclohexanediaminetetraacetic Acid [*Also, DCTA*] [*Organic chemistry*]
OCTA	Outsized Cargo Tanker Aircraft
OCTAHDR	Octahedral
OCTAHDR	Octahedron (SAUS)
OCTANE	Operations Control Technique for Actuals Number Extraction (MCD)
OCTAP	Of Concern to Air Passengers [*Group affiliated with PATCO*] (EA)
OCTB	Oxford Church Textbooks [*A publication*]
OCTC	O-Chlorobenzotrichloride (SAUS)
OCTC	Operators Console Transfer Channel (SAUS)
OCTC	Operator's Control Transfer Channel [*Electronics*] (ECII)
OCTD	Observation, Conclusion, Temporary Data (SAUS)
OCTD	Orange County Transit District (SAUS)
OCTD	Ornithine Carbamoyltransferase Deficiency [*Medicine*]
OCTD	Other Connective Tissue Diseases [*Medicine*]
OCTD	Overlap Connective Tissue Disease [*Medicine*] (DMAA)
octe	Optical Component Testing and Evaluation (AD)
Octel	Octel Communications [*Associated Press*] (SAG)
October	October and November (AD)
OCTG	Oil Country Tubular Goods [*Metal industry*]
OCTH	Town of Haldimand Public Libraries, Caledonia, Ontario [*Library symbol*] [*National Library of Canada*] (NLC)
OCTHB	Office, Chief of Transportation, Historical Branch [*Army*]
OCTI	Office Central des Transports Internationaux par Chemins de Fer [*Central Office for International Railway Transport*] (EAIO)
OCTI	Ordnance Corps Technical Instruction
OCTL	Octel Communications Corp. [*NASDAQ symbol*] (NQ)
OCTL	One-Channel-to-Line (SAUS)
OCTL	Open-Circuited Terminating Line (IAA)
OCTL	Open-Circuited Transmission Line
OCTLA	Out of Control Area (SAUS)
OCTM	Organization Concepts for Top Management (SAUS)
Octn	Octanus [*Constellation*]
OCTO	October Oil Co. (SAUS)
OCTOPUS	Ocean Colour Techniques for Observation, Processing and Utilization Systems (SAUS)
oct pars	Octava Pars [*Eighth Part*] [*Latin*] (AD)
OCTR	Octoraro Railway, Inc. [*AAR code*]
O/CTR	Over Center [*Automotive engineering*]
OCTRF	Ontario Cancer Treatment and Research Foundation [*Canada*] (BUAC)
octr prot	Octrooi Protectie [*Patent Protected*] [*Dutch*] (AD)
OCT/RR	Off Course Target/Remote Reference Display (NG)
OCT/RR Display	Off-Course Target/Remote Reference Display (SAUS)
OCTS	Japanese Ocean Color Temperature Scanner (SAUS)
OCTS	Occupational Carpal-Tunnel Syndrome (SAUS)
OCTS	Ocean Color and Temperature Scanner (SAUS)
OCTS	Ocean Color and Temperature Sensor (ACAE)
OCTS	Ocean Color and Temperature Sounder (SAUS)
OCTS	Ocean Colour and Temperature Sensor (SAUS)
OCTS	Ocean Colour and Thermal Scanner (SAUS)
OCTS	Open Cooperative Test System [*Trademark of NCR Corp.*]
OCTS	Optical Cable Transmission System (MCD)
OC/TS Output	Open Collector/Tri-State Output (SAUS)
Oct Str	Octavo Strange [*Strange's Select Cases on Evidence*] [*A publication*] (DLA)
OCTU	Officer Cadet Training Unit [*Military*] [*British*]
octup	Octuplus [*Eightfold*] [*Latin*] (MAE)
octupl	Octuplicate (AD)
octv	Open-Circuit Television (AD)
OCTV	Open-Circuit Television
OCTW	Optical Communications Through the shuttle Window (SAUS)
OCU	Observation Care Unit [*Medicine*] (DAVI)
OCU	Oceanroutes, Inc., Palo Alto, CA [*OCLC symbol*] (OCLC)
OCU	Office Channel Unit (IAA)
OCU	Oklahoma City University
OCU	Ontario Council of Universities (SAUS)
OCU	Operational Capability Upgrade (ACAE)
OCU	Operational Control Unit
ocu	Operational Conversion Unit (AD)
OCU	Operational Conversion Unit (NATG)
OCU	Order of Christian Unity [*British*]
OCU	Orderwire Operator Control Unit (MCD)
OCU	Osaka City University (SAUS)
OCU	Oscillator Clock Unit (SAUS)
OCU	Over-the-Counter Control Unit [*Stock exchange term*] (MHDW)
OCU	University of Cincinnati, Cincinnati, OH [*Library symbol*] [*Library of Congress*] (LCLS)
OCUA	Ontario Council on University Affairs [*Canada*] (AD)
OCUB	Osmium Collidine Uranylenbloc (SAUS)
OCU-B	University of Cincinnati, Biology Library, Cincinnati, OH [*Library symbol*] [*Library of Congress*] (LCLS)
OCUC	Oxford and Cambridge Universities Club [*British*] (DAS)
OCU-DA	University of Cincinnati, Design, Architecture, and Art Library, Cincinnati, OH [*Library symbol*] [*Library of Congress*] (LCLS)

OCU-E.......... University of Cincinnati, Engineering Library, Cincinnati, OH [*Library symbol*] [*Library of Congress*] (LCLS)

OCUFA......... Ontario Confederation of University Facility Associations [*Canada*] (AD)

OCUG........... Union Gas Ltd., Chatham, Ontario [*Library symbol*] [*National Library of Canada*] (NLC)

OCUG........... Union Graduate School, Cincinnati, OH [*Library symbol*] [*Library of Congress*] (LCLS)

OCU-Geo...... University of Cincinnati, Geology-Geography Library, Cincinnati, OH [*Library symbol*] [*Library of Congress*] (LCLS)

ocul............ Oculis [*To the Eyes*] [*Latin*] (AD)

OCUL........... Oculo [*To the Eye*] [*Pharmacy*]

OCUL........... Ocurest Laboratories, Inc. [*NASDAQ symbol*] (SAG)

OCUL........... Ontario Council on University Libraries (SAUS)

OCU-L.......... University of Cincinnati, Law Library, Cincinnati, OH [*Library symbol*] [*Library of Congress*] (LCLS)

OCULA........ Ontario College and University Library Association (SAUS)

OCULENT...... Oculentum [*Eye Ointment*] [*Pharmacy*]

oculent....... Oculentum [*Eye Ointment*] [*Latin*] (AD)

OCU-M.......... University of Cincinnati, School of Medicine, Cincinnati, OH [*Library symbol*] [*Library of Congress*] (LCLS)

OCU-Math.... University of Cincinnati, Mathematics Library, Cincinnati, OH [*Library symbol*] [*Library of Congress*] (LCLS)

OCuME........ Milton Elementary School, Custar, OH [*Library symbol*] [*Library of Congress*] (LCLS)

OCU-Mu...... University of Cincinnati, College Conservatory of Music, Cincinnati, OH [*Library symbol*] [*Library of Congress*] (LCLS)

OCU-N......... University of Cincinnati, College of Nursing, Cincinnati, OH [*Library symbol*] [*Library of Congress*] (LCLS)

OCU-Ph........ University of Cincinnati, Physics Library, Cincinnati, OH [*Library symbol*] [*Library of Congress*] (LCLS)

OCUS........... Oblate Conference of the United States (EA)

OCUSI.......... United States Industrial Chemicals Co., Research Center Library, Cincinnati, OH [*Library symbol*] [*Library of Congress*] (LCLS)

OCV............. Bering Sea, AK [*Location identifier*] [*FAA*] (FAAL)

OCV............. Consultative Committee for Exploratory Studies (SAUS)

OCV............. Ocana [*Colombia*] [*Airport symbol*] (OAG)

OCV............. Oil Check Valve

OCV............. Old Aircraft Carrier [*Navy symbol*]

OCV............. Onsite Calibration Van (SAUS)

ocv............. Open-Circuit Voltage (AD)

OCV............. Open-Circuit Voltage

OCV............. Operational Compliance Value (SAUS)

OCV............. Opimian California Vineyards Corp. [*Toronto Stock Exchange symbol*]

OCV............. Ordinary Conversational Voice [*Medicine*]

OCV............. Ordre des Chevaliers du Verseau [*Knights of Aquarius Order*] (EAIO)

OCV............. Overriding Cam Valve

OCV............. Overseas Cooperation Volunteers (SAUS)

OCV............. United States Veterans Administration Hospital, Cincinnati, OH [*Library symbol*] [*Library of Congress*] (LCLS)

OCVD........... Open-Circuit Voltage Decay [*In silicon devices*]

OCV-L.......... Oil Control Valve - Low-Speed

OCVR........... Open Circuit Voltage Response (SAUS)

OCVRA........ Overseas Citizens Voting Rights Act

oc vu.......... Ocean View (AD)

OCW............ Oklahoma College for Women

OCW............ Old Cars Weekly [*A publication*]

OCW............ Operation Command Word [*Computer science*] (VLIE)

OCW............ Orange Cyan Wideband (IAA)

OCW............ Washington, NC [*Location identifier*] [*FAA*] (FAAL)

OCW............ Waterloo Regional Library, Waterloo, Ontario [*Library symbol*] [*National Library of Canada*] (NLC)

OCWCIB....... Organizing Committee of the World Congress on Implantology and Bio-Materials [*See also COCMIB*] [*Rouen, France*] (EAIO)

OCWCT........ West Carleton Township Public Library, Carp, Ontario [*Library symbol*] [*National Library of Canada*] (BIB)

OCWFLU...... Operative Coachmakers' and Wheelwrights' Federal Labour Union [*British*]

OCWG.......... Ocean Color Working Group (SAUS)

OCWN.......... Ocwen Financial Corp. [*NASDAQ symbol*] (SAG)

OcwnFin...... Ocwen Financial Corp. [*Associated Press*] (SAG)

OCWP.......... Operational Control Work Post (SAUS)

OCX............. Object Linking and Embedding Control Extension [*Computer science*] (IGQR)

OCX............. OLE Control Extensions (SAUS)

OCX............. OLE Custom Control (SAUS)

OCX............. Onex Corp. [*Toronto Stock Exchange symbol*]

OCX............. Open Compact Exchange (VLIE)

OCX............. Xavier University, Cincinnati, OH [*Library symbol*] [*Library of Congress*] (LCLS)

OCXO........... Oven-Controlled Crystal Oscillator

OCXO........... Oven-temperature Controlled Crystal Oscillator (SAUS)

OCY............. Organization Country (SAUS)

OCY............. Young Men's Mercantile Library Association, Cincinnati, OH [*Library symbol*] [*Library of Congress*] (LCLS)

OCYF........... Office for Children, Youth & Families (SAUS)

OCZ............. Lincoln, NE [*Location identifier*] [*FAA*] (FAAL)

OCZ............. Ocean Container Zebrugge (AD)

OCZ............. Operational Control Zone (MCD)

OCZM........... Office of Coastal Zone Management [*National Oceanic and Atmospheric Administration*]

OD............. Aerovias Condor de Colombia Ltda. (AEROCONDOR) [*Colombia*] [*ICAO designator*] (ICDA)

OD............. Delaware County District Library, Delaware, OH [*Library symbol*] [*Library of Congress*] (LCLS)

OD............. Doctor of Ophthalmology (WDAA)

OD............. Doctor of Optometry

OD............. Doctor of Osteopathy (WDAA)

OD............. Drug Overdose [*Emergency Medicine*] (DAVI)

OD............. Dundas Public Library, Ontario [*Library symbol*] [*National Library of Canada*] (NLC)

OD............. Emerald Airlines [*ICAO designator*] (AD)

OD............. Obiter Dicta [*Legal term*] [*Latin*] (DLA)

OD............. Object Data (SAUS)

OD............. Observable Difference

OD............. Observation Data (SAUS)

OD............. Observed Drift

O-D............. Obstacle-Dominance [*Medicine*] (DMAA)

OD............. Occupational Disease

OD............. Oceanographic Data (SAUS)

OD............. Oceanographic Datastation [*Telecommunications*] (TEL)

od............. Och Dylika [*And the Like*] [*Swedish*] (AD)

OD............. Octal-to-Decimal [*Computer science*] (BUR)

OD............. Ocular Density [*Ophthalmology*]

OD............. Ocular Dominance [*Opthalmology*]

OD............. Oculus Dexter [*Right Eye*] [*Ophthalmology*]

od............. Oculus Dexter [*Right Eye*] [*Latin*] (AD)

Od............. Odeon [*Record label*] [*Europe, etc.*]

Od............. Odericus [*Flourished, 1166-1200*] [*Authority cited in pre-1607 legal work*] (DSA)

Od............. Odofredus [*Deceased, 1265*] [*Authority cited in pre-1607 legal work*] (DSA)

od............. Odur [*or*] [*German*] (AD)

Od............. Odyssey [*of Homer*] [*Classical studies*] (OCD)

OD............. Office Decision [*United States Internal Revenue Bureau*] [*A publication*] (DLA)

OD............. Office of Disability [*Department of Health and Human Services*] (GFGA)

OD............. Office of the Director

OD............. Officer of the Day [*or Deck*] [*Also, OOD*] [*Navy*]

OD............. Ohio Decisions [*A publication*] (DLA)

OD............. Oil Desurger

OD............. Oil Distribution (DNAB)

OD............. Oil Drainage

OD............. Oildroplet (SAUS)

OD............. Oktal Dump (SAUS)

OD............. Old Dutch [*Language, etc.*]

OD............. Oldest Dryas (SAUS)

od............. Olive Drab (WDAA)

OD............. Olive Drab [*Color often used for military clothing and equipment*]

OD............. Omnes Dies [*Every Day*] [*Pharmacy*]

OD............. Once a Day [*or Daily*] (DAVI)

OD............. Once Daily (SAUS)

O/D............. On Deck (KSC)

od............. On Demand (AD)

OD............. On Demand [*Business term*]

O/D............. On Dock (MCD)

OD............. On Duty

OD............. One Day (SAA)

od............. Only Daughter (WDAA)

OD............. Onrechtmatige Daad [*Tort or Tortious Act*] [*Netherlands*] (ILCA)

OD............. Opendoc, Open Document (SAUS)

OD............. Open Drain (IAA)

OD............. Open Drop

OD............. Operational Data (SAUS)

OD............. Operational Decoder (SAUS)

OD............. Operational Demonstration (SAUS)

O/D............. Operational Difficulty (ACAE)

OD............. Operational Directive (SAUS)

OD............. Operational Downlink (SAUS)

OD............. Operational Downlink/Downlist (NASA)

OD............. Operational DownList

OD............. Operation Description

OD............. Operations Directive [*or Director*]

OD............. Operations Director (SAUS)

OD............. Operations Division

OD............. Opioid Dependence [*Medicine*] (MELL)

od............. Optical Density (AD)

OD............. Optical Density

OD............. Optical Detection (ABAC)

OD............. Optical Disc (SAUS)

OD............. Optical Disk [*Computer science*] (TELE)

OD............. Opus Dei (EA)

OD............. Orbit Determination

OD............. Orbiter (Operational) Downlink [*NASA*]

OD............. Order Dienst [*Netherlands first organized resistance group, 1940*] [*World War II*]

OD............. Order of Daedalians (EA)

OD............. Order of Death (SAUS)

OD............. Order of DeMolay (EA)

O/D............. Order of Deportation

OD............. Order of the Day (SAUS)

OD............. Ordinary (SAUS)

OD............. Ordinary Seaman [*British*] (DMA)

OD............. Ordnance (ACAE)

OD............. Ordnance Corps [*Army*] (GFGA)

OD............. Ordnance Data [*Inspection and test data*]

OD............. Ordnance Delivery (SAUS)

OD	Ordnance Department [*or Division*]
OD	Ordnance Depot (SAUS)
OD	Ordnance Disposal (SAUS)
OD	Ordnance Document [*Navy*]
OD	Ordnance Drawing
OD	Ordnungsdienst [*Military Police Service*] [*German military - World War II*]
od	Organizational Development (AD)
OD	Organization Development [*Human resources*] (WYGK)
OD	Original Data (SAUS)
od	Original Design (AD)
OD	Original Design
OD	Original Dirac [*Vacuum model*] [*Physics*]
OD	Originally Derived
OD	Origin and Destination [*Aviation*] (AFM)
O/D	Origin and Destination [*OST*] (TAG)
OD	Orphan Drug [*Medicine*] (MELL)
OD	Osseous Defect [*Medicine*]
OD	Other Denomination [*British military*] (DMA)
OD	Out Diffusion (SAUS)
OD	Outer Detector
od	Outer Diameter (SHCU)
OD	Outer Diameter [*Mechanical engineering*]
OD	Out-of-Date
OD	Output Data (IEEE)
OD	Output Diode (SAUS)
OD	Output Disable
OD	Output Display [*Computer science*] (IAA)
od	Outside Diameter (AD)
OD	Outside Dimension
OD	Outstanding Debt [*Finance*] (MHDB)
od	Oven Dried (AD)
OD	Oven Dry
OD	Overall Depth [*Typography*] (DGA)
OD	Overburden Drill (PDAA)
od	Overdose (AD)
OD	Overdose [*of narcotics*]
OD	Overdraft [*or Overdrawn*] [*Banking*]
OD	Overdrawn [*Banking*] (WDAA)
OD	Overdrive (AAG)
od	Overdrive (AD)
Od	Overdue
OD	Overload Detection [*Telecommunications*] (TEL)
OD	Overtly Diabetic [*Medicine*]
OD	Oxford Dictionary (SAUS)
OD	Oxygen Drain (MCD)
O-D	Zero Dimensional (AAEL)
OD3	Operational Data Dictionary/Directory (SAUS)
OD3	Optical Digital Data Disk
ODA	Civic Democratic Alliance [*Czech Republic*] [*Political party*] (BUAC)
ODa	Dayton and Montgomery County Public Library, Dayton, OH [*Library symbol*] [*Library of Congress*] (LCLS)
ODA	Iso-Octyldecyladipinat (SAUS)
oda	Occipito-Dextra Anterior (AD)
ODA	Occipitodextra Anterior [*A fetal position*] [*Medicine*] (AAMN)
ODA	Octadecylamine (SAUS)
ODA	Octal Debugging Aid [*Computer science*]
ODA	Octyldecyladipat (SAUS)
Oda	Odessa (AD)
ODA	Offa's Dyke Association [*British*] (DBA)
ODA	Office Data Architecture (SAUS)
ODA	Office Document Architecture [*Telecommunications*] (TSSD)
ODA	Office of Debt [*or Depreciation*] Analysis [*Department of the Treasury*]
ODA	Office of Drug Abuse (AD)
ODA	Office of the Defense Attache [*Foreign Service*]
ODA	Office of the Deputy Administrator (COE)
ODA	Office of the District Administrator (AD)
ODA	Office of the District Attorney (AD)
ODA	Official Development Aid [*or Assistance*]
ODA	Ohio Dental Association (SAUS)
ODA	Oklahoma Dental Association (SAUS)
ODa	Old Danish (AD)
ODA	Omni Deployment Actuator (ACAE)
ODA	Omnidirectional Aerial (SAUS)
ODA	Omnidirectional Antenna
ODA	One-Digit Adder (SAUS)
ODA	Online Delivery Acknowledgement (SAUS)
ODA	Ontario Dental Association [*Canada*] (BUAC)
ODA	Open Document Architecture (SAUS)
ODA	Operational Data Analysis
ODA	Operational Design and Analysis (IEEE)
ODA	Optical Diffraction Analyser (SAUS)
ODA	Optical Diffraction Analyses (SAUS)
ODA	Optical Diffraction Analysis [*Microscopy*]
ODA	Oronite Fuel Additive (SAUS)
ODA	Orphan Drug Ace [*1983*] (BARN)
ODA	Oscillating Doublet Antenna
ODA	Oscillator/Doubler/Amplifier
ODA	Other Design Activity (MSA)
ODA	Ouadda [*Central African Republic*] [*Airport symbol*] (AD)
ODA	Output Data Acknowledge (SAUS)
ODA	Overseas Development Administration [*British*] (EAIO)
ODA	Overseas Development Agency [*British*]
ODA	Overseas Development Aid

ODA	Overseas Development Assistance (AD)
ODA	Overseas Doctors Association in the United Kingdom [*British*]
ODA	Oxydianiline [*Organic chemistry*]
ODAA	Aden/International [*People's Democratic Republic of Yemen*] [*ICAO location identifier*] (ICLI)
ODaA	Dayton Art Institute, Dayton, OH [*Library symbol*] [*Library of Congress*] (LCLS)
ODAA	Office of Dependent Area Affairs [*Department of State*]
ODAB	Beihan [*People's Democratic Republic of Yemen*] [*ICAO location identifier*] (ICLI)
ODAC	Old Dominion Athletic Conference (PSS)
ODAC	On Demand Analyzer Computer
ODAC	Open Document Architecture Consortium (SAUS)
ODAC	Operations Distribution Administration Center (SAUS)
ODACA	Original Doll Artists Council of America (EA)
ODaCox	Cox Coronary Heart Institute, Dayton, OH [*Library symbol*] [*Library of Congress*] (LCLS)
ODADAS	Ohio Department of Alcohol and Drug Addiction Services
ODADC	Omnidirectional Air Data Computer (MCD)
ODaE	Engineers' Club of Dayton, Dayton, OH [*Library symbol*] [*Library of Congress*] (LCLS)
ODAF	Aden [*People's Democratic Republic of Yemen*] [*ICAO location identifier*] (ICLI)
ODAG	Al-Gheida [*People's Democratic Republic of Yemen*] [*ICAO location identifier*] (ICLI)
ODaGH	Grandview Hospital, Dayton, OH [*Library symbol*] [*Library of Congress*] (LCLS)
ODaGL	Church of Jesus Christ of Latter-Day Saints, Genealogical Society Library, Dayton Ohio Branch, Dayton, OH [*Library symbol*] [*Library of Congress*] (LCLS)
ODaGMI	General Motors Corp., Inland Manufacturing Division, Engineering Library, Dayton, OH [*Library symbol*] [*Library of Congress*] (LCLS)
ODaGMI	General Motors Corp., Inland Manufacturing Division, Engineering Library, Dayton (SAUS)
ODaGS	Good Samaritan Hospital, Dayton, OH [*Library symbol*] [*Library of Congress*] (LCLS)
ODAI	Origin/Destination Address Assignor Indicator (SAUS)
ODAI	Origin-Destination Assignor Identifier (SAUS)
ODAL	Octadecenal (SAUS)
ODALC	Ogden Air Logistics Center (MCD)
ODALE	Office of Drug Abuse Law Enforcement [*Later, Drug Enforcement Administration*] [*Department of Justice*]
ODALS	Omnidirectional Approach Lighting System [*Aviation*] (FAAC)
ODAM	Mukeiras [*People's Democratic Republic of Yemen*] [*ICAO location identifier*] (ICLI)
ODAM	Open Distributed Application Model (SAUS)
ODaMC	Barney Children's Medical Center, Dayton, OH [*Library symbol*] [*Library of Congress*] (LCLS)
ODaMCo	Mead Corp., Dayton, OH [*Library symbol*] [*Library of Congress*] (LCLS)
ODaMNH	Dayton Museum of Natural History, Dayton, OH [*Library symbol*] [*Library of Congress*] (LCLS)
ODaMR	Monsanto Research Corp., Dayton Laboratory, Dayton, OH [*Library symbol*] [*Library of Congress*] (LCLS)
ODAMS	Open Water Disposal Area Management Simulation [*US Army Corps of Engineers*]
ODaMVH	Miami Valley Hospital, Dayton, OH [*Library symbol*] [*Library of Congress*] (LCLS)
ODAN	Kamaran [*People's Democratic Republic of Yemen*] [*ICAO location identifier*] (ICLI)
ODaN	National Cash Register Co., NCR Library, Dayton, OH [*Library symbol*] [*Library of Congress*] (LCLS)
ODan	Old Danish (BEE)
ODAN	Old Danish [*Language, etc.*]
O'D & Br Eq Dig	O'Donnell and Brady's Irish Equity Digest [*A publication*] (DLA)
OD and MC	Operational Direction and Management Control (NATG)
OD & RD	Overseas Discharge and Replacement Depot
ODaNR	North Research Stillwater Pioneers, Dayton, OH [*Library symbol*] [*Library of Congress*] (LCLS)
ODaNT	National Cash Register Co., Technical Library, Dayton, OH [*Library symbol*] [*Library of Congress*] (LCLS)
ODA/ODIF	Office Document Architecture/Office Document Interchange Format (DOMA)
ODAP	Office of Drug and Alcohol Programs (SAUS)
O-DAP	Oncovin [*Vincristine*], Dianhydrogalactitol, Adriamycin, Platinol [*Cisplatin*] [*Antineoplastic drug regimen*]
ODAP	Operation Data Analysis Program (IAA)
ODAP	Perim [*People's Democratic Republic of Yemen*] [*ICAO location identifier*] (ICLI)
ODAPI	Omnidirectional Approach Path Indicator (SAUS)
ODAPI	Open Database Applications Program Interface [*Microsoft Corp.*]
ODAPS	Oceanic Display and Planning System [*Air traffic control*]
ODAPS	Operational OGE [*Operational Ground Equipment*] Data Acquisition and Patch Subsystem (GAVI)
ODAQ	Qishn [*People's Democratic Republic of Yemen*] [*ICAO location identifier*] (ICLI)
ODAR	Omnidirectional Airborne Radar (SAUS)
ODAR	Optical Detection and Ranging (DNAB)
ODAR	Riyan [*People's Democratic Republic of Yemen*] [*ICAO location identifier*] (ICLI)
ODAS	OCA-DLR Asteroid Survey (SAUS)
ODAS	Ocean Data Acquisition Systems, Aids and Devices [*Marine science*] (OSRA)
ODAS	Ocean Dynamics Advisory Subcommittee [*NASA*] (MSC)

ODAS	Oceanic Data Assimilation System (SAUS)
ODAS	Offshore Data Acquisition System (SAUS)
ODAS	Oral Deaf Adults Section [*Later, OHIS*] (EA)
ODAS	Socotra [*People's Democratic Republic of Yemen*] [*ICAO location identifier*] (ICLI)
ODaSC	Sinclair Community College, Dayton, OH [*Library symbol*] [*Library of Congress*] (LCLS)
ODASD	Office of the Deputy Assistant Secretary of Defense
ODaSR	Standard Register Co., Engineering and Research Library, Dayton, OH [*Library symbol*] [*Library of Congress*] (LCLS)
ODaStE	Saint Elizabeth Hospital, Dayton, OH [*Library symbol*] [*Library of Congress*] (LCLS)
ODaStL	Saint Leonard College, Dayton, OH [*Library symbol*] [*Library of Congress*] (LCLS)
ODAT	Ataq [*People's Democratic Republic of Yemen*] [*ICAO location identifier*] (ICLI)
odat	One Day at a Time (AD)
ODATS	Office Director Assignment Tracking System (SAUS)
ODaTS	United Theological Seminary, Dayton, OH [*Library symbol*] [*Library of Congress*] (LCLS)
ODaU	University of Dayton, Dayton, OH [*Library symbol*] [*Library of Congress*] (LCLS)
ODaU-L	University of Dayton, Law Library, Dayton, OH [*Library symbol*] [*Library of Congress*] (LCLS)
ODaUM	United Methodist Church, Commission on Archives and History, Dayton, OH [*Library symbol*] [*Library of Congress*] (LCLS)
ODaU-M	University of Dayton, Marian Library, Dayton, OH [*Library symbol*] [*Library of Congress*] (LCLS)
ODaV	United States Veterans Administration Center, Library Services, Dayton, OH [*Library symbol*] [*Library of Congress*] (LCLS)
ODaWU	Wright State University, Dayton, OH [*Library symbol*] [*Library of Congress*] (LCLS)
ODaWU-H	Wright State University, School of Medicine, Fordham Library, Dayton, OH [*Library symbol*] [*Library of Congress*] (LCLS)
ODaWU-W	Wright State University, Western Ohio Branch Campus, Celina, OH [*Library symbol*] [*Library of Congress*] (LCLS)
O Day	Organization Day (SAUS)
ODB	Air Service [*Mali*] [*ICAO designator*] (FAAC)
ODB	Cordoba [*Spain*] [*Airport symbol*] (OAG)
ODB	Ocean Data Buoy [*Marine science*] (MSC)
ODB	O-Dichlorobenzene (SAUS)
ODB	Odontoblast
ODB	Office of Dependency Benefits
ODB	Oil-Degrading Bacteria
ODB	Operational Database (SSD)
ODB	Operational Data Book [*NASA*] (NAKS)
odb	Opiate-Directed Behavior (AD)
odb	Opiate-Directed Behavior
ODB	Orbit Determination Beacon (SAUS)
ODB	Output Data Buffer
ODB	Output Data Bulk (SAUS)
ODB	Output Display Branch [*Computer science*] (IAA)
odb	Output to Display Buffer [*Computer science*] (AD)
ODB	Output to Display Buffer [*Computer science*]
ODB	Oven Dry Basis
ODB	Overseas Development Bank [*Investors' Overseas Services*]
ODB	Oxydibenzil [*Organic chemistry*]
ODBA	Ocean Dumping Ban Act [*1988*]
ODBA	Oregon Dairy Breeders Association (BUAC)
ODBC	Object-Oriented Database Connectivity (SAUS)
ODBC	Official Doctor of Broken Computers
ODBC	Open Database Connectivity [*Computer science*]
ODBMS	Object Database Management System (SAUS)
ODBMS	Object-Oriented Database Management System
ODBMS	On-Board Database Management System (SSD)
OD Boat	One-Design Boat (SAUS)
ODBR	Output Data Buffer Register (SAUS)
ODBTS	United Theological Seminary, Dayton (SAUS)
ODC	Ocean Dynamics and Climate (SAUS)
ODC	Oceanographic Data Center (MCD)
ODC	Odometer Data Computer [*Developed by Mileage Validator, Inc.*]
ODC	Office of Defense Cooperation (DOMA)
ODC	Office of Defense Co-ordination (SAUS)
ODC	Office of Deputy Chief of Staff Programs and Resources [*Air Force*]
ODC	Officer Data Card
ODC	Ohio Dominican College, Columbus, OH [*OCLC symbol*] (OCLC)
ODC	Oil-Dri Corp. of America [*NYSE symbol*] (SPSG)
ODC	Old Dominion College (SAUS)
ODC	Oligodendrocyte [*Also, OLG*] [*Cytology*]
ODC	One-Directional Control [*Engineering*]
ODC	Online Data Capture
ODC	Ontario Development Corporation (SAUS)
ODC	Operational Data Center [*Deep Space Network, NASA*]
ODC	Operational Document Control
ODC	Operation Desert Capture [*DoD*]
ODC	Operation Design Criteria (MCD)
ODC	Optical Data Collecting (SAUS)
ODC	Optical Disc Controller (NITA)
ODC	Optical Disc Corporation (SAUS)
ODC	Orbital Data Collector
ODC	Order of Discalced Carmelites [*Roman Catholic religious order*]
ODC	Ordinary Decent Criminal [*British prison slang for other than a political prisoner*]
ODC	Organization Development Council [*Defunct*] (EA)
ODC	Original Design Cutoff (AAG)
ODC	Oritidine Decarboxylase (DMAA)
ODC	Ornithine Decarboxylase [*An enzyme*]
ODC	Orotidylate Decarboxylase (SAUS)
ODC	Oscilloscope Digital Control
ODC	Other Data Center (SAUS)
ODC	Other Direct Charge (ACAE)
odc	Other Direct Costs (AD)
ODC	Other Direct Costs [*Accounting*]
odc	Outer Dead Center (AD)
ODC	Outer Dead Center (DNAB)
ODC	Outpatient Diagnostic Center (STED)
ODC	Output Data Carrier (SAUS)
ODC	Output Data Control
ODC	Overseas Development Corporation (NADA)
ODC	Overseas Development Council (EA)
ODC	Overseas Diplomacy Coordinator (DNAB)
ODC	Oxford Decimal Classification
ODC	Oxygen Dissociation Curve [*Medicine*] (DMAA)
ODC	Oxyhaemoglobin Dissociation Curve (PDAA)
ODC	Ozone-Depleting Compound [*Environmental chemistry*]
ODCA	Ocean Dumping Control Act [*Canada*]
ODCA	Organizacion Democrata Cristiana de America [*Christian Democratic Organization of America - CDOA*] [*Caracas, Venezuela*]
ODCARP	Operational Data Collection, Analysis and Reporting Program (ACAE)
ODCBA	Oxford and District Cattle Breeders Association (SAUS)
ODCC	Ohio Decisions, Circuit Court [*Properly cited Ohio Circuit Decisions*] [*A publication*] (DLA)
ODCC	On-Board Digital Computer Control
ODCC	One-Design Class Council (EA)
ODCC	Oxford Dictionary of the Christian Church
ODCC	United States One-Design Class Council (EA)
ODCCP	United Nations Office for Drug Control and Crime Prevention (SAUS)
ODCDR	Orbiter Delta CDR [*NASA*] (GFGA)
ODCF	One-Dimensional Compressible Flow (SAUS)
ODCH	Ordinary Disease of Childhood (STED)
OD Class	One-Design Class (SAUS)
ODCM	Office of Defense and Civilian Mobilization [*See also OCDM*] (MUGU)
ODCM	Office of the Director of Civilian Marksmanship (ACAE)
ODCM	Off-Site Dose Calculation Manual [*Nuclear energy*] (NRCH)
ODC of S	Office of the Deputy Chief of Staff [*World War II*]
ODCOPS	Office of the Deputy Chief of Staff for Operations & Plans (SAUS)
ODCP	Office of the Deputy Commissioner for Programs (SAUS)
ODCP	One-Digit Code Point [*Telecommunications*] (TEL)
ODCPC	Order of Descendants of Colonial Physicians and Chirurgiens [*Defunct*] (EA)
ODCR	Officer Distribution Control Report [*Navy*] (NG)
ODCR	Operations Deputies Conference Room (SAUS)
ODCS	Office of the Deputy Chief of Staff [*World War II*]
ODCS	Online Data Compression System (PDAA)
ODCS	Open Distributed Computing Structure (SAUS)
ODCS	Operational Data Collection System (SAUS)
ODCSCD	Office of the Deputy Chief of Staff, Combat Developments [*Army*]
ODCSI	Office of the Deputy Chief of Staff for Intelligence
ODCSLOG	Office of the Deputy Chief of Staff for Logistics [*Army*] (AABC)
ODCSO	Office of Data Collection and Survey Operations [*Bureau of Labor Statistics*]
ODCSOPS	Office of the Deputy Chief of Staff for Operations and Plans [*Army*]
ODCSPER	Office of the Deputy Chief of Staff for Personnel [*Army*]
ODCSRDA	Office of the Deputy Chief of Staff for Research, Development, and Acquisition [*Army*] (AABC)
ODCTI	Old Dominion College Technical Institute (AD)
ODD	Obsessive-Deductive Disorder [*Facetious term for a malady affecting some taxpayers*]
ODD	Obstacle Detection Device
ODD	Ocean Disposal Database [*US Army Corps of Engineers*]
odd	oculodentodigital (SAUS)
ODD	Oculodentodigital Dysplasia [*Medicine*] (MAE)
ODD	Offboard Deception Device [*Navy*] (CAAL)
ODD	Old Destroyer [*Navy symbol*]
ODD	Oodnadatta [*Australia*] [*Airport symbol*] (OAG)
ODD	Open Data Desktop (SAUS)
ODD	Operational Detachment Delta [*Antiterrorist unit*] [*Military*] (LAIN)
odd	Operator Distance Dialing (AD)
ODD	Operator Distance Dialing
ODD	Oppositional Defiant Disorder
ODD	Oppositional Developmental Disorder (SAUS)
ODD	Optical Data Digitizer [*Computer science*]
ODD	Optical Data Disc (NITA)
ODD	Optical Digital Data Disk
ODD	Optical Digital Disc (NITA)
ODD	Optical Downconverter Demultiplexer (ACAE)
ODD	Order and Dispatch Desk for SAR data products (SAUS)
ODD	Organizing District Delegate [*British labor*]
ODD	Ouchterlony Double Diffusion Test [*Immunogel assay*]
ODD	Outside Design and Development
ODD	Overdetermined Dual-Doppler (SAUS)
ODD	Overseas Deployment Data [*Military*]
ODD	Oxalate Deposition Disease [*Medicine*] (MELL)
ODDA	Office of Deputy Director for Administration [*Marshall Space Flight Center*] (KSC)
ODDD	Operator Direct Distance Dialing (SAUS)
ODDD	Optical Digital Data Disk
ODDDR & R	Office of the Deputy Director of Defense Research and Engineering (RDA)
ODDH	On-Board Digital Data Handling

ODDL	Onboard Digital Data Load (ACAE)
ODDO	Operation Description Distribution Order
ODDP	Office of the Director of Development Planning [*Air Force*] (MCD)
ODDR & E	Office of the Director of Defense Research and Engineering [*Later, Office of the Under Secretary of Defense for Research and Engineering*] [*Army*]
ODDRD	Office of Deputy Director for Research and Development [*Marshall Space Flight Center*] (KSC)
ODDRE	Office of the Director of Defense Research and Engineering [*Later, Office of the Under Secretary of Defense for Research and Engineering*] [*Army*]
ODDS	Oceanographic Digital Data System [*Navy*]
ODDS	Online Data Entry and Display System [*Job Service*] (OICC)
ODDS	Operational Data Delivery Services (MCD)
ODDS	Optical Disk Data System (NITA)
ODDS	Optional Delivery Dispenser System (MCD)
ODE	Delhi Public Library, Ontario [*Library symbol*] [*National Library of Canada*] (NLC)
ODE	Odense [*Denmark*] [*Airport symbol*] (OAG)
ODE	O-Desmethylencainide (STED)
ODE	Odessa [*Former USSR*] [*Geomagnetic observatory code*]
ODE	Office 97 Developer Edition [*Microsoft*]
ODE	Office of Device Evaluation [*U.S. Food and Drug Administration*]
ODE	Oil Drilling and Exploration (AD)
ODE	Old-Dog Encephalitis (SAUS)
ODE	Omicron Delta Epsilon [*Fraternity*]
ODE	One Day Event [*Horse-riding*] [*British*] (DI)
ode	One-Day Event (AD)
ODE	One-Dimensional Equilibrium (MCD)
ODE	Online Data Entry (ADA)
ODE	Optical Designation Evaluation (MCD)
ODE	Optimally Designed Experiments
ODE	Orbit Data Editor Assembly [*Space Flight Operations Facility, NASA*]
ODE	Ordinary Differential Equation [*Mathematics*]
ODE	Ordnance Development & Engineering (SAUS)
ODE	Ortho-Demethylencainide [*Biochemistry*]
ODE	OSF Development Environment (SAUS)
ODE	Oxford Dictionary of the English Language (SAUS)
ODE	Oxygen Defect Electron (SAUS)
ODEA	Oxygen Enriched Air (ACAE)
ODEAG	Research Station, Agriculture Canada [*Station de Recherches, Agriculture Canada*] Delhi, Ontario [*Library symbol*] [*National Library of Canada*] (NLC)
O'Dea Med Exp	O'Dea's Medical Experts [*A publication*] (DLA)
ODE Assembly	Orbit Data Editor Assembly (SAUS)
ODEC	Ocean Data Equipment Corporation (SAUS)
ODEC	Ocean Design Engineering Corp. (AD)
ODECA	Organizacion de los Estados Centroamericanos [*Organization of Central American States - OCAS*] [*San Salvador, El Salvador*] (EAIO)
ODECO	Ocean Drilling & Exploration Company, New Orleans (SAUS)
O Dec Rep	Ohio Decisions Reprint [*A publication*] (DLA)
ODEE	[*The*] Oxford Dictionary of English Etymology [*A publication*]
ODef	Defiance Public Library, Defiance, OH [*Library symbol*] [*Library of Congress*] (LCLS)
ODefC	Defiance College, Defiance, OH [*Library symbol*] [*Library of Congress*] (LCLS)
ODelp	Delphos Public Library, Delphos, OH [*Library symbol*] [*Library of Congress*] (LCLS)
OdeM	Order of Our Lady of Mercy (TOCD)
odem	Order of Our Lady of Mercy (TOCD)
ODEND	OR Optical Detected ENDOR (SAUS)
ODENDOR	Optical Detected Electron Nuclear Double Resonance (AAEL)
OD-ENDOR	Optically Detected Electron Nuclear Double Resonance [*Spectroscopy*]
Odeneal	Odeneal's Reports [*9-11 Oregon*] [*A publication*] (DLA)
ODEP	Oxford Dictionary of English Proverbs (SAUS)
ODEPA	Organizacion Deportiva Panamericana [*Pan American Sports Organization - PASO*] [*Mexico City, Mexico*] (EAIO)
ODEPA	Oxapentamethylenediethylenephosphoramide [*Pharmacology*]
ODEPLAN	Oficina de Planificacion Nacional [*Office of National Planning*] [*Spain*] (AD)
ODEPR	Optical Detected Electron Paramagnetic Resonance (AAEL)
O Dep Rep	Ohio Department Reports [*A publication*] (DLA)
ODEQ	Oklahoma Department of Environmental Quality (SAUS)
Oderi	Odericus [*Flourished, 1166-1200*] [*Authority cited in pre-1607 legal work*] (DSA)
ODES	Deseronto Public Library, Ontario [*Library symbol*] [*National Library of Canada*] (NLC)
ODES	Ocean Data Evaluation System [*Environmental Protection Agency*] (AEPA)
ODES	Optical Discrimination Evaluation Study [*NASA*] (NASA)
OD-ESR	Optically Detected Electron Spin Resonance [*Spectroscopy*]
ODESSA	Ocean Data Environmental Science Services Acquisition [*Buoy*]
ODESSA	Oceanographic Data & Environmental Satellite System Application (SAUS)
ODESSA	Oceanographic Data for the Environmental Science Services Administration (GFGA)
ODESSA	Organisation der Ehemaligen Schutzstaffel Angehoeriggen [*Organization of Former Members of the Elite Guard*] [*Founded after World War II to smuggle war criminals out of Germany and provide them with false identities*]
Odes Sol	Odes of Solomon [*Biblical*] (RION)
ODESUR	Organizacion Deportiva Sudamericana [*An association*] (EAIO)
ODESY	Online Data Entry System [*Burroughs Corp.*]
ODET	Odetics, Inc. [*NASDAQ symbol*] (SAG)
ODETA	Odetics, Inc. 'A' [*NASDAQ symbol*] (TTSB)
ODETB	Odetics, Inc. 'B' [*NASDAQ symbol*] (TTSB)
Odetics	Odetics, Inc. [*Associated Press*] (SAG)
ODETTE	Organisation for Data Exchange by Tele-Transmission in Europe (SAUS)
ODEX	Optical Dynamics Experiment (SAUS)
ODF	Oceanographic Data Facility (SAUS)
Odf	Odofredus [*Deceased, 1265*] [*Authority cited in pre-1607 legal work*] (DSA)
ODF	Official Development Finance
ODF	Old Dominion Foundation (AD)
ODF	One-Dimension Flow
ODF	Opacity Distribution Function [*Spectroscopy*]
ODF	Opendoc Development Framework (SAUS)
ODF	Opendoc Part Framework (SAUS)
ODF	Operational Deployment Force (AD)
ODF	Operations Data File
ODF	Optimal Decision Function
ODF	Optoelectronic Data Filter (SAUS)
ODF	Orbit Determination Facility (MCD)
ODF	Orientation Distribution Function
ODF	Original Data File (NITA)
ODF	Output Data File
odfc	Outside Diameter of Female Coupling (AD)
ODFFU	Organization for Defense of Four Freedoms for Ukraine (EA)
ODFI	Open Die Forging Institute (EA)
ODFL	Old Dominion Freight Lines, Inc. [*NASDAQ symbol*] (SPSG)
ODFR	Oxygen-Derived Free Radicals [*Biochemistry*]
OD-FSR	Optically Detected Electron Spin Resonance (SAUS)
ODFT	Odd Discrete Fourier Transform (MCD)
ODFW	Oregon Department of Fish and Wildlife Research and Development Section [*Oregon State University*] [*Research center*] (RCD)
ODG	Enid, OK [*Location identifier*] [*FAA*] (FAAL)
ODG	Offline Data Generator
ODG	Ontario Drive & Gear Ltd (SAUS)
ODG	Operational Data Group (MCD)
ODG	Operational Design Group
ODG	Orbit Data Generator [*NASA*]
Odgers	Odgers on Libel and Slander [*A publication*] (DLA)
ODGF	Osteosarcoma-Derived Growth Factor [*Biochemistry*]
Odg Lib	Odgers on Libel and Slander [*A publication*] (DLA)
ODGP	Osborne Division of General Practice (AD)
Odg Pl	Odgers on Principles of Pleading [*20th ed.*] [*1975*] [*A publication*] (DLA)
ODGRT	Oman Directorate General of Radio and Television (SAUS)
ODGSE	Operational Deployment Ground Support Equipment (AAG)
ODGSO	Office of Domestic Gold and Silver Operations [*Department of the Treasury*]
ODH	Highland Secondary School, Dundas, Ontario [*Library symbol*] [*National Library of Canada*] (NLC)
ODH	Octanol Dehydrogenase [*An enzyme*]
ODH	Octopine Dehydrogenase [*An enzyme*]
ODH	Ontario Department of Health [*Canada*] (AD)
ODH	Operations Directive Handbook (SAUS)
ODHS	Dundas Historical Society Museum, Ontario [*Library symbol*] [*National Library of Canada*] (BIB)
ODHT	Hagerman Township Public Library, Ontario [*Library symbol*] [*National Library of Canada*] (NLC)
ODHWS	Office of Defense Health and Welfare Services [*World War II*]
ODI	Nodine, MN [*Location identifier*] [*FAA*] (FAAL)
ODI	Odin Industry Ltd. [*Vancouver Stock Exchange symbol*]
ODI	Office Document Index
ODI	Office of Defense Investigation (SAUS)
ODI	Office of Director of Intelligence [*Military*]
ODI	Oil Drain Interval
ODI	Open Datalink Interface [*Computer science*]
ODI	Open Device Interconnect
ODI	Open-Door International [*An association*] (AD)
ODI	Open Door International for the Economic Emancipation of the Woman Worker [*Brussels, Belgium*] (EAIO)
ODI	Open Driver Interface [*Computer science*] (CIST)
ODI	Operational Development Inspection (SAA)
ODI	Optical Digital Image (SAUS)
ODI	Optical Digital Imagery
ODI	Optonics Devices Incorporated
ODI	Organization Development Institute (SAUS)
ODI	Overseas Development Institute (EA)
O Dia	Outer Diameter (AD)
ODIC	Oceanographic Data and Information Centre (SAUS)
ODIC	Office of the Director of Information Control (SAUS)
ODIC	Outside Diameter of Inner Conductor
ODID	Office of the Director of Industrial Demobilization
ODID	Operational Display and Input Development (SAUS)
ODIF	Office Document Interchange Format (HGAA)
ODIF	Open Document Interchange Format (SAUS)
ODIFF	Oil Differential
ODIHR	Office for Democratic Institutions & Human Rights [*British*] (WDAA)
ODIL	Overseas Development Institute Ltd. (AD)
ODIMS	Open Distributed Information Management System (SAUS)
ODIN	Ocean Data and Information Network (SAUS)
ODIN	Onboard Data Interfaces and Network [*NASA*] (SPST)
ODIN	Online Dakota Information Network [*Information service or system*] (IID)
ODIN	On-line Documentation and Information Network (SAUS)

ODIN .... Online Dokumentations- und Informationsverbund [*Online Documentation and Information Affiliation*]
ODIN .... Operational Data Interface (SAUS)
ODIN .... Operational Display Information Network (MCD)
ODIN .... Optical Design Integration (SAUS)
ODIN .... Optimal [*or Orbital*] Design Integration [*Computer program*]
ODIN .... Orbital Design Integration [*NASA*] (NAKS)
ODINEA .... Ocean Data and Information Network for Eastern Africa (SAUS)
Oding .... Overdosing (SAUS)
OD Input ...... Output Disable Input (SAUS)
OD Institu .... Organization Development Institute (NTPA)
Odinsup .... ODI-NDIS Supplementary Driver (SAUS)
ODINSUP ..... Open Data link Interface-Network driver interface specification Support (SAUS)
ODIRP .... Office, Director of Personnel [*Air Force*]
ODIS .... Object Design, Inc. [*NASDAQ symbol*] (SAG)
ODIS .... Ocean Dynamics Information System [*Marine science*] (MSC)
ODIS .... Oceanographic Data Information System (SAUS)
ODIS .... Online Data Information System (SAUS)
ODIS .... Onsite Discharge Information System (SAUS)
ODIS .... Optical Disk Interface System [*Computer science*]
ODIS .... Orbital Design Integration System
ODIS .... Origin Destination Information System [*US Postal Service*]
ODISC4 .... Office of the Director of Informantion Systems for Command, Control, Communications, and Computers [*Army*]
ODISS .... Optical Digital Image Storage System (ACAE)
ODISTA .... Oceanographic Data in Subtrial Areas
O Div .... Ontario Division (SAUS)
ODJ .... Ouanda Djalle [*Central African Republic*] [*Airport symbol*] (AD)
ODJB .... Original Dixieland Jazz Band
ODJS .... Office of the Director, Joint Staff (MCD)
ODK .... Kodiak, AK [*Location identifier*] [*FAA*] (FAAL)
ODK .... Office Develoment Kit (SAUS)
ODK .... Omicron Delta Kappa [*Fraternity*]
ODK .... One-Dimensional Kinetics [*Computer program*] (MCD)
ODK .... Orlop Deck (SAUS)
ODL .... Cordillo Downs [*South Australia*] [*Airport symbol*] (AD)
ODL .... Object Definition Language [*Computer science*]
ODL .... Object Description Language (SAUS)
ODL .... Object Design Language (SAUS)
ODL .... Oceanic Data Link [*FAA*] (TAG)
ODL .... Office Document Language [*Telecommunications*]
ODL .... Office of Defense Lending [*Department of the Treasury*]
ODL .... Office of the Duchy of Lancaster [*British*]
ODL .... Officer Deficiency Letter [*Navy*] (NVT)
ODL .... Oklahoma Department of Libraries
ODL .... Open and Distance Learning (AIE)
ODL .... Open Discrepancy List (ACAE)
ODL .... Open Document Language (SAUS)
ODL .... Optical Disc Library (SAUS)
ODL .... Ostwald Dilution Law [*Chemistry*]
ODL .... Overseas Drilling Ltd. (SAUS)
ODL .... University of Dayton, Law Library, Dayton, OH [*OCLC symbol*] (OCLC)
ODLAMP ...... One-Dimensional LASER and Mixing Program
ODLB .... Dwight Branch, Lake Of Bays Township Public Library, Ontario [*Library symbol*] [*National Library of Canada*] (BIB)
ODLB .... Optical Dispensers' Licensing Board [*New South Wales, Australia*]
ODLC .... Outboard Data Link Control
ODLI .... Open Data Link Interface [*Computer science*]
ODLIS .... Online Dictionary of Library and Information Science
ODLRO .... Off-Diagonal Long-Range Order [*Physics*]
odlsq .... Odalisque (VRA)
ODLY .... Orderly (WGA)
ODM .... Methodist Theological School in Ohio, Delaware, OH [*Library symbol*] [*Library of Congress*] (LCLS)
ODM .... Object Database Manager (SAUS)
ODM .... Object Data Manager (SAUS)
ODM .... Odiham FTU [*British*] [*ICAO designator*] (FAAC)
ODM .... Office of Defense Mobilization [*Transferred to Office of Defense and Civilian Mobilization, 1958*]
ODM .... Oil Debris Monitor
ODM .... One Day Mission [*NASA*] (KSC)
ODM .... Operational Data Management (KSC)
ODM .... Operational Development Memorandum (AAG)
ODM .... Operational Development Model (ACAE)
ODM .... Operations Data Message (MCD)
odm .... Ophthalmodynamometry [*Ophthalmology*] (AD)
odm .... Ophthalmodynamometry [*Ophthalmology*] (MAE)
ODM .... Optical Diffractogram
ODM .... Optical Disk Memory
ODM .... Optical Display Memory [*Computer science*]
ODM .... Optical Driver Modem (SAUS)
ODM .... Optimized Delivery Model [*Compaq*] [*Computer science*]
ODM .... Optimized Distribution Model [*Compaq Computer Corp.*] [*Computer science*]
ODM .... Orbital Determination Module
ODM .... Order of De Molay (AD)
ODM .... Original Design Manufacturer (AGLO)
ODM .... Outboard Data Manager [*Computer science*] (BUR)
ODM .... Overseas Development Ministry [*British*]
ODMA .... Office of the Director of Military Assistance [*Air Force*] (AFM)
ODMA .... Open Document Management API [*Application Programming Interface*] [*Computer science*]
ODMA .... Optical Disc Manufacturing Association (IGQR)

ODMA .... Optical Distributors and Manufacturers Association (AD)
ODMC .... Office for Dependents' Medical Care [*Army*] (AABC)
odmc .... Outside Diameter of Male Coupling (AD)
ODMD .... Delcan, Don Mills, Ontario [*Library symbol*] [*National Library of Canada*] (NLC)
ODMF .... Ortho-Demethylfortimicin [*Biochemistry*]
ODMG .... Object Database Management Group [*Computer science*] (CDE)
ODMH .... Ohio Department of Mental Health
ODMIBM ..... IBM Canada Ltd., Don Mills, Ontario [*Library symbol*] [*National Library of Canada*] (NLC)
ODMII .... Optical Detected Microwave Induced Impact Ionization (AAEL)
ODMN .... National Research Council, Don Mills, Ontario [*Library symbol*] [*National Library of Canada*] (NLC)
ODMO .... Office of Defense Management and Organization [*Military*]
ODMR .... Optical Detection of Magnetic Resonance (SAUS)
ODMR .... Optical Double Magnetic Resonance (SAUS)
ODMR .... Optically Deflected Magnetic Resonance (SAUS)
ODMR .... Optically Detected Magnetic Resonance [*Spectroscopy*]
ODMRJ .... Rolf Jensen & Associates Ltd., Don Mills, Ontario [*Library symbol*] [*National Library of Canada*] (NLC)
ODMS .... Odesta Document Management System (SAUS)
ODMS .... Operational Data Management System [*FAA*] (TAG)
ODMT .... Office of the Director of Military Training
ODMWS .... Wyda Systems Canada, Inc., Don Mills, Ontario [*Library symbol*] [*National Library of Canada*] (NLC)
ODN .... Company of Mary [*Roman Catholic women's religious order*]
ODN .... Dalton-Dalton-Newport, Cleveland, OH [*OCLC symbol*] (OCLC)
ODN .... Long Seridan [*Malaysia*] [*Airport symbol*] (OAG)
ODN .... Obligation Document Number (SAUS)
ODN .... Octadecennitril (SAUS)
Odn .... Odense (AD)
Odn .... Odin (AD)
ODN .... Oligodeoxynucleotide [*Biochemistry*]
ODN .... Ophthalmodynamometry [*Ophthalmology*]
ODN .... Optical Data Network (SAUS)
ODN .... Organization Development Network (EA)
ODN .... Out Dial Notification (SAUS)
ODN .... Overseas Development Network (EA)
odn .... Own Doppler Nullifer (AD)
ODN .... Own Doppler Nullifier
ODN .... Oxbridge Directory of Newsletters [*A publication*]
ODNA .... Operational Data and Notices to Airmen [*FAA*]
ODNMR .... Optically-Detected Nuclear Magnetic Resonance [*Spectroscopy*]
ODNP .... Ohio Decisions [*A publication*] (DLA)
ODNR .... Ohio Department of Natural Resources (SAUS)
ODNR .... Oxford Dictionary of Nursery Rhymes [*A publication*]
ODNRI .... Overseas Development Natural Resources Institute [*British*] [*Information service or system*] (IID)
ODNS .... Operations Division of Naval Staff [*British*]
Odo .... Odofredus [*Deceased, 1265*] [*Authority cited in pre-1607 legal work*] (DSA)
ODO .... Odometer [*Automotive engineering*]
ODO .... Offensive Duty Officer (SAUS)
ODO .... Office of Disability Operations [*Social Security Administration*] [*Began in 1979*] (OICC)
ODO .... Opeongo High School, Douglas, Ontario [*Library symbol*] [*National Library of Canada*] (NLC)
ODO .... Operations Duty Officer (MUGU)
ODO .... Outdoor Officer [*Customs*] [*British*]
ODOB .... Dobie Public Library, Ontario [*Library symbol*] [*National Library of Canada*] (BIB)
ODOD .... Oculodento-Osseous Dysplasia (STED)
ODOE .... Oregon Department of Energy (AD)
OD/OE .... Organizational Development/Organizational Effectiveness (MCD)
ODOF .... Dowling Branch, Onaping Falls Public Library, Ontario [*Library symbol*] [*National Library of Canada*] (NLC)
Odof .... Odofredus [*Deceased, 1265*] [*Authority cited in pre-1607 legal work*] (DSA)
Odofr .... Odofredus [*Deceased, 1265*] [*Authority cited in pre-1607 legal work*] (DSA)
Odofre .... Odofredus [*Deceased, 1265*] [*Authority cited in pre-1607 legal work*] (DSA)
ODOM .... Odometer (AAG)
odom .... Odometer (AD)
Odonel Mercandil ... Odonellus Mercandilis [*Authority cited in pre-1607 legal work*] (DSA)
odont .... Odontogenic (STED)
odont .... Odontology (AD)
Odont .... Odontology (STED)
ODONT .... Odontology
OdoorS .... Outdoor Systems, Inc. [*Associated Press*] (SAG)
odop .... Offset Doppler (AD)
ODOP .... Offset Doppler
ODOP .... Orbital Doppler (IAA)
ODOPA .... Publications. Dominion Observatory (SAUS)
ODOP System ... Orbital Doppler System (SAUS)
ODOR .... Dorion Public Library, Ontario [*Library symbol*] [*National Library of Canada*] (NLC)
odoram .... Odoramentum [*Perfume*] [*Latin*] (MAE)
odorat .... Odoratus [*Odorous*] [*Latin*] (MAE)
odorl .... Odorless [*Latin*]
ODOT .... Oregon Department of Transportation
ODOTS .... One-Day One-Trial System (AD)
ODOU .... Douro Public Library, Ontario [*Library symbol*] [*National Library of Canada*] (BIB)

ODOW...........	Ohio Division of Wildlife
O'Dowd Sh...	O'Dowd's Merchant Shipping Act [*A publication*] (DLA)
ODP	Iso-Octyldecylphthalat (SAUS)
odp	Occipito-Dextra Posterior (AD)
ODP	Occipitodextra Posterior [*A fetal position*] [*Medicine*] (AAMN)
ODP	Ocean Drilling Program [*Texas A & M University*] [*Research center*] (RCD)
ODP	Octyldecylphthalat (SAUS)
ODP	Octyl Isodecyl Phthalate [*Organic chemistry*]
ODP	Oekologisch-Demokratische Partei [*Ecological Democratic Party*] [*Germany*] [*Political party*] (PPW)
ODP	Office Data Processing (TIMI)
ODP	Office Depot, Inc. [*NYSE symbol*] (SPSG)
ODP	Office Development Permit (SAUS)
ODP	Office of Defense Planning [*of FRS*]
ODP	Office of Disability Programs [*Social Security Administration*] (OICC)
ODP	Office of Disaster Preparedness (AD)
ODP	Office of Disclosure Policy (SAUS)
ODP	Officer Distribution Plan [*Army*]
ODP	Official Development Planning (SAUS)
ODP	Offshore Drilling Platform
ODP	Offspring of Diabetic Parent [*Medicine*] (MELL)
ODP	Onboard Data Processor (SAUS)
ODP	On-Demand Publishing (SAUS)
ODP	Open Data Path (MCD)
ODP	Open Distributed Processing [*Telecommunications*] (OSI)
ODP	Open Door Policy
ODP	Open Dripproof
ODP	Operational Development Phase (SAUS)
ODP	Operational Development Plan [*or Program*]
ODP	Operational Development Program (SAUS)
ODP	Operational Display Procedure [*NASA*] (NAKS)
ODP	Optical Data Processing
ODP	Optical Data Processor (SAUS)
ODP	Orbit Determination Program
ODP	Order Despatched (SAUS)
odp	Order-Despatched (AD)
ODP	Orderly Departure Program [*for Vietnamese refugees*] [*United Nations*]
ODP	Order of the Sons of Divine Providence
ODP	Organic Development Problem (SAA)
ODP	Organization Department (SAUS)
ODP	Organized Reservists in Drill Pay Status [*Military*]
ODP	Original Departure Point
ODP	Original Document Processing
O/DP	Originating/Destination Point (SAUS)
ODP	Outline Development Plan [*Army*] (AFIT)
ODP	Output-to-Display Parity Error [*Computer science*] (SAA)
ODP	Overall Development Planning (SAUS)
ODP	Overall Documentation Plan [*NATO*] (NATG)
ODP	Overdrive Processor (SAUS)
ODP	Overlay Demonstration Program [*Military*]
ODP	Oviposition-Determining Pheromone
ODP	Ozone-Depleting [*or Depletion*] Potential [*Environmental science*]
ODP	Ozone Depletion Potential [*Meteorology*]
ODPA	Octylated Diphenyl Amine (SAUS)
ODPA	Organization of Democratic and Popular Action [*Morocco*] [*Political party*] (BUAC)
OD (PA & E)...	Office of the Director (Program Analysis and Evaluation) (MCD)
ODPC	ODP Council (SAUS)
ODPCS........	Oceanographic Data Processing and Control System (OA)
ODPEX	Offshore Drilling and Production Exhibition (PDAA)
ODPHP........	Office of Disease Prevention and Health Promotion [*US Public Health Service*] [*Information service or system*] (IID)
ODPI	Office of Director Public Information [*Military*]
ODP/MT	Organisation pour la Democratie Populaire/Mouvement du Travail [*Burkina Faso*] [*Political party*] (EY)
ODPN	Oxydipropionitrile (SAUS)
ODPP	Office of the Director of Public Prosecutions [*Australia*]
ODPP	Open Dripproof Protected
ODPPP	Operating Division Project Product Policy (SAUS)
ODPR	Office of the Data Protection Registrar (BUAC)
ODPR	OverDrive Processor Replacement (SAUS)
O'D Pr & Acc...	O'Dedy's Principal and Accessory [*1812*] [*A publication*] (DLA)
ODPRF........	Operating Documents Preliminary Review Form (SAUS)
ODPS	Operational Data Processing Squadron
ODPSK........	Oil Dipstick
ODQ	On Direct Questioning (DMAA)
ODQ	Opponens Digiti Quinti [*Muscle*] [*Anatomy*] (DAVI)
ODQ	[*The*] Oxford Dictionary of Quotations [*A publication*]
ODQM........	Office of the Division Quartermaster
ODR	Dryden Public Library, Ontario [*Library symbol*] [*National Library of Canada*] (NLC)
ODR	Ocean Drilling & Exploration Co. (SAUS)
ODR	Oculomotor Delayed Response [*Performance test task*]
ODR	Office of Defense Representative (COE)
ODR	Office of Defense Resources [*Civil Defense*]
ODR	Office of Dissemination and Resources [*HEW*]
ODR	Officer of Defense Resources (SAUS)
ODR	Official Discount Rate [*Finance*] (ECON)
ODR	Oil Droplet Reflex [*Medicine*] (MELL)
ODR	Omnidirectional Range
ODR	Omnidirection Range (SAUS)
ODR	On Display Racks [*Freight*]
ODR	Ontrack Data Recovery (SAUS)
ODR	Operational Design Resolution (SAA)
ODR	Operator Data Register [*Telecommunications*] (TEL)
ODR	Optical Data Recognition [*Computer science*]
ODR	Optical Digital Reference (SAUS)
ODR	Optical Double Resonance (SAUS)
ODR	Optically-Detected Resonance (SAUS)
ODR	Optimized Dynamic Routing (SAUS)
ODR	ORDALT [*Ordnance Alterations*] Deficiency Review (MCD)
odr	Order (AD)
ODR	Ordnance Difficulty Report (MCD)
ODR	Original Data Record
ODR	Oscillating Disk Rheometer (AAEL)
ODR	Output Data Redundancy (MCD)
ODR	Output Data Request (SAUS)
ODR	Output Definition Register
ODR	Overland Downlook Radar (SAUS)
ODR	Oxygen Diffusion Rate (OA)
ODR	Roanoke, VA [*Location identifier*] [*FAA*] (FAAL)
ODRAN	Operational Drawing Revision Advance Notice (NASA)
ODRC	Office of Disaster Relief Coordinator [*United Nations*] (WDAA)
ODRC	Orbiter Data Reduction Center [*NASA*] (MCD)
OD Re..........	Ohio Decisions Reprint [*A publication*] (DLA)
OD Rep........	Ohio Decisions Reprint [*A publication*] (DLA)
ODRES........	Old Dominion Real Estate (SAUS)
ODRI	Deep River Public Library, Ontario [*Library symbol*] [*National Library of Canada*] (NLC)
ODRI	Office of United States Defense Representative, India [*Army*] (AABC)
ODRL	Delta Branch, Rideau Lakes Union Library, Ontario [*Library symbol*] [*National Library of Canada*] (BIB)
ODRM..........	Operations Design Reference Mission (MCD)
ODRN..........	Orbiting Data Relay Network
ODRP..........	Office of Defense Representative, Pakistan [*Army*]
ODRS	Orbiting Data Relay System (MCD)
ODRS	Ore Deposits Research Section [*Pennsylvania State University*] [*Research center*] (RCD)
ODRSS........	Orbiting Data Relay Satellite System (MCD)
O/DRV.........	Over Drive [*Automotive engineering*]
ODS	Obstacle Detection System
ODS	Occupational Demand Schedule (ADA)
ODS	Ocean Data Station [*Marine science*] (MSC)
ODS	Octadecylsilane [*Organic chemistry*]
ODS	Octadecyltrimethyloxysilane (SAUS)
ODS	Octadeyl(dimethyl)chlorosilane [*Organic chemistry*]
ODS	Odessa [*Ukraine*] [*Airport symbol*] (OAG)
ODS	Odessa [*Washington*] [*Seismograph station code, US Geological Survey*] (SEIS)
ODS	Odessa Explorations Ltd. [*Vancouver Stock Exchange symbol*]
ODS	Odometer Disclosure Statement
ODS	Office Dialog System [*Computer science*]
ODS	Office for Domestic Shipping [*Department of Commerce*]
ODS	Office of Defender Services (AD)
ODS	Office of Dietary Supplements (SAUS)
ODS	Office of Disability Services (SAUS)
ODs............	Oildroplets (SAUS)
ODS	Old Dominion Speedway [*Auto racing*]
ODS	One Digit Subtractor (SAUS)
ODS	Open Database Server [*Computer science*]
ODS	Open Data Service [*Electronics systems testing*]
ODS	Open Data Services
ODS	Open Distributed System (RALS)
ODS	Operating-Differential Subsidy [*Authorized by Merchant Marine Act of 1936*]
ODS	Operational Data Store [*Computer science*] (ITCA)
ODS	Operational Data Summary (AAG)
ODS	Operational Display System (SAUS)
ODS	Operation Desert Storm [*Military*] (RDA)
ODS	Operations Directorate Station (SAA)
ODS	Optical Data Systems (SAUS)
ODS	Optical Design System [*Automotive lighting*]
ODS	Optical Discrimination System (SAUS)
ODS	Optical Disk Storage (SAUS)
ODS	Optical Disk System (SAUS)
ODS	Optical Display System (SAUS)
ODS	Optical Docking System
ODS	Optical Document Sorter (SAUS)
ODS	Optimal Decisions System
ODS	Orbiter Docking System [*NASA*]
ODS	Orbiter Dynamic Simulator [*NASA*]
ODS	Ordnance Delivery Schedule [*Navy*] (NG)
ODS	Orton Dyslexia Society (EA)
ODS	Osric Dining Society (EA)
ODS	Output Data Set (SAUS)
ODS	Output Data Store [*Computer science*] (TIMI)
ODS	Output Data Strobe
ODS	Overall Distance Standard [*for golf balls*] [*Adopted by the United States Golf Association in 1976*]
ODS	Overhead Data Stream
ODS	Oxidative-Desulfurization [*Fuel technology*]
ods.............	Oxide Dispersion Strengthened (AD)
ODS	Oxide Dispersion Strengthened [*Ferrous metallurgy*]
ODS	Oxygen Depletion Sensor
ODS	Oxygen Dispersion Strengthening (SAUS)
ODS	Ozone-Depleting Substance (AAGC)
ODSA	Oil-Dri Corp. of America (EFIS)
ODSA	Open Distributed Systems Architecture [*British*]

ODSA.........	Operating Deflection Shape Analysis
ODSA..........	Operating-Differential Subsidy Agreement [*MARAD*] (TAG)
ODSA.........	Overseas Development Service Association (BUAC)
ODSAS.........	Officer Dual Specialty Allocation System
ODSB.........	Ocean Data Station Buoy
ODSBA........	Oxford Down Sheep Breeders Association [*British*] (DBA)
ODSD.........	Oversea Duty Selection Date [*Air Force*]
odsd...........	Overseas Duty Selection Date (AD)
ODSDG	Dalkeith Branch, Stormont, Dundas, and Glengarry County Library, Ontario [*Library symbol*] [*National Library of Canada*] (BIB)
ODSE	Open Door Student Exchange (EA)
ODS/FRODS...	Observable Differences/Functionally Related Observable Differences (MCD)
ODSG..........	Ophthalmic Doppler Sonogram [*Medicine*] (MELL)
ODSI...........	Ocean Data Systems, Inc. [*Information service or system*] (IID)
ODSI...........	ODS Networks [*NASDAQ symbol*] (SG)
ODSI...........	Old Dominion Systems, Inc. (SAUS)
ODSI...........	Optical Data Systems, Inc. [*NASDAQ symbol*] (SAG)
ODSR..........	Office of the Director of Scientific Research (AD)
ODSRS........	Orbiting Deep Space Relay Station (MCD)
ODSS..........	Ocean Dumping Surveillance System [*Coast Guard*] (MSC)
ODSS	Order Delivery Schedule Summary (MCD)
ODST	Online Depression Screening Test (SAUS)
OD Structure...	Order-Disorder Structure (SAUS)
ODSY	Sayun [*People's Democratic Republic of Yemen*] [*ICAO location identifier*] (ICLI)
ODT	Occipitodextra Transversa [*A fetal position*] [*Medicine*] (AAMN)
odt	Occipito-Dextra Transverse (AD)
ODT	Ocean Data Transmitter
odt	Octal Debugging Technique (AD)
ODT	Octal Debugging Technique [*Computer science*] (IEEE)
odt	Odor Detection Threshold (AD)
ODT	Odor Detection Threshold (PDAA)
ODT	Office of Defense Transportation [*Within Office for Emergency Management*] [*World War II*]
ODT	Oklahoma Department of Transportation
ODT	Omnidirection Transmission (NVT)
ODT	On Demand Technologies
odt	One-Day Trials (AD)
odt	On-Line Debugging Technique [*Computer science*] (AD)
ODT	Online Debugging Technique
ODT	Open Desktop (SAUS)
ODT	Operational Demand Time [*Military*] (CAAL)
ODT	Operational Demonstration Test
ODT	Operational Development Team (IAA)
ODT	Operator Display Terminal (SAUS)
ODT	Optical Data Transmission
ODT	Order-Disorder Transformation
ODT	Order-Disorder Transition
ODT	Otago Daily Times [*A publication*] (AD)
ODT	Outdoor Trainer (SAUS)
ODT	Outside Diameter Tube (MSA)
ODT	Overseas Deployment Training [*Army*]
ODTAA	One Damn Thing After Another [*Title of book by John Masefield*]
ODTACCS	Office of the Director, Telecommunications, and Command and Control Systems [*DoD*] (PDAA)
ODTC	Office of Defense Trade Controls (AAGC)
ODTC	Optic Display Test Chamber
ODTF	Operational Development Test Facility (AAG)
ODTM	n-Octyldecyltrimellitat (SAUS)
ODTM	Optical Time Division Multiplexing (SAUS)
ODTM	Orbiter Dynamic Test Model [*NASA*]
ODTS	Offset Doppler Tracking System (KSC)
ODTS	Operational Development Test Site (AAG)
ODTS	Optical Data Transmission System
ODTS	Optical Discrimination and Tracking System [*Army*]
ODTS	Organic Dust Toxic Syndrome [*Medicine*]
ODTW	Oppositely-Directed Travelling Wave (PDAA)
ODU	Dunnville Public Library, Ontario [*Library symbol*] [*National Library of Canada*] (NLC)
ODU	Old Dominion University [*Virginia*]
ODU	Old Dutch [*Language, etc.*]
ODU	Optical Density Unit
ODU	Optical Display Unit [*Computer science*] (MCD)
ODU	Output Display Unit [*Computer science*]
ODUB	Bibliotheque Publique de Dubreuilville, Ontario [*Library symbol*] [*National Library of Canada*] (NLC)
ODUC	Ohio Data Users Center [*Columbus*] [*Information service or system*] (IID)
ODUM	Association of American Youth of Ukrainian Descent (EA)
ODUMP........	Ocean Dumping Permits [*Database*] [*Environment Canada*] [*Information service or system*] (CRD)
ODUN	Dundalk Public Library, Ontario [*Library symbol*] [*National Library of Canada*] (NLC)
od units	Optical-Density Units (AD)
ODUR..........	Durham Public Library, Ontario [*Library symbol*] [*National Library of Canada*] (NLC)
ODURF........	Old Dominion University Research Foundation [*Old Dominion University*] [*Research center*] (RCD)
ODUSD(ES)...	Office of the Deputy Under Secretary of Defense (Environmental Security) [*DoD*] (RDA)
ODUSD (R & AT)...	Office of the Deputy Under Secretary of Defense for Research and Advanced Technology [*DoD*] (RDA)
ODUSM........	Office, Deputy Under Secretary for Manpower [*Navy*]
ODUSN	Office, Deputy Under Secretary of the Navy

ODV	Eau-de-Vie [*Taken from the French pronunciation and used to refer to brandy*]
ODVA..........	Open DeviceNet Vendors Association (ACII)
ODVAR........	Orbit Determination and Vehicle Attitude Reference
ODVP..........	Optimal Digital Voice Processor (MCD)
ODW	Oak Harbor [*Washington*] [*Airport symbol*] (OAG)
ODW	Office of Drinking Water [*Environmental Protection Agency*]
ODW	Ohio Wesleyan University, Delaware, OH [*Library symbol*] [*Library of Congress*] (LCLS)
ODW	Omega Dropwindsonde [*Meteorology*]
ODW	Oregon Draymen & Warehousemen's Association, Portland OR [*STAC*]
ODW	Organic Dry Weight
ODW	Our Developing World [*An association*] (EA)
ODW	Output Discrete Word (MCD)
ODW	Oven-Dried Weight
ODW	Workers Health and Safety Centre, Don Mills, Ontario [*Library symbol*] [*National Library of Canada*] (BIB)
ODWA	Odwalla, Inc. [*NASDAQ symbol*] (SAG)
Odwalla	Odwalla, Inc. [*Associated Press*] (SAG)
ODWC	West Carleton Secondary School, Dunrobin, Ontario [*Library symbol*] [*National Library of Canada*] (BIB)
ODWG.........	Offset Drilling Working Group (SAUS)
ODWIN........	Opening Doors Wider in Nursing [*Project*]
ODWSA.......	Office of the Directorate of Weapon Systems Analysis [*Army*] (AABC)
O'Dwyer......	Jack O'Dwyer's Newsletter [*A publication*] [*New York, NY*] (WDMC)
ODX	Ord, NE [*Location identifier*] [*FAA*] (FAAL)
ODXT	Omnidentix Systems (SAUS)
ODY	Odyssey Industries, Inc. [*Toronto Stock Exchange symbol*]
ODY	Odyssey International [*Canada*] [*ICAO designator*] (FAAC)
ODYY	Odyssey Entertainment Ltd. (SAUS)
ODZ	Outer Defense Zone
OE..............	Austria [*International civil aircraft marking*] (ODBW)
OE..............	Exeter Public Library, Ontario [*Library symbol*] [*National Library of Canada*] (NLC)
O/E.............	Observed versus Expected
OE..............	Occupied by Enemy (SAUS)
OE..............	Oceanic Engineering (SAUS)
OE..............	OE, Inc. [*Toronto Stock Exchange symbol*]
oe	Oersted (AD)
Oe	Oersted [*Unit of magnetizing intensity*]
OE..............	Offensive End [*Football*]
OE..............	Office Equipment
OE..............	Office of Education [*HEW*]
OE..............	Office of Emergency Planning and Operations (SAUS)
OE..............	Office of Energy [*Department of Agriculture*] (GFGA)
OE..............	Office of Enforcement [*Environmental Protection Agency*] (GFGA)
OE..............	Oil Emulsion [*Microbiology*]
OE..............	Oil Equivalent
OE..............	Old England (GEAB)
OE..............	Old English [*Typeface*] (WDMC)
OE..............	Old English [*Language, etc.*] [*i.e., before 1150 or 1200*]
OE..............	Old Etonian [*British*]
OE..............	Omission Excepted (IAA)
oe	Omissions Excepted (WDAA)
oe	Omissions Expected (AD)
OE..............	One Edge (SAUS)
o/e.............	On Examination (AD)
OE..............	On Examination [*Medicine*]
OE..............	Opened Edges [*Publishing*] (DGA)
OE..............	Open Edition (SAUS)
oe	Open End (AD)
OE..............	Open End (MSA)
OE..............	Operating Engineer (NRCH)
OE..............	Operating Environment (CTAS)
OE..............	Operating Expense
OE..............	Operational Efficiency (SAUS)
OE..............	Operational Evaluation [*Army*]
OE..............	Operation Enterprise [*Hamilton, NY*] (EA)
OE..............	Operation Enterprise Newsletter [*A publication*]
OE..............	Operations Engineering (AAG)
OE..............	Opportunity Evaluation (SAUS)
OE..............	Optical/Electrical Conversion [*Telecommunications*]
OE..............	Optical Emission (MCD)
OE..............	Optical Engineering
O/E.............	Optical-to-Electrical (SAUS)
OE..............	Optoelectronics (SAUS)
OE..............	Orbital Engine ADS [*NYSE symbol*] (SPSG)
OE..............	Order Entry (DMAA)
O/E.............	Order/Entry System [*Computer science*] (DHSM)
OE..............	Ordnance Electrician [*British military*] (DMA)
OE..............	Ordnance Engineer [*British military*] (DMA)
OE..............	Oregon Electric Railway Co. [*AAR code*]
oe	Organizational Effectiveness (AD)
OE..............	Organizational Effectiveness
OE..............	Organizational Entity
OE..............	Organizational Error [*Engineering*]
OE..............	Organo Espressivo [*Swell Organ*] [*Music*]
oe	Organo Espressivo [*Swell Organ*] [*Italian*] (AD)
OE..............	Orientalium Ecclesiarum [*Decree on the Eastern Catholic Churches*] [*Vatican II document*]
OE..............	Original Entry [*Computer science*]
OE..............	Original Equipment [*Automobile industry*]
OE..............	Original Error [*Navigation*]
OE..............	Originating Exchange (SAUS)

OE .... Orthoenstatite [*Mineral*]
OE .... Orthopedic Examination (SAUS)
OE .... Other Essays [*Literature*] (ROG)
o/e .... Otitis Externa (AD)
OE .... Otitis Externa [*Medicine*] (DMAA)
oe .... Outdoor Education (AD)
OE .... Out Island Airways (OAG)
OE .... Outlook Express [*Computer science*] (PCM)
O/E .... Output Electronics (SAUS)
OE .... Output Enable [*Semiconductor memory*] (IEEE)
OE .... Overrun Error (SAUS)
OE .... Over-the-Horizon Expanded (MCD)
OE .... Own Exchange [*Telecommunications*] (TEL)
OE .... Oxide Electrode (SAUS)
OE .... Samoan [*ICAO designator*] (AD)
OEA .... Archives, City of Etobicoke, Ontario [*Library symbol*] [*National Library of Canada*] (BIB)
OEA .... Eastern Oklahoma District Library, Muskogee, OK [*OCLC symbol*] (OCLC)
OEA .... Oahu Education Association [*Hawaii*] (AD)
OEA .... Oblate Education Association [*Defunct*] (EA)
OEA .... OEA, Inc. [*NYSE symbol*] (SPSG)
OEA .... Office Education Association (EA)
OEA .... Office Executives Association (AD)
OEA .... Office of Economic Adjustment [*Air Force*] (AFM)
OEA .... Office of Economic Analysis [*Formerly, Office of Business Economics*] [*Department of Commerce*]
OEA .... Office of Environmental Affairs (AD)
OEA .... Office of Environmental Analysis [*Oak Ridge National Laboratory*]
OEA .... Office of Ethnic Affairs [*Victoria, Australia*]
OEA .... Office of European Associations in Higher Education [*Belgium*] (BUAC)
OEA .... Office of Export Administration [*Formerly, OEC*] [*Department of Commerce*]
OEA .... Office of External Affairs [*Environmental Protection Agency*] (GFGA)
OEA .... Ohio Education Association (AD)
OEA .... Ohio Environmental Agency (SAUS)
OEA .... Operational Effectiveness Analysis (MCD)
OEA .... Operator Error Analysis
OEA .... Ophthalmic Exhibitors' Association [*British*] (DBA)
OEA .... Optometric Editors Association (EA)
OEA .... Orchestral Employers' Association [*British*] (BI)
OEA .... Ordnance Electrical Artificer [*British military*] (DMA)
OEA .... Oregon Education Association (AD)
OEA .... Organisation of Europe Aluminium-Smelters (BUAC)
OEA .... Organizacion de los Estados Americanos [*Organization of American States - OAS*] [*Spanish*]
OEA .... Organizational Expense Accounts [*Army*]
OEA .... Original Equipment Assembler [*Automotive engineering*]
OEA .... Outdoor Education Association (EA)
OEA .... Overseas Education Association (EA)
OEA .... Oxygen Enriched Atmosphere (SAUS)
OEA .... Vincennes, IN [*Location identifier*] [*FAA*] (FAAL)
OEAA .... Oil Engineering Apprentices Association (AD)
OEAB .... Abha [*Saudi Arabia*] [*ICAO location identifier*] (ICLI)
OEac .... East Cleveland Public Library, East Cleveland, OH [*Library symbol*] [*Library of Congress*] (LCLS)
OEAH .... Al-Ahsa [*Saudi Arabia*] [*ICAO location identifier*] (ICLI)
OEal .... East Liverpool Carnegie Public Library, East Liverpool, OH [*Library symbol*] [*Library of Congress*] (LCLS)
OEALC .... Oficina Regional de Educacion para America Latina y el Caribe [*Regional Office for Education in Latin America and the Caribbean-Chile*] (IID)
OEalK .... Kent State University, East Liverpool Regional Campus, East Liverpool, OH [*Library symbol*] [*Library of Congress*] (LCLS)
OE & TB .... Officer Education and Training Branch [*BUPERS*]
OEAP .... Operational Error Analysis Program
OEAQ .... Outdoor Educators' Association of Queensland [*Australia*]
OEAS .... Orbital Emergency Arresting System [*NASA*] (NASA)
OEAS .... Organisation Europaischer Aluminium Schmelzhutten [*Organization of European Aluminium Foundries*] (PDAA)
OEAS .... Oxygen Enriched Air System (MCD)
OEASA .... Outdoor Educators Association of South Australia (SAUS)
OEB .... Officers' Organization for Economic Benefits [*Commercial firm*] (EA)
OEB .... Ontario Energy Board (SAUS)
OEB .... Open Electronic Book (SAUS)
OEB .... Oregon Educational Broadcasting (AD)
OEB .... Organic Electrolyte Battery
OEBA .... El-Baha [*Saudi Arabia*] [*ICAO location identifier*] (ICLI)
OEBA .... Office for Economic and Business Affairs [*Department of State*]
OeBF .... Open eBook Forum
OEBH .... Bisha [*Saudi Arabia*] [*ICAO location identifier*] (ICLI)
OE-BR .... Oil Extended Butadiene Rubber (SAUS)
OEBR .... Optical Edge Bead Removal (AAEL)
OEBS .... Office of Employee Benefits Security [*Department of Labor*]
OEBS .... Organic Electrolyte Battery System
OEC .... Observed Effect Concentration [*Environmental science*] (ERG)
OEC .... Odd-Even Check
Oec .... Oeconomica [*of Aristotle*] [*Classical studies*] (OCD)
Oec .... Oeconomicus [*of Xenophon*] [*Classical studies*] (OCD)
OEC .... Oesterreichischer Aero-Club [*Austrian Aero Club*] [*German*] (AD)
OEC .... Office of Electronics and Control (SAUS)
OEC .... Office of Emergency Communications [*FCC*] (NTCM)
OEC .... Office of Energy Conservation [*Functions transferred to Federal Energy Administration*]

OEC .... Office of Environmental Compliance (SAUS)
OEC .... Office of Export Control [*Later, OEA*] [*World War II*]
OEC .... Office on Educational Credit [*Later, OECC*] (EA)
OEC .... Ohio Edison Co. [*NYSE symbol*] (SPSG)
OEC .... Ohio Edison Financing Trust [*NYSE symbol*] (SAG)
OEC .... Oil Exporting Countries (AD)
OEC .... Ontario Economic Council (SAUS)
OEC .... Ontario Election Decisions [*A publication*] (DLA)
OEC .... Ontario Energy Corporation (SAUS)
OEC .... Open-End Company [*Business term*] (MHDW)
OEC .... Open-End Credit [*Business term*] (MHDW)
OEC .... Open Enterprise Computing (TIMI)
OEC .... Open Environment Corporation (SAUS)
OEC .... Operational Employment Concept [*Army*] (AABC)
OEC .... Operational Evaluation Command [*Army*] (DOMA)
OEC .... Optical Effect Code
OEC .... Optic-Electronic Corp. (RDA)
OEC .... Opto-Electronics Center (MCD)
OEC .... Orange Empire Conference (PSS)
OEC .... Orbital Electron Capture
OEC .... Orbiting Experimental Capsule
OEC .... Ordnance Equipment Chart
OEC .... Organizational Effectiveness Consultants (INF)
oec .... Organizational Entity Code (AD)
OEC .... Organizational Entity Code
OEC .... Oribital Engine Corporation (SAUS)
OEC .... Other Early Capability (ACAE)
OEC .... Output Edge Control (SAUS)
OEC .... Overpaid Entry Certificate (DS)
OEC .... Overseas Employment Corp. [*Pakistan*] (BUAC)
OEC .... Oxygen Equilibrium Curve (DB)
OEC .... Oxygen-Evolving Complex [*Photosynthesis*]
OECA .... Office of Enforcement and Compliance Assurance [*Environmental Protection Agency*] (AEPA)
OECA .... Ontario Educational Communications Authority [*Canada*]
OEC & S .... Organizational Effectiveness Center and School [*Army*]
OECC .... Office on Educational Credit and Credentials (EA)
OECC .... Oregon Educational Computing Consortium (EDAC)
OECCNU .... Organizacion para la Educacion la Ciencia, y la Cultura [*Organization for Education, Science, and Culture*] [*United Nations*] (AD)
OECD .... Organization for Economic Cooperation and Development [*Formerly, OEEC*]
OECD .... Organization for European Community Development (SAUS)
OECD/ENC .... Organization for Economic Cooperation and Development/ Environment Committee [*Marine science*] (MSC)
OECD/MEI .... OECD Main Economics Indicators (NITA)
OECD/NIA .... OECD National Income Accounts (NITA)
OECE .... Organisation Europeenne de Cooperation Economique [*Organization for European Economic Cooperation - OEEC*] [*Later, OECD*] [*See also OCDE*] [*France*] (MSC)
OECE .... Organizacion Europea de Cooperacion Economica [*Organization for European Economic Cooperation - OEEC*] [*Later, OECD*] [*Spain*]
OECF .... Overseas Economic Cooperation Fund (AD)
OECF .... Overseas Economic Cooperation Fund of Japan (BUAC)
OECIC .... Open-End Contract Information Circulars (AAGC)
OECM .... Office of Enforcement and Compliance Monitoring [*Environmental Protection Agency*] (GFGA)
OEC Md .... OEC Medical [*Associated Press*] (SAG)
oeco .... Outboard Engine Cutoff (AD)
OECO .... Outboard Engine Cutoff [*NASA*]
OECO .... Oxygen Enrichment Company Ltd. (SAUS)
OECON .... Offshore Engineering Conference (MCD)
OECON .... Offshore Exploration Conference
OECOS .... Organizational Engineering for Communications and Organizational Systems (SAUS)
OECPrA .... Ohio Edison 3.90% Pfd [*NYSE symbol*] (TTSB)
OECPrB .... Ohio Edison, 4.40% Pfd [*NYSE symbol*] (TTSB)
OECPrC .... Ohio Edison 4.44% Pfd [*NYSE symbol*] (TTSB)
OECPrT .... Ohio Edison Fin Tr 9.00% Pfd [*NYSE symbol*] (TTSB)
OECQ .... Organisation Europeene pour la Controle de la Qualite GG1 European Quality-Control Organization GG2 [*France*] (AD)
OECQ .... Organisation Europeenne pour la Qualite [*European Organization for Quality -EOQC*] [*Switzerland*]
OECS .... Optics of Excitons in Confined Systems (SAUS)
OECS .... Organisation of Eastern Caribbean States (EAIO)
OECS .... Organization for the Enforcement of Child Support (EA)
OECSEAS .... Organisation of Eastern Caribbean States, Economic Affairs Secretariat [*St. Johns, Antigua*] (EAIO)
OECT .... European Association of the Textile Wholesale Trade [*EC*] (ECED)
OECT .... Oxford Editions of Cuneiform Texts [*A publication*] (BJA)
oecu .... Outboard Engine Cutoff (AD)
OED .... Ocean Engineering Division [*Coast Guard*]
OED .... Office Equipment Division (SAUS)
OED .... Office of Economic Development [*Bureau of Indian Affairs*]
OED .... Operational Engineering Detachment (MCD)
OED .... Operational Engineering Division [*Central Electricity Generating Board*] [*British*] (IRUK)
OED .... Operational Evaluation Demonstration (MCD)
OED .... Operation Effectiveness Demonstration (RDA)
OED .... Optoelectronic Device (SAUS)
OED .... Opto Electronic Display [*Computer science*] (ELAL)
OED .... Orbiting Energy Depot
OED .... Oscillating Electron Discharge (SAUS)
OED .... Otto Erich Deutsch [*Music cataloger*]

OED .... Oxford English Dictionary [Information service or system] [A publication]
OED .... Oxidation-Enhanced Diffusion (SAUS)
OEDA .... Office of Energy Data and Analysis [Functions transferred to Federal Energy Administration]
OEDC .... Office of Engineering Design and Construction [Tennessee Valley Authority]
OEDC .... Offshore Energy Development Corp. [NASDAQ symbol] (SAG)
OEDC .... Ontario Engineering Design Competition (SAUS)
OEDIPUS..... Oxford English Dictionary Inputting, Proofing, and Updating Service
OEDIT .... Octal Editor [Computer science] (MHDi)
OEDO .... Ordnance Engineering Duty Officer
OEDP .... Office of Employment Development Programs (AD)
OEDP .... Overall Economic Development Program [Bureau of Indian Affairs]
OEDR .... Dhahran/International [Saudi Arabia] [ICAO location identifier] (ICLI)
OEDRC........ Optico-Electronic Device for Registering Coincidences (PDAA)
OEDSF........ On-Board Experimental Data Support Facility
OEE............. Ernst & Whinney, Cleveland, OH [OCLC symbol] (OCLC)
OEE............. Essex County Public Library, Essex, Ontario [Library symbol] [National Library of Canada] (NLC)
OEE............. Odd-Even Effect (SAUS)
OEE............. Office of Educational Exchange [Department of State]
OEE............. Office of the Assistant Secretary for Export Enforcement [Department of Commerce] (GFGA)
OEE............. Ordre de l'Etoile de l'Europe [Huy, Belgium] (EAIO)
oee............. Outer Enamel Epithelium (AD)
OEE............. Outer Enamel Epithelium [Dentistry]
OEE............. Overall Equipment Effectiveness (AAEL)
OEEC.......... Organization for European Economic Cooperation [Later, OECD]
OEED .... Oxford Encyclopedic English Dictionary [A publication]
OEEO .... Office of Equal Educational Opportunities [Office of Education]
OEEO .... Office of Equal Employment Opportunity [Department of Labor] (OICC)
OE-EPDM.... Oil Extended Ethylene-Propylene Diene Monomer (SAUS)
OEEPE........ Organisation Europeenne d'Etudes Photogrammetriques Experimentales [European Organisation for Experimental Photogrammetric Research] [Research Center] [Netherlands] (PDAA)
OEER .... Oceanographic Equipment Evaluation Range (NOAA)
OEES.......... Interagency Committee on Ocean Exploration and Environmental Services [Terminated, 1971] (EGAO)
OEES.......... Organization for Equal Education of the Sexes (EA)
OE-E-SBR ... Oil Extended Emulsion Styrene Butadiene Rubber (SAUS)
OEET.......... Office of Environmental Engineering and Technology [Environmental Protection Agency] (EPA)
OEETD .... Office of Environmental Engineering and Technology Demonstration [Washington, DC] [Environmental Protection Agency] (GRD)
OEF............. Ear Falls Public Library, Ontario [Library symbol] [National Library of Canada] (NLC)
OEF............. Oceanic Educational Foundation (EA)
OEF............. Officeholders Expense Funds [Slush money]
OEF............. Oil Emersion Field [Biochemistry] (DAVI)
OEF............. Online Education Facility [Computer science] (VLIE)
OEF............. Open-End Funds [Investment term]
OEF............. Operational Efficiency Factor (SAUS)
OEF............. Optical Evaluation Facility (RDA)
OEF............. Order Entry Form (TIMI)
OEF............. Organization of Employers Federations (SAUS)
OEF............. Origin Element Field [Computer science] (ELAL)
OEF............. Origin Element Field (SAUS)
OEF............. Osteopathic Educational Foundation (AD)
OEF............. Overseas Education Fund [Later, OEFI] (EA)
OEF............. Oxford Economic Forecasting (BUAC)
OEF............. Oxygen Extraction Fraction [Medicine] (DMAA)
OEFD .... Orbiter Electric Field Detector [NASA]
OEFE.......... Flos-Elmvale Public Library, Elmvale, Ontario [Library symbol] [National Library of Canada] (BIB)
OEFI........... OEF [Overseas Educational Fund] International (EA)
OEFS........... Interagency Committee on Ocean Exploration and Environmental Services (SAUS)
OEFS........... Organisation for Equal Education of the Sexes (SAUS)
OEG .... Eganville Public Library, Ontario [Library symbol] [National Library of Canada] (NLC)
OEG .... Occluded Eye Gunsight [Military] (INF)
Oeg............. Oestrogene (SAUS)
OEG .... Office of Environmental Guidance (SAUS)
OEG .... Open-End Guide (SAUS)
OEG .... Operational Exposure Guidance [Military] (INF)
OEG .... Operational Exposure Guide
OEG .... Operations Evaluation Group [Military]
OEG .... Organization and Equipment Guide [Army] (AABC)
OEG .... Outdoor Ethics Guild (EA)
OEG .... Public Library of Enid and Garfield County, Enid, OK [OCLC symbol] (OCLC)
OEGCA........ Old English Game Club of America (EA)
OEGCMJ...... Officer Exercising General Court-Martial Jurisdiction
OEGN.......... Gizan [Saudi Arabia] [ICAO location identifier] (ICLI)
OEGS .... Gassim [Saudi Arabia] [ICAO location identifier] (ICLI)
OEGT .... Guriat [Saudi Arabia] [ICAO location identifier] (ICLI)
oegt............. Observable Evidence of Good Teaching (AD)
OEGT .... Observable Evidences of Good Teaching
OEGT .... Office of Education for the Gifted and Talented [HEW]
OEH .... Baltimore, MD [Location identifier] [FAA] (FAAL)
OEH .... Occupational & Environmental Health Library (SAUS)
OEH .... Orient Express Hotels (EFIS)

OEHA.......... Office of Environmental and Health Affairs [World Bank] (BUAC)
OEHL .... Hail [Saudi Arabia] [ICAO location identifier] (ICLI)
OEHL .... Hoffman-La Roche Ltd., Etobicoke, Ontario [Library symbol] [National Library of Canada] (NLC)
OEHL .... Occupational and Environmental Health Laboratory [Brooks Air Force Base, TX] [Air Force]
OEHMO........ Open-Ended Health Maintenance Organization [Insurance] (WYGK)
OEHS .... Office of Environmental Health & Safety (SAUS)
OEI............. Ocean Energy [NYSE symbol] [Formerly, Flores & Rucks] (SG)
OEI............. Officers Efficiency Index (SAUS)
OEI............. Official Establishment Inventory
OEI............. Offshore Ecology Investigation [Oil study]
OEI............. Oficina de Educacion Iberoamericana [Ibero-American Bureau of Education - IABE] [Madrid, Spain] (EAIO)
OEI............. One Engine Inoperative [Aviation]
OEI............. One Essential Ingredient (SAUS)
OEI............. Open Enterprise Infrastructure (TIMI)
OEI............. Options Exchange Index
OEI............. Optoelectronic Isolator
OEI............. Order and Equipment Installed (VLIE)
OEI............. Organizacion de Estados Iberoamericanos para la Educacion, la Ciencia, y la Cultura [Organization of Ibero-American States for Education, Science, and Culture] (EAIO)
oei............. Organizational Entity Identity (AD)
OEI............. Organizational Entity Identity
OEI............. Overall Efficiency Index
OEI............. Own Equipment Inventory (VLIE)
OEIAA .... Office Equipment Industry Association of Australia
OEIC........... Ocean Engineering Information Centre [Memorial University of Newfoundland] [Information service or system] (IID)
OEIC........... Open-End Investment Co. [Investment term]
OEIC........... Optoelectronic Integrated Circuit [Computer science]
OEIC........... Opto-Electronic Integrated Circuits
OEIC........... Overseas Economic Intelligence Committee [Military]
OEID........... Office of Engineering Infrastructure Development [Washington, DC] [National Science Foundation] (GRD)
OEII............ O'Neill Educational Ideologies Inventory (EDAC)
OEII............ Operation Everest II [Army] (RDA)
OEIMC .... Oklahoma Environmental Information and Media Center (SAUS)
OEIO .... Odds and Ends Input/Output (MCD)
OEIPS .... Office of Engineering and Information Processing Standards [National Bureau of Standards]
OEIS .... Office of Energy Information Services [Department of Energy] (IID)
OEIS .... Orbiter Electrical Interface Simulator [NASA]
OEIT............ Open-End Investment Trust [Investment term]
OEITFL........ Organisation Europeenne des Industries Transformatrices de Fruits et Legumes [European Organization of Fruit and Vegetable Processing Industries] [Common Market] [Belgium]
OEIU .... Office Employes International Union [Later, OPEIU]
OEJ............. Office of Environmental Justice [Environmental Protection Agency] (AEPA)
OEJB........... Jubail [Saudi Arabia] [ICAO location identifier] (ICLI)
OEJD........... Jeddah [Saudi Arabia] [ICAO location identifier] (ICLI)
OEJH........... Office of Environmental Justice Hotline [Environmental Protection Agency] (AEPA)
OEJN........... Jeddah/King Abdul Aziz International [Saudi Arabia] [ICAO location identifier] (ICLI)
OEKJ........... Al-Kharj [Saudi Arabia] [ICAO location identifier] (ICLI)
OEKM.......... Khamis Mushait [Saudi Arabia] [ICAO location identifier] (ICLI)
OEL............. Elliot Lake Public Library, Ontario [Library symbol] [National Library of Canada] (NLC)
OEL............. Eugene Public Library, Eugene, OR [OCLC symbol] (OCLC)
OEL............. Oakley, KS [Location identifier] [FAA] (FAAL)
OEL............. Occupational Exposure Limit
OEL............. Ontario Electrical League (SAUS)
OEL............. Ontario Express Ltd. [Canada] [ICAO designator] (FAAC)
OEL............. Ordered Edge List (SAUS)
OEL............. Ordnance Engineering Laboratory
OEL............. Ordnance Equipment List [Navy] (NG)
OEL............. Organic Electroluminescent (AEBE)
OEL............. Organizational Equipment List [Army]
OE LASE ..... Optics, Electro-Optics and Laser Applications in Science and Engineering (SAUS)
OELB........... Oertlicher Landwirtschaftsbetrieb [Local Agricultural Enterprise] [German]
OELD .... Office of the Executive Legal Director [Nuclear Regulatory Commission] (GFGA)
OELF........... Fort Hope Band Library, Eabamet Lake, Ontario [Library symbol] [National Library of Canada] (BIB)
OELK........... Elk Lake Public Library, Ontario [Library symbol] [National Library of Canada] (BIB)
OELM.......... Elmwood Branch, Bruce County Public Library, Ontario [Library symbol] [National Library of Canada] (NLC)
OELMA........ Ohio Educational Library Media Association (EDAC)
OEL/MA....... Ohio Educational Library/Media Association (SAUS)
OELMN(A)..... Ordnance Electrical Mechanician (Air) [British military] (DMA)
OELRR........ Office of Economic Liaison and Regulatory Review [Western Australia]
OELS........... Elliot Lake Secondary School, Ontario [Library symbol] [National Library of Canada] (NLC)
OELS........... Operationally Efficient Launch Site Study (SAUS)
OEly............ Elyria Library, Elyria, OH [Library symbol] [Library of Congress] (LCLS)
OElyL.......... Lorain County Community College, Elyria, OH [Library symbol] [Library of Congress] (LCLS)

OEM	Emo Public Library, Ontario [*Library symbol*] [*National Library of Canada*] (NLC)
OEM	Occupational and Environmental Medicine
OEM	Odd Even Merge (SAUS)
OEM	Office & Electronic Machines Lt.d (SAUS)
OEM	Office Equipment Maintenance
OEM	Office for Emergency Management [*World War II*]
OEM	Office of Electronic Machines [*Commercial firm*] [*British*]
OEM	Office of Environmental Mediation
OEM	Office of Executive Management
oem	Oil-Emulsion Mud (AD)
OEM	On Equipment Materiel [*Army*] (AABC)
OEM	Open-End Marriage
OEM	Optical Electronic Microscope (WDAA)
oem	Optical Electron Microscope (AD)
OEM	Optical Electron Microscope (PDAA)
OEM	Ordnance Electrical Mechanic [*British military*] (DMA)
OEM	Organizational Element Model
oem	Original Equipment Manufacturer (AD)
OEM	Original Equipment Manufacturer
OEM	Original Equipment Manufacturing (SAUS)
OEM	Original Equipment Market (SAUS)
OEM	Other Equipment Manufacturer (IAA)
OEM	Other Equipment Manufacturers (CMD)
OEM	Own Equipment Material
OEMA	Madinah [*Saudi Arabia*] [*ICAO location identifier*] (ICLI)
OEMA	Office Equipment Manufacturers Association (AD)
OEMA	Office of Educational and Manpower Assistance (OICC)
OEMA	Office of Export Marketing Assistance [*Department of Commerce*]
OEMA	Oregon Educational Media Association
oemcp	Optical Effects Module Electronic Controller and Processor (AD)
OEMCP	Optical Effects Module Electronic Controller and Processor [*NASA*]
OEMI	Office Equipment Manufacturers Institute [*Later, CBEMA*]
OEMI	Office of Energy, Minerals, and Industry [*Environmental Protection Agency*]
OEMI	Original Equipment Manufacture Interface (SAUS)
OEMI	Original Equipment Manufacturers Information (VLIE)
OEMI	Other Equipment Manufacturer's Information (IAA)
OEMM	Operational Experiment on Mesoscale Meteorology (SAUS)
OEMN	Ordnance Electrical Mechanician [*British military*] (DMA)
OEMO	One-Electron Molecular Orbital (DB)
OEMP	Office of Environmental Monitoring and Prediction [*Marine science*] (OSRA)
OEMP	Operational Environmental Monitoring Program (SAUS)
OEMP	Oral Evaluation of Mechanical Proficiency (SAUS)
OEMS	Optical Emission under Mechanical Stress
OEMSA	Optical Equipment Manufacturers and Suppliers Association (BUAC)
OEMT	Operational Emergency Management Team [*Environmental science*] (COE)
OEN	Ennismore Township Public Library, Ontario [*Library symbol*] [*National Library of Canada*] (BIB)
OEN	Odd-Even Nuclei
oen	Oenanthic (AD)
oen	Oenanthyl (AD)
oen	oenological (SAUS)
oen	oenologist (SAUS)
OEN	Oenology (SAUS)
oen	oenolyn (SAUS)
oen	oenomancy (AD)
oen	oenomel (AD)
oen	oenometer (AD)
oen	oenophilist (AD)
oen	oenophobist (AD)
oen	oenopoetic (AD)
OEN	Ohio Environmental Protection Agency Library, Columbus, OH [*OCLC symbol*] (OCLC)
OEN	Operating Environment (SAUS)
OEN	Organizational Entity Name
OEN	Oxford Energy Co. (SAUS)
OENCO	Organizational Effectiveness Noncommissioned Officer [*Military*]
OENG	Englehart Public Library, Ontario [*Library symbol*] [*National Library of Canada*] (BIB)
OENG	Nejran [*Saudi Arabia*] [*ICAO location identifier*] (ICLI)
OENLA	Enterprise Branch, Lennox and Addington County Library, Ontario [*Library symbol*] [*National Library of Canada*] (NLC)
OENR	Oil-Extended Natural Rubber
OE-NR	Oil Extended Nitrile Rubber (SAUS)
OENR	Organization for European Nuclear Research
OEO	Office of Economic Opportunity [*Functions transferred to other federal agencies, 1973-75*]
OEO	Office of Equal Opportunity [*NASA*]
oeo	Officer's Eyes Only (AD)
OEO	Officers' Eyes Only [*Military*] (NVT)
OEO	Operational Equipment Objective (VLIE)
OEO	Ordnance Engineer Overseer (AD)
OEO	Ordnance Executive Officer [*Military*] [*British*]
OEO	Osceola, WI [*Location identifier*] [*FAA*] (FAAL)
OEO	Oversea Employment Office [*Air Force*] (AFM)
OEOA	Office for Emergency Operations in Africa [*United Nations*] (EY)
OEOB	Old Executive Office Building [*Washington, DC*]
OE/OE	Open Entry/Open Exit (OICC)
OE/OEM	Original Equipment/Original Equipment Manufacturer (SAUS)
OEP	Occupational Education Project
OEP	Occupational Exploration Program (OICC)
OEP	Ocean Education Project (EA)

OEP	Octaethylporphine (SAUS)
OEP	Octaethyl Porphyrin (SAUS)
OEP	Odd-Even Predominance [*Organic chemistry*]
OEP	Office of Economic Planning (SAUS)
OEP	Office of Economic Policy (SAUS)
OEP	Office of Economic Programs [*of BDSA*]
OEP	Office of Emergency Planning (AD)
OEP	Office of Emergency Preparedness [*formerly, Planning*] [*Terminated, 1973*]
OEP	Office of Energy Planning (COE)
OEP	Office of Energy Programs [*NASA*]
OEP	Office of Enforcement Policy (SAUS)
OEP	Office of Environmental Policy [*White House*] [*Marine science*] (OSRA)
OEP	Office of External Programs [*Environmental Protection Agency*] (GFGA)
OEP	Office of Extramural Programs (MELL)
OEP	Officer Education Program (SAUS)
OEP	Oil-Extended Polymer (IAA)
OEP	Open-Ended Plan [*Human resources*] (WYGK)
OEP	Operand Execution Pipeline [*Computer science*]
OEP	Operational Employment Plan [*Army*]
OEP	Optional Educational Programs (AD)
OEP	Optoelectronic Packaging (SAUS)
OEP	Organization, Education and Personnel (SAUS)
OEP	Original Element Processor (MHDB)
OEP	Outside Engineering Personnel (MCD)
OEP	Overall Economic Perspective (SAUS)
OEP	Overseas Employment Program [*DoD*]
OEP	Owen Electric Pictures [*Telecommunications service*] (TSSD)
OEP	Preble County District Library, Eaton, OH [*Library symbol*] [*Library of Congress*] (LCLS)
OEP	United States Environmental Protection Agency, Cincinnati (SAUS)
OEPA	Hafr Al-Batin Airport [*Saudi Arabia*] [*ICAO location identifier*] (ICLI)
OEPA	Ohio Environmental Protection Agency
OEPA	Vincristine, Etoposide, Prednisone, and Doxorubicin [*Medicine*]
OEPAC	Office of the Economic Planning Advisory Council [*Australia*]
OEP&GR	Office of Employment Policy and Grievance Review (ACAE)
OEPER	Office of Environmental Processes and Effects Research [*Environmental Protection Agency*] [*Washington, DC*] (GRD)
OEPF	Optometric Extension Program Foundation (EA)
OEPFC	Official Elvis Presley Fan Club (EAIO)
OEP Off Equip Prod	OEP Office Equipment and Products (SAUS)
OEPP	Organisation Europeenne et Mediterraneenne pour la Protection des Plantes [*European and Mediterranean Plant Protection Organization - EPPO*] (EAIO)
OEPR	Office of Environmental Project Review [*Department of the Interior*]
OEPR	Office of Extramural Program Review [*Department of Health and Human Services*] (GRD)
OEPS	Office of Educational Programs and Services [*NASA*]
OEPSS	Operationally Efficient Propulsion System Study (SAUS)
OEPT	Perry Township Public Library Emsdale, Ontario [*Library symbol*] [*National Library of Canada*] (NLC)
OEQ	Order of Engineers of Quebec [*Canada*] (PDAA)
OEQ	Organisation Europeenne pour la Qualite [*Switzerland*] (EAIO)
OEQC	Office of Environmental Quality Control (AD)
OER	Odd-Even Rule
OER	Oersted [*Unit of magnetizing intensity*]
OER	Offensive Efficiency Ratio [*Basketball*]
OER	Office of Aerospace Research [*Air Force*] (AD)
OER	Office of Economic Research [*Department of Commerce*]
OER	Office of Energy Research [*Department of Energy*] [*Washington, DC*] (GRD)
OER	Office of Energy Research [*University of Illinois*] [*Research center*] (RCD)
OER	Office of Environmental Restoration (AUEG)
OER	Office of Evaluation Research [*University of Illinois at Chicago*] [*Research center*] (RCD)
OER	Office of Exploratory Research [*Environmental Protection Agency*] [*Washington, DC*] (GRD)
OER	Officer Effectiveness Report [*Air Force*] (AFM)
OER	Officer Efficiency Report [*Military*]
OER	Officer Engineering Reserve (AD)
OER	Officer Evaluation Report [*Military*] (INF)
OER	Officers Effectiveness Report (SAUS)
OER	Officers Efficiency Report (SAUS)
OER	Officers' Emergency Reserve [*British*]
OER	Officers Evaluation Report (SAUS)
OER	Oil Extended Rubber (EDCT)
OER	Operating Equipment Requirements (VLIE)
OER	Operational Effectiveness Rate (SAUS)
OER	Operational ELINT Requirements (MCD)
OER	Operational Equipment Requirement (AAG)
OER	Operations Engineering Report (AAG)
OER	Organization for European Research (AD)
oer	Original Equipment Replacement (AD)
OER	Original Equipment Request (AAG)
OER	Ornskoldsvik [*Sweden*] [*Airport symbol*] (OAG)
OER	Osmotic Erythrocyte Resistance
O'ER	Over (ROG)
OER	Overhead Expenditure Request
OER	Oxygen Enhancement Ratio
OER	Oxygen Evolution Reaction (PDAA)
OERA	Omnibus Education Reconciliation Act of 1981

OERAHA....... Organisation Europeenne pour des Recherches Astronomiques dans l'Hemisphere Austral [*European Southern Observatory - ESO*] (EAIO)
OERC .... Ontario Educational Research Council [*Canada*] (EDAC)
OERC .... Optimum Earth Reentry Corridor [*Aerospace*]
oerc .... Optimum Earth-Reentry Corridor (AD)
OERCPrD ..... Ohio Edison 4.56% Pfd [*NYSE symbol*] (TTSB)
OERD .... Erin District High School, Erin, Ontario [*Library symbol*] [*National Library of Canada*] (NLC)
OERD .... Ocean Environment Research Division [*Formerly, MARD, Marine Assessment Research Division and MRRD, Marine Resources Research Division*] [*Marine science*] (OSRA)
OERD .... Office of Economic and Regional Development (SAUS)
OERD .... Office of Energy Research and Development (SAUS)
OERF .... Orthodontic Education and Research Foundation (EA)
OERF .... Rafha [*Saudi Arabia*] [*ICAO location identifier*] (ICLI)
OERI .... Office of Educational Research and Improvement [*Department of Education*] [*Washington, DC*]
OERI .... Office of Energy-Related Inventions [*Gaithersburg, MD*] [*National Institute of Standards and Technology*]
OERK .... Riyadh/King Khalid International [*Saudi Arabia*] [*ICAO location identifier*] (ICLI)
OERL .... Elgin Branch, Rideau Lakes Union Library, Ontario [*Library symbol*] [*National Library of Canada*] (NLC)
OERL .... Officer Education Research Laboratory [*Air Force*]
OERL .... Overall Echo Return Loss
OERP .... Overseas Expenditure Reduction Program [*Military*] (AFM)
OERPA .... Office of Exploratory Research and Problem Assessment [*National Science Foundation*] (AD)
OERR .... Arar [*Saudi Arabia*] [*ICAO location identifier*] (ICLI)
OERR .... Office of Emergency and Remedial Response [*Environmental Protection Agency*] (GFGA)
OERR .... Office of Environmental Regulatory Research (SAUS)
OERS .... Officer Evaluation Reporting System [*Army*]
OERS .... Operational Earth Resources System (SAUS)
OERS .... Organisation Europeenne de Recherches Spatiales
OERT .... Succursale d'Embrun, Bibliotheque Publique du Canton de Russell [*Embrun Branch, Russell Township Public Library*] Ontario [*Library symbol*] [*National Library of Canada*] (BIB)
OERWM .... Office of Environmental Restoration and Waste Management [*U.S. Department of Energy*] (BARN)
OERY .... Riyadh [*Saudi Arabia*] [*ICAO location identifier*] (ICLI)
OES .... Bureau of Oceans and International Environmental and Scientific Affairs [*Department of State*]
OES .... Espanola Public Library, Ontario [*Library symbol*] [*National Library of Canada*] (NLC)
OES .... Occupational Employment Statistics [*Department of Labor*]
OES .... Occupational Exposure Standard [*Environmental chemistry*]
OES .... Oceanic Engineering Society (SAUS)
OES .... Odd Even Sort (SAUS)
OES .... Office Evaluation System (SAUS)
OES .... Office of Earthquake Studies (SAUS)
OES .... Office of Economic Stabilization [*World War II*]
OES .... Office of Emergency Service [*Federal disaster planning*]
OES .... Office of Employment Security [*Department of Labor*]
OES .... Office of Endangered Species [*Department of the Interior*]
OES .... Office of Examinations and Supervision [*Federal Home Loan Bank Board*]
OES .... Office of Executive Support [*Environmental Protection Agency*] (GFGA)
OES .... Officer Education System [*Army*] (RDA)
OES .... Officer Evaluation System (SAUS)
OES .... Official Experimental Station [*Amateur radio*]
OES .... Offshore Engineering Society (BUAC)
OES .... Olympus Endoscopy System [*Gastroenterology*] (DAVI)
OES .... Open-Ended Spinning [*Textile industry*]
OES .... Open-Ended System [*Computer science*]
OES .... Operations and Engineering Squadron
OES .... Operations and Equipment Section (SAA)
OES .... Optical Emission Spectroscopy [*Laboratory science*] (DAVI)
OES .... Orbital-Escape System [*NASA*]
OES .... Orbiter Emergency Site [*NASA*] (NASA)
OES .... Order Entry System (SAUS)
OES .... Order/Entry System [*Computer science*] (OA)
OES .... Order of the Eastern Star [*Freemasonry*] (EA)
OES .... Organisation Europeenne des Scieries [*European Sawmills Organization*] [*EC*] (ECED)
OES .... Organizacion de Estados Americanos [*Organization of American States*] [*Spain*] (AD)
OES .... Organization of European Saw-Mills (BUAC)
OES .... Organization of European States (AD)
OES .... Ostrich Eggshell [*Archeological material*]
OES .... Outgoing Echo Suppressor [*Telecommunications*] (TEL)
OES .... Output Enable Serial [*Computer science*] (VLIE)
OES .... Overseas Educational Service [*Defunct*]
OES .... San Antonio Oeste [*Argentina*] [*Airport symbol*] (OAG)
OESA .... Office of Earth Sciences Applications [*Department of the Interior*] (GRD)
OESA .... Office of Employment Service Administration [*US Employment Service*] [*Department of Labor*]
OESBR .... Oil Extended Styrene Butadiene Rubber (PDAA)
oesbr .... Oil-Extended Styrene-Butadiene Rubber (AD)
OESC .... Open-Ended Systems Corp.
OESCA .... Old English Sheepdog Club of America (EA)
OESCAND .... Old East Scandinavian [*Language, etc.*]

OESD .... Ocean Engineering System Development
OESD .... Opto-Electronic Semiconductor Device (SAUS)
OESE .... Office of Elementary and Secondary Education [*Department of Education*]
OES/E .... Office of the Environment (US Department of) State/Environment, Health and Natural Resources (GNE)
OES/EGC ...... Office of the Environment (US Department of) State/Office of Global Change (GNE)
OES/EHC ...... Office of the Environment (US Department of) State/Office of Ecology, Health and Conservation (GNE)
OES/ENP ...... Bureau of Oceans and International Environmental and Scientific Affairs/Environmental and Population Affairs [*Department of State*] (MSC)
OES/ENV ...... Office of the Environment (US Department of) State/Office of Environmental Protection (GNE)
OESH .... Office of Environment, Safety, and Health (COE)
OESH .... Shared Library Services, South Huron Hospital, Exeter, Ontario [*Library symbol*] [*National Library of Canada*] (BIB)
OESH .... Sharurah [*Saudi Arabia*] [*ICAO location identifier*] (ICLI)
OESK .... Al-Jouf [*Saudi Arabia*] [*ICAO location identifier*] (ICLI)
OESK .... Osteuropeiska Solidaritetskommitten [*East European Solidarity Committee*] (EAIO)
OESL .... Oceanographic and Environmental Service Laboratory [*Raytheon Co.*]
OESL .... Sulayel [*Saudi Arabia*] [*ICAO location identifier*] (ICLI)
OESLA .... Office of Engineering Standards Liaison and Analysis [*National Bureau of Standards*] (IAA)
OESM .... Occupational and Environmental Safety Management
OES/N .... Office of the Environment (US Department of) State/Nuclear Energy and Energy Technology Affairs (GNE)
OES/NED ..... Office of the Environment (US Department of) State/Office of Export and Import Control (GNE)
OES/NEP ..... Office of the Environment (US Department of) State/Office of Non-Proliferation and Export Policy (GNE)
OES/NTS ..... Office of the Environment (US Department of) State/Office of Nuclear Technology and Safeguards (GNE)
OES/O .... Office of the Environment (US Department of) State/Oceans and Fisheries Affairs (GNE)
OESO .... Organisation Internationale d'Etudes Statistiques pour les Maladies de l'Oesophage [*International Organization for Statistical Studies on Diseases of the Esophagus*] (EAIO)
OESO .... Organizational Effectiveness Staff Officer [*Military*]
OESOC .... Organizational Effectiveness Staff Officer Course [*Army*]
OES/OFA ...... Bureau of Oceans and International Environmental and Scientific Affairs/Ocean and Fishery Affairs [*Department of State*] (MSC)
OES/OFA ...... Office of the Environment (US Department of) State/Office of Fisheries Affairs (GNE)
OES/OLP ...... Office of the Environment (US Department of) State/Office of Ocean Law and Policy (GNE)
oesoph .... Oesophagus (AD)
OESOPH ...... Oesophagus
OES/OSP ...... Office of the Environment (US Department of) State/Office of Marine Science and Polar Affairs (GNE)
OESP .... O Estado de Sao Paulo [*State of Sao Paulo*] [*Brazil*] [*A publication*] (AD)
OESP .... Ontario Export Support Programme (SAUS)
OESPCMJ .... Officer Exercising Special Court-Martial Jurisdiction
OE Spinning... Open End Spinning (SAUS)
OESR .... Oil Extended Synthetic Rubber (PDAA)
OESS .... O/ET [*Orbiter/External Tank*] Separation System [*NASA*] (MCD)
OESS .... Office of Engineering Standards Services [*National Bureau of Standards*]
OES/S .... Office of the Environment (US Department of) State/Science and Technology Affairs (GNE)
OESS .... Organizational Effectiveness Survey System [*Army*]
OES/SAT ..... Office of the Environment (US Department of) State/Office of Advanced Technology (GNE)
OES/SCI ...... Bureau of Oceans and International Enviromental and Scientific Affairs/Scientific and Technological Affairs [*Department of State*] (MSC)
OES/SCT ..... Office of Environment (US Department of) State/Office of Cooperative Science and Technology Programs (GNE)
OEST .... Outline European Staff Target (SAUS)
OET .... Objective End Time
OET .... Office of Economic Transition (SAUS)
OET .... Office of Education and Training (AD)
OET .... Office of Emergency Transportation [*FAA*]
OET .... Office of Employment Training (SAUS)
OET .... Office of Engineering and Technology [*Washington, DC*] [*FCC*] (GRD)
OET .... Official English Title
OET .... Official Establishments Trust [*Australia*]
OET .... Oldest English Texts
OET .... On Equipment Training (MCD)
OET .... Open Epicutaneous Test (SAUS)
OET .... Optic-Electronic Transducer (SAUS)
OET .... Oral Esophageal Tube [*Medicine*] (MELL)
O/ET .... Orbiter/External Tank [*NASA*] (NASA)
OET .... Organ Extract Therapy [*Medicine*] (MELL)
OET .... Organizacao para Estudios Tropicales [*Organization for Tropical Studies*] (EAIO)
OET .... Organizational Effectiveness Team (TIMI)
OET .... Overseas Exchange Transactions (AD)
OETA .... Occupied Enemy Territory Administration [*World War II*]
OETA .... Original Estimated Time of Arrival (CTAS)

OETA	Township of Armstrong Public Library [*Bibliotheque Publique Canton Armstrong*], Earlton, Ontario [*Library symbol*] [*National Library of Canada*] (BIB)
OET & E	Operational Employment Testing and Evaluation (AFM)
OETB	Ocean Economics and Technology Branch [*United Nations*] (MSC)
OETB	Offshore Energy Technology Board [*British*]
OETB	Tabuk [*Saudi Arabia*] [*ICAO location identifier*] (ICLI)
OETB	United Nations Ocean Economics and Technology Branch (SAUS)
OETC	Optoelectronics Technology Consortium [*Sponsored by the Department of Defense*]
OETC	Oregon Educational Technology Consortium
OETC	Organizational Effectiveness Training Center [*Army*] (MCD)
OETF	Taif [*Saudi Arabia*] [*ICAO location identifier*] (ICLI)
OETLC	Office of Economic Trends and Labor Conditions [*Department of Labor*]
OETO	United Nations Ocean Economics and Technology Office (SAUS)
OETP	Operations Experimental Test Plan (IAA)
OETP	Orbiter Electron Temperature Probe [*NASA*]
OETR	Turaif [*Saudi Arabia*] [*ICAO location identifier*] (ICLI)
OETT	Oral Endotracheal Tube [*Medicine*] (STED)
OEu	Euclid Public Library, Euclid, OH [*Library symbol*] [*Library of Congress*] (LCLS)
OEU	Operational Evaluation Unit (SAUS)
OEU	Operation Eyesight Universal [*Canada*] (EAIO)
OEUNAH	Econometrics and Operations Research (journ.) (SAUS)
OEVE	Office of Earthquakes, Volcanoes, and Engineering [*US Geological Survey*] (AD)
OEW	Offensive Electronic Warfare (SAUS)
OEW	Office of Economic Warfare [*World War II*]
OEW	Old English White [*Automobile classified advertising*]
OEW	Open-End Wrench
OEW	Operating Empty Weight (SAUS)
OEW	Operational Empty Weight [*Aviation*]
OEW	Ordinary Electromagnetic Wave
OEW	Ordnance and Explosive Waste [*Military*]
OEWG	Open-Ended Working Group (NATG)
OEWG	Open-End Waveguide (SAUS)
OEWG	Operation, Evaluation Wartime Group (NATG)
OEWGP	Operational Experiments Working Group (SAUS)
OEWJ	Wejh [*Saudi Arabia*] [*ICAO location identifier*] (ICLI)
OEX	Office of Educational Exchange [*Department of State*]
OEX	Oklahoma City, OK [*Location identifier*] [*FAA*] (FAAL)
OEX	Options Exchange [*Finance*]
OEX	Orbiter Experiments [*NASA*] (MCD)
OEX	Standard & Poor's 100 Stock Index (DFIT)
OEXP	Office of Exploration [*NASA*]
OEYN	Yenbo [*Saudi Arabia*] [*ICAO location identifier*] (ICLI)
OEZ	Osteuropaeische Zeit [*East European Time*] [*German*] (AD)
OF	Degrees Fahrenheit
OF	Fast Airways BV [*Netherlands*] [*ICAO designator*] (ICDA)
OF	Fitted for Oil Fuel [*Ships*]
OF	Frankford Public Library, Ontario [*Library symbol*] [*National Library of Canada*] (BIB)
OF	Noosa Air [*ICAO designator*] (AD)
OF	Occipitalfrontal [*Diameter of skull*]
OF	Occupations Finder [*A publication*] (DHP)
OF	Oceanographic Facility
OF	Odd Fellows [*An association*]
OF	Off Course (SAUS)
Of	Official (DAVI)
of	Official (ELAL)
OF	Official Files
Of	Offizier (SAUS)
OF	Offset Printing Program [*Association of Independent Colleges and Schools specialization code*]
OF	Offshore Funds [*Investment term*]
OF	Offshore Oil International (SAUS)
OF	Oil Facility [*International Monetary Fund*]
OF	Oil-Filled (IAA)
OF	Oil Fired (ADA)
OF	Oil Fuel [*British military*] (DMA)
of	Old Face (AD)
OF	Old Face [*Typography*]
OF	Old Field [*Botany*]
OF	Old French [*Language, etc.*]
OF	One of the Finn (SAUS)
OF	One of the Firm [*Telecommunications*] (TEL)
O/F	On File (SAUS)
OF	Open Forum [*An association*] (EA)
OF	Open Fracture [*Medicine*] (MELL)
OF	Open Full [*Container*] (DCTA)
OF	Operand Field
OF	Operating Forces [*Navy*]
OF	Operational Fixed
OF	Operational Functionality (SAUS)
OF	Operation Friendship (BUAC)
OF	Operations and Food Analysis
OF	Operations Following (MCD)
OF	Ophthalmological Foundation [*Later, NSPB*]
OF	Optical Fibre (EECA)
OF	Optical Flat (SAUS)
OF	Optical Fluorescence (SAUS)
OF	Optical Frequency
OF	Optic Fundi (STED)
OF	Optimal Feedback (SAUS)

OF	Optimal Filtering (SAUS)
OF	Optional Feature (IAA)
OF	Optional File (SAUS)
of	Optional Form (AD)
OF	Optional Form
OF	Orbital Facilities (SAUS)
OF	Orbital Facility (IAA)
O/F	Orbital Flight [*NASA*] (KSC)
OF	Orbitofrontal
OF	Order of the Founder [*Salvation Army*]
OF	Ordnance Factory (SAUS)
OF	Oriented Film (SAUS)
OF	Orphan Foundation [*Later, OFA*] (EA)
OF	Orthochromatic Film [*Photography*] (DGA)
OF	Oscillator Frequency [*Telecommunications*] (IAA)
OF	Osfriends (EA)
Of	Osmond Tape Exchange [*An association*] (EA)
OF	Osmotic Fragility Test
OF	Osseointegration Foundation (SAUS)
OF	Osteitis Fibrosa [*Medicine*] (MAE)
OF	Osteopathic Foundation [*Later, NOF*]
OF	Ostrum-Furst [*Syndrome*] [*Medicine*] (STED)
OF	Other Medical/Surgical Facility (MEDA)
OF	Outer Flame (SAUS)
OF	Outfield [*Baseball*]
OF	Outfielder [*Baseball term*] (NDBD)
O/F	Outfit [*Doll collecting*]
OF	Output Factor [*Computer science*] (IEEE)
OF	Output File (SAUS)
of	Outside Face (AD)
OF	Outside Face [*Technical drawings*]
Of	Ovenstone Factor (AD)
OF	Ovenstone Factor [*Medicine*] (MAE)
of	Overflow (ELAL)
OF	Overflow
OF	Overflow Flag (SAUS)
OF	Overfrequency (MSA)
OF	Oxbow Falls (AD)
OF	Oxenstierna Foundation (AD)
OF	Oxford Foundation (AD)
O-F	Oxidation-Fermentation [*Growth medium*]
o/f	Oxidation/Fermentation (AD)
OF	Oxide Film (SAUS)
O/F	Oxidizer-to-Fuel [*Ratio*]
o/f	Oxidizer to Fuel Ratio (AD)
of	Oxidizing Flame (AD)
OF	Oxidizing Flame
OF	Oxydizer-to-Fuel [*Ratio*]
OF	Oxygen Fill (NASA)
OF	Oxygen-Free (ACAE)
OF/2	Operator Facility/2 (SAUS)
OFA	Fairfield County District Library, Lancaster, OH [*OCLC symbol*] (OCLC)
OFA	Object Free Area [*FAA*] (TAG)
OFA	Office for the Aging (BARN)
OFA	Office of Family Assistance [*Department of Health and Human Services*] (GFGA)
OFA	Office of Federal Activities [*Environmental Protection Agency*] (GFGA)
OFA	Office of Financial Analysis [*Department of the Treasury*]
OFA	Office of Flight Assurance (SAUS)
OFA	Oficina Alemania [*Chile*] [*Seismograph station code, US Geological Survey*] (SEIS)
OFA	Oil-Immersed Forced-Air-Cooled [*Transformer*] (IEEE)
OFA	Oklahoma Forestry Association (WPI)
OFA	Old Farmers Almanac (SAUS)
OFA	Old Folks Association (AD)
OFA	Omnite Fuel Additive (SAUS)
OFA	Oncofetal Antigen [*Immunology*]
OFA	Ontario Federation of Agriculture [*Canada*]
OFA	Ontario Film Association [*Canada*] (BUAC)
OFA	Optimal Flexible Architecture (SAUS)
OFA	Optimized Fuel Assembly [*Nuclear energy*] (NRCH)
OFA	Order for Assignment [*Military*] (CAAL)
OFA	Organic Food Alliance (EA)
OFA	Organization of Flying Adjusters (NTPA)
OFA	Organized Flying Adjusters (EA)
OFA	Orienteering Federation of Australia
OFA	Oronite Fuel Additive
OFA	Orphan Foundation of America (EA)
OFA	Orthopedic Foundation for Animals (EA)
OFA	Other Federal Agencies (ABAC)
OFA	Over Fifties Association [*Australia*]
OFA	Over Fire Air [*Combustion technology*]
OFA	Overseas Family Allowance [*British military*] (DMA)
OFA	Owen Family Association (EA)
OFA	Oxygenated Fuels Association (EA)
OFAA	Oyster Farmers' Association of Australia
OFAAP	Ontario Farm Adjustment Assistance Program (SAUS)
OFAB	Fort Albany Band Library, Ontario [*Library symbol*] [*National Library of Canada*] (BIB)
OFAC	Owens Fine Arts Center (SAUS)
OFACS	Overseas-Foreign Aeronautical Communications Station (MUGU)
O-Factor	Oscillation Factor (SAUS)

OFAD	Ocean Floor Analysis Division [*Later, Sea Floor Division*] [*NORDA*] (EA)
OFAED	Organization Forecast Authorization Equipment Data [*Military*] (AFIT)
OFAES	Oriental Fine Arts Exchange Society [*China*] (BUAC)
OFAF	Metallurgical Research Library, Falconbridge Nickel Mines Ltd., Falconbridge, Ontario [*Library symbol*] [*National Library of Canada*] (NLC)
OFAGE	Orthogonal-Field-Alternation Gel Electrophoresis [*Analytical biochemistry*]
OFALF	Omega First Amendment Legal Fund (EA)
OFAM	Office of Financial and Administrative Management [*Department of Labor*]
OFANC	Falconbridge Branch, Nickel Centre Public Library, Ontario [*Library symbol*] [*National Library of Canada*] (NLC)
OFANSW	Oyster Farmers' Association of New South Wales [*Australia*]
OFAP	Observing Facilities Advisory Panel (SAUS)
OFAR	Office of Foreign Agricultural Relations [*Department of Agriculture*]
OFARS	Overseas-Foreign Aeronautical Receiver Station
OFAS	Overseas Flight Assistance Service
OFATS	Overseas-Foreign Aeronautical Transmitter Station
OFavp	Fairview Park Regional Library, Fairview Park, OH [*Library symbol*] [*Library of Congress*] (LCLS)
OFB	Oil Forced Blast (IAA)
OFB	Operational Facilities Branch [*NASA*] (MCD)
OFB	Output Feedback (NITA)
OFBM	Oxidation-Fermentation Basal Medium (STED)
OFC	Conference on Optical Fiber Communication [*Optical Society of America*] [*Washington, DC*] (TSSD)
OFC	Corporate Office Prop Tr SBI [*NYSE symbol*] (SG)
OFC	Foleyet Community Library, Ontario [*Library symbol*] [*National Library of Canada*] (NLC)
OFC	High Court Reports, Orange Free State [*A publication*] (DLA)
OFC	Occipitofrontal Circumference [*Anatomy*]
OFC	Oceania Football Confederation
OFC	Oceanography and Fisheries Committee (ASF)
ofc	Office (AD)
OFC	Office [*or Officer*] (AFM)
Ofc	Office (TBD)
OFC	Office of Fishery Coordination [*World War II*]
OFC	Oil-Filled Cable (SAUS)
OFC	Oil Free Compressor
OFC	Oldest Finest Canadian [*Whiskey*] (IIA)
OFC	Old Fired Copper [*Initialism once used as brand name for bourbon*]
OFC	Old French Canadian [*Initialism used in Schenley brand of Canadian whisky*]
OFC	One Flow Cascade Cycle (IAA)
OFC	Open Financial Connectivity [*Microsoft Computer Software*] [*Computer Science*]
OFC	Operational Flight Control [*NASA*]
OFC	Opposing Force Component (MCD)
OFC	Optical Fiber Communication (CIST)
OFC	Optical Fiber Control (DCDG)
OFC	Optical File Cabinet [*Computer science*]
OFC	Optical Formatter Controller (NITA)
OFC	Optical Frequency Conversion
OFC	Orbitofacial Cleft [*Medicine*] (STED)
OFC	Orthonormal Function Coding (SAUS)
OFC	Oscillation Frequency Control (CIST)
OFC	Osteitis Fibrosa Cystica [*Medicine*] (DMAA)
OFC	Outside Front Cover [*Publishing*] (NTCM)
OFC	Overflow Card (SAUS)
OFC	Overflow Control (SAUS)
OFC	Overhead Foxhole Cover (SAUS)
OFC	Overseas Food Corp. (AD)
OFC	Oxford First Corporation (SAUS)
OFC	Oxyfuel-Gas Cutting [*Welding*]
OFC	Oxygen-Free Copper (SAUS)
OFCA	Ontario Federation of Construction Associations [*Canada*] (AD)
OFCA	Organisation des Fabricants de Produits Cellulosiques Alimentaires de la CEE [*Organization of Manufacturers of Cellulose Products for Foodstuffs in the European Economic Community*]
OFC-A	Oxyfuel-Gas Cutting - Acetylene [*Welding*]
OFCAPPDE	Office Application Descriptons (SAUS)
OFCAPPE	Office Application Entries (SAUS)
OFCATS	Optical Fiber Cable Assembly Automatic Test System (ACAE)
OFCC	Office of Federal Contract Compliance [*Later, OFCCP*] [*Department of Labor*]
OFCCP	Office of Federal Contract Compliance Programs [*Formerly, OFCC*] [*Department of Labor*]
OFCCP Fed Cont Compl Man	OFCCP Federal Contract Compliance Manual [*A publication*] (AAGC)
OFCE	Office [*or Officer*]
OFCF	Overseas Farmers Co-Operative Federation Ltd. (BUAC)
OFC-H	Oxyfuel-Gas Cutting - Hydrogen [*Welding*]
ofcl	Official (AD)
Ofcl	Official (TBD)
OFCL	Official
Of Cl Pac	Officium Clerici Pacis [*A publication*] (DLA)
OFCM	Office of the Federal Coordinator for Meteorological Services and Research
OFCM	Office of the Federal Coordinator for Meteorology (SAUS)
OFCN	Organization for Community Networks (IGQR)
OFC-N	Oxyfuel Cutting - Natural Gas [*Welding*]
OFC-N	Oxynatural Gas Cutting (SAUS)
OFCO	Offensive Counterintelligence Operations (MCD)
OFCO	Office of the Federal Coordinating Officer (SAUS)
OFCOFASSTSECNAV	Office of the Assistant Secretary of the Navy (DNAB)
OFCOFASSTSECNAV(FINMGMT)	Office of the Assistant Secretary of the Navy (Financial Management) (DNAB)
OFCOFASSTSECNAV(INSTALLOG)	Office of the Assistant Secretary of the Navy (Installations and Logistics) (DNAB)
OFCOFASSTSECNAV(PERSRESFOR)	Office of the Assistant Secretary of the Navy (Personnel and Reserve Force) (DNAB)
OFCOFASSTSECNAV(RSCHDEV)	Office of the Assistant Secretary of the Navy (Research and Development) (DNAB)
OFCOFINFO	Office of Information (DNAB)
OFCP	Ontario Federation for Cerebral Palsy [*Canada*] (NRGU)
OFCP	Ottawa Financial [*NASDAQ symbol*] (TTSB)
OFCP	Ottawa Financial Corp. [*NASDAQ symbol*] (SAG)
OFC-P	Oxyfuel-Gas Cutting - Propane [*Welding*]
OFC-P	Oxypropane Cutting (SAUS)
OFCR	Officer
OFCS	Office of Foreign Commercial Services [*Abolished 1970, functions transferred to Bureau of International Commerce*]
OFCS	Operational Flight Control System [*NASA*] (KSC)
OFCSAV	Orchardists and Fruit Cool Stores Association of Victoria [*Australia*]
OFCT	Order Fulfillment Cycle Time (TIMI)
OFD	Object Film Distance [*Optics*]
OFD	Objective Force Designator (MCD)
OFD	Occipitofrontal Diameter [*of the skull*]
OFD	Ocean Floor Drilling
OFD	Ocean Freight Differential [*MARAD*] (TAG)
Ofd	Offered [*Stock exchange term*]
OFD	Ohio Federal Decisions [*A publication*] (DLA)
ofd	One-Function Diagram (AD)
OFD	One-Function Diagram
OFD	Open-Face Dectector [*Instrumentation*]
ofd	Optical Fire Detector (AD)
OFD	Optical Fire Director (SAUS)
OFD	Optical Frequency Division Demultiplexer (or Demultiplexing) (SAUS)
OFD	Optical Gun Fire Director [*Military*] (PDAA)
OFD	Oral-Facial-Digital [*Genetics*] (DAVI)
OFD	Ordnance Field Depot (SAUS)
OFD	Orofacial Dyskinesia (DIPS)
OFD	Oro-Facio-Digital [*Syndrome*] [*Medicine*]
OFD	Oued Fodda [*Algeria*] [*Seismograph station code, US Geological Survey*] (SEIS)
OFD	Overflow Data (SAUS)
OFDA	Office Foreign Disaster Assistance (SAUS)
OFDA	Office Furniture Distribution Association (EA)
OFDA	Office of Foreign Disaster Assistance (COE)
OFDA	Office of United States Foreign Disaster Assistance [*Agency for International Development*]
OFDAP	Office of the Field Directorate of Ammunition Plants
OFDC	Official First Day Cover [*Canada Post Corp.*]
OFDC	Ontario Film Development Corp. [*Canada*]
OFDG	Operator Fractionation Decision Guide [*Process control*]
OFDI	Office of Foreign Direct Investments [*Department of Commerce*]
OFDM	Orthogonal Frequency Division Modulation (SAUS)
OFDM	Orthogonal Frequency Division Multiplex (SAUS)
OFDR	Off-Frequency Decoupling Resonance [*Physical chemistry*]
OFDS	Optimal Financial Decision Strategy (MHDI)
OFDS	Orbiter Flight Dynamics Simulator [*NASA*] (NASA)
OFDS	Oxygen Fluid Distribution System [*NASA*] (NASA)
OFE	Odds for Effectiveness [*Navy*]
OFE	Office of Federal Elections [*Later, FEC*]
OFE	Office of Fossil Energy (COE)
OFE	Office of Fuels and Engergy (AD)
OFE	Office of Fusion Energy [*Oak Ridge National Laboratory*]
OFE	Open Finance Exchange (SAUS)
OFE	Operative Functional Element (SAUS)
OFE	Optical Flight Evaluation
OFE	Order for Engagement [*Military*] (CAAL)
OFE	Osteogenic Factor Extract (DB)
OFE	Other Further Education
OFE	Ottawa Fundraising Executives [*Ontario, Canada*]
OFE	Overall Factory Effectiveness (SAUS)
OFEA	Office of Foreign Economic Administration [*Lend-Lease*] [*World War II*]
OFEA	Officer Front End Analysis (MCD)
OFEC	Office of Federal Employees Compensation [*Department of Labor*]
OFEC	Office of Foreign Economic Coordination [*World War II*]
OFEC	Wellington County Museum, Fergus, Ontario [*Library symbol*] [*National Library of Canada*] (BIB)
OFEHM	Fort Erie Historical Museum, Ontario [*Library symbol*] [*National Library of Canada*] (BIB)
OFEMA	Office Francais d'Exportation de Materiel Aeronautique [*French Office for theExportation of Aeronautical Materiel*] (AD)
OFEP	Fort Erie Public Library, Ontario [*Library symbol*] [*National Library of Canada*] (NLC)
OFER	Fergus Public Library, Ontario [*Library symbol*] [*National Library of Canada*] (NLC)
OFER	Ohio Ferro-Alloys Corp. (SAUS)
OFERC	Centre Wellington District High School, Fergus, Ontario [*Library symbol*] [*National Library of Canada*] (NLC)
OFERRA	Office of Foreign Economic Relief and Rehabilitation Administration
OFERW	Wellington County Public Library, Fergus, Ontario [*Library symbol*] [*National Library of Canada*] (NLC)
OFERWM	Wellington County Museum and Archives, Fergus, Ontario [*Library symbol*] [*National Library of Canada*] (BIB)

OFF.............	Challenge Air Transport, Inc. [*ICAO designator*] (FAAC)
Off...............	De Officiis [*of Cicero*] [*Classical studies*] (OCD)
OFF.............	Fort Frances Public Library, Ontario [*Library symbol*] [*National Library of Canada*] (NLC)
OFF.............	Offensive
OFF.............	Offer
off...............	Offertory (GROV)
OFF.............	Offertory
OFF.............	Office [*or Officer*] (AFM)
off...............	Office (DD)
OFF.............	Office for Families (DICI)
OFF.............	Office of Facts and Figures [*Later, Office of War Information*] [*Military*]
Off..............	Officer (AD)
off...............	Officer (SHCU)
OFF.............	Officers' Family Fund
off...............	Official (MILB)
Off..............	Official (STED)
OFF.............	Official
OFF.............	Offretite [*A zeolite*]
OFF.............	Omaha, NE [*Location identifier*] [*FAA*] (FAAL)
OFF.............	Organization for Femininity
OFF.............	State of Being Powered Down (SAUS)
OFFA...........	One Fund for All [*An association*] (BUAC)
Off Abr........	Official Abbreviation (SAUS)
Off&WO.......	Officers and Warrant Officers (SAUS)
OFFAR........	Office of Fuel and Fuel Additive Registration [*Environmental Protection Agency*]
Off Br.........	Officina Brevium [*1679*] [*A publication*] (DLA)
Off Brev.......	Officina Brevium [*1679*] [*A publication*] (DLA)
OFF BUS ONLY...	Official Business Only (DNAB)
OFFC.........	Office
OffcDpt.......	Office Depot [*Associated Press*] (SAG)
OFFEE.........	Offeree [*Legal shorthand*] (LWAP)
OFFEG.........	Offshore Fossil-Fueled Electric Generators
OFFEN.........	Offensive [*Ammunition*] (AAG)
offen...........	Offensive (AD)
OFFENS.......	Offensive
Off Environ...	Office Environment (SAUS)
offeq...........	Office Equipment (AD)
Off Equip Index...	Office Equipment Index (SAUS)
Off Equip Methods...	Office Equipment and Methods (SAUS)
Off Equip News...	Office Equipment News (SAUS)
offer...........	Offertories (AD)
Offer...........	Office of Electricity Regulation [*British*] (WA)
OFFER.........	Office of Electricity Regulation [*British*]
Off Ex.........	Wentworth's Office of Executors [*A publication*] (DLA)
Off Exec.......	Wentworth's Office of Executors [*A publication*] (DLA)
offg...........	Offering (AD)
OFFG.........	Officiating
Off Gaz Pat Office...	Official Gazette. United States Patent and Trademark Office [*A publication*] (DLA)
Off Home.....	Office at Home (SAUS)
OFFI...........	Official
OFFI...........	Old Fashion Foods, Inc. (SAUS)
offic..........	Official (AD)
OFFIC.........	Official
OFFIC.........	Officiate
Office A&A...	Office Administration and Automation (SAUS)
Office Adm&Automation...	Office Administration and Automation (SAUS)
Office Pubns...	Office Publications (SAUS)
Officer........	Officer's Reports [*1-9 Minnesota*] [*A publication*] (DLA)
Official J Ind Comm Prop...	Official Journal of Industrial and Commercial Property [*Eire*] [*A publication*] (DLA)
Official Rep III Courts Commission...	Official Reports, Illinois Courts Commission [*A publication*] (DLA)
Officmx.......	Officemax, Inc. [*Associated Press*] (SAG)
Off Inf Manage Int...	Office and Information Management International (SAUS)
OFFINTAC....	Offshore Installations Technical Advisory Committee (BUAC)
Off J Eur Communities Inf Not...	Official Journal of the European Communities. Information and Notices (SAUS)
OFFL..........	Official (AFM)
OFFM..........	Fort Frances Museum and Cultural Centre, Ontario [*Library symbol*] [*National Library of Canada*] (BIB)
Off Mag......	Office Magazine (SAUS)
OFFMAUTSYS...	Officer Master File Automated System (DNAB)
OFFNAVHIST...	Office of Naval History [*Also, ONH*]
OFFNAVWEASERV...	Office of Naval Weather Service
Off Nom.......	Official Nomenclature (SAUS)
OFFOR........	Offeror [*Legal shorthand*] (LWAP)
OFFP..........	Fenelon Falls Public Library, Ontario [*Library symbol*] [*National Library of Canada*] (BIB)
OFFP..........	Ovarian Follicular Fluid Peptide [*Endocrinology*]
OFF PREM...	Off Premises (SAUS)
Off Prod News...	Office Products News (SAUS)
OFFPROMSYS...	Officer Promotion System (DNAB)
Off Publ Assoc Am Plant Food Control Off...	Official Publication Association of American Plant Food Control Officials (SAUS)
Offr...........	Officer (AL)
OFFR..........	Officer
Off Rep.......	Official Reports of the High Court of the Transvaal [*A publication*] (DLA)
OFFS..........	Optical Fiber Field Sensor (ACAE)
Offset Print Reprogr...	Offset Printing and Reprographics (SAUS)
OffshEnr.......	Offshore Energy Development Corp. [*Associated Press*] (SAG)
OFFSHR.......	Offshore (NVT)
OffsLog.......	Offshore Logistics, Inc. [*Associated Press*] (SAG)
OFF STA......	Officer Status (DNAB)
off-st pkg.....	Off-Street Parking (AD)
Off Syst Res J...	Office Systems Research Journal (SAUS)
OFFV.........	Order of First Families of Virginia, 1607-1624/5 (EA)
Off World News...	Office World News (SAUS)
OFG..........	Opferfuersorgegesetz (BJA)
OFG..........	Optical Frequency Generator
OFG..........	Ordnance Field Guide (SAUS)
OFG..........	Organic Farmers and Growers Ltd. (BUAC)
OFG..........	Organic Functional Group (SAUS)
OFGA........	Oxyacetylene Cutting (SAUS)
OFGAS.......	Office of Gas Service [*Government body*] [*British*]
Ofgas.........	Office of Gas Supply [*British*] (WA)
OFGH........	Oxyhydrogen Cutting (SAUS)
OFGR........	Objective Force Gross Requirement [*Army*] (AABC)
OFGSA.......	Organic Farming and Gardening Society of Australia
OFGST.......	Organic Farming and Gardening Society of Tasmania [*Australia*]
OFH..........	Odd Fellows Hall (ROG)
OFH..........	Oil Field Haulers Association Inc., Austin TX [*STAC*]
OFH..........	Rutherford B. Hayes Library, Fremont, OH [*Library symbol*] [*Library of Congress*] (LCLS)
OFHA........	Occipitofrontal Headache [*Medicine*] (DMAA)
OFHA........	Oil Field Haulers Association (EA)
OFHA........	Oilfield Haulers Association
OFHC........	Oxygen Free Hard Copper (IAA)
ofhc.........	Oxygen-Free High-Carbon (AD)
ofhc.........	Oxygen-Free High Conductivity (AD)
OFHC........	Oxygen-Free, High-Conductivity [*Copper*]
OFHC........	Oxygen-Free High-Conductivity Copper [*Electronics*] (AAEL)
OFHC Copper...	Oxygen-Free High Conductivity Copper (SAUS)
OFHEO........	Office of Federal Housing Enterprise Oversight (SAUS)
OFHIC........	Oxygen-Free High Conductivity Copper (SAUS)
OFi............	Findlay-Hancock County District Public Library, Findlay, OH [*Library symbol*] [*Library of Congress*] (LCLS)
OFI...........	Office of Foreign Investment [*Department of Commerce*]
OFI...........	Office of the Federal Inspector (AD)
OFI...........	Omni Films International, Inc. (EFIS)
OFI...........	On-Line Free Form Input [*Computer science*] (MHDI)
OFI...........	Operational Flight Instrumentation [*NASA*] (NASA)
OFI...........	Opportunity for Improvement (ACAE)
OFI...........	Optical Fiber Identifier (SAUS)
OFI...........	Orangutan Foundation International (SAUS)
OFI...........	Orbital Flight Instrumentation (SAUS)
OFI...........	Ornamental Fish International (EAIO)
OFI...........	Overflow Incontinence [*Medicine*] (MELL)
OFI...........	Overflow Indicator (SAUS)
OFI...........	Oxford Forestry Institute [*University of Oxford*] [*British*] (IRUK)
OFIA.........	Ontario Forest Industries Association (SAUS)
OFIA.........	Optical Frame Importers' Association [*British*] (DBA)
OFiC.........	Findlay College, Findlay, OH [*Library symbol*] [*Library of Congress*] (LCLS)
ofic.........	Oficial [*Official*] [*Spanish*] (AD)
OFIC.........	Ohio Foundation of Independent Colleges (AD)
OFID.........	OPEC [*Organization of Petroleum Exporting Countries*] Fund for International Development (EAIO)
OFID.........	Optical Free Induction Decay (SAUS)
O-FID........	Oxygen-Flame Ionization Detector
OFIG.........	Operational Forces Interface Group [*US Army Natick Research, Development, and Engineering Center*] [*Natick, MA*] (RDA)
OFII..........	Omni Films International, Inc. (SAUS)
OFII..........	Organization for International Investment (NTPA)
OFII..........	Otto Fuel II [*Military*] (DNAB)
OFINDMAN...	Office of Industrial Management [*Navy*] (DNAB)
OFINTAC......	Offshore Installations Technical Advisory Committee [*British*] [*Marine science*] (MSC)
OFIR.........	Oceanic Flight Information Region (IAA)
OFIS.........	Office Information System (NITA)
OFIS.........	Office of Transportation Security (SAUS)
OFIS.........	Operational Flight Information Service [*ICAO*] (DA)
OFIS.........	US Office Products Co. [*NASDAQ symbol*] (SAG)
OFIX.........	Office of the Future Information Exchange (NITA)
OFIX.........	Orthofix International [*NASDAQ symbol*] (SAG)
OFIXF........	Orthofix International [*NASDAQ symbol*] (TTSB)
OFJ..........	Olafsfjordur [*Iceland*] [*Airport symbol*] (OAG)
OFK..........	Norfolk [*Nebraska*] [*Airport symbol*] (OAG)
OFK..........	Norfolk, NE [*Location identifier*] [*FAA*] (FAAL)
OFK..........	Oberfeldkommandantur [*Military government area headquarters*] [*German military - World War II*]
OFK..........	Official Flight Kit [*NASA*] (NASA)
OFK..........	Optical Flight Kit (NASA)
OFL..........	Flesherton Public Library, Ontario [*Library symbol*] [*National Library of Canada*] (NLC)
OFL..........	Official (AABC)
ofl..........	Official (AD)
OFL..........	Ontario Federation of Labour (SAUS)
OFL..........	Open Fault Locater
OFL..........	Optical Fault Locator (SAUS)
OFL..........	Optic Fiber Layer
OFL..........	Overflow [*Computer science*]
OFL..........	Own Front Line (SAUS)
OFL..........	Oxidizer Fill Line (AAG)
Oflag.........	Offizierlager [*Officer's Prison Camp*] [*German*] (AD)

OFLAG .... Offizierslager [*Permanent Prison Camp for Captured Officers*] [*German military - World War II*]
OFLC .... Office of Foreign Liquidation Commission
OFLD .... Off-Load (NVT)
OFlem .... Old Flemish [*Language, etc.*] (BARN)
OFLIC .... Office of Foreign Liquidation Commission
OFLINPS ...... Open Frame Linear Power Supply [*Electronics*] (EECA)
OFLOT .... Office of the National Lottery (BUAC)
OFLP .... Oxygen-Free Low-Phosphorus (SAUS)
OFLPC .... Oxygen-Free Low-Phosphorus Copper (SAUS)
OFLT .... Office of Foreign Labor and Trade [*Department of Labor*]
OFLTR .... Oil Filter
OFLUSE ...... For Official Use Only [*Army*]
OFLW .... Overflow (SAUS)
Ofly .... Offaly (AD)
ofm .... Conventual Franciscans, Friars Minor (TOCD)
OFM .... Franciscan Friars (TOCD)
ofm .... Franciscan Friars, Order of Friars Minor (TOCD)
OFM .... Observation File Maintenance
OFM .... Office of Finance and Management [*Department of Agriculture*] (GFGA)
OFM .... Office of Financial Management [*Bureau of the Budget; later, OMB*]
OFM .... Office of Flight Missions [*NASA*] (MCD)
OFM .... Office of Foreign Missions [*Department of State*]
OFM .... Open Face Mask [*Medicine*] (MELL)
OFM .... Open Frame Motor
OFM .... Optical Frequency Division Multiplexer (or Multiplexing) (SAUS)
OFM .... Optofiber Metric Switch
OFM .... Ordnance Field Manual [*Military*]
OFM .... Ordo Fratrum Minorum [*Order of Friars Minor*] [*Observant Franciscans*] [*Roman Catholic religious order*] (EA)
OFM .... Organization Field Maintenance
OFM .... Oriental Fruit Moth [*Entomology*]
OFM .... Original Equipment Manufacturer (SAUS)
OFM .... Orofacial Malformation
OFM .... Otto Fuel Monitor (SAUS)
OFM .... Our First Men [*Slang*]
OFM .... Out for Maintenance [*Aviation*] (FAAC)
OFM .... Outlet Feature Model (SAUS)
OFM .... Oxygen Fill to Missile (AAG)
OFMC .... Operational Fixed Microwave Council (IAA)
OFMC .... Order of Friars Minor Conventual [*Conventuals*] [*Roman Catholic religious order*]
OFMCap .... [*The*] Capuchin Friars (TOCD)
ofmcap .... [*The*] Capuchin Friars, Franciscan Fathers (TOCD)
OFM Cap .... Order of Friars Minor Capuchin [*Capuchins*] [*Roman Catholic religious order*]
OFMConv ..... Conventual Franciscans (TOCD)
OFM Conv.... Order of Friars Minor Conventual [*Conventuals*] [*Roman Catholic religious order*]
OFMConv .... Ordo Fratrum Minorum Conventualium (SAUS)
OFMIS .... Office of Financial and Management Information Systems (OICC)
OFMP .... Organization of Facility Managers and Planners [*Later, OMERF*] (EA)
OFMS .... Office of Financial and Management Services [*Department of Labor*]
OFMS .... Organic-Functionalized Molecular Sieve [*Organic chemistry*]
OFM Switch... Opto-Fibre Metric Switch (SAUS)
OFMT .... Output Format (SAUS)
OFN .... Open File Number (SAUS)
OFN .... Organization for Flora Neotropica (EA)
OFN .... Ottawa Fundraisers Network [*Ontario, Canada*]
OFN .... Overfull Employment [*Economics*]
OFNCS .... Orange Field Naturalist and Conservation Society [*Australia*]
OFNPS .... Outstate Facility Network Planning System [*Telecommunications*] (TEL)
OFNS .... Observer Foreign News Service (AD)
OFO .... Office of Field Operations [*Employment and Training Administration*] [*Department of Labor*]
OFO .... Office of Flight Operations [*NASA*]
OFO .... Orbiting Frog Otolith [*NASA experimental spacecraft*]
Ofo .... Orfeo [*Record label*]
OFOBA .... Oils, Fats, and Oilseeds Brokers Association [*Netherlands*] (BUAC)
OFOC .... Old Free Order of Chaldeans [*Freemasonry*] (ROG)
OFOD .... On-Flight Origin and Destination [*International Civil Aviation Organizati on*] [*Information service or system*] (DUND)
OFOFLEGAFFAIRS... Office of Legal Affairs [*Navy*] (DNAB)
OFOM .... Operational Figure of Merit [*Military*] (CAAL)
OFOS .... Opening Filled Other State [*Employment*]
OFP .... Ashland, VA [*Location identifier*] [*FAA*] (FAAL)
OFP .... Occluded Frontal Passage (SAUS)
OFP .... Offensive Firepower (SAUS)
OFP .... Office of Family Planning (SAUS)
OFP .... Office of Federal Policy (COE)
OFP .... Offshore Pipelines (SAUS)
OFP .... Oil Filter Pack
OFP .... On-the-Fly Printer
OFP .... Open Fireplace [*Classified advertising*] (ADA)
OFP .... Operating Force Plan
OFP .... Operational Flight Profile [*NASA*] (NASA)
OFP .... Operational Flight Profit
OFP .... Operational Flight Program [*NASA*] (NASA)
OFP .... Operational Format Program [*NASA*] (KSC)
OFP .... Operations Gerions Funded Project (SAUS)
OFP .... Operative Federal Plasterers [*A union*] [*British*]
OFP .... Orbiter Flight Program [*NASA*] (NASA)

OFP .... Order of Friars Preachers [*Dominicans*] (ADA)
OFP .... Ordnance Field Park [*British*]
OFP .... Organizations, Functions, and Programs [*IRS*]
OFP .... Original Flight Plan
OFP .... Oscilloscope Face Plane
OFP .... Ozone Forming Potential [*Exhaust emissions*] [*Automotive engineering*]
OFPA .... Federal Office of Armament Production (SAUS)
OFPA .... Ontario Food Protection Association (SAUS)
OFPA .... Order of the Founders and Patriots of America (EA)
OFPA .... Organic Foods Production Act
OFPANA ...... Organic Foods Production Association of North America (EA)
OFPCP .... Organization of Fitness and Personal Care Professionals [*Defunct*] (EA)
OFPF .... Optical Fiber-Pulling Facility (SSD)
OFPM .... Office of Fiscal Plans and Management [*Bureau of Indian Affairs*]
OFP-MIR ...... Ozone-Forming Potential-Maximum Incremental Reactivity [*Exhaust emissions*] [*Automotive engineering*]
OFPP .... Office of Federal Procurement Policy [*Executive Office of the President*] (MCD)
OFPP .... Office of Procurement & Policy (SAUS)
OFPPA .... Office of Federal Procurement Policy Act (COE)
OFPPL .... Office of Federal Procurement Policy Letters (SAUS)
OFPS .... Office of Field Project Support (SAUS)
OFPS .... Open Frame Power Supply [*Electronics*] (EECA)
OFPSD .... Office of Financial Policy and Systems Design (SAUS)
OFPU .... Optical Fiber Production Unit
OFr .... Franklin Public Library, Franklin, OH [*Library symbol*] [*Library of Congress*] (LCLS)
OFR .... Ocean Freight Reimbursement (SAUS)
OFR .... Ocular Following Reflex [*Ophthalmology*]
OFR .... Offer
ofr .... Off Frequency Rejection (AD)
OFR .... Off Frequency Rejection [*Radio communications*]
OFR .... Office for Recruitment [*American Library Association*]
OfR .... Office for Research
OFR .... Office for Research [*American Library Association*]
OFR .... Office of the Federal Register
Ofr .... Officer (PHSD)
OFR .... Officer Fitness Report [*Navy*] (NVT)
OFR .... Official Failure Rate [*Military*] (AFIT)
OFR .... Oil-Filled Resistor
OFR .... Oil-Resistant, Flame-Retardant (SAUS)
O Fr .... Old French (AD)
OFR .... Old French [*Language, etc.*]
OFR .... On-Frequency Repeater (IEEE)
OFR .... Open Failure Report [*NASA*] (KSC)
OFR .... Open File Report (MCD)
OFR .... Operational Failure Report (IAA)
OFR .... Operational Fleet Requirements (MCD)
OFR .... Optical Film Reader (SAUS)
OFR .... Ordering Function Register
OFR .... Over-Flow Register (SAUS)
OFR .... Over Frequency Relay
OFR .... Overfrequency Relay (SAUS)
OFR .... Overseas Fuel Region (AFIT)
OFR .... Oxidation-Fluorination Ratio (MCD)
OFR .... Oxygen Free Radical (SAUS)
OFR .... United Front of Workers (BUAC)
OFRA .... O'Dochartaigh Family Research Association (EA)
OFRAC .... On Farm Research Advisory Committee [*Australia*]
OFR-ALA ...... Office of Recruitment-American Library Association (AD)
O/F Ratio .... Oxidant/Fuel Ratio (SAUS)
OFRF .... Organic Farming Research Foundation
OFRF .... Overland Flow Research Facility [*Army*]
OFRID .... Outline of Factors Relating to Industry Development (SAUS)
OFris .... Old Frisian (AD)
OFRIS .... Old Frisian [*Language, etc.*]
O Frk .... Old Frankish (AD)
OFRP .... Overseas Family Residence Program [*Military*] (NVT)
OFRR .... Office of Foreign Relief and Rehabilitation [*Obsolete*]
OFRRO .... Office of Foreign Relief and Rehabilitation Operation [*Obsolete*]
OFrS .... Franklin City Schools, Franklin, OH [*Library symbol*] [*Library of Congress*] (LCLS)
OFRW .... Oklahoma Federation of Republican Women
OFS .... Fauquier-Strickland Public Library, Fauquier, Ontario [*Library symbol*] [*National Library of Canada*] (BIB)
OFS .... Object File System [*Computer science*] (VLIE)
OFS .... Octave Filter Set
OFS .... Office of Field Service [*OSRD*] [*World War II*]
OFS .... Office of Field Services [*Later, Bureau of Domestic Commerce*] [*Department of Commerce*]
OFS .... Office of Oceanographic Facilities and Support [*National Science Foundation*] (USDC)
OFS .... Office of the Foreign Secretary (SAUS)
OFS .... Offset (MSA)
OFS .... Oil from Sludge
OFS .... One Finger Salute (SAUS)
ofs .... One-Function Sketch (AD)
OFS .... One-Function Sketch
OFS .... Ontario Federation of Students [*Canada*] (AD)
OFS .... Operating Functional Summary (VLIE)
OFS .... Operational Fixed-microwave Service (SAUS)
OFS .... Operational Fixed Service (SAUS)
OFS .... Operational Flight Simulator (SAUS)

OFS............. Operational Flight Software (ACAE)
OFS............. Operational Flying School (SAUS)
OFS............. Operations Fixed Service [Microwave service] (NTCM)
OFS............. Optical Fiber Sensor
OFS............. Optical Fuzing System
OFS............. Orange Free State Reports, High Court [1879-83] [South Africa] [A publication] (DLA)
OFS............. Orbital [or Orbiter] Flight System [NASA] (MCD)
OFS............. Orbiter Flight System (SAUS)
OFS............. Orbiter Functional Simulator (NASA)
OFS............. Order of Free State (SAUS)
OFS............. Organofunctional Silanes (SAUS)
OFS............. Output Field Separator [Computer science] (VLIE)
OFS............. Output Format Specification (SAUS)
OFS............. Oxygen-Free with Silver (SAUS)
OFSA .... Optical Fire Sensor Assembly (SAUS)
OFSA .... Ordo Fratrum Sancti Augustini [Order of St. Augustine - OSA] [Rome, Italy] (EAIO)
OFSB .... Fort Severn Band Library, Ontario [Library symbol] [National Library of Canada] (BIB)
OFSB .... Ordnance Field Service Bulletin [Military]
OFSB .... Oriental Federal Savings Bank (EFIS)
OFSC .... Ordnance Field Service Circular [Military]
OFSC .... Organization and Finance Subcommittee
OFSCC .... Orbiter Functional Simulator Control Center (MCD)
OFSD .... Operating Flight Strength Diagram
OFSDG .... Finch Branch, Stormont, Dundas, and Glengarry County Public Library, Ontario [Library symbol] [National Library of Canada] (BIB)
OFSE .... Operating Forces Support Equipment (DNAB)
OFSH .... Ovine Follicle Stimulation Hormone (SAUS)
OFSH .... Shared Library Services, South Huron Hospital, Exeter, Ontario (SAUS)
OFSI............ OESI Power (SAUS)
OFSL .... Orange Free State Investment Ltd. (SAUS)
OFSM .... Operational Flight Safety Monitor (SAA)
OFSMPS ..... Open Frame Switch Mode Power Supply [Electronics] (EECA)
OFSO .... Oracle Field Sales Online [Computer science] (VLIE)
OFSO .... Overfill Shutoff Sensor (KSC)
OFSOC .... Organizational Effectiveness Staff Officer Course (SAUS)
OFS/OFA ...... Bureau of Oceans and International Environmental and Scientific Affairs/ Ocean and Fishery Affairs (SAUS)
OFSP .... Office of Federal Statistical Policy [Later, OFSPS] [Department of Commerce]
OFSPCMJ .... Officer Exercising Special Court-Martial Jurisdiction (SAUS)
OFSPS .... Office of Federal Statistical Policy and Standards [Formerly, OFSP] [Department of Commerce]
OFSSA .... Orange Free State, South Africa (ILCA)
OFST .... Lateral Offset Active Light (GAVI)
OFST .... Office of the Secretary of the Air Force (AD)
ofst .... Offset (VRA)
OFST .... Operational Flight Simulator Trainer (SAUS)
Ofsted .... Office for Standards in Education [British] (WA)
OFSTED ...... Office for Standards in Education [British] (WDAA)
OFSTNO...... Offset Switch Number (SAUS)
OFT............. Field Township Public Library, Ontario [Library symbol] [National Library of Canada] (NLC)
OFT............. Observed Fire Trainer [Army] (RDA)
OFT............. Office of Fair Trade (SAUS)
OFT............. Office of Fair Trading [British]
oft.............. Often (GEAB)
OFT............. Often
OFT............. Ohio Federation of Teachers (AD)
OFT............. Operational Feasibility Testing (MCD)
OFT............. Operational Flight Trainer
OFT............. Optical Fiber Thermometry [Instrumentation]
OFT............. Optical Fiber Tube
OFT............. Optical Fibre Technology
OFT............. Optical Fourier Transform
OFT............. Optimal Foraging Theory [Animal behavior]
OFT............. Orbital Flight Test [NASA] (NASA)
OFT............. Orbiter Flight Test (SAUS)
OFT............. Outer Fix Time [FAA] (TAG)
OFT............. Outfit (MSA)
OFT............. Outline Feasibility Test [Army]
OFTA .... Office for the Aged [Australia]
OFTA .... Office of the Telecommunications Authority (SAUS)
OFTA .... Operational Flight Transfer Airframe
OFTB .... Offshore Technology Board [British]
OFTC .... Overseas Finance and Trade Corporation (SAUS)
OFTD .... Oxygen Furnace Tilt Drive
OFTDA .... Office of Flight Tracking and Data Acquisition [NASA]
OFTDA .... Office of Right Tracking and Data Acquisition (SAUS)
OFTDS .... Orbital Flight Test Data System [NASA] (MCD)
OFTEC......... Oil Firing Technical Association for the Petroleum Industry (BUAC)
OFTEL......... Office of Director General of Telecommunications (SAUS)
Oftel .... Office of Telecommunications [British] (WDAA)
OFTEL......... Office of Telecommunications [Independent government agency] [British]
OFTF .... Optical Fibre Transfer Function (EECA)
OFTM.......... On-Orbit Flight Technique Meeting [NASA] (MCD)
OFTMS........ Output Format Table Modification Submodule
OFTP.......... Odette File Transfer Protocol (SAUS)
OFTR .... Orbital Flight Test Requirement [NASA] (NASA)
OFTS.......... Office of Technical Services (AD)

OFTS........... Office of Transportation Security (AD)
OFTS........... Officers Training School (AD)
OFTS........... Operational Flight and Tactics Simulator (MCD)
OFTS........... Optical Fibre Transmission System (NITA)
OFTS........... Overseas Fixed Telecommunications System (AD)
OFTT.......... Federal Office of Transport Troops (SAUS)
OFTT.......... Operational Flight and Tactics Trainer (MCD)
OFTT.......... Organic Failure to Thrive [Medicine] (MEDA)
OF Type....... Old Face Type (SAUS)
OFU .... Floating Units Division [Coast Guard]
OFU .... Franklin University, Columbus, OH [OCLC symbol] (OCLC)
OFU .... Ofu Island [American Samoa] [Airport symbol] (OAG)
OFU .... Ofunato [Japan] [Seismograph station code, US Geological Survey] (SEIS)
OFUS .... Orbit Frequency Utilization Simulation (SAUS)
OFUS-M....... Orbit Frequency Utilization Simulation-Mobile (SAUS)
OFV............. Opposing Forces Vehicle [Military]
OFV............. Orchid Fleck Virus [Plant pathology]
OFV............. Overflow Valve (SAUS)
OFW............ Objective Family of Weapons
OFW............ Off Watch [Aviation] (FAAC)
OFW............ Operation Fish Watch [National Oceanic and Atmospheric Administration] (MSC)
OFW............ Opportunities for Women (BUAC)
OFW............ Oxyfuel-Gas Welding
Ofwat.......... Office of Water Services [British] (WDAA)
OFWAT .... Office of Water Services [British]
OFWN .... Ontario Library Service - Nipigon, Thunder Bay, Ontario [Library symbol] [National Library of Canada] (NLC)
OF/WST ...... Operational Flight/Weapons System Trainer (NG)
OFX............. Open Financial Exchange [Computer science]
OFX............. Outer Fix (CTAS)
OFXLP .... Oxygen-Free Extra-Low-Phosphorus (SAUS)
OFXLPC ...... Oxygen-Free Extra-Low-Phosphorus Copper (SAUS)
OFXT .... Outer Fix Time [Aviation] (FAAC)
OFY............. Operation Feed Yourself [Ghana] (BUAC)
OFY............. Opportunities for Youth [Canada] (AD)
OFY............. Opportunities for Youth Program [Canada]
OFZ............. Fort Sill, OK [Location identifier] [FAA] (FAAL)
OFZ............. Obstacle Free Zone
OG .... Air Guadeloupe [ICAO designator] (AD)
OG .... Guelph Public Library, Ontario [Library symbol] [National Library of Canada] (NLC)
OG .... Obergericht [Court of Appeal] [German] (DLA)
OG .... Oberstes Gericht [Supreme Court] [German]
OG .... Object Glass (MSA)
OG .... Obscure Glass
OG .... Observation Group (SAUS)
OG .... Obstetrics-Gynecology [Medicine]
OG .... Occlusogingival [Dentistry]
OG .... Ocean Going (SAUS)
OG .... Octyl Glucoside [Organic chemistry]
OG .... Oesterreichische Galerie [Austrian Gallery] (AD)
OG .... Offensive Guard [Football]
OG .... Off-Gas [Nuclear energy] (NRCH)
OG .... Office of Geography [Functions transferred to Geographic Names Division of Army Topographic Command] [Department of the Interior]
OG .... Officer of the Guard [Army]
OG .... Official Gazette [PTO] [A publication] (AAGC)
OG .... Ogasawara Trench
OG .... Ogden Corp. [NYSE symbol] (SPSG)
OG .... Ogdensburg [Diocesan abbreviation] [New York] (TOCD)
OG .... Ogee [A molding] [Architecture] (ROG)
og .... Oh Gee (AD)
OG .... Oil Gauge
og .... Oil Gland (AD)
OG .... Oil Glands [In propeller shaft]
OG .... Old Gaelic (AD)
OG .... Old German [Language, etc.]
og .... Old Girl (AD)
OG .... Old Girl [A wife] [Slang]
OG .... Old Greasybeard: Tales from the Cumberland Gap [A publication]
OG .... Old Greek (SAUS)
OG .... Oligodendrocyte (DMAA)
OG .... Olive Green [Army] (ADDR)
OG .... Olympic Games
OG .... Ongoing (ADA)
OG .... On Grade (DAC)
og .... On Ground (AD)
OG .... On Ground [Aviation]
og .... On Guard (AD)
OG .... Openly Gay [An association] (BUAC)
OG .... Operational Group [World War II]
OG .... Operation Greenhouse [Atomic weapons testing]
OG .... Operations Guide (VLIE)
OG .... Optical Generation
OG .... Optical Glass (SAUS)
OG .... Optic Ganglion
o/g .... Opto-Graphic (AD)
O/G .... Opto/Graphic (AD)
OG .... Orange Green [Stain] [Medicine]
o-g .... Orange-Green (AD)
OG .... Ordinary Goods (SAUS)
OG .... Organic Gardening [A publication]

OG .... Organic Geochemistry (SAUS)
OG .... Organisation Gestosis [*Basel, Switzerland*] (EAIO)
OG .... OR Gate [*Electronics*] (ECII)
OG .... Orientation Group [*Air Force*]
OG .... Original Gravity (BARN)
og .... Original Gum (AD)
OG .... Original Gum [*Philately*]
OG .... Orogastric [*Feeding*] [*Gastroenterology*] (DAVI)
OG .... Outdoor Girl [*Max Factor cosmetic line*]
OG .... Outer Gimbal
o/g .... Outgoing (AD)
OG .... Outgoing (VLIE)
O/G .... Outgoing [*Computer science*]
OG .... Outguard (SAUS)
OG .... Output Gate [*Computer science*] (IAA)
OG .... Outside Guard
OG .... Outside Guardian [*Freemasonry*] (ROG)
OG .... Oxygen Gage (NAKS)
OG .... Oxygen Gas Process (SAUS)
OG .... Oxygen Gauge (NASA)
OG .... Zero Gravity
OGA .... Obergurgl [*Austria*] [*Seismograph station code, US Geological Survey*] (SEIS)
OGA .... Oesterreichische Gesellschaft fur Akupunktur [*Austrian Society of Acupuncture and Auricular Therapy*] (EAIO)
OGA .... Office of Government Affairs (SAUS)
OGA .... Ogallala, NE [*Location identifier*] [*FAA*] (FAAL)
O/GA .... Oil Gauge [*Automotive engineering*]
OGA .... Omega Ltd. [*Ukraine*] [*FAA designator*] (FAAC)
OGA .... Option Generation Aid (SAUS)
OGA .... Organic Growers Association [*British*] (DBA)
OGA .... Ornamental Growers Association (EA)
OGA .... Orogastric Aspirate [*Medicine*] (AAMN)
OGA .... Other Government Agencies (COE)
OGA .... Outer Gimbal Angle (NASA)
OGA .... Outer Gimbal Assembly (NASA)
OGA .... Outer Gimbal Axis [*NASA*] (IAA)
OGAC .... Galt Collegiate Institute, Cambridge, Ontario [*Library symbol*] [*National Library of Canada*] (NLC)
OGAC .... Organizational Governance Advisory Committee [*NERComP*]
OGAE .... Oklahoma Gas and Electric, Co. (SAUS)
O Gael .... Old Gaelic (AD)
OGalG .... Gallia County District Library, Gallipolis (SAUS)
OGAL .... Cambridge Public Library, Ontario [*Library symbol*] [*National Library of Canada*] (NLC)
OGalG .... Gallia County District Library, Gallipolis, OH [*Library symbol*] [*Library of Congress*] (LCLS)
OGALL .... Cavendish Public Library (G. Galloway), Ontario [*Library symbol*] [*National Library of Canada*] (BIB)
OGAMA .... Ogden Air Material Area [*AFLC*]
OGAMM ...... Optical Glass and Macromolecular Materials [*Imaging*]
OGAN .... Gananoque Public Library, Ontario [*Library symbol*] [*National Library of Canada*] (NLC)
OGANSW .... Organic Growers' Association of New South Wales [*Australia*]
OGAR .... OGara Co. (The) [*NASDAQ symbol*] (SAG)
OGaraCo ..... OGara Co. (The) [*Associated Press*]
OGAWA .... Organic Growers' Association of Western Australia [*Australia*]
OGB .... Beriault Branch, Gloucester Public Library, Ontario [*Library symbol*] [*National Library of Canada*] (NLC)
OGB .... Oesterreichischer Gewerkschaftsbund [*Austrian Trade Union Federation*] [*German*] (AD)
OGB .... Old Government Buildings (SAUS)
OGB .... Orangeburg, SC [*Location identifier*] [*FAA*] (FAAL)
OGB .... Overseas Golden Bar (SAUS)
OGBD .... Orbiter Gamma Burst Detecter [*NASA*]
OGBG .... Official Gazette Reports, British Guiana [*A publication*] (DLA)
OGBH .... Blackburn Hamlet Branch, Gloucester Public Library, Ontario [*Library symbol*] [*National Library of Canada*] (NLC)
OGBKT .... Blessed Kateri Tekakwitha School, Gloucester, Ontario [*Library symbol*] [*National Library of Canada*] (NLC)
OGBU .... Gore Bay Union Public Library, Ontario [*Library symbol*] [*National Library of Canada*] (NLC)
OGC .... Centennial Collegiate Vocational Institute, Guelph, Ontario [*Library symbol*] [*National Library of Canada*] (NLC)
OGC .... Grove City Public Library (SAUS)
OGc .... Grove City Public Library, Grove City, OH [*Library symbol*] [*Library of Congress*] (LCLS)
OGC .... Oculogyric Crisis [*Medicine*] (DMAA)
OGC .... Office of General Counsel
OGC .... Office of the General Counsel (SAUS)
OGC .... On-Going Care [*Medicine*] (MELL)
OGC .... Open GIS Consortium (SAUS)
OGC .... Order of the Golden Chain (EA)
OGC .... Oregon Graduate Center for Study and Research [*Research center*] (RCD)
OGC .... Ore Grain Carrier (SAUS)
OGC .... Other Government Costs (ACAE)
OGC .... Outgoing Trunk Circuit (SAUS)
OGCA .... Ohio Gun Collectors Association
OGCA .... Ontario General Contractors Association (SAUS)
OGCF .... Canadian Farm Management Data System, Agriculture Canada [*Systeme Canadien deDonnees sur la Gestion Agricole, Agriculture Canada*] Guelph, Ontario [*Library symbol*] [*National Library of Canada*] (NLC)

OGCH .... College Heights Secondary School, Guelph, Ontario [*Library symbol*] [*National Library of Canada*] (NLC)
OGCM .... Ocean General Circulation Model [*Atmospheric science*]
OGCM .... Oceanic General Circulation Model (SAUS)
OGCMD .... Ogden Contract Management District (SAA)
OGC-N .... Office of General Counsel - NASA
OGCV .... Guelph Collegiate Vocational Institute, Ontario [*Library symbol*] [*National Library of Canada*] (NLC)
OGCW .... Cairine Wilson Secondary School, Gloucester, Ontario [*Library symbol*] [*National Library of Canada*] (BIB)
OGCWS........ Office of Government Contract Wage Standards (AAGC)
OGD .... Oesophogogastroduodenoscopy [*Medicine*] (WDAA)
OGD .... Ogden [*Utah*] [*Airport symbol*] (AD)
Ogd .... Ogdensburg (AD)
OGD .... Ogdensburg [*New Jersey*] [*Seismograph station code, US Geological Survey*] (SEIS)
Ogd .... Ogden's Reports [*12-15 Louisiana*] [*A publication*] (DLA)
OGD .... Ogden, UT [*Location identifier*] [*FAA*] (FAAL)
OGD .... Old Granulomatus Disease (DAVI)
OGD .... Omega Gamma Delta [*Fraternity*] (EA)
OGD .... Open Government Document (PDAA)
OGD .... Other Government Departments (HEAS)
OGDA .... Oyster Growers and Dealers Association (EA)
OGDC .... Office of Geographic Data Coordination (SAUS)
OGDC .... Oil and Gas Development Corp. (AD)
OGDD .... Outgoing/Delay Dial [*Telecommunications*] (TEL)
Ogden .... Ogden Corp. [*Associated Press*] (SAG)
Ogden .... Ogden's Reports [*12-15 Louisiana*] [*A publication*] (DLA)
OGDH .... Oxoglutarate Dehydrogenase [*An enzyme*]
Ogdn .... Ogden Corp. [*Associated Press*] (SAG)
OGDR .... Uniroyal Research Laboratories, Guelph, Ontario [*Library symbol*] [*National Library of Canada*] (NLC)
OGE .... Entomological Society of Ontario, Guelph, Ontario [*Library symbol*] [*National Library of Canada*] (NLC)
OGE .... Objective Grating Electronics (SPST)
OGE .... Observer Group Egypt [*UN Truce Supervisor Organization*]
OGE .... Office of Government Ethics
OGE .... OGE Energy Corp. [*NYSE symbol*] (SAG)
OGE .... Oklahoma Gas & Electric Co. [*NYSE symbol*] (SPSG)
OGE .... Omaha Grain Exchange [*Defunct*] (EA)
OGE .... On-Gimbal Electronics (ACAE)
OGE .... Operating [*or Operational*] Ground Equipment
oge .... Operational Ground Equipment (AD)
OGE .... Optional Ground Equipment (AAGC)
OGE .... Optogalvanic Effect (MCD)
OGE .... Oregon Graduate Center, Beaverton, OR [*OCLC symbol*] (OCLC)
OGE .... Osaka Grain Exchange [*Japan*] (NUMA)
OGE .... Out-of-Ground Effect
OGEC .... Organization of Gas Exporting Countries [*Proposed gas cartel*]
OGEDJ .... E. D. Jones Branch, Gloucester Public Library, Ontario [*Library symbol*] [*National Library of Canada*] (NLC)
OGE Engy.... OGE Energy Corp. [*Associated Press*] (SAG)
OGEG .... Georgetown District High School, Ontario [*Library symbol*] [*National Library of Canada*] (NLC)
OGEH .... Georgetown Branch, Halton Hills Public Libraries, Ontario [*Library symbol*] [*National Library of Canada*] (BIB)
OGELR .... Ecole Secondaire Louis-Riel, Gloucester, Ontario [*Library symbol*] [*National Library of Canada*] (BIB)
OGELS .... Observer Group in El Salvador
OGEO .... Georgetown Public Library, Ontario [*Library symbol*] [*National Library of Canada*] (NLC)
OGeo .... Mary P. Shelton Library, Georgetown, OH [*Library symbol*] [*Library of Congress*] (LCLS)
OGEPrA....... Okla Gas & Elec,4% Pfd [*NYSE symbol*] (TTSB)
OGER .... Geraldton Public Library, Ontario [*Library symbol*] [*National Library of Canada*] (NLC)
OGer .... Germantown Public Library, Germantown, OH [*Library symbol*] [*Library of Congress*] (LCLS)
OGE/RPIE .... Operating Ground Equipment/Real Property Installed Equipment (AFM)
OGES .... Operating Ground Equipment Specification [*Italian*] (AD)
OGEV .... Varian Canada, Inc., Georgetown, Ontario [*Library symbol*] [*National Library of Canada*] (NLC)
ogf .... Option Growth Fund (AD)
OGF .... Orogastric Feeding [*Gastroenterology*] (DAVI)
OGF .... Ovarian Growth Factor [*Medicine*]
OGF .... Oxygen Gain Factor [*Medicine*] (DMAA)
OGFC .... Official Gumby Fan Club (EA)
OGFP .... Obtaining Goods by False Pretense
OGFS .... Oil and Gas Field Study [*Department of the Interior*]
OGG .... GasTOPS Ltd., Gloucester, Ontario [*Library symbol*] [*National Library of Canada*] (NLC)
OGG .... Kahului, HI [*Location identifier*] [*FAA*] (FAAL)
ogg .... Oggetto [*Object*] [*Italian*] (AD)
OGG .... Orchard Grubbing Grant (SAUS)
OGG .... Organic Geochemistry Group
OGH .... Opera-Glass Hand (MELL)
OGH .... Ovine Growth Hormone (DB)
OGHC .... Hart Chemicals Ltd., Guelph, Ontario [*Library symbol*] [*National Library of Canada*] (NLC)
OGHS .... Gloucester High School, Ontario [*Library symbol*] [*National Library of Canada*] (BIB)
OGHS .... Orbit Gas Co. (SAUS)
OGI .... Gould Information Center, Cleveland, OH [*OCLC symbol*] (OCLC)

OGI .... Oceanic Gamefish Investigations [*National Oceanic and Atmospheric Administration*] (MSC)
OGI .... Oculogyral Illusion [*NASA*]
OGI .... Oesterreichische Gesseleschaft fuer Informatik [*Austrian Society for Information Processing*] [*German*] (AD)
OGI .... Off-Gas Isolation [*Nuclear energy*] (NRCH)
OGI .... Ontario Government Information [*Database*] [*Ministry of Culture and Communications*] [*Information service or system*] (CRD)
OGI .... Opera Guilds International (AD)
OGI .... Oregon Graduate Institute (SAUS)
OGI .... Orientis Graeci Inscriptiones Selectae [*A publication*] (OCD)
OGI .... Outer Grid Injection
OGI .... Oxygen-Glucose Index [*Medicine*] (DMAA)
OGIB .... Occult Gastrointestinal Bleeding [*Medicine*]
OGICSE .... Oregon Graduate Institute Computer Science and Engineering (SAUS)
OGID .... Outgoing/Immediate Dial [*Telecommunications*] (TEL)
OGIFC .... Original Gilligan's Island Fan Club (EA)
OGIL .... Open General Import Licence [*British*] (DS)
Ogilvie Dict... Ogilvie's Imperial Dictionary of the English Language [*A publication*] (DLA)
OGIP .... Office of Guest Investigator Programs (SAUS)
OGIP .... Original Gas in Place [*Natural resources*]
OGIRS .... Oklahoma Geographic Information Retrieval System (SAUS)
OGIS .... Open Geodata Interoperability Specification (SAUS)
OGIS .... Open Geographic Information System
OGJ .... Oil and Gas Journal [*A publication*] (AD)
OGJ .... Outgoing Junction [*Telecommunications*] (TEL)
OGJFR .... John F. Ross Collegiate Vocational Institute, Guelph, Ontario [*Library symbol*] [*National Library of Canada*] (NLC)
OGK .... Kenyon College, Gambier, OH [*Library symbol*] [*Library of Congress*] (LCLS)
OGL .... Obscure Glass (AAG)
ogl .... Obscure Glass (AD)
OGL .... Open General License [*Import license*] (DS)
OGL .... Oral Glucose Loading [*Endocrinology*]
OGL .... Outgoing Line
OGLA .... Officer Grade Limitations Act of 1954
OGLA .... Officers Grade Limitation Action (SAUS)
Oglbay .... Oglebay Norton Co. [*Associated Press*] (SAG)
OGLE .... Oglebay Norton [*NASDAQ symbol*] (TTSB)
OGLE .... Oglebay Norton Co. [*NASDAQ symbol*] (NQ)
OGLE .... Optical Gravitational Lens Experiment [*Astronomy*]
OGLE .... Optical Gravitational Lensing Experiment
OGLE .... Organization for Getting Legs Exposed [*Group opposing below-the-knee fashions introduced in 1970*]
Oglethorpe U... Oglethorpe University (GAGS)
OGLPFC .... Official Gary Lewis and the Playboys Fan Club (EA)
OGM .... Office of Grants Management [*Public Health Service*]
OGM .... Office of Guided Missile (IAA)
OGM .... Ontonagon, MI [*Location identifier*] [*FAA*] (FAAL)
OGM .... Optimum Gradient Method
OGM .... Ordinary General Meeting
OGM .... Organic Gaseous Mercury [*Environmental chemistry*]
OGM .... Outgoing Message [*Telecommunications*]
OGM .... Outgrowth Medium [*Microbiology*] (DAVI)
OGM .... Outside Gage Marks (SAA)
OGMB .... Mattagami Band Public Library, Gogama, Ontario [*Library symbol*] [*National Library of Canada*] (NLC)
OGMC .... Ordnance Guided Missile Center (MCD)
OGMH .... Morrison Hershfield Ltd., Guelph, Ontario [*Library symbol*] [*National Library of Canada*] (NLC)
OGMS .... Ordnance Guided Missile School
OGMSD .... Glen Morris Branch, South Dumfries Township Public Library, Ontario [*Library symbol*] [*National Library of Canada*] (BIB)
OGMT .... Orbiter Greenwich Mean Time [*NASA*] (MCD)
OGN .... Obstetric, Gynecologic, and Neonatal
OGN .... Yonagunijima [*Japan*] [*Airport symbol*] (OAG)
OGNB .... Orange National Bancorp [*NASDAQ symbol*] (SAG)
OGNB .... Orange Natl Bancorp [*NASDAQ symbol*] (TTSB)
OGNC .... Garson Branch, Nickel Centre Public Library, Ontario [*Library symbol*] [*National Library of Canada*] (NLC)
OGNC .... Organic, Inc. [*NASDAQ symbol*] (SG)
OGNP .... Obstetrical Gynecological Nurse Practitioner (NUJO)
OGNR .... Oribi Gorge Nature Reserve [*South Africa*] (AD)
OGO .... Abengourou [*Ivory Coast*] [*Airport symbol*] (OAG)
OGO .... City Hall Branch, Gloucester Public Library, Ontario [*Library symbol*] [*National Library of Canada*] (NLC)
OGO .... Gould, Inc., Ocean Systems Information Center, Cleveland, OH [*OCLC symbol*] (OCLC)
OGO .... Officer Grade Objectives
OGO .... Oliver Gold Corp. [*Vancouver Stock Exchange symbol*]
OGO .... Orbiting Geophysical Observatory [*NASA*]
OG/OB .... Office Group/Office Branch [*IRS*]
OGOD .... One Gene One Disorder [*Hypothesis*]
OGOG .... Gogama Community Library, Ontario [*Library symbol*] [*National Library of Canada*] (NLC)
OGOH .... Huron County Public Library, Goderich, Ontario [*Library symbol*] [*National Library of Canada*] (NLC)
OGOHC .... Huron County Pioneer Museum, Goderich, Ontario [*Library symbol*] [*National Library of Canada*] (BIB)
OGOR .... Goulais River Community Library, Ontario [*Library symbol*] [*National Library of Canada*] (NLC)
OGOS .... Outward Grade of Service (DNAB)

OGP .... Office of Global Programs [*National Oceanic and Atmospheric Administration*] (USDC)
OGP .... Oncogenic Potential (MELL)
OGP .... Original Gross Premium [*Insurance*] (AIA)
OGP .... Outgoing Message Process [*Telecommunications*] (TEL)
OGPA .... Office of Governmental and Public Affairs [*Department of Agriculture*] (GFGA)
OGPA .... Office of the General Purchasing Agent [*Military*]
OGPI .... Optical Glide Path Indicator
OGPr .... Ogden Corp. $1.875 cm Cv Pfd [*NYSE symbol*] (TTSB)
OGPS .... Office of Grants and Program Systems [*Department of Agriculture*]
OGPU .... Obiedinennoye Gosudartsvennoye Politicheskoye Upravlenie [*United State Political Administration*] [*Russian*] (AD)
OGPU .... Otdelenie Gosudarstvenni Politcheskoi Upravi [*Special Government Political Administration*] [*Former Soviet secret service organization, also known as GPU*] [*Later, KGB*]
OGR .... B. F. Goodrich Co., Information Center, Brecksville, OH [*OCLC symbol*] (OCLC)
OGr .... Greenville Public Library, Greenville, OH [*Library symbol*] [*Library of Congress*] (LCLS)
OGR .... Grimsby Public Library and Art Gallery, Ontario [*Library symbol*] [*National Library of Canada*] (NLC)
OGR .... Oak Ridge Graphite Reactor (SAUS)
OGR .... Office of Geologic Repositories (SAUS)
OGR .... Office of Government Relations [*Environmental Protection Agency*] (GFGA)
OGR .... Office of Government Reports [*New Deal*]
OGR .... Officer Grade Requirements (ACAE)
OGR .... Official Guide of the Railways [*A publication*] (AD)
OGR .... Old Garden Rose [*Pre-1870*] [*Horticulture*]
OGR .... Ontario Government Railway [*Canada*] (AD)
OGR .... Operation Grass Roots [*Small communities employment service*]
OGR .... Order of the Golden Rule (EA)
OGR .... Ordnance, Gunnery, and Readiness Division [*Coast Guard*]
OGR .... Original Gross Rate [*Insurance*] (AIA)
OGR .... ORNL [*Oak Ridge National Laboratory*] Graphite Reactor
OGR .... Outgoing Repeater
OGR .... Oxygen-Gas Recovery System (SAUS)
OGRA .... Gravenhurst Public Library, Ontario [*Library symbol*] [*National Library of Canada*] (NLC)
OGraD .... Denison University, Granville, OH [*Library symbol*] [*Library of Congress*] (LCLS)
OGRAN .... Open Gate-Router Access Node (SAUS)
OGraO .... Owens-Corning Fiberglas Corp., Granville, OH [*Library symbol*] [*Library of Congress*] (LCLS)
OGRC .... Office of Grants and Research Contracts [*NASA*]
OGRE .... Greely Public Library, Ontario [*Library symbol*] [*National Library of Canada*] (NLC)
OGRE .... Optical Grating Reflectance Evaluator (PDAA)
OGRE .... Organization of Generally Rotten Enterprises [*Evil organization in television cartoon series "The Drak Pack"*]
OGRL .... Outgoing Rural Line [*Telecommunications*] (IAA)
OGRM .... Grimsby Museum, Ontario [*Library symbol*] [*National Library of Canada*] (BIB)
OGRS .... Outgoing Relay Set [*Telecommunications*] (IAA)
OGRS .... Outgoing Rural Selector [*Telecommunications*] (IAA)
OGRV .... Grand Valley Public Library, Ontario [*Library symbol*] [*National Library of Canada*] (NLC)
OGS .... Oakland Growth Study [*1932-1964*] [*Sociology*]
OGS .... Obsolete General Supplies [*Military*]
OGS .... Off-Gas System [*Nuclear energy*] (NRCH)
OGS .... Ogdensburg [*New York*] [*Airport symbol*] (OAG)
OGS .... Ogdensburg, NY [*Location identifier*] [*FAA*] (FAAL)
OGS .... Ohio Genealogical Society (EA)
OGS .... Ontario Geological Survey [*Ontario Ministry of Northern Development and Mines*] [*Canada*] (IRC)
OGS .... Ontario Graduate Scholarship (SAUS)
OGS .... Operative Glovers' Society [*A union*] [*British*]
O-GS .... Operator-to-General Support [*Maintenance*] (MCD)
OGS .... Optical Grating Spectrometer (SAUS)
OGS .... Optical Guidance System
OGS .... Oratory of the Good Shepherd [*British*]
OGS .... Original Ground Surface
OGS .... Osteogenic Sarcoma (MELL)
OGS .... Osteogenic Scoliosis (MELL)
OGS .... Other Government Securities (SAUS)
OGS .... Outer Glidescope
OGS .... Outer Glide Slope [*Aviation*] (NASA)
OGS .... Outgoing Secondary Switch (IAA)
OGS .... Outgoing Secondary Switches (SAA)
OGS .... Overseas Geological Survey (SAUS)
OGS .... Overseas Ground Station (MCD)
OGS .... Oxford GlycoSciences
OGS .... Oxogenic Steroid (MAE)
OGS .... Oxygen Generation System (NASA)
OGSE .... Operational Ground Support Equipment (AAG)
ogse .... Operational Ground-Support Equipment (AD)
OGSEL .... Operational Ground Support Equipment List (AAG)
OGSESS ...... Operational Ground Support Equipment Systems Specification (SAA)
OGSGS .... Orangeburgh German Swiss Genealogical Society (EA)
OGSI .... Ongard Sys [*NASDAQ symbol*] (TTSB)
OGSI .... On Gard Systems [*NASDAQ symbol*] (SAG)
OGSM .... Office of the General Sales Manager [*Department of Agriculture*]
OGSM .... Stone Shop Museum, Grimsby, Ontario [*Library symbol*] [*National Library of Canada*] (NLC)

Ogs Med Jur...   Ogston's Medical Jurisprudence [*1878*] [*A publication*] (DLA)
OGSO ....   O-Anon General Service Office [*An association*] (EA)
OGSR ....   Office of Graduate Studies and Research (AD)
OGST ....   Overthread Guide Sleeve Tool [*Nuclear energy*] (NRCH)
o-g stain ......   Orange-Green Stain (AD)
OGSTM ....   St. Matthew High School, Gloucester, Ontario [*Library symbol*] [*National Library of Canada*] (BIB)
OGT ....   MIS Division, Turnelle Productions Ltd., Gloucester, Ontario [*Library symbol*] [*National Library of Canada*] (BIB)
OGT ....   Office for Gifted and Talented [*Education*]
ogt ....   On-Going Thing (AD)
OGT ....   Oppenheimer Multi-Government Trust [*NYSE symbol*] (SPSG)
OGT ....   Outgoing Toll (SAUS)
OGT ....   Outgoing Trunk
ogt ....   Outlet Gas Temperature (AD)
OGT ....   Outlet Gas Temperature (MSA)
OGTC ....   Outgoing Toll Center [*Telecommunications*] (IAA)
OGTC ....   Outgoing Toll Circuit [*Telecommunications*] (IAA)
OGTC ....   Tudor and Cashel Public Library, Gilmour, Ontario [*Library symbol*] [*National Library of Canada*] (BIB)
OGTM ....   Official Gazette. United States Patent and Trademark Office [*A publication*] (DLA)
OGTT ....   Oral Glucose Tolerance Test [*Medicine*]
OGU ....   Occupational Guidance Unit [*Department of Employment*] [*British*]
OGU ....   Ogden Bay [*Utah*] [*Seismograph station code, US Geological Survey*] (SEIS)
OGU ....   Orogenital Ulceration [*Medicine*] (DB)
OGU ....   Outgoing Unit [*Telecommunications*] (IAA)
OGU ....   Outgoing Unit [*Military*]
OGU ....   University of Guelph, Ontario [*Library symbol*] [*National Library of Canada*] (NLC)
ogv ....   Outlet Guide Vane (AD)
OGV ....   Outlet Guide Vane
OGV ....   Oxygen Gauge Valve (NASA)
OGW ....   Overhead Ground Wire
OGW ....   Overload Gross Weight (NG)
OGWE ....   Education Library, Wellington County Board of Education, Guelph, Ontario [*Library symbol*] [*National Library of Canada*] (NLC)
OGWMN ......   Operational Groundwater Monitoring Network (SAUS)
OGWP ....   Office of Ground Water Protection [*Environmental Protection Agency*] (GFGA)
OGWS ....   Outgoing/Wink Start [*Telecommunications*] (TEL)
OGX ....   Ouargla [*Algeria*] [*Airport symbol*] (OAG)
OGY ....   O'Gyalla [*Later, HRB*] [*Czechoslovakia*] [*Geomagnetic observatory code*]
OGY ....   OGY Petroleum [*Vancouver Stock Exchange symbol*]
OH ....   Comair [*ICAO designator*] (AD)
OH ....   Finland [*International civil aircraft marking*] (ODBW)
OH ....   Hamilton Public Library, Ontario [*Library symbol*] [*National Library of Canada*] (NLC)
oh ....   Hospitaller Brothers of St. John of God (TOCD)
OH ....   Hospitaller Order of St. John of God [*Roman Catholic men's religious order*]
OH ....   Hydroxy [*As substituent on nucleoside*] [*Also, HO*] [*Biochemistry*]
OH ....   Hydroxycorticosteroid [*Endocrinology*] (DAVI)
OH ....   Hydroxyl (SAUS)
OH ....   Hydroxyl ion of water (SAUS)
OH ....   Hydroxyl Radical (AD)
OH ....   Oakwood Homes Corp. [*NYSE symbol*] (SPSG)
OH ....   Observation Helicopter
OH ....   Obstructive Hypopnea (DMAA)
OH ....   Occipital Horn [*Brain anatomy*]
OH ....   Occupational Health
OH ....   Occupational History [*Medicine*]
O-H ....   Octal-to-Hexadecimal [*Computer science*] (IEEE)
OH ....   Ocular Herpes [*Medicine*] (AD)
OH ....   Ocular Hypertension (MELL)
OH ....   Off Hook [*Computer science*]
oh ....   Office Hours (AD)
OH ....   Office Hours
OH ....   Office of Hydrology (SAUS)
OH ....   Office of the Handicapped
OH ....   Official Hostess (BARN)
OH ....   Ohio [*Postal code*]
Oh ....   Ohio Courts of Appeals Reports [*A publication*] (DLA)
OH ....   Ohio Field Office (SAUS)
OH ....   Ohmic Heating
Oh ....   Oholoth (BJA)
OH ....   Oil Hardened (SAUS)
OH ....   Oil Hardening (SAUS)
OH ....   Old Harrovian (WDAA)
OH ....   Olduvai Hominid [*Paleoanthropology*]
OH ....   Oligomer Hybridization (DMAA)
OH ....   Omega House (AD)
OH ....   Omni Hora [*Every Hour*] [*Pharmacy*]
oh ....   Omni Hora [*Hourly*] [*Latin*] (AD)
oh ....   On Hand (AD)
OH ....   On Hand
o-H ....   On-Hudson (AD)
OH ....   Ontario Hydro (SAUS)
OH ....   Ontario Hydroelectric [*Canada*]
oh ....   Open Hearth (AD)
OH ....   Open Hearth
OH ....   Open Heart Surgery [*Medicine*]
OH ....   Opera House (AD)

OH ....   Operand Holen (SAUS)
OH ....   Operating Hours (MCD)
OH ....   Operational Handbook [*Marine Corps*] (INF)
OH ....   Operational Hardware (KSC)
OH ....   Operator's Handbook
OH ....   Opposite Hand (OA)
OH ....   Optical Harness (SAUS)
OH ....   Orah Hayyim Shulhan 'Arukh (BJA)
OH ....   Oral Hygiene [*Dentistry*] (DAVI)
OH ....   Originating Hospital [*Aeromedical evacuation*]
OH ....   Orthohydrogen (SAUS)
OH ....   Orthostatic Hypotension [*Medicine*]
OH ....   Osteopathic Hospital (DAVI)
OH ....   Otago Hussars [*British military*] (DMA)
OH ....   Outer Housing (COE)
oh ....   Out Home (AD)
OH ....   Out Home [*Men's lacrosse position*]
OH ....   Outlaw HAWK [*Naval Air Development Center*]
OH ....   Out of Hospital (DMAA)
OH ....   Outpatient Hospital [*Medicine*]
oh ....   Oval Head (AD)
OH ....   Overall Height [*of the Vehicle*] [*TII*] (TAG)
o/h ....   Overhaul (AD)
OH ....   Overhaul
oh ....   Overhead (AD)
OH ....   Overhead
O/H ....   Over-the-Horizon Transmission
O/H ....   Overzuche Handels Maatschappij [*Foreign Trade Company*] [*Dutch*] (ILCA)
O/h ....   Ovulation-producing Hormone (SAUS)
OH ....   Ozar Hatorah (EA)
OH ....   San Francisco and Oakland Helicopter Airlines (SAUS)
OH ....   SFO [*San Francisco and Oakland*] Helicopter Airlines, Inc. [*ICAO designator*] (OAG)
OHA ....   Chicago, IL [*Location identifier*] [*FAA*] (FAAL)
OHA ....   Havelock Public Library, Ontario [*Library symbol*] [*National Library of Canada*] (BIB)
OHA ....   Hydroxyandrostenedione [*Antineoplastic drug*] (CDI)
OHa ....   Lane Public Library, Hamilton, OH [*Library symbol*] [*Library of Congress*] (LCLS)
OHA ....   Occupational Health Administration (AD)
OHA ....   Office of Health Affairs [*U.S. Food and Drug Administration*]
OHA ....   Office of Hearings and Appeals [*In various federal departments*]
OHA ....   Officers' Home Advance (ADA)
OHA ....   Off-station Housing Allowance (DOMA)
Oha ....   Ohaloth (BJA)
OHA ....   OH Aviationa [*France*] [*ICAO designator*] (FAAC)
Oh A ....   Ohio Appellate Reports [*A publication*] (DLA)
OHA ....   Ontario Homeopathic Association (SAUS)
OHA ....   Ontario Horticultural Association (SAUS)
OHA ....   Ontario Hospital Association (SAUS)
OHA ....   Operational Hazard Analysis (NASA)
OHA ....   Oral History Association (EA)
OHA ....   Oral Hypoglycemic Agent [*Medicine*] (CPH)
OHA ....   Oral Hypoglycemic Agents [*Medicine*] (DMAA)
OHA ....   Orbital Height Adjustment Maneuver (MCD)
OHA ....   Oriental Herb Association (AD)
OHA ....   Oscillator Housing Assembly
oha ....   Outside Helix Angle (AD)
OHA ....   Outside Helix Angle
OHA ....   Overseas Housing Allowance
OHA ....   Owner Handler Association of America (EA)
OHA ....   Oxygen Hemoglobin Affinity (OA)
Oh A 2d .....   Ohio Appellate Reports, Second Series [*A publication*] (DLA)
OHaBHi ....   Butler County Historical Society, Hamilton, OH [*Library symbol*] [*Library of Congress*] (LCLS)
OHAD ....   Dysart Branch, Haliburton County Public Library, Ontario [*Library symbol*] [*National Library of Canada*] (BIB)
OHADOE ......   Office of Hearings and Appeals, Department of Energy (SAUS)
OHADOI ......   Office of Hearings and Appeals, Department of the Interior (SAUS)
OHAG ....   Art Gallery of Hamilton, Ontario [*Library symbol*] [*National Library of Canada*] (NLC)
OHAI ....   Haileybury Public Library, Ontario [*Library symbol*] [*National Library of Canada*] (NLC)
OHAINC ....   Haileybury School of Mines Campus, Northern College of Applied Arts and Technology, Ontario [*Library symbol*] [*National Library of Canada*] (BIB)
OHAL ....   Haliburton County Public Library, Ontario [*Library symbol*] [*National Library of Canada*] (NLC)
OHALM ....   Haliburton Highlands Museum, Haliburton, Ontario [*Library symbol*] [*National Library of Canada*] (BIB)
OHaMH ....   Mercy Hospital, Health Science Library, Hamilton, OH [*Library symbol*] [*Library of Congress*] (LCLS)
OHAN ....   Hanover Public Library, Ontario [*Library symbol*] [*National Library of Canada*] (NLC)
OH&T ....   Oil Hardened and Tempered (SAUS)
Oh Ap ....   Ohio Appellate Reports [*A publication*] (DLA)
OHAPT ....   Orleans-Hanna Algebra Prognosis Test (EDAC)
OHARAG ......   Research Station, Agriculture Canada [*Station de Recherches, Agriculture Canada*] Harrow, Ontario [*Library symbol*] [*National Library of Canada*] (NLC)
OhArt ....   [*The*] Ohio Art Co. [*Associated Press*] (SAG)
OHAS ....   Occupational Health and Safety
OHaU ....   Miami University, Hamilton Campus, Hamilton, OH [*Library symbol*] [*Library of Congress*] (LCLS)

OHB .... L'Equilbre Biologique [France] [Research code symbol]
OH-B .... Ocean Hill-Brownsville (AD)
OHB .... O-Hydroxybenzamide (SAUS)
OHB .... Orleans Homebuilders [Montreal Stock Exchange] [Formerly, FPA Corp.]
OHBC .... Ohio Bancorp (SAUS)
OHBC .... Oregon Highland Bentgrass Commission (EA)
OHBES .... Schools, Hamilton Board of Education, Ontario [Library symbol] [National Library of Canada] (NLC)
OHBFS .... Schools, Hamilton Board of Education, Ontario (SAUS)
OHBHU .... Hilton Union Public Library, Hilton Beach, Ontario [Library symbol] [National Library of Canada] (NLC)
OHBMS .... On His [or Her] Britannic Majesty's Service
OHBP .... Pic Heron Bay Band Public Library, Heron Bay, Ontario [Library symbol] [National Library of Canada] (BIB)
OHC .... Hydroxycholcalciferol [A form of vitamin D] (DAVI)
OHC .... Occupational Health Center (KSC)
OHC .... Ocean Heat Convergence
OHC .... Office of Humanities Communication (AD)
OHC .... Office of HUMINT [Human Intelligence] Collection [Military]
OHC .... O'Higgins [Antarctica] [Seismograph station code, US Geological Survey] (SEIS)
OHC .... On Board Hard Copier (NASA)
OHC .... Ontario Housing Corporation (SAUS)
OHC .... Optics Hand Controller (KSC)
OHC .... Oral History Collection (SAUS)
OHC .... Order of the Holy Cross [Episcopalian religious order]
OHC .... Oriole Homes Corporation (SAUS)
OHC .... Other Hanford Contractor (SAUS)
OHC .... Ottumwa Heights College [Iowa]
ohc .... Outer Hair Cells (AD)
OHC .... Outer Hair Cells [of cochlea] [Anatomy]
OHC .... Over-Head-Cam [TII] (TAG)
ohc .... Overhead Cam (AD)
OHC .... Overhead Camshaft [Automotive term]
OHC .... Overhead Cupboards [Classified advertising] (ADA)
OHC .... Overseas Hotel Corp. (AD)
OHC .... Oxygen Hole Centers (SAUS)
OHC.A .... Oriole HomesCv'A' [AMEX symbol] (TTSB)
OHC.B .... Oriole Homes 'B' [AMEX symbol] (TTSB)
OHCA .... Otter Hound Club of America [Later, OCA] (EA)
OHCA .... Out-of-Hospital Cardiac Arrest [Medicine] (DMAA)
OH-Cbl .... Hydroxycobalamin [Medicine] (BABM)
OHCC .... Ordinary High Current Configuration [Magnetic field]
OHCEN .... Ontario Health Care Evaluation Network (SAUS)
OHCI .... Open Host Controller Interface (SAUS)
Oh Cir Ct ..... Ohio Circuit Court Reports [A publication] (DLA)
Oh Cir Ct NS... Ohio Circuit Court Reports, New Series [A publication] (DLA)
Oh Cir Dec.... Ohio Circuit Decisions [A publication] (DLA)
OHC-OHP.... Overhead Camshaft-Overhead Pushrod [Automotive engines]
OHCS .... Hydroxycorticosteroid [Endocrinology] (AAMN)
OHCS .... Office of Home Care Services (AD)
OHCU .... College Universitaire de Hearst, Ontario [Library symbol] [National Library of Canada] (NLC)
OHD .... Hydroxycholcalciferol (STED)
OHD .... Hydroxyvitamin D (DMAA)
OHD .... Occupational Health Division (COE)
OHD .... Office of Human Development [Later, OHDS] [HEW]
OHD .... Ohrid [Former Yugoslavia] [Airport symbol] (OAG)
OHD .... Old Hickory Dam [TVA]
OHD .... Ondine-Hirschprung Disease [Medicine] (DMAA)
OHD .... One-Hour Duty (IAA)
OHD .... Optical Heterodyne Detection
OHD .... Ordinary Hydrodynamic
ohd .... Organic Hearing Disease [Medicine] (AD)
ohd .... Organic Heart Disease [Medicine] (AD)
OHD .... Organic Heart Disease [Medicine]
OHD .... Overhead Display
OHD .... Overhead Door Corp. (EFIS)
OHD .... Overhead Drive (SAUS)
OHD .... Over-the-Horizon Detector [RADAR]
OHDA .... Hydroxydopamine [Also, HDA, HDM] [Biochemistry]
OH/D&D-G ... Ontario Hydro/Design and Development Division-Generation (SAUS)
OHD & W..... Outer Harbor Dock and Wharf (AD)
OHD-B .... Over-the-Horizon Detection RADAR-Backscatter (MCD)
OHDDD .... Ontario Hydro Design and Development Division (SAUS)
Oh Dec .... Ohio Decisions [A publication] (DLA)
Oh Dec Rep... Ohio Decisions Reprint [A publication] (DLA)
OHDET .... Over-the-Horizon Detection [RADAR] (SAA)
OHDETS....... Over-the-Horizon Detection System [RADAR]
OHDF .... Dofasco, Inc., Hamilton, Ontario [Library symbol] [National Library of Canada] (NLC)
OHDFR........ Research Information Center, DOFASCO, Inc., Hamilton, Ontario [Library symbol] [National Library of Canada] (NLC)
OHDMS........ Operational Hydromet Data Management System (PDAA)
OH-DOC ..... Hydroxydeoxycorticosterone [Endocrinology] (DAVI)
OHDS .... Office of Human Development Services [Formerly, OHD] [Department of Health and Human Services]
OHE .... Hearst Public Library, Ontario [Library symbol] [National Library of Canada] (NLC)
OHE .... Office of Hanford Environment (SAUS)
OHE .B .... Office of Health Economics [British]
OHE .... Office of the Housing Expediter [Terminated, 1951] (GPO)
OHE .... Oxidizer Heat Exchange (MCD)

OHEA .... Office of Health and Environmental Assessment [Environmental Protection Agency] (GFGA)
OHEA .... Office of Health Effects Assessment (SAUS)
oheat .... Overheat (AD)
OHEAT .... Overheat
OHEC .... Dr. Harry Paikin Library, Hamilton Board of Education, Ontario [Library symbol] [National Library of Canada] (NLC)
OHEC .... Hamilton Education Centre, Ontario [Library symbol] [National Library of Canada] (NLC)
OhEd .... Ohio Edison Co. [Associated Press] (SAG)
OhEd .... Ohio Edison Financing Trust [Associated Press] (SAG)
OHEF .... Oral Health Education Foundation (SAUS)
OHEP .... Hepworth Branch, Bruce County Public Library, Ontario [Library symbol] [National Library of Canada] (NLC)
OHER .... Office of Health and Environmental Research [Department of Energy] [Washington, DC]
OHESC........ Ontario Library Service - Escarpment, Hamilton, Ontario [Library symbol] [National Library of Canada] (NLC)
OHET .... Erin Township Public Library, Hillsburgh, Ontario [Library symbol] [National Library of Canada] (NLC)
OHF .... Occupational Health Facility [NASA] (KSC)
OHF .... Old Hydrofracture Facility (SAUS)
ohf .... Omsk Hemorrhagic Fever (AD)
OHF .... Omsk Hemorrhagic Fever [Medicine]
OHF .... O'Neill Hull Form (ACAE)
OHF .... Ordnance Historical Files [Military]
ohf .... Overhaul Factor (AD)
OHF .... Overhead Fire (MCD)
OHF .... Overhead Frame (MEDA)
OHF .... Oxalosis and Hyperoxaluria Foundation (EA)
OHFA .... Hydroxy Fatty Acid [Biochemistry] (AAMN)
OHFC .... Hartington Branch, Frontenac County Library, Hartington, Ontario [Library symbol] [National Library of Canada] (BIB)
OHFC .... Owen Hart Fan Club (EA)
Oh F Dec .... Ohio Federal Decisions [A publication] (DLA)
OH/FH......... Operating Hour/Flight Hour [Ratio]
OHFR.......... Objective High Frequency Radio (ACAE)
OHFS .... Optimized Hartree-Fock-Slater (SAUS)
OHFT .... Overhead Frame Trapeze (STED)
OHG .... Banco OHiggins [NYSE symbol] (SAG)
OHG .... Banco O'Higgins ADS [NYSE symbol] (TTSB)
OHG .... Offene Handelsgesellschaft [General Partnership] [German]
OHG .... Official Hotel Guide (TRID)
OHG .... Old High German [Language, etc.]
OHG .... Oral Hypoglycemic [Endocrinology] (DAVI)
OHGI .... Over the Hill Gang, International (EA)
OHGS .... Omega Hyperbolic Grid System
OHGVT....... Orbital Horizontal Ground Vibration Test [NASA] (NASA)
OHH .... Herrold Hall Learning Resource Center, Zanesville (SAUS)
OHH .... Ohio Household Goods Carriers Bureau Inc., Warren OH [STAC]
OHH .... Orthopedia Head Halter (MELL)
OHH .... Owen Harrison Harding [of the James W. Ellison novel, "I'm Owen Harrison Harding"]
OHHA .... Occupational Health Hazard Assessment
OHI .... HUNA International (EA)
OHI .... Occupational Health Institute [Defunct] (EA)
ohi .... Ocular Hypertension Indicator (AD)
OHI .... Ocular Hypertension Indicator
OHi .... Ohio Historical Society, Columbus, OH [Library symbol] [Library of Congress] (LCLS)
OHI .... Oil-Heat Institute of America [Later, PMAA]
OHI .... Omega Healthcare Investors [NYSE symbol] (SPSG)
OHI .... Open Head Injury [Medicine] (PAZ)
OHI .... Oral Hygiene Index (STED)
OHI .... Ordnance Handling Instructions
OHI .... Organisation Hydrographique Internationale [International Hydrographic Organization - IHO] [Monte Carlo, Monaco]
OHI .... Other Health Impaired [Education]
OHI .... State Library of Ohio, Columbus, OH [OCLC symbol] (OCLC)
OHIA .... Oil-Heat Institute of America [Later, PMAA] (KSC)
OHIAA.......... Hydroxyindolacetic Acid [Oncology] (DAVI)
OH-IAA....... Hydroxyindoleacetic Acid (STED)
OHIC .... ODPHP Health Information Center (EA)
OHICU .... Open Heart Intensive Care Unit (NUJO)
OHiIH......... Highland County District Library, Hillsboro, OH [Library symbol] [Library of Congress] (LCLS)
OHiIS .... South Hillsboro City Schools, Hillsboro, OH [Library symbol] [Library of Congress] (LCLS)
OHIMA....... Ohio Health Information Management Association (SAUS)
Ohio............ College Library Center (SAUS)
Ohio............ Ohio Supreme Court Reports [1821-51] [A publication] (DLA)
OHIO............ Over the Hill in October [Used prior to the bombing of Pearl Harbor to typify a recruit's view of US Army life]
Ohio Abs...... Ohio Law Abstract [A publication] (DLA)
Ohio Abstract... Ohio Law Abstract [A publication] (DLA)
Ohio Admin Code... Ohio Administrative Code [Official compilation published by Banks-Baldwin] [A publication] (DLA)
Ohio Ag Exp... Ohio. Agricultural Experimental Station. Publications (SAUS)
Ohio Agric Exp Stn Res Bull... Ohio. Agricultural Experimental Station. Research Bulletin (SAUS)
Ohio Agric Exp Stn Res Circ... Ohio. Agricultural Experimental Station. Research Circular (SAUS)
Ohio Agric Exp Stn Spec Circ... Ohio. Agricultural Experimental Station. Special Circular (SAUS)
Ohio App ..... Ohio Appellate Reports [A publication] (DLA)

Ohio App 2d... Ohio Appellate Reports, Second Series [*A publication*] (DLA)
Ohio Apps.... Ohio Appellate Reports [*A publication*] (DLA)
Ohio BTA..... Ohio Board of Tax Appeals Reports [*A publication*] (DLA)
OhioCa........ Ohio Casualty Corp. [*Associated Press*] (SAG)
Ohio CA........ Ohio Courts of Appeals Reports [*A publication*] (DLA)
OhioCas....... Ohio Casualty Corp. [*Associated Press*] (SAG)
Ohio CC .... Ohio Circuit Court Reports [*A publication*] (DLA)
Ohio CC Dec... Ohio Circuit Court Decisions [*A publication*] (DLA)
Ohio CC NS... Ohio Circuit Court Reports, New Series [*A publication*] (DLA)
Ohio CCR..... Ohio Circuit Court Reports [*A publication*] (DLA)
Ohio CCR NS... Ohio Circuit Court Reports, New Series [*A publication*] (DLA)
Ohio CD .... Ohio Circuit Decisions [*A publication*] (DLA)
Ohio C Dec... Ohio Circuit Decisions [*A publication*] (DLA)
Ohio Circ Dec... Ohio Circuit Decisions [*A publication*] (DLA)
Ohio Cir Ct... Ohio Circuit Court Decisions [*A publication*] (DLA)
Ohio Cir Ct (NS)... Ohio Circuit Court Reports, New Series [*A publication*] (DLA)
Ohio Cir Ct R... Ohio Circuit Court Reports [*A publication*] (DLA)
Ohio Cir Ct R NS... Ohio Circuit Court Reports, New Series [*A publication*] (DLA)
Ohio Circuits... Ohio Circuit Court Decisions [*A publication*] (DLA)
Ohio Cir Dec... Ohio Circuit Decisions [*A publication*] (DLA)
Ohio Cond ... Wilcox's Condensed Ohio Reports [*A publication*] (DLA)
Ohio Cond R... Wilcox's Condensed Ohio Reports [*A publication*] (DLA)
Ohio Ct App... Ohio Courts of Appeals Reports [*A publication*] (DLA)
Ohio Dec ..... Ohio Decisions [*A publication*] (DLA)
Ohio Dec NP... Ohio Decisions Nisi Prius [*A publication*] (DLA)
Ohio Dec R... Ohio Decisions Reprint [*A publication*] (DLA)
Ohio Dec Re... Ohio Decisions Reprint [*A publication*] (DLA)
Ohio Dec Rep... Ohio Decisions Reprint [*A publication*] (DLA)
Ohio Dec Repr... Ohio Decisions Reprint [*A publication*] (DLA)
Ohio Dep't... Ohio Department Reports [*A publication*] (DLA)
Ohio Div WaterTech Rep... Ohio. Division of Water. Technical Report (SAUS)
OhioEd......... Ohio Edison Co. [*Associated Press*] (SAG)
Ohio FD .... Ohio Federal Decisions [*A publication*] (DLA)
Ohio F Dec... Ohio Federal Decisions [*A publication*] (DLA)
Ohio Fed Dec... Ohio Federal Decisions [*A publication*] (DLA)
Ohio Gov't... Ohio Government Reports [*A publication*] (DLA)
Ohio GSB..... Ohio. Geological Survey. Bulletin (SAUS)
Ohio Jur ..... Ohio Jurisprudence [*A publication*] (DLA)
Ohio Jur 2d... Ohio Jurisprudence, Second Series [*A publication*] (DLA)
Ohio L Abs... Ohio Law Abstract [*A publication*] (DLA)
Ohio Law Abs... Ohio Law Abstract [*A publication*] (DLA)
Ohio Law Abst... Ohio Law Abstract [*A publication*] (DLA)
Ohio Law Bull... Weekly Law Bulletin [*Ohio*] [*A publication*] (DLA)
Ohio Law J... Ohio Law Journal [*A publication*] (DLA)
Ohio Law R... Ohio Law Reporter [*A publication*] (DLA)
Ohio Law Rep... Ohio Law Reporter [*A publication*] (DLA)
Ohio Law Repr... Ohio Law Reporter [*A publication*] (DLA)
Ohio Laws ... State of Ohio: Legislative Acts Passed and Joint Resolutions Adopted [*A publication*] (DLA)
Ohio LB .... Weekly Law Bulletin [*Ohio*] [*A publication*] (DLA)
Ohio L Bull... Ohio Law Bulletin [*A publication*] (DLA)
Ohio Legal N... Ohio Legal News [*A publication*] (DLA)
Ohio Legis Bull... Ohio Legislative Bulletin (Anderson) [*A publication*] (DLA)
Ohio Legis Serv... Ohio Legislative Service [*A publication*] (DLA)
Ohio Leg N... Ohio Legal News [*A publication*] (DLA)
Ohio Leg News... Ohio Legal News [*A publication*] (DLA)
OhioLINK ..... Ohio Library and Information Network
Ohio LJ .... Ohio Law Journal [*A publication*] (DLA)
Ohio Low Dec... Ohio Lower Court Decisions [*A publication*] (DLA)
Ohio Lower Dec... Ohio Lower Court Decisions [*A publication*] (DLA)
Ohio LR .... Ohio Law Reporter [*A publication*] (DLA)
Ohio LR & Wk Bul... Ohio Law Reporter and Weekly Bulletin [*A publication*] (DLA)
Ohio L Rep... Ohio Law Reporter [*A publication*] (DLA)
OHIO M......... Ohio Magazine [*A publication*] (ROG)
Ohio Misc.... Ohio Miscellaneous Reports [*A publication*] (DLA)
Ohio Misc 2d... Ohio Miscellaneous Reports, Second Series [*A publication*] (DLA)
Ohio Misc 3d... Ohio Miscellaneous Reports, Third Series [*A publication*] (DLA)
Ohio Misc Dec... Ohio Miscellaneous Decisions [*A publication*] (DLA)
Ohio Monthly Rec... Ohio Monthly Record [*A publication*] (DLA)
Ohio Nat ...... Ohio Naturalist (SAUS)
OHIONET...... Ohio Network (NITA)
Ohio (New Series)... Ohio State Reports, New Series [*A publication*] (DLA)
Ohio Nisi Prius... Ohio Nisi Prius Reports [*A publication*] (DLA)
Ohio Nisi Prius (NS)... Ohio Nisi Prius Reports, New Series [*A publication*] (DLA)
Ohio No U ... Ohio Northern University (GAGS)
Ohio NP ...... Ohio Nisi Prius Reports [*A publication*] (DLA)
Ohio NP NS... Ohio Nisi Prius Reports, New Series [*A publication*] (DLA)
Ohio NS....... Ohio State Reports, New Series [*A publication*] (DLA)
Ohio O .... Ohio Opinions [*A publication*] (DLA)
Ohio O .... Ohio Opinions, Annotated [*A publication*] (DLA)
Ohio O 2d... Ohio Opinions, Second Series [*A publication*] (DLA)
Ohio Op .... Ohio Opinions [*A publication*] (DLA)
Ohio Op 2d... Ohio Opinions, Second Series [*A publication*] (DLA)
Ohio Op 3d... Ohio Opinions, Third Series [*A publication*] (DLA)
Ohio Ops ..... Ohio Opinions [*A publication*] (DLA)
Ohio Prob ... Ohio Probate Reports, by Goebel [*A publication*] (DLA)
Ohio Prob Ct... Goebel's Probate Reports [*Ohio*] [*A publication*] (DLA)
Ohio R .... Ohio Report [*A publication*] (DLA)
Ohio R Cond... Ohio Reports Condensed [*A publication*] (DLA)
Ohio Rep Res Develop... Ohio Report on Research and Development. Ohio Agricultural Experiment Station (SAUS)
Ohio Rev Code Ann... Ohio Revised Code, Annotated [*A publication*] (DLA)
Ohio Rev Code Ann (Anderson)... Ohio Revised Code, Annotated (Anderson) [*A publication*] (DLA)

Ohio Rev Code Ann (Baldwin)... Ohio Revised Code, Annotated (Baldwin) [*A publication*] (DLA)
Ohio Rev Code Ann (Page)... Ohio Revised Code, Annotated (Page) [*A publication*] (DLA)
Ohio S......... Ohio State Reports [*A publication*] (DLA)
Ohio S & CP... Ohio Superior and Common Pleas Decisions [*A publication*] (DLA)
Ohio S & CP Dec... Ohio Superior and Common Pleas Decisions [*A publication*] (DLA)
Ohio SBA Bull... Ohio State Bar Association. Bulletin [*A publication*] (DLA)
Ohio SR....... Ohio State Reports [*A publication*] (DLA)
Ohio S Rep... Ohio State Reports [*A publication*] (DLA)
Ohio St .... Ohio State Reports [*A publication*] (DLA)
Ohio St 2d... Ohio State Reports, Second Series [*A publication*] (DLA)
Ohio St 3d... Ohio State Reports, Third Series [*A publication*] (DLA)
Ohio State... Ohio State Reports [*A publication*] (DLA)
Ohio State Rep... Ohio State Reports [*A publication*] (DLA)
Ohio State R (NS)... Ohio State Reports, New Series [*A publication*] (DLA)
Ohio St R.... Ohio State Reports [*A publication*] (DLA)
Ohio St Rep... Ohio State Reports [*A publication*] (DLA)
Ohio St Report... Ohio State Reports [*A publication*] (DLA)
Ohio St R (NS)... Ohio State Reports, New Series [*A publication*] (DLA)
Ohio St U.... [*The*] Ohio State University (GAGS)
Ohio SU .... Ohio Supreme Court Decisions, Unreported Cases [*A publication*] (DLA)
Ohio Sup & CP Dec... Ohio Superior and Common Pleas Decisions [*A publication*] (DLA)
Ohio Supp ... Ohio Supplement [*A publication*] (DLA)
Ohio Turn .... Ohio Turnpike (AD)
Ohio U .... Ohio University (GAGS)
Ohio Unrep... Ohio Supreme Court Decisions, Unreported Cases [*A publication*] (DLA)
Ohio Unrep Jud Dec... Pollack's Ohio Unreported Judicial Decisions Prior to 1823 [*A publication*] (DLA)
Ohio Unrept Cas... Ohio Supreme Court Decisions, Unreported Cases [*A publication*] (DLA)
Ohio U Pr ... Ohio University Press (AD)
OhioVal........ Ohio Valley Banc Corp. [*Associated Press*] (SAG)
OHIP .... Office of Health and Industry Programs [*U.S. Food and Drug Administration*]
OHIP .... Ontario Health Insurance Plan [*Canada*] (CMD)
OHIP .... Ontario Hospital Insurance Plan [*Canada*] (AD)
OHIR .... Operating House of III Repute
OHirC .... Hiram College, Hiram, OH [*Library symbol*] [*Library of Congress*] (LCLS)
OHirP .... Portage County District Library, Hiram, OH [*Library symbol*] [*Library of Congress*] (LCLS)
OHIS .... Oral Hearing-Impaired Section [*of the Alexander Graham Bell Association for the Deaf*] (EA)
OHI-S .... Oral Hygiene Index-Simplified
OHJ.......... Old-House Journal [*A publication*]
OHJD .... John Deere Ltd., Hamilton, Ontario [*Library symbol*] [*National Library of Canada*] (NLC)
Oh Jur .... Ohio Jurisprudence [*A publication*] (DLA)
OHK .... Hawkesbury Public Library, Ontario [*Library symbol*] [*National Library of Canada*] (NLC)
OHKAC........ Resource Centre, Algonquin College of Applied Arts and Technology [*Centre de Documentation, College Algonquin des Arts Appliques et de la Technologie*], Hawkesbury, Ontario [*Library symbol*] [*National Library of Canada*] (BIB)
OHKC .... CIP Research Ltd., Hawkesbury, Ontario [*Library symbol*] [*National Library of Canada*] (NLC)
OHKGH .... Hawkesbury General Hospital, Ontario [*Library symbol*] [*National Library of Canada*] (BIB)
OHL .... Oberste Herresleitung [*Supreme Headquarters*] [*German*] (AD)
OHL .... Occupational Health Laboratory (SAUS)
OHL .... Occupational Hygiene Laboratory (SAUS)
OHL .... Ontario Hydro Library [*UTLAS symbol*]
OHL .... Oral Hairy Leukoplakia [*Medicine*]
OHL .... Overhaul
OHL .... Oxford Higher Local Examination [*British*] (ROG)
OHLA .... Anthony Pape Memorial Law Library, Hamilton Law Association, Ontario [*Library symbol*] [*National Library of Canada*] (BIB)
Oh L Bul .... Ohio Law Bulletin [*A publication*] (DLA)
Oh L Ct D .... Ohio Lower Court Decisions [*A publication*] (DLA)
OHLEG .... East Gwillimbury Public Libraries, Holland Landing, Ontario [*Library symbol*] [*National Library of Canada*] (NLC)
Oh Leg N .... Ohio Legal News [*A publication*] (DLA)
OHLH .... Overhead Heavy Load Handling [*Nuclear energy*] (NRCH)
Ohlinger Fed Practice... Ohlinger's Federal Practice [*A publication*] (DLA)
Oh LJ .... Ohio Law Journal [*A publication*] (DLA)
Oh L Rep .... Ohio Law Reporter [*A publication*] (DLA)
OHM .... McMaster University, Hamilton, Ontario [*Library symbol*] [*National Library of Canada*] (NLC)
OHM .... Miami University, Hamilton Campus, Hamilton, OH [*OCLC symbol*] (OCLC)
OHM .... Office of Hazardous Materials [*Department of Transportation*]
OHM .... OHM Corp. [*NYSE symbol*] (SPSG)
OHM .... Ohmmeter [*Engineering*] (AAG)
ohm .... Ohmmeter (AD)
OHM .... Oil and Hazardous Materials (SAUS)
OHM .... Oil and Hazardous Materials Incidence
OHMA .... Archives and Special Collections Division, McMaster University, Hamilton, Ontario [*Library symbol*] [*National Library of Canada*] (NLC)
OHMA .... Office of Health and Medical Affairs (GHCT)

OHMAH........ Department of Art and Art History, McMaster University, Hamilton, Ontario [*Library symbol*] [*National Library of Canada*] (NLC)
OHMAR........ Oral History in the Mid-Atlantic Region [*An association*]
OHMB.......... Health Sciences Library, McMaster University, Hamilton, Ontario [*Library symbol*] [*National Library of Canada*] (NLC)
OHMC.......... Mohawk College of Applied Arts and Technology, Hamilton, Ontario [*Library symbol*] [*National Library of Canada*] (NLC)
OHMcGF...... Odyssey House McGrath Foundation [*Australia*]
OHMCI........ Office of Her Majesty's Chief Inspector of Schools [*British*] (DET)
OHMCL........ Library Technician Program, Mohawk College of Applied Arts & Technology, Hamilton, Ontario [*Library symbol*] [*National Library of Canada*] (NLC)
OHM-CM...... Ohm-Centimeter (AAG)
ohm-cm........ Ohm-Centimeter (AD)
OHM Cp....... OHM Corp. [*Associated Press*] (SAG)
OHMDBA..... Canadian Baptist Archives, McMaster Divinity College, McMaster University, Hamilton, Ontario [*Library symbol*] [*National Library of Canada*] (NLC)
OHMEA........ Office of Hazardous Materials Exemptions and Approvals [*RSPA*] (TAG)
OHMES........ Occupational Health Monitoring and Evaluation System (PDAA)
OHMIS........ Occupational Health Management Information System [*Military*] (GFGA)
Oh Misc....... Ohio Miscellaneous Reports [*A publication*] (DLA)
OHMM.......... Map Library, McMaster University, Hamilton, Ontario [*Library symbol*] [*National Library of Canada*] (NLC)
OHMM.......... Ohmmeter [*Engineering*]
ohm/m.......... Resistence per Meter
OHMO.......... Office of Hazardous Materials Operations [*Department of Transportation*] (DLA)
OHMO.......... Office of Health Maintenance Organization [*Insurance*] (DHSM)
OHMP.......... Occupational Health Maintenance Program (SARE)
OHMP.......... Oral Health Maintenance Program [*Army*] (AABC)
OHMP.......... United States Army Oral Health Maintenance Program (SAUS)
OHMR.......... Office of Hazardous Materials Regulation [*Department of Transportation*] (OICC)
OHMS.......... Office of Hazardous Materials Safety (SAUS)
OHMS.......... Office of Hazardous Materials Standards [*RSPA*] (TAG)
OHMS.......... Onboard Health Monitoring System (AD)
OHMS.......... On His [*or Her*] Majesty's Service
OHMS.......... Our Helpless Millions Saved [*Title of early film*]
OHMS.......... Overhead Machine Screw [*Technical drawings*]
OHMSB........ Oil and Hazardous Materials Spills Branch [*Environmental Protection Agency*] (GRD)
OHMSETT ... Oil and Hazardous Materials Simulated Environmental Test Tank [*Leonardo, NJ*] [*Environmental Protection Agency*]
OHMT.......... Office of Hazardous Materials Transportation [*Department of Transportation*] (GFGA)
OHM-TADS... Oil and Hazardous Materials Technical Assistance Data System [*Databank*] [*Environmental Protection Agency*] (IID)
OHMTADS.... Oil and Hazardous Material Technical Assistance Data System [*Environmental Protection Agency*] (AEPA)
OHMVR........ Off-Highway Motor Vehicle Recreation (SAUS)
OHN............ Hastings Branch, Northumberland County Public Library, Ontario [*Library symbol*] [*National Library of Canada*] (BIB)
OHN............ Memphis, TN [*Location identifier*] [*FAA*] (FAAL)
OHN............ Occupational Health Nurse [*Government classification*]
OHN............ OHIONET, Columbus, OH [*OCLC symbol*] (OCLC)
OHNC.......... Occupational Health Nursing Certificate [*British*]
OH/NMMD ... Ontario Hydro/Nuclear Materials Management Department (SAUS)
OHNN.......... Otorhinolaryngology and Head/Neck Nurses (EA)
OHNO.......... Occupational Health Nursing Officer (AD)
Oh NP......... Ohio Nisi Prius Reports [*A publication*] (DLA)
Oh NP (NS)... Ohio Nisi Prius Reports, New Series [*A publication*] (DLA)
OHNS.......... Occupational Health Nursing Sister (AD)
Oh NU Intra LR... Ohio Northern University. Intramural Law Review [*A publication*] (DLA)
OHO............ Ohio Hospice Organization (SAUS)
OHO............ Ohio Resources Corp. [*Vancouver Stock Exchange symbol*]
Oho............ Oholoth (BJA)
OHO............ Order Holding Office
OHO............ Ordnance Handling Officer [*Navy*] (DOMA)
oho .... Out-of-House Operation (AD)
OHOB.......... O'Neill House Office Building [*U.S. House of Representatives*] [*Washington, D.C.*]
OHOC.......... Oregon Hanford Oversight Committee (SAUS)
OHOHS........ Canadian Centre for Occupational Health and Safety [*Centre Canadien d'Hygieneet de Securite au Travail*] Hamilton, Ontario [*Library symbol*] [*National Library of Canada*] (NLC)
Ohol............ Oholoth (BJA)
OHP............ Hydroxypyroline [*Biochemistry*] (AAMN)
OHP............ Oban-Heliport [*Scotland*] [*Airport symbol*] (OAG)
OHP............ Occupational Health Physician (SAUS)
OHP............ Ocean History Panel (SAUS)
OHP............ Office of Health Physics [*U.S. Food and Drug Administration*]
OHP............ Open Hypertext Protocol (RALS)
OHP............ Operational Health Physics (SAUS)
OHP............ Operational Hit Probabilities (SAUS)
OHP............ Operational Hydrology Program [*World Meteorological Organization*] (GFGA)
OHP............ Order of the Holy Paraclete [*Anglican religious community*]
OHP............ Outer Helmholtz Plane [*Physics*]
ohp .... Overhead Projection (AD)
OHP............ Overhead Projector (ADA)
OHP............ Overhead Transparency Panel (SAUS)

OHP .... Oxygen at High Pressure [*Also, HBO, HPO*] (MCD)
OHP .... Oxygen under Hyperbaric Pressure [*For hyperbaric oxygen therapy*] [*Medicine*] (DAVI)
OhP25........ Ohio Power Co. [*Associated Press*] (SAG)
OH PED....... Ohne Pedal [*Without Pedal*] [*Music*]
oh Ped........ Ohne Pedale [*Without Pedals*] [*German*] (AD)
OHPO.......... Organization Health Program Officer (AFM)
OHPR.......... Outstanding Hardware Problem Report (MCD)
Oh Prob....... Ohio Probate [*A publication*] (DLA)
OHPS.......... Oil Hydraulic Power Switch
OHPSS........ Operational Health Physics Site Surveillance (SAUS)
OHQ........... Originating Headquarters (SAUS)
OHQ........... Overseas Headquarters [*British military*] (DMA)
OHR........... Office of Health Research [*Environmental Protection Agency*] [*Washington, DC*] (GRD)
OHR........... Office of Human Resources (SAUS)
OHR........... Of Human Rights (EA)
OHR........... O'Hara Resources Ltd. [*Vancouver Stock Exchange symbol*]
OHR........... Ohrid [*Yugoslavia*] [*Seismograph station code, US Geological Survey*] (SEIS)
OHR........... Ontario Hydro-Research (SAUS)
OHR........... Operating House of Ill Repute (SAUS)
OHR........... Operational Hazard Report [*Air Force*] (AFM)
OHR........... Over-the-Horizon RADAR
OHRB.......... Royal Botanical Gardens, Hamilton, Ontario [*Library symbol*] [*National Library of Canada*] (NLC)
OHRC.......... Redeemer College, Ancaster, Ontario [*Library symbol*] [*National Library of Canada*] (NLC)
OHRD.......... Ontario Hydro Research Division (SAUS)
OHRDP .... Ontario Health Resources Development Program (SAUS)
OHRD/TSTA... Ontario Hydro Research Division/Tritium Systems Test Assembly (SAUS)
OHRE.......... Department of Energy, Office of Human Radiation Experiments (SAUS)
OHRE.......... Office of Human Radiation Experiments. Department of Energy (SAUS)
ohrf............ Overhaul Replacement Factor (AD)
OHRG.......... Official Hotel and Resort Guide [*A publication*] (AD)
OHRI.......... Occupational Health & Rehabilitation, Inc. [*NASDAQ symbol*] (SAG)
OHRI.......... Oral Health Research Institute [*Indiana University*] [*Research center*] (RCD)
OHRI.......... Overhaul Recurrent Item (CINC)
OHRI.......... Overhaul Removal Interval [*Military*] (AFIT)
OHRI.......... Overhaul Removal Item (CINC)
OHRIM........ Office of Human Resource Information Management [*Department of Health and Human Services*] (GFGA)
OHRM.......... Office of Human Resources Management [*Environmental Protection Agency*] (GFGA)
OHRR.......... Open Heart Recovery Room [*Cardiology*] (DAVI)
OHRS.......... Overflow Heat Removal System [*Nuclear energy*] (NRCH)
OHS .... Hamilton Spectator, Ontario [*Library symbol*] [*National Library of Canada*] (NLC)
OHS .... Hydroxy-Steroids (SAUS)
OHS .... Obesity Hypoventilation Syndrome
OHS .... Occupational Health and Safety
OHS .... Occupational Health Services, Inc. [*Secaucus, NJ*] [*Medical databank originator*] [*Information service or system*]
OHS .... Occupational Hearing Service
OHS .... Oceanography & Hydrographic Ship (SAUS)
OHS .... Octadecylhydrogensuccinate (SAUS)
OHS .... Ocular Histoplasmosis Syndrome (SAUS)
OHS .... Ocular Hypofusion Syndrome (MELL)
OHS .... Off-Hook Service [*Telecommunications*] (TEL)
OHS .... Office of Highway Safety [*of BPR*]
OHS .... Oil Hydraulic Assembly (SAUS)
OHS .... Ontario Historical Society (SAUS)
OHS .... Ontario Humane Society [*Canada*] (AD)
OHS .... Open-Health Steel (SAUS)
ohs............ Open-Hearth Steel (AD)
OHS .... Open-Hearth Steel
OHS .... Open Heart Surgery [*Medicine*]
OHS .... Optometric Historical Society (EA)
OHS .... Oral Hygiene Service (AD)
OHS .... Oral Hygiene Society (NADA)
OHS .... Oregon Historical Society (SAUS)
OHS .... Organ Historical Society (EA)
OHS .... Organization Health Survey [*Test*]
OHS .... Organization of Historical Studies (EA)
OHS .... Oval-Headed Screw (DAC)
OHS .... Ovarian Hyperstimulation Syndrome [*Medicine*] (DMAA)
OHS .... Overland Highway Society (SAUS)
OHS .... Oxford High School (SAUS)
OHS .... Oxford Historical Society [*British*] (ODCC)
OHS .... University of Oregon, Health Sciences Library, Portland, OR [*OCLC symbol*] (OCLC)
OHSA.......... Occupational Health and Safety Act (SAUS)
OHSA.......... Occupational Health and Safety Authority [*Victoria, Australia*]
Oh S & CP... Ohio Superior and Common Pleas Decisions [*A publication*] (DLA)
OHSB.......... Occupational Health and Safety Branch (SAUS)
OHSC.......... Oak Hill Sportswear Corp. [*NASDAQ symbol*] (NQ)
OHSC.......... Occupational Health and Safety Commission (SAUS)
OHSCC........ Steel Company of Canada, Hamilton, Ontario [*Library symbol*] [*National Library of Canada*] (NLC)
Oh SCD....... Ohio Supreme Court Decisions, Unreported Cases [*A publication*] (DLA)

OH Screw	Oval Head Screw (SAUS)
OHSCSA......	Occupational Health and Safety Commission of South Australia
OHSD...........	Occupational Health and Safety Division (SAUS)
OhSEA.........	Ohio Society of Enrolled Agents (SAUS)
OHSGT........	Office of High-Speed Ground Transportation [Department of Transportation]
OHSI...........	Omega Health Systems [NASDAQ symbol] (TTSB)
OHSI...........	Omega Health Systems, Inc. [NASDAQ symbol] (SAG)
OHSI...........	Oral Health Status Index [Dentistry]
OHSIP.........	Ontario Health-Services Insurances Plan [Canada] (AD)
OHSL..........	OHSL Financial Corp. [NASDAQ symbol] (SAG)
OHSL Fn......	OHSL Financial Corp. [Associated Press] (SAG)
OHS MSDS...	Occupational Health Services Material Safety Data Sheets [Database]
OHSPAC.......	Occupational Health-Safety-Programs Accreditation Commission (AD)
OHSPC........	Oil and Hazardous Substance Pollution Contingency (SAUS)
OHSRC........	Occupational Health Safety and Rehabilitation Council [New South Wales, Australia]
OHSS..........	Occupational Health and Safety Staff [Environmental Protection Agency] (GFGA)
OHSS..........	Occupation Health and Safety Staff (SAUS)
OHSS..........	Ovarian Hyperstimulation Syndrome [Medicine] (DMAA)
OHST..........	Occupational Health & Safety Technicians (SAUS)
OHST..........	Occupational Health and Safety Technologist
Oh St..........	Ohio State Reports [A publication] (DLA)
OHST..........	Overhead Storage Tank [Nuclear energy] (NRCH)
OHSU..........	Oregon Health Sciences University (IID)
OHT...........	Hornepayne Township Public Library, Ontario [Library symbol] [National Library of Canada] (NLC)
OHT...........	Ocean Heat Transport
OHT...........	Ocular Hypertensive [Ophthalmology]
OHT...........	Office of Housing Technology [National Bureau of Standards]
OHT...........	Ohio Historical Society, Columbus, OH [OCLC symbol] (OCLC)
OHT...........	Ohio Tank Truck Carriers Bureau, Worthington OH [STAC]
oht.............	Overheating Temperature (AD)
OHT...........	Overheating Temperature (PDAA)
OHT...........	Oxygen at High Temperature (OA)
OHTA..........	Office of Health Technology Assessment [HHS]
OHTA..........	Organ Historical Trust of Australia
OHTB..........	Ontario Highway and Transport Board (SAUS)
OHTCS........	Outer Head Temperature Control System [Nuclear energy] (NRCH)
OHTDC........	Ontario Hydro Tritium Dispersion Code (SAUS)
OHTE..........	Ohmically-Heated Toroidal Experiment (SAUS)
OHTE..........	Ohmic Heating Toroidal Experiment [Nuclear fusion device]
OHTEX........	Ocean Heat Transport Experiment [Japan] [Marine science] (OSRA)
OHTR..........	Theological College of the Canadian Reformed Churches, Hamilton, Ontario [Library symbol] [National Library of Canada] (NLC)
O/H Transmission...	Over-the-Horizon Transmission (SAUS)
OHTS..........	Oil-Hardened Tool Steel
OHu	Hubbard Public Library, Hubbard, OH [Library symbol] [Library of Congress] (LCLS)
OHU...........	Huntsville Public Library, Ontario [Library symbol] [National Library of Canada] (NLC)
ohu............	Ohio [MARC country of publication code] [Library of Congress] (LCCP)
OHU...........	Optical Head Unit (SAUS)
OHU...........	Overseas Homeported Units [Navy] (NVT)
OHUM.........	Muskoka Pioneer Village, Huntsville, Ontario [Library symbol] [National Library of Canada] (BIB)
OHur..........	Huron Public Library, Huron, OH [Library symbol] [Library of Congress] (LCLS)
OHV	Off-Highway Vehicle
ohv............	Overhead Valve (AD)
OHV	Overhead Valve
OHV	Overhead Valve Engine (SAUS)
OHV	Overhead Vent (WDAA)
OHVE.........	Hanmer Branch, Valley East Public Library [Succursale Hanmer, Bibliotheque Publique de Valley-East], Ontario [Library symbol] [National Library of Canada] (NLC)
OHW	Electronic Systems Library, Westinghouse Canada Ltd., Burlington, Ontario [Library symbol] [National Library of Canada] (NLC)
OHW	Oak Harbor [Washington] [Seismograph station code, US Geological Survey] (SEIS)
OHW	Oxygen-Hydrogen Welding (SAUS)
OHW	Oxyhydrogen Welding
OHWL.........	Wentworth Public Library, Hamilton, Ontario [Library symbol] [National Library of Canada] (NLC)
OHWM........	Office of Hazardous Waste Management (SAUS)
OHWM........	Open Heart World Mission (EA)
OHWM........	Ordinary High Water Mark (SAUS)
OHWS.........	Offensive Handgun Weapon System (SAUS)
OHWS.........	Overhead Wood Screw [Technical drawings]
OHY	Onur Hava Tasimacilik AWMS [Turkey] [ICAO designator] (FAAC)
OI..............	Ingersoll Public Library, Ontario [Library symbol] [National Library of Canada] (NLC)
OI..............	Object Interface (SAUS)
OI..............	Obturator Internus [Muscle] (MELL)
OI..............	Occipito Iliacus (SAUS)
OI..............	Occult Injury (MELL)
OI..............	Odyssey Institute [Later, OIC] (EA)
OI..............	Office Information (SAUS)
OI..............	Office Instruction (AFM)
OI..............	Office of Automation (AFM)
OI..............	Office of Investigations [Environmental Protection Agency] (GFGA)

OI..............	Ohashi Institute (EA)
oi..............	Oil-Immersed (AD)
OI..............	Oil-Immersed
OI..............	Oil Immersion (SAUS)
OI..............	Oil-Insulated
OI..............	Oil Insulation (SAUS)
OI..............	Old Icelandic [Language] (BARN)
OI..............	Omega Inertial (SAUS)
OI..............	ONE, Inc. (EA)
OI..............	On Instruments [Aviation]
OI..............	Opener Inhibitor
OI..............	Opening of Intestine
OI..............	Open Issue (SAUS)
OI..............	Operating Income [Accounting]
OI..............	Operating Instructions
OI..............	Operational Instrumentation (NASA)
OI..............	Operational Intelligence
OI..............	Operational Issue [Military]
OI..............	Operation Identity (EA)
OI..............	Operation Interface (SAUS)
OI..............	Operations Instruction (SAUS)
OI..............	Operations Intelligence (SAUS)
OI..............	Operations Interface (MCD)
OI..............	Operator Input
OI..............	Operator Interface (ACII)
OI..............	Opportunistic Illness (MELL)
OI..............	Opportunistic Infection [Medicine]
OI..............	Opsconic Index [Laboratory science] (DAVI)
o/i.............	Opsonic Index (AD)
o/i.............	Opsonic Index [Medicine]
OI..............	Optical Isolator [Nuclear energy] (NRCH)
O/I.............	Optimal Interpolation (SAUS)
OI..............	Optimist International (EA)
OI..............	Optimum Interpolation [Marine science] (OSRA)
OI..............	Opto Isolator (AAEL)
OI..............	Orbiter Instrumentation [NASA] (NASA)
OI..............	Orbit [or Orbital] Insertion
OI..............	Ordinary Interest [Banking]
OI..............	Organizational/Intermediate (MCD)
OI..............	Organization Integration [Military]
o-i.............	Orgasmic Impairment (AD)
OI..............	Orgasmic Impairment [Medicine]
OI..............	Oriental Institute (AD)
OI..............	Orientation Inventory [Psychology]
OI..............	Orthopedically Impaired
OI..............	Osteogenesis Imperfecta [Medicine]
OI..............	Ote Iwapo [All That Is Must Be Considered] [of OI Committee International, a third-world lobby opposing systematic birth control] [Swahili]
OI..............	Otitis Interna [Medicine] (MELL)
OI..............	Ours, Inc. (EA)
O-I.............	Outer and Inner (DMAA)
OI..............	Output Impedance
O/I.............	Output/Input (SAUS)
OI..............	Ovarian Insufficiency [Medicine] (MELL)
O/I.............	Overseas Investment [Economics]
OI..............	Owens-Illinois, Inc. [NYSE symbol] (SPSG)
OI..............	Oxide Isolated (TIMI)
OI..............	Oxygen Income [or Intake] [Medicine]
OI..............	Oxygen Index [Medicine] (DAVI)
OI..............	Oxygen Intact [Medicine] (DAVI)
OI..............	Oxygen Intake (SAUS)
OIA.............	Municipal Income Opportunity Trust [Formerly, Allstate Municipal Income Opportunities Trust] [NYSE symbol] (SPSG)
OIA.............	Ocean Industries Association (AD)
OIA.............	Office Information Architecture (SAUS)
OIA.............	Office of Impact Analysis [Environmental Protection Agency] (BARN)
OIA.............	Office of Industrial Associates (AD)
OIA.............	Office of Inspector and Auditor [Nuclear Regulatory Commission] (NRCH)
OIA.............	Office of International Activities [American Chemical Society]
OIA.............	Office of International Administration [Department of State]
OIA.............	Office of International Affairs [NASA, HUD]
OIA.............	Official Information Act (SAUS)
OIA.............	Oil Import Administration [Later, Office of Oil and Gas] [Department of the Interior]
OIA.............	Oil Insurance Association [Later, Industrial Risk Insurance] (EA)
OIA.............	Oishiyama A [Japan] [Seismograph station code, US Geological Survey] (SEIS)
OIA.............	Operations Intelligence Automation (SAUS)
OIA.............	Operative Ironmoulders' Association [A union] [British]
OIA.............	Operator Information Area (SAUS)
OIA.............	Optical Immunoassay [Clinical chemistry]
OIA.............	Optics Inertial Analyzer (SAA)
OIA.............	Orbiter Interface Adapter [NASA] (NASA)
OIA.............	Organizacion Internacional del Azucar [International Sugar Organization - ISO] (EAIO)
OIA.............	Outboard Industry Association [Later, NMMA] (EA)
OIAA..........	Abadan/International [Iran] [ICAO location identifier] (ICLI)
OIAA..........	Office of Inter-American Affairs [Later, BIAA]
OIAA..........	Office of International Aviation Affairs [FAA]
OIA & TU ...	Office of Industry Affairs and Technology Utilization [NASA]
OIAB	Boostan [Iran] [ICAO location identifier] (ICLI)
OIAB	Oil Import Appeals Board (AD)

OIAC	Organizacion Internacional de la Aviacion Civil [International Civil AviationOrganization] [Spanish] (AD)
OIAD	Dezful [Iran] [ICAO location identifier] (ICLI)
OIAF	Office of Information for the Armed Forces (DNAB)
OIAG	Aghajari [Iran] [ICAO location identifier] (ICLI)
OIAH	Gachsaran [Iran] [ICAO location identifier] (ICLI)
OIAI	Masjed Soleiman [Iran] [ICAO location identifier] (ICLI)
OIAI	OIA, Inc. (SAUS)
OIAJ	Office for Improvements in the Administration of Justice (AD)
OIAJ	Omidyeh [Iran] [ICAO location identifier] (ICLI)
OIAK	Haft-Gel [Iran] [ICAO location identifier] (ICLI)
OIAL	Lali [Iran] [ICAO location identifier] (ICLI)
OIAM	Bandar Mahshahr [Iran] [ICAO location identifier] (ICLI)
OIAN	Andimeshk [Iran] [ICAO location identifier] (ICLI)
OI & C	Office of Investigation and Compliance [Employment and Training Administration] [Department of Labor]
OI & I	Office of Invention and Innovation [Disbanded] [National Institute of Standards and Technology]
OIAO	Ogaden Islamic Alliance Organization (SAUS)
OIAS	Observer Impression Assessment Scale
OIAS	Occupational Information Access System (WDAA)
OIAT	Abadan [Iran] [ICAO location identifier] (ICLI)
OIAT	Osteopathic Institute of Applied Technique (SAUS)
OIATU	Office of Industry Affairs and Technology Utilization [NASA]
OIAW	Ahwaz [Iran] [ICAO location identifier] (ICLI)
OIB	Briggs-Lawrence County Public Library, Ironton, OH [Library symbol] [Library of Congress] (LCLS)
OIB	Iron Bridge Public Library, Ontario [Library symbol] [National Library of Canada] (NLC)
OIB	Municipal Income Opportunity Trust [Formerly, Allstate Municipal Income Opportunities Trust] [NYSE symbol] (SPSG)
OIB	Oceanic Island Basalt [Geology]
OIB	Official Information Base
OIB	Ohio Inspection Bureau (AD)
OIB	Oishiyama B [Japan] [Seismograph station code, US Geological Survey] (SEIS)
OIB	Oklahoma Inspection Bureau (AD)
OIB	Oligoclonal Immunoglobulin Bands [Clinical chemistry]
OIB	Olympic Installations Board
OIB	Operating Impedance Bridge (IAA)
OIB	Operation Instruction Block (NITA)
OIB	Operation Instruction Book (SAUS)
OIB	Operations Integration Branch [NASA] (KSC)
OIB	Operations Intelligence Branch (SAUS)
OIB	Orbiter Interface Box [NASA] (NASA)
OIB	Ortho-Iodobenzoic (Acid) [Biochemistry]
OIBA	Abumusa Island [Iran] [ICAO location identifier] (ICLI)
OIBA	Office of Industrial Base Assessment (DOMA)
OIBB	Bushehr/Bushehr [Iran] [ICAO location identifier] (ICLI)
OIBD	Bandar Deylam [Iran] [ICAO location identifier] (ICLI)
OIBF	Forouz Island [Iran] [ICAO location identifier] (ICLI)
OIBG	Ganaveh [Iran] [ICAO location identifier] (ICLI)
OIBH	Bastak [Iran] [ICAO location identifier] (ICLI)
OIBI	Golbandi [Iran] [ICAO location identifier] (ICLI)
OIBK	Kish Island [Iran] [ICAO location identifier] (ICLI)
OIBL	Bandar Lengeh [Iran] [ICAO location identifier] (ICLI)
OIBN	Borazjan [Iran] [ICAO location identifier] (ICLI)
OIBQ	Khark Island [Iran] [ICAO location identifier] (ICLI)
OIBS	Siri Island [Iran] [ICAO location identifier] (ICLI)
OIBT	Bushehr [Iran] [ICAO location identifier] (ICLI)
OIBV	Lavan Island [Iran] [ICAO location identifier] (ICLI)
OIBX	Tonb Island [Iran] [ICAO location identifier] (ICLI)
OIC	Municipal Income Opportunity Trust [Formerly, Allstate Municipal Income Opportunities Trust] [NYSE symbol] (SPSG)
OIC	Norwich, NY [Location identifier] [FAA] (FAAL)
OIC	Objective Individual Combat Weapon
OIC	Ocean Information Center (SAUS)
OIC	Oceanographic Instrumentation Center [Navy]
OIC	Oceans Institute of Canada (IRC)
OIC	Octyl Isocyanate [Organic chemistry]
OIC	Odyssey Institute Corp. (EA)
OIC	Offer in Compromise [IRS]
OIC	Office of Independent Counsel [U.S. Department of Justice] (BARN)
OIC	Office of Industrial Cooperation [AEC]
OIC	Office of International Conferences [Department of State]
OIC	Office of International Cooperation [in CAA]
OIC	Office of the Independent Counsel (SAUS)
OIC	Office of the Insurance Commissioner (AD)
Oic	Officer-in-Charge (WDAA)
OIC	Officer-in-Charge
OIC	Ohio Improved Chesters [Initialism itself now used as name of breed of swine]
OIC	Oh, I See [Online dialogue] (IGQR)
OIC	Oil Cooler (SAUS)
OIC	Oil Industry Commission (AD)
OIC	Oil Information Committee (SAUS)
OIC	Oil-Insulated Cable (SAUS)
OIC	Oishiyama C [Japan] [Seismograph station code, US Geological Survey] (SEIS)
OIC	Okinawa Interboard Committee [Absorbed by Interboard Committee for Christian Work in Japan] (EA)
OIC	Oklahoma Intercollegiate Conference (PSS)
OIC	On-line Instrument and Control (SAUS)
OIC	Online Instrument and Control Program [Computer science] (NRCH)
OIC	On-line Instrumentation Coordinator (SAUS)

OIC	Only-in-Chain (ELAL)
OIC	Ontario International Corporation (SAUS)
OIC	Operational Intelligence Centre [British military] (DMA)
OIC	Operations Instrumentation Coordinator [NASA] (KSC)
OIC	Operator's Instruction Chart
OIC	Opportunities Industrialization Center (OICC)
OIC	Optical Integrated Circuit (IEEE)
OIC	Optimized Image Compression (PCM)
oic	Orbiter Integrated Checkout [NASA] (NAKS)
OIC	Orbiter Integrated Checkout [NASA] (NASA)
O-I-C	Order-in-Council [Canada]
OIC	Order of the Imitation of Christ (TOCD)
oic	Order of the Imitation of Christ (TOCD)
O-I-C	Organisation Interafricaine du Cafe [Inter-African Coffee Organization] [French] (AD)
OIC	Organisation Internationale Catholique
OIC	Organisation Internationale du Commerce [International Organization for Commerce] [France]
OIC	Organization for International Cooperation (EA)
OIC	Organization of Islamic Countries [Intergovernmental group]
OIC	Organization of the Islamic Conference [See also OCI] [Jeddah, Saudi Arabia] (EAIO)
OIC	Overseas Investment Commission (AD)
OICA	Azna [Iran] [ICAO location identifier] (ICLI)
OICA	Ontario Institute of Chartered Accountants [Canada] (DD)
OICA	OPLAN Implementation Capabilities Report (SAUS)
OIC/A	Opportunities Industrialization Centers of America (EA)
OICA	Oregon Independent Colleges Association (SAUS)
OICA	Organisation Internationale des Constructeurs d'Automobiles (EAIO)
OICAP	Ocean Industries Capital Assistance Program (SAUS)
OICB	Baneh [Iran] [ICAO location identifier] (ICLI)
OICC	Bakhtaran [Iran] [ICAO location identifier] (ICLI)
OICC	Officer-in-Charge of Construction [Navy]
OICC	Ontario Institute of Chartered Cartographers (SAUS)
OICC	Operational Intelligence Coordination Center (COE)
OICC	Operational Intelligence Crisis Center [Defense Intelligence Agency] (DOMA)
OICC	Operations Interface Control Chart (KSC)
OICC	Organization of Islamic Capitals and Cities (EA)
OICCD	Oblique Imaging Charged Couple Device (ACAE)
OICCFE	Officer-in-Charge of Construction, Far East [Navy]
OICCSOWESPAC	Officer-in-Charge of Construction, South Western Pacific (DNAB)
OICCSW	Objective Individual Combat & Crew Served Weapon (SAUS)
OICD	Abdanan [Iran] [ICAO location identifier] (ICLI)
OICD	Office of International Cooperation and Development [Department of Agriculture]
OICD	On-Board Information Compression Device [Aerospace]
OICE	Bijar [Iran] [ICAO location identifier] (ICLI)
O ICE	Old Icelandic [Language, etc.] (ROG)
OIcel	Old Icelandic [Language] (BARN)
OICETS	Optical Inter-Orbit Communications Engineering Test Satellite [Sponsored by European Space Agency and Japan Space Agency]
OICF	Naft-E-Shah [Iran] [ICAO location identifier] (ICLI)
OICF	Oklahoma Independent College Foundation (AD)
OICF	Oregon Independent College Foundation (AD)
OICG	Ghasre-Shirin [Iran] [ICAO location identifier] (ICLI)
OICH	Islam Abad [Iran] [ICAO location identifier] (ICLI)
OICI	Ilam [Iran] [ICAO location identifier] (ICLI)
OICI	Oficina Internacional Catolica de la Infancia [International Catholic Child Bureau]
OICI	Organizacion Ibero-Americana de Cooperacion Intermunicipal [Ibero-American Municipal Organization] (EAIO)
OICI	Organizacion Interamericana de Cooperacion [Inter-American Cooperation Organ ization] [Spanish] (AD)
OICI	Organizacion Interamericana de Cooperacion Intermunicipal [Interamerican Municipal Organization]
OICJ	Boroujerd [Iran] [ICAO location identifier] (ICLI)
OICJ	Office of International Criminal Justice (AD)
OICK	Khorram Abad [Iran] [ICAO location identifier] (ICLI)
OICL	Sare Pole Zahab [Iran] [ICAO location identifier] (ICLI)
OICM	Mehran [Iran] [ICAO location identifier] (ICLI)
OICM	Organisation Internationale pour la Cooperation Medicale [International Organization for Medical Cooperation]
OICMA	Organisation Internationale Contre le Criquet Migrateur Africain [International African Migratory Locust Organization] (EAIO)
OICMATU	Officer-in-Charge, Marine Air Traffic Control Unit (DNAB)
OICMILDEPT	Officer-in-Charge, Military Department (DNAB)
OICNA	Overseas Indian Congress of North America [Defunct] (EA)
OICO	Office of Integration and Checkout
OICO	OI Corp. [NASDAQ symbol] (NQ)
OICO	OI Corporation (SAUS)
OICO	Songhor [Iran] [ICAO location identifier] (ICLI)
OI Corp	OI Corp. [Associated Press] (SAG)
OICP	Office of International Communications Policy (NITA)
OICP	Paveh [Iran] [ICAO location identifier] (ICLI)
OICQ	Takab [Iran] [ICAO location identifier] (ICLI)
OICR	Dehloran [Iran] [ICAO location identifier] (ICLI)
OICR	Office of International Commercial Relations [Department of State]
OICR	Ontario Institute for Computer Research (SAUS)
OICR	Operational Intelligence Collection Requirement (SAUS)
OICR	Operation, Implementation, Capabilities Report (SAUS)
OICS	Office of Interoceanic Canal Studies [National Oceanic and Atmospheric Administration] (NOAA)

OICS .... Operational Intelligence Collection System
OICS .... Organe International de Controle des Stupefiants [*International Narcotics Control Board*] (EAIO)
OICS .... Sanandaj [*Iran*] [*ICAO location identifier*] (ICLI)
OICT .... Bakhtaran [*Iran*] [*ICAO location identifier*] (ICLI)
OICTP .... Outline Individual and Collective Training Plan [*Army*]
OICW .... Objective Individual Combat Weapon [*Army*] (INF)
OICW .... Opportunities Industrial Center West (SAUS)
OICY .... Malavi [*Iran*] [*ICAO location identifier*] (ICLI)
OICZ .... Aligoodarz [*Iran*] [*ICAO location identifier*] (ICLI)
OID .... Object Identification (AAEL)
OID .... Object Identifier [*Computer science*]
OID .... Object Interaction Diagram (AAEL)
OID .... Octal Identifier [*Computer science*] (KSC)
OID .... Ofensiva de Izquierda Democratica [*Offensive of the Democratic Left*] [*Bolivia*] (PPW)
OID .... Operator Instruction Document (TIMI)
OID .... Optoelectronic Imaging Device
OID .... Order Initiated Distribution
OID .... Organism Identification Number [*Microbiology*] (DAVI)
oid .... Original Issue Discount (AD)
OID .... Original Issue Discount [*Business term*]
OID .... Original Issue Discount Obligations (TDOB)
OID .... Outline and Installation Drawing
OID .... Ovine Interdigital Dermatitis (SAUS)
OIDA .... Optoelectronics Industry Development Association (SAUS)
OIDA .... Ordnance Industrial Data Agency
OIDA .... Original Image Data Array (SAUS)
OIDC .... Object Identifier Component (SAUS)
OIDC .... Oil Importing and Developing Country
OIDC .... Ontario Industrial Development Council (SAUS)
OIDI .... Optically Isolated Digital Input
OI DIV .... Operations/Combat Information Center Division (DNAB)
OIDL .... Object Interface Definition Language [*Computer science*]
OIDMM .... Office Internationale de Documentation de Medecine Militaire [*International Office of Documentation on Military Medicine - IODMM*] (EAIO)
OIDO .... Ocean Industries Development Office (SAUS)
OIDO .... Original Issue Discount Obligations (EBF)
OIDP .... Oracle Internet Development Pack (SAUS)
OIDP .... Oversea Internal Defense Policy [*Army*] (AABC)
OIDPS .... Oversea Intelligence Data Processing System
OIDT .... Operator Interactive Display Terminal (SAUS)
OIE .... Central Library, Albright & Wilson Americas, Islington, Ontario [*Library symbol*] [*National Library of Canada*] (NLC)
OIE .... Office International des Epizooties [*International Office of Epizootics*] [*Research center*] [*France*] (IRC)
OIE .... Office of Indian Education [*Department of Education*] (GFGA)
OIE .... Office of Inspection and Enforcement [*Nuclear Regulatory Commission*]
OIE .... Office of International Epizootics (AD)
O/I/E .... Offsites/Infrastructure/Establishment [*Engineering*]
OIE .... Operational Independent Evaluator
OIE .... Optical Incremental Encoder
OIE .... Optical Infrared Equipment
OIE .... Organisation Internationale des Employeurs [*International Organization of Employers*]
OIE .... Overseas Investment Exchange (NUMA)
OIEA .... Office of Integrated Environmental Analysis (SAUS)
OIEA .... Organismo Internacional de Energia Atomica [*International Atomic Energy Agency*] [*Spanish*] [*United Nations*] (DUND)
OIEC .... Office International de l'Enseignement Catholique [*Catholic International Education Office - CIEO*] (EAIO)
OIEO .... Ocean Instrumentation Engineering Office [*National Oceanic and Atmospheric Administration*] (MSC)
OIER .... Office of International Economic Research (AD)
OIER .... Official Intermodal Equipment Register [*Intermodal Publishing Co.*] [*Information service or system*] (IID)
OIER .... Operational Information Exchange Requirement (SAUS)
OIES .... Office of Interdisciplinary Earth Studies (SAUS)
OIES .... Oxford Institute for Energy Studies [*British*]
OIESA .... Office of International Economic and Social Affairs [*Department of State*]
OIF .... American Opportunity Income [*NYSE symbol*] (SPSG)
OIF .... Amer Opportunity Income [*NYSE symbol*] (TTSB)
OIF .... Iroquois Falls Public Library, Ontario [*Library symbol*] [*National Library of Canada*] (NLC)
OIF .... Observed Intrinsic Frequency [*Medicine*] (DMAA)
OIF .... Office for Intellectual Freedom [*American Library Association*]
OIF .... Office Interconnect Facility [*Computer science*] (BTTJ)
OIF .... Office of International Finance [*Department of the Treasury*]
OIF .... Oil Immersion Field (MAE)
OIF .... Optimum Index Factor (SAUS)
OIF .... Option Institute and Fellowship (EA)
OIF .... Osteogenesis Imperfecta Foundation (EA)
OIF .... Osteoinductive Factor [*Biochemistry*]
OIF .... Other Intelligence File (MCD)
OIFB .... Boroujen [*Iran*] [*ICAO location identifier*] (ICLI)
OIFC .... Ghamsar [*Iran*] [*ICAO location identifier*] (ICLI)
OIFC .... Oil-Insulated, Fan-Cooled
OIFC .... Osmonds International Fan Club (EA)
OIFD .... Ardestan [*Iran*] [*ICAO location identifier*] (ICLI)
OIFE .... Outside-In Flow Element [*Automotive engineering*]
OIFF .... Soffeh [*Iran*] [*ICAO location identifier*] (ICLI)
OIFG .... Golpaygan [*Iran*] [*ICAO location identifier*] (ICLI)
OIFH .... Esfahan [*Iran*] [*ICAO location identifier*] (ICLI)
OIFI .... Semirom [*Iran*] [*ICAO location identifier*] (ICLI)
OIFIG .... Official Irish FORTH [*Programming language*] Interest Group (EAIO)
OIFJ .... Najaf Abad [*Iran*] [*ICAO location identifier*] (ICLI)
OIFK .... Kashan [*Iran*] [*ICAO location identifier*] (ICLI)
OIFL .... Felavarjan [*Iran*] [*ICAO location identifier*] (ICLI)
OIFM .... Esfahan [*Iran*] [*ICAO location identifier*] (ICLI)
OIFN .... Naein [*Iran*] [*ICAO location identifier*] (ICLI)
OIFO .... Khomeini Shahr [*Iran*] [*ICAO location identifier*] (ICLI)
OIFOC .... Oil-Immersed, Forced-Oil-Cooled (SAUS)
OIFR .... Ghomsheh [*Iran*] [*ICAO location identifier*] (ICLI)
OIFS .... Shahrekord [*Iran*] [*ICAO location identifier*] (ICLI)
OIFT .... Esfahan [*Iran*] [*ICAO location identifier*] (ICLI)
OIFU .... Fereidan [*Iran*] [*ICAO location identifier*] (ICLI)
OIFW .... Khomein [*Iran*] [*ICAO location identifier*] (ICLI)
OIFY .... Meymeh [*Iran*] [*ICAO location identifier*] (ICLI)
OIFZ .... Natanz [*Iran*] [*ICAO location identifier*] (ICLI)
OIG .... Ignace Public Library, Ontario [*Library symbol*] [*National Library of Canada*] (NLC)
OIG .... Office of the Inspector General [*Army*]
OIG .... Operations Interface Group (SAUS)
OIG .... Optically Isolated Gate (IEEE)
OIG .... Organisation Intergouvernementale [*Inter-Governmental Organization*] [*French*] (AD)
OIGA .... Astara [*Iran*] [*ICAO location identifier*] (ICLI)
OIGF .... Fouman [*Iran*] [*ICAO location identifier*] (ICLI)
OIGG .... Rasht [*Iran*] [*ICAO location identifier*] (ICLI)
OIGH .... Hashtpar [*Iran*] [*ICAO location identifier*] (ICLI)
OIGIS .... Office of the Inspector-General of Intelligence and Security [*Australia*]
OIGK .... Khailkhal [*Iran*] [*ICAO location identifier*] (ICLI)
OIGL .... Langerood [*Iran*] [*ICAO location identifier*] (ICLI)
OIGM .... Manjil [*Iran*] [*ICAO location identifier*] (ICLI)
OIGN .... Lahijan [*Iran*] [*ICAO location identifier*] (ICLI)
OIGP .... Bandar Anzali [*Iran*] [*ICAO location identifier*] (ICLI)
OIGR .... Office of Industrial Growth and Research [*of BDSA*]
OIGR .... Office of Intergovernmental Relations [*US Congress*] [*Washington, DC*] (GRD)
OIGR .... Roodsar [*Iran*] [*ICAO location identifier*] (ICLI)
OIGS .... On Indian Government Service (SAUS)
OIGT .... Rasht [*Iran*] [*ICAO location identifier*] (ICLI)
OIGU .... Roodbar [*Iran*] [*ICAO location identifier*] (ICLI)
OIH .... Oceanic Institute of Hawaii
OIH .... Oceanographic Institute of Hawaii (SAUS)
OIH .... Office of International Health [*Department of Health and Human Services*]
OIH .... Oil in Hole (SAUS)
OIH .... Ortho-Iodohippurate [*Clinical chemistry*] (AAMN)
OIH .... Ovulation-Inducing Hormone [*Endocrinology*]
OIH .... Ovulation-Producing Hormone [*Medicine*] (AD)
OIHA .... Orthoiodohippuric Acid [*Clinical chemistry*] (DAVI)
OIHA .... Takestan [*Iran*] [*ICAO location identifier*] (ICLI)
OIHB .... Asad Abad [*Iran*] [*ICAO location identifier*] (ICLI)
OIHD .... Shahzand [*Iran*] [*ICAO location identifier*] (ICLI)
OIHF .... Tafresh [*Iran*] [*ICAO location identifier*] (ICLI)
OIHG .... Kharaghan [*Iran*] [*ICAO location identifier*] (ICLI)
OIHH .... Hamadan [*Iran*] [*ICAO location identifier*] (ICLI)
OIHJ .... Avaj [*Iran*] [*ICAO location identifier*] (ICLI)
OIHM .... Malayer [*Iran*] [*ICAO location identifier*] (ICLI)
OIHN .... Nahavand [*Iran*] [*ICAO location identifier*] (ICLI)
OIHP .... Office International d'Hygiene Publique [*United Nations*]
OIHQ .... Kangavar [*Iran*] [*ICAO location identifier*] (ICLI)
OIHR .... Arak [*Iran*] [*ICAO location identifier*] (ICLI)
OIHS .... Hamadan [*Iran*] [*ICAO location identifier*] (ICLI)
OIHT .... Hamadan [*Iran*] [*ICAO location identifier*] (ICLI)
OIHU .... Tooyserkan [*Iran*] [*ICAO location identifier*] (ICLI)
OII .... Occupational Injury/Illness (SAUS)
OII .... Oceaneering International, Inc. [*NYSE symbol*] (SPSG)
OII .... Office of International Investment [*Department of Commerce*]
OII .... Office of Invention and Innovation (AD)
OII .... Oil Investment Institute [*Washington, DC*] (EA)
OII .... Open Information Interchange (SAUS)
OII .... Operations Integration Instruction [*NASA*] (NASA)
OII .... Operations-Intelligence Interface (SAUS)
OII .... Optical Imaging Instrument (SAUS)
OII .... Ourobourus Institute (EA)
OIIA .... Abe-Ali [*Iran*] [*ICAO location identifier*] (ICLI)
OIIC .... Kushke Nosrat [*Iran*] [*ICAO location identifier*] (ICLI)
OIIC .... Oil Industry Industrial Committee [*Australia*]
OIIC .... Oil Industry Information Committee (SAUS)
OIID .... Tehran/Doshan Tappeh [*Iran*] [*ICAO location identifier*] (ICLI)
OIIE .... Abyek [*Iran*] [*ICAO location identifier*] (ICLI)
OIIF .... Firouzkouh [*Iran*] [*ICAO location identifier*] (ICLI)
OIIFDRES .... Oficina Internacional de Informacion del Frente Democratico Revolucionario de ElSalvador [*International Information Office of the Democratic Revolutionary Front of El Salvador - IIODRFES*] [*San Jose, Costa Rica*] (EAIO)
OIIG .... Tehran/Ghaleh Morghi [*Iran*] [*ICAO location identifier*] (ICLI)
OIIH .... Mahallat [*Iran*] [*ICAO location identifier*] (ICLI)
OIII .... Tehran/Mehrabad International [*Iran*] [*ICAO location identifier*] (ICLI)
OIIJ .... Karaj [*Iran*] [*ICAO location identifier*] (ICLI)
OIIK .... Ghazvin [*Iran*] [*ICAO location identifier*] (ICLI)
OIIM .... Khoram Dareh [*Iran*] [*ICAO location identifier*] (ICLI)
OIIM .... Overseas Issues Identification Meeting (DNAB)
OIIN .... Delijan [*Iran*] [*ICAO location identifier*] (ICLI)
OIIQ .... Ghom [*Iran*] [*ICAO location identifier*] (ICLI)

OIIR	Garmsar [*Iran*] [*ICAO location identifier*] (ICLI)
OIIS	Semnan [*Iran*] [*ICAO location identifier*] (ICLI)
OIIT	Tehran [*Iran*] [*ICAO location identifier*] (ICLI)
OIIU	Damghan [*Iran*] [*ICAO location identifier*] (ICLI)
OIIV	Seveh [*Iran*] [*ICAO location identifier*] (ICLI)
OIIW	Varamin [*Iran*] [*ICAO location identifier*] (ICLI)
OIIX	Tehran [*Iran*] [*ICAO location identifier*] (ICLI)
OIJ	Octarius Duos [*Two Pints*] [*Pharmacy*] (ROG)
OIJ	Organisation Internationale des Journalistes [*International Organization of Journalists - IOJ*] (EAIO)
OIJSS	Octarios Duobus cum Semisse [*Two and a Half Pints*] [*Pharmacy*] (ROG)
OIK	Ocean City, MD [*Location identifier*] [*FAA*] (FAAL)
OIKA	Shahre Babak [*Iran*] [*ICAO location identifier*] (ICLI)
OIKB	Bandar Abbas [*Iran*] [*ICAO location identifier*] (ICLI)
OIKD	Darband/Ravar [*Iran*] [*ICAO location identifier*] (ICLI)
OIKE	Anar [*Iran*] [*ICAO location identifier*] (ICLI)
OIKF	Baft [*Iran*] [*ICAO location identifier*] (ICLI)
OIKI	Bandar Khamir [*Iran*] [*ICAO location identifier*] (ICLI)
OIKJ	Jiroft [*Iran*] [*ICAO location identifier*] (ICLI)
OIKK	Kerman [*Iran*] [*ICAO location identifier*] (ICLI)
OIKM	Bam [*Iran*] [*ICAO location identifier*] (ICLI)
OIKN	Narmashir [*Iran*] [*ICAO location identifier*] (ICLI)
OIKO	Minab [*Iran*] [*ICAO location identifier*] (ICLI)
OIKQ	Gheshm Island [*Iran*] [*ICAO location identifier*] (ICLI)
OIKR	Rafsanjan [*Iran*] [*ICAO location identifier*] (ICLI)
OIKS	Shahdad [*Iran*] [*ICAO location identifier*] (ICLI)
OIKT	Kerman [*Iran*] [*ICAO location identifier*] (ICLI)
OIKU	Hengam Island [*Iran*] [*ICAO location identifier*] (ICLI)
OIKW	Kahnooj [*Iran*] [*ICAO location identifier*] (ICLI)
OIKX	Hormoz Island [*Iran*] [*ICAO location identifier*] (ICLI)
OIKY	Sirjan [*Iran*] [*ICAO location identifier*] (ICLI)
OIKZ	Zarand [*Iran*] [*ICAO location identifier*] (ICLI)
OIL	Ocelot Industries Ltd. [*Toronto Stock Exchange symbol*]
OIL	Office of Intergovernmental Liaison [*Environmental Protection Agency*] (GFGA)
OIL	Oil City, PA [*Location identifier*] [*FAA*] (FAAL)
OIL	Oklahoma Information Lines [*Oklahoma State Department of Libraries*] [*Oklahoma City*] [*Information service or system*] (IID)
OIL	Only Input Line (MHDI)
OIL	Open Individual License (SAUS)
OIL	Operation Inspection Log (AAG)
OIL	Operator Identification Language (SAUS)
OIL	Orange Indicating Lamp (SAUS)
OIL	Orange Indicating Light (MSA)
OIL	Orbital International Laboratory
OIL	Ordnance Investigation Laboratory
OIL	Outside Independent Laboratory (SAUS)
OIL	Triton Energy Corp. [*NYSE symbol*] (SPSG)
OILA	Office of International Labor Affairs [*Department of Labor*]
Oil & Gas	Oil and Gas Reporter [*A publication*] (DLA)
Oil & Gas LR	Oil and Gas Law Review [*A publication*] (DLA)
Oil & Gas Reptr	Oil and Gas Reporter [*A publication*] (DLA)
Oil & Gas Rptr	Oil and Gas Reporter [*A publication*] (DLA)
OILB	Organisation Internationale de Lutte Biologique Contre les Animaux et les Plantes Nuisibles [*International Organization for Biological Control of Noxious Animals and Plants - IOBC*] (EAIO)
OILC	Oil-Dri Corporation of America (SAUS)
Oil Colour Chemist Assoc J	Oil and Colour Chemists Association. Journal (SAUS)
OILCOM	Oil Company of Malawi (SAUS)
OILD	Occupational Immunologic Lung Disease (MELL)
OILD	Occupationally Induced Lung Disease
OilDri	Oil-Dri Corp. of America [*Associated Press*] (SAG)
OILF	Oromo Islamic Liberation Front (SAUS)
Oil Gas Compact Bull	Interstate Oil and Gas Compact Commission. Committee Bulletin (journ.) (SAUS)
Oil Gas Petrochem Equip	Oil, Gas and Petrochem Equipment (SAUS)
Oilgear	[*The*] Oilgear Co. [*Associated Press*] (SAG)
OILHM	Oil and Hazardous Material Information System (SAUS)
Oilman Wkly Newsl	Oilman Weekly Newsletter (SAUS)
OILN	Oil International Ltd. (SAUS)
oiloff	Oil Ripoff (AD)
Oil Paint Drug Rep	Oil, Paint and Drug Reporter (SAUS)
OILPOL	Convention for the Prevention of Pollution of the Sea by Oil (SAUS)
OILPOL	Convention for the Prevention of Pollution of the Sea by Oil (SAUS)
OILPOL	International Convention for the Prevention of Pollution of the Sea by Oil (SAUS)
OILREC	Oil Recovery (RIMS)
OILS	Oil Securities, Inc. (SAUS)
OILSAR	Ocean-Ice-Land Synthetic Aperture Radar (SAUS)
OILSR	Office of Interstate Land Sales Registration (AD)
OILT	Oiltight (SAUS)
OIL TURP	Oil of Turpentine (SAUS)
OIM	Office of Industrial Managers [*Navy*]
OIM	Office of Industrial Mobilization [*of BDSA*]
OIM	Office of Intergovernmental Management (OICC)
OIM	Offshore-Installation Manager [*Oil well drilling*]
OIM	On Its Merits [*British*] (ROG)
OIM	Open Information Model (VLIE)
OIM	Open systems interconnections Internet Management (SAUS)
OIM	Optical Index Modulation (VLIE)
OIM	Orbit Insertion Maneuver
OIM	Organic Insulating Material
OIM	Organizational Intermediate Maintenance [*Military*] (AFIT)

OIM	Oriental Institute Museum [*University of Chicago*] (AD)
OIM	Orientational Imaging Microscopy (AAEL)
OIM	Oshima Island [*Japan*] [*Airport symbol*] (OAG)
OIMA	Torbat-E-Jam [*Iran*] [*ICAO location identifier*] (ICLI)
OIMB	Birjand [*Iran*] [*ICAO location identifier*] (ICLI)
OIMC	Office of Information Services (AAGC)
OIMC	Sarakhs [*Iran*] [*ICAO location identifier*] (ICLI)
OIMD	Goonabad [*Iran*] [*ICAO location identifier*] (ICLI)
OIME	Esfarayen [*Iran*] [*ICAO location identifier*] (ICLI)
OIMF	Ferdous [*Iran*] [*ICAO location identifier*] (ICLI)
OIMG	Ghaen [*Iran*] [*ICAO location identifier*] (ICLI)
OIMH	Torbat-E-Heidarieh [*Iran*] [*ICAO location identifier*] (ICLI)
OIMJ	Emam Shahr [*Iran*] [*ICAO location identifier*] (ICLI)
OIMK	Nehbandan [*Iran*] [*ICAO location identifier*] (ICLI)
OIML	Janat Abad [*Iran*] [*ICAO location identifier*] (ICLI)
OIML	Organisation Internationale de Metrologie Legale [*International Organization of Legal Metrology*] (EAIO)
OIMM	Mashhad [*Iran*] [*ICAO location identifier*] (ICLI)
OIMN	Bojnord [*Iran*] [*ICAO location identifier*] (ICLI)
OIMO	Ghoochan [*Iran*] [*ICAO location identifier*] (ICLI)
OIMP	Taybad [*Iran*] [*ICAO location identifier*] (ICLI)
OIMQ	Kashmar [*Iran*] [*ICAO location identifier*] (ICLI)
OIMR	Fariman [*Iran*] [*ICAO location identifier*] (ICLI)
OIMS	Orbiter Ion Mass Spectrometer [*NASA*]
OIMS	Oscillator Instability Measurement System
OIMS	Sabzevar [*Iran*] [*ICAO location identifier*] (ICLI)
OIMSJ	Micropower/St. Joseph's High School, Islington, Ontario [*Library symbol*] [*National Library of Canada*] (NLC)
OIMT	Tabas [*Iran*] [*ICAO location identifier*] (ICLI)
OIMV	Mashhad [*Iran*] [*ICAO location identifier*] (ICLI)
OIMW	Shirvan [*Iran*] [*ICAO location identifier*] (ICLI)
OIMX	Shahr Abad [*Iran*] [*ICAO location identifier*] (ICLI)
OIMY	Neishaboor [*Iran*] [*ICAO location identifier*] (ICLI)
OIMYFC	Official International Michael York Fan Club (EA)
OIN	Oberlin, KS [*Location identifier*] [*FAA*] (FAAL)
OI-N	Office of Information, Navy
OIN	Ointment (SAUS)
OIN	Organisation Internationale de Normalisation [*International Organization for Standardization*]
OIN	Organization of International Numismatists
OIN	Osrodek Informacji Naukowej [*Scientific Information Center*] [*Polish Academy of Sciences*] [*Warsaw*] [*Information service or system*] (IID)
OINA	Amol [*Iran*] [*ICAO location identifier*] (ICLI)
OINA	Oyster Institute of North America [*Later, SINA*] (EA)
OINB	Babolsar [*Iran*] [*ICAO location identifier*] (ICLI)
OINC	Chalous [*Iran*] [*ICAO location identifier*] (ICLI)
O in C	Officer-in-Charge
OINC	Officer-in-Charge [*Navy*]
OINCABCCTC	Officer-in-Charge, Advanced Base Combat Communication Training Center [*Pearl Harbor*] [*Navy*]
OIND	Minoo Dasht [*Iran*] [*ICAO location identifier*] (ICLI)
OINE	Kalaleh [*Iran*] [*ICAO location identifier*] (ICLI)
OInF	Ferro Corp., Independence, OH [*Library symbol*] [*Library of Congress*] (LCLS)
OING	Gorgan [*Iran*] [*ICAO location identifier*] (ICLI)
OING	Organisation Internationale Non-Gouvernementale [*Non-Governmental International Organization*] [*French*] (AD)
OINH	Behshahr [*Iran*] [*ICAO location identifier*] (ICLI)
OINI	Ghaem Shahr [*Iran*] [*ICAO location identifier*] (ICLI)
OINK	Gonbad Ghabous [*Iran*] [*ICAO location identifier*] (ICLI)
Oink	One Income, No Kids [*Lifestyle classification*]
OINL	Alamdeh [*Iran*] [*ICAO location identifier*] (ICLI)
OINM	Mahmood Abad [*Iran*] [*ICAO location identifier*] (ICLI)
OINN	Noshahr [*Iran*] [*ICAO location identifier*] (ICLI)
OINO	Noor [*Iran*] [*ICAO location identifier*] (ICLI)
OINP	Azad Shahr [*Iran*] [*ICAO location identifier*] (ICLI)
OINQ	Kelardasht [*Iran*] [*ICAO location identifier*] (ICLI)
OINR	Ramsar [*Iran*] [*ICAO location identifier*] (ICLI)
OINS	Sari [*Iran*] [*ICAO location identifier*] (ICLI)
oint	Ointment (AD)
OINT	Ointment
OINT	Omni-Intersection (SAUS)
OINV	Tonkabon [*Iran*] [*ICAO location identifier*] (ICLI)
OINY	Bandar Torkaman [*Iran*] [*ICAO location identifier*] (ICLI)
OINZ	Dasht-E-Naz [*Iran*] [*ICAO location identifier*] (ICLI)
OIO	Obligated Involuntary Officers [*Used in movie "Spies Like Us"*]
OIO	Office of International Operations [*of IRS*]
OIO	Oklahomans for Indian Opportunity (AD)
OIO	Operations Integration Officer [*NASA*] (MCD)
OIOPSWL	Old Input/Output Program Status Word Location [*Computer science*] (MHDB)
OIP	Eastland, TX [*Location identifier*] [*FAA*] (FAAL)
OIP	Offical Index Period (SAUS)
OIP	Office for Information Programs (SAUS)
OIP	Office of Import Programs [*Functions transferred to Domestic and International Business Administration*] [*Department of Commerce*]
OIP	Office of Industrial Programs [*Department of Energy*]
OIP	Office of International Programs [*National Science Foundation*]
oip	Oil in Place (AD)
OIP	Oil-in-Place
OIP	Ontario Institute of Painters, Toronto [*1958*] [*Canada*] (NGC)
OIP	Operating Internal Pressure [*Nuclear energy*] (NRCH)
OIP	Operational Improvement Plan [*or Program*] [*Navy*]

OIP............	Operational Improvement Program (SAUS)
OIP............	Operational Instruction Pamphlet
OIP............	Operations Improvement Program (SAUS)
OIP............	Operations Interface Procedure (SAUS)
OIP............	Optical Image Processing (SAUS)
OIP............	Optical Image Processor
OIP............	Optical Improvement Program [Army]
OIP............	Orbital Improvement Program
OIP............	Ordnance Installation Plan (MCD)
OIP............	Organic Insulative Plastic
OIP............	Organisation Internationale de la Paleobotanique [International Organization of Paleobotany]
OIP............	Organisation Internationale de Psychophysiologie [International Organization of Psychophysiology - IOP] (EAIO)
OIP............	Organisation Internationale pour le Progres [Austria] (EAIO)
OIP............	Organizacion Iberoamericana de Pilotos [Ibero-American Organization of Pilots - IOP] [Mexico City, Mexico] (EAIO)
OIP............	Organizing Interstitial Pneumonia [Medicine]
oip............	Oxford India Paper (AD)
OIPA..........	Ortho-Isopropylaniline [Organic chemistry]
OIPAAR.......	Office of Industrial Personnel Access Authorization Review [Army] (AABC)
OIPC.........	Organisation Internationale de Police Criminelle [International Criminal Police Organization] [French] (AD)
OIPC	Organisation Internationale de Protection Civile [International Civil Defense Organization - ICDO] (EAIO)
OIPCFC......	Official International Peter Coyote Fan Club (EA)
OIPD	Operations Interface Procedure Document (ACAE)
OIPEEC	Organisation Internationale pour l'Etude de l'Endurance des Cables [International Organization for the Study of the Endurance of Wire Ropes - IOSEWR] (EAIO)
OIPH	Office of International Public Health (AD)
Oipi...........	One Income plus Inheritance [Lifestyle classification]
OIPMT	Optimum Insect Pest Management Trial [Department of Agriculture]
OIPO	Optimum Installation Position Only (MCD)
OIPR	Office of Information, Publications, and Reports [Department of Labor]
OIPR	Office of Intelligence Policy and Review [U.S. Department of Justice] (BARN)
OIPS	Optical Image Processing System
OIPT..........	Overarching Integrated Product Team [Army]
OIQ	Ordre des Ingenieurs du Quebec [Canada] (DD)
OIQ	Sioux City, IA [Location identifier] [FAA] (FAAL)
OIR	Iroquois Public Library, Ontario [Library symbol] [National Library of Canada] (BIB)
OIR	Office of Indian Rights [Department of Justice]
OIR	Office of Industrial Relations [Superseded, 1966, by Office of Civilian Manpower] [Navy]
OIR	Office of Industrial Research [University of Manitoba] [Canada] [Research center] (RCD)
OIR	Office of Industry Relations (SAUS)
OIR	Office of Institutional Relations [Energy Research and Development Administration]
OIR	Office of Inter-American Radio (AD)
OIR	Office of International Research [National Institutes of Health]
OIR	Office of International Resources [Department of State]
OIR	Official Information Request (SAUS)
OIR	Okushiri [Japan] [Airport symbol] (OAG)
OIr	Old Irish (AD)
OIr	Old Irish [Language, etc.]
OIR	Online Information Retrieval Ltd. [Information service or system] [Defunct] (IID)
OIR	Open Item Review (KSC)
OIR	Operational and Information Requirements (SAUS)
OIR	Operations Integration Review (NASA)
OIR	Orbiter Infrared Radiometer [NASA]
OIR	Organisation Internationale de Radiodiffusion [International Radio Organization] [Later, OIRT]
OIR	Other Intelligence Requirements [Army] (MCD)
OIR	Slov-Air [Slovakia] [ICAO designator] (FAAC)
OIRA	Office of Industrial Resource Administration (AAGC)
OIRA	Office of Information and Regulatory Affairs [Office of Management and Budget]
OIRA	Officials of the Irish Republican Army [Northern Ireland]
OIran	Old Iranian (SAUS)
OIRB	Oregon Insurance Rating Bureau (AD)
OIRCA	Ontario Industrial Roofing Contractors Association (SAUS)
OIRD	Object-to-Image Receptor Distance [Radiology] (DAVI)
OIRE	Optical Infrared Equipment
OIRM	Office and Industrial Records Management (AD)
OIRM	Office of Information Resources Management [General Services Administration]
OIR-N.........	Office of Industrial Relations, Navy [Superseded, 1966, by Office of Civilian Manpower]
OIRS	Occupational Interest Rating Scale [Vocational guidance test]
OIRS	Operation and Inspection Route Sheet (DNAB)
OIRSA	Organismo Internacional Regional de Sanidad Agropecuaria [Regional International Organization of Plant Protection and Animal Health] [El Salvador]
OIRT	Organisation Internationale de Radiodiffusion et Television [International Radio and Television Organization] [Formerly, OIR] (EAIO)
OIRTD	Office of Industrial Relations and Technology Development (SAUS)
OIS...........	Obstacle Identification Surface [Aviation] (DA)
OIS...........	Occupational Information System [Department of Labor]

OIS...........	Occupational Interest Survey [Aptitude test]
OIS...........	Office of Industrial Security [DoD]
OIS...........	Office of Information Services [Council of State Governments] [Lexington, KY]
OIS...........	Office of Information Systems [Social and Rehabilitation Service, HEW]
OIS...........	Office of International Services [Red Cross]
OIS...........	Office of Investigatory Services (SAUS)
OIS...........	Officer of Information Service (SAUS)
OIS...........	Oishiyama [Japan] [Seismograph station code, US Geological Survey] (SEIS)
OIS...........	OIS Optical Imaging Systems, Inc. [Associated Press] (SAG)
OIS...........	Oncology Information Service [University of Leeds] [England] [Information service or system] (IID)
OIS...........	Operating Information System [Army]
OIS...........	Operational Information Service (SAUS)
OIS...........	Operational Insertion System
OIS...........	Operational Instruction Sheet (ACAE)
OIS...........	Operational Instrumentation System
OIS...........	Operational Intercommunication System [NASA] (KSC)
ois...........	Operational Intercommunication System (NAKS)
OIS...........	Opium Investigation Service (SAUS)
OIS...........	Optical Image Sensor
OIS...........	Optical Imaging Systems (RDA)
OIS...........	Optical Information Storage (SAUS)
OIS...........	Optical Information System [Computer science]
OIS...........	Orbiter Insertion Stage (SAUS)
ois...........	Orbiter Instrumentation System [NASA] (NAKS)
OIS...........	Orbiter Instrumentation Systems [NASA] (MCD)
OIS...........	Orbit Injection System (ACAE)
OIS...........	Osteopathic Information Service (SAUS)
OIS...........	Ounce-Inches per Second (IAA)
OIS...........	Output Information Signal (SAUS)
OIS...........	Overseas Investors Services (AD)
OIS...........	Oxford Institute of Statistics (SAUS)
OIS...........	Oxygen Isotope Stage (QUAC)
OIS...........	WWW Operational Information Service (SAUS)
OISA	Abadeh [Iran] [ICAO location identifier] (ICLI)
OISA	Office of International Science Activities [National Science Foundation]
OISA	Office of International Scientific Affairs (AD)
OIS & T.......	Office of Information Systems and Telecommunications [Veterans Administration] (TSSD)
OISB	Bavanat [Iran] [ICAO location identifier] (ICLI)
OISC	Ardakan-E-Fars [Iran] [ICAO location identifier] (ICLI)
OISC	Oil-Insulated, Self-Cooling
OISCA	Organization for Industrial, Spiritual and Cultural Advancement (SAUS)
OISCA	Organization for Industrial, Spiritual, and Cultural Advancement International [Tokyo, Japan] (EAIO)
OISD	Darab [Iran] [ICAO location identifier] (ICLI)
OISDG.........	Ingleside Branch, Stormont, Dundas, and Glengarry County Library, Ontario [Library symbol] [National Library of Canada] (BIB)
OISE..........	Estahbanat [Iran] [ICAO location identifier] (ICLI)
OISE..........	Office Information System Equipment (SAUS)
OISE..........	Office of Industrial Security, Europe [DoD]
OISE..........	Ontario Institute for Studies in Education [University of Toronto] [Research center] (RCD)
OISF..........	Fasa [Iran] [ICAO location identifier] (ICLI)
OISH	Farashband [Iran] [ICAO location identifier] (ICLI)
OISI	Dehbid [Iran] [ICAO location identifier] (ICLI)
OISI	Office of Industrial Security, International [DoD] (MCD)
OISI	Ophthalmic Imaging Sys [NASDAQ symbol] (TTSB)
OISI	Ophthalmic Imaging Systems, Inc. [NASDAQ symbol] (SAG)
OIS/IGP.......	Office Information System Intelligent Gateway Processor (SAUS)
OISILGR.......	Office of Industry and State and Local Government Relations (SAUS)
OISJ..........	Jahrom [Iran] [ICAO location identifier] (ICLI)
OISK	Kazeroun [Iran] [ICAO location identifier] (ICLI)
OISL	Lar [Iran] [ICAO location identifier] (ICLI)
OISLGR........	Office of Industry and State and Local Government Relations [Energy Research and Development Administration]
OISM	Mamassani [Iran] [ICAO location identifier] (ICLI)
OISN	Neiriz [Iran] [ICAO location identifier] (ICLI)
OISP	Overseas Internal Security Program [Army]
OISP	Persepolis/Marvdasht [Iran] [ICAO location identifier] (ICLI)
OISQ	Ghir/Karzin [Iran] [ICAO location identifier] (ICLI)
OISR	Lamerd [Iran] [ICAO location identifier] (ICLI)
OISR	Office of Interstate Sales Registration [HUD]
OISR	Open Item Status Report (NASA)
OISRU........	Office of Intergovernmental Science and Research Utilization [National Science Foundation]
OISS	Office of Information Systems and Services (AAGC)
OISS	Online Information Search Service [Computer science] (AD)
OISS	Operational Intelligence Support System (MCD)
OISS	Organizacion Iberoamericana de Seguridad Social [Ibero-American Social Security Organization]
OISS	Shiraz/International [Iran] [ICAO location identifier] (ICLI)
OISSP	Office of Interim Space Station Program [NASA]
OIST..........	Operator Integration Shakedown Test
OIST..........	Shiraz [Iran] [ICAO location identifier] (ICLI)
OISTV	Organisation Internationale pour la Science et la Technique du Vide [International Organization for Vacuum Science and Technology] [French] (AD)
OISU	Abarghou [Iran] [ICAO location identifier] (ICLI)
OISW	Kohkiloyeh [Iran] [ICAO location identifier] (ICLI)

OISX	Khonj [*Iran*] [*ICAO location identifier*] (ICLI)
OISY	Yasouj [*Iran*] [*ICAO location identifier*] (ICLI)
OISZ	Firouzabad [*Iran*] [*ICAO location identifier*] (ICLI)
OIT	Object Identification Test
OIT	Object Identifier Tree (SAUS)
OIT	Oblique-Incidence Transmission
OIT	Office of Industrial Technologies (SAUS)
OIT	Office of International Trade [*Department of Commerce*]
O i T	Officer in Training (AD)
OIT	Office Software Development & Information Technology (SAUS)
OIT	Oil Immersion Test (MELL)
OIT	Oil Interceptor Trap
OIT	Oita [*Japan*] [*Airport symbol*] (OAG)
OIT	Oita [*Japan*] [*Seismograph station code, US Geological Survey*] (SEIS)
O It	Old Italian (AD)
O IT	Old Italian [*Language, etc.*] (ROG)
OIT	Ontario Ministry of Industry, Trade, and Technology [*UTLAS symbol*]
OIT	Operational Instruction Title (ACAE)
OIT	Operator Interface Terminal (MCD)
OIT	Optical Image Terminal [*Computer science*] (VLIE)
OIT	Optical Information Transfer (SAUS)
OIT	Optimum Insulation Thickness (DICI)
OIT	Orbiter Integrated Test [*NASA*] (NASA)
OIT	Oregon Institute of Technology, Klamath Falls, OR [*OCLC symbol*] (OCLC)
OIT	Organic Integrity Test [*Psychology*]
OIT	Organisation Internationale du Travail [*International Labor Organization*] [*French United Nations*] (EAIO)
OIT	Organizacion Internacional del Trabajo [*International Labor Organization*] [*Spanish*] [*United Nations*] (DUND)
OIT	Organization Iberoamericaine de Television (NTCM)
OITA	Office of International Tax Affairs [*Department of the Treasury*]
OITA	Sarab [*Iran*] [*ICAO location identifier*] (ICLI)
OITAF-NACS	Organizzazione Internazionale dei Trasporti a Fune [*International Organization for Transportation by Rope*] - North American Continental Section (EA)
OITB	Mahabad [*Iran*] [*ICAO location identifier*] (ICLI)
OITC	Officer-in-Tactical Command (SAUS)
OITC	Sardasht [*Iran*] [*ICAO location identifier*] (ICLI)
OITD	Marand [*Iran*] [*ICAO location identifier*] (ICLI)
OITDA	Optoelectronic Industry and Technology Development Association [*Japan*]
OITDS	Operations and Intelligence Tactical Data Systems (MCD)
OITF	Office of International Trade and Finance [*Department of State*]
OITF	Office of International Trade Fairs [*Department of Commerce*]
OITF	Organisation Intergouvernementale pour les Transports Internationaux Ferroviaires [*Intergovernmental Organization for International Carriage by Rail*] (EAIO)
OITG	Naghadeh [*Iran*] [*ICAO location identifier*] (ICLI)
OITH	Khaneh/Piranshahr [*Iran*] [*ICAO location identifier*] (ICLI)
OITI	Mianeh [*Iran*] [*ICAO location identifier*] (ICLI)
OITJ	Julfa [*Iran*] [*ICAO location identifier*] (ICLI)
OITK	Khoy [*Iran*] [*ICAO location identifier*] (ICLI)
OITL	Outdoor-Indoor Transmission Loss (SAUS)
OITM	Maragheh [*Iran*] [*ICAO location identifier*] (ICLI)
OITN	Meshgin Shahr [*Iran*] [*ICAO location identifier*] (ICLI)
OITO	Mian Do Ab [*Iran*] [*ICAO location identifier*] (ICLI)
OITP	Office for Information Technology Policy [*American Library Association*]
OITP	Office of International Trade Promotion [*Department of State*]
OITP	Ohio Industrial Training Program
OITP	Parsabad/Moghan [*Iran*] [*ICAO location identifier*] (ICLI)
OITQ	Ahar [*Iran*] [*ICAO location identifier*] (ICLI)
OITR	Uromiyeh [*Iran*] [*ICAO location identifier*] (ICLI)
OITS	Saghez [*Iran*] [*ICAO location identifier*] (ICLI)
OITT	Outpulser, Identifier, Trunk Test
OITT	Tabriz [*Iran*] [*ICAO location identifier*] (ICLI)
OITT Frame	Outpulse Identifier Trunk Test Frame (SAUS)
OITU	Makou [*Iran*] [*ICAO location identifier*] (ICLI)
OITV	Tabriz [*Iran*] [*ICAO location identifier*] (ICLI)
OITW	Azar Shahr [*Iran*] [*ICAO location identifier*] (ICLI)
OITX	Sareskand [*Iran*] [*ICAO location identifier*] (ICLI)
OITY	Marivan [*Iran*] [*ICAO location identifier*] (ICLI)
OITZ	Zanjan [*Iran*] [*ICAO location identifier*] (ICLI)
OIU	Office Interface Unit [*Computer science*] (VLIE)
OIU	Ogaden Islamic Union (SAUS)
OIU	Operator Interface Unit [*Computer science*]
OIU	Optical Image Unit [*Computer science*] (VLIE)
OIUC	Optical Infrared Ultraviolet Communications (ACAE)
OIUC	Oriental Institute of the University of Chicago (SAUS)
OIUCSAOC	Oriental Institute. University of Chicago. Studies in Ancient Oriental Civilization (SAUS)
OIUS	Optical Infrared Ultraviolet Surveillance (ACAE)
OIV	Object Idenitfier Value (SAUS)
OIV	Octarios Quatior [*Four Pints*] [*Pharmacy*] (ROG)
OIV	Office International de la Vigne et du Vin [*International Vine and Wine Office*] (EAIO)
OIV	Overhead Inlet Valve [*Automotive engineering*]
OIV	Oxidizer Isolation Valve (MCD)
oiv	Oxidizer Isolation Valve (NAKS)
OIVA	127th Infantry Veterans Association (EA)
oivs	Orbiter Interface Verification Set [*NASA*] (NAKS)
OIVS	Orbiter Interface Verification Set [*NASA*] (NASA)
OIVV	Office Internationale de la Vigne et du Vin [*International Office of Vines and Wines*] [*French*] (AD)
OIW	Oceanographic Institute of Washington [*Marine science*] (MSC)
OIW	Oceanographic Institute Wellington New Zealand (AD)
OIW	Office of Indigenous Women [*Australia*]
OIW	Oiwake [*Japan*] [*Seismograph station code, US Geological Survey*] [*Closed*] (SEIS)
OIW	Open Information Warehouse (SAUS)
OIW	Open systems environment Implementors Workshop (SAUS)
OIW	Order of the Indian Wars (EA)
OIW	OSI Implementors Workshop (SAUS)
OIWC	Oil-Immersed, Water-Cooled (SAUS)
OIWC	Oil-Insulated, Water-Cooled
OIWG	Operations-Intelligence Working Group (SAUS)
OIWG	Operations Interface Working Group (ACAE)
OIWP	Oil Industry Working Party (AD)
OIWR	Office of Indian Water Rights [*Bureau of Indian Affairs*]
OIX	Ottawa, IL [*Location identifier*] [*FAA*] (FAAL)
OIYA	Ardakan-E-Yazd [*Iran*] [*ICAO location identifier*] (ICLI)
OIYB	Bafgh [*Iran*] [*ICAO location identifier*] (ICLI)
OIYD	Dehshir [*Iran*] [*ICAO location identifier*] (ICLI)
OIYF	Taft [*Iran*] [*ICAO location identifier*] (ICLI)
OIYK	Khor/Jandagh [*Iran*] [*ICAO location identifier*] (ICLI)
OIYM	Mehriz [*Iran*] [*ICAO location identifier*] (ICLI)
OIYN	Khore Beyabanak [*Iran*] [*ICAO location identifier*] (ICLI)
OIYQ	Khezr Abad [*Iran*] [*ICAO location identifier*] (ICLI)
OIYT	Yazd [*Iran*] [*ICAO location identifier*] (ICLI)
OIYY	Yazd [*Iran*] [*ICAO location identifier*] (ICLI)
OIYZ	Ashkezar [*Iran*] [*ICAO location identifier*] (ICLI)
OIZA	Jalagh [*Iran*] [*ICAO location identifier*] (ICLI)
OIZB	Zabol [*Iran*] [*ICAO location identifier*] (ICLI)
OIZC	Chah Bahar/Konarak [*Iran*] [*ICAO location identifier*] (ICLI)
OIZD	Dashtyari [*Iran*] [*ICAO location identifier*] (ICLI)
OIZG	Ghasre Ghand [*Iran*] [*ICAO location identifier*] (ICLI)
OIZH	Zahedan [*Iran*] [*ICAO location identifier*] (ICLI)
OIZI	Iran Shahr [*Iran*] [*ICAO location identifier*] (ICLI)
OIZJ	Jask [*Iran*] [*ICAO location identifier*] (ICLI)
OIZK	Khash [*Iran*] [*ICAO location identifier*] (ICLI)
OIZL	Zabolee [*Iran*] [*ICAO location identifier*] (ICLI)
OIZM	Mirjaveh [*Iran*] [*ICAO location identifier*] (ICLI)
OIZN	Bazman [*Iran*] [*ICAO location identifier*] (ICLI)
OIZO	Sarbaz [*Iran*] [*ICAO location identifier*] (ICLI)
OIZP	Bampoor [*Iran*] [*ICAO location identifier*] (ICLI)
OIZR	Bask [*Iran*] [*ICAO location identifier*] (ICLI)
OIZS	Saravan [*Iran*] [*ICAO location identifier*] (ICLI)
OIZT	Zahedan [*Iran*] [*ICAO location identifier*] (ICLI)
OIZY	Nik-Shahr [*Iran*] [*ICAO location identifier*] (ICLI)
OJ	Air Texana [*ICAO designator*] (AD)
OJ	Jackson Public Library, Jackson, OH [*Library symbol*] [*Library of Congress*] (LCLS)
OJ	Obstructive Jaundice [*Medicine*] (MELL)
OJ	Official Journal (HEAS)
OJ	Ohne Jahr [*Without Date of Publication*] [*Bibliography*] [*German*]
OJ	Ohne Jahr [*Without Year*] [*German*] (AD)
OJ	Open Joint (SAUS)
oj	Open-Joint (AD)
OJ	Open-Joisted [*Technical drawings*]
OJ	Open Web Joist [*Technical drawings*]
OJ	Operation Joshua (EA)
OJ	Opium Joint [*Slang*]
OJ	Orange Co. [*NYSE symbol*] (SPSG)
oj	Orange Juice (AD)
OJ	Orange Juice
OJ	Order of Jamaica
OJ	Orenthal James [*Given names of football player O. J. Simpson*]
OJ	Oriental Pearl Airways Ltd. (SAUS)
OJ	Originating Junctor [*Telecommunications*] (TEL)
OJ	Orthomode Junction [*Electronics*]
OJ	Orthoplast Jacket [*Orthopedics*] (DAVI)
OJ	Outer Jacket
OJ	Outgoing Junctor (SAUS)
OJA	Onklos-Jonathan Aramaic (BJA)
OJA	Oriental Pearl Airways Ltd. [*British*] [*ICAO designator*] (FAAC)
OJA	Weatherford, OK [*Location identifier*] [*FAA*] (FAAL)
OJAC	Amman [*Jordan*] [*ICAO location identifier*] (ICLI)
OJ Act	Ontario Judicature Act [*A publication*] (DLA)
OJAF	Amman [*Jordan*] [*ICAO location identifier*] (ICLI)
OJA-G	Office of the Judge Advocate General [*British*]
OJAI	Amman/Queen Alia [*Jordan*] [*ICAO location identifier*] (ICLI)
OJAJ	October, January, April, and July [*Denotes quarterly payments of interest or dividends in these months*] [*Business term*]
OJAM	Amman/Marka [*Jordan*] [*ICAO location identifier*] (ICLI)
OJapan	Order of Japan (DD)
OJAQ	Aqaba [*Jordan*] [*ICAO location identifier*] (ICLI)
OJARS	Office of Justice Assistance, Research, and Statistics [*Department of Justice*]
OJAY	Orange Julius International, Inc. (SAUS)
OJBD	Irbid [*Jordan*] [*ICAO location identifier*] (ICLI)
OJC	North Central Regional Library, Ojibway Cree Project [*UTLAS symbol*]
OJC	Occupied Japan Club (EA)
OJC	Office of Job Corps [*Department of Labor*]
OJC	Olathe, KS [*Location identifier*] [*FAA*] (FAAL)
OJC	Operation Job Card (TIMI)
OJC	Order of Jacques-Cartier [*Canada*] (BARN)

OJC.............	Organisation Juive de Combat [*Jewish Combat Organization*] [*French*] (AD)
OJC.............	Orlando Junior College [*Florida*]
OJC.............	Otero Junior College [*La Junta, CO*]
OJC.............	Overseas Jazz Club (EA)
OJCAC	Ohio Junior College Athletic Conference (PSS)
OJCCT.........	On-Line Journal of Current Clinical Trends (TELE)
OJCCT.........	Online Journal of Current Clinical Trials [*A publication*]
OJCE...........	Orchestre des Jeunes de la Communaute Europeenne [*European Community Youth Orchestra - ECYO*] (EAIO)
OJCN	Jarvis Branch, City of Nanticoke Public Library, Ontario [*Library symbol*] [*National Library of Canada*] (BIB)
OJCS...........	Office of the Joint Chiefs of Staff (AFM)
OJCS...........	Organization of the Joint Chiefs of Staff
OJD.............	Order of Job's Daughters
OJDYD	Office of Juvenile Delinquency and Youth Development [*Later, Youth Development Bureau*] [*HEW*]
OJE.............	Okumenischer Jugendrat in Europa [*Ecumenical Youth Council in Europe - EYCE*] (EAIO)
OJE.............	On-the-Job Education
OJE.............	On-the-Job Evaluation (OICC)
OJE.............	On-the-Job Evaluator (SAUS)
OJE.............	On-the-Job Experience
OJE.............	Operation Joint Endeavor [*Army*]
OJE.............	Orthodox Job Enrichment (PDAA)
OJEC...........	Official Journal of the European Communities [*A publication*] (AD)
OJG.............	Operation Joint Guard [*Army*]
OJG.............	Ordnance Job Guide
OJHF..........	Hotel Five [*Jordan*] [*ICAO location identifier*] (ICLI)
OJHR	Hotel Four [*Jordan*] [*ICAO location identifier*] (ICLI)
oji..............	Ojibwa [*MARC language code*] [*Library of Congress*] (LCCP)
oji..............	On-the-Job Injuries (AD)
OJI..............	On-the-Job Injuries
OJIN...........	Online Journal of Issues in Nursing (SAUS)
OJJ.............	Office of Juvenile Justice (AD)
OJJDP.........	Office of Juvenile Justice and Delinquency Prevention [*Department of Just ice*] [*Washington, DC*]
OJJO...........	Jericho [*Jordan*] [*ICAO location identifier*] (ICLI)
OJJR...........	Jerusalem [*Jordan*] [*ICAO location identifier*] (ICLI)
OJKSN	Online Journal of Knowledge Synthesis for Nursing (SAUS)
OJL.............	Josephine County Library System, Grants Pass, OR [*OCLC symbol*] (OCLC)
OJL.............	Office Journal (SAUS)
OJMF..........	Mafraq [*Jordan*] [*ICAO location identifier*] (ICLI)
OJNI...........	On-line Journal of Nursing Informatics (SAUS)
OJNRF	O. J. Noer Research Foundation (EA)
OJOP..........	Olympic Job Opportunities Program
OJP.............	Office of Justice Programs [*Department of Justice*]
OJP.............	Ontong Java Plateau [*Geology*]
OJP.............	Orlando, FL [*Location identifier*] [*FAA*] (FAAL)
OJPR	Office for Jewish Population Research [*Defunct*] (EA)
OJQ.............	Objective Judgment Quotient
oJr..............	Old Jamaica Rum (AD)
OJR.............	Old Jamaica Rum (ROG)
OJRL...........	Optoelectronics Joint Research Laboratory [*Japan*]
OJS.............	Las Oblatas de Jesus Sacerdote [*Oblates of Jesus the Priest*] [*Roman Catholic women's religious order*]
OJS.............	Optical Jammer Source
OJS.............	Organization Jointly Shared (SAUS)
OJS.............	Output Job Stream [*Computer science*] (VLIE)
OJSA..........	Orthomode Junction and Switching Assembly [*Electronics*]
ojt..............	On-the-Job Training (AD)
OJT.............	On-the-Job Training
OJT.............	Over-Water Jet Transport (MCD)
OJTA..........	Officer Job/Task Analysis [*Military*]
OJTC..........	Outgoing Junctor Test Circuit (SAUS)
O Jur	Ohio Jurisprudence [*A publication*] (DLA)
OJVR	Online Journal of Veterinary Research (SAUS)
OJW...........	Otjiwarongo [*South-West Africa*] [*Airport symbol*] (AD)
OJY.............	Florida Air, Inc. [*ICAO designator*] (FAAC)
OJZ.............	White Plains, NY [*Location identifier*] [*FAA*] (FAAL)
OJZZ	Amman [*Jordan*] [*ICAO location identifier*] (ICLI)
ok	all correct (SAUS)
OK.............	All Right [*From Oll Korrect; or from Old Kinderhook, a political club that supported the 1840 presidential campaign of Martin Van Buren*]
OK.............	Approved (EBF)
OK.............	Correct (EBF)
OK.............	Czechoslovak Airlines [*ICAO designator*] (AD)
OK.............	Kingston Public Library, Ontario [*Library symbol*] [*National Library of Canada*] (NLC)
O-K............	Object-Kowal [*Object in the solar system*]
OK.............	Odorless Kerosene
OK.............	Ohne Kosten [*Without Cost*] [*German*]
ok	Ohne Kosten [*Without Cost*] [*German*] (AD)
OK.............	Okay [*International telex abbreviation*] (WDMC)
OK.............	Okinawa [*Japan*]
OK.............	Oklahoma [*Postal code*]
Ok..............	Oklahoma Department of Libraries, Oklahoma City, OK [*Library symbol*] [*Library of Congress*] (LCLS)
OK.............	Okonite (IAA)
OK.............	Oktal (IAA)
OK.............	Ola Kala [*All Is Well*] [*Greek*]
ok	Ola Kala [*All is Fine*] [*Greek*] (AD)
OK.............	Old Kent Financial [*NYSE symbol*]

OK.............	Old Kinderhook (IIA)
OK.............	Old Kingdom [*Egyptology*] (ROG)
ok..............	Optical Klystron (AD)
OK.............	Optical Klystron (PDAA)
OK.............	Order of Knights (ADA)
OK.............	Oskar Kokoschka [*Austrian painter*] [*1886-1980*]
OK.............	Our King (SAUS)
ok..............	Outer Keel (AD)
OK.............	Outer Keel
OKA	Bethany Nazarene College, Bethany, OK [*OCLC symbol*] (OCLC)
OKA	Kingston Laboratories, Alcan International Ltd., Ontario [*Library symbol*] [*National Library of Canada*] (NLC)
OKA	Okayama [*Japan*] [*Seismograph station code, US Geological Survey*] (SEIS)
OKA	Okinawa [*Japan*] [*Airport symbol*] (OAG)
oka.............	Otherwise Known As (AD)
OKA	Otherwise Known As
OKA	Out-of-Kilter Algorithm [*Mathematics*]
OKAA	Kuwait Directorate General of Civil Aviation [*Kuwait*] [*ICAO location identifier*] (ICLI)
OKAAN	Optokinetic After-After-Nystagmus [*Ophthalmology*]
OKAB	Beaverbrook Branch, Kanata Public Library, Ontario [*Library symbol*] [*National Library of Canada*] (NLC)
OKAC	Kuwait [*Kuwait*] [*ICAO location identifier*] (ICLI)
OkAd	Ada Public Library, Ada, OK [*Library symbol*] [*Library of Congress*] (LCLS)
OkAdE.........	East Central State College [*Later, East Central Oklahoma State University*], Ada, OK [*Library symbol*] [*Library of Congress*] (LCLS)
OKAER	Radiochemical Co., Atomic Energy of Canada Ltd., [*Societe Radiochimique, L'Energie Atomique du Canada Ltee.*], Kanata, Ontario [*Library symbol*] [*National Library of Canada*] (NLC)
OKAF	Kuwait Air Force [*Kuwait*] [*ICAO location identifier*] (ICLI)
OKAH	Hazeldean Branch, Kanata Public Library, Ontario [*Library symbol*] [*National Library of Canada*] (NLC)
OKAI	Research & Technology Centre, AMCA International Ltd., Kanata, Ontario [*Library symbol*] [*National Library of Canada*] (NLC)
OKAKS	Synod Office, Diocese of Keewatin, Anglican Church of Canada, Kenora, Ontario [*Library symbol*] [*National Library of Canada*] (NLC)
OkAl............	Altus Library, Altus, OK [*Library symbol*] [*Library of Congress*] (LCLS)
OKAL	Aluminum Co. of Canada Ltd., Kingston, Ontario [*Library symbol*] [*National Library of Canada*] (NLC)
OkAlS..........	Southern Prairie Library System, Altus, OK [*Library symbol*] [*Library of Congress*] (LCLS)
OkAlvN........	Northwestern State College, Alva, OK [*Library symbol*] [*Library of Congress*] (LCLS)
OKAMA	Okinawa Air Materiel Area (SAUS)
OKAN	Kanata Public Library, Ontario [*Library symbol*] [*National Library of Canada*] (BIB)
OKAN	Optokinetic After-Nystagmus [*Ophthalmology*]
OKANA	Arctec Canada Ltd., Kanata, Ontario [*Library symbol*] [*National Library of Canada*] (NLC)
OKAOS	Synod Office, Diocese of Ontario, Anglican Church of Canada, Kingston, Ontario [*Library symbol*] [*National Library of Canada*] (NLC)
OKAP	Kapuskasing Public Library, Ontario [*Library symbol*] [*National Library of Canada*] (NLC)
OkArC	Chickasaw Library System, Ardmore, OK [*Library symbol*] [*Library of Congress*] (LCLS)
OKASG........	St. George's Cathedral, Anglican Church of Canada, Kingston, Ontario [*Library symbol*] [*National Library of Canada*] (NLC)
Okayama Univ Inst Therm Spring Res Pap...	Okayama University. Institue for Thermal Spring Research. Papers (SAUS)
OKAYJ	A. Y. Jackson High School, Kanata, Ontario [*Library symbol*] [*National Library of Canada*] (BIB)
OkB.............	Bartlesville Public Library, Bartlesville, OK [*Library symbol*] [*Library of Congress*] (LCLS)
OKB.............	Design Bureau (SAUS)
OKB.............	Kashechewan Band Library, Ontario [*Library symbol*] [*National Library of Canada*] (BIB)
OKB	Missile design bureau (SAUS)
OKB.............	Oklahoma Baptist University, Shawnee, OK [*OCLC symbol*] (OCLC)
OKB	Orchid Beach [*Australia*] [*Airport symbol*]
OkBERDA.....	United States Energy Research Development Administration, Energy Research Center, Bartlesville, OK [*Library symbol*] [*Library of Congress*] (LCLS)
OkBetC........	Bethany Nazarene College, Bethany, OK [*Library symbol*] [*Library of Congress*] (LCLS)
OKBK	Kuwait/International [*Kuwait*] [*ICAO location identifier*] (ICLI)
OkBP...........	Phillips Petroleum Co., Research and Development Department, Bartlesville, OK [*Library symbol*] [*Library of Congress*] (LCLS)
OkBP-NR......	Philips Petroleum Co., Exploration and Production Library, Bartlesville, OK [*Library symbol*] [*Library of Congress*] (LCLS)
OkBr............	Bristow Public Library, Bristow, OK [*Library symbol*] [*Library of Congress*] (LCLS)
OKBT	Billings Township Public Library, Kagawong, Ontario [*Library symbol*] [*National Library of Canada*] (NLC)
OkBUSM	United States Bureau of Mines, Petroleum Research Center, Bartlesville, OK [*Library symbol*] [*Library of Congress*] [*Obsolete*] (LCLS)
OKC	Cameron University, Lawton, OK [*OCLC symbol*] (OCLC)

OKC .... Canadian Forces School of Communications and Electronics, Kingston, Ontario [*Library symbol*] [*National Library of Canada*] (BIB)

OKC .... Odontogenic Keratocyst [*Medicine*] (DMAA)

OKC .... Okanagan College Learning Resources Centre [*UTLAS symbol*]

OKC .... Oklahoma City [*Oklahoma*] [*Airport symbol*] (OAG)

OKC .... Will Rogers World Airport [*FAA*] (TAG)

OKCAA .... Archives, Archdiocese of Kingston, Catholic Church, Ontario [*Library symbol*] [*National Library of Canada*] (NLC)

OkChicW ..... Oklahoma College of Liberal Arts, Chickasha, OK [*Library symbol*] [*Library of Congress*] (LCLS)

OKCHN .... Pan-National Congress of the Chechen People [*Russian Federation*]

OKCKT .... King Township Public Library, King City, Ontario [*Library symbol*] [*National Library of Canada*] (NLC)

OkCl .... Clinton Public Library, Clinton, OK [*Library symbol*] [*Library of Congress*] (LCLS)

OkClaW .... Will Rogers Library, Claremore, OH [*Library symbol*] [*Library of Congress*] (LCLS)

OkClW .... Western Plains Library System, Clinton, OK [*Library symbol*] [*Library of Congress*] (LCLS)

OKCM .... Canadian Marconi Co., Kanata, Ontario [*Library symbol*] [*National Library of Canada*] (NLC)

OKCO .... Oakbrook Consolidated (SAUS)

OKCS .... Oklahoma Climatological Survey (SAUS)

OKD .... Oklahoma Department of Libraries, Oklahoma City, OK [*OCLC symbol*] (OCLC)

OKD .... Research Centre Library, Du Pont Canada, Inc., Kingston, Ontario [*Library symbol*] [*National Library of Canada*] (NLC)

OKD .... Sapporo/Okadama [*Japan*] [*Airport symbol*] (OAG)

OKDBMS ...... Operations Knowledge Data Base Management System [*NASA*]

OKDC .... Du Pont Canada, Inc., Kingston, Ontario [*Library symbol*] [*National Library of Canada*] (NLC)

OkDurS .... Southeastern State College, Durant, OK [*Library symbol*] [*Library of Congress*] (LCLS)

OKE .... Kenora Public Library, Ontario [*Library symbol*] [*National Library of Canada*] (NLC)

OKE .... Metropolitan Library System, Capitol Hill Branch, Oklahoma City, OK [*OCLC symbol*] (OCLC)

OKE .... Okino Erabu [*Japan*] [*Airport symbol*] (OAG)

OKE .... ONEOK, Inc. [*NYSE symbol*] (SPSG)

OKE .... Optical Kerr Effect [*Birefringence induced in an electrical field*]

OkE .... Public Library of Enid and Garfield County, Enid, OK [*Library symbol*] [*Library of Congress*] (LCLS)

OKEA .... Kearney and Area Public Library, Kearney, Ontario [*Library symbol*] [*National Library of Canada*] (NLC)

OKED .... Okinawa Engineer District (SAUS)

OkEdT .... Central State University, Edmond, OK [*Library symbol*] [*Library of Congress*] (LCLS)

OKEE .... Keewatin Public Library, Ontario [*Library symbol*] [*National Library of Canada*] (NLC)

O'Keefe Ord ... O'Keefe's Order in Chancery [*Ireland*] [*A publication*] (DLA)

Oke Fish L ... Oke. Fisher Laws [*4th ed.*] [*1924*] [*A publication*] (DLA)

OkEG .... Phillips University, Graduate Seminary, Enid, OK [*Library symbol*] [*Library of Congress*] (LCLS)

Oke Game L ... Oke. Game Laws [*5th ed.*] [*1912*] [*A publication*] (DLA)

OKEH .... Okehampton [*England*]

OKEM .... Kemptville Public Library, Ontario [*Library symbol*] [*National Library of Canada*] (NLC)

OKEMAF ...... Ontario Ministry of Agriculture and Food, Kemptville, Ontario [*Library symbol*] [*National Library of Canada*] (NLC)

Oke Mag Form ... Oke. Magisterial Formulist [*19th ed.*] [*1978*] [*A publication*] (DLA)

Oke Mag Syn ... Oke. Magisterial Synopsis [*14th ed.*] [*1893*] [*A publication*] (DLA)

OKEMC .... Kemptville College of Agricultural Technology, Ontario [*Library symbol*] [*National Library of Canada*] (BIB)

OKEMS .... Earl of March Secondary School, Kanata, Ontario [*Library symbol*] [*National Library of Canada*] (NLC)

OKEN .... Old Kent Financial Corp. [*NASDAQ symbol*] (NQ)

OKEN .... Old Kent Finl [*NASDAQ symbol*] (TTSB)

OKentU .... Kent State University, Kent, OH [*Library symbol*] [*Library of Congress*] (LCLS)

OkEP .... Phillips University, Enid, OK [*Library symbol*] [*Library of Congress*] (LCLS)

OkErC .... El Reno Junior College Learning Resource Center, El Reno, OK [*Library symbol*] [*Library of Congress*] (LCLS)

OKES .... Georgina Township Public Library, Keswick, Ontario [*Library symbol*] [*National Library of Canada*] (NLC)

OKET .... Euphrasia Township Public Library, Kimberley, Ontario [*Library symbol*] [*National Library of Canada*] (NLC)

OKetBD .... BDM International, Information Service Center, Kettering, OH [*Library symbol*] [*Library of Congress*] (LCLS)

OKetH .... Kettering Memorial Hospital, Kettering, OH [*Library symbol*] [*Library of Congress*] (LCLS)

OKetK .... Charles F. Kettering Foundation, Kettering, OH [*Library symbol*] [*Library of Congress*] (LCLS)

Oke Turn ...... Oke. Turnpike Laws [*2nd ed.*] [*1861*] [*A publication*] (DLA)

OKF .... Fort Frontenac Library, Canada Department of National Defence [*Bibliotheque Fort Frontenac, Ministere de la Defense Nationale*] Kingston, Ontario [*Library symbol*] [*National Library of Canada*] (NLC)

OKFC .... Frontenac County Library, Kingston, Ontario [*Library symbol*] [*National Library of Canada*] (NLC)

OKFCSM ...... Frontenac County Schools Museum Association, Kingston, Ontario [*Library symbol*] [*National Library of Canada*] (BIB)

OKFI .... Siltronics Ltd., Kanata, Ontario [*Library symbol*] [*National Library of Canada*] (NLC)

OkFsAGM .... United States Army, Artillery and Guided Missile School, Fort Sill, OK [*Library symbol*] [*Library of Congress*] (LCLS)

OKG .... Oak Grove [*Tennessee*] [*Seismograph station code, US Geological Survey*] (SEIS)

OKG .... Okoyo [*Congo*] [*Airport symbol*] (OAG)

OKG .... Phillips University, Graduate Seminary Library, Enid, OK [*OCLC symbol*] (OCLC)

OKGH .... Kingston General Hospital, Ontario [*Library symbol*] [*National Library of Canada*] (NLC)

OkGoP .... Panhandle State College, Goodwell, OK [*Library symbol*] [*Library of Congress*] (LCLS)

OkGuC .... Catholic College of Oklahoma for Women, Guthrie, OK [*Library symbol*] [*Library of Congress*] [*Obsolete*] (LCLS)

OkGuy .... Guymon City Library, Guymon, OK [*Library symbol*] [*Library of Congress*] (LCLS)

OKH .... Oberkommando des Heeres [*Army High Command*] [*German military - World War II*]

OKH .... Okha [*Former USSR*] [*Seismograph station code, US Geological Survey*] (SEIS)

OKH .... University of Oklahoma, Health Science Center Library, Oklahoma City, OK [*OCLC symbol*] (OCLC)

OKHD .... Hotel-Dieu Hospital, Kingston, Ontario [*Library symbol*] [*National Library of Canada*] (NLC)

OkHenn .... Hennessey Public Library, Hennessey, OK [*Library symbol*] [*Library of Congress*] (LCLS)

OkHi .... Oklahoma Historical Society, Oklahoma City, OK [*Library symbol*] [*Library of Congress*] (LCLS)

OKI .... Choctaw Nation Multi-County Library, McAlester, OK [*OCLC symbol*] (OCLC)

OKI .... Kincardine Branch, Bruce County Public Library, Ontario [*Library symbol*] [*National Library of Canada*] (NLC)

OKI .... Ohio-Kentucky-Indiana Regional Planning Authority

OKI .... Oki Island [*Japan*] [*Airport symbol*] (OAG)

OKI .... Okijuku [*Japan*] [*Seismograph station code, US Geological Survey*] [*Closed*] (SEIS)

OKI .... Oko Electric Industry Company (SAUS)

OKIESMO ...... Oklahoma Machismo [*Term coined by author Mark Singer*]

OKIL .... Killaloe Public Library, Ontario [*Library symbol*] [*National Library of Canada*] (NLC)

OkIM .... McUrtain County High Education Program, Idabel, OK [*Library symbol*] [*Library of Congress*] (LCLS)

Okin .... Okinawa (AD)

OKIT .... Kitchener Public Library, Ontario [*Library symbol*] [*National Library of Canada*] (NLC)

OKI-TAC ...... Oki Transistorized Computer (SAUS)

OKITAI .... Okinawa-Taiwan Submarine Cable (SAUS)

OKITC .... Learning Resource Centre, Conestoga College of Applied Arts and Technology, Kitchener, Ontario [*Library symbol*] [*National Library of Canada*] (NLC)

OKITD .... Doon Pioneer Village, Kitchener, Ontario [*Library symbol*] [*National Library of Canada*] (BIB)

Oki Tech Rev ... Oki Technical Review (SAUS)

OKITM .... Ontario Library Service - Saugeen, Kitchener, Ontario [*Library symbol*] [*National Library of Canada*] (NLC)

OKITW .... Kitchener-Waterloo Record, Kitchener, Ontario [*Library symbol*] [*National Library of Canada*] (NLC)

OKITWC ...... Waterloo County Board of Education, Kitchener, Ontario [*Library symbol*] [*National Library of Canada*] (NLC)

OKJ .... Okada Airlines Ltd. [*Nigeria*] [*ICAO designator*] (FAAC)

OKJ .... Okayama [*Japan*] [*Airport symbol*] (OAG)

OKJ .... Oklahoma City Community College, Oklahoma City, OK [*OCLC symbol*] (OCLC)

OKK .... Charles F. Kettering Foundation, Dayton, OH [*OCLC symbol*] (OCLC)

OKK .... Kokomo [*Indiana*] [*Airport symbol*] (OAG)

OKK .... Kokomo, IN [*Location identifier*] [*FAA*] (FAAL)

OKKBWP ...... One Kind Kiss Before We Part [*Slang*]

OKL .... Lake Ontario Regional Library System, Kingston, Ontario [*Library symbol*] [*Obsolete*] [*National Library of Canada*] (NLC)

OkL .... Lawton Public Library, Lawton, OK [*Library symbol*] [*Library of Congress*] (LCLS)

OKL .... Oberkommando der Luftwaffe [*Air Force High Command*] [*German military - World War II*]

Okl .... Oklahoma (DLA)

OKL .... Oklahoma City [*Diocesan abbreviation*] [*Oklahoma*] (TOCD)

Okl .... Oklahoma Reports [*A publication*] (DLA)

OKL .... On Key Label (SAUS)

OKL .... University of Oklahoma, Law Library, Norman, OK [*OCLC symbol*] (OCLC)

Okla .... Oklahoma (AD)

OKLA .... Oklahoma (AFM)

Okla .... Oklahoma Criminal Reports [*A publication*] (DLA)

Okla .... Oklahoma Supreme Court Reports [*A publication*] (DLA)

OklaAgric Exp Stn Prog Rep ... Oklahoma. Agricultural Experiment Station. Progress Report (SAUS)

Okla Ap Ct Rep ... Oklahoma Appellate Court Reporter [*A publication*] (DLA)

OklaC .... Oklahoma City (AD)

OklaChronicles ... Chronicles of Oklahoma (journ.) (SAUS)

Okla City U ... Oklahoma City University (GAGS)

Okla Cr .... Oklahoma Criminal Reports [*A publication*] (DLA)

Okla Crim ..... Oklahoma Criminal Reports [*A publication*] (DLA)

Okla CULR .... Oklahoma City University. Law Review [*A publication*] (DLA)

OklaG .... Oklahoma Gas & Electric Co. [*Associated Press*] (SAG)

Okla Gaz ...... Oklahoma Gazette [*A publication*] (DLA)

OklaGE .... Oklahoma Gas & Electric Co. [*Associated Press*] (SAG)

Okla GS .... Oklahoma. Geological Survey (SAUS)

Oklahoma	Oklahoma Reports [*A publication*] (DLA)
Okla ICR	Oklahoma Industrial Commission Reports [*A publication*] (DLA)
Okla Lawy ...	Oklahoma Lawyer [*A publication*] (DLA)
Okla LJ........	Oklahoma Law Journal [*A publication*] (DLA)
Okla Mil Dist...	Oklahoma Military District (SAUS)
Okl App........	Oklahoma Court of Appeals (DLA)
Okla SBJ.....	Oklahoma State Bar Journal [*A publication*] (DLA)
Okla Sess Laws...	Oklahoma Session Laws [*A publication*] (DLA)
Okla Sess Law Serv...	Oklahoma Session Law Service (SAUS)
Okla Sess Law Serv...	Oklahoma Session Law Service (West) [*A publication*] (DLA)
Okla Stat	Oklahoma Statutes [*A publication*] (DLA)
Okla Stat Ann (West)...	Oklahoma Statutes, Annotated (West) [*A publication*] (DLA)
Okla St U.....	Oklahoma State University (GAGS)
OkLaU..........	Langston University, Langston, OK [*Library symbol*] [*Library of Congress*] (LCLS)
OkLC............	Cameron University, Lawton, OK [*Library symbol*] [*Library of Congress*] (LCLS)
Okl City UL Rev...	Oklahoma City University. Law Review [*A publication*] (DLA)
OkLC-M........	Cameron College, Medical Library Resource Center, Lawton, OK [*Library symbol*] [*Library of Congress*] (LCLS)
Okl Cr	Oklahoma Criminal Reports [*A publication*] (DLA)
Okl Cr R	Oklahoma Criminal Reports [*A publication*] (DLA)
OKLEM	McMichael Canadian Collection, Kleinburg, Ontario [*Library symbol*] [*National Library of Canada*] (NLC)
OKLFC	Official Kate Linder Fan Club (EA)
OKLN	Northeastern Regional Library, Kirkland Lake, Ontario [*Library symbol*] [*National Library of Canada*] (NLC)
OKLN	Ontario Library Service - James Bay, Kirkland Lake, Ontario [*Library symbol*] [*National Library of Canada*] (NLC)
OKLNC	Kirkland Lake Campus, Northern College, Ontario [*Library symbol*] [*National Library of Canada*] (NLC)
Okl St Ann ...	Oklahoma Statutes, Annotated [*A publication*] (DLA)
OKLT............	Teck Centennial Public Library, Kirkland Lake, Ontario [*Library symbol*] [*National Library of Canada*] (NLC)
OKLU	Lumonics, Inc., Kanata, Ontario [*Library symbol*] [*National Library of Canada*] (NLC)
OKM............	Mitel Corp., Kanata, Ontario [*Library symbol*] [*National Library of Canada*] (NLC)
OKM............	Oberkommando der Kriegsmarine [*Navy High Command*] [*German military - World War II*]
OKM............	Oklahoma Mesonet (SAUS)
OKM............	Okmulgee, OK [*Location identifier*] [*FAA*] (FAAL)
OKM............	Pioneer Multi-County Library, Norman, OK [*OCLC symbol*] (OCLC)
OKMC	Miller Communications Systems Ltd., Kanata, Ontario [*Library symbol*] [*National Library of Canada*] (NLC)
OkMcC	Choctaw Nation Multi-County Library, McAlester, OK [*Library symbol*] [*Library of Congress*] (LCLS)
OkMcO	Oscar Rose Junior College, Midwest City, OK [*Library symbol*] [*Library of Congress*] (LCLS)
OKMD	Digital Equipment of Canada Ltd., Kanata, Ontario [*Library symbol*] [*National Library of Canada*] (NLC)
OKME..........	Metro Canada Ltd., Kingston, Ontario [*Library symbol*] [*National Library of Canada*] (NLC)
OKMM	Marine Museum of the Great Lakes at Kingston, Ontario [*Library symbol*] [*National Library of Canada*] (NLC)
OkMu	Muskogee Public Library, Muskogee, OK [*Library symbol*] [*Library of Congress*] (LCLS)
OkMuE	Eastern Oklahoma District Library, Muskogee, OK [*Library symbol*] [*Library of Congress*] (LCLS)
OkMuV........	United States Veterans Administration Hospital, Muskogee, OK [*Library symbol*] [*Library of Congress*] (LCLS)
OKMV	Okra Mosaic Virus [*Plant pathology*]
OKN	Northeastern Oklahoma State University, Tahlequah, OK [*OCLC symbol*] (OCLC)
OKN	Okmulgee Northern Railway Co. [*AAR code*]
OKN	Okondja [*Gabon*] [*Airport symbol*] (OAG)
OKN	Optokinetic Nystagmus [*Ophthalmology*]
OkN	Pioneer Multi-County Library, Norman, OK [*Library symbol*] [*Library of Congress*] (LCLS)
OKNC..........	Newbridge Communication Network Corp., Kanata, Ontario [*Library symbol*] [*National Library of Canada*] (BIB)
OKNeoAC....	Neo-American Church, the Original Kleptonian [*An association*] (EA)
OkNNS	National Severe Storms Laboratory, Norman, OK [*Library symbol*] [*Library of Congress*] (LCLS)
OKNO	Kuwait International NOTAM Office [*Kuwait*] [*ICAO location identifier*] (ICLI)
OKO	Oral Roberts University, Tulsa, OK [*OCLC symbol*] (OCLC)
OKOH..........	Penrose Division, Ongwanada Hospital, Kingston, Ontario [*Library symbol*] [*National Library of Canada*] (NLC)
OkOk	Oklahoma County Libraries, Oklahoma City, OK [*Library symbol*] [*Library of Congress*] (LCLS)
OkOkB.........	Oklahoma Library for the Blind and Physically Handicapped, Oklahoma City, OK [*Library symbol*] [*Library of Congress*] (LCLS)
OkOkC.........	Oklahoma Christian College, Oklahoma City, OK [*Library symbol*] [*Library of Congress*] (LCLS)
OkOkCGS	Oklahoma City Geological Survey, Inc., Oklahoma City, OK [*Library symbol*] [*Library of Congress*] (LCLS)
OkOkD	Deaconess Hospital, Oklahoma City, OK [*Library symbol*] [*Library of Congress*] (LCLS)
OkOke.........	Okemah Public Library, Okemah, OK [*Library symbol*] [*Library of Congress*] (LCLS)
OkOkFA........	United States Federal Aviation Administration, Civil Aeromedical Institute, Oklahoma City, OK [*Library symbol*] [*Library of Congress*] (LCLS)
OkOkGS	Church of Jesus Christ of Latter-Day Saints, Genealogical Society Library, Oklahoma City Branch, Oklahoma City, OK [*Library symbol*] [*Library of Congress*] (LCLS)
OkOkK.........	Kerr-McGee Corp., Oklahoma City, OK [*Library symbol*] [*Library of Congress*] (LCLS)
OkOkM	Mid-America Bible College, Oklahoma City, OK [*Library symbol*] [*Library of Congress*] (LCLS)
OkOkSO	Oklahoma City Community College, Learning Resources Center, Oklahoma City, OK [*Library symbol*] [*Library of Congress*] (LCLS)
OkOkU	Oklahoma City University, Oklahoma City, OK [*Library symbol*] [*Library of Congress*] (LCLS)
OkOkU-L.......	Oklahoma City University, Law Library, Oklahoma City, OK [*Library symbol*] [*Library of Congress*] (LCLS)
OkOkV.........	United States Veterans Administration Hospital, Oklahoma City, OK [*Library symbol*] [*Library of Congress*] (LCLS)
OKOT	Otonabee Township Library, Keen, Ontario [*Library symbol*] [*National Library of Canada*] (NLC)
OKP	Citizens' Parliamentary Club [*Poland*] [*Political party*]
OKP	Oksapmin [*Papua New Guinea*] [*Airport symbol*] (OAG)
OKP	O'Okiep Copper Co. Ltd. [*AMEX symbol*] (SPSG)
OKP	Optimized Kill Probability
OKP	Southern Prairie Library System, Altus, OK [*OCLC symbol*] (OCLC)
OkPo	Ponca City Public Library, Ponca City, OK [*Library symbol*] [*Library of Congress*] (LCLS)
OkPoC.........	Continental Oil Co., R and D Technical Information Service, Ponca City, OK [*Library symbol*] [*Library of Congress*] (LCLS)
OkPot.........	Buckley Public Library, Poteau, OK [*Library symbol*] [*Library of Congress*] (LCLS)
OKQ	Okaba [*Indonesia*] [*Airport symbol*] (OAG)
OKQ	Queen's University, Kingston, Ontario [*Library symbol*] [*National Library of Canada*] (NLC)
OKQA	Agnes Etherington Art Centre, Queen's University, Kingston, Ontario [*Library symbol*] [*National Library of Canada*] (NLC)
OKQAR.........	Archives, Queen's University, Kingston, Ontario [*Library symbol*] [*National Library of Canada*] (NLC)
OKQCI	Canadian Institute of Guided Ground Transport, Queen's University, Kingston, Ontario [*Library symbol*] [*National Library of Canada*] (NLC)
OKQG	Department of Geography, Queen's University, Kingston, Ontario [*Library symbol*] [*National Library of Canada*] (NLC)
OKQGS	Department of Geological Sciences, Queen's University, Kingston, Ontario [*Library symbol*] [*National Library of Canada*] (NLC)
OKQH	Bracken Library, Queen's University, Kingston, Ontario [*Library symbol*] [*National Library of Canada*] (NLC)
OKQL	Law Library, Queen's University, Kingston, Ontario [*Library symbol*] [*National Library of Canada*] (NLC)
OKQM	McArthur College of Education, Queen's University, Kingston, Ontario [*Library symbol*] [*National Library of Canada*] (NLC)
OKQMA........	Map Collection, Douglas Library, Queen's University, Kingston, Ontario [*Library symbol*] [*National Library of Canada*] (NLC)
OKR	Optical Key Reader [*Automotive engineering*]
OKR	Royal Military College of Canada, Kingston, Ontario [*Library symbol*] [*National Library of Canada*] (NLC)
OKRC..........	Regiopolis - Notre Dame High School, Kingston, Ontario [*Library symbol*] [*National Library of Canada*] (NLC)
Ok Reg	Oklahoma Register [*A publication*] (AAGC)
OKRGI.........	Rutherford and George Island Township Public Library, Killarney, Ontario [*Library symbol*] [*National Library of Canada*] (NLC)
OKRS	Science Engineering Library, Royal Military College of Canada, Kingston, Ontario [*Library symbol*] [*National Library of Canada*] (BIB)
OKS	Ohio Kache Systems Corp.
OKS	Okanagan Skeena Group Ltd. [*Vancouver Stock Exchange symbol*] [*Toronto Stock Exchange symbol*]
OkS	Oklahoma State University, Stillwater, OK [*Library symbol*] [*Library of Congress*] (LCLS)
OKS	Old King's Scholars Association [*Canterbury, England*]
OKS	Oshkosh, NE [*Location identifier*] [*FAA*] (FAAL)
OKSB	Southwest Bancorp [*NASDAQ symbol*] (SAG)
OKSBP........	Southwest Bcp 9.2% cm 'A'Pfd [*NASDAQ symbol*] (TTSB)
OkSEA........	Oklahoma Society of Enrolled Agents (SAUS)
OkShB........	Oklahoma Baptist University, Shawnee, OK [*Library symbol*] [*Library of Congress*] (LCLS)
OKSL	St. Lawrence College of Applied Arts and Technology, Kingston, Ontario [*Library symbol*] [*National Library of Canada*] (NLC)
OKSMG........	Gibson Medical Library, St. Mary's of the Lake Hospital, Kingston, Ontario [*Library symbol*] [*National Library of Canada*] (NLC)
OkS-T..........	Oklahoma State University Technical Institute Library, Oklahoma City, OK [*Library symbol*] [*Library of Congress*] (LCLS)
OkSt..........	Stillwater Public Library, Stillwater, OK [*Library symbol*] [*Library of Congress*] (LCLS)
OkS-TBO	Oklahoma State University Technical Branch, Okmulgee, OK [*Library symbol*] [*Library of Congress*] (LCLS)
OKT	Oakite Products, Inc. (SAUS)
OKT	[*The*] Oakland Terminal Railway [*Later, OTR*] [*AAR code*]
okt	Oktober [*October*] [*GRM*] (AD)
okt	Oktyab [*October*] [*Russian*] (AD)
OKT	Ollier-Klippel-Trenaunay [*Syndrome*] [*Medicine*] (DB)
OKT............	Oslo Kommune Tunnelbanekontoret [*Oslo Subway System*] (AD)
OkT	Tulsa City-County Library System, Tulsa, OK [*Library symbol*] [*Library of Congress*] (LCLS)
OKT............	University of Tulsa, Tulsa, OK [*OCLC symbol*] (OCLC)

OKT.............	Yoakum, TX [*Location identifier*] [*FAA*] (FAAL)
OkTA............	American Association of Petroleum Geologists, Energy Resources Library, Tulsa, OK [*Library symbol*] [*Library of Congress*] (LCLS)
OkTahN.........	Northeastern State College, Tahlequah, OK [*Library symbol*] [*Library of Congress*] (LCLS)
OkTAm.........	AMOCO Production Co., Research Center Geology Library, Tulsa, OK [*Library symbol*] [*Library of Congress*] (LCLS)
OkTC...........	Ceja Corp., Tulsa, OK [*Library symbol*] [*Library of Congress*] (LCLS)
OKTc...........	Ortho-Kung T-cell (SAUS)
OkTCS.........	Cities Service Co., Energy Resources Group, E & P Library, Tulsa, OK [*Library symbol*] [*Library of Congress*] (LCLS)
OkTG..........	Thomas Gilcrease Institute of American History and Art, Tulsa, OK [*Library symbol*] [*Library of Congress*] (LCLS)
OkTGS	Church of Jesus Christ of Latter-Day Saints, Genealogical Society Library, TulsaBranch, Tulsa, OK [*Library symbol*] [*Library of Congress*] (LCLS)
OkTo	Tonkawa Public Library, Tonkawa, OK [*Library symbol*] [*Library of Congress*] (LCLS)
OkTOR	Oral Roberts University, Learning Resources Center, Tulsa, OK [*Library symbol*] [*Library of Congress*] (LCLS)
OkTPA.........	Pan American Oil Corp., Research Library, Tulsa, OK [*Library symbol*] [*Library of Congress*] (LCLS)
OkTPh.........	Philbrook Art Center, Tulsa, OK [*Library symbol*] [*Library of Congress*] (LCLS)
Oktronics	Oklahoma Electronics (AD)
OkTU...........	University of Tulsa, Tulsa, OK [*Library symbol*] [*Library of Congress*] (LCLS)
OkTU-L	University of Tulsa, College of Law, Tulsa, OK [*Library symbol*] [*Library of Congress*] (LCLS)
oku.............	Oklahoma [*MARC country of publication code*] [*Library of Congress*] (LCCP)
OKU	Omicron Kappa Upsilon [*Fraternity*]
OkU............	University of Oklahoma, Norman, OK [*Library symbol*] [*Library of Congress*] (LCLS)
OkU-C	University of Oklahoma, Communication Department, Political Communications Center, Political Commercial Archives, Norman, OK [*Library symbol*] [*Library of Congress*] (LCLS)
OkU-L	University of Oklahoma, Law School, Norman, OK [*Library symbol*] [*Library of Congress*] (LCLS)
OkU-M	University of Oklahoma, Health Sciences Center, Oklahoma City, OK [*Library symbol*] [*Library of Congress*] (LCLS)
OkU-P	University of Oklahoma, College of Pharmacy, Norman, OK [*Library symbol*] [*Library of Congress*] (LCLS)
OKUTD.........	Urban Transportation Development Corp., Kingston, Ontario [*Library symbol*] [*National Library of Canada*] (NLC)
OkU-TM	University of Oklahoma, Tulsa Medical College, Tulsa, OK [*Library symbol*] [*Library of Congress*] (LCLS)
OkU-W	University of Oklahoma, Western History Collections, Norman, OK [*Library symbol*] [*Library of Congress*] (LCLS)
OKV	University of Oklahoma, Library School, Norman, OK [*OCLC symbol*] (OCLC)
OKW	Brookwood, AL [*Location identifier*] [*FAA*] (FAAL)
OKW	Oberkommando der Wehrmacht [*Armed Forces High Command*] [*German military - World War II*]
OKW	University of Tulsa, College of Law, Tulsa, OK [*OCLC symbol*] (OCLC)
OK W/C.......	Okay Except for [*with*] the Corrections [*Proofreading*] (WDMC)
OkWeaT.......	Southwestern State College, Weatherford, OK [*Library symbol*] [*Library of Congress*] (LCLS)
OkWo..........	Woodward Carnegie Library, Woodward, OK [*Library symbol*] [*Library of Congress*] (LCLS)
OKX	Central State University, Edmond, OK [*OCLC symbol*] (OCLC)
OKXS	Xenotech Systems, Inc., Kitchener, Ontario [*Library symbol*] [*National Library of Canada*] (NLC)
OKY	Oakey [*Queensland*] [*Airport symbol*] (AD)
OKY	Oklahoma City University, Law Library, Oklahoma City, OK [*OCLC symbol*] (OCLC)
OKZ...........	Phillips University, Zollars Memorial Library, Enid, OK [*OCLC symbol*] (OCLC)
OKZ...........	Sandersville, GA [*Location identifier*] [*FAA*] (FAAL)
OL.............	London Public Library, Ontario [*Library symbol*] [*National Library of Canada*] (NLC)
OL.............	Object Language (SAUS)
O/L.............	Observation/Losing [*Army*] (ADDR)
OL.............	Observer, Left (SAUS)
OL.............	Occupational Level
OL.............	Ocean Letter
OL.............	October League (AD)
OL.............	Oculus Laevus [*Left Eye*] [*Ophthalmology*]
ol.............	Oculus Laevus [*Left Eye*] [*Latin*] (AD)
OL.............	Odd Lot [*Stock exchange term*]
OL.............	Offering Line (SAUS)
OL.............	Office Lady [*Japan*] (ECON)
OL.............	Office of Labor
OL.............	Officer of the Order of Leopold
OL.............	Official Liquidator [*British*] (ROG)
OL.............	Ohio Laws [*A publication*] (DLA)
ol.............	Oil [*Pharmacy*] (CPH)
OL.............	Oil Level (AAG)
ol.............	Oil Level (AD)
OL.............	Oil Lighter [*Shipping*] [*British*]
OL.............	Oiseau-Lyre [*Record label*] [*France*]
OL.............	Oldham [*Postcode*] (ODBW)
OL.............	Old Latin [*Language, etc.*]
OL.............	Old Leysian (WDAA)

Ol.............	Oldradus da Ponte de Laude [*Deceased, 1335*] [*Authority cited in pre-1607 legal work*] (DSA)
OL.............	Oleum [*Oil*] [*Pharmacy*]
ol.............	Oleum [*Oil*] [*Latin*] (AD)
OL.............	Oligoblastic Leukemia [*Oncology*]
Ol.............	Olivary [*Neurology*]
Ol.............	Olive [*Political party*] (AD)
ol.............	Olive [*Philately*]
OL.............	Oliver [*Tire retread brand*]
ol.............	Olivine [*CIPW classification*] [*Geology*]
Ol.............	Olsen Line (AD)
Ol.............	Olympian [*of Pindar*] [*Classical studies*] (OCD)
OL.............	Olympic
OL.............	Olympic Lift [*Sports*]
OL.............	Online
OL.............	Only Loadable [*Computer science*] (IAA)
OL.............	Open Learning (AIE)
OL.............	Open Light (SAUS)
OL.............	Open Loop
OL.............	Operating Level (IEEE)
O/L.............	Operating Level
ol.............	Operating License (AD)
OL.............	Operating License
OL.............	Operating Limit (COE)
OL.............	Operating Location [*Army*]
OL.............	Operating Log
OL.............	Operating Loss
OL.............	Operational Left [*NASA*] (NAKS)
OL.............	Operational Left DSC or MDM (SAUS)
OL.............	Operational Semantics (SAUS)
OL.............	Operation Liftoff (EA)
OL.............	Operation Limits (SAUS)
O/L.............	Operations and Logistics (SAUS)
o/l.............	Operations/Logistics (AD)
OL.............	Optical Limiter (SAUS)
OL.............	Orbital Launch
OL.............	Ordered List (SAUS)
OL.............	Order of Lafayette (EA)
OL.............	Ordinary Leave [*Military*] (AFM)
OL.............	Ordinary Letter (WDAA)
OL.............	Ordnance Lieutenant [*Navy*] [*British*]
OL.............	Organization List (MCD)
OL.............	Organizing Language (SAUS)
OL.............	Original Learning [*Psychometrics*]
ol.............	Or Less (AD)
OL.............	Or Less
OL.............	Oscillating Limiter (IAA)
OL.............	Ostfriesische Lufttransport GmbH [*Germany*] [*ICAO designator*] (ICDA)
OL.............	Other Line [*Telecommunications*] (TEL)
OL.............	Outgoing Letter
o/l.............	Outlook (AD)
OL.............	Output Latch
OL.............	Output List (SAUS)
OL.............	Output Logic (SAUS)
OL.............	Outside Left [*Soccer position*]
OL.............	Overflow Level
OL.............	Overhead Line
OL.............	Overlap
OL.............	Overlay (NASA)
OL.............	Overload
OLA.............	Lakefield Public Library, Ontario [*Library symbol*] [*National Library of Canada*] (NLC)
OLA.............	National Oceanic and Atmospheric Administration, Rockville, MD [*OCLC symbol*] (OCLC)
OLA.............	Oaklahoma Lumbermen's Association (WPI)
ola.............	Occipito-Laeva Anterior (AD)
OLA.............	Occipitolaeva Anterior [*A fetal position*] [*Medicine*] (AAMN)
OLA.............	Occupiers' Liability Act [*1957*] [*British*] (DCTA)
OLA.............	Office of Legislative Affairs
OLA.............	Office of Legislative Analysis [*Environmental Protection Agency*] (GFGA)
OLA.............	Official Languages Act [*Canada*]
OLA.............	Ohio Law Abstract [*A publication*] (DLA)
OLA.............	Ohio Library Association (AD)
OLA.............	Oklahoma Library Association (AD)
OLA.............	Oligonucleotide Ligation Assay [*Analytical biochemistry*]
OLA.............	On-Line AUTODIN (SAUS)
OLA.............	Ontario Library Association [*Canada*] (AD)
OL-A.............	Operating Location-A (SAUS)
OLA.............	Optical Laboratories Association (EA)
OLA.............	Optical Link in the Atmosphere (PDAA)
OLA.............	Optimally Localized Averages [*Mathematics*]
OLA.............	Orbital Lock Assembly
OLA.............	Original Language (SAUS)
OLA.............	Orland [*Norway*] [*Airport symbol*] (OAG)
OLA.............	Osteopathic Libraries Association [*Defunct*] (EA)
OLA.............	Overview Latin America (EA)
OLAA.............	Office of Legal Aid Administration
OLABS	Offshore Labrador Biological Studies (SAUS)
OL Abs........	Ohio Law Abstract [*A publication*] (DLA)
OLA Bulletin...	Ohio Library Association. Bulletin (SAUS)
OLAC.............	Offline Adaptive Computer [*Computer science*]
OLAC	On-Line Accelerated Cooling (SAUS)
OLAC.............	Online Audiovisual Catalogers [*An association*] (EA)

OLAD .... Operating Location Alert Detachment (SAUS)
OLADE .... Organizacion Latin-Americana de Energia [*Latin American Energy Organization*] [*Spanish*] (AD)
OLAF .... Operand Lattice File (SAUS)
OLAFL .... Front of Leeds and Lansdowne Public Library, Lansdowne, Ontario [*Library symbol*] [*National Library of Canada*] (NLC)
OLAFS .... Office of Legal Aid and Family Services
OLAFS .... Orbiting and Launch Approach Flight Simulator
OLAG .... London Research Center, Agriculture Canada [*Centre de Recherches de London, Agriculture Canada*] London, Ontario [*Library symbol*] [*National Library of Canada*] (NLC)
OLAG .... Oesterreichische Luftverkehrs Aktiengesellschaft [*Austrian Airlines*]
O-Lager .... Ortslager (SAUS)
OLak .... Lakewood Public Library, Lakewood, OH [*Library symbol*] [*Library of Congress*] (LCLS)
OLakB .... Lakewood Board of Education, Lakewood, OH [*Library symbol*] [*Library of Congress*] (LCLS)
OLAL .... Bibliotheque Publique du Canton d'Alfred [*Alfred Township Public Library*],Lefaivre, Ontario [*Library symbol*] [*National Library of Canada*] (BIB)
OLAM .... Online Alpha Monitor (SAUS)
OLAMINE ..... Ethanolamine [*Also, EA, Etn*] [*USAN*] [*Organic chemistry*]
OLAN .... Landsdowne Public Library, Ontario [*Library symbol*] [*National Library of Canada*] (BIB)
OLA-N .... Office of Legislative Affairs, Navy (MUGU)
OLAN .... On-Board Local Area Network [*Aviation*]
O/LAND .... Overland
O/LANDED .. Overlanded
ol & t .... Owners, Landlords, and Tenants (AD)
OL & T .... Owners, Landlords, and Tenants [*Liability insurance*]
OL&T .... Owners, Landlords, and Tenants [*Insurance*]
OLanF .... Fairfield County District Library, Lancaster, OH [*Library symbol*] [*Library of Congress*] (LCLS)
OLanU .... Ohio University, Lancaster Branch Campus, Lancaster, OH [*Library symbol*] [*Library of Congress*] (LCLS)
OLAP .... Online Analytical Processing [*Computer science*] (CDE)
OLAPEC ..... Organization of Latin American Petroleum Exporting Countries (AD)
OLAR .... On-Line Analytical Processing [*Computer science*]
OLAS .... Office of Arid Land Studies [*University of Arizona*] (AD)
OLAS .... On-Line Acquisitions Systems [*Brodart, Inc.*] [*Book acquisition system*] [*Information service or system*] (IID)
OLAS .... Organizacion Latino-Americana de Solidaridad [*Latin American Solidarity Organization*] [*Spanish*] (AD)
OLAS .... Organization of Latin American Students (AD)
OLATN .... Township of Norfolk Public Library, Langton, Ontario [*Library symbol*] [*National Library of Canada*] (NLC)
OLAU .... Lanark Union Public Library, Lanark, Ontario [*Library symbol*] [*National Library of Canada*] (BIB)
Olav Tryg..... Olav Trygvason (AD)
OLB .... London Board of Education, Ontario [*Library symbol*] [*National Library of Canada*] (NLC)
OLB .... Odd-Lot Broker [*Finance*] (MHDW)
OLB .... Oertlicher Landwirtschaftsbetrieb [*Local Agricultural Enterprise*] [*German*]
OLB .... Official Log Book [*Ship's diary*] (DS)
OLB .... Ohio Law Bulletin [*A publication*] (DLA)
OLB .... Olbia [*Italy*] [*Airport symbol*] (OAG)
OLB .... Omaha, Lincoln & Beatrice Railway Co. [*AAR code*]
OLB .... Online Batch (NITA)
OLB .... Open Liver Biopsy [*Medicine*] (DMAA)
OLB .... Open-Loop Bandwidth [*Also, OLBW*]
OLB .... Open Lung Biopsy
OLB .... Outer Lead Bond [*Integrated circuit technology*]
OLB .... Outside Linebacker [*Football*]
OLBA .... Beirut/International [*Lebanon*] [*ICAO location identifier*] (ICLI)
OLBGFC ...... Official Lane Brody Global Fan Club (EA)
OLBIEN .... Olsen's Biomass Energy [*G. V. Olsen Associates*] [*Information service or system*] (CRD)
olbm .... Orbital Launched Ballistic Missile (AD)
OLBM........... Orbital Launched Ballistic Missile [*Military*] (WDAA)
OLBM .... Overlay Battle Manager
OLBR .... Brescia College, London, Ontario [*Library symbol*] [*National Library of Canada*] (NLC)
OlBr .... Olive Brown (AD)
OLBR .... Operational LASER Beam Recorder
OLBS .... OnLine Bookstore
OLBV .... Beirut [*Lebanon*] [*ICAO location identifier*] (ICLI)
OLBW .... Open-Loop Bandwidth [*Also, OLB*]
olc .... Brothers of Our Lady of Providence (TOCD)
OLC............. Catholic Central High School, London, Ontario [*Library symbol*] [*National Library of Canada*] (NLC)
OLC............. Linfield College, McMinnville, OR [*OCLC symbol*] (OCLC)
OLC............. Oak Leaf Cluster [*Military decoration*]
OLC............. Occupation Level Crossing (HEAS)
OLC............. Office of Legal Counsel [*Department of Justice*]
Ol C .... Oil Cable (SAUS)
Olc .... Olcott's United States District Court Reports, Admiralty [*A publication*] (DLA)
OLC............. Olema [*California*] [*Seismograph station code, US Geological Survey*] (SEIS)
OLC............. Oneida, TN [*Location identifier*] [*FAA*] (FAAL)
OLC............. One Level Code (SAUS)
OLC............. On-Line Classifier (SAUS)
olc .... On-Line Computer (AD)
OLC............. Online Computer [*System*] [*Computer science*]

OLC............. Ontario Ladies College
OLC............. Ontario Land Corporation (SAUS)
OLC............. Ontario Library Co-Operative [*UTLAS symbol*]
OLC............. Ontario Library Council (SAUS)
OLC............. Open-Loop Control (CIST)
OLC............. Operating Location Clerk (SAUS)
OLC............. Operational Logical Circuit (SAUS)
OLC............. Operation Load Code (MCD)
OLC............. Operator-Level Chan (SAUS)
OLC............. Operator-Level Chart (AFIT)
OLC............. Optical Link Card (SAUS)
OLC............. Optical Loop Carrier (SAUS)
OLC............. Order Location and Control (MCD)
OLC............. Oubain-Like Compound [*Biochemistry*]
OLC............. Outgoing Line Circuit
OLC............. Overload Class (CGWS)
OLC............. Overseas Liaison Committee [*of the American Council on Education*] [*Later, Division of International Educational Relations of the American Council on Education*] (EA)
OLC............. Sisters of Our Lady of Charity (TOCD)
OLCA .... Office of Legislation and Congressional Affairs (SAUS)
OLCA .... Online Circuit Analysis [*System*] [*Computer science*]
OLCA .... Orifice of Left Coronary Artery [*Medicine*] (MELL)
Olc Adm ..... Olcott's United States District Court Reports, Admiralty [*A publication*] (DLA)
OLCAO .... Orthogonalized Linear Combination of Atomic Orbitals [*Optics*]
OLCA System... One-Line Circuit Analysis System (SAUS)
OLCA System... On-Line Circuit Analysis System (SAUS)
OLCC .... Olympus Capital Corp. (SAUS)
OLCC .... On-Line Card Catalog (SAUS)
OLCC .... Ontario Cancer Clinic, London, Ontario [*Library symbol*] [*National Library of Canada*] (NLC)
OLCC .... Optimum Life Cycle Costing (PDAA)
olcc............. Optimum Life-Cycle Costing (AD)
OLCC .... Ordinary Low Current Configuration [*Magnetic field*]
OLCC .... Our Lady of Cincinnati College [*Ohio*]
OLCC .... Overseas Labour Consultative Committee [*British*] (DCTA)
OLCD .... Overseas Liaison and Consultancy Department (NITA)
OLCG .... Clarkson Gordon, London, Ontario [*Library symbol*] [*National Library of Canada*] (BIB)
OLCM.......... Olicom AS [*NASDAQ symbol*] (SAG)
OLCMF........ Olicom A/S [*NASDAQ symbol*] (TTSB)
OLCMS .... On-Line Cargo Movement System (SAUS)
Ol Conv....... Oliver's Conveyancing [*A publication*] (DLA)
Olcott.......... Olcott's United States District Court Reports, Admiralty [*A publication*] (DLA)
Olcott Adm (F)... Olcott's United States District Court Reports, Admiralty [*A publication*] (DLA)
Olcott's Adm... Olcott's United States District Court Reports, Admiralty [*A publication*] (DLA)
OLCP .... Oil City Petroleum, Inc. (SAUS)
OLCP .... Online Complex Processing [*Computer science*] (CDE)
OLCP .... Open-Loop Conjugate Point (SAUS)
OLCPR .... Canadian Peace Research Institute, London, Ontario [*Library symbol*] [*National Library of Canada*] (NLC)
OLCR .... Clark Road Secondary School, London, Ontario [*Library symbol*] [*National Library of Canada*] (NLC)
OLCR .... On-Line Character Recognition (SAUS)
O L Cr.......... Ordinance Lieutenant-Commander (AD)
OLCR .... Ordnance Lieutenant-Commander [*Navy*] [*British*]
OLCR .... Sisters of Our Lady of Charity of Refuge [*Roman Catholic religious order*]
OLCS .... On-Line Computer System (AD)
OLCS .... On-Line Cover System (SAUS)
OLCSSCP..... Children's Psychiatric Research Institute, Ontario Ministry of Community and Social Services, London, Ontario [*Library symbol*] [*National Library of Canada*] (NLC)
OLC System... One-Line Computer System (SAUS)
OLCT............ Tax Services, Canada Trust Co., London, Ontario [*Library symbol*] [*National Library of Canada*] (BIB)
OLCV .... Century Village, Lang, Ontario [*Library symbol*] [*National Library of Canada*] (BIB)
OLD .... Obstructive Lung Disease [*Medicine*] (DMAA)
OLD .... Odd Lot Dealer
OLD .... Office of Legislative Development [*Bureau of Indian Affairs*]
OLD .... Ohio Lower Court Decisions [*A publication*] (DLA)
Old.............. Oldradus da Ponte de Laude [*Deceased, 1335*] [*Authority cited in pre-1607 legal work*] (DSA)
Old.............. Oldright's Nova Scotia Reports [*A publication*] (DLA)
OLD .... Old Town, ME [*Location identifier*] [*FAA*] (FAAL)
OLD .... Online Debug [*Computer science*] (IAA)
OLD .... On-Line Tests and Diagnostics [*Environmental science*] (COE)
OLD .... Onsite Licensing Office (SAUS)
OLD .... Open-Loop Damping
OLD .... Open Loop Drive (SAUS)
OLD .... Operating Level Days
OLD .... Operations and Liquidations Division [*Federal Savings and Loans Insurance Corporation*]
OLD .... Oral Lethal Dose [*Medicine*]
OLD .... Orthochromatic Leukodystrophy [*Medicine*] (DMAA)
OLD .... Our Lady of Deliverance Syriac, Union City [*Diocesan abbreviation*] [*New Jersey*] (TOCD)
OLD .... Oxford Latin Dictionary [*A publication*]
OldAmer ...... Old America Stores, Inc. [*Associated Press*] (SAG)
OLDAP .... Online Data Processor (PDAA)

OLDB .... Old Natl Bancorp(Ind) [*NASDAQ symbol*] (TTSB)
OLDB .... On-Line Data Bank [*NASA*] (NAKS)
OLDB .... Online Database [*or Data Bank*]
Old Bailey ... London's Central Criminal Court [*England*] (AD)
Old Bailey Chr... Old Bailey Chronicle [*A publication*] (DLA)
Old Ben ...... Benloe in Benloe and Dalison's English Common Pleas Reports [*A publication*] (DLA)
Old Benloe... Benloe in Benloe and Dalison's English Common Pleas Reports [*A publication*] (DLA)
OLDC .... Off-Line Data Collection (SAUS)
OLDC .... One-Line Data Collecting (SAUS)
OLDC .... Online Data Collection [*Computer science*] (MCD)
OLDD .... Beirut [*Lebanon*] [*ICAO location identifier*] (ICLI)
OldDom ...... Old Dominion Freight Lines, Inc. [*Associated Press*] (SAG)
Old Dom U... Old Dominion University (GAGS)
OLD ECC...... Ordinary Linear Differential Equations with Constant Coefficients [*Mathematics*]
Old Ent ...... Rastell's Old Entries [*A publication*] (DLA)
OLDERT ...... On-Line Executive for Real-Time [*Computer science*] (MHDB)
old-fash ...... Old Fashioned (AD)
Oldfos......... Old Established Forces (AD)
OLDFOS ...... Old Established Forces [*Military*] (CINC)
OldGBI .... Oldenburgisches Gesetzblatt (SAUS)
OLDHM .... Oldham [*City in England*]
OLDI .... On-Line Data Input (SAUS)
OLDI .... Online Data Interchange (DA)
OLDIV .... Operations/Lookout and Recognition Division (DNAB)
OldKent....... Old Kent Financial Corp. [*Associated Press*] (SAG)
Old Maid's... Old Maid's Day [*June 4*] (AD)
Old Nat Brev... Old Natura Brevium [*A publication*] (DLA)
OldNB .... Old National Bancorp Industries [*Associated Press*] (SAG)
Oldn Pr ...... Oldnall's Sessions Practice [*A publication*] (DLA)
OLDO .... On-Line Data Output (SAUS)
OLDP .... Off-Line Data Processing (SAUS)
Oldr .... Oldradus da Ponte de Laude [*Deceased, 1335*] [*Authority cited in pre-1607 legal work*] (DSA)
Oldr .... Oldright's Nova Scotia Reports [*A publication*] (DLA)
OLDR .... On-Line Data Reduction (SAUS)
OLDR .... On-Time Data Reduction (SAUS)
OLDR .... Quick Look Data Reference [*NASA*] (NAKS)
Oldra .... Oldradus da Ponte de Laude [*Deceased, 1335*] [*Authority cited in pre-1607 legal work*] (DSA)
Oldra de Lau... Oldradus da Ponte de Laude [*Deceased, 1335*] [*Authority cited in pre-1607 legal work*] (DSA)
old rep......... Old Repertory (AD)
OldRep .... Old Republic International Corp. [*Associated Press*] (SAG)
Oldr NS....... Oldright's Nova Scotia Reports [*A publication*] (DLA)
OldRp .... Old Republic International Corp. [*Associated Press*] (SAG)
OLDS .... Off-Axis LASER Detection System (MCD)
OLDS .... Offshore Lease Data System [*Department of the Interior*] [*Information service or system*] (IID)
Olds .... Oldsmobile (AD)
OLDS .... Oldsmobile [*Automotive engineering*]
OLDS .... On-Line Detection System [*Nuclear energy*]
OLDS .... Online Display System [*Computer science*]
OLDS .... Open Loop Drive System (SAUS)
Old SC .... Old Select Cases [*Oudh, India*] [*A publication*] (DLA)
OldSecBc..... Old Second Bancorp, Inc. [*Associated Press*] (SAG)
OLDSS .... Online Database Search Services Directory [*A publication*]
Old Territorial... Old Territorial Penitentiary (SAUS)
Old Test...... Old Testament (AD)
OLDU .... On-Line Distillation Unit (SAUS)
Old Vetern ... Caring for the Older Veteran (journ.) (SAUS)
OLE .... Lane Community College, Eugene, OR [*OCLC symbol*] (OCLC)
OLE............ Leamington Public Library, Ontario [*Library symbol*] [*National Library of Canada*] (NLC)
OLe............ Lebanon Public Library, Lebanon, OH [*Library symbol*] [*Library of Congress*] (LCLS)
OLE .... Object-Linked Environment (SAUS)
OLE .... Object Linking and Embedding [*Windows*] [*Computer science*]
OLE .... Office for Library Education [*American Library Association*]
OLE .... Olean [*New York*] [*Airport symbol*] (AD)
OLE .... Olean, NY [*Location identifier*] [*FAA*] (FAAL)
OLE .... On-Line Edit (SAUS)
OLE .... On-Line Encyclopedia [*Hypergraphics Corp.*]
OLE .... Online Enquiry [*System*]
OLE .... On-Line Equipment (SAUS)
OLE .... Ontario Land Economist [*Canada*] (DD)
OLE .... Optical Logic Etalon (ACAE)
OLE .... Oral Language Evaluation [*English and Spanish test*]
OLE .... Organizational Leadership for Executives [*Military*] (RDA)
OLE .... Oriole Communication [*Vancouver Stock Exchange symbol*]
OLE .... Outside Location Engineer (MCD)
OLEA .... Office of Law Enforcement Assistance (AD)
OLEASS ...... Organic Long Endurance Airborne Area Surveillance System (ACAE)
OLeC.......... Lebanon Correctional Institution Library, Lebanon, OH [*Library symbol*] [*Library of Congress*] (LCLS)
OLEC .... Other Local Exchange Carrier (SAUS)
Oleck Corporations... Oleck's Modern Corporation Law [*A publication*] (DLA)
OLED .... Organic Light Emitting Device (SAUS)
OLED .... Organic Light-Emitting Device [*Photonics*]
OLED .... Organic Light-Emitting Diode [*Electronics*]
OLED .... Organic Light Emitting Display (SAUS)
OLE DB ...... OLE Database [*Computer science*]
OLEDS .... Object Linking and Embedding Directory Services (SAUS)

O Legal News... Ohio Legal News [*A publication*] (DLA)
OLEI............ Point Pelee National Park, Parks Canada [*Parc National de la Pointe-Pelee, Parcs Canada*] Leamington, Ontario [*Library symbol*] [*National Library of Canada*] (NLC)
OLELB......... Lyn Branch, Elizabethtown Township Public Library, Ontario [*Library symbol*] [*National Library of Canada*] (BIB)
OLEM.......... Other Loans Especially Mentioned (EBF)
oleo............ Oleomargarine [*Dietetics*] (DAVI)
oleo............ Oleoresins (AD)
OLEO .... Open Linking and Embedding of Objects (SAUS)
OLEO .... Orbiting Large Engineering Observatory (SAUS)
OLEP .... Office of Law Enforcement and Planning (AD)
OLEP......... Office of Law Enforcement Programs [*Federal government*]
OLEP......... Office of Legal Enforcement Policy [*Environmental Protection Agency*] (EPA)
OLEP.......... Organization for the Lifelong Establishment of Paternity (EA)
OLEP.......... Osculating Lunar Elements Program (SAUS)
OLER .... Olericulture
olericult....... Olericulture (AD)
OLERT .... Online Executive for Real Time [*Computer science*] (IEEE)
OLES .... Online Editorial System [*Computer science*] (DGA)
OLESS .... Open Learning Electronic Support Services [*Australia*]
OLETC .... Office of Law Enforcement Technology Commercialization (SAUS)
O level........ Ordinary Level (ODBW)
O-level........ Ordinary Level Examination [*Education*] (WDAA)
O-levels....... Ordinary Levels [*of educational tests*] (AD)
OLeWHi....... Warren County Historical Society, Lebanon, OH [*Library symbol*] [*Library of Congress*] (LCLS)
OLEX .... Ontario Livestock Exchange (SAUS)
OLF .... Ohio Library Foundation (AD)
OLF .... Old Low Franconian [*Language, etc.*]
olf .... Olfactory [*Medicine*] (DAVI)
OLF .... One Hundred Linear Feet (SAUS)
olf .... On-Line Filing (AD)
OLF .... Online Filing [*Computer science*] (PDAA)
OLF .... Only Living Father [*of Newfoundland's confederation with Canada in 1949*] [*Epithet for Joseph R. Smallwood*]
OLF .... Open Learning Federation [*British*] (DI)
OLF .... Open-Loop Feedback (SAUS)
OLF .... Orbital Launch Facility
OLF .... Orbiter Landing Facility [*NASA*] (NASA)
OLF .... Organ Literature Foundation (EA)
OLF .... Oromo Liberation Front [*Ethiopia*] [*Political party*] (PD)
OLF .... Outline Font [*Computer science*] (PCM)
OLF .... Outlying Field [*Army*]
OLF .... Overland Flow (SAUS)
OLF .... Wolf Point [*Montana*] [*Airport symbol*] (OAG)
OLF .... Wolf Point, MT [*Location identifier*] [*FAA*] (FAAL)
OLFC.......... Fanshawe College of Applied Arts and Technology, London, Ontario [*Library symbol*] [*National Library of Canada*] (NLC)
OLFDEMO .... Outline Font Demonstration [*Computer science*]
OLFO .... Open-Loop Feedback Optimal (PDAA)
OLFR .... Olfactory Receptor [*Medicine*] (DMAA)
OLG .... Nordmaling [*Sweden*] [*Airport symbol*] (AD)
OLG .... Oberlandesgericht [*District Court of Appeal*] [*German*] (DLA)
OLG .... Ohio Legislative Service Commission, Columbus, OH [*OCLC symbol*] (OCLC)
OLG .... Old Low German [*Language, etc.*]
OLG .... Oligodendrocyte [*Also, ODC*] [*Cytology*]
OIG .... Olive Green (AD)
OLG .... Open Level Generation (SAUS)
OLG .... Open-Loop Gain
OLG .... Operation Landing Ground (SAUS)
OLG .... Sisters of Guadalupe [*Roman Catholic religious order*]
OLG .... Sisters of Our Lady of the Garden [*Roman Catholic religious order*]
OLGA .... On-line Guitar Archive [*Internet site*]
OLGC.......... Orthologic Corp. [*NASDAQ symbol*] (SAG)
OLGR.......... [*The*] Oilgear Co. [*NASDAQ symbol*] (NQ)
OLH .... Huron College, London, Ontario [*Library symbol*] [*National Library of Canada*] (NLC)
OLH .... Old Harbor [*Alaska*] [*Airport symbol*] (OAG)
OLH .... Old Harbor, AK [*Location identifier*] [*FAA*] (FAAL)
OLH .... Orpen's Light Horse [*British military*] (DMA)
OLH .... Ovine Lactogenic Hormone [*Endocrinology*] (MAE)
OLH .... Ovine Luteinizing Hormone [*Endocrinology*]
OLH .... Oxfordshire Light Horse [*British military*] (DMA)
OLHC.......... Old Lyme Holding Corp. [*NASDAQ symbol*] (SAG)
OLHI .... Ovine Luteinizing Hormone (SAUS)
OLHM .... London Historical Museums, Ontario [*Library symbol*] [*National Library of Canada*] (BIB)
OLHMIS .... On-Line Hospital Management Information System [*Computer science*]
Ol Horse ..... Oliphant's Law of Horses [*6th ed.*] [*1908*] [*A publication*] (DLA)
OLI .... Lindsay Public Library, Ontario [*Library symbol*] [*National Library of Canada*] (NLC)
OLI............ Ocean Living Institute [*Defunct*] (EA)
OLI............ Olafsvik [*Iceland*] [*Airport symbol*] (OAG)
OLI............ Oliktok, AK [*Location identifier*] [*FAA*] (FAAL)
Oli............ Oliver (AD)
OLI............ Online Information
OLI............ On-Line Input (SAUS)
OLI............ Open Learning Institute [*UTLAS symbol*]
OLI............ Open Link Interface (TNIG)
OLI............ Operation Lifesaver [*An association*] (EA)
OLI............ Optical Line Interface (SAUS)

OLI............. Optical Phone Line Interface (SAUS)
OLI............. Originating Line Information (SAUS)
OLI............. Out-of-Line Igniter [*Military*] (CAAL)
OLI............. Out-of-Line Interrupter (MCD)
OLI............. Out-of-Lock Indicator (SAUS)
OLI............. Overlay Interceptor
OLI............. Oxfordshire Light Infantry [*Military unit*] [*British*]
OLiC........... Columbiana County Court House, Lisbon, OH [*Library symbol*]
      [*Library of Congress*] (LCLS)
OLIC.......... Online Information Centre (NITA)
OLIC.......... On-Line Inspection Centre [*British Gas*] (WDAA)
OL-IC......... Operating Location-Iceland (DNAB)
O-Licence.... Operators Licence (SAUS)
O-license.... Operator's License (AD)
Olicom........ Olicom AS [*Associated Press*] (SAG)
OLICU......... Little Current Public Library, Ontario [*Library symbol*] [*National
      Library of Canada*] (NLC)
OLICUS........ Sucker Creek Indian Band Public Library, Little Current, Ontario
      [*Library symbol*] [*National Library of Canada*] (NLC)
OLID .... On-Line Identification (SAUS)
OLIDS......... Open Loop Insulin Delivery System [*Medicine*] (DMAA)
OLIF........... Orbiter Landing Instrumentation Facilities [*NASA*] (NASA)
OLIFLM....... Online Image Forming Light Modulator
Olig............ Oligocene (AD)
OLIH.......... Lion's Head Branch, Bruce County Public Library, Ontario [*Library
      symbol*] [*National Library of Canada*] (NLC)
OLI/HMD..... Online Images from the History of Medicine Division (SAUS)
OLIM.......... Olimpiadas [*Ministerio de Cultura*] [*Spain*] [*Information service or
      system*] (CRD)
OLima........ Lima Public Library, Lima, OH [*Library symbol*] [*Library of
      Congress*] (LCLS)
OLimaAL...... Allen County Law Library, Lima, OH [*Library symbol*] [*Library of
      Congress*] (LCLS)
OLIMCH ...... Open Learning Information and Materials Clearing House [*Australia*]
OLIN .... Oklahoma Library Information Network (SAUS)
Olin............ Olin Corp. [*Associated Press*] (SAG)
OLIP........... Online Instrument Package [*Computer science*] (NRCH)
OLIPaC....... Office of Land Information Policy and Coordination (SAUS)
OLIPAC....... Oligotrophic Pacific (SAUS)
Oliph Hor.... Oliphant's Law of Horses [*6th ed.*] [*1908*] [*A publication*] (DLA)
OLIPS .... Open Literature Information Processing System (ACAE)
OLIPSE ...... Optizon Liquid Phase Sintering Experiment [*NASA*] (SPST)
OLIS........... Listowel Public Library, Ontario [*Library symbol*] [*National Library of
      Canada*] (NLC)
OLIS........... Online Information Services [*Mercer County Community College
      Library*] (OLDSS)
OLIS........... On-Line Information System (SAUS)
OLIS........... Oregon Legislative Information System [*Information service or
      system*]
OLIS........... Oxford Library Information System (TNIG)
OLIS........... Oxford Library Integrated System [*British*] (TELE)
OLIS........... Oxide Layer Isolation Structure
OLISF.......... Frost Campus Library, Sir Sandford Fleming College, Lindsay,
      Ontario [*Library symbol*] [*National Library of Canada*] (NLC)
OLIT........... Open Look Interface Toolkit (SAUS)
OLIT........... OPEN LOOK Intrinsic Toolkit
OLitW .... Wagnalls Memorial Library, Lithopolis, OH [*Library symbol*] [*Library of
      Congress*] (LCLS)
OLIV........... Oleum Olivae [*Olive Oil*] [*Pharmacy*] (ROG)
OLIV........... Victoria County Public Library, Lindsay, Ontario [*Library symbol*]
      [*National Library of Canada*] (NLC)
Oliv B & L ... Oliver, Beavan, and Lefroy's English Railway and Canal Cases
      [*A publication*] (DLA)
Oliv Conv.... Oliver's Conveyancing [*A publication*] (DLA)
Olive.......... Olivera (AD)
OLIVER .... Online Instrumentation via Energetic Radioisotopes [*Computer
      science*] (PDAA)
OLIVER .... Online Interactive Variable Editing Reporter [*Computer science*] (IAA)
Olivet Naz U... Olivet Nazarene University (GAGS)
Oliv Prec ..... Oliver's Precedents [*A publication*] (DLA)
OLIVR .... Online Interactive Virtual Reality (SAUS)
OLIVW .... Walden Public Library, Lively, Ontario [*Library symbol*] [*National
      Library of Canada*] (BIB)
OLJ............. Ohio Law Journal [*A publication*] (DLA)
OLJ............. Order of St. Lazarus of Jerusalem [*British*]
OLJ............. Oudh Law Journal [*India*] [*A publication*] (DLA)
OLJ............. Spokane, WA [*Location identifier*] [*FAA*] (FAAL)
OL Jour....... Ohio Law Journal [*A publication*] (DLA)
OL Jour....... Oudh Law Journal [*India*] [*A publication*] (DLA)
OLK............ King's College, London, Ontario [*Library symbol*] [*National Library of
      Canada*] (NLC)
OLK............ Salomon, Inc. [*AMEX symbol*] (SPSG)
OLK............ Salomon Inc, 7.25% ORCL'ELKS' [*AMEX symbol*] (TTSB)
OLK............ Wolf Lake, IN [*Location identifier*] [*FAA*] (FAAL)
OLKK .... Tripoli [*Lebanon*] [*ICAO location identifier*] (ICLI)
OLKV .... Tripoli [*Lebanon*] [*ICAO location identifier*] (ICLI)
OLL............ Larder Lake Public Library, Ontario [*Library symbol*] [*National Library
      of Canada*] (BIB)
OLL............ Oceaneering International, Inc. (SAUS)
OLL............ Office of Legislative Liaison
OLL............ Ollague [*Chile*] [*Seismograph station code, US Geological Survey*]
      [*Closed*] (SEIS)
OLL............ Open-Loop Loss (SAUS)
OLL............ Organic Liquid LASER

OLL............. Our Lady of Lebanon of Los Angeles [*Diocesan abbreviation*]
      [*California*] (TOCD)
OLL............. Output Logic Level
OLLA.......... Office of Lend-Lease Administration [*World War II*]
OLLA.......... Oil Lands Leasing Act
Oll B & F..... Ollivier, Bell, and Fitzgerald's New Zealand Reports [*A publication*]
      (DLA)
OLLC.......... Office of the Liquor Licensing Commissioner [*South Australia*]
OLLC.......... Our Lady of the Lake College [*Texas*]
OLLCR .... Labatt's Central Research Library, London, Ontario [*Library symbol*]
      [*National Library of Canada*] (NLC)
OLLE.......... Lake Erie Regional Library System, London, Ontario [*Library symbol*]
      [*National Library of Canada*] (NLC)
OLLE.......... Ontario Library Service - Thames, London, Ontario [*Library symbol*]
      [*National Library of Canada*] (NLC)
OLLFSC....... Open-Loop Leader-Follower Speed Control [*Hydraulics*]
OLLI........... Online Library Index [*Western Michigan University*]
OLLI........... Online Library Information (SAUS)
OLLIE.......... Operation Last Laugh Independence Expenditure [*Political Action
      Committee opposed to Oliver North's candidacy for United States
      Senator of Virginia*]
OL LINI SI ... Oleum Lini sine Igne [*Cold-Drawn Linseed Oil*] [*Pharmacy*] (ROG)
Olliv B & F... Ollivier, Bell, and Fitzgerald's New Zealand Reports [*A publication*]
      (DLA)
OLLL........... Beirut [*Lebanon*] [*ICAO location identifier*] (ICLI)
OLLS........... Online Logical Simulation System [*Computer science*] (KSC)
OLLS........... Operational Logistics Support Summary (SAUS)
OLLS........... Optical Locator Laser Station (SAUS)
OLLT........... Office of Libraries and Learning Technologies (NITA)
OLLU........... Our Lady of the Lake University [*Texas*]
OLM............ Lloyd Library and Museum, Cincinnati, OH [*OCLC symbol*] (OCLC)
OLM............ Office for Laboratory Management [*DoD*] (MCD)
OLM............ Olympia [*Washington*] [*Airport symbol*] (AD)
OLM............ Olympia, WA [*Location identifier*] [*FAA*] (FAAL)
OLM............ Olympic Financial Ltd [*NYSE symbol*] (TTSB)
OLM............ On-Line Measurement (SAUS)
OLM............ Online Monitor [*Computer science*]
OLM............ Optical Light Microscopy (SAUS)
OLM............ Optical Link Modul (SAUS)
OLM............ Organic Leach Model [*Landfill technology*]
OLM............ Sisters of Charity of Our Lady of Mercy [*Roman Catholic religious
      order*]
OLMA.......... Ontario Lumber Manufacturers Association (SAUS)
OLMAT........ Otis Lennon Mental Ability Test (EDAC)
OLMC.......... Olivier Management Corporation (SAUS)
OLMC.......... On-Line Machine Control (SAUS)
OLMC.......... Output Logic Macrocell [*Computer science*]
OLMCPR...... Operating Limit of MCPR (SAUS)
OLMR .... Office of Labor Management Relations (AD)
OLMR .... Organic Liquid Moderated Reactor
olmr........... Organic Liquid-Moderator Reactor (AD)
Olms........... Decisions of the Judicial Committee of the Privy Council re the British
      North American Act, 1867, and the Canadian Constitution
      [*A publication*] (DLA)
OLMS.......... Office of Labor-Management Standards [*Department of Labor*]
OLMS.......... Osborn Laboratories of Marine Sciences [*New York Zoological
      Society*] [*Research center*] (RCD)
OLMSA........ Office of Life & Microgravity Sciences & Applications [*NASA*]
Olmsted....... Olmsted's Privy Council Decisions [*1867-1954*] [*A publication*] (DLA)
OLMT.......... Organizational Level Maintenance Timer
OLMUG........ Online Librarian's Microcomputer User Group [*Teleconferencing
      system*]
OLMWPR..... Office of Labor-Management and Welfare-Pension Reports
      [*Department of Labor*]
OLN .... Colonia Sarmiento [*Argentina*] [*Airport symbol*] (AD)
OLN .... Lane Public Library, Hamilton, OH [*OCLC symbol*] (OCLC)
OLN .... Ohio Legal News [*A publication*] (DLA)
OLN .... Old Man, AK [*Location identifier*] [*FAA*] (FAAL)
OLN .... Oleylnitril (SAUS)
OLN .... Olin Corp. [*NYSE symbol*] (TTSB)
OLN .... Online News (NITA)
OLN .... Operator's License Number (SARE)
OLO .... Longlac Public Library, Ontario [*Library symbol*] [*National Library of
      Canada*] (NLC)
OLO .... Off-Line Operation (SAUS)
OLO .... Olomouc [*Czechoslovakia*] [*Airport symbol*] (AD)
OLO .... Olotillo [*Race of maize*]
OLO .... Online Operation [*Computer science*]
OLO .... On-Line Output (SAUS)
OLO .... Oologah [*Oklahoma*] [*Seismograph station code, US Geological
      Survey*] [*Closed*] (SEIS)
OLO .... Operations Launch Order (MUGU)
OLO .... Orbital Launch Operation
OLOC .... Old Lesbians Organizing for Change [*An association*] (EA)
OLOE .... Online Order Entry
OLOF .... Levack Branch, Onaping Falls Public Library, Ontario [*Library
      symbol*] [*National Library of Canada*] (NLC)
Olofson........ Olofsson Corp. [*Associated Press*] (SAG)
OLOFV........ Olofsson Corp. [*NASDAQ symbol*] (SAG)
OLOG.......... Offshore Logistics [*NASDAQ symbol*] (TTSB)
OLOG.......... Offshore Logistics, Inc. [*NASDAQ symbol*] (NQ)
OLogC........ Logan-Hocking County District Library, Logan, OH [*Library symbol*]
      [*Library of Congress*] (LCLS)
OLOGP........ Offshore Logistics, Inc. (MHDW)
OLOGS........ Open-Loop Oxygen-Generating System [*Air Force*]

ol ol	Olive Oil (AD)
ol oliv	Oleum Olivae [*Olive Oil*] [*Pharmacy*]
OLOM	Orbiter Lift-Off Mass [*NASA*] (KSC)
OLor	Lorain Public Library, Lorain, OH [*Library symbol*] [*Library of Congress*] (LCLS)
OLOS	Oakridge Secondary School, London, Ontario [*Library symbol*] [*National Library of Canada*] (NLC)
OLOS	Observer Line of Sight (SAUS)
OLOS	Office for Library Outreach Service [*American Library Association*]
OLOS	Office for Literacy and Outreach Services (AL)
OLOS	Operational Land Observation System (SAUS)
olos	Out of Line of Sight (AD)
OLOS	Out of Line of Sight (NATG)
OLou	Loudonville Public Library, Loudonville, OH [*Library symbol*] [*Library of Congress*] (LCLS)
OLOW	Orbiter Lift-Off Weight [*NASA*]
olow	Orbiter Liftoff Weight (AD)
O Lower D	Ohio Lower Court Decisions [*A publication*] (DLA)
OLP	Brothers of Our Lady of Providence (TOCD)
OLP	Lewis and Clark College, Portland, OR [*OCLC symbol*] (OCLC)
OLP	Missionaries of the Third Order of St. Francis of Our Lady of the Prairies [*Roman Catholic women's religious order*]
OLP	Objective Lens Power Supply
OLP	Observation Landplane [*Coast Guard*]
olp	Occipito-Laeva Posterior
OLP	Occipitolaeva Posterior [*A fetal position*] [*Medicine*] (AAMN)
OLP	Office of Labor Production [*WPB*] [*World War II*]
OLP	Off-Line Processing (SAUS)
OLP	Off-Line Program [*Computer science*]
OLP	Olympic Dam [*Australia*] [*Airport symbol*] (OAG)
OLP	One Liberty Properties, Inc. [*AMEX symbol*] (SPSG)
OLP	On-Line Processing (SAUS)
OLP	Online Processor (TEL)
OLP	Online Programming
OLP	Open Learning Programme (AIE)
OLP	Optical Line Pair
OLP	Oral Lichen Plannus [*Medicine*]
OLP	Order Load Print (SAUS)
OLP	Organizacion para la Liberacion Palestina [*Palestinian Liberation Organization*] [*Spanish*] [*Political party*] (AD)
olp	Original List Price (AD)
OLP	Outside Left Position [*Dancing*]
OLP	Oxygen at Low Pressure (KSC)
OLP	Oxygen Lance Powder (IAA)
OLP	Oxygen Lime Powder [*Steelmaking process*]
OLP	Oxygen Low Pressure (SAUS)
OLP	Sisters of Our Lady of Providence [*Roman Catholic religious order*]
olpar	Other Large Phased-Array RADAR (AD)
OLPARS	Online Pattern Analysis and Recognition System [*Computer science*] (MCD)
OLPBAR	On-Line Patient Billing and Accounts Receivable (SAUS)
OL/PBAR	Online Patient Billing and Accounts Receivable System [*Computer science*] (PDAA)
OLPBAR System	On-Line Patient Billing and Accounts Receivable System (SAUS)
OLPH	London Psychiatric Hospital, Ontario [*Library symbol*] [*National Library of Canada*] (NLC)
OLPHS	Parkwood Hospital Services, London, Ontario [*Library symbol*] [*National Library of Canada*] (BIB)
OLPP	One Liberty Prop $1.60 Cv Pfd [*AMEX symbol*] (TTSB)
OLP Process	Oxygen Lime Powder Process (SAUS)
OLPR	Office of Library Personnel Resources [*American Library Association*]
Ol Prec	Oliver's Precedents [*A publication*] (DLA)
OLPS	Online Programming System [*Computer science*]
OLPT	Oxford Library of Practical Theology [*A publication*]
OLPT	Pinchas Troester Library, Congregation B'Nai Israel, London, Ontario [*Library symbol*] [*National Library of Canada*] (NLC)
OLQ	Biloxi, MS [*Location identifier*] [*FAA*] (FAAL)
olq	Officer-Like Qualities (AD)
OLQ	Officer-Like Qualities [*British military*] (DMA)
OLQ	Olsobip [*Papua New Guinea*] [*Airport symbol*] (OAG)
OLQ	On-Line Query (SAUS)
OLR	Oak-Leaf Roller [*Moth*] [*Entomology*]
OLR	Objective Loudness Rating [*of telephone connections*] (IEEE)
OLR	Objective Loudness Ratio (SAUS)
OLR	Office Loop Regenerator (ACAE)
OLR	Office Loop Repeater (MHDB)
OLR	Office of Labor Racketeering [*Department of Labor*]
OLR	Office of Legislative Reference [*Bureau of the Budget; later, OMB*]
OLR	Offline Reader [*Bulletin board*]
OLR	Offline Recovery [*Telecommunications*] (TEL)
OLR	Off Load Route [*Aviation*] (DA)
OLR	Off Load Routes (SAUS)
OLR	Ohio Law Reporter [*A publication*] (DLA)
O-LR	Ohio Legislative Reference Bureau, Columbus, OH [*Library symbol*] [*Library of Congress*] (LCLS)
OLR	On-Line Research, Inc. [*Information service or system*] (IID)
OLR	On Location Repair (MCD)
OLR	Ontario Law Reporter [*A publication*] (DLA)
OLR	Ontario Law Reports [*A publication*] (DLA)
OLR	Open-Loop Receiver [*or Response*]
OLR	Open Loop Response (CIST)
OLR	Operator's Local Representative (AIA)
OLR	Organisation pour la Liberation du Rwanda [*Organization for the Liberation of Rwanda*]

OLR	Oudh Law Reports [*India*] [*A publication*] (DLA)
OLR	Outer Lindblad Resonance [*Planetary science*]
OLR	Outgoing Long-Wave Radiation [*Satellite sensed*]
OLR	Overall Loudness Rating (SAUS)
olr	Overload Relay (AD)
OLR	Overload Relay
OLR	Robarts School Library, London, Ontario [*Library symbol*] [*National Library of Canada*] (BIB)
OLRA	Ontario Labour Relations Act (SAUS)
OLRAG	London Regional Art Gallery, Ontario [*Library symbol*] [*National Library of Canada*] (NLC)
OLRB	Ontario Labor Relations Board [*Canada*] (AD)
OLRB	Ontario Labour Relations Board Monthly Report [*A publication*] (DLA)
O/L-RC	Overload-Reverse Current (NASA)
OL Rep	Ohio Law Reporter [*A publication*] (DLA)
ol res	Oleoresin (AD)
Ol Res	Oleoresin [*Also, OR*] [*Pharmacy*]
OLRI	Office & Factory, Rochevert Industrie, Inc., Lindsay, Ontario [*Library symbol*] [*National Library of Canada*] (NLC)
OL RIC	Oleum Ricine (SAUS)
OL RIC	Oleum Ricini [*Castor Oil*] [*Pharmacy*] (ROG)
OLRL	Lyndhurst Branch, Rideau Lakes Union Library, Ontario [*Library symbol*] [*National Library of Canada*] (BIB)
OLRM	Medical Library, Ross Memorial Hospital, Lindsay, Ontario [*Library symbol*] [*National Library of Canada*] (BIB)
OLRP	On-Line Report Processor (SAUS)
OLRS	Optical LASER Ranging System
olrt	On-Line Real Time [*Computer science*] (AD)
OLRT	Online Real Time [*Computer science*]
OLRT Computer	On-Line Real Time Computer (SAUS)
OLRV	Olive Latent Ringspot Virus [*Plant pathology*]
OLS	Nogales, AZ [*Location identifier*] [*FAA*] (FAAL)
OLS	Oceanographic Lidar System (SAUS)
OLS	Office of Legal Services [*of Office of Economic Opportunity*]
OLS	Office of Library Services (AAGC)
OLS	Off-Line Storage (SAUS)
OLS	OLS Asia Holdings Ltd. [*Associated Press*] (SAG)
OLS	Olsten Corp. [*NYSE symbol*] (SAG)
OLS	Online Library System (AEPA)
OLS	Online Scan [*Computer science*] (CAAL)
OLS	Online Search (NITA)
OLS	Online System [*Computer science*]
OLS	Ontario Land Surveyor [*Canada*] (ASC)
OLS	Open-Loop System [*Chemical engineering*]
OLS	Operational Launch Station (AAG)
OLS	Operational License Stage (CARB)
OLS	Operational Line Scanner (CARB)
OLS	Operational Linescan System [*Navy*] (ANA)
OLS	Operational Lines of Succession [*Defense readiness*]
OLS	Operation Lifeline Sudan
OLS	Operation...Life Support [*Online lobbying for the television show "My So-Called Life"*]
OLS	Operation Line Scanner (SAUS)
OLS	Optical Landing System
OLS	Optical Line Scanner (EOSA)
OLS	Orbiting Lunar Station [*NASA*]
OLS	Ordinary Least Squares [*Statistics*]
OLS	Original Line of Sight
OLS	Overlap Shear
OLS	Sisters of Our Lady of Sorrows [*Roman Catholic religious order*]
OLS	Spartan of Canada Ltd., London, Ontario [*Library symbol*] [*National Library of Canada*] (NLC)
OLSA	Off-Line Selectric Analyser [*Computer science*] (IAA)
OLSA	OLS Asia Holdings Ltd. [*NASDAQ symbol*] (SAG)
OLSA	Orbiter Logistics Support Plan [*NASA*]
OLSA	Orbiter/LPS [*Launch Processing System*] Signal Adapter [*NASA*] (NASA)
OLS AH	OLS Asia Holdings Ltd. [*Associated Press*] (SAG)
OL'SAM	Online Database Search Assistance Machine [*Franklin Institute*] [*Information service or system*] [*Defunct*] (IID)
OL'SAM	Online Search Assistance Machine (NITA)
OLSASS	Online System Availability and Service Simulation [*Computer science*] (PDAA)
OLSA-T	Off-Line Selectric Analyzer-Transistorized (SAUS)
OLSAT	Otis-Lennon School Ability Test [*Education*]
OLSAY	OLS Asia Hlds ADS [*NASDAQ symbol*] (TTSB)
olsc	On-Line Scientific Computer (AD)
OLSC	Online Scientific Computer [*Computer science*]
OLSCA	Orientation Linkage for a Solar Cell Array
OLSCG	Latchford Senior Citizens Group, Ontario [*Library symbol*] [*National Library of Canada*] (BIB)
OLSD	Office for Library Service to the Disadvantaged [*American Library Association*]
OLSDG	Lancaster Branch, Stormont, Dundas, and Glengarry County Library, Ontario [*Library symbol*] [*National Library of Canada*] (BIB)
OLSDMS	On-Line Strain and Damage Measurement System (SAUS)
OLSE	Ordinary Least-Squares Estimators [*Statistics*]
OLSF	Olson Farms, Inc. (SAUS)
OLSF	Online Subsystem Facility [*Computer science*] (MCD)
OLSH	Our Lady of the Sacred Heart (ADA)
OLSIDI-F	Oral Language Sentence Imitation Diagnostic Inventory Format Revised (SAUS)
OLSILC	On the Lighter Side, International Lighter Collectors (EA)
OLSIST-F	Oral Language Sentence Imitation Screening Test - Format Revised [*Educational test*]

OLSJ .... St. Joseph's Hospital, London, Ontario [*Library symbol*] [*National Library of Canada*] (NLC)
OLSN .... Olson Industries, Inc. (SAUS)
OLSNA .... Orthopaedic Laser Society of North America (SAUS)
OLSOR .... Object Location and Small Object Recovery [*Military*] (DNAB)
OLSP .... Office of Life Science Programs [*Obsolete*] [*NASA*]
OLSP .... Operational Logistic Support Plan
OLSP .... Orbiter Logistics Support Plan [*NASA*] (NASA)
OLSP .... St. Peter's Seminary, London, Ontario [*Library symbol*] [*National Library of Canada*] (NLC)
OLSS .... On-Line Sodium Sampling (SAUS)
OLSS .... Online Software System [*Computer science*] (IEEE)
OLSS .... On-Line Support Software (SAUS)
OLSS .... Operational Logistic Support Summary [*Military*] (CAAL)
OLSS .... Overseas Limited Storage Site [*Army*]
OLSSDG ...... Long Sault Branch, Stormont, Dundas, and Glengarry County Public Library, Ontario [*Library symbol*] [*National Library of Canada*] (BIB)
Olsten .... Olsten Corp. [*Associated Press*] (SAG)
OLSUS .... Online System Use Statistics (NITA)
OLSWF .... OLS Asia HLDS ADS Wrrt [*NASDAQ symbol*] (TTSB)
OLT .... Occipitolaeva Transversa [*A fetal position*] [*Medicine*] (AAMN)
olt .... Occipito-Laeva Transverse (AD)
OLT .... Oddity-Learning Task [*Psychology*]
OLT .... Official Latin Title
OLT .... Off-Line Transmission (SAUS)
Olt .... Old Italian (AD)
OLT .... On-Line Teller (SAUS)
OLT .... Online Test [*Computer science*]
OLT .... On-Line Testing (SAUS)
OLT .... On-Line Transmission (SAUS)
OLT .... Optical Line Termination (SAUS)
OLT .... Orange Light
OLT .... Orthotopic Liver Transplantation [*Medicine*]
OLT .... Ostfriesische Lufttransport GmbH [*Germany*] [*ICAO designator*] (FAAC)
OLT .... Oxford Library of Translations [*A publication*]
OLT .... United Lodge of Theosophists, London, Ontario [*Library symbol*] [*National Library of Canada*] (NLC)
OLTC .... On-Load Tap Changer (SAUS)
OLTE .... Online Test (NITA)
OLTE .... On-Line Test Equipment (SAUS)
OLTE .... Online Test Executive Program [*Computer science*] (PDAA)
OLTE .... Optical Line Terminating Equipment (SAUS)
OLTE .... Organizational Level Test Equipment (MCD)
OLTEP .... On-Line Test Executive Program [*IBM Corp.*] [*Computer science*]
OLTL .... One Life to Live [*Television program*]
OLTM .... Optical Line Terminating Multiplexer (SAUS)
OLTMC .... Technical Information Centre, 3M Canada, Inc., London, Ontario [*Library symbol*] [*National Library of Canada*] (NLC)
OLTP .... Off-Line Tape Preparation (SAUS)
OLTP .... On-Line Transaction Processing [*Tandem Computers*]
OLTP .... On-Line Transaction Processor (SAUS)
OLTS .... On-Line Mainframe Testing System [*Computer science*] (IAA)
OLTS .... On-Line Tape System [*Computer science*] (VLIE)
OLTS .... On-Line Testing System (SAUS)
OLTS .... Online Test Section (NITA)
OLTS .... Online Test System [*Computer science*] (BUR)
OLTS .... Online Time Share [*Computer science*]
OLTS .... On Line Tracking System (SAUS)
OLTS .... On-Line Tracking System [*Environmental Protection Agency*] (EPAT)
OLTS .... Online Transaction System [*Computer science*] (IAA)
OLTSEP .... On-Line Test Stand-Alone Executive Program [*Computer science*] (VLIE)
oltt .... On-Line Teller Terminal [*Computer science*] (AD)
OLTT .... Online Teller Terminal
OLTT .... Online Terminal Test [*Computer science*] (IBMDP)
OLTU .... Optical Line Terminating Unit (SAUS)
OLU .... Columbus [*Nebraska*] [*Airport symbol*] (OAG)
OLU .... On-Line Unit (SAUS)
OLU .... Outdoing Line Unit (IAA)
OLU .... Outgoing Line Unit (SAUS)
OLU .... University of Western Ontario, London, Ontario [*Library symbol*] [*National Library of Canada*] (NLC)
OLUC .... Lucknow Branch, Bruce County Public Library, Ontario [*Library symbol*] [*National Library of Canada*] (NLC)
OLUC .... Office of Land Use Coordination [*Abolished, 1944*] [*Department of Agriculture*]
OLuUC .... Online Union Catalog [*Online Computer Library Center, Inc.*] [*Information service or system*] (CRD)
OLuCF .... Southern Ohio Correctional Facility, Lucasville, OH [*Library symbol*] [*Library of Congress*] (LCLS)
OLUD .... Online Update (TEL)
OLUE .... Engineering Library, University of Western Ontario, London, Ontario [*Library symbol*] [*National Library of Canada*] (BIB)
OLUG .... Department of Geography, University of Western Ontario, London, Ontario [*Library symbol*] [*National Library of Canada*] (NLC)
OLUG .... Office Landscape Users Group [*Later, OPUG*] (EA)
OLUH .... University Hospital, London, Ontario [*Library symbol*] [*National Library of Canada*] (NLC)
OLUHO .... Okinawa-Luzon-Hong Kong Submarine Cable (SAUS)
OLUIT .... Object Oriented Librarian User Interface Tool (TELE)
OLUL .... Law Library, University of Western Ontario, London, Ontario [*Library symbol*] [*National Library of Canada*] (NLC)
OLUM .... Online Update Control Module (TEL)

OLUM .... Sciences Library, Natural Sciences Centre, University of Western Ontario, London, Ontario [*Library symbol*] [*National Library of Canada*] (NLC)
OLUMG .... MacIntosh Gallery, University of Western Ontario, London, Ontario [*Library symbol*] [*National Library of Canada*] (NLC)
OLUNO .... Northern Outreach Library Service, University of Western Ontario, London, Ontario [*Library symbol*] [*National Library of Canada*] (BIB)
OLURC .... London Urban Resource Centre, Ontario [*Library symbol*] [*National Library of Canada*] (NLC)
OLUS .... Online Update System (RDA)
OLUS .... On-Line User Services (SAUS)
OLUS .... School of Library and Information Science, University of Western Ontario, London, Ontario [*Library symbol*] [*National Library of Canada*] (NLC)
OLuS .... Scioto Technical College, Lucasville, OH [*Library symbol*] [*Library of Congress*] [*Obsolete*] (LCLS)
OLUVA .... Visual Arts Department, University of Western Ontario, London, Ontario [*Library symbol*] [*National Library of Canada*] (NLC)
OLUWP .... Office of Land Use and Water Planning [*Abolished, 1976*] [*Department of the Interior*]
olv .... Olivaceous (AD)
olv .... Olive (AD)
OLV .... Olive Branch, MS [*Location identifier*] [*FAA*] (FAAL)
OLV .... Oliver Resources [*Vancouver Stock Exchange symbol*]
OLV .... One-Lung Ventilation [*Medicine*]
olv .... On-Line Validation [*Computer science*] (AD)
OLV .... Onze Lieve Vrouw [*Our Lady*] [*Dutch*] (AD)
OLV .... Open-Frame Low Voltage (IEEE)
OLV .... Orbital Launch Vehicle
OLVG .... Open-Loop Voltage Gain
OLVH .... Medical Library, South Street Campus, Victoria Hospital Corp., London, Ontario [*Library symbol*] [*National Library of Canada*] (NLC)
OLVIMS .... On-Line Vehicle Interactive Management System (SAUS)
OLVL .... Oil Level
O-LVL .... Organizational Level (MCD)
OLVM .... Our Lady of Victory Missionary Sisters [*Roman Catholic religious order*]
olvn .... Olivine [*Philately*]
OLVP .... Office of Launch Vehicle Programs [*Obsolete*] [*NASA*]
OLVP .... Office of Launch Vehicles and Propulsion (SAUS)
OLVWM .... Open Look Virtual Window Manager [*Computer science*] (VLIE)
OLWI .... Organic Liquid Waste Incinerator (SAUS)
Olwine's LJ (PA)... Olwine's Law Journal [*Pennsylvania*] [*A publication*] (DLA)
OLWM .... Open Look Window Manager (VLIE)
OLWM .... Open-Look Window Manager (SAUS)
OLWM .... Ordinary Low Water Mark (SAUS)
OLX .... Linn-Benton Community College, Albany, OR [*OCLC symbol*] (OCLC)
OLX .... Off-Line Express [*Mustang Software, Inc.*] (PCM)
OLX .... On-Line Executive [*Computer science*] (MHDB)
OLY .... Olney-Noble, IL [*Location identifier*] [*FAA*] (FAAL)
Oly .... Olympia (AD)
Oly .... Olympic (AD)
OLY .... Olympic Aviation SA [*Greece*] [*ICAO designator*] (FAAC)
OLY .... Olympic Cascade Finl. [*AMEX symbol*]
Olym .... Olympia (AD)
OLYM .... Olympiad
OLYM .... Olympic Financial Ltd. [*NASDAQ symbol*] (NQ)
OLYM .... Olympic National Park
OlymF .... Olympic Financial Ltd. [*Associated Press*] (SAG)
OlymFn .... Olympic Financial Ltd. [*Associated Press*] (SAG)
Olymp .... Olympic (DIAR)
OLYMP .... Olympic Finl Cv Exch Pfd [*NASDAQ symbol*] (TTSB)
Olympic .... Olympic National Park, Washington (AD)
OlympStl ...... Olympic Steel, Inc. [*Associated Press*] (SAG)
OLZ .... Oelwein, IA [*Location identifier*] [*FAA*] (FAAL)
OM .... Air Mongol [*ICAO designator*] (AD)
Om .... Book of Omni (TOCD)
OM .... Member of the Order of Merit [*Canada*] (DD)
OM .... Minim Fathers (TOCD)
om .... Minim Fathers (TOCD)
OM .... Mississauga Public Library, Ontario [*Library symbol*] [*National Library of Canada*] (NLC)
OM .... Obermanual [*Upper Manual*] [*Music*]
OM .... Object Machine (SAUS)
OM .... Object Manager (SAUS)
OM .... Object Module (SAUS)
OM .... Observer's Mate [*British military*] (DMA)
OM .... Obtuse Marginal [*Medicine*] (MAE)
OM .... Occipitomental [*Diameter of skull*]
OM .... Occupational Medal [*as used with special reference to Germany or Japan*] [*Military decoration*]
OM .... Occupational Medicine
OM .... Ocean Mapping (SAUS)
OM .... Oceanographic and Meteorological (SAUS)
OM .... Oceanography and Meteorology
OM .... Ochsner-Mahorner [*Echocardiogram*] (DAVI)
OM .... Oculomotor (DB)
OM .... Oduma Magazine [*A publication*]
OM .... Odyssey of the Mind
OM .... Oesterreichische Monatsschrift fuer den Orient (BJA)
OM .... Office Management (SAUS)
OM .... Office Manager
OM .... Office Master (ELAL)

OM	Office Messenger [*Military*]
OM	Office Model (SAUS)
OM	Officer Messenger (SAUS)
OM	Officine Meccaniche [*Italian auto manufacturer*]
om	Old Man (AD)
om	Old Measurement (AD)
OM	Old Measurement
OM	Olympus Mons [*A filamentary mark on Mars*]
OM	Omaha [*Diocesan abbreviation*] [*Nebraska*] (TOCD)
OM	Oman (AD)
OM	Oman [*IYRU nationality code*] [*ANSI two-letter standard code*] (CNC)
om	Omit
OM	Omni Mane [*Every Morning*] [*Pharmacy*]
om	Omni Mane [*Every Morning*] [*Latin*] (AD)
OM	On Margin [*Investment term*]
OM	Opaque Media [*X-ray microscopy*]
OM	Open Market
OM	Open Matching [*Parapsychology*]
OM	Open Mouth [*Doll collecting*]
OM	Opera di Maria [*Work of Mary*] [*An association*] (EAIO)
OM	Opera Mundi [*Book-packaging firm based in Paris*]
OM	Operand Manipulation (SAUS)
OM	Operating Memorandum
OM	Operating Memory (KSC)
OM	Operating Method (COE)
OM	Operational Maintenance (SAUS)
OM	Operational Management [*Computer science*] (IAA)
OM	Operational Mid DSC or MDM (SAUS)
OM	Operational Modeling (AAEL)
om	Operational Monitor (AD)
OM	Operational Monitor (IAA)
OM	Operation Mainstream (OICC)
OM	Operation Memorandum (SAUS)
OM	Operation Minute (HEAS)
OM	Operation Mobilisation [*Religious movement*] [*British*]
OM	Operation Monkees (EA)
O/M	Operations and Maintenance (SAUS)
OM	Operations Maintenance
OM	Operations Manager
OM	Operations Manual (NITA)
OM	Operations Memorandum [*Department of Agriculture*] (GFGA)
OM	Operations Module (SAUS)
OM	Operator's Manual
OM	Optical Man (SAUS)
OM	Opticalman [*Navy*] (DAVI)
OM	Optical Master (KSC)
OM	Optical Media [*Computer graphics*]
OM	Optical Metallography (SAUS)
OM	Optical Microscope (ECII)
OM	Optical Microscopy
OM	Optical Modulation (SAUS)
OM	Optical Modulator (VLIE)
OM	Optimal Mismatch (SAUS)
OM	Optimus Maximus [*Greatest and Best*] [*Latin*]
OM	Options for Men [*A publication*]
OM	Options Market [*Finance*]
OM	Orbital Maneuvering Engine [*NASA*] (NAKS)
OM	Orbiter Main Engine [*NASA*] (NAKS)
OM	Orbit Modification (IAA)
OM	Order of Merit
Om	Ordinance Map (AD)
OM	Ordnance Map (SAUS)
OM	Ordnance Mission (AAG)
OM	Ordo [*Fratrum*] Minimorum [*Minims of St. Francis of Paul*] [*Roman Catholic men's religious order*]
om	Organic Matter (AD)
OM	Organic Matter
OM	Organizational Maintenance (MCD)
OM	Organized Militia (GEAB)
OM	Organo Metallic (ACAE)
OM	Organometallic
OM	Orifice Meter (SAUS)
OM	Orthogonal Memory (MHDB)
OM	Osborne Mendel Rat [*Medicine*] (DMAA)
OM	Osmiophilic Layer [*Botany*]
OM	Osteomalacia [*Medicine*] (MAE)
OM	Osteomyelitis [*Medicine*]
OM	Osteopathic Manipulation (SAUS)
OM	Ostmark [*Monetary unit*] [*Germany*]
OM	Otitis Media [*Medicine*]
OM	Otolitic Membrane [*Otology*]
om	Our Memo (AD)
OM	Our Message
OM	Outboard Marine [*NYSE symbol*] (TTSB)
om	Outer Marker (AD)
OM	Outer Marker [*Part of an instrument landing system*] [*Aviation*]
OM	Outer Membrane [*Biochemistry*]
OM	Out for Maintenance (SAUS)
OM	Out of Memory [*Computer science*] (VLIE)
OM	Output Machine (SAUS)
OM	Output Memory (SAUS)
OM	Output Module
OM	Outside Manufacturing
O/M	Outside of Metal (MSA)
OM	Overall Modernity [*Sociological scale*]
OM	Overhaul Manual (MCD)
OM	Overland Monthly [*A publication*] (ROG)
OM	Overseas Mail [*British*]
OM	Overseas Minister [*World War I*] [*Canada*]
OM	Overt Meditation
OM	Overturning Moment
OM	Ovulation Method [*Birth control*]
OM	Owners Manual
O/M	Oxygen-to-Metal [*Ratio*] (NRCH)
OM1	Open MPEG consortium 1 (SAUS)
OM1	Opticalman, First Class [*Navy rating*]
OM2	Opticalman, Second Class [*Navy rating*]
OM3	Opticalman, Third Class [*Navy rating*]
OMA	Eppley Airfield [*FAA*] (TAG)
OMA	Markham Public Library, Ontario [*Library symbol*] [*National Library of Canada*] (NLC)
OMA	Object Management Architecture [*Computer science*] (CDE)
OMA	Ocean Mining Administration (AD)
OMA	Oceanography and Marine Assessment [*Marine science*] (OSRA)
OMA	Ocular Motor Apraxia
OMA	Office of Management and Administration [*Social Security Administration*] (OICC)
OMA	Office of Maritime Administration [*Navy*]
OMA	Office of Maritime Affairs (AD)
OMA	Office of Military Affairs
OMA	Office of Military Applications [*Department of Energy*]
OMA	Office of Military Assistance
OMA	Office of Mine Awareness (SAUS)
OMA	Office of Minority Affairs [*Department of Agriculture*] (GFGA)
OMA	Oilskin Manufacturers' Association of Great Britain Ltd. (BI)
OMA	Oklahoma Military Academy
OMA	Omaezaki [*Japan*] [*Seismograph station code, US Geological Survey*] (SEIS)
OMA	Omaha [*Nebraska*] [*Airport symbol*]
Oma	Omaha, Nebraska (AD)
OMA	Ontario Medical Association [*Canada*] (AD)
OMA	Ontario Mining Act (SAUS)
OMA	Ontario Mining Association (SAUS)
OMA	Ontario Ministry of Agriculture (SAUS)
OMA	Ontario Museums Association (SAUS)
OMA	Open Management Architecture (SAUS)
OMA	Operational Maintenance Activity (NVT)
OMA	Operation and Maintenance, Army (SAUS)
OMA	Operation Medicare Alert
OMA	Operations and Maintenance Appopriation [*Army*]
OMA	Operations and Maintenance, Army
OMA	Operations Maintenance Area (NASA)
OMA	Operations Management Application (SSD)
OMA	Operations Management Society (NTPA)
OMA	Operations Monitor Alarm
OMA	Optical Manufacturers Association (EA)
OMA	Optical-Mechanical Assembly [*Apollo*] [*NASA*]
OMA	Optical Multichannel Analyzer [*Spectrometry*]
OMA	Orbiter Maintenance Area [*NASA*] (MCD)
OMA	Orderly Marketing Agreement
oma	Orderly Marketing Arrangement (AD)
OMA	Organizational Maintenance Activity
OMA	Oriental Merchants Association [*Defunct*] (EA)
OMA	Output Message Area (SAUS)
OMA	Outstanding Merchandising Achievement Award
OMA	Outstanding Merchandising Awards (SAUS)
OMA	Overall Manufacturers' Association
OMA	Overall Manufacturers' Association of Great Britain (BI)
OMA	Overseas Mining Association (SAUS)
OMAA	Abu Dhabi/International [*United Arab Emirates*] [*ICAO location identifier*] (ICLI)
OMAA	Occupational Medical Administrators' Association (EA)
OMAA	Office of Management Analysis and Audit [*Civil Service Commission*]
OMAAEEC	Organisation Mondiale des Anciens et Anciennes Eleves de l'Enseignement Catholique [*World Organization of Former Pupils of Catholic Schools*] (EAIO)
OMAB	Buhasa [*United Arab Emirates*] [*ICAO location identifier*] (ICLI)
OMABP	Abitibi-Price, Inc., Mississauga, Ontario [*Library symbol*] [*National Library of Canada*] (NLC)
OMAC	Alkaril Chemicals Ltd., Mississauga, Ontario [*Library symbol*] [*National Library of Canada*] (NLC)
OMAC	Asab [*United Arab Emirates*] [*ICAO location identifier*] (ICLI)
OMAC	Occupational Medical Association of Canada (SAUS)
OMAC	Old Man's Aircraft Company (ACAE)
OMAC	Online Manufacturing, Accounting, and Control System
OMAC	Online Manufacturing Control (NITA)
OMAC	Open Modular Architecture Controller (ACII)
OMAC	Operator Measures and Criteria (MCD)
OMAC	Otitis Media, Acute Catarrhal [*Medicine*] (MELL)
OMA CCD	Optical Multichannel Analyzer Charge-Coupled Device (SAUS)
OMACON	Optimized Magnetohydrodynamic Conversion
OMACS	Online Manufacturing and Control System [*Computer science*] (PDAA)
OMAD	Abu Dhabi/Bateen [*United Arab Emirates*] [*ICAO location identifier*] (ICLI)
OMAD	Madoc Public Library, Ontario [*Library symbol*] [*National Library of Canada*] (BIB)
OMAD	Oncovin [*Vincristine*], Methotrexate, Adriamycin, Dactinomycin [*Actinomycin D*] [*Antineoplastic drug regimen*]
OMAD	Optical Mark and Automatic Dialing [*Facsimile transmission*] (DGA)

OMADA........ Airway Centre, AES Data Ltd., Mississauga, Ontario [*Library symbol*] [*National Library of Canada*] (NLC)

OMAE.......... Emirates Flight Information Region [*United Arab Emirates*] [*ICAO location identifier*] (ICLI)

OMAE.......... Offshore Mechanics and Arctic Engineering (SAUS)

OMAECL...... AECL International, Mississauga, Ontario [*Library symbol*] [*National Library of Canada*] (NLC)

OMAF........... Ontario Ministry of Agriculture and Food [*Canada*]

OMAF........... Operations and Maintenance, Air Force

OMAFRA..... Ontario Ministry of Agriculture, Food and Rural Affairs

OMAG.......... Geac Computers International, Markham, Ontario [*Library symbol*] [*National Library of Canada*] (NLC)

OMAG.......... Orbiter Magnetometer [*NASA*]

OMAH.......... Al Hamra [*United Arab Emirates*] [*ICAO location identifier*] (ICLI)

OMAH.......... Markham High School, Ontario [*Library symbol*] [*National Library of Canada*] (NLC)

Omaha System... Omaha System for Community Health Nursing (SAUS)

OMAHM....... Markham District Historical Museum, Ontario [*Library symbol*] [*National Library of Canada*] (BIB)

OMAI........... Allelix, Inc., Mississauga, Ontario [*Library symbol*] [*National Library of Canada*] (NLC)

OMAI........... Organisation Mondiale Agudath Israel [*Agudas Israel World Organization - AIWO*] (EAIO)

OMAJ........... Jebel Dhana [*United Arab Emirates*] [*ICAO location identifier*] (ICLI)

OMAL........... Al Ain [*United Arab Emirates*] [*ICAO location identifier*] (ICLI)

OM-AI.......... Organic Monomeric Aluminum (SAUS)

O'Mal & H... O'Malley and Hardcastle's Election Cases [*England*] [*A publication*] (DLA)

OMAM......... Abu Dhabi/Al Dhafra [*United Arab Emirates*] [*ICAO location identifier*] (ICLI)

OMAN.......... Manitouwadge Public Library, Ontario [*Library symbol*] [*National Library of Canada*] (NLC)

O-MAN......... Overhead Manipulator [*For handling loads in a nuclear environment*]

OM/A/N/AF/M... Operation and Maintenance, Army/Navy/ Air Force/USMC (SAUS)

OMancAH..... Alfred Holbrook College, Manchester, OH [*Library symbol*] [*Library of Congress*] [*Obsolete*] (LCLS)

OMancO....... Ohio Valley Local District Free Public Library, Manchester, OH [*Library symbol*] [*Library of Congress*] (LCLS)

OM&F.......... Organization, Mission and Functions Manual (SAUS)

O'M & H....... O'Malley and Hardcastle's Election Cases [*England*] [*A publication*] (DLA)

O'M & H El Cas... O'Malley and Hardcastle's Election Cases [*England*] [*A publication*] (DLA)

OM & MG .... Organizational Manual and Management Guide

OM & S .... Osteopathic Medicine and Surgery

OMANO........ Manotick Public Library, Ontario [*Library symbol*] [*National Library of Canada*] (NLC)

OMans .... Mansfield Public Library, Mansfield, OH [*Library symbol*] [*Library of Congress*] (LCLS)

OMansK....... Kingwood Center Library, Mansfield, OH [*Library symbol*] [*Library of Congress*] (LCLS)

OMansU....... Ohio State University, Mansfield Regional Campus, Mansfield, OH [*Library symbol*] [*Library of Congress*] (LCLS)

OMAP .... Object Module Assembly Program

OMAP .... Oceanic Monitoring, Assessment and Prediction (SAUS)

OMAP .... Office of Military Assistance Programs (SAUS)

OMAP .... Operations and Maintenance Application Pan (SAUS)

OMAP .... Operations and Maintenance Application Part [*Telecommunications*]

OMAP .... Operations, Maintenance and Administration Part (SAUS)

OMAP .... Vaughan Public Library, Maple, Ontario [*Library symbol*] [*National Library of Canada*] (NLC)

OMAPC .... Astra Pharmaceuticals Canada Ltd., Mississauga, Ontario [*Library symbol*] [*National Library of Canada*] (NLC)

OMAPFW .... Ontario Ministry of Natural Resources, Maple, Ontario [*Library symbol*] [*National Library of Canada*] (NLC)

OMAQ .... Quarmain [*United Arab Emirates*] [*ICAO location identifier*] (ICLI)

OMAR .... Arzana [*United Arab Emirates*] [*ICAO location identifier*] (ICLI)

OMar .... Congregation of Maronite Monks (TOCD)

omar........... Congregation of Maronite Monks (TOCD)

OMAR .... Marathon Public Library, Ontario [*Library symbol*] [*National Library of Canada*] (NLC)

OMAR .... Office of Medical Applications of Research [*Bethesda, MD*] [*Department of Health and Human Services*] [*National Institutes of Health*]

OMAR .... Operations and Maintenance, Army Reserve (AABC)

OMAR .... Optical Mark Reader [*Computer science*]

OMAR .... Order Maintenance Analysis Report (VLIE)

OMAR .... Order Management and Routing (VLIE)

OMAR .... Ozone Monitoring and Research (ACAE)

omarb.......... Omarbetad [*Revised*] [*Swedish*] (AD)

OMarion ...... Marion Carnegie Public Library, Marion, OH [*Library symbol*] [*Library of Congress*] (LCLS)

OMarionU .... Ohio State University, Marion Campus, Marion, OH [*Library symbol*] [*Library of Congress*] (LCLS)

OMARK........ Markdale Public Library, Ontario [*Library symbol*] [*National Library of Canada*] (NLC)

OMARNG ..... Operation and Maintenance, Army National Guard (AABC)

OMARS .... Outstanding Media Advertising by Restaurants (AD)

OMAS .... Assiginack Public Library, Manitowaning, Ontario [*Library symbol*] [*National Library of Canada*] (NLC)

OMAS .... Das Island [*United Arab Emirates*] [*ICAO location identifier*] (ICLI)

OMas .... Massillon Public Library, Massillon, OH [*Library symbol*] [*Library of Congress*] (LCLS)

OMAS .... Off-Magic-Angle-Spinning [*Spectroscopy*]

OMAS .... One-Man Atmospheric Submersible (PDAA)

OMAS .... Operational Miscellaneous Audio Subsystem

OMASD........ Office of Management Appraisal and Systems Development (SAUS)

OMAST .... Massey and Township Public Library, Ontario [*Library symbol*] [*Library network*]

OMAT.......... Matheson Public Library, Ontario [*Library symbol*] [*National Library of Canada*] (NLC)

OMAT.......... Ocean Measurement and Array Technology [*Navy*] (CAAL)

OMAT.......... Office of Manpower, Automation, and Training [*See also OAM*] [*Department of Labor*]

OMAT.......... Optimal Modified Adaptive Test (SAUS)

OMATT........ Mattawa Public Library, Ontario [*Library symbol*] [*National Library of Canada*] (NLC)

OMAU .... Magnetawan Area Union Public Library, Magnetawan, Ontario [*Library symbol*] [*National Library of Canada*] (NLC)

OMAZ.......... Zirku [*United Arab Emirates*] [*ICAO location identifier*] (ICLI)

OMB............. Midhurst Branch Library, Ontario [*Library symbol*] [*National Library of Canada*] (NLC)

OMB............. Object Management Architecture [*Computer science*]

OMB............. Office of Management and Budget [*Executive Office of the President*] [*Formerly, Bureau of the Budget*] [*Washington, DC*]

OMB............. Office of Money and Banking (WPI)

OMB............. Omboue [*Gabon*] [*Airport symbol*] (OAG)

Omb............. Ombudsman (AD)

OMB............. Ombudsperson-Faculty (SAUS)

OMB............. Ombudsperson-Student (SAUS)

OMB............. Ontario Municipal Board (SAUS)

OMB............. Operational Maintenance Battalion [*Army*] (DOMA)

OMB............. Ordnance Maintenance Bulletin

OMB............. Outboard Motorboat

OMB............. Outer Marker Beacon [*Part of an instrument landing system*] [*Aviation*]

OMB............. Out-of-Home Measurement Bureau [*Later, TABMM*] (EA)

OMBAC .... Old Mission Beach Athletic Club (AD)

OMBC .... Beak Consultants, Mississauga, Ontario [*Library symbol*] [*National Library of Canada*] (NLC)

OMB Circular... Office of Management and Budget Circular (AAGC)

OMBE........... Office of Minority Business Enterprise [*Later, MBDA*] [*Department of Commerce*]

OMBE........... Oxford Mission Brotherhood of the Epiphany [*Anglican religious community*]

OMB/FPPO... Office of Management and Budget/Federal Procurement Policy Office (OICC)

OMBI .... Observation-Measurement-Balancing and Installation [*Production analysis*]

OMBI .... Overcoming Mobility Barriers International (EA)

om bid.......... Omnibus Bidendis [*Every Two Days*] [*Latin*] (AD)

OMBK .... OmniBank of Connecticut, Inc. (SAUS)

OMBO .... One man Bridge Operation (SAUS)

OMBR .... Ontario Municipal Board Reports [*A publication*] (DLA)

OMBUU....... Orbiter Midbody Umbilical Unit [*NASA*] (NASA)

OMBVT .... Minesing Branch, Vespra Township Public Library, Ontario [*Library symbol*] [*National Library of Canada*] (BIB)

OMBW .... Bangor, Wicklow, McClure, and Monteagle Union Public Library, Maynooth, Ontario [*Library symbol*] [*National Library of Canada*] (BIB)

OMBW .... OMB [*Office of Management and Budget*] Watch (EA)

OMC............. Chief Opticalman [*Navy rating*]

OMc............. Herbert Wescoat Memorial Library, McArthur, OH [*Library symbol*] [*Library of Congress*] (LCLS)

OMC............. Marietta College, Marietta, OH [*Library symbol*] [*Library of Congress*] (LCLS)

OMC............. Mayo Clinic Library, Rochester, MN [*OCLC symbol*] (OCLC)

OMC............. Occupational Measurement Center (SAUS)

OMC............. Occupational Medical Center (EFIS)

OMC............. Office of Military Cooperation [*Foreign Service*]

OMC............. Office of Motor Carriers [*FHWA*] [*NHSTA*] [*RSPA*] (TAG)

OMC............. Office of Munitions Control [*Department of State*]

OMC............. Official Mail Center [*Air Force*] (AFM)

OMC............. Off-Machine Coated [*Paper*] (DGA)

OMC............. Omnicom Group, Inc. [*NYSE symbol*] (SPSG)

OMC............. One-Man Control (DNAB)

OMC............. Opel Motorsport Club AG (EA)

OMC............. Open Magnetic Circuit [*Computer science*] (ELAL)

OMC............. Open Market Committee [*Also, FOMC*] [*Federal Reserve System*]

OMC............. Operating and Maintenance Costs

OMC............. Operation and Maintenance Center (VLIE)

OMC............. Operations and Maintenance Center (SAUS)

OMC............. Operations Management Consultant [*Department of Emergency Management*] (DEMM)

OMC............. Operations Monitoring Computer

OMC............. Opticalman, Chief [*Navy rating*] (DNAB)

OMC............. Optical Memory Card [*Computer science*] (CIST)

OMC............. Optimum Moisture Content (SAUS)

omc............. Orbiter Maintenance and Checkout [*NASA*] (NAKS)

OMC............. Orbiter Maintenance and Checkout [*NASA*] (NASA)

OMC............. Ordnance Missile Command [*Later, Missile Command*]

OMC............. Ordo Minorum Cappucinorum [*Capuchins*] [*Roman Catholic men's religious order*]

OMC............. Ordo Minorum Conventualium [*Conventual Franciscans*] [*Roman Catholic men's religious order*]

OMC............. Organic Matrix Composite (SAUS)

OMC............. Organic Molecular Crystal

OMC............. Organometallic Chemistry (SAUS)

OMC............. Organometallic Compound (SAUS)

OMC............. Orion Molecular Cloud [*Astronomy*]

OMC............ Outboard Marine Corp.
OMC............ Oxford Military College (ROG)
OMC............ Oxford Mission to Calcutta [*British*] (ROG)
OMC............ Oxidized Microcrystalline (SAUS)
OMC............ Oxidized Microcrystalline Waxes (EDCT)
OMC............ TOGA XBT Operations and Management Committee (SAUS)
OMC1.......... Orion Molecular Cloud 1 [*Astronomy*]
OMCA .... Occupational Medical Corp. of America, Inc. (SAUS)
OMCA .... Ontario Motor Coach Association
OMCA .... Organic-Moderated Critical Assembly [*Nuclear energy*] (NRCH)
OMCA .... Otitis Media, Catarrhal, Acute [*Medicine*] (MAE)
OMCB .... Off-Machine Coated Board [*Paper*] (DGA)
OMCC .... Open Minded Comics Club [*Defunct*] (EA)
OMCF.......... Operations and Maintenance Control File [*NASA*] (NASA)
OMCF.......... Orbiter Maintenance and Checkout Facility [*NASA*] (NASA)
OMCFP .... Optimized MAC Computer Flight Plan (SAUS)
OMCG .... Ciba/Geigy Canada Ltd., Mississauga, Ontario [*Library symbol*] [*National Library of Canada*] (NLC)
OMCHE .... Organic Material Hydrocarbon Equivalent [*Materials science*]
OMChS .... Otitis Media, Chronic, Suppurating [*Medicine*] (STED)
OMCI .... Organisation Maritime Consultatif Intergouvernementale [*Intergovernmental Maritime Consultative Organization*]
OMCILCR..... Chemical Research Laboratory, CIL, Inc., Mississauga, Ontario [*Library symbol*] [*National Library of Canada*] (NLC)
OMcL.......... Herbert Wescoat Memorial Library, McArthur, OH [*Library symbol*] [*Library of Congress*] (LCLS)
OMCM .... Master Chief Opticalman [*Navy rating*]
OMCM .... Omnicom Group, Inc. (MHDW)
OMCO .... Official Mail Control Officer (MCD)
OMCO .... Overmyer Corporation (SAUS)
OMCR .... Chippewa Resource Centre, Muncey, Ontario [*Library symbol*] [*National Library of Canada*] (NLC)
OMC-R........ Operation and Maintenance Center Radio (SAUS)
OMCR .... Organic-Moderated Cooled Reactor
OMCR .... Organized Marine Corps Reserve
OMCS .... Office of Motor Carrier Standards [*Federal Highway Administration*]
OMC-S........ Operation and Maintenance Center Switch (SAUS)
OMCS .... Operations and Maintenance Communications System (ACAE)
OMCS .... Ozone Monitor Comparison System (CARB)
OMCS .... Senior Chief Opticalman [*Navy rating*]
OMCS .... Sheridan Park Research Community, Cominco Ltd., Mississauga, Ontario [*Library symbol*] [*National Library of Canada*] (NLC)
OMCSDG...... Moose Creek Branch, Stormount, Dundas, and Glengarry County Public Library, Ontario [*Library symbol*] [*National Library of Canada*] (NLC)
OMCSG........ Canada Systems Group, Mississauga, Ontario [*Library symbol*] [*National Library of Canada*] (NLC)
OMCT.......... Carnarvon Township Public Library, Mindemoya, Ontario [*Library symbol*] [*National Library of Canada*] (NLC)
OMCT.......... Office of Motor Carrier Transportation [*Federal Highway Administration*]
OMCT.......... Organisation Mondiale Contre la Torture [*World Organization Against Torture*] [*Switzerland*] (EAIO)
OMCTS .... Octamethylcyclotetrasiloxane [*Organic chemistry*]
OMCT/SOST... Organisation Mondiale Contre la Torture/SOS-Torture [*World Organization Against Torture/SOS-Torture*] [*Geneva, Switzerland*] (EAIO)
OMCU .... Ontario Ministry of Colleges and Universities (SAUS)
OM-CVD ...... Organometallic Chemical Vapor Deposition [*Also, OM-VPE, MO-CVD, MO-VPE*] [*Semiconductor technology*]
OMCVD .... Organo-Metallic Chemical Vapour Deposition (SAUS)
OMCVD .... OrganoMetallic CVD (SAUS)
OMCVH .... Credit Valley Hospital, Mississauga, Ontario [*Library symbol*] [*National Library of Canada*] (NLC)
OMC Wax .... Oxidized Microcrystalline Wax (SAUS)
OMD .... Doctor of Oriental Medicine
OMD .... Du Pont Canada, Inc., Maitland, Ontario [*Library symbol*] [*National Library of Canada*] (NLC)
OMD .... Ocean Margin Drilling [*Program*] [*National Science Foundation*]
OMD .... Ocean Movement Designator
OMD .... Ocular Muscle Dystrophy [*Ophthalmology*] (MAE)
OMD .... Oculoman Dibulodyscephaly (STED)
OMD .... Office of Management Development [*Later, OMPR*] [*NASA*]
omd .... Off-Market Date (AD)
OMD .... Oldsmobile Motor Division [*General Motors Corp.*]
OMD .... O-Methyldopa [*Biochemistry*]
OMD .... On-line Medical Dictionary (SAUS)
OMD .... Open Macrodefinition
OMD .... Operations and Maintainer Decision
OMD .... Operations and Maintenance Documentation [*NASA*] (NASA)
OM/D .... Orbital Mode/Data (SAUS)
OMD .... Orbiter Mating Device [*NASA*]
OMD .... Orchestral Manoeuvres in the Dark [*Pop music group*]
OMD .... Ordnance Medical Department [*British military*] (DMA)
OMD .... Organic Mental Disorder [*Neurology*] (CPH)
OMD .... Oriental Medicine Doctor [*Medicine*]
OMD .... Ormand Industries, Inc.
OMDB .... Dubai [*United Arab Emirates*] [*ICAO location identifier*] (ICLI)
OMDB .... Over My Dead Body
OMDC .... Du Pont Canada, Inc., Mississauga, Ontario [*Library symbol*] [*National Library of Canada*] (NLC)
OMDCPL...... Patent & Legal Library, DuPont Canada, Inc., Mississauga, Ontario [*Library symbol*] [*National Library of Canada*] (NLC)
OMDEAC...... Dearborn Chemical Co. Ltd., Mississauga, Ontario [*Library symbol*] [*National Library of Canada*] (NLC)

OMDG......... Dominion Glass Co. Ltd., Mississauga, Ontario [*Library symbol*] [*National Library of Canada*] (NLC)
OMDIR........ Research Library, Duracell, Inc., Mississauga, Ontario [*Library symbol*] [*Obsolete*] [*National Library of Canada*] (NLC)
OMDL .... Marmora, Deloro, and Lake Union Public Library, Marmora, Ontario [*Library symbol*] [*National Library of Canada*] (BIB)
OMDM .... Optomechanical Display Module
OMDO .... Corporate Library, Domglas, Inc., Mississauga, Ontario [*Library symbol*] [*National Library of Canada*] (NLC)
OMDP .... Ocean Margin Drilling Program [*National Science Foundation*]
OMDP .... Orbiter Maintenance Down Period (SAUS)
OMDR .... Dunlop Research Centre, Sheridan Park, Mississauga, Ontario [*Library symbol*] [*National Library of Canada*] (NLC)
omdr.......... Off-Market Date Received (AD)
OMDR .... Operation and Maintainability Data Record
OMDR .... Operation and Maintenance Deficiency Report (SAUS)
OMDR .... Operations and Maintenance Data Record [*NASA*] (KSC)
OMDR .... Optical Memory Disk Recorder Animation System (SAUS)
OMDR .... Optic Memory Disk Recorder
OMDR1 .... Operations and Maintainability Data Record (SAUS)
OMDS .... Delphax Systems, Mississauga, Ontario [*Library symbol*] [*National Library of Canada*] (NLC)
OMDS .... Online Diver Monitoring System
OMDS .... Optical Mass Data Storage (SAUS)
OMDW........ Diversey Wyandotte, Inc., Mississauga, Ontario, [*Library symbol*] [*National Library of Canada*] (NLC)
OME........... Erindale College, University of Toronto, Mississauga, Ontario [*Library symbol*] [*National Library of Canada*] (NLC)
OME........... Nome [*Alaska*] [*Airport symbol*] (OAG)
OME........... Object Management Extension
OME........... Office of Management Engineer
OME........... Office of Manpower Economics [*Department of Employment*] [*British*]
OME........... Office of Minerals Exploration [*Functions transferred to Geological Survey*] [*Department of the Interior*]
OME........... Office of the Medical Examiner (DAVI)
Ome........... Omega [*Record label*] [*Belgium, etc.*]
OME........... Omega Protein [*NYSE symbol*] (SG)
OME........... Ometepe [*Nicaragua*] [*Seismograph station code, US Geological Survey*] (SEIS)
O-Me .... O-Methyl Diisopropyl (SAUS)
OME........... On-board Modul Extension (SAUS)
OME........... One-Meson Exchange (SAUS)
OME........... Ontario Ministry of Education (SAUS)
OME........... Ontario Ministry of Energy (SAUS)
OME........... Ontario Ministry of the Environment (SAUS)
OME........... Open Messaging Environment [*Computer science*] (CDE)
OME........... Operational Mission Environment (MCD)
OME........... Optimum Mineral Extraction (SAUS)
OME........... Orbital [*or Orbiter*] Main Engine [*NASA*] (NASA)
OME.\.......... Orbital Maneuvering Engine [*NASA*] (KSC)
OME........... Ordnance Mechanical Engineer [*British military*] (DMA)
OME........... Oregon Microcomputer Engineering (SAUS)
OME........... Organisation Mondiale de l'Emballage [*World Packaging Organization - WPO*] (EAIO)
OME........... Organizational Maintenance Equipment (SAUS)
OME........... Ormont Explorations Ltd. [*Vancouver Stock Exchange symbol*]
OME........... Otitis Media with Effusion [*Medicine*]
OMEA......... Meaford Public Library, Ontario [*Library symbol*] [*National Library of Canada*] (NLC)
OMEA......... Office of Multicultural and Ethnic Affairs [*Australia*]
OMEA......... Ontario Municipal Electric Association (SAUS)
OMEC......... Online Medical Employment Center (SAUS)
OMEC......... Optimized Microminiature Electronic Circuit
OMEC......... Organization of Mineral Exporting Countries [*Proposed*]
OMED......... Oxboro Medical International, Inc. [*NASDAQ symbol*] (SAG)
OMED......... Oxboro Med Intl. [*NASDAQ symbol*] (TTSB)
OMEE......... Ontario Ministry of Environment and Energy [*Canada*]
OMEF......... Office Machines and Equipment Federation [*British*] (DIT)
OMEF......... Omega Financial [*NASDAQ symbol*] (TTSB)
OMEF......... Omega Financial Corp. [*NASDAQ symbol*] (SAG)
OMEG......... Omega Environmental [*NASDAQ symbol*] (SPSG)
OMEG......... Omega Optical Co. (SAUS)
OMEGA....... Observing and Modelling of Eddy Scale Geostrophic and Ageostrophic Circulation (SAUS)
OMEGA....... Octanoyl-N-Methylglucamide (SAUS)
OMEGA....... Off-Road Mobility Evaluation and Generalized Analysis [*Army*]
OMEGA....... Operation Model Evaluation Group, Air Force (MCD)
OMEGA....... Optimal Missile Engagement Guidance Algorithm (AD)
OmegaEn..... Omega Environmental, Inc. [*Associated Press*] (SAG)
Omega-Int J.. Omega-The International Journal of Management Science (SAUS)
Omega Rho... Operations Research Honor Society (SAUS)
OmegFn...... Omega Financial Corp. [*Associated Press*] (SAG)
OmegHlt ...... Omega Healthcare Investors [*Associated Press*] (SAG)
OMeH .... Holden Arboretum, Mento, OH [*Library symbol*] [*Library of Congress*] (LCLS)
OM/EH .... Occupational Medicine/Environmental Health Evaluation Center [*Emory University*]
OMEI.......... Office of Minority Economic Impact [*Department of Energy*]
OMEI.......... Other Major End Item [*Military*] (AFIT)
OMEI.......... Other Major Equipment Items (SAUS)
OMEL......... Orient Mid-East Lines (AD)
OMEN .... Ohio Medical Education Network [*Ohio State University*] [*Columbus*] (TSSD)
OMEN .... Orthogonal Mini-Embedment (MHDI)

OMEP	Office of Marine and Estuarine Protection [*Environmental Protection Agency*] (EPA)
OMEP	One-Meson Exchange Potential (SAUS)
OMEP	Ontario Mineral Exploration Program (SAUS)
OMEP	Organisation Mondiale pour l'Education Prescolaire [*World Organization for Early Childhood Education*] (EAIO)
OMER	Merrickville Public Library, Ontario [*Library symbol*] [*National Library of Canada*] (NLC)
OMER	Operations Management Education and Research Foundation (EA)
OMERAD	Office of Medical Education Research and Development [*Michigan State University*] [*Research center*] (RCD)
OMerc	Order of Mercedarians [*Also, MMB*] [*Roman Catholic women's religious order*]
OME-RESA	Ohios Mid-Eastern Regional Education Services Agency (SAUS)
OMERF	Operations Management Education and Research Foundation [*Formerly, OFMP*] (EA)
O-Mess	Officer's Mess [*Military*] (AD)
OMET	Orbiter Mission Elapsed Time [*NASA*] (MCD)
OMET	Ordnance Middle East Tasks [*Military*]
OMET	Organization Manning Equipment Table (MCD)
OMETA	Ordnance Management Engineering Training Agency [*Army*]
OMEW	Office of Missile Electronic Warfare [*Army*] (RDA)
OMEWG	Orbiter Maintenance Engineering Working Group [*NASA*] (NASA)
OMEX	Ocean Margin Exchanges (CARB)
OMF	Moose Factory Library, Ontario [*Library symbol*] [*National Library of Canada*] (BIB)
OMF	Object Management Facility [*Computer science*]
OMF	Object Management Framework (SAUS)
OMF	Object Module File [*Computer science*] (IAA)
OMF	Object Module Format
OMF	Office of Management and Finance (AD)
OMF	Office of Marketing Facilities (SAUS)
OMF	Officer Master File [*Army*] (INF)
OMF	Old Master File
OMF	Omniflys SA de CV [*Mexico*] [*ICAO designator*] (FAAC)
OMF	Open Media Framework (DOM)
OMF	Open Message Format (SAUS)
OMF	Open Modeling Forum (SAUS)
OMF	Operational Mission Failure (MCD)
OMF	Operation and Maintenance of Facilities [*Army*]
OMF	Operations Management Forum (HEAS)
OMF	Optical Matched Filter
OMF	Order Materials For
OMF	Organizational Master File [*Army*]
OMF	Organization Master File (SAUS)
OMF	Oscillatory Magnetic Field
OMF	Osteomyelofibrose (SAUS)
OMF	Overseas Missionary Fellowship, USA Headquarters (EA)
OMFBAA	Operation and Maintenance of Facilities Budget Activity Account [*Army*] (AABC)
OMFBR	Organic-Moderated Fluidized Bed Reactor
OMFC	Overseas Military Forces of Canada [*World War I*]
OMFCA	Operation and Maintenance of Facilities Cost Account [*Army*] (AABC)
OMFCU	Outboard Message Format Conventional Unit (SAUS)
OMFCU	Outboard Message Format Conversion Unit (MCD)
OMFD	Mount Forest District High School, Mount Forest, Ontario [*Library symbol*] [*National Library of Canada*] (NLC)
OMFE	Front of Escott Public Library, Mallorytown, Ontario [*Library symbol*] [*National Library of Canada*] (NLC)
OMFG	Official Meeting Facilities Guide (TVEL)
OMFG	Optimum Manufacturing, Inc. (SAUS)
OMFI	Open Media Framework Interchange (SAUS)
OMFJ	Fujeirah/International [*United Arab Emirates*] [*ICAO location identifier*] (ICLI)
OMFP	Obtaining Money by False Pretense
omfp	Obtaining Money by False Pretenses (AD)
OMFP	Ortho-Methylfluorescein Phosphate [*Biochemistry*]
OMFS	Office Master Frequency Supply [*Telecommunications*] (TEL)
OMFS	Optimum Metric Fastener System
OMFSCA	Operation and Maintenance of Facilities Summary Cost Account [*Army*] (AABC)
OMFT	Optical Matched Filter Technique
OMFTS	Operational Maneuver from the Sea [*Marine Corps*] (DOMA)
OMFUG	Other Music for Urban Gormandizers [*Acronym used as subtitle to the New York City nightclub name, CBGB*]
OMFY	Front of Yonge Township Public Library, Mallorytown, Ontario [*Library symbol*] [*National Library of Canada*] (BIB)
OMG	Aeromega Ltd. [*British*] [*ICAO designator*] (FAAC)
OMG	Object Management Group [*Computer science*]
OMG	Ocean Mapping Group (SAUS)
OMG	Office Machines Group [*Business Equipment Manufacturers Association*]
OMG	Office of Marine Geology [*United States Geological Survey*]
OMG	Office of Military Government
OMG	Older Metamorphic Group [*Geology*]
OMG	Oligodendrocyte-Myelin Glycoprotein (DMAA)
OMG	Omega [*Namibia*] [*Airport symbol*] (OAG)
OMG	Omni Multimedia Group, Inc. [*AMEX symbol*] (SAG)
OMG	Open Management Group (SAUS)
OMG	Operational-Maneuver Group [*Military*]
OMG	Opthalmology Medical Group (AD)
OMG	Osteopathic Medical School Graduate (DMAA)
OMG	Outlaw Motorcycle Gang
OMGA	Golder Associates, Mississauga, Ontario [*Library symbol*] [*National Library of Canada*] (NLC)
OMGA	Operations Management Ground Application (SSD)
OmgaHI	Omega Health Systems, Inc. [*Associated Press*] (SAG)
OMGB	Georgian Bay Township Public Library, Mactier, Ontario [*Library symbol*] [*National Library of Canada*] (BIB)
OMGB	Office of Military Government for Bavaria [*US Military Government, Germany*]
OMGBS	Office of Military Government for Berlin Sector [*US Military Government, Germany*]
OMGCR	Research & Development, Gulf Canada Ltd., Mississauga, Ontario [*Library symbol*] [*National Library of Canada*] (NLC)
OMGCR	Technical Library, Petro-Canada Products, Mississauga, Ontario [*Library symbol*] [*National Library of Canada*] (NLC)
OMGE	Organisation Mondiale de Gastroenterologie [*World Organization of Gastroenterology - WOG*] [*Edinburgh, Scotland*] (EAIO)
OMGH	Office of Military Government for Hesse [*US Military Government, Germany*]
OMGI	OM Group [*NASDAQ symbol*] (TTSB)
OMGI	OM Group, Inc. [*NASDAQ symbol*] (SAG)
OMGL	Gartner Lee Associates Ltd., Markham, Ontario [*Library symbol*] [*National Library of Canada*] (NLC)
OMGR	Omni Insurance Group [*NASDAQ symbol*] (TTSB)
OMGR	Omni Insurance Group, Inc. [*NASDAQ symbol*] (SAG)
OM Grp	OM Group, Inc. [*Associated Press*] (SAG)
OMGT	Overall Missile Guidance Tests (MCD)
OMGUS	Office of Military Government, United States
OMGWB	Office of Military Government for Wuerttemberg-Baden [*US Military Government, Germany*]
OMH	Health Sciences Library, Mississauga Hospital, Ontario [*Library symbol*] [*National Library of Canada*] (BIB)
OMH	Office of Mental Health (DMAA)
OMH	Office of Minority Health (SAUS)
OMH	Omaha Aviation, Inc. (SAUS)
OMH	Omega Hydrocarbons Ltd. [*Toronto Stock Exchange symbol*]
OMH	Omohyoid [*Muscle*] (MELL)
OMH	Ontario Ministry of Health (SAUS)
OMH	Orumieh [*Iran*] [*Airport symbol*] [*Obsolete*] (OAG)
OMHCE	Organic Material Hydrocarbon Equivalent [*Automotive emissions control*]
OMHL	Occupational Medicine and Hygiene Laboratory [*British*] (IRUK)
OMH-RC	Office of Minority Health Resource Center
OMHSA	Ontario Municipal Health and Safety Association (SAUS)
OMHT	Hagar Township Public Library, Markstay, Ontario [*Library symbol*] [*National Library of Canada*] (NLC)
OMI	Middletown Public Library, Middletown, OH [*OCLC symbol*] (OCLC)
OMI	Midland Public Library, Ontario [*Library symbol*] [*National Library of Canada*] (NLC)
OMI	Oblate of Mary Immaculate (SAUS)
OMI	Oblates of Mary Immaculate (TOCD)
omi	Oblates of Mary Immaculate (TOCD)
OMI	Oblats de Marie Immaculee [*Oblates of Mary Immaculate*] [*Rome, Italy*] (EAIO)
OMI	Office of Management Improvement [*Department of Agriculture*]
OMI	Office of Management Information [*Military*] (AFIT)
OMI	Office of Medical Investigator (DMAA)
OMI	Office of Multicultural Interests [*Western Australia*]
OMI	Ogilvy & Mather International, Inc. (EFIS)
OMI	Ohio Mechanics Institute
OMI	Old Myocardial Infarction [*Medicine*]
OMI	Olympic Media Information (AD)
OMI	OMI Corp. [*Associated Press*] (SAG)
OMI	Omni-bearing Magnetic Indicator (SAUS)
OMI	Omnibus Computer Graphics, Inc. [*Toronto Stock Exchange symbol*]
OMI	Oocyte Maturation Inhibitor [*Endocrinology*]
OMI	Open Market, Inc. (IGQR)
OMI	Open Messaging Interface [*Lotus Development Corp.*] (PCM)
OMI	Open Microprocessor (SAUS)
OMI	Open Microprocessor Initiative (SAUS)
OMI	Open Microprocessorsystems Initiative (SAUS)
OMI	Open Modelling Interface (SAUS)
OMI	Operating Memorandum - Information
OMI	Operational Maintenance Instruction (AAG)
OMI	Operation Move-In [*New York City*]
omi	Operations and Maintenance Instruction (NAKS)
OMI	Operator Message Input (SAUS)
OMI	Opinions about Mental Illness [*A questionnaire*]
OMI	Optical Mapping Instrument (SAUS)
OMI	Optical Measurement Instrument (SAA)
OMI	Optical Mode Interference (SAUS)
OMI	Opto Mechanik Inc. (SAUS)
OMI	Ordnance Modifications Instructions
OMI	Organisation Maritime Internationale [*International Maritime Organization - IMO*] (EAIO)
OMI	Organisation Meteorologique Internationale
OMI	Organizacion Maritima Internacional [*International Maritime Organization*] [*Spanish*] [*United Nations*] (DUND)
OMI	Organization for Microinformation
OMI	Organizations Master Index [*A publication*]
OMI	Other Manufacturing Industries [*Department of Employment*] [*British*]
OMI	Our Main Interest (LAIN)
OMI	Owens & Minor, Inc. [*NYSE symbol*] (SPSG)
OMI	Ozone Monitoring Instrument
OMI	Systems Initiative (SAUS)
OMIA	Online Mendelian Inheritance in Animals (SAUS)
OMIA	Operating, Maintenance, Interest, and Adaptability
OMIAA	Orientation and Mobility Instructors Association of Australasia (SAUS)

OMiabM...... Monsanto Research Corp., Mound Laboratory, Miamisburg, OH [*Library symbol*] [*Library of Congress*] (LCLS)
OMiabMI..... Mead Imaging, Miamisburg, OH [*Library symbol*] [*Library of Congress*] (LCLS)
OMiabMM.... Monarch Marking Systems, Pitney Bowes, Chemical Research and Development Library, Miamisburg, OH [*Library symbol*] [*Library of Congress*] (LCLS)
OMIBAC ...... Ordinal Memory Inspecting Binary Automatic Calculator (RALS)
OMIBAC ...... Ordinal Memory Inspecting Binary Automatic Computer (IEEE)
OMIBM .... IBM Canada Ltd., Markham, Ontario [*Library symbol*] [*National Library of Canada*] (NLC)
OMICA .... Organized Migrants in Community Action [*Florida*] [*Defunct*]
OMid............ Middletown Public Library, Middletown, OH [*Library symbol*] [*Library of Congress*] (LCLS)
OMidAR .... Armco, Inc., Research Center, Technical Library, Middletown, OH [*Library symbol*] [*Library of Congress*] (LCLS)
OMidH .... Middletown Hospital Association, Ada Leonard Memorial Library, Middletown, OH [*Library symbol*] [*Library of Congress*] (LCLS)
OMidU .... Miami University, Middletown Campus, Middletown, OH [*Library symbol*] [*Library of Congress*] (LCLS)
OMIH .... Huronia Historical Park, Midland, Ontario [*Library symbol*] [*National Library of Canada*] (NLC)
OMIHM .... Halton Region Museum, Milton, Ontario [*Library symbol*] [*National Library of Canada*] (BIB)
OMIHS .... Institute for Hydrogen Systems, Mississauga, Ontario [*Library symbol*] [*National Library of Canada*] (NLC)
OMII............. Oxy Metal Industries International (AD)
OMIKK .... Orszagos Muszaki Informacios Kozpont es Konyvtar [*National Technical Information Center and Library*] [*Information service or system*] (IID)
OMIL............ Milton Public Library, Ontario [*Library symbol*] [*National Library of Canada*] (NLC)
OMILD .... Mildmay Branch, Bruce County Public Library, Ontario [*Library symbol*] [*National Library of Canada*] (NLC)
OMill .... Holmes County Public Library, Millersburg, OH [*Library symbol*] [*Library of Congress*] (LCLS)
OMILL........... Millbrook Public Library, Ontario [*Library symbol*] [*National Library of Canada*] (BIB)
OMILV .... Milverton Public Library, Ontario [*Library symbol*] [*National Library of Canada*] (NLC)
OMiM........... Megis Local School District Public Library, Middleport Branch, Middleport, OH [*Library symbol*] [*Library of Congress*] (LCLS)
OMIM.......... Online Mendelian Inheritance in Man [*Genetics*]
OMiM.......... Outer Mitochondrial Membrane [*Also, OMM*] [*Cytology*]
OMIN .... Inco Ltd., Mississauga, Ontario [*Library symbol*] [*National Library of Canada*] (NLC)
OMIOM .... Original Meaning Is the Only Meaning [*Writing term*]
omiom.......... Original Meaning is the Only Meaning (AD)
OMIP .... Ocean Model Intercomparison Project (SAUS)
OMIP .... Office of Minority Institutions Program [*U.S. Department of the Interior*] (BARN)
OMIS .... Office, Management Information System (SAUS)
OMIS .... Office of Management Information Systems [*Office of Administration and Management*] [*Department of Labor*]
OMIS .... Office of Media and Information Services (SAUS)
OMIS .... Omission (AAG)
OMiS .... Operational Management Information System [*NASA*] (NAKS)
OMIS .... Operational Management Information System [*Computer science*]
OMIS .... Operational Multi-Spectral Imager Suite (ACAE)
OMIS .... Operations Management Information System (SAUS)
OMIS .... Optical Microscope Inspection System (SAUS)
O Misc......... Ohio Miscellaneous Reports [*A publication*] (DLA)
OMiSS .... Operation and Maintenance Instruction Summary Sheet [*NASA*] (NAKS)
OMISTN .... Optical Mode Interface Super Twisted Nematic (SAUS)
OMIT............ Mitchell Public Library, Ontario [*Library symbol*] [*National Library of Canada*] (NLC)
OMIT............ Orienthine-decarboxylase, Motility, Indole, Tryptophandeaminase (SAUS)
omit............. Orinthine-Decarboxylase, Motility, Indole, Trytophandeaminase (AD)
OMIT............ Orinthine-decarboxylase, Motility, Indole, Trytophandeandeaminase (SAUS)
OMITT......... Omittatur [*Let It Be Omitted*] [*Pharmacy*] (ROG)
OMJ............. Ohmine [*Japan*] [*Seismograph station code, US Geological Survey*] (SEIS)
OMJ............. Orthomode Junction [*Electronics*]
OMJ............. Osler Medical Journal (SAUS)
OMJAT......... J. A. Turner Professional Library, H. J. A. Brown Education Centre, Mississauga,Ontario [*Library symbol*] [*National Library of Canada*] (NLC)
OMK............. Omak, WA [*Location identifier*] [*FAA*] (FAAL)
OMK............. Owl Monkey Kidney [*Cell line*]
omkr............ Omdring [*About*] [*Norwegian*] (AD)
OMKR .... Outer Marker [*Part of an instrument landing system*] [*Aviation*]
OMKT.......... Open Market [*NASDAQ symbol*] (TTSB)
OMKT.......... Open Market, Inc. [*NASDAQ symbol*] (SAG)
OML............. Object Manipulation Language (SAUS)
OML............. Object Module Library [*Computer science*] (VLIE)
OML............. Ocean Mixed Layer (SAUS)
OML............. One-conductor Many-turn Loop (SAUS)
OML............. One-Man-LAN [*Linked Access Network*] [*PC Interconnect, Inc.*] [*Telecommunications*] (PCM)
OML............. Ontario Ministry of Labour (SAUS)
OML............. Ontario Ministry of Labour Library [*UTLAS symbol*]
OML............. Ontario Motor League [*Canada*] (AD)

OML........... Ontology Markup Language (IDAI)
OML............. Open Modelling Language [*Computer science*] (VLIE)
OML............. Operations Manual Letter [*National Weather Service*] (NOAA)
OML............. Orbiter Mold Line [*NASA*] (NASA)
OML............. Orbiting Military Laboratory (AAG)
OML............. Orbitomeatal Line (STED)
OML............. Orbitomental Line (DMAA)
OML............. Order of Merit List [*Army*] (AABC)
OML............. Ordnance Material Letter (SAA)
OML............. Ordnance Missile Laboratories (KSC)
OML............. Ordnance Muzzle Loading [*British military*] (DMA)
OML............. Organic Materials Laboratory [*Watertown, MA*] [*Army*] (GRD)
OML............. Organizational Maintenance Level (NVT)
OML............. Outer Mold Line (NASA)
OML............. Outgoing Matching Loss [*Telecommunications*] (TEL)
oml............. Outside Mold Line (AD)
OML............. Outside Mold Line [*Technical drawings*]
OML............. University of Cincinnati, Marx Law Library, Cincinnati, OH [*OCLC symbol*] (OCLC)
OMLA .... Organizational Maintenance Level Activity (MCD)
OMLAC .... Oxfordshire Modern Languages Achievement Certificate [*British*] (AIE)
OMLCSA ..... Old Mine Lamp Collectors Society of America (EA)
OMLE.......... Organization of Spanish Marxist-Leninists (PD)
OMLET........ Ocean Mixed Layer Experiment (SAUS)
OMLF.......... Oromo Muslim Liberation Front (SAUS)
OMLIT........ One-Man Live Interception Test (SAA)
OMLJ.......... Officer of Merit, Order of St. Lazarus of Jerusalem (DD)
OMLP.......... Ohio Midland Light & Power [*AAR code*]
OMLRS .... Operations, Maintenance and Logistics Resources Simulation (SAUS)
OMLS .... Office of Management Information Systems (SAUS)
OMLT .... [*The*] Learning Tree, Mississauga, Ontario [*Library symbol*] [*National Library of Canada*] (NLC)
OMLTA .... Ohio Modern Language Teachers Association (EDAC)
OMLX......... London Securities and Derivatives Exchange (SAUS)
OMM .... Miami University, Middletown Campus, Middletown, OH [*OCLC symbol*] (OCLC)
OMM........... Office of Marine Minerals
OMM........... Office of Minerals Mobilization [*Later, OMSF*] [*Department of the Interior*]
OMM........... Officer Message Mail [*Military*]
OMM........... Officer Messenger Mail (SAUS)
OMM........... Officer of the Order of Military Merit [*Canada*] (DD)
OMM........... Offshore Minerals Management Program
OMM........... Oil Market Module [*Department of Energy*] (GFGA)
OMM........... OMI Corp. [*NYSE symbol*] (TTSB)
OMM........... Ommatidium [*Arthropod eye anatomy*]
OMM........... Operation and Maintenance Manual
omm........... ophchalmomandibulomelic (SAUS)
OMM........... Ophthalmomandibulomelic [*Dysplasia Syndrome*] [*Medicine*] (STED)
OMM........... Orbicular Muscle of Mouth (MELL)
OMM........... Orbital Maintenance Mission [*NASA*] (SSD)
OMM........... Organisation Meteorologique Mondiale [*World Meteorological Organization - WMO*] (EAIO)
OMM........... Organizacion Meteorologica Mundial [*World Meteorological Organization - WMO*] [*Spanish*]
OMM........... Organometallic Material
OMM........... Outer Mitochondrial Membrane [*Also, OMiM*] [*Cytology*]
OMM........... Output Message Manual [*Computer science*] (VLIE)
OMM........... Oxford Medical Manuals [*A publication*]
OMMA .... Outboard Motor Manufacturers Association [*Later, MEMA*] (EA)
OMMB .... Information Centre, Molson Breweries of Canada Ltd., Mississauga, Ontario [*Library symbol*] [*National Library of Canada*] (NLC)
OMMB .... Ontario Milk Marketing Board (SAUS)
OMMC .... Officer Message Mail Center [*Military*]
OMMC .... Officer Messenger Mail Center (SAUS)
OMMCS ...... Ordnance Missile and Munitions Center and School [*Army*]
Om Mer Sh... Omond's Merchant Shipping Acts [*1877*] [*A publication*] (DLA)
OMMH .... Orbiter Maintenance Man-Hours [*NASA*] (NASA)
OMMI .... Magna International, Inc., Markham, Ontario [*Library symbol*] [*National Library of Canada*] (BIB)
OMMI .... Oblate Missionaries of Mary Immaculate (TOCD)
OMMIC .... Ordnance Maintenance Management Information Center [*Navy*]
OMMLT .... Murchison Lyell Township Community Library, Madawaska, Ontario [*Library symbol*] [*National Library of Canada*] (NLC)
OMMM........ Moore Museum, Mooretown, Ontario [*Library symbol*] [*National Library of Canada*] (BIB)
OMMMSA .... Oil Mill Machinery Manufacturers and Supply Association (EA)
OMMS .... Office of Merchant Marine Safety [*Coast Guard*]
OMMS .... Organizational Missile Maintenance Squadron [*Air Force*]
OMMS .... Oxygen Mask-Mounted Sight (SAUS)
OMM(S)C .... Officer Messenger Mail (Sub) Center [*Navy*]
OMMSC ...... Officer Messenger Mail Sub-Center (SAUS)
OMMSQA .... Office of Modeling, Monitoring Systems, and Quality Assurance [*Environmental Protection Agency*]
OMN .... Mansfield-Richland County Public Library, Mansfield, OH [*OCLC symbol*] (OCLC)
OMN .... Octamethylnaphthalene [*Organic chemistry*]
OMN .... Oculomotor Nerve [*Medicine*] (STED)
OMN .... Oman [*ANSI three-letter standard code*] (CNC)
OMN .... Omnivorous
OMN .... Ormond Beach, FL [*Location identifier*] [*FAA*] (FAAL)
OMN .... Orthomin
omn 2 hor .... Omni Secunda Hora [*Every Two Hours*] [*Latin*] [*Pharmacy*] (DAVI)
OMN BID ..... Omni Bidus [*Every Two Days*] [*Pharmacy*] (ROG)

OMN BIH	Omni Bihora [*Every Two Hours*] [*Pharmacy*]
omn bih	Omni Bihora [*Every Two Hours*] [*Latin*] (AD)
Omncre	Omnicare, Inc. [*Associated Press*] (SAG)
OMNCS	Office of the Manager National Communications System [*GSA*]
OMNDM	Ontario Ministry of Northern Development and Mines (SAUS)
OMNET	Organizational Maintenance New Equipment Training [*Army*] (INF)
OMNG	Operations and Maintenance, National Guard [*Army*]
OMN H	Omni Hora [*Every Hour*] [*Pharmacy*]
OMN HOR	Omni Hora [*Every Hour*] [*Pharmacy*]
omni	Omnidirectional [*Microphone*] (WDMC)
OMNI	Omnidirectional
Omni	Omni Multimedia Group, Inc. [*Associated Press*] (SAG)
OMNI	Omni-Range (NAKS)
omni	Omnirange (AD)
omni	Omnivisual (AD)
omni	Onmidirectional (AD)
OMNI	On-Site Multiple Network Installation [*Thomas & Betts Corp.*]
OMNI	Optimum Management with Necessary Information (SAUS)
OMNI	Organizing Medical Networked Information [*British*] (TELE)
Omnicm	Omnicom Group, Inc. [*Associated Press*] (SAG)
OmniIns	Omni Insurance Group, Inc. [*Associated Press*] (SAG)
OmniMult	Omni Multimedia Group, Inc. [*Associated Press*] (SAG)
Omnipt	Omnipoint Corp. [*Associated Press*] (SAG)
OMNIRANGE	Omnidirectional Radio Range (MSA)
OMNITAB	Omnibus Program with Tabular Numerical Functions [*Programming language*] [*1965*] (CSR)
OMNITENNA	Omnirange Antenna
OmniUSA	Omni USA, Inc. [*Associated Press*] (SAG)
OMNIX	Onyx Microcomputer Unix (SAUS)
OMN MAN	Omni Mane [*Every Morning*] [*Pharmacy*]
omn man	Omni Mane [*Every Morning*] [*Latin*] (AD)
OMNMHCE	Organic Material Non-Methane Hydrocarbon Equivalent (EEVL)
OMNMPS	Operative Machine Needle Makers' Protection Society [*A union*] [*British*]
OMN NOCT	Omni Nocte [*Every Night*] [*Pharmacy*]
omn noct	Omni Nocte [*Every Night*] [*Latin*] (AD)
omn quad hor	Omni Quadrante Hora [*Every quarter of An Hour*] [*Latin*] [*Pharmacy*] (DAVI)
OMN QUADR HOR	Omni Quadrante Horae [*Every Quarter of an Hour*] [*Pharmacy*] (ROG)
OMNR	Ontario Ministry of Natural Resources [*Canada*]
OMNRF	Omni Resources, Inc. (SAUS)
OMNS	Open Network Management System [*Computer science*] (VLIE)
OMNT	Northern Telecom, Mississauga, Ontario [*Library symbol*] [*National Library of Canada*] (NLC)
OMNTS	Over Mountains (WEAT)
OMNU	Orthomolecular Nutrition Institute (SAUS)
OMNX	Omni Exploration, Inc. (SAUS)
OMNY	Omni Sky Corp. [*NASDAQ symbol*]
OMO	Moonbeam Public Library, Ontario [*Library symbol*] [*National Library of Canada*] (BIB)
OMO	Mostar [*Yugoslavia*] [*Airport symbol*] (AD)
OMO	Oblates of the Mother of Orphans (TOCD)
OMO	Occupational Medicine Office (SAUS)
OMO	Office of Management and Organization (SAUS)
OMO	Office of Marine Operations [*Marine science*] (OSRA)
OMO	Office of Meteorological Observations (SAUS)
OMO	Office of the Director of Manpower and Organization [*Air Force*]
OMO	Old Man's Out [*Facetious translation of Omo, a brand of detergent*] [*British*]
OMO	Omoco Holdings [*Vancouver Stock Exchange symbol*]
OMO	One-Man Operated (SAUS)
OMO	One-Man-Operated Bus [*London, England*]
OMO	One Man Operation [*Railroad*] [*British*]
OMO	Open Market Operations [*Economics*]
OMO	Operator Message Output (SAUS)
OMO	Oral Malodor [*Medicine*] (MELL)
OMO	Orbiting Meteorological Observatory (SAUS)
OMO	Ordinary Money Order
OMO	Singly-Occupied Molecular Orbital [*Physical chemistry*]
OMOAM	Ontario Agricultural Museum, Milton, Ontario [*Library symbol*] [*National Library of Canada*] (NLC)
OMOB	Offensive Missile Order of Battle (MCD)
OMODE	Ordinary Mode (MCD)
OMOL	Oliver Township Public Library, Murillo, Ontario [*Library symbol*] [*National Library of Canada*] (BIB)
OMOO	Moosonee Public Library, Ontario [*Library symbol*] [*National Library of Canada*] (BIB)
omor	One Man, One Responsibility (AD)
OMorS	Salem Township Public Library, Morrow, OH [*Library symbol*] [*Library of Congress*] (LCLS)
OMORSDG	Morewood Branch, Stormont, Dundas, and Glengarry County Public Library, Ontario [*Library symbol*] [*National Library of Canada*] (BIB)
OMOSC	Organisation des Musiciens d'Orchestres Symphoniques du Canada [*Organization of Canadian Symphony Musicans - OCSM*]
OMOSDG	Morrisburg Branch, Stormont, Dundas, and Glengarry County Public Library, Ontario [*Library symbol*] [*National Library of Canada*] (NLC)
OMOT	Metcalfe Branch, Osgoode Township Library, Ontario [*Library symbol*] [*National Library of Canada*] (BIB)
OMOTH	Osgoode Township High School Library, Metcalfe, Ontario [*Library symbol*] [*National Library of Canada*] (BIB)
OMOV	One Member, One Vote [*System to select parliamentary candidates*] [*British*]
OMP	Espe [*Germany*] [*Research code symbol*]
OMP	Marion Public Library, Marion, OH [*OCLC symbol*] (OCLC)
OMP	Obstetrical Measuring Plate [*Medicine*] (MELL)
OMP	Ocean Margins Program (SAUS)
OMP	Ocean Microwave Package (SSD)
OMP	Office of Metric Programs [*Department of Commerce*]
OMP	Olfactory Marker Protein [*Biochemistry*]
OMP	Oligo-N-methylmorpholinopropylene Oxide [*Pharmacology*]
OMP	OM Group, Inc. [*NYSE symbol*] (SAG)
OMP	Operating Maintenance Panel (IAA)
OMP	Operating Maintenance Procedure (IAA)
OMP	Operating Memorandum - Policy
OMP	Operations and Maintenance Plan [*NASA*] (NASA)
OMP	Optical Mark Printer (NITA)
omp	Organo-Metallic Polymer (AD)
OMP	Organometallic Polymer (CAAL)
OMP	Ormetoprim [*Potentiator for antibacterials*] [*Veterinary medicine*]
OMP	Ornithine Monophosphate (DMAA)
OMP	Orotidine Monophosphate [*Organic chemistry*]
OMP	Outer Membrane Protein [*Biochemistry*]
OMP	Output Makeup
OMP	Overseas Manpower [*British*]
OMP	Oxford Medical Publications [*A publication*]
OMpA	American Society for Metals Library, Metals Park, OH [*Library symbol*] [*Library of Congress*] (LCLS)
OMPA	Octamethylpyrophosphoramide [*Insecticide*]
OMPA	Octamethylpyrophosphoramide, Schradan (EDCT)
OMPA	Office of Marine Pollution Assessment [*National Oceanic and Atmospheric Administration*] (ASF)
ompa	One-Man Pension Arrangement (AD)
OMPA	One-Man Pension Arrangement [*Management*]
OMPA	Operating Memorandum - Personnel Assignment
OMPA	Otitis Media, Purulent, Acute [*Medicine*]
OMPA	Outer Membrane Protein A [*Biochemistry*]
OMPC	Office of Municipal Pollution Control [*Environmental Protection Agency*] (GFGA)
OMPC	Overseas Military Personnel Charter (MCD)
OMPD	Office of Mineral Policy Development [*Department of the Interior*]
OMPE	Office of Management Planning and Evaluation [*Environmental Protection Agency*] (EPA)
OMPE & R	Office of Manpower Policy, Evaluation, and Research [*Department of Labor*]
OMPEC	Offshore Mechanics and Polar Engineering Council
OMPER	Office of Manpower Policy, Evaluation, and Research [*Department of Labor*]
OMPF	Official Military Personnel File [*Army*] (AABC)
OMPF	Official Military Police File (SAUS)
ompf	Omphaloskepsis (AD)
OMPF	Operation and Maintenance Processor Frame [*Computer science*] (VLIE)
OMPI	Ordnance Master Publication Index (MCD)
OMPI	Organisation Mondiale de la Propriete Intellectuelle [*World Intellectual Property Organization - WIPO*] [*Information service or system*] (IID)
OMPI	Organizacion Mundial de la Propiedad Intelectual [*World Intellectual Property Organization*] [*Spanish*] [*United Nations*] (DUND)
OMPI	Oxo(mercaptoethyl)(phenyl)imidazolidine [*Biochemistry*]
OMPLA	Outer Membrane Phospholipase A
OMPO	Oahu Metropolitan Planning Organization [*Hawaii*] (AD)
OMPR	Office of Management Planning and Review [*Formerly, OMD*] [*NASA*]
OMPR	Operational Maintainability Problem Reporting (NASA)
OMPR	Optical Mark Page Reader [*Computer science*] (AABC)
ompr	Optical Mark Page Reader (AD)
OMPR	Optical Mark Printer (CIST)
OMPR	Optimal Multiple Point Reassignment (SAUS)
OMPRA	Office of Minerals Policy and Research Analysis (AD)
OMPRA	One-Man Propulsion Research Apparatus [*NASA*]
OMPS	On-orbit Maneuvering Propulsion System (SAUS)
OMPS	Orbit Maneuvering Propulsion System [*NASA*] (KSC)
OMPSA	Organisation Mondiale pour le Promotion Sociale des Aveugles [*World Council for the Welfare of the Blind - WCWB*] (EAIO)
OMPT	Observed Man [*or Mass*] Point Trajectory [*NASA*] (KSC)
OMPT	Omnipoint Corp. [*NASDAQ symbol*] (TTSB)
OMPU	Oficina Municipale de Planeamiento Urbano [*Municipal Office of Urban Planning*] [*Spain*] (AD)
OMPUS	Official Munitions Production United States
OMPW	Pratt & Whitney Aircraft Ltd., Mississauga, Ontario [*Library symbol*] [*National Library of Canada*] (NLC)
OMPX	OCLC Microcomputer Program Exchange (NITA)
OM QUAR HOR	Omni Quarta Hora [*Every Quarter of An Hour*] [*Latin*] [*Pharmacy*] (DAVI)
OMR	Midland-Ross Corp., Library, Cleveland, OH [*OCLC symbol*] (OCLC)
omr	Office Methods Research (AD)
OMR	Office Methods Research
OMR	Office of Marine Resources [*Department of the Interior*] (NOAA)
OMR	Officer Master Record [*Air Force*] (AFM)
OMR	Offsite Methods Retrieval (SAUS)
OMR	Oligomycin-Resistant (DMAA)
OMR	Online Medical Record (HCT)
OMR	Operational Microwave Receiver (SAUS)
OMR	Operational Modification Report (IAA)
OMR	Operation Management Room [*NASA*] (KSC)
OMR	Operations and Maintenance Requirements (NASA)
OMR	Operations Management Room [*NASA*]

OMR	Operations Manager's Report
OMR	Operative Morality Rate [*Statistics*] [*Medicine*] (DAVI)
OMR	Optical Mark and Read (SAUS)
OMR	Optical Mark Read (SAUS)
omr	Optical Mark Reader (AD)
OMR	Optical Mark Reader [*Computer science*]
OMR	Optical Mark Reading (SAUS)
omr	Optical Mark Recognition (AD)
OMR	Optical Mark Recognition [*Computer science*] (MCD)
OMR	Optical Meter Relay
OMR	Orad [*Romania*] [*Airport symbol*] (OAG)
OMR	Orbiter Management Review [*NASA*] (NASA)
OMR	Organic Magnetic Resonance
OMR	Organic-Moderated Reactor [*Nuclear energy*]
OMR	Our Material Returned (AAG)
OMR	Output Message Report (SAUS)
OMR	Overhaul, Maintenance, and Repair (MCD)
OMR	Overhead Materials Requirement [*Manufacturing*]
OMRA	135th Medical Regiment Association (EA)
OMRB	Operating Material Review Board [*NASA*] (NASA)
OMRB	Outstanding National Resource Waters (SAUS)
OMRC	Operational Maintenance Requirements Catalog [*NASA*] (MCD)
OMRC	Optical Mark Reader Card [*Computer science*] (MHDI)
OMRCA	Organic-Moderated Reactor Critical Assembly [*Nuclear energy*]
OMRD	Office of Manpower Research and Development [*National Academy of Sciences*]
OMRD	Overseas Mineral Resource Development (AD)
OMRE	Organic-Moderated Reactor Experiment [*Nuclear energy*]
OMRF	Oklahoma Medical Research Foundation [*University of Oklahoma*] [*Research center*]
OMRF	Orbiter Maintenance and Refurbishment Facility (SAUS)
OMRF	Orbiter Modification and Refurbishment Facility [*NASA*] (NAKS)
OMRI	Oklahoma Medical Research Institute
OMRI	Open Media Research Institute [*Non-profit news and analysis organization covering Eastern Europe and the former Soviet Union*] (ECON)
OMRK	Ras Al Khaimah/International [*United Arab Emirates*] [*ICAO location identifier*] (ICLI)
OMRM	Manitou Library (Ojibway of Manitou Rapids Indian Band), Manitou Rapids, Ontario [*Library symbol*] [*National Library of Canada*] (BIB)
OMRO	Ordnance Materials Research Office [*Later, AMMRC*] [*Army*] (MCD)
OMR/P	Operations and Maintenance Requirements/Plan [*NASA*] (NASA)
OMRR	Ordnance Material Research Reactor [*Nuclear energy*]
OMRS	Onsite Management Records System (SAUS)
OMRS	Operations and Maintenance Requirements Specifications (NASA)
OMRS	Optical Mark Reader Sheet [*Computer science*] (MHDI)
OMRS	Orders and Medals Research Society (EA)
OMRSD	O&M Requirements and Specification Documentation (SAUS)
OMRSD	Operational Maintainability Reporting Systems Document [*NASA*] (NASA)
OMRSD	Operational Maintenance Requirements and Specifications Document [*NASA*] (NASA)
OMRSD	Operations and Maintenance Requirements and Specification Documentation (NASA)
OMRSD	Operations and Maintenance Requirements and Specifications Documentation
OMRSP	Operations and Maintenance Requirements and Specification Document (SAUS)
OMRV	Operational Maneuvering Reentry Vehicle (MCD)
OMRW	Optical MASER [*Microwave Amplification by Stimulated Emission of Radiation*] Radiation Weapon (AAG)
OMS	Margin System on OMLX (SAUS)
OMS	Object Management Services (SAUS)
OMS	Object Management System [*Computer science*] (VLIE)
OMS	Ocean Minesweeper
OMS	Octahedral Molecular Sieve [*Inorganic chemistry*]
OMS	Office Mail System [*Computer science*] (VLIE)
OMS	Office Management System [*Computer science*] (IAA)
OMS	Office of Management Services [*Department of Agriculture*]
OMS	Office of Management Studies (EA)
OMS	Office of Management Support [*Environmental Protection Agency*] (EPA)
OMS	Office of Marketing Services [*of BDSA*]
OMS	Office of Mobile Sources [*Environmental Protection Agency*] (GFGA)
OMS	Off-Line Management System (SAUS)
OMS	Oil Market Simulation Model [*Department of Energy*] (GFGA)
OMS	Omsk [*Former USSR*] [*Airport symbol*] (OAG)
OMS	On-Board Maintenance System [*Aviation*]
OMS	One-Minute Superstar [*Actor whose bit part in a television series results in instant stardom*]
OMS	Opcode MIDI [*Musical Instrument Digital Interface*] System
OMS	Open Mail System [*Raindrop Software Co.*] (PCM)
OMS	Open Management System [*Vitalink Communicatons Corp.*]
OMS	Open Measurement Solution
OMS	Open Music System (SAUS)
OMS	Operational Maintenance System
OMS	Operational Meteorological Satellite [*NASA*]
OMS	Operational Mission Summary [*Army*]
OMS	Operational Mode Summary
OMS	Operational Monitoring System (MCD)
OMS	Operation and Maintenance Subsystem (SAUS)
OMS	Operations Management System (SSD)
OMS	Opocode MIDI System
OMS	Oppenheimer Multi-Sector Income Trust [*NYSE symbol*] (SPSG)

OMS	Opsocionus-Myocionus Support Network, Inc. (NRGU)
OMS	Opsocionus-Myocionus Syndrome [*Medicine*] (MELL)
OMS	Optical MASER [*Microwave Amplification by Stimulated Emission of Radiation*] System
OMS	Optical Mass Spectroscopy (AAEL)
OMS	Optical Modulation System
OMS	Optimum Mode Selector (CAAL)
OMS	Optoelectronic Measuring System (SAUS)
OMS	Optronic Mast Sensor (SAUS)
OMS	Oral and Maxillofacial Surgery
OMS	Oral Morphine Sulfate [*Medicine*] (MELL)
oms	Orbital Maneuvering Subsystem [*NASA*] (NAKS)
OMS	Orbital Maneuvering System [*or Subsystem*] [*NASA*]
OMS	Orbital Mapping System (SAUS)
OMS	Orbital Multifunction Satellite
OMS	Orbit Mode Software (ACAE)
OMS	Ordnance Machine Shop
OMS	Ordnance Management System (SAUS)
OMS	Ordnance Mounting System (SAUS)
OMS	Organic Mass Spectroscope (SAUS)
OMS	Organic Mass Spectroscopy
OMS	Organic Mental Syndrome [*Medicine*] (DMAA)
OMS	Organisation Mondiale de la Sante [*World Health Organization - WHO*] [*Switzerland*]
OMS	Organizacion Mundial de la Salud [*World Health Organization*] [*Spanish*] [*United Nations*] (DUND)
OMS	Organizational Maintenance Shop [*Army*]
OMS	Organizational Maintenance Squadron [*Air Force*] (MCD)
OMS	Organizational Maintenance Support
OMS	Oriental Missionary Society [*Later, OMS International*] (EA)
OMS	Other Members Score (SAUS)
OMS	Otomandibular Syndrome [*Medicine*] (DMAA)
OMS	Outcomes Management System (AMHC)
OMS	Outdoor Microphone System
OMS	Output Multiplex Synchronizer
oms	Output per Man Shift (AD)
OMS	Output per Man Shift
OMS	Overnight Message Service [*Diversified Data Processing and Consulting, Inc.*] [*Oak Park, MI*] [*Telecommunications*] (TSSD)
OMS	Overseas Mission Society [*Defunct*] (EA)
OMS	Ovonic Memory Switch (PDAA)
OMS	Spectravac Power Conversion Systems, Inc., Mississauga, Ontario [*Library symbol*] [*National Library of Canada*] (NLC)
OMSA	Offshore Marine Service Association [*New Orleans, LA*] (EA)
OMSA	Ontario Medical Secretaries Association (SAUS)
OMSA	Orders and Medals Society of America (EA)
OMSA	Ordnance Missile Support Agency (SAA)
OMSA	Otitis Media, Suppurative, Acute [*Medicine*]
OMSA	Seaman Apprentice, Opticalman, Striker [*Navy rating*]
OMSA	Simcoe County Archives, Minesing, Ontario [*Library symbol*] [*National Library of Canada*] (NLC)
OMS&A	Office of Mission Safety and Assurance (SAUS)
OMSAP	Occupational Medicine Self-Assessment Program (SAUS)
OMSAPC	Office of Mobile Source Air Pollution Control [*Environmental Protection Agency*]
OMSB	Outcomes Management System Information Board
OMSC	Organisation Mondiale pour la Systemique et la Cybernetique [*World Organization of Systems and Cybernetics*] (EAIO)
OMSC	Otitis Media, Secretory, Chronic [*Medicine*] (DAVI)
OMSC	Otitis Media, Suppurative, Chronic [*Medicine*]
OMSD	Organization and Management Services Division (SAUS)
OMSDG	Maxville Branch, Stormont, Dundas, and Glengarry County Public Library, Ontario [*Library symbol*] [*National Library of Canada*] (NLC)
OMSE	Office of Management Systems and Evaluation [*Environmental Protection Agency*] (GFGA)
Om Sea	Omond's Law of the Sea [*1916*] [*A publication*] (DLA)
OMSF	Office of Manned Space Flight [*NASA*]
OMSF	Office of Minerals and Solid Fuels [*Formerly, OMM*] [*Abolished, 1971*] [*Department of the Interior*]
OMSG	Official Mail Study Group [*Defunct*] (EA)
OMSG	Our Message [*Aviation*] (FAAC)
OMSI	Oregon Museum of Science and Industry
OMSIP	Ontario Medical Surgical Insurance Plan [*Canada*] (AD)
OMSITE	Oral and Maxillofacial Surgery In-Training Examination
OMSJ	Sharjah/International [*United Arab Emirates*] [*ICAO location identifier*] (ICLI)
OMSJB	St. Jean Bosco Library, Matachewan, Ontario [*Library symbol*] [*National Library of Canada*] (BIB)
OMSK	Smith, Kline & French Canada Ltd., Mississauga, Ontario [*Library symbol*] [*National Library of Canada*] (NLC)
OMSLMSq	Organizational Missile Maintenance Squadron [*Air Force*]
OMSM	Medical Library, Syntex, Inc., Mississauga, Ontario [*Library symbol*] [*National Library of Canada*] (NLC)
OMS/MP	Operational Mode Summary/Mission Profiles (MCD)
OMS/MP	Opmode Summary/Mission Profile (SAUS)
OMSMT	South Marysburgh Township Public Library, Milford, Ontario [*Library symbol*] [*National Library of Canada*] (BIB)
OMsn	Mason Public Library, Mason, OH [*Library symbol*] [*Library of Congress*] (LCLS)
OMSN	Seaman, Opticalman, Striker [*Navy rating*]
OMSP	Operational Maintenance Support Plan [*NASA*] (MCD)
OMSq	Organizational Maintenance Squadron [*Air Force*] (AFM)
OMSQA	Office of Monitoring Systems and Quality Assurance [*Environmental Protection Agency*] (EPA)

OMSRADS ... Optimum Mix of Short Range Air Defense Systems
OMSS .... Operational Meteorological Satellite System (SAUS)
OMST .... Object Manipulation Speed Test
OMSWG ...... Operations and Maintenance Security Working Group (SSD)
OMT .... McKellar Township Public Library, Ontario [*Library symbol*] [*National Library of Canada*] (NLC)
OMT .... Metropolitan Toronto Library, Multilanguage Service [*UTLAS symbol*]
OMT .... Object Management Technique (SAUS)
OMT .... Object Modeling Technique (AAEL)
OMT .... Object Modeling Technology [*Ungermann-Bass, Inc.*]
OMT .... Object Model Template (SAUS)
OMT .... Ocean Marine Technology [*Vancouver Stock Exchange symbol*]
OMT .... Oceanography and Marine Technology [*Defunct*] (USDC)
OMT .... Office of Manufacturing Technology [*DARCOM*] [*Army*] (RDA)
OMT .... Officiating Minister to the Troops [*British*]
OMT .... Ohio Mattress Co. (EFIS)
OMT .... Old Merchant Taylors [*School*] [*British*] (ROG)
OMT .... Oleoyl Methyl Taurate [*Organic chemistry*]
OMT .... O-Methylthreonine [*Biochemistry*]
OMT .... O-Methyl Transferase [*An enzyme*]
OMT .... Ophthalmic Medical Assistant (DAVI)
OMT .... Ophthalmic Medical Technician [*or Technologist*] (HCT)
OMT .... Oral Mucosal Transudate [*Clinical chemistry*]
OMT .... Ordnance Maintenance Truck [*British*]
OMT .... Organizational Maintenance Technician [*Army*] (AABC)
OMT .... Organizational Maintenance Trainer (MCD)
OMT .... Oriental Movement Therapy (MELL)
OMT .... Orthogonal Mode Transducer (IAA)
omt .... Orthomode Transducer (AD)
OMT .... Orthomode Transducer [*Electronics*]
OMT .... Ortho-Mycaminosyltylonolide [*Antibacterial compound*]
OMT .... Orthotropic Multicell Tank
OMT .... Osteopathic Manipulative Therapy (CPH)
OMT .... Other Military Target
OMTA .... Office of Management and Technical Assessment [*Environmental Protection Agency*] (GFGA)
OMTA .... Ovulation Method Teachers Association (EA)
OMTBP .... Octamethyltetrabenzporphyrin [*Organic chemistry*]
OMTC .... Ontario Ministry of Transportation and Communications [*Downsview, ON*] [*Telecommunications*] (TSSD)
OMTD .... Omitted (SAUS)
OMTD .... Operator/Maintenance Task Description (DNAB)
OMTE .... Organizational Maintenance Test Equipment (SAUS)
OMTF .... Officers Master Tape File (SAUS)
OMTF .... Optical Modulation Transfer Function (ACAE)
OMTF .... Overall Missile Test Facility (SAUS)
OMTL .... Optical Mechanical Tube Length (SAUS)
OMTN .... Other Military Teletypewriter Network (CET)
OMTNS .... Over Mountains [*NWS*] (FAAC)
OMTR .... Officer Master Tape Record [*Army*] (AABC)
OMTR .... Officer Master Tape Recorder (SAUS)
OMTS .... Organizational Maintenance Test Station [*Army*]
OMtsjC .... College of Mount St. Joseph-On-The-Ohio, Mount St. Joseph, OH [*Library symbol*] [*Library of Congress*] (LCLS)
OMTSS .... Ordnance Multiple-Purpose Tactical Satellite System
OMTU .... Organizational Maintenance Trainer Unit (ACAE)
OMtv .... Mount Vernon Public Library, Mount Vernon, OH [*Library symbol*] [*Library of Congress*] (LCLS)
OMtvN .... Mount Vernon Nazarene College, Mount Vernon, OH [*Library symbol*] [*Library of Congress*] (LCLS)
OMU .... Operational Mock-Up
OMU .... Operative Mechanics' Union [*British*]
OMU .... Optical Measuring Unit (KSC)
omu .... Optical Measuring Unit (NAKS)
OMU .... Optical Memory Unit (SAUS)
OMU .... Orbital Maneuvering Unit (ACAE)
OMUA .... Office Machinery Users Association (SAUS)
OMUC .... Upper Canada Village, Morrisburg, Ontario [*Library symbol*] [*National Library of Canada*] (NLC)
OMUP .... Operating and Maintenance User Part (SAUS)
OMUP .... Organization and Management User Parts [*Telecommunications*] (OSI)
OMV .... Oat Mosaic Virus [*Plant pathology*]
OMV .... Oblates of the Virgin Mary (TOCD)
omv .... Oblates of the Virgin Mary (TOCD)
OMV .... Office Machines Vocabulary (SAUS)
OMV .... Orbital Maneuvering Vehicle [*NASA*]
OMV .... Overseas Media Visitor
omv .... Oxygen Manual Valve (NAKS)
OMV .... Oxygen Manual Valve (NASA)
OMVC .... Mattice-Val Cote Public Library, Mattice, Ontario [*Library symbol*] [*National Library of Canada*] (BIB)
OMVC .... Open Mitral Valve Commissurotomy [*Medicine*]
OMVCC .... Orbital Maneuvering Vehicle Control Center [*NASA*] (SSD)
OMVD .... Operator Multi-Valued Dependency
OMVG .... Gambia River Development Organization (SAUS)
OMVG .... Organisation pour la Mise en Valeur du Fleuve Gambie [*Gambia River Basin Organisation*] (EAIO)
OMVI .... Operating a Motor Vehicle Intoxicated (MEDA)
OMVPE .... Organo-Metallic Vapor-Phase Epitaxy (SAUS)
OM-VPE ...... Organometallic Vapor Phase Epitaxy [*Also, OM-CVD, MO-CVD, MO-VPE*] [*Semiconductor technology*]
OMVPE .... Organometallic Vapour Phase Epitaxy (AAEL)
OMVS .... Senegal River Development Organization (SAUS)
OMVTO .... Office Motor Vehicle Transportation Officer [*Army*] (AABC)

OMVUIL ...... Operating Motor Vehicle under the Influence of Liquor [*Traffic offense charge*]
OMVWI .... Operating Motor Vehicle while Intoxicated [*Traffic offense charge*]
OMW .... Office of the Mining Warden [*Victoria, Australia*]
OMW .... Olds Motor Works [*Precursor of Oldsmobile Division of General Motors*]
OMW .... Omak [*Washington*] [*Seismograph station code, US Geological Survey*] (SEIS)
OMW .... Ordnance Mobile Workshop (SAUS)
OMWG .... Object Model Working Group
OMWIL .... Operating Motor Vehicle under the Influence of Liquor (SAUS)
OMWM .... Open Marsh Water Managed [*Ecology*]
OMWOG ..... Ocean-based Measurements Working Group (SAUS)
OMWOG ..... Oceans-based Measurements Working Group (SAUS)
OMX .... Officemax, Inc. [*NYSE symbol*] (SAG)
OMX .... Option Market Index [*Sweden*] (NUMA)
OMX .... Xerox Research Centre of Canada, Mississauga, Ontario [*Library symbol*] [*National Library of Canada*] (NLC)
OMY .... Output per Man-Year (SAUS)
OMZ .... Oamaru [*New Zealand*] [*Seismograph station code, US Geological Survey*] (SEIS)
OMZ .... Oxygen-Minimum Zone [*Oceanography*]
OMZ .... Oxymorphonazine [*An analgesic*]
ON .... Air Nauru [*ICAO designator*] (AD)
ON .... Central Branch, Nepean Public Library, Ontario [*Library symbol*] [*National Library of Canada*] (NLC)
ON .... McKinley Memorial Library, Niles, OH [*Library symbol*] [*Library of Congress*] (LCLS)
ON .... New Order [*Revolutionary group*] [*Italy*]
ON .... Obstructive Nephropathy [*Medicine*] (MELL)
ON .... Occupational Nursing (SAUS)
on .... Octane Number (AD)
ON .... Octane Number [*Fuel terminology*]
ON .... Oculonasal [*Anatomy*]
ON .... Office Nurse
ON .... Officer's Name (NITA)
ON .... Official Number (DS)
ON .... Off Normal
ON .... Ogden Nash (AD)
ON .... Oil-Immersed Natural-Colled Transformer (IAA)
ON .... Oil-immersed Natural-cooled (or cooling) (SAUS)
ON .... Old Norse [*Language, etc.*]
ON .... Olfactory Nerve [*Neuroanatomy*]
ON .... Oligonucleotide [*Chemistry*]
ON .... Omega Navigation (PDAA)
ON .... Omega Neuron [*Neuroanatomy*]
ON .... Omni Nocte [*Every Night*] [*Pharmacy*]
on .... Omni Nocte [*Every Night*] [*Latin*] (AD)
ON .... Oncology [*Medical specialty*] (DHSM)
ON .... Oncor [*Tire retread brand*]
ON .... Onions (ROG)
on .... Onomastikon [*Lexicon*] [*Greek*] (AD)
ON .... Onorevole [*Honorable*] (EY)
ON .... Onorevole [*Honorable*] [*Italian*] (AD)
On .... Onsdag [*Wednesday*] [*Danish*] (AD)
on .... Onstage [*Theater*] (WDMC)
ON .... Ontario [*Canadian province*] [*Postal code*]
ON .... Ontario Northland Railway [*Canada*] (AD)
ON .... Opera News [*A publication*] (BRI)
ON .... Operation Notice (AAG)
ON .... Operation Number (ELAL)
ON .... Optic Nerve [*Anatomy*]
ON .... Optic Neuritis (SAUS)
ON .... Optic Neuropathy (SAUS)
O/N .... Order Notify [*Bill of lading*] [*Shipping*]
ON .... Order Number (NITA)
ON .... Ordre Nouveau [*New Order*] [*France*] [*Political party*] (WDAA)
ON .... Oregon [*Obsolete*] (ROG)
ON .... Original Negative (MCD)
ON .... Ortho-Novum [*A contraceptive*] [*Ortho Pharmaceutical Corp.*] (DAVI)
ON .... Orthopedic Nurse
ON .... Other Networks (SAUS)
ON .... Our Neighbours [*A publication*]
ON .... Overnighter (SAUS)
o/n .... Own Name (AD)
O/N .... Own Name
ON .... Oxidation Number (IAA)
O/N .... Oxygen-to-Nitrogen ratio (SAUS)
ONA .... Nakina Public Library, Ontario [*Library symbol*] [*National Library of Canada*] (BIB)
ONA .... Office of National Assessments [*Australia*]
ONA .... Ohio Nurses Association (SAUS)
ONA .... Oklahoma Nurses Association (SAUS)
ONA .... Onahama [*Japan*] [*Seismograph station code, US Geological Survey*] (SEIS)
ONA .... Oneita Industries [*NYSE symbol*] (SAG)
ONA .... O-Nitroaniline (SAUS)
ONA .... Ontario Nurses Association (SAUS)
ONA .... Open Network Architecture [*Computer science*]
ONA .... Optical Navigation Attachment (WDAA)
ONA .... Oregon Nurses Association (SAUS)
ONA .... Orthonitroaniline (DICI)
ONA .... Overseas National Airways [*Belgium*] [*ICAO designator*] (FAAC)
ONA .... Overseas National Airways, Inc.
ONA .... Overseas News Agency

ONA	Oxides of Nitrogen Analysis [*Automotive emissions*]
ONA	Winona [*Minnesota*] [*Airport symbol*] (AD)
ONA	Winona, MN [*Location identifier*] [*FAA*] (FAAL)
ONAC	Office of Noise Abatement and Control [*Environmental Protection Agency*]
On a/c	On Account (EBF)
ONAC	Operating Network Advisory Committee [*NERComP*]
ONAC	Operations Network Administration Center (SAUS)
ONAIS	Organization of North American Indian Students [*Defunct*] (EA)
ONA J	Orthopedic Nurses Association. Journal (SAUS)
ONAL	Off-Net Access Line [*Telecommunications*] (TEL)
ONAP	Orbit Navigation Analysis Program
ONAP	Organisation Nationale d'Anti-Pauvrete [*Canada*]
ON APPROV	On Approval (SAUS)
ONARP	Occurrence Notification and Report Program (SAUS)
ONAS	Office of Naval Acquisition Support (SAUS)
ONAS	Outpatient Nonavailability Statement [*DoD*]
OnAssign	On Assignment, Inc. [*Associated Press*] (SAG)
ONAT	Off-Network Access Trunk (SAUS)
on av	on average (SAUS)
O-NAV	On-Board Navigation (MCD)
ONAX	Overseas National Airways, Inc. [*Air carrier designation symbol*]
ONB	Monkey Bay [*Malawi*] [*Airport symbol*] (AD)
ONb	New Breman Public Library, New Breman, OH [*Library symbol*] [*Library of Congress*] (LCLS)
ONB	North Bay Public Library, Ontario [*Library symbol*] [*National Library of Canada*] (NLC)
ONB	Obturator Nerve Block [*Medicine*] (MELL)
ONB	Octane Number Barrel [*Fuel terminology*]
ONB	Old Natura Brevium [*A publication*] (DLA)
ONB	O-Nitrobiphenyl (SAUS)
ONB	Ortho-Nitrobiphenyl [*Organic chemistry*]
ONBA	Centre de Ressources, Ecole Secondaire Algonquin, North Bay, Ontario [*Library symbol*] [*National Library of Canada*] (NLC)
ONBC	Ouachita National Bancshares (SAUS)
ONBCC	Canadore College, North Bay, Ontario [*Library symbol*] [*National Library of Canada*] (NLC)
Onbcp	ONBANcorp, Inc. [*Associated Press*] (SAG)
ONBD	On Board (NASA)
ONBK	Onbancorp, Inc. [*NASDAQ symbol*] (NQ)
ONBKP	ONBANCorp 6.75% Cv 'B' Pfd [*NASDAQ symbol*] (TTSB)
ONBM	Belmont and Methuen Township Public Library, Nephton, Ontario [*Library symbol*] [*National Library of Canada*] (BIB)
ONBNU	Nipissing University College, North Bay, Ontario [*Library symbol*] [*National Library of Canada*] (NLC)
O-N Border	Oder-Neisse Border (SAUS)
ONBOSUB	On Board a Submarine [*Navy*]
ONBOWCOM	Duty on Board that Vessel when Placed in Commission [*Navy*]
ONBOWSERV	Duty on Board that Vessel when Placed in Service [*Navy*]
ONBP	Staff Library, North Bay Psychiatric Hospital, Ontario [*Library symbol*] [*National Library of Canada*] (NLC)
ONBT	Orbiter Neutral Buoyancy Trainer [*NASA*] (MCD)
ONBT	Regroupement des Organisations Nationales Benevoles [*Also, National Voluntary Organizations*] (AC)
ONBWF	West Ferris Secondary School, North Bay, Ontario [*Library symbol*] [*National Library of Canada*] (NLC)
ONC	Confederation High School, Nepean, Ontario [*Library symbol*] [*National Library of Canada*] (NLC)
ONC	Occurrence Notification Center (SAUS)
ONC	Office of Narcotics Coordinator [*Later, NARCOG*] [*CIA*]
ONC	Office of New Careers [*HEW*]
ONC	Olivet Nazarene College [*Kankakee, IL*]
ONC	Oncology (DAVI)
ONC	Oncor, Inc. [*AMEX symbol*] (SAG)
ONC	On-Site Container (DOMA)
onc	Ontario [*MARC country of publication code*] [*Library of Congress*] (LCCP)
ONC	Open Network Computing [*Computer science*] (PCM)
ONC+	Open Network Computing Plus [*Computer science*] (PCM)
ONC	Open Networking Consortium (SAUS)
ONC	Operational Navigation Charts [*Air Force*]
ONC	Optimists National Corps [*British military*] (DMA)
ONC	Ordinary National Certificate [*British*]
ONC	Oregon-Nevada-California [*Truck line*] (IIA)
ONC	Organization of Nigerian Citizens
ONC	Orthopaedic Nurse Certified (NUJO)
ONC	Orthopedic Nursing Certificate
ONC	Overall NATO Command (NATG)
ONCB	Centennial Branch, Nepean Public Library, Ontario [*Library symbol*] [*National Library of Canada*] (NLC)
ONCB	Office of the Narcotics Control Board, Thailand (SAUS)
ONCC	Oncology Nursing Certification Corporation (SAUS)
ONC/D	Ordinary National Certificate/Diploma (ACII)
ONCE	Office of National Cost Estimates [*Department of Health and Human Services*] (GFGA)
ONCF	Office National des Chemins de Fer [*Moroccan Railways*]
ONCFM	Office National des Chemins de Fer du Maroc [*Moroccan Railways*] (DCTA)
ONCG-A	Oncogenic Virus Battery - Acute [*Oncology*] (DAVI)
ONcM	Muskingum College, New Concord, OH [*Library symbol*] [*Library of Congress*] (LCLS)
ONCMM	Cosby, Mason, and Martland Public Library, Noelville, Ontario [*Library symbol*] [*National Library of Canada*] (NLC)
ONCN	[*An*] O'Neill Concordance [*A publication*]

ONCO	Office of NOAA [*National Oceanic and Atmospheric Administration*] Corps Operations [*Marine science*] (OSRA)
ONCO	On Command Corp. [*NASDAQ symbol*] (SAG)
OnCo	On Command Corp. [*Associated Press*] (SAG)
Onco	OncoRx, Inc. [*Associated Press*] (SAG)
ONCO	Operations Non-Commissioned Officer (SAUS)
Oncogn	Oncogene Science, Inc. [*Associated Press*] (SAG)
oncol	oncologic (SAUS)
ONCOL	Oncologist
oncol	oncolysis (SAUS)
OnCom	On Command Corp. [*Associated Press*] (SAG)
OnComm	On Command Corp. [*Associated Press*] (SAG)
Oncor	Oncor, Inc. [*Associated Press*] (SAG)
ONCORE	On-Command Restartable (MCD)
Oncormd	OncorMed, Inc. [*Associated Press*] (SAG)
OncoRx	OncoRx, Inc. [*Associated Press*] (SAG)
ONCRC	Central Resource Centre, Carleton Roman Catholic School Board, Nepean, Ontario [*Library symbol*] [*National Library of Canada*] (NLC)
ONCS	Oncogene Science [*NASDAQ symbol*] (TTSB)
ONCS	Oncogene Science, Inc. [*NASDAQ symbol*] (NQ)
ONCU	Cumberland Township Library, Navan, Ontario [*Library symbol*] [*National Library of Canada*] (BIB)
ONCXDR	Open Network Computing External Data Representation (SAUS)
OND	Office for Network Development [*Ottawa, ON*] [*National Library of Canada*] [*Telecommunications service*] (TSSD)
OND	Office of Neighborhood Development (OICC)
OND	Office of the Nominal Defendant [*Australia*]
OND	Ondangua [*Namibia*] [*Airport symbol*] (OAG)
OND	Operator Need Dale (SAUS)
OND	Operator Need Date (NASA)
OND	Ophthalmic Nursing Diploma
OND	Optical Neural Device (SAUS)
OND	Ordinary National Diploma [*British*]
OND	Organic Nervous Disease [*Medicine*] (MELL)
OND	Orthopaedic Nursing Diploma [*British*]
OND	Other Neurological Disorders
OND	Own Number Dialing [*Telecommunications*] (OA)
ONDA	Norwich and District Archives, Norwich, Ontario [*Library symbol*] [*National Library of Canada*] (BIB)
ONDC	Office of National Drug Control (SAUS)
ONDCP	Office of National Drug Control Policy [*Executive Office of the President*]
ONDE	Office of Naval Disability Evaluation (NVT)
OnderstJ V	Onderstepoort Journal of Veterinary Research (SAUS)
ONDI	Ontrack Data International, Inc. [*NASDAQ symbol*] (SAG)
ONDO	ODP Nankai Downhole Observatory (SAUS)
ONDS	Dipix Systems Ltd., Nepean, Ontario [*Library symbol*] [*National Library of Canada*] (NLC)
ONDS	Open Network Distribution Services (SAUS)
ONDS	Optic Nerve Decompression Surgery
ONDS	Oriental Nocturnal Death Syndrome [*Neurology*] (DAVI)
ONE	Bank One Corp. [*NYSE symbol*] (SG)
ONE	Current Tech [*Vancouver Stock Exchange symbol*]
ONE	Current Technology [*VS, exchange symbol*] (TTSB)
ONe	Nelsonville Public Library, Nelsonville, OH [*Library symbol*] [*Library of Congress*] (LCLS)
ONE	Newmarket Public Library, Ontario [*Library symbol*] [*National Library of Canada*] (NLC)
ONE	Northeastern Ohio University, College of Medicine, Rootstown, OH [*OCLC symbol*] (OCLC)
ONE	Office National de l'Energie [*National Energy Board - NEB*] [*Canada*]
ONE	Office Network Exchange [*Honeywell, Inc.*]
ONE	Office of National Estimates (SAUS)
ONE	Onepusu [*Solomon Islands*] [*Airport symbol*] [*Obsolete*] (OAG)
ONE	Onerahi [*Whangarei*] [*New Zealand*] [*Seismograph station code, US Geological Survey*] (SEIS)
ONE	OPAC Network in Europe (SAUS)
ONE	Open Network Environment [*Netscape network*] [*Computer science*]
ONE	Optimum Network Executive (SAUS)
ONE	Optimum Nutritional Effectiveness [*Brand name of dog food*] [*Ralston Purina Co.*]
ONeA	Organization Number of Employees (SAUS)
ONeA	Newark Public Library, Newark (SAUS)
O'Neal Neg L	O'Neal's Negro Law of South Carolina [*A publication*] (DLA)
ONEB	Office of National Environmental Board (SAUS)
ONEC	OneComm Corp. [*NASDAQ symbol*] (SAG)
OneCm	OneComm Corp. [*Associated Press*] (SAG)
ONEG	O Negative [*Blood type*] [*Hematology and laboratory*] (DAVI)
ONeH	Hocking Technical College, Nelsonville, OH [*Library symbol*] [*Library of Congress*] (LCLS)
Oneida	Oneida Ltd. [*Associated Press*] (SAG)
Oneita	Oneita Industries [*Associated Press*] (SAG)
ONELAC	Newburgh Branch, Lennox and Addington County, Ontario [*Library symbol*] [*National Library of Canada*] (BIB)
OneLb	One Liberty Properties, Inc. [*Associated Press*] (SAG)
Onelibt	One Liberty Properties, Inc. [*Associated Press*] (SAG)
ONEMRCM	BCC Library, CANMET, Energy, Mines, and Resources Canada [*Bibliotheque du CBC, CANMET, Energie, Mines, et Ressources Canada*], Nepean, Ontario [*Library symbol*] [*National Library of Canada*] (NLC)
ONEO	Office of Navajo Economic Opportunity
ONEOK	ONEOK, Inc. [*Associated Press*] (SAG)
ONEP	Office National d'Edition et de Presse [*News agency*] [*Niger*] (EY)

ONEP .... Pickering College, Newmarket, Ontario [*Library symbol*] [*National Library of Canada*] (NLC)

ONEPI .... Office National d'Edition, de Presse, et d'Imprimerie [*Publisher*] [*Benin*] (EY)

OnePrice ...... One Price Clothing Stores, Inc. [*Associated Press*] (SAG)

ONER .... Oceanic Navigational Error Report [*Aviation*] (FAAC)

ONE-R .... One Time and Revisions as Required (ACAE)

ONet .... Ontario Network [*Canada*]

Onet .... Ontario Regional Network [*Canada*] [*Computer science*] (TNIG)

ONEU .... Neustadt Village Public Library, Ontario [*Library symbol*] [*National Library of Canada*] (NLC)

OneVall .... One Valley Bancorp of West Virginia, Inc. [*Associated Press*] (SAG)

ONew .... Newark Public Library, Newark, OH [*Library symbol*] [*Library of Congress*] (LCLS)

ONewU .... Ohio State University, Newark Campus, Newark, OH [*Library symbol*] [*Library of Congress*] (LCLS)

OneWve ...... OneWave, Inc. [*Associated Press*] (SAG)

ONF .... Niagara Falls Public Library, Ontario [*Library symbol*] [*National Library of Canada*] (NLC)

ONF .... Offensive Nuclear Forces (SAUS)

ONF .... Office National du Film du Canada [*National Film Board of Canada - NFB*]

ONF .... Old Norman French [*Language, etc.*]

ONF .... Old Northern French [*Language, etc.*]

ONF .... Oncology Nursing Forum (SAUS)

ONF .... Oncology Nursing Foundation

ONF .... On File (SAUS)

ONF .... Optic Nerve Fiber [*Anatomy*]

ONFA .... Acres Consulting Services Ltd., Niagara Falls, Ontario [*Library symbol*] [*National Library of Canada*] (NLC)

ONFCY .... Cyanamid, Niagara Falls, Ontario [*Library symbol*] [*National Library of Canada*] (NLC)

ONFJC .... John Coutts Library Services Ltd., Niagara Falls, Ontario [*Library symbol*] [*National Library of Canada*] (NLC)

ONFLC .... Lanmer Consultants Ltd., Niagara Falls, Ontario [*Library symbol*] [*National Library of Canada*] (NLC)

ONFM .... On Nearest Full Moon (SAUS)

ONFM .... On or Nearest Full Moon [*Freemasonry*] (ROG)

ONFR .... Old Northern French [*Language, etc.*]

ONFWM .... Willoughby Historical Museum, Niagara Falls, Ontario [*Library symbol*] [*National Library of Canada*] (BIB)

ONFWPL ...... W. P. London & Associates, Niagara Falls, Ontario [*Library symbol*] [*National Library of Canada*] (NLC)

ONG .... Donalsonville, GA [*Location identifier*] [*FAA*] (FAAL)

ONG .... Mornington Island [*Australia*] [*Airport symbol*] (OAG)

ONG .... Old North German (SAUS)

ONG .... Oneok, Inc. (EFIS)

ONG .... Ongar [*England*]

ONG .... Ongoro [*Peru*] [*Seismograph station code, US Geological Survey*] [*Closed*] (SEIS)

ONG .... Osteopathic and Naturopathic Guild [*British*] (DBA)

ONGA .... Overseas Number Group Analysis [*Telecommunications*] (TEL)

ONGC .... Office des Normes Generales du Canada

ONGC .... Oil & Natural Gas Commission (SAUS)

OnGrd .... On Gard Systems [*Associated Press*] (SAG)

OnGrdSy ...... On Gard Systems [*Associated Press*] (SAG)

ONGRT .... North Gower Branch, Rideau Township Library, Ontario [*Library symbol*] [*National Library of Canada*] (BIB)

ONGS .... Office of National Geodetic Survey [*National Ocean Survey*]

ONH .... Office of Naval History [*Also, OFFNAVHIST*]

ONH .... Oneonta [*New York*] [*Airport symbol*] (OAG)

ON/H .... On the Hatch Cover [*Stowage*] (DNAB)

ONHI .... Niagara Historical Society, Niagara-On-The-Lake, Ontario [*Library symbol*] [*National Library of Canada*] (NLC)

ONHIC .... ODPHP [*Office of Disease Prevention and Health Promotion*] National Health Information Center (IID)

ONHN .... OnHealth Network [*NASDAQ symbol*] (SG)

ONI .... Moanamani [*Indonesia*] [*Airport symbol*] (OAG)

ONI .... Nipigon Public Library, Ontario [*Library symbol*] [*National Library of Canada*] (NLC)

ONI .... Office of National Waste Terminal Storage Integration (SAUS)

ONI .... Office of Naval Intelligence

ONI .... Office of NWTS Integration (SAUS)

ONI .... Oficina Nacional de Informacion [*National Information Office*] [*Press agency*] [*Peru*]

ONI .... Oni [*Former USSR*] [*Seismograph station code, US Geological Survey*] (SEIS)

ONI .... Operator Number Identification [*Bell System*]

ONI .... Optical Network Interface [*Telecommunications*] (DCDG)

ONI .... Optical Networks, Inc.

ONIO .... Office of Naval Inspectors of Ordnance

ONIP .... Office of National Industry Promotion [*Bureau of Apprenticeship and Training*] [*Department of Labor*]

ONIP .... Perry County District Library, New Lexington (SAUS)

ONIS .... ONI Systems [*NASDAQ symbol*]

OnIssues ...... On the Issues [*A publication*] (BRI)

ONIX .... Online Information Exchange [*Association of American Publishers*]

ONJ .... Olivia Newton-John [*Singer*]

ONJSW .... J. S. Woodsworth Secondary School, Nepean, Ontario [*Library symbol*] [*National Library of Canada*] (NLC)

Onk .... Targum Onkelos (BJA)

ONL .... New Liskeard Public Library, Ontario [*Library symbol*] [*National Library of Canada*] (NLC)

ONL .... Office of Naval Liaison [*NASA*] (KSC)

ONL .... Ohio Northern University, Law Library, Ada, OH [*OCLC symbol*] (OCLC)

ONL .... O'Neill, NE [*Location identifier*] [*FAA*] (FAAL)

ONL .... On-Line (SAUS)

ONL .... Outer Nuclear Layer [*Anatomy*]

ONL .... Overnight Loan (ADA)

ONLAC .... Lennox and Addington Counties Public Library, Napanee, Ontario [*Library symbol*] [*National Library of Canada*] (NLC)

ONLAH .... Lennox and Addington Historical Society, Napanee, Ontario [*Library symbol*] [*National Library of Canada*] (BIB)

ONLAM .... Lennox and Addington Museum, Napanee, Ontario [*Library symbol*] [*National Library of Canada*] (NLC)

ONLAS .... Optical Night Landing Approach System [*Aviation*] (PDAA)

ONLEXCRT .... Online Exercise Critique System (SAUS)

ONLF .... Ogaden National Liberation Front [*Ethiopia*]

ONLICATS .... Online Shared Cataloging System [*Computer science*]

Online Bus Inf ... Online Business Information

Online Libr Microcomput ... Online Libraries and Microcomputers (SAUS)

ONLP .... On-Line Program Development [*Computer science*] (MHDB)

ONIP .... Perry County District Library, New Lexington, OH [*Library symbol*] [*Library of Congress*] (LCLS)

ONLS .... Sunnidale Township Public Library, New Lowell, Ontario [*Library symbol*] [*National Library of Canada*] (BIB)

ONLY .... Online Yield [*Computer science*]

ONM .... Condamine [*Queensland*] [*Airport symbol*] (AD)

ONM .... Ocmulgee National Monument (SAUS)

ONM .... Office of Naval Material [*Later, NMCOM*]

ONM .... OncorMed, Inc. [*AMEX symbol*] (SAG)

ONM .... Open Network Management (SAUS)

ONM .... Organization Name (SAUS)

ONM .... Socorro, NM [*Location identifier*] [*FAA*] (FAAL)

ONMB .... Merivale Road Branch, Nepean Public Library, Ontario [*Library symbol*] [*National Library of Canada*] (BIB)

ONMINST ..... Office of Naval Material Publication Type Instruction

ONMM .... On-Board Microwave MODEM [*Telecommunications*] (LAIN)

ONMP .... Office of Nuclear Materials Processing (SAUS)

ONMPC .... Office of Naval Material - Permanent Cadre

ONMS .... Open Network Management System (SAUS)

ONMS .... Orbiter Neutral Mass Spectrometer [*NASA*]

ONMSS .... Office of Nuclear Materials Safety and Safeguards [*Nuclear Regulatory Commission*]

ONN .... Enkabe Contact (journ.) (SAUS)

ONN .... Fort Meade, MD [*Location identifier*] [*FAA*] (FAAL)

ONN .... National Standardisation Office (SAUS)

ONN .... O'Nyong-Nyong Virus

ONN .... Open Network Node (SAUS)

ONNA .... Oh No, Not Again! [*Computer hacker terminology*]

ONNI .... Office of National Narcotics Intelligence [*Later, Drug Enforcement Administration*] [*Department of Justice*]

ONNM .... On or Nearest New Moon [*Freemasonry*] (ROG)

ONNN .... SCG Holdings [*NASDAQ symbol*] (SG)

ONO .... Norwood Public Library, Ontario [*Library symbol*] [*National Library of Canada*] (BIB)

ONO .... Office of Naval Operations

ONO .... Ontario [*Oregon*] [*Airport symbol*] (AD)

ONO .... Ontario, OR [*Location identifier*] [*FAA*] (FAAL)

ONO .... Organization of News Ombudsmen (EA)

ONO .... Or Nearest [*or Near*] Offer [*Business term*] (ADA)

ONO .... Oxide-Nitride-Oxide (SAUS)

ONOC .... Oceania National Olympic Committee [*Australia*]

ONocHE .... Hoover Co., Engineering Division, North Canton, OH [*Library symbol*] [*Library of Congress*] (LCLS)

ON-OFF .... Oscillatory, Nonoscillatory Flip-Flop [*Computer science*]

ONOL .... Niagara-On-The-Lake Public Library, Ontario [*Library symbol*] [*National Library of Canada*] (BIB)

Onom .... Onomasticon [*of Eusebius*] (BJA)

onomast ...... onomastics (SAUS)

onomast ...... onomatologist (SAUS)

onomat .... onomatology (SAUS)

ONOMAT ..... Onomatopoeia (ROG)

onomat .... onomatopoeical (SAUS)

ONOO .... Outline NATO Operational Objective (MCD)

ONOP .... Office of Naval Officer Procurement

ONOP .... Officer-in-Charge, Branch Office of Naval Officer Procurement (DNAB)

O Norw .... Old Norwegian (SAUS)

ONowdM ...... Athenaeum of Ohio, Norwood, OH [*Library symbol*] [*Library of Congress*] (LCLS)

ONOZ .... Oil Nozzle

ONP .... Newport [*Oregon*] [*Airport symbol*] [*Obsolete*] (OAG)

ONP .... Office of National Programs [*Employment and Training Administration*] [*Department of Labor*]

ONP .... Ohio Nisi Prius Reports [*A publication*] (DLA)

ONP .... Old Newspaper [*Recycling*]

ONP .... Olympic National Park (SAUS)

ONP .... Onex Packaging, Inc. [*Toronto Stock Exchange symbol*]

ONP .... Open Networking Platform

ONP .... Open Network Provision

ONP .... Operating Nursing Procedure

ONP .... Optical Nuclear Polarization (AAEL)

ONP .... Original Net Premium [*Insurance*] (AIA)

ONP .... Ortho-Nitrophenol [*Organic chemistry*]

ONPA .... Office of National Projects Administration [*Department of Labor*]

ONPG .... O-Nitrophenyl-a-D-Galactoside (SAUS)

ONPG .... O-Nitrophenyl-beta-D-galactopyranoside [*Test*] [*Microbiology*]

ONPG	O-Nitrophenyl Galactoside (DOG)
ONPG	Operational Nuclear Planning Group [*Military*]
ONPG	Operations Nuclear Planning Group (SAUS)
ONPG	Ortho-Nitrophenyl-a-D-Galactopyranoside (SAUS)
ONP-GAL	Ortho-Nitrophenyl-B-Galactosidase [*Organic chemistry*] (MAE)
ONPI	Office of News and Public Information (SAUS)
ONpK	Kent State University, Tuscarawas County Regional Campus, New Philadelphia, OH [*Library symbol*] [*Library of Congress*] (LCLS)
ONPNS	Ohio Nisi Prius Reports, New Series [*1903-13*] [*A publication*] (DLA)
OnPointT	On-Point Technology Systems, Inc. [*Associated Press*] (SAG)
ONPOSR	Office of Naval Petroleum and Oil Shale Reserves
ONPR	Office of New Production Reactors [*U.S. Department of Energy*] (BARN)
ONPR	One Price Clothing Stores, Inc. [*NASDAQ symbol*] (NQ)
ONPR	One Price Clothing Strs [*NASDAQ symbol*] (TTSB)
ONPT	On-Point Technology Systems, Inc. [*NASDAQ symbol*] (SAG)
ONQ	Order of Nurses of Quebec (SAUS)
ONR	Monkira [*Queensland*] [*Airport symbol*] (AD)
ONR	Oboz Narodowo-Radykalny [*Radical Nationalist Camp*] [*Poland*] [*Political party*] (PPE)
ONR	Octane Number Requirement [*Automotive engineering*]
ONR	Office of Naval Research [*Arlington, VA*]
ONR	Official Naval Reporter [*British*]
ONR	Ontario Northland Railway
ONR	Operational NonRADAR Directed Flights (NATG)
ONR	Original Net Rate [*Insurance*] (AIA)
ONR	Phillips Petroleum Co., Exploration and Product Library, Bartlesville, OK [*OCLC symbol*] (OCLC)
ONRARO	Office of Naval Research, Area Research Office (DNAB)
ONR/BO	Office of Naval Research/Branch Office (SAUS)
ONR BR	Branch Office, Office of Naval Research
ONRBRO	Office of Naval Research Branch Research Office
ONRC	Office of Naval Research, Chicago
ONRDB	Ruth E. Dickinson Branch, Nepean Public Library, Ontario [*Library symbol*] [*National Library of Canada*] (BIB)
ONRDET	Office of Naval Research Detachment (DNAB)
ONREAST	Office of Naval Research, East Coast Regional Office (DNAB)
ONRFE	Office of Naval Research, Far East Regional Office (DNAB)
ONRI	Octane Number Requirement Increase [*Automotive engineering*]
ONRL	Office of Naval Records and Library (SAUS)
ONRL	Office of Naval Research, London
ONRO	ODA Natural Resources Office
ONRR	Office of Nuclear Regulatory Research (SAUS)
ONRRR	Office of Naval Research Resident Representative
ONRS	Oceanic Navigation Research Society (EA)
ONRS	Office of National Range Support (SAA)
ONRT	Office of Naval Research, Tokyo
ONRT	Online Real Time [*Computer science*] (ADA)
ONRW	Outstanding National Resource Waters (EEVL)
ONRWEST	Office of Naval Research, West Coast Regional Office (DNAB)
ONRY	Ogdensburg Bridge & Port Authority [*AAR code*]
ONS	Northwestern School of Law, Lewis and Clark College, Portland, OR [*OCLC symbol*] (OCLC)
ONS	Oconee Nuclear Station (NRCH)
ONS	Office for National Statistics [*British*]
ONS	Office of National Statistics (SAUS)
ONS	Office of Nuclear Systems (SAA)
ONS	Off-Normal Switch
ONS	Omega Navigation System
ONS	Oncology Nursing Society (EA)
ONS	One Night Stand (SAUS)
ONS	Onslow [*Australia*] [*Airport symbol*] [*Obsolete*] (OAG)
ONS	Open Network Server [*Tylink Corp.*]
ONS	Operational Needs Statement [*Army*]
ONS	Oriental Numismatic Society [*Reading, Berkshire, England*] (EAIO)
ONS	Overseas News Service (SAUS)
ONSAM	Onsala Atmospheric Measurements (SAUS)
ONSD	Optic Nerve Sheath Decompression (SAUS)
ONSDG	Newington Branch, Stormont, Dundas, and Glengarry County Library, Ontario [*Library symbol*] [*National Library of Canada*] (BIB)
On Serv	On Service [*A publication*]
ONSHR	On Shore [*NWS*] (FAAC)
ONSI	Orion Network Systems [*NASDAQ symbol*] (TTSB)
ONSI	Orion Network Systems, Inc. [*NASDAQ symbol*] (SAG)
ONSIDIV	On-Sight Surveys Division
OnSiteS	On-Site Sourcing, Inc. [*Associated Press*] (SAG)
Onsl NP	Onslow's Nisi Prius [*A publication*] (DLA)
ONSOD	Omega Navigation System Operations Detail
ONSPS	Office of Nuclear Safety Policy and Standards (SAUS)
ONSR	Ozark National Scenic Riverways (SAUS)
ONSR	Sir Robert Borden High School, Nepean, Ontario [*Library symbol*] [*National Library of Canada*] (BIB)
ONSS	On-Site Sourcing, Inc. [*NASDAQ symbol*] (SAG)
ONST	Office of National Security Technology (SAUS)
ONST	On Stage Entertainment [*NASDAQ symbol*] (SG)
ONST	Outline NATO Staff Target
On Sta	On Station (SAUS)
ONT	Air Ontario Ltd. [*Canada*] [*ICAO designator*] (FAAC)
ONT	Office Nationale du Tourisme [*Algeria*] (EY)
ONT	Office of Naval Technology (MCD)
ONT	Ombudsman of the Northern Territory [*Australia*]
ONT	O-Nitrotoluene (SAUS)
Ont	Ontario [*Canada*] (DD)
ONT	Ontario [*Canadian province*]
ONT	Ontario [*California*] [*Airport symbol*]

ONT	Ontario City Library, Ontario, CA [*OCLC symbol*] (OCLC)
ONT	Ontario Northland Railway [*AAR code*]
Ont	Ontological (SAUS)
Ont	Ontologist (SAUS)
Ont	Ontology (SAUS)
ONT	Ordinary Neap Tide (WDAA)
ONT	Orthogonal Noise Tuning (SAUS)
ONT	Our New Thread [*Clark thread designation*]
Ont 2d	Ontario Reports, Second Series [*Canada*] [*A publication*] (DLA)
Ont A	Ontario Appeals [*A publication*] (DLA)
ONTAP	Online Training and Practice (NITA)
ONTAP	On-Line Training and Practice File [*Lockheed*] [*Computer science*]
Ont App	Ontario Appeal Reports [*A publication*] (DLA)
Ontario Cons Reg	Ontario Consolidated Regulations [*Canada*] [*A publication*] (DLA)
Ontario Technol	Ontario Technologist (SAUS)
ONTC	Ontario Northland Transportation Commission (SAUS)
ONTC	ON Technology Corp. [*NASDAQ symbol*] (SAG)
ON Tch	ON Technology Corp. [*Associated Press*] (SAG)
Ont Dig	Digest of Ontario Case Law [*A publication*] (DLA)
Ont Dig	Digest of Ontario Case Law (journ.) (SAUS)
Ont Div Mines Missc Pap	Ontario. Division of Mines. Miscellaneous Paper (SAUS)
Ont El Cas	Ontario Election Cases [*1884-1900*] [*Canada*] [*A publication*] (DLA)
Ont Elec	Ontario Election Cases [*1884-1900*] [*Canada*] [*A publication*] (DLA)
Ont Elec C	Ontario Election Cases [*1884-1900*] [*Canada*] [*A publication*] (DLA)
Ont Elect	Ontario Election Cases [*1884-1900*] [*Canada*] [*A publication*] (DLA)
ONTERIS	Ontario Educational Research Information System (SAUS)
ONTERIS	Ontario Education Resources Information System [*Ontario Ministry of Education*] [*Toronto*] [*Information service or system*] (IID)
ONTG	Oral Nitroglycerine [*Medicine*]
ONTK	OnTrak Systems [*NASDAQ symbol*] (TTSB)
ONTK	On Trak Systems, Inc. [*NASDAQ symbol*] (SAG)
Ont L	Ontario Law Reports [*A publication*] (DLA)
Ont LJ	Ontario Law Journal [*A publication*] (DLA)
Ont LJ (NS)	Ontario Law Journal, New Series [*A publication*] (DLA)
Ont LR	Ontario Reports [*A publication*] (DLA)
Ont L Rep	Ontario Law Reports [*A publication*] (DLA)
ONTOLT	Onion, Tomato, or Lettuce [*Notation on restaurant checks*]
Ont Pen	Ontario Penitentiary (SAUS)
Ont Pr	Ontario Practice [*A publication*] (DLA)
Ont PR	Ontario Practice Reports [*A publication*] (DLA)
Ont Pr Rep	Ontario Practice Reports [*A publication*] (DLA)
Ont R	Ontario Reports [*A publication*] (DLA)
ONTR	Orders Not to Resuscitate [*Medicine*]
OnTrak	OnTrak Systems, Inc. [*Associated Press*] (SAG)
Ont R & WN	Ontario Reports and Ontario Weekly Notes [*Canada*] [*A publication*] (DLA)
OntrDta	Ontrack Data International, Inc. [*Associated Press*] (SAG)
Ont Reg	Ontario Regulations [*Canada*] [*A publication*] (DLA)
Ont Regs	Ontario Regulations [*Canada*] [*A publication*] (DLA)
Ont Rev Regs	Ontario Revised Regulations [*Canada*] [*A publication*] (DLA)
Ont Rev Stat	Ontario Revised Statutes [*Canada*] [*A publication*] (DLA)
Ont Rgt	Ontario Regiment [*Canada*] (DMA)
Ont Sci Cen	Ontario Science Center (SAUS)
Ont Stat	Ontario Statutes [*Canada*] [*A publication*] (DLA)
Ont Tax Rep (CCH)	Ontario Tax Reporter (Commerce Clearing House) [*A publication*] (DLA)
Ont Week N	Ontario Weekly Notes [*A publication*] (DLA)
Ont Week R	Ontario Weekly Reporter [*A publication*] (DLA)
Ont Wkly N	Ontario Weekly Notes [*A publication*] (DLA)
Ont Wkly Rep	Ontario Weekly Reporter [*A publication*] (DLA)
Ont WN	Ontario Weekly Notes [*A publication*] (DLA)
Ont WR	Ontario Weekly Reporter [*A publication*] (DLA)
Ont WR Op	Ontario Weekly Reporter. Opinions of United States Attorneys General [*A publication*] (DLA)
ONU	Kongoussi [*Upper Volta*] [*Airport symbol*] (AD)
ONU	Ohio Northern University [*Ada, OH*]
ONU	Ohio Northern University, Ada, OH [*OCLC symbol*] (OCLC)
ONU	Ono-I-Lau [*Fiji*] [*Airport symbol*] [*Obsolete*] (OAG)
ONU	Optical Network Unit [*Telecommunications*]
ONU	Organisation des Nations Unies [*United Nations*] [*French*]
ONU	Organizacion de las Naciones Unidas [*United Nations*] [*Spanish*] (DUND)
ONU	Organizzazione Nazioni Unite [*United Nations*] [*Italian*]
ONUC	Organisation des Nations Unies au Congo [*United Nations Organization in the Congo*]
ONUDI	Organisation des Nations Unies pour le Developpement Industriel [*United Nations Industrial Development Organization*]
ONUDI	Organizacion de las Naciones Unidas para el Desarrollo Industrial [*United Nations Industrial Development Organization*] [*Spanish*] (DUND)
ONU Intra LR	Ohio Northern University. Intramural Law Review [*A publication*] (DLA)
ONULP	Ontario New Universities Library Project
Onuphr De Interp Voc Eccles	Onuphrius. De Interpretatione Vocum Ecclesiae [*A publication*] (DLA)
ONV	Organisations Nationales Volontaires [*Canada*]
ON-VA	Operator Network Validation Area (SAUS)
ONVI	Onvia.com, Inc. [*NASDAQ symbol*] (SG)
ONVL	Over-the-Nose Vision Line (PDAA)
ONW	Office of Naval Weapons
ONW	Onwards (RIMS)
ONW	On Watch
ONW	Oregon & Northwestern Railroad Co. [*AAR code*]

ONWARD ..... Organization of Northwest Authorities for Rationalized Design (SAUS)
ONWB .... Oregon Nuclear Waste Board (SAUS)
ONWI .... Office of Nuclear Waste Isolation (MCD)
ONWL .... Whitefish Lake Band Public Library, Naughton, Ontario [*Library symbol*] [*National Library of Canada*] (NLC)
ONWM .... Office of Nuclear Waste Management (SAUS)
ONWR .... Okefinokee National Wildlife Refuge (SAUS)
ONWR .... Ottawa National Wildlife Refuge (SAUS)
ONWR .... Ouray National Wildlife Refuge (SAUS)
ONWS .... Office of Naval Weather Service
ONX .... Colon [*Panama*] [*Airport symbol*] (OAG)
ONX .... Mount Olive, NC [*Location identifier*] [*FAA*] (FAAL)
onx .... Onyx (VRA)
ONX .... Onyx Petroleum Exploration Co. Ltd. [*Toronto Stock Exchange symbol*]
ONXX .... ONYX Pharmaceuticals [*NASDAQ symbol*] (TTSB)
ONXX .... Onyx Pharmaceuticals, Inc. [*NASDAQ symbol*] (SAG)
ONY .... Olney, TX [*Location identifier*] [*FAA*] (FAAL)
ony............. onymous (SAUS)
ONYX .... Onyx Acceptance [*NASDAQ symbol*] (TTSB)
ONYX .... Onyx Acceptance Corp. [*NASDAQ symbol*] (SAG)
OnyxAcc...... Onyx Acceptance Corp. [*Associated Press*] (SAG)
OnyxPh .... Onyx Pharmaceuticals, Inc. [*Associated Press*] (SAG)
OO .... Belgium [*International civil aircraft marking*] (ODBW)
OO .... Naval Oceanographic Office [*Also known as NOO; formerly, HO, NHO, USNHO*]
OO .... Oakly, Inc. [*NYSE symbol*] (SAG)
OO .... Oberlin College, Oberlin, OH [*Library symbol*] [*Library of Congress*] (LCLS)
OO .... Object-Oriented (BYTE)
OO .... Observation Officer [*Military*]
OO .... Oceanic Operators (SAUS)
OO .... Oceanographic Office
OO .... Ocean Outlook (EA)
O/O .... Office of Oceanography (SAUS)
OO .... Office of Operations [*Department of Agriculture*] (GFGA)
O/O .... Office of Origin (AFM)
O/O .... Off Ocean (SAA)
OO .... Ohio Opinions [*A publication*] (DLA)
OO .... Ohne Ort [*Without Place of Publication*] [*Bibliography*] [*German*]
O/O .... Oil/Ore [*Ship*] (DS)
OO .... Old Orkney [*Whisky*] (ROG)
OO .... Once Over [*To examine cursorily*] [*Slang*]
o-o .... Once-Over [*Theater*] [*Slang*] (WDMC)
O/O .... Only to Order (DGA)
O/O .... On Orbit (MCD)
OO .... On Order
OO .... Oophorectomized [*Gynecology*]
OO .... Open Order
OO .... Operation Office (SAUS)
OO .... Operation Order [*Military*]
OO .... Operations Office [*Environmental Protection Agency*] (GFGA)
OO .... Operations Officer [*Navy*] [*British*]
OO .... Optical Orientation (SAUS)
OO .... Oral Order (SAUS)
OO .... Orbiting Observatory (SAUS)
OO .... Orderly Officer [*British*]
O/O .... Order Of [*Business term*]
O/o .... Order of (EBF)
o/o .... Order of (EBF)
OO .... Ordnance Office [*or Officer*]
O/O .... Ore/Oil (SAUS)
OO .... Orthopaedics Overseas (EA)
OO .... Osobyi Otdel [*Counterintelligence surveillance unit in military formation until 1943*] [*Former USSR*]
O/O .... Owner/Operator
O/O .... Owner or Operator (COE)
OO .... Owner's Option (RIMS)
OO .... Own Occupation [*Banking*]
OO .... Skywest Airlines (SAUS)
OO .... Sunaire Lines [*ICAO designator*] (AD)
OO 2d .... Ohio Opinions, Second Series [*A publication*] (DLA)
OOA .... Object of Affections [*Slang*]
OOA .... Object-Oriented Analysis [*Computer science*]
OOA .... Office of Ocean Affairs [*Navy*]
OOA .... Office of the Americas [*An association*] (EA)
OOA .... Olive Oil Association (EA)
OOA .... On or About (WDAA)
OOA .... Open Ocean Area (SAA)
OOA .... Optimum Orbital Altitude (AAG)
OOA .... Optimum Orbital Attitude (SAUS)
OOA .... Oskaloosa, IA [*Location identifier*] [*FAA*] (FAAL)
OOA .... Outer Otic Anlage (DMAA)
OOA .... Out of Action (MCD)
OOA .... Out of Area (NVT)
OOA .... Owner Operators of America [*Boston, NY*] (EA)
OOA .... Public Archives [*Archives Publiques*] Ottawa, Ontario [*Library symbol*] [*National Library of Canada*] (NLC)
OOAA .... Olive Oil Association of America [*Later, OOA*] (EA)
OOAC .... Algonquin College of Applied Arts and Technology, Ottawa, Ontario [*Library symbol*] [*National Library of Canada*] (NLC)
OOACC......... Colonel By Campus, Algonquin College of Applied Arts and Technology, Ottawa, On tario [*Library symbol*] [*National Library of Canada*] (NLC)

OOACF .... Alta Vista Branch, Ontario Cancer Foundation, Ottawa, Ontario [*Library symbol*] [*National Library of Canada*] (NLC)
OOACH......... Heron Park Campus, Algonquin College of Applied Arts and Technology, Ottawa, Ontario [*Library symbol*] [*National Library of Canada*] (BIB)
OOACL......... Library Technician Program, Algonquin College of Applied Arts & Technology, Ottawa, Ontario [*Library symbol*] [*National Library of Canada*] (NLC)
OOACR......... Rideau Campus, Algonquin College of Applied Arts and Technology, Ottawa, On tario, [*Library symbol*] [*National Library of Canada*] (NLC)
OOAD .... Object-Oriented Analysis & Design [*Computer science*] (CDE)
OOAD .... Object Oriented Application Design (SAUS)
OOAD .... Object Oriented Application Development (SAUS)
OOADE......... Archives Deschatelets (Oblats de Marie-Immaculee), Ottawa, Ontario [*Library symbol*] [*National Library of Canada*] (NLC)
OOAEA......... Ethnic Archives of Canada, Public Archives [*Archives Ethniques du Canada, Archives Publiques*] Ottawa, Ontario [*Library symbol*] [*National Library of Canada*] (NLC)
OOAECB....... Atomic Energy Control Board [*Commission de Controle de l'Energie Atomique*]Ottawa, Ontario [*Library symbol*] [*National Library of Canada*] (NLC)
OOAER......... Research Co., Atomic Energy of Canada Ltd. [*Societe de Recherches, L'Energie Atomique du Canada Ltee*] Ottawa, Ontario [*Library symbol*] [*National Library of Canada*] (NLC)
OOAF .... Bibliotheque de l'Ambassade de France, Ottawa, Ontario [*Library symbol*] [*National Library of Canada*] (BIB)
OOAFN......... Assembly of First Nations, Ottawa, Ontario [*Library symbol*] [*National Library of Canada*] (NLC)
OOAG .... Libraries Division, Agriculture Canada [*Division des Bibliotheques, Agriculture Canada*] Ottawa, Ontario [*Library symbol*] [*National Library of Canada*] (NLC)
OOAGA......... Animal Diseases Research Institute, Agriculture Canada [*Institut de Recherches Veterinaires, Agriculture Canada*] Ottawa, Ontario [*Library symbol*] [*National Library of Canada*] (NLC)
OOAGAR...... Animal Research Institute, Agriculture Canada [*Institut de Recherches Zootechniques, Agriculture Canada*] Ottawa, Ontario [*Library symbol*] [*National Library of Canada*] (NLC)
OOAGB......... Plant Research Library, Biosystematics Research Institute, Agriculture Canada [*Bibliotheque de Recherches sur les Vegetaux, Institut de Recherches Biosystematiques, Agriculture Canada*] Ottawa, Ontario [*Library symbol*] [*National Library of Canada*] (NLC)
OOAGCH ...... Neatby Library, Agriculture Canada [*Bibliotheque Neatby, Agriculture Canada*] Ottawa, Ontario [*Library symbol*] [*National Library of Canada*] (NLC)
OOAGE......... Entomology Research Library, Biosystematics Research Institute, Agriculture Canada [*Bibliotheque de Recherches Entomologiques, Institut de Recherches Biosytematiques, Agriculture Canada*] Ottawa, Ontario [*Library symbol*] [*National Library of Canada*] (NLC)
OOAGER ...... Engineering and Statistical Research Centre, Agriculture Canada [*Centre de Recherche Technique et de Statistique, Agriculture Canada*] Ottawa, Ontario [*Library symbol*] [*National Library of Canada*] (NLC)
OOAGFP....... Laboratory Services Section, Food Production and Marketing Branch, Agriculture Canada [*Section des Services d'Analyse, Direction de la Production et de la Commercialisation des Aliments, Agriculture Canada*] Ottawa, Ontario [*Library symbol*] [*National Library of Canada*] (NLC)
OOAGFR ...... Food Research Centre, Agriculture Canada [*Centre de Recherches sur les Aliments,Agriculture Canada*], Ottawa, Ontario [*Library symbol*] [*National Library of Canada*] (BIB)
OOAGO .... Research Station, Agriculture Canada [*Station de Recherches, Agriculture Canada*] Ottawa, Ontario [*Library symbol*] [*National Library of Canada*] (NLC)
OOAGSR ...... Soil Research Institute, Agriculture Canada [*Institut de Recherches sur les Sols, Agriculture Canada*] Ottawa, Ontario [*Library symbol*] [*National Library of Canada*] (NLC)
OOAI .... AMCA International Ltd., Ottawa, Ontario [*Library symbol*] [*National Library of Canada*] (NLC)
OOAK .... Oakville Public Library, Ontario [*Library symbol*] [*National Library of Canada*] (NLC)
OOAKA......... Appleby College, Oakville, Ontario [*Library symbol*] [*National Library of Canada*] (NLC)
OOAKG......... G. D. Searle Co. of Canada Ltd., Oakville, Ontario [*Library symbol*] [*National Library of Canada*] (BIB)
OOAKM........ Oakville Museums, Ontario [*Library symbol*] [*National Library of Canada*] (BIB)
OOAKS......... Shell Research Centre, Oakville, Ontario [*Library symbol*] [*National Library of Canada*] (NLC)
OOAKSC....... Sheridan College, Oakville, Ontario [*Library symbol*] [*National Library of Canada*] (NLC)
OOAKSCL..... Library Techniques, Sheridan College, Oakville, Ontario [*Library symbol*] [*National Library of Canada*] (NLC)
OOAMA........ National Map Collection, Public Archives [*Collection Nationale des Cartes et Plans, Archives Publiques*] Ottawa, Ontario [*Library symbol*] [*National Library of Canada*] (NLC)
OOAMA........ Office, Ogden Air Material Area [*AFLC*]
OOAM & S... On-Orbit Assembly, Maintenance, and Service [*NASA*] (SSD)
OOAMS........ Manuscript Division, Public Archives [*Division des Manuscrits, Archives Publiques*] Ottawa, Ontario [*Library symbol*] [*National Library of Canada*] (NLC)

OOANF......... National Film Archives, Public Archives [*Archives Nationales du Film, Archives Publiques*] Ottawa, Ontario [*Library symbol*] [*National Library of Canada*] (NLC)

OOAOA......... Archives, Diocese of Ottawa, Anglican Church of Canada, Ontario [*Library symbol*] [*National Library of Canada*] (NLC)

OOAR........... Canadian Broadcasting Corp. [*Societe Radio-Canada*] Ottawa, Ontario [*Library symbol*] [*National Library of Canada*] (NLC)

OOASH........ Ashbury College, Ottawa, Ontario [*Library symbol*] [*National Library of Canada*] (NLC)

OOB .... Bank of Canada [*Banque du Canada*] Ottawa, Ontario [*Library symbol*] [*National Library of Canada*] (NLC)

OOB .... Offensive Operations Branch (SAUS)

OOB .... Off-Off Broadway [*Theater*]

OOB .... Off Our Backs [*A publication*] (BRI)

OOB .... Old Orchard Beach (SAUS)

OOB .... Opening of Business (MCD)

OOB .... Operations Operating Budget [*Military*] (AFIT)

OOB .... Order of Battle [*Military*] (NVT)

OOB .... Ordnance Office Bulletin [*Military*]

OOB .... Out of Balance (SAUS)

OOB .... Out of Band [*Telecommunications*] (TEL)

OOB .... Out of Bed [*Medicine*]

OOB .... Out of Body [*Parapsychology*]

OOB .... Out of Bounds (IIA)

OOB .... Outs on Base (SAUS)

OOBA .... Brewers Association of Canada, [*Association des Brasseurs du Canada*], Ott awa, Ontario [*Library symbol*] [*National Library of Canada*] (NLC)

OOBA .... Off Off Broadway Alliance [*Later, ART/NY*]

OOBBRP ...... Out of Bed with Bathroom Privileges [*Medicine*] (DAVI)

OOBC .... Bowmar Canada Ltd., Ottawa, Ontario [*Library symbol*] [*National Library of Canada*] (NLC)

OOBE .... Ottawa Board of Education, Ontario [*Library symbol*] [*National Library of Canada*] (NLC)

OOBE .... Out-of-Body Experience [*Parapsychology*]

OOBE .... Out-Of-Box Experience [*Computer hacker's terminology*] (PCM)

OOBH .... Information Library, British High Commission, Ottawa, Ontario [*Library symbol*] [*National Library of Canada*] (BIB)

OOBLA .... Onset of Blood Lactose Accumulation [*Metabolism*]

OOBM .... Bartonian Metaphysical Society, Ottawa, Ontario [*Library symbol*] [*National Library of Canada*] (NLC)

OOBMC........ Bureau of Management Consulting, Department of Supply and Services [*Bureau des Conseillers en Gestion, Ministere des Approvisionnements et Services*] Ottawa, Ontario [*Library symbol*] [*National Library of Canada*] (NLC)

OOBMI .... Bell Canada Market Information Centre, Ottawa, Ontario [*Library symbol*] [*National Library of Canada*] (NLC)

OOBMM ...... Medical Library, Bristol-Myers Pharmaceutical Group, Ottawa, Ontario [*Library symbol*] [*National Library of Canada*] (NLC)

OOBP .... Opponents on-base Percentage (SAUS)

OOBR........... Buraimi [*Oman*] [*ICAO location identifier*] (ICLI)

OOC .... Junior Optimist Octagon International [*Formerly, Optimist Octagon Clubs*] (EA)

OOC .... Oberlin College, Conservatory of Music, Oberlin, OH [*Library symbol*] [*Library of Congress*] (LCLS)

OOC .... OEC Compression [*AMEX symbol*] (SG)

OOC .... Office of Censorship [*Terminated, 1945*] [*Military*]

OOC .... Office of Corrections [*Victoria, Australia*]

OOC .... Office of Olympic Coordination [*New South Wales, Australia*]

OOC .... Off-On Control

OOC .... On-Off Control (SAUS)

OOC .... Operating Vehicle without Owner's Consent [*Traffic offense charge*]

OOC .... Operating without Owners Consent (SAUS)

OOC .... Operational Oceanography Center (USDC)

OOC .... Operation Oceanography Center [*Marine science*] (OSRA)

OOC .... Ore/Oil Carrier (SAUS)

OOC .... Organized Occupational Curricula

OOC .... Ottawa Public Library [*Bibliotheque Publique d'Ottawa*] Ontario [*Library symbol*] [*National Library of Canada*] (NLC)

OOC .... Out of Characters (SAUS)

OOC .... Out of Commission (NVT)

OOC .... Out of Control

OOC .... Over-Ocean Communications

OOC .... Overseas Operating Committee [*World War II*]

OOCAA........ Canadian Astronautics, Ottawa, Ontario [*Library symbol*] [*National Library of Canada*] (NLC)

OOCAAS....... Canadian Automobile Association, Ottawa, Ontario [*Library symbol*] [*National Library of Canada*] (BIB)

OOCAB........ Canadian Association of Broadcasters [*Association Canadienne des Radiodiffuseurs*] Ottawa, Ontario [*Library symbol*] [*National Library of Canada*] (NLC)

OOCAC........ Canada Council [*Conseil des Arts du Canada*] Ottawa, Ontario [*Library symbol*] [*National Library of Canada*] (NLC)

OOCACR ...... Research and Evaluation Section, Canada Council [*Service de Recherche et d'Evaluation, Conseil des Arts du Canada*], Ottawa, Ontario [*Library symbol*] [*National Library of Canada*] (BIB)

OOCACSW ... Documentation Centre, Canadian Advisory Council on the Status of Women [*Centre de Documentation, Conseil Consultatif Canadien de la Situation de la Femme*]Ottawa, Ontario [*Library symbol*] [*National Library of Canada*] (NLC)

OOCAM........ Canadian Association of Medical Radiation Technologists, Ottawa, Ontario [*Library symbol*] [*National Library of Canada*] (BIB)

OOCANM...... Canadian Museum Association [*Association des Musees Canadiens*], Ottawa, Ontario [*Library symbol*] [*National Library of Canada*] (NLC)

OOCAR......... Canadian Arctic Resources Committee, Ottawa, Ontario [*Library symbol*] [*National Library of Canada*] (NLC)

OOCARE....... Care Canada, Ottawa, Ontario [*Library symbol*] [*National Library of Canada*] (BIB)

O/O Carrier... Ore/Oil Carrier (SAUS)

OOCAS......... Children's Aid Society of Ottawa-Carleton, Ottawa, Ontario [*Library symbol*] [*National Library of Canada*] (NLC)

OOCB .... Colonel By Secondary School, Ottawa, Ontario [*Library symbol*] [*National Library of Canada*] (NLC)

OOCBC......... Conference Board of Canada, Ottawa, Ontario [*Library symbol*] [*National Library of Canada*] (NLC)

OOCBE......... Carleton Board of Education, Ottawa, Ontario [*Library symbol*] [*National Library of Canada*] (NLC)

OOCBH........ Human Resources Department, Canadian Broadcasting Corp. [*Departement des Ressources Humaines, Societe Radio-Canada*], Ottawa, Ontario [*Library symbol*] [*National Library of Canada*] (BIB)

OOCC .... Carleton University, Ottawa, Ontario [*Library symbol*] [*National Library of Canada*] (NLC)

OOCCAH ...... Department of Art History, Carleton University, Ottawa, Ontario [*Library symbol*] [*Obsolete*] [*National Library of Canada*] (NLC)

OOCCFA....... Canadian Centre for Films on Art [*Centre Canadien du Film sur l'Art*] Ottawa, Ontario [*Library symbol*] [*National Library of Canada*] (NLC)

OOCCG........ Geography Department, Carleton University, Ottawa, Ontario [*Library symbol*] [*Obsolete*] [*National Library of Canada*] (NLC)

OOCCJ .... Church Council on Justice and Correction [*Conseil des Eglises pour la Justiceet la Criminologie*], Ottawa, Ontario [*Library symbol*] [*National Library of Canada*] (BIB)

OOCCL .... County of Carleton Law Library, Ottawa, Ontario [*Library symbol*] [*National Library of Canada*] (NLC)

OOCCR........ Canada Centre for Remote Sensing, Energy, Mines and Resources Canada [*Centre Canadien de Teledetection, Energie, Mines et Ressources Canada*] Ottawa, Ontario [*Library symbol*] [*National Library of Canada*] (NLC)

OOCCU........ Canadian Commission for UNESCO, Ottawa, Ontario [*Library symbol*] [*National Library of Canada*] (BIB)

OOCD .... Canadian International Development Agency [*Agence Canadienne de DeveloppementInternational*] Ottawa, Ontario [*Library symbol*] [*National Library of Canada*] (NLC)

OOCDA........ Canadian Dental Association, Ottawa, Ontario [*Library symbol*] [*National Library of Canada*] (NLC)

OOCDC........ Computing Devices of Canada, Ottawa, Ontario [*Library symbol*] [*National Library of Canada*] (NLC)

OOCDP........ College Dominicain de Philosophie et de Theologie, Ottawa, Ontario [*Library symbol*] [*National Library of Canada*] (NLC)

OOCEEC ...... Delegation of the Commission of the European Communities [*Delegation de la C ommission des Communautes Europeennes*], Ottawa, Ontario [*Library symbol*] [*National Library of Canada*] (BIB)

OOCES .... Combustion Engineering Superheater Ltd., Ottawa, Ontario [*Library symbol*] [*National Library of Canada*] (NLC)

OOCESC....... Centre d'Animation Pedagogique, Conseil des Ecoles Separees Catholiques d'Ottawa, Ontario [*Library symbol*] [*National Library of Canada*] (BIB)

OOCF .... Canadian Film Institute [*Institut Canadien du Film*] Ottawa, Ontario [*Library symbol*] [*National Library of Canada*] (NLC)

OOCFB .... Canadian Forces Base, Ottawa, Ontario [*Library symbol*] [*National Library of Canada*] (BIB)

OOCFS .... Combustion Engineering Superheater Ltd., Ottawa, Ontario (SAUS)

OOCH .... Orient Overseas Container Holdings (SAUS)

OOCHA .... Canadian Hospital Association [*Association des Hopitaux du Canada*] Ottawa,Ontario [*Library symbol*] [*National Library of Canada*] (NLC)

OOCHAC ...... Catholic Health Association of Canada [*Association Catholique Canadienne de la Sante*], Ottawa, Ontario [*Library symbol*] [*National Library of Canada*] (NLC)

OOCHC........ Canadian Horticultural Council [*Conseil Canadien de l'Horticulture*], Ottawa, Ontario [*Library symbol*] [*National Library of Canada*] (BIB)

OOCHEO ...... Children's Hospital of Eastern Ontario [*Hopital pour Enfants de l'Est de l'Ontario*] Ottawa, Ontario [*Library symbol*] [*National Library of Canada*] (NLC)

OOCHI.......... Chreod International, Ottawa, Ontario [*Library symbol*] [*National Library of Canada*] (NLC)

OOCHP........ Common Heritage Programme, Ottawa, Ontario [*Library symbol*] [*National Library of Canada*] (BIB)

OOCHR .... Canadian Human Rights Commission [*Commission Canadienne des Droits de la Personne*] Ottawa, Ontario [*Library symbol*] [*National Library of Canada*] (NLC)

OOCI .... Department of Consumer and Corporate Affairs [*Ministere de la Consommation etdes Corporations*] Ottawa, Ontario [*Library symbol*] [*National Library of Canada*] (NLC)

OOCIC.......... Documentation Centre, Canadian Intergovernmental Conference Secretariat [*Centre de Documentation, Secretariat des Conferences Intergouvernementales Canadiennes*], Ottawa, Ontario [*Library symbol*] [*National Library of Canada*] (NLC)

OOCIFE........ Field Exploration Library, Inco Ltd., Copper Cliff, Ontario [*Library symbol*] [*National Library of Canada*] (NLC)

OOCIHM...... Canadian Institute for Historical Microreproductions [*Institut Canadien de Microreproductions Historiques*] Ottawa, Ontario [*Library symbol*] [*National Library of Canada*] (NLC)

OOCIIPS....... Canadian Institute for International Peace and Security [*Institut Canadien pour la Paix et la Securite Mondiales*] Ottawa, Ontario [*Library symbol*] [*National Library of Canada*] (NLC)

OOCIRS........ Canadian Institute for Radiation Safety, Ottawa, Ontario [*Library symbol*] [*National Library of Canada*] (NLC)

OOCITT........ Canadian International Trade Tribunal [*Tribunal Canadien du Commerce Exterieur*], Ontario [*Library symbol*] [*National Library of Canada*] (BIB)

OOCL.......... Capital Library Wholesale, Ottawa, Ontario [*Library symbol*] [*National Library of Canada*] (NLC)

OOCLA........ Canadian Library Association, Ottawa, Ontario [*Library symbol*] [*National Library of Canada*] (BIB)

OOCLC........ Canadian Labour Congress [*Congres du Travail du Canada*] Ottawa, Ontario [*Library symbol*] [*National Library of Canada*] (NLC)

OOCLCG....... Coopers & Lybrand Consulting Group, Ottawa, Ontario [*Library symbol*] [*National Library of Canada*] (BIB)

OOCLM........ Canadian Labour Market and Productivity Centre [*Centre Canadien du Marche du Travail et de la Productivite*], Ottawa, Ontario [*Library symbol*] [*National Library of Canada*] (NLC)

OOCM.......... Canadian Housing Information Centre, Canada Mortgage and Housing Corp. [*Centre Canadien de Documentation sur l'Habitation, Societe Canadienne d'Hypotheques et de Logement*] Ottawa, Ontario [*Library symbol*] [*National Library of Canada*] (NLC)

OOCMA........ Canadian Medical Association, Ottawa, Ontario [*Library symbol*] [*National Library of Canada*] (NLC)

OOCMC........ Children's Environments Advisory Service, Canada Mortgage and Housing Corp. [*Service Consultatif sur l'Environnement de l'Enfant, Societe Canadienne d'Hypotheques et de Logement*] Ottawa, Ontario [*Library symbol*] [*National Library of Canada*] (NLC)

OOCMF........ Office of the Commissioner for Federal Judicial Affairs [*Bureau du Commissaire a la Magistrature Federale*], Ottawa, Ontario [*Library symbol*] [*National Library of Canada*] (BIB)

OOCN.......... Canadian Nurses' Association [*Association Canadienne des Infirmieres*] Ottawa, Ontario [*Library symbol*] [*National Library of Canada*] (NLC)

OOCNET....... Office of Corrections Network

OOCNP......... CNP Resource Centre, Energy, Mines, and Resources Canada [*Centre d'Information EESP, Energie, Mines, et Ressources Canada*] Ottawa, Ontario [*Library symbol*] [*National Library of Canada*] (NLC)

OOCO.......... Department of Communications [*Ministere des Communications*] Ottawa, Ontario [*Library symbol*] [*National Library of Canada*] (NLC)

OOCOAC ...... Consumer's Association of Canada, Ottawa, Ontario [*Library symbol*] [*National Library of Canada*] (BIB)

OOCOG .... COGLA [*Canada Oil and Gas Lands Administration*] Ocean Mining Resource Centre , Ottawa, Ontario [*Centre de Ressources sur l'Extraction de Minerais Oceaniques, Administration du Petrole et du Gaz des Terres du Canada*] [*Library symbol*] [*National Library of Canada*] (NLC)

OOCOI......... Cognos, Inc., Ottawa, Ontario [*Library symbol*] [*National Library of Canada*] (BIB)

OOCOL........ Commissioner of Official Languages [*Commissaire aux Langues Officielles*] Ottawa, Ontario [*Library symbol*] [*National Library of Canada*] (NLC)

OOCOT........ Competition Tribunal [*Tribunal de la Concurrence*], Ottawa, Ontario [*Library symbol*] [*National Library of Canada*] (BIB)

OOCOW........ Cowater International, Inc., Ottawa, Ontario [*Library symbol*] [*National Library of Canada*] (BIB)

OOCP.......... Community Planning Association of Canada [*Association Canadienne d'Urbanisme*] Ottawa, Ontario [*Library symbol*] [*National Library of Canada*] (NLC)

OOCPA........ Canadian Payments Association, Ottawa, Ontario [*Library symbol*] [*National Library of Canada*] (BIB)

OOCPB........ Planning and Development Library, City of Ottawa, Ontario [*Library symbol*] [*National Library of Canada*] (BIB)

OOCPR........ Canadian Public Relations Society [*Societe Canadienne des Relations Publiques*], Ottawa, Ontario [*Library symbol*] [*National Library of Canada*] (BIB)

OOCRC........ Canadian Red Cross Society [*Societe Canadienne de la Croix-Rouge*] Ottawa, Ontario [*Library symbol*] [*National Library of Canada*] (NLC)

OOCRI......... Canadian Research Institute for the Avancement of Women [*Institut Canadien deRecherches sur les Femmes*] Ottawa, Ontario [*Library symbol*] [*National Library of Canada*] (NLC)

OOCRLF....... Canadian Rights and Liberties Federation, Ottawa, Ontario [*Library symbol*] [*National Library of Canada*] (NLC)

OOCRM........ Canadian Royal Mint [*Monnaie Royale Canadienne*] Ottawa, Ontario [*Library symbol*] [*National Library of Canada*] (NLC)

OOCS.......... Public Service Commission [*Commission de la Fonction Publique*] Ottawa, Ontario [*Library symbol*] [*National Library of Canada*] (NLC)

OOCSC........ Canada Safety Council [*Conseil Canadien de la Securite*] Ottawa, Ontario [*Library symbol*] [*National Library of Canada*] (NLC)

OOCT.......... Canadian Teachers Federation, Ottawa, Ontario [*Library symbol*] [*National Library of Canada*] (NLC)

OOCTG........ Object Orientated COBOL Task Group (SAUS)

OOCTI......... Canadian Textiles Institute [*Institut Canadien des Textiles*], Ottawa, Ontario [*Library symbol*] [*National Library of Canada*] (BIB)

OOCU.......... Association of Universities and Colleges of Canada [*Association des Universites et Colleges du Canada*], Ottawa, Ontario [*Library symbol*] [*National Library of Canada*] (NLC)

OOCUI......... Canadian Unity Information Office [*Centre d'Information sur l'Unite Canadienne*] Ottawa, Ontario [*Library symbol*] [*National Library of Canada*] (NLC)

OOCUS......... CUSO [*Canadian University Service Overseas*], Ottawa, Ontario [*Library symbol*] [*National Library of Canada*] (NLC)

OOCVB......... Central Volunteer Bureau of Ottawa-Carleton [*Bureau Central des Benevoles d'Ottawa-Carleton*] Ottawa, Ontario [*Library symbol*] [*National Library of Canada*] (BIB)

OOCW......... Canadian Council on Social Development [*Conseil Canadien de Developpement Social*] Ottawa, Ontario [*Library symbol*] [*National Library of Canada*] (NLC)

OOCWC........ Canadian Wood Council [*Conseil Canadien du Bois*] Ottawa, Ontario [*Library symbol*] [*National Library of Canada*] (NLC)

OOCZ.......... Ottawa Citizen, Ontario [*Library symbol*] [*National Library of Canada*] (NLC)

OOD .... Object-Oriented Design [*Computer science*]

OOD .... Object Oriented Development (SAUS)

OOD .... Office of Disability [*Australia*]

OOD .... Office Operations Department

OOD .... Officer of the Day [*or Deck*] [*Also, OD*] [*Navy*]

OOD .... Operations Orientation Director [*NASA*]

OOD .... Opposite Oriented Diffusion (SAUS)

OOD .... Orbiter on Dock [*NASA*] (KSC)

OOD .... Woodstown, NJ [*Location identifier*] [*FAA*] (FAAL)

OODA .... Observation, Orientation, Decision, Action

OODB .... Dominion Bridge Co. Ltd., Ottawa, Ontario [*Library symbol*] [*National Library of Canada*] (NLC)

OODB .... Object-Oriented Database [*Computer science*] (CDE)

OODBMS..... Object-Oriented Database Management System [*Objectivity, Inc.*] [*Computer science*]

OODBS........ DOBIS (Dortmunder Bibliothekssystem), Ottawa, Ontario [*Library symbol*] [*National Library of Canada*] (NLC)

OODBS........ Object-Oriented Database System (SAUS)

OODCH .... DCH Consultants, Inc., Ottawa, Ontario [*Library symbol*] [*National Library of Canada*] (NLC)

OODE .... Office of Overseas Dependent Education [*Military*]

OODEP......... Owner, Officer, Director, or Executive Personnel (MCD)

OODF .... Officer-of-the-Deck (Fleet Task Force Operations) [*Navy*] (DNAB)

OODI .... Officer-of-the-Deck (Independent) [*Navy*] (DNAB)

OODL .... Object-Oriented Dynamic Language [*Computer science*] (PCM)

OODLAC....... Odessa Branch, Lennox and Addington County Library, Ontario [*Library symbol*] [*National Library of Canada*] (NLC)

OODLC........ Library Education Services, Data Logic Canada, Ottawa, Ontario [*Library symbol*] [*National Library of Canada*] (NLC)

OODM .... Dali Management [*Gestion Dali*], Ottawa, Ontario [*Library symbol*] [*National Library of Canada*] (BIB)

OODMR........ DMR Group, Inc., Ottawa, Ontario [*Library symbol*] [*National Library of Canada*] (BIB)

OODMS........ Object Oriented Database Management System [*Computer science*] (VLIE)

OODP.......... Department of Supply and Services [*Ministere des Approvisionnements et Services*] Ottawa, Ontario [*Library symbol*] [*National Library of Canada*] (NLC)

OODP.......... Out-of-Detent Pitch [*Aviation*] (MCD)

OODPS......... Superannuation Division, Compensation Services Branch, Department of Supply and Services [*Division des Pensions de Retraite, Direction des Services de Renumeration, Ministere des Approvisionnements et Services*] Ottawa, Ontario [*Library symbol*] [*National Library of Canada*] (NLC)

OODQ.......... Oliver Organization Description Questionnaire [*Test*]

OODR.......... Out-of-Detent Roll [*Aviation*] (MCD)

OODRC .... Defence Research Establishment Ottawa, Department of National Defence [*Centrede Recherches pour la Defense Ottawa, Ministere de la Defense Nationale*] Ontario [*Library symbol*] [*National Library of Canada*] (NLC)

OODR-MPI ... Optical-Optical Double Resonance Multiphonton Ionization [*Spectrocopy*]

OODSIS........ Directorate of Scientific Information Services, Department of National Defence [*Services d'Information Scientifique, Ministere de la Defense Nationale*] Ottawa, Ontario [*Library symbol*] [*National Library of Canada*] (NLC)

OODV.......... Orbit-on-Demand Vehicle

OOD/W......... Officer of the Day/Watch (SAUS)

OOE .... Department of External Affairs [*Ministere des Affaires Exerieures*] Ottawa,Ontario [*Library symbol*] [*National Library of Canada*] (NLC)

OOE .... Odd-Odd Effect (SAUS)

OOE .... Office of Employment [*Victoria, Australia*]

OOE .... Office of Energy [*New South Wales, Australia*]

OOE .... Office of Ocean Engineering [*National Oceanic and Atmospheric Administration*] (MSC)

OOE .... Opening of Oesophagus

OOE .... Out-of-Ecliptic Mission [*NASA*] (EGAO)

OOEA .... Embassy of Argentina, Ottawa, Ontario [*Library symbol*] [*National Library of Canada*] (BIB)

OOEAB......... Archaeological Research, Environment Canada [*Recherches Archeologiques, Environnement Canada*] Ottawa, Ontario [*Library symbol*] [*National Library of Canada*] (NLC)

OOEAPT .... River Road Environmental Technology Centre, Environment Canada [*Centre de Techologie Environnementale de River Road, Environnement Canada*] Ottawa, Ontario [*Library symbol*] [*National Library of Canada*] (NLC)

OOEB .... Elisabeth Bruyere Health Center [*Centre de Sante Elisabeth Bruyere*] Ottawa, Ontario [*Library symbol*] [*National Library of Canada*] (NLC)

OOEC .... Economic Council of Canada [*Conseil Economique du Canada*] Ottawa, Ontario [*Library symbol*] [*National Library of Canada*] (NLC)

OOEC	Oxford Orthopaedic Engineering Centre [*British*] (IRUK)
OOECS	ECS [*Energy Conversion Systems*] Power Systems, Inc., Ottawa, Ontario [*Library symbol*] [*National Library of Canada*] (NLC)
OOECW	Canadian Wildlife Service, Environment Canada [*Service Canadien de la Faune, Environnement Canada*] Ottawa, Ontario [*Library symbol*] [*National Library of Canada*] (NLC)
OOECWN	National Wildlife Research Centre, Canadian Wildlife Service, Environment Canada[*Centre National de Recherche sur la Faune, Service Canadien de la Faune, En vironnement Canada*] Ottawa, Ontario [*Library symbol*] [*National Library of Canada*] (NLC)
OOEDC	Export Development Corp. [*Societe pour l'Expansion des Exportations*] Ottawa, Ontario [*Library symbol*] [*National Library of Canada*] (NLC)
OOEE	Engineering and Economic Research Technologies, Inc., Ottawa, Ontario [*Library symbol*] [*National Library of Canada*] (BIB)
OOEIB	Interpretation Division, Environment Canada - Parks [*Direction de l'Interpretation, Environnement Canada - Parcs*] Ottawa, Ontario [*Library symbol*] [*National Library of Canada*] (NLC)
OOEK	Embassy of Korea, Ottawa, Ontario [*Library symbol*] [*National Library of Canada*] (BIB)
OOELB	Legal Branch, Department of External Affairs [*Direction des Operations Juridiques, Ministere des Affaires Exterieures*] Ottawa, Ontario [*Library symbol*] [*National Library of Canada*] (NLC)
OOELC	Elections Canada, Ottawa, Ontario [*Library symbol*] [*National Library of Canada*] (BIB)
OOELS	Legal Services, Environment Canada [*Services Juridiques, Environnement Canada*] Ottawa, Ontario [*Library symbol*] [*National Library of Canada*] (NLC)
OOEMB	Embassy of Brazil, Ottawa, Ontario [*Library symbol*] [*National Library of Canada*] (BIB)
OOEN	Cameco Research Center, Ottawa, Ontario [*Library symbol*] [*National Library of Canada*] (NLC)
OOEO	Eastern Ontario Regional Library, Ottawa, Ontario [*Library symbol*] [*National Library of Canada*] (NLC)
OOEO	Ontario Library Service - Rideau, Ottawa, Ontario [*Library symbol*] [*National Library of Canada*] (NLC)
OOEOB	Conservation Division, Environment Canada [*Division de la Conservation, Environnement Canada*] Ottawa, Ontario [*Library symbol*] [*National Library of Canada*] (NLC)
OOEPC	Emergency Planning Canada [*Planification d'Urgence Canada*] Ottawa, Ontario [*Library symbol*] [*National Library of Canada*] (NLC)
OOEPSE	Socio-Economic Research Division, Parks Canada Program, Environment Canada [*Division de la Recherche Socio-Economique, Programme Parcs Canada, Environnement Canada*] Ottawa, Ontario [*Library symbol*] [*National Library of Canada*] (NLC)
OOESC	Ecole Secondaire Champlain, Ottawa, Ontario [*Library symbol*] [*National Library of Canada*] (NLC)
OOEU	Euroline, Ottawa, Ontario [*Library symbol*] [*National Library of Canada*] (BIB)
OOEY	Eyretechnics Ltd., Ottawa, Ontario [*Library symbol*] [*National Library of Canada*] (NLC)
OOF	Department of Finance [*Ministere des Finances*] Ottawa, Ontario [*Library symbol*] [*National Library of Canada*] (NLC)
OOF	Offense Only Fighter (MCD)
OoF	Office of Facilitation (SAUS)
OOF	Office of Fisheries [*National Oceanic and Atmospheric Administration*] (GFGA)
OOF	Office of the Family [*Western Australia*]
OOF	Office of the Future (IAA)
OOF	Open Order File (TIMI)
OOF	Orbiting Quarantine Facility [*A proposed Earth-orbiting laboratory*]
OOF	Other Official Flows (ADWA)
OOF	Out of Frame [*Telecommunications*] (ITD)
OOFA	Documentation Centre, Family Action [*Centre de Documentation, Action Famille*], Ottawa, Ontario [*Library symbol*] [*National Library of Canada*] (NLC)
OOFA	Oblinger/Oplinger Family Association (EA)
O of A	Office of Administration (SAUS)
O of A	Order of Amaranth (EA)
O of B	Order of Battle (SAUS)
OOFC	Federal Court of Canada [*Cour Federale du Canada*] Ottawa, Ontario [*Library symbol*] [*National Library of Canada*] (NLC)
O of C	Order of the Chief (SAUS)
O of C	Order of the Coif (SAUS)
OOFCC	Farm Credit Corp., Ottawa, Ontario [*Library symbol*] [*Obsolete*] [*National Library of Canada*] (NLC)
OOFD	Fahud [*Oman*] [*ICAO location identifier*] (ICLI)
OOFE	Federal Environmental Assessment Review Office [*Bureau Federal d'Examen des Evaluations Environnementales*], Ottawa, Ontario [*Library symbol*] [*National Library of Canada*] (BIB)
OOFF	Departmental Library, Environment Canada [*Bibliotheque du Ministere, Environnemet Canada*] Ottawa, Ontario [*Library symbol*] [*National Library of Canada*] (NLC)
O Offr	Orderly Officer (SAUS)
OOFI	Fisheries and Oceans Canada [*Peches et Oceans Canada*] Ottawa, Ontario [*Library symbol*] [*National Library of Canada*] (NLC)
OOFL	Federal Liberal Agency of Canada, Ottawa, Ontario [*Library symbol*] [*National Library of Canada*] (NLC)
OOFM	Mining Library, Falconbridge Ltd., Onaping, Ontario [*Library symbol*] [*National Library of Canada*]
O of O	Order of Owls (SAUS)

OOFP	Forintek Canada Corp., Ottawa, Ontario [*Library symbol*] [*National Library of Canada*] (NLC)
OOFQ	Firq [*Oman*] [*ICAO location identifier*] (ICLI)
O of R	Office for Research
OOFS	Sport Information Resource Centre [*Centre de Documentation de Reference pour le Sport*] Ottawa, Ontario [*Library symbol*] [*National Library of Canada*] (NLC)
O of SC	Order of Scottish Clans (SAUS)
OOG	Geological Survey of Canada [*Commission Geologique du Canada*] Ottawa, Ontario [*Library symbol*] [*National Library of Canada*] (NLC)
OOG	Office of Gambling [*Victoria, Australia*]
OOG	Office of Oil and Gas [*Functions transferred to Energy Research and Development Administration*] [*Department of the Interior*]
OOG	Officer of the Guard [*Navy*] [*British*]
OOG	Olive Oil Group [*Later, OOA*] (EA)
OOG	Oscillating Output Geneva
OOG	Out of Gauge [*Shipping*] (DCTA)
OOGB	Ghaba Central [*Oman*] [*ICAO location identifier*] (ICLI)
OOGDC	Gandalf Data Ltd., Ottawa, Ontario [*Library symbol*] [*National Library of Canada*] (NLC)
OOGE	Canadian Government Expositions Centre, Department of Supply and Services [*Centre des Expositions du Gouvernement Canadien, Ministere des Approvisionnements et Services*] Ottawa, Ontario [*Library symbol*] [*National Library of Canada*] (NLC)
OOGG	Documentation Centre, Goss, Gilroy & Associates, Ottawa, Ontario [*Library symbol*] [*National Library of Canada*] (BIB)
OOGGH	Grace General Hospital, Ottawa, Ontario [*Library symbol*] [*National Library of Canada*] (NLC)
OOGH	Reference Library, Government House [*Salle de Reference, Residence du Gouverneur-General*] Ottawa, Ontario [*Library symbol*] [*National Library of Canada*] (NLC)
OOGKS	Gottlieb Kaylor & Stocks, Ottawa, Ontario [*Library symbol*] [*National Library of Canada*] (BIB)
OOGOH	Gowling & Henderson, Ottawa, Ontario [*Library symbol*] [*National Library of Canada*] (NLC)
OOGUI	Object-Oriented Graphical User Interface [*Computer science*]
OOH	Heraldry Society of Canada [*Societe Heraldique du Canada*], Ottawa, Ontario [*Library symbol*] [*National Library of Canada*] (BIB)
OOH	Occupational Outlook Handbook [*A publication*] (OICC)
OOH	Other Overhead (TIMI)
OOH	Out-of-Hospital (DMAA)
OOHA	Haima [*Oman*] [*ICAO location identifier*] (ICLI)
OOHA	Operation Oil Heat Associates (SAUS)
OOHC	Heritage Canada Foundation [*Fondation Canadienne pour la Protection du Patrimoine*] Ottawa, Ontario [*Library symbol*] [*National Library of Canada*] (NLC)
OOHG	Ottawa General Hospital [*Hopital General d'Ottawa*] Ontario [*Library symbol*] [*National Library of Canada*] (NLC)
OOHI	Historical Society of Ottawa Library and the Bytown Historical Museum, Ontario [*Library symbol*] [*National Library of Canada*] (NLC)
OOH-OOH	On the One Hand, On the Other Hand
OOHUR	Huronia Regional Centre, Orillia, Ontario [*Library symbol*] [*National Library of Canada*] (NLC)
OOI	Informetrica Ltd., Ottawa, Ontario [*Library symbol*] [*National Library of Canada*] (NLC)
OOI	Memphis, TN [*Location identifier*] [*FAA*] (FAAL)
OOI	Object Oriented Implementation (SAUS)
OOI	Out of Interest (ADWA)
OOI	Oxygen/Ozone Indicator
OOIA	Ibra [*Oman*] [*ICAO location identifier*] (ICLI)
OOIB	Imperial Ballet of Canada, Ottawa, Ontario [*Library symbol*] [*National Library of Canada*] (NLC)
OOIC	Information Centre, Investment Canada [*Centre d'Information, Investissement Canada*] Ottawa, Ontario [*Library symbol*] [*National Library of Canada*] (NLC)
OOICC	Indian Claims Commission [*Commission d'Etude des Revendications des Indiens*] Ottawa, Ontario [*Library symbol*] [*National Library of Canada*] (NLC)
OOICCS	International Council for Canadian Studies [*Conseil International d'Etudes Canadiennes*], Ottawa, Ontario [*Library symbol*] [*National Library of Canada*] (BIB)
OOICP	Phototheque, National Film Board [*Phototheque, Office National du Film*] Ottawa, Ontario [*Library symbol*] [*National Library of Canada*] (NLC)
OOID	International Development Research Centre [*Centre de Recherches pour le Developpement International*] Ottawa, Ontario [*Library symbol*] [*National Library of Canada*] (NLC)
OOIDA	Owner-Operator Independent Drivers Association
OOIHC	India High Commission, Ottawa, Ontario [*Library symbol*] [*National Library of Canada*] (BIB)
OOII	Ibri [*Oman*] [*ICAO location identifier*] (ICLI)
OOIJC	International Joint Commission [*Commission Mixte Internationale*], Ottawa, Ontario [*Library symbol*] [*National Library of Canada*] (NLC)
OOIL	Osage Energy, Inc. (SAUS)
OOIN	Office of the Superintendent of Financial Institutions Canada [*Bureau du Surintendant des Institutions Financieres Canada*] Ottawa, Ontario [*Library symbol*] [*National Library of Canada*] (NLC)
OOIP	Original Oil in Place [*Petroleum*]
OOIPC	Offices of the Information and Privacy Commissioners of Canada [*Bureaux des Commissaires a l'Information et a la Protection de la Vie Privee du Canada*] Ottawa, Ontario [*Library symbol*] [*National Library of Canada*] (NLC)

OOIRB.......... Immigration and Refugee Board [*Commission d'Immigration et du Status de Refugie*], Ottawa, Ontario [*Library symbol*] [*National Library of Canada*] (BIB)

OOIRP.......... Institute for Research on Public Policy [*Institut de Recherches Politiques*], Ottawa, Ontario [*Library symbol*] [*National Library of Canada*] (NLC)

OOIRS.......... Irving R. Silver Associates Library [*IRSA*], Ottawa, Ontario [*Library symbol*] [*National Library of Canada*] (NLC)

OOIT .... Inuit Tapirisat of Canada, Ottawa, Ontario [*Library symbol*] [*National Library of Canada*] (NLC)

OOIZ .... Izki [*Oman*] [*ICAO location identifier*] (ICLI)

OOJ.............. Department of Justice [*Ministere de la Justice*] Ottawa, Ontario [*Library symbol*] [*National Library of Canada*] (NLC)

OOJ.............. Obstruction of Justice

OOJN .... Jarf North [*Oman*] [*ICAO location identifier*] (ICLI)

OOK .... On-Off Keying [*Computer science*] (IEEE)

OOK .... Toksook [*Alaska*] [*Airport symbol*] (OAG)

OOKB .... Khasab [*Oman*] [*ICAO location identifier*] (ICLI)

OOkiep......... O'Okiep Copper Co. Ltd. [*Associated Press*] (SAG)

OOL .... Coolangatta [*Queensland*] [*Airport symbol*] (AD)

OOL .... Gold Coast [*Australia*] [*Airport symbol*] (OAG)

OOL .... Labour Canada [*Travail Canada*] Ottawa, Ontario [*Library symbol*] [*National Library of Canada*] (NLC)

OOL .... Oberlin Public Library, Oberlin, OH [*Library symbol*] [*Library of Congress*] (LCLS)

OOL .... Object-Oriented Language [*Computer science*] (BYTE)

OOL .... Odessa Ocean Line (SAUS)

OOL .... Office of Oceanography and Limnology [*Smithsonian Institution*] (MCD)

Ool.............. Oology (SAUS)

OOL .... Open Objects Library (SAUS)

OOL .... Operator-Oriented Language [*Computer science*]

OOL .... Optimized Optical Link

OOL .... Out of Lock (SAUS)

OOL .... Out of Orbit Launch [*NASA*] (LAIN)

OOLAP .... Occupational Safety and Health Branch, Labour Canada [*Direction de la Securite et de l'Hygiene, Travail Canada*] Ottawa, Ontario [*Library symbol*] [*National Library of Canada*] (NLC)

OOLC .... Labour College of Canada, Ottawa, Ontario [*Library symbol*] [*National Library of Canada*] (NLC)

OOLHMD...... Optimized Optical Link Helmet-Mounted Display

OOLK .... Lekhwair [*Oman*] [*ICAO location identifier*] (ICLI)

OOLM .... Computing Department, Loeb's MIS, Ottawa, Ontario [*Library symbol*] [*National Library of Canada*] (BIB)

OOLML .... Lang, Michener, Lash & Johnston, Ottawa, Ontario [*Library symbol*] [*National Library of Canada*] (BIB)

Oologists Rec... Oologists Record (SAUS)

OOLP .... Object-Oriented Literate Programming (SAUS)

OOLR .... Law Reform Commission [*Commission de Reforme du Droit*] Ottawa, Ontario [*Library symbol*] [*National Library of Canada*] (NLC)

OOLR .... Ophthalmology, Otology, Laryngology, Rhinology

OOLR .... Overall Objective Loudness Rating [*of telephone connections*] (IEEE)

OOLRB......... Canada Labour Relations Board [*Conseil Canadien des Relations de Travail*] Ottawa, Ontario [*Library symbol*] [*National Library of Canada*] (NLC)

OOLRS......... Research Library, LRS Trimark Ltd., Ottawa, Ontario [*Library symbol*] [*National Library of Canada*] (BIB)

OOLUG......... Oklahoma On Line Users Group (NITA)

OOLWB........ Women's Bureau, Labour Canada [*Bureau de la Main-d'Oeuvre Feminine, Travail Canada*] Ottawa, Ontario [*Library symbol*] [*National Library of Canada*] (NLC)

OOM .... CANMET [*Canada Centre for Mineral and Energy Technology*] Library, Energy, Mines, and Resources Canada , Ottawa, Ontario [*Bibliotheque CANMET, Energie, Mines, et Ressources Canada*] [*Library symbol*] [*National Library of Canada*] (NLC)

OOM .... Cooma [*Australia*] [*Airport symbol*] (OAG)

OOM .... Object-Oriented Methodology (SAUS)

OOM .... Office of Ocean Management [*Marine science*] (MSC)

OOM .... Office of Organization and Management [*NASA*]

OOM .... Officers' Open Mess [*Military*] (AFM)

OOM .... Oomiya [*Japan*] [*Seismograph station code, US Geological Survey*] [*Closed*] (SEIS)

OOM .... Open Ocean Mining

OOM .... Open Order Master (MCD)

OOM .... Order of March (SAUS)

OOM .... Organized Organic Monolayer [*Organic chemistry*]

OOM .... Original Online Module [*Computer science*] (PDAA)

OOM .... Outside Office Memo (SAUS)

OOMA .... Masirah [*Oman*] [*ICAO location identifier*] (ICLI)

OOMAD........ Michael A. Dagg Associates [*Michael A. Dagg Associes*], Ottawa, Ontario [*Library symbol*] [*National Library of Canada*] (NLC)

OOMFC........ Ompah Branch, Frontenac County Library, Ontario [*Library symbol*] [*National Library of Canada*] (BIB)

OOMHC........ Malaysia High Commission, Ottawa, Ontario [*Library symbol*] [*National Library of Canada*] (NLC)

OOMHS........ Merivale High School, Ottawa, Ontario [*Library symbol*] [*National Library of Canada*] (NLC)

OOMI .... Employment and Immigration Canada [*Emploi et Immigration Canada*] Ottawa, Ontario [*Library symbol*] [*National Library of Canada*] (NLC)

OOMIL .... MIL Systems Engineering, Inc., Ottawa, Ontario [*Library symbol*] [*National Library of Canada*] (BIB)

OOMJ........... Macera & Jarzyna, Ottawa, Ontario [*Library symbol*] [*National Library of Canada*] (BIB)

OOML .... Metropolitan Life Insurance Co., Ottawa, Ontario [*Library symbol*] [*National Library of Canada*] (NLC)

OOMM .... Muscat [*Oman*] [*ICAO location identifier*] (ICLI)

oomm .... Organizational Operations and Maintenance Manual (NAKS)

OOMM .... Organizational Operations and Maintenance Manual (NASA)

OOMNA....... National Air Photo Library, Energy, Mines, and Resources Canada [*BibliothequePhotographie Aerienne Nationale, Energie, Mines, et Ressources Canada*], Otta wa, Ontario [*Library symbol*] [*National Library of Canada*] (BIB)

OOMO .... Oxford Mills Branch, Oxford-On-Rideau Township Public Library [*Library symbol*] [*National Library of Canada*] (BIB)

OOMP .... Physical Metallurgy Division, Energy, Mines and Resources Canada [*Division dela Metallurgie Physique, Energie, Mines et Ressources Canada*] Ottawa, Ontari o [*Library symbol*] [*National Library of Canada*] (NLC)

OOMPR .... Microtel Pacific Research Ltd., Ottawa, Ontario [*Library symbol*] [*National Library of Canada*] (NLC)

OOMR .... Headquarters Library, Energy, Mines and Resources Canada [*Bibliotheque Centrale, Energie, Mines et Ressources Canada*] Ottawa, Ontario [*Library symbol*] [*National Library of Canada*] (NLC)

OOMS .... Muscat/Seeb International [*Oman*] [*ICAO location identifier*] (ICLI)

OOMS .... On-Orbit Maintenance/Servicing (ACAE)

OOMSD........ Ministry of State for Social Development [*Ministere d'Etat au Developpement Social*] Ottawa, Ontario [*Library symbol*] [*National Library of Canada*] (NLC)

OOMSS .... Ministry of State for Science and Technology [*Ministere d'Etat pour les Sciences et la Technologie*], Ottawa, Ontario [*Library symbol*] [*National Library of Canada*] (NLC)

OON .... Canada Institute for Scientific and Technical Information, National Research Council (CISTI) [*Institut Canadien de l'Information Scientifique et Technique, Conseil National de Recherches (ICIST)*] Ottawa, Ontario [*Library symbol*] [*National Library of Canada*] (NLC)

OON .... Object Oriented Nonsens (SAUS)

OON .... Odd-Odd Nuclei

OON .... Officer of the Order of Niger

OON .... Out-of-Network (SAUS)

OONAB........ Administration Building Library, Canada Institute for Scientific and Technical Information [*Bibliotheque de l'Edifice de l'Administration, Institut Canadien de l'Information Scientifique et Technique*] Ottawa, Ontario [*Library symbol*] [*National Library of Canada*] (NLC)

OONAM........ Aeronautical and Mechanical Engineering Branch, Canada Institute for Scientific and Technical Information [*Division du Genie Aeronautique et Mecanique, Institut Canadien de l'Information Scientifique et Technique*] Ottawa, Ontario [*Library symbol*] [*National Library of Canada*] (NLC)

OONAMC..... NABU Manufacturing Corp., Ottawa, Ontario [*Library symbol*] [*National Library of Canada*] (NLC)

OONBR .... IRC [*Institute for Research in Construction*] Library, National Research Council Canada Ottawa, Ontario [*Bibliotheque IRC (Institut de Recherche en Construction), Conseil National de Recherches Canada*] [*Library symbol*] [*National Library of Canada*] (NLC)

OONC .... Chemistry Library, Canada Institute for Scientific and Technical Information [*Division de Chimie, Institut Canadien de l'Information Scientifique et Technique*] Ottawa, Ontario [*Library symbol*] [*National Library of Canada*] (NLC)

OONCC........ National Capital Commission [*Commission de la Capitale Nationale*] Ottawa, Ontario [*Library symbol*] [*National Library of Canada*] (NLC)

OOND.......... Department of National Defence [*Ministere de la Defense Nationale*] Ottawa,Ontario [*Library symbol*] [*National Library of Canada*] (NLC)

OONDAT ...... Air Technical Library, Department of National Defence [*Bibliotheque Techniquede l'Aviation, Ministere de la Defense Nationale*] Ottawa, Ontario [*Library symbol*] [*National Library of Canada*] (NLC)

OONDC .... Communications and Electronics Engineering Library, Department of National Defence [*Bibliotheque du Genie Electronique et des Communications, Ministere de laDefense National*] Ottawa, Ontario [*Library symbol*] [*National Library of Canada*] (NLC)

OONDCP ...... Chief, Construction and Properties, Library, Department of National Defence [*Bibliotheque, Chef - Construction et Immeubles, Ministere de la Defense Nationale*] Ottawa, Ontario [*Library symbol*] [*National Library of Canada*] (NLC)

OONDCS ...... Communications Security Establishment, Department of National Defence [*Centrede la Securite des Telecommunications, Ministere de la Defense Nationale*] Ot tawa, Ontario [*Library symbol*] [*National Library of Canada*] (NLC)

OONDH .... Directorate of History, Department of National Defence [*Bureau du Service Historique, Ministere de la Defense Nationale*] Ottawa, Ontario [*Library symbol*] [*National Library of Canada*] (NLC)

OONDIS .... Directorate of Information Services, Department of National Defence [*Servicesd'Information, Ministere de la Defense Nationale*] Ottawa, Ontario [*Library symbol*] [*National Library of Canada*] (NLC)

OONDJ........ Judge Advocate General, Department of National Defence [*Jugeavocat General, Ministere de la Defense Nationale*] Ottawa, Ontario [*Library symbol*] [*National Library of Canada*] (NLC)

OONDLT....... Land Technical Library, Department of National Defence [*Bibliotheque Technique (Terre), Ministere de la Defense Nationale*] Ottawa, Ontario [*Library symbol*] [*National Library of Canada*] (NLC)

OONDM........ National Defence Medical Centre, Department of National Defence [*Centre Medical de la Nationale, Ministere de la Defense Nationale*] Ottawa, Ontario [*Library symbol*] [*National Library of Canada*] (NLC)

OONDMC ..... Mapping and Charting Establishment, Department of National Defence [*Service de la Cartographie, Ministere de la Defense Nationale*] Ottawa, Ontario [*Library symbol*] [*National Library of Canada*] (NLC)

OONDMT...... Maritime Technical Library, Department of National Defence [*Bibliotheque Technique (Mer), Ministere de la Defense Nationale*] Ottawa, Ontario [*Library symbol*] [*National Library of Canada*] (NLC)

OONDORAE... Operational Research and Analysis Establishment, Department of National Defence [*Centre d'Analyse et de Recherche Operationnelle, Ministere de la Defense Nationale*] Ottawa, Ontario [*Library symbol*] [*National Library of Canada*] (NLC)

OONDT......... Secretary of State Library at National Defence [*Bibliotheque du Secretariat d'Etat a la Defense Nationale*], Ottawa, Ontario [*Library symbol*] [*National Library of Canada*] (NLC)

OONE........... National Energy Board [*Office National de l'Energie*] Ottawa, Ontario [*Library symbol*] [*National Library of Canada*] (NLC)

OONFP......... National Farm Products Marketing Council [*Conseil National de Commercialisation des Produits Agricoles*], Ottawa, Ontario [*Library symbol*] [*National Library of Canada*] (BIB)

OONG........... National Gallery of Canada [*Galerie Nationale du Canada*] Ottawa, Ontario [*Library symbol*] [*National Library of Canada*] (NLC)

OONH........... Department of National Health and Welfare [*Ministere de la Sante Nationale etdu Bien-Etre Social*] Ottawa, Ontario [*Library symbol*] [*Obsolete*] [*National Library of Canada*] (NLC)

OONHAC ...... Federal Centre for AIDS [*Acquired Immune Deficiency Syndrome*], Health Protection Branch, Health and Welfare Canada , Ottawa, Ontario [*Centre Federal du SIDA, Direction Generale de la Protection de la Sante, Sante et Bien-Etre Social Canada*] [*Library symbol*] [*National Library of Canada*] (BIB)

OONHBR ...... Banting Research Centre Library, Department of National Health and Welfare [*Bibliotheque du Centre de Recherches Banting, Ministere de la Sante Nationale et du Bien-Etre Social*] Ottawa, Ontario [*Library symbol*] [*National Library of Canada*] (NLC)

OONHFV ...... National Clearinghouse on Family Violence, Health and Welfare Canada [*Centre National d'Information sur la Violence dans la Famille, Sante et Bien-Etre Social Canada*], Ottawa, Ontario [*Library symbol*] [*National Library of Canada*] (BIB)

OONHHP ...... Library Services Division, Health Protection Branch, Health and Welfare Canada [*Service de Bibliotheque, Direction Generale de la Protection de la Sante, Sante et Bien-Etre Social Canada*] Ottawa, Ontario [*Library symbol*] [*National Library of Canada*] (NLC)

OONHHS ...... Health Services and Promotion Branch, Department of National Health and Welfare [*Direction Generale des Services et de la Promotion de la Sante, Ministere dela Sante Nationale et du Bien-Etre Social*] Ottawa, Ontario [*Library symbol*] [*National Library of Canada*] (NLC)

OONHP .... Vanier Reading Room, Place Vanier, Health Protection Branch, Health and Welfare Canada [*Salle de Lecture de Vanier, Place Vanier, Direction Generale de la Protection de la Sante, Sante et Bien-Etre Social Canada*], Ottawa, Ontario [*Library symbol*] [*National Library of Canada*] (NLC)

OONHPP ...... Library Services, Policy, Communications, and Information Branch, Health and Welfare Canada [*Services de Bibliotheque, Direction Generale de la Politique, des Communications, et de l'Information, Sante et Bien-Etre Social Canada*] Ottawa, Ontario [*Library symbol*] [*National Library of Canada*] (NLC)

OONIN .... National Institute of Nutrition [*Institut National de la Nutrition*], Ottawa, Ontario [*Library symbol*] [*National Library of Canada*] (BIB)

OONL........... National Library of Canada [*Bibliotheque Nationale du Canada*] Ottawa, Ontario [*Library symbol*] [*National Library of Canada*] (NLC)

OONLB......... Union Catalogue of Books, National Library of Canada [*Catalogue Collectif desLivres, Bibliotheque Nationale du Canada*] Ottawa, Ontario [*Library symbol*] [*National Library of Canada*] (NLC)

OONLC......... Canadiana Acquisitions, National Library of Canada [*Acquisitions pour Canadiana, Bibliotheque Nationale du Canada*] Ottawa, Ontario [*Library symbol*] [*National Library of Canada*] (NLC)

OONLD......... Information Technology Services, National Library of Canada [*Services de Technologie de l'Information, Bibliotheque Nationale de Canada*], Ottawa, Ontario [*Library symbol*] [*National Library of Canada*] (NLC)

OONLD......... Library Systems Centre, National Library of Canada [*Centre des Systemes de Bibliotheque, Bibliotheque Nationale du Canada*] Ottawa, Ontario [*Library symbol*] [*National Library of Canada*] (NLC)

OONLG......... Official Publications, National Library of Canada [*Publications Officielles, Bibliotheque Nationale du Canada*] Ottawa, Ontario [*Library symbol*] [*National Library of Canada*] (NLC)

OONLI.......... ISDS Canada, National Library of Canada [*ISDS Canada, Bibliotheque Nationale du Canada*], Ottawa, Ontario [*Library symbol*] [*National Library of Canada*] (BIB)

OONLMBS.... Multilingual Biblioservice, National Library of Canada [*Biblioservice Multilingue, Bibliotheque Nationale du Canada*] Ottawa, Ontario [*Library symbol*] [*National Library of Canada*] (NLC)

OONLN......... Newspaper Division, National Library of Canada [*Division des Journaux Bibliotheque Nationale du Canada*] Ottawa, Ontario [*Library symbol*] [*National Library of Canada*] (NLC)

OONLP......... Serials Record, National Library of Canada [*Enregistrement des Publications en Serie, Bibliotheque Nationale du Canada*] Ottawa, Ontario [*Library symbol*] [*National Library of Canada*] (NLC)

OONLR......... Retrospective Bibliography, National Library of Canada [*Bibliographie Retrospective, Bibliotheque Nationale du Canada*] Ottawa, Ontario [*Library symbol*] [*National Library of Canada*] (NLC)

OONLS......... Union Catalogue of Serials, National Library of Canada [*Catalogue Collectif des Periodiques, Bibliotheque Nationale du Canada*] Ottawa, Ontario [*Library symbol*] [*National Library of Canada*] (NLC)

OONM.......... National Museums of Canada [*Musees Nationaux du Canada*] Ottawa, Ontario [*Library symbol*] [*National Library of Canada*] (NLC)

OONMA........ National Aviation Museum [*Musee National de l'Aviation*], Ottawa, Ontario [*Library symbol*] [*National Library of Canada*] (NLC)

OONMC........ Canadian War Museum [*Musee de Guerre du Canada*] Ottawa, Ontario [*Library symbol*] [*National Library of Canada*] (NLC)

OONMCC...... Canadian Conservation Institute, National Museums of Canada [*Institut Canadien de Conservation, Musees Nationaux du Canada*] Ottawa, Ontario [*Library symbol*] [*National Library of Canada*] (NLC)

OONMM....... Canadian Museum of Civilization, National Museums of Canada [*Musee Canadien des Civilisations, Musees Nationaux du Canada*] Ottawa, Ontario [*Library symbol*] [*National Library of Canada*] (NLC)

OONMNS ..... National Museum of Natural Sciences [*Musee National des Sciences Naturelles*], Ottawa, Ontario [*Library symbol*] [*National Library of Canada*] (NLC)

OONMS........ National Museum of Science and Technology [*Musee National des Sciences et de la Technologie*] Ottawa, Ontario [*Library symbol*] [*National Library of Canada*] (NLC)

OONORE ...... Bell Northern Research, Ottawa, Ontario [*Library symbol*] [*National Library of Canada*] (NLC)

OONP........... Division of Physics, Canada Institute for Scientific and Technical Information [*Division de Physique, Institute Canadien de l'Information Scientifique et Technique*] Ottawa, Ontario [*Library symbol*] [*National Library of Canada*] (NLC)

OONR........... Customs and Excise Division, Department of National Revenue [*Division des Douanes et de l'Accise, Ministere du Revenu National*] Ottawa, Ontario [*Library symbol*] [*National Library of Canada*] (NLC)

OONR........... Marmul/Nasir [*Oman*] [*ICAO location identifier*] (ICLI)

OONRE......... Electrical Engineering Division, Canada Institute for Scientific and Technical Information [*Division de Genie Electrique, Institut Canadien de l'Information Scientifique et Technique*] Ottawa, Ontario [*Library symbol*] [*National Library of Canada*] (NLC)

OONRT......... Taxation Division, Department of National Revenue [*Division de l'Impot, Ministere du Revenu National*] Ottawa, Ontario [*Library symbol*] [*National Library of Canada*] (NLC)

OONRTC ...... Centre for Career Development, Revenue Canada - Taxation [*Centre de Developpement Professionnel, Revenu Canada - Impot*] Ottawa, Ontario [*Library symbol*] [*National Library of Canada*] (NLC)

OONS........... Sussex Library, Canada Institute for Scientific and Technical Information [*Bibliotheque Sussex, Institut Canadien de l'Information Scientifique et Technique*] Ottawa, Ontario [*Library symbol*] [*National Library of Canada*] (NLC)

OONSE......... Natural Sciences and Engineering Research Council of Canada [*Conseil de Recherches en Sciences Naturelles et en Genie du Canada*], Ottawa, Ontario [*Library symbol*] [*National Library of Canada*] (NLC)

OONSF......... National Science Film Library [*Cinematheque Nationale Scientifique*] Ottawa, Ontario [*Library symbol*] [*National Library of Canada*] (NLC)

OONSI.......... North-South Institute [*L'Institut Nord-Sud*], Ottawa, Ontario [*Library symbol*] [*National Library of Canada*] (NLC)

OOnt .... Order of Ontario [*Decoration*] [*Canada*] (CMD)

OONU........... Uplands Library, Canada Institute for Scientific and Technical Information [*Bibliotheque d'Uplands, Institut Canadien de l'Information Scientifique et Technique*] Ottawa, Ontario [*Library symbol*] [*National Library of Canada*] (NLC)

OONUL........ Union List of Scientific Serials in Canadian Libraries [*Catalogue Collectif des Publications Scientifiques dans les Bibliotheques Canadiennes*] Ottawa, Ontario [*Library symbol*] [*National Library of Canada*] (NLC)

OONVRC ...... National Victims Resource Centre [*Centre National de la Documentation sur lesVictimes*] Ottawa, Ontario [*Library symbol*] [*National Library of Canada*] (NLC)

OONY........... Opera Orchestra of New York

OONZ........... Nizwa [*Oman*] [*ICAO location identifier*] (ICLI)

OOO............. Earth Physics Branch, Energy, Mines and Resources Canada [*Direction de la Physique du Globe, Energie, Mines et Resources Canada*] Ottawa, Ontario [*Library symbol*] [*National Library of Canada*] (NLC)

OOO............. Geophysics Collection, Geological Survey of Canada [*Collection de la Geophysique, Commission Geologique du Canada*], Ottawa, Ontario [*Library symbol*] [*National Library of Canada*] (NLC)

OOO............. Grants Pass, OR [*Location identifier*] [*FAA*] (FAAL)

OOO............. Office of the Ombudsman

OOO............. Oleum Olivae Optimum [*Best Olive Oil*] [*Pharmacy*] (ROG)

OOO............. Order of Owls (EA)

OOO............. O Sapientia, O Radix, O Adonai [*Three anthems sung in Roman Catholic churches before Christmas*] (ROG)

OOO............. Out of Order [*Telecommunications*] (TEL)

OOOA........... City of Ottawa Archives, Ontario [*Library symbol*] [*National Library of Canada*] (NLC)

OOOAG........ Office of the Auditor General [*Bureau du Verificateur General*] Ottawa, Ontario [*Library symbol*] [*National Library of Canada*] (NLC)

OOOCF........ Ottawa Clinic, Ontario Cancer Foundation, Ontario [*Library symbol*] [*National Library of Canada*] (NLC)

OOOCH .... Ottawa Civic Hospital, Ontario [*Library symbol*] [*National Library of Canada*] (NLC)

OOOCM........ Information Services, Ontario Centre for Microelectronics, Nepean, Ontario [*Library symbol*] [*National Library of Canada*] (NLC)

OOOF........... Onaping Branch, Onaping Falls Public Library, Ontario [*Library symbol*] [*National Library of Canada*] (NLC)

OOOI............ Out-Off-On-In [*Telecommunications*]

OOOL........... Optotek Ltd., Ottawa, Ontario [*Library symbol*] [*National Library of Canada*] (NLC)

OOOS........... Object-Oriented Operating System [*Computer science*] (CDE)

OOOTQFUE... Omnipotent Overseer of the Quest for Unsurpassable Excellence [*Rank in the Junior Woodchucks organization mentioned in Donald Duck comic by Carl Barks*]

OOP .... Library of Parliament [*Bibliotheque du Parlement*] Ottawa, Ontario [*Library symbol*] [*National Library of Canada*] (NLC)

OOP .... Object Oriented Pleasure (SAUS)

OOP .... Object-Oriented Programming [*Computer science*]

OOP .... Oceanographic Observations of the Pacific

OOP .... Office of Organization Planning

OOP .... Offline Orthophoto Printer [*Computer science*] (PDAA)

OOP .... Optimum Optical Pump

OOP .... Ounce of Prevention [*A publication*]

OOP .... Out of Pelvis [*Obstetrics*] (DAVI)

OOP .... Out-of-Phase [*Gynecology*]

OOP .... Out of Plane

OOP .... Out of Plant

OOP .... Out of Plaster [*Orthopedics*] (DAVI)

OOP .... Out Of Pocket (SAUS)

OOP .... Out of Pocket Cost

OOP .... Out of Pocket Expense

OOP .... Out of Position (MCD)

OOP .... Out of Print [*Also, OP*] [*Publishing*]

OOP .... Out on Pass (DAVI)

OOPA........... National Arts Centre [*Centre National des Arts*] Ottawa, Ontario [*Library symbol*] [*National Library of Canada*] (NLC)

OOPA........... One and Only Parents Association (EA)

OOPAC........ Chaudiere Branch, Departmental Library, Environment Canada [*Succursale Chaudiere, Bibliotheque du Ministere, Environnement Canada*] Ottawa, Ontario [*Library symbol*] [*National Library of Canada*] (NLC)

OOPART....... Out of Place Artifact [*Archeology*]

OOPC........... Management Information Centre, Privy Council Office [*Regie Interne de l'Information, Bureau du Conseil Prive*] Ottawa, Ontario [*Library symbol*] [*National Library of Canada*] (NLC)

OOPC........... Ocean Observations Panel for Climate (SAUS)

OOPC........... Office of Operational Planning and Control [*Social Security Administration*]

OOPC........... Owners & Officers of Private Companies [*A publication*]

OOPCF........ Parliamentary Centre for Foreign Affairs and Foreign Trade [*Centre Parlementaire pour les Affaires Etrangeres et le Commerce Exterieur*], Ottawa, Ontario [*Library symbol*] [*National Library of Canada*] (NLC)

OOPEC........ Office for Official Publications of the European Communities (ECED)

OOPEC........ Petro-Canada, Ottawa, Ontario [*Library symbol*] [*National Library of Canada*] (NLC)

OOPED........ Pylon Electronic Development Co. Ltd., Ottawa, Ontario [*Library symbol*] [*National Library of Canada*] (NLC)

OOPF........... Resource Centre, Ottawa Police Force, Ontario [*Library symbol*] [*National Library of Canada*] (BIB)

OOPH........... Perley Hospital, Ottawa, Ontario [*Library symbol*] [*National Library of Canada*] (NLC)

OOPI........... Petroleum Incentives Program, Energy, Mines and Resources Canada [*Programmes d'Encouragement Petrolier, Energie, Mines et Ressources Canada*] Ottawa, Ontario [*Library symbol*] [*National Library of Canada*] (NLC)

OOPIP......... Professional Institute of the Public Service of Canada [*Institut Professionnel de la Fonction Publique au Canada*], Ottawa, Ontario [*Library symbol*] [*National Library of Canada*] (BIB)

OOPL........... Object-Oriented Programming Language [*Computer science*] (PCM)

OOPLFC & A.. Only Official Peggy Lee Fan Club and Archives (EA)

OOPM........... National Postal Museum [*Musee National des Postes*] Ottawa, Ontario [*Library symbol*] [*National Library of Canada*] (NLC)

OOPMF........ Marten Falls Band Library, Ogoki Post, Ontario [*Library symbol*] [*National Library of Canada*] (BIB)

OOPMP........ Peat, Marwick & Partners, Ottawa, Ontario [*Library symbol*] [*National Library of Canada*] (NLC)

O Opns .... Overseas Operations (SAUS)

OOPO........... Canada Post [*Postes Canada*] Ottawa, Ontario [*Library symbol*] [*National Library of Canada*] (NLC)

OOPO........... Out of Position Occupant [*Automotive safety*]

OOPOM........ Meriline Branch, Canada Post [*Postes Canada*], Ottawa, Ontario [*Library symbol*] [*National Library of Canada*] (BIB)

OOPOR .... Ports Canada, Ottawa, Ontario [*Library symbol*] [*National Library of Canada*] (NLC)

OOPS........... Object-Oriented Pieces of Something [*Computer science*]

OOPS........... Object-Oriented Programming (BYTE)

OOPS........... Object-Oriented Programming Software (SAUS)

OOPS........... Object-Oriented Programming System (AAEL)

OOPS .... Object Oriented Program Support (SAUS)

OOPS .... O'Brien's Oil Pollution Service of New Orleans [*Oil spill cleanup service*]

OOPS .... Office for Operations in Political Systems

OOPS .... Off-Line Operating Simulator [*Computer science*]

OOPS .... Offshore Oil Pollution Sleeve (SAUS)

OOPS .... Online Object Patching System [*Computer science*] (PDAA)

OOPS .... Operational Ozone Processing System (SAUS)

OOPS .... Operational Ozone Product System (SAUS)

OOPS .... Operator Oriented Problem Source (VLIE)

OOPS .... Organization of Oil Producing States (SAUS)

OOPS .... Originals on Permanent Sale

OOPS .... Public Service Staff Relations Board [*Commission des Relations de Travail dans la Fonction Publique*] Ottawa, Ontario [*Library symbol*] [*National Library of Canada*] (NLC)

OOPSAC...... Public Service Alliance of Canada [*Alliance de la Fonction Publique du Canada*] Ottawa, Ontario [*Library symbol*] [*National Library of Canada*] (NLC)

OOPSLA....... Object-Oriented Programming Systems, Languages, and Applications [*Computer conference*]

OOPSTAD .... Object Orientated Programming for Small Talk Application Development association (SAUS)

OOPSTAD .... Object Oriented Programming for Smalltalk Application Developers Association (SAUS)

OOPW......... Public Works Canada [*Travaux Publics Canada*] Ottawa, Ontario [*Library symbol*] [*National Library of Canada*] (NLC)

OOPWC....... Capital Region Library, Public Works Canada [*Bibliotheque de la Region de la Capitale, Travaux Publics Canada*] Ottawa, Ontario [*Library symbol*] [*National Library of Canada*] (NLC)

OOPWR....... Research and Development Laboratories, Public Works Canada [*Laboratoires de Recherche et de Developpement, Travaux Publics Canada*] Ottawa, Ontario [*Library symbol*] [*Obsolete*] [*National Library of Canada*] (NLC)

OOQ .... Officer of the Quarters

OOQ .... Original Order Quantity (SAUS)

OOQA........... Director-General, Quality Assurance Library, Department of National Defence [*Bibliotheque du Directeur General-Assurance de la Qualite, Ministere de la Defense Nationale*], Ottawa, Ontario [*Library symbol*] [*National Library of Canada*] (NLC)

OOQC........... Queensway-Carleton Hospital, Ottawa, Ontario [*Library symbol*] [*National Library of Canada*] (NLC)

OOQM........... Queen Mary Street School, Ottawa, Ontario [*Library symbol*] [*National Library of Canada*] (BIB)

OOR............ Mooraberrie [*Queensland*] [*Airport symbol*] (AD)

OOR............ Office for Ordnance Research [*Later, Army Research Office*]

OOR............ Office of Ordnance Research (SAUS)

OOR............ Open Ocean Release

OOR............ Operator Override [*Telecommunications*] (TEL)

OOR............ Out of Range (VLIE)

OOR............ Out of Room (DAVI)

OOR............ Out-of-Roundness [*Manufacturing term*]

OOR............ Oxygen/Ozone Recorder

OOR............ RCMP Headquarters [*Direction Generale de la GRC*] Ottawa, Ontario [*Library symbol*] [*National Library of Canada*] (NLC)

OOR............ RCMP [*Royal Canadian Mounted Police*] Law Enforcement Reference Centre , Ottawa, Ontario [*Centre de Documentation Policiere, Gendarmerie Royale du Canada*] [*Library symbol*] [*National Library of Canada*] (NLC)

OORA........... Oligoarticular Onset Rheumatoid Arthritis [*Medicine*] (MELL)

OORA........... Orangeville Public Library, Ontario [*Library symbol*] [*National Library of Canada*] (NLC)

OORASS ...... Object Oriented Role Analysis, Synthesis and Structuring (SAUS)

OORCS......... Ottawa Roman Catholic Separate School Board, Ontario [*Library symbol*] [*National Library of Canada*] (NLC)

OORD........... Indian and Northern Affairs Canada [*Affaires Indiennes et du Nord Canada*] Ottawa, Ontario [*Library symbol*] [*National Library of Canada*] (NLC)

OORDBMS ... Object-Oriented Relational Database Management System (SAUS)

OORH........... Riverside Hospital, Ottawa, Ontario [*Library symbol*] [*National Library of Canada*] (NLC)

OORI............ Orillia Public Library, Ontario [*Library symbol*] [*National Library of Canada*] (NLC)

OORIA........... J. L. Richard & Associates Ltd., Ottawa, Ontario [*Library symbol*] [*National Library of Canada*] (NLC)

OORIGC .... Learning Resources Centre, Georgian College of Applied Arts and Technology, Orillia, Ontario [*Library symbol*] [*National Library of Canada*] (NLC)

OORIMT....... Mara Township Public Library, Orillia, Ontario [*Library symbol*] [*National Library of Canada*] (BIB)

OORISMH .... OSMH Health Sciences Library, Orillia Soldiers' Memorial Hospital, Ontario [*Library symbol*] [*National Library of Canada*] (NLC)

OORM........... Planning Department Library, Regional Municipality of Ottawa-Carleton, Ottawa, Ontario [*Library symbol*] [*National Library of Canada*] (NLC)

OORM......... Rima [*Oman*] [*ICAO location identifier*] (ICLI)

OORMT........ Transportation-Works Department, Regional Municipality of Ottawa-Carleton, Ottawa, Ontario [*Library symbol*] [*National Library of Canada*] (NLC)

OORO........... Royal Ottawa Hospital, Ontario [*Library symbol*] [*National Library of Canada*] (NLC)

OORORR...... Royal Ottawa Regional Rehabilitation Centre, Royal Ottawa Hospital, Ontario [*Library symbol*] [*National Library of Canada*] (NLC)

OORP........... Rockliffe Park Public Library, Ottawa, Ontario [*Library symbol*] [*National Library of Canada*] (BIB)

OORPL......... Communications Research Centre, Department of Communications [*Centre de Recherches sur les Communications, Ministere des Communications*] Ottawa, Ontario [*Library symbol*] [*National Library of Canada*] (NLC)

OORQ........... Rostaq [*Oman*] [*ICAO location identifier*] (ICLI)

OORR........... Regional Realty Ltd., Ottawa, Ontario [*Library symbol*] [*National Library of Canada*] (BIB)

OOrrW........ Wayne General and Technical College, Orrville, OH [*Library symbol*] [*Library of Congress*] (LCLS)

OORS........... RCMP Scientific Information Centre [*Centre d'Information Scientifique de la GRC*] Ottawa, Ontario [*Library symbol*] [*National Library of Canada*] (NLC)

OORSFC...... Only Official Rolling Stones Fan Club (EAIO)

OORSS......... CSIS [*Canadian Security Intelligence Service*] Open Information Centre Ontario [*Bibliotheque du SCRS (Service Canadien du Renseignement de Securite), Ottawa*] [*Library symbol*] [*National Library of Canada*] (NLC)

OORT........... Canadian Radio-Television and Telecommunications Commission [*Conseil de la Radiodiffusion et des Telecommunications Canadiennes*] Ottawa, Ontario [*Library symbol*] [*National Library of Canada*] (NLC)

OORTA........ Roads and Transportation Association of Canada [*Association des Routes et Transports du Canada*] Ottawa, Ontario [*Library symbol*] [*National Library of Canada*] (NLC)

OOS .... Object Oriented Software [*Computer science*] (VLIE)

OOS .... Object-Oriented Systems (SAUS)

OOS .... Occupational Overuse Syndrome

OOS .... Ocean Observing System [*Marine science*] (OSRA)

OOS .... Office of Operations Support [*Law Enforcement Assistance Administration*]

OOS .... Off-Line Operating Simulator [*Computer science*] (VLIE)

OOS........... On-Orbit Station [*NASA*] (NAKS)

OOS........... On-Orbit Station [*NASA*] (NASA)

OOS .... On-Orbit Support

OOS .... Operational Operating System [*Telecommunications*] (TEL)

OOS........... Orbit-to-Orbit Shuttle [*NASA*] (NAKS)

OOS .... Orbit-to-Orbit Shuttle [*NASA*]

OOS........... Orbit-to-Orbit Stage [*NASA*] (NAKS)

OOS .... Orbit-to-Orbit Stage [*NASA*] (NASA)

OOS .... Orbit to Orbit Unmanned System (ACAE)

OOS .... Ore/Oil Ship (SAUS)

OOS .... Out of School (OICC)

OOS .... Out of Sequence (NRCH)

OOS .... Out of Service (NRCH)

OOS .... Out-of-Shot [*Photography*] (ADA)

OOS .... Out-of-Sight (SAUS)

OOS .... Out of Stock

OOS .... Statistics Canada [*Statistique Canada*] Ottawa Ontario [*Library symbol*] [*National Library of Canada*] (NLC)

OOSA .... National Social Services Consultant and Government Relations Officer, Salvation Army Library, Ottawa, Ontario [*Library symbol*] [*National Library of Canada*] (BIB)

OOSA .... Object Orientated System Analysis (SAUS)

OOSA .... Object-Oriented Software Architecture (SAUS)

OOSA .... Salalah [*Oman*] [*ICAO location identifier*] (ICLI)

OOSAR......... Government Relations Office, Spar Aerospace Ltd., Ottawa, Ontario [*Library symbol*] [*National Library of Canada*] (BIB)

OOSB .... Smart & Biggar, Ottawa, Ontario [*Library symbol*] [*National Library of Canada*] (BIB)

OOSC........... Olfactronics and Odor Sciences Center (SAUS)

OOSC........... Out-of-Sight Control (MUGU)

OOSC........... Supreme Court of Canada [*Cour Supreme du Canada*] Ottawa, Ontario [*Library symbol*] [*National Library of Canada*] (NLC)

OOSCA......... Archives des Soeurs de la Charite d'Ottawa, Ontario [*Library symbol*] [*National Library of Canada*] (NLC)

OOSCAC...... Scanada Consultants Ltd., Ottawa, Ontario [*Library symbol*] [*National Library of Canada*] (NLC)

OOSCC......... Out-of-Site Control Center (SAA)

OOSCC......... Science Council of Canada [*Conseil des Sciences du Canada*] Ottawa, Ontario [*Library symbol*] [*National Library of Canada*] (NLC)

OOSCL......... Census Library, Statistics Canada [*Bibliotheque du Recensement, Statistique Canada*] Ottawa, Ontario [*Library symbol*] [*National Library of Canada*] (NLC)

OOSCM........ Census Map Library, Statistics Canada [*Cartotheque du Recensement, Statistique Canada*] Ottawa, Ontario [*Library symbol*] [*National Library of Canada*] (NLC)

OOSD........... Object Oriented Structured Design [*Computer science*]

OOSDG........ Ontario Secondary School Graduation Diploma (SAUS)

OOSDP......... On-Orbit Station Distribution Panel [*NASA*] (MCD)

OOSE........... Object-Oriented Software Engineering (SAUS)

OOSG........... Ministry of the Solicitor General [*Ministere du Solliciteur General*] Ottawa, Ontario [*Library symbol*] [*National Library of Canada*] (NLC)

OOSGO .... Osgoode Public Library, Ontario [*Library symbol*] [*National Library of Canada*] (BIB)

OOSH........... Object Oriented Shell (SAUS)

OOSH........... Oshawa Public Library, Ontario [*Library symbol*] [*National Library of Canada*] (NLC)

OOSH........... Out of School Hours

OOSH........... Sohar [*Oman*] [*ICAO location identifier*] (ICLI)

OOSHD........ Durham College of Applied Arts and Technology, Oshawa, Ontario [*Library symbol*] [*National Library of Canada*] (NLC)

OOSHH .... Education Resource Centre, Oshawa General Hospital, Ontario [*Library symbol*] [*National Library of Canada*] (BIB)

OOSHR .... Robert McLaughlin Gallery, Oshawa, Ontario [*Library symbol*] [*National Library of Canada*] (NLC)

OOSHT........ Technical Library, Systemhouse Ltd., Ottawa, Ontario [*Library symbol*] [*National Library of Canada*] (NLC)

OOSJ ....: La Bibliotheque Deschatelets Peres Oblats [*Closed to the public*] Ottawa, Ontario [*Library symbol*] [*National Library of Canada*] (NLC)

OOSLM......... Montfort Hospital [*Hopital Montfort*] Ottawa, Ontario [*Library symbol*] [*National Library of Canada*] (NLC)

OOSLR......... S. L. Ross Environmental Research, Ottawa, Ontario [*Library symbol*] [*National Library of Canada*] (BIB)

OOSM .... Sahma [*Oman*] [*ICAO location identifier*] (ICLI)

OOSMM .... Map Library, Energy, Mines and Resources Canada [*Cartotheque, Energie, Mines et Ressources Canada*] Ottawa, Ontario [*Library symbol*] [*National Library of Canada*] (NLC)

OOSN........... Six Nations Public Library, Ohsweken, Ontario [*Library symbol*] [*National Library of Canada*] (BIB)

OOSP........... Patent and Copyright Office, Department of Consumer and Corporate Affairs [*Bureau des Brevets et du Droit d'Auteur, Ministere de la Consommation et des Corporations*] Ottawa, Ontario [*Library symbol*] [*National Library of Canada*] (NLC)

OOSPD......... Ocean Observing System Development Panel [*Marine science*] (OSRA)

OOSPX......... St.-Pius X High School, Ottawa, Ontario [*Library symbol*] [*National Library of Canada*] (BIB)

OOSQ........... Saiq [*Oman*] [*ICAO location identifier*] (ICLI)

OOSR........... Sur [*Oman*] [*ICAO location identifier*] (ICLI)

OOSS .... Department of the Secretary of State [*Secretariat d'Etat*] Ottawa, Ontario [*Library symbol*] [*National Library of Canada*] (NLC)

OOSS .... Outpatient Ophthalmic Surgery Society (EA)

OOSS .... Overseas Operational Storage Site [*Army*]

OOSSHRC ... Social Sciences and Humanities Research Council of Canada [*Conseil de Recherches en Sciences Humaines du Canada*] Ottawa, Ontario [*Library symbol*] [*National Library of Canada*] (NLC)

OOSSTE ...... Terminology and Documentation Branch, Translation Bureau, Department of the Secretary of State [*Direction generale de la Terminologie et de la Documentation, Bureau des Traductions, Secretariat d'Etat*] Ottawa, Ontario [*Library symbol*] [*National Library of Canada*] (NLC)

OOSSTE ...... Terminology Library, Information Resource Services Directorate, Secretary of State [*Bibliotheque de la Terminologie, Direction Info-Ressources, Secretariat d'Etat*], Ottawa, Ontario [*Library symbol*] [*National Library of Canada*] (NLC)

OOSSTM ...... Multilingual Services Directorate, Translation Bureau, Department of the Secretary of State [*Direction des Services Multilingues, Bureau des Traductions, Secretariat d'Etat*] Ottawa, Ontario [*Library symbol*] [*National Library of Canada*] (NLC)

OOSSTR....... Translation Services Branch, Translation Bureau, Department of the Secretary of State [*Direction Generale des Services de Traduction, Bureau des Traductions, Secretariat d'Etat*] Ottawa, Ontario [*Library symbol*] [*National Library of Canada*] (NLC)

OOST .... Standards Council of Canada, Ottawa, Ontario [*Library symbol*] [*National Library of Canada*] (BIB)

OOSTM .... Careerware Reference Centre, STM Systems Corp., Ottawa, Ontario [*Library symbol*] [*National Library of Canada*] (BIB)

OOSU .... St. Paul University [*Universite St-Paul*] Ottawa, Ontario [*Library symbol*] [*National Library of Canada*] (NLC)

OOSUA........ Archives, St. Paul University [*Archives, Universite St-Paul*] Ottawa, Ontario [*Library symbol*] [*National Library of Canada*] (NLC)

OOSV .... St. Vincent Hospital [*Hopital St-Vincent*] Ottawa, Ontario [*Library symbol*] [*National Library of Canada*] (NLC)

OOSW .... Status of Women Canada [*Condition Feminine Canada*] Ottawa, Ontario [*Library symbol*] [*National Library of Canada*] (NLC)

OOSWH........ Soloway, Wright & Houston Law Firm, Ottawa, Ontario [*Library symbol*] [*National Library of Canada*] (BIB)

OOT .... Object-Oriented Technology [*Computer science*] (CDE)

OOT .... Office of Operational Testing (SAUS)

OOT .... Oil Out Temperature

OOT .... Onotoa [*Kiribati*] [*Airport symbol*] (OAG)

OOT .... Ootomari [*Former USSR*] [*Seismograph station code, US Geological Survey*] [*Closed*] (SEIS)

OOT .... Out of Oxygen Tent

OOT .... Out of Territory (VLIE)

OOT .... Out of Tolerance (FAAC)

OOT .... Out-of-Town [*Word processing*]

OOT .... Transport Canada [*Transports Canada*] Ottawa, Ontario [*Library symbol*] [*National Library of Canada*] (NLC)

OOTA .... Airworthiness Library, Transport Canada [*Bibliotheque de la Navigabilite Aerienne, Transports Canada*], Ottawa, Ontario [*Library symbol*] [*National Library of Canada*] (NLC)

OOTAC......... Airports and Construction Services, Transport Canada [*Service des Aeroports et de la Construction, Transports Canada*] Ottawa, Ontario [*Library symbol*] [*National Library of Canada*] (NLC)

OOTAS......... Canadian Aviation Safety Board [*Bureau Canadien de la Securite Aerienne*] Ottawa, Ontario [*Library symbol*] [*National Library of Canada*] (NLC)

OOTB .... Out of the Box (ADWA)

OOTB .... Tourism Reference and Documentation, Regional Industrial Expansion [*Centre deReference et de Documentation Touristique, Expansion Industrielle Regionale*] , Ottawa, Ontario [*Library symbol*] [*National Library of Canada*] (NLC)

OOTC .... Department of Regional Industrial Expansion [*Ministere de l'Expansion Industrielle Regionale*] Ottawa, Ontario [*Library symbol*] [*National Library of Canada*] (NLC)

OOTC .... Obligatory On-Topic Comment [*Computer hacker terminology*]
OOTC .... Oceania Olympic Training Center [*Australia*]
OOTC .... Old Old Timers Club (EA)
OOTCI .... Documentation Centre, Communications and Informatics, Transport Canada [*Centre de Documentation, Communications et Informatique, Transports Canada*], Ottawa, Ontario [*Library symbol*] [*National Library of Canada*] (BIB)
OOTCO .... Telecommunications Library, Transport Canada [*Bibliotheque de Telecommunications, Transports Canada*], Ottawa, Ontario [*Library symbol*] [*National Library of Canada*] (NLC)
OOTCT .... TransCanada Telephone System, Ottawa, Ontario [*Library symbol*] [*National Library of Canada*] (NLC)
OOTE .... Out-of Town Executive (SAUS)
OOTE .... Out-of-Town Executive
OOTEL .... Telesat Canada, Ottawa, Ontario [*Library symbol*] [*National Library of Canada*] (NLC)
OOTFS .... Technical Library AAFBAA, Flight Services Directorate, Transport Canada [*Bibliotheque Technique AAFBAA, Direction Generale du Service des Vols, Transports Canada*], Ottawa, Ontario [*Library symbol*] [*National Library of Canada*] (NLC)
OOTG .... One of the Greats (SAUS)
OOTH .... Thumrait [*Oman*] [*ICAO location identifier*] (ICLI)
OOTI .... Technical Information Centre, Transport Canada Training Institute [*Centre d'Information Technique, Institut de Formation Transports Canada*], Cornwall, Ontario [*Library symbol*] [*National Library of Canada*] (NLC)
OOTIR .... Traffic Injury Research Foundation of Canada [*Fondation de Recherches sur lesBlessures de la Route au Canada*] Ottawa, Ontario [*Library symbol*] [*National Library of Canada*] (NLC)
OOTN .... Trade Negotiations Office, External Affairs Canada [*Affaires Exterieures Canada*] Ottawa, Ontario [*Library symbol*] [*National Library of Canada*] (NLC)
OOTR .... Tax Court of Canada [*Cour Canadienne de l'Impot*] Ottawa, Ontario [*Library symbol*] [*National Library of Canada*] (NLC)
OOTRAT ...... Les Traductions Tessier SCC (Division de Multiscript International), Ottawa, Ontario [*Library symbol*] [*National Library of Canada*] (BIB)
OOTRS .... Road Safety and Motor Vehicle Regulation Branch, Transport Canada [*Direction de la Securite Routiere et de la Reglementation Automobile, Transports Canada*], Ottawa, Ontario [*Library symbol*] [*National Library of Canada*] (NLC)
OOTRT .... Railway Transportation Directorate, Transport Canada [*Direction du Transport Ferroviaire, Transports Canada*] Ottawa, Ontario [*Library symbol*] [*National Library of Canada*] (NLC)
OOTSSA ...... St. Lawrence Seaway Authority, Transport Canada [*Administration de la Voie Maritime du Saint-Laurent, Transports Canada*] Ottawa, Ontario [*Library symbol*] [*National Library of Canada*] (NLC)
OOTT .... National Transportation Agency of Canada [*Office National des Transports du Canada*], Ottawa, Ontario [*Library symbol*] [*National Library of Canada*] (NLC)
OOTTD .... Technical Data Resource Centre, Transport Canada [*Centre de la Documentation Technique, Transports Canada*], Ottawa, Ontario [*Library symbol*] [*National Library of Canada*] (NLC)
OOTTE .... Telecommunications and Electronics Directorate, Transport Canada [*Direction des Telecommunications et de l'Electronique, Transports Canada*] Ottawa, Ontario [*Library symbol*] [*Obsolete*] [*National Library of Canada*] (NLC)
OOTW .... Operations Other Than War [*Army*] (INF)
Ooty .... Ootacamund Madras (SAUS)
OOU .... Out of Use (IAA)
OOU .... University of Ottawa [*Universite d'Ottawa*] Ontario [*Library symbol*] [*National Library of Canada*] (NLC)
OOUA .... Archives, Universite d'Ottawa [*Archives, University of Ottawa*], Ontario [*Library symbol*] [*National Library of Canada*] (BIB)
OOUC .... Department of Criminology, University of Ottawa [*Departement de Criminologie,Universite d'Ottawa*] Ontario [*Library symbol*] [*National Library of Canada*] (NLC)
OOUD .... Faculty of Civil Law, University of Ottawa [*Faculte de Droit Civil, Universite d'Ottawa*] Ontario [*Library symbol*] [*National Library of Canada*] (NLC)
OOUG .... Oregon Online User Group (NITA)
OOUH .... Health Sciences Library, University of Ottawa [*Bibliotheque des Sciences de la Sante, Universite d'Ottawa*] Ontario [*Library symbol*] [*National Library of Canada*] (NLC)
OOUI .... Object-Oriented User Interface [*Computer science*]
OOUIC .... Institute of International Cooperation, University of Ottawa [*Institut de Cooperation Internationale, Universite d'Ottawa*] Ontario [*Library symbol*] [*National Library of Canada*] (NLC)
OOUM .... Vanier Library, University of Ottawa [*Bibliotheque Vanier, Universite d'Ottawa*] Ontario [*Library symbol*] [*National Library of Canada*] (NLC)
OOUMA .... Map Library, University of Ottawa [*Cartotheque, Universite d'Ottawa*] Ontario [*Library symbol*] [*National Library of Canada*] (NLC)
OOURC .... Centre de Recherche en Civilisation Canadienne-Francaise, Universite d'Ottawa [*Centre for Research on French Canadian Culture, University of Ottawa*], Ontario [*Library symbol*] [*National Library of Canada*] (BIB)
OOUSA .... United States Information Service, Ottawa, Ontario [*Library symbol*] [*National Library of Canada*] (NLC)
OOUSC .... Unitarian Service Committee of Canada, Ottawa, Ontario [*Library symbol*] [*National Library of Canada*] (BIB)
OOV .... Objects of Verification [*Arms control*] (DOMA)
OOV .... Orbit-to-Orbit Vehicle (MCD)
OOV .... Out of View (IAA)
OOV .... Out of Vision [*Films, television, etc.*]

OOVIF .... Vanier Institute of the Family [*Institut Vanier de la Famille*] Ottawa, Ontario [*Library symbol*] [*National Library of Canada*] (NLC)
OOVV .... Versatile Vickers Systems, Inc., Ottawa, Ontario [*Library symbol*] [*National Library of Canada*] (NLC)
OOW .... Officer of the Watch [*Navigation*]
OOW .... Out-of-Warranty (TIMI)
OOW .... Out of Wedlock (MELL)
OOW .... Owen Sound Public Library, Ontario [*Library symbol*] [*National Library of Canada*] (NLC)
OOW .... Versatile Vickers Systems, Inc., Ottawa, Ontario (SAUS)
OOWC .... Wordcount, Creative Writing Services, Inc., Ottawa, Ontario [*Library symbol*] [*National Library of Canada*] (NLC)
OOWD .... Western Diversification [*Diversification de l'Ouest*], Ottawa, Ontario [*Library symbol*] [*National Library of Canada*] (BIB)
OOWGC .... Georgian College Resource Centre, Owen Sound, Ontario [*Library symbol*] [*National Library of Canada*] (NLC)
OOWGM ...... Health Sciences Library, General & Marine Hospital, Owen Sound, Ontario [*Library symbol*] [*National Library of Canada*] (NLC)
OOWGM ...... Health Sciences Library, Grey Bruce Regional Health Centre, Owen Sound, Ontario [*Library symbol*] [*National Library of Canada*] (NLC)
OOWIC .... West Island College of Ontario, Ottawa [*Library symbol*] [*National Library of Canada*] (BIB)
OOWLS .... Sir Wilfrid Laurier High School Library, Carleton Board of Education, Ottawa, Ontario [*Library symbol*] [*National Library of Canada*] (BIB)
OOWM .... Owen Sound Museum, County of Grey, Ontario [*Library symbol*] [*National Library of Canada*] (BIB)
OOWSRA ..... Omnibus Oregon Wild and Scenic Rivers Act of 1988 (COE)
OOWT .... Tom Thomson Memorial Gallery, Owen Sound, Ontario [*Library symbol*] [*National Library of Canada*] (NLC)
OOWU .... Briefing Centre, World University Services of Canada [*Centre de Ressources, Entraide Universitaire Mondiale du Canada*], Ottawa, Ontario [*Library symbol*] [*National Library of Canada*] (NLC)
OOX .... XIOS Research Corp., Ottawa, Ontario [*Library symbol*] [*National Library of Canada*] (BIB)
OOxM .... Miami University, Oxford, OH [*Library symbol*] [*Library of Congress*] (LCLS)
OOxM-S ...... Miami University, Scripps Foundation for Research in Population Problems, Oxford, OH [*Library symbol*] [*Library of Congress*] (LCLS)
OOYB .... Yibal [*Oman*] [*ICAO location identifier*] (ICLI)
OOZ .... Open Ocean Zone [*Oceanography*]
OOZE .... Object-Oriented Z Environment [*Computer science*]
OP .... Air Panama Internacional [*ICAO designator*] (AD)
Op .... De Opficio Mundi [*Philo*] (BJA)
OP .... Dominican Contemplative Nuns (Cloistered) (TOCD)
OP .... Dominican Rural Missionaries (TOCD)
OP .... Dominican Sisters (Adrian, MI) (TOCD)
OP .... Dominican Sisters (Akron, OH) (TOCD)
OP .... Dominican Sisters (Amityville, NY) (TOCD)
OP .... Dominican Sisters (Blauvelt, NY) (TOCD)
OP .... Dominican Sisters (Caldwell, PA) (TOCD)
OP .... Dominican Sisters (Colombia) (TOCD)
OP .... Dominican Sisters (Columbus, OH) (TOCD)
OP .... Dominican Sisters (Ecuador) (TOCD)
OP .... Dominican Sisters (Edmonds, WA) (TOCD)
OP .... Dominican Sisters (Fall River, MA) (TOCD)
OP .... Dominican Sisters (Grand Rapid, MI) (TOCD)
OP .... Dominican Sisters (Great Bend, KS) (TOCD)
OP .... Dominican Sisters (Hawthorne, NY) (TOCD)
OP .... Dominican Sisters (Houston, TX) (TOCD)
OP .... Dominican Sisters (Justice, IL) (TOCD)
OP .... Dominican Sisters (Kenosha, WI) (TOCD)
OP .... Dominican Sisters (Media, PA) (TOCD)
OP .... Dominican Sisters (Nashville, TN) (TOCD)
OP .... Dominican Sisters (Newburgh, NY) (TOCD)
OP .... Dominican Sisters (New Orleans, LA) (TOCD)
OP .... Dominican Sisters of Carondelet (TOCD)
OP .... Dominican Sisters of Charity of the Presentation of the Blessed Virgin (TOCD)
OP .... Dominican Sisters of Mt. Thabor (TOCD)
OP .... Dominican Sisters of Our Lady of the Most Holy Rosary (TOCD)
OP .... Dominican Sisters of Our Lady of the Rosary and of Saint Catherine of Siena, Cabra (TOCD)
OP .... Dominican Sisters of the Roman Congregation (TOCD)
OP .... Dominican Sisters (Ossining, NY) (TOCD)
OP .... Dominican Sisters (Oxford, MI) (TOCD)
OP .... Dominican Sisters (Oxford, South Africa) (TOCD)
OP .... Dominican Sisters (Racine, WI) (TOCD)
OP .... Dominican Sisters (San Jose, CA) (TOCD)
OP .... Dominican Sisters (San Rafael, CA) (TOCD)
OP .... Dominican Sisters (Sinsinawa, WI) (TOCD)
OP .... Dominican Sisters (Sparkill, NY) (TOCD)
OP .... Dominican Sisters (Spokane, WA) (TOCD)
OP .... Dominican Sisters (Springfield, IL) (TOCD)
OP .... Dominican Sisters (St. Catherine, KY) (TOCD)
OP .... Dominican Sisters (Tacoma, WA) (TOCD)
OP .... Dominican Sisters (Vietnam) (TOCD)
OP .... Eucharistic Missionaries of St. Dominic (TOCD)
OP .... Hermanas Dominicanas de la Doctrine Cristiana (TOCD)
OP .... Marian Society of Dominican Catechists (TOCD)
OP .... Object Program (IAA)
OP .... Obligated Position [*Civil Service*]

OP	Observation Patrol (SAUS)	
OP	Observation Plane	
OP	Observation Point [or Post]	
OP	Observation Post [Military]	
OP	Observed Position [Navigation]	
OP	Obstructive Pancreatitis [Medicine] (MELL)	
OP	Occasional Paper	
OP	Occipitoparietal [Medicine] (AAMN)	
OP	Occiput Posterior [Medicine]	
OP	Occupational Psychologist	
OP	Oceanus Procellarum [Lunar area]	
OP	Octapeptide [Biochemistry]	
OP	Offering Price	
OP	Office of Personnel [Department of Agriculture] (GFGA)	
OP	Office of Pesticides [Public Health Service]	
OP	Office of Planning (SAUS)	
OP	Office of Policy [NASA]	
OP	Office of Preparedness (DNAB)	
OP	Office of Protocol (SAUS)	
OP	Office of the president (SAUS)	
OP	Office Pass (AAG)	
OP	Office Power (SAUS)	
OP	Office Printer (SAUS)	
OP	Office Processor (SAUS)	
OP	Office Product (IAA)	
OP	Officer Program [Military] (DNAB)	
OP	Official Publication (ADA)	
O/P	Off Peak (WDAA)	
O-P	Off-Price [A retail outlet selling discounted merchandise]	
o/p	Oil on Panel (VRA)	
OP	Oil Pressure	
OP	Oilproof	
OP	Oil Pump	
OP	Old Particular [Marsala]	
OP	Old [Previously seen] Patient	
OP	Old Pattern [British military] (DMA)	
OP	Old Persean (WDAA)	
OP	Old Persian [Language, etc.]	
OP	Old Price [Riots] [Occurred for 67 nights, beginning December 30, 1808, opening night of rebuilt Covent Garden Theatre, London, because of new and higher prices]	
OP	Old Process (SAUS)	
OP	Olfactory Peduncle [Medicine] (DMAA)	
OP	Omega Project (EA)	
O/P	On Proof [Publishing] (DGA)	
OP	Opaque [Envelopes]	
OP	Open [Stock exchange term]	
OP	Opening Pressure [Medicine]	
OP	Opening Price [Stock exchange term]	
OP	Opening Purchase [Stock exchange term]	
OP	Open Pit (SAUS)	
OP	Open Policy	
OP	Open Position [Dancing]	
OP	Opera	
op	Opera [Works] [Italian]	
Op	Opera et Dies [of Hesiod] [Classical studies] (OCD)	
OP	Operand [Computer science]	
op	Operate (IDOE)	
OP	Operate	
OP	Operating Plan [Management term] (MCD)	
OP	Operating Point (IAA)	
OP	Operating Policy [Military]	
OP	Operating Potential (SAUS)	
OP	Operating Procedure [Management term] (KSC)	
OP	Operating Profit [DoD]	
OP	Operation (AFM)	
op	Operation (ELAL)	
op	Operation (NTIO)	
OP	Operational (CAAL)	
op	Operational (IDOE)	
OP	Operational Performance (SAUS)	
OP	Operational Priority	
OP	Operational Procedure (MCD)	
OP	Operational Process (SAUS)	
OP	Operational Project [Army] (AABC)	
OP	Operation Overlord Preparations [World War II]	
OP	Operation Part (SAUS)	
OP	Operation Plans	
OP	Operations (KSC)	
OP	Operations Order (MCD)	
OP	Operations Plan (IAA)	
OP	Operative Procedure	
op	Operator (IDOE)	
OP	Operator [Computer science]	
OP	Operator Panel (SAUS)	
OP	Operator Performance (SAUS)	
OP	Operator Position (SAUS)	
OP	Operator Precedence (SAUS)	
OP	Ophthalmology	
OP	Opinion (ADA)	
OP	Opium (SAUS)	
O-P	Oppenheimer-Phillips [Process]	
OP	Opposed (NVT)	
op	Opposite (WDMC)	
OP	Opposite	

OP	Opposite Prompt [i.e., the left side] [A stage direction]	
OP	Optical Probe (AAG)	
OP	Optical Properties (SAUS)	
OP	Optical Technician Program [Association of Independent Colleges and Schools specialization code]	
OP	Optime [Best] [Latin] (ROG)	
OP	Optimum Programming (SAUS)	
op	Optional (ELAL)	
OP	Optional	
OP	Optional Flag [Navy] [British]	
op	Opus (WDMC)	
OP	Opus [Work] [Latin]	
Op	Opus	
OP	Orange Pekoe [Tea]	
OP	Orbital Period (AAG)	
OP	Orbital Probe [NASA]	
OP	Ordering Possibility (SAUS)	
op	Order of Preachers, Dominican Fathers (TOCD)	
OP	Order of Preachers (Dominicans) (TOCD)	
OP	Order of Preceptors	
OP	Order Parameter (SAUS)	
OP	Order Policy [Insurance]	
OP	Ordinary Pay (SAUS)	
OP	Ordinis Praedicatorum [Of the Order of Preachers, or Dominicans] [Latin]	
OP	Ordnance Pamphlets	
OP	Ordnance Personnel	
OP	Ordnance Publications [Navy] (MCD)	
OP	Ordo Praedicatorum [Order of Preachers] [Dominicans] [Roman Catholic religious order]	
Op	Oregon pine (SAUS)	
OP	Organic Phosphates (GNE)	
OP	Organization Problem (SAUS)	
OP	Organophoshate (LDT)	
OP	Organophosphorus [Organic chemistry]	
OP	Oriented Polymer (SAUS)	
OP	Orient Press [Press agency] [South Korea]	
OP	Original Pack (DB)	
OP	Original Policy (ADA)	
OP	Original Premium [Insurance]	
OP	Orthogonal Polynomial (OA)	
OP	Orthogonal Processor (SAUS)	
OP	Orthomat Plot (MCD)	
OP	Ortho-Phosphate (SAUS)	
OP	Oscillatory Potentials (SAUS)	
OP	Osmotic Pressure	
OP	Osteopoetin [Biochemistry]	
OP	Osteoporosis [Orthopedics] (DAVI)	
OP	Osterogenic Protein	
OP	Other Papers (ROG)	
OP	Other People's [Borrowed money, cigarettes, etc.] [Slang]	
OP	Other Person (TRID)	
OP	Other Procurement	
OP	Other than Psychotic	
OP	Outer Panel (AAG)	
OP	Out-of-Press [Recordings]	
op	Out of Print [Publishing] (WDMC)	
OP	Out of Print [Also, OOP] [Publishing]	
OP	Outpatient [Medicine]	
op	Outport (SAUS)	
OP	Outpost	
OP	Out Primary (SAUS)	
OP	Output (AAG)	
O/P	Output (PIPO)	
o/p	Output	
OP	Output Point (SAUS)	
OP	Output Port (CCCA)	
O/P	Output Power (ACAE)	
OP	Output Primary [Electronics]	
OP	Output Printer (SAUS)	
OP	Output Processor (SAUS)	
OP	Output Puncher (SAUS)	
OP	Outside Production	
OP	Overall Position [Tertiary entrance]	
OP	Overflow Position (ELAL)	
OP	Overpotential (SAUS)	
OP	Over Pressure (AAG)	
OP	Overpressure (SAUS)	
O/P	Overpriced (WDAA)	
op	Overprint [Journalism] (WDMC)	
OP	Overprint	
OP	Over Proof (SAUS)	
OP	Overproof [Distilling]	
OP	Overprune (SAUS)	
OP	Overpuff (SAUS)	
OP	Overseas Post (ADA)	
OP	Overtime Pay (MHDB)	
OP	Ovine Prolactin [Endocrinology]	
O/P	Ownership Purpose Code [Army] (AABC)	
OP	Own Protection (WDAA)	
OP	Oxazolinylphenoxy [Organic radical]	
OP	Oxygen Point (SAUS)	
OP	Oxygen Pressure Process [Ore leach process]	
OP	Oxygen Purge [NASA] (NASA)	
OP	Ozone Protection [Environmental science] (COE)	

OP................ Paulding County Carnegie Public Library, Paulding, OH [*Library symbol*] [*Library of Congress*] (LCLS)

OP................ Perth Public Library, Ontario [*Library symbol*] [*National Library of Canada*] (NLC)

OP................ Religious Missionaries of St. Dominic (Spanish Prov.) (TOCD)

OPA .... Isopropyl Alcohol (SAUS)

OPA .... Kopasker [*Iceland*] [*Airport symbol*] (OAG)

OPa.............. Morley Library, Painesville, OH [*Library symbol*] [*Library of Congress*] (LCLS)

OPA .... Obscene Publications Act [*British*]

OPA .... Occupational Personality Assessment [*Test*] (TMMY)

OPA .... Office of Performance Assessment (SAUS)

OPA .... Office of Petroleum Allocation [*Federal Energy Administration*]

OPA .... Office of Planning and Analysis (SAUS)

OPA .... Office of Policy Analysis [*Environmental Protection Agency*] (GFGA)

OPA .... Office of Population Affairs [*HEW*]

OPA .... Office of Population Affairs Clearinghouse (EA)

OPA .... Office of Price Administration [*World War II*]

OPA .... Office of Producer Affairs [*Federal Telecommunications Commission*]

OPA .... Office of Program Analysis [*Department of Energy*] [*Washington, DC*]

OPA .... Office of Program Appraisal [*Navy*]

OPA .... Office of Public Affairs [*in various government agencies*]

OPA .... Office of Public Assistance (SAUS)

OPA .... Office of the Pardon Attorney [*Department of Justice*]

OPA .... Officer Personnel Act

o/pa .... Oil on Paper (VRA)

OPA .... Oil Pollution Act of 1990 [*MARAD*] (TAG)

OPA .... Onafhankelijke Partij [*Independent Party*] [*Netherlands*] [*Political party*] (PPW)

OPA .... One-Photon Absorption (SAUS)

OPA .... Ontario Paramedic Association (SAUS)

OPA .... Ontario Pharmacists Association (SAUS)

OPA .... Ontario Physiotherapists Association (SAUS)

OPA .... Opal Air Pty Ltd. [*Australia*] [*FAA designator*] (FAAC)

OPA .... Opana [*Hawaii*] [*Seismograph station code, US Geological Survey*] (SEIS)

OPA .... Opaque [*Type of ice formation*]

OPA .... Open Protocol Architecture (SAUS)

OPA .... Open Publishing Architecture (SAUS)

Opa.............. Opera of the Month Club [*Record label*]

OPA .... Operations Planning Analysis [*NASA*] (MCD)

OPA .... Operator Priority Access (NITA)

OPA .... O-Phthalaldehyde

OPA .... Optical Parametric Amplifier (SAUS)

OPA .... Optical Parametric Oscillator [*Physics*]

OPA .... Optical Plotting Attachment (WDAA)

OPA .... Optical Publishing Association (EA)

OPA .... Optoelectric Pulse Amplifier

OPA .... Optoelectronic Pulse Amplifier

OPA .... Orbiter Plasma Analyzer [*NASA*]

OPA .... Organophosphorous Acid [*Organic chemistry*]

OPA .... Organ Procurement Agency [*Department of Health and Human Services*] (GFGA)

OPA .... Oropharyngeal Airway (SAUS)

OPA .... Ortho-Phthaldehyde [*Organic chemistry*]

OPA .... Ortho-Propylaniline

OPA .... Other Procurement, Army (AABC)

OPA .... Output and Performance Analysis (HEAS)

OPA .... Output Plate Assembly (MCD)

OPA .... Ovarian Papillary Adenocarcinoma [*Oncology*]

OPA .... Overall Paid Attendance [*Sports*] (GOBB)

OPA .... Overall Pavments Agreement (SAUS)

OPA .... Overall Probability of Attack (DNAB)

OPA .... Overhead Precautionary Approach

OPA .... Overview Pac Attribute (SAUS)

OPAA .... Organophosphorous Acid Anhydrase [*An enzyme*]

OPAAER .... Archaeological Survey of Alberta. Occasional Papers (journ.) (SAUS)

OPAAS .... Optimum Aircraft Armament System (SAUS)

OPAAW .... Organization of Pan Asian-American Women (EA)

OPAB .... Abbottabad [*Pakistan*] [*ICAO location identifier*] (ICLI)

OPAC .... Online Public Access Catalog [*Silicon Valley Information Center - SVIC*] [*San Jose, CA*] [*Information service or system*] (IID)

Op A/C .... Operational Aircraft (SAUS)

OPAC .... Operation of Aircrafts (SAUS)

OPAC .... Operations Planning Advisory Committee (SAUS)

OPAC .... Overall Performance Appraisal Certification [*Environmental Protection Agency*] (GFGA)

OPAC .... Resource Centre, School of Lanark County, Algonquin College of Applied Arts & Technology, Perth, Ontario [*Library symbol*] [*National Library of Canada*] (NLC)

OPACK .... Operation Acknowledge [*Computer science*] (MHDI)

OPACS .... Office of Price Administration and Civilian Supply [*Name changed to Office of Price Administration*] [*World War II*]

OPACS .... Order Planning and Control System (MCD)

OPACT .... Organization of Professional Acting Coaches and Teachers (EA)

OPaD .... Diamond Shamrock Corp., Research Library, Painesville, OH [*Library symbol*] [*Library of Congress*] (LCLS)

OPADEC ...... Optical Partial Decoy (IAA)

OPADEC ...... Optical Particle Decoy

OPADR .... Operand Address [*Computer science*] (IAA)

OPAE .... Office of Program Analysis and Evaluation [*DoD*]

OPAEP .... Organisation des Pays Arabes Exportateurs de Petrole [*Organization of Arab Petroleum Exporting Countries*] (EAIO)

OPAFD7 ...... Allan Hancock Foundation. Occasional Papers (journ.) (SAUS)

OPA/FMOCCl... Orthophthalaldehyde/Fluorenylmethoxycarbonyl Chloride (SAUS)

OPAG .... Operations and Planning Group (SAUS)

Op AG .... Opinions of the Attorney General [*A publication*] (DLA)

OPAGREE.... Operational Agreement (DNAB)

OPAGY .... Operating Agency [*Military*]

OPAH .... Oil Pump Assembly Housing (MCD)

OPAI .... Paisley Branch, Bruce County Public Library, Ontario [*Library symbol*] [*National Library of Canada*] (NLC)

OPAIT .... Ontario Program for the Advancement of Industrial Technology (SAUS)

OPaL .... Lake Erie College, Painesville, OH [*Library symbol*] [*Library of Congress*] (LCLS)

OPAL .... Lakehead University, Thunder Bay, Ontario [*Library symbol*] [*National Library of Canada*] (NLC)

OPAL .... Ocean Process Analysis Laboratory [*University of New Hampshire*] [*Research center*] (RCD)

OPAL .... Older People with Active Lifestyles [*Lifestyle classification*]

OPAL .... Omni Purpose Apparatus for LEP (SAUS)

OPAL .... Oncovin [*Vincristine*], Prednisolone, Adriamycin, L-Asparaginase [*Antineoplastic drug regimen*]

OPAL .... One People of Australia League (SAUS)

OPAL .... Opal, Inc. [*NASDAQ symbol*] (SAG)

OPAL .... Operation Alert [*Designed to test ability to recover from an enemy attack*]

OPAL .... Operational Performance Analysis Language [*Computer science*]

OPAL .... Operation Plan Analysis Logic [*Search technology*]

OPAL .... Optical Platform Alignment Linkage

OPAL .... Order Processing Automated Line (SAUS)

OPAL .... Orientation Program in American Law [*of AALS*]

OPALE .... Faculty of Education, Lakehead University, Thunder Bay, Ontario [*Library symbol*] [*National Library of Canada*] (NLC)

OPALE .... French bibliographic database (SAUS)

OPALG .... Department of Geography, Lakehead University, Thunder Bay, Ontario [*Library symbol*] [*National Library of Canada*] (NLC)

OPALs.......... Older People with Active Lifestyles [*Lifestyle classification*]

Opals .... Older People with an Active Lifestyle [*Lifestyle classification*]

OPALS .... Optical Parallel Array Logic System (SAUS)

OpAmp........ Operational Amplifier (AAEL)

op amp........ Operational Amplifier (IDOE)

OP AMP ...... Operational Amplifier [*Computer science*]

OP/A/N/AF... Other Procurement, Army/Navy/Air Force (SAUS)

OPANAL...... Agency for the Prohibition of Nuclear Weapons in Latin America and the Caribbean (SAUS)

OPANAL....... Operations Analysis [*Navy*] (NG)

OPANAL....... Organismo para la Proscripcion de las Armas Nucleares en la America Latina [*Agency for the Prohibition of Nuclear Weapons in Latin America*] (EAIO)

OP&C.......... Operations Planning and Control (SAUS)

OP&CMIA... Operative Plasterers and Cement Masons International Association

OP & I .... Office of Patents and Inventions

OP & I .... Office of Publications and Information [*Department of Commerce*]

OP & PB ...... Oceanographic Plans and Policy Board (SAA)

OP & R........ Offset Printing and Reprographics [*A publication*] (DGA)

OPAP .... Operational Performance Acceptance Procedures (SAUS)

OPAPE .... Organisation Pan-Africaine de la Profession Enseignante [*All Africa Teachers' Organization*] (EAIO)

OPAQ .... Offer Parent-Adolescent Questionnaire [*Personality development test*] [*Psychology*]

OPAQUE...... Optical Atmospheric Quality in Europe (MCD)

OPAR .... Office of Policy Analysis and Review [*Environmental Protection Agency*] (GFGA)

OPAR .... Operation Plans Assessment Report [*Environmental science*] (COE)

OPAR .... Paris Public Library, Ontario [*Library symbol*] [*National Library of Canada*] (NLC)

Op Arch ...... Opuscula Archaeologica [*A publication*] (OCD)

OPAREA...... Operating Area (CAAL)

OPARI......... Occasional Publications. African and Afro-Amerian Research Institute. University of Texas, Austin (SAUS)

OPARS........ Optimum Path Aircraft Routing System (SAUS)

op art.......... Optical Art (ODBW)

OPAS .... Occupation Pensions Advisory Service (WDAA)

OPAS .... Operational Assignment (DA)

OPAS .... Operational Assistance [*United Nations Development Program*]

OPAS .... Operational Public Address System

OPAS .... Overpass [*Postal Service standard*] (OPSA)

OPASTCO.... Organization for the Promotion and Advancement of Small Telephone Companies (CGWS)

OPASTCO.... Organization for the Protection and Advancement of Small Telephone Companies (EA)

OPat........... Pataskala Public Library, Pataskala, OH [*Library symbol*] [*Library of Congress*] (LCLS)

OPATSS ...... Offshore Product Acceptance Tests Specification System (TIMI)

Op Att Gen... Opinions of the Attorneys-General [*United States*] [*A publication*] (DLA)

OPATTI .... Office de Promotion et d'Animation Touristique de Tahiti et ses Iles (EY)

Op Att'y Gen... Opinions of the Attorney General [*A publication*] (DLA)

Op Attys Gen... Opinions of the Attorneys-General [*United States*] [*A publication*] (DLA)

OPB .... Observation Preparation Branch (SAUS)

OPB .... Occupational Pensions Board [*British*] (DCTA)

OPB .... Office of Plans and Budget (SAUS)

OPB .... Office of the Publication Board [*Department of Commerce*]

OPB .... Open Bay [*Papua New Guinea*] [*Airport symbol*] (OAG)

OPB .... Oregon Public Broadcasting (SAUS)

OPB .... Other People's Butts [*Cigarette butts garnered from ash trays*] [*Slang*]
OPB .... Outpatient Basis [*Medicine*]
OPB .... Oxidizer Preburner (KSC)
OPB .... Pikangikum Band Library, Ontario [*Library symbol*] [*National Library of Canada*] (BIB)
OPBA .... Ontario Public Buyers Association (SAUS)
OPBAT .... Operation Bahamas, Antilles, and Turks [*Air Force*]
OPBCT .... Providence Bay Branch, Carnarvon Township Public Library, Ontario [*Library symbol*] [*National Library of Canada*] (NLC)
OPBDR........ Office of Program and Budget Development and Review [*Bureau of Apprenticeship and Training*] [*Department of Labor*]
OPBE .... Office of Planning, Budgeting, and Evaluation [*National Institute of Education*]
OPBG .... Bhagtanwala [*Pakistan*] [*ICAO location identifier*] (ICLI)
OPBL .... Bela [*Pakistan*] [*ICAO location identifier*] (ICLI)
Opble........... Operable (SAUS)
OPBMA ...... Ocean Pearl Button Manufacturers Association [*Defunct*]
OPBN .... Bannu [*Pakistan*] [*ICAO location identifier*] (ICLI)
OPBOV........ Oxidizer Preburner Oxidizer Valve (NASA)
OPBR .... Bahawalnagar [*Pakistan*] [*ICAO location identifier*] (ICLI)
OPBU .... Operating Budget
OPBW .... Bahawalpur [*Pakistan*] [*ICAO location identifier*] (ICLI)
OPC .... Committee on Ocean Processes and Climate (SAUS)
OPC .... Occult Papillary Carcinoma [*Oncology*]
OPC .... Ocean Policy Committee [*Marine science*] (MSC)
OPC .... Ocean Products Center [*Marine science*] (OSRA)
OPC .... Oculopalatocerebral [*Syndrome*] [*Medicine*] (DMAA)
OPC .... Odd Parity Check (SAUS)
OPC .... Office de la Protection du Consommateur [*Quebec, PQ*]
OPC .... Office of Peoples Counsel (SAUS)
OPC .... Office of Policy Coordination (LAIN)
OPC .... Office of Price Control [*World War II*]
OPC .... Office of Primary Concern [*DoD*]
OPC .... Office of Private Cooperation [*Department of State*]
OPC .... Office of Procurement and Contracts [*Department of Housing and Urban Development*] (GFGA)
OPC .... Office of Program Coordination (SAUS)
OPC .... Office of Public Communication (SAUS)
OPC .... Office of the Parliamentary Counsel (SAUS)
OPC .... Office of the Protective Commissioner [*Australia*]
OPC .... Office Percentage (SAUS)
OPC .... Ogren, Paul C., South Bend IN [*STAC*]
OPC .... Ohio Power Co. (SAUS)
OPC .... Oil Policy Committee [*Office of Emergency Preparedness*] [*Obsolete*]
OPC .... Old People's Center (GOBB)
OPC .... Oldsmobile Performance Chapter (EA)
OPC .... OLE [*Object Linking and Embedding*] for Process Control (ACII)
OPC .... Oligonucleotide Purification Cartridge [*Chromatography*]
OPC .... Olivetti Personal Computers
OPC .... One Pound Charge (MCD)
OPC .... Online Plotter Controller [*California Computer Products, Inc.*]
OPC .... Ontario Press Council (SAUS)
OPC .... Ontario Prevention Clearinghouse (SAUS)
OPC .... Open GL performance Characterization (SAUS)
OPC .... Open Printed Circuit (IAA)
OPC .... Open Promoter Complex [*Genetics*]
OPC .... Operated Preference Controls
OPC .... Operating Center (SAUS)
OPC .... Operation Code
Op C .... Operation Complete (SAUS)
OPC .... Operation Planning and Control (SAUS)
OPC .... Operations Code [*Army*] (IAA)
OPC .... Operations Control (IAA)
OPC .... Operator Position Controller [*Telecommunications*]
OPC .... Optical Particle Counter (PDAA)
OPC .... Optical Phase Conjugator [*LASER-aiming device*]
OPC .... Optical Photoconductor (PCM)
OPC .... Optical Photo Coupler
OPC .... Optical Propagation Conference (SAUS)
OPC .... Optical Proximity Correct (AAEL)
OPC .... Optional Calling (SAUS)
OPC .... Optional Calling Plans [*Telecommunications*] (TEL)
OPC .... Orange Pigment Cell
OPC .... Ordinary Portland Cement
OPC .... Ordnance Procurement Center [*Army*]
OPC .... Organic Photoconducting Cartridge (RALS)
OPC .... Organic Photoconductor
OPC .... Organizational Point of Contact (SAUS)
OPC .... Organization Postcode (SAUS)
OPC .... Origination Point Code (SAUS)
OPC .... Orion Pictures Corporation (SAUS)
OPC .... Other Parks Corrector (SAUS)
OPC .... Other Project Costs (ABAC)
OPC .... Outer Passenger Cabin
OPC .... Outer Proliferative Center [*Brain anatomy*]
opc.............. Out of Print and Cancelled [*Publishing*] (WDMC)
OPC .... Out of Print, Canceled [*Publishing*]
OPC .... Outpatient Catheterization [*Medicine*] (MELL)
OPC .... Outpatient Clinic [*Medicine*]
OPC .... Outpatient Psychiatric Care [*Health insurance*] (GHCT)
OPC .... Output Control (SAUS)
OPC .... Output Punched Card (SAUS)
OPC .... Ovamboland Peoples Congress (SAUS)
OPC .... Overall Performance Category

OPC .... Overseas Press Club of America (EA)
OPC .... Ownership Purpose and Condition Code [*Navy*] (DNAB)
OPC .... Oxford Pocket Classics [*A publication*] (ROG)
OPC .... Oxypneumocardiogram [*Cardiology*] (DAVI)
OPC .... Perth Courier, Ontario [*Library symbol*] [*National Library of Canada*] (NLC)
OPC .... QC Optics [*AMEX symbol*] (SAG)
OPCA .... Occupational Program Consultants Association (EA)
OPCA .... Olivopontocerebellar Atrophy [*Neurology*]
OPCA .... Opium Poppy Control Act of 1942
OPCA .... Ornamental Plant Collection Association (SAUS)
OPCA .... Ornamental Plant Collectors Association (SAUS)
OPCA .... Overseas Press Club of America (WDAA)
OP-CAL .... Operation California (EA)
Op Cal Att'y Gen... Opinions of the Attorney General of California [*A publication*] (DLA)
OPCC .... Office of Preschool and Child Care [*Victoria, Australia*]
OPCC .... Offutt Air Force Base Processing and Correlation Center (MCD)
OPCC .... Offutt Processing and Correlation Center (SAUS)
OPCC .... Optical Product Code Council (EA)
OPCC .... Outpatient Psychiatric Care Coverage
Op CCCG ..... Opinion, Chief Counsel, United States Coast Guard [*A publication*] (DLA)
OP-CCK .... Octapeptide of Cholecystokinin (SAUS)
OPCD .... Operational Planning and Coordination Directorate (SAUS)
OPCE .... Operator Control Element [*Computer science*] (IBMDP)
OPCEN........ Operations Center [*INTELSAT*]
OPC/ESA..... Operations, Planning & Control/ESA (SAUS)
OPCG .... Organic Polymer Crystal Growth (SAUS)
OPCG .... Original Print Collectors Group (EA)
OPCGE........ Organic/Polymer Crystal Growth Experiment (SSD)
OPCGF........ Organic/Polymer Crystal Growth Facility (SSD)
OPCH .... Chitral [*Pakistan*] [*ICAO location identifier*] (ICLI)
op cit .... Opere Citato [*In the work cited*] [*Latin*] (WDMC)
OP CIT .... Opere Citato [*In the Work Cited*] [*Latin*]
OPCIT .... Opus Citatum (IAA)
OPCL .... Chilas [*Pakistan*] [*ICAO location identifier*] (ICLI)
OPCM .... Operative Plasterers and Cement Masons International Association of the US and Canada
OPC/MCA..... Optical Particle Counter/Multi-Channel Analyzer (SAUS)
OPCMIA....... Operative Plasterers and Cement Masons International Association of US and Canada (EA)
OPCML .... Township of Muskoka Lakes Public Library Board, Port Carling, Ontario [*Library symbol*] [*National Library of Canada*] (BIB)
OPCNM .... Organ Pipe Cactus National Monument (SAUS)
OPCO .... Operating Company (SAUS)
OPCO .... Operating Plan Change Orders [*Coast Guard publication*]
OPCO .... Outside Production Consignment Order
OPCOCM Symposium... Symposium on the Occurrence, Prediction and Control of Outbursts in Coal Mines (SAUS)
OP-COD .... Operating Code [*Computer science*]
Opcode .... Operating Code [*Computer science*] (ITCA)
OPCODE...... Operational Code (SAUS)
op code .... Operation Code (IDOE)
OPCODE...... Operations Code [*Army*] (AABC)
O/P Code ..... Ownership Purpose Code (SAUS)
OP-COM...... Opera-Comique [*Comic Opera*] [*Music*]
OPCOM .... Operational Command [*Military*] (MCD)
OP-COM...... Operations-Communications
OPCOM .... Operator Communications (SAUS)
op-com .... Optical Communication (MED)
OPCOM .... Optical Communications (ACAE)
OPCOMCTR... Operational Command Center [*Navy*] (NVT)
OPCOM System... Operator Communication System (SAUS)
OPCON........ Operational Control [*Army*] (NVT)
OPCON........ Operation and Control (SAUS)
OPCON........ Operation Control [*Military*] (VNW)
OPCON........ Operations and Control System (IAA)
OPCON........ Operator's Console
OPCON........ Optimizing Control [*Military*]
OPCONCEN... Operational Control Center [*Navy*]
OPCONCTR... Operational Control Center [*Navy*] (NVT)
OPCONCTR... Operations Control Center [*Navy*]
OPCON System... Operation and Control System (SAUS)
OPCOSAL..... Optimum Coordinated Shipboard [*or Shorebased*] Allowance List
OPCPL .... Port Colborne Public Library, Ontario [*Library symbol*] [*National Library of Canada*] (NLC)
OPCR .... Chachro [*Pakistan*] [*ICAO location identifier*] (ICLI)
OPCR .... One-Pass Cold-Rolled [*Steel sheets*]
OPCR .... Original Program Clock Reference (SAUS)
OPCS .... Office of Population Census and Surveys [*British*] (ECON)
OPCS .... Office of Population Censuses and Surveys [*Department of Employment*] [*British*]
OPCS .... Operational Planning and Control System [*Department of Labor*] (OICC)
OPCT .... Chirat [*Pakistan*] [*ICAO location identifier*] (ICLI)
OPCTR .... Operation Counter (IAA)
OPCTR .... Operations Center [*Military*]
OPCV .... Office of Planning, Control, and Validation [*Social Security Administration*]
OPCW .... Office of Petroleum Coordination for War [*New Deal*]
OPCW .... Organization for the Prohibition of Chemical Weapons [*Proposed, 1992*]
OPD .... Audit Programs Division (AAGC)
OPD .... Chemical Marketing Reporter (journ.) (SAUS)

OPD	Delayed Opening
OPD	Observed Position Data
OPD	Obstetric Prediabetic [*Medicine*] (DMAA)
OPD	Office of Policy Development [*Executive Office of the President*]
OPD	Office of Program Development [*Environmental Protection Agency*] (GFGA)
OPD	Office of Public Defender (SAUS)
OPD	Office Product Division (ELAL)
OPD	Office Products Division (SAUS)
OPD	Officer Personnel Directorate [*Army*]
OPD	Officer Professional Development [*Military*] (INF)
OPD	Ohio College of Podiatric Medicine, Cleveland, OH [*OCLC symbol*] (OCLC)
OPD	One Per Desk (NITA)
OPD	Open Distributed Processing [*Computer science*] (TELE)
OPD	Opened [*Stock exchange term*] (SPSG)
OPD	Opening Delayed (SAUS)
OPD	Opening Posterior Digestive [*Gland*]
OPD	Operand [*Computer science*]
OPD	Operational Programming Department [*Telecommunications*] (TEL)
OPD	Operations Division [*War Department General Staff*] [*World War II*]
OPD	Operations Planning Division [*Manned Spacecraft Center*]
OPD	O-Phenylenediamine (SAUS)
OPD	Optical Particle Detector [*for evaluating film quality*]
OPD	Optical Path Difference (MCD)
OPD	Optical Phase Distortion (PDAA)
OPD	Optical Proximity Detector
OPD	Oral and Pharyngeal Development [*Section*] [*National Institute of Dental Research*]
OPD	Orbiting Propellant Depot [*NASA*]
OPD	Original Pack Dispensing [*For drugs*] [*Packaging*]
OPD	Original Point of Distribution (SAUS)
OPD	Ortho-Phenylenediamine [*Organic chemistry*]
OPD	'Osef Piskei Din shel ha-Rabanut ha-Rashit le-'Erets Yisrael (BJA)
OPD	Oto-Palato-Digital [*Syndrome*]
OPD	Outpatient Department [*or Dispensary*] [*Medicine*]
OPD	Outpatient Dispensary [*Medicine*] (DMAA)
OPD	Output Driver (SAUS)
OPD	Overall Program Design (OICC)
OPD	Overcurrent Protective Device (ELAL)
O/PD	Overpaid (ROG)
OPD	Over Pin Diameter (SAUS)
OPD	Overseas Policy Defence Committee [*British*]
OPD	Oxford Paperback Dictionary [*A publication*]
OPD	Port Dover Centennial Public Library, Ontario [*Library symbol*] [*National Library of Canada*] (NLC)
OPDAC	Optical Data Converter (NOAA)
OPDAG	Original Paper Doll Artists Guild (EA)
OPDAR	Optical Detection and Ranging
OPDAR	Optical Direction and Ranging (SAUS)
OPDAR	Optical Radar (SAUS)
OPDARS	Optical Detection and Ranging System (IAA)
OPDAT	Office of Professional Development and Training (SAUS)
OPDATS	Operational Performance Data System
OPDB	Dalbandin [*Pakistan*] [*ICAO location identifier*] (ICLI)
OPDC	Overseas Policy Defence Committee [*British*] (DI)
OPDD	Dadu [*Pakistan*] [*ICAO location identifier*] (ICLI)
OPDD	Operational Plan Data Document [*Military*] (AFM)
OPDD	Overall Plant Design Description (SAUS)
O,p-DDD	Ortho, Para-Dichloro-Diphenyldichlorethane [*Mitotane*] [*Antineoplastic drug regimen*] (DAVI)
OPDEC	Operational Deception [*Navy*] (NVT)
OPDEF	Operational Defect (SAUS)
OPDEFSYS...	Operational Defects System (SAUS)
OPDEM	Operational Demand (SAUS)
OpDent	Operative Dentistry (BABM)
Opdent	Operative Dentistry (DAVI)
OPDESC	Operation Description (SAUS)
OPDET	Operational Detachment (MCD)
OPDEVFOR...	Operational Development Forces
OPDF	Omo Peoples Democratic Front (SAUS)
OPDF	Output Data Funnel (SAUS)
OPDG	Dera Ghazi Khan [*Pakistan*] [*ICAO location identifier*] (ICLI)
OPDG	Ocular Plethysmodynamography (DB)
OPD Gland...	Opening of Posterior Digestive Gland (SAUS)
OPDI	Dera Ismail Khan [*Pakistan*] [*ICAO location identifier*] (ICLI)
OPDI	Operator Please Deliver Immediately
OP DIAP	Open Diapason [*Organ stop*] [*Music*]
OPDIF	Operational Planning Identification File [*Military*]
OPDIN	Ocean Pollution Data and Information Network [*Washington, DC*] [*Department of Commerce*] (GRD)
OPDIN	Ocean Pollution Data Center [*Marine science*] (OSRA)
OPDIR	Operational Directive (SAUS)
OP DIV	Operations/Air Intelligence Photography Division (DNAB)
OPDK	Daharki [*Pakistan*] [*ICAO location identifier*] (ICLI)
OPDL	Office of Production and Defense Lending [*Department of the Treasury*]
OPDO	Oromo People's Democratic Organization [*Ethiopia*] [*Political party*] (EY)
OPDOC	Operational Documentation [*Military*]
OPDP	Officer Professional Development Program [*Pronounced "opey-dopey"*] [*Canadian Navy*]
OPDPE	Office of Policy Development Planning and Evaluation [*Pronounced "opey dopey"*] [*NIMH*]
OPDR	Office of Primary Development Responsibility (AFM)
OPDS	Occupant Position Detection System [*Automotive safety systems*]
OPDS	Office Professional Development System (MCD)
OPDS	Officer Professional Development Seminar (SAUS)
OPDS	Offshore Petroleum Distribution System
OPDS	Overall Plant Design Specification (SAUS)
OPD Syndrome...	Oto-Palato-Digital Syndrome (SAUS)
OPDU	Operation Protocol Data Unit [*Telecommunications*] (OSI)
OPDU	Powassan and District Union Public Library, Powassan, Ontario [*Library symbol*] [*National Library of Canada*] (NLC)
OPDUA........	Operative Painters amd Decorators' Union of Australia
OPD WDGS...	Operations Division, War Department General Staff [*World War II*]
OPE	Eldorado Nuclear Ltd., Port Hope, Ontario [*Library symbol*] [*National Library of Canada*] (NLC)
OPE	Office of Planning and Environment (ABAC)
OPE	Office of Planning and Evaluation [*Office of Personnel Management*] (GRD)
OPE	Office of Policy Evaluation [*Nuclear energy*] (NRCH)
OPE	Office of Postsecondary Education [*Department of Education*] (GFGA)
OPE	Office of Program Eligibility (AAGC)
OPE	Office of Program Evaluation [*Office of Policy, Evaluation, and Research*] [*Department of Labor*]
OPE	Olivetti Peripheral Equipment (SAUS)
OPE	One-Particle Exchange (SAUS)
OPE	One-Pion Exchange [*Nuclear energy*]
OPE	Open Point Expanding [*Bullet*] (DICI)
OPE	Operational Planning Estimate
OPE	Operational Proficiency Examination (SAUS)
OPE	Operations Project Engineer [*NASA*] (KSC)
OPE	Optical Pointing Error
OPE	Optical-Probe Experiment [*Giotto probe of Halley's comet*] [*European Space Agency*]
OPE	Optimized Processing Element
OPE	Oral Proficiency Examination (SAUS)
OPE	Orbiting Primate Experiment (MCD)
OPE	Oregon, Pacific & Eastern Railway Co. [*AAR code*]
OPE	Other Plant Equipment [*DoD*]
OPE	Other Project Element (NASA)
OPE	Outer Planets Explorer [*NASA*]
OPE	Oxygen Plasma Etching (SAUS)
OPE	Societe 3S Aviation (Aerope) [*France*] [*ICAO designator*] (FAAC)
OPE	Topeka, KS [*Location identifier*] [*FAA*] (FAAL)
OPEAA	Outdoor Power Equipment Aftermarket Association (EA)
OPEB	Bruce County Public Library, Port Elgin, Ontario [*Library symbol*] [*National Library of Canada*] (NLC)
OPEC	Oil Producers' Economic Cartel (NADA)
OPEC	Oil Producers Equipment (SAUS)
OPEC	One-Pion Exchange Contribution (SAUS)
Opec	Organisation of Petroleum Exporting Countries (SAUS)
OPEC	Organization of Petroleum Exporting Countries (NADA)
OPECNA	OPEC [*Organization of Petroleum Exporting Countries*] News Agency [*See also APOPEC*] [*Vienna, Austria*] (EAIO)
OPECNA	Organization of Petroleum Exporting Countries News Agency (SAUS)
OPECO	Operations Coordinator [*Marine science*] (MSC)
OP-ED	Opinion-Editorial (SAUS)
OP-ED	Opposite Editorial Page [*in a newspaper*] [*Usually consists of opinion columns by various guest writers or syndicated columnists*]
Op-Ed.........	Opposite the Editorial (ADWA)
op ed	Opposite - the Editorial Page [*Newspapers*] (WDMC)
OPED	Other Pay Entry Date [*Army*] (AABC)
OPED	Point Edward Public Library, Ontario [*Library symbol*] [*National Library of Canada*] (NLC)
OPEDA	Organization of Professional Employees of the United States Department of Agriculture (EA)
OPEDA	Outdoor Power Equipment Distributors Association (EA)
OPEDC	Overseas Private Enterprise Development Corp. [*Proposed successor to Agency for International Development*]
OPeeO	Ohio Valley Local District Free Public Library, Peebles Branch, Peebles, OH [*Library symbol*] [*Library of Congress*] (LCLS)
OPEF	Overall Plume Enhancement Factor [*Space Shuttle*] [*NASA*]
OPEI...........	Office of Public Education and Information [*NASA*]
OPEI...........	Outdoor Power Equipment Institute (EA)
OPEI...........	Outdoor Power Equipment Institute, Inc.
OPEIU	Office and Professional Employees International Union (EA)
OPE Language...	Office Procedures by Example Language (SAUS)
OPEM..........	One-Pion Exchange Model [*Nuclear energy*]
OPEM..........	Pembroke Public Library, Ontario [*Library symbol*] [*National Library of Canada*] (NLC)
OPEMA	Oilfield Production Equipment Manufacturers Association [*Defunct*] (EA)
OPEMAC	Upper Ottawa Valley Campus Resource Centre, Algonquin College, Pembroke, Ontario [*Library symbol*] [*National Library of Canada*] (NLC)
OPEMO	Ottawa Valley Historical Society, Pembroke, Ontario [*Library symbol*] [*National Library of Canada*] (BIB)
OPEN	Fund for an Open Society (EA)
OPEN	Ocean Production Enhancement Network (SAUS)
OPen	Olympic Peninsula (SAUS)
OPEN	Oncovin, Prednisone, Etopside, Mitoxantrone [*Antineoplastic drug*] (CDI)
OPEN	Online Public Education Network
OPEN	Open Environment Corp. [*NASDAQ symbol*] (SAG)
OPEN	Opening (SAUS)
OPEN	Open Protocol Enhanced Network [*Northern Telecom communications network*] [*Canada*]

OPEN	Open ROUTE Network [*NASDAQ symbol*] [*Formerly, Proteon, Inc.*]
OPEN	Optical Pan-European Network (SAUS)
OPEN	Organisation des Producteurs d'Energie Nucleaire [*Paris, France*] (EAIO)
OPEN	Origins of Plasma in the Earth's Neighborhood [*Ad Hoc Advisory Committee terminated, 1981*]
OPEN	Penetanguishene Public Library, Ontario [*Library symbol*] [*National Library of Canada*] (BIB)
OPENAH	Operational Evaluation of Armed Helicopters (MCD)
OPENE	Ecole Secondaire le Caron, Penetanguishene, Ontario [*Library symbol*] [*National Library of Canada*] (BIB)
OPENGL	Open Graphics Language (SAUS)
OPENHCI	Open Host Controller Interface (SAUS)
OPENM	Mental Health Centre, Penetanguishene, Ontario [*Library symbol*] [*National Library of Canada*] (NLC)
OpenMkt	Open Market, Inc. [*Associated Press*] (SAG)
OpenPln	Open Plan Systems, Inc. [*Associated Press*] (SAG)
Open Syst Softw	Open Systems and Software (SAUS)
OpenTxt	Open Text Corp. [*Associated Press*] (SAG)
OpenVis	OpenVision Technologies, Inc. [*Associated Press*] (SAG)
OpenVMS	Open Virtual Memory System (SAUS)
OPEO	Oakland-Pontiac Enthusiast Organization (EA)
OPEO	Octylphenol Polyethoxylate [*Organic chemistry*]
OPEOS	Outside Plant Planning, Engineering, and Construction Operations System (MCD)
OPEP	One-Pion Exchange Potential (SAUS)
OPEP	Orbital-Plane Experiment Package [*NASA*]
OPEPB	Eastern Pentecostal Bible College, Peterborough, Ontario [*Library symbol*] [*National Library of Canada*] (NLC)
OPER	Coin Phones, Inc. (SAUS)
OPER	Office of Policy and Economic Research [*Federal Home Loan Bank Board*] [*Washington, DC*] (GRD)
OPER	Office of Policy, Evaluation, and Research [*Employment and Training Administration*] [*Department of Labor*]
OPer	Old Persian [*Language*] (BARN)
OPER	Operating [*Automotive engineering*]
oper	Operation (DD)
OPER	Operation [*or Operational*] (KSC)
Oper	Operation (TBD)
OPER	Operations, Operate, Operator (SAUS)
OPER	Operator
OPERA	Operational Analysis (IAA)
OPERA	Ordnance Pulses Experimental Research Assembly [*Nuclear reactor*]
OPERA	Out-of-Pile Expulsion and Reentry Apparatus [*Nuclear energy*]
OPERA	Outpatient Endometrial Resection and Ablation [*Medicine*]
OPERATORS	Optimization Program for Economical Remote Trunk Arrangement and TSPS [*Traffic Service Positions System*] Operator Arrangements [*Telecommunications*] (TEL)
OPERG	Operating (MDG)
Oper Geogr	Operational Geographer (SAUS)
Oper Manage Rev	Operations Management Review (SAUS)
Oper Off	Operations Officer (TBD)
O-PERS	Officer Personnel Office (DNAB)
OPers	Old Persian [*Language*] (BARN)
OPERSCRS	Officer Personnel Course [*Air Force*]
OPersLex	Old Persian Grammar Texts Lexicon [*A publication*] (BJA)
OPERSUN	Operation Planning and Execution System for Railway Unified Network (SAUS)
Oper Syst Netw	Operating Systems and Networks (SAUS)
OPERUN	Operation Planning and Execution System for Railway Unified Network (PDAA)
OPES	Centre de Documentation, Ecole Secondaire de Plantagenet [*Documentation Centre, Plantagenet Secondary School*], Ontario [*Library symbol*] [*National Library of Canada*] (BIB)
OPEST	Oil Protection of Emissions System Test [*Lubricants*]
OPET	Organization, Personnel Equipment and Training [*Group*]
OPET	Oriented Polyester (SAUS)
OPET	Oriented Polyethylene Terephthalate [*Organic chemistry*]
OPET	Trent University, Peterborough, Ontario [*Library symbol*] [*National Library of Canada*] (NLC)
OPETA	Trent University Archives, Peterborough, Ontario [*Library symbol*] [*National Library of Canada*] (NLC)
OPETAL	Trent Audio Library Services, Trent University, Peterborough, Ontario [*Library symbol*] [*National Library of Canada*] (NLC)
OPETC	Trent Canal Office, Peterborough, Ontario [*Library symbol*] [*National Library of Canada*] (BIB)
OPETCG	Canadian General Electric Co. Ltd., Peterborough, Ontario [*Library symbol*] [*National Library of Canada*] (NLC)
OPETCM	Peterborough Centennial Museum and Archives, Ontario [*Library symbol*] [*National Library of Canada*] (BIB)
OPETHS	Hutchison House Museum, Peterborough Historical Society, Ontario [*Library symbol*] [*National Library of Canada*] (BIB)
OPETM	Map Library, Trent University, Peterborough, Ontario [*Library symbol*] [*National Library of Canada*] (NLC)
OPETP	Peterborough Public Library, Ontario [*Library symbol*] [*National Library of Canada*] (NLC)
OPETSF	Brealy Library, Sir Sandford Fleming College, Peterborough, Ontario [*Library symbol*] [*National Library of Canada*] (NLC)
OPETSFD	Daniel Library, Sir Sandford Fleming College, Peterborough, Ontario [*Library symbol*] [*National Library of Canada*] (BIB)
OPEV	Petawawa Village and Township Union Public Library, Ontario [*Library symbol*] [*National Library of Canada*] (NLC)
OPEVAL	Operational Evaluation [*Navy*] (NG)
OPEX	Operational and Executive (SAUS)
OPEX	Operational Executive (CIST)
OPEX	Operational, Executive, and Administrative Personnel Program [*United Nations*]
OPEX	Operational Experience (SAUS)
OPEX	Operational Extension
OPF	Miami, FL [*Location identifier*] [*FAA*] (FAAL)
OPf	Office of Promotion and Tourism (SAUS)
OPF	Official Personnel File (MCD)
OPF	Official Personnel Folder [*Military*]
OPF	One-Piece Folder [*Publishing*] (WDMC)
OPF	Open-Pore Foam [*Plastic*]
OPF	Operations Flight [*Military*]
OPF	Optical Propagation Facility
OPF	Orbiter Processing Facility [*NASA*] (NASA)
OPF	Osmium Potassium Ferrocyanide (SAUS)
OPF	Output Filter (SAUS)
OPF	Overseas Project Fund [*British Overseas Trade Board*] (DS)
OPFA	Faisalabad [*Pakistan*] [*ICAO location identifier*] (ICLI)
OPFAC	Operating Facilities [*Coast Guard publication*]
OPFAC	Operational Facility (RDA)
OPFAD	Outer-Perimeter Fleet Air Defense
OPFAEI	Freshwater Biological Association. Occasional Publication (journ.) (SAUS)
OPFC	Hinchinbrooke Public Library, Frontenac County Library, Parkham, Ontario [*Library symbol*] [*National Library of Canada*] (BIB)
OPFC	Orbiter Preflight Checklist [*NASA*] (MCD)
OPFCA	Ornamental Pool and Fountain Constructors Association [*British*] (DBA)
OPFCDIN	Great Britain. Forestry Commission. Occasional Paper (journ.) (SAUS)
OPFCO	Operational Program Functional Checkout (MCD)
OPFET	Optical Field-Effect Transistor (SAUS)
OPFI	Office of Program and Fiscal Integrity (USGC)
OPFM	Outlet Plenum Feature Model [*Nuclear energy*] (NRCH)
OPFOR	Opportunity to Confront the Best Opposing Force [*Army*] (INF)
OPFOR	Opposing Force [*Military*] (INF)
OpFor	Opposing Force
OPFOR	Opposing Force Program (SAUS)
OPFOR	Opposition Force (SAUS)
OPFRC	Clarendon-Miller Branch, Frontenac County Library, Plevna, Ontario [*Library symbol*] [*National Library of Canada*] (NLC)
OPFT	Other than Permanent Full-Time (GFGA)
OPFTE	Other than Permanent Full-Time Equivalent (GFGA)
OPG	Ocular Pneumoplethysmography (DB)
OPG	Oculoplethysmograph [*Instrumentation*]
OPG	Office Of Global Programs [*Marine science*] (OSRA)
OPG	Office of the Postmaster General [*Obsolete*]
O Pg	Old Portuguese (SAUS)
OPG	Opening
OPG	Operating
OPG	Operational Performance Goals
OPG	Operational Planning Grant (OICC)
OPG	Operations Planning Group [*Military*]
OPG	Original Proof Gallon
OPG	Outside Production Group
OPG	Overseas Products Group [*Department of Trade*] [*British*]
OPG	Overseas Project Group (SAUS)
OPG	Oxalate, Peroxide and Gluconic Acid (SAUS)
OPG	Oxypolygelatin [*Plasma extender*]
OPGA	Ohio Personnel and Guidance Association (SAUS)
OPGA	Oregon Personnel and Guidance Association (SAUS)
OPGA	Outpatient General Anesthesia (MELL)
Op GA Att'y Gen	Opinions of the Attorney General of Georgia [*A publication*] (DLA)
OPG/CPA	Oculoplethysmography/Carotid Phonoangiography [*Medicine*] (DAVI)
Op GCT	Opinion, General Counsel, United States Treasury Department [*A publication*] (DLA)
OPGD	Gwadar [*Pakistan*] [*ICAO location identifier*] (ICLI)
OPGE	OEEC [*Organization for European Economic Cooperation*] Petroleum Industry Emergency Group (NATG)
OPGEN	Operation Plan Generation (SAUS)
OPGEN	Operations General Message (SAUS)
OP/GSA	Office of Preparedness, General Services Administration [*Later, Federal Preparedness Agency*]
OPGSX	Oppenheimer Gold & Spl. Minerals [*Mutual fund ticker symbol*] (SG)
OPGT	Gilgit [*Pakistan*] [*ICAO location identifier*] (ICLI)
OPGT	Outer Planets Grand Tour [*NASA*]
OPGUID	Optimum Guidance [*Technique*] (NASA)
OPGW	Optical Groundwire [*Telecommunications*] (TSSD)
OPH	Obliterative Pulmonary Hypertension [*Medicine*]
OPH	Office Phone (SAUS)
OPH	Old Parliamentary Hand [*Political*] [*British*]
OPh	Old Phoenician (BJA)
OPH	Operational Propellant Handling [*NASA*] (AAG)
oph	Ophicleide (WDAA)
OPH	Ophicleide [*Musical instrument*]
Oph	Ophiuchus [*Constellation*]
OPH	Ophthalmodynamometry [*Ophthalmology*]
OPH	Ophthalmolgist
OPH	Ophthalmology [*or Ophthalmoscopy*]
OPH	[*The*] Ophthalmoscope [*London*] [*A publication*] (ROG)
Oph	Ophthalmoscope [*or Ophthalmoscopic*] [*Ophthalmology*] (DAVI)
OPH	Ophthalmoscopic (SAUS)
OPH	Opposite Hand [*Technical drawings*]
OPH	Organophosphorus Hydrolase [*An enzyme*]

OPH .... Public Library, Port Hope, Ontario [*Library symbol*] [*National Library of Canada*] (NLC)
OPHA .... Ontario Public Health Association (SAUS)
OPHC .... Office of Prepaid Health Care [*Department of Health and Human Services*] (GFGA)
Oph D .... Doctor of Ophthalmology
OPHELIOS.... Optronic Passive Highly-sensitive Light IR Optical Sensor (SAUS)
OPHF .... Orbital Polarized Hartree-Fock [*Atomic physics*]
Ophi .... Ophiuchus [*Constellation*]
ophidiol .... ophidiologist (SAUS)
ophidiol .... ophtidiology (SAUS)
OPHIR .... Organic Power and Heat Industrial Reactor
OPHM .... OraPharma, Inc. [*NASDAQ symbol*] (SG)
OPhn .... Orpheon [*Record label*] [*Poland*]
OPHQ .... Karachi [*Pakistan*] [*ICAO location identifier*] (ICLI)
OPHR .... Olympic Project for Human Rights
Op Hrs .... Operation Hours (DA)
OPHS .... Office of Public Health and Science
OPHS .... Operational Propellant Handling System [*NASA*] (AAG)
OPHT .... Ophthalmic
OPHTH .... Ophthalmology (AABC)
OPHTHAL..... Ophthalmology
Ophthal........ Ophthalmoscope (SAUS)
OphtImg....... Ophthalmic Imaging Systems [*Associated Press*] (SAG)
OPHTS .... Operational Propellant Handling Test Site [*NASA*] (AAG)
OPHWA........ Nuclear Products Department, Westinghouse Canada, Inc., Port Hope, Ontario [*Library symbol*] [*National Library of Canada*] (NLC)
OPi.............. Flesh Public Library, Piqua, OH [*Library symbol*] [*Library of Congress*] (LCLS)
OPI.............. Oculoparalytic Illusion [*Ophthalmology*]
OPI.............. Office of Planning and Integration (ABAC)
OPI.............. Office of Primary Interest
OPI.............. Office of Programs Integration [*Energy Research and Development Administration*]
OPI.............. Office of Protective Intelligence (SAUS)
OPI.............. Office of Public Information [*NASA*]
OPI.............. Office of Public Information [*UNESCO*]
OPI.............. Office of Public Inquiry (SAUS)
OPI.............. Off-Site Production Inspection (AAG)
OPI.............. Ogden Projects (SAUS)
OPI.............. Oil Patch Group, Inc. [*Toronto Stock Exchange symbol*]
OPI.............. Oil Pressure Indicator
OPI.............. Omnibus Personality Inventory [*Psychology*]
OPI.............. One Person's Impact [*An association*] (EA)
OPI.............. Open for Public Inspection [*Patent applications*]
OPI.............. Open Information Interchange (SAUS)
OPI.............. Open Prepress Interface [*Computer science*] (PCM)
OPI.............. Open Prepress Standard (SAUS)
OPI.............. Open Protocol Interface [*Telecommunications*]
OPI.............. Operator Interface (SAUS)
OPI.............. Optical Publishing, Inc. [*Information service or system*] (IID)
OPI.............. Orbital Position Indicator
OPI.............. Orbiter Payload Interface (ACAE)
OPI.............. Orbiter Payload Interrogator [*NASA*] (MCD)
OPI.............. Ordnance Procedure Instrumentations (AAG)
OPI.............. Ordnance Procurement Instructions [*Army*]
OPI.............. Organophosphate Insecticide
OPI.............. Other Party Identifier (SAUS)
OPI.............. Output Productivity Index
OPI.............. Outside Procurement [or Purchase] Inspection (AAG)
OPI.............. Outside Production Inspection (SAUS)
OPI.............. Outside Purchase Inspection (SAUS)
OPI.............. Overall Performance Index [*Finance*]
OPI.............. Picton Public Library, Ontario [*Library symbol*] [*National Library of Canada*] (NLC)
OPIA .... Opto-Precision Instruments Association (NTPA)
OPIAT .... Opiates [*Chemical dependency*] [*Pharmacology*] (DAVI)
OPIC .... Oficina Permanente Internacional de la Carne [*Permanent International Meat Office*] (EAIO)
OPIC .... Open Programmable Interrupt Controller (SAUS)
OPIC .... Overseas Private Investment Corp. [*US International Development Cooperatio n Agency*] [*Washington, DC*]
OPIC .... Overseas Processing and Interpretation Center (SAUS)
OPIC .... Pickering Public Library, Ontario [*Library symbol*] [*National Library of Canada*] (NLC)
OPID .... Operational Procedures Interface Document (MCD)
OPIDF......... Operational Planning Identification File (MCD)
OPIDN......... Organophosphate Induced Delayed Neural Toxicity
OPiE........... Edison State Community College, Piqua, OH [*Library symbol*] [*Library of Congress*] (LCLS)
OPIE........... Ohio Program of Intensive English (EDAC)
OPIET.......... Eco-Tec Ltd., Pickering, Ontario [*Library symbol*] [*National Library of Canada*] (NLC)
OPIEW .... Older People in Europe Week (WDAA)
OPIG .... Picton Gazette, Ontario [*Library symbol*] [*National Library of Canada*] (NLC)
OPIL........... Opalescent Indicating Light
Op III Att'y Gen... Illinois Attorney General's Opinion [*A publication*] (DLA)
Op III Atty Gen... Illinois Attorney Generals Opinion (journ.) (SAUS)
OPIM .... Operations & Information Management (SAUS)
OPIM .... Order Processing and Inventory Monitoring [*Computer science*]
OPIM .... Other Potentially Infectious Material (AMHC)
Opin............ Opinions of the Attorneys-General [*United States*] [*A publication*] (DLA)

Opinc........... Options Income (BARN)
OPINDOC .... Operational Indoctrination (ACAE)
OPINE .... Operations in a Nuclear Environment [*DoD*]
Opine .... Option Income [*Business term*]
OPINM......... North Marysburgh Museum, Picton, Ontario [*Library symbol*] [*National Library of Canada*] (BIB)
OpinRsh....... Opinion Research Corp. [*Associated Press*] (SAG)
OPINS .... Oakland Planning Information System (SAUS)
OPINT......... Optical Intelligence
OPINTEL ..... Operational Intelligence
OPIO .... Office of Policy, Integration and Outreach (SAUS)
OPIR .... Office of Program and Integrity Reviews (SAUS)
OPIRI .... Osaka Prefectural Industrial Research Institute (SAUS)
OPIRL .... Operator Interface Rolling Loop
OPIS .... Operational Priority Indicating System (NATG)
opis .... opisometer (SAUS)
OPIS .... Orbiter Prime Item Specification [*NASA*] (NASA)
OPIS .... Pelee Island Public Library, Ontario [*Library symbol*] [*National Library of Canada*] (NLC)
OP(IT)......... Operation Overlord Preparations, Inland Transport [*World War II*]
OPIT........... Operator Interface Table (MCD)
OPIT........... Oxide-Powder-in-Tube
OPIVITA...... Outpatient Intravenous Infusion Therapy Association (NTPA)
OPiWU........ Wright State University, Piqua Branch Campus, Piqua, OH [*Library symbol*] [*Library of Congress*] (LCLS)
OPJ............. Ohio Power 8.16% Jr Sub Debs [*NYSE symbol*] (TTSB)
OPJA........... Jacobabad [*Pakistan*] [*ICAO location identifier*] (ICLI)
Op JAGAF ... Opinion, Judge Advocate General, United States Air Force [*A publication*] (DLA)
Op JAGN...... Opinion, Judge Advocate General, United States Navy [*A publication*] (DLA)
OPJC........... Jacobabad [*Pakistan*] [*ICAO location identifier*] (ICLI)
OPJI........... Jiwani [*Pakistan*] [*ICAO location identifier*] (ICLI)
Op Judge Adv Gen... Opinion of the Judge Advocate General (AAGC)
OPK .... Operative Personenkontrolle [*Operational Person Control*] [*German*]
OPK .... Optokinetic
OPK .... Ovulation Prediction Kit
OPK .... Ovulation Predictor Kit
OPKA........... Cape Monze [*Pakistan*] [*ICAO location identifier*] (ICLI)
Op Kan Att'y Gen... Opinions of the Attorney General of Kansas [*A publication*] (DLA)
OPKC .... Karachi/International [*Pakistan*] [*ICAO location identifier*] (ICLI)
OPKD .... Hyderabad [*Pakistan*] [*ICAO location identifier*] (ICLI)
OPKE .... Chore [*Pakistan*] [*ICAO location identifier*] (ICLI)
OPKE .... Knudsen Engineering Ltd., Perth, Ontario [*Library symbol*] [*National Library of Canada*] (BIB)
OPKF .... Gharo [*Pakistan*] [*ICAO location identifier*] (ICLI)
OPKH .... Khuzdhar [*Pakistan*] [*ICAO location identifier*] (ICLI)
OPKK .... Karachi/Korangi Creek [*Pakistan*] [*ICAO location identifier*] (ICLI)
OPKL .... Kalat [*Pakistan*] [*ICAO location identifier*] (ICLI)
OPKN .... Kharan [*Pakistan*] [*ICAO location identifier*] (ICLI)
OPKO .... Kohat [*Pakistan*] [*ICAO location identifier*] (ICLI)
OPKR .... Karachi [*Pakistan*] [*ICAO location identifier*] (ICLI)
OPKT .... Kohat [*Pakistan*] [*ICAO location identifier*] (ICLI)
Op KY Att'y Gen... Opinion of Attorney General, State of Kentucky [*A publication*] (DLA)
OPL............. Air Cote d'Opale [*France*] [*ICAO designator*] (FAAC)
OPL............. Oberlin Public Library, Oberlin, OH [*OCLC symbol*] (OCLC)
OPL............. Obvious Panty Line (SAUS)
OPL............. Ocean Pressure Laboratory
OPL............. Office of Presidential Libraries [*National Archives*] (BARN)
OPL............. Official Publications Library [*The British Library*]
OPL............. Old Product Line (IAA)
OPL............. Omaha Public Library (SAUS)
OPL............. One-Person Library
OPL............. Opelousas, LA [*Location identifier*] [*FAA*] (FAAL)
OPL............. Open Problem List (NASA)
OPL............. Operational (AFM)
OPL............. Operations Plan (KSC)
OPL............. Optically Pumped LASER (AAEL)
OPL............. Optical Path Length
OPL............. Organizer Programming Language [*Computer science*]
OPL............. Orient-Pacific Line [*Shipping*] (ROG)
OPL............. Orlando Public Library (SAUS)
OPL............. Other Party Liability [*Insurance*] (DMAA)
OPL............. Ottawa Public Library [*UTLAS symbol*]
OPL............. Outer Plexiform Layer [*Retina*]
OPL............. Out-of-Phase Loading
OPL............. Outpost Line
OPL:........... Overpaid Last Account
OPL:........... Ovine Placental Lactogen [*Medicine*] (DMAA)
OPLA .... Lahore [*Pakistan*] [*ICAO location identifier*] (ICLI)
OPLA .... Offshore Pollution Liability Agreement (SAUS)
OPLA .... Ontario Public Library Association (SAUS)
Op LA Att'y Gen... Opinions of the Attorney General of Louisiana [*A publication*] (DLA)
OPLAC........ Argyle Community Library, Port Loring, Ontario [*Library symbol*] [*National Library of Canada*] (NLC)
OPLAC........ Ontario Public Libraries Advisory Committee (SAUS)
OPLAN........ Operation Plan [*Army*]
OPLAN REV... Operation Plan Review (SAUS)
OPLANS....... Operations Plans (ACAE)
OPLAN SEA... Operation Plan, Southeast Asia [*Military*]
OPLAW .... Operational Law (COE)
OPLB .... Ontario Public Libraries Board (SAUS)

OPLC	Ontario Provincial Libraries Council (SAUS)
OPLC	Organizacion para la Liberacion de Cuba [*Organization for the Liberation of Cuba*] (PD)
OPLC	Overpressure Layer Chromatography
OPLE	Omega Position Location Equipment (SAUS)
OPLE	Omega Position Location Experiment [*NASA*]
Op Let	Opinion Letter [*A publication*] (DLA)
OPLF	Orbiter Processing and Landing Facility [*NASA*] (MCD)
OPLF	Oromo Peoples Liberation Front (SAUS)
OPLG	Oil Plug
OPLH	Lahore/Walton [*Pakistan*] [*ICAO location identifier*] (ICLI)
OP/LIM	Operational Limitation (SAUS)
OPLIN	Ohio Public Library Information Network
OPLIN	Ontario Public Libraries Information Network (SAUS)
OPLK	Oplink Communications [*NASDAQ symbol*]
OPLL	Loralai [*Pakistan*] [*ICAO location identifier*] (ICLI)
OPLL	Optical Phase-Locked Loop (SAUS)
OPLL	Ossification of Posterior Longitudinal Ligament [*Orthopedics*] (DAVI)
OPLO	Oromo Peoples Liberation Organization (SAUS)
OPLP	Office of Program and Legislative Planning (SAUS)
OPLP	Pickle Pat Public Library, Pickle Lake, Ontario [*Library symbol*] [*National Library of Canada*] (NLC)
OPLR	Lahore [*Pakistan*] [*ICAO location identifier*] (ICLI)
OPLR	Outpost Line of Resistance
OPLSS	Optimized Portable Life-Support System [*NASA*]
OPM	Object Properties Manager
OPM	Occult Primary Malignancy [*Oncology*]
OPM	Office of Personnel Management [*Supersedes Civil Service Commission*]
OPM	Office of Planning and Management [*DoD*]
OPM	Office of Policy and Management [*Environmental Protection Agency*] (GFGA)
OPM	Office of Procurement and Materiel [*Army*]
OPM	Office of Production Management [*Superseded by WPB, 1942*]
OPM	Office of Program Management [*Environmental Protection Agency*] (GFGA)
OPM	Office of Program Management [*Unemployment Insurance Service*] [*Department of Labor*]
OPM	Office of the Program Manager (SAUS)
OPM	Office, Personnel Manager [*Army*] (MUGU)
OPM	Open Pit Mining (SAUS)
OPM	Operating Plane Months [*Navy*] (NG)
OPM	Operating Procedure for Ministers
OPM	Operations Message (SSD)
OPM	Operations per Minute [*Performance measure*]
OPM	Operator Master (SAUS)
OPM	Operator Programming Method [*Computer science*]
OPM	Ophthalmodynamometry [*Ophthalmology*]
OPM	Ophthalmoplegic Migraine [*Medicine*] (DB)
OPM	Optically Projected Map
OPM	Optical Power Meter
OPM	Options Pricing Model
OPM	Orbits per Minute (SAUS)
OPM	Ordnance Proof Manual (SAA)
OPM	Organisasi Papua Merdeka [*Papua Independent Organization*] [*Indonesia*] (PD)
OPM	Organisation Papua Merduka (SAUS)
OPM	Organizacion Politico-Militar [*Politico-Military Organization*] [*Paraguay*] (PD)
OPM	Organization & Procedures Manual (SAUS)
OPM	Original Program Model (SAUS)
OPM	Orthophoto Map (SAUS)
OPM	Oscillating Pressure Method
OPM	Other People's Money
OPM	Outer Planet Mission
OPM	Output and Performance Measures (HEAS)
OPM	Output per Man (ODBW)
OPM	Output Processor Map [*Computer science*] (OA)
OPM	Output Processor Module (MCD)
OPM	Outside Plant Module (SAUS)
OPM	Owner President Management Program (DD)
OPM	Oxford Policy Management [*British*]
OPM	Perth Museum, Ontario [*Library symbol*] [*National Library of Canada*] (NLC)
OPMA	Mangla [*Pakistan*] [*ICAO location identifier*] (ICLI)
OPMA	Office Products Manufacturers Association (EA)
OPMA	Open Pit Mining Association (EA)
OPMA	Ophthalmic Prescription Manufacturers Association [*British*] (DBA)
OPMA	Overseas Press and Media Association [*British*] (EAIO)
OPMAC	Operations for Military Assistance to the Community (PDAA)
OPMACC	Operation Military Aid to the Civil Community [*British military*] (DMA)
OPMARV	Operational Maneuvering Reentry Vehicle (MCD)
OPMC	Office of Professional Medical Conduct (SAUS)
OPMC	One Player Median Competitive (PDAA)
OPMCS	Otto Pre-Marital Counseling Schedules [*Psychology*]
OPMD	Officer Personnel Management Directorate [*Military*]
OPME	Office of Personnel Management Evaluation (DNAB)
OPME	Office of Program Management and Evaluation [*Environmental Protection Agency*] (GFGA)
OPMEM	Operand Memory (SAUS)
OPMET	Operational Meteorological Information [*ICAO*] (FAAC)
OPMF	Muzaffarabad [*Pakistan*] [*ICAO location identifier*] (ICLI)
OPMG	Office of the Provost Marshal General [*Army*]
OpMG	Oppenheimer Multi-Government Trust [*Associated Press*] (SAG)
OPMH	Occupations for Patients in Mental Hospitals [*British*]

OPMI	Mianwali [*Pakistan*] [*ICAO location identifier*] (ICLI)
OPMI	Open Perfusion Micro-Incubator
OPMI	Operation Microscope [*Surgery*]
Op Minn Att'y Gen	Opinions of the Attorney General of Minnesota [*A publication*] (DLA)
OPMIS	Optical Propulsion Management Interface System
OPMJ	Moenjodaro [*Pakistan*] [*ICAO location identifier*] (ICLI)
OPMK	Mir Pur Khas [*Pakistan*] [*ICAO location identifier*] (ICLI)
OPMN	Miranshah [*Pakistan*] [*ICAO location identifier*] (ICLI)
OPMN	Port McNicoll Public Library, Ontario [*Library symbol*] [*National Library of Canada*] (NLC)
OPMO	Office of Program Management Operations [*Environmental Protection Agency*] (GFGA)
OPMOPLAN	Operation Missouri Plan [*Program for five-day state funeral planned several years in advance for ex-President Harry Truman*] [*Army*]
OPMOR	Operations Materiel and Organization Review (SAUS)
OPMPR	Office of Personnel Management Procurement Regulations [*A publication*] (AAGC)
OPMR	Karachi/Masroor [*Pakistan*] [*ICAO location identifier*] (ICLI)
OPMR	Optimal Robotics Corp. [*NASDAQ symbol*] (SAG)
OPMS	Miranshah [*Pakistan*] [*ICAO location identifier*] (ICLI)
OPMS	Office of Physical Measurement Services [*Gaithersburg, MD*] [*National Institute of Standards and Technology*] (GRD)
OPMS	Office of Program Management and Support [*Environmental Protection Agency*] (GFGA)
OPMS	Officer Personnel Management System [*Army*]
OPMS	On-the-machine Probe Measuring System (SAUS)
OPMS	Outplant Procurement Manufacturing Specification (SAA)
OPMSO	Outside Production Material Sales Order
OPMT	Multan [*Pakistan*] [*ICAO location identifier*] (ICLI)
OPMT	Office of Program Management and Technology (SAUS)
OPMW	Mianwali [*Pakistan*] [*ICAO location identifier*] (ICLI)
OPMX	Optimax Industries, Inc. [*NASDAQ symbol*] (SAG)
OPMX	Otimax Industries [*NASDAQ symbol*] (TTSB)
OPMXZ	Optimax Inds Wrrt'BB' [*NQS*] (TTSB)
OPN	Norwell District Secondary School, Palmerston, Ontario [*Library symbol*] [*National Library of Canada*] (NLC)
OPN	Office of the Chief of Naval Operations
OPN	Office Productivity Network [*Computer science*]
OPN	Oil Pan
OPN	One-Port Network (SAUS)
OPN	Open (AAG)
opn	Open
OPN	Operation
OPN	Opercular Nerve
OPN	Ophthalmic Nurse (DAVI)
OPN	Opinion (ROG)
OPN	Optimised-Profile Navigation (SAUS)
OPN	Option (ADA)
OPN	Ora pro Nobis [*Pray for Us*] [*Latin*]
OPN	Organ Pipe National Monument (SAUS)
OPN	Osteopontin (DMAA)
OPN	Other Procurement, Navy
OPNAV	Chief of Naval Operations (AAGC)
OPNAV	Office of the Chief of Naval Operations
OPNAVCOMMO	Office of the Chief of Naval Operations, Communications Office (DNAB)
OPNAVINST	Office of the Chief of Naval Operations Instruction
OPNAVINST	OPNAV Instruction (SAUS)
OPNAVO	Office of the Chief of Naval Operations
OPNAVSUPPACT	Office of the Chief of Naval Operations, Support Activity (DNAB)
OPNAVSUPPACTDET	Office of the Chief of Naval Operations, Support Activity Detachment (DNAB)
OPNAVSUPPACT FIG	Office of the Chief of Naval Operations, Support Activity Flight Information Group (DNAB)
OPNAVSUPPACT TCC	Office of the Chief of Naval Operations, Support Activity Telecommunications Center (DNAB)
OPNAVSUPPACT WWMCCS DP	Office of the Chief of Naval Operations, Support Activity, Worldwide Military Command Control System, Data Processing (DNAB)
OPNAVSUPPACT WWMCCS EMPSKED	Office of the Chief of Naval Operations, Support Activity, Worldwide Military Command Control System, Employment Schedule (DNAB)
OPNAVSUPPACT WWMCCS FORSTAT	Office of the Chief of Naval Operations, Support Activity, Worldwide Military Command Control System, Force Status (DNAB)
OPNAVSUPPACT WWMCCS MOVREP	Office of the Chief of Naval Operations, Support Activity, Worldwide Military Command Control System, Movement Reports (DNAB)
OPNAVTCC	Office of the Chief of Naval Operations, Telecommunications Center (DNAB)
OPN CEN	Operation Center (SAUS)
Op N Cplt	Operation Not Complete (SAUS)
OPND	Operand (ECII)
Op ND Att'y Gen	Opinions of the Attorney General of North Dakota [*A publication*] (DLA)
OpnEnv	Open Environment Corp. [*Associated Press*] (SAG)
OPNET	Operator's Training New Equipment Training [*Army*] (INF)
OPNET	WWMCCS Operational Network (SAUS)
Op Nev Att'y Gen	Official Opinions of the Attorney General of Nevada [*A publication*] (DLA)
OPNG	Opening (AAG)
OPNH	Nawabshah [*Pakistan*] [*ICAO location identifier*] (ICLI)
OpnhCa	Oppenheimer Capital Ltd. [*Associated Press*] (SAG)

OPNJC .... Ora pro Nobis Jesu Christe [*Pray for Us, Jesus Christ*] [*Motto of Ernst, Duke of Bavaria (1554-1612)*] [*Latin*]
OPNK .... Naushki [*Pakistan*] [*ICAO location identifier*] (ICLI)
opnl .... Operational (ELAL)
OPNL .... Operational
OPNL .... Osaka Prefectural Nakanoshima Library (SAUS)
OPNL RPTS... Operational Reports (SAUS)
OPNML .... Operations Normal (FAAC)
OPNMR .... Optically Pumped Nuclear Magnetic Resonance [*Physics*]
Op no .... Opus number (SAUS)
OPNO .... Originating Public Network Operator (SAUS)
OPNOTE ...... Operational Note (MCD)
OPNS .... Operational Phase [*NASA*] (NAKS)
OPNS .... Operations (NASA)
OPNSEVAL & TNGSq... Operational Evaluation and Training Squadron [*Air Force*]
OP Nurse ...... Ophthalmic Nurse (SAUS)
opnwndo ...... Open Window
Op NY Atty Gen... Opinions of the Attorneys-General of New York [*A publication*] (DLA)
OPo .... Megis Local School District Public Library, Pomeroy, OH [*Library symbol*] [*Library of Congress*] (LCLS)
OPO .... Office of Personnel Operations [*Army*]
OPO .... Officer of the Post Office [*British*]
OPO .... Oil Pressure Out
OPO .... One-Person Operation [*Slang*] [*Business term*] (DCTA)
OPO .... One Point Operation (VLIE)
OPO .... One Price Only (WDAA)
OPO .... Online Process Optimization [*Computer science*] (VLIE)
OPO .... Operational Performance Objectives (SAUS)
OPO .... Oporto [*Portugal*] [*Airport symbol*] (OAG)
OPO .... Optical Parametric Oscillator [*Tunable LASER device*]
OPO .... Orbiter Project Office [*NASA*] (MCD)
OPO .... Orbiting Planetary Observatory
OPO .... Ordnance Personnel Office [*Army*]
OPO .... Organ Procurement Organization [*Generic term*] [*Medicine*]
OPO .... Oropharyngeal Candidiasis [*Medicine*] (MELL)
OPO .... Other Programmed Operations (IAA)
OPO .... Outside Production Order (SAA)
OPO .... Outside Purchase Order (SAA)
OPO .... Ovamboland Peoples Organization (SAUS)
OPO .... Overseas Press Club (NADA)
OPOA .... Office Products of America, Inc. (SAUS)
OPOC .... On-Board Pilot-Observer Camera (SAA)
OPOCX .... Oppenheimer Discovery [*Mutual fund ticker symbol*] (SG)
OPOEB .... Port Elgin Branch, Bruce County Public Library, Ontario [*Library symbol*] [*National Library of Canada*] (NLC)
Op Off Legal Counsel... Opinions of the Office of Legal Counsel [*A publication*] (DLA)
Op Offr .... Operations Officer (SAUS)
Op Ohio Att'y Gen... Opinions of the Attorney General of Ohio [*A publication*] (DLA)
OPOK .... Okara [*Pakistan*] [*ICAO location identifier*] (ICLI)
Op Okla Att'y Gen... Opinions of the Attorney General of Oklahoma [*A publication*] (DLA)
OPOL .... Offshore Pollution Liability Association Ltd. (EA)
O Pol .... Old Polish (SAUS)
OPOL .... Optimization-Oriented Language
OPOL Agreement... Offshore Pollution Liability Agreement (SAUS)
OPOMP .... Overall Planning and Optimization and Machining Process (MHDI)
OPON .... Opinion (ROG)
OPOP .... Operation (SAUS)
op/ops .... Operational/Operations (MILB)
OPOR .... Office of Public Opinion Research (SAUS)
OPOR .... Ormara [*Pakistan*] [*ICAO location identifier*] (ICLI)
Op Or Att'y Gen... Opinions of the Attorney General of Oregon [*A publication*] (DLA)
OPORC .... Port Carling Public Library, Ontario [*Library symbol*] [*National Library of Canada*] (BIB)
OPORD .... Operations Order [*Army*]
OPORPL .... Opposed Replenishment (SAUS)
OPORPL .... Oppose Replenishment [*Navy*] (NVT)
O Port .... Old Portuguese (SAUS)
OPOS .... Optical Property of Orbiting Satellite [*NASA*] (PDAA)
OPOS .... Outside Production Operation Sheet (MCD)
O-POS .... Oxygen-Dope Polysilicon (PDAA)
OPOSENT ...... Opposed Entry (SAUS)
OPOSENT ...... Oppose Entry [*Navy*] (NVT)
OPOS-Film... Oxygen-doped Polysilicon Film (SAUS)
OPosm .... Portsmouth Public Library, Portsmouth, OH [*Library symbol*] [*Library of Congress*] (LCLS)
OPosmG .... Goodyear Atomic Corp., Portsmouth, OH [*Library symbol*] [*Library of Congress*] (LCLS)
OPosmS .... Shawnee State College, Portsmouth, OH [*Library symbol*] [*Library of Congress*] (LCLS)
OPosmU ...... Ohio University, Portsmouth Branch Campus, Portsmouth, OH [*Library symbol*] [*Library of Congress*] [*Obsolete*] (LCLS)
OPOSORT ...... Oppose Sortie [*Navy*] (NVT)
OPOSS .... Office of Personnel Operations Standards and Systems Office [*Army*]
OPOSSMS.... Options to Purchase or Sell Specific Mortgage-Backed Securities [*Merrill Lynch & Co.*] [*Finance*]
OPOSTOR .... Oppose Sortie [*Navy*]
OPOV .... Oxidizer Preburner Oxidizer Valve (MCD)
OPOVA .... Oxidizer Preburner Oxidizer Valve Actuator (SAUS)
OPowS .... Scioto Village High School, Powell, OH [*Library symbol*] [*Library of Congress*] (LCLS)

OPP .... Occiput Posterior Position (DAVI)
OPP .... Octal Print Punch [*Computer science*]
OPP .... Office of Pesticide Programs [*Environmental Protection Agency*]
OPP .... Office of Plans and Policy (LAIN)
OPP .... Office of Polar Programs [*Later, Division of Polar Programs*] [*National Science Foundation*]
OPP .... Office of Policy and Planning [*Office of Policy, Evaluation, and Research*] [*Department of Labor*]
OPP .... Office of Productivity Programs [*Office of Personnel Management*] (GRD)
OPP .... Office of Program Planning (AAGC)
OPP .... Office of Public Programs [*National Archives*] (BARN)
OPP .... Office of Public Prosecutions [*Northern Territory, Australia*]
OPP .... Off-Load Preparation Party [*Navy*] (ANA)
OPP .... Off-Peak Power (SAUS)
OPP .... Oncovin [*Vincristine*], Procarbazine, Prednisone [*Antineoplastic drug regimen*]
OPP .... Ontario Provincial Police [*UTLAS symbol*]
OPP .... Open Pore (SAUS)
OPP .... Open-Pore Polyurethan [*Plastic*]
OPP .... Operator Preparation Program (IAA)
OPP .... Opponent
OPP .... Opportunity (ADA)
opp .... Opposed (DAVI)
OPP .... Opposed To
OPP .... Opposing (GOBB)
OPP .... Opposite (AAG)
opp .... Opposite (WDMC)
OPP .... Oppure [*Otherwise*] [*Music*]
OPP .... Optical Precipitate Profiler (SAUS)
OPP .... Optical Printer Projector (VLIE)
OPP .... Order Processing Pipeline (AGLO)
OPP .... Organizational Project Plan [*Civil Defense*]
OPP .... Organization and Personnel Plan [*Army*]
OPP .... [*The*] Organization of Plastics Processors
OPP .... Organophosphorous Poisoning [*Medicine*] (MELL)
OPP .... Oriented Polypropylene [*Plastics technology*]
OPP .... Ortho-Phenylphenol [*Disinfectant*]
OPP .... Otago Press and Produce (SAUS)
OPP .... Other Physical Principles [*Defense system*]
OPP .... Other Programme Participation (SAUS)
OPP .... Outer Planet Project
opp .... Out of Print at Present [*Publishing*] (WDMC)
OPPCX .... Out of Print at Present [*Publishing*]
OPP .... Oxidative Pentose Phosphate (PDAA)
OPP .... Oxygen Partial Pressure
OPPA .... Octylphenyl Phosphoric Acid (EDCT)
OPPA .... Octylpyrophosphoric Acid [*Organic chemistry*]
OPPA .... Office of Publications and Public Affairs [*National Endowment for the Humanities*] (BARN)
OPPA .... Operation Plan Package Appraisal (AFM)
Op PA Att'y Gen... Opinions of the Attorney General of Pennsylvania [*A publication*] (DLA)
OPPAR .... Orbiter Project Parts Authorization Request [*NASA*] (NASA)
OPPAS .... OPP Administrative Support Systems (SAUS)
OPPAX .... Oppenheimer Global Cl.A [*Mutual fund ticker symbol*] (SG)
OPPC .... Optima Petroleum Corp. [*NASDAQ symbol*] (SAG)
OPPC .... Outpatient Professional Psychiatric Clinic [*Health insurance*] (GHCT)
OPPC .... Parachinar [*Pakistan*] [*ICAO location identifier*] (ICLI)
OPPCE .... Opposite Commutator End (IEEE)
OPPCF .... Optima Petroleum [*NASDAQ symbol*] (TTSB)
OPPD .... Omaha Public Power District
OPPE .... Office of Plans and Program Evaluation (SAA)
OPPE .... Office of Policy, Planning, and Evaluation [*Environmental Protection Agency*] (GFGA)
OPPE .... Office of Programming, Planning and Evaluation (SAUS)
OPPE .... Office of Program Planning and Evaluation [*National Institutes of Health*]
OPPE .... Operational Propulsion Plant Examination [*Navy*] (NVT)
OPPE .... Operations Planning Project Engineer [*Deep Space Instrumentation Facility, NASA*]
OPPE .... Organic and Polymer Processing Experiment (SAUS)
OPPEX .... Oppenheimer Equity Inc. Cl.A [*Mutual fund ticker symbol*] (SG)
OPPF .... Operation of Property and Pressurization Facility (SAUS)
OPP Film .... Orientated Polypropylene Film (SAUS)
OPPG .... Oculopneumoplethysmography (DAVI)
OPPG .... Office of Propulsion and Power Generation (SAA)
OPPG .... Panjgur [*Pakistan*] [*ICAO location identifier*] (ICLI)
OPP HND .... Opposite Hand (MSA)
OPPHX .... Oppenheimer High Yield Cl.A [*Mutual fund ticker symbol*] (SG)
OPPI .... Office of Policy, Planning, and Information [*Environmental Protection Agency*] (GFGA)
OPPI .... Organization of Pharmaceutical Producers of India (SAUS)
OPPI .... Pasni [*Pakistan*] [*ICAO location identifier*] (ICLI)
oppies .... Older Professional Parents (ADWA)
Opp Int L .... Oppenheim's International Law [*A publication*] (DLA)
OPPL .... Orbiter Project Parts List [*NASA*] (NASA)
OPPLAN ...... Operations Plan (KSC)
OPPM .... Office of Policy and Program Management [*Environmental Protection Agency*] (GFGA)
OPPM .... Outside Principal Period of Maintenance (SAUS)
OppMS .... Oppenheimer Multi-Sector Income Trust [*Associated Press*] (SAG)
OPPMSA ...... Ontario Pulp and Paper Makers Safety Association (SAUS)
OPPN .... Pishin [*Pakistan*] [*ICAO location identifier*] (ICLI)
OPPOR .... Opportunity (AABC)

OPPORT...... Opportunity (ADA)

OPPOSIT...... Optimization of a Production Process by an Ordered Simulation and Iteration Technique (IEEE)

OPPOSSMS... Options to Purchase or Sell Specified Mortgage-Backed Securities (EBF)

OPPP .... Office of Program Policy and Planning [Social Security Administration] (OICC)

OPPP .... Order Point and Peak Point (VLIE)

OPPP .... Port Perry High School, Ontario [Library symbol] [National Library of Canada] (NLC)

OPP PE .... Opposite Pulley End (SAUS)

OPPR .... Offset Printing Press

OPPR .... Oil Pollution Preparedness and Response (SAUS)

OPPR .... Operating Program

OPPRC .... International Convention on Oil Pollution, Preparedness, Response and Cooperation (SAUS)

OPPROC ...... Operation Procedures (TIMI)

O-P Process... Oppenheimer-Phillips Process (SAUS)

OPPS .... Office of Planning and Program Services [Office of Field Operations] [Department of Labor]

OPPS .... Overpressurization Protection Switch (IEEE)

OPPS .... Overpressurization Protection System (IEEE)

OPPS .... Oxygen Partial Pressure Sensor

OPPS .... Peshawar [Pakistan] [ICAO location identifier] (ICLI)

OPPSD .... Organic Peroxide Producers Safety Division (SAUS)

OPPSL .... Office of Private and Public Sector Liaison [Environmental Protection Agency] (GFGA)

OPPSX .... Oppenheimer Growth Cl.A [Mutual fund ticker symbol] (SG)

OPPT .... Office of Pollution Prevention and Toxics [Environmental Protection Agency] (AEPA)

OPPTS .... EPA Office of Prevention, Pesticides and Toxic Substances (SAUS)

OPPTS .... Office of Prevention, Pesticides, and Toxic Substances [Environmental Protection Agency] (AEPA)

OPPWFA ...... Operative Plasteres amd Plaster Workers' Federation of Australia

OPPY .... Opportunity (ROG)

OPQ .... Occupational Personality Questionnaires [Employment test]

OPQ .... Occupying Public Quarters [Military]

OPQ .... Opaque (SAUS)

OPQC .... Office Professional Quality Council (SAUS)

OPQS .... Qasim [Pakistan] [ICAO location identifier] (ICLI)

OPQT .... Quetta/Samungli [Pakistan] [ICAO location identifier] (ICLI)

OPR .... Lifts Operating [Skiing]

OPR .... Office of Planning and Research [International Trade Administration] (GRD)

OPR .... Office of Population Research (SAUS)

OPR .... Office of Pre-Claims Requirements [Social Security Administration]

OPR .... Office of Primary Responsibility [Air Force]

OPR .... Office of Private Resources [Department of State]

OPR .... Office of Professional Responsibility [Department of Justice]

OPR .... Office of Public Relations [Later, PUBINFO] [Navy]

OPR .... Offsite Procurement Request (IEEE)

OPR .... Oil Production Rate (SAUS)

OPR .... Old Prussian [Language, etc.]

OPR .... Ontario Practice Reports [A publication] (DLA)

OPR .... Opener (MSA)

OPR .... Open Pool Reactor [Nuclear energy] (NRCH)

OPR .... Operand [Computer science]

OPR .... Operate [or Operator] (AAG)

OPR .... Operated (SAUS)

OPR .... Operating (SAUS)

OPR .... Operational Preference (DA)

OPR .... Operational Project Requirements (AABC)

OPR .... Operation Planning Report (SAUS)

OPR .... Operations Planning Review (NASA)

OPR .... Operations Procedure (MUGU)

OPR .... Operative (SAUS)

OPR .... Operator

OPR .... Operator Request (SAUS)

OPR .... OP Resources Ltd. [Vancouver Stock Exchange symbol]

OPR .... Optical Page Reader [Computer science]

OPR .... Optical Page Reading (SAUS)

OPR .... Optical Pattern Recognition

OPR .... Optimized Palette Reduction [Algorithm] [Computer Presentations, Inc.] (PCM)

OPR .... Optional Parts Request (SAA)

OPR .... Orbit/Payload Recorder [NASA] (MCD)

OPR .... Order Point Recognition (ADA)

OPR .... Ordnance Property Regulations (SAUS)

OPR .... Outpatient Rate [Medicine] (AFM)

OPR .... Outstanding Performance Rating [Military] (RDA)

OPR .... Overall Pressure Ratio

OPR .... Over-Pressure Relief [Automotive emissions]

OPR .... Oxygen Pressure Regulator (MCD)

OPR .... Oxygen Production Rate [Biochemistry]

OPR .... Port Rowan Public Library, Ontario [Library symbol] [National Library of Canada] (NLC)

OPR .... Santander Overseas Bank [NYSE symbol] (SPSG)

OPRA .... Observation Post Royal Artillery [British military] (DMA)

OPRA .... Office Products Representatives Association (SAUS)

OPRA .... Ohio Penal Racing Association (EA)

OPRA .... Options Price Reporting Authority [Information service or system] (IID)

OPRAD......... Operations Research and Development Management (PDAA)

OPraem .... Canons Regular of Premontre (TOCD)

opraem .... Canons Regular of Premontre, Premonstratensians, Norbetines (TOCD)

OPraem .... Ordo Canonicorum Regularium Praemonstatenstium [Order of the Canons Regular of Premontre] [Norbertines] [Roman Catholic men's religious order]

OPRAF .... Office of Passenger Rail Franchising [British] (ECON)

OPRC .... International Convention for Oil Pollution Preparedness, Response and Cooperation (SAUS)

OPRC .... Oil Pollution Preparedness, Response and Co-operation (SAUS)

OPRC .... Oil Pollution Preparedness, Response and Cooperation Convention (SAUS)

OPRD .... Office of Production Research and Development

OPRD .... Organic Process Research & Development [A publication]

OPRDY .... Operationally Ready [Army] (AABC)

OPRE .... Prescott Public Library, Ontario [Library symbol] [National Library of Canada] (NLC)

OPRED .... Operations Reduction [Government term]

OPREDS....... Operational Performance Recording and Evaluation Data System [Military] (CAAL)

OPREG .... Operation Register (IAA)

OPrem .... Ordre de Premontre [Order of the Canons Regular of Premontre] [Rome, Italy] (EAIO)

OPREP .... Operational Reporting [Army]

OPREPS....... Operational Reporting System [Military]

OPREQ .... Operation Request [Computer science] (MHDI)

OPRES .... Operations Research (ACAE)

OPREX .... Operational Exercise [NATO] (NATG)

OPRFLT .... Operator Fault (AAG)

oprg .... Operating (STED)

OPRG .... Oxygenated Fuels Program Reformulated Gasoline

OPRI .... Office de la Propriete Industrielle [Department of Industrial Property] [Ministry of Economic Affairs] (IID)

OPRI .... Office de Protection contre les Rayonnements Ionisants [France]

OPRIC .... Operator in Charge (IAA)

Opr i/C .... Operator-in-Charge (SAUS)

OPRIS .... Ohio Project for Research in Information Service (NITA)

OPRK .... Opiate Receptor Kappa (DMAA)

OPRK .... Rahimyarkhan [Pakistan] [ICAO location identifier] (ICLI)

OPRL .... Ovine Prolactin [Endocrinology]

OPRL .... Portland Branch, Rideau Lakes Union Library, Ontario [Library symbol] [National Library of Canada] (BIB)

OPRLFT .... Operator Fault [Computer science] (MHDI)

OPRN .... Islamabad/Chaklala [Pakistan] [ICAO location identifier] (ICLI)

OPRN .... Operation

Opr N Compl... Operation Not Complete (SAUS)

OPRND .... Operand (VLIE)

OPRNL .... Operational (AAG)

OPRNTL .... Operational

OPRO .... Operations Order (SAUS)

OPRO .... Output Processing (SAUS)

Opro............. Oxyprolin (SAUS)

OpRobt .... Optimal Robotics Corp. [Associated Press] (SAG)

OPROM........ Optical Programmable Read-Only Memory [Disk] (BYTE)

OProv........... Old Provencal [Language] (BARN)

OPRPrC........ Santander Overseas Bk'C'Pfd [NYSE symbol] (TTSB)

OPRPrD........ Santander Overseas Bk 'D'Pfd [NYSE symbol] (TTSB)

OPRQ .... Shorekote/Rafiqui [Pakistan] [ICAO location identifier] (ICLI)

OPRR .... Office for Protection from Research Risks [Bethesda, MD] [National Institutes of Health] (GRD)

OPRR .... Outside Production Requirement Record (SAA)

OPRRB......... Officer Personnel Record Review Board [Air Force] (AFM)

OPRRE......... Office of Public Roads and Rural Engineering [Later, Bureau of Public Roads]

OPRS .... Office of Professional Research Services [American Occupational Therapy Association]

OPRS .... Oil Pressure

OPRS .... Operational Planning and Review Systems [Employment and Training Administration] [Department of Labor]

OPRS .... Risalpur [Pakistan] [ICAO location identifier] (ICLI)

OpRsch........ Operations Research (SAUS)

OPRT .... Operator Table

OPRT .... Orotate Phosphoribosyltransferase (STED)

OPRT .... Rawalakot [Pakistan] [ICAO location identifier] (ICLI)

OPRTNTY...... Opportunity

OPRU.......... Oil Pollution Research Unit [British] (ARC)

OPruss.......... Old Prussian [Language] (BARN)

OPRV.......... Oxygen Pressure Relief Valve (MCD)

OPS .... Oblique Photo Sketcher

OPS .... Obscene Publications Squad [British] (DI)

OPS .... Obstacle Planner Software (RDA)

OPS .... Occupational Preparation Scheme (AIE)

OPS .... Ocean Patrol Ship (SAUS)

OPS .... Ocean Platform Station [National Data Buoy Office] (NOAA)

OPS .... Office of Pipeline Safety [Department of Transportation]

OPS .... Office of Population Surveys [British]

OPS .... Office of Price Stabilization [Terminated, 1953]

OPS .... Office of Products Safety [FDA]

OPS .... Office of Product Standards [Department of Commerce] (WDAA)

OPS .... Office of Programmatic Systems [Social Security Administration]

OPS .... Office of Program Services [US Employment Service] [Department of Labor]

OPS .... Office of Public Service [British] (WA)

OPS .... Office of Publishing Services (AAGC)

OPS .... Office Procedure Specification (VLIE)

OPS .... Official Phone Station [Amateur radio]

OPS .... Official Production System [*Production-system language*]
OPS .... Official Public Service Reports [*New York*] [*A publication*] (DLA)
OPS .... Off-Premise Station [*Telecommunications*] (TEL)
OPS .... Offshore Power Systems, Inc. (SAUS)
OPS .... Oil Pressure Switch
OPS .... Oil Production Stock
OPS .... Omnidirectional Point Source (PDAA)
OPS .... On-Line Process Synthesis [*Computer science*]
OPS .... On-line Process Synthesizer (SAUS)
OPS .... Online Programming and Simulation (SAUS)
OPS .... On-Site Inspection Agency [*DoD*] [*ICAO designator*] (FAAC)
OPS .... Open Pan Sulphitation [*Sugar production*]
OPS .... Open Price System (SAUS)
OPS .... Open Profiling Standard [*Firefly Network*] [*Computer science*]
OPS .... Operating hours (SAUS)
OPS .... Operating Plans Summary (VLIE)
OPS .... Operating System (SAUS)
OPS .... Operational Paging System [*NASA*] (KSC)
OPS .... Operational Performance Standard [*Aviation*] (DA)
OPS .... Operational Power Supply
OPS .... Operational Protection System [*Nuclear energy*] (NRCH)
OPS .... Operational Sequence [*NASA*] (NAKS)
OPS .... Operational Station (SAA)
OPS .... Operational Support (MCD)
OPS .... Operation and Support (MCD)
ops............ Operations (ELAL)
OPS .... Operations (MCD)
OPS .... Operations Division [*NATO*] (NATG)
OPS .... Operations Group (SAUS)
OPS .... Operations Officer (SAUS)
OPS .... Operations per Second (IAA)
ops............ Operations per Second (VLIE)
OPS .... Operations Planning System (VLIE)
OPS .... Operations Processing System (SAUS)
OPS .... Operations Sequence [*NASA*] (MCD)
OPS .... Operations Squadron
OPS .... Operations Staff [*Military*] [*British*]
OPS .... Operator's Subsystem [*Telecommunications*] (TEL)
OPS .... Operator System Program [*Manufacturing engineering*] [*Computer science*]
OPS .... Ophthalmic Photographers' Society (EA)
Ops............ Opinions [*Legal term*] (DLA)
OPS .... Opposite Prompters' Side [*i.e., the left side*] [*Stage direction*] (ROG)
OPS .... Opposite Surface [*Technical drawings*]
OPS .... OPSEC [*Operations Security*] Professional Society (EA)
OPS .... Optical Power Spectrum (PDAA)
OPS .... Optical Processing System
OPS .... Optical Propagation Study (SAUS)
OPS .... Optical Sensor (EOSA)
OPS .... Oracle Parallel Server [*Computer science*]
OPS .... Orbiter Project Schedules [*NASA*] (NASA)
OPS .... Orbiting Primate Spacecraft (MCD)
OPS .... Organisation Panamericaine de la Sante [*Pan American Health Organization*] (MSC)
OPS .... Oriented Polystyrene [*Plastics technology*]
OPS .... Ortho-Phosphoserine [*Biochemistry*]
O-Ps............ Ortho-Positronium (SAUS)
OPS .... Other Personal Services
OPS .... Outlet Pipe Space (SAUS)
ops............ Out of Print and Searching [*Publishing*] (WDMC)
OPS .... Out of Print, Searching [*Publishing*]
OPS .... Out of Production Spares (MCD)
OPS .... Outpatient Section (DAVI)
OPS .... Outpatient Service [*Medicine*]
OPS .... Outpatient Supervision [*Medicine*] (DHP)
OPS .... Outpatient Surgery [*Health insurance*] (GHCT)
OPS .... Outside Production Service (SAA)
OPS .... Overhead Positioning System [*AEC*]
OPS .... Overpressure [*or Overpressurization*] Protection System [*Nuclear energy*] (NRCH)
OPS .... Oxidized Porous Silicon [*Materials science*]
OPS .... Oxidizer Particle Size
OPS .... Oxygen Purge Subsystem (SAUS)
OPS .... Oxygen Purge System [*or Subsystem*] [*NASA*]
OPS .... Parry Sound Public Library, Ontario [*Library symbol*] [*National Library of Canada*] (NLC)
OPS .... Phillips Petroleum Co., Research and Development Department, Bartlesville, OK [*OCLC symbol*] (OCLC)
OPS .... P-Octylphenylsalicylat (SAUS)
OpS............ Specialist in Optical Science (GAGS)
OPSA .... Algonquin Regional Library, Parry Sound, Ontario [*Library symbol*] [*Obsolete*] [*National Library of Canada*] (NLC)
OPSA .... Optimal Pneumatic Systems Analysis (PDAA)
OPSA .... Ovarian Papillary Serous Adenocarcinoma [*Medicine*] (DMAA)
Ops AAG POD... United States Post Office Department. Official Opinions of the Solicitor [*A publication*] (DLA)
OPSADT........ Optically Programmable Semi-Automatic Direct-current Tester (SAUS)
Ops AG .... Opinions of the Attorney General [*A publication*] (DLA)
OPSAM .... Optical Storage Access Method [*Computer science*] (PDAA)
OPSAN .... Operations Analysis System
Ops Analysis... Operations Analysis (SAUS)
OP(S)ARMYJAG.. Opinion(s) of the Army Judge Advocate General
OPSAS .... Office of Program Support and Advanced Systems (SAA)
OPSATCOM... Optical Satellite Communications (MCD)

Ops Atts Gen... Opinions of the Attorneys-General of the United States (SAUS)
Ops Atty Gen... Opinions of the Attorney General [*A publication*] (DLA)
Ops Atty Gen Wisc... Wisconsin Attorney General Reports [*A publication*] (DLA)
OPSB .... Orbiter Processing Support Building [*NASA*] (NASA)
OPSB .... Sibi [*Pakistan*] [*ICAO location identifier*] (ICLI)
OPSC .... Office of Planning Standards and Coordination [*HUD*]
OPSC .... Office of the Public Service Commissioner [*Australia*]
OPSC .... Optical Security Group [*NASDAQ symbol*] (TTSB)
OPSC .... Optical Security Group, Inc. [*NASDAQ symbol*] (SAG)
OpScan........ Optical Scanning [*Medicine*] (STED)
OPSCAN....... Optical Scanning [*Computer science*] (WDAA)
OPSCO .... Operations Co-ordinator (SAUS)
OPSCOM...... Operational Secure Communications (SAUS)
OPSCOMM.... Operational Communications (SAUS)
OPSCOMM.... Operations Communications (MCD)
Ops Comms... Opinions of the Commissioners (SAUS)
OPSCON ...... Operations Control [*NASA*] (KSC)
OPSCOP....... Operations Control [*Monitor*] Program
OPSCT .... Christie Township Public Library, Parry Sound, Ontario [*Library symbol*] [*National Library of Canada*] (NLC)
OPSD .... Office of Placement Support and Development [*US Employment Service*] [*Department of Labor*]
OPSD .... Openside
OPSD .... O Products and Services Division (SAUS)
OPSD .... Skardu [*Pakistan*] [*ICAO location identifier*] (ICLI)
OPSDEP .... Operations Deputy [*In JCS system*] [*Military*]
OPSDEPS...... Operations Deputies (SAUS)
OPS DIV ...... Operations Division (SAUS)
OPSE .... Optically Pumped Stimulated Emission (AAEL)
OPSEC .... Open Platform for Secure Enterprise Connectivity (SAUS)
OPSEC .... Operational Security
OPSEC .... Operations per Second (IAA)
OPSEC .... Operations security (SAUS)
OPSEC .... Operations Security Program (AAGC)
OPSEC .... OPSEC Professionals Society [*Later, OPS*] (EA)
OPSEC M&A... Operations Security Management and Analysis Section (SAUS)
OPSER .... Operator Service (CIST)
OPSET .... Operation Set (SAUS)
OPSET .... Optimal Set [*of Parameters*] [*Hydrology*]
OPSET .... Optional Set (SAUS)
OPSF .... Karachi/Shara-E-Faisal [*Pakistan*] [*ICAO location identifier*] (ICLI)
OP SF .... Office of Preparedness, General Services Administration [*later, Federal Preparedness Agency*], Special Facility
OPSF .... Orbital Propellant Storage Facility (MCD)
OPSG .... Operation Plans Steering Group (DOMA)
OPSHT........ Humphrey Township Public Library, Parry Sound, Ontario [*Library symbol*] [*National Library of Canada*] (NLC)
OPSI .... Optical Sensors, Inc. [*NASDAQ symbol*] (SAG)
OPSI .... Ordnance Publications for Supply Index [*Military*]
OPSI .... Overwhelming Post-Splenectomy Infection [*Medicine*]
OPSIM .... Officer Planning and Simulation Model (ACAE)
OPSIM .... Operational Simulator [*Coast Guard*]
OPSIMS ...... Operational Simulation Subsystem (MCD)
OPSIX .... Oppenheimer Strategic Inc. Cl.A [*Mutual fund ticker symbol*] (SG)
Ops JAG ...... Opinions of the Judge Advocate General, United States Army [*A publication*] (DLA)
OPSK .... Optimum Phase-Shif Keying (SAUS)
OPSK .... Sukkur [*Pakistan*] [*ICAO location identifier*] (ICLI)
OPSKIP........ Optional Skip (SAUS)
OPSKS .... Optimum Phase Shift Keyed Signals [*Telecommunications*]
OPSM .... Office of Public Sector Management [*Australian Capital Territory*]
OPSM .... Optical Prescriptions Spectacle Makers (SAUS)
OPSM .... Outside Plant Subscriber Module (SAUS)
OPSMB .... Organization of Progressive Socialists of the Mediterranean Basin
OPSMOD...... Operations Planning Module (SAUS)
OPSNET .... Operations System Network (SAUS)
OPSNOTE..... Operations Note (SAUS)
OPSO .... Office of Pipeline Safety Operations [*Department of Transportation*] (DLA)
OPS O......... Operations Officer [*Navy*] (DOMA)
Op Sol Dept... Opinions of the Solicitor for the Department of Labor [*United States*] [*A publication*]
Op Sol Dept Labor... Opinions of the Solicitor for the Department of Labor Dealing with Workmen's Compensation [*A publication*] (DLA)
Op Solic PO Dep't... Official Opinions of the Solicitor for the Post Office Department [*A publication*] (DLA)
Op Sol POD... Opinions of the Solicitor for the Post Office Department [*United States*] [*A publication*] (DLA)
OPSORD ...... Operations Order (SAUS)
OPSP .... Office of Product Standards Policy [*Gaithersburg, MD*] [*Department of Commerce*] (GRD)
OPSP .... Operations Panel [*ICAO*] (DA)
OPSP .... Shekhupura [*Pakistan*] [*ICAO location identifier*] (ICLI)
OPSPA .... Oleandomycin-Polymyxin-Sulphadiazine-Perfringens Agar (SAUS)
OPSR .... Office of Pipeline Safety Regulation [*Department of Transportation*] (OICC)
OPSR .... Office of Professional Standards Review [*Medicare and Medicaid*] [*HEW*]
OPSR .... Operations Supervisor [*NASA*] (MCD)
OPSR .... Ordnance Provision System Regulations (SAUS)
OPSR .... Sargodha [*Pakistan*] [*ICAO location identifier*] (ICLI)
OPSRDY ...... Operations Readiness (MCD)
OPSREP ...... Operations Report [*NATO*] (NATG)
OPSRO........ Office of Professional Standards Review [*Medicare and Medicaid*] Organization [*HEW*]

OPSS	Intelligent Occupant Position and Sensing System [*Automotive safety*]
OPSS	Office of Principal Staff Support (SAUS)
OPSS	Orbital Propellant Storage Subsystem (MCD)
OPSS	Overweight & Pregnant Support (SAUS)
OPSS	Saidu Sharif [*Pakistan*] [*ICAO location identifier*] (ICLI)
OP(ST)	Operation Overlord Preparations, Service Leave and Travel [*World War II*]
OPST	Out-of-Pile Systems Test [*Nuclear energy*] (NRCH)
OPSTACOM	Optical Satellite Communications
OPSTAT	Operational Status [*Navy*] (NVT)
OPSTATUSREP	Operations Status Report (NATG)
OPST-BQA	Office of Professional Standards Review-Bureau of Quality Assurance (STED)
OPSTOP	Optional Stop (SAUS)
OPSTR	Operating Strength [*Army*] (AABC)
OPSU	Sui [*Pakistan*] [*ICAO location identifier*] (ICLI)
OPSUB	Operational SUBPAY (DNAB)
OPSUM	Operational Summary [*Navy*] (NVT)
OPSUPPFAC	Operational Support Facility (MCD)
OPSW	Sahiwal [*Pakistan*] [*ICAO location identifier*] (ICLI)
OPSWL	Old Program Status Word Location
OPS-X	Operational Teletype Message
OPSYS	Operating System [*Computer science*]
OPT	International Finance Corp. [*NYSE symbol*] (SAG)
OPT	Office of the Public Trustee [*Australian Capital Territory*]
OPT	Oil Point [*Alaska*] [*Seismograph station code, US Geological Survey*] (SEIS)
OPT	Oil Pressure Transmitter
OPT	Open Pneumothorax [*Medicine*] (MELL)
OPT	Open Protocol Technology [*Computer science*] (AGLO)
OPT	Operability Testing [*Military*] (CAAL)
OPT	Operate (WGA)
OPT	Operational Pressure Transducer (MCD)
OPT	Operation Prime Time [*Television*]
OPT	Operations and Telling (SAA)
OPT	Operations Planning Team [*Air Force*] (DOMA)
OPT	Opportunities for Professional Transition [*An association*] (EA)
OPT	Optative [*Grammar*]
OPT	Optic (IAA)
OPT	Optical (AAG)
opt	Optical (NTIO)
OPT	Optical Point Transfer
OPT	Optician
OPT	Optics
opt	optimal (SAUS)
OPT	Optimization (SAUS)
OPT	Optimization Study [*Nuclear energy*] (NRCH)
OPT	Optimization Under Uncertainty Project (SAUS)
OPT	Optimized Production Technology
OPT	Optimizer (SAUS)
OPT	Optimum (AAG)
OPT	Optimus [*Best*] [*Latin*]
Opt	Option (EBF)
OPT	Option [*Shares*]
OPT	Optional (AAG)
Opt	Optional (EBF)
opt	Optional (IDOE)
OPT	Options (SAUS)
Opt	Optometrist (STED)
OPT	Ortho-Phthaladehyde (DB)
OPT	Other People's Tobacco [*Slang*]
OPT	Outpatient [*Medicine*] (AAMN)
OPT	Outpatient Physical Therapy [*Health insurance*] (GHCT)
OPT	Outpatient Therapy (DAVI)
OPT	Outpatient Treatment [*Medicine*]
OPT	Output Position Transducer [*Electronics*]
OPT	Output Punched Tape (SAUS)
OPT	Output Transformer (IAA)
OPT	Overhead Projection Transparency (MCD)
OPT	Ovulation Predictor Test (SAUS)
OPT	Pakenham Township Public Library, Ontario [*Library symbol*] [*National Library of Canada*] (BIB)
OPT	Payne Theological Seminary, Wilberforce, OH [*OCLC symbol*] (OCLC)
Opta	Opta Food Ingredients, Inc. [*Associated Press*] (SAG)
OPTA	Optimal Performance Theoretically Attainable (IEEE)
OPTA	Optimum Performance Theoretically Obtainable (SAUS)
OPTA	Organ and Piano Teachers Association [*Defunct*] (EA)
OPTA	Terbela [*Pakistan*] [*ICAO location identifier*] (ICLI)
OPTAC	Optical Target Acquisition and Cueing (ACAE)
OPTACON	Optical-to-Tactile Converter [*Electronic reader for the blind*]
OPTADS	Operations Tactical Data Systems [*Army*] (RDA)
OPTAG	Optical Aimpoint Guidance System [*Weaponry*]
OPTAG	Optical Pickoff Two-Axis Gyroscope (SAA)
OPTAL	Olivetti Press Tool Automation Language (SAUS)
OPTAN	Operations Target Analysis [*of strike missions in North Vietnam*]
OPTAR	Operating Target
OPTAR	Optical Automatic Ranging
OPTARE	Office of Planning, Technical Assistance, Research, and Evaluation [*Washington, DC*] [*Department of Commerce*] (GRD)
OPTASK	Operational Tasking (DOMA)
OPTAX	Oppenheimer Municipal Bond Cl.A [*Mutual fund ticker symbol*] (SG)
OPT AX	Optical Axis (SAUS)
OPTB	Operational Program Time Base [*NASA*] (MCD)
OPTC	Optelecom, Inc. [*NASDAQ symbol*] (NQ)
OptCble	Optical Cable Corp. [*Associated Press*] (SAG)
OptclData	Optical Data Systems [*Associated Press*] (SAG)
OptclDt	Optical Data Systems, Inc. [*Associated Press*] (SAG)
Opt Clm	Optional Claiming Race (WGA)
OPTCN	Optician
Opt Commun	Optical Communication (SAUS)
Opt County Gov't	Optional County Government [*A publication*] (DLA)
Opt D	Doctor of Optometry
OPT'D	Optioned [*Automotive advertising*]
OPTE	Operational Proficiency Training Equipment [*Roland International Corp.*] (MCD)
OPTEC	Operational Test and Evaluation Command [*Army*] (RDA)
OPTEC	Optical Properties Technical Evaluation Center
Opt Electron Microsc	Optical and Electron Microscopy (SAUS)
OPTEMPO	Operational Tempo [*Military*]
OPTEMPO	Tempo of Operations (MCD)
Opt Eng Rep	Optical Engineering Report (SAUS)
Op Tenn Att'y Gen	Opinions of the Attorney General of Tennessee [*A publication*] (DLA)
OPTEV	Operational Test and Evaluation [*Military*]
OPTEVFOR	Operational Test and Evaluation Force [*Norfolk, VA*] [*Navy*]
OPTEVFORDET	Operational Test and Evaluation Force Detachment (DNAB)
OPTEVG	Operational Test and Evaluation Group (SAUS)
OPTEX	Optical Exploder (TIMI)
OptEx	Optional Exchange [*Dietetics*]
Op Tex Att'y Gen	Opinions of the Attorney General of Texas [*A publication*] (DLA)
OPTG	Operating (SAUS)
OPTH	Ophthalmic (ROG)
OPTH	Talhar [*Pakistan*] [*ICAO location identifier*] (ICLI)
OPTI	Office of Productivity, Technology, and Innovation [*Department of Commerce*]
OPTI	OPTI, Inc. [*NASDAQ symbol*] (SAG)
OPTI	Optimize (SAUS)
OPTI	Optimum Holding Corp. (SAUS)
OPTIC	Ophthalmological Products Trade and Industry Conference [*British*] (DBA)
OPTIC	Optical
OPTIC	Optical Procedural Task Instruction Compiler
optic	opticociliary (SAUS)
optic	opticopupillary (SAUS)
OPTIC	Oryx Pecos Test Inquiry and Control System (NITA)
Opticam	Optics Automation and Management (RDA)
OpticC	Optical Coating Laboratory, Inc. [*Associated Press*] (SAG)
OPTICIMP	Optimization of Computer Integrated Materials Processing (SAUS)
OPTICON	Optical Tactical Converter (SAUS)
OPTIM	Occupational Projections and Training Information for Michigan [*Information service or system*] (IID)
OPTIM	Order Point Technique for Inventory Management (BUR)
Optima	Optima Petroleum Corp. [*Associated Press*] (SAG)
OPTIMA	Optimization of Policies for Transport Integration in Metropolitan Areas
OPTIMA	Organization for the Phyto-Taxonomic Investigation of the Mediterranean Area [*Berlin, Federal Republic of Germany*] (EAIO)
OptImag	Optika Imaging Systems, Inc. [*Associated Press*] (SAG)
Optimax	Optimax Industries, Inc. [*Associated Press*] (SAG)
OPTIMOS	Optimized Metal Oxide Semiconductor (SAUS)
OPTIMUM	Obtain Increased Productivity through Improved Modernization of Facilities and Updating Maintenance Tools, Equipment, and Methods [*Military*]
OPTIMUS	Office of Public Trustee Information Management User System [*Canada*]
Opt Inf Syst	Optical Information Systems (SAUS)
OPTINT	Optical Intelligence (MCD)
OPTIPARES	Optical Processing of Airborne Remote Sensing (SAUS)
OPTIR	Optical Infrared (ACAE)
OPTIS	Oxfordshire Project for the Training of Instructors and Supervisors [*British*] (AIE)
OptiSG	Optical Security Group, Inc. [*Associated Press*] (SAG)
OPTK	Optika Imaging Systems, Inc. [*NASDAQ symbol*] (SAG)
OPTL	Optional (MSA)
OPTLC	Overpressurized Thin-Layer Chromatography
OptIcm	Optelecom, Inc. [*Associated Press*] (SAG)
OPTM	Optometry
Opt Mater	Optical Materials (SAUS)
Opt Min	Optical Mineralogy (SAUS)
OPTMRST	Optometrist (SAUS)
OPTMTRC	Optometric
Optmx	Optimax Industries, Inc. [*Associated Press*] (SAG)
OPTN	[*The*] National Organ Procurement and Transplantation Network [*Information service or system*] (IID)
OPTN	Optician (SAUS)
OPTN	Option [*Legal shorthand*] (LWAP)
OPTN	Option Care, Inc. [*NASDAQ symbol*] (SAG)
OptnCr	Option Care, Inc. [*Associated Press*] (SAG)
OPTNET	Optimum Private Trunk Network Embodying Tandems (PDAA)
Opt News	Optical News (SAUS)
OPT-NSC	Outpatient Treatment/Nonservice-Connected [*Veterans Administration*] (DAVI)
OPTO	Optometry Library (SAUS)
OPTOEL	Optoelectronics (SAUS)
Optoelectron Instrum Data Process	Optoelectronics, Instrumentation and Data Processing (SAUS)

OPTOL .... Optimized Test-Oriented Language [*Computer science*] (PDAA)
OPTOM .... Optometer (SAUS)
OPTOM .... Optometrist
Optom .... Optometry
OPTOM .... Optomyometer (SAUS)
OPTOMA ...... Ocean Prediction through Observation, Modeling, and Analysis [*Experimental program*]
OPT/OSP ...... Outpatient Physical Therapy/Outpatient Speech Pathology Services [*Department of Health and Human Services*] (GFGA)
OPTQ .... Ocean Optique Distributors, Inc. [*NASDAQ symbol*] (SAG)
OPTQ .... Ocean Optique Dstr [*NASDAQ symbol*] (TTSB)
OPTR .... Optical Punched Tape Reader (SAUS)
O/P Tr .... Output Transformer (SAUS)
OPTRA .... Operational Training (DNAB)
OPTRAK ...... Optical Tracking and Ranging Kit (PDAA)
OPTRAN ...... Operational Transit (GAAI)
OPTRAN ...... Optical Transmission (SAUS)
OPTRARON... Operational Training Squadron (DNAB)
OPTRONICS... Optical Electronics
OPTRX .... Oppenheimer Total Return Cl.A [*Mutual fund ticker symbol*] (SG)
OPTS .... Office of Pesticides and Toxic Substances [*Environmental Protection Agency*]
OPTS .... Office of Program and Technical Services [*Employment and Training Administration*] [*Department of Labor*]
OPTS .... Online Peripheral Test System
OPTS .... Online Program Testing System [*Computer science*] (IAA)
OPTS .... Operations (SAUS)
OPTS .... Opta Food Ingredients, Inc. [*NASDAQ symbol*] (SAG)
Opt S .... Optical Sight (SAUS)
OPTS .... Organization of Parents through Surrogacy (EA)
OPT-SC .... Outpatient Treatment/Service Connected [*Veterans Administration*] (DAVI)
OptSens ...... Optical Sensors, Inc. [*Associated Press*] (SAG)
OPTS RTS.... OPTS Regulation Tracking System (SAUS)
OPTT .... Optek Technology [*NASDAQ symbol*] (TTSB)
OPTT .... Taftan [*Pakistan*] [*ICAO location identifier*] (ICLI)
OPTU .... Turbat [*Pakistan*] [*ICAO location identifier*] (ICLI)
OPTUL .... Optical Pulse Transmitter Using LASER
OPTV .... Operative
OPTX .... Optek Technology, Inc. (SAUS)
OPTX .... Optex Biomedical [*NASDAQ symbol*] (TTSB)
OPTYP .... Opalotype (VRA)
OPTZU .... Optical-Pan-Tilt-Zoom Unit (SAA)
OPU .... Balimo [*Papua New Guinea*] [*Airport symbol*] (OAG)
OPU .... Operational Performance Unit (ADA)
OPU .... Operations Priority Unit
OPU .... Operator Processing Unit (SAUS)
OPU .... Out-Plant Usage (VLIE)
OPU .... Overseas Plexiglas Unit
OPU .... Pacific University, Forest Grove, OR [*OCLC symbol*] (OCLC)
OPU .... Unemployed Peoples Union (NADA)
OP/UCOP ..... Office of the President/UC Office of the President (SAUS)
OPUG.......... Office Planners and Users Group (NTPA)
OPUR .... Object Program Utility Routine
OPURD7 ...... Institute of Arctic and Alpine Research. University of Colorado. Occasional Paper (journ.) (SAUS)
OPUS .... Obvious Password Utility System [*Computer science*] (VLIE)
OPUS .... Octal Program Updating System [*Computer science*]
OPUS .... Officer Planning Utilization System (SAUS)
OPUS .... Offshore Persistent Upwelling Structure
OPUS .... Older People United for Service (SAUS)
OPUS .... Open University System (SAUS)
OPUS .... Operating Utility System (SAUS)
OPUS .... Optical Prism Uniformity System
OPUS .... Opus 360 Corp. [*NASDAQ symbol*] (SG)
OPUS .... Opus Computer Products, Inc. (SAUS)
OPUS .... Organisation of Professional Users of Statistics
OPUS .... Organization for Promoting the Understanding of Society (SAUS)
OPUS .... Organization of Persistant Upwelling Structure
OPUS .... Organization of Professional Users of Statistics (SAUS)
OPUSA........ Operation U.S.A. [*An association*] (EA)
OPUSC........ Opuscula [*Minor Works*] [*Latin*] (ROG)
OPV .... Bedarfsflugunternehmen Dr. L. Polsterer [*Austria*] [*ICAO designator*] (FAAC)
OPV .... Observation Post Vehicle (SAUS)
OPV .... Offshore Patrol Vessel (DOMA)
OPV .... Ohms per Volt
OPV .... Optical Path-Length Variation (PDAA)
OPV .... Optionally Piloted Vehicle (SAUS)
OPV .... Oral Polio Vaccine [*Also, Sabin vaccine*] (PAZ)
OPV .... Oral Poliovirus [*Infectious diseases*] (DAVI)
OPV .... Oral Polio Virus Vaccine
OPV .... Organic PhotoVoltaic (SAUS)
Op VA Att'y Gen... Opinions of the Attorney General and Report to the Governor of Virginia [*A publication*] (DLA)
OPVN .... OpenVision Technologies, Inc. [*NASDAQ symbol*] (SAG)
OPVN .... Open Vision Technology [*NASDAQ symbol*] (TTSB)
OPW .... Objective Personal Weapon
OPW .... Oboz Polski Walczacej [*A publication*] (BJA)
OPW .... Office of Public Works
OPW .... Opawica Explorations, Inc. [*Toronto Stock Exchange symbol*]
OPW .... Open Pilot Warranty [*Insurance*] (AIA)
OPW .... Operating Weight [*Air Force*]
OPW .... Optical Window
OPW .... Opuwa [*Namibia*] [*Airport symbol*] (OAG)

OPW .... Orthogonalized Plane Wave
OPW .... Orthogonal Plane Wave (SAUS)
OPW .... Porter Public Library, Westlake, OH [*OCLC symbol*] (OCLC)
OPW .... Whitney Public Library, Porcupine, Ontario [*Library symbol*] [*National Library of Canada*] (NLC)
OPWA .... Office Products Wholesalers Association (NTPA)
Op Wash Att'y Gen... Office of the Attorney General (State of Washington) Opinions [*A publication*] (DLA)
OPWC .... Old Peoples Welfare Centre (SAUS)
OPWI .... Opiate Withdrawal [*Medicine*] (DMAA)
Op Wis Att'y Gen... Opinions of the Attorney General of Wisconsin [*A publication*] (DLA)
OpWldBd ...... Oppenheimer World Bond Fund [*Associated Press*] (SAG)
OPWN .... Wana [*Pakistan*] [*ICAO location identifier*] (ICLI)
OPWS .... Occupant Position and Weight Sensor [*Automotive safety*]
OPWS .... Orbiter Payload Work Station (MCD)
OPWSA....... Ontario Prader-Willi Syndrome Association (SAUS)
Op Wyo Att'y Gen... Opinions of the Attorney General of Wyoming [*A publication*] (DLA)
OPX .... Off-Premise Exchange Operation (AGLO)
OPX .... Off-Premise Extension [*Nuclear energy*] (NRCH)
OPX .... Online Performance Monitor Destination (SAUS)
OPX .... Orthopyroxene [*A silicate mineral*]
OPY .... Salomon, Inc. [*AMEX symbol*] (SAG)
OP Year...... Original Production Year (EEVL)
OPZ .... Opsonized Zymosan [*Biochemistry*]
OPZB .... Zhob [*Pakistan*] [*ICAO location identifier*] (ICLI)
OPZONE...... Operation Zone (COE)
OQ .... Officers' Quarters [*Military*]
OQ .... Officier de l'Ordre du Quebec [*French*] (CPGU)
OQ .... Oil Quench (IAA)
OQ .... Oil Quenching (SAUS)
OQ .... Operational Qualification (ACII)
OQ .... Optical Quality
OQ .... Order Quantity (DNAB)
OQ .... Ordre du Quebec [*Order of Quebec*] [*Canada*] (DD)
OQ .... Output Quantity (SAUS)
OQ .... Output Queue [*Computer science*] (VLIE)
oq .... overmation quotient (SAUS)
OQ .... Royale Airlines [*ICAO designator*] (AD)
OQ .... Tropical Air Services (SAUS)
OQA .... Operations Quality Assurance [*Nuclear energy*] (NRCH)
OQA .... Optical Quantum Amplifier (PDAA)
OQA .... Reidsville, NC [*Location identifier*] [*FAA*] (FAAL)
OQ&A.......... Oil Quenched and Annealed (SAUS)
OQAP .... Oil Quality Assessment Program [*Society of Automotive Engineers, Inc.*]
O-QAR .... Optical Quick Access Recorder (GAVI)
OQC .... Office of Quality Control [*Social and Rehabilitation Service, HEW*]
OQC .... Officers Qualification Card (SAUS)
OQC .... Operator Quality Control [*RADAR*]
OQC .... Outgoing Quality Control (SAUS)
OQC .... Outside Quality Control (KSC)
OQD .... Optical Quantum Detector
OQE .... Objective Quality Evidence (MCD)
OQG .... Optical Quantum Generator
OQI .... Oil Quantity Indicator
OQL .... Oberserved Quality Level (SAUS)
OQL .... Object Query Language [*Computer science*] (VLIE)
OQL .... Observed Quality Level
OQL .... Online Query Language
OQL .... Outgoing Quality Level
OQL .... Outgoing Quality Limit
OQM .... Office of the Quartermaster [*Military*]
OQMG .... Office of the Quartermaster General [*Military*]
OQP .... Optimum Qualification Procedure
OQPSK....... Offset Quadrature Phase Shift Keying (SAUS)
O-QPSK....... Offset Quaternary Phase Shift Keying (SAUS)
OQQ .... Officer Qualification Questionnaire [*Navy*] (DOMA)
OQR .... Officer's Qualification Record [*Army*]
OQS .... Offsite Quality Surveillance (SAUS)
OQSMAT...... Otis Quick Scoring Mental Abilities Tests [*Psychology*] (DAVI)
OQT .... Officer Qualification Test
OQTD .... Operational Qualifications Test Deficiency [*Air Force*]
OQU .... North Kingstown, RI [*Location identifier*] [*FAA*] (FAAL)
OQW .... Maquoketa, IA [*Location identifier*] [*FAA*] (FAAL)
OQZ .... Union City, TN [*Location identifier*] [*FAA*] (FAAL)
OR .... Air Comores [*ICAO designator*] (AD)
OR .... Beginning of Record (SAUS)
Or .... Indian Law Reports, Orissa Series [*A publication*] (DLA)
OR .... Oak Ridge Complex [*Department of Energy*] [*Oak Ridge National Laboratory*] (GAAI)
OR .... Oak Ridge Operations Office (DOGT)
OR .... Objective Reliability (MCD)
OR .... Object Routine (SAUS)
OR .... Observed Ratio (MCD)
OR .... Observer, Right (SAUS)
OR .... Occurrence Report (ABAC)
OR .... Octane Rating [*Automotive engineering*]
OR .... Octane Requirement [*Mechanical engineering*]
OR .... Odds Ratio [*Statistics*]
O/R .... Office of Record (AFM)
OR .... Officer of Reserve (SAUS)
OR .... Officer Records [*Military*] (AFM)
OR .... Official Receiver

OR	Official Records	
OR	Official Referee	
OR	Official Reports, South Africa [*A publication*] (DLA)	
OR	Official Requirement (SAUS)	
OR	Off-Radial (RDA)	
OR	Off-Route [*Telecommunications*] (OTD)	
OR	Ohms, Resistance (SAUS)	
OR	Oil Rehabilitation Committee [*British*]	
OR	Oil Resistance (SAUS)	
OR	Oil Retention [*Enema*] [*Medicine*]	
OR	Oil Ring (MSA)	
OR	Old Roman (ADA)	
OR	Oleoresin [*Also, Ol Res*] [*Pharmacy*]	
OR	Oleoresinous (SAUS)	
OR	Olfactory Receptor [*Biochemistry*]	
OR	Oligomer Restriction [*Genetics*]	
OR	Olympic Range (SAUS)	
OR	Olympic Record (SAUS)	
OR	Omega Rho (SAUS)	
OR	Omnidirectional Radio Range (MCD)	
OR	On Rail (SAUS)	
o/r	On Request (PIAV)	
O/R	On Request	
OR	On Return	
OR	Ontario Reports [*A publication*] (DLA)	
OR	Open Reduction [*Orthopedics*] (DAVI)	
OR	Open Registry [*Flag of convenience*] [*Shipping*] (DS)	
OR	Open Routine (SAUS)	
OR	Operand Register (VLIE)	
OR	Operating Reactor [*Nuclear energy*] (NRCH)	
OR	Operating Resources (AFM)	
OR	Operating Revenue (SAUS)	
OR	Operating Room [*Medicine*]	
OR	Operational Equipment Requirement (IAA)	
OR	Operationally Ready (MCD)	
OR	Operational Readiness [*Army*]	
OR	Operational Recorder (SAUS)	
OR	Operational Reliability [*Army*] (AABC)	
OR	Operational Report (AAG)	
OR	Operational Requirement	
OR	Operational Research	
OR	Operational Right	
OR	Operational Right DSC or MDM (SAUS)	
OR	Operation Rate (SAUS)	
OR	Operation Reach-Out [*Department of Labor*]	
OR	Operation Record	
OR	Operation Rescue (EA)	
OR	Operation Research (SAUS)	
OR	Operations and Regulations (SAUS)	
OR	Operations Request [*Military*]	
OR	Operations Requirements	
OR	Operations Research [*Computer science*]	
OR	Operations Review [*NASA*] (MCD)	
OR	Operations Room	
OR	Operator (IAA)	
OR	Operator Register (SAUS)	
OR	Operator Routine (SAUS)	
OR	Operculum Ridge	
OR	Ophthalmic Rete [*Bird anatomy*]	
OR	Opponents' Runs [*Baseball*]	
OR	Optical Reader [*Computer science*] (BUR)	
OR	Optical Receiver (SAUS)	
OR	Optic Radiation (DB)	
O+R	Optiram, St. Helier, Jersey, Channel Islands, United Kingdom [*Library symbol*] [*Library of Congress*] (LCLS)	
OR	Oral Rehydration [*Medicine*] (MELL)	
OR	Orange	
Or	Oratio [*A publication*] (OCD)	
Or	Orationes [*of Julian*] [*Classical studies*] (OCD)	
Or	Orationes [*of Dio Chrysostomus*] [*Classical studies*] (OCD)	
OR	Oratorians	
OR	Ordered Recorded	
OR	Ordering Register (IAA)	
OR	Orderly Room	
OR	Order of the Road [*British*] (DBA)	
OR	Order Pennant [*Navy*] [*British*]	
OR	Order [*or Ordering*] Register (SAA)	
OR	Order Release (SAUS)	
OR	Ordinance Report (SAUS)	
OR	Ordnance Requirement	
Or	Oregon (NTIO)	
OR	Oregon [*Postal code*]	
Or	Oregon State Library, Salem, OR [*Library symbol*] [*Library of Congress*] (LCLS)	
Or	Oregon Supreme Court Reports [*A publication*] (DLA)	
OR	Ore Reserve	
Or	Orestes [*of Euripides*] [*Classical studies*] (OCD)	
OR	Organizational Representative (SAUS)	
OR	Organizational Research (SAUS)	
OR	Organized Reserves [*Military*]	
OR	Organ Recovery (EA)	
OR	OR Gate (SAUS)	
OR	Orient	
OR	Oriental (ROG)	
OR	Orientation Ratio (VLIE)	

OR	Orientaed Response (SAUS)	
OR	Oriented (SAUS)	
OR	Orienting Reflex [*Medicine*] (MELL)	
OR	Orienting Response [*Psychology*]	
Or	Origen [*Deceased circa 254*] [*Authority cited in pre-1607 legal work*] (DSA)	
OR	Origin (VLIE)	
OR	Original (ADA)	
OR	Originating Register (VLIE)	
O/R	Originator or Recipient [*Telecommunications*] (OSI)	
OR	O-Ring [*Automotive engineering*]	
'Or	'Orlah (BJA)	
OR	Orosomucoid [*Biochemistry*]	
or	Orthoclase [*CIPW classification*] [*Geology*]	
OR	Orthopedic	
OR	Orthopedic Research [*Medicine*]	
OR	Orthophthalic Resin [*Plastics*]	
OR	Oswestry Rangers [*British military*] (DMA)	
OR	Other (ROG)	
OR	Other Ranks [*Ranks other than officers*] [*Military*]	
OR	Outer Roll [*Aviation*] (MCD)	
OR	Out of Range	
OR	Output Record (SAUS)	
OR	Output Register (MSA)	
OR	Output Routine (SAUS)	
OR	Outside Radius [*Technical drawings*]	
OR	Outside Right [*Soccer position*]	
OR	Overall Report	
OR	Overall Resistance (IAA)	
OR	Overflow Register (SAUS)	
OR	Overhaul and Repair	
OR	Overload Relay (KSC)	
O/R	Overrange [*System or element*] (IEEE)	
O/R	Override (KSC)	
OR	Over Run (MHDW)	
OR	Overrun (SAUS)	
OR	Oversea Requisition (SAUS)	
OR	Overseas Replacement [*Military*]	
OR	Owasco River [*AAR code*]	
or	Owner's Risk (WDAA)	
OR	Owner's Risk [*Shipping*]	
OR	Own Recognizance [*Legal term*]	
O-R	Oxidation-Reduction	
OR	Oxidation Resistance (SAUS)	
OR	Oxide Removal (SAUS)	
OR	Oxygen Enchancement Ratio (IAA)	
OR	Oxygen Relief (NASA)	
OR	Renfrew Public Library, Ontario [*Library symbol*] [*National Library of Canada*] (NLC)	
OR2000	Ocean Rescue 2000 (SAUS)	
ORA	Montauk Caribbean Airways, Inc. [*ICAO designator*] (FAAC)	
ORA	Occultation Radiometer (SAUS)	
ORA	Office of Records Administration [*National Archives*] (BARN)	
ORA	Office of Redress Administration [*Department of Justice*]	
ORA	Office of Regulatory Affairs [*U.S. Food and Drug Administration*]	
ORA	Office of Regulatory Analysis [*Federal Energy Regulatory Commission*]	
ORA	Office of Research Administration [*University of Hawaii*] [*Research center*] (RCD)	
ORA	Office of Research Administration [*St. Louis University*] [*Research center*] (RCD)	
ORA	Office of Research Administration [*University of Pennsylvania*] [*Research center*] (RCD)	
ORA	Office of Research Administration [*North Carolina A & T State University*] [*Research center*] (RCD)	
ORA	Office of Research Analysis [*Air Force*]	
ORA	Office of Research and Applications (SAUS)	
ORA	Office of Rural Affairs [*Victoria, Australia*]	
ORA	Official Records of the Admiralty (SAUS)	
ORA	Oil Refiners Association (NADA)	
ORA	Operating Room Attendant [*British military*] (DMA)	
ORA	Operational RADAR Directed Flights (NATG)	
ORA	Operational Readiness Assessment	
ORA	Operational Requirements Analysis (SPST)	
ORA	Operation Response Area (MCD)	
ORA	Operations Research Analyst [*Army*] (AABC)	
ORA	Operations Research Appreciation (SAUS)	
ORA	Opiate Receptor Agonist [*Medicine*] (MELL)	
ORA	Opportunity Resources for the Arts (EA)	
ORA	Optical Reference Axis	
ORA	Option Revision Agreement (VLIE)	
ORA	Oran [*Argentina*] [*Airport symbol*] (AD)	
ORA	Order for Reinforced Alert (NATG)	
Or A	Oregon Court of Appeals Reports [*A publication*] (DLA)	
ORA	Organisation de Resistance de l'Armee [*France*]	
ORA	Organisation Revolutionnaire Anarchiste [*Revolutionary Anarchist Organization*] [*France*] [*Political party*] (PPE)	
ORA	Organizacao Revolucionaria Armada [*Terrorist group*] [*Portugal*] (EY)	
ORA	Organizational Role Analysis (PDAA)	
ORA	Orifice Rod Assembly [*Nuclear energy*] (NRCH)	
ORA	Oromo Relief Association [*Ethiopia*]	
ORA	Orthopaedic Rehabilitation Association (SAUS)	
ORA	OR to Accumulator (SAUS)	
ORA	Output Reference Axis (IAA)	
ORA	Output Register Address	

ORA .... Ramore Library, Ontario [*Library symbol*] [*National Library of Canada*] (BIB)
ORA .... Ross Laboratory Library, Columbus, OH [*OCLC symbol*] (OCLC)
ORAAP .... Outstanding Reserve Airman Appointment Program
ORAC .... Optical Reference for Azimuth Correction (SAUS)
ORAC .... Oxygen Radical Absorbance Capacity [*Analytical Chemistry*]
ORACBA ...... Office of Risk Assessment and Cost-Benefit Analysis
ORACLE ...... Oak Ridge Automatic Computer and Logical Engine
ORACLE .... Observational Research and Classroom Learning Evaluation [*British*] (DET)
ORACLE ...... On-Line Retrieval and Computational Language for Economists [*Computer science*]
ORACLE ...... Operational Research and Critical Link Evaluation (SAUS)
ORACLE ...... Operations Research and Critical Link Evaluator (SAUS)
ORACLE ...... Optical Reception of Announcements by Coded Line Electronics
ORACLE ...... Optimized Reliability and Component Life Estimate
ORACLE ...... Optimum Record Automation for Court and Law Enforcement
ORACLE .... Optional Reception of Announcements by Coded Line Electronics [*Independent Television "newspaper"*] [*British*] (DI)
ORACLE .... Optional Recovery of Announcements by Coded Line Electronics (NITA)
Oracle .... Oracle Systems Corp. [*Associated Press*] (SAG)
ORACLE ...... Ordnance Rapid Area Clearance [*Military*] (CAAL)
ORACLE ...... Organic Rankine Cycle
ORACLE .... Oversight of Resources and Capability for Logistics Effectiveness (PDAA)
ORACT .... Operational Readiness and Confidence Test
OrAd .... Adams Public Library, Adams, OR [*Library symbol*] [*Library of Congress*] (LCLS)
ORAD .... Office of Rural Areas Development [*Later, Rural Community Development Service*] [*Department of Agriculture*]
ORad .... Officer Radar (SAUS)
ORAD .... Orbiter RADAR [*NASA*]
ORAD .... Outbound Radian (SAUS)
ORAD .... Outhound Radial (SAUS)
Or Admin R... Oregon Administrative Rules [*A publication*] (DLA)
Or Admin R Bull... Oregon Administrative Rules Bulletin [*A publication*] (DLA)
ORADS .... Optical Ranging and Detection System
Or Ad Sh ..... Supreme Court of the State of Oregon Advance Sheets [*A publication*] (DLA)
ORAE .... Aerospace Industries Association of Canada (SAUS)
ORAE .... Office de Repartition des Approvisionnements d'Energie [*Canada*]
ORAE .... Operational Research and Analysis Establishment (MCD)
OrAg .... Agness Community Library, Agness, OR [*Library symbol*] [*Library of Congress*] (LCLS)
ORaH .... Robinson Memorial Hospital, Ravenna, OH [*Library symbol*] [*Library of Congress*] (LCLS)
OrAh .... Washington County Cooperative Library Services, Aloha, OR [*Library symbol*] [*Library of Congress*] (LCLS)
ORAIS .... Opportunities and Risks of Artificial Intelligent Systems (SAUS)
OrAl .... Albany Public Library, Albany, OR [*Library symbol*] [*Library of Congress*] (LCLS)
ORAL .... Oral Access to Library
OrAlBM .... United States Bureau of Mines, Education and Training Center, Albany, OR [*Library symbol*] [*Library of Congress*] (LCLS)
OrAlC .... Linn-Benton Community College, Albany, OR [*Library symbol*] [*Library of Congress*] (LCLS)
ORALFORE... Opposed Rates of Advance of Large Forces in Europe (SAUS)
OrAlH .... Albany General Hospital, Albany, OR [*Library symbol*] [*Library of Congress*] (LCLS)
Oral Roberts U... Oral Roberts University (GAGS)
Oral Surg Oral Med Oral Pathol... Oral Surgery, Oral Medicine and Oral Pathology (SAUS)
OrAIT .... Teledyne-Wah Chang Albany, Albany, OR (LCLS)
ORALTOX..... Acute Oral Toxicity for Birds, Mice, Rats (SAUS)
OrAm .... Amity Public Library, Amity, OR [*Library symbol*] [*Library of Congress*] (LCLS)
ORAM .... Office for Research in Academic Methods (SAUS)
ORAM .... Orbital Repair and Maintenance (SAUS)
ORAN .... Orange [*Laboratory science*] (DAVI)
ORAN .... Orbital Analysis
ORAN .... Organisation Regionale Africaine de Normalisation [*African Regional Organization for Standardization - AROS*] (EAIO)
OR&E .... Office of Research and Engineering (SAUS)
OR&F .... Open Reduction and Fixation (DMAA)
OR&F .... Operations, Research and Facilities [*Marine science*] (OSRA)
OR&IE .... Operations Research and Industrial Engineering (SAUS)
OR & N .... Oregon Railroad & Navigation Co.
OR & SP ..... Office of Research and Sponsored Programs [*Research center*] (RCD)
ORANG .... Oregon Air National Guard (MUSM)
Orange......... Orange PLC [*Associated Press*] (SAG)
Orange Cty Dent Soc Bull... Orange County Dental Society. Bulletin (SAUS)
Orange Light... Change Approaching (SAUS)
OrangN .... Orange National Bancorp [*Associated Press*] (SAG)
OranRk .... Orange & Rockland Utilities, Inc. [*Associated Press*] (SAG)
ORANS .... Oak Ridge Analytical Systems
ORAP .... Originator/Recipient Address Prefix (VLIE)
ORAPA .... Ontario Retail Accident Prevention Association (SAUS)
Or App .... Oregon Reports, Court of Appeal [*A publication*] (DLA)
ORAQI .... Oak Ridge Air Quality Index (SAUS)
OrAr .... Arlington Public Library, Arlington, OR [*Library symbol*] [*Library of Congress*] (LCLS)
Or-Ar........... Oregon State Archives, Salem, OR [*Library symbol*] [*Library of Congress*] (LCLS)

ORAR .... Rainy River Public Library, Ontario [*Library symbol*] [*National Library of Canada*] (NLC)
ORAS .... Oil Recovery and Separation Technology [*Jastram Werke*]
ORASA .... Operational Research and Systems Analysis (PDAA)
OrAshS .... Southern Oregon College, Ashland, OR [*Library symbol*] [*Library of Congress*] (LCLS)
ORASS .... Offender Risk Assessment Scoring System (SAUS)
OrAst .... Astor Library, Astoria, OR [*Library symbol*] [*Library of Congress*] (LCLS)
OrAstC .... Clatsop Community College, Astoria, OR [*Library symbol*] [*Library of Congress*] (LCLS)
OrAstM .... Columbia River Maritime Museum, Astoria, OR [*Library symbol*] [*Library of Congress*] (LCLS)
ORAT .... Oralorical (SAUS)
Orat .... Oration [*or Orator or Oratorio*]
Orat .... Orator ad M. Brutum [*of Cicero*] [*Classical studies*] (OCD)
ORAT .... Oratorical
Orat .... Oratorio (SAUS)
Orat .... Oratory (SAUS)
ORATE .... Ordered Random Access Talking Equipment
ORATMS...... Off-Route Antitank Mine System (MCD)
ORATOS...... Orbit & Attitude Operations System (SAUS)
ORATS .... Operational Readiness Assessment and Training System (MCD)
ORAU .... Oak Ridge Associated Universities (EA)
OraVax........ OraVax, Inc. [*Associated Press*] (SAG)
ORAW......... Oil Remaining after Waterflooding [*Petroleum technology*]
OrB .... Beaverton City Library, Beaverton, OR [*Library symbol*] [*Library of Congress*] (LCLS)
ORB .... Object Request Broker [*Computer science*]
ORB .... Oceanic Ridge Basalts
ORB .... Oceanographic Research Buoy
ORB .... Ocean Research Buoy (IAA)
ORB .... Offenders' Review Board [*New South Wales, Australia*]
ORB .... Office Repeater Bay (SAUS)
ORB .... Officer Record Brief [*Army*] (AABC)
ORB .... Offsets Review Board [*New South Wales, Australia*]
ORB .... Omnidirectional Radio Beacon
ORB .... Omnidirectional Research Beacon (SAUS)
ORB .... Online Reference Book for Medieval Studies [*Internet resource*]
ORB .... Operational Research Branch [*Canada*]
ORB .... Operational Review Board (ACAE)
ORB .... Operations Record Book [*Air Ministry*] [*British*] [*World War II*]
ORB .... Optometrists' Registration Board [*Victoria, Australia*]
ORB .... Orbe [*Switzerland*] [*Seismograph station code, US Geological Survey*] [*Closed*] (SEIS)
Orb............. Orbis [*Record label*] [*Germany, etc.*]
ORB .... Orbit
ORB .... Orbital (KSC)
ORB .... Orbital Sciences Corp. [*NYSE symbol*]
ORB .... Orbiter [*NASA*] (NASA)
ORB .... Orbit Oil & Gas Ltd. [*Toronto Stock Exchange symbol*]
ORB .... Order
ORB .... Orebro [*Sweden*] [*Airport symbol*] (OAG)
ORB .... Organitzational Records Branch (SAUS)
ORB .... Organizational Records Branch [*Army*]
ORB .... Orr, MN [*Location identifier*] [*FAA*] (FAAL)
ORB .... Outer Radiation Belt
ORB .... Outside Reactor Building [*Nuclear energy*] (NRCH)
Orb............. Owners Risk of Breakage (EBF)
ORB .... Owners Risk of Breakage (or Breaking) (SAUS)
ORB 1-G ..... Orbiter One-G Trainer [*NASA*] (NASA)
OrBa .... Banks Community Library, Banks, OR [*Library symbol*] [*Library of Congress*] (LCLS)
ORBA .... Erbil [*Iraq*] [*ICAO location identifier*] (ICLI)
ORBA .... Ontario Road Builders Association (SAUS)
ORBACT....... Optometrists' Registration Board of the Australian Capital Territory
OrBak.......... Baker County Public Library, Baker, OR [*Library symbol*] [*Library of Congress*] (LCLS)
OrBakSE...... Saint Elizabeth Hospital, Baker, OR [*Library symbol*] [*Library of Congress*] (LCLS)
OrBan .... Bandon Public Library, Bandon, OR [*Library symbol*] [*Library of Congress*] (LCLS)
ORBANCO.... Oregon Bank (EFIS)
Or Bar Bull... Oregon Bar Bulletin [*A publication*] (DLA)
ORBAT........ Order of Battle (SAUS)
ORBAT........ Order of Battle Report [*Military*] (NATG)
ORBATREP... Order of Battle Report (SAUS)
ORBATTOA.. Order of Battle-Transfer of Authority (SAUS)
ORBB .... Sirsenk/Bamarni [*Iraq*] [*ICAO location identifier*] (ICLI)
ORBC .... Baghdad/Soica Headquarters [*Iraq*] [*ICAO location identifier*] (ICLI)
ORBC .... Ox Red Blood Cell [*Medicine*] (DMAA)
ORBD .... Object Relational Database
ORBD-NRC... Osteoporosis and Related Bone Diseases-National Resource Center (SAUS)
OrBe .... Deschutes County Library, Bend, OR [*Library symbol*] [*Library of Congress*] (LCLS)
ORBE .... Open Reciprocating Brayton Engine (PDAA)
OrBeBR........ Bend Research, Inc., Bend, OR [*Library symbol*] [*Library of Congress*] (LCLS)
OrBeC .... Central Oregon Community College, Bend, OR [*Library symbol*] [*Library of Congress*] (LCLS)
OrBeCJ .... Cascade Junior High School, Bend, OR [*Library symbol*] [*Library of Congress*] (LCLS)
OrBeHS....... Bend Senior High School, Bend, OR [*Library symbol*] [*Library of Congress*] (LCLS)

OrBeMC	Saint Charles Medical Center, Medical Library, Bend, OR [*Library symbol*] [*Library of Congress*] (LCLS)
OrBeMH	Mountain View High School, Bend, OR [*Library symbol*] [*Library of Congress*] (LCLS)
OrbEng	Orbital Engine Corp. Ltd. [*Associated Press*] (SAG)
OrBeOHM	Oregon High Desert Museum, Bend, OR [*Library symbol*] [*Library of Congress*] (LCLS)
OrBePJ	Pilot Butte Junior High School, Bend, OR [*Library symbol*] [*Library of Congress*] (LCLS)
ORBF	Ordinary Radial Basis Function (IDAI)
OrBFP	Floating Point Systems, Inc., Beaverton, OR [*Library symbol*] [*Library of Congress*] (LCLS)
OrBG	Oregon Graduate Center, Beaverton, OR [*Library symbol*] [*Library of Congress*] (LCLS)
OrBGS	Church of Jesus Christ of Latter-Day Saints, Genealogical Society Library, Beaverton Branch, Beaverton, OR [*Library symbol*] [*Library of Congress*] (LCLS)
ORBI	Orbital Sciences Corp. [*NASDAQ symbol*] (SAG)
ORBI	Rocky Band No. 1 Indian Band Library, Ontario [*Library symbol*] [*National Library of Canada*] (BIB)
orbic	orbicular (SAUS)
orbic	orbicularis (SAUS)
ORBID	On-line Retrieval of Bibliographic Data (SAUS)
ORBIFC	Oak Ridge Boys International Fan Club (EA)
ORBIS	Orbiting Radio Beacon Ionospheric Satellite [*NASA*]
ORBIS	Ordering and Billing System
ORBIS	Oregon Business Information System [*Oregon State Economic Development Department*] [*Information service or system*] [*Defunct*] (IID)
ORBIS CAL	Orbiting Radio Beacon Ionosphere Satellite for Calibration [*NASA*] (PDAA)
ORBISCAL	Orbiting Radio Beacon Ionospheric Satellite for Calibration (SAUS)
ORBIT	Oak Ridge Binary Internal-Translator
ORBIT	Objectives-Referenced Bank of Items and Tests (TES)
ORBIT	Office Research into Buildings and IT (NITA)
ORBIT	On-Line, Real-Time, Branch Information Transmission [*IBM Corp.*] [*Computer science*]
ORBIT	On-Line Reduced Bandwidth Information Transfer [*Computer science*]
ORBIT	On-line Retrieval of Bibliographic Information Timeshared (SAUS)
ORBIT	On-Line Retrieval of Bibliographic Text [*Search system*] [*Computer science*]
ORBIT	ORACLE Binary Internal Translator [*Algebraic programming system*]
ORBIT	Orbit, Ballistic Impact, and Trajectory [*Computer*] (MUGU)
Orbit	Orbit International Corp. [*Associated Press*] (SAG)
ORBIT	Order Billing Inventory Technique (PDAA)
ORBITSIM	Orbit Simulation (ACAE)
ORBK	Orbotech Ltd. [*Formerly, Optrotech Ltd.*] [*NASDAQ symbol*] (SPSG)
ORBKF	Orbotech Ltd Ord [*NASDAQ symbol*] (TTSB)
ORBL	Outline Raised Black Letter [*Tire design*]
ORBM	Mosul [*Iraq*] [*ICAO location identifier*] (ICLI)
ORBN	Orbanco Financial Services Corp. (SAUS)
OrBo	Boardman Public Library, Boardman, OR [*Library symbol*] [*Library of Congress*] (LCLS)
Orbotch	Orbotech [*Associated Press*] (SAG)
OrBP	Oregon Regional Primate Research Center, Beaverton, OR [*Library symbol*] [*Library of Congress*] (LCLS)
Or-BPH	Oregon State Library, Services for the Blind and Physically Handicapped, Salem, OR [*Library symbol*] [*Library of Congress*] (LCLS)
ORBR	Baghdad/Rasheed [*Iraq*] [*ICAO location identifier*] (ICLI)
OrBroo	Chetco Community Public Library, Brookings, OR [*Library symbol*] [*Library of Congress*] (LCLS)
ORBS	Baghdad/Saddam International [*Iraq*] [*ICAO location identifier*] (ICLI)
ORBS	Off Reservation Boarding School (EDAC)
ORBS	Orbital Rendezvous Base System
ORBS	Orbiting Rendezvous Base System (SAUS)
OrbSci	Orbital Sciences Corp. [*Associated Press*] (SAG)
ORBT	Orbit International Corp. [*NASDAQ symbol*] (NQ)
OrBT	Tektronix, Inc., Beaverton, OR [*Library symbol*] [*Library of Congress*] (LCLS)
OrbtSemi	Orbit Semiconductor Co. [*Associated Press*] (SAG)
Or Bull	Oregon Bulletin [*A publication*] (AAGC)
ORBV	Optometrists' Registration Board of Victoria [*Australia*]
ORBW	Baghdad/Muthenna [*Iraq*] [*ICAO location identifier*] (ICLI)
ORBWA	Optometrists' Registration Board of Western Australia
ORBZ	Ain Zalah [*Iraq*] [*ICAO location identifier*] (ICLI)
OrC	Corvallis Public Library, Corvallis, OR [*Library symbol*] [*Library of Congress*] (LCLS)
ORC	Occupational Research Centre [*Hatfield Polytechnic*] [*British*] (CB)
ORC	Oculo-Reno-Cerebellar [*Syndrome*] [*Medicine*] (DMAA)
ORC	Office of Regional Counsel [*Environmental Protection Agency*] (GFGA)
ORC	Office of Reserve Components [*Army*]
ORC	Office of the Regional Commissioner [*Social Security Administration*] (OICC)
ORC	Officers' Reserve Corps [*Later, Army Reserve*]
ORC	Offshore Racing Council
ORC	Oilseeds Research Council [*Australia*]
ORC	On-Line Reactivity Computer [*Nuclear energy*] (NRCH)
ORC	On-Road Costs [*Motor vehicles*]
ORC	Operarios del Reina de Cristo (TOCD)
orc	Operarios del Reina de Cristo (TOCD)
ORC	Operational Readiness Check
ORC	Operational Reports Control [*Military*] (AFM)

ORC	Operational Requirements Committee [*Ministry of Defence*] [*British*]
ORC	Operational Research Committee (SAUS)
ORC	Operations Research Center [*Massachusetts Institute of Technology*] [*Research center*] (KSC)
ORC	Operations Review Committee (COE)
ORC	Opinion Research Center
ORC	Opinion Research Corp. (SAUS)
ORC	Optical Radiation Corp.
ORC	Optical Recording Corp.
ORC	Optical Recording Corporation (SAUS)
ORC	Orange City, IA [*Location identifier*] [*FAA*] (FAAL)
ORC	Orange River Colony [*Later, Orange Free State*] [*South Africa*]
ORC	Orbital Research Centrifuge [*NASA*] (KSC)
ORC	Orcadas Del Sur [*Argentina*] [*Geomagnetic observatory code*]
ORC	Orcatech, Inc. [*Toronto Stock Exchange symbol*]
ORC	Orderly Room Corporal [*British*]
ORC	Order of the Red Cross
ORC	Ordnance Rocket Center (KSC)
ORC	Organic Rankine Cycle [*for power generation*] (PDAA)
ORC	Organization Requirements Clerk [*Defense Supply Agency*]
ORC	Organization Resources Counselors (MCD)
ORC	Organized Reserve Corps [*Later, Army Reserve*]
ORC	Origin Recognition Complex [*Genetics*]
ORC	Orthogonal Row Computer
ORC	Outbound RADAR Control
ORC	Overrun Clutch
ORC	Overseas Reconstruction Committee [*British*] [*World War II*]
ORC	Overseas Replacement Center (SAUS)
ORC	Overseas Research Center [*Wake Forest University*] [*Research center*] (RCD)
ORC	Overseas Research Council (SAUS)
ORC	Owner's Risk of Chafing [*Shipping*]
ORC	Oxidation Reduction Cycle (SAUS)
ORC	Oxidation-Resistant Coating
ORC	Oxidized Regenerated Cellulose [*Hemostatic*] [*Organic chemistry*]
ORC	Ozarks Regional Commission [*Department of Commerce*]
ORC	Reed College, Portland, OR [*OCLC symbol*] (OCLC)
ORC	Reports of the High Court of the Orange River Colony [*South Africa*] [*A publication*] (DLA)
ORCA	Ocean Resource Coordination and Assessment [*National Oceanic and Atmospheric Administration*]
ORCA	Ocean Resources Conservation Association [*British*]
ORCA	Official Receiver under the Companies Act (SAUS)
ORCA	Oldtime Radio-Show Collector's Association (EA)
ORCA	Online Resource Control Aid [*Computer science*] (HGAA)
ORCA	Ontario Royal Commission on Asbestos (SAUS)
ORCA	Operations Requirements Continuity Assessment (SAUS)
ORCA	Oregon Caves National Monument
ORCA	Organisme Europeen de Recherche sur la Carie [*European Organization for Caries Research*] (EAIO)
ORCA	Organized Resistance to Capture in Alaska [*Defunct*] (EA)
ORCA	Regional Office for Central America (SAUS)
Orcad	Orcad, Inc. [*Associated Press*] (SAG)
ORCAL	Orange County Manufacturing and Metalworking Conference and Exposition (SAUS)
ORCALMIS	Ordnance Calibration Management Information System [*Navy*] (DNAB)
OrCan	Canby Public Library, Canby, OR [*Library symbol*] [*Library of Congress*] (LCLS)
OrCanHS	Canby Union High School, Canby, OR [*Library symbol*] [*Library of Congress*] (LCLS)
ORCATS	Oldtime Radio Collectors and Traders Society (EA)
OrCb	Coos Bay Public Library, Coos Bay, OR [*Library symbol*] [*Library of Congress*] (LCLS)
ORCB	Order of Railway Conductors and Brakemen [*Later, United Transportation Union*] (EA)
OrCbS	Southwestern Oregon Community College, Coos Bay, OR [*Library symbol*] [*Library of Congress*] (LCLS)
OrCC	Corvallis Clinic, Corvallis, OR [*Library symbol*] [*Library of Congress*] (LCLS)
ORCC	Ohio Regional Campus Conference (PSS)
ORCC	Online Resources Communications Co.
ORCC	Operational Requirements Committee (SAUS)
ORCC	Orangutan Research and Conservation Center (SAUS)
ORCC	Outward-Rectifying Chloride Channel [*Biochemistry*]
ORCCA	Open Road Camper Clubs of America [*Later, ORSAC*] (EA)
ORCEF	Oak Ridge Critical Experimental Facility (SAUS)
ORCEN	Overseas Records Center [*Military*]
OrCEPA	United States Environmental Protection Agency, Corvallis Environmental Research Laboratory, Corvallis, OR [*Library symbol*] [*Library of Congress*] (LCLS)
OrCg	W. A. Woodward Memorial Library, Cottage Grove, OR [*Library symbol*] [*Library of Congress*] (LCLS)
OrCGS	Church of Jesus Christ of Latter-Day Saints, Genealogical Society Library, Corvallis Branch, Corvallis, OR [*Library symbol*] [*Library of Congress*] (LCLS)
OrCGSH	Good Samaritan Hospital, Corvallis, OR [*Library symbol*] [*Library of Congress*] (LCLS)
ORCH	Orchard
orch	Orchestra (WDAA)
ORCH	Orchestra
Orch	Orchestra
orch	Orchestral (GROV)
ORCH	Orchiectomy [*Medicine*] (MELL)
ORCHARD	Orchard [*Commonly used*] (OPSA)

Orch Circ	Orchestra Circle (SAUS)
orchd	Orchestrated (GROV)
ORCHD	Orchestrated (By) [*Music*]
Orch H	Orchestra Hall (SAUS)
ORCHIS.........	Oak Ridge Computerized Hierarchical Information System [*AEC*] (IID)
ORCHL	Orchestral [*Music*]
ORCHRD	Orchard [*Commonly used*] (OPSA)
OrchSHw......	Orchard Supply Hardware Stores Corp. [*Associated Press*] (SAG)
ORCI	Office for the Research and Collection of Information (SAUS)
ORCI	Opinion Research [*NASDAQ symbol*] (TTSB)
ORCID..........	Optical Readout Cherenkov Imaging Detector [*Computer science*] (PDAA)
OrckitCo.......	Orckit Communications Ltd. [*Associated Press*] (SAG)
ORCL	Oracle Systems Corp. [*NASDAQ symbol*] (NQ)
OrCIS	Sunnyside Medical Library, Clackamas, OR [*Library symbol*] [*Library of Congress*] (LCLS)
ORCMD	Orlando Contract Management District (SAA)
OrCMG........	Mid-Valley Genealogical Society, Corvallis, OR [*Library symbol*] [*Library of Congress*] (LCLS)
ORCO	Central Ontario Regional Library, Richmond Hill, Ontario [*Library symbol*] [*National Library of Canada*] (NLC)
OrCo	Coquille Public Library, Coquille, OR [*Library symbol*] [*Library of Congress*] (LCLS)
ORCO	Ontario Library Service - Trent, Richmond Hill, Ontario [*Library symbol*] [*National Library of Canada*] (NLC)
ORCO..........	Optical Radiation Corporation (SAUS)
ORCO..........	Organization Committee (SAUS)
ORCODO	Annual Research Reviews. Oral Contraceptives (journ.) (SAUS)
OrColHS.......	Colton High School, Colton, OR [*Library symbol*] [*Library of Congress*] (LCLS)
OrCon	Condon Public Library, Condon, OR [*Library symbol*] [*Library of Congress*] (LCLS)
ORCON	Observation Report Conversion [*Program*]
ORCON	Organic Control
ORCON	Originator Controlled [*Information dissemination*]
ORCON	Originator Control of Information Release (SAUS)
ORCON Program...	Observation Report Conversion Program (SAUS)
OrCor..........	Cornelius Public Library, Cornelius, OR [*Library symbol*] [*Library of Congress*] (LCLS)
ORCP	Ocean Ridge Crest Processes (SAUS)
ORCP	Optical Reader Card Punch (SAUS)
ORCS	Omnitronics Research Corporation (SAUS)
ORCS	On-line Remote Compile System (SAUS)
OrCS	Oregon State University, Corvallis, OR [*Library symbol*] [*Library of Congress*] (LCLS)
ORCS	Organic Rankine Cycle System [*For power generation*]
ORCS	Organic Reactions Catalysis Society (EA)
ORCSA........	Orange River Colony, South Africa (ILCA)
OrCS-Ar	Oregon State University Archives, Corvallis, OR [*Library symbol*] [*Library of Congress*] (LCLS)
OrCS-MB......	Oregon State University, Institute of Marine Biology, Coos Bay, OR [*Library symbol*] [*Library of Congress*] (LCLS)
OrCS-MSC ...	Oregon State University, Hatfield Marine Science Center, Newport, OR [*Library symbol*] [*Library of Congress*] (LCLS)
ORCT	Orckit Communications Ltd. [*NASDAQ symbol*] (SAG)
OrCuHS.......	Culver Senior High School, Culver, OR [*Library symbol*] [*Library of Congress*] (LCLS)
ORCUP........	Ontario Region Canadian University Press (SAUS)
ORCUS........	Operational Research Co., Universal Systems
ORCV..........	Outdoor Recreation Center Victoria [*Australia*]
ORCV..........	Overriding Cam Valve
ORC youth ...	Opinion Research Corporation Youth (NITA)
ORD	CAP PA Gutierrez [*Hernando R.*] Ordonez [*Mexico*] [*ICAO designator*] (FAAC)
ORD	Chicago [*Illinois*] O'Hare Airport [*Derived from former name: Orchard Field*] [*Airport symbol*]
ORD	Office for Research and Development [*American Library Association*] (AEBS)
ORD	Office of Rare Diseases, National Institutes of Health (SAUS)
ORD	Office of Regional Development [*Organization of American States*]
ORD	Office of Research and Development [*National Oceanic and Atmospheric Administration*] (GFGA)
ORD	Office of Research and Development [*Washington, DC*] [*Environmental Protection Agency*] (GRD)
ORD	Office of Research Development [*Office of Policy, Evaluation, and Research*] [*Department of Labor*]
ORD	Office of Rubber Director [*WPB*] [*World War II*]
ORD	Officers Replacement Depot (SAUS)
ORD	Off-Range Distance (MCD)
ORD	Ohio River Division [*Army Corps of Engineers*]
ORD	Once-Run Distillate (PDAA)
ORD	Operational Readiness Date
ORD	Operational Readiness Demonstration [*FAA*] (TAG)
ORD	Operational Ready [*or Readiness*] Data [*NASA*] (GFGA)
ORD	Operational Ready Data (or Date) (SAUS)
ORD	Operational Requirements Document (COE)
ORD	Operational Research Division [*Department of National Defence*] [*Canada*]
ORD	Operational Suitability (SAUS)
ORD	Operation Readiness Demonstration (SAUS)
ORD	Operations [*or Operational*] Requirement Document
ORD	Optical Reference Device
ORD	Optical Rotary Dispersion
ORD	Oral Radiation Death (MELL)
ORD	Orbital Requirements Document
ord	Ordained (GEAB)
ord	Ordained
Ord.	Order (EBF)
ord	Order (WDAA)
ORD	Order
ORD	Orderly
ord	Ordinal (NTIO)
ORD	Ordinal
ord	Ordinance (WDAA)
ORD	Ordinance
Ord.	Ordinary (EBF)
ord	Ordinary (ELAL)
ORD	Ordinary (MSA)
ORD	Ordinary Seaman [*British*]
ORD	Ordinary Share (SAUS)
Ord.	Ordinate (SAUS)
ORD	Ordnance (AAG)
ORD	Ordovician [*Period, era, or system*] [*Geology*]
Ord.	Orotidine [*Also, O*] [*A nucleoside*]
ORD	Overseas Replacement Depot [*Military*]
ORD	Owner's Risk of Damage [*Shipping*]
ORD	Oxidation-Reduced Diffusion (SAUS)
ORDA	NIH Office of Recombinant DNA Activities (SAUS)
ORDA	Ober Ramstadt Depot Activity [*Germany*] [*Army*]
ORDA	Oceanographic Research for Defense Application (SAUS)
ORDA	Office of Recombinant DNA Activities [*Bethesda, MD*] [*National Institute of Allergy and Infectious Diseases*]
ORDA	Office of Research Development Administration (SAUS)
ORDAC........	Overrange Detection and Correction [*Analytical chemistry*]
OrDal	Dallas Public Library, Dallas, OR [*Library symbol*] [*Library of Congress*] (LCLS)
ORDAL........	Operations Research Direct Access Language (SAUS)
ORD-ALA	Office of Research and Development-American Library Association (SAUS)
ORDALT.......	Ordnance Alterations
Ord Amst	Ordinance of Amsterdam [*A publication*] (DLA)
Ord Antw	Ordinance of Antwerp [*A publication*] (DLA)
Ord Austl Cap Terr...	Ordinances of the Australian Capital Territory (SAUS)
ORD BBS	Office of Research and Development Electronic Bulletin Board System [*Environmental Protection Agency*] (AEPA)
Ord BD	Ordnance Board [*Military*] (WDAA)
Ord Bilb	Ordinance of Bilboa [*A publication*] (DLA)
ORDBMS......	Object-Relational Database Mangement System (SAUS)
ORDBN	Ordnance Battalion
OrdBrd	Ordnance Board [*British*]
ORDC..........	Orbiter Data Reduction Center [*NASA*]
ORDC..........	Ordnance Corps [*Army*]
ORDC..........	Ordnance Research and Development Center [*Aberdeen Proving Ground, Maryland*] [*Navy*]
ORDCAL.......	Ordnance Calibration [*Navy*] (NVT)
ORDCAN	Orders Canceled [*Air Force*]
ORDCIT........	Ordnance Department and California Institute of Technology [*Army*] (RDA)
ORDCONCAN...	Orders Considered Canceled [*Air Force*]
ORDCONTECH...	Ordnance Control Technician (DNAB)
Ord Copen ...	Ordinance of Copenhagen [*A publication*] (DLA)
ORDCOR	Orders Corrected [*Air Force*]
ORDCORPS...	Ordnance Corps [*Army*]
ORDCU	Occupational Research and Development Coordinating Unit
ORDD	Office of Research, Development, and Demonstrations [*Federal Railroad Administration*]
ORDD..........	Ordered (ROG)
OrdDep	Ordnance Depot (SAUS)
ORD DEPT ...	Ordnance Department [*Military*] (WDAA)
ORDDIS	Ordinary Discharge [*Military*]
ORDDIST	Ordnance District
ORDEAL.......	Oak Ridge Data Evaluation and Analysis Language [*Department of Energy*] (PDAA)
ORDEAL......	Orbital Rate Drive Electronics for Apollo and LM [*NASA*]
ORDEAL......	Orbit Rate Display - Earth and Lunar [*NASA*]
ORDEF	Ontario Research Development Foundation (SAUS)
OrdEng........	Ordnance Engineer (SAUS)
ORDENG	Ordnance Engineering
ORDER.........	On-Line Order Entry System [*Computer science*] (MHDB)
ORDER.........	Organization and Retrieval of Data for Efficient Research (SAUS)
ORDER........	Outstanding Requisitions Defeat Endurance Readiness (DNAB)
ORDET	Orbit Determination Group
ORDet	Owner's Risk of Deterioration [*Shipping*]
ORDFAC.......	Ordnance Facility
OrdFdPk.......	Ordnance Field Park (SAUS)
ORDFIAC......	Ordnance Fiscal and Inventory Automatic Computer (SAUS)
ORDFIN........	Ordinary Finish (SAUS)
Ord Flor.......	Ordinance of Florence [*A publication*] (DLA)
OrdFuzeLab...	Ordnance Fuze Laboratory (SAUS)
Ord Gen	Ordinance of Genoa [*A publication*] (DLA)
ORDHAC......	Ordnance Systems Command Hydroballistics Advisory Committee [*Obsolete*] [*Navy*]
Ord Hamb....	Ordinance of Hamburg [*A publication*] (DLA)
ORD/HWERL...	Office of Research and Development/ Hazardous Waste Environmental Research Laboratory (SAUS)
OrdInsp........	Ordnance Inspector (SAUS)
ORDINST	Ordnance Instruction
ORDIP	Ordnance Alteration Installation Plan [*Navy*]
ORDIR	Omnirange Digital RADAR

ORDIS......... Office of Research and Development Information Systems (SAUS)
ORDIS......... Optical Reading Direct Input System (IAA)
ORDIS......... Ordnance Discharge (DNAB)
Ord Konigs... Ordinance of Konigsberg [*A publication*] (DLA)
ORDL........... Ohio River Division Laboratory [*Army Corps of Engineers*] (KSC)
ORDL-EC...... Ohio River Division Laboratory, Engineer Corps [*Army*] (MCD)
Ord Leg ...... Ordinance of Leghorn [*A publication*] (DLA)
ORDLIS........ Ordnance Logistics Information System [*Navy*]
ORDLIX........ Organized Design for Line and Crew System (SAUS)
ORDM.......... Ordnance Corps Manual (AAG)
ORDMAINTCO... Ordnance Maintenance Company [*Navy*] (DNAB)
Ord Man ...... Ordnance Manual (SAUS)
Ord Med Jur... Ordronaux's Medical Jurisprudence [*A publication*] (DLA)
ORDMOD...... Orders Modified [*Navy*]
OrdMslComd... Ordnance Missile Command (SAUS)
ordn............ Ordinance (WDAA)
ORDN.......... Ordnance (KSC)
ORDNA .... Organismes de Radiodiffusion des Pays NonAlignes [*Broadcasting
                  Organizations of Non-Aligned Countries - BONAC*] (EAIO)
ORDNG .... Ordering
Ordn Surv .... Ordnance Survey (SAUS)
ORDNTR ...... Ordinator
ORDO.......... Ordinario [*Ordinarily*] [*Music*] (ROG)
OrdO .... Ordnance Officer (SAUS)
Ordo Nob Urb... Ordo Nobilium Urbium [*of Ausonius*] [*Classical studies*] (OCD)
ORDP.......... Office of Rural Development Policy [*Department of Agriculture*]
ORDP.......... Ordnance Corps Pamphlet [*Army*] (MCD)
ORDPDS...... Offender Rehabilitation Division of the Public Defender Service (EA)
OrdPG......... Ordnance Proving Ground (SAUS)
Ord Port...... Ordinance of Portugal [*A publication*] (DLA)
OrdProcDist... Ordnance Procurement District (SAUS)
Ord Prus...... Ordinance of Prussia [*A publication*] (DLA)
ORDR........... Order
ORDRAT....... Ordnance Dial Reader and Translator
OrdRepSh .... Ordnance Repair Shop (SAUS)
ORDREV ...... Ordnance Procedures Review [*Military*] (NVT)
Ordr Jud Ins... Ordronaux on Judicial Aspects of Insanity [*A publication*] (DLA)
Ordr Med Jur... Ordronaux's Medical Jurisprudence [*A publication*] (DLA)
Ord Rott...... Ordinance of Rotterdam [*A publication*] (DLA)
ORDRPT ...... Ordnance Report
ORDS.......... Observation Requirements Data Sheet (IAA)
ORDS........... Office of Research, Demonstrations, and Statistics [*Health Care
                  Financing Administration*]
ORDS.......... Ordinary Shares (WDAA)
OrdSch........ Ordnance School (SAUS)
ORDSER ...... Ordnance Support Element Review (NVT)
Ord Sgt .... Ordnance Sergeant [*Military*] (DMA)
Ords NZ ...... Ordinances of the Legislative Council of New Zealand
                  [*A publication*] (DLA)
OrdSpActv.... Ordnance Special Activity (SAUS)
ORDSTA....... Ordnance Station
OrdSupDep... Ordnance Supply Depot (SAUS)
Ord Swe ...... Ordinance of Sweden [*A publication*] (DLA)
ORDSYSCOM... Ordnance Systems Command [*Formerly, Bureau of Naval
                  Weapons; later, Naval Sea Systems Command*]
ORDT........... Office of Research, Demonstrations, and Training [*Social and
                  Rehabilitation Service, HEW*]
OrdTestSta... Ordnance Test Station (SAUS)
OrdTTC .... Ordnance Technical Training Center (SAUS)
Ord Us......... Ord on Usury [*A publication*] (DLA)
ORDVAC...... Ordinance Variable Automatic Computer (RALS)
OrdVAC .... Ordnance Variable Automatic Computer (SAUS)
OrdWpnComd... Ordnance Weapons Command (SAUS)
ORDY.......... Ordinary (AABC)
OrE............. Eugene Public Library, Eugene, OR [*Library symbol*] [*Library of
                  Congress*] (LCLS)
ORE .... Greendale Aviation Co. [*Nigeria*] [*FAA designator*] (FAAC)
ORE .... Greenfield [*Massachusetts*] [*Airport symbol*] (AD)
ORE .... Obtained Radiation Emittance
ORE .... Occupational Radiation Exposure (NRCH)
ORE .... Oceanographic Research Equipment
ORE .... Ocean Research Equipment (SAUS)
ORE .... Ocean Resources Engineering (SAUS)
ORE .... Office of Regional Economics [*Department of Commerce*]
ORE .... Office of Research and Evaluation [*Bureau of Labor Statistics*] (GRD)
ORE .... Officer Responsible for the Exercise [*Navy*] (NVT)
ORE .... On-Orbit Repair Experiment [*NASA*] (NASA)
ORE .... Operational Readiness [*Navy*] (NG)
ORE .... Operational Readiness Evaluation [*Army*]
ORE .... Operational Readiness Exercise (MCD)
ORE .... Operational Research Establishment (SAUS)
ORE .... Operational Research Executive (SAUS)
ORE .... Optimum Resource Extraction (PDAA)
ORE .... Orange, MA [*Location identifier*] [*FAA*] (FAAL)
ORE .... Oregon (AAG)
Ore.............. Oregon (ODBW)
ORE .... Oregon Resources Corp. [*Vancouver Stock Exchange symbol*]
ORE .... Oregon State University, Corvallis, Corvallis, OR [*OCLC symbol*]
                  (OCLC)
ORE .... Organization Region (SAUS)
ORE .... Ornitologia Rondo Esperantlingva [*Esperantist Ornithologists'
                  Association*] (EAIO)
ORE .... Orthophoto Resolution Enhancer [*Army*]
ORE .... Output Register Empty (MHDB)
ORE .... Overall Reference Equivalent (NITA)

ORE .... Overhaul, Rebuild, and Exchange (MCD)
ORE .... Overtraining Reversal Effect
OREALC...... Regional Office for Education in Latin America and the Caribbean
                  [*UNESCO*] [*Acronym is based on foreign phrase*]
Ore App .... Oregon Court of Appeals Reports [*A publication*] (DLA)
OrEc............ Echo Public Library, Echo, OR [*Library symbol*] [*Library of
                  Congress*] (LCLS)
OREC .... Eramosa Community Library, Rockwood, Ontario [*Library symbol*]
                  [*National Library of Canada*] (NLC)
OREC .... Optimises Rectangles [*AERE Harwell*] [*Software package*] (NCC)
OREC .... Oxidation-Resistant Elemental Carbon [*Chemistry*]
ORECHL...... Centre Hospitalier Le Gardeur, Repentigny, Quebec [*Library symbol*]
                  [*National Library of Canada*] (NLC)
OrECoAr...... Lane County Archives, Eugene, OR [*Library symbol*] [*Library of
                  Congress*] (LCLS)
OrECoL........ Lane County Law Library, Eugene, OR [*Library symbol*] [*Library of
                  Congress*] (LCLS)
ORE/ERO...... Organisation Regionale de la Federation Internationale Dentaire pour
                  l'Europe [*European Regional Organization of the International
                  Dental Federation*] (EAIO)
OREF .... Orthopedic Research and Education Foundation [*Medicine*] (DMAA)
OREG .... Operation Register (IAA)
OREG .... Ordinary Multiple Regression [*Statistics*]
OREG .... Oregon (AFM)
Oreg............ Oregon (ODBW)
Oreg Fish Comm Contrib... Oregon Fish Commission Contributions (SAUS)
Oreg Fish Comm Res Briefs... Oregon Fish Commission Research Briefs (SAUS)
OregMt .... Oregon Metallurgical Corp. [*Associated Press*] (SAG)
Oregon........ Oregon Reports [*A publication*] (DLA)
Oreg Rev Stat... Oregon Revised Statutes [*A publication*] (DLA)
OrEGS......... Church of Jesus Christ of Latter-Day Saints, Genealogical Society
                  Library, Eugene Branch, Eugene, OR [*Library symbol*] [*Library of
                  Congress*] (LCLS)
Oreg SB Bull... Oregon State Bar Bulletin [*A publication*] (DLA)
Ore Health Sci U... Oregon Health Sciences University (GAGS)
OreHSocQuar... Oregon Historical Society Quarterly (SAUS)
Ore-Ida pots... Oregon-Idaho potatoes (SAUS)
OReilyAu ..... O'Reilly Automotive [*Associated Press*] (SAG)
OrEL........... Lane Community College, Eugene, OR [*Library symbol*] [*Library of
                  Congress*] (LCLS)
OREL .... Ocean Research and Engineering Laboratory (SAA)
ORELA .... Oak Ridge Electron Linear Accelerator [*Oak Ridge, TN*] [*Department
                  of Energy*]
OREM .... Objective Reference Equivalent Measurement (IAA)
OREM .... Objective Reference Equivalent Meter (SAUS)
OREM .... Office of Research and Evaluation Methods [*National Institute of
                  Justice*] (GRD)
OREM .... Oregon Metallurgical Corp. [*NASDAQ symbol*] (NQ)
OREM .... Overall Reference Equivalence Measurement (SAUS)
OREM-B....... Overall Reference Equivalance Measurement, Method B (SAUS)
OREN .... Orthorhombic Enstatite [*Geology*]
OrENC .... Northwest Christian College, Eugene, OR [*Library symbol*] [*Library of
                  Congress*] (LCLS)
OrEnW .... Wallowa County Library, Enterprise, OR [*Library symbol*] [*Library of
                  Congress*] (LCLS)
OrEnWM ...... Wallowa Memorial Hospital, Burton Carlock Memorial Library,
                  Enterprise, OR [*Library symbol*] [*Library of Congress*] (LCLS)
OREO .... Operations Response Engineering Order (SAUS)
OREO .... Orbiting Radio Emission Observatory [*Satellite*]
OREO .... Other Real Estate Owned (EBF)
O Rep .... Ohio Reports [*A publication*] (DLA)
OREP .... Optical Repeater Equipment (SAUS)
OrEPM .... Lane County Museum [*Formerly, Lane County Pioneer Museum*],
                  Eugene, OR [*Library symbol*] [*Library of Congress*] (LCLS)
OREPS .... Operational Research in Electrical Power Systems (PDAA)
ORER .... Official Railway Equipment Register [*National Railway Publication
                  Co.*] [*Information service or system*] (IID)
ORE RES...... Ore Reserve (SAUS)
Ore Rev Stat... Oregon Revised Statutes [*A publication*] (DLA)
ORERP........ Off-Site Radiation Exposure Review Project [*Department of Energy*]
OrEs............ Estacada Public Library, Estacada, OR [*Library symbol*] [*Library of
                  Congress*] (LCLS)
ORES .... Office of Research and Engineering Services (SAUS)
ORESCO...... Overseas Research Council (SAUS)
OrESH .... Sacred Heart General Hospital, Eugene, OR [*Library symbol*] [*Library
                  of Congress*] (LCLS)
OrEsHS .... Estacada High School, Estacada, OR [*Library symbol*] [*Library of
                  Congress*] (LCLS)
Ore St B Bull... Oregon State Bar Bulletin [*A publication*] (DLA)
OreStl .... Oregon Steel Mills [*Associated Press*] (SAG)
Ore St U ...... Oregon State University (GAGS)
Ore Tax Ct ... Oregon Tax Court Reports [*A publication*] (DLA)
ORETF .... Outdoor Residential Exposure Task Force [*A consortium of pesticide
                  manufacturers*]
OREX .... Isolyser Co. [*NASDAQ symbol*] (TTSB)
OREX .... Isolyser Company, Inc. [*NASDAQ symbol*] (SAG)
OREX .... Orbital Reentry Vehicle (IGSL)
ORF .... Norfolk/Virginia Beach [*Virginia*] [*Airport symbol*] (OAG)
ORF .... Obesity Research Foundation [*British*] (DI)
ORF .... Oceanic Research Foundation [*Australia*]
ORF .... Oesterreichischer Rundfunk [*Radio and television network*] [*Austria*]
ORF .... Officers' Recreation Facility
ORF .... Olfactory Research Fund
ORF .... Oman Royal Flight [*ICAO designator*] (FAAC)
ORF .... Ontario Research Foundation [*Canada*] [*Research center*] (RCD)

ORF .... Open Reading Frame [*Genetics*]
ORF .... Operational Readiness Fleet (SAUS)
ORF .... Operational Readiness Float (AABC)
ORF .... Optical Rangefinder
ORF .... Oral Rehydration Fluid
ORF .... Oratorum Romanorum Fragmenta [*A publication*] (OCD)
Orf .... Orfeo [*Record label*]
ORF .... Orifice (NASA)
ORF .... Ortho Pharmaceutical Corp. [*Research code symbol*]
ORF .... Overhaul Replacement Factor (MCD)
ORF .... Owner's Risk of Fire [*Shipping*]
ORF .... Owner's Risk of Freezing [*Shipping*]
OrF .... Rogers City Public Library, Forest Grove, OR [*Library symbol*] [*Library of Congress*] (LCLS)
OrFc .... Falls City Public Library, Falls City, OR [*Library symbol*] [*Library of Congress*] (LCLS)
ORFC .... Orifice (AAG)
ORFCOM ...... Oak Ridge Facility Comparison Study (SAUS)
ORFEUS ...... Orbiting Far and Extreme Ultraviolet Spectrometer [*Telescope*]
OrFFM .... Oregon Masonic Grand Lodge, Forest Grove, OR [*Library symbol*] [*Library of Congress*] (LCLS)
OrFl .... Florence Public Library, Florence, OR [*Library symbol*] [*Library of Congress*] (LCLS)
ORFLS .... Oak Ridge Full Matrix Least Squares
ORFM .... Outlet Region Feature Model [*Nuclear energy*] (NRCH)
Orf ML .... Orfila's Medecine Legale [*A publication*] (DLA)
OrFP .... Pacific University, Forest Grove, OR [*Library symbol*] [*Library of Congress*] (LCLS)
OrFS .... Orange Free State (DAS)
ORFS .... Origin Rail Freight [*MARAD*] (TAG)
ORG .... Glen Robertson Branch, Stormont, Dundas, and Glengarry County Public Library, Ontario [*Library symbol*] [*National Library of Canada*] (BIB)
org .... Nonprofit Organization
ORG .... Office of Racing and Gaming [*Western Australia*]
ORG .... Official Recreation Guide (TRID)
ORG .... Olympics Research Group [*University of Calgary*] [*Canada*] [*Research center*] (RCD)
ORG .... Operations Research Group
ORG .... Orange [*Diocesan abbreviation*] [*California*] (TOCD)
org .... Orange [*Philately*]
ORG .... Orange, TX [*Location identifier*] [*FAA*] (FAAL)
org .... Organ (WDAA)
ORG .... Organ
org .... Organic (NTIO)
ORG .... Organic
ORG .... Organism (ADA)
ORG .... Organization [*or Organizational*] (AAG)
Org. .... Organization (AAGC)
org .... Organization (GEAB)
Org. .... Organizational (AL)
ORG .... Organize (SAUS)
Org. .... Organizer (SAUS)
ORG .... Organogenesis, Inc. [*AMEX symbol*] (SPSG)
ORG .... Organon [*Netherlands*] [*Research code symbol*]
ORG .... Oriental Airlines (Gambia) Ltd. [*ICAO designator*] (FAAC)
ORG .... Origin (MDG)
Org. .... Original (TBD)
ORG .... Original New York Seltzer of Canada Ltd. [*Vancouver Stock Exchange symbol*]
ORG .... Origination (SAUS)
org .... Originator [*MARC relator code*] [*Library of Congress*] (LCCP)
ORG .... Paramaribo [*Surinam*] Zorg En Hoop Airport [*Airport symbol*] (OAG)
ORGA .... Organizacion Regional Gallega Autonoma [*Regional Galician Autonomy Organization*] [*Spain*] [*Political party*] (PPE)
ORGALIME... Liaison Group of the European Mechanical, Electrical, Electronic and Metal Working Industries (SAUS)
ORGALIME... Organisme de Liaison des Industries Metalliques Europeennes [*Liaison Group for the European Engineering Industries*] [*Brussels, Belgium*] (EAIO)
ORGAN .... Organisation Regionale Africaine de Normalisation [*African Regional Organization for Standardization - AROS*] (EA)
ORGAN .... Organization
Organ Am Stats Ann... Organization of American States. Annals (SAUS)
Organik....... Organik Technologies, Inc. [*Associated Press*] (SAG)
organiz .... Organization [*or Organizational*] (DAVI)
OrGb .... Curry Public Library, Gold Beach, OR [*Library symbol*] [*Library of Congress*] (LCLS)
OrgBehav.... Organizational Behaviour (DD)
Orgburo .... Organizational Bureau of the Central Committee (SAUS)
ORgC .... Rio Grande College, Rio Grande, OH [*Library symbol*] [*Library of Congress*] (LCLS)
Org Chem .... Organic Chemistry (SAUS)
ORGD .... Organized
ORGDP .... Oak Ridge Gaseous Diffusion Plant [*Department of Energy*]
ORGEL .... Organique et Eau Lourde [*Organic liquid and heavy water nuclear reactor*]
Org Exp .... Organo Espressivo [*Swell Organ*] [*Music*]
OrGH........... Josephine Memorial Hospital, Grants Pass, OR [*Library symbol*] [*Library of Congress*] (LCLS)
ORGK .... Organik Technologies [*NASDAQ symbol*] (TTSB)
ORGK .... Organik Technologies, Inc. [*NASDAQ symbol*] (SAG)
ORGKL .... Organik Tech Wrrt [*NASDAQ symbol*] (TTSB)
ORGKW ...... Organik Technologies Wrrt'A' [*NASDAQ symbol*] (TTSB)
ORGKZ........ Organik Technologies Wrrt'B' [*NASDAQ symbol*] (TTSB)

OrGl .... Gladstone Public Library, Gladstone, OR [*Library symbol*] [*Library of Congress*] (LCLS)
ORGL .... Organizational (AFM)
ORGL .... Overall Reading Grade Level (MCD)
OrGIHS .... Gladstone High School, Gladstone, OR [*Library symbol*] [*Library of Congress*] (LCLS)
ORGM .... Outdoor Recreation Grants-in-Aid Manual
Org-Man ...... Organization Man (SAUS)
ORGN .... Organization (AFM)
Orgngn........ Organogenesis, Inc. [*Associated Press*] (SAG)
Orgnik......... Organik Technologies, Inc. [*Associated Press*] (SAG)
ORGNL .... Organizational
Org No........ Originators Number (SAUS)
ORGO......... Organo [*Organ*] [*Music*] (ROG)
OrGR........... Rogue Community College, Grants Pass, OR [*Library symbol*] [*Library of Congress*] (LCLS)
OrGrC.......... Mount Hood Community College, Gresham, OR [*Library symbol*] [*Library of Congress*] (LCLS)
Org React .... Organic Reactivity (SAUS)
OrGrGS .... Church of Jesus Christ of Latter-Day Saints, Genealogical Society Library, Gresham Branch, Gresham, OR [*Library symbol*] [*Library of Congress*] (LCLS)
ORGS.......... Operational Research Group of Scotland (SAUS)
ORGSBS ..... Oak Ridge Graduate School of Biomedical Sciences [*Tennessee*]
ORGSC........ Oregon Ryegrass Growers Seed Commission (EA)
Orgst.......... Organist (SAUS)
ORGT .... Organist
ORGY .... Organization for the Rational Guidance of Youth [*Fictitious organization in film, "The Man from ORGY"*]
ORH .... Occupational Role History [*Psychology*]
ORH .... Office of Rural Health (MEDA)
ORH .... Operational Requirements Handbook
ORH .... Orchard Supply Hardware Strs [*NYSE symbol*] (TTSB)
o-rh. .... Orthorhombic [*Crystallography*]
ORH .... Richmond Hill Public Library, Ontario [*Library symbol*] [*National Library of Canada*] (NLC)
ORH .... Worcester [*Massachusetts*] [*Airport symbol*] (OAG)
OrHe .... Hermiston Public Library, Hermiston, OR [*Library symbol*] [*Library of Congress*] (LCLS)
OrHeGS....... Good Shepherd Hospital, Hermiston, OR [*Library symbol*] [*Library of Congress*] (LCLS)
OrHep .... Heppner Public Library, Heppner, OR [*Library symbol*] [*Library of Congress*] (LCLS)
OrHepPM..... Pioneer Memorial Hospital, Heppner, OR [*Library symbol*] [*Library of Congress*] (LCLS)
ORHFC........ Official Rocky Horror Fan Club (EA)
OrHi .... Oregon Historical Society, Portland, OR [*Library symbol*] [*Library of Congress*] (LCLS)
OrHil .... Hillsboro Public Library, Hillsboro, OR [*Library symbol*] [*Library of Congress*] (LCLS)
OrHilHI .... Tuality Health Information Resource Center, Hillsboro, OR [*Library symbol*] [*Library of Congress*] (LCLS)
OrHilT......... Tuality Community Hospital, Hillsboro, OR [*Library symbol*] [*Library of Congress*] (LCLS)
OrHilW........ Washington County Law Library, Hillsboro, OR [*Library symbol*] [*Library of Congress*] (LCLS)
ORHP .... Office of Rural Health Policy
OrHr............ Hood River County Library, Hood River, OR [*Library symbol*] [*Library of Congress*] (LCLS)
OrHx .... Helix Pubic Library, Helix, OR [*Library symbol*] [*Library of Congress*] (LCLS)
Orl .... Independence Public Library, Independence, OR [*Library symbol*] [*Library of Congress*] (LCLS)
ORI .... Occurrence of Reinforcing Information (SAUS)
ORI .... Ocean Research Institute (WDAA)
ORI .... Ocean Resources Institute (COE)
ORI .... Octane Requirement Increase [*Mechanical engineering*]
ORI .... Ocurrence of Reinforcing Information (PDAA)
ORI .... Office of Research and Inventions
ORI .... Office of Research Integrity [*Department of Health and Human Services*]
ORI .... Office of Road Inquiry [*Later, Bureau of Public Roads*]
ORI .... Office Research Institute (NADA)
ORI .... Old Republic International Corp. [*NYSE symbol*] (SPSG)
ORI .... Omni Resources, Inc. [*Vancouver Stock Exchange symbol*]
ORI .... Online Retrieval Interface (SAUS)
ORI .... Operating and Repair Instruction
ORI .... Operational Readiness Inspection [*Army*]
ORI .... Operational Readiness Instruction [*Military*]
ORI .... Operations Research and Industrial Engineering (SAUS)
ORI .... Operations Research and Information Systems (SAUS)
ORI .... Operations Research, Inc. [*Information service or system*]
ORI .... Ophthalmic Research Institute (EA)
ORI .... Orders and Requests for Information (SAUS)
ORI .... Oregon Research Institute
ORI .... Orient Air Ltd. [*British*] [*ICAO designator*] (FAAC)
ORI .... Orientation Inventory [*Vocational guidance test*]
ORI .... Originating Body (SAUS)
Ori .... Oriole [*Record label*] [*Great Britain*]
Ori .... Orion [*Constellation*]
ori .... Oriya [*MARC language code*] [*Library of Congress*] (LCCP)
ORI .... Outdoor Recreation Institute (EA)
ORI .... Overhaul and Repair Instruction
ORI .... Overriding Royalty Interest (SAUS)
ORI .... Port Lions [*Alaska*] [*Airport symbol*] (OAG)

ORIA	Office of Regulatory and Information Affairs (SAUS)
ORIA	Oriental Rug Importers Association of America (EA)
ORIAC	CERN Accounting System (SAUS)
ORIADOC	Orientation and Access to Information and Documentation Sources in France [*Commission de Coordination de la Documentation Administrative*] [*Database*]
ORIC	Oak Ridge Isochronous Cyclotron [*Department of Energy*]
ORIC	Operational Readiness Inspection Committee [*NASA*]
ORICAT	Original Cataloguing System (NITA)
ORICS	Optical Ranging, Identification, and Communications System (ACAE)
ORICS	Optical Ranging Identification Friend or Foe Communication System (ACAE)
ORIDE	Override (KSC)
ORIE	Operational Radiation Instrumentation Equipment (SAA)
ORIEL	Oriel College, Oxford (SAUS)
ORIEN	Orientation (AABC)
ORIENT	Orient Airways (SAUS)
Orient	Oriental (DIAR)
ORIENT	Orientation
OrientB	Oriental Bank & Trust [*Associated Press*] (SAG)
Ori Exp	Orient Express (SAUS)
ORIF	Open Reduction with Internal Fixation [*Medicine*]
Orig	Origen [*Deceased circa 254*] [*Authority cited in pre-1607 legal work*] (DSA)
ORIG	Origin [*or Original*] (AAG)
orig	Origin (VRA)
orig	Original (BEE)
Orig	Original
orig	Originally (NTIO)
Orig	Originally (SAUS)
ORIG	Originated (TVEL)
ORIG	Originator (MSA)
ORIGAN	Origanum [*Marjoram*] [*Pharmacology*] (ROG)
ORIG BDS	Original Boards [*Graphic arts*] (DGA)
Orig Ed	Original Edition (SAUS)
ORIGEN2	Oak Ridge Isotope Generation and Depletion Code [*Department of Energy*] (GAAI)
Orig Enl	Original Enlistment (SAUS)
ORIGINATG	Originating (ROG)
ORIGINS	Oklahoma Resources Integrated General Information Network System
ORIGL	Original (ROG)
Orig Publ	Original Publication (SAUS)
Orig Publ	Original Publisher (SAUS)
ORIN	Orleans Installation (SAUS)
O Ring	O-shaped Ring (SAUS)
ORINS	Oak Ridge Institute of Nuclear Studies [*Later, ORAU*] (EA)
ORINT	Oriented Integrator (SAUS)
ORIO	Oak Ridge Regional Inspections Office (SAUS)
Orio	Orion [*Constellation*]
OriolH	Oriole Homes Corp. [*Associated Press*] (SAG)
ORION	Online Retrieval of Information over a Network
ORION	Operational Radio Interferometry Observing Network (MCD)
OrionCap	Orion Capital Corp. [*Associated Press*] (SAG)
OrionNS	Orion Network Systems, Inc. [*Associated Press*] (SAG)
ORIP	Ripley Branch, Bruce County Public Library, Ontario [*Library symbol*] [*National Library of Canada*] (NLC)
ORIPrH	Old Republic Int 8.75% Pfd'H' [*NYSE symbol*] (TTSB)
Oris	All India Reporter, Orissa [*A publication*] (DLA)
ORIS	Object Recognition and Identification System (VLIE)
ORIS	Office of Regulatory Information Systems [*Energy Regulatory Commission*] (IID)
ORIS	Officeworker Reader Information Services [*British*]
oris	orismological (SAUS)
Oris	Orismologist (SAUS)
Oris	Orismology (SAUS)
ORIS	Overlapped Rank-Intervals Set (VLIE)
ORIS	South Carleton High School, Richmond, Ontario [*Library symbol*] [*National Library of Canada*] (NLC)
ORISE	Oak Ridge Institute for Science and Education [*Oak Ridge Associated Universities*] [*Research center*] (RCD)
Orissa	All India Reporter, Orissa [*A publication*] (DLA)
ORIT	Operational Readiness Inspection Team [*Air Force*]
ORIT	Operational Readiness Inspection Test [*Air Force*]
ORIT	Organization Regional Interamericana de Trabdjadores [*Inter-American Labor Organization*] [*Spanish*] (BARN)
ORJ	Corry, PA [*Location identifier*] [*FAA*] (FAAL)
ORJ	Ohio Power Co. [*NYSE symbol*] (SAG)
ORJ	Oneida Resources, Inc. [*Vancouver Stock Exchange symbol*]
OrJ	Orange Juice
ORJ	Orinduik [*Guyana*] [*Airport symbol*] (OAG)
OrJc	Junction City Public Library, Junction City, OR [*Library symbol*] [*Library of Congress*] (LCLS)
OrJe	Jefferson Public Library, Jefferson, OR [*Library symbol*] [*Library of Congress*] (LCLS)
ORJETS	On-Line Remote Job Entry Terminal System [*Computer science*]
OrJM	Jacksonville Museum, Jacksonville, OR [*Library symbol*] [*Library of Congress*] (LCLS)
OrJvHS	Jordan Valley High School, Jordan Valley, OR [*Library symbol*] [*Library of Congress*] (LCLS)
ORK	Air Orkney [*British*] [*ICAO designator*] (FAAC)
ORK	Cork [*Ireland*] [*Airport symbol*] (OAG)
OrK	Klamath County Library, Klamath Falls, OR [*Library symbol*] [*Library of Congress*] (LCLS)
ORK	Office Resource Kit (SAUS)
ORK	Orkney [*County in Scotland*] (ROG)
ORKID	Open Real-Time Kernel Interface Definition [*Computer science*] (VLIE)
ORKID	Orientation Determination from Kikuchi Diagrams (SAUS)
OrKM	Merle West Medical Center Library, Klamath Falls, OR [*Library symbol*] [*Library of Congress*] (LCLS)
OrKT	Oregon Technical Institute, Klamath Falls, OR [*Library symbol*] [*Library of Congress*] (LCLS)
ORL	Journal for Oto-Rhino-Laryngology and its related specialties (SAUS)
ORL	Observed Range Limit
ORL	Olivetti Research Laboratory Ltd. [*British*] (IRUK)
ORL	On Air Ltd. [*Canada*] [*ICAO designator*] (FAAC)
ORL	Optimum Repair Level Analysis
ORL	Orbital Research Laboratory [*NASA*]
ORL	Orbiting Research Laboratory (SAUS)
ORL	Ordnance Research Laboratory [*Later, Applied Research Laboratory*] [*Pennsylvania State University*] (MCD)
ORL	Orion Resources Ltd. [*Vancouver Stock Exchange symbol*]
'Orl	'Orlah (BJA)
ORL	Orlando [*Florida*] [*Airport symbol*] (OAG)
ORL	Orlando Public Library, Orlando, FL [*OCLC symbol*] (OCLC)
ORL	Otorhinolaryngologist
ORL	Otorhinolaryngology [*Medicine*]
ORL	Outlook on Research Libraries (SAUS)
ORL	Overrun Lights (SAUS)
ORL	Owner's Risk of Leakage [*Shipping*]
ORL	Red Lake Public Library, Ontario [*Library symbol*] [*National Library of Canada*] (NLC)
ORLA	Optical Remote Sensing of the Land (SAUS)
ORLA	Optimum Repair Level Analysis [*Air Force*]
ORLA	Optimum Repair Level Authorization (MCD)
ORLA	Optimum Report Level Analysis [*Military*]
Orla	Orde Lama (SAUS)
OrLak	Lake County Library, Lakeview, OR [*Library symbol*] [*Library of Congress*] (LCLS)
OrLan	Langlois Public Library, Langlois, OR [*Library symbol*] [*Library of Congress*] (LCLS)
Or Laws	Oregon Laws and Resolutions [*A publication*] (DLA)
Or Laws Adv Sh	Oregon Laws Advance Sheets [*A publication*] (DLA)
Or Laws Spec Sess	Oregon Laws and Resolutions [*A publication*] (DLA)
Orl Bridg	Orlando Bridgman's English Common Pleas Reports [*A publication*] (DLA)
Orl Bridgman	Orlando Bridgman's English Common Pleas Reports [*A publication*] (DLA)
Orleans App	Orleans Court of Appeals [*Louisiana*] (DLA)
Orleans TR	Orleans Term Reports [*1, 2 Martin*] [*Louisiana*] [*A publication*] (DLA)
OrLeH	Lebanon Community Hospital, Lebanon, OR [*Library symbol*] [*Library of Congress*] (LCLS)
OrLg	La Grande Public Library, La Grande, OR [*Library symbol*] [*Library of Congress*] (LCLS)
OrLgE	Eastern Oregon College, La Grande, OR [*Library symbol*] [*Library of Congress*] (LCLS)
OrLgFS	United States Forest Service, Range and Wildlife Habitat Laboratory, La Grande, OR [*Library symbol*] [*Library of Congress*] (LCLS)
OrLgGRH	Grande Ronde Hospital, LaGrande, OR [*Library symbol*] [*Library of Congress*] (LCLS)
OrLgGS	Church of Jesus Christ of Latter-Day Saints, Genealogical Society Library, La Grande Branch, La Grande, OR [*Library symbol*] [*Library of Congress*] (LCLS)
ORLIS	Orts-, Regional-, und Landesplanung Literaturinformationssystem [*Literature Information System for Town and Regional Planning*] [*1974-1978*] [*Database*]
ORLL	Operational Reports - Lessons Learned [*Army*] (AABC)
OrLo	Lake Oswego Public Library, Lake Oswego, OR [*Library symbol*] [*Library of Congress*] (LCLS)
OrLoHS	Lake Oswego High School, Lake Oswego, OR [*Library symbol*] [*Library of Congress*] (LCLS)
OrLoJS	Lake Oswego Junior High School, Lake Oswego, OR [*Library symbol*] [*Library of Congress*] (LCLS)
OrLoLHS	Lakeridge High School, Lake Oswego, OR [*Library symbol*] [*Library of Congress*] (LCLS)
OrLpHS	La Pine Senior High School, La Pine, OR [*Library symbol*] [*Library of Congress*] (LCLS)
OrlPID	Industrial Design Corp., Portland, OR [*Library symbol*] [*Library of Congress*] (LCLS)
ORLPP	Office of Research, Legislation, and Program Policies [*Unemployment Insurance Service*] [*Department of Labor*]
ORLRAPS	Online Remedial Action Progress System (SAUS)
ORLS	Selco Mining Corp., Red Lake, Ontario [*Library symbol*] [*National Library of Canada*] (NLC)
Or LSJ	Oregon Law School Journal [*1902-03*] [*A publication*] (DLA)
ORLSTJ	St. Joseph Township Public Library, Richards Landing, Ontario [*Library symbol*] [*National Library of Canada*] (NLC)
Orl TR	Orleans Term Reports [*1, 2 Martin*] [*Louisiana*] [*A publication*] (DLA)
ORLY	O'Reilly Automotive [*NASDAQ symbol*] (SAG)
ORLY	Overload Relay (IEEE)
ORM	Northampton [*England*] [*Airport symbol*] (AD)
ORM	Object Role Modeling (SAUS)
ORM	Object Role Modelling (VLIE)
ORM	Office of Recycled Materials [*National Bureau of Standards*]
ORM	Office of Regional Management [*Employment and Training Administration*]
ORM	Office of Regulated Material [*Environmental Protection Agency*] (GFGA)
ORM	Office of Resource Management (SAUS)

ORM .... Off-Road Mobility
ORM .... Off-Route Mine
ORM .... Ohio Reformatory for Men (SAUS)
ORM .... On Request from Manufacturer (SAUS)
ORM .... Operators Reference Manual (IAA)
ORM .... Optically Remote switching Module (SAUS)
ORM .... Optical Reference Manual
ORM .... Optical Remote Module [Computer science] (VLIE)
ORM .... Optimal Replacement Method (SAUS)
ORM .... Opytnyi Reaktivnyi Motor [Experimental Reaction Motor] [Former USSR]
orm .... Ormolu (VRA)
ORM .... Other Regulated Material
ORM .... Outside Rearview Mirror [Automotive engineering]
ORM .... Overhaul and Repair Manual
ORM .... Overlapping Resolution Mapping [Computer science]
ORMA .... Office of Refugee and Migration Affairs [Department of State]
ORMA .... Regional Office for Meso-America (SAUS)
OrMaC .... Marylhurst College, Marylhurst, OR [Library symbol] [Library of Congress] (LCLS)
ORMAC .... Oral Response Machine (VLIE)
OrMad .... Jefferson County Library, Madras, OR [Library symbol] [Library of Congress] (LCLS)
OrMadHS .... Madras High School, Madras, OR [Library symbol] [Library of Congress] (LCLS)
OrMadJH ..... Madras Junior High School, Madras, OR [Library symbol] [Library of Congress] (LCLS)
ORMAK .... Oak Ridge TOKAMAK [Energy Research and Development Administration]
ORMAS .... Operational Resource Management Assessment Plan (SAUS)
ORMAS .... Operational Resource Management Assessment System [Military]
OrMc .... McMinnville Public Library, McMinnville, OR [Library symbol] [Library of Congress] (LCLS)
ORMC .... Off-Route [Smart] Mine Clearance [Military]
OR/MC .... Operational Requirements/Military Characteristics (NG)
OrMcL .... Linfield College, McMinnville, OR [Library symbol] [Library of Congress] (LCLS)
OrMeGS ...... Church of Jesus Christ of Latter-Day Saints, Genealogical Society Library, Medford Branch, Medford, OR [Library symbol] [Library of Congress] (LCLS)
OrMeJ .... Jackson County Library System, Medford, OR [Library symbol] [Library of Congress] (LCLS)
OrMePH ...... Providence Hospital, Medford, OR [Library symbol] [Library of Congress] (LCLS)
OrMeRM ...... Rogue Valley Medical Center, Medford, OR [Library symbol] [Library of Congress] (LCLS)
OrMf .... Milton-Freewater Public Library, Milton-Freewater, OR [Library symbol] [Library of Congress] (LCLS)
ORMH .... Office of Research on Minority Health (SAUS)
OrMi .... Milwaukie Public Library, Milwaukie, OR [Library symbol] [Library of Congress] (LCLS)
ORMI .... Oak Ridge Military Institute
OrMiCHS ..... Clackamas High School, Media Center, Milwaukie, OR [Library symbol] [Library of Congress] (LCLS)
OrMiD .... Dwyer Community Hospital, Medical Library, Milwaukie, OR [Library symbol] [Library of Congress] (LCLS)
OrMiHS .... Milwaukie High School, Milwaukie, OR [Library symbol] [Library of Congress] (LCLS)
OrMiLHS ..... La Salle High School, Milwaukie, OR [Library symbol] [Library of Congress] (LCLS)
OrMiPHS ..... Rex Putnam High School, Milwaukie, OR [Library symbol] [Library of Congress] (LCLS)
ORML .... Oriental Meal (TVEL)
ORMM .... Basrah/Magal [Iraq] [ICAO location identifier] (ICLI)
ORMOA .... Office for Relations with Military and Occupation Authorities
OrMol .... Molalla Public Library, Molalla, OR [Library symbol] [Library of Congress] (LCLS)
OrMolHS ..... Molalla Senior High School, Molalla, OR [Library symbol] [Library of Congress] (LCLS)
OrMolMS .... Molalla Mid-High School, Molalla, OR [Library symbol] [Library of Congress] (LCLS)
OrMon .... Monmouth Library, Monmouth, OR [Library symbol] [Library of Congress] (LCLS)
Ormond .... Ormond's Reports [19-107 Alabama] [A publication] (DLA)
OrMonO ...... Oregon College of Education, Monmouth, OR [Library symbol] [Library of Congress] (LCLS)
ORMONS ..... Operational Readiness Monitoring System (MCD)
OrMonW ...... Western Oregon State College, Monmouth, OR [Library symbol] [Library of Congress] (LCLS)
OrMp .... Myrtle Point Public Library (Flora M. Laird Library), Myrtle Point, OR [Library symbol] [Library of Congress] (LCLS)
ORMS .... Basrah/Shaibah [Iraq] [ICAO location identifier] (ICLI)
ORMS .... Office Resources Management System (SAUS)
ORMS .... Operating Resource Management System (VLIE)
ORMS .... Operational Readiness Management System
OR/MS .... Operational Research/Management Systems (SAUS)
OR/MS .... Operations Research or Management Science
ORMS .... Operative Roller Makers' Society [A union] [British]
ORMS .... Other Regulated Materials (GNE)
ORMSS .... Ohio River Main Stem Study (SAUS)
OrMta .... Mount Angel Public Library, Mount Angel, OR [Library symbol] [Library of Congress] (LCLS)
OrMtaC .... Mount Angel College [Later, Cesar Chavez College], Mount Angel, OR [Library symbol] [Library of Congress] (LCLS)
ORMU .... Orbital Remote Maneuvering Unit

ORMWH .... Office of Research on Minority and Womens Health (SAUS)
OrN .... Newberg Library Association, Newberg, OR [Library symbol] [Library of Congress] (LCLS)
ORN .... Oak Ridge National Laboratory, Oak Ridge, TN [OCLC symbol] (OCLC)
ORN .... Olfactory Receptor Neuron [Biochemistry]
ORN .... Operating Room Nurse [Medicine]
ORN .... Oran [Algeria] [Airport symbol] (OAG)
ORN .... Orange (AAG)
ORN .... Organization of Revolutionaries of the North [Lebanon] (PD)
ORN .... Orient Airways [Pakistan] [ICAO designator] (FAAC)
ORN .... Orion Power Hldgs. [NYSE symbol]
ORN .... Ornament (MSA)
orn .... ornamental (SAUS)
ORN .... Ornamentation (SAUS)
ORN .... OrNda Healthcorp [NYSE symbol] (TTSB)
ORN .... Ornithine (DB)
Orn .... Ornithine [Same as DAV] [An amino acid]
ORN .... Ornithology
Orn .... Ornithyl (SAUS)
ORN .... Orthopedic Nurse
ORN .... Osteoradionecrosis [Medicine] (MELL)
ORN .... Output Reconfiguration Network (SAUS)
ORNAC .... Operating Room Nurses Association of Canada (SAUS)
ornam .... Ornament (VRA)
ORNAM .... Ornamental
ORNAME ...... Originator/Recipient Name (VLIE)
Ornam/Misc Met Fabr... Ornamental/Miscellaneous Metal Fabricator (SAUS)
OrNb .... North Bend Public Library, North Bend, OR [Library symbol] [Library of Congress] (LCLS)
OrNbGS .... Church of Jesus Christ of Latter-Day Saints, Genealogical Society Library, Coos Bay Stake Branch, North Bend, OR [Library symbol] [Library of Congress] (LCLS)
ORND .... Ornda Healthcorp [Formerly, Republic Health Corp.] [NASDAQ symbol] (SPSG)
Ornda .... Ornda Healthcorp [Associated Press] (SAG)
OrNep .... Newport Public Library, Newport, OR [Library symbol] [Library of Congress] (LCLS)
OrNepH .... Pacific Communities Hospital Library, Newport, OR [Library symbol] [Library of Congress] (LCLS)
ORNG .... Orange
ORNG .... Orange PLC [NASDAQ symbol] (SAG)
OrngCo .... Orange-Co., Inc. [Associated Press] (SAG)
OrNGF .... George Fox College, Newberg, OR [Library symbol] [Library of Congress] (LCLS)
ORNGY .... Orange PLC ADR [NASDAQ symbol] (TTSB)
ornith .... ornithological (SAUS)
ornith .... Ornithology (NTIO)
ORNITH .... Ornithology
ornithol .... ornithologic (SAUS)
ornithol .... Ornithology (BEE)
ORNITHOL ... Ornithology
ORNL .... Oak Ridge National Laboratory [Oak Ridge, TN] [Department of Energy]
ORNL .... Ordnance Navy Laboratory (SAUS)
ORNL-CF...... Oak Ridge National Laboratory Critical Facility (SAUS)
ORNL/DAAC... Oak Ridge National Laboratory Distributed Active Archive Center for Biogeochemical Dynamics
ORNLL .... Oak Ridge National Laboratory Library (SAUS)
ORNL-PCA .... Oak Ridge National Laboratory Pool Critical Assembly (SAA)
ORNLY-NDP... Oak Ridge National Laboratory Nuclear Data Project [Database producer]
ORNMT .... Ornament
ORNTL .... Ornamental
OrNyGS .... Church of Jesus Christ of Latter-Day Saints, Genealogical Society Library, NyssaBranch, Nyssa, OR [Library symbol] [Library of Congress] (LCLS)
OrNyMH ...... Malheur Memorial Hospital, J. J. Sarazin Memorial Library, Nyssa, OR [Library symbol] [Library of Congress] (LCLS)
ORO .... Oak Ridge Operations Office (MCD)
ORO .... Office of Regional Operations [Environmental Protection Agency] (GFGA)
ORO .... Office of Regional Operations [Office of Field Operations] [Department of Labor]
ORO .... Official Receiver's Office [Australia]
ORO .... Oil Red O [A stain]
ORO .... Operations Research Office
ORO .... Orapouche [An arbovirus] [Laboratory science] (DAVI)
OrO .... Oregon City Public Library, Oregon City, OR [Library symbol] [Library of Congress] (LCLS)
ORO .... Orofino Resources Ltd. [Toronto Stock Exchange symbol] [Vancouver Stock Exchange symbol]
ORO .... Oropa [Italy] [Seismograph station code, US Geological Survey] [Closed] (SEIS)
ORO .... Oropouche [An arbovirus]
Oro .... Orotate [Biochemistry]
Oro .... Orotic Acid [Biochemistry]
ORO .... Orthicon Read-Out
ORO .... Porto Seguro [Brazil] [Airport symbol] (AD)
ORO .... Rockland Public Library, Ontario [Library symbol] [National Library of Canada] (NLC)
OrOa .... Oakridge Public Library, Oakridge, OR [Library symbol] [Library of Congress] (LCLS)
OROA .... Oroamerica, Inc. [NASDAQ symbol] (SAG)
Oroamer ...... Oroamerica, Inc. [Associated Press] (SAG)

OROAP.........	Organizacion Regional del Oriente para la Administracion Publica [*Eastern Regional Organization for Public Administration*] (EAIO)
OrOC............	Clackamas County Public Library, Oregon City, OR [*Library symbol*] [*Library of Congress*] (LCLS)
OrOCC.........	Clackamas Community College, Oregon City, OR [*Library symbol*] [*Library of Congress*] (LCLS)
OROCS........	Optical Recognition of Chemical Structures Program [*IBM Almaden Research Center*] [*San Jose, CA*]
OR/OD	Operations requirements/Operations Directive (SAUS)
Orog............	Orographer (SAUS)
Orog............	Orography (SAUS)
OrOgCL	Cooperative Library Network of Clackamas County, Oak Grove, OR [*Library symbol*] [*Library of Congress*] (LCLS)
OrOHS	Oregon City Senior High School, Oregon City, OR [*Library symbol*] [*Library of Congress*] (LCLS)
OROM	Optical Read-Only Memory [*Computer science*]
OrOn	Malheur County Library, Ontario, OR [*Library symbol*] [*Library of Congress*] (LCLS)
OrOnHR	Holy Rosary Hospital, Weise-Biggs Memorial Medical Library, Ontario, OR [*Library symbol*] [*Library of Congress*] (LCLS)
OrOnT	Treasure Valley Community College, Ontario, OR [*Library symbol*] [*Library of Congress*] (LCLS)
ORootN........	Northeastern Ohio Universities, College of Medicine, Basic Medical Sciences Library, Rootstown, OH [*Library symbol*] [*Library of Congress*] (LCLS)
OROS...........	Optical Read-Only Storage [*Computer science*]
OROS...........	Oral Osmotic [*System for delivering drugs into the bloodstream*] [*Alza Corp. trademark*]
OROS...........	Rosseau Public Library, Ontario [*Library symbol*] [*National Library of Canada*] (NLC)
OROSS........	Operational Readiness-Oriented Supply System [*Army*] (PDAA)
OrOWH	Willamette Falls Community Hospital, Oregon City, OR [*Library symbol*] [*Library of Congress*] (LCLS)
OrP	Library Association of Portland [*Public Library for Portland and Multnomah County*], Portland, OR [*Library symbol*] [*Library of Congress*] (LCLS)
ORP	Objective Rallying Point (SAUS)
ORP	Objective Rally [*or Rallying*] Point [*Military*]
ORP	Objective Release Point [*Army*] (INF)
ORP	Occiput Right Posterior Fetal position [*Medicine*] (STED)
ORP	Occurrence Reporting Program (SAUS)
ORP	Office of Radiation Programs [*Environmental Protection Agency*]
ORP	Office of Regulatory Programs [*Federal Energy Administration*] [*Obsolete*]
ORP	Officer Requirements Plan (DNAB)
ORP	OFS [*Orbital Flight System*] Retransmission Processor [*NASA*] (GFGA)
ORP	OFS [*Orbiter Functional Simulator*] Retransmission Processor [*NASA*]
ORP	Operational Readiness Panel
ORP	Operational Readiness Platform [*Aviation*] (DA)
ORP	Operational Readiness Program (SAUS)
ORP	Opioid-Resistant Pain [*Medicine*] (MELL)
ORP	Optical Response Poll (SAUS)
ORP	Optical Rotary Power
ORP	Optional Response Poll (VLIE)
ORP	Optional Retirement Program (SAUS)
ORP	Oranje River Project (SAUS)
ORP	Orapa [*Botswana*] [*Airport symbol*] [*Obsolete*] (OAG)
ORP	Orbital Radiation Program (ACAE)
ORP	Orbital Rendezvous Procedure (AAG)
ORP	Ordinary, Reasonable, and Prudent [*Legal term*] (BARN)
ORP	Organ Recovery Program (EA)
ORP	Ormara [*Pakistan*] [*Airport symbol*] (AD)
ORP	Outside Right Position [*Dancing*]
ORP	Oxidation-Reduction Potential
ORP	Oxidation-Reduction Probe (SAUS)
ORP	Oxygen-Regulated Protein [*Biochemistry*]
ORP	Phelps Community Library, Redbridge, Ontario [*Library symbol*] [*National Library of Canada*] (NLC)
ORPA...........	Office of Regional and Political Affairs (SAUS)
ORPA...........	Orbiter Retarding Potential Analyzer [*NASA*]
ORPA...........	Organizacion Revolucionaria del Pueblo en Armas [*Revolutionary Organization of the People in Arms*] [*Guatemala*] [*Political party*] (PD)
OrP-A...........	Portland City Archives, Portland, OR [*Library symbol*] [*Library of Congress*] (LCLS)
OrPAA.........	Arthur Anderson & Co., Portland, OR [*Library symbol*] [*Library of Congress*] (LCLS)
OrPAB.........	Academic Book Center, Portland, OR [*Library symbol*] [*Library of Congress*] (LCLS)
ORP Amp.....	Oxidation-Reduction Potential Amplifier (SAUS)
OrPB...........	Bonneville Power Administration, Portland, OR [*Library symbol*] [*Library of Congress*] (LCLS)
OrPBC.........	Blue Cross/Blue Shield of Oregon, Portland, OR [*Library symbol*] [*Library of Congress*] (LCLS)
OrPBK.........	Bess Kaiser Foundation Hospital, Medical Library, Portland, OR [*Library symbol*] [*Library of Congress*] (LCLS)
OrPC...........	Cascade College, Portland, OR [*Library symbol*] [*Library of Congress*] (LCLS)
ORPC...........	Office of Rail Public Counsel [*Terminated, 1979*] [*Affiliated with Interstate Commerce Commission*]
ORPC...........	Old Radio Program Collectors Club (EA)
OrPCA.........	Roman Catholic Archdiocese of Portland in Oregon, Chancery Office, Portland, OR [*Library symbol*] [*Library of Congress*] (LCLS)
OrPCC...........	Concordia College, Portland, OR [*Library symbol*] [*Library of Congress*] (LCLS)
OrPCM	Cedar Mill Community Library, Portland, OR [*Library symbol*] [*Library of Congress*] (LCLS)
OrPCNM.......	National College of Naturopathic Medicine, Portland, OR [*Library symbol*] [*Library of Congress*] (LCLS)
OrPCol	Columbia Christian College, Portland, OR [*Library symbol*] [*Library of Congress*] (LCLS)
OrPD...........	Protestant Episcopal Church, Diocesan Library, Portland, OR [*Library symbol*] [*Library of Congress*] (LCLS)
ORPE	Oleum Ricine Polyoxyaethylat (SAUS)
OrPeB	Blue Mountain Community College, Pendleton, OR [*Library symbol*] [*Library of Congress*] (LCLS)
OrPeCH........	Pendleton Community Hospital, Pendleton, OR [*Library symbol*] [*Library of Congress*] (LCLS)
OrPEH	Emanuel Hospital, Portland, OR [*Library symbol*] [*Library of Congress*] (LCLS)
OrPeSA	Saint Anthony Hospital, Pendleton, OR [*Library symbol*] [*Library of Congress*] (LCLS)
OrPeU	Umatilla County Library, Pendleton, OR [*Library symbol*] [*Library of Congress*] (LCLS)
OrPFW	United States Fish and Wildlife Service, Portland, OR [*Library symbol*] [*Library of Congress*] (LCLS)
OrPGE.........	Portland General Electric Co., Portland, OR [*Library symbol*] [*Library of Congress*] (LCLS)
OrPGF.........	Genealogical Forum of Portland, Portland, OR [*Library symbol*] [*Library of Congress*] (LCLS)
OrPGH	Good Samaritan Hospital and Medical Center, Portland, OR [*Library symbol*] [*Library of Congress*] (LCLS)
OrPGS.........	Church of Jesus Christ of Latter-Day Saints, Genealogical Society Library, Portland Branch, Portland, OR [*Library symbol*] [*Library of Congress*] (LCLS)
OrPGSE.......	Church of Jesus Christ of Latter-Day Saints, Genealogical Society Library, Portland East Branch, Portland, OR [*Library symbol*] [*Library of Congress*] (LCLS)
ORPH...........	Orphan [*or Orphanage*]
orph............	orphanage (SAUS)
orph............	orphaned (SAUS)
ORPH...........	Orphan Medical, Inc. [*NASDAQ symbol*] (SAG)
orph............	orphans (SAUS)
OrphanM.......	Orphan Medical, Inc. [*Associated Press*] (SAG)
Orph Frag.....	Orphica Fragmenta [*A publication*] (OCD)
ORPHIC.......	Organized Projected Hypotheses for Innovations in Curriculum [*Educational planning*]
OrPHP.........	Holladay Park Hospital, Medical Library, Portland, OR [*Library symbol*] [*Library of Congress*] (LCLS)
OrPHS-D	Oregon Health Sciences University, Dental Library, Portland, OR [*Library symbol*] [*Library of Congress*] (LCLS)
ORPI...........	Organ Pipe Cactus National Monument
ORPICS........	Orbital Rendezvous Positioning, Indexing, and Coupling System
OrPK...........	Bess Kaiser Foundation Hospital, Medical Library, Portland, OR [*Library symbol*] [*Library of Congress*] (LCLS)
OrPKF.........	Kaiser Foundation Hospitals, Health Services Research Center, Portland, OR [*Library symbol*] [*Library of Congress*] (LCLS)
OrPL	Lewis and Clark College, Portland, OR [*Library symbol*] [*Library of Congress*] (LCLS)
ORPL	Office de Protection contre les Rayonnements Ionisants [*Office for Protecti on Against Ionizing Radiation*] [*France*]
ORPL	Overseas Replacement [*Military*]
OrPL-L.........	Northwestern School of Law, Lewis and Clark College, Portland, OR [*Library symbol*] [*Library of Congress*] (LCLS)
ORPM.........	Office of Research Program Management [*Environmental Protection Agency*] (GFGA)
ORPM.........	Orthorhythmic Pacemaker [*Medicine*] (STED)
OrPMB.........	Multnomah School of the Bible, Portland, OR [*Library symbol*] [*Library of Congress*] (LCLS)
OrPML.........	Multnomah County Law Library, Portland, OR [*Library symbol*] [*Library of Congress*] (LCLS)
OrPNA.........	Northwest Association of Private Colleges and Universities, Microform Center, Portland, OR [*Library symbol*] [*Library of Congress*] (LCLS)
OrPNR	Northwest Regional Educational Laboratory, Information Center Library, Portland, OR [*Library symbol*] [*Library of Congress*] (LCLS)
OrPO...........	Oregonian Publishing Co. Library, Portland, OR [*Library symbol*] [*Library of Congress*] (LCLS)
OrPOF.........	Oregon Odd Fellows Grand Lodge, Portland, OR [*Library symbol*] [*Library of Congress*] (LCLS)
OrPOj.........	Oregon Daily Journal, Portland, OR [*Library symbol*] [*Library of Congress*] (LCLS)
OrPoL.........	Hazel M. Lewis Library (Powers Public Library), Powers, OR [*Library symbol*] [*Library of Congress*] (LCLS)
ORPOS.........	Office of Regulatory Policy, Oversight, and Supervision [*Federal Home Loan Bank Board*]
OrPP	Port of Portland Library, Portland, OR [*Library symbol*] [*Library of Congress*] (LCLS)
OrPPC.........	Portland Community College, Portland, OR [*Library symbol*] [*Library of Congress*] (LCLS)
OrPPCP.......	Precision Cast Parts, Portland, OR [*Library symbol*] [*Library of Congress*] (LCLS)
OrPPL.........	Pacific Power & Light Co., Portland, OR [*Library symbol*] [*Library of Congress*] (LCLS)
OrPPM.........	Providence Medical Center, Portland, OR [*Library symbol*] [*Library of Congress*] (LCLS)

OrPPS........... Portland Public School District, Portland, OR [*Library symbol*] [*Library of Congress*] (LCLS)

OrPr............. Crook County Library, Prineville, OR [*Library symbol*] [*Library of Congress*] (LCLS)

OrPR............ Reed College, Portland, OR [*Library symbol*] [*Library of Congress*] (LCLS)

OrPRAM....... Oregon Royal Arch Masons Grand Chapter Archives, Portland, OR [*Library symbol*] [*Library of Congress*] (LCLS)

OrPrC........... Crook County Library, Prineville, OR [*Library symbol*] [*Library of Congress*] (LCLS)

OrPrH.......... Pioneer Memorial Hospital Library, Prineville, OR [*Library symbol*] [*Library of Congress*] (LCLS)

OrPrK.......... Pilot Rock Public Library, Pilot Rock, OR [*Library symbol*] [*Library of Congress*] (LCLS)

OrPRP.......... Riverside Psychiatric Hospital, Portland, OR [*Library symbol*] [*Library of Congress*] (LCLS)

ORPS........... Occurrence Reporting and Processing System [*Environmental science*] (COE)

ORPS........... Overseas Return Placement System [*Military*]

OrPS............ Portland State University, Portland, OR [*Library symbol*] [*Library of Congress*] (LCLS)

OrPSMA....... Saint Mary's Academy, Portland, OR [*Library symbol*] [*Library of Congress*] (LCLS)

OrPS-MI....... Metropolitan Instructional Support Laboratory, Portland State University, Portland, OR [*Library symbol*] [*Library of Congress*] (LCLS)

OrPStV......... Saint Vincent Hospital and Medical Center, Portland, OR [*Library symbol*] [*Library of Congress*] (LCLS)

ORPSU......... Organized Reserve Port Security Unit [*Military*]

OrPT............ Temple Beth Israel, Portland, OR [*Library symbol*] [*Library of Congress*] (LCLS)

OrPTC.......... Town Center Library at Tanasbourne, Portland, OR [*Library symbol*] [*Library of Congress*] (LCLS)

OrPto........... Port Orford Public Library, Port Orford, OR [*Library symbol*] [*Library of Congress*] (LCLS)

OrPU............ University of Portland, Portland, OR [*Library symbol*] [*Library of Congress*] (LCLS)

OrPUCA....... United States Court of Appeals, Portland, OR [*Library symbol*] [*Library of Congress*] (LCLS)

Or PUC Ops... Oregon Office of the Public Utilities Commissioner. Opinions and Decisions [*A publication*] (DLA)

OrPUDC....... United States District Court, Central Library, Portland, OR [*Library symbol*] [*Library of Congress*] (LCLS)

OrPV............ United States Veterans Administration Hospital, Portland, OR [*Library symbol*] [*Library of Congress*] (LCLS)

OrPW........... Western Evangelical Seminary, Portland, OR [*Library symbol*] [*Library of Congress*] (LCLS)

OrPWB......... Western Conservative Baptist Theological Seminary, Portland, OR [*Library symbol*] [*Library of Congress*] (LCLS)

OrPWP......... Warner Pacific College, Portland, OR [*Library symbol*] [*Library of Congress*] (LCLS)

OrPWS........ Western States Chiropractic College, Portland, OR [*Library symbol*] [*Library of Congress*] (LCLS)

OrPWsC....... West Slope Community Library, Portland, OR [*Library symbol*] [*Library of Congress*] (LCLS)

ORQ............. Norwalk, CT [*Location identifier*] [*FAA*] (FAAL)

ORQ............. Outstanding Performance Rating with Quality Step Increase [*Military*] (DNAB)

ORQMC....... Orderly Room Quartermaster-Corporal [*British military*] (DMA)

ORQMS........ Orderly Room Quartermaster-Sergeant [*British military*] (DMA)

ORR............. Oak Ridge Reactor (SAUS)

ORR............. Oak Ridge Research Reactor [*ORNL*] (NRCH)

ORR............. Oak Ridge Reservation

ORR............. Office of Ready Reserve [*Army*]

ORR............. Office of Refugee Relief [*Department of Health and Human Services*]

ORR............. Office of Refugee Resettlement (USGC)

ORR............. Office of the Rail Regulator [*British*] (WA)

ORR............. Omnidirectional RADAR Range (IAA)

ORR............. Omnidirectional Radio Range (IAA)

ORR............. Onsager Reciprocal Relations [*Thermodynamics*]

ORR............. Operational Radar Replacement (SAUS)

ORR............. Operational Readiness Report (SAUS)

ORR............. Operational Readiness Reporting

ORR............. Operational Readiness Review (NASA)

ORR............. Operational Ready Rate (MCD)

ORR............. Operational Research Research (SAUS)

ORR............. Operations Requirements Review (NASA)

ORR............. Operations Research Research (SAUS)

ORR............. Optical Ratio Reflector

ORR............. Orbital Rendezvous RADAR (AAG)

ORR............. Orroval Valley, Australia, Tracking Station [*NASA*] (NASA)

ORR............. Orthographic RADAR Restitutor

ORR............. Oudh and Rohilkand Railway Rifles [*British military*] (DMA)

ORR............. Overhaul Replacement Rate

ORR............. Overseas Research Reports (SAUS)

ORR............. Owner's Risk Rates [*Shipping*]

ORR............. Red Rock Public Library, Ontario [*Library symbol*] [*National Library of Canada*] (NLC)

ORR............. Rogue Community College Library, Grants Pass, OR [*OCLC symbol*] (OCLC)

ORRA......... Orbit Semiconductor [*NASDAQ symbol*] (SAG)

ORRA......... Oriental Rug Retailers of America (EA)

ORRAS......... Optical Research Radiometrical Analysis System (IEEE)

ORRB.......... Organic Radio Review Board (SAUS)

ORRCAT...... Ridgetown College of Agricultural Technology, Ontario [*Library symbol*] [*National Library of Canada*] (NLC)

OrRed .... Redmond Public Library, Redmond, OR [*Library symbol*] [*Library of Congress*] (LCLS)

OrRedDH ..... Central Oregon District Hospital, Medical Library, Redmond, OR [*Library symbol*] [*Library of Congress*] (LCLS)

OrRedHS...... Redmond Senior High School, Redmond, OR [*Library symbol*] [*Library of Congress*] (LCLS)

OrRedOJ ...... Obsidian Junior High School, Redmond, OR [*Library symbol*] [*Library of Congress*] (LCLS)

OrRedTE ..... John Tuck Elementary School, Redmond, OR [*Library symbol*] [*Library of Congress*] (LCLS)

O-R Release... Own-Recognizance Release (SAUS)

Or Rep......... Oregon Reports [*A publication*] (DLA)

Or Rev Stat... Oregon Revised Statutes [*A publication*] (DLA)

ORRIO .... Oak Ridge Regional Investigation Office (SAUS)

ORRMIS...... Oak Ridge Regional Modeling Information System

OrRoD.......... Douglas County Library, Roseburg, OR [*Library symbol*] [*Library of Congress*] (LCLS)

OrRoM......... Douglas County Museum, Roseburg, OR [*Library symbol*] [*Library of Congress*] (LCLS)

OrRoMM...... Mercy Medical Center, Roseburg, OR [*Library symbol*] [*Library of Congress*] (LCLS)

OrRoU.......... Umpqua Community College, Roseburg, OR [*Library symbol*] [*Library of Congress*] (LCLS)

OrRoV.......... United States Veterans Administration Hospital, Roseburg, OR [*Library symbol*] [*Library of Congress*] (LCLS)

ORRPB......... Ottawa River Regulation Planning Board (SAUS)

ORRR.......... Oak Ridge Research Reactor [*Department of Energy*] (NRCH)

ORRRC....... Outdoor Recreation Resources Review Commission [*Terminated, 1962*] [*Department of the Interior*]

ORRS.......... Outer Radial Reflector Surveillance (SAUS)

ORRSR........ Onsite Routine Radioactive Shipment Record (SAUS)

ORRT........... Operational Readiness and Reliability Test

ORRTA......... Office of the Registrar of Restrictive Trading Agreements (PDAA)

ORRV........... Off-Road Recreation Vehicle

ORS............. Object Recognition Systems (SAUS)

ORS............. Obligated Reserve Section [*Air Force*] (AFM)

ORS............. Oceanographic Research Ship

ORS............. Octahedral Research Satellite [*NASA*]

ORS............. Offensive Radar System (ACAE)

ORS............. Office for Research & Statistics [*American Library Association*]

ORS............. Office of Radiation Standards [*AEC*]

ORS............. Office of Refugee Settlement (SAUS)

ORS............. Office of Regulatory Support [*Environmental Protection Agency*] (GFGA)

ORS............. Office of Rent Stabilization [*Functions transferred to Office of Defense Mobilization, 1953*]

ORS............. Office of Research and Statistics [*Social Security Administration*]

ORS............. Office of Research Services (SAUS)

ORS............. Office of Revenue Sharing [*Department of the Treasury*]

ORS............. Official Rate Standard (SAUS)

ORS............. Official Relay Station [*Amateur radio*]

ORS............. Off-Site Repair and Support (MCD)

ORS............. Oil Recovery System

ORS............. Old Red Sandstone

ORS............. Olfactory Reference Syndrome [*Medicine*] (DMAA)

ORS............. Omnidirectional Range Station (SAUS)

ORS............. Online Reference Service [*Thunder Bay Public Library*] [*Canada*] (OLDSS)

ORS............. Online Research Systems [*Information service or system*] (IID)

ORS............. On-Line Retrieval System [*Computer science*] (TELE)

ORS............. On-Site Reclamation System (SAUS)

ORS............. Operating Review System (SAUS)

ORS............. Operational Reactor Safeguards (DNAB)

ORS............. Operational Reports Section (SAUS)

ORS............. Operational Research Society [*British*]

ORS............. Operational Research Station [*Air Ministry*] [*British*] [*World War II*]

ORS............. Operations Research Society

ORS............. Optical Rendezvous System (ACAE)

ORS............. Optimal Real Storage (CMD)

ORS............. Optional Remittance Scheme (SAUS)

ORS............. Oral Electrolyte Solution [*Nutrition*]

ORS............. Oral Rehydration Salts [*or Solution*]

ORS............. Oral Rehydration Solution (SAUS)

ORS............. Oral Surgeon

ORS............. Orbital Refueling System [*NASA*] (NASA)

ORS............. Orbiter Refueling System [*NASA*]

ORS............. Orbiter Relay Simulator [*NASA*]

ORS............. Orbiting Research Satellite [*NASA*]

ORS............. Orderly Room Sergeant [*British*]

ORS............. Ordnance Repair Shop (SAUS)

ORS............. Oregon Radiological Society (SAUS)

ORS............. Oregon Revised Statutes [*A publication*] (AAGC)

ORS............. Organization Rating Scale

ORS............. Originating Register Sender

ORS............. O-Ring Seal (SAUS)

ORS............. Orpheus Island [*Australia*] [*Airport symbol*]

ORS............. Orsett [*England*]

ORS............. Orsina Resources [*Vancouver Stock Exchange symbol*]

ORS............. Orthopedic Research Society (EA)

ORS............. Orthopedic Surgeon

ORS............. Orthopedic Surgery (STED)

ORS............. OR to Storage (SAUS)

ORS............. Oscillographic Recording System

ORS	Others
ORS	Outboard Rotating Shield
ORS	Outdoor Research Surveys (SAUS)
ORS	Output Record Separator
ORS	Outstanding Requisition System (DNAB)
ORS	Oval Ring Seal
ORS	Ovarian Remnant Syndrome [Medicine] (MELL)
ORS	Overlay Reproducer System
ORS	Over Range Station (SAUS)
ORS	Overrange Station (SAUS)
ORS	Ownership Reporting System [Securities and Exchange Commission] (GFGA)
ORS	Owner's Risk of Shifting [Shipping]
ORS	Oxfordshire Record Society [British] (DBA)
ORS	Research and Development Library, Shaw Industries, Rexdale, Ontario [Library symbol] [National Library of Canada] (BIB)
ORSA	Oceanic Remote Sensing Assembly (SAUS)
ORSA	Ogive Recovery System Assembly (SAUS)
ORSA	Operational Research System Analysts
ORSA	Operations Research Society of America (EA)
OR/SA	Operations Research/Systems Analysis [Army]
ORSA	Order of Recollects of St. Augustine
ORSA	Oregon Revised Statutes Annotated [A publication]
ORSA	Osteoclast Resorption Stimulating Activity (DMAA)
OrSa	Salem Public Library, Salem, OR [Library symbol] [Library of Congress] (LCLS)
OrSaC	Chemeketa Community College, Salem, OR [Library symbol] [Library of Congress] (LCLS)
ORSAC	Oak Ridge Systems Analysis Code
ORSAC	Open Road "See America" Club [Defunct] (EA)
OR/SAEC	Operations Research/Systems Analysis Executive Course [Army]
OrSaGS	Church of Jesus Christ of Latter-Day Saints, Genealogical Society Library, SalemBranch, Salem, OR [Library symbol] [Library of Congress] (LCLS)
OrSaH	Salem Hospital, Salem, OR [Library symbol] [Library of Congress] (LCLS)
OrSaMHi	Marion County Historical Society, Salem, OR [Library symbol] [Library of Congress] (LCLS)
OrSan	Sandy Public Library, Sandy, OR [Library symbol] [Library of Congress] (LCLS)
ORSANCO	Ohio River Valley Water Sanitation Commission
OrSanHS	Sandy Union High School, Sandy, OR [Library symbol] [Library of Congress] (LCLS)
ORSAR	Official Reports, South African Republic [A publication] (DLA)
OrSaSH	Oregon State Hospital, Medical Library, Salem, OR [Library symbol] [Library of Congress] (LCLS)
OrSaT	Oregon Department of Transportation, Salem, OR [Library symbol] [Library of Congress] (LCLS)
OrSaW	Willamette University, Salem, OR [Library symbol] [Library of Congress] (LCLS)
OrSaWB	Western Baptist Bible College, Salem, OR [Library symbol] [Library of Congress] (LCLS)
OrSaW-L	Willamette University, Law Library, Salem, OR [Library symbol] [Library of Congress] (LCLS)
Or SB Bull	Oregon State Bar. Bulletin [A publication] (ILCA)
ORS(BC)	Operational Research Section (Bomber Command) [British] [World War II]
ORS-BR	O-Ring Seal, Braze Type (SAUS)
ORS-BT	O-Ring Seal, Bite Type (SAUS)
Or-SC	Oregon Supreme Court, Salem, OR [Library symbol] [Library of Congress] (LCLS)
ORSDI	Oak Ridge Selective Dissemination of Information [Department of Energy] (NASA)
ORSE	Operational Reactor Safeguard Examination (NVT)
ORSE	Otherwise
OrSEA	Oregon Society of Enrolled Agents (SAUS)
ORSEP	Operational Reentry Systems Evaluation Program (SAA)
ORSEP	Organic Separation (SAUS)
ORSER	Office for Remote Sensing of Earth Resources [Pennsylvania State University] [Research center]
OrSh	Sherwood Public Library, Sherwood, OR [Library symbol] [Library of Congress] (LCLS)
OrShe	Sheridan Public Library, Sheridan, OR [Library symbol] [Library of Congress] (LCLS)
ORSI	Office of Retirement and Survivors Insurance (SAUS)
ORSI	Operations Research Society of India (SAUS)
OrSi	Sisters Public Library, Sisters, OR [Library symbol] [Library of Congress] (LCLS)
OrSibyll	Sibylline Oracles (Pseudepigrapha) (BJA)
OrSil	Silverton Public Library, Silverton, OR [Library symbol] [Library of Congress] (LCLS)
ORSIP	Office of Research, Statistics, and International Policy [Later, ORS] [Social Security Administration] (IID)
ORSIS	Oak Ridge Sector Isotope Separator (SAUS)
ORSL	Order of the Republic of Sierra Leone
ORSoc	Operational Research Society [British] (DBA)
ORSociety	Operational Research Society (ACII)
ORSON	Orient, Spell Out, Nail Down [Method for organizing and communicating information, proposed by Barry Tarshis in his book "How to Write without Pain"]
ORSORT	Oak Ridge School of Reactor Technology [Department of Energy]
OrSp	Springfield Public Library, Springfield, OR [Library symbol] [Library of Congress] (LCLS)
ORSR	Offsite Radioactive Shipment Record (SAUS)
ORSR	Onsite Radioactive Shipment Record (SAUS)
ORS(S)	Operational Research Section (Singapore) [Military]
ORSSA	Office of Regulatory Support and Scientific Analysis [Environmental science] (COE)
ORSST	Operating Review System Support Team (SAUS)
OrSt	Stayton Public Library, Stayton, OR [Library symbol] [Library of Congress] (LCLS)
OR St B	Operation Rescue Saint Bernard [Test given to Junior Woodchucks in Donald Duck comic by Carl Barks]
Or St B Bull	Oregon State Bar Bulletin [A publication] (DLA)
OrStbM	Mount Angel College, Mount Angel Abbey, St. Benedict, OR [Library symbol] [Library of Congress] (LCLS)
OrStf	Stanfield Public Library, Stanfield, OR [Library symbol] [Library of Congress] (LCLS)
OrSthDH	Columbia District Hospital, Medical Library, St. Helens, OR [Library symbol] [Library of Congress] (LCLS)
ORSTOM	Office de la Recherche Scientifique et Technique Outre-Mer (USDC)
ORSV	Odontoglossum Ringspot Virus [Plant pathology]
O-R system	Oxidation Reduction System (ADWA)
ORT	Northway, AK [Location identifier] [FAA] (FAAL)
ORT	Oak Ridge [Tennessee] [Seismograph station code, US Geological Survey] (SEIS)
ORT	Object Relations Technique [Psychology]
ORT	Odor Recognition Threshold (SAUS)
ORT	Ongoing Reliability Test (SAUS)
ORT	Ooty Radio Telescope [India]
ORT	Open Radiator Tank [Automotive engineering]
ORT	Operating Room Technician [Medicine]
ORT	Operationally Ready Time
ORT	Operational Readiness Test
ORT	Operational Readiness Training [Army]
ORT	Operational Reliability Test joint (SAUS)
ORT	Optical Relay Tube (MCD)
ORT	Optical Rotary Table
ORT	Optimum Resolution Technique
ORT	Oral Rehydration Therapy
ORT	Orbital Rendezvous Technique (AAG)
ORT	Orbit Readiness Test [NASA] (NASA)
ORT	Order of Railroad Telegraphers [Later, Transportation-Communication Employees Union] (EA)
ORT	Ordnance Repair Truck [British]
ORT	Organization for Rehabilitation through Training [Acronym is used in names of several Jewish social welfare organizations]
ORT	Orient-Avia [Former USSR] [FAA designator] (FAAC)
ORT	Original Running Time [Movies] (CDAI)
Ort	Ortho Diagnostics
ORT	Overage Retirement Training (SAUS)
ORT	Overhaul RADAR Technology
ORT	Overland RADAR Technology (MCD)
ORT	Owner Requirements Table (HLLA)
ORT	Registered Occupational Therapist (STED)
ORTA	Office of Research and Technology Applications [Gaithersburg, MD] [National Institute of Standards and Technology] (GRD)
ORTA	Office of Research and Technology Applications [Berkeley, CA] [Lawrence Berkeley Laboratory] [Department of Energy] (GRD)
ORTA	Office of Research and Technology Applications [Army] (RDA)
ORTA	Optical Relay Tube Assembly (MCD)
ORTAG	Operations Research Technical Assistance Group [Army] (PDAA)
ORTAI	Orbit-to-Air Intercept (IAA)
ORTC	Organized Reserve Training Center [Military]
ORTC	Ortec International, Inc. [NASDAQ symbol] (SAG)
ORTC	Ortec Intl. [NASDAQ symbol] (TTSB)
ORTC	Ortec Intl. Wrrt'B' [NASDAQ symbol] (TTSB)
ORT/CTL	Operational Readiness Training - Combat Training Launch [Military] (SAA)
ORTCW	Ortec Intl. Wrrt'A' [NASDAQ symbol] (TTSB)
ORTE	Operational Readiness Training Equipment [Military] (SAA)
ORTEC	Oak Ridge Technical Enterprises Corp.
ORTECH	Ontario Research and Technology Foundation (SAUS)
OR tech	Operating Room Technician (DAVI)
OrtecInt	Ortec International, Inc. [Associated Press] (SAG)
Ortel	Ortel Corp. [Associated Press] (SAG)
ORTEP	Oak Ridge Thermal Ellipsoid Program (SAUS)
ORTF	Office de la Radio et de la Television Francaise [State-owned radio and television network] [France]
ORTF	Office de Radiodiffusion-Television Francaise [National Broadcasting Organization] [France] (NTCM)
ORTF	Organization Radio Television France (IAA)
Orth	Orthodox (WDAA)
ORTH	Orthodox
ORTH	Orthography
orth	Orthopedic (NTIO)
ORTH	Orthopedic
ORTH	Orthopedic Technology, Inc. [NASDAQ symbol] (SAG)
Orthdx	Orthodox (DIAR)
Orthfx	Orthofix International [Associated Press] (SAG)
orthg	Orthogonals (VRA)
Ort Hist	Ortolan's History of the Roman Law [A publication] (DLA)
Orthlog	Orghologic Corp. [Associated Press] (SAG)
ORTHO	American Orthopsychiatric Association (EA)
ORTHO	Orthochromatic [Photography] (ROG)
ortho	orthographical (SAUS)
ORTHO	Orthopedic
Ortho	Orthopedics [Medicine] (AMHC)
Orthodon	Orthodontic Centers of America, Inc. [Associated Press] (SAG)
ORTHOG	Orthagonal

ORTHOG ...... Orthogonal (NASA)
ortho-k .... orthokeratologist (SAUS)
Ortho-K .... Orthokeratology [*Medicine*]
orthokera ..... orthokeratologist (SAUS)
orthokera ..... orthokeratology (SAUS)
orthomol ...... orthomolecular (SAUS)
ORTHOMOL.. Orthomolecularologist (SAUS)
ORTHOMOL.. Orthomolecularology (SAUS)
orthop .... Orthopnea [*Medicine*] (DAVI)
ORTHOPHOS... Orthophosphoric acid (SAUS)
orthopod ...... Orthopedist [*Orthopedic Physician*] (DAVI)
OrthopT .... Orthopedic Technology, Inc. [*Associated Press*] (SAG)
orthor .... orthorhombic (SAUS)
OrTig .... Tigard Public Library, Tigard, OR [*Library symbol*] [*Library of Congress*] (LCLS)
Ort Inst .... Ortolan's Justinian's Institutes [*A publication*] (DLA)
OrtInt .... Ortec International, Inc. [*Associated Press*] (SAG)
ORTL .... Ortel Corp. [*NASDAQ symbol*] (SAG)
ORTM .... On-orbit Right Technique Meeting (SAUS)
ORTN .... Officie Radiodiffusion Television du Niger [*Radio and television network*] [*Niger*]
ORTO .... Occupational Rehabilitation Training for Overseas (SAUS)
ORTO .... Olympics Radio and Television Organization [*Organisme de Radio-Television des Olympiques*] [*Canada*]
ORTP .... Operational Readiness Training Program [*Military*] (AABC)
ORTPA .... Oven-Ready Turkey Producers Association (SAUS)
Or TR .... Oregon Tax Reporter [*A publication*] (DLA)
Or T Rep ...... Oregon Tax Reporter [*A publication*] (ILCA)
Or T Rep ...... Orleans Term Reports [*1, 2 Martin*] [*Louisiana*] [*A publication*] (DLA)
Ort Rom Law... Ortolan's History of the Roman Law [*A publication*] (DLA)
ORTS .... Occurrence Reporting and Tracking System (SAUS)
ORTS .... Operational Readiness Test System [*Military*] (CAAL)
ORTS .... Operational Test and Readiness System (SAUS)
ORTS .... Optional Residence (or Residential) Telephone Service (SAUS)
ORTS .... Optional Residential Telephone Service [*Telecommunications*] (TEL)
ORTT .... Operational Readiness Training Test [*Army*] (AABC)
ORTT .... Overreaching Transfer Trip (IAA)
ORTU .... Organized Reserve Training Unit [*Military*]
ORTU .... Other Ranks Training Unit (SAUS)
OrTua .... Tualatin Public Library, Tualatin, OR [*Library symbol*] [*Library of Congress*] (LCLS)
ORTUAG ...... Organized Reserve Training Unit, Vessel Augmentation [*Military*]
OrTuaM .... Meridian Park Hospital, Medical Library, Tualatin, OR [*Library symbol*] [*Library of Congress*] (LCLS)
ORTUAM ...... Organized Reserve Training Unit, Administration of Mobilization [*Military*]
ORTUAV ...... Organized Reserve Training Unit, Aviation Support [*Military*]
ORTUEL ...... Organized Reserve Training Unit, Electronics [*Military*]
ORTUF .... Organized Reserve Training Unit, Coastal Force [*Military*]
ORTUPS ...... Organized Reserve Training Unit, Port Security [*Military*]
ORTUPS(O)... Organized Reserve Training Unit, Port Security (Operational) [*Military*]
ORTUR .... Organized Reserve Training Unit, Rescue Coordination Center [*Military*]
OrTW .... Wasco County Library, The Dalles, OR [*Library symbol*] [*Library of Congress*] (LCLS)
ORTX .... Ortner Air Service [*Air carrier designation symbol*]
ORU .... On-Line Replacement Unit [*Computer science*] (MCD)
ORU .... Operational Readiness Unit
ORU .... Operational Research Unit (SAUS)
ORU .... Operator Radio Unit (SAUS)
ORU .... Optical Reference Unit
ORU .... Optimal Replaceable Unit (IAA)
ORU .... Oral Roberts University [*Oklahoma*]
ORU .... Orange & Rockland Utilities, Inc. [*NYSE symbol*] (SPSG)
ORU .... Orbital Replaceable Unit (SSD)
ORU .... Orbit Replaceable Unit (SAUS)
oru .... Oregon [*MARC country of publication code*] [*Library of Congress*] (LCCP)
ORU .... Organization for Rebirth of Ukraine (EA)
ORU .... Organized Research Unit (SAUS)
ORU .... Oruro [*Bolivia*] [*Airport symbol*] (AD)
ORU .... Other than Ship or Squadron Reinforcement Unit [*Naval Reserve*] (DNAB)
ORU .... Russell Branch, Russell Township Public Library, Ontario [*Library symbol*] [*National Library of Canada*] (BIB)
OrU .... University of Oregon, Eugene, OR [*Library symbol*] [*Library of Congress*] (LCLS)
ORU .... University of Oregon Library, Eugene, OR [*OCLC symbol*] (OCLC)
ORUC .... Orbital Replacement Unit Carrier (SAUS)
OrU-C .... University of Oregon, Computing Center, Eugene, OR [*Library symbol*] [*Library of Congress*] (LCLS)
OrU-D .... University of Oregon, Dental School, Portland, OR [*Library symbol*] [*Library of Congress*] (LCLS)
ORUEF .... Oral Roberts University Educational Fellowship (EA)
ORUFE .... Operational Research Unit, Far East
OrUk .... Ukiah Public Library, Ukiah, OR [*Library symbol*] [*Library of Congress*] (LCLS)
OrU-L .... University of Oregon, Law Library, Portland, OR [*Library symbol*] [*Library of Congress*] (LCLS)
OrU-M .... University of Oregon, Medical School, Portland, OR [*Library symbol*] [*Library of Congress*] (LCLS)
OrUma .... Umatilla Public Library, Umatilla, OR [*Library symbol*] [*Library of Congress*] (LCLS)

OrUmaH .... Umatilla Hospital, Umatilla, OR [*Library symbol*] [*Library of Congress*] (LCLS)
OrUmH .... Umatilla Hospital, Umatilla, OR [*Library symbol*] [*Library of Congress*] (LCLS)
OrUn .... Carnegie Public Library, Union, OR [*Library symbol*] [*Library of Congress*] (LCLS)
O/RUNN .... Overrunning [*Automotive engineering*]
OrU-O .... University of Oregon, Ocean and Coastal Law Center, Eugene, OR [*Library symbol*] [*Library of Congress*] (LCLS)
OrU-Or .... University of Oregon, Oriental Museum, Portland, OR [*Library symbol*] [*Library of Congress*] (LCLS)
ORUP .... Ocean Resource Utilization Program (ASF)
ORUS .... Official Register of the United States
ORUS .... Orbital Replacement Units (SAUS)
OrU-S .... University of Oregon, Science Division Library, Eugene, OR [*Library symbol*] [*Library of Congress*] (LCLS)
ORuss .... Old Russian [*Language*] (BARN)
OrV .... Fern Ridge Community Library, Veneta, OR [*Library symbol*] [*Library of Congress*] (LCLS)
ORV .... Noorvik [*Alaska*] [*Airport symbol*] (OAG)
ORV .... Oceanographic Research Vessel
ORV .... Ocean Range Vessel [*Air Force*]
ORV .... Off-Road Vehicle
ORV .... Operational Range Vessels (ACAE)
ORV .... Orbital Reentry Vehicle [*NASA*] (IAA)
ORV .... Orbital Rescue Vehicle [*NASA*] (KSC)
ORV .... Orbital Return Vehicle [*NASA*] (IAA)
ORV .... Oroville [*California*] [*Seismograph station code, US Geological Survey*] (SEIS)
ORVAT .... Organizational Vehicle Automatic Tester
ORVC .... River Valley Community Library, Ontario [*Library symbol*] [*National Library of Canada*] (NLC)
ORVID .... Online X-ray Evaluation over Video-Display Including Documentation (PDAA)
ORVR .... On-Board Refueling Vapor Recovery [*Automotive engineering*]
ORVX .... OraVax, Inc. [*NASDAQ symbol*] (SAG)
ORW .... Norwich, CT [*Location identifier*] [*FAA*] (FAAL)
ORW .... Ohio Reformatory for Women (SAUS)
ORW .... Orange Walk [*British Honduras*] [*Airport symbol*] (AD)
ORW .... Orwell Resources Ltd. [*Vancouver Stock Exchange symbol*]
ORW .... Orwex [*Poland*] [*ICAO designator*] (FAAC)
ORW .... Outstanding Resource Waters [*Water quality standards*] [*Environmental Protection Agency*]
ORW .... Owner's Risk of Becoming Wet [*Shipping*]
ORW .... Raymond Walters General and Technical College, Blue Ash, OH [*OCLC symbol*] (OCLC)
OrWe .... Weston Public Library, Weston, OR [*Library symbol*] [*Library of Congress*] (LCLS)
OrWel .... West Linn Public Library, West Linn, OR [*Library symbol*] [*Library of Congress*] (LCLS)
OrWelH .... West Linn High School, West Linn, OR [*Library symbol*] [*Library of Congress*] (LCLS)
ORWG .... Operational Requirements Working Group (DOMA)
ORWH .... Office of Research on Women's Health [*National Institutes of Health*]
OrWi .... Willamina Public Library, Willamina, OR [*Library symbol*] [*Library of Congress*] (LCLS)
ORWISE....... Otherwise (ROG)
ORWL .... Outline Raised White Letter [*Tire design*]
OrWo .... Woodburn Public Library, Woodburn, OR [*Library symbol*] [*Library of Congress*] (LCLS)
ORWP .... Optical Radiation Weapon Program (AAG)
ORX .... Oriximina [*Brazil*] [*Airport symbol*] (AD)
ORX .... Oryx Aviation [*South Africa*] [*ICAO designator*] (FAAC)
ORX .... Oryx Energy Co. [*NYSE symbol*] (SPSG)
ORY .... Paris [*France*] Orly Airport [*Airport symbol*] (OAG)
Oryx .... Oryx Energy Co. [*Associated Press*] (SAG)
ORYX .... Oryx Technology [*NASDAQ symbol*] (TTSB)
ORYX .... Oryx Technology Corp. [*NASDAQ symbol*] (SAG)
OryxTc .... Oryx Technology Corp. [*Associated Press*] (SAG)
ORYXW .... Oryx Technology Wrrt [*NASDAQ symbol*] (TTSB)
ORZ .... Omnirange Zero (IAA)
ORZ .... Omnirange Zone
ORZ .... Orange Walk [*Belize*] [*Airport symbol*] [*Obsolete*] (OAG)
ORZ .... Outer Radiation Zone
OS .... Austrian Airlines [*ICAO designator*] (AD)
OS .... By Mouth [*Pharmacy*] (DAVI)
Os .... Oberseminar (SAUS)
OS .... Obese Strain [*White leghorn*]
OS .... Object-Subject [*Education of the hearing-impaired*]
OS .... Oblique Sounding [*Telecommunications*] (OA)
OS .... Observation-Scouting Plane [*When first two letters in Navy designation*]
OS .... Observation Squadron (SAUS)
OS .... Observation Station (SAUS)
OS .... Observer School (SAUS)
OS .... Observing Station [*Marine science*] (MSC)
OS .... Occupational Safety (DAVI)
OS .... Oceanic Society (EA)
OS .... Oceanography Section (SAUS)
OS .... Ocean Station [*Maps and charts*]
OS .... Ocean Surveillance (ACAE)
OS .... Octavian Society (EA)
OS .... Oculus Sinister [*Left Eye*] [*Ophthalmology*]
OS .... Odd Symmetric
OS .... Offensive Support (SAUS)

OS............... Office of Supply (SAUS)
OS............... Office of Systems [*NASA*] (KSC)
OS............... Office of the Secretary
OS............... Officers' Steward [*Ranking title*] [*British Women's Royal Naval Service*]
OS............... Office Surgery (SAUS)
OS............... Office System
OS............... Official Scorer [*Baseball term*] (NDBD)
OS............... Official Station
OS............... Off Scale (IAA)
OS............... Off Screen [*or Stage*]
OS............... Offset
OS............... Off Stage (SAUS)
OS............... Ohio State (SAUS)
OS............... Ohio State Reports [*A publication*] (DLA)
OS............... Oil Sand (SAUS)
OS............... Oil Shale (SAUS)
OS............... Oil Solenoid
OS............... Oil Solubility (SAUS)
OS............... Oil-Soluble (SAUS)
OS............... Oil Solvent (SAUS)
OS............... Oil Switch
OS............... Old Saxon [*Language, etc.*]
OS............... Old School
OS............... Old Series
OS............... Old Side
OS............... Old Standard [*Currency*] (ROG)
OS............... Old Style [*Printing*] (NTCM)
OS............... Old Style [*Calendar, previous to 1752*]
OS............... Old Style date (SAUS)
OS............... Omega Society [*Defunct*] (EA)
OS............... Omnibus Society [*British*]
OS............... One Shot
OS............... One Side
OS............... One-Stop [*Aviation*]
os............... Only Son (WDAA)
OS............... Only Son
OS............... On-Orbit Station [*NASA*] (MCD)
os............... On-Orbit Station [*NASA*] (NAKS)
OS............... On Sale
OS............... On Sample
OS............... On Schedule
O/S............... On Sea [*In place names*] [*British*] (ROG)
o-S............... on-Sea (SAUS)
OS............... On Sheet (WGA)
OS............... On Side
OS............... On-Site
OS............... On Spot (ROG)
OS............... On Station [*Military*]
OS............... On Switch
OS............... Opening Snaps [*Cardiology*]
OS............... Open Shop (SAUS)
OS............... Open Side (SAUS)
OS............... Open Statement (SAUS)
OS............... Open Subroutine (SAUS)
OS............... Open System (SAUS)
os............... Opera Seria [*Music*] (GROV)
OS............... Operating Schedule [*Field stations*] (MCD)
OS............... Operating Software (MCD)
OS............... Operating System [*Computer science*] (BUR)
O/S............... Operational Assist Project/Shipborne Application
OS............... Operational Sequence (KSC)
OS............... Operational Sheets
OS............... Operational Software (SAUS)
OS............... Operational Specialist [*Navy*]
OS............... Operational Suitability
OS............... Operational Supplements [*Air Force*] (MCD)
OS............... Operation Sandstone [*Atomic weapons testing*]
O/S............... Operations and Support (SAUS)
OS............... Operation Sheet (SAUS)
OS............... Operation Smile (EA)
OS............... Operation Snapper [*Atomic weapons testing*]
OS............... Operations Specialist [*Navy*] (DNAB)
OS............... Operations Superintendent (SAUS)
OS............... Operations Support [*Office of U.S. Foreign Disaster Assistance*]
OS............... Operations System (SAUS)
OS............... Operation Suburbia [*Defunct*] (EA)
OS............... Operator Service (SAUS)
OS............... Operator's Set
OS............... Optical Scanner (SAUS)
OS............... Optical Scanning [*Computer science*]
OS............... Optical Society (NADA)
OS............... Optical Spectroscopy (SAUS)
OS............... Optical System (SAUS)
OS............... Optics Subsystem
OS............... Optimum Size (ELAL)
OS............... Option Spreading [*Investment term*]
OS............... Oral Surgery
OS............... Oral Suspension [*Pharmacy*]
OS............... Orbital Servicing
AS............... Orbiter CEI [*Contract End Item*] Specification [*NASA*] (NASA)
OS............... Orderly Sergeant (SAUS)
OS............... Order of Servites
OS............... Order Sheet
OS............... Ordinary Seaman [*British*]

OS............... Ordnance School [*Army*] (MCD)
OS............... Ordnance Server (SAUS)
OS............... Ordnance Services [*Military*] [*British*]
OS............... Ordnance Specifications [*Navy*]
OS............... Ordnance Survey
OS............... Oregon State (SAUS)
OS............... Oregon Steel Mills [*NYSE symbol*] (SPSG)
OS............... Organic Solvent (SAUS)
OS............... Organic Synthesis (SAUS)
OS............... Organizational Source [*Online database field identifier*] [*Computer science*]
OS............... Organizational Support (SAUS)
OS............... Organizations System (IAA)
OS............... Organization System (SAUS)
OS............... Organosilicon (SAUS)
OS............... Original Series
OS............... Ornamental Stitching (DNAB)
OS............... Oro Sellado [*Standard Gold*] [*Business term*] [*Spanish*]
OS............... Orthogonal System (SAUS)
O/S............... Orthopaedic Surgery [*Medical Officer designation*] [*British*]
OS............... Orthopedics (DAVI)
OS............... Orthopedic Surgery (DAVI)
OS............... Orton Society [*Later, ODS*] (EA)
OS............... Osgood-Schlatter's Disease [*Medicine*]
Os............... Osmium [*Chemical element*]
OS............... Osmotic Shock
OS............... Osteogenic Sarcoma [*Medicine*]
OS............... Osteosarcoma [*Oncology*]
OS............... Osteosclerosis [*Medicine*] (DAVI)
OS............... Oszillator im Sender (SAUS)
OS............... Other Side [*A publication*] (BRI)
OS............... Other Sources
OS............... Otherwise Specified (MSA)
OS............... Outer Segment
OS............... Outer Sheath [*Botany*]
OS............... Outer Space (SAUS)
OS............... Outlaw Shark [*RADAR surveillance*] [*Naval Electronic Systems Command*]
OS............... Outline Square Condition [*Vision*]
O/S............... Out of Service (AFM)
O/S............... Out-of-Shot [*Photography*]
O/S............... Out of State (SAUS)
OS............... Out of Stock (NTCM)
OS............... Output Secondary [*Electronics*]
OS............... Output Signal (SAUS)
OS............... Output Source (SAUS)
OS............... Output Specification (SAUS)
OS............... Output Store (SAUS)
OS............... Output System (SAUS)
OS............... Out Secondary (SAUS)
OS............... Outside
OS............... Outside Sales (TRID)
OS............... Outside Sentinel
OS............... Outsize [*Of clothes*]
os............... Outstanding (ELAL)
O/S............... Outstanding
OS............... Outstate (SAUS)
OS............... Outstation (MCD)
OS............... Out Stealing [*Baseball*]
OS............... Overall Size (SAUS)
OS............... Overall Survival [*Medicine*]
OS............... Overlong Sentence [*Used in correcting manuscripts, etc.*]
OS............... Overscene [*Films, television, etc.*]
OS............... Oversea [*Military*]
OS............... Overseas Service (SAUS)
O/S............... Overshipped (MCD)
OS............... Overshoot (SAUS)
OS............... Oversize (AAG)
OS............... Overspecificity [*Psychometrics*]
OS............... Overstressing (SAUS)
OS............... Over-the-Horizon Targeting System (MCD)
OS............... Over-the-Shoulder Cinematography (NTCM)
OS............... Over the State [*Regarding distribution*]
OS............... Own Ship [*Navy*] (CAAL)
OS............... Oxygen Saturation (DB)
OS............... Oxygen Sensor [*Automotive engineering*]
OS............... Oxygen Service (DNAB)
OS............... Sarnia Public Library, Ontario [*Library symbol*] [*National Library of Canada*] (NLC)
OS............... Shell Development Co. [*Research code symbol*]
OS............... Test Oscilloscope [*JETDS nomenclature*] [*Military*] (CET)
OS............... Warder Public Library of Springfield and Clark County, Springfield, OH [*Library symbol*] [*Library of Congress*] (LCLS)
OS/2............ IBMs Operating System (SAUS)
OS/2............ Operating System 2 [*Computer science*]
OS 2d.......... Ohio State Reports, Second Series [*A publication*] (DLA)
OS9............. Operating System-9
OS/390........ Open Server/390 (SAUS)
OS/400........ Operationg System/400 (SAUS)
OS/400........ Optimized Server for AS/400 computers (SAUS)
OSA .... Aero Astra [*Mexico*] [*ICAO designator*] (FAAC)
OSA .... Augustinian Nuns of Contemplative Life (TOCD)
OSA .... [*The*] Augustinians (TOCD)
osa............. [*The*] Augustinians (TOCD)
OSA .... Augustinian Sisters of Our Lady of Consolation (TOCD)

OSA .... Congregation of Augustinian Sisters Servants of Jesus and Mary (TOCD)
OSA .... Object System Adaptor (SAUS)
OSA .... Obstructive Sleep Apnea [*Medicine*]
OSA .... Occupational Safety Aid
OSA .... Ocean Shipping Act (SAUS)
OSA .... Office of Safety Assessment (ABAC)
OSA .... Office of Savings Associations [*Formerly, FHLIC*]
OSA .... Office of Services to the Aging (DAVI)
OSA .... Office of Special Activities (CINC)
OSA .... Office of Special Applications (SAUS)
OSA .... Office of State Administration [*Australia*]
OSA .... Office of Student Affairs (SAUS)
OSA .... Office of Student Aid (SAUS)
OSA .... Office of the Secretary of the Army
OSA .... Office of the Special Assistant to the Ambassador
OSA .... Office Systems Administrator (SAUS)
OSA .... Office Systems Architecture (SAUS)
OSA .... Official Secrets Act [*British*]
OSA .... Offshore Acquisition [*Army*] (AABC)
OSA .... Oil-Soluble Acid (SAUS)
OSA .... Oklahoma Statutes Annotated [*A publication*] (DLA)
OSA .... Old South Arabic (BJA)
OSA .... Old Style Antique [*British*]
OSA .... Olefin-Modified Styrene-Acrylonitrile (SAUS)
OSA .... Omnibus Society of America (EA)
OSA .... On-Stream Analysis (SAUS)
OSA .... Ontario Society of Artists [*Canada*] (BARN)
OSA .... Open Scripting Architecture (SAUS)
OSA .... Open Solutions Architecture (SAUS)
OSA .... Open Storage Architecture (SAUS)
OSA .... Open System Adapter (SAUS)
OSA .... Open Systems Architecture [*Computer science*]
OSA .... Operational Safety Analysis (SAUS)
OSA .... Operational Safety Assessment (SAUS)
OSA .... Operational Support Aircraft [*or Airlift*]
OSA .... Operational Support Airlift [*Air Force*] (DOMA)
OSA .... Operational Support Area
OSA .... Operation Sciences Appliquees [*Quebec*]
OSA .... Optical Society of America (EA)
OSA .... Optimization by Simulated Annealing [*Mathematics*]
OSA .... Order for Simple Alert (NATG)
OSA .... Order of St. Anne [*Anglican religious community*]
OSA .... Order of St. Augustine [*See also OFSA*] [*Rome, Italy*] (EAIO)
OSA .... Order-Sorting Aperture [*Instrumentation*]
OSA .... Organic Soil Association (SAUS)
OSA .... Organisation for Strategic Labour Markets (SAUS)
OSA .... Ormec Serro Analyst (NITA)
OSA .... Orthodox Society of America
osa .... Osage [*MARC language code*] [*Library of Congress*] (LCCP)
OSA .... Oscilloquartz SA (SAUS)
OSA .... Ossa Resources, Inc. [*Vancouver Stock Exchange symbol*]
OSA .... Osteosarcoma (SAUS)
OSA .... Outfit Supply Activity (MCD)
OSA .... Ovarian Sectional Area [*Medicine*] (DMAA)
OSA .... Overall System Attenuation (SAUS)
OSA .... Overseas Sterling Area (SAUS)
OSA .... Overseas Supply Agency [*Military*]
OSA .... Overspenders Anonymous (EA)
OSA .... Oyster Shell Association (SAUS)
OSa .... Sabina Public Library, Sabina, OH [*Library symbol*] [*Library of Congress*] (LCLS)
OSA .... Sisters of St. Augustine (TOCD)
OSA .... Sisters of St. Rita (TOCD)
OSAA .... Operational Satellite Active Archive [*Marine science*] (OSRA)
OSA (ABCMR)... Office, Secretary of the Army (Army Board for Correction of Military Records)
OSAC .... Open Space Action Committee (SAUS)
OSAC .... Operator Services Assistance Center (SAUS)
OSAC .... Orifice Spark Advance Control [*Valve*] [*Automotive technology*]
OSAC .... Overseas Schools Advisory Council [*Department of State*] [*Washington, DC*] (EGAO)
OSAC .... Overseas Security Advisory Council [*Department of State*] [*Washington, DC*] (EGAO)
OSAC .... Oxford System of Automated Cartography (SAUS)
OSACA .... Open System Architecture for Controls within Automation systems (SAUS)
OSACI .... Ecumenical Study and Action Centre on Investment [*Netherlands*]
OSAD .... Outer Space Affairs Division (SAUS)
OSAD A & L... Office of the Secretary of the Army for Development / Acquisition and Logistics
OSADBU ...... Office of Small and Disadvantaged Business Utilization (AAGC)
OS/AEL .... Operating Space/Allowance Equipage List
OSAF .... Office of the Secretary of the Air Force
OSAF .... Origin Subarea Address Field (SAUS)
OSAF .... Origin Subarea Field (SAUS)
OSAFO .... Office of the Special Assistant for Field Operations [*Formerly, CORDS*] (VNW)
OSAFU .... Oromo Students Association of Finfine University [*Ethiopia*]
OSAH .... Health Sciences Library, Sudbury Algoma Hospital, Sudbury, Ontario [*Library symbol*] [*National Library of Canada*] (NLC)
OSAHRC ...... Occupational Safety and Health Review Commission [*Department of Labor*]
OSAI .... Office of Systems Analysis and Information [*Department of Transportation*]

OSAIS .... Oil Spillage Analytical and Identification Service [*Laboratory of the Government Chemist*] (PDAA)
OSAIS .... Oil Spillage Analytical Information Service (NITA)
OSAK .... Open Systems Application Kernel (SAUS)
OSAK .... OSI [*Open Systems Interconnection*] Applications Kernel [*Computer science*] (TNIG)
Osaka Pref Bull... Osaka Prefecture. University. Bulletin [*A publication*] (DLA)
Osaka ULR... Osaka University. Law Review [*A publication*] (DLA)
Osaka UL Rev... Osaka University. Law Review [*A publication*] (DLA)
Osaka Univ L Rev... Osaka University. Law Review [*Osaka, Japan*] [*A publication*] (DLA)
OSAL .... Opening of Salivary [*Gland*]
OSal .... Salem Public Library, Salem, OH [*Library symbol*] [*Library of Congress*] (LCLS)
OSALC .... Savant Lake Community Library, Ontario [*Library symbol*] [*National Library of Canada*] (NLC)
OSalK .... Kent State University, Columbiana Regional Campus, Salem, OH [*Library symbol*] [*Library of Congress*] (LCLS)
OSALSAA.... Office, Special Assistant for Logistical Support of Army Aircraft (AABC)
OSALSTC.... Office, Special Assistant for Logistical Support of Tactical Communications (AABC)
OSAM .... Overflow Sequential Access Method [*Computer science*]
OSAMM ...... Optimum Supply and Maintenance Model [*Army*] (RDA)
OSAMS .... Synod Office, Diocese of Moosonee, Anglican Church of Canada, Schumacher, Ontario [*Library symbol*] [*National Library of Canada*] (NLC)
OSand......... Sandusky Library Association, Sandusky, OH [*Library symbol*] [*Library of Congress*] (LCLS)
OS & CP Dec... Ohio Superior and Common Pleas Decisions [*A publication*] (DLA)
OS & D....... Over, Short, and Damaged [*Report*] [*Shipping*] (MSA)
OS&D........ Over, Short and Damage Report (SAUS)
OS & DR...... Over, Short, and Damaged Report [*Shipping*]
OS and D Report... Over, Short and Damaged Report (SAUS)
OS&E.......... Ocean Science and Engineering (SAUS)
OS & FM ..... Office of Systems and Financial Management [*DoD*]
OS&M......... Operational Support and Maintenance (SAUS)
OS & RP...... On-Board Spares and Repair Parts [*Navy*] (DNAB)
OS & TD ...... Ocean Science and Technology Division [*Office of Naval Research*] (DNAB)
OS & W....... Oak, Sunk, and Weathered [*Construction*]
OS & Y .... Outside Screw and Yoke
OS&Y.......... Outside Screw and Yolk (SAUS)
OSAP .... Aleppo/Neirab [*Syria*] [*ICAO location identifier*] (ICLI)
OSAP .... Ocean Surveillance Air Patrol (CINC)
OSAP .... Ocean Survey Advisory Panel [*Marine science*] (MSC)
OSAP .... Office of Scientific and Academic Publications (SAUS)
OSAP .... Office of Substance Abuse Prevention [*Department of Agriculture*] (EGAO)
OSAP .... Office Space Allocation Plan (MCD)
OSAP .... Ontario Student Assistance Program (SAUS)
OSAP .... Ontario Student Awards Program (SAUS)
OSAPI .... Operating System/Application Program Interface [*Computer science*]
OSAR .... Operational Safety Analysis Report (ABAC)
OSAR .... Operations Suitability Assessment Report (SSD)
OSAR .... Optical Storage and Retrieval [*Computer science*]
OSAR .... Overhead Systems Apprearance Research (IAA)
OSarS .... Southern State Community College, Sardinia, OH [*Library symbol*] [*Library of Congress*] (LCLS)
OSART .... Operational Safety Review Team [*International Atomic Energy Agency*]
OSAS .... Obstructive Sleep Apnea Syndrome [*Medicine*] (DMAA)
OSAS .... Ohio Social Acceptance Scale (EDAC)
OSAS .... Open Systems Accounting Software [*Computer science*]
OSAS .... Overseas Service Aid Scheme
OSASA .... Obstructive Sleep Apnea Sydrome (SAUS)
OSASF .... Overseas Supply Agency, San Francisco [*Military*] (CINC)
OSASN........ Office of Special Assistant, Secretary of the Navy
OSAT .... Office for the Study of Automotive Transportation [*Department of Transportation*]
OSAT .... Office of the Special Assistant for Training [*Army*] (RDA)
OSAT .... Optical Sensor and Tracker
OSAT .... Optimized Sustained Action Technology (DB)
OSATA .... Order of Saint Andrew the Apostle (EA)
OSATRMS.... Operational Resource Tracking and Management System (SAUS)
OSA-UCS .... Optical Society of America Uniform Color Scales (SAUS)
OSAY .... Outside Screw and Yoke (IAA)
OSB .... Benedictine Congregation of Our Lady of Monte (TOCD)
OSB .... Benedictine Monks (TOCD)
osb .... Benedictine Monks, Olivetan Benedictines, Sylvestrine Benedictines (TOCD)
OSB .... Benedictine Nuns (TOCD)
OSB .... Benedictine Nuns of the Congregation of Solesmes (TOCD)
OSB .... Benedictine Nuns of the Primitive Observance (TOCD)
OSB .... Benedictine Sisters (TOCD)
OSB .... Benedictine Sisters of Liberty (TOCD)
OSB .... Benedictine Sisters of Pontifical Jurisdiction (TOCD)
OSB .... Benedictine Sisters of Sacred Heart (TOCD)
OSB .... Congregation of Jesus Crucified (TOCD)
OSB .... Congregation of the Benedictine Sisters of Perpetual Adoration of Pontifical Jurisdiction (TOCD)
OSB .... Congregation of the Benedictine Sisters of the Sacred Heart (TOCD)
OSB .... Contemplative Sisters of St. Benedict (TOCD)
OSB .... Missionary Benedictine Sisters (TOCD)
OSB .... Occupational Safety Bulletin (SAUS)

OSB	Ocean Sciences Board [*NASA*] (MSC)
OSB	Ocean Studies Board (SAUS)
OSB	Office of Savings Bonds [*Navy*]
OSB	Office of Surveillance and Biometrics [*U.S. Food and Drug Administration*]
OSB	Officer Selection Battery [*Military*]
OSB	Officer Selection Board
OSB	Officer Selection Brief (SAUS)
OSB	Olivetan Benedictine Sisters (TOCD)
OSB	One-Statement Banking (MHDB)
OSB	Operational Stations Book (SAUS)
OSB	Operational Status BIT [*Binary Digit*]
OSB	Operations and Services Building (SAUS)
OSB	Operations Software Branch (SAUS)
OSB	Operations Stations Book [*Navy*]
OSB	Operations Support Building [*NASA*] (KSC)
OSB	Operation Support Building
OSB	Operative Society of Bricklayers [*A union*] [*British*]
OSB	Orangeburg [*South Carolina*] [*Seismograph station code, US Geological Survey*] (SEIS)
OSB	Orbital Solar Observation (IAA)
OSB	Order of Saint Benedict (SAUS)
OSB	Order of Shepherds of Bethlehem (EA)
OSB	Order of St. Benedict (SAUS)
OSB	Order of the Stars and Bars [*Later, MOSB*] (EA)
OSB	Ordinis Sancti Bernardi [*Order of St. Bernard*] [*Latin*] (ROG)
OSB	Ordnance Supply Bulletin
OSB	Ordo Sancti Benedicti [*Order of St. Benedict*] [*Roman Catholic religious order*]
OSB	Oriented-Strand Board [*A plywood panel composition*]
OSB	Orthopedic Seat Backrest [*Automotive engineering*]
OSB	Osage Beach [*Missouri*] [*Airport symbol*] [*Obsolete*] (OAG)
OSB	Output Signal Balance (SAUS)
OSB	Overseas Brats
OSB	Overseas Service Bureau (SAUS)
OSB	Sauble Beach Branch, Bruce County Public Library, Ontario [*Library symbol*] [*National Library of Canada*] (NLC)
OSBA	Ohio School Boards Association (SAUS)
OSBA	Oregon School Boards Association (SAUS)
OSBA	Outlet and Switch Box Association [*Defunct*] (EA)
OSBA Bull	Ohio State Bar Association. Bulletin [*A publication*] (DLA)
OSBC	Old Second Bancorp [*NASDAQ symbol*] (TTSB)
OSBC	Old Second Bancorp, Inc. [*NASDAQ symbol*] (SAG)
OSBCam	Camaldolese Benedictine Sisters (TOCD)
OSBCam	Camaldolese Hermits (TOCD)
osbcam	Camaldolese Hermits (TOCD)
OSBE	Organization of State Broadcasting Executives (SAUS)
OSBF	Damascus [*Syria*] [*ICAO location identifier*] (ICLI)
OSBF	OSB Financial [*NASDAQ symbol*] (SAG)
OSBF	OSB Finl Corp. [*NASDAQ symbol*] (TTSB)
OSB Fn	OSB Financial [*Associated Press*] (SAG)
OSBL	Outside Battery Limits [*Chemical engineering*]
OSB Loss	Output Signal Balance Loss (SAUS)
OSBM	Morrison Library Outpost, Severn Bridge, Ontario [*Library symbol*] [*National Library of Canada*] (NLC)
OSBM	Office of Space Biology and Medicine [*Proposed for NASA*]
osbm	Order of St. Basil the Great (TOCD)
OSBM	Ordo Sancti Basil Magni [*Order of St. Basil the Great*] [*Roman Catholic religious order*]
OSBM	Sisters of the Order of St. Basil the Great (TOCD)
OSBN	Osborn Communications [*NASDAQ symbol*] (TTSB)
OSBN	Osborn Communications Corp. [*NASDAQ symbol*] (NQ)
Osborn	Osborn Communications [*Associated Press*] (SAG)
Osborn	Osborne Communications Corp. [*Associated Press*] (SAG)
OSBP	Office of Small Business Programs
OSBP	Ontario Special Bursary Plan (SAUS)
OSBR	Seeley's Bay Branch, Rideau Lakes Union Library, Ontario [*Library symbol*] [*National Library of Canada*] (BIB)
OSBRB	Overhead/Support Budget Review Board (SAUS)
OSBRD	Office of Small Business Research and Development [*National Science Foundation*] (GRD)
OSBS	Oblate Sisters of the Blessed Sacrament [*Roman Catholic religious order*]
OSBT	Officer Selection Battery Test [*Military*]
OSC	Canonici Regulares Ordinis Sanctae Crucis [*Canons Regular of the Order of the Holy Cross*] [*Crosier Fathers*] [*Roman Catholic religious order*]
osc	Canons Regular of the Order of the Holy Cross, Crosier Fathers (TOCD)
OSC	Clan Grant No. 17, Order of Scottish Clans (EA)
OSC	Clark County Technical Institute, Springfield, OH [*Library symbol*] [*Library of Congress*] (LCLS)
OSC	Complete Operational Software [*Telecommunications*] (TEL)
OSC	Oak Satellite Corp. (NITA)
OSC	Obedience Stewards Club (EA)
OSC	Objective Supply Capability [*Army*] (RDA)
OSC	Oblate of Saint Charles (SAUS)
OSC	Oblate Spherical Coordinates
OSC	Oblati Sancti Caroli [*Oblate Fathers of St. Charles*] [*Roman Catholic religious order*]
OSC	Occupational Standards Council (AIE)
OSC	Ocean Science Committee [*National Academy of Sciences/Ocean Affairs Board*] (NOAA)
OSC	Ocean Sciences Center [*Memorial University of Newfoundland*] [*Canada*]
OSC	Offence against Sine Condition (SAUS)
OSC	Office of Scientific Computing (SAUS)
OSC	Office of Space Communications [*NASA*] (BARN)
OSC	Office of Special Counsel [*Federal agency*]
OSC	Office of the Security Council
OSC	Officer Specialty Code [*Army*] (INF)
OSC	Offshore Survival Centre [*Robert Gordon's Institute of Technology*] [*British*] (CB)
OSC	Ogden [*Utah*] Service Center [*IRS*]
OSC	Ohio Soybean Council (SAUS)
OSC	Ohio Supercomputer Center (SAUS)
O-SC	Ohio Supreme Court, Columbus, OH [*Library symbol*] [*Library of Congress*] (LCLS)
OSC	One Shoe Crew [*An association*] (EA)
OSC	Online Scenario Controller (SAUS)
OSC	On-Scene Commander [*Navy*] (NVT)
OSC	On-Scene Coordinator [*Environmental Protection Agency*] (FFDE)
OSC	On-Site Safety Committee (IAA)
OSC	Ontario Science Center (SAUS)
OSC	Ontario Securities Commission (HGAA)
OSC	Open System Center (SAUS)
OSC	Operating Switching Cabinet (SAUS)
OSC	Operating System Command (SAUS)
OSC	Operating System Control (VLIE)
OSC	Operational Simulator Console
OSC	Operational Summary Console
OSC	Operational Support Center (NRCH)
OSC	Operational Support Chart [*Nuclear energy*] (NUCP)
OSC	Operational Switching Cabinet
OSC	Operational System Control (SAUS)
OSC	Operations Sequence Chart (MCD)
OSC	Operations Support Center (SAUS)
OSC	Operation Switching Cabinet (SAUS)
OSC	Operator Services Center (VLIE)
OSC	Operator Services Complex [*Telecommunications*] (TEL)
OSC	Optically Sensitive Controller (SAUS)
OSC	Optical Sciences Center [*University of Arizona*] [*Research center*] (RCD)
OSC	Optical Signature Code
OSC	Optical String Switch Controller (NITA)
OSC	Options Selection Committee (COE)
OSC	Orangeburg [*South Carolina*] [*Seismograph station code, US Geological Survey*] [*Closed*] (SEIS)
OSC	Orbital Sciences Corporation (SAUS)
OSC	Orbit Shift Coil
OSC	Orbit-Spin Coupling (SAUS)
OSC	Order of St. Clare [*Roman Catholic women's religious order*]
OSC	Order to Show Cause
OSC	Order to Show Cause and Notice of Hearing (SAUS)
OSC	Ordnance Store Corps [*British military*] (DMA)
OSC	Ordnance Systems Command [*Formerly, Bureau of Naval Weapons; later, Naval Sea Systems Command*]
OSC	Oregon State College [*Later, OSU*]
OSC	Organic Solderability Coating [*Electronics*] (AAEL)
OSC	Organic Sulfur Compound [*Organic chemistry*]
OSC	Organizational Structure Code [*Air Force*] (AFIT)
OSC	Organizational Supply Code [*Army*] (AABC)
OSC	Organosilicon Compound (SAUS)
OSC	Orthosubstitution Compound (SAUS)
OSC	Oscillate [*or Oscillation, Oscillator, Oscillograph, Oscilloscope*] (KSC)
OSC	Oscillation (SAUS)
OSC	Oscillator (ACAE)
osc	Oscillator (IDOE)
OSC	Oscoda, MI [*Location identifier*] [*FAA*] (FAAL)
OSC	Osmotically Sensitive Cell
OSC	Outer Space Committee (SAUS)
OSC	Outer Space Contact
OSC	Out of Stock, Canceled [*Business term*]
OSC	Output State Check [*Electronics*]
OSC	Out, See Copy [*Proofreader's note*]
OSC	Overlapping Spreading Centers [*Geology*]
OSC	Overlap Slotted Container [*Packaging*]
OSC	Overseas Settlement Committee [*World War I*] [*British*]
OSC	Overseas Shipping Company (SAUS)
OSC	Overseas Staff College [*British*]
OSC	Overseas Supply Committee [*World War II*]
OSC	Own Ship's Course [*Navy*]
OSC	Oxidatively Solubilized Coal [*Fuel technology*]
OSC	Oxygenated Sterol Compound [*Biochemistry*]
OSC	Oxygen Storage Capacity [*Automotive emissions control*]
OSC	Royal Clan, Order of Scottish Clans [*Later, Independent Order of Foresters*] (EA)
OSC	Scugog Public Library, Ontario [*Library symbol*] [*National Library of Canada*] (NLC)
OSC	Sisters of St. Clare (TOCD)
OSC	Southern State Community College, Wilmington, OH [*OCLC symbol*] (OCLC)
OSCA	Office of Saver and Consumer Affairs [*Federal Reserve Board*]
OSCA	Office of Senior Citizens Affairs (NADA)
OSCA	Office of State Corporate Affairs [*Western Australia*]
OSCA	Operations Systems Computing Architecture (SAUS)
OSCA	Optical Sensors Collaborative Association [*British*] (DBA)
OSCA	OSCA, Inc. [*NASDAQ symbol*]
OSCA	Out-of-School Childcare Association (WDAA)
OSCAA	Oil Spill Control Association of America [*Later, SCAA*] (EA)

OSCAD........ Office of the Scientific Advisor (SAUS)
oscam.......... Camillian Fathers and Brothers (TOCD)
OS Cam ...... Order of St. Camillus [*Camillians*] [*Roman Catholic religious order*]
OSCAND ...... Old Scandinavian [*Language, etc.*]
OSCAP........ Operating System Communication Application Program [*Computer science*]
OSCAR........ Observation Schedule and Records
OSCAR........ Oil Spill Computer Aided Response (SAUS)
OSCAR........ Omnium System Car [*Research vehicle*]
OSCAR........ Online Serials Control at Ratcliffe (NITA)
OSCAR........ Online System for Controlling Activities and Resources (SAUS)
OSCAR........ OnScreen Configuration & Activity Reporting (SAUS)
OSCAR........ On-Site Computer Assisted Research [*Oscar, Inc.*] [*Information service or system*] (IID)
OSCAR........ Operating Sequence Control Array [*NASA*]
OSCAR........ Operational System Characteristics
OSCAR........ Operations, Scheduling, Control, and Reporting (MCD)
OSCAR........ Optically Scanned Character Automatic Reader [*Computer science*] (DIT)
OSCAR........ Optical Submarine Communications by Aerospace Relay
OSCAR........ Optimum Survival Containment and Recovery (AAG)
OSCAR........ Optimum System for the Control of Aircraft Retardation
OSCAR........ Optimum Systems Covariance Analysis Results (IEEE)
oscar .... Orbital-Satellite-Carrying Amateur Radio (SAUS)
OSCAR........ Orbiting Satellite Carrying Amateur Radio [*Telecommunications*] (TEL)
OSCAR........ Order Status Control and Reporting [*Telecommunications*] (TEL)
OSCAR........ Oregon State Conversational Aid to Research [*Computer science*] (CSR)
OSCAR........ Organisation for Sickle Cell Anemia Research [*British*]
OSCAR........ Organization for Scientific Coordination in AIDS [*Acquired Immune Deficiency Syndrome*] Research, Inc. [*New York, NY*]
OSCAR........ Oscillogram Scan and Recorder System (PDAA)
OSCAR........ Outside Cable Rehabilitation (SAUS)
OSCAR........ Overnight Statewide Customer Accounting Reporting (IAA)
OSCAR........ Oxidant-Scavenging Characteristics of April Rains (SAUS)
OSCAR........ Oxygen Steelmaking Computer and Recorder (SAUS)
OSCAR II .... Outside Cable Rehabilitation II [*Army*] (RDA)
OSCARS...... One-way Synchronous Collision Avoidance and Ranging System (SAUS)
OSCARS...... Order Status Control and Reporting System [*Telecommunications*]
OSCAS........ Office of Statistical Coordination and Standards (SAUS)
OSCB .... College Bibliocentre, Scarborough, Ontario [*Library symbol*] [*National Library of Canada*] (BIB)
OSCCap ...... Capuchin Poor Clares (TOCD)
OSCCB .... On-Site Change Control Board [*Military*] (CAAL)
OSCCJA ...... Casimir, Jennings, and Appleby Public Library, St. Charles, Ontario [*Library symbol*] [*National Library of Canada*] (NLC)
OSCD .... Ohio Supreme Court Decisions, Unreported Cases [*A publication*] (DLA)
OSCD .... Ontario Securities Commission Decisions [*QL Systems Ltd.*] [*Information service or system*] [*Canada*] (CRD)
OSCD .... Operations Support Computing Division (ACAE)
OSCE .... Office of Child Support Enforcement (USGC)
OSCE .... Office Statistique des Communautes Europeennes [*Statistical Office of the European Communities - EUROSTAT*] [*Commission of the European Communities*]
OSCE .... Organisation for Security and Co-Operation in Europe (ECON)
OSCE .... Organization on Security and Cooperation in Europe (SAUS)
OSCER........ Offshore Survival Craft Emergency Radiotelephone [*Telecommunications*] (PDAA)
OSCF .... Operations Support Computing Facility (MCD)
OSCG .... Information Resource Centre, Consumers Gas, Scarborough, Ontario [*Library symbol*] [*National Library of Canada*] (NLC)
OSCG .... Oscillating
OSCG .... Oscillograph, String
OSCGRM...... Oscillogram [*Engineering*]
OSCH .... Schreiber Public Library, Ontario [*Library symbol*] [*National Library of Canada*] (NLC)
OSCIA .... Ontario Soil and Crop Association [*Canada*]
OSCILAB ...... Ocean Science Laboratory [*Oceanography*]
OSCILLOSC.. Oscilloscope (IAA)
OSCL .... Operating System Control Language (NITA)
OSCL .... Own Ship's Centerline [*Navy*]
OSCMF .... Oxygen Scavenging Cell Membrane Fragment [*Biochemistry*]
OSCMIS ...... Operating and Support Costs Management Information System (MCD)
OS/CMP ...... Operational Support/Configuration Management Plan (SAUS)
OSC-MULT... Oscillator-Multiplier [*Telecommunications*] (TEL)
OSCO .... Oil Shipment Corp. (NITA)
OSCO .... Organizational Source Code (NITA)
OSCOM .... Oslo Commission (EAIO)
OSCOM .... Oslo Commission for the Prevention of Marine Pollution by Dumping from Ships and Aircraft (SAUS)
OSCON/M .... Oslo Convention/Commission (SAUS)
OSCOT........ Overall Systems Combat Operability Test [*Navy*] (ANA)
OSCP .... Ocean Sediment Coring Program [*National Science Foundation*]
OSCP .... Off Shore Centrally Procured (SAUS)
OSCP .... On-Site Computer Programmer (SAUS)
OSCP .... Oscilloscope (AAG)
OSCP .... Oscilloscope Panel
OSCPS........ Oxygen Supply and Cabin Pressurization Section [*Apollo*] [*NASA*]
OSCR .... Ocean Surface Current RADAR
OSCR .... Off Standard Condition Report (SAUS)
OSCR.......... Online Service Center Response [*Computer science*] (VLIE)

OSCR .... Operating and Support Cost Reduction [*Army*]
OSCR .... Operations and Sustainment Cost Reduction Strategy (RDA)
OSCRL........ Operating System Command and Response Language
OSCRN........ Oil Screen
OSCRO........ Oglala Sioux Civil Rights Organization [*South Dakota*]
OSCRS........ Orbital Spacecraft Consumables Resupply System (SAUS)
OSCT .... Office of Scholarly Communication and Technology (SAUS)
OSCUT........ Oil Spill Clean-Up Technology (ASF)
OSD .... Dow Chemical Co., Sarnia, Ontario [*Library symbol*] [*National Library of Canada*] (NLC)
OSD .... Office of Standards Development [*Abolished*] [*Nuclear Regulatory Commission*]
OSD .... Office of Student Detachment [*Navy*]
OSD .... Office of Systems Development [*Social Security Administration*]
OSD .... Office of the Secretary of Defense
OSD .... Officer Service Date [*Air Force*] (AFM)
OSD .... Officers Service Dress [*British military*] (DMA)
OSD .... Office Systems Design (SAUS)
OSD .... On-line System Driver (SAUS)
OSD .... Online System Drivers [*NCR Corp.*]
OSD .... Online Systems Driver (SAUS)
OSD .... On-Screen Digital (SAUS)
OSD .... On Screen Display [*Computer science*] (AAEL)
OSD .... Open Shelter Deck [*Shipping*] (DS)
OSD .... Open Software Description [*Computer science*]
OSD .... Open Software Description standard (SAUS)
OSD .... Open Software Distribution [*Computer science*] (VLIE)
OSD .... Open System Direction (SAUS)
OSD .... Operating Safety Document (SAUS)
OSD .... Operating Specification Document (SAUS)
OSD .... Operational Sea Vehicle Diagram (MCD)
OSD .... Operational Sequence Diagram (IEEE)
OSD .... Operational Service Date (VLIE)
OSD .... Operational Specification Document (SAUS)
OSD .... Operational Support Directive [*Military*] (AFM)
OSD .... Operational System Diagram (SAUS)
OSD .... Operational Systems Development (MCD)
OSD .... Operations Subdirective
OSD .... Optical Scanning Device [*Computer science*]
OSD .... Ordinis Sancti Dominici [*Order of St. Dominic*] [*Latin*] (ROG)
OSD .... Ordnance Safing Device
OSD .... Ordnance Store Department [*British*] (ROG)
OSD .... Ordnance Sub-Depot (SAUS)
OSD .... Ordnance Supply Depot
OSD .... Organization Subject Details (SAUS)
OSD .... Organosilicon Device (SAUS)
OSD .... Original Sponsoring Distributor (SAUS)
OSD .... Osgood-Schlatter Disease
OSD .... Osgood Semantic Differential [*Occupational therapy*]
OSD .... Ostersund [*Sweden*] [*Airport symbol*] (OAG)
OSD .... Outer Sleeve and Dome (SAUS)
OSD .... Out-of-Station Designation (SAUS)
OSD .... Out of Stock for the Duration [*Business term*] (DGA)
OSD .... Overseas Duty
OSD .... Overseas Settlement Department [*World War I*] [*British*]
OSD .... Overseas Shipping Directive (SAUS)
OSD .... Overseas Standards Digest [*A publication*] (ADA)
OSD .... Overseas Supply Division [*Military*]
OSD .... Over, Short, and Damaged [*Report*] [*Shipping*] (MCD)
OSD .... Overside Drainage [*Medicine*] (DAVI)
OSD .... Own Ship's Distance [*Navy*] (MCD)
OSD .... Oxygen Selective Detector [*Chromatography*]
OSDA .... Oceanic System Development and Support [*FAA*] (TAG)
OSDA .... Onsite Sewage Disposal Act (SAUS)
OSDA .... Original Subimage Data Array (SAUS)
OSDB .... Ocean Surveillance Data Base (SAUS)
OSDBMC...... Office of the Secretary of Defense, Ballistic Missile Committee
OSDBU........ Office of Small and Disadvantaged Business Utilization [*See also SDBU/CR*] [*Agency for International Development*]
OSD/CSD .... Open Shelter Deck/Closed Shelter Deck [*Shipping*] (DS)
OSD/DSAA ... Office of the Secretary of Defense, Defense Security Assistance Agency (MCD)
OSDH.......... Oklahoma State Department of Health (SAUS)
OSDH.......... Optical Shubnikhov-de Haas [*Effect*] (AAEL)
OSDH.......... Orbiter System Definition Handbook [*NASA*] (NASA)
OSDI .... Damascus/International [*Syria*] [*ICAO location identifier*] (ICLI)
OSDI .... Own Ships Data Interface (SAUS)
OSDIDBAD... Office of the Secretary of Defense Identification Badge [*Military decoration*] (GFGA)
OSDIdentBad... Office of the Secretary of Defense Identification Badge (AABC)
OSD/ISA...... Office of the Secretary of Defense for International Security Affairs
OSDIT .... Office of Software Development and Information Technology [*General Services Administration*]
OSDIU.......... Over-the-Horizon Targeting System Digital Interface Unit
OSDM .... Optical Space-Division Multiplexing (EECA)
OSDMT........ Organization for the Support of Democratic Movement of Taiwan (EA)
OSDNRL ...... Ocean Science Division-Naval Research Laboratory (SAUS)
OSDOC........ Offshore Discharge of Container-Ships (RDA)
OSDOC........ Over-the-Shore Discharge of Cargo [*Navy*] (CAAL)
OSDOCS...... Over-the-Shore Discharge of Container Ships (SAUS)
OSDOC Ship.. Offshore Discharge of Container Ship (SAUS)
OSDOC Ship.. Over-the-Store Discharge of Container Ship (SAUS)
OS/DOS........ Operating System/Disk Operating System [*Software*]
OSDP.......... On-Site Data Processing [*or Processor*] [*NASA*]

OSDP	On-Site Data Processor (SAUS)
OSDP	Operational System Development Program
OSDP	Operations System Development Program [*Marine science*] (OSRA)
OSD(PA & E)	Office of the Secretary of Defense for Program Analysis and Evaluation (MCD)
OSDPD	Office of Satellite Data Processing and Distribution (SAUS)
OSDPT	Optimization of Systems for Data Processing and Transmission (PDAA)
OSDR	Oil Slick Detection RADAR
OS/D Report	Over, Short and Damaged Report (SAUS)
OSDS	Operating System for Distributed Switching [*Computer science*] (VLIE)
OSD-SA	Office of the Secretary of Defense - Systems Analysis
OSDSA	Office of the Secretary of Defense Systems Analysis (SAUS)
OSDSAC	Office of the Secretary of Defense, Scientific Advisory Committee
OSDT	Damascus [*Syria*] [*ICAO location identifier*] (ICLI)
OSDU	Output Signal Distribution Unit (MCD)
OSDV	Oat Sterile Dwarf Virus [*Plant pathology*]
OSDZ	Deir Ez Zor [*Syria*] [*ICAO location identifier*] (ICLI)
OSE	Bethel, AK [*Location identifier*] [*FAA*] (FAAL)
OSE	Edwardsburg Township Public Library, Spencerville, Ontario [*Library symbol*] [*National Library of Canada*] (BIB)
OSE	Oblique Seismic Experiment (SAUS)
OSE	Occupational Supplies and Equipment [*Red Cross*]
OSE	Ocean and Science Engineering Inc.
OSE	Oceanic Society Expeditions (EA)
OSE	Ocean Shipping and Enterprises (SAUS)
OSE	Office of Science Education (SAUS)
OSE	Office of Sex Equity (SAUS)
OSE	Office of Systems Engineering [*Social Security Administration*]
OSE	Officer Scheduling the Exercise [*Navy*] (NVT)
OSE	Office Server Extension
OSE	Olefin Strain Energy [*Organic chemistry*]
OSE	Omniforce Spatial Environment (AAG)
OSE	On Scene Endurance [*Environmental science*] (COE)
OSE	Open Software Environment (SAUS)
OSE	Open Systems Environment [*Computer science*] (CIST)
OS/E	Operating System/Environment [*Computer science*] (BYTE)
OSE	Operational Security Evaluation (MCD)
OSE	Operational Support Equipment
OSE	Operations Simulations Engineer (ADWA)
OSE	Operation Status Equipment
OSE	Operation Support Equipment (SAUS)
OSE	Optical Science and Engineering (SAUS)
OSE	Orbital Sequence of Events [*NASA*] (IAA)
OSE	Orbiter Support Equipment [*NASA*] (NASA)
OSE	Order of the Star in the East [*A theosophical organization*]
OSE	Organizational Support Equipment [*Army*]
OSE	Osage Systems Group [*AMEX symbol*] (SG)
OSE	Osaka Securities Exchange (SAUS)
OSE	Osaka Stock Exchange [*Japan*]
OSE	Osec Petroleum [*Vancouver Stock Exchange symbol*]
OSE	Overall System Effectiveness (IAA)
OSE	Overseas Security Eligibility [*DoD*]
OSE	Salem Public Library, Salem, OR [*OCLC symbol*] (OCLC)
OSE	Union Mondiale pour la Protection de la Sante des Populations Juives et Oeuvres de Secours aux Enfants
OSEA	Oregon School Employees Association
OSEAP	Oil Shale Environmental Advisory Panel [*Department of the Interior*]
OSEAS	Ocean Sampling and Environmental Analysis System (PDAA)
O/SEAS	Overseas
OSEC	Office of the Secretary
OSEC	Office Systems Education and Counseling (HGAA)
OSECCA	Old Sleepy Eye Collectors' Club of America (EA)
OSECY	Office of the Secretary to the Staff [*NATO*] (NATG)
OSEDA	Office of Social and Economic Data Analysis (VLIE)
OSEDS	Operational Support Equipment Design Specification
OSEE	Optically Stimulated Electron Emission [*Also, PEE*] [*Physics*]
OSEE	Optically Stimulated Exoelectron Emission (SAUS)
O/SEER	Overseer
OSEH	Order of St. Elizabeth of Hungary [*Anglican religious community*]
OSEIA	Open System Environment profile for Imminent Acquisitions (SAUS)
OSEM	Office of Systems Engineering Management [*Department of Transportation*]
OSEOS	Operational Synchronous Earth Observatory Satellite [*Telecommunications*] (TEL)
OSEP	Office of Scientific and Engineering Personnel [*National Academy of Sciences*] [*Information service or system*] (IID)
OSEP	Office of Special Education Programs [*Also, SEP*] [*Department of Education*]
O Serb	Old Serbian (SAUS)
OSERP	Oil Sands Environmental Research Program (SAUS)
OSERS	Office of Special Education and Rehabilitative Services [*Department of Education*]
OSES	Operations Systems Engineering Support (MCD)
OSESG	Oil Sands Environmental Study Group [*Canada*]
OSETI	Optical Search for Extraterrestrial Intelligence (SAUS)
OSETNO	Offset Number (SAUS)
OSEXT	Operating System Extensions [*Computer science*] (VLIE)
OSF	Bernardine Sisters of the Third Order of St. Francis (TOCD)
OSF	Congregation of the Religious Brothers of the Third Order Regular of St. Francis (TOCD)
OSF	Congregation of the Sisters of the Third Order of St. Francis Oldenburg, IN (TOCD)
OSF	Congregation of the Third Order of St. Francis of Mary Immaculate, Joliet IL (TOCD)
OSF	Franciscan Brothers of Christ the King (TOCD)
OSF	Franciscan Brothers of Christ the King (TOCD)
osf	Franciscan Brothers of the Third Order Regular (TOCD)
OSF	Franciscan Missionaries of Our Lady (TOCD)
OSF	Franciscan Missionary Brothers of the Sacred Heart of Jesus (TOCD)
osf	Franciscan Missionary Brothers of the Sacred Heart of Jesus (TOCD)
OSF	Franciscan Missionary Sisters for Africa (TOCD)
OSF	Franciscan Missionary Sisters of Our Lady of Sorrows (TOCD)
OSF	Franciscan Missionary Sisters of the Immaculate Conception (TOCD)
OSF	Franciscan Sister, Daughters of the Sacred Hearts of Jesus and Mary (TOCD)
OSF	Franciscan Sisters of Allegany, New York (TOCD)
OSF	[*The*] Franciscan Sisters of Baltimore (TOCD)
OSF	Franciscan Sisters of Chicago (TOCD)
OSF	Franciscan Sisters of Christian Charity (TOCD)
OSF	Franciscan Sisters of Christ the Divine Teacher (TOCD)
OSF	Franciscan Sisters of Little Falls, Minnesota (TOCD)
OSF	Franciscan Sisters of Our Lady of Perpetual Help (TOCD)
OSF	Franciscan Sisters of St. Paul (TOCD)
OSF	Franciscan Sisters of the Immaculate Conception and St. Joseph for the Dying (TOCD)
OSF	Franciscan Sisters of the Sacred Heart (TOCD)
OSF	Fransciscan Brothers of the Third Order Regular (TOCD)
OSF	Hospital Sisters of the Third Order of St. Francis (TOCD)
OSF	Missionary Franciscan Sisters of the Immaculate Conception (TOCD)
OSF	Obtain Service From [*Navy*] (NVT)
OSF	Ocean Simulation Facility [*Naval Coastal Systems Laboratory*] (DNAB)
OSF	Odd Side Flat
OSF	Office of Space Flight [*NASA*] [*Washington, DC*] (NASA)
OSF	Office Systems Family (HGAA)
OSF	Official Statistics for Finland (SAUS)
OSF	One Hundred Square Feet (SAUS)
OSF	Open Software Foundation
OSF	Open Systems Foundation
OSF	Operational Service Fee (WDAA)
OSF	Operations System Function (SAUS)
OSF	Operations Systems Function Block (SAUS)
OSF	Operation Support Facility [*National Weather Service*] (USDC)
OSF	Oppose Sun Forever (SAUS)
OSF	Optically-Shaped Film
OSF	Optronic Sector System (SAUS)
OSF	Order of St. Francis [*Franciscans*] [*Roman Catholic religious order*]
OSF	Ordinary Shareholders Fund (WDAA)
OSF	Ordnance Storage Facility (KSC)
OSF	Organic Storage Facility (SAUS)
OSF	Organizational Status File (SAUS)
OSF	Organ System Failure [*Medicine*]
OSF	Osaka Stock Futures [*Japan*] (ECON)
OSF	Outer Spiral Fibers [*Ear anatomy*]
OSF	Out of Stock, To Follow [*Business term*]
OSF	Overgrowth Stimulating Factor [*Cancer cause*]
OSF	Oxidation-Induced Stacking Fault (PDAA)
osf	Religious Brothers of the Third Order Regular of St. Francis (TOCD)
OSF	School Sisters of St. Francis (TOCD)
OSF	School Sisters of the Third Order of St. Francis (Bethlehem, PA) (TOCD)
OSF	School Sisters of the Third Order of St. Francis (Panhandle, TX) (TOCD)
OSF	School Sisters of the Third Order of St. Francis (Pittsburgh, PA) (TOCD)
OSF	Servants of the Holy Infancy of Jesus (TOCD)
OSF	Sisters of Saint Francis, Clinton, Iowa (TOCD)
OSF	Sisters of Saint Francis of Milvale, Pennsylvania (TOCD)
OSF	Sisters of Saint Francis of the Providence of God (TOCD)
OSF	Sisters of St. Francis (TOCD)
OSF	Sisters of St. Francis of Christ the King (TOCD)
OSF	Sisters of St. Francis of Penance and Christian Charity (TOCD)
OSF	Sisters of St. Francis of Perpetual Adoration (TOCD)
OSF	Sisters of St. Francis of Savannah, MO (TOCD)
OSF	Sisters of St. Francis of the Congregation of Our Lady of Lourdes, Sylvania, Ohio (TOCD)
OSF	Sisters of St. Francis of the Holy Cross (TOCD)
OSF	Sisters of St. Francis of the Holy Eucharist (TOCD)
OSF	Sisters of St. Francis of the Holy Family (TOCD)
OSF	Sisters of St. Francis of the Immaculate Conception (TOCD)
OSF	Sisters of St. Francis of the Immaculate Heart of Mary (Hankinson, North Dakota) (TOCD)
OSF	Sisters of St. Francis of the Martyr St. George (TOCD)
OSF	Sisters of St. Francis of the Third Order Regular (Williamsville, New York) (TOCD)
OSF	Sisters of the Third Franciscan Order (TOCD)
OSF	Sisters of the Third Order of St. Francis of Penance and Charity (TOCD)
OSF	Sisters of the Third Order of St. Francis (Peoria, IL) (TOCD)
OSF	Sisters of the Third Order Regular of St. Francis of the Congregation of Our Lady of Lourdes (TOCD)
OSF	St. Francis Mission Community (TOCD)
OSF	[*The*] Sisters of St. Francis of Assisi (TOCD)
OSF	[*The*] Sisters of St. Francis of Philadelphia (TOCD)
OSFA	Office of Student Financial Assistance [*Department of Education*] (GFGA)
OSFA	Offshore Shrimp Fisheries Act of 1973

OSFAR.......... Sturgeon Falls Branch of the Algonquin Regional Library System, Ontario [*Library symbol*] [*National Library of Canada*] (NLC)

OSFAS.......... Overseas Students Fee Awards Scheme (SAUS)

OSFC.......... Fiberglas Canada, Inc., Sarnia, Ontario [*Library symbol*] [*National Library of Canada*] (NLC)

OSFC.......... Ordinis Sancti Francisci Capuccini [*Franciscan Capuchins*] [*Roman Catholic men's religious order*]

OSFCO.......... Office of Solid Fuels Coordinator [*Military*] (DNAB)

OSFCSR....... Rideau Regional Centre, Ministry of Community and Social Services, Smiths Falls,Ontario [*Library symbol*] [*National Library of Canada*] (NLC)

OSFCW.......... Office of Solid Fuels Coordinator for War [*World War II*]

OSFD.......... Office of Space Flight Development [*Obsolete*] [*NASA*]

OSF/DCF........ Open Software Foundation/Distributed Computing Environment [*Computer science*] (AGLO)

OSF/DME........ Operation System Function/Distributed Management Environment (SAUS)

OSFET.......... Oxide Semiconductor Field Effect Transistor (SAUS)

OSFI.......... Office of the Superintendent of Financial Institutions [*Department of Insurance*] [*Ottawa, ON*] [*Information service or system*] (IID)

OSFI.......... Open Steel Flooring Institute [*Defunct*]

OSFM.......... Office of Spacecraft and Flight Missions [*NASA*]

OSFM.......... Office of Surplus Facility Management (SAUS)

OSFP.......... Office of Space Flight Programs [*Obsolete*] [*NASA*]

OSFS.......... Oblate of Saint Francis of Sales (SAUS)

OSFS.......... Oblates of St. Francis de Sales (TOCD)

osfs.......... Oblates of St. Francis de Sales (TOCD)

OSFS.......... Oblati Sancti Francisci Salesii [*Oblate Fathers or Sisters of St. Francis of Sales*] [*Roman Catholic religious orders*]

OSFT.......... ObjectSoft Corp. [*NASDAQ symbol*] (SAG)

OSG.......... Occupations Study Group [*British*]

OSG.......... Office of Sea Grant [*National Oceanic and Atmospheric Administration*]

OSG.......... Office of the Secretary General [*United Nations*]

OSG.......... Office of the Solicitor General [*Department of Justice*]

OSG.......... Office of the Surgeon General [*of Public Health Service; later, absorbed by office of Assistant Secretary for Health and Scientific Affairs*]

OSG.......... Official Steamship Guide (SAUS) ·

OSG.......... Open Service Gateway (RALS)

OSG.......... Operand Select Gate [*Computer science*]

OSG.......... Operations Support Group [*Nuclear energy*] (NRCH)

OSG.......... Organization and Staffing Guide [*Department of Labor*] (OICC)

OSG.......... Osphradial Ganglion [*In mollusks*]

OSG.......... Otosclerosis Study Group (EA)

OSG.......... Overseas Shipholding Group, Inc. [*NYSE symbol*] (SPSG)

OSG.......... Overspeed Generator (SAUS)

OSG.......... South Gillies Library, Ontario [*Library symbol*] [*National Library of Canada*] (BIB)

OSGB.......... Orchid Society of Great Britain (EAIO)

OSGD.......... Office of Sea Grant Development [*National Oceanic and Atmospheric Administration*] (MSC)

OSGI.......... Open-Service Gateway Interface

OSGLI.......... Office of Servicemen's Group Life Insurance

OSGP.......... Office of Sea Grant Programs [*National Oceanic and Atmospheric Administration*]

OSGP.......... Ontario Study Grant Plant (SAUS)

OSGP.......... Operations Support Group Prototype (SAUS)

OSGR.......... Oscillator Single Gain Region (PDAA)

OSGS.......... Office of the Secretary of the General Staff

OSGS.......... On Sudan Government Service (SAUS)

OSGS.......... Stittsville Branch, Goulbourn Township Public Library, Ontario [*Library symbol*] [*National Library of Canada*] (NLC)

OSH.......... Community Hospital of Springfield, Springfield, OH [*Library symbol*] [*Library of Congress*] (LCLS)

OSH.......... National Institute for Occupational Safety and Health, Cincinnati, OH [*OCLC symbol*] (OCLC)

OSH.......... Occupational Safety and Health [*Department of Labor*]

OSH.......... Office on Smoking and Health Database [*Centers for Disease Control*] [*Information service or system*] (CRD)

OSH.......... Omni Singula Hora [*Every Hour*] [*Pharmacy*]

OSH.......... Ordo Sancti Hieronymi [*Hieronymites*]

OSH.......... Oshawa Group Ltd. [*Toronto Stock Exchange symbol*]

OSH.......... Oshima [*Japan*] [*Seismograph station code, US Geological Survey*] (SEIS)

OSH.......... Oshkosh [*Wisconsin*] [*Airport symbol*] (OAG)

OSH.......... Oshman's Sporting Goods, Inc. [*AMEX symbol*] (SAG)

OSH.......... Own Ship's Heading [*Navy*]

OSh.......... Shaker Heights Public Library, Shaker Heights, OH [*Library symbol*] [*Library of Congress*] (LCLS)

OSH.......... Shelburne Public Library, Ontario [*Library symbol*] [*National Library of Canada*] (NLC)

OSHA.......... Occupational Safety and Health Act [*1970*]

OSHA.......... Occupational Safety and Health Administration [*Department of Labor*] [*Washington, DC*]

OSHA.......... Occupational Safety Hazards Act (AAEL)

OSHA.......... Office of Special Housing Assistance [*HUD*]

OSHAct.......... Occupational Safety and Health Act (EEVL)

Oshap.......... OSHAP Technologies Ltd. [*Associated Press*] (SAG)

OSHB.......... One-Sided Height Balanced [*Telecommunications*]

OshB.......... Oshkosh B'Gosh [*Associated Press*] (SAG)

OSHB.......... Sheshegwaning Band Public Library, Ontario [*Library symbol*] [*National Library of Canada*] (NLC)

OSHC.......... Orchard Supply Hardware Stores Corp. [*NASDAQ symbol*] (SAG)

OSHC.......... Outside School Hours Care

OSHC.......... Overseas Student Health Coverage

OSH Cas...... Occupational Safety and Health Cases [*A publication*] (DLA)

OSHD.......... Occupational Safety and Health Decisions [*A publication*] (DLA)

OSH Dec...... Occupational Safety and Health Decisions [*A publication*] (DLA)

o/sheep.......... odd sheep (SAUS)

OShelS.......... Sacred Heart Seminary, Shelby, OH [*Library symbol*] [*Library of Congress*] (LCLS)

OSHI.......... Occupational, Safety, and Health Institute [*University of Houston*] [*Research center*] (RCD)

OSHI.......... Office of Special Health Issues (SAUS)

O/SHIP.......... Ownership (SAUS)

OSHJ.......... Oblate Sisters of the Sacred Heart of Jesus [*Roman Catholic religious order*]

OshkT.......... Oshkosh Truck Corp. [*Associated Press*] (SAG)

OShL.......... Shaker Heights Public Library, Shaker Heights, OH [*Library symbol*] [*Library of Congress*] (LCLS)

Oshmn.......... Oshman's Sporting Goods, Inc. [*Associated Press*] (SAG)

OSHPD.......... Office of Statewide Health Planning and Development (SAUS)

OSHR.......... Occupational Safety and heal Review Commission (EBF)

OSHRC.......... Occupational Safety and Health Review Commission [*Department of Labor*]

OSHS.......... Occupational Safety and Health Scheme (SAUS)

OSHS.......... Occupational Safety and Health Statistics [*Bureau of Labor Statistics*] (GFGA)

OSHS.......... OSHAP Technologies Ltd. [*NASDAQ symbol*] (NQ)

OShS.......... Shaker Heights City School District, Shaker Heights, OH [*Library symbol*] [*Library of Congress*] (LCLS)

OSHSA.......... Occupational Safety and Health Standards Act (SAUS)

OSHSF.......... Oshap Technologies Ltd. [*NASDAQ symbol*] (TTSB)

OSHT.......... Grand Lodge Order of the Sons of Hermann in Texas [*San Antonio, TX*] (EA)

OSHT.......... Sharon Temple, Sharon, Ontario [*Library symbol*] [*National Library of Canada*] (NLC)

OSI.......... Aerosi SA de CV [*Mexico*] [*ICAO designator*] (FAAC)

OSI.......... National Institute for Occupational Safety and Health, Rockville, MD [*OCLC symbol*] (OCLC)

OSI.......... Office of Samoa Information [*Press agency*]

OSI.......... Office of Scientific Information [*National Science Foundation*] (MCD)

OSI.......... Office of Scientific Integrity [*National Institutes of Health*]

OSI.......... Office of Scientific Intelligence [*Fictitious government agency on TV series "The Six Million Dollar Man"*]

OSI.......... Office of Seniors' Interests [*Australia*]

OSI.......... Office of Special Investigation [*Air Force*]

OSI.......... Office of Strategic Information [*DoD*]

OSI.......... Office of Strategic Intelligence [*Air Force*] (INF)

OSI.......... Office of Systems Integration [*Social Security Administration*]

OSI.......... Officer Skill Identifiers [*Army*]

OSI.......... Office Systems Interconnection [*Telecommunications*] (TSSD)

OSI.......... Offshore Islands (CINC)

OSI.......... Off Site Instruction (SAUS)

OSI.......... Ohio Scientific Inc. (SAUS)

OSI.......... Online Software International (SAUS)

OSI.......... On-Site Inspection

OSI.......... Opening Shock Inhibitor (SAUS)

OSI.......... Open Society Institute [*Russia*]

OSI.......... Open Space Institute (EA)

OSI.......... Open Standards Interconnection [*International Standards Organisation*]

OSI.......... Open System Interconnections [*Networking technique*]

OSI.......... Open System Interface (SAUS)

OSI.......... Open Systems Interconnect

OSI.......... Open Systems Interface (SAUS)

OSI.......... Operating Space Item [*Military*] (CAAL)

OSI.......... Operating System Interface

OSI.......... Operating Systems, Inc. (MCD)

OSI.......... Operational Status Indicator (MUGU)

OSI.......... Operation Smile International (EA)

OSI.......... Optical Sciences Institute (SAUS)

OSI.......... Optical Society of India (SAUS)

OSI.......... Optimum Scale Integration (SAUS)

OSI.......... Optional Stop Instruction (SAUS)

OSI.......... ORDALT [*Ordnance Alterations*]/SHIPALT Inspector [*Ship Alteration*] (MCD)

OSI.......... Organic Sign Index [*Psychology*]

OSI.......... Oriental Shorthairs International (EA)

OSI.......... OR Storage to Indicators (SAUS)

OSI.......... Osijek [*Former Yugoslavia*] [*Airport symbol*] (OAG)

OSI.......... Other Service Information (TRID)

OSI.......... Other Service Investigation (SAUS)

OSI.......... Other Support Items

OSI.......... Otto-Suhr-Institut (SAUS)

OSI.......... Outback Steakhouse [*NYSE symbol*]

OSI.......... Out of Stock, Indefinite [*Business term*]

OSI.......... Out of Stock Indefinitely (ADWA)

OSI.......... Overhead Supply Inventory (MCD)

OSI.......... Owner Satisfaction Index (SAUS)

OSI.......... Oyster Shell Institute (EA)

OSI.......... Ozark Society (EA)

OSI.......... Research Technical Information Centre, ESSO Petroleum Canada, Sarnia, Ontario [*Library symbol*] [*National Library of Canada*] (NLC)

OSI.......... Woodside, CA [*Location identifier*] [*FAA*] (FAAL)

OSIA.......... Office, Services and Information Agency [*Military*] (AABC)

OSIA.......... On-Site Inspection Agency [*DoD*]

OSIA.......... Open Systems Interconnection Association (SAUS)

OSIA	Open Systems Interconnections Architecture (SAUS)
OSIA	Order Sons of Italy in America (EA)
OSIA	Outdoor Systems, Inc. [*NASDAQ symbol*] (SAG)
OSIASL	Order Sons of Italy in America Supreme Lodge [*Later, OSIA*] (EA)
OSIC	Ocean Science Information Center [*University of Hawaii*] (NOAA)
OSIC	Offshore Suppliers Information Centre (SAUS)
OSIC	Oil Spill Information Center [*Santa Barbara, CA*]
OSIC	Optimization of Subcarrier Information Capacity
OSICOM	Open Systems Interconnections Division [*Now Open Systems Interconnection Division*] (ACII)
Osicom	Osicom Technologies, Inc. [*Associated Press*] (SAG)
OSICS	Commission Scolaire de Sept-Iles, Quebec [*Library symbol*] [*National Library of Canada*] (NLC)
OSI/CS	Open Systems Interconnection/Communications Subsystem (SAUS)
OSI/CS	OSI/Communications Subsystem (SAUS)
OSICS	OSI Communication Systems (SAUS)
OSID	Open Systems Interconnection Division (ACII)
OSID	Operational System Interface Document (MCD)
OSID	Origination Signaling Identifier (SAUS)
OSIDM	Eva Brook Donly Museum, Simcoe, Ontario [*Library symbol*] [*National Library of Canada*] (NLC)
OSIE	Office of Software Improvement and Engineering [*Social Security Administration*]
OSIE	Open Systems Interconnection Environment [*Telecommunications*] (OSI)
OSIE	Operational Support Integration Engineering
OS/IES	On-Site Integrated Energy System
OSIFA	Operational Sequence and Information Flow Analysis (SAUS)
OSI/FS	OSI File Services (SAUS)
OSIGA	Ohio State Inventory of Guidance Awareness
OSIGO	Office of the Chief Signal Officer
OSIGO	Office of the Signal Officer (SAUS)
OSII	Objective Sys Integrators [*NASDAQ symbol*] (TTSB)
OSII	Objective Systems Integrators, Inc. [*NASDAQ symbol*] (SAG)
OSIL	Lynwood Arts Centre, Simcoe, Ontario [*Library symbol*] [*National Library of Canada*] (NLC)
OSIL	Operating System Implementation Language
OSINET	Open System Interconnection Network (SAUS)
OSINET	Open Systems Interconnection Network (SAUS)
OSInet	OSI Network (SAUS)
OSINH	Norfolk Historical Society, Simcoe, Ontario [*Library symbol*] [*National Library of Canada*] (NLC)
OSINLCP	OSI Network Layer Control Protocol (SAUS)
OSI/NMF	Open Systems Interconnect Network Management Forum [*Computer science*] (BTTJ)
OSI/NMF	OSI Network Management Forum (SAUS)
OSINT	Open Source Intelligence (SAUS)
OSIP	Operational and Safety Improvement Program (NVT)
OSIP	Operational Satellite Improvement Program (ACAE)
OSIP	Operational Suitability Improvement Program [*Aviation*]
OSIP	OSI Pharmaceuticals [*NASDAQ symbol*] [*Formerly, Oncogene Science*] (SG)
OSIP	Simcoe Public Library, Ontario [*Library symbol*] [*National Library of Canada*] (NLC)
OS/IPC	Operating System/Inter-Process Communications (DOMA)
OSIQ	Offer Self-Image Questionnaire
OSIQA	Offer Self-Image Questionnaire for Adolescents (EDAC)
OSIR	Office of Scientific Integrity Review [*US Secretary of Health*]
OSIR	Oil Spill Intelligence Report
Os-Ir	Osmiridium (IDOE)
OSIR	Out of Service in Reserve [*Military*] (CINC)
OSIRIS	Online Search Information Retrieval Information Storage [*Computer science*] (PDAA)
OSIRIS	Online Serials Information Registration and Inquiry System (SAUS)
OSIRIS	Optical Simulation for Imaging Reconnaissance and Intelligence Sensors (SAUS)
OSI/RM	Open System Interconnection/Reference Model (SAUS)
OSIRM	Open Systems Interconnection Reference Model (SAUS)
OSI/RM	OSI Reference Model (SAUS)
OSIS	Ocean Surveillance Information System [*Navy*] (MCD)
OSIS	Office of Science Information Service [*National Science Foundation*]
OSIS	On-Site Inspection System (SAUS)
OSIS	Operating Systems Installation Support (SAUS)
OSIS	Organization Structure Information System (SAUS)
OSITOP	Open Systems Interconnection Technical and Office Protocols [*Telecommunications*] (OSI)
osj	Oblates of St. Joseph (TOCD)
OSJ	Oblates of St. Joseph [*Roman Catholic religious order*]
OSJ	Office of Supervisory Jurisdiction [*Investment term*]
OSJ	Sovereign Order of Saint John of Jerusalem (EA)
OSJD	Ordinis Sancti Joannis de Deo [*Order of St. John of God*]
OS-JTF	Open Systems Joint Task Force (SAUS)
OSK	Osaka [*Takayasuyama*] [*Japan*] [*Seismograph station code, US Geological Survey*] (SEIS)
OSK	Oskarshamn [*Sweden*] [*Airport symbol*] (OAG)
OSKAR	Outstanding Superior Kitchen All-Rounder [*Trademark of Sunbeam Corp.*]
OSKL	Kamishly [*Syria*] [*ICAO location identifier*] (ICLI)
OSKL	Swastika Branch, Kirkland Lake Public Library, Ontario [*Library symbol*] [*National Library of Canada*] (BIB)
OSKNC	Skead Branch, Nickel Centre Public Library, Ontario [*Library symbol*] [*National Library of Canada*] (NLC)
OSKY	Mahaska Investment [*NASDAQ symbol*] (TTSB)
OSKY	Mahaska Investment Co. [*NASDAQ symbol*] (SAG)
OSL	International Order of Saint Luke the Physician (EA)

OSL	Object Script Language (SAUS)
OSL	Observed Significance Level (SAUS)
OSL	Office of the Secretary of Labor (SAUS)
OSL	Oil Seal
OSL	Old [*Church*] Slavonic [*Language, etc.*]
OSL	Old Style Latin (ADA)
OSL	Ontario Safety League (SAUS)
OSL	Open/Short Locator
OSL	Operand Specification List (SAUS)
OSL	Operating Safety Limit (SAUS)
OSL	Operating System Language
OSL	Operational Safety Limit (SAUS)
OSL	Operator Set Loop [*Electronics*] (ECII)
OSL	Optically Stimulated Luminescence [*Analytical Chemistry*]
OSL	Optical Storage Ltd.
OSL	Orbital Space Laboratory (SAUS)
OSL	Orbiting Solar Laboratory (SAUS)
OSL	Orbiting Space Laboratory
OSL	Order of St. Luke the Physician of America (EA)
OSL	Ordnance Sub-Lieutenant [*British military*] (DMA)
OSL	Oregon Short Line Railroad [*of Union Pacific Railroad Co.*]
OSL	Organic Semiconductor LASER [*Materials science*]
OSL	Osgood-Schlatter Lesion [*Medicine*] (STED)
OSL	Osler Resources, Inc. [*Vancouver Stock Exchange symbol*]
OSL	Oslo [*Norway*] [*Airport symbol*] (OAG)
OSL	O'Sullivan Corp. [*AMEX symbol*] (SPSG)
OSL	Outer Structured Layer (SAUS)
OSL	Outstanding Leg [*NASA*] (KSC)
OSL	Sioux Lookout Public Library, Ontario [*Library symbol*] [*National Library of Canada*] (NLC)
OSL	University of Oregon, School of Librarianship, Eugene, OR [*OCLC symbol*] (OCLC)
OSLA	Ontario Association of Speech-Language Pathologists and Audiologists (SAUS)
OSLA	Stella Branch, Lennox and Addington County Library, Ontario [*Library symbol*] [*National Library of Canada*] (NLC)
OS Language	Old Saxon Language (SAUS)
O Slav	Old [*Church*] Slavic [*Language*] (BARN)
OSLB	Operational Search Lower Bound [*RADAR*]
OSLC	Lambton College of Applied Arts and Technology, Sarnia, Ontario [*Library symbol*] [*National Library of Canada*] (NLC)
OSLEAS	Association Sectorielle de Fabrication d'Equipement de Transport et de Machines, St.-Leonard, Quebec [*Library symbol*] [*National Library of Canada*] (NLC)
OSLFC	Sharbot Lake Branch, Frontenac County Library, Ontario [*Library symbol*] [*National Library of Canada*] (BIB)
OSLI	Office of Servicemen's Life Insurance (OICC)
OSLJ	Law Journal. Student Bar Association. Ohio State University [*A publication*] (DLA)
OSLK	Latakia/Latakia [*Syria*] [*ICAO location identifier*] (ICLI)
OSLM	Operations Shop/Laboratory Manager [*NASA*] (MCD)
O-SLM	Optically addressed Spatial Light Modulator (SAUS)
OSLO	Other Six Leases Operation (SAUS)
OSLP	Ontario Student Loans Plan (SAUS)
OSLR	Intergovernmental Committee for Ocean Science and Living Resources [*Marine science*] (OSRA)
OSLR	Ocean Sciences and Living Resources (SAUS)
OSLT	On-Site Logistics Team (MCD)
OSM	Mantellate Sisters, Servants of Mary of Blue Island (TOCD)
OSM	Mental Health Services for Clark County, Springfield, OH [*Library symbol*] [*Library of Congress*] (LCLS)
OSM	Mosul [*Iraq*] [*Airport symbol*] (AD)
OSM	Oblates of St. Martha (TOCD)
OSM	Office of Sample Management (SAUS)
OSM	Office of Spectrum Management [*US National Telecommunications and Information Administration*] (TSSD)
OSM	Office of Surface Mining Reclamation and Enforcement [*Department of the Interior*]
OSM	Office Service Manual (SAUS)
OSM	Off-Screen Model [*Computer science*]
OSM	Oil-Sands Mining (SAUS)
OSM	Omnispectra Miniature
OSM	Oncostatin [*Antibiotic*]
OSM	One of the Swinish Multitude (SAUS)
OSM	On-Screen Manager [*Computer science*]
OSM	On Screen Menue (SAUS)
OSM	On-Site Maintenance
OSM	On Station Mode
OSM	Open System Module (SAUS)
OSM	Operating Service Month
OSM	Operating System Manual (MCD)
OSM	Operating System Monitor
OSM	Operating System Service Module (SAUS)
OSM	Operating System Specific Module (SAUS)
OSM	Operations Sampling Management (SAUS)
OSM	Operations Systems Manager (SAUS)
OSM	Operator's Service Manual
OSM	Opisu Struktur Mikroprogramownych [*Programming language*] (CSR)
OSM	Optical Section Microscope
OSM	Optical Storage Manager (SAUS)
OSM	Optical Support Measures (SAUS)
OSM	Option Select Mode [*Computer science*] (OA)
OSM	Orbital Service Module [*NASA*] (MCD)
osm	Orbital Service Module [*NASA*] (NAKS)
OSM	Ordnance Safety Manual [*Military*]

OSM............ Ordnance Supply Manual (SAUS)
OSM............ Ordo Servorum Mariae [*Order of Servants of Mary*] [*Servites*] [*Roman Catholic religious order*]
OSM............ Organization Structure Model (TIMI)
OSM............ Orr-Schelen-Mayeron & Associates (EFIS)
OSM............ Oscillating Secondary Mirror [*Telescope*]
Osm............ Osmania (SAUS)
OSM............ Osmol (SAUS)
osM............ Osmolar [*Chemistry*] (DAVI)
OSM............ Osmolarity (STED)
Osm............ Osmole [*Physical chemistry*]
OSM............ Osmonics, Inc. [*NYSE symbol*] (SPSG)
OSM............ Osmosis (SAUS)
osm............ Osmotic (STED)
OSM............ Osmotic
OSM............ Output Switch Module [*Automotive engineering*]
OSM............ Outside Mail (AFM)
OSM............ Outside of Metal
OSM............ Ovine Submaxillary Mucin [*Medicine*] (DMAA)
OSM............ Oxygen Saturation Meter (MAE)
OSM............ Oxygen Steel Making
OSM............ Schumacher Memorial Library, Ontario [*Library symbol*] [*National Library of Canada*] (BIB)
OSM............ Servants of Mary (TOCD)
osm .... Servite Fathers (TOCD)
OSM............ Servites (TOCD)
OSMA .... Occidental Society of Metempiric Analysis (EA)
OSMA .... Office of Small Manufacturers Assistance [*FDA*]
OSMA .... Optical Spectrometric Multichannel Analyzer [*Instrumentation*]
OSMA .... Orthopedic Surgical Manufacturers Association (EA)
OSMA .... Otago-Southland Manufacturers Association (SAUS)
OSMA .... Overseas Sales and Marketing Association of America [*Lake Bluff, IL*] (EA)
OSMA/CD..... Optical Sense Multiple Access with Collision Detection (SAUS)
OSMAS .... Oil Spill Modelling for the Antarctic Seas (SAUS)
OSMC .... Object Storage Management Component (SAUS)
OSM Connector... Omni Spectra Miniature Connector (SAUS)
OSM Connector... Omnispectra Miniature Connector (SAUS)
OSME.......... Open Systems Message Exchange [*Computer science*] (CIST)
OSME.......... Oral Speech Mechanism Screening Examination [*Educational test*]
OSME.......... Ornithological Society of the Middle East (EAIO)
OSMED .... Otospondylomegaepiphyseal Dystrophy [*Medicine*] (DAVI)
OSMF.......... Oral Submucous Fibrosis [*Medicine*] (STED)
OSMF.......... Smith Falls Public Library, Ontario [*Library symbol*] [*National Library of Canada*] (NLC)
OS/MFT........ Operating System/Multiprogramming Fixed Task (NITA)
OS/MFT........ Operating System/Multiprogramming with a Fixed Number of Tasks [*IBM Corp.*] [*Computer science*]
OSML.......... McNeil Laboratories (Canada) Ltd., Stouffville, Ontario [*Library symbol*] [*National Library of Canada*] (NLC)
OSML.......... Operating System Machine Level (VLIE)
OSMM .... Mercy Medical Center, Springfield, OH [*Library symbol*] [*Library of Congress*] (LCLS)
OSMM .... Office of Safeguards and Materials Management [*AEC*]
OSMM .... Optimum Supply and Maintenance Model
osmo .... Osmolality [*Chemistry*]
osmol .... Osmole [*Measurement*] (DAVI)
Osmonic ...... Osmonics, Inc. [*Associated Press*] (SAG)
OSMOS........ Own Ship's Motion Simulator [*Navy*]
OSMOS........ Own Ship's Motion System [*Navy*]
OSMP.......... Operational Support Maintenance Plan [*NASA*] (MCD)
OSMR.......... Office of Systems Modernization Requirements [*Social Security Administration*]
OSMRE........ Office of Surface Mining Reclamation and Enforcement [*Also, OSM*] [*Department of the Interior*]
OSMS .... Organizational Supply Management System [*Army*] (INF)
OSM S .... Osmolarity Serum [*Biochemistry*] (DAVI)
OSMSE-R..... Oral Speech Mechanism Screening Examination-Revised [*St. Louis and Ruscello*] (TES)
OSMU .... Oesterreichische Schuhmusterschau [*Austrian Footwear Exhibition*] [*Wiener Messen und Kongress GmbH*] (TSPED)
OSM U .... Osmolarity Urine [*Biochemistry*] (DAVI)
OSMV .... Oat Striate Mosaic Virus [*Plant pathology*]
OSMV .... One Shot Multivibrator (MSA)
OS/MVS ...... Operating System/Multiprogramming with Virtual Storage [*Computer science*]
OS/MVT ...... Operating System/Multiprogramming with a Variable Number of Tasks [*Computer science*]
OSN .... Ocean Science News [*Marine science*] (OSRA)
OSN .... Ocean Seismic Network (SAUS)
OSN .... Ocular Surgery News (SAUS)
OSN .... Office of the Secretary of the Navy
OSN .... Office Systems Node (VLIE)
OSN .... Off Service Note [*Medicine*] (DAVI)
OSN .... Open Systems Network [*Computer science*] (VLIE)
OSN .... Osphradial Nerve [*In mollusks*]
OSN .... Output Sequence Number
OSN .... Sioux Narrows Public Library, Ontario [*Library symbol*] [*National Library of Canada*] (NLC)
OSNAP........ Object Snap [*Auto CAD*] [*Computer science*]
OSNC.......... Orient Steam Navigation Company (SAUS)
OSNC.......... Sarnia Northern Collegiate, Ontario [*Library symbol*] [*National Library of Canada*] (NLC)
OSNI .... Ordinance Survey of Northern Island (SAUS)

OSNLR........ Ocean Science in Relation to Non-Living Resources [*Marine science*] (OSRA)
OSNS .... Open Systems Network Support [*Computer science*] (VLIE)
OSNS .... Shedden Public Library, Spanish, Ontario [*Library symbol*] [*National Library of Canada*] (NLC)
OSNSW....... Office of the Sheriff of New South Wales [*Australia*]
OSNY .... Oratorio Society of New York (SAUS)
OSNZ .... Ornithological Society of New Zealand (SAUS)
OSO .... Objective and Strategies Overview (SAUS)
oso............. Ocean Systems Operation [*NASA*] (NAKS)
OSO .... Ocean Systems Operation [*NASA*]
OSO .... Offensive System Operator (ACAE)
OSO .... Offensive Systems Operator (SAUS)
OSO .... Office of Satellite Operations (SAUS)
OSO .... Office of Space Operations (ACAE)
OSO .... Office of Systems Operations [*Social Security Administration*]
OSO .... Officer Selection Office (DNAB)
OSO .... Offshore Suppliers Office [*British*]
OSO .... Offshore Supply Office (SAUS)
OSO .... Omaha Symphony Orchestra (SAUS)
OSO .... One-Shot Operation (SAUS)
OSO .... One Side Only (SAUS)
OSO .... Onsala Space Observatory [*Sweden*]
OSO .... Onsite Office (SAUS)
OSO .... Operations Scheduling Office (SSD)
OSO .... Orbital Solar Observation (SAUS)
OSO .... Orbital Solar Observatory (SAUS)
OSO .... Orbiting Satellite Observer (IEEE)
OSO .... Orbiting Scientific Observatory (IAA)
OSO .... Orbiting Solar Observatory [*A satellite*]
OSO .... Ordnance Supply Office
OSO .... Oregon State Library, Salem, OR [*OCLC symbol*] (OCLC)
OSO .... Oregon Symphony Orchestra (SAUS)
O/S/O .... Ore/Slurry/Oil [*Supertanker*]
OSO .... Originating Screening Office (SAUS)
OSO .... Originating Signaling Office (SAUS)
OSO .... Originating Signalling Office (VLIE)
OSO .... Origination Screening Office [*Telecommunications*] (TEL)
OSO .... Overscan Operation (SAUS)
OSO .... Overseas Security Operations (SAUS)
OSO .... Southampton Branch, Bruce County Public Library, Ontario [*Library symbol*] [*National Library of Canada*] (NLC)
OSO 1-8...... Orbiting Solar Observatories 1-8 (SAUS)
OSOB .... Old Senate Office Building [*Also, RSOB*] [*Washington, DC*] (DLA)
OSOC.......... Off-Site Originated Change (AAG)
OSOCC........ On-Site Operations Coordination Center
OSODS........ Office of Strategic Offensive and Defensive Systems [*Navy*]
OSOG.......... Office Systems Owners Group (HGAA)
OSOIPB........ Ordnance Supply Office Illustrated Parts Breakdown [*Navy*]
OSol........... Odes of Solomon (BJA)
OSOL .... Office of the Solicitor [*Department of Labor*]
OS/OLM ...... On-Site/On-Line Maintenance
OSOM .... Bruce County Museum, Southampton, Ontario [*Library symbol*] [*National Library of Canada*] (BIB)
OSOP .... Off-Site Operations Plan (SSD)
OSOP .... Orbiter Systems Operating Procedures [*NASA*] (NASA)
OSOR.......... Operational Standoff Range (NVT)
OSOS .... Ore/Slurry/Oil Ship (SAUS)
OSOS .... Oxide Silicon Oxide Semiconductor (SAUS)
OSoSJ.......... Saint Joseph's Priory, Somerset, OH [*Library symbol*] [*Library of Congress*] (LCLS)
OSOT .... Oakland Township Public Library, Scotland, Ontario [*Library symbol*] [*National Library of Canada*] (BIB)
OSOTM .... Sombra Township Museum, Ontario [*Library symbol*] [*National Library of Canada*] (BIB)
OSP .... Obiit sine Prole [*Died without Issue*] [*Latin*]
OSP .... Objective and Strategies Plan (SAUS)
OSP .... Oblate Sisters of Providence [*Roman Catholic religious order*]
OSP .... Occupational Safety Programs Branch (SAUS)
OSP .... Ocean Surveillance Product (DOMA)
OSP .... Ocean Survey Plan [*or Program*] [*Navy*]
OSP .... Ocean Survey Program (SAUS)
OSP .... Office of Science Policy [*National Science Foundation*]
OSP .... Office of Scientific Personnel [*NAS-NRC*]
OSP .... Office of Special Projects (COE)
OSP .... Office of Special Technology [*Formerly, Office of Special Projects*] [*Washington, DC*] [*Department of Energy*] (GRD)
OSP .... Office of Sponsored Projects (SAUS)
OSP .... Office of Staffing Policy [*Office of Personnel Management*] [*Washington, DC*] (GRD)
OSP .... Office of Statistical Policy (SAUS)
OSP .... Office of Surplus Property [*Superseded by War Assets Corporation*] [*World War II*]
OSP .... Office of the Special Prosecutor [*Queensland, Australia*]
OSP .... Offshore Patrol (SAUS)
OSP .... Off-Shore Procedure (SAUS)
OSP .... Offshore Procurement [*Army*]
O-SP .... Off-Street Parking (WDAA)
OSP .... Oficina Sanitaria Panamericana [*Pan-American Sanitary Bureau - PASB*] [*Washington, DC*]
OSP .... Oil Suction Pump (MSA)
OSp............ Old Spanish (BEE)
OSP .... OLE-DB Simple Provider (SAUS)
OSP .... Online Service Provider
OSP .... On-Screen Programming (SAUS)

OSP	On-Site Programmer	(SAUS)
OSP	On-Site Service Provider [*Computer science*]	(VLIE)
OSP	On Station Position	(MUGU)
OSP	Open-Space Program	(SAUS)
OSP	Operating Steam Pressure	(MSA)
OSP	Operating System Plan	(SAA)
OS/P	Operating Systems for People	(SAUS)
OSP	Operational Safety Procedures	(COE)
OSP	Operational Surveillance Program [*Nuclear Regulatory Commission*]	(NRCH)
OSP	Operational Survival Plan [*Civil Defense*]	
OSP	Operations Special Procedures	(SAUS)
OSP	Operations Support Plan [*Navy*]	(NG)
OSP	Operator Service Provider	
OSP	Operator Station Processor [*Computer science*]	(VLIE)
OSP	Optical Signal Processing	(SAUS)
OSP	Optical Signature Program [*Military*]	(CAAL)
OSP	Optical Storage Processor [*Computer science*]	(VLIE)
OSP	Optical Surveillance Platform	(SAUS)
OSP	Optimum Sustainable Population [*Marine science*]	(MSC)
OSP	Optoelectronic Systems Programme [*British*]	
OSP	Orbital/Suborbital Program	(IGSL)
OSP	Orbital Support Plan	(MCD)
OSP	Orbiting Standards Platform	(ACAE)
OSP	Order of St. Paul [*Anglican religious community*]	
OSP	Order of St. Paul the First Hermit [*Pauline Fathers*] [*Roman Catholic religious order*]	
OSP	Ordinary Superphosphate	(EDCT)
OSP	Organic Solderability Perservative [*Electronics*]	(AAEL)
OSP	Original Set Pattern [*Ice dancing*]	
OSP	Outer Surface Protein [*Cytology*]	
OSP	Outfitting Stock Point	
OSP	Outside Plant [*Telecommunications*]	(TEL)
OSP	Outside Procured Stores	(AAG)
OSP	Outside Purchase	(WDAA)
OSP	Own Ship's Position [*Navy*]	(MCD)
OSP	Polysar Ltd., Sarnia, Ontario [*Library symbol*] [*National Library of Canada*]	(NLC)
OSP	Slupsk [*Poland*] [*Airport symbol*]	(OAG)
OSPA	Open Signal Coprocessing Architecture [*Computer science*]	
OSPAAAL	Organization of Solidarity of the Peoples of Africa, Asia, and Latin America	
OSPAR	Oslo and Paris Convention for Protection of the Marine Environment of the North-East Atlantic	(SAUS)
OSPARCOM	Oslo-Paris Commission	
OSPC	Off-Site Property Control	(SAUS)
OSPC	Options Service of Project Concern [*An association*]	(EA)
OSPCS	Charles M. Shields Centennial Library, South Porcupine, Ontario [*Library symbol*] [*National Library of Canada*]	(BIB)
OSPD	Office of Sponsored Program Development [*State University of New York at Binghamton*] [*Research center*]	(RCD)
OSPD	Official Scrabble Players Dictionary [*A publication*]	
OSPDS	Ocean Surveillance Product Dissemination Service	(SAUS)
OSPE	Organizational Spare Parts and Equipment [*Army*]	
OSPENEA	Conventions for the protection of the marine environment of the North-East Atlantic	(SAUS)
OSPES	Outer Shell Photoelectron Spectroscopy	
OSPF	Internes Routingprotokoll	(SAUS)
OSPF	Open Shortest Path First [*Communications routing protocol*]	
OSPG	Original Society of Painters and Glaziers [*A union*] [*British*]	
OSPI	Office of Strategic Planning and Integration	(SAUS)
OSPI	Office of Superintendent of Public Instruction	
OSPI	Operating System Programming Interface	(SAUS)
OSPIC	Oil Spill Public Information Center	(SAUS)
OSPIC	Overseas Patent Information Center	(SAUS)
OS-PIF	Office of the Secretary of Defense Productivity Investment Funding	
OSPIRG	Oregon State Public Interest Research Group [*Research center*]	(RCD)
OSPJ	Offshore Procurement, Japan	
OSpM	Mental Health Services for Clark County, Springfield, OH [*Library symbol*] [*Library of Congress*]	(LCLS)
OSPM	Operating System directed Power Management	(SAUS)
OSPNC	Porcupine Campus, Northern College of Applied Arts and Technology, South Porcupine, Ontario [*Library symbol*] [*National Library of Canada*]	(NLC)
OSPPE	Pauline Fathers	(TOCD)
osppe	Pauline Fathers	(TOCD)
OSPR	Office of Oil Spill Prevention and Response	
OSPR	Palmyra [*Syria*] [*ICAO location identifier*]	(ICLI)
OSPRDS	Oblate Spheroid	(PDAA)
OSPREY	Ocean Swell Powered Renewable Energy [*United Kingdom*]	
OSPRO	Ocean Shipping Procedures	
OSPS	Operator Service Position System	(SAUS)
OSPS	Operator Services Position System	(SAUS)
OSPTM	Timmins Museum, South Porcupine, Ontario [*Library symbol*] [*National Library of Canada*]	(BIB)
OSQ	Officer Separation Questionnaire	(DNAB)
OSQ	Officer Student Quarters	(DNAB)
OS Q	Operating System Q	(SAUS)
OSQ	San Antonio, TX [*Location identifier*] [*FAA*]	(FAAL)
OSQL	Object Structured Query Language	(SAUS)
OSR	Occupational Survey Report	
OSR	Oceanographic Survey Recorder	(SAUS)
OSR	OEM Service Release	(SAUS)
OSR	Offender Status Register	(SAUS)
OSR	Office for Scientific Research	(SAUS)
OSR	Office of Scientific Research [*AFSC*]	
OSR	Office of Security Review [*Obsolete*] [*DoD*]	
OSR	Office of Sponsored Research	(SAUS)
OSR	Office of Sport and Recreation [*Australian Capital Territory*]	
OSR	Office of Standards and Regulations [*Environmental Protection Agency*]	(GFGA)
OSR	Office of Strategic Research	(SAUS)
OSR	Office of Systems Requirements [*Social Security Administration*]	
OSR	Official Visitors Spot Report	(SAUS)
OSR	Ohio State Reports [*A publication*]	(DLA)
OSR	Oil Shale Reserves	(SAUS)
OSR	Oil/Steam Ratio	(SAUS)
OSR	Old Style Roman	(ADA)
OSR	Onsite Review [*Military*]	
OSR	Operand Storage Register [*Computer science*]	
OSR	Operating Safety Requirements	(SAUS)
OSR	Operational Safety Requirements	(COE)
OSR	Operational Scanning Recognition	
OSR	Operational Status Release [*Navy*]	(NG)
OSR	Operational Support Readiness	
OSR	Operational Support Requirement [*Military*]	
OSR	Operations Safety Requirement	(SAUS)
OSR	Operations Support Room [*NASA*]	
OSR	Optical Scanner Reader	(SAUS)
OSR	Optical Scanning Recognition [*Computer science*]	
OSR	Optical Solar Reflector	
OSR	Optical Sound Recorder	
OSR	Optical Spectral Reflector	(SAUS)
OSR	Optical Still Recorder [*LASER-disc technology*]	
OSR	Optical Surface Reflector	(SAUS)
OSR	Optimum Ship Routing [*Obsolete*]	
OSR	Ordnance Status Report	(NG)
OSR	Original Stock Requisition	(TIMI)
OSR	Originators Status Report [*Army*]	
OSR	OR with Switch Register	(SAUS)
OSR	Oscar Resources Ltd. [*Vancouver Stock Exchange symbol*]	
OSR	Ostrava [*Former Czechoslovakia*] [*Airport symbol*]	(OAG)
OSR	Output Shift Register	
OSR	Output Signal Range	
OSR	Output Status Register	
OSR	Oversea Returnee [*Military*]	
OSR	Overseas Service Ribbon [*Military decoration*]	
OSR	Over-the-Shoulder Rating	
OSR	Own Ship's Roll [*Navy*]	
OSR	Oxide-Stable Resin	
OSRA	Office Systems Research Association [*Cleveland, OH*]	(EA)
OSRA	Oil Spill Risk Analysis	(SAUS)
OSRA	Operational Software Release Approval	(SAUS)
OSRA	Overseas Shipping Representatives Association	(SAUS)
OSRAC	Ocean Shipping Requirements and Capabilities	
OSRADP	Oil Spill Research and Development Program [*Louisiana*]	
Osram	Osmium und Wolfram	(SAUS)
OSRAP	Optimum Stockage Requirements Analysis Program	
OSRB	Overseas Service Resettlement Bureau	(SAUS)
OSRC	Oil Sands Research Centre [*Alberta*]	
OSRD	Office of Scientific Research and Development [*World War II*]	
OSRD	Office of Standard Reference Data [*Gaithersburg, MD*] [*National Institute of Standards and Technology*]	
OSRDB	Office of Standard Reference Data Bibliography [*National Institute of Standards and Technology*]	
OS Rep	Ohio State Reports [*A publication*]	(DLA)
OSREPL	Oversea Replacement [*Army*]	
OSRET	Oversea Returnee [*Army*]	
OSRF	Smooth Rock Falls Public Library, Ontario [*Library symbol*] [*National Library of Canada*]	(NLC)
OSRI	Originating Station Routing Identifier	
OSRI	Originating Station Routing Indicator	(SAUS)
OSRL	Organizations and Systems Research Laboratory [*Army*]	(RDA)
OSRM	Office of Standard Reference Materials [*Gaithersburg, MD*] [*National Institute of Standards and Technology*]	(GRD)
OSRM	South River-Machar Union Public Library, South River, Ontario [*Library symbol*] [*National Library of Canada*]	(NLC)
OSRMD	Office of Scientific Research, Mechanics Division	(SAUS)
OSRMS	Ocean Surface Roughness Measurement System	(SAUS)
OSRO	Office for the Sahelian Relief Operation [*UN Food and Agriculture Organization*]	
OSRO	Operations Support Requirements Office [*NASA*]	(KSC)
OSROK	Office of Supply Republic of Korea	(SAUS)
OSRP	Occupant Safety Research Partnership	
OSRP	Occupant Safety Research Project	(SAUS)
OSRP	Oil Spill Response Plan [*Pollution prevention*]	
OSRPA	Offices, Shops, and Railway Premises Act [*1963*] [*British*]	
OSRR	Spanish River Reserve Band Public Library, Ontario [*Library symbol*] [*National Library of Canada*]	(NLC)
OSRS	Oceanic Satellites and Remote Sensing	(SAUS)
OSRS	Operational Status Recording Subsystem	
OSRS	Organization of Senegal River States	(SAUS)
OSRS	Subgroup on Ocean Satellites and Remote Sensing	(SAUS)
OSRTN	Office of the Special Representative for Trade Negotiations [*Later, Office of the United States Trade Representative*] [*Executive Office of the President*]	
OSRU	Optical Sensors Research Unit	(NITA)
OSRV	Oil Spill Response Vehicle	
OSRV	Outside Rear View [*Mirrors*] [*Automotive features*]	

OSS	Los Angeles, CA [*Location identifier*] [*FAA*] (FAAL)
OSS	Objective Supply System [*Army*]
OSS	Object Services Standard (AAEL)
OSS	Object Sorting Scales [*Psychology*]
OSS	Observatory of the Sahara and the Sahel (SAUS)
OSS	Observing Simulation System (USDC)
OSS	Observing Stimulation System [*Marine science*] (OSRA)
OSS	Occupant Sensing System [*Automotive safety systems*]
OSS	Occupational Superannuation Standard
OSS	Oceanic Scanning Spectrophotometer
OSS	Oceanic Space Subcommittee [*Congressional committee*] (MSC)
OSS	Ocean Science and Surveys (SAUS)
OSS	Ocean Surveillance Satellite (MCD)
OSS	Ocean Surveillance System [*Navy*] (SAA)
OSS	Ocean Survey Ship (NOAA)
OSS	OEX [*Orbiter Experiments*] Support System [*NASA*]
OSS	Office of Safeguards and Security [*Department of Energy*] [*Washington, DC*] (GRD)
OSS	Office of Secret Services (SAUS)
OSS	Office of Senate Security [*Congress*]
oss	Office of Space Science [*NASA*] (NAKS)
OSS	Office of Space Science [*NASA*]
OSS	Office of Space Station (ACAE)
OSS	Office of Space Systems [*Air Force*]
OSS	Office of Statistical Standards [*Bureau of the Budget; later, OMB*]
OSS	Office of Strategic Services [*Facetiously translated as "Oh So Social" because some of its staff were socially prominent*] [*World War II*]
OSS	Office of Support Services [*Army*]
OSS	Office of Systems Operations [*National Weather Service*] (USDC)
OSS	Office of the Space Station (SAUS)
OSS	Office Skills Series [*Test*] (TMMY)
OSS	Office Support System (SAUS)
OSS	Offshore Surveillance System
OSS	Old Submarine [*Navy symbol*]
OSS	One Stop Shop [*Small business advice*] [*British*] (ECON)
OSS	Online Service System (SAUS)
OSS	Online Support System von SAP (SAUS)
OSS	Ontario Secondary School Teachers' Federation [*UTLAS symbol*]
OSS	Open Sound System (SAUS)
OSS	Open Source Software (SAUS)
OSS	Open Source Solution (SAUS)
OSS	Open-Source Spectrometer (SAUS)
oss	Opera Semiseria [*Music*] (GROV)
oSS	operates Saturday and Sunday (SAUS)
OSS	Operating Supply Specification (SAUS)
OSS	Operating System Software [*Personal computers*]
OSS	Operating System Supervisor
OSS	Operating System Support (NITA)
OSS	Operational Storage Site [*Army*]
OSS	Operational Support Squadron (SAUS)
OSS	Operational Support System [*Computer science*]
OSS	Operation Safe Streets (SAUS)
OSS	Operations Support Services (SAUS)
OSS	Operations Support Squadron (SAUS)
OSS	Operations Support System (DOMA)
OSS	Operator Service Switch (SAUS)
OSS	Operator Service System (SAUS)
OSS	Operator Support System (SAUS)
OSS	Optical Sensor Subsystem [*Military*] (CAAL)
OSS	Optical Sight System
OSS	Optical Subsystem (KSC)
OSS	Optical Surveillance System (AAG)
OSS	Optics Subsystems (SAUS)
OSS	Optimized Systems Software [*San Jose, CA*]
OSS	Orbital Space Station Study [*NASA*] (IAA)
OSS	Orbital Stabilization System (MCD)
oss	Orbiting Space Station [*NASA*] (NAKS)
OSS	Orbiting Space Station [*NASA*]
OSS	Order Short Shipped (SAUS)
OSS	Ordnance Safety Switch [*Military*] (IAA)
OSS	Organised Science Series [*A publication*]
OSS	Organization for Cooperation of Socialist Countries in the Domain of Posts and Telecommunications [*Defunct*] (EAIO)
OSS	Orient Shipping Services (SAUS)
OSS	Osisko Lake Mines Ltd. [*Toronto Stock Exchange symbol*]
oss	Ossetic [*MARC language code*] [*Library of Congress*] (LCCP)
OSS	Ossory [*Ireland*] (ROG)
OSS	Outer Solar System
OSS	Overhead Speaker System [*Automotive engineering*]
OSS	Overseas Shipping Services (SAUS)
OSS	Overseas Switch [*Military*]
OSS	Over-the-Shoulder Shot [*Photography*] (WDMC)
OSS	Over-the-Shoulder Strap (DMAA)
OSS	Own Ship's Speed [*Navy*]
OSS	Oxygen Sleep Starvation
OSS	Religious of the Order of the Blessed Sacrament and Our Lady [*Sacramentine Nuns*] [*Roman Catholic religious order*]
OSS	Sacramentine Nuns (TOCD)
OSS	Sahara and Sahel Observatory (SAUS)
OSS	Shawnee State Community College, Portsmouth, OH [*OCLC symbol*] (OCLC)
OSSA	Office of Space Science and Applications [*Washington, DC*] [*NASA*]
OSSA	Order Scheduled Shipment Analysis (MCD)
OSSA	Order Secular of St. Augustine [*See also ASAS*] [*Rome, Italy*] (EAIO)
OSSBA	Oklahoma State School Boards Association (SAUS)

OSSC	Oblati Sacratissimi Cordis [*Oblate Fathers of the Sacred Heart*] [*Roman Catholic religious order*]
OSSC	Office of Stationary Source Compliance (COE)
OSSC	Ordnance Storage and Shipment Chart [*Army*] (MCD)
OSSC	Oregon School Study Council (SAUS)
OSSD	Office of Space Systems Development [*NASA*]
OSSD	Off-Site Surveillance Data [*Military*]
OSSD	Ontario Secondary School Diploma (SAUS)
OSSE	Object/Surface/Special Effect
OSSE	Observation Simulation System Experiments (SAUS)
OSSE	Observation System Simulation Experiments (SAUS)
OSSE	Observing System Sensitivity Experiments (SAUS)
OSSE	Observing Systems Simulation Experiments [*National Center for Atmospheric Research*]
OSSE	Oriented Scintillation Spectrometer Experiment [*Instrumentation in Gamma Ray Observatory*] [*NASA*]
OSSEs	Observing Systems Simulation Experiments (SAUS)
OSSF	Operating System Storage Facility (SAUS)
OSSF	Operating System Support Facility (MHDI)
OSSF	Other Services Stock Fund (ACAE)
OSSF	Overseas Services Storage Facility
OSShD	Organisation fur die Zusammenarbeit der Eisenbahnen [*Organisation for the Collaboration of Railways - OCR*] (EAIO)
OSSHE	Oregon State System of Higher Education (SAUS)
OSSHGD	Ontario Secondary School Honour Graduation Diploma (SAUS)
OSSI	Office of Supplemental Security Income (SAUS)
OSSI	Open Storage Systems Interconnection (RALS)
OSSI	Outback Steakhouse, Inc. [*NASDAQ symbol*] (SPSG)
OSSJ	St. Joseph's Hospital, Sarnia, Ontario [*Library symbol*] [*National Library of Canada*] (BIB)
OSSKC	Operative Society of Spring Knife Cutlers [*A union*] [*British*]
OSSL	Operating Systems Simulation Language (SAUS)
OSSM	Office of Safety Surface Mining [*Department of the Interior*] (COE)
OSSM	Oil Spill Simulation Model
OSSM	Optimum Shipboard Spares Model (SAUS)
OSSM Connector	Omnispectra Subminiature Connector (SAUS)
OSSMJ	Order of the Societies of Mary and Joseph (ROG)
OSSN	Operational Specialist Supervisor, Night [*Navy*]
OSSN	Originating Station Serial Number (SAUS)
OSSN	Other Specialty Serial Numbers [*Air Force*]
OSSN	Outside Sales Support Network Association (TVEL)
OSSNSS	Ordnance Supply Segment of the Navy Supply System
OSSO	Office of State Systems Operations [*Social and Rehabilitation Service, HEW*]
OSSO	Open Source Solutions Operation (SAUS)
OSSP	Operational Supply Support Plan (MCD)
OSSP	Oregon Small Schools Program (SAUS)
OSSP	Outer Solar System Probe
OS-SPT	Osmolality Urin-Spot [*Test*] [*Biochemistry*] (DAVI)
OSSR	Oblates [*or Order*] of the Most Holy Redeemer [*Roman Catholic women's religious order*]
OSSR	Order of the Most Holy Redeemer (TOCD)
OSSR	Own Ship's Speed Repeater [*Navy*]
OSSRH	Orbiter Subsystem Requirements Handbook [*NASA*] (NASA)
OSSRS	Optimum Step Size Random Search [*Computer science*] (IAA)
osss	Brigittine Monks (TOCD)
OSSS	Damascus [*Syria*] [*ICAO location identifier*] (ICLI)
OSSS	Optical Space Surveillance Subsystem (AAG)
OSSS	Optical Space Surveillance System [*or Subsystem*] (IAA)
OSSS	Orbital Space Station Studies (or Study) (SAUS)
OSSS	Orbital Space Station Study
OSSS	Orbital Space Station System [*of NASA*]
OSSS	Orbiting Space Station Study (SAUS)
OSSS	Order of the Most Holy Savior [*Bridgettine Sisters*] [*Roman Catholic religious order*]
OSSS	The Brigittine Sisters (TOCD)
OSST	Ocean Ship Surveillance Training
OSST	Official Summary of Security Transactions and Holdings
OSST	Offshore Storage Tank
OSST	Operating System Symbol Table (SAUS)
OSST	Operational Site System Test (SAUS)
OSST	Order of the Holy Trinity (TOCD)
osst	Order of the Most Holy Trinity, Trinitarian Fathers (TOCD)
OSsT	Ordo Sanctissimae Trinitatis Redemptionis Captivorum [*Order of the Most Holy Trinity*] [*Trinitarians*] [*Roman Catholic religious order*]
OSST	Sisters of the Most Holy Trinity (TOCD)
OSSTF	Ontario Secondary School Teachers Federation (SAUS)
OSSU	Operator Services Switching Unit [*Telecommunications*] (TEL)
OSSU	Sundridge & Strong Union Public Library, Sundridge, Ontario [*Library symbol*] [*National Library of Canada*] (NLC)
OSSup	Overseas Supply (SAUS)
OS Supp	Oklahoma Statutes, Supplement [*A publication*] (DLA)
OST	Austria Fund [*NYSE symbol*] (SPSG)
OST	Objectives, Strategy, and Tactics [*Management system*]
OST	Objective Start Time
OST	Object Sorting Test [*Psychology*]
OST	Observation Skills Test
OST	Observatoire des Sciences et des Techniques [*France*]
OST	Occlusal Splint Therapy [*Medicine*] (MELL)
OST	Ocean Surface Temperature [*Marine science*] (OSRA)
OST	Office of Science and Technology [*Terminated 1973, functions transferred to National Science Foundation*] [*Later, CSTD*]
OST	Office of Strategic Trade (SAUS)
OST	Office of Systems Operations [*Marine science*] (OSRA)

OST............	Office of the Secretary of Transportation [*Department of Transportation*]
OST............	Office of the Special Trustee
OST............	Offshore Storage and Treatment (SAUS)
O St	Ohio State Reports [*A publication*] (DLA)
OST............	Old Spanish Trail (SAUS)
OST............	One-Station Training
OST............	On Same Terms (WDAA)
OST............	On-Shift Test (IEEE)
OST............	On-Site Test (IAA)
OST............	Operating System Toolbox (SAUS)
OST............	Operating System Trap (SAUS)
OST............	Operational Sea Training (SAUS)
OST............	Operational Suitability Test [*Aviation*]
OST............	Operational System Test (KSC)
OST............	Operations Support Team [*NASA*] (MCD)
OST............	Operator Station Task (ELAL)
OST............	Optical Sensing Trigger
OST............	Optical Star Tracker
OST............	Optic Support Table
OST............	Orbiter Support Trolley [*NASA*] (NASA)
OST............	Orbit Stay Time
OST............	Order Shipping Time (SAUS)
OST............	Order Ship Time [*DoD*]
OST............	Ordinary Spring Tides
OST............	Ordnance Shock Test [*Military*]
OST............	Ordnance Special Training (AAG)
OST............	Ordnance Suitability Test
OST............	Organisation Socialiste des Travailleurs [*Socialist Workers' Organization*] [*Senegal*] [*Political party*] (PPW)
OST............	Organizacion Socialista de los Trabajadores [*Socialist Workers' Organization*] [*Bolivia*] [*Political party*] (PPW)
OST............	Organizacion Socialista de los Trabajadores [*Socialist Workers' Organization*] [*Costa Rica*] [*Political party*] (PPW)
OST............	Originating Station Treatment [*Telecommunications*] (TEL)
OST............	Ostend [*Belgium*] [*Airport symbol*] (OAG)
OST............	Osteopathic (WGA)
Ost.............	Osteotomy [*Orthopedics*] (DAVI)
OST............	Osterhout Free Library, Wilkes-Barre, PA [*OCLC symbol*] (OCLC)
OST............	Outer Space Treaty (SAUS)
OST............	Out of Stock, Temporary [*Business term*]
OST............	Output Stage Tube (SAUS)
OST............	Overseas Students Trust [*British*] (AEBS)
OST............	Over Stress Testing
OST............	Oxford Superconductive Technology [*Manufacturing company*] [*British*]
OST............	Stratford Public Library, Ontario [*Library symbol*] [*National Library of Canada*] (NLC)
OSTA	Office of Space and Terrestrial Applications [*NASA*] (GRD)
OSTA	Optical Storage Technology Association (CDE)
OSTA	Stayner Public Library, Ontario [*Library symbol*] [*National Library of Canada*] (NLC)
OSTAC	Bibliotheque Publique Cambridge-St.-Albert, St.-Albert, Ontario [*Library symbol*] [*National Library of Canada*] (NLC)
OSTAC	Ocean Science Technology Advisory Committee [*Terminated, 1976*] [*National Security Industrial Association*] (MSC)
OSTAG	Gallery Stratford, Ontario [*Library symbol*] [*National Library of Canada*] (NLC)
OSTAR	Observer Single-Handed Transatlantic Race [*Sailing*]
OSTARE	Old Scientific Technical Aerospace Reports Extended
OSTARS.......	Orbiting Surveillance and Target Acquisition Relay [*Army*] (RDA)
OSTASDG	St. Andrews Branch, Stormount, Dundas, and Glengarry County Library, Ontario [*Library symbol*] [*National Library of Canada*] (BIB)
O State	Ohio State Reports [*A publication*] (DLA)
OSTB	Office of the State Training Board [*Australia*]
OSTC	Office for Scientific, Technical and Cultural affairs (SAUS)
OSTC	Open Systems Testing Consortium (TELE)
OSTC	St. Catharines Public Library, Ontario [*Library symbol*] [*National Library of Canada*] (NLC)
OStcB.........	Belmont Technical Institute, St. Clairsville, OH [*Library symbol*] [*Library of Congress*] (LCLS)
OSTCB	Brock University, St. Catharines, Ontario [*Library symbol*] [*National Library of Canada*] (NLC)
OSTCBG.......	Department of Geography, Brock University, St. Catharines, Ontario [*Library symbol*] [*National Library of Canada*] (NLC)
OSTCG	Grantham High School, St. Catharines, Ontario [*Library symbol*] [*National Library of Canada*] (NLC)
OSTCGL	Genaire Ltd., St. Catharines, Ontario [*Library symbol*] [*National Library of Canada*] (NLC)
OSTCH	Hotel-Dieu Hospital, St. Catharines, Ontario [*Library symbol*] [*National Library of Canada*] (BIB)
OSTCM	St. Catharines Historical Museum, Ontario [*Library symbol*] [*National Library of Canada*] (BIB)
OSTCMEC	Monenco Consultants Ltd., St. Catharines, Ontario [*Library symbol*] [*National Library of Canada*] (NLC)
OSTCOOP	Office of the Secretary of Transportation Continuity of Operations Plan
OSTCT	St. Catharines Teachers' College, Ontario [*Library symbol*] [*National Library of Canada*] (NLC)
OSTCTR.......	St. Catharines Teachers' Reference Library, Ontario [*Library symbol*] [*National Library of Canada*] (NLC)
OStcU	Ohio University, Belmont County Branch Campus, St. Clairsville, OH [*Library symbol*] [*Library of Congress*] (LCLS)
OSTD	Office of Supersonic Transport Development [*Department of Transportation*] [*Obsolete*]
OSTD	Off-Site Technical Director (MHDI)
OSTD	Ontario Society for Training and Development [*Canada*] (EDAC)
OSTD	Ordnance Standards
OSTD	Ordnance Standard Technical Directives [*Obsolete*]
OSTDS.........	Office of Space Tracking and Data Systems [*NASA*] (NASA)
OSTE..........	Osteotech, Inc. [*NASDAQ symbol*] (SAG)
OSte...........	Public Library of Steubenville and Jefferson County, Steubenville, OH [*Library symbol*] [*Library of Congress*] (LCLS)
OSteC	College of Steubenville, Steubenville, OH [*Library symbol*] [*Library of Congress*] (LCLS)
osteo	Osteoarthritis [*Medicine*]
Osteo	Osteomyelitis [*Orthopedics*] (DAVI)
OSTEO	Osteomyelitis [*Medicine*]
OSTEO	Osteopathic
osteoart	osteoarthritic (SAUS)
Osteoart.......	Osteoarthritis (SAUS)
Osteoarthritis Cartilage...	Osteoarthritis and Cartilage (SAUS)
OSTEOL	Osteology (SAUS)
OSTEOPORO...	Osteoporosus (SAUS)
OSTEOPTH...	Osteopath
Osteotch	Osteotech, Inc. [*Associated Press*] (SAG)
OSTEST.......	Operating System Test [*Telecommunications*] (TEL)
Ostex	Ostex International, Inc. [*Associated Press*] (SAG)
OSTF	Off-Site Test Facility (SAUS)
OSTF	Operational Silo Test Facility
OSTF	Operational Suitability Test Facility [*Aviation*]
OSTF	Operational System Test Facility [*Air Force*]
OSTF	Optical, Sensor, Test, Facilities (ACAE)
OSTF	Ordnance Survey Transfer Format (SAUS)
OSTFC	Storrington Branch, Frontenac County Library, Ontario [*Library symbol*] [*National Library of Canada*] (BIB)
OSTG	Ocean Science and Technology Group [*Navy*] (MCD)
OSTG	St. Georges Branch, South Dumfries Public Library, Ontario [*Library symbol*] [*National Library of Canada*] (BIB)
OSTI	Bibliotheque Publique de St.-Isidore, Ontario [*Library symbol*] [*National Library of Canada*] (NLC)
OSTI	Office of Science and Technology
OSTI	Office of Scientific and Technical Information [*Later, BLR & DD*] [*British Library*]
OSTI	Office of Scientific and Technical Information [*Department of Energy*] [*Information service or system*] (IID)
OSTI	Organization for Social and Technical Innovation
OSTI	Organization for Social and Technological Innovation (SAUS)
OSTIR	Stirling Public Library, Ontario [*Library symbol*] [*National Library of Canada*] (BIB)
OSTIV	Organisation Scientifique et Technique Internationale du Vol a Voile [*International Technical and Scientific Organization for Soaring Flight*]
OStJ...........	Officer of the Order of Saint John of Jerusalem (SAUS)
OStJ...........	Officer of the Order of St. John of Jerusalem [*British*]
OStJ...........	Officer, Venerable Order of St. John of Jerusalem [*Decoration*] (CMD)
ostk...........	Oilstick (VRA)
OSTL..........	Operating System Table Loader [*Telecommunications*] (TEL)
OSTL..........	Ovary Style Length [*Botany*]
OSTM..........	Open System Transaction Management (SAUS)
OSTM..........	Sault Ste. Marie Public Library, Ontario [*Library symbol*] [*National Library of Canada*] (NLC)
OSTMA	Algoma College, Sault Ste. Marie, Ontario [*Library symbol*] [*National Library of Canada*] (NLC)
OSTMAAS	Synod Office, Diocese of Algoma, Anglican Church of Canada, Sault Ste. Marie, Ontario [*Library symbol*] [*National Library of Canada*] (NLC)
OStmaC	Chatfield College, St. Martin, OH [*Library symbol*] [*Library of Congress*] (LCLS)
OSTMAS	Research Library, Algoma Steel Corp. Ltd., Sault Ste. Marie, Ontario [*Library symbol*] [*National Library of Canada*] (NLC)
OSTMB	Batchewana Indian Band, Sault Ste. Marie, Ontario [*Library symbol*] [*National Library of Canada*] (NLC)
OSTMEF.......	Sea Lamprey Control Centre, Fisheries and Oceans Canada [*Centre de Controle des Lamproies de Mer, Peches et Oceans Canada*] Sault Ste. Marie, Ontario [*Library symbol*] [*National Library of Canada*] (NLC)
OSTMF........	Great Lakes Forest Research Centre, Canadian Forestry Service [*Centre de Recherches Forestieres des Grands Lacs, Service Canadien des Forets*] Sault Ste. Marie, Ontario [*Library symbol*] [*National Library of Canada*] (NLC)
OSTMFF.......	Forest Pest Management Institute, Canadian Forestry Service [*Institut pour laRepression des Ravageurs Forestiers, Service Canadien des Forets*], Sault-Ste .-Marie, Ontario [*Library symbol*] [*National Library of Canada*] (NLC)
OSTMGH......	General Hospital, Sault Ste. Marie, Ontario [*Library symbol*] [*National Library of Canada*] (NLC)
OSTMH	Sault Ste. Marie and 49th (SSM) Field Regiment RCA Historical Society, Ontario [*Library symbol*] [*National Library of Canada*] (NLC)
OSTMM.......	Strathroy Middlesex Museum, Strathroy, Ontario [*Library symbol*] [*National Library of Canada*] (BIB)
OSTMNA	Aviation and Fire Management Centre, Ontario Ministry of Natural Resources, Sault Ste. Marie [*Library symbol*] [*National Library of Canada*] (BIB)
OSTMPH	Plummer Public Hospital, Sault Ste. Marie, Ontario [*Library symbol*] [*National Library of Canada*] (NLC)

OSTMSC	Sault College of Applied Arts and Technology, Sault Ste. Marie, Ontario [*Library symbol*] [*National Library of Canada*] (NLC)
OSTMY	St. Mary's Public Library, Ontario [*Library symbol*] [*National Library of Canada*] (NLC)
OSTMYM	St. Mary's District Museum, St. Mary's, Ontario [*Library symbol*] [*National Library of Canada*] (BIB)
OSTNPS	Operator Services Traffic Network Planning System (SAUS)
OSTO	Office of Space Transportation Operations [*NASA*] (NASA)
OST-ONA	Office of the Secretary of Transportation Office of Noise Abatement
OSTP	Office of Science and Technology Policy [*Executive Office of the Presiden t*] [*Washington, DC*]
OSTP	Office of Scientific and Technical Personnel (SAUS)
OSTP	Onboard Short Term Plan [*NASA*] (SPST)
OSTP	On-Site Test Procedure
OSTP	Orbiting System Test Plan [*NASA*] (NASA)
OSTP	Strathroy Public Library, Ontario [*Library symbol*] [*National Library of Canada*] (NLC)
OSTPA	Stratford-Perth Archives Board, Ontario [*Library symbol*] [*National Library of Canada*] (BIB)
O St R	Ohio State Reports [*A publication*] (DLA)
OSTR	Oregon State Triga Reactor (SAUS)
OSTR	Streetsville Public Library, Ontario [*Library symbol*] [*National Library of Canada*] (NLC)
OSTRE	Objective Sidetone Reference Equivalent (SAUS)
O St Rep	Ohio State Reports [*A publication*] (DLA)
OSTRO	Stroud Branch, Township of Innisfil Public Library, Ontario [*Library symbol*] [*National Library of Canada*] (NLC)
OSTS	Office of Space Transportation System [*NASA*]
OSTS	Office of Space Transportation Systems [*NASA*] (GRD)
OSTS	Office of State Technical Services [*Also, STS*] [*Abolished, 1970*] [*Department of Commerce*]
OSTS	Official Seed Testing Station (WDAA)
OSTS	Operational Suitability Test Site [*Aviation*] (AAG)
OST/SS	Open Systems Transport/Session Support (SAUS)
OST System	Objectives-Strategy-Tactics System (SAUS)
OSTT	Damascus [*Syria*] [*ICAO location identifier*] (ICLI)
OSTT	Open Systems Technology Transfer Programme [*British*]
OSTT	St. Thomas Public Library, Ontario [*Library symbol*] [*National Library of Canada*] (NLC)
OSTTE	Elgin County Public Library, St. Thomas, Ontario [*Library symbol*] [*National Library of Canada*] (NLC)
OSTTP	St. Thomas Psychiatric Hospital, Ontario [*Library symbol*] [*National Library of Canada*] (NLC)
OSTV	Operational Support Television [*Military*] (AFM)
OSTX	Ostex International, Inc. [*NASDAQ symbol*] (SAG)
OSTX	Ostex Intl. [*NASDAQ symbol*] (TTSB)
OSU	Columbus, OH [*Location identifier*] [*FAA*] (FAAL)
OSU	Irish Ursuline Union (TOCD)
OSU	Officially Sanctioned User (SAUS)
OSU	Ohio State University, Columbus, OH [*OCLC symbol*] (OCLC)
O Su	Ohio Supplement [*A publication*] (DLA)
OSU	Ohio Supreme Court Decisions, Unreported Cases [*A publication*] (DLA)
OSU	Oklahoma State University
OSU	Older-Worker Service Unit [*US Employment Service*] [*Department of Labor*]
OSU	Omega VLF Sensor Unit (SAUS)
OSU	Open Systems Unit [*British*]
OSU	Operational Strategy Unit (HEAS)
OSU	Operational Switching Unit
OSU	Operation Sisters United (EA)
OSU	Optical Scanning Unit (DNAB)
OSU	Optical Service Unit [*Telecommunications*]
OSU	Order of St. Ursula [*Roman Catholic women's religious order*]
OSU	Ordnance Support Unit (SAUS)
OSU	Oregon State University [*Formerly, OSC*]
OSU	Osaka Sangyo University (SAUS)
OSU	O'Sullivan Industries Holding [*NYSE symbol*] (SPSG)
OSU	Own Ship's Use [*Navy*] (DNAB)
OSU	Sudbury Public Library, Ontario [*Library symbol*] [*National Library of Canada*] (NLC)
OSU	Ursuline Nuns of the Congregation of Paris (Cincinnati, OH) (TOCD)
OSU	Ursuline Nuns of the Congregation of Paris (Cleveland, OH) (TOCD)
OSU	Ursuline Nuns of the Congregation of Paris (Kansas City, KS) (TOCD)
OSU	Ursuline Nuns of the Congregation of Paris (Louisville, KY) (TOCD)
OSU	Ursuline Nuns of the Congregation of Paris (Owensboro, KY) (TOCD)
OSU	Ursuline Nuns of the Congregation of Paris (St. Martin, OH) (TOCD)
OSU	Ursuline Nuns of the Congregation of Paris (Toledo, OH) (TOCD)
OSU	Ursuline Nuns of the Congregation of Paris (Youngstown, OH) (TOCD)
OSU	Ursuline Sisters of Belleville (TOCD)
OSU	Ursuline Sisters of the Congregation of Tildonk, Belgium (TOCD)
OSUAS	Ohio State University Administrative Science (SAUS)
OSUBE	Educational Media Centre, Sudbury Board of Education, Ontario [*Library symbol*] [*National Library of Canada*] (NLC)
OSUC	Cambrian College, Sudbury, Ontario [*Library symbol*] [*National Library of Canada*] (NLC)
OSU-CISRC	Ohio State University-Computer and Information Science Research Center (SAUS)
OSUCS	Civic Square, Information and Reference, Sudbury Public Library, Ontario [*Library symbol*] [*National Library of Canada*] (NLC)
OSUE	On-Site User Evaluation (MCD)
OSUGH	Sudbury General Hospital, Ontario [*Library symbol*] [*National Library of Canada*] (NLC)
OSUHRF	Ohio State University Heat Release Calorimeter (SAUS)
OSUK	Ophthalmological Society of the United Kingdom
OSUL	Laurentian University [*Universite Laurentienne*] Sudbury, Ontario [*Library symbol*] [*National Library of Canada*] (NLC)
OSUL	Ohio State University Libraries (NITA)
OSUL	Oklahoma State University Library (SAUS)
OSUL	Oregon State University Library (SAUS)
OSULH	Medical Library, Laurentian Hospital, Sudbury, Ontario [*Library symbol*] [*National Library of Canada*] (BIB)
OSullvnC	O'Sullivan Corp. [*Associated Press*] (SAG)
OSulvInd	O'Sullivan Industries Holdings [*Associated Press*] (SAG)
OSUM	Ohio State University Museum of Zoology [*Research center*] (RCD)
OSUME	Ontario Ministry of Education, Sudbury, Ontario [*Library symbol*] [*National Library of Canada*] (BIB)
OSUN	North Central Regional Library, Sudbury, Ontario [*Library symbol*] [*National Library of Canada*] (NLC)
OSUN	Ontario Library Service - Voyageur, Sudbury, Ontario [*Library symbol*] [*National Library of Canada*] (NLC)
OSUNB	Brock Township Public Library, Sunderland, Ontario [*Library symbol*] [*National Library of Canada*] (NLC)
OSUOP	Northeastern Ontario Oncology Program [*Programme d'Oncologie du Nord-Est de l'Ontario*], Sudbury, Ontario [*Library symbol*] [*National Library of Canada*] (NLC)
OSUP	Ohio State University Press (DGA)
OSUPE	Ohio State University Psychological Exam (EDAC)
O Supp	Ohio Supplement [*A publication*] (DLA)
OSUR	Ohio State University Reactor
OSUREP	Overseas Unit Replacement System [*Military*] (AFIT)
OSU Research Review	Ohio State University Research Review (SAUS)
OSURF	Ohio State University Research Foundation
OSURO	Ohio State University Radio Observatory
OSUS	Ocean Surveillance (SAUS)
OSUT	One-Station-Unit Training [*Army*]
OSUT	On-Site User Test
OSUT	On-Site User Training
OSUT	Ordinary Seamen Under Training [*Canadian Navy*]
OSUTCB	Ohio State University Theatre Collection Bulletin (SAUS)
OSUT-COFT	One-Station-Unit Training - Conduct of Fire Trainer [*Army*] (MCD)
OSUU	University of Subury [*Universite de Sudbury*] Ontario [*Library symbol*] [*National Library of Canada*] (NLC)
OSV	Object-Subject-Verb (ADWA)
OSV	Ocean Station Vessel
OSV	Office of Space Vehicles
OSV	Offscreen Voice [*Films, television, etc.*]
OSV	Offset Scan Voting (AAEL)
OSV	Offshore Supply Vessel [*Coast Guard*] (GFGA)
OSV	Offshore Support Vessel (SAUS)
OSV	On-Site Vendor (TIMI)
OSV	On-Site Verification (SAUS)
OSV	On Station Vehicle (MCD)
OSV	OPFOR Surrogate Vehicle (SAUS)
OSV	Orbital Servicing Vehicle (ACAE)
OSV	Orbital Support Vehicle
OSV	Orbiting Servicing Vehicle (SAUS)
OSV	Order of St. Vincent (EA)
OSV	Ordnance Spare Vehicle (SAUS)
OSV	Oriented Space Vehicle
OSV	Output Serving Voltage
OSV	Over-Sand Vehicle
OSVA	Off-Site Vital Area (MCD)
OSVC	Outgoing Switched Virtual Circuit (SAUS)
OS/VS	Operating Schedule/Virtual System
OS/VS	Operating System/Virtual Storage [*Computer science*] (MDG)
OS/VS1	Operating System/Virtual Storage 1 [*Computer science*] (ITCA)
OS/VS2	Operating System/Virtual Storage 2 [*Computer science*] (ITCA)
OSW	Oblique Shock Wave
OSW	Office of Saline Water [*Later, OWRT*] [*Department of the Interior*]
OSW	Office of Secretary of War [*Obsolete*]
OSW	Office of Solid Waste [*Environmental Protection Agency*] (EPA)
OSW	Office Saline Water (SAUS)
OSW	Old Swedish [*Language, etc.*]
OSW	Olique Shock Wave (SAUS)
OSW	Operational Switching Unit
OSW	Operations Support Wing [*NASA*]
OSW	Orbital Weapon System (SAUS)
OSW	Order of the Sacred Word [*Affiliate of the magical society, Aurum Solis*]
OSW	Ordnance Weapon Systems (SAUS)
OSW	Oswego, KS [*Location identifier*] [*FAA*] (FAAL)
OSW	Oswestry [*British depot code*]
OSW	Wittenberg University, Springfield, OH [*Library symbol*] [*Library of Congress*] (LCLS)
OSWA	Off-Shift Work Authorization (AAG)
OSWA	Orchid Society of Western Australia
OSWA	Organ Society of Western Australia
OSWAC	Ordnance Special Weapons Ammunition Command [*Later, Weapons Command*]
OSWC	Ordnance Special Weapons Command [*Merged with Missile Command*] [*Army*]
OSWD	Office of Special Weapons Development [*Army*]
OSWEP	Overseas Student Welfare Expansion Programme (SAUS)
OSWER	Office of Solid Waste and Emergency Response [*Environmental Protection Agency*] [*Washington, DC*]
OSWG	Optical Systems Working Group (MUGU)
OSWI	Old Spaghetti Warehouse, Inc. (MHDW)

OSWMP	Office of Solid Waste Management Programs [*Environmental Protection Agency*]
OSWR	Office of Solid Waste Research (SAUS)
OSWS	Operating System Workstation [*Computer science*]
OSWS	Whitchurch-Stouffville Public Library, Stouffville, Ontario [*Library symbol*] [*National Library of Canada*] (NLC)
OSWV	Osteryoung Square Wave Voltammogram [*Electrochemistry*]
OSX	Kosciusko, MS [*Location identifier*] [*FAA*] (FAAL)
OSY	Namsos [*Norway*] [*Airport symbol*] (OAG)
OSY	National Institute for Occupational Safety and Health, Morgantown, WV [*OCLC symbol*] (OCLC)
OSY	Odyssey Resources Ltd. [*Vancouver Stock Exchange symbol*]
OSY	Optimum Sustainable Yield (SAUS)
OSYC	Officer Supervising Yardcraft [*Canadian Navy*]
OSYFC	Sydenham Branch, Frontenac County Library, Ontario [*Library symbol*] [*National Library of Canada*] (BIB)
OSYS	OccuSystems, Inc. [*NASDAQ symbol*] (SAG)
OSyS	Sylvania Schools, Sylvania, OH [*Library symbol*] [*Library of Congress*] (LCLS)
OSZ	Koszalin [*Poland*] [*Airport symbol*] (OAG)
OSZ	Offshore Surf Zone
OSZ	Washington, DC [*Location identifier*] [*FAA*] (FAAL)
OSzK	Orszagos Szechenyi Konyvtar [*National Szechenyi Library*] [*Information service or system*] (IID)
OT	Evergreen Helicopters of Alaska [*ICAO designator*] (AD)
OT	Objective Test [*Psychology*]
OT	Object Technology [*Computer science*] (CDE)
OT	Object Track (ACAE)
OT	Observer Target [*Army*]
OT	Occipitotransverse [*Obstetrics*]
OT	Occlusion Time (MAE)
OT	Occupational Therapist [*or Therapy*] [*Medicine*]
OT	Occupational Therapy (SAUS)
OT	Occupational Therapy Technician [*Navy*]
OT	Occupational Training (AIE)
OT	Occupied Territories (BJA)
OT	Ocean Systems Technician [*Navy*] (DNAB)
OT	Ocean Transportation [*Military*]
OT	Ocular Tension [*Medicine*]
OT	Oedipus Tyrannus [*of Sophocles*] [*Classical studies*] (OCD)
OT	Oesterreicher-Turner [*Syndrome*] [*Medicine*] (DB)
OT	Offensive Tackle [*Football*]
OT	Offensive Threat (ACAE)
OT	Office of Telecommunications [*Department of Commerce*]
OT	Office of Territories [*Department of the Interior*]
OT	Office of Transportation [*Department of Agriculture*]
OT	Off Time (WDAA)
OT	Off Topic (SAUS)
OT	Oil Tanker (SAUS)
OT	Oil Temperature [*Automotive engineering*]
OT	Oil-Tempered (IAA)
OT	Oil-Tight
OT	Old Term
OT	Old Terminology
OT	Old Testament [*of the Bible*]
OT	Old Timer [*Communications operators' colloquialism*]
OT	Old Tom [*British slang term for gin*] (ROG)
OT	Old Top [*Communications operators' colloquialism*]
OT	Old [*or Original*] Tuberculin [*Also, TO*] [*Medicine*]
OT	Olfactory Threshold
OT	Olfactory Tubercle [*Neuroanatomy*]
OT	On a Track [*Rail*] [*Shipping*] (DCTA)
OT	Once-Through [*Nuclear reactor technology*]
OT	One Time
OT	On Target [*Military*] (CAAL)
O/T	On Thames [*In place names*] [*British*] (ROG)
o-T	on-Thames (SAUS)
OT	On Time
OT	Ontological Theory (VLIE)
OT	On Track (SAUS)
OT	On Track (VLIE)
OT	On Trajectory (ACAE)
O/T	On Trent [*In place names*] [*British*] (ROG)
OT	On Truck [*Shipping*]
OT	Onward Transfer (SAUS)
OT	Opening Time (SAUS)
OT	Open Topped [*Container*] [*Packaging*] (DCTA)
OT	Open Transport [*Computer science*]
OT	Operability Test (SAUS)
OT	Operating Temperature [*Nuclear energy*]
OT	Operating Theater
OT	Operating Thetan (SAUS)
OT	Operating Time
OT	Operational Instrumentation MDM-Tank (SAUS)
OT	Operational Instrumentation Tank [*NASA*] (NAKS)
OT	Operational Technology [*Nuclear energy*] (NRCH)
OT	Operational Test (AFM)
OT	Operational Testing (SAUS)
OT	Operational Training (MCD)
OT	Operational Trajectory [*Aerospace*] (KSC)
OT	Operations Team (MCD)
OT	Operation Time (SAUS)
OT	Opportunity Target (SAUS)
OT	Optatam Totius [*Decree on Priestly Formation*] [*Vatican II document*]
OT	Optical Techniques group (SAUS)
OT	Optical Technology (SAUS)
OT	Optical Thickness (ADWA)
OT	Optical Tool
OT	Optical Tracker [*NASA*] (NAKS)
OT	Optical Tracking [*NASA*] (KSC)
OT	Optical-Transient [*Astronomy*]
OT	Optic Tectum [*Anatomy*]
O/T	Oral Temperature (DAVI)
OT	Oral Testimony (BJA)
OT	Oral Thrush [*Medicine*] (MEDA)
OT	Ordering Table (SAUS)
OT	Oregon Territory [*Prior to statehood*]
OT	Oregon Trunk Railway [*AAR code*]
OT	Organizational Table
OT	Organization Table
OT	Organization Theory (SAUS)
OT	Orienteering Tasmania [*Australia*] [*An association*]
OT	Orifice Tube [*Automobile air conditioning system*]
OT	Original Transposed (SAUS)
OT	Original Tuberculin [*Medicine*] (DMAA)
OT	Orotracheal [*Medicine*]
OT	Orthite (SAUS)
OT	Orthogonal Trees (SAUS)
O-T	Orthohombic-Tetragonal [*Temperature transition*]
OT	Ortho Tolidine (SAUS)
OT	Oscillation Transformer [*Radio*]
OT	Osmium Tetroxide [*Inorganic chemistry*]
OT	Other (VLIE)
OT	Other Than
OT	Other Time
o/t	Other Times (PIAV)
O/T	Other Times (PIPO)
OT	Otis Elevator (SAUS)
OT	Otis Test [*Psychiatry*] (DAVI)
Ot	Otolaryngologist (SAUS)
OT	Otolaryngology [*Medicine*]
OT	Otology [*Medicine*]
OT	O'Toole's Group, Inc. [*Toronto Stock Exchange symbol*]
Ot	Otto Papiensis [*Flourished, 12th century*] [*Authority cited in pre-1607 legal work*] (DSA)
Ot	Otto's United States Supreme Court Reports [*91-107 United States*] [*A publication*] (DLA)
OT	Ought (ROG)
OT	Outer Table (MCD)
OT	Outer Tube
OT	Outfit
OT	Out of Territory (VLIE)
OT	Out of Tolerance
OT	Out of Town (GOBB)
OT	Output [*Computer science*] (IAA)
OT	Output Tape (SAUS)
OT	Output Terminal
OT	Outside Test (SAUS)
OT	Out Temperature (MCD)
OT	Overall Test (KSC)
OT	Overhead Transparencies
OT	Overlap Technician
OT	Overlap Telling (MCD)
OT	Overseas Tankship (SAUS)
OT	Overseas Territories (MCD)
OT	Overseas Trade
OT	Overseas Trading [*A publication*]
OT	Overseas Transportation (SAUS)
O/T	Overtemperature (KSC)
OT	Over There (ADA)
OT	Overtime
OT	Overtone
OT	Ovotransferrin [*Biochemistry*]
OT	Ovum Transfer (SAUS)
OT	Oxygen Therapy (MELL)
OT	Oxytocin [*Endocrinology*]
OT	Stations Open Exclusively to Operational Traffic of the Services Concerned [*ITU designation*] (CET)
OT	Tara Branch, Bruce County Public Library, Ontario [*Library symbol*] [*National Library of Canada*] (NLC)
OT	Toledo-Lucas County Public Library, Toledo, OH [*Library symbol*] [*Library of Congress*] (LCLS)
OT1H	On The One Hand (SAUS)
OTA	Academy of Medicine, Toronto, Ontario [*Library symbol*] [*National Library of Canada*] (NLC)
OTA	Congressional Office of Technology Assessment (SAUS)
OTA	Mota [*Ethiopia*] [*Airport symbol*] (AD)
OTA	Occupational Therapists Association (NADA)
OTA	Occupied Territory Administration [*World War II*]
OTA	Office of Tax Analysis [*Department of the Treasury*]
OTA	Office of Technical Assistance (USGC)
OTA	Office of Technology Assessment [*Congressional study group*] [*Washington, DC*]
OTA	Office of Technology Assistance [*General Services Administration*]
OTA	Office of Telecommunications Applications [*US National Telecommunications and Information Administration*] (TSSD)
OTA	Office of Territorial Affairs (SAUS)
OTA	Officer Training Allowance [*Naval Reserve*]
OTA	Official Test Aerosol (SAUS)
OTA	Off-the-Air Record Club [*Record label*]

OTA.............. Oil Trades Association of New York (EA)
OTA.............. Old Testament Abstracts [*A publication*] (BJA)
OTA.............. Omnidirectional Transmitter Antenna
OTA.............. Ontario Trucking Association (SAUS)
OTA.............. Open Terminal Architecture (RALS)
OTA.............. Open Test Assembly [*Nuclear energy*] (NRCH)
OTA.............. Operational Test Agency (DOMA)
OTA.............. Operational Transconductance Amplifier (IEEE)
OTA.............. Operational Transconductance Array (SAUS)
OTA.............. Operation Town Affiliations [*An association*] (EA)
OTA.............. Operation-Triggered Architecture [*Computer science*]
OTA.............. Optical Telescope Assembly [*NASA*]
OTA.............. Optical Tracking Aid [*Deep Space Instrumentation Facility, NASA*]
OTA.............. Organic Trade Association
OTA.............. Organisation Mondiale du Tourisme et de l'Automobile [*World Touring and Automobile Organization*]
OTA.............. Ornithine Transaminase (DB)
OTA.............. Orthodontic Technicians Association [*British*] (DBA)
OTA.............. Orthopaedic Trauma Association (SAUS)
OTA.............. Ortho-Tolidine Arsenite [*Organic chemistry*]
OTA.............. Other Talk Address (IAA)
OTA.............. Other than Air (CINC)
ota .... Ottoman Turkish [*MARC language code*] [*Library of Congress*] (LCCP)
OTA.............. Outer Transport Area
OTA.............. Output Transformerless Amplifier (DICI)
OTA.............. Outside-Wheel Turning Angle [*Automotive engineering*]
OTA.............. Ovarian Tumor-Associated Antigen [*Medicine*] (MELL)
OTA.............. Overflight Top Attack (SAUS)
OTA.............. U. S. Congress Office of Technology Assessment (SAUS)
OTAA........... AASTRA Aerospace, Inc., Downsview, Ontario [*Library symbol*] [*National Library of Canada*] (BIB)
OTAA........... Office of Trade Adjustment Assistance [*Department of Labor*]
OTABN......... Ortho-Tolueno-Azo-Beta-Naphthol [*Medicine*] (MELL)
OTAC .... Acres Consulting Services Ltd., Toronto, Ontario [*Library symbol*] [*National Library of Canada*] (NLC)
OTAC .... Oceanic Trade Alliance Council International
OTAC .... Ordnance Tank-Automotive Command [*Merged with Weapons and Mobility Command*] [*Army*]
OTACS .... Old Timer Assay Commissioners Society [*Defunct*] (EA)
OTAD .... Addiction Research Foundation, Toronto, Ontario [*Library symbol*] [*National Library of Canada*] (NLC)
OTAD .... Office of Tributary Area Development [*Tennessee Valley Authority*]
OTAD .... Oversea Terminal Arrival Date [*Army*] (AABC)
OTADA .... Office of Tracking and Data Acquisition [*NASA*]
OTADL .... Outer Target Azimuth Datum Line
OTAE .... Atomic Energy of Canada [*L'Energie Atomique du Canada*] Toronto, Ontario [*Library symbol*] [*National Library of Canada*] (NLC)
OTAE .... [*The*] Old Testament in the Light of the Ancient East [*A publication*] (BJA)
OTAF .... Office of Technology Assessment and Forecast [*Patent and Trademark Office*] [*Washington, DC*]
OTAF .... Ontario Ministry of Agriculture and Food, Toronto, Ontario [*Library symbol*] [*National Library of Canada*] (NLC)
OTAF .... Operating Time at Failure (MCD)
OTAF Data Base... Office of Technology Assessment and Forecasts Data Base (NITA)
OTAG .... Art Gallery of Ontario, Toronto, Ontario [*Library symbol*] [*National Library of Canada*] (NLC)
OTAG .... Office of the Adjutant General [*Military*]
OTAG .... Operations & Training Analysis Group (SAUS)
OTAG .... Ozone Transport Assessment Group
OTAGAV....... Audiovisual Library, Art Gallery of Ontario, Toronto, Ontario [*Library symbol*] [*National Library of Canada*] (NLC)
Otago Pol Gaz... Otago Police Gazette [*1861-64*] [*New Zealand*] [*A publication*] (DLA)
OTAL .... Arts and Letters Club, Toronto, Ontario [*Library symbol*] [*National Library of Canada*] (NLC)
OTAN .... Organisation du Traite de l'Atlantique Nord [*North Atlantic Treaty Organization - NATO*] [*Brussels, Belgium*]
OTAN .... Organizacao do Tratado do Atlantico Norte [*North Atlantic Treaty Organization*] [*Portuguese*]
OT&A .... Operational Test and Acceptance (SAUS)
OT & E .... Operational Test and Evaluation [*Military*] (AFM)
OT&E .... Operational Testing and Evaluation (USDC)
OTANS .... Offshore Trade Association of Nova Scotia (SAUS)
OTANY .... Oil Trades Association of New York (EA)
OTANZ .... Output Tape Analyzer [*Computer science*] (VLIE)
OTAP .... Alternative Press Centre, Toronto, Ontario [*Library symbol*] [*National Library of Canada*] (NLC)
OTAQ .... Offer Therapist-Adolescent Questionnaire [*Personality development test*] [*Psychology*]
OTAR .... Archives of Ontario, Toronto, Ontario [*Library symbol*] [*National Library of Canada*] (NLC)
OTAR .... Overseas Tariffs and Regulations (DS)
OTAR .... Over-the-Air Rekey (SAUS)
OTARC .... Centennial College of Applied Arts and Technology, Scarborough, Ontario [*Library symbol*] [*National Library of Canada*] (NLC)
OTAS .... Observers Target Acquisition System (SAUS)
OTAS .... Observer Target Acquisition Subsystem (MCD)
OTAS .... On Top and Smooth [*NWS*] (FAAC)
OTASO .... Organizacao do Tratado da Asia Sul-Oriental [*South-East Asia Treaty Organization*] [*Portuguese*]
OTAT .... Office of Technical Assistance and Training (SAUS)
OTATO .... One Trip Air Travel Orders (SAUS)

O T AUTIC ... Other than Automatic [*Freight*]
OTAWA .... Occupational Therapy Association of Western Australia
O-TAWCS.... Okinawa-Tactical Air Weapons Control System (SAUS)
Otb.............. October (CDAI)
OTB............. Office Track Betting (SAUS)
OTB............. Off the Board [*Investment term*]
OTB............. Off-Track Betting
OTB............. Old Tired Broads
OTB............. On the Bow [*Nautical*]
OTB............. Open to Buy
OTB............. Operations Training Branch (SAUS)
OTB............. Orbiting Tanker Base [*NASA*] (NASA)
OTB............. Ordnance and Terminal Ballistics
OTB............. Ortho-Toluidine Boric Acid [*Organic chemistry*]
OTB............. Oval Fat Body (SAUS)
OTB............. Overseas Trust Bank [*Hong Kong*]
OTB............. Waverly Resource Library, Thunder Bay Public Library, Ontario [*Library symbol*] [*National Library of Canada*] (NLC)
OTBA .... Ocean Thermal Boundary Analysis Charts [*Marine science*] (MSC)
OTBA .... Owners, Traders, Breeders Association (NADA)
OTBA .... Terrace Bay Public Library, Ontario [*Library symbol*] [*National Library of Canada*] (NLC)
OTBBR .... Brodie Resource Library, Thunder Bay, Ontario [*Library symbol*] [*National Library of Canada*] (NLC)
OTBC .... Canadian Broadcasting Corp. [*Societe Radio-Canada*] Toronto, Ontario [*Library symbol*] [*National Library of Canada*] (NLC)
OTBCC .... Confederation College, Thunder Bay, Ontario [*Library symbol*] [*National Library of Canada*] (NLC)
OTBCG .... Blake, Cassels & Graydon, Toronto, Ontario [*Library symbol*] [*National Library of Canada*] (NLC)
OTBCGC....... Staff Library, Baycrest Centre for Geriatric Care, Toronto, Ontario [*Library symbol*] [*National Library of Canada*] (BIB)
OTBCIR .... Bell Canada Information Resource Centre, Toronto, Ontario [*Library symbol*] [*National Library of Canada*] (NLC)
OTBCO .... Technical Information Facility, Canadien Imperial Bank of Commerce, Toronto, Ontario [*Library symbol*] [*National Library of Canada*] (NLC)
OTBCP .... Program Archives, Canadian Broadcasting Corp. [*Archives des Emissions, Societe Radio-Canada*] Toronto, Ontario [*Library symbol*] [*National Library of Canada*] (NLC)
OTBD .... Doha/International [*Qatar*] [*ICAO location identifier*] (ICLI)
OTBD .... Outboard (ADA)
OTBDHC....... Thunder Bay District Health Council, Thunder Bay, Ontario [*Library symbol*] [*National Library of Canada*] (NLC)
OTBE .... Ontario Ministry of Education, Thunder Bay, Ontario [*Library symbol*] [*National Library of Canada*] (NLC)
OTBE........... Out of the Body Experiences [*Parapsychology*] (ECON)
OTBE........... Overtaken by Events [*Military*]
OTBGH........ General Hospital of Port Arthur, Thunder Bay, Ontario [*Library symbol*] [*National Library of Canada*] (NLC)
OTBH .... Thunder Bay Historical Museum Society, Ontario [*Library symbol*] [*National Library of Canada*] (NLC)
OTBhd.......... Oil-Tight Bulkhead (SAUS)
OTBHS .... Hammarskjold High School, Thunder Bay, Ontario [*Library symbol*] [*National Library of Canada*] (NLC)
OTBLA .... Audio Library Services of Northwestern Ontario, Lakehead University, Thunder Bay, Ontario [*Library symbol*] [*National Library of Canada*] (NLC)
OTBLL......... School of Library Technology, Lakehead University, Thunder Bay, Ontario [*Library symbol*] [*National Library of Canada*] (NLC)
OTBLP .... Staff Library, Lakehead Psychiatric Hospital, Thunder Bay, Ontario [*Library symbol*] [*National Library of Canada*] (NLC)
OTBM .... Technical Information Centre, Bank of Montreal, Willowdale, Ontario [*Library symbol*] [*National Library of Canada*] (NLC)
OTBMB .... Mary J. L. Black Library, Thunder Bay, Ontario [*Library symbol*] [*National Library of Canada*] (NLC)
OTBMBI .... Business Information Centre, Bank of Montreal, Toronto, Ontario [*Library symbol*] [*National Library of Canada*] (BIB)
OTBMC .... Medical Library, McKellar General Hospital, Thunder Bay, Ontario [*Library symbol*] [*National Library of Canada*] (NLC)
OTBML .... Music Library, Canadian National Institute for the Blind, Toronto, Ontario [*Library symbol*] [*National Library of Canada*] (BIB)
OTBNL .... National Library Division, Canadian National Institute for the Blind, Toronto, Ontario [*Library symbol*] [*National Library of Canada*] (NLC)
OTBNR........ Learning Resource Centre, BNR Ltd., Toronto, Ontario [*Library symbol*] [*National Library of Canada*] (NLC)
OTBNS .... Bell Northern Software Research, Toronto, Ontario [*Library symbol*] [*National Library of Canada*] (NLC)
OTBOC .... Ontario Cancer Treatment and Research Foundation, Thunder Bay, Ontario [*Library symbol*] [*National Library of Canada*] (NLC)
OTBP .... Blaney, Pasternak, Smela, Eagleson & Watson, Toronto, Ontario [*Library symbol*] [*National Library of Canada*] (NLC)
OTBQ .... Occupational Therapists' Board of Queensland [*Australia*]
OTBR .... Barringer Research Ltd., Rexdale, Ontario [*Library symbol*] [*National Library of Canada*] (NLC)
OTBS .... One True Bracketing Style (VLIE)
OTBS .... On-the-Bottom Sonobuoy (MCD)
OTBSL .... Bassel, Sullivan & Leake, Toronto, Ontario [*Library symbol*] [*National Library of Canada*] (NLC)
OTBSSC ...... Over Thirty but Still Swinging Club
OTBV .... Oxidizer Turbine Bypass Valve (KSC)
OTBV .... Victoriaville Branch, Thunder Bay Public Library, Ontario [*Library symbol*] [*National Library of Canada*] (BIB)
OTC............. Bol [*Chad*] [*Airport symbol*] (AD)

OTC............ Faculty of Education, University of Toronto, Ontario [*Library symbol*] [*National Library of Canada*] (NLC)
OTC............ Objective, Time, and Cost
OTC............ Ocean Transshipment Cargo (SAUS)
OTC............ Office of Technical Cooperation [*United Nations*]
OTC............ Office of Telecommunications (SAUS)
OTC............ Office of Temporary Controls
OTC............ Office of Transport and Communications (SAUS)
OTC............ Officer in Tactical Command [*Air Force*]
OTC............ Officers' Training Camp [*World War I*]
OTC............ Officers' Training Corps
OTC............ Officers Transit Camp [*British military*] (DMA)
OTC............ Officer Training Center [*Navy*]
OTC............ Office Telecommunication Commission (SAUS)
OTC............ Offshore Technology Conference
OTC............ Ohio Motor Freight Tariff Committee Inc., Columbus OH [*STAC*]
OTC............ Old Testament Commentary [*A publication*] (BJA)
OTC............ Old Timers' Club (EA)
OTC............ Once-Through Cooling [*Nuclear energy*] (NRCH)
OTC............ One-Stop Charter (SAUS)
OTC............ One-Stop Tour Charter [*Airline fare*]
OTC............ One-Time Carbon [*Paper*] (PDAA)
OTC............ One-Time Charge (VLIE)
OTC............ Online Training Center (MELL)
OTC............ Open Tubular Column [*For gas chromatography*]
OTC............ Operado de Terminal de Contenedores [*Container Terminal Operator*] [*Shipping*] [*Spanish*]
OTC............ Operador de Transporte Combinado [*Combined Transport Operator*] [*Spanish*] [*Business term*]
OTC............ Operating Telephone Company (SAUS)
OTC............ Operational Techniques Conference
OTC............ Operational Test Center [*NASA*] (KSC)
OTC............ Operational Test Command [*Army*]
OTC............ Operational Test Coordinator [*Military*] (CAAL)
OTC............ Operational Training Capability [*Air Force*] (AFM)
OTC............ Operational Training Centre (SAUS)
OTC............ Operational Training Command (MCD)
OTC............ Operational Training Course (SAUS)
OTC............ Operatore di Trasporto Combinato [*Combined Transport Operator*] [*Italian*] [*Business term*]
OTC............ Orbiter Test Conductor [*NASA*] (NASA)
OTC............ Orbiting Trajectory Computations
OTC............ Order of Three Crusades (EA)
OTC............ Ordnance Technical Committee [*Military*] (MUGU)
OTC............ Ordnance Training Command [*Army*]
OTC............ Oregon Technical Council (SAUS)
OTC............ Organization for Trade Cooperation [*GATT*]
OTC............ Organize Training Center (EA)
OTC............ Organotin Compound [*Organic chemistry*]
OTC............ Orginating Toll Center (SAUS)
OTC............ Orginating Toll Circuit (SAUS)
OTC............ Orginating Trunk Center (SAUS)
OTC............ Original Trenton Cracker Co. [*Maker of Chowder & Oyster Crackers, claimed by some to be the oldest continuously manufactured American food product*]
OTC............ Originating Toll Center [*Telecommunications*] (TEL)
OTC............ Originating Toll Circuit [*Telecommunications*] (IAA)
OTC............ Originating Trunk Center [*Telecommunications*] (IAA)
OTC............ Ornithine Transcarbamoylase [*Also, OCT*] [*An enzyme*]
OTC............ Orthogonal Transform Coding (CCCA)
OTC............ Orthogonal Tree Cycles (SAUS)
OTC............ Osaka Transformer Co. Ltd. (SAUS)
OTC............ Oshkosh Truck Corp.
OTC............ Ottawa Transit Commission (SAUS)
OTC............ Otterbein College, Westerville, OH [*OCLC symbol*] (OCLC)
OTC............ Outcrop (SAUS)
OTC............ Outer Tube Centerline
OTC............ Output Technology Corporation (VLIE)
OTC............ Oval Target Cell (DMAA)
OTC............ Overhead Travelling Crane (SAUS)
OTC............ Overseas Telecommunications Commission (NITA)
OTC............ Overseas Telecommunications Commission of Australia (BARN)
OTC............ Overseas Telecommunications Corporation (SAUS)
OTC............ Over-the-Calf [*Women's fashions*] (IIA)
OTC............ Over-the-Capacitor [*Sockets*]
OTC............ Over-the-Counter [*Pharmacy*]
OTC............ Over-the-Counter [*Also, O/C*] [*Stock exchange term*]
OTC............ Ownership Transfer Corporation (SAUS)
OTC............ Oxygen Transfer Compressor
OTC............ Oxytetracycline [*Antibiotic*]
OTCA.......... Ozone Transport Commission [*State environmental agencies*]
OTCA.......... Olson 30 Class Association (EA)
OTCA.......... Omnibus Trade and Competitiveness Act of 1988 (JAGO)
OTCA.......... Ontario College of Art, Toronto, Ontario [*Library symbol*] [*National Library of Canada*] (NLC)
OTCA.......... Oxothiazolidinecarboxylic Acid [*Biochemistry*]
OTCAG........ Canada Arctic Gas Study Ltd., Toronto, Ontario [*Library symbol*] [*National Library of Canada*] (NLC)
OTCAS........ Canadian Association in Support of the Native Peoples, Toronto, Ontario [*Library symbol*] [*National Library of Canada*] (NLC)
OTCBS......... Central Baptist Seminary and Bible College, Toronto, Ontario [*Library symbol*] [*National Library of Canada*] (NLC)
OTCC.......... Operator Test Control Console (MCD)
OTCC.......... Organic Thermal Control Coating

OTCC.......... United Church of Canada Archives, Toronto, Ontario [*Library symbol*] [*National Library of Canada*] (NLC)
OTCCC........ Cross Cultural Communication Centre, Toronto, Ontario [*Library symbol*] [*National Library of Canada*] (NLC)
OTCCC........ Open Type Control Circuit Contacts (MSA)
OTCCL......... Currie, Coopers & Lybrand Ltd., Toronto, Ontario [*Library symbol*] [*National Library of Canada*] (NLC)
OTCCP........ Canadian Centre for Philanthropy, Toronto, Ontario [*Library symbol*] [*National Library of Canada*] (NLC)
OTCCRT....... Technical Standards Division, Ontario Ministry of Consumer and Commercial Relations, Toronto, Ontario [*Library symbol*] [*National Library of Canada*] (NLC)
OTCD.......... Ornithine Carbomoyltransferase Deficiency (DMAA)
OTCD.......... Over-the-Counter-Drug (MEDA)
OTCE.......... Central Library, North York, Ontario [*Library symbol*] [*National Library of Canada*] (NLC)
OTCEA........ [*The*] Canadian Education Association [*L'Association Canadienne d'Education*] Toronto, Ontario [*Library symbol*] [*National Library of Canada*] (NLC)
OTCF.......... H. Ward Smith Library, Centre of Forensic Sciences, Toronto, Ontario [*Library symbol*] [*National Library of Canada*] (NLC)
OTCFA........ Occupational Therapy Comprehensive Functional Assessment
OTCFX........ Price T. Rowe: Small-Cap Stock [*Mutual fund ticker symbol*] (SG)
OTCGL........ Campbell, Godfrey & Lewtas, Toronto, Ontario [*Library symbol*] [*National Library of Canada*] (NLC)
OTCGR........ Canadian Gas Research Institute, Don Mills, Ontario [*Library symbol*] [*National Library of Canada*] (NLC)
OTCGW....... Clarkson, Gordon, Woods, Gordon, Toronto, Ontario [*Library symbol*] [*National Library of Canada*] (NLC)
OTCH.......... Anglican Church House, Toronto, Ontario [*Library symbol*] [*National Library of Canada*] (NLC)
OTCH.......... Obedience Trial Champion [*Dog training*]
OTCh.......... Obedience Trial Champion [*Prefix*]
OTCHA........ Canadian Hospital Association [*Association des Hopitaux du Canada*] Toronto, Ontario [*Library symbol*] [*National Library of Canada*] (NLC)
OTCHAR....... Anglican Church of Canada Archives, Toronto, Ontario [*Library symbol*] [*National Library of Canada*] (NLC)
OTCI.......... OTC [*Overseas Telecommunications Commission*] International Ltd. [*Australia*] [*Telecommunications service*] (TSSD)
OTCIA........ Canadian Institute of International Affairs [*Institut Canadien des Affaires Internationales*] Toronto, Ontario [*Library symbol*] [*National Library of Canada*] (NLC)
OTCIB........ Canadian Imperial Bank of Commerce, Toronto, Ontario [*Library symbol*] [*National Library of Canada*] (NLC)
OTCIL......... Central Library, C-I-L, Inc., North York, Ontario [*Library symbol*] [*National Library of Canada*] (NLC)
OTCILL........ Law Library, C-I-L, Inc., North York, Ontario [*Library symbol*] [*National Library of Canada*] (NLC)
OTCIXS .... Officer in Tactical Command Information Exchange Subsystem [*Navy*] (ANA)
OTCJC........ Genealogical Society Library, Church of Jesus Christ of Latter-Day Saints, Etobicoke, Ontario [*Library symbol*] [*National Library of Canada*] (NLC)
OTCL.......... Connaught Laboratories Ltd., Willowdale, Ontario [*Library symbol*] [*National Library of Canada*] (NLC)
OTCLA........ Confederation Life Association, Toronto, Ontario [*Library symbol*] [*National Library of Canada*] (NLC)
OTCLANT .... Fleet Operational Training Command, Atlantic [*Usually, COTCLANT*]
OTCLEV....... Ozone Transport Commission Low-Emissions Vehicle
OTCLH........ Research and Information Library, Canadian Life and Health Insurance Association, Toronto, Ontario [*Library symbol*] [*National Library of Canada*] (BIB)
OTCM.......... Canadian School of Missions and Ecumenical Institute, Toronto, Ontario [*Library symbol*] [*National Library of Canada*] (NLC)
OTCM.......... Ocean Systems Technician, Master Chief [*Navy rating*] (DNAB)
OTCM.......... Orbiter Thermal Control Model [*NASA*]
OTCM.......... Ordnance Technical Committee Minutes [*Military*]
OTCM.......... Royce Micro-Cap Tr [*NASDAQ symbol*] (TTSB)
OTCM.......... Royce OTC [*Over the Counter*] Micro Capital Fund [*NASDAQ symbol*] (SAG)
OTCMC .... Canadian Memorial Chiropractic College, Toronto, Ontario [*Library symbol*] [*National Library of Canada*] (NLC)
OTCMCC..... Old Time Country Music Club of Canada (EA)
OTCMH....... Saul A. Silverman Library, C. M. Hincks Treatment Centre, Toronto, Ontario [*Library symbol*] [*National Library of Canada*] (BIB)
OTCMHA..... Canadian Mental Health Association, Toronto, Ontario [*Library symbol*] [*National Library of Canada*] (BIB)
OTCMLA ..... Canadian Music Library Association [*Association Canadienne des Bibliotheques Musicales*] Toronto, Ontario [*Library symbol*] [*National Library of Canada*] (NLC)
OTCMS .... Operations Training Certification Management System [*NASA*]
OTCOM .... Cominco Ltd., Toronto, Ontario [*Library symbol*] [*National Library of Canada*] (NLC)
OTCOP........ Olympic Training Center Outreach Program
OTCOS......... Concord Scientific Corp., Downsview, Ontario [*Library symbol*] [*National Library of Canada*] (NLC)
OTCOU........ Council of Ontario Universities, Toronto, Ontario [*Library symbol*] [*National Library of Canada*] (NLC)
OTCP .... Canada Packers Ltd., Toronto, Ontario [*Library symbol*] [*National Library of Canada*] (NLC)
OTCPAC....... Fleet Operational Training Command, Pacific [*Usually, COTCPAC*]
OTC Paper... One-Time Carbon Paper (SAUS)
OTCPB......... Toronto City Planning Board Library, Ontario, [*Library symbol*] [*National Library of Canada*] (NLC)

OTCQM .... Office of the Theater Chief Quartermaster [*World War II*]

OTCR .... Office of Technical Cooperation and Research [*Department of State*]

OTCR .... Ontario Ministry of Culture and Communications, Toronto, Ontario [*Library symbol*] [*National Library of Canada*] (NLC)

OTCRC .... National Office Library, Canadian Red Cross Society [*Bibliotheque du Siege Social, Societe Canadienne de la Croix-Rouge*] Toronto, Ontario [*Library symbol*] [*National Library of Canada*] (NLC)

OTCRx .... Over-the-Counter Drug (MEDA)

OTCS .... Ocean Systems Technician, Senior Chief [*Navy rating*] (DNAB)

OTCS .... Ontario Ministry of Correctional Services, Toronto, Ontario [*Library symbol*] [*National Library of Canada*] (NLC)

OTCS .... Operational Teletype Communications Subsystem

OTCS .... Optical Transient Current Spectroscopy

OTCSA .... Canadian Standards Association, Rexdale, Ontario [*Library symbol*] [*National Library of Canada*] (NLC)

OTCSAO .... Construction Safety Association of Ontario, Toronto, Ontario [*Library symbol*] [*National Library of Canada*] (NLC)

OTCSC .... Civil Service Commission of Ontario, Toronto, Ontario [*Library symbol*] [*National Library of Canada*] (NLC)

OTCSE .... Canadian Selection, Toronto, Ontario [*Library symbol*] [*National Library of Canada*] (NLC)

OTCSS .... CANEBSCO Subscription Service Ltd., Toronto, Ontario [*Library symbol*] [*National Library of Canada*] (NLC)

OTCT .... Canadian Tax Foundation [*Association Canadienne d'Etudes Fiscales*] Toronto, Ontario [*Library symbol*] [*National Library of Canada*] (NLC)

OTCTA .... Canadian Telebook Agency, Toronto, Ontario [*Library symbol*] [*National Library of Canada*] (NLC)

OTCTAR ...... Division of Records and Archives, City of Toronto (NLC)

OTCTH .... Town Hall, Collins Canada, Toronto, Ontario [*Library symbol*] [*National Library of Canada*] (NLC)

OTCTVN ...... CTV News Research Library, CTV Television Network, Toronto, Ontario [*Library symbol*] [*National Library of Canada*] (NLC)

OTCW .... Canada Wire & Cable Co. Ltd., Toronto, Ontario [*Library symbol*] [*National Library of Canada*] (NLC)

OTCWB .... Welding Institute of Canada, Oakville, Ontario [*Library symbol*] [*National Library of Canada*] (NLC)

OTCWT .... Canadian Waste Technology, Inc., Toronto, Ontario [*Library symbol*] [*National Library of Canada*] (NLC)

OTD .... Contadora [*Panama*] [*Airport symbol*] (OAG)

OTD .... Doctor of Occupational Therapy (PGP)

OTD .... Ocean Technology Division (SAUS)

OTD .... Ocean Travel Development (DS)

OTD .... Oculotrichodysplasia (DMAA)

OTD .... Office of Technology Development (COE)

OTD .... Official Table of Distances (AFM)

OTD .... Official Tour Directory (TRID)

OTD .... Offset, Tilted Dipole [*Model of Uranus' magnetic field*]

OTD .... Oil Turbine Drive

OTD .... Old Total Depth (SAUS)

OTD .... On the Deck

OTD .... On-Time Delivery (SAUS)

OTD .... Operational Technical Documentation [*NASA*] (NASA)

OTD .... Operational Test Director [*Navy*]

OTD .... Operations and Technical Data [*Engineering*]

OTD .... Operator Training Device (SAUS)

OTD .... Optical Technology Development (ACAE)

OTD .... Optical Time Division (SAUS)

OTD .... Optical Time Domain (EECA)

OTD .... Optical Tracking Device

OTD .... Optical Transient Detector

OTD .... Optimal Terminal Descent (PDAA)

OTD .... Oral Temperature Device (MCD)

OTD .... Orbital Test Direction (SAUS)

OTD .... Orbital Test Directive (SAUS)

OTD .... Orbiter Test Director [*NASA*] (NASA)

OTD .... Orbit Test Direction [*or Directive*] (IAA)

OTD .... Order to Delivery [*Automotive manufacturing*]

OTD .... Organ Tolerance Dose [*Medicine*] (DMAA)

OTD .... Original Transmission Density (OA)

OTD .... Ortho-Toluenediamine [*Organic chemistry*]

OTD .... Out the Door (DAVI)

OTD .... Overseas-Trained Doctors

OTDA .... DSMA Acton Ltd., Toronto, Ontario [*Library symbol*] [*National Library of Canada*] (NLC)

OTDA .... Office of Tracking and Data Acquisition [*NASA*]

OTDA .... Other-Than-Defined Adult (SAUS)

OTD&C .... Offshore Technology Development & Consulting (EFIS)

OTD&SP ...... Office of Technical Data and Standardization Policy (SAUS)

OTDAR .... Alexander Raxlen Memorial Library, Doctors Hospital, Toronto, Ontario [*Library symbol*] [*National Library of Canada*] (NLC)

OTDB .... Operations Tasking Data Base (SAUS)

OTDC .... Dominion Colour Ltd., Toronto, Ontario [*Library symbol*] [*National Library of Canada*] (NLC)

OTDC .... Observational Test and Development Center [*National Weather Service*] (NOAA)

OTDC .... Optical Target Designation Computer

OTDCB .... Dictionary of Canadian Biography, Toronto, Ontario [*Library symbol*] [*National Library of Canada*] (BIB)

OTDD .... Optical Target Detecting Device

OTDE .... Ontario Ministry of Education, Toronto, Ontario [*Library symbol*] [*National Library of Canada*] (NLC)

OTDH .... Ontario Ministry of Health, Toronto, Ontario [*Library symbol*] [*National Library of Canada*] (NLC)

OTDHA .... De Havilland Aircraft of Canada Ltd., Downsview, Ontario [*Library symbol*] [*National Library of Canada*] (NLC)

OTDHC .... Oceanographic Technical Data Handling Committee

OTDHL .... Laboratory Services, Ontario Ministry of Health, Toronto, Ontario [*Library symbol*] [*National Library of Canada*] (NLC)

OTDL .... Ontario Ministry of Labour, Toronto, Ontario [*Library symbol*] [*National Library of Canada*] (NLC)

OTDM .... Mines Library, Ontario Ministry of Natural Resources, Toronto, Ontario [*Library symbol*] [*National Library of Canada*] (NLC)

OTDM .... Optical Time Division Multiplexer (SAUS)

OTDM .... Optical Time Division Multiplexing (SAUS)

OTDO .... Donwood Institute, Toronto, Ontario [*Library symbol*] [*National Library of Canada*] (BIB)

OTDR .... Optical Fiber Time-Domain Reflectometer [*Computer science*]

OTDR .... Optical Test Data Receiver (SAUS)

OTDR .... Optical Time Domain Reflectometer (NITA)

OTDR .... Optical Time Domain Reflectometry (SAUS)

OTDR .... Outdoor

OTDRE .... Ontario Ministry of Treasury and Economics, Toronto, Ontario [*Library symbol*] [*National Library of Canada*] (NLC)

OTDT .... Ontario Ministry of Transportation and Communications, Toronto, Ontario [*Library symbol*] [*National Library of Canada*] (NLC)

OTDT .... Operational Test, Development Test

OTDT .... Operations Training Development Team [*Air Force*]

OTDT .... Over Temperature Delta T (SAUS)

OTDU .... Ontario Ministry of Colleges and Universities, Toronto, Ontario [*Library symbol*] [*National Library of Canada*] (NLC)

OTDW .... Day-Wilson-Campbell, Toronto, Ontario [*Library symbol*] [*National Library of Canada*] (BIB)

OTE .... Emmanuel College, Victoria University, Toronto, Ontario [*Library symbol*] [*National Library of Canada*] (NLC)

OTE .... Odd Transversal Electrical (SAUS)

OTE .... On-Target Earnings [*Sales industry*] (ODBW)

OTE .... Ontario Ministry of Treasury and Economics Library [*UTLAS symbol*]

OTE .... Operational Test and Evaluation [*Army*] (AABC)

OTE .... Operational Test Equipment [*NASA*] (KSC)

OTE .... Operator Training Equipment (SAUS)

OTE .... Optically Transparent Electrode

OTE .... Optical Tracking Electronics

OTE .... Organismos Tilepikoinonion Ellados [*Hellenic Telecommunications Organization*] [*Greek*]

OTE .... Other Technical Effort

OTE .... Outer Tube Equipment

OTE .... Overtaken by Events [*US Congress*]

OTE .... Oxalyl Thiolester [*Biochemistry*]

OTEA .... Office of Trade & Economic Analysis [*U.S. Department of Commerce*] [*Internet resource*]

OTEA .... Operational Test and Evaluation Agency [*Army*]

OTEA .... Oval Track Equipment Association (EA)

OTEAOW ...... Atmospheric Environment Service (ODIT Ontario Weather Centre), Environment Canada [*Service de l'Environnement Atmospherique (Centre Meteorologique de l'Ontario), Environnement Canada*] Toronto, Ontario [*Library symbol*] [*National Library of Canada*] (NLC)

OTEBE .... Resource Library, Board of Education for the City of Etobicoke, Ontario [*Library symbol*] [*National Library of Canada*] (NLC)

OTEC .... Education Centre, Toronto Board of Education, Ontario [*Library symbol*] [*National Library of Canada*] (NLC)

OTEC .... Ocean Thermal Energy Conservation (SAUS)

OTEC .... Ocean Thermal Energy Conversion

OTEC .... Ontario Teacher Education Colleges (SAUS)

OTEC .... Operational Test and Evaluation Center (SAUS)

OTEC .... Operational Test and Evaluation Command [*Army*] (AAGC)

OTEC .... Oriental Telephone and Electric Company (SAUS)

OTEC .... Osage Tribal Education Committee [*Department of the Interior*] [*Muskogee, OK*] (EGAO)

OTECA .... Ocean Thermal Energy Conversion Act of 1980

OTECH .... Oceaneering Technology Integration (ABAC)

OTEC R&D ... Ocean Thermal Energy Conversion Research and Development (SAUS)

OTECS .... Ocean Thermal Energy Conversion Systems [*Department of Energy*]

OTECU .... Colleges and Universitites, Ontario Ministry of Education, Toronto, Ontario [*Library symbol*] [*National Library of Canada*] (NLC)

OTEE .... Teeswater Branch, Bruce County Public Library, Ontario [*Library symbol*] [*National Library of Canada*] (NLC)

OTEF .... Operational Test and Evaluation Facility (ACAE)

OTEF .... Operational Training and Evaluation Facility

OTEF .... Overseas Troop Entertainment Fund (SAUS)

OTEM .... ESSO [*Standard Oil*] Minerals of Canada, Toronto, Ontario [*Library symbol*] [*National Library of Canada*] (NLC)

OTEMAC ...... Temagami Community Library, Ontario [*Library symbol*] [*National Library of Canada*] (NLC)

OTEMAS ...... Osaka International Textile Machinery Show

OTEMC .... Elizabeth McRae Associates, Toronto, Ontario [*Library symbol*] [*Obsolete*] [*National Library of Canada*] (NLC)

OTEMP .... Overtemperature (NASA)

OTEMPO ...... Operating Temporaries

OTEMR .... Conservation and Renewable Energy Office, Energy, Mines, and Resources Canada [*Bureau de la Conservation de l'Energie et de l'Energie Renouvelable, Energie, Mines, et Ressources Canada*] Toronto, Ontario [*Library symbol*] [*National Library of Canada*] (NLC)

OTEP .... Office of Transportation Energy Policy [*Department of Transportation*]

OTEP .... Operational Test and Evaluation Plan [*Military*] (AFM)

OTEPL.......... Etobicoke Public Library, Ontario [*Library symbol*] [*National Library of Canada*] (NLC)

OTEPS .... Environmental Protection Service, Environment Canada [*Service de la Protection de l'Environnement, Environnement Canada*] Toronto, Ontario [*Library symbol*] [*National Library of Canada*] (NLC)

OTEPSE....... Environmental Emergency Library, Environmental Protection Service, Environment Canada [*Bibliotheque des Incidences Environnementales, Service de la Protection de l'Environnement, Environnement Canada*] Toronto, Ontario [*Library symbol*] [*National Library of Canada*] (NLC)

OTER .... Ontario Institute for Studies in Education, Toronto, Ontario [*Library symbol*] [*National Library of Canada*] (NLC)

OTES........... Operational Test and Evaluation Squadron [*Military*]

OTES........... Optical Technology Experiment Study (SAUS)

OTES........... Optical Technology Experiment System

OTES........... Orbiter Thermal Effects Simulator [*NASA*]

OTET .... Ontario Educational Communications Authority, Toronto, Ontario [*Library symbol*] [*National Library of Canada*] (NLC)

OTET .... TVOntario, Toronto, Ontario [*Library symbol*] [*National Library of Canada*] (NLC)

OTEU .... Office and Technical Employees (International) Union

O TEUT .... Old Teutonic [*Language, etc.*] (ROG)

OTEVFOR.... Operational Test & Evaluation for Operational Requirements (SAUS)

OTEX .... Open Text Corp. [*NASDAQ symbol*] (SAG)

OTEXA .... Office of Textiles and Apparel [*Department of Commerce*] (GFGA)

OTEXF......... Open Text [*NASDAQ symbol*] (TTSB)

OTEY........... East York Public Library, Toronto, Ontario [*Library symbol*] [*National Library of Canada*] (NLC)

OTEYBE....... Professional Library, Board of Education for the Borough of East York, Toronto, Ontario [*Library symbol*] [*National Library of Canada*] (NLC)

OTF............. Institute of Environment Studies, University of Toronto, Ontario [*Library symbol*] [*National Library of Canada*] (NLC)

OTF............. Ocean Test Fixture (SAUS)

OTF............. Octamer Transcription Factor [*Genetics*]

OTF............. Off-the-Film [*Photography*] (WDMC)

OTF............. Off-the-Film Metering [*Olympus cameras*]

OTF............. Ontario Teachers Federation (AEBS)

OTF............. Ontario Technology Fund (SAUS)

OTF............. On the Floor [*Computer language*] [*Computer science*]

OTF............. On-the-Fly [*Computer compression program*] (PCM)

OTF............. Open Token Foundation (BTTJ)

OTF............. Operational Test Flight (ACAE)

OTF............. Optical Transfer Function

OTF............. Optimum Traffic Condition [*Radio*] (IAA)

OTF............. Optimum Traffic Frequency [*Radio*]

OTF............. Oral Transfer Factor [*Virology*]

OTF............. Orbital Test Flight (MCD)

OTF............. Ordered Triangular Factorization (SAUS)

OTF............. Order to Fire (SAUS)

OTF............. Organ Transplant Fund (SAUS)

OTF............. Other than Flat [*Freight*]

OTFA........... Office of Technical Financial Assistance (ABAC)

OTFC........... Official 3 Stooges Fan Club [*Defunct*] (EA)

OTFC........... Ontario Ministry of Consumer and Commercial Relations, Toronto, Ontario [*Library symbol*] [*National Library of Canada*] (NLC)

OTFC........... Overflight Traffic [*Aviation*] (FAAC)

OTFCS......... On-Target Fire Control System (MCD)

OTFE........... Optical Terminal Flight Evaluation

OTFE........... Oscillatory Thermocapillary Flow Experiment (SAUS)

OTFEC......... Fenco Consultants Ltd., Toronto, Ontario [*Library symbol*] [*National Library of Canada*] (NLC)

OTFH .... Forest Hill Public Library, Toronto, Ontario [*Library symbol*] [*National Library of Canada*] (NLC)

OTFM........... Fire Marshal of Ontario, Toronto, Ontario [*Library symbol*] [*National Library of Canada*] (NLC)

OTFN........... Information Centre, Falconbridge Nickel Mines Ltd., Toronto, Ontario [*Library symbol*] [*National Library of Canada*] (NLC)

OT/FOT .... Operational Test/Follow-On Operational Test

OTFP........... Fisons Corp. Ltd., Markham, Ontario [*Library symbol*] [*National Library of Canada*] (NLC)

OTFP........... Octylthio(trifluoro)propanone [*Biochemistry*]

OTFP........... Operational Traffic Flow Planning (GAVI)

OTFP........... Other than Full Paid [*IRS*]

OTFR........... Overall Transfer Function Response

OTF Reporter... Ontario Teachers Federation Reporter (SAUS)

OTFT........... Financial Times, Don Mills, Ontario [*Library symbol*] [*National Library of Canada*] (NLC)

OTFT........... Observer Tit for Tat [*Gene theory*]

OT/FT.......... Operational Test/Follow-On Test [*Missiles*] (DOMA)

OTFTS......... Outfits

OTG............. Information Centre, Glaxo Canada, Inc., Toronto, Ontario [*Library symbol*] [*National Library of Canada*] (BIB)

OTG............. Objective Transmission Grating (SAUS)

OTG............. Oil Temperature Gauge (MSA)

OTG............. OPTEVFOR [*Operational Test and Evaluation Force*] Tactics Guide [*Navy*] (CAAL)

OTG............. Option Table Generator

OTG............. Otolith Test Goggles [*NASA*] (KSC)

OTG............. Worthington [*Minnesota*] [*Airport symbol*] (OAG)

OTGA........... Information Centre, Giffels Associates Ltd., Rexdale, Ontario [*Library symbol*] [*National Library of Canada*] (NLC)

OTGAR......... Engineering Library, Garrett Canada, Rexdale, Ontario [*Library symbol*] [*National Library of Canada*] (BIB)

OTGB .... Library and Audio-Visual Services, George Brown College of Applied Arts and Technology, Toronto, Ontario [*Library symbol*] [*National Library of Canada*] (BIB)

OTGFM......... Management Science Department, General Foods, Inc.; Don Mills, Ontario [*Library symbol*] [*National Library of Canada*] (NLC)

OTGG........... Goodman & Goodman, Toronto, Ontario [*Library symbol*] [*National Library of Canada*] (BIB)

OTGH .... Fudger Medical Library, Toronto General Hospital, Ontario [*Library symbol*] [*National Library of Canada*] (NLC)

OTGHPP....... Ocean Thermal Gradient Hydraulic Power Plant

OTGM........... Globe and Mail, Toronto, Ontario [*Library symbol*] [*National Library of Canada*] (NLC)

OTGMC .... Gulf Minerals Canada Ltd., Toronto, Ontario [*Library symbol*] [*National Library of Canada*] (NLC)

OTGOH......... Gowling & Henderson, Toronto, Ontario [*Library symbol*] [*National Library of Canada*] (NLC)

OTGS .... Gore & Storrie Ltd., Toronto, Ontario [*Library symbol*] [*National Library of Canada*] (NLC)

OTGS .... Ocean Thermal Gradient System [*National Science Foundation*]

OTGS .... OTG Software [*NASDAQ symbol*] (SG)

OTGSB .... Bibliographic Centre, Ontario Ministry of Government Services, Toronto, Ontario [*Library symbol*] [*National Library of Canada*] (NLC)

OTGSI .... CTS Information Resource Centre, Ontario Ministry of Government Services, Toronto [*Library symbol*] [*National Library of Canada*] (BIB)

OTH .... Independent Institute, NAD, Dublin, OH [*OCLC symbol*] (OCLC)

OTH .... North Bend [*Oregon*] [*Airport symbol*] (OAG)

OTH .... Oil-Tight Hatch [*Shipfitting*]

OTH .... Ontario Hydro, Toronto, Ontario [*Library symbol*] [*National Library of Canada*] (NLC)

OTH .... Optical Time History (MCD)

OTH .... Othello [*Washington*] [*Seismograph station code, US Geological Survey*] (SEIS)

Oth............. Othello [*Shakespearean work*]

OTH .... Other (DAVI)

oth .... Other (VRA)

OTH .... Other than Hand [*Freight*]

OTH .... Other than Honorable Conditions [*Military*] (AABC)

OTH .... Over-the-Horizon [*RADAR*]

OTHA .... Hatch Associates Ltd., Toronto, Ontario [*Library symbol*] [*National Library of Canada*] (NLC)

OTHB .... Over-the-Horizon Back-Scatter [*RADAR*]

OTHB .... Toronto Historical Society, Ontario [*Library symbol*] [*National Library of Canada*] (BIB)

OTHB Radar... Over-the-Horizon Backscatter Radar (SAUS)

OTH-B WCRS... Over-the-Horizon Backscatter West Coast Radar System (SAUS)

OTHC .... Humber College of Applied Arts and Technology, Rexdale, Ontario [*Library symbol*] [*National Library of Canada*] (NLC)

OTH/DA........ Over-the-Horizon/Damage Assessment [*Navy*] (CAAL)

OTHDC & T... Over-the-Horizon Detection, Classification, and Targeting (NVT)

OTH-DC&T... Over-the-Horizon Detection, Classification and Tracking (SAUS)

OTHDT .... Over-The-Horizon Detection & Targeting (SAUS)

OTH-E .... Over-the-Horizon - Expanded

OTHE .... Thessalon Union Public Library, Ontario [*Library symbol*] [*National Library of Canada*] (NLC)

OTHER .... Open Tubular Heterogeneous Enzyme Reactor [*Biochemical engineering*]

OTHF .... Over the Horizon Forwardscatter (SAUS)

OTH-F .... Over-the-Horizon - Forward Scatter

OTHG .... Over the Hill Gang, International (EA)

OTHL .... Advanced Technology Centre, Honeywell Ltd., Willowdale, Ontario [*Library symbol*] [*National Library of Canada*] (NLC)

OTHMC .... Information Resources, Hay Management Consultants, Toronto, Ontario [*Library symbol*] [*National Library of Canada*] (NLC)

OTHMH .... Humber Memorial Hospital, Weston, Ontario [*Library symbol*] [*National Library of Canada*] (NLC)

OTHO .... Thornbury Public Library, Ontario [*Library symbol*] [*National Library of Canada*] (NLC)

OTHOP......... Quebec & Ontario Paper Co. Ltd., Thorold, Ontario [*Library symbol*] [*National Library of Canada*] (NLC)

OTHOR......... Thornhill Public Library, Ontario [*Library symbol*] [*National Library of Canada*] (NLC)

OTHORF....... Metallurgical Laboratory, Falconbridge Nickel Mines Ltd., Thornhill, Ontario [*Library symbol*] [*National Library of Canada*] (NLC)

OTHORO ...... Thorold Public Library, Ontario [*Library symbol*] [*National Library of Canada*] (BIB)

OTHR .... Ontario Hydro Research, Toronto, Ontario [*Library symbol*] [*National Library of Canada*] (NLC)

OTHR .... Over-the-Horizon RADAR (MCD)

OTHS .... Other Services (TVEL)

OTHSA .... Orphan Train Heritage Society of America (EA)

OTHSC .... Hospital for Sick Children, Toronto, Ontario [*Library symbol*] [*National Library of Canada*] (NLC)

OTHSSM...... Over-the-Horizon Ship-to-Ship Missile

OTH-SW........ Over-The-Horizon, Surface Wave (SAUS)

OTH-T .... Over the Horizon-Targeting (ACAE)

OTHT .... Over-the-Horizon Targeting (NVT)

OTH-T .... Over-the-Horizon-Targeting (SAUS)

OTHT-G........ Over the Horizon Targeting Gold (SAUS)

OTHU .... Huntec Ltd., Toronto, Ontario [*Library symbol*] [*National Library of Canada*] (NLC)

OTI............. Morotai Island [*Indonesia*] [*Airport symbol*] (OAG)

OTI............. Newport, RI [*Location identifier*] [*FAA*] (FAAL)

OTI............. Office of Technical Information (MUGU)

OTI.............	Office of Technology Integration (ABAC)
OTI.............	Office of Trade and Investment [Victoria, Australia]
OTI.............	Office of Transition Initiative (SAUS)
OTI.............	Office of Treatment Improvement [U.S. Public Health Service] (BARN)
OTI.............	Official Test Insecticide
OTI.............	Open Technology Interface (SAUS)
OTI.............	Optimum Time Invariant (IAA)
OTI.............	Ordnance Technical Instructions [Navy]
OTI.............	Oregon Technical Institute
OTI.............	Original Title [Online database field identifier]
OTI.............	Original Transmitter Identification (SAUS)
OTI.............	Otiai [Former USSR] [Seismograph station code, US Geological Survey] [Closed] (SEIS)
OTI.............	OT Industries, Inc. [Vancouver Stock Exchange symbol]
OTI.............	Ovomucoid Trypsin Inhibitor [Medicine] (DMAA)
OTI.............	Oxide Throat Insert
OTI.............	Timmins Public Library, Ontario [Library symbol] [National Library of Canada] (NLC)
OTIA.............	Office of Technical Information Agency [Army] (MCD)
OTIA.............	Ordnance Technical Intelligence Agency (AAG)
OTIAP	IAPA [Industrial Accident Prevention Association] Library, Toronto, Ontario [Library symbol] [National Library of Canada] (NLC)
OTIBI	IBI Group, Toronto, Ontario [Library symbol] [National Library of Canada] (BIB)
OTIC.............	Idea Corp., Toronto, Ontario [Library symbol] [National Library of Canada] (NLC)
OTIC.............	Innovation Ontario Corp., Toronto, Ontario [Library symbol] [National Library of Canada] (NLC)
OTICA	Institute of Chartered Accountants of Ontario, Toronto, Ontario [Library symbol] [National Library of Canada] (NLC)
OTICS	Offset Target Indicator System (SAUS)
OTID	Industrial Disease Standards Panel, Toronto, Ontario [Library symbol] [National Library of Canada] (BIB)
OTID	Office of Talented Identification and Development [Johns Hopkins University] (EDAC)
OTID	Office of Talented Indentification and Development [Johns Hopkins Institute] (WDAA)
OTIEP.........	Office of Technical Information and Educational Programs [Terminated] [NASA]
OTIF.............	Organisation Intergouvernementale pour les Transports Internationaux Ferrovaires [Intergovernmental Organization for International Carriage by Rail] (EAIO)
OTif.............	Tiffin Seneca Public Library, Tiffin, OH [Library symbol] [Library of Congress] (LCLS)
OTifH	Heidelberg College, Tiffin, OH [Library symbol] [Library of Congress] (LCLS)
OTI Filtering...	Optimum Time-Invariant Filtering (SAUS)
OTIG	Office of the Inspector General [Army] (AABC)
OTIHM	Tillsonburg and District Historical Museum Society, Tillsonburg, Ontario [Library symbol] [National Library of Canada] (NLC)
OTII.............	Our Torah Institutions of Israel (EA)
OTIL.............	Tilbury Public Library, Ontario [Library symbol] [National Library of Canada] (NLC)
OTIM.............	Pontifical Institute of Mediaeval Studies, University of Toronto, Ontario [Library symbol] [National Library of Canada] (NLC)
OTIME.........	One Time (ACAE)
OTIN	International Nickel Co. of Canada Ltd., Toronto, Ontario [Library symbol] [National Library of Canada] (NLC)
OTINF	Infomart, Toronto, Ontario [Library symbol] [National Library of Canada] (NLC)
OTINP	Information Plus Library, Toronto, Ontario [Library symbol] [National Library of Canada] (BIB)
OTIO	United Kingdom Information Office, Toronto, Ontario [Library symbol] [National Library of Canada] (NLC)
OTIOL	Imperial Oil Ltd., Toronto, Ontario [Library symbol] [National Library of Canada] (NLC)
OTIP.............	Occupational Therapist in Independent Practice
OTIP.............	Offense Technology Interaction Program (ACAE)
OTIP.............	Ontario Training Incentive Program (SAUS)
OTIP.............	Tillsonburg Public Library, Ontario [Library symbol] [National Library of Canada] (NLC)
OTIR.............	Operational Test Incident Report (MCD)
OTIS.............	Observer's Thermal Imaging System (PDAA)
OTIS.............	Occupational Training Information System
OTIS.............	Offset Target Indicator System (MCD)
OTIS.............	Oklahoma Telecommunications Interlibrary System (AUEG)
OTIS.............	Oklahoma Teletype Interlibrary System [Library network]
OTIS.............	Once-Through Integral System [Nuclear energy] (NRCH)
OTIS.............	One Term In-Service Course (AIE)
OTIS.............	Online Telecommunications Information Service [Connections Telecommunications, Inc.] [West Bridgewater, MA] [Telecommunications service] (TSSD)
OTIS.............	Operational Test Instrumentation Ship [Navy]
OTIS.............	Operation, Transport, Inspection, Storage (MHDB)
OTIS.............	Optimum Thermal Interpolation System (SAUS)
OTIS.............	Order Trend Information System (SAUS)
OTIS.............	Ordnance Telemetry Instrumentation Station [Army] (AABC)
OTIS.............	Oregon Total Information System [Eugene] [Information service or system] (IID)
OTIS.............	Other than Iron or Steel [Freight]
OTIS.............	Overhead Travel Information System [Automotive electronics]
OTIS.............	Overstayer Tracing and Intelligence System [British]
Otis Art Inst...	Otis Art Institute of Parsons School of Design (GAGS)

OT/ITS	Office of Telecommunications Institute for Telecommunication Sciences [Boulder, CO] [Department of Commerce]
OT/ITSRR....	Office of Telecommunications/Institute for Telecommunications Sciences Research (SAUS)
OTIU	Overseas Technical Information Unit [Department of Trade] [British]
OTIV.............	Tiverton Branch, Bruce County Public Library, Ontario [Library symbol] [National Library of Canada] (NLC)
OTJ.............	Off-the-Job
OTJ.............	On the Job
OTJ.............	Toronto Regional Office, Department of Justice Canada [Bureau Regional de Toronto, Ministere de la Justice du Canada] Toronto, Ontario [Library symbol] [National Library of Canada] (NLC)
OTJAE.........	John Arpin Enterprises, Inc., Toronto, Ontario [Library symbol] [National Library of Canada] (NLC)
OTJAG.........	Office of the Judge Advocate General [Army] (AABC)
OTJFM.........	James F. MacLaren Ltd., Willowdale, Ontario [Library symbol] [National Library of Canada] (NLC)
OTJL.............	Judges Library, Ontario Ministry of the Attorney General, Toronto, Ontario [Library symbol] [National Library of Canada] (NLC)
OTJPS.........	Sands Pharmaceutical Division, Jerram Pharmaceuticals Ltd., Toronto, Ontario [Library symbol] [National Library of Canada] (NLC)
OTJT	On the Job Training
OTJWT.........	Information Centre, J. Walter Thompson Co. Ltd., Toronto, Ontario [Library symbol] [National Library of Canada] (NLC)
OTK.............	Knox College, University of Toronto, Ontario [Library symbol] [National Library of Canada] (NLC)
OTK.............	Oil Tank
OTK.............	Old Tuberculin Koch (SAUS)
OTK.............	One-Time Key (SAUS)
OTK.............	Over the Knee (SAUS)
OTK.............	Oxidizer Tank (MCD)
OTKC.............	Kidd Creek Mines Ltd., Toronto, Ontario [Library symbol] [National Library of Canada] (NLC)
OTKDF.........	Other than Knocked Down Flat [Freight]
OTKE.............	Kilborn Engineering Ltd., Toronto, Ontario [Library symbol] [National Library of Canada] (NLC)
OTL.............	Boutilimit [Mauritania] [Airport symbol] (AD)
OTL.............	Legislative Library of Ontario, Toronto, Ontario [Library symbol] [National Library of Canada] (NLC)
OTL.............	Libbey-Owens-Ford Glass Co., Technical Library, Toledo, OH [Library symbol] [Library of Congress] (LCLS)
OTL.............	Observer Target Line (NVT)
OTL.............	Office Technology Ltd. (NITA)
OTL.............	Ogden Technology Laboratories [NASA] (KSC)
OTL.............	Ohio Theological Librarians [Library network]
OTL.............	Oil-Tight Light
OTL.............	[The] Old Testament Library [A publication] (BJA)
OTL.............	Online Task Loader
OTL.............	Operating Temperature Limit
OTL.............	Operating Time Log (AAG)
OTL.............	Opportunity to Learn
OTL.............	Oracle Teletext Ltd. (NITA)
OTL.............	Order Trunk Line [Telecommunications] (OA)
OTL.............	Ordnance Test Laboratory (NASA)
OTL.............	OSI Testing Liaison Group (SAUS)
OTL.............	Outer Tube Limit [Chemical engineering]
OTL.............	Outland Resources [Vancouver Stock Exchange symbol]
OTL.............	Output-Transformerless (SAA)
OTL.............	Out to Lunch
OTL.............	Over the Line (WDAA)
OTL.............	Ovine Testicular Lymph [Endocrinology]
OTL.............	Oxidizer Tapping Line (SAUS)
OTL.............	Oxidizer Topping Line (AAG)
OTLAC	Tamworth Branch, Lennox and Addington County Library, Ontario [Library symbol] [National Library of Canada] (BIB)
OTLAMR	Ocean Temperature Large Antenna Microwave Radiometer (SAUS)
OTLC.............	Information Section, Ontario Ministry of Natural Resources, Toronto, Ontario [Library symbol] [National Library of Canada] (NLC)
OTLC.............	Open Tubular Liquid Chromatography
OTLC.............	Orbiter Timeline Constraints [NASA] (NASA)
OTLCC	Lummus Co. Canada Ltd., Willowdale, Ontario [Library symbol] [National Library of Canada] (NLC)
OTLF.............	Natural Resources Library, Ontario Ministry of Natural Resources, Toronto, Ontario [Library symbol] [National Library of Canada] (NLC)
OTLF.............	One-Time License Fee (SAUS)
OTLH.............	Laventhol & Horwath, Toronto, Ontario, [Library symbol] [National Library of Canada] (BIB)
OTLK.............	Outlook [NWS] (FAAC)
OTLMO	Orde des Technologistes de Laboratoire Medical de l'Ontario (AC)
OTLN	Outline (SAUS)
OTLO	Libbey-Owens-Ford Glass Co., Corporate Library, Toledo, OH [Library symbol] [Library of Congress] (LCLS)
OTLP.............	Ledbury Park Junior High School, Toronto, Ontario [Library symbol] [National Library of Canada] (NLC)
OTLR	Research Branch, Ontario Ministry of Natural Resources, Toronto, Ontario [Library symbol] [National Library of Canada] (NLC)
OTLS	Law Society of Upper Canada, Toronto, Ontario [Library symbol] [National Library of Canada] (NLC)
OTLSC	Litton Systems Canada Ltd., Rexdale, Ontario [Library symbol] [National Library of Canada] (NLC)
OTLT	Outlet (SAUS)

OTM............ Atmospheric Environment Service, Environment Canada [*Service de l'Environnement Atmospherique, Environnement Canada*] Downsview, Ontario [*Library symbol*] [*National Library of Canada*] (NLC)

OTM............ Office of Telecommunications Management [*Later, OTP*] [*FCC*]

OTM............ Office of Transportation Materials (SAUS)

OTM............ Office Technology Management Association (SAUS)

OTM............ Old Turkey Mill (SAUS)

OTM............ Once-through-Methanol [*Fuel technology*]

OTM............ On the Mark - Mark Hamill Fan Club (EA)

OTM............ On-the-Move (SAUS)

OTM............ On-Time Marker [*Computer science*]

OTM............ Operational Test Models (SAUS)

OTM............ Optical Tool Master (MCD)

OTM............ Orbit Trim Maneuver (ACAE)

OTM............ Organo-Transition-Metal (PDAA)

OTM............ Original Turkey Mill [*Paper*] (DGA)

OTM............ Ortho-Tolidine Manganese Sulphate

OTM............ Other than Mexican [*Term applied by US Border Patrol to certain illegal immigrants*]

otm............ other track material (SAUS)

OTM............ Ottumwa [*Iowa*] [*Airport symbol*] (OAG)

OTM............ Out of the Money [*Options*] [*Investment term*] (NUMA)

OTM............ Overseas Trade Mission (JAGO)

OTM............ Timken Co., Research Library, Canton, OH [*OCLC symbol*] (OCLC)

OTM............ Toledo Museum of Art, Toledo, OH [*Library symbol*] [*Library of Congress*] (LCLS)

OTMA.......... Office Technology Management Association [*Defunct*] (EA)

OTMA.......... Oilfield Tank Manufacturers Association (EA)

OTMAG........ Ontario Ministry of the Attorney General [*Ministere du Procureur-General*],Toronto [*Library symbol*] [*National Library of Canada*] (BIB)

OTMB.......... McMillan, Binch, Toronto, Ontario [*Library symbol*] [*National Library of Canada*] (NLC)

OTMC.......... Massey College, Toronto, Ontario [*Library symbol*] [*National Library of Canada*] (NLC)

OTMC.......... Medical College of Ohio at Toledo, Toledo, OH [*Library symbol*] [*Library of Congress*] (LCLS)

OTMCL........ Metropolitan Toronto Library, Ontario [*Library symbol*] [*National Library of Canada*] (NLC)

OTME.......... Ontario Ministry of Energy, Toronto, Ontario [*Library symbol*] [*National Library of Canada*] (NLC)

OTMEN........ Ontario Ministry of the Environment, Toronto, Ontario [*Library symbol*] [*National Library of Canada*] (NLC)

OTMENL...... Laboratory, Ontario Ministry of the Environment, Rexdale, Ontario [*Library symbol*] [*National Library of Canada*] (NLC)

OTMF.......... McIntyre-Falconbridge Library, Toronto, Ontario [*Library symbol*] [*National Library of Canada*] (NLC)

OTMH.......... Financial Post, Toronto, Ontario [*Library symbol*] [*National Library of Canada*] (NLC)

OTMI.......... Royal Canadian Military Institute, Toronto, Ontario [*Library symbol*] [*National Library of Canada*] (NLC)

OTMIO........ Employment and Immigration Canada [*Emploi et Immigration Canada*] Toronto, Ontario [*Library symbol*] [*National Library of Canada*] (NLC)

OTMIO........ Ontario Region Library, Employment and Immigration Canada [*Bibliotheque de laRegion de l'Ontario, Emploi et Immigration Canada*], North York, Ontario [*Library symbol*] [*National Library of Canada*] (NLC)

OTMIP........ One-Time Mortgage Insurance Premium (GFGA)

OTMIR........ Office of Tropical Medicine and International Research (SAUS)

OTMIS........ Medical Information Services, Toronto, Ontario [*Library symbol*] [*National Library of Canada*] (BIB)

OTMJ.......... Outgoing Trunk Message Junction [*Telecommunications*] (OA)

OTML.......... Law Library, Manufacturers Life Insurance Co., Toronto, Ontario [*Library symbol*] [*National Library of Canada*] (BIB)

OTML.......... Oatmeal [*Freight*]

OTMM.......... Mary Manse College, Toledo, OH [*Library symbol*] [*Library of Congress*] (LCLS)

OTMM.......... McCarthy & McCarthy, Barristers & Solicitors, Toronto, Ontario [*Library symbol*] [*National Library of Canada*] (NLC)

OTMMB........ Ontario Milks Marketing Board, Toronto, Ontario [*Library symbol*] [*National Library of Canada*] (NLC)

OTMML........ Micromedia Ltd., Toronto, Ontario [*Library symbol*] [*National Library of Canada*] (NLC)

OTMMM....... Marshall-Macklin-Monaghan Library, Don Mills, Ontario [*Library symbol*] [*National Library of Canada*] (NLC)

OTMN.......... Oxotremorine [*Cholinergic agent*]

OTMO.......... Monopros Ltd., Toronto, Ontario [*Library symbol*] [*National Library of Canada*] (BIB)

OTMOF........ MacDonald Ophthalmic Foundation, Toronto, Ontario [*Library symbol*] [*National Library of Canada*] (NLC)

OTMS.......... Mount Sinai Hospital, Toronto, Ontario [*Library symbol*] [*National Library of Canada*] (NLC)

OTMS.......... [*The*] Old Testament and Modern Study [*A publication*] (BJA)

OTMS.......... Operational Technical Managerial System (NVT)

OTMS.......... Over Thirty Months Slaughter scheme (SAUS)

OTMSM........ Management Services Department Library, Municipality of Metropolitan Toronto, Ontario [*Library symbol*] [*National Library of Canada*] (BIB)

OTMSS........ Professional Library, Metropolitan Separate School Board, Willowdale, Ontario [*Library symbol*] [*National Library of Canada*] (NLC)

OTM Sulphate... Orthotolidine Manganese Sulphate (SAUS)

OTMT.......... Monetary Times, Toronto, Ontario [*Library symbol*] [*National Library of Canada*] (NLC)

OTMTC........ Economic Development Division, Metro Toronto Chairman's Office, Toronto, Ontario [*Library symbol*] [*National Library of Canada*] (BIB)

OTMTS........ Metropolitan Toronto School Board, Ontario [*Library symbol*] [*National Library of Canada*] (NLC)

OTMTSS...... Secondary Schools, Metropolitan Toronto School Board, Ontario [*Library symbol*] [*National Library of Canada*] (NLC)

OTMW........ Department of Works, Municipality of Metropolitan Toronto, Ontario [*Library symbol*] [*National Library of Canada*] (BIB)

OTN............ Lastp-Linhas Aereas de Sao Tome e Principe [*ICAO designator*] (FAAC)

OTN............ Newtonbrook Secondary School, Willowdale, Ontario [*Library symbol*] [*National Library of Canada*] (NLC)

OTN............ Oaktown, IN [*Location identifier*] [*FAA*] (FAAL)

OTN............ Octal Track Number [*Computer science*]

OTN............ Operational Teletype Network

OTN............ Operational Test, Non-Major Systems (MCD)

OtN............ Order to Negotiate (SAUS)

OTN............ Orthogonal Tree Network (SAUS)

OTN............ Over the Nose [*Aviation*]

OTN............ Own-the-Night [*Technology*] [*Army*] (INF)

OTNA.......... Ontario Ministry of Northern Development and Mines, Toronto, Ontario [*Library symbol*] [*National Library of Canada*] (NLC)

OTNC.......... International Council for Adult Education, Toronto, Ontario [*Library symbol*] [*National Library of Canada*] (BIB)

OTNG.......... Observer Training [*Army*] (AABC)

OTNGH........ Health Sciences Library, Northwestern General Hospital, Toronto, Ontario [*Library symbol*] [*National Library of Canada*] (BIB)

OTNH.......... National Heritage Ltd., Toronto, Ontario [*Library symbol*] [*National Library of Canada*] (NLC)

OTNHH........ Health Protection Branch, Canada Department of National Health and Welfare [*Direction Generale de la Protection de la Sante, Ministere de la Sante Nationale et du Bien-Etre Social*] Toronto, Ontario [*Library symbol*] [*National Library of Canada*] (NLC)

OTNI.......... Industrial Development Office, National Research Council Canada [*Bureau du Developpement Industriel, Conseil National de Recherches Canada*], Scarborough, Ontario [*Library symbol*] [*National Library of Canada*] (NLC)

OTNIMR...... G. Allan Roeher Institute, Downsview, Ontario [*Library symbol*] [*National Library of Canada*] (NLC)

OTNIMR...... National Institute on Mental Retardation [*Institut National pour la Deficience Mentale*] Toronto, Ontario [*Library symbol*] [*National Library of Canada*] (NLC)

OTNM.......... Northern Mines, Toronto, Ontario [*Library symbol*] [*National Library of Canada*] (NLC)

OTNM.......... Over-Thirty-Never-Married [*Lifestyle classification*]

OTNO.......... Our Telegram Number (SAUS)

OTNP.......... Other than New Procurement [*Navy*] (DNAB)

OTNR.......... Survey Records Branch, Ontario Ministry of Natural Resources, Toronto, Ontario [*Library symbol*] [*National Library of Canada*] (BIB)

OTNS.......... Bank of Nova Scotia [*Banque de Nouvelle-Ecosse*], Toronto, Ontario [*Library symbol*] [*National Library of Canada*] (NLC)

OTNY.......... North York Public Library, Willowdale, Ontario [*Library symbol*] [*National Library of Canada*] (NLC)

OTNYE........ F. W. Minkler Library, North York Board of Education, Willowdale, Ontario [*Library symbol*] [*National Library of Canada*] (NLC)

OTO............ Oblique Takeoff (SAUS)

OTO............ Oil Temperature Out

OTO............ One-Time-Only

OTO............ Operational Testing Office (SAUS)

OTO............ Operator-to-Operator [*Military*] (CAAL)

OTO............ Optical Tracker Operator (MUGU)

OTO............ Ordo Templi Orientis [*Order of the Oriental Templars*] [*A mystical lodge*] [*Latin*] (ADA)

Oto............ Otolaryngology [*Medicine*]

Oto............ Otology [*Medicine*] (AMHC)

OTO............ Otology [*Medicine*]

oto............ Otomian [*MARC language code*] [*Library of Congress*] (LCCP)

OTO............ Otorhinolaryngologist (SAUS)

OTO............ Otorhinolaryngology [*Medicine*] (DHSM)

OTO............ Otto, NM [*Location identifier*] [*FAA*] (FAAL)

OTO............ Out-to-Out (AAG)

OTO............ Owens-Illinois, Inc., Technical Information Service-NTC, Toledo, OH [*Library symbol*] [*Library of Congress*] (LCLS)

OTO............ Tottenham Public Library, Ontario [*Library symbol*] [*National Library of Canada*] (NLC)

OTOB.......... Tobermory Branch, Bruce County Public Library, Ontario [*Library symbol*] [*National Library of Canada*] (NLC)

OTOC.......... Ontario Cancer Institute, Toronto, Ontario [*Library symbol*] [*National Library of Canada*] (NLC)

OTOCTA...... Optimum Technical Operational Concept to Accomplish

OTOD.......... Organization of Teachers of Oral Diagnosis (EA)

OTOE.......... Omnispace Environments Ltd., Toronto, Ontario [*Library symbol*] [*National Library of Canada*] (NLC)

OTOEB........ Ontario Energy Board, Toronto, Ontario [*Library symbol*] [*National Library of Canada*] (NLC)

OTO EPROM... One-Time-Only Erasable Read-Only Memory [*Computer science*] (MED)

OTOGR.......... Canadian Geriatrics Research Society, Toronto, Ontario [*Library symbol*] [*National Library of Canada*] (NLC)

OTOH.......... Ontario Ministry of Municipal Affairs and Housing, Toronto, Ontario [*Library symbol*] [*National Library of Canada*] (NLC)

OTOH .... On The One Hand (SAUS)

OTOH .... On the Other Hand [*Internet language*] [*Computer science*]

OTOHCR ...... Central Records, Ontario Hydro, Toronto, Ontario [*Library symbol*] [*National Library of Canada*] (NLC)

OTOL .... Ontario Lottery Corporation, Toronto, Ontario [*Library symbol*] [*National Library of Canada*] (BIB)

otol .... otological (SAUS)

Otol .... Otologist (STED)

OTOL .... Otology [*Medicine*]

Otolar .... Otolaryngology [*Medicine*] (DAVI)

Otolaryngol Head Neck Surg... Otolaryngology-Head and Neck Surgery (SAUS)

OTOLR .... Ontario Labour Relations Board [*Commission des Relations de Travail de l'Ontario*], Toronto, Ontario [*Library symbol*] [*National Library of Canada*] (NLC)

OTOLRC ...... Ontario Law Reform Commission, Toronto, Ontario [*Library symbol*] [*National Library of Canada*] (BIB)

OTOMA .... Ontario Medical Association, Toronto, Ontario [*Library symbol*] [*National Library of Canada*] (NLC)

OTOME .... Information Resource Centre, Ontario Municipal Employees Retirement Board, Toronto [*Library symbol*] [*National Library of Canada*] (BIB)

OTOMR .... Ontario Ministry of Revenue, Toronto, Ontario [*Library symbol*] [*National Library of Canada*] (NLC)

OTONA .... Ontario Nurses Association, Toronto, Ontario [*Library symbol*] [*National Library of Canada*] (NLC)

OTO NAVSUPPACT... Overseas Transportation Office, Naval Support Activity (DNAB)

OTO/Neth ..... Only to Order from Netherlands (SAUS)

O to O .... Out to Out [*Technical drawings*]

O to O .... Out-to-Out (SAUS)

OTOPC .... Ortho Pharmaceutical Canada Ltd., Don Mills, Ontario [*Library symbol*] [*National Library of Canada*] (NLC)

OTOPCT :...... Planning and Research Library, Technical Services Branch, Ontario Police Commission, Toronto, Ontario [*Library symbol*] [*National Library of Canada*] (NLC)

OTORHINOL... Otorhinolaryngology (SAUS)

Otorhinol ...... Otorhinology (SAUS)

OTOS .... Orbit-to-Orbit Stage [*NASA*] (MCD)

OTOSC .... Ontario Securities Commission, Toronto, Ontario [*Library symbol*] [*National Library of Canada*] (NLC)

OTOSS .... Ontario Secondary School Teachers Federation, Toronto, Ontario [*Library symbol*] [*National Library of Canada*] (NLC)

OTOW .... Resource Centre, Ontario Women's Directorate [*Library symbol*] [*National Library of Canada*] (BIB)

OTP .... Obstacle to Progress (SAUS)

OTP .... Ocean Test Platform [*Marine science*] (MSC)

OTP .... Office of Telecommunications Policy [*Terminated, 1978*] [*Executive Office of the President*]

OTP .... Office of Territorial Programs (COE)

OTP .... Office of Trade Promotion [*Department of Commerce*]

OTP .... Office Technology Plus [*General Services Administration*]

OTP .... Off True Position (SAUS)

OTP .... Of This Parish

OTP .... Of True Position (MSA)

OTP .... One-Time Pad [*Navy*] [*British*]

OTP .... One Time Password (SAUS)

OTP .... One-Time Process (SAUS)

OTP .... One-Time Programmable [*Computer science*]

OTP .... On Top [*Aviation*]

OTP .... On Top Position (SAUS)

OTP .... Open Top [*Freight*]

OTP .... Open Trade Protocol (SAUS)

OTP .... Operational Test Plan

OTP .... Operational Test Procedure (KSC)

OTP .... Operations Turnaround Plan (NASA)

OTP .... Order to Plan (SAUS)

OTP .... Oscillation Test Point [*British military*] (DMA)

OTP .... Otepa [*Tuamotu Archipelago*] [*Seismograph station code, US Geological Survey*] (SEIS)

OTP .... Other than Portable [*Freight*]

Ot P .... Otto Papiensis [*Flourished, 12th century*] [*Authority cited in pre-1607 legal work*] (DSA)

OTP .... Outline Test Plan [*Army*]

OTP .... Overhead Trickle Purification (PDAA)

OTP .... Overtemperature Protection (SAUS)

OTP .... Overtime Premium (MCD)

OTP .... Ovine Trophoblast Protein [*Biochemistry*]

OTP .... Oxidizer Tanking Panel (AAG)

OTP .... Oxygen Tanking Panel (SAUS)

OTP .... Ozone Trends Panel [*NASA*]

OTP .... Toronto Public Libraries, Ontario [*Library symbol*] [*National Library of Canada*] (NLC)

OTPA .... Institute of Public Administration of Canada [*Institut d'Administration Publique du Canada*] Toronto, Ontario [*Library symbol*] [*National Library of Canada*] (NLC)

OTPAL .... PAL Reading Service, Toronto, Ontario [*Library symbol*] [*National Library of Canada*] (NLC)

OTPEC .... Officer Training Program Examining Center [*Air Force*]

OTP-EPROM... One-Time Programmable-Electrically Programmable Read-Only Memory (SAUS)

OTPFA .... Fine Arts Library, Northern District, Toronto Public Libraries, Ontario [*Library symbol*] [*National Library of Canada*] (NLC)

OTPG .... Polar Gas Library, Toronto, Ontario [*Library symbol*] [*National Library of Canada*] (NLC)

OTPH .... History Section, Metropolitan Toronto Library, Ontario [*Library symbol*] [*National Library of Canada*] (NLC)

OTPHC .... Prentice Hall Canada, Inc., Scarborough, Ontario [*Library symbol*] [*National Library of Canada*] (NLC)

OTPHR .... Resource Centre, Department of Public Health, City of Toronto, Ontario [*Library symbol*] [*National Library of Canada*] (BIB)

OTPI .... On Top Position Indicator [*Navy*] (NG)

OTPI .... Operational Test Program Instruction (MCD)

OTPM .... Peat, Marwick & Partners, Toronto, Ontario [*Library symbol*] [*National Library of Canada*] (NLC)

OTPMG .... Office of the Provost Marshal General [*Army*]

OTPNL .... Outer Pane [*Aerospace*] (IAA)

OTPNL .... Outer Panel (SAUS)

OTPP .... Ocean Thermal Power Plant

OTPP .... Office of Transport, Policy and Planning [*South Australia*]

OTPP .... Ontario Provincial Police, Toronto, Ontario [*Library symbol*] [*National Library of Canada*] (NLC)

OTPP .... Operational Transfer Point Plan (SAUS)

Ot Pp .... Otto Papiensis [*Flourished, 12th century*] [*Authority cited in pre-1607 legal work*] (DSA)

OTPPC .... Ontario Provincial Police College, Toronto, Ontario [*Library symbol*] [*National Library of Canada*] (NLC)

OTPPP .... Open Transport/Point-to-Point Protocol (SAUS)

OTPR .... Proctor & Redfern Group, Don Mills, Ontario [*Library symbol*] [*National Library of Canada*] (NLC)

OTPROM...... One-Time Programmable Read Only Memory [*Computer science*]

OTP/RS .... Outline Test Plan/Resume Sheet (MCD)

OTPRW .... National Office Library, Price Waterhouse & Co., Toronto, Ontario [*Library symbol*] [*National Library of Canada*] (BIB)

OTPS .... Oceanic Traffic Planning System [*FAA*] (TAG)

OTPS .... One-Time Process System (SAUS)

OTPS .... Operational Test Program Set (MCD)

OTPT .... Operational Test Program Tape (MCD)

OTPT .... Output (KSC)

O-TPV .... Olefinic Thermoplastic Vulcanizate (SAUS)

OTPV2 .... Operational Test Perspective View and Visualization (SAUS)

OTPW .... Ontario Ministry of Community and Social Services, Toronto, Ontario [*Library symbol*] [*National Library of Canada*] (NLC)

OTPWC .... Ontario Regional Library, Public Works Canada [*Bibliotheque Regionale de l'Ontario, Travaux Publics Canada*] Toronto, Ontario [*Library symbol*] [*National Library of Canada*] (NLC)

OTQ .... On the Quarter

OTQE .... Queen Elizabeth Hospital, Toronto, Ontario [*Library symbol*] [*National Library of Canada*] (NLC)

OTQL .... Quaere Legal Resources Ltd., Toronto, Ontario [*Library symbol*] [*National Library of Canada*] (NLC)

OTQRM .... [*The*] Queen's Own Rifles of Canada Regimental Museum, Toronto, Ontario [*Library symbol*] [*National Library of Canada*] (NLC)

OTQSM .... Queen Street Mental Health Centre, Toronto, Ontario [*Library symbol*] [*National Library of Canada*] (NLC)

OTR .... Coto 47 [*Costa Rica*] [*Airport symbol*] (OAG)

OTR .... [*The*] Oakland Terminal Railway [*Formerly, OKT*] [*AAR code*]

OTR .... Observed Temperature Rise

OTR .... Occupational Therapist, Registered

OTR .... Oceanic Transition Route [*FAA*] (TAG)

OTR .... Office of Technical Resources

OTR .... Office of Testing and Research [*Drug evalution*]

OTR .... Off-the-Road

OTR .... Old Time Radio

OTR .... One Touch Recording

OTR .... On The Rag (SAUS)

OTR .... Open-Tubular Reactor

OTR .... Operating Temperature Range

OTR .... Operating Time Record (SAUS)

OTR .... Operational Time Record (AAG)

OTR .... Operational Turn-Round (SAUS)

OTR .... Optical Tracking [*NASA*] (KSC)

OTR .... Optical Transition Radiation [*Physics*]

OTR .... Oregon Tax Reports [*A publication*] (DLA)

OTR .... Organic Test Reactor [*Nuclear energy*]

OTR .... Organ Transplant Rejection [*Medicine*] (MELL)

OTR .... Orotek Resources Corp. [*Vancouver Stock Exchange symbol*]

OTR .... Other-Total Ratio [*B. Mullen*] (DIPS)

OTR .... Outer (MSA)

OTR .... Out-Turn Report (SAUS)

OTR .... Ovarian Tumor Registry [*Medicine*]

OTR .... Overload Time Relay (SAUS)

OTR .... Over-the-Road [*Automotive engineering*]

OTR .... Owning-the-Realty (SAUS)

OTR .... Oxygen Transfer Rate [*Chemical engineering*]

OTR .... Oxygen Transmission Rate (SAUS)

OTR .... Oxytocin Receptor [*Endocrinology*]

OTR .... Ozone Transport Region [*Environmental Protection Agency*] (EPAT)

OTR .... Registered Occupational Therapist (SAUS)

OTR .... Ryerson Polytechnical Institute, Toronto, Ontario [*Library symbol*] [*National Library of Canada*] (NLC)

OTr.............. Troy-Miami County Public Library, Troy, OH [*Library symbol*] [*Library of Congress*] (LCLS)

OTRA .... Other than Regular Army (AABC)

OTRA .... Oversea Theater Requisitioning Authority [*Military*]

OTRA .... Royal Astronomical Society [*Societe Royale d'Astronomie*] Toronto, Ontario [*Library symbol*] [*National Library of Canada*] (NLC)

OTRAC .... Oscillogram Trace Reader [*Non-Linear Systems, Inc.*] [*Computer science*]

OTRAG........ Orbital Transport and Rocket AG (SAUS)

OTRAG......... Orbital Transport- und Raketen-Aktiengesellschaft [Rocket company] [Germany]
OTRAL .... Rio Algom Ltd., Toronto, Ontario [Library symbol] [National Library of Canada] (NLC)
OTRAN........ Ocean Testing Ranges and Instrumentation Conference
OTRAN........ Ocean Test Range and Instrumentation (SAUS)
O/Trans....... Output Transformer
OTRAR......... Other than Regular Army
OTRBI .... Information Resources, Royal Bank of Canada, Toronto, Ontario [Library symbol] [National Library of Canada] (NLC)
OTRBSA .... Occupational Therapists' Registration Board of South Australia
OTRC .... Canadian Forces College, Toronto, Ontario [Library symbol] [National Library of Canada] (NLC)
OTRCF .... Royal Commission on the Future of the Toronto Waterfront, Toronto, Ontario [Library symbol] [National Library of Canada] (BIB)
OTRCL .... Reichhold Chemicals Ltd., Weston, Ontario [Library symbol] [National Library of Canada] (NLC)
OTRCR .... Trout Creek Community Library, Ontario [Library symbol] [National Library of Canada] (NLC)
OTRCS .... Canadian Forces Staff School, Canada Department of National Defence [College d'Etat-Major des Forces Canadiennes, Ministere de la Defense Nationale] Toronto, Ontario [Library symbol] [National Library of Canada] (NLC)
OTRE .... Trenton Public Library, Ontario [Library symbol] [National Library of Canada] (NLC)
OTREC .... Regis College, Toronto, Ontario [Library symbol] [National Library of Canada] (NLC)
OTReg .... Occupational Therapist Registered [Canada] (DAVI)
OTREN .... Northumberland County Public Library, Warkworth, Ontario [Library symbol] [National Library of Canada] (NLC)
OTREX .... Canada Department of Regional Industrial Expansion [Ministere de l'Expansion Industrielle Regionale] Toronto, Ontario [Library symbol] [National Library of Canada] (NLC)
OTR Ex .... OTR Express, Inc. [Associated Press] (SAG)
OTRF .... Ontario Research Foundation, Sheridan Park, Mississauga, Ontario [Library symbol] [National Library of Canada] (NLC)
OTRG .... Office Technology Research Group [Defunct] (EA)
OTRG .... Old Testament Reading Guide [Collegeville, MN] [A publication] (BJA)
OTRHNLRGYNGY... Otorhinolaryngology
OTRIC .... Collins Canada Division, Rockwell International, Toronto, Ontario [Library symbol] [National Library of Canada] (NLC)
OTRK .... Oshkosh Truck Corp. [Oshkosh, WI] [NASDAQ symbol] (NQ)
OTRKB .... Oshkosh Truck'B' [NASDAQ symbol] (TTSB)
OTRL .... Reed Ltd., Toronto, Ontario [Library symbol] [National Library of Canada] (NLC)
OTrL........... Troy-Miami County Public Library, Troy, OH [Library symbol] [Library of Congress] (LCLS)
OTRM .... Royal Ontario Museum, Toronto, Ontario [Library symbol] [National Library of Canada] (NLC)
OTRMC .... Canadiana Department, Royal Ontario Museum, Toronto, Ontario [Library symbol] [National Library of Canada] (NLC)
OTRMF .... Far Eastern Department, Royal Ontario Museum, Toronto, Ontario [Library symbol] [National Library of Canada] (NLC)
OTRO .... Overhaul Test Requirement Outline
OTROT .... Corporate Information Centre, Royal Trust, Toronto, Ontario [Library symbol] [National Library of Canada] (BIB)
OTRPM .... Rothmans of Pall Mall Ltd., Don Mills, Ontario [Library symbol] [National Library of Canada] (NLC)
OTRR .... Operation Test Readiness Review [Army]
OTRR .... Organisation for the Total Redemption of Rwandese (SAUS)
OTRS .... Operational Test Readiness Statement
OT/RT .... Occupational Therapy/Recreational Therapy (STED)
OTRT .... Operating Time Record Tag (AAG)
OTRT .... Rose Technology Group Ltd., Toronto, Ontario [Library symbol] [National Library of Canada] (NLC)
OTRX .... OTR Express [NASDAQ symbol] (TTSB)
OTRX .... OTR Express, Inc. [NASDAQ symbol] (SAG)
OTS............. Oakhanger Tracking Station (ACAE)
OTS............. Object Time System (MHDB)
OTS............. Object Transaction Service (VLIE)
OTS............. Occipital Temporal Sulcus [Medicine] (DMAA)
OTS............. Octadecyltrichlorosilane [Organic chemistry]
OTS............. Office of Technical Services [Later, CFSTI, NTIS] [National Institute of Standards and Technology]
OTS............. Office of Technical Support [US Employment Service] [Department of Labor]
OTS............. Office of Technological Services (SAUS)
OTS............. Office of Thrift Supervision [Department of the Treasury] [Superseded Federal Home Loan Bank Board, 1989]
OTS............. Office of Toxic Substances [Environmental Protection Agency]
OTS............. Office of Traffic Safety (SAUS)
OTS............. Office of Transportation Security [Department of Transportation]
OTS............. Office of Treaty Settlements (SAUS)
OTS............. Officers' Tactical School [Navy] (NVT)
OTS............. Officers' Training School
OTS............. Officer Training School (SAUS)
OTS............. Office TeleSystem (SAUS)
OTS............. Off the Shelf
OTS............. Ohio Carriers Tariff Service Inc., Cleveland OH [STAC]
OTS............. Omega Tau Sigma [An association] (NTPA)
OTS............. One-man operated Ticketing System (SAUS)
OTS............. One-Time Source (MCD)
OTS............. On-Line Terminal System [Computer science] (MHDB)
OTS............. On the Spot (VLIE)

OTS............. Open Two Seater [Style of automobile]
OTS............. Operational Test Site (AAG)
OTS............. Operational Time Synchronization (VLIE)
OTS............. Operational Training Squadron (MCD)
OTS............. Operational Training System [HAWK]
OTS............. Operator Telephone System (SAUS)
OTS............. Opportunities to See [Business term]
OTS............. Optical Technology Satellite
OTS............. Optical Tracking Satellite [NASA] (IAA)
OTS............. Optical Tracking System (SAUS)
OTS............. Optical Transport Systems (IEEE)
OTS............. Orbital Technical Satellite (SAUS)
OTS............. Orbital Technology Satellite (SAUS)
OTS............. Orbital Test Satellite [Communications satellite] [European Space Agency]
OTS............. Orbital Transport Systems (MCD)
OTS............. Orbiter Test Conductor (SAUS)
OTS............. Organization for Tropical Studies (EA)
OTS............. Organized Track Structure (SAUS)
OTS............. Organized Track System [Aviation]
OTS............. Orotracheal Suction [Medicine] (DAVI)
OTS............. Ortho-Toluenesulfonamide [Used in manufacture of saccharin]
OTS............. O-Toluenesulfonamide (SAUS)
OTS............. Out-of-house Time Sharing (SAUS)
OTS............. Out of Service (PIPO)
OTS............. Outside Temperature Sensor [Automotive engineering]
OTS............. Overlap Technician Supervisor (SAA)
OTS............. Overlap Telling and Surveillance (SAA)
OTS............. Overseas Telecommunications Services (SAUS)
OTS............. Overseas Telephone Services (DAS)
OTS............. Over-the-Shoulder [Cinematography]
OTS............. Over-the-Side [Navy] (CAAL)
OTS............. Ovionic Threshold Switch (SAUS)
OTS............. Ovonic Threshold Switch
OTS............. Own Time Switch [Connection or call] [Telecommunications] (TEL)
OTS............. Oxford Text System (NITA)
OTS............. Oxygen Test Stand (KSC)
OTS............. Statistics Canada [Statistique Canada] Toronto, Ontario [Library symbol] [National Library of Canada] (NLC)
OTSA .... Ocean Systems Technician, Seaman Apprentice [Navy rating] (DNAB)
OTSA .... Orthodox Theological Society in America (EA)
OTSA .... Salvation Army, Toronto, Ontario [Library symbol] [National Library of Canada] (NLC)
OTSAA .... Officer Training School Alumni Association (EA)
OTSAC .... Sanco Consultants Ltd., Toronto, Ontario [Library symbol] [National Library of Canada] (NLC)
OTS-AES ...... Optical Technology Satellite - Apollo Extension System (DNAB)
OTSAP .... Spar Aerospace Products, Toronto, Ontario [Library symbol] [National Library of Canada] (NLC)
OTSC .... Officials Treaty Strategy Committee (SAUS)
O/TSC .... Other than Special Consultants [Military]
OTSC .... Seneca College, Willowdale, Ontario [Library symbol] [National Library of Canada] (NLC)
OTSCC .... Scarborough College, Ontario [Library symbol] [National Library of Canada] (NLC)
OTSCI .... Sulzer Canada, Inc., Toronto, Ontario [Library symbol] [National Library of Canada] (NLC)
OTSCL .... Shell Canada Ltd., Toronto, Ontario [Library symbol] [National Library of Canada] (NLC)
OTSCLT........ Library Techniques, Seneca College of Applied Arts and Technology, Willowdale, Ontario [Library symbol] [National Library of Canada] (NLC)
OTSD .... Operational Test Supportability Demonstration
OTSDG .... Outstanding (SAUS)
OTSE........... Toronto Stock Exchange Library, Ontario [Library symbol] [National Library of Canada] (BIB)
OTS/ECS ...... Orbital Test Satellite/European Communications Satellite (SAUS)
OTSED .... Scarborough Borough Board of Education, Toronto, Ontario [Library symbol] [National Library of Canada] (NLC)
OTSF........... Open Telephony Server Forum [Computer science] (VLIE)
OTSG .... Office of the Surgeon General [Public Health Service]
OTSG .... Once-Through Steam Generator [Nuclear energy]
OTSGS .... Once-Through Steam Generating System [Nuclear energy] (IEEE)
OTSI .... Over-The-Shoulder Inspection (SAUS)
OTSLI.......... Sun Life of Canada, Toronto, Ontario [Library symbol] [National Library of Canada] (NLC)
OTSM.......... St. Michael's Hospital, Toronto, Ontario [Library symbol] [National Library of Canada] (NLC)
OTSMC .... Sunnybrook Medical Centre, Toronto, Ontario [Library symbol] [National Library of Canada] (NLC)
OTSMG .... St. Mary's General Hospital, Timmins, Ontario [Library symbol] [National Library of Canada] (NLC)
OTSML......... Selco Mining Corp., Toronto, Ontario [Library symbol] [National Library of Canada] (NLC)
OTS MTS ..... OTS Milestone Tracking System (SAUS)
OTSN .... Ocean Systems Technician, Seaman [Navy rating] (DNAB)
OTSO .... Office of Telecommunications Systems Operations [Social Security Administration]
OTSOA .... Overseas Telegraph Superintending Officers' Association [A union] [British]
OTSOG......... On the Shoulders of Giants [Literature]
OTSP .... Office of Technology Support Programs [Washington, DC] [Department of Energy] (GRD)

OTSP .... Office of Transportation Systems and Planning [*Battelle Memorial Institut e*] [*Department of Energy*] [*Also, an information service or system*] (IID)

OTSP .... Scarborough Public Library, Ontario [*Library symbol*] [*National Library of Canada*] (NLC)

OTSPA .... Albert Campbell Branch, Scarborough Public Library, Ontario [*Library symbol*] [*National Library of Canada*] (NLC)

OTSPC .... Cedarbrae Branch, Scarborough Public Library, Ontario [*Library symbol*] [*National Library of Canada*] (NLC)

OTS-PST ...... Orbiting Transition State-Phase Space Theory [*Physical chemistry*]

OTSQ .... Offer Teacher-Student Questionnaire [*Personality development test*] [*Psychology*]

OTSR .... Once-Through Superheat Reactor [*Nuclear energy*]

OTSR .... Optics Technology for Stand-Off Reconnaissance (ACAE)

OTSR .... Optimum Track Ship Routing [*Navy*] (NVT)

OTSS .... Office of Technical and Special Services [*Office of Field Operations*] [*Department of Labor*]

OTSS .... Off-the-Shelf System [*Bell System*]

OTSS .... Ontario Regional Library, Secretary of State Canada [*Bibliotheque Regionale de l'Ontario, Secretariat d'Etat*], Toronto, Ontario [*Library symbol*] [*National Library of Canada*] (NLC)

OTSS .... Open Systems Transport and Session Support [*Computer science*] (VLIE)

OTSS .... Open Transport and Session Support (NITA)

OTSS .... Operational Telecommunications Switching System (SAUS)

OTSS .... Operational Test Support System

OTSS .... Optical Tracking Servo

OTS SB .... Office of Technical Service, Selective Bibliographies [*US government*]

OTS SB .... Office of Technical Service, Selective Biographies (SAUS)

OTST .... Ontario Science Centre, Toronto, Ontario [*Library symbol*] [*National Library of Canada*] (NLC)

OTSTA .... St. Augustine's Seminary, Toronto, Ontario [*Library symbol*] [*National Library of Canada*] (NLC)

OTSTB .... St. Basil's Seminary [*Collection transferred to OTSTM*] Ontario [*Library symbol*] [*National Library of Canada*] (NLC)

OTSTF .... Ontario Film Institute, Ontario Science Centre Library, Don Mills, Ontario [*Library symbol*] [*National Library of Canada*] (NLC)

OTSTG .... St. George's College, Toronto, Ontario [*Library symbol*] [*National Library of Canada*] (NLC)

OTSTJ .... George Pennal Library, St. Joseph's Health Centre, Toronto, Ontario [*Library symbol*] [*National Library of Canada*] (BIB)

OTSTM......... University of Saint Michael's College, Toronto, Ontario [*Library symbol*] [*National Library of Canada*] (NLC)

OTSU .... Open Technology Support Unit (HEAS)

OTSZH .... Other than Steel or Zinc Heads [*Freight*]

OTT.............. Nottingham, MD [*Location identifier*] [*FAA*] (FAAL)

OTT.............. Ocean Transport and Trading [*British*]

OTT.............. Office of Technology Transfer [*University of Illinois*]

OTT.............. Office of Traffic and Transportation (SAUS)

OTT.............. Office of Transportation Technologies

OTT.............. One Terminal per Task (SAUS)

OTT.............. One-Time Tape

OTT.............. Operational Training Test (NVT)

OTT.............. Operations Team Trainer (SAUS)

OTT.............. Operator Tactics Trainer [*Patriot air defense system*] (MCD)

OTT.............. Optional Team Targeting (MCD)

OTT.............. Oral Trade Tests [*Department of Labor*]

OTT.............. Orotracheal Tube [*Medicine*] (DAVI)

OTT.............. Ottava [*Octave*] [*Music*]

OTT.............. Ottawa [*Ontario*] [*Seismograph station code, US Geological Survey*] (SEIS)

OTT.............. Ottery Saint Mary [*Urban district in England*]

Ott................ Ottoman (DIAR)

Ott................ Otto's United States Supreme Court Reports [*91-107 United States*] [*A publication*] (DLA)

OTT.............. Outgoing Teletype

OTT.............. Outgoing Trunk Terminal [*Telecommunications*] (IAA)

OTT.............. Outlet Tank Temperature [*Automotive engineering*]

OTT.............. Outside Trim Template (MSA)

OTT.............. Over the Top [*British*] [*Slang*]

OTT.............. Over-the-Top [*Marshall-MacIntosh knee operation*]

OTT.............. Over the Transom (ADWA)

OTT.............. Oxygen Tolerance Test

OTT.............. Teledyne CAE Engineering Library, Toledo, OH [*Library symbol*] [*Library of Congress*] (LCLS)

OTT.............. Toronto Transit Commission, Ontario [*Library symbol*] [*National Library of Canada*] (NLC)

OTT.............. University of Ottawa Library [*UTLAS symbol*]

OTT&E .... Operational Test Training & Evaluation (SAUS)

OttawFn .... Ottawa Financial Corp. [*Associated Press*] (SAG)

OTTB........... Optically-Thin Thermal Bremsstrahlung [*Astrophysics*]

OTTB........... Owner to Take Back

OTTC........... University of Trinity College, Toronto, Ontario [*Library symbol*] [*National Library of Canada*] (NLC)

OTTCA .... University of Trinity College Archives, Toronto, Ontario [*Library symbol*] [*National Library of Canada*] (NLC)

OTTDB .... Toronto-Dominion Bank, Toronto, Ontario [*Library symbol*] [*National Library of Canada*] (NLC)

OTTE........... Operational Testing, Training, and Evaluation

OTTEC.......... Toronto Teachers' College, Ontario [*Library symbol*] [*National Library of Canada*] (NLC)

OTTER .... Operational Training, Test, and Evaluation RADAR

OTTER .... Oregon Transect Ecosystem Research (SAUS)

OTTER .... Organized Techniques for Theorem-Proving and Effective Research (RALS)

OTTEX.......... Texaco Canada, Inc., Don Mills, Ontario [*Library symbol*] [*National Library of Canada*] (NLC)

OTTFC.......... Official Tim Topper Fan Club [*Defunct*] (EA)

OTTH........... On the Third Hand (ADWA)

OTTI............ Ontario Ministry of Industry and Trade, Toronto [*Library symbol*] [*National Library of Canada*] (NLC)

OTTLE .... Optically Transparent Thin-Layer Electrode

OTTO .... Olympic Technology Trailer Operations

OTTO .... Once Through, Then Out [*Fuel management system*]

OTTO .... Optical-to-Optical (IAA)

Otto.............. Otto's United States Supreme Court Reports [*91-107 United States*] [*A publication*] (DLA)

OTTOA .... Ontario Region, Canadian Air Transportation Administration, Transport Canada [*Region de l'Ontario, Administration Canadienne des Transports Aeriens, Transports Canada*] Toronto, Ontario [*Library symbol*] [*National Library of Canada*] (NLC)

OTTOMH...... Off the Top of My Head (VLIE)

OTTR .... Otter Tail Power [*NASDAQ symbol*] (TTSB)

OTTR .... Otter Tail Power Co. [*NASDAQ symbol*] (NQ)

OTTR .... Thomson, Rogers, Barristers & Solicitors, Toronto, Ontario [*Library symbol*] [*National Library of Canada*] (NLC)

OTTRAC .... Travelers Canada, Toronto, Ontario [*Library symbol*] [*National Library of Canada*] (BIB)

OTTRC......... Thistletown Regional Centre for Children and Adolescents, Rexdale, Ontario [*Library symbol*] [*National Library of Canada*] (NLC)

OTTRC......... Touche Ross & Co., Toronto, Ontario [*Library symbol*] [*National Library of Canada*] (NLC)

OttrTP .... Otter Tail Power Co. [*Associated Press*] (SAG)

OTTS........... Operations Training and Technical Services [*Nuclear Regulatory Commission*] (NRCH)

OTTS........... Organisation of Teachers of Transport Studies [*British*]

OTTS........... Outgoing Trunk Testing System [*Telecommunications*] (TEL)

OTTST.......... Toronto School of Theology, Toronto, Ontario [*Library symbol*] [*National Library of Canada*] (NLC)

OTTSU .... Open Tech Training Support Unit (AIE)

Ott's US Sup Ct R... Otto's United States Supreme Court Reports [*91-107 United States*] [*A publication*] (DLA)

OTTT............ Tory, Tory, DesLauriers & Binnington, Toronto, Ontario [*Library symbol*] [*National Library of Canada*] (BIB)

OTTW........... Optical Telescope Technology Workshop [*NASA*] (PDAA)

OTTWH .... Health Sciences Library, Toronto Western Hospital, Ontario [*Library symbol*] [*National Library of Canada*] (NLC)

OTU .... Odometer Transducer Unit (SAUS)

OTU .... Office of Technology Utilization [*NASA*]

OTU .... Officers' Training Unit [*Air Force*] [*British*]

OTU .... Ogden Test Unit (SAA)

OTU .... Olfactory Tubercle (STED)

OTU .... One-Time Use

OTU .... Operating Time Update

OTU .... Operational Taxonometric Unit (SAUS)

OTU .... Operational Taxonomic Unit [*Numerical taxonomy*]

OTU .... Operational Test Unit (KSC)

OTU .... Operational Training Unit [*Military*]

OTU .... Opetus-ja Tutkimusalan Unioni [*Teaching and Research Employees Union*] [*Finalnd*] (EY)

OTU .... Organization Turnover (SAUS)

OTU .... Orthopedic Transcription Unit

OTU .... Otu [*Colombia*] [*Airport symbol*] (OAG)

OTU .... Output Terminal Unit (SSD)

OTU .... Oxygen Toxicity Unit (SAUS)

OTU .... University of Toledo, Toledo, OH [*Library symbol*] [*Library of Congress*] (LCLS)

OTUA .... Institute for Aerospace Studies, University of Toronto, Ontario [*Library symbol*] [*National Library of Canada*] (NLC)

OTUAN......... Department of Anatomy, University of Toronto, Ontario [*Library symbol*] [*National Library of Canada*] (NLC)

OTUAP......... Department of Applied Physics, University of Toronto, Ontario [*Library symbol*] [*National Library of Canada*] (NLC)

OTUAR......... University of Toronto Archives, Ontario [*Library symbol*] [*National Library of Canada*] (NLC)

OTUAV......... Audio-Visual Library, University of Toronto, Ontario [*Library symbol*] [*National Library of Canada*] (NLC)

OTUB .... Department of Biochemistry, University of Toronto, Ontario [*Library symbol*] [*National Library of Canada*] (NLC)

OTUBP......... Banting-Best Physiology Library, University of Toronto, Ontario [*Library symbol*] [*National Library of Canada*] (NLC)

OTUC .... Department of Chemistry, University of Toronto, Ontario [*Library symbol*] [*National Library of Canada*] (NLC)

OTUCC......... Institute of Computer Science, University of Toronto, Ontario [*Library symbol*] [*National Library of Canada*] (NLC)

OTUCE......... Department of Chemical Engineering and Applied Chemistry, University of Toronto, Ontario [*Library symbol*] [*National Library of Canada*] (NLC)

OTUCI......... Department of Civil Engineering, University of Toronto, Ontario [*Library symbol*] [*National Library of Canada*] (NLC)

OTUCR......... Centre of Criminology, University of Toronto, Ontario [*Library symbol*] [*National Library of Canada*] (NLC)

OTUCS......... Institute of Child Study, University of Toronto, Ontario [*Library symbol*] [*National Library of Canada*] (NLC)

OTUD .... David Dunlap Observatory, University of Toronto, Ontario [*Library symbol*] [*National Library of Canada*] (NLC)

OTUDB......... Department of Botany, University of Toronto, Ontario [*Library symbol*] [*National Library of Canada*] (NLC)

OTUDM........ Department of Mathematics, University of Toronto, Ontario [*Library symbol*] [*National Library of Canada*] (NLC)

OTUDP......... Clarke Institute of Psychiatry, University of Toronto, Ontario [*Library symbol*] [*National Library of Canada*] (NLC)

OTUE .... Engineering Library, University of Toronto, Ontario [*Library symbol*] [*National Library of Canada*] (NLC)

OTUEE .... Department of Electrical Engineering, University of Toronto, Ontario [*Library symbol*] [*National Library of Canada*] (NLC)

OTUFA .... Department of Fine Art, University of Toronto, Ontario [*Library symbol*] [*National Library of Canada*] (NLC)

OTUFD .... Faculty of Dentistry, University of Toronto, Ontario [*Library symbol*] [*National Library of Canada*] (NLC)

OTUFM .... Faculty of Music, University of Toronto, Ontario [*Library symbol*] [*National Library of Canada*] (NLC)

OTUFP .... Faculty of Pharmacy, University of Toronto, Ontario [*Library symbol*] [*National Library of Canada*] (NLC)

OTUG .... Department of Geological Sciences, University of Toronto, Ontario [*Library symbol*] [*National Library of Canada*] (NLC)

OTUGL .... Geophysics Laboratory, University of Toronto, Ontario [*Library symbol*] [*National Library of Canada*] (NLC)

OTUH .... Operational Training Unit, Helicopter (SAUS)

OTUH .... Science and Medicine Library, University of Toronto, Ontario [*Library symbol*] [*National Library of Canada*] (NLC)

OTUHO .... Occupational & Environment Health Unit, Science and Medicine Library, Universityof Toronto, Ontario [*Library symbol*] [*National Library of Canada*] (NLC)

OTUINC........ Innis College, University of Toronto, Ontario [*Library symbol*] [*National Library of Canada*] (NLC)

OTUIRN........ [*The*] Jean and Dorothy Newman Industrial Relations Library, Center for Industrial Relations, University of Toronto, Ontario [*Library symbol*] [*National Library of Canada*] (NLC)

OTUL .... Faculty of Law, University of Toronto, Ontario [*Library symbol*] [*National Library of Canada*] (NLC)

OTU-L .... University of Toledo, Law Library, Toledo, OH [*Library symbol*] [*Library of Congress*] (LCLS)

OTULAS ...... UTLAS [*University of Toronto Library Automation System*] International Canada, Toronto, Ontario [*Library symbol*] [*National Library of Canada*] (NLC)

OTULS .... Faculty of Library Science, University of Toronto, Ontario [*Library symbol*] [*National Library of Canada*] (NLC)

OTUM .... Department of Mechanical Engineering, University of Toronto, Ontario [*Library symbol*] [*National Library of Canada*] (NLC)

OTUMA .... Map Library, University of Toronto, Ontario [*Library symbol*] [*National Library of Canada*] (NLC)

OTUME .... Department of Metallurgical Engineering, University of Toronto, Ontario [*Library symbol*] [*National Library of Canada*] (NLC)

OTUMI .... Department of Mining Engineering, University of Toronto, Ontario [*Library symbol*] [*National Library of Canada*] (NLC)

OTUMS .... Faculty of Management Studies, University of Toronto, Ontario [*Library symbol*] [*National Library of Canada*] (NLC)

OTUN .... Faculty of Nursing, University of Toronto, Ontario [*Library symbol*] [*National Library of Canada*] (NLC)

OTUNC .... Union Carbide Canada Ltd., Toronto, Ontario [*Library symbol*] [*National Library of Canada*] (NLC)

OTUNWC...... New College, University of Toronto, Ontario [*Library symbol*] [*National Library of Canada*] (NLC)

OTUP .... Department of Physics, University of Toronto, Ontario [*Library symbol*] [*National Library of Canada*] (NLC)

OTUPA .... Department of Pathology, Banting-Best Institute, University of Toronto, Ontario [*Library symbol*] [*National Library of Canada*] (NLC)

OTUPG .... Information Centre, Programme in Gerontology, University of Toronto, Ontario [*Library symbol*] [*National Library of Canada*] (NLC)

O Turk .... Old Turkish (SAUS)

OTUS .... Office of the Treasurer of the United States

OTUSA .... School of Architecture, University of Toronto, Ontario [*Library symbol*] [*National Library of Canada*] (NLC)

OTUSP .... School of Physical and Health Education (Women), University of Toronto, Ontario [*Library symbol*] [*National Library of Canada*] (NLC)

OTUSW .... School of Social Work, University of Toronto, Ontario [*Library symbol*] [*National Library of Canada*] (NLC)

OTUTD .... Urban Transportation Development Corp., Toronto, Ontario [*Library symbol*] [*National Library of Canada*] (NLC)

OTUTF .... Thomas Fisher Rare Book Library, University of Toronto, Ontario [*Library symbol*] [*National Library of Canada*] (NLC)

OTUTP .... University of Toronto Press, Ontario [*Library symbol*] [*National Library of Canada*] (NLC)

OTUUC .... University College, University of Toronto, Ontario [*Library symbol*] [*National Library of Canada*] (NLC)

OTUZ .... Department of Zoology, University of Toronto, Ontario [*Library symbol*] [*National Library of Canada*] (NLC)

OTV............. Operational Television (KSC)

OTV............. Operational Test Vehicle (IAA)

OTV............. Optimum Time Varying (IAA)

OTV............. Orbiter Transfer Vehicle [*NASA*]

OTV............. Otavi [*South-West Africa*] [*Airport symbol*] (AD)

OTV............. Outer Television (SAUS)

OTV............. Victoria University, Toronto, Ontario [*Library symbol*] [*National Library of Canada*] (NLC)

OTVC .... Open Top Vapor Cleaner [*Engineering*]

OTVCT .... Outer Tube Vertical Centerline Target

OTVL............ V & L Enterprises, Downsview, Ontario [*Library symbol*] [*National Library of Canada*] (NLC)

OTV System... Operational Television System (SAUS)

OTW............. Off the Wall [*Slang*]

OTW............. On the Whole (VLIE)

OTW............. Over the Wing [*Aircraft*]

OTW............. Owner's Tank Wagons [*Shipping*]

OTW............. Owning the Weather [*Army*] (RDA)

OTW............. Wycliffe College, Toronto, Ontario [*Library symbol*] [*National Library of Canada*] (NLC)

OTWC .... Ontario Workmen's Compensation Board, Toronto, Ontario [*Library symbol*] [*National Library of Canada*] (NLC)

OTWCA......... Ontario Workers' Compensation Appeals Tribunal, Toronto, Ontario [*Library symbol*] [*National Library of Canada*] (NLC)

OTWCH .... Medical Library, Women's College Hospital, Toronto, Ontario [*Library symbol*] [*National Library of Canada*] (NLC)

OTWD .... Out-The-Window Display (SAUS)

OTWE .... Tweed Public Library, Ontario [*Library symbol*] [*National Library of Canada*] (BIB)

OTWEN .... Ontario Ministry of Northern Development and Mines, Tweed [*Library symbol*] [*National Library of Canada*] (BIB)

OTWFC .... Old Time Western Film Club (EA)

OTWG .... Operational Test Working Group (SAUS)

OTWH .... Wellesley Hospital, Toronto, Ontario [*Library symbol*] [*National Library of Canada*] (NLC)

OTWL........... William Lyon Mackenzie Collegiate Institute, Downsview, Ontario [*Library symbol*] [*National Library of Canada*] (NLC)

OTWLC .... Warner-Lambert Canada Ltd., Scarborough, Ontario [*Library symbol*] [*National Library of Canada*] (NLC)

OTWM .... William M. Mercer Ltd., Toronto, Ontario [*Library symbol*] [*National Library of Canada*] (NLC)

OTWR .... Oblique Tape Wound Refrasil

OTWRC .... Weston Research Centre, Toronto, Ontario [*Library symbol*] [*National Library of Canada*] (NLC)

OTWY .... Medical Library, Wyeth Ltd., Downsview, Ontario [*Library symbol*] [*National Library of Canada*] (BIB)

OTX............. Oiltex International Ltd. [*Toronto Stock Exchange symbol*]

OTXRA .... X-Ray Assay Laboratories Ltd., Don Mills, Ontario [*Library symbol*] [*National Library of Canada*] (NLC)

OTY............. Organization Type (SAUS)

OTY............. Oria [*Papua New Guinea*] [*Airport symbol*] [*Obsolete*] (OAG)

OTY............. York University, Toronto, Ontario [*Library symbol*] [*National Library of Canada*] (NLC)

OTYA .... York University Archives, Toronto, Ontario [*Library symbol*] [*National Library of Canada*] (NLC)

OTYBE .... Professional Library, Board of Education for the City of York, Toronto, Ontario [*Library symbol*] [*National Library of Canada*] (NLC)

OTYBE .... York Borough Board of Education, Toronto, Ontario [*Library symbol*] [*National Library of Canada*] (NLC)

OTYBES ...... Schools, Board of Education for the City of York, Toronto, Ontario [*Library symbol*] [*National Library of Canada*] (NLC)

OTYF........... Hospital Library, York-Finch General Hospital, Downsview, Ontario [*Library symbol*] [*National Library of Canada*] (BIB)

OTYL........... Law Library, York University, Toronto, Ontario [*Library symbol*] [*National Library of Canada*] (NLC)

OTYLR .... Listening Room, York University, Toronto, Ontario [*Library symbol*] [*National Library of Canada*] (NLC)

OTYP .... City of York Public Library, Toronto, Ontario [*Library symbol*] [*National Library of Canada*] (NLC)

OTZ............. Kotzebue [*Alaska*] [*Airport symbol*] (OAG)

OTZ............. Ortiz [*New Mexico*] [*Seismograph station code, US Geological Survey*] (SEIS)

OTZ............. Oxothiazolidine [*Biochemistry*]

OU.............. City Express [*ICAO designator*] (AD)

OU .... Oat Unit (SAUS)

OU .... Object Unit (NITA)

OU .... Observation Unit

OU .... Observation Unknown (SAUS)

OU .... Oculi Unitas [*Both Eyes Together*] [*Ophthalmology*]

OU .... Oculus Uterque [*Each Eye*] [*Ophthalmology*]

OU .... Odense University (SAUS)

OU .... Odor Unit [*Air pollution*]

OU .... Official Use (WDAA)

OU .... Oglethorpe University (SAUS)

OU .... Ohio State University, Columbus, OH [*Library symbol*] [*Library of Congress*] (LCLS)

OU .... Ohio University [*Athens*]

OU .... Okayama University (SAUS)

OU .... Oklahoma University

OU .... Open University [*British*]

OU .... Operable Unit (BCP)

OU .... Operation Unit

OU .... Oppenheim-Urbach [*Disease*] [*Medicine*] (DB)

OU .... Opposition Unie [*United Opposition*] [*The Comoros*] [*Political party*] (EY)

OU .... Osaka University (SAUS)

OU .... Otago University (SAUS)

OU .... Otonabee Airways [*ICAO designator*] (AD)

OU .... Ottawa University (SAUS)

OU .... Otterbein University (SAUS)

ou .... Ounce [*Unit of weight*] (CDAI)

OU .... Outlook Unusual (VLIE)

OU .... Output Unit [*Computer science*] (IAA)

O/U............. Over and Under (GOBB)

OU	Owen University (SAUS)
OU	Owosso University (SAUS)
OU	Oxford University [England]
OU	University of Oklahoma (SAUS)
OU	University of Oklahoma, Norman [USA] [Marine science] (OSRA)
OUA	Office of University Affairs [NASA]
OUA	Order of United Americans (NADA)
OUA	Organisation de l'Unite Africaine [Organization of African Unity - OAU] (EAIO)
OUA	Ouagadougou [Burkina Faso] [Airport symbol] (OAG)
OUA	Ouanaham [Loyalty Islands] [Seismograph station code, US Geological Survey] (SEIS)
OUa	Upper Arlington Public Library, Upper Arlington, OH [Library symbol] [Library of Congress] (LCLS)
OUAA	Ontario Universities Athletic Association (SAUS)
OUAC	Ontario University Application Center (SAUS)
OUAC	Oxford University Appointments Committee (SAUS)
OUADP	Operational Utility of ADP (SAUS)
OUAM	Order of United American Mechanics
OUAS	Oxford University Air Squadron [British] (DI)
OUASS	Omega Upper Atmospheric Sounding Systems (SAUS)
OUAT	Once upon a Time (The Prisoner Fan Club) (EA)
OUB	Occasional-Use Bands (SAUS)
OUBD	Outbound [ICAO designator] (FAAC)
OU-BP	Ohio State University, Byrd Polar Research Center, Goldthwait Polar Library, Columbus, OH [Library symbol] [Library of Congress] (LCLS)
OUBS	Open University Business School [British]
OUC	Ocracoke, NC [Location identifier] [FAA] (FAAL)
OUC	Ohio University, Chillicothe Branch Campus, Chillicothe, OH [OCLC symbol] (OCLC)
OUCA	Chemical Abstracts, Ohio State University, Columbus, OH [Library symbol] [Library of Congress] (LCLS)
OUCA	Ontario University Council on Admissions (SAUS)
OUCC	Ohio University Cartographic Center [Research center] (RCD)
OUCD	Operations Utilization and Capability Development (SAUS)
OUCH	Off-Line Universal Command History [Computer science] (KSC)
OUCH	Organised Unitary Content Hypothesis (SAUS)
OUCL	Oxford University Computing Laboratory (SAUS)
OUCTA	Order of United Commercial Travelers of America (EA)
OUD	AMOCO Production Co., Library, Tulsa, OK [OCLC symbol] (OCLC)
OUD	Operational Use Data
OUD	Oujda [Morocco] [Airport symbol] (OAG)
Oud C	Oudh Code [India] [A publication] (DLA)
Oudh C	Oudh Code [India] [A publication] (DLA)
Oudh LJ	Oudh Law Journal [India] [A publication] (DLA)
Oudh LR	Oudh Law Reports [India] [A publication] (DLA)
Oudh Rev Sel Cas...	Revised Collection of Selected Cases Issued by Chief Commissioner and Financial Commissioner of Oudh [A publication] (DLA)
Oudh Wkly N...	Oudh Weekly Notes [India] [A publication] (DLA)
Oudh WN	Oudh Weekly Notes [India] [A publication] (DLA)
OUDP	Officer Undergraduate Degree Program [Army] (AABC)
OUDS	Oxford University Dramatic Society [British] (AIE)
OUE	National Oceanic and Atmospheric Administration, National Severe Storms Laboratories, Norman, OK [OCLC symbol] (OCLC)
OUE	Operational Utility Evaluation
OUE	Orbital Uncertainty Estimate
OUE	Ouesso [Congo] [Airport symbol] (OAG)
OUE	Ouvriers Unis de l'Electricite, de la Radio, et de la Machinerie d'Amerique [United Electrical, Radio, and Machine Workers of America - UE]
OUEL	Oxford University Engineering Laboratory (SAUS)
OUF	Northwestern Oklahoma State University, Library, Alva, OK [OCLC symbol] (OCLC)
OUF	Optimum Usable (or Usual) Frequency (SAUS)
OUF	Optimum Usual Frequency Radio (IAA)
OUF	Order of Use File (MCD)
OUF	Oxygen Utilization Factor
OUG	Occam User Group (SAUS)
OUG	Oklahoma Children's Memorial Hospital, Library, Oklahoma City, OK [OCLC symbol] (OCLC)
OUG	On-line Users Group (SAUS)
OUG	Organisation de l'Unite Guineenne [Organization of Guinean Unity] (PD)
OUG	Ouahigouya [Upper Volta] [Airport symbol] (AD)
Ought	Oughton's Ordo Judiciorum [Order of Judgments] [A publication] (DLA)
OUG/I	Online Users' Group/Ireland (EAIO)
OU-H	Ohio State University, Health Sciences Library, Columbus, OH [Library symbol] [Library of Congress] (LCLS)
OUH	Oklahoma College of Osteopathic Medicine and Surgery, Library, Tulsa, OK [OCLC symbol] (OCLC)
OUH	Oudtshoorn [South Africa] [Airport symbol] (OAG)
OUHK	Open University of Hong Kong
OUHS	Oxford University Historical Society (SAUS)
OUHSC	Oklahoma University Health Sciences Center
OUI	Ban Houei Sai [Laos] [Airport symbol] (AD)
OUI	Office of Unemployment Insurance [Employment and Training Administration] [Department of Labor]
OUI	Oklahoma Osteopathic Hospital, Library, Tulsa, OK [OCLC symbol] (OCLC)
OUI	Operating under the Influence (GOBB)
OUI	Organisation Universitaire Interamericaine [Inter-American Organization for Higher Education] (EAIO)
OUI	Organizationally Unique Identifier (SAUS)
OUI	Organizational Unit Identifier (SAUS)
OUI	Outdoors Unlimited (EA)
OUI	Outer Integument [Botany]
OUIC	Operational Unit Identification Code (SAUS)
OUIL	Operating a Vehicle while under the Influence of Liquor [Traffic offense charge]
OUJ	Oklahoma State University, Technical Institute Library, Oklahoma City, OK [OCLC symbol] (OCLC)
OUK	Operation Upshot-Knothole [Atomic weapons testing]
OUK	Oscar Rose Junior College Library, Midwest City, OK [OCLC symbol] (OCLC)
OUL	Air Atonabee Ltd. [Canada] [ICAO designator] (FAAC)
OU-L	Ohio State University, College of Law, Columbus, OH [Library symbol] [Library of Congress] (LCLS)
OUL	Ohio University, Lancaster Branch Campus, Lancaster, OH [OCLC symbol] (OCLC)
OUL	Orbital Utility Light
OUL	Oulu [Finland] [Airport symbol] (OAG)
OUL	Oulu [Finland] [Seismograph station code, US Geological Survey] (SEIS)
OULC	Oxford University Lacrosse Club (SAUS)
OULCS	Ontario University Libraries Cooperative System (NITA)
Oult Ind	Oulton's Index to Irish Statutes [A publication] (DLA)
Oult Laws Ir...	Oulton's Laws of Ireland [A publication] (DLA)
OUM	Oxford University Mission (SAUS)
OUM	Philbrook Art Center Library, Tulsa, OK [OCLC symbol] (OCLC)
OUMC	Otago University Medical Corps [British military] (DMA)
OUN	Norman, OK [Location identifier] [FAA] (FAAL)
OUN	Ohio University, Athens, OH [OCLC symbol] (OCLC)
OUNPSA	Office of United Nations Political and Security Affairs [Department of State]
OUNS	Office of Urban Neighborhood Services [HUD]
OUNSAF......	Office of the Under Secretary of the Air Force
OUNSPI.......	Ontario Universities Non Salary Price Index (SAUS)
OUO	Official Use Only
OUO	United States Army, Morris Swett Library, Fort Sill, OK [OCLC symbol] (OCLC)
OUP	Official Unionist Party [Northern Ireland] (PPW)
OUP	OFS [Orbiter Functional Simulator] Uplink Processor [NASA]
OU-P	Ohio State University, Pharmacy and Bacteriology Library, Columbus, OH [Library symbol] [Library of Congress] (LCLS)
OUP	Operative United Painters [A union] [British]
OUP	Operative United Plumbers [A union] [British]
OUP	Oxford University Press, Inc. [New York, NY]
OUP	University of Portland, Portland, OR [OCLC symbol] (OCLC)
OUPID	Ontario Universities Program for Instructional Development (SAUS)
OUPID	Ontario University Program for Instructional Development (SAUS)
OUPT	Output (AAG)
OUQ	Ocean University of Qingdao (SAUS)
OUQ	United States Army, Nye Library, Fort Sill, OK [OCLC symbol] (OCLC)
OUR	Batouri [Cameroon] [Airport symbol] (OAG)
OUR	Office of the University Registrar (SAUS)
OUR	Office of University Research (SAUS)
OUR	Organizacion de Unidad Revolucionaria [Organization of Revolutionary Unity] [Bolivia] [Political party] (PPW)
OUR	Oxygen Uptake Rate [Biochemistry]
OUR	Oxygen Utilization Rate [Photosynthesis]
OUR	United States Federal Aviation Administration, Aeronautical Center Library, Oklahoma City, OK [OCLC symbol] (OCLC)
OURAD	Our Radiogram (SAUS)
OUrC	Urbana College, Urbana, OH [Library symbol] [Library of Congress] (LCLS)
OURD	[The] Ogden Union Railway & Depot Co. [AAR code]
OURD Co	Overseas Uranium Resources Development Company (SAUS)
OURI	Oklahoma University Research Institute
Our Lady Lake U...	Our Lady of the Lake University (GAGS)
OURQ	Outer Upper Right Quadrant [Anatomy]
OURS	Open Users Recommended Solutions (SAUS)
OURS	Orangutan Recovery Service [Later, IUCN]
OURS	Organization for United Response [Later, AFA (Adoptive Families of America)] (PAZ)
OURTEL	Our Telegram (NATG)
OUS	Oculo Urethro Synovite (SAUS)
OUS	Okayama University of Science (SAUS)
OUS	Oklahoma Union List of Serials Project, Stillwater, OK [OCLC symbol] (OCLC)
OUS	Ourinhos [Brazil] [Airport symbol] (OAG)
OUS	Outdoor Unit Substation
O/US	Over-Under Shotgun (SAUS)
OUS	Oxford Union Society (SAUS)
OUSA	Office of the Under Secretary of the Army
OUSA	Omni USA, Inc. [NASDAQ symbol] (SAG)
OUSA	Open University Students' Association [British]
OUSA	Operation USA [An association] (EA)
OUSA	Organisation de l'Unite Syndicale Africaine [Organisation of African Trade Union Unity - OATUU] [Accra, Ghana] (EAIO)
OUSAF	Office of the Under Secretary of the Air Force
OUSAIRA	Office of the United States Air Attache (CINC)
OUSARMA ...	Office of the United States Army Attache
OUSCS	Office of Urban Studies and Clearinghouse Services [HUD]
OUSD	Office of the Under Secretary of Defense (MCD)
OUSDA........	Office of the Under Secretary of Defense for Acquisition

OUSD(A & T)...	Office of the Under Secretary of Defense (Acquisition and Technology) (RDA)
OUSD(P)......	Office of the Under Secretary of Defense (Policy) (MCD)
OUSDRE	Office of the Under Secretary of Defense for Research and Engineering
OUSF	Oxford University School of Forestry (SAUS)
OUSH...........	Uxbridge-Scott Historical Society, Uxbridge, Ontario [Library symbol] [National Library of Canada] (BIB)
OUSL	Office of the Undersecretary of Labor (SAUS)
OUSN	Office of the Under Secretary of the Navy
OUSOFA......	Office of the Under Secretary of the Army
OUST	Office of Underground Storage Tanks [Environmental Protection Agency]
OUSW	Office of the Under Secretary of War [Obsolete]
OUT	Bousso [Chad] [Airport symbol] (AD)
OUT	Check-Out Date (TVEL)
OUT	Operational Utilization Test (ACAE)
OUT	Orbiter Utilities Tray [NASA] (NASA)
OUT	Organizacao Unida de Trabalhadores [United Organization of Workers] [Portugal] [Political party] (PPE)
OUT	Organization for Unemployed Teachers
OUT	Organization for Use of the Telephone (EA)
Out..............	Outerbridge's State Reports [97, 98 Pennsylvania] [A publication] (DLA)
out	Outgoing (ELAL)
OUT	Outgoing
OUT	Outing (ROG)
OUT	Outlet [Hawaii] [Seismograph station code, US Geological Survey] (SEIS)
OUT	Outlines (SAUS)
OUT	Output (NASA)
OUT	Outsize Cargo (COE)
OUT	United States Federal Aviation Administration, CAMI Library, Oklahoma City, OK [OCLC symbol] (OCLC)
OUT	Uxbridge Township Public Library, Uxbridge, Ontario [Library symbol] [National Library of Canada] (NLC)
OUTA	Ontario Urban Transit Association (SAUS)
OUTA	Ouvriers Unis des Textiles d'Amerique [United Textile Workers of America - UTWA]
Out Aer.......	Outdoor Aerial (SAUS)
Out Ant	Outdoor Antenna (SAUS)
OUTBD........	Outboard
OUTBD........	Outbound
OutbdM.......	Outboard Marine Corp. [Associated Press] (SAG)
OUTBGS.....	Outbuildings (ROG)
OutbkStk.....	Outback Steakhouse, Inc. [Associated Press] (SAG)
OUTC	Ordnance Unit Training Center [Military]
OUTC	Outbound Cargo (SAUS)
OUTCONUS...	Outside Continental Limits of the United States [Military] (DNAB)
OUTDA	Ontario Urban Transportation Development Agency (SAUS)
OUTG	Outage (KSC)
OUTHO........	Outhouse (ROG)
OUTL	Outlet
outl	Outline (VRA)
OUTL	Outlook Group Corp [NASDAQ symbol] (SPSG)
Outlet.........	Outlet Communications, Inc. [Associated Press] (SAG)
OUTLIM	Output Limiting (SAUS)
OUTLIM	Output Limiting Facility [Computer science] (MDG)
OUTLIM Facility...	Output Limiting Facility (SAUS)
OutlkGrp	Outlook Group Corp. [Associated Press] (SAG)
Outlook Res Libr...	Outlook on Research Libraries (SAUS)
OUTLT	Outlet
Out of Sync...	Out of Synchronization (SAUS)
OUTPUTM....	Output Measures for Public Libraries [Clarion University of Pennsylvania] [Information service or system] (IID)
OUTRAN	Outlet
OUTRAN	Output
OUTRAN	Output Translator [IBM Corp.]
OUTREG.......	Output Register (IAA)
OUTS	Operational Unit Transportable System (MCD)
OUTS	Output String (SAUS)
Outstdg	Outstanding (EBF)
OUTSTDG	Outstanding [Business term]
outstg	Outstanding [Business term] (MHDW)
OUTUS	Outside the United States
OUTWATS....	Outgoing Wide-Area Telephone Service [Telecommunications] (TEL)
OUTWATS....	Outward Wide Area Telephone Service (SAUS)
OUTWD........	Outward (ROG)
OUTXLTR....	Output Translator [IBM Corp.] (MSA)
OUU	University of Oklahoma, Tulsa Medical College Library, Tulsa, OK [OCLC symbol] (OCLC)
OUUI............	Decisions Given by the Office of the Umpire (Unemployment Insurance) Respecting Claims to Out-of-Work Donation [England] (DLA)
OUUIBD	Benefit Decisions of the British Umpire [A publication] (DLA)
OUUID	Umpire Decisions, Benefit Claims [England] [A publication] (DLA)
OUUISD	Benefit and Donation Claims, Selected Decisions of Umpire [England] [A publication] (DLA)
OUV	University of Science and Arts of Oklahoma Libraries, Chickasha, OK [OCLC symbol] (OCLC)
OUVB..........	Oxford University Volunteer Battalion [British military] (DMA)
OUVS	Orbiter Ultraviolet Spectrometer [NASA]
OUW	Elkins, WV [Location identifier] [FAA] (FAAL)
OUW	Western Oklahoma State College, Library, Altus, OK [OCLC symbol] (OCLC)
OUZ	Zouerate [Mauritania] [Airport symbol] (OAG)
OV	Observed Vehicle (WDAA)
OV	Observed Velocity (SAUS)
OV	Obvious (AAMN)
OV	Offense Variable [Criminal sentencing]
OV	Office of Volunteers [Red Cross]
OV	Office Visit [Medicine]
OV	Ohio Valley
OV	Oil of Vitriol
OV	Olivine (SAUS)
OV	One Village [An association] (EAIO)
OV	One Voice: a Magazine about Church Music [A publication] (APTA)
OV	Open Valve [Automotive fuel systems]
OV	Open Ventilated (MSA)
OV	Open Visit (WDAA)
OV	Operational Verification (SAUS)
OV	Operation Venus (EA)
OV	Optimum Value (SAUS)
OV	Orbital [or Orbiter] Vehicle [NASA]
ov	Orbiter Vehicle [NASA] (NAKS)
OV	Orbiting Vehicle (ACAE)
OV	Organic Variable (DIPS)
OV	Organismic Variable (DIPS)
OV	Orientation Visit (SAUS)
OV	Orphan Voyage (EA)
OV	Osler-Vaquez [Disease] [Medicine] (DB)
OV	Output Voltage
OV	Oval
OV	Ovalbumin [Also, OA, OVA, OVAL] [Biochemistry]
OV	Ovarian Volume [Gynecology]
OV	Ovary (ADA)
OV	Oven [Refers to the open space below the stage in a theater] [Slang] (DSUE)
OV	Over (AAG)
ov	Over (VRA)
OV	Overflow
OV	Overruled [Legal shorthand] (LWAP)
OV	Overseas National Airways (GAVI)
ov	Overture (GROV)
OV	Overture (ROG)
OV	Overventilation [Medicine]
OV	Overvoltage
OV	Ovid [Roman poet, 43BC-17AD] [Classical studies] (ROG)
OV	Ovulate [Gynecology] (DAVI)
OV	Ovum [Egg] [Latin]
OV	Owner's Vans [Shipping]
ov	Oxygen Vent (NAKS)
OV	Oxygen Vent (NASA)
OVA	Bekily [Madagascar] [Airport symbol] (OAG)
OVA	Office of Veterans' Affairs
OVA	Offshore Valve Association (EA)
OVA	Ontario Veterinary Association (SAUS)
OVA	Operational Voltage-controlled Amplifier (SAUS)
OVA	Optical Visual Analysis (SAUS)
OVA	Organic Vapor Analyzer [Chromatography]
OVA	Original Video Animation (SAUS)
OVA	Ottava [Octave] [Music]
OVA	Ovalbumin [Also, OA, OV, OVAL] [Biochemistry]
OVAB	Overhead Value Analysis (ADA)
OVAB	Orbiting Vehicle Assembly Building [Later, OVSB]
OVAC	Organisation Value Analysis Chart (PDAA)
OVAC	Overseas Visual Aids Centre [British]
OVAE	Office of Vocational and Adult Education [Department of Education] (OICC)
OVAG	Horticultural Research Institute of Ontario Ministry of Agriculture and Food, Vineland Station, Ontario [Library symbol] [National Library of Canada] (NLC)
OVAGR........	Research Station, Agriculture Canada [Station de Recherches, Agriculture Canada] Vineland Station, Ontario [Library symbol] [National Library of Canada] (NLC)
Ovako Steel Tech Rep...	Ovako Steel Technical Report (SAUS)
OVAL	Object-Based Virtual Application Language (SAUS)
OVAL	Oval [Postal Service standard] (OPSA)
OVAL	Ovalbumin [Also, OA, OV, OVA]
OVAL	Ovalocytes [Laboratory science] (DAVI)
OVAL	Overalls [Freight]
OVALO........	Ovalocytosis [Laboratory science] (DAVI)
OVAM	Orbital Vehicle Assembly Mode [NASA]
OVAMS	Office of Vulnerability Assessment and Management Services [Department of Commerce]
OVAN	Vanier Public Library, Ontario [Library symbol] [National Library of Canada] (NLC)
OVAR	Off Vertical Axis Rotation (SAUS)
OVAS	Offshore Vessels Availability System [Alpha Asia Systems Pte. Ltd.] [Defunct] [Information service or system] (CRD)
OVATE	Okumenische Vereinigung der Akademien und Tagungzentren in Europa [Ecumenical Association of Laity Centres and Academies in Europe - EALCAE] [Bad Boll, Federal Republic of Germany] (EAIO)
OVAX	Ovariectomized [Gynecology]
OVB	Novosibirsk [Former USSR] [Airport symbol] (OAG)
OVB	Overseas Visitors Bureau [Department of Trade] [British]
OVBC	Ohio Valley Banc Corp. [NASDAQ symbol] (SAG)
OVBD	Overboard (AAG)
OVC	Occupational Violent Crime (HEAS)

OVC .... Office for Victims of Crime [Department of Justice]
OVC .... Ohio Valley Conference [Collegiate sports]
OVC .... Ontario Veterinary College
OVC .... Optimized Valence Configuration [Air Force]
ovc............. Other Valuable Considerations [Commerce] (BARN)
OVC .... Ovarian Cancer (MELL)
OVC .... Overcast
OVC .... Oxidizer Vent Control
OVC .... Valley East Public Library, Val Caron, Ontario [Library symbol] [National Library of Canada] (NLC)
OVCA .... Ovarian Carcinoma [Oncology]
OVCO .... Operational Voice Communication Office [NASA] (MCD)
ovco........... Operational Voice Communication Office [NASA] (NAKS)
OVCP .... Orbiting Vehicle Checkout Procedure
OVCS .... Operational Voice Communication Subsystem
OVCSEL .... Organic Vertical-Cavity Surface-Emitting LASER [Materials science]
OVCST .... Overcast (AFM)
OVCT .... Caldwell Township Public Library, Verner, Ontario [Library symbol] [National Library of Canada] (NLC)
OVD .... Occlusal Vertical Dimension [Dentistry]
OV/D .... Operational Verification/Demonstration
OVD .... Optically Variable Device
OVD .... Optical Video Disk
OVD .... Optimum Velocity Distribution (SAUS)
OVD .... Outer Vapor Phase Deposition [Coating technology]
OVD .... Outside Vapor Deposition [Coating technology]
OVD .... Overdue (ACAE)
OVD .... Oviedo [Spain] [Airport symbol] (OAG)
OVDED .... Overdeduction
OVDF .... Official Visitors to Departmental Facilities [New South Wales, Australia]
OVDP .... Outside Vapor-Deposition Process (SAUS)
OVDR .... Observed Vertical Detection Range
OVE .... Ohio Valley Electric Railroad
OVE .... On Vehicle Equipment
OVE .... Optimum Value Engineered (Home)
OVE .... Orator Verbis Electric (IAA)
OVE .... Oroville, CA [Location identifier] [FAA] (FAAL)
OVE .... Overton [Nevada] [Seismograph station code, US Geological Survey] [Closed] (SEIS)
OVE .... Owen Vapor Engine
OVEATP ..... Ohio Vocational Education Achievement Test Program (EDAC)
OVEC .... Ohio Valley Electric Corporation (SAUS)
OVEN .... Italian Oven [NASDAQ symbol] (TTSB)
OVEN .... [The] Italian Oven, Inc. [NASDAQ symbol] (SAG)
OVER .... Optimum Vehicle for Effective Reconnaissance [Air Force] (PDAA)
OVER .... Oversize (SAUS)
OVER .... Oversize Cargo (COE)
Over............ Overtone [Record label]
Over............ Overton's Tennessee Supreme Court Reports [1791-1816] [A publication] (DLA)
Overl.......... Overland [A publication]
OVERMATION... Over-Instrumentation (SAUS)
OVERPASS... Overpass [Commonly used] (OPSA)
Overr.......... Overruled In [or Overruling] [Legal term] (DLA)
OVERS .... Orbital Vehicle Reentry Simulator [NASA]
OVERS .... Overplus (DGA)
Overs......... Overshoes (SAUS)
Overseas Devt Nat Resourc Inst Newsl... Overseas Development Natural Resources Institute Newsletter (SAUS)
Overseas Trade Stat... Overseas Trade Statistics (SAUS)
Overt.......... Overton's Tennessee Supreme Court Reports [1791-1816] [A publication] (DLA)
Overt Pr....... Overton's Iowa and Wisconsin Practice [A publication] (DLA)
OVF............ Overfill (NASA)
OVF............ Overflow [Computer science]
OVF............ Overhead Fire (SAUS)
OVF............ Overvoltage Factor (IAA)
OVF............ Oxygen Vent Fill
OVF Bit....... Overflow Bit (SAUS)
OVFF.......... Orbital Valence Force Field (SAUS)
OVFL.......... Overflow (AAG)
ovflo.......... Overflow (HGAA)
OVG .... Oberverwaltungsgericht [Provincial Administrative Court of Appeal] [German] (DLA)
OVG .... Office of the Valuer-General [Northern Territory, Australia]
OVGWU ...... Orange Vaal General Workers Union (SAUS)
OVH .... Vankleek Hill Public Library, Ontario [Library symbol] [National Library of Canada] (NLC)
OVHD.......... Oval Head
OVHD.......... Overhead (AAG)
OVHDLD ..... Overhandled [Freight]
OVHD PWR CAB... Overhead Power Cable [Nautical charts]
OVHG.......... Overhanging
OVHL .... Overhaul (AAG)
OVHT .... Overheat (NASA)
OVHT .... Tay-Victoria Harbour Union Library, Victoria Harbour, Ontario [Library symbol] [National Library of Canada] (BIB)
OVI............. Office of Volunteerism Initiatives (BARN)
OVI............. Open Verilog International (SAUS)
OVI............. Operational Validation Inspection (MCD)
ovi .... Operational Validation Inspection (NAKS)
OVIC .... Orbiting Vehicle Integrating Contractor
OVID .... Object, View, and Interaction Design (SAUS)
OVID .... On-line Visual Display (SAUS)

OVID .... Optical Visible and near Infrared Detector (SAUS)
OVID .... Ovid Technologies [NASDAQ symbol] (SAG)
OvidTec....... Ovid Technologies [Associated Press] (SAG)
OVIFT......... Ohio Valley Institute of Food Technology (SAUS)
OVIR.......... Office of Visas and Registrations [Former USSR]
OVIS .... Ohio Vocational Interest Survey [Vocational guidance test]
OVK .... Overkill (SAUS)
OVKOT....... On Various Kinds of Thinking (SAUS)
OVL .... Office of Volunteer Liaison [ACTION]
OVL .... Optically Void Liquid
OVL .... Oval [Commonly used] (OPSA)
OVL .... Overhead Line (SAUS)
OVL .... Overlap (IAA)
OVL .... Overlay (IAA)
OVL .... Overlay File [Computer science]
OVL .... Program Overlay (SAUS)
OVLA .... Oblique Vein of Left Atrium [Medicine] (MELL)
OVLA .... Optical Very Large Array (SAUS)
OVLAY .... Overlay
OVLBI .... Orbital Very-Long Baseline Interferometer [Communications satellite] [Telecommunications] (IEEE)
OVLD .... Overload (AAG)
ovld .... Overload (ELAL)
OVLMA .... Orbiting Vehicle Limited Maintenance Area
OVLO .... Over-Voltage Lock-Out (CIST)
OVLP .... Overvoltage Load Protection
OVLT .... Organum Vasculosum of the Lamina Terminalis [Medicine]
OVM.......... Congregation of the Oblates of the Virgin Mary [Rome, Italy] (EAIO)
OVM.......... Department of Computational Mathematics, Academy of Sciences, Moscow (SAUS)
OVM.......... McGarry Public Library, Virginiatown, Ontario [Library symbol] [National Library of Canada] (BIB)
OVM.......... Online Vacation Mall [Computer site]
OVM.......... On Vehicle Materiel [Military]
OVM.......... Operator-Valued Measure (SAUS)
OVM.......... Orbiting Velocity Meter
OVN .... Oxygen Ventilation Network (SAUS)
OVNGT....... Overnight (FAAC)
OVO .... North Vernon, IN [Location identifier] [FAA] (FAAL)
OVO .... Orbiting Volcanological Observatory (ACAE)
Ovolactos..... Ovolactovegetarians (SAUS)
OVON .... OIS Optical Imaging Sys [NASDAQ symbol] (TTSB)
OVON .... OIS Optical Imaging Systems, Inc. [NASDAQ symbol] (SAG)
OVONIC....... Ovshinsky and Electronic [Excitation processing term formed by combining name of Stanford Ovshinsky, energy researcher, and "electronic"]
Ovos .... Ovovegetarians (SAUS)
OVOT .... Vernon Branch, Osgoode Township Library, Ontario [Library symbol] [National Library of Canada] (NLC)
OVP .... Oesterreichische Volkspartei [Austrian People's Party] [Political party] (PPW)
OVP .... Office of the Vice-President
OVP .... Oil-Vapor Pump
OVP .... Outside Vendor Personnel
OVP .... Oval Paint
OVP .... Ovarian Vein Plasma [Endocrinology]
OVP .... Overplay (SAUS)
OVP .... Overseas Private Investment Corp., Washington, DC [OCLC symbol] (OCLC)
OVP .... Overvoltage Protection
OVPC .... Ovary Pubescence - Curly [Botany]
OVPD .... Overpaid (AFM)
OVPG .... Ovary Pubescence, Glandular [Botany]
OVPLOT...... Over Plot (SAUS)
OVPO .... Outside Vapor Phase Oxidation [Glass technology]
OVPR .... Over-Voltage Protection Relay [Electrical engineering]
OVPRESS.... Overpressurized
OVPRT .... Overprinted (SAUS)
OVPT .... Overprint (SAUS)
OVPU .... Over-Voltage Protection Unit [Computer science] (EECA)
OVPUS .... Office of the Vice President of the United States (BARN)
OVPWR....... Overpower
OVR .... Office of Vocational Rehabilitation [Later, Vocational Rehabilitation Administration] [HEW]
OVR .... Operable Vehicle Rate (SAUS)
OVR .... Orbiting Vehicle Requirements
OVR .... Oudtshoorn Volunteer Rifles [British military] (DMA)
OVR .... Overlay File [Computer science]
OVR .... Overvoltage Relay
OVR .... Program Overlay (SAUS)
OVRA .... Organizzazione Vigilanza Repressione Antifascismo [Italian Organisation for Vigilance & Repression of Anti-Fascism] [Political party] (WDAA)
OVRD .... Override (AAG)
OVRH .... Val Rita-Harty Public Library, Val Rita, Ontario [Library symbol] [National Library of Canada] (BIB)
OVRHD .... Overhead
OVRMP .... Ohio Valley Regional Medical Program (SAUS)
OVRN .... Overrun (AFM)
OVRN .... Overrun Standard Approach Lighting System [Aviation] (DA)
OVRNG .... Overrunning (DA)
OVRO .... Owens Valley Radio Observatory [California Institute of Technology] [Research center] (RCD)
OVRO Millimeter Array... Owens Valley Radio Observatory Millimeter Array (SAUS)

OVRP	Organizacion de Voluntarios para la Revolucion Puertorriquena [*Organization of Volunteers for the Puerto Rican Revolution*] (PD)
OVRR	Office of Veterans Reemployment Rights [*Department of Labor*]
OVRS	Operational Voice Recording Subsystem
OVRSGHT	Oversight
OVRSTK	Overstrike (SAUS)
OVRWGT	Overweight (SAUS)
OVS	Object-Verb-Subject (ADWA)
OVS	Official Visitors' Scheme
OVS	Online Version Storage [*Computer science*] (PDAA)
OVS	Operational Voice System (MCD)
ovs	Operational Voice System (NAKS)
OVS	Optical Viewing System
OVS	Orbiting Vehicle System
OVS	Ovarian Vein Serum [*Endocrinology*]
OVS	Overhaul Specification (NG)
OVS	Oversize
OVSB	Overvoltage Sensing (MCD)
OVSB	Orbiting Vehicle Support Building [*Formerly, OVAB*]
OVSC	Office of Vehicle Safety Compliance [*Automotive safety*]
OVSEA	Overseas [*Aviation*] (FAAC)
OvShip	Overseas Shipholding Group, Inc. [*Associated Press*] (SAG)
OVSL	Overslow (SAUS)
OVSP	Overspeed (AAG)
OVSR	Office of Vehicle Systems Research [*Later, Safety System Laboratory*] [*National Institute of Standards and Technology*]
OVSTFD	Overstuffed [*Freight*]
OVT	Occupational-Vocational-Technical Training
OVT	Oceonics Vehicle Technology (SAUS)
OVT	Operational Validation Test (SAUS)
OVT	Operational Verification Test
OVT	Optical Van Trailer
OVTK	Overtake (FAAC)
OVTR	Operational Video Tape Recorder [*Air Force*] (MCD)
OVTR	Overtravel
OVUIL	Operating Vehicle under Influence of Liquor or Narcotic Drugs [*FBI standardized term*]
OVUREP	Overseas Unit Replacement [*System*] [*Army*]
OVUREP	Oversea Unit Replacement System (SAUS)
OVUREP System	Overseas Units Replacement System (SAUS)
O/V-U/V	Over Voltage - Under Voltage (MCD)
OVV	Optically Violently Variable [*QUASAR*]
ovv	Overvoltage (NAKS)
OVV	Overvoltage
OVV	Ovvero [*Otherwise*] [*Music*]
OVW	Open-View Windows (SAUS)
OVWA	On-Line Voltammetric Wastewater Analyzer [*Biochemistry*]
OVWD	Operating Vehicle while Drunk [*Traffic offense charge*]
OVWV	One Valley Bancorp [*NASDAQ symbol*] (TTSB)
OVWV	One Valley Bancorp of West Virginia, Inc. [*NASDAQ symbol*] (NQ)
OVX	Ovariectomized [*Gynecology*] (DAVI)
OVX	Ovariectomy [*Medicine*] (MELL)
OVXO	Oven-controlled, Voltage-controlled Crystal Oscillator (SAUS)
OW	Obere Winkelgruppe [*Angles above 45*] [*German military - World War II*]
OW	Observation Ward [*British*]
OW	Ocellus Width
OW	Offer Wanted
OW	Office of Water [*Environmental Protection Agency*] (GFGA)
OW	Officer's Writer [*British military*] (DMA)
OW	Off White (SAUS)
OW	Ohne Wert [*Without Value*] [*German*]
O/W	Oil-dispersed-in-Water [*Emulsion*]
OW	Oil-Immersed Water-Cooled [*Transformer*] (IEEE)
O/W	Oil in Water
O/W	Oil-Water [*Ratio*] [*Laboratory science*] (DAVI)
OW	Older Worker
OW	Old Well (SAUS)
OW	Old Wellingtonian [*Wellington College*] [*British*]
OW	Old Welsh [*Language, etc.*]
OW	Old Woman [*A wife*] [*Slang*]
OW	One Way [*Fare*]
OW	Open Web (SAUS)
OW	Open Wedge [*Osteotomy*] [*Orthopedics*] (DAVI)
OW	Open Wheel [*A publication*]
OW	Open-Window (SAUS)
OW	Open Wire (NATG)
OW	Open Work (SAUS)
OW	Open Wound (SAUS)
OW	Operand Word (SAUS)
ow	Optical Window (NAKS)
OW	Optical Window (NASA)
O/W	Optional With [*Automotive engineering*]
OW	Optional Word (SAUS)
OW	Options for Women [*Later, Options*] (EA)
OW	Order Wire [*Military*] (AABC)
OW	Order Writing (IAA)
OW	Ordinary Warfare
O-W	Ordinary Wave (MCD)
OW	Ordinary Welfare (BABM)
OW	Ordnance Workshop (SAUS)
OW	Outer Wing
OW	Out of Wedlock
OW	Oval Window (MELL)
OW	Over-Achieving Women
OW	Overall Width [*of the Vehicle*] [*TII*] (TAG)
OW	Overseas Writers (EA)
OW	Over Water (WDAA)
OW	Over Write (SAUS)
Ow	Owen's English Common Pleas Reports [*A publication*] (DLA)
Ow	Owen's English King's Bench Reports [*1556-1615*] [*A publication*] (DLA)
OW	Owners (RIMS)
OW	Owner's Wagons [*Shipping*]
OW	Trans Mountain Airlines [*ICAO designator*] (AD)
OW	Warren Public Library, Warren, OH [*Library symbol*] [*Library of Congress*] (LCLS)
OW	Windsor Public Library, Ontario [*Library symbol*] [*National Library of Canada*] (NLC)
OWA	Optical Wholesalers Association [*Later, OLA*] (EA)
OWA	Organics-in-Water Analyzer [*Instrumentation*]
OWA	Other Weird Arrangements (AMHC)
OWA	Outlook Web Access [*Computer science*] (VLIE)
OWA	Owase [*Japan*] [*Seismograph station code, US Geological Survey*] (SEIS)
OWA	Owatonna, MN [*Location identifier*] [*FAA*] (FAAL)
OWA	University of Windsor, Ontario [*Library symbol*] [*National Library of Canada*] (NLC)
OWAA	Anderson Associates Ltd., Willowdale, Ontario [*Library symbol*] [*National Library of Canada*] (NLC)
OWAA	Outdoor Writers Association of America (EA)
OWAAD	Organisation of Women of Asian and African Descent [*British*] (DI)
OWAB	Wasaga Beach Public Library, Ontario [*Library symbol*] [*National Library of Canada*] (BIB)
OWAEC	Organization for West African Economic Co-operation
OWAG	Art Gallery of Windsor, Ontario [*Library symbol*] [*National Library of Canada*] (NLC)
OWAIT	Airy Township Public Library, Whitney, Ontario [*Library symbol*] [*National Library of Canada*] (NLC)
OWAL	Law Library, University of Windsor, Ontario [*Library symbol*] [*National Library of Canada*] (NLC)
OWALK	Walkerton Branch, Bruce County Public Library, Ontario [*Library symbol*] [*National Library of Canada*] (NLC)
OWALL	Wallaceburg Public Library, Ontario [*Library symbol*] [*National Library of Canada*] (NLC)
OWAP	Overhead Warning Annunciator Panel (MCD)
OWaP	Pike County Free Public Library, Waverly, OH [*Library symbol*] [*Library of Congress*] (LCLS)
OWAP	Waterford Public Library, Ontario [*Library symbol*] [*National Library of Canada*] (NLC)
OWAR	Warkworth Public Library, Ontario [*Library symbol*] [*National Library of Canada*] (NLC)
OWARNP	Percy Township Branch, Northumberland County Public Library, Warkworth, Ontario [*Library symbol*] [*National Library of Canada*] (BIB)
OWas	Carnegie Public Library, Washington Court House, OH [*Library symbol*] [*Library of Congress*] (LCLS)
OWASU	Old World Archaeological Study Unit (EA)
OWAT	Wainfleet Township Library, Ontario [*Library symbol*] [*National Library of Canada*] (NLC)
OWAV	OneWave, Inc. [*NASDAQ symbol*] (SAG)
OWAVE	Ordinary Wave (MSA)
OWay	Mary L. Cook Public Library, Waynesville, OH [*Library symbol*] [*Library of Congress*] (LCLS)
OWB	Oppenheimer World Bond Fund [*NYSE symbol*] (SAG)
OWB	Oscillating Waterbed (MELL)
OWB	Owensboro [*Kentucky*] [*Airport symbol*] (AD)
OWB	West Bay Public Library, Ontario [*Library symbol*] [*National Library of Canada*] (NLC)
OWBA	Office of Women's Business Ownership (EBF)
OW Bailey Chr	Old Bailey Chronicle (SAUS)
OWBC	Health Sciences Library, Bloorview Children's Hospital, Willowdale, Ontario [*Library symbol*] [*National Library of Canada*] (BIB)
OWBE	Office of Women's Business Enterprise [*Federal government*]
OWBE	Windsor Board of Education, Ontario [*Library symbol*] [*National Library of Canada*] (NLC)
OWBL	Beaver Lake Branch, Walden Public Library, Ontario [*Library symbol*] [*National Library of Canada*] (NLC)
OWBL	Office of Work-Based Learning [*U.S. Department of Labor*] (BARN)
OWBMS	Manitoulin Secondary School Library, West Bay, Ontario [*Library symbol*] [*National Library of Canada*] (BIB)
OWBO	Office of Women's Business Ownership [*Small Business Administration*]
OWBPA	Older Workers Benefit Protection Act of 1990 (WYGK)
OWBR	Bartlet & Richardes, Windsor, Ontario [*Library symbol*] [*National Library of Canada*] (BIB)
OWC	Centennial Secondary School, Windsor, Ontario [*Library symbol*] [*National Library of Canada*] (NLC)
OWC	Officers' Wives Club [*Military*]
OWC	Oil Well Cement (SAUS)
OwC	Omniwest Corporation, Salt Lake City, UT [*Library symbol*] [*Library of Congress*] (LCLS)
OWC	One Way Communication (ELAL)
OWC	Ontario Workers' Compensation Appeals Tribunal [*UTLAS symbol*]
OWC	Order of Woodcraft Chivalry [*British*] (DBA)
OWC	Ordinary Wave Component
OWC	Ordnance Weapons Command [*Later, Weapons Command*]
OWC	Outline of World Cultures [*Human Relations Area Files*] [*Information retrieval*]

OWC .... Owner Will Carry [*Banking*]
OWC .... Owning Work Center [*Military*] (AFIT)
OWC .... Wood County District Public Library, Bowling Green, OH [*OCLC symbol*] (OCLC)
OWCA .... Canadian Automobile Workers Union, Willowdale, Ontario [*Library symbol*] [*National Library of Canada*] (BIB)
OWCC .... Cape Croker Public Library, Wiarton, Ontario [*Library symbol*] [*National Library of Canada*] (NLC)
OWCF .... Canadian Federation of Independent Business, Willowdale, Ontario [*Library symbol*] [*National Library of Canada*] (BIB)
OWCL .... Octane Weekly Cost Ledger (MCD)
OWCL .... Old World Cutaneous Leishmaniasis [*Medicine*] (MELL)
OWCP .... Office of Workers' [*formerly, Workmen's*] Compensation Programs [*Formerly, Bureau of Employees' Compensation*] [*Department of Labor*]
OWCS .... Outer Wing Canted Station (MCD)
OWCSC .... Old Water Colour Society's Club (EA)
OWD .... Norwood, MA [*Location identifier*] [*FAA*] (FAAL)
OWD .... Oil-in-Water Dispersion [*Pollution*]
OWD .... One-Way Doppler (MCD)
OWD .... On-Line Wholesale Distribution System [*Computer science*] (BUR)
OWDC .... Office of Water Data Coordination [*US Geological Survey*] [*Reston, VA*]
OWDD .... Old Well Drilling Deeper (SAUS)
OWDE .... One-Way Doppler Extraction
OWDM .... Original Water Depth Mine (SAUS)
OWE .... Eagle, CO [*Location identifier*] [*FAA*] (FAAL)
OWE .... Office of Water Enforcement [*Environmental Protection Agency*] (ERG)
OWE .... Operating Weight Empty [*of space shuttle*] [*NASA*]
OWE .... Optimum Working Efficiency
OWE .... Outer Window Envelope [*Business stationery*]
OWE .... Welland Public Library, Ontario [*Library symbol*] [*National Library of Canada*] (NLC)
OWE .... Western Plains Library System, Clinton, OK [*OCLC symbol*] (OCLC)
OWe .... Westerville Public Library, Westerville, OH [*Library symbol*] [*Library of Congress*] (LCLS)
OWEB .... Webbwood Public Library, Ontario [*Library symbol*] [*National Library of Canada*] (NLC)
OWEC .... Centennial Secondary School, Welland, Ontario [*Library symbol*] [*National Library of Canada*] (NLC)
OWel .... Sylvester Memorial Wellston Public Library, Wellston, OH [*Library symbol*] [*Library of Congress*] (LCLS)
OWEL .... Wellington Public Library, Ontario [*Library symbol*] [*National Library of Canada*] (BIB)
OWelsh .... Old Welsh (ADWA)
O/W Emulsion... Oil/Water Emulsion (SAUS)
OWEN .... Niagara College of Applied Arts and Technology, Welland, Ontario [*Library symbol*] [*National Library of Canada*] (NLC)
OWEN .... Owen Healthcare, Inc. [*NASDAQ symbol*] (SAG)
Owen .... Owen's English King's Bench Reports [*1556-1615*] [*A publication*] (DLA)
OWEN .... Science & Engineering Library (SAUS)
Owen Bankr... Owen on Bankruptcy [*A publication*] (DLA)
OwenC .... Owens-Corning Fiberglas Corp. [*Associated Press*] (SAG)
OWENC .... Westport-North Crosby Public Library, Westport, Ontario [*Library symbol*] [*National Library of Canada*] (NLC)
OwenHlt .... Owen Healthcare, Inc. [*Associated Press*] (SAG)
OWENL .... Library Technician Program, Niagara College of Applied Arts & Technology, Welland, Ontario [*Library symbol*] [*National Library of Canada*] (NLC)
OwensIll ...... Owens Illinois [*Associated Press*] (SAG)
OwensM ...... Owens & Minor Inc. Holding Co. [*Associated Press*] (SAG)
OWeO .... Otterbein College, Westerville, OH [*Library symbol*] [*Library of Congress*] (LCLS)
OWEP .... Office of Water Enforcement and Permits [*Environmental Protection Agency*] (GFGA)
OWEP .... Oily Waste Extraction Program (SAUS)
OWERP .... Open Window Early Retirement Plans
OWESBC ...... Borden Chemical, Westhill, Ontario [*Library symbol*] [*National Library of Canada*] (NLC)
OWEST .... Asphodel Township Public Library, Westwood, Ontario [*Library symbol*] [*National Library of Canada*] (BIB)
OWF .... Object World Frankfurt (SAUS)
OWF .... Oceania Weightlifting Federation [*Australia*] (EA)
OWF .... One-Way Function (VLIE)
OWF .... On Weight of Fiber
OWF .... Optimal Work Function (SAUS)
OWF .... Optimum Working Facility (NITA)
OWF .... Optimum Working Frequency [*Telecommunications*]
OWF .... Orbital, Weightless Flight (IAA)
OWF .... Overwing Fairing (SAUS)
OWFEA .... Ontario Wholesale Farm Equipment Association (SAUS)
OWFS .... Optical WORM File System (SAUS)
OWG .... Oil, Water, Gas
OWG .... Open Waveguide (SAUS)
OWG .... Optical Waveguide (SAUS)
OWG .... Washington, DC [*Location identifier*] [*FAA*] (FAAL)
OWGL .... Obscure Wire Glass
OWH .... CDCs Office of Womens Health (SAUS)
OWH .... Herman Collegiate Institute, Windsor, Ontario [*Library symbol*] [*National Library of Canada*] (NLC)
OWH .... Office of the War on Hunger (SAUS)
OWH .... Ordinary Working Hours (SAUS)

OWH .... Warren General Hospital, Warren, OH [*Library symbol*] [*Library of Congress*] (LCLS)
OWHA .... Oliver Wendell Holmes Association
OWHD .... Medical Library, Hotel-Dieu of St. Joseph Hospital, Windsor, Ontario [*Library symbol*] [*National Library of Canada*] (NLC)
OWHM .... Hiram Walker Historical Museum, Windsor, Ontario [*Library symbol*] [*National Library of Canada*] (BIB)
OWHM .... Office of Water and Hazardous Materials (OICC)
OWHN .... One Word Host Name (SAUS)
OWHP .... Whitby Public Library, Ontario [*Library symbol*] [*National Library of Canada*] (NLC)
OWI .... Ocellus Width Index
OWI .... Office of War Information [*World War II*]
OWI .... Office of Waste Isolation [*Department of Energy*]
OWI .... OneWorld Internet [*Global Village Communication*] [*Internet gateway service*]
OWI .... Open Work Items (KSC)
OWI .... Operating Vehicle while Intoxicated [*Traffic offense charge*]
OWI .... Operating While Intoxicated (SAUS)
OWI .... Ottawa, KS [*Location identifier*] [*FAA*] (FAAL)
OWI .... Owens-Illinois, Inc., Technical and Business Information Services, Toledo, OH [*OCLC symbol*] (OCLC)
OWI .... Wiarton Branch, Bruce County Public Library, Ontario [*Library symbol*] [*National Library of Canada*] (NLC)
OWIB .... Wikwemikong Band Public Library, Ontario [*Library symbol*] [*National Library of Canada*] (NLC)
OWibfC .... Central State University, Wilberforce, OH [*Library symbol*] [*Library of Congress*] (LCLS)
OWibfP .... Payne Theological Seminary, Wilberforce, OH [*Library symbol*] [*Library of Congress*] (LCLS)
OWibfU .... Wilberforce University, Wilberforce, OH [*Library symbol*] [*Library of Congress*] (LCLS)
OWicB .... Borromeo Seminary of Ohio, Wickliffe, OH [*Library symbol*] [*Library of Congress*] (LCLS)
OWIFC .... Wolfe Island Branch, Frontenac County Public Library, Ontario [*Library symbol*] [*National Library of Canada*] (NLC)
OWIJC .... International Joint Commission [*Commission Mixte Internationale*] Windsor, Ontario [*Library symbol*] [*National Library of Canada*] (NLC)
OWil .... Willard Memorial Library, Willard, OH [*Library symbol*] [*Library of Congress*] (LCLS)
OWillo .... Willoughby-Eastlake Public Library, Willowick, OH [*Library symbol*] [*Library of Congress*] (LCLS)
OWilm .... Wilmington Public Library, Wilmington, OH [*Library symbol*] [*Library of Congress*] (LCLS)
OWilmC .... Wilmington College, Wilmington, OH [*Library symbol*] [*Library of Congress*] (LCLS)
OWilmH .... Clinton Memorial Hospital, Health Resource Center, Wilmington, OH [*Library symbol*] [*Library of Congress*] (LCLS)
OWilm-O....... Southwestern Ohio Rural Library, Wilmington, OH [*Library symbol*] [*Library of Congress*] (LCLS)
OWilmS .... Southern State Community College, Wilmington, OH [*Library symbol*] [*Library of Congress*] (LCLS)
OWin .... Adams-Brown County Bookmobile, Winchester, OH [*Library symbol*] [*Library of Congress*] (LCLS)
OWIN .... Office of Work Incentive Program [*Office of Comprehensive Employment Development*] [*Department of Labor*]
OWINF .... F. E. Madill Secondary School, Wingham, Ontario [*Library symbol*] [*National Library of Canada*] (NLC)
OWISDG ...... Williamstown Branch, Stormount, Dundas, and Glengarry County Library, Ontario [*Library symbol*] [*National Library of Canada*] (NLC)
owise .... otherwise (SAUS)
OWIT .... Organization of Women in International Trade (NTPA)
OWIU .... Oil Workers International Union [*Later, OCAW*]
OWJ .... Orthodontics Web Journal (SAUS)
OWK .... Kent State University, Trumbull Regional Campus, Warren, OH [*Library symbol*] [*Library of Congress*] [*OCLC symbol*] (LCLS)
OWK .... Norridgewock, ME [*Location identifier*] [*FAA*] (FAAL)
OWL .... Lowe Technical School, Windsor, Ontario [*Library symbol*] [*National Library of Canada*] (NLC)
OWL .... Maui Airlines, Inc. [*ICAO designator*] (FAAC)
OWL .... National Order of Women Legislators (EA)
OWL .... Object Windows Library [*Borland International*] [*Computer science*] (PCM)
OWL .... Ocotillo Water League (SAUS)
OWL .... Office Workstations Ltd. (NITA)
OWL .... Older Women's League (EA)
OWL .... Older Women's Liberation [*Feminist group*] [*Defunct*]
OWL .... Olympic-Wallowa Lineament [*Geology*]
OWL .... One Watt Linear (ACAE)
OWL .... On-line Without Limitation (SAUS)
OWL .... Online without Limits
OWL .... Online Writing Lab [*Purdue University*] [*Computer science*]
OWL .... Open Windows Library [*Computer science*] (VLIE)
OWL .... Optimal Waste Loading (ABAC)
OWL .... Orbiting Wide-Angle Light Collectors (SAUS)
OWL .... Orthopaedic Web Links (SAUS)
OWL .... Other Woman Limited [*An association*]
OWL .... Outlined-White Letter (SAUS)
OWL .... Outlined White Letters [*Tire design*]
OWL .... Overland Western Limited (SAUS)
OWL .... Over Water Line (SAUS)
OWL .... Overwhelmingly Large (SAUS)

OWL.............	Westerville Public Library, Westerville, OH [*OCLC symbol*] (OCLC)
OWLA	Organization of Women for Legal Awareness (EA)
OWLaw........	Trumbull County Law Library, Warren, OH [*Library symbol*] [*Library of Congress*] (LCLS)
OWLB	Wunnummin Lake Band Library, Ontario [*Library symbol*] [*National Library of Canada*] (BIB)
OWL/D	Optical Warning Locator/Detector (MCD)
OWLEF.........	Older Women's League Educational Fund (EA)
OWIGS.........	Church Jesus Christ of Latter-Day Saints, Genealogical Society Library, Cleveland Branch, Westlake, OH [*Library symbol*] [*Library of Congress*] (LCLS)
OWIGS.........	Church of Jesus Christ of Latter-Day Saints, Genealogical Society Library, Cleveland Branch, Westlake, OH [*Library symbol*] [*Library of Congress*] (LCLS)
OWLI	Lively Branch, Walden Public Library, Ontario [*Library symbol*] [*National Library of Canada*] (NLC)
OWLS	Office Workers Link Shift [*After-hours production workers*] [*World War II*]
OWLS	Operation Work Load Scheduling (MCD)
OWLS	Outagamie-Waupaca Counties Federated Library System [*Library network*]
OWLS	Overseas Weapons, Logistically Supported (MCD)
OWLS	Oxford Word and Language Service [*A service of the Oxford English Dictionary group*]
OWLT..........	One-Way Light Time
OWM	Office of War Mobilization [*Succeeded by OWMR, 1944*]
OWM	Office of Weights and Measures [*National Institute of Standards and Technology*]
OWM	Office Work Measurement (CIST)
OWM	Optical Waveguide Microscopy (SAUS)
OWM	Over Without Marks (SAUS)
OWMA	Oscar Wells Museum of Art (SAUS)
OWMC	Ontario Waste Management Corporation (SAUS)
OWMMD	M. M. Dillon Ltd., Willowdale, Ontario [*Library symbol*] [*National Library of Canada*] (NLC)
OWMR	Office of War Mobilization and Reconversion [*Succeeded OWM, 1944; became part of Office of Temporary Controls, 1946*]
OWMR	Other War Materiel Requirements [*Army*]
OWMT	Michipicoten Township Public Library, Wawa, Ontario [*Library symbol*] [*National Library of Canada*] (NLC)
OWN	Naughton Branch, Walden Public Library, Ontario [*Library symbol*] [*National Library of Canada*] (NLC)
OWN	Ontario Weekly Notes [*A publication*] (DLA)
OWN	Oudh Weekly Notes [*India*] [*A publication*] (DLA)
OWN	Overwintered Nest [*Ornithology*]
OWN	Owen Healthcare [*NYSE symbol*] (TTSB)
OWN	Owensboro [*Diocesan abbreviation*] [*Kentucky*] (TOCD)
OWN	Owens Group Ltd. [*New Zealand*] [*ICAO designator*] (FAAC)
OWN	Owen Ventures Ltd. [*Vancouver Stock Exchange symbol*]
OWN	Owner (MCD)
OWN	Sunterra Corp. [*NYSE symbol*] [*Formerly, Signature Resorts*]
OWN	Wise, VA [*Location identifier*] [*FAA*] (FAAL)
OWNR..........	Owner
OWO	On Work Order [*Military*] (AFIT)
OWO	OWI Washington Office (SAUS)
OWo.............	Wayne County Public Library, Wooster, OH [*Library symbol*] [*Library of Congress*] (LCLS)
OWO	Woodstock Public Library, Ontario [*Library symbol*] [*National Library of Canada*] (NLC)
OWoA	Ohio Agricultural Research and Development Center, Wooster, OH [*Library symbol*] [*Library of Congress*] (LCLS)
OWOBC.......	J. William Horsey Library, Ontario Bible College, Ontario Theological College, Willowdale, Ontario [*Library symbol*] [*National Library of Canada*] (NLC)
OWoC	College of Wooster, Wooster, OH [*Library symbol*] [*Library of Congress*] (LCLS)
OWOH..........	Huron Park Secondary School, Woodstock, Ontario [*Library symbol*] [*National Library of Canada*] (NLC)
OWoH	Wooster Community Hospital, Wooster, OH [*Library symbol*] [*Library of Congress*] (LCLS)
OWOL	Ontario Library Co-Operative, Wyoming, Ontario [*Library symbol*] [*National Library of Canada*] (NLC)
OWOM..........	Woodstock Museum, Ontario [*Library symbol*] [*National Library of Canada*] (BIB)
OWOO..........	Oxford County Public Library, Woodstock, Ontario [*Library symbol*] [*National Library of Canada*] (NLC)
OWor...........	Worthington Public Library, Worthington, OH [*Library symbol*] [*Library of Congress*] (LCLS)
OWorNW......	National Water Wall Association, Ground Water Library/Information Center, Worthington, OH [*Library symbol*] [*Library of Congress*] (LCLS)
OWorP.........	Pontifical College Josephinum, Worthington, OH [*Library symbol*] [*Library of Congress*] (LCLS)
OWOS..........	Owosso Corp. [*NASDAQ symbol*] (SAG)
Owosso......	Owosso Corp. [*Associated Press*]
OWOW.........	Office of Wetlands, Oceans, and Watersheds (WPI)
OWoWCL....	Wayne County Law Library, Wooster, OH [*Library symbol*] [*Library of Congress*] (LCLS)
OWP	Oboz Wielkiej Polski [*Camp of Great Poland*] (PPE)
OWP	Office of Water Policy [*Department of the Interior*]
OWP	Office of Water Programs [*Abolished*] [*Environmental Protection Agency*]
OWP	Office of Wetlands Protection [*Office of Water*] (COE)
OWP	Oil Well Pumper (SAUS)
OWP	One-Way Polar [*Telegraph*]
OWP	One-Write Plus [*Computer software*]
OWP	Operations Work Procedure [*Nuclear energy*] (NRCH)
OWP	Orange Washed Pulp [*Citrus processing*]
OWP	Organization of Wildlife Planners (EA)
OWP	Outer Wing Panel
OWP	Overall Work Programs (EEVL)
OWP	Warner Pacific College, Portland, OR [*OCLC symbol*] (OCLC)
OWpAR........	United States Air Force, Aerospace Research Laboratories, Wright-Patterson Air Force Base, OH [*Library symbol*] [*Library of Congress*] (LCLS)
OWPB..........	Old Well Plugging Back (SAUS)
OWpDI........	United States Air Force, Defense Institute of Security Administration Management, Wright-Patterson Air Force Base, OH [*Library symbol*] [*Library of Congress*] (LCLS)
OWPE	Office of Waste Programs Enforcement [*Environmental Protection Agency*] (EPA)
OWPH..........	Whitby Psychiatric Hospital, Ontario [*Library symbol*] [*National Library of Canada*] (NLC)
OWpIT.........	United States Air Force Institute of Technology, Wright-Patterson Air Force Base, OH [*Library symbol*] [*Library of Congress*] (LCLS)
OWpL..........	United States Air Force, Air Force Logistics Command, Wright-Patterson Air ForceBase, OH [*Library symbol*] [*Library of Congress*] (LCLS)
OWpM..........	United States Air Force, Medical Center Library, SGEL, Wright Patterson AFB, OH [*Library symbol*] [*Library of Congress*] (LCLS)
OWPO..........	Office of Water Program Operations [*Environmental Protection Agency*] (EPA)
OWPP	Office of Welfare and Pension Plans [*Department of Labor*]
OWPR	Ocean Wave Profile Recorder (IEEE)
OWPS	Offshore Windpower System [*Proposed system to generate electricity by wind turbines mounted on offshore platforms*]
OWPT..........	Overpaid Windfall Profits Tax (SAUS)
OWpT..........	United States Air Force, Wright-Patterson Technical Library, Wright-Patterson Air Force Base, OH [*Library symbol*] [*Library of Congress*] (LCLS)
OWQ	Output Work Queue (SAUS)
OWR	Obligated War Reserves [*Army*] (AABC)
OWR	Office of Worship Resources [*Later, WRO*] (EA)
OWR	Old World Realm (SAUS)
OWR	Omega West Reactor [*Los Alamos, NM*] [*Department of Energy*]
OWR	Ontario Weekly Reporter [*A publication*] (DLA)
OWR	Order of the White Rose of Finland (DD)
OWR	Ouse Washes Reserve (SAUS)
OWR	Riverside Secondary School, Windsor, Ontario [*Library symbol*] [*National Library of Canada*] (NLC)
OWR	Worthington Public Library, Worthington, OH [*OCLC symbol*] (OCLC)
OWRAP........	Office of Worker Retraining and Adjustment Programs [*U.S. Department of Labor*] (BARN)
OWRB..........	RC Reid-Bicknell Eng. Ltd., Woodbridge, Ontario [*Library symbol*] [*National Library of Canada*] (NLC)
OWRC..........	Office of Water Resource Center [*Environmental Protection Agency*] (AEPA)
OWRC..........	Old West Regional Commission [*Department of Commerce*]
OWRC..........	Ontario Water Resources Commission (SAUS)
OWRC..........	White River Community Library, Ontario [*Library symbol*] [*National Library of Canada*] (NLC)
OWRD..........	Ratter and Dunnet Public Library, Warren, Ontario [*Library symbol*] [*National Library of Canada*] (NLC)
OWRHS........	Ontario and Western Railroad Historical Society (EA)
OWRL	One-Way Radio Link [*Telecommunications*] (LAIN)
OWRM	Office of Weather Research and Modification [*National Oceanic and Atmospheric Administration*] (GRD)
OWRM	Other War Reserve Materiel
OWRMR.......	Other War Reserve Materiel Requirement (AFIT)
OWRMS	Other War Reserve Materiel Stocks [*Army*] (AABC)
OWRR..........	Office of Water Resources Research [*Later, OWRT*] [*Department of the Interior*]
OWRRI.........	Oklahoma Water Resources Research Institute [*Stillwater, OK*] [*Department of the Interior*] (GRD)
OWRS..........	Office of Water Regulations and Standards [*Environmental Protection Agency*] (GFGA)
OWRT..........	Office of Water Research and Technology [*Formerly, OSW, OWRR*] [*Abolished, 1982*] [*Department of the Interior*]
OWRTS	Open-Wire Radio Transmission System (VLIE)
OWS	Cargosur [*Spain*] [*ICAO designator*] (FAAC)
OWS	Obstacle Warning System (SAUS)
OWS	Occupational Wage Survey
OWS	Ocean Weather Service (SAUS)
OWS	Ocean Weather Ship
OWS	Ocean Weather Station (MCD)
OWS	Oil Water Separator [*Navy*] (CAAL)
OWS	Old West Saxon [*Language, etc.*] (ROG)
OWS	Oliphant Washington Service [*Information service or system*] (IID)
OWS	One-Way Simultaneous (VLIE)
OWS	Operational Weapon Satellite (SAUS)
OWS	Operational Weather Support
OWS	Operations Weather Support (SAUS)
OWS	Operators Workstation (SAUS)
OWS	Optical Witness Sample (SAUS)
OWS	Orbital Weapon System (AAG)
OWS	Orbital Workshop [*NASA*]
OWS	Ordnance Weapon Systems [*Army*]
OWS	Outerwear Syndrome [*Medicine*] (DMAA)
OWS	Outer Wing Station (MCD)
OWS	Overhead Weapon Station (SAUS)

OWS .... Overload Warning System (MCD)
OWS .... Overwear Syndrome [*Of contact lens*]
OWS .... Southwestern Regional Library, Windsor, Ontario [*Library symbol*] [*Obsolete*] [*National Library of Canada*] (NLC)
OWS .... Willamette University, Salem, OR [*OCLC symbol*] (OCLC)
OWSA .... Spar Aerospace Ltd., Weston, Ontario [*Library symbol*] [*National Library of Canada*] (NLC)
OWSAH........ Salvation Army Grace Hospital, Windsor, Ontario [*Library symbol*] [*National Library of Canada*] (BIB)
OWSC .... Old West Scandinavian [*Language, etc.*]
OWSC .... St. Clair College, Windsor, Ontario [*Library symbol*] [*National Library of Canada*] (NLC)
OWSCC........ Simon-Carves of Canada Ltd., Willowdale, Ontario [*Library symbol*] [*National Library of Canada*] (NLC)
OWSCL........ Senes Consultants Ltd., Willowdale, Ontario [*Library symbol*] [*National Library of Canada*] (NLC)
OWSDG........ Winchester Branch, Stormount, Dundas, and Glengarry County Public Library, Ontario [*Library symbol*] [*National Library of Canada*] (NLC)
OWSE .... Otherwise
OWSG.......... Older Worker Specialists Group
OWSJ .... Off the Wall Street Journal [*Parody of the Wall Street Journal*]
OWSM .... Seagram Museum, Waterloo, Ontario [*Library symbol*] [*National Library of Canada*] (BIB)
OWS Meteorological Summary... Ocean Weather Ship Meteorological Summary (SAUS)
OWSP .... One Word Storage Programmer (SAUS)
OWSS .... Ocean Weather Ship Service (SAUS)
OWT............ Organic Weather Team
OWT............ Waterloo Public Library, Ontario [*Library symbol*] [*National Library of Canada*] (NLC)
OWT............ Willamette University, Law Library, Salem, OR [*OCLC symbol*] (OCLC)
OWTA .... Kitchener-Waterloo Academy of Medicine, Kitchener, Ontario [*Library symbol*] [*National Library of Canada*] (NLC)
OWTAI .... Airworthiness Library, Ontario Region, Transport Canada [*Bibliotheque de la Navigabilite Aerienne, Region de l'Ontario, Transports Canada*], Willowdale, Ontario [*Library symbol*] [*National Library of Canada*] (NLC)
OWTD .... Office of Waste Technology Development (SAUS)
OWTG .... Kitchener-Waterloo Hospital, Kitchener, Ontario [*Library symbol*] [*National Library of Canada*] (NLC)
OWTL........... Open-Wire Transmission Line [*Telecommunications*] (VLIE)
OWTL........... Wilfrid Laurier University [*Formerly, Waterloo Lutheran University*] Waterloo, Ontario [*Library symbol*] [*National Library of Canada*] (NLC)
OWTM .... Legal Reference Centre, Manufacturers' Life Insurance Co., Waterloo, Ontario [*Library symbol*] [*National Library of Canada*] (BIB)
OWTML........ Corporate Library, Mutual Life of Canada, Waterloo, Ontario [*Library symbol*] [*National Library of Canada*] (BIB)
OWTO .... Ontario Library Services Center, Waterloo, Ontario [*Library symbol*] [*National Library of Canada*] (NLC)
OWTS .... St. Mary's General Hospital, Kitchener, Ontario [*Library symbol*] [*National Library of Canada*] (NLC)
OWTTE......... Or Words to That Effect (VLIE)
OWTU .... Oilfields Workers Trade Union (SAUS)
OWTU .... University of Waterloo, Ontario [*Library symbol*] [*National Library of Canada*] (NLC)
OWTUE........ Environmental Studies Library, University of Waterloo, Ontario [*Library symbol*] [*National Library of Canada*] (NLC)
O/W Type..... Oil/Water Type (SAUS)
OWU .... Office of War Utilities [*War Production Board*]
OWU .... Office Workers Union (SAUS)
OWU .... Ohio Wesleyan University, Delaware, OH [*OCLC symbol*] (OCLC)
OWU .... Open-Window Unit (MSA)
OWU .... Overload Warning Unit (MCD)
OWU .... Woodward, OK [*Location identifier*] [*FAA*] (FAAL)
OW-USS ...... Our World-Underwater Scholarship Society (EA)
OWV .... Ocean Weather Vessel [*Shipping*] (AIA)
OWVL........... One-Way Voice Link (GOBB)
OWVM .... Vincent Massey Secondary School, Windsor, Ontario [*Library symbol*] [*National Library of Canada*] (NLC)
OWW .... Organic Wash Waste (ABAC)
OWW .... Walkerville Collegiate Institute, Windsor, Ontario [*Library symbol*] [*National Library of Canada*] (NLC)
OWWA......... Waters Branch, Walden Public Library, Ontario [*Library symbol*] [*National Library of Canada*] (NLC)
OWWH......... Whitefish Branch, Walden Public Library, Ontario [*Library symbol*] [*National Library of Canada*] (NLC)
OWWM .... Office of Water and Waste Management (ERG)
OWWS .... Office of World Weather Systems
OWX .... Office of the Assistant for Weather [*Air Force*]
OWX .... Ottawa, OH [*Location identifier*] [*FAA*] (FAAL)
OWY .... Owyhee, NV [*Location identifier*] [*FAA*] (FAAL)
OWYL .... Lambton County Public Library, Wyoming, Ontario [*Library symbol*] [*National Library of Canada*] (NLC)
OW/YM .... Older Woman / Younger Man (WDAA)
OX .... Air Atlantic Airlines [*ICAO designator*] (AD)
Ox .... Odd Oxygen (SAUS)
OX............... Optic Chiasm (STED)
OX............... Optic Chiasma [*Medicine*] (MELL)
OX............... Order Crossover (VLIE)
OX............... Orthopedic Examination (STED)
OX............... Ottawa Exchange (SAUS)

OX .... Overnight eXpress (SAUS)
OX............... Oxacillin [*Medicine*] (MELL)
OX............... Oxford [*England*]
Ox .... Oxford [*Record label*]
OX............... Oxidant [*Photochemical*] (ERG)
OX............... Oxidation (EEVL)
OX............... Oxide [*or Oxidizer*] (AAG)
ox .... Oxides (VRA)
ox .... Oxidizer (NAKS)
OX............... Oxygen [*Chemical element*] (IAA)
ox .... Oxygen (IDOE)
Ox .... Oxygen (STED)
OX............... Oxymel [*Syrup of vinegar and honey*] [*Pharmacy*]
OX............... Oxytocin [*Medicine*] (MELL)
Ox .... Total Oxidants (SAUS)
OXA .... Oxalic Acid [*Organic chemistry*]
OXA .... Oxaprotiline (DMAA)
OXAL........... Oxalate (SAUS)
OXB .... Baldwin-Wallace College, Berea, OH [*OCLC symbol*] (OCLC)
OxboroM..... Oxboro Medical International, Inc. [*Associated Press*] (SAG)
Oxbridge..... Oxford and Cambridge Universities (NTIO)
OXBRIDGE ... Oxford/Cambridge [*England*]
OXC .... Oxford, CT [*Location identifier*] [*FAA*] (FAAL)
OXC .... Oxidizing Catalyst [*Automotive engineering*]
OXC .... Waterbury [*Connecticut*] [*Airport symbol*] (AD)
OXCI .... Oxford Consolidated, Inc. [*NASDAQ symbol*] (NQ)
OXD .... Oxford [*England*] [*Seismograph station code, US Geological Survey*] [*Closed*] (SEIS)
OXD .... Oxidation (SAUS)
O-X-D........... Oxidative Dehydrogenation (SAUS)
OXD .... Oxide (NAKS)
OXD .... Oxidized (MSA)
OXDZR .... Oxidizer (NASA)
OXe.............. Greene County District Library, Xenia, OH [*Library symbol*] [*Library of Congress*] (LCLS)
OXE.............. OEC Medical Sys [*NYSE symbol*] (TTSB)
OXE.............. OEC Medical Systems [*Formerly, Diasonics, Inc.*] [*NYSE symbol*] (SPSG)
OXE.............. Oxaero [*British*] [*FAA designator*] (FAAC)
OXEA .... Ox Erythrocyte Antibody [*Medicine*] (STED)
OXeGH......... Greene Memorial Hospital, Health Resource Library, Xenia, OH [*Library symbol*] [*Library of Congress*] (LCLS)
OXERA .... Oxford Economic Research Associates Ltd
OXF............. Open Exchange Format (SAUS)
OXF............. Oxford [*England*] [*Airport symbol*] (AD)
OXF............. Oxford [*Mississippi*] [*Seismograph station code, US Geological Survey*] [*Closed*] (SEIS)
OXF............. Oxford [*British depot code*]
OXF............. Oxford [*England*]
OXF............. Oxford Properties Canada Ltd. [*Toronto Stock Exchange symbol*]
OXFAM .... Oxford Committee for Family Relief (SAUS)
OXFAM .... Oxford Committee for Famine Relief [*Acronym is now organization's official name*] [*British*] (EA)
Oxfam .... Oxford Committee for Famine Relief (NTIO)
OXFD .... Oxford Resources CI'A' [*NASDAQ symbol*] (TTSB)
OXFD .... Oxford Resources Corp. [*NASDAQ symbol*] (SAG)
OxfdHlt .... Oxford Health Plans, Inc. [*Associated Press*] (SAG)
OxfdRsc ...... Oxford Resources Corp. [*Associated Press*] (SAG)
Oxf Lawy .... Oxford Lawyer [*1958-61*] [*A publication*] (DLA)
Oxford......... Oxford Industries, Inc. [*Associated Press*] (SAG)
Oxford Law... Oxford Lawyer [*1958-61*] [*A publication*] (DLA)
OxfrdC......... Oxford Consolidated, Inc. [*Associated Press*] (SAG)
OXGN.......... Oxigene, Inc. [*NASDAQ symbol*] (SAG)
OXGNW....... OXIGENE Inc. Wrrt [*NASDAQ symbol*] (TTSB)
OXH .... Oxygen Heat Exchanger (KSC)
OXHP .... Oxford Health Plans [*NASDAQ symbol*] (SPSG)
OXI .... Knox, IN [*Location identifier*] [*FAA*] (FAAL)
OXI .... Orbex Industries, Inc. [*Vancouver Stock Exchange symbol*]
Oxi .... Oximeter (STED)
OXID .... Oxidizer (AAG)
OXIDN......... Oxidation
Oxigene....... Oxigene, Inc. [*Associated Press*] (SAG)
Oxign .... Oxigene, Inc. [*Associated Press*] (SAG)
OXIL........... Oxid Insulated (or Insulation) Logic (SAUS)
OXIM .... Oxide-Isolated Mask (SAUS)
OXIM .... Oxide-Isolated Monolith
OXIM Technology... Oxide-Isolated Monolithic Technology (SAUS)
OXINE .... Oxyquinoline [*Organic chemistry*]
OXIS .... Oxide Insulation (SAUS)
OXIS .... Oxide Isolated (NITA)
OXIS .... Oxide Isolation (IAA)
OXIS .... Oxis International, Inc. [*NASDAQ symbol*] (SAG)
OXK .... Belleville, IL [*Location identifier*] [*FAA*] (FAAL)
OXLAT .... Oxalate [*Laboratory science*] (DAVI)
Oxley.......... Oxley's Railway Cases [*1897-1903*] [*A publication*] (DLA)
Oxley.......... Young's Nova Scotia Vice-Admiralty Decisions, Edited by Oxley [*A publication*] (DLA)
OXM............ Oxford Indus [*NYSE symbol*] (TTSB)
OXM............ Oxford Industries, Inc. [*NYSE symbol*] (SPSG)
OXM............ Oxtotitlan [*Mexico*] [*Seismograph station code, US Geological Survey*] (SEIS)
Ox M OUP ... Oxford Medical Oxford University Press (SAUS)
OXN .... Oxin Industries Ltd. [*Vancouver Stock Exchange symbol*]
OXO .... Million Air, Inc. [*ICAO designator*] (FAAC)
OXO .... Orbiting X-Ray Observatory [*NASA*]

OXO	Orientos [*Queensland*] [*Airport symbol*] (AD)
OXOCO	Offshore Exploration Oil Company (SAUS)
Oxon	Oxfordshire (DIAR)
OXON	Oxfordshire [*County in England*]
Oxon	Oxoiensis [*Academic degree*] (WDAA)
OXON	Oxonia [*Oxford University*] [*Latin*]
OXON	Oxoniensis [*Of Oxford University*] [*Latin*]
OXP	Oxford Poets [*A publication*]
OXP	Oxprenolol [*Vasodilator*]
OXP	Oxypressin [*Medicine*] (MELL)
OXPHOS	Oxidative Phosphorylation [*Medicine*]
OXR	Oxidizer (SAUS)
OXR	Oxnard [*California*] [*Airport symbol*] (OAG)
OXRB	Oxygen Replacement Bottles
OXRO	Orbiting X-Ray Observatory (ACAE)
OXS	Objective X-ray Crystal Spectrometer (SAUS)
OXS	Oxygen Sensor (ACAE)
OXSOME	Oxford County Soil Moisture Experiment (SAUS)
OXT	Oxytocin [*Medicine*] (MELL)
OXV	Knoxville, IA [*Location identifier*] [*FAA*] (FAAL)
OXWLD	Oxyacetylene Weld (SAUS)
Oxy	Occidental College (SAUS)
Oxy	Occidental Petroleum Corporation (SAUS)
OXY	Oxley [*British depot code*]
OXY	Oxygen [*Chemical element*] [*Symbol is O*] (AAG)
OXY	Oxytocin [*Endocrinology*]
oxycephs	oxycephalics (SAUS)
OXYCOD	Oxycodone Hydrochloride (SAUS)
OXYCOD TER	Oxycodone Terephthalate (SAUS)
OXYG	Oxygen [*Chemical element*] [*Symbol is O*]
OXYG	Oxygon (SAUS)
OXYM	Oxymel [*Syrup of vinegar and honey*] [*Pharmacy*] (ROG)
OXYPrA	Occidental Petr $3 Cv Pfd [*NYSE symbol*] (TTSB)
OXZ	Oxazepam [*Medicine*] (MELL)
Oy	Both Eyes (SAUS)
OY	Denmark [*International civil aircraft marking*] (ODBW)
OY	New Jersey Airways [*ICAO designator*] (AD)
OY	Operating Year (COE)
OY	Optimum Yield
OY	Orange Yellow
Oy	Osakeyhtioe [*Limited Company*] [*Finland*]
Oy	Oyster (SAUS)
OY	Public Library of Youngstown and Mahoning County, Youngstown, OH [*Library symbol*] [*Library of Congress*] (LCLS)
OYA	Goya [*Argentina*] [*Airport symbol*] (OAG)
OYA	Orthodox Youth of America [*Later, SOYO*]
Oya Cur	Oyashio Current (SAUS)
OYAP	Outstanding Young American Pianist
OYAS	Abbs [*Yemen*] [*ICAO location identifier*] (ICLI)
OYBI	Al-Beida [*Yemen*] [*ICAO location identifier*] (ICLI)
OYBO	Al-Bough [*Yemen*] [*ICAO location identifier*] (ICLI)
OYBT	Barat [*Yemen*] [*ICAO location identifier*] (ICLI)
OYC	Conair AS [*Denmark*] [*ICAO designator*] (FAAC)
OYC	Corpus Christi, TX [*Location identifier*] [*FAA*] (FAAL)
OYC	Out Year Costs (MCD)
OYCV	Optimum Yaw Control Vertical (SAA)
OYD	Office of Youth Development (SAUS)
OYD	Rome, GA [*Location identifier*] [*FAA*] (FAAL)
OYDV	Onion Yellow Dwarf Virus [*Plant pathology*]
OYE	Old Yellow Enzyme [*Biochemistry*]
OYE	Oyem [*Gabon*] [*Airport symbol*] (OAG)
OYesA	Antioch College, Yellow Springs, OH [*Library symbol*] [*Library of Congress*] (LCLS)
OYesF	Fels Research Institute, Yellow Springs, OH [*Library symbol*] [*Library of Congress*] (LCLS)
OYesK	Charles F. Kettering Foundation, Research Laboratory Library, Yellow Springs, OH [*Library symbol*] [*Library of Congress*] (LCLS)
OYG	Operating Year Guidance (GFGA)
OYHD	Hodeidah [*Yemen*] [*ICAO location identifier*] (ICLI)
OYK	Oiapoque [*Brazil*] [*Airport symbol*] (AD)
OYKM	Kamaran [*Yemen*] [*ICAO location identifier*] (ICLI)
OYM	Outstanding Young Man (DICI)
OYM	Oyama [*Japan*] [*Seismograph station code, US Geological Survey*] (SEIS)
OYM	St. Mary's, PA [*Location identifier*] [*FAA*] (FAAL)
OYMB	Marib [*Yemen*] [*ICAO location identifier*] (ICLI)
OYMC	Mokha [*Yemen*] [*ICAO location identifier*] (ICLI)
OYMHi	Mahoning Valley Historical Society, Arms Museum, Youngstown, OH [*Library symbol*] [*Library of Congress*] (LCLS)
OYMV	Ononis Yellow Mosaic Virus [*Plant pathology*]
OYO	Own Your Own (SAUS)
OYO	Tres Arroyos [*Argentina*] [*Airport symbol*] (OAG)
OYOC	One-Year-On-Campus (SAUS)
OYOG	OYO Geospace Corp. [*NASDAQ symbol*] (SAG)
OYOGeo	OYO Geospace Corp. [*Associated Press*] (SAG)

OYP	Office of Youth Programs [*Department of Labor*]
OYP	Opportunities for Youth Program [*Canada*]
OYS	Otsar Yehude Sefarad (BJA)
OYS	Outstanding Young Singaporeans (SAUS)
Oys	Oysters [*Quality of the bottom*] [*Nautical charts*]
OYS	Yosemite National Park [*California*] [*Airport symbol*] [*Obsolete*] (OAG)
OYSH	Saada [*Yemen*] [*ICAO location identifier*] (ICLI)
OYSN	Sanaa/International [*Yemen*] [*ICAO location identifier*] (ICLI)
OYSREA	Office of Youth, Sport, Recreation and Ethnic Affairs [*Northern Territory, Australia*]
OYSTER	Optical Yardsticks Toward Error Reduction (ACAE)
OYTZ	Taiz/Ganad [*Yemen*] [*ICAO location identifier*] (ICLI)
OYU	Youngstown State University, Youngstown, OH [*Library symbol*] [*Library of Congress*] (LCLS)
OYY	Columbus, OH [*Location identifier*] [*FAA*] (FAAL)
OYZM	Al-Hazm [*Yemen*] [*ICAO location identifier*] (ICLI)
Oz	Ooze [*Quality of the bottom*] [*Nautical charts*]
OZ	Ounce [*Unit of weight*] (AAG)
oz	Ounce (IDOE)
OZ	Outer Zone (HEAS)
OZ	Ozark Airlines, Inc. [*ICAO designator*] (OAG)
OZ	Ozonation (SAUS)
oz	Ozone (IDOE)
OZ	Ozone
OZA	Ozark (MCD)
OZA	Ozark Airlines (MHDB)
OZA	Ozona, TX [*Location identifier*] [*FAA*] (FAAL)
OZ AP	Apothecaries' Ounce (WDAA)
oz ap	ounze, apothecaries (SAUS)
oz apoth	Apothecaries Ounce (BARN)
OZAR	Ozark National Scenic Riverways [*National Park Service designation*]
OZARC	Ozone ARCAS [*All-Purpose Rocket for Collecting Atmospheric Soundings*] [*Navy*]
OZav	John McIntire Public Library, Zanesville, OH [*Library symbol*] [*Library of Congress*] (LCLS)
OZavU	Ohio University, Zanesville Branch Campus, Zanesville, OH [*Library symbol*] [*Library of Congress*] (LCLS)
OZC	Cleveland Heights-University Heights Public Library, Cleveland Heights, OH [*OCLC symbol*] (OCLC)
OZC	Ozamis City [*Philippines*] [*Airport symbol*] (OAG)
OZ-CCA	Danmark-Cross-Country Award (SAUS)
OZD	Observed Zenith Distance [*Navigation*]
OZE	Outer Zone Electron
OZEM	OzMail Ltd. [*NASDAQ symbol*] (SAG)
OzEmail	OZEmail Ltd. [*Associated Press*] (SAG)
OZEMY	OzEmail Ltd ADR [*NASDAQ symbol*] (TTSB)
OZEP	Outer Zone Electron Precipitation
ozf	ounce-force (SAUS)
oz ff	Fluid Ounce (SAUS)
ozf-in	ounce-force-inch (SAUS)
oz fl	ounze, fluid ounce (SAUS)
OZFLUX	Australian Flux Measurement Network (SAUS)
OZ-FT	Ounce Foot (AAG)
oz ft	ounce-foot (SAUS)
OZ/FT²	Ounces per Square Foot
OZ/GAL	Ounces per Gallon
OZH	Zaporozh'ye [*Former USSR*] [*Airport symbol*] [*Obsolete*] (OAG)
OZ-IN	Ounce Inch (AAG)
oz-in	Ounce-Inch (IDOE)
oz-in	Ounce-Inches (IDOE)
OZ/IN²	Ounces per Square Inch
OZ/IN³	Ounces per Cubic Inch
OZIPP	Ozone Isopleth Plotting Package (GFGA)
OZIPPM	Ozone Isopleth Plotting Package, Modified (GFGA)
OZN	St. George, UT [*Location identifier*] [*FAA*] (FAAL)
OZO	Orbiting Zoological Observatory to Track Animals
OZON	Cyclc3PSS Corp. [*NASDAQ symbol*] (SAG)
OZON	Cyclopss Corp. [*NASDAQ symbol*] (TTSB)
Ozone Sci Eng	Ozone Science and Engineering (SAUS)
OZ/PT	Ounces per Pint
OZR	Ozark, Fort Rucker, AL [*Location identifier*] [*FAA*] (FAAL)
OZRF	Opposed Zone Reheating Furnace (PDAA)
OZRK	Ozark Plateaus (SAUS)
oz/t	ounces per ton (SAUS)
OZT	Ounces Troy [*Unit of weight*]
oz t	ounce troy (SAUS)
OZ TR	Ounce Troy (GOBB)
oz tr	ounze,troy (SAUS)
ozws	otherwise (SAUS)
OZX	Oneonta, NY [*Location identifier*] [*FAA*] (FAAL)
Ozy	Ozzie (SAUS)
OZ/YD²	Ounces per Square Yard
OZZ	Ouarzazate [*Morocco*] [*Airport symbol*] (OAG)
OZZ	Ozark, AR [*Location identifier*] [*FAA*] (FAAL)

P
By Acronym

P .... Aircraft [*Wind triangle problems*]
P .... All India Reporter, Patna [*A publication*] (DLA)
P .... Armour Pharmaceutical Co. [*Research code symbol*]
P .... Assistant in Private Practice [*Chiropody*] [*British*]
P .... Asta Werke AG [*Germany*] [*Research code symbol*]
P .... Bristol Laboratories [*Research code symbol*]
P .... cis-Platinum [*Cisplatin*] [*Also, cis-DDP, CDDP, CPDD, CPT, DDP*] [*Antineoplastic drug*]
P .... Dainippon Pharmaceutical Co. [*Japan*] [*Research code symbol*]
P .... Democratic People's Republic of Korea [*Aircraft nationality and registration mark*] (FAAC)
p .... Density [*Heat transmission symbol*]
P .... Departure
p .... Difficulty [*of a test item*] [*Psychology*]
p .... Druck (SAUS)
P .... Electric Dipole Moment (BARN)
P .... Farbenfabriken Bayer [*Germany*] [*Research code symbol*]
P .... Farmitalia [*Italy*] [*Research code symbol*]
P .... Faulty Punctuation [*Used in correcting manuscripts, etc.*]
P .... first class premium (SAUS)
p .... fluid density (SAUS)
P .... Force of Concentrated Load
P .... Games [*or Matches*] Played [*Sports statistics*]
p .... gas pressure in blood (SAUS)
P .... Hole P-Type Semiconductor Material
P .... Indian Law Reports, Patna Series [*A publication*] (DLA)
P .... Law Reports, Probate, Divorce, and Admiralty [*Since 1890*] [*England*] [*A publication*] (DLA)
P .... Lepetit [*Italy*] [*Research code symbol*]
P .... Mainsail Hoist Lenght [*IOR*]
p .... Momentum [*Symbol*] [*IUPAC*]
P .... Office of Personnel [*Coast Guard*]
p .... On Probation [*Navy*] [*British*]
P .... Orbital Period [*of a comet*] [*In years*]
P .... Pacer
P .... Pacific Coast Stock Exchange [*Later, PSE*]
p---- .... Pacific Ocean [*MARC geographic area code*] [*Library of Congress*] (LCCP)
P .... Pacific Reporter [*A publication*] (DLA)
P .... Pacific Stock Exchange (SG)
P .... Pack [*JETDS*]
P .... Packed Lunches [*School meals*] [*British*]
P .... Pad (SAA)
P .... Paddington Railway Station (ROG)
P .... Paddle (DS)
P .... Page
P .... Paid This Year [*In stock listings of newspapers*]
P .... Pain [*Medicine*]
P .... Pair (IAA)
P .... Paired [*for or against*] [*Votes in Congress*]
P .... Paise [*Monetary unit*] [*India*]
P .... Palace (ROG)
P .... Pale (ADA)
p .... Pallet (NAKS)
P .... Pallet [*Spacelab*] [*NASA*] (NASA)
P .... Pamphlet
P .... Panama Line (SAUS)
P .... Pancreas (MELL)
P .... Pancuronium [*A muscle relaxant*]
P .... Pandects [*A publication*] [*Authority cited in pre-1607 legal work*] (DSA)
P .... Panel (NFPA)
P .... Papa [*Phonetic alphabet*] [*International*] (DSUE)
P .... Papa [*Pope*] [*Latin*]
P .... Paper
P .... Paperback (WGA)
P .... Papilla [*Optic*] [*Medicine*]
P .... Papillate [*A type of seed*] [*Botany*]
P .... Para [*Monetary unit*] [*Former Yugoslavia*]
p .... Para [*Chemistry*]
P .... Parabellum (GOBB)
P .... Parachutist [*Army skill qualification identifier*] (INF)
P .... Paragraph (ADA)
P .... Paralegal Program [*Association of Independent Colleges and Schools specialization code*]
P .... Parallax

P .... Parallel
P .... Paramecin [*A protozoan toxin*]
P .... Parashah (BJA)
P .... Pardon (ADA)
P .... Parenchyma [*Botany*]
P .... Parent (CPH)
P .... Parental
P .... Parentalgeneration (SAUS)
P .... Parietal Electrode Placement in Electroencephalography [*Medicine*] (DMAA)
P .... Parish (ROG)
P .... Parity [*Obstetrics*] (DAVI)
P .... Parity [*Atomic physics*]
P .... Park
P .... Parking Place [*Traffic sign*] [*British*]
P .... Parlophone [*Record label*] [*Great Britain, Italy, Australia, etc.*]
P .... Parous (STED)
P .... Parson
p .... Part (WDMC)
P .... Part
P .... Parthian [*Language, etc.*]
P .... Partial [*Astronomy*]
P .... Partial Pressure (MAE)
P .... Partial Tension [*Medicine*] (DAVI)
p .... Participle (NTIO)
P .... Participle [*Grammar*]
P .... Partim [*In Part*]
P .... Partnership
P .... Party
P .... Parve [*or Pareve*] [*In food labeling, indicates food is kosher and can be used with either meat or dairy products*]
P .... Pass (SAUS)
P .... Passable (SAUS)
P .... Passed [*Examination*]
P .... Passenger [*Automotive tire designation*]
P .... Passing Showers [*Meteorology*]
p .... Past (WDMC)
P .... Past
P .... Paste
P .... Pasteboard (DGA)
P .... Pasteurella [*Genus of bacteria*]
P .... Pastor
P .... Patella (MELL)
P .... Patent
P .... Pater [*Father*] [*Latin*]
P .... Paternal (STED)
P .... Paternally Contributing [*Genetics*] (DAVI)
P .... Patient
P .... Patrol [*Designation for all US military aircraft*]
P .... Patrol Service Gunnery Instructor [*Officer's rating*] [*British Royal Navy*]
P .... Patron
P .... Pattern
P .... Paulus de Liazaris [*Deceased, 1356*] [*Authority cited in pre-1607 legal work*] (DSA)
P .... Paused Program [*Computer science*]
P .... Paved Surface [*Aviation*] (DA)
P .... Pavilion (ROG)
P .... Pawn [*Chess*]
P .... Pax [*Peace*] [*Latin*]
P .... Pay
P .... Payee
P .... Paymaster [*Military*] (ROG)
p .... P-Doped Semiconductor [*Photovoltaic energy systems*]
P .... Peak
P .... Pear (SAUS)
P .... Peat (ROG)
P .... Pebbles [*Quality of the bottom*] [*Nautical charts*]
P .... Pectoral [*Anatomy*] (ROG)
p .... Peculiar [*Astronomy*]
P .... Pedal (WDAA)
P .... Pedestrian (WDAA)
P .... Peg [*Telecommunications*] (IAA)
P .... Pelagius [*Deceased, 1232*] [*Authority cited in pre-1607 legal work*] (DSA)
P .... Pellagra [*Medicine*] (MELL)

P	Pelvis (STED)
P	Pen [*Sports*]
p	Pence [*Monetary unit*] [*British*]
P	Pencil Tube (MDG)
P	Pengo [*Monetary unit in Hungary until 1946*]
P	Penicillin
p	Penni(a) [*Penny or Pence*] [*Monetary unit*] [*Finland*] (GPO)
P	Pennsylvania (DLA)
P	Pennsylvania State Library, Harrisburg, PA [*Library symbol*] [*Library of Congress*] (LCLS)
p	Penny (ODBW)
P	Penny
P	Pennzoil (SAUS)
P	Pentachlorophenol [*Also, PCP*] [*Wood preservative*] [*Organic chemistry*] (TEL)
P	Pentode [*Electronics*] (OA)
P	Peony [*Horticulture*]
P	People
P	Pepper (DICI)
p	Per (WDMC)
P	Per
P	Percent (STED)
P	Percentile
P	Perceptual
P	Perceptual Speed [*A factor ability*] [*Psychology*]
P	Perch
P	Perchloroethylene [*Also, TCE*] [*Dry cleaning*]
P	Percussion
P	Pere [*Father*] [*French*]
P	Perforateur Honeywell Bull (IAA)
P	Perforating (SAUS)
P	Perforation
P	Performance [*Army*] (INF)
P	Performer
P	Perfusionist [*Medicine*] (DAVI)
P	Perianth
P	Pericardium [*Medicine*]
P	Perimeter
p	Period (NAKS)
P	Period
P	Peripheral (DAVI)
P	Periphery (SAUS)
P	Perishable
P	Peritoneum [*Medicine*] (MELL)
P	Permanent [*Inks*] (DGA)
P	Permanent Stay [*in hospital*] [*British*]
P	Permeability (STED)
P	Permeance (IDOE)
P	Permutation (NITA)
P	Perpetuus [*Uninterrupted*] [*Latin*]
p	Perseverate [*Psychology*]
P	Persian (DLA)
P	Persimmon
P	Persistence [*Medicine*]
P	Person
P	Personal (DA)
P	Personality Organization and Stability [*Eysenck*] [*Psychology*]
P	Personnel
P	Person to Person [*Telecommunications*] (TEL)
P	Perstetur [*Continue*] [*Pharmacy*] (ROG)
P	Persuasion [*Novel by Jane Austen*]
P	Peseta [*Monetary unit*] [*Spain and Latin America*]
P	Pesewa [*Monetary unit*] [*Ghana*]
P	Pesher (BJA)
P	Peshitta (BJA)
p	Peso (NTIO)
P	Peso [*Monetary unit*] [*Spain and Latin America*]
P	Peta [*A prefix meaning multiplied by 10^15*] [*SI symbol*]
P	Peter [*Phonetic alphabet*] [*World War II*] (DSUE)
P	Peter [*New Testament book*]
P	Peters' United States Supreme Court Reports [*26-41 United States*] [*A publication*] (DLA)
P	Petiole [*Botany*]
P	Petite (WGA)
P	Petrol [*British Waterways Board sign*]
P	Petrus Hispanus [*Authority cited in pre-1607 legal work*] (DSA)
P	Peyote
P	Pfizer, Inc. [*Research code symbol*]
P	Pharmacopoeia
P	Pharmacy (WDAA)
P	Pharynx (MELL)
P	Phenacetin (STED)
P	Phencyclidine [*An anesthetic*]
P	Phenolphthalein [*Chemical indicator*]
P	Philadelphia [*Pennsylvania*] [*Mint mark, when appearing on US coins*]
P	Philadelphia Stock Exchange, Inc.
P	Phillips Petroleum [*NYSE symbol*] (TTSB)
P	Phillips Petroleum Co. [*NYSE symbol*] (SPSG)
P	Phoenician (BJA)
P	Phon [*Unit of loudness level*]
P	Phone (IAA)
p	Phosphate [*One-letter symbol*] [*Biochemistry*]
P	Phosphorescence (SAUS)
p	Phosphoric Residue [*As substituent on nucleoside*] [*Biochemistry*]

P	Phosphorus [*Chemical element*]
P	Photographic Reconnaissance Capability [*When suffix to Navy aircraft designation*]
P	Phototropism [*Botany*]
P	Phrase Structure Rule [*Linguistics*]
P	Physics [*Secondary school course*] [*British*]
P	Physiology [*Medical Officer designation*] [*British*]
P	Phytophthora [*A fungus*]
P	Piaggio Rinaldo [*Industria Aeronautiche & Meccaniche SpA*] [*Italy*] [*ICAO aircraft manufacturer identifier*] (ICAO)
P	Pianissimo [*Very Softly*] [*Music*]
P	Piano [*Softly*] [*Music*]
P	Piaster [*Monetary unit*] [*Spain, Republic of Vietnam, and some Middle Eastern countries*]
p	Pica [*Typography*] [*Also, P*] (WDMC)
P	Pick (IAA)
P	Pickering's Massachusetts Reports [*18-41 Massachusetts*] [*A publication*] (DLA)
P	Pico
p	Pico [*A prefix meaning divided by one trillion*] [*SI symbol*]
P	Picot [*Crochet*] (ROG)
P	Pie
P	Pied [*Foot*] [*French*]
P	Pierced [*Quilting*]
P	Pigs (ROG)
P	Pilaster [*Technical drawings*]
P	Pillar [*Buoy*]
P	Pilot
P	Pilotage (SAUS)
P	Pilotless (SAUS)
P	Pincherle Catalogue [*Vivaldi*] (GROV)
P	Pink
P	Pinnule
P	Pint
P	Pip [*Phonetic alphabet*] [*Pre-World War II*] (DSUE)
P	Pipe
P	Pipe Rolls [*British*]
P	Pique; Inclusions [*Diamond clarity grade*]
p	Pitch (NAKS)
P	Pitch [*Technical drawings*]
P	Pitch [*or Pitcher*] [*Baseball*]
P	Pitcher (NTIO)
P	Pith [*Botany*]
P	Pitman Examination Institute [*British*]
P	Pitman-Moore Co. [*Research code symbol*]
P	Pius [*Dutiful*] [*Latin*]
P	Placebo [*Medicine*]
P	Placentinus [*Deceased, 1192*] [*Authority cited in pre-1607 legal work*] (DSA)
P	Placitum [*or Placita*] [*Agreeable, Agreed Upon*] [*Latin*] [*Legal term*] (DLA)
P	Plaintiff [*Legal shorthand*] (LWAP)
P	Plan (CPH)
P	Planed
P	Planning
P	Plasma
P	Plasmodium [*Biology*] (MAE)
P	Plastid [*Botany*]
P	Plate [*Electron tube*] [*Technical drawings*]
P	Platform (DCTA)
P	Players League [*Major league in baseball, 1890*]
P	Pleasant
P	Pleinsbachian [*Geology*]
P	Pleyel (SAUS)
P	Plotter [*British military*] (DMA)
P	Plug
P	Plus [*More*]
P	Poco [*Somewhat*] [*Music*]
P	Point [*Lacrosse position*]
P	Point-to-Point Radio [*FAA designator*] (CET)
P	Poise [*Unit of dynamic viscosity*]
P	Poise [*Unit of measure*]
P	Poison
P	Polar Distance [*Navigation*]
P	Polarizability (SAUS)
P	Polarization
p	Pole (NAKS)
p	Pole
P	Political Division [*Geography*]
P	Polka [*Music*]
P	Pollen [*Botany*]
P	Pollicis (MELL)
P	Poll rate (SAUS)
P	Polymorphic [*Biology*]
P	Polymyxin [*An antibiotic*] (DAVI)
P	Polyneuropathy [*Medicine*]
P	Polynomial Time (IAA)
P	Polyphagous [*Biology*]
P	Polytechnic (AIE)
P	Pond [*Maps and charts*]
P	Pondere [*By Weight*] [*Latin*]
p	Pondus [*Weight*] [*Latin*] (MAE)
P	Ponendum [*To Be Placed*] [*Latin*]
P	Pontifex [*Bishop*] [*Latin*]
P	Pool

P .... Poop [Portion of a ship]
P .... Poorly Organized, Unstable Personality [Eysenck] [Psychology]
P .... Poor Skiing Conditions
P .... Pope
P .... Popular Response [Rorschach] [Psychology]
P .... Population
p .... Populus (GEAB)
P .... Populus [People] [Latin]
P .... Porcelain
P .... Porphyrin [Medicine] (DAVI)
P .... Port [Maps and charts]
P .... Portable [JETDS nomenclature]
P .... Portion
P .... Portland [Diocesan abbreviation] [Oregon] (TOCD)
P .... Portugal [IYRU nationality code]
P .... Position
P .... Positive (IAA)
P .... Positive [Crystal]
P .... Positive Conducting [Electronics] (IAA)
P .... Post [After] [Latin]
P .... Post [Surgery laboratory work] (DAVI)
P .... Postage
P .... Posten [Sentry] [German military]
P .... Posterior
P .... Postpartum [Medicine]
P .... Pouce [Inch] [French]
P .... Pound (IDOE)
P .... Pounds [As measurement of total stress] [Aerospace] (AAG)
P .... Pour [For] [French]
P .... Power [Symbol] [IUPAC]
P .... Poynting Vector [Electromagnetism] (DEN)
P .... Practical
p .... Practical Intelligence (DIPS)
P .... Practical Intelligence
P .... Pre-1920 [Deltiology]
P .... Preceding
p .... pre-cell (SAUS)
P .... Precipitation Static
P .... Precise Code [Computer science] (RDA)
P .... Precision (SAUS)
P .... Precursor (MELL)
P .... Predators Present [Ecology]
P .... Predicate
P .... Predictor [British military] (DMA)
P .... Prednisolone [Endocrinology]
P .... Prednisone [Also, PDN, Pr, Pred, Pro] [Endocrinology]
                    [Antineoplastic drug]
P .... Preferred
P .... Prefix [Indicating a private radiotelegram]
P .... P-Register [Computer science]
P .... Preliminary
P .... Premolar [Dentistry]
P .... Presbyopia [Ophthalmology]
P .... Presbyterian
P .... Prescribing
P .... Present
P .... Present BIT [Binary Digit] [Computer science]
P .... Preset
P .... President
P .... Press [Publishing]
P .... Pressure (NAKS)
p .... Pressure [or p] [Symbol] [IUPAC]
P .... Pressurized Tank [Liquid gas carriers]
P .... Preview
P .... Prey [Zoology]
P .... Price [Economics]
P .... Pridie [The Day Before] [Latin]
P .... Priest
P .... Priestly (SAUS)
P .... Priestly Source [Biblical scholarship]
P .... Prilled
p .... Primary (NAKS)
P .... Primary
P .... Primary [or Push] Wave [Earthquakes]
p .... Prime (NAKS)
P .... Prime
P .... Primipara [Woman bearing first child] [Medicine] (MAE)
P .... Primitive
P .... Primus [First] [Latin]
P .... Prince
P .... Princeps [First Edition] [French]
P .... Princess (ROG)
P .... Principal
P .... Print
P .... Prions [Medicine] (MELL)
P .... Priority [Telecommunications] (TEL)
P .... Priority Precedence (SAUS)
P .... Priory
P .... Prismatic Joint (IAA)
P .... Prisoner [Military]
P .... Private
P .... Private Trust [Includes testamentary, investment, life insurance,
                    holding title, etc.] [Legal term] (DLA)
P .... Private Venture
P .... Privy (ROG)

P .... Pro [For] [Latin]
p .... Probability (DIPS)
P .... Probability [or Probability Ratio] [Statistics]
P .... Probate
P .... Probe (MSA)
P .... Probucol [Anticholesteremic]
P .... Procarbazine [Also, PC, PCB, Pr] [Antineoplastic drug]
P .... Procedure
P .... Proceedings (IAA)
P .... Processor [Computer science]
P .... Proconsul
P .... Producer [Films, television, etc.]
P .... Product
P .... Production [of Energy]
P .... Profession
P .... Professional [Civil Service employees designation]
P .... Professor
P .... Proficiency
P .... Profit
P .... Progesterone [A hormone]
P .... Program (KSC)
P .... Programmable
P .... Progressive
P .... Prohibited Area [Followed by identification]
P .... Prolactin (MELL)
P .... Proliferation [Biology]
P .... Proline [One-letter symbol; see Pro]
P .... Promoter [Genetics]
P .... Prompt [i.e., the right side] [A stage direction]
P .... Proof [Philately]
P .... Prop (DS)
P .... Propagation Distribution [Broadcasting]
P .... Propionic [Bacteriology] (DAVI)
P .... Proportional (IAA)
P .... Proportion in a Specific Class
P .... Propulsion (AAG)
P .... Protein
P .... Proteinuria [Clinical chemistry]
P .... Protestant
P .... Protet [Protest] [French]
P .... Proteus [Genus of bacteria] (MAE)
P .... Proto [Linguistics]
p .... Proton [A nuclear particle]
P .... Protoplasmic [Freeze etching in microscopy]
P .... Prototroch
P .... Prototype (AAG)
P .... Provisional
p .... Proximum [Near] [Latin] (MAE)
P .... Psychiatry
P .... Psychometrist [Psychology]
P .... Public (AL)
P .... Publications
P .... Public Houses [Public-performance tariff class] [British]
P .... Public Safety [FCC] (NTCM)
P .... Pudding [Phonetic alphabet] [Royal Navy] [World War I] (DSUE)
P .... Pugillus [A Handful] [Pharmacy] (ROG)
P .... Pula [Monetary unit] (ODBW)
P .... Pull (NFPA)
P .... Pulled Up [Horse racing]
P .... Pulmonary (MELL)
P .... Pulse
P .... Pump (AAG)
P .... Punch
P .... Punic (BJA)
P .... Punkt [Point] [German military]
P .... Punter [Football]
P .... Pupil
P .... Purchased (AAG)
P .... Purified [Animal breeding]
P .... Purinethol [Mercaptopurine] [Also, M, MP] [Antineoplastic drug]
P .... Purkinje Cell [Neuroanatomy]
P .... Purl [Knitting]
P .... Purple
P .... Purpure [Purple] [Heraldry]
P .... Pursuit [Airplane designation]
P .... Put [In options listings of newspapers]
P .... Pya [Monetary unit] [Myanmar]
P .... Pylon (SAUS)
p .... Pyranose [One-letter symbol] [Biochemistry]
P .... Pyroxene Subgroup [Acmite, sodium metasilicate, potassium
                    metasilicate, diopside, wollastonite, hypersthene] [CIPW
                    classification] [Geology]
P .... RADAR [JETDS nomenclature]
P .... Rank Correlation (DIPS)
P .... Reproducing [JETDS nomenclature]
P .... Roll Rate
P .... Single Paper [Wire insulation] (AAG)
P .... Soft Pad [Missile launch environment symbol]
P .... Warner-Lambert Pharmaceutical Co. [Research code symbol]
P00 .... Program Zero-Zero (SAUS)
P1 .... Form to arrange payment to an outside body (SAUS)
P$_1$ .... Inorganic Phosphate [Chemistry] (DAVI)
p-1 .... Page 1 [Also, P-1] (WDMC)
P-1 .... Page One [Broadcasting] (WDMC)
p1 .... Para 1 [Unipara - having borne one child] (DAVI)

P₁	Parental Generation (MAE)
P1	Pershing 1 [*Missile*] (GFGA)
P₁	Pulmonic First Heart Sound [*Medicine*] (DAVI)
P₁	Pulmonic First Sound [*Medicine*] (MEDA)
P1a	Pershing 1a [*Missile*] (GFGA)
P1E	Planed One Edge [*Technical drawings*] (DAC)
P1MG	P1 [*Code*] for Multigroup [*Method*] [*Nuclear energy*] (NRCH)
P1S	Planed One Side [*Technical drawings*] (DAC)
P1S2E	Planed One Side and Two Edges [*Technical drawings*] (DAC)
P2	Papua New Guinea [*Aircraft nationality and registration mark*] (FAAC)
P2	Pollution Prevention
P-2	Propaganda Due [*Secret Italian Masonic organization, allegedly tied to the Roman Catholic church*]
P₂	Pulmonic Second Sound [*Medicine*]
P2	Second Parental Generation (EES)
P2	Second Pilot [*Aviation*] (AIA)
P2C4I	Power Projection C4I (SAUS)
P2d	Pacific Reporter, Second Series [*West*] [*A publication*] (AAGC)
P2I	Planned Product Improvement
P²NBC2	Physiological and Psychological Effects of NBC [*Nuclear, Biological, and Chemical Warfare*] and Extended Operations [*Army study project*] (INF)
P2P	Peer-to-Peer
P2S	Panoramic Periscope System (SAUS)
P-3	Fixed wing ASW aircraft (SAUS)
P3	Industry Composites and Polymer Processing Program [*Massachusetts Institute of Technology*] [*Research center*] (RCD)
P3	Pacific Project Phoenix
P3	Phillips Post Processor
P3	Platform for Privacy Preferences (SAUS)
P3	Polluter-Pays-Principle (SAUS)
P3	Portable Plotting Package [*Nuclear energy*] (NRCH)
P/3	Proximal Third [*of bone*] [*Orthopedics*] (DAVI)
P3FE	Polytrifluoroethylene (EDCT)
P₃I	Planned Program Product Improvement [*Army*]
P3I	Precision Plan Position Indication (SAUS)
P3I	Precision Plan Position Indicator (SAUS)
P³I	Preplanned Product Improvement [*DoD*]
P3P	Platform for Privacy Preferences
P3P	Platform for Privacy Preferences Project [*Computer science*]
P3RDB	Prelaunch/Postlanding Processing Requirements Data Base (SAUS)
P4	Aruba [*Aircraft nationality and registration mark*] (FAAC)
P4	Production Process Prove-Out Program
P 4 CAST Model	Probabilistic Forecasting Model (SAUS)
P4P	Pagans for Peace Network [*Canada*] (EAIO)
P4S	Planed Four Sides [*Technical drawings*] (DAC)
P4SR	Predicted Four Hour Sweat Rate (PDAA)
P6ROC	P6 Rover Owners Club (EAIO)
P08	German marking denoting the so-called luger service pistol (SAUS)
P 14	Pattern 14 Rifle [*Made in the US for Great Britain, beginning in 1914*]
P 32	Radioactive Phosphorus (DAVI)
P38	German 9mm service pistol (SAUS)
P₅₀	Partial pressure of oxygen at 50% hemoglobin saturation [*Medicine*]
P-55	Hydroxypregnanedione [*Endocrinology*] (DAVI)
P-88/ARA	Project '88: Americans for the Reagan Agenda [*Defunct*] (EA)
P450	P450-Aromatase (SAUS)
P_A	Alveolar Pressure [*Medicine*] (DAVI)
PA	B. F. Jones Memorial Library, Aliquippa, PA [*Library symbol*] [*Library of Congress*] (LCLS)
PA	Office of Public Affairs [*DoD*]
P-A	Pacific-Atlantic Line (SAUS)
PA	Package Application (SAUS)
PA	Pack Area (SAUS)
PA	Packet Adapter [*Telecommunications*] (IAA)
PA	Pad Abort [*NASA*] (KSC)
PA	Paging Algorithm (SAUS)
PA	Paging and Area Warning (MCD)
P/A	Paid Annually (SAUS)
Pa	Paine's United States Circuit Court Reports [*A publication*] (DLA)
PA	Paintmakers Association [*British*] (DBA)
PA	Paired Associates [*Psychometrics*]
PA	Pakistan Army
PA	Palaeontology Association (SAUS)
PA	Paleopathology Association
PA	Palestine Affairs [*New York*] [*A publication*] (BJA)
PA	Palestinian (SAUS)
PA	Palestinian Authority [*Political movement*] (ECON)
PA	Palladium [*Chemical element*] (ROG)
PA	Panama [*ANSI two-letter standard code*] (CNC)
PA	Panama Area (SAUS)
PA	Pan American (SAUS)
PA	Pan American World Airways, Inc. [*See also PAA, PAN-AM, PN*] [*ICAO designator*] (MCD)
P-A	Pan-Atlantic Line (SAUS)
P-A	Pan-Atlantic Steamship Corp. (MHDW)
PA	Panatlas Energy, Inc. [*Toronto Stock Exchange symbol*]
PA	pancreatic Ascites [*Medicine*] (MELL)
PA	Panel Absorber (SAUS)
PA	Panic Alarm (SAUS)
PA	Panic Attack [*Medicine*] (MEDA)
PA	Panniculus Adiposus [*Medicine*] (MELL)
PA	Pantothenic Acid [*Biochemistry*] (DB)
pa	Paper (VRA)
PA	Paper (WGA)
PA	Paper Advance (BUR)
PA	Para-Amps (EA)
Pa	Parachutist [*British military*] (DMA)
PA	Parallel Access (SAUS)
PA	Parallel Adder (SAUS)
PA	Parallel Algorithm (SAUS)
PA	Paralysis Agitans
PA	Parameter Address (SAUS)
PA	Parametric Amplifier
PA	Par Amitie [*By Favor*] [*French*]
Pa	Paranoia [*Psychology*]
PA	Parapsychological Association (EA)
PA	Parasitic Antenna (SAUS)
PA	Parathion (LDT)
PA	Par Autorite [*By Authority*] [*French*]
PA	Parental Advisory (WDMC)
PA	Parenteral Alimentation [*Medicine*] (MELL)
PA	Parents Anonymous (EA)
PA	Parents' Association
PA	Parish
Pa	Paris Stock Exchange [*France*]
PA	Parti Affectae [*To the Affected Part*] [*Pharmacy*]
PA	Partial Application [*Military*] (AFIT)
P_A	Partial Pressure in Arterial Blood [*Medicine*] (DAVI)
PA	Participating Activity [*Responsible for standardization efforts*] [*DoD*]
PA	Participial Adjective [*Grammar*]
PA	Particle Accelerator (SAUS)
PA	Particular Average
PA	Parti de l'Action [*Party of Action*] [*Morocco*] [*Political party*] (PPW)
PA	Partido Andalucista [*Spain*] [*Political party*] (ECED)
PA	Partido Arnulfista [*Panama*] [*Political party*] (EY)
PA	Partners of the Americas (EA)
PA	Pascal [*Unit of measure*]
Pa	Pascal [*Symbol*] [*SI unit of pressure*]
PA	Passenger Address System [*Aviation*] (DA)
PA	Passenger Agent
PA	Passenger Ship
PA	Passive Aggressive (DMAA)
PA	Patent Assignee (NITA)
PA	Patents (NITA)
PA	Pathfinder Association (EAIO)
PA	Pathology (AAMN)
PA	Patient
PA	Patient's Advocate [*Medicine*] (DMAA)
PA	Patrol Aircraft (NATG)
PA	Pattern Analysis [*Test*]
PA	Pay and Allowances
PA	Paying Agent [*Legal term*] (DLA)
PA	Payload Accommodations (SAUS)
P/A	Payment Authority [*Business term*]
PA	Peak-Aged (SAUS)
PA	Peak Amplitude [*Medicine*] (DMAA)
P-A	Peak-to-Average (SAUS)
PA	Pedestrians Association [*British*] (DBA)
PA	Pending Availability
PA	Pendulous Axis [*Accelerometer*] (IEEE)
Pa	Pennsylvania (ODBW)
PA	Pennsylvania [*Postal code*]
PA	Pennsylvania Railroad Co. (SAUS)
Pa	Pennsylvania Reports [*A publication*] (AAGC)
PA	Pennsylvania Supreme Court Reports [*1845-date*] [*A publication*] (DLA)
PA	People's Alliance [*Althydubandalag*] [*Iceland*] [*Political party*] (PPW)
PA	Peptide Absorption
PA	Per Abdomen
PA	Per Adresse [*Care Of*] [*German*]
PA	Per Annum [*By the Year*] [*Latin*]
pa	Per annum (EBF)
PA	Per Auguri [*Used on visiting cards to express congratulations, birthday wishes, etc.*] [*Italian*]
PA	Percentage Activity [*Measurement*] (DAVI)
PA	Performance Alertness (AEBS)
PA	Performance Analysis
PA	Performance Analysts (SAUS)
PA	Performance Appraisal
PA	Performance Appraisal Required [*Civil Service*]
PA	Performance Assessment (DOGT)
PA	Performing Arts [*US Copyright Office class*]
PA	Periapical [*Anatomy*] (DAVI)
PA	Periarteritis [*Medicine*] (DMAA)
PA	Peridural Artery [*Medicine*] (DMAA)
PA	Periodic Acid [*Inorganic chemistry*]
PA	Periodontal Abscess [*Medicine*] (MELL)
pA	Periplanone A [*Biochemistry*]
PA	Peritoneal Adhesions [*Medicine*] (MELL)
PA	Permanent Abeyance [*FDA*]
PA	Permanent Address (ROG)
PA	Permanent Appointment
PA	Permanently Assigned (ACAE)
PA	Permanently Associated [*Telecommunications*] (TEL)
PA	Pernicious Anemia [*Hematology*]
PA	Personal Accident [*Insurance*] (AIA)
P/A	Personal Account (WDAA)
PA	Personal Adjutant (SAUS)
PA	Personal Affairs (AFM)
PA	Personal Appearance

PA	Personal Assistant [*British*]
PA	Personal Audit [*Psychological testing*]
PA	Personnel Administrator [*American Society for Personnel Administration*] [*A publication*] [*Information service or system*]
PA	Personnel Area (NRCH)
PA	Personnel Assistant
PA	Personnel Association
PA	Perturbation Analysis (SAUS)
PA	Petroleum Association (SAUS)
PA	Pfizer, Inc. [*Research code symbol*]
PA	Phakic-Aphakic [*Ophthalmology*] (MAE)
PA	Pharmacology, Clinical [*Medical specialty*] (DHSM)
PA	Phase Angle (IAA)
PA	Phased Array (SAUS)
PA	Phenol Alcohol [*Chemistry*] (DAVI)
PA	Phentolamine [*Antiadrenergic*]
PA	Phenylalanine (SAUS)
PA	Philippine Army
PA	Philippine Association (EA)
PA	Phobics Anonymous (MELL)
PA	Phonocardiogram Amplifier [*Cardiology*]
PA	Phosphatidic Acid [*Biochemistry*]
PA	Phosphoarginine [*Biochemistry*]
PA	Phosphoric Acid (ECON)
PA	Photoallergenic [*Response*] [*Medicine*]
PA	Photodiode Amplifier
PA	Photoinduced Anisotropy [*Physics*]
PA	Phthalic Anhydride [*Organic chemistry*]
PA	Physical Activity (MCD)
PA	Physical Address (SAUS)
PA	Physician Advisor (HCT)
PA	Physician's Assistant
PA	Physics Abstracts [*Institution of Electrical Engineers*] [*Information service or system*] [*A publication*] (CRD)
PA	Phytoalexin [*Plant pathology*]
PA	Piaster [*Monetary unit*] [*Spain, Republic of Vietnam, and some Middle Eastern countries*]
PA	Picatinny Arsenal [*New Jersey*] [*Later, Armament Development Center*] [*Army*]
pA	Picoampere [*One trillionth of an ampere*]
PA	Pierre Allain [*Lightweight rock-climbing boot named after its designer*]
PA	Pierre Arpels [*Jewelry designer*]
PA	Pills Anonymous [*Later, DA*] [*An association*] (EA)
PA	Pilot Amplifier (SAUS)
PA	Pilot Approval [*Automotive project management*]
PA	Pilotless Aircraft
PA	PIMCO Advisors'A' [*NYSE symbol*] (TTSB)
PA	Pimco Advisors Ltd. [*NYSE symbol*] (SAG)
PA	Pipeline Authority [*Australia*]
PA	Piper Aircraft Corp. [*ICAO aircraft manufacturer identifier*] (ICAO)
PA	Pirke Avot (BJA)
PA	Pitch Angle
PA	Pituitary-Adrenal [*Endocrinology*] (DAVI)
PA	Placenta Accreta [*Medicine*] (MELL)
P/A	Planetary Atmosphere (SAA)
PA	Planning Assistance (EA)
PA	Planning Authority (HEAS)
PA	Plasma Adsorption [*Medicine*] (DMAA)
PA	Plasma Aldosterone [*Endocrinology*]
PA	Plasma-Arc (SAUS)
PA	Plasminogen Activator [*Biochemistry*]
PA	Plate Appearance [*Baseball term*] (NDBD)
PA	Platelet Adhesiveness [*Hematology*]
PA	Platelet-Associated (DB)
PA	Platform Assembly (MCD)
PA	Play Aid (SAUS)
PA	Podiatry Association [*British*] (DBA)
PA	Point of Aim [*Military*]
PA	Points Against [*Football*]
PA	Polar Atlantic [*American air mass*]
PA	Polarization Approximation [*Physical chemistry*]
PA	Polarographic Analyzer
PA	Polar to Analog
PA	Police Academy
PA	Police Agent (WDAA)
PA	Policy Analyst (GNE)
PA	Polled Angus (SAUS)
PA	Polyacetal [*Organic chemistry*]
PA	Polyacrylate (EDCT)
PA	Polyacrylic [*Organic chemistry*]
PA	Polyallomer (SAUS)
PA	Polyamide [*Organic chemistry*]
PA	Polyanhydride [*Organic chemistry*]
PA	Polyarteritis [*Medicine*]
PA	Polyarthritis [*Medicine*] (DMAA)
PA	Polyarylate (SAUS)
PA	Polymer Adhesive
PA	Port Agency [*Army*]
PA	Port Authority [*Western Australia*]
PA	Port of Arrival (SAUS)
PA	Position Accuracy
PA	Position Angle [*Astronomy*]
PA	Position Approximate [*Nautical charts*]
P/A	Positioner/Actuator (SAUS)
PA	Position of Assembly (SAUS)
PA	Positive Addiction [*Self-improvement method developed by William Glasser, MD*]
PA	Positive Attitude
PA	Postacceleration (SAUS)
PA	Post Adjutant
PA	Postal Assistant (DCTA)
PA	Post Amplifier
PA	Post-Aural [*Medicine*] (DMAA)
PA	Post Award Contract [*Department of Defense*]
PA	Posterior Anterior [*Medicine*]
PA	Posterior Aorta
PA	Postero-Anterior (SAUS)
PA	Postmortem Aging [*of meat*]
PA	Post-Secondary Accreditation (SAUS)
PA	Potato Agar [*Microbiology*]
PA	Potsmokers Anonymous (EA)
PA	Power Alarm (SAUS)
PA	Power Amplification (SAUS)
PA	Power Amplifier
PA	Power Antenna [*Automotive term*]
PA	Power Approach [*Aerospace*]
PA	Power of Attorney
P/A	Power of Authority
PA	Practice Amendment (AAG)
PA	Preacceleration (SAUS)
PA	Prealbumin [*Biochemistry*]
PA	Prealloying (SAUS)
PA	Preamble (SAUS)
PA	Preamplifier
PA	Preapproved
PA	Prearm
PA	Preavailability
PA	Precision-Acrobatics (DOMA)
PA	Precision Angle (IAA)
PA	Precision Approach (SAUS)
PA	Precision Architecture [*Hewlett-Packard Co.*] [*Computer science*]
PA	Precomputed Altitude
PA	Predictive Accuracy [*Medicine*] (DMAA)
PA	Predictive Analyzer [*Computer science*] (DIT)
PA	Prefect-Apostolic [*Roman Catholic*]
PA	Preferential Adsorption (SAUS)
PA	Pregnancy-Associated [*Gynecology*] (MAE)
PA	Preliminary Acceptance (KSC)
PA	Preliminary Amplifier (IAA)
PA	Preliminary Assessment (ERG)
PA	Preliminary Award
PA	Preparing Activity [*Responsible for Federal document and study projects*]
PA	Preplaced Aggregate (SAUS)
P/A	Presence or Absence
PA	Present Again (ADA)
PA	Presentation Architecture (SAUS)
PA	Preservation Action (EA)
PA	Presidents Association [*New York, NY*] (EA)
PA	Press Agency (WDAA)
PA	Press Agent
PA	Press Association Ltd. (IID)
PA	Pressure Actuated [*Switch*]
PA	Pressure Alarm [*Nuclear energy*] (NRCH)
PA	Pressure Altitude [*Aviation*]
PA	Pressure Angle (MSA)
PA	Pressure Anomaly (SAUS)
PA	Pressure Area [*Medicine*]
PA	Presumptive Address (SAUS)
PA	Price Analyst
PA	Price Availability (SAUS)
PA	Primary Aerospace Vehicle [*or Aircraft*]
PA	Primary Amenorrhea [*Gynecology*] (MAE)
PA	Primary Anemia [*Medicine*]
PA	Prince Albert (ACAE)
PA	Prince Albert Coat [*Slang*]
PA	Principal Applicant (SAUS)
PA	Principal Assistant (NOAA)
PA	Principal Axes
PA	Principle of Adding [*New math*]
PA	Priority A (MCD)
PA	Priority Aggregate
PA	Prior to Admission [*Medicine*]
PA	Prison Auxiliary (WDAA)
PA	Privacy Act
PA	Privacy Act of 1974 (COE)
PA	Private Account [*Banking*]
PA	Private Architect [*British*]
Pa	Proactinium (IDOE)
PA	Proactivator [*Medicine*]
PA	Pro Anno [*For the Year*] [*Latin*]
PA	Proanthocyanidin (Assay) [*Analytical chemistry*]
PA	Pro Applicatione [*To Be Applied*] [*Pharmacy*] (ROG)
PA	Probability of Acceptance (KSC)
PA	Probability of Acquisition [*Military*]
PA	Probability of Arrival (SAUS)
PA	Problem Analysis
PA	Problem Area (ACAE)
PA	Probleme der Agyptologie [*A publication*] (BJA)
PA	Procainamide [*Cardiac depressant*]

PA .... Procedure Administrator (SAUS)
PA .... Process Alert (SAUS)
PA .... Process Allocator [*Telecommunications*] (TEL)
PA .... Process Automation (CMD)
PA .... Procurement Agency (MCD)
PA .... Procurement Appropriations [*Army*] (AABC)
PA .... Procurement, Army
PA .... Procurement Authorization
PA .... Procuring Activity [*Military*]
PA .... Product Acceptance [*Automotive engineering*]
PA .... Product Administration (HCT)
PA .... Product Analysis (IEEE)
PA .... Product Analyst (SAUS)
PA .... Product Assortment (MHDB)
PA .... Product Assurance (NASA)
PA .... Product Attention (ELAL)
PA .... Production Adjustment
PA .... Production Agency (COE)
PA .... Production Analysis (SAUS)
PA .... Production Assistant
PA .... Professional Administrator [*Australia*] [*A publication*]
PA .... Professional Agent [*Professional Insurance Agents*] [*A publication*]
PA .... Professional Archeologist (SAUS)
PA .... Professional Association [*Telecommunications*]
PA .... Profile Analysis [*Medicine*]
PA .... Profile Angle (MSA)
PA .... Program Access
PA .... Program Account (NG)
PA .... Program Action (SAUS)
PA .... Program Address
PA .... Program Administrator (MCD)
PA .... Program Agent (OICC)
PA .... Program Aid [*A publication*]
PA .... Program Amount (NITA)
PA .... Program Analysis [*Computer science*]
PA .... Program Announcement
PA .... Program Application (SAUS)
PA .... Program Application Instructions [*Telecommunications*] (TEL)
PA .... Program Assessment (MCD)
PA .... Program Attention [*Computer science*] (IAA)
PA .... Program Attention Key [*Computer science*]
PA .... Program Authorization (AFM)
PA .... Program for the Aging (OICC)
PA .... Programmable Automation
PA .... Programmatic Agreement (SAUS)
PA .... Programmed Addressing (SAUS)
PA .... Programmed Algorithm (SAUS)
PA .... Programmed Arithmetic (IAA)
P/A .... Programmer/Analyst [*Computer science*] (VLIE)
PA .... Programming Address (SAUS)
PA .... Programming Aid (SAUS)
PA .... Progressive Alliance [*Defunct*] (EA)
PA .... Prohibited Area (SAUS)
PA .... Project Administration (MCD)
PA .... Project Analysis (MHDB)
PA .... Project Authorization
PA .... Proliferating Angioendotheliomatosis
PA .... Prologue Auditor (ACAE)
PA .... Prolonged-Action [*Pharmacy*]
PA .... Prolotherapy Association (EA)
PA .... Property Administrator [*DoD*]
PA .... Prophylactic Antibiotic
PA .... Propionic Acid (DMAA)
PA .... Proponent Agency [*Army*]
PA .... Proportional Action (AAG)
PA .... Proposal Authorization
PA .... Proposed Algorithm (SAUS)
PA .... [*The*] Proprietary Association [*Later, NDMA*] (EA)
PA .... Propulsion Assistance (DS)
PA .... Propulsion Assisted (SAUS)
P/A .... Propulsion/Avionics (SAUS)
PA .... Prosecuting Attorney
PA .... Prospecting Authority [*Australia*]
PA .... Prostitutes Anonymous (EA)
PA .... Protactinium
Pa .... Protactinium [*or Protoactinium*] [*Chemical element*]
PA .... Protected Area [*Nuclear energy*] (NRCH)
PA .... Protective Action (COE)
PA .... Protective Agent (SAUS)
PA .... Protective Antigen
PA .... Protestant Alliance [*British*] (DBA)
PA .... Prothonotary Apostolic
PA .... Protocol Adapter [*Communications*]
PA .... Proton Affinity [*Surface ionization*]
PA .... Protrusio Acetabuli [*Medicine*] (DMAA)
PA .... Provisional Acceptance (SAUS)
PA .... Provisional Allowance
PA .... Pseudo Address (SAUS)
PA .... Pseudoaneurysm [*Medicine*]
PA .... Pseudo-Astronomy
PA .... Pseudomonas aeruginosa [*Bacterium*]
PA .... Psoriasis Association [*Australia*]
PA .... Psoriatic Arthritis
PA .... Psychiatric Aide (DAVI)
PA .... Psychoacoustics (SAUS)

PA .... Psychoanalyst
PA .... Psychogenic Aspermia [*Medicine*]
PA .... Psychological Age
PA .... Public Accountant
PA .... Public Act
PA .... Public Address [*Amplification equipment*] [*Communications*]
PA .... Public Address System (WDMC)
PA .... Public Administration
PA .... Public Advocate (EA)
PA .... Public Affairs
PA .... Public Agent (WDAA)
PA .... Public Archives [*of Canada*]
PA .... Public Art (SAUS)
PA .... Public Assistance
PA .... Publication Announcement
PA .... Public Awareness (SAUS)
PA .... Publicity Agent (WDAA)
PA .... Published Author (CPGU)
PA .... Publishers' Alliance [*Defunct*] (EA)
PA .... Publishers' Association [*London, England*] (DIT)
PA .... Pull and Adjust [*Brace*] [*Medicine*]
PA .... Pulmonary Angiography [*Medicine*]
pa .... Pulmonary Artery [*Medicine*] (ADWA)
PA .... Pulmonary Artery [*Medicine*]
PA .... Pulmonary Atresia [*Medicine*]
PA .... Pulpoaxial [*Dentistry*]
PA .... Pulsating Arc (IAA)
PA .... Pulse Amplifier
PA .... Pulse Analyzer (SAUS)
PA .... Puppeteers of America (EA)
PA .... Purchase Agreement (VLIE)
PA .... Purchasing Agent
PA .... Purge Alarm [*Nuclear energy*] (NRCH)
PA .... Puromycin Aminonucleoside [*Biochemistry*] (OA)
PA .... Purpose and Activities (NITA)
PA .... Put Away [*Papers*] [*British*]
PA .... Puumala [*Vole virus*]
PA .... Pyro Ammonia (ROG)
PA .... Pyrrolizidine Alkaloid [*Toxicology*]
PA .... Pythium aphanidermatum [*A fungus*]
PAO$_2$ .... Arterial Oxygen Pressure (MAE)
PAA .... Pa-An [*Myanmar*] [*Airport symbol*] (OAG)
PAA .... Pacific Alaska Airways (SAUS)
PAA .... Pacific Arts Association (EA)
PAA .... Pan Am Corp. [*AMEX symbol*] (SAG)
PAA .... Pan American Minerals Corp. [*Toronto Stock Exchange symbol*] [*Vancouver Stock Exchange symbol*]
PAA .... Pan American World Airways, Inc. [*See also PA, PAN-AM, PN*]
PAA .... Pancretan Association of America (EA)
PAA .... Pancyprian Association of America [*Defunct*] (EA)
PAA .... Panguna [*Solomon Islands*] [*Seismograph station code, US Geological Survey*] (SEIS)
PAA .... Paper Agents Association [*British*] (DBA)
paa .... Papuan-Australian [*MARC language code*] [*Library of Congress*] (LCCP)
PAA .... Para-Azoxyanisole [*Organic chemistry*]
PAA .... Parke, Davis & Co. [*Research code symbol*]
PAA .... Parti Affectae Applicandus [*Apply to the Affected Part*] [*Pharmacy*]
PAA .... Partial Agonist Activity (DB)
PAa .... Passive Acoustic Analysis (ACAE)
PAA .... Patriot Airlines, Inc. [*ICAO designator*] (FAAC)
PAA .... Pay Adjustment Authorization
PAA .... Payload Attach Assembly (IGSL)
PAA .... P-azoxyanisole (SAUS)
PAA .... Peer Access Approval (VLIE)
PAA .... Per Acetic Acid (SAUS)
PAA .... Peracetic Acid [*Organic chemistry*]
PAA .... Peri-Appendicular Abscess [*Medicine*] (MELL)
PAA .... Peroxyacetic Acid (SAUS)
PAA .... Peruvian American Association (EA)
PAA .... Petroleum Administration Act [*Canada*]
PAA .... Phase Antenna Array (SAUS)
PAA .... Phased Array Aerial (or Antenna) (SAUS)
PAA .... Phased Array Antenna
PAA .... Phenanthrene Amino Alcohol [*Organic chemistry*]
PAA .... Phenanthrylacetamide [*Organic chemistry*]
PAA .... Phenylacetic Acid [*Organic chemistry*]
PAA .... Phonetic Alphabet Association (DGA)
PAA .... Phosphonoacetic Acid [*Antiviral compound*]
PAA .... Phosphoric Acid Aluminum Treatment (SAUS)
PAA .... Photographers Association of America [*Later, Professional Photographers of America*]
PAA .... Photon Activation Analysis
PAA .... Physiological Amino Acid (SAUS)
PAA .... Pi Alpha Alpha (EA)
PAA .... Pill Addicts Anonymous (EA)
PAA .... Plains All Amer Pipeline [*NYSE symbol*] (SG)
PAA .... Planar Array Aerial (or Antenna) (SAUS)
PAA .... Planar Array Antenna
PAA .... Plasma Amino Acid (SAUS)
PAa .... Plasma Angiotensinase Activity [*Medicine*] (MELL)
PAA .... Plasminogen Activator Activity [*Biochemistry*]
PAA .... Platelet Associated Activity [*Pharmacology*]
PAA .... Polish Association of America [*Later, NFLI*] (EA)
PAA .... Polocrosse Association of Australia

PAA............	Poly Acetic Acid (SAUS)
PAA............	Polyacrylamide [Also, PAAM, PAM] [Organic chemistry]
PAA............	Polyacrylic Acid [Organic chemistry]
PAA............	Polyammino Acid [Medicine] (MELL)
PAA............	Polyaspartic Acid [Biochemistry]
PAA............	Polycyclic Aromatic Amine [Organic chemistry]
PAA............	Population Association of America (EA)
PAA............	Port Autonome d'Abidjan [The Ivory Coast] (EY)
PAA............	Post Award Action
PAA............	Potato Association of America (EA)
PAA............	Power Amplifier Assembly
PAA............	Pre-Apprenticeship Allowance
PAA............	Pre-arrangement Association of America (SAUS)
PAA............	Primary Aircraft Assigned (ACAE)
PAA............	Primary Aircraft Authorized [Air Force]
PAA............	Primary Aromatic Amine (ABAC)
PAA............	Primary Authorized Aircraft
PAA............	Primary Auxiliary Area [Nuclear energy] (NRCH)
PAA............	Print Advertising Association [Defunct] (EA)
PAA............	Priority Abatement Areas [Environment] (GNE)
PAA............	Priority Problem Areas
PAA............	Prisoners Aid Association (SAUS)
PAA............	Procurement Appropriation, Army (MCD)
PAA............	Procurement of Ammunition, Army (AABC)
PAA............	Professional Apparel Association
PAA............	Professional Archers Association (EA)
PAA............	Program Assistant Administrator (SAUS)
PAA............	Programme d'Aide aux Athletes [Athlete Assistance Program] [Canada]
PAA............	Provincial Archives of Alberta (SAUS)
PAA............	Pulse-Amplitude Analyzer (SAUS)
PAA............	Purchasing Agents Association (NADA)
PAA............	Pyridineacetic Acid [Organic chemistry]
P/AA3............	Probationary Aircraft Artificer 3rd Class [British military] (DMA)
PAAA............	Polyaminoamido Acid (SAUS)
PAAA	Premium Advertising Association of America [Later, PMAA] (EA)
PAAA	Price Anderson Amendments Act (SAUS)
P/AAA2	Probationary Aircraft Artificer, Acting, 2nd Class [British military] (DMA)
PAAAC	Pan-American Agricultural Aviation Center (SAUS)
PAAAR	Pioneers Across America for Alzheimer's Research [An association]
PAAAS	Proceedings of the American Academy of Arts and Sciences (SAUS)
PAAB	PERSCOM [Personnel Command] Acquisition Accession Board [Army] (INF)
PAAB	Public Arts Advisory Board (SAUS)
PAABA	P-Acetamidobenzoic Acid (SAUS)
PAABA	Para-Acetamidobenzoic Acid [Biochemistry]
PAABS	PanAmerican Association of Biochemical Societies (EA)
PAAC	Pacific and Asian Affairs Council
PAAC	Payments and Administrative Communication Corp. (SAUS)
PAAC	Pennsylvania Athletic Conference (PSS)
PAAC	Product Assurance Action Center (SAUS)
PAAC	Program Analysis Adaptable Control [Computer science]
PAAC	Public Arts Advisory Council (SAUS)
PAACE	Precision Aircraft Armament Control Experiment (RDA)
PAACS	Prior Active Army Commissioned Service
PAACT	Patient Advocates for Advanced Cancer Treatments
PAAD	Private Automatic Answering Device [Telecommunications] (VLIE)
PAAD	Program Assistance Approval Document (SAUS)
PAAD	Project Army Aviation Data (SAUS)
PAADAR	Passive Airborne Detection and Ranging (MSA)
PAADC	Principal Air Aide-de-Camp [RAF] [British]
PA Admin Bull...	Pennsylvania Bulletin [A publication] (DLA)
PA Admin Code...	Pennsylvania Administrative Code [A publication] (DLA)
PAAE	Pennsylvania Association for Adult Education (SAUS)
PAAECI	Pan American Association of Educational Credit Institutions [See also APICE] (EAIO)
PAAES	Prior Active Army Enlisted Service
PAAES	Publications. American Archaeological Expedition to Syria [A publication] (BJA)
PAAF	Professional Actors Association of Florida (SAUS)
PAAFB	Patrick Auxiliary Air Force Base [Florida] (SAA)
PAAFCS	Prior Active Air Force Commissioned Service
PAAFES.......	Prior Active Air Force Enlisted Service
PAAG	Portable Airfield Arrestor Gear (SAUS)
PAAGE	Panel on Alternate Approaches to Graduate Education (EA)
PAAGE	Polyacryl-Amide Gel Electrophoresis (SAUS)
PAAH	Polyacrylamide-Hydrazide [Organic chemistry]
PAAHA	Para-Acetamidohippuric Acid [Biochemistry]
PAAJR	Proceedings of the American Academy for Jewish Research (SAUS)
PAAJR	Proceedings of the American Academy of Jewish Research (SAUS)
PAAL	Paleolimnology of Alpine-Adriatic Lakes (SAUS)
PAAM..........	Physicians Association for Anthroposophical Medicine (EA)
PAAM..........	Polyacrylamide [Also, PAA, PAM] [Organic chemistry]
PAAM..........	Projective Assessment of Aging Method [Personality development test] [Psychology]
P/AAMHRC...	Pacific/Asian American Mental Health Research Center [University of Illinois at Chicago] [Research center] (RCD)
PAAMS	Principal Anti-Air Missile System (MILB)
PAAN	Physician Assistant AIDS Network (SAUS)
PAAN	Product Assurance Alert Notice (MCD)
PA/A/N/AF...	Procurement of Ammunition, Army/Navy/Air Force (SAUS)
PA&C	Plessey Avionics & Communications (SAUS)
PA&D	Purchase Authorization and Directive (SAUS)
PA & E.........	Program Analysis and Evaluation

PA & F........	Percussion, Auscultation, and Fremitus [Medicine]
PA & I	Planning, Analysis, and Integration
PA&I	Project Analysis and Integration (SAUS)
PA and SP...	Positioner Antenna and Solar Panel (SAUS)
PA & T........	Product Assurance and Test
PAANG........	Pennsylvania Air National Guard (MUSM)
PAANS	Pan African Association of Neurological Sciences (EAIO)
PAANSW......	Prisoners' Aid Association of New South Wales [Australia]
PAAO	Pan-American Association of Ophthalmology (EA)
P(A-a)O₂ ...	Alveolar-Arterial Pressure Difference [For A-aDO₂] [Medicine] (DAVI)
PAAORLBE..	Pan-American Association of Oto-Rhino-Laryngology and Broncho-Esophagology [Mexico City, Mexico] (EAIO)
PAAP	Peaceful Alternatives to the Atlantic Pact
PAAP	Plastic Area Array (SAUS)
PAAP	Provisional Algal Assay Procedure [Test measuring impact of chemicals on algal growth]
PAA-PS	Polyacrylic Acid-Polysulfone (SAUS)
PAAQ	Palmer [Alaska] [ICAO location identifier] (ICLI)
PAAR	Pioneers Across America for Alzheimer's Research [An association]
PAAR	Precision Approach Airfield RADAR [Aviation] (IAA)
PAAR	Product Assurance Analysis Report (SAUS)
PAAS	Pakistan Association for the Advancement of Science (SAUS)
PAAS	Pan American Allergy Society (EA)
PAAS	Passive Active All Weather System (ACAE)
PAAS	Passive-Active Attack System (ACAE)
PAAS	Performance Assessment and Appraisal System
PAAS	Phased Array Aerial (or Antenna) System (SAUS)
PAAS	Phased Array Analysis System
PAAS	Phased Array Antenna System
PAAS	Proceedings of the American Antiquarian Society (SAUS)
PAAS	Region 10 External Affairs Labels System (SAUS)
PAASF	Pan American Silver Corp. [NASDAQ symbol] (SAG)
PAASF	Pan Amer Silver [NASDAQ symbol] (TTSB)
PAAT	Parent as a Teacher Inventory [Psychology]
PAAT	Passive Acoustics Analysis Trainer (SAUS)
PAAT	Personnel and Administrative Assistance Team [Navy] (NVT)
PAAT	Personnel Assistance and Audit Team [Military]
PAAT	Professional Association of Alexander Teachers [British] (DBA)
PAAT	Programmer Analyst Aptitude Test
PAAT	Public Affairs Assist Team [Hazardous substance emergency response]
PAATI	Phased Array Antenna Technology Investigation
PAATLANT ...	Personnel and Administration Assistance Team, Atlantic [Navy] (DNAB)
PAATPAC	Personnel and Administration Assistance Team, Pacific [Navy] (DNAB)
PAATS	Precision Approach Area Tracking System (ACAE)
PAAWA	Pakistan Australia Association of Western Australia
PAAWA	Progressive Axemen's Association of Western Australia
P(A-awo)	Pressure Gradient from Alveolus to Airway Opening [Medicine] (DAVI)
PAAWS	Precision Advanced All Weather Strike (ACAE)
PAAWS	Principal Anit-Air Warfare System (ACAE)
PAAWWW...	Pacific Asian American Women Writers West (EA)
PAAXOP......	Pan-Dodecanesian Association of America "Xanthos O Philikos" (EA)
PAb............	Abington Free Library, Abington, PA [Library symbol] [Library of Congress] (LCLS)
PAb............	Cabrini College, Library, Radnor, PA [OCLC symbol] (OCLC)
PAB&I........	PAB Bankshares, Inc. [AMEX symbol] (SAG)
PAB............	Pacific Air Boats Ltd. [Canada] [ICAO designator] (FAAC)
PAB............	Panair do Brasil, SA
PAB............	Para-Aminobenzoate (DB)
PAB............	Para-Aminobenzoic Acid [Also, PABA] [Biochemistry]
PAB............	Para-Aminobenzyl
PAB............	Paramaribo [Suriname] [Geomagnetic observatory code]
PAB............	Parti des Paysans, Artisans, et Bourgeois [Farmers', Artisans', and Burghers' Party] [Switzerland] [Political party] (PPE)
PAB............	Passenger Air Bag [Automotive safety systems]
PAB............	Patent Abstracts Bibliography [NASA]
PAB............	Patrick Air Force Base [Florida]
PAB............	Peanut Advisory Board (EA)
PAB............	Pedro Afonso [Brazil] [Airport symbol] (AD)
PAB............	Pension Appeals Board [Canada]
pab............	per acre bonus (SAUS)
PAB............	Performance Assesment Battery [Medicine] (DMAA)
PAB............	Personal Address Book [MAPI - Mail Applications Program Interface] [Microsoft Corp.] [Computer science]
PAB............	Pes Anserinus Bursa [Medicine] (MELL)
PAB............	Petroleum Administrative Board [Terminated, 1936]
PAB............	Pharmacologic Autonomic Block [Medicine] (DMAA)
PAB............	Plastic Assault Boat [Navy]
PAB............	Plumbing Advisory Board [South Australia]
PAB............	Police Administration Building
PAB............	Police Appeal Board [South Australia]
PAB............	Policies Allotment Board [Navy] (DNAB)
PAB............	Policy Advisory Body
PAB............	Polyclonal Antibody [Immunochemistry]
PAB............	Polymer Alloys and Blends (SAUS)
P/AB...........	Port Side Abreast (DNAB)
PAB............	Potter & Brumfield, Inc. (IAA)
PAB............	Poultry Advisory Board [Queensland, Australia]
PAB............	Power-Assisted Brakes
PAB............	Prealbumin [Biochemistry]
PAB............	Precision Aneroid Barometer (DNAB)
PAB............	Preliminary As-Built [Nuclear energy] (NRCH)

PAB.............	Premature Anti-Berninghausenite (SAUS)
PAB.............	Premature Atrial Beat [Cardiology] (AAMN)
PAB.............	Price Adjustment Board
PAB.............	Price Agreement Bulletin
PAB.............	Primary Application Block [Computer science] (ELAL)
PAB.............	Primary Auxiliary Building [Nuclear energy] (NRCH)
PAB.............	Priorities Allotment Board
PAB.............	Priority Assignment Base (MCD)
PAB.............	Private Activity Bond (AAGC)
PAB.............	Problems Analysis Branch of the CIA (SAUS)
PAB.............	Product Application Bulletins [A publication] (EAAP)
PAB.............	Program Advisory Board (MCD)
PAB.............	Programmer Aptitude Battery [Terence R. Taylor] (TES)
PAB.............	Promotions Appeal Board [Victoria, Australia]
PAB.............	Psychiatric Attitudes Battery [Psychology]
PAB.............	Psychology of Addictive Behaviors [An association] (EA)
PAB.............	Public Affairs Bureau (SAUS)
PAB.............	Pulmonary Artery Banding [Cardiology]
PAB.............	Pulsed Adsorption Bed [Process]
PAB.............	Pulsed Air Blast
PAB.............	Purple Agar Base [Media] [Microbiology]
PABA	Barter Island [Alaska] [ICAO location identifier] (ICLI)
PABA	Para-Aminobenzoic Acid [Also, PAB] [Biochemistry]
PA BA	Pennsylvania Bar Association. Reports [A publication] (DLA)
PABA	Pro-Am Bowfishing Association
PABA	Progressive Angus Breeders Association
PAB Bk	PAB Bankshares, Inc. [Associated Press] (SAG)
PA B Brief ...	Pennsylvania Bar Brief [A publication] (DLA)
PABC	Pacific Bancorp (EFIS)
PABC	Pan American Basketball Confederation [See also CPB] (EAIO)
PABC	Physiotherapy Association of British Columbia (SAUS)
PABD	Precise Access Block Diagram
PABD	Predeposited Autologous Blood Donation [Medicine] (MELL)
PABE..........	Bethel [Alaska] [ICAO location identifier] (ICLI)
PABE..........	Program and Budget Estimate (MCD)
PABF	Precision Air-Bearing Floor (SSD)
PABFSA	Pediatric Association of Black French-Speaking Africa (EAIO)
PABG	Big Delta [Alaska] [ICAO location identifier] (ICLI)
PABI...........	Delta Junction/Allen Army Air Field [Alaska] [ICAO location identifier] (ICLI)
PA Bk Cas ...	Pennsylvania Bank Cases [A publication] (DLA)
PABLA	Problem Analysis by Logical Approach
PABLE	Payable (ROG)
PABLI..........	Pages Bleues Informatisees [Commission of the European Communities] [Information service or system] (CRD)
PABLOS	Program to Analyse the Block System [Computer science] (PDAA)
PABM..........	Big Mountain Air Force Station [Alaska] [ICAO location identifier] (ICLI)
PABMI	Performing Arts Biography Master Index [A publication]
PABN	Pacific Capital Bancorp [NASDAQ symbol] (SAG)
PABP	Poly(A)-Binding Protein
PABP	Pulmonary Artery Ballon Pump [Medicine] (DMAA)
PAB Process...	Pulsed Adsorption Bed Process (SAUS)
PAB-PTC	Promotion Appeal Board, Postal and Telecommunications Commission [Australia]
PAB(Q)........	Poultry Advisory Board (Queensland) [Australia]
PABR	Barrow [Alaska] [ICAO location identifier] (ICLI)
PABR	Planning Appeals Board. Reports [A publication]
P Abr	Pulton's Abridgment of the Statutes [A publication] (DLA)
PA Browne (PA)...	Browne's Reports (Pennsylvania) [A publication] (DLA)
PA Browne R...	Browne's Reports [Pennsylvania] [A publication] (DLA)
PABRX	Phoenix-Engemann Balanced Return Cl.A [Mutual fund ticker symbol] (SG)
PABS	Pan-American Biodeterioration Society (EA)
PABS	Para-Aminobenzensulfonamide [Antibiotic]
PABST	Primary Adhesively Bonded Structural Technology [Aviation]
PABST	Primary Adhesively Bonded Structure Techniques
PABT	Bettles [Alaska] [ICAO location identifier] (ICLI)
PABV	Percutaneous Aortic Balloon Valvuloplasty [Medicine] (HCT)
PABV	Pyroactuated Ball Valve
PABX	Private Access Branch Exchange (SAUS)
PABX	Private Automatic Branch Exchange [Telecommunications] (DEN)
PABX	Public-Area Branch Exchange (AEBE)
PAC.............	cis-Platinum [Cisplatin], Adriamycin, Cyclophosphamide [Antineoplastic drug regimen]
PAC.............	P1 Artificial Chromosome (SAUS)
PAC.............	Pacific (AFM)
Pac.............	Pacific [Record label] [France]
Pac.............	Pacifica: Australian Theological Studies [A publication] (APTA)
PAC.............	Pacific Accreditation Cooperation (SAUS)
PAC.............	Pacific Aerospace Corp. Ltd. (SAUS)
PAC.............	Pacific Air Command [Air Force]
PAC.............	Pacific Airmotive Corporation
PAC.............	Pacific Automotive Corp. (SAUS)
PAC.............	Pacific Command [Military] (GFGA)
PAC.............	Pacific Ocean
PAC.............	Pacific Region [USTTA] (TAG)
Pac.............	Pacific Reporter [A publication] (DLA)
PAC.............	Pacific Telesis Group [NYSE symbol] (SPSG)
PAC.............	Pacific Telesis Group Financing I [NYSE symbol] (SAG)
PAC.............	Pacific Telesis Group Financing II [NYSE symbol] (SAG)
PAC.............	Package Assembly Circuit (SAUS)
PAC.............	Package Attitude Control [NASA]
PAC.............	Packaged Assembly Circuit
PAC.............	Packaged Attitude Control (SAUS)
PAC.............	Packaging Association of Canada (SAUS)
PAC.............	Packard Automobile Classics (EA)
PAC.............	Packed Memory [Computer science] (IAA)
PAC.............	Packet Autopiloted Cruiseway
PAC.............	Pacto de Alianza de Centro [Chile] [Political party] (EY)
PAC.............	Pad Air Conditioner (SAUS)
PAC.............	Paging Area Controller (VLIE)
PAC.............	Pakistan Aeronautical Complex (SAUS)
PAC.............	Pak-Man Resources, Inc. [Vancouver Stock Exchange symbol]
PAC.............	Palestine Affairs Center (EA)
PAC.............	Palo Alto - Branner [California] [Seismograph station code, US Geological Survey] [Closed] (SEIS)
PAC.............	Palo Alto Clinic (SAUS)
PAC.............	Pan African Congress (SAUS)
PAC.............	Pan-Africanist Congress [South Africa]
PAC.............	Panama City [Panama] Paitilla Airport [Airport symbol] (OAG)
PAC.............	Pan American College [Texas]
PAC.............	Pan-American Congress
PAC.............	Papular Acrodermatitis of Childhood
PAC.............	Para-Aminoclonidine [Biochemistry]
PAC.............	Para-Aminosalicylic Acid Calcium Salt [Pharmacology]
PAC.............	Parachute and Cable (SAUS)
PAC.............	Parachute and Cable Defence [British military]
PAC.............	Parallel Alternate Curriculum (EDAC)
PAC.............	Parametric Amplifier Converter
P-A-C	Parent-Adult-Child [Transactional analysis]
PAC.............	Parent Advisory Committee [Migrant education] (AEE)
PAC.............	Parent Advisory Council (EDAC)
PAC.............	Parker Aircraft Corp. (MCD)
PAC.............	Partido Autentico Constitucional [Authentic Constitutional Party] [El Salvador] [Political party]
PAC.............	Parts Allocation Chart (MCD)
PAC.............	Pascagoula, MS [Location identifier] [FAA] (FAAL)
PAC.............	Passed the Final Examination of the Advanced Class [Military College of Science] [British]
PAC.............	Passive Acoustic Classification (NVT)
PAC.............	Patents Advisory Committee [British]
PAC.............	Patient Airlift Center [Aeromedical evacuation]
PAC.............	Patriot Advanced Capability [Missile technology] [Military] (PS)
PAC.............	Patriot Antimissile Capability [Army]
PAC.............	Patriot ATM Capability (SAUS)
PAC.............	Payment after Closing [Insurance]
PAC.............	Peace Action Center [Defunct] (EA)
PAC.............	Pedagogic Automatic Computer (IEEE)
PAC.............	Pediatric AIDS [Acquired Immune Deficiency Syndrome] Coalition (EA)
PAC.............	Penal Affairs Consortium (WDAA)
PAC.............	Penalty Assessment Criteria [Environmental Protection Agency]
PAC.............	Penetration Aid Carrier (SAUS)
PAC.............	Penetration Aids Deployment Concept (SAA)
PA C	Pennsylvania Commonwealth Court Reports [A publication] (DLA)
PAC.............	People Against Cancer
PAC.............	People's Army Congress
PAC.............	Peptide Acid [Organic chemistry]
PAC.............	Perceptual Audio Coding (VLIE)
PAC.............	Performance Analysis and Control
PAC.............	Performance Assured Certification
PAC.............	Performing Arts Center (SAUS)
PAC.............	Periapical Cyst [Medicine] (MELL)
PAC.............	Peripheral Autonomous Control (NITA)
PAC.............	Permanent Accomodation Complex (SAUS)
PAC.............	Permanent Agricultural Committee (SAUS)
PAC.............	Personal Access Code
PAC.............	Personal Accident Coverage [Travel industry] (TRID)
PAC.............	Personal Analog Computer
PAC.............	Personal Authentication Code (VLIE)
PAC.............	Personal Authenticator Card (SAUS)
PAC.............	Person in Addition to Crew [Sailing]
PAC.............	Personnel Action Center [Army] (INF)
PAC.............	Personnel Action Code
PAC.............	Personnel Administrative Center
PAC.............	Personnel and Administration Center [Army] (AABC)
PAC.............	Personnel Assistance Center [Military] (INF)
PAC.............	Perturbation Angular Correlation (SAUS)
PAC.............	Perturbed Angular Correlation
PAC.............	Pesticides Advisory Committee [Tasmania, Australia]
PAC.............	Petroleum Advisory Committee [of Organization for Economic Cooperation and Development] [Terminated, 1976] (EGAO)
PAC.............	Pharmaceutical Advertising Council [New York, NY] (EA)
PAC.............	Phenacetin [Acetophenetidin], Aspirin, Caffeine [Pharmacology]
PAC.............	Phenacetin-Aspirin-Caffeine (SAUS)
PAC.............	Phenacetin, Aspirin, Coffeine (SAUS)
PAC.............	Philbrook Art Center (SAUS)
PAC.............	Photoacoustic [Spectroscopy]
PAC.............	Photoactive Compound [Chemistry]
PAC.............	Photo Aperture Card (SAA)
PAC.............	Phototypesetting Automatic Controller (DGA)
PA-C	Physician's Assistant-Certified (WGA)
PAC.............	Pilotless Aircraft [Navy] (IAA)
PAC.............	Piper Aircraft Corp.
PAC.............	Pittsburgh Activated Carbon (SAUS)
PAC.............	Place Complement of Address in Index Register (SAA)
PAC.............	Planned Amortization Class [Investment term] (DFIT)
PAC.............	Planned-Amortization-Class Bond [Investment term]
PAC.............	Planned Amortization Credit [Investment term] (ECON)

PAC............. Planned Availability Concept (MHDI)
PAC............. Planning Advisory Committee (OICC)
PAC............. Plasma Aldosterone Concentration [*Hematology*] (DMAA)
PAC............. Plasma Arc Chamber
PAC............. Plasma Arc Cutting [*Welding*]
PAC............. Platelet-Associated Complement [*Medicine*] (DMAA)
PAC............. Platinol [*Cisplatin*], Adriamycin, Cyclophosphamide [*Antineoplastic drug regimen*]
PAC............. Player Access Control (SAUS)
PAC............. Plowshare Advisory Committee [*AEC*]
PAC............. Pneumatic Analog Computer
PAC............. Pneumatic Auxiliary Console (AAG)
PAC............. Pod Air Conditioner (AAG)
PAC............. Poisons Advisory Committee [*Australia*]
PAC............. Polar Air Cargo, Inc. [*FAA designator*] (FAAC)
PAC............. Polar Atmospheric Chemistry (CARB)
PAC............. Policy Advisory Center
PAC............. Policy Advisory Committee [*National Cancer Institute*] [*Department of Health and Human Services*] (GFGA)
PAC............. Policy Advisory Committee [*Office of Economic Opportunity*]
PAC............. Polish American Congress (EA)
PAC............. Political Action Caucus [*Superseded by LPAC*] (EA)
PAC............. Political Action Committee [*Generic term*]
PAC............. Polled Access Circuit
PAC............. Pollution Abatement and Control
PAC............. Pollution Abatement Control (SAUS)
PAC............. Polyacrylat (SAUS)
PAC............. Polyalkene Carbonate (SAUS)
PAC............. Polyaluminum Chloride [*Inorganic chemistry*]
PAC............. Polyanionic Cellulose [*Organic chemistry*]
PAC............. Polycyclic Aromatic Compound [*Organic chemistry*]
PAC............. Population Action Council (EA)
PAC............. Portable Air Compressor (SAUS)
PAC............. Porterfield Airplane Club (EA)
PAC............. Post-Adoption Centre [*British*] (CB)
PAC............. Post Award Conference (MCD)
PAC............. Post Award Contract
PAC............. Potentially Adverse Condition (SAUS)
PAC............. Powder Air Conveyor (SAUS)
PAC............. Powdered Activated Carbon [*Adsorbent*]
PAC............. Pre-Action Calibration [*Gunnery*] (NVT)
PAC............. Pre-Admission Certification [*Medicine*] (MEDA)
PAC............. Prearrival Confirmation (SAUS)
PAC............. Preauthorized Checking (SAUS)
PAC............. Preauthorized Check Plan [*Insurance*]
PAC............. Pre-Authorized Chequing [*Canada*]
PAC............. Premature Atrial Contraction [*Medicine*]
PAC............. Premature Auricular Contraction [*Cardiology*] (AAMN)
PAC............. Preservation and Conservation [*IFLA Core Program*]
PAC............. President of the Air Council (SAUS)
PAC............. President's Advisor for Science
PAC............. Presidents Advisory Council (SAUS)
PAC............. Presidents' Athletic Conference (PSS)
PAC............. Pressure Alpha Center (MCD)
PAC............. Primary Address Code (AFM)
PAC............. Prime [*or Principal*] Associate Contractor (MCD)
PAC............. Principal Associate Contractor (MCD)
PAC............. Printing Accountants Club (EA)
PAC............. Printing Automatic Calculator (SAUS)
PAC............. Priority Area Children (AIE)
PAC............. Privacy Act Coordinator [*Navy*] (DNAB)
PAC............. Privilege Access Certificate (SAUS)
PAC............. Privilege Attribute Certificate (SAUS)
PAC............. Probably Approximately Correct (IDAI)
PAC............. Probe Aerodynamic Center [*NASA*]
PAC............. Problem Action Center [*NASA*] (NASA)
PAC............. Problem Assessment Center (SAUS)
PAC............. Process Analytical Chemistry
PAC............. Process Automation Computer (SAUS)
PAC............. Procurement and Contract (IAA)
PAC............. Production Acceleration Capacity [*Manufacturing*]
PAC............. Product of Ambulatory Care [*Medicine*] (HCT)
PAC............. Professional Activities Committee (SAUS)
PAC............. Professional Activities Survey [*Medicine*]
PAC............. Professional Advisory Committee (DIPS)
PAC............. Program Acquisition Cost (MCD)
PAC............. Program Address Counter [*Computer science*] (EECA)
PAC............. Program Adjustment Committee
PAC............. Program Administration and Control (SAUS)
PAC............. Program Advisory Committee
PAC............. Program Allocation Checker
PAC............. Program Application Code (DNAB)
PAC............. Program Assembly Card (NITA)
PAC............. Program Authorized Credentials [*Computer science*]
PAC............. Programmable Analogical Controller (NITA)
PAC............. Programmable Armament Control (SAUS)
PAC............. Programmable Automatic Comparator
PAC............. Programmable Automotive Controller (SAUS)
PAC............. Programme Activity Center [*Advisory Committee on Pollution of the Sea*]
PAC............. Progress Assessment Chart [*Psychology*]
PAC............. Project Advisory Committee (EGAO)
PAC............. Project Analysis and Control (IAA)
PAC............. Promoting Achievement through Communications [*Education*]
PAC............. Protect America's Children [*An association*] (EA)

PAC............. Protection Against Aircraft (SAUS)
PAC............. Protection Auxiliary Cabinet [*Nuclear energy*] (NRCH)
PAC............. Prudential Assurance Co. Ltd. [*Australia*]
PAC............. Public Access Catalogue (ADA)
PAC............. Public Access Control
PAC............. Public Accounts Committee [*British government*]
PAC............. Public Affairs Committee [*Defunct*] (EA)
PAC............. Public Affairs Coordinator [*Nuclear energy*] (NRCH)
PAC............. Public Affairs Council (EA)
PAC............. Public Archives of Canada
PAC............. Public Assistance Cooperative (SAUS)
PAC............. Public Authority Contribution [*Australia*]
PAC............. Public Awareness Committee [*American Library Association*]
PAC............. Publishers' Ad Club [*New York, NY*] (EA)
PAC............. Pulmonary Artery Catheter [*Medicine*]
PAC............. Purchasing and Contracting [*Army*] (IAA)
PAC............. Pure and Applied Chemistry [*IUPAC*]
p A c............. pure Argentinian cocaine (SAUS)
PAC............. Pursuant to Authority Contained (SAUS)
PAC............. Pursuant to Authority Contained In [*Army*]
PAC............. Put and Call [*Stock exchange term*]
Pac 2d......... Pacific Reporter, Second Series [*A publication*] (DLA)
PAC-3 .... Patriot Advanced Capability-3 [*Army*]
PAC-10 .... Pacific 10 Conference (EA)
Pac A........... Pacific Affairs [*A publication*] (BRI)
PACA .... Perishable Agricultural Commodities Act, 1930
PACA .... Physics and Chemistry of the Atmosphere (SAUS)
PACA .... Picture Agency Council of America (EA)
PACA .... Polyamide Carboxylic Acid (SAUS)
PACA .... Principal Assistant County Architect [*British*]
PACA .... Proceedings of the African Classical Association (SAUS)
PACA .... Propulsion and Control Assembly
PACA .... Proyecto Ambiental para Centro America [*Environmental Project for Central America*] [*Spanish*] (ECON)
PACAACS... Pacific Area Airways and Air Communications (IAA)
PACAACS.... Pacific Area Airways and Air Communications Service (SAUS)
PacA & E.... Pacific Aerospace & Electronics, Inc. [*Associated Press*] (SAG)
PACADIV..... Pacific Fleet Advance Headquarters Division (DNAB)
PACADV..... Pacific Fleet Advance Headquarters [*Guam*]
PACAF .... Pacific Air Command Air Forces (SAUS)
PACAF .... Pacific Air Forces
PACAFBASECOM... Pacific Air Forces Base Command
PACAF-OA.... Pacific Air Forces Operations Analysis
PACAF-OA.... Pacific Air Forces Operations Analysis Office [*Hickam Air Force Base, HI*]
PACAH........ Pitch Attitude Command/Attitude Hold [*Aviation*] (MCD)
PACAMS..... Pacific Aircrew Management System (SAUS)
PacAni........ Pacific Animated Imaging Corp. [*Associated Press*] (SAG)
PACAP .... Pituitary Adenylate Cyclase Activating Polypeptide [*Biochemistry*]
PACAP .... Pituitary Adenylyl Cyclase-Activating Polypeptide [*Endocrinology*]
Pacar........... PACCAR, Inc. [*Associated Press*] (SAG)
PAC Area.... Pacific Area (SAUS)
PacAS......... Pacific American Income Shares, Inc. [*Associated Press*] (SAG)
PACAS........ Patient Care System [*Army*] (AABC)
PA Cas........ Pennsylvania Supreme Court Cases (Sadler) [*A publication*] (DLA)
PACAS........ Personnel Access Control Accountability System [*NASA*] (MCD)
PACAS........ Psychological Abstracts Current Awareness Service (IID)
PACB .... Pan-American Coffee Bureau [*Defunct*] (EA)
PACB .... Pennsylvania Association of Community Bankers (TBD)
PACB .... Poppy Advisory and Control Board [*Tasmania, Australia*]
PACBA .... Pan-African Christian Broadcast Associaton (SAUS)
PACBAR...... Pacific Barrier RADAR (MCD)
PacBB......... Pacific Basin Bulk Shippers Ltd. [*Associated Press*] (SAG)
PacBBS....... Pacific Basin Bulk Shippers Ltd. [*Associated Press*] (SAG)
Pac Bch ...... Pacific Beach (SAUS)
Pac Bell...... Pacific Bell (SAUS)
PacBio .... Pacific Biometrics, Inc. [*Associated Press*] (SAG)
PacBiom..... Pacific Biometrics, Inc. [*Associated Press*] (SAG)
PACC .... Pacific Airlift Control Center (ACAE)
PACC .... Pacific Coast [*Railroad*] (MHDB)
PA CC .... Pennsylvania County Court Reports [*A publication*] (DLA)
PACC .... PERT [*Program Evaluation and Review Technique*] Associated Cost Control [*Computer science*] (IAA)
PACC .... Portable Arm Control Console (KSC)
PACC .... Primary Alternative Command Centre (SAUS)
PACC .... Primary Ambulatory Care Center [*Medicine*] (DMAA)
P(ACC)........ Probability of Acceptance
PACC .... Problem Action Control Center [*NASA*] (NASA)
PACC .... Product Administration and Contract Control (IAA)
PACC .... Professional Association of Custom Clothiers (EA)
PACC .... Programmable Array Combinatorial Circuit (NITA)
PACC .... Project Administration Contact Control (SAUS)
PACC .... Promoting Aphasics' Communicative Competence [*Medicine*] (DMAA)
PACC .... Propulsion and Auxiliary Control Console [*NASA*] (DNAB)
PACC .... Protected Air-Cooled Condenser [*Nuclear energy*] (NRCH)
PACC .... Protein A Immobilized in Collodion Charcoal (DAVI)
PACC .... Public Arts Advisory Council (NADA)
PACCA .... Airfield Capabilities Application (SAUS)
PACCA .... Policy Alternatives for the Caribbean and Central America (EA)
PACCALL..... Pacific Fleet Calls [*Radio call signs*]
PacCapB..... Pacific Capital Bancorp [*Associated Press*] (SAG)
PACCAR...... Pacific Car and Foundry
PACCAT ...... Pacific Area Command & Control AUTODIN Terminal (SAUS)
PACCE .... Providing Professional Development, Assessment, and Coordination of Competency-Based Education Project [*Illinois*] (EDAC)

PACCIOS...... Pan American Council of International Committee of Scientific Management

PACCO......... Cisplatin, Adriamycin, Cyclophosphamide, CCNU [*Lomustine*], Oncovin [*Vincristine*] [*Antineoplastic drug regimen*]

Pac Coast Int... Pacific Coast International [*A publication*] (ILCA)

Pac Coast LJ... Pacific Coast Law Journal [*A publication*] (DLA)

PACCOM...... Pacific Command [*Military*]

PACCOM...... Pacific Communications Network [*Computer science*] (TNIG)

PACCOM...... Pacific Computer Communications

PACCOM...... Pacific Fleet Communications Instructions

PACCOMMAREA... Pacific Communications Area (SAUS)

PACCOMOPCONCEN... Pacific Fleet Command Operational Control Center (DNAB)

PA CCR....... Pennsylvania County Court Reports [*A publication*] (DLA)

PA CC Reps... Pennsylvania County Court Reports [*A publication*] (DLA)

PacCrst...... Pacific Crest Capital [*Associated Press*] (SAG)

PACCS........ Pan American Cancer Cytology Society [*Defunct*] (EA)

PACCS........ Post-Attack Command and Control System [*Military*]

PACCS........ Product Administration and Contract Control System (SAUS)

PACCS/ADA... Post-Attack Command and Control System/Airborne Data Automation [*Military*]

PACCSq....... Post-Attack Command Control Squadron [*Air Force*]

PACCT........ PERT [*Program Evaluation and Review Technique*] and Cost Correlation Technique

PACCT........ Political Action Committee for Cable Television (NTCM)

PACD......... Cold Bay [*Alaska*] [*ICAO location identifier*] (ICLI)

PACD......... Pacific Division [*Military*]

PACD......... Parachute and Cable Defence [*British military*] (DMA)

PACD......... Plan of Action to Combat Desertification (SAUS)

PACDA....... Personnel and Administration, Combat Development Activity [*Army*] (AABC)

PA C Dec WCC... Pennsylvania Courts, Decisions in Workmen's Compensation Cases [*A publication*] (DLA)

PACDIGS..... Pacific Digital Graphics System (SAUS)

PACDIV...... Pacific Division [*Military*]

PacDunl...... Pacific Dunlop Ltd. [*Associated Press*] (SAG)

PACE........ Ampace Corp. [*NASDAQ symbol*]

PACE........ Pacific Agricultural Cooperative for Export [*Corte Madera, CA*] (EA)

PACE........ Pacific Airlift Center (SAUS)

PACE........ Pacific Alternate Command Element (CINC)

PACE........ Pacific America Container Express (MHDB)

PACE........ Pacific Atoll Cratering Experiment [*Military*] (DNAB)

PACE........ Pacing and Clinical Electrophysiology (SAUS)

PACE........ Packaged CRAM [*Card Random-Access Memory*] Executive [*NCR Corp.*] [*Computer science*]

PACE........ Package for Architectural Computer Evaluation (PDAA)

PACE........ Packet of Accelerated Christian Education [*Educational material marketed by fundamentalist company, Accelerated Christian Education*]

PACE........ Paging Access Control Equipment (SAUS)

PACE........ Paper, Allied-Industrial, Chemical and Energy Workers International

PACE........ Parental Alliance for Choice in Education (AIE)

PACE........ Parents and Children's Equality [*An association*] (PAZ)

PACE........ Parts Automated Control through Electronics (SAUS)

PACE........ Passive Attitude Control Experimental [*Satellite*]

PACE........ Patient Advise and Consent Encounter

PACE........ Patrol Airship Concept Evaluation

PACE........ People with Arthritis Can Exercise [*Medical program*]

PACE........ Performance Advantage with Cummins Electronics [*Automotive engineering*]

PACE........ Performance and Cost Evaluation

PACE........ Performing Arts, Culture, and Entertainment [*Proposed cable television system*]

PACE........ Perigee Augmentation Control Electronics (ACAE)

PACE........ Peripheral Automatic Channel Emulator [*Computer science*]

PACE........ Permafrost and Climate in Europe (SAUS)

PACE........ Personal Audio Computer Editing (SAUS)

PACE........ Personalized Aerobics for Cardiovascular Enhancement

PACE........ Petroleum Association for Conservation of the Canadian Environment

PACE........ Phased Array Control Electronics

PACE........ Philippine Association of Civil Engineers (SAUS)

PACE........ Physics and Chemistry Experiment

PACE........ Planetary Association for Clean Energy (EA)

PACE........ Plan for Action by Citizens in Education

PACE........ Planned Action with Constant Evaluation [*Computer science*]

PACE........ Planning and Control Made Easy (PDAA)

PACE........ Plant Acquisition and Construction Equipment [*Nuclear energy*] (NRCH)

PACE........ Plant and Capital Equipment (MCD)

PACE........ Plasma-Assisted Chemical Etching [*Metallurgy*]

PACE........ Platinol [*Cis-Platinum*] [*Antineoplastic drug regimen*] (DAVI)

PACE........ Plessey Adaptive Compass Equipment (SAUS)

PACE........ Polar Anglo-American Conjugate Experiment (SAUS)

PACE........ Police and Criminal Evidence Act [*1964*] [*British*]

PACE........ Policy Analysis for California Education [*Research center*] (RCD)

PACE........ Political Action for Candidate Election [*National Association*]

PACE........ Pollution Abatement Capital Expense (EDCT)

PACE........ Portable Acoustic Collection Equipment (MCD)

PACE........ Power at Combined Efficiency (SAUS)

PACE........ Precipitation Augmentation for Crops Experiment (SAUS)

PACE........ Precision Analog Computing Equipment

PACE........ Preflight Acceptance Checkout Equipment

PACE........ Preflight Automatic Checkout Equipment (SAUS)

PACE........ Prelaunch Automatic Checkout Equipment [*NASA*]

PACE........ Premier Automotive Supplier Contribution to Excellence

PACE........ Priority Access Control Enabled [*Telecommunications*]

PACE........... Priority Activities in Cancer Education

PACE........... Prisoners Accelerated Creative Exposure [*An association*]

PACE........... Procedural Approach to the Composition of Essays [*In book title*]

PACE........... Process and Assembly Computerized Environment (SAUS)

PACE........... Process Automation and Control Extecutive (SAUS)

PACE........... Processing and Classification of Enlistees (SAUS)

PACE........... Processing and Control Element [*Computer science*] (IAA)

PACE........... Processing Control Element (SAUS)

PACE........... Producers of Associated Components for Electronics (IAA)

PACE........... Producible Alternative to Cadmium telluride for Epitaxy (SAUS)

PACE........... Product Assurance Confidence Evaluator (SAUS)

PACE........... Professional Activities Committees for Engineers (SAUS)

PACE........... Professional Activities for Continuing Education [*AEC*]

PACE........... Professional and Administrative Career Examination [*Formerly, FSEE*] [*Civil Service*]

PACE........... Professional and Career Education for Early Childhood

PACE........... Professional Application Creation Environment (NITA)

PACE........... Professional Association of Christian Educators (EA)

PACE........... Professional Association of Consulting Engineers

PACE........... Professional Athletes Career Enterprises (SAUS)

PACE........... Professional Automotive Career Education [*Automotive industry training*]

PACE........... Program Acquisition Cost Estimate (SAUS)

PACE........... Program Analysis Control and Evaluation [*Computer science*] (IAA)

PACE........... Program for Acquiring Competence in Entrepreneurship (EDAC)

PACE........... Program for Afloat College Education [*Navy*] (NVT)

PACE........... Program for Arrangement of Cables and Equipment (SAUS)

PACE........... Programmable Aerospace Checkout Equipment (ACAE)

PACE........... Programmable Autonomously-Controlled Electrode [*Instrumentation*]

PACE........... Programmed Automatic Communications Equipment

PACE........... Programmed Automatic Customer Engineer (SAUS)

PACE........... Programming Analysis Consulting Education (IEEE)

PACE........... Program of Adult College Education (SAUS)

PACE........... Program of All-Inclusive Care for the Elderly

PACE........... Programs Advancing Citizenship Education [*Institute*]

PACE........... Program to Advance Creativity in Education (SAUS)

PACE........... Progressive Aerobic Circuit Exercise [*Fitness training*]

PACE........... Project for the Advancement of Church Education

PACE........... Projects to Advance Creativity in Education [*HEW*]

PACE........... Promoting Aphasics Communicative Effectiveness [*Australia*]

PACE........... Providing Avenues for Continuing Encouragement [*Scholarship awarded by Fraternity of Recording Executives*]

PACE........... Proving & Adjustment for Communications Efficiency (SAUS)

PACE........... Provisioning Action Control Evaluation [*Military*] (AFIT)

PACE........... Public Access Cabletelevision by and for the Elders (SAUS)

PACE........... Public Affairs Council for Education [*Canada*]

PACE........... Public Awareness Communication Exchange (SAUS)

PACE........... Pulsed Analog-to-Digital Converter and Encoder (SAUS)

PACE........... Pulse-Synthesized Advanced Conversion Equipment

P/ACEA2....... Probationary Control Electrical Artificer, Acting, 2nd Class [*British military*] (DMA)

PACECO .... Pacific Coast Engineering Co. (SAUS)

PACED .... Program for Advanced Concepts in Electronic Design

PACEE......... Propulsion and Auxiliary Control Electronic Enclosure (DNAB)

PaceHlt....... Pace Health Management Systems, Inc. [*Associated Press*] (SAG)

PACE-LV ...... Preflight Acceptance Checkout Equipment-Launch Vehicle [*NASA*]

PACEM........ Physics and Chemistry of Earth Materials (SAUS)

PACEMAKER... Public Agency Career Employment Maker [*OEO project*]

PACEN .... Public Affairs Center [*Navy*] (DNAB)

PACENLANT... Public Affairs Center, Atlantic [*Navy*] (DNAB)

PACENPAC... Public Affairs Center, Pacific [*Navy*] (DNAB)

PACENS .... Patient Census

PacEnt .... Pacific Enterprises [*Associated Press*] (SAG)

PACEO .... Professional Application Creation Environment (HGAA)

PACER .... Parent Advocacy Coalition for Educational Rights [*Minnesota*] (EDAC)

PACER .... Part and Component Evaluation Report [*NASA*]

PACER .... Planning and Control of Engineering Resources (SAUS)

PACER .... Planning Automation and Control for Evaluating Requirements

PACER .... Portable Aircraft Condition Evaluation Recorder (SAUS)

PACER .... Portable Aircraft Condition Evaluator Recorder

PACER .... Portfolio Analysis, Control, Evaluation and Reporting (SAUS)

PACER .... Postadoption Center for Education and Research

PACER .... Post-Operational Analysis and Exercise Review [*Program*]

PACER .... Postoperational Analysis Critique and Exercise Report [*Military*] (CAAL)

PACER .... Prescriptive Analysis for Curriculum Evaluation [*Vocational guidance*]

PACER .... Prescriptive Analysis for Curriculum Evaluation and Review (SAUS)

PACER .... Priority for Allocation/Application of COMSEC Equipment Resources (MCD)

PACER .... Private Access to Court Electronic Records (AAGC)

PACER .... Process Assembly Case Evaluator Routine [*Computer science*]

PACER .... Professional Association of Comics Entertainment Retailers (NTPA)

PACER .... Program-Assisted Console Evaluation and Review [*Air Force*]

PACER .... Program for the Acceleration of Commercial Energy Research (SAUS)

PACER .... Programmed Automatic Circuit Evaluator and Recorder

PACER .... Programmed Automatic Communications Equipment Requirements

PACER .... Program of Active Cooling Effects and Requirements

PACER .... Purpose, Agenda, Code of Conduct, Expectations/Introductions and Roles (SAUS)

PACER ACQUIRE... AFLC Management System Acquisition (SAUS)

PACERS .... Pacing and Cardiac Electrophysiology Retrieval System [*Intermedics, Inc.*] [*Information service or system*] (IID)

PACES .... Parent Attitude Toward Child Experssiveness Scale (EDAC)

PACES .... Patient as Customer Evaluation Survey
PACES .... Political Action Committee for Engineers and Scientists
PACE-S/C ..... Preflight Acceptance Checkout Equipment for Spacecraft
Pace U .... Pace University (GAGS)
PAC-EX .... Canadian National Packaging Exposition [Packaging Association of Canada] (TSPED)
PACEX .... Pacific Exchange [System] [Military] (AFM)
PACEX System... Pacific Exchange System (SAUS)
PACf .... Pacific
Pacf .... PacifiCorp [Associated Press] (SAG)
PACF .... Partial Autocorrelation Function [Statistics]
PACF .... Periodic Autocorrelation Function (SAUS)
PAC-FACS .... Programmed Appropriation Commitments-Fixed Asset Control System (SAUS)
PACFAST ..... Pacific Forward Area Support Team (DNAB)
PACFASTDET.. Pacific Forward Area Support Team Detachment (DNAB)
PACFASTREP.. Pacific Forward Area Support Team Representative (DNAB)
PacFIN .... Pacific Fishery Information Network [Database] [National Marine Fisheries Service]
PACFLAP ..... Pacific Fleet Augmentation Plan [Navy] (NVT)
PACFLT .... Pacific Fleet
PACFLTCOM... Pacific Fleet Command
PACFLTMOPHOTOU... Pacific Fleet Mobile Photographic Unit (MUGU)
PACFLTPROPEXAMBD... Pacific Fleet Propulsion Examining Board (DNAB)
PACFORNET... Pacific Coast Forest Research Information Network [Later, WESTFORNET] [Forest Service] (IID)
PACFW .... President's Advisory Committee for Women [Terminated, 1980] (EGAO)
Pac Gas&El... Pacific Gas and Electric (SAUS)
PacGate....... Pacific Gateway Properties [Associated Press] (SAG)
PACGCS ...... Prior Active Coast Guard Commissioned Service
PacGE.......... Pacific Gas & Electric Co. [Associated Press] (SAG)
PACGEEIA.... Pacific Area Ground Environment Electronic Installation Agency (CINC)
PACGES....... Prior Active Coast Guard Enlisted Service
PACGO......... President's Advisory Committee on Government Organization [Abolished, 1961]
PACGSR....... Pan American Center for Geographical Studies and Research [See also CEPEIGE] (EAIO)
PacGul........ Pacific Gulf Properties, Inc. [Associated Press] (SAG)
PacGulf....... Pacific Gulf Properties [Associated Press] (SAG)
PACH .... Performing Arts Center for Health [New York University/Bellevue Hospital, New York, NY] [Superseded by Center for Dance Medicine -CDM]
PACH .... Pipers to After Coming Head [Obstetrics] (DAVI)
PACH .... Public Administration Clearing House [1931-1956]
PACH .... Publishers' Accounts Clearing House [British] (BI)
PACHACH.... Partizanim-Chayalim-Chalutzim (BJA)
PACHEDPEARL... Pacific Headquarters, Pearl Harbor, Hawaii [Navy]
PACHEM ...... Point Area Chemical Effects Model (ACAE)
PACHG .... Program Advisory Committee on the Human Genome (HGEN)
PACI........... Partnerships for Advanced Computational Infrastructure [National Science Foundation]
PACIA .... Particle Counting Immunoassay
PACICOM..... Pacific Coastal Marine Productivity [Marine science] (OSRA)
Pacif........... Pacific (NTIO)
PACIF.......... Pacific
Pacif........... PacifiCorp [Associated Press] (SAG)
PacifBnk...... Pacific Bank NA [Associated Press] (SAG)
PacifC......... PacifiCare Health Systems, Inc. [Associated Press] (SAG)
PacifCp....... PacifiCorp [Associated Press] (SAG)
Pacif Defence Reporter... Pacific Defence Reporter [A publication]
PACIFIC .... Peripheral Audio Chip for Improved Features in Cellular Phones (TIMI)
PACIFIC .... Planning, Accounting and Control Information for use in Construction (SAUS)
Pacific Basin Countries... Australia, China, Hong Kong, Indonesia, Japan, Malaysia, New Zealand, Philippines, Singapore, South Korea, Taiwan, Thail (SAUS)
Pacific CLJ... Pacific Coast Law Journal [San Francisco] [A publication] (DLA)
Pacific Law Mag... Pacific Law Magazine [A publication] (DLA)
Pacific Rep... Pacific Reporter [A publication] (DLA)
Pacif Is Mon... Pacific Islands Monthly [A publication]
Pacif Rep..... Pacific Reporter [A publication] (DLA)
PACIFY .... Parents and Alumni Committee Involved for Youth [Brown University]
PAC II .... CCSC Project Management System (SAUS)
PACIMS .... Passive Chemical Ionization Mass Spectrometry
PACINTCEN... Pacific Intelligence Center (DNAB)
PacIntl......... Pacific International Services Corp. [Associated Press] (SAG)
PAC IO......... Planned Amortization Class Interest-Only (SAUS)
PACIR .... Practical Approach to Chemical Information Retrieval
PACIR .... Propulsion, Aerodynamics, Control, Integration, Research (SAUS)
PACIS .... Pilot Aid & Close-In Surveillance (SAUS)
PACIT.......... Passive and Active Interface Test [Electronic warfare]
PACIT.......... Process Automation for Cable Interface Tape (VLIE)
Pac J Math... Pacific Journal of Mathematics (SAUS)
PACK .... Gibraltar Packaging Group, Inc. [NASDAQ symbol] (SAG)
pack........... Packed
PACK .... Packing (SAUS)
PACK .... Packing and Allocation for a COMPOOL [Communications Pool] Kaleidoscope (SAA)
PACK .... Parents and Cataract Kids [An association] (PAZ)
PACK .... Pontoon Air Cushion Kit [Army] (RDA)
PACKAGE/.... Planned Aids for Cross-Culture Knowledge, Action and Growth in Effectiveness

PackRs .... Packaging Research Corp. [Associated Press] (SAG)
PackRsh ...... Packaging Research Corp. [Associated Press] (SAG)
PACL........... Clear [Alaska] [ICAO location identifier] (ICLI)
Pac Law Mag... Pacific Law Magazine [A publication] (DLA)
Pac Law Reptr... Pacific Law Reporter [San Francisco] [A publication] (DLA)
Pac Leg N ... Pacific Legal News [A publication] (DLA)
Pac Luth U... Pacific Lutheran University (GAGS)
PACM......... Parts and Components Manual (SAUS)
PACM......... Passive Access Control Module (SAUS)
PACM......... Passive Countermeasures (MSA)
PACM......... Pulse Amplitude Code Modulation [Electronics]
PACMAR..... Pacific Management Resources (SAUS)
Pac Mar Fish Comm Bull/Annu Rep... Pacific Marine Fisheries Commission Bulletin/Annual Report (SAUS)
PACMD .... Philadelphia Contract Management District (SAA)
PACMEDS... Pacific Meteorological Distribution Systems (SAUS)
PACMETNET... Pacific Meteorological Network (AAG)
PACMI .... President's Advisory Committee on Management Improvement [Terminated, 1973]
PACMISCEN... Pacific Missile Center [Marine science] (DNAB)
PACMISRAN... Pacific Missile Range [Later, WTR] (MUGU)
PACMISRANFAC... Pacific Missile Range Facility [Obsolete]
PACMISRANFACDET... Pacific Missile Range Facility Detachment [Obsolete] (DNAB)
PACMISRANFACREP... Pacific Missile Range Facility Representative [Obsolete] (DNAB)
PACMISTESTCEN... Pacific Missile Test Center [Navy]
PACMISTESTCEN LO... Pacific Missile Test Center Liaison Office [Navy] (DNAB)
PACMS .... Pacific Crisis Management System (SAUS)
PACMS .... Psycho-Acoustical Measuring System (PDAA)
PA Cmwlth... Pennsylvania Commonwealth Court Reports [A publication] (DLA)
PACN.......... Pacific Area Communications Network (SAA)
PACNAVCONSTFOR... Pacific Naval Construction Force (DNAB)
PACNAVFACENGCOM... Pacific Division Naval Facilities Engineering Command
PACNCF ...... Pacific Naval Construction Force (DNAB)
PACNCO ...... Personnel Assistance Center Noncommissioned Officer (INF)
PACNET .... OCLC Pacific Network [Claremont, CA] [Information service or system] (IID)
PACNET .... Plymouth Audioconferencing Network [Plymouth Polytechnic] [Plymouth, England] [Telecommunications] (TSSD)
PACNET .... POCC [Payload Operations Control Center] Automated Computer Network
PacNoRGG... Pacific Northwest Regional Genetics Group (SAUS)
PACNY .... Pawnbrokers' Association of the City of New York (EA)
PACO .... Accounting Policy Division (AAGC)
PacO .... Pacific Ocean
PACO .... Peak Aboriginal Community Organisation [Australia]
PACO .... Pivot Ambulating Crutchless Orthosis [Medicine]
PACO .... Polaris Accelerated Change Operation [Missiles]
PACO .... Primary Administrative Contracting Officer [Military] (AFIT)
PACO .... Principal Administrative Contracting Officer (AAGC)
PA_{CO2}.......... Alveolar Carbon Dioxide Pressure [in blood gases] [Medicine] (DAVI)
$PaCO2$.......... Arterial Carbon Dioxide Pressure (SAUS)
$Paco_2$.......... Arterial Carbon Dioxide Pressure, Tension [Medicine] (MAE)
$PaCO2$ .... Pressure of Carbon Dioxide (SAUS)
PACOB........ Propulsion Auxiliary Control Box (AAG)
Pac Ocean Terr... Pacific Ocean Territories (SAUS)
PA Co Ct..... Pennsylvania County Court Reports [A publication] (DLA)
PA Co Ct R... Pennsylvania County Court Reports [A publication] (DLA)
PACOM .... Pacific Command [Military]
PACOM .... Pacific Communications Group
PACOMBPO... Pacific Command Blood Program Office [Military] (DNAB)
PACOMDET... Pacific Command Detachment [Military] (DNAB)
PACOMEP ... Pacific Command Emergency Procedures (CINC)
PACOMEW... Pacific Command Electronic Warfare (CINC)
PACOMINTS... Pacific Command Intelligence School (CINC)
PACOMJRO... Pacific Command Joint Medical Regulating Office (DNAB)
PA Commw... Pennsylvania Commonwealth Court Reports [A publication] (DLA)
Pa Commw... Pennsylvania Commonwealth Reports [A publication] (AAGC)
PA Commw Ct... Pennsylvania Commonwealth Court Reports [A publication] (DLA)
PA Com Pl... Pennsylvania Common Pleas Reporter [A publication] (DLA)
PA Cons Stat... Pennsylvania Consolidated Statutes [A publication] (DLA)
PA Cons Stat Ann... Pennsylvania Consolidated Statutes, Annotated [A publication] (DLA)
PA Cons Stat Ann (Purdon)... Pennsylvania Consolidated Statutes, Annotated (Purdon) [A publication] (DLA)
PACOPS....... Pacific Air Combat Operations Staff
PACOPS....... Pacific Air Force Operations (MCD)
PACOR........ Packet Processor (ADWA)
PACOR........ Passive Correlation and Ranging
PACOR........ Passive Correlation and Ranging Station (IAA)
PACORE ...... Parabolic Corner Reflector
PACORNALOG... Pacific Coast Coordinator of Naval Logistics
PA Corp ...... Pennsylvania Corp. Reporter [A publication] (DLA)
PA Corp R ... Pennsylvania Corp. Reporter [A publication] (DLA)
PA Corp Rep... Pennsylvania Corp. Reporter [A publication] (DLA)
PACOS......... Package Operating System (PDAA)
PACOS......... Procedure for Automatic Computing Steps (SAUS)
PACOS......... Process Automation Control Operating System (VLIE)
PACOSS....... Passive and Active Control of Space Structure (ACAE)
PA County Ct... Pennsylvania County Court Reports [A publication] (DLA)
PA CP .... Pennsylvania Common Pleas Reporter [A publication] (DLA)
PACP.......... Photo Aperture Card Program (SAA)
PACP.......... Propulsion Auxiliary Control Panel [NASA] (KSC)
PACP.......... Pulmonary Alveolar-Capillary Permeability [Medicine] (MELL)

PACP	Pulmonary Artery Counter-Pulsation [*Cardiology*] (MAE)
PacPhy	Pacific Physician Services, Inc. [*Associated Press*] (SAG)
PACPIP	Public Advocate - Coalition of Public Interest Professionals (EA)
PACPrT	Pac Telesis Fin I 7.56%'TOPrS' [*NYSE symbol*] (TTSB)
PACQI	Probability of Acquisition [*Military*]
Pac R	Pacific Reporter [*Commonly cited as P*] [*A publication*] (DLA)
PA CR	Pennsylvania County Court Reports [*A publication*] (DLA)
PACR	Performance and Compatibility Requirements
PACR	Perimeter Acquisition RADAR (MSA)
PACRAD	Practical Absolute Cavity Radiometer (PDAA)
PacR & E.	Pacific Research & Engineering Corp. [*Associated Press*] (SAG)
PACRAO	Pacific Association of Collegiate Registrars and Admission Officers
PACRED	Pacific Area Cooperative Renewable Energy Development [*University of Hawaii*]
PacRehab	Pacific Rehabilitation & Sports Medicine, Inc. [*Associated Press*] (SAG)
Pac Rep	Pacific Reporter [*Commonly cited as P*] [*A publication*] (DLA)
PACREP	Port Activities Report [*Navy*]
PACREPCOMNAVSURFRES...	Pacific Representative for Commander Naval Surface Reserve Force (DNAB)
PACREPNAVRES..	Pacific Representative of the Chief of Naval Reserve (DNAB)
Pac Repr	Pacific Reporter [*A publication*] (DLA)
PACRESFLT...	Pacific Reserve Fleet
PacRim	Pac Rim Holding Corp. [*Associated Press*] (SAG)
PACRNB	Presidents Advisory Commission on Recreation and Natural Beauty (SAUS)
PACS	Cape Sarichef Air Force Station [*Alaska*] [*ICAO location identifier*] (ICLI)
PACS	Pacific Area Communications Service (SAUS)
PACS S	Pacific Area Communications System (MCD)
Pac S	Pacific Studies [*A publication*] (BRI)
PACS	Pan America Climate Studies [*Marine science*] (OSRA)
PACS	Pan American Climate Studies (SAUS)
PACS	Particle Analysis Cameras for the Shuttle [*NASA*]
PACS	Passenger Automated Check-In System (SAUS)
PACS	Patient Accounting, Census, and Statistics
PACS	Patient Care and Services (DMAA)
PACS	Payload Actuation and Control System (SAUS)
PACS	Payroll Accounting and Cost System (SAUS)
PACS	Peace and Common Security [*Defunct*] (EA)
PACS	Pentagon Automated Communications System (SAUS)
PACS	Personal Access Communications System (VLIE)
PACS	Photo Aperture Card System (SAA)
PACS	Physics and Astronomy Classification Scheme
PACS	Physics and Chemistry Classification Scheme (SAUS)
PACS	Picture Archival and Communication System
PACS	Picture Archiving and Communication System (ADWA)
PACS	Pitch Augmentation Control System (PDAA)
PACS	Plant Automation Communication System [*IBM Corp.*]
PACS	Pointing and Attitude Control System [*Aerospace*] (NASA)
PACS	Pointing and Control System (SAUS)
PACS	Polar Acquisition and Control Subsystem (SAUS)
PACS	Post-Attack Communication System
PACS	Press and Automation Control System [*Metal Stamping*]
PACS	Principal Appreciation Conversion Security [*Finance*]
PACS	Process Automation & Computer Systems
PACS	Program Authorization Control System (MCD)
PACS	Programmable Armament Control Set (DOMA)
PACS	Public-Access Computing Systems (SAUS)
Pa CSA	Pennsylvania Consolidated Statutes, Annotated [*A publication*] (DLA)
PACSAT	Packet Satellite [*Telecommunications*]
PACSAT	Passive Communications Satellite
PACSBB	Phased Array Concept Study and Brass Board (ACAE)
PA/CSC	Payload Accommodation/Carrier Support Center [*NASA*] (SSD)
PACSC	Pesticides and Agricultural Chemicals Standing Committee (SAUS)
PACSCAT	Pacific Ionospheric Scatter (CINC)
Pac Sci	Pacific Science (SAUS)
PacSci	Pacific Scientific Co. [*Associated Press*] (SAG)
PACS DB	Picture Archiving and Communication System Data Base (DMAA)
PacSen	Pacific Sentinel Gold Corp. [*Associated Press*] (SAG)
PACSICOM	Pan African Conference on Sustainable Integrated Coastal Management (SAUS)
PACSIM	Performance Achievement Computer Model for Waste Package (SAUS)
PACS-L	Public Access Computers in Libraries-Listservice (SAUS)
PACS-L	Public Access Computer Systems List (VLIE)
PACS Review...	Public-Access Computer Systems Review [*A publication*]
PACSUBDSEC..	Pacific Submarine Direct Support Element Coordinator (DNAB)
PacSun	Pacific Sunwear of California, Inc. [*Associated Press*] (SAG)
Pac Sym	Pacific Symphony (SAUS)
PacT	Pacific Telesis Group Financing I [*Associated Press*] (SAG)
PacT	Pacific Telesis Group Financing II [*Associated Press*] (SAG)
PACT	Pan American Commission of Tampa (EA)
PACT	Pandick Computerized Typesetting (NITA)
PACT	Papillary Carninoma of Thyroid [*Medicine*] (DMAA)
PACT	Parents, Children, and Teachers (AIE)
PACT	Participating and Assertive Consumer Training [*Health education*]
PACT	Partnership for Capacity Building in Africa
PACT	Partnership in Advanced Computing Technologies (SAUS)
PACT	Passive Active Correlation Techniques (ACAE)
PACT	Paved Concrete Track [*Railways*]
PACT	Pay Actual Computer Time
PACT	Performing Arts for Crisis Training [*In association name, PACT Training*] (EA)
PACT	Personal Air Communications Technology (CGWS)
PACT	Perturbed-Anisotropic-Chain Theory [*Chemistry*]
PACT	Phased Control Technique (PDAA)
PACT	Philadelphia Association for Clinical Trials (DAVI)
PACT	Philco Automatic Circuit Tester
PACT	Plan of Action for Challenging Times (EA)
PACT	Plasma Arc Centrifugal Treatment
PACT	Portable Aircraft Calibration Tracker [*NASA*]
PACT	Portable Automatic Calibration Tracker (ACAE)
PACT	Poseidon Automatic Cable Tester [*Missiles*] (DNAB)
PACT	Powdered Activated Carbon Treatment [*For wastewater*] [*E. I. Du Pont De Nemours & Co., Inc.*]
PACT	Precision Aircraft Control Technology (MCD)
PACT	Precordial Acceleration Tracing [*Medicine*] (DMAA)
PACT	Predictive Analysis and Crash Testing [*Automotive safety research*]
PACT	Prefix Access Code Translator (VLIE)
PACT	Prepaid Accountable Care Term [*Medicine*] (DMAA)
PACT	Print Active Computer Tables (SAA)
PACT	Prisoners and Community Working Together [*Institute*]
PACT	Private Agencies Collaborating Together (EA)
PACT	Processing and Communications Terminal (MCD)
PACT	Producers Alliance for Cinema & Television
PACT	Production Action Control Technique (SAA)
PACT	Production Analysis Control Technique [*Navy*]
PACT	Professional Association of Canadian Theatres
PACT	Program for Advancement of Commercial Technology (SAUS)
PACT	Program for Automatic Coding Techniques [*Computer science*]
PACT	Programmable Asynchronous Clustered Teleprocessing
PACT	Programmable Automatic Continuity Tester (SAUS)
PACTT	Programmed All-purpose Communications Terminal (SAUS)
PACT	Programmed Analysis Computer Transfer (KSC)
PACT	Programmed Automatic Circuit Tester
PACT	Progress in Advanced Circuit Technology (SAUS)
PACT	Progress in Advanced Component Technology (IAA)
PACT	Project Accounting by Cost and Time (SAUS)
PACT	Project Analysis and Control Technique (SAUS)
PACT	Project for the Advancement of Coding Techniques
PACT	Protective Action for Children's Television (NTCM)
PACT	Provide Addict Care Today [*Later, NADAP*]
PACT	Public Access Cordless Telephony (VLIE)
PACT	Public Action Coalition on Toys [*Opposes sexist toys*]
PACTA	Packed Tape Assembly
PACTAIS	Pacific Theater Air Intelligence System (SAUS)
PACTCU	Pacific Area Communications Message Traffic Control Unit (IAA)
PacTec	Pacer Technology [*Associated Press*] (SAG)
Pac Tel	Pacific Telephone (SAUS)
PACTEL	Pacific Telesis (NITA)
PacTel	Pacific Telesis Group [*Associated Press*] (SAG)
PACTEL	PA Computers & Telecommunications [*Information service or system*] (IID)
PACTEL	Planning Associates for Computers and Telecommunications (NITA)
PACTEX	Pacific-Texas [*Pipeline*]
PACTG	Pediatric AIDS Clinical Trials Group (SAUS)
PACTIDS	Pacific TAC Intelligence Data System (SAUS)
PACTIV	Principos Activos [*Ministerio de Sanidad y Consumo*] [*Spain*] [*Information service or system*] (CRD)
PACTO	Professional, Administrative, Clerical, Technical, and Other (BARN)
PACTOA	Pacific Technical Operations Area [*Military*]
PacTOP	Pacific Tsunami Observation Program [*Marine science*] (OSRA)
PACTS	Parents, Administrators, Community, Teachers, and Students [*School-community groups*]
PACTS	Programmer Aptitude Competence Test System
PACTS	Public Access Cordless Telephone Service [*Australia*]
PACTT	Planning the Australian Capital Territory Together
Pac U	Pacific University (GAGS)
PACU	Pennsylvania Association of Colleges and Universities (SAUS)
PACU	Post-Anesthesia Care Unit (MEDA)
PACUIT	Packet + Circuit (MHDI)
Pac Union C..	Pacific Union College (GAGS)
PACUSA	Pacific Air Command, United States Army
PACV	Cordova [*Alaska*] [*ICAO location identifier*] (ICLI)
PACV	Patrol Air-Cushion Vehicle [*Also called Hovercraft*] [*Navy*]
PACV	Personnel Air-Cushion Vehicle
PACV	Post-Accident Containment Venting [*Nuclear energy*] (NRCH)
PACVD	Plasma-Assisted Chemical Vapor Deposition [*Coating technology*]
PACVIS	Pathological Cardiovascular Ischemic States [*Medicine*] (DB)
PACWP	Pulmonary Arterial Capillary Wedge Pressure [*Medicine*] (DMAA)
PACX	Private Automatic Computer Exchange [*Telecommunications*]
PACZ	Cape Romanzof Air Force Station [*Alaska*] [*ICAO location identifier*] (ICLI)
PAD	Accounting Policy Division (AAGC)
PAD	Anthropology of Development Programme [*McGill University*] [*Canada*] [*Research center*] (RCD)
PAD	Packet Assembler/Disassembler [*Switching technique*] [*Computer science*]
PAD	Packet Assembly Disassembly (NITA)
PAD	Padder [*Capacitor*] [*Electronics*]
PAD	Padding (SAUS)
PAD	Paddling (SAUS)
PAD	Paderborn [*Germany*] [*Airport symbol*] (OAG)
PAD	Padlock (SAUS)
PAD	Padova [*Italy*] [*Seismograph station code, US Geological Survey*] (SEIS)
PAD	Padstow [*Town in England*]
PAD	Paducah Gaseous Diffusion Plant [*Department of Energy*] [*Paducah, KY*] (GAAI)

PAD	Palestine Arab Delegation (EA)
PAD	Panama Air Depot (SAUS)
PAD	Panama District (SAUS)
PAD	Para-Amino Benzoic Acid (SAUS)
PAD	Partido Accion Democratica [*Democratic Action Party*] [*El Salvador*] [*Political party*] (PPW)
PAD	Partido de Accion Democrata [*Democratic Action Party*] [*Spain*] [*Political party*] (PPW)
PAD	Passenger Airbag Disable
PAD	Passive Acoustic Detection [*Military*] (CAAL)
PAD	Passive Air Defense [*British*]
PAD	Patient Accounts Department (SAUS)
PAD	Patriot Arm Decoy [*Weaponry*] (DWSG)
PAD	Payable after Death [*Insurance*] (ADA)
PAD	Pedagogischer Austauschdienst [*Pedagogical Exchange Service*] [*German*]
PAD	Penetration Aids Deployment [*Weaponry*] (DWSG)
PAD	People Against Displacement (NADA)
PAD	Percutaneous Abscess Drainage [*Surgery*] (DAVI)
PAD	Percutaneous Automated Diskectomy [*Neurology*] (DAVI)
PAD	Percutaneous Device (SAUS)
PAD	Performance Analysis and Design [*Nuclear energy*] (NRCH)
PAD	Performance Analysis Department (SAUS)
PAD	Performing Arts Directory [*A publication*]
PAD	Peripheral Adaptor (SAUS)
PAD	Peripheral Arterial Disease [*Medicine*]
PAD	Permissible Accumulated Dose
PAD	Personal Articulation Device [*Facetious term for pre-word-processing equipment*]
PAD	Personnel Armoured Devices (SAUS)
PAD	Perturbed Angular Distribution [*Nuclear physics*]
PAD	Peters' United States District Court Reports, Admiralty Decisions [*A publication*] (DLA)
PAD	Petroleum Administration for Defense [*Abolished, 1954*]
PAD	Phenacetin [*Acetophenetidin*], Aspirin, Deoxyephedrine [*Pharmacology*]
PAD	Phenacetin, Aspirin, Desoxyephedrine (SAUS)
PAD	Phi Alpha Delta [*An association*] (NTPA)
PAD	Phonological Acquisition Device (DAVI)
PAD	Photon Absorption Densitometry [*Medicine*] (DMAA)
pad	Photoshop File [*Computer science*]
PAD	Physical Acoustics/Dunnegan (SAUS)
PAD	Physician-Assisted Death (MELL)
PAD	Pilotless Aircraft Division [*Navy*]
PAD	Pitch Angle Distribution
PAD	Pitch Axis Definition
PAD	Pitless Adapter Division
PAD	Pitless Adapter Division of Water Systems Council (EA)
PAD	Pixel Access Definition (SAUS)
PAD	Planning Action Directive [*Military*] (AFIT)
PAD	Planning Analysis Document (SAUS)
PAD	Planning and Analysis Division [*Environmental Protection Agency*] (GFGA)
PAD	Plant Apparatus Division (SAUS)
PAD	Plastics Analysis Division (SAUS)
PAD	Player Assessment Device
PAD	Pododermatitis Aseptica Diffusa (SAUS)
PAD	Point Air Defence (SAUS)
PAD	Polar and Auroral Dynamics [*Meteorology*]
PAD	Polyaperture Device [*NASA*] (KSC)
PAD	Pontoon Assembly Depot (NVT)
PAD	Pontoon Assembly Detachment
PAD	Poor Acquisition Data (AAG)
PAD	Port Air Defense (SAUS)
PAD	Port of Aerial Debarkation [*Air Force*]
PAD	Positioning Arm Disk
PAD	Post-Activation Diffusion (IEEE)
PAD	Post Alloy Diffused (SAUS)
PAD	Post Alloy Diffusion (IAA)
PAD	Potential Area of Danger [*Navigation*]
PAD	Power Amplifier Device [*or Driver*]
PAD	Power Amplifier Driver
PAD	Preadvisory Data (KSC)
PAD	Pre-Authorized Debit (EBF)
PAD	Precise Access Diagram
PAD	Preferential Adaptive Defense (ACAE)
PAD	Preferred Arrival Date (AFM)
PAD	Preliminary Advisory Data (MCD)
PAD	Preliminary Analysis Document (SAUS)
PAD	Presence and Amplitude Detector
PAD	Pressure Alarm Detector (SAUS)
PAD	Pressure Anomaly Difference (PDAA)
PAD	Preventive Aggressive Device [*Restraint*] [*Medicine*]
PAD	Primary Aeronautical Designation (DNAB)
PAD	Primary Affective Disorder [*Psychiatry*] (DAVI)
PAD	Primary Afferent Depolarization [*Electrophysiology*]
PAD	Prime Contractor Address (SAUS)
PAD	Principal Associate Director (SAUS)
PAD	Procurement Acquisition Directive
PAD	Product Assembly Document
PAD	Product Assembly Drawing [*Automotive project management*]
PAD	Product Assurance Directorate [*Armament, Munitions, and Chemical Command*] [*Army*]
PAD	Professional Administrative Development [*Medicine*]
PAD	Professional Express Courier Service, Inc. [*ICAO designator*] (FAAC)

PAD	Program Action Directive (AFM)
PAD	Program Analysis Division (AAGC)
PAD	Program Analysis for Documentation [*Computer science*]
PAD	Program and Acquisition Division (ACAE)
PAD	Program Approval Document [*NASA*] (KSC)
PAD	Programmable Algorithm for Drafting (SAUS)
PAD	Project Approval Document [*NASA*]
PAD	Propellant Acquisition Device (NASA)
PAD	Propellant-Actuated Device
PAD	Property Accountability Document (ACAE)
PAD	Provisional Acceptance Date (NATG)
PAD	Provisional Air Division (SAUS)
PAD	Provisional Assembly Date (SAUS)
PAD	Pseudoachondroplastic Spondyloepiphysial Dysplasia (DIPS)
PAD	Psychoaffective Disorder [*Psychiatry*] (DAVI)
PAD	Public Access Device (VLIE)
PAD	Public Affairs Department (SAUS)
PAD	Public Affairs Detachment
PAD	Public Affairs Division [*Military*] (AABC)
PAD	Public Assistance Director [*Federal disaster planning*]
PAD	Pueblo Army Depot [*Colorado*]
PAD	Pulmonary Artery Diastolic [*Pressure*] [*Cardiology*]
PAD	Pulsatile Assist Device [*Cardiology*]
PAD	Pulse amplifier discriminator (SAUS)
PAD	Pulse Amplitude Density (SAUS)
PAD	Pulse Averaging Discriminator
PAD	Pulsed Activation Doppler (MCD)
PAD	Pulsed Amperometric Detection [*Electroanalytical chemistry*]
PADA	Payroll Automation for Department of Agriculture
PADA	Pharmacists Against Drug Abuse (EA)
PADA	Poly(adipicanhydride) [*Organic chemistry*]
PADA	Prespin Automatic Dynamic Alignment
PADA	Public Address Assembly [*Ground Communications Facility, NASA*]
PADA	Pyridine-2-Azo-P-Dimethylaniline (SAUS)
PADA	(Pyridylazo)dimethylaniline [*Organic chemistry*]
PADAC	Professional Art Dealers Association of Canada
PADAF	Pacific Command Air Defense Analysis Facility (CINC)
PADAL	Pattern for Analysis, Decision, Action, and Learning
PA D & C	Pennsylvania District and County Reports [*A publication*] (DLA)
PA D & C 2d	Pennsylvania District and County Reports, Second Series [*A publication*] (DLA)
PA D & C 3d	Pennsylvania District and County Reports, Third Series [*A publication*] (DLA)
PA D & C Rep	Pennsylvania District and County Reports [*A publication*] (DLA)
PADAR	Passive Airborne Detection and Ranging
PADAR	Passive Detection and Ranging [*Electronics*] (IAA)
PADAR	Photoacoustic Detection and Ranging (SAUS)
PADAR	Program Approval Disposal and Redistribution [*Army*] (AABC)
PADAT	Psychological Abstracts Direct Access Terminal
PADAT	Psychological Abstracts Direct Action Terminal (SAUS)
PADC	Pennsylvania Avenue Development Corp. [*Washington, DC*] [*Federal corporation*]
PADC	Piccole Apostole della Carita [*Ponte Lambro, Italy*] (EAIO)
PADCO	Pan American Development Corp. (SAUS)
PADCP	Paul Andrew Dawkins Children's Project (EA)
PADD	Passive Antidrown Device (DWSG)
PADD	Pedestrians Against Dangerous Drivers (SAUS)
PADD	Pedestrians Against Drunken Drivers (SAUS)
PADD	Personal Access Display Device (VLIE)
PADD	Petroleum Administration for Defense District [*Department of Energy*]
PADD	Planned Active Duty Date [*Military*]
PADD	Political Art Documentation and Distribution (SAUS)
PADD	Portable Acoustic Doppler Detector
PADDS	Procurement Automated Data Document System [*Military*] (RDA)
PADE	Pad Automatic Data Equipment (PDAA)
PADEL	Pattern Description Language
PA Dep L & I Dec	Pennsylvania Department of Labor and Industry Decisions [*A publication*] (DLA)
PA Dep Rep	Pennsylvania Department Reports [*A publication*] (DLA)
PADER	Pennsylvania Department of Environmental Resources
PADF	Driftwood Bay Air Force Station [*Alaska*] [*ICAO location identifier*] (ICLI)
PADF	Pan American Development Foundation (EA)
PAD Facility	Packet Assembly/Disassembly Facility (SAUS)
PAD Facility	Paket Assembly/Disassembly Facility (SAUS)
PADFAR	Program for Air Defense Forward Area (SAUS)
PADGEM	Platelet Activation-Dependent Granulocyte External Membrane Protein [*Biochemistry*]
PADGERC	PACOM [*Pacific Command*] Air Defense Ground Environment Requirements Committee (CINC)
PADGT	Past Assistant Deputy Grand Treasurer [*Freemasonry*]
PADI	Parti pour l'Avancement de la Democratie en Ituri [*Party for Democratic Advancement in Ituri*] [*Political party*]
PADI	Personal Alarm Dose Integrator (SAUS)
PADI	Professional Association of Diving Instructors (EA)
PADIA	Patrol Diagnosis (NITA)
PADIE	Prevention and Detection of Illegal Entry [*Military*] (DNAB)
PADIL	Patriot Air Defense Information Language [*Army*]
Padin	Partido de Integracion Nacional [*National Integration Party*] [*Peru*] [*Political party*] (PPW)
PADIRT	Platform for Atmospheric Data in Real-Time (SAUS)
PADIS	Pan African Development and Information System (SAUS)
PADIS	Pan-African Documentation and Information System [*Economic Commission for Africa*] [*United Nations*] (IID)
PA Dist	Pennsylvania District Reporter [*A publication*] (DLA)

PA Dist & Co R... Pennsylvania District and County Reports [*A publication*] (DLA)
PA Dist & Co Repts... Pennsylvania District and County Reports [*A publication*] (DLA)
PA Dist & C Rep... Pennsylvania District and County Reports [*A publication*] (DLA)
PA Dist R.... Pennsylvania District Reporter [*A publication*] (DLA)
PA Dist Rep... Pennsylvania District Reports [*A publication*] (DLA)
PADK .... Adak/Davis [*Alaska*] [*ICAO location identifier*] (ICLI)
PADL .... Dillingham [*Alaska*] [*ICAO location identifier*] (ICLI)
PADL .... Part and Assembly Description Language [*Computer science*]
PADL .... Parts and Design Language (NITA)
PADL .... Parts Application Data List (SAUS)
PaDL .... Pattern Development Language (SAUS)
PADL .... Performing and Captive Animals Defence League [*British*] (BI)
PADL .... Personal Activities of Daily Living (DMAA)
PADL .... Pilotless Aircraft Development Laboratory [*Navy*]
PADL .... Polycell and Device Library (SAUS)
PADLA .... Programmable Asynchronous Dual Line Adapter
PADLOC .... Passive Active Detection and Location (IEEE)
PADLOC .... Passive Detection and Location [*Air Force*] (IAA)
PADLOC .... Passive Detection and Location of Countermeasures [*Air Force*]
PADLOCC .... Passive Active Detection and Location Countermeasures (SAUS)
PADLOCC .... Passive Detection and Location of Countermeasures [*Air Force*] (IAA)
PADM .... Product Assurance Directives Manual (ACAE)
PAdm .... Professional Administrator (DD)
PADMIS .... Patient Administration Information System [*Army*] (AABC)
PADO .... Passive Air Defence Officer (SAUS)
PADO .... Proposed Advanced Development Objective [*Army*] (AABC)
PADOC .... Pay Adjustment Document [*Army*]
PADP .... Physicians Against the Death Penalty (EA)
PADP .... Proposal for Advanced Development Program
PADP .... Pulmonary Artery Diastolic Pressure [*Cardiology*] (AAMN)
PADPAO .... Philippine Agency Detective Protective Association (SAUS)
PADQ .... Kodiak [*Alaska*] [*ICAO location identifier*] (ICLI)
PADR .... Parts and Data Record System (MCD)
PaDR .... Payload Design Review (SAUS)
PA DR .... Pennsylvania District Reports [*A publication*] (DLA)
PADR .... Product Assurance Discrepancy Report
PADR .... Production Administration Deficiency Report [*DoD*]
PADRA .... Pass to Air Defense RADAR [*Aviation*] (FAAC)
PADRE .... Packaging Administration & Inventory Services (SAUS)
PADRE .... Particle Analysis and Data Reduction [*Environmental Protection Agency*] (GFGA)
PADRE .... Particulate Data Reduction (EPA)
PADRE .... Patient Automatic Data Recording Equipment (IEEE)
PADRE .... Pilot Automatic Dead-Reckoning Equipment (SAUS)
PADRE .... Portable Automatic Data Recording Equipment
PADS .... Parametric Array Doppler SONAR (PDAA)
PADS .... Passive-Active Data Simulation
PADS .... Passive Advanced Sonobuoy
PADS .... Pen Application Development System [*Computer software*] [*Slate Corp.*] (PCM)
PADS .... Penetration Aid Deployment System (SAUS)
PADS .... People Against Dioxins in Sanitary Products [*An association*] [*Australia*]
PADS .... Performance Analysis and Design Synthesis [*Computer program*] [*NASA*]
PADS .... Performance Analysis Display System (NITA)
PADS .... Peroxylaminedisulfonate [*Organic chemistry*]
PADS .... Personnel Automated Data System [*TIMMS*] [*Navy*]
PADS .... Planned Arrival and Departure System [*FAA*] (TAG)
PADS .... Plant Alarm and Display System [*Nuclear energy*] (NRCH)
PADS .... Point Air Defense System
PADS .... Port and Airport Development Strategy (SAUS)
PADS .... Position and Azimuth Determining System [*Aviation*]
PADS .... Position Attack Defence System (SAUS)
PADS .... Positioning Azimuth Determining System
PADS .... Precision Aerial Delivery System
PADS .... Precision Aerial Display System
PADS .... Precision Antenna Display System (IAA)
PADS .... Precision Azimuth Determination System (SAUS)
PADS .... Product Assurance Data System (SPST)
PADS .... Professional Application Development System [*Slate*] [*Computer science*]
PADS .... Program Allocator to Drum Storage (VLIE)
PADS .... Programmer Advanced Debugging System [*Computer science*]
PADS .... Publications of the American Dialect Society (SAUS)
PADS .... Punch and Drill System (SAUS)
PADS System... Parametric Array Doppler Sonar System (SAUS)
PADT .... Point Air Defence Trainer (SAUS)
PADT .... Post Allow Diffused Transistor (VLIE)
PADT .... Postalloy Diffusion Technique (IAA)
PADT .... Postalloy Diffusion Transistor
PADT .... Preliminary Aircraft Design Technology (ACAE)
PADU .... Dutch Harbour [*Alaska*] [*ICAO location identifier*] (ICLI)
PADU .... Protected Areas Data Unit (SAUS)
PADUA .... Pennsylvania Analysis of Decompression for Undersea and Aerospace (SAUS)
PADUA .... Progressive Augmentation by Dilating the Urethra Anterior [*Medicine*] (DMAA)
PADUD .... Program of Advanced Professional Development, University of Denver College of Law (DLA)
PADWSS ...... Pulsed Acoustic Doppler Wind Shear Sensing System (PDAA)
PAE .... Everett, WA [*Location identifier*] [*FAA*] (FAAL)

PAE .... Paea [*Society Islands*] [*Seismograph station code, US Geological Survey*] (SEIS)
PAE .... Paisajes Espanoles SA [*Spain*] [*ICAO designator*] (FAAC)
PAE .... Parachutust Adjustable Equipment Bag [*Army*] (VNW)
PAE .... Park Air Electronics Ltd. (SAUS)
P AE .... Partes Aequales [*Equal Parts*] [*Pharmacy*]
PAE .... Passed Assistant Engineer [*British*]
PAE .... Payload Accomodations Equipment [*NASA*] (SSD)
PAE .... Payload Attach Equipment [*NASA*] (SSD)
PAE .... Peace Arch Entertainment 'B' [*AMEX symbol*] (SG)
PAE .... Peoria & Eastern Railway [*Absorbed into Consolidated Rail Corp.*] [*AAR code*]
PAE .... Personal Arms and Equipment [*Army*] (ADDR)
PAE .... Phase Angle Error
PAE .... Photo-Anodic Engraving (PDAA)
PAE .... Phthalic Acid Esters [*Organic chemistry*]
PAE .... Physical Aptitude Examination (AFM)
PAE .... Planning and Estimating (IAA)
PAE .... Polyarylene Ether (SAUS)
PAE .... Polyarylene Ethylene (SAUS)
PAE .... Polyaryl Ether (SAUS)
PAE .... Polyarylether [*Organic chemistry*]
PAE .... Polyaspartic Ester [*Organic chemistry*]
PAE .... Port of Aerial Embarkation [*Air Force*]
PAE .... Positive Affect Enhancement (MELL)
PAE .... Post-Accident Environment [*Nuclear energy*] (IEEE)
PAE .... Postantibiotic Effect [*Medicine*] (MELL)
PAE .... Power-Added Efficiency (SAUS)
PAE .... Precision Attack Enhancement (ACAE)
PAE .... Preliminary Airworthiness Evaluations
PAE .... Preliminary Army Evaluation (MCD)
PAE .... Preventive Action Engineer (NASA)
PAE .... Problem Assessment Engineer (SAUS)
PAE .... Problem Assessment Engineering (NASA)
PAE .... Products-Activities-End Products (SAUS)
PAE .... Progress Aerospace Enterprises (SAUS)
PAE .... Project Assurance Engineer (SAUS)
PAE .... Projets pour une Agriculture Ecologique [*Ecological Agriculture Projects - EAP*] [*Sainte Anne De Bellevue, PQ*] (EAIO)
PAE .... Public Affairs Event (NVT)
PAEA .... Pakistan Atomic Energy Authority (SAUS)
PAEAC .... Parliamentary Association for Euro-Arab Cooperation (EA)
PAEB .... Pan American EDIFACT Board (SAUS)
PAEC .... Pakistan Army Education Corps [*British military*] (DMA)
PAEC .... Pakistan Atomic Energy Commission (or Council) (SAUS)
PAEC .... Philippine Atomic Energy Commission (SAUS)
PAECI .... Pan American Association of Educational Credit Institutions [*Bogota, Colombia*] (EAIO)
PAECT .... Pollution Abatement and Environmental Control Technology [*Army*] (AABC)
PAED .... Anchorage/Elmendorf Air Force Base [*Alaska*] [*ICAO location identifier*] (ICLI)
PAED .... Paediatric [*or Paediatrics*]
PAED .... Plans, Analysis, and Evaluation Division [*Army*] (MCD)
PAEDP .... Pulmonary Artery End-Diastolic Pressure [*Cardiology*]
PAEF .... Peace Action Education Fund (SAUS)
PAEG .... Prueba de Admisiones para Estudios Graduados (GAGS)
PAEH .... Cape Newenham Air Force Station [*Alaska*] [*ICAO location identifier*] (ICLI)
PAEI .... Fairbanks/Eielson Air Force Base [*Alaska*] [*ICAO location identifier*] (ICLI)
PAEI .... Periscope Azimuth Error Indicator
PAEI .... Plane Avionic Enterprises Inc. (SAUS)
PAEI .... Purchasing Agents of the Electronic Industry [*Rosedale, NY*] (EA)
PAEK .... Polyarylether Ketone (SAUS)
PAEK .... Polyaryletherketone [*Organic chemistry*]
PAEL .... Preliminary Allowance Equipage List [*Military*] (CAAL)
PAEM .... Program Analysis and Evaluation Model (IEEE)
PAEMST ...... Presidential Awards for Excellence in Math and Science Teaching
PAEN .... Kenai [*Alaska*] [*ICAO location identifier*] (ICLI)
PAEN .... Performance Analysis of Electrical Networks (SAUS)
PAEP .... Preliminary Annual Engineering Plan [*Military*] (AFIT)
P AEQ .... Partes Aequales [*Equal Parts*] [*Pharmacy*]
PAES .... Phenyl(aminoethyl)sulfide [*Biochemistry*]
PAES .... Planning Analysis Evaluation System
PAES .... Positron annihilation Auger Electron Spectroscopy (SAUS)
PAESP .... Pennsylvania Association of Elementary School Principals (SAUS)
PAET .... Planetary Atmosphere Experimental [*or Experiments*] Test [*NASA*]
PAETS .... Product Assurance Estimating Techniques System (ACAE)
PAET Vehicle... Planetary Atmosphere Experiments Test Vehicle (SAUS)
PAEW .... Personnel and Equipment Working [*Aviation*] (FAAC)
PAEWCC ...... Peace Activists East and West Coordinating Committee (EA)
PAF .... Pacific Air Forces
PAF .... Pacific Aqua Foods Ltd. [*Toronto Stock Exchange symbol*]
PAF .... Page Address Field
PAF .... Pakistan Air Force
PAF .... Panaf Airways Ltd. [*Gambia*] [*ICAO designator*] (FAAC)
PAF .... Pan American Foundation [*Defunct*] (EA)
PAF .... Paraburdoo [*Western Australia*] [*Airport symbol*] (AD)
PAF .... Paroxysmal Atrial [*or Auricular*] Fibrillation [*Medicine*] (MAE)
PAF .... Particle and Field Package (SAUS)
PAF .... Partitive Analytical Forecasting (PDAA)
PAF .... Payload Attach Fitting (SAUS)
PAF .... Payload Attachment Fitting [*NASA*]
PAF .... Peak Annual Funding (NASA)

PAF	Pediatric AIDS Foundation (PAZ)
PAF	Performing Arts Foundation (EA)
PAF	Peripheral Address Field
PAF	Peripheral Airfield (SAUS)
PAF	Permanent Air Force [Australia]
PAF	Peroxisome Assembly Factor [Biochemistry]
PAF	Personal Achievement Formula [Test] (TES)
PAF	Personal Ancestry File [Computer science] (PCM)
PAF	Personal Article Floater [Air baggage insurance]
PAF	Personnel Action Form (SAUS)
PAF	Pet Assistance Foundation (SAUS)
PAF	Philippine Air Force
PAF	Phosphodiesterase-Activating Factor [Medicine] (DMAA)
PAF	Photoactivated Fluorescence Molecules [Analytical biochemistry]
PAF	Picric Acid Formaldehyde
PAF	Pilotage Aerodynamique Fort (SAUS)
PAF	Pilots Active File (SAUS)
PAF	Platelet-Activating Factor [Hematology]
PAF	Platelet Aggregation Factor [Hematology]
PAF	Polaris Accelerated Flight [Chamber] [Missiles]
PAF	Polish Air Force (SAUS)
PAF	Pollen Adherence Factor [Immunology] (DMAA)
PAF	Portable Arc Furnace
PAF	Port-Aux-Francais [Kerguelen Islands] [Seismograph station code, US Geological Survey] [Closed] (SEIS)
PAF	Ports Authority of Fiji (SAUS)
PAF	Portuguese Air Force
PAF	Postcode Address File [Computer science] (TELE)
PAF	Posterior Auditory Field
PAF	Preadmission Assessment Form [Health Care Financing Administration]
PAF	Prearranged Fire
PAF	Preatomized Fuel [Trademark] [Petroform product]
PAF	Premature Anti-Fascist [World War II designation used by Army Counterintelligence Department]
PAF	Preprocessing and Archiving Facility (ACAE)
PAF	Price Analysis File (AFIT)
PAF	Printed and Fired (SAUS)
PAF	Printed and Fired Circuit
PAF	Pro-American Forum [Defunct] (EA)
PAF	Processing and Archiving Facility (SAUS)
PAF	Processor Availability Facility (SAUS)
PAF	Production Assembly Facility [Manufacturing]
PAF	Pseudoamniotic Fluid [Gynecology]
PAF	Pseudo-Archaic Forgery
PAF	Psychoanalytic Assistance Fund (EA)
PAF	Public Agenda Foundation (EA)
PAF	Public Art Fund (EA)
PAF	Publication Authority Form (AAG)
PAF	Pulmonary Arteriovenous Fistula [Medicine]
PAF	Pulse-Air Feeder [Automotive engineering]
PAF	Punishment and Fine (SAUS)
PAFA	Fairbanks/International [Alaska] [ICAO location identifier] (ICLI)
PAFA	Pakistan Australia Friendship Association [Australia]
PAFA	Pan-American Festival Association (EA)
PAFA	Pennsylvania Academy of the Fine Arts
PAFA	Presidential Academic Fitness Award [Department of Education] (GFGA)
PAFA	Priority Based Assessment of Foot Additives [Medicine] (DMAA)
PAFAC	Plastic and Failure Analysis of Composites (SAUS)
PAFAM	Performance and Failure Assessment Monitor (MCD)
PAFAMS	Pan American Federation of Associations of Medical Schools [See also FEPAFEM] [Caracas, Venezuela] (EAIO)
PAFATU	Pan-African Federation of Agricultural Trade Unions (EA)
PAFB	Fairbanks/Wainwright Army Air Field [Alaska] [ICAO location identifier] (ICLI)
PAFB	Patrick Air Force Base [Florida]
PAFC	Paul Anka Fan Club (EA)
PAFC	Phase-Locked Automatic Frequency Control [Telecommunications]
PAFC	Philippine-American Financial Commission (SAUS)
PAFC	Phosphoric-Acid Fuel Cell (SAUS)
PAFC	Public Affairs Field Center (SAUS)
PAFCO	Pacific Fishing Co. (SAUS)
PAFCOMNET	Pacific Air Forces Communications Network (SAA)
PAFCS	Prior Active Foreign Commissioned Service
PAFD	Percutaneous Abscess and Fluid Drainage [Medicine] (DMAA)
PAFDEFNET	Pacific Air Forces Defense Network (SAA)
PAFE	Place Accepted for Enlistment
PAFEC	Program for Automatic Finite Element Calculation (IAA)
PAFES	Prior Active Foreign Enlisted Service (DNAB)
PAFI	Platelet-Aggregation Factor Inhibitor [Medicine] (DMAA)
PAFIB	Paroxysmal Atrial [or Auricular] Fibrillation [Medicine] (MAE)
PA Fid	Pennsylvania Fiduciary Reporter [A publication] (DLA)
PA Fiduc	Pennsylvania Fiduciary Reporter [A publication] (DLA)
PA Flow	Pulmonary Artery Flow (SAUS)
PAFLU	Philippine Association of Free Labour Unions (SAUS)
PAFMECA	Pan-African Freedom Movement of East and Central Africa (SAUS)
PAFMECSA	Pan African Freedom Movement for East, Central, and Southern Africa [Superseded in 1963 by the liberation committee of the Organization of African Unity] (PD)
PAFP	Photochemical Aerosol-Forming Potential of Polluted Air [Environmental chemistry]
PAFP	Pre-Achilles Fat Pad [Medicine] (DMAA)
PAFR	Fort Richardson/Bryant Army Air Field [Alaska] [ICAO location identifier] (ICLI)

PAF Resistor	Printed and Fired Resistor (SAUS)
PAFS	Primary Air Force Specialty
PAFS	Publication of the American Folklore Society (SAUS)
PAFSC	Primary Air Force Specialty Code
PAFT	Polish American Folk Theatre
PAFT	Programme for Alternative Fluorocarbon Toxicity Testing [British]
PAFTA	Pacific Free Trade Area
PAFTA	Pacifiic Area Free Trade Association (SAUS)
PAFTAD	Pacific Trade and Development Conference
PA-FTIR	Photoacoustic Fourier Transform Infrared Spectroscopy (AAEL)
PAFTT	Program for Alternative Fluorocarbon Toxicity Testing [Environmental science]
PAFU	Patriot Arm Fire Unit [Weaponry] (MCD)
PAFU	Propulsion Arming and Firing Unit [Military]
PAFVA	Polish Air Force Veterans Association (EA)
PAFW	Farewell [Alaska] [ICAO location identifier] (ICLI)
PAG	I Pagliacci [Opera] (DSUE)
PAG	Pacific Gulf Properties, Inc. [AMEX symbol] (SAG)
PAG	Pagadian [Philippines] [Airport symbol] (OAG)
Pag	Page's Three Early Assize Rolls, County of Northumberland [Surtees Society Publications, Vol. 88] [A publication] (ILCA)
PAG	Paget Resources Ltd. [Vancouver Stock Exchange symbol]
PAG	Paging (SAUS)
Pag	Pagoda
PAG	Pamphlet Antigas (SAUS)
PAG	Panagjuriste [Bulgaria] [Geomagnetic observatory code]
PAG	Panjim [India] [Airport symbol] (AD)
PAG	Pariaqueductal Grey Matter [Neurology] (DAVI)
PAG	Parts Acquisition Group
PAG	Party for the Autonomy of Gibraltar [Political party] (PPW)
PAG	Pentaacetylglucose [Laundry bleach activator]
PAG	Periaqueductal Gray Matter [Brain anatomy]
PAG	Perimeter Aviation Ltd. [Canada] [ICAO designator] (FAAC)
PAG	Pesticide Assessment Guideline [Environmental Protection Agency]
PAG	Photoacid Generator
Pag	Piper [Airplane code]
PAG	Planning Advisory Group (SAUS)
PAG	Plant Advisory Group (SAUS)
PAG	Plasma-Arc-Based Gasifier (SAUS)
PAG	Pneumatic Antishock Garment (MELL)
PAG	Polyacrylamide Gel [Analytical chemistry]
PAG	Polyalkylene Glycol [Organic chemistry]
PAg	Poultry-Related Antigens [Immunology]
PAG	Poverty Advisory Group
PAG	Prealbumin Globulin [Biochemistry] (OA)
PAG	Precision Alignment Gyrocompass
PAG	Precursor Active Galaxies
PAG	Pregnancy-Associated alpha-Glycoprotein [Gynecology]
PAG	Pregnancy-Associated Globulin [Medicine] (MELL)
PAG	Preliminary Analysis Group (NATG)
PAG	Primary Analysis Group (SAUS)
PAG	Prince Albert's Guard [British military] (DMA)
PAG	Prior Austenite Grain (SAUS)
PAG	Priorities Analysis Group
PAG	Professional Activities Group
PAg	Professional Agrologist (DD)
PAG	Professional Auto Group, Inc.
PAG	Program Advisory Group
PAG	Program Assessment Guide [Department of Labor] (OICC)
PAG	Progress Analysis Group [Navy] (MCD)
PAG	Project Advisory Group [Army]
PAG	Property Advisory Group [British] (DCTA)
PAG	Protection Against Gas
PAG	Protection Anti-Gas (SAUS)
PAG	Protective Action Guide [Nuclear energy]
PAG	Protein A colloidal Gold
PAG	Protein Advisory Group [United Nations]
pAg	Protein A-Gold Technique [Medicine] (DMAA)
PAG	Public Affairs Guidance [Environmental science] (COE)
PAG	Spring Garden College, Philadelphia, PA [OCLC symbol] (OCLC)
PAGA	Galena [Alaska] [ICAO location identifier] (ICLI)
PAGA	Pan American Grace Airways, Inc. [Also, PANAGRA]
PAGA	Proliferation-Associated Gene A (DMAA)
PAGAD	People Against Gangsterism and Drugs [South Africa]
PAGAN	Pattern Generation Language [Computer science]
PAGAN	People Against Goodness & Normalcy (WDAA)
PAGB	Poultry and Egg Producers Association of Great Britain (SAUS)
PAGB	Proprietary Association of Great Britain
PAGB Yearbook	Poultry Association of Great Britain Yearbook (SAUS)
PAGCH	Paging and Access Grant Channel (CGWS)
PAGDC	Past Assistant Grand Director of Ceremonies [Freemasonry] (ROG)
PAGE	Page Generation [or Generator] (PDAA)
Page	Page's Three Early Assize Rolls, County of Northumberland [Surtees Society Publications, Vol. 88] [A publication] (DLA)
PAGE	Paging Network [NASDAQ symbol] (SPSG)
PAGE	Permanent Automatic Ground Environment (SAUS)
PAGE	PERT [Program Evaluation and Review Technique] Automated Graphical Extension (KSC)
PAGE	Philatelic Association of Government Employees
PAGE	Piston Arrestment Gas Entrapment System [SPRINT launch cell] [Army] (AABC)
PAGE Resistor	Polyacrylamide Gel Electrophoresis [Analytical chemistry]
PAGE	Preliminary Automated Ground Environment
PAGE	Preview and Graphics Editing [Computer science] (MHDI)
PAGE	Program for Automated Gated Evaluation [Cardiology] (DAVI)

PAGE	Programmable Aerospace Ground Equipment (SAUS)	
PAGE	Publish Australia Group Enterprise	
PageAm	Page America Group, Inc. [*Associated Press*] (SAG)	
Page Contr.	Page on Contracts [*A publication*] (DLA)	
Page Div.	Page on Divorce [*A publication*] (DLA)	
PAGEL	Priced Aerospace Ground Equipment List	
PAGEN	Pattern Generation (SAUS)	
PAGEN	Pattern Generator (SAUS)	
PAGEN Language	Pattern Generation Language (SAUS)	
PAGEOS	Passive Geodetic Earth-Orbiting Satellite [*NASA*]	
PAGER	Pediatric/Adolescent Gastroesophageal Reflux Association, Inc. (NRGU)	
Pa Ger Soc.	Pennsylvania German Society (SAUS)	
Pages	Pages, Inc. [*Associated Press*] (SAG)	
PAGES	Past Global Changes [*Marine science*] (OSRA)	
PAGES	Past Global Environmental Changes (SAUS)	
PAGES	Print and Graphics Express Station (ACAE)	
PAGES	Program Affinity Grouping and Evaluation System	
PAGES/CPO	PAGES/Core Project Office (SAUS)	
PAGES-EXCOMM	PAGES Executive Committee (SAUS)	
PAGES-SSC	PAGES Scientific Steering Committee (SAUS)	
PAGE System	Pharmacia Gel Electrophoresis System (SAUS)	
PAGE System	Piston Arrestment Gas Entropment System (SAUS)	
PAGI	Penn America Group [*NASDAQ symbol*] (SAG)	
PAGICEP	Petroleum and Gas Industry Communications Emergency Plan [*FCC*]	
PAGIF	Polyacrylamide Gel Isoelectric Focusing (DB)	
Paging	Paging Network, Inc. [*Associated Press*] (SAG)	
Paging	Paging Partners Corp. [*Associated Press*] (SAG)	
PagingN	Paging Network Inc. [*Associated Press*] (SAG)	
PagingP	Paging Partners Corp. [*Associated Press*] (SAG)	
PAGIS	Pastoral and Agricultural Geographic Information System (SAUS)	
PAGIS	Performance Assessment of Geological Isolation System [*Nuclear energy*] (NUCP)	
Pag Jud Puz	Paget's Judicial Puzzles [*A publication*] (DLA)	
PAGK	Gulkana [*Alaska*] [*ICAO location identifier*] (ICLI)	
PAGL	Pulsed Argon Gas LASER	
PAGM	Permit Applicants Guidance Manual (COE)	
PAGMK	Primary African Green Monkey Kidney [*Cells*]	
PAGN	Pagnall [*England*]	
PAGOS	Program for the Analysis of General Optical Systems (SAUS)	
PAGS	Parti de l'Avant-Garde Socialiste [*Socialist Vanguard Party*] [*Algeria*] [*Political party*] (PD)	
PAGS	Polish-American Guardian Society (EA)	
PAGS	Prior Austenite Grain Size (SAUS)	
PAGSE	Partnership Group for Science and Engineering (SAUS)	
PAGT	Port Authority Grain Terminal (SAUS)	
PAGT	Provincial Association of Geography Teachers (SAUS)	
PAGTU	Pan-American Ground Training Unit	
PAGZ	Pages, Inc. [*NASDAQ symbol*] (SAG)	
PAH	Paducah [*Kentucky*] [*Airport symbol*] (OAG)	
PAH	Pahoa [*Hawaii*] [*Seismograph station code, US Geological Survey*] [*Closed*] (SEIS)	
PAH	Pan American Highway (SAUS)	
PAH	Panorama Air Tour, Inc. [*ICAO designator*] (FAAC)	
PAH	Para-Aminohippurate [*Clearance Test*] [*Urology*] (DAVI)	
PAH	Para-Aminohippuric [*Biochemistry*]	
PAH	Para-Aminohippuric Acid (SAUS)	
PAH	Para-Amino-Hyppurate (SAUS)	
PAH	Parts Application Handbook	
PAH	Pathtechnics Ltd. [*Vancouver Stock Exchange symbol*]	
PAH	Patriot American Hospitality, Inc. [*NYSE symbol*] (SAG)	
PAH	Payload Accommodations Handbook [*NASA*] (NASA)	
PAH	Phase Adjusting Hub	
PAH	Phenylalanine Hydroxylase [*An enzyme*]	
Pah	Piper Pressurised Prop-Jet [*Airplane code*]	
PAH	Pitch Attitude Hold [*Aviation*] (MCD)	
PAH	Polyaromatic Hydrocarbon (EDCT)	
PAH	Polycyclic [*or Polynuclear*] Aromatic Hydrocarbon [*Organic chemistry*]	
PAH	Polycyclic Aromatic Hydrocarbons [*Automotive emissions*] [*Organic chemistry*]	
PAH	Polynuclear Aromatic Hydrocarbon (EEVL)	
PAH	Pulmonary Artery Hypertension [*Medicine*]	
PAH	Pulmonary Artery Hypotension [*Cardiology*] (DAVI)	
PAH	Push and Hold [*Push button*]	
PAHA	P-Aminohippuric Acid (SAUS)	
PAHA	Para-Aminohippuric Acid	
PAHA	Polish American Historical Association (EA)	
PAHA	Procainamide-Hydroxylamine (DMAA)	
PAHBAH	Para-Hydroxybenzoic Acid Hydrazide [*Organic chemistry*]	
PAHC	Pan American Highway Congresses (EA)	
PAHC	Pontifical Association of the Holy Childhood (EA)	
PAHCOM	Professional Association of Health Care Office Managers	
PAHEF	Pan American Health and Education Foundation (EA)	
PAHEL	Pay Records and Health Records	
PAHEO	Particle Accelerators in High Earth Orbit [*Proposed*]	
PAHEP	Plasma and High Energy Physics (IAA)	
PAHF	Pan American Hockey Federation [*Winnipeg, MB*] (EAIO)	
PAHL	Pressure Alarm, High-Limit [*Nuclear energy*] (NRCH)	
PAHO	Homer [*Alaska*] [*ICAO location identifier*] (ICLI)	
PAHO	Pan American Health Organization (EA)	
PAHOCENDES	Pan-American Health Organization Center for Development Studies (SAUS)	
PAHR	Post-Accident Heat Removal [*Nuclear energy*]	
PAHRI	Pakistan Animal Husbandry Research Institute (SAUS)	
PAHS	Passive Annual Heat Storage [*Housing technology*]	

PAHVC	Pulmonary Alveolar Hypoxic Vasoconstriction [*Medicine*] (STED)	
PAHVC	Pulmonary Alveolar Hypoxic Vasoconstrictor [*Medicine*] (MELL)	
PAHZ	Panzer Abwewp Hubschrauber [*Attack Helicopter*]	
PAI	Kitty Hawk Aircargo, Inc. [*ICAO designator*] (FAAC)	
PAI	Pacific Aerospace Index (DIT)	
PAI	Pacific American Income Shares, Inc. [*NYSE symbol*] (SPSG)	
PAI	Pacific American Institute (EA)	
PAI	Pacoima, CA [*Location identifier*] [*FAA*] (FAAL)	
Pai	Paige's New York Chancery Reports [*A publication*] (DLA)	
Pai	Paine's United States Circuit Court Reports [*A publication*] (DLA)	
PAI	Pair Attraction Inventory [*Premarital, marital, and family counseling test*] [*Psychology*]	
PAI	Panama Airways Inc. (SAUS)	
PAI	Parachute Association of Ireland (EAIO)	
PAI	Paradise Airways, Inc. [*FAA designator*] (FAAC)	
PAI	Parti Africain de l'Independance [*African Independence Party*] [*Senegal*] [*Political party*] (PPW)	
PAI	Partido Aragones Independiente [*Spain*] [*Political party*] (EY)	
PAI	Parts Application Information [*Manufacturing*]	
PAI	Passive-Aggressive Index [*Psychology*]	
PAI	Patient Assesment Instrument [*Medicine*] (DMAA)	
PAI	Percent Adherence Index	
PAI	Performance Audit Inspection [*Environmental Protection Agency*] (GFGA)	
PAI	Personal Accident Insurance	
PAI	Personal Adjustment Inventory [*Psychology*]	
PAI	Personnel Accreditation Institute (EA)	
PAI	Pesticide Active Ingredient (EEVL)	
PAI	Phosphate Adsorption Index [*Analytical chemistry*]	
PAI	Photographic Administrators, Inc. (EA)	
PAI	Piedmont Aviation, Inc. [*Air carrier designation symbol*]	
PAI	Pilot Attack Instructor (SAUS)	
PAI	Piping and Instrumentation [*Nuclear energy*] (IAA)	
PAI	Pirchei Agudath Israel (EA)	
PAI	Place Accumulator in Indicators (IAA)	
PAI	Plasminogen-Activator Inhibitor [*Biochemistry*]	
PAI	Platelet Accumulation Index [*Medicine*] (MELL)	
PAI	Please Airmail Immediately (SAUS)	
PAI	Plunger Actuated Indexer	
PAI	Poale Agudath Israel of America (EA)	
PAI	Polar Area Index [*Palynology*] (QUAC)	
PAI	Polish Assistance, Inc. (EA)	
PAI	Polyamide-Imide [*Organic chemistry*]	
PAI	Population Action International (SAUS)	
PAI	Prearrival Inspection	
PAI	Precise Angle Indicator	
PAI	Primary Aerospace Vehicle [*or Aircraft*] Inventory	
PAI	Primary Aircraft Inventory (SAUS)	
PAI	Process After Input (SAUS)	
PAI	Process Analytical Instrument	
PAI	Process Analytical Instrumentation (SAUS)	
PAI	Process Automation Interface (IAA)	
PAI	Processed Apples Institute (EA)	
PAI	Product Assurance Instruction (ACAE)	
PAI	Production Acceptance Inspection (IAA)	
PAI	Production Adjustment Index [*Word processing*]	
PAI	Professional Athletes International [*Later, NFLPA*] (EA)	
PAI	Programmer Appraisal Instrument [*Computer science*] (IEEE)	
PAI	Project Assignment Instruction (MCD)	
PAI	Property Agents International	
PAI	Protected Area Information (SAUS)	
PAI	Protocol Addressing Information [*Telecommunications*] (OSI)	
PAI	Provisional Acceptance Inspection (SAUS)	
PAI	Public Affairs Information, Inc. [*Sacramento, CA*] [*Database producer*] [*Information service or system*]	
PAI	Public Affairs Institute [*Defunct*] (EA)	
PAI	Public Assistance Information [*A publication*]	
PAI	Pure Active Ingredient (EEVL)	
PAI	Pure Active Ingredient compound (SAUS)	
PAIA	Pan American Implant Association (EA)	
PAIAW	Philadelphia Association of Intercollegiate Athletics for Women (PSS)	
PAIB	Polish-American Information Bureau [*Later, PATIB*] (EA)	
PAIC	Persia and Iraq Command [*World War II*]	
PAIC	Personal Attribute Inventory for Children (EDAC)	
PAIC	Procedures, Alternatives, Indications, and Complications [*Medicine*] (DMAA)	
PAIC	Public Address Intercom System (NRCH)	
PAICC	Professional Association of the Interstate Commerce Commission	
Pai Ch	Paige's New York Chancery Reports [*A publication*] (DLA)	
PAID	Pacific Animated Imaging [*NASDAQ symbol*] (TTSB)	
PAID	Pacific Animated Imaging Corp. [*NASDAQ symbol*] (SAG)	
PAID	Pan African Institute for Development (EAIO)	
PAID	Parked Aircraft Intrusion Detector (PDAA)	
PAID	Personnel and Accounting Integrated Data [*System*] [*Veterans Administration*]	
PAID	Piping and Instrumentation Diagram [*or Design*] [*Nuclear energy*] (IAA)	
PAID	Piping and Instrumentation Drawing (SAUS)	
PAID	Plutonium Air Inhalation Dose (SAUS)	
PAID	Price and Item Display [*British*]	
PAID	Problem Areas in Diabetes [*Scale*] [*Medicine*] (DMAA)	
PAID	Programmers Aid in Debugging [*Computer science*] (MHDI)	
PAIDS	Paralyzed Academic Investigator's Disease Syndrome [*Medicine*] (DMAA)	
PAIDS	Pediatric Acquired Immune Deficiency Syndrome [*Medicine*]	

PAIDS .... Pediatric Acquired Immunodeficiency Syndrome [*Medicine*] (STED)
PAID System... Personnel and Accounting Integrated Data System (SAUS)
PAIF.... Persia and Iraq Force [*World War II*]
PAIFORCE.... Persia and Iraq Force [*World War II*] (DMA)
PAIg............ Platelet-Associated Immunoglobulin [*Hematology*]
PAIGC .... Partido Africano da Independencia da Guine e do Cabo Verde [*African Party for the Independence of Guinea and Cape Verde*] [*Political party*] (PPW)
Paige........... Paige's New York Chancery Reports [*A publication*] (DLA)
PAIGE .... Patient Instruction Generator (ADWA)
Paige Ch...... Paige's New York Chancery Reports [*1828-45*] [*A publication*] (DLA)
Paige Ch Rep... Paige's New York Chancery Reports [*A publication*] (DLA)
Paige's Ch.... Paige's New York Chancery Reports [*A publication*] (DLA)
PAIgG .... Platelet-Associated Immunoglobulin G [*Hematology*]
PAIGH......... Pan American Institute of Geography and History [*Research center*] [*Mexico*] (IRC)
PAIH .... Public-Access Internet Host [*Computer science*] (VLIE)
PAII.............. Professional Association of Innkeepers International (NTPA)
PAIL............. Iliamna [*Alaska*] [*ICAO location identifier*] (ICLI)
PAIL............. Post-Attack Intercontinental Link
PAIL............. Procedural Aspects of International Law Institute (SAUS)
PAILS........... Projectile Airburst and Impact Location System
PAILS........... Projectile and Impact Location System (SAUS)
PAILS........... Publication Automated Information Locator System [*Army*]
PAIM............ Indian Mountain Air Force Station [*Alaska*] [*ICAO location identifier*] (ICLI)
PAIM............ Parti Africain pour l'Independance des Masses [*African Party for the Independence of the Masses*] [*Senegal*] [*Political party*] (PPW)
PAIM............ Primary Air Inlet Muffler (MCD)
PAIMEG .... Pan American Institute of Mining, Engineering, and Geology [*Defunct*]
PAIN .... Pan American Institute of Neurology (SAUS)
PAIN .... Parents Against Injustice (WDAA)
PAIN .... Prisoners' Advice & Information Network (WDAA)
Paine........... Paine's United States Circuit Court Reports [*A publication*] (DLA)
Paine & D Pr... Paine and Duer's Practice [*A publication*] (DLA)
Paine CC ..... Paine's United States Circuit Court Reports [*A publication*] (DLA)
Paine CCR ... Paine's United States Circuit Court Reports [*A publication*] (DLA)
Paine Cir Ct R... Paine's United States Circuit Court Reports [*A publication*] (DLA)
PAINS .... Patient Information System (SAUS)
PAINT .... Painter (SAUS)
PAINT .... Painting (ROG)
PAINT .... Post-Attack Intelligence
Painters Union... International Brotherhood of Painters and Allied Trades of the United States and Canada (SAUS)
Paint Resin... Paint and Resin (SAUS)
PainWeb....... PaineWebber Group, Inc. [*Associated Press*] (SAG)
PainWP....... Paine Webber Premier Tax Free Income [*Associated Press*] (SAG)
PAIP............ Preverbal Assessment-Intervention Profile [*Test*]
PAIP............ Production Acceleration Insurance Program
PAIP............ Public Affairs and Information Program [*Atomic Industrial Forum*] (NRCH)
PAIR .... Pairgain Technologies [*NASDAQ symbol*] (SAG)
PAIR .... Performance Accountability and Improvement Report
PAIR .... Performance and Improved Reliability
PAIR .... Performance and Integration Retrofit
PAIR .... Performance Assessment in Reading [*Educational test*]
PAIR .... Personal Assessment of Intimacy in Relationships (STED)
PAIR .... Personnel Administration and Industrial Relations
PAIR .... Polarization-Agile Instrumentation Radar (SAUS)
PAIR .... Precision Approach Interferometer RADAR (MCD)
PAIR .... Preliminary Assessment Information Rule [*Environmental Protection Agency*]
PAIR .... Procurement Automated Integrated Requirements (MCD)
PAIR .... Product Analysis Incident Report (VLIE)
PAIR .... Product Analysis Information Report (SAUS)
PAIR .... Psychological Audit for Interpersonal Relations [*Psychology*]
PAIR .... Pulse-Air Injection Reactor [*Automotive engineering*]
PAIRC.......... Polish American Immigration and Relief Committee (EA)
PAIRMEM .... Paired Word Memory Task (TES)
PAIRO......... Professional Association of Interns and Residents (SAUS)
PAIRS .... Pain and Impairment Relationship Scale (MELL)
PAIRS .... Parent Assisted Instruction in Reading and Spelling (AIE)
PAIRS .... Private Aircraft Inspection Reporting System (PDAA)
PAIRS .... Product Assurance Information Retrieval System [*Boeing*]
PAIRS .... Program for the Analysis of Infrared Spectra [*Computer program*] [*Analytical chemistry*]
PAIRS .... Pushbroom Airborne Infrared Remote Sensor (SAUS)
PairTch........ Pairgain Technologies [*Associated Press*] (SAG)
PAIS............ Padre Island National Seashore [*National Park Service designation*]
PAIS............ PAIS International in Print
PAIS............ Partido Amplio de Izquierda Socialista [*Chile*] [*Political party*] (EY)
PAIS............ Partido Autentico Institucional Salvadoreno [*Salvadoran Authentic Institutional Party*] [*Political party*] (PPW)
PAIS............ Pennsylvania Association of Independent Schools (SAUS)
PAIS............ Personnel Authentication Identification System (MCD)
PAIS............ Petroleum Abstracts Information Services [*University of Tulsa*] [*Oklahoma*] [*Information service or system*] (IID)
PAIS............ Project Analysis Information System [*Agency for International Development*]
PAIS............ Prototype Advanced Indicator System (MCD)
PAIS............ Psychological Abstracts Information Services [*American Psychological Association*]
PAIS............ Psychosocial Adjustment to Illness Scale [*Personality development test*] [*Psychology*]

PAIS............ Public-Access Internet Site [*Computer science*] (VLIE)
PAISA .... Partido Autentico Institucional Salvadoreno [*Salvadoran Authentic Institutional Party*] [*Political party*] (EY)
PAIS FLI ...... PAIS Foreign Language Index (NITA)
PAIS FLI ...... Public Affairs Information Service-Foreign Language Index (SAUS)
PAIT............ Passive Adoptive Immunotherapy [*Medicine*] (MELL)
PAIT............ Program for Advancement of Industrial Technology [*Canada*]
PAIV............ Power as an Integral Variable
PAIVM .... Passive Accessory InterVertebral Movement (SAUS)
PAIVS .... Pulmonary Atresia with Intact Ventricular Septum [*Cardiology*] (DAVI)
PAIX............ Pacific Alaska Airlines [*Air carrier designation symbol*]
PAJ............. Kansas City, MO [*Location identifier*] [*FAA*] (FAAL)
PAJ............. Paralysis Agitans Juvenilis [*Medicine*] (DMAA)
PAJ............. Performing Arts Journal [*A publication*]
PAJ............. Petroleum Association of Japan (SAUS)
PAJA .... Parachute Jumping Activities [*Aviation*] (FAAC)
PAJAR .... Parti Rakyat Jati Sarawak [*Sarawak Native People's Party*] [*Malaysia*] [*Political party*] (PPW)
PAJES .... Parents of Adult Jewish Singles
PAJHS .... Publications of the American Jewish Historical Society (SAUS)
PAJN........... Juneau [*Alaska*] [*ICAO location identifier*] (ICLI)
PAK............. Hanapepe, HI [*Location identifier*] [*FAA*] (FAAL)
PAK............. Pacific Alaska Airlines [*ICAO designator*] (FAAC)
PAK............. Packed (SAUS)
PAK............. Packet (SAUS)
PAK............. Pakistan [*ANSI three-letter standard code*] (CNC)
Pak............. Pakistan (VRA)
PAK............. Panzer Abwehr Kanone [*Cannon Against Armor*] [*German antitank gun*]
PAK............. Performance Advantage Kit [*Personal computers*]
PAK............. Polycyclic Aromatic Ketone [*Organic chemistry*]
PAK............. Polyester Alkyd (SAUS)
PAK............. Power Amplifier Klystron
PAK............. Product Authorization Key (VLIE)
PAK............. Program Attention Key [*Computer science*] (BUR)
PAK............. Projector Alignment Kit (SAUS)
PAK............. Pseudomonas Aeruginosa Strain K (DB)
Pak Bar J..... Pakistan Bar Journal [*A publication*] (DLA)
Pak Crim LJ.. Pakistan Criminal Law Journal [*A publication*] (DLA)
PakE........... Pakistani English (SAUS)
Pakete .... Daten-Pakete (SAUS)
PAKEX .... International Packaging Exhibition [*British*] (ITD)
PA KEY .... Program Extension Key [*Computer science*] (ITCA)
PakisInv...... Pakistan Investment Fund, Inc. [*Associated Press*] (SAG)
Pak J Sci..... Pakistan Journal of Science (SAUS)
Pak J Sci Res... Pakistan Journal of Scientific Research (SAUS)
PakLibrAssQJ... Pakistan Library Association Quarterly Journal (SAUS)
PakLibrRev... Pakistan Library Review (SAUS)
Pak LR........ Pakistan Law Reports [*India*] [*A publication*] (DLA)
Pak L Rev.... Pakistan Law Review [*A publication*] (DLA)
PAKN.......... King Salmon [*Alaska*] [*ICAO location identifier*] (ICLI)
PAKOMIN..... Pakistan Oxygen Minimum (SAUS)
PAKSI .... Pakistan Standards Institute (SAUS)
Pak Sup Ct Q... Pakistan Supreme Court Law Quarterly [*Lahore, Pakistan*] [*A publication*] (DLA)
PAKT........... Ketchikan [*Alaska*] [*ICAO location identifier*] (ICLI)
PAL............. Allegheny County Law Library, Pittsburgh, PA [*OCLC symbol*] (OCLC)
PAL+........... Enhanced-fidelity PAL (SAUS)
PAL............. North Amer. Palladium [*AMEX symbol*]
PAL............. Pacific Aeronautical Library
PAL............. Pacific Aerospace Library (SAUS)
PAL............. Pacific Air Lines
PAL............. Pacific Aluminium (SAUS)
pal............. Pahlavi [*MARC language code*] [*Library of Congress*] (LCCP)
PAL............. Paired-Associates Learning [*Task*] [*Psychology*]
PAL............. Pakistan Airlines (SAUS)
PAL............. Palace
Pal............. Palamedes [*of Gorgias*] [*Classical studies*] (OCD)
pal............. Palate (DMAA)
PAL............. Palatine [*or Palatinate*] [*Genealogy*]
PAL............. Paleography (ROG)
PAL............. Paleontology
PAL............. Paleozoic [*Period, era, or system*] [*Geology*]
Pal............. Palestine (NTIO)
PAL............. Palestine
pal............. Palette (VRA)
PAL............. Palisades [*New York*] [*Seismograph station code, US Geological Survey*] (SEIS)
PAL............. Pallet (VLIE)
PAL............. Pallor (KSC)
Pal............. Palmer's Assizes at Cambridge [*England*] [*A publication*] (DLA)
Pal............. Palmer's English King's Bench Reports [*1619-29*] [*A publication*] (DLA)
Pal............. Palmer's Reports [*53-60 Vermont*] [*A publication*] (DLA)
PAL............. Paloma Petroleum Ltd. [*Toronto Stock Exchange symbol*]
PAL............. Pan Asia Line (SAUS)
PAL............. Paradox Application Language [*ANSA*] [*Computer science*]
PAL............. Parcel Air Lift [*US Postal Service*]
PAL............. Parents Anonymous Lifeline [*British*] (DI)
PAL............. Parser Assembly Language [*Computer science*]
PAL............. Partition Allocation Utility (SAUS)
PAL............. Parts and Assemblies Locator [*ADP/CES*]
PAL............. Parts Authorization List (KSC)
PAL............. Passive Activity Loss [*Investment term*] (DFIT)

PAL............	Patent Associated Literature
PAL............	Pathology Laboratory [Test]
PAL............	Pectin Acid Lyase [An enzyme]
PAL............	Pedagogic Algorithmic Language [Computer science]
PAL............	Pensioners Advancement League (SAUS)
PAL............	People Against Chlordane (EA)
PAL............	People-Animals-Love (EA)
PAL............	Peptidyl-Alpha-Hydroxyglycine Alpha-Amidating Lysine Phase Alteration Plane [Medicine] (DMAA)
PAL............	Perceptual Alternatives Laboratory [University of Louisville] [Research center] (RCD)
PAL............	Performance Assessment Logic
PAL............	Peripheral Access Lattices
PAL............	Permanent Artificial Lighting (IEEE)
PAL............	Permissive Action Link [Army]
PAL............	Permissive Arming Line [or Link]
PAL............	Peroxide Assisted Leach [Ore processing]
PAL............	Personal Answer Line [Telecommunications] (VLIE)
PAL............	Personal Assets Line
PAL............	Personnel Accounting Level [Air Force] (AFM)
PAL............	Personnel Address Listing (SAA)
PAL............	Personnel Airlock [Nuclear energy] (NRCH)
PAL............	Personnel Augmentation List [Military]
PAL............	Phase Alternate Line (NITA)
PAL............	Phase Alternating Line [Telecommunications] (MLOA)
PAL............	Phase Alternating Loop (SAUS)
PAL............	Phase Alternation Line [West German color television system]
PAL............	Phase Alternation Standard (SAUS)
PAL............	Phase-Alternation System [A color TV format] [Also, phase alternate each line] (WDMC)
PAL............	Phase Attenation by Line (SAUS)
PAL............	Phenylalanine Ammonia-Lyase [An enzyme]
PAL............	Philippine Air Lines
PAL............	Philippine Air Lines, Inc. [ICAO designator] (FAAC)
PAL............	Philips Air Liquefier (SAUS)
PAL............	Philips Assembler Language (IAA)
PAL............	Physical Activity Level (WDAA)
PAL............	Pipe Analysis Log [Gas well]
PAL............	Plasma Ammonia Level [Medicine] (MELL)
PAL............	Platform Abstraction Layer (VLIE)
PAL............	Podiatry Arts Laboratory (SAUS)
PAL............	Point, Area, and Line Source Air Quality Model [Environmental Protection Agency] (GFGA)
PAL............	Police Athletic League
PAL............	Police Attendance Line
PAL............	Polyacrylnitril (SAUS)
PAL............	Polyaniline (SAUS)
PAL............	Poly-DL-alanine Poly-L-lysine [Biochemical analysis]
PAL............	Polynesian Airlines Ltd. (SAUS)
PAL............	Portable, Accurate, Lightweight (SAUS)
PAL............	Portable Advanced Laser (SAUS)
PAL............	Positive Arming Link [Military] (DNAB)
PAL............	Postal Answer Line [US Postal Service automated telephone information service]
PAL............	Posterior Axillary Line [Medicine]
PAL............	Power and Light (IAA)
PAL............	Power Assist Lathe
PAL............	Pre-Academic Learning Inventory [Child development test]
PAL............	Preapproved Loan [Business term]
PAL............	Precision Artwork Language [Computer science]
PAL............	Preliminary Allowance List [Military] (DNAB)
PAL............	Premier Automobiles Ltd. [India]
PAL............	Prescribed Action Link [DoD]
PAL............	Present Atmospheric Level
PAL............	Price and Availability List (CINC)
PAL............	Princeton Accelerator Laboratory
PAL............	Princeton Air Link
PAL............	Prison Atheist League (SAUS)
PAL............	Prisoner-at-Large
PAL............	Privileged Architecture Library (SAUS)
PAL............	Privileged Architecture Library Code
PAL............	Problem Action Log (AAG)
PAL............	Process Assembler Language
PAL............	Process Assembly Languages
PAL............	Process Asset Library
PAL............	Process Audit List (MCD)
PAL............	Process Automation Language [Computer science] (AAEL)
PAL............	Processing and Analytical Laboratories (SAUS)
PAL............	Production and Application of Light (MCD)
PAL............	Product of Activated Lymphocytes [Medicine] (DMAA)
PAL............	Products and Area Locator (SAUS)
PAL............	Professional Adjustable Ladder (SAUS)
PAL............	Profile Automobile League (EA)
PAL............	Profile of Aptitude for Leadership [Test] (TMMY)
PAL............	Program Array Logic (SAUS)
PAL............	Program Assembler (or Assembly) Language (SAUS)
PAL............	Programmable Algorithm Machine Assembly Language [Computer science]
PAL............	Programmable Array Logic [Computer science] (IEEE)
PAL............	Programmed Application Library [IBM Corp.]
PAL............	Programmed Array Logic (SAUS)
PAL............	Programmed Audit Library
PAL............	Programmer Assistance and Liaison [Computer science] (NRCH)
PAL............	Programming Application Language (SAUS)
PAL............	Programming Assembly Language (SAUS)
PAL............	Progressive Alliance of Liberia [Political party] (PPW)
PAL............	Prototype Application Loop [Nuclear energy] (NRCH)
PAL............	Protuberance Aerodynamic Load
PAL............	Psycho-Acoustic Laboratory [Harvard University] (MCD)
PAL............	Public Archives Library (SAUS)
PAL............	Public Archives of Canada Library [UTLAS symbol]
PAL............	Publication Applicability List [Navy]
PAL............	Publications Allowance List [Military] (CAAL)
PAL............	Pulmonary Air Leak [Medicine] (DB)
PAL............	Pulsed Argon LASER
PAL............	Push and Latch [Push button]
PAL............	Pyogenic Abscess of the Liver [Medicine] (DMAA)
PALA..........	N-(Phosphoacetyl)-L-aspartate [Biochemistry]
pala............	Palace (VRA)
pala............	Palazzo (VRA)
Pala..........	Partido Laborista [Labor Party] [Panama] [Political party] (PPW)
PALA..........	Partition Affinity Ligand Assay [Analytical microbiology]
PALA..........	Passenger Acceptance and Load Accumulation [Aviation]
PaLA..........	Pennsylvania Library Associaton
PALA..........	Phosphonoacetyl-L-Aspartate [Biochemistry]
PALA..........	Polish American Librarians Association (EA)
PALA..........	Prison Atheist League of America (EA)
PALAAS	Property and Liability Agency Accounting System (SAUS)
PALACE.......	Profiling ALACE [Autonomous Lagrangian Circulation Explorer] [Marine science] (OSRA)
palaeob	Palaeobotanical (SAUS)
PALAEOB	Palaeobotany
palaeog	palaeographical (SAUS)
PALAEOG	Palaeography
Palaeogeogr Palaeoclimatol Palaeoecol...	Palaeogeography Palaeoclimatology Palaeoecology (SAUS)
Palaeo III....	Palaeogeography, Palaeoclimatology, Palaeoecology (SAUS)
PALAEONT...	Palaeontology
Palaeontol...	Palaeontological (DIAR)
Pal Ag	Paley on Principal and Agent [3rd ed.] [1833] [A publication] (DLA)
PAL APA	Indonesian Communications Satellite (SAUS)
PALASM	Programmable Array Logic Assembler [Computer science] (IEEE)
Palat...........	Palatinate (SAUS)
PA Law J	Pennsylvania Law Journal [A publication] (DLA)
PA Law Jour...	Pennsylvania Law Journal [Philadelphia] [A publication] (DLA)
PA Laws	Laws of the General Assembly of the Commonwealth of Pennsylvania [A publication] (DLA)
PA Law Ser...	Pennsylvania Law Series [A publication] (DLA)
PALC..........	Palace
PALC..........	Passenger Acceptance and Load Control [Aviation]
PALC..........	Plasma-Addressed Liquid Crystal (SAUS)
PALC..........	Point Arguello Launch Complex
PALC..........	Precastable Autoclaved Lightweight Concrete [Residential construction]
PAL-C	Profile of Adaptation to Life - Clinical [Personality development test] [Psychology]
PALCD	Plasma Addressable Liquid Crystal Display (SAUS)
PALCO	Pacific Lumber Co. (EFIS)
PALCO	Pan American Liaison Committee of Women's Organizations (EA)
PALCON.......	Pallet-Size Container (MCD)
Pal Conv......	Paley on Summary Convictions [10th ed.] [1953] [A publication] (DLA)
PALCR	Propulsion Auxiliaries Local Control Rack (DNAB)
PALCRU.......	Pay and Allowances Accrue From [Air Force]
PALCS	Permissive Action Link Cypher System (MCD)
PALC System...	Passenger Acceptance and Load Control System (SAUS)
PALCTS........	Processing Analytical Laboratories Commitment Tracking System (SAUS)
PAL-D	Phase Alternation Line Delay (IEEE)
PALD	Phase Alternation Line Delay
PALDS	Point, Area, and Line Source with Deposition and Settling of Pollutants [Air quality model] [Environmental Protection Agency] (GFGA)
PALE	Palaeoclimate from Arctic Lakes and Estuaries (SAUS)
Pale...........	Palestine (VRA)
PALE	Pelvis and Legs Elevating [Pilot seat]
PALE	Popular Army for the Liberation of Eritrea (SAUS)
PA Leg Gaz...	Legal Gazette (Pennsylvania) [A publication] (DLA)
PA Leg Gaz...	Legal Gazette Reports (Campbell) [Pennsylvania] [A publication] (DLA)
PA Legis Serv...	Pennsylvania Legislative Service (Purdon) [A publication] (DLA)
Paleo..........	Paleolithic (SAUS)
paleob	Paleobotany (BARN)
Paleoclim Res...	Paleoclimate Research (SAUS)
PALEOECOL...	Paleoecologic
paleog	Paleography
PALEOGEOG...	Paleogeographic
Paleol	Paleolithic (VRA)
paleon	Paleontology
PALEONT	Paleontologic
PALEONT	Paleontological (SAUS)
PALEONT	Paleontologist (SAUS)
Paleontol.....	Paleontology (BEE)
PALE Seat ...	Pelvis and Legs Elevating Seat (SAUS)
Palest.........	Palestinian (DIAR)
PALEX.........	Pacific Armies Look Exercise
Paley Ag......	Paley on Principal and Agent [A publication] (DLA)
Paley Princ & Ag...	Paley on Principal and Agent [3rd ed.] [1833] [A publication] (DLA)
Palfed.........	PALFED, Inc. [Associated Press] (SAG)

PA LG	Legal Gazette (Pennsylvania) [*A publication*] (DLA)
PA LG	Legal Gazette Reports (Campbell) [*Pennsylvania*] [*A publication*] (DLA)
Palg Ch.......	Palgrave's Proceedings in Chancery [*A publication*] (DLA)
Palgrave......	Palgrave's Proceedings in Chancery [*A publication*] (DLA)
Palgrave......	Palgrave's Rise and Progress of the English Commonwealth [*A publication*] (DLA)
Palg Rise & Prog...	Palgrave's Rise and Progress of the English Commonwealth [*1832*] [*A publication*] (DLA)
Palg Rise Etc...	Palgrave's Rise and Progress of the English Commonwealth [*A publication*] (DLA)
PAL-H	Profile of Adaptation to Life - Holistic [*Personality development test*] [*Psychology*]
PALI	Pacific and Asian Linguistics Institute [*University of Hawaii*]
Pali.............	Partido Liberal [*Nicaragua*] [*Political party*] (EY)
PALI...........	Prince Albert's Light Infantry [*Military unit*] [*British*]
PALIKA	Parti de Liberation Kanak [*New Caledonia*] [*Political party*] (EY)
palin	palindromic (SAUS)
PALINET......	Pennsylvania Area Library Network
PALINET	Philadelphia Area Library Network (SAUS)
PALINET/ULC...	PALINET and Union Library Catalogue of Pennsylvania [*Philadelphia, PA*] [*Library network*]
PALIS.........	Polarized Airborne Laser Imaging Sensor (SAUS)
PALIS.........	Programmable Adapter Logic Sequence (SAUS)
PALIS..........	Property and Liability Information System
PA LJ	Pennsylvania Law Journal [*A publication*] (DLA)
PA LJ	Pennsylvania Law Journal Reports [*1842-52*] [*A publication*] (DLA)
PA LJR	Clark's Pennsylvania Law Journal Reports [*A publication*] (DLA)
PALL.........	Pallet [*Freight*]
Pall............	Pallium (SAUS)
PallCp.........	Pall Corp. [*Associated Press*] (SAG)
PALLNIC	Palladium-Nickel (EECA)
PALM........	PALFED, Inc. [*NASDAQ symbol*] (NQ)
Palm............	Palmer's Assizes at Cambridge [*England*] [*A publication*] (DLA)
Palm............	Palmer's English King's Bench Reports [*1619-29*] [*A publication*] (DLA)
Palm............	Palmer's Reports [*53-60 Vermont*] [*A publication*] (DLA)
PALM........	Palm, Inc. [*NASDAQ symbol*] (SG)
PALM.........	Palmistry (ADA)
Palm...........	Palmyrene (BJA)
PALM.........	Personalized Automated Life Management (SAUS)
PALM.........	Philips Automated Laboratory Management (SAUS)
PALM........	Philips Automated Laboratory Management System (NITA)
PALM.........	Precision Altitude and Landing Monitor [*Aircraft location*]
PALM.........	Pro Audio, Light & Music (SAUS)
Palma.........	Palma de Mallorca
Palm Comp L...	Palmer's Company Law [*22nd ed.*] [*1976*] [*A publication*] (DLA)
Palm Comp Prec...	Palmer's Company Precedents [*17th ed.*] [*1956-60*] [*A publication*] (DLA)
Palmer.........	Palmer's Assizes at Cambridge [*England*] [*A publication*] (DLA)
Palmer.........	Palmer's English King's Bench Reports [*A publication*] (DLA)
Palmer.........	Palmer's Reports [*53-60 Vermont*] [*A publication*] (DLA)
Palmer Co Prec...	Palmer's Company Precedents [*16 eds.*] [*1877-1952*] [*A publication*] (DLA)
PALMER FLD...	Palmer Field (SAUS)
Palmer Pr Comp...	Palmer's Private Companies [*41st ed.*] [*1950*] [*A publication*] (DLA)
PALMES.......	Pulsed Appendage Large Mobile Electromagnetic-Pulse Simulator (PDAA)
PalmHH	Palm Harbor Homes, Inc. [*Associated Press*] (SAG)
PALMNET......	Protocol for Automotive Local Area Network
Palm Pr Lords...	Palmer's Practice in the House of Lords [*1830*] [*A publication*] (DLA)
PalmrMd......	Palomar Medical Technologies [*Associated Press*] (SAG)
PALMS........	Propulsion Alarm and Monitoring System (PDAA)
PALMS........	Provisioning Automated Logistics Material System (MCD)
Palm Sh	Palmer's Shareholders [*34th ed.*] [*1936*] [*A publication*] (DLA)
Palm Wr	Palmer's Law of Wreck [*1843*] [*A publication*] (DLA)
PALN	Para-Aortic Lymph Node [*Anatomy*] (DAVI)
PALO	Phosphonoacetyl-L-Ornithine [*Biochemistry*]
PALO	Port Amenities Liaison Officer [*British*] (DSUE)
Pal Obs........	Palomar Observatory (SAUS)
PALOS	Pacific Logistic Operations - Streamline [*Army*]
PA Loudspeaker...	Public Address Loudspeaker (SAUS)
PALP...........	Palpable [*Medicine*]
palp	Palpitation [*Cardiology*] (DAVI)
PALP..........	Protected Areas and Landscapes Programme (SAUS)
PALP..........	Pyridoxal Phosphate [*Also, PLP*] [*Biochemistry*]
PALPI..........	Palpitation [*Medicine*]
palpit	Palpitation [*Medicine*]
PALR	Permissive Action Link Report [*Army*] (AABC)
PA L Rec	Pennsylvania Law Record [*A publication*] (DLA)
PALS...........	Paediatric Advanced Life Support [*Medicine*] (WDAA)
PALS...........	Paired Associate Learning Subtest [*Speech and language therapy*] (DAVI)
PALS...........	Patient Advocacy Legal Service [*An association*] [*Defunct*] (EA)
PALS...........	Pediatric Advanced Life Support [*Medicine*] (ADWA)
PALS...........	Pediatric Advanced Life Support (NUJO)
PA LS	Pennsylvania Law Series [*A publication*] (DLA)
PALS...........	People Against Lenient Sentences [*An association*] [*Australia*]
PALS...........	People Against Loneliness [*British*] (DI)
PALS...........	Periarteriolar Lymphocyte Sheath (AAMN)
PALS...........	Permissive Action Link System [*Army*]
PALS...........	Phase Alternation Line Simple [*TV decoding system*]
PAL-S	Phase Alternation Line-Simple

PALS...........	Photo Area and Location System (NASA)
PALS...........	Photographic Area and Location System
PALS...........	Point Arguello Launch Site (AAG)
PALS...........	Portable Airfield Lighting System (SAUS)
PALS...........	Portable Airfield Light Set (SAUS)
PALS...........	Positioning and Locating System [*Aviation*] (PDAA)
PALS...........	Pre-Announcement Level System (SAUS)
PALS...........	Precision Approach and Landing System (NASA)
PALS...........	Precision Approach Lighting System [*Aviation*] (FAAC)
PALS...........	Preliminary Award Letter System
PALS...........	Prestaged Ammunition Loading System [*Army*] (RDA)
PALS...........	Principle of the Alphabet Literacy System [*Software*] [*IBM Corp.*]
PALS...........	Principles of Adult Learning Scale (EDAC)
PALS...........	Prison-Acquired Lymphoproliferative Syndrome [*Medicine*] (DMAA)
PALS...........	Program for Address List Supplementation (SAUS)
PALS...........	Protection Against Limited Strikes [*Military defence system*]
PALS...........	Public Access Library System (SAUS)
PA L Ser.	Pennsylvania Law Series [*A publication*] (DLA)
PALS-G	Passive Artillery Locating System - Ground Based (MCD)
PALSG	Personnel and Logistics Systems Group [*Army*] (AABC)
PA-LS-ID....	Pernicious Anemia-Like Syndrome and Immunoglobulin Deficiency [*Hematology*] (AAMN)
PALST........	Picture Articulation and Screening Test
PAL System...	Phase Alternating (or Alternation) Line System (SAUS)
PAlt............	Altoona Area Public Library, Altoona, PA [*Library symbol*] [*Library of Congress*] (LCLS)
PALT...........	Procurement Acquisition Lead Times (SAUS)
PALT...........	Procurement Administrative Lead Time
PALTC........	Pacific Asian and Latino Training Center (SAUS)
PALU	Cape Lisburne Air Force Station [*Alaska*] [*ICAO location identifier*] (ICLI)
PALU	Progressive Arbeiders- en Landbouwersunie [*Progressive Workers' and Farm Laborers' Union*] [*Surinam*] [*Political party*] (PPW)
Palud	Paludonus [*Pierre de la Palu*] [*Deceased, 1342*] [*Authority cited in pre-1607 legal work*] (DSA)
PALV:	Passiflora Latent Virus [*Plant pathology*]
PALW.........	Plasma Arc-augmented Laser Welding
PALX..........	Private Automatic Loudspeaking Exchange [*Telecommunications*] (IAA)
PAM............	Pacific Armies Management
PAM............	Package for Analogue Modeling (SAUS)
PAM............	Page Allocation Map (SAUS)
PAM............	Paging Area Memory (SAUS)
PAM............	Palermo [*California*] [*Seismograph station code, US Geological Survey*] (SEIS)
PAM............	Pamida Holdings Corp. [*AMEX symbol*] (SPSG)
PAM............	Pamour, Inc. [*Toronto Stock Exchange symbol*]
Pam	Pampa [*Record label*] [*Brazil*]
PAM............	Pamphlet (AFM)
pam	Pamphlet (WDMC)
PAM............	PAM Transportation Services, Inc. [*Associated Press*] (SAG)
PAM............	Pan Africanist Movement (SAUS)
PAM............	Panama City, FL [*Location identifier*] [*FAA*] (FAAL)
PAM............	Panel Monitor (MHDI)
PAM............	Panoramic
PAM............	Panvalet Access Method (IAA)
PAM............	Parallel Associative Memory (SAUS)
PAM............	Parameter Adjusting Mechanism
PAM............	Parametric Amplifier (NATG)
PAM............	Parents Against Molesters (EA)
PAM............	Parititioned Access Method (SAUS)
PAM............	Partial Mobilization Expansion Plan [*Army*] (GFGA)
PAM............	Particle Anticoincidence Mantle (SAUS)
PAM............	Partitioned Access Method [*Computer science*]
PAM............	Pasadena Art Museum (SAUS)
PAM............	Payload Accommodation Manager (SAUS)
PAM............	Payload Assist Module [*NASA*] (MCD)
PAM............	Peachtree Accounting-Macintosh (SAUS)
PAM............	Penetration Augmented Munition
PAM............	Penicillin Aluminum Monostearate [*Antibiotic*]
PAM............	People's Action Movement [*Nevis*] [*Political party*] (PPW)
PAM...........	People's Anti-War Mobilization (EA)
PAM............	Performance Analysis Model (MCD)
PAM............	Performance Assessment Matrix (SARE)
PAM............	Performance Assessment Monitoring (MCD)
PAM............	Performing Arts Medicine
PAM............	Perigee Assist Motor (ACAE)
PAM............	Peripheral Adapter Module
PAM............	Personal Accounting Management
PAM............	Personal Application Monitor (SAUS)
PAM............	Personal Applications Manager [*Hewlett-Packard Co.*]
PAM............	Personnel Action Memorandum [*Military*]
PAM............	Personnel Availability Model (PDAA)
PAM............	Pesticide Analytical Manual (EEVL)
PAM............	Phase-Amplitude Modulation
PAM............	Phased Array Module
PAM............	Phenylacetamidomethyl (SAUS)
PAM............	Phenylalanine Mustard (AAMN)
PAM............	Philosophies, Ancient and Modern [*A publication*]
PAM............	Phoenix Airborne Missile
PAM............	Phoenix Air Service GmbH [*Germany*] [*ICAO designator*] (FAAC)
PAM............	Phone Activities Manager (SAUS)
PAM............	Phono Amplifier (SAUS)
PAM............	Photoacoustic Microscopy (SAUS)
PAM............	Pittsburgh, Allegheny & McKees Rocks Railroad Co. [*AAR code*]

PAM	Plan-Applier Mechanism (SAUS)
PAM	Planning, Activation, Modification [Army reorganization]
PAM	Plant Available Moisture (SAUS)
PAM	Plasma-Arc Machining [Manufacturing term]
PAM	Pledged Account Mortgage
PAM	Pluggable Authentication Module (RALS)
PAM	Pole Amplitude Modulation (IEEE)
PAM	Policies and Measures (SAUS)
PAM	Polyacrylamide [Also, PAA, PAAM] [Organic chemistry]
PAM	Portable Activity Monitor
PAM	Portable Alpha Meter (SAUS)
PAM	Portable Alpha Monitor
PAM	Portable Automated Mesonet [Meteorology]
PAM	Portland Art Museum
PAM	Position and Altitude Monitor (MCD)
PAM	Post-Accident Monitoring [Nuclear energy] (NRCH)
PAM	Postauricular Myogenic [Medicine] (DMAA)
PAM	Potential Acuity Meter [Instrumentation]
PAM	Potential Available Market (TIMI)
PAM	Power Assist Module [NASA]
PAM	Pozzolan Aggregate Mixture (OA)
PAM	Pralidoxime [Pharmacology] (DAVI)
PAM	Pralidoxime Chloride [Pharmacology] (DAVI)
PAM	Pralidoxime Methiodide [Biochemistry]
PAM	Precision Angular Mover (SAUS)
PAM	Preliminary Aerosol Monitor (SAUS)
PAM	Presbyterian Association of Musicians (EA)
PAM	Pressure-Acoustic-Magnetic [Minesweeping system] (DNAB)
PAM	Primary Access Method [Sperry UNIVAC]
PAM	Primary Acquired Melanosis [Oncology]
PAM	Primary Amoebic Meningitis [or Meningoencephalitis] [Medicine]
PAM	Primary Amoebic Meningoencephalitis (SAUS)
PAM	Primary Auxiliary Memory [Unit] [Computer science] (MCD)
PAM	Printer Authorization Matrix (VLIE)
PAM	Priorities and Allocations Manual [Army] (AABC)
PAM	Process Application Module (AAEL)
PAM	Process Automatic Monitor (SAUS)
PAM	Process Automation Monitor [Texas Instruments, Inc.]
PAM	Processor and Memory [Computer science]
PAM	Procurement Aids Man [Marine Corps]
PAM	Procurement Aircraft and Missiles (SAUS)
PAM	Procurement and Acquisition Management (SAUS)
PAM	Procurement of Aircraft and Missiles
PAM	Product Assurance Manager (ACAE)
PAM	Profit Analysis Model (MHDI)
PAM	Program Analysis Memorandum (MCD)
PA-M	Program Authorization - Map [Military] (AFIT)
PAM	Program Automated Method [Computer science]
PAM	Programmable Active Memory [Computer science] (VLIE)
PAM	Programmable Algorithmic Machine (SAUS)
PAM	Programmable Algorithm Machine [Computer science]
PAM	Programmed Accounting Machine (SAUS)
PAM	Programmed Associative Memory [Computer science] (VLIE)
PAM	Project Assurance Manager (SAUS)
PAM	Project Assurance Manual (SAUS)
PAM	Propulsion Assistance Module (MCD)
PAM	Protopan Chloride [Medicine] (BARN)
PAM	Provincial Archives of Manitoba (SAUS)
PAM	Pulmonary Alveolar Macrophage [Attacks inhaled particles]
PAM	Pulmonary Alveolar Microlithiasis [Medicine] (MAE)
PAM	Pulse Amplification Modulation (SAUS)
PAM	Pulse Amplified Modulation (SAUS)
PAM	Pulse Amplifier Modulation (NAKS)
PAM	Pulse Amplitude Modulated (SAUS)
PAM	Pulse Amplitude Modulation [Electronics]
PAM	Pulse Amplitude Modulator (SAUS)
PAM	Pyridine Aldoxime Methiodide [Biochemistry]
PAM	Pyridine Aldoxime Methyl [Pharmacology]
PAM	Pyridine-Aldoxine-N-Methyliodide (SAUS)
PAM	University of Pennsylvania, School of Medicine, Philadelphia, PA [OCLC symbol] (OCLC)
PAm	Wissahickon Valley Public Library, Ambler, PA [Library symbol] [Library of Congress] (LCLS)
PAM 250	Accepted Point Mutation 250 (SAUS)
PAM-A	PAM [Payload Assist Module] Atlas-Centaur Class Spacecraft (NASA)
PAMA	Pan American Medical Association [Also known as Association Medica Pan Americana] (EA)
PAMA	Para-Dimethylaminophenylazopyridine [An indicator] [Chemistry]
PAM-A	Payload Assist Module - Atlas Class Spacecraft (MCD)
PAMA	Philippines Air Materiel Area (SAUS)
PAMA	Polish Alma Mater of America (EA)
PAMA	Polyalkylmethacrylate (IAA)
PAMA	Pre-Assigned Multiple Access [Telecommunications] (LAIN)
PAMA	Preferred Acquisition Method of Analysis (SAUS)
PAMA	Press Advertisement Managers' Association (DGA)
PAMA	Processing Algorithm for Maintenance Actions (SAUS)
PAMA	Professional Aviation Maintenance Association (EA)
PAMA	Publishers Advertising and Marketing Association (SAUS)
PAMA	Pulse-Address Multiple Access [Satellite communications]
PAMAC	Parts and Materials Accountability Control
PAMAD	Parents Against Middle-Aged Discrimination [British] (DI)
PAMAI	Program of Action for Mediation, Arbitration, and Inquiry [American Library Association]
PAMAM	Polyamidoamine [Organic chemistry]

PAMB	Pressure Ambient (NASA)
PAMBA	Para-Aminomethylbenzoic Acid (SAUS)
PAmbT	Trinity Episcopal School, Ambridge, PA [Library symbol] [Library of Congress] (LCLS)
PAMBU	Pacific Manuscripts Bureau (SAUS)
PAMC	McGrath [Alaska] [ICAO location identifier] (ICLI)
PAMC	Pakistan Army Medical Corps
PAMC	Progressive Aircraft Maintenance Concept (SAUS)
PAMC	Provident American Corp. [Norristown, PA] [NASDAQ symbol] (NQ)
PAMC	Provisional Acceptable Means of Compliance (MCD)
PAMC	Pterygoarthromyodysplasia Congenital [Medicine] (DMAA)
PAmC	Temple University, Ambler Campus, Ambler, PA [Library symbol] [Library of Congress] (LCLS)
PAMCCS	Prior Active Marine Corps Commissioned Service
PAMCES	Prior Active Marine Corps Enlisted Service
PAMCI	Pyridinealdoxime Methochloride [Organic chemistry]
PAMCO	Pacific Annuity Marketing Co.
PAMCS	Panel on Air Space Management & Control System (SAUS)
PAMCS	Phoenix Airborne Missile Control System
PAM-D	PAM [Payload Assist Module] Delta Class Spacecraft (NASA)
PAMD	Parallel Access Multiple Distribution (PDAA)
PAM-D	Payload Assist Module - Delta Class Spacecraft (MCD)
PAMD	Periodic Acid Mixed Diamine (OA)
PAMD	Prelingually Acquired Meningitic Deafness [Medicine] (MELL)
PAMD	Price and Management Data
PAMD	Primary Adrenocortical Micronodular Dysplasia [Medicine] (DMAA)
PAM/D	Process Automation Monitor/Disc Version (NITA)
PAMD	Process Automation Monitor/Disk Version [Texas Instruments, Inc.]
PAMD	Public Access Machine Readable Documents (NITA)
PAM-DII	Payload Assist Module-Delta Class 2 (SAUS)
PAMDS	Price and Management Data Section [of a stock list] [Navy]
PAME	Pandemokratiki Agrotikon Metapon Ellados [Pan-Democratic Agrarian Front of Greece] [Political party] (PPE)
PAME	Primary Amoebic Meningoencephalitis [Medicine]
P/AMEA2	Probationary Marine Engineering Artificer, Acting, 2nd Class [British military] (DMA)
Pa Med	Pennsylvania Medicine (SAUS)
PAMEE	Philippine Association of Mechanical and Electrical Engineers (SAUS)
PAMELA	Patient Automatic Monitoring Endless Loop Attachment (SAUS)
PAMELA	Plan-Applier Mechanism for English Language Analysis (SAUS)
PAMELA	Process Abstraction Method for Embedded Large Applications (SAUS)
PAMETON	Paracetamol and Methionine [Pain-relief drug]
PAMETRADA	Parsons Marine Experimental Turbine Research and Development Association (SAUS)
PAMF	Portable Arc Melting Furnace
PAMF	Programmable Analogue Matched Filter (PDAA)
PAM FILE	Pamphlet File (SAUS)
PAM/FM	Pulse Amplitude Modulated-Frequency Modulated (SAUS)
PAM-FM	Pulse Amplitude Modulation - Frequency Modulation [Electronics]
PAmh	Amherst Papyri [A publication] (OCD)
PamHld	Pamida Holdings Corp. [Associated Press] (SAG)
PAMI	Performing Arts Management Institute (SAUS)
PAMI	Personnel Accounting Machine Installation
PAMI	Prairie Agricultural Machinery Institute [Canada]
PAMI	Primary Angioplasty in Myocardial Infarction [Cardiology study]
PAMI	Professional Arts Management Institute (EA)
PAMICONUS	Personnel Accounting Machine Installation, Continental United States (SAUS)
PA Microphone	Public Address Microphone (SAUS)
PAMIE	Physical and Mental Impairment of Function Evaluation [Medicine] (DMAA)
PAMIF	Physical and Mental Impairment-of-Function [Scale] [Medicine] (DB)
PAMII	Protection and Advocacy for Mentally Ill Individuals Act [1986]
PAMIPAC	Personnel Accounting Machine Installation Pacific Fleet (SAUS)
PAMIR	Passive Airborne Modular Infra-Red (SAUS)
PAMIR	Passive and Active Microwave and Infrared Radiometer (SAUS)
PAMIRASAT	Passive Microwave Radiometer Satellite (PDAA)
PAMIRASAT	Primary Afferent Depolarization (PDAA)
PAMIS	Processing and Manufacturing in Space [European Space Agency]
PAMIS	Psychological Operations Automated Management Information System (MCD)
PAMIS	PSYOP Automated Manpower Information System (SAUS)
PA Misc	Pennsylvania Miscellaneous Reports [A publication] (DLA)
PAML	Pan American Mail Line
PAML	Program Authorized Materials List (SAUS)
PAML	Publicly Accessible Mailing Lists (SAUS)
PAMLPU	Pianoforte Action Makers' Labour Protection Union [British]
PAMM	Payload and Mission Model
PAMM	Precision Automatic Measuring Machine (VLIE)
PAMM	Procurement, Accounts payable and Materials Management (SAUS)
PAMM	Program Against Micronutrient Malnutrition (SAUS)
PAMN	Procurement Aircraft and Missiles, Navy [An appropriation]
PAMN	Propiono Atropine Methyl Nitrate (SAUS)
PAMNET	Public Affairs Management Network [Air Force]
PAMO	Pacific Airlift Management Office [Military]
PAMO	Port Air Materiel Office
PAMP	Pampero [River Plate gale] [Nautical term] (DSUE)
PAMP	Plasma-Assisted Materials Processing (SAUS)
PAMP	Precision-Aimed Mortar Projectile (SAUS)
PAMP	Public Art Master Plan (SAUS)
PAMP2	Pulmonary Artery Mean Pressure [Medicine] (MEDA)
PAMPA	Pulmonary Artery Medium Pressure [Medicine]
PAMPA	Pacific Area Movement Priority Agency [Military]
PAMPA	Precision Aerobatics Model Pilots Association (EA)

PamPAC	Pamela's Political Action Committee [Nickname of "Democrats for the '80's," a committee founded by Pamela Harriman]
PAM-PDM....	Product and Machine Performance (SAUS)
PAM-PDM....	Pulse Amplitude Modulation-Pulse Duration Modulation (SAUS)
PAMPER	Practical Application of Mid-Points for Exponential Regression
PAMPH	Pamphlet [Freight]
Pamph Laws...	Pamphlet Laws, Acts [A publication] (DLA)
Pamphl Laws...	Pamphlet Laws, Acts [A publication] (DLA)
PAMPS	Poly(Acrylamidomethyl Propane) Sulphonic Acid [Organic chemistry]
PAMPUS	Photons for Atomic and Molecular Processes and Universal Studies [Physics]
PAMR	Anchorage/Merrill Field [Alaska] [ICAO location identifier] (ICLI)
PAMR	Public Access Mobile Radio (VLIE)
Pamrapo	Pamrapo Bancorp, Inc. [Associated Press] (SAG)
PAMRF	Palo Alto Medical Research Foundation [Research center] (RCD)
PAMRI	Peripheral Adapter Module Replacement Item (CTAS)
PAMRS	Parameter Adaptive Model Reference System
PAMS..........	Pacific Advanced Media Studies [Australia]
PAMS..........	Pacific Armies Management Seminar
PAMS..........	Pacific AUTODIN Multiplex System (SAUS)
PAMS..........	Pad Abort Measuring System [NASA] (KSC)
PAMS..........	Paging Area Memory Space [Computer science] (IAA)
PAMS..........	Parallel Application Management System (SAUS)
PAMS..........	Parts Management System
PAMS..........	Passive Multifrequency Microwave Scanner Radiometer (SAUS)
PAMS..........	Pentax Analytical Measurement System (SAUS)
PAMS..........	Photo and Audio/visual Management System (SAUS)
PAMS..........	Photochemical Assessment Monitoring Station (EEVL)
PAMS..........	Photogrammetric Analytical Measurement System (SAUS)
PAMS..........	Plan Analysis and Modeling System (MHDB)
PAMS..........	Point Anti-Missile System (SAUS)
PAMS..........	Portable Acoustic Monitoring System
PAMS..........	Post-Accident Monitoring System [Nuclear energy] (NRCH)
PAMS..........	Predictive Aircraft Maintenance System
PAMS..........	Preselected Alternate Master-Slave [Telecommunications] (TEL)
PAMS..........	Printing Advisory and Management Service (DGA)
PAMS..........	Proceedings of the American Mathematical Society [A publication]
PAMS..........	Procurement Action Management System (MCD)
PAMS..........	Public Access Message System
PAM SCAD...	Program of Action To Mitigate the Social Cost of Adjustment (SAUS)
PAM Signal...	Pulse-Amplitude-Modulated Signal (SAUS)
PAMT..........	Port Authority Marine Terminal (SAUS)
PAMTGG	Pan Am Makes the Going Great [Title of ballet choreographed by George Balanchine, taken from Pan American World Airways' slogan] [Pronounced "pam-ti-guh-guh"]
PAMUSA......	Post-Attack Mobilization of the United States Army
PAMUX	Parallel Addressable Multiplexer [Telecommunications] (IAA)
PAMV..........	Petunia Asteroid Mosaic Virus [Plant pathology]
PAMWA	Pan American Medical Women's Alliance (EA)
PAMX..........	Pancho's Mexican Buffet [NASDAQ symbol] (TTSB)
PAMX..........	Pancho's Mexican Buffet, Inc. [NASDAQ symbol] (NQ)
PAN	National Action Party [Mexico] [Political party] (PD)
PAN	Pagans Against Nukes [British] (DI)
PAN	Paladin Fuel Technology [Vancouver Stock Exchange symbol]
PAN	Pan African Congress (SAUS)
PAN	Panama [ANSI three-letter standard code] (CNC)
Pan	Panama (VRA)
PAN	Pan American Navigation (SAUS)
PAN	Panartriitis Nodosa (SAUS)
PAN	Panchromatic (DEN)
pan	Panchromatic [Photography] (WDMC)
pan .../......	Pancreas (STED)
Pan	Panegyricus [of Pliny the Younger] [Classical studies] (OCD)
PAN	Panel (SAUS)
PAN	Paneled (WGA)
PAN	Panimavida [Chile] [Seismograph station code, US Geological Survey] [Closed] (SEIS)
PAN	Panis [Bread] [Pharmacy] (ROG)
pan	Panjabi [MARC language code] [Library of Congress] (LCCP)
pan	Panorama
PAN	Panoramic (MSA)
Pan	Panormitanus [Nicholas de Tudeschis] [Deceased, 1445] [Authority cited in pre-1607 legal work] (DSA)
Pan	Pantheon [Record label] [France, etc.]
pan	Pantomime (GROV)
PAN	Pantry (MSA)
PAN	Parents Against Narcotics (SAUS)
PAN	Partido de Accion Nacional [Nicaragua] [Political party] (EY)
PAN	Pattani [Thailand] [Airport symbol] (OAG)
PAN	Peace Action Network (EA)
PAN	Pennsylvania Animal Network [Coalition operated by Trans-Species Unlimited]
PAN	Pennsylvania Association of Notaries (EA)
PAN	Percussion Actuated Nonelectric [An explosive disrupter]
PAN	Performing Artists Network [Electronic network]
PAN	Periaortic Nodes [Medicine] (MELL)
PAN	Periarteritis Nodosa [Also, PN] [Medicine]
PAN	Periodic Alternating Nystagmus [Ophthalmology]
PAN	Peripheral Area Network (VLIE)
PAN	Peroxyacetyl Nitrate [Lacrimator]
PAN	Peroxyacetylnitrate (SAUS)
PAN	Personal Account Number (VLIE)
PAN	Personal Area Network [Computer science]
PAN	Personnel Advice Notes (HEAS)
PAN	Pesticides Action Network (EA)
PAN	Phase Advance Network [Computer science] (VLIE)
PAN	Physical Association Number (SAUS)
PAN	Polled Access Network
PAN	Pollution Abatement Notice [Environmental science] (COE)
PAN	Polska Akademia Nauk [Polish Academy of Sciences] [Also, an information service or system] (IID)
PAN	Polyacrylonitrile [Organic chemistry]
PAN	Polyarteritis Nodosa [Medicine]
PAN	Porte-Avion Nucleaire
PAN	Positional Alcohol Nystagmus [Physiology]
PAN	Practical Active Network [Computer science] (VLIE)
PAN	Preauricular Node (SAUS)
PAN	Primary Access Network [Computer science] (VLIE)
PAN	Primary Account Number [Business term]
PAN	Primary Alerting Network (SAUS)
PAN	Project Authorization Notice (MCD)
PAN	Propodial Anlage [Zoology]
PAN	Publications Account Number [DoD]
PAN	Puromycin Aminonucleoside [Medicine] (DMAA)
PAN	Pyridineazohydroxynaphthalene (SAUS)
PAN	Pyridylazonaphthol [An indicator] [Chemistry]
PAN	Switchboard Panel [Telecommunications] (TEL)
PA$_{N20}$	Mean Alveolar Nitrous Oxide Tension [Medicine] (DAVI)
PANA	Panaco, Inc. [NASDAQ symbol] (SAG)
PANA	PanAfrican News Agency (EAIO)
PANA	Pan-African Press Agency (SAUS)
PANA	Pan-Asia News Agency Ltd. [Also, PANASIA] [Hong Kong]
PANA	Pan-Asia Newspaper Alliance (SAUS)
PANA	Pan-Asian Newspaper Alliance [Also, PANANEWS] (NADA)
PANA	Panorama (VRA)
PANA	Polish-American Numismatic Association (EA)
PANABANK...	Banco Panamericano [Panama] (EY)
PanaBev	Panamerican Beverages [Commercial firm] [Associated Press] (SAG)
PANACEA	Package for Analysis of Networks of Asynchronous Computers with Extended Asymptotics (SAUS)
Panaco	Panaco, Inc. [Associated Press] (SAG)
PANAFTEL ...	Pan-African Telecommunications (BARN)
PANAFTEL ...	Pan-African Telecommunications Network (TELE)
PANAFTEL Network...	Pan-African Telecommunications Network (SAUS)
PANAFU	Pan African Union (SAUS)
PANAGRA	Pan American Grace Airways, Inc. [Also, PAGA]
PANAIR........	Panama Air Lines
PANAL	Papuan National Alliance [Political party] (PPW)
PANALU	Parti National Lumumba [Lumumba National Party] [Political party]
PANALYZER...	Peroxyacetyl Nitrate Analyzer (SAUS)
Pan-Am........	Pan American (SAUS)
PANAM	Pan American World Airways (SAUS)
PAN-AM.......	Pan American World Airways, Inc. [See also PA, PAA, PN]
PANAMAC....	Pan American World Airways Communications System
PANAMAC System...	Pan-American Airways Communications System (SAUS)
PanAmC.......	Pan Am Corp. [Associated Press] (SAG)
PANAMIN.....	Presidential Arm for National Minorities (SAUS)
PanAmSat....	Pan American Satellite [Greenwich, CT] [Telecommunications service] (TSSD)
Pan-Am TS..	Pan-American Treaty Series [A publication] (DLA)
PANANEWS...	Pan-Asia Newspaper Alliance (SAUS)
PANANEWS...	Pan-Asian Newspaper Alliance [Also, PANA] (NADA)
PANAR.........	Panoramic RADAR
PANASH.......	Palaeoclimates of the Northern and Southern Hemispheres (SAUS)
PANASH.......	Paleoclimates of the Northern and Southern Hemisphere (SAUS)
PANASIA......	Organization of Pan Asian American Women (EA)
PANASIA......	Pan-Asia News Agency Ltd. [Also, PANA] [Hong Kong]
PanASlv......	Pan American Silver Corp. [Associated Press] (SAG)
Panax	Panax Pharmaceutical Co. Ltd. [Associated Press] (SAG)
PanaxP.......	Panax Pharmaceutical Co. Ltd. [Associated Press] (SAG)
PANB	Panic Bolt
PANC	Anchorage/International [Alaska] [ICAO location identifier] (ICLI)
panc...........	pancreas (SAUS)
PANC	Power Amplifier Neutralizing Capacitor (DEN)
P-ANCA	Perinuclear Anti-Neutrophilic Cytoplasmic Antibody [Medicine] (DMAA)
PANCAN.......	[The] Panama Canal
PANCANCO...	Panama Canal Co. [Superseded by Panama Canal Commission]
PANCAP......	Practical Annual Capacity [FAA]
panchr	Panchromatic (VRA)
PancMx.......	Pancho's Mexican Buffet, Inc. [Associated Press] (SAG)
PANCO	Procurement Aids Noncommissioned Officer [Marine Corps]
Pand	[The] Pandects [A publication] (DLA)
PAND	Pandering [FBI standardized term]
PAND	Passive Air Navigation Device
PAND	Performing Artists for Nuclear Disarmament (EA)
PAND	Primary Adrenocortical Nodular Dysplasia [Endocrinology] (DMAA)
P & A	Page and Adams' Code [1912] [A publication] (DLA)
P & A	Pay and Allowances
P & A	Pennsylvania & Atlantic Railroad Co. (IIA)
P & A	Percussion and Auscultation [Medicine] (AMHC)
P and A	Percussion and Auscultation (SAUS)
P & A	Percussion and Auscultation [Medicine]
PANDA	Performance and Demand Analyser (PDAA)
P & A	Personnel and Administration [Army] (AABC)
P and A	Personnel and Administration (SAUS)
P and A	Pioneer and Ammunition (SAUS)
P & A	Pioneer and Ammunition
P&A...........	Planning and Analysis (ABAC)
P & A..........	Plans and Analysis

PANDA........	Portable Array for Numerical Data Acquisition [*Instrumentation*]	P&FA	Program and File Analysis [*Computer science*] (CIST)
PANDA........	Portable Atmospheric Noise Data Acquisition (SAUS)	Pand Flo....	Pandectae Florentinae [*A publication*] (DSA)
P&A	Precision and Accuracy (COE)	P & FM	Programs and Financial Management [*Navy*]
P and A	Prediction and Allocation (SAUS)	P & F Radio Reg...	Pike and Fischer's Radio Regulation Reporter [*A publication*] (DLA)
P & A	Prediction and Allocation		
PANDA........	Prestel Advanced Network Design Architecture	P & FS	Particles and Fields Subsatellite [*NASA*] (KSC)
PANDA........	Prevent Abuse and Neglect Dental Awareness (SAUS)	P & G	Post and Girder [*Lumber*] (DAC)
P and A	Price and Availability (SAUS)	P & G	Procter & Gamble Co.
P & A	Price and Availability	P & G News...	Plants and Gardens News [*A publication*]
P & A...........	Pricing and Acceptability Claims Processing System [*Health insurance*] (GHCT)	P & H	Patton, Jr., and Heath's Reports [*Virginia Special Court of Appeals*] [*A publication*] (DLA)
P & A...........	Print and Advertising [*Marketing*] (ECON)	p&h..........	Postage and Handling (NTIO)
P & A...........	Priorities and Allocations (MUGU)	P&H..........	Postage and Handling (WDMC)
P&A..........	Prizes and Awards Committee (ACII)	P&HEP......	Plasma and High Energy Physics (SAUS)
P & A	Procedures and Analysis	P&HTGR...	Peach Bottom High-Temperature Gas-Cooled Reactor (SAUS)
P and A	Procurement and Assignment (SAUS)	P & I	Passenger and Immigration Lists [*A publication*]
P & A	Procurement and Assignment	P & I	Performance and Interface [*Specification*] [*NASA*] (NASA)
P & A	Professional and Administrative (AAG)	P&I..........	Physics & Irradiation (SAUS)
P and A	Professional and Administrative (SAUS)	P & I	Piping and Instrumentation [*Nuclear energy*] (NRCH)
P&A..........	Program and Acquisition (ACAE)	P&I..........	Planning & Integration (SAUS)
PANDA........	Programmers Analysis and Development Aid (SAUS)	P & I	Pneumonia and Influenza (MELL)
P&A..........	Programming and Analysis (SAUS)	P & I	Postage and Insurance
P & A	Protection and Advocacy [*System*] [*To protect the rights of developmentally disabled persons*]	P&I..........	Principal and Interest [*Finance*] (DFIT)
		P and I	Principal and Interest (SAUS)
PandaPrj....	[*The*] Panda Project, Inc. [*Associated Press*] (SAG)	p&i...........	Principal and Interest (SHCU)
P & AR	Pacific & Arctic Railway (MHDB)	P & I	Privileges and Immunities [*Legal shorthand*] (LWAP)
P & AW	Paging and Area Warning	P&I..........	Probe and Irrigate (SAUS)
P&B..........	Pain & Burning [*Medicine*] (DMAA)	P & I	Properties and Installations
P & B	Phenobarbital and Belladonna [*A drug regimen*]	P & I	Protection and Indemnity [*Insurance*]
P & B	Planning and Budgeting [*Military*] (AFIT)	P and I club...	Protection and Indemnity club (SAUS)
P & B	Price and Budgeting (MCD)	P&ID.........	Piping and Instrumentation Design (SAUS)
P & B	Printing and Binding [*Publishing*]	P & ID	Piping and Instrumentation Diagram [*or Design or Drawing*] [*Calcomp Ltd.*] [*Software package*] [*Nuclear energy*] (NRCH)
P & B	Pugsley and Burbridge's New Brunswick Reports [*A publication*] (DLA)		
		P & ID	Process and Instrumentation Diagram [*Engineering*] (NRCH)
P&C..........	Parents and Citizens Association (SAUS)	P&II.........	Personalization and Identification Institute (NTPA)
P & C	Parge and Core [*Construction*]	P&IM Rev...	Production Inventory Management Reviews (SAUS)
P & C	Performance and Control (SSD)	PANDIT......	Produce an Adjusted Nuclear Data Input Tape (SAUS)
P & C	Physical and Chemical (AAG)	P & J	Plaza y Janes [*Publisher*] [*Spain*]
P&C..........	Precautions and Contraindications [*Medicine*] (MELL)	P&J..........	Protection and Indemnity (EBF)
P & C	Prideaux and Cole's English Reports [*4 New Sessions Cases*] [*A publication*] (DLA)	P & K	Perry and Knapp's English Election Cases [*1833*] [*A publication*] (DLA)
P & C	Prism and Cover (Test) [*Ophthalmology*]	P & KI	Promisel & Korn, Inc. [*Information service or system*] (IID)
P & C	Procurement and Contracting (AFM)	P & L	Paul and Lisa (EA)
P&C..........	Procurement and Contracting (or Contracts) (SAUS)	P & L	Pioneer & Labour (SAUS)
P&C..........	Property or Casualty	P & L	Points and Lines [*Military*] (CAAL)
P and C	Purchases and Contracts (SAUS)	P&L..........	Power and Light (SAUS)
P & C	Purchasing and Contracting	P & L	Power and Lighting (MSA)
P & C	Put and Call [*Stock exchange term*]	P & L	Pratt & Lambert, Inc.
P & CA	Paying and Collecting Area (AFM)	P & L	Profit and Loss [*Accounting*]
P&CG........	Planning and Coordination Group (SAUS)	P&L..........	Profit and Loss Statement [*Finance*] (DFIT)
P & CO	Plans and Combat Operations	P&L..........	Projects and Logistics (SAUS)
P & CP	Plate and Cylinder Production (DGA)	PANDLCHAR...	Pay and Allowances Chargeable
P & CR	Performance and Compatibility Requirements	P & L Dig Laws...	Pepper and Lewis' Digest of Laws [*Pennsylvania*] [*A publication*] (DLA)
P & CR	Planning and Compensation Reports [*British*]		
P & CR	Property and Compensation Reports [*A publication*] (DLA)	P&L DISTR...	Power and Lighting Distribution (SAUS)
P & CYC	Police and Citizens' Youth Club [*Australia*]	P & LERR	[*The*] Pittsburgh & Lake Erie Railroad Co.
P & D	Law Reports, Probate and Divorce [*England*] [*A publication*] (DLA)	P & L Laws...	Private and Local Laws [*A publication*] (DLA)
P&D..........	Performance and Demonstration	P & M...........	Law Reports, Probate and Matrimonial Cases [*England*] [*A publication*] (DLA)
P & D	Perry and Davison's English Queen's Bench Reports [*1834-44*] [*A publication*] (DLA)		
		P&M..........	Performance Monitor (SAUS)
P & D	Pick Up and Delivery [*Business term*]	P&M..........	Phase Modulated (or Modulation) (SAUS)
P and D	Pickup and Delivery (SAUS)	P&M..........	Planetary Mission (SAUS)
P & D	Pioneer and Demolition Section [*Army*]	P & M...........	Pollock and Maitland's History of English Common Law [*A publication*] (DLA)
P&D..........	Plug and Display [*Computer science*]		
P & D	Pressing and Distribution (WDMC)	P & M	Probate and Matrimonial [*Legal*] [*British*]
P&D..........	Price and Delivery (SAUS)	P&M..........	Processes and Materials (NASA)
P & D	Probate and Divorce [*Legal*] [*British*]	P&M..........	Program Milestone (SAUS)
P & D	Procurement and Distribution [*Military*]	P&MC........	Procurement and Material Control (SAUS)
P&D..........	Production and Deployment	P & MHEL ...	Pollock and Maitland's History of English Common Law [*A publication*] (DLA)
P & D	Promote and Develop Fishery Products Pertaining to American Fisheries Account [*National Oceanic and Atmospheric Administration*] (GFGA)		
		P & MP.......	Paris & Mount Pleasant Railroad (IIA)
		P & N	Piedmont and Northern Railroad (AD)
P & DD	Plumbing and Deck Drain (MSA)	p & n	Psychiatry and Neurology (AD)
P & DR........	Price and Delivery Request	P&N..........	Psychiatry and Neurology (SAUS)
P & DSEC ...	Pioneer and Demolition Section [*Army*]	P & N	Psychiatry and Neurology
P & E.........	Pike and Eel [*A pub at Cambridge University*] [*British*] (DSUE)	p & o	Paints and Oil (AD)
P&E..........	Planning and Estimating (AAG)	p & o	Paints and Oil
P&E..........	Planning and Evaluation (ACAE)	P & O	Parasites and Ova [*Gastroenterology*] (DAVI)
P&E..........	Pneumonia and Empyema (MELL)	P & O	Peninsular & Occidental Steamship Co. (AD)
P & E	Privileges and Elections Subcommittee [*US Senate*]	P&O..........	Peninsular & Oriental Line (SAUS)
P & E	Procurement and Expedition	P & O	Peninsular & Oriental Steam Navigation Co. [*Steamship line*]
P & E.........	Propellants and Explosives [*Military*] (AABC)	P & O	Performance and Operational [*Test or reports*]
P & E.........	Pyrotechnical and Explosive [*NASA*] (KSC)	p & o	Pickled and Oiled (AD)
Pandect Flor...	Pandectae Florentinae [*A publication*] (DSA)	P&O..........	Pickled and Oiled (SAUS)
P & EE........	Proof and Experimental Establishments (RDA)	P & O	Pickled and Oiled
P & EML.......	Personnel and Equipment Modification List [*Air Force*]	P&O..........	Pipe and Operating (SAUS)
P & ESI	Physical and Engineering Sciences Division [*Army Research Office*]	P & O	Planning and Operations
P & F..........	P & F Industries, Inc. [*Associated Press*] (SAG)	P & O	Planning and Organization
P & F..........	Petroleum and Fuel	P & O	Plans and Operations Division [*War Department*] [*World War II*]
P & F..........	Pike and Fischer's Administrative Law [*A publication*] (DLA)	P & O	Portland & Ogdensburgh Railroad
P & F..........	Pike and Fischer's Federal Rules Service [*A publication*] (DLA)	P & O	Positioning and Orientation
P & F..........	Pike and Fischer's OPA Price Service [*A publication*] (DLA)	P&O..........	Prosthetic and Orthotic [*Health insurance*] (GHCT)
P & F..........	Planning and Forecasting (MCD)	P & OC	Peninsular & Oriental (Steam Navigation) Co. Ltd. (ROG)
P & F..........	Plant and Facilities	P & O Div....	Planning and Operations Division [*Military*]
P&F..........	Program and Financial Plan (SAUS)	p & oo........	Pianistic and Orchestral Orgasm [*Music*] (AD)

PANDORA.... Passive and Active Signal Digital Correlator Analyzer (MCD)
PANDORA.... Preserving and Accessing Networked Documentary Resources of Australia (SAUS)
PANDORA.... Prototyping a Navigation Database of Road Network Attributes (SAUS)
P & OSCC.... Plans and Operations for the Safeguard Communications Command [Army] (RDA)
P & OSNCo.. Peninsular & Oriental Steam Navigation Co. [Steamship line]
P&OT........ Physical & Occupational Therapy (CMD)
P & P........ Packing and Preservation
P & P........ Pam and Peter Fisher [Commercial firm] [British]
p & p........ Parsimonious and Penurious (AD)
P&P......... Past and Present (SAUS)
P&P......... Pay & Privileges (WDAA)
p&p......... Payments and Progress (AD)
P and P...... Payments and Progress Committee [NATO] (NATG)
P & P........ Peace and Prosperity Issue [Politics]
P & P........ Pins and Plaster [Orthopedics] (DAVI)
P&P......... Planning and Programming (SAUS)
P & P........ Plans and Policies
P & P........ Plans and Programs
P&P......... Policy and Procedure Statements (SAUS)
p&p......... Postage & Packing (WDAA)
P&P......... Postage and Packing (SAUS)
P & P........ Postage and Packing [Shipping]
P&P......... Preservation and Packing
P & P........ Pride and Prejudice [Novel by Jane Austen]
P & P........ Procurement and Production [Military]
P & P........ Production and Procurement [Military]
P & P/CT..... Prothrombin and Proconvertin Control [Hematology] (DAVI)
P & PD...... Percussion and Postural Drainage
P&P Intnl.... Pulp and Paper International Annual Review (SAUS)
P&P Jrl...... Pulp and Paper Journal (SAUS)
P & PM....... Packing and Packaging Manual (MCD)
p & pp....... Pull and Push Plate (AD)
P & PP....... Pull and Push Plate
P&P Qtly..... Pulp and Paper Quarterly Statistics (SAUS)
P&PR........ Psychoanalysis and the Psychoanalytic Review (SAUS)
P & PU...... Peoria and Pekin Union [Railroad] (AD)
P & PW...... Publicity and Psychological Warfare
p & q......... Peace and Quiet (AD)
P & Q........ Peace and Quiet
P and Q....... Prime Quality [Slang]
p & r......... Parallax and Refraction (AD)
P&R.......... Parks & Recreation [A publication] (BRI)
P & R........ Pelvic and Rectal [Medicine]
P & R........ Performance and Resources (NASA)
P & R........ Philadelphia & Reading Railway
P & R........ Picture and Resume [Theatre slang]
P & R........ Pigott and Rodwell's Reports in Common Pleas [1843-45] [A publication] (DLA)
P&R.......... Planning & Research Ltd. (SAUS)
P & R........ Planning and Review (MCD)
P&R.......... Plans and Requirements (SAUS)
P & R........ Post and Rail
P & R........ Pulse and Respiration [Medicine]
P and RD..... Decisions of the Department of the Interior, Pension and Retirement Claims [United States] [A publication] (DLA)
P&RF........ Personnel and Reserve Force (ACAE)
P&RP........ Production and Research Property [Department of Defense]
P & RT....... Physical and Recreational Training [Navy] [British]
P & S........ Packers and Stockyards
P & S........ Pain and Suffering (DAVI)
P&S......... Panel and Shelf
P & S........ Paracentesis and Suction [Medicine]
P & S........ Pay and Supply [Coast Guard]
P & S........ Perkins & Squier [Paper manufacturer]
P&S......... Permanent and Stationary (SAUS)
P&S......... Personnel and Security (SAUS)
P & S........ Physicians and Surgeons (DAVI)
P & S........ [The] Pittsburg & Shawmut Railroad Co.
P & S........ Planking and Strutting [Construction]
P&S......... Planning and Scheduling (CIST)
P and S...... Plugged and Suspended (SAUS)
P & S........ Port and Starboard
PANDS........ Print and Search Processor [Computer science]
P & S........ Purchase and Sale [Business term]
P & SA....... Packers and Stockyards Administration [Department of Agriculture]
P&SA......... Payload and Servicing Accommodations [NASA] (SPST)
P&SA......... Program and Systems Analysis (SAUS)
P&SB......... Portland & South Bend (SAUS)
P & SF....... Panhandle & Santa Fe Railway Co.
P & SI....... Pay and Supply Instruction [Coast Guard]
P & SM...... Procurement and Subcontract Management [NASA] (NASA)
P & SNP..... Pay and Subsistence of Naval Personnel [Budget appropriation title]
P&SS......... Provost & Security Services (SAUS)
P&T.......... Packaging and Transportation (SAUS)
P & T........ Permanent and Total [Disability] [Medicine]
P & T........ Personnel and Training [Military] (MUGU)
P & T........ Pharmacy and Therapeutics
P & T........ Plans and Training [Military] (IIA)
P&T.......... Pointing and Tracking (ACAE)
P&T.......... Pope and Talbot (SAUS)
P & T........ Posts and Timbers [Technical drawings]
P&T.......... Privilege & Tenure Committee (SAUS)

P & T......... Professional and Technology [Category] [British]
P & T......... Pugsley and Trueman's New Brunswick Reports [A publication] (DLA)
P & T......... Purge-and-Trap [Technique] [Environmental Protection Agency]
P & TD ...... Parts and Tool Disposition (SAA)
P & T Div .... Plans and Training Division [Military]
P&U.......... Pharmacia & Upjohn AB [Commercial firm] [Sweden]
P & V .... Percuss and Vibrate [Medicine] (DAVI)
P&V.......... Pressure and Velocity (SAUS)
P & V .... Pyloroplasty and Vagotomy [Medicine]
P&V.......... Pyloroplasty and Vagtomy (SAUS)
P & VE....... Propulsion and Vehicle Engineering [A Marshall Space Flight Center laboratory] (MCD)
P & VE-ADM... Propulsion and Vehicle Engineering - Administrative [Marshall Space Flight Center Laboratory] (SAA)
P & VE-DIR... Propulsion and Vehicle Engineering - Director [Marshall Space Flight Center Laboratory] (SAA)
P & VE-E .... Propulsion and Vehicle Engineering - Vehicle Engineering [Marshall Space Flight Center Laboratory] (SAA)
P & VE-F .... Propulsion and Vehicle Engineering - Advanced Flight Systems [Marshall Space Flight Center Laboratory] (SAA)
P & VE-M .... Propulsion and Vehicle Engineering - Engineering Materials [Marshall Space Flight Center Laboratory] (SAA)
P & VE-N .... Propulsion and Vehicle Engineering - Nuclear Vehicle Projects [Marshall Space Flight Center Laboratory] (SAA)
P & VE-P .... Propulsion and Vehicle Engineering - Propulsion and Mechanics [Marshall Space Flight Center Laboratory] (SAA)
P & VE-PC... Propulsion and Vehicle Engineering - Program Coordination [Marshall Space FlightCenter Laboratory] (SAA)
P & VE-REL... Propulsion and Vehicle Engineering - Reliability [Marshall Space Flight Center Laboratory] (SAA)
P & VE-S .... Propulsion and Vehicle Engineering - Structures [Marshall Space Flight Center Laboratory] (SAA)
P & VE-TS ... Propulsion and Vehicle Engineering - Technical and Scientific Staff [Marshall Space Flight Center Laboratory] (SAA)
P & VE-V .... Propulsion and Vehicle Engineering - Vehicle Systems Integration [Marshall Space Flight Center Laboratory] (SAA)
P&VIR......... Pure and Vulcanized India Rubber (SAUS)
P & VIR ...... Pure and Vulcanized Rubber Insulation
P&VR......... Pure and Vulcanized Rubber (SAUS)
P&W.......... Particles and Waves (SPST)
P & W .... Penrose and Watts' Pennsylvania Reports [1829-32] [A publication] (DLA)
P & W .... Pension and Welfare (WDMC)
P & W .... Post and Wire (ADA)
P & W .... Pratt & Whitney [Aircraft]
P&W.......... Pratt and Whitney Aircraft Division, United Aircraft Corp. (SAUS)
P & WA ...... Pratt & Whitney Aircraft (KSC)
P&W I........ Poets and Writers Inc. (SAUS)
P&WV......... Pittsburgh & West Virginia (SAUS)
P & WV ...... Pittsburgh & West Virginia Railroad
P&Y.......... Pitch and Yaw
P&Z.......... Planning and Zoning (PA)
PANE .... Performance Analysis of Networks, Electrical
PanEC......... Panhandle Eastern Corp. [Associated Press] (SAG)
PANEC .... Performance Analysis of Electrical Circuits (SAUS)
PANEES ...... Professional Association of Naval Electronics Engineers and Scientists (SAUS)
Paneg......... Panegyricus [of Isocrates] [Classical studies] (OCD)
panendo ...... Panendoscopy [Medicine]
PANES .... Prior Active Navy Enlisted Service
PANES .... Program for Analysis of Nonlinear Equilibrium and Stability [NASA]
PANESS ...... Physical and Neurologic Examination for Soft Signs [Medicine] (MELL)
PA News Letter... Physical Anthropology News Letter (SAUS)
PANF......... Plan Account Number File [IRS]
PANFERT ..... Pregnancy After Infertility [Medicine]
PANFI .... Precision Automatic Noise Figure Indicator
PANFX .... Phoenix-Engemann Nifty Fifty Cl.A [Mutual fund ticker symbol] (SG)
PANGAEA.... Paleo-Network for Geological and Environmental Data (SAUS)
PANGCS...... Prior Active National Guard Commissioned Service
PANGES...... Prior Active National Guard Enlisted Service
PANGIS........ Pan-African Network for a Geological Information System [UNESCO] (DUND)
PANGLOSS... Parallel Architecture for Networking Gateways Linking OSI Systems (NITA)
PAngV......... Preisangabenverordnung (SAUS)
PANH .... Panhandling [FBI standardized term]
PANH .... Picolinaldehyde Nicotinoylhydrazone [Reagent]
Pan-Hd .... Pan Head (SAUS)
PANHONLIB... Panama, Honduras, and Liberia [Acronym used to refer to merchant ships operating under "flags of convenience"]
PANI .... Patriarch Athenagoras National Institute (EA)
PAni.......... Polyaniline (SAUS)
PANIC .... Parameter Analysis of Integrated Circuits (SAUS)
PANIC .... Planned Attack on Nine Inner Cities [to build education parks]
PANIC .... Potential and Needs, Investments and Capabilities (SAUS)
Panj C .... Panjab Code [India] [A publication] (DLA)
Pank Jur .... Pankhurst's Jurisprudence [A publication] (DLA)
PAnL......... Lebanon Valley College, Annville, PA [Library symbol] [Library of Congress] (LCLS)
PANL .... Universal Display [NASDAQ symbol] (TTSB)
PANL .... Universal Display Corp. [NASDAQ symbol] (SAG)
PANLAR....... PanAmerican League Against Rheumatism [Canada] (EAIO)

PANLIBHON...   Panama, Liberia, and Honduras [*Acronym used to refer to merchant ships operating under "flags of convenience"*]
PANLIBHONCO...   Panama-Liberia-Honduras-Costa Rica
PANLW ....   Universal Display Wrrt [*NASDAQ symbol*]   (TTSB)
Pan Met.......   Pan American Meteorological Station   (SAUS)
PANMV ....   Panicum Mosaic Virus [*Plant pathology*]
PANN ....   Professional Association of Nursery Nurses [*British*]   (DBA)
PAN NA......   Pesticides Action Network, North America   (GNE)
PANNAP.......   Panavia New Aircraft Project   (MCD)
PANNA RC ...   Pesticide Action Network North America Regional Center   (EA)
PANNDA ......   Precedent Analysis by Nearest Neighbor Discriminant Analysis
PANNR.........   Previous Applicants Need Not Reapply [*Civil Service*]
pano ....   Panoramic   (ADWA)
panograms....   panoramas   (SAUS)
Panol ....   Panology   (SAUS)
PANOPO ......   Pacific to Atlantic via North Pole   (SAUS)
PANOR........   Panoramic   (IAA)
Panor...........   Panormitanus [*Nicholas de Tudeschis*] [*Deceased, 1445*] [*Authority cited in pre-1607 legal work*]   (DSA)
PANOS........   Panos Institute [*An association*]   (EA)
PA NP ....   Brightly's Pennsylvania Nisi Prius Reports [*A publication*]   (DLA)
PANPA ....   Pacific Area Newspaper Publishers Association   (EAIO)
Pan Phot......   Panoramic Photograph   (SAUS)
PANPRA......   Parti Nationaliste Progressiste Revolutionnaire [*Haiti*] [*Political party*]   (EY)
PANPUB.......   Panel Publishers   (DLA)
PANR ....   Panhandle Royalty Co. [*NASDAQ symbol*]   (SAG)
PANRA ....   Panhandle Rty [*NASDAQ symbol*]   (TTSB)
PanRoyl ......   Panhandle Royalty Co. [*Associated Press*]   (SAG)
PANS ....   Peripheral Autonomic Nervous System [*Medicine*]   (MELL)
PANS ....   Personal-Area Networks
PANS ....   Pest Articles News Summaries [*Commonwealth Mycological Institute*] [*Kew, England*] [*A publication*]
PANS ....   Position and Navigation System   (SAUS)
PANS ....   Positioning and Navigation System
PANS ....   Potentially Attractive New Services   (SAUS)
PANS ....   Pretty Advanced New Stuff   (SAUS)
PANS ....   Pretty Amazing New Services   (NITA)
PANS ....   Pretty Amazing New Stuff   (SAUS)
PANS ....   Priority Admission to Nursery Schools   (AIE)
PANS ....   Procedures for Air Navigation Services [*ICAO*]
PANS ....   Programmable Augmented Noise Source [*Military*]   (CAAL)
PANS ....   Public Archives of Nova Scotia   (SAUS)
PANS ....   Puromycin Aminonucleoside [*Biochemistry*]
PANSDOC ....   Pakistan National Scientific and Documentation Center [*Later, PASTIC*]
PANSDOC ....   Pakistan National Scientific and Technology Documentation Centre   (NITA)
PANSEAFRON...   Panama Sea Frontier
PANSIP ....   Propulsion and Airframe Structural Integration Program   (SAUS)
PANSMET ....   Procedures for Air Navigation Services - Meteorology   (IEEE)
PANS/OPS ...   Procedures for Air Navigation Services/ Aircraft Operations   (SAUS)
PANS/RAC ...   Procedures for Air Navigation Services/ Rules of the Air Traffic Services   (SAUS)
PANSS ....   Positive and Negative Syndrome Scale [*Medicine*]   (DMAA)
PANSW.......   Playgroup Association of New South Wales [*Australia*]
PANSW.......   Police Association of New South Wales [*Australia*]
PANSY ....   Program Analysis System   (PDAA)
PANT ....   Annette Island [*Alaska*] [*ICAO location identifier*]   (ICLI)
PANT ....   Pantex Plant [*Department of Energy*] [*Amarillo, TX*]   (GAAI)
PANT ....   Pantograph   (KSC)
pant ....   Pantomine
PANT ....   Police Association of the Northern Territory [*Australia*]
Pantch ....   Panatech Research & Development Corp. [*Associated Press*]   (SAG)
Pantes ....   Panel Tester   (SAUS)
Pantex ....   Pantex Site
Pantex EIS...   Pantex Site Environmental Impact Statement
panth ....   pantheism   (SAUS)
panth ....   pantheist   (SAUS)
PANTHEON...   Public Access by New Technology to Highly Elaborate Online Networks [*Computer science*]   (PDAA)
PANTIES ......   Passive Automatic Nighttime Tracking Investigation and Evaluation Studies [*DoD*]
PAntin..........   [*The*] Antinoe Papyrus of Theocritus [*Classical studies*]   (OCD)
PAntinoop....   Antinoopolis Papyri [*A publication*]   (OCD)
PantiP.........   Peroxidase-Antiperoxidase [*Immunochemistry*]
Panto ....   Pantographic   (SAUS)
panto ....   Pantomime [*British*] [*Slang*]   (WDMC)
PANTO ....   Pantomime
panto ....   pantomimic   (SAUS)
Pan trog ......   Pan troglodytes   (SAUS)
pantrop........   Pantropical [*Botany*]
PANTS ....   Pantaloons   (DSUE)
PANTS ....   Public Acceptance of New Technologies   (SAUS)
PANVALET ...   Direct Access Library Maintenance Package [*Pansophic Systems*]
PANX ....   Panax Pharmaceutical [*NASDAQ symbol*]   (TTSB)
PANX ....   Panax Pharmaceutical Company Ltd. [*NASDAQ symbol*]   (SAG)
PANXU ....   Panax Pharmaceutical Unit [*NASDAQ symbol*]   (TTSB)
PANXW ....   Panax Pharmaceutical Wrrt [*NASDAQ symbol*]   (TTSB)
PANY ....   Platinumsmiths Association of New York   (EA)
PANY ....   Port Authority of New York [*Later, PANYNJ*]
PANYNJ.......   Port Authority of New York and New Jersey [*Formerly, PANY*]
PANZ ....   Public Access New Zealand   (SAUS)
Pao.............   Ascending Aortic Pressure [*Medicine*]   (STED)
PAO ....   Palo Alto, CA [*Location identifier*] [*FAA*]   (FAAL)

PAO ....   Paotow [*Republic of China*] [*Seismograph station code, US Geological Survey*]   (SEIS)
PAO ....   Paragon Group [*NYSE symbol*]   (TTSB)
PAO ....   Paragon Group, Inc. [*NYSE symbol*]   (SAG)
PAO ....   Paramount Resources, Inc. [*Vancouver Stock Exchange symbol*]
PaO.............   Paranoia Obvious [*Psychology*]
PAO ....   Parts Assembly Order   (IAA)
PAO ....   Peacetime Acquisition Objective [*DoD*]   (AFIT)
PAO ....   Peak Acid Output [*Physiology*]
PAO ....   Pediatric Assessment Online   (SAUS)
PAO ....   Penalty Appeals Officer [*IRS*]
PAO ....   Performance Assessment and Oversight   (SAUS)
PA/O ....   Performing Arts/Omaha [*Nebraska*]
PAO ....   Peripheral Airway Obstruction [*Medicine*]   (DMAA)
PAO ....   Personnel Administration Office   (SAUS)
PAO ....   Phenylarsine Oxide
PAO ....   Pinellas Area Office [*Energy Research and Development Administration*]
PAO ....   Plasma Amine Oxidase [*Hematology*]   (DMAA)
PAO ....   Polyalkaline Oxide   (SAUS)
PAO ....   Polyalkyleneoxide [*Organic chemistry*]
PAO ....   Polyalphaolefin [*Organic chemistry*]
PAO ....   Polyamine Oxidase   (STED)
PAO ....   Polynesian Airline Operations Ltd. [*Western Samoa*] [*ICAO designator*]   (FAAC)
PAO ....   Poultry Advisory Officer   (SAUS)
PAO ....   Primary Action Office [*or Officer*] [*Army*]
PAO ....   Prince Albert's Own [*Military unit*] [*British*]
PAO ....   Princeton Area Office   (SAUS)
PAO ....   Principal Administrative Officer
PAO ....   Pro Athletes Outreach   (EA)
PAO ....   Procurement Assistance Office   (AAGC)
PAO ....   Product Activity/Operational Code   (MCD)
PAO ....   Product Assurance Operations [*Army*]
PAO ....   Program Action Officer [*Navy*]   (CAAL)
PAO ....   Project Action Officer [*Air Force*]   (AFIT)
PAO ....   Project Administration Officer [*Military*]   (AFIT)
PAO ....   Property Accountable Officer   (SAUS)
PAO ....   Property Accounting Office   (SAUS)
PAO ....   Property Action Order
PAO ....   Public Affairs Office [*NASA*]
PAO ....   Public Affairs Officer [*Embassies*]
PAO ....   Public Assistance Officer   (DEMM)
PAO ....   Pulmonary Artery Occlusion [*Medicine*]   (DMAA)
PAO ....   Pulsed Avalanche Diode Oscillator [*Telecommunications*]   (IEEE)
PAO ....   Pustulotic Arthroosteitis [*Medicine*]   (DMAA)
PAO2 ....   Alveolar Oxygen Pressure   (WDAA)
PAO2 ....   Arterial Oxygen Pressure   (WDAA)
PaO$_2$ ....   Arterial Partial Pressure of Oxygen [*Medicine*]   (DAVI)
pAO$_2$ ....   Oxygen Pressure on Room Air [*Medicine*]   (DAVI)
PAOA ....   Pan American Odontological Association   (EA)
PAOC ....   Pacific Air Operations Center   (SAUS)
PAOC ....   Pakistan Army Ordnance Corps [*British military*]   (DMA)
PAOC ....   Pan-African Ornithological Congress
PAOC ....   Pentacostal Assemblies of Canada
PAOC ....   Pollution Abatement Operations Center   (MCD)
PAOC ....   Post Award Orientation Conference   (ACAE)
PAOC ....   Principal Administrative Officers Committee [*Chiefs of Staff*] [*World War II*]
PAOCCS 2...   Portuguese Air Command & Control Systems 2   (SAUS)
PAOD ....   Peripheral Arterial Occlusive Disease [*Medicine*]   (MELL)
PAOD ....   Peripheral Arteriosclerotic Occlusive Disease [*Medicine*]   (MAE)
PAODAP.......   Plant and Animal Products Department   (SAUS)
PAODAP.......   Presidents Action Office for Drug Abuse Prevention   (SAUS)
P/AOEA2 ......   Probationary Ordnance Electrical Artificer, Acting, 2nd Class [*British military*]   (DMA)
PA of W ......   Pentecostal Assemblies of the World   (EA)
PAOI ....   Peak Acid Output Insulin-Induced   (STED)
PAOL ....   Poly-alpha-olefin [*Organic chemistry*]
PAOM ....   Nome [*Alaska*] [*ICAO location identifier*]   (ICLI)
PAOP ....   Pulmonary Artery Occlusion Pressure [*Cardiology*]
PAOR ....   Northway [*Alaska*] [*ICAO location identifier*]   (ICLI)
PAOS ....   Physician Assistants in Orthopaedic Surgery   (SAUS)
PAOS ....   Proceedings of American Oriental Society   (SAUS)
PAOT ....   Kotzebue [*Alaska*] [*ICAO location identifier*]   (ICLI)
PAOT ....   Persons at One Time
PAOTS ....   Power and Ordnance Test Set   (ACAE)
PAP.............   Asia Pulp & Paper ADS [*NYSE symbol*]   (TTSB)
PAP.............   Asia Pulp and Paper Co. Ltd. [*NYSE symbol*]   (SAG)
PAP.............   Langtry Flying Group Ltd. [*British*] [*FAA designator*]   (FAAC)
PAP.............   Pacific Automation Products   (IAA)
PAP.............   Packet-level Procedure   (SAUS)
P/AP ....   Painter/Apprentice Painter   (AAG)
PAP.............   Pancreatitis-Associated Protein [*Medicine*]   (DMAA)
PAP.............   Papain [*An enzyme*]
pap ....   papal [*British*]
PAP.............   Papanicolaou [*Diagnosis, smear, stain, or test*] [*Medicine*]
Pap.............   Paper   (DIAR)
PAP.............   Paper   (DSUE)
PAP.............   Paper Bound [*Books*]   (ROG)
pap ....   Papilla [*Medicine*]
Pap ....   Papist   (SAUS)
Pap ....   Pappie   (SAUS)
Pap ....   Papua [*New Guinea*]   (BARN)
Pap ....   Papyrus   (BJA)

pap .... Papyrus (VRA)
PAP .... Para-Aminophenol [Organic chemistry]
PAP .... Parallel Applications Programme [British]
PAP .... Participatory Anthropic Principle [Term coined by authors John Barrow and Frank Tipler in their book, "The Anthropic Cosmological Principle"]
PAP .... Parti d'Action Paysanne [Farmers Actions Party] [Burkina Faso] [Political party]
PAP .... Partido Accion Popular [Popular Action Party] [Peru] [Political party]
PAP .... Partido Accion Popular [Popular Action Party] [Ecuador] [Political party]
PAP .... Password Authentication Protocol [Computer science] (PCM)
PAP .... Patient Assesment Program [Medicine] (DMAA)
PAP .... Patrol Amphibian Plane
PAP .... Paulin [H.] & Co. Ltd. [Toronto Stock Exchange symbol]
PAP .... Payload Activity Planner [NASA]
PAP .... Peak Airway Pressure [Physiology]
PAP .... Pension Administration Plan [Insurance]
PAP .... Pentyl-alpha-pyrone [Organic chemistry]
PAP .... People's Action Party [Papua New Guinea] [Political party] (EY)
PAP .... People's Action Party [Singapore] [Political party] (PPW)
PAP .... People's Action Party [Malaya] [Political party]
PAP .... People's Alliance Party [Solomon Islands] [Political party] (PPW)
PAP .... Performance Assessment Plan
PAP .... Periphery Access Processor [Computer science] (IAA)
PAP .... Peroxidase-Antibody to Peroxidase (DB)
PAP .... Peroxidase-Antiperoxidase [Immunochemistry]
PAP .... Personal Auto Policy [Insurance]
PAP .... Personnel Allocation Plan [Navy]
PAP .... Personnel Assistance Point [Army] (AABC)
PAP .... Phase Advance Pulse
PAP .... Phenolphthalein in Paraffin [Emulsion]
PAP .... Phenyl Acid Phosphate [Organic chemistry]
PAP .... Philippine Aid Plan
PAP .... Phosphoadenosine Phosphate [Biochemistry]
PAP .... Photodiode Array Processing (MCD)
PAP .... Photon-Assisted Processing (SAUS)
PAP .... Photonic Array Processor [Device for manipulating light beams in an optical computer]
PAP .... Physics and Astronomy (SAUS)
PAP .... Physics and Astronomy Programs [NASA]
PAP .... Phytolacca Americana Protein (DB)
PAP .... Pierced Aluminum Plank [Technical drawings]
PAP .... Pilotless Aircraft Program (NG)
PAP .... Placental Alkaline Phosphatase (DB)
PAP .... Plans Activation Party (SAUS)
PAP .... Plant Acquisition Plan (SAUS)
PAP .... Plant Air Package (IAA)
PAP .... Plasma-Assisted Processing (SAUS)
PAP .... Platelet Aggregation Profiler [Hematology]
PAP .... Platelet Alkaline Phosphatase [An enzyme]
P a P .... Poco a Poco [Little by Little] [Music]
PAP .... Point Authorization Protocol (SAUS)
PAP .... Pokeweed Antiviral Protein [Immunochemistry]
PAP .... Political Asylum Project [Defunct] (EA)
PAP .... Politiki Aneksartitos Parataksis [Independent Political Front] [Greek] [Political party] (PPE)
PAP .... Polska Agencja Prasowa [Polish Press Agency]
PAP .... Poly(acryloylpyrrolidine) [Organic chemistry]
PAP .... Poly-a-polymerase [An enzyme]
PAP .... Popular Alliance Party
PAP .... Port-Au-Prince [Haiti] [Airport symbol] (OAG)
PAP .... Positive Airway Pressure (MAE)
PAP .... Post Apollo Program (SAUS)
PAP .... Pouchou and Pichoir (SAUS)
PAP .... Prealloyed Powder (SAUS)
PAP .... Preapproved Payment (SAUS)
PAP .... Pre-Approved Procedures (SAUS)
PAP .... Prearranged Payments [Business term]
PAP .... Preauthorized Payment (SAUS)
pAP .... Presynaptic Action Potential [Neurochemistry]
PAP .... Primary Atypical Pneumonia [Medicine]
PAP .... Printer Access Protocol (BYTE)
PAP .... Priority Action Programme (SAUS)
PAP .... Prison-Ashram Project (EA)
PAP .... Process/Application Protocol (SAUS)
PAP .... Procurement and Production (AFIT)
PAP .... Product Assurance Plan [Army] (AABC)
PAP .... Production Allocation Program
PAP .... Production Assurance Program (SAUS)
PAP .... Program Advanced Planning (SAUS)
PAP .... Project Aerospace Plane (AAG)
PAP .... Projected Average Progress (NG)
PAP .... Propagation Analysis Package (SAUS)
PAP .... Prostatic Acid Phosphatase [An enzyme]
PAP .... Proton Attenuation Procedure
PAP .... Public Access Profile (SAUS)
PAP .... Public Affairs Program [of the American Friends Service Committee] (EA)
PAP .... Public Assistance Program
PAP .... Public Awareness Program
PAP .... Pulmonary Alveolar Proteinosis [Medicine]
PAP .... Pulmonary Arterial [or Artery] Pressure [Medicine]
PAP .... Purple Acid Phosphatase [An enzyme]
PAPA .... Back Bay Restaurant Group, Inc. [NASDAQ symbol] (SAG)

PAPA .... Parallax Aircraft Parking Aid (PDAA)
PAPA .... Parents As Partners Associated (SAUS)
PAPA .... Pesticide Applicators Professional Association (SAUS)
PAPA .... Philippines Alien Property Administration
PAPA .... Pizza and Pasta Association [British] (DBA)
PAPA .... Pollution Abatement and Prevention Analysis [Environmental science] (BCP)
PAPA .... Polyazelaic Polyanhydride (EDCT)
PAPA .... Probabilistic Automatic Pattern Analyzer [Computer science]
PAPA .... Programmer and Probability Analyzer [Computer science] (IEEE)
PAPA .... Psychiatrists Against Psychiatric Abuse [Canada] (EAIO)
PapaJohn .... Papa Johns International, Inc. [Associated Press] (SAG)
Pap & Disc Vic Inst Eng... Papers and Discussions. Victorian Institute of Engineers [Australia] [A publication]
Pap & Proc Roy Soc Tas... Papers and Proceedings. Royal Society of Tasmania [A publication]
PAPAS .... Pennsylvania Association of Private Academic Schools (SAUS)
PAPAS .... Pin and Pellet Assay System [Nuclear energy] (NRCH)
Papav .... Papaverine (SAUS)
PAPAV .... Papaver Poppy [Botany] (ROG)
PAPB .... Point Barrow [Alaska] [ICAO location identifier] (ICLI)
PAPC .... Presidents Accident Prevention Council (SAUS)
PAPC .... Processed Apple and Pear Committee [Victoria, Austrial]
PAPCA .... Pan-American Progressive Consumers Alliance [Later, NPCA] (EA)
PAPCAPS .... Publicly Available Price Cap Agreements (AAGC)
PapclS .... Paperclip Imaging Software, Inc. [Associated Press] (SAG)
PAPCNY ...... Portuguese American Progressive Club of New York (EA)
PAPD .... Passive-Agressive Personality Disorder (MELL)
PAPD .... Periodate Dimethylphenylenediamine (SAUS)
Pap Diag .... Papanicolaou Diagnosis (SAUS)
PAPE .... Photoactive Pigment Electrophotography (IEEE)
PAPER .... People and Physical Environmental Research (SAUS)
PAPER .... Prairie Association of Publishers Education Representatives [Canada]
Paperboard Packag... Paperboard Packaging (SAUS)
PAPERCHEM... Paper Chemistry [Institute of Paper Chemistry] [Appleton, WI] [Bibliographic database]
Paper Conserv News... Paper Conservation News (SAUS)
PAPERMAN... Payroll and Accounting, Personnel Management, Manpower Utilization [Air Force]
Paper Technol... Paper Technology (SAUS)
Paper Twine J... Paper and Twine Journal (SAUS)
Paper Yearb... Paper Yearbook (SAUS)
PAPF .... Platelet Adhesiveness Plasma [Hematology] (DMAA)
PAPH .... (Pyridinealdehyde)pyridylhydrazone [Organic chemistry]
Papi .... Papi [Aemilius] Papinianus [Deceased, 212] [Authority cited in pre-1607 legal work] (DSA)
Papi .... Papirius Justus [Flourished, 2nd century] [Authority cited in pre-1607 legal work] (DSA)
PAPI .... Polymethylene Polyphenyl Isocyanate (EDCT)
PAPI .... Precision Approach Path Indicator [FAA] (TAG)
PAPI .... Professional Association of Pet Industries (EA)
Papil .... Papilla (SAUS)
Pap Inf ...... Papal Infallability (SAUS)
PapJohn .... Papa Johns International, Inc. [Associated Press] (SAG)
PaPL .... Pennsylvania Power & Light Co. [Associated Press] (SAG)
PAPL .... Preliminary Allowance Parts List [Military] (CAAL)
PaPL .... W. and F. Pascoe Proprietory Ltd., Milsons Point, NSW, Australia [Library symbol] [Library of Congress] (LCLS)
Pap Lab Tree Ring Res... Papers of the Laboratory of Tree Ring Research (SAUS)
Pap Lib ...... Paperback Library (SAUS)
PAPM .... Pall Aircraft Porous Media
PAPM .... Passed Assistant Paymaster [British]
PAPM .... Port Moller Air Force Station [Alaska] [ICAO location identifier] (ICLI)
PAPM .... Pulse Amplitude and Phase Modulation (PDAA)
Pap Mich Acad Sci Arts Lett... Papers of the Michigan Academy of Science, Arts and Letters (SAUS)
PAPMOP ...... Product Assurance Program Management Operations Plan (MCD)
PAPMV .... Papaya Mosaic Virus [Plant pathology]
Papo .... Partido de Accion Popular [Popular Action Party] [Panama] [Political party] (PPW)
PAPOC .... Parents' Alliance to Protect Our Children (EA)
PAPOILA ...... Pacis Amico, Persecutionis Osore, Joanne Lockio Anglo [Pseudonym used by John Locke]
PAPOVA ...... Papilloma Virus, Polyoma Virus, Vacuolating Virus
PAPP .... Pappenheimer Bodies [Hematology] (DAVI)
PAPP .... Para-Aminopropiophenone [Pharmacology]
PAPP .... Parametric Aircraft Performance Program (MCD)
PAPP .... Pre-Approved Payment Plan (SAUS)
PAPP .... Pregnancy-Associated Plasma Protein
PAPP .... Product Assurance Program Plan (ACAE)
PAPP .... Pull and Push Plate (IAA)
PAPPA .... Pulp and Paper Prepackaging Association [Later, SSI] (EA)
PAPPGM ...... Preliminary Army Planning and Program Guidance Memorandum (MCD)
Pa Pple ...... Passive Participle (SAUS)
Pa Pple ...... Past Participle (SAUS)
PAPR .... Powered Air Purifying Respirator (ERG)
PAP/RAC ..... Priority Action Programme/Regional Activity Centre (SAUS)
PA Prac ...... Standard Pennsylvania Practice [A publication] (DLA)
PAPRICAN .. Pulp and Paper Research Institute of Canada [McGill University] [Research center] (RCD)
PA Projection... Posterior Anterior Projection (SAUS)
PAPROS .... Parallel Processing System (SAUS)
Paps .... Papillomas [Medicine] (DMAA)

PAPS	Performance Analysis and Prediction Study (PDAA)
PAPS	Periodic Acid Phenylhydrazine Schiff (SAUS)
PAPS	Periodic Acid-Schiff with Phenylhydrazine Interposition [*A stain*]
PAPS	Periodic Armaments Planning System (MCD)
PAPS	Periodic Arrays of Pinning Sites [*Solid state physics*]
PAPS	Permissive Arming and Protection System [*AEC*]
PAPS	Phased Armaments Programme Systems (SAUS)
PAPS	Phosphoadenosine Diphosphosulfate [*Phosphoadenosyl-Phosphosulfate*] [*Biochemistry*] (DAVI)
PAPS	Phosphoadenosine Phosphosulfate [*Also, APPS*] [*Biochemistry*]
PAPS	Phosphoadenylyl Sulfate [*Biochemistry*]
PAPS	Physics Auxiliary Publication Service (SAUS)
PAPS	Portable Ada Programming System (SAUS)
PAPS	Procurement and Production Status System
PAPS	Public Assistance Processing System
PA/PS	Pulmonary Atresia/Pulmonary Stenosis [*Cardiology*] (DAVI)
PAPSB	Patent Attorneys' Professional Standards Body [*Australia*]
PA PSC	Pennsylvania Public Service Commission Annual Report [*A publication*] (DLA)
PA PSC Dec...	Pennsylvania Public Service Commission Decisions [*A publication*] (DLA)
PAPSI	Pregnancy-Associated Prostaglandin Synthetase Inhibitor [*Endocrinology*]
Pap smear...	Papanicolaou smear (SAUS)
Papsom	Papaver somniferum (SAUS)
PAPSS	Procurement and Production Status System (SAUS)
Pap Sta	Papal States (SAUS)
PAPT	Palladium Print (VRA)
PAPTC	Pakistan Army Physical Training Corps [*British military*] (DMA)
PAPTC	Paper Tape Controller (NITA)
PAPTE	President's Advisory Panel on Timber and the Environment
Pap Ter	Papua Territory (SAUS)
Pap Test	Papanicolaou Test (SAUS)
PAPUFA	Physiologically Active Polyunsaturated Fatty Acid [*Nutrition*]
Pa-Pv	Pulmonary Arterial Pressure-Pulmonary Venous Pressure [*Medicine*] (STED)
PAPVC	Partial Anomalous Pulmonary Venous Connection (MAE)
PAPVR	Partial Anomalous Pulmonary Venous Return
PAPW	Papworth [*England*]
PAPW	Posterior Aspect of the Pharyngeal Wall [*Medicine*] (STED)
Papy	Papy's Reports [*5-8 Florida*] [*A publication*] (DLA)
PAQ	Palmer, AK [*Location identifier*] [*FAA*] (FAAL)
PAQ	Partially Allocated Quotas [*Ocean fishery management*]
PAQ	Passive Asynchronous Quenching (SAUS)
PAQ	Pending Action Queue (SAUS)
PAQ	Personal Attributes Questionnaire
PAQ	Port Authorities Queensland [*Australia*]
PAQ	Position Analysis Questionnaire
PAQ	Preliminary Allowance Quantity [*Military*] (CAAL)
PAQ	Process Average Quality
PAQ	Production, Accounting, Quality (SAUS)
PAQAB	President's Air Quality Advisory Board [*Environmental Protection Agency*]
PAQR	Polyacene Quinone Radical (SAUS)
PAQR	Polyacenequinone Radical [*Organic chemistry*]
PAQS	Pacific Association of Quantity Surveyors [*Australia*]
PAQSS	Pennsylvania Air Quality Surveillance System (SAUS)
PAR	Coastcast Corp. [*NYSE symbol*] (SPSG)
Par	Guiraudus Pargues [*Authority cited in pre-1607 legal work*] (DSA)
PAR	Pacific-Antarctic Ridge [*Geology*]
PAR	Page Address Register
PAR	Panama Canal Commission Acquisition Regulation (AAGC)
PAR	Parabolic Aluminized Reflector [*Lamp*]
PAR	Paracel Islands [*ANSI three-letter standard code*] (CNC)
PAR	Parachute
par	Paraffin [*Chemistry*] (DAVI)
PAR	Paraffin (STED)
PAR	Paragon Resources Ltd. [*Vancouver Stock Exchange symbol*]
PAR	Paragraph (AAG)
par	Paragraph (WDMC)
Par	Paraguay
Par	Parah (BJA)
PAR	Paralipomenon [*Old Testament book*] [*Douay version*]
PAR	Parallax
PAR	Parallax and Refraction (IAA)
Par	Parallaxe (SAUS)
PAR	Parallel (KSC)
par	Parallel (WDMC)
PAR	Parallelogram [*Geometry*] (ADA)
PAR	Parameter
PAR	Parameter Request (SAUS)
PAR	Parametric Amplifier
Par	Paranoid [*Psychiatry*] (DAVI)
PAR	Paraphrase (ADA)
PAR	Parcel
Par	Parenchesis (SAUS)
PAR	Parental Awareness and Responsibility (SAUS)
par	Parenthesis (WDMC)
PAR	Parenthesis
Par	Parents Magazine [*A publication*] (BRI)
PAR	Parimeter Array Radar
PAR	Paris [*France*] [*Airport symbol*] (OAG)
par	Parish (GEAB)
PAR	Parish

PAR	Paris - Parc St. Maur [*France*] [*Seismograph station code, US Geological Survey*] (SEIS)
PAR	Parity (ADA)
Par	Parker's English Exchequer Reports [*A publication*] (DLA)
Par	Parker's New York Criminal Reports [*A publication*] (DLA)
PAR	Parochial
PAR	Parole Assessment Report (WDAA)
PAR	Parole Services for Adults [*Public human service program*] (PHSD)
Par	Parsons' Reports [*65-66 New Hampshire*] [*A publication*] (DLA)
par	Part (BARN)
PAR	Partheite [*A zeolite*]
Par	Participating (AMHC)
PAR	Participating [*Health insurance*] (GHCT)
PAR	Participating Provider [*Health insurance*] (DMAA)
PAR	Participation-Achievement-Reward (PDAA)
PAR	Partido Aragones Regionalista [*Aragonese Regional Party*] [*Spain*] [*Political party*] (PPW)
PAR	Partito Anti-Reformista [*Anti-Reform Party*] [*Malta*] [*Political party*] (PPE)
PAR	Parts Approval Request (MCD)
PAR	Passive Avoidance Reaction [*Medicine*] (DMAA)
PAR	Payload Accommodations Requirements (SAUS)
PAR	Payload Adapter Ring
PAR	[*The*] Payment Analysis Report [*Dun & Bradstreet Credit Services*] [*Information service or system*] (CRD)
PAR	Peacetime Airborne Reconnaissance (AFM)
PAR	Peak Accelerometer Recorder (IEEE)
PAR	Peak Area Ratio [*Chromatographic analysis*]
PAR	Peak Average Rectified (SAUS)
PAR	Peak-to-Average Ratio [*Telecommunications*]
PAR	Peak-to-Average Reading (SAUS)
PAR	Pennsylvania Advanced Reactor
PAR	People Against Racism [*Civil rights organization*]
PAR	People Against Rape (EA)
PAR	Per Acre Rental (WDAA)
PAR	Perennial Allergic Rhinitis [*Medicine*]
PAR	Performance Analysis and Review
PAR	Performance Analysis Report
PAR	Performance Analysis Routine [*Computer science*]
PAR	Performance and Availability Report (SAUS)
PAR	Performance Appraisal Report [*Nuclear energy*] (NRCH)
PAR	Performance Assessment Report [*Small Cities Community Development Block Grant*] [*Department of Housing and Urban Development*] (GFGA)
PAR	Performance Augmentation Ring (MCD)
PAR	Perimeter Acquisition RADAR [*Army*]
PAR	Perimeter Array RADAR (MCD)
PAR	Personal Animation Recorder (SAUS)
PAR	Personnel Activity Report [*Office of Management and Budget*]
PAR	Personnel Activity Request
PAR	Personnel Advancement Requirement [*Navy*] (NVT)
PAR	Personnel At Risk (SAUS)
PAR	PERT [*Program Evaluation and Review Technique*] Analysis Report (KSC)
PAR	Phased Array RADAR
PAR	Phosphoric Acid-Resistant
PAR	Photosynthetically Active Radiation
PAR	Photosynthetically Active Radiometer
PAR	Photosynthetically Active Range
PAR	Photosynthetically Available Radiation (CARB)
PAR	Physical Activity Ratio (WDAA)
PAR	Physiological Aging Rate
PAR	Pilot Action Request
PAR	Plain Abdominal Radiograph [*Medicine*] (DMAA)
PAR	Planed All Around (SAUS)
PAR	Planed All Round (DAC)
PAR	Planning Action Request [*NASA*] (MCD)
PAR	Planning Activity Report
PAR	Planning and Allocation of Resources (SAUS)
PAR	Plasma-Arc Reduction (SAUS)
PAR	Plasma-Arc Remelting (SAUS)
PAR	Platelet Aggregate Ratio [*Hematology*]
PAR	Point Address Register (SAUS)
PAR	Police Accident Report [*NHTSA*] (TAG)
PAR	Policy and Administrative Reform (SAUS)
PAR	Pollen Accumulation Rate [*Botany*]
PAr	Polyarteritis (STED)
PAR	Polyarylate [*Resin*]
PAR	Population at Risk (FFDE)
PAR	Positive Acknowledgment and Retransmission [*Telecommunications*] (IAA)
PAR	Positive Attitudinal Reinforcement [*In George Lee Walker novel "The Chronicles of Doodah"*]
PAR	Post Adjudicative Review [*Social Security Administration*] (OICC)
PAR	Postanesthesia [*or Postanesthetic*] Room [*Medicine*]
PAR	Postanesthetic Recovery [*Medicine*]
PAR	Post Attach Requirements (AAG)
PAR	Potassium-Adsorption-Ratio
PAR	Power Analyser & Recorder (SAUS)
PAR	Power Analysis Report [*Automobile testing*]
PAR	Practical Accounts Receivable (SAUS)
PAR	Preadmission Review (WYGK)
PAR	Precedent, Action, and Result
PAR	Precision Aerotech (EFIS)
PAR	Precision Aircraft Reference

PAR	Precision Approach RADAR [*Aviation*]
PAR	Preferential Arrival Route [*Aviation*] (DA)
PAR	Preferred Arrival Route (CTAS)
PAR	Preliminary Analysis Review (SAUS)
PAR	Preparedness Assessment Report [*Environmental science*] (COE)
PAR	Price-Adjusted Rate Preferred [*Investment term*] (MHDW)
PAR	Prime Assets Ratio
PAR	Princeton Applied Research Corp. [*Princeton University*]
PAR	Print Area Reader (DGA)
PAR	Priority Action Report (AAG)
PAR	Priority Action Request (AAG)
PAR	Probabilistic Analysis of Risk (KSC)
PAR	Probable Allergic Rhinitis [*Medicine*] (DAVI)
PAR	Problem Accountability Record (NASA)
PAR	Problem Action Record (KSC)
PAR	Problem Action Request (NASA)
PAR	Problem Analysis and Resolution
PAR	Problem Analysis and Response (SAUS)
PAR	Problem Analysis and Response Program (IAA)
PAR	Problem Analysis Report (MCD)
PAR	Process Action Request
PAR	Processor Address Register (SAUS)
PAR	Procurement Advisory Release (SAUS)
PAR	Product Acceptance & Research [*Commercial firm*] (WDMC)
PAR	Product Acceptance Review (NASA)
PAR	Product Assurance Requirements (ACAE)
PAR	Production Acceptance Review
PAR	Production Action Request (MCD)
PAR	Production Analysis Report
PAR	Production, Augmentation, and Reliability (NG)
PAR	Production Automated Riveting
PAR	Product of Antigenic Recognition [*Immunochemistry*]
PAR	Professional Abstracts Registries [*Database Innovations, Inc.*]
PAR	Profile of Average Reflectivity
PAR	Program Acquisition Request (SAUS)
PAR	Program Acquisition Review (ACAE)
PAR	Program Action Request (SSD)
PAR	Program Activity Recording [*Computer science*] (IAA)
PAR	Program Address Register
PAR	Program Adjustment Request [*Navy*]
PAR	Program Administrator's [*Progress*] Report [*DoD*]
PAR	Program-Aid Routine [*Computer science*]
PAR	Program Allocation and Reimbursements (AFIT)
PAR	Program Analysis and Review
PAR	Program Analysis Report
PAR	Program Appraisal and Review (IEEE)
PAR	Program Appraisal Report
PAR	Program Assessment Report [*or Review*] (MCD)
PAR	Program Audience Rating
PAR	Program for Alcohol Recovery
PAR	Programmed and Remote (SAUS)
PAR	Progressive Aircraft Repair [*or Rework*]
PAR	Progressive Airframe Rework
PAR	Project Activity Report (SAUS)
PAR	Project Analysis and Reporting system (SAUS)
PAR	Project Anthorization Request (SAUS)
PAR	Project Appraisal Report (SAUS)
PAR	Project Approval Review (SAUS)
PAR	Project Audit Report
PAR	Project Authorization Request (IAA)
PAR	Projected Automation Requirement
PAR	Proposal Analysis Report (AAGC)
PAR	Propulsion and Aeroballistics Research (SAA)
PAR	Protease-Activated Receptor [*Hematology*]
PAR	Protect Abortion Rights (SAUS)
PAR	Protection Action Recommendation [*Department of Emergency Management*] (DEMM)
PAR	Protective Action Recommendation (COE)
PAR	Provisioning Allowance Record (SAUS)
PAR	Proximal Alveolar Region [*Medicine*] (DMAA)
PAR	Pseudoautosomal Region [*Genetics*]
PAR	Psychological Assessment Resources, Inc. (DHP)
PAR	Public Accounting Report (SAUS)
PAR	Public Administration Review [*A publication*] (BRI)
PAR	Public Affairs Research Council [*Research center*] (RCD)
PAR	Publication Analysis Report (SAA)
PAR	Pulmonary Arteriolar Resistance [*Medicine*] (MAE)
PAR	Pulse Acquisition RADAR [*Military*] (NG)
PAR	Pulse Address Register (VLIE)
PAR	Punch Address Register (SAUS)
PAr	Punta Arenas (SAUS)
PAR	Purchasing Approval Request (NRCH)
PAR	Push and Release [*Push button*]
PAR	Pyridinazo-Resorcin (SAUS)
PAR	(Pyridylazo)resorcinol [*Organic chemistry*]
PAR	Spair [*Russian Federation*] [*ICAO designator*] (FAAC)
PARA	Parabellum (GOBB)
PARA	Parabolic (IAA)
para	Paracentesis [*Medicine*] (MAE)
PARA	Parachute
PARA	Parachutist (SAUS)
PARA	Paragraph (AFM)
para	Paragraph (DIAR)
PARA	Paraguay
PARA	Parallel (WDAA)

PARA	Paramagnetic (SAUS)
PARA	Paramedic (SAUS)
PARA	Paramount Financial [*NASDAQ symbol*] (TTSB)
PARA	Paramount Financial Corp. [*NASDAQ symbol*] (SAG)
para	Paraphrase (BARN)
para	Paraplegic
PARA	Parasite (SAUS)
para	Parathy Roidectomy [*Medicine*] (DMAA)
para	Paratroop (MILB)
PARA	Paratrooper (GOBB)
para	Parity [*Gynecology and obstetrics*] (DAVI)
para	Parquet (BARN)
PARA	Particle Aiding Replication of Adenovirus [*Virology*]
PARA	Perceiving and Recognition Automation (SAUS)
PARA	Policy Analysis and Resource Allocation [*Department of State*]
PARA	Polyarylamid [*Organic chemistry*]
PARA	Problem Analysis and Recommended Action (IAA)
PARA	Professional Audiovideo Retailers Association (EA)
PARA	Program for At-Risk Addicts (SAUS)
Para 1	Unipara [*Having borne one child*] [*Gynecology and obstetrics*] (DAVI)
Para-A	Paratyphoid A [*Medicine*] (DAVI)
PARAB	Parabola [*Mathematics*] (IAA)
Para-B	Paratyphoid B [*Medicine*] (DAVI)
PARABAT	Parachute Battalion [*Army*]
PARABOL	Parabolic (IAA)
PARABOLA	Portable Apparatus for Rapid Acquisition of Bidirectional Observations of Land and Atmosphere (SAUS)
Para-C	Paratyphoid C [*Medicine*] (DAVI)
Paracels	Paracelsus Healthcare Corp. [*Associated Press*] (SAG)
paracent	Paracentesis [*Medicine*]
PARACOMPT	Parameter Analysis of Respiration Agents Considering Operations Motivation Protection and Time Model (MCD)
PARACS	Perimeter Acquisition RADAR Attack Characterization System (MCD)
PARAD	Paradichlorobenzene (SAUS)
parad	paradisal (SAUS)
parad	paradise (SAUS)
parad	paradoxicalness (SAUS)
PARADA	Preparatory Academy for the Royal Academy of Dramatic Art [*British*] (BI)
PARADE	Passive-Active Range Determination
Paradl	Paradise, Inc. [*Associated Press*] (SAG)
PARADISE	Phased Array RADAR and Divers Integrated Semiconductor Elements (PDAA)
Par Adm	Parsons on the Law of Shipping and Admiralty [*A publication*] (DLA)
PARADROP	Parachute Airdrop (SAUS)
PAR AFF	Pars Affecta [*The Part Affected*] [*Pharmacy*]
PARAFRAG	Parachute Fragmentation Bomb [*Air Force*]
PARAFRAG Bomb	Parachute Fragmentation Bomb (SAUS)
PARAG	Paraguay [*or Paraguayan*] (WDAA)
Parag	Paraguayan (DIAR)
ParagGg	Paragon Group, Inc. [*Associated Press*] (SAG)
ParagGp	Paragon Group, Inc. [*Associated Press*] (SAG)
PARAGON	Processing and Archiving of Radar and Gauge Data Off-Line and in Near Real Time (SAUS)
ParagTr	Paragon Trade Brands [*Associated Press*] (SAG)
Para II	Bipara [*Having borne two children*] [*Gynecology and Obstetrics*] (DAVI)
Para III	Tripara [*having borne three children*] [*Gynecology and obstetrics*] (DAVI)
PARAKU	Pasokan Rakyat Kalimantan Utara [*North Kalimantan People's Forces*] [*Malaya*]
Parallel Comput	Parallel Computing (SAUS)
PARAM	Parameter (KSC)
PARAM	Parametric (SAUS)
ParaMed	Paradigm Medical Industries, Inc. [*Associated Press*] (SAG)
Parameters	Parameters: US Army War College Quarterly [*A publication*] (BRI)
PARAMI	Parsons Active Ring-Around Miss Indicator
PARAMIS	Parsons Passive Miss Distance Indicating System (SAA)
Par Am Law	Parsons' Commentaries on American Law [*A publication*] (DLA)
Par Am Law Comm	Parsons' Commentaries on American Law [*A publication*] (DLA)
Paramnt	Paramount Financial Corp. [*Associated Press*] (SAG)
PARAMP	Parametric Amplifier
paramp	Parametric Amplifier (VLIE)
ParamrkE	Paramark Enterprises, Inc. [*Associated Press*] (SAG)
Paramt	Paramount Financial Corp. [*Associated Press*] (SAG)
PARAN	Perimeter Array Antenna (PDAA)
Par & Fonb Med Jur	Paris and Fonblanque's Medical Jurisprudence [*A publication*] (DLA)
Par Ant	Parochial Antiquities [*A publication*] (DLA)
Parapsy	Parasychologist (SAUS)
PARAPSYCH	Parapsychologist (SAUS)
PARAPSYCH	Parapsychology
PARAQUAD	Paraplegic and Quadriplegic Association of New South Wales [*Australia*]
ParaQuad NSW	Paraplegic and Quadriplegic Association of NSW (SAUS)
PARARESCUE	Rescue by Individuals Parachuted to Distressed Persons [*Air Force*]
PARAS	Parasitic (IAA)
Paras	Parasitism (SAUS)
PARAS	Pye Automatic Roadside Alarm System (SAUS)
PARASAIL	Parachute Sail (SAUS)
PARASEV	Paraglider Research Vehicle [*NASA*]
parasit	Parasitology [*Medicine*] (DMAA)
PARASITOL	Parasitologic (SAUS)

Parasitol...... Parasitologist (SAUS)
PARASITOL... Parasitology
parasym ...... Parasympathetic [*Division of autonomic nervous system*] [*Neurolgoy*] (DAVI)
parasym div... Parasympathetic Division [*of autonomic nervous system*] [*Neurology*] (DAVI)
PARASYN .... Parametric Synthesis [*Computer science*]
PARATHORMONE... Parathyroid Hormone [*Endocrinology*]
PARATROOPS... Parachute Infantry [*Military*]
para VIII ...... Octipara [*Having borne eight children*] [*Gynecology and obstetrics*] (DAVI)
Paravnt........ Paravant Computer Systems, Inc. [*Associated Press*] (SAG)
PARAW........ Paramount Financial Wrrt [*NASDAQ symbol*] (TTSB)
PARB .... Perimeter Acquisition RADAR Building [*Army*] (AABC)
PARB .... Public Accountants Registration Board [*Australia*]
Parbhani AgricCollMag.. Parbhani Agricultural College Magazine (SAUS)
PARBICA...... Pacific Regional Branch of the International Council on Archives (EAIO)
Par Bills & N... Parsons on Bills and Notes [*A publication*] (DLA)
PARC .... Pacific Air Rescue Center [*or Command*] (CINC)
PARC .... Pacific-Asia Resources Center [*Japan*] (EAIO)
PARC .... Palo Alto Research Center [*Xerox Corp.*]
PARC .... Pan-African Resource Center (EA)
PARC .... Pan-African Rinderpest Campaign [*Organization of African Unity*]
PARC .... Parcelas
parc .... Parchment (VRA)
PARC .... Pennsylvania Association for Retarded Children (EDAC)
PARC .... Performing Arts Research Center (SAUS)
PARC .... Pericardial Fluid [*Cardiology*] (DAVI)
PARC .... Periodic Aircraft Reconditioning Cycle (DNAB)
PARC .... Polarimetric Active Radar Calibrator (SAUS)
PARC .... Predator and Rodent Control [*US Fish and Wildlife Service*] (IIA)
PARC .... President's Appalachian Regional Commission
PARC .... Princeton Applied Research Corp.
PARC .... Principal Assistant Responsible for Contracting [*Army*]
PARC .... Prison Activist Resource Center (SAUS)
PARC .... Profile Analysis and Recording Control (PDAA)
PARC .... Program on the Analysis & Resolution of Conflicts (SAUS)
PARC .... Progressive Aircraft Reconditioning [*or Repair*] Cycle
PARC .... Progressive Aircraft Repair Cycle (SAUS)
PARC .... Protected Area Resource Centres (SAUS)
PARC .... Public Affairs Research Council (SAUS)
PARC .... Public Archives Records Centre (SAUS)
PARCA.......... Pan American Railway Congress Association
PARCA.......... Patient Access to Responsible Care Act
PARCAC...... Polar Amateur Radio Club of Alaska Certificate (SAUS)
Par Car Ret... Partial Carriage Return (SAUS)
PARCC......... Precision, Accuracy, Representativeness, Completeness, Comparability (SAUS)
PARCH........ Parchment (ADA)
Par Ch........ Parents' Choice [*A publication*]
PARCHM...... Parchment (ROG)
PARCHT...... Parchment
PaRCL .... Parsec Research Control Language [*Pronounced "parkul"*] [*Parsec Reseach*] [*Robotics*]
Parcls .... Paracelsian, Inc. [*Associated Press*] (SAG)
Parclsn .... Paracelsian, Inc. [*Associated Press*] (SAG)
PARCOM...... Paris Commission [*See also CP*] (EAIO)
PARCOM...... Paris Commission for the Environmental Protection of the North East Atlantic (SAUS)
Par Cont ...... Parsons on Contracts [*A publication*] (DLA)
PARCOR ...... Partial Correlation (SAUS)
Par Costs..... Parsons on Costs [*A publication*] (DLA)
PARCP......... PEMARS [*Procurement of Equipment and Missiles, Army Management and AccountingReporting System*] Accounting and Reporting Control Point [*Army*]
ParcPplce .... Parcplace Systems, Inc. [*Associated Press*] (SAG)
PARCS......... Parking and Revenue Control System (SAUS)
PARCS......... Perimeter Acquisition RADAR Attack Characterization System [*Army*]
PARCS......... Pesticide Analysis Retrieval and Control System (NITA)
PARC System... Profile Analysis and Recording Control System (SAUS)
PARD .... Parts Application Reliability Data (IEEE)
PARD .... Periodic and Random Deviation
PARD .... Personal Alarm Radiation Dose (SAUS)
PARD .... Personnel Actions and Records Directorate [*Military Personnel Center*] (AABC)
PARD .... Phased Array Radar Detection/Track (SAUS)
PARD .... Pilot Airborne Recovery Device [*A balloon-parachute*]
PARD .... Pilotless Aircraft Research Division [*Later, Applied Materials and Physics Division*] [*Langley Research Center*]
PARD .... Post-Accident Radioactivity Depletion [*Nuclear energy*] (NRCH)
PARD .... Precision Annotated Retrieval Display [*System*] [*Computer science*]
PARD .... Project Activities Relationship Diagram (PDAA)
PARD .... Protect as Restricted Data
PARDAC...... Parallel Digital-to-Analog Converter
Par Dec ...... Parsons' Decisions [*2-7 Massachusetts*] [*A publication*] (DLA)
PARDEM...... Participatory Democracy (SAUS)
PARDENTL... Paradental
Pardgm........ Paradigm Technology, Inc. [*Associated Press*] (SAG)
Pard Lois Mar... Pardessus' Lois Maritimes [*A publication*] (DLA)
PARDON ..... Pastors' Anonymous Recovery-Directed Order for Newness [*Rehabilitation program for troubled clergymen*] [*Defunct*]
PARDOP ..... Passive Ranging Doppler
PARDP......... Perimeter Acquisition RADAR Data Processor [*Army*] (AABC)
PARDPS....... PAR Data Processing System (SAUS)

PARDS......... Phased Array RADAR Detection System (PDAA)
Pard Serv ... Pardessus' Traites des Servitudes [*A publication*] (DLA)
PARE .... People Against Racism in Education
PARE .... Physical Ability Requirement Evaluation (SAUS)
PARE .... Physiological and Anatomical Rodent Experiment (SAUS)
PARE .... Price Adjusted Rates of Exchange [*Monetary conversion rate*] (ECON)
PARE .... Program Analysis and Resouces Evaluation (IAA)
PARE .... Program for Analytical Reliability Estimation (VLIE)
P/AREA ...... Probationary Acting Radio Electrical Artificer [*British military*] (DMA)
PAREC .... Pay Record
PA Rec .... Pennsylvania Record [*A publication*] (DLA)
PAREN .... Parenthesis [*or Parentheses*] (AFM)
paren .... Parenthesis (WDMC)
PAREN .... Progressive Aircraft Engine Repair
PARENS...... Parentheses (NTCM)
parent .... parentally (SAUS)
PARENT ..... Parenteral
PARENTS ..... People of America Responding to Educational Needs of Today's Society (EA)
Parents Cit Guide... Parents and Citizens Guide [*A publication*]
PARENTS FLAG... Parents and Friends of Lesbians and Gays [*An association*]
PARENTSQ.. Parent Squadron Base [*Military*] (NVT)
PA Rep .... Pennsylvania Reports [*A publication*] (DLA)
Par Eq Cas.. Parsons' Select Equity Cases [*1842-51*] [*Pennsylvania*] [*A publication*] (DLA)
Par Eq Cases... Parsons' Select Equity Cases [*Pennsylvania*] [*A publication*] (DLA)
pares .... paresthesia (SAUS)
PARES .... Passive Radar ESM System (SAUS)
PARES .... Preprocessing of Airborne Remote Sensing Data (SAUS)
PARESEV .... Paraglider Research Vehicle [*NASA*] (MCD)
Par Ess........ Parsons' Essays on Legal Topics [*A publication*] (DLA)
PARET .... Parallel Architecture Research and Evaluation Tool [*Computer science*]
PARET .... Program for the Analysis of Reactor Transients (SAUS)
PAREX .... Programmed Accounts Receivable Extra Service [*Computer science*]
Parexel........ Parexel International Corp. [*Associated Press*] (SAG)
PARF .... Paradise, Inc. [*NASDAQ symbol*] (SAG)
PARF .... Polymorphic Amplifiable Restriction (Endonuclease) Fragment [*Genetics*]
PARF .... Practical Allergy Research Foundation (EA)
PARFAS ...... Passive Radio Frequency Acquisition System
PARFC .... Power Amplifier Radio Frequency Coil (SAUS)
par for .... par for the course (SAUS)
PARFORCE... Parallel Formal Computing Environment (VLIE)
PARFOX...... Parapet Foxhole
PARFR .... Program for Applied Research on Fertility Regulation [*Northwestern University*] [*Research center*]
Parg............ Paraguay (SAUS)
PARG .... Polytechnic Academic Registrars' Group (AIE)
Pargs .... Guiraudus Pargues [*Authority cited in pre-1607 legal work*] (DSA)
PARGS......... Parks and Recreation Girls Service
PARI .... Parent Attitude Research Instrument [*A questionnaire*]
pari .... parietal (SAUS)
PARI .... Pre-Columbian Art Research Institute
PARIET .... Parietal Cell Antibody [*Immunology*] (DAVI)
PARIF .... Program for Automatic Retrieval Improvement by Feedback (SAUS)
PARIF .... Program for Automation Retrieval Improvement by Feedback (NITA)
PARIMPS.... Professional Association of Residents in the Maritime Provinces (SAUS)
PARIS .... Passenger Routing and Information System [*FTA*] (TAG)
PARIS .... Passive Active Ranging & Intercept System (SAUS)
PARIS .... Passive/Activity Radar Identification System (ACAE)
PARIS .... Persantin/Aspirin Reinfarction Study [*Medicine*] (DB)
PARIS .... Pictorial and Artifact Retrieval and Information System [*Canadian Heritage Information Network*] [*Information service or system*]
PARIS .... Planning Aid for Retail Information System [*IBM Corp.*]
PARIS .... Polarized Angle-Resolved Infrared Spectroscopy (SAUS)
PARIS .... Portable Automated Remote Inspection System [*Failure Analysis Associates*] (RDA)
PARIS .... Postal Address Reader Indexer System (PDAA)
PARIS .... Pour l'Amenagement et le Renouveau Institutionel et Social [*France*] [*Political party*]
PARIS .... Pulse Analysis-Recording Information System
ParisBu....... Paris Business Forms, Inc. [*Associated Press*] (SAG)
PA-RISC...... Precision Architecture-Reduced Instruction Set Computing (SAUS)
Paris O .... Paris Opera Computing (SAUS)
PARK .... Park [*Postal Service standard*] (OPSA)
PARK .... Parkerized [*Metallurgy*] [*Tradename*]
Park .... Parker's English Exchequer Reports [*1743-67*] [*A publication*] (DLA)
Park .... Parker's New Hampshire Reports [*A publication*] (DLA)
Park .... Parker's New York Criminal Cases [*1823-68*] [*A publication*] (DLA)
PARK .... Parking
PARK .... Photorefractive Astigmatic Keratectomy (SAUS)
PARK .... Premier Parks, Inc. [*NASDAQ symbol*] (SAG)
PARKA .... Pacific Acoustic Research (SAUS)
PARKA .... Pacific Acoustic Research Kaneohe-Alaska [*Navy*]
Park Arb ...... Parker on Arbitration [*1820*] [*A publication*] (DLA)
Park Ch....... Parker's Practice in Chancery [*A publication*] (DLA)
Park CR....... Parker's New York Criminal Reports [*A publication*] (DLA)
Park Cr Cas.. Parker's New York Criminal Cases [*A publication*] (DLA)
Park Crim L.. Parker's New York Criminal Reports [*A publication*] (DLA)
Park Crim (NY)... Parker's New York Criminal Cases [*A publication*] (DLA)
Park Crim R.. Parker's New York Criminal Reports [*A publication*] (DLA)
Park Crim Rep... Parker's New York Criminal Reports [*A publication*] (DLA)

Park Cr Rep...	Parker's New York Criminal Reports [*A publication*] (DLA)
Park Dig	Parker's California Digest [*A publication*] (DLA)
Park Dow.....	Park. Dower [*1819*] [*A publication*] (DLA)
ParkDrl	Parker Drilling Co. [*Associated Press*] (SAG)
ParkEl	Park Electrochemical Corp. [*Associated Press*] (SAG)
Parker.........	Parker on the Laws of Shipping and Insurance [*England*] [*A publication*] (DLA)
Parker.........	Parker's English Exchequer Reports [*A publication*] (DLA)
Parker.........	Parker's New Hampshire Reports [*A publication*] (DLA)
Parker.........	Parker's New York Criminal Reports [*6 vols.*] [*A publication*] (DLA)
Parker Cr Cas...	Parker's New York Criminal Reports [*A publication*] (ILCA)
Parker Cr Cas (NY)...	Parker's New York Criminal Reports [*A publication*] (ILCA)
Parker Cr R...	Parker's New York Criminal Reports [*A publication*] (ILCA)
Parker Cr R (NY)...	Parker's New York Criminal Reports [*A publication*] (ILCA)
Parker's Crim R...	Parker's New York Criminal Reports [*A publication*] (DLA)
Parker's Crim Rep (NY)...	Parker's New York Criminal Reports [*A publication*] (DLA)
Parker's Cr R...	Parker's New York Criminal Reports [*A publication*] (DLA)
Park Exch	Parker's English Exchequer Reports [*1743-67*] [*A publication*] (DLA)
Park Hist Ch...	Parkes' History of Court of Chancery [*1828*] [*A publication*] (DLA)
ParkHn.........	Parker-Hannifin Corp. [*Associated Press*] (SAG)
Park Ins.......	Parker's Insurance [*8 eds.*] [*1787-1842*] [*England*] [*A publication*] (DLA)
ParkMed	Park Meditech, Inc. [*Associated Press*] (SAG)
ParkNatl	Park National Corp. [*Associated Press*] (SAG)
Park NH	Parker's New Hampshire Reports [*A publication*] (DLA)
ParkOh.........	Park Ohio Industries [*Associated Press*] (SAG)
ParkOh.........	Park-Ohio Industries, Inc. [*Associated Press*] (SAG)
ParkPar.......	Parker & Parsley Petroleum [*Associated Press*] (SAG)
Park Pr Ch...	Parker's Practice in Chancery [*A publication*] (DLA)
Park Rev Cas...	Parker's English Exchequer Reports (Revenue Cases) [*A publication*] (DLA)
Parkrvsn......	Parkervision, Inc. [*Associated Press*] (SAG)
PARKS........	Parks [*Commonly used*] (OPSA)
Parks&Rec...	Parks and Recreation (SAUS)
ParkvF........	Parkvale Financial Corp. [*Associated Press*] (SAG)
PARKWAY...	Parkway [*Commonly used*] (OPSA)
PARKWAYS...	Parkways [*Commonly used*] (OPSA)
PARKWY...	Parkway [*Commonly used*] (OPSA)
Parkwy........	[*The*] Parkway Co. [*Associated Press*] (SAG)
PARL	Palo Alto Research Laboratory (SAUS)
PARL	Parallel
Parl..............	Parliament (DIAR)
parl..............	Parliament (NTIO)
PARL	Parliament
PARL	Parliamentary (SAUS)
PARL	Parlux Fragrances, Inc. [*NASDAQ symbol*] (NQ)
Par L	Parsons' Law by Hughes [*A publication*] (DLA)
PARL	Preferential Arrival Route [*Aviation*] (PIPO)
PARL	Prince Albert RADAR Laboratory
Parlacen......	Central American Parliament (SAUS)
Parl Agt	Parliamentary Agent (SAUS)
PARLARS.....	Particulars
Par Laws Bus...	Parsons' Laws of Business [*A publication*] (DLA)
PARLB	Parliamentary Borough
Parl Cas	Parliamentary Cases [*House of Lords Reports*] [*A publication*] (DLA)
Parl Const ...	Parliamentary Constituency
PARLE	Parallel Architectures and Languages Europe (SAUS)
Parlex.........	Parlex Corp. [*Associated Press*] (SAG)
Parl Hist Eng...	Parliamentary History of England [*Pre-1803*] [*A publication*] (DLA)
PARLIGAES...	Parliamentary Liaison Group for Alternative Energy Strategies [*British*]
PAR Light	Parabolic Aluminized Reflector Lamp (SAUS)
PARLIKDER...	Partiya Litsom k Derevne [*The Party Face to Face with the Countryside*] [*Given name popular in Russia after the Bolshevik Revolution*]
PARLIQ.......	Phase Partitioning in Liquids (SAUS)
PARLO	Parlando [*Music*] (ROG)
parl proc.....	Parliamentary Procedure [*British*] (WDAA)
Parl Reg......	Parliamentary Register [*England*] [*A publication*] (DLA)
PARLT	Parliament
PARLTY	Parliamentary
Parlux.........	Parlux Fragrances, Inc. [*Associated Press*] (SAG)
PARLV	Parsley Latent Virus [*Plant pathology*]
PARLY	Parliamentary
PARM	Parallelogram [*Geometry*] (ROG)
parm...........	Parameter (ELAL)
PARM	Parameter [*Computer science*]
PARM	Participating Manager
PARM	Partido Autentico de la Revolucion Mexicana [*Authentic Party of the Mexican Revolution*] [*Political party*] (PPW)
PARM	Persistent Antiradiation Missile (MCD)
PARM	Post-Attack Resource Management System (MCD)
PARM	Precision Anti-Radiation Missile [*Military*] (PDAA)
PARM	Primary Alignment Reference Mirror (ACAE)
PARM	Program Analysis for Resource Management
PARMA	Program for Analysis, Reporting, and Maintenance [*Computer science*]
PARMA	Public Agency Risk Managers Association [*San Jose, CA*] (EA)
Par Mar Ins...	Parsons on Marine Insurance and General Average [*A publication*] (DLA)
Par Mar L....	Parsons on Maritime Law [*A publication*] (DLA)
ParMd........	Paradigm Medical Industries, Inc. [*Associated Press*] (SAG)
PARMEDL...	Paramedical
Par Merc Law...	Parsons on Mercantile Law [*A publication*] (DLA)
PARMIS	Planning and Resource Management Information System (SAUS)
PARMLIB	Parameter Library (VLIE)
PARMOD.....	Progressive Aircraft Rework Modification (SAUS)
ParmTch	Parametric Technology Corp. [*Associated Press*] (SAG)
PARMV	Parsnip Mosaic Virus [*Plant pathology*]
Par N & B...	Parsons' Notes and Bills [*A publication*] (DLA)
Parnassus...	Parnassus: Poetry in Review [*A publication*] (BRI)
PARO	Patent Royalties (AAGC)
Paroch	Parochial (DIAR)
PAROCH	Parochial (ROG)
Paroch Ant...	Kennett's Parochial Antiquities [*A publication*] (DLA)
Parod Epic Gr Rel...	Parodorum Epicorum Graecorum Reliquiae [*A publication*] (OCD)
PAROS	Passive Ranging on Submarines [*Navy*]
PAROS	Programmed Automated Replenishment Ordering System (IAA)
PAROSS......	Passive/Active Reporting Ocean Surveillance System [*Navy*] (NVT)
parot...........	parotid (SAUS)
PAROX........	Paroxysmal [*Medicine*]
PARP	Partially Acidulated Rock Phosphate (OA)
PARP	Pre-Engineered AUTOVON Restoral Plan Pacific (SAUS)
PARP	Procyclic Acidic Repetitive Protein [*Biochemistry*]
PARP	Production Assistance Report to Pricing [*DoD*]
Par Part......	Parsons on Partnership [*1889*] [*A publication*] (DLA)
ParPet	Parallel Petroleum Corp. [*Associated Press*] (SAG)
ParPf2	Partners Preferred Yield II [*Associated Press*] (SAG)
ParPf3	Partners Perferred Yield III [*Associated Press*] (SAG)
ParPfd	Partners Preferred Yield [*Associated Press*] (SAG)
PARPRO......	Peacetime Aerial Reconnaissance Program [*Military*] (NVT)
PARPRO......	Peacetime Airborne Reconnaissance Program
PAR Program...	Problem Analysis and Response Program (SAUS)
PARQ	ParcPlace-Digitalk [*NASDAQ symbol*] [*Formerly, ParcPlace Systems*] (SG)
PARQ	Parcplace Systems, Inc. [*NASDAQ symbol*] (SAG)
PARQ	Parental Acceptance-Rejection Questionnaire [*Psychology*]
parq...........	parquet (SAUS)
PAR-Q.........	Physical Activity Readiness Questionnaire
PARR	Bullet Sports International, Inc. [*NASDAQ symbol*] (SAG)
PARR	Pakistan Atomic Research Reactor
Par R	Parsons' Select Equity Cases [*Pennsylvania*] [*A publication*] (DLA)
PARR	Performance Analysis Reliability Reporting (DNAB)
PARR	Post-Accident Radioactivity Removal [*Nuclear energy*] (NRCH)
PARR	Postanesthesia Recovery Room [*Medicine*] (DAVI)
PARR	Procurement Authorization and Receiving Report [*NASA*] (KSC)
PARR	Program Analysis and Resources Review
PARR	Program Assessment Review Report [*Military*] (GFGA)
PARRAS.......	Prototype Army Rapid Reprogramming System (SAUS)
PARRC........	Pacific Aerospace Rescue and Recovery Center [*Air Force*]
Parres plot...	Partial Residual Plot
PARREV......	Paraglider Research Vehicle
Par Rights Cit...	Parsons on the Rights of a Citizen of the United States [*A publication*] (DLA)
PAR Room...	Postanesthetic Recovery Room (SAUS)
PARROT.......	Position Adjustable Radar Range and Orientation Transponder (ACAE)
PARRS........	Postal Analysis Response and Reporting System [*Computer system designed to track mail through the US Postal Service*] [*R. R. Donnelley & Sons Co.*]
PARRS........	Psychological Abstracts Reference Retrieval System [*Syracuse University*]
PARS	Paging and Radiotelephone Service [*Telecommunications*] (OTD)
PARS	Parachute Altitude Recognition System (MCD)
Pars	Parsons' Select Equity Cases [*1842-51*] [*Pennsylvania*] [*A publication*] (DLA)
PARS	Passenger Airlines Reservation System
PARS	Patrol Analysis Recording System [*British*]
PARS	Pedestrians Association for Road Safety [*British*] (DI)
PARS	Performance Analysis and Reporting System (VLIE)
PARS	Performance Analysis Reports System (SAUS)
PARS	Perimeter Acquisition RADAR [*Characterization*] System (MCD)
PARS	Pershing Audio Reproduction System (PDAA)
PARS	Personal Adjustment and Role Skills Scale [*Medicine*] (DMAA)
PARS	Pharmos Corp. [*NASDAQ symbol*] (SAG)
PARS	Photoacoustic Raman Spectroscopy
PARS	Pilotless Aircraft Research Station [*NASA*]
PARS	Portable Analyzer for Residual Stresses (SAUS)
PARS	Precision and Accuracy Reporting System [*Environmental Protection Agency*] (GFGA)
PARS	Primary Attitude Reference Systems (SAUS)
PARS	Prisoner Aid and Rehabilitation Society (NADA)
PARS	Private Advanced Radio Service (SAUS)
PARS	Private Aircraft Reporting System [*FAA*] (PDAA)
PARS	Procurement Accounting and Reporting System [*Navy*] (NVT)
PARS	Procurement Action Reporting System (ACAE)
PARS	Program Analysis and Review System (EDAC)
PARS	Programmed Airline Reservation System
PARS	Project Analysis Reporting System (SAUS)
PARS	Property Accountability Record System (NASA)
PARS	Provincial Archives and Records Service [*Canada*]
PARSA........	Parasitological Society of Southern Africa (EAIO)
PARSA........	Postgraduate and Research Students' Association [*Australian National University*]
PARSAC......	Particle Size Analog Computer (IAA)
Pars Ans.....	Parsons' Answer to the Fifth Part of Coke's Reports [*A publication*] (DLA)
PARSAVAL...	Pattern Recognition System Application Evaluation (IAA)

Pars Bills & N...	Parsons on Bills and Notes [*A publication*] (DLA)
Pars Cont.....	Parsons on Contracts [*A publication*] (DLA)
Pars Dec.....	Parsons' Decisions [*2-7 Massachusetts*] [*A publication*] (DLA)
parsec	Parallax Second (SHCU)
PARSEC	Parallax Second [*Unit of interstellar-space measure*]
PARSEC......	Parallel State Event Condition (VLIE)
PARSEC......	Parliament Secretariat (SAUS)
PARSEC......	Parser and Extensible Compiler [*Programming language*] (CSR)
PARSECS.....	Program for Astronomical Research and Scientific Experiments Concerning Space
Pars Eq Cas...	Parsons' Select Equity Cases [*1842-51*] [*Pennsylvania*] [*A publication*] (DLA)
PARSET	Precision Askania Range System of Electronic Timing (MUGU)
PARSEV......	Paraglider Research Vehicle [*NASA*] (KSC)
PARS-F......	Programmed Airlines Reservation System-Financial (SAUS)
Par Sh & Adm...	Parsons on the Law of Shipping and Admiralty [*A publication*] (DLA)
PARSIM	Perimeter Acquisition RADAR Simulation [*Missile system evaluation*] (RDA)
PARSIM.......	Plant Appropriation Request Simulation (IAA)
PARSIP.......	Point Arguello Range Safety Impact Predictor (MUGU)
Pars Mar Ins...	Parsons on Marine Insurance [*A publication*] (DLA)
Pars Mar Law...	Parsons on Maritime Law [*A publication*] (DLA)
Pars Merc Law...	Parsons on Mercantile Law [*A publication*] (DLA)
Parsons'......	Parsons' Select Equity Cases [*Pennsylvania*] [*A publication*] (DLA)
PARSQ.......	Pararescue
Pars Sel Eq Cas (PA)...	Parsons' Select Equity Cases [*Pennsylvania*] [*A publication*] (DLA)
Pars S Eq Cas...	Parsons' Select Equity Cases [*Pennsylvania*] [*A publication*] (DLA)
Pars Shipp & Adm...	Parsons on Shipping and Admiralty [*A publication*] (DLA)
PARSYM......	Partial Symmetry
PARSYN.......	Parametric Synthesis [*Computer science*]
part.......	palticiple (SAUS)
PART	Pan American Round Tables in the USA [*Defunct*] (EA)
PART	Part Allocation Requirements Technic (SAUS)
Part..........	Parterre (SAUS)
PART	Partial (MSA)
part..........	Partial (VRA)
PART	Participate (AABC)
Part..........	Participating (EBF)
part..........	Participle (NTIO)
PART	Participle [*Grammar*]
PART	Particle (IAA)
PART	Particular
PART	Partis [*A Part*] [*Pharmacy*]
PART	Partition [*Ballistics*]
PART	Partner (ADA)
PART	Partnership (SAUS)
PART	Parts Allocation Requirements Technique
PART	People Against Racist Terror (EA)
PART	Performing Arts Repertory Theater
PART	Pressure Altitude Reporting Transponder (SAUS)
PART	Production Allocation and Requirements Technique (MHDB)
PART	Professional Audit Review Team (AAGC)
PARTAC.......	Precision Askania Range Target Acquisition and Control (MUGU)
Part Adj......	Participle Adjective (SAUS)
PART AEQ...	Partes Aequales [*Equal Parts*] [*Pharmacy*]
PART AEQUAL...	Partes Aequales [*Equal Parts*] [*Pharmacy*] (ROG)
Part An	De Partibus Animalium [*of Aristotle*] [*Classical studies*] (OCD)
PARTAN.......	Parallel Tangents (SAUS)
PARTAN/SD...	Parallel Tangents and Steepest Descent (SAUS)
PARTAS	Precision Asrania Range Target Acquisition and Control
ParTch	PAR Technology Corp. [*Associated Press*] (SAG)
Part Charact...	Particle Characterization (SAUS)
PART DOLENT...	Partes Dolentes [*Painful Parts*] [*Pharmacy*]
PARTEI	Purchasing Agents of the Radio, Television, and Electronics Industries [*An association*] (IAA)
PARTEQ	Partners in Technology at Queens (SAUS)
PARTES	Piece-Wise Application of Radiation through the Electromagnetic-Pulse Simulator (PDAA)
Parth...........	Parthenius [*First century BC*] [*Classical studies*] (OCD)
Parth...........	Parthenogenesis (SAUS)
PARTIAL......	Participation in Architectural Layout (PDAA)
parti bd........	Particle Board (VRA)
Partic..........	Participating [*or Participation*] (DLA)
PARTIC	Participial [*Grammar*]
PARTIC	Particle
PARTIC	Particular
PARTIC EXH...	Particulate Exhaust (SAUS)
PARTICO.......	Parti d'Interets Congolais [*Party for Congolese Interests*] [*Political party*]
PARTIC PHYS...	Particle Physics (SAUS)
Partidas........	Moreau-Lislet and Carleton's Laws of Las Siete Partidas in Force in Louisiana [*A publication*] (DLA)
PARTIE	People's Alliance to Reform, Transform and Improve Everything (EA)
Partit	Partitive (SAUS)
PARTN	Partnership (ADA)
PARTNER.....	Proof of Analog Results through a Numerical Equivalent Routine [*Computer science*]
PartnerR.......	PartnerRe Ltd. [*Associated Press*] (SAG)
PARTNO......	Part Number (SAUS)
Part Or........	Partitiones Oratoriae [*of Cicero*] [*Classical studies*] (OCD)
Part Part Syst Charact...	Particle and Particle Systems Characterization (SAUS)
PARTR	Particular (ROG)

PARTS	Parts Analysis and Review Technique for Spares (SAUS)
PARTS	Parts Assembly and Reuse Tool Set [*Computer software*] [*Digitalk, Inc.*] (PCM)
PARTS	Parts Automated Repairable Tracking System (SAUS)
PARTS	Precision Approach RADAR Training System (MCD)
PARTS	Price Analysis and Review Technique for Spares
Part Sci Technol...	Particulate Science and Technology (SAUS)
PARTSHIP....	Partnership [*Legal shorthand*] (LWAP)
PartsS.........	Parts Source, Inc. (The) [*Associated Press*] (SAG)
PART VIC....	Partitis Vicibus [*In Divided Parts*] [*Pharmacy*]
Part World....	Particle World
PARU	Personnel Applied Research Unit [*Canadian military*]
PARU	Photographic and Reproduction Unit
PARU	Police Aerial Reinforcement [*or Resupply*] Unit [*Thailand*] (CINC)
PARU	Postanesthetic Recovery Unit [*Medicine*]
Par Uni.......	Party Unity (SAUS)
PARV	Paravane [*Anti-moored-mine device*] (KSC)
PARV	Parvus [*Small*] [*Pharmacy*]
PARV3	Parsnip Virus 3 [*Plant pathology*]
ParVec.........	Purdue Center for Parallel and Vector Computing [*Purdue University*] [*Research center*] (RCD)
Parvnt.........	Paravant Computer Systems, Inc. [*Associated Press*] (SAG)
PARVO........	Professional and Academic Regional Visits Organization (SAUS)
PARVSTRCRA...	Paravane and Stores Crane [*Engineering*]
PARW	Professional Association of Resume Writers (EA)
Par WC	Parish Will Case [*A publication*] (DLA)
Par Wills	Parsons on Wills [*1854*] [*A publication*] (DLA)
PAS.............	National Postsecondary Agriculture Student Organization (EA)
PAS.............	Pakistan Academy of Sciences (SAUS)
PAS.............	Palestine Aid Society of America (EA)
PAS.............	P-Aminosalicylic Acid (SAUS)
PAS.............	Para-Aminosalicylic [*Acid*] [*Organic chemistry*]
PAS.............	Parallel Assignment Statement (SAUS)
PAS.............	Parametric Amplifier System
PaS.............	Paranoia Subtle [*Psychology*]
PAS.............	Parent Attitude Scale
PAS.............	Paros [*Greece*] [*Airport symbol*] (OAG)
PAS.............	Partido de Accion Socialista [*Socialist Action Party*] [*Costa Rica*] [*Political party*] (PPW)
PAS.............	Parti Islam se Malaysia [*Islamic Party of Malaysia*] [*Political party*] (PPW)
PAS.............	Partition Alternate Sector (SAUS)
PAS.............	Partito de Azione de Sardegna [*Sardinian Action Party*] [*Italy*] [*Political party*] (PPW)
PAS.............	Pasadena [*California*] [*Seismograph station code, US Geological Survey*] (SEIS)
PA S	Pascal Second
PAS.............	PASCAL source code (SAUS)
PAS.............	Pascal Source File [*Computer science*]
PAS.............	Passage (AABC)
PAS.............	Passed to the Adjacent Sector
PAS.............	Passing Aid System (IAA)
Pas	Passipoverus [*Flourished, 13th century*] [*Authority cited in pre-1607 legal work*] (DSA)
PAS.............	Passive (WDAA)
PAS.............	Passive Alcohol Sensor (SAUS)
PAS.............	Patent Applicant Service (NITA)
PAS.............	Patient Administration System [*British*]
PAS.............	Patient Appointments and Scheduling [*Medicine*] (DMAA)
PAS.............	Patients' Aid Society
PAS.............	Pattern Analysis System (SAUS)
PAS.............	Payload Accommodations Studies [*NASA*] (NASA)
PAS.............	Payload Analysis Section (SAUS)
PAS.............	Payload Assist Stage (ACAE)
PAS.............	Payload Assist System (SAUS)
PAS.............	Payload Attach Structure (SAUS)
PAS.............	Pelita Air Service PT [*Indonesia*] [*ICAO designator*] (FAAC)
PAS.............	Penetration Aids System (ACAE)
PA S	Pennsylvania Superior Court Reports [*A publication*] (DLA)
PAS.............	Perceptual Aberration Scale (SAUS)
PAS.............	Percussive Arts Society (EA)
PAS.............	Performance Abatement Services, Inc. (EFIS)
PAS.............	Performance Advisory System (SAUS)
PAS.............	Performance Analysis and Systems development (SAUS)
PAS.............	Performance Assessment System (ACAE)
PAS.............	Perigee-Apogee Satellite [*Aerospace*]
PAS.............	Perigee-Apogee Stage [*Aerospace*]
PAS.............	Perigee-Apogee System [*Aerospace*]
PAS.............	Periodic Acid Schiff (SAUS)
PA/S...........	Periodic Acid/Schiff [*A stain*]
PAS.............	Peripheral Anterior Synechia [*Ophthalmology*]
PAS.............	Persistent Atrial Standstill [*Medicine*] (DMAA)
PAS.............	Personal Acquaintance Service
PAS.............	Personal Attitude Survey (EDAC)
PAS.............	Personnel Accounting Symbol [*Air Force*] (AFM)
PAS.............	Personnel Accounting System [*Marine Corps*]
PAS.............	Personnel Activity Sequence (AAG)
PAS.............	Personnel Administration Section [*Library Administration Division of ALA*]
PAS.............	Personnel Assignment Survey (MCD)
PAS.............	Phase Address System
PAS.............	Phase Array System
PAS.............	Philanthropic Advisory Service
PAS.............	Phosphatase Acid Serum [*Medicine*] (MELL)
PAS.............	Phosphoric Acid-Sensitive

PAS	Photoabsorption Spectroscopy [Chemistry]
PAS	Photoacoustic Spectrometry [Also, OAS]
PAS	Physician-Assisted Suicide
PAS	Physicians for Automotive Safety [Defunct] (EA)
PAS	Pierce-Arrow Society (EA)
PAS	Pilots Advisory Service
PAS	Pilot's Attack Sight [British]
PAS	Pioneer Aerodynamic Systems
PAS	Pioneer Air System (SAUS)
PAS	Pioneer America Society (EA)
PAS	Planning Advisory Service (GNE)
PAS	Planning and Scheduling (SAUS)
PAS	Plant Alarms Sum (ECII)
PAS	Plasma Arc Spraying (SAUS)
PAS	Plasma Arc System
PAS	Plessey Assessment Services (NITA)
PAS	Pneumatic Actuation System (ACAE)
PAS	Pneumatic Air Saw
PAS	Police Aviation Services Ltd (SAUS)
PAS	Policy Analysis Staff [Environmental Protection Agency] (GFGA)
PAS	Polish Academy of Sciences
PAS	Polish Astronautical Society [See also PTA]
PAS	Pollution Abatement Seminar (SAUS)
PAS	Poly(alkyl Sulfone) [Organic chemistry]
PAS	Polyaminosiloxane [Organic chemistry]
PAS	Polyarylsulfone [Organic chemistry]
PAS	Pontifical Academy of Science (SAUS)
PAS	Positron Annihilation Spectroscopy (MCD)
PAS	Post Abortion Syndrome
PAS	Postacoustic Spectroscopy
PAS	Posterior Airway Space [Medicine] (DMAA)
PAS	Posterior Area of [Loose] Skin
PAS	Postponed Accounting System [Banking]
PAS	Power Apparatus and Systems (MCD)
PAS	Power-Assisted Steering [Automotive feature]
PAS	Power-Assist System [Motorcycle steering]
PAS	Power Available Shaft (SAUS)
PAS	Pre-Admission Screening [Medicine] (MEDA)
PAS	Preaward Survey [To determine a contractor's capability] [DoD]
PAS	Precategorical Acoustic Storage (DIPS)
PAS	Precise Acquisition System
PAS	Precision Acquisition System
PAS	Preconscious Activity Scale (EDAC)
PAS	Pregnancy Advisory Service [British]
PAS	Premature Atrial Stimulus [Medicine] (DMAA)
PAS	Premorbid Adjustment Scale (SAUS)
PAS	Presidential Appointee Subject
PAS	President's Advisor for Science
PAS	Pressure Alarm Switch (SAUS)
PAS	Pressure-Assisted Sintering [Forging] [Automotive engineering]
PAS	Pressurized Air Subsystem
PAS	Price Analysis Sheet
PAS	Primary Alerting System
PAS	Primary Ascent System [Aerospace] (NASA)
PAS	Princeton Aqua Science, New Brunswick (SAUS)
PAS	Principal Assistant Secretary
PAS	Prisoners' Advice Service (WDAA)
PAS	Prisoners' Aid Society [Australia]
PAS	Privacy Act Statement (NRCH)
PAS	Probation and Aftercare Service (SAUS)
PAS	Problem Appraisal Scales [Personality development test] [Psychology]
PAS	Problem Assessment System (SAUS)
PAS	Process Analysis Services (SAUS)
PAS	Process Automation System (SAUS)
PAS	Processed Array Signal
PAS	Procurement Action System (MCD)
PAS	Procurement Appropriation, Secondary (MCD)
PAS	Product Acceptance Standard [Automotive engineering]
PAS	Product Acceptance Test Specification (SAUS)
PAS	Product Assurance Survey
PAS	Product Availability Search (MCD)
PAS	Professional Activity Study [Later, CPHA]
PAS	Professional Advancement Series [National Court Reporters Association]
PAS	Professor of Aerospace Studies [Air Force] (AFIT)
PAS	Professor of Air Science [Air Force]
PAS	Program Activity Structure
PAS	Program Address Storage (IEEE)
PAS	Program Allowance Schedule
PAS	Program Alternative Simulation (IAA)
PAS	Programmable Audio Synthesiser (SAUS)
PAS	Program of Advanced Studies
PAS	Progressive Accumulated Stress [Psychiatry]
PAS	Propellant Acquisition System (IGSL)
PAS	Propulsion and Auxiliary Systems Department [David W. Taylor Naval Ship Research and Development Center]
PAS	Protocol Analysis System (ABAC)
PAS	Pseudo Aircraft Simulation (CTAS)
PAS	Psychiatric Assessment Scale (SAUS)
PAS	Psychopathological Assessment Scale (DB)
PAS	Public Address System
PAS	Public Administration Service (EA)
PAS	Public Affairs Specialist
PAS	Public Announcement Service (SAUS)

PAS	Public Automobile System (SAUS)
PAS	Publicly Available Specification (RALS)
PAS	Pulmonary Artery Stenosis [Medicine]
PAS	Pulmonary Aspiration Syndrome [Medicine] (MELL)
PAS	Pulsating Air System [Automotive engineering]
PAS	Pulse Analysis System (SAUS)
PAS	Pump Actuator Set
PAS	Pyrotechnics Arming Switch
Pas	Terminus Paschae [Easter Term] [Latin] [Legal term] (DLA)
PASA	Pacific American Steamship Association [Later, AIMS]
PASA	Para-Aminosalicylic Acid [Organic chemistry]
PASA	Participating Agency Service Agreement (GNE)
PASA	PCR [Polymerase Chain Reaction] Amplification of Specific Alleles [Genetics]
PASA	Pennsylvania Association of School and Administrators (SAUS)
PASA	Personnel Administrative Services Agency [Army]
PASA	Pioneers' Association of South Australia
PASA	Pipelines Authority of South Australia
PASA	Playgroup Association of South Australia
PASA	Police Association of South Australia
PASA	Polymerase Chain Reaction Amplification of specific alleles (SAUS)
PASA	Primary Acquired Sideroblastic Anemia [Medicine]
PASA	Proximal Articular Set Angle [Orthopedics] (DAVI)
PASA	Quepass.com, Inc. [NASDAQ symbol]
PAS&T	Particle Accelerator Science and Technology (SAUS)
PASAR	Philippine Associated Smelting and Refining (SAUS)
PASAR	Psychological Abstracts Search and Retrieval
PASARR	Preadmission Screening and Annual Resident Review [Medicare]
PASARS	Podded Advanced Synthetic Aperture Radar System (SAUS)
PASAT	Particle Accelerator Science and Technology (IAA)
PASAT	Poppleton-Allen Sales Aptitude Test
PASB	Pan American Sanitary Bureau
PASB	Perpetual Savings Bank FSB (MHDW)
PASb	Predneaziatskii Sbornik Voprosy Khattologii i Khurritologii [A publication] (BJA)
PASB	Proceedings of the Anthropological Society of Bombay (SAUS)
PASB	Proceedings of the Asiatic Society of Bengal (SAUS)
P-as-B	Program as Broadcast [Radio] (DEN)
PASB	Public Authorities Superannuation Board [New South Wales, Australia]
PASBI	Palo Alto Social Background Inventory [Psychology]
PASBO	Pennsylvania Association of School Business Officials (SAUS)
PASC	Deadhorse [Alaska] [ICAO location identifier] (ICLI)
PASC	Pacific Air Service Command (SAUS)
PASC	Pacific Area Standards Congress [American National Standards Institute]
PASC	Palestine Armed Struggle Command (PD)
PASC	Panama Area Service Command (SAUS)
PASC	Pan American Sanitary Conference
PASC	Pan-American Standardization Conference (SAUS)
PASC	Pan American Standards Commission [See also COPANT] (EAIO)
PASC	Pan American Standards Committee
PAS-C	Para-Aminosalicylic Acid Crystallized with Ascorbic Acid [Organic chemistry] (MAE)
Pasc	Paschal [Easter Term] [Legal term] (DLA)
Pasc	Paschal's Reports [25, 28-31 Texas] [A publication] (DLA)
PASC	Planning Advisory Subcommittee (SAUS)
PASC	Polar Air and Snow Chemistry Programme (SAUS)
PASC	Polar Atmospheric and Snow Chemistry (CARB)
PASC	Portable Application Standards Committee (SAUS)
PASC	Precision Adaptive Sub-Band Coding [Electronics]
PASC	Primitive Art Society of Chicago (EA)
PASCA	Positron Annihilation Spectroscopy for Chemical Analysis
PASCAL	Philips Automatic Sequence Calculator
PASCAL	Program Applique a la Selection et a la Compilation Automatique de la Litterature [Centre National de la Recherche Scientifique-Informascience] [Bibliographic database]
PASCALS	Projected Antisubmarine Classification and Location System (DNAB)
PASCH	Pascha [Easter] [Church calendars] (ROG)
Pasch	Paschal [Easter Term] [Legal term] (DLA)
Paschal	Paschal's Reports [28-31 Texas] [Supplement to Vol. 25] [A publication] (DLA)
Paschal's Ann Const	Paschal's United States Constitution, Annotated [A publication] (DLA)
Pasch Dig	Paschal's Texas Digest of Decisions [A publication] (DLA)
PASCO	Pan American Sulfur Corp. (SAUS)
PASCOSS	Passive and Active Control of Space Structures
PASCT	Pan American Society for Chemotherapy of Tuberculosis [See also SAQT] [Buenos Aires, Argentina] (EAIO)
PASD	After Diastase Digestion [Biochemistry] (DAVI)
p'ase	Alkaline Phosphatase [Biochemistry] (DAVI)
PASE	Passive Start and Entry System
PASE	Polar Air-Snow Experiment (CARB)
PASE	Post-Apollo Space Electrophoresis [European Space Agency]
PASE	Power-Assisted Storage Equipment (IEEE)
PASE	Product Acceptance Exceptions
PASE	Programs in the Arts for Special Education Project (EDAC)
PaSEA	Pennsylvania Society of Enrolled Agents (SAUS)
PASECT	Panama Sector (SAUS)
PASEM	Program of Assistance to Solar Equipment Manufacturers (SAUS)
PASEM System	Partial Analysis by Scanning Electron Microscopy System (SAUS)
PASEP	Passed Separately [Military]
PASEP	Pass Separately

PASES	Performance Assessment of Syntax: Elicited and Spontaneous [*Educational test*]
Pas Ex	Passive Exercise [*Physical Therapy*] (DAVI)
PASEX	Polar Atmosphere Snow Experiment (SAUS)
PASF............	Photographic Art and Science Foundation (EA)
PASFIS	Philippines Aquatic Sciences and Fisheries Information System [*Marine science*] (OSRA)
PASG	Patent Abstracts Section, Official Gazette [*Federal government*] [*A publication*]
PASG	Pneumatic Antishock Garment [*Roentgenology*]
PASG	Programs Activities and Services Guide (SAUS)
PASG	Pulse Amplifier/Symbol Generator
PASG	Pulse Analyzer Signal Generator
PASGAP	Pacific Sea Grant Advisory Program (SAUS)
PASGT	Personnel Armor System for Ground Troops (RDA)
PASGX	Phoenix-Engemann Growth Cl.A [*Mutual fund ticker symbol*] (SG)
PASH	Palaeoclimates of the Southern Hemisphere (SAUS)
PASI............	Pikunas Adult Stress Inventory [*Psychology*]
PA/SI	Preliminary Assessment and Site Inspection [*Environmental Protection Agency*] (FFDE)
PA/SI	Preliminary Assessment/Site Investigation (SAUS)
PASI............	Professional Associate, Chartered Surveyors' Institution [*Later, ARICS*]
PASI............	Psoriasis Area and Severity Index [*Medicine*]
PASI............	Sitka [*Alaska*] [*ICAO location identifier*] (ICLI)
PASIC	Percussive Arts Society International Convention [*Percussive Arts Society*]
PasifSat.......	Pasifik Satelit Nusantara (PT) [*Associated Press*] (SAG)
pasim	paimological (SAUS)
Pasim	Pasimologist (SAUS)
PASIM	Pasimology (SAUS)
PASIN	Particle-Matter Airborne Sampling Inlet Experiment (SAUS)
PAS-INAH	Para-Aminosalicylic Acid and Isonicotinic Acid Hydrazide (BARN)
PASIPS	Parallel Signal and Image Processing System (SAUS)
PASITAM	Program of Advanced Studies of Institution Building and Technical Assistance Methodologies [*MUCIA*]
PASJ............	Publications of the Astronomical Society of Japan (SAUS)
PASL............	Physical Activity Sciences Laboratory (SAUS)
PASL............	Polish Americans for the Statue of Liberty [*Defunct*] (EA)
PASLA	Programmable Asynchronous Line Adapter
PASLIB	Pakistan Association of Special Libraries (NITA)
Pas Lux	Pasicrisie Luxembourgeoise [*Luxembourg Law Reports*] [*A publication*] (ILCA)
PASM..........	Partitionable SIMD/MIMD [*Single Instruction, Multiple Data/Multiple Instruction, Multiple Data*] (MCD)
PASM..........	Periodic Acid - Silver Methenamine [*Biological stain*]
PA-SM	Periodic Acid-Silver Methenamine (SAUS)
PASM..........	Preaward Survey Monitor [*DoD*]
PASMA	Prefabricated Aluminium Scaffold Manufacturers Association [*British*] (DBA)
PASN	St. Paul Island [*Alaska*] [*ICAO location identifier*] (ICLI)
PASO	Pan Africanist Students Organization (SAUS)
PASO	Pan American Sanitary Organization
PASO	Pan American Sports Organization [*See also ODEPA*] [*Mexico City, Mexico*] (EAIO)
PA/SO	Port Antisubmarine Officer [*Navy*]
PASO	Principal Armament Supply Officer [*British military*] (DMA)
PASOC	Partido de Accion Socialista [*Party of Socialist Action*] [*Spain*] [*Political party*] (PPW)
PASOCO.......	Parti Socialiste des Comores [*Socialist Party of Comoros*] [*Political party*] (EY)
PASOH........	Partido de Accion Socialista de Honduras [*Political party*] (EY)
PASOH........	Partido Socialista de Honduras [*Honduran Socialist Party*] [*Political party*]
PASOK	Panellinion Sosialistikon Kinema [*Pan-Hellenic Socialist Movement*] [*Greek*] [*Political party*] (PPE)
PASOK........	Pan-Hellenic Socialist Commune (SAUS)
PASOLS	Pacific Area Senior Officer Logistics Seminar (MCD)
PASOS	Paperless Shop-Order System (SAUS)
PASP	Pancreas-Specific Protein [*Medicine*] (DMAA)
PASP	Port Autonome de San Pedro [*The Ivory Coast*] (EY)
PA/SP	Positioner Antenna and Solar Panel [*NASA*]
PASP	Price Adjusting Sampling Plan (PDAA)
PASP	Program in Aegean Scripts and Prehistory (SAUS)
PASP	Publications of the Astronomical Society of the Pacific (SAUS)
PASP	Pulmonary Artery Systolic Pressure [*Medicine*] (DMAA)
PAS(PR)	Principal Assistant Secretary (Priority)
PAS procedure...	Periodic Acid Schiff Procedure (DOG)
P-as-R	Program as Recorded [*Radio*] (DEN)
PASR	Project Authorization Status Report (SAUS)
PASRB	Preaward Survey Review Board [*DoD*]
PAS Reaction...	Periodic Acid Schiff Reaction (SAUS)
PASS	Panic Attack Sufferers' Support Groups (EA)
PASS	Parameterization of Subgrid Scale (SAUS)
PASS	Parents Against Secondhand Smoke (SAUS)
PASS	Parents Against Subliminal Seduction [*Defunct*] (EA)
PASS	Parked Aircraft Security System (PDAA)
PASS	Parts Analysis Summary Sheet
PASS	Pass [*Postal Service standard*] (OPSA)
Pass............	Passage (DD)
PASS	Passage [*Maps and charts*] (KSC)
PASS	Passenger (KSC)
PASS	Passenger Automated Selection System (ADA)
PASS	Passim [*Everywhere*] [*Latin*]
PASS	Passitive (SAUS)

PASS	Passivate [*Metallurgy*] (IAA)
PASS	Passivated (SAUS)
pass............	Passive (NTIO)
PASS	Passive
PASS	Passive Acquisiton Surveillance System (SAUS)
PASS	Passive-Active Surveillance System (MCD)
PASS	Passive Aircraft Surveillance System
PASS	Passive & Active Sensor Subsystem (SAUS)
Pass............	Passover (BARN)
PASS	Passport (SAUS)
PASS	Patrol Advanced Surveillance System (MCD)
PASS	Pay/Personnel Administrative Support System (NVT)
PASS	Penetration Aids/Strike System (NG)
PASS	Performance Analysis Software System (SAUS)
PASS	Performance Analysis Subsystem [*Military*] (CAAL)
PASS	Performance Assessment Scientific Support (ABAC)
PASS	Personal Access Satellite System [*NASA*] (CIST)
PASS	Personalized Automotive Security System [*In product name, PASS-Key*] [*Delco Electronics*] [*Automotive engineering*]
PASS	Personnel Accounting & Skills System (SAUS)
PASS	Petroleum Abstracts Search Service [*Online information service*]
PASS	Petroleum Abstracts Search System (SAUS)
PASS	Phased Array Sector Scanner [*Instrument for measuring ultrasound*] [*Trademark of General Electric Co.*]
PASS	Phoenix Ability Survey System [*Test*]
PASS	Photo-Access Security System
PASS	Photogrammetric Archival Storage System (SAUS)
PASS	Pilot Aerial Survival System (PDAA)
PASS	Pirelli Active Safety System
PASS	Planning and Scheduling Session
PASS	Planning and Scheduling System (NASA)
PASS	Planning and Specification Software (SAUS)
PASS	Policyowner Attitude Survey Service [*LIMRA*]
PASS	Polish Assembler (SAUS)
PASS	Polymeric Aluminum Silicate Sulfate [*Inorganic chemistry*]
PASS	Pooled Analytical Stereoplotter System (PDAA)
PASS	Portable Analysis/Synthesis System (TIMI)
PASS	Portable Analyze/Synthesize System (SAUS)
PASS	Portable Assisted Study Sequence Program [*California*] (EDAC)
PASS	Position and Surveyance System (SAUS)
PASS	Positioning and Surveying System (MCD)
PASS	Post-Accident Sampling Systems [*Nuclear energy*]
PASS	Precision Angulation and Support System (SAUS)
PASS	Precision Autocollimating Solar Sensor
PASS	Prenotification Analysis Support System (SAUS)
PASS	Pressurized Air Starter System (MCD)
PASS	Price Adjusted Single Sampling (PDAA)
PASS	Primary Academic Sentiment Scale [*Child development test*]
PASS	Primary Avionics Software System (NASA)
PASS	Prince Albert Satellite Station (SAUS)
PASS	Priority Academic Student Skills
PASS	Private Alarm Signalling System
PASS	Private Automatic Switching System [*Telecommunications*]
PASS	Procurement Aging and Staging System [*Army*] (AABC)
PASS	Procurement and Acquisition Support System (SAUS)
PASS	Procurement Automated Source System [*Small Business Administration*] [*Washington, DC*] [*Information service or system*] (IID)
PASS	Production Automated Scheduling System (IEEE)
PASS	Professional Accounting System for Schools (AIE)
PASS	Professional Airways Systems Specialists (EA)
PASS	Professional Airways Systems Specialists Division [*An association*] (EA)
PASS	Professional Amateur Sports Systems [*Cable-television network*]
PASS	Professional Association of Secretarial Services [*Later, NASS*] (EA)
PASS	Program Aid Software Systems [*Computer science*] (IEEE)
PASS	Program Alternative Simulation System (KSC)
PASS	Program Analysis of Service Systems [*Procedure to evaluate human service programs*]
PASS	Programmed Access/Security System [*Card Key Systems*]
PASS	Programming Aid Software System (SAUS)
PASS	Project Activating Signal System (SAUS)
PASS	Prototype Artillery Sub-System (SAUS)
PASS	Purchasing Activities Support System (SAUS)
PASS	Pure Acoustic Sounder (SAUS)
PASSA	Pacific American Steamship Association [*Later, AIMS*] (EA)
PASSAGE......	Passage [*Commonly used*] (OPSA)
PASSAT	PASCAL Subset for Application in Test Computers (NITA)
PASSCAL	Program for Array Seismic Studies of the Continental Lithosphere (SAUS)
PASSEX	Passing Exercise (DOMA)
PASSIM	President's Advisory Staff on Scientific Information Management
PASS-IN-REVIEW...	Priority Aircraft Subsystem Suitability Intensive Review (MCD)
PASSION......	Program for Algebraic Sequences Specifically of Input-Output Nature [*Computer science*]
PASSMAN....	Pay/Personnel Administrative Support System Manual (DNAB)
PAssn	Postassistentin (SAUS)
PASSP	Pennsylvania Association of Secondary School Principals (SAUS)
PASSR........	Passenger (DCTA)
Pass Tr	Passenger Train (SAUS)
PASSWD.....	Password [*Computer science*]
PAST...........	Pacific/Asian Strategy for Tomorrow (SAUS)
PAST...........	Pasteurella [*Genus of bacteria*]
PAST...........	Pastillus [*A Lozenge, Troch, Pastil*] [*Pharmacy*] (ROG)
Past	Pastoral Epistles (BJA)

PAST............	Pastorate
PA St............	Pennsylvania State Reports [A publication] (DLA)
PAST............	Periodic Acid-Schiff Technique [Medicine] (DMAA)
PAST............	Portable Arming System Trainer (MCD)
PAST............	Process Accessible Segment Table
PAST............	Professor of Air Science and Tactics
PAST............	Propulsion and Associated Systems Test (MCD)
PA Stat Ann...	Pennsylvania Statutes, Annotated [A publication] (DLA)
PA Stat Ann (Purdon)...	Pennsylvania Statutes, Annotated (Purdon) [A publication] (DLA)
PA State	Pennsylvania State Reports [A publication] (DLA)
PA State R...	Pennsylvania State Reports [A publication] (DLA)
PASTIC	Pakistan Scientific and Technological Information Center [Formerly, PANSDOC] [Quaid-I-Azan University Campus] [Islamabad, Pakistan]
PAstO...........	Our Lady of Angels College, Aston, PA [Library symbol] [Library of Congress] (LCLS)
PA St R.......	Pennsylvania State Reports [A publication] (DLA)
PASTRAM...	Passenger Traffic Management (SAUS)
PASTRAM...	Passenger Traffic Management System [Army]
PASTRAM System...	Passenger Traffic Management System (SAUS)
PA St Tr.......	Pennsylvania State Trials (Hogan) [A publication] (DLA)
PASU	Pan-African Socialist Union [Southern Rhodesia]
PASU	Patrol Aircraft Service Unit
PASU	Performing Arts Study Unit (EA)
PASU	Polyarylsulfone [Organic chemistry]
PASU	Preliminary Approval for Service Use [Military]
PASU	Provisional Approval for Service Use [Navy] (NVT)
PA Summary...	Summary of Pennsylvania Jurisprudence [A publication] (DLA)
PA Super	Pennsylvania Superior Court Reports [A publication] (DLA)
PA Super Ct...	Pennsylvania Superior Court Reports [A publication] (DLA)
PA Superior Ct...	Pennsylvania Superior Court Reports [A publication] (DLA)
PASUS........	Pan American Society of the United States (EA)
PASV	Pangola Stunt Virus [Plant pathology]
PASV	Sparrevohn Air Force Station [Alaska] [ICAO location identifier] (ICLI)
PASW	Personal Assistance Service Worker [Medicine] (DMAA)
PASW	Pure Atria [NASDAQ symbol] [Formerly, Pure Software] (SG)
PASW	Pure Atria Corp. [NASDAQ symbol] (SAG)
PASWEPS....	Passive Antisubmarine Warfare Environmental Protection System [Navy] (NATG)
PASY	Shemya Air Force Base [Alaska] [ICAO location identifier] (ICLI)
PAt..............	Allentown Public Library, Allentown, PA [Library symbol] [Library of Congress] (LCLS)
Pat..............	All India Reporter, Patna Series [A publication] (ILCA)
PAT.............	Athenaeum of Philadelphia (EA)
PAT.............	Athenaeum of Philadelphia, Philadelphia, PA [OCLC symbol] (OCLC)
Pat..............	Indian Law Reports, Patna Series [A publication] (DLA)
Pat..............	Indian Rulings, Patna Series [A publication] (DLA)
PAT.............	International Brotherhood of Painters and Allied Trades
PAT.............	National Patents Appeal Tribunal [England] (DLA)
PAT.............	Pacific Air Transport (SAUS)
PAT.............	Pacific Automobile Train (SAUS)
PAT.............	Packed Tower Aeration (EEVL)
PAT.............	Palleted Automated Transport (PDAA)
PAT.............	Parametric Artificial Talker
PaT.............	Parents as Teachers (BARN)
PAT.............	Paroxysmal Atrial [or Auricular] Tachycardia [Medicine]
PAT.............	Parts Accountability Technique (MCD)
PAT.............	Passive Acoustic Target [Military]
PAT.............	Passive Acoustic Torpedo [Military]
PAT.............	Passive Acting Tracking (SAUS)
PAT.............	Passive Angle Attack
PAT.............	Passive Angle Track (NVT)
pa t.............	Past Tense [Grammar] (BARN)
PAT.............	Patch (SAUS)
PAT.............	Patelet Aggregation Test (SAUS)
pat.............	Patella (STED)
Pat.............	Patent (AAGC)
pat.............	Patent (STED)
PAT.............	Patent (KSC)
PAT.............	Patent Rolls [British]
Pat.............	Paternal (SAUS)
pat.............	Paternal Origin [Medicine] (DMAA)
PAT.............	Paterson [Diocesan abbreviation] [New Jersey] (TOCD)
PAT.............	Patersons [Publisher]
Pat.............	Paterson's Scotch Appeals, House of Lords [A publication] (DLA)
Pat.............	Pathe [Record label] [France]
PAT.............	Patient
pat.............	Patina (VRA)
PAT.............	Patio
PAT.............	Patna [India] [Airport symbol] (OAG)
Pat.............	Paton's Scotch Appeal Cases, House of Lords [A publication] (DLA)
PAT.............	Patras [Greece] [Seismograph station code, US Geological Survey] (SEIS)
PAT.............	Patriarch [Greek Church] (ROG)
PAT.............	Patrick Air Force Base [Florida] (KSC)
PAT.............	Patrol
PAT.............	Patten Corp. [NYSE symbol] (SPSG)
PAT.............	Pattern
PAT.............	Pattern Analysis Test [Army]
PAT.............	Peninsulator Air Transport (SAUS)
PAT.............	People's Action Team [South Vietnam]
PAT.............	Performance Acceptance Test (SAA)
PAT.............	Performance Alignment Tester (SAUS)
PAT.............	Performance Appraisal Team [Nuclear energy] (NRCH)

PAT.............	Performance Assessment Team (SAUS)
PAT.............	Peripheral Allocation Table (NITA)
PAT.............	Peripheral Assignment Table (CMD)
PAT.............	Permit Assistance Team [Environmental Protection Agency] (GFGA)
PAT.............	Person Activity Tracker (VLIE)
PAT.............	Personalized Array Translator (IEEE)
PAT.............	Personnel Assistance Team [Military]
PAT.............	Personnel Authorization Table [Air Force]
PAT.............	Pesticide Applicator Training [Environmental Protection Agency] (AEPA)
PAT.............	Pets as Therapy (WDAA)
PAT.............	Phenylaminotetrazole [Psychology]
PAT.............	Phenylazotriphenylmethane (SAUS)
PAT.............	Philippine Aerial Taxi (SAUS)
PAT.............	Phosphinothricin Acetyl Transferase [An enzyme]
PAT.............	Photo Articulation Test
PAT.............	Physics Achievement Test
PAT.............	Picric Acid Turbidity Test
PAT.............	Picture Arrangement Test
PAT.............	Planar Assembly and Test System (VLIE)
PAT.............	Plasma Arc Tunnel
PAT.............	Plastic Apply Template (MCD)
PAT.............	Platelet Aggregation Test [Medicine] (MELL)
PAT.............	Platoon Anti-Tank (SAA)
PAT.............	Plenum Air Tread [Army amphibian vehicle]
PAT.............	Plutonium Air Transportable [Nuclear energy] (NRCH)
PAT.............	Point after Touchdown [Football]
PAT.............	Point-After Try (SAUS)
PAT.............	Polar Adjectives Test (AEBS)
PAT.............	Polar Auxin Transport [Botany]
PAT.............	Polaris Acceleration Test [Military] (SAA)
PAT.............	Police Association of Tasmania [Australia]
PAT.............	Political Action Teams
PAT.............	Polyamine Acetyltransferase (DB)
PAT.............	Polyaminotriazole [Organic chemistry]
PAT.............	Polyarlterephthalate [Organic chemistry]
PAT.............	Population, Affluence and Technology (SAUS)
PAT.............	Portable Audio Terminal (VLIE)
PAT.............	Port Address Translation [Computer science] (VLIE)
PAT.............	Port and Address Translation (SAUS)
PAT.............	Port Authority Transit (SAUS)
PAT.............	Position Adjusting Type
PAT.............	Postavailability Trials
PAT.............	Power Alarm Test (SAUS)
PAT.............	Power Ascension Testing (IEEE)
PAT.............	Power-Assisted Traverse (SAUS)
PAT.............	Practical, Available Technology (SAUS)
PAT.............	Preadmission Screening and Assessment Team [Medicine] (DB)
PAT.............	Preadmission Testing
PAT.............	Prearranged Transfers
PAT.............	Pre-Authorized Transfer (SAUS)
PAT.............	Precision Aim Technique [for helicopters] [Army] (RDA)
PAT.............	Prediction Analysis Techniques
PAT.............	Pregnancy at Term [Gynecology]
PAT.............	Preliminary Acceptance Tests
PAT.............	Preliminary Acceptance Trials [Navy]
PAT.............	Prescription Athletic Turf [Trademark for an artificial turf]
PAT.............	Pressure Assembled Thyristor
PAT.............	Printer Action Table [Computer science] (HGAA)
PAT.............	Prioirty Access Timer [Telecommunications] (OSI)
PAT.............	Priority Air Transport [Army] (FAAC)
PAT.............	Priority Air Travel [Army]
PAT.............	Prism Adaptation Test [Ophthalmology]
PAT.............	Problem Action Team [NASA] (NASA)
PAT.............	Procedure for Automatic Testing (IAA)
PAT.............	Procedures Authorized Task (MCD)
PAT.............	Process Action Team [Army] (RDA)
PAT.............	Process-Activation Table [Computer science]
PAT.............	Process Analysis Team
PAT.............	Product Acceptance Test [Advertising] (DOAD)
PAT.............	Product Adaption Tool (VLIE)
PAT.............	Production Acceptance Test [NASA] (KSC)
PAT.............	Production Acceptance Testing (SAUS)
PAT.............	Production Assessment (SAUS)
PAT.............	Production Assessment Test
PAT.............	Professional, Administrative, and Technical (OICC)
PAT.............	Professional Association of Teachers [British]
PAT.............	Proficiency Analytical Testing [National Institute on Occupational Safety and Health]
PAT.............	Profit After Tax (SAUS)
PAT.............	Program Activity Transmission
PAT.............	Program Analysis Table (VLIE)
PAT.............	Program Analysis Team (KSC)
PAT.............	Program Analyzer Tool (VLIE)
PAT.............	Program Attitude Test (IEEE)
PAT.............	Programmable Actuator-Transducer [Automotive engineering]
PAT.............	Programmable Automatic Tester (SAUS)
PAT.............	Programmed Activity Transmission (MCD)
PAT.............	Programmer Aptitude Test
PAT.............	Progressive Achievement Test of Listening Comprehension (TMMY)
PAT.............	Project Action Team [Acquisition Reform] (AAGC)
PAT.............	Property and Accounting Technician [Navy]
PAT.............	Proportional to Absolute Temperature (IAA)
PAT.............	Prototype Adaptation Toolkit (CTAS)
PAT.............	Pseudoadder Tree [Computer science]

PAT............	Psychoacoustic Testing
PAT.............	PSYOP [*Psychological Operation*] Automated Terminal (RDA)
PAT............	Public Access Terminal (SAUS)
PAT............	Public Administration Times [*A publication*] (EAAP)
PAT............	Public Affairs Team (COE)
PAT............	Pulsed Amplifier Tube
PAT............	Pump Algebra Tutor [*Computer program*]
PaT............	Purge-and-Trap [*Technique*] [*Environmental Protection Agency*]
PAtA............	Air Products & Chemicals, Inc.; Allentown, PA [*Library symbol*] [*Library of Congress*] (LCLS)
PATA............	Pacific American Tankship Association [*Defunct*] (EA)
PATA............	Pacific Area Travel Association [*San Francisco, CA*]
PATA............	Pacific Asia Travel Association (EA)
PATA............	Patagonia [*Region of South America*] (ROG)
PATA............	Pensions Appeal Tribunals Act (SAUS)
PATA............	Plenum Air Tread, Amphibious [*Army vehicle*]
PATA............	Pneumatic All-Terrain Amphibian (IEEE)
PATA............	Professional Aeromedical Transport Association (EA)
PATA............	Proprietary Articles Trade Association [*British*] (BI)
PATA............	Tanana [*Alaska*] [*ICAO location identifier*] (ICLI)
Pat Abr........	Paterson's Abridgment of Poor Law Cases [*1857-63*] [*A publication*] (DLA)
PATAFIL......	Policies of Author Affiliation Listing (SAUS)
PAT & E.......	Product Acceptance Testing and Evaluation [*Marketing*] (MCD)
PAT&E.........	Product Assurance Test and Evaluation
PAT&E.........	Production Acceptance Test and Evaluation
Pat & H........	Patton, Jr., and Heath's Reports [*Virginia Special Court of Appeals*] [*A publication*] (DLA)
Pat & Mr	Paterson and Murray's Reports [*1870-71*] [*New South Wales*] [*A publication*] (DLA)
Pat App........	Craigie, Stewart, and Paton's House of Lords Appeals from Scotland [*1726-1857*] [*A publication*] (DLA)
Pat App Cas...	Paterson's Scotch Appeal Cases [*A publication*] (DLA)
Pat App Cas...	Paton's Scotch Appeal Cases [*Craigie, Stewart, and Paton*] [*A publication*] (DLA)
PAT/ARM.....	Passive Angle Tracking/Anti-Radiation Missile system (SAUS)
PATAS	Portable Air-Launched Missile Telemetry Acquisition System (MCD)
PATAS	Publications Automated Task Analysis System (SAUS)
PATASWDEVGRU...	Patrol Antisubmarine Warfare Development Group
PATBOMRON...	Patrol-Bombing Squadron
PatBt..........	Patrol Boat (SAUS)
PATBX	Private Automatic Telegraph Branch Exchange [*Telecommunications*]
PATBX	Private Automatic Telex Branch Exchange (NITA)
PAtC...........	Cedar Crest College, Allentown, PA [*Library symbol*] [*Library of Congress*] (LCLS)
PATC..........	Page Address Translation Cache (SAUS)
PATC..........	Pain-Anxiety-Tension Cycle (MELL)
PATC..........	Paroxysmal Atrial [*or Auricular*] Tachycardia [*Medicine*]
PATC..........	PATCLASS [*Pergamon ORBIT InfoLine, Inc.*] [*No longer available online*] [*Information service or system*] (CRD)
PATC..........	Pioneer Automobile Touring Club (EA)
PAT-C.........	Position, Attitude, Trajectory-Control [*Aerospace*] (AAG)
PATC..........	Potomac Appalachian Trail Club (EA)
PATC..........	Professional, Administrative, Technical, and Clerical [*Bureau of Labor Statistics survey*]
PATC..........	Professional Air Traffic Controller (SAUS)
PATC..........	Tin City Air Force Station [*Alaska*] [*ICAO location identifier*] (ICLI)
PATCA	Panama Air Traffic Control Area
PATCA	Phase Lock Automatic Tuned Circuit Adjustment [*Telecommunications*]
PATCA	Printing and Allied Trades Christian Association (DGA)
PATCA	Professional and Technical Consultants Association (EA)
Pat Cas........	Reports of Patent, Design, and Trade Mark Cases [*England, Scotland, Ireland*] [*A publication*] (DLA)
PATCENT	Patching Central [*Army*] (AABC)
PATCH	People Against Toxic Chemical Hazards [*An association*] [*Australia*]
PATCH	Planned Approach to Community Health
PATCH	Precision Approach To Coupled Hover (SAUS)
PA-TCH-SP...	Periodic Acid-Thiocarbohydrazide-Silver Proteinate [*Test*] [*Cytology*]
PATCO	Port Authority Transit Corp. (SAUS)
PATCO	Prednisone, ara-C [*Cytarabine*], Thioguanine, Cyclophosphamide, Oncovin [*Vincristine*] [*Antineoplastic drug regimen*]
PATCO	Professional, Administrative, Technical, Clerical, and Other [*Bureau of Labor Statistics survey*] (DNAB)
PATCO	Professional Air Traffic Controllers Association (SAUS)
PATCO	Professional Air Traffic Controllers Organization [*Defunct*] (EA)
PATCOM	Patriot Communications Model (MCD)
Pat Comp.....	Paterson's Compendium of English and Scotch Law [*A publication*] (DLA)
PATCRA	Papua New Guinea Australia Trade and Commercial Relations Agreement (SAUS)
PATD	Parts and Tool Disposition (IAA)
patd	Patented (NTIO)
PATD	Patented
Pat Dec.......	Decisions of the Commissioner of Patents [*A publication*] (DLA)
Pat Des & TM Rev...	Patent, Design, and Trade Mark Review [*India*] [*A publication*] (DLA)
PAT Device...	Parametric Artificial Talking Device (SAUS)
Pat Dig	Pattison's Missouri Digest [*A publication*] (DLA)
PATDPA	Deutsche Patent Datenbank [*German Patent Database*] [*German Patent Office*] [*Information service or system*] (IID)
PATE...........	Philippine Association of Technological Education (SAUS)
PATE...........	Pointing and Tracking Experiment (SAUS)
PATE...........	Production Acceptance Test and Evaluation
PATE...........	Programmed Automatic Telemetry Evaluator

PATE...........	Programmed Automatic Test Equipment
PATE...........	Psychodynamics and Therapeutic Education
PATE...........	Pulmonary Artery Thromboembolectomy [*Cardiology*] (DAVI)
Pate...........	Pulmonary Artery Thromboembolism [*Medicine*] (STED)
PATEC........	Pacific Technica Corp. (EFIS)
PATEFA News...	Printing and Allied Trades Employers' Federation. News [*A publication*]
PATELL	Psychological Abstracts Tape Edition Lease or Licensing
PatEng	Patterson Energy, Inc. [*Associated Press*] (SAG)
Pater...........	Paterson's New South Wales Reports [*A publication*] (DLA)
Pater...........	Paterson's Scotch Appeal Cases [*A publication*] (DLA)
Pater Ap Cas...	Paterson's Scotch Appeal Cases [*A publication*] (DLA)
Pater App	Paterson's Scotch Appeal Cases [*A publication*] (DLA)
Paters App...	Paterson's Appeal Cases [*A publication*] (ILCA)
Paters Comp...	Paterson's Compendium of English and Scotch Law [*A publication*] (DLA)
Paterson	Paterson on the Game Laws [*A publication*] (DLA)
Paterson	Paterson on the Liberty of the Subject [*A publication*] (DLA)
Paterson	Paterson's Compendium of English and Scotch Law [*A publication*] (DLA)
Paterson	Paterson's Law and Usages of the Stock Exchange [*A publication*] (DLA)
Paterson	Paterson's Scotch Appeal Cases [*A publication*] (DLA)
Paterson Sc App Cas...	Paterson's Scotch Appeal Cases [*A publication*] (DLA)
PATF...........	Program Activation Task Force [*Military*] (AFIT)
PATF...........	Property Accountability Task Force [*Army*] (MCD)
PATFOR	Patrol Force
Pat Game L...	Paterson on the Game Laws [*1861*] [*A publication*] (DLA)
PATGC	Purge-and-Trap Gas Chromatography [*Environmental Protection Agency*]
PATH	Partnership Approach to Health (MEDA)
PATH	Path [*Postal Service standard*] (OPSA)
path	Pathogen (STED)
PATH	Pathological (GOBB)
PATH	Pathology (AABC)
path	Pathology (STED)
PATH	Peer Attitudes Toward the Handicapped Scale [*Psychology*] (EDAC)
PATH	Performance Analysis and Test Histories (KSC)
PATH	Performing Arts Theater of the Handicapped (SAUS)
PATH	Physicians at Teaching Hospitals [*Program*]
PATH	Pituitary Adrenotrophic Hormone [*Endocrinology*]
PATH	Port Authority Trans-Hudson [*New York*]
PATH	Postflight Attitude and Trajectory History (SAUS)
PATH	Preserve American Patriotic Holidays Committee (EA)
PATH	Professional Association of Traditional Healers (SAUS)
PATH	Program for Appropriate Technology in Health (EA)
PATH	Program on Advanced Technology for the Highway
PATH	Prospectors and Treasure Hunters Guild (EA)
PATHAT	Precision Aim-Technique Heliborne Antitank [*Gun system concept*] [*Ballistic Research Laboratory*] (RDA)
PATHE	Positive Action Through Holistic Evaluation Program (EDAC)
PATHFINDER...	Pathological Element Finder (SAUS)
Pat HL Sc	Paterson's Scotch Appeal Cases [*A publication*] (DLA)
Pat HL Sc	Paton's Scotch Appeal Cases [*A publication*] (DLA)
PathoG........	PathoGenesis Corp. [*Associated Press*] (SAG)
PATHOGEN...	Pathogenic (SAUS)
PATHOL	Pathologic (SAUS)
PATHOL	Pathological (MSA)
PATHOL	Pathologically (SAUS)
Pathol Int....	Pathology International (SAUS)
Pathol Res Pract...	Pathology, Research and Practice (SAUS)
PATHOMORPH...	Pathomorphologic (SAUS)
PATHOMORPH...	Pathomorphologist (SAUS)
PATHOMORPH...	Pathomorphology (SAUS)
PATHS	Pacific Transport of Heat and Salt [*Canada-Japan-USA*] [*Marine science*] (OSRA)
PATHS	Path [*Commonly used*] (OPSA)
PATHS	Peer Attitudes Toward the Handicapped Scale [*Educational testing*]
PATHS	Precursor above the Horizon Sensor [*Strategic Defense Initiative*]
PATI...........	Passive Airborne Time-Difference Intercept [*Navy*]
PATI...........	Patient Infosystems, Inc. [*NASDAQ symbol*] (SAG)
PATI...........	Penetrating Abdominal Trauma Index (MELL)
PATIA	Pacific Area Trading and Investment Area
Patiala........	Indian Law Reports, Patiala Series [*A publication*] (DLA)
PATIB........	Polish-American Travel Information Bureau (EA)
PATIE	Pointing and Tracking Integrated Experiment (SAUS)
PATINA	Potomac Antique Tools and Industries Association (EA)
PatInfo........	Patient Infosystems, Inc. [*Associated Press*] (SAG)
Pat Ins........	Paton on Insurance [*1962*] [*A publication*] (DLA)
PATIO	Program Addressable Table Index Operation [*Computer science*] (VLIE)
Pat J..........	Patent Journal, Including Trademarks and Models [*South Africa*] [*A publication*] (DLA)
PATK..........	Patrick Indus [*NASDAQ symbol*] (TTSB)
PATK..........	Patrick Industries, Inc. [*NASDAQ symbol*] (NQ)
PATK..........	Talkeetna [*Alaska*] [*ICAO location identifier*] (ICLI)
PAtL..........	Lehigh County Historical Society, Allentown, PA [*Library symbol*] [*Library of Congress*] (LCLS)
PATL..........	Tatalina Air Force Station [*Alaska*] [*ICAO location identifier*] (ICLI)
PATLAW	Patent Law (NITA)
Pat Law Rev...	Patent Law Review [*A publication*] (DLA)
PATLC........	Progessive Achievement Tests of Listening Comprehension (STED)
Patlex	Patlex Corp. [*Associated Press*] (SAG)
Pat Licens...	Paterson's Licensing Acts Annual [*A publication*] (DLA)
Pat LJ........	Patna Law Journal [*India*] [*A publication*] (DLA)

Pat LR .... Patent Law Review [*A publication*] (DLA)
Pat LR .... Patna Law Reports [*India*] [*A publication*] (DLA)
Pat L Reptr... Patna Law Reporter [*India*] [*A publication*] (DLA)
Pat L Rev ... Patent Law Review [*A publication*] (DLA)
Pat LT......... Patna Law Times [*India*] [*A publication*] (DLA)
Pat LW ...... Patna Law Weekly [*A publication*] (DLA)
PAtM......... Muhlenberg College, Allentown, PA [*Library symbol*] [*Library of Congress*] (LCLS)
pat med ...... Patent Medicine (STED)
PAT MED ..... Patent Medicine (WDAA)
PATMI......... Powder Actuated Tool Manufacturers' Institute (EA)
PATMI......... Power Actuated Tool Manufacturers Institute (SAUS)
PATMKG ...... Patternmaking (WGA)
PATMO .... Patent and Trademark Office (SAUS)
Pat Mort ...... Patch on Mortgages [*1821*] [*A publication*] (DLA)
PATMRG ...... PACOM [*Pacific Command*] Air Target Materials Review Group (CINC)
PATN .... Pattern (MDG)
PATN .... Pattern Analysis Package (SAUS)
PATN .... Promotional Port Access Telephone Number (SAUS)
PATNT .... Patent
PATNT .... Playgroup Association of the Northern Territory [*Australia*]
PATO .... Pacific-Asian Treaty Organization (NADA)
PATO .... Partial Acceptance and Takeover Date [*Telecommunications*] (TEL)
PATO .... Pattetico [*Pathetically*] [*Music*] (ROG)
PATO .... Principal Ammunition Technical Officer [*British military*] (DMA)
Pat Off .... Patent Office (DLA)
Pat Off J ...... Patent Office Journal [*India*] [*A publication*] (DLA)
Pat Off Rec.. Patent Office Record (SAUS)
Pat Off Rep... Patent Office Reports [*A publication*] (DLA)
PATOLIS ...... Patent Online Information System [*Database*] [*Japan*]
Paton .... Craigie, Stewart, and Paton's Scotch Appeal Cases [*1726-1821*] [*A publication*] (DLA)
Paton App Cas... Paton's Scotch Appeal Cases [*A publication*] (DLA)
Paton Sc App Cas... Paton's Scotch Appeal Cases [*A publication*] (DLA)
PATOOMB.... Phage and the Origins of Molecular Biology
PATOS .... Patent-Online-System [*Bertelsmann Datenbankdienste GmbH*] [*Database*]
PATOS .... Payment at Time of Service (ADWA)
PATOUSA..... Police and Traffic Officers Union of South Africa (SAUS)
PATP........... Poets and the Pub [*Programme*] [*Australia*]
PATP........... Preliminary Authority to Proceed (NASA)
PATP........... Production Acceptance Test Procedure (MCD)
PATP........... (Pyridylcarbonylamino)tetrahydropyridine [*Biochemistry*]
Pat Pend...... Patent Pending (SAUS)
patpend ...... Patent Pending (SHCU)
PATPEND ..... Patent Pending
PAT Personnel... Professional-Administrative-Technical Personnel (SAUS)
PAT-PTR ...... US Patent Data Base - Patent Technology Reports [*Patent and Trademark Office*] [*Database*]
patr............. Patriarch (RION)
PATR .... Patriarch
PATR .... Patriotic (ROG)
Patr............. Patrol (SAUS)
PATR .... Patron
PATR .... Production Acceptance Test Requirement (MCD)
PATRA......... Packaging and Allied Trades Research Association (SAUS)
PATRA......... Printing, Packaging, and Allied Trades Research Association
PATRA......... Professional and Technical Role Analyses [*Occupational therapy*]
PatrAH .... Patriot American Hospitality, Inc. [*Associated Press*] (SAG)
Patra Journal... Printing, Packaging and Allied Trades Research Association Journal (SAUS)
PATRAM ...... Packaging and Transport of Radioactive Materials (HEAS)
PATRDL .... Pan American Tung Research and Development League [*Defunct*] (EA)
Patr Elect Cas... Patrick's Election Cases [*1824-49*] [*Upper Canada*] [*A publication*] (DLA)
Patriarch...... Patriarchate (DIAR)
PATRIC .... Pattern Recognition and Information Correlations [*Police crime-detection computer*]
PATRIC .... Pattern Recognition Interpretation and Correlation (CET)
PATRIC .... Position and Time-Resolved Ion Counting [*Detector*]
PATRICIA..... Practical Algorithm to Receive Information Coded in Alphanumeric [*Information retrieval*]
Patrick El Cas... Patrick's Election Cases [*Canada*] [*A publication*] (DLA)
PATRIC System... Pattern Recognition, Information and Correlation System (SAUS)
Patrida Seybolds Off Comput Res... Partricia Seybolds Office Computing Report (SAUS)
Patriot .... Patriotic (DIAR)
PATRIOT...... Pesticide Assessment Tool for Rating Investigations for Transport [*Environmental Protection Agency*] (AEPA)
PATRIOT...... Phased Array Tracking to Intercept of Target [*Air defense system unit*] [*Army*] (RDA)
PatriotB .... Patriot Bank Corp. (PA) [*Associated Press*] (SAG)
PATRIOT ICC... Patriot Information Control Center
PatrkInd...... Patrick Industries, Inc. [*Associated Press*] (SAG)
Patrm.......... Patrimony (DIAR)
PatrNBk .... Patriot National Bank CT [*Associated Press*] (SAG)
PATROL .... Program for Administrative Traffic Reports On-Line [*Computer program*] [*Bell System*]
PatrolGr....... Patrologia Graeca (BJA)
PatrolLat...... Patrologia Latina (BJA)
PATRON .... Patrol Squadron
PATS........... Pacific Animal Therapy Society (SAUS)
PATS........... Parameterized Abstract Test Suite (VLIE)

PATS........... Parametrized Abstract Test Suite (SAUS)
PATS........... Passive Angle Tracking System (SEWL)
PATS........... Passive Auto Theft System [*Automotive security*]
PATS........... Payload Avionics Test Station [*NASA*] (SSD)
PATS........... Payment and Telecommunication Services Corp. [*New York, NY*] [*Telecommunications*] [*Defunct*] (TSSD)
PATS........... People Against Tobacco Smoke (EA)
PATS........... Personnel Assistance Teams [*Military*]
PATS........... Personnel in an Awaiting Training Status [*Air Force*] (AFM)
PATS........... Pesticide Action Tracking System (EEVL)
PATS........... Pesticides Analytical Transport Solution (EEVL)
PATS........... Plant Action Tracking System [*Environmental science*] (COE)
PATS........... Portable Acoustic Tracking System for Divers (MCD)
PATS........... Preacademic Training Student [*Military*]
PATS........... Preauthorized Automatic Transfer Scheme [*Banking*]
PATS........... Precise Automated Tracking System (PDAA)
PATS........... Precision Aircraft Tracking System (SAUS)
PATS........... Precision Altimeter Techniques Study
PATS........... Precision Automated Tracking System [*FAA*] (TAG)
PATS........... Predicasts Abstract Terminal System [*Computer science*]
PATS........... Primary Aircraft Training System (MCD)
PATS........... Priority Activity Tracking System (DB)
PATS........... Product Acceptance Test Specification (TIMI)
PATS........... Program for Analysis of Time Series (NASA)
PATS........... Programmable Automatic Test System (SAUS)
PATS........... Programmatic and Technical Support [*Army*]
PATS........... Proliferation of Antitank Systems (SAUS)
PATS........... Proof and Transit System (SAUS)
PATS........... Propulsion Analysis Trajectory Simulation [*Computer program*] [*NASA*]
PATS........... Prototype Automated Telecommunications System (SAUS)
PATS........... Prototype Automatic Target Screener (SAUS)
PATS Corporation... Payment and Telecommunication Services Corp. (SAUS)
PATSEARCH... Patent Search [*Computer science*]
PATSEARCH... Patent Search System (NITA)
Pat Ser .... Indian Law Reports, Patna Series [*A publication*] (DLA)
PA-T-SP .... Periodic Acid-Thiocarbohydrazide-Silver Proteinate (STED)
Pat St Tr ...... Paton on Stoppage in Transitu [*1859*] [*A publication*] (DLA)
PATSU .... Patrol Aircraft Service Unit
PATSY .... Parametric Test Synthesis [*Computer science*]
PATSY .... Picture Animal Top Star of the Year [*or Performing Animal Television Star of the Year*] [*American Humane Association award*]
PATSY .... Programmed Automatic Testing System (SAUS)
PATSY .... Programmer's Automatic Testing System
PATSY .... Pulse-Amplitude Transmission System (PDAA)
PAT System... Planar Assembly and Test System (SAUS)
PATT........... Partial Automatic Translation Technique
pat T........... Patellar Tenderness [*Medicine*] (STED)
PATT........... Patent (ROG)
PATT........... Pattern (AAG)
patt............ Pattern (ELAL)
PATT........... Programmable Automatic Transistor Tester (PDAA)
PATT........... Project for the Analysis of Technology Transfer [*NASA*]
Patt & H ...... Patton, Jr., and Heath's Reports [*Virginia*] [*A publication*] (DLA)
Patt & Heath R... Patton, Jr., and Heath's Reports [*Virginia*] [*A publication*] (DLA)
Patt & H (VA)... Patton, Jr., and Heath's Reports [*Virginia*] [*A publication*] (DLA)
PattDntl .... Patterson Dental Co. [*Associated Press*] (SAG)
Patten......... Patten Corp. [*Associated Press*] (SAG)
PATTERN ..... Planning Assistance Through Technical Evaluation of Relevance Numbers [*RAND Corp.*]
Pattern Recognit... Pattern Recognition (SAUS)
Pattern Recognit Lett... Pattern Recognition Letters (SAUS)
PAT Test...... Picric Acid Turbidity Test (SAUS)
PATTH .... People Against Telephone Terrorism and Harassment (EA)
PATTI.......... Pneumatic Adhesion Tensile Testing Instrument (SAUS)
PATTI.......... Precise and Accurate Time and Time Interval [*An experiment aboard the Spacelab*] [*NASA*] (PDAA)
PATTI.......... Prompt Action to Telephone Inquiries (SAA)
PAT/TM....... Patient's Time (DAVI)
Pat TM & Copyr J of R & Educ... Patent, Trademark, and Copyright Journal of Research and Education [*A publication*] (DLA)
Patton & H... Patton, Jr., and Heath's Reports [*Virginia Special Court of Appeals*] [*A publication*] (DLA)
Patton & Heath... Patton, Jr., and Heath's Reports [*Virginia*] [*A publication*] (DLA)
Patton & H (VA)... Patton, Jr., and Heath's Reports [*Virginia Special Court of Appeals*] [*A publication*] (DLA)
Pat Trademark & Copyright J (BNA)... Patent, Trademark, and Copyright Journal (Bureau of National Affairs) [*A publication*] (DLA)
PATTS.......... Programmed Auto Trim/Test System (SAUS)
PATU .... PanAfrican Telecommunications Union (EAIO)
PATU .... Pan American Taekwondo Union (EA)
PATWA .... Playgroup Association of Western Australia
PATWA .... Professional and Technical Workers Aliyah [*British*] (BI)
PATWAS ...... Pilots Automatic Telephone Weather Answering Service
PATWING.... Patrol Wing [*Later, Fleet Air Wing*]
PATWINGDET... Patrol Wing [*Later, Fleet Air Wing*] Detachment (DNAB)
PATWINGLANTFLT... Patrol Wing [*later, Fleet Air Wing*] Atlantic Fleet
PATWINGSCOFOR... Patrol Wing [*later, Fleet Air Wing*] Scouting Force
PATX........... Private Automatic Telegraph Exchange (PDAA)
PATX........... Private Automatic Telex Exchange (NITA)
PATY........... Private Annuity for Term of Years (SAUS)
PAU .... Pacific Command Frequency Allocation and Uses (CINC)
PAU .... Pan American Union [*Central organ and permanent secretariat of the OAS*]
PAU .... Pan American University (SAUS)

PAU	Parallel Arithmetic Unit (SAUS)
PAU	Pattern Articulation Unit [*Computer science*]
PAU	Pauk [*Myanmar*] [*Airport symbol*] (OAG)
PAU	Paulingite [*A zeolite*]
Pau	Paulus de Liazaris [*Deceased, 1356*] [*Authority cited in pre-1607 legal work*] (DSA)
PAU	Pauzhetka [*Former USSR*] [*Seismograph station code, US Geological Survey*] (SEIS)
pau	Pennsylvania [*MARC country of publication code*] [*Library of Congress*] (LCCP)
PAU	Phenol-Acetic Acid-Urea [*Medicine*] (DMAA)
PAU	Pilotless Aircraft Unit
PAU	Police Airborne Unit (SAUS)
PAU	Portable Annotation Unit [*Military*] (CAAL)
PAU	Position Analog Unit [*Manufacturing term*]
PAU	Power and Alarm Unit (SAUS)
PAU	Present Address Unknown
PAU	Probe Aerodynamic Upper [*NASA*] (MCD)
PAU	Production Assurance Unit (MCD)
PAU	Programmes Analysis Unit [*British*] (MCD)
PAU	Public Awareness Unit (SAUS)
PAU	University of Pennsylvania, Philadelphia, PA [*OCLC symbol*] (OCLC)
PAUB	Platform Access Under Bridge (SAUS)
PAUBM	Pan American Union of Baptist Men [*Defunct*] (EA)
PAUC	Program Acquisition Unit Cost (AAGC)
PAUCA	Providence Association of Ukrainian Catholics in America (EA)
Pau de Cast...	Paulus de Castro [*Deceased, 1441*] [*Authority cited in pre-1607 legal work*] (DSA)
Pau de La....	Paulus de Liazaris [*Deceased, 1356*] [*Authority cited in pre-1607 legal work*] (DSA)
Pau de Montep...	Paulus Ruinus de Montepico [*Flourished, 15th century*] [*Authority cited in pre-1607 legal work*] (DSA)
PAUDGET....	Photometer, Automated Universal Distribution Gonielectric Type
PAUH	Harris [*Paul*] Stores [*NASDAQ symbol*] (SAG)
PAUH	Paul Harris Stores [*NASDAQ symbol*] (SAG)
Pau Hunga...	Paulus Hungarus [*Deceased, 1242*] [*Authority cited in pre-1607 legal work*] (DSA)
Pau Hungar...	Paulus Hungarus [*Deceased, 1242*] [*Authority cited in pre-1607 legal work*] (DSA)
PAUKO	Pan-American Union of Karatedo Organizations [*Later, PUKO*] (EA)
PAUL	Parallel-Axis Ultraprecision Lathe (SAUS)
PAUL	Paullum [*A Little*] [*Pharmacy*]
PAULA	Port, Audio, Uart and Logic (SAUS)
Paul de Cast...	Paulus de Castro [*Deceased, 1441*] [*Authority cited in pre-1607 legal work*] (DSA)
Paul de Castr...	Paulus de Castro [*Deceased, 1441*] [*Authority cited in pre-1607 legal work*] (DSA)
Pau Leon....	Paulus Leonius [*Flourished, 16th century*] [*Authority cited in pre-1607 legal work*] (DSA)
Paul Liaz....	Paulus de Liazaris [*Deceased, 1356*] [*Authority cited in pre-1607 legal work*] (DSA)
PAULS	Pennsylvania Union List of Serials
Paulson	Paulson Capital Corp. [*Associated Press*] (SAG)
PaulSon	Paul-Son Gaming Corp. [*Associated Press*] (SAG)
Paulus	Julius Paulus. Sententiae Receptae [*A publication*] (DLA)
PAU Message...	Pause Message (SAUS)
PAUMV	Potato Aucuba Mosaic Virus [*Plant pathology*]
PAUN	Peoples Assembly for the United Nations (EA)
PAUN	Unalakleet [*Alaska*] [*ICAO location identifier*] (ICLI)
PAUP	Phylogenic Analysis Using Parsimony [*Biology*]
PAUS	Pale Amber Unsmoked Sheet (SAUS)
Paus	Pausanias [*Second century AD*] [*Classical studies*] (OCD)
PAUS	Piedmontese Association of the United States (EA)
PAUS	Planning and Analysis for Uncertain Situations (MHDI)
PAUS	Public Advocate of the United States (EA)
PAUSE	People Against Unconstitutional Sex Education
PAUT	Pennsylvania & Atlantic Railroad Co. [*Absorbed into Consolidated Rail Corp.*] [*AAR code*]
PAUT	Profit After Ultimate Tax (TIMI)
PAUX	Pauxillum [*A Little*] [*Pharmacy*]
P/AV	Particular Average
PaV	Pathe-Vox [*Record label*] [*France*]
PAV	Paulo Afonso [*Brazil*] [*Airport symbol*] (OAG)
PAV	Pavia [*Italy*] [*Seismograph station code, US Geological Survey*] (SEIS)
Pav	Pavilion (DIAR)
PAV	Pavilion
Pav	Pavillon (SAUS)
Pav	Pavo [*Constellation*]
PAV	Pay Adjustment Voucher [*Military*]
PAV	Personnel Allotment Voucher [*Army*]
PAV	Phase Angle Voltmeter
PAV	Pneumatic Actuated Valve (SAUS)
PA(V)	Police Association (Victoria) [*Australia*]
PAV	Position and Velocity
PAV	Position and Velocity Tracking (IAA)
PAV	Poste-Avion [*Airmail*] [*French*]
PAV	Potential Acquisition Valuation Method [*Management*]
PAV	Potential AIDS [*Acquired Immune Deficiency Syndrome*] Victim
PAV	Pressure Actuated Valve (SAUS)
PAV	Pressure-Actuated Valve (NASA)
PAV	Pressure Ageing Vessel (ABAC)
PAV	Pressure Altitude Variation [*Aviation*]
PAV	Program Activation Vector [*Computer science*] (ELAL)
PAV	Propellant-Actuated Valve
PAV	Prototype Availability (SAUS)
PAV	Public Access Videotex
PAV	Public Against Violence [*Former Czechoslovakia*] [*Political party*]
PAV	Puella Americana Vallensis [*Valley Girl*] [*Teenaged girl who follows the fads, fashions, and slang originated among teenagers in California's San Fernando Valley*]
PAV	Pyrotechnically Activated Venting [*Automotive safety systems*]
PAV	Stock Pavilion (SAUS)
PAVA	Polish Army Veterans Association of America (EA)
PAVAS	Performing and Visual Arts Society (EA)
PAVD	Valdez [*Alaska*] [*ICAO location identifier*] (ICLI)
PAVE	Parents Active for Vision Education [*An association*] (EA)
PAVE	Paving
PAVE	Performance-Based Adult Vocational Education (EDAC)
PAVE	Philippine Association for Vocational Education (SAUS)
PAVE	Position and Velocity Extraction
PAVE	Precision Acquisition Vehicle Entry (SEWL)
PAVE	Preparing for AIDS/HIV Vaccine Evaluation [*National Institutes of Health project*]
PAVE	Primary Auditory Visual Experience [*National Visitor Center*]
PAVE	Principles and Applications of Value Engineering
PAVe	Procarbazine, Alanine Nitrogen Mustard [*L-Phenylanine mustard, L-PAM*], Velban [*Vinblastine*] [*Antineoplastic drug regimen*]
PAVE	Professional Audiovisual Education Study
PAVE	Programmed Analysis for Value Engineering (or Engineers) (SAUS)
PAVE	Programmed Analysis for Value Engineers
PAVE	Programmed Assistance to Vocational Education (SAUS)
PAVE-PAWS...	Phased-Array Radars (SAUS)
PAVE-PAWS...	Precision Acquisition of Vehicle Entry and Phased Array Warning System
PAVE PAWS...	Precision Acquisition of Vehicle Entry Phased Array Warning System
PAVE Study...	Professional Audiovisual Education Study (SAUS)
PAVF	Pulmonary Arteriovenous Fistula [*Medicine*]
PAVFC	Princeton Azimuthally-Varying-Field Cyclotron
PAVG	Prince Albert's Volunteer Guards [*British military*] (DMA)
PAVGX	One Group: Value Growth Cl.A [*Mutual fund ticker symbol*] (SG)
pavl	Pavilion (VRA)
PAVL	Protected Areas Virtual Library (SAUS)
PAVLA	Papal Volunteers for Latin America [*Defunct*]
PAVM	Patrons of the Arts in the Vatican Museum (EA)
PAVM	Phase Angle Voltmeter
PAVM	Potential Acquisition Valuation Method (SAUS)
PAVM	Proximity Automatic Vehicle Monitoring (PDAA)
PAVM	Pulmonary Arteriovenous Malformation [*Medicine*] (DMAA)
PAVMT	Pavement
PAVN	People's Army of Vietnam
PAVO	Prince Albert Victor's Own [*British military*] (DMA)
PAVOC	Prince Albert Victor's Own Cavalry [*British military*] (DMA)
PA/VR	Public Assistance/Vocational Rehabilitation
PAVR Insulation...	Pure and Vulvanized Rubber Insulation (SAUS)
PAVS	Passive Aided Visual Sensor (ACAE)
PAVS	Pulmonary Arterial Vasconstrictor Substance [*Medicine*]
PA/VSI	Preliminary Assessment and Visual Site Inspection [*Environmental science*] (BCP)
PAVT	Position and Velocity Tracking
PAVUS	Post Attack Viability of the US (SAUS)
PAW	Florida Panthers Hlds [*NYSE symbol*] (SG)
PAW	Pambwa [*Papua New Guinea*] [*Airport symbol*] (OAG)
PAW	Panel of American Women (EA)
PAW	Peachtree Accounting for Windows (SAUS)
PAW	Peak Airway Pressure [*Medicine*] (DAVI)
PAW	Pentanol Acedic-acid Water (SAUS)
PAW	Pentecostal Assemblies of the World (EA)
PAW	People for the American Way (EA)
PAW	Percussive Arc Welder
PAW	Performance Analysis Workstation [*Computer science*]
PAW	Performance Automotive Warehouse (SAUS)
PAW	Peripheral Airways [*Medicine*] (DMAA)
PAW	Petroleum Administration for War [*World War II*]
PAW	Pets and Wildlife (SAUS)
PAW	Physics Around the World (SAUS)
PAW	Plant-Available Water [*Botany*]
PAW	Plasma Arc Welding
PAW	Poetic Allusion Watch
PAW	Portable Auxiliary Workroom (SAUS)
PAW	Port Angeles Western Railroad (IIA)
PAW	Powered All the Way
Paw	Pressure in the Airway [*level to be specified*] (DAVI)
PAW	Primary Affective Witzelsucht [*Medicine*] (CPH)
PAW	Princeton Alumni Weekly (SAUS)
PAW	Programmed Automatic Welding (SAUS)
PAW	Protect Appalachian Wilderness [*An association*] (WPI)
PAW	Public Administered Whipping [*Slang*]
PAW	Pulmonary Artery Wedge [*Pressure*] [*Cardiology*] (DAVI)
PAW	Pulmonary Artery Wedge Pressure [*Cardiology*]
PAWA	Pan American Women's Association (EA)
PAWA	Pan-American World Airways (NADA)
PAWA	Power and Water Authority [*Northern Territory, Australia*]
PAWAF	Polish American Workmen's Aid Fund (EA)
PAWBP	Pension and Welfare Benefit Programs [*Labor-Managment Services Administration*] (IAA)
PAWC	Pacific West Conference (PSS)
PAWC	Pan-African Womens Conference (SAUS)
PAWC	Pan-American Weightlifting Confederation (EA)

PA WC Bd Dec... Pennsylvania Workmen's Compensation Board Decisions [*A publication*] (DLA)
PA WC Bd Dec Dig... Digest of Decisions, Pennsylvania Workmen's Compensation Board [*A publication*] (DLA)
PA WC Bd (Dep Rep Sup)... Workmen's Compensation Supplement to Department Reports of Pennsylvania [*A publication*] (DLA)
PAWD .... Kodiak/Municipal [*Alaska*] [*ICAO location identifier*] (ICLI)
PAWE .... Program for Analysis of the World Ecosystem
PAWES .... Performance Assessment and Workload Evaluation (GAVI)
PAWLC .... Pan-American Weightlifting Confederation (EA)
PAWLS .... Passive Artillery Weapons Locating System (ACAE)
PAWN .... First Cash [*NASDAQ symbol*] (TTSB)
PAWN .... First Cash, Inc. [*NASDAQ symbol*] (SAG)
PAWN .... Photon Adjoint with Neutron (PDAA)
PAWN .... Poole, Aberley, Worthington, and Nolen [*Four early residents of Pawn, Oregon. The city derives its name from the initial letters of their surnames*]
PAWNW .... First Cash Wrrt [*NASDAQ symbol*] (TTSB)
PAWO .... Pan-African Women's Organization [*Commercial firm*] (NADA)
Pawo .... Pressure at the Airway Opening [*Medicine*] (DAVI)
PAWOB .... Passenger Arriving Without Baggage
PAWOS .... Portable Automatic Weather Observing Station (MCD)
PAWP .... Pulmonary Artery Wedge Pressure [*Medicine*]
PAWRS .... Private Aviation Weather Research Station (SAUS)
PAWS .... Parachute Altitude Wind Sensor
PAWS .... Passive Airborne Warning System [*Military*] (SEWL)
PAWS .... Performing Animal Welfare Society (EA)
PAWS .... Pet Animal Welfare Scheme [*British*] (DI)
PAWS .... Pets Are Worth Safeguarding [*An association*]
PAWS .... Phased Array Warning System
PAWS .... Polar Automatic Weather Station (NG)
PAWS .... Portable Acoustic Wave Sensor (AAEL)
PAWS .... Portable AN/UYS-1 Work Station (SAUS)
PAWS .... Portable ASAS/ENSCE Work Station (SAUS)
PAWS .... Portable Automatic Weather Station (MUGU)
PAWS .... Pro-Active World Suspension [*Automotive engineering*]
PAWS .... Program for Avionics & Weapon Systems (SAUS)
PAWS .... Programmed Automatic Welding System
PAWS .... Progressive Animal Welfare Society (GNE)
PAWS .... Protection Against Wrapped Sequence numbers (SAUS)
PAWS .... Prototype Analyst Work Station (SAUS)
PAWS .... Psychological Abuse Warriors and Survivors (SAUS)
PAWS .... Psychological, Atmospheric, and Weather Sciences (SAUS)
PAWT .... Wainwright [*Alaska*] [*ICAO location identifier*] (ICLI)
PAWW .... Wildwood [*Alaska*] [*ICAO location identifier*] (ICLI)
PAX .... OPTEVFOR [*Operational Test and Evaluation Force*] Detachment, Patuxent River, MD [*Navy*] (CAAL)
PAX .... Pan Air, Inc. [*ICAO designator*] (FAAC)
PAX .... Pan Central Explorations Ltd. [*Toronto Stock Exchange symbol*]
PAX .... Parallel Architecture Extended [*Computer science*]
PAX .... Passenger (AFM)
PAX .... Passenger Aircraft (SAUS)
pax .... Passengers (PIAV)
PAX .... Passengers
PAX .... Patuxent River [*Maryland*] (MCD)
PAX .... Patuxent River Office Field Support (SAUS)
PAX .... Paxson [*Alaska*] [*Seismograph station code, US Geological Survey*] (SEIS)
PAX .... Paxson Communications 'A' [*AMEX symbol*] (SG)
Pax .... Paxton [*Record label*] [*Great Britain*]
PAX .... Person-to-Person Accelerated Xerography [*Office technology*] [*British*]
PAX .... Photoemission of Adsorbed Xenon [*Physics*]
PAX .... Physical Address Extension
PAX .... Pixel Addressing Extension (SAUS)
PAX .... Place Address in Index (SAUS)
PAX .... Place Address in Index Register (SAA)
PAX .... Portable Archive Exchange (SAUS)
PAX .... Private Area Exchange (SAUS)
PAX .... Private Automatic Exchange [*Telecommunications*]
Paxar .... Paxar Corp. [*Associated Press*] (SAG)
PAXCON....... Passenger Airlift Contract [*Military*]
PAX DOC ..... Passenger Documentation (SAUS)
PAX Register... Place Address in Index Register (SAUS)
PaxsnC .... Paxson Communications Corp. [*Associated Press*] (SAG)
PAXWX .... Pax World Fund [*Mutual fund ticker symbol*] (SG)
PAY .... Pamol [*Malaysia*] [*Airport symbol*] (OAG)
PAY .... SPS Transaction Services [*NYSE symbol*] (SAG)
PAYA .... Yakutat [*Alaska*] [*ICAO location identifier*] (ICLI)
PAYABL .... Payable
Pay & Iv Carr... Payne and Ivamy's Carriage by Sea [*10th ed.*] [*1976*] [*A publication*] (DLA)
PAYC .... Payco American Corp. [*NASDAQ symbol*] (NQ)
Paychx .... Paychex, Inc. [*Associated Press*] (SAG)
Pay Cmdr...... Paymaster Commander (SAUS)
Payco .... Payco American Corp. [*Associated Press*] (SAG)
PAYCOM ...... Payload Command [*NASA*] (MCD)
PayCsh .... Payless Cashways, Inc. [*Associated Press*] (SAG)
PAYDAT .... Payload Data [*NASA*] (MCD)
PAYE .... Pay As You Earn
PAYE .... Pay As You Enter
PAYE .... Pitch and Yaw Engine (MCD)
PAYERS .... Program Accomplishment Year to Date Evaluation Reviews
PAYES .... Program for Assessing Youth Employment Skills [*Vocational guidance test*]

PAYG .... Pay-As-You-Go
PAYGO......... Pay-As-You-Go
PAYLD .... Payload
PAYLL .... Payroll (SAUS)
PaylSh .... Payless ShoeSource, Inc. [*Associated Press*] (SAG)
PAYM .... Pan African Youth Movement (BUAC)
PAYM .... Paymaster [*Military*] [*British*] (ROG)
PAYMARCORPS... Paymaster, Marine Corps
PAYMR .... Paymaster
PAYMT........ Payment
PAYMTR ...... Paymaster [*Military*] [*British*] (ROG)
PAYR .... Paymaster (WGA)
PAYS .... Patriotic American Youth Society
PAYSOP .... Payroll-Based Stock Option Plan [*Human resources*] (WYGK)
PAYSOP .... Payroll/Stock Ownership Plan
PAYSU .... P'Eylim-American Yeshiva Student Union (EA)
Payt .... Payment (EBF)
payt .... Payment (WDAA)
PAYT .... Payment
Paytel .... Pay Television (SAUS)
PAY-TV .... Pay-Television (SAUS)
PAYX .... Paychex, Inc. [*NASDAQ symbol*] (NQ)
PAZ .... Palaeozoic Axial Zone [*Geophysics*]
PAZ .... Partial Annealing Zone [*Geology*]
PAZ .... PM Air, Inc. [*ICAO designator*] (FAAC)
PAZ .... Pollen Assemblage Zone (QUAC)
PAZ .... Poza Rica [*Mexico*] [*Airport symbol*] (OAG)
PAZA .... Anchorage [*Alaska*] [*ICAO location identifier*] (ICLI)
PAZA .... Pan American Zebu Association [*Later, IZBA*] (EA)
PAZA .... Press Association of Zambia (BUAC)
PAZF .... Fairbanks [*Alaska*] [*ICAO location identifier*] (ICLI)
PB .... Air Burundi [*ICAO designator*] (AD)
PB .... Bachelor of Philosophy (WDAA)
PB .... Barometric Pressure [*Medicine*] (STED)
PB .... Bethlehem Public Library, Bethlehem, PA [*Library symbol*] [*Library of Congress*] (LCLS)
PB .... Dr. Karl Thomae GmbH [*Germany*] [*Research code symbol*]
PB .... Lead [*BTS*] (TAG)
Pb .... Lead
PB .... Pacific Beach (SAUS)
PB .... Packard Bell (SAUS)
P/B............. Pad and Boom [*Refueling*] [*Aerospace*] (MSA)
PB .... Page Buffer (NITA)
PB .... Painted Base (AAG)
PB .... Panama Basin
PB .... Panamerican Beverages [*NYSE symbol*] (SPSG)
PB .... Panamerican Beverages 'A' [*NYSE symbol*] (TTSB)
PB .... Panic Bar [*Technical drawings*]
PB .... Paperback (CDAI)
PB .... Paper Base (MSA)
PB .... Paperboard Industries Corp. [*Toronto Stock Exchange symbol*]
PB .... Papua Besena [*Papua New Guinea*] [*Political party*] (FEA)
PB .... Parabellum (GOBB)
PB .... Paraffin Bath [*Medicine*]
PB .... Parallel Binary (ACAE)
PB .... Paris Bourse [*The French stock exchange*]
PB .... Parity BIT [*Binary Digit*] [*Data communications*] (IAA)
PB .... Parke-Bernet [*Later, SPB*] [*Manhattan art auction house*]
PB .... Parliamentary Bill [*British*] (ROG)
PB .... Parole Board [*Australian Capital Territory*]
PB .... Particle Beam
PB .... Particle-Beam Weapon
PB .... Parts Breakdown
PB .... Passband (SAUS)
P/B............. Pass Book (SAUS)
PB .... Passbook [*Banking*]
PB .... Passed Ball
PB .... Patch Bay (SAUS)
PB .... Patrol Base [*Army*] (VNW)
PB .... Patrol Boat [*Navy symbol*]
PB .... Patrol Bomber
PB .... Paul-Bunnell [*Test*] [*Immunology*] (AAMN)
PB .... Pawnbroker
PB .... Pay Board
PB .... Peaceful Beginnings (EA)
PB .... Peach Bottom (SAUS)
P/B............. Peak-to-Background (SAUS)
PB .... Peanut Butter [*Brand name of the Red Wing Co.*]
PB .... Pending Bid (TIMI)
PB .... Pennsylvania Ballet
PB .... Pentaborane [*Rocket fuel*]
PB .... Pentobarbital [*Organic chemistry*]
PB .... Peribrachialis [*Anatomy*]
PB .... Peripheral Blood [*Medicine*] (AAMN)
PB .... Peripheral Buffer
PB .... Permanent Ballast (DS)
PB .... Permanent Base (SAUS)
PB .... Permanent Bunkers
PB .... Permanently Blind
PB .... Permian Basis (SAUS)
PB .... Peroneus Brevis [*Muscle*] [*orthopedics*] (DAVI)
PB .... Personnel Board (SAUS)
PB .... Petabyte (SAUS)
PB .... Petrus Brito [*Flourished, 13th century*] [*Authority cited in pre-1607 legal work*] (DSA)

PB	Phalangeal Bracket [*i.e., cup handle*] [*Slang*]
PB	Pharmacopoeia Britannica [*British Pharmacopoeia*]
PB	Phase Boundary (SAUS)
Pb	Phenobarbital (STED)
PB	Phenobarbital [*A drug*]
PB	Philosophiae Baccalaureus [*Bachelor of Philosophy*]
PB	Phonetically Balanced [*With reference to word lists*]
PB	Phosphate Buffer
PB	Phosphoribosyl
PB	Photon Barrier [*Astrophysics*]
PB	Physics Briefs [*Physikalische Berichte*] [*American Institute of Physics*] [*Database*] [*Information service or system*] (IID)
PB	Physiotherapists Board [*Australian Capital Territory*]
PB	Picket Boat [*Navy*]
PB	Piebald
P/B	Piggy Back (SAUS)
PB	Piggyback (IAA)
PB	Pilot Balloon (SAUS)
PB	Pilotless Bomber [*Air Force*]
PB	Pinchbeck [*Jewelry*] (ROG)
PB	Pinch Biopsy [*Medicine*] (MEDA)
PB	Pine Bark
PB	Pink Bollworm [*Cotton pest*]
PB	Pipe Break [*Nuclear energy*] (NRCH)
PB	Pipeline Burst (SAUS)
PB	Piperonyl Butoxide [*Organic chemistry*]
PB	Pit Border [*Paleobotany*]
PB	Pitney-Bowes, Inc.
PB	Planning Board
PB	Plasma reactor, Barrel type (SAUS)
PB	Plasminogen Binding [*Hematology*]
PB	Plastic Banded (SAUS)
PB	Plate Block [*Philately*]
PB	Playback (KSC)
PB	Plot Board (KSC)
PB	Plotboard (SAUS)
PB	Plotting Board (SAUS)
PB	Plugboard
PB	Plugged Back (SAUS)
PB	Plugging Back [*Computer science*] (IAA)
Pb	Plumbum [*Lead*] [*Chemical element*]
PB	Plymouth Brethren (ROG)
PB	Pocket Book
PB	Police Band (SAUS)
PB	Police Boat (SAUS)
PB	Police Burgh
PB	Policy Board (OICC)
PB	Polished Buckram (DGA)
PB	Pollen Body [*Botany*]
PB	Polybenzene [*Organic chemistry*]
PB	Polybutadiene (SAUS)
PB	Polybutylene [*Organic chemistry*]
PB	Polymer Blend (SAUS)
PB	Polymyxin B [*An antibiotic*]
PB	Polystyrene Base (DGA)
PB	Pony Baseball (EA)
PB	Pony Baseball/Softball [*An association*] (EA)
PB	Poop and Bridge [*of a ship*] (DS)
PB	Poor Box
PB	Population Biology
PB	Portable (SAUS)
PB	Ports and Beaches (NATG)
PB	Post Bag (SAUS)
PB	Post Boost (ACAE)
PB	Powder Bed (DAVI)
PB	Powder Board (DAVI)
PB	Power Boiler
PB	Power Box (IAA)
PB	Power Brakes [*Automotive engineering*]
PB	Power Builder [*Computer software*] (CDE)
PB	Prayer Book
PB	Pre-Boreal (SAUS)
PB	Preburner [*NASA*] (NASA)
PB	Precipitation Body (SAUS)
PB	Preliminary Breakdown
PB	Premature Beat [*Medicine*] (CPH)
PB	Premium Bond (ODBW)
Pb	Presbyopia [*Ophthalmology*]
PB	Presentation Brothers [*See also FPM*] (EAIO)
PB	Presidents Budget (SAUS)
PB	Presiding Bishop [*Episcopal Church*]
PB	Pressure-Barometer [*Automotive emissions*]
PB	Pressure Breathing
PB	Primary Buffer [*Chemistry*]
PB	Primary Bus [*Computer science*] (CAAL)
PB	Primitive Baptist
PB	Printed Board (AAEL)
PB	Prisoners' Barracks (ADA)
PB	Private Bus (SAUS)
PB	Private Business [*Slang*] [*British*]
PB	Privately Bonded
Pb	Probability (PCM)
Pb	Probenecid (STED)
PB	Process Basic (ECII)
PB	Process Bulletin
PB	Procurement Board (SAUS)
PB	Product Baseline (SAUS)
PB	Product Bulletin (SAUS)
PB	Production Base (MCD)
pB	product of polarization and brightness (SAUS)
PB	Professional Books Ltd. (ILCA)
PB	Profile Block (MCD)
PB	Program Base [*Computer science*] (ELAL)
PB	Program Baseline (DOMA)
PB	Program Block (IAA)
PB	Program Breakdown
PB	Program Budgeting (ADA)
PB	Programming Block (SAUS)
PB	Property Book [*Army*] (AABC)
PB	Proportional Band
PB	Protein-Binding (MAE)
PB	Protein-Bound [*Clinical chemistry*] (DAVI)
PB	Provisional Battalion [*Military*] [*A publication*] (ROG)
PB	Pseudo Boolean (SAUS)
PB	Pseudoterminal Bud [*Botany*]
PB	Ptychodiscus brevis [*An alga, the cause of the red tide*]
PB	Public (DSUE)
PB	Publication Bulletin (SAUS)
PB	Publications (NITA)
PB	Publications Board [*Later, CFSTI, NTIS*]
PB	Publications Bulletin
PB	Public Buildings (SAUS)
PB	Publisher (NITA)
PB	Publishers' Binding (DGA)
PB	Publisher's Name [*Online database field identifier*]
PB	Pull Back (NTCM)
PB	Pull Box (AAG)
PB	Pulse Beacon (KSC)
PB	Pulse Bonded (SAUS)
PB	Punch Buffer (SAUS)
PB	Punching Block (SAUS)
PB	Pure Binary (SAUS)
PB	Purl into Back of Stitch [*Knitting*] (WDAA)
PB	Purplish Blue
PB	Push Button
PB4	Plate Block of Four [*Philately*]
PBa	Academy of the New Church, Bryn Athyn, PA [*Library symbol*] [*Library of Congress*] (LCLS)
Pba	Brachial Arterial Pressure [*Medicine*] (MAE)
PBA	Pacific Broadcasting Association (EAIO)
PBA	Paid by Agent [*Business term*] (DCTA)
PBA	Partial-Birth Abortion (MELL)
PBA	Partido Barrientista Autentico [*Bolivia*] [*Political party*] (PPW)
PBA	Patrol Boat, Air Cushion (MCD)
PBA	Patrolmen's Benevolent Association
PBA	Pencil Beam Aerial (or Antenna) (SAUS)
PBA	Pencil Beam Antenna
PBA	Percutaneous Bladder Aspiration [*Urology*] (DAVI)
PBA	Permanent Budget Account
PBA	Phenylboronate Agarose [*Biochemistry*] (DAVI)
PBA	Phenylboronic Acid [*Organic chemistry*]
PBA	Phenylbutyric Acid [*Organic chemistry*]
PBA	Philadelphia Bar Association
PBA	Physical Block Address (SAUS)
PBA	Physical Blowing Agent [*Plastics technology*]
PBA	Pill Box Aerial (or Antenna) (SAUS)
PBA	Pill Box Antenna
PBA	Pine Bluff Arsenal [*Army*] (AABC)
PBA	Plant Breeding Abstracts [*A publication*]
PBa	Plasmodium Berghei Anka [*Bacteriology*]
PBA	Plastic Bag Association (EA)
PBA	Polar Bear Association (EA)
PBA	Polish Beneficial Association (EA)
PBA	Polybenzamide [*Organic chemistry*]
PBA	Polybutyl Acrylate [*Organic chemistry*]
PBA	Polyclonal B Cell Activator [*Hematology*]
PBA	Port Blair [*Andaman Islands*] [*Seismograph station code, US Geological Survey*] (SEIS)
PBA	Port of Brisbane Authority (SAUS)
PBA	Port of Bristol Authority [*British*]
PBA	Poultry Bowling Association
PBA	Poultry Breeders of America (EA)
PBA	Power-Book Army [*Computer science*]
PBA	Powered Battle Armor [*A computer game*] (PCM)
PBA	Preliminary Benefit Analysis [*Environmental Protection Agency*] (EPAT)
PBA	Prescott Builders Association (EA)
PBA	President of the British Academy
PBA	Pressure Breathing Assister [*Medicine*] (STED)
PBA	Pressure Breathing Assistor [*Medicine*]
PBA	Principal Business Activity (GFGA)
PBA	Printed Board Assembly (IAA)
PBA	Printing Brokerage Association (EA)
PBA	Production Base Analysis (MCD)
PBA	Professional Bookmen of America [*Later, Pi Beta Alpha*] (EA)
PBA	Professional Bowlers Association of America (EA)
PBA	Prolactin-Binding Assay (STED)
PBA	Proportional Band Adjustment (SAUS)
PBA	Provincetown-Boston Airlines, Inc.
PBA	Prune Belly Anomaly [*Medicine*] (DMAA)

PBA	Public Buildings Administration [*Functions transferred to PBS, 1949*]
PBA	Published by Arrangement (SAUS)
PBA	Pudendal Block Anesthesia [*Medicine*] (MELL)
PBA	Pulpobuccoaxial [*Dentistry*]
PBA	Pyrene Butyric Acid (SAUS)
PBA	Pyrenebutyric Acid [*Organic chemistry*]
PBAA	Periodical and Book Association of America (EA)
PBAA	Polybatadieneacrylic Acid (SAUS)
PBAA	Poly(butadiene-acrylic Acid) [*Organic chemistry*]
PBAA	Polybutadiene Acrylic Acid (SAUS)
PBAA	Polybutadiene Acrylic Acid Copolymer (EDCT)
PBAA	Private Businesses Association of Australia
PBAAC	Polybutadiene Acrylic Acid Copolymer (SAUS)
PBAC	Pacific Bantam Austin Club (EA)
PBAC	Peach Belt Athletic Conference (PSS)
PBAC	Program Budget Advisory Committee [*Army*]
PB-AESRS	Property Book - Army Equipment Status Reporting System (AABC)
PBAFB	Palm Beach Air Force Base (SAUS)
P Bag	Paper Bag (SAUS)
PBAL	Protected Bronchoalveolar Lavage [*Medicine*] (DMAA)
PBAM	Problem Billing Analysis Module (VLIE)
P-BAMS	Programming-Budgeting and Accounting Management System (SAUS)
PBAN	Pheromone Biosynthesis-Activating Neuropeptide [*Biochemistry*]
PBAN	Poly(butadiene-acrylonitrile) [*Organic chemistry*]
PBAN	Polybutadiene Acrylonitrile Copolymer (EDCT)
P-BAND	225-390 Megacycles per Second
PB&D	Piano, Bass & Drums (WDAA)
PB and J	Peanut Butter and Jelly
PB-AP	Plastic Banded, Armour Piercing (SAUS)
PBA Package	Public Budgeting and Accounting Package (SAUS)
PB-APDS	Plastic Banded, Armour Piercing, Discarding Sabot (SAUS)
PBAPRS	Program/Budget Accounting and Progress Reporting System [*Proposed*] [*Navy*]
PBAPS	Peach Bottom Atomic Power Station (NRCH)
PBAPS	Pipe Break Air Piping System (IEEE)
PBAPS	Pipe Break Automatic Protective System (IEEE)
PBAR	Baker Island Army Air Field [*Baker Island*] [*ICAO location identifier*] (ICLI)
PBAR	Post-Balloon Angioplasty Restenosis [*Medicine*] (MELL)
PBAR	Print Buffer Address Register [*Computer science*] (VLIE)
PBAR	Programming, Budgeting, Accounting and Reporting (SAUS)
PBAS	Program Budget Accounting System [*Military*] (GFGA)
PBASCO	Puritan-Bennett Aero Systems Co. (SAUS)
PBAT	Pyro Battery (KSC)
PBATS	Portable Battlefield Attack System (SAUS)
PBATS	Professional Baseball Athletic Trainers Society (EA)
PBAV	Percutaneous Balloon Aortic Valvuloplasty [*Cardiology*] (CPH)
PBAV	Power Boat Association of Victoria [*Australia*]
PBAX	Private Automatic Branch Exchange [*Computer science*] (ITCA)
PBB	Bloomsburg State College, Bloomsburg, PA [*OCLC symbol*] (OCLC)
PBB	Parallel by Bit
PBB	Paranaiba [*Brazil*] [*Airport symbol*] (OAG)
PBB	Parti Pesaka Bumiputera Bersatu Sarawak [*United Bumiputra Party*] [*Malaysia*] [*Political party*] (FEA)
PBB	Please Be Brief [*Internet dialog*]
PBB	Polybrominated Biphenyl [*Flame retardant, toxic chemical*]
PBB	Posterior Basal Body [*Botany*]
PBB	Private Boxes and Bags
PBB	Program Plan Budgeting (TDOB)
PBB	Project Blue Book [*An association*] (EA)
PBB	Push-Button Banking (SAUS)
PBBA	Printing Brokerage Buyers Association (NTPA)
PBBA	Pro-Bessarabia and Bukovina Association [*Romania*] (BUAC)
PBBATU	Pastrycooks, Bakers, Biscuitmakers, and Allied Trades Union [*Australia*]
PBBCAS	Program-Based Budget Classification and Analysis System [*Pronounced "pib-kaz"*] [*Office of Management and Budget*]
PBbCHi	Columbia County Historical Society, Bloomsburg, PA [*Library symbol*] [*Library of Congress*] (LCLS)
PBBFI	Pearl S. Buck Birthplace Foundation, Inc. (EA)
PBBH	Peter Bent Brigham Hospital [*Boston*]
PBBI	Polybutadiene Bisimide (SAUS)
PBBL	Project Budget Baseline Log (SAUS)
PBBO	Phenylbiphenylylbenzoxazole (SAUS)
PBBP	Passive Beamformer Broadband Processor (ACAE)
PBbS	Bloomsburg State College, Bloomsburg, PA [*Library symbol*] [*Library of Congress*] (LCLS)
PBBS	Pertubuhan Bumiputera Bersatu Sarawak [*United Sarawak National Association*] [*Malaysia*] [*Political party*] (FEA)
PBBS	Physical Baseline Build Standard (SAUS)
PBBs	Polybromated Biphenyls [*Organic chemistry*] (DAVI)
PBBS	Public Bulletin Board System (ACAE)
PBBSF	Pacific Basin Bulk [*NASDAQ symbol*] (TTSB)
PBBSF	Pacific Basin Bulk Shippers Ltd. [*NASDAQ symbol*] (SAG)
PBBWF	Pacific Basin Blk Shipng Wrrt [*NASDAQ symbol*] (TTSB)
PBBWF	Pacific Basin Bulk Shippers Ltd. [*NASDAQ symbol*] (SAG)
PBC	Columbia/Mt. Pleasant, TN [*Location identifier*] [*FAA*] (FAAL)
PBC	Pacific Basin Conference (EEVL)
PBC	Pacific Bible College [*California*]
PBC	Packed Bed Condenser (EEVL)
PBC	Packed by Carrier
PBC	Pakistan Broadcasting Corp. (IMH)
PBC	Panamerican Badminton Confederation (EAIO)
PBC	Parallel by Character
PBC	Parent Behavior Checklist [*Test*] (TMMY)
PBC	Pedal Branch of Columellar [*Muscle*]
PBC	Pen and Brush Club (EA)
PBC	People's Bank of China (ECON)
PBC	People's Bicentennial [*later, Business*] Commission
PBC	Period Batch Control [*Computer science*] (VLIE)
PBC	Periodic Binary Convolutional [*Computer science*] (VLIE)
PBC	Periodic Bond Chain (IAA)
PBC	Periodic Boundary Conditions (SAUS)
PBC	Peripheral Blood Cells [*Medicine*]
PBC	Peripheral Board Controller (SAUS)
PBC	Peripheral Buffer Computer (SAUS)
PBC	Peripheral Bus Computer [*Bell System*]
PBC	Personal Business Computer (VLIE)
PBC	Personnel/Burden Carrier Manufacturers Association [*Defunct*] (EA)
PBC	Philadelphia Blood Clinic (SAUS)
PBC	Philadelphia Book Clinic (SAUS)
PBC	Plain Bond Copier [*Pitney Bowes*]
PBC	Planning and the Black Community (EA)
PBC	Point of Basal Convergence
PBC	Practice Bomb Carrier (SAUS)
PBC	Practice Bomb Contained (NG)
PBC	Practice Bomb Container (SAUS)
PBC	Prebed Care [*Medicine*] (MAE)
PBC	Prefix Block Code (SAUS)
PBC	Pregnancy and Birth Complications (STED)
PBC	Presbyterians for Biblical Concerns (EA)
PBC	Primary Biliary Cirrhosis [*Medicine*]
PBC	Processor Bus Controller [*Computer science*] (VLIE)
PBC	Produce Buying Co. (SAUS)
PBC	Progestin-Binding Complement (STED)
PBC	Program Booking Center [*Telecommunications*] (TEL)
PBC	Program Breakdown Code (ACAE)
PBC	Program Budget Committee [*Military*]
PBC	Psychometric Behavior Checklist [*Psychology*]
PBC	Public Broadcasting Corp. (SAUS)
PBC	Public Buildings Commission [*Functions transferred to PBA, 1939*]
PBC	Pure Binary Code [*Computer science*] (VLIE)
pBc	pure Bolivian cocaine (SAUS)
PBCA	Pacific Bible College of Azusa [*California*]
PBCA	Paperboard Butter Chip Association
PBCA	Professional Business Colleges of Australia
PBCB	Pierce-Blank Die (Class B) (MCD)
PBCB	Plugboard Circuit Breaker (SAUS)
PBCB	Professional Boxing Control Board [*Victoria, Australia*]
PBCC	Packard Bell Computer Corp. (IAA)
PBCC	Palm Beach Computer Consultants (SAUS)
PBCC	Pigmented Basal Cell Carcinoma [*Medicine*] (MELL)
PBCC	Pitney Bowes Credit Corp.
PBCCH	Pentabromochlorocyclohexane [*Flame retardant*] [*Organic chemistry*]
PBCD	Packed Binary Coded Decimal [*Computer science*] (VLIE)
PBCE	Pine Bluff Cotton Exchange [*Defunct*] (EA)
PBCF	Prudential-Bache Capital Funding
PBCH	Primitive Bose Chaudhuri-Hocquenghem (SAUS)
PBCI	Pamrapo Bancorp [*NASDAQ symbol*] (TTSB)
PBCI	Pamrapo Bancorp, Inc. [*NASDAQ symbol*] (NQ)
PBCLS	Palm Beach County Library System [*Florida*]
PBCMO	Poly(bis(chloromethyl)oxetane) [*Organic chemistry*]
PBCO	Praseodymium Barium Copper Oxide [*Inorganic chemistry*]
PB/COC	Plymouth Barracuda/Cuda Owners Club (EA)
PbCoNA	Publishing Co. of North America, Inc. (The) [*Associated Press*] (SAG)
PBCP	Political Bureau of the Communist Party (BUAC)
PBCS	Persian Bicolor and Calico Society (EA)
PBCS	Post Boost Control System [*Aerospace*]
PBCT	People's Bank [*Bridgeport, CT*] [*NASDAQ symbol*] (NQ)
PBCT	Polybutadiene Carboxyl-Terminated (SAUS)
PBCT	Proposed Boundary Crossing Time [*Aviation*]
PBCTP	People's Bank 8.5% Cv 'A' Pfd [*NASDAQ symbol*] (TTSB)
PBCU	Predominately Black Colleges and Universities
PBC-USA	Polar Bear Club - USA (EA)
PBC Vector	Periodic Bond Chain Vector (SAUS)
PBC-WS	Polar Bear Club - Winter Swimmers [*Later, PBC-USA*] (EA)
PBD	Pacific Basin Development Corp. [*Vancouver Stock Exchange symbol*]
PBD	Pacific Bell Directory (SAUS)
PBD	Paperboard (MSA)
PBD	Parallel Blade Damper (OA)
PBD	Particle Board [*Technical drawings*]
PBD	Paul-Bunnell-Davidsohn [*Test*] [*Immunology*]
PBD	Payload Bay Door [*NASA*] (NASA)
PBD	Percutaneous Biliary Drainage [*Gastroenterology*] (DAVI)
PBD	Phenylbiphenylyloxadiazole [*Analytical biochemistry*]
PBD	Pierce-Blank Die (MCD)
PBD	Pigeon Breeder's Disease [*Medicine*] (MELL)
PBD	Place Bearing/Distance [*Way point*] (GAVI)
PBD	Plans and Budget Division (SAUS)
PBD	Plasterboard
PBD	Plenum Bleed Duct [*Hovercraft*]
PBD	Polybutadiene [*Organic chemistry*]
PBD	Porbandar [*India*] [*Airport symbol*] (OAG)
PBD	Postburn Day [*Medicine*] (DMAA)
PBD	Power Building (NATG)
PBD	Prayer Book Dictionary [*A publication*] (ODCC)
PBD	Precise Block Diagram

PBD .... Pressboard (MSA)
PBD .... Primary Blistering Disorder [*Medicine*] (MELL)
PBD .... Production Buy Decision (SAUS)
PBD .... Professional Building Designer [*Accreditation from the American Institute of Building Designers*]
PBD .... Program Budget Decision [*DoD*]
PBD .... Program Budget Directive (MCD)
PBD .... Program Budget Document (MCD)
PBD .... Programmer Brain Damage [*Computer hacker terminology*] (NHD)
PBD .... Proliferative Breast Disease [*Medicine*]
PBD .... Public Buildings Department (SAUS)
PBDB .... Provisional Base Defense Battalion [*Marine Corps*] (VNW)
PBDBM .... Peripheral Backup Detailed Billing Control Element (SAUS)
PBDC .... Pacific Basin Development Council (EA)
PBDE .... Polybrominated Diphenyl Ether [*Flame retardant*]
PBDF .... Payload Bay Door Forward [*NASA*] (MCD)
PBDG .... Push-Button Data Generator (IEEE)
PBDI .... Position Bearing and Distance Indicator (MCD)
PBDM .... Payload Bay Door Mechanism [*NASA*] (NASA)
PBDMA .... Poly(butadiene-malic Acid) [*A polymer*]
PBDNDB ...... Perceived Barking Dog Noise Decibels (SAUS)
PBDP .... Protective Barrier Development Program (SAUS)
Pbd Pkg ..... Paperboard Packaging (SAUS)
PBDR .... Push Button Dialing Receiver (SAUS)
PBDS .... Parti Bansa Dayak Sarawak [*Malaysia*] [*Political party*] (FEA)
PBDS .... Photothermal Beam Deflection Spectroscopy (SAUS)
PBDU .... Pancreaticobiliary Ductal Union [*Anatomy*]
PBDU .... Protocol Bridge Data Unit (SAUS)
PBe .... Beaver Memorial Library, Beaver, PA [*Library symbol*] [*Library of Congress*] (LCLS)
PBE .... Paint, Body, and Equipment [*Automotive engineering*]
PBE .... Paschen-Back Effect [*Spectroscopy*]
PBE .... Pemberton Exploration [*Vancouver Stock Exchange symbol*]
PBE .... Perlsucht Bacillary Emulsion [*Medicine*]
PBE .... Piggyback Experiment
PBE .... Plain Both Ends (SAUS)
PBE .... Poison-Boltzmann Equation [*Physical chemistry*]
PBE .... Polybutene [*Organic chemistry*]
PBE .... Pool Boiling Experiment (SAUS)
PBE .... Present-Barrel-Equivalent
PBE .... Probability of Bit Error (CCCA)
PBE .... Prompt Burst Experiments [*Nuclear energy*] (NRCH)
PBE .... Prompt-by-Example [*Computer science*]
PBE .... Proton Balance Equation
PBE .... Proton Binding Energy
PBE .... Puerto Berrio [*Colombia*] [*Airport symbol*] (OAG)
PBE .... Pulsed Bridge Element [*Telecommunications*] (OA)
PBEA .... Paint, Body, and Equipment Association (EA)
PBEB .... Pentabromoethylbenzene [*Flame retardant*] [*Organic chemistry*]
PBeC .... Beaver County Court House, Beaver, PA [*Library symbol*] [*Library of Congress*] (LCLS)
PBEC .... Pacific Basin Economic Committee (or Council) (SAUS)
PBEC .... Pacific Basin Economic Council (FEA)
PBEC .... Public Broadcasting Environment Center [*Corporation for Public Broadcasting*]
PBECL .... Performance-Based Exposure Control Limit [*Environmental science*]
PBECS .... Pacific Basin Extended Climate Study (SAUS)
PBEI .... Performance-Based Evaluation Instrument (EDAC)
PBEIC .... Point Beach Energy Information Center (SAUS)
PBEIST ...... Planning Board European Inland Surface Transport [*Army*] (AABC)
PBel .... Centre County Library, Bellefonte, PA [*Library symbol*] [*Library of Congress*] (LCLS)
PBelC .... Centre County Court House, Bellefonte, PA [*Library symbol*] [*Library of Congress*] (LCLS)
PBEM .... Play by Electronic Mail [*Computer science*]
PBER .... Program Budget Execution Review [*Army*]
PBerol .... Berlin Papyri [*A publication*] (OCD)
PBET .... Performance-Based Equipment Training (AAEL)
PBf .... Carnegie Free Library, Beaver Falls, PA [*Library symbol*] [*Library of Congress*] (LCLS)
PBF .... Fast Patrol Boat [*Ship symbol*] [*NATO*] (NATG)
PBF .... Patriotic Burmese Forces [*World War II*]
PBF .... Patrol Boat, Fast [*British military*] (DMA)
PBF .... Peribronchial Fibrosis [*Medicine*]
PBF .... Permalloy-Bar File (SAUS)
PBF .... Pilot Briefing Facility (SAUS)
PBF .... Pilot Bypass Filter (IAA)
PBF .... Pine Bluff [*Arkansas*] [*Airport symbol*] [*Obsolete*] (OAG)
PBF .... Plastic Bottle Feeder
PBF .... Plates for Beam Forming (DEN)
PBF .... Poop, Bridge, and Forecastle [*of a ship*] (DS)
PBF .... Portal Blood Flow [*Physiology*]
PBF .... Potential Benefit Factor (OA)
PBF .... Power Burst Facility [*Nuclear energy*]
PBF .... Pulmonary Blood Flow [*Medicine*]
PBFA .... Particle Beam Fusion Accelerator
PBFA .... Provincial Booksellers' Fairs Association [*British*] (DI)
PBFC .... Peter Breck Fan Club (EA)
PBFC .... Pierce Brosnan Fan Club (EA)
PBFC .... Portland Blast-Furnace Cement (SAUS)
PBFD .... Pierce Bland and Form Die (MSA)
PBFD .... Psittacine beak and feather disease (SAUS)
PBFE .... Peroxisomal Bifunctional Enzyme (DMAA)
PB-Fe .... Protein-Bound Iron (MAE)

PBfG .... Geneva College, Beaver Falls, PA [*Library symbol*] [*Library of Congress*] (LCLS)
PBFG .... Guided Missile Fast Patrol Boat [*Ship symbol*] (NATG)
PBFG .... Patrol Boat, Fast, Guided Weapon [*British military*] (DMA)
PBFI .... Paris Business Forms, Inc. [*Burlington, NJ*] [*NASDAQ symbol*] (NQ)
PBFI .... Paris Corp. [*NASDAQ symbol*] (TTSB)
PBFL .... Planning for Better Family Living [*UN Food and Agriculture Organization*]
PBFP .... Provisioning Budget Forecast Procedure (MCD)
PBF/WR ..... Presiding Bishop's Fund for World Relief (EA)
PBG .... Phenylbiguanide [*Biochemistry*]
PBG .... Phorphobilinogen (SAUS)
PBG .... Photonic Bandgap [*Physics*]
PBG .... Plattsburgh, NY [*Location identifier*] [*FAA*] (FAAL)
PBG .... Poly(benzyl Glutamate) [*Organic chemistry*]
PBG .... Porphobilinogen [*Clinical chemistry*]
PBG .... Powszechny Bank Gospodarczy [*Poland*]
PBG .... Program and Budget Guidance [*Army*]
PBGA .... Plastic Ball Grid Arrays
PBGC .... Pension Benefit Guaranty Corp. [*Government agency*]
PBGD .... Porphobilinogen Deaminase [*An enzyme*]
PBGI .... Piedmont BankGroup, Inc. [*NASDAQ symbol*] (NQ)
PBGM .... Brazilian Marine Geology Programme (SAUS)
PBG-QN ...... Porphobilinogen - Quantitative [*Genetics*] (DAVI)
PBG-S .... Porphobilinogen Synthase [*Medicine*] (DMAA)
PBH .... Partial Bulkhead (DS)
PBH .... Patrol Boat, Hydrofoil (MCD)
PBH .... Phillips, WI [*Location identifier*] [*FAA*] (FAAL)
PBH .... Planar-Buried Heterostructure (SAUS)
PBH .... Post Biblical Hebrew [*Language, etc.*] (BJA)
PBH .... Primary Borehole (SAUS)
PBH .... Primordial Black Hole [*Astrophysics*]
PBH .... Pulling Boat Hands (DMAA)
PBHB .... Poly-Beta-Hydroxybutyrate (DMAA)
PB-HEPI ..... Plastic Banded, High Explosive, Penetrating Incendiary (SAUS)
PBHF .... President Benjamin Harrison Foundation (EA)
PBHGX .... PBHG Growth Fund [*Mutual fund ticker symbol*] (SG)
PBHP .... Pounds per Brake Horsepower
PB-HTGR .... Peach Bottom High-Temperature Gas-Cooled Reactor
PBI .... Pacific Bell Internet
PBI .... Palm Beach International Airport [*FAA*] (TAG)
PBI .... Paper Bag Institute (EA)
PBI .... Parental Bonding Index (SAUS)
PBI .... Parental Bonding Instrument
PBI .... Partial Background Investigation [*Army*]
PBI .... Partial Bony Impaction [*Orthopedics*] (DAVI)
PBI .... Paving Block Institute (SAUS)
PBI .... Paving Brick Institute
PBI .... Peace Brigades International (EA)
PBI .... Pen and Brush, Inc. (EA)
PBI .... Penile-Brachial Index [*Medicine*] (DAVI)
PBI .... Peterson Builders Inc. (SAUS)
PBI .... Phenformin [*An oral hypoglycemic*] [*Obsolete*] (DAVI)
PBI .... Philadelphia Bible Institute [*Pennsylvania*]
PBI .... Phillips Business Information, Inc. (IID)
PBI .... Phone Based Interface (SAUS)
PBI .... Pitch Boundary Indicator (MCD)
PBI .... Pitney-Bowes, Inc. [*NYSE symbol*] (SPSG)
PBI .... Plant Biological Institute [*University of Saskatchewan*] [*Canada*]
PBI .... Plant Biotechnology Institute [*National Research Council of Canada*] [*Research center*] (RCD)
PBI .... Plant Breeding Institute [*British*]
PBI .... Plastic Bottle Institute (EA)
PBI .... Please Book Immediately (SAUS)
PBI .... Plumbing Brass Institute [*Later, PMI*] (EA)
PBI .... Polybenzimidazole [*Organic chemistry*] (NATG)
PBI .... Poly(phenylenebibenzimidazole) [*Organic chemistry*]
PBI .... Poor Bloody Infantry [*British military slang*]
PBI .... Post-Bonding Inspection (VLIE)
PBI .... Post Boost Intercept (ACAE)
PBI .... Post, Buckley International
PBI .... Power Base Inventory [*Test*] (TMMY)
PBI .... Process Branch Indicator
PBI .... Program Baseline Integration (SAUS)
PBI .... Programme Biologique Internationale [*International Biological Program - IBP*] (MSC)
PBI .... Projected Books, Inc. [*Defunct*] (EA)
PBI .... Prophylactic Brain Irradiation [*Oncology*]
PBI .... Protein-Bound Iodine [*Clinical chemistry*]
PBI .... Public Benevolent Institution [*Australia*]
PBI .... Pupil Behavior Inventory [*Psychology*]
PBI .... Push Button Indicator (NAKS)
PBI .... Puzzle Buffs International (EA)
PBI .... West Palm Beach [*Florida*] [*Airport symbol*]
PBIA .... Pacific Brain Injury Association (SAUS)
PBiB .... Paperback Books in Print (SAUS)
PBIB .... Partially-Balanced Incomplete Block (PDAA)
PBIB Design... Partially Balanced Incomplete Block Design (SAUS)
PBIC .... Plant Breeding International Cambridge (BUAC)
PBIC .... Poly(butyl Isocyanate) [*Organic chemistry*]
PBIC .... Polybutylisocyanate (SAUS)
PBIC .... Programmable Buffer Interface Card [*Computer science*] (NASA)
PBICSGH...... Permanent Bureau of International Congresses for the Sciences of Genealogy and Heraldry (EA)
PBIF .... Pacific Bible Institute of Fresno [*California*]

PBIL............ Polybenzimidazolone [*Organic chemistry*]
PBIM......... Programmable Buffer Interface Module (MCD)
PBIMR .... Push Broom Imaging Microwave Radiometer (SAUS)
PBIO........... PerSeptive Biosystems [*NASDAQ symbol*] (TTSB)
PBIO........... PerSeptive Biosystems, Inc. [*NASDAQ symbol*] (SAG)
PBIOZ .... PerSeptive Biosystems Wrrt [*NASDAQ symbol*] (TTSB)
PBIP........... Paperbound Books in Print [*A publication*]
PBIP........... Pulse Beacon Impact Predictor (AAG)
PBIPr......... Pitney Bowes $2.12 Cv Pref [*NYSE symbol*] (TTSB)
PBIS........... Peachtree Business Internet Suit (SAUS)
PBIS........... Performance-Based Incentive System (AAGC)
PBISTP....... Peter Burwash International Special Tennis Programs (EA)
PBIT........... Parity BIT [*Binary Digit*] [*Data communications*]
PBI-USA..... Peace Brigades International-United States of America (EA)
PB/IWT....... Ports and Beaches and Inland Waterways Transports [*Military*] (NATG)
PBIX........... Patriot Bank [*NASDAQ symbol*] (TTSB)
PBIX........... Patriot Bank Corp. (PA) [*NASDAQ symbol*] (SAG)
PBJ............ Paper-Braided Jute (IAA)
PBJ............ Partial-Band Jammer (SAUS)
PBJ............ Peanut Butter and Jelly
PBJ............ Peanut Butter and Jelly Sandwich (TAG)
PBJ............ Presa Benito Juarez [*Mexico*] [*Seismograph station code, US Geological Survey*] (SEIS)
PBJC.......... Palm Beach Junior College [*Lakeworth, FL*]
PBJ Cable.... Paper, Braided Jute Cable (SAUS)
PBK........... Palm Beach, Inc. (EFIS)
PBK........... Paperback
PBK........... Payload Bay Kit [*NASA*] (NASA)
PBK........... Phi Beta Kappa [*Honorary society*]
PB (k)........ Phonetically Balanced (Kindergarten) [*Speech and language therapy*] (DAVI)
PBK........... Phosphorylase B Kinase [*An enzyme*] (MAE)
PBK........... Poncebank [*NYSE symbol*] (SAG)
PBK........... Pseudophakic Bullous Keratopathy (SAUS)
PBKAL....... Paris, Brussels, Koln [*Cologne*], Amsterdam, London [*High-speed rail network*] (ECON)
PBKB .... Peoples Bancshares, Inc. [*NASDAQ symbol*] (SAG)
PBKB .... People's Savings Bank of Brockton [*Brockton, MA*] [*NASDAQ symbol*] (NQ)
PBKC .... Premier Bankshares [*NASDAQ symbol*] (TTSB)
PBKC .... Premier Bankshares Corp. [*NASDAQ symbol*] (NQ)
PBKS .... Provident Bankshares [*NASDAQ symbol*] (TTSB)
PBKS .... Provident Bankshares Corp. [*NASDAQ symbol*] (NQ)
PBKTOA .... Printing, Bookbinding and Kindred Trades Overseers Association (SAUS)
PBL........... Bethlehem Public Library, Bethlehem, PA [*OCLC symbol*] (OCLC)
PBl............ Blairsville Public Library, Blairsville, PA [*Library symbol*] [*Library of Congress*] (LCLS)
PBL........... Lehigh University, Bethlehem, PA [*Library symbol*] [*Library of Congress*] (LCLS)
PBL........... Pacific Beach Library (SAUS)
PBL........... Parachute-Braked Landing [*Military*] (IAA)
PBL........... Payload Bay Liner [*NASA*] (MCD)
PBL........... Peripheral Blood Leukocyte [*or Lymphocyte*] [*Hematology*]
PBL........... Peripheral Blood Lymphocyte [*Medicine*] (MELL)
PBL........... [*The*] Philadelphia Belt Line Railroad Co. [*AAR code*]
PBL........... Photo Butt Line (MSA)
PBL........... Pigeon Breeder's Lung [*Medicine*] (MELL)
PBL........... Planetary Boundary Layer [*Aerospace*]
PBL........... Plateau Black-Bladed Letters [*Tire design*]
PBL........... Poly-Buffered Local Oxidation of Silicon (AAEL)
PBL........... Potential Binding Level [*Of natural waters for metal ions*]
PBL........... Problem Based Learning [*Education*]
PBL........... Product Baseline (MCD)
PBL........... Prune Brownline [*Plant pathology*]
PBL........... Public Broadcasting Laboratory (NTCM)
PBL........... Public Broadcast Laboratory
pbl............ Publisher [*MARC relator code*] [*Library of Congress*] (LCCP)
PBL........... Pueblo [*Diocesan abbreviation*] [*Colombia*] (TOCD)
PBL........... Puerto Cabello [*Venezuela*] [*Airport symbol*] (OAG)
PBlbM.......... Montgomery County Community College, Blue Bell, PA [*Library symbol*] [*Library of Congress*] (LCLS)
PBLD .... Progressive Base Line Dimensioning (SAA)
PBLG .... Polybenzyl-L-glutamate [*Biochemistry*]
PBLI .... Premature Birth, Live Infant [*neonatology*] (DAVI)
PBIP........... Blairsville Public Library, Blairsville, PA [*Library symbol*] [*Library of Congress*] (LCLS)
PBLS.......... Production Baseline Set (MCD)
pblsh .... publish (SAUS)
PBLSHNG .... Publishing
PBm........... Bryn Mawr College, Bryn Mawr, PA [*Library symbol*] [*Library of Congress*] (LCLS)
PBM........... Paramaribo [*Surinam*] [*Airport symbol*] (OAG)
PBM........... Parrot Beak-Micromelia (SAUS)
PBM........... Patrol Boat Multi-Mission (ACAE)
PBM........... Patrol Search Plane [*Navy designation for Mariner aircraft*]
PBM........... Pay By Mail (SAUS)
PBM........... Peak Bone Mass [*Medicine*] (DMAA)
PBM........... Performance-Based Management (AAGC)
PBM........... Performance Based Method [*Environmental Protection Agency*] [*Analytical chemistry*]
PBM........... Peribacteriod Membrane (CARB)
PBM........... Peripheral Basement Membrane [*Medicine*] (DMAA)
PBM........... Peripheral Blood Mononuclear [*Cells*] [*Hematology*]

PBM........... Permanent Bench Mark
PBM........... Pharmaceutical Benefit Manager [*or Management*] [*Managed health care*]
PBM........... Pharmacy Benefit Managers (ECON)
PBM........... Pipelined Burst Mode (SAUS)
PBM........... PIXEL Block Mode [*Computer science*] (BYTE)
PBM........... Placental Basement Membrane [*Medicine*] (DMAA)
PBM........... Play By Mail (SAUS)
PBM........... Portable BIT [*Binary Digit*] Map [*Computer science*]
PBM........... Port Bypass Module (SAUS)
PBM........... Poskanzer Portable Bitmap (SAUS)
PBM........... Potential Barrier Method (IAA)
PBM........... Power Balance Model (SAUS)
PBM........... Prescription Benefit Manager (ADWA)
PBM........... Pressure Bias Modulation (MCD)
PBM........... Principal Beach Master [*RAF*] [*British*]
PBM........... Probability Based-Matched [*Database search techniques*]
PBM........... Production Base Modernization (MCD)
PBM........... Production Bill of Material (SAUS)
PBM........... Program Budget Manager (MCD)
PBM........... Program Business Management (NASA)
PBM........... Pulse Burst Modulation (IAA)
PBmA.......... American College of Life Underwriters, Bryn Mawr, PA [*Library symbol*] [*Library of Congress*] (LCLS)
PBMA......... Peanut Butter Manufacturers Association [*Later, PBNPA*] (EA)
PBMA......... Plastic Bath Manufacturers Association [*British*] (DI)
PBMA......... Plumbers and Builders Merchants Association [*Australia*]
PBMA......... Polybutyl Methacrylate [*Organic chemistry*]
PBMA......... Pressed Brick Makers' Association Ltd. [*British*] (BI)
PBMA......... Public Broadcasting Management Association (SAUS)
PBMASA ..... Paper Bag Manufacturers' Association of South Australia
PBMC......... Moravian College and Theological Seminary, Bethlehem, PA [*Library symbol*] [*Library of Congress*] (LCLS)
PBMC......... Peripheral Blood Mononuclear Cells [*Hematology*]
PBMCA .... Archives of the Moravian Church, Bethlehem, PA [*Library symbol*] [*Library of Congress*] (LCLS)
PBMCHRC... Pacific Basin Maternal and Child Health Resource Center [*Guam*] (BUAC)
PBMD-Bull... PBMD-Bulletin (SAUS)
PBME......... Physiology and Biomedical Engineering [*Program*] (DAVI)
PBME......... Physiology and Biomedical Engineering Program (BABM)
PBMI.......... Pacific Biometrics, Inc. [*NASDAQ symbol*] (SAG)
PBMI.......... Polybismaleinimid (SAUS)
PBMI.......... Purchase Base Machine Inventory (SAUS)
PBmL.......... Ludington Public Library, Bryn Mawr, PA [*Library symbol*] [*Library of Congress*] (LCLS)
PBMNC .... Peripheral Blood Mononuclear Cell [*Hematology*] (DAVI)
PBMR .... Pennsylvania Bureau of Municipal Research (MCD)
PBMR .... Provisional Basic Military Requirements (NATG)
PBMR .... Push Broom Microwave Radiometer (SAUS)
PBMR .... Pushbroom Microwave Radiometer (SAUS)
PBMS......... Pacific Bell Mobile Services (SAUS)
PBMS......... Parcel Business Machine System (NITA)
PBMS......... Performance-Based Measurement System [*Environmental Protection Agency*]
PBMS......... Photonburst Mass Spectrometry
PBMS......... Pitney Bowes Management Services
PBM/STIRS... Probability Based Matching and Self-Trained Interpretive and Retrieval Systems [*Database*] [*John Wiley & Sons, Inc.*] [*Information service or system*] (CRD)
PBMV......... Percutaneous Balloon Mitral Valvoplasty [*Medicine*] (MELL)
PBMW .... Moravian College, Bethlehem, PA [*Library symbol*] [*Library of Congress*] (LCLS)
PBN .... Northampton County Area Community College, Bethlehem, PA [*Library symbol*] [*Library of Congress*] (LCLS)
PBN .... Paralytic Brachial Neuritis [*Medicine*] (MAE)
PBN .... PE Ben Oilfield Services Ltd. [*Toronto Stock Exchange symbol*]
PBN .... Peribrachialis Nuclei [*Neurology*]
PBN .... Peroxybutryl Nitride (SAUS)
PBN .... Phenyl(butyl)nitrone [*Organic chemistry*]
PBN .... Physical Block Number
PBN .... Pilatus Britten-Norman Ltd. [*British*] [*ICAO designator*] (FAAC)
PBN .... PointCast Business Network
PBN .... Polybutylene Napthalate (SAUS)
PBN .... Polymixin-B Sulfate/Bacitracin/Neomycin [*Antibacterial regime*]
PBN .... Porto Amboin [*Angola*] [*Airport symbol*] (OAG)
PBN .... Posteriobuccal Nerve (SAUS)
PBN .... Primary Block Number [*Computer science*]
PBN .... Provisional Buy Notice (SAUS)
PBN .... Pyrolytic Boron Nitride [*Inorganic chemistry*]
PBNA .... Partial Body Neutron Activation [*Radiology*]
PBNA .... Phenyl-beta-naphthylamine [*Organic chemistry*]
PBNB .... People's Savings Financial Corp. [*Formerly, People's Savings Bank New Britain*] [*NASDAQ symbol*] (NQ)
PBNB .... Peoples Svgs Finl [*NASDAQ symbol*] (TTSB)
PBND .... Pollybeak Nasal Deformity [*Medicine*] (MELL)
PBNE .... Philadelphia, Bethlehem & New England Railroad Co. [*AAR code*]
PBNI .... PacBell Networking Integration
PBNM .... Parallel Bar Noise Maker [*Antiacoustic torpedo device*]
PBNP .... Phipps Bend Nuclear Plant (NRCH)
PBNP .... Point Beach Nuclear Plant (NRCH)
PBNP .... Porcine Brain Natriuretic Peptide [*Biochemistry*]
PBNPA .... Peanut Butter and Nut Processors Association (EA)
PBNS .... Proceedings of the Bristol Naturalists Society (SAUS)
PBNSC .... Peripheral Backup NSC Control Element (SAUS)

PBNSW........ Pharmacy Board of New South Wales [*Australia*]
PBNSW........ Police Board of New South Wales [*Australia*]
PBNT .... Parole Board of the Northern Territory [*Australia*]
PBO .... Packed by Owner
PBO .... Paleobioclimatic Operator
PBO .... Paraburdoo [*Australia*] [*Airport symbol*] (OAG)
PBO .... Pauling Bond Order [*Physical chemistry*]
PBO .... Penicillin in Beeswax [*Medicine*] (DMAA)
PBO .... Penicillin in Beeswax and Oil [*Medicine*] (DMAA)
PBO .... Performance-Based Organization
PBO .... Personal Banking Officer (TBD)
P Bo............. Petrus Boaterius [*Flourished, 1285-1321*] [*Authority cited in pre-1607 legal work*] (DSA)
PBO .... Piperonylbutoxid (SAUS)
pbo .... Placebo [*Medicine*]
PBO .... Plotting Board Operator (MUGU)
PBO .... Polite Brush-Off (SAUS)
PBO .... Poly(p-phenylene Benzobisoxazole) (RDA)
PBO .... Poor Bloody Observer [*British World War I military slang*] (DSUE)
PBO .... Print Business Opportunities [*A publication*] (EAAP)
PBO .... Priority Back Order (TIMI)
PBO .... Process Before Output (SAUS)
PBO .... Projected Benefit Obligation (TDOB)
PBO .... Property Book Officer [*Army*] (AABC)
PBO .... Push-Button Operation
PBoC........... People's Bank of China
PBOCST....... Poly(butoxycarbonyloxystyrene) [*Organic chemistry*]
PBOD .... Phytoplankton Biochemical Oxygen Demand [*Oceanography*]
PBOI .... Public Board of Inquiry
PBOIP .... Preliminary Basis of Issue Plan [*Military*] (MCD)
PBOS .... Planning Board for Ocean Shipping [*Army*] [*NATO*]
PBOT .... Philiadelphia Board of Trade (NUMA)
PBP............. Packet Burst Protocol (SAUS)
PBP............. [*The*] Paper Bag Players (EA)
PBP............. Para-(Benzyloxy)phenol [*Organic chemistry*]
PB/P............ Particleboard/Plywood
PBP............. Pay-Back Period [*Finance*]
PBP............. Pay by Phone [*Business term*]
PBP............. Payrole, Budgeting, Personnel-System (SAUS)
PBP............. Peak Blood Pressure [*Cardiology*] (DAVI)
PBP............. Pellin-Broca Prism [*Physics*]
PBP............. Penicillin-Binding Protein [*Biochemistry*]
PBP............. Performance-Based Pay
PBP............. Periplasmic Binding Protein [*Biochemistry*]
PBP............. Person Before Place [*Library cataloguing*] (DGA)
PBP............. Pheromonebinding Proteins [*Biochemistry*]
PBP............. Phosphate-Binding Protein [*Biochemistry*]
PBP............. Picnic Basket Porphyrin [*Organic chemistry*]
PBP............. Picture-by-Picture [*Television technology*] (PS)
PBP............. Play-by-Play (WDMC)
PBP............. Plotting Board Plot (MUGU)
PBP............. Point by Point
PBP............. Porphyrin Biosynthetic Pathway [*Biochemistry*] (AAMN)
PBP............. Post Boost Phase (ACAE)
PBP............. Postural Back Pain (MELL)
PBP............. Power Bias Panel
PBP............. Preburner Pump (SAUS)
PBP............. Pregnenolone Binding Protein [*Endocrinology*]
PBP............. Private Brand Proneness [*Marketing*]
PBP............. Production Base Plan (MCD)
PBP............. Program and Budget Planning
PBP............. Program Board Panel
PBP............. Progressive Bulbar Palsy [*Medicine*] (MEDA)
PBP............. Provider Based Physician
PBP............. Pulse Burst Period (PDAA)
PBP............. Purified Brucella Protein [*Biochemistry*] (DAVI)
PBP............. Push-Button Panel
PBPA .... Pharmaceutical Benefits Pricing Authority [*Australia*]
PBPB .... Para-bromophenacyl Bromide [*Organic chemistry*]
PBPB .... Pyridinium Bromide Perbromide [*Inorganic chemistry*]
PBPC .... Passenger and Baggage Processing Committee [*IATA*] (DS)
PBPE .... Population Biology/Physiological Ecology [*Program*] [*National Science Foundation*]
PBPITMT...... Production Base Productivity Improvement through Manufacturing Technology (MCD)
PBPK .... Physiologically Based Pharmacokinetics [*Biochemistry*]
PBPM........... Poultry Byproduct Meal
PBPS .... Painting Brushmakers' Provident Society [*A union*] [*British*]
PBPS .... Paulist Bible Pamphlet Series [*Glen Rock, NJ*] [*A publication*] (BJA)
PBPS .... Performance-Based Payment System
PBPS .... Post-Boost Propulsion System [*Aerospace*]
PB/PS .... Power Brakes/Power Steering (SAUS)
PBPS .... Program Budgeting and Planning System (SAUS)
PBPTC .... Palm Beach Psychotherapy Training Center (EA)
PBPV .... Percutaneous Balloon Pulmonary Valvuloplasty [*Medicine*] (DMAA)
PBQ .... Pharmacy Board of Queensland [*Australia*]
PBQ .... Physiotherapists' Board of Queensland [*Australia*]
PBQ .... Podiatrists' Board of Queensland [*Australia*]
PBQ .... Poste De La Baleine [*Quebec*] [*Seismograph station code, US Geological Survey*] (SEIS)
PBQ .... Preschool Behavior Questionnaire
PBr.............. Carnegie Public Library, Bradford, PA [*Library symbol*] [*Library of Congress*] (LCLS)
PBR .... Pabst Blue Ribbon [*Beer*]
PBR .... Packed Bed Reactor

PBR .... Particle Bed Reactor [*Department of Energy*]
PBR .... Patapsco & Back Rivers Railroad Co. [*AAR code*]
PBR .... Patient's Bill of Rights (MELL)
PBR .... Patrol Boat, River [*Navy symbol*]
PBR .... Patrol Boat Roadstead [*Navy*]
PBR .... Payment by Results [*Payment system*]
PBR .... Pebble-Bed Reactor [*Nuclear energy*]
PBR .... Pembroke, NH [*Location identifier*] [*FAA*] (FAAL)
PBR .... Pencil Beam RADAR
PBR .... Performance-Based Regulation (SAUS)
PBR .... Permit by Rule [*Pollution control*]
PBR .... Photobioreactor (ADWA)
PBR .... Pigment-Binder Ratio [*Weight*]
PBR .... Pittsburgh Byzantine [*Diocesan abbreviation*] [*Pennsylvania*] (TOCD)
PBR .... Plant Breeders' Rights
PBR .... Plum Brook Reactor [*Nuclear energy*]
PBR .... Polar Biomedical Research (SAUS)
PBR .... Pole Broken [*Telecommunications*] (TEL)
PBR .... Polished-Bore Receptacle (SAUS)
PBR .... Power Breeder Reactor (AAG)
PBR .... Precision Bombing Range [*Army*]
PBR .... Pressurized Ballistic Range [*NASA*]
PBR .... Price-to-Book Value Ratio [*Investment term*] (DFIT)
PBR .... Procedure Base Register (IAA)
PBR .... Procion Brilliant Red (DB)
PBR .... Professional Bull Riders [*An association*]
PBR .... Program Budgetary Review (SAUS)
PBR .... Program Business Representative (SAUS)
PBR .... Puerto Barrios [*Guatemala*] [*Airport symbol*] (AD)
PBR .... Pyridine-Butadiene Rubber
PBR .... Vinylpyridine-Butadiene Rubber (SAUS)
PBra............ Carnegie Free Library, Braddock, PA [*Library symbol*] [*Library of Congress*] (LCLS)
PBRA .... Practical Bomb Rack Adapter (NG)
PBRA .... Professional Bicycle Racers Association [*Defunct*] (EA)
PBracAL....... Allegheny International, Inc., Brackenridge, PA [*Library symbol*] [*Library of Congress*] (LCLS)
Pb-RBC....... Lead Red Blood Count [*For lead poisoning*] [*Medicine*] (DAVI)
PBR Beer..... Pabst Blue Ribbon Beer (SAUS)
PBRC .... Program Budget Review Committee (SAUS)
PBRE .... Pebble-Bed Reactor Experiment [*Nuclear energy*]
PB Report ... Publications Board Report (SAUS)
PBRERP....... Permanent Board for Review of the Enlisted Retention Program
PBRERS....... Permanent Board for Review of the Enlisted Rating Structure
PBRESD....... Polar Branch, Research Environmental Science Division [*Army*]
PBRF .... Plant Breeding Research Forum [*Defunct*] (EA)
PBRF .... Plum Brook Reactor Facility [*Lewis Research Center*]
PBriR .... Rohm & Haas Co., Bristol, PA [*Library symbol*] [*Library of Congress*] (LCLS)
P/BRK .... Power Brake [*Automotive engineering*]
PBroGS........ Church of Jesus Christ of Latter-Day Saints, Genealogical Society Library, Philadelphia Branch, Broomall, PA [*Library symbol*] [*Library of Congress*] (LCLS)
PBRS .... Polybromostyrene [*Organic chemistry*]
PBRS .... Prison Behavior Rating Scale
PBRS .... Pupil Behavior Rating Scale [*Psychology*]
PBRS .... Push-Button Rotary Switch
PBRV .... Potato Black Ringspot Virus [*Plant pathology*]
PBS............. Bethlehem Steel Corp., Charles H. Herty, Jr., Memorial Library, Bethlehem, PA [*Library symbol*] [*Library of Congress*] (LCLS)
PbS............. Lead Sulphide (SAUS)
PBS............. Pacific Biological Station [*Department of Fisheries and Oceans*] [*Canada*] [*Research center*] (RCD)
PBS............. Packed Bed Scrubber (EEVL)
PBS............. Paginated By Sections (SAUS)
PBS............. Palestine Broadcasting Service (BJA)
PBS............. Panama Bureau of Shipping (SAUS)
PBs............. Paperback Books (SAUS)
PBS............. Parenchymatous Bundle Sheath [*Botany*]
PBS............. Parimutuel Betting System
PBS............. Parti Bersatu Sabah [*Malaysia*] [*Political party*] (ECON)
PBS............. Particulate Biogenic Silica [*Environmental science*]
PBS............. Parts Breakdown Structure
PBS............. Path Between the Seas (SAUS)
PBS............. Peninsular Base Section [*Military*]
PBS............. Percent Bone Solids (SAUS)
PBS............. Periscope Bombsight Stabilizer
PBS............. Permanent Building Societies (SAUS)
PBS............. Personal Bibliographic Software, Inc. [*Information service or system*] (IID)
PBS............. Peterborough Board of Education [*UTLAS symbol*]
PBS............. Philippine Broadcasting Service (NADA)
PBS............. Philips Business Systems (NITA)
PBS............. Phosphate-Buffered Saline
PBS............. Phosphate-Buffered Sodium (MAE)
PBS............. Photon Backscattering (AAEL)
PBS............. Phycobilisome [*Biochemistry*]
PBS............. Picture Building System (NITA)
PBS............. Pigeon Bay [*South Carolina*] [*Seismograph station code, US Geological Survey*] (SEIS)
PBS............. Pilgrim Amer Bk & Thrift [*NYSE symbol*] (TTSB)
PBS............. Pilgrim American Bank & Thrift Fund, Inc. [*NYSE symbol*] (SAG)
PBS............. Pilgrim Regional Bank Shares, Inc. [*NYSE symbol*] (SPSG)
PBS............. Place Before Subject [*Library cataloguing*] (DGA)
PBS............. Plant Breeding Station (SAUS)

PBS............. Plettenberg Bay [*South Africa*] [*Airport symbol*] (AD)
PBS............. Podiatry Bibliographical Society [*Defunct*] (EA)
PBS............. Polarization Beam Splitter
PBS............. Polarizing Beamsplitter (SAUS)
PBS............. Polybutadiene Styrene (SAUS)
PBS............. Poly(butenesulfone) [*Organic chemistry*]
PBS............. Polysteel Building Systems Ltd. [*Toronto Stock Exchange symbol*]
PBS............. Portable Base Station (SAUS)
PBS............. Portable Batch System (SAUS)
PBS............. Potere Battericida del Sangue [*Bactericidal Property of the Blood*] [*Medicine*]
PBS............. Poverty Budget Share [*Bureau of the Census*] (GFGA)
PBS............. Power Blending System (SAUS)
PBS............. Power Breakfast Syndrome [*Suffered by late-risers forced to attend breakfast meetings*]
PBS............. Prayer Book Society [*British*] (DBA)
PBS............. Prefabricated Bituminous Surfacing
PBS............. Press-Button Signalling (PDAA)
Pbs............. Pressure at the Body Surface [*Medicine*] (DAVI)
PBS............. Pressure Boundary Subsystem [*Nuclear energy*] (NRCH)
PBS............. Prevent Blindness Society (SAUS)
PBS............. Primer Binding Site [*Genetics*]
PBS............. Procedure Branching Statement (SAUS)
PBS............. Process Batch Size (SAUS)
PBS............. Production Base Support [*Army*] (AABC)
PBS............. Professional Bibliographic System [*Database manager package*] [*Personal Bibliographic Software, Inc.*] [*Ann Arbor, MI*]
PBS............. Professional Bowhunters Society (EA)
PBS............. Professional Business Solutions (ACAE)
PBS............. Program and Budgeting System (OICC)
PBS............. Program Board Stowage
PBS............. Program Breakdown Structure [*Nuclear energy*]
PBS............. Program Buffer Storage (IAA)
PBS............. Project Breakdown Structure [*Nuclear energy*] (NRCH)
PBS............. Protective Breathing System (NAKS)
PBS............. Protestant Big Sisters
PBS............. Prune Belly Syndrome [*Medicine*] (DMAA)
PBS............. Public Brand Software (PCM)
PBS............. Public Broadcasting Service [*Facetious translation: Primarily British Shows*] (EA)
PBS............. Public Broadcasting System
PBS............. Public Buildings Service [*of General Services Administration*]
PBS............. Punch Barrier Strip (SAUS)
PBS............. Push-Button Switch
PBSA .... Parole Board of South Australia
PBSA .... Partially Blinded Soldiers Association (SAUS)
PBSA .... Pastoral Board of South Australia
PBSA .... Permanent Building Societies Association (SAUS)
PBSA .... Pharmacy Board of South Australia
PBSA .... Phosphate-Buffered Saline Azide [*Culture medium*]
PBSA .... Phylloxera Board of South Australia
PBSA .... Physiotherapists' Board of South Australia
PBSA .... Publication of the Bibliographical Society of America (SAUS)
PBSAA .... Partially Blinded Soldiers' Association of Australia
PBSC .... Packard BioScience [*NASDAQ symbol*] (SG)
PBSC .... Panelized Building Systems Council (EA)
PBSC .... Performance-Based Service Contracting (AAGC)
PBSC .... Peripheral-Blood Stem-Cell [*Biochemistry Medicine*]
PBSCMA ...... Peanut Butter Sandwich and Cookie Manufacturers Association [*Later, PBNPA*] (EA)
PBSCT .... Peripheral Blood Stem Cell Transplant [*Medicine*]
PBSCT .... Peripheral Blood Stem Cell Transplantation (SAUS)
PBSE............ Philadelphia-Baltimore Stock Exchange [*Later, Philadelphia-Baltimore-Washington Stock Exchange*]
PBSF............ Pacific Bank NA [*NASDAQ symbol*] (SPSG)
PBshBrc....... Peoples Bancshares, Inc. [*Associated Press*] (SAG)
PBSI............ Philips Business Systems, Inc. (SAUS)
PBS/IS .... Public Buildings Service/Information System (SAUS)
PBSM........... Plastic Bonded Starter Mix
PBSP .... Prognostically Bad Sign During Pregnancy [*Obstetrics*] (MAE)
PBSR .... Papers of the British School at Rome (SAUS)
PBSR .... Permanent Building Societies Registrar [*New South Wales, Australia*]
PB SRAM..... Pipeline Burst SRAM [*Static Random-Access Memory*] [*Computer science*]
PBSS .... Phosphate-Buffered Saline Solution (SAUS)
PbSt9........... Public Storage Properties IX [*Associated Press*] (SAG)
PbSt 10........ Public Storage Properties X, Inc. [*Associated Press*] (SAG)
PbSt 11........ Public Storage Properties XI, Inc. [*Associated Press*] (SAG)
PbSt 12........ Public Storage Properties XII, Inc. [*Associated Press*] (SAG)
PbSt14......... Public Storage Properties XIV, Inc. [*Associated Press*] (SAG)
PbSt15......... Public Storage Properties XV, Inc. [*Associated Press*] (SAG)
PbSt16......... Public Storage Properties XVI, Inc. [*Associated Press*] (SAG)
PbSt17......... Public Storage Properties XVII, Inc. [*Associated Press*] (SAG)
PbSt18......... Public Storage Properties XVIII, Inc. [*Associated Press*] (SAG)
PbSt19......... Public Storage Properties XIX, Inc. [*Associated Press*] (SAG)
PbSt20......... Public Storage Properties XX, Inc. [*Associated Press*] (SAG)
PBSTA .... Push-Button Station (IAA)
PBSteel........ Bethlehem Steel Corp., Charles M. Schwab Memorial Library, Bethlehem, PA [*Library symbol*] [*Library of Congress*] (LCLS)
PBSU .... Portable Beacon and Scoring Unit (MCD)
PBSV .... Plum Bark Split Virus (SAUS)
PBSW .... Push-Button Switch
PBT............. Pacific Ballet Theatre
PBT............. Para-Bandit Target
PBT............. Parity BIT [*Binary Digit*] Test

PBT............. Party of Businessmen and Tradesmen [*Czech Republic*] (BUAC)
PBT............. Passband Tuning
PBT............. Passenger Boarding Total (SAUS)
PBT............. Peoria Board of Trade (EA)
PBT............. Performance-Based Teaching (SAUS)
PBT............. Performance-Based Training (SAUS)
PBT............. Permeable Base Transistor [*Electronics*]
PBT............. Permian Basin Royalty Trust [*NYSE symbol*] (SPSG)
PBT............. Persistent, Bioaccumulative, and Toxic [*Chemistry*]
PBT............. Philippine Ballet Theater (ECON)
PBT............. Pierce-Blank Tool (MCD)
PBT............. Piggyback Tape [*or Twistor*] [*Computer science*]
PBT............. Pittsburgh Ballet Theatre
PB-T............ Plastic Banded, Tracer (SAUS)
PBT............. Polybay Tier
PBT............. Polybenzothiazole [*Organic chemistry*]
PBT............. Polybutylene Terephthalate [*Organic chemistry*]
PBT............. Portable Breathalyzer Test (SARE)
PBT............. Preferred Body Temperature [*Physiology*]
PBT............. Preliminary Bearing Training (SAUS)
PBT............. Preliminary-Breath-Test [*Device used by police to determine whether or not a driver is legally intoxicated*]
PBT............. President of the Board of Trade (SAUS)
PBT............. Professional Billiards Tour [*An association*]
PBT............. Profile-Based Therapy [*Medicine*] (DB)
PBT............. Profit before Tax [*Finance*] (WDAA)
PBT............. Push-Button Telephone
PBT............. Red Bluff, CA [*Location identifier*] [*FAA*] (FAAL)
PBT₄ .... Protein-Bound Thyroxine [*Endocrinology*] (DAVI)
PBTB........... Paper Bag Trade Board (SAUS)
PBTB........... Parsons Brinckerhoff-Tudor-Bechtel
PBTC.......... Peoples Banctrust [*NASDAQ symbol*] (TTSB)
PBTC.......... Peoples BancTrust Company Inc. [*NASDAQ symbol*] (SAG)
PBTC.......... Postal Business Training Centre [*British*]
PBTE.......... Performance-Based Teacher Education (OICC)
PBTF.......... Polybromotrifluoroethylene (SAUS)
PBTF.......... Protective Barrier Test Facility (SAUS)
PBTF.......... Pump Bearing Test Facility [*Nuclear energy*]
PBTI........... Pancreatic Basic Trypsin Inhibitor (DB)
P/BTN .... Push Button [*Automotive engineering*]
PBTP.......... Polybutylene Terephthalate [*Organic chemistry*]
PBT-PAR..... Polybutylene Terephthalate-Polyarylate (SAUS)
PBT-PET .... Polybutylene Terephthalate-Polyethylene Terephthalate (SAUS)
PBTS.......... Business-Oriented Technology Promotion Programme (SAUS)
PBTS.......... Proton Beam Transport System
PBTX.......... Ptychodiscus brevis Toxin [*Florida red-tide toxin*]
PBU .... Air-Burundi [*ICAO designator*] (FAAC)
PBU .... Bucknell University, Lewisburg, PA [*OCLC symbol*] (OCLC)
PBU .... Page Buffer Unit (SAUS)
PBU .... Pali Buddhist Union (BUAC)
PBU .... Palm Beach County Utility Corp. [*Toronto Stock Exchange symbol*]
PBU .... Peribacteroid Unit (SAUS)
PBU .... Peripheral Buffer Unit (SAUS)
PBU .... Perry Basin [*Utah*] [*Seismograph station code, US Geological Survey*] (SEIS)
PBU .... Photo Blow-up (SAUS)
PBU .... Premature Baby Unit [*National Health Service*] [*British*] (DI)
PBU .... Primary Beam Unit (SAUS)
PBU .... Progil-Bayer-Ugine (SAUS)
PBU .... Push Button Unit (NITA)
PBU .... Pushbutton Unit (SAUS)
PBU .... Putao [*Myanmar*] [*Airport symbol*] (OAG)
P Buoy........ Pillar Buoy (SAUS)
PBUP.......... Perforated Backup Plate
PBUS .... Professional Bail Agents of the United States (NTPA)
PBut........... Butler Public Library, Butler, PA [*Library symbol*] [*Library of Congress*] (LCLS)
PButV......... United States Veterans Administration Hospital, Butler, PA [*Library symbol*] [*Library of Congress*] (LCLS)
PBV............. English Prayer Book Version (BJA)
PBV............. Peach Blotch Virus (SAUS)
PBV............. Pedal Blood Vessel
PBV............. Pharmacy Board of Victoria [*Australia*]
PBV............. Platinol [*Cisplatin*], Bleomycin, Vinblastine [*Antineoplastic drug regimen*]
PBV............. Post Boost Vehicle [*Missiles*] (AFM)
PBV............. Predicted Blood Volume [*Medicine*]
PBV............. Proportioning and Bypass Valve
PBV............. Pulmonary Blood Volume [*Medicine*]
PBVCO........ Post Boost Vehicle Cutoff (ACAE)
PBVM......... Presentation of the Blessed Virgin Mary [*Roman Catholic women's religious order*]
PBVM......... Presentation of the Blessed Virgin Mary Sisters (TOCD)
PBVM......... Sisters of the Presentation of the B.V.M. (TOCD)
PBVM......... Union of the Sisters of the Presentation of the Blessed Virgin Mary (TOCD)
PBVP.......... Post Boost Vehicle Propulsion [*Missiles*] (MCD)
PBVR.......... [*The*] Port Bienville Railroad [*AAR code*]
PBvu .... Andrew Bayne Memorial Library, Bellevue, PA [*Library symbol*] [*Library of Congress*] (LCLS)
PBW............ Particle-Beam Weapon
PBW............ Parts by Weight (IEEE)
PBW............ Percussive Butt Welder
PBW............ Pink Bollworm [*Cotton pest*]
PBW............ Posterior Bite Wing [*Dentistry*]

PBW............	Power by Wire [*Flight control*]
PBW............	Proportional Bandwidth (MCD)
PBW............	Pulse Burst Wave
PBWA.........	Plasma Beat Wave Accelerator [*Physics*]
PBWA.........	Plasma Beta-Wave Accelerator [*Plasma physics*]
PBWA.........	Professional Basketball Writers Association (NTPA)
PBWAA........	Professional Basketball Writers' Association of America (EA)
PBWEE........	Pilot Boll Weevil Eradication Experiment [*Department of Agriculture*]
PBWF..........	Pulse Burst Waveform
PBWG	Pakistan Bibliographical Working Group (BUAC)
PBWS..........	Performance-Based Work Statement
PBWSE	Philadelphia-Baltimore-Washington Stock Exchange [*Later, Philadelphia Stock Exchange*]
PBWT..........	Parts by Weight (WDAA)
PBWU	Projektgruppe Bayern zur Erforschung der Wirkung von Umweltschadstoffen (SAUS)
PBX............	PBX Resources [*Vancouver Stock Exchange symbol*]
PBX............	Pillbox (SAUS)
PBX............	Plastic Bonded Explosive
PBX............	Polymer Bonded Explosive (SAUS)
PBX............	Private Branch Exchange [*Telecommunications*]
PBx............	Prostate Biopsy [*Medicine*] (MELL)
PBX............	Public Branch Exchange (SAUS)
PBXFS	Private Branch Exchange Final Selector [*Telecommunications*] (IAA)
PBX-M	Princeton Beta Experiment Modified (SAUS)
PBXs...........	Personal Business Exchanges (SAUS)
PBY............	Kayenta, AZ [*Location identifier*] [*FAA*] (FAAL)
PBY............	Patrol Bomber [*Navy designation for Catalina aircraft*]
PBY............	Pearl Air Services (U) Ltd. [*Uganda*] [*ICAO designator*] (FAAC)
PBY............	Pep Boys-Man,Mo,Ja [*NYSE symbol*] (TTSB)
PBY............	Pep Boys - Manny, Moe & Jack [*NYSE symbol*] (SPSG)
PBY............	Pillars Bay [*Alaska*] [*Airport symbol*] (AD)
PBY............	Postgraduate Year (MELL)
PBYP	Play-By-Play Toys&Novelties [*NASDAQ symbol*] (TTSB)
PBYP	Play By Play Toys & Novelties, Inc. [*NASDAQ symbol*] (SAG)
PBZ............	Khortitsa-Air Ltd. [*Ukraine*] [*FAA designator*] (FAAC)
PBZ............	Peoples Bank of Zanzibar [*Tanzania*] (BUAC)
PBZ............	Personal Breathing Zone (HEAS)
PBZ............	Phenoxybenzamine [*Also, POB*] [*Adrenergic blocking agent*]
PBZ............	Phenylbutazone [*Anti-inflammatory compound*]
PBZ............	Plettenberg [*South Africa*] [*Airport symbol*] (OAG)
PBZ............	Pyribenzamine [*Antihistamine*] [*Trademark*]
PBzMA........	Polybenzylmethacrylate (SAUS)
PBzN..........	Peroxybenzoyl Nitrate [*Lacrimator*]
PBZT...........	Polyphenylene Benzalthiazole (SAUS)
PBZT...........	Poly-P-Phenylene Benzobesthiazole
PC............	All India Reporter, Privy Council [*1914-50*] [*A publication*] (DLA)
PC............	British and Colonial Prize Cases [*A publication*] (DLA)
Pc............	Chamber Pressure
PC............	Civilian Personnel Division [*Coast Guard*]
PC............	Coastal Escort [*Ship symbol*] (NATG)
PC............	Communist Party [*Peru*] [*Political party*] (PD)
PC............	diacyl-glyceroPhosphoCholine (SAUS)
PC............	Fiji Air [*ICAO designator*] (AD)
PC............	Indian Rulings, Privy Council [*1929-47*] [*A publication*] (DLA)
PC............	J. Lewis Crozer [*Chester Public*] Library, Chester, PA [*Library symbol*] [*Library of Congress*] (LCLS)
PC............	Judicial Committee of the Privy Council (DLA)
PC............	Paccinian Corpuscle [*Medicine*] (MELL)
PC............	Pace College (SAUS)
PC............	Pacific Airlines (SAUS)
PC............	Pacific Coast Railroad [*AAR code*] [*Terminated*]
PC............	Pacific College (SAUS)
PC............	Pacific Command [*Department of Defense*] (BARN)
PC............	Package Control [*or Controller*]
PC............	Packed Cell [*Hematology*] (MAE)
PC............	Pad Coordinator [*NASA*]
PC............	Page Copy (SAUS)
PC............	Pain Control (MELL)
PC............	Paine College (SAUS)
PC............	Paired Comparisons [*Education*] (EDAC)
PC............	Palmer College (SAUS)
PC............	Palmitoyl Carnitine [*Biochemistry*]
PC............	Palomar College (SAUS)
PC............	[*The*] Panama Canal
PC............	Pancreatic Carcinoma [*Medicine*] (MELL)
PC............	Pancreatic Cholera [*Medicine*] (MELL)
Pc............	Pancuronium [*A muscle relaxant*]
PC............	Panola College (SAUS)
PC............	Panoramic Camera
PC............	Paper Chromatography
PC............	Paper Copy
PC............	Paper Core (IAA)
PC............	Paper/Cotton (SAUS)
PC............	Paper or Cloth [*Freight*]
PC............	Paracortex (DMAA)
PC............	Paracortical Hyperplasia [*Oncology*]
PC............	Parallax Computer (SAUS)
pc	Parallax Second (NTIO)
PC............	Parallax Second [*Unit of interstellar-space measure*]
PC............	Parallel Circuit
PC............	Parallel Connection (SAUS)
PC............	Parameter Card (SAUS)
PC............	Parameter Checkout [*Computer science*] (IAA)
PC............	Parametric Cubic [*Computer science*] (OA)

PC............	Parental Control [*Channel lockout*] [*Video technology*]
PC............	Parent Care (EA)
PC............	Parent Cells
PC............	Parents' Charter (AIE)
PC............	Paris College (SAUS)
PC............	Parish Church [*British*] (ROG)
PC............	Parish Council
PC............	Parish Councillor (WDAA)
PC............	Parity Check [*Computer science*] (IAA)
PC............	Park College (SAUS)
PC............	Parliamentary Cases [*A publication*] (DLA)
PC............	PARSEC [*Parallax Second*] [*Unit of interstellar-space measurement*]
PC............	Parsons College (SAUS)
PC............	Part Card [*Computer science*] (IAA)
PC............	Participation Certificate
PC............	Parti Communiste [*Communist Party*] [*Luxembourg*] [*Political party*] (PPW)
PC............	Particulate Component (DMAA)
PC............	Partly Cloudy (ADWA)
PC............	Partido Colorado [*Colorado Party*] [*Uruguay*] [*Political party*] (PPW)
PC............	Partido Conservador [*Conservative Party*] [*Nicaragua*] [*Political party*] (EY)
PC............	Partido Conservador [*Conservative Party*] [*Ecuador*] [*Political party*] (PPW)
PC............	Partition Coefficient
PC............	Parts Catalog (KSC)
PC............	Pasadena College (SAUS)
PC............	Passenger Cargo (SAUS)
PC............	Passenger Certificate [*Shipping*] (DS)
PC............	Past Commander
PC............	Patch Card (SAUS)
PC............	Patch Conversion (SAUS)
PC............	Patent Cases [*A publication*] (DLA)
PC............	Patent Classification (NITA)
PC............	Patent Committee (MCD)
PC............	Patentee/Company Code (NITA)
PC............	Path Carrier (SAUS)
PC............	Path Consistency (SAUS)
PC............	Path Control [*Computer science*] (IBMDP)
PC............	Path Controller (NITA)
PC............	Patient Cancellation [*Medicine*] (DHP)
PC............	Patres Conscripti [*Senators*] [*Latin*]
PC............	Patrol Car [*British military*] (DMA)
PC............	Patrol Carrier (SAUS)
PC............	Patrol Commander (SAUS)
PC............	Patrol Corvette (SAUS)
PC............	Patrol Craft
PC............	Patrol Vessel, Submarine Chaser [*Navy symbol*]
PC............	Pay Card (SAUS)
PC............	Paycheck (SAUS)
PC............	Pay Clerk
PC............	Paymaster-Captain [*Navy*] [*British*]
PC............	Paymaster-Commander [*Navy*] [*British*]
PC............	Paymaster-in-Chief
PC............	Payment Center (MHDB)
PC............	PC Holdings ADS [*NYSE symbol*] (SG)
PC............	Peace Commissioner [*Ireland*]
PC............	Peace Corps (EA)
PC............	Peak Capacity
PC............	Peg Count [*Telecommunications*] (TEL)
PC............	Pembroke College (SAUS)
PC............	Penal Code [*A publication*] (DLA)
PC............	Penetrating Cell
Pc............	Penicillin (STED)
PC............	Penn Central Transportation Co. [*Subsidiary of Penn Central Corp.*] [*Absorbed into Consolidated Rail Corp.*] [*AAR code*]
PC............	Penny Cyclopoedia [*British*] [*A publication*] (ROG)
PC............	Penske Car [*Racing model*]
PC............	Pentose Cycle [*Biochemistry*] (MAE)
PC............	People for a Change [*An association*] [*Defunct*] (EA)
PC............	People's Conference [*India*] [*Political party*] (PPW)
PC............	Pepperdine College (SAUS)
PC............	Percent [*or Percentage*] (IAA)
pc............	Percent (WDMC)
PC............	Percent Correct
PC............	Percentile (SAUS)
PC............	Per Centum [*By the Hundred*] [*Latin*]
PC............	Perciconia circinata [*A toxin-producing fungus*]
PC............	Per Compass (IAA)
PC............	Per Condoglianza [*Used on visiting cards to express condolence*] [*Italian*]
PC............	Percutaneous Cholecystostomy [*Medicine*]
PC............	Perfins Club (EA)
PC............	Performance Code
PC............	Performance Contract (OICC)
PC............	Pericarditis [*Avian pathology*]
PC............	Pericentral
PC............	Pericynthion [*Perilune, or low point, in lunar orbit*]
PC............	Period Contract
PC............	Peripheral Cell
PC............	Peripheral Control (BUR)
PC............	Peripheral Controller (NITA)
PC............	Peritoneal Cell (DMAA)
PC............	Permanently Connected (ELAL)
PC............	Permeance Coefficient (IAA)

PC	Perpetual Curate
PC	Personal Call (OA)
PC	Personal Care
PC	Personal Communication (SAUS)
pc	Personal Computer (WDMC)
pc	Personal Computer
PC	Personal Computing (SAUS)
PC	Personal Copier [In product name, PC-10] [Canon Inc.]
PC	Personal Corporation (BARN)
PC	Personal Correction
PC	Personality Card (SAUS)
PC	Personnel Carrier [A vehicle]
PC	Personnel Coordinator (SAUS)
PC	Personnel Council (ACAE)
PC	Perspective control [Photography]
PC	Petro-Canada
PC	Petrochemistry (SAUS)
pc	Petty Cash (WDMC)
PC	Petty Cash
PC	Pfeiffer College (SAUS)
PC	Pharmacology [Medicine] (DMAA)
PC	Pharmacy Corps [Army]
PC	Phase Change (SAUS)
PC	Phase-Change [Physics]
PC	Phase Code (NITA)
PC	Phase Coherent (CET)
PC	Phase Conjugate (SAUS)
PC	Phase Conjugation (SAUS)
PC	Phase Contrast (SAUS)
PC	Phase Control (IAA)
PC	Phase Converter (SAUS)
PC	Phase Current (SAUS)
PC	Phenol Coefficient (IIA)
PC	Pheochromocytoma [Oncology]
PC	Philadelphia College (SAUS)
PC	Philco Corp. (IAA)
Pc	Philips curve (SAUS)
PC	Philosophical Classics [A publication]
P-C	Phlogistic Corticoid (STED)
PC	Phobia Clinic (EA)
PC	Phoenix College (SAUS)
PC	Phone Call (SAUS)
PC	Phosphate Crown (SAUS)
PC	Phosphate Cycle [Chemistry] (MAE)
PC	Phosphatidylcholine [Lecithin] [Biochemistry]
PC	Phosphocholine [Biochemistry]
PC	Phosphocreatine [Also, PCr] [Creatine phosphate; see CP] [Biochemistry]
PC	Phosphorylcholine [Biochemistry]
PC	Photo Cathode (SAUS)
PC	Photo Cell (SAUS)
PC	Photocell
PC	Photochemical (SAUS)
PC	Photochromatic (SAUS)
PC	Photochromic (SAUS)
PC	Photocomposing (SAUS)
PC	Photoconductance (SAUS)
PC	Photoconduction (SAUS)
PC	Photoconductive
PC	Photoconductivity (SAUS)
pc	Photoconductor (ELAL)
PC	Photoconductor
PC	Photocounting
PC	Photocurrent (SAUS)
PC	Photographic Camera (SAUS)
PC	Photonic Crystal (SAUS)
PC	Photostatic Copy (SAUS)
Pc	Phthalocyanine [Organic chemistry]
PC	Phycocyanin (DB)
PC	Physical Conditioning (SAUS)
PC	Physical Contact (SAUS)
PC	Physicians's Corporation [Medicine] (DMAA)
PC	Physocyanin [Biochemistry]
PC	Phytophthora Cinnamoni [A fungus]
PC	Pica [Typography] (WDMC)
PC	Pick Up Cargo (AFM)
pC	Picocoulomb [One trillionth of a coulomb]
pc	Picocurie (IDOE)
pC	Picocurie [Also, pCi] [One trillionth of a curie]
PC	Picture (MDG)
PC	Piece (AAG)
pc	Piece (VRA)
PC	Piece of Crap (SAUS)
pc	Pied Carre [Square Foot] [French]
pc	Pied Cube [Cubic Foot] [French]
PC	Piedmont College (SAUS)
PC	Pierre Cardin [Fashion designer]
PC	Pikeville College (SAUS)
PC	Pill Counter [Medicine] (DMAA)
PC	Pilotage Charts [Air Force]
PC	Pilot Card (SAUS)
PC	Pin Cutting (SAUS)
PC	Pineland College (SAUS)
PC	Pioneer Clubs (EA)
PC	Pioneer Conference (PSS)

PC	Pioneer Corps [British military] (DMA)
PC	Piriform Cortex (DMAA)
pc	Pitcairn [MARC country of publication code] [Library of Congress] (LCCP)
PC	Pitch Channel
PC	Pitch Circle [Technical drawings]
PC	Pitch Class (SAUS)
PC	Pitch Control (KSC)
PC	Pitch Cycle (DNAB)
PC	Pitting Corrosion (PDAA)
PC	Pittsburgh Commerce Institute
PC	Pittsburgh Corning (SAUS)
PC	Plaid Cymru [Welsh national liberation party] [Political party]
P/C	Plane Captain (MUGU)
PC	Plane Change (MCD)
PC	Plane Commander
PC	Planetary Camera (SAUS)
PC	Planetary Citizens (EA)
PC	Planned Commitment (COE)
PC	Planning Card (AAG)
PC	Planning Commission (PA)
PC	Planning Commitee (SAUS)
PC	Planning Concept (MCD)
PC	Plant Computer (NRCH)
PC	Plant computer-performance monitoring and Calculations (SAUS)
PC	Planting Council (EA)
PC	Plasma Cell [Oncology]
PC	Plasma Chromatography
PC	Plasma Cortisol (DB)
PC	Plasmacytoma [Medicine]
PC	Plasmatic Cell (SAUS)
P-C	Plastic-Carbon (SAUS)
PC	Plastic Core
Pc	Plastocyanin
PC	Plate Circuit (DEN)
PC	Platelet Concentrate [Hematology]
PC	Platelet Count [Hematology]
PC	Platform/Crane (DCTA)
PC	Platoon Commander (SAUS)
PC	Player Character (SAUS)
PC	Pleas of the Crown [A publication] (DLA)
P/C	Pledges/Cost (WDMC)
p/c	Pledges/Cost [Fundraising] (WDMC)
PC	Plenum Chamber
PC	Plotting Chart (SAUS)
PC	Plug Care [Computer science] (IAA)
PC	Plug Cock (AAG)
PC	Plug Compatible [Computer science] (BUR)
PC	Pluggable Card (SAUS)
PC	Pneumatic Circuit (SAUS)
PC	Pneumatic Controller (SAUS)
PC	Pneumotoxic Center (AAMN)
PC	Pocket Calculator (SAUS)
PC	Pocket Computer
PC	Poetry Criticism [A publication]
PC	Point Cathode (SAUS)
PC	Point Clause (SAUS)
PC	Point Contact (IDOE)
PC	Point of Curve [Technical drawings]
P-C	Polar-Cartesian (SAUS)
PC	Polar Component [Food science]
PC	Polar Continental [American air mass]
PC	Polar Crane [Nuclear energy] (NRCH)
PC	Polarity Coefficient (SAUS)
P-C	Polar to Cartesian
PC	Polar-to-Cartesian (SAUS)
PC	Pole Cell [Insect embryology]
P/C	Police Car
PC	Police College (SAUS)
PC	Police Commissioner (WGA)
PC	Police-Constable [Scotland Yard]
PC	Police Court [British] (ROG)
PC	Policy Control (ADA)
PC	Polish Council [Czech Republic] (BUAC)
PC	Political Code [A publication] (ILCA)
PC	Political Correctness
PC	Politically Correct
P/C	Polizza di Carico [Bill of Lading] [Shipping] [Italian]
PC	Pollution Control (MHDB)
PC	Polycarbonate [Organic chemistry]
PC	Polycarbosilane [Organic chemistry]
PC	Polycomb (SAUS)
PC	Polymer Chemistry (SAUS)
PC	Polymer-Concrete (KSC)
PC	Polyposis Coli [Medicine] (DMAA)
PC	Pomona College (SAUS)
PC	Pondus Civile [Civil (Avoirdupois) Weight] [Pharmacy] (ROG)
PC	Poni Curavit [Caused to Be Placed] [Latin]
PC	Poor Clares [Roman Catholic women's religious order]
PC	Poor Classes [British] (DSUE)
PC	Poor Condition [Medicine] (DMAA)
PC	Poor Coordination [Medicine] (DMAA)
pc	Pop Corn [Crochet]
PC	Popular Coalition (BUAC)
PC	Popular Cult

PC...............	Population Census
PC...............	Population Communication (EA)
PC...............	Population Concern [*British*] (EAIO)
PC...............	Population Council (EA)
PC...............	Portable Computer
PC...............	Portacaval [*Medicine*]
PC...............	Portal Cirrhosis [*Medicine*] (DB)
PC...............	Port Call [*Army*]
PC...............	Port Charles [*Television program title*]
PC...............	Port Committee (NATG)
PC...............	Port Control [*Telecommunications*] (TEL)
PC...............	Porterville College (SAUS)
PC...............	Portion Control [*Food service*]
PC...............	Portland Cement
PC...............	Position Classification (GFGA)
PC...............	Position Control (SAUS)
PC...............	Positive Column (IAA)
PC...............	Positive Control
Pc...............	Positive Wave in Children [*Neurophysiology*]
PC...............	Postal & Courier
PC...............	Postal Clerk [*Navy rating*]
PC...............	Post Card (SAUS)
PC...............	Postcard
pc...............	Postcard (ODBW)
PC...............	Post-Chlorinated (IAA)
PC...............	Post Cibum [*After Meals*] [*Pharmacy*]
PC...............	Postcode (ADA)
PC...............	Postcoital [*Medicine*]
PC...............	Post Commander [*Military*]
PC...............	Post Consulatum [*After the Consulate*] [*Latin*]
PC...............	Posterior Capsule (SAUS)
PC...............	Posterior Cervical [*Medicine*] (DMAA)
PC...............	Posterior Chamber [*Ophthalmology*]
PC...............	Posterior Circumflex [*Artery*] [*Anatomy*] (DAVI)
PC...............	Posterior Commissure [*Neuroanatomy*]
PC...............	Posterior Cortex [*Medicine*] (DMAA)
PC...............	Postinflammatory Corticoid [*Medicine*]
PC...............	Potential Carcinogen (SAUS)
PC...............	Potential Complications [*Medicine*] (DMAA)
pc...............	Pottery Cache (BJA)
PC...............	Pour Condoler [*To Offer Sympathy*] [*French*]
PC...............	Power Cartesian (IAA)
PC...............	Power Center (SAUS)
PC...............	Power Circuit (IAA)
PC...............	Power Component (IAA)
PC...............	Power Contactor
PC...............	Power Control [*System*] (NG)
P-C...............	Power Conversion (CET)
PC...............	Power Conversion
PC...............	Power Converter (SAUS)
pc...............	Power Cord (BARN)
PC...............	Practice Cases [*A publication*] (DLA)
PC...............	Pre-Carrier (SAUS)
PC...............	Precast
PC...............	Precast Chair (SAUS)
PC...............	Precaution Category [*For clinical laboratories*]
PC...............	Precedents in Chancery [*A publication*] (DLA)
PC...............	Pre-Chamber [*Automotive engineering*]
PC...............	Precinct (GOBB)
PC...............	Precision Control [*Computer programming*] (BYTE)
PC...............	Preconditioning [*Medicine*] (DMAA)
PC...............	Precordia [*Anatomy*]
PC...............	Predictable Computation (SAUS)
PC...............	Prediction Computer (SAUS)
PC...............	Predictor Control (SAUS)
PC...............	Pre-Emphasis Circuit (OA)
PC...............	Preliminary Commendation (SAUS)
PC...............	Preliminary Commitment (IMH)
PC...............	Prenatal Care [*Medicine*] (DMAA)
PC...............	Preparatory Commission
PC...............	Preparatory Committee
PC...............	Prepunched Card (SAUS)
PC...............	Presbyterian College (SAUS)
PC...............	Present Complaint [*Medicine*]
PC...............	Presidents Club [*Commercial firm*] (EA)
PC...............	Press Club (NTCM)
PC...............	Press Council [*British*]
PC...............	Pressure Cable (SAUS)
PC...............	Pressure Chamber (NAKS)
PC...............	Pressure Circuit (SAUS)
PC...............	Pressure Controller [*Nuclear energy*]
PC...............	Pressure Cooker (SAUS)
PC...............	Prestressed Concrete (BARN)
PC...............	Previous Convictions (WDAA)
pc...............	Price (WDAA)
PC...............	Price Commission [*Cost of Living Council*]
PC...............	Price Control Cases [*A publication*] (DLA)
P/C...............	Price/Cost
P/C...............	Price Current (SAUS)
PC...............	Price per Copy [*of books*]
pc...............	Prices Current (WDMC)
PC...............	Prices Current
PC...............	Priest Confessor
PC...............	Primary Center
PC...............	Primary Circuit (MCD)

PC...............	Primary Closure [*Medicine*] (DMAA)
PC...............	Primary Code
PC...............	Primary Contributor
PC...............	Primary Control (MCD)
PC...............	Prime Contractor
PC...............	Prime Cost
PC...............	Prince Consort (IIA)
PC...............	Prince Edward Island Provincial Library, Charlottetown, Prince Edward Island [*Library symbol*] [*National Library of Canada*] (NLC)
PC...............	Principal Chaplain (ADA)
PC...............	Principal Component
PC...............	Principia College (SAUS)
PC...............	Print Check (SAUS)
PC...............	Print Club (EA)
PC...............	Print Command [*Computer science*] (IAA)
PC...............	Print Complement (SAUS)
PC...............	Print Contrast (DGA)
PC...............	Print Control (SAUS)
PC...............	Print Cycle [*Computer science*] (IAA)
PC...............	Printed Card (IAA)
PC...............	Printed Character (SAUS)
PC...............	Printed Circuit
PC...............	Printer Control
PC...............	Printing Cylinder (DGA)
PC...............	Printmakers' Council (BUAC)
PC...............	Print of Curve (IAA)
PC...............	Priority Code (VLIE)
PC...............	Priority Control (MLOA)
PC...............	Prisoner of Conscience (BJA)
PC...............	Privacy Commission
PC...............	Private Circuit (SAUS)
PC...............	Private Code (VLIE)
PC...............	Private Concerns [*An association*] [*Defunct*] (EA)
PC...............	Private Contract [*Tea trade*] (ROG)
PC...............	Private Corporation
PC...............	Privatization Council [*New York, NY*] (EA)
PC...............	Privilege Car [*on a train*] [*Theatre slang*]
PC...............	Privileged Character [*A favored student*] [*Teen slang*]
PC...............	Privy Council [*or Councillor*] [*British*]
PC...............	Privy Counselor (SAUS)
PC...............	Prize Court (DLA)
PC...............	Probable Cause [*Legal term*]
PC...............	Probate Court [*British*] (ROG)
PC...............	Procaer SpA [*Italy*] [*ICAO aircraft manufacturer identifier*] (ICAO)
PC...............	Procarbazine [*Also, P, PCB, Pr*] [*Antineoplastic drug*]
PC...............	Procedure Coordinator (VLIE)
PC...............	Procerebral Lobe [*Neuroanatomy*]
PC...............	Process Change (SAUS)
PC...............	Process Chemistry
PC...............	Process Computer (NRCH)
PC...............	Process Condensate (SAUS)
PC...............	Process Control (DEN)
PC...............	Process Controller (SAUS)
PC...............	Processing Center [*Telecommunications*] (TEL)
PC...............	Processing Conditions [*Food*] (DICI)
PC...............	Processor Cluster (SAUS)
PC...............	Processor Code (SAUS)
PC...............	Processor Controller [*Computer science*] (MDG)
PC...............	Procollagen [*Medicine*] (DMAA)
PC...............	Procurement Command [*Army*]
PC...............	Procurement Communication [*Military*]
PC...............	Producers' Council [*Later, CPMC*] (EA)
PC...............	Product Code (NITA)
PC...............	Production Certificate (MCD)
PC...............	Production Company [*Films, television, etc.*]
P-C...............	Production-Consumption (SAUS)
PC...............	Production Control (MCD)
PC...............	Production Costs
PC...............	Productive Cough [*Medicine*] (DMAA)
PC...............	Professional Communication (MCD)
PC...............	Professional Computer (VLIE)
PC...............	Professional Consultant (SAUS)
PC...............	Professional Corporation
PC...............	Professors of Curriculum (EA)
PC...............	Profile Component (DET)
PC...............	Profit Center (MHDB)
PC...............	Progenitor Cryptocides (SAUS)
PC...............	Program Card [*Computer science*] (IAA)
PC...............	Program Change
PC...............	Program Check [*Computer science*] (IAA)
PC...............	Program Committee [*UN Food and Agriculture Organization*]
PC...............	Program Communications [*Military*] (AFIT)
PC...............	Program Contract (SAUS)
PC...............	Program Control
PC...............	Program Controller (NITA)
PC...............	Program Coordination (IEEE)
PC...............	Program Coordinator
PC...............	Program Council (SAUS)
PC...............	Program Counter
PC...............	Programmable Channel (SAUS)
PC...............	Programmable Computer
PC...............	Programmable Controller (ACII)
PC...............	Programmable Logic Control [*Computer science*] (IAA)
PC...............	Programmable Machine Control (IAA)

PC	Programmed Channel (SAUS)
PC	Programmed Check (AAG)
PC	Programmed Computation (SAUS)
PC	Programmed Console (SAUS)
PC	Programmed Control (SAUS)
PC	Programming Change (VLIE)
PC	Programming Cost (SAUS)
PC	Programming Course (SAUS)
PC	Progressive Conservative [Canada] [Political party]
PC	Progressive Conservative Party [Canada] [Political party] (BUAC)
PC	Prohormone Convertase [Medicine] (DMAA)
PC	Project Censored (EA)
PC	Project Children (EA)
PC	Project Control (NASA)
PC	Project Coordinator (NG)
PC	Project Cuddle [An association] (EA)
PC	Projector Charge
PC	Prompt Corner (WDAA)
PC	Proof Coins [Numismatics]
PC	Propellant Control (SAUS)
P/C	Property/Casualty [Insurance]
PC	Prophylactic Center (SAUS)
PC	Proportional Counter [Instrumentation]
PC	Proposed Category [Lubricants]
PC	Proposed Change
PC	Propositional Calculus [Logic]
PC	Propulsive Coefficient
PC	Propylene Carbonate [Organic chemistry]
PC	Prospectors Club [Later, PCI]
PC	Prostatic Carcinoma [Medicine] (DB)
PC	Prosthetics Center [Veterans Administration]
PC	Protective Climate [Solar heating]
PC	Protective Clothing (SAUS)
PC	Protective Cover (MCD)
PC	Protein C [Medicine] (DMAA)
PC	Protein Convertase [Medicine] (DMAA)
PC	Proto-Canaanite (BJA)
PC	Protocol Configuration (SAUS)
PC	Protocol Control (SAUS)
PC	Protocol Converter (MCD)
PC	Providence College (SAUS)
PC	Provincial Commissioner [British government]
PC	Provisional Costs
PC	Provisional Cut [Television] (NTCM)
PC	Provocative Concentration [Immunology]
PC	Pseudo Code (SAUS)
PC	Pseudocode (AAG)
PC	Pseudoconditioning Control [Neurophysiology]
PC	Psychodevelopment Checklist [Psychology] (DAVI)
PC	Publications Committee (SAUS)
PC	Publications in Climatology (MCD)
PC	Public Charter (TRID)
PC	Public Citizen (EA)
PC	Public Contract
PC	[The] Publishers' Circular [A publication] (ROG)
PC	Pubococcygeus [Muscle] [Anatomy]
PC	Pull Chain [Technical drawings] (DAC)
PC	Pulmonary Capillary [Medicine]
PC	Pulmonary Contusions (SAUS)
PC	Pulmonic Closure [Medicine] (MAE)
PC	Pulsating Current
PC	Pulse Circuit (SAUS)
PC	Pulse Cleaned [Dust filtration]
PC	Pulse Code [Telecommunications] (IAA)
PC	Pulse Comparator (AAG)
PC	Pulse Compression
PC	Pulse Controller
PC	Pulse Counter [Computer science] (MDG)
PC	Pulverized Coal [Fuel technology]
PC	Pumice Concrete (SAUS)
PC	Punch Card (NITA)
PC	Punch Code (SAUS)
PC	Punch Column (SAUS)
PC	Punch Control (SAUS)
PC	Punched Card [Computer science]
PC	Punched Code (SAUS)
PC	Punjab Cavalry [British military] (DMA)
PC	Puns Corps (EA)
PC	Purchase Card
PC	Purchasing and Contracting [Army]
PC	Pure Clairvoyance [Psychical research]
PC	Purified Concentrate
PC	Purkinje Cell [Neuroanatomy]
PC	Pyrochlore (SAUS)
PC	Pyrrolinecarboxylic Acid [Biochemistry]
PC	Pyruvate Carboxylase [An enzyme] (MAE)
PC	Single Paper Single Cotton [Wire insulation] (AAG)
PC	Submarine Chaser [173 foot] [Navy symbol] [Obsolete]
PC	Sumitomo Chemical Co. [Japan] [Research code symbol]
PC	Veterans of the US Posse Comitatus (EA)
pc1	Platelet Count Pretransfusion [Medicine] (STED)
PC1	Postal Clerk, First Class [Navy rating]
PC1	Power Control One [Hydraulic] (MCD)
pc2	Platelet Count Posttransfusion [Medicine] (STED)
PC2	Postal Clerk, Second Class [Navy rating]
PC2	Power Control Two [Hydraulic] (MCD)
PC3	Phoenix Conference on Computers and Communications (SAUS)
PC3	Postal Clerk, Third Class [Navy rating]
PC97	Personal Computer 97 (SAUS)
PCA	Acts of the Privy Council [England] [A publication] (DLA)
PCA	Calgon Corp., Pittsburgh, PA [OCLC symbol] (OCLC)
PCA	Pacific Communications Area [Air Force] (MCD)
PCA	Packaging Council of Australia (BUAC)
PCA	Panama Canal Authority
PCA	Paper Converters Association [Defunct] (EA)
PCA	Paperweight Collectors' Association (EA)
PCA	Papillary Cystadenoma [Medicine] (MELL)
PCA	Papillon Club of America (EA)
PCA	Para-Chloramphetamine (STED)
PCA	Para-Chloroaniline [Organic chemistry]
PCA	Parachute Club of America [Later, USPA] (EA)
PCA	Para-Coumaric Acid [Organic chemistry]
PCA	Parallel Channel Adapter (SAUS)
PCA	Parallel Computer Architecture (SAUS)
PCA	Parietal Cell Antibodies [Immunology]
PCA	Parietal Cell Antibody (DB)
PCA	Parliamentary Candidates Association (BUAC)
PCA	Parliamentary Commissioner for Administration [British]
PCA	Parochial Clergy Association [British] (DBA)
PCA	Parti Communiste Algerien [Algerian Communist Party] [Political party]
PCA	Partido Comunista de Argentina [Communist Party of Argentina] [Political party] (PD)
PCA	Partition Control Area (SAUS)
PCA	Parts Control Area [NASA] (KSC)
PCA	Party of the Civic Alliance [Romania] [Political party] (EY)
PCA	Passive Cutaneous Anaphylaxis [Immunochemistry]
PCA	Patient Care Aide [or Assistant] (DAVI)
PCA	Patient Care Audit (HCT)
PCA	Patient-Controlled Analgesia
PCA	Patient Support Associate [Medicine]
PCA	Patriotic Catholic Association [Name given to nationalized Catholic Church in China]
PCA	Payload Clamp Assembly (SAUS)
PCA	P-Chlorophenylalanine (SAUS)
PCA	Peachtree Complete Accounting (SAUS)
PCA	Peak Clipping Amplifier
PCA	Pekingese Club of America (EA)
PCA	Pennsylvania Coal Association (SAUS)
PCA	Pennsylvania Council on the Arts (SAUS)
PCA	Pentachloraniline [Organic chemistry]
PCA	Pentachloroanisole [Organic chemistry]
PCA	Percent Cortical Area [Neurology]
PCA	Perchloric Acid [Inorganic chemistry]
PCA	Percutaneous Carotid Arteriogram [Medicine] (MAE)
PCA	Percutaneous Coronary Agioplasty (STED)
PCA	Performance and Code Analysis (VLIE)
PCA	Performance and Coverage Analyzer (SAUS)
PCA	Pericruciate Association [Cortex, of cat]
PCA	Period Contract Acceptance
PCA	Peripheral Circulatory Assist [Medicine]
PCA	Peritoneal Carcinomatosis [Oncology]
PCA	Permanent Change of Assignment [Army]
PCA	Permanent Court of Arbitration [See also CPA] [Hague, Netherlands] (EAIO)
PCA	Personal Care Aide [or Assistant or Attendant]
PCA	Personal Cash Allowance
PCA	Personal Computer Analyzer (SAUS)
PCA	Personal Computers Association (SAUS)
PCA	Pest Control Association (NADA)
PCA	Petro-Chemical Associates, Inc. (EFIS)
PCA	Pharmacy Corporation of America
PCA	Phenylcarboxylic Acid [Chemistry] (DAVI)
PCA	Photo Cell Assembly (SAUS)
PCA	Photocontact Allergic (STED)
PCA	Photocurrent Amplifier (SAUS)
PCA	Photogrammetric Consultants Association (SAUS)
PCA	Photon Counting Array [Instrumentation]
PCA	Photon-Coupled Amplifier (VLIE)
PCA	Photovoltaic Cell Array (SAUS)
PCA	Physical Configuration Audit [Military, NASA]
PCA	Physicians Corp. of America (ECON)
PCA	Piezo-Ceramic Accelerometer [Electronics]
PCA	Pinnacle [Alaska] [Seismograph station code, US Geological Survey] (SEIS)
PCA	Pitcairn Cierva Autogiro [Aeronautics]
PCA	Pitch Control Assembly (MCD)
PCA	Plane Circular Aperture
PCA	Plasma Catecholamine [Biochemistry]
PCA	Plasma Catecholamine Concentration (STED)
PCA	Plasma Covered Aerial (or Antenna) (SAUS)
PCA	Plasma-Covered Antenna
PCA	Plaster Contractors Association (SAUS)
PCA	Plate Count Agar [Microbiology]
PCA	Pneumatic Control Assembly (NASA)
PCA	Point of Closest Approach
PCA	Polar Cap Absorption
PCA	Polarizer-Compensator-Analyzer (PDAA)
PCA	Police Complaint Authority [British]
PCA	Policy Certification Authority

PCA............. Polish Community in Australia
PCA............. Pollution Control Agency (COE)
PCA............. Polycaproamide (SAUS)
PCA............. Polycrystalline Alumina
PCA............. Polycycliche Aromaten (SAUS)
PCA............. Poodle Club of America (EA)
PCA............. Pool Critical Assembly [Nuclear reactor]
PCA............. Popular Culture Association (EA)
PCA............. Pork Council of Australia
PCA............. Porous-Coated Anatomical [Prosthesis]
PCA............. Porsche Club of America (EA)
PCA............. Portacaval Anastomosis [Animal model of chronic liver disease]
PCA............. Portage Creek [Alaska] [Airport symbol] (OAG)
PCA............. Port Communications Area [Telecommunications] (TEL)
PCA............. Portland Cement Association (EA)
PCA............. Ports Canada
PCA............. Positive Control Area
PCA............. Positive Controlled Airspace
PCA............. Postconstruction Availability (NVT)
PCA............. Posterior Cerebral Artery [Brain anatomy]
PCA............. Posterior Communicating Artery [Anatomy]
PCA............. Posterior Cricoarytenoid [A muscle of the larynx]
PCA............. Potash Co. of America, Inc. [Toronto Stock Exchange symbol]
PCA............. Potato Carrot Agar [Culture Media]
PCA............. Potentially Contaminated Area (DNAB)
PCA............. Poultrymen's Cooperative Association (EA)
PCA............. Power Calibration Area (SAUS)
PCA............. Power Conditioning Assembly
PCA............. Power Control Assembly (NASA)
PCA............. Power Controller Assemblies (SAUS)
PCA............. Precipitation with a Compressed Fluid Antisolvent [Chemical engineering]
PCA............. Precision Cleaning Agent (SAUS)
PCA............. Precision Clearing Agent (DNAB)
PCA............. Pre-Conditioned Air System [Aviation] (DA)
PCA............. Precontractual Authorization
PCA............. Prescribed Concentration of Alcohol (ADA)
PCA............. Presidency of Civil Aviation [Saudi Arabia] (BUAC)
PCA............. President's Council on Aging [Inactive]
PCA............. Pressure Control Assembly
PCA............. Prestressed Concrete Association [British] (DBA)
PCA............. Primary Carbon Assimilation [Botany]
PCA............. Primary Communication Attachment [Computer science] (ELAL)
PCA............. Primary Control Assembly [Nuclear energy] (NRCH)
PCA............. Primary Coolant Activity [Nuclear energy] (NRCH)
PCA............. Primary Coverage Area (SAUS)
PCA............. Prime Candidate Alloy (MCD)
PCA............. Prime Condition Aircraft
PCA............. Principal Component Analysis
PCA............. Principal Control Authority (NATG)
PCA............. Prindle Class Association (EA)
PCA............. Print Council of America (EA)
PCA............. Printed Circuit Analyzer (ELAL)
PCA............. Printed Circuit Assembly [Telecommunications] (TEL)
PCA............. Printed Circuit Association (BUAC)
PCA............. Printer Communications Adapter
PCA............. Printers' Costing Association [British] (BI)
PCA............. Printing Corp. of America
PCA............. Private Care Association (SAUS)
PCA............. Private Communications Association [Later, NCA]
PCA............. Procedure Change Authorization (SAUS)
PCA............. Proceedings of the Classical Association (SAUS)
PCA............. Process Change Authorization (SAUS)
PCA............. Process Control Analyzer
PCA............. Pro-Choice Alliance (BUAC)
PCA............. Procoagulant Activity
PCA............. Procrastinators' Club of America (EA)
PCA............. Producers Commission Association (EA)
PCA............. Production Code Administration (BARN)
PCA............. Production Compliance Audit [Automotive emissions standards]
PCA............. Production Credit Association (BUAC)
PCA............. Professional Chess Association (EA)
PCA............. Professional Comedians' Association (EA)
PCA............. Professional Cycling Association [British] (DBA)
PCA............. Program Calibration Area [Computer science] (DOM)
PCA............. Program Change Analysis [DoD]
PCA............. Program Coupler Assembly (KSC)
PCA............. Program Cumulative Audience [Advertising] (DOAD)
PCA............. Programmable Communications Adapter [Computer science]
PCA............. Progress Change Authority
PCA............. Progressive Citizens of America
PCA............. Progressive Cultural Association (BUAC)
PCA............. Project Control Analyst (ACAE)
PCA............. Propellant Control Assembly (ACAE)
PCA............. Property Clearance Assessment (SARE)
PCA............. Proprietary Cremation Association (SAUS)
PCA............. Proprietary Crematoria Association [British] (DBA)
PCA............. Propulsion-Controlled Aircraft (SEWL)
PCA............. Protective Clothing Arrangement [Telecommunications] (TEL)
PCA............. Protective Connecting Arrangement [Telecommunications] (TEL)
PCA............. Prototype Protein C Activator [Biochemistry]
PCA............. Public Archives, Charlottetown, Prince Edward Island [Library symbol] [National Library of Canada] (NLC)
PCA............. Puli Club of America (EA)
PCA............. Pulp Chemicals Association (EA)

PCA............. Pulse Code Adaptor (NITA)
PCA............. Pulse Counter Adapter
PCA............. Punched Card Accounting (SAUS)
PCA............. Putnam California Investment Grade Municipal [AMEX symbol] (SPSG)
PCA............. Pyrotechnic Control Assembly [NASA]
PCA............. Pyrrolidonecarboxylic Acid [Organic chemistry]
PCAA........... Pancretan Association of America (EA)
PCAA........... Particulate Combined Amino Acid [Marine biology]
PCaab.......... Parietal Cell Autoantibody [Immunology]
PcA&E......... Pacific Aerospace & Electronics, Inc. [Associated Press] (SAG)
PCAAS........ Proceedings of the Connecticut Academy of Arts and Sciences (SAUS)
PC-ABS....... Polycarbonate-Acrylonitrile-Butadiene-Styrene (SAUS)
PCAC.......... Partially Conserved Axial Current [Electronics] (IAA)
PCAC.......... Partially Conserved Axial-Vector Current
PCAC.......... Personal Computer Acquisition Contracts (SAUS)
PCAC.......... Poultry Costings Advisory Council (BUAC)
PCAC.......... Primary Control and Analysis Center (SAUS)
PCAC.......... Private College Admissions Center [Later, NAAPHE]
PCAC.......... Professional Classes Aid Council (AIE)
PCACIAS..... Personal Computer Automated Calibration Interval Analysis System (SAUS)
PC Act .... Probate Court Act [A publication] (DLA)
PCAD.......... Package Computer-Aided Design [Computer science]
PCAD.......... Packaging Computer-Aided Design (SAUS)
P-CAD......... Personal Computer-Aided Design (SAUS)
PCAD.......... Premature Coronary Artery Disease (MELL)
PCAD.......... Program Change Approval Document (DOMA)
PCAD.......... Programs in Computer Applications Development (SAUS)
PCADS........ Panoramic Control and Display System (MCD)
PCAE.......... Parts Control and Expediting (SAUS)
PCAE.......... Polar Cap Absorption Event
PC-AEO....... Personal Computer - Annual Energy Outlook Forecasting Model [Department of Energy] (GFGA)
PCAFB........ Pinecastle Air Force Base (SAUS)
PCAFV........ Physicians Campaign Against Family Violence (SAUS)
PCAG.......... Pentobarbital-Chlorpromazine-Alcohol Group [Medicine]
PCAG.......... Petroleum Conservation Action Group [India] (BUAC)
PCAG.......... Research Station, Agriculture Canada [Station de Recherches, Agriculture Canada] Charlottetown, Prince Edward Island [Library symbol] [National Library of Canada] (NLC)
PCAI........... Parliamentary Commissioner for Administrative Investigations [Western Australia]
PCAI........... PCA International, Inc. [NASDAQ symbol] (NQ)
PCAI........... PCA Intl [NASDAQ symbol] (TTSB)
PCAI........... Personal Care Assessment Instrument [Australia]
PCA Int ...... PCA International, Inc. [Associated Press] (SAG)
P Cal .... Petrus Calvelli [Flourished, 14th century] [Authority cited in pre-1607 legal work] (DSA)
PCalS.......... California State College, California, PA [Library symbol] [Library of Congress] (LCLS)
PCAM......... Partitioned Content Addressable Memory
PCAM......... Physician Corp. of America [NASDAQ symbol] (SAG)
PCAM......... Probe Card Assembly Machine (SAUS)
PCAM......... Punched Card Accounting Machine [Computer science]
PCamA........ Alliance College, Cambridge Springs, PA [Library symbol] [Library of Congress] (LCLS)
PCAMIC ...... People Concerned about MIC [Methyl Isocyanate] (EA)
PCAMP .... Protective Coatings and Metalizing Process (DNAB)
PCAN.......... Potential Child Abuse and Neglect (MELL)
PCAN.......... Program Change Action Notice (DNAB)
PC and A..... Project Control and Administration (SAUS)
PC & A .... Project Control and Administration [NASA]
PC&A......... Property Classification and Accounting (SAUS)
PC & B .... Personnel Compensation and Benefits (GFGA)
PC & D .... Priest, Confessor, and Doctor (ROG)
PC&E.......... Parts Control and Expediting (SAUS)
PC & H .... Packing, Crating, and Handling [Shipping] (AFM)
PC & IC ...... Polaris Control and Information Center [Missiles]
PC & OR .... Procurement, Commitment, and Obligation Record [Navy]
PC&PS........ Professional Credentials and Personnel Service (SAUS)
PC&R.......... Post Construction and Repair (SAUS)
PC & S .... Posts, Camps, and Stations [Military]
PC & S .... Preliminary Command and Sequencing [Viking lander mission] [NASA]
PCANSW...... Pest Control Association of New South Wales [Australia]
PCAO .... Pollution Control Association of Ontario (SAUS)
PCAO .... President's Commission on Americans Outdoors
PCAP .... Physical Correlation Analysis Program [Military]
P-CAP .... Physically-Challenged Assistance Program [Chrysler Motors Corp.] [Detroit, MI] [Information service or system] (IID)
PCAP .... Post Commercial Action Plan [International Trade Administration]
PCAP .... Process Characterization Analysis Package (SAUS)
PCAP .... Programmer Capacity
PCAPA .... Pacific Coast Association of Port Authorities (SAUS)
PCAPI .... Pollution Control Association of the Philippines, Inc. (SAUS)
PCAPK .... Presidents Commission on the Assassination of President Kennedy (SAUS)
PC App .... Law Reports, Privy Council, Appeal Cases [England] [A publication] (DLA)
PCAPS .... Plant Control and Protection System (SAUS)
PCAPS .... Production Control and Planning System (MCD)
PCAQ .... Pony Club Association of Queensland [Australia]
PCAR .... PACCAR, Inc. [NASDAQ symbol] (NQ)

PCAR .... Parent-Child Activity Rating Scale [*Education*] (EDAC)
PCAR .... Process Characterization Analysis Package (MHDI)
P/Carb .... Polycarbonate (SAUS)
P (Card) .... Personal Card [*Containing person's name, address, age, description, job, habits, haunts, movements*] [*Used in Belfast, Northern Ireland*]
PCarl .... Bosler Free Library, Carlisle, PA [*Library symbol*] [*Library of Congress*] (LCLS)
PCarlA .... United States Army War College, Carlisle Barracks, PA [*Library symbol*] [*Library of Congress*] (LCLS)
PCarlD .... Dickinson College, Carlisle, PA [*Library symbol*] [*Library of Congress*] (LCLS)
PCarlD-L ...... Dickinson School of Law, Sheeley-Lee Law Library, Carlisle, PA [*Library symbol*] [*Library of Congress*] (LCLS)
PCarlH .... Cumberland County Historical Society and Hamilton Library Association, Carlisle,PA [*Library symbol*] [*Library of Congress*] (LCLS)
PCarlMH ...... United States Army, Military History Research Collection, Carlisle Barracks, PA [*Library symbol*] [*Library of Congress*] (LCLS)
PCarlPL ...... United States Army, Carlisle Barracks Post Library, Carlisle Barracks, PA [*Library symbol*] [*Library of Congress*] (LCLS)
PCARR .... Philippines Council for Agricultural Resources and Research (BUAC)
PCARS .... Partially Coherent Anti-Stokes Raman Scattering (SAUS)
PCARS .... Point Credit Accounting and Reporting System (AFM)
PCAS .... Patient Care Algorithm System [*Medicine*] (DMAA)
PCAS .... Persistent Chemical Agent Stimulant
PCAS .... Personnel Cost Accounting System (SAUS)
PCAS .... Polytechnics Central Admissions System [*British*] (DET)
PCAS .... Possible Carotid Artery System [*Medicine*]
PCas .... Primary Central Alarm Station [*Nuclear energy*] (NRCH)
P Cas .... Prize Cases [*1914-22*] [*England*] [*A publication*] (DLA)
P Cas .... Prize Cases (Trehearn and Grant) [*England*] [*A publication*] (DLA)
PCAS .... Proceedings of the Cambridge Antiquarian Society (SAUS)
PCAS .... Programming Components Announcement Summary (SAUS)
PCAS .... Punch Card Accounting System [*Computer science*]
PCASA .... Pony Club Association of South Australia
PCAS/CADS... Persistent Chemical Agent Stimulant/Chemical Agent Disclosure Solution [*Army*]
PCASO .... Pilot Classification and Screening Operation (ACAE)
PCASP .... Passive Cavity Aerosol Spectrometer Probe (SAUS)
PCASS .... Parts Control Automated Support System [*Database*]
PCASS .... Program Compliance Assurance and Status System (SAUS)
PCAST .... President's Committee of Advisors on Science and Technology
PCAST .... President's Council of Advisers on Science and Technology [*1989*]
PC/AT .... Personal Computer/Advanced Technology (DCDG)
PCAT .... Pharmacy College Admissions Test (GAGS)
PCAT .... Philippine College of Arts and Trades (SAUS)
pCAT .... Plasmid Chloramphenicol Acetyltransferase [*An enzyme*]
PCAT .... Procedures for the Control of Air Traffic (SAA)
PCAT .... Product Category (SAUS)
PCAT .... Punched Card Accounting Technique (SAUS)
PCATD .... Personal Computer Aircraft Training Device
PCAU .... Parachute Course Administrative Unit [*Military*] [*British*] (INF)
PCAU .... Philippine Civil Affairs Unit [*Army unit which supplied emergency subsistence after end of Japanese dominance*] [*World War II*]
PCAV .... Pony Club Association of Victoria [*Australia*]
PCAV .... Principal Component Analysis with Varimax Rotation
PCAWA .... Pony Club Association of Western Australia
PCB .... Central Pennsylvania District Library Center, Bellefonte, PA [*OCLC symbol*] (OCLC)
PcB .... Near Point of Convergence [*Ophthalmology*]
PCB .... Page Control Block [*Computer science*] (IBMDP)
PCB .... Pancuronium Bromide [*A muscle relaxant*] (DAVI)
PCB .... Paracervical Block [*Anesthesiology*]
PCB .... Paracolon Bacilli [*Medicine*] (MELL)
PCB .... Particle Count Blank [*Automotive testing*]
PCB .... Parti Communiste de Belgique [*Communist Party of Belgium*] [*See also KPB*] [*Political party*] (PPE)
PCB .... Partido Comunista de Bolivia [*Communist Party of Bolivia*] [*Political party*] (PPW)
PCB .... Partido Comunista do Brasil [*Communist Party of Brazil*] [*Pro-Albanian*] [*Political party*] (PPW)
PCB .... Parts Control Board
PCB .... Patent Compensation Board [*Energy Research and Development Administration*]
PCB .... Percutaneous Biopsy [*Medicine*] (CPH)
PCB .... Pest Control Bureau (SAUS)
PCB .... Petty Cash Book [*Business term*]
PCB .... Placebo [*Medicine*] (MELL)
PCB .... Planning Change Board (AAG)
PCB .... Please Call Back (SAUS)
PCB .... Plenum Chamber Burning
PCB .... Point-Contact Breakdown (SAUS)
PCB .... Polychlorinated Biphenyl [*Organic chemistry*]
PCB .... Polychlorobenzene
PCB .... Polychlorobiphenyl (SAUS)
PCB .... Portacaval Bypass [*Cardiology*] (DMAA)
PCB .... Port Check BIT [*Binary Digit*] [*Telecommunications*] (TEL)
PCB .... Possibly Carcinogenic Substance (SAUS)
PCB .... Postcoital Bleeding [*Medicine*] (DMAA)
PCB .... Power Circuit Breaker (MSA)
PCB .... Power Control Board (SAUS)
PCB .... Power Control Box (NASA)
PCB .... Precambrian Shield Resources Ltd. [*Toronto Stock Exchange symbol*]

PCB .... Precommit Boost (ACAE)
PCB .... Premier Commercial Bank Ltd. [*Nigeria*]
PCB .... Pressure Core Barrel (SAUS)
PCB .... Primary Carpet Backing
PCB .... Printed Circuit Board (MCD)
pcb .... Printed-Circuit Board (IDOE)
PCB .... Printed Control Board
PCB .... Prix de Cession de Base [*Basic Wholesale Price*] [*French*]
PCB .... Procarbazine [*Also, P, PC, Pr*] [*Antineoplastic drug*]
PCB .... Process Control Block
PCB .... Processor Command Bus (NITA)
PCB .... Processor Control Block (SAUS)
PCB .... Product Configuration Baseline (NASA)
PCB .... Professional Capacity Building
PCB .... Program Change Board (SAUS)
PCB .... Program Communication Block
PCB .... Program Control Block [*Computer science*] (BUR)
PCB .... Project Change Board (AAG)
PCB .... Project Control Branch [*Social Security Administration*]
PCB .... Projected Control Board
PCB .... Property Control Branch [*of Allied Military Government*] [*Post-World War II*]
PCB .... Proposed Committee Bill (WPI)
PCB .... Proprietor of Copyright on a Work by a Corporate Body
PCB .... Propulsion [*Ground*] Control Box (AAG)
PCB .... Protocol Control Block (SAUS)
PCB .... Public Coin Box [*Telecommunications*] (TEL)
PCB .... Publisher's Central Bureau
PCB .... Punch Circuit Breaker (SAUS)
PCBA .... Para-Chlorobenzoic Acid [*Organic chemistry*]
PCBA .... P-Chlorobenzoic Acid (SAUS)
PCBA .... Pepsi-Cola Bottlers Association (EA)
PCBA .... Pioneer Citizens Band Association (IAA)
PCBA .... Polyclonal B Cell Activation [*Hematology*]
PCBA .... Printed Circuit Board Assembly (MCD)
PCBB .... Power Conditioning Brass Board (MCD)
PCBB .... Primary Commercial Blanket Bond [*Insurance*]
PCBC .... Para-Chlorobenzyl Chloride [*Organic chemistry*]
PCBC .... Partially Conserved Baryon Current (IEEE)
PCBC .... Perry County Financial [*NASDAQ symbol*] (TTSB)
PCBC .... Perry County Financial Corp. [*NASDAQ symbol*] (SAG)
PCBC .... Plain Cipher Block Chaining (SAUS)
PCBC .... Platoon Commander Battle Course (SAUS)
PCBC .... Polk County Biomedical Consortium [*Library network*]
PCBC .... Pretoria Consumer Boycott Committee (SAUS)
PCBC .... Progressive Conservative Broadcasting Corp. [*Fictional version of the Cana dian Broadcasting Corp.*]
PCBC .... Propagating Cipher Block Chaining (SAUS)
PCBC .... Punched Card Blank Column (SAUS)
PCBCI .... Pedigree Cattle Breeders' Council of Ireland (BUAC)
PCBCL .... Printed Circuit Board Configuration List (MCD)
PCBD .... Polychlorinated Benzodioxin [*Organic chemistry*]
PCBDA .... Put and Call Brokers and Dealers Association [*Inactive*] (EA)
PCBG .... Primary Care Block Grant
p cbm .... Per Cubic Meter (or Metre) (SAUS)
PCB-ML ...... Partido Comunista Marxista-Leninista de Bolivia [*Marxist-Leninist Communist Party of Bolivia*] [*Political party*] (PPW)
PC-BMP ...... Phosphorylcholine-Binding Myeloma Protein [*Medicine*] (DMAA)
PCBN .... Para-Chlorobenzonitrile [*Organic chemistry*]
PCBN .... Pentachlorobenzonitrile (EES)
PCBN .... Polycrystalline Cubic Boron Nitrite
PCBPA .... Personal Computer Board Panel Assembly (DWSG)
PCBPS .... Printed Circuit Board Power Supply (SAUS)
PCBR .... Printed Circuit Board Repair (MCD)
PC/BRD .... Printed Circuit Board [*Automotive engineering*]
PCBS .... Plastic Connector Backing Shell
PCBS .... Portable Cascade Bottle System (SAUS)
PCBS .... Portland Cement British Standard (SAUS)
PCBS .... Positive Control Bombardment System [*Air Force*]
PCBS .... Printed Circuit Board Socket
PCBS .... Pupil Classroom Behavior Scale
PCBTF .... Para-Chlorobenzotrifluoride [*Organic chemistry*]
PCBTS .... Portable Cesium Beam Time Standard
PCBU .... Passenger Car Business Unit
PC Bus Softw... PC Business Software (SAUS)
PCBW .... Provisional Combat Bomb Wing (SAUS)
PCBZ .... Polychlorobenzene [*Medicine*] (MELL)
PCC .... Acts of the Privy Council, Colonial Series [*A publication*] (DLA)
PCC .... Chief Postal Clerk [*Navy rating*]
PCC .... Order of St. Clare (TOCD)
PCC .... Pacific Coast Conference (PSS)
PCC .... Pacific Conference of Churches (BUAC)
PCC .... Pacific Cruise Conference [*Formerly, TPPC*] [*Defunct*] (EA)
PCC .... Package Carrier Committee (EA)
PCC .... Pad Control Center [*NASA*] (NASA)
PCC .... Paid Collection Council [*Later, ASCMP*]
PCC .... Palestine Liberation Organisation's Central Council
PCC .... Palestinian Ceramic Chronology [*200BC-70AD*] [*A publication*] (BJA)
PCC .... Palmer Community College (SAUS)
PCC .... Panama Canal Co. [*Superseded by Panama Canal Commission*]
PCC .... Panama Canal Commission [*Independent government agency*]
PCC .... Panamerican Cultural Circle (EA)
PCC .... Papas Computer-Club (SAUS)
PCC .... Parametric Channel Controller (SAUS)
PCC .... Parent and Child Center [*Project Head Start*]

PCC	Parity Check Circuit (SAUS)
PCC	Parklawn Health Library Computer Center [Department of Health and Human Services] (GFGA)
PCC	Parks and Cemeteries Committee (SAUS)
PCC	Parochial Church Council [Church of England]
PCC	Partial Crystal Control (IEEE)
PCC	Partido Comunista Chileno [Communist Party of Chile] [Political party] (PD)
PCC	Partido Comunista Cubano [Communist Party of Cuba] [Political party] (PPW)
PCC	Partido Conservador Colombiano [Conservative Party of Colombia] [Political party] (PPW)
PCC	Party of Catalan Communists [Political party] (PPW)
PCC	Pasadena City College [California]
PCC	Patient Care Coordinator [Medicine]
PCC	Payload Control and Checkout [NASA] (NASA)
PCC	Peak Cathode Current
PCC	Penn Central Corp. (EFIS)
PCC	Pennsylvania Crime Commission (SAUS)
PCC	People's Caretakers' Council [Rhodesian]
PCC	People's Christian Coalition [Later, Sojourners] (EA)
PCC	Peoples Computer Co. (SAUS)
PCC	Pepper Community [Later, IPC]
PCC	Per-Command Course (MCD)
PCC	Per Copia Conforme [True Copy] [Italian]
PCC	Performance Certification Component [SQT] (MCD)
PCC	Performance Criteria Categories (MCD)
PCC	Pericardial Constriction [Medicine] (MELL)
PCC	Peripheral Control Computer
PCc	Periscopic Concave [Ophthalmology]
PCC	Permanent Consultative Committee
PCC	Permanently Crewed Capability
PCC	Perry Como Circle (EA)
PCC	Personal Care Clinic (DAVI)
PCC	Personal Code Calling (NITA)
PCC	Personal Communication Computer (VLIE)
PCC	Personal Communications Controller (NITA)
PCC	Personal Computer Coprocessor
PCC	Personnel Control Center [Air Force] (AFM)
PCC	Personnel Coordination Center [Army]
PCC	Pertec Computer Corp. (EFIS)
PCC	Perth Chamber of Commerce [Western Australia]
PCC	Peters' United States Circuit Court Reports [A publication] (DLA)
PCC	Petroleum Compensation Charge (SAUS)
PCC	Phaeochromocytoma [Medicine] (BABM)
PCC	Phase Correction Circuit (SAUS)
PCC	Phenylchlorocarbene [Organic chemistry]
PCC	Pheochromocytoma [Oncology]
PCC	Philippine Christian College (AEBS)
PCC	Philippine Cotton Corp. (BUAC)
PCC	Philips Consumer Communications
PCC	Phosphate Carrier Compound
PCC	Photoelectric Counter Chronometer (IAA)
PCC	Physical Coal Cleaning [Fuel technology]
PCC	Pilarcitos Creek [California] [Seismograph station code, US Geological Survey] (SEIS)
PCC	Pilot Control Console
PCC	Piperidinocyclohexanecarbonitrile [Organic chemistry]
PCC	Pitch of Cone to Cone (SAUS)
PCC	Planning Coordination Conference [NATO] (NATG)
PCC	Plastic Chip Carrier (AEBE)
PCC	Plastics in Construction Council [Later, CCS]
PCC	Platform Control Center [NASA] (SSD)
PCC	Platoon Command Center [Army]
PCC	Plug Compatible Computer (ADA)
PCC	Plutonium Concentrator Concentrate [Nuclear energy] (NRCH)
PCC	PMC Commercial Trust [AMEX symbol] (SAG)
PCC	Pointe Claire Public Library [UTLAS symbol]
PCC	Point of Common Coupling (SAUS)
PCC	Point of Compound Curve (KSC)
PCC	Poison Control Center
PCC	Polarity Coincidence Correlation receiver (SAUS)
PCC	Polarity Coincidence Correlator
PCC	Pole-Changing Control (SAUS)
PCC	Police Compact Carbine (SAUS)
PCC	Policy Coordination Council (USDC)
PCC	Political Consultative Committee [Warsaw Pact]
PCC	Political Consultative Council [Russia] (BUAC)
PCC	Polychlorinated Camphene (SAUS)
PCC	Polycore Composite Construction [Automotive engineering]
PCC	Polymer-Cement Concrete (KSC)
PCC	Polynesian Cultural Center (EA)
PCC	Pontifical Council for Culture [Vatican City] (EAIO)
PCC	Poor Clares of St. Colette [Roman Catholic women's religious order]
PCC	Population Action International [An association] (EA)
PCC	Population Crisis Committee (EA)
PCC	Portable Cable Checker
PCC	Portable C Compiler (VLIE)
PCC	Port Controller Chip [Computer science] (VLIE)
PCC	Portland Cement Concrete
PCC	Portland Community College (SAUS)
PCC	Portland Concrete Cement (SAUS)
PCC	Port of Corpus Christi (SAUS)
PCC	Positive Control Communication
PCC	Postal and Courier Communications [British]
PCC	Postal Concentration Center [Army]
PCC	Postal Customer Council (SAUS)
PCC	Posting Control Code (SAUS)
PCC	Pour Copie Conforme [Certified True Copy] [French]
PCC	Power Conditioning and Control (SAUS)
PCC	Power Consumption Charge (SAUS)
PCC	Power Control Center
PCC	Power Control Console [Diving apparatus]
PCC	Precast Concrete [Technical drawings]
PCC	Precipitated Calcium Carbonate [Inorganic chemistry]
PCC	Pre-Command Course [Military]
PCC	Precompressor Cooling (MCD)
PCC	Pregnancy Crisis Centre [Australia]
PCC	Premature Chromosome Condensation [Genetics]
PCC	Prematurely Condensed Chromosome (DB)
PCC	Prerogative Court of Canterbury [English court previously having jurisdiction over wills]
PCC	Presbyterian Charismatic Communion [Later, PRR] [An association] (EA)
PCC	President of the Canteen Committee [Military] [British]
PCC	President's Conference Committee
PCC	Press Complaints Commission (ECON)
PCC	Price Control Council (NADA)
PCC	Primary Care Center [Health care] (HCT)
PCC	Primary Care Clinic (DAVI)
PCC	Primary Category Code (NITA)
PCC	Primary Combustion Chamber (EEVL)
PCC	Primary Command Center (SAUS)
PCC	Primary Component Cooling (COE)
PCC	Primary Control Center (COE)
PCC	Print Character Counter (SAUS)
PCC	Print Collectors' Club [British] (DBA)
PCC	Print Control Character [Computer science] (VLIE)
PCC	Printed Circuit Card
PCC	Printed Circuit Conference
PCC	Printer Carriage Control (SAUS)
PCC	Printers' Charitable Corp. (DGA)
PCC	Private Carrier Conference [of ATA] (EA)
PCC	Privy Council Cases [British]
PC(C)	Privy Councillor (Canada)
PCC	Problem Control and Contact Unit [IRS]
PCC	Process Change Control (VLIE)
PCC	Process Chemistry Cell (NRCH)
PCC	Process Control Computer
PCC	Processor Control Cards [Computer science] (IAA)
PCC	Processor Control Console [Telecommunications] (TEL)
PCC	Procurement Coordination Committee
PCC	Producers Council of Canada (SAUS)
PCC	Product Control Center [DoD]
PCC	Product-Customer Center (TIMI)
PCC	Production Compression Capability
PCC	Production Control Centers
PCC	Productivity Communication Center [Defunct] (EA)
PCC	Professional Computer Corp. (SAUS)
PCC	Program Control Card (IAA)
PCC	Program Control Center (SAUS)
PCC	Program Control Counter
PCC	Program-Controlled Computer (DIT)
PCC	Program Coordinating Centre (SAUS)
PCC	Program Coordination Committee (SSD)
PCC	Program for Cooperative Cataloging [American Library Association]
PCC	Progress Control Clerk [DoD]
PCC	Progressive Coronary Care [Medicine] (AMHC)
PCC	Project Change Control (SAUS)
PCC	Project Control Center
PCC	Project Coordination Centre [Defence Research Board] [Canada]
PCC	Project Coordination Committee (SAUS)
PCC	Propionyl CoA Carboxylase [An enzyme]
PCC	Protein-Conducting Channel [Biochemistry]
PCC	Prothrombin Complex Concentrates [Hematology]
PCC	Protocol Communications (SAUS)
PCC	Protocol Converter Concentrator [Telecommunications] (IAA)
PCC	Provincial Congress Committee
PCC	Provisioning Control Code [Military] (AFIT)
PCC	Psychometric Colorimeter Chamber (MCD)
PCC	Puerto Rico [Colombia] [Airport symbol] (AD)
PCC	Pulse Counter Chain
PCC	Pulse Counting Circuit (SAUS)
PCC	Pulverized Coal Combustion [or Combustor]
PCC	Punched Card Code (SAUS)
PCC	Punched Card Control (SAUS)
PCC	Punched Card Counting (SAUS)
PCC	Pure Car Carrier [Shipping] (DS)
pCc	pure Colombian cocaine (SAUS)
PCC	Put Control Call (SAUS)
PCC	Pyridinium Chlorochromate [Organic chemistry]
PCC	Pyroconvective Cooling
PC(C)	Submarine Chaser (Control) [173 foot] [Navy symbol] [Obsolete]
PCCA	Confederation Art Gallery and Museum, Charlottetown, Prince Edward Island [Library symbol] [National Library of Canada] (NLC)
PCCA	Pacific Class Catamaran Association (EA)
PCCA	Pattern-Contingent Chromatic Aftereffects
PCCA	Pediatric Crohn's and Colitis Association, Inc. (NRGU)
PCCA	Personal Computer Communications Associations (SAUS)

PCCA .... Pewter Collectors Club of America (EA)
PCCa............ Pheochromocytoma (SAUS)
PCCA .... Pipe Collectors Club of America [Defunct] (EA)
PCCA .... Playing Card Collectors' Association (EA)
PCCA .... Police Car Collectors Association (EA)
PCCA .... Polymerized Crystalline Colloidal Array [Materials science]
PCCA .... Portable Computer and Communications Association (CGWS)
PCCA .... Portable Computer and Community Association
PCCA .... Postcard Collector's Club of America [Defunct] (EA)
PCCA .... Power and Communication Contractors Association (EA)
PCCA .... Professional Compounding Centers of America
PCCA .... Promotion of Community and Cultural Awareness [Australia]
PC Cable ..... Paper Core Cable (SAUS)
PC-CAD....... Personal Computer-Computer-Aided Design (SAUS)
PCCADS....... Panoramic Cockpit Control and Display System (MCD)
PCCAF .... Procedure Change Control Action Form (AAG)
PCCAF .... Procedure Committee Change Authorization Form (AAG)
PCCAL .... Pharmacy Consortium for Computer Aided Learning (ADWA)
P/C/C Alert... Polymers/Ceramics/Composites Alert
PcCAp......... Pacific Coast Apparel Co., Inc. [Associated Press] (SAG)
PcCap......... Pacificorp Capital [Associated Press] (SAG)
PCCAP .... Physicians' Continued Competence Assessment Program
               [Medicine] (DMAA)
PcCApp........ Pacific Coast Apparel Co., Inc. [Associated Press] (SAG)
PC CARP..... Personal Computer/Cluster Analysis and Regression Program
               (SAUS)
PCCB .... Payload Configuration Control Board [NASA] (MCD)
PCCB .... Process Communication Control Block (SAUS)
PCCB .... Program Configuration Control Board [NASA] (NASA)
PCCB .... Project Configuration Control Board [Army] (AABC)
PCCC .... Pacific Coast Collegiate Conference (PSS)
PCCC .... Pakistan Central Cotton Committee (BUAC)
PCCC .... Participating College Correspondence Course (MUGU)
PCCC .... Penang Chinese Chamber of Commerce [Malaysia] (BUAC)
PCCC .... Phoenix Conference on Computers and Communications (SAUS)
PCCC .... Polytechnics and Colleges Computer Committee (AIE)
PCCD .... Peristaltic Charge-Coupled Device (IEEE)
PCCDS........ Patrol Craft Combat Direction System [Navy] (SAA)
PCCE.......... Pacific Coast Coin Exchange
PCCE.......... Particle Cloud Combustion Experiment (SAUS)
PCCE.......... Payload Common Communication Equipment [NASA] (NASA)
PCCEI......... Permanent Charities Committee of the Entertainment Industries (EA)
PCCEMRSP... Permanent Commission for the Conservation and Exploitation of the
               Maritime Resources of the South Pacific
PCCES .... Planning and Coordinating Committee for Environmental Studies
               [National Research Council]
PCCF.......... Plan Case Control File [IRS]
PCCF.......... Prostate Cancer Cure Foundation Ltd.
PCCF.......... Protein C Cofactor (DMAA)
PCCG .... PCC Group [NASDAQ symbol] (TTSB)
PCCG .... PCC Group, Inc. [NASDAQ symbol] (SAG)
PCCG .... Protestant Cinema Critics Guild [Later, PCG] (EA)
PCCGB........ Photographic Collectors Club of Great Britain (DBA)
PCC Gp ...... PCC Group, Inc. [Associated Press] (SAG)
PCCh......... Partido Comunista de Chile [Chilean Communist Party] [Political
               party] (EY)
PCCH .... Pentachlorocyclohexene [Organic chemistry]
PCCH .... Physical Control Channel (SAUS)
PCCH .... Program Control Channel (VLIE)
PCCI.......... Pacific Crest Capital [NASDAQ symbol] (SAG)
PCCI.......... Paper Cup and Container Institute [Later, SSI] (EA)
PCCI.......... President's Committee on Consumer Interests [Terminated, 1971]
PCCIE......... Power Conditioning and Continuation Interfacing Equipment (SAUS)
PCC/I/O/R/H... Patrol Craft, Coastal/Inshore/Offshore/Riverine/Harbour (MILB)
PCCL.......... People's Community Civic League (EA)
PCCL.......... Precontract Cost Letter [Navy] (NG)
PCCL.......... Pulse Coupled Complementary Logic (SAUS)
PCCLAS ...... Pacific Coast Council on Latin American Studies (BUAC)
PCCM.......... Master Chief Postal Clerk [Navy rating]
PCCM.......... Pediatric Critical Care Medicine (DMAA)
PCCM.......... Portuguese Cultural Centre of Melbourne [Victoria, Australia]
PCCM.......... Primary Care Case Management [Medicine] (DMAA)
PCCM.......... Primary Care Case Manager [Medicine] (DMAA)
PCCM.......... Private Circuit Control Module [Telecommunications] (TEL)
PCCM.......... Program Change Control Management (NASA)
PCCM.......... Program Control Contract Manager (MCD)
PCC (M-L) ... Parti Communiste Canadien (Marxiste-Leniniste) [Marxist-Leninist
               Communist Party of Canada] [Political party]
PCCN .... Part Card Change Notice (KSC)
PCCN .... Port Call Control Number [Army] (AABC)
PCCN .... Preliminary Configuration Control Number (AAG)
PCCN .... Provisioning Contract Control Number (NASA)
PCCNA........ Pentecostal Charismatic Churches of North America (EA)
PCCNL........ Pacific Coast Coordinator of Naval Logistics
PCCNY........ Penal Code of the City of New York (SAUS)
PCCO .... Plant Clearance Contracting Officer [DoD]
PCCO .... Production Control Close Out (VLIE)
PCCOA........ Coles Associates Ltd., Charlottetown, Prince Edward Island [Library
               symbol] [National Library of Canada] (NLC)
PCC/OES..... Policy Coordinating Committee for Oceans and International
               Environmental and Scientific Affairs (SAUS)
PCCP .... Canadian Pension Commission [Commission Canadienne des
               Pensions], Charlottetown, Prince Edward Island [Library symbol]
               [National Library of Canada] (BIB)
PCCP .... Preliminary Contract Change Proposal [NASA] (KSC)

PCCP .... Private Child Care Provider (EDAC)
PCCP .... Product Cost Curve Picture (VLIE)
PCCPS .... Pacific Coast Canned Pear Service (EA)
PCCR .... Procurement Code Change Request (IAA)
PCCR .... Publishing Center for Cultural Resources [Defunct] (EA)
PCCS .... Pad-Circuit Center Spacing (SAUS)
PCCS .... Parti Conservateur Chretien-Social [Conservative Christian-Social
               Party] [Switzerland] [Political party] (PPE)
PCCS .... Personnel Command and Control System (SAUS)
PCCS .... Photographic Camera Control System (KSC)
PCCS .... Ported Coax Cable Sensor [Military] (DWSG)
PCCS .... Ported Coaxial Cable System (VLIE)
PCCS .... Positive Control Communications System
PCCS .... Primate Captive Care Society (BUAC)
PCCS .... Process Control Computer System (SAUS)
PCCS .... Processor Common Communications System
PCCS .... Production Change Control System (TIMI)
PCCS .... Program and Cost Control System [Army] (RDA)
PCCS .... Program Change Control System (NG)
PCCS .... Project Change Control System
PCCS .... Project Cost Control System
PCCS .... Publications Contract Coverage Schedule (MCD)
PCCS .... Senior Chief Postal Clerk [Navy rating]
PCCT........... Percept and Concept Cognition Test [Psychology]
PCCT........... Punched Card Controlled Typewrite (SAUS)
PCCTV .... Portable Closed-Circuit Television (SAUS)
PCCU .... Postal & Courier Communications Unit (SAUS)
PCCU .... Post-Coronary Care Unit [Medicine] (STED)
PCCU .... Power Conditioning and Cover Control Unit (ACAE)
PCCU .... President's Commission on Campus Unrest (EA)
PCCU .... Progressive Coronary Care Unit (SAUS)
PCCU .... Psychiatric Criminal Care Unit (WDAA)
PCCU .... Punched Card Control Unit [Computer science] (AABC)
PCC Unit..... Power Conditioning and Control Unit (SAUS)
PCCW .... Price/Costco, Inc. [NASDAQ symbol] (SPSG)
PCCW .... Public Citizens Congress Watch (COE)
PCD .... Democratic Conservative Party [Nicaragua] [Political party] (PD)
PCD .... Pacific Car Demurrage Bureau, San Francisco CA [STAC]
PCD .... Pacific Communications Division [Military]
PCD .... Pacing Cardioverter/Defibrillator (SAUS)
PCD .... Panama Canal Defense (SAUS)
PCD .... Panama Canal Department
PCD .... Panama Canal District (SAUS)
PCD .... Papillary Collecting Duct [Medicine] (DMAA)
PCD .... Paroxysmal Cerebral Dysrhythmia [Medicine] (STED)
PCD .... Partial Cooldown Drive [Automotive testing]
PCD .... Parti Communiste du Dahomey [Communist Party of Dahomey]
               [Benin] [Political party]
PCD .... Partido Comunista Dominicano [Dominican Communist Party]
               [Dominican Republic] [Political party] (PPW)
PCD .... Partition Control Descriptor [Computer science] (ELAL)
PCD .... Party of Christian Democrats [Poland] [Political party] (BUAC)
PCD .... Patriotic Coalition for Democracy [Political group] [Guyana]
PCD .... Payload Correction Data (SAUS)
PCD .... PCD, Inc. [Associated Press] (SAG)
PCD .... Perceptual-Communicative Disorder [Education] (EDAC)
PCD .... Personal Communication Device [FTA] (TAG)
PCD .... Phase-Change Drive (SAUS)
PCD .... Phenylchlorodiazirine [Organic chemistry]
PCD .... Phosphate-Citrate-Dextrose Polycystic Disease (MAE)
PCD .... Photo Compact Disk [Eastman Kodak Co.] (PCM)
PCD .... Photoconductive Decay [Semiconductor material]
PCD .... Photoconductive Device
PCD .... Pincushion Distortion (SAUS)
PCD .... Pine Channel Gold [Vancouver Stock Exchange symbol]
PCD .... Pioneer-Central Division [Bendix]
PCD .... Pitch Circle Diameter [Technical drawings] (IAA)
PCD .... Planned Commercial Development (PA)
PCD .... Planned Community Development (SAUS)
PCD .... Planned Completion Date (TEL)
PCD .... Planned Continuation Date (SAUS)
PCD .... Plasma Cell Dyscrasia [Medicine]
PCD .... Plasma-Coupled Device
PCD .... Plutonium Concentrator Distillate [Nuclear energy] (NRCH)
PCD .... Pneumatic Control Distributors (KSC)
PCD .... Point Chemical Detector (SEWL)
PCD .... Polar Cap Disturbance (DNAB)
PCD .... Polycarbodiimide (SAUS)
PCD .... Polychlorinated Dibenzo (BARN)
PCD .... Polycrystalline Diamond (ECON)
PCD .... Polycystic Disease [of kidneys] [Medicine]
PCD .... Polymeric Carrier Delivery System [Nuclear energy] (NUCP)
PCD .... Port Control Diagnostic [Telecommunications] (TEL)
PCD .... Positive Control Document (MCD)
PCd .... Post Card [Philately]
Pcd .... Postcard (BJA)
PCD .... Postcode (SAUS)
PCD .... Posterior Corneal Deposit [Ophthalmology] (MAE)
PCD .... Postmortem Cesarean Delivery (STED)
PCD .... Pounds per Capita per Day (AAG)
PCD .... Power Circle Diagram (SAUS)
PCD .... Power Control and Distribution
PCD .... Power Control Device [Nuclear energy] (NRCH)
PCD .... Power Conversion Distributor
PCD .... Precision Course Direction [Aerospace] (MCD)

PCD	Pre Congfigured Definition [*Computer science*] (ELAL)
PCD	Preliminary Conceptual Design (SAUS)
PCD	Presentation Capabilities Descriptor (SAUS)
PCD	Pressure Control Distributor (KSC)
PCD	Primary Ciliary Dyskinesia [*Medicine*]
PCD	Primary Current Distribution [*Electroplating*]
PCD	Prime Contractor Department (SAUS)
PCD	Principal Criteria Document (SAUS)
PCD	Problem Control and Display
PCD	Procedural Change Directive (KSC)
PCD	Proceed [*ICAO designator*] (FAAC)
PCD	Process Control Device (SAUS)
PCD	Process Control Division (SAUS)
PCD	Procurement and Contracts Division [*NASA*]
PCD	Procurement Control Document [*NASA*] (MCD)
PCD	Product Configuration Documentation (AAGC)
PCD	Production Common Digitizer
PCD	Program Change Decision [*Army*]
PCD	Program Control Display System [*NATO Air Defense Ground Environment*] (NATG)
PCD	Program Control Document (KSC)
PCD	Programmed Cell Death [*Cytology*]
PCD	Programmed Cutting Director (SAUS)
PCD	Project Control Drawing (AAG)
PCD	Projected Charge Density (PDAA)
PCD	Prolonged Contractile Duration (STED)
PCD	Protocatechuatedioxygenase [*An enzyme*]
PCD	Pulmonary Clearance Delay [*Medicine*]
PCD	Punched Card Data (SAUS)
PCDA	Post Card Distributors Association
PCDA	Power Control and Distribution Assembly (SAUS)
PCDA	Process Control and Data Acquisition (SAUS)
PCDA	Professional Currency Dealers Association (EA)
PCDA	Program Controlled Data Acquisition (SAUS)
PCDA	Protective Clothing Distributors Association [*British*] (DBA)
PCDANA	Post Card Distributors Association of North America (NTPA)
PCDB	Poison Control Data Base [*Database*]
PCDB	Product Cost Data Base (TIMI)
PCDC	Diagnostic Chemicals Ltd., Charlottetown, Prince Edward Island [*Library symbol*] [*National Library of Canada*] (NLC)
PCDC	Plasma Clot Diffusion Chamber [*Medicine*] (DMAA)
PCDC	Plutonium Canister Decontamination Cell [*Nuclear energy*] (NRCH)
PCDC	Professionals Committee for Democratic Change (SAUS)
PCDD	Pentachlorodioxin [*Organic chemistry*]
PCDD	Polychlorinated Dibenzodioxin [*Organic chemistry*]
PCDD	Polychlorinated Dibenzodioxins [*Automotive emissions*] [*Organic chemistry*]
PCDDS	Private Circuit Digital Data Service [*Telecommunications*] (TEL)
PCDE	Parent Council for Deaf Education [*Australia*]
PCDE	Photon-induced Chemical Dry Etching (SAUS)
PCDESIG	Plane Captain Designated [*or Designation*] (DNAB)
PCDF	Polychlorinated Dibenzofuran [*Organic chemistry*]
PCDF	Polychlorinated Dibenzofurans [*Automotive emissions*] [*Organic chemistry*]
PCDG	Prestressed Concrete Development Group (SAUS)
PCDH	Polychlorinated Diaromatic Hydrocarbon [*Organic chemistry*]
PCDHi	Delaware County Historical Society, Chester, PA [*Library symbol*] [*Library of Congress*] (LCLS)
PCDI	PCD, Inc. [*NASDAQ symbol*] (SAG)
PCDI	Per Capita Disposable Income [*Economics*]
PCDI	Pierce Die
PCDI	Printed Circuit Design Interface (NITA)
PCDJ	Pakistan Committee for Democracy and Justice [*Defunct*] (EA)
PCDL	Pro-Choice Defense League (EA)
PCDMA	Personal Computer Direct Marketers Association (BUAC)
PCDN	Production Development Change Notice (SAUS)
PCdoB	Partido Comunista do Brasil [*Communist Party of Brazil*] [*Political party*] (PPW)
PC DOCS	PC DOCS Group International [*Associated Press*] (SAG)
PC-DOS	Personal Computer-Disk Operating System (DOM)
PCDP	Parti Comorien pour la Democratie et le Progres [*Political party*] (EY)
PCDP	Pilot Control and Display Panel
PCDP	Punched Card Data Processing
PCDP Equipment	Punched Card Data Processing Equipment (SAUS)
PCDPPP	Pan Caribbean Disaster Preparedness and Prevention Project (BUAC)
PCD-PRP	Pueblo, Cambio, y Democracia - Partido Roldosista Popular [*People, Change, and Democracy - Popular Roldosista Party*] [*Ecuador*] [*Political party*] (PPW)
PCDR	Preconceptual Design Report (SAUS)
PCDR	Preliminary Conceptual Design Report (SAUS)
PCDR	Procedure (AAG)
PCDS	Patient Care Data Set (SAUS)
PCDS	Payload Command Decoder Subunit [*NASA*] (KSC)
PCDS	Pilot Climate Data System (SAUS)
PCDS	Power Conversion and Distribution System
PCDS	Precision Course Direction System (SAUS)
PCDS	Procurement Congressional Descriptive Summary [*Army*] (RDA)
PCDS	Program Control Display System (SAUS)
PCDS	Project Control Drawing System (AAG)
PCDT	Pacific Coast Dog Tick (MELL)
PCDU	Payload Command Decoder Unit [*NASA*] (NASA)
PCDUS	Plasma Cell Dyscrasias of Unknown Significance [*Medicine*]
PCE	Page Communications Engineers, Inc. [*Canada*] (MCD)
PCE	Painter Creek, AK [*Location identifier*] [*FAA*] (FAAL)

PCE	Palm Island [*Queensland*] [*Airport symbol*] (AD)
PCE	Parameter Checkout Engineer [*Computer science*] (IAA)
PCE	Parliamentary Commissioner for the Environment (SAUS)
PCE	Partido Comunista de Espana [*Communist Party of Spain*] [*Political party*] (PPE)
PCE	Partido Comunista Ecuatoriano [*Communist Party of Ecuador*] [*Political party*] (PPW)
PCE	Passenger Car Equivalence [*TRB*] (TAG)
PCE	Patrol Escort [*Patrol Craft Escort*] [*Navy symbol*]
PCE	Pedco Energy Ltd. [*Vancouver Stock Exchange symbol*]
PCE	Perchloroethylene [*Organic chemistry*]
PCE	Pericardial Effusion [*Medicine*] (MELL)
PCE	Peripheral Control Element
PCE	Peripheral Controller Enclosure (NITA)
PCE	Personal Consumption Expenditure
PCE	Petrozavodsk Commodity Exchange [*Russian Federation*] (EY)
PCE	Phase Change Erasable (SAUS)
PCE	Photocell Emitter (IAA)
PCE	Physical Capacities Evaluation [*Test of hand skills*]
PCE	Physical Completion Estimate (SAUS)
PCE	Piece [*Numismatics*]
PCE	Plasma Chamber Evacuation Subsystem (MCD)
PCE	Platinol [*Cis-Platinum*] Cyclophosphamide, Vindesine [*Antineoplastic drug regimen*] (DAVI)
PCE	Plug Compatible Ethernet
PCE	Pollution Control Ecology (SAUS)
PCE	Pollution Control Equipment (GFGA)
PCE	Polyarthrite Chronique Evolutive [*Chronic Evolutive Polyarthritis*] [*Medicine*] [*French*]
PCE	Polychloroethylene (BARN)
PCE	Polymer-Coated Erythromycin [*An antibiotic*] (DAVI)
PCE	Ponce [*Diocesan abbreviation*] [*Puerto Rico*] (TOCD)
PCE	Pool Control Error (IAA)
PCE	Positive Continuous Engagement [*Automotive engineering*]
PCE	Post-Communist Europe (SAUS)
PCE	Posterior Chamber of Eye [*Medicine*] (MELL)
PCE	Potentially Compensable Event (DICI)
PCE	Power Conditioning Electronics (SAUS)
PCE	Power Conditioning Equipment
PCE	Power Conversion Equipment (DNAB)
PCE	Preliminary Closure Estimate (SAUS)
PCE	Present Company Excluded (SAUS)
PCE	Pressure to Clutch Engage [*Aerospace*] (AAG)
PCE	Prince Edward Island Department of Education, Charlottetown, Prince Edward Island [*Library symbol*] [*National Library of Canada*] (NLC)
PCE	Private Ciphering Equipment (SAUS)
PCE	Privy Councillor, England (ROG)
PCE	Probability of Character Error (CCCA)
PCE	Process [*or Processor*] Control Element [*Computer science*] (IAA)
PCE	Process Control Engineering
PCE	Processor Control Element (SAUS)
PCE	Production Check Equipment (MCD)
PCE	Professional Continuing Education (DOMA)
PCE	Program Cost Estimate (AFM)
PCE	Prohormone-Converting Endopeptidase
PCE	Project Coordination Center Europe (SAUS)
PCE	Project Cost Estimate (SAUS)
PCE	Pseudocholinesterase [*Same as ACAH*] [*An enzyme*]
PCE	Pulmocutaneous Exchange
PCE	Punch Card Equipment [*Computer science*] (AFM)
PCE	Pyrometric Cone Equivalent [*Refractory industry*]
PCE	Submarine Chaser Escort
PCEA	Pacific Coast Electrical Association
PCEA	Patient-Controlled Epidural Analgesia
PCEA	Phosphate Chemicals Export Association (EA)
PCEA	Presbyterian Church of Eastern Australia
PCEA	Presidents Council of Economic Advisors (SAUS)
PCEA	Professional Construction Estimators Association of America (NTPA)
P/CEA3	Probationary Control Electrical Artificer 3rd Class [*British military*] (DMA)
PCEAA	Professional Construction Estimators Association of America (EA)
PCEB	PCI to EISA Bridge (SAUS)
PCEC	Patrol Craft Escort Control (SAUS)
PCE(C)	Patrol Vessel, Escort (Control) [*180 feet*] [*Navy symbol*] [*Obsolete*]
PCEC	Personal Computer Enhanced Connectivity (SAUS)
PCEC	Pollution Control and Ecology Commission (SAUS)
PCEDURE	Procedure (ROG)
PCEE	Presidents Commission on Executive Exchange (SAUS)
PCEEDGS	Proceedings (ROG)
PCEEO	President's Committee on Equal Employment Opportunity [*Later, OFCCP*] [*Department of Labor*]
PCEH	President's Committee on Employment of the Handicapped [*Washington, DC*]
PCEI	Prime Contract End Item (MCD)
PCEK	Pappas Carter Evans & Koop (SAUS)
PCEM	Parliamentary Council of the European Movement
PCEM	Process Chain Evaluation Model (IEEE)
PCEM	Program Committee on Education for Mission (EA)
PCEM	Propulsion Contamination Effects Module [*NASA*]
PcEn	Pacific Enterprises [*Associated Press*] (SAG)
PCEN	Paracentesis Fluid [*Medicine*] (DAVI)
PCEO	Personal Computer Enhancement Operation [*Intel Corp.*] (CIST)
PCEQ	President's Commisssion on Environmental Quality (GNE)
PCEQ	Presidents Council on Environmental Quality (SAUS)

PCE-R .... Partido Comunista de Espana - Reconstituido [*Reconstituted Spanish Communist Party*] [*Political party*] (PD)
PCER .... Patrol Craft, Escort Rescue (SAUS)
PCER .... Patrol Rescue Escort [*Patrol Craft Escort Rescue*] [*Navy symbol*]
PCER .... Rescue Escort (SAUS)
PCERT .... Purdue Computer Emergency Response Team (SAUS)
P Cert Ed ..... Professional Certificate in Education
PCES .... Pace Health Management Systems, Inc. [*NASDAQ symbol*] (SAG)
PCES .... Phase Change Energy Storage (SAUS)
PCES .... President's Committee on Economic Security [*New Deal*]
PCES .... Product Cost Estimate System (SAUS)
PCES .... Production Control Experimental System (SAUS)
PCET .... Personal Computer Extended Technology [*Computer bus*]
PCETF .... Power Conversion Equipment Test Facility [*Nuclear energy*]
PCEU .... Partido Comunista de Espana Unificado [*Unified Communist Party of Spain*] [*Political party*] (PPW)
PCEU .... Pulse Compression/Expansion Unit
PCF .... Pacific Air Express [*ICAO designator*] (FAAC)
PCF .... Pacific Car and Foundry
PCF .... Pacific Ridge Resources [*Vancouver Stock Exchange symbol*]
PCF .... Pacificulture Foundation (EA)
PCF .... Palliative Care Foundation [*Canada*] (EAIO)
PCF .... Parallel Computing Forum (ACAE)
PCF .... Parents' Choice Foundation (EA)
PCF .... Parliamentary Christian Fellowship [*British*] (WDAA)
PCF .... Partial Correction Function (SAUS)
PCF .... Partial Correlation Function (SAUS)
PCF .... Parti Communiste Francais [*French Communist Party*] [*Political party*] (PPW)
PCF .... Parts Conditioning Facility (TIMI)
PCF .... Patrol Craft Fast (SAUS)
PCF .... Payload Control Facility [*NASA*] (MCD)
PCF .... Peace Centers Foundation [*Later, UDC*] (EA)
PCF .... Pentagon Counterintelligence Force
PCF .... Peripheral Circulatory Failure [*Medicine*] (DMAA)
PCF .... Peripheral Control Facility (SAUS)
PCF .... Personal Card File
PCF .... Personal Computing Facility (SAUS)
PCF .... Personnel Control Facility [*Army*] (AABC)
PCF .... Pharyngoconjunctival Fever [*Medicine*]
PCF .... Pistol Centre Fire (SAUS)
PCF .... Plan Characteristics File [*IRS*]
PCF .... Planning Cable Fill (SAUS)
PCF .... Planning Coordination Facility (SAUS)
PCF .... Plutonium Chemistry Facility (SAUS)
PCF .... Point Coordination Function (SAUS)
PCF .... Polycationized Ferritin [*Biochemistry*]
PCF .... Portable Compiled Font (SAUS)
PCF .... Postcard Club Federation [*Defunct*] (EA)
PCF .... Posterior Carotid Foramen [*Anatomy*]
PCF .... Posterior Cervical Fusion [*Medicine*] (MELL)
PCF .... Posterior Cranial Fossa [*Anatomy*] (MAE)
PCF .... Potential Conflict Forecasts [*Army*]
PCF .... Potential Controlled Flotation (SAUS)
PCF .... Potentially Critical Failures
pcf .... Pounds per Cubic Foot (WPI)
PCF .... Pounds per Cubic Foot
PCF .... Power Cathode Follower
PCF .... Power Coupling Factor (SAUS)
PCF .... Power per Cubic Foot
PCF .... Prairie Chicken Foundation (EA)
PCF .... Primary Checkpoint File
PCF .... Primary Control Field (SAUS)
PCF .... Probability of Consequence Factor
PCF .... Procedure Completion Form (SAUS)
PCF .... Process Control File (SAUS)
PCF .... Processed Citation File
PCF .... Procoagulant Factor [*Medicine*] (MELL)
PCF .... Program Change Factor
PCF .... Program Characteristics File [*Medicaid*] (GFGA)
PCF .... Program Checkout Facility
PCF .... Program Complex File [*Computer science*] (MHDI)
PCF .... Program Control Facility
PCF .... Programmed Cryptographic Facility [*Computer science*]
PCF .... Proposed Change File (SAUS)
PCF .... Prothrombin Conversion Factor [*Hematology*]
PCF .... Public Concern Foundation (EA)
PCF .... Pulse Compression Filter
PCF .... Pulse-to-Cycle Fraction
PCF .... Pulverized Coal-Fired Plant
PCF .... Punched Card Feed (SAUS)
PCF .... Putnam High Income Convertible & Bond Fund [*NYSE symbol*] (SPSG)
PCFA .... Fast Patrol Craft, Air Cushion [*Navy*]
PCFA .... Pin, Clip, and Fastener Association [*Later, PCFS*] (EA)
PCFA .... Polytechnics and Colleges Funding Council (BUAC)
PCFA .... Precast Concrete Frame Association [*British*] (DBA)
PCFC .... Phil Collins Fan Club (EA)
PCFC .... Phil Collins Information [*Formerly, Phil Collins Fan Club*] (EA)
PCFC .... Pioneer Commercial Funding Corp. [*NASDAQ symbol*] (SAG)
PCFC .... Polytechnics and Colleges Funding Council [*British*]
Pcfcp25 .... Pacificorp [*Associated Press*] (SAG)
Pcfcp35 .... Pacificorp [*Associated Press*] (SAG)
PCFE .... Polytrifluorochloroethylene [*Organic chemistry*]
PCFE .... Prime Contractor Furnished Equipment (MCD)

PCFFA .... Pacific Coast Federation of Fishermen's Associations (EA)
PCFFF .... Post-Collision Fuel-Fed Fire [*Automotive safety engineering*]
PCFG .... Probabilistic Context Free Grammar (IDAI)
PC/FGD .... Pulverized Coal / Flue Gas Desulfurization [*Energy technology*]
PCFH .... Fast Patrol Craft, Hydrofoil [*Navy*]
PCFIA .... Particle Concentration Fluorescence Immunoassay
PCFLIS .... Presidents Commission on Foreign Language and International Studies (SAUS)
PCFlot .... Patrol Craft Flotilla (SAUS)
PCFM .... Production Control File Manager (IAA)
PCFN .... PC Financial Network (PCM)
PCFO .... Position Classification Field Office
PCFP .... Predicted Comparative Failure Probability
PCFR .... Programmatic Center for Fire Research [*National Institute of Standards and Technology*]
PCFRE .... Professional Council of Religious Education [*British*] (DBA)
PCFS .... Pacific Coast Fertility Society (SAUS)
PCFS .... Pin, Clip, and Fastener Services (EA)
PCFT .... Information Centre, Prince Edward Island Food Technology Centre, Charlottetown [*Library symbol*] [*National Library of Canada*] (BIB)
PCG .... Guided Missile Coastal Escort [*Ship symbol*] (NATG)
PCG .... Pacific Gas & Elec [*NYSE symbol*] (TTSB)
PCG .... Pacific Gas & Electric Co. [*AMEX symbol*] (SPSG)
PCG .... Paracervical Ganglion [*Anatomy*]
PCG .... Parti Communiste de Guadeloupe [*Communist Party of Guadeloupe*] [*Political party*] (PPW)
PCG .... Period Costume Group (BUAC)
PCG .... PezCorona Gold Corp. [*Vancouver Stock Exchange symbol*]
PCG .... PG & E Capital I [*AMEX symbol*] (SAG)
PCG .... PG & E Corp. Holdings Co. [*NYSE symbol*] (SAG)
PCG .... Phonocardiogram [*Cardiology*]
pcg .... Picogram [*Measurement*] (DAVI)
P/CG .... Pilot Controller Glossary [*Aviation*] (FAAC)
PCG .... Plain Clothes Gratuity [*British military*] (DMA)
PCG .... Plains Cotton Growers (EA)
PCG .... Planning and Control Guide
PCG .... Planning Career Goals [*Vocational guidance test*]
PCG .... Policy Coordination Group (DOGT)
PCG .... Power Conditioning Group (MCD)
PCG .... Power Converter Group (SAUS)
PCG .... Preconditioned Gradient (SAUS)
PCG .... Primary Congenital Glaucoma (MELL)
PCG .... Primate Chorionic Gonadotropin [*Medicine*] (DMAA)
PCG .... Printed Circuit Generator
PCG .... Programmable Character Generator
PCG .... Protein Crystal Growth (SAUS)
PCG .... Protestant Cinema Guild [*Formerly, PCCG*] [*Defunct*]
PCG .... Pubococcygeus [*Muscle*] [*Anatomy*] (DAVI)
PCG .... Pulsed Coaxial Gun
PCG2 .... Preconditioned Conjugate Gradient
PCGA .... Pacific Coast Gas Association (SAUS)
PCGD .... Pollution Control Guidance Document
PCGE .... Protein Crystal Growth Experiment (SAUS)
PCGF .... Protein Crystal Growth Facility (SSD)
PCGG .... PCG Glovebox (SAUS)
PCGG .... Philippine Commission on Good Government (BUAC)
PCGG .... Primary Care Group in Gynaecology (BUAC)
PCGL .... Printed Circuit Generated Level (SAUS)
PCGM .... Pacific Coast Garment Manufacturers [*Later, AAMA*] (EA)
PCGM .... Preconditioned Gradient Method (SAUS)
PCGN .... Permanent Committee of Geographical Names [*Later, BGN*]
PCGOV .... Port Charges Paid by Foreign Government (DNAB)
PCGPrA .... Pacific Gas & El 6% Pfd [*AMEX symbol*] (TTSB)
PCGPrB .... Pacific Gas & El 5 1/2% Pfd [*AMEX symbol*] (TTSB)
PCGPrC .... Pacific Gas & El 5% Pfd [*AMEX symbol*] (TTSB)
PCGPrCA .... PG&E Cap I 7.90%'QUIPS' [*AMEX symbol*] (TTSB)
PCGPrD .... Pacific Gas & El 5% Pfd [*AMEX symbol*] (TTSB)
PCGPrE .... Pac G&E 5%cmRed1stA Pfd [*AMEX symbol*] (TTSB)
PCGPrG .... Pacific Gas & El 4.80% Pfd (TTSB)
PCGPrH .... Pacific Gas & El 4.50% Pfd [*AMEX symbol*] (TTSB)
PCGPrI .... Pacific Gas & El 4.36% Pfd [*AMEX symbol*] (TTSB)
PCGPrQ .... Pacific Gas & El 7.44% Pfd [*AMEX symbol*] (TTSB)
PCGPrU .... Pacific Gas & El 7.04% Pfd [*AMEX symbol*] (TTSB)
PCGPrX .... Pacific Gas & El 6.875% Pfd [*AMEX symbol*] (TTSB)
PCGPrY .... Pacific Gas & El 6.57% Pfd [*AMEX symbol*] (TTSB)
PCGPrZ .... Pacific Gas & El 6.30% Pfd [*AMEX symbol*] (TTSB)
PCGRIDS .... Personal Computer Gridded Interactive Display and Diagnostic System [*Marine science*] (OSRA)
PCGRX .... Pioneer Capital Growth Cl.A [*Mutual fund ticker symbol*] (SG)
PCGS .... Professional Coin Grading Service (BARN)
PCGS .... Protein Crystal Growth System
PCGU .... Protein Crystal Growth Unit (SSD)
PCGVB .... Pairwise Correlated Generalized Valence Bond [*Physics*]
PCH .... Cheyney State College, Cheyney, PA [*OCLC symbol*] (OCLC)
PCH .... Packing, Crating, and Handling [*Shipping*]
PCH .... Paging Channel (CGWS)
PCH .... Paper Clearing House (TBD)
PCH .... Parallel Channel (VLIE)
PCH .... Parent Compound Handbook [*Later, Ring Systems Handbook*] [*American Chemical Society*]
PCH .... Pari-Cachoeira [*Brazil*] [*Airport symbol*] (AD)
PCH .... Paroxysmal Cold Hemoglobinuria [*Medicine*]
PCH .... Partido Comunista de Honduras [*Communist Party of Honduras*] [*Political party*] (PD)
PCH .... Patrol Craft (Hydrofoil) [*Navy symbol*]

P-Ch	P-Channel (SAUS)
PCH	PCH Post Career [Vancouver Stock Exchange symbol]
PCh	Phosphocholine [Biochemistry]
PCH	Physicochemical Hydrodynamics [A publication]
PCH	Pitch
PCH	Polycyclic Hydrocarbon (DMAA)
pch	Porch (VRA)
PCH	Porch (WGA)
PCH	Porous Clay Heterostructure [Materials science]
PCH	Positive Channel [Telecommunications] (IAA)
PCH	Potlatch Corp. [Formerly, PFI] [NYSE symbol] (SPSG)
PCH	Prepare Chassis
PCH	Presbyterian Church House [British] (BI)
PCH	Prince Charles Hospital [Australia]
Pch	Principal Chaplain [Navy] [British]
PCH	Program Critical Hardware (SAUS)
PCH	Proton Channeling (SAUS)
pch	Punch (ELAL)
PCH	Punch (KSC)
pch	punched (SAUS)
PCH	Purchase (DCTA)
PCH & T	Packaging, Crating, Handling, and Transportation [Shipping] (CINC)
PCHAR	Printing Character [Computer science]
PCHB	Pollution Control Hearings Board (SAUS)
PCHBD	Patchboard (MSA)
PCHC	Holland College, Charlottetown, Prince Edward Island [Library symbol] [National Library of Canada] (NLC)
PCHC	People's Center for Housing Change (EA)
p Ch c	pure Chilean cocaine (SAUS)
PChCo	Conococheague District Library, Chambersburg, PA [Library symbol] [Library of Congress] (LCLS)
PCHCY	Parents Campaign for Handicapped Children and Youth (EA)
pchd	Purchased (GEAB)
PCHD	Purchased (ROG)
Pch Del	Punch Delay (SAUS)
Pch Dir	Punch Direct (SAUS)
PCHDMT	Polycyclohexane Dimethylene Terephthalate (SAUS)
PChE	Plasma Cholinesterase (SAUS)
PCHE	Poor Clare Nuns of the Holy Eucharist [Roman Catholic religious order]
PC HE	Pseudocholinesterase [An enzyme] (DAVI)
PCHE	Purchase (ROG)
PCheS	Cheyney State College, Cheyney, PA [Library symbol] [Library of Congress] (LCLS)
PCHG	Punching
P Chgs	Particular Charges (SAUS)
PCHIS	Population Clearing House and Information System (NITA)
PCHK	Parity Check [Data communications] (TEL)
PCHL	Pacific Coast Hockey League [Later, Western Hockey League] (EA)
Pchl	Protochlorophyll (SAUS)
Pchlide	Protochlorophyllide (SAUS)
PCHLT	Pressurized Cabin Hydraulic Leakage Tester (DWSG)
PCHM	PharmChem Laboratories [NASDAQ symbol] (SPSG)
PCHMOS	Positive-Channel Metal-Oxide Semiconductor [Electronics] (IAA)
PCHN	Programmed Course, Home Nursing [Red Cross]
Pch Off	Punch Off (SAUS)
PCHR	Panamanian Committee for Human Rights (EA)
PCHR	Paraguay Committee for Human Rights [British]
PCHR	Pentecostal Coalition for Human Rights [Defunct] (EA)
PCHR	Purchaser (ROG)
PCHRG	Public Citizen Health Research Group (EA)
P Chr N	Post Christum Natum [After the Birth of Christ] [Latin]
PChS	Proceedings of the Chemical Society (SAUS)
PCHS	Purchase (WGA)
PCHSR	Purchaser
Pch Sup	Punch Suppress (SAUS)
PCHT	Packaging, Crating, Handling, and Transportation [Shipping] (AABC)
PCHT	Parchment (MSA)
PChW	Wilson College, Chambersburg, PA [Library symbol] [Library of Congress] (LCLS)
Pch X	Punch X (SAUS)
PCI	Packer Collegiate Institute (SAUS)
PCI	Packet/Circuit Interface (SAUS)
PCI	Packet Communications, Inc.
PCI	Panel Call Indicator
PCI	Pantone Color Institute (EA)
PCI	Paramount Communications (EFIS)
PCI	Parti Communiste Internationaliste [Internationalist Communist Party] [France] [Political party] (PPE)
PCI	Partito Comunista Italiano [Italian Communist Party] [Political party]
PCI	Patent Citation Index (SAUS)
PCI	Paterson Candy International [British]
PCI	Pattern Correspondence Index
PCI	Pattern of Cockpit Indication
PCI	Pavement Condition Index [Aviation] (DA)
PCI	Pax Christi International (EAIO)
PCI	PCL Industries Ltd. [Toronto Stock Exchange symbol]
PCI	Pellet Clad Interaction [Nuclear energy] (NRCH)
PCI	Per Column Inch [Publishing]
PCI	Periodic Conformance Inspection (MCD)
PCI	Periodic Convolutional Interleaving (ACAE)
PCI	Peripheral Command Indicator
PCI	Peripheral Component Interconnect [Telecommunications] (PCM)
PCI	Peripheral Component Interface (PCM)
PCI	Peripheral Connection Interface
PCI	Peripheral Control Instruction (SAUS)
PCI	Peripheral Controller Interface
PCI	Perpetual Cost Index (SAUS)
PCI	Personal Computer Interconnect (VLIE)
PCI	Personal Computer Interface [Varitronics Systems, Inc.]
PCI	Phase-Conjugate Interferometry (SAUS)
PCI	Photographic Credit Institute (EA)
PCI	Photon-Coupled Isolator (SAUS)
PCI	Physical Configuration Inspection (AFIT)
PCI	Physical Configuration Item [Military]
PCI	Physico-Chemical Institute (SAUS)
Pci	Phytophthora Citricola [A fungus]
pCi	Picocurie [Also, pC] [One trillionth of a curie]
PCI	Pilot Club International (EA)
PCI	Pilot Controller Integration (IEEE)
PCI	Pilots for Christ International (EA)
PCI	Pipe Collectors International [Later, PCCA] (EA)
PCI	Planning Card Index (AAG)
PCI	Plant Control Interface
PCI	Pneumatic Circuit Indicator
PCI	Pneumatosis Cystoides Intestinorum [Medicine] (AAMN)
PCI	Polar Circulation Index [Climatology]
PCI	Political Campaign Institute [Commercial firm] (EA)
PCI	Polycrystal Isolation (IAA)
PCI	Population Communications International [An association] (EA)
PCI	Population Council of India (BUAC)
PCI	Portable Cesium Irradiator
PCI	Portable Compass Indicator
PCI	Possible Criminal Informant
PCI	Post Cure Inflation (SAUS)
PCI	Potato Chip Institute, International [Later, PC/SFA] (EA)
PCI	Potential Criminal Informant (SAUS)
PCI	Powder Coating Institute (EA)
PCI	Power Conversion International (SAUS)
PCI	Precast/Prestressed Concrete Institute (NTPA)
PCI	Pre-Chamber Ignition [Automotive engineering]
PCI	Precision Cascade Impactor (SAUS)
PCI	Precision Components, Inc. [Addison, IL] [Telecommunications service] (TSSD)
PCI	Precombat Checks and Inspections [Army]
PCI	Pre-Combat Inspection (INF)
PCI	Pre-Counseling Inventory [Psychology]
PCI	Premarital Communication Inventory [Psychology] (DHP)
PCI	Presentation Context Identifier [Computer science] (TNIG)
PCI	Press Control, Inc.
PCI	Press Council of India (BUAC)
PCI	Prestressed Concrete Institute (EA)
PCI	Price Cap Index (OTD)
PCI	Prime Ceiling Incentive
PCI	Printed Circuits, Inc. (SAUS)
PCI	Printer Command Language [Computer science] (AGLO)
PCI	Private Citizen, Inc. [An association] (EA)
PCI	Privy Council Decisions [India] [A publication] (DLA)
PCI	Privy Councillor, Ireland (ROG)
PCI	Procedure Change Unit (SAUS)
PCI	Process Capability Index (SAUS)
PCI	Process Control Interface
PCI	Product Change Information
PCI	Product Configuration Identification (KSC)
PCI	Product Configuration Item
PCI	Product Cost Index
PCI	Production Configuration Identification (SAUS)
PCI	Production, Configuration, Integration
PCI	Production Control Information [Software supplier] [Sheffield, England] (NCC)
PCI	Production Cost Information (SAUS)
PCI	Program Check Interruption [Computer science] (MDG)
PCI	Program Control Input (NASA)
PCI	Program-Controlled Interruption [Computer science] (IBMDP)
PCI	Program Controlled Interuption (SAUS)
PCI	Program in Correctional Institutions (OICC)
PCI	Programmable Communications Interface
PCI	Programmable Controller Interface (SAUS)
PCI	Programmed Control Interrupt (SAUS)
PCI	Project Concern International (EA)
PCI	Project Control Information (SAUS)
PCI	Prophylactic Cranial Irradiation [Oncology]
PCI	Proportional Change Index [Occupational therapy]
PCI	Prospectors Club International [Defunct] (EA)
PCI	Protein C Inhibitor [Organic chemistry]
PCI	Prothrombin Consumption Index (PDAA)
PCI	Protocol Capability Indicator (CGWS)
PCI	Protocol Computers Inc. (NITA)
PCI	Protocol Control Indicator (SAUS)
PCI	Protocol Control Information [Telecommunications]
PCI	Pseudo-Code Instruction (SAUS)
PCI	Pulverised Coal Injection [Coal industry]
PCI	Punched Card Input (SAUS)
PCI	Pupil Control Ideology Form [Education] (EDAC)
PCI	Put Control Instruction (SAUS)
PCIA	Personal Communications Industry Association (DDC)
PCIA	Person Communications Industry Association (NTPA)
PCIAC	Petro-Canada International Assistance Corp.
PCIAOH	Permanent Commission and International Association on Occupational Health (EAIO)

PCIB............	Pacific Cargo Inspection Bureau (SAUS)
PCIB............	Personal Computer Instruments Bus (NITA)
PCIC............	Petroleum and Chemical Industry Conference (SAUS)
PCIC............	Pittsburgh Chemical Information Center (SAUS)
PCIC............	Poison Control Information Center
PCIC............	Polaris Control and Information Center (SAUS)
PCIC............	Program Control Information Card (VLIE)
PCICP..........	Primary Control Inventory Control Point [Navy]
PCICS	Permanent Council of the International Convention of Stresa on Cheeses (EAIO)
PCID............	Pontifical Council for Inter-Religious Dialogue (BUAC)
PCIE............	Period of Central Inspiratory Excitability (SAUS)
PCIE............	President's Council on Integrity and Efficiency (AAGC)
PCIE............	President's Council on Integrity and Efficiency in Government (EPA)
PCIEC..........	Permanent Committee for International Eucharistic Congresses (EA)
PCIF............	Personal Computing Internal Fanout (TIMI)
PCIF............	Printed Circuit Interconnection Federation [British] (DBA)
PCIF............	Programmable Controller Interface Facility (SAUS)
PCIFC..........	Patsy Cline International Fan Club (EA)
PCIFC..........	Permanent Commission of the International Fisheries Convention
pCi/g...........	Picocuries per Gram (SAUS)
PCII.............	Potato Chip Institute International (SAUS)
PCIJ............	Permanent Court of International Justice (BUAC)
PCIJ............	Permanent Court of International Justice Cases [A publication] (DLA)
PCIJ Ann R...	Permanent Court of International Justice Annual Reports [A publication] (DLA)
pCi/L...........	Picocuries per Liter [Measure of radioactivity]
PCIL............	Pilot-Controlled Instrument Landing [Aviation] (NASA)
PCIL............	Private Core Image Library (VLIE)
PCIL............	Programmable Current-Injection Logic (SAUS)
PCI LBS	Peripheral Component Interconnect Local Bus Specification (SAUS)
PCILO	Perturbative Configuration Interaction [Based on] Localized Orbitals [Quantum mechanics]
PCILOCC	Perturbative Configuration Interaction Using Localized Orbitals for Crystal Calculation (SAUS)
PCIM............	Packet Channel Interface Module [Telecommunications]
PCIM............	Parallel Character Input Module (SAUS)
PCIM............	Parti du Congres de l'Independance de Madagascar [Party of the Congress for Malagasy Independence]
PCIM............	Power Conversion and Intelligent Motion (SAUS)
PCIM............	Presidential Commission on Income Maintenance (SAUS)
PCIMP	President's Commission on Income Maintenance Programs (EA)
PCIMR	Centre for Information and Technical Assistance, Institute of Man and Resources, Charlottetown, Prince Edward Island [Library symbol] [National Library of Canada] (NLC)
PCIMS	Positive Chemical Ionization Mass Spectroscopy
PCIN	Program Change Identification Number (NASA)
PCIN	Program Change Incorporation Notice (SAUS)
PCIN	Program Change Integration (NASA)
PCIO	PC Information Officer (SAUS)
PCI/O	Program-Controlled Input-Output
PC-IOC........	Posterior Chamber - Intraocular Lens [Ophthalmology]
PC I/O Channel...	Personal Computer Input/Output Channel (SAUS)
PCIOL..........	Posterior Chamber Intraocular Lens [Ophthalmology] (DAVI)
PCIOMR.......	Preconditioning Interim Operating Management Recommendation [Nuclear energy] (NRCH)
PCIOS	Processor Common Input/Output System [Computer science] (VLIE)
PCIP............	Permitting Compliance Implementation Plan (SAUS)
PCIP............	Personal Computer, Instrument Product
PCIP............	Poseidon [Missile] Communication Improvement Program [Navy]
PCIPI	Permanent Committee on Industrial Property [World Intellectual Property Organization] [Switzerland] [Information service or system] (IID)
PCIPS	Paris Conversational Image Processing System (SAUS)
PCIPS	Personal Computer Image Processing System (SAUS)
PCIR	Post-Contract Implementation Report (AAGC)
PCIRI	Paint and Coatings Industry Research Institute [China] (BUAC)
PCIRO	Preparatory Commission for International Refugee Organization
PCIS............	Canton Island [Phoenix Islands] [ICAO location identifier] (ICLI)
PCIS............	Patient Care Information System (IID)
PCIS............	PCI Services [NASDAQ symbol] (TTSB)
PCIS............	PCI Services, Inc. [NASDAQ symbol] (SAG)
PCIS............	Period Cottage Improvement Society (BUAC)
PCIS............	Personal Computer Information Service (NITA)
PCIS............	Pinnacles Component Information Standard [Computer science] (AGLO)
PCIS............	Portable Common Interface Set (SAUS)
PCIS............	Post-Cardiac Injury Syndrome (MELL)
PCIS............	Primary Containment Isolation System [Nuclear energy] (NRCH)
PCIS............	Process Control Information System [Computer science] (VLIE)
PCIS............	Processed Commodities Inventory System [Department of Agriculture] (GFGA)
PCIS............	Production Control Information System (NVT)
PCIS............	Professional Career Information Service [Department of Labor]
PCIS............	Proposals and Contracts Information System (SAUS)
PCI Sv	PCI Services, Inc. [Associated Press] (SAG)
PCI/SWCI.....	Product Configuration Item/Software Configuration Item (SAUS)
PCITF..........	Positive Combat Identification Task Force (SAUS)
PCIU	Parts Controlled by Indentifiable Unit
PCIU	Parts Controlled by Indentifiable Unit (VLIE)
PCIU	Programmable Communications Interface Unit
PCIV............	Prestressed Cast Iron Vessel (SAUS)
PC/IX	Personal Computer / Interactive Executive (HGAA)
PCIYRA........	Pacific Coast Intercollegiate Yacht Racing Association

PCIZC..........	Permanent Committee of International Zoological Congresses (BUAC)
PCJ.............	Pax Christi Institute (TOCD)
PCJ.............	Peoples Jewellers Ltd. [Toronto Stock Exchange symbol]
PCJ.............	Petroleum Corporation of Jamaica (BUAC)
PCJ.............	Planning Commissioners Journal (SAUS)
PCJ.............	Pontifical College Josephinum, Worthington, OH [OCLC symbol] (OCLC)
PCJ.............	Pulsed Combustion Jet
PCJ.............	Sisters of the Poor Child Jesus [Roman Catholic religious order]
PCJC...........	Pakistan Central Jute Committee (BUAC)
PCJC...........	Parliamentary Criminal Justice Committee [Queensland, Australia]
PCJE...........	Program on Criminal Justice and the Elderly (DICI)
PCJILMCC	Philip C. Jessup International Law Moot Court Competition (EAIO)
PCjr............	Personal Computer-Junior (NITA)
PCJRI..........	Pakistan Central Jute Research Institute (SAUS)
PC Judg.......	Privy Council Judgments [India] [A publication] (DLA)
pck.............	Peacock [Philately]
PCK............	Peacock H.E. and Son (Thorney) Ltd. [British] [FAA designator] (FAAC)
PCK............	Peck (IAA)
PCK............	Pedagogical Content Knowledge
PCK............	Phase Control Keyboard
PCK............	Pilot Check (SAUS)
PCK............	Polycystic Kidney [Medicine] (DMAA)
PCK............	Porcupine Creek, AK [Location identifier] [FAA] (FAAL)
PCK............	Premarital Counseling Kit [Psychology]
PCK............	Primary Chicken Kidney [Cell line]
PCK............	Printed Circuit Keyboard
PCK............	Printed Control Keyboard [Computer science] (CIST)
PCK............	Processor Controlled Keying [Computer science] (DCTA)
PCKB	Phase Control Keyboard [Computer science] (VLIE)
PCKB	Printed Circuit Keyboard
PCKD	Polycystic Kidney Disease [Medicine]
PCKRR........	Pine Creek Railroad [An association] (EA)
PCKT..........	Printed Circuit [Computer science] (CIST)
PCL............	Alberta Attorney General, Provincial Court Libraries [UTLAS symbol]
PCI.............	Clarion Free Library, Clarion, PA [Library symbol] [Library of Congress] (LCLS)
PCL............	Confederation Centre Library, Charlottetown, Prince Edward Island [Library symbol] [National Library of Canada] (NLC)
PCL............	Pachaco Lake [California] [Seismograph station code, US Geological Survey] (SEIS)
PCL............	Pacific Coast League [Baseball]
PCL............	Pacific Coast Line (SAUS)
PCL............	Pallet Coolant Loop (NASA)
PCL............	Parallel Communications Link
PCL............	Parcel
PCL............	Paroxysmal Choreathetois Dystonia [Medicine]
PCL............	Partial Core Loading (SAUS)
PCL............	Parti Communiste de Luxembourg [Communist Party of Luxembourg] [Political party] (PPE)
PCL............	Parti Communiste Libanais [Lebanese Communist Party] [Political party] (PPW)
PCL............	Parts Complement List (ACAE)
PCL............	Passive Coherent Location (SEWL)
PCL............	Patch-Constrained Layer [Insulation]
PCL............	Pencil (MSA)
PCL............	Peoples College of Law (SAUS)
PCL............	Peripheral Control Line (SAUS)
PCL............	Permissible Contamination Limits [Nuclear energy] (NRCH)
PCL............	Persistent Corpus Luteum [Medicine]
PCL............	Personnel Security Clearance
P CI	Petrus Calvelli [Flourished, 14th century] [Authority cited in pre-1607 legal work] (DSA)
PCL............	Phase Correction Loop (SAUS)
PCL............	Philippine Cultural League [Australia]
PCL............	Phillips Cables Ltd. [Toronto Stock Exchange symbol]
PCL............	Photo Chemical Laboratories (SAUS)
PCL............	Pilot Controlled Lighting [Aviation] (FAAC)
PCL............	Planning and Conservation League (EA)
PCL............	Planning Configuration List
PCL............	Planning Consultancy Ltd. (NITA)
PCL............	Plasma Cell Leukemia [Oncology]
PCL............	Plasma Cholesterol Level (MELL)
PCL............	Playboy Club of London
PCL............	Plum Creek Timber Co., Inc. [NYSE symbol] (SPSG)
PCL............	Plum Creek Timber L.P. [NYSE symbol] (TTSB)
PCL............	Plutonium-Contaminated Liquid [Nuclear energy] (NUCP)
PCL............	Pocket Checklist (MCD)
PCL............	Police Crime Laboratory (SAUS)
PCL............	Polycaprolactone [Organic chemistry]
PCL............	[The] Polytechnic of Central London
PCL............	Pontifical Council for the Laity (BUAC)
PCL............	Portable Common Loops (SAUS)
PCL............	Positive Control Launch (CCCA)
PCL............	Positive Control Line
PCL............	Post Conference List
PCL............	Posterior Chamber Lens [Ophthalmology] (DAVI)
PCL............	Posterior Cruciate Ligament [Anatomy]
PCL............	PostScript and LASERJet-Type [LASER printer]
PCL............	Power Control Lever (DNAB)
PCL............	Power Control List (MCD)
PCL............	Power Conversion Loop (SAUS)
PCL............	Precancel (SAUS)

PCL............	Precancerous Lesion (MELL)
PCL............	Preliminary Change Letter [*Navy*] (NG)
PCL............	Premier Cruise Lines
PCL............	Prescribed Chemical Load (SAUS)
PCL............	Primary Coolant Line (NASA)
PCL............	Primary Coolant Loop (NASA)
PCL............	Primary Copy Locking (SAUS)
PCL............	Princess Cruise Line (TVEL)
PCL............	Print Control Language (NITA)
PCL............	Printed Circuit Lacquer (SAUS)
PCL............	Printed Circuit Lamp
PCL............	Printer Command Language [*Hewlett Packard*] [*Computer science*]
PCL............	Printer Control Language
PCL............	Priority Chemicals List (SAUS)
PCL............	Procedural Control Language [*1971*] [*Computer science*] (CSR)
PCL............	Process Capability Laboratory
PCL............	Process Communications Link (ECII)
PCL............	Process Control Laboratory (ABAC)
PCL............	Process Control Language [*Texas Instruments, Inc.*] [*Computer science*] (IAA)
PCL............	Prodedure Change List
PCL............	Product Computing Module Load (SAUS)
PCL............	Programmable Command Language [*Computer science*] (VLIE)
PCL............	Programming Checklist (MCD)
PCL............	Programming Control Language [*Computer science*] (PCM)
PCL............	Project Control Ledgers [*Navy*] (NG)
PCL............	Pseudocleistogamous [*Botany*]
PCL............	Pucallpa [*Peru*] [*Airport symbol*] (OAG)
PCL............	Pulse Compression Loop
PCL............	Punch Card Lever (SAUS)
PCL............	Purkinje Cell Layer [*Cytology*]
PCLA...........	Polish Canadian Librarians Association
PCLA...........	Power Control Linkage Assembly
PCLA...........	Process Control Language [*Texas Instruments, Inc.*]
PCLA...........	Project Coordination and Liaison Administration (OICC)
PCLC...........	Pest Control Licensing Committee [*New South Wales, Australia*]
PCLD..........	Dependent Political Entity [*Board on Geographic Names*]
PCLD..........	Polycystic Liver Disease (MELL)
PCLDI.........	Prototype Closed-Loop Development Installation [*Nuclear energy*] (NRCH)
PCLE..........	Pinnacle Systems [*NASDAQ symbol*] (TTSB)
PCLE..........	Pinnacle Systems, Inc. [*NASDAQ symbol*] (SAG)
PCLEAJ.......	Presidents Commission on Law Enforcement and the Administration of Justice (SAUS)
P-C Lens......	Perspective-Correction Lens (SAUS)
PCLFC........	Projected Consequences of Less Than Full Control (COE)
PCLG	Public Citizen Litigation Group (EA)
PCLI...........	Independent Political Entity [*Board on Geographic Names*]
PCLI...........	Parti de la Convergence pour les Libertes et l'Integration [*Burkina Faso*] [*Political party*] (EY)
PCLI...........	Plasma Cell Labeling Index [*Medicine*] (DMAA)
PC-LITE......	Processor, Laptop Imagery Transmission Equipment (DOMA)
PCLJ..........	Pacific Coast Law Journal [*A publication*] (DLA)
PCLK..........	Pay Clerk
PCLK..........	Program Clock [*Computer science*] (CIST)
PCLLG	Ollennu's Principles of Customary Land Law in Ghana [*A publication*] (DLA)
PCLLRC	Post-Colonial Literatures and Languages Centre [*Macquarie University*] [*Australia*]
PCLMP........	President's Advisory Committee on Labor-Management Policy [*Abolished, 1973*]
PCLN	Personalcomputer Literaturnachweis [*Datendienst Weiss*] [*Database*]
PCLN	Priceline.com
PCLN	priceline.com, Inc. [*NASDAQ symbol*] (SG)
PC-LNIM	Personal Computer Local Network Interface Module (TSSD)
PCLO	Passenger Control Liaison Office [*or Officer*] [*Army*] (AABC)
PCLO	Printed Circuit Layout (SAUS)
PCLP	PaperClip Imaging Software [*NASDAQ symbol*] (TTSB)
PCLP..........	Paperclip Imaging Software, Inc. [*NASDAQ symbol*] (SAG)
PCLP..........	Process Control Laboratory Procedures (TIMI)
PCLPW	Paperclip Imaging Softw'r Wrrt [*NASDAQ symbol*] (TTSB)
PCLR	Parallel Communications Link Receiver (NITA)
P Cl R	Parker's New York Criminal Reports [*A publication*] (DLA)
PCLR	PR [*Public Relations*] Committee for Licensing and Registration (EA)
P Cl R........	Privy Council Reports [*A publication*] (DLA)
PCL-R........	Psychopathy Checklist-Revised [*R. Hare*] (DIPS)
PCIS..........	Clarion State College, Clarion, PA [*Library symbol*] [*Library of Congress*] (LCLS)
PCLS..........	Law Society of Prince Edward Island, Charlottetown, Prince Edward Island [*Library symbol*] [*National Library of Canada*] (NLC)
PCLS..........	Passive Coherent Locating System (CCCA)
PCLS..........	People's Committee for Libyan Students (EA)
PCLS..........	Pressure-Compensated Load Sensing [*Hydraulics*]
PCLS..........	Prototype Closed-Loop System [*Nuclear energy*] (NRCH)
PCLST........	Polychlorstyrene [*Organic chemistry*]
PCLT..........	Portable Coded LASER Target
PCLT..........	Prototype Closed-Loop Test [*Nuclear energy*] (NRCH)
PCLTT........	Permanent Committee on Land Transportation and Telecommunications (SAUS)
PCLU	Pioneer Civil Labour Unit [*British*]
PClvU..........	Ursinus College, Collegeville, PA [*Library symbol*] [*Library of Congress*] (LCLS)
PCLW..........	Platinum Compensating Lead Wire (PDAA)
PCLX..........	Parallel Communications Link Transmitter (SAUS)
PCLX..........	Section of Independent Political Entity [*Board on Geographic Names*]
PCM............	Coastal Escort Medium [*200-500 tons*] [*Ship symbol*] (NATG)
PCM............	Pacific Comox Resources [*Vancouver Stock Exchange symbol*]
PCM............	Packet Compress when Matched bit in DCR2 (SAUS)
PCM............	Parabolic Collimator Mirror
PCM............	Paragraph Completion Method [*Education*] (EDAC)
PCM............	Parallel Calculating Mechanism (SAUS)
PCM............	Parallel Cutter Mechanism
PCM............	Parity Check Matrix (MCD)
PCM............	Parti Communiste Marocain [*Moroccan Communist Party*] [*Political party*]
PCM............	Parti Communiste Martiniquais [*Communist Party of Martinique*] [*Political party*] (PPW)
PCM............	Parti des Classes Moyennes [*Middle Class Party*] [*Luxembourg*] [*Political party*] (PPE)
PCM............	Partido Comunista Mexicano [*Mexican Communist Party*] [*Political party*] (PPW)
PCM............	Passive Countermeasure
PCM............	Patient Care Manager
PCM............	Patient Management Category (HCT)
PCM............	Peabody Conservatory of Music (SAUS)
PCM............	Penalty Cost Model
PCM............	Pending Contractual Matters (NRCH)
PCM............	Per Calendar Month [*Business term*] (ADA)
pcm	Per Calendar Month [*Business term*] (ODBW)
PCM............	Percentage of Completion Method (AAGC)
PCM............	Percentage of Moisture (SAUS)
PCM............	Percent Milli (NRCH)
PCM............	Peregrine Capital Myanmar
PCM............	Performance Capability Measure (IAA)
PCM............	Pericentriolar Material [*Biochemistry*]
PCM............	Peripheral Computer Manufacturer (SAUS)
PCM............	Personal Computer Manufacturer (SAUS)
PCM............	Personnel Contamination Monitor (SAUS)
PCM............	Phase Change Materials [*Solar energy*]
PCM............	Phase Comparison Monopulse (SAUS)
PCM............	Phase Conjugate Mirror
PCM............	Phase Contrast Microscopy
PCM............	Philippine Campaign Medal
PCM............	Photochemical Machining [*Desktop manufacturing*]
PCM............	Photoformed Ceramic Modules [*Du Pont process for making microconductors*]
PCM............	Physical Connection Management (SAUS)
PCM............	Piezo-Ceramic Material (SAUS)
PCM............	PIMCO Commercial Mortgage Security Trust [*NYSE symbol*] (SPSG)
PCM............	PIPES Buffer with Calcium and Magnesium
PCM............	Pitch Control Motor
PCM............	Planar Camping Model (SAUS)
PCM............	Planning and Control Memorandum [*Army*]
PCM............	Plasma Cell Myeloma [*Medicine*] (MELL)
PCM............	Plug Compatible Machine (SAUS)
PCM............	Plug Compatible Mainframe [*Computer science*]
PCM............	Plug Compatible Manufacturer [*Computer science*]
PCM............	Plug Compatible Memory
PCM............	Plug Compatible Module [*Computer science*] (IAA)
PCM............	Plug Control Module (SAUS)
PCM............	Plutonium Contaminated Material
PCM............	Pneumococcal Meningitis [*Medicine*] (MELL)
PCM............	Police Court Mission [*British*] (ROG)
PCM............	Polyimide Composite Material
PCM............	Polymer Coated Material (SAUS)
PCM............	Portable Conformable Mask [*Microlithography*]
PCM............	Port Command Area [*Telecommunications*] (TEL)
PCM............	Port Command Module (SAUS)
PCM............	Postal [*Service*] Contracting Manual [*A publication*] (AAGC)
PCM............	Post Column Method [*Chromatography*]
PCM............	Postgraduate Committee in Medicine [*Australia*]
PCM............	Postmammillary Caudal Magnocellular Nuclei [*Neuroanatomy*]
PCM............	Power Center Multiplexer (SAUS)
PCM............	Power Control Mission (NASA)
PCM............	Power Control Module (SAUS)
PCM............	Power-Cooling Mismatch [*Nuclear energy*]
PCM............	Powertrain Control Module [*Automotive engineering*]
PCM............	Precision Capacitor Microphone (SAUS)
PCM............	Precision Condenser Microphone
PCM............	President's Certificate of Merit [*Military decoration*] (AFM)
PCM............	Primary Care Manager (HCT)
PCM............	Primary Code Modulation [*Computer science*] (IAA)
PCM............	Printer Cartridge Metric (SAUS)
PCM............	Process Communication Monitor [*Telecommunications*] (IAA)
PCM............	Process Control Manual (SAUS)
PCM............	Process Control Module [*Telecommunications*] (TEL)
PCM............	Process Control Monitor (SAUS)
PCM............	Processor Communication Monitor (SAUS)
PCM............	Production Control Master (SAUS)
PCM............	Productive Cost Management (ADA)
PCM............	Profiling Current Meter [*Oceanography*] (MSC)
PCM............	Program Configuration Manager
PCM............	Program Continuity Memorandum [*Military*]
PCM............	Program Cost Management (MCD)
PCM............	Project Cost Model [*Project Software Ltd.*] [*Software package*] (NCC)
PCM............	Proposed Corrective Measures (SAUS)
PCM............	Protein-Calorie Malnutrition [*Medicine*]
PCM............	Protein-Carboxyl Methylase [*Biochemistry*] (DAVI)
PCM............	Pulse Code Modulation [*Telecommunications*] (OSI)
PCM............	Pulse Code Modulation Microwave [*System*]

PCM............ Pulse Code Modulator (NAKS)
PCM............ Pulse Compression Modulation (SEWL)
PCM............ Punch Card Machine [Computer science]
PCM............ Punched Card Method (SAUS)
PCM............ Pyrotechnic Countermeasure [Military] (SDI)
PCM............ WestAir Industries, Inc. [ICAO designator] (FAAC)
PCMA......... Paired Carrier Multiple Access (SAUS)
PCMA......... Pennsylvania Coal Mining Association (EA)
PCMA......... Personal Computer Management Association [Orange, CA] [Commercial firm] [Information service or system] (EA)
PCMA......... Phenylcyclopropanemethylamine [Organic chemistry]
PCMA......... Plaited Cordage Manufacturers Association [British] (BI)
PCMA......... Plasmacytoma (SAUS)
PCMA......... Plastic Crate Manufacturers Association (BUAC)
PCMA......... Post Card Manufacturers Association [Defunct] (EA)
PCMA......... Potato Chips Manufacturers Association (BUAC)
PCMA......... Power Cooling Mismatch Accident [Nuclear energy] (NUCP)
PCMA......... Precision Chain Manufacturers Association (BUAC)
PCMA......... Prince Edward Island Department of Municipal Affairs, Charlottetown, Prince Edward Island [Library symbol] [National Library of Canada] (NLC)
PCMA......... Professional Convention Management Association [Birmingham, AL] (EA)
PCMA......... Provincial Carters' and Motormen's Association [A union] [British]
PC Mag....... PC Magazine (SAUS)
PCMANSW... Precast Concrete Manufacturers' Association of New South Wales [Australia]
PCMAS ...... Portable Computer-Based Maintenance Aid System (ACAE)
PCMAS ...... Portable Computer-Based Maintenance System (SAUS)
PCMAV ...... Precast Concrete Manufacturers' Association of Victoria [Australia]
PCMB......... Para-Chloromercuribenzoate [Organic chemistry]
PCMB......... Parachloro-Mercuric Benzoic (SAUS)
PCMB......... P-Chloromercuribenzoate (SAUS)
PCMB......... P-Chloromercuribenzoic Acid (SAUS)
PCMB Acid... Parachloro-Mercury Benzoic Acid (SAUS)
PCMC......... Para-Chloro-meta-cresol [Organic chemistry]
PCMC......... PCI, Cache, Memory Controller (SAUS)
PCMC......... Pirmasens Communications and Electronics Maintenance Center
PCMC......... Postal [Service] Contracting Manual Circular (AAGC)
PCMC......... Preparatory Commission for Metric Conversion (SAUS)
PCMC......... Primary Children's Medical Center (STED)
PCMC......... Provided Chief of Mission Concurs [Army]
PCMCIA ...... People Can't Memorize Computer Industry Acronyms (PS)
PCMCIA ...... Personal Computer Memory Card International Association (PCM)
PCMCIA ...... Personal Computer Miniature Communications Interface Adapter [Computer science] (VLIE)
PCMCIA ...... Personal Comuter Memory Card Interface Adapter (DDC)
PCMCIA ...... Portable Computer Memory Card Industry Association (DOM)
PCMD .... Particle Count Monitoring Device (KSC)
PCMD .... Passive Count Monitoring Device (KSC)
PCMD .... Procurement and Contracts Management Division [Environmental Protection Agency] (GFGA)
PCMD .... Pulse Code Modulation, Digital
PCMDHS...... Pulse Code Modulation Data Handling System [Telecommunications] (IAA)
PCM-DHS .... Pulse Code Modulation-Data Handling System (SAUS)
PCMDI .... Program for Climate Model Diagnosis and Intercomparison [Department of Energy]
PCME.......... Pulse Code Modulation Event
PCMF.......... Perceptual Cognitive Motor Function (STED)
PCMF.......... Phi Chi Medical Fraternity (EA)
PCM-FM ...... Pulse Code Modulation-Frequency Modulation (SAUS)
PCM/FSK/AM... Pulse Code Modulation/Frequency Shift Keying/Amplitude Modulation (SAA)
PCMGS .... Pulse Code Modulated Ground Station
PCMH .... Para-Cresol Methylhydroxylase [An enzyme]
PCMH .... Postgraduate Center for Mental Health (EA)
PCMH .... Professional Certified in Materials Handling (SAUS)
PCMI........... Pellet Cladding Mechanical Interaction (SAUS)
PCMI........... Photo-Chemical Machining Institute (EA)
PCMI........... Photochromic Microimage [Microfiche]
PCMI........... Photochromic Microimage System (IAA)
PCMI........... Plastic Container Manufacturers Institute [Defunct] (EA)
PCMI........... President's Council on Management Improvement [Executive Office of the President] (GFGA)
PCMIA .... Personal Computer Manufacturer Interface Adapter (VLIE)
PCMIA .... Personal Computer Manufacturer Interface Adaptor
PCMIA .... Pittsburgh Coal Mining Institute of America (EA)
PCMIA .... Plasterers and Cement Masons International Association (SAUS)
PCMI Film ... Photo Chromic Micro Image Film (SAUS)
PCMIM........ Personal Computer Media Interface Module (SAUS)
PCMIP........ Pontifical Commission for Migrants and Itinerant Peoples [See also PCMT] [Vatican City, Vatican City State] (EAIO)
PCMI Process... Photo Chromic Micro Image Process (SAUS)
PCMI System... Photochromic Micro-Image System (SAUS)
PCMK......... Piece Mark
PC-ML .... Marxist-Leninist Communist Party [Bolivia] [Political party] (PPW)
PCML.......... Parti Communiste Marxiste-Leniniste [Marxist-Leninist Communist Party] [France] [Political party] (PPW)
PCML.......... Partito Comunista Marxista-Leninista [Marxist-Leninist Communist Party] [San Marino] [Political party] (PPE)
PCML.......... President's Committee on Migratory Labor [Terminated, 1964]
PCML.......... Pseudo Current Mode Logic (SAUS)

PCMLF........ Parti Communiste Marxiste-Leniniste Francais [French Marxist-Leninist Communist Party] [Dissolved, 1978] [Political party] (PPW)
PC(ML)I....... Partito Comunista (Marxista-Leninista) de Italia [Communist Party of Italy (Marxist-Leninist)] [Political party] (PPE)
PCMM......... Plug Compatible Mainframe Manufacturer (NITA)
PCMM......... Professional Certified in Materials Management (SAUS)
PCMMU ...... PCM [Punch Card Machine] Master Unit [Computer science] (GFGA)
PCMMU ...... Pulse Code Modulation Master Unit [Electronics] (NASA)
PCMNA .... Provisions for Carbon Monoxide Nonattainment Areas [Environmental science] (COE)
PCM/NRZ .... Pulse Code Modulation/Non-Return to Zero (SAUS)
PCMO .... Passenger Car Motor Oil
PCMO .... Principal Clinical Medical Officer [British]
PCMO .... Principal Colonial Medical Officer [British]
PCMOD ...... Personal Computer Modification Program
PC-MOS ..... Personal Computer-Modular Operating System (SAUS)
PCMP .... Packed Computational (IAA)
PCMP .... Pennsylvania Comprehensive Mathematics Plan (EDAC)
PCMP .... (Phenylcyclohexyl)methylpiperidine [Organic chemistry]
PCMP .... Post Chemical-Mechanical Polishing (AAEL)
PCMP .... Preliminary Configuration Management Plan (MCD)
PCMP .... Progressive Car Manufacturing Program (SAUS)
PCM/PAM .... Pulse Code Modulation/Pulse Amplitude Modulation (SAUS)
PCM/PL....... Pulse Code Modulated/Polarized Light (SAUS)
PCM-PM ...... Pulse Code Modulation-Phase Modulation (SAUS)
PCMPM ...... Pulse Code Modulation-Phase-Modulation (IAA)
PCMPN .... Pulse Code Modulation Pseudonoise [Telecommunications] (IAA)
PCM-PN ...... Pulse Code Modulation-Pseudo-Noise (SAUS)
PCMPS .... Para-Chloromercuriphenylsulfonic Acid [Organic chemistry]
PCM-PS ...... Pulse Code Modulation-Phase-Shift (SAUS)
PCMR .... Patient Computer Medical Record
PCMR .... Photochromic Microreproduction (DIT)
PCMR .... President's Committee on Mental Retardation [Washington, DC]
PCMR .... Probability of Correct Message Receipt (CCCA)
PCMS .... Pad-Circuit Minimum Spacing (SAUS)
PCMS .... Para-Chloromercuriphenyl Sulfonate [or Sulfonic Acid] [Organic chemistry]
PCMS .... Pattern Card Makers' Society [British] (BI)
PCMS .... P-Chloromercurphenylsulfonic Acid (SAUS)
PCMS .... P-Com, Inc. [NASDAQ symbol] (SAG)
PCMS .... Photographic Cabinet Makers' Society [A union] [British]
PCMS .... Plasma Chemistry Monte-Carlo Simulation (AAEL)
PCMS .... Plasma Chromatography Mass Spectroscopy
PCMS .... Process Control Management System (TIMI)
PCMS .... Production Control Monitoring System (NVT)
PCMS .... Project & Configuration Management System (SAUS)
PCMS .... Pulse Code Modulation Shared (MCD)
PCMS .... Punch Card Machine System [Computer science]
PCMSB .... Phased-Array Contiguous Multi-Spot Barrage (SEWL)
PCMSER ..... Presidents Commission on Marine Science, Engineering and Resources (SAUS)
PCMSIGNAL... Pulse Code Modulated Signal (SAUS)
PCMT .... Personal Computer Message Terminal (SAUS)
PCMT.......... Pontificia Commissione Migrazioni e Turismo [Pontifical Commission for Migrants and Itinerant Peoples - PCMIP] [Vatican City, Vatican City State] (EAIO)
PCMTE........ Pulse Code Modulation and Timing Electronics (SAUS)
PCMTE........ Pulse Code Modulation and Timing Equipment (KSC)
PCMTEA...... Pulse Code Modulation and Timing Electronics Assembly
PCMTS........ Pulse Code Modulation Telemetry System (AAG)
PCMU .... Physico-Chemical Measurements Unit [British]
PCMU .... Propellant Calibration Measuring Unit (KSC)
PCMV......... Plug Compatible Mainframe Vendor [Computer science] (VLIE)
PCMV......... Porcine Cerebral Microvascular [Cell line]
PCMX......... Para-Chloro-meta-xylenol [Organic chemistry]
PCMX......... P-Chlorodimethylphenol (SAUS)
PCN .... Pacific Communications Network [Air Force] (IAA)
PCN .... Package Control Number
PCN .... Page Change Notice (MCD)
PCN .... Pameco Corp'A' [NYSE symbol] (SG)
PCN .... PanCana Minerals [Toronto Stock Exchange symbol]
PCN .... Parent Country National (PDAA)
PCN .... Part Control Number (AAG)
PCN .... Partido Comunista de Nicaragua [Communist Party of Nicaragua] [Political party] (PD)
PCN .... Partido Conservador Nicaraguense [Nicaraguan Conservative Party] [Political party] (PPW)
PCN .... Partido de Conciliacion Nacional [National Reconciliation Party] [El Salvador] [Political party] (PPW)
PCN .... Parts Change Notice (MCD)
PCN .... Parts Control Number (SAUS)
PCN .... Pavement Classification Number [Aviation] (DA)
PCN .... Payroll Change Notice (GOBB)
PCN .... Penicillin [Antibiotic]
PCN .... Percutaneous Nephrostomy (DAVI)
PCN .... Permanent Control Number (MCD)
PCN .... Personal Communications Network [British]
PCN .... Personal Computer Network [Telecommunications]
PCN .... Personal Computer News (NITA)
PCN .... Personnel Change Notice (TIMI)
PCN .... Pharmaceutical Case Network (SAUS)
PCN .... Piacenza [Italy] [Seismograph station code, US Geological Survey] [Closed] (SEIS)
PCN .... Pitcairn Islands [ANSI three-letter standard code] (CNC)

PCN	Planning Change Notice
PCN	PointCast Network [*Internet news service*]
PCN	Point Comfort & Northern Railway Co. [*AAR code*]
PCN	Policy Criteria Notice [*Environmental Protection Agency*] (EPAT)
PCN	Polychlorinated Naphthalene [*Organic chemistry*]
PCN	Popcorn Noise (SAUS)
PCN	Position Control Number (AFM)
PCN	Post Christum Natum [*After the Birth of Christ*] [*Latin*] (ROG)
PCN	Potato Cyst Nematode [*Plant pathology*]
PCN	Pregnenolone Carbonitril [*Pharmacology*] (DAVI)
PCN	Prelaunch Channel Number [*NASA*] (IAA)
PCN	Primary Care Network [*Insurance*] (AMHC)
PCN	Primary Care Network [*Medical insurance*]
PCN	Primary Care Nurse (SAUS)
PCN	Primary Care Nursing
PCN	Princeton Aviation Corp. [*ICAO designator*] (FAAC)
PCN	Printed Control Number (SAUS)
PCN	Procedure Change Notice
PCN	Process Change Notice (VLIE)
PCN	Processing Control Number
PCN	Procurement Control Number (AFM)
PCN	Product Control Number (AFM)
PCN	Production Change Number (KSC)
PCN	Production Control Number (SAUS)
PCN	Program Change Notice (MCD)
PCN	Program Change Number (SAUS)
PCN	Program Composition Notation [*Computer science*]
PCN	Program Control Number (AFM)
PCN	Project Control Number (AAG)
PCN	Proposal Control Number (AAG)
PCN	Publication Change Notice (MCD)
PCN	Publication Code Number (SAUS)
PCN	Public Communications Network (SAUS)
PCN	Public Convenience and Necessity [*Department of Transportation*]
PCN	Pulse Compression Network
PCNA	Palestine Congress of North America [*Defunct*] (EA)
PCNA	P-Chloro-0-Nitroaniline (SAUS)
PCNA	Porsche Cars North America, Inc.
PCNA	Proliferating Cell Nuclear Antigen [*Cytology, immunology*]
PCNA	Publishing Co. of North America, Inc. (The) [*NASDAQ symbol*] (SAG)
PCNAC	Professionals Coalition for Nuclear Arms Control (EA)
PCNB	Pentachloronitrobenzene [*Agricultural fungicide*]
PCNB	Permanent Control Narcotics Board
PCNC	Projected Consequences of No Control [*Environmental science*] (COE)
PCNE	Protocol Converter for Native Equipment [*Telecommunications*] (IAA)
PCNET	Personal Computer Network
PCNF	Pacific Central NOTAM [*Notice to Airmen*] Facility [*Military*]
PCN(Fr.)	Physics, Chemistry & Natural Science-France (CMD)
PCNFS	Personal Computer Network File System (VLIE)
PCNG	Presidents Commission on National Goals (SAUS)
PCNI	Physician Computer Network [*NASDAQ symbol*] (SPSG)
PCNI	Physician Computer Ntwk [*NASDAQ symbol*] (TTSB)
PCNI	Physicians Computer Network [*NASDAQ symbol*] (SAG)
PCNM	Polymer-Immobilised Clusters of the Noble Metals [*Catalytic chemistry*]
PCNP	Personal Computer Network Program (HGAA)
PCNR	Part Control Number Request (AAG)
PCNR	Planning Change Notice Request
PCNS	Polar Coordinates Navigation System
PCNSL	Polymerised Cashew Nut Shell Liquid (PDAA)
PCNV	Postchemotherapy Nausea and Vomiting [*Medicine*] (MELL)
PCNV	Provisional Committee on Nomenclature of Viruses (DAVI)
PCNY	Proofreaders Club of New York (EA)
P$_{co}$	Carbon Monoxide Tension (DAVI)
PCO	Conococheague District Library, Chambersburg, PA [*OCLC symbol*] (OCLC)
PCO	Pacific Chamber Opera (SAUS)
PCO	Pacific Coastal Airline [*Canada*] [*ICAO designator*] (FAAC)
PCO	Parcel Concentration Office [*British*]
PCO	Parent Company (SAUS)
PCO	Parliamentary Counsel's Office [*Australia*]
PCO	Passport Control Office [*British*]
PCO	Patient Complains Of [*Medicine*]
PCO	Peacetime Contingency Operation [*Army*] (ADDR)
PCO	Peak Conservation Organization (SAUS)
PCO	Peg Count and Overflow (SAUS)
PCO	Pest Control Officer (SAUS)
PCO	Pest Control Operator
PCO	Philadelphia College of Osteopathy [*Pennsylvania*]
PCO	Phoenix Canada Oil Co. Ltd. [*Toronto Stock Exchange symbol*]
PCO	Photocatalytic Oxidation (AAEL)
PCO	Photosynthetic Carbon Oxidation [*Plant metabolism*]
PCO	Picture Control Oscilloscope (IAA)
PCO	Pittston Co. (EFIS)
PCO	Placement Contracting Officer [*Army*] (AABC)
PCO	Plant Clearance Officer [*DoD*]
PCO	Plant Clearance Order
PCO	Plant Control Office (SAUS)
PCO	Playcore, Inc. [*AMEX symbol*] [*Formerly, Swing-N-Slide Corp.*]
PCO	Point of Control and Observation [*Telecommunications*] (OSI)
PCO	Polar Cap Observatory (SAUS)
PCO	Police Commissioner's Office
PCO	Polycarbonate (EDCT)
PCO	Polycystic Ovary [*Gynecology*]

PCO	Ponca City [*Oklahoma*] [*Seismograph station code, US Geological Survey*] (SEIS)
PCO	Port Communications Office (SAUS)
PCO	Port Convey Officer (SAUS)
PCO	Post Central Office (SAUS)
PCO	Post Checkout
PCO	Postcheckout Operations
PCO	Potassium Channel Opener [*Vasodilator*]
PCO	Predicted Cardia Output [*Medicine*] (DMAA)
PCO	Primary Communications-Oriented (IAA)
PCO	Primary Contracting Officer (MCD)
PCO	Prime Contracting Officer (SAA)
PCO	Prince Consort's Own [*Military unit*] [*British*]
PCO	Principal Careers Officer (AIE)
PCO	Principal Coast Officer [*Customs*] [*British*] (ROG)
PCO	Principal Conservation Officer (SAUS)
PCO	Principal Contracting Officer [*Air Force*]
PCO	Printer Control Option (SAA)
PCO	Printing Control Officer [*Air Force*] (AFM)
PCO	Prison Custody Officer (WDAA)
PCO	Privy Council Office [*British*]
PCO	Proceedings of the Congress of Orientalists (SAUS)
PCO	Process Change Order (VLIE)
PCO	Procurement Change Order (MCD)
PCO	Procurement Contracting Officer (AAGC)
PCO	Procuring Contracting Office [*or Officer*] [*Military*]
PCO	Procuring Contrast Offer
PCO	Procuring Contrast Officer (SAUS)
PCO	Procytoxid (STED)
PCO	Professional Conference Organizer
PCO	Professional Congress Organizer (TVEL)
PCO	Program Change Order [*Computer science*] (ELAL)
PCO	Program Comparator
PCO	Program Contracting Officer (SAUS)
PCO	Program-Controlled Output (NASA)
PCO	Program Control Output
PCO	Program Coordination Office (AAG)
PCO	Program Counterpart Office
PCO	Project Control Office (MCD)
PCO	Property Control Office [*of Allied Military Government*] [*Post-World War II*]
PCO	Proposed Change Order (AFIT)
PCO	Prospective Commanding Officer [*Navy*]
PCO	Provisioning Contracting Officer [*Military*] (AFIT)
PCO	Publications Control Officer [*DoD*]
PCO	Public Call Office (DAS)
PCO	Public Communications Office
PCO	Punched Card Order (SAUS)
PCO	Punched Card Output (SAUS)
PCO	Purchase Change Order (MCD)
PCO	Purchasing and Contracting Officer (SAUS)
P/CO	Purser/Catering Officer (SAUS)
PCO$_2$	Carbon Dioxide Tension [*in blood gases*] (DAVI)
pCO$_2$	Partial Pressure of Carbon Dioxide (AAMN)
pCO$_2$	Pressure of Carbon Dioxide (HGAA)
PCoA	Principal Co-Ordinates Analysis
PCO/ACO	Procuring Contracting Officer/Administrative Contracting Officer
PCOAS	Permanent Council of the Organization of American States
P Coast LJ ..	Pacific Coast Law Journal [*A publication*] (DLA)
PCOB	Permanent Central Opium Board [*United Nations*] (BUAC)
PCOB(UN)	Permanent Central Opium Board (United Nations)
PCOC	Partit Comunista Obrero de Catalunya [*Communist Workers' Party of Catalonia*] [*Political party*] (PPW)
PCOC	Primary Care Organization Consortium [*Health insurance*] (DMAA)
PCOCA	Parti-Colour Oriental Cat Association (BUAC)
PCOD	Permanent Change of Duty [*Navy*] (DNAB)
PCOD	Polycystic Ovarian Disease [*Medicine*]
P-Code	Precision Code (SEWL)
P-CODE	Program Code [*Computer science*] (AGLO)
PCOE	Partido Comunista Obrero de Espana [*Communist Workers' Party of Spain*] [*Political party*] (PPW)
PCOF	Probable Cause of Failure (MCD)
PC of E	Presbyterian Church of England
PCOFT	Patriot Conduct of Fire Trainer (SAUS)
P-COFT	Platoon COFT (SAUS)
PCOGA	Pacific Coast Oyster Growers Association (EA)
PCOI	Preconstruction Operating Instruction [*Environmental Protection Agency*]
PCOIT	Putnam Convertible Opportunities & Income Trust [*Associated Press*] (SAG)
PCOL	Procuring Contracting Officer Letter (ACAE)
PCOL	Protocol Systems [*NASDAQ symbol*] (TTSB)
PCOL	Protocol Systems, Inc. [*NASDAQ symbol*] (SAG)
PCOLA	Pulse-Coded Optical Landing Aid [*Aviation*] (PDAA)
PCOM	Parallel Character Output Module (SAUS)
P-Com	P-Com, Inc. [*Associated Press*] (SAG)
PCOM	Philadelphia College of Osteopathic Medicine
PCOM	Photocomm, Inc. [*NASDAQ symbol*] (NQ)
PCOM	Planning Committee (SAUS)
PCOM	Posterior Communicating [*Artery*] [*Medicine*] (DMAA)
PCOMP	Packet Compression Pin (SAUS)
PCON	Para-Chloro-ortho-nitroaniline [*Also, PCONA*] [*Organic chemistry*]
PCON	Personnel Continuity
PCON	Platelet Concentration [*hematology*] (DAVI)
PCON	Potential Contractor (COE)

PCON	Primary Care Optometry News [*A publication*] (ADWA)
PCON	Primary Care Organization Network [*Health insurance*] (DMAA)
PCONA	Para-Chloro-ortho-nitroaniline [*Also, PCON*] [*Organic chemistry*]
PCONNECT	Presentation Connect (VLIE)
P Contr LJ	Public Contract Law Journal [*A publication*] (AAGC)
PCOOS	Pacific Coast Oto Ophthalmological Society (SAUS)
PCOP	Pharmacopeia Inc. [*NASDAQ symbol*] (TTSB)
PCOP	Port Charges Operator (DNAB)
PCOP	Port Charges Paid by Commercial Operator (DNAB)
PCOP	President's Commission on Obscenity and Pornography (DGA)
PCOPF	President's Council on Physical Fitness [*Later, PCPFS*] (KSC)
PCOR	pcOrder.com, Inc.'A' [*NASDAQ symbol*] (SG)
PCOR	Pressure Compensator Over-Ride (PDAA)
PCOR	Profit Commission on Renewal [*Insurance*] (AIA)
PCOR	PSICOR, Inc. [*NASDAQ symbol*] (NQ)
PCOR	Purchase Change Order Request
PCoR	Robert Morris College, Coraopolis, PA [*Library symbol*] [*Library of Congress*] (LCLS)
PCORN	Perpetual Convertible or Redeemable Note [*Economics*]
PCOS	Polycystic Ovarian Syndrome [*Also, POS*] [*Gynecology*]
PCOS	Primary Communication Operating System (SAUS)
PCOS	Primary Communications-Oriented System (IEEE)
PCOS	Process Control Operating System
PCOS	Production Control Operating System (SAUS)
PCOS	Project Concern's Options Service (EA)
PCOS	Punched Card Oriented System (SAUS)
P-COSWA	Pugwash Conferences on Science and World Affairs
PCOT	Payload Center Operations Team [*NASA*] (MCD)
PCOTES	Prototype Carrier Operational Test and Evaluation Site [*Military*] (CAAL)
PCOUNT	Parameter Count [*Computer science*]
PCOV	Precombustor Oxidizer Valve (KSC)
P(COV)	Probability of No Covariate Effect [*Statistics*]
PCOYO	President's Council on Youth Opportunity [*Defunct*] (EA)
PCP	Centre for Personal Construct Psychology [*British*] (CB)
PCP	Packet Control Panel (SAUS)
PCP	Packet Control Process (SAUS)
PCP	Paired Cone Pigments [*Vision physiology*]
PCP	Palestinian Communist Party [*Political party*] (PD)
PCP	PanCanadian Petroleum [*TS, Exchange Symbol*] (TTSB)
PCP	PanCanadian Petroleum Ltd. [*Toronto Stock Exchange symbol*] [*Vancouver Stock Exchange symbol*]
PCP	Para-Chlorophenol [*Organic chemistry*]
PCP	Paraguayan Communist Party
PCP	Parallel Cascade Processor (IEEE)
PCP	Parallel Circular Plate (IEEE)
PCP	Parker Consultant Panel (SAUS)
PCP	Parliamentary Conservative Party [*British*] (BARN)
PCP	Partial Cleft Palate (MELL)
PCP	Partido Comunista Paraguayano [*Paraguayan Communist Party*] [*Political party*] (PD)
PCP	Partido Comunista Peruano [*Peruvian Communist Party*] [*Political party*] (PPW)
PCP	Partido Comunista Portugues [*Portuguese Communist Party*] [*Political party*] (PPE)
PCP	Partido Comunista Puertorriqueno [*Puerto Rican Communist Party*] [*Political party*] (PPW)
PCP	Passenger Control Point [*Army*] (AABC)
PCP	Past Chief Patriarch [*Freemasonry*]
PCP	Patient Care Publications
PCP	Payload Control Processor [*NASA*]
PCP	Peace Corps Physician
PCP	PeaCe Pill [*Slang for Phencyclidine*] (DIPS)
PCP	Peking Central Philharmonic (SAUS)
PCP	Pentachlorophenate [*A topical antibacterial*] (DAVI)
PCP	Pentachlorophenol [*Wood preservative*] [*Organic chemistry*]
PCP	Pentachlorophenyl (SAUS)
PCP	Pentachlorophenol (SAUS)
PCP	Peptidyl Carrier Protein [*Biochemistry*]
PCP	Pericardial Pressure [*Medicine*] (MELL)
PCP	Pericyclic Process (SAUS)
PCP	Peridinin-Chlorophyll-Protein [*Botany*]
PCP	Peripheral Circumflex Pressure (SAUS)
PCP	Peripheral Control Program
PCP	Peripheral Control Pulse [*Computer science*]
PCP	Peripheral Coronary Pressure [*Cardiology*] (AAMN)
PCP	Personal Communications Programme [*British*]
PCP	Personal Credit Plan (SAUS)
PCP	Personnel Control Point (SAUS)
PCP	Peter Collins Publishing [*British*]
PCP	Phencyclidine (NTIO)
PCP	Phencyclidine Hydrochloride [*Medicine*] (AMHC)
PCP	Phencyclidine Palmitate [*Organic chemistry*] (DAVI)
PCP	(Phenylcyclohexyl)piperidine [*or Phencyclidine*] [*Anesthetic*] [*A street drug*]
PCP	Philadelphia College of Pharmacy and Science, Philadelphia, PA [*OCLC symbol*] (OCLC)
PCP	Phosphor Coated Paper
PCP	Photochemical Processing (SAUS)
PCP	Photon-Coupled Pair (IEEE)
PCP	Picture Check Print (SAUS)
PCP	Pilot Control Panel
PCP	Planar Combat Problem
PCP	Plant Control Plan (SAUS)
PCP	Plasma Cell Pneumonia [*Medicine*] (MELL)

PCP	Plastic Clad Plastic [*Materials science*]
PCP	Platoon Command Post [*Military*] (RDA)
PCP	Plug Compatible Peripheral [*Computer science*] (EECA)
PCP	Pneumatics Control Panel (AAG)
PCP	Pneumocystic Pneumonia [*Medicine*] (DAVI)
PCP	Pneumocystis Carinii Pneumonia [*Microbiology*]
PCP	Polaroid Color Pack Camera
PCP	Polychloroprene [*Organic chemistry*]
PCP	Poorly Characterized Phase [*Mineralogy*]
PCP	Portable Code Processor
PCP	Port Call Processing (SAUS)
PCP	Portuguese Communist Party
PCP	Post-Construction Permit [*Nuclear energy*] (NRCH)
PCP	Posted County Price [*Agriculture*]
PCP	Postgraduate Center for Psychotherapy [*Later, Postgraduate Center for Mental Health*] (EA)
PCP	Potential Contractor Program (MCD)
PCP	Power Control Panel [*Aerospace*] (AAG)
PCP	Preassembled Cable in Pipe
PCP	Precision Castparts [*NYSE symbol*] (TTSB)
PCP	Precision Castparts Corp. [*NYSE symbol*] (SPSG)
PCP	Preliminary Cost Proposal (MCD)
PCP	Pressurization Control Panel [*NASA*] (KSC)
PCP	Primary Care Physician
PCP	Primary Care Provider (SAUS)
PCP	Primary Command Point [*Military*] (CAAL)
PCP	Primary Control Program [*Computer science*]
PCP	Primary Coolant Pump [*Nuclear energy*] (NRCH)
PCP	Primary Cross-Connection Point (NITA)
PCP	Principal Care Provider [*For a patient*] (DAVI)
PCP	Printed Circuit Patchboard
PCP	Printing Card Punch (SAUS)
P(CP)	Process Control Package (SAUS)
PCP	Process Control Plan (SAUS)
PCP	Process Control Processor (IEEE)
PCP	Process Control Program [*Nuclear energy*] (NRCH)
PCP	Processor Control Panel
PCP	Processor Control Program
PCP	Procollagen Peptide (DB)
PCP	Product Change Proposal (MCD)
PCP	Product Chassis Package
PCP	Production Change Point
PCP	Program Change Package (SAUS)
PCP	Program Change Procedure
PCP	Program Control Plan (AAG)
PCP	Program Control Procedure [*Nuclear energy*] (NRCH)
PCP	Program Control Program (SAUS)
PCP	Programmable Circuit Process (SAUS)
PCP	Programmable Circuit Processor (SAUS)
PCP	Programmable Communication Processor
PCP	Progressive Conservative Party [*Canada*] [*Political party*] (PPW)
PCP	Progressive Conservative Party [*Australia*] [*Political party*]
PCP	Progressive Constitutionalist Party [*Malta*] [*Political party*] (PPE)
PCP	Progressive Constitutional Party [*Malta*] [*Political party*] (BUAC)
PCP	Project Change Proposal (NAKS)
PCP	Project Control Plan (IEEE)
PCP	Project Cost Plan (NASA)
PCP	Prototype Communications Processor
PCP	Psilcybin [*Medicine*] (MEDA)
PCP	Pulmonary Capillary Pressure [*Medicine*] (CPH)
PCP	Pulse Comparator
PCP	Pulse Cytophotometry [*Hematology*]
PCP	Pump Cavitation Pressure [*Automotive engineering*]
PCP	Punch Card Programming (SAUS)
PCP	Punch Control Panel (SAUS)
PCP	Punched Card Perforator (SAUS)
PCP	Punched Card Processing (SAUS)
PCP	Punched Card Programming (SAUS)
PCP	Punched Card Punch [*Computer science*] (IEEE)
PcP	Reflected P Wave [*Earthquakes*]
PCPA	Pacific Conservatory of the Performing Arts
PCPA	Panama Canal Pilots Association (SAUS)
PCPA	Panel of Consultants for the Performing Arts [*of CFC*]
PCPA	Para-Chlorophenoxyacetic Acid [*Organic chemistry*]
PCPA	Para-Chlorophenylacetic Acid [*Organic chemistry*]
PCPA	Parachlorophenylalanin (SAUS)
PCPA	Para-Chlorophenylalanine [*Biochemistry*]
PCPA	P-Chlorophenylacetic Acid (SAUS)
PCPA	P-Chlorophenylalanine (SAUS)
PCPA	Philadelphia College of the Performing Arts (SAUS)
PCPA	Plan for Congressional and Public Affairs
PCPA	Poor Clares of Perpetual Adoration [*Roman Catholic women's religious order*]
PC/PA	Process Control/Product Acceptance (SAUS)
PCPA	Protestant Church-Owned Publishers Association (EA)
PCPAC	Parker-Coltrane Political Action Committee [*Defunct*] (EA)
PCPAV	Pensioners-Combined Pensioners Association of Victoria [*Australia*]
PCPB	P-Chlorophenylbenzene
PCPBMA	Pacific Coast Paper Box Manufacturers' Association (EA)
PCPBS	Para-Chlorophenyl-Benzenesulphonate (SAUS)
PCPBS	P-Chlorophenylbenzenesulfonate (SAUS)
PCPC	Personal Computers Peripheral Corp. (SAUS)
PCPC	Power Conversion Products Council [*Later, PCPCI*] (EA)
PCPC	Principal Conical Polar Curve (SAUS)
PCPCA	Pairpoint Cup Plate Collectors of America (EA)

PCPCI	Power Conversion Products Council International (EA)
PCPCN	Part Card Procurement Change Notice (KSC)
PCPCU	Pontifical Council for Promoting Christian Unity (BUAC)
PCPD	Portland Commission of Public Docks (SAUS)
PCPE	Partido Comunista de los Pueblos de Espana [Communist Party of the Peoples of Spain] [Political party] (EY)
PCPEA	Pennsylvania Cooperative Program in Educational Administration (SAUS)
PC Perspect Newsl	PC Perspectives Newsletter (SAUS)
PC/PET	Polycarbonate/Polyethylene Terephthalate (SAUS)
PCPF	Percutaneous Pin Fixation [Medicine] (MELL)
PCPF	President's Council on Physical Fitness [Later, PCPFS]
PCPFS	President's Council on Physical Fitness and Sports (EGAO)
PCPG	Primary Clock Pulse Generator
PCPhS	Proceedings of the Cambridge Philological Society (SAUS)
PCPI	Parent Cooperative Pre-Schools International (EA)
PCPI	Permanent Committee on Patent Information [World Intellectual Property Organization] [Information service or system] (IID)
PCPI	President's Commission on Personnel Interchange [Later, President's Commission on Executive Exchange]
P-CPIB Acid	P-2,4-dichlorophenoxyisobutyric Acid (SAUS)
PCPJ	Peoples Coalition for Peace and Justice [Defunct]
PCPL	Government Services Library, Charlottetown, Prince Edward Island [Library symbol] [National Library of Canada] (NLC)
PCPL	Pentachlorophenyl Laurate (SAUS)
PCPL	Planning Library, Charlottetown, Prince Edward Island [Library symbol] [National Library of Canada] (NLC)
PCPL	Production Control Priority List (MCD)
PCPL	Proposed Change Point Line [NASA] (KSC)
PCPL	Pulmonary Capillary Protein Leakage [Medicine] (DMAA)
PCPM	Per Contract per Month
PCPM	PERT [Program Evaluation and Review Technique] Cost Performance Measurement
PCPM	Program Control Procedures Manual (SAUS)
PCP M-L	Partido Comunista de Portugal, Marxista-Leninista [Marxist-Leninist Communist Party of Portugal] [Political party] (PPE)
pcpn	Precipitation (DAVI)
PCPP	(Para-Chlorophenoxy)propionic Acid [Organic chemistry]
PCPP	Parts Control Program Plan (SAUS)
PCPP	Peace Corps Partnership Program (EA)
PCPP	Presidents Commission on Pension Policy (SAUS)
PCPP	Printing Card Proof Punch (SAUS)
PCPS	Percutaneously-Introduced Cardiopulmonary Support System [Medicine]
PCPS	Philadelphia College of Pharmacy and Science [Pennsylvania]
PCPS	Pool Cooling and Purification System [Nuclear energy] (NRCH)
PCPS	Portable Collective Protection Shelter (ACAE)
PCPS	Private Carrier Paging System (SAUS)
PCPS	Private Companies Practice Section
PCPS	Proceedings of the Cambridge Philological Society [A publication] (OCD)
PCPS	Prodat Communication and Processing System (SAUS)
PCPS	Program Change Package (IAA)
PCPS	Pulse-Coded Processing System
PCPS	Pulverized-Coal Power System [Environmental science] (COE)
PCPT	Para-Chlorophenylthio [Organic chemistry]
PCPT	Perception
PCPT	Physical Combat Proficiency Test [Army]
PCPT	Post Conference Provisioning Tape (MCD)
PCPT	Prostate Cancer Prevention Trial [Medicine]
PCPV	Partido Comunista del Pais Valenciano [Spain] [Political party] (EY)
PCPV	Point-Contact Photo-Voltaic [Solar cells]
PCPV	Prestressed Concrete Pressure Vessel
PCQ	Pacificorp [NYSE symbol] (SAG)
PCQ	PacifiCorp 8.375% 'QUIDS' [NYSE symbol] (TTSB)
PCQ	Personal Control Questionnaire (SAUS)
PCQ	Production Control Quantometer
PCQ	Productivity Criteria Quotient
PCQ	Professional Capabilities Questionnaire [Jet Propulsion Laboratory, NASA]
PCQ	Yuma, AZ [Location identifier] [FAA] (FAAL)
PCQEH	Queen Elizabeth Hospital, Charlottetown, Prince Edward Island [Library symbol] [National Library of Canada] (NLC)
PCQT	Paper-Core Quad Trunk (PDAA)
PCQT	Personal Computer Query Tool [Military software package] (INF)
PC Quote	PC Quote, Inc. [Associated Press] (SAG)
PCR	Pacific Amber Resources [VS, Exchange Symbol] (TTSB)
PCR	Page Control Register
PCR	Parker's Criminal Reports [New York] [A publication] (DLA)
PCR	Partial Carriage Return (IAA)
PCR	Partially Coherent Receiver (SAUS)
PCR	Parti Communiste Reunionnais [Communist Party of Reunion] [Political party] (PPW)
PCR	Partido Comunista Revolucionario [Revolutionary Communist Party] [Peru] [Political party] (PPW)
PCR	Partidul Comunist Roman [Romanian Communist Party] [Political party] (PPE)
PCR	Pass Card Reader [Telecommunications] (TEL)
PCR	Patient Charge Ratio
PCR	Patient Contact Record [Medicine] (DMAA)
PCR	Payload Certification Review (SSD)
PCR	Payload Changeout Room [NASA] (NASA)
PCR	Payload Checkout Room [NASA] (NASA)
P Cr	Paymaster-Commander [Navy] [British] (DMA)
PCR	PC Resource [A publication]

PCR	Peak Cell Rate (MLOA)
PCR	Pearson Aviation Corp. [ICAO designator] (FAAC)
PCR	Pedestrian Crossings Regulations (SAUS)
PCR	Peer Code Review (IAA)
PCR	Peninsular Chemresearch [Calgon Corp.]
PCR	Pennsylvania Corp. Reporter [A publication] (DLA)
PCR	Pennsylvania County Court Reports [A publication] (DLA)
PCR	Per Call Rate [Telecommunications] (IAA)
PCR	Perini Corp. [AMEX symbol] (SPSG)
PCR	Period Contract Request
PCR	Periodic Current Reversal [Electrochemistry]
PCR	Peripheral Control Routine (CMD)
PCR	Personal Care Residence (DAVI)
PCR	Personal Communications Report [FutureComm Publications, Inc.] [Information service or system] [Defunct] (CRD)
PCR	Phase Change Recording (SAUS)
PCR	Phase Controlled Rectifier (SAUS)
PCr	Phosphocreatine [Also, CP, PC] [Biochemistry]
PCR	Photoconductive Relay (IEEE)
PCR	Photoconductive Resonance [Physics]
PCR	Photosynthetic Carbon Reduction [Plant metabolism]
PCR	Physician Contingency Reserve
PCR	Pickled and Cold Rolled (SAUS)
PCR	Pilot Chute Controlled (SAUS)
PCR	Pine Creek Railroad [An association] (EA)
PCR	Planned Component Replacement [Predictive maintenance schedule]
PCR	Planning Change [or Check] Request (AAG)
PCR	Planning Check Request (SAUS)
PCR	Plant Control Room [Nuclear energy] (IAA)
PCR	Plasma Clearance Rate [Medicine] (DMAA)
Pcr	Plasma Creatinine (DAVI)
PCR	Pneumatic Checkout Rack (KSC)
PCR	Pneumatic Control Regulator (KSC)
PCR	Polar Cap Radar (SAUS)
PCR	Pollution Control Report [Navy]
PCR	Pollution Control Revenue
PCR	Polychromatic Color Removal [Printing technology]
PCR	Polymerase Chain Reaction [Genetics]
PCR	Polymerase Chain Technology (SAUS)
PCR	Population Census Report (OICC)
PCR	Positive Control Route [Aviation] (OA)
PCR	Post-Column Reaction (SAUS)
PCR	Post-Compression Remodeling [Medicine] (DMAA)
PCR	Post-Consumer Recyclate (SAUS)
PCR	Post-Consumer Recycle [or Reclaim] [Plastics industry]
PCR	Post-Consumer Resin [Plastic recycling]
PCR	Postconviction Remedy
PCR	Postinfarction Cardiac Rehabilitation [Medicine] (MELL)
PCR	Powell Cycle Registry (EA)
PCR	Power Change Request [NASA] (NASA)
PCR	Power Control Register
PCR	Power Control Room [Nuclear energy] (IAA)
PCR	Power Conversion Room
PCR	Precision Control Relay (SAUS)
PCR	Pressure Check Range
PCR	Prestressed Ceramic RADOME
PCR	Preventative Cyclic Retransmission [Telecommunications] (TEL)
PCR	Primary Chemotherapy-Radiotherapy [Oncology]
PCR	Primary Control Rod (SAUS)
PCR	Primary Cosmic Radiation
PCR	Principal Components Regression
PCR	Principle Component Regression (SAUS)
PCR	Print-Command Register
PCR	Print Contrast Ratio (TIMI)
PCR	Probable Causal Relationship [Medicine] (MEDA)
PCR	Problem/Change Report (SAUS)
PCR	Procedure Change Request [NASA]
PCR	Procedure Comment Record (SAUS)
PCR	Process Control Rack (SAUS)
PCR	Processor Configuration Register (SAUS)
PCR	Procurement Center Representative [Small Business Administration]
PCR	Product Change Request (SAUS)
PCR	Production & Casting Report (WDAA)
PCR	Production Capability Review [Army]
PCR	Production Change Request (MCD)
PCR	Production Control Record [NASA] (KSC)
PCR	Program Change Request [DoD]
PCR	Program Clock Reference (SAUS)
PCR	Program-Controlled Request (SAUS)
PCR	Program Control Register
PCR	Program Control Report
PCR	Program Control Room (ACAE)
PCR	Program Counter [Computer science] (IAA)
PCR	Program Counter Register
PCR	Programmer in Charge of Records [Computer science] (IAA)
PCR	Program to Combat Racism [British] (DI)
PCR	Progress Curve Report
PCR	Project Control Room [NASA] (NASA)
PCR	Project Cost Record [or Report] [NASA] (KSC)
PCR	Project Cost Report (SAUS)
PCR	Projected Communications Requirement (SAUS)
PCR	Project on Corporate Responsibility (EA)
PCR	Protein Catabolic Rate [Biochemistry] (DAVI)
PCR	Proven Commercial Registration [Advertising] (WDMC)
PCR	Publication Change Request (MCD)

PCR	Publication Contract Requirements
PCR	Puerto Carreno [Colombia] [Airport symbol] (OAG)
PCR	Pulse Compression RADAR
PCR	Pulse Compression Ratio (ACAE)
PCR	Punch Card Register (SAUS)
PCR	Punched Card Reader [Computer science] (BUR)
PCR	Punched Card Request
PCR	Punched Card Requisition [Computer science] (MCD)
PCR	Put Control Read (SAUS)
PCRA	Phantom Class Racing Association (EA)
PCRA	Poland China Record Association (EA)
PCRAM	Page Composition Random Access Memory (NITA)
PCR & A	Picked Cold, Rolled, and Annealed [Metallurgy] (ROG)
PCR&DC	Pomona Colleges Research and Development Center (SAUS)
PCRAP	Personal Computer Response Analysis Program
PCRB	Personnel and Control Room Building [Nuclear energy] (NRCH)
PCRB	Pollution Control Revenue Bond [Environmental Protection Agency]
PCRB	Program Change Review Board [NASA]
PCRC	Pacific Concerns Resource Center (EA)
PCRC	Paraffined Carton Research Council [Later, Paperboard Packaging Council]
PCRC	Perinatal Clinical Research Center [Case Western Reserve University] [Research center] (RCD)
PCRC	Poor Clergy Relief Corp. [British] (BI)
PCRC	Primary Communications Research Centre [University of Leicester] [Canada]
PCRCA	Pickled, Cold-Rolled, and Close-Annealed [Metal]
PCRD	Primary Control Rod Driveline [Nuclear energy] (NRCH)
PCRDM	Primary Control Rod Drive Mechanism [Nuclear energy] (NRCH)
PCR/DNA	Polymerase Chain Reaction/Deoxyribonucleic Acid (SAUS)
PC Rep	English Privy Council Reports [A publication] (DLA)
PCRF	Parallel Computing Research Facility (SAUS)
PCRF	Paralysis Cure Research Foundation (EA)
PCRF	Parker Chiropractic Resource Foundation (EA)
PCRGA	Precipitation Chemistry, Reactive Gases, and Aerosols Section (SAUS)
PCRH	Provincial Cities and Rural Highways Program [Australia]
PCRI	Papanicolaou Cancer Research Institute [University of Miami] [Research center]
PCRI	Parent-Child Relationship Inventory [Test] (TMMY)
PCRM	Physicians Committee for Responsible Medicine (EA)
PCRM	Primary Certified Reference Material [Nuclear energy] (NRCH)
PCRMGPS	Poor Clerks Regular of the Mother of God of the Pious Schools [Rome, Italy] (EAIO)
PCRML	Parti Communiste Revolutionnaire - Marxiste-Leniniste [Revolutionary Marxist-Leninist Communist Party] [France] [Political party] (PPW)
PCRMSL	Pacific Coast Rocky Mountain Shooting League (PSS)
PC-ROM	Personal Computer Read-Only Memory
PCRP	Pennsylvania Comprehensive Reading Program (EDAC)
Pcr/Pi	Phosphocreatine to Inorganic Phosphate Ratio
PCRPr	Perini Corp. Dep Cv Exch Pfd [AMEX symbol] (TTSB)
PCRPS	Program for Collaborative Research in the Pharmaceutical Sciences [University of Illinois at Chicago] [Information service or system] (IID)
PCRR	Pennsylvania Central Railroad (ROG)
PCRS	Poor Clergy Relief Society [British]
PCRS	Precision Chiropractic Research Society [Also known as Spinal Stress Research Society] (EA)
PCRS	Primary Casualty Receiving Ship (SAUS)
PCRS	Primary Control Rod System [Nuclear energy] (NRCH)
PCRS	Primary CRITICOMM [Critical Intelligence Communications System] Relay Station (CET)
PCRS	Punched Card Reading System (SAUS)
PCR test	Polymerase Chain Reaction Test [Medicine] (TAD)
PCRV	Poinsettia Cryptic Virus [Plant pathology]
PCRV	PowerCerv Corp. [NASDAQ symbol] (SAG)
PCRV	Pressurized Concrete Reactor Vessel [Nuclear energy]
PCRV	Prestressed Concrete Reactor Vessel [Nuclear energy]
PCRW	Phase Change Rewritable (SAUS)
PCS	IEEE Professional Communication Society (EA)
PCS	Pace Car Society [Defunct] (EA)
PCS	Pacific Command Ship
PCS	Package Checking System (SAUS)
PCS	Packaging and Checkup System (SAUS)
PCS	Palliative Care Service
PCS	Paracas [Peru] [Seismograph station code, US Geological Survey] [Closed] (SEIS)
PCS	Parents' Confidential Statement [Education]
PCS	Parti Chretien-Social [Christian Social Party] [Luxembourg] [Political party] (PPW)
PCS	Particle Counting System
PCS	Parti Communiste Suisse [Communist Party of Switzerland] [Political party] (PPE)
PCS	Particulates, Condensables, and Solubles [In gases]
PCS	Partido Comunista Salvadoreno [Salvadoran Communist Party] [Political party] (PPW)
PCS	Partito Comunista Sammarinese [Communist Party of San Marino] [Political party] (PPE)
PCS	Part Number Configuration Summary
PCS	Parts Collection Survey (SAUS)
PCS	Parts, Components, Subassemblies
PCS	Parts Control System [DoD]
PCS	Passive Containment System [Nuclear energy] (NRCH)
PCS	Patchable Control Store (SAUS)

PCS	Patent Classification Service (SAUS)
PCS	Patient Care System
PCS	Patrol Craft, Submarine-chaser (SAUS)
PCS	Patrol Craft Sweeper (SAUS)
PCS	Patrol Vessel, Submarine Chaser (Control) [136 feet] [Navy symbol] [Obsolete]
PCS	Patterns of Care Study [Roentgenography]
PCS	Paul Claudel Society (EA)
PCS	Payless Cashways, Inc. [NYSE symbol] (SPSG)
PCS	Payload Checkout System [NASA] (NASA)
PCS	Payload Control Supervisor [NASA] (MCD)
PCS	Payload Correction Subsystem (SAUS)
PCS	PCL State (SAUS)
PCS	PC Service (SAUS)
PCS	Pelvic Congestion Syndrome [Medicine] (MELL)
PCS	Perforated Card System (SAUS)
PCS	Performance Command System (SAUS)
PCS	Pergamon Compact Solution [CD-ROM publisher] (IT)
PCS	Periodical Control System [Libraries]
PCS	Peripheral Computer System (IAA)
PCS	Peripheral Control System (SAUS)
PCS	Permanent Change of Station [Army]
PCS	Permanent Committee on Shipping (SAUS)
PCS	Permanent Cruiser Service [British military] (DMA)
PCS	Permit Compliance System [Environmental Protection Agency] (GFGA)
PCS	Personal Care Subsidy [Australia]
PCS	Personal Clerk of Session (SAUS)
PCS	Personal Communications Service [Provided by Personal Communications Network]
PCS	Personal Communications Services [Telecommunications]
PCS	Personal Communications System
PCS	Personal Composition System (DGA)
PCS	Personal Computer System
PCS	Personal Computing System
PCS	Personal Conferencing Specification [Telecommunications] (CDE)
PCS	Personnel Capabilities System [Jet Propulsion Laboratory, NASA]
PCS	Personnel Change of Station
PCS	Personnel Consultancy Services Ltd. [British]
PCS	Petrochemical Corp. of Singapore
PCS	Pharmaceutical Card System (MCD)
PCS	Pharmacogenic Confusional Syndrome [Medicine] (DMAA)
PCS	Phase Combining System [Trademark] [A solubilizer in scintillation counting]
PCS	Phase Compensator System
PCS	Philippine Collectors Society (EA)
PCS	Philips Car Systems
PCS	PhonoCardioScan [Cardiology]
PCS	Photo Correlation System (SAUS)
PCS	Photoformed Ceramic Substrates [Du Pont process for making microconductors]
PCS	Photon Correlation Spectroscopy
PCS	Physical-Chemical System (SAA)
PCS	Physical Coding Signalling (SAUS)
PCS	Physical Control Space (SAUS)
PCS	Physical Control System
PCS	Physically Controlled Space [Military] (GFGA)
PCS	Physics of Colloids in Space (SAUS)
pCs	Picocoulombs (SAUS)
PCS	Pictorial Cancellation Society [Defunct] (EA)
pcs	Picture File [Computer science]
pcs	Pieces (EBF)
PCS	Pieces
PCS	Piezoelectric Crystal Sensor (DB)
PCS	Pilot Control System (MCD)
PCS	Pinball Construction Set (SAUS)
PCS	Pitch Control System (MCD)
PCS	Planning Control Sheet
PCS	Plant Computer System (NRCH)
PCS	Plant Control System [Nuclear energy] (NRCH)
PCS	Plastic-Clad Silica [Optics]
PCS	Plastic Coated Silica (NITA)
PCS	Plastic-Coated Silica (SAUS)
PCS	Plastic Coding System (SAUS)
PCS	Plastic Connector Shell
PCS	Platoon Combat Skills [Army] (INF)
PCS	Plausible Conflict Situations [Army]
PCS	Plessey Commercial Software (SAUS)
PCS	Pluto-Charon System [Planetary science]
PCS	Pneumatic Control System [Gas chromatography]
PCS	Pocket Computer System (SEWL)
PCS	Pointing-Control System [Aerospace]
PCS	Polycarbosilane (EDCT)
PCS	Polymer-Clad Silica [Chemistry]
PCS	Polytechnic Certificate in Shipping (SAUS)
PCS	Portable Communications System
PCS	Portable Computer System (SAUS)
PCS	Portable Control Station (SAUS)
PCS	Portacaval Shunt [Medicine]
PCS	Port Command Store [Telecommunications] (TEL)
PCS	Port Concentrator Shelf (SAUS)
PCS	Port Control Store [Telecommunications] (TEL)
PCS	Port Control System [Telecommunications] (TEL)
PCS	Position Classification Standard [Civil Service]
PCS	Position Control System

PCS............	Position, Course, and Speed
PCS............	Positive Concatenation Structures [Mathematics]
PCS............	Postal & Courier Service (SAUS)
PCS............	Postal Church Service
PCS............	Postal Commemorative Society (EA)
PCS............	Postcardiotomy Syndrome [Medicine]
PCS............	Postcaval [or Portacaval] Shunt [Medicine]
PCS............	Posterior Concave Side
PCS............	Posts, Camps, and Stations [Military]
PCS............	Postural Control System (SAUS)
PCS............	Potash Corp. of Saskatchewan [Canada]
PCS............	Power Center Substation (SAUS)
PCS............	Power Conditioning System
PCS............	Power Conductor System (SAUS)
PCS............	Power Conversion System
PCS............	Powered Causeway Section [Military] (CAAL)
PCS............	Practical Computer Solutions (NITA)
PCS............	Precedence Charting System (IAA)
PCS............	Precision Casting Standard (MCD)
Pcs............	Preconscious [Medicine] (STED)
PCS............	Preconscious
PCS............	Pre-Crash Sensor [Automotive safety systems]
PCS............	Preferred Capital Stock [Investment term]
PCS............	Preferred Character Set (SAUS)
PCS............	Pregnancy Counselling Service [Australia]
PCS............	Preliminary Component Specification
PCS............	Press Computer System (DGA)
PCS............	Pressure Control System
PCS............	Pressure Core Sampler (SAUS)
PCS............	Pressure Cycling Switch [Automotive engineering]
PCS............	Previous Condition of Servitude (SAUS)
PCS............	Primary Calibration System
PCS............	Primary Cancer Site [Oncology]
P c/s........	Primary Cesarian Section (STED)
PCS............	Primary Conditioning Solution
PCS............	Primary Control Ship [Navy]
PCS............	Primary Coolant System (MSA)
PCS............	Prime Compatible Set (PDAA)
PCS............	Principal Clerk of Session
PCS............	Principal Coordinating Scientist [NASA] (KSC)
PCS............	Print Contrast Scale (IEEE)
PCS............	Print Contrast Signal [Computer science]
PCS............	Print Contrast System (BUR)
PCS............	Probabilistic Clock Synchronization (SAUS)
PCS............	Probability of Command Shutdown (MCD)
PCS............	Probability of Correct Selection [Statistics]
PCS............	Probability of Crew Survival (AAG)
PCS............	Probable Carcinogenic Substances (EEVL)
PCS............	Procedure Coding System (SAUS)
PCS............	Procedure Completion Sheet [NASA] (MCD)
PCS............	Process Communication Supervisor (IAA)
PCS............	Process Communication System (SAUS)
PCS............	Process Computer System (NRCH)
PCS............	Process Control Sheet [Nuclear energy] (NRCH)
PCS............	Process Control Specification (SAUS)
PCS............	Process Control Station
PCS............	Process Control System
PCS............	Pro Computer Services (NITA)
PCS............	Production Control Section
PCS............	Production Control System (BUR)
PCS............	Production Cost Savings (AAEL)
PCS............	Professional Careers Sourcebook [A publication]
PCS............	Professional Car Society (EA)
PCS............	Program Center Store (SAUS)
PCS............	Program Control System (SAUS)
PCS............	Program Coordination Staff [Environmental Protection Agency] (GFGA)
PCS............	Program Cost Status [Report] (MCD)
PCS............	Program Counter Store
PCS............	Programmable Character Set [Computer science] (VLIE)
PCS............	Programmable Communications Subsystem
PCS............	Programmable Communications System (SAUS)
PCS............	Programmed Control Sequencer (SAUS)
PCS............	Project Control Sheet [Computer science]
PCS............	Project Control System [Computer science]
PCS............	Project Coordination Staff [NASA] (KSC)
PCS............	Promotion of Chemical Safety (SAUS)
PCS............	Property Consultants Society [British] (DBA)
PCS............	Property Control System
PCS............	Proprietary Computer Systems, Inc. [Information service or system] (IID)
PCS............	Propulsion Control System (ACAE)
PCS............	Prostate Cancer Society (WDAA)
PCS............	Protected Cable System
PCS............	Provision Coordinate Schedule (MCD)
PCS............	Proxy Cache Server (SAUS)
PCS............	Pseudo-Code System (SAUS)
PCS............	Pseudotumor Cerebri Syndrome [Medicine] (DMAA)
PCS............	Public and Commercial Services Union (HEAS)
PCS............	Publication Control Sheet (MCD)
PCS............	Public Choice Society (EA)
PCS............	Pulse Compression System
PCS............	Pump Control Sensor
PCS............	Punch Card System (NITA)
PCS............	Punch Column Skip (SAUS)

PCS............	Punched Card Selector (SAUS)
PCS............	Punched Card System [Computer science]
PCS............	Punjab Cooperative Society (SAUS)
PCS............	Pyrotechnics Circuit Simulator
PCS............	Sabah Chinese Party [Malaysia] [Political party] (FEA)
PCS............	Submarine Chaser
PCS............	Sun Shipbuilding & Dry Dock Co., Chester, PA [Library symbol] [Library of Congress] (LCLS)
PCS-1900	Personal Communication Service in 1.9GHz band (SAUS)
PCSA	Palm and Cycad Societies of Australia
PCSA	Patrol Craft Sailors Association (EA)
PCSA	Personal Computer Systems Architecture (SAUS)
PCSA	Personal Computing Systems Architecture
PCSA	Polish Cultural Society of America (SAUS)
PCSA	Power Crane and Shovel Association (EA)
PCSA	Seaman Apprentice, Postal Clerk, Striker [Navy rating]
PCS(A)	Submarine Chaser (Air Cushion) (MCD)
PCSAS	Policy Committee for Scientific Agricultural Society (BUAC)
PCsB	Baptist Bible College of Pennsylvania, Clarks Summit, PA [Library symbol] [Library of Congress] (LCLS)
PCSB	Pulse-Code Scanning Beam (SAUS)
PCSC	Control Submarine Chaser [136 feet] [Navy symbol] [Obsolete]
PCSC	Pacific Coast Science Center (SAUS)
PCSC	Pacific Coast Swimming Conference (PSS)
PCSC	Plant Cell Suspension Cultures [Biotechnology]
PCSC	Power Conditioning, Switching, and Control
PCSC	Principal Commonwealth Supply Committee [World War II]
PCSCA	Permanent Committee on Socio-Cultural Affairs (SAUS)
PCS-CSS......	Parents' Confidential Statement of the College Scholarship Service [Education] (IIA)
PCSD	Partido Cristao Social Democratico [Christian Social Democratic Party] [Portugal] [Political party] (PPE)
PCSD	Polychloro(chloromethylsulfonamido)diphenyl Ether [Insectproofing agent for wool]
PCSD	President's Council on Sustainable Development [1993]
PCSD	Printer Control Sequence Description (SAUS)
PCSDC........	Pacific Collegiate Swim/Dive Conference (PSS)
PCSDS.........	Pump Controls and Data System (SAUS)
PCSE..........	Pacific Coast Stock Exchange [Later, PSE] (EA)
PCSE..........	President's Committee on Scientists and Engineers [Expired, 1958]
PCSE..........	Printed Circuit Soldering Equipment
PC/SFA	Potato Chip/Snack Food Association [Formerly, NPCI, PCI] [Later, SFA]
PCSFSK	Phase Coherent Sinusoidal Frequency Shift Keying (CCCA)
PCSFSK	Phase Comparison Sinusoidal Frequency Shift Keying
PCSG	Public Cryptography Study Group [Defunct] (EA)
PCSH	Pierce Shell
PCS(H)........	Submarine Chaser (Hydrofoil) (MCD)
PCSI..........	Pacific Communication Sciences, Inc. (SAUS)
PCSI..........	Public Cleansing and Salvage Inspection (SAUS)
PCSIG	Personal Computer-Software Interest Group (EA)
PCSIR	Pakistan Council of Scientific and Industrial Research
PCSJ..........	All-Party Parliamentary Committee for the Release of Soviet Jewry (EAIO)
PCSL..........	Procurement Component Supplier List (VLIE)
PCSM..........	Percutaneous Stone Manipulation [Medicine]
PCSMQC......	Polish Committee for Standardization, Measures and Quality Control (SAUS)
PCSN	PC Satellite Network
PCSN	Precision Standard [NASDAQ symbol] (TTSB)
PCSN	Precision Standard, Inc. [NASDAQ symbol] (NQ)
PCSN	Private Circuit-Switching Network [Telecommunications] (OSI)
PCSN	Seaman, Postal Clerk, Striker [Navy rating]
PCSO	Presidential Communications Support Office (CCCA)
PCSP	Partial Constraint Satisfaction Problem (SAUS)
PCSP	Permanent Commission for the South Pacific (WDAA)
PCSP	Polar Continental Shelf Project [Canada] (QUAC)
PCSP	Preliminary Cruise Sampling Plan (SAUS)
PCSP	Princeton Cooperative School Program (SAUS)
PCSP	Programmed Communications Support Program [Air Force] (AFM)
PCSPS	Principal Civil Service Pension Scheme [British]
PCSR	Program Cost and Schedule Report (TIMI)
PCS/REAL	Project Control System/Resource Allocation (VLIE)
PCSS	PC Service Source [NASDAQ symbol] (TTSB)
PCSS	PC Service Source, Inc. [NASDAQ symbol] (SAG)
PCSS	Personal Computer Support Service (VLIE)
PCSS	Photo-Conductive Semiconductor Switch (VLIE)
PCSS	Platform Check Subsystem
PCSS	Princess (ROG)
PCSSD........	Philippines Council for Sustainable Development (SAUS)
PCST..........	Pakistan Council for Science and Technology (BUAC)
PCST..........	Permanent Commission on Science and Technology (SAUS)
PCST..........	Precision Castparts Corp. (MHDW)
PCST..........	President's Committee on Science and Technology
PCSU	Peripheral Control Switching Unit (VLIE)
PC Svc.......	PC Service Source, Inc. [Associated Press] (SAG)
PCSW	Police Chiefs Spouses - Worldwide [An association] (EA)
PCSW	President's Commission on the Status of Women
PC System...	Power Control System (SAUS)
PCT............	Pacific Coast Tariff Bureau, San Francisco CA [STAC]
PCT............	Pacific Coast Terminals (SAUS)
PCT............	Pacific Crest Trail
PCT............	Page Copy Teleprinter (SAUS)
PCT............	Painful Cervical Trauma [Medicine] (MELL)
PCT............	Paper Crepe Tape

PCT	Para-Chlorotoluene [Organic chemistry]
PCT	Parity, Charge conjugation, Time-reversal (SAUS)
PCT	Parti Communiste Tunisien [Tunisian Communist Party] [Political party] (PD)
PCT	Parti Congolais du Travail [Congolese Labor Party] [Political party] (PPW)
PCT	Partido Conservador Tradicional [Traditionalist Conservative Party] [Nicaragua] [Political party]
PCT	Partition Control Table [Computer science] (ELAL)
PCT	Partition Control Table (SAUS)
PCT	Patent Cooperation Treaty [World Intellectual Property Organization, 1978]
PCT	Patient Care Technician (MELL)
PCT	Patient Clotting Time (SAUS)
PCT	Peace Air Togo [ICAO designator] (FAAC)
PCT	Peak Centerline Temperature [Nuclear energy] (NRCH)
PCT	Peak Cladding Temperature [Nuclear energy] (NRCH)
PCT	Per Cent (SAUS)
pct	Percent (NTIO)
pct	Percent (SHCU)
PCT	Percent [or Percentage]
PCT	Percentage [Used instead of "average"] [Baseball]
PCT	Perfect Crystal Technology (IAA)
PCT	Performance Correlation Technique
PCT	Periodic Confidence Test
PCT	Peripheral Control Terminal
PCT	Personal Communications Technology (AGLO)
PC/T	Personal Computer/Technology (HGAA)
PCT	Personality Completion Test [Psychology]
PCT	Pest Control Team (SAUS)
PCT	Pharmacy and Chemistry Technician [Navy]
PCT	Philadelphia College of Textiles and Science, Philadelphia, PA [OCLC symbol] (OCLC)
PCT	Photochemical Transfer (SAUS)
PCT	Photoinduced Charge Transfer [Electrochemistry]
PCT	Photometric Calibration Target (ACAE)
PCT	Photometric Calibration Test (ACAE)
PCT	Photon-Coupled Transistor (IEEE)
PCT	Physical Correlate Theory [Psychophysics]
PCT	Physiognomic Cue Test [Psychology] (STED)
PCT	Picrotoxin [Biological stimulant]
PCT	Picture
PCT	Pitch Centering Torque (SAUS)
PCT	Pitch Centering Torquer (SAA)
PCT	Planning and Control Techniques
PCT	Plasma Clotting Time [Medicine] (STED)
PCT	Plasmacrit Test [Medicine]
PCT	Plasmacytoma [Medicine]
PCT	Platelet Count [Hematology]
PCT	Platelet Hematocrit (STED)
PCT	Point-Contact Transistor [Electronics] (IAA)
PCT	Polychemotherapy [Oncology]
PCT	Polychlorinated Terphenyl [Pesticide]
PCT	Polychlorinated Triphenyl (STED)
PCT	Polychloroterphenyl [Organic chemistry]
PCT	Polycyclohexane Dimethylene Terephthalate (SAUS)
PCT	Polycyclohexyl Terephthalate (SAUS)
PCT	Porcine Calcitonin [Biochemistry] (AAMN)
PCT	Porphyria Cutanea Tarda [Disease] [Medicine]
PCT	Portable Camera-Transmitter
PCT	Portable Conference Telephone [Bell Laboratories]
PCT	Portacaval Transportation (STED)
PCT	Portacaval Transposition [Medicine] (MAE)
PCT	Portsmouth College of Technology (SAUS)
PCT	Positron Computed Tomography
PCT	Postcoital Test [Medicine] (DAVI)
PCT	Potato Curly Top Disease [Plant pathology]
PCT	Potential Current Transformer
PCT	Power Control Test (SAUS)
PCT	Precinct
PCT	Preliminary Change Transmittal (AAG)
PCT	Prepared Childbirth Training (MELL)
PCT	Pressure Concentration Temperature
PCT	Pressure Controlled Test (SAUS)
PCT	Prime Contract Termination (AAG)
PCT	Princeton [New Jersey] [Airport symbol] [Obsolete] (OAG)
PCT	Principal Component Transform (SAUS)
PCT	Printed Circuit Tester (VLIE)
PCT	Printer Carriage Tape (SAUS)
PCT	Prism Cover Test [Ophthalmology] (CPH)
PCT	Private Communications Technology [Microsoft Corp.] [Computer science]
P Ct	Probate Court (DLA)
PCT	Probe Control Table (SAUS)
PCT	Process Change Teams (AAEL)
PCT	Processing Control Table (SAUS)
PCT	Product Consistency Test (ABAC)
PCT	Production Confirmatory Test (MCD)
PCT	Progestin Challenge Test (STED)
PCT	Programa de Cooperacion Tecnica [Program of Technical Cooperation - PTC] [Organization of American States] [Washington, DC]
PCT	Program Controlled Transfer (SAUS)
PCT	Program Control Table [Computer science]
PCT	Program Counter Timer (IAA)

PCT	Project Control Tool (BUR)
PCT	Property Capital Trust [AMEX symbol] (SPSG)
PCT	Prophyria Catanba Tarda [Medicine]
PCT	Propulsion Component Technology (ACAE)
PCT	prothrombin Consumption Test (SAUS)
PCT	Prothrombin Consumption Time [Hematology] (DAVI)
PCT	Proximal Convoluted Tubule [of a nephron]
PCT	Puangchon Chao Thai [Thai Mass Party] [Thailand] [Political party]
PCT	Pulmonary Care Team Medicine (STED)
PCT	Pulse Compression Test (SAUS)
PCT	Pulse Compression Tube
PCT	Pulse Count [Telecommunications] (TEL)
PCT	Pump Cavitation Temperature [Automotive engineering]
PCT	Punched Card Technique (SAUS)
PCT	Pure Chance Traffic (SAUS)
PCT	Wesman Personnel Classification Test
PCTA	Pentachlorothioanisole [Organic chemistry]
PCTA	Percutaneous Transluminal Angioplasty [Medicine] (MELL)
PCTA	Personal Computer Terminal Adapter (SAUS)
PCTA	Plastic-Cased Telescoped Ammunition (SAUS)
PCTA	Polymer of Cyclohexanedimethanol Terephthalic Acid (SAUS)
PCTA	Provisional Collection of Taxes Act (SAUS)
PCT&S	Philadelphia College of Textiles and Science (SAUS)
PCTAP	Positive Control Turnaround Point (CCCA)
PCTB	Pacific Coast Tariff Bureau
PCTC	Panama Canal Transition Commission (SAUS)
PCTC	Payload Crew Training Complex (SAUS)
PCTC	Penn Central Transportation Co.
PCTC	Pentagon Consolidated Telecommunications Center (SAUS)
PCTC	Portable Common Tool Environment (SAUS)
PCTC	Pure Car Truck Carrier [Shipping] (DS)
PCTC	Pyrotechnic Circuit Test Console (KSC)
PCTDS	Problem and Change Tracking Directory System
PCTE	Portable Commercial Test Equipment (NASA)
PCTE	Portable Common Test Environment [British]
PCTE	Portable Common Tools Environment (IAA)
PCTE Bulletin	Pennsylvania Council of Teachers of English, Bulletin (SAUS)
PCTF	Plant Component Test Facility [Nuclear energy]
PCTF	Power Conversion Test Facility (SAA)
PCTF	Premiers Council Technology Fund (SAUS)
PCTF	Process Condensate Treatment Facility (SAUS)
PCTFE	Polychlorotrifluoroethylene [Organic chemistry]
PCTFE	Polymonochlorotrifluoroethyle [Organic chemistry] (IAA)
PCTFE	Polymonochlorotrifluoroethylene (SAUS)
PCTG	glycol-modified PCT copolymer (SAUS)
PCTG	Programmable Channel Termination Group (SAUS)
PCT-GF	Plasmacytoma Growth Factor [Oncology]
PCTH	Pacific Aerospace & Electronics, Inc. [NASDAQ symbol] (SAG)
PCTH	PCT Holdings [NASDAQ symbol] (TTSB)
PCTH	PCT Holdings, Inc. [NASDAQ symbol] (SAG)
PCTHold	PCT Holdings, Inc. [Associated Press] (SAG)
PCTIS	Preston Commercial and Technical Information Service (NITA)
PCTL	Picture Tel Corp. [NASDAQ symbol] (TTSB)
PC/TM	Performance Criteria and Test Methods Task
PCTM	Pulse-Count Modulation (MSA)
PCTMSL	Permanent Committee on Tides and Mean Sea-Level (SAUS)
PCTO	Payload Cost Tradeoff Optimization [NASA] (NASA)
PCTOJ	Passive Correlation Track-On-Jam [Department of Defense]
PCTP	Partido Comunista dos Trabalhadores Portugueses [Portuguese Workers' Communist Party] [Political party] (PPW)
PCTP	Pierce Template
PCTP	Plant Completion Task Proposal (SAUS)
PCTR	Pad Connection Terminal Room [NASA] (NAKS)
PCTR	Physical Constant Test Reactor [Nuclear energy]
PCTR	Program Counter
PCTR	Property Control Transaction Report
PCTR	Protocol Conformance Test Report (SAUS)
PCTR	Pulsed Column Test Rig [Chemical engineering]
PCTs	Panama Canal Treaties (SAUS)
PCTS	Pentagon Consolidated Telecommunications System (MCD)
PC/TS	Performance Criteria/Test Standard (SAUS)
PCTS	Photocapacitance Transient Spectroscopy (SAUS)
PCTS	Portable Cesium Time Standard
PCTS	President's Committee for Traffic Safety (EA)
PCTSCM	Piezoelectric, Continuously Twisted, Structurally Chiral Medium (SAUS)
PCTT	Precommit Track Time [DoD]
PCT Theorem	Parity, Charge-conjugation, Time-reversal Theorem (SAUS)
PCTUULAW	Permanent Congress of Trade Union Unity of Latin American Workers [See also CPUSTAL] [Mexico City, Mexico] (EAIO)
PCTV	Peoples Choice TV Corp. [NASDAQ symbol] (SAG)
PCTV	Personal Computer Television (SAUS)
PCTV	Printed Circuit Test Vehicle (SAUS)
PCTV	Private Channel Television
PCTV	Program Controlled Transverters (SAUS)
PCtvL	Lukens Steel Co., Coatesville, PA [Library symbol] [Library of Congress] [Obsolete] (LCLS)
PCtvVA	United States Veterans Administration Hospital, Medical Library, Coatesville, PA [Library symbol] [Library of Congress] (LCLS)
PCTWin	PC [Personal Computer] Tools for Windows (PCM)
PCTY	Party City [NASDAQ symbol] (TTSB)
PCTY	Party City Corp. [NASDAQ symbol] (SAG)
PCU	Packet Communications Unit
PCU	Page Clean-up (SAUS)
PCU	Paging Control Unit [Telecommunications] (TEL)

PCU	Pain Control Unit
PCU	Palliative Care Unit [*Medicine*] (CPH)
PCU	Parachute Control Unit (SAUS)
PCU	Parallel Computation Unit (SAUS)
PCU	Partido Conservador Unido [*Chilean Catholic political party*]
PCU	Passenger Car Unit (SAUS)
PCU	Passenger Control Unit (MCD)
PCU	Patient Care Unit (HCT)
PCU	Payload Checkout Unit [*NASA*] (MCD)
PCU	Peripheral Control Unit (CMD)
PCU	Photocopy Unit (SAUS)
PCU	Physical Control Unit (SAUS)
PCU	Picayune, MS [*Location identifier*] [*FAA*] (FAAL)
pcu............	Platinum Cobalt Unit [*Water analysis*]
PCU	Pneumatic Checkout Unit (AAG)
PCU	Pod Cooling Unit (AAG)
PCU	Ponable Checkout Unit (SAUS)
PCU	Portable Checkout Unit
PCU	Portable Communications Unit (SAUS)
PCU	Portable Computer Unit
PCU	Portable Control Unit (SAUS)
PCU	Port-Contention Unit (SAUS)
PCU	Portuguese Continental Union of the United States of America (EA)
PCU	Post-Coronary Care Unit [*Cardiology*] (DAVI)
PCU	Pound Centigrade Unit
PCU	Power and Controller Unit (SAUS)
PCU	Power Conditioning Unit
PCU	Power Control Unit
PCU	Power Conversion Unit (IEEE)
PCU	Power Convulsion Unit
PCU	Premises Control Unit (SAUS)
PCU	Pressure Control Unit (MCD)
PCU	Pressurization Control Unit (SAUS)
PCU	Price [*Utah*] [*Seismograph station code, US Geological Survey*] (SEIS)
PCU	Primary Care Unit [*Medicine*] (DMAA)
PCU	Primary Control Unit (IAA)
PCU	Printed Control Unit [*Military*] (GFGA)
PCU	Printer Control Unit (SAUS)
PCU	Priority Control Unit (SAUS)
PCU	Prisoner Casework Unit (WDAA)
PCU	Procedure Change Unit
PCU	Process Control Unit (NAKS)
PCU	Processor Control Unit
PCU	Product Co-Ordination Unit [*British Overseas Trade Board*] (DS)
PCU	Program Control Unit [*Computer science*]
PCU	Programmable Control Unit (SAUS)
PCU	Progress Control Unit (KSC)
PCU	Progressive Care Unit [*Medicine*]
PCU	Propellant Control Unit (SAA)
PCU	Protective Care Unit [*Medicine*]
PCU	Protective Custody Unit (SAUS)
PCU	Protein-Calorie Undernutrition [*Medicine*]
PCU	Pulmonary Care Unit [*Medicine*] (DMAA)
PCU	Punched Card Unit (NITA)
PCU	Punched Card Utility [*Computer science*]
PCU	Southern Peru Copper [*NYSE symbol*] (TTSB)
PCU	Southern Peru Copper Corp. [*NYSE symbol*] (SAG)
PCU	University of Prince Edward Island, Charlottetown, Prince Edward Island [*Library symbol*] [*National Library of Canada*] (NLC)
PCUA	Power Controller Unit Assembly (IEEE)
PCUA	Pressure Control Unit, Atlas (MCD)
PCUA	Profit Control Users Association (SAUS)
PCUC	Positive Continuous Ullage Control
PCUCDGIS ...	Personal Computer University College Dublin Geographic Information System (SAUS)
PCUD	Peripheral Control Unit Diagnostic [*Program*]
PCU/HDR	Primary Control Unit, Hydraulics (AAG)
PCUI	Partito Comunista Unificado de Italia [*Unified Communist Party of Italy*] [*Political party*] (PPE)
PCUR	Pulsating Current
PCUS	Peace Corps of the United States (EA)
PCUs	Peripheral Control Units (SAUS)
PCUS	Port Charges Paid by United States Army, Navy, or Air Force (DNAB)
PCUS	Propeller Club of the United States (EA)
PC-USA	Pax Christi - USA (EA)
PCUSA	Presbyterian Church in the U.S.A. (SAUS)
PCUSAW	Pen Center USA West (EA)
PCUSEQ	Pressure Control Unit Sequencer (AAG)
pcut...........	Percutaneous [*Medicine*] (AAMN)
PCUUS	Polish Council of Unity in the United States [*Defunct*] (EA)
PCU-USA	Portuguese Continental Union of the U.S.A. (SAUS)
PCU Value...	Passenger Car Unit Value (SAUS)
PCV............	Pacific Concord Resources Corp. [*Vancouver Stock Exchange symbol*]
PCV............	Packed Cell Volume [*Hematology*] (CPH)
PCV............	Parietal Cell Vagotomy [*Medicine*] (AAMN)
PCV............	Partido Comunista Venezolana [*Venezuelan Communist Party*] [*Political party*] (PPW)
PCV............	Passenger Carrying Vehicle [*Military*] (GFGA)
PCV............	Passenger Control Vehicle (WDAA)
PCV............	Path Coding Violation (SAUS)
PCV............	P-bit Coding Violation (SAUS)
PCV............	Peace Corps Volunteer
PCV............	Peach Calico Virus (SAUS)

PCV............	Peanut Clump Virus [*Plant pathology*]
PCV............	Penciclovir [*Antiherpetic*]
PCV............	Pestalozzi Childrens Village (SAUS)
PCV............	Petty Cash Voucher (MCD)
PCV............	Physical Control Volume (SAUS)
PCV............	Pneumatic Control Valve
PCV............	Pollution Control Valve (IEEE)
PCV............	Polychlorinated Vinyl (MELL)
PCV............	Polycythemia Vera [*Also, PV*] [*Hematology*]
PCV............	Porcine Cirovirus
PCV............	Positive Crankcase Ventilation [*For automotive antipollution systems*]
PCV............	Positive Crankcase Ventilator
PCV............	Postcapillary Venule [*Medicine*] (DMAA)
PCV............	Precheck Verification [*NASA*] (NASA)
PCV............	Precursor Vehicle (SAUS)
PCV............	Presidents Commission on Violence (SAUS)
PCV............	Pressure [*or Pressurizer*] Control Valve (AAG)
PCV............	Pressure-Control Ventilation [*Medicine*] (DMAA)
PCV............	Primary Containment Vessel
PCV............	Primary Control Vessel (DNAB)
PCV............	Primate Calicivirus
PCV............	Printed Circuit Vehicle (SAUS)
PCV............	Procarbazine, CCNU [*Lomustine*], Vincristine [*Antineoplastic drug regimen*] (DAVI)
PCV............	Process Cell Ventilation (SAUS)
PCV............	Proportional Cartridge Valve [*Hydraulics*]
PCV............	Proportioning Control Valve [*Automotive brakes*]
PCV............	Protocol Converter [*Electronics*] (ECII)
PCV............	Pump Control Valve [*Hydraulics*]
PCV............	Purge Control Valve (NASA)
PCV............	Putnam Convertible Opportunities & Income Trust [*NYSE symbol*] (SAG)
PCV............	Pyrocatechol Violet [*Also, PV*] [*An indicator*] [*Chemistry*]
PCV............	Veterans Affairs, Canada [*Affaires des Anciens Combattants Canada*] Charlottetown, Prince Edward Island [*Library symbol*] [*National Library of Canada*] (NLC)
PCvA...........	Allentown College of Saint Francis De Sales, Center Valley, PA [*Library symbol*] [*Library of Congress*] (LCLS)
PCVB	Pyro Continuity Verification Box [*NASA*] (NASA)
PCVC	Partially Conserved Vector Current (IAA)
PCVC	Public Citizens Visitors Center [*An association*] [*Defunct*] (EA)
PCVD	Plasma Chemical Vapor Deposition
PC virus......	Port Chalmers type of influenza virus (SAUS)
PCVL..........	Pilot-Controlled Visual Landing [*Aviation*] (NASA)
PCV-M	Myeloid Metaplasia with Polycythemia Vera [*Hematology*] (MAE)
PCVN	Precracked Charpy V-Notch (PDAA)
PCVS	Point-to-point Switched Virtual Connections (SAUS)
PCVS	Professional Credentials Verification Service (ADWA)
PCV system...	Positive Crankcase Ventilation System
PCV Valve ...	Positive Crankcase Ventilation Valve (SAUS)
PCW............	Personal Computer World Show [*Montbuild Ltd.*] (TSPED)
PCW............	Plate Control Wedge [*Printing technology*]
PCW............	Point Calculation Worksheet [*Army*] (INF)
PCW............	PortaCom Wireless [*VS, Exchange Symbol*] (TTSB)
PCW............	Port Clinton, OH [*Location identifier*] [*FAA*] (FAAL)
PCW............	Post Consumer Waste (EG)
PCW............	Previously Complied With
PCW............	Primary Cooling Water [*Reactor*]
PCW............	Princess Charlotte of Wales [*Military unit*] [*British*]
PCW............	Principal Conductor of the Works [*Freemasonry*]
PCW............	Program Control Word
PCW............	Proprietor of Copyright on a Composite Work
PCW............	Pulmonary Capillary Wedge [*Medicine*]
PCW............	Pulsed Continuous Wave (IEEE)
PCW............	Put Control Write (SAUS)
PCW............	Widener College, Chester, PA [*Library symbol*] [*Library of Congress*] (LCLS)
PCWA	Pharmaceutical Council of Western Australia
PCWBS	Preliminary Contract Work Breakdown Structure (MCD)
PCWCA	Poured Concrete Wall Contractors Association (EA)
PCWF	Philippine Communications Workers Federation (SAUS)
PCWG	Personal Conferencing Work Group (SAUS)
PC-WNIM.....	Personal Computer Wide Area Network Interface Module (TSSD)
PCWO	Production Control Work Order (MCD)
PCWP	Pulmocapillary Wedge Pressure (SAUS)
PCWP	Pulmonary Capillary Wedge Pressure [*Medicine*]
PCWPC	Permanent Committee of the World Petroleum Congress (BUAC)
PCWPC	Permanent Council of the World Petroleum Congress (SAUS)
PCW Reactor...	Primary Cooling Water Reactor (SAUS)
PCWTU	Philippine Woman's Christian Temperance Union (BUAC)
PCWU	Port Commissioners Workers' Union [*India*]
PCX............	Pacificorp [*NYSE symbol*] (SAG)
PCX............	PacifiCorp 8.55%'QUIDS' [*NYSE symbol*] (TTSB)
PCX............	Peripheral Channel Exchange (SAUS)
PCx............	Periscopic Convex [*Ophthalmology*]
PCX............	Picture Exchange (SAUS)
PCX............	Picture Image (SAUS)
PCX............	Plasma Confinement Experiment [*Physics*]
PCX............	Process Control Executive (MHDI)
PCXR	Portable Chest X-Ray (CPH)
PC-XT.........	Personal Computer-Extended Technology (SAUS)
PCX Unit......	Peripheral Computer Exchange Unit (SAUS)
PCY............	Aquila Air, Inc. [*ICAO designator*] (FAAC)
PCY............	Pacific Cypress Minerals Ltd. [*Vancouver Stock Exchange symbol*]
PCY............	Pittsburgh, Chartiers & Youghiogheny Railway Co. [*AAR code*]

PCY............	Plastocyanin
PCY............	Prerogative Court of York [*English court previously having jurisdiction over wills*]
PCYC..........	Pharmacyclics, Inc. [*NASDAQ symbol*] (SAG)
PCYF..........	President's Council on Youth Fitness (EA)
PCYF..........	Progressive Conservative Youth Federation of Canada
PCZ............	Canal Zone [*ANSI three-letter standard code*] [*Obsolete*] (CNC)
PCZ............	Panama Canal Zone [*Panama*] [*Airport symbol*] (AD)
PCZ............	Paracomp Technology, Inc. [*Vancouver Stock Exchange symbol*]
PCZ............	Petro-Canada [*NYSE symbol*] (SAG)
PCZ............	Petro-Canada Variable Vtg [*NYSE symbol*] (TTSB)
PCZ............	Physical Control Zone (NASA)
PCZ............	Positive Control Zone (DNAB)
PCZ............	Procarbazine [*Antineoplastic drug*] (DAVI)
PCZ............	Prochlorperazine [*Antiemetic*]
PCZ............	Waupaca, WI [*Location identifier*] [*FAA*] (FAAL)
PCZPP........	Petro-Canada Installm't Vtg [*NYSE symbol*] (TTSB)
PCZST........	Panama Canal Zone Standard Time (SAUS)
PD.............	Cleveland Plain Dealer (SAUS)
PD.............	Democratic Party [*Ecuador*] [*Political party*] (PD)
PD.............	Doctor of Pedagogy
PD.............	Doctor of Pharmacy
PD.............	Doctor of Philosophy (WDAA)
Pd.............	Dorsal Pressure Neuron [*of a leech*]
PD.............	Dublin Pharmacopoeia
PD.............	Interpupillary Distance
PD.............	Law Reports, Probate, Divorce, and Admiralty Division [*1875-90*] [*England*] [*A publication*] (DLA)
PD.............	Packed Data (SAUS)
PD.............	Packet Driver (SAUS)
PD.............	Packetization Delay (SAUS)
PD.............	Packing Density (SAUS)
p/d............	Packs per Day [*Cigarettes*] [*Medicine*]
PD.............	Pad (MCD)
PD.............	Page Directory (SAUS)
PD.............	Paget's Disease [*Medicine*]
Pd.............	Paid (EBF)
pd.............	Paid (ODBW)
PD.............	Paid
PD.............	Paid Daily (SAUS)
PD.............	Palisade Diabase [*Geology*]
PD.............	Palladium
Pd.............	Palladium [*Chemical element*]
PD.............	Pallet Decoupler (SAUS)
PD.............	Pancreatic Divisum [*Medicine*]
PD.............	Pancreatic Duct [*Anatomy*]
PD.............	Panel Display (ELAL)
PD.............	Panic Disorder (DIPS)
PD.............	Pants Down [*At a disadvantage*] [*Slang*] (DSUE)
pd.............	Papilla Diameter [*Medicine*]
PD.............	Papillary Distance
PD.............	Papillary Duct [*Medicine*] (MELL)
PD.............	Paralytic Dose (SAUS)
PD.............	Paralyzing Dose [*Pharmacology*] (DAVI)
PD.............	Parental Ditype [*Genetics*]
PD.............	Parish District (SAUS)
PD.............	Parity Digit (SAUS)
PD.............	Parke-Davis [*Commercial firm*] (DAVI)
PD.............	Parkinsonism Dementia [*Medicine*]
PD.............	Parkinson's Disease [*Medicine*]
PD.............	Pars Distalis [*Medicine*]
PD.............	Part Damaged (ROG)
PD.............	Partial Delivery (SAUS)
PD.............	Partial Denture (MELL)
PD.............	Partial Depletion (SAUS)
PD.............	Partial Derivative (SAUS)
PD.............	Partial Discharge [*High-voltage testing*] (IEEE)
PD.............	Participatory Design (SEWL)
PD.............	Particle-Density [*Forensic science*]
PD.............	Particle Dynamics (SAUS)
PD.............	Parti Democratique [*Democratic Party*] [*Luxembourg*] Political party] (EAIO)
PD.............	Partido Democrata [*Democratic Party*] [*Costa Rica*] [*Political party*] (PPW)
PD.............	Partido Democrata [*Democratic Party*] [*Chile*] [*Political party*]
pd.............	Passed (ODBW)
PD.............	Passed
PD.............	Passive Defence (SAUS)
PD.............	Passive Detection [*Electronics*]
PD.............	Past Due
PD.............	Paste-Down [*Album*] [*Photography*] (ROG)
PD.............	Patent Ductus [*Cardiology*] (MAE)
PD.............	Pattern Detection (SAUS)
PD.............	Pavement Design (SAUS)
PD.............	Pay Department [*Army*] [*British*] (ROG)
PD.............	Pay Dirt
PD.............	Payload Developer (SAUS)
PD.............	Payload Diameter
PD.............	Peak Detector
PD.............	Pedestal (IAA)
PD.............	Pediatric [*or Pediatrics*]
Pd.............	Pediatrics (DMAA)
PD.............	Pem Air [*ICAO designator*] (AD)
PD.............	Pen Down (SAUS)
P/D............	Penetration Diameter [*Military*]
PD.............	People's Democracy [*Ireland*] [*Political party*]
PD.............	Pepper Dust [*An adulterating element*]
PD.............	Percent Difference (SAUS)
PD.............	Percutaneous Drain [*Surgery*] (DAVI)
PD.............	Per Day (SAUS)
pd.............	Per Diem [*By the day*] [*Latin*] (WDMC)
PD.............	Per Diem [*By the Day*] [*Latin*]
PD.............	Per Diluquim [*By Deliquescence*] [*Pharmacy*] (ROG)
PD.............	Perfect Diffuser [*Optics*]
PD.............	Performance Data (SAUS)
PD.............	Performance Demonstration (MCD)
PD.............	Performer Diploma (PGP)
PD.............	Periderm [*Botany*]
PD.............	Period (AABC)
PD.............	Periodic Duty (IAA)
PD.............	Peripheral Decoder (SAUS)
PD.............	Peripheral Device (BUR)
PD.............	Periscope Depth (IAA)
PD.............	Peritoneal Dialysis [*Medicine*]
PD.............	Permanent Deactivation
PD.............	Permanent Dunnage (SAUS)
PD.............	Permissible Dose
PD.............	Permits Division [*Environmental Protection Agency*] (GFGA)
PD.............	Perphenazine Decanoate (SAUS)
PD.............	Personal Disposition [*G. W. Allport*] (DIPS)
PD.............	Personality Disorder (MELL)
PD.............	Personnel Department
PD.............	Personnel Depot (SAUS)
PD.............	Personnel Development
PD.............	Personnel Distribution [*Army*]
PD.............	Perthes' Disease (MELL)
PD.............	Peyronie's Disease (MELL)
PD.............	Pharmacopoeia of Dublin (SAUS)
PD.............	Pharmacy Director
PD.............	Pharmacy Dispenser [*British military*] (DMA)
PD.............	Phase-Change Dual (SAUS)
PD.............	Phase Detection (SAUS)
PD.............	Phase Discriminator
PD.............	Phase Distortion (SAUS)
PD.............	Phelps Dodge [*NYSE symbol*] (TTSB)
PD.............	Phelps Dodge Corp. [*NYSE symbol*] (SPSG)
PD.............	Phenyldichlorarsine [*A war gas*]
PD.............	Philosophiae Doctor [*Doctor of Philosophy*]
PD.............	Philosophy Doctor (SAUS)
PD.............	Phosphate Dehydrogenase
PD.............	Phosphate Dextrose (DAVI)
PD.............	Phosphodiester [*Organic chemistry*]
PD.............	Photodesorption (SAUS)
PD.............	Photo-Detection (or Detector) (SAUS)
PD.............	Photodielectric (SAUS)
PD.............	Photodiode
PD.............	Photo Distance (SAUS)
PD.............	Photosensitivity Dermatitis [*Medicine*] (DMAA)
PD.............	Phyllis Dorothy James White [*In name P. D. James*] [*Author*]
PD.............	Physical Damage [*Insurance*]
PD.............	Physical Development (IAA)
PD.............	Physical Disabilities
PD.............	Physical Distribution (ADA)
PD.............	Physically Disabled (SAUS)
PD.............	Physics Department
PD.............	Picknick Dam [*TVA*]
PD.............	Picks Disease (SAUS)
P/D............	Pickup and Deposit
PD.............	Pictorial Display (MCD)
PD.............	Piece Dyed (SAUS)
PD.............	Pierce's Disease [*Plant pathology*]
PD.............	Pilot Dogs (EA)
PD.............	Piskei Din Shel Bet ha-Mishpat ha-'Elyon le-Yisrael (BJA)
PD.............	Pitch Circle Diameter [*Technical drawings*] (IAA)
PD.............	Pitch Diameter
PD.............	Pitch Down (MCD)
PD.............	Pitcher Defense (SAUS)
P/D............	Pitch-to-Diameter (SAUS)
PD.............	Pivoted Door (AAG)
PD.............	Planar-Doped (SAUS)
PD.............	Plane Disagreement [*Telecommunications*] (TEL)
PD.............	Planned Derating [*Electronics*] (IEEE)
PD.............	Planning Directive (NG)
PD.............	Planning Document
PD.............	Plans Division [*Military*]
PD.............	Plant Deficiency (SAUS)
PD.............	Plasma Defect [*Hematology*] (DAVI)
PD.............	Plasma Deposited (IAA)
PD.............	Plasma Desorption [*of ions for analysis*]
PD.............	Plasma Display
PD.............	Plasmodesmata [*Botanical cytology*]
PD.............	Plastic Drum Institute
PD.............	Plate Dissipation
PD.............	Platelet Deaggregation [*Hematology*]
PD.............	Plausible Deniability
PD.............	Plotting Display (SAUS)
PD.............	Plug & Display (SAUS)
PD.............	Plumbing Damage (ADWA)
PD.............	Point Defense
PD.............	Point Delay Fuze [*Army*]

PD	Point Detonating [*Projectile*]		PD	Probate Division (SAUS)
PD	Polar Distance [*Navigation*]		PD	Problem Definition [*Army*]
P/D	Polarizer/Diplexer (SAUS)		PD	Problem Determination (SAUS)
PD	Police Department		PD	Procedure Division (SAUS)
PD	Policy Determination (GNE)		PD	Procedure Division (VLIE)
pd	Pond [*Pound*] [*Monetary unit*] [*Afrikaans*]		PD	Procedures Description (COE)
PD	Pontoon Dock		PD	Procesing Data (SAUS)
PD	Pool Density [*Pisciculture*]		PD	Process Data (NITA)
PD	Poor Decals		PD	Process Descriptor [*Computer science*] (ELAL)
PD	Poorly Differentiated [*Medicine*]		PD	Process Descriptor [*Telecommunications*] (IAA)
PD	Population Density (NRCH)		PD	Process Diagnostic [*Interpersonal skills and attitudes test*]
PD	Population Distribution (NRCH)		PD	Procurement Data
PD	Population Doubling		PD	Procurement Directive [*Army*]
PD	Porak-Durante [*Disease*] [*Medicine*] (DB)		PD	Procurement District [*Air Force*] (AFIT)
PD	Pore Diameter		PD	Procurement Division
PD	Porphobilinogen Deaminase [*Clinical chemistry*] (MAE)		PD	Procurement Document (NASA)
PD	Porsche Design		PD	Procurement Drawing
PD	Port Director		pd	Pro Defendente [*On Behalf of Defendant*] [*Latin*] [*Legal term*] (DLA)
PD	Port Du [*Carriage Forward*] [*French*]		PD	Product Definition (SAUS)
PD	Port Dues		PD	Product Design [*Phase*]
PD	Porting Demonstration (SAUS)		P/D	Product Development
PD	Port of Debarkation [*Navy*]		PD	Production and Deployment Phase [*Military*] (MCD)
PD	Position Description		PD	Production Department
PD	Position Document		PD	Production Director (NTCM)
PD	Position Doubtful [*Nautical charts*]		PD	Professional Development (ADA)
PD	Positive Definite (SAUS)		PD	Professional Digital [*Recording*] (NTCM)
PD	Positive Density (SAUS)		PD	Professional Diploma [*Education*] (AEE)
PD	Positive Displacement		PD	Profile Descent (GAVI)
PD	Positives and Deposition (DGA)		PD	Programa Democratico [*Democratic Program*] [*Spain*] [*Political party*] (PPE)
PD	Postage Due			
PD	Postal District		PD	Program Deceleration (KSC)
PD	Post Dated (WDAA)		PD	Program Decoder
PD	Post Diluvium [*After the Flood*] [*Latin*] (ROG)		PD	Program Development (SAUS)
PD	Post District (SAUS)		PD	Program Directive (NG)
PD	Postdoctorate		PD	Program Director [*Television*]
PD	Posterior Deltoid [*Myology*]		PD	Program Document (SAUS)
PD	Posterior Digestive [*Gland*]		PD	Programmable Device (SAUS)
PD	Postnasal Drainage [*Medicine*]		PD	Programming Device (SAUS)
PD	Postural Drainage [*Medicine*] (MAE)		PD	Progression of Disease [*Medicine*]
PD	Potassium Dichromate (SAUS)		PD	Progressive Democrats [*Ireland*] [*Political party*]
pd	Potential Difference (MELL)		PD	Project Definition (SAUS)
PD	Potential Difference [*Electricity*]		PD	Project Description (EEVL)
PD	Pound (ROG)		PD	Project Development (ABAC)
PD	Power Density (SAUS)		PD	Project Directive (NASA)
PD	Power Dissipation (VLIE)		PD	Project Director
PD	Power Distribution		PD	Project Document
PD	Power Divider (IAA)		PD	Project Documentation (SAUS)
PD	Power Doubler (IAA)		PD	Projected Decision Date (NRCH)
PD	Power Driven (IAA)		PD	Projected Display
PD	Precision Device [*British military*] (DMA)		PD	Projection Distance (SAUS)
PD	Precision Drilling (1987) Ltd. [*Toronto Stock Exchange symbol*]		PD	Promotion Director
PD	Predeployment		PD	Promotion Dossier (HEAS)
P/D	Predicted [*NASA*] (KSC)		PD	Propagation Delay (MLOA)
PD	Pre-Digital (SAUS)		PD	Propellant Dispersal (NAKS)
PD	Predilute		PD	Propellant Dispersion (KSC)
PD	Preference for Duty		PD	Property Damage
PD	Pregnanediol [*Biochemistry*]		PD	Property Disposition [*FHA*] (EMRF)
PD	Preliminary Design		PD	Propodite-Dactylopodite (SAUS)
PD	Prescription Drug		PD	Proportional Derivative (IAA)
PD	Present Disease (SAUS)		PD	Proportional-Differential (SAUS)
PD	Presidential Determination		PD	Proportional Plus Derivative (IAA)
PD	Presidential Directive		PD	Proposal Development (AAG)
PD	Press Division [*Environmental Protection Agency*] (GFGA)		PD	Prostatodynia [*Medicine*]
PD	Pressor Dose [*Medicine*]		PD	Protective Device (BUR)
PD	Pressure Demand (SAUS)		PD	Protective Dose (SAUS)
PD	Pressure Destillate (SAUS)		PD	Protein Diet (DMAA)
Pd	Pressure, Diastolic [*Cardiology*]		PD	Protocol Driver (SAUS)
PD	Pressure Difference (SAUS)		PD	Prototype Demonstration
PD	Pressure Distillate (IAA)		PD	Provisioning Document
PD	Pressure Dose (SAUS)		PD	Provocation Dose [*Medicine*] (MEDA)
PD	Pressure Drop (KSC)		PD	Proximity Detector
PD	Presumptive Disability [*Title XVI*] [*Social Security Administration*] (OICC)		PD	Prussian Dollar [*Monetary unit*] (ROG)
			PD	Pseudohomogeneous Axial Dispersion Model [*Fluid dynamics*]
PD	Pretty Disgusting (WDAA)		PD	Psychodynamic
PD	Prevention Detention [*Scotland Yard*]		Pd	Psychopathic Deviate [*Psychology*]
PD	Preventive Dentistry (DAVI)		PD	Psychotic Depression [*Medicine*]
PD	Preventive Detention (SAUS)		PD	Psychotic Deviate [*Psychiatry*] (DAVI)
PD	Prime Depot (SAUS)		PD	Publication Date [*Online database field identifier*]
PD	Prime Driver		PD	Public Defender [*Australia*]
PD	Primer Driver (SAUS)		PD	Public Domain
PD	Principal Directorate (SAUS)		PD	Published Document (SAUS)
PD	Principal Distance [*Graphic arts*] (OA)		PD	Publisher's Directory [*Formerly, BPD*] [*A publication*]
PD	Printer Driver		PD	Pulley Drive (IAA)
PD	Printer's Devil (ROG)		PD	Pulmonary Disease [*Medicine*]
PD	Priority Designator [*Army*]		PD	Pulpodistal [*Dentistry*]
PD	Priority Directive		PD	Pulsed Doppler (SAUS)
PD	Prism Diopter		PD	Pulse Detector [*Spectroscopy*]
PD	Prisoner's Dilemma [*Psychology*]		PD	Pulse Doppler
PD	Privatdozent [*Tutor*] [*German*]		PD	Pulse Driver
PD	Private Detective		PD	Pulse Duration
PD	Probability Density [*Statistics*] (IAA)		PD	Punch Delay (SAUS)
PD	Probability of Damage (MCD)		PD	Punch Die (SAUS)
PD	Probability of Death [*Biology*]		P-D	Punch-Die (MSA)
PD	Probability of Destruction (SAUS)		PD	Punch Driver
PD	Probability of Detection		PD	Punched Data (SAUS)

PD	Punching Device (SAUS)
pd	Pupillary Distance [*Medicine*]
PD	Purchase Description
PD	Pushdown (SAUS)
PD	Pyloric Dilator [*Neuron*]
PD1	Pyramidal Decussation [*Neuroanatomy*]
PD1	Portable Dictionary 1 [*English/Japanese electronic dictionary*] [*Sanyo Electric*]
PDA	Pacific Dance Association (EA)
PDA	Pacific Dermatologic Association (EA)
PDA	Packaging Distributors Association [*British*] (DBA)
PDA	Paediatric Allergy (SAUS)
PDA	Panhellenic Dental Association (BUAC)
PDA	Parallel Data Adapter
PDA	Parallel Drive Array [*Computer science*] (CIST)
PDA	Parametric Design Analysis (RDA)
PDA	Parenteral Drug Abuser (STED)
PDA	Parenteral Drug Association (MELL)
PdA	Partei der Arbeit [*Labor Party*] [*Switzerland*] [*Political party*] (PPE)
PDA	Parti Democratico da Angola [*Democratic Party of Angola*] [*Political party*]
PDA	Partido Democratico Arubano [*Democratic Party of Aruba*] [*Political party*] (EY)
PDA	Parti Dolonti Applicandum [*Apply to Painful Part*] [*Pharmacy*] (ROG)
PDA	Partit Democrata d'Andorra [*Andorran Democratic Party*] [*Political party*] (PPW)
Pd'A	Partito d'Azione [*Action Party*] [*Italy*] [*Political party*] (PPE)
PdA	Parts Disposal Area (MCD)
PDA	Party of Democratic Action [*Bosnia-Herzegovina*] [*Political party*] (EY)
PDA	Pasadena Energy [*Vancouver Stock Exchange symbol*]
PDA	Patent Ductus Arteriosus [*Cardiology*]
PDA	Patents and Designs Act (SAUS)
PDA	Patient Data Automation
PDA	Patient Distress Alarm (STED)
PDA	Payload Accommodations (SAUS)
PDA	Payroll Deduction Authorization (MCD)
PDA	Peak Distribution Analyzer
PdA	Pediatric Allergy [*Medicine*] (DMAA)
PDA	Pediatric Allergy
PDA	Pentadecanoic Acid [*Organic chemistry*]
PDA	Percent Defective Allowable (MHDB)
PDA	Perdigao SA ADS [*NYSE symbol*]
PDA	Periodontal Abscess (MELL)
PDA	Peripheral Data Acquisition (SAUS)
PDA	Permanent Duty Assignment [*Air Force*] (AFM)
PDA	Personal Data Assistant
PDA	Personal Death Awareness (SAUS)
PDA	Personal Deposit Account [*Banking*]
PDA	Personal Digital Assistant [*Computer science*]
PDA	Petrol Dealers' Association [*British*]
PDA	Phased-Doppler Anemometer (SAUS)
PDA	Phenylenediamine [*Chemistry*]
PDA	Philadelphia Dance Alliance
PDA	Phorbol Diacetate [*Organic chemistry*]
PDA	Photodiode Array [*Instrumentation*]
PDA	Photographic Dealers' Association [*British*] (BI)
PDA	Photon Detector Assembly (MCD)
PDA	Physical Device Address [*Computer science*] (IBMDP)
PDA	Piperidinedicarboxylic Acid [*Organic chemistry*]
PDA	Pisatin Demethylase [*An enzyme*]
PDA	Plywood Distributors Association (SAUS)
PDA	Point Density Analysis [*Mathematics*]
PDA	Point Director Array
PDA	Pointing Device Adapter [*Computer science*]
PDA	Poise Distribution Amplifier (AFM)
PDA	Polarization Diversity Array
PDA	Polydiacetylene [*Organic chemistry*]
PDA	Polydiarylamine (SAUS)
PDA	Poly(dimethylacrylamide) [*Organic chemistry*]
PDA	Polydrug Abuse (MELL)
PDA	Ponta Delgada [*Azores*] [*Seismograph station code, US Geological Survey*] (SEIS)
PDA	Population and Community Development Association [*Thailand*] (BUAC)
PDA	Population Drainage Area [*Civil Defense*]
PDA	Portable Diagnostic Analyzer (SSD)
PDA	Portable Digital Assistant (SEWL)
PDA	Port Defence Area (SAUS)
PDA	Port Development Authority (SAUS)
PDA	Post Acceleration (IAA)
PDA	Post-Deflection Accelerator (DEN)
PDA	Post-Delivery Availability [*Military*] (NVT)
PDA	Post-Design Analysis
PDA	Post Diffused Alloyed (SAUS)
PDA	Posterior Descending Artery [*Anatomy*] (DAVI)
PDA	Potato Dextrose Agar [*Culture media*]
PDA	Pour Dire Adieu [*To Say Farewell*] [*On visiting cards*] [*French*]
PDA	Power Distribution Assembly (KSC)
PDA	Precision Drive Axis (KSC)
PDA	Predelivery Acceptance Test [*NASA*]
PDA	Predialyzed Human Albumin [*Medicine*] (MAE)
PDA	Predicted Drift Angle [*Navigation*]
PDA	Predocketed Application (NRCH)
PDA	Pregnancy Discrimination Act [*An amendment to Title VII of the Civil Rights Act of 1964*] (PAZ)
PDA	Pregnancy Discrimination Act of 1978 (WYGK)
PDA	Preliminary Damage Assessment [*Department of Emergency Management*] (DEMM)
PDA	Preliminary Design Acceptance (NRCH)
PDA	Preliminary Design Activity (LAIN)
PDA	Preliminary Design Approval [*or Authorization*] (NRCH)
PDA	Preliminary Design Assessment [*Nuclear energy*] (NRCH)
PDA	Preliminary Design Audit (SAUS)
PDA	Preliminary Design Authorization (SAUS)
PDA	Prescription Drug Abuse (MELL)
PDA	Present Duty Assignment Option [*Military*]
PDA	Primary Data Acquisition (SAUS)
PDA	Principal Decision Authority (DOMA)
PDA	Principal Deputy for Acquistion [*Army*] (RDA)
PDA	Principal Development Activity [*Navy*]
PDA	Principal Development Authority (MCD)
PDA	Principal Diagonal Artery [*Anatomy*] (DAVI)
PDA	Principal DOD Executive (AAGC)
PDA	Private Doctors of America [*Defunct*] (EA)
PDA	Private Doctors of Australia (SAUS)
PDA	Probabilistic Decision Algorithm [*Artificial intelligence job performance aid*] [*Army*]
PDA	Probabilities Decision Analysis (SAUS)
PDA	Probability Density Analyzer (SAUS)
PDA	Probability Discrete Automata (IEEE)
PDA	Probability Discrete Automation
PDA	Probability Distribution Analyzer [*Statistics*]
PDA	Probably Disappointed Again (PCM)
PDA	Probate, Divorce, and Admiralty [*British*] (DLA)
PDA	Problem Determination Aid (EECA)
PDA	Problem Determination Application (VLIE)
PDA	Procedure Departure Authorization (SAUS)
PDA	Process Defect Average [*Quality management*]
PDA	Process Design Analysis [*Program*]
PDA	Processor and Distribution Assembly [*Viking lander analysis equipment*] [*NASA*]
PDA	Procurement Defense Agencies [*DoD*]
PDA	Product Departure Authorization
PDA	Production Data Acquisition [*Computer science*] (VLIE)
PDA	Professional Designers' Association (BUAC)
PDA	Professional Drivers Association
PDA	Program Developing Agency [*Military*] (CAAL)
PDA	Prolonged Depolarizing Afterpotential [*Neurophysiology*]
PDA	Propanediamine [*Organic chemistry*]
PDA	Propellant Drain Area (NASA)
PDA	Property Disposal Account [*Military*] (NG)
PDA	Property Disposal Agency
PDA	Property Disposal Agent [*Military*] (NG)
PDA	Property Disposal Authorization (SAUS)
PDA	Property Disposition Authorization
PDA	Proposed Development Approach [*Navy*]
PDA	Propylenediamine [*Organic chemistry*]
PDA	Prospectors' and Developers' Association [*Canada*]
PDA	Prototype Development Associate
PDA	Public Display of Affection [*Slang*]
PDA	Puerto Inirida [*Colombia*] [*Airport symbol*] (OAG)
PDA	Pulmonary Disease Anemia [*Medicine*] (STED)
PDA	Pulse Demodulation Analysis
PDA	Pulse Discrimination Analysis (SAUS)
PDA	Pulse Distribution Amplifier
PDA	Pump Distributors Association [*British*] (DBA)
PDA	Pump Distributors Association of Great Britain (BUAC)
PDA	Pump Drive Assembly
PDA	Punch Die Assembly (SAUS)
PDA	Push Down Acceptor (SAUS)
PDA	Pushdown Automation [*Computer science*] (HGAA)
PDAAP	Plume Data Analysis of Advanced Propellants (MCD)
PDAB	Para-(Dimethylamino)benzaldehyde [*Organic chemistry*]
PDAB	P-Dimethyl Amino Benzaldehyde (SAUS)
PDAB	Physical Disability Appeals Board [*Military*] (AFM)
PDAC	Professional Development Advisory Committee [*American Occupational Therapy Association*]
PDAC	Prospectors and Developers Association of Canada (EAIO)
PDAD	Photodiode Array Detector [*Spectrophotometry*]
PDAD	Probate, Divorce, and Admiralty Division [*Legal*] [*British*] (ROG)
PDAD	Proposed Draft Addendum (SAUS)
PDAES	Proceedings of the Devon Archaeological Exploration Society (SAUS)
PDAF	Provincial Department of Agriculture and Forestry (SAUS)
PDAFSC	Projected Duty Air Force Specialty Code (AFM)
PDAID	Problem Determination Aid [*Computer science*] (MDG)
PDA J Pharm Sci Technol	PDA Journal of Pharmaceutical Science and Technology (SAUS)
PDAK	Party of Democratic Action for Kosovo [*Serbia*] [*Political party*] (BUAC)
PDA-KM	Party of Democratic Action of Kosovo-Metohija [*Serbia*] [*Political party*] (EY)
PDAL	Post-Deflection Acceleration Lens (SAUS)
PDalCM	College Misericordia, Dallas, PA [*Library symbol*] [*Library of Congress*] (LCLS)
PDAM	Periodontal Disease-Associated Microbiotae [*Dentistry*]
PDAM	Proposed Draft Amendment (SAUS)
PD&C	Plug Drive and Control (SAUS)
PD & C	Postural Drainage and Clapping [*Medicine*] (DAVI)

PD&C	Power Distribution and Control
PD & D	Product Design & Development [*Radnor, PA*] [*A publication*]
PD & E	Provisioning Documentation and Effort [*Military*] (AFIT)
PD & P	Postural Drainage and Percussion [*Medicine*] (DAVI)
PD&P	Project Definition and Planning (CIST)
PD & PL	Property Damage and Public Liability [*Insurance*] (IIA)
PD & R	Policy Development and Research
PD & RS	Payload Deployment and Retrieval Subsystem [*NASA*] (NASA)
PDanMHi	Montour County Historical Society, Danville, PA [*Library symbol*] [*Library of Congress*] (LCLS)
PDanSH	Danville State Hospital, Danville, PA [*Library symbol*] [*Library of Congress*] (LCLS)
PDAP	Palmer Drug Abuse Program (DMAA)
PDAP	Program Data Analysis Plan (SAUS)
PDAP	Programmable Digital Autopilot (MCD)
PDAP	Provincial Development Assistance Program [*Agency for International Development*]
PDAP	Publication Design and Ad Placement (DGA)
PDAPS	Pollution Detection and Prevention System (SAUS)
PDAR	Parts Drawing Approval Request (MCD)
PD/AR	Photosensitivity Dermatitis and Actinic Reticuloid Syndrome [*Medicine*] (DMAA)
PDAR	Preferential Departure [*Aviation*] (DA)
PDAR	Preferential Departure and Arrival Route [*FAA*] (TAG)
PDAR	Producibility Design Analysis Report (AAG)
PDAR	Product Disposition Authorization Report (SAUS)
PDAR	Program Description and Requirements [*NASA*] (NASA)
PDA Rec	PDA Recorder (SAUS)
PDARR	Production Drawing and Assembly Release Record (AAG)
PDARS	Pulsed Doppler Acoustic Radar System (SAUS)
PDAS	Paid Associate (SAUS)
PDA-S	Party of Democratic Action of the Sandjak [*Serbia*] [*Political party*] (EY)
PDAS	Photo Data Analysis System [*Navy*]
PDAS	Photodiode Array Spectrophotometer [*Marine science*] (OSRA)
PDAS	Physiological Data Acquisition System (SAUS)
PDAS	Plant Data Acquisition System (NRCH)
PDAS	Police Department American Samoa (SAUS)
PDAS	[*A*] Popular Dictionary of Australian Slang [*A publication*]
PDAS	Portable Data Acquisition System (MCD)
PDAS	Process Design Analysis System (CIST)
PDAS	Programmable Data Acquisition System (IDOE)
PDAS	Programming and Design Assist System (SAUS)
PDAS	Pulmonary Disease-Anemia Syndrome (MELL)
PDASD	Principal Deputy Assistant Secretary of Defense
PDAT	Portable Digital Access Transceiver (ACAE)
PDate	Pay Date
PDATE	Production Date [*Computer science*]
PDA Tube	Post-Deflection Accelerated Tube (SAUS)
PDAU	Physical Data Access Unit (SAUS)
PDAU	Physical Delivery Access Unit (VLIE)
PDAV	Parkinson's Disease Association of Victoria [*Australia*]
P (Day)	Production Day [*Army*] (AABC)
Pd B	Bachelor of Pedagogy
PDB	Isotope Standard for Carbon (SAUS)
PDB	Packard Data Bank (EA)
PDB	Paget's Disease of Bone (MELL)
PDB	Para-Dichlorobenzene [*Insecticide for moths, etc.*]
PDB	Parallel Data Base (SAUS)
PDB	Parametric Data Base
PDB	Partei der Deutschsprachigen Belgier [*Party of German-Speaking Belgians*] [*Political party*] (PPW)
PDB	Pedro Bay [*Alaska*] [*Airport symbol*] (OAG)
PDB	Pee Dee Belemnite [*An isotopic standard for oxygen and carbon*]
PDB	Pentadecylbenzene [*Organic chemistry*]
PDB	Performance Data Base (GAVI)
PDB	Performance Data Book (NASA)
PDB	Periodical Directories and Bibliographies [*A publication*]
PDB	Personality Data Base
PDB	Phorbol Dibutyrate [*Also, PDBu*] [*Organic chemistry*]
PDB	Phosphorus-Dissolving Bacteria [*Microbiology*]
PDB	Physical Data Base [*Computer science*] (VLIE)
PDB	Piedmont Bancorp, Inc. [*AMEX symbol*] (SAG)
PDB	Pierce's Disease Bacterium [*Plant pathology*]
PDB	Pilot Database
PDB	Planar-Doped Barrier (SAUS)
PDB	Plant Damage Bin [*Environmental science*] (COE)
PDB	Plasma Diagnostic Base
PDB	Police Discipline Board [*New South Wales, Australia*]
PDB	Positive Displacement Blower
PDB	Potato Dextrose Broth [*Microbiology*]
PDB	Power Disc Brakes [*Automotive term*]
PDB	Power Distribution Box (NASA)
PDB	President's Daily Brief
PDB	Price Decontrol Board [*Post-World War II*]
PDB	Primary Data Bus [*Computer science*]
PDB	Primary Dispersal Base (CCCA)
PDB	Process Data Base (SAUS)
PDB	Process Descriptor Base [*Telecommunications*] (TEL)
PDB	Process Display Data Base [*Computer science*] (ECII)
PDB	Product Description Block (SAUS)
PDB	Program Definition Block (NITA)
PDB	Project Data Base (SAUS)
PDB	Project Development Brochure [*Military*]
PDB	Protein Data Bank [*Brookhaven National Laboratory*] [*Information service or system*] (CRD)
PDB	Psychic Detective Bureau (EA)
PDB	Public Debt Bureau (SAUS)
PDBA	Personnel Database Application (MCD)
PDBA/SIPM	Personnel Database Application / Student Instructor Performance Module (DNAB)
PDBH	Production Broach (AAG)
PDBIN	Processor Data Bus In (MHDI)
PDBM	Pulse Delay Binary Modulation (MCD)
PDBMI	Periodical Directories and Bibliographies Master Index [*A publication*]
PDBP	Powered Disposal Bomb Pod (AAG)
PDBR	Page-Directory Base Register [*Computer science*] (BYTE)
PDBR	Physical Data Base Record [*Computer science*] (VLIE)
PDBS	Pictorial Data Base System
PDBU	Pesticides Documentation Bulletin
PDBu	Phorbol Dibutyrate [*Also, PDB*] [*Organic chemistry*]
PD Bus	Process Data Bus (SAUS)
PDBz	Phorbol Dibenzoate [*Organic chemistry*]
PDC	Center for Parallel Computers (SAUS)
PDC	Community College of Philadelphia, Philadelphia, PA [*OCLC symbol*] (OCLC)
PDC	Mueo [*New Caledonia*] [*Airport symbol*] (OAG)
PDC	Pacific Defense College (CINC)
PDC	Pacific Development Corp. (SAUS)
PDC	Pacific Digital Cellular (CGWS)
PDC	Pacific Disaster Center
PDC	Package Design Council [*New York, NY*] (EA)
PDC	Packaging Design Criteria (SAUS)
PDC	Pacte Democratica per Catalunya [*Democratic Pact for Catalonia*] [*Spain*] [*Political party*] (PPE)
PDC	Page Description Communications [*Microsoft Corp.*] (PCM)
PDC	Paleoenvironmental Database of China (SAUS)
PDC	Paper Distribution Centers
PDC	Paper Distribution Council (EA)
PDC	Paper Double Cotton (SAUS)
PDC	Parallel Data Communicator (AAG)
PDC	Parallel Data Controller
PDC	Parallel Digital Computer (SAUS)
PDC	Parametric Defense Coverage
PDC	Park Distance Control [*Automotive electronics*]
PDC	Parti Democrate Chretien [*Christian Democratic Party*] [*Burundi*] [*Political party*]
PDC	Parti Democrate-Chretien Suisse [*Christian Democratic Party of Switzerland*] [*Political party*] (PPE)
PDC	Parti des Democrates Camerounais [*Political party*] (EY)
PDC	Partido da Democracia Cristao [*Christian Democratic Party*] [*Portugal*] [*Political party*] (PPW)
PDC	Partido Democracia Cristiana [*Christian Democratic Party*] [*Guatemala*] [*Political party*] (PPW)
PDC	Partido Democrata Cristiana [*Christian Democratic Party*] [*Panama*] [*Political party*] (PPW)
PDC	Partido Democrata Cristiano [*Christian Democratic Party*] [*Bolivia*] [*Political party*] (PPW)
PDC	Partido Democrata Cristiano [*Christian Democratic Party*] [*Costa Rica*] [*Political party*] (PPW)
PDC	Partido Democrata Cristiano [*Christian Democratic Party*] [*Honduras*] [*Political party*] (PPW)
PDC	Partido Democrata Cristiano [*Christian Democratic Party*] [*Paraguay*] [*Political party*] (PPW)
PDC	Partido Democrata Cristiano [*Christian Democratic Party*] [*Peru*] [*Political party*] (PPW)
PDC	Partido Democrata Cristiano [*Christian Democratic Party*] [*El Salvador*] [*Political party*]
PDC	Partido Democrata de Confianza Nacional [*Nicaragua*] [*Political party*] (EY)
PDC	Partido Democratico Cristao [*Christian Democratic Party*] [*Brazil*] [*Political party*]
PDC	Partido Democratico Cristiano [*Christian Democratic Party*] [*Argentina*] [*Political party*] (PPW)
PDC	Partido Democratico Cristiano [*Christian Democratic Party*] [*Chile*] [*Political party*] (PPW)
PDC	Partisan Defence Committee (BUAC)
PDC	Partito della Democrazia Cristiana [*Christian Democratic Party*] [*Italy*] [*Political party*]
PDC	Partners for Democratic Change [*An association*] (EA)
PDC	Parts Distribution Center (SAUS)
PDC	Passive Data Collection
PDC	Pediatric Cardiology [*Medical specialty*] (DHSM)
PDC	Penang Development Corp. (SAUS)
PDC	Pentadecylcatechol [*An allergen*]
PDC	Peoples Defense Committee (SAUS)
PDC	Per Diem, Travel and Transportation Allowance Committee for Departments of the Army, Navy, and Air Force
PDC	Performance Data Computer
PDC	Performance Development Corp. (SAUS)
PDC	Period and Damping Controlled (SAUS)
PDC	Periodical Distributors of Canada (SAUS)
PDC	Peripheral Device Controller [*Computer science*] (VLIE)
PDC	Permanent Data Call (SAUS)
PDC	Personal Digital Cellular (SAUS)
PDC	Personnel Data Card
PDC	Personnel Despatch Centre (SAUS)
PDC	Personnel Dispersal Centre (SAUS)
PDC	Personnel Distributing Center (SAUS)

PDC	Personnel Distribution Command
PDC	Peru Debt Campaign (BUAC)
PDC	Petroleum Development Corp. (EFIS)
PDC	Petroleum Distribution Command (SAUS)
PDC	Philosophy Documentation Center
PDC	Photo-Data Card [Trademark] [Computer science]
PDC	Photonuclear Data Center [National Institute of Standards and Technology]
PDC	Physical Development Centre (SAUS)
PDC	Pieve Di Cadore [Italy] [Seismograph station code, US Geological Survey] [Closed] (SEIS)
PDC	Piston-Driven Compaction (MCD)
PDC	Plastic Dielectric Capacitor
PDC	Pneumatic Damping Control
PDC	Polaris Documentation Control [Missiles]
PDC	Policy Determination Committee (AAG)
PDC	Polycrystalline Diamond Compact [Well drilling technology]
PDC	Polycrystalline Diamond Compact Drill Bit
PDC	Polystyrene Dielectric Capacitor
PDC	Population Documentation Center [Food and Agriculture Organization] [United Nations] [Information service or system] (IID)
PDC	Portable Data Carrier
PDC	Portable Data Communications [British]
PDC	Position Depth Charge
PDC	Power Demand Charges (SAUS)
PDC	Power Disk Cartridge (SAUS)
PDC	Power Distribution and Control
PDC	Power Distribution Center [Automotive engineering]
PDC	Power Distribution Control (SAUS)
PDC	Power Distribution Cubiale (NATG)
PDC	Practice Depth Charge
PDC	Prairie Du Chien, WI [Location identifier] [FAA] (FAAL)
PDC	Predecessors and Defunct Companies (NITA)
PDC	Predefined Command (MCD)
PDC	Predeparture Check [Aviation] (AIA)
PDC	Pre-Departure Clearance [FAA] (TAG)
PDC	Predetection Combining (IAA)
PDC	Predocketed Construction (NRCH)
PDC	Pregnancy Distress Center (SAUS)
PDC	Preliminary Diagnostic Clinic
PDC	Premission Documentation Change [NASA] (KSC)
PDC	Premium and Dispersion Credits [Insurance]
PDC	Prescott Development Corp. [Vancouver Stock Exchange symbol]
PDC	Presely Cos. 'A' [NYSE symbol] (TTSB)
PDC	Presley Co. [NYSE symbol] (SPSG)
PDC	Pressure Die Casting [Commercial firm] [British]
PDC	Prevention of Deterioration Center [Defunct] (EA)
PDC	Price Decontrol Board [Post-World War II] [A publication] (DLA)
PDC	Primary Development Contract (SAUS)
PDC	Primary Domain Controller [Computer science] (VLIE)
PDC	Primary Dtstribution Course (SAUS)
PDC	Printing Density Controller (SAUS)
PDC	Printing Desk Calculator (SAUS)
PDC	Private Diagnostic Clinic
PDC	Probability of Detection and Conversion [Military]
PDC	Process Data Collector (TIMI)
PDC	Procurement Document Change (NASA)
PDC	Production Decision Criteria
PDC	Production Drawing Control
PDC	Productivity and Development Center [Philippines] (BUAC)
PDC	Professional Developers Conference (SAUS)
PDC	Professional Development Center (SAUS)
PDC	Professional Development Committee (SAUS)
PDC	Proficiency Data Card [Army]
PDC	Program Data Cards (OICC)
PDC	Program Data Coordinator (MCD)
PDC	Program Development Computer (COE)
PDC	Programmable Data Controller (SAUS)
PDC	Programmable Desk Calculator (ELAL)
PDC	Programmable Digital Clock (SAUS)
PDC	Programmable Digital Controller (PDAA)
PDC	Programmes Directorate Committee [British]
PDC	Programming, Design & Construction System (SAUS)
PDC	Project Data Card
PDC	Project Data Control (MCD)
PDC	Project Data Coordinator
PDC	Project Design Criteria (SAUS)
PDC	Project Development Corp. (SAUS)
PDC	Prolog Development Center (SAUS)
PDC	Prolonged Detention Care (CPH)
PDC	Proposal Development Center (SAUS)
PDC	Prosthetic Distribution Center [Veterans Administration]
PDC	Proteus Digital Channel (SAUS)
PDC	Psychodevelopment Checklist [Psychology] (DAVI)
PDC	Publications Distribution Center [Military] (AFM)
PDC	Public Disclosure Commission
PDC	Public Dividend Capital (PDAA)
PDC	Public Documents Commission [Government agency]
PDC	Publishers' Data Center, Inc.
PDC	Pulse Discharge Cleaning (SAUS)
PDC	Pulse-Duration Commutator
PDC	Punched Data Carrier (SAUS)
PDC	Pure Direct Current [Electronics] (IAA)
PDC	Pyridinium Dichromate [Organic chemistry]
PDC	Pyrotechnic Devices Checker
PDC	Pyruvate Decarboxylase [An enzyme]
PDC	Pyruvate Dehydrogenase Complex [Also, PDHC] [Biochemistry]
PDC	Single Paper Double Cotton [Wire insulation] (AAG)
PDCA	Painting and Decorating Contractors of America (EA)
PDCA	Pile Driving Contractors Association (NTPA)
PDCA	Pioneer Dairymen's Club of America (EA)
PDCA	Plan-Do-Check-Act [Medicine] (DMAA)
PDCA	Posterior Descending Coronary Artery [Medicine] (MELL)
PDCA	Primary Degenerative Cerebral Disease [Medicine] (MELL)
PDCA	Pug Dog Club of America (EA)
PDCA	Purebred Dairy Cattle Association (EA)
PDCA	United States Professional Diving Coaches Association (EA)
PDCAB	Packet Services Compatibility Advisory Board (SAUS)
PDCAU	Pete Duel - Clube da Amizade do Universo [Pete Duel Universal Friendship Club - PDUFC] (EAIO)
PDCC	Print and Drawing Council of Canada [1976] (NGC)
PDCD	Primary Degenerative Cerebral Disease [Medicine] (DMAA)
PD-CD Drive	Phase Change Dual Compact Disk Drive [Computer science] (ITCA)
PDCE	Paramagnetic Design and Cost Effectiveness (SAUS)
PDCE	Parametric Design and Cost Effectiveness (SAUS)
PDCE	Parametric Design/Cost Effectiveness (SAUS)
PDCE	Passive Defence Control Element (SAUS)
PDCG	Partido Democracia Cristiana Guatemalteca [Guatemalan Christian Democratic Party] [Political party] (PPW)
PDCH	Parti Democratique Chretien d'Haiti [Political party] (EY)
PDCH	Physical Data Channel (SAUS)
PDCI	Package Design Council International (SAUS)
PDCI	Parti Democratique de la Cote-D'Ivoire [Democratic Party of the Ivory Coast] [Political party] (PPW)
PDCI	Product Data Call-In (EEVL)
Pdck	Probability of Detection Conversion and Kill [for an interceptor system] [Military]
PDCL	Provisioning Data Check List [NASA] (KSC)
PDCM	Positive Displacement Coring Motor (SAUS)
PDCN	Partido Democratico de Cooperacion Nacional [Democratic Party of National Cooperation] [Guatemala] [Political party]
PDCN	Production Development Change Notice
PDCN	Public Data Communications Network [Library science]
PDC Newsletter	Prevention of Deterioration Center Newsletter (SAUS)
PDCO	Patterson Dental [NASDAQ symbol] (TTSB)
PDCO	Patterson Dental Co. [NASDAQ symbol] (SAG)
PDCO	Property Disposal Contracting Officer [Military]
PDCP	Pilot's Display Control Panel
PDCP	Private Development Corp. of the Philippines
PDCPD	Polydicyclopentadiene [Organic chemistry]
PDCR	Project Data Compliance Report (MCD)
PDCR	Proprietary Data Control Record (NASA)
PDCRC	Periodontal Disease Clinical Research Center [State University of New York at Buffalo] [Research center] (RCD)
PDCS	Parallel Digital Computing System
PDCS	Partito Democratico Cristiano Sammarinese [Christian Democratic Party of San Marino] [Political party] (PPE)
PDCS	Performance Data Computer System (MCD)
PDCS	Power Distribution and Conditioning System (SAUS)
PDCS	Power Distribution and Control System [or Subsystem] [NASA] (NASA)
PDCS	Processing Distribution and Control System
PDCS	Product Data Control System (TIMI)
PDCS	Programmable Data Collection System [Military] (CAAL)
PDCS	Propellant Development & Characterization Subcommittee [Joint Army, Navy, NASA, Air Force]
PDCS	Prototype Die Casting Service
PD-CSE	Pulsed Doppler Cross-Sectional Echocardiography [Medicine] (DMAA)
PDCSTBL	Peripheral Device Control and Status Table (SAUS)
PDC System	Pre-Detection Combining System (SAUS)
PDCU	Plotting Display Control Unit
PDCU	Power Distribution and Control Unit
Pd D	Doctor of Pedagogy
PDD	Package Designation and Description File (DOMA)
PDD	Packed Decimal Data (SAUS)
PDD	Pancreatic Dorsal Duct [Anatomy]
PDD	Partial Discharge Detector (SAUS)
PDD	Participacion Democratica de Tzquierda [Chile] [Political party] (EY)
PDD	Past Due Date
PDD	Patients Dental Dictionary (SAUS)
PDD	Percent Depth Dose [Medicine] (MELL)
PDD	Peridontal Disease (MELL)
PDD	Personal Digital Devices (AGLO)
PDD	Personnel Detection Device (SEWL)
PDD	Pervasive Developmental Disorder [Medicine]
PDD	Petty Delinquency Detention (SAUS)
PDD	Phenyldodecane [Organic chemistry]
PDD	Phorbol Didecanoate [Organic chemistry]
PDD	Physical Damage Division [Navy]
PDD	Physical Data Description (VLIE)
PDD	Physical Defense Division [Army]
PDD	Physical Device Driver [Computer science] (VLIE)
PDD	Platinum Diamminodichloride [Cisplatin and cis-platinum] [Antineoplastic drug] (DAVI)
PDD	Player Detection Device (SAUS)
PDD	Plotting Data Distributor (MCD)
PDD	Portable Digital Document (SAUS)

PDD .... Post Dialing Delay [*Telecommunications*] (TEL)
PDD .... Post Due Date (SAUS)
PDD .... Precision Depth Digitizer [*Oceanography*]
PDD .... Pre-Dental Discomfort (SAUS)
PDD .... Preferred Delivery Date (AFM)
PDD .... Preliminary Design and Development (MCD)
PDD .... Premenstrual Dysphoric Disorder [*Proposed psychiatric diagnosis*]
PDD .... Premodulation Processor - Deep Space - Data
PDD .... Presidential Decision Directive
PDD .... Primary Degenerative Dementia [*Medicine*]
PDD .... Principal Distribution Depot [*DoD*]
PDD .... Priority Delivery Date (AFM)
PDD .... Probability Density Distribution [*Statistics*]
PDD .... Process Distillate Discharge (SAUS)
PDD .... Processor Description Database [*Computer science*] (VLIE)
PDD .... Procurement Description Data [*DoD*]
PDD .... Product Definition Data [*Computer science*] (VLIE)
PDD .... Product Delivery Device (SAUS)
PDD .... Professional Development Degree (SAUS)
PDD .... Professional Development Division [*American Occupational Therapy Association*]
PDD .... Program Description Document [*Military*] (CAAL)
PDD .... Program Design Data
PDD .... Program Design Document (ADWA)
PDD .... Program Development Department (SAUS)
PDD .... Program Dimension Drawing (MCD)
PDD .... Program Directive Document (RDA)
PDD .... Progressive Diaphyseal Dysplasia [*Medicine*] (MELL)
PDD .... Projected Data Display
PDD .... Projected Decision Date (NRCH)
PDD .... Proposal Due Date (SAUS)
PDD .... Prospective Decision Date (NRCH)
PDD .... Protable Digital Document (SAUS)
PDD .... Provisioning Description Data
PDD .... Public Documents Department [*Government Printing Office*]
PDD .... Pulse Delay Device
PDD .... Puy-De-Dome [*France*] [*Seismograph station code, US Geological Survey*] [*Closed*] (SEIS)
PDD .... Pyridoxine-Deficient Diet (MAE)
PDDA .... Power-Driven Decontaminating Apparatus (SAUS)
PDDA .... Power Driver Decontamination Apparatus (NATG)
PDDAIO .... Parts for Direct Discrete Analog Input/Output (MCD)
PDDB .... Phenododecinium [*or Phenoxyethyldimethyl-dodecylammonium*] Bromide [*Antiseptic*]
PDDB .... Product Definition Database (MCD)
PDD Base .... Processor Description Data Base (SAUS)
PDDC .... Proceed Directly on Course [*Aviation*] (FAAC)
PDDC .... Progressive Die Design by Computer (SAUS)
PDD/CRASH... Problem Drinking Driver/Court Referred Action for Safer Highways (SAUS)
PDDD .... Program Demonstration and Development Division [*ACTION*]
PDDF .... Portable Document Delivery Format (SAUS)
PDDF .... Post-Decision Document File (SAUS)
PDDF .... Propargyl(dideaza)folic Acid [*Biochemistry*]
PDDGM .... Past District Deputy Grand Master [*Freemasonry*]
PDDI .... Product Data Definition Interface
PDDI .... Product Definition Data Interface (MCD)
PD Div'l Ct... Probate, Divorce, and Admiralty Divisional Court [*England*] (DLA)
PDDL .... Perpendicular Diffraction Delay Line (PDAA)
PDDLS .... Post D-Day Logistic Support [*Army*] (AABC)
PDDM .... Disciples of the Divine Master [*Roman Catholic women's religious order*]
PDDM .... Pious Disciples of the Divine Master (TOCD)
PDD/NOS ..... Pervasive Developmental Disorder, Not Otherwise Specified
PDDP .... Parallel Data Distribution Preprocessor (SAUS)
PDDP .... Product Design and Development Program (SAUS)
PDDR .... Product Definition Data Requirements (SPST)
PDD/RDD .... Priority Delivery Date/Required Delivery Date (AFM)
PDDS .... Parasitic Disease Drug Service (MAE)
PDDS .... Peoria District Dental Society (SAUS)
PDDS .... Program Definition Data Sheet
PDD Sheet... Program Definition Data Sheet (SAUS)
PDDT .... Page Device Description Table (VLIE)
PDDU .... Process Development and Demonstration Unit (SAUS)
PDE .... Page-Directory Entry [*Computer science*] (BYTE)
PDE .... Pandie Pandie [*Australia*] [*Airport symbol*] [*Obsolete*] (OAG)
PDE .... Parade
Pde .... Parade [*Record label*]
PDE .... Paroxysmal Dyspnea on Exertion [*Medicine*]
PDE .... Partei fuer Deutschland und Europa [*Party for Germany and Europe*] [*Germany*] [*Political party*] (PPW)
PDE .... Partial Differential Equation
PDE .... Particle Dispersion Experiment (SAUS)
PDE .... Paste Down Ends [*Graphic arts*] (DGA)
PDE .... Pediatric Endocrinology [*Medical specialty*] (DHSM)
PDE .... Personnel Development and Education (MCD)
PDE .... Phosphatidyl(dimethyl)ethanolamine [*Biochemistry*]
PDE .... Phosphodiesterase [*An enzyme*]
PDE .... Photon Drag Effect (SAUS)
PDE .... Pilot's Discrete Encoder
PDE .... Plain Deckle Edges [*Graphic arts*] (DGA)
PDE .... Portable Development Environment [*Computer science*] (VLIE)
PDE .... Position-Determining Equipment
PDE .... Post-test Disassembly Examination (SAUS)
PDE .... Preliminary Determination of Epicenter [*Seismology*]

PDE .... Pride Resources Ltd. [*Vancouver Stock Exchange symbol*]
PDE .... Principal DOD [*Department of Defense*] Executive
PDE .... Producers' Durable Equipment (GFGA)
PDE .... Product Data Exchange [*Computer science*] (VLIE)
PDE .... Production Design Engineers
PDE .... Professional Development Education [*Military*] (RDA)
PDE .... Progressive Dialysis Encephalopathy [*Medicine*] (MELL)
PDE .... Projectile Development Establishment [*British*]
PDE .... Propellant Disposition Effects
PDE .... Propulsion Driver Electronics (ACAE)
PDE .... Prospective Data Element [*Army*] (AABC)
PDE .... Pulsed Doppler Echocardiography [*Medicine*] (DMAA)
PDE .... Pulse Detonation Engine (SEWL)
PDEA .... Phenyldiethanolamine [*Organic chemistry*]
P de Ancha... Petrus de Ancharano [*Deceased, 1416*] [*Authority cited in pre-1607 legal work*] (DSA)
P de B .... Petrus de Bellapertica [*Deceased, 1308*] [*Authority cited in pre-1607 legal work*] (DSA)
P de Bp ...... Petrus de Bellapertica [*Deceased, 1308*] [*Authority cited in pre-1607 legal work*] (DSA)
PDECS .... Portable Detector and Cueing System
PDED .... Partial Double Error Detecting (NITA)
PDED .... Partial Double Error Detection
PDED .... Program Development and Evaluation Division [*Environmental Protection Agency*] (GFGA)
PDEF .... Protean Data Exchange Format (SAUS)
PDEGF .... Platelet-Derived Epidermal Growth Factor [*Medicine*] (MELL)
PDEI .... Phosphodiesterase Inhibitor [*Biochemistry*]
PDEIS .... Preliminary Draft Environmental Impact Statement (SAUS)
PDEISEC ..... Permanent Directory of Energy Information Sources in the European Community (SAUS)
PDEL .... Partial Differential Equation Language [*Computer science*]
P de L .... Paulus de Liazaris [*Deceased, 1356*] [*Authority cited in pre-1607 legal work*] (DSA)
PDELAN ...... Partial Differential Equation Language [*Computer science*] (CSR)
PDELB .... Plumbers and Drainers' Examination and Licensing Board [*Queensland, Australia*]
PDELS .... Parallel-Detection Electron Loss Spectrometer (SAUS)
PDEM .... Personal Dust Exposure Monitor (PDAA)
P Dent J ..... Pennsylvania Dental Journal (SAUS)
P de Orfi..... Petrus de Orfila [*Deceased, 1307*] [*Authority cited in pre-1607 legal work*] (DSA)
PDEP .... Preliminary Draft Equipment Publication (MCD)
PDEQ .... Profile of DARCOM Environmental Quality (MCD)
PDES .... Phase Image of Poly(diethylsiloxane) [*Organic chemistry*]
PDES .... Preliminary Draft Environmental Statement (NRCH)
PDES .... Product Data Exchange Specification (NITA)
PDES .... Product Data Exchange Standard [*Computer science*] (VLIE)
PDES .... Product Data Exchange using STEP [*Sequentially Timed Events Plotting*]
PDES .... Product Definition Exchange Specification [*Army*]
PDES .... Product Definition Exchange Standards (SAUS)
PDES .... Product Description Exchange Standard (SAUS)
PDES .... Pulse-Doppler Elevation Scan (PDAA)
P de Sal ..... Petrus de Salinis [*Flourished, 13th century*] [*Authority cited in pre-1607 legal work*] (DSA)
P de Sam .... Petrus de Sampsone [*Flourished, 1246-58*] [*Authority cited in pre-1607 legal work*] (DSA)
P de Samp... Petrus de Sampsone [*Flourished, 1246-58*] [*Authority cited in pre-1607 legal work*] (DSA)
P Det .... Port Detachment [*British military*] (DMA)
PDET .... Post-Diapause Eclosion Time [*Entomology*]
PDET .... Probability of Detection, Evaluation, and Transfer (MCD)
PDEX .... Pro-Dex, Inc. [*NASDAQ symbol*] (NQ)
PDF .... Hancock [*John*] Patriot Premium Dividend Fund I [*NYSE symbol*] (SAG)
PDF .... John Hancock Patr Prem Dv Fd [*NYSE symbol*] (TTSB)
PDF .... LAR Transregional, Linhas Aereas Regionais SA [*Portugal*] [*ICAO designator*] (FAAC)
PDF .... Pacific Dentistry Association (BUAC)
PDF .... Package Definition File [*Computer science*] (VLIE)
PDF .... Paget's Disease Foundation (EA)
PDF .... Pair Distribution Function [*Physical chemistry*]
PDF .... Pakistan Democratic Front
PDF .... Panama Defense Forces [*Later, Public Forces*]
PDF .... Parallel Data Field (SAUS)
PDF .... Parallel Disk File (SAUS)
PDF .... Parkinson's Disease Foundation (EA)
PDF .... Particle Distribution Function
PDF .... Parti Democrate Francais [*French Democratic Party*] [*Political party*] (PPW)
PDF .... Passive Direction Finding
PDF .... Patient Data Form (SAUS)
PDF .... Pavement Depth Factor (ADA)
PDF .... Peace Development Fund (EA)
PDF .... Pele Defense Fund (EA)
PDF .... People's Democratic Force [*The Bahamas*] [*Political party*] (EY)
PDF .... Peritoneal Dialysis Fluid [*Medicine*] (DMAA)
PDF .... Piecewise Data Flow (SAUS)
PDF .... Pigmented Dermatofibroma [*Medicine*] (MELL)
PDF .... Planar Deformation Feature [*Geology*]
PDF .... Planet Drum Foundation (EA)
PDF .... Plant Design Factor [*Nuclear energy*] (NRCH)
PDF .... Plant Design Flood [*Nuclear energy*] (GFGA)
PDF .... Platform Independent File Format [*Computer science*]

PDF.............	Point Detonating Fuze [Army]
PDF.............	Polar Density Function (SAUS)
PDF.............	Pooled Development Funds [Economics]
PDF.............	Popular Defence Force (SAUS)
PDF.............	Popular Defence Forces [Sudan] [Political party]
PDF.............	Popular Democratic Front [Jordan] [Political party]
PDF.............	Porsche Dual-Function Transmission [Automotive engineering]
PDF.............	Portable Document File [Computer science] (PCM)
PDF.............	Portable Document Format [Computer science]
pdf..............	Portable Document Format [Computer science]
PDF.............	Post Defense Force
PDF.............	Post Detection Filter [Telecommunications] (TEL)
PDF.............	Postdoctoral Fellow (SAUS)
PDF.............	Powder Diffraction File (DICI)
PDF.............	Power Diffraction File (NITA)
PDF.............	Power Distribution Frame (SAUS)
PDF.............	Precision Direction Finder (SAUS)
PDF.............	Primary Direction of Fire (SAUS)
PDF.............	Primordial Density Fluctuation [Cosmology]
PDF.............	Principal Direction of Fire [Military]
PDF.............	Printer Description File (SAUS)
PDF.............	Private Database Facility [Computer science]
PDF.............	Probability Density Function [Statistics]
PDF.............	Probability Distribution Function [Statistics]
PDF.............	Problem Data Field (SAUS)
PDF.............	Processor Defined Function
PDF.............	Production and Distribution of Foodstuffs [British]
PDF.............	Program Data File
PDF.............	Program Data Form [Army]
PDF.............	Program Development Facility [Computer science] (MHDI)
PDF.............	Project Design Flood (NRCH)
PDF.............	Protected Difference Fat (OA)
PDF.............	Pyruvate Dehydrogenase (DMAA)
PDFA	Partnership for a Drug Free America (SAUS)
PDF Architecture...	Piecewise Data Flow Architecture (SAUS)
PDFC	Power Dissipation Factor per Column (SAUS)
PDFC	Premature Dead Female Child (DAVI)
PDFCS	Pennsylvania Dutch Folk Culture Society (EA)
PDFD	Predemonstration Fusion Device
PDFD	Pulsed Doppler Frequency Diversity (NG)
PDFES	Pitch-Synchronous Digital Feature Extraction System (PDAA)
PDFG	Planar Distributed Function Generator (PDAA)
PDFG	Platelet-Derived Growth Factor [Endocrinology] (DAVI)
PDFI	Probability of Detected Fault Isolation (SAUS)
PDFIB	Piecewise Data Flow Instruction Block (SAUS)
PDFID	Preconstruction Direct Flame Ionization Detection (EEVL)
PDFLP	Popular Democratic Front for the Liberation of Palestine
PDFM	Phillips and Drew Fund Management [England] [British]
PDFRR	Program Directors Flight Readiness Review [NASA] (KSC)
PDFSR	Proposed Detailed Functional System Requirement (SAUS)
PDFT	Programmable Data Formatter (SAUS)
PDFWPR	Physical Disabilities Fieldwork Performance Report [Occupational therapy]
PDG	Padang [Indonesia] [Airport symbol] (OAG)
PDG	Padding
PDG	Parachute Drop Glider
PDG	Paradigm (WGA)
PDG	Parkinsonism-Dementia Complex of Guam [Medicine] (DMAA)
PDG	Parti Democratique de Guinee [Democratic Party of Guinea] [Political party] (PPW)
PDG	Parti Democratique Gabonais [Gabonese Democratic Party] [Political party] (PPW)
PDG	Passive Defense Group (MUGU)
PDG	Patent Documentation Group (DIT)
PDG	Patient Dependency Groups (SAUS)
PDG	Paymaster Director General (SAUS)
PDG	PDG Remediation, Inc. [Associated Press] (SAG)
PDG	Peak Detector, Gated (SAUS)
PDG	Pendant Drop Growth (SAUS)
PDG	Personalistic Discussion Group - Eastern Division (EA)
PDG	Phosphate-Dependent Glutaminase (STED)
PDG	Phosphogluconate Dehydrogenase [Organic chemistry] (MAH)
PDG	Placer Dome, Inc. [NYSE symbol] [Toronto Stock Exchange symbol] [Vancouver Stock Exchange symbol] (SPSG)
PDG	Precision Drop Glider [Army]
PDG	Pregnanediol Glucuronide [Endocrinology]
PDG	President Directeur General [President Director General] [French]
PDG	Production Development Group (IAA)
PDG	Professional Dyers Guild [Defunct]
PDG	Program Decision Group (ACAE)
PDG	Program Documentation Generator [Computer science] (MHDI)
PDG	Programmable Display Generator (SAUS)
PDG	Programs Development Group (MUGU)
PDG	Proposal Development Group [Aerospace] (AAG)
PDG	Psychiatric Diagnostic Groups (SAUS)
PDG	Pyruvate Dehydrogenase (DB)
PDGA	Professional Disc Golf Association
PDGA	Pteroyldiglutamic Acid [Pharmacology]
PDGDL........	Plasma Dynamics and Gaseous Discharge Laboratory [MIT] (MCD)
PDGE	Partido Democratico de Guinea Ecuatorial [Democratic Party of Equatorial Guinea] [Political party] (EY)
PDGE	PDG Environmental [NASDAQ symbol] (TTSB)
PDGE	PDG Environmental, Inc. [NASDAQ symbol] (SAG)
PDG En	PDG Environmental, Inc. [Associated Press] (SAG)
PDGF	Platelet-Derived Growth Factor [Genetics]

PDGF	Power Data Grapple Fixture (SAUS)
PDGFA	Platelet-Derived Growth Factor [Medicine] (DMAA)
PDGFR.........	Platelet-Derived Growth Factor Receptor [Genetics]
PD Gland....	Posterior Digestive Gland (SAUS)
PDGMS	Peabody Developmental Gross Motor Scale
PDGS	PDG Remediation [NASDAQ symbol] (TTSB)
PDGS	PDG Remediation, Inc. [NASDAQ symbol] (SAG)
PDGS	Precision Delivery Glider System
P-DGs	Presidents-Directeurs Generaux
PDGS	Probe Drill Guidance System
PDGS	Product Design Graphics System [Prime Computer Ltd.] [Software package] (NCC)
PDGSW........	PDG Remediation Wrrt [NASDAQ symbol] (TTSB)
PDGW..........	Principal Director of Guided Weapons (SAUS)
PDGW..........	Principle Directorate of Guided Weapons [British] (SAA)
PDGXT........	Predischarge Graded Exercise Test [Cardiology] (DAVI)
PDH	Packaged Disaster Hospital [Public Health Service]
PDH	Pain Drug Hypnosis (SAUS)
PDH	Passive Defense Handbook [Navy] (MCD)
PDH	Past Dental History
PDH	Phosphate Dehydrogenase (MAE)
PDH	Plaiochronous Digital Hierarchies (SAUS)
PDH	Planned Derated Hours [Electronics] (IEEE)
PDH	Plesiochronous Digital Hierarchy (SAUS)
PDH	Pocket Dosimeter High (NAKS)
PDH	Project Development History (SAUS)
PDH	Puromycin Dihydrochloride (SAUS)
PDH	Pyruvate Dehydrogenase [An enzyme]
PDH & DS ...	Plant Data Handling and Display System [Nuclear energy] (NRCH)
PDHC	Pyruvate Dehydrogenase Complex [Biochemistry]
PDHF	Postdilution Hemofiltration [Medicine]
PDHI	Palmer Drought Hydrological Index
PDHL	Peak Design Heat Loss (PDAA)
PdHO	Pediatric Hematology-Oncology (STED)
PDHV-RDA...	Parti Democratique de la Haute Volta-Rassemblement Democratique Africain [Democratic Party of Upper Volta-African Democratic Rally]
PDI..............	Packet Driver Interface (SAUS)
PDI..............	Pain Disability Index [Medicine] (DMAA)
PDI..............	Palmer Drought Index
PDI..............	Panel Data Interface [Computer science] (IAA)
PDI..............	Paradise Island Airlines, Inc. [ICAO designator] (FAAC)
PDI..............	Partai Demokrasi Indonesia [Indonesian Democratic Party] [Political party] (PPW)
PDI..............	Partial Delivery Injection [Materials science]
PDI..............	Particle Displacement Interferometry (SAUS)
PDI..............	Parti Democratique de l'Independance [Democratic Independence Party] [Morocco] [Political party]
PDI..............	Partito Democratica Italiana [Italian Democratic Party] [Political party] (PPE)
PDI..............	Payload Data Interleaver [NASA] (NASA)
PDI..............	Percentage Difference Index
PDI..............	Perfect Digital Invariant (OA)
PDI..............	Periodontal Disease Index [Dentistry] (DMAA)
PDI..............	Peripheral Dynamics, Inc. (SAUS)
PDI..............	Personal Data Interchange (SAUS)
PDI..............	Personal Disposable Income [Economics]
PDI..............	Pharmacy Dedication Information (SAUS)
PDI..............	Pictorial Deviation Indicator (AAG)
PDI..............	Picture Description Instruction [Telecommunications]
PDI..............	Pilot Direction Indicator [Electronic communications]
PDI..............	Plan-Do Intergration [Medicine] (DMAA)
PDI..............	Plastic Drum Institute (NTPA)
PDI..............	Plumbing and Drainage Institute (EA)
PDI..............	Point-Diffraction Interferometer (SAUS)
PDI..............	Polydispersity Index (SAUS)
PDI..............	Polymer Dispersion Industries (SAUS)
PDI..............	Porto D'Ischia [Italy] [Seismograph station code, US Geological Survey] [Closed] (SEIS)
PDI..............	Positive Displacement Injector (SAUS)
PDI..............	Post Detection Integration (MCD)
PDI..............	Potential Determining Ions
PDI..............	Powder for Injection (SAUS)
PDI..............	Power and Data Interface (SAUS)
PDI..............	Power Data Interface (TIMI)
PDI..............	Power Dissipation Index (IAA)
PDI..............	Powered Descent Initiation [Aerospace]
PDI..............	Practice Development Institute (SAUS)
PDI..............	Pre-Delivery Inspection (DCTA)
PDI..............	Predeployment Inspection [Navy] (NVT)
PDI..............	Premdor, Inc. [Toronto Stock Exchange symbol]
PDI..............	Preschool Development Inventory [Test] (TMMY)
PDI..............	Pressure Differential Indicator (SAUS)
PDI..............	Prevalence, Duration and Intensity (SAUS)
PDI..............	Primary Depressive Illness (SAUS)
PDI..............	Prise Ombilicale Derniers Instants
PDI..............	Privately Developed Item (AAGC)
PDI..............	Process Data Input (SAUS)
PDI..............	Product Data Interchange (SAUS)
PDI..............	Professional Development Institute [Canada]
PDI..............	Program Design, Inc. [Commercial firm]
PDI..............	Program with Developing Institutions (EA)
PDI..............	Project Data Index [Jet Propulsion Laboratory, NASA]
PDI..............	Protein Dispersibility Index [Analytical chemistry]
PDI..............	Protein Disulfide-Isomerase [An enzyme]

PDI..............	Psychiatric Diagnostic Interview [*Personality development test*] [*Psychology*]
PDI..............	Psychological Distress Inventory [*Student personality test*]
PDI..............	Psychomotor Development Index [*Bayley Scales of Infant Development*]
PDI..............	Public Debt Interest (ADA)
PDI..............	Public Demographics, Inc. (IID)
PDI..............	Putnam Dividend Income [*NYSE symbol*] (SPSG)
PDI..............	Pyronetics Devices, Incorporated (ACAE)
Pdi..............	Transdiaphragmatic [*Pressure*]
PDIAL	Public Dialup Internet Access List [*Computer science*] (CDE)
PDIC	Periodic (AFM)
PDIC	Professional Diving Instructors Corp. (SAUS)
PDIC	Professional Driver Improvement Course
PDIC	Protection Development International Corp. (SAUS)
PDID	Public Disorder Intelligence Department (SAUS)
PDID	Public Disorder Intelligence Division (SAUS)
PDID	Pulse Doppler Identification (SEWL)
PDIE	Phosphodiesterase (DMAA)
PDIF............	Product Definition Interchange Format (SAUS)
PDIF............	Putnam Dividend Income Fund [*Associated Press*] (SAG)
PDII	Pusat Dokumentasi dan Informasi Ilmiah [*Indonesian Center for Scientific Documentation and Information*] [*Information service or system*] (IID)
PDIIS	Priority Defense Items Information System
PDIL...........	Power-Dependent Insertion Limit [*Nuclear energy*] (NRCH)
PDIN	Pusat Dokumentasi Ilmiah Nasional (NITA)
PDIO	Parallel Digital Input/Output
PDIO	Photodiode
P-DIOL........	Pregnanediol [*Biochemistry*]
PDIP	Plastic Dual In-Line Packaging (AAEL)
PDIP	Preflight Data Insertion Program (NVT)
PDIP	Program Development Increment Package [*Military*]
PDIP	Program Development Integration Plan (SAUS)
PDIR...........	Peripheral Data Set Information Record (SAUS)
PDIR...........	Priority Disassembly and Inspection Report
PDIR...........	Program Directive
PDIS	Parts Dissection Information System
PDIS	Payload Data Interleaver System [*NASA*] (MCD)
PDIS	Pressure Differential Switch (IAA)
PDIS	Proceedings of the National Symposia [*A publication*]
PDIS	Product Description Information Standards [*or System*]
PDISCH........	Pump Discharge
PDISP	Page Displacement (SAUS)
pDISP	Proposed Draft International Standardized Profile (SAUS)
PDISPL	Positive Displacement [*Engineering*]
PDIT............	Product Development Improvement Team (ACAE)
PDIT............	Provision for Deferred Income Tax
PDIUM	Partito Democratico Italiano di Unita Monarchica [*Italian Democratic Party of Monarchical Unity*] [*Political party*] (PPE)
P Div	Law Reports, Probate Division [*England*] [*A publication*] (DLA)
PDIWT	Planning and Design Institute for Water Transportation [*China*] (BUAC)
PDJ..............	Plaine Des Jarres [*South Vietnam*]
PDJ..............	Precision Drill Jig
PDJB...........	Precision Drill Jig Bushing
PD/JV..........	Project Definition/Joint Validation (MCD)
PDK	Atlanta [*Georgia*] De Kalb/Peachtree Airport [*Airport symbol*] [*Obsolete*] (OAG)
PDK	Party of Democratic Kampuchea [*Cambodia*] [*Political party*] (BUAC)
PDK	PDK Labs, Inc. [*Associated Press*] (SAG)
PDK	Personal Decontamination Kit (SAUS)
PDK	Phase-Delay Keying [*Computer science*]
PDK	Phi Delta Kappa [*Fraternity*]
PDK	Phileleftheron Demokratikon Kendron [*Liberal Democratic Union*] [*Greek*] (PPE)
PDK	Phileleftheron Demokratikon Komma [*Liberal Democratic Party*] [*Greek*] [*Political party*] (PPE)
PDK	Polycystic Kidney Disease (MELL)
PDK	Poop Deck [*Naval engineering*]
PDK	Promenade Deck [*of a ship*] (DS)
PDK	Science Foods, Inc. [*AMEX symbol*] (SAG)
PDKL	PDK Labs [*NASDAQ symbol*] (TTSB)
PDKL	PDK Labs, Inc. [*NASDAQ symbol*] (SAG)
PDKLM........	PDK Labs Wrrt'C' [*NASDAQ symbol*] (TTSB)
PDKLP........	PDK Labs $0.49 Cv'A' Pfd [*NASDAQ symbol*] (TTSB)
PDL.............	Page Description Language [*Computer graphics*]
PDL.............	Page Design Language (SAUS)
PDL.............	Parameter Data Load (ACAE)
PDL.............	Particle Dynamics Laboratory (SAUS)
PDL.............	Particle Physics Laboratory (SAUS)
PDL.............	Partido Democrata Liberal [*Liberal Democratic Party*] [*Spain*] [*Political party*] (EY)
PDL.............	Parts Deletion List (MSA)
PDL.............	Parts Difference List (MCD)
PDL.............	Parts Documentation List (MCD)
PDL.............	Party of Democratic Left [*Slovakia*] [*Political party*] (BUAC)
PDL.............	Pass Down the Line [*Book*] [*Navy*] (MUGU)
PDL.............	Patent Depository Library [*Designated by the Patent and Trademark Office*]
PDL.............	People's Democracy of Laos [*Political party*] (VNW)
PDL.............	Periodontal Ligament [*Dentistry*]
PDL.............	Permanent Duty Location
PDL.............	Photodissociation Dye LASER
PDL.............	Picture Description Language [*Computer science*] (MHDI)

PDL..............	Placer Development Ltd. [*Toronto Stock Exchange symbol*] [*Vancouver Stock Exchange symbol*]
PDL..............	Pocket Dosimeter-Low (MCD)
PDL..............	Polarization Diversity LIDAR
PDL..............	Ponce De Leon
PDL..............	Ponta Delgada [*Portugal*] [*Airport symbol*] (OAG)
PDL..............	Poorly Differentiated Lymphocytic [*Oncology*]
PDL..............	Population Doubling Level [*Cytology*]
PDL..............	Portable Data Loader [*Aviation*]
PDL..............	Positive Diode Logic (VLIE)
pdl..............	Poundal [*Unit of force*]
PDL..............	Poverty Datum Line
PDL..............	Power Door Locks
PDL..............	Precision Delay Line
PDL..............	Preliminary Design Language [*Computer science*] (VLIE)
PDL..............	Presidential Realty Corp. [*AMEX symbol*] (SPSG)
PDL..............	Primary Defect List (SAUS)
PDL..............	Print Definition Language [*Computer science*] (EECA)
PDL..............	Procedure Definition Language [*Computer science*] (BUR)
PDL..............	Procedure Description Language
PDL..............	Procedure Distribution List (MCD)
PDL..............	Process Description Language (SAUS)
PDL..............	Process Design Language [*Computer science*] (MHDI)
PDL..............	Processor Data Load (ACAE)
PDL..............	Procurement Data List
PDL..............	Product Disaster Loans [*Small Business Administration*]
PDL..............	Professional Development League (EA)
PDL..............	Program Description Language (MCD)
PDL..............	Program Design Language (NASA)
PDL..............	Program Development Language (SAUS)
PDL..............	Program Device Librarian [*Computer science*]
PDL..............	Programmable Data Language (NITA)
PDL..............	Programmable Data Logger [*Computer science*] (VLIE)
PDL..............	Programmable Definition Logic (SAUS)
PDL..............	Programmable Digital Logic (SAUS)
PDL..............	Progressively Diffused Leukoencephalopathy [*Medicine*] (MELL)
PDL..............	Project Document List
PDL..............	Protocol Description Language [*Telecommunications*] (IAA)
PDL..............	Publishers' Databases Ltd. [*Publishing consortium*] [*British*]
pdl..............	Pudendal [*Anatomy*] (MAE)
PDL..............	Pulsed Dye LASER
PDL..............	Pumped Dye LASER
PDL..............	Push Down List [*Computer science*] (MHDI)
PDL..............	Sierra Leone Peoples Democratic League (SAUS)
PDL A...........	Presidential Rlty Cl'A' [*AMEX symbol*] (TTSB)
PD(LAO)	Public Defender (Legal Aid Office) [*Australia*]
PDLB	Pass Down the Line Book (SAUS)
PDL B	Presidential Rlty Cl'B' [*AMEX symbol*] (TTSB)
PDLC	North American Palladium [*NASDAQ symbol*] (SAG)
PDLC	Partido Liberal de Cataluna [*Liberal Democratic Party of Catalonia*] [*Political party*] (PPW)
PDLC	Polymer Dispersed Liquid Crystal [*Physical chemistry*]
PDLC	Poorly Differentiated Lung Cancer [*Medicine*] (DMAA)
PDLCF	North Amer Palladium [*NASDAQ symbol*] (TTSB)
PDLD	Polymer-Dispersed Liquid-crystal Display (SAUS)
PDLD	Poorly Differentiated Lymphocytic-Diffuse [*Oncology*] (DMAA)
PDLE	Process Development Laboratory East (SAUS)
PDLF...........	Pakistan Democratic Labour Federation (BUAC)
pdl-ft...........	foot-poundal (SAUS)
PDL/FT²	Poundals per Square Foot
PDLI	Protein Design Labs [*NASDAQ symbol*] (TTSB)
PDLI	Protein Design Labs, Inc. [*NASDAQ symbol*] (SAG)
PDLL...........	Poorly Differentiated Lymphatic [*or Lymphocytic*] Lymphoma [*Oncology*]
PDLM..........	Periodic Depot Level Maintenance
PDLM..........	Planned Depot Level Maintenance (MCD)
PDLM..........	Programmed Depot Level Maintenance [*Air Force*]
PDLN	Poorly Differentiated Lymphocytic-Nodular [*Oncology*] (DMAA)
PDLP...........	Pacific Dunlop Ltd. [*NASDAQ symbol*] (NQ)
PDLP...........	Patent Depository Library Program (SAUS)
PDLPY	Pacific Dunlop Ltd. (MHDW)
PDLPY	Pacific Dunlop Ltd. ADR [*NASDAQ symbol*] (TTSB)
PDLR...........	Power Deck Lid Release
PDLS	Party of the Democratic Left of Slovakia [*Former Czechoslovakia*] [*Political party*] (EY)
PDL S/FT²	Poundal Seconds per Square Foot
PDLT...........	P-Channel Depletion-Load Triode Inverter
PD/LT.........	Program Design and Learning Tool (NITA)
PDLW	Process Development Laboratory West (SAUS)
Pd M	Master of Pedagogy
PDM...........	Parallel-Port Data Module [*Computer communications*]
PDM...........	Parlance Document Manager (SAUS)
PDM...........	Partial Descriptive Method
PDM...........	Parti Democratique Malgache [*Malagasy Democratic Party*]
PDM...........	Partido de los Democratas Melillenses [*Spanish North Africa*] [*Political party*] (MENA)
PDM...........	Patient Data Management
PDM...........	Pay Duties Manual (SAUS)
PDM...........	Pendant Drop Method
PDM...........	People's Democratic Movement [*Guyana*] [*Political party*] (EY)
PDM...........	People's Democratic Movement [*Papua New Guinea*] [*Political party*] (FEA)
PDM...........	People's Democratic Movement [*Turks and Caicos Islands*] [*Political party*] (PPW)
PDM...........	Percent Deviation from the Median

PDM............ Periodic Depot Maintenance (SAUS)
PDM............ Permanent Data Memory (SAUS)
PDM............ Phase Difference Modulation (SAUS)
PDM............ Phase Displacement (IAA)
PDM............ Photographic Data Memory (SAUS)
PDM............ Physical Distribution Management
PDM............ Physiological Data Monitor
PDM............ Pilot Decision Making [Aviation] (DA)
PDM............ Pinch Design Method [Heat exchange design]
PDM............ Pipework Design Management (SAUS)
PDM............ Pitt-DesMoines Inc. [AMEX symbol] (TTSB)
PDM............ Pittsburgh - Des Moines, Inc. [AMEX symbol] (SPSG)
PDM............ Planned Depot Maintenance
pdm............ Podium (VRA)
PDM............ Point Defence Missile (SAUS)
PDM............ Point Distribution Model (DMAA)
PDM............ Polarization Division Multiplexing (SAUS)
PDM............ Polynomial Discriminant Method (PDAA)
PDM............ Portable Differential Magnetometer
PDM............ Positive Displacement Motor (SAUS)
PDM............ Possible Duplicate Message (TRID)
PDM............ Power Density Meter
PDM............ Power Density Monitor [Environmental science] (COE)
PDM............ Practical Data Manager [Hitachi Ltd.] [Japan]
PDM............ Practical Dental Monographs (SAUS)
PDM............ Precedence Diagraming Method (MCD)
PDM............ Predictive Maintenance
PDM............ Prehospital and Disaster Medicine (SAUS)
PDM............ Preliminary Development Model
PDM............ Preliminary Draft Manuscript
PDM............ Presidential Decision Memorandum [Jimmy Carter Administration]
PDM............ Primary Data Management (SAUS)
PDM............ Print Down Module
PDM............ Probabilistic Dilution Model (SAUS)
PDM............ Process Decision Model (VLIE)
PDM............ Processor Data Monitor (NASA)
PDM............ Product and Document Management (SAUS)
PDM............ Product Data Management
PDM............ Product Data Manager (SAUS)
PDM............ Product Development Manual [Automotive project management]
PDM............ Production Decision Criteria Matrix
PDM............ Program Data Manager (MCD)
PDM............ Program Debugging Mode [Computer science] (VLIE)
PDM............ Program Decision Meeting (SAUS)
PDM............ Program Decision Memorandum [Military]
PDM............ Program Design Manual (VLIE)
PDM............ Program Development Manager (SAUS)
PDM............ Program Development Manual (ACAE)
PDM............ Programmable Data Monitor (SAUS)
PDM............ Programmable Data Mover (SAUS)
PDM............ Programmed Depot Maintenance (MCD)
PDM............ Programmer Defined Macro [Computer science] (VLIE)
PDM............ Progres et Democratie Moderne [Progress and Modern Democracy] [France] [Political party] (PPE)
PDM............ Project Data Manual (ACAE)
PDM............ Project Design Memo
PDM............ Project Development Methodology (SAUS)
PDM............ Propellant Dispersion Munition (ACAE)
PDM............ Propellant Distribution Module (ACAE)
PDM............ Protected Difference Milk (OA)
PDM............ Publications Distribution Manager [Military] (AFM)
PDM............ Pulse Data Modulation [Computer science] (IAA)
PDM............ Pulse Delay Mechanism [British military] (DMA)
PDM............ Pulse Delta Modulation (IEEE)
PDM............ Pulse Duration Modulation [Data transmission]
PDM............ Pursuit Deterrent Mine
PDM............ Pursuit Deterrent Munition
PDM............ Push Down Memory [Computer science]
PDMA.......... Peninsula Drafting Management Association
PDMA.......... Pipelined Direct Memory Access [Computer science] (CIST)
PDMA.......... Plumbing and Drainage Manufacturers Association (SAUS)
PDMA.......... Polarization Division Multiple Access (VLIE)
PDMA.......... Prescription Drug Marketing Act [1987]
PDMA.......... Product Development and Management Association [Indianapolis, IN] (EA)
PDMAC........ Prescription Drug Maximum Allowable Cost
PDMAMS..... Product Design Minuteman Airborne Mechanical System (SAA)
PDMC.......... Premature Dead Male Child (DAVI)
PDMC.......... Princeton Dental Management Corp. [NASDAQ symbol] (SAG)
PDMC.......... Princeton Dental Mgmt [NASDAQ symbol] (TTSB)
PDMC.......... Product Development & Manufacturing Center
PDMCW....... Princeton Dental Mgmt Wrrt [NASDAQ symbol] (TTSB)
PDME.......... Peak Distortion Monitoring Equipment (SAUS)
PDME.......... Pendant-Drop Melt Extraction [Metal fiber technology]
PDME.......... Precision Distance Measuring Equipment (MCD)
PDM-FM...... Pulse-Duration Modulation - Frequency Modulation (CET)
PDMFM....... Pulse-Duration Modulation-Frequency Modulation
PDMG......... Perspective Digital Map Generator
PDMLR....... Post-Development Maintainability Logistics Review (MCD)
PDMM........ Push Down Memory MODEM [Computer science]
PDMMS..... Product Design Minuteman Mechanical System (IAA)
PDMNT....... Piedmont
PDMO......... Production Mold (AAG)
PDMP......... Positive Displacement Mechanical [or Metering] Pump
PDMP......... Positive Displacement Metering Pump (SAUS)

PDMP......... Product Development Management Program (SAUS)
PDMP......... Project Data Management Plan (ACAE)
PDM/PM...... Pulse-Duration Modulation on Phase Modulation (MED)
PDMPO....... Polydimethyl Phenylene Oxide [Organic chemistry]
PDM-PSK.... Pulse Duration Modulation-Phase Shift Keying (SAUS)
PDMR......... Provisioning Data Master Record (MCD)
PDMS......... Particle Desorption Mass Spectrometry
PDMS......... Patient Data Management Systems [Medical records] (DAVI)
PDMS......... Payload Data Management System (SAUS)
PDMS......... Personal Data Management System (SAUS)
PDMS......... Pesticide Document Management System [Environmental Protection Agency] (GFGA)
PDMS......... Pharmacokinetic Drug Monitoring Services [Medicine] (DMAA)
PDMS......... Photodissociation Mass Spectrometry
PDMS......... Physiological Data Monitoring System
PDMS......... Pipework Design Management System (SAUS)
PDMS......... Plant Design and Management System [Computer Aided Design Centre] [Software package] (NCC)
PDMS......... Plasma-Desorption Mass Spectrometry (ABAC)
PDMS......... Plasma Desorption Mass Spectroscopy
PDMS......... Point Defense Missile System [NATO] (NATG)
PDMS......... Polydimethylsiloxane [Organic chemistry]
PDMS......... Postal Direct Marketing Service (WDAA)
PDMS......... Power-Plant and Process Design Management System [Computer science]
PDMS......... Product Data Management System (ACAE)
PDMS......... Program Data and Management System (SAUS)
PDMS......... Program Definition and Management System (MCD)
PDM System... Point-Designed Memory System (SAUS)
PDMT......... Predominant [National Weather Service] (FAAC)
PDMU......... Passive Data Memory Unit
PDMU......... Production Mock-Up (AAG)
PDMV......... Pressure Differential Monitoring Valve
PDN............ Packet Data Network [Computer science] (IGQR)
PDN............ Partido Democratico Nacional [National Democratic Party] [Chile] [Political party]
PDN............ Partido Democratico Nacional [National Democratic Party] [Venezuela] [Political party]
PDN............ Partito Democratico Nazionalista [Democratic Nationalist Party (1921-1926)] [Malta] [Political party] (PPE)
PDN............ Partnerships Data Net [Defunct] (EA)
PDN............ Petition Denied
PDN............ Phased-Array Doppler Noise (SEWL)
PDN............ Physics Data Notebook (SAUS)
PDN............ Portable Data Network [Computer science] (VLIE)
PDN............ Port Heiden, AK [Location identifier] [FAA] (FAAL)
PDN............ Positive Delivery Notification (SAUS)
PDN............ Power Dividing Network [Telecommunications] (LAIN)
PDN............ Pre-Discharge Notification (SAUS)
PDN............ Prednisone [Also, P, Pr, Pred, Pro] [Endocrinology] [Antineoplastic drug]
PDN............ Premises Distribution Network [Computer science] (IGQR)
PDN............ Private Duty Nurse (DAVI)
PDN............ Problem Documentation Number (AAG)
PDN............ Procedure Departure Notice (SAUS)
PDN............ Production (AFM)
PDN............ Properly Driven Net
PDN............ Public Data Network [Packet-switching network] [British Telecommunications Ltd.] [London]
PDN............ Putnam Diversified Premium (EFIS)
PDNC......... Parallel Digital Network Computer (VLIE)
PDNC......... Presidents' Day National Committee (EA)
PDNES....... Pulse-Doppler Non-Elevation Scan (PDAA)
PDNF......... Prime Disjunctive Normal Form (PDAA)
PD/NSC...... Presidential Directives/National Security Council
PDO........... Pacific Decadal Oscillation [Climatology]
PDO........... Packet Data Optimized (SAUS)
PDO........... Petroleum Development Oman (BUAC)
PDO........... Philips & Du Pont Optical Co. [Wilmington, DE]
PDO........... Phthalate Dioxygenase [An enzyme]
PDO........... Plasma-Deposited Oxide (SAUS)
PDO........... Portable Distributed Object (SAUS)
PDO........... Port Dry Out [Nuclear energy] (NUCP)
PDO........... Postman's Delivery Office (DCTA)
PDO........... Prado [Brazil] [Airport symbol] (AD)
PDO........... Printer Direction Optimizer (BUR)
PDO........... Procedure Description Overview (SAUS)
PDO........... Process Data Output (SAUS)
PD-O.......... Program Directive - Operations (KSC)
PDO........... Program Directive Operations (SAUS)
PDO........... Property Disposal Office [Environmental science] (BCP)
PDO........... Property Disposal Officer [Army]
PDO........... Property Disposal Organization
PdO........... Psychopathic Deviate Obvious [Psychology]
PDO........... Publications Distribution Officer [Military]
PDO........... Public Defender's Office (LAIN)
PDoB......... Bucks County Free Library, Doylestown, PA [Library symbol] [Library of Congress] (LCLS)
PDoBHi........ Bucks County Historical Society, Doylestown, PA [Library symbol] [Library of Congress] (LCLS)
PDOC......... Particulate and/or Dissolved Organic Carbon [Chemistry]
PDOC......... Proceed Directly on Course (SAUS)
PDOD......... Phytoplankton Dissolved Oxygen Deficit [Oceanography]
PDOF......... Principal Direction of Force [Mechanical engineering]

PDOIS .... People's Democratic Organisation for Independence and Socialism [*Senegambia*] [*Political party*]
PDOL .... Publishers Discount Option List
PDoN .... Delaware Valley College of Science and Agriculture, Doylestown, PA [*Library symbol*] [*Library of Congress*] (LCLS)
PDOP .... Position Dilution of Position [*Navigation systems*]
PDOP .... Position Dilution of Precision
PDOP .... Prospective Designated Overhaul Point (MCD)
PDOS .... Parallel and Distributed Operating System (SAUS)
PDOS .... Parent Diabetes Opinion Survey [*Test*]
PDOS .... Process Disk Operating System (SAUS)
PDOS .... Professional Development of Officers Study
PDOS .... Publishing Distribution Office System (SAUS)
PDOS .... Purple Dinosaur Operating System (SAUS)
PDowN .... Newcomen Society in North America, Downingtown, PA [*Library symbol*] [*Library of Congress*] (LCLS)
P/DOZ .... Per Dozen (WDAA)
PDP .... Packaging Development Plan
PDP .... Pakistan Democratic Party [*Political party*] (PD)
PDP .... Pan-African Democratic Party (SAUS)
Pdp .... Paradip (SAUS)
PDP .... Parallel Data Processing [*Computer science*]
PDP .... Parallel Detection Polychromator [*Instrumentation*]
PDP .... Parallel Distributed Processing [*A simulation of mental processes*]
PDP .... Parker & Parsley Petrol [*NYSE symbol*] (TTSB)
PDP .... Parker & Parsley Petroleum [*NYSE symbol*] (SAG)
PDP .... Parliamentary Democratic Party [*Myanmar*] [*Political party*]
PDP .... Parti Democrate Populaire [*Popular Democratic Party*] [*France*] [*Political party*] (PPE)
PDP .... Partido da Direita Portuguesa [*Party of the Portuguese Right*] [*Political party*] (PPE)
PDP .... Partido Democrata Popular [*Popular Democratic Party*] [*Dominican Republic*] [*Political party*] (PPW)
PDP .... Partido Democrata Popular [*Popular Democratic Party*] [*Spain*] [*Political party*] (PPW)
PDP .... Partido Democratico para o Progresso [*Democratic Progressive Party*] [*Guinea-Bissau*] [*Political party*] (EY)
PDP .... Partito Democratico Populare [*Popular Democratic Party*] [*San Marino*] [*Political party*] (PPE)
PDP .... Party for Democratic Prosperity [*Macedonia*] [*Political party*]
PDP .... Passive Driving Periscope [*Military*] (PDAA)
PDP .... Pasture Development Plan (SAUS)
PDP .... Pattern Disruption Point [*Medicine*] (DMAA)
PDP .... Payload Distribution Panel [*NASA*] (MCD)
PDP .... Payload Distribution Plan
PDP .... Pentadecylphenol [*Organic chemistry*]
PDP .... People Data Planning (SAUS)
PDP .... People's Democratic [*Saint Christopher and Nevis*] [*Political party*] (EY)
PDP .... People's Democratic Party [*Montenegro*] [*Political party*] (BUAC)
PDP .... People's Democratic Party [*Uzbekistan*] [*Political party*] (BUAC)
PDP .... People's Democratic Party [*Netherlands Antilles*] [*Political party*] (EY)
PDP .... People's Democratic Party [*Sierra Leone*] [*Political party*] (EY)
PDP .... People's Democratic Party [*South Korea*] [*Political party*] (EY)
PDP .... People's Democratic Party [*Sudan*] [*Political party*]
PDP .... Peripheral Data Processing (SAUS)
PDP .... Personal Development Program (MCD)
PDP .... Pesticide Data Program [*Environmental Protection Agency*]
PDP .... Phenyl-Dichlorophosphine (PDAA)
PDP .... Phi Delta Phi [*An association*] (NTPA)
PDP .... Philadelphia, PA [*Location identifier*] [*FAA*] (FAAL)
PDP .... Philippine Democratic Party [*Pilipino Lakas Ng Bayan*] [*Political party*] (PPW)
PDP .... Pilot District Project [*Office of Economic Opportunity*] [*Defunct*] (EA)
PDP .... Piperidino-Pyrimidine [*Biochemistry*] (MAE)
PDP .... Pitch-Depitch (AAG)
PDP .... Planning Development Program (OICC)
PDP .... Plasma Diagnostics Package [*NASA*]
PDP .... Plasma Display Panel [*Computer science*]
PDP .... Plasma Display Processor [*Computer science*]
PDP .... Polysilicon Dielectric Polysilicon [*Organic chemistry*] (IAA)
PDP .... Popular Democratic Party [*Puerto Rico*] [*Political party*]
PDP .... Positive Displacement Pump
PDP .... Post Detection Processor [*Military*] (CAAL)
PDP .... Post-Drug Potentiation
PDP .... Post-Insertion Deorbit Preparation [*NASA*] (MCD)
PDP .... Power Delay Product (SAUS)
PDP .... Power Distribution Panel
PDP .... Power Distribution Plan (SAUS)
PDP .... Power Drain Protection [*Automotive engineering*]
PDP .... Preconceptual Design Phase (SAUS)
PDP .... Preliminary Definition Plan (NASA)
PDP .... Preliminary Design Phase
PDP .... Preliminary Design Proposal (MCD)
PDP .... Preprototype Demonstration
PDP .... Prescription Drug Plan [*Insurance*] (WYGK)
PDP .... Prescription Drug Program [*Health insurance*] (GHCT)
PDP .... Present-Day Primers [*A publication*]
PDP .... Pressure Distribution Panel (AAG)
PDP .... Principal Display Panel [*Packaging*]
PDP .... Procedure Definition Processor [*Computer science*]
PDP .... Process Data Processing (IAA)
PDP .... Process Development Pile [*Nuclear energy*]
PDP .... Procurement Data Package [*Military*] (AABC)
PDP .... Product Development Pressure (SAUS)
PDP .... Product Development Process [*Automotive engineering*]
PDP .... Product Development Program (SAUS)
PDP .... Product Development Protocol [*U.S. Food and Drug Administration*]
PDP .... Product Documentation Procedures (SAUS)
PDP .... Production Data Package (MCD)
PDP .... Productivity Development Program (SAUS)
PDP .... Professional Data Processor (SAUS)
PDP .... Professional Developers Program (SAUS)
PDP .... Professional Development Document (SAUS)
PDP .... Professional Development Program [*Military*]
PDP .... Program Decision Package [*Military*]
PDP .... Program Definition Phase [*Army*]
PDP .... Program Development Paper (MCD)
PDP .... Program Development Plan [*NASA*]
PDP .... Programmable Data Processor (IAA)
PDP .... Programmable Digital Processor (SAUS)
PDP .... Programmable Display Pushbuttons
PDP .... Programmed Data Processor
PDP .... Programmed Digital Processor
PDP .... Progressive Democratic Party [*Romania*] [*Political party*] (BUAC)
PDP .... Progressive Democratic Party [*Montserrat*] [*Political party*] (PPW)
PDP .... Progressive Democratic Party [*St. Vincent*] [*Political party*] (PPW)
PDP .... Project Data Package (SAUS)
PDP .... Project Definition Phase (NRCH)
PDP .... Project Development Plan
PDP .... Psychopharmacology Demonstration Project [*Department of Defense*] (DIPS)
PDP .... Punta Del Este [*Uruguay*] [*Airport symbol*] (OAG)
PDPA .... People's Democratic Party of Afghanistan [*Political party*] (PPW)
PDPA .... Production Pattern (AAG)
PDPA .... Project Data Processing Authorization (ACAE)
PDPC .... Position Display Parallax Corrected
PDPC .... Post Detection Pulse Compression [*Military*] (CAAL)
PDP-CVS .... Positive Displacement Pump-Constant Volume Sampler (ERG)
PDPD .... Prolonged-Dwell Peritoneal Dialysis [*Medicine*] (DMAA)
PDPE .... Profit Dollar per Employee (SAUS)
Pd-PEI .... Palladium-Polyethylenimine (SAUS)
PDPF .... Packet Data Processing Facility (MCD)
PDPF .... Project Data Processing Facility (SAUS)
PDPGM .... Past Deputy Provincial Grand Master [*Freemasonry*]
PDPH .... Postdural Puncture Headache [*Medicine*] (DMAA)
PDPI .... Primer-Dependent Deoxynucleic Acid Polymerase Index [*Medicine*] (DMAA)
PDPI .... Product Development Pressure Index (SAUS)
PDPIC .... Professional Development Program Improvement Center (EDAC)
PDPL .... Property Damage, Personal Liability [*Insurance*]
PDPM .... Preliminary Draft Presidential Memo
PDPM .... Programmable Data Processing Machine (SAUS)
PDPOA .... Proposal Directive Plan of Action (MCD)
PDPR .... Per Day Pro-Rata (RIMS)
PDPR .... Present-Day Preachers [*A publication*]
PD Projectile ... Point Detonating Projectile (SAUS)
PDPS .... Parts Data Processing System [*Bell Telephone*]
PDPS .... Planning and Data Production System (SAUS)
PDPS .... Problem Driver Pointer System [*NHTSA*] (TAG)
PDPS .... Program Data Processing Section (AAG)
PDPS .... Program Data Processing System (IAA)
PDPS .... Program Definition Phase Studies [*Navy*]
PDPS .... Project Data Processing System (MCD)
PDPT .... Parti Democratique des Populations Togolaises [*Togolese Democratic People's Party*] [*Political party*]
PD PT .... Production Pattern (SAUS)
PDPUB .... Pedicel Pubescence [*Botany*]
PDPVF .... Presidential and Democratic Party Victory Fund (EA)
PDQ .... Packages Delivered Quick [*Allegheny Airlines service*]
PDQ .... Parallel Data Query [*Computer science*] (CDE)
PDQ .... Parental Diagnostic Questionnaire [*Speech evaluation test*]
PDQ .... Parodies Done Quirkily [*Humorous translation of Peter Schickele's PDQ Bach*]
PDQ .... Passed Data-set Queue (SAUS)
PDQ .... PDQ Air Service, Inc. [*ICAO designator*] (FAAC)
PDQ .... Peachtree Data Query (SAUS)
PDQ .... Permanent Durable Quality [*Paper*]
PDQ .... Personal Data Query (SAUS)
PDQ .... Personal Description Questionnaire
PDQ .... Personality Diagnostic Questionnaire (SAUS)
PDQ .... Personality Disorders Questionnaire (SAUS)
PDQ .... Pertinent Data Quest (MCD)
PDQ .... Photo Data Quantizer
PDQ .... Physician Data Query (SAUS)
PDQ .... Physician's Data Query [*NIH*]
PDQ .... Please Draw Quickly [*Initialism used as title of TV series*]
PDQ .... Point, Digital, Qualifier [*In automobile name Opel PDQ*]
PDQ .... Position Description Questionnaire (SAUS)
PDQ .... Prescreening Developmental Questionnaire [*Child development test*]
PDQ .... Pretty Darn Quick (TAG)
PDQ .... Price and Delivery Quotations
PDQ .... Price Delivery Quality
PDQ .... Prime Hospitality [*NYSE symbol*] (SPSG)
PDQ .... Product Demand Quotation (SAUS)
PDQ .... Program for Descriptive Query (SAUS)
PDQ .... Programmed Data Quantizer
PDQ .... Protocol Data Query [*Database*] [*National Institutes of Health*]
PDQC .... Physicians Data Query: Cancer Information File [*Database*]

PDQD	Physicians Data Query: Directory File [Database]
PDQP	Physicians Data Query: Protocol File [Database]
PDR	Packet Drop Rate (SAUS)
PDR	Page Data Register
PDR	Parent Daily Telephone Report [Education] (EDAC)
PDR	Particulate Data Reduction (EPA)
PDR	Parti Democratique Progressif [Algeria] [Political party] (EY)
PDR	Party of Democratic Reform [Slovenia] [Political party] (EY)
PDR	Pattern Delayed-Response [Ophthalmology]
PDR	Peak Dose Rate [Radiation] (AAG)
PDR	Pediatric Radiology [Medical specialty] (DHSM)
PDR	Pendaries Petroleum [AMEX symbol] (SG)
PDR	Peninsula Development Road (SAUS)
PDR	People's Democratic Republic (TVEL)
PDR	Performance Data Rate (SAUS)
P/DR	Performance/Development Review (SAUS)
PDR	Peripheral Diabetic Retinopathy [Medicine] (MELL)
PDR	Periscope Depth Range [SONAR]
PDR	Periscope Detection RADAR (NG)
PDR	Pharma-Dokumentationsring [Pharma Documentation Ring] [Information service or system] (IID)
PDR	Phase Data Recorder (KSC)
PDR	Phase Delay Rectifier
PDR	Philippine Defense Ribbon [Military decoration]
PDR	Photodissociation [or Photodominated] Region [Galactic science]
PDR	Photon-Dominated Region (SAUS)
PD-R	Physical Development by Reduction (SAUS)
PDR	Physicians' Desk Reference [Also, an information service or system] [A publication]
PDR	Pilot's Display Recorder
PDR	Piskei Din Shel Batei ha-Din ha-Rabaniyim be-Yisrael (BJA)
PDR	Pitch-to-Diameter Ratio (SAUS)
PDR	Plasma-Developed Resist Processing [Lithography]
PDR	Polarization Differential Reflectance (AAEL)
PDR	Portable Data Recorder (SAUS)
PDR	Position Distribution Report [DoD]
PDR	Post-Drug Repetition (SAUS)
PDR	Potential-Drop Ratio (SAUS)
pdr	Pounder (MILB)
PDR	Pounder (MSA)
PDR	Powder
PDR	Powder for Reconstitution (SAUS)
PDR	Power Deck Release
PDR	Power Directional Relay
PDR	Precision Depth Recorder
PDR	Predetection Recording
PDR	Predetermined Demand Rate
PDR	Pre-Determined Route [Aviation] (DA)
PDR	Preferential Departure Route [FAA] (TAG)
PDR	Preliminary Data Report
PDR	Preliminary Data Requirements (NASA)
PDR	Preliminary Design Report (NRCH)
PDR	Preliminary Design Review (NASA)
PDR	Pressurized Deuterium Reactor [Nuclear energy]
PDR	Previous Document Reference (SAUS)
PDR	Price Description Record [Computer science] (IBMDP)
PDR	Price-Dividend Ratio (WDAA)
PDR	Primary Data Recording (SAUS)
PDR	Primary Demographic Report [A. C. Nielsen Co.] (NTCM)
PDR	Priority Data Reduction
PDR	Procedure Development Request (SAUS)
PDR	Process Description Report (SAUS)
PDR	Process Dynamics Recorder
PDR	Processed Data Recorder
PDR	Processing Data Rate (IEEE)
PDR	Processing, Distribution and Retailing (SAUS)
PDR	Procurement Data Reference
PDR	Procurement Data Reporting (SAUS)
PDR	Product Design Review [Army]
PDR	Production, Distribution and Retailing (SAUS)
PDR	Program Design Review (MCD)
PDR	Program Director's Review [NASA] (NASA)
PDR	Program Discrepancy Report (IEEE)
PDR	Program Document Requirement (BUR)
PDR	Program Drum Recording
PDR	Proliferative Diabetic Retinopathy [Ophthalmology]
PDR	Property Disposal Request (ABAC)
PDR	Publications Data Request
PDR	Public Document Room (NRCH)
PDR	Pulse Doppler RADAR
PDR	Pulse Duty Ratio
PDR	Purchase of Development Rights (PA)
PDRA	Professional Drag Racing Association (EA)
PDRB	Permanent Diability Rating Board (DMAA)
PDRC	Clinical Research Center for Periodontal Disease [University of Florida] [Research center] (RCD)
PDRC	Personnel Despatch and Reception Centre [British military] (DMA)
PDRC	Peter Duel Remembrance Club (EA)
PDRC	Positron Diagnostic Research Center (SAUS)
PDRC	Poultry Disease Research Center [University of Georgia] [Research center] (RCD)
PDRC	Preliminary Design Review Commercial (MCD)
PDRC	Pressure Difference Recording Controller
PDRC	Professional Development and Recruitment Career Program [Military]
PDRC	Program Development Review Committee [Navy] (CAAL)
PDRCA	Participatory Development Resource Centre for Africa (SAUS)
PDRD	Procurement Data Requirements Document (NASA)
PDRD	Program Definition and Requirements Document (SSD)
PDRE	People's Democratic Republic of Ethiopia
PDRF	Parts Data Record File (SAUS)
PDRF	Passive Defense Recovery Force (MUGU)
PDRF	Presbyterians for Democracy and Religious Freedom (EA)
PDRH	Partido Democratico Revolucionario Hondureno [Revolutionary Democratic Party of Honduras] [Political party]
PDRJ	Pulse-Doppler Radar Jammer (SAUS)
PDRK	Peoples Democratic Republic of Korea (SAUS)
PdRK	Pesikta de-Rav Kahana (BJA)
PDRL	Permanent Disability Retired List
PDRL	Procurement Data Requirements List (NASA)
pDRLMS	Programmable Digital Radar Land Mass Simulation (SAUS)
PDRM	Payload Deployment and Retrieval Mechanism [NASA]
PDRM	Payload Distribution and Retrieval Mechanism (SAUS)
PDRM	Portable Dose Rate Meter
PDRM	Post-Depositional Remanent Magnetization [Geophysics]
PDRM	Postdetrital Remanent Magnetization [Geophysics]
PDRMA	Portable Drilling Rig Manufacturers Association [Defunct] (EA)
PDRP	Power Distribution Reactor Program (SAUS)
PDRP	Program Data Requirement Plan [Nuclear Regulatory Commission] (NRCH)
PDRP	Program Document Requirement Plan (SAUS)
PDRR	Program Definition and Risk Reduction (SAUS)
PDRS	Payload Data and Retrieval System [NASA] (NAKS)
PDRS	Payload Deployment and Retrieval System [NASA] (NAKS)
PDRS	Pulse Doppler Radar Simulation (SAUS)
PDRSS	Payload Deployment and Retrieval System Simulation [NASA] (SSD)
PDRSS	Payload Development and Retrieval System Simulator [NASA] (NAKS)
PDRSTA	Payload Deployment and Retrieval System Test Article [NASA] (NASA)
PDRY	People's Democratic Republic of Yemen [Political party]
PDS	Auburn/Lewiston, ME [Location identifier] [FAA] (FAAL)
PDS	Pacific Data Services (SAUS)
PDS	Pacific Data System (IAA)
PDS	Pacific Data Systems, Inc. (SAUS)
PDS	Pacific Distribution System (SAUS)
PDS	Package Data System (NASA)
PDS	Packaging Data Sheet (SAUS)
PDS	Packet Data Satellites [Telecommunications] (TSSD)
PDS	Packet Driver Specification (SAUS)
PDS	Paid-during-Service [Billing]
PDS	Pain Dysfunction Syndrome [Medicine] (AAMN)
PDS	Parkinson's Disease Society [British]
PDS	Paroxysmal Depolarizing Shift [Physiology]
PDS	Partei des Demokratischen Sozialismus [Party of Democratic Socialism] [Germany Political party] (EAIO)
PDS	Parti Democratique Senegalais [Senegalese Democratic Party] [Political party] (PPW)
PDS	Partido Democrata Socialista [Socialist Democratic Party] [Panama] [Political party] (PPW)
PDS	Partitioned Data Set [or System] [Computer science] (NASA)
PDS	Partito Democratico della Sinistra [Democratic Party of the Left] [Formerly, Italian Communist Party] [Political party] (EY)
PDS	Partito di Democrazia Socialista [Socialist Democracy Party] [San Marino] [Political party] (PPW)
PDS	Party of Democratic Socialism [Germany] [Political party]
PDS	Passenger Documentation System (SAUS)
PDS	Passive Defense System (SAUS)
PDS	Passive Detection System (NVT)
PDS	Patient Data System [Pharmacology] (DAVI)
PDS	Patient Decontamination Site [Army] (INF)
PDS	Patient Distribution System (SAUS)
PDS	Payload Data Subsystem (ACAE)
PDS	Pediatric Surgery [Medical specialty] (DHSM)
PdS	Pediatric Surgery [Medicine] (DMAA)
PDS	Penultimate Digit Storage [Telecommunications] (TEL)
PDS	Performer Design Sheet
PDS	Perimeter Defense System (MCD)
PDS	Periodicals Data System (NITA)
PDS	Peritoneal Dialysis System [nephrology] (DAVI)
PDS	Permanent Duty Station [Air Force] (AFM)
PDS	Permanent Dynamic Speaker (SAUS)
PDS	Permissible Data Symbol (SAUS)
PDS	Perry Drug Stores, Inc. (EFIS)
PDS	Persistent Data Services (SAUS)
PDS	Persistent Data Store (SAUS)
PDS	Personal Data System (NITA)
PDS	Personal Decision Series (HGAA)
PDS	Personal Development Study [Psychology]
PDS	Personnel Daily Summary [Army] (AABC)
PDS	Personnel Data Summary (SAUS)
PDS	Personnel Data System [Air Force]
PDS	Personnel Decontamination Station (MCD)
PDS	Personnel Delivery System
PDS	Petroleum Data System [University of Oklahoma] [Databank] (IID)
PDS	Pharma-Dokumentations-Service [Pharma Documentation Service] [Information service or system] (IID)
PDS	Phased Development Shuttle [NASA] (KSC)
PDS	Philadelphia Divinity School (SAUS)
PDS	Philips Data Systems (SAUS)
PDS	Philips Development System (SAUS)

PDS .... Photo Densitometer System (SAUS)
PDS .... Photo-Digital Store
PDS .... Photodischarge Spectroscopy (MCD)
PDS .... Photo Document Sensor (SAUS)
PDS .... Photographic Display System (SAUS)
PDS .... Photometric Data System (SAUS)
PDS .... Photothermal Deflection Spectroscopy (MCD)
PDS .... Physician Data Services
PDS .... Physician Depression Scale (SAUS)
PDS .... Piedras Negras [Mexico] [Airport symbol] (AD)
PDS .... Planar Diffusion Source (SAUS)
PDS .... Planar Dopant Source (SAUS)
PDS .... Planetary Data System (ACAE)
PDS .... Planning Data Sheet (KSC)
PDS .... Planning Data Systems [Information service or system] (IID)
PDS .... Plant Damage State
PDS .... Plant Data System [Nuclear energy] (NRCH)
PDS .... Plasma-Derived Serum
PDS .... Plasma Display (MCD)
PDS .... Plasma Display System
PDS .... Plotter Display System (DNAB)
PDS .... Pneumatic Distribution System
PDS .... Polydimethylsiloxane [Organic chemistry]
PDS .... Polydioxanone [Organic chemistry]
PDS .... Poly-P-Dioxanone
PDS .... Portable Data Store (SAUS)
PDS .... Portable Data System (MCD)
PDS .... Portable Display Shell (SAUS)
PDS .... Portable Document Software [Computer science] (DDC)
PDS .... Portable Duress Sensor (MCD)
PDS .... Positional Data System (SAUS)
PDS .... Position-Determining System
PDS .... Post Design Services [British] (RDA)
PDS .... Post Design Support (SAUS)
PDS .... Power Density Spectra (IEEE)
PDS .... Power Distribution Specification (IAA)
PDS .... Power Distribution Subsystem (SAUS)
PDS .... Power Distribution System [or Subsystem]
PDS .... Power Drive System
PDS .... Preadsorb-Dilute-Shake [Phage growth method]
PDS .... Precision Drilling Corp. [NYSE symbol] (SAG)
PDS .... Predialyzed Human Serum [Medicine] (MAE)
PDS .... Predocketed Special Project (NRCH)
PDS .... Predocketed Special Report (SAUS)
PDS .... Premises Distribution System [AT & T Corp.]
PDS .... Primary Data Set (SAUS)
PDS .... Primary Data Store (SAUS)
PDS .... Priority Decision System (NITA)
PDS .... Priority Distribution System [Military] (AFM)
PDS .... Prison Disciplinary System (WDAA)
PDS .... Prisoner Detention System
PDS .... Private Database Service (NITA)
PDS .... Probability Distribution Subprogram [Computer science] (BUR)
PDS .... Problem Data System (MCD)
PD/S .... Problem Definition/Solution
PDS .... Problem Descriptor System
PDS .... Procedures Development Simulator (KSC)
PDS .... Processing and Display System (CCCA)
PDS .... Processor Direct Slot [Computer science]
PDS .... Processor Direct Socket (SAUS)
PDS .... Procurement Data Sheet
PDS .... Product Data Sheet (SAUS)
PDS .... Product Demand Structure (SAUS)
PDS .... Product Design Standard
PDS .... Product Development System (SAUS)
PDS .... Production Data Sheet (MCD)
PDS .... Professional Development Scheme (HEAS)
PDS .... Professional Development School
PDS .... Professional Development Seminar (HGAA)
PDS .... Professional Development System [PC software] [Microsoft, Inc.] (PCM)
PDS .... Program Data Set (SAUS)
PDS .... Program Data Sheets [Army] (AABC)
PDS .... Program Data Source (BUR)
PDS .... Program Design Specification (CAAL)
PDS .... Program Development Section (SAUS)
PDS .... Program Development Specialist
PDS .... Program Development System [Computer science]
PDS .... Program Distribution System
PDS .... Programmable Data Station [or System]
PDS .... Programmable Data System (SAUS)
PDS .... Programmable Device Support
PDS .... Programmable Distribution System (SAUS)
PDS .... Programming Documentation Standards [Computer science] (WDAA)
PDS .... Progressive Deterioration Scale
PDS .... Project Data Sheet (SAUS)
PDS .... Project Definition Study (SAUS)
PDS .... Project Designation Study (SAUS)
PDS .... Propellant Delivery System
PDS .... Propellant Dispersion System (MCD)
PDS .... Proposed Delivery Schedule
PDS .... Protected Distribution System [Military] (GFGA)
PDS .... Protection and Defence Systems (SAUS)
PDS .... Proximity Defense Systems [Military] (INF)
PdS .... Psychiatric Deviate, Subtle (DAVI)

PdS .... Psychopathic Deviate Subtle [Psychology]
PDS .... Public Domain Software (SAUS)
PDS .... Pulse Doppler Search (SAUS)
PDS .... Pulse Doppler Seeker
PDS .... Punch Driver Selectric
PDS .... Purchasing Department Specification (MSA)
PDS .... Pyrotechnic Devices Simulator (SAA)
PDSA .... Paid Scientific Associates (SAUS)
PDSA .... People's Dispensary for Sick Animals [British]
PDSA .... Peroxydisulfuric Acid (AAEL)
PDS-A .... Personnel Data System - Airmen [Air Force]
PDSA .... Predesign and Systems Analysis [NASA] (KSC)
PDSA .... Private Doctors' Society of South Australia
PDSA Associate... Peoples Dispensary for Sick Animals Associate (SAUS)
PDS-A(I) ...... Personnel Data System - Airmen (Interim) [Air Force] (AFM)
PDSAR .... Public Document Status of Assessment Report (SAUS)
PDSB .... Physical Distribution Standards Board (SAUS)
PDSC .... PACOM [Pacific Command] Data Systems Center (MCD)
PDSC .... Parti Democrate et Social Chretien [Zaire] [Political party] (EY)
PDS-C .... Personnel Data System - Civilian [Air Force] (AFM)
PDSC .... Pressure Differential Scanning Calorimetry [Analytical technique]
PDSC .... Public Disaster Service Committee (SAUS)
PDSC .... Publishers Data Service Corp. [Monterey, CA]
PDSD .... Point Detonating Self-Destroying [Projectile]
PDSDD .... Plotting Display Subchannel Data Distributor (MCD)
PDSE .... Production Sample (AAG)
PDSF .... Parallel Distributed Simulation Facility (SAUS)
PDSF .... PDS Financial [NASDAQ symbol] (TTSB)
PDSF .... PDS Financial Corp. [NASDAQ symbol] (SAG)
PDS Fin ...... PDS Financial Corp. [Associated Press] (SAG)
PDSG .... Pick's Disease Support Group [British] (NRGU)
PDSI .... Palmer Drought Severity Index [Meteorology]
PDSI .... Performance Data Services, Inc. [Falls Church, VA] [Software manufacture r]
PDSI .... Portable Digital Strain Indicator
PDSI .... Professional Data Service, Incorporated
PDSK .... Petroleum Distribution System - Korea [Army] (MCD)
PDSL .... Pressure Differential Switch Load (SAUS)
PDSM .... Powder Diffraction Search-Match System [International Data Center]
PDS/MAGEN... Problem Descriptor System/Matrix Generation [Programming language] [1965] (CSR)
PDSMAN...... Partitioned Data Set Management System (SAUS)
PDSMS .... Point Defense Surface Missile System
PDSMS .... Power Diffraction Search and Match System (PDAA)
PDSN .... Plasma-Deposited Silicon Nitride (SAUS)
PDS-O......... Personnel Data System - Officers [Air Force] (AFM)
PDSOC........ Police Department Superior Officers Council (SAUS)
PDSOF........ Public Domain Software on File [Facts on File, Inc.] [Information service or system] (IID)
PDSOR........ Positive Definitive Successive Over-Relaxation (PDAA)
PDSP .... Peripheral Data Storage Processor
PDSP .... Personnel Data System - Planning [Air Force] (AFM)
PDSPI .... Polyurethane Division, Society of the Plastics Industry (EA)
PDSQ .... Point Detonating Super-Quick Fuze (NATG)
PDSQDL ...... Point Detonating, Superquick and Delay (SAUS)
PDSQ Fuze... Point Detonating Superquick Fuze (SAUS)
PDS-R......... Parti Democratique Senegalais - Renovation [Senegalese Democratic Party - Reform] [Political party]
PDSR .... Principal Director of Scientific Research (SAUS)
PDSS .... Particle Doppler Shift Spectrometer (PDAA)
PDSS .... Payload Data Services System (SPST)
PDSS .... Payload Development Support System (SAUS)
PDSS .... Physical Disabilities Special Interest Section [American Occupational Therapy Association]
PDSS .... Post Deployment Software Support (ACAE)
PDSS .... Post-Deployment Software System (MCD)
PDSS .... Post Development Support System (SAUS)
PDSS .... Procurement Decision Support System (ACAE)
PDSS .... Program Development Support System (SAUS)
PDSS .... Propulsion-Derived Ship Service (SAUS)
PDSSC........ Post Deployment Software Support Center
PDST .... Pacific Daylight Saving Time (KSC)
PDST .... Personnel Data System for Training (SAUS)
pdstl .... Pedestal (VRA)
PDSTT .... Pulse Doppler Single Target Track [Military] (CAAL)
PDSU .... Plant Data System Upgrade (SAUS)
PD Supp ...... Per Diem Supplement (AAGC)
PDSZ .... Party of Convinced Social Democrats of Zaire (SAUS)
PDT............. Hancock [John] Patriot Premium Dividend, Inc. II [NYSE symbol] (SPSG)
PDT............. John Hancock Patr Prem Dv II [NYSE symbol] (TTSB)
PDT............. Pacific Daylight Time
PDT............. Panoramic Design Technique
PDT............. Parallel Data Transmission
PDT............. Parameter Descriptor Table (SAUS)
PdT .... Parti du Travail [Labor Party] [Switzerland] [Political party] (PPE)
PDT............. PDT, Inc. [Associated Press] (SAG)
PDT............. Pendleton [Oregon] [Airport symbol] (OAG)
PDT............. Performance Demonstration Test
PDT............. Performance Diagnostic Tool (SAUS)
PDT............. Peripheral Data Transfer [Telecommunications] (IAA)
PDT............. Peripheral Device Type (CIST)
PDT............. Personal Data Transmitter [From the movie "Aliens"]
PDT............. Phenyldimethyltriazine [Organic chemistry] (AAMN)
PDT............. Photodynamic Therapy [Oncology]

PDT............	Physical Device Table (NITA)
PDT............	Picture Description Test (PDAA)
PDT............	Piedmont Airlines, Inc. [ICAO designator] (FAAC)
PDT............	Planned Data to Transportation [DoD]
PDT............	Plasma Display Terminal [Computer science]
PDT............	Pollable Data Terminal [Bell System]
PDT............	Population Doubling Time [Cytology]
PDT............	Portable Data Terminal (SEWL)
PDT............	Positive Displacement Turbine (SAUS)
PDT............	Post Alloy Diffused Transistor [Electronics] (IAA)
PDT............	Posting Data Transfer [Air Force] (AFM)
PDT............	Potentially Dangerous Taxpayer (AFM)
PDT............	Power Distribution Trailer (NATG)
PDT............	Practice Delivery Torpedo (SAUS)
PDT............	Predelivery Test (MCD)
PDT............	Predictor Display Technique
PDT............	President Mines [Vancouver Stock Exchange symbol]
PDT............	Pressure Decay Test [Automotive emissions]
PDT............	Printer Definition Table (SAUS)
PDT............	Processed Directional Transmission [Military] (NVT)
PDT............	Processor Diagnostic Test (ACAE)
PDT............	Procurement Data Transmittal (SAUS)
PDT............	Product (SAUS)
PDT............	Product Development Team [Automotive project management]
PDT............	Professional Development and Teaching (SAUS)
PDT............	Programmable Data Terminal [Digital Equipment Corp.] (IEEE)
PDT............	Programmable Drive Table
PDT............	Propagation Delay Time (SAUS)
PDT............	Published Data Tape [A. C. Nielsen Co.] [A publication] (WDMC)
PDT............	Pulse Delay Time
PDT............	Pushdown Transducer (CIST)
PDT............	(Pyridyl)diphenyltriazine [Analytical chemistry]
PDT-1	Picatinny Arsenal Detonation Trap Number 1 [Army] (AABC)
PDTA	Production Tape (AAG)
PDTA	Professional Dance Teachers Association (EA)
PDTA	Propylenediaminetetraacetic Acid [Organic chemistry]
PDTAG	Product Data Technology Advisory Group (SAUS)
PDT & T	Post-Delivery Test and Trials [Military] (CAAL)
PDTC	Philadelphia Depository Trust Co.
PDTE..........	Packet-mode Data Terminal Equipment (SAUS)
PDTE..........	Packet-mode DTE (SAUS)
PD Technique...	Physical Development Technique (SAUS)
PDTF..........	Program Development and Test Facility [Social Security Administration]
PDTI..........	PDT, Inc. [NASDAQ symbol] (SAG)
PDTM..........	PD Technical Mouldings plc (SAUS)
PDTMR	Phalloidin Tetramethylrhodamine [Biochemistry]
PDTP..........	Plasma Display Touch Panel [Computer science]
PDTRST.......	Podiatrist
PDTS	Police Detective Training School (SAUS)
PDTS	Procurement Document Tracking System (MCD)
PDTS	Program Development Tracking System [Computer science]
PDTS	Programmable Data Terminal Set [Military] (CAAL)
PDTTT.........	Post-Delivery Test and Trial Team (MCD)
PDU	Pacific Democrat Union (EAIO)
PDU	Packet Data Unit (MLOA)
PDU	Parti Dahomeen de l'Unite [Dahomean Unity Party] [Benin] [Political party]
PDU	Parti Democrate Unifie [Unified Democratic Party] [Name replaced by Section Voltaique de Rassemblement] [Burkina Faso] [Political party]
PDU	Paysandu [Uruguay] [Airport symbol] (OAG)
PDU	Performance Diagnostic Unit (SAUS)
PDU	Phase Demodulation Unit
PDU	Philippines Digital Upgrade (SAUS)
PDU	Photomultiplier Detector Unit (KSC)
PDU	Pilot's Display Unit (MCD)
PDU	Plasma Display Unit (SAUS)
PDU	Plug Distribution Unit (SAUS)
PDU	Positive Displacement Unit [Mechanical pumps]
PDU	Power Distribution Unit (AAG)
PDU	Power Drive Unit (MCD)
PDU	Pressure Distribution Unit
PDU	Process Demonstration Unit [Chemical engineering]
PDU	Process Development Unit [Chemical engineering]
PDU	Product Distribution Unit (SAUS)
PDU	Production Distribution Unit (AAG)
PDU	Programmable Delay Unit
PDU	Programmable Diagnostic Unit [TACOM] [Army] (RDA)
PDU	Project Development Unit [Chemical engineering]
PDU	Projection Display Unit
PDU	Protocol Data Unit [Telecommunications]
PDU	Pulsed Doppler Ultrasonography [Radiology] (DAVI)
PDU	Pulse Detection Unit (NASA)
PDUFA	Prescription Drug User Fee Act
PDUFC	Pete Duel Universal Friendship Club (EAIO)
PdUP	Partito di Unita Proletaria per il Comunismo [Democratic Party of Proletarian Unity for Communism] [Italy] [Political party] (PPE)
PDUPE........	Protocol Data Unit Programming Environment (SAUS)
PDur	Papyri Durani (BJA)
PDUR	Predischarge Utilization Review [Medicine]
PDUS	Primary Data User Station [Computer science] (PDAA)
PDV	Parcel Delivery Van
PDV	Path Delay Value (SAUS)
PDV	Phocine Distemper Virus

PDV	Photorealistic Data Visualization (SAUS)
PDV	Polyhedra Derived Virus
PDV	Ponderosa Ventures, Inc. [Vancouver Stock Exchange symbol]
PDV	Premodulation Processor - Deep Space - Voice
PDV	Pressure Disconnect Valve (MCD)
PDV	Probability of Detection and Verification [Military] (CAAL)
PDV	Prune Dwarf Virus
PDV	Pure Dried Vacuum (SAUS)
PDV	Pyrotechnic Development Vehicle (PDAA)
PDVC	Phase-Dependent Voltage Contrast (AAEL)
PDVF	Payload Design Verification Facility (ACAE)
PDVM	Printing Digital Voltmeter (SAUS)
PDVN	Power-Driven
PDW	Evansville, IN [Location identifier] [FAA] (FAAL)
PDW	Partially Delactosed Whey (OA)
PDW	Personal Damage Waiver (TRID)
PDW	Personal Defense Weapon [Army] (INF)
PDW	Personal Design Workstation (DGA)
PDW	Physical Damage Waiver [Insurance] (TVEL)
PDW	Planar Dielectric Waveguide (SAUS)
PDW	Platelet Distribution Width [Hematology]
PDW	Priority Delayed Weather [NWS] (FAAC)
PDWE	Pulse Detonation Wave Engine (SAUS)
PDWHF........	Platelet-Derived Wound-Healing Factor [Biochemistry]
PD Work	Public Domain Work (SAUS)
PDWP	Partially Delactosed Whey Powder (OA)
PDWR	Primary Drinking Water Regulation (COE)
PDWS	Passive Doppler Wind Sensor (SAUS)
PDWS	Primary Drinking Water Standards (SAUS)
PDX	Paradox files (SAUS)
PDX	Passive Dosimeter Experiment (KSC)
PDX	Place Decrement in Index
PDX	Poloidal Divertor Experiment [Princeton University]
PDX	Portland [Oregon] [Airport symbol] (OAG)
PDX	Prado Explorations Ltd. [Toronto Stock Exchange symbol]
PDX	Printer Description Extension (SAUS)
PDX	Private Digital Exchange
PDX	Probable Diagnosis (DAVI)
PDX	Processor-controlled Digital Exchange (SAUS)
PDX	Program Development Executive (MHDI)
PDY	Piccadilly Resources Ltd. [Vancouver Stock Exchange symbol]
PDY	Principal Duty [Military]
PDYN	Prodynorphin [Biochemistry]
PDZ............	Ontario, CA [Location identifier] [FAA] (FAAL)
PDZ............	Parachute Dropping Zone (SAUS)
PDZ............	Pedernales [Venezuela] [Airport symbol] (OAG)
PDZC	Pathfinder Drop-Zone Control (SAUS)
PE	British Aircraft Corp. Ltd. [ICAO aircraft manufacturer identifier] (ICAO)
PE	Easton Area Public Library, Easton, PA [Library symbol] [Library of Congress] (LCLS)
PE	Edinburgh Pharmacopoeia [British] (DAVI)
Pe	episcleral venous Pressure (SAUS)
PE...............	Ice Pellets [Meteorology]
PE	Pacific Electric Railway [AAR code]
PE	Page-End (SAUS)
PE	Page-End Character [Computer science]
PE	Paleoecology (SAUS)
PE	Paper Electrophoresis [Medicine] (MAE)
PE	Parabolic Equation
PE	Parallel Element (SAUS)
PE	Parity Error
PE	Parity Even (SAUS)
PE	Partes Aequales [Equal Parts] [Pharmacy]
PE	Partial Evaluation (VLIE)
PE	Patrol Vessel, Eagle [Eagle boat] [Navy symbol] [Obsolete]
PE	Peace Establishment (SAUS)
PE	Peacetime Establishment [Military] (NATG)
Pe	Peclet Number [IUPAC]
PE	PECO Energy [Formerly, Philadelphia Electric Co.] [NYSE symbol] (SPSG)
PE	Pectinesterase [Also, PME] [An enzyme]
PE	Pediatrics (DAVI)
Pe	Pelagius [Deceased, 1232] [Authority cited in pre-1607 legal work] (DSA)
PE	Pel-Ebstein [Disease] [Medicine] (DB)
pe	Pen (VRA)
PE	Penile Erection [Medicine] (DMAA)
PE	Pentaeythrol (IAA)
Pe	Pentyl [Biochemistry]
PE	People Express [ICAO designator] (AD)
PE	Percent Bit Error Probability (SAUS)
PE	Percent Error (ACAE)
PE	Performance Enhancement [Computer science] (VLIE)
PE	Performance Evaluation (ABAC)
PE	Pericardial Effusion [Cardiology] (DAVI)
PE	Period Ending
PE	Period Entry (SAUS)
PE	Periodic (AAG)
PE	Peripheral Equipment (AAG)
PE	Periscope
PE	Peritoneal Exudate [Medicine]
PE	Perkin Elmer Corp.
PE	Permanent Echo [RADAR]
PE	Permanent Error (IAA)

PE	Permissible Error (ADA)
PE	Perry Ellis [*Fashion designer, 1940-86*]
PE	Persistent Estrus [*Endocrinology*]
PE	Personal Effects
PE	Personal Electronics (VLIE)
PE	Personal Equipment
PE	Personnel Division (SAUS)
PE	Personnel, Enlisted [*or Enlisted Personnel Division*] [*Coast Guard*]
PE	Personnel Equipment [*Air Force*] (AFM)
PE	Personnel Equivalent [*DoD*]
PE	Peru [*ANSI two-letter standard code*] (CNC)
pe	Peru [*MARC country of publication code*] [*Library of Congress*] (LCCP)
Pe	Peru (MILB)
Pe	Perylene [*Organic chemistry*] (AAMN)
Pe	Peterborough [*Postcode*] (ODBW)
PE	Petroleum Economist [*London*] [*A publication*] (BJA)
PE	Petroleum Engineer
PE	Petroleum Engineering (SAUS)
Pe	Petrus de Bellapertica [*Deceased, 1308*] [*Authority cited in pre-1607 legal work*] (DSA)
Pe	Petrus Hispanus [*Authority cited in pre-1607 legal work*] (DSA)
PE	Phakoemulsification [*Ophthalmology*] (DAVI)
PE	Pharmacopaeia Edinensis [*Edinburgh Pharmacopoeia*] [*A publication*] (ROG)
PE	Pharmacopoeia of Edinburgh (SAUS)
PE	Pharyngoesophageal [*Medicine*]
PE	Phase Encoded (SAUS)
PE	Phase Encoding [*Magnetic tape recording*] [*Computer science*] (MDG)
PE	Phenylephrine
PE	Philadelphia Electric (SAUS)
PE	Philadelphia Stock Exchange (CDAI)
PE	Philips Electric (SAUS)
PE	Phorbol Ester (SAUS)
PE	Phosphatidylethanolamine [*Biochemistry*]
PE	Photoelectric
PE	Photoelectron (IAA)
pe	Photoelectron
PE	Photoemission [*Physics*]
PE	Photoengraving (SAUS)
PE	Photographic Effect (MAE)
PE	Photon Echo [*Spectroscopy*]
PE	Phycoerythrin [*Biochemistry*]
PE	Physical Education
PE	Physical Evaluation [*Medicine*] (MAE)
PE	Physical Examination
PE	Physiological Ecology
PE	Pictorial Element (SAUS)
PE	Pictorial Eleven [*Later, PES*] [*An association*] (EA)
PE	Picture Element (ELAL)
PE	Piezoelectric (AAEL)
PE	Piezoelectricity (SAUS)
PE	Pigment Epithelium [*of the retina*]
PE	Pilot Equalizer (IAA)
PE	Pilot Error
PE	Pinion End
PE	Pistol Expert
PE	Plain Edged (SAUS)
PE	Plain Edges [*Graphic arts*] (DGA)
PE	Plain End [*Lumber*] (DAC)
PE	Planetary Explorer [*NASA*]
PE	Planification de l'Emploi [*Canadian Jobs Strategy - CJS*]
P/E	Planning Economics Group, Boston [*Information service or system*] (IID)
PE	Planning Engineer (SAUS)
PE	Planning Estimate
PE	Plant Engineering (AAG)
PE	Plant Equipment (MCD)
PE	Plant Extrusion (OA)
PE	Plasma Emission [*Spectrophotometry*]
PE	Plasma Exchange [*Medicine*]
PE	Plastic Engine (SAUS)
PE	Plastic Explosive (NATG)
PE	Plating Efficiency (DB)
PE	Platinum Electrode (SAUS)
PE	Pleural Effusion [*Medicine*]
PE	Plutonium Equivalent (SAUS)
PE	Pneumatic Equalization [*Tube*] [*Otorhinolaryngology*] (DAVI)
PE	Pocket Edition (WDAA)
PE	Point of Entry (SAUS)
PE	Pollen Equivalent [*Immunology*]
PE	Polyelectrolyte [*Organic chemistry*]
PE	Polyester [*Tire design*]
PE	Polyether (SAUS)
PE	Polyethylene [*Organic chemistry*]
PE	Ponton Equipment (SAUS)
PE	Population Equivalent (FFDE)
PE	Porcelain Enamel [*Technical drawings*]
PE	Portable Error (SAUS)
PE	Portable Executable
PE	Portable Executable File [*Computer science*]
PE	Port Engineer (DNAB)
PE	Port of Embarkation [*Military*]
PE	Positional Efficiency (SAUS)
PE	Position Effect [*Parapsychology*]
PE	Position Error
PE	Positive Expulsion (SAA)
PE	Positives and Etching (DGA)
PE	Post Edit (SAUS)
PE	Post Engineer [*Army*] (AABC)
PE	Post Exchange [*Marine Corps*]
PE	Postexposure [*Medicine*]
PE	Potato Eaters (EA)
PE	Potential Electrode (SAUS)
PE	Potential Energy
PE	Potential Evaporation (SAUS)
PE	Potential Evapotranspiration (DICI)
PE	Potential Excess [*of stock*] [*DoD*]
PE	Powdered Extract [*Pharmacy*]
PE	Power, Electric (SAUS)
PE	Power Equipment [*Military*] (IAA)
PE	Power Exchange (SAUS)
PE	Practical Exercise
PE	Precipitation Efficiency (SAUS)
P-E	Precipitation-Environment (SAUS)
P-E	Precipitation-Evaporation
PE	Pre-Eclampsia [*Medicine*]
PE	Pre-Emption [*Telecommunications*] (TEL)
PE	Preliminary Evaluation
PE	Preliminary Exploitation (MCD)
PE	Prepaid Expense [*Finance*] (MHDW)
PE	Presidential Exemption [*Environmental Protection Agency*]
PE	Presiding Elder
PE	Pressure Enclosure (MCD)
PE	Pressure Equalization [*Tube*] [*Otorhinolaryngology*] (DAVI)
PE	Pressure Equalizing [*Tube*] [*Otorhinolaryngology*] (DAVI)
Pe	Pressure on Expiration [*Medicine*]
PE	Pressurized Element (SAUS)
PE	Priced Exhibit (MCD)
P/E	Price [*or Profit*]/Earnings Ratio [*Relation between price of a company's stock and its annual net income*]
PE	Price Earnings Ratio [*Investment term*] (DFIT)
P/E	Price-to-Earnings
PE	Primary Education (AIE)
PE	Primary Electricity
PE	Primary Electron (SAUS)
PE	Prime Equipment
PE	Primitive Endoderm [*Cytology*]
PE	Primitive Equation
PE	Prince Edward Island [*Canadian province*] [*Postal code*]
PE	Principal Engineer (AAG)
PE	Principle Engineer (SAUS)
PE	Print End [*Computer science*] (VLIE)
pe	Printer's Error (WDAA)
PE	Printer's Error
PE	Private Eye (SAUS)
PE	Probability of Error (CCCA)
pe	Probable Error (DIPS)
PE	Probable Error [*Statistics*]
PE	Procedures Evaluation [*DoD*]
PE	Process Engineer (SAUS)
PE	Process Engineering (SAUS)
PE	Processing Element [*of central processing unit*]
PE	Processor Element
PE	Procurement Executive [*British*]
PE	Production Engineer (SAUS)
PE	Production Engineering
PE	Production Engineering Division [*Frankford Arsenal*] [*Philadelphia, PA*]
PE	Production Executive [*British*]
P/E	Professional and Executive [*Employment register*] [*British*]
PE	Professional Ecologist (SAUS)
PE	Professional Edition
PE	Professional Education (AFM)
PE	Professional Engineer
PE	Professional Engraver (SAUS)
PE	Professional Equipment (SAUS)
PE	Professional Estimator (SAUS)
PE	Program Element (AFM)
PE	Program Evaluation (OICC)
PE	Programmed Exciter
PE	Programming Environment (SAUS)
PE	Programming Error (SAUS)
PE	Project Engineer
PE	Project Equality (EA)
PE	Prometheus-Europe [*Paris, France*] (EAIO)
PE	Propellants and Explosives
PE	Proponent Evaluation (MCD)
PE	Proposed Endangered (SAUS)
PE	Protected Environment
PE	Protect Enable [*Computer science*] (PCM)
PE	Protection Earth (SAUS)
PE	Protection Enabled (SAUS)
PE	Protective Earth (SAUS)
PE	Protective Entrance (SAUS)
PE	Protein Electrophoresis [*Biochemistry*] (DAVI)
PE	Protein Equivalent (SAUS)
PE	Protestant Episcopal
PE	Proteus Engine [*Hovercraft*]

PE...............	Protocol Elements (SAUS)
PE...............	Proton Event
PE...............	Prototype Event (SAUS)
PE...............	Pseudomonas Exotoxin [Bacterial toxin]
PE...............	Public Eye [Internet Site]
PE...............	Pulled Elbow (MELL)
PE...............	Pulley End
PE...............	Pulmonary Edema [Medicine]
PE...............	Pulmonary Effusion [Medicine]
PE...............	Pulmonary Embolism [Medicine]
PE...............	Pulmonary Embolus (SAUS)
PE...............	Pulmonary Emphysema [Medicine] (MELL)
PE...............	Pulse Echo [Materials research]
P/E.............	Pulse-Echo Testing (SAUS)
PE...............	Pulse Encoding [Computer science]
PE...............	Purchased Equipment
P/E.............	Purchase Enquiry (RIMS)
PE...............	Pyramidal Eminence [Medicine] (MELL)
PE...............	Pyroelectric
PE...............	Pyroelectricity (SAUS)
Pe...............	Warner-Lambert Pharmaceutical Co. [Research code symbol]
PE2.............	Secondary Plating Efficiency (STED)
PEA.............	Palmitylethanolamide [Organic chemistry]
PEA.............	Pan Europeenne Air Service [France] [ICAO designator] (FAAC)
PEA.............	Papillary Eccrine Adenoma [Oncology]
PEA.............	Parking Enforcement Aide (ECON)
PEA.............	Pattern Error Analysis
PEA.............	Patterson Experimental Array (MCD)
PEA.............	Payload Enclosure Assembly (MCD)
Pea.............	Peake's English Nisi Prius Reports [1790-1812] [A publication] (DLA)
PEA.............	Pella, IA [Location identifier] [FAA] (FAAL)
PEA.............	Penneshaw [Australia] [Airport symbol] (OAG)
PEA.............	Pennsylvania Electric Association
PEA.............	People Express Airlines (SAUS)
PEA.............	Percentage Electrical Activity (SAUS)
PEA.............	Phenethyl Alcohol [Organic chemistry]
PEA.............	Phenylethanolamine [Organic chemistry]
PEA.............	Phenylethylamine [Biochemistry]
PEA.............	Phosphoethanolamine [Organic chemistry]
PE(A).........	Physical Education (Association) [British]
PEA.............	Piezoelectric Accelerometer [Electronics]
PEA.............	Pilot's Employment Agency
PEA.............	Pitch Error Amplifier
PEA.............	Plant Engineering Agency
PEA.............	Plastics Engineers Association [Defunct] (EA)
PEA.............	Platform Electronics Assembly (KSC)
PEA.............	Pocket Ethernet Adapter [Computer science] (VLIE)
PEA.............	Polish Ex-Servicemen's Association [Australia]
PEA.............	Poly(ethyl Acrylate) [Organic chemistry]
PEA.............	Polysaccharide Egg Antigen (STED)
PEA.............	Portuguese East Africa [Mozambique]
PEA.............	Positive Electron Affinity (SAUS)
PEA.............	Potash Export Association (EA)
PEA.............	Poultry Education Association [British] (BI)
PEA.............	Power Excursion Accident [Nuclear energy] (NUCP)
PEA.............	Preliminary Endangerment Assessment (SARE)
PEA.............	Preliminary Environmental Assessment (MCD)
PEA.............	Primary Expense Account
PEA.............	Private Employment Agency (OICC)
PEA.............	Process Environmental Analysis
PEA.............	Process Equipment Accessory (MCD)
PEA.............	Procurement Executives Association (AAGC)
PEA.............	Program Element Administrator [Navy] (NG)
PEA.............	Progressive Education Association [Defunct]
PEA.............	Proposal Expansion Award (TELE)
PEA.............	Publication Effectiveness Audit (SAUS)
PEA.............	Public Education Association
PEA.............	Pulseless Electrical Activity (SAUS)
PEA.............	Push-Effective Address [Computer science] (IEEE)
PEA.............	Pyridylethylamine [Organic chemistry]
Pea (2).......	Peake's Additional Cases Nisi Prius [170 English Reprint] [1795-1812] [A publication] (DLA)
PEAA...........	Program Elements Activity Accounts (MCD)
P/EA(A)3.....	Probationary Electrical Artificer (Air) 3rd Class [British military] (DMA)
Pea Add Cas...	Peake's English Nisi Prius Reports [Vol. 2] [A publication] (DLA)
PEAB...........	Professional Engineers Appointments Bureau (SAUS)
Peab L Rev...	Peabody Law Review [A publication] (DLA)
Peabody Inst...	Peabody Institute of The Johns Hopkins University (GAGS)
PEAC...........	Peripheral Array Computer (SAUS)
PEAC...........	Pharmaceutical Education Advisory Committee [Australia]
PEAC...........	Photoelectric Alignment Collimator (IAA)
PEAC...........	Photoelectric Auto Collimator
PEAC...........	Photoelectroanalytical Chemistry
PEAC...........	Police Education Advisory Council [New South Wales, Australia]
PEAC...........	Program Evaluation and Audit Committee (SAUS)
PEAC...........	Public Education Awards Competition (SAUS)
PEACAMPOT...	Perturbation by East Asia Continental Air Mass to Pacific Oceanic Troposphere (SAUS)
PEACE.........	People Emerging Against Corrupt Establishments [Underground military newspaper]
PEACE.........	Plan for Excellence in a Collaborative Environment [School project]
PEACE.........	Plasma Electron and Current Analyzer (SAUS)
PEACE.........	Project Evaluation and Assistance, Civil Engineering [Air Force]
PEACE.........	Protection of Environment for Assuring Cleaner Earth (SAUS)
PEACER.......	Petroleum Employers Advisory Council on Employ Relations (SAUS)

PEACESAT ...	Pan-Pacific Editing and Communication Experiment by Satellite (NITA)
PEACESAT ...	Pan-Pacific Educational and Cultural Exchange by Satellite Program [University of Hawaii, Manoa] [Research center] (RCD)
PEACESAT ...	Pan-Pacific Education and Communication Experiments by Satellites [University of Hawaii] [NASA]
PEACH	Preschool Evaluation and Assessment for Children with Handicaps (STED)
PEACU	Plastic Energy Absorption in Compression Unit (IEEE)
PEAD	Presidential Emergency Action Document
PEADS	Presidential Emergency Action Direction System (MCD)
PEAF...........	Print Evaluation and Acceptance Form (TIMI)
PEAI...........	Physical Education Association of Ireland (EAIO)
PEAK...........	Peak Technologies Group, Inc. [NASDAQ symbol] (SAG)
PEAK...........	Peak Technologies Grp [NASDAQ symbol] (TTSB)
PEAK...........	Pricing Electronic Access to Knowledge
Peake	Peake's Cases [1790-1812] [A publication] (DLA)
Peake Add Cas...	Peake's Additional Cases Nisi Prius [1795-1812] [A publication] (DLA)
Peake Ev	Peake on the Law of Evidence [A publication] (DLA)
Peake NP	Peake's English Nisi Prius Cases [170 English Reprint] [A publication] (DLA)
Peake NP Add Cas...	Peake's Additional Cases Nisi Prius [170 English Reprint] [England] [A publication] (DLA)
Peake NP Add Cas (Eng)...	Peake's Additional Cases Nisi Prius [170 English Reprint] [England] [A publication] (DLA)
Peake NP Cas...	Peake's English Nisi Prius Cases [170 English Reprint] [1790-1812] [A publication] (DLA)
Peake NP Cas (Eng)...	Peake's English Nisi Prius Cases [170 English Reprint] [A publication] (DLA)
PeakTch.......	Peak Technologies Group, Inc. [Associated Press] (SAG)
PEAL	Professional Engineers Association Ltd. (SAUS)
PEAM..........	Personal Electronic Aid for Maintenance [Military]
Pea MS.......	Peachey on Marriage Settlements [1860] [A publication] (DLA)
Pea Mus......	Peabody Museum (SAUS)
PEAMUSE.....	Peabody Museum of Archaeology and Ethnology [Harvard University] [Research center] (RCD)
PE&D	Plant engineering and design (SAUS)
PE & M	Plant Engineering and Maintenance (MCD)
PE&R	Policy, Evaluation and Research (SAUS)
PE&S	Parts Engineering and Standardization (SAUS)
PEANZ	Petroleum Exploration Association of New Zealand (SAUS)
PEAO	Phenylethylamine Oxidase (STED)
PEAP..........	Pad Emergency Air Pack [NASA] (KSC)
PEAP..........	Personal Egress Air Pack (NAKS)
PEAP..........	Pesticide Education and Action Project (EA)
PEAP..........	Positive End-Airway Pressure [Medicine] (DMAA)
PEAP..........	Principal Error Axis for Position
PEAP..........	Program Evaluation Analysis Plan (MCD)
PEAQ	Personal Experience and Attitude Questionnaire (STED)
PeAR..........	Die Provinzeinteilung des Assyrischen Reiches [A publication] (BJA)
PEAR	Plasma Extended Arc Reactor (SAUS)
PEAR	Polyetheramide [Plastics]
PEAR	Production Error Analysis Report (SAUS)
PEAR	Program Error Analysis Report [Computer science] (VLIE)
Pearce CC ...	Pearce's Reports in Dearsley's English Crown Cases [A publication] (DLA)
PEARL	Committee for Public Education and Religious Liberty (EA)
PEARL	Parts Explosion and Retrieval Language (SAUS)
pearl..........	pearl white (SAUS)
PEARL	Performance Evaluation of Amplifiers from a Remote Location
PEARL	Periodical Enquiry Acquisition and Registration Locally (NITA)
PEARL	Periodicals Automation, Rand Library
PEARL	Personal Equipment and Rescue/Survivable Lowdown (MCD)
PEARL	Personnel Expertise and Resource Listing (COE)
PEARL	Portable Environmental Assessment and Research Laboratory (SAUS)
PEARL	Process and Experiment Automation Real-Time Language [Computer science]
PEARL	Processor and Experiment Automation Realtime Language (SAUS)
PEARL	Program for EPS [Electrical Power System] Analysis and Rapid Look-Ahead [NASA computer program]
PEARL	Programmed Editor and Automated Resources for Learning
PEARL	Public Education and Religious Liberty (SAUS)
PEARL	Pupils Equal and React to Light [Medicine] (MELL)
PEARLA	Pupils Equal and React to Light and Accomodation [Medicine]
PEARLNAVSHIPYD...	Pearl Harbour Naval Shipyard (SAUS)
Pears	Pearson's Reports [1850-80] [Pennsylvania] [A publication] (DLA)
PEARS	Porcine Epidemic Abortion and Respiratory Syndrome (SAUS)
Pearson	Pearson's Common Pleas [Pennsylvania] [A publication] (DLA)
Pears (PA)...	Pearson's Reports [1850-80] [Pennsylvania] [A publication] (DLA)
PEART	Passive Electronic Advanced Receiver (MCD)
pearwd	Pear Tree Wood (VRA)
PEAS..........	Pacific's Electronics Acquisition Service (NITA)
PEAS..........	Physical Estimation and Attraction Scales
PEAS..........	Policy and External Affairs Staff [Environmental Protection Agency] (GFGA)
PEAS..........	Practical Engineering Applications Software (NITA)
PEAS..........	Presbyterian Educational Association of the South [Defunct] (EA)
Pease	Pease Oil & Gas Co. (SAG)
PeaseOG......	Pease Oil & Gas Co. [Associated Press] (SAG)
PEAS/SOAS...	PSYOP Effects and Analysis/SOAS (SAUS)
PEAT..........	Phenylethanolaminotetralin [Organic chemistry]
PEAT..........	Pricing Evaluation for Audit Technique [Finance]

PEAT	Programme Elargi d'Assistance Technique [*Expanded Program of Technical Assistance*] [*United Nations*]
PEAT	Programmer Exercised Autopilot Test (AAG)
PEATMOS	Primitive Equation and Trajectory Model Output Statistics (SAUS)
PEAV	Principal Error Axis for Velocity
PE B	Bachelor of Pedagogy (ROG)
Pe B	Bachelor of Pediatrics
PEB	Parametric Empirical Bayes [*Statistics*]
PEB	Partial Etch-Back (SAUS)
PEB	Party Election Broadcast [*British*] (BARN)
PEB	Pebble [*Jewelry*] (ROG)
PEB	Pebble Gold Resources [*Vancouver Stock Exchange symbol*]
PEB	Pensioners' Employment Bureau [*British*]
PEB	Performance Evaluation Board [*NASA*] (MCD)
PEB	Phosphate Ester Base (PDAA)
PEB	Phototype Environment Buoy (PDAA)
PEB	Phycoerythrobilin [*Biochemistry*]
PE B	Physical Education Building (SAUS)
PEB	Physical Evaluation Board [*Military*]
PEB	Plasma Electron Beam (PDAA)
PEB	Population-Environment Balance (EA)
PEB	Porcelain Enamel Bath [*Classified advertising*] (ADA)
PEB	Positive Expulsion Bladder
PEB	Post-Election Briefing (SAUS)
PEB	Post Exposure Bake (SAUS)
PEB	Postexposure Baking [*Microlithography*]
PEB	Pre-Expanded Bin (DNAB)
PEB	Presidential Emergency Board
PEB	Production Efficiency Board [*British*] [*World War II*]
PEB	Program Element Breakdown [*Computer science*] (IAA)
PEB	Propulsion Examining Board [*Navy*] (NVT)
PEB	Prototype Environmental Buoy [*Marine science*] (MSC)
PEB	Psycho-Educational Battery [*Educational test*]
PEB	Public Examination Board (SAUS)
PEB	Pulmonary Ectopic Beat [*Cardiology*]
PEB	Pulsed Electron Beam (IEEE)
PEBA	Polyether Block Amide [*Plastics technology*]
PEBA	Polyether Block Polyamide (SAUS)
PEBA	Pulsed Electron Beam Annealer [*Photovoltaic energy systems*]
PEBA	Purified Extract of Brucella Abortus (SAUS)
PEBAB	Para-(Ethoxybenzylidene)aminobenzonitrile [*Also, EBCA*] [*Organic chemistry*]
PEB & B	Porcelain Enamel Bath and Basin [*Classified advertising*] (ADA)
PEBB	Power Electronic Building Block [*Electric vehicle engineering*]
PEBB	Public Employees Blanket Bond
PEBBLE	Probe Encapsulated by BioListic Embedding [*Biosensor*]
PEBBLE	Probe-Encapsulated by Biologically Localized Embedding
PEBCAK	Problem Exists Between Chair and Keyboard (ADWA)
PeBcCH	Peoples Bancorp, Inc. (Ohio) [*Associated Press*] (SAG)
PEBCO	Port Elizabeth Black Civic Organization South Africa (SAUS)
PEBCO	Program Evaluation and Budget Committee [*American Library Association*]
PEBD	Pay Entry Base Date
PEBES	Personal Earning and Benefit Estimate Statement [*Social Security Administration*]
PEBG	Phenethylbiguanide [*Same as PEDG*] [*Antidiabetic compound*]
PEBH	Physical Evaluation Board Hospital [*Military*]
PEBK	Peoples Bank [*Catawba, NC*] [*NASDAQ symbol*] (NQ)
PEBL	Port Everglades Belt Line Railway [*AAR code*] [*Obsolete*]
PEBLDS	Pan-European Biological and Landscape Diversity Strategy (SAUS)
PEBLO	Physical Evaluation Board Liaison Officer [*Air Force*] (AFM)
PEBO	Peoples Bancorp [*NASDAQ symbol*] (TTSB)
PEBO	Peoples Bancorp, Inc. (Ohio) [*NASDAQ symbol*] (SAG)
PEBP	Patient Escorted by Police (DMAA)
PEBS	Pulsed Electron Beam Source (MCD)
PEBU	Peripheral Equipment Buffer Unit
PEBV	Pea Early-Browning Virus [*Plant pathology*]
PEBW	People's Bancorp Worcester (EFIS)
PEBX	Private Electronic Branch Exchange (SAUS)
PEC	American Irish Political Education Committee (EA)
PEC	Chlorinated Polyethylene (SAUS)
PEc	Ellwood City Area Public Library, Ellwood City, PA [*Library symbol*] [*Library of Congress*] (LCLS)
PEC	IEEE Power Electronics Council (EA)
PEC	Pacific Command Electronic Intelligence Center (MCD)
PEC	Pacific East Asia Cargo Airline, Inc. [*Philippines*] [*ICAO designator*] (FAAC)
PEC	Pacific Economic Community (FEA)
PEC	Packaged Electronic Circuit [*Computer science*] (IAA)
PEC	Page End Character [*Computer science*] (ELAL)
PEC	Palestine Economic Commission
PEC	Panasonic Energy Corp. [*Vancouver Stock Exchange symbol*]
PEC	Panel Electronic Circuit (EECA)
PEC	Parents Education Committee (SAUS)
PEC	Passive Equipment Cabinet [*Military*] (CAAL)
PEC	Patient Evaluation Center (DAVI)
PEC	Peak Electrode Current
PEC	PEC Israel Economic Corp. [*Associated Press*] (SAG)
PEC	Pectoral [*Lungs and Chest*] [*Medicine*] (ROG)
PEC	Pedal Excretory Cell
PEC	Peduncle of Cerebrum (DB)
PEC	Pelican [*Alaska*] [*Airport symbol*] (OAG)
PEC	Pelvic Cramps [*Medicine*] (MELL)
PEC	Penelec Capital Ltd. [*NYSE symbol*] (SAG)
PEC	Perfect Electric Conductor (SAUS)
PEC	Perfil de Evaluacion del Comportamiento [*Standardized test of elementary through high school students' behavior at school, at home, and with peers*]
PEC	Performance Evaluation Committee (SAUS)
PEC	Peripheral Equipment Corp. (SAUS)
PEC	Peripheral Expansion Chassis (TIMI)
PEC	Peritoneal Exudate Cells [*Hematology*]
PEC	Perkin-Elmer Corp. (MCD)
PEC	Perris [*California*] [*Seismograph station code, US Geological Survey*] (SEIS)
PEC	Persistent Early Curvature
PEC	Personal Education Counseling (DNAB)
PEC	Personal Effects Coverage [*Insurance*]
PEC	Petro-Canada
PEC	Phenylene Ether Copolymer [*Organic chemistry*]
PEC	Photoelectric Cell
PEC	Photoelectrochemical Cell [*Energy conversion device*]
PEC	Photoelectrochromic [*Chemistry*]
PEC	Photoemissive Cell (SAUS)
PEC	Physical Education Centre (SAUS)
PEC	Physics, Engineering, and Chemistry (AAG)
PEC	Pigmented Emulsified Creosote
PEC	Pigmented Epithelial Cell [*Ophthalmology*]
PEC	Pilot Error Correction (IAA)
PEC	Pin Electronic Card (SAUS)
PEC	Plain English Campaign [*British*] (DBA)
PEC	Planetary Entry Capsule [*Aerospace*]
PEC	Plant Equipment Codes [*DoD*]
PEC	Plastics Environment Council (SAUS)
PEC	Platform Electron Card [*Electronics*] (OA)
PEC	Platform Electronic Cards (SAUS)
PEC	Platform Evaluation Confidence (SEWL)
PEC	Political Education Committee [*American Ireland Education Foundation*] (EA)
PEC	Polyester Carbonate (SAUS)
PEC	Polyestercarbonate [*Organic chemistry*]
PEC	Polyphenylene Ether Copolymer (SAUS)
PEC	Position Error Correction (DA)
PEC	Positive Engagement Clutch
PEC	Potasse et Engrais Chimiques
PEC	Potential Enviromental Concentration [*Pollution technology*]
PEC	Power Electronics Council (NTPA)
PEC	Predicted Environmental Concentration (DCTA)
PEC	Pre-Existing Condition [*Health Insurance*]
PEC	Presbyterian Evangelical Coalition (EA)
PEC	Presidential Ethics Commission (SAUS)
PEC	President's Export Council (JAGO)
PEC	Previous Element Coding
PEC	Primary Environment Care (SAUS)
PEC	Print Error Check (SAUS)
PEC	Production Equipment Code [*Military*]
PEC	Production Executive Committee
PEC	Program Element Code (AFM)
PEC	Program Environment Control
PEC	Program Evaluation Center [*Navy*] (AFIT)
PEC	Program Exception Code [*Computer science*] (ELAL)
PEC	Program Execution Control (SAUS)
PEC	Program Executive Council (SAUS)
PEC	Projected Effective Coverage (SAUS)
PEC	Propulsion Environmental Chamber
PEC	Protestant Episcopal Church (WDAA)
PEC	Protocol Engineering Center (SAUS)
PEC	Prova Elementi Combustibili [*An Italian fast reactor*]
PEC	Psychology Examining Commission (or Committee) (SAUS)
PEC	Public Extension Circuit (SAUS)
PEC	Pugwash Etudiant du Canada
PEC	Pulsed Eddy Current (SAUS)
p E c	pure Ecuadoran cocaine (SAUS)
PEC	Pyridylethylcysteine [*Biochemistry*]
PEC	Pyrogenic Exotoxin C [*Medicine*]
PECA	Petroleum Equipment Contractors Association (EA)
Peca	Petrus de Bellapertica [*Deceased, 1308*] [*Authority cited in pre-1607 legal work*] (DSA)
PECA	Pre-Engineering Change Action (SAUS)
PECA	Preliminary Engineering Change Analysis (SAUS)
PECA	Process Engineers and Constructors' Association [*Australia*]
PECA	Proposed Engineering Change Assessment (SAUS)
PECAM	Platelet-Endothelial Cell Adhesion Molecule [*Cytology*]
PECAN	Pulse Envelop Correlation Air Navigation
PECANS	Poughkeepsie Engineering Circuit Analysis System (SAUS)
PE CARD	Production Estimate Card (MSA)
PE CARD	Production-Estimate Card (SAUS)
PECBI	Professional Engineers Conference Board for Industry (EA)
PECC	Pacific Economic Cooperation Conference (DOMA)
PECC	Panel of Experts on Climatic Change [*WMO*] (MSC)
PECC	Precanceled Envelope Collectors Club (EA)
PECC	Product Engineering Control Center [*Telecommunications*] (TEL)
PECDAR	Palestine Economic Council for Development and Reconstruction (ECON)
PECDS	Professional Engineering Career Development Series [*Book series*]
PECE	Presidents Emergency Committee for Employment (SAUS)
PECE	Proposed Engineering Change Estimate
PECF	Pseudoextracellular Fluid [*for biocompatibility testing*]
PECFA	Presidential Election Campaign Fund Act of 1966
PECH	Polyepichlorohydrin (SAUS)

Pecho	Prostatic Echogram [*Medicine*] (AAMN)
PECHORA	Paleo Environment and Climate History of the Russian Arctic (SAUS)
PE-CI	Plutonium Equivalent Curies (SAUS)
PECI	Preliminary Equipment Component Index [*or Inventory*]
PECI	Preliminary Equipment Component Inventory (SAUS)
PECI	Productivity Enhancing Capital Investment [*DoD*]
PECI	Projects and Equipment Corporation of India (SAUS)
PECIACESC	Permanent Executive Committee of the Inter-American Council for Education, Science, and Culture
PECIAECOSOC	Permanent Executive Committee of the Inter-American Economic and Social Council
PECIP	Productivity Enhancing Capital Investment Program (MCD)
Peck	Peck's Reports [*7 Tennessee*] [*1921-24*] [*A publication*] (DLA)
Peck	Peck's Reports [*24-30 Illinois*] [*A publication*] (DLA)
Peck	Peckwell's English Election Cases [*1802-06*] [*A publication*] (DLA)
Peck El Cas	Peckwell's English Election Cases [*A publication*] (DLA)
Peck Elec Cas	Peckwell's English Election Cases [*1802-06*] [*A publication*] (DLA)
Peck (III)	Peck's Reports, Illinois Supreme Court Reports [*11-22, 24-30*] [*A publication*] (DLA)
Peck (Tenn)	Peck's Reports [*7 Tennessee*] [*A publication*] (DLA)
Peck Tr	Peck's Trial (Impeachment) [*A publication*] (DLA)
Peckw	Peckwell's English Election Cases [*A publication*] (DLA)
PECL	Plessey Electron Coupled Logic (SAUS)
PECL	Positive Emitter-Coupled Logic (AEBE)
PECL	Preliminary Engineering Configuration List
PECM	Passive Electronics Countermeasures [*Military*] (NG)
PECM	Preliminary Engineering Change Memorandum [*Air Force*] (CET)
PECN	Process Equipment Change Notification (SAUS)
PECO	Pays d'Europe Centrale et Orientale (ECON)
PECO	PECO Energy [*Associated Press*] (SAG)
PECO	Pecos National Monument
PECo	Philadelphia Electric Company
PECO$_2$	Mixed Expired Carbon Dioxide Tension [*Medicine*] (DAVI)
PECOS	Pays D'Europe Centrale et Orientale
PECOS	Pentagon Computer Operations Support (MCD)
PECOS	Picture Enhancement Computer Operating System (SAUS)
PECOS	Program Environment Checkout System
PECOS	Project Evaluation and Control System (MCD)
PECOS	Project Evaluation and Cost Optimization System (IAA)
PECP	Preliminary Engineering Change Proposal
PECPrZ	Penelec Capital L.P. 'MIPS' [*NYSE symbol*] (TTSB)
PECR	Photo-Electric Card Reader (SAUS)
PECR	Program Error Correction Report
Pe Cri	Petrus Crispanus [*Authority cited in pre-1607 legal work*] (DSA)
PECS	Picture Exchange Communication System
PECS	Plant Engineering Check Sheet (AAG)
PECS	Portable Environmental Control System [*NASA*]
PECS	Printers' Estimating and Costing System (DGA)
PECS	Programmable Electronic Call Simulator (SAUS)
PECSS	Presorted Emergency Cooling System Sampling [*Environmental science*] (COE)
PECT	Pectori [*To the Chest*] [*Pharmacy*]
PECT	Progestin-Estrogen Cyclic Therapy [*Medicine*] (MELL)
PECTFE	Polyethylene-Chlorotrifluoroethylene [*Organic chemistry*]
pecto	pectoral (SAUS)
PECTS	Performance Evaluation Commitment Tracking System (SAUS)
PECU	Print Edit Control Unit (SAUS)
pecul	peculated (SAUS)
pecul	peculating (SAUS)
pecul	peculation (SAUS)
pecul	peculator (SAUS)
PECUL	Peculiar (ROG)
PECUS	Personal Engineering Computer User's Society [*Defunct*] (EA)
PECUSA	Presidential Ethics Commission (NADA)
PECUSA	Protestant Episcopal Church in the United States
PECUSA	Protestant Episcopal Church of the U.S.A. (SAUS)
PECUY	Pecuniary (ROG)
PECVD	Plasma-Enhanced Chemical Vapor Deposition [*Coating technology*]
PECWBS	Proposed Extended Contract Work Breakdown Structure [*Military*]
PECWG	Piaster Expenditure Control Working Group [*Military*]
PED	Doctor of Physical Education (PGP)
PED	Parole Eligibility Date (WDAA)
PED	Patient Examined by Doctor (DMAA)
PED	Payload Element Developer (SAUS)
PED	Pedagogue
Ped	Pedagogy (SAUS)
PED	Pedal
PED	Peddler [*or Peddling*] [*FBI standardized term*]
PED	Pedestal (AAG)
Ped	Pedestrian (ADWA)
PED	Pedestrian
PED	Pediatric Emergency Department (DMAA)
PED	Pediatrician
PED	Pediatrics (AABC)
PED	Pedlary (ROG)
PED	Pedro Aguirre Cerda [*Antarctica*] [*Seismograph station code, US Geological Survey*] [*Closed*] (SEIS)
PED	Period End Date (MCD)
PED	Personal Equipment Data [*Computer science*] (IAA)
PED	Personnel Equipment Data [*Army*] (IAA)
PED	Phosphorus Enhanced Diffusion (IAA)
PED	Photoelectric Device (SAUS)
PED	Photoelectron Energy Distribution (SAUS)
PED	Photoemission Diode
PEd	Physical Education
PED	Pigment Epithelial Detachment (SAUS)
PED	Pink-Eyed Dilution [*Medicine*] (DMAA)
PED	Plastic-Encapsulated Device (SAUS)
PED	Platform Equipment Deck
PED	Polymer Engineering Directive (WDAA)
PED	Polymer Engineering Directorate (SAUS)
PED	Positive Expulsion Device
PED	Power Equipment Division (SAUS)
PED	Processing, Exploitation and Dissemination (ACAE)
PED	Production Eligibility Date (MUGU)
PED	Production Engineering Division [*University of Wisconsin - Madison*] [*Research center*] (RCD)
PED	Program Element Description
PED	Program Element Directive
PED	Program Evaluation Division [*Environmental Protection Agency*] (GFGA)
PED	Program Execution Directive (AAG)
PED	Promotion Eligibility Date [*Military*]
PED	Protective Equipment Decontamination (SAUS)
PED	Proton-Enhanced Diffusion
PED	Proton-Excited Diffusion (SAUS)
PED	Public Employee Department (of AFL-CIO) (EA)
PEd	Pulmonary Edema [*Medicine*]
PED	Pulse Edge Discrimination (OA)
PED	Purchase Early Development (SAUS)
PED	Pure Edge Dislocation
PED	Pyramid Element Designator
PED	Springfield, TN [*Location identifier*] [*FAA*] (FAAL)
PEDA	Pedal Artery
PEDA	Personnel Equipment Data Analysis
PEDANT	Preprogrammable Evaluations based on a Data Normalizing Technique (SAUS)
Ped B	Bachelor of Pedagogy
PED B	Bachelor of Pediatrics (WDAA)
PEDB	Page Element Data Base [*Printing*] (DGA)
PEDB	Payload Engineering Data Base [*NASA*] (SSD)
PEDB	Planning and Execution Data Base (COE)
PEDB	Process Engineering Database
PEDBASE	Pediatric Database (SAUS)
PEDC	Personal Effects Distribution Center
PEDC	Professional Educational Development Corp. [*An association*] (EA)
PEDCUG	Planning Engineers Desktop Computer Users Group (EA)
Ped D	Doctor of Pedagogy
PEDD	Program Element Descriptive Data (CAAL)
PEDDRO	Network of information in the field of drug abuse prevention through education (SAUS)
PEddyB	Baldwin Locomotive Works, Eddystone, PA [*Library symbol*] [*Library of Congress*] [*Obsolete*] (LCLS)
Pe de Ancar	Petrus de Ancharano [*Deceased, 1416*] [*Authority cited in pre-1607 legal work*] (DSA)
Pe de Anch	Petrus de Ancharano [*Deceased, 1416*] [*Authority cited in pre-1607 legal work*] (DSA)
Pe de Ancha	Petrus de Ancharano [*Deceased, 1416*] [*Authority cited in pre-1607 legal work*] (DSA)
Pe de Bel	Petrus de Bellapertica [*Deceased, 1308*] [*Authority cited in pre-1607 legal work*] (DSA)
Pe de Belper	Petrus de Bellapertica [*Deceased, 1308*] [*Authority cited in pre-1607 legal work*] (DSA)
Pe de Bepe	Petrus de Bellapertica [*Deceased, 1308*] [*Authority cited in pre-1607 legal work*] (DSA)
Pe de Blpti	Petrus de Bellapertica [*Deceased, 1308*] [*Authority cited in pre-1607 legal work*] (DSA)
Pe de Pal	Pierre de la Palu [*Deceased, 1342*] [*Authority cited in pre-1607 legal work*] (DSA)
Pe de Sal	Petrus de Salinis [*Flourished, 13th century*] [*Authority cited in pre-1607 legal work*] (DSA)
Pe de Samp	Petrus de Sampsone [*Flourished, 1246-58*] [*Authority cited in pre-1607 legal work*] (DSA)
PEDET	Pedetemptim [*Gradually*] [*Pharmacy*]
PEDF	Pigment Epithelium-Derived Factor [*Medicine*] (DMAA)
PEDF	Potential-Energy Distribution Function [*Physical chemistry*]
PEDF	Protective Equipment Decontamination Facility (SAUS)
PEDG	Phenethyldiguanide [*Same as PEBG*] [*Antidiabetic compound*]
PEDI	Pediatrics [*Medicine*] (DHSM)
PEDIAT	Pediatric (SAUS)
PEDIAT	Pediatrician (SAUS)
Pediatric	Pediatric Services of America, Inc. [*Associated Press*] (SAG)
Pediatr Rev	Pediatrics in Review (SAUS)
PEDIN	National Petroleum Exploration Database [*Australia*]
PEDIN	Peapod Dinghy
PEDIN	Petroleum Exploration Data Index (SAUS)
PE Dir	Director of Physical Education (PGP)
PE Dir	Physical Education Director
PEdiS	Edinboro State College, Edinboro, PA [*Library symbol*] [*Library of Congress*] (LCLS)
PEDITOR	Portable Editor (SAUS)
PEDL	Pedicel Length [*Botany*]
PEDL	Prototype Equipment Development Laboratory (SAUS)
Ped M	Master of Pedagogy
pedm	Pediment (VRA)
PEDMAN	PACFLT [*Pacific Fleet*] Enlisted Personnel Distribution Manual (CINC)
PEDMS	Portable and Extensible Data Management System (IAA)
PEDN	Planned Event Discrepancy Notification [*NASA*] (KSC)
PedNSS	Pediatric Nutrition Surveillance System (ADWA)

pedobap	pedobaptism (SAUS)
pedobap	pedobaptist (SAUS)
pedog	pedography (SAUS)
pedogen	pedogenesis (SAUS)
PEDOL	Pedology
pedom	pedometer (SAUS)
PEDONT.......	Pedodontic (SAUS)
pedop	pedophile (SAUS)
PEDP	Pacific Energy Development Program [*Fiji*] [*United Nations*]
PEDP	Performance Evaluation and Development Plan (TIMI)
PEDRA........	Palestine Economic Development and Reconstruction Agency (ECON)
PEDRO........	Perkins Engineering Data Retrieval Organization (SAUS)
PEDRO........	Pneumatic Energy Detector with Remote Optics
PEDRO........	Pride, Efficiency, Dedication, Reliability, and Order (DNAB)
PEDRS........	Process Evaluation and Defect Reporting System (ACAE)
PEDRTC.......	Pediatric
PEDS	Packaging Engineering Data System (AFM)
PeDS	Pediatric Drug Surveillance [*Program*] (DAVI)
Peds	Pediatrics [*Medicine*] (AMHC)
PEDS	Pediatrics
PEDS	Peltier Effect Diffusion Separation [*Physical chemistry*]
PEDS	Philips Engineering and Development System (NITA)
PEDS	Pilgrim Edward Doty Society (EA)
PEDS	Planning, programming, budget, and execution Electronic Delivery System (SAUS)
PEDS	Plasma-Enhanced Deposition System (AAEL)
PEDS	Precise Engineering and Deformation Survey (SAUS)
PEDS	Program Element Descriptive Summary (CAAL)
PEDS	Protective Equipment Decontamination Section [*Nuclear energy*] (NRCH)
PEDSTL.......	Pedestal [*Freight*]
PEDT..........	Pendant [*Jewelry*] (ROG)
PEDT..........	Peridot [*Jewelry*] (ROG)
PEDTRC.......	Pediatric
PEDUC.........	Professeurs d'Economie Domestique des Universites Canadiennes [*Canadian University Teachers of Home Economics - CUTHE*]
PEDX	Pediatrix Medical Group [*NASDAQ symbol*] (TTSB)
PEDX	Pediatrix Medical Group, Inc. [*NASDAQ symbol*] (SAG)
PED XING ...	Pedestrian Crossing (SAUS)
PEE	Phosphate-Eliminating Enzyme (DMAA)
PEE	Photo-Electric Emission (SAUS)
PEE	Photoelectron Emission [*Also, OSEE*]
PEE	Photoemission Effect
PEE	Photoferroelectric Effect (SAUS)
PEE	Polycrystalline Electrode with Epitaxy (SAUS)
PEE	Pressure Environmental Equipment (NVT)
PEE	Program Estimating Equation
PEE	Proof and Experimental Establishment [*British*]
PEE	Punctate Epithelial Erosions (SAUS)
PEE	Talkeetna, AK [*Location identifier*] [*FAA*] (FAAL)
PEEA............	(Phenyl)(ethyl)ethanolamine [*Organic chemistry*]
PEEC...........	Partial Element Equivalent Circuit (SAUS)
PEEC...........	Personnel Emergency Estimator Capability
PEEC...........	Programmable Electronic Engine Control [*Automotive engineering*]
PEEC...........	Project for an Energy-Enriched Curriculum [*Department of Energy*]
PEECP.........	Pilot Expedited Environmental Cleanup Program (BCP)
PEEIC..........	Programme des Economies d'Energie dans l'Industrie Canadienne
PEEK	Partners Early Experience Kit (SAUS)
PEEK	Peekskill Financial [*NASDAQ symbol*] (TTSB)
PEEK	Peekskill Financial Corp. [*NASDAQ symbol*] (SAG)
PEEK	People for the Enjoyment of Eyeballing Knees [*Group opposing below-the-knee fashions introduced in 1970*]
PEEK	Periodically Elevated Electronic Kibitzer
PEEK	Polyetheretherketone (DMAA)
PEEK	Polyetherketone [*Organic chemistry*]
PEEKK........	Poly Ether Ether Ketone Ketone (EDCT)
PEEKKK......	Polyetherether Ketone Ketone Ketone (SAUS)
Peekskill......	Peekskill Financial Corp. [*Associated Press*] (SAG)
PEEL	Programmable Electrically Erasable Logic (SAUS)
PE Element...	Parallel Elastic Element (SAUS)
PEELS.........	Parallel [*Detection*] Electron Energy Loss Spectroscopy
PEEM	Panel of Experts on Environmental Management (GNE)
PEEM	Photoelectron Emission Electron Microscopy (SAUS)
PEEM	Photoelectron Emission Microscopy (SAUS)
PEEM	Photoemission Electron Microscope
PEEP...........	Panel of Experts on Environmental Pollution [*WMO*] (MSC)
PEEP...........	Pilot's Electronic Eyelevel Presentation [*British*]
PEEP...........	Porous Electrode Electrostatic Precipitation
PEEP...........	Positive End Expiratory Pressure [*Medicine*]
PEEP...........	Production Electronic Equipment Procurement Status Report
Peeples & Stevens...	Peeples and Stevens' Reports [*80-97 Georgia*] [*A publication*] (DLA)
PEER...........	Partnerships for Environmental Education and Research (SAUS)
PEER...........	Pediatric Examination of Educational Readiness [*Child development test*]
Peer............	Peerless [*Record label*] [*USA, Mexico*]
PEER...........	Performance Efficiency Evaluation Report (SAUS)
PEER...........	Planned Environment and Education Research Institute (SAUS)
PEER...........	Planned Experience for Effective Relating
PEER...........	Price Escalation Estimated Rates
PEER...........	Professional Engineers Employment Registry (SAUS)
PEER...........	Program of Equal Employment Opportunity Evaluation Reports
PEER...........	Project Engineer Evaluation Report (HGAA)
PEER...........	Project on Equal Education Rights [*Defunct*] (EA)

PEERAMID...	Pediatric Examination of Educational Readiness at Middle Childhood [*Child development test*] [*Psychology*]
PEERC	Production Engineering Education and Research Center
Peere Wms...	Peere-Williams' English Chancery and King's Bench Cases [*1695-1736*] [*A publication*] (DLA)
PeerMf........	Peerless Manufacturing Co. [*Associated Press*] (SAG)
PEET	Partnerships for Enhancing Expertise in Taxonomy [*National Science Foundation*]
PEET	Printing Equipment Education Trust [*British*]
PEETPACK...	Process Engineering Evaluation Techniques Package (PDAA)
PEETSA.......	Parents, Educators and Environmentalists to Save Anchoives [*An association*]
PEEX	Pediatric Early Elementary Examination [*Child development test*] [*Psychology*]
PEF	Pacific-Euro Growth Fund (EFIS)
PEF	Packaging Education Foundation (EA)
PEF	Palestine Endowment Funds [*Later, PEF Israel Endowment Funds*] (EA)
PEF	Palestine Exploration Fund
PEF	Particulate Emission Factor (EEVL)
PEF	Pathway-Exposure Factor [*Environmental chemistry*]
PEF	Peak Expiratory Flow [*Pulmonary function*]
PEF	PEF Israel Endowment Funds [*An association*] (EA)
PEF	Performance Efficiency Factor (AFIT)
PEF	Personal Effects Floater [*Insurance*]
PEF	Personality Evaluation Form [*Psychology*]
PEF	Pharyngo-Epiglottic Fold [*Medicine*] (MELL)
PEF	Phil Esposito Foundation [*Defunct*] (EA)
PEF	Physical Electronics Facility (MCD)
PEF	Plastics Education Foundation (EA)
PEF	Polyethylene Foam
PEF	Potential-Energy Function [*Physical chemistry*]
PEF	Powerhouse Exhaust Facility (IAA)
PEF	Prediction Error Filter [*Wave frequency and phase modifier*]
PEF	Presbyterian Evangelistic Fellowship [*Defunct*] (EA)
PEF	Presidential Election Fund (SAUS)
PEF	Pro Ecclesia Foundation (EA)
PEF	Program Estimating Factor (AFM)
PEF	Proposal Evaluation Form (AAG)
PEF	Psychiatric Evaluation Form [*Psychology*]
PEF	Pulmonary Edema Fluid [*Medicine*] (DMAA)
PEF	Pulsed-Electric-Field
PEF	Pulse Eliminating Filter (IAA)
PEFC...........	Private Export Funding Corp. (IMH)
PEFCO	Private Export Funding Corp.
Peff.............	Effective Filtration Pressure [*Medicine*] (MELL)
Pe Fi..........	Petrus Filipi [*Authority cited in pre-1607 legal work*] (DSA)
Pe Fili	Petrus Filipi [*Authority cited in pre-1607 legal work*] (DSA)
PEF/NET.......	Public Education Fund Network (EA)
PEFO...........	Payload Effects Follow-On Study [*NASA*] (NASA)
PEFO...........	Petrified Forest National Park
PEFOS	Program Evaluation and Field Operations Staff [*Environmental Protection Agency*] (GFGA)
PEFQS	Palestine Exploration Fund. Quarterly Statement [*London*] [*A publication*] (BJA)
PEFQST........	Palestine Exploration Fund. Quarterly Statement [*London*] [*A publication*] (BJA)
PEFR...........	Peak Expiratory Flow Rate
PEFR/PIFR....	Peak Expiratory Flow/Peak Inspiratory Flow Rate [*Medicine*] (DAVI)
PEFSR.........	Partial Expiratory Flow-Static Recoil Curve [*Physiology*] (MAE)
PEFST.........	Palestine Exploration Fund. Quarterly Statement (SAUS)
PEFT...........	Peripheral Equipment Functional Test (CAAL)
PEFT...........	Preschool Embedded Figures Test [*Child development test*]
PEFTOK.......	Philippine Expeditionary Force to Korea [*United Nations*]
PEFTP.........	Parent Education Follow Through Program (EDAC)
PEFU..........	Panel of Experts on Fish Utilization [*FAO*] (ASF)
PEFV..........	Partial Expiratory Flow-Volume [*Physiology*]
PEG............	General Analine & Film Co., General Research Laboratory, Easton, PA [*Library symbol*] [*Library of Congress*] [*Obsolete*] (LCLS)
PEG............	Pac Engo Materials [*Vancouver Stock Exchange symbol*]
PEG............	Pacific Environmental Group [*Marine science*] (MSC)
PEG............	Patient Evaluation Grid [*Medicine*] (DMAA)
Peg............	Pegasus [*Constellation*]
PEG............	Pelangi Air Sdn. Bhd. [*Malaysia*] [*FAA designator*] (FAAC)
PEG............	Percutaneous Endoscopic Gastrostomy [*Medicine*] (CPH)
PEG............	Performance Evaluation Group (CINC)
PEG............	Petrochemical Energy Group (EA)
PEG............	Photo Exploitation Group
PEG............	Pittsburgh Elderly Gay (SAUS)
PEG............	Pneumatic Explosion Generator
PEG............	Pneumoencephalogram [*Medicine*]
PEG............	Polyethylene Glycol [*Organic chemistry*]
PEG............	Powered Explicit Guidance (NAKS)
PEG............	Previous Endorsement(s) Guaranteed [*Banking*]
PEG............	Prime Event Generation (VLIE)
PEG............	Principle of the Equivalent Generator
PEG............	Prior Endorsement Guaranteed (HGAA)
PEG............	Priorities Exploitation Group
PEG............	Process Evaluation Guide [*Graphic Communications Association*]
PEG............	Production Entitlement Guarantee [*International Agricultural Trade Research Consortium*] (ECON)
PEG............	Professional Emphasis Group [*National Audience Board*] (NTCM)
PEG............	Program Evaluation Group [*Air Force*]
PEG............	Program Execution Guidance (SAUS)
PEG............	Project Engineering Guide (MCD)

PEG............ Project Execution Guidelines (ABAC)
PEG............ Protected Employee Group [*Program*]
PEG............ Protection Engineers Group [*United States Telephone Association*] [*Telecommunications*]
PEG............ PSE & G Capital Trust [*NYSE symbol*] (SAG)
PEG............ Public, Educational, Government [*Cable television access channels*] (NTCM)
PEG............ Public Service Elec & Gas Co. [*NYSE symbol*] (SAG)
PEG............ Public Service Enterprise Group, Inc. [*NYSE symbol*] (SPSG)
PEG............ Pyrotechnic Electron Generator (MCD)
PEGA.......... Pegasystems, Inc. [*NASDAQ symbol*] (SAG)
PEGA.......... Polyethylene Glycol Adipate [*Organic chemistry*]
PEGA.......... Precision Engineering Grinding Apparatus (SAUS)
PegaCm...... Pegasus Communications Corp. [*Associated Press*] (SAG)
PEGAD........ Permission Granted to Add (SAUS)
PEG-ADA..... Polyethylene Glycol-Adenosine Deaminase [*A modified enzyme*]
PEGASUS.... People, Goods, and Services Urban System [*Texas*] [*FHWA*] (TAG)
PEGASUS.... Precision Engineering Grinding Apparatus for Superfinishing Ultrahard Surfaces (SAUS)
Pegasys...... Pegasystems, Inc. [*Associated Press*] (SAG)
PEGBB........ Polyester-Glass Bias-Belted (SAUS)
PEGDE........ Pentaethylene Glycol Dodecyl Ether [*Organic chemistry*]
PEGE.......... Program for Evaluation of Ground Environment
PEG-ELS..... Polyethylene Glycol and Iso-Osmolar Electrolyte Solution (STED)
PegGld........ Pegasus Gold, Inc. [*Associated Press*] (SAG)
PEGLN........ Petiole Gland Pairs, Number Of [*Botany*]
PEGPrA....... Pub Sv E&G 4.08% Pfd [*NYSE symbol*] (TTSB)
PEGPrC....... Pub Sv E&G 4.30% Pfd [*NYSE symbol*] (TTSB)
PEGPrD....... Pub Sv E&G 5.05% Pfd [*NYSE symbol*] (TTSB)
PEGPrE....... Pub Sv E&G 5.28% Pfd [*NYSE symbol*] (TTSB)
PEGPrG....... Pub Sv E&G 6.80% Pfd [*NYSE symbol*] (TTSB)
PEGPrI........ Public Sv E&G 7.40% cm Pfd [*NYSE symbol*] (TTSB)
PEGPrJ........ Pub Sv E&G 7.52% Pfd [*NYSE symbol*] (TTSB)
PEGPrV....... Pub Sv E&G 7.44% Pfd [*NYSE symbol*] (TTSB)
PEGPrW...... Pub Sv E&G 5.97% Pfd [*NYSE symbol*] (TTSB)
PEGPrX....... Public Svc E&G Cap 8.00%'MIPS' [*NYSE symbol*] (TTSB)
PEGPrY....... Pub Sv E&G 6.75% Pfd [*NYSE symbol*] (TTSB)
PEGPrZ....... Public Svc E&G Cap 9.375% 'MIPS' [*NYSE symbol*] (TTSB)
PEGR.......... Proportional Exhaust Gas Recirculation [*Engines*]
PEGS.......... Parametric Evaluation Geometric System (VLIE)
PEGS.......... Parametric Evaluation of Generalized Systems (SAUS)
Pegs........... Pegasus [*Constellation*]
PEGS.......... Pesticide Exposure Group of Sufferers (HEAS)
PEGS.......... Polyethylene Glycol Succinate [*Organic chemistry*]
PEGS.......... Program for the Exchange of Generative Studies (SAUS)
PEGS.......... Project Engineering Graphics System [*Computer Aided Design Centre*] [*Software package*] (NCC)
PEGS.......... Project Engineering System
PEGS.......... Publication of the English Goethe-Society (SAUS)
PEH............ Papillary Endothelial Hyperplasia [*Medicine*] (MELL)
PEH............ Pehpei [*Republic of China*] [*Seismograph station code, US Geological Survey*] (SEIS)
PEH............ Pehuajo [*Argentina*] [*Airport symbol*] (OAG)
PEH............ Periods of European History [*A publication*]
PEH............ Planning Estimate Handbook (SAA)
PEH............ Plus Each Hour (SAUS)
PEH............ Polyphenylene Ether Homopolymer (SAUS)
PEH............ Promotion of Environmental Health (SAUS)
PEHA.......... Pentaethylenehexamine [*Organic chemistry*]
PEHA.......... Pony Express Historical Association (EA)
PE-HD......... PolyEthylene-High Density (AGLO)
PEHD.......... Polyethylene-High Density [*Organic chemistry*]
PEHi........... Northampton County Historical and Genealogical Society, Mary Illick Memorial Library, Easton, PA [*Library symbol*] [*Library of Congress*] (LCLS)
Pe His......... Petrus Hispanus [*Authority cited in pre-1607 legal work*] (DSA)
PEI............. Parity Error Interrupt (VLIE)
PEI............. Patriotic Education, Inc. (EA)
PEI............. Peine [*Chile*] [*Seismograph station code, US Geological Survey*] [*Closed*] (SEIS)
pe/i............ Pen and Ink (VRA)
PEI............. Penna RE Inv Tr SNI [*AMEX symbol*] (TTSB)
PEI............. Pennsylvania Real Estate Investment Trust [*AMEX symbol*] (SPSG)
PEI............. People Effectiveness Index (TIMI)
PEI............. Pereira [*Colombia*] [*Airport symbol*] (OAG)
PEI............. Petrocel Industries, Inc. [*Vancouver Stock Exchange symbol*]
PEI............. Petroleum Educational Institute (SAUS)
PEI............. Petroleum Equipment Institute (EA)
PEI............. Phosphate Excretion Index [*Biochemistry*] (DAVI)
PEI............. Phosphorous Excretion Index [*Medicine*] (MEDA)
PEI............. Phosphorus Excretion Index [*Biochemistry*] (DAVI)
PEI............. Physical Education Instructor (WDAA)
PEI............. Physical Efficiency Index [*Medicine*] (DMAA)
PEI............. Planning Executives Institute [*Later, PF*]
PEI............. Plant Engineering Inspection (AAG)
PEI............. Plant Engineering Introduction (SAUS)
PEI............. Playboy Enterprises, Inc.
PEI............. Pointless Electronic Ignition (SAUS)
PEI............. Polyetherimide
PEI............. Polyethylenimine [*Organic chemistry*]
PEI............. Porcelain Enamel Institute (EA)
PEI............. Postejaculatory Interval [*Physiology*]
PEI............. Precipitation-Efficiency Index
PEI............. Preferred Equipment Identifier (VLIE)
PEI............. Preliminary Engineering Inspection [*NASA*] (KSC)
PEI............. Preparedness Exercise Issue (SAUS)
PEI............. Prince Edward Island [*Canadian province*]
PEI............. Prince Edward Island Provincial Library [*UTLAS symbol*]
PEI............. Prince Edward Island Reports (Haviland's) [*A publication*] (DLA)
PEI............. Professional Engineers in Industry
PEI............. Pupil Evaluation Inventory [*Education*] (EDAC)
PEI-A......... Personal Experience Inventory for Adults [*Test*] (TMMY)
PEIA........... Poultry and Egg Institute of America (EA)
PEIAS......... Phenylephrine-Activated Isolated Aortic Strip (DB)
PEIC........... Periodic Error Integrating Controller
PEICOST...... Probability of Incurring Estimated Cost (SAUS)
PEID........... Program Element Identifier [*Military*] (AFIT)
PEIEC......... Prince Edward Island Energy Corp. (SAUS)
PEIF........... Productivity Enhancing Incentive Fund (DNAB)
PEIFL......... Prince Edward Island Federation of Labour (SAUS)
PEILS......... PACOM [*Pacific Command*] Executive Intelligence Summary (MCD)
PEILS......... Prince Edward Island Land Surveyors (SAUS)
PEIN........... Pan European Intelligent Network (SAUS)
PEINFS....... Pan European Intelligent Network Freephone Service (SAUS)
PEIP........... Presidential Executive Interchange Program [*Federal government*]
PEIR........... Performance Evaluation and Information Reduction (IAA)
PEIR........... Problem Equipment Indicator Reports (MCD)
PEIR........... Process Evaluation and Information Reduction (IAA)
PEIR........... Project Equipment Inspection Record [*NASA*] (KSC)
PEI Rep...... Prince Edward Island Reports (Haviland's) [*1850-1914*] [*A publication*] (DLA)
PEI Rev Stat... Prince Edward Island Revised Statutes [*Canada*] [*A publication*] (DLA)
PEIRS......... Pathology Expert Interpretative Reporting System (IDAI)
PEIS........... Polyethylene Isopthalate [*Organic chemistry*]
PEIS........... Preliminary Environmental Impact Statement (SAUS)
PEIS........... Programmatic Environmental Impact Statement (NRCH)
PEISC......... Prince Edward Island Safety Council (SAUS)
PEI Stat...... Prince Edward Island Statutes [*Canada*] [*A publication*] (DLA)
PEITA......... Professional Equestrian Instructors and Trainers Association [*Defunct*] (EA)
PEITV......... Preliminary Encapsulated Inert Test Vehicle (MCD)
PEJ............ Percutaneous Endoscopic Jejunostomy [*Medicine*] (DMAA)
PEJ............ Premolded Expansion Joint [*Technical drawings*]
Pe Ja.......... Petrus Jacobi [*Flourished, 14th century*] [*Authority cited in pre-1607 legal work*] (DSA)
PEJO.......... Plant Engineering Job Order (AAG)
PEK............ Beijing [*China*] [*Airport symbol*] (OAG)
PEK............ Jacksonville, FL [*Location identifier*] [*FAA*] (FAAL)
PEK............ Peak Aviation, PLC [*British*] [*FAA designator*] (FAAC)
PEK............ Peking [*China*] [*Airport symbol*] (AD)
PEK............ Peking [*Republic of China*] [*Seismograph station code, US Geological Survey*] (SEIS)
PEK............ Pekoe [*Tea trade*] (ROG)
PEK............ Phase-Exchange Keying [*Computer science*] (IEEE)
PEK............ Phi Epsilon Kappa [*Fraternity*]
PEK............ Pig Embryo Kidney (SAUS)
PEK............ Polyetherketone [*Organic chemistry*]
PEKEKK...... Polyetherketone Etherketone Ketone (SAUS)
PEKK.......... Polyether Ketone Ketone (SAUS)
PEKK.......... Polyetherketoneketone [*Materials science*]
PEL............ Aeropelican Air Services Pty Ltd. [*Australia*] [*ICAO designator*] (FAAC)
Pel............. Elastic Recoil Pressure of Lung [*Medicine*] (STED)
PEL............ Lafayette College, Easton, PA [*Library symbol*] [*Library of Congress*] (LCLS)
PEL............ Paid Educational Leave (AIE)
PEL............ PanEnergy Corp. [*NYSE symbol*] [*Formerly, Panhandle Eastern*] (SG)
PEL............ Panhandle Eastern Pipe Line Co. [*NYSE symbol*] (SPSG)
PEL............ Payroll Expenditure Listing (SAUS)
Pel............. Pelagius [*Deceased, 1232*] [*Authority cited in pre-1607 legal work*] (DSA)
PEL............ Pelaneng [*Lesotho*] [*Airport symbol*] (OAG)
PEL............ Peldehue [*Chile*] [*Seismograph station code, US Geological Survey*] (SEIS)
Pel............. Pelopidas [*of Plutarch*] [*Classical studies*] (OCD)
PEL............ Pelvis (SAUS)
PEL............ Peritoneal Exudate Lymphocytes [*Hematology*]
PEL............ Permissible Exposure Level
PEL............ Permissible Exposure Limit [*OSHA*]
PEL............ Personal Effectiveness Inventory (AIE)
PEL............ Personal Exposure Level [*or Limit*]
PEL............ Personal Exposure Limit (SAUS)
PEL............ Personnel Exposure Limit (SAUS)
PEL............ Personnel Licensing (SAUS)
PEL............ Personnel Licensing and Training [*ICAO*] (AIA)
PEL............ Petroleum Exploration License (SAUS)
PEL............ Philatelic Esperanto League [*See also ELF*] [*Solna, Sweden*] (EAIO)
PEL............ Photoelectron Layer
PEL............ Photographic Element (SAUS)
PEL............ Physics & Engineering Laboratory (SAUS)
PEL............ Picture Element [*Single element of resolution in image processing*] (IBMDP)
PEL............ Plant Engineers Language (SAUS)
PEL............ Portable Event Logger (SAUS)
PEL............ Precision Elastic Limit
PEL............ President Electric Ltd. (SAUS)
PEL............ Pressure Exposure Limit (SAUS)
PEL............ Priests Eucharistic League (EA)

PEL .... Primary Effusion Lymphoma [*Oncology*]
PEL .... Production Error Log (NITA)
PEL .... Professional Education Libraries [*UTLAS symbol*]
PEL .... Programmable Electronics Load (SAUS)
PEL .... Proportional Elastic Limit
PEL .... Public Exposure Limit (MCD)
PEIC .... Elizabethtown College, Elizabethtown, PA [*Library symbol*] [*Library of Congress*] (LCLS)
PELC .... Professional Engineers' Legislative Committee
PELCO .... Polyester-Caprolactone Copolymer [*Plastics*]
PE-LD .... PolyEthylene-Low Density (AGLO)
PELEC .... Photoelectric (MSA)
PEIeph .... Elephantine Papyri [*A publication*] (OCD)
PELG .... Pelger Muet Anomaly [*Laboratory science*] (DAVI)
PELG .... Poly(ethyl L-Glutamate) [*Organic chemistry*]
PELI .... Production, Engineering and Logistics Information (AAGC)
PELICON ...... Project for Estimation of Long-Term Variability in Ice Concentration (SAUS)
PELISA .... Paper Enzyme-Linked Immunosorbent Assay (STED)
PELJ .... Pyrotechnical Expendable Laser Jammer (ACAE)
PELL .... Papers on English Language and Literature [*A publication*]
PELL .... Publications in English Language and Literature (SAUS)
PELP .... Poland Efficient Lighting Project
PELR .... Peeler
PELR .... Pelsart Resources NL [*NASDAQ symbol*] (NQ)
PELRV .... Pea Leafroll Virus [*Plant pathology*]
PELRY .... Pelsart Resources ADR [*NASDAQ symbol*] (TTSB)
PELS .... P-channel Enhancement Load in Saturation (SAUS)
PELS .... Precision Emitter Location System [*Air Force*] (MCD)
PELS .... Propionyl Erythromycin Lauryl Sulfate [*Antimicrobial agent*]
Pelsart .... Pelsart Resources NL [*Associated Press*] (SAG)
PELSS .... Precision Emitter Location Strike System [*Air Force*]
PELT .... P-channel Enhancement Load in Triode (SAUS)
Pelt .... Peltier's Orleans Appeals [*1917-23*] [*A publication*] (DLA)
PELT .... Princeton American [*NASDAQ symbol*] (TTSB)
PELT .... Princeton Electronic Products, Inc. [*NASDAQ symbol*] (NQ)
PELTP .... Personnel Licensing and Training Panel (SAUS)
PELTS .... Personal Emergency Locator Transmitter Service [*Telecommunications*] (CIST)
PELV .... Pepino Latent Virus [*Plant pathology*]
PELV .... Protected Extra Low Voltage (SAUS)
PEM .... Pacific Exploratory Measurements (SAUS)
PEM .... Pacific Exploratory Mission (ACAE)
PEM .... Parametric Earth Model [*Geodynamics*]
PEM .... Parasitic Encephalitis Meningitis [*Medicine*]
PEM .... Partial Equilibrium Multimarket Model (EEVL)
PEM .... Particle Environmental Monitor (MCD)
PEM .... Particle Modulator Radiometer (CARB)
PEM .... Partido Ecologista Mexicano [*Political party*] (EY)
PEM .... Payload Ejection Mechanism
PEM .... Payload Electronics Module (SAUS)
PEM .... PEM-AIR Ltd. [*Canada*] [*ICAO designator*] (FAAC)
PEM .... Pembrokeshire [*County in Wales*] (ROG)
PEM .... Performance Enhancement Module (VLIE)
PEM .... Performance Evaluation Missile (ACAE)
PEM .... Performance Evaluation Model
PEM .... Peritoneal Exudate Macrophage [*Hematology*]
PEM .... Perrot Memorial Library, Old Greenwich, CT [*OCLC symbol*] (OCLC)
PEM .... Personal-E Mailbox [*Computer software*] (PCM)
PEM .... Personal Exposure Model (EEVL)
PEM .... Personal Exposure Monitor [*Environmental chemistry*]
PEM .... Petite Ensemble Model (MCD)
PEM .... Petrox Energy & Mineral Corp. [*Toronto Stock Exchange symbol*]
PEM .... Phased Equipment Modernization [*Army*] (AABC)
PEM .... Philco Electronic Module
PEM .... Photoelastic Modulator [*Instrumentation*]
PEM .... Photoelectromagnetic
PEM .... Photoelectron Microscopy
PEM .... Photoemission Microscope
PEM .... Photographic Equipment and Materials (NATG)
PEM .... Plant Engineering and Maintenance (NASA)
PEM .... Plant Engineer Mechanical (AAG)
PEM .... Plastic-Encapsulated Microcircuit [*Telecommunications*]
PEM .... Plastic-Envelope Method (SAUS)
PEM .... Plastic Epoxy Molded (SAUS)
PEM .... Polaris Evaluation Missile
PEM .... Polioencephalomalacia (SAUS)
PEM .... Polyethylene Matrix (DB)
PEM .... Polymer Electrolyte Membrane [*Fuel technology*]
PEM .... Position Encoding Module (CAAL)
PEM .... Precordial Electrocardiographic Mapping (STED)
PEM .... Prescription-Event Monitoring
PEM .... Primary Enrichment Medium [*Microbiology*]
PEM .... Primitive Equation Model
PEM .... Privacy-Enhanced Mail [*Software package*]
PEM .... Privacy Enhanced Message (SAUS)
PEM .... Probable Error of Measurement
PEM .... Process Execution Module (NITA)
PEM .... Processing Element Memory [*Computer science*]
PEM .... Processing Element Module [*Computer science*] (IAA)
PEM .... Processor Element Memory
PEM .... Procurement Equipment and Missiles (SAUS)
PEM .... Product Effectiveness Manual
PEM .... Product Engineering Measure (SAUS)
PEM .... Product Engineering Memo (SAUS)

PEM .... Product Error Message (SAUS)
PEM .... Production Engineering Measure [*Army*] (MCD)
PEM .... Production Evaluation Missile [*Military*] (CAAL)
PEM .... Program and Environmental Management (SAUS)
PEM .... Program Element Manager (MCD)
PEM .... Program Element Monitor (AFM)
PEM .... Program Endorsement Memorandum (AAGC)
PEM .... Program Execution Monitor [*Computer science*] (ELAL)
PEM .... Project Engineering Memorandum
PEM .... Properties/Events/Methods (SAUS)
PEM .... Proposal Evaluation Manager
PEM .... Protein Energy Malnutrition [*Medicine*]
PEM .... Proto-Environmental Model (SAUS)
PEM .... Proton Exchange Membrane [*Fuel technology*] (PS)
PEM .... Puerto Maldonado [*Peru*] [*Airport symbol*] (OAG)
PEM .... Pulmonary Embolus [*Medicine*] (DAVI)
PEM .... Pulse Electromagnetic (SAUS)
PEMA .... Pheny(ethyl)malonamide [*Organic chemistry*]
PEMA .... Polyethyl Methacrylate [*Organic chemistry*]
PEMA .... Process Equipment Manufacturers Association (EA)
PEMA .... Procurement Equipment and Missiles-Army (SAUS)
PEMA .... Procurement Equipment Maintenance, Army (MCD)
PEMA .... Procurement, Equipment, Missiles, Army
PEMA .... Procurement of Equipment and Munitions, Appropriations (SAUS)
PEMA .... Production-Equipment-Missile Agency [*Army*]
PEMAC .... Professional Engineers Manpower Assessment Committee (SAUS)
PEMAP .... President's Environmental Merit Award Program [*Environmental Protection Agency*]
PEMARS ...... Procurement of Equipment and Missiles, Army Management and Accounting Reporting System (AABC)
PEMB .... Pembroke College [*Oxford and Cambridge Universities*] (ROG)
Pemb .... Pembroke College, Oxford (SAUS)
PEMB .... Pembrokeshire [*County in Wales*]
Pemb Coll ... Pembroke College-Cambridge (SAUS)
Pemb Eq .... Pemberton's Practice in Equity by Way of Revivor and Supplement [*1867*] [*A publication*] (ILCA)
Pemb Judg.. Pemberton's Judgments and Orders [*A publication*] (DLA)
Pembs .... Pembrokeshire (DIAR)
PEMBS .... Pembrokeshire [*County in Wales*]
PEM-Central.. Pacific Exploratory Mission-Central (SAUS)
PEMCONS.... Photographic Equipment Management Control System
PEMD .... Personalized Educational Materials Development (SAUS)
PEMD .... Program Evaluation and Methodology Division [*General Accounting Office*] [*Federal government*] (GFGA)
PEMD .... Program for Export Market Development [*Canada*]
PEME .... Pulsed Electromagnetic Energy [*Diathermy*] (CPH)
PEMF .... Pulsating Electromagnetic Field
PEM-FC....... Polymer Electrolyte Membrane Fuel Cell (SEWL)
PEMFC .... Proton Exchange Membrane Fuel Cell [*Energy source*]
PEMISA .... Proficiency Battery in English and Mathematics for Indian South Africans (TES)
PEMN .... Program Engineering Management Network [*Computer science*] (RDA)
Pe Mo .... Petrus Morini [*Authority cited in pre-1607 legal work*] (DSA)
PEMO .... Plant Engineering Maintenance Order
PEMO .... Production Engineering and Manufacturing Organization (AAG)
PEMO .... Prospective Electronics Material Officer (SAUS)
PE-MOCVD... Plasma-Enhanced Metalorganic Chemical Vapor Deposition [*Coating technology*]
Pe Mori .... Petrus Morini [*Authority cited in pre-1607 legal work*] (DSA)
PEMOV .... Peanut Mottle Virus [*Plant pathology*]
PEM Process Eng Mag... PEM Process Engineering Magazine (SAUS)
PEMR .... Petroleum Engineering Monthly Report (SAUS)
PEMRam ...... Precision Electromagnetic Ram [*Denne Developments*] (PS)
PEMRC .... Program Executive Management Review Committee (SAUS)
PEMS .... Paris Evangelical Missionary Society (SAUS)
PEMS .... Pesticide Enforcement Management System (NITA)
PEMS .... Physical, Emotional, Mental, Safety [*Model for charting procedure*] [*Medicine*]
PEMS .... Policy and Expenditure Management System (SAUS)
PEMS .... Porcelain-Enamelled Metal Substrate (EECA)
PEMS .... Portable Environmental Measuring System
PEMS .... Predictive Emission Monitoring System [*Environmental science*]
PEMS .... Professional Education of the Media Specialist
PEMS .... Propulsion Energy Management Study (MCD)
PEMT .... Phosphatidylethanolamine Methyltransferase [*An enzyme*]
PE Mus .... Port Elizabeth Museum (SAUS)
PEMV .... Pea Enation Mosaic Virus [*Plant pathology*]
PeMV .... Pepper Mottle Virus
PEM-West.... Pacific Exploratory Mission-West [*Western Pacific Tropospheric Chemistry Experiment*] [*Marine science*] (OSRA)
Pem Yeo...... Pembroke Yeomanry [*British military*] (DMA)
PEN .... Astoria, OR [*Location identifier*] [*FAA*] (FAAL)
PEN .... International PEN [*Official name; PEN, never spelled out in use, is said to stand for poets, playwrights, editors, essayists, novelists*] (EAIO)
PEN .... Pacific Exchange Network [*Marine science*] (OSRA)
PEN .... Parenteral and Enteral Nutrition [*Gastroenterology*] (DAVI)
PEN .... Peace Education Network (EA)
pen .... penal (SAUS)
PEN .... Penang [*Malaysia*] [*Airport symbol*] (OAG)
PEN .... Pendeli [*Greece*] [*Geomagnetic observatory code*]
PEN .... Penetration (AFM)
Pen .... Penicillin [*Medicine*] (DMAA)
PEN .... Penicillin [*Antibiotic*]

pen	Peninsula (NTIO)
PEN...........	Peninsula [Maps and charts]
PEN...........	Peninsula Airways, Inc. [ICAO designator] (FAAC)
PEN...........	Peninsula Environmental Network (SAUS)
PEN.............	Penitent
pen	Penitentiary (ADWA)
PEN...........	Penitentiary (WDAA)
pen	penmanship (SAUS)
Pen	Pennewill's Delaware Reports [A publication] (DLA)
Pen	Pennington's New Jersey Reports [2, 3 New Jersey] [A publication] (DLA)
PEN...........	Pensacola [Florida] [Seismograph station code, US Geological Survey] [Closed] (SEIS)
PEN..............	Pentazocine [An analgesic]
PEN...........	Pentegra Dental Group [AMEX symbol] (SG)
PEN...........	Pentobarbital [Sedative]
PEN...........	Pentode (DEN)
PEN...........	Permanent Entry Number [Computer science]
PEN...........	Pharmacology Equivalent Name
PEN...........	Pharmacy Equivalent Name [Medicine] (DMAA)
PEN...........	Physicians Education Network (EA)
PEN...........	Plasma-Enhanced silicon Nitride (SAUS)
PEN...........	Polyethylene Naphthalate [Organic chemistry]
PEN...........	Professional Enrichment News [Portuguese] (BJA)
PEN...........	Program Element Number [Computer science] (KSC)
PEN...........	Program Error Note [Computer science]
PEN...........	Protection Earth Neutral (SAUS)
PEN...........	Public Education Network (SAUS)
PEN...........	Public Electronic Network [Information service or system] (IID)
PEN...........	Purchasing Electronic Notebook (HGAA)
PENA.........	Primary Emission Neuron Activation (IEEE)
PENAID.......	Penetration Aid [Weaponry]
PENAIDS.....	Penetration Aids
Pen & W.....	Penrose and Watts' Pennsylvania Reports [1829-32] [A publication] (DLA)
PEN-B	Penicillin, Benzalthine Salt (SAUS)
PENB	Poultry and Egg National Board [Later, AEB] (EA)
PENBAL.......	Peninsular Spain-Balearic Islands Submarine Cable (SAUS)
PENBASE.....	Peninsular Base Section [Military]
Pen Bse.......	Peninsular Base (SAUS)
Pen C...........	Penal Code [A publication] (DLA)
PENC	Pen Interconnect [NASDAQ symbol] (TTSB)
PENC	Pen Interconnect, Inc. [NASDAQ symbol] (SAG)
PENCAN.....	Peninsular Spain-Canary Islands Submarine Cable (SAUS)
PENCE	Protein Engineering Network of Centres of Excellence (SAUS)
Penchk........	Pennichuck Corp. [Associated Press] (SAG)
PENCIL	Pictorial Encoding Language [Computer science] (IEEE)
PENCIL	Portable Encoder/Illustrator [Facetious term for pre-word-processing equipment]
PENCIL	Public Education Needs Civic Involvement in Learning
Pencp	Penncorp Financial Group [Associated Press] (SAG)
PencpFn......	Penncorp Financial Group [Associated Press] (SAG)
PENCPR......	PEN [Poets, Playwrights, Essayists, Editors, and Novelists] Club of PuertoRico (EA)
PENCW	Pen Interconnect Wrrt [NASDAQ symbol] (TTSB)
Pend	Pendant (ROG)
pend	Pendant (VRA)
PEND	Pendens [Weighing] [Pharmacy]
PEND	Pending
Pen Dec......	Pension Decisions [Department of the Interior] [A publication] (DLA)
PENDOR	Photon Echo-Nuclear Double Resonance (SAUS)
PENDORF	Penetrate Dorfman [FBI investigation of Teamster leader Allen Dorfman]
PENDWN......	Pen Down (SAUS)
Penedrm......	Penederm, Inc. [Associated Press] (SAG)
Penelc	Penelec Capital Ltd. [Associated Press] (SAG)
PenEM	Penn Engineering & Manufacturing Corp. [Associated Press] (SAG)
PenEMA.......	Penn Engineering & Manufacturing Corp. [Associated Press] (SAG)
P/E News.....	Petroleum Energy Business News Index (SAUS)
P/E NEWS....	Petroleum/Energy Business News Index [American Petroleum Institute] [New York, NY] [Bibliographic database]
P/E News.....	Petroleum/Energy News (SAUS)
PenG...........	Penicillin G [Antibacterial agent]
PenG...........	Pennsylvania Gas & Water Co. [Associated Press] (SAG)
PENG	Photo-Electro-Nystagmogram (SAUS)
PENG	Photo-Electro-Nystagmography [Medicine]
PENG	Prima Energy [NASDAQ symbol] (TTSB)
PENG	Prima Energy Corp. [NASDAQ symbol] (NQ)
PEng	Professional Engineer
PEng	Registered Professional Engineer (DD)
PENGEM	Penetrate Gray Electronics Markets [FBI "sting" operation, 1982, where employees of Japanese computer firms were caught trying to obtain proprietary information illegally from IBM Co.]
P Engine	Port Engine (SAUS)
PENGUIN	Polar Experiment Network for Geophysical Upper-atmosphere Investigations (SAUS)
PENIC	Penicillin [Antibiotic]
Penic Cam...	Penicillum Camelinum [A Camel's-Hair Brush] [Pharmacy]
Penin	Peninsula (BEE)
penin	Peninsula
PenInt.........	Pen Interconnect, Inc. [Associated Press]
PenInter......	Pen Interconnect, Inc. [Associated Press] (SAG)
PeninTst.....	Peninsula Trust Bank, Inc. [Associated Press] (SAG)
PENIT..........	Penitentiary
PENJERDEL...	Pennsylvania, New Jersey, Delaware
PENK	Proenkephalin [Biochemistry]
PENMS	Pan European Network Management System (SAUS)
Penn	Pennewill's Delaware Reports [A publication] (DLA)
Penn	Pennington's New Jersey Reports [A publication] (DLA)
PENN	Penn National Gaming [NASDAQ symbol] (TTSB)
PENN	Penn National Gaming, Inc. [NASDAQ symbol] (SAG)
Penn..........	Pennsylvania (ODBW)
PENN	Pennsylvania
PENN	Pennsylvanian [Period, era, or system] [Geology]
Penn	Pennsylvania State Reports [A publication] (DLA)
Penn	Pennypacker's Unreported Pennsylvania Cases [A publication] (DLA)
Penna	Pennsylvania (ODBW)
PENNA	Pennsylvania
Penna Law Journal...	Pennsylvania Law Journal [A publication] (DLA)
Penna LJ	Pennsylvania Law Journal [A publication] (DLA)
PennAm......	Penn America Group [Associated Press] (SAG)
Penna R......	Pennsylvania State Reports [A publication] (DLA)
Penna SR	Pennsylvania State Reports [A publication] (DLA)
Penna St.....	Pennsylvania State Reports [A publication] (DLA)
Penna State Rep...	Pennsylvania State Reports [A publication] (DLA)
PennBc	PennFirst Bancorp [Associated Press] (SAG)
PennBcp	PennFirst Bancorp [Associated Press] (SAG)
Penn Central...	Pennsylvania New York Central Transportation Co. (SAUS)
Penn Co Ct Rep...	Pennsylvania County Court Reports [A publication] (DLA)
Penn C Opt...	Pennsylvania College of Optometry (GAGS)
Penn Corp Rep...	Pennsylvania Corporation Reporter [A publication] (DLA)
Penn Del.....	Pennewill's Delaware Reports [A publication] (DLA)
Penn Dist & Co Rep...	Pennsylvania District and County Reports [A publication] (DLA)
Penn Dist Rep...	Pennsylvania District Reports [A publication] (DLA)
PennDOT......	Pennsylvania Department of Transportation (SAUS)
Penne	Pennewill's Delaware Reports [17-23 Delaware] [1897-1909] [A publication] (DLA)
PennEn........	Penn Enterprises, Inc. [Associated Press] (SAG)
Pennew........	Pennewill's Delaware Reports [A publication] (DLA)
Pennewill	Pennewill's Delaware Supreme Court Reports [1897-1909] [A publication] (DLA)
Penney	Penney [J. C.] Co., Inc. [Associated Press] (SAG)
PennFed	PennFed Financial Services, Inc. [Associated Press] (SAG)
Penn German...	Pennsylvania-German (SAUS)
PenNGm......	Penn National Gaming, Inc. [Associated Press] (SAG)
Penning	Pennington's New Jersey Reports [2, 3 New Jersey] [A publication] (DLA)
Pen NJ........	Pennington's New Jersey Reports [2, 3 New Jersey] [A publication] (DLA)
Penn Law Jour...	Pennsylvania Law Journal [A publication] (DLA)
Penn LG	Pennsylvania Legal Gazette [A publication] (DLA)
Penn LG	Pennsylvania Legal Gazette Reports (Campbell) [A publication] (DLA)
Penn LJ	Pennsylvania Law Journal [A publication] (DLA)
Penn LJR.....	Pennsylvania Law Journal Reports, Edited by Clark [1842-52] [A publication] (DLA)
Penn L Rec...	Pennsylvania Law Record [Philadelphia] [A publication] (DLA)
Penn L Rev...	Pennsylvania Law Review [A publication] (DLA)
Penn Mil Dist...	Pennsylvania Military District (SAUS)
PennOct......	Penn Octane Corp. [Associated Press] (SAG)
PENNORTH...	Pennyworth [British] (ROG)
Penn R	Pennsylvania State Reports [A publication] (DLA)
Penn Rep....	Pennsylvania State Reports [A publication] (DLA)
Penn Rep....	Penrose and Watts' Pennsylvania Reports [A publication] (DLA)
PennSAHIC...	Pennsylvania Substance Abuse and Health Information (SAUS)
Penn St......	Pennsylvania State Reports [A publication] (DLA)
PENNSTAC...	Penn State University Automatic Digital Computer
Penn Stat...	Pennsylvania State Reports [A publication] (DLA)
Penn State Rep...	Pennsylvania State Reports [A publication] (DLA)
Penn St R....	Pennsylvania State Reports [A publication] (ILCA)
Penn St Rep...	Pennsylvania State Reports [A publication] (DLA)
Penn St U....	Pennsylvania State University (GAGS)
Penn St U Harrisburg...	Pennsylvania State University at Harrisburg (GAGS)
Penn Super...	Pennsylvania Superior Court Reports [A publication] (DLA)
PENNTAP.....	Pennsylvania Technical Assistance Program [Pennsylvania State University] [University Park, PA]
PennTr........	Penn Traffic Co. [Associated Press] (SAG)
PennTrty......	Penn Treaty American [Associated Press] (SAG)
Penn Turn....	Pennsylvania Turnpike (SAUS)
PennVa.......	Penn Virginia Corp. [Associated Press] (SAG)
Pennwd.......	Pennwood Savings Bank [Associated Press] (SAG)
PENNX	Pennsylvania Mutual [Mutual fund ticker symbol] (SG)
Penny	Pennypacker's Pennsylvania Colonial Cases [A publication] (DLA)
Penny	Pennypacker's Unreported Pennsylvania Cases [A publication] (DLA)
Penny Col Cas...	Pennypacker's Pennsyulvania Colonial Cases [A publication] (DLA)
Pennyp	Pennypacker's Unreported Pennsylvania Cases [A publication] (DLA)
Pennyp Col Cas...	Pennypacker's Pennsylvania Colonial Cases [A publication] (DLA)
Pennyp (PA)...	Pennypacker's Unreported Pennsylvania Cases [A publication] (DLA)
Pennzol.......	Pennzoil Co. [Associated Press] (SAG)
PEN-O........	Penner Serotype-O [Laboratory science] (DAVI)
Penob.........	Penobscot Shoe Co. [Associated Press] (SAG)
penol	penological (SAUS)
PENOL	Penologist (SAUS)
PENOL	Penology
Pen P	Penault's Prerosti de Quebec [A publication] (DLA)
PEN-P	Penicillin, Procain Salt (SAUS)

PENR .... Penryn [*England*]
PENRAD....... Penetration RADAR
Penr Anal .... Penruddocke's Short Analysis of Criminal Law [*2nd ed.*] [*1842*]
        [*A publication*] (DLA)
Penr & W .... Penrose and Watts' Pennsylvania Reports [*1829-32*] [*A publication*]
        (DLA)
PenRE......... Pennsylvania Real Estate Investment Trust [*Associated Press*] (SAG)
Pen Ref .... Penal Reformer [*1934-39*] [*A publication*] (DLA)
Pen Ref League M Rec... Penal Reform League Monthly Record [*1909-12*]
        [*A publication*] (DLA)
Pen Ref League Q Rec... Penal Reform League Quarterly Record [*1912-20*]
        [*A publication*] (DLA)
PENREP....... Penetration Report [*National Security Agency*]
Penril.:........ Penril Corp. [*Associated Press*] (SAG)
PENS .... Partido Espanol Nacional Sindicalista [*Political party*] [*Spain*]
PENS .... Pediatric Endocrinology Nursing Society (SAUS)
PENS .... Pensacola Naval Air Station (SAUS)
PENS .... Percutaneous Electrical Nerve Stimulation
PENS .... Percutaneous Epidural Nerve Stimulator [*neurology*] (DAVI)
PENS .... Polymer Ejection for Noise Suppression
PENS .... Provisions of Engineer Support (SAUS)
PENSAD...... Pension Administration (SAUS)
PENSADS..... Pension Administration System (SAUS)
PENSAD System... Pensions Administration System (SAUS)
PENSAM ...... Penetration Survivability Assessment Model (MCD)
Pens & Profit Sharing (P-H)... Pension and Profit Sharing (Prentice-Hall, Inc.)
        [*A publication*] (DLA)
PensCr......... Pensamiento Cristiano. Tribuna de Exposicion del Pensamiento
        Evangelico [*Cordoba, Argentina*] [*A publication*] (BJA)
PEN SDK..... Pen Computing Software Development Kit (SAUS)
Pension Rep... Pension Reporter [*Bureau of National Affairs*] [*A publication*] (DLA)
PenskeM...... Penske Motorsports, Inc. [*Associated Press*] (SAG)
Pens Rep (BNA)... Pension Reporter (Bureau of National Affairs) [*A publication*]
        (DLA)
PenST.......... Penicillin Skin Test [*Immunology*]
Pen St R...... Pennsylvania State Reports [*A publication*] (DLA)
PENT........... Penetrate (AABC)
PENT........... Pentagon
Pent............ Pentagonal (SAUS)
PENT........... Pentameter
Pent............ Pentateuch (BJA)
PENT........... Pentecost
PENT........... Pentode (AAG)
Pent............ Pentothal [*Anesthetic*] (AAMN)
PENT........... Phenylethanolamine N-Methyltransferase (DMAA)
PENT........... Project for the Education of Native Teachers (SAUS)
Penta........... Pentachlorophenol [*Wood preservative*] (WPI)
PENTAC ...... Penetration for Tactical Aircraft [*Air Force*]
PENTAFLUX... Fifth Flux Experiment (USDC)
Pentair........ Pentair, Inc. [*Associated Press*] (SAG)
Pentch .... Pentech International, Inc. [*Associated Press*] (SAG)
PENTE......... Pentecostal
PENTENG.... Pentagon English [*Pseudotechnical language*]
PENTIUM ..... Produces Erroneous Numbers Through Incorrect Understanding of
        Mathematics (SAUS)
Pentl........... Pentelic (VRA)
PENTOBARB... Pentobarbital Sodium (SAUS)
PenTrt......... Penn Treaty American Corp. [*Associated Press*] (SAG)
pentu.......... Pentateuch (VRA)
PENULT....... Penultimate (SAUS)
PENV .... Philip Environmental [*NASDAQ symbol*] (SAG)
PENVAL...... Penetration Evaluation [*Military*] (NVT)
Pen VK .... Penicillin V Postassium [*An antibiotic*] (DAVI)
PENW .... Penetrating Wound
PENW .... PENWEST Ltd. [*Bellevue, WA*] [*NASDAQ symbol*] (NQ)
PENW .... Penwith [*England*]
Penwst........ PENWEST Ltd. [*Associated Press*] (SAG)
PENZ........... Penzance [*City in England*] (ROG)
PEO............ Paalsgard Emulsion Oil (SAUS)
PEO............ Pacific Economic Outlook
PEO............ Pankypria Ergatiki Omospondia [*Pancyprian Federation of Labour*]
        [*The "Old Trade Unions"*] [*Cyprus*]
PEO............ Patrol Emergency Officer [*Nuclear energy*] (NRCH)
PEO............ Patrol Emergency Operator (SAUS)
peo............ People (GEAB)
PEO............ People
PEO............ Peoria [*Diocesan abbreviation*] [*Illinois*] (TOCD)
peo............ Persian, Old [*MARC language code*] [*Library of Congress*] (LCCP)
PEO............ Petroleum & Resources [*NYSE symbol*] (TTSB)
PEO............ Petroleum & Resources Corp. [*NYSE symbol*] (SPSG)
PEO............ Petrolia Oil & Gas [*Vancouver Stock Exchange symbol*]
PEO............ Philanthropic and Educational Organization [*Facetious translation
        "Pop Eats Out"*]
PEO............ Photographic Eye Oximeter (SAUS)
PEO............ Piezoelectric Oscillator (SAUS)
PEO............ Planners for Equal Opportunity [*Defunct*] (EA)
PEO............ Plant Engineering Order
PEO............ Plant Equipment Operator [*Nuclear energy*] (NRCH)
PEO............ Poly(ethylene oxide) [*Acronym is trade name owned by Seitetsu
        Kagaku Co.*]
PEO............ Polymer Electrolyte (SAUS)
PeO............ President ex-Oficio (SAUS)
PEO............ President's Export Council (AAGC)
PEO............ Principal Embarkation Officer (SAUS)
PEO............ Principal Establishment Officer (SAUS)

PEO............ Principal Executive Officer [*Civil Service*] [*British*]
PEO............ Process Engineering Order
PEO............ Product Engineering Office
PEO............ Production Engineering Order
PEO............ Program Enrichment Office (COE)
PEO............ Program Evaluation Office [*Army*]
PEO............ Program Executive Office [*or Officer*]
PEO............ Progressive External Ophthalmoplegia
PEO............ Propulsion Engineering Officer (MCD)
PEO............ Prospective Engineer Officer
PEO............ Protect Each Other [*An association*] (NADA)
PEO............ Public Employment Office [*State Employee Security Agency*] (OICC)
PEO-ASM..... Program Executive Office - Armored Systems Modernization [*Army*]
        (RDA)
PeoBkIN...... Peoples Bank Corp. Indianapolis [*Associated Press*] (SAG)
PEOC .... Presidential Emergency Operations Room (SAUS)
PEOC .... Publishing Employees Organizing Committee [*AFL-CIO*]
PEO-C3S..... Program Executive Office, Command, Control, and Communications
        Systems [*Army*]
PEO CCS..... Program Executive Officer, Command and Control Systems (SAUS)
PEO COMM... Program Executive Office for Communications (SAUS)
PEO-FAS..... Program Executive Office - Field Artillery System [*Army*] (RDA)
PEO-GPALS... Program Executive Officer, Global Protection Against Limited Strikes
        [*Army*] (RDA)
PEO-IEW...... Program Executive Office - Intelligence and Electronic Warfare
        [*Army*] (RDA)
Peo L Adv.... People's Legal Advisor [*Utica, NY*] [*A publication*] (DLA)
PEOLE......... Preliminary Eole (SAUS)
PEO-MD...... Program Executive Office - Missile Defense [*Military*] (RDA)
PEON .... Polar Environmental Officers Network (SAUS)
Peop .... People's (AL)
PeopBcp ...... Peoples Bancorp [*Dekalb County*] [*Associated Press*] (SAG)
PeopBcT ...... Peoples BancTrust Co. [*Associated Press*] (SAG)
PeopBk .... Peoples Bank [*Catawba, NC*] [*Associated Press*] (SAG)
PEOPC .... Polyethylene Oxide/Polycarbonate (SAUS)
PeopChc ...... Peoples Choice TV Corp. [*Associated Press*] (SAG)
PeopCT....... Peoples Bank [*Bridgeport, CT*] [*Associated Press*] (SAG)
PeopEn .... Peoples Energy Corp. [*Associated Press*] (SAG)
PEOPET....... Polyethylene Oxide/Polyethylene Terephthalate (SAUS)
PeopFin ...... Peoples Financial Corp. [*Associated Press*] (SAG)
PeopFst ...... People First Corp. [*Associated Press*] (SAG)
PeopHld...... Peoples Holding Co. [*Associated Press*] (SAG)
PeopHrt ...... People's Heritage Financial Group, Inc. [*Associated Press*] (SAG)
Peoples ...... Peoples' Reports [*77-97 Georgia*] [*A publication*] (DLA)
PeopleTel .... Peoples Telephone Co. [*Associated Press*] (SAG)
Peopsft .... Peoplesoft, Inc. [*Associated Press*] (SAG)
PeopTel ...... People's Telephone Co., Inc. [*Associated Press*] (SAG)
PEOS .... Propulsion and Electrical Operating System (IEEE)
PEO-SD....... Program Executive Officer-Ship Defense
PEO-STAMIS... Program Executive Office, Standard Army Management Information
        Systems
PeoSvFn ...... People's Savings Financial Corp. [*Associated Press*] (SAG)
PEOT.......... Physical End of Tape (VLIE)
PEOX .... Polyethyleneoxide [*Organic chemistry*]
PEP............ All India Reporter, Patiala and East Punjab States Union Series
        [*A publication*] (ILCA)
PEP............ Charlotte, NC [*Location identifier*] [*FAA*] (FAAL)
PEP............ Cyclophosphamide, VM-26 Prednisolone [*Antineoplastic drug
        regimen*] (DAVI)
PEP............ Packet Exchange Protocol [*Computer science*] (CDE)
PEP............ Packetized Ensemble Protocol [*Computer science*]
PEP............ Paper Electrophoresis (MELL)
PEP............ Paperless Electronic Payment [*Business term*]
PEP............ Paperless Entry Processing (SAUS)
PEP............ Paperless Entry Processing User Group [*Defunct*] (CSR)
PEP............ Parametric Element Processor (SAUS)
PEP............ Parent Effectiveness Program (SAUS)
PEP............ Parenting, Education, and Political Involvement [*Jack and Jill of
        America*]
PEP............ Parkinsons Educational Program (SAUS)
PEP............ Parti Ecologiste pour le Progres [*Burkina Faso*] [*Political party*] (EY)
PEP............ Parti Evangelique Populaire [*Popular Protestant Party*] [*Switzerland*]
        [*Political party*] (PPE)
PEP............ Partitioned Emulation Program [*Computer science*] (BUR)
PEP............ Patent Examining Procedure (IAA)
PEP............ Patient Educational Program (MELL)
PEP............ Patient Environment Program [*Medicine*]
PEP............ Pauli Exclusion Principle [*Physics*]
PEP............ Peak Effective Power
PEP............ Peak Energy Product
PEP............ Peak Envelope Power [*Telecommunications*]
PEP............ Peer Evaluation Program [*College of American Pathologists*]
PEP............ People for Energy Progress [*Defunct*] (EA)
PEP............ Pepitilla [*Race of maize*]
Pep............ Pepper (SAUS)
PEP............ Peppermint (DSUE)
pep............ pep pill (SAUS)
PEP............ PepsiCo Inc. [*NYSE symbol*] (SPSG)
Pep............ Peptidase (DB)
PEP............ Peptide [*Biochemistry*]
PEP............ Performance Effectiveness [*or Evaluation*] Program [*Navy*]
PEP............ Performance Evaluation Procedure [*Joint Commission on
        Accreditation of Hospitals*] (DHSM)
PEP............ Performance Evaluation Process (SAUS)
PEP............ Peripheral Event Processor [*Computer science*]

PEP............	Perkin-Elmer Processor [Computer]
PEP............	Personal Effects Protection (SAUS)
PEP............	Personal Employee Profiling [Information service or system] (IID)
PEP............	Personal Empowerment Program (WDAA)
PEP............	Personal Equity Plan [Finance]
PEP............	Personal Exam Prep (SAUS)
PEP............	Personal Exemption Phase-Out [Income tax]
PEP............	Personal Exercise Programmer
PEP............	Personal Financial Planner
PEP............	Personality-Profile Exam
PEP............	Personnel Exchange Program [Military] (NVT)
PEP............	Petroleum Electric Power (SAUS)
PEP............	Pfizer, Inc., Research Center Library, Easton, PA [Library symbol] [Library of Congress] (LCLS)
PEP............	Phenethyl Propionate [Insect attractant] [Organic chemistry]
PEP............	Philips Environmental Protection (SAUS)
PEP............	Phosphoenolpyruvate [Biochemistry]
PEP............	Phosphoenolpyruvic Acid (SAUS)
PEP............	Photoelectric Potential
PEP............	Photo-Electron Plasma (SAUS)
PEP............	Photoelectrophoresis
PEP............	Photographic Exploitation Products (MCD)
PEP............	Physical Education for Progress [Act]
PEP............	Physical Education Program
PEP............	Physiological Education of Primates (SAUS)
PEP............	Physiological Evaluation of Primates
PEP............	Pictorial End-Papers [Publishing]
PEP............	Pigmentation, Edema and Plasma Cell Dyscrasia (MELL)
PEP............	Pipeline Expanding Polymer
PEP............	Piping Efficiency Program
PEP............	Planar Epitaxial Passivated
PEP............	Planetary Ephemeris Program (IEEE)
PEP............	Planetary Exploration Plan [NASA]
PEP............	Planner Epitaxiel Passivated
PEP............	Plant Equipment Package [DoD]
PEP............	Plasma Exhaust Process (SAUS)
PEP............	Platform Electronic Package
PEP............	Platform Environment Profile [Computer science] (VLIE)
PEP............	Platform Evaluation Program
PEP............	Plessey Electronic Payroll (DEN)
PEP............	Plume Exposure Pathway [Nuclear emergency planning]
PEP............	Point, Edge, Polygon [Computer science]
PEP............	Pole-Equator-Pole (QUAC)
PEP............	Political and Economic Planning [A British organization] [Later, Policy Studies Institute]
PEP............	Polyestradiol Phosphate [Endocrinology]
PEP............	Polyethylene Polyamine (SAUS)
PEP............	Polyethylene Powder
PEP............	Polymorphic Eruption of Pregnancy (SAUS)
PEP............	Polynominal Error Protection (MCD)
PEP............	Pool Exercise Program [Arthritis Foundation]
PEP............	Porsche Experimental Prototype [Automotive engineering]
PEP............	Portable Energy Provision (SSD)
PEP............	Portfolio Evaluation Plan [Australia]
PEP............	Positive Energy [Vancouver Stock Exchange symbol]
PEP............	Positron-Electron Project [High-energy accelerator]
PEP............	Positron Electron Proton [Physics]
PEP............	Postal Efficiency Plan (SAA)
PEP............	Postencephalitic Parkinsonism [Medicine] (DB)
PEP............	Postexposure Prophylaxis [Medicine]
PEP............	Power Evaluation Program
PEP............	Power Extension Package (MCD)
PEP............	Power Extension Plant (MCD)
PEP............	Practical Engineering Paperwork
PEP............	Pratt & Whitney Engine Program [Aviation] (NG)
PEP............	Preamplifier Extension Plug
PEP............	Precipitation Enhancement Program (SAUS)
PEP............	Pre-Ejection Period [Cardiology]
PEP............	Pre-Employment Program
PEP............	Preferred Equipment Package [Automotive retailing]
PEP............	Preliminary Evaluation Plan (SAUS)
PEP............	Preschool Education Program [Sesame Street TV program]
PEP............	President's Economy Program
PEP............	Preventive Enforcement Patrol [New York City police]
PEP............	Primary Education Program [Child development test]
PEP............	Primary Entry Point System (OTD)
PEP............	Primate Equilibrium Platform
PEP............	Princeton Electronic Products, Inc. (IAA)
PEP............	Princeton Experiment Package [NASA]
PeP............	Principal of Pedagogy [Academic degree]
PEP............	Printer-Emulation Package [Software]
PEP............	Priority Energy Policy [Environmental Protection Agency]
PEP............	Probability Encoding Program (SAUS)
PEP............	Process Evaluation Program (VLIE)
PEP............	Processing Enhancing Protein [Biochemistry]
PEP............	Procurement Evaluation Panel [Air Force] (MCD)
PEP............	Procytox [Cyclophosphamide], Epipodophyllotoxin Derivative , Prednisolone [VM-26] [Antineoplastic drug regimen]
PEP............	Producibility Engineering and Planning [Army] (AABC)
PEP............	Producibility Engineering Plan [Air Force]
PEP............	Product Engineering and Production (MCD)
PEP............	Production EAGLE [Elevation Angle Guidance Landing Equipment] Package
PEP............	[The] Production Engineering and Productivity Exhibition and Conference [British] (ITD)
PEP............	Production Engineering Planning
PEP............	Production Equipment Package
PEP............	[The] Productivity Effectiveness Program [Title of a pamphlet by Robert Gedaliah that describes sedentary exercises for desk-bound workers]
PEP............	Productivity Enhancement Program (SAUS)
PEP............	Productivity Enhancement Project (SAUS)
PEP............	Professional Enhancement Program (SAUS)
PEP............	Professional Enhancement Project [American Occupational Therapy Association]
PEP............	Professional Experience Program [Australia]
PEP............	Proficiency Examination Program (MCD)
PEP............	Proficiency in English Program (SAUS)
PEP............	Program Element Plan (AFIT)
PEP............	Program Evaluation Procedure [Air Force]
PEP............	Program Evaluation Program [Air Force] (IAA)
PEP............	Programmable Extension Package (IAA)
PEP............	Programmed Emulation Partition (SAUS)
PEP............	Programmed End Point (SAUS)
PEP............	Program to Enhance Productivity (SAUS)
PEP............	Progressive Exercise Program
PEP............	Project Element Plan (SAUS)
PEP............	Projects and Exports Policy [Board of Trade] [British]
PEP............	Prolyl Endopeptidase
PEP............	Promoting Enduring Peace (EA)
PEP............	Promotion Evaluation Pattern
PEP............	Propellant, Explosive, and Pyrotechnic
PEP............	Property Estimation Program [Utah Water Research Laboratory]
PEP............	Proposal Equipment Packages (MCD)
PEP............	Proposal Evaluation Panel (MCD)
PEP............	Proposal Evaluation Plan [or Program] (MCD)
PEP............	Proposal Evaluation Program
PEP............	Proposal Exploitation Product
PEP............	Propulsion and Energetics Panel (SAUS)
PEP............	Propulsion Evaluation Plan
PEP............	Protection in Evaluation Procedures
PEP............	Protein Electrophoresis [Medicine] (DMAA)
PEP............	Protocol Extension Protocol (SAUS)
PEP............	Protocol on Environmental Protection (SAUS)
PEP............	Proton-Electron-Positron (SAUS)
PEP............	Proton Electron Positron Colliding Beams (IAA)
PEP............	Proton-Electron-Proton [Nuclear physics]
PEP............	Prototyping, Evaluation and Programming (SAUS)
PEP............	Psychiatric Evaluation Profile [Psychology] (MAE)
PEP............	Psychoeducational Profile [Test for autistic children]
PEP............	Psychoepistemological Profile [Student personality test]
PEP............	Public Employment Program (EBF)
PEP............	Pulse Echo Pattern
PEP............	Pulse Effective Power [Telecommunications] (IAA)
PEP............	Pupil Evaluation Program
PEPA........	Peptidase A [An enzyme]
PEPA........	Per Employee per Annum
PEPA........	Petroleum Electric Power Association [Later, EUIPA] (EA)
PEPA........	Pitch Fibre Pipe Association of Great Britain (BI)
PEPA........	Polyether-Polyamide Block Copolymer (EDCT)
PEPA........	Polyethylene Polyamide (SAUS)
PEPA........	Protected Environment plus Prophylactic Antibiotics [Oncology]
PEPA........	Pulse Echo Pattern Analyzer
PEPAE......	Permanent Entry Permit After Entry
PEPAG	Physical Electronics and Physical Acoustics Group [MIT] (MCD)
PEPAOP	(Phenylethyl)phenylacetoxypiperidine [Organic chemistry]
PEPAS	WHO [World Health Organization] Western Pacific Regional Centre for the Promotion of Environmental Planning and Applied Studies (EAIO)
PEPAT........	Protocol on Environment Protection of the Antarctic Treaty (SAUS)
Pep-Bis.......	Pepto-Bismol (SAUS)
PEPBNC	Peninsula Enrichment Program for Bright Needy Children [Queensland, Australia]
PepBoy.......	Pep Boys-Manny, Moe & Jack [Associated Press] (SAG)
PEPC...........	Peptidase C [An enzyme]
PEPC...........	Phosphoenolpyruvate Carboxylase [An enzyme]
PEPC...........	Polynomial Error Protection Code [Computer science]
PEPC...........	Postsecondary Education Planning Commission [Florida] (EDAC)
PEPC...........	Potomac Electric Power Co.
PEPCase......	Phosphenol-Pyruvate Carboxylase (SAUS)
PEPCI.........	Providing Emergency Presidential Communications Interface (SAUS)
PEPCK........	Phosphoenolopyruvate Carboxkinase [An enzyme]
PEPCK	Phosphoenolpyruvate Carboxykinase [An enzyme]
PEPCO........	Potomac Electric Power Co.
PEPCOM	Pacific Engineering Production Company (AAGC)
PEPCOM	Pepsi-Cola Bottling Companies (EFIS)
PEPD...........	Peptidase D [An enzyme]
PEPE..........	Parallel Element Processing Element (SAUS)
PEPE..........	Parallel Element Processing Ensemble [Burroughs Corp.] (BUR)
PEPE..........	People Persecuted by Pablo Escobar [Colombia] (ECON)
PEPE..........	Pepe Est Presque Emacs (SAUS)
PEPE..........	Perkin-Elmer Performance Evaluation (SAUS)
PEPE..........	Persistant Elevated Pollution Episodes (SAUS)
PEPE..........	Prolonged Elevated-Pollution Episode [Environmental Protection Agency]
PEP/EP.......	Pre-Ejection Period to Ejection Period [Cardiology] (DAVI)
PEPES.........	People Persecuted by Pablo Escobar
PEPG..........	Piezoelectric Power Generation
PEPG..........	Port Emergency Planning Group [NATO] (NATG)
PEPGB	Plasma Exhaust Pumping Glove Box (SAUS)

PEPI............	Physical Education Public Information [Film]
PEPI............	Post-Menopausal Estrogen and Progestin Intervention [Medicine] (BARN)
	Postmenopausal Estrogen/Progestin Interventions
PEPI............	Pre-Ejection Period Index [Cardiology]
PEPIC..........	Public Education Project on the Intelligence Community (SAUS)
PEPICO........	Photoelectron Photoion Coincidence (SAUS)
PE Pipe.......	Polyethylene Pipe (SAUS)
PEP-L.........	Partitioned Emulation Programming-Local (SAUS)
PEPL..........	Preliminary Engineering Parts List
PEPLAN	Polaris Executive Plan [British]
PEP-LR........	Partitioned Emulation Programming-Local/Remote (SAUS)
PEP/LVET.....	Pre-Ejection Period/Left Ventricular Ejection Time [Medicine] (MEDA)
PEPMC........	Printing Estimators and Production Men's Club [New York, NY] (EA)
PEPMIS.......	Plant Equipment Packages Management Information System (MCD)
PEPMOV	Pepper Mottle Virus [Plant pathology]
PEPMV........	Pepino Mosaic Virus [Plant pathology]
PEPP..........	Permanent-Equity Pension Plan [Human resources] (WYGK)
PEPP..........	Planetary Entry Parachute Program [NASA]
PEPP..........	Positive Expiratory Pressure Plateau [Medicine] (MAE)
PEPP..........	Professional Engineers in Private Practice
PEPPA	Preparedness for Emergency Plant Pest Action [In Animal and Plant Health Inspection Service publication PEPPA Pot]
PEPPARD.....	Propellant, Explosive, Pyrotechnic Pollution Abatement Research and Development (DNAB)
PEPPER	Photo-Electric Portable Probe Reader (PDAA)
PEPPER	Photo-Electro Portable Probe Reader (SAUS)
Pepper & L Dig...	Pepper and Lewis' Digest of Laws [Pennsylvania] [A publication] (DLA)
Pepper & L Dig Laws...	Pepper and Lewis' Digest of Laws [Pennsylvania] [A publication] (DLA)
Pepperdine U...	Pepperdine University (GAGS)
PEPPI..........	Program to Encorage Product and Process Innovation (SAUS)
PEPPI..........	Projected Elevation of Product Performance Indices (SAUS)
PEPPRE	Photo Electric Portable Probe Reader (IAA)
PEP Programme...	Philips Environmental Protection Programme (SAUS)
PEP-PTS	Phosphoenolpyruvate-dependent Phosphotransferase System (SAUS)
PEPR	Precision Encoding and Pattern Recognition Device [Computer science]
PEP-R.........	Psychoeducational Profile-Revised (TES)
PEPrA	PECO Energy, $3.80 Pfd [NYSE symbol] (TTSB)
PEPrB	PECO Energy, $4.30 Pfd [NYSE symbol] (TTSB)
PEPrC	PECO Energy, $4.40 Pfd [NYSE symbol] (TTSB)
PEPrD	PECO Energy, $4.68 Pfd [NYSE symbol] (TTSB)
PEPR Device...	Precision Encoding and Pattern Recognition Device (SAUS)
PEPrF.........	PECO Energy Dep Pfd [NYSE symbol] (TTSB)
PEPrY.........	PECO En Cap Tr I 8.72% 'TOPrS' [NYSE symbol] (TTSB)
PEPrZ.........	PECO Energy L.P. MIPS'A' [NYSE symbol] (TTSB)
PEPS..........	National Committee on Public Employee Pension Systems (EA)
PEPS..........	Peperomia and Exotic Plant Society (EA)
Peps...........	Pepsin (SAUS)
PEPS..........	Peptidase S [An enzyme]
PEPS..........	Pesticide Enforcement Policy Statement [Environmental Protection Agency]
PEPS..........	Pinion Electric Power Steering
PEPS..........	Plasma Electron Profiles, Symmetric
PEPS..........	Positive-Expulsion Propellant System (SAUS)
PEPS..........	Preliminary Evaluation Programme for SPOT (SAUS)
PEPS..........	Priced Exhibit Preliminary System (SAUS)
PEPS..........	Priced Exhibit Processing System
PEPS..........	Primary Earnings per Share (TDOB)
PEPS..........	Primary Environmental Prediction System
PEPS..........	Primary Environmental Processing Systems [Navy] (GFGA)
PEPS..........	Production Engineering Productivity System [Camtek Ltd.] [Software package]
PEPS..........	Productivity Environmental Preference Survey [Test]
PEPS..........	Program Element Plan Supplement
PEPS..........	Psychological, Economic, Political and Sociological (SAUS)
PEP-SEP	Peptide Separation [Biochemistry]
PEP Service...	Pan European Paging Service (SAUS)
PEPSI..........	Plasma Electron Profiles, Symmetric Integrals (MCD)
PepsiC........	PepsiCo, Inc. [Associated Press] (SAG)
PEPSICO......	Pepsi-Cola Co. (EFIS)
PepsiPR.......	Pepsi Cola Puerto Rico Bottling [Associated Press] (SAG)
PEPSS........	Preschool and Early Primary Skills Survey [Child development test]
PEPSS........	Programmable Equipment for Personnel Subsystem Simulation
PEPSU	All India Reporter, Patiala and East Punjab States Union [1950-57] [A publication] (DLA)
PEPSU	Patiala and East Punjab States Union
PEPSY	Precision Earth-Pointing System (MCD)
PEPSY	Scandinavian pedagogical publications bibliography (SAUS)
PEP Technique...	Planar Epitaxial Passivated Technique (SAUS)
PEPTP	(Phenylethyl)Phenyltetrahydropyridine [Organic chemistry]
PEP Train	Prototype Electro-Pneumatic Train (SAUS)
PEP Transistor...	Planar Epitaxial Passivated Transistor (SAUS)
PEP/USA	Parkinson's Educational Program - USA (EA)
PEPUSL	Pepperdine University School of Law (DLA)
PEpW..........	Westinghouse Electric Corp., East Pittsburgh, PA [Library symbol] [Library of Congress] (LCLS)
PEPWG	Pressurized Element Working Group (SAUS)
PEQ............	Pecos City, TX [Location identifier] [FAA] (FAAL)
PEQ............	Personal Experience Questionnaire [Psychology]
PEQ............	Petroquin Resources Ltd. [Vancouver Stock Exchange symbol]
PEQ............	Potomac Edison [NYSE symbol] (SAG)

PEQ............	Potomac Edison 8.00% 'QUIDS' [NYSE symbol] (TTSB)
PEQC	Presidents Environmental Quality Council (SAUS)
PEQC	Production Engine Quality Control (SAUS)
PEQI...........	Perceived Environmental Quality Indices (EEVL)
PEQIX	Pioneer Equity-Income Cl.A [Mutual fund ticker symbol] (SG)
PEQUA	Production Equipment Agency [Army]
PEQUOD	Pacific Equatorial Ocean Dynamics [Project] [USA] [Marine science] (OSRA)
PEr............	Erie Public Library, Erie, PA [Library symbol] [Library of Congress] (LCLS)
PER............	For Each (DAVI)
PER............	Packed Encoding Rules (ACII)
PER............	Paraelectric Resonance (SAUS)
PER............	Paramagnetic Electron Resonance (SAUS)
PER............	Par Exchange Rate [Business term]
PER............	Parity Error Rate
PER............	Parole Evidence Rule [Legal shorthand] (LWAP)
PER............	Partido Estadista Republicano [Puerto Rico] [Political party]
PER............	Path Extension Ratio (MCD)
PER............	Peak Ejection Rate [Cardiology]
PER............	Peak Expiration Rate [Medicine]
Per............	Pediatric Emergency Room (DAVI)
Pe R...........	Pennewill's Delaware Reports [A publication] (DLA)
Per............	Perchlorethylen (SAUS)
per............	Perennial [Botany]
Per............	Perera's Select Decisions [Ceylon] [A publication] (DLA)
PER............	Per Exchange Rate [Finance] (MHDW)
PER............	Performance (DA)
PER............	Performance Energy Ratio (SAUS)
PER............	Performance Evaluation Report [DoD]
PER............	Performance Evaluation Routine (SAUS)
PER............	Perhaps (ROG)
Per............	Pericles [Shakespearean work]
Per............	Pericles [of Plutarch] [Classical studies] (OCD)
PER............	Perigee (KSC)
per............	Perineal [Gynecology] (MAE)
Per............	Periochae [of Livy] [Classical studies] (OCD)
Per............	Period (VRA)
Per............	Period [Record label]
PER............	Period
per............	Periodic (AAMN)
Per............	Periodical (AL)
per............	Periodical
PER............	Periodical (ROG)
PER............	Periodic Evaluation Record (DIPS)
PER............	Periodicity (DMAA)
Per............	Periodogram (DMAA)
PER............	Peritoneum (SAUS)
PER............	Permission (AABC)
PER............	Perodicity (SAUS)
PER............	Perot Systems'A' [NYSE symbol] (SG)
Per............	Perseus [Constellation]
Per............	Persia (VRA)
PER............	Persia [Obsolete]
per............	Persian, Modern [MARC language code] [Library of Congress] (LCCP)
per............	Person (WDMC)
PER............	Person
PER............	Personate (SAUS)
PER............	Personnel (KSC)
PER............	PERT [Program Evaluation and Review Technique] Event Report
PER............	Perth [Australia] [Airport symbol] (OAG)
PER............	Perth [Australia] [Seismograph station code, US Geological Survey] [Closed] (SEIS)
PER............	Peru [ANSI three-letter standard code] (CNC)
PER............	Perylene (SAUS)
PER............	Pharmaceutical Evaluation Report [Australia]
PER............	Phase Encoding Recording (SAUS)
PER............	Phase Engineering Report
PER............	Photo-Electric Reader (or Reading) (SAUS)
PER............	Physical Examination Rate [Military] (AFM)
PER............	Planning, Evaluation, and Reporting [Education-improvement system]
PER............	Pominex Ltd. [Toronto Stock Exchange symbol]
PER............	Ponca City, OK [Location identifier] [FAA] (FAAL)
PER............	Port Everglades Railway [AAR code]
PER............	Postelectrophoresis Relaxation
PER............	Post Engineer Request
PER............	Post-Execution Reporting (MHDI)
PER............	Potential Excess Report
PER............	Preedited Region [Genetics]
PER............	Pre-Emptive Right (MHDW)
PER............	Preliminary Engineering Report (KSC)
PER............	PressNet Environmental Reports [Information service or system] (IID)
PER............	Price Earnings Ratio [Relation between price of a company's stock and its annual net income]
PER............	Printing Executive Register (DGA)
PER............	Probable Error Radial [Statistics] (IAA)
PER............	Process Energy Requirement (SAUS)
PER............	Product Engineering Recommendation [Automotive engineering]
PER............	Product Engineering Release (SAUS)
PER............	Production Engineering and Research (SAUS)
PER............	Production Engine Remanufacturers Program [Automotive engineering]
PER............	Professional and Executive Recruitment Service [British]

PER............. Professional Employment Register [British] (ODBW)
PER............. Proficiency Evaluation Review
PER............. Program Error Report (MHDI)
PER............. Program Event Recording [Computer science] (MDG)
PER............. Program Execution Request
PER............. Program for Ecological Research (SAUS)
PER............. Program for Ecosystem Research (SAUS)
PER............. Pronated External Rotation [Medicine] (MELL)
PER............. Proposal Evaluation Report (MCD)
PER............. Protein Efficiency Ratio [Nutrition]
PER............. Pseudoequilibrium Ratio (SAUS)
PER............. Public Employees Roundtable (EA)
PER7........... Region 7 Personnel System (SAUS)
PERA .... Planning and Engineering for Repair and Alteration [Navy]
PERA .... Production Engineering Research Association [Research center] [British] (IRC)
PERA .... Production Engine Remanufacturers Association (EA)
PERA .... Production Equipment Rental Association (NTPA)
PERA .... Project Engineering Research Association (SAUS)
Per A J .... Performing Arts Journal [A publication] (BRI)
PERAM .... Personnel Action Memorandum [Military]
PER AN........ Per Annum [By the Year] [Latin]
Per & Dav ... Perry and Davison's English King's Bench Reports [1838-41] [A publication] (DLA)
Per & Kn ..... Perry and Knapp's English Election Reports [1838] [A publication] (DLA)
per ann........ Per Annum (EBF)
PER ANN ...... Per Annum [By the Year] [Latin]
PERA system... Project Engineering Research Association system (NITA)
P/E ratio ...... Price/Earnings Ratio (WDAA)
Pe Rave....... Petrus Ravennas [Flourished, 1468-1508] [Authority cited in pre-1607 legal work] (DSA)
PERB .... Personnel Evaluation Research Bureau (SAUS)
PERB .... Planning and Environmental Review Board (SAUS)
PERB .... Professional Engineers Registration Board (SAUS)
PERB .... Public Employment Relations Board (EDAC)
PERC .... Parents Educational Resource Center
PERC .... Peace on Earth Research Center
PERC .... Perchloroethylene (SAUS)
PERC .... Perclose, Inc. [NASDAQ symbol] (SAG)
PERC .... Percolate (SAUS)
PERC .... Percolator (DSUE)
PERC .... Percussion (AAG)
perc .... Percussion (WDAA)
PERC .... Pittsburgh Energy Research Center [Later, PETC] [Energy Research and Development Administration]
PERC .... Plasma Energy Recycle and Conversion
PERC .... Political & Economic Risk Consultancy [Commercial firm] [Hong Kong]
PERC .... Political Economy Research Center [Research center] (RCD)
PERC .... Preliminary Editorial Review Checklist (SAUS)
PERC .... Private Enterprise Research Center (EA)
PERC .... Processor Emergency Recovery Circuit [Bell System]
PERC .... Professional Engineering and Research Consultants
PERC .... Psoriasis Education and Research Centre [University of Toronto] [Canada] [Research center] (RCD)
PERC .... Public Employment Relations Commission (EDAC)
PERC .... Public Enterprises Reform Commission [Sri Lanka]
PERCAM ...... Performance and Cost Analysis Model (MCD)
Per cap....... Per Capita (EBF)
Per Cap .... Per Capita [By the Individual] [Latin]
PERCAP....... Persian Gulf Requirements and Capabilities [Military]
PERCASREPT... Personnel Casualty Report [Military] (NVT)
PERC DR ..... Percussion Drilling (SAUS)
PERCENT ..... Per Centum [By the Hundred] [Latin]
Percep........ Perceptions (DIAR)
PERCHLOR... Perchloride [Chemistry] (ROG)
PERCI......... Personnel Contamination Instrumentation
Perclose ..... Perclose, Inc. [Associated Press] (SAG)
PERCO .... Percobarg (SAUS)
PERCO .... Percodan (SAUS)
PERCOM ...... Peripheral Communications (SAUS)
PERCOM...... Personnel Command [Army] (MCD)
PERCOMP.... Personal Computing Conference (MHDI)
PERCOMPASIA... South East Asian Personal Computer Hardware and Software Show
PERCOMP Conference... Personal Computing Conference (SAUS)
Percon........ Percon, Inc. [Associated Press] (SAG)
Per con...... Per Contra [On the Other Side] [Latin]
PERCON....... Peripheral Converter (SAUS)
PERCOS...... Performance Coding System
Percptr........ Perceptron, Inc. [Associated Press] (SAG)
Per CS .... Perrault's Conseil Superieur [Canada] [A publication] (DLA)
PERCS .... Preference Equity Redemption Cumulative Stock (ECON)
PERCS .... Preferred Equity Redemption Cumulative Stock
PERCUSS ..... Percussion [Medicine] (DAVI)
PERCUSS & AUSC... Percussion and Auscultation [Medicine] (DHSM)
PERCY .... Photo Electronic Recognition Cybernetics (SAUS)
PERD .... Panel for Energy Research and Development (SAUS)
PERD .... Payload Element Requirements Document (SAUS)
PERD .... Perdendo [or Perdendosi] [Softer and Slower] [Music]
PERD .... Periodic (MSA)
PERD .... Perused (ROG)
PERDA........ Per Diem [By the Day] [Latin] (NOAA)

PERDDiMS... Personnel Deployment and Distribution Management System [Military] (AABC)
PERDEN ...... Perdendo [or Perdendosi] [Softer and Slower] [Music]
PERDEX ...... Permuted Formula Index [Molecular formula indexing]
PerDia .... Personal Diagnostics, Inc. [Associated Press] (SAG)
PERECORDING... Phase Encoded Recording (SAUS)
PEREF .... Personal Effects
PEREF .... Propellant Engine Research Environmental Facility
Pereg.......... Peregrinus Fabius [Authority cited in pre-1607 legal work] (DSA)
PERF.......... Peak Expiratory Flow Rate [Medicine] (DMAA)
perf............ Perfect (WDAA)
PERF.......... Perfect
PERF.......... PerfectData Corp. [NASDAQ symbol] (NQ)
PERF.......... Perfection (SAUS)
perf............ perfectum (SAUS)
PERF.......... Perforate [or Perforator]
PERF.......... Perforation (DSUE)
perf............ Perforation (WDMC)
PERF.......... Perform (KSC)
PERF.......... Performance (KSC)
perf............ Performance (VRA)
PERF.......... Performer (SAUS)
PERF.......... Perfusionist [Medicine] (HCT)
PerF........... Perma Fix Environmental Services [Associated Press] (SAG)
PERF.......... Petroleum Environmental Research Forum (SAUS)
PERF.......... Planetary Entry Radiation Facility [Langley Research Center] [NASA] (PDAA)
PERF.......... Police Executive Research Forum (EA)
PERF.......... Police Executive Resource Form (SAUS)
PER FA ATK SYS ANAL... Perform Field Artillery Attack System Analysis (SAUS)
PER FA PERS CNTRL... Perform Field Artillery Personnel Control (SAUS)
PER FA SPL CNTRL... Perform Field Artillery Supply Control (SAUS)
PERFCE....... Performance
PERFD........ Performed (ROG)
Perfdta........ PerfectData Corp. [Associated Press] (SAG)
PERFECT.... Performance Evaluation for Cost Effective Transformations (SAUS)
PERFECT...... Productivity Erosion Runoff Functions to Evaluate Conservation Techniques (SAUS)
PERFINS ..... Perforated Insignia [Philately]
PERFM....... Perform (ROG)
PERFMON.... Performance Monitoring (SAUS)
PerFood....... Performance Food Group [Commercial firm] [Associated Press] (SAG)
PERFORM.... Performance
Perform Chem... Performance Chemicals (SAUS)
Perform Eval... Performance Evaluation (SAUS)
Perform Eval Rev... Performance Evaluation Review (SAUS)
PERFR........ Perforator (IAA)
PERF RM ..... Perfect Ream (DGA)
PERFS .... Perfumers (SAUS)
PerfSys .... Performance Systems International, Inc. [Associated Press] (SAG)
PerfTech ...... Performance Technologies, Inc. [Associated Press] (SAG)
Perfum........ Perfumania, Inc. [Associated Press] (SAG)
PERFW .... Perforating Wound
PErG .... Gannon University, Erie, PA [Library symbol] [Library of Congress] (LCLS)
PERG......... Pattern Electroretinogram (SAUS)
PERG......... Pergola [Classified advertising] (ADA)
PERG......... Production Emergency Redistribution Group
PERG......... Production Equipment Redistribution Group [Army]
PERGO........ Project Evaluation and Review with Graphic Output (IEEE)
PERGRA...... Permission Granted [Military]
PERGS....... Portable Earth Resources Ground Station (SAUS)
perh........... Perhaps (GEAB)
PERH .... Perhaps
PerHi .... Erie County Historical Society, Erie, PA [Library symbol] [Library of Congress] (LCLS)
PERI........... Pea Ridge National Military Park
peri............ Pericardium [Medicine] (ADWA)
PERI........... Perigee
Peri............ Perigeum (SAUS)
PERI........... Perimeter (AABC)
peri............ Perineal [Anatomy] (DAVI)
PERI........... Periodical
PERI........... Periphonics Corp. [NASDAQ symbol] (SAG)
PERI........... Periscope
PERI........... Peritoneal Fluid (DAVI)
PERI........... Pharmaceutical Education & Research Institute (SAUS)
PERI........... Photoengravers Research Institute (SAUS)
PERI........... Platemakers Educational and Research Institute [Later, IAP]
PERI........... Production Equipment Redistribution Inventory [Army]
PERI........... Production Equipment Reserve Inventory [Navy] (NG)
PERI........... Protein Engineering Research Institute [Japanese governmental and industrial consortium] [Later, BERI]
PERI........... Psychiatric Epidemiology Research Interview
PERIAP .... Periapical [Dentistry]
peric .... Pericope (VRA)
Pericom....... Pericom Semiconductor Corp. [Associated Press] (SAG)
PERIF......... Peripheral
perig........... Perigee (BARN)
Pe Rigal ...... Petrus Rigaldi [Flourished, 14th century] [Authority cited in pre-1607 legal work] (DSA)
perih........... perihelion (SAUS)
PERIM .... Perimeter (KSC)
PERI/M .... Perimortem (DAVI)

PeriniC .... Perini Corp. [*Associated Press*] (SAG)
PERINTREP... Periodic Intelligence Report (NATG)
PERINTREPT... Periodic Intelligence Report
PERINTSUM... Periodic Intelligence Summary [*Army*] (AABC)
perio........... Periodontist [*Dentistry*] (DAVI)
Period.......... Periodical (DIAR)
Periodentol... Periodentology (SAUS)
PERIODONTOL... Periodontology (SAUS)
Period Polytech... Periodica Polytechnica (SAUS)
Period Polytech\ Chem Eng... Periodica Polytechnica, Chemical Engineering (SAUS)
Period Polytech\ Electr Eng... Periodica Polytechnica, Electrical Engineering (SAUS)
Period Polytech\ Mech Eng... Periodica Polytechnica, Mechanical Engineering (SAUS)
Peripad........ Perineal Pad [*Medicine*] (AMHC)
PERIPH........ Periphery (KSC)
Periphn........ Periphonics Corp. [*Associated Press*] (SAG)
Periphony .... Peripheral Phony (SAUS)
Peripl M Eux... Periplus Maris Euxini [*of Arrian*] [*Classical studies*] (OCD)
PERIS .... Periscope (KSC)
PERJ............ Perjury [*FBI standardized term*]
PERJY.......... Perjury (ROG)
PERK .... Payroll Earnings Record Keeping
PERK .... Percolate (GOBB)
Perk............ Perkins on Conveyancing [*A publication*] (DLA)
Perk............ Perkins on Pleading [*A publication*] (DLA)
Perk............ Perkins' Profitable Book (Conveyancing) [*A publication*] (DLA)
PERK .... Perquisite
PERK .... Prospective Evaluation of Radial Keratotomy [*Protocol*] [*Ophthalmology*] (DAVI)
PERKARA..... Parti Perdapuan Kebangsaan Ra'ayat Brunei [*Brunei People's National United Party*] [*Political party*] (EY)
PerkEl.......... Perkin-Elmer Corp. [*Associated Press*] (SAG)
PerkF.......... Perkins Family Restaurants Ltd. [*Associated Press*] (SAG)
Perkin-Elmer Tech News... Perkin-Elmer Technical News (SAUS)
Perk Pr Bk... Perkins' Profitable Book (Conveyancing) [*A publication*] (DLA)
perks.......... Perquisites (MHDB)
PERL........... Pacific Estuarine Research Laboratory (SAUS)
PERL........... Pathologically Eclectic Rubbish Lister
PERL........... Perception Enhanced Resolution Logic (SAUS)
PERL........... Perkin-Elmer Robot Language
PERL........... Perle Systems Ltd. [*Scarborough, ON*] [*NASDAQ symbol*] (NQ)
PERL........... Perusal (ROG)
PERL........... Pictorial Engineering and Research Laboratory
PERL........... Portable Electronic Runway Lighting (PDAA)
Perl............ Practical Extraction and Report Language [*Computer science*]
PERL........... Practice Extraction and Report Language [*Facetious translation: Pathologically Eclectic Rubbish Lister*] [*Computer science*] (NHD)
PERL........... Prepositioned Equipment Requirements List [*Navy*] (MCD)
PERL........... principal Exchange Rate Linked (SAUS)
PERL........... Public Employee Relations Library [*of International Personnel Management Association*]
PERL........... Pupils Equal and Reactive to Light (DAVI)
PERL........... Pupils Equal, Regular, and Reactive to Light (DAVI)
PERLA .... Pupils Equal, React to Light and Accommodation [*Medicine*]
PERLA .... Pupils Equal, Regular and Reactive to Light and Accommodation (DAVI)
PerleSys....... Pearle Systems Ltd. [*Associated Press*] (SAG)
PERLF.......... Perle System [*NASDAQ symbol*] (TTSB)
PERLS .... Principal Exchange-Rate-Linked Securities [*Investment term*]
Perm........... Permanence (SAUS)
perm........... Permanent (ELAL)
PERM.......... Permanent
PERM.......... Permanent Bancorp [*NASDAQ symbol*] (SAG)
PERM.......... Permanent Employee (DSUE)
PERM.......... Permanent Material (SAUS)
PERM.......... Permanent Wave (SAUS)
PERM.......... Permeability
PERM.......... Permian [*Period, era, or system*] [*Geology*]
PERM.......... Permission (MSA)
PERM.......... Permutation (DSUE)
PERM.......... Pre-Embossed Rigid Magnetic [*Electronics*] (AAEL)
PERM.......... Pre-Embossed Rigid Magnetic Media [*Computer science*]
PERM.......... Program Evaluation for Repetitive Manufacture (IEEE)
PERM.......... Programmed Evaluation for Repetitive Manufacture (VLIE)
PERMACAP... Personnel Management and Accounting Card Processor [*Military*]
PERMACAPS... Personnel Management and Accounting Card Processing System (MCD)
PERMAFLOWERS... Permanent Flowers (SAUS)
PERMAFROST... Permanent Frost
PERMAFRUIT... Permanent Fruit (SAUS)
PER MAINT CNTRL... Perform Maintenance Control (SAUS)
PERMAS ..... Persatuan Rakyat Malaysian Sarawak [*Political party*] (EY)
PERMAS ..... Personnel Management Assistance System [*Military*] (AABC)
PERMB .... Permeability
PermBcp..... Permanent Bancorp [*Associated Press*] (SAG)
PErMC........ Mercyhurst College, Erie, PA [*Library symbol*] [*Library of Congress*] (LCLS)
PERM C of Sta... Permanent Change of Station (SAUS)
Perm Ct of Arb... Permanent Court of Arbitration (SAUS)
PERMDATA... PERMDATA Management System (SAUS)
PerMdw...... Perpetual Midwest Financial, Inc. [*Associated Press*] (SAG)
PERME........ Propellants, Explosives, and Rocket Motors Establishment [*British Ministry of Defense*] [*Research center*] (RDA)

PERMED ...... Permanently Waved (SAUS)
PermF........ Perma Fix Environmental Services [*Associated Press*] (SAG)
PermFix...... Perma Fix Environmental Services [*Associated Press*] (SAG)
PERMIC ...... Personnel Management Information Center [*Navy*] (NVT)
PERMINVAR... Permeability Invariable
PERMINVAR... Permeability Invariant
PERMIS ...... Preference Management Information System (SAUS)
PERMIS ...... Public Employees Retirement Management Information System (SAUS)
PERMIT....... Polar Orbiter Effective Rainfall Monitoring Integrative Technique
PERMIXT ..... Permixtus [*Mixed*] [*Pharmacy*] (ROG)
PERMLY ..... Permanently
Perm Med Mbr... Permanent Medical Member (SAUS)
PERMR .... Permanent Residence
PERMREP... Permanent Representation to North Atlantic Council [*NATO*] (NATG)
PERMS ...... Personnel Electronic Record Management System [*Army*] (RDA)
PERMS ...... Process and Effluent Radiological Monitoring System [*Nuclear energy*] (NRCH)
PERMSS ..... Process and Effluent Radiological Monitoring and Sampling System [*Nuclear energy*] (NRCH)
PERMT........ Permanent (ROG)
PERMT........ Permanently (SAUS)
PERMU .... Permit (VLIE)
PERMU .... Permanent Magnet Users Association [*Defunct*] (EA)
PER MVMT C2... Perform field artillery Movement Control and Coordination (SAUS)
PernC........ Perini Corp. [*Associated Press*] (SAG)
PERNOGRA.. Permission Not Granted [*Military*]
PERO .... President's Emergency Relief Organization (NADA)
PEROM ...... Programmable and Erasable Read-Only Memory (SAUS)
PEROM .... Programmable Erasable Read Only Memory (SAUS)
PER OP EMET... Peracta Operatione Emetici [*When the Operation of the Emetic is Finished*] [*Pharmacy*] (ROG)
Per Or Cas... Perry's Oriental Cases [*Bombay*] [*A publication*] (DLA)
PEROX........ Peroxidase Stain [*Biochemistry*] (DAVI)
PEROX........ Peroxide
PERP......... Pan-Ethnic Republican Party of Australia [*Political party*]
PERP......... Peak Effective Radiated Power [*Telecommunications*] (OTD)
PERP......... Perpendicular (AAG)
perp........... Perpendicular (VRA)
perp........... Perpetrator (ADWA)
PERP......... Perpetrator (WDAA)
PERP......... Perpetual (ADA)
Perp......... Perpetual (EBF)
Perp......... Perpignan (SAUS)
Per P........ Perrault's Prevoste de Quebec [*A publication*] (DLA)
PERP......... Personnel Processing (MUGU)
PERP......... Process Evaluation/Research Planning (SAUS)
perpad........ Perineal Pad [*Gynecology*] (MAE)
PerpBnk...... Perpetual Bank Federal Savings Bank [*Associated Press*] (SAG)
Perpet....... Perpetual (DLA)
Per Pro ...... Per Procuration (EBF)
per pro .... Per Procurationem [*By Proxy, By the Action Of*] [*Legal term*] [*Latin*] (BARN)
PER PROC ... Per Procurationem [*By Proxy, By the Action Of*] [*Legal term*] [*Latin*]
PERPS .... Police Executive Forum (SAUS)
PerpSB ...... Petpetual State Bank [*North Carolina*] [*Associated Press*] (SAG)
Per Psy ...... Personnel Psychology [*A publication*] (BRI)
PERR .... Patter-Evoked Retinal Response [*neurology and ophthalmology*] (DAVI)
PERR .... Premature Engine Removal Rate (AAG)
Perrault ..... Perrault's Conseil Superieur [*Canada*] [*A publication*] (DLA)
Perrault ...... Perrault's Prevoste de Quebec [*A publication*] (DLA)
Perrault ...... Perrault's Quebec Reports [*A publication*] (DLA)
Perrigo .... Perrigo Co. [*Associated Press*] (SAG)
PERRL .... Pupils Equal, Round and Reactive to Light (DAVI)
PERRL .... Pupils Equal, Round, Regular and Reactive to Light (DAVI)
PERRLA ...... Pupils Equal, Round, React to Light and Accommodation [*Medicine*]
PERRLA (DC)... Pupils Equal, Round, and Reactive to Light and Accommodation (Directly and Consensually) (DAVI)
Perry........... Perry's Oriental Cases [*Bombay*] [*A publication*] (DLA)
Perry & D ... Perry and Davison's English King's Bench Reports [*A publication*] (DLA)
Perry & D (Eng)... Perry and Davison's English King's Bench Reports [*A publication*] (DLA)
Perry & K ... Perry and Knapp's English Election Cases [*A publication*] (DLA)
Perry & Kn... Perry and Knapp's English Election Cases [*A publication*] (DLA)
PerryCF....... Perry County Financial Corp. [*Associated Press*] (SAG)
Perry Ins..... Perry's English Insolvency Cases [*1831*] [*A publication*] (DLA)
Perry OC..... Perry's Oriental Cases [*Bombay*] [*A publication*] (DLA)
PERS .... Patient Evaluation Rating Scale [*Medicine*] (DMAA)
PERS .... Performance Evaluation Reporting System [*DoD*]
PERS .... Periodical Source Index [*A publication*]
Pers........... Persae [*of Aeschylus*] [*Classical studies*] (OCD)
Pers........... Perseus [*Constellation*]
PERS .... Persia [*Obsolete*]
Pers........... Persian (BEE)
PERS .... Persian Leather [*Bookbinding*] (DGA)
Pers........... Persius [*34-62AD*] [*Classical studies*] (OCD)
PERS .... Person
Pers........... Personal (TBD)
pers........... Personal (WDMC)
PERS .... Personal
PERS .... Personal Emergency Response System [*Telecommunications*]
PERS .... Personality (SAUS)

PERS .... Personnel (AFM)
Pers .... Personnel (AL)
pers .... Personnel (DD)
PERS .... Personnel Squadron
pers .... Persons (WDMC)
PERS .... Perspective (WDAA)
PERS .... Preliminary Engineering Reports (MUGU)
PERS .... Proactive Error Reduction System (SAUS)
PERS .... Program for Evaluation of Rejects and Substitutions [Computer
                   science] (IAA)
PERS .... Public Employees Retirement System (DICI)
PERSACLIT... Peritus in Sacred Liturgy [Roman Catholic]
PERSACS..... Personnel Structure and Accounting System [Army]
PERSACS..... Personnel Structure and Composition System [Military]
PERS & TRACOMD... Personnel and Training Command
PERSAS .... Personnel Accounting System (ACAE)
PERSC .... Public Education Religion Studies Center [Defunct] (EA)
PERS CASREP... Personnel Casualty Report [Navy] (ANA)
PERSCEN..... Personnel Center
PERSCO..... Personnel Support of Contingency Operations [Military]
PersCom... Personnel Command [Army] (INF)
PERSCOM..... Personnel Command [Army]
Pers Comput Mag... Personal Computer Magazine (SAUS)
Pers Comput World... Personal Computer World (SAUS)
PERSCON ..... Personnel Control [Military]
PERSD .... Personnel Department [Marine Corps]
PERSDEP .... Personnel Deployment (SAUS)
PERSDEP ..... Personnel Deployment Report [Military]
PERSDEP Report... Personnel Deployment Report (SAUS)
PerSep........ PerSeptive Technologies II Corp. [Associated Press] (SAG)
PERSEP .... Pershing Survivability Evaluation Program [Military] (MCD)
PERSEPCOMD... Personnel and Separation Command (DNAB)
PERSERVDEPSERVS... Personal Services and Dependents' Services Support
                   System [Navy] (DNAB)
PERSET........ Personnel Standardization and Evaluation Team [Military]
PERSEVCE ... Perseverance (ROG)
PERSEXP ..... Personal Expense Money [Army]
PersGp........ Personnel Group of America [Associated Press] (SAG)
PERSH .... Perishable (WGA)
Pershad....... Privy Council Judgments [1829-69] [India] [A publication] (DLA)
persian white... fantanyl (SAUS)
PERSID........ Personnel Seismic Intruder Detector (ACAE)
PERSIL .... Peroxide Silicate [Detergent and bleach]
Pers Inj Comment'r... Personal Injury Commentator [A publication] (DLA)
Pers Inj LJ... Personal Injury Law Journal [A publication] (DLA)
PERSINS...... Personnel Information System [Army]
PERSINSCOM... Personnel Information Systems Command [Army] (AABC)
PERSINSD ... Personnel Information Systems Directorate [Military Personnel
                   Center] (AABC)
PERSIR........ Personnel Inventory Report [Army] (AABC)
PERSIS .... Personnel Information System (MHDB)
PERSITREP... Personnel Situation Report (SAUS)
PERSL .... Personal
Persl .... Personnel (TBD)
Pers Man..... Personnel Management [A publication]
Pers Manage... Personnel Management (SAUS)
PERSMAR... Personnel Manning Assistance Report (DNAB)
Pers N .... Personal Noun (SAUS)
PERSNET..... Personnel Network [Army]
PersnMg ...... Personnel Management, Inc. [Associated Press] (SAG)
PERSO .... Personnel Officer [Air Force]
PERSOF .... Personnel Officer [Navy]
PERSON....... Personnel Simulation On-Line [Department of State] [Computer
                   program]
personi .... personification (SAUS)
personi .... personified (SAUS)
personi .... personifier (SAUS)
Personnel&Guid J... Personnel and Guidance Journal (SAUS)
PERSP .... Perspective (MSA)
persp .... Perspective (VRA)
Persp .... Perspective [Record label]
PERSPAY ..... Personnel and Pay [Project] [Navy]
Pers Prac B... Personnel Practice Bulletin [A publication]
PERSPROC... Personnel Processing [Army]
Pers Pron .... Personal Pronoun (SAUS)
PERSPROP... Personal Property Data Entry and Report System (SAUS)
Pers PS .... Perspectives on Political Science [A publication] (BRI)
PerSptv........ PerSeptive Biosystems, Inc. [Associated Press] (SAG)
PERSRSCHSYSTM... Personnel Management and Training Research Statistical
                   Data System [Navy] (DNAB)
PERSRU....... Personnel Reporting Unit
PERSSEPCENT... Personnel Separation Center
PERSSO........ Personnel System Staff Officer
PERSTAT ..... Personnel Status Report [Military]
PERSTATREP... Personnel Status Report [Military]
PERSTEMPO... Personnel Tempo (SEWL)
PERSTRAN... Personal Transportation [Navy]
PERT........... Patients Experience of the Relationship with the Therapist Method
PERT........... Performance Evaluation Review Technique
PERT........... Perpetual Bank Federal Savings Bank [NASDAQ symbol] (SAG)
PERT........... Pertain (AABC)
pert............ Pertaining (ADWA)
PERT........... Pertinent (SAUS)
PERT........... Pertussis [Whooping cough]
PERT........... Phenol Enhanced Reassociation Technique [Clinical chemistry]

PERT........... Pollution Emergency Response Team (SAUS)
PERT........... Printing Economy Remote Terminal (SAUS)
PERT........... Production and Evaluation Review Technique (SAUS)
PERT........... Program Estimation Revaluation Technique [Computer science] (IAA)
PERT........... Program Evaluation and Reporting Technique (SAUS)
PERT........... Program Evaluation and Review Technique [Computer science]
PERT........... Program Evaluation Research Task (IEEE)
PERT........... Program Evaluation Research Test (SAUS)
PERT........... Program Evaluation Review Technique (SAUS)
PERT........... Program Evolution and Review Technique (SAUS)
PERT........... Project Evaluation Review Technique (SAUS)
PERT........... Project on Education, Research and Training (SAUS)
PERTCO ...... Program Evaluation and Review Technique with Cost
PERT COST... Program Evaluation and Review Techniques Costs
PERT/CPM... Program Evaluation and Review Technique/Critical Path Method
                   [Computer science] (DOM)
PERT-CS...... Program Evaluation and Review Technique - Cost System (DNAB)
PER TDA RPT... Perform TDA Reporting (SAUS)
PER TGT PRC... Perform Target Processing (SAUS)
PERTHS....... Perthshire [County in Scotland]
PERT-NAP.... Program Evaluation and Review Technique - Network Automatic
                   Plotting (SAA)
PERTO .... Pertaining To (NVT)
Per Tr......... Perry on Trusts [A publication] (DLA)
PERTRAN... Perturbation Transport [NASA]
PERTSIM...... Program Evaluation and Review Technique Simulation [Game]
PERT-TAM... Program Evaluation and Review Technique Task, Action, and
                   Milestone Items
PERT/TIME... Program Evaluation and Review Technique/Time Analyzer [Sperry
                   UNIVAC]
PERTVS .... Perimeter Television System (SAUS)
Peru........... Peruvian (DIAR)
PERU .... Production Equipment Records Unit (IEEE)
PERU BAL.... Peruvian Balsam (SAUS)
Peru Cur...... Peruvian Current (SAUS)
PERUG........ Perusing (ROG)
PERUPEC... Peruvian National Committee for Pacific Economic Cooperation
PERUSA...... Perspectives - United States of America [History course]
PERUV .... Peruvian
PERV .... Perversion (SAUS)
PERV .... Pervert [or Perverted] [FBI standardized term]
perv .... Pervious (SAUS)
PERV .... Porcine Endogenous Provirus
PERV .... Porcine Endogenous Retrovirus
PErV .... United States Veterans Administration Hospital, Erie, PA [Library
                   symbol] [Library of Congress] (LCLS)
PERVAL ...... Performance/Valuation (VLIE)
PErVM .... Villa Maria College, Erie, PA [Library symbol] [Library of Congress]
                   (LCLS)
PERY .... Ellis, Perry, Intl. [NASDAQ symbol] (SG)
PERYLENE ... Peri-Dinaphthalene [A fluorophore] [Organic chemistry]
Pes .... Esophageal Pressure [Used to estimate intrapleural pressure] (DAVI)
PES............. IEEE Power Engineering Society (EA)
PES............. Pacific Environmental Services, Inc. (EFIS)
PES............. Paid Educational Services [British]
PES............. Pan European Survey [A publication]
PES............. Paper End Signal (VLIE)
PES............. Paraendocrine Syndrome [Endocrinology]
PES............. Parent Egg Seed
PES............. Partial Energy Service [Electric power]
PES............. Partido Ecuatoriano Socialista [Ecuadorean Socialist Party] [Political
                   party]
PES............. Parts Engineering Support
PES............. Passive Electromagnetic System (IAA)
PES............. Patent Examining System
PES............. P-bit Errored Seconds (SAUS)
PES............. Pecos Resources [Vancouver Stock Exchange symbol]
PES............. People Effectiveness Survey (TIMI)
PES............. Personal Earth Stations (ACAE)
PES............. Personalized Exercise System (SAUS)
Pes............. Pesahim (BJA)
PES............. Peshawar [Pakistan] [Seismograph station code, US Geological
                   Survey] [Closed] (SEIS)
PES............. Philosophy of Education Society (EA)
PES............. Photo-Electret State (SAUS)
PES............. Photoelectric Scanner
PES............. Photo-Electric Scanner (or Scanning) (SAUS)
PES............. Photoelectric Scanning [Electronics] (ECII)
PES............. Photoelectron Spectroscope (or Spectroscopy) (SAUS)
PES............. Photo-Electron-Spectroscopy (SAUS)
PES............. Photoelectron Spectroscopy
PES............. Photoelectron Spectrum (SAUS)
PES............. Photoemission Spectroscopy
PES............. Photojet Edge Sensor
PES............. Physicians Equity Services
PES............. Pictorial Eleven Society [Formerly, PE] [PCS] [Absorbed by] (EA)
PES............. Planning and Evaluation Staff (COE)
PES............. Pointing Error Sensor (MCD)
PES............. Polyethersulfone [Organic chemistry]
PES............. Polyethylene Sodium Sulfonate [Anticoagulant]
PES............. Polyphenylene Sulfide [Plastics]
PES............. Porsche Engineering Services
PES............. Positioning Error Signal (VLIE)
PES............. Post Ejection Sequencer (ACAE)
PES............. Post-Enumeration Survey [Bureau of the Census]

PES............. Postextrasystolic Potentiation [*Cardiology*]
PES............. Potential Energy Source [*Physiology*]
PES............. Potential-Energy Surface [*Chemical kinetics*]
PES............. Poultry and Egg Situation
PES............. Power Electronics Society (SAUS)
PES............. Power Engineering Society
PES............. Power Engineering Specification
PES............. Preexcitation Syndrome [*Cardiology*]
PES............. Preparedness Evaluation System (COE)
PES............. Preschool Evaluation Scale [*Test*] (TMMY)
Pes............. Pressure, End-Systole [*Cardiology*]
PES............. Pressure Equalization System [*Nuclear energy*] (NUCP)
PES............. Private Express Statutes (DICI)
P(ES)........... Probability of Equal Regressive Slopes [*Statistics*]
PES............. Probe Entry Site [*Instrumentation*]
PES............. Problem-Etiology-Signs [*or Symptoms*] [*Nursing*]
PES............. Processed Eucheuma Seaweed
PES............. Processor Enhancement Socket [*Computer science*] (PCM)
PES............. Production Engineering Service
PES............. Production Engineering Specification (NG)
PES............. Professional Examination Service
PES............. Program Element Summary
PES............. Program Emphasis Statement [*US Employment Service*] [*Department of Labor*]
PES............. Program Execution System
PES............. Programmable Electronic System [*Engineering*]
PES............. Programmed Electrical Stimulation [*Neurophysiology*]
PES............. Programmer Electronic Switch (SAUS)
PES............. Projected Engagement Scheduler [*Military*] (CAAL)
PES............. Proposed Encryption Standard (SAUS)
PES............. Public Enquiry System (SAUS)
PES............. Public Expenditure Survey [*British*]
PESA........... Percutaneous Epididymal Sperm Aspiration [*Medicine*] (MELL)
PESA........... Petroleum Electric Supply Association [*Defunct*] (EA)
PESA........... Petroleum Equipment Suppliers Association (EA)
PESA........... Propellant Expulsion and Storage Assembly
PESA........... Proton Elastic-Scattering Analysis
PESABC....... Permanent Executive Secretariat of the Andres Bello Convention [*See also SECAB*] (EAIO)
PESAM........ Penetration Survivability Assessment Model (ACAE)
PESC........... Passivated Emitter Solar Cell (SAUS)
PESC........... Physical and Engineering Sciences Committee (SAUS)
PESc........... Poly Ethylene Succinate (EDCT)
PESC........... Pool Energy Services [*NASDAQ symbol*] (TTSB)
PESC........... Pool Energy Services Co. [*NASDAQ symbol*] (SAG)
PESC........... Public Expenditure Survey Commission (SAUS)
PESC........... Public Expenditure Survey Committee [*British*] (ODBW)
PESCGB...... Provincial Electric Supply Committee of Great Britain (SAUS)
PESD.......... Pacific Electronic Security Division [*Military*]
PESD.......... Post-Employment Services Demonstration
PESD.......... Postsecondary Education Statistics Division [*Department of Education*] (GFGA)
PESD.......... Private and Executive Secretary's Diploma (AIE)
PESD.......... Program Element Summary Data [*DoD*]
PESD.......... Program Execution Subdirective (AABC)
PESDA........ Printing Equipment Supply Dealers Association (SAUS)
PESDC........ Properties of Electrolyte Solutions Data Center [*National Institute of Standards and Technology*]
PESDS........ Program Element Summary Data Sheet [*DoD*]
PESGB........ Petroleum Exploration Society of Great Britain
Pesh........... Peshitta [*Syriac translation of the Bible*] (BJA)
Peshawar.... All India Reporter, Peshawar [*1933-50*] [*A publication*] (DLA)
Peshawar.... Indian Rulings, Peshawar Series [*1933-47*] [*A publication*] (DLA)
PESI........... Perma Fix Environmental Services [*NASDAQ symbol*] (SAG)
PESI........... Perma Fix Enviro Svcs [*NASDAQ symbol*] (TTSB)
PESIA......... Postal Employees Salary Increase Act of 1960
PESIC......... Parti du Progres Economique et Social des Independants Congolais Luluabourg [*Party for Economic and Social Progress of the Congolese Independents in Luluabourg*] [*Political party*]
Pesik........... Pesikta de-Rav Kahana (BJA)
Pesikt......... Pesikta de-Rav Kahana (BJA)
PesiktR....... Pesikta Rabbati (BJA)
PESIS......... Photo-Electron Spectroscopy of Inner-Shell (PDAA)
PESIW........ Perma-Fix Envir'l Svcs Wrrt [*NASDAQ symbol*] (TTSB)
PESIZ......... Perma-Fix Envir'l Svcs Wrrt'B' [*NASDAQ symbol*] (TTSB)
PESKI......... Probabilities Expert Systems Knowledge and Inference (IDAI)
PESM.......... Photoelectron Spectromicroscope
PESM.......... Photoelectron Spectromicroscopy (SAUS)
PESM.......... Precision Electronic Support Measures (SEWL)
PeSMoT....... Penn State Microoxidation Test [*Analytical chemistry*]
PESO.......... Participation Enriches Science, Music, and Art Organizations [*Orlando, Florida*]
PESO.......... Performance Evaluation Support Office
PESO.......... Plant Engineering Shop Order (AAG)
PESO.......... Product Engineering Services Office [*DoD*]
PESOS........ Perkin-Elmer Solvent Optimization System [*Chemistry*]
PESOS........ Photo-Electron Spectroscopy of Outer-Shell (PDAA)
PESOS........ Prepare, Explain, Show, Observe, Supervise [*Formula*] [*LIMRA*]
PESP.......... Postextrasystolic Potentiation [*Medicine*] (DMAA)
PesR.......... Pesikta Rabbati (BJA)
PESR.......... Planning Element System Report (NATG)
PESR.......... Precision Echo Sounder Recorder
PESR.......... Pseudoequivalent Service Rounds [*Military*] (NVT)
PEsS.......... East Stroudsburg State College, East Stroudsburg, PA [*Library symbol*] [*Library of Congress*] (LCLS)

PESS........... Pessus [*Pessary*] [*Pharmacy*]
PESS........... Private Electronic Switching System (SAUS)
PESS........... Problem, Etiology, Signs, and Symptoms [*Medicine*] (DMAA)
PESS........... Product Evaluation and Selection System (VLIE)
PE SS & RM... Department of Physical Education, Sports Science and Recreation Management (SAUS)
PESSO......... Personnel System Staff Officer
PEST............ Parameter Entity Symbol Translator [*Elstree Computing Ltd.*] [*Software package*] (NCC)
PEST............ Parameter Estimation by Sequential Testing [*Computer*]
PEST............ Patterned Elicitation Syntax Test [*Educational test*]
PEST............ People for Environmentally Sustainable Transport (SAUS)
PEST............ Pesticide Evaluation Summary Tabulation
PEST............ Planning and Evaluation of Sequential Trials [*Statistics*]
PEST............ Political, Environmental, Social, and Technological [*Business term*] (ODBW)
PEST............ Pressure for Economic and Social Toryism [*Tory Reform Group*] [*British*] (DI)
PEST............ Production Evaluation Surveillance Test
PEST............ Project Engineer Scheduling Technique (SAUS)
PEST............ Region 7 Nebraska Pesticide (SAUS)
PESTAB....... Pesticides Abstracts (NITA)
PESTAN...... Pesticide Analytical Model Version [*Environmental Protection Agency*] (AEPA)
PESTAN...... Pesticides Analytical Transport Solution (SAUS)
Pest Contr ... Pest Control (SAUS)
PESTDOC.... Pest Control Literature Documentation [*Derwent Publications Ltd.*] [*Bibliographic database*] [*Information service or system*] (IID)
PESTDOC.... Pesticide Documentation (NITA)
PESTF......... Proton Event Start Forecast [*Solar weather information*]
PESTIC........ Pesticide
PESU.......... Polyethersulfone [*Organic chemistry*]
PESV.......... Pea Streak Virus [*Plant pathology*]
PESY.......... Pheripheral Exchange Synchronization (IAA)
PET............. Aeropetrel [*Chile*] [*ICAO designator*] (FAAC)
PET............. Pacific Enterprises [*AMEX symbol*] (SAG)
PET............. Panel on Educational Terminology [*Office of Education*]
PET............. Panel on Education and Training [*COSATI*]
PET............. Paper Equilibrium Tester (BARN)
PET............. Parent Effectiveness Training [*A course of study*]
PET............. Particle Electrostatic Thruster
PET............. Patterned Epitaxial Technology (IEEE)
PET............. Payroll Expense Transfer
PET............. Pelotas [*Brazil*] [*Airport symbol*] (OAG)
PET............. Pentaerythritol [*Organic chemistry*]
PET............. Pentaerythritol Tetranitrate [*Also, PETN*] [*Explosive, vasodilator*]
PET............. Pentaerythritol Tetrastearate (SAUS)
PET............. Penthouse Entertainment Network [*Cable television system*]
PET............. Performance Efficiency Test [*Employee screening and placement test*]
PET............. Performance Evaluation Team [*Nuclear energy*] (NRCH)
PET............. Performance Evaluation Test
PET............. Periodic Environmental Test
PET............. Periodic Evaluation Test
PET............. Peripheral Equipment Tester [*Computer science*] (BUR)
PET............. Peritoneal Equilibration Test (SAUS)
PET............. Permeation Enhancement Technology (SAUS)
PET............. Personal Effectiveness Training (MCD)
PET............. Personal Electronic Transaction Computer (NITA)
PET............. Personal Electronic Transactor [*Computer*] [*Commodore Business Machines*]
PET............. Personal Electronic Translator (SAUS)
PET............. Personal Employee Time (DHSM)
PET............. Personnel Experimentation and Testing Device (SAUS)
Pet............. Peter [*New Testament book*]
Pet............. Peterhouse College, Oxford (SAUS)
Pet............. Peters' Prince Edward Island Reports [*1850-72*] [*Canada*] [*A publication*] (DLA)
Pet............. Peters' United States Circuit Court Reports [*A publication*] (DLA)
Pet............. Peters' United States District Court Reports, Admiralty Decisions [*A publication*] (DLA)
Pet............. Peter's United States Reports [*1828-42*] [*A publication*] (AAGC)
Pet............. Peters' United States Supreme Court Reports [*26-41 United States*] [*A publication*] (DLA)
Pet............. Petihta (BJA)
PET............. Pet, Inc., Corporate Information Center, St. Louis, MO [*OCLC symbol*] (OCLC)
PET............. Petition
PET............. Petrine [*Of, or relating to, Peter the Apostle or Peter the Great*]
Pet............. Petrol (SAUS)
PET............. Petrolatum (WGA)
Pet............. Petroleum (DD)
PET............. Petroleum
PET............. Petropavlovsk [*Kazakhstan*] [*Seismograph station code, US Geological Survey*] (SEIS)
PET............. Petrotech, Inc. [*Toronto Stock Exchange symbol*]
Pet............. Petrus [*Authority cited in pre-1607 legal work*] (DSA)
Pet............. Petrus de Bellapertica [*Deceased, 1308*] [*Authority cited in pre-1607 legal work*] (DSA)
PET............. Phase Elapsed Time (NASA)
PET............. Philco Epoxy Transistor (IAA)
PET............. Photoelectric Transducer (PDAA)
PET............. Photoemission Tube
PET............. Photographic Equipment Technician (SAUS)
PET............. Photoinduced Electron Transfer

PET .... Phototropic Energy Transfer
PET .... Physical Equipment Table
PET .... Pierre Elliott Trudeau [*Canadian prime minister*] [*Acronymic designation considered derogatory*]
PET .... Pilot-Line Experiment Technology (SAUS)
PET .... Plasma Edge Technique (SAUS)
PET .... Plastic Engine Technology (SAUS)
PET .... Point of Equal Time [*Aviation*]
PET .... Polyester
PET .... Polyethylene [*Organic chemistry*] (IAA)
PET .... Poly(ethylene Terephthalate) [*Organic chemistry*]
PET .... Polyethylene Tubing [*Medicine*] (MELL)
PET .... Polyethylenterephtalatester, Polyester (SAUS)
PET .... Portable Earth Terminal [*NASA*]
PET .... Portable Electric Tool, Inc. (SAUS)
PET .... Portable Electronic Telephone
PET .... Portable Electronic Translator
PET .... Portable Executive Telephone (SAUS)
PET .... Position-Event-Time
PET .... Positive-Emission Tomography (SAUS)
PET .... Positron Electron Tomography (SAUS)
PET .... Positron Emission Computed Tomography (SAUS)
PET .... Positron-Emission Tomography
PET .... Post Endurance Test (SAUS)
PET .... Post-Etch Treatment (AAEL)
PET .... Potential-Effect Transistor (SAUS)
PET .... Potential Evapotranspiration
PET .... Potentially Exempt Transfer (ODBW)
PET .... Precision End Trimmed (SAUS)
PET .... Prediction Error Transform (PDAA)
PET .... Pre-Eclamptic Toxemia [*Medicine*]
PET .... Pre-Employment Training (OICC)
PET .... Preliminary Evaluation Team
PET .... Preliminary Examination Team [*NASA*]
PET .... Preprimary Evaluation and Training
PET .... Pressure Equalization [*Tubes or Equalizing*] [*Otorhinolaryngology*] (DAVI)
PET .... Pressurization Events Trainer
PET .... Print Enhancement Technology (VLIE)
PET .... Prisoner's Education Trust (WDAA)
PET .... Privacy Enhancing Technology (VLIE)
PET .... Probe Ephemeris Tape
PET .... Process Evaluation Tester
PET .... Producibility Evaluation Task [*Army*] (RDA)
PET .... Production Environmental Testing
PET .... Production Environmental Tests
PET .... Production Evaluation Test
PET .... Production Experimental Test (SAA)
PET .... Program Evaluation Team
PET .... Program Evaluation Test
PET .... Program Evaluator and Tester [*Computer science*]
PET .... Program Execution Time (VLIE)
PET .... Progressive Educational Technology (SAUS)
PET .... Property Enterprise Trust [*Investment term*] [*British*] (ECON)
PET .... Proposal Evaluation Team (ACAE)
PET .... Propulsion Experimental Test (SAA)
PET .... Prototype Evaluation Test
PET .... Prototype Evaluation Testing (SAUS)
PET .... Psychiatric Emergency Team
PET .... Pulsed Electrothermal (MCD)
PET .... Pupil Evaluation Team [*Education*]
PETA .... Parabolic Expandable Truss Antenna (ACAE)
PETA .... Pentaerythritol Triacrylate [*Organic chemistry*]
PETA .... People for the Ethical Treatment of Animals (EA)
PETA .... Performance Evaluation and Trend Analysis (NASA)
PETA .... Plutonium Equipment Transfer Area [*Nuclear energy*] (NRCH)
PETA .... Portable Electronic Traffic Analyzer [*British*]
Pet Ab ...... Petersdorff's Abridgment [*A publication*] (DLA)
Pet Abr ...... Petersdorff's Abridgment [1660-1823] [*A publication*] (DLA)
Pet Ad .... Peters' United States District Court Reports, Admiralty Decisions [*A publication*] (DLA)
Pet Ad Dec... Peters' United States District Court Reports, Admiralty Decisions [*A publication*] (DLA)
Pet Adm ...... Peters' United States District Court Reports, Admiralty Decisions [*A publication*] (DLA)
Pet Adm App... Peters' United States District Court Reports, Admiralty Decisions (Appendix) [*A publication*] (DLA)
Pet Ad R ..... Peters' United States District Court Reports, Admiralty Decisions [*A publication*] (DLA)
PET & S ...... Performance Evaluation, Test, and Simulation [*Air Force*]
PETANS .... Petroleum Training Association-North Sea (SAUS)
Pet Aret ...... Petrus Aretinus [*Flourished, 1088-91*] [*Authority cited in pre-1607 legal work*] (DSA)
PETAT .... Periodic Inspection Turn-Around Time [*Military*] (AFIT)
PETB .... Preflight Test Bus
Pet Bail ...... Petersdorff on Bail [1824] [*A publication*] (DLA)
Pet Br .... Bellewe's Cases Tempore Henry VIII [*Brooke's New Cases*] [*England*] [*A publication*] (DLA)
Pet Br .... Brooke's New Cases (Petit Brooke) [1515-58] [*A publication*] (DLA)
PETC .... Parent Effectiveness Training Course [*Australia*]
PETC .... Petco Animal Supplies [*NASDAQ symbol*] (SAG)
PETC .... Pet in Cabin [*Travel industry*] (TRID)
PETC .... Pittsburgh Energy Technology Center [*Formerly, PERC*] [*Department of Energy*] [*Pittsburgh, PA*] (GRD)
PETC .... Polyethylene Tetrachloride [*Organic chemistry*] (IAA)

PETC .... Portable Equipment Test Chamber (MCD)
Pet CC .... Peters' United States Circuit Court Reports [*A publication*] (DLA)
Pet Chem ... Petroleum Chemistry (SAUS)
Pet Cir CR ... Peters' Condensed United States Circuit Court Reports [*A publication*] (DLA)
PetcoAn ...... Petco Animal Supplies [*Associated Press*] (SAG)
PETCOCK ...... Proposal Evaluation Technique Conditioned on Contract Kind (SAUS)
PET Computer... Personal Electronic Transaction Computer (SAUS)
Pet Cond...... Peters' Condensed Reports, United States Supreme Court [*A publication*] (DLA)
Pet Cond Rep... Peters' Condensed United States Circuit Court Reports [*A publication*] (DLA)
PETD .... Petroleum Development [*NASDAQ symbol*] (TTSB)
PETD .... Petroleum Development Corp. [*NASDAQ symbol*] (NQ)
Pet de Anch... Petrus de Ancharano [*Deceased, 1416*] [*Authority cited in pre-1607 legal work*] (DSA)
Pet de Bel ... Petrus de Bellapertica [*Deceased, 1308*] [*Authority cited in pre-1607 legal work*] (DSA)
Pet de Bellap... Petrus de Bellapertica [*Deceased, 1308*] [*Authority cited in pre-1607 legal work*] (DSA)
Pet de Belper... Petrus de Bellapertica [*Deceased, 1308*] [*Authority cited in pre-1607 legal work*] (DSA)
Pet de Mont... Petrus Piccoli de Monteforte [*Flourished, 14th century*] [*Authority cited in pre-1607 legal work*] (DSA)
Pet de Sam... Petrus de Sampsone [*Flourished, 1246-58*] [*Authority cited in pre-1607 legal work*] (DSA)
Pet de Samp... Petrus de Sampsone [*Flourished, 1246-58*] [*Authority cited in pre-1607 legal work*] (DSA)
Pet Dig .... Peters' United States Digest [*A publication*] (DLA)
Pet Dig .... Peticolas' Texas Digest [*A publication*] (DLA)
PetDv .... Petroleum Development Corp. [*Associated Press*] (SAG)
PETE .... Parliamentary Education for Teacher Education [*Australia*]
PETE .... Partnership for Environmental Technology Education [*Nonprofit organization of 400 community colleges*]
PETE .... Petersburg National Battlefield
PETE .... Pneumatic End to End
PETE .... Pneumatic End-to-End (SAUS)
PETE .... Portable Educational Tools Environment (AIE)
PETE .... Portable Electronics Test Equipment (DNAB)
PETE .... Portable Emergency Thermal Environment
PETE .... Primary Bank [*NASDAQ symbol*] (SAG)
PETE .... Product Engineering Tribute to Excellence
PETE .... Proof and Experimental Test Establishment [*Canada*] (MCD)
PETEOS .... Plasma-Enhanced Tetraethylosilicate (AAEL)
Peter .... Analysis and Digest of the Decisions of Sir George Jessel, by A. P. Peter [*England*] [*A publication*] (DLA)
Peters .... Haviland's Prince Edward Island Chancery Reports, by Peters [1850-72] [*Canada*] [*A publication*] (DLA)
Peters .... Peters' United States Supreme Court Reports [26-41 United States] [*A publication*] (DLA)
Peters' Ad ... Peters' United States District Court Reports, Admiralty Decisions [*A publication*] (DLA)
Peters Adm... Peters' United States District Courts Reports, Admiralty Decisions [*A publication*] (DLA)
Peters' Adm Dec... Peters' United States District Court Reports, Admiralty Decisions [*A publication*] (DLA)
Peters' Admiralty Dec... Peters' United States District Court Reports, Admiralty Decisions [*A publication*] (DLA)
Peters' Adm R... Peters' United States District Court Reports, Admiralty Decisions [*A publication*] (DLA)
Peters Adm Rep... Peters' United States District Court Reports, Admiralty Decisions [*A publication*] (DLA)
Peters CC .... Peters' United States Circuit Court Reports [*A publication*] (DLA)
Petersd Ab... Petersdorff's Abridgment [*A publication*] (DLA)
Petes .... Petes Brewing Co. [*Associated Press*] (SAG)
PETFE .... Polyethylene-Co-Tetrafluoroethylene (SAUS)
PETFE .... Polyethylenetetrafluoroethylene [*Organic chemistry*]
PETFEM .... Postsecondary Education Task Force on Energy Management [*Canada*]
PetFood ...... Pet Food Warehouse [*Commercial firm*] [*Associated Press*] (SAG)
PETG .... Phenylethyl(thiogalactoside) [*Organic chemistry*]
PETG .... Polyethylene Terephthalate, G Copolymer (SAUS)
PETG .... Polyethylene Terephthalate Glycol (SAUS)
PETG .... Proposal Editing Task Group (SAUS)
Pet Geol ...... Petroleum Geology (SAUS)
Petg Pr & Ag... Petgrave's Principal and Agent [1857] [*A publication*] (DLA)
Pet Greg ...... Petrus Gregorius [*Deceased, 1617*] [*Authority cited in pre-1607 legal work*] (DSA)
PETH .... Pink-Eyed, Tan-Hooded Rat [*Medicine*] (DMAA)
Peth Dis ...... Petheram's Discovery by Interrogations [1864] [*A publication*] (DLA)
PETI .... Percent of Travel Involved (SAUS)
PETI .... Phenyl-Ethynyl Terminated Imide [*Plastics*]
PETI .... Portable Electronic Typewriter Interface [*Applied Creative Technology, Inc.*]
PETIA .... Particle-Enhanced Turbidometric Immunoassay [*Clinical chemistry*]
Pet Intell Wkly... Petroleum Intelligence Weekly (SAUS)
Petit Br .... Petit Brooke, or Brooke's New Cases, English King's Bench [1515-58] [*A publication*] (DLA)
PETITN........ Petition
PETLES .... Peritoneal Exudate T-Lymphocyte-Enriched System (DB)
Pet L Nat ...... Petersdorff's Law of Nations [*A publication*] (DLA)
PETM .... Petsmart, Inc. [*NASDAQ symbol*] (SAG)
PETMA .... Portable Electric Tool Manufacturers' Association [*British*] (BI)
Pet Manage... Petroleum Management (SAUS)
Pet M & S ..... Petersdorff's Master and Servant [1876] [*A publication*] (DLA)

PETMS..........	Phenethyltrimethoxy Silane [*Organic chemistry*]
PETN..........	Pentaerythritol Tetraniconitate [*Niceritrol*] [*Pharmacology*] (DAVI)
PETN..........	Pentaerythritol Tetranitrate [*Also, PET*] [*Explosive, vasodilator*]
PETN..........	Petaerythrite Tetranitrate (NAKS)
PETN..........	Petition
PETNAIS........	Pacific Essential Telecommunications Network and Information System (SAUS)
PETNR..........	Petitioner
PETOS	Perkin Elmer Terminal Operating System (SAUS)
PETP..........	(Phenylethyl)phenyltetrahydropyridine [*Organic chemistry*]
PETP..........	Poly(ethylene Terephthalate) [*Organic chemistry*]
PETP..........	Preliminary Engineering Technical Proposal
Pet Peck Zir...	Petrus Peckius (Ziricaeus) [*Deceased, 1589*] [*Authority cited in pre-1607 legal work*] (DSA)
Pet PM	Petersen's Photographic Magazine [*A publication*] (BRI)
PETPrA........	Pacific Ent $4.36 Pfd [*AMEX symbol*] (TTSB)
PetPrac........	[*The*] Pet Practice, Inc. [*Associated Press*] (SAG)
PETPrB........	Pacific Ent $4.40 Pfd [*AMEX symbol*] (TTSB)
PETPrC........	Pacific Ent $4.50 Pfd [*AMEX symbol*] (TTSB)
PETPrD........	Pacific Ent $4.75 Pfd [*AMEX symbol*] (TTSB)
PetPRO........	Pet Professional Retailers Organization [*Defunct*] (EA)
Pet Pt	Petrol Point (SAUS)
PETQI..........	Patient Education Total Quality Improvement [*Medicine*] (DMAA)
petr..........	Petitioner (GEAB)
PETR..........	Petitioner
Petr..........	Petrification (SAUS)
petr..........	petrified (SAUS)
petr..........	Petrify (SAUS)
PETR..........	PetroCorp [*NASDAQ symbol*] (TTSB)
PETR..........	Petrocorp, Inc. [*NASDAQ symbol*] (SAG)
petr..........	Petroleum [*Chemistry*] (DAVI)
PETR..........	Photo-Electric Tape Reader (SAUS)
PETR..........	Post Environmental Test Review (ACAE)
PETRA.........	Positron-Electron Tandem Ring Accelerator [*Nuclear*]
PETRA	Program for the Vocational Training of Young People and their Preparation for Adult and Working Life [*EC*] (ECED)
PETRA.........	Project for Evaluation and Treatment of Radioactive Waste [*Nuclear energy*] (NUCP)
Petr Bellug...	Petrus Belluga [*Flourished, 1446-68*] [*Authority cited in pre-1607 legal work*] (DSA)
Petr de Benint...	Petrus de Benintendis [*Flourished, 16th century*] [*Authority cited in pre-1607 legal work*] (DSA)
PETREL........	Professional Education and Training for Research Librarianship Program (EDAC)
PETRES........	Petroleum Reserves [*Navy*]
PETRESO	Petroleum Reserves Office [*or Officer*]
petrgly........	Petroglyph (VRA)
Petr Greg.....	Petrus Gregorius [*Deceased, 1617*] [*Authority cited in pre-1607 legal work*] (DSA)
PETRIBURG...	Petriburgensis [*Signature of the Bishops of Peterborough*] [*Latin*] (ROG)
Petrie..........	Petrie Stores Corp. [*Associated Press*] (SAG)
PETRL..........	Petroleum (AABC)
Petrl..........	Petroleum (TBD)
PetrlGeo	Petroleum Geo Services [*Associated Press*] (SAG)
PetrLng.......	Petersburg Long Distance [*Commercial firm*] [*Associated Press*] (SAG)
Petrlte..........	Petrolite Corp. [*Associated Press*] (SAG)
Petrmn........	Petrominerals Corp. [*Associated Press*] (SAG)
Petr Nuni.....	Petrus Nunius de Avendano [*Flourished, 16th century*] [*Authority cited in pre-1607 legal work*] (DSA)
Petro..........	Petrochemical (SAUS)
PETRO	Petroleum
PetroC........	Petro-Canada [*Associated Press*] (SAG)
PetroC2........	Petro-Canada [*Associated Press*] (SAG)
PETROCH.....	Rock Chemical Database [*Ontario Geological Survey*] [*Canada*] [*Information service or system*] (CRD)
petro-chem...	petroleum-chemical (SAUS)
Petrocp........	Petrocorp, Inc. [*Associated Press*] (SAG)
PETRODEG...	Petroleum Degrading [*Agent*]
Petrodollars...	Petroleum-controlled Dollars (SAUS)
PETRO ENG...	Petroleum Engineering (SAUS)
PETROEX......	Petroleum Products Exchange Data Clearing House (NITA)
Petrog..........	Petrographer (SAUS)
PETROG.......	Petrographic
PETROGAL...	Petroleos de Portugal, EP [*Portuguese Petroleum Co.*]
PETROGR ...	Petrography
PETROL	Petroleum
PETROL	Petrology
PETROL RAM...	Petroleum Resource Automated Management (SAUS)
PETROMIN...	General Petroleum & Mineral Organization [*Saudi Arabia state-owned oil company*]
PETROMIN...	General Petroleum and Minerals Organization (SAUS)
Petromt........	Petromet Resouces Ltd. [*Associated Press*] (SAG)
Petron........	Petronius [*First century AD*] [*Classical studies*] (OCD)
PETRONET ...	Petroleum Network [*Distribution and interdiction model*] (MCD)
Petron Satyric...	Petronius' [*Titus*] Arbiter, Satyricon, Etc. [*A publication*] (DLA)
PETROPHIL...	Petroleum Philatelic Society International (EAIO)
PETROPOL...	Petropolis [*St. Petersburg*] [*Imprint*] [*Latin*] (ROG)
PetroUn	Petro Union, Inc. [*Associated Press*] (SAG)
Petr Rave	Petrus Ravennas [*Flourished, 1468-1508*] [*Authority cited in pre-1607 legal work*] (DSA)
PetRs..........	Petroleum & Resources Corp. [*Associated Press*] (SAG)
PETS..........	Pacific Electronics Trade Show
PETS..........	Parameterised Executable Test Suite (SAUS)

PETS..........	Parameterized Executable Test Suite (VLIE)
PETS..........	Payload Environmental Transportation System [*NASA*] (NASA)
PETS..........	Peripheral Equipment Test Set
PETS..........	Photographic Equipment Test System (ACAE)
PETS..........	Plastic Education and Troubleshooting System (SAUS)
PETS..........	P/L Experiment Test System [*NASA*] (GFGA)
PETS..........	POCC [*Payload Operations Control Center*] Experiments Timeline System [*Ground Data Systems Division and Spacelab*] [*NASA*] (NASA)
PETS..........	Polaris Engineering Technical Service [*Missiles*]
PETS..........	Portable Engine Test Stand (MCD)
PETS..........	Positions Equipment Task Summary (AAG)
PETS..........	Posting and Enquiry Terminal System (SAUS)
PETS..........	Pre-Eclampsia Society [*British*] (NRGU)
PETS..........	Prior to Expiration of Term of Service [*Reenlistments*] [*Military*]
PETS..........	Procedures for Evaluating Technical Specifications Program (COE)
PETS..........	Programmed Extended Time Sharing [*Computer science*]
PETS..........	Property and Evidence Tracking System (SEWL)
PETS..........	Proximity Effect Tunneling Spectroscopy (MCD)
Pet SC	Peters' United States Supreme Court Reports [*26-41 United States*] [*A publication*] (DLA)
PET scan	Positron Emission Transaxial Tomography [*Also, PETT*] (PAZ)
PETSEC.......	Petroleum Section [*Allied Force Headquarters*]
PetsMrt.......	Petsmart, Inc. [*Associated Press*] (SAG)
PET/SPECT...	Positron-Emission Tomography/Single Photon-Emission-Computed Tomography (SAUS)
Pet Sta	Petrol Station (SAUS)
Pet Suppl.....	Supplement to Petersdorff's Abridgment [*A publication*] (DLA)
PETT..........	Pendular Eye-Tracking Test [*Medicine*] (DMAA)
PETT..........	Phototropic Energy Transfer Technique
PETT..........	Portable Ethernet Transceiver Tester (SAUS)
PETT..........	Positron Emission Transaxial [*or Transverse*] Tomography [*Roentgenography*]
PETT..........	Project Engineering and Technology for Tomorrow (SAUS)
PETT..........	Purkinje Fiber [*Medicine*] (DMAA)
PETT..........	Purpura Fulminans [*Medicine*] (DMAA)
PETT..........	Push Fluids [*Medicine*] (DMAA)
PETV..........	Planar Epitaxial Tuning Varactor
PETV..........	Process Evaluation Test Vehicle
PEU..........	Paneuropa-Union [*Paneuropean Union*] (EAIO)
PEU..........	Plasma Equivalent Unit [*Medicine*] (DMAA)
PEU..........	Polyether Urethane (STED)
PEU..........	Port Expander Unit
PEU..........	Protected Environment Unit [*Medicine*]
PEUA..........	Pelvic Exam under Anesthesia [*Medicine*]
PEURX........	Pioneer Europe Cl.A [*Mutual fund ticker symbol*] (SG)
PEUU..........	Polyether Polyurethane Urea [*Organic chemistry*]
PeV..........	Parameter Equals Value (SAUS)
pev..........	Peak Electron Volt (STED)
PEV..........	Peak Envelope Voltage [*Telecommunications*] (TEL)
PEV..........	Peak Expiratory Velocity [*Medicine*] (DMAA)
PeV..........	Peripheral Vein [*Medicine*] (STED)
PEV..........	Permanent Entry Visa
PEV..........	Perpetual Electric Vehicle [*Hybrid vehicles*]
PeV..........	Petaelectron Volt (SAUS)
PEV..........	Philip Environmental [*NYSE symbol*] (SAG)
PEV..........	Pleasant Valley [*California*] [*Seismograph station code, US Geological Survey*] (SEIS)
PEV..........	Position-Effect Variegation [*Genetics*] [*Botany*]
PEV..........	Positive Expected Value
PEV..........	Pressure Equalization Valves (SAUS)
PEV..........	Propeller-Excited Vibration (PDAA)
PEV..........	Pulmonary Extravascular Fluid Volume [*Medicine*] (STED)
PEV..........	Pyroelectric Vidicon (PDAA)
PEVCV........	Petunia Vein Clearing Virus [*Plant pathology*]
PEVE..........	Post Experience Vocational Education (AIE)
PEVE..........	Prensa Venezolana [*Press agency*] [*Venezuela*]
PEVI..........	Perry's Victory and International Peace Memorial National Monument
PEVL..........	Polyethylene Expanded Video Longitudinal Cable (MCD)
PEVM..........	Personal'naia Elektronnaia Vychislitel'naia Mashina [*Personal Computer*] [*Russian*]
PEVM.....	Professional'naia Elektronnaia Vychislitel'naia Mashina [*Professional Computer*] [*Russian*]
PEVN..........	Periventricular Nucleus (STED)
PEVR	Power-Enrichment Vacuum Regulator [*Automotive engineering*]
PEW..........	Passive Electronics Warfare (NG)
PEW..........	Percussion Welding
PEW..........	Peshawar [*Pakistan*] [*Airport symbol*] (OAG)
pew..........	Pewter (VRA)
PEW..........	Pulmonary Extravascular Water [*Medicine*] (DMAA)
PEWD..........	Platoon Early Warning Device [*Military*] (SEWL)
PEWO	Plant Engineering Work Order (MCD)
PEWR	Plant Engineering Work Release (AAG)
PEWS..........	Parts Early Warning System (IAA)
PEWS..........	Platoon Early Warning System (RDA)
PEWS..........	Plutonium Equipment Warm Shop [*Nuclear energy*] (NRCH)
PEWS..........	Preliminary Early Warning System (SAUS)
PEWS..........	Professional Engineering Workstation (TIMI)
PEWSS..........	Portable Electronic Warfare Signal Simulator [*Military*] (SEWL)
PEWSX........	PEWS Q-D Subsystem (SAUS)
PEWV..........	Pulmonary Extravascular Water Volume [*Physiology*]
Pex..........	Peak Exercise (DMAA)
PEX..........	Per Example
PEX..........	PetroCorp, Inc. [*AMEX symbol*] (SG)
PEX..........	Phenazine Ethosulfate [*Biochemistry*]

PEx	Physical Examination (MAE)
PEX	Pituitary Extract (SAUS)
PEX	Private Electronic Exchange [Telecommunications] (IAA)
PEX	Projectable Excitation (SAUS)
PEX	Pronto Explorations Ltd. [Vancouver Stock Exchange symbol]
PEX	Pseudoexfoliation (SAUS)
PEX	World Aircraft Flight Operation, Inc. [ICAO designator] (FAAC)
PEXA	Pre-Edge X-Ray Absorption [For study of solids]
PEXAFS	Photoelectron Extended X-Ray Absorption Fine Structure
PEXRA	Programmed Electronic X-Ray Automatic Diffractometer (IAA)
PEXRAD	Programmed Electronic X-Ray Automatic Diffractometer
PEX-SI	PEX-Sample Implementation (SAUS)
PEY	Pengelly Mines Ltd. [Vancouver Stock Exchange symbol]
PEY	Photoelectric Yield
PEYS	Photoelectron Yield Spectroscopy (MCD)
PEZ	Pezgold Resource Corp. [Vancouver Stock Exchange symbol]
PEZ	Pleasanton, TX [Location identifier] [FAA] (FAAL)
PEZV	Prime Equities International [NASDAQ symbol] (SAG)
PEZVF	Prime Equities Intl [NASDAQ symbol] (TTSB)
PF	Amer First Prep Fd 2 L.P. [AMEX symbol] (TTSB)
PF	American First PREP [Preferred Real Estate Participation] Fund 2 Ltd. [AMEX symbol] (SPSG)
PF	Frankford Public Library, Frankford, PA [Library symbol] [Library of Congress] (LCLS)
PF	French Polynesia [ANSI two-letter standard code] (CNC)
PF	frigate-patrol escort vessel (SAUS)
PF	L-Phenylalanine Mustard and 5-Fluorouracil [Antineoplastic drug regimen] (DAVI)
PF	Pacemaker Failure (MELL)
PF	Pacifica Foundation (EA)
PF	Package Freighter [Shipping]
PF	Packaging Facility (SAUS)
PF	Packing Factor (EECA)
PF	Packing Fraction (EECA)
PF	Paderewski Foundation [Defunct] (EA)
PF	Page Fault (IAA)
PF	Page Footing (BUR)
PF	Page Formatter (MDG)
PF	Pair Feeding (DMAA)
PF	Paling Fence
PF	Panchromatic Film (ADA)
PF	Paper and Foil [Capacitor] (DEN)
pf	Paracel Islands [MARC country of publication code] [Library of Congress] (LCCP)
PF	Parachute Facility (NASA)
PF	Parachute Flare (NVT)
PF	Parafascicular Nucleus [Neuroanatomy]
PF	Parallel Feed (ELAL)
PF	Parallel Fiber [Neuroanatomy]
PF	Parallel Fold
PF	Paramount Funding Corp. [Toronto Stock Exchange symbol]
PF	Parapsychology Foundation (EA)
PF	Parity Flag (SAUS)
PF	Park Factor (SAUS)
PF	Partial Function (IAA)
PF	Partition Factor (NRCH)
PF	Passage Free (ROG)
P/F	Pass-Fail [System] (MAE)
PF	Patellofemoral Joint [Anatomy] (DAVI)
PF	Path Finder [British military] (DMA)
PF	Pathfinder Fund (EA)
PF	Patriotic Front [Zimbabwe] [Political party] (PPW)
PF	Patrol Vessel, Frigate [Navy symbol]
P/F	Pattern Flight [Also, P/FLT] (MUGU)
PF	Paved Flume (COE)
PF	Payload Forward [NASA] (MCD)
PF	Payload Function [NASA] (MCD)
PF	Payload operational instrumentation MDM-FWD (SAUS)
PF	Peace and Freedom Party [Political party] (DLA)
PF	Peak Flow [Medicine]
PF	Peak Frequency
PF	Peanut Flour
PF	Pedal Furrow
PF	Penetration Fracture (IAA)
PF	Pen Fanciers (EA)
PF	Pen Friends [Defunct] (EA)
PF	Pension Fund
PF	Perchloryl Fluoride (SAUS)
PF	Peregrine Fund (EA)
pf	Perfect (WDAA)
PF	Perfect
PF	Perfect Fluid (SAUS)
PF	Performance Factor
PF	Perfusion Fixation [Histology]
PF	Perfusion Fluid [Medicine] (DMAA)
PF	Pericardial Fluid [Medicine] (DMAA)
PF	Peritoneal Fluid [Medicine] (MAE)
PF	Permanent Fireman
PF	Permanent Force [Canadian Militia before 1940]
PF	Permeability Factor
pf	Perofskite [CIPW classification] [Geology]
PF	Personal Finance (SAUS)
PF	Personal Fouls [Basketball]
PF	Personality Factor
PF	Personal Security File Number [British Secret Service]
Pf	Pfeifferella [Genus of bacteria]
PF	Pfennig [Penny] [Monetary unit] [German]
PF	Phenol-Formaldehyde [Organic chemistry]
PF	Phenylalanine and Methotrexate [Antineoplastic drug regimen] (DAVI)
PF	Philatelic Foundation (EA)
PF	Photofluorography (SAUS)
PF	Photogrammetric Facility [Army]
PF	Photon Factory
PF	Physical File (SAUS)
PF	Physicians Forum (EA)
pf	Pianoforte (WDAA)
PF	Pianoforte [Soft, then Loud] [Music]
PF	Pico Farad (ACAE)
PF	Picofarad
pF	Picofarad
PF	Picture Frequency (SAUS)
PF	Picture Frustration [Study] (MAE)
PF	Piedmont Fracture (MELL)
PF	Piled Fathom (SAUS)
PF	Pilgrim Fellowship (EA)
PF	Pilot Flying (GAVI)
PF	Pilot Stop Filter (IAA)
PF	Pininfarina [Automotive coachworks]
PF	[The] Pioneer & Fayette Railroad Co. [AAR code]
PF	Pipkin Fracture (MELL)
PF	Pistonfon (SAUS)
PF	Piu Forte [A Little Louder] [Music]
PF	Plain Face [Construction]
PF	Plane Frame [Camutek] [Software package] (NCC)
PF	Planning Forum (EA)
PF	Plantar Fasciaitis [Medicine]
PF	Plantar Flexion [Medicine]
PF	Plasma Factor (DMAA)
PF	Plasticity Index [Soil] (DICI)
PF	Platelet Factor [Hematology]
PF	Platform (SSD)
PF	Plentiful Foods [Department of Agriculture] [A publication]
PF	Pleural Fluid [Medicine] (DB)
PF	Plot Function [Computer science]
PF	Plug-Flow Transport (SAUS)
PF	Pneumatic Float
PF	Poco Forte [Rather Loud] [Music]
PF	Poe Foundation (EA)
PF	Point Foundation (EA)
PF	Point of Frog [Electronics] (MSA)
PF	Points For [Football]
PF	Polar Front [Climatology]
PF	Polarization Fraction (SAUS)
PF	Polarizing Filter (SAUS)
PF	Pole Figure (SAUS)
PF	Pole Fittings [JETDS nomenclature] [Military] (CET)
PF	Police Forces [British]
PF	Police Foundation (EA)
PF	POLISARIO [Frente Popular para la Liberacion de Saguia El Hamra y Rio De Oro] [Popular Front for the Liberation of Saguia El Hamra and Rio De Oro] [Morocco] (PD)
P/F	Poll/Final [Computer science] (TNIG)
PF	Poloidal Field (MCD)
PF	Polycenter Framework (SAUS)
PF	Polyurethane Foam
PF	Pool Frequency [Pisciculture]
PF	Poop and Forecastle [of a ship] (DS)
PF	Poor Foam
PF	Popular Forces [South Vietnam]
PF	Pore Free (IAA)
PF	Por Favor [Please] [Portuguese]
PF	Portal Fibrosis [Medicine]
PF	Portfolio [A publication]
PF	Position Failure
PF	Position Finder [British military] (DMA)
PF	Postage Free (ROG)
PF	Posterior Fontanelle [Anatomy] (DAVI)
P/F	Post Flight (AFIT)
PF	Postman's Federation [A union] [British]
PF	Posture Foundation [Initialism is used in brand of sneaker shoe, PF Flyers]
PF	Potency Factor (GNE)
PF	Potential Flow (SAUS)
PF	Pott's Fracture [Medicine] (MELL)
PF	Powered Flight (NASA)
pf	Power Factor (IDOE)
PF	Power Factor [Radio]
PF	Power Focus [Photography]
PF	Power Frame [Telecommunications] (TEL)
PF	Power Frequency (SAUS)
P/F	Practical Factors
PF	Precursor Fluid [Medicine] (MEDA)
PF	Pred Forte (SAUS)
PF	Preference
PF	Preferred
PF	Prefetch [Computer science]
P/F	Pre-Flight
PF	Preflight
PF	Preformed Fragment (SAUS)
PF	Presbyterian Foundation [Australia]

PF	Pressure Fan (AAG)
PF	Preterm Foundation [*Australia*]
PF	Primary Fibrinolysin [*Medicine*] (DMAA)
PF	Primary File (SAUS)
PF	Primary Filter [*Automotive engineering*]
PF	Prime Function (NASA)
PF	Principles of Flight (SAUS)
PF	Prison Fellowship Ministries (EA)
PF	Private File (SAUS)
PF	Probability Factor (SAUS)
PF	Probability of Failure (NASA)
PF	Probability of Fool (ACAE)
PF	Probability of Fratricide (ACAE)
PF	Procurator Fiscal
PF	Pro Female [*International Bowhunting Organization*] [*Class Equipment*]
PF	Profile (KSC)
pf	profiled (SAUS)
Pf	Pro Forma (EBF)
pf	Pro Forma [*As a Matter of Form*] [*Latin*] (WGA)
PF	Program Function [*Computer science*] (IBMDP)
PF	Programmable Format [*Perforating keyboard*]
PF	Programmable Function (NITA)
PF	Programmed Function (SAUS)
PF	Programming Fault (SAUS)
PF	Progressive Foundation (EA)
PF	Project Friend (EA)
PF	Projectile Fragment
PF	Proof
PF	Prop Forward
PF	Proposed Finding [*Nuclear energy*] (NRCH)
PF	Prostatic Fluid [*Medicine*] (DMAA)
PF	Prostatitis Foundation (SAUS)
PF	Protection Factor
PF	Protein Factor (SAUS)
PF	Protein-Free
PF	Protoflight (ACAE)
PF	Protoplasmic Fracture [*Freeze etching in microscopy*]
PF	Proximity Fuze [*Bomb, rocket, or shell*]
PF	PsychoHistory Forum (EA)
PF	Psynetics Foundation (EA)
P/F	Pteropod/Foraminifera [*Ratio in coastal waters*]
PF	Public Funding [*Finance*] (WDAA)
PF	Pulmonary Blood-Flow [*Medicine*] (DB)
PF	Pulmonary Factor [*Medicine*]
PF	Pulmonary Function [*Medicine*] (DMAA)
PF	Pulse Feedback [*Telecommunications*] (IAA)
PF	Pulse Frequency
PF	Pulverized Fuel
P F	Pump-Out Facilities [*Nautical charts*]
PF	Punch Feed (SAUS)
PF	Punch Off [*Computer science*] (BUR)
PF	Purge Fan [*Nuclear energy*] (NRCH)
PF	Purkinje Fibers [*Cardiology*] (DAVI)
PF	Purple Finch [*Ornithology*]
PF	Purpura Fulminans (DB)
PF	Pygmy Fund (EA)
PF	Pyrolysis Fluorescence (SAUS)
PF	Trans Pennsylvania Airlines [*ICAO designator*] (AD)
PF3a	Platelet Factor 3 Availability [*Hematology*] (DAVI)
PFA	Alliance Forest Prod [*NYSE symbol*] (SG)
PFA	Pacific Football Alliance (PSS)
PFA	Palmdale Final Assembly [*NASA*] (NASA)
PFA	Panarcadian Federation of America (EA)
PFA	Papermakers Felt Association (EA)
PFA	Para-Fluorophenylalanine [*Biochemistry*]
PFA	Parallel Full Adder (SAUS)
PFA	Parameter Field Address (SAUS)
PFA	Parametric Ferrite Amplifier (SAUS)
PFA	Participating Field Activity [*DoD*]
PFA	Parti de la Federation Africaine [*African Federation Party*] [*Political party*]
PFA	Peachtree First Accounting (SAUS)
PFA	Pedorthic Footwear Association (NTPA)
PFA	Pellet-Fired Appliance [*Heating system*]
PFA	Pension Fund Association [*Japan*] (ECON)
PFA	Perfluoroalkoxy [*Organic chemistry*]
PFA	Personal Fall Arrest [*Safety systems*]
PFA	Personnel Functional Assessment [*Of the Army Acquisition Corps*] (RDA)
PFA	Pesticide Formulators Association (SAUS)
PFA	Petroflame International [*Vancouver Stock Exchange symbol*]
PFA	Phosphofructoaldolase
PFA	Phosphonoformic Acid [*Antiviral compound*]
PFA	Phosphor-Fruct-Aldolase (SAUS)
PFA	Pianists Foundation of America [*Defunct*] (EA)
PFA	Pierce Ferry [*Arizona*] [*Seismograph station code, US Geological Survey*] [*Closed*] (SEIS)
PFA	Pierre Fauchard Academy (EA)
PFA	Pioneer Fraternal Association (EA)
PFA	Pitch Follow-Up Amplifier
PFA	Plan for Action (MCD)
PFA	Plant Functional Attributes (SAUS)
PFA	Polish Falcons of America (EA)
PFA	Polyfluoroalkoxy (SAUS)

PFA	Polyformaldehyde (SAUS)
PFA	Polyfurfuryl Alcohol [*Organic chemistry*]
PFA	Polymeric Fatty Acid [*Food science*]
PFA	Polyurethane Foam Association (EA)
PFA	Pontius Family Association (EA)
PFA	Popular Flying Association [*British*]
PFA	Post Flight Analysis
PFA	Post-Flight Annex (SAUS)
PFA	Power Fastenings Association [*British*] (DBA)
PFA	Predictive Failure Analysis (SAUS)
PFA	Prescription Footwear Association (EA)
PFA	Presidential Families of America (EA)
PFA	Prevention of Food Adulteration (SAUS)
PFA	Principal Financial Analyst (SAUS)
PFA	Prison Families Anonymous (EA)
PFA	Prison Fellowship of Australia
PFA	Private Fliers Association (SAUS)
PFA	Probability of False Alarm [*Department of Defense*]
PFA	Product and Field Activity (SAUS)
PFA	Production Flow Analysis (PDAA)
PFA	Professional Farmers of America (EA)
PFA	Professional Fishermen's Association [*Tasmania, Australia*]
PFA	Professional Footballers' Association [*British*] (BI)
PFA	Professional Fraternity Association (EA)
PFA	Profunda Femoris Artery [*Anatomy*] (DAVI)
PFA	Program and File Analysis
PFA	Proportional Fluid Amplifier
PFA	Provincial Forestry Administration (SAUS)
PFA	Psychologic Flight Avoidance (SAUS)
PFA	Pulverized Fuel Ash (IEEE)
PFA	Pure Fluid Amplification
PFA	Pure Food Act (SAUS)
PFAA	Phelps Family Association of America (EA)
PFAA	Prairie Farm Assistance Act
PFAB	Prefabricated
PFAC	Panepirotic Federation of America and Canada [*Later, PFACA*] (EA)
PFAC	People for a Change (EA)
PFACA	Panepirotic Federation of America, Canada, and Australia (EA)
P/FACCTL	Pad Facility Controls [*Aerospace*] (AAG)
PFACP	Pro-Fac Cooperative, Inc. [*NASDAQ symbol*] (SAG)
PFACP	Pro-Fac Co-op 'A' Pfd [*NASDAQ symbol*] (TTSB)
P Factor	Preservation Factor (SAUS)
PFAD	Palm Fatty Acid Distillate [*Organic chemistry*]
PFADS	Physical Operators Foreign Area Data System
PFAE	Perfluoroalkyl Ether [*Organic chemistry*]
PFAG	Pulse Field Alternating Gradient (SAUS)
PFAM	Programmed Frequency Amplitude Modulation
PFANZ	Police Federation of Australia and New Zealand
PFAP	Poly(fluoroalkoxyphosphazene) [*Organic chemistry*]
PFAPC	Psychological Factor Affecting Physical Condition (SAUS)
PFAR	Popular Front for Armed Resistance [*Pakistan*]
PFAR	Power Fail Automatic Restart [*Computer science*]
PFAR	Preliminary Failure Analysis Report [*NASA*] (KSC)
PFA Rules	Prevention of Food Adulteration Rules (SAUS)
PFAS	Performic Acid-Schiff Reaction [*Medicine*] (MAE)
PFAS	Planar Flank Array Sonar (SAUS)
PFAS	President of the Faculty of Architects and Surveyors [*British*] (DBQ)
PFASC	PATRIOT [*Phased Array Tracking to Intercept Target*] Field Army Suppor t Center [*Army*]
PFAT	Pre-First Article Test
PFAT	Pre-Flight Acceptance Test (SAUS)
PFAT	Preliminary Flight Appraisal Test (MCD)
PFAT	Private Forestry Association of Tasmania [*Australia*]
PFATS	Professional Football Athletic Trainers Society (NTPA)
PFAVC	Pacific Fleet Audio-Visual Command (DNAB)
PFAW	People for the American Way (EA)
PFAWA	Parents and Friends Association of Western Australia
PFAWA	Poultry Farmers' Association of Western Australia
PFB	Parallel Filter Bank (CIST)
PFB	Partei Freier Buerger [*Free Citizens' Party*] [*Germany*] [*Political party*] (PPW)
PFB	Passo Fundo [*Brazil*] [*Airport symbol*] (OAG)
PFB	Patellofemoral Knee Brace [*Medicine*]
PFB	Payload Feedback [*NASA*] (MCD)
PFB	Payload Forward Bus [*NASA*] (MCD)
PFB	Pentafluorobenzyl [*Organic radical*]
PFB	Pentafluorobenzyl Bromide [*Organic chemistry*]
PFB	Photo Flash Battery
PFB	Plasti-Fab Ltd. [*Toronto Stock Exchange symbol*]
PFB	Pneumatic Float Bridge
PFB	Position Feedback (MCD)
PFB	Postscript Font Binary (SAUS)
PFB	Prefabricated [*Technical drawings*]
PFB	Prefetch Buffer (CIST)
PFB	Preformed Beams [*SONAR*]
PFB	Pressure Fed Booster (NASA)
PFB	Pressurized Fluid-Bed [*Chemical engineering*]
PFB	Printer Font Binary [*Computer science*] (CDE)
PFB	Provincial Food Bureau (SAUS)
PFB	Provisional Frequency Board [*ITU*]
PFB	Pseudofolliculitis Barbae [*Medicine*]
PFBA	Poly(perfluorobutyl Acrylate) [*Organic chemistry*]
PFBC	Pentaflurobenzoyl Chloride [*Organic chemistry*]
PFBC	Pressurized Fluidized-Bed Combustion
PFBCA	Pennsylvania Farm Bureau Cooperative Association (SAUS)

PFBHA .... Pentafluorobenzylhydroxylamine Hydrochloride [*Analytical biochemistry*]
PFBI .... Premier Financial Bancorp, Inc. [*NASDAQ symbol*] (SAG)
PFBI .... Premier Finl Bancorp [*NASDAQ symbol*] (TTSB)
P/F Bit .... Poll/Final Bit (SAUS)
PFBMF .... Polaris Fleet Ballistic Missile Force (SAUS)
PFBR .... Plutonium Fast Breeder Reactor (SAUS)
PFBR .... Prototype Fast Breeder Reactor (SAUS)
PFBRG .... Pneumatic Float Bridge
PFBT .... Performance Functional Board Tester (SAUS)
PFBV .... Pelargonium Flower Break Virus [*Plant pathology*]
PFC .... Pacific City, OR [*Location identifier*] [*FAA*] (FAAL)
PFC .... Pacific Forestry Center (SAUS)
PFC .... Pack Feed and Converter (SAUS)
PFC .... Panama Ferrying Command (SAUS)
PFC .... Paper Format Control (SAUS)
PFC .... Parallel-Flow Condenser [*Air conditioning systems*]
PFC .... Parapet Foxhole Cover (SAUS)
PFC .... Parti Feministe du Canada
PFC .... Partnerships for Change (SAUS)
PFC .... Passed Flying College [*British*]
PFC .... Passenger Facility Charge [*Airports*]
PFC .... Patellofemoral Chondrosis [*Medicine*] (MELL)
PFC .... Pathfinder Industries Ltd. [*Formerly, Pathfinder Financial Corporation*] [*Toronto Stock Exchange symbol*]
PFC .... Patient Focused Care [*Medicine*]
PFC .... Peak Follower Circuit
PFC .... Peculiar Facility Change (AAG)
PFC .... Pelvic Flexion Contracture [*Orthopedics*] (DAVI)
PFC .... Pen Fancier's Club (EA)
PFC .... Pennsylvania Public Library Film Center, University Park, PA [*OCLC symbol*] (OCLC)
PFC .... Perfluorocarbon [*Organic chemistry*]
PFC .... Perfluorochemical [*Organic chemistry*]
PFC .... Perfluorocompound (AAEL)
PFC .... Performance Flight Certification [*NASA*] (NASA)
PFC .... Permanent Families for Children [*Defunct*] (EA)
PFC .... Persistent Fetal Circulation [*Medicine*]
PFC .... Personal Finance Center [*Information service or system*]
PFC .... Phase Frequency Characteristics (SAUS)
PFC .... Phenylacetamidotrifluoromethylcoumarin (SAUS)
PFC .... Photofinish Camera (SAUS)
PFC .... Physicians for Choice (EA)
PFC .... Planar Flow Casting (SAUS)
PFC .... Plan Filing Cabinet
PFC .... Plaque-Forming Cell [*Immunochemistry*]
PFC .... Plow-Furrow-Cover [*Waste*] (DICI)
PFC .... Pneumatic Function Controller
PFC .... Point Focusing and Centering [*Optics*]
PFC .... Police Forces [*British*]
PFC .... Portable Four Channel (SAUS)
PFC .... Port Flow Control (SAUS)
PFC .... Positive Feedback Circuit
PFC .... Postflight Checklist (MCD)
PFC .... Postflight Checkout (SAUS)
PFC .... Power Factor Capacitor [*Radio*] (IAA)
PFC .... Power Factor Compensation (SAUS)
PFC .... Power Factor Controller (SAUS)
PFC .... Power Factor Correction
PFC .... Prairie Fiction Collection, Alberta Culture [*UTLAS symbol*]
PFC .... Praying for Corporal [*Private First Class desirous of promotion, or female in wartime desirous of a boyfriend*]
PFC .... Preflight Certification (SAUS)
PFC .... Preflight Console (MCD)
PFC .... Prefrontal Cortex [*Anatomy*]
PFC .... Preliminary Flight Certification [*NASA*]
PFC .... Presley-ites Fan Club (EA)
PFC .... Press-Fit Component (MELL)
PFC .... Pressure Function Controller
PFC .... Primary Flight Control
PFC .... Priority Foreign Country [*International trade*] (ECON)
Pfc .... Private First Class [*Military*] (NTIO)
PFC .... Private, First Class [*Army*]
PFC .... Private Forestry Council [*Australia*]
PFC .... Privately Financed Consumption (MHDW)
PFC .... Processing Figure Channel [*Electronics*] (ECII)
PFC .... Professional Fee Costing (SAUS)
PFC .... Programmed Fuel Computer [*Automotive engineering*]
PFC .... Progreso y Futuro de Ceuta [*Political party*] (EY)
PFC .... Progressive Fish Culturist (SAUS)
PFC .... Protocol Field Compression (SAUS)
PFC .... Pulsed Flame Combustor
PFC .... Pulse-Flow Coulometry
PFC .... Pusan Fisheries College (SAUS)
PFCA .... Performance Ford Club of America (EA)
PFCA .... Plastic Food Container Association [*Defunct*]
PFCB .... Page Frame Control Block (SAUS)
PFCC .... Power Factor Corrector Capacitor [*Radio*] (IAA)
PFCCG .... Pacific Fleet Combat Camera Group (DNAB)
PFCCT .... Pennsylvania Federation of Community College Trustees (SAUS)
PFCD .... Primary Flight Control Display
PFCDA .... Photographers & Friends United Against AIDS-Canadian Chapter (SAUS)
PFCE .... Performance (WGA)
PFCE .... Preface (ROG)
PFCE .... Preference (AAG)
PFCF .... Payload Flight Control Facility [*NASA*] (MCD)
PFCF .... Producer Fixed Capital Formation (MCD)
PFCG .... Pulse Field Constant Gradient (SAUS)
PFCH .... Prefilled Clutch Hydraulic Actuation [*Automotive Products, Inc.*] [*Automotive engineering*]
PFCM .... Pittsburgh Festival of Contemporary Music [*Record label*]
PFCO .... Position Field Classification Officer
PFCO .... Principal Fire Control Officer (WDAA)
PFCP .... Primary Familial and Congenital Polycythemia [*Medicine*]
PFCR .... Plaque-Forming Cell Response [*Immunochemistry*] (OA)
PFCRA .... Program Fraud Civil Remedies Act
PFCRN .... Partido del Frente Cardenista de Reconstruccion Nacional [*Mexico*] [*Political party*] (EY)
PFCS .... Primary Flight Control System [*NASA*] (MCD)
PFCS .... Primary Flow Control System [*Nuclear energy*] (NRCH)
PFCS .... Process Floor Control System (TIMI)
PFCS .... Program and Funds Control System (MCD)
PFCS .... Public Facsimile Communication System (SAUS)
PFCT .... Pre-Flight Certification Test
PFCU .... Parallel File Control Unit (SAUS)
PFCU .... Power Flying Control Unit [*Aviation*] (DA)
PFCV .... Patriotic Funds Council of Victoria [*Australia*]
PFCWKS .... Pogo Fan Club and Walt Kelly Society (EA)
PFCWTS .... Pogo Fan Club and Walt Kelly Society (EA)
PFD .... Paraffined (SAUS)
PFD .... Particle [*or Proton*] Flux Density
PFD .... Particle Flux Detector (ACAE)
PFD .... Partnership for Democracy [*An association*] (EA)
PFD .... Perfluorodecalin [*Organic chemistry*]
PFD .... Personal, Fatigue, and Delay [*Work measurement factors*]
PFD .... Personal Flotation Device [*Life jacket*]
PFD .... Phase Frequency Distortion [*Telecommunications*] (IAA)
PFD .... Planned Flight Data [*Aviation*] (DA)
PFD .... Planning Factors Development (MCD)
PFD .... Policy Formulation Division (AAGC)
PFD .... Polyostotic Fibrous Dysplasia [*Medicine*] (DMAA)
PFD .... Position Fixing Device (ADA)
PFD .... Power Flux Density [*Telecommunications*] (TEL)
PFD .... Preferred (AAG)
pfd .... Preferred (ELAL)
Pfd .... Preferred (SG)
pfd .... Preferred
PFD .... Preferred Income Fund [*NYSE symbol*] (SPSG)
PFD .... Preferred Stock [*Investment term*] (DFIT)
PFD .... Preliminary Functional Description (CINC)
PFD .... Present for Duty
PFD .... Primary Flash Distillate [*Chemical technology*]
PFD .... Primary Flight Display
PFD .... Probability of Error/Fault Detection (SAUS)
PFD .... Probability of Failure on Demand (ACII)
PFD .... Process Flow Diagram (NRCH)
PFD .... Programming Facility for Display users (SAUS)
PFD .... Proton Flux Density (SAUS)
PFD .... Proximity Fuze Disconnector (SAUS)
PFD .... Pseudoinflammatory Fundus Disease [*Medicine*] (DMAA)
PFD .... Puffed [*Freight*]
PFD .... Pulse-Frequency Diversity [*Electronics*] (NG)
PFDA .... Perfluorodecanoic Acid [*Organic chemistry*]
PFDA .... Post Flight Data Analysis
PFDA .... Precision Frequency Distribution Amplifier
PFDA .... Pulse-Frequency Distortion Analyzer
PFDA .... Pure Food and Drug Administration (SAUS)
PFDAR .... Post-Flight Data Analysis Review (SAUS)
PFDBAD .... Pathfinder Badge [*Military decoration*] (GFGA)
PFDC .... Peoples Bancorp (Dekalb County) [*NASDAQ symbol*] (SAG)
PFDC .... Peoples Bancorp(IN) [*NASDAQ symbol*] (TTSB)
PFDC .... Peoples Federal Savings Bank of DeKalb City [*NASDAQ symbol*] (NQ)
PFDC .... Pole Figure Data Collection (SAUS)
PFDCCA .... Prodemca: Friends of the Democratic Center in the Americas [*Defunct*] (EA)
PFDF .... Pacific Fisheries Development Foundation [*Defunct*] (EA)
PFDF .... Petroleum Fuel Development Facility (SAUS)
PFDI .... Preferred Funeral Directors International (NTPA)
PF DI .... Progressive Die (SAUS)
PfdInco .... Preferred Income Fund [*Associated Press*] (SAG)
PFDJ .... People's Front for Democracy and Justice [*Formerly, EPLF*] [*Eritrea*] [*Political party*] (ECON)
PFDJ .... Popular Front for Democracy and Justice [*Eritrea*]
PFDL .... Parameterized Format Description Language (SAUS)
PfDL .... Pflegedienstleitung (SAUS)
PFDM .... Preliminary Final Draft Manuscript
PF/DOS .... Product Improvement (SAUS)
PFDR .... Pathfinder [*Aircraft*]
PfdrBad .... Pathfinder Badge [*Military decoration*] (AABC)
PFDS .... Pergamon Financial Data Services [*Pergamon Orbit Infoline Ltd.*] [*British*] [*Information service or system*] (IID)
PFDS .... Priority Freight Distribution System (SAUS)
PFD SP .... Preferred Spelling (WDAA)
PFDTM .... Preliminary Flightweight Demonstration Test Motor (MCD)
PFE .... Pacific Fruit Express Co. [*AAR code*]
PFE .... Page Fault Error (SAUS)
PFE .... Partido Feminista de Espana [*Feminist Party of Spain*] [*Political party*] (PPW)

PFE............. Pelvic Floor Exercise (DMAA)
PFE............. Performance Fitness Examination [*Military*] (DNAB)
PFE............. Pfizer, Inc. [*NYSE symbol*] (SPSG)
PFE............. Photoferroelectric Effect [*Physics*]
PFE............. Physics of Failure in Electronics [*A publication*] (MCD)
PFE............. Plenum Fill Experiment [*Nuclear energy*] (NRCH)
PFE............. Popular Front of Estonia [*Political party*]
PFE............. Portable Fire Extinguisher (SPST)
PFE............. Post Fire Evaluation [*Military*] (CAAL)
PFE............. Post Flight Evaluation
PFE............. Pressure Feedback Exhaust [*Automotive engineering*]
PFE............. Priests for Equality (EA)
PFE............. Primary Feedback Element (IAA)
PFE............. Process Fuel Equivalent (MCD)
PFE............. Program for Executives (SAUS)
PFE............. Programmers File Editor (SAUS)
PFE............. Pulsed Field Electrophoresis [*Analytical biochemistry*]
PFE............. Purchaser Furnished Equipment (NATG)
PFEAAC....... Posterior Fossa Extra-Axial Arachnoid Cyst [*Medicine*] (DAVI)
PFEC........... Philatelic Friends Exchange Circuit (EA)
PFEFES....... Pacific and Far East Federation of Engineering Societies
PfeifVac...... Pfeiffer Vacuum Technology AG [*Associated Press*] (SAG)
PFEL.......... Pacific Far East Line
PFEP.......... Polyfluoroethylene Propylene (SAUS)
PFEP.......... Programmable Front-End Processor [*Computer science*]
PFES.......... Pan American Federation of Engineering Societies
PFES.......... Pelvic Floor Electrical Stimulation [*Medicine*] (MELL)
PFES.......... Portable Field Emission Spectrometer (SAUS)
PFES.......... Proposed Final Environmental Statement [*Department of Energy*]
PFES.......... Pure Fluid Encoder System
PFET.......... P-Channel Junction Field-Effect Transistor (IDOE)
PFET.......... Prototype Flight Evaluation Tests (SAUS)
PFF............. Page Fault Frequency [*Computer science*] (MHDI)
PFF............. Partial-Flow Filter [*Automotive engineering*]
PFF............. Pathfinder Force [*British RADAR designation which became overall synonym for RADAR*] [*Military*]
PFF............. Permanent Family File [*Navy*] (NG)
PFF............. Phenolfurfural [*Organic chemistry*]
PFF............. Planning Factors File (MCD)
PFF............. Plaque-Forming Factor (PDAA)
PFF............. Pluto Express Mission [*Space exploration*]
PFF............. Pluto Fast Flyby [*NASA*] (PS)
PFF............. Police Field Force (CINC)
PFF............. Porcine Follicular Fluid [*Endocrinology*]
PFF............. Precast Flooring Federation [*British*] (DBA)
PFF............. Pre-Formed Fragmentation (MUSM)
PFF............. Presbyterian Frontier Fellowship (EA)
PFF............. Presidential Faculty Fellow (SAUS)
PFF............. Primary Focus Feed [*Satellite communications*]
PFF............. Prisoners' Families & Friends (WDAA)
PFF............. Project Formulation Framework (SAUS)
PFF............. Proposed Fabric Flammability Standard [*Consumer Product Safety Commission*]
PFF............. Protein Fat-Free [*Food technology*]
PFF............. Punjab Frontier Force [*British military*] (DMA)
PFFB.......... PFF Bancorp [*NASDAQ symbol*] (TTSB)
PFFB.......... PFF Bancorp, Inc. [*NASDAQ symbol*] (SAG)
PFFBcp....... PFF Bancorp, Inc. [*Associated Press*] (SAG)
PFFBI......... Pacific Fire Fighters Burn Institute (SAUS)
PFFC.......... Parallel-Flow Film Cooling
PFFC.......... Peoples Financial Corp. [*NASDAQ symbol*] (SAG)
PFFC.......... Philadelphia Flyers Fan Club (EA)
PFFD.......... Proximal Femoral Focal Deficiency [*Orthopedics*] (DAVI)
PFFF.......... Polypropylene Fibrillated Film Fiber (or Fibre) (SAUS)
PFF Inc...... Police-FBI Fencing, Incognito [*Phony fencing ring operated by Washington, DC, law enforcement agents during 1976 to identify and arrest area thieves*]
PFFT.......... Parallel Fast Fourier Transform (SAUS)
PFFX.......... Profiling Fixture
PFG........... Pacific Rim Mining Corp. [*Vancouver Stock Exchange symbol*]
PFG........... Paeoniflorigenone [*Biochemistry*]
PFG........... Paper Flow Group [*Nuclear Regulatory Commission*] (GFGA)
PFG........... Peak Flow Gauge [*Medicine*] (AAMN)
PFG........... PennCorp Financial Group [*NYSE symbol*] (SPSG)
PFG........... Pfennig [*Penny*] [*Monetary unit*] [*German*]
PFG........... Piping and Filter Gallery [*Nuclear energy*] (NRCH)
PFG........... Primary Frequency Generator
PFG........... Principal Financial Group (SAUS)
PFG........... Programmable Frequency Generator (SAUS)
PFG........... Pulsed-Field Gel Electrophoresis (DMAA)
PFG........... Pulsed Field Gradient [*Electroanalytical chemistry*]
PFG........... Purple Flower Gang (EA)
PFGC.......... Parameters from Group Contribution [*Equation of state*]
PFGC.......... Performance Food Group [*NASDAQ symbol*] (SAG)
PFGE.......... Pulsed Field Gel Electrophoresis
PFGE.......... Pulsed-Field Gel Electrophresis (HGEN)
PFGE.......... Pulsed Field Gradient Gel Electrophoresis
PFGI.......... Provident Financial Group [*NASDAQ symbol*] [*Formerly, Provident Bancorp.*] (SG)
PFGM.......... Guided Missile Patrol Escort [*Ship symbol*] (NATG)
PFGPr........ PennCorp Finl $3.375 Pfd [*NYSE symbol*] (TTSB)
PFGX.......... Pacific Fruit Growers Express
PFH............. Hudson, NY [*Location identifier*] [*FAA*] (FAAL)
PFH............. Pafco Financial Holdings Ltd. [*Toronto Stock Exchange symbol*]
PFH............. Perifornical Hypothalamus (DB)

PFH............. Pressurized Fluidized-Bed Hydroretorting [*Chemical engineering*]
PFHA.......... Paso Fino Horse Association (EA)
PFHE.......... Pre-Fragmented High Explosive (SAUS)
PFHM.......... Protein-Free Hybridoma Medium
PFHS.......... Precipitation from Homogeneous Solution [*Catalyst preparation process*]
PFI............. Pacific Forest Industries (EA)
PFI............. Pack File Indexer (NITA)
PFI............. People First International (EA)
PFI............. Pet Food Institute (EA)
PFI............. Photo Finishing Institute [*Defunct*] (EA)
PFI............. Photon Flow Integrating (IAA)
PFI............. Photon Flux Integration (IAA)
PFI............. Physical Fault Insertion (SAUS)
PFI............. Physical Fitness Index
PFI............. Picture and Frame Institute [*Defunct*] (EA)
PFI............. Pie Filling Institute [*Defunct*] (EA)
PFI............. Pipe Fabrication Institute (EA)
PFI............. Police Foundation Institute (NADA)
PFI............. Port Fuel Injector [*Automotive engines*]
PFI............. Position Finding Instrument (DS)
PFI............. Power Factor Indicator (IAA)
PFI............. Power Failure Indicator [*NASA*] (KSC)
PFI............. Prison Fellowship International (EA)
PFI............. Private Finance Initiative [*British*]
PFI............. Product Features Index (SAUS)
PFIA.......... Police and Firemen's Insurance Association (EA)
PFIA.......... Prevention of Fraud Investments Act [*British*]
PFIAB........ President's Foreign Intelligence Advisory Board (AFM)
PFI & R....... Part Fill In and Ram [*Construction*]
PFIB.......... Pentafluoroiodosylbenzene [*Organic chemistry*]
PFIB.......... Perfluoroisobutene [*Organic chemistry*]
PFIB.......... Perfluoroisobutylene [*Organic chemistry*] (MAE)
PFIC.......... Passive Foreign Investment Company [*IRS*]
PFIC.......... Processed Food Industry Council [*Australia*]
PFID.......... Perturbed Free Induction Decay
PFIEP........ Perfluorinated Ion-Exchange Polymer [*Organic chemistry*]
PFIM.......... Pure Fluid Impact Modulator
PFIMF........ Preferred Income Management Fund, Inc. [*Associated Press*] (SAG)
PFI Mode.... Photon-Flow Integration Mode (SAUS)
PFIN.......... P & F Industries, Inc. [*NASDAQ symbol*] (NQ)
PFINA........ P&F Indus'A' [*NASDAQ symbol*] (TTSB)
PFINP........ P & F Ind $1 Pfd [*NASDAQ symbol*] (TTSB)
PFIR.......... People for Internet Responsibility (SAUS)
PFIRS........ Paperless Fax Image Reporting System (SAUS)
PFIS.......... Personnel Feedback Information System (SAUS)
PFIS.......... Property Fabric Information System (SAUS)
PFIU.......... Plot File Import Utility [*IBM Corp.*]
PFIX.......... Power Failure Interrupt (SAUS)
Pfizer........ Pfizer, Inc. [*Associated Press*] (SAG)
PFJ........... Patreksfjordur [*Iceland*] [*Airport symbol*] (OAG)
PFJ........... Polar Front Jet Stream (ADA)
PFJR.......... Patellofemoral Joint Reaction [*Physiology*]
PFK........... Pay for Knowledge (TIMI)
PFK........... Payload Function Key [*NASA*] (MCD)
PFK........... Perfluorokerosene [*Heat transfer agent*]
PFK........... Phosphofructokinase [*An enzyme*]
PFK........... Plastic Fluted Knob (SAUS)
PFK........... Program Function Keyboard
PFK........... Programmed Function Key (NITA)
PFK........... Programmed Function Keyboard [*Computer science*]
PF KEY...... Program Function Key [*Computer science*] (ITCA)
PFKM.......... Phosphofructokinase, Muscle Type [*Medicine*] (DMAA)
PFKY.......... People First Corp. [*NASDAQ symbol*] (SAG)
PFKY.......... Peoples First [*NASDAQ symbol*] (TTSB)
PFL........... Fort Sill, OK [*Location identifier*] [*FAA*] (FAAL)
PFL........... Pacific Cassiar Ltd. [*Toronto Stock Exchange symbol*]
PFL........... Pacific Freight Lines (SAUS)
PFL........... Pennsylvania Folk Life (SAUS)
PFL........... People for Life (EA)
PFL........... Pharmacists for Life (EA)
PFL........... Pioneer Football League (PSS)
PFL........... Pol-Fly [*Poland*] [*ICAO designator*] (FAAC)
PFL........... Pounds per Lineal Foot [*Technical drawings*]
PFL........... Pre-Fade Listen (SAUS)
PFL........... Pressed-For-Life (SAUS)
PFL........... Primary Freon Loop (NASA)
PFL........... Propulsion Field Laboratory
PFL........... Public Facility Loans
PFLA.......... Popular Front for the Liberation of Ahvaz [*Iran*]
P-FLAG....... Federation of Parents and Friends of Lesbians and Gays (EA)
PFLAG........ Parents, Families, and Friends of Lesbians and Gays [*An association*] (EA)
PFLF.......... People, Food and Land Foundation (EA)
PFLI.......... Pharmacists for Life International (EA)
PFLL.......... Phase and Frequency Locked Loop [*Telecommunications*] (IAA)
P Flo......... Pandectae Florentinae [*A publication*] (DSA)
PFLO.......... Popular Front for the Liberation of Oman [*Political party*] (PD)
PFLOAG...... Popular Front for the Liberation of Oman and the Arabian Gulf [*Political party*] (PD)
PFLOAG...... Popular Front for the Liberation of the Occupied Arabian Gulf
PFLOLS....... Portable Fresnel-Lens Optical-Landing System (NG)
P Florent.... Pandectae Florentinae [*A publication*] (DSA)
PFLP.......... Popular Front for the Liberation of Palestine [*Political party*] (PD)

PFLP-GC ...... Popular Front for the Liberation of Palestine - General Command [*Political party*] (PD)

PFLP-SC ...... Popular Front for the Liberation of Palestine-Special Command (SAUS)

PFLT .... Paint Filter Liquids Test [*Environmental science*] (FFDE)

P/FLT .... Pattern Flight [*Also, P/F*] (MUGU)

PFLT .... People's Front of the Liberation Tigers [*Sri Lanka*] [*Political party*] (EY)

PFLT .... Photographic Flight (SAUS)

PFLTS .... Parquet Floor Layers' Trade Society [*A union*] [*British*]

PFLV .... Pressure Fed Launch Vehicle [*NASA*] (KSC)

PFM .... Little Franciscan Sisters of Mary [*Roman Catholic religious order*]

PFM .... Pacific Minesearch Ltd. [*Vancouver Stock Exchange symbol*]

PFM .... Package Feasibility Model (SAUS)

PFM .... Patient Flow Model (SAUS)

PFM .... Patriots of Fort McHenry (EA)

PFM .... Peak Flow Meter [*Medicine*] (AAMN)

PFM .... Performance Monitor (SAUS)

PFM .... Personnel File Management (TIMI)

PFM .... Physiological Flow Model [*For simulating medical conditions*]

PFM .... Pitch Follow-Up Motor

PFM .... Plan for Maintenance [*Navy*]

PFM .... Planning Factors Management (MCD)

PFM .... Platform (NASA)

PFM .... Political Freedom Movement [*British*]

PFM .... Pont Flottant Motorise [*French*]

PFM .... Porcelain Fused to Metal [*Dentistry*]

PFM .... Porsche Flug Motor [*Automotive engineering*]

PFM .... Potato Futures Market [*Finance*]

PFM .... Poultry Feather Meal [*Fisheries*]

PFM .... Power Factor Meter

PFM .... Precise Frequency Measurement (SEWL)

PFM .... Precision Frequency Multivider (KSC)

PFM .... Predictor Frame Memory

PFM .... Preferred Income Management Fund [*NYSE symbol*] (SPSG)

PFM .... Pre-Finished Metal (SAUS)

PFM .... Preliminary Flight Motor (MCD)

PFM .... Pressure Flow Meter

PFM .... Printer Font Metrics [*Computer science*] (CDE)

PFM .... Prison Fellowship Ministries (EA)

PFM .... Process Facility Modification (ABAC)

PFM .... Proto Flight Model (ACAE)

PFM .... Proto-Flight Model (SAUS)

PFM .... Pulse-Forming Machine

PFM .... Pulse-Frequency Modulation [*RADAR*] [*Telecommunications*]

PFM .... Pure Fantastic Magic (SAUS)

P/FM .... Pylon/Fin Movement

PFM .... University of Pittsburgh, Falk Library - Health Professions, Pittsburgh, PA [*OCLC symbol*] (OCLC)

PFMA .... Pet Food Manufacturers Association [*British*] (DBA)

PFMA .... Phenolic Foam Manufacturers Association [*British*] (DBA)

PFMA .... Pipe Fittings Manufacturers Association [*Later, APFA*] (EA)

PFMA .... Plumbing Fixture Manufacturers Association [*Defunct*] (EA)

PFMA .... Pressed Felt Manufacturers' Association [*British*] (BI)

PFMAA .... Pet Food Manufacturers' Association of Australia

PFMC .... Pacific Fishery Management Council (EA)

PFMEA .... Process for Failure Mode and Effects Analysis

PFMGO .... Pre-Flight Message-Generating Officer (SAUS)

PFMO .... Planning Factors Management Office

PFMP .... Personal Finance Management Program (SAUS)

PFMPG .... Pacific Fleet Mobile Photographic Group (DNAB)

PFMR .... Pasadena Foundation for Medical Research [*California*]

PFMR .... Plug-Flow Membrane Reactor [*Chemical engineering*]

PFMR .... Project Funds Management Record (MCD)

PFMS .... Plant Facilities Management System (SAUS)

PFN .... Page Frame Number (TIMI)

PFN .... Panama City [*Florida*] [*Airport symbol*] (OAG)

PFN .... Pantyffynnon [*British depot code*]

PFN .... Partially Functional Neutrophil (DMAA)

PFN .... Parti des Forces Nouvelles [*New Forces Party*] [*France*] [*Political party*] (PPW)

PFN .... Passamaquoddy Ferry & Navigation Co. [*AAR code*]

PFN .... Permanent File Name

PFN .... Peroxyformyl Nitrate (SAUS)

PFN .... Plasma Fibronectin [*Biochemistry*]

PFN .... PMC Corp. [*Toronto Stock Exchange symbol*]

PFN .... Prefinished [*Technical drawings*]

PFN .... Prime Fanout Node (SAUS)

PFN .... Profilin (DMAA)

PFN .... Pulse-Forming Network

PFNA .... Pentecostal Fellowship of North America (EA)

PFNA .... Pulsed Fast Neutron Analysis [*for detection of explosives*] (PS)

PFNC .... Progress Financial Corp. [*Plymouth Meeting, PA*] [*NASDAQ symbol*] (NQ)

PFNC .... Progress Finl [*NASDAQ symbol*] (TTSB)

PFNM .... Petrified Forest National Monument (SAUS)

PFNP .... Partido Federalista Nacionalista Popular [*Panama*] [*Political party*] (EY)

PFNP .... Petrified Forest National Park (SAUS)

PFNS .... Position Fixing Navigation System (AABC)

PFNT .... Police Force of the Northern Territory [*Australia*]

PFNT .... Preferred Networks [*NASDAQ symbol*] (TTSB)

PFNTU .... Pathfinder Navigation Training Unit [*Military*]

PFO .... Pacific Food Outlook

PFO .... Paphos [*Cyprus*] [*Airport symbol*] (OAG)

PFO .... Partly Filled Out [*Questionnaire*]

PFO .... Patent Foramen Ovale [*Cardiology*]

PFO .... Personal Freedom Outreach (EA)

PFO .... Physical Fitness Officer [*British military*] (DMA)

PFO .... Pitch Follow-Up Operation

PFO .... Pomona Public Library, Pomona, CA [*OCLC symbol*] (OCLC)

PFO .... Postal Finance Officer [*Army*]

PFO .... Preferred Income Opportunity Fund [*NYSE symbol*] (SAG)

PFO .... Procurement Field Office

PFO .... Procurement Field Officer (SAUS)

PFO .... Pyrolysis Fuel Oil [*Petroleum refining*]

PFO .... Pyruvate: Ferredoxin Oxidoreductase [*An enzyme*]

PFO .... Spofford, TX [*Location identifier*] [*FAA*] (FAAL)

PFOA .... Perfluorooctanoic Acid [*Organic chemistry*]

PFOB .... Perfluorocytylbromide (DMAA)

PFOBA .... Paso Fino Owners and Breeders Association [*Later, PFHA*] (EA)

PFOC .... Prairie Fire Organizing Committee (SAUS)

PFOD .... Presumed Finding of Death [*DoD*]

PFOE .... Percentage of Frames recovered with Zero Error (SAUS)

PFoI .... Ridley Township Public Library, Folsom, PA [*Library symbol*] [*Library of Congress*] (LCLS)

PFOM .... Preformed Fragmentation OTO Munition (SAUS)

PFORM .... Print Format (SAUS)

PFOS .... Perfluorooctane Sulfonate

PFouad .... Les Papyrus Fouad I [*A publication*] (OCD)

PFP .... Partnership for Peace [*An organization of non-member countries which have established military cooperation with NATO*] (ECON)

PFP .... Partnership for Productivity International (EA)

PFP .... Pattern Factoring Program (TIMI)

PFP .... Peace and Freedom Party (EA)

PFP .... Pensions for Professionals, Inc.

PFP .... Pentafluoropropionate [*or Pentafluoropropionyl*] [*Organic chemistry*]

PFP .... Performic Acid Phosphotungsite (SAUS)

PFP .... Peripheral Facial-Paralysis [*Medicine*] (MELL)

PFP .... Personal Financial Planning (ADA)

PFP .... Pet-Facilitated Psychotherapy [*Psychiatry*]

PFP .... Plastic Faced Plaster (SAUS)

PFP .... Platelet-Free Plasma [*Hematology*]

PFP .... Pleiades Foundation for Peace [*Later, PFPSE*] (EA)

PFP .... Plutonium Finishing Plant

PFP .... Policy-Framework Paper (ECON)

PFP .... Popular Front Party [*Ghana*] [*Political party*] (PPW)

PFP .... Pore Forming Protein [*Biochemistry*]

PFP .... Postage Forward Parcels [*Shipping*]

PFP .... Post Flight Processor

PFP .... Prefetch Processor (SAUS)

PFP .... Premier Farnell PLC [*NYSE symbol*] (SAG)

PFP .... Premier Farnell PLC ADS [*NYSE symbol*] (TTSB)

PFP .... Primary Failed Part (DNAB)

PFP .... Probability of Failure, Performance [*NASA*] (SAA)

PFP .... Products for Power [*Automotive components manufacturer*]

PFP .... Program File Processor

PFP .... Program Financial Plan (NASA)

PFP .... Program Forecast Period [*Military*] (AFIT)

PFP .... Programmable Function Panel (NASA)

PFP .... Progressiewe Federale Party [*Progressive Federal Party*] [*South Africa*] [*Political party*] (PPW)

PFP .... Progressive Federal Party (SAUS)

PFP .... Proton Flare Project (PDAA)

PFP .... Proving for Production (MCD)

PFP .... Proximity Fuze Programmer (SAUS)

PFP .... Publishers for Peace [*An association*]

PFPA .... Pentafluoropropionic Anhydride [*Organic chemistry*]

PFPA .... Pitch Fiber Pipe Association

PFPC .... Pro-Family Press Association [*Defunct*] (EA)

PFPC .... Passenger Form and Procedures Committee [*IATA*] (DS)

PFPDBRD .... Paget Foundation for Paget's Disease of Bone and Related Disorders [*Formerly, Paget's Disease Foundation (PDF)*] (PAZ)

PFPE .... Perfluorinated Polyether [*Organic chemistry*]

PFPE .... Perfluoropolyether (SAUS)

PFPE .... Polyfluorinated Polyether [*Lubricants, polymers*]

PFP EIS ...... Plutonium Finishing Plant Environmental Impact Statement

PFPH .... Pentafluorophenylhydrazine [*Organic chemistry*]

PFPI .... Partnership for Productivity International (EA)

PFPI .... Pentafluoropropionyl Imidazole [*Organic chemistry*]

PFPM .... Production Flight Procedures Manual (MCD)

PFPPr .... Premier Farnell $1.35 Pref ADS [*NYSE symbol*] (TTSB)

PFP/PTP ...... Pensions for Professionals/Pensions for Technical Professionals (SAUS)

PFPPX .... Pre-Fragmented Programmable Proximity Fuzed (SAUS)

PFPS .... Patellofemoral Pain Syndrome [*Medicine*] (DMAA)

PFPS .... Potential for Foster Parenthood Scale [*Psychology*]

PFPS .... Progressive French Polishers' Society [*A union*] [*British*]

PFPSE .... Pleiades Foundation for Peace and Space Education (EA)

PFPU .... Processor Frame Power Unit

PFPUT .... Pension Fund Property Unit Trust [*British*]

PFPX .... Pre-Fragmented Proximity Fuzed (SAUS)

PFQ .... Personality Factor Questionnaire (MAE)

PFQ .... Preflight Qualification

PFQT .... Preliminary Flight Qualification Test (SAUS)

PFr .... Franklin Public Library, Franklin, PA [*Library symbol*] [*Library of Congress*] (LCLS)

PFR .... Parotid Flow Rate [*otorhinolaryngology*] (DAVI)

PFR .... Part Failure Rate

PFR .... Patriot Field Report [*Army*]

PFR.............. Peak Flow Rate [or Reading] [Medicine]
PFR.............. Peak Flow Reading (SAUS)
PFR.............. Percentage of Frames Recovered (SAUS)
PFR.............. Perforator (DEN)
PFR.............. Pericardial Friction Rub [Medicine] (MEDA)
PFR.............. Perkins Family Restaurants Ltd [NYSE symbol] (SPSG)
PFR.............. Permanent Factory Repairable (MCD)
PFR.............. Permanent Fix Request (TIMI)
PFR.............. Permitted Flying Route [Aviation] (DA)
PFR.............. Persistent Fat Retention [Syndrome]
PFR.............. Personal Financial Record [Army] (AABC)
PFR.............. Pfarrer [Pastor] [German] (EY)
PFR.............. Phase Failure Relays [Environmental science] (COE)
PFR.............. Photoflash Relay
PFR.............. Pike Fry Rhabdovirus
PFR.............. Planning for Results [A publication]
PFR.............. Plug-Flow Reactor [Engineering]
PFR.............. Plutonium-fueled Fast Reactor (SAUS)
PFR.............. Polarized Field Frequency Relay (IAA)
PFR.............. Polarized Frequency Relay
PFR.............. Portable Font Resource (SAUS)
PFR.............. Portable Foot Restraint (NASA)
PFR.............. Port Francqui [Zaire] [Airport symbol] (AD)
PFR.............. Post-Fielding Review [DoD]
PFR.............. Power Fail Recovery System [Computer science] (MDG)
PFR.............. Power Fail/Restart
PFR.............. Power Failure Release
PFR.............. Precision Fathometer Recorder [Raytheon Co.]
PFR.............. Preferred Resources, Inc. [Vancouver Stock Exchange symbol]
PFR.............. Preflight Review [NASA] (KSC)
PFR.............. Preheating, Falling-Film, Rising-Film [Sections of a concentrator] [Chemical engineering]
PFR.............. Preliminary Flight Rating [Air Force]
PFR.............. Problem/Failure Report
PFR.............. Procedure for Rework (SAUS)
PFR.............. Program Financial Review (ACAE)
PFR.............. Programmable Film Reader (SAUS)
PFR.............. Programmed Film Reader [System]
pfr.............. Proofreader [MARC relator code] [Library of Congress] (LCCP)
PFR.............. Prototype Fast Reactor
PFR.............. Pulmonary Blood Flow Redistribution [Medicine]
PFR.............. Pulmonary Flow Rate [Medicine] (DAVI)
PFR.............. Pulsed Fast Reactor (SAUS)
PFR.............. Pulse Frequency (MDG)
PFR.............. Punch Feed Read (CMD)
PFRA............ Percent of Females Reproductively Active [Ecology]
PFRA............ Prairie Farm Rehabilitation Act (SAUS)
PFRA............ Prairie Farm Rehabilitation Administration [Canada]
PFRA............ Prairie Farm Rehabilitation Association (SAUS)
PFRA............ Problem-Focused Research Applications [of ASRA] [National Science Foundation]
PFRA............ Professional Football Referees Association (EA)
PFRA............ Professional Football Researchers Association (EA)
PFRB............ Pacific Fire Rating Bureau (SAUS)
PFRB............ Publications and Films Review Board [Western Australia]
PFRC............ Pacific Forest Research Centre [Canada] (ARC)
PFRD............ Preferred Stock [Investment term]
PFredY........ Joseph A. Yablonski Memorial Clinic, Fredericktown, PA [Library symbol] [Library of Congress] (LCLS)
PFR Film..... Preheat Falling-Rising Film (SAUS)
PFRMG........ Performing (ROG)
PFRS........... Portable Field Recording System [NASA] (KSC)
PFRS........... Portable Field Reflectance Spectrometer (SAUS)
PFRT........... Performance Flight Rating Test (SAUS)
PFRT........... Pre-Flight Rating Test (SAUS)
PFRT........... Preliminary Field Rating Test (SAUS)
PFRT........... Preliminary Flight Rated Test
PFRT........... Preliminary Flight Rating Test
PFRT........... Preliminary Flight Readiness Test [NASA] (KSC)
PFRX........... Preflight Relmat (SAUS)
PFS.............. Page Format Selection (SAUS)
PFS.............. Parallel Filter System
PFS.............. Particles and Fields Subsatellite [NASA]
PFS.............. Path Fault Secure (MHDI)
PFS.............. Pay for Skills [Human resources] (WYGK)
PFS.............. Payload Feasibility Study (ACAE)
PFS.............. Percent Full Scale (KSC)
PFS.............. Performance Funding System [Department of Housing and Urban Development] (GFGA)
PFS.............. Periodic Feature Selection (SAUS)
PFS.............. Peripheral Fixed Shim [Nuclear energy] (NRCH)
PFS.............. Personal and Family Survival [Civil Defense]
PFS.............. Personal Filing System [Data-base program] [Software Publishing Corp.]
PFS.............. Personal Financial Specialist
PFS.............. Photofragment Spectroscopy
PFS.............. Physical File System (IAA)
PFS.............. Pioneer Financial Svcs [NYSE symbol] (TTSB)
PFS.............. Pitch Follow-Up System
PFS.............. Pittsburgh, PA [Location identifier] [FAA] (FAAL)
PFS.............. Planned Flying and Servicing
PFS.............. Plasterers' Friendly Society [A union] [British]
PFS.............. Platform Functional Specification [Computer science]
PFS.............. Porous Friction Surface [Airfield pavement]
PFS.............. Portable File System (SAUS)

PFS.............. Positive Fuel Stop
PFS.............. Power Fuel Steamship (SAUS)
PFS.............. Prairie Flying Service (1976) Ltd. [Canada] [ICAO designator] (FAAC)
PFS.............. Precision Frequency Source
PFS.............. Pre-Feasability Study (SAUS)
PFS.............. Preflight School [Military]
PFS.............. Press Fit Socket
PFS.............. Primary Fibromyalgia Syndrome [Medicine] (DMAA)
PFS.............. Primary Flight System (NASA)
PFS.............. Primary Flying Squadron (SAUS)
PFS.............. Primary Frequency Supply [Telecommunications] (TEL)
PFS.............. Probability of Failure, Stress [NASA] (SAA)
PFS.............. Professional Software (SAUS)
PFS.............. Pro-Forma Statement (MHDI)
PFS.............. Programmable Frequency Standard
PFS.............. Progression Free Survival [Medicine]
PFS.............. Propellant Feed System
PFS.............. Propellant Field System
PFS.............. Pulmonary Function Score [Physiology]
PFS.............. Pure Fluid System
PFSA........... Pilot to Forecaster Service Available (SAUS)
PFSB........... PennFed Financial Services, Inc. [NASDAQ symbol] (SAG)
PFSB........... PennFed Financial Svcs [NASDAQ symbol] (TTSB)
PFSDR........ Parts Failure Service Difficulties Report (ACAE)
PFSh.......... Partia Fashismit e Shqiperise [Fascist Party of Albania] [Political party] (PPE)
PFSH .... Porcine Follicle Stimulating Hormone [Endocrinology]
PFSK .... Permutation Frequency-Shift Keying (SAUS)
PFSL........... Pocahontas Federal Savings & Loan Association [NASDAQ symbol] (SAG)
PFSL........... Pocahontas Fed Svg& L A Ark [NASDAQ symbol] (TTSB)
PFSO .... Postal Finance and Supply Office (AFM)
PFSP.......... Polyfactorial Study of Personality [Psychology] (AEBS)
PFS/PRS...... Patent Family Service/Patent Register Service [Database] [International Patent Documentation Center] [Information service or system] (CRD)
PFSR.......... Program Financial Status Report (AAG)
PFSS........... Particles and Fields Subsatellite [Telecommunications] (OA)
PFSS........... Patellofemoral Stress Syndrome [Medicine]
PFSS........... Pesticide Farmworker Safety Staff [Office of Pesticides and Toxic Substances] (COE)
pfst .... pianofortist (SAUS)
P-F Study.... Picture-Frustration Study (SAUS)
PFT.............. Pacific Asia Tech [Vancouver Stock Exchange symbol]
PFT.............. Pacific Fisheries Technologists [An association]
PFT.............. Page Frame Table (BUR)
PFT.............. Pancreatic Function Test [Medicine]
PFT.............. Paper, Flat Tape
PFT.............. Parachute Familiarization Training (SAUS)
PFT.............. Parafascicular Thalamotomy [Medicine]
PFT.............. Parallel Fourier Transform (MCD)
PFT.............. People For Trees (SAUS)
PFT.............. Permanent Full-Time (GFGA)
PFT.............. Pet-Facilitated Therapy [Psychiatry]
PFT.............. Phenylalanine mustard [Melphalan], Fluorouracil, Tamoxifen [Antineoplastic drug regimen]
PFT.............. Physical Fitness Test
PFT.............. Pittsburgh, Fort Wayne & Chicago Railway Co. (IIA)
PFT.............. Plant Functional Type (QUAC)
PFT.............. Plastic Fuel Tank
PFT.............. Platelet-Fibrin-Thrombi [Medicine] (MELL)
PFT.............. Portable Flame Thrower [Army]
PFT.............. Positive Flight Termination (MUGU)
PFT.............. Posterior Fossa Tumor [Anatomy] (MAE)
PFT.............. Prefabricate Foxhole Twin (SAUS)
PFT.............. Preflight Team [Air Force] (AFM)
PFT.............. Preflight Tool (MCD)
PFT.............. Prime Factor Transform (IAA)
PFT.............. Prism Fiber-reading Tube (SAUS)
PFT.............. Professional Football Trainers (EA)
PFT.............. Program Flying Training [Air Force] (AFM)
PFT.............. Projective Field Theory
PFT.............. Pulmonary Function Test [Medicine]
PFT.............. Pulse Fourier Transform
PFTA........... Payload Flight Test Article [NASA] (MCD)
PFTA........... Post-Fielding Training Analysis
pft acct ...... pianoforte accompaniment (SAUS)
PFTB.......... Preflight Test Bus (MCD)
PFTBA........ Perfluorotributylamine (SAUS)
PFTBE........ Progressive Form of Tick-Borne Encephalitis [Medicine] (DMAA)
PFTC.......... Pestalozzi-Froebel Teachers College [Illinois]
PFTC.......... Plesetsk Flight Test Centre (SAUS)
PFTE.......... Permanent Full-Time Equivalent (GFGA)
pfte .... Pianoforte (WDAA)
PFTE.......... Pianoforte [Soft, then Loud] [Music]
PFTE.......... Polytetrafluoroethylene [Teflon]
PFTE.......... Portable Field Trainer/Evaluator (MCD)
PFTEA........ Post-Fielding Training Effectiveness Analysis
PFTM.......... Preliminary Flight Test Memo
PFTQ.......... Partnering for Total Quality (AAEL)
PFTR.......... Preliminary Flight Test Report
PFTs.......... Perfluorocarbon Tracers (SAUS)
PFTS.......... Permanent Field Training Site
PFTS........... Primary Flying Training School (SAUS)

PFTs	Pulmonary Function Tests	(SAUS)
PFU	Passive Filtration Unit	
PFU	Physical Fitness Uniform [*Army*]	(INF)
PFU	Plan for Use	(DNAB)
PFU	Plaque-Forming Unit [*Immunochemistry*]	
PFU	Please Follow Up	
PFU	Pock-Forming Unit	
PFU	Preparation for Use	
PFU	Prepared for Use	(SAUS)
PFUA	Pitch Follow-Up Amplifier	
PFUEI	Prime Focus Universal Extragalactic Instrument [*Astronomy*]	
P Fuel	Patent Fuel	(SAUS)
PFUM	Pitch Follow-Up Motor	
PFUND	Program for Understanding Neurological Diseases	
PFUO	Pitch Follow-Up Operation	
PFUO	Prolonged Fever of Unknown Origin [*Medicine*]	(DMAA)
PFUS	Pitch Follow-Up System	
PFV	Peak Flow Velocity [*Cardiology*]	
PFV	Peak Forward Voltage	(IAA)
PFV	Pestalozzi-Froebel-Verband [*Pestalozzi-Froebel Association*]	
PFV	Philippine Forces, Vietnam	
PFV	Physiological Full Value	
PFV	Probability of Failure, Vehicle [*NASA*]	(SAA)
PFVEA	Professional Film and Video Equipment Association	(EA)
PFW	Power, Fulcrum, Weight	
PFW	Predicted Fire Weapon	
PFW	Progressive Free Wave	
PFW	Punch Feed Write	(SAUS)
PFWA	Pet Food Warehouse [*NASDAQ symbol*]	(SAG)
PFWA	Professional Football Writers of America	(EA)
PFwB	Budd Co., Fort Washington, PA [*Library symbol*] [*Library of Congress*]	(LCLS)
PFWOAD	Place from Which Ordered to Active Duty [*Military*]	
PFwR	William H. Rorer, Inc., Fort Washington, PA [*Library symbol*] [*Library of Congress*]	(LCLS)
PFWS	Predicted Fire Weapon System [*Army*]	
PFX	Pacific Fruit Express	(SAUS)
PFX	Pilgrim American Capital [*NYSE symbol*]	
PFX	Prefix	(ROG)
PFX	Proflex Ltd. [*Vancouver Stock Exchange symbol*]	
PFXP	Plan Failure explanation Pattern	(SAUS)
PFY	Prior Fiscal Year	(AFIT)
PFYA	Predicted First-Year Average [*Law school*]	
PFZ	Polar Front Zone [*Marine science*]	(MSC)
PFZ	Potassium Hexafluorozirconate [*Inorganic chemistry*]	
PFZ	Precipitate-Free Zone	(MCD)
PF-ZAPU	Patriotic Front - Zimbabwe African People's Union [*Political party*]	(PD)
PG	Florida Commuter [*ICAO designator*]	(AD)
PG	Glycerate-3-Phosphate [*Biochemistry*]	(DAVI)
pg	Page	(WDMC)
PG	Page [*or Pagination*] [*Online database field identifier*]	
PG	Pan American Grace Airways	(SAUS)
PG	Paper Gain	(MHDW)
PG	Papua New Guinea [*ANSI two-letter standard code*]	(CNC)
PG	Paralysie Generale [*General Paralysis*] [*Medicine*] [*French*]	
PG	Paregoric [*Slang*]	
PG	Parental Guidance Suggested [*Formerly, GP*] [*Some material may not be suitable for preteenagers*] [*Movie rating*]	
PG	Paris Granite	
PG	Paris Group [*See also GP*] [*France*]	(EAIO)
PG	Parity Generate	(SAUS)
PG	Parotid Gland [*Medicine*]	(DMAA)
PG	Partial Gum [*Philately*]	
PG	Parti Quebecois [*Canada*] [*Political party*]	(WDAA)
PG	Pass Gas	(SAUS)
PG	Paste Grain [*Bookbinding*]	
PG	Past Grand [*Freemasonry*]	
PG	Patrol Combatant [*Gunboat*] [*Navy symbol*]	
PG	Patrol Escort [*Navy*]	
PG	Patrol Gunboat, Motorized [*Navy symbol*]	(VNW)
PG	Patrologiae Cursus. Series Graeca [*A publication*]	(OCD)
PG	Patrol Vessel Gunboat [*Navy*]	
PG	Pattern Generator	(TIMI)
PG	Pay Grade	
PG	Pay Group	
PG	Paying Guest	
PG	PEACE [*Program for Emergency Assistance, Cooperation, and Education*] for Guatemala	(EA)
PG	Pedal Ganglion	
PG	Pedal Groove	
PG	Pelham Grenville Wodehouse [*British humorist, 1881-1975*]	
PG	Pelvic Girdle [*Medicine*]	(MELL)
PG	Pentagastrin	(DMAA)
Pg	Pentagram [*One billion metric tons*]	
PG	Pepsinogen [*Medicine*]	(MEDA)
PG	Peptidoglycan [*Biochemistry*]	
PG	Periodic Group	(SAUS)
PG	Permanent Glow [*Telecommunications*]	(TEL)
PG	Permanent Grade	
PG	Persian Gulf	(MCD)
PG	Persistent Gas	(SAUS)
Pg	Petagram	(SAUS)
PG	Petrogenesis	(SAUS)
PG	Pharmaceutical Guide	(SAUS)

PG	Pharmacopoeia Germanica [*German Pharmacopoeia*]	
PG	Phase Gradient	(SAUS)
PG	Phosphatidylglycerol	
PG	Phosphogluconate [*Biochemistry*]	
PG	Phosphogypsum [*Inorganic chemistry*]	
PG	Photogrammetry	
PG	Physical Geography	(SAUS)
pg	Picogram [*One trillionth of a gram*]	
PG	Picture Generation	
PG	Picture Generator	(SAUS)
PG	Pilot Generator	(IAA)
PG	Pine Grosbeak [*Ornithology*]	
PG	Pin Grid	(SAUS)
PG	Pipers Guild	(EA)
PG	Pistol Grip	(SAUS)
PG	Pituitary Gonadotropin [*Endocrinology*]	(MAE)
PG	Pivot Gun	(SAUS)
PG	Placebo Group [*Medicine*]	
PG	Plagioclase	(SAUS)
PG	Planning Group [*DoD*]	
PG	Planning Guidance	(SAUS)
PG	Planning Guide [*HUD*]	
PG	Plant Genome	(HGEN)
PG	Plant Growth	(SAUS)
PG	Plasma Gastrin [*Endocrinology*]	(AAMN)
PG	Plasma Glucose [*Hematology*]	
PG	Plasma Triglyceride [*Hematology*]	(DAVI)
PG	Plate Glass	
PG	Plate-Glazed [*Paper*]	
PG	Pointer Game	(AEBS)
PG	Point Group	(SAUS)
PG	Pollen Grain [*Botany*]	
PG	Polyethylene Glycol [*Organic chemistry*]	
PG	Polygalacturonase [*An enzyme*]	
PG	Polyglycine [*Biochemistry*]	
PG	Polypropylene Glycol	(EDCT)
PG	Pontius Guillelmi [*Authority cited in pre-1607 legal work*]	(DSA)
PG	Port Group [*Telecommunications*]	(TEL)
Pg	Portugal	(ODBW)
PG	Portugal	
Pg	Portuguese	(ODBW)
PG	Portuguese [*Language, etc.*]	
pg	Portuguese Guinea [*Guinea-Bissau*] [*MARC country of publication code*] [*Library of Congress*]	(LCCP)
PG	Position Guide	(MCD)
P/G	Postagram [*British military*]	(DMA)
PG	Postgraduate [*Refers to courses or students*] [*Slang*]	
PG	Power Gain	
PG	Power Gate [*Electronics*]	(OA)
PG	Power Generation	(MCD)
PG	Powerglide [*Automatic transmission*]	
PG	Preacher General	
PG	Precision Ground [*Electronics*]	(IAA)
PG	Predicted Grade [*IRS*]	
PG	Pregnanediol Glucuronide [*Endocrinology*]	
pg	Pregnant	(DMAA)
PG	Pregnant	
PG	Pregnant Guppy [*Reference to Boeing 377 aircraft*]	(SAA)
PG	Press Gallery [*US Senate*]	
PG	Pressure Gauge	(KSC)
PG	Priority Group	
PG	Prisonnier de Guerre [*Prisoner of War - POW*] [*French*]	
PG	Processed Gas	(COE)
PG	Processing Gain	(SAUS)
PG	Procter & Gamble Co. [*NYSE symbol*]	(SPSG)
PG	Procureur Generaal [*Public Attorney*] [*Dutch*]	(ILCA)
PG	Producers Group	(EA)
PG	Product Group	(SAUS)
PG	Professional Geologist	
PG	Professional Geophysicist	(SAUS)
PG	Professional Group	(MCD)
PG	Pro-German [*Prisoner of war term*] [*World War I*]	(DSUE)
PG	Program [*Telecommunications*]	
PG	Program Generator	(IAA)
PG	Program Generic [*Computer science*]	(TEL)
PG	Program Guidance	
PG	Program Management Assistance Group	
PG	Programmer	(AAG)
PG	Programmer Group	(IAA)
PG	Project Group	
PG	Prompt Gamma Ray	(SAUS)
PG	Proof Gallon [*Wines and spirits*]	
PG	Propylene Glycol	
PG	Propyl Gallate [*Antioxidant*] [*Organic chemistry*]	
PG	Prostaglandin [*Also, Pg*] [*Biochemistry*]	
PG	Protective Ground [*Electronics*]	(IAA)
PG	Protein Granule	
PG	Proteoglycan [*Biochemistry*]	
PG	Prothoracic Gland [*Insect anatomy*]	
PG	Province Guard [*Cambodia*]	(CINC)
PG	Proving Ground [*Army*]	
P-G	Prudential Grace Lines [*Steamship*]	(MHDB)
PG	Public Gaol [*British*]	
PG	Pulse Gate	
PG	Pulse Generator	

PG............ Pure Gum [of envelopes]
PG............ Pyoderma Gangrenosum [Medicine]
PG............ Pyogenic Granuloma (SAUS)
PG............ Pyrolytic Graphite (MCD)
PG............ Pyrotechnic Gyro (AAG)
PG-13 .... Parental Guidance Suggested [Now: Parents Strongly Cautioned. Some material may be inappropriate for children under 13] [Movie rating]
PGA .... Page [Arizona] [Airport symbol] (OAG)
PGA .... Paragould [Arkansas] [Seismograph station code, US Geological Survey] (SEIS)
PGA .... Parliamentarians for Global Action [An association] (EA)
PGA .... Pega Capital Resources Ltd. [Toronto Stock Exchange symbol]
PGA .... Pendulous Gyro Accelerometer
PGA .... Pepsinogen A (DMAA)
PGA .... Personnel Group of America [NYSE symbol] (SAG)
PGA .... PGI, Inc. [AMEX symbol] (SPSG)
PGA .... Phosphoglyceric Acid [Biochemistry]
PGA .... Phosphoglyzerinaldehyd (SAUS)
PGA .... Pin-Grid-Array [Motorola, Inc.]
PGA .... Pin Grip Array [Computer science] (DDC)
PGA .... Pistachio Growers' Association [Australia]
PGA .... Plate Glass Association [British] (BI)
PGA .... Polyglandular Autoimmune Syndrome [Medicine] (DMAA)
PGA .... Polyglycolic Acid [Organic chemistry] (RDA)
PGA .... Poly(L-glutamic Acid) [Organic chemistry]
PGA .... Port of Geelong Authority [Victoria, Australia]
PGA .... Portugalia, Companhia Portuguesa de Transportes Aeros SA [Portugal] [ICAO designator] (FAAC)
PGA .... Potato Growers of Australia
PGA .... Power Gain Antenna
PGA .... Power Generating Assembly (KSC)
PGA .... Pressure Garment Assembly
PGA .... Prison Governors' Association [British] (WDAA)
PGA .... Producers Guild of America (EA)
PGA .... Production Go-Ahead (SAUS)
PGA .... Professional Golfers Association (NADA)
PGA .... Professional Graphics Adapter [IBM Corp.]
PGA .... Professional Group Audio
PGA .... Program Global Area (SAUS)
PGA .... Programmable Gain Amplifier (MCD)
PGA .... Programmable Gate Array
PGA .... Propane Gas Association (SAUS)
PGA .... Prostaglandin A [Biochemistry]
PGA .... Prostaglandin Analog [Biochemistry]
PGA .... Pteroylglutamic Acid (WDAA)
PGA .... Pteroylmonoglutamic Acid [Folic acid] [Also, FA, PteGlu] [Biochemistry]
PGA .... Puppetry Guild of Australia
PGA .... Purchased Gas Adjustment
PGA .... Pure Grain Alcohol
PGA .... Pyrolysis Gas Analysis
PGA .... Upjohn Co. [Research code symbol]
PGAA .... Pin Grid Array Adapter (SAUS)
PGAA .... Professional Guides Association of America (EA)
PGAA .... Prompt Gamma-Ray Activation Analysis
P-GABA....... Phenyl-gamma-aminobutryic Acid [Tranquilizer]
PGAC .... Guam/Taguac [Mariana Islands] [ICAO location identifier] (ICLI)
PG-AC .... Phenylglycine Acid Chloride [Biochemistry] (AAMN)
PGAC .... Professional Group - Automatic Control
PGAE .... Pacific Gas and Electric (SAUS)
PGAH .... Pineapple Growers Association of Hawaii (EA)
PGAM .... Phosphoglyceromutase [An enzyme]
PG & E .... Pacific Gas and Electric [Rock music group]
PG & E .... Pacific Gas & Electric Co.
PG & E Cp... PG & E Corp. Holdings Co. [Associated Press] (SAG)
PGANE .... Professional Group on Aeronautical and Navigational Electronics
PGA-NOC .... Permanent General Assembly of National Olympic Committees
PGANSW...... Potato Growers' Association of New South Wales [Australia]
PGAP .... Pilot Geriatric Arthritis Program [Medicine] (DMAA)
PGAP .... Professional Group - Antennas and Propagation
PGAPL .... Preliminary Group Assembly Parts List
PGAR .... Provisional Government of the Algerian Republic
PGAS .... Persisting Galactorrhea-Amenorrhea Syndrome [Medicine] (DMAA)
PGase......... Polygalacturonase [An enzyme]
PGAWA....... Pastoralists and Graziers' Association of Western Australia
PGAWA....... Potato Growers' Association of Western Australia
Pg B........... Bachelor of Pedagogy
PGB .... Paravertebral Ganglion Block [Medicine] (MELL)
PGB .... Patrol Gunboat [Navy symbol] (NATG)
PGB .... Personal Guidance Base (AIE)
PGB .... Phoenix Global [Vancouver Stock Exchange symbol]
PGB .... Portland General Electric Co. [NYSE symbol] (SAG)
PGB .... Portland Genl Elec 8.25% 'QUIDS' [NYSE symbol] (TTSB)
PGB .... Program Budget Guidance
PGB .... Prostaglandin B [Biochemistry]
PGB .... Protestant Guild for the Blind (EA)
PGB .... Pyrographalloy Boron
PGBA .... Piece Goods Buyers Association [Defunct] (EA)
PGBA .... Possum Growers and Breeders Association (EA)
PGBBX........ PaineWebber Global Income Cl.B [Mutual fund ticker symbol] (SG)
PGBD .... Pegboard [Freight]
PGBD .... Plugboard (VLIE)
PGBL .... Pluggable (VLIE)
PGBM .... Pulse Gate Binary Modulation (MCD)

PGbSH .... Seton Hill College, Greensburg, PA [Library symbol] [Library of Congress] (LCLS)
PGBTR .... Professional Group - Broadcast and Television Receivers
PG-BTS .... Professional Group-Broadcast Transmission System (SAUS)
PGBTS .... Professional Group - Broadcast Transmission Systems
PGbU .... University of Pittsburgh at Greensburg, Greensburg, PA [Library symbol] [Library of Congress] (LCLS)
PGC .... Geneva College, Beaver Falls, PA [OCLC symbol] (OCLC)
PGC .... Gettysburg College, Gettysburg, PA [Library symbol] [Library of Congress] (LCLS)
PGC .... Pacific Geoscience Center (SAUS)
PGC .... Pagurian Corp. [Toronto Stock Exchange symbol]
PGC .... Parents of Galactosemic Children [An association]
PGC .... Past Grand Commander [Freemasonry] (ROG)
PGC .... Peapack-Gladstone Fin'L. [AMEX symbol]
PGC .... Peoples Gas Co. (SAUS)
PGC .... Percentage of Goblet Cells (STED)
PGC .... Per Gyro Compass [Navigation]
PGC .... Persian Gulf Command [World War II]
PGC .... Phillips Gas [NYSE symbol] (SPSG)
PGC .... Plant Growth Chamber (SAUS)
PGC .... Policy Guidance Council (DOMA)
PGC .... Polynomial Generator Checker (IAA)
PGC .... Pontine Gaze Center [Eye anatomy]
PGC .... Poorly Graphitized Carbon [Physical chemistry]
PGC .... Port Group Control [Telecommunications] (TEL)
PGC .... Post-Graduate Certificate (PGP)
PGC .... Potassium Gold Cyanide [Inorganic chemistry]
PGC .... Potential Gas Committee
PGC .... Power Generation Committee (SAUS)
PGC .... Preliminary General Catalogue (SAUS)
PGC .... Primordial Germ Cell
PGC .... Process Gas Chromatography
PGC .... Process Gas Consumers Group (EA)
PGC .... Professional Graphics Controller [IBM Corp.]
PGC .... Program Chain [Computer science] (DCDG)
PGC .... Program Counter (VLIE)
PGC .... Program Generation Center [Military] (CAAL)
PGC .... Program Grande Carajas (SAUS)
PGC .... Program Group Control (VLIE)
PGC .... Programmable Guidance Controller [Military]
PGC .... Programmed Gain Control
PGC .... Prostaglandin C [A prostoglandin endoperoxide] [Biochemistry] (DAVI)
PGC .... Proving Ground Command [Air Force]
PGC .... Pulsed Gas Crymotography
PGC .... Pure Glycollide (DB)
PGC .... Pyrolysis Gas Chromatography
PGCA .... Patent Glazing Contractors Association [British] (DBA)
PGcC.......... Grove City College, Grove City, PA [Library symbol] [Library of Congress] (LCLS)
PGCC .... Power Generation Control Complex [Nuclear energy] (NRCH)
PGCCM .... Pure Garbage Collection Contour Machine (SAUS)
PGCE .... Post Graduate Certificate of Education
PGCh .... Past Grand Chaplain [Freemasonry]
PGCI .... Program Chain Information [Computer science] (DCDG)
PG Clamp .... Parallel-Groove Clamp (SAUS)
PGCML .... Prince George's County Memorial Library [Maryland]
PGCOA .... Pennsylvania Grade Crude Oil Association (EA)
PGCP .... Particles and Gases Contamination Panel (SAUS)
PGCP .... Professional Group - Component Parts
PGCPr......... Phillips Gas 9.32% Pfd [NYSE symbol] (TTSB)
PGCR .... Portable Gas-Cooled Reactor (SAUS)
PGCRA .... Professional Golf Club Repairmen's Association (EA)
PGCS .... Photogrammetric Graphics Compiling System (SAUS)
PGCS .... Professional Group - Communications Systems
PGCT .... Precision Gunnery Crew Trainer (SAUS)
PGCT .... Professional Group - Circuit Theory
PGCU .... International Printing and Graphic Communications Union
PGCVS .... Postgraduate Committee in Veterinary Science [Australia]
PGD .... Hancock [John] Patriot Global Dividend Fund [NYSE symbol] (SPSG)
PGD .... John Hancock Patr Gl Div Fd [NYSE symbol] (TTSB)
pgd .... paged (SAUS)
PGD .... Pango Gold Mines Ltd. [Toronto Stock Exchange symbol]
PGD .... Paradigm (SAUS)
PGD .... Past Grand Deacon [Freemasonry]
PGD .... Phosphogluconate Dehydrogenase [Also, PGDH] [An enzyme]
PGD .... Phosphoglyceraldehyde Dehydrogenase [An enzyme] (MAE)
PGD .... Pikwitonei Granulite Domain [Geology]
PGD .... Pinion Gear Drive
PGD .... Planar Gas Discharge (VLIE)
PGD .... Planetary Gear Drive
PGD .... Policy and Grants Division [Environmental Protection Agency] (GFGA)
PGD .... Preimplantation Genetic Diagnosis [For in vitro fertilization] [Medicine]
PGD .... Program for Geographical Display (IAA)
PGD .... Prostaglandin D [Biochemistry]
PGD .... Pulse Generator Display
PGD .... Punta Gorda [Florida] [Airport symbol] (OAG)
PGDA .... Piercing Pagoda [NASDAQ symbol] (TTSB)
PGDA .... Piercing Pagoda, Inc. [NASDAQ symbol] (SAG)
PGDB .... Propylene Glycol Dibenzoate [Organic chemistry]
PGDC .... Provincial Grand Director of Ceremonies [Freemasonry]
PGDCS........ Power Generation, Distribution, and Control Subsystem (MCD)

PGDF	Pilot Guide Dog Foundation (EA)
PGDF	Product Generation and Distribution Facility (ACAE)
PGDH	Phosphogluconate Dehydrogenase [*Also, PGD*] [*An enzyme*]
PGDip	Postgraduate Diploma [*Australia*]
PGDipA	Postgraduate Diploma in Arts [*Australia*]
PGDipAgrSc..	Postgraduate Diploma in Agricultural Science [*Australia*]
PGDipDevTech...	Postgraduate Diploma in Development Technology [*Australia*]
PGDipEdSt	Postgraduate Diploma in Educational Studies [*Australia*]
PGDipForSc..	Postgraduate Diploma in Forest Science [*Australia*]
PGDipIEM....	Postgraduate Diploma in Irrigation Engineering Management [*Australia*]
PGDipMath & MathEd...	Postgraduate Diploma in Mathematics and Mathematics Education [*Australia*]
PGDipMgtSt..	Postgraduate Diploma in Management Studies [*Australia*]
PGDipPhysio...	Postgraduate Diploma in Physiotherapy [*Australia*]
PGDipSc	Postgraduate Diploma in Science [*Australia*]
PgDn	Page Down [*Computer science*] (CDE)
PGDN	Page Down [*Computer science*] (VLIE)
PGDN	Propylene Glycol Dinitrate [*Organic chemistry*]
PGDP	Paducah Gaseous Diffusion Plant
PGD Press...	Progressive Die Press (SAUS)
PGDR	Plasma-Glucose Disappearance Rate [*Hematology*] (MAE)
PGDRB	Plumbers, Gasfitters, and Drainers Registration Board [*Victoria, Australia*]
PGDS	Pioneer Ground Data System
PGDS	Pulse Generator Display System
PGDT	Portable Ground Data Terminal
PGE	Pacific Gas & Electric Co. [*Associated Press*] (SAG)
PGE	Pacific Great Eastern Railway Co. [*Nicknames: Prince George Eventually, Please Go Easy*] [*Later, British Columbia Railway*] [*AAR code*]
PGE	Page Petroleum Ltd. [*Toronto Stock Exchange symbol*] (SPSG)
PGE	Persian Gulf Evacuee (SAUS)
PGE	Petroleum and Geosystems Engineering (SAUS)
PGE	Phenyl Glycidyl Ether [*Organic chemistry*]
PGE	Platelet Granule Extract [*Hematology*] (MAE)
PGE	Platinum Group Element [*Chemistry*]
PGE	Polyglycerol Esters of Fatty Acids
PGE	Population Growth Estimation
PGE	Pore Gradient Electrophoresis
PGE	Portland General Electric Co., Library, Portland, OR [*OCLC symbol*] (OCLC)
PGE	Portland Grain Exchange (EA)
PGE	Posterior Gastroenterostomy [*Medicine*] (MELL)
PGE	Precision Gimbal Experiment
PGE	Preliminary Gunners Examination (SAUS)
PGE	Primary Ground Electrode (SAUS)
PGE	Prime Group Engineer (AAG)
PGE	Product Generation Executive (SAUS)
PGE	Professional Group - Education
PG-E	Professional Group Education (SAUS)
PGE	Prostaglandin E [*Biochemistry*]
PGE	Provisional Government of Eritrea
PGE	Purge (NASA)
PG-EC	Professional Group-Electronic Computers (SAUS)
PGEC	Professional Group on Electronic Computers [*IEEE*]
PGECap	PG & E Capital I [*Associated Press*] (SAG)
PGECP	Professional Group Electronic Component Parts (IAA)
PGED	Point-contact Germanium Diode (SAUS)
PGED	Professional Group - Electronic Devices
PG-ED	Professional Group-Electronic Devices (SAUS)
PGEM	Professional Group - Engineering Management
PGEM	Prostaglandin E Metabolite (STED)
PGEner	PG Energy, Inc. [*Associated Press*] (SAG)
P-generation...	Parental Generation (WDAA)
P-Generation...	Parental-Generation (SAUS)
PGeol	Professional Geologist (DD)
PGeoph	Professional Geophysicist (DD)
PGER	Pacific Great Eastern Railway (SAUS)
PGEU	Pharmaceutical Group of the European Union (SAUS)
PGEWS	Professional Group on Engineering Writing and Speech [*Institute of Radio Engineers; now IEEE*]
PGEX	Pacific Gateway Exchange, Inc. [*NASDAQ symbol*] (SAG)
PGF	Pacific Gamefish Foundation (EA)
PGF	Paternal Grandfather (STED)
pgf	Paternal Grandfather (STED)
PGF	Patrol Ship [*Navy*]
PGF	Pengrowth Gas Income Fund Trust Units [*Toronto Stock Exchange symbol*]
PGF	Peptide Growth Factor [*Biochemistry*]
PGF	Perpignan [*France*] [*Airport symbol*] (OAG)
PGF	Plant Growth Facility (SAUS)
PGF	Plerocercoid Growth Factor [*Endocrinology*]
PGF	Portugal Fund [*NYSE symbol*] (SPSG)
PGF	Postglacial Fault [*Biology*]
PGF	Presentation Graphic Feature [*Computer science*]
PGF	Pressure Gradient Force (SAUS)
PGF	Prostaglandin F [*Biochemistry*]
PGFC	Periodical Guide for Computerists [*Applegate Computer Enterprises*] [*Information service or system*] [*Defunct*] (IID)
PGFEL	Preliminary Government-Furnished Equipment List (MCD)
PGFM	Prostaglandin F and its Metabolite [*Dihydro-keto-prostaglandin*] [*Medicine*] (BABM)
PGFNA	Prince George Free-Net Association (SAUS)
PGFR	Power-Generating Fusion Reaction

PGFVS	Postgraduate Federation in Veterinary Science [*Australia*]
PGFW	Guam [*Mariana Islands*] [*ICAO location identifier*] (ICLI)
PGG	Guided Missile Patrol Combatant [*Navy*]
PGG	Page America Group, Inc. [*AMEX symbol*] (SPSG)
PGG	Petrogold Financial Corp. [*Vancouver Stock Exchange symbol*]
PGG	Pneumatic Ground Group
PGG	Polyclonal Gamma Globulin [*Medicine*] (STED)
PGG	Power Generation Group [*Nuclear Regulatory Commission*] (NRCH)
PGG	Prostaglandin G [*A prostaglandin endoperoxide*] [*Biochemistry*]
PG/GAG	Proteoglycans/Glyosaminoglyans
PGGO	Prescribed Goods (General) Order
PGH	Pantnagar [*India*] [*Airport symbol*] (AD)
PGH	Paragraph (ADWA)
PGH	Patrol Gunboat (Hydrofoil) [*Navy symbol*]
PGH	Per Geard Hatch (RIMS)
PGH	Philadelphia General Hospital (SAUS)
PGH	Philippine General Hospital (SAUS)
PGH	Phosphoglycolohydroxamate [*Biochemistry*]
PGH	Pituitary Growth Hormone [*Endocrinology*]
PGH	Plasma Growth Hormone [*Hematology*] (MAE)
PGH	Polymer Group, Inc. [*NYSE symbol*] (SAG)
PGH	Porcine Growth Hormone [*Biochemistry*]
PGH	Port Group Highway [*Telecommunications*] (TEL)
PGH	Prostaglandin H [*A prostaglandin endoperoxide*] [*Biochemistry*]
PGHA	Park Gallatin Hereford Association (EA)
PGHFE	Professional Group - Human Factors in Electronics
Pgh Leg Journal...	Pittsburgh Legal Journal [*Pennsylvania*] [*A publication*] (DLA)
PGHM	Payload Ground Handling Mechanism [*NASA*] (MCD)
PGHS	Prostaglandin Hydrogen Synthase [*An enzyme*]
PGHS	Public-General Hospital Section [*American Hospital Association*] (EA)
PGHTS	Port Group Highway Timeslot [*Telecommunications*] (TEL)
PGI	Chitato [*Angola*] [*Airport symbol*] [*Obsolete*] (OAG)
PGI	General Information Programme [*UNESCO*] [*Acronym is based on foreign phrase*]
PGI	Panagra Airways, Inc. [*FAA designator*] (FAAC)
PGi	Paragigantocellularis [*Neuroanatomy*]
PGI	Parameter Group Identifier [*Computer science*] (TNIG)
PGI	Paris Gestion Informatique [*Paris Informatics Administration*] [*France*] [*Information service or system*] (IID)
PGI	Parking Guidance and Information [*Traffic management*]
PGI	Peripheral Graphics, Inc.
PGI	Peripherals General Inc. (SAUS)
PGI	Personalized Gift Institute (NTPA)
PGI	Phosphoglucoisomerase [*An enzyme*]
PGI	Phosphoglucose-Isomerase (SAUS)
PGI	Physicians Guide to the Internet (SAUS)
PGI	Pilot Gunnery Instructor (SAUS)
PGI	Ply-Gem, Inc. [*NYSE symbol*] (SAG)
PGI	Ply Gem Industries Inc. [*NYSE symbol*] (TTSB)
PGI	Polar Geophysical Institute [*Murmansk Region*] [*Russia*]
PGI	Port Group Interface [*Telecommunications*] (TEL)
PGI	Potassium, Glucose, and Insulin (MAE)
PGI	Power Generators, Incorporated
PGI	Professional Group - Instrumentation
PG-I	Professional Group Instrumentation (SAUS)
PGI	Project Group, Inc. [*Advertising agency*] [*Acronym now used as official n ame of agency*]
PGI	Prostaglandin I [*Biochemistry*]
PGI	Provigo, Inc. [*Toronto Stock Exchange symbol*]
PGI	Purge Gas Inlet (AAEL)
PGI	Pyrotechnics Guild International (EA)
PGIA	Pendulous Gyro Integrating Accelerometer (IAA)
PGIA	Programmable Gain Instrumentation Amplifier (IAA)
PGIE	Professional Group - Industrial Electronics
PG-IE	Professional Group Industrial Electronics (SAUS)
PGiess	Griechische Papyri im Museum des Oberhessischen Geschichtsvereins zu Giessen [*A publication*] (OCD)
P-GILD	Projection Gas Immersion LASER Doping (AAEL)
PGIM	Professional Group on Instrumentation and Measurement [*National Bureau of Standards*]
PGIP	Polygalacturonase-Inhibiting Protein [*Biochemistry*]
PGIP	Post Graduate Intelligence Program (DOMA)
PGIS	Parking Guidance Information System
PGIS	Project Grant Information System
PGIT	Professional Group - Information Theory
PGJ	Pipeline Girth Joint
PG/JAP	Persian Gulf to Japan (SAUS)
PGJD	Past Grand Junior Deacon [*Freemasonry*]
PGJN	Pomegranate Guild of Judaic Needlework (EA)
PGJW	Past Grand Junior Warden [*Freemasonry*] (ROG)
PGK	Pangkalpinang [*Indonesia*] [*Airport symbol*] (OAG)
PGK	Phosphoglycerate Kinase [*An enzyme*]
PGK	Phosphoglyceric Phosphokinase (SAUS)
PGI	Glenside Free Library, Glenside, PA [*Library symbol*] [*Library of Congress*] (LCLS)
PGL	Lutheran Theological Seminary, Gettysburg, PA [*Library symbol*] [*Library of Congress*] (LCLS)
PGL	Paraglossa of Labium [*Entomology*]
PGL	Partnership in Global Learning
PGL	Pascagoula, MS [*Location identifier*] [*FAA*] (FAAL)
PGL	Peer Group Leader (SAUS)
PGL	Peoples Energy [*NYSE symbol*] (TTSB)
PGL	Peoples Energy Corp. [*NYSE symbol*] (SPSG)
PGL	Persistent Generalized Lymphadenopathy [*Medicine*]
PGL	Peter Group Leader

PGL.............. Phenolic Glass Laminate
PGL.............. Phosphating Granulating Liquid (VLIE)
PGL.............. Phosphoglycolipid
PGL.............. Polyglutaraldehyde [*Organic chemistry*]
PGL.............. Portable Gas LASER
PGL.............. Professional Games League (SAUS)
PGL.............. Professional Graphics Language [*Software*] [*IBM Corp.*] (BYTE)
PGL.............. Provincial Grand Lodge [*Freemasonry*]
PGL.............. Pulsed Gas LASER
PGladM......... Mary J. Drexel Home, Gladwyne, PA [*Library symbol*] [*Library of Congress*] [*Obsolete*] (LCLS)
PGLAF .... Progen Industries [*NASDAQ symbol*] (SG)
PGLAX .... One Group: Louisiana Municipal Cl.A [*Mutual fund ticker symbol*] (SG)
PGIB .... Beaver College, Glenside, PA [*Library symbol*] [*Library of Congress*] (LCLS)
PGLC .... Pyrolysis Gas Liquid Chromatography
PGLD .... Phoenix Gold International, Inc. [*NASDAQ symbol*] (SAG)
PGLD .... Phoenix Gold Intl [*NASDAQ symbol*] (TTSB)
PGL-Hi........ Lutheran Historical Society, Gettysburg, PA [*Library symbol*] [*Library of Congress*] (LCLS)
PGLIN .... Page and Line [*Computer science*] (VLIE)
PGIL........... Glenside Free Library, Glenside, PA [*Library symbol*] [*Library of Congress*] (LCLS)
PGLN .... Page and Line (IAA)
PGlu........... Pyroglutamyl (SAUS)
PGlyM......... Phosphoglyceromutase (DB)
PGM............ Messiah College Learning Center, Grantham, PA [*OCLC symbol*] (OCLC)
PGM............ Palenque [*Mexico*] [*Airport symbol*] (AD)
PGM............ Paleogeomorphology (SAUS)
PGM............ Papyri Graecae Magicae [*A publication*] (OCD)
PGM............ Past Grand Master [*Freemasonry*]
PGM............ Paternal Grandmother (MEDA)
PGM............ Patrol Vessel, Motor Gunboat [*Navy symbol*] [*Obsolete*]
PGM............ Periaqueductal Grey Matter (SAUS)
PGM............ Perron Gold Mines [*Vancouver Stock Exchange symbol*]
PGM............ Persatuan Geologi Malaysia [*Geological Society of Malaysia*] (EAIO)
PGM............ PGM-11 Redstone Missile (SAUS)
PGM............ Phosphoglucomutase [*An enzyme*]
PGM............ Planetary Gearhead Motor [*Aerospace*]
PGM............ Planning Guidance Memorandum (DOMA)
PGM............ Plant Genetic Materials
PGM............ Platinum Group Metal [*In meteorites*]
PGM............ Platinum-Group Minerals (SAUS)
PGM............ Poly-Gel Mitigator
PGM............ Porous Glass Matrix (SAUS)
PGM............ Portable Greymap [*Image format*] (AAEL)
PGM............ Port Graham, AK [*Location identifier*] [*FAA*] (FAAL)
PGM............ Precision Guided Missile
PGM............ Precision-Guided Munition (MCD)
PGM............ Processing Graph Methodology (SAUS)
pgm............ Program (ELAL)
PGM............ Program
PGM............ Programable (SAUS)
PGM............ Program Guidance Memorandum
PGM............ Putnam Investment Grade Municipal Trust [*NYSE symbol*] (SPSG)
PGMA .... Phosphoglycerate Mutase A (DMAA)
PGMA .... Poly(glyceryl Methacrylate) [*Organic chemistry*]
PGMA .... Private Grocers' Merchandising Association [*British*] (BI)
PGMA .... Public Golf Management Association (NTPA)
PGMA .... Pulsed Gas Metal Arc (KSC)
PGMA-EA .... Polyglycidal Methacrylate-Ethyl Acrylate [*Organic chemistry*] (PDAA)
PGMARV...... Precision Guided Maneuvering Re-Entry Vehicle (PDAA)
P-GMAW..... Pulsed-Current Gas Metal-Arc Welding (SAUS)
PGMB .... Phosphoglycerate Mutase B (DMAA)
PGMC .... Primary Glass Manufacturers Council (NTPA)
PGmc........... Proto-Germanic (SAUS)
PGME.......... Professional Group - Medical Electronics
PG-ME .... Professional Group-Medical Electronics (SAUS)
PGMEA .... Propylene Glycol Monomethyl Ether Acetate [*Organic chemistry*]
PGM-FI .... Programmed Fuel Injection [*Automotive engineering*]
PGMIL......... Professional Group - Military Electronics (MUGU)
PGMILE....... Professional Group - Military Electronics (AAG)
PG-MITT ..... Professional Group-Microwave Theory and Technics (SAUS)
PGML.......... Precision Graphics Markup Language [*Computer science*]
PGMM .... Precision Guided Mortar Munition
PGMOT .... Pollution Generation Multiplier from Output Table (PDAA)
PGMP .... Preliminary Guaranteed Minimum Price
PGMR .... Programmer (SAUS)
PGMS .... Professional Grounds Management Society (EA)
PGMS .... Stillwater Mining [*NASDAQ symbol*] (TTSB)
PGMS .... Stillwater Mining Co. [*NASDAQ symbol*] (SAG)
PGMSJ......... Professional Group of Mathematical Symbol Jugglers (MUGU)
PGMT......... Pigment (MSA)
PGMTT....... Professional Group - Microwave Theory and Techniques
PGMV......... Pea Green Mottle Virus [*Plant pathology*]
PGN .... Paragon Health Network [*NYSE symbol*] [*Formerly, Living Centers of America*] (SG)
PGN .... Paragon Petroleum Ltd. [*Toronto Stock Exchange symbol*]
PGN .... Performance Group Number (SAUS)
PGN .... Perigeniculate Nucleus [*Anatomy*]
PGN .... Phi Gamma Nu [*Fraternity*]
PGN .... Pigeon (ADA)
PGN .... Platinum Group Nugget [*In meteorites*]

PGN .... Portland General Corp. [*NYSE symbol*] (SPSG)
PGN .... Proliferative Glomerulonephritis [*Medicine*]
PGN .... Pulse Generator
PGNAA........ Prompt Gamma Neutron Activation Analysis [*Analytical chemistry*]
PGNC .... Payload Guidance Navigation and Control (SAUS)
PGNCS........ Primary Guidance, Navigation, and Control System [*or Subsystem*] [*Apollo*] [*NASA*] (MCD)
PGND .... Propaganda (AABC)
PGNP .... Pagsanjan Gorge National Park (SAUS)
PGNR .... Page Number (VLIE)
PGNS .... PathoGenesis Corp. [*NASDAQ symbol*] (SAG)
PGNS .... Primary Guidance and Navigation System [*Apollo*] [*NASA*]
PGNS .... Professional Group - Nuclear Science
PGNT .... Sabanettan, Tinian Island [*Mariana Islands*] [*ICAO location identifier*] (ICLI)
PGNW........ Ritidian Point, Guam Island [*Mariana Islands*] [*ICAO location identifier*] (ICLI)
PGO .... Pagecorp, Inc. [*Toronto Stock Exchange symbol*]
PGO .... Page, OK [*Location identifier*] [*FAA*] (FAAL)
PGO .... Past Grand Orient [*Freemasonry*] (ROG)
PGO .... Peroxidase-Glucose Oxidase [*Also, GOD-POD*] [*Enzyme mixture*]
PGO .... Pontine Geniculate Occipital (DIPS)
PGO .... Ponto-Geniculate-Occipital [*Electroencephalography*]
PGO .... Positive Grid Oscillator
PGO .... Pyrolysis Gas Oil (SAUS)
PGOC .... Payload Ground Operation Contract (SAUS)
PGOC .... Payload Ground Operations Contractor [*NASA*] (SSD)
PGOC .... Payload Ground Operations Control (SAUS)
PGOC .... Philadelphia Grand Opera Co. (SAUS)
PGOR .... Payload Ground Operation Requirements [*NASA*] (NASA)
PGORS........ Payload Ground Operation Requirements Study [*NASA*] (MCD)
PGOS .... Petroleum, Gas and Oil Shale (SAUS)
PGOWG....... Payload Ground Operations Working Group (SAUS)
PGP .... Pacific Gateway Properties [*Formerly, Perini Investment Properties, Inc.*] [*AMEX symbol*] (SPSG)
PGP .... Parti Gabonais du Progres [*Political party*] (EY)
PGP .... Peace Garden Project [*Later, NPG*] (EA)
PGP .... Phagocyte Glycoprotein [*Biochemistry*]
PGP .... Phosphoglycolate Phosphatase [*An enzyme*]
PGP .... Pico Glass Pellet
PGP .... Planning Grant Program
PGP .... Postgamma Proteinuria [*Medicine*] (MAE)
PGP .... Precision Gas Products [*Commercial firm*]
PGP .... Prepaid Group Practice [*Insurance*]
PGP .... Pretty Good Piracy (SAUS)
PGP .... Pretty Good Privacy [*Telecommunications*]
PGP .... Programmable Graphics Processor
PGP .... Progressive General Paralysis (MELL)
PGP .... Project on Government Procurement (EA)
PGP .... Prostaglandin Production
PGP .... Puerta Galera [*Philippines*] [*Seismograph station code, US Geological Survey*] (SEIS)
PGP .... Pulsed Glide Path (IAA)
PGP .... University of Southern Maine at Portland, Portland, ME [*OCLC symbol*] (OCLC)
PGPEP .... Professional Group - Product Engineering and Production
PGPH .... Peptidylglutamyl-Peptide Hydrolyzing [*Biochemistry*]
PGPI .... Protein Grain Products International (EA)
PGP Landing System... Pulsed Glide Path Landing System (SAUS)
PGPR .... Plant-Growth-Promoting Rhizobacteria
PGPR .... Provincial Guild of Printers Readers (SAUS)
PGPS .... Packaged Gas Pressure System
PGPT .... Professional Group - Production Techniques
PGQC .... Professional Group-Quality Control (IAA)
PGR .... Paragould, AR [*Location identifier*] [*FAA*] (FAAL)
PGR .... Parental Guidance Recommended [*Movie rating*] [*Australia*]
PGR .... Paternal Grandfather (DAVI)
PGR .... Peregrine Petroleum [*Vancouver Stock Exchange symbol*]
PGR .... Petition Granted (DNAB)
PGR .... PGR. Press Gallery Report [*A publication*] (ADA)
PGR .... Planning and Ground Rule (SAUS)
PGR .... Plant Genetic Resources (SAUS)
PGR .... Plant Growth Regulator
PGR .... Polymerized Grass Extract [*Immunology*]
PGR .... Population Growth Rate
PGR .... Postglacial Rebound (SAUS)
PGR .... Precision Graphic Recorder
PgR............ Progesterone Receptor [*Endocrinology*]
PGR .... Progressive Corp., Ohio [*NYSE symbol*] (TTSB)
PGR .... Psychogalvanic Reaction (SAUS)
PGR .... Psychogalvanic Reflex [*or Response*] [*Psychology*]
PGR .... Psychogalvanic Response (SAUS)
PGR .... Pulsed Graphite Reactor (SAUS)
PGR .... Pyrogallol Red [*Also, PR*] [*An indicator*] [*Chemistry*]
PGR .... Reconnaissance Patrol Combatant [*Navy*]
PGR .... Spacelab Planning and Ground Rule [*NASA*] (NAKS)
PGraM......... Messiah College, Grantham, PA [*Library symbol*] [*Library of Congress*] (LCLS)
PG Rating.... Parental Guidance Rating (SAUS)
PGRC .... Plant Gene Resources of Canada [*See also RPC*]
PGRC.......... Privacy Global Resource Center (EA)
PGRC.......... Program Guidance and Review Committee [*Army*] (AABC)
PGrev.......... Greenville Area Public Library, Greenville, PA [*Library symbol*] [*Library of Congress*] (LCLS)

PGrevT.........	Thiel College, Greenville, PA [Library symbol] [Library of Congress] (LCLS)
PGRF	Pacific Gamefish Research Foundation [Later, PORF] (EA)
PGRF	Pulse Group Repetition Frequency
PGRFA	Plant Genetic Resources for Food and Agriculture (SAUS)
PGRFI	Professional Group - Radio Frequency Interference
PGRG..........	Potomac General Research Group
PGRM	Parti Gerakan Rakyat Malaysia [People's Action Party of Malaysia] [Political party] (PPW)
P-GRN	Progranulocytes [Hematology] (DAVI)
PGRO	Pea Growing Research Organisation Ltd. [British] (BI)
PGRO	Processors and Growers Research Organisation [British] (IRUK)
PGRO	Rota/International [Mariana Islands] [ICAO location identifier] (ICLI)
PGRQC.........	Professional Group - Reliability and Quality Control
PGRS	Pergerakan Guerilja Rakyat Sarawak [Sarawak People's Guerrilla Forces] [Malaya]
PGRS	Plume Groundwater Recovery System [Environmental science] (BCP)
PGRS	Precision Guided Rocket System (SEWL)
PGRSA	Plant Growth Regulator Society of America (EA)
PGRT	Petroleum Gas and Revenue Tax [Canada]
PGRTRC.........	Professional Group-Radio Telemetry and Remote Control (IAA)
PGRV	Photogravure (VRA)
PGRV	Precision Guided Reentry Vehicle
PGRVT.........	Precisely Guided Reentry Test Vehicle (SAA)
PGRWG.........	Payload Ground Requirements Working Group [NASA] (NASA)
PGRWG.........	Plant Growth Regulator Working Group (SAUS)
PGS	Naval Postgraduate School
PGS	Pagosa Springs [Colorado] [Seismograph station code, US Geological Survey] [Closed] (SEIS)
PGS	Papergram System [Military] (CAAL)
PGS	Parallel Gap Soldering
PGS	Parser-Generating System (SAUS)
PGS	Passive Geodetic Satellite [NASA]
PGS	Passive Gravity Stabilization
PGS	Peach Springs, AZ [Location identifier] [FAA] (FAAL)
PGS	Pennsylvania German Society [Later, TPGS] (EA)
PGS	Physicians for Global Survival
PGS	Pidaung Game Sanctuary (SAUS)
PGS	Pikunas Graphoscopic Scale [Personality development test] [Psychology]
PGS	Plane Grating Spectrograph
PGS	Plan Graphics Support (SAUS)
PGS	Plant Growth Substance
PGS	Plasma Generator System
PGS	Platoon Gunnery Simulator (SAUS)
PGS	Polish Genealogical Society (EA)
PGS	Polymer Glass Sealant
PGS	Portable Ground Station
PGS	Postsurgical Gastroparesis Syndrome [Medicine] (MELL)
PGS	Power Generation Satellite (HGAA)
PGS	Power Generation Section
PGS	Power Generation System [or Subsystem]
PGS	Power Generator Section (KSC)
PGS	Practical Guide Series (ACII)
PGS	Precision Gunnery System [Army training device] (INF)
PGS	Predicted Ground Speed [Navigation]
PGS	President of the Geographical Society [British] (ROG)
PGS	President of the Geological Society [British]
PGS	Pressed Glassmakers Society [British] (DBA)
PGS	Pressure-Gradient Single-Ended [Microphone] (DEN)
PGS	Pretty Good Signature [Computer science]
PGS	Pretty Good Stuff [Liquor]
PGS	Primary Guidance Subsystem (MCD)
PGS	Primary Guidance System (SAUS)
PGS	Proceedings of the Geological Society (SAUS)
PGS	Process Guiding System (SAUS)
PGS	Product Generation System (EOSA)
PGS	Professional Guidance Systems, Inc. [Information service or system] (IID)
PGS	Progenitor Genealogical Society (EA)
PGS	Program Generation System [Computer science] (MDG)
PGS	Program Generator System (SAUS)
PGS	Propellant Gauging System
PGS	Prostaglandin Synthase [An enzyme]
PGS	Provincial Grand Secretary [Freemasonry]
PGS	Publications Gravure Server (SAUS)
PGS	Public Service Co. North Carolina [NYSE symbol] (SAG)
PGS	Tauranga Aero Club, Inc. [New Zealand] [ICAO designator] (FAAC)
PGSA	Petroleum Geo Services [NASDAQ symbol] (SAG)
PGSA	Polish Genealogical Society of America (EA)
PGSAY	Petroleum Geo-Svcs A/S ADS [NASDAQ symbol] (TTSB)
PGSB	Past Grand Sword Bearer [Freemasonry] (ROG)
PGSB	Provincial Grand Sword-Bearer [Freemasonry]
PGSC	Panel on Geological Site Criteria (SAUS)
PGSC	Payload and General Support Computer [NASA]
PGSC	Persian Gulf Service Command
PGSC	Portable Gas Supply Cart (SAUS)
PGSCOL.......	Naval Postgraduate School
PGSD	Past Grand Senior Deacon [Freemasonry]
PGSE	Payload Ground Support Equipment [NASA] (MCD)
PGSE	Peculiar Ground Support Equipment [DoD]
PGSE	Processing Graph Support Environment (SAUS)
PGSE	Pulsed Field Gradient Spin-Echo
PGSE	Pulsed Gradient Spin Echo [Physics]

PGSEL	Priced Ground Support Equipment List (AAG)
PGSET	Professional Group on Space Electronics and Telemetry (AAG)
PGSF	Public Good Science Fund [New Zealand]
PGSGX........	One Group: Small Cap. Cl.A [Mutual fund ticker symbol] (SG)
PGSI	Prostaglandin Synthetase Inhibitor (DMAA)
PGSM	Payload Gimbal Separation Mechanism (SAUS)
PGSM	Precision Guided Submunition (SAUS)
PGSN	Saipan Island (Obyan)/International [Mariana Islands] [ICAO location identifier] (ICLI)
PGSR	Psychogalvanic Skin Resistance [Otolaryngology]
PGSS	Paget-Gorman Sign System (AIE)
PGSTAP........	Pressure, Gas, Start, Turbine, Auxiliary Pump-Drive Assembly [Pronounced "pigstap"]
PGSU	Propellant [or Propulsion] Gas Supply Unit
PGSW	Past Grand Senior Warden [Freemasonry]
PGT............	Pacific Gas Transmission (SAUS)
PGT............	Page Table [Computer science] (IBMDP)
PGT............	Partido Guatemalteco del Trabajo [Guatemalan Labor Party] [Political party] (PD)
PGT............	Passenger and Goods Transport (SAUS)
PGT............	Past Grand Treasurer [Freemasonry]
PGT............	Pegasus Hava Tasimaciligi AS [Turkey] [ICAO designator] (FAAC)
PGT............	Per Gross Ton [Shipping]
PGT............	Photo Glow Tube
PGT............	Pigtail (MSA)
PGT............	Planetary Gear Train (SAUS)
PGT............	Planned Giving Today [A publication]
PGT............	Platoon Gunnery Trainer (DOMA)
PGT............	Pollen Grain Trajectory [Botany]
PGT............	Polymer Grid Triode [Imaging technology]
PGT............	Porangatu [Brazil] [Airport symbol] (AD)
PGT............	Potato Extract-Glucose-Thiamine Hydrochloride [Growth medium]
PGT............	Power Grid Tube
PGT............	Princeton Gamma Tech (AAEL)
PGT............	Program Global Table (CIST)
PGT............	Putnam Intermediate Government Income [NYSE symbol] (SPSG)
PGTA	Pharmaceutical Grade Transfer Adhesive (SAUS)
PGTE	Precision Gunnery Training Equipment (SAUS)
PGTO	Portuguese Government Trade Office (EA)
PGTR	Plasma-Glucose Tolerance Rate [Hematology] (MAE)
PGTRC........	Professional Group-Telemetry and Remote Control (IAA)
PGTS	Precision Gunnery Training System [Army] (INF)
PGTSND.....	Puget Sound (FAAC)
PGTT..........	Prednisolone Glucose Tolerance Test [Medicine] (DMAA)
PGTTT........	Precision Gear Train Tools and Test
PGTV	Pegasus Communications Corp. [NASDAQ symbol] (SAG)
PGTW	Guam [Mariana Islands] [ICAO location identifier] (ICLI)
PGTZ	Praegitzer Industries [NASDAQ symbol] (TTSB)
PGTZ	Praegitzer Industries, Inc. [NASDAQ symbol] (SAG)
PGU	Gannon University, Nash Library, Erie, PA [OCLC symbol] (OCLC)
PGU	Pegasus Gold, Inc. [AMEX symbol] [Toronto Stock Exchange symbol]
PGU	Peripheral Glucose Uptake [Medicine] (MELL)
PGU	Plant Growth Unit [NASA] (MCD)
PGU	Pontifical Gregorian University (SAUS)
PGU	Postgonococcal Urethritis [Medicine]
PGU	Power Generator Unit (IAA)
PGU	Pressure Gas Umbilical (KSC)
PGU	Propulsion Gas Umbilical
PGUA	Andersen Air Force Base, Guam Island [Mariana Islands] [ICAO location identifier] (ICLI)
PGUE	Professional Group - Ultrasonic Engineering
PGUM..........	Agana Naval Air Station, Guam Island [Mariana Islands] [ICAO location identifier] (ICLI)
PgUp..........	Page Up [Computer science] (BARN)
PGUT	Phosphogalactose Uridyltransferase [Known as Galactose-1-phosphate Uridyl yltransferase] [An enzyme]
PGV	Greenville [North Carolina] [Airport symbol] (OAG)
PGV	Proximal Gastric Vagotomy [Medicine]
PGVC	Professional Group - Vehicular Communications
PGW	Parallel Gap Welding
PGW	Past Grand Warden [Freemasonry]
PGW	Periodic Gravity Wave (SAUS)
PGW	Persian Gulf War (SAUS)
PGW	Practice Guided Weapon (MCD)
PGW	Pressure Gas Welding
PGW	Pressurized Stone Groundwood [Pulp and paper technology]
PGW	United Plant Guard Workers of America
PGWA	Pottery and Glass Wholesalers Association (NADA)
PGWB	Psychological General Well Being [Index] (DMAA)
PGWC	Pennsylvania Gas & Water Co. [NASDAQ symbol] (SAG)
PGWC	PG Energy, Inc. [NASDAQ symbol] (SAG)
PGWCX........	PIMCO: Growth Cl.C [Mutual fund ticker symbol] (SG)
PGWCZ........	P G Energy $2.25 Dep Pfd [NASDAQ symbol] (TTSB)
PGWD	Pesticides in Ground Water Database [Environmental Protection Agency]
PGWG	Parliamentary Group for World Government
PGWG	Particles and Gases Working Group [NASA] (NASA)
PGWR	Pressurised Gas-Cooled Water Reactor [Nuclear energy] (NUCP)
PGWS	Peak Gust Wind Speed (SAUS)
PGWS	P. G. Wodehouse Society (EA)
PGWT	Peipeinimaru, Tinian Island [Mariana Islands] [ICAO location identifier] (ICLI)
PGWV	Persian Gulf War Veteran (MELL)

PGwvG......... Gwynedd-Mercy College, Gwynedd, PA [*Library symbol*] [*Library of Congress*] (LCLS)
PGX .... Prostaglandin X [*or Prostacyclin*] [*Biochemistry*]
PGY .... Global Yield Fund, Inc. [*NYSE symbol*] (SPSG)
PGY .... Postgraduate Year
PGY .... San Diego, CA [*Location identifier*] [*FAA*] (FAAL)
PGYE .... Peptone, Glucose Yeast Extract [*Medium*] [*Biochemistry*] (DAVI)
PGZ .... Ponta Grossa [*Brazil*] [*Airport symbol*] (OAG)
PG/ZD .... Group Propogate / Zero Detect (MHDI)
PH............... Czechoslovakia [*License plate code assigned to foreign diplomats in the US*]
Ph................ Hit Probability
pH............... Hydrogen Ion Concentration (MAE)
Ph................ [*The*] New Testament in Modern English [*1958*] [*J. B. Phillips*] [*A publication*] (BJA)
PH............... Packet Handler (or Handling) (SAUS)
PH............... Page Heading (BUR)
PH............... Pan Head [*Screw Head*] (ECII)
PH............... Parachute Handler (SAUS)
PH............... Parathyroid Hormone (STED)
PH............... Parity High bit (SAUS)
PH............... Parker-Hannifin Corp. [*NYSE symbol*] (SPSG)
PH............... Parotid Hormone [*Biochemistry*]
PH............... Partial Hysterectomy [*Medicine*] (MELL)
PH............... Partially Hepatectomized (DB)
PH............... Passive Hemagglutination (STED)
PH............... Past History [*Medicine*]
PH............... Patient History (SAUS)
PH............... Pauling and Harrischfeger
PH............... Pearl Harbor, Hawaii
PH............... Peliosis Hepatitis (STED)
PH............... Penthouse
pH............... Percent Hydrogen (SSD)
PH............... Performance History
PH............... Per Hour (IAA)
PH............... Period Hours (IAA)
PH............... Pershing II
PH............... Persistent Hepatitis [*Medicine*]
PH............... Personal History [*Medicine*] (AAMN)
PH............... Personal Hygiene (MCD)
PH............... Perth [*Postcode*] (ODBW)
PH............... Pest Hospital (SAUS)
Ph................ Phallacidin [*Biochemistry*]
PH............... Phantom (IAA)
PH............... Phantom Circuit [*Telecommunications*] (TEL)
Ph................ Pharmacia AB [*Sweden*] [*Research code symbol*]
Ph................ Pharmacopoeia
PH............... Phase (KSC)
ph................ Phase (WDMC)
Ph................ Phenanthrene [*Organic chemistry*] (AAMN)
Ph................ Phenyl [*Organic chemistry*]
PH............... Phenylalanine Hydroxylase (STED)
PH............... Phiala [*Bottle*] [*Pharmacy*]
PH............... Philadelphia [*Diocesan abbreviation*] [*Pennsylvania*] (TOCD)
Ph................ Philadelphia Stock Exchange (SG)
PH............... Philharmonic Hall (NADA)
Ph................ Philippians [*New Testament book*] (BJA)
PH............... Philippines [*ANSI two-letter standard code*] (CNC)
ph................ Philippines [*IYRU nationality code*] [*MARC country of publication code*] [*Library of Congress*] (LCCP)
Ph................ Philippus [*Flourished, 13th century*] [*Authority cited in pre-1607 legal work*] (DSA)
Ph................ Phillimore's English Ecclesiastical Reports [*A publication*] (DLA)
Ph................ Phillips' English Chancery Reports [*1841-49*] [*A publication*] (DLA)
Ph................ Phillips' English Election Cases [*1780-81*] [*A publication*] (DLA)
PH............... Phillips Head (DAC)
PH............... Philosophy (GOBB)
PH............... Phone (MDG)
Ph................ Phosphate
PH............... Phosphor (SAUS)
PH............... Phosphorylase (SAUS)
PH............... Phot [*Electronics*] (DEN)
PH............... Photographer's Mate [*Navy rating*]
PH............... Photography Program [*Association of Independent Colleges and Schools specialization code*]
Ph................ Photoreceptor
Ph................ Photostat (BJA)
PH............... Phrase (ADA)
Ph................ Physica [*of Aristotle*] [*Classical studies*] (OCD)
PH............... Physically Handicapped (OICC)
Ph................ Phytane [*Organic chemistry*]
PH............... Piano Type Hinge
PH............... Picohenry [*One trillionth of a henry*]
P/H............... Pier to House [*Classified advertising*] (ADA)
Ph................ Pilot-Helicopter [*Navy*] [*British*]
PH............... Pilot House
PH............... Pinch Hitter [*Baseball*]
PH............... Pin Hole [*Eye examination*] (CPH)
PH............... Plane Handler [*Navy*]
PH............... Plant Height [*Botany*]
PH............... Plateholder (SAUS)
PH............... Pleckstrin-Homology [*Domain*] [*Biochemistry*]
PH............... Polynesian Airlines [*Airline code*] [*Australia*]
pH............... Pondus Hydrogenii (SAUS)
PH............... Poor Health (DAVI)

PH............... Porphyria Hepatica (STED)
PH............... Porta Hepatis [*Anatomy*]
PH............... Porter House [*Initials often used as a pattern on clothing designed by this firm*]
P/H............... Postage and Handling [*Shipping*]
PH............... Posterior Hypothalamus (STED)
PH............... Post History (STED)
PH............... Postural Hypotension [*Medicine*] (MELL)
pH............... Potential Hydrogen (WDAA)
pH............... Pouvoir Hydrogene [*Hydrogen Power*] [*Negative logarithm of effective H ion concentration*] [*Chemistry*]
PH............... Power Hood [*Automobile classified advertising*]
PH............... Power House (SAUS)
PH............... Powerhouse
PH............... Power of Hydrogen (IAA)
PH............... Practitioner's Handbooks [*A publication*]
PH............... Precipitation Hardening
P-H............... Prentice-Hall, Inc. [*Publishers*]
PH............... Presidential Medal of Honour [*Botswana*]
PH............... Pressure Head (SAUS)
PH............... Previous Hardening (SAUS)
PH............... Previous History [*Medicine*]
PH............... Primary Hyperparathyroidism
PH............... Private Hotel
PH............... Probability of Hit [*Military*] (MCD)
PH............... Process Hold (SAUS)
PH............... Professional Hydrologist
PH............... Prohibited area (SAUS)
PH............... Project Handclasp (EA)
PH............... Prolactin Hormone (SAUS)
PH............... Prolyl Hydroxylase (STED)
PH............... Prospect Hill [*Vole virus*]
PH............... Prostatic Hypertrophy [*Medicine*] (MAE)
PH............... Public Health
PH............... Public Holiday (DA)
PH............... Public House [*A drinking establishment*] [*British*]
PH............... Pulmonary Hypertension [*Medicine*] (MAE)
PH............... Punctate Hemorrhage [*Medicine*] (STED)
PH............... Purple Heart [*Given to personnel wounded in military service*] [*Military decoration*]
PH............... Purpura Hyperglobulinemia [*Medicine*] (DAVI)
pH$_1$............... Isoelectric Point [*Chemistry*] (DAVI)
PH1............... Phase I Environmental Inspection (COE)
Ph^1............... Philadelphia Chromosome (MAE)
PH1............... Photographer's Mate, First Class [*Navy rating*]
Ph^{1}c............ Philadelphia Chromosome
PH2............... Phase II Environmental Inspection (COE)
PH2............... Photographer's Mate, Second Class [*Navy rating*]
Ph$_2$0............ Partial Pressure of Water Vapor [*Chemistry*] (DAVI)
PH3............... Phase III Environmental Inspection (COE)
PH3............... Phosphine (AAEL)
PH3............... Photographer's Mate, Third Class [*Navy rating*]
PHA .... Arterial pH [*Hydrogen ion concentration*] [*Medicine*] (DAVI)
PHA .... Chicago, IL [*Location identifier*] [*FAA*] (FAAL)
PHa .... Hazelton Public Library, Hazelton, PA [*Library symbol*] [*Library of Congress*] (LCLS)
PHA .... Pachena Industries Ltd. [*Vancouver Stock Exchange symbol*]
PHA .... Pacific Pharmaceuticals [*AMEX symbol*] [*Formerly, Xytronyx, Inc.*] (SG)
PHA .... Palomino Horse Association (EA)
PHA .... Parallel Half Adder (SAUS)
PHA .... Parts per Hundred of Asphalt [*Chemical technology*]
PHA .... Passive Hemagglutination [*Immunology*]
PHA .... Peak Horizontal Acceleration
PHA .... Peripheral Hyperalimentation (Solution) [*Medicine*]
PHA .... Peruvian Heart Association (EA)
PHA .... Phenylalanine [*Medicine*] (MEDA)
PHA .... Physics and Astronomy (SAUS)
PHA .... Phytohemagglutinin [*Immunology*]
PHA .... Phytohemagglutinin Antigen [*A skin test for cellular based immunity*] (DAVI)
PHA .... Polomino Horse Association (SAUS)
PHA .... Polyhydroxyalkanoate [*Organic chemistry*]
PHA .... Poly(hydroxystearic Acid) [*Organic chemistry*]
PHA .... Port Health Authority (SAUS)
PHA .... Port Heiden [*Alaska*] [*Seismograph station code, US Geological Survey*] [*Closed*] (SEIS)
PHA .... Potentially Hazardous Asteroids
PHA .... Poultry Husbandry Adviser [*Ministry of Agriculture, Fisheries, and Food*] [*British*]
PHA .... Preferred Hotels Association [*Also known as Preferred Hotel Worldwide*] (EA)
PHA .... Prelaunch Hazard Area (MUGU)
PHA .... Preliminary Hazard Analyses (NASA)
PHA .... Preliminary Hazards Assessment [*Environmental science*] (COE)
PHA .... Primary Human Amnion [*Biology*] (BARN)
PHA .... Pritikin Health Association of Australia
PHA .... Process Hazard Analysis [*Environmental science*]
PHA .... Process Hazards Analysis [*Chemical engineering*]
PHA .... Professional Hairdressers' Association [*Australia*]
PHA .... Professional Handlers Association (EA)
PHA .... Professional Horsemen's Association of America (EA)
PHA .... Programmable Host Access [*Computer science*] (IAA)
PHA .... Pseudohypoaldosteronism [*Medicine*]
PHA .... Public Health Act (DAS)

PHA	Public Health Agency (DMAA)
PHA	Public Housing Administration [*or HHFA; disbanded 1965*]
PHA	Public Housing Agency [*Department of Housing and Urban Development*] (GFGA)
PHA	Pulmonary Hypertension Association (NRGU)
PHA	Pulse Height Analysis [*Spectroscopy*]
PHA	Pulse Height Analyzed
PHA	State Library of Pennsylvania, Harrisburg, PA [*OCLC symbol*] (OCLC)
PHAA	Airman Apprentice, Photographer's Mate, Striker [*Navy rating*]
PHAA	Percheron Horse Association of America (EA)
PHAA	Photographer's Airman Apprentice [*Navy*]
PHAA	Positive High-Angle of Attack
PHAA	Pritikin Health Association of Australia (SAUS)
PHAA	Professional Horsemen's Association of America [*Later, PHA*] (EA)
PHAABO	Purebred Hanoverian Association of American Breeders and Owners (EA)
PHAB	Physically Handicapped and Able Bodied [*Charitable organization*] [*British*]
PHABSIM	Physical Habitat Simulation Model [*Ecology*]
PHABY	Pharmacia AB [*Commercial firm*] (MHDW)
PHACO	Phacoemulsification [*Medicine*] (MELL)
PHADA	Public Housing Authorities Directors Association (EA)
PHADS	Phoenix Air Defense Sector (SAA)
phaeo	Phaeochromocytoma [*Pheochromocytoma*] [*Endocrinology*] (DAVI)
PHAID	Positive Hostile Aircraft Identification
PHAL	Phalange (WDAA)
PHAL	Phalanx (WDAA)
PHAL	Phytohemagglutinin-Stimulated Lymphocyte [*Medicine*] (DMAA)
Phal CC	Phalen's Criminal Cases [*A publication*] (DLA)
PHALCM	Phytohemagglutinin Stimulated Leukocyte Conditioned Medium
PHALSE	Phreakers, Hackers, and Laundry Service Employees [*East Coast group of computer trespassers raided by the FBI*]
PHAM	Phamis, Inc. [*NASDAQ symbol*] (SAG)
PHAM	Phase Amplitude Monopulse (PDAA)
PHA-M	Phytohemagglutinin M [*Immunology*] (MAE)
PHAM	Project: Hearts and Minds [*An association*] (EA)
Phamis	Phamis, Inc. [*Associated Press*] (SAG)
P-H Am Lab Arb Awards	American Labor Arbitration Awards (Prentice-Hall, Inc.) [*A publication*] (DLA)
P-H Am Lab Cas	American Labor Cases (Prentice-Hall, Inc.) [*A publication*] (DLA)
PHAMOS	Philips Application Modular Software (SAUS)
PHAMOS	Premote Hemodynamics and Metabolism in an Orbiting Satellite (KSC)
PHAN	Airman, Photographer's Mate, Striker [*Navy rating*]
PH and P	Peace, Health, and Prosperity
PH&P	Peace, Heath and Prosperity (SAUS)
PHANT	Phantom-Glass [*Theater term*] (DSUE)
PHAOMU	Pianoforte, Harmonium, and American Organ Makers' Union [*British*]
PHAP	Palmitoyl Hydrolyzed Animal Protein [*Organic chemistry*]
PHAP	Phytohemagglutinin Protein [*Medicine*] (MELL)
PHAP	Provincial Health Assistance Program [*Vietnam*]
PHAQ	Private Hospitals' Association of Queensland [*Australia*]
PHAR	Pharmaceutical (WDAA)
PHAR	Pharmacology
PHAR	Pharmacopoeia (ROG)
PHAR	Pharmacy [*or Pharmacist*] (MSA)
phar	Pharmacy (WDAA)
PHaR	Photosynthetically Active Radiation (EES)
PHarA	AMP, Inc., Harrisburg, PA [*Library symbol*] [*Library of Congress*] (LCLS)
Phar B	Pharmaciae Baccalaureus [*Bachelor of Pharmacy*]
PHarC	Harrisburg Area Community College, Harrisburg, PA [*Library symbol*] [*Library of Congress*] (LCLS)
PharC	Pharmaceutical Chemist [*British*]
PHarD	Dauphin County Library System, Harrisburg, PA [*Library symbol*] [*Library of Congress*] (LCLS)
Phar D	Doctor of Pharmacy (SAUS)
Phar D	Pharmaciae Doctor [*Doctor of Pharmacy*]
PHARE	Action Plan for Coordinated Aid to Poland and Hungary (SAUS)
PHARE	Poland and Hungary Assistance for Economic Restructuring [*EC*] (ECED)
PHARE	Program for Harmonized ATC [*Air Traffic Control*] Research in Europe (GAVI)
PharER-T	Pennsylvania Department of Environmental Resources, Bureau of Topographic and Geologic Survey, Harrisburg, PA [*Library symbol*] [*Library of Congress*] (LCLS)
Phar G	Graduate in Pharmacy (AAMN)
PHarH	Pennsylvania Historical and Museum Commission, Harrisburg, PA [*Library symbol*] [*Library of Congress*] (LCLS)
PHarH-Ar	Pennsylvania Historical and Museum Commission, Division of Archives and Manuscript, Harrisburg, PA [*Library symbol*] [*Library of Congress*] (LCLS)
PharLb	Pharmchem Laboratories, Inc. [*Associated Press*] (SAG)
PHARM	Pharmaceutical
Pharm	Pharmaceutist (SAUS)
Phar M	Pharmaciae Magister [*Master of Pharmacy*]
PHARM	Pharmacist [*or Pharmacy*]
PHARM	Pharmacology
Pharm	Pharmacy (DD)
pharm	Pharmacy (SHCU)
PHARM	Pharmacy
PHARM	Pharmacy Building (SAUS)
PhARMA	Pharmaceutical Research and Manufacturers Association of America (SAUS)
PHARMAC	Pharmacology
PHARMACOL	Pharmacological (MSA)
Pharmacol & Toxicol	Pharmacology and Toxicology (MEC)
Pharmacol Biochem Behav	Pharmacology, Biochemistry and Behavior (SAUS)
Pharmacol Toxicol	Pharmacology and Toxicology (SAUS)
Pharma Int	Pharma International (SAUS)
Pharm C	Pharmaceutical Chemist (MEDA)
PHARM CHEM	Pharmaceutical Chemistry (WDAA)
PHARMCL	Pharmaceutical
PharmD	Doctor of Pharmacology [*Canada*] (ASC)
Pharm D	Doctor of Pharmacy
PHARMDOC	Pharmaceutical Documentation (SAUS)
Pharm Eng	Pharmaceutical Engineering (SAUS)
Pharm G	Graduate in Pharmacy (MEDA)
PHARML	Pharmaceutical
Pharm M	Master of Pharmacy
PharMor	Phar-Mor, Inc. [*Associated Press*] (SAG)
PharmoS	Pharmos Corp. [*Associated Press*] (SAG)
PharmP	Pharmaceutical Product Development, Inc. [*Associated Press*] (SAG)
PHARM PAT	Pharmaceutical Patent (SAUS)
Pharm Tech Jpn	Pharm Tech Japan (SAUS)
Pharm Technol	Pharmaceutical Technology (SAUS)
Pharm World Sci	Pharmacy World and Science (SAUS)
PHAROS	Phased Array Radar for Overland Surveillance (ACAE)
PHAROS	Phased Array RADAR Operational Simulation [*Army*] (AABC)
PHAROS	Plan Handling and RADAR Operating System [*Aviation*] (DA)
PHarP	Harrisburg Polyclinic Hospital, Harrisburg, PA [*Library symbol*] [*Library of Congress*] (LCLS)
PHarris	Paul Harris Stores [*Associated Press*] (SAG)
PharUpj	Pharmacia & Upjohn, Inc. [*Associated Press*] (SAG)
PHARUS	Phased Array Universal Sar (SAUS)
PHAS	Pollution Hazard Assessment System [*Environmental science*]
PHAS	Pulse Height Analyzer System
PHASE	Package for Hospital, Appraisal, Simulation and Evaluation (SAUS)
PHaSE	Physics of Hard Spheres Experiment (SAUS)
PHASE	Pre-Hospital Arrest Survival Evaluation [*Cardiology study*]
PHASE IV	Base Level Data Automation Program (SAUS)
Phase Transit	Phase Transition (SAUS)
PHASR	Personnel Hazards Associated with Space Radiation [*Satellite*]
PHatfB	Biblical School of Theology, Hatfield, PA [*Library symbol*] [*Library of Congress*] (LCLS)
PHATOX	Pharmacological and Toxicological (SAUS)
PHatU	Union Library Co., Hatboro, PA [*Library symbol*] [*Library of Congress*] [*Obsolete*] (LCLS)
PHav	Haverford Township Free Library, Havertown, PA [*Library symbol*] [*Library of Congress*] (LCLS)
PHAV	Private Hospitals' Association of Victoria [*Australia*]
PHAWA	Private Hospitals' Association of Western Australia
PHAXSCAN	Philips High-Speed Automatic X-Ray Analysis System (SAUS)
Ph B	Bachelor of Pharmacy
PhB	Bachelor of Philosophy (DAVI)
Ph B	Bachelor of Physical Culture
PhB	British Pharmacopoeia (DAVI)
PHB	Para-Hexadecylaminobenzoate [*Clinical chemistry*]
PHB	Para-Hydroxybenzoate [*Organic chemistry*]
PHB	Parahydroxy Benzoic Acid (EDCT)
PHB	Parliament House Book [*Scotland*] [*A publication*] (DLA)
PHB	Parnaiba [*Brazil*] [*Airport symbol*] (OAG)
PHB	Per Hop Behaviour (SAUS)
PhB	Pharmacopoeia of Britain (SAUS)
Ph B	Philosophiae Baccalaureus [*Bachelor of Philosophy*]
PHB	Photochemical Hole Burning [*Spectrometry*]
PHB	Photographic Bulletin (MCD)
PHB	Pioneer Hi-Bred Intl [*NYSE symbol*] (TTSB)
PHB	Pointy Haired Boss
PHB	Poly(hydroxybenzoate) [*Organic chemistry*]
PHB	Polyhydroxybutyrate [*Organic chemistry*]
PHB	Pre-Homeobox [*Genetics*]
PHB	Preventive Health Behavior [*Medicine*] (DMAA)
PHB	Program Header Block [*Computer science*] (ELAL)
PHB	Public Health Bibliography
PHB	Public Health Service Building
PHBA	Palomino Horse Breeders of America (EA)
PHBA	Para-Hydroxybenzoic Acid [*Organic chemistry*]
PHBA	P-Hydroxybenzoic Acid
PHB Acid	Poly-a-Hydroxybutyric Acid (SAUS)
PHBB	Propylhydroxybenzyl Benzimidazole [*Organic chemistry*] (MAE)
Ph BD	Doctor of Bible Philosophy
PHBH	Para-Hydroxybenzoate Hydroxylase [*An enzyme*]
Ph B in Arch	Bachelor of Philosophy in Architecture
Ph B in Com	Bachelor of Philosophy in Commerce
Ph B in Ed	Bachelor of Philosophy in Education
PhBJ	Bachelor of Philosophy in Journalism (NADA)
PHBK	Barking Sands, Kauai Island [*Hawaii*] [*ICAO location identifier*] (ICLI)
PHBK	People's Heritage Financial Group, Inc. [*NASDAQ symbol*] (NQ)
PHBK	Peoples Heritage Finl Gr [*NASDAQ symbol*] (TTSB)
PHBLX	Phoenix Balanced [*Mutual fund ticker symbol*] (SG)
PHB/PHBV	Poly-3-Hydroxybutyric Acid
Ph-Br	Phenyl-Bromide (SAUS)
PHBRZ	Phosphor Bronze
PhBSp	Bachelor of Philosophy in Speech (NADA)
PHBV	Hydroxy Butyric Valeric Acid [*Polymer*]
PHBV	Poly(hydroxybutyrate-Valerate) [*Organic chemistry*]

ph bz .... Phosphor Bronze (BARN)
PHC .... Chief Photographer's Mate [Navy rating]
PHC .... Children's Hospital of Pittsburgh, Pittsburgh, PA [OCLC symbol] (OCLC)
PHC .... Haverford College, Haverford, PA [Library symbol] [Library of Congress] (LCLS)
PHC .... Pacific Holding Corp. (EFIS)
PHC .... Pacific Hurricane Centers [National Weather Service]
PHC .... Palmitoyl Homocysteine [Biochemistry]
PHC .... Panhandle Conference (PSS)
PHC .... Pathonic Network, Inc. [Toronto Stock Exchange symbol]
PHC .... Patrick Henry College (SAUS)
PHC .... Personal Health Costs [Medicine] (DMAA)
PHC .... Personal Holding Company [Generic term]
PHC .... Perturbed-Hardness Chain [Molecular thermodynamics]
PHC .... Petroleum Helicopters de Colombia SA [ICAO designator] (FAAC)
PHC .... Petroleum Hydrocarbon (SAUS)
Ph C .... Pharmaceutical Chemist
PHC .... PHC, Inc. [Associated Press] (SAG)
Ph C .... Philosopher of Chiropractic
PHC .... Photographic Change (MCD)
PHC .... Physical Hydrogen Cracking (SAUS)
PHC .... Population Housing Census (OICC)
PHC .... Port Harcourt [Nigeria] [Airport symbol] (OAG)
PHC .... Port Hardy [British Columbia] [Seismograph station code, US Geological Survey] (SEIS)
PHC .... Posthospital Care [Medicine]
PHC .... [A] Prairie Home Companion [National Public Radio program]
PHC .... Pratt Hotel Corp. [AMEX symbol] (SPSG)
PHC .... Premature Hereditary Canities [Medicine]
PHC .... Premolar Hypodontia, Hyperhidrosis, Canities Prematura [Syndrome] [Medicine] (DMAA)
PHC .... Primary Health Care
PHC .... Primary Health Centre [British]
PHC .... Primary Hepatic Carcinoma [Medicine]
PHC .... Primary Hepatocellular Carcinoma [Oncology] (DAVI)
PHC .... Principal Hazardous Constituent (GNE)
PHC .... Proliferative Helper Cells [Immunology]
PHC .... Public Health Committee (SAUS)
PHCA .... Philippine Heart Center for Asia (PDAA)
PHCA .... Pig Health Control Association [British]
PHCA .... Pleasure Horse Club of America (EA)
PHCAA .... Public Health Cancer Association of America [Defunct] (EA)
P-H Cas ...... American Federal Tax Reports (Prentice-Hall, Inc.) [A publication] (DLA)
PHCB .... Page Header Control Bit (SAUS)
PHCC .... Patients Encountered at [Primary] Health Care Centers
P-HCC .... Piston-Hand Control Clutch (DNAB)
PHCC .... Plumbing, Heating, Cooling Contracters (SAUS)
PHCC .... Primary Hepatocellular Carcinoma [Medicine] (DMAA)
PHCC .... Punjab High Court Cases [India] [A publication] (DLA)
PHCDS .... Public Health Common Data Set (SAUS)
PHCF .... Pituitary Growth Hormone Cell Function (SAUS)
Ph Ch .... Phillips' English Chancery Reports [1841-49] [A publication] (DLA)
PHCIB .... Plumbing-Heating-Cooling Information Bureau (EA)
PHC Inc ...... PHC, Inc. [Associated Press] (SAG)
PH Circuit.... Phantom Circuit (SAUS)
Ph-Cl .... Phenyl-Chloride (SAUS)
PHCLIS .... Protected Home Circle Life Insurance Society (EA)
PHCM .... Master Chief Photographer's Mate [Navy rating]
PHCM .... Phone.com, Inc. [NASDAQ symbol]
PHCO .... Peoples Holding [NASDAQ symbol] (TTSB)
PHCO .... Peoples Holding Co. [NASDAQ symbol] (SAG)
PHCONST .... Phase Constant (IAA)
P-H Corp..... Corporation [Prentice-Hall, Inc.] [A publication] (DLA)
PHCP .... Physically Handicapped Children's Program
PHCP .... Prehospital Care Provider [Health insurance] (DMAA)
PHCS .... Private Healthcare Systems
PHCS .... Senior Chief Photographer's Mate [Navy rating]
PHCSC .... Piers-Harris Children's Self-Concept Scale [Child development test] [Psychology]
PHCSG........ Primary Health Care Specialist Group (SAUS)
PHCT .... Perturbed Hard Chain Theory [Equation of state]
PHCVD........ Photochemical Chemical Vapor Deposition (SAUS)
PHCVD........ Photon-induced CVD (SAUS)
PHCVD........ Photosensitized Chemical Vapor Deposition (SAUS)
PHCV-SD .... Phase Conversion and Step-Down (MSA)
PHD .... Chesapeake Biological Laboratories, Inc. [AMEX symbol] (SAG)
PHD .... Dixmont State Hospital, Sewickley, PA [OCLC symbol] (OCLC)
Ph D .... Doctor of Pharmacy
PhD............ Doctor of Philosophy (GAGS)
PHD .... Doctor of Public Health [British] (DAS)
PHD .... Duncan Aviation, Inc. [ICAO designator] (FAAC)
PHD .... New Philadelphia, OH [Location identifier] [FAA] (FAAL)
PHD .... Panty-Hose Distributor (SAUS)
PHD .... Parallel Head Disk
PhD............ Perfect Hard Disk [Century Data Systems] [Computer science]
Phd .... Phaedo [of Plato] [Classical studies] (OCD)
PhD............ Pharmaciae Doctor [Doctor of Pharmacy] (DAVI)
PHD .... Phase Detector (SAUS)
PHD .... Phase-Shift Driver (CET)
Ph D .... Philosophiae Doctor [Doctor of Philosophy] [Facetious translation: Piled Higher and Deeper]
PHD .... Photoelectron Diffraction [Spectroscopy]
PHD .... Photohydrodynamic [Astrophysics]

PHD .... Physical Hydrology Division (SAUS)
PHD .... Piled Higher and Deeper (SAUS)
PHD .... Pilot's Horizontal Display [Aviation] (CAAL)
PHD .... Poly Harnstoff Dispersion [Organic chemistry]
PHD .... Port Hueneme Division [Naval Surface Warfare Center]
PHD .... Port Huron & Detroit Railroad Co. [AAR code]
PHD .... Positioning-Head Drum (DNAB)
PHD .... Potential Harmful Drug (SAUS)
PHD .... Precision High Dose
PH D .... Pre-Pearl Harbor Dad [A humorous wartime degree]
PHD .... Pride, Hustle, and Drive
PHD .... Public Health Department
PHD .... Public Health Director
PHD .... Public Health Doctor (SAUS)
PHDr .... Public Housing Development [Department of Housing and Urban Development] (GFGA)
PHD .... Pulsed Holograpy Development [Department of Energy]
PHD .... Pulse Height Discrimination
PHD .... Pulse Height Discriminators (ADWA)
PHD.EC........ Chesapeake Bio Labs 'A' [ECM, Symbol] (TTSB)
PHDAN........ Pharmacopoeia Danica (SAUS)
PHDAN........ Physically Dangerous (DNAB)
PhD cameras... Push-here-Dummy cameras (SAUS)
PHDD .... Personal History of Depressive Disorders (MEDA)
PHDDS........ PSRO [Professional Standards Review Organization] Hospital Discharge Data Set
PHDE .... Poly(heptadiester) [Organic chemistry]
PHDEA .... Public Housing Drug Elimination Act [1988]
PhDEd......... Doctor of Philosophy in Education [British] (ADA)
PHDH.......... Dillingham Air Force Base, Oahu Island [Hawaii] [ICAO location identifier] (ICLI)
PHDI .... Palmer Hydrological Drought Index
PhD(Med).... Doctor of Philosophy (Medicine) (ADA)
PhDMH........ Doctor of Philosophy in Mechanics and Hydraulics
PhD Otol...... Doctor of Philosophy in Otolaryngology (PGP)
PhDPM Rehab... Doctor of Physical Medicine and Rehabilitation (PGP)
PHDr........... Doctor of Philosophy
Phdr .... Phaedrus [of Plato] [Classical studies] (OCD)
PHDR.......... Preliminary Hardware Design Review
PhD(RCA).... Doctor of Philosophy (Royal College of Art) [British] (DBQ)
PHDS.......... Post-Harvest Documentation Service [Kansas State University] (IID)
PhD Surg..... Doctor of Philosophy in Surgery (PGP)
PHE............ Aviation POL [Petroleum, Oil, and Lubrication] Handling Equipment (NATG)
PHE............ Eastern State School and Hospital, Trevose, PA [OCLC symbol] (OCLC)
PHE............ Packaging and Handling Engineer (SAUS)
PHE............ Pawan Hans Ltd. [India] [ICAO designator] (FAAC)
PHE............ Periodic Health Examination
PHE............ Petroleum Handling Equipment (MCD)
phe .... Phenylalanine [Also, F] [An amino acid] (DOG)
Phe .... Phenylalanine [Also, F] [An amino acid]
PHE............ Phenylephrine [Medicine] (DMAA)
PHE............ Pheophytin [Biochemistry]
Phe .... Phoenix [Constellation]
PHE............ Photo Engravers & Electrotypers Ltd. [Toronto Stock Exchange symbol]
PHE............ Plate Heat Exchanger [Chemical engineering]
PHE............ Port Hedland [Australia] [Airport symbol] (OAG)
PHE............ Post-Heparin Esterase [Medicine] (MAE)
PHE............ Preflight Heat Exchanger [NASA] (KSC)
PHE............ Public Health Evaluation (SAUS)
PHEA.......... Public Health Engineering Abstracts [A publication]
PHEAA .... Pennsylvania Higher Education Assistance Agency (EDAC)
Phear Wat ... Phear's Rights of Water [1859] [A publication] (DLA)
PHED .... Physical & Health Education (SAUS)
PHEEM........ Photoelectron-Emission Microscopy (AAEL)
PhEEM........ Photoemission Electron Microscopy [Medicine] (DMAA)
Ph Eg.......... Pharmacopoeia of Egypt (SAUS)
PHEI........... Penetrator, High-Explosive, Incendiary (MCD)
PHEL.......... Petroleum Helicopters, Inc. [NASDAQ symbol] (NQ)
PHEL.......... Petroleum Helicopters (Vtg) [NASDAQ symbol] (TTSB)
PHELK......... Petroleum Helicopters [NASDAQ symbol] (TTSB)
PHELM........ Pulsed High Energy Laser Countermeasures (ACAE)
PhelpD......... Phelps Dodge Corp. [Associated Press] (SAG)
PHeM.......... Hershey Medical Center, Hershey, PA [Library symbol] [Library of Congress] (LCLS)
PHEM.......... Primitive Helium Mantle [Geology]
PHEM.......... Public Health Evaluation Manual (SAUS)
PHEMA .... Poly(hydroxyethyl Methacrylate) [Organic chemistry]
pHEMT........ Psedomorphic High Electron Mobility Transistor [Electronics] (AAEL)
phen .... o-Phenanthroline [Organic chemistry]
PHEN .... Phenanthroline Monohydrate (SAUS)
PHEN .... Phenolic (AAG)
PHEN .... Phenotype [Microbiology] (DAVI)
Pheney Rep... Pheney's New Term Reports [England] [A publication] (DLA)
PHENG......... Photoengraving (VRA)
PH Eng .... Public Health Engineer
PHENIR........ Pheniramine Maleate (SAUS)
PHENO .... Phenobarbital [A drug]
pheno .... Phenotype
PHENO .... Precise Hybrid Elements for Nonlinear Operation (IEEE)
PHENOB........ Phenobarbital [A Drug] (DAVI)
phenobarb ... Phenobarbital [A drug] (DAVI)
PHENO/D ..... Phenomenological Death (SAUS)

PHENOLP..... Phenolphthalein (SAUS)
PHENOLPHT... Phenolphthalein (SAUS)
PHENOM....... Phenomena (SAUS)
phenom .... Phenomenon (BARN)
PHENOM....... Phenomenon (GOBB)
PHENOS...... Precise Hybrid Elements for Nonlinear Operations (IAA)
PHEN SAL.... Phenyl Salicylate
PHENTH....... Phenothiazine [A drug] (DAVI)
PHENYL....... Phenylpropanol [A drug] (DAVI)
PHENYLEPH... Phenylephrine Hydrochloride (SAUS)
PHENYLEPH BIT... Phenylephrine Bitartrate (SAUS)
PHENYLEPH TAN... Phenylephrine Tannate (SAUS)
PHENYLTOL... Phenyltoloxamine Citrate (SAUS)
PHEO .... Pheochromocytoma [Oncology]
PHER .... Photographic Mechanical Equipment Repair [Course] (DNAB)
PHER .... Plate Heat Exchanger [Chemical Engineering] (DNAB)
PHERMEX.... Pulsed High-Energy Radiographic Machine Emitting X-Rays
PHERP .... Public Health Education and Research Program (ADWA)
PHET .... Photoetching (VRA)
Ph Ev .... Phillips on Evidence [A publication] (DLA)
PHEWA ...... Presbyterian Health, Education, and Welfare Association (EA)
PHF............. Fairview State Hospital, Waymart, PA [OCLC symbol] (OCLC)
PHF............. Newport News [Virginia] [Airport symbol] (OAG)
PHF............. Paired Helical Filaments [Neuroanatomy] [Term coined by Dr. Robert Terry to describe the components of neurofibrillary tangles in the brains of Alzheimer's Disease patients]
PHF............. Patrick Henry Foundation [Liberty, NY] (EA)
PHF............. Patrol Hydrofoil [Missile] (HGAA)
PHF............. Payload Handling Fixture [NASA] (NAKS)
PHF............. Peak Hour Factor [Transportation]
PHF............. Peanut Hull Flour
PHF............. Pergamon Holding Foundation [Liechtenstein]
PHF............. Personal Hygiene Facility [NASA] (NASA)
Ph-F........... Phenyl-Fluoride (SAUS)
PHF............. Phoenix House Foundation (EA)
PHF............. Plug Handling Fixture (NRCH)
PHF............. Potomac Horse Fever [Veterinary science] (DB)
PHF............. Procedure History File (COE)
PHF............. Process Holding Fixture (MCD)
PHF............. Procurement History File [DoD]
PHF............. Public Health Foundation [Information service or system] (IID)
PHF............. USF&G Pacholder Fd [AMEX symbol] (TTSB)
PHF............. USF & G Pacholder Fund, Inc. [AMEX symbol] (CTT)
PHFA .... Potomac Horse Fever Agent
PHFC .... Pittsburgh Home Finl [NASDAQ symbol] (TTSB)
PHFE.......... Pulsed High-Frequency Electroporation [Analytical biochemistry]
P-H Fed Taxes... Federal Taxes (Prentice-Hall, Inc.) [A publication] (DLA)
PHFENN...... Pharmacopoeia Fennica (SAUS)
PHFET......... Photosensitive Field Effect Transistor (SAUS)
PHFF.......... Oahu [Hawaii] [ICAO location identifier] (ICLI)
PHFG.......... Primary Human Fetal Glial [Cytology]
PHFPrA....... USF&G $4.10cm Cv Exch A Pfd [NYSE symbol] (TTSB)
PHFTX .... Prentice-Hall Federal Taxes [Database] (IT)
Ph G .... Graduate in Pharmacy
PhG........... Pharmacopoeia Germanica [German Pharmacopeia] (MAE)
PHG .... Phenate-Hexamine Goggle [British World War I anti-poison-gas helmet]
PHG .... Philips Electronics NV [Formerly, Philips NV] [NYSE symbol] (SPSG)
PHG .... Phillipsburg, KS [Location identifier] [FAA] (FAAL)
PHG .... Phosphatidylglycerol [Test used to determine fetal lung maturity] (DAVI)
Phg .... Phytophthora Megasperma Glycinea [A fungus]
PHG .... Postman, Higher Grade [British] (DI)
PHG .... Prototype Hydrofoil Gunboat
PHG .... Scranton State General Hospital, Scranton, PA [OCLC symbol] (OCLC)
PHGA......... Pteroylhexaglutamylglutamic [or Pteroylheptaglutamic] Acid [Biochemistry]
PhGABA..... Phenyl-gamma-aminobutyric Acid [Tranquilizer]
PHGALL...... Pharmacopoeia Gallica (SAUS)
PHGLTF...... Physiological Training Flight [Air Force]
Phgly .... Phenylglycine [An amino acid]
PHGM........ Patrol Hydrofoil Guided Missile [Navy] (DNAB)
Phgn .... Physiognomonica [of Aristotle] [Classical studies] (OCD)
PHGNDWG.. Photogenic (VRA)
PHGRM....... Photogram (VRA)
P HGT .... Package Height [Freight]
PHGY .... Physiology (SAUS)
PHH .... Andrews, SC [Location identifier] [FAA] (FAAL)
PHH .... Haverford State Hospital, Haverford, PA [OCLC symbol] (OCLC)
PHH .... Peterson, Howell & Heather, Inc. (EFIS)
PHH .... Phan Thiet [South Vietnam] [Airport symbol] (AD)
PHH .... PHH Corp. [NYSE symbol] [Toronto Stock Exchange symbol] (SPSG)
PHH .... Phillips Head [Screw]
PHH .... Posthemorrhagic Hydrocephalus [Neurology] (DAVI)
PHH .... Puu Huluhulu [Hawaii] [Seismograph station code, US Geological Survey] [Closed] (SEIS)
PHHA .... Pearl Harbor History Associates (EA)
PHHC .... Programmable Hand-Held Calculator (RDA)
PHHGSIA .... Pamphlet-Household Goods Shipment Information (SAUS)
PHHI .... Persistent Hyperinsulinemic Hypoglycemia of Infancy [Medicine]
PHHI .... Wheeler Air Force Base, Oahu Island [Hawaii] [ICAO location identifier] (ICLI)
PHHM......... Palm Harbor Homes [NASDAQ symbol] (TTSB)

PHHM......... Palm Harbor Homes, Inc. [NASDAQ symbol] (SAG)
PHHN.......... Hana, Maui Island [Hawaii] [ICAO location identifier] (ICLI)
PHHS .... Patrick Henry High School (SAUS)
PHHS .... Precise Helicopter Hovering System (SAUS)
PHHSA .... Protestant Health and Human Services Assembly (EA)
PHI .... Archie Phinny Hall (SAUS)
PHi .... Historical Society of Pennsylvania, Philadelphia, PA [Library symbol] [Library of Congress] (LCLS)
PhI .... International Pharmacopoeia
PHI .... Pacific Health Information Network (SAUS)
PHI .... Packard Humanities Institute (SAUS)
PHI .... Passive Hemagglutination Inhibitor (DB)
PHI .... Past History of Illness (MELL)
PHI .... Permanent Health Insurance [British]
PHI .... Petroleum Helicopters, Inc. (MCD)
PhI .... Pharmacopoeia Internationalis [International Pharmacopoeia] (DAVI)
Ph-I........... Phenyl-Iodide (SAUS)
PHI .... Philadelphia [Pennsylvania] [Seismograph station code, US Geological Survey] [Closed] (SEIS)
Phi .... Philadelphia Eagles [National Football League] [1933-42, 1944-present] (NFLA)
PHI .... Philadelphia White Stockings (SAUS)
PHI .... Philippine Long Distance Telephone Co. [NYSE symbol] (SAG)
PHI .... Philippine Long D Tel ADS [NYSE symbol] (TTSB)
Phi .... Philippus [Flourished, 13th century] [Authority cited in pre-1607 legal work] (DSA)
Phi .... Philips [Holland & International] [Record label]
PHI .... Philips Aviation Services [Netherlands] [ICAO designator] (FAAC)
PHI .... Philipsburg State General Hospital, Philipsburg, PA [Inactive] [OCLC symbol] (OCLC)
PHI .... Phillipsite [A zeolite]
PHI .... Philosophie Informationsdienst [Philosophy Information Service] [University of Dusseldorf] [Information service or system] (IID)
PHI .... Philosophy (WGA)
PHI .... Phosphine (LDT)
PHI .... Phosphohexose Isomerase [An enzyme]
Phi .... Physeptone [A narcotic substitute]
PHI .... Physiological Hyaluronidase Inhibitor [Biochemistry]
PHI .... Polarity Health Institute (EA)
PHI .... Position & Heading Indicator (SAUS)
PHI .... Position and Homing Indicator
PHI .... Precision Homing Indicator (SAUS)
PHI .... Pre-Harvest Interval (EPAT)
PHI .... Prentice-Hall International [Publisher]
PHI .... Programme Hydrologique International [International Hydrological Program - IHP] [UNESCO] (MSC)
PHI .... Provincial House, Inc. (EFIS)
PHI .... Public Health Inspector [British]
PHI .... Public Health Institute (SAUS)
PHIA .... Pharmaceutical Ingredients Asia [Conference]
PHIA .... Phenylalanine (MAE)
PHIA .... Profoundly Hearing Impaired Adult (MELL)
PHIAL .... Phiala [Bottle] [Pharmacy]
PHIB .... Amphibious
PHib........... Hibeh Papyri [A publication] (OCD)
PHIBB .... Project for Historical Biobibliography [A publication]
PHIBCB .... Amphibious Construction Battalion [Also, ACB] (NVT)
PhibComd .... Amphibious Forces Command (SAUS)
PHIBCORPAC... Amphibious Corps, Pacific Fleet [Marine Corps]
PHIBCORPS... Amphibious Corps [Marine Corps]
PHIBDET ...... Amphibious Detachment
PHIBDETIND... Amphibious Detachment, India
PHIBEU .... Amphibious Forces, Europe
PHIBEX .... Amphibious Exercise [NATO]
PHIBFOR...... Amphibious Forces
PHIBGROUP... Amphibious Group
PHIBGRU ..... Amphibious Group
PHIBLANT.... Amphibious Forces, Atlantic Fleet
PHIBLEX ..... Amphibious Landing Exercise [Navy] (NVT)
PHIBNAW .... Amphibious Forces, Northwest African Waters
PHIBOPS..... Amphibious Operations [Navy] (NVT)
PHIBPAC..... Amphibious Forces, Pacific Fleet
PHIBRAIDEX... Amphibious Raid Exercise [Navy] (NVT)
PHIBRECONEX... Amphibious Reconnaissance Exercise [Navy] (NVT)
PHIBREFTRA... Amphibious Refresher Training [Navy] (CAAL)
PHIBRFT...... Amphibious Refresher Training [Navy] (NVT)
PHIBRON ..... Amphibious Squadron [Army]
PHIBSEU ..... Amphibious Forces, Europe
PHIBSFORPAC... Amphibious Forces, Pacific Fleet
PHIBSKDN ... Amphibious Ship Shakedown Cruise [Navy] (NVT)
PHIBSLANT... Amphibious Forces, Atlantic Fleet
PHIBSPAC.... Amphibious Forces, Pacific Fleet
PHIBSS .... Amphibious Schoolship [Navy] (NVT)
PhibsTraLant... Amphibious Forces Training Command, Atlantic Fleet (SAUS)
PhibsTraPac... Amphibious Forces Training Command, Pacific Fleet (SAUS)
PHIBSTRAPAC... Training Command Amphibious Forces, US Pacific Fleet
PHIBSUKAY... Amphibious Bases, United Kingdom
PHIBTF .... Amphibious Task Force [Navy] (NVT)
Phibtra........ Amphibious Training (SAUS)
PHIBTRA...... Training Command Amphibious Forces
PHIBTRABASE... Amphibious Training Base [Navy]
PHIBTRAEX... Amphibious Training Exercise [Navy] (NVT)
PHIBTRAINLANT... Training Command Amphibious Forces, US Atlantic Fleet
PHIBTRAINPAC... Training Command Amphibious Forces, US Pacific Fleet
PhibTraLant... Amphibious Training Command, Atlantic (SAUS)

PHIBTRALANT... Training Command Amphibious Forces, US Atlantic Fleet
PHIBTRANS... Amphibious Transport [*Navy*]
PHIB Transistor... Phosphor Inverted Bipolar Transistor (SAUS)
PHIBTRAPAC... Training Command Amphibious Forces, US Pacific Fleet
PHIBTRBASE... Amphibious Training Base [*Navy*]
PHIBUF........ Performance Buffet Limit (GAVI)
PHIBWARTRACEN... Amphibious Warfare Training Center [*Navy*]
PHIC Poly(hexyl Isocyanate) [*Organic chemistry*]
PHICB .... Putnam High Income Convertible & Bond Fund [*Associated Press*] (SAG)
PHICT .... Philips Inventory Control Technique [*Computer science*] (IAA)
Phi D .... Doctor of Philanthropy
PHID .... Positive Hostile Identification Device [*Air Force*]
PHID .... Project for Health Information Dissemination (ADWA)
PHIDAS .... Philips Data Systems (SAUS)
Phi Dex .... Phi Delta Chi [*An association*] (NTPA)
PHIG .... Programmers Hierarchical Interactive Graphics (SAUS)
PHIGS PLUS... Programmers Hierarchical Interactive Graphics System Plus Lumiere Und Surfaces (SAUS)
PHII Planet Hollywood International, Inc. [*NASDAQ symbol*] (SAG)
PHII Planet Hollywood Intl'A' [*NASDAQ symbol*] (TTSB)
PHIK Honolulu/Hickam Air Force Base, Oahu Island [*Hawaii*] [*ICAO location identifier*] (ICLI)
PhiKaps .... Phi Kappa Theta National (EA)
Phil.............. Orationes Philippicae [*of Cicero*] [*Classical studies*] (OCD)
Phil.............. Philadelphia (ODBW)
PHIL .... Philadelphia [*Pennsylvania*]
PHIL .... Philadelphia Exchange (EBF)
Phil.............. Philadelphia Reports [*A publication*] (DLA)
phil.............. Philanthropic (PROS)
Phil.............. Philemon [*New Testament book*]
Phil.............. Philharmonia [*Record label*]
PHIL .... Philharmonic
PHIL .... Philippians [*Biblical*]
Phil.............. Philippians [*New Testament book*]
Phil.............. Philippine (SAUS)
Phil.............. Philippine Island Reports [*A publication*] (DLA)
PHIL .... Philippines (AFM)
Phil.............. Philippines (VRA)
Phil.............. Phillimore's English Ecclesiastical Reports [*A publication*] (DLA)
Phil.............. Phillips' English Chancery Reports [*1841-49*] [*A publication*] (DLA)
Phil.............. Phillips' English Election Cases [*1780-81*] [*A publication*] (DLA)
Phil.............. Phillips' Illinois Reports [*152-245 Illinois*] [*A publication*] (DLA)
Phil.............. Phillips' North Carolina Law Reports [*A publication*] (DLA)
Phil.............. Phillips' Treatise on Insurance [*A publication*] (DLA)
Phil.............. Philoctetes [*of Sophocles*] [*Classical studies*] (OCD)
PHIL .... Philology
Phil.............. Philopoemen [*of Plutarch*] [*Classical studies*] (OCD)
Phil.............. Philosophy (DD)
phil.............. Philosophy (SHCU)
PHIL .... Philosophy
PHIL .... Philosophy Library (SAUS)
PHIL .... Potential Host Institures List [*European Commission*]
PHIL .... Programmable Algorithm Machine High-Level Language [*Computer science*]
PHILA .... Philadelphia [*Pennsylvania*]
Phila............ Philadelphia Reports [*Pennsylvania*] [*A publication*] (DLA)
Phila C Pharmacy... Philadelphia College of Pharmacy and Science (GAGS)
Philad.......... Philadelphia Reports [*Pennsylvania*] [*A publication*] (DLA)
PHILADA...... Philadelphia (ROG)
Philada R .... Philadelphia Reports [*Pennsylvania*] [*A publication*] (DLA)
Philada Rep... Philadelphia Reports [*Pennsylvania*] [*A publication*] (DLA)
PHILADEL...... Philadelphia (ROG)
Philadelphia Leg Int... Philadelphia Legal Intelligencer [*Pennsylvania*] [*A publication*] (DLA)
Philadelphia Rep... Philadelphia Reports [*Pennsylvania*] [*A publication*] (DLA)
Phila Free Lib... Philadelphia Free Library (SAUS)
PHILAG .... Public Health Institute-London Action Group (SAUS)
PHILAGRP .... Philadelphia Group (DNAB)
Phila Leg Int... Philadelphia Legal Intelligencer [*Pennsylvania*] [*A publication*] (DLA)
Phila LJ .... Philadelphia Law Journal [*A publication*] (DLA)
PHILAMCHAM... Philippine-American Chamber of Commerce (NTPA)
philan .... Philanthropical (BJA)
PHILANTHR... Philanthropic (ROG)
Phila (PA)... Philadelphia Reports [*Pennsylvania*] [*A publication*] (DLA)
Phila QM Depot... Philadelphia Quartermaster Depot (SAUS)
Phila Reports... Philadelphia Reports [*Pennsylvania*] [*A publication*] (DLA)
PHILASAG.... Philippine Association of Agriculturists (SAUS)
PHILASHIPYD... Philadelphia Shipyard (SAUS)
philat .... Philately
Philbro........ Philipp Brothers Ltd. [*Commercial firm*]
Phil C .... Philosophy in Chiropractic
PHILCAG...... First Philippine Civic Action Group [*Deployed in 1964 to assist South Vietnam*] (VNW)
Phil Civ & Can Law... Phillimore's Civil and Canon Law [*A publication*] (DLA)
PHILCOA...... Philippine Coconut Administration (SAUS)
PHILCOM...... Philippine Global Communications, Inc. [*Manila*] [*Telecommunications*]
PhilCon........ Philadelphia Consolidated Holding [*Commercial firm*] [*Associated Press*] (SAG)
PHILCON...... Philippine Contingent [*Military*]
Phil Cop ...... Phillips' Law of Copyright Designs [*A publication*] (DLA)
Phil D .... Philosophiae Doctor [*Doctor of Philosophy*] [*See also Ph D*] [*Latin*]
PHILDANCO... Philadelphia Dance Company

Phil Dec ...... Philippus Decius [*Deceased circa 1537*] [*Authority cited in pre-1607 legal work*] (DSA)
Phil Dom ..... Phillimore's Law of Domicil [*A publication*] (DLA)
Phil Ecc .... Phillimore's Ecclesiastical Judgments [*A publication*] (DLA)
Phil Ecc .... Phillimore's English Ecclesiastical Law [*2 eds.*] [*1873, 1895*] [*A publication*] (DLA)
Phil Ecc .... Phillimore's English Ecclesiastical Reports [*1809-21*] [*A publication*] (DLA)
Phil Ecc Judg... Phillimore's Ecclesiastical Judgments [*1867-75*] [*A publication*] (DLA)
Phil Ecc Law... Phillimore's English Ecclesiastical Law [*2 eds.*] [*1873, 1895*] [*A publication*] (DLA)
Phil Ecc R ... Phillimore's English Ecclesiastical Reports [*1809-21*] [*A publication*] (DLA)
Phil El Cas... Phillips' English Election Cases [*1780-81*] [*A publication*] (DLA)
Philem......... Philemon [*New Testament book*]
PhilEnv .... Philip Environmental [*Commercial firm*] [*Associated Press*] (SAG)
Phil Eq........ Phillips' North Carolina Equity Reports [*A publication*] (DLA)
Phil Ev........ Phillips on Evidence [*A publication*] (DLA)
Phil Ev Cow & H & Edw Notes... Phillips on Evidence, Notes by Cowen, Hill, and Edwards [*A publication*] (DLA)
PHILEX .... Philadelphia Stock Exchange
Phil Fam Cas... Phillipps' Famous Cases in Circumstantial Evidence [*A publication*] (DLA)
Phil Grand... Phillips' Grandeur of the Law [*A publication*] (DLA)
Phil Hung .... Philharmonica Hungarica (SAUS)
PHIL I .... Philippine Islands (WDAA)
Phili Fran .... Philippus Francus [*Deceased, 1471*] [*Authority cited in pre-1607 legal work*] (DSA)
Phil ILJ........ Philippine International Law Journal [*A publication*] (DLA)
Phil Ins........ Phillips on Insurance [*A publication*] (DLA)
Phil Insan.... Phillips on Lunatics [*1858*] [*A publication*] (DLA)
Phil Int Law... Phillimore's International Law [*A publication*] (DLA)
Phil Int LJ ... Philippine International Law Journal [*A publication*] (DLA)
Phil Int Rom Law... Phillimore's Introduction to the Roman Law [*A publication*] (DLA)
Philip .... Philippines
Philip Fran... Philippus Franchus [*Deceased, 1471*] [*Authority cited in pre-1607 legal work*] (DSA)
Philipp......... Philippines (BARN)
Philippine .... Philippine Reports [*A publication*] (DLA)
Philippine Co... Philippine Code [*A publication*] (DLA)
Philippine Internat LJ... Philippine International Law Journal [*Manila, Philippines*] [*A publication*] (DLA)
Philippine Int'l LJ... Philippine International Law Journal [*A publication*] (DLA)
Philippine LJ... Philippine Law Journal [*A publication*] (DLA)
Philippine L Rev... Philippine Law Review [*A publication*] (DLA)
PhilipsEl ...... Philips Electronics NV Holding Co. [*Associated Press*] (SAG)
Philips J Res... Philips Journal of Research (SAUS)
Philips Res Rept... Philips Research Reports (SAUS)
Philips Telecommun Data Syst Rev... Philips Telecommunication and Data Systems Review (SAUS)
Philips Weld Rep... Philips Welding Reporter (SAUS)
PHILIRAN .... Philips Petroleum Iran (SAUS)
Phil Jud....... Phillimore's Ecclesiastical Judgments [*1867-75*] [*England*] [*A publication*] (DLA)
Phil Judg..... Phillimore's Ecclesiastical Judgments [*1867-75*] [*A publication*] (DLA)
Phill.............. Phillips' English Chancery Reports [*1841-49*] [*A publication*] (DLA)
Phill.............. Phillips' English Election Cases [*1780-81*] [*A publication*] (DLA)
Phill.............. Phillips' Illinois Reports [*152-245 Illinois*] [*A publication*] (DLA)
Phill.............. Phillips' North Carolina Equity Reports [*A publication*] (DLA)
Phill.............. Phillips' North Carolina Law Reports [*A publication*] (DLA)
Phil Lab Rel J... Philippine Labour Relations Journal [*A publication*] (DLA)
Phil Law...... Phillips' North Carolina Law Reports [*A publication*] (DLA)
Phill Ch ...... Phillips' English Chancery Reports [*1841-49*] [*A publication*] (DLA)
Phill Ch (Eng)... Phillips' English Chancery Reports [*1841-49*] [*A publication*] (DLA)
Phil LD .... Doctor of Lithuanian Philology
Phill Ecc Judg... Phillimore's Ecclesiastical Judgments [*1867-75*] [*A publication*] (DLA)
Phill Ecc R... Phillimore's English Ecclesiastical Reports [*1809-21*] [*A publication*] (DLA)
Phill Eq (NC)... Phillips' North Carolina Equity Reports [*A publication*] (DLA)
Phil Lic........ Licentiate of Philosophy [*British*]
Phillim......... Phillimore's English Ecclesiastical Reports [*1809-21*] [*A publication*] (DLA)
Phillim Dom... Phillimore's Law of Domicil [*A publication*] (DLA)
Phillim Eccl... Phillimore's Ecclesiastical Judgments [*1867-75*] [*A publication*] (DLA)
Phillim Eccl... Phillimore's English Ecclesiastical Reports [*1809-21*] [*A publication*] (DLA)
Phillim Ecc Law... Phillimore's English Ecclesiastical Law [*A publication*] (DLA)
Phillim Int Law... Phillimore's International Law [*A publication*] (DLA)
Phill Ins........ Phillips on Insurance [*A publication*] (DLA)
PHILLIPS ...... Philips Petroleum Co. (SAUS)
Phillips .... Phillips' English Chancery Reports [*1841-49*] [*A publication*] (DLA)
Phillips .... Phillips' English Election Cases [*1780-81*] [*A publication*] (DLA)
Phillips .... Phillips' Illinois Reports [*152-245 Illinois*] [*A publication*] (DLA)
Phillips .... Phillips' North Carolina Equity Reports [*A publication*] (DLA)
Phillips .... Phillips' North Carolina Law Reports [*A publication*] (DLA)
Phillips U ..... Phillips University (GAGS)
Phil Lit R...... Philatelic Literature Review [*A publication*]
Phil LJ .... Philippine Law Journal [*Manila*] [*A publication*] (DLA)
Phill L (NC)... Phillips' North Carolina Law Reports [*A publication*] (DLA)
Phil L Rev ... Philippine Law Review [*A publication*] (DLA)
PHILLS .... Portable Hyperspectral Imager for Low Light Spectroscopy (SEWL)

Phil Lun......... Phillips on Lunatics [1858] [A publication] (DLA)
Philly............ Philadelphia
PhilM........... Master of Philosophy (GAGS)
Phil Mag..... Philips Magazine (SAUS)
Phil Mech Liens... Phillips on Mechanics' Liens [A publication] (DLA)
PhilMr......... Philip Morris Companies, Inc. [Associated Press] (SAG)
philn........... Philanthropy
Phil NC....... Phillips' North Carolina Law Reports [A publication] (DLA)
Philo........... Philo Judaeus [First century AD] [Classical studies] (OCD)
philo........... Philology (WDAA)
Philocrit....... Philosopher Critic (SAUS)
Philocrit....... Philosophical Criticism (SAUS)
Philol......... Philological (SAUS)
Philol......... Philologus [A publication] (OCD)
Philol......... Philology (DIAR)
Philol......... Philology (SAUS)
PHILOL........ Philology
Philol Suppl... Philologus. Supplement [A publication] (OCD)
PHILOM....... Philomathes [Lover of Learning] (ROG)
PHILOMATH... Philomathematicus [Lover of Mathematics] (ROG)
Phil Orch ..... Philadelphia Orchestra (SAUS)
Philos........ Philosophic (SAUS)
Philos......... Philosophy (BEE)
PHILOS .... Philosophy (EY)
Philos Educ... Philosophy of Education (SAUS)
Philos Mag A\ Phys Condens Matter Defects Mech... Philosophical Magazine A, Physics of Condensed Matter, Defects and Mechanical Properties (SAUS)
Philos Mag B\ Phys Condens Matter ElectronOpt... Philosophical Magazine B, Physics of Condensed Matter, Electronic, Optical and Magnetic Properties (SAUS)
Philos Mag Lett... Philosophical Magazine Letters (SAUS)
Philos Pub... Philosophical Publishing Co (SAUS)
Philos Res... Philosophical Research Society (SAUS)
Philostr........ Philostratus [Second century AD] [Classical studies] (OCD)
Philos Trans R Soc London... Philosophical Transactions of the Royal Society of London (SAUS)
Philos Trans R Soc London A Math Phys Sci... Philosophical Transactions of the Royal Society of London A, Mathematical and Physical Sciences (SAUS)
Phil (PA)..... Philadelphia Reports [Pennsylvania] [A publication] (DLA)
Phil Pat .... Phillips on Patents [A publication] (DLA)
PhilPet........ Phillips Petroleum Co. [Associated Press] (SAG)
PHILPUC...... Philippine Presidential Unit Citation Badge [Military decoration]
PHILPUC Badge... Philippine Presidential Unit Citation Badge (SAUS)
PHILQA........ Philips Question Answering System (NITA)
Phil R........ Philadelphia Reports [Pennsylvania] [A publication] (DLA)
Phil R......... Philosophical Review [A publication] (BRI)
Phil Rep ..... Philadelphia Reports [Pennsylvania] [A publication] (DLA)
PhilRH........ Phillips [R.H.], Inc. [Associated Press] (SAG)
Phil Rom Law... Phillimore's Private Law among the Romans [A publication] (DLA)
PHILSEAFRON... Philippine Sea Frontier
PHILSIN........ Philippines-Singapore Submarine Cable (SAUS)
PHIL SOC... Philharmonic Society (WDAA)
PHILSOM..... Periodical Holdings in the Library of the School of Medicine [Washington University School of Medicine] [Library network]
PHILSOM Network... Periodical Holdings in the Library of the School of Medicine Network (SAUS)
Phil Sp .... Philippine Spanish (SAUS)
Phil St Leg R... Phillips' Studii Legalis Ratio [A publication] (DLA)
Phil St Tr...... Phillipps' State Trials [Prior to 1688] [A publication] (DLA)
PhilSub........ Philadelphia Suburban Corp. [Associated Press] (SAG)
PHILSUGIN... Philipine Sugar Institute (SAUS)
Phil Unters... Philologische Untersuchungen [A publication] (OCD)
Phil US Pr... Phillips' United States Practice [A publication] (DLA)
Phil Wochenschr... Philologische Wochenschrift [A publication] (OCD)
Phil Yb Int'l L... Philippine Yearbook of International Law [Manila, Philippines] [A publication] (DLA)
PHIM........... Posthypoxic Intention Myoclonus [Medicine] (DMAA)
PHIN .... Pharmaceutical and Healthcare Industry News (SAUS)
PHIN .... Position and Homing Inertial Navigator
PHIND.......... Pharmaceutical and Healthcare Industries News Database [PJB Group Publications Ltd.] [Information service or system] (IID)
P-H Ind Rel Lab Arb... Industrial Relations, American Labor Arbitration (Prentice-Hall, Inc.) [A publication] (DLA)
P-H Ind Rel Union Conts... Industrial Relations, Union Contracts, and Collective Bargaining (Prentice-Hall,Inc.) [A publication] (DLA)
PHINet......... Prentice-Hall Information Network [Prentice-Hall Information Services] [Information service or system] (IID)
PHINTS........ Phase locked Interferometric Tracking System (SAUS)
Phip............ Phipson's Digest, Natal Reports [South Africa] [A publication] (DLA)
Phip............ Phipson's Reports, Natal Supreme Court [South Africa] [A publication] (DLA)
Phip Ev........ Phipson on Evidence [12th ed.] [1976] [A publication] (DLA)
PHIPrA......... Philippine L-D Tel Pfd GDS [NYSE symbol] (TTSB)
PHIPS .... Professional Hi-Resolution Image Processing System [TerraVision, Inc.] (PCM)
Phipson .... Reports of Cases in the Supreme Court of Natal [A publication] (DLA)
PHIRB......... Public Health Inspectors' Registration Board [British] (BI)
PHIS .... Physically Handicapped in Science (BABM)
PHIS .... Population and Housing Information System (SAUS)
PHIS .... Program Hardware Interface Specification (CAAL)
pH/ISE .... pH Value/Ion-Selective Electrode (SAUS)

PHITAP .... Predesigned [or Priority] High-Interest Tactical Air Prediction [Acoustic forecast] (MCD)
PHITAP .... Priority High Interest Tactical Air Acoustic Forecast Prediction
PHITAR .... Predesignated High-Interest Tactical Area [Navy] (NVT)
PhIUS .... Pharmaceutical Ingredients U.S.
PHJ............. Danville State Hospital, Danville, PA [OCLC symbol] (OCLC)
PHJC........... Penn Hall Junior College [Pennsylvania] [Closed, 1973]
PHJC........... Poor Handmaids of Jesus Christ [Ancilla Domini Sisters] [Roman Catholic religious order]
PHJC........... Port Huron Junior College [Michigan]
PH/JO .... Photojournalist (DNAB)
PHK .... Pahokee, FL [Location identifier] [FAA] (FAAL)
PHK .... Personal Hygiene Kit (MCD)
PhK .... Phosphorylase Kinase [An enzyme]
PHK .... Platelet Phosphohexokinase (MAE)
PHK .... Postmortem Human Kidney [Cells]
PHK Cells .... Postmonem Human Kidney Cells (SAUS)
PHK Cells .... Post-mortem Human Kidney Cells (SAUS)
PHKO .... Kona/Ke-Ahole, Hawaii Island [Hawaii] [ICAO location identifier] (ICLI)
PHKP .... Kaanapali, Maui Island [Hawaii] [ICAO location identifier] (ICLI)
PHKU .... Kunia [Hawaii] [ICAO location identifier] (ICLI)
PHKW .... Powerhouse Resources, Inc. [NASDAQ symbol] (SAG)
PHKWE .... Powerhouse Resources [NASDAQ symbol] (TTSB)
PHL .... Allentown State Hospital, Allentown, PA [OCLC symbol] (OCLC)
Ph L .... Licentiate in Philosophy
Ph L .... Licentiate of Pharmacy
PHL .... Packaging, Handling and Logistics (SAUS)
PHL .... Periodical Holdings List [Libraries]
PHL .... Philadelphia [Pennsylvania] [Airport symbol]
PHL .... Philippines [ANSI three-letter standard code] (CNC)
PHL .... Phillips Michigan City Flying Service, Inc. [ICAO designator] (FAAC)
PHL .... Philosophy (SAUS)
PHL .... Planet Hollywood Intl'A' [NYSE symbol] (SG)
PHL .... Preliminary Hazards List (ACAE)
PHL .... Pressure to Horizontal Locks [Missiles] (AAG)
PHL .... Public Health Law
PHLA .... Plasma Postheparin Lipolytic Activity [Clinical chemistry]
PHLA .... Postheparin Lipolytic Activity [Medicine] (DMAA)
PHLAG .... Philips Load and Go (NITA)
PHLAG .... Phillips Petroleum Load and Go [System]
PHLAGS ...... Phillips Petroleum Load and Go System (DNAB)
PHLAG System... Philips Load and Go System (SAUS)
Phlb .... Philebus [of Plato] [Classical studies] (OCD)
Phld .... Philodemus [First century BC] [Classical studies] (OCD)
phleg .... phlegmaticalness (SAUS)
phleg .... phlegmaticness (SAUS)
phleg .... phlegmier (SAUS)
phleg .... phlegmiest (SAUS)
PHLEGM ...... People's Hayfever Listener Examiner Gazette Magazine [A publication] (WDAA)
Phlgr........... Photolithographer (SAUS)
PHLH .... Phillips Head [Screw]
PHLH Screw... Philips Head Screw (SAUS)
PHLI........... Lihue, Kauai Island [Hawaii] [ICAO location identifier] (ICLI)
PHLI........... Public Health Leadership Institutes (SAUS)
PHLIS .... Public Health Laboratory Information System (SAUS)
PHLITHO...... Photolithographic (VRA)
PhILD.......... Philippine Long Distance Telephone Co. [Associated Press] (SAG)
PHILDis .... Philadelphia Procurement District (SAUS)
Phlm........... Philemon [New Testament book]
PHLO .... Phloretin [Biochemistry]
PHLODOT .... Phase Lock Doppler Tracking [System] (MUGU)
PHLODOT System... Phase Lock Doppler Tracking System (SAUS)
PhlpGs......... Phillips Gas [Associated Press] (SAG)
PHLS .... Public Health Laboratory Service [British]
PHLSB......... Public Health Laboratory Service Board [British]
PhlVH .... Phillips-Van Heusen Corp. [Associated Press] (SAG)
PHLWR........ Pressurized Heavy and Light Water Reactor (SAUS)
PHLX .... Philadelphia Stock Exchange
PHLY .... Philadelphia Consol Hldg [NASDAQ symbol] (TTSB)
PHLY .... Philadelphia Consolidated Holding [NASDAQ symbol] (SAG)
Ph M........... Master in Pharmacy
Ph M........... Master of Philosophy
PHM........... Mayview State Hospital, Bridgeville, PA [OCLC symbol] (OCLC)
PHM........... Patrol Combatant Missile Hydrofoil [Navy]
PHM........... Patrol Hydrofoil Missile [Navy symbol]
PHM........... Patrol Hydrofoil Missileship [Navy]
PHM........... Patterson-Harker Method [Physics]
PHM........... Per Hundred Million (NASA)
PHM........... Petroleum Helicopters, Inc. [ICAO designator] (FAAC)
PHM........... Phantom (MSA)
PhM........... Pharmaciae Magister [Master of Pharmacy] (DAVI)
PHM........... Pharmacist's Mate [Navy rating]
PHM........... Phase Meter
PHM........... Phase Modulation [Radio data transmission] (DEN)
Phm........... Philemon [New Testament book] (BJA)
PHM........... Philemon [Biblical]
PhM........... Philips Minigroove [Record label]
PHM........... Posterior Hyaloid Membrane [Eye anatomy]
PHM........... Post-Holiday Movie
PHM........... Power Hybrid Microcircuit
PHM........... Pulmonary Hyaline Membrane [Syndrome] [Medicine] (DB)
PHM........... Pulte Corp. [NYSE symbol] (SPSG)
PHM........... Pulte Home Corp. (EFIS)

PHM	Pyroheliometer (SAUS)
PHMA	Plastic Houseware Manufacturers Association
PHMA	Polyhexyl Methacrylate [Organic chemistry]
PHMA	Professional Housing Management Association (NTPA)
Phm B	Bachelor of Pharmacy
PHMB	Para-Hydroxymercuribenzoate [Biochemistry]
PHMC	Pennsylvania Historical and Museum Commission (SAUS)
PHMC	Probe Heater Motor Controller [NASA] (MCD)
Phmcyc	Pharmacyclics, Inc. [Associated Press] (SAG)
PHMD	Pseudohypertrophic Muscular Dystrophy (CPH)
PHMDP	Pharmacist's Mate, Dental Prosthetic Technician [Navy rating]
PhMeSFl	Phenylmethylsulfonylfluoride (SAUS)
Phm G	Graduate in Pharmacy
PHMK	Molokai, Molokai Island [Hawaii] [ICAO location identifier] (ICLI)
PHMO	Partially Hydrogenated Menhaden Oil [Food science]
PhMor	Phar-Mor, Inc. [Associated Press] (SAG)
PHMOV	Phleum Mottle Virus [Plant pathology]
PHMP	Primordial Hot Mantle Plume (PDAA)
PhmRes	Pharmaceutical Resources, Inc. [Associated Press] (SAG)
PHMS	Para-Hydroxymercuriphenylsulfonate [Organic chemistry]
PHMS	Patrol Hydrofoil Missile Ship [Navy/NATO]
PHMS	Polish Historical Military Society (EA)
PHMU	Waimea-Kohala, Kamuela, Hawaii Island [Hawaii] [ICAO location identifier] (ICLI)
PhMV	Phleum Mottle Virus
pH/mV	pH Value versus Millivolts (SAUS)
PHMV	Physalis Mosaic Virus [Plant pathology]
PHMWO	Prospect Hill Millimeter Wave Observatory [Waltham, MA] [Air Force]
PHMX	PhyMatrix Corp. [NASDAQ symbol] (SAG)
PHN	Norristown State Hospital, Norristown, PA [OCLC symbol] (OCLC)
PHN	Passive Heymann Nephritis [Medicine] (DMAA)
PHN	Phoenix Resource Companies, Inc. [AMEX symbol] (SAG)
PHN	Phone (KSC)
PHN	Population, Health and Nutrition (SAUS)
PHN	Port Huron [Michigan] [Airport symbol] (AD)
PHN	Port Huron, MI [Location identifier] [FAA] (FAAL)
PHN	Postherpetic Neuralgia [Medicine]
PHN	Public Health Network [Information service or system] (IID)
PHN	Public Health Nurse
PHNA	Barbers Point Naval Air Station, Oahu Island [Hawaii] [ICAO location identifier] (ICLI)
PHNBR	Phone Number (SAUS)
PHNC	Pearl Harbor, Oahu Island [Hawaii] [ICAO location identifier] (ICLI)
PHNG	Kaneohe Bay Marine Corps Air Station, Oahu Island [Hawaii] [ICAO location identifier] (ICLI)
PHNL	Honolulu/International, Oahu Island [Hawaii] [ICAO location identifier] (ICLI)
PHNORD	Pharmacopoeia Nordica (SAUS)
PHNS	Pearl Harbor Naval Shipyard
PHNSY	Pearl Harbor Navy Ship Yard (SAUS)
PHNX	Phoenix Shannon Ltd. [NASDAQ symbol] (SAG)
PhnxRs	Phoenix Resource Companies, Inc. [Associated Press] (SAG)
PhnxShn	Phoenix Shannon Ltd. [Associated Press] (SAG)
PhnxTc	Phoenix Technologies Ltd. [Associated Press] (SAG)
PHNXY	Phoenix Shannon plc ADR [NASDAQ symbol] (TTSB)
PHNY	Lanai City, Lanai Island [Hawaii] [ICAO location identifier] (ICLI)
PHNY	Pearl Harbor Navy Yard [Later, Pearl Harbor Naval Shipyard]
P-H NYETR	Prentice-Hall New York Estate Tax Reports [A publication] (DLA)
PHO	Pediatric Hematology-Oncology [Medical specialty] (DHSM)
PHO	Peoples Telephone Co. [AMEX symbol] (SAG)
PHO	Phenolic Heavy Oil
PHO	Philco Houston Operations (SAA)
PHO	Phoenix Airways (Pfy) [South Africa] [FAA designator] (FAAC)
Pho	Phoenix Cardinals [National Football League] [1988-93] (NFLA)
PHO	Phone List (SAUS)
Pho	Photographer [British military] (DMA)
Pho	Photonic (SAUS)
PHO	Physician Hospital Organization (AMHC)
PHO	Physician-Hospital Organization [Information service or system] (HCT)
PHO	Point Hope [Alaska] [Airport symbol] (OAG)
PHO	Polk State School and Hospital, Polk, PA [OCLC symbol] (OCLC)
PHO	Port Health Officer
PHO	Potentially Hazardous Object
PHO	Principal House Officer [Australia]
PHO	Public Hazard Office [Environmental science] (COE)
PHO	Public Health Officer Inspector (HEAS)
PHO	Puu Honuaula [Hawaii] [Seismograph station code, US Geological Survey] (SEIS)
PHOAC	Photographer's Mate, Combat Aircrewman [Navy rating] [Obsolete]
Phob	Previous Highroller, on a Budget [Lifestyle classification]
PHOBOS	Photometric Instrument for Biological Optical Sections
PHOC	Photo Control [NASDAQ symbol] (TTSB)
PHOC	Photo Control Corp. [NASDAQ symbol] (NQ)
PHOC	Photocopy (MSA)
PHOCAS	Photo Optical Cable Controlled Submersible (PDAA)
PHOCIS	Photogrammetric Circulatory Survey (PDAA)
PHOCL	Photo-initiated Chemical Laser (SAUS)
PHOD	Philadelphia Ordnance Depot [Military] (AAG)
PHODEC	Photometric Determination of Equilibrium Constants [Computer science]
Phoe	Phoenix [Constellation]
Phoen	Phoenician (BJA)
Phoen	Phoenissae [of Euripides] [Classical studies] (OCD)

PHOENIX	Plasma Heating Obtained by Energetic Neutral Injection Experiment (IEEE)
Phoenix Voice Scrap Ind	Phoenix. Voice of the Scrap Industries (SAUS)
PHOFEX	Photofragment Excitation [Spectroscopy]
PHOFL	Photoflash (AAG)
PHOG	Kahului, Maui Island [Hawaii] [ICAO location identifier] (ICLI)
PHOINT	Photographic Intelligence
PHOLAS	Philips Host Language System (SAUS)
PHOM	Photographer's Mate [Navy rating] [Obsolete]
PHON	Phoenician
phon	Phonetic (NTIO)
PHON	Phonetics
PHON	Phonogram (ROG)
PHON	Phonograph (AAG)
phon	Phonology (SHCU)
PHONCON	Telephone Conversation [or Conference]
PHONE	Telephone (NTCM)
PHONEBOOK	Region 3 Telephone Directory (SAUS)
Phones	Earphones (SAUS)
PHONET	Phonetics (ROG)
Phonetel	Phonetel Technologies [Commercial firm] [Associated Press] (SAG)
P HONG	Ponchong [Tea trade] (ROG)
Phono	Phonocardiogram [Cardiology] (DAVI)
PHONO	Phonograph (MSA)
PHONOG	Phonography
phonol	Phonology (WDAA)
PHONOL	Phonology
PHONORECORD	Phonograph Record (SAUS)
Phonos	Phonoscopy (SAUS)
PHONOVISION	Telephone Television (SAUS)
PHOPT	Pseudohypoparathyroidism [Endocrinology]
Phor	Phoronida (SAUS)
Phorm	Phormio [of Terence] [Classical studies] (OCD)
PHOS	Phosphate (KSC)
PHOS	Phosphorescent (KSC)
Phos	Phosphorous (SAUS)
PHOS	Phosphorus [Chemical symbol is P]
PhosBro	Phosphor Bronze
PHOSCHEM	Phosphate Chemicals Export Association (EA)
PHOSI	Preliminary Handbook of Operations and Service Instructions
PHOSIAC	Photographically Stored Information Analog Comparator
PHosp	Post Hospital [Army]
PHOS-S	Phosphorus Spot [Urine Test] [Chemistry] (DAVI)
PHOST	Poly(hydroxystyrene) [Organic chemistry]
Phot	Photius [Ninth century AD] [Classical studies] (OCD)
PHOT	Photograph
PHOT	Photographer [Navy rating] [British]
Phot	Photography (BEE)
PHOTABS	Photographic Abstracts [Pergamon] [Database]
PHOTAC	Phototypesetting and Composing [AT & T]
Photcm	Photocomm, Inc. [Associated Press] (SAG)
PHOTEX	Photographic Exercise (SAUS)
PHOTINT	Photographic Intelligence [Military]
photmur	Photo Mural (VRA)
PHOTO	Photograph (AAG)
photo	Photograph (VRA)
PHOTO	Photographic
Photo	Photogravure [Philately]
Photobiochem Photobiophys	Photobiochemistry and Photobiophysics (SAUS)
PhotoC	Photo-Control Corp. [Associated Press] (SAG)
PHOTOCD	Photographic Compact Disk (SAUS)
Photochem Photobiol	Photochemistry and Photobiology (MEC)
PHOTOCOMP	Photocomposed (SAUS)
PHOTOCOMP	Photocomposition (SAUS)
PHOTOG	Photographic
photog	Photography (SHCU)
Photogeog	Photogeography (SAUS)
PHOTOGEOL	Photographic Geology (SAUS)
PHOTOGR	Photographer
Photogr	Photographical (SAUS)
PHOTOGR	Photography
Photogramm Eng Remote Sens	Photogrammetric Engineering and Remote Sensing (SAUS)
Photogramm Rec	Photogrammetric Record (SAUS)
Photogr Appl Sci Technol	Photographic Applications in Science. Technology and Medicine (SAUS)
Photogr Sci Eng	Photographic Science and Engineering (SAUS)
PHOTOINT	Photo Intelligence (ACAE)
PHOTOLITH	Photolithographic
PHOTOM	Photometry
photomon	Photomontage (VRA)
PHOTON	Paneuropean Photonic Transport Overlay Network (SAUS)
Photon	Photon Dynamics, Inc. [Associated Press] (SAG)
PHOTONICS	Photo Electronics (ACAE)
PHOTONS	Photometric Thermospheric Oxygen Nightglow Study (SAUS)
Photo Op	Photo Opportunity (SAUS)
Photophysiol Curr Top	Photophysiology, Current Topics (SAUS)
PHOTOSYN	Photosynthesis (SAUS)
Photosynth Res	Photosynthesis Research (SAUS)
PHOTOTRIGULANT	Photographic Triangulation Group, Atlantic [Military] (DNAB)
PHOTOTRIGUPAC	Photographic Triangulation Group, Pacific [Military] (DNAB)
PHOTOX	Photochemical Vapor Deposition Process (ACAE)
PHOTOXE	Pathfinder and Helicopter Operation in a Toxic Environment (SAUS)
PhotrIn	Photronic Labs [Associated Press] (SAG)
PHOTRIPART	Photo Triangulation Party [Military]

PHOTRON	Photographic Squadron [*Navy*]
PHOTUB.......	Phototube (KSC)
PHO/TY	Photo Type [*Deltiology*]
P How..........	Pack Howitzer (SAUS)
PHOXA.........	Photochemical Oxidant and Acid Deposition Model Application within the Framework of PIC (SAUS)
PHP	Pacific Hawaiian Products Co. [*Later, PHP Co.*]
PHP	Packing-House Products [*Food industry*]
PHP	Parents Helping Parents [*An association*] (EA)
PHP	Parts, Hybrids, and Packaging (MCD)
PHP	Passive Hyperpolarizing Potential [*Neurochemistry*]
PHP	Payload Handling Panel [*NASA*] (MCD)
PHP	Pennhurst State School and Hospital, Spring City, PA [*OCLC symbol*] (OCLC)
PHP	Peoples Heritage Party (SAUS)
PHP	Performance, Hermeticity and Price (SAUS)
PHP	Personal Handy Phone [*Telecommunications*]
PHP	Personal Home Page (SAUS)
PHP	Petroleum Heat & Power (EFIS)
PHP	Philip, SD [*Location identifier*] [*FAA*] (FAAL)
PHP	Phillip Resources, Inc. [*Vancouver Stock Exchange symbol*]
PHP	Philosophia Patrum [*A publication*] (BJA)
PHP	PHP Healthcare Corp. [*Associated Press*] (SAG)
PHP	PHP Hypertext Preprocessor (SAUS)
PHP	Physician's Health Plan
PHP	Physicians Home Page (SAUS)
PHP	Pinane Hydroperoxide [*Organic chemistry*]
PHP	Planetary Horizon Platform [*Aerospace*]
PHP	Pooled Human Plasma (MELL)
PHP	Post-Heparin Phospholipase [*Medicine*] (MAE)
PHP	Postheparin Plasma (DAVI)
PHP	Post-Hostilities Planning Subcommittee of the Chiefs of Staff Committee [*World War II*]
PHP	Pounds per Horsepower
PHP	Prentice Hall Press [*Publisher*]
PHP	Prepaid Health Plan [*Insurance*]
PHP	Presbyterian Hunger Program (EA)
PHP	Primary Hyperparathyroidism (MAE)
PHP	Propeller Horsepower
PHP	Pseudohyperbolic Particle [*Astrophysics*]
PHP	Pseudohypoparathyroidism [*Endocrinology*]
PHP	Psychologists Helping Psychologists (SAUS)
PHP	Public Health Plan (SAUS)
PHP	Pump Horsepower
PHPA	Pacific Herring Packers Association (EA)
PHPA	Partially-Hydrolyzed Polyacrylamide [*Well drilling technology*]
PHPC	Post-Hostilities Planning Committee [*Navy*] [*World War II*]
PHPD	Per Hatch per Day (RIMS)
PHPES	Program for Health Policy in Economies under Stress (ADWA)
PHPFI	Personal Home Page/Form Interpreter (SAUS)
PHPG	Poly(hydroxypropylglutamine) [*Organic chemistry*]
PHPHB.........	P-heptyl-p-hydroxy Benzoate [*A preservative used in the making of American and British beer*]
PHPK	Probability of Hit to Probability of Kill (INF)
PHPL	Parallel Hardware Processing Language [*1977*] [*Computer science*] (CSR)
PHPO	Private Health Plan Option [*Medicare*] (GFGA)
PHPPO.........	Public Health Practice Program Office (SAUS)
PHPS	Post-Hostilities Planning Staff [*World War II*]
PHPT	Portable High-Potential Tester
pHPT...........	Primary Hyperparathyroidism [*Medicine*] (STED)
PHPT	Primary Hyperparathyroidism
PHPT	Pseudohypoparathyroidism [*Medicine*] (DB)
PHPV	Persistent Hyperplastic Primary Vitreous [*Ophthalmology*]
PHQ	Peacetime Headquarters (SAUS)
PHQ	Personnel History Questionnaire (MHDB)
PHQ	Phenylhydroquinone [*Organic chemistry*]
PHQ	Port Headquarters (SAUS)
PHQ	Postal Headquarters [*British*]
PHQ Card.....	Phase Qualification Card (SAUS)
PHR	Pacific Harbour [*Fiji*] [*Airport symbol*] (OAG)
PHR	Pacific Historical Review [*A publication*] (BRI)
PHR	Parts per Hundred of Resin (SAUS)
PHR	Parts per Hundred of Rubber [*Chemical technology*]
PHR	Payload Hazardous Report (NASA)
PHR	Peak Heart Rate [*Cardiology*]
PHR	Peak Height Ratio
PHR	Per Hour (SAUS)
PHR	Pharmacy (SAUS)
PHR	Phorbol [*Organic chemistry*]
PHR	Photographic Reconnaissance
PHR	Photoreactivity (DMAA)
phr	Phrase (ELAL)
phr	Phrase (NTIO)
Phr.............	Phrase (SAUS)
PHR	Phrase
phr	Phrase Book
PHR	Phraseology (SAUS)
Phr.............	Phrenomena: an Annual Review [*A publication*] (APTA)
PHR	Physical Record [*Computer science*]
PHR	Physicians for Human Rights (EA)
PHR	Point-Hour Ratio (DIPS)
PHR	Pound-Force per Hour (MCD)
PHR	Pounds per Hour (AAG)
PHR	Preheater (KSC)
PHR	Process Hazardous Review [*Environmental science*]
PHR	Process Heat Reactor Program [*Nuclear Regulatory Commission*]
PHR	Professional in Human Resources
PHR	Public Health Reports [*A publication*]
PHR	Pulse-Height Resolution [*By photomultiplier tubes*]
PHR	Retreat State Hospital, Hunlock Creek, PA [*OCLC symbol*] (OCLC)
PHRA...........	Principal Human Resources Advisor (SAUS)
PHRACT.......	Print-Handicapped Radio, Australian Capital Territory
PHRAN.........	Phrasal Analyzer (SAUS)
PHRASEO.....	Phraseogram (SAUS)
phraseo	phraseograph (SAUS)
PHRASEO.....	Phraseologist (SAUS)
PHRASEO.....	Phraseology (SAUS)
PHRC	Palestine Human Rights Campaign (EA)
PHRED........	Phrasal English Diction (SAUS)
PHRED........	Public Health Risk Evaluation Data [*Environmental Safety*]
Phren.........	Phrenic (SAUS)
Phren.........	Phrenological (SAUS)
Phren.........	Phrenologist (SAUS)
PHREN........	Phrenology
Ph Rep	Philadelphia Reports [*Pennsylvania*] [*A publication*] (DLA)
PHRF..........	Performance Handicap Racing Fleet [*Boating*]
PHRF..........	Performance Handicap Racing Formula [*Sailing*]
PHRG..........	Park Home Residents Guild [*British*] (DBA)
PHRG..........	Parliamentary Human Rights Group (EAIO)
PHRHD	Pump, Hydraulic Ram, Hand-Driven (MSA)
PHRI	Pittsburgh Health Research Institute (SAUS)
PHRI	Public Health Research Institute (NADA)
PHRI	Public Health Research Institute of the City of New York, Inc. [*Research center*] (RCD)
PHRIC.........	Palestine Human Rights Information Center (EA)
PHRIR.........	Pointable High Resolution Imaging Radiometer (SAUS)
PHRK..........	Power and Heat Rejection Kit [*NASA*]
PHRM.........	Pharmaceutical (SAUS)
PhRMA	Pharmaceutical Research and Manufacturers of America (NTPA)
Phrmhse......	Pharmhouse Corp. [*Associated Press*] (SAG)
PhrmMkt......	Pharmaceutical Marketing Services, Inc. [*Associated Press*] (SAG)
PHRMST......	Pharmacist
PHR Program...	Process Heat Reactor Program (SAUS)
PHRR..........	Parenchymal Hepatic Resection Rate [*Medicine*]
PHRS..........	Portable Heat Rejection System
PHRT..........	Procarbazine, Hydroxyurea, Radiotherapy Protocol (DAVI)
PHRU..........	Population Health Research Unit (SAUS)
PHRW.........	Preferred Hotels and Resorts Worldwide (NTPA)
PHS	Packaging, Handling, and Storage (MCD)
PHS	Pallottine House of Studies
PHS	Pan Head Steel (IAA)
PHS	Parallel Half Subtracter (SAUS)
PHS	Partial Hospitalization Program (STED)
PHS	Paternal Half Sister (OA)
PHS	Pathological Human Serum [*Serology*]
PHS	Patient-Heated Serum (STED)
PHS	Payload Handling Station [*NASA*] (MCD)
PHS	Pennsylvania Historical Society (SAUS)
PHS	Personal Handyphone System [*Telecommunications*]
PHS	Personal Health Summary (SAUS)
PHS	Personal Health Survey [*Psychology*]
PHS	Personal Hygiene Subsystem [*NASA*] (KSC)
PHS	Phenylalanine Hydroxylase Stimulator (STED)
PhS	Philosophical Society [*British*] (DBA)
Ph S	Philosophical Society of England (SAUS)
PHS	Phitsanuloke [*Thailand*] [*Airport symbol*] (OAG)
PHS	Photographic Historical Society (EA)
PHS	Photo Hydrography System (SAUS)
PHS	Physicians Health Services
PHS	Physicians' Health Study
PHS	Plated Heat Sink (SAUS)
PHS	Police History Society [*British*] (DBA)
PHS	Polyhydroxystyrene [*Also, PHOST*] [*Organic chemistry*]
PHS	Pooled Human Serum [*Hematology*] (DMAA)
PHS	Postal History Society (EA)
PHS	Postcard History Society (EA)
PHS	Posthypnotic Suggestion [*Psychology*]
PHS	Precision Hover Sensor (PDAA)
PHS	Prepared Hessian Surfacing [*Air Force*]
PHS	Presbyterian Historical Society (EA)
PHS	Price History System (MCD)
PHS	Printing Historical Society [*British*]
PHS	Printing House Square (DGA)
PHS	Prison Health Services (SAUS)
PHS	Probability of Having a Space
PHS	Progressive Hongkong Society [*Political party*]
PHS	Prostaglandin H Synthase [*An enzyme*] (GNE)
PHS	ProVantage Health Svcs. [*NYSE symbol*] (SG)
PHS	Public Health Service [*Department of Health and Human Services*]
PHS	Public Health Standards (SAUS)
PHS	Pulmonary Hypertension Syndrome (SAUS)
PHS	Pulse Height Selection (SAUS)
PHS	Pumped Hydro Storage [*Power source*]
PHS	Somerset State Hospital, Somerset, PA [*OCLC symbol*] (OCLC)
PHSA..........	Pearl Harbor Survivors Association (EA)
PHSA..........	Polyhydroxystearic Acid [*Organic chemistry*]
PHSA..........	Polymerized Human Serum Albumin [*Biochemistry*]
PHSA..........	Provincial Hospital Services Association [*British*] (DBA)
PHSA..........	Public Health Service Act (GFGA)

PHS&T.........	Packaging, Handling, Storage, and Transportability
PHS & T........	Packaging, Handling, Storage, and Transportation [*Shipping*]
PhSAP.........	Physical Service Access Point [*Telecommunications*] (OSI)
PHSAR.........	Public Health Service Acquisition Regulations [*Department of Health and Human Services*] (GFGA)
PHSBG.........	Preventive Health Services Block Grant [*Public human service program*] (PHSD)
PHSC	Pluripotent Hematopoietic Stem Cells [*Cytology*]
PHSC	Postal History Society of Canada (EA)
PHSC	Posterior Horn of Spinal Cord [*Medicine*] (MELL)
PHSC	Private Hospital Supplementary Charges (ADA)
PHSCS.........	Pier-Harris Self-Concept Scale (EDAC)
PHSE	Pharmhouse Corp. [*NASDAQ symbol*] (SAG)
PHSE	Phase [*Computer science*]
PHSE	Piedmont Health Survey of the Elderly [*Department of Health and Human Services*] (GFGA)
PHSF	Bradshaw Field, Hawaii Island [*Hawaii*] [*ICAO location identifier*] (ICLI)
PHSF	Payload Hazardous Servicing Facility [*NASA*] (NAKS)
PHSG	Postal History Study Group (EA)
PHSI	Plant Health and Seeds Inspectorate [*Ministry of Agriculture, Fisheries, and Food*] [*British*]
PHSIG	Pan Hellenic Society Inventors of Greece in USA [*Defunct*] (EA)
PHSKX	Phoenix Aggressive Growth Cl.A [*Mutual fund ticker symbol*] (SG)
PHSNZ........	Postal History Society of New Zealand [*Auckland*] (EA)
PHSO	Partially Hydrogenated Soybean Oil [*Cooking fat*]
PHSO	Postal History Society of Ontario [*Later, PHSC*] (EA)
PHSOC........	Photographical Historical Society of Canada
P-H Soc Sec Taxes...	Social Security Taxes (Prentice-Hall, Inc.) [*A publication*] (DLA)
PHS of A........	Postal History Society of the Americas (EA)
PHSP	Phase-Splitter (MSA)
PHSP	Public Health Service Publications
PHSPS.........	Preservation, Handling, Storage, Packaging, and Shipping (NRCH)
PHSS	Physician Support Systems, Inc. [*NASDAQ symbol*] (SAG)
PHSS	Population Health Summary System (ADWA)
PHST	Packaging, Handling, Storage, and Transportation [*Shipping*]
Ph St Tr........	Phillipps' State Trials [*A publication*] (DLA)
PHSV	Physicians Health Services, Inc. [*NASDAQ symbol*] (SAG)
PHSV	Physicians Health Svcs'A' [*NASDAQ symbol*] (TTSB)
PHSY	PacifiCare Health Systems, Inc. [*Cypress, CA*] [*NASDAQ symbol*] (NQ)
PHSYA.........	PacifiCare Health Sys'A' [*NASDAQ symbol*] (TTSB)
PHT.............	Managed High Yield Fd [*NYSE symbol*] (TTSB)
PHT.............	Packaging, Handling and Transportability (ACAE)
PHT.............	Packaging, Handling & Transportation (SAUS)
PHT.............	PaineWebber Premium High Income [*NYSE symbol*] (SPSG)
PHT.............	Paired Hands Test [*Education*] (EDAC)
PHT.............	Paris, TN [*Location identifier*] [*FAA*] (FAAL)
PHT.............	Passive Haemagglutination Test (SAUS)
PHT.............	Passive Hemagglutination Technique [*Immunology*]
PHT.............	Peak Hour Traffic (PA)
PHT.............	Peak Hour Trips (PA)
PHT.............	Peroxide Hemolysis Test [*Medicine*] (STED)
PHT.............	Phenylhydantoin [*Pharmacology*] (CPH)
PhT.............	[*The*] Phoenix and the Turtle [*Shakespearean work*]
pht.............	Photographer [*MARC relator code*] [*Library of Congress*] (LCCP)
PHT.............	Phototube
Pht.............	Phthaloyl [*Also, Phth*] [*Organic chemistry*]
PHT.............	Physical Therapy Technician [*Navy*]
PHT.............	Pitch, Hit, and Throw [*Youth competition sponsored by professional baseball*]
PHT.............	Poly-Hexylthiophene [*Organic chemistry*]
PHT.............	Portal Hypertension [*Medicine*]
PHT.............	Port Hold Time (SAUS)
PHT.............	Preheat
PHT.............	Primary Hyperthyroidism [*Medicine*] (STED)
PHT.............	Pulmonary Hypertension [*Cardiology*] (CPH)
PHT.............	Putting Hubby Through [*College "degree" earned by some wives*]
PHT.............	Pyridohomotropane [*Organic chemistry*]
PHT.............	Pyrrolidone Hydrotribromide (SAUS)
PHTab.........	Torrance State Hospital, Torrance, PA [*OCLC symbol*] (OCLC)
PHTab.........	President's Hundred Tab [*Military decoration*] (AABC)
PHTAT	Para-Hydroxytriamterene [*Biochemistry*]
PHTATS	Para-Hydroxytriamterene Sulfate [*Biochemistry*]
P-H Tax	Federal Taxes (Prentice-Hall, Inc.) [*A publication*] (DLA)
P-H Tax Ct Mem...	Tax Court Memorandum Decisions (Prentice-Hall, Inc.) [*A publication*] (DLA)
P-H Tax Ct Rep & Mem Dec...	Tax Court Reported and Memorandum Decisions (Prentice-Hall, Inc.) [*A publication*] (DLA)
PHTBX	Phoenix Tax Exempt Bond [*Mutual fund ticker symbol*] (SG)
PHTC	Pneumatic Hydraulic Test Console (KSC)
PHTC	Pulse Height to Time Converter (OA)
PhTD..........	Physical Therapy Doctor
PHTF..........	Pearl Harbor Training Facility [*Navy*]
Phth	Phthaloyl [*Also, Pht*] [*Organic chemistry*]
PHTK	Prompt Hard Target Kill (SAUS)
PHTLS	Pre Hospital Trauma Life Support (SAUS)
PHTM	Public Health and Tropical Medicine (ADWA)
PHTN	Photon Dynamics [*NASDAQ symbol*] (TTSB)
PHTN	Photon Dynamics, Inc. [*NASDAQ symbol*] (SAG)
PHTN	Public Health Training Network
PHTO	Hilo/General Lyman Field, Hawaii Island [*Hawaii*] [*ICAO location identifier*] (ICLI)
PHTP	Priority Health Training Programs (SAUS)

PHTS	Packaging, Handling, Transportation, Storage (SAUS)
PHTS	Primary Heat Transport System [*Nuclear energy*] (NRCH)
PHTS	Psychiatric Home Treatment Service (DAVI)
PHU	Philadelphia Ukrainian [*Diocesan abbreviation*] [*Pennsylvania*] (TOCD)
PHU	Power Holdover Unit (SAUS)
PHU	Pressure, Hydraulic Unit
PHU	Public Health Unit (SAUS)
PHuJ	Juniata College, Huntingdon, PA [*Library symbol*] [*Library of Congress*] (LCLS)
PHUN	Phreakers and Hackers Underground Network (SAUS)
P-H Unrep Tr Cas...	Prentice-Hall Unreported Trust Cases [*A publication*] (DLA)
Phus Plu......	Philippus Puldericus [*Authority cited in pre-1607 legal work*] (DSA)
PHV	Pahlavi [*Iran*] [*Airport symbol*] (AD)
PHV	Parallel Hybrid Vehicle
PHV	Paramount Home Video
PHV	Peak Height Velocity (DMAA)
PHV	Peak Horizontal Velocity
PHV	Persistent Hypertrophic Vitreous [*Ophthalmology*] (DAVI)
PHV	Phase Velocity
PHV	Pro Haec Vice [*For This Turn*] [*Latin*] (ROG)
PHV	Prospect Hill Virus [*Medicine*] (DMAA)
PHV	Prosthetic Heart Valve (MELL)
PHV	Wernersville State Hospital, Wernersville, PA [*OCLC symbol*] (OCLC)
PHVA	Plasma Homovanillic Acid [*Biochemistry*]
PHVA Level...	Plasma Level of HomoVanillic Acid (SAUS)
pH Value	Pondus Hydrogenii Value (SAUS)
PH Valve	Pressure Holding Valve (SAUS)
PHVPS	Primary High-Voltage Power Supply
PHW	Pemberton Houston Willoughby Investment Corp. [*Toronto Stock Exchange symbol*] [*Vancouver Stock Exchange symbol*]
PHW	Phalaborwa [*South Africa*] [*Airport symbol*] (OAG)
PHW	Philatelic Hobbies for the Wounded (EA)
PHW	Pressurized Heavy Water (SAUS)
PHW	Prime Hard Wheat
PHW	Warren State Hospital, Warren, PA [*OCLC symbol*] (OCLC)
PHWA	Professional Hockey Writers' Association (EA)
PHWA	Protestant Health and Welfare Assembly [*Later, PHHSA*] (EA)
PHWC	Polish Helsinki Watch Committee (EAIO)
PHWFJD......	Partners in Harmony, World Family of John Denver (EA)
PHWR.........	Hickam United States Air Force Automatic Weather Switch, Oahu Island [*Hawaii*] [*ICAO location identifier*] (ICLI)
PHWR.........	Pressurized Heavy Water-Moderated and Cooled Reactor [*Nuclear energy*] (IAA)
PHWR.........	Pressurized Heavy Water Reactor [*Nuclear energy*]
PHWRH.......	Pressurized Heavy Water Reactor-Homogenized (SAUS)
PHX	Partial Hepectomy [*Medicine*]
PHx	Past History [*Medicine*] (MAE)
Phx	Pharynx [*Anatomy*] (DAVI)
PHX	Phoenix [*Arizona*] [*Airport symbol*] (OAG)
PHX	Phoenix 2000 Airtaxi Ltd. [*Hungary*] [*ICAO designator*] (FAAC)
PHX	Phoenix Network, Inc. [*AMEX symbol*] (SPSG)
PHX	Woodville State Hospital, Carnegie, PA [*OCLC symbol*] (OCLC)
PhxDffP......	Phoenix Duf & Phelps Corp. [*Associated Press*] (SAG)
PhxDfP.......	Phoenix Duff & Phelps Corp. [*Associated Press*] (SAG)
PhxDuffP....	Phoenix Duff & Phelps Corp. [*Associated Press*] (SAG)
PhxGold......	Phoenix Gold International, Inc. [*Associated Press*] (SAG)
PhxNet.......	Phoenix Network, Inc. [*Associated Press*] (SAG)
PHY	C. Howard Marcy State Hospital, Pittsburgh, PA [*OCLC symbol*] (OCLC)
PHY	Norman, OK [*Location identifier*] [*FAA*] (FAAL)
PHY	Pharyngitis
Phy	Physalaemin [*Biochemistry*]
PHY	Physical
PHY	Physical Access (SAUS)
PHY	Physical Layer (AAEL)
PHY	Physical Layer Control (SAUS)
PHY	Physician
PHY	Physics
PHY	Physiology (DMAA)
PHY	Phytohemagglutinin [*Immunology*] (AAMN)
PHY	Prospect Street High Income Portfolio, Inc. [*NYSE symbol*] (SPSG)
PHYC	PhyCor, Inc. [*NASDAQ symbol*] (SPSG)
phyce	Photocopy-Control Electronics unit (SAUS)
PHYCOM......	Physicians Communications Service [*Fisher-Stevens, Inc.*] [*Merged into BRS/COLLEAGUE*]
PhyCor........	PhyCor, Inc. [*Associated Press*] (SAG)
PhyCpt........	Physicians Computer Network [*Associated Press*] (SAG)
PHYCUS......	Physical Custody [*of Records*] (MHDB)
PHY ED........	Physical Education (WGA)
PHYL	Physiological
PHYLIP	Phylogeny Inference Package [*Botany*]
PHYLIS	Physics Online Information System [*Computer science*] (PDAA)
PHYLO	Phylogeny (SAUS)
PHYM	Putnam High Yield Municipal Trust [*Associated Press*] (SAG)
PhyMatr......	PhyMatrix Corp. [*Associated Press*] (SAG)
PHYN	Physician Reliance Network [*NASDAQ symbol*] (TTSB)
PHYN	Physician Reliance Network, Inc. [*NASDAQ symbol*] (SAG)
PHYS	Physic (SAUS)
PHYS	Physical (AFM)
Phys..........	Physical (DIAR)
phys..........	Physical (NTIO)
phys..........	Physical (SHCU)
PHYS	Physically (SAUS)
Phys..........	Physician (CMD)

phys............ Physician (SHCU)
PHYS .... Physician
PHYS .... Physicist [or Physics] (ADA)
phys............ Physicist (SHCU)
Phys............ Physics (DD)
PHYS .... Physics (GOBB)
phys............ Physics (SHCU)
PHYS .... Physio-Control Intl [NASDAQ symbol] (TTSB)
PhyS .... Physiological Saline [Pharmacology] (DAVI)
PHYS .... Physiology
PhySale....... Physician Sales & Service, Inc. [Associated Press] (SAG)
PHY-SAP...... Physical Layer Service Access Point (SAUS)
PHYSB........ PacifiCare Health Sys'B' [NASDAQ symbol] (TTSB)
PHYSBE....... Physiological Simulation Benchmark Experiment
Phys Briefs.... Physics Briefs (SAUS)
Phys Bull ..... Physics Bulletin (SAUS)
Phys Chem... Physiological Chemistry and Physics (MEC)
Phys Chem Glasses... Physics and Chemistry of Glasses (SAUS)
Phys Chem Mater Treat... Physics and Chemistry of Materials Treatment (SAUS)
Phys Chem Mech Surf... Physics, Chemistry and Mechanics of Surfaces (SAUS)
Phys Chem Miner... Physics and Chemistry of Minerals (SAUS)
PHYSCL....... Physical
PhysCpA ...... Physician Corp. of America [Associated Press] (SAG)
Phys Dis...... Physical Disability (CPH)
Phys Dsabl... Physical Disability (SAUS)
Phys Earth Planet Inter... Physics of the Earth and Planetary Interiors (SAUS)
PHYSEC....... Physical Security (MCD)
PHYS ED...... Physical Education
Phys Educ.... Physics Education (SAUS)
Phys Eng ..... Physical Engineer
PHYSEXAM... Physical Examination
Phys Fluids A Fluid Dyn... Physics of Fluids A, Fluid Dynamics (SAUS)
Phys Fluids B Plasma Phys... Physics of Fluids B, Plasma Physics (SAUS)
PHYSH........ Physicians and Surgeons Hospital (SAUS)
Phys Hndcpd... Physically Handicapped (AL)
PHYSIAT...... Physiatrical (SAUS)
PHYSIAT...... Physiatrist (SAUS)
PhysicHlt..... Physicians Health Services, Inc. [Associated Press] (SAG)
Physicochem Hydrodyn... Physicochemical Hydrodynamics (SAUS)
Physik Chem... Physikalisch-Chemische Trenn- und Messmethoden (MEC)
PhysIn .... Physicians Insurance Co. of Ohio [Associated Press] (SAG)
Physio .... Physiology (DAVI)
physio.......... Physiotherapy [Medicine] (DMAA)
PHYSIO....... Physiotherapy [Medicine]
Physiog....... Physiognomy (DIAR)
PHYSIOG ..... Physiognomy [Slang] (DSUE)
Physiog....... Physiognomy (SAUS)
PHYSIOG ..... Physiographic
PHYSIOL...... Physiological (MSA)
Physiol .... Physiology (BEE)
PHYSIOL...... Physiology (ROG)
Physiol Biochem Cultiv Plan... Physiology and Biochemistry of Cultivated Plants (SAUS)
Physiol Chem Phys... Physiological Chemistry and Physics (SAUS)
Physiol Ecol Jpn... Physiology and Ecology Japan (SAUS)
Physiol Plant Pathol... Physiological Plant Pathology (SAUS)
PHYSL .... Physiological (AFM)
PHYSLAC.... Physical Sciences Library Advisory Committee (SAUS)
Phys Med .... Physical Medicine (CPH)
PHYS MET.... Physical Metallurgy (SAUS)
Phys Met ..... Physics of Metals (SAUS)
Physmet ...... Physiometrix, Inc. [Associated Press] (SAG)
Phys Met Metallogr... Physics and Metallography (SAUS)
Phys Met Metallogr... Physics of Metals and Metallography (SAUS)
PHYSN......... Physician
PHYSNET..... Physics Network (ACAE)
PHYSOCEAN... Physical Oceanography (SAUS)
PHYSOG ...... Physiognomy [Slang] (DSUE)
Phys Pap .... Physics Papers (SAUS)
PhysPRC ..... Physician's Payment Review Commission (HCT)
PHYSQUAL... Physical Disqualification [Military] (DNAB)
PhysRel .... Physician Reliance Network, Inc. [Associated Press] (SAG)
Phys Rep ..... Physics Reports (SAUS)
Phys Rev ..... Physical Review (SAUS)
PhysRev ..... Physical Review Journal (SAUS)
Phys Rev .... Physical Revue (SAUS)
Phys Rev .... Physiological Review (MEC)
Phys Rev A... Physical Review A (MEC)
Phys Rev A At Mol Opt Phys... Physical Review A, Atomic, Molecular and Optical Physics (SAUS)
Phys Rev Abstr... Physical Review, Abstracts (SAUS)
Phys Rev A Stat Phys Plasmas Fluids Relat In... Physical Review A, Statistical Physics, Plasmas, Fluids and Related Interdisciplinary Topics (SAUS)
Phys Rev B Condens Matter... Physical Review B, Condensed Matter (SAUS)
Phys Rev C... Physical Review C: Nuclear Physics (MEC)
Phys Rev C Nucl Phys... Physical Review C, Nuclear Physics (SAUS)
Phys Rev D Part Fields... Physical Review D, Particles and Fields (SAUS)
Phys Rev Lett... Physical Review Letters (MEC)
PhysRs .... Physician Resources Group, Inc. [Associated Press] (SAG)
PHYS SC...... Physical Science (WDAA)
Phys Solid Earth... Physics of the Solid Earth (SAUS)
PhysSup ...... Physician Support Systems, Inc. [Associated Press] (SAG)
PHYST .... Physicist
Phys Teach... Physics Teaching (SAUS)

Phys-Tech.... Physico-Technical (SAUS)
PHYSTER..... Physical Therapy (AABC)
Phys Test Chem Anal Chem Anal... Physical Testing and Chemical Analysis, Chemical Analysis (SAUS)
Phys Ther .... Physical Therapist (DMAA)
Phys Today... Physics Today [A publication] (BRI)
Phys World... Physics World (SAUS)
PHYSY........ Physiology
Phytochem... Phytochemistry (SAUS)
Phytogeog ... Phytogeography (BARN)
PHYTOPATH... Phytopathology
PHYX.......... Physiometrix, Inc. [NASDAQ symbol] (SAG)
PHZ........... Ashland State General Hospital, Ashland, PA [OCLC symbol] (OCLC)
PHZ............ Phenylhydrazine (LDT)
PHZH .... Honolulu Air Traffic Control Center [Hawaii] [ICAO location identifier] (ICLI)
PI............ Division of Plant Industry (SAUS)
Pi............ Inorganic Phosphate (SAUS)
pi............ irregular pulsations (SAUS)
pI................ Isoelectric Point (MAE)
PI................ Pacific Islands (SAUS)
PI................ Pacing Impulse [Cardiology] (DAVI)
PI................ Pacing Indicator (SAUS)
PI................ Pacing Item (MCD)
PI................ Package Insert [Instructional leaflet distributed with certain prescription drugs] [Also, PPI]
PI................ Packaging Institute [Later, PI/USA] (EA)
PI................ Packing Index (SAUS)
PI................ Paducah & Illinois Railroad [AAR code]
PI................ Paleo-Indian (QUAC)
PI................ Palmaris Longus (DMAA)
PI................ Pancreatic Insufficiency [Gastroenterology]
PI................ Pancreatic Lipase [Medicine] (DMAA)
PI................ Pandectae (Pisanae) Florentinae [A publication] (DSA)
PI................ Panel Input
PI................ Pansophic Institute [Defunct] (EA)
PI................ Pantera International (EA)
PI................ Paper Insulated
PI................ Paper Insulation (SAUS)
PI................ Paracel Islands [ANSI two-letter standard code] (CNC)
PI................ Parachute Infantry (SAUS)
PI................ Paradoxical Intention [V. E. Frankl] (DIPS)
PI................ Parainfluenza (MELL)
PI................ Parallel Importation (DB)
PI................ Parallel Input [Computer science] (BUR)
PI................ Parallel Interface (SAUS)
PI................ Parameter Identifier [Computer science] (TNIG)
PI................ Parametric Industry (IAA)
Pi................ Paranoid Ideation (DAVI)
Pi................ Parental Generation [Medicine] (DMAA)
PI................ Parental Investment [Biology]
PI................ Parity Index [EEO]
PI................ Parity Insert (SAUS)
PI................ Partial Interchangeability (SAUS)
PI................ Particle Integration (CAAL)
PI................ Particular Integral (SAUS)
PI................ Partido Independente [Independent Party] [Costa Rica] [Political party]
PI................ Partido Intransigente [Intransigent Party] [Argentina] [Political party] (PD)
PI................ Parti Independantiste [Quebec]
PI................ Passeport International [International Passport] [An association] [France] (EAIO)
PI................ Passive Immunity [Medicine] (MELL)
PI................ Pasteur Institute (SAUS)
PI................ Pathfinder International (EA)
PI................ Patient's Interests [Medicine]
PI................ Patrol Inspector [Immigration and Naturalization Service]
PI................ Payload Interrogator [NASA] (MCD)
PI................ Payload Interrogator [NASA] (NAKS)
Pi................ Pen and Ink (NAKS)
PI................ Pen and Ink
PI................ Penetration Index (IAA)
PI................ Pepsin Inhibitor (OA)
PI................ Peptide Inhibitor (DB)
PI................ Perceptions, Inc. (EA)
PI................ Perceptual Isolation
PI................ Perfect Initials [Philately]
PI................ Performance Improvement
PI................ Performance Index
PI................ Performance Indicator (MCD)
PI................ Performance Intensity (MAE)
PI................ Perinatal Injury [Neonatology] (DAVI)
PI................ Per Inhalation (SAUS)
pi................ Per Inquiry (WDMC)
PI................ Per Inquiry [Advertising]
PI................ Periodical Index Term (NITA)
PI................ Periodicals Institute (EA)
PI................ Periodic Inspection [Military] (AFM)
PI................ Peripheral Interface [Computer science] (PCM)
PI................ Peripheral Inventory (SAUS)
PI................ Peripheral Iridectomy [Medicine]
PI................ Perlite Institute (EA)
PI................ Permaculture International [Australia]
PI................ Permeability Index [Clinical chemistry]

PI	Perpetual Inventory (SAUS)
PI	Personal Identification
PI	Personal Identity (SAUS)
PI	Personal Income
PI	Personal Injury [*Insurance*]
PI	Personal Injury Accident [*British police term*]
PI	Personal Investment [*A publication*] (ADA)
PI	Personality Inventory [*Psychology*]
PI	Petroleum Information Corp. (IID)
PI	Petrol Injection [*British*]
PI	Pharmacopoeia Internationalis [*International Pharmacopoeia*]
PI	Phase-In
PI	Phenanthroimidazole [*Organic chemistry*]
PI	Phenyl Isocyanate [*Organic chemistry*]
PI	Philippines (MILB)
PI	Phonographic Institute (SAUS)
PI	Phosphate, Inorganic [*Chemistry*]
PI	Phosphatidylinositol [*Also, PtdIns*] [*Biochemistry*]
PI	Photoelectric Inspection (ELAL)
P-I	Photogrammetric Instrumentation (AAG)
PI	Photographic Institute (SAUS)
PI	Photographic Intelligence (SAUS)
PI	Photographic Interpretation
PI	Photographic Interpreter
PI	Photo Intelligence (SAUS)
PI	Photo International [*Defunct*] (EAIO)
PI	Photo Interpretation
PI	Photointerpretation [*or Photointerpreter*]
PI	Photo Interpreter (SAUS)
PI	Photointerpreter (IAA)
PI	Photoionization [*Physical chemistry*]
PI	Physical Instruction (SAUS)
PI	Physical Inventory (NRCH)
PI	Physically Impaired
PI	Physics International
PI	Piaster [*Monetary unit*] [*Spain, Republic of Vietnam, and some Middle Eastern countries*]
pi	Pica [*Typesetting*] [*Also called pie*] (WDMC)
PI	Piedmont Aviation, Inc. [*ICAO designator*] (OAG)
PI	Pigeon Trainer [*Navy*]
PI	Pig Iron
Pi	Pillius Medicinensis [*Flourished, 1165-1207*] [*Authority cited in pre-1607 legal work*] (DSA)
PI	Pilot International (EA)
PI	Pilot Item (MCD)
PI	Pilotless Intercepter [*Air Force*]
PI	Pineal Body (DB)
PI	Pinedale [*Wyoming*] [*Seismograph station code, US Geological Survey*] [*Closed*] (SEIS)
PI	Pin Insulator (SAUS)
PI	Pink (ROG)
PI	Pipe [*Freight*]
PI	Pirelli [*Tire casing code*]
PI	Planetary Interior (SAUS)
PI	Planet Imager (SAUS)
PI	Plan Information (SAUS)
PI	Planning Index (SAUS)
PI	Plant Industry (SAUS)
PI	Plant Inspection
PI	Plant Introduction [*Botany*]
PI	Plaque Index [*Dentistry*]
PI	Plasma Iron [*Hematology*]
PI	Plastic Index
PI	Plasticity Index (SAUS)
PI	Plastics Institute (NADA)
PI	Plastochron Index [*Botany*]
PI	Plug-in (SAUS)
PI	Plug-In Instrument (IAA)
P/I	Pneumatic-to-Current (SAUS)
PI	Pneumatosis Intestinalis [*Medicine*]
PI	Point Initiating
PI	Point Insulating
PI	Point Interception (SAUS)
PI	Point of Impact (AFM)
PI	Point of Interception [*Navigation*]
PI	Point of Intersection
PI	Point of Inversion (SAUS)
PI	Poison Ivy [*Campers' slang*]
PI	Polar Inductor (SAUS)
PI	Polling Interrupt (SAUS)
PI	Polyimide [*Organic chemistry*]
PI	Polyisoprene [*Organic chemistry*]
PI	Polymer International (NS), Inc. [*Toronto Stock Exchange symbol*]
PI	Pompeiiana, Inc. (EA)
PI	Ponderal Index [*Measurement*] (DAVI)
PI	Poni Iussit [*Ordered to Be Placed*] [*Latin*]
PI	Popcorn Institute (EA)
PI	Population Indication (SAUS)
PI	Population Institute (EA)
PI	Population Inversion (SAUS)
PI	Porch Index [*Psychiatry*] (DAVI)
PI	Portfolio Insurance [*Finance*]
PI	Position Indicating (SAUS)
PI	Position Indication (SAUS)
PI	Position Indicator [*Army*]
PI	Positive Identification Feature
PI	Positive Input (SAUS)
PI	Positive Intelligence (LAIN)
PI	Positive Interlace [*Television*]
PI	Postal Instruction (IAA)
PI	Post-Impressionist (SAUS)
PI	Postimpressionist Movement [*Art*]
PI	Postinfection [*Medicine*] (DB)
PI	Postinoculation [*Medicine*]
PI	Postischemic [*Medicine*]
PI	Potash Institute [*Later, PPI*] (EA)
PI	Potomac Institute [*Defunct*] (EA)
PI	Power Indicator (IAA)
PI	Power Injection
PI	Power Input
PI	Power Interlock (IAA)
PI	Practice Interception (SAUS)
PI	Pratt Institute (SAUS)
PI	Precision Instrument (NVT)
PI	Predicted Impact (MCD)
PI	Pregnancy Induced [*Gynecology*]
PI	Preinduction [*Medicine*]
PI	Preliminary Incubation (OA)
PI	Preliminary Injunction [*Legal term*] (HGAA)
PI	Preliminary Input (SAUS)
PI	Preliminary Inspection (MCD)
PI	Preliminary Investigation (NAKS)
PI	Preliminary Investigation (NASA)
PI	Preliminary Issue
PI	Premdor, Inc. [*NYSE symbol*] (SPSG)
PI	Premium Income (MARI)
PI	Preparatory Interval [*Psychometrics*]
PI	Prepositioned Instruction [*DoD*]
PI	Present Illness [*Medicine*]
PI	Pressure Indicator [*Nuclear energy*]
Pi	Pressure of Inspiration [*Medicine*]
P/I	Pressure to Current (SAUS)
PI	Presumptive Instruction (SAUS)
PI	Primacord Interstage
PI	Primary Infarction [*Medicine*]
PI	Primary Infertility (SAUS)
PI	Primary Input (IAA)
PI	Primary Item (ACAE)
PI	Prime Implicant (SAUS)
PI	Prime Interest Rate [*Banking*]
PI	Prime Item (SAUS)
PI	Principal Investigator (MCD)
Pi	Principal Investigator (NAKS)
PI	Printer [*Navy*]
PI	Printers Ink (SAUS)
PI	Print Image (IAA)
PI	Printing Impressions [*A publication*] (DGA)
PI	Priority Interrupt (IEEE)
PI	Private Institution [*British*]
PI	Private Investigator
PI	Priviledged Information (SAA)
PI	Privileged Instruction (SAUS)
PI	Proactive Inhibition [*Psychology*]
PI	Proactive Interference (EDAC)
PI	Problem Input (SAA)
PI	Procedure Interface (SAUS)
PI	Process Image (NITA)
PI	Process Instruction (SAUS)
PI	Process Instrumentation [*Nuclear energy*] (NRCH)
PI	Process Interface (SAUS)
PI	Process Interrupt (SAUS)
PI	Processor Interface [*Computer science*] (IAA)
PI	Procurement Inspection (MCD)
PI	Procurement Item (NASA)
PI	Prodigy Internet
PI	Product Improved
PI	Product Improvement (MCD)
P/I	Production Illustration (MSA)
PI	Production Index (SAUS)
PI	Production Interval
PI	Productivity Index (IEEE)
pi	Professional Indemnity [*Insurance*] (ODBW)
PI	Professional Indemnity [*Insurance*]
PI	Profibus International (SAUS)
PI	Program Indicator (IEEE)
PI	Program Information
PI	Program Innovations (ADA)
PI	Program Instruction [*Computer science*] (BUR)
PI	Program Integrator [*Military*] (RDA)
PI	Program Interface (SAUS)
PI	Program Interrupt
PI	Program Interrupter
Pi	Program Introduction (NAKS)
PI	Program Introduction
PI	Program Isolation [*Computer science*] (ELAL)
PI	Program Issuances [*Assistance Payments Administration, HEW*]
PI	Programmed Information [*Computer science*]
PI	Programmed Instruction
PI	Programmed Interrupt (SAUS)
PI	Programmed Introduction (MCD)

PI	Program of Instrumentation (MUGU)
PI	Project Inform (EA)
PI	Project Intrex [*Massachusetts Institute of Technology*] (EA)
PI	Prolactin Inhibitor [*Endocrinology*]
PI	Property Index [*British police term*]
PI	Propidium Iodide [*Fluorescent dye*]
PI	Proportional Integral (AAEL)
PI	Proportional-Plus Integral [*Digital control*]
PI	Proprietary Information (SAA)
PI	Propyl Isome (OA)
PI	Protamine Insulin
PI	Protease Inhibitor
PI	Proteinase Inhibitor [*Biochemistry*]
PI	Protocol International (SAUS)
PI	Protocol Interpreter (SAUS)
PI	Pseudo-Instruction (SAUS)
PI	Psychiatric Institute
PI	Psychosynthesis Institute (EA)
PI	Publication Instructions
PI	Public Information
PI	Public Investigation (SAUS)
PI	Public Involvement (ABAC)
PI	Puebla Institute (EA)
PI	Pulmonary Incompetence [*Medicine*]
PI	Pulmonary Indices [*Medicine*]
PI	Pulmonary Infarction [*Medicine*]
PI	Pulmonary Intervertebral Disc [*Medicine*]
PI	Pulse Induction (ADA)
PI	Pulse Input (SAUS)
PI	Purge Isolation [*Nuclear energy*] (NRCH)
PI	Pyritization Index [*Geoscience*]
PI	Sunshine Airlines [*Airline code*] [*Australia*]
PI1	State Correctional Institute at Camp Hill, Camp Hill, PA [*OCLC symbol*] (OCLC)
PI2	State Correctional Institute at Dallas, Dallas, PA [*OCLC symbol*] (OCLC)
PI3	State Correctional Institute at Grateford, Grateford, PA [*OCLC symbol*] (OCLC)
PI-3-Virus	Parainfluenza-3-Virus (SAUS)
PI4	State Correctional Institute at Huntingdon, Huntingdon, PA [*OCLC symbol*] (OCLC)
PI5	State Correctional Institute at Muncy, Muncy, PA [*OCLC symbol*] (OCLC)
PI6	State Correctional Institute at Pittsburgh, Pittsburgh, PA [*OCLC symbol*] (OCLC)
PI7	State Regional Correctional Facility, Greensburg, PA [*OCLC symbol*] (OCLC)
PI-3-3	Parainfluenza-3 (SAUS)
PIA	Municipal Premium Income Trust [*Formerly, Allstate Municipal Premium Fund*] [*NYSE symbol*] (SPSG)
PIA	National Association of Professional Insurance Agents (NTPA)
PIA	Pacific Islands Association (EA)
PIA	Packaged Ice Association (EA)
PIA	Paid in Advance (WDMC)
PI/A	Pakistan Institute of International Affairs (SAUS)
PIA	Pakistan International Airlines (SAUS)
PIA	Pakistan International Airlines Corp. [*ICAO designator*] (FAAC)
PIA	Panel-Information-Air Operation
PIA	Parallel Interface Adapter (SAUS)
PIA	Parapsychology Institute of America (EA)
PIA	Particle Impact Analyzer [*Astrophysics*]
PIA	Partitioning Industry Association [*British*] (DBA)
PIA	Passive Immunological Agglutination
PIA	Payload Interface Adapter [*NASA*] (SSD)
PIA	Payload Interface Agreement (SAUS)
PIA	Peoria [*Illinois*] [*Airport symbol*] (OAG)
PIA	Perfumery Importers Association [*Defunct*] (EA)
PIA	Peril Insured Against (MARI)
PIA	Peripheral Interface Adapter [*Computer science*]
PIA	Personal Information Appliance [*Telecommunications*] (PCM)
PIA	Personal Intelligent Agent (SAUS)
PIA	Personal Investment Authority [*British*] (ECON)
PIA	Personnel Inventory Analysis [*Army*]
PIA	Perspective Inversion Algorithm [*Computer science*]
PIA	Petervin Information Associates [*Also, an information service or system*] (IID)
PIA	Petroleum Incentives Administration [*Canada*]
PIA	Pharmaceutical Industries Association (SAUS)
PIA	Phenylisopropyladenosine [*Biochemistry*]
PIA	Philippine Institute of Architects (SAUS)
PIA	Phosphoroimmunoassays
PIA	Photoelectric Intravenous Angiography [*Medicine*] (DMAA)
PIA	Photographic Importers Association [*British*] (BI)
PIA	Piano [*Softly*] [*Music*]
PIA	Pilots International Association (EA)
PIA	Pine Institute of America (SAUS)
PIA	Pitten [*Austria*] [*Seismograph station code, US Geological Survey*] (SEIS)
PIA	Place Indicator in Accumulators (SAA)
PIA	Plasma Insulin Activity [*Clinical chemistry*]
PIA	Plastics Industries Association [*Ireland*]
PIA	Plastics Institute of America (EA)
PIA	Plug-in Administrator (SAUS)
PIA	Plug-In Amplifier
PIA	Pointed Instrument Assembly (ACAE)
PIA	Polycultural Institution of America
PIA	Positive Ion Accelerator
PIA	Positron Intensity Accumulator (MCD)
PIA	Postal Inspectors' Association [*A union*] [*British*]
PIA	Potentiometric Immunoassay [*Clinical chemistry*]
PIA	Predominant Interest Agency (AAGC)
PIA	Preferential Trade Area (EBF)
PIA	Preinfarction Angina [*Cardiology*] (DMAA)
PIA	Pre-Inspection Acceptance (SAA)
PIA	Preinstallation Acceptance
PIA	Pressure Indicating Alarm [*Engineering*]
PIA	Primary Inspection Agency [*Federal Manufactured Housing Construction and Safety Standards*] [*Department of Housing and Urban Development*] (GFGA)
PIA	Primary Insurance Account [*Social Security Administration*] (OICC)
PIA	Principal Industry Activity [*IRS*]
PIA	Printing Industries Association (SAUS)
PIA	Printing Industries of America (EA)
PIA	Printing Institute of America (SAUS)
PIA	Prison Industry Authority (SAUS)
PIA	Proceedings of the Irish Academy (SAUS)
PIA	Production Inventory Analysis (AAG)
PIA	Professional Insurance Agents [*Alexandria, VA*] (EA)
PIA	Program Implementation Agency (SAUS)
PIA	Program Initiation Agreement (SSD)
PIA	Programmable Interconnect Array [*Computer science*] (CIST)
PIA	Project Impact Analysis (NASA)
PIA	Project Initiation Agreement (SAUS)
PIA	Project Interface Adapter (SSD)
PIA	Propellant Isolation Assembly (ACAE)
PIA	Proprietary Industries Association (AAGC)
PIA	Psychiatric Institute of America [*For-profit network of private psychiatric hospitals*] (EA)
PIA	Public and International Affairs [*USCG*] (TAG)
PIA	Public Information Act
PIA	Public Information Adviser [*NATO*] (NATG)
PIA	Public Information and Awareness (SAUS)
PIA	Public Intoxication Act [*Australia*]
PIA	Pulse-Interval Analyzer (SAUS)
PIA	Pumice Institute of America (EA)
PIA	Purified Isophthalic Acid
PIA	White Haven Center, White Haven, PA [*OCLC symbol*] (OCLC)
PIAA	Pacific Index of Abbreviations and Acronyms (SAUS)
PIAA	Physician Insurers Association of America
PIAA	Pre-Arrangement Interment Association of America [*Later, PAA*] (EA)
PIAC	Partido de Integracion de America Central [*Nicaragua*] [*Political party*] (EY)
PIAC	Peak Instantaneous Airborne Count (DA)
PIAC	Permanent International Altaistic Conference (EA)
PIAC	Petroleum Industry Advisory Committee [*British*]
PIAC	Printing Industry Advisory Committee (HEAS)
PIAC	Problem Identification and Correction [*DoD*] (AFIT)
PIACCS	Pacific Integrated Automatic Command and Control System [*Military*] (DNAB)
PIACS	Pacific Integrated Automatic Communications Systems [*Military*]
PIACT	Program for the Introduction and Adaptation of Contraceptive Technology (EA)
PIAD	Plastics in Automotive Design (SAUS)
PIADC	Plum Island Animal Disease Center [*Formerly, PIADL*]
PIADL	Plum Island Animal Disease Laboratory [*of ARS, Department of Agriculture*] [*Later, PIADC*]
PIAF	Piege a Fibre Optique (SAUS)
PIAGET	Promoting Intellectual Adaptation Given Experiential Transforming Project (EDAC)
PIAI	Printing Industry of America, Inc. (SAUS)
PIAM	Petroleum Industry Application of Microcomputer (SAUS)
PIAM	PIA Merchandising Services, Inc. [*NASDAQ symbol*] (SAG)
PIAMA	Professional Institute for the American Management Association (OICC)
PIA Mer	PIA Merchandising Services, Inc. [*Associated Press*] (SAG)
PIANC	Permanent International Association of Navigation Congresses [*Brussels, Belgium*] (EAIO)
PIand	Papyri Iandanae [*A publication*] (OCD)
PIANEC	Planning of the Implementation of an Improved AFTN/AFS Network (SAUS)
PIANG	Piangendo [*Plaintive*] [*Music*]
PIANISS	Pianissimo [*Very Softly*] [*Music*]
PIANO	Propulsion Integration of Aero-Control Nozzles (SAUS)
PIAP	Pesticides Incidents Appraisal Panel (HEAS)
PIAP	Psychologists Interested in the Advancement of Psychotherapy [*Later, APA*] (EA)
PIAPACS	Psychophysiological Information Acquisition, Processing, and Control System
PIAR	Problem Identification and Analysis Report [*Military*] (CAAL)
PIAR	Project Impact Analysis Report (MCD)
PIARC	Permanent International Association of Road Congresses [*See also AIPCR*] [*Paris, France*] (EAIO)
PIARR	Product Independent Automatic Routing and Release (SAUS)
PIARy	Product Independent Automatic Routing and Release (SAUS)
PIAS	Photographic Inventory and Accountancy System
PIAS	Piaster [*Monetary unit*] [*Spain, Republic of Vietnam, and some Middle Eastern countries*]
PIAS	Prague Institute of Advanced Studies
PIAS	Precision Intelligence Augmentation System
PIAS	Precision Locator Strike System Intelligence Augmentation System

PIAS............ Pressure Indicating Alarm Switching [Engineering]
PIAS............ Program Impact Analysis Scenario
PIASA.......... Polish Institute of Arts and Sciences of America (EA)
PIASS......... Paris International Aviation and Space Salon (MCD)
PIAT............ Peabody Individual Achievement Test [Education]
PIAT............ Platoon Infantry Anti-Tank (WDAA)
PIAT............ Project Integrity Assurance Team (WDAA)
PIAT............ Projector Infantry, Antitank [British shoulder-controlled weapon]
PIAT............ Public Information Assist Team [Environmental Protection Agency]
                  (ERG)
PIAT-R........ Peabody Individual Achievement Test-Revised (TES)
PIAVA .... Polydactyly-Imperforate Anus-Vertebral Anomalies [Syndrome]
                  [Medicine] (DMAA)
PIB............. George Junior Republic, Grove City, PA [OCLC symbol] (OCLC)
PIB............. Laurel/Hattiesburg [Mississippi] [Airport symbol] (OAG)
PIB............. Pacific Inland Tariff Bureau, Portland OR [STAC]
PIB............. Papuan Infantry Battalion
PIB............. Parachute Infantry Battalion [Army]
PIB............. Partial Ileal Bypass [Medicine]
PIB............. Particle in a Box (SAUS)
PIB............. Partido Indio de Bolivia [Political party]
PIB............. Payload Integration Bay [NASA] (KSC)
PIB............. Pender Island [British Columbia] [Seismograph station code, US
                  Geological Survey] (SEIS)
PIB............. Periodic Information Briefing (MCD)
PIB............. Personal Information Briefing [of returning POW's] [Air Force]
PIB............. Petroleum Information Board (SAUS)
PIB............. Petroleum Information Bureau
PIB............. Photo Intelligence Brief (AFM)
PIB............. Photo Interpretation Brief (MCD)
PIB............. Plans Intelligence Branch (SAUS)
PIB............. Polar Ionosphere (or Ionospheric) Beacon (SAUS)
PIB............. Polar Ionospheric Beacon
PIB............. Polyisobuten (SAUS)
PIB............. Polyisobutylene [Organic chemistry]
PIB............. Polytechnic Institute of Brooklyn [Later, PINY] (MCD)
PIB............. Potential-Induced Breathing (SAUS)
PIB............. Power Ionosphere Beacon (SAUS)
PIB............. Pre-Flight Information Bulletin [Aviation] (DA)
PIB............. Preliminary Instruction Book
PIB............. Prices and Incomes Board [British]
PIB............. Prison Industry Board (SAUS)
PIB............. Processor Interface Buffer [Telecommunications] (TEL)
PIB............. Product Improvement Bulletin
PIB............. Program Information Block (IAA)
PIB............. Program Information Briefing
PIB............. Programmable Input Buffer
PIB............. Propellant Inspection Building [NASA] (KSC)
PIB............. Public Investments Board (SAUS)
PIB............. Publishers Information Bureau [New York, NY] (EA)
PIB............. Publishing Information Bulletin
PIB............. Pulse Interference Blanker
PIB............. Pyrotechnic Installation Building [NASA] (KSC)
PIBA............ Primary Industry Bank of Australia Ltd. (ADA)
PIBAC .... Permanent International Bureau of Analytical Chemistry of Human
                  and Animal Food
PIBAL............ Pilot Balloon Observation
PIBAL............ Polytechnic Institute of Brooklyn Aeronautical Laboratory (MCD)
PIBALS .... Pilot Balloon Soundings
PIBC............ Pacific Institute of Bio-Organic Chemistry
PIBC............ Percutaneous Intraaortic Balloon Counterpulsation [Catheter]
                  [Medicine] (DMAA)
PIBD .... Point Initiating, Base Detonating Projectile [Army]
PIBD .... Portable Interface Bond Detector (IAA)
PIBD Projectile.... Point Initiating, Base Detonating Projectile (SAUS)
PIBEB............ Polytechnic Institute of Brooklyn, Electrophysics Branch (SAUS)
PIBEE.......... Polytechnic Institute of Brooklyn, Department of Electrical
                  Engineering (SAUS)
PIBEP........... Polytechnic Institute of Brooklyn, Department of Electrophysics
                  (SAUS)
PIBI............ butyl rubber (SAUS)
PIBL............ PEMA Item Baseline List [Army] (AABC)
PIBMM......... Permanent International Bureau of Motorcycle Manufacturers
PIBMRI .... Polytechnic Institute of Brooklyn, Microwave Research Institute
                  (IEEE)
PIBO .... Poly Isobutylene Oxide (EDCT)
PIBOL .... Pilot Back Up Control
PIBOL .... Pilot in Booster Loop (SAA)
PIBOR........ Paris Interbank Offered Rank (ODBW)
PIBOR......... Paris Interbank Offered Rate (SAUS)
PIBS............ Permanent Interest-Bearing Shares [Finance] (WDAA)
PIBS............ Polar Ionospheric Beacon Satellite [NASA]
PIBUC .... Pilot Back Up Control
PIC............... Calverton, NY [Location identifier] [FAA] (FAAL)
PIC............... Craig House Technoma Workshop, Pittsburgh, PA [OCLC symbol]
                  (OCLC)
PIC............... Pacific Airlines Holding Co. [Vietnam] [ICAO designator] (FAAC)
PIC............... Pacific Imagery Processing and Interpretation Center (SAUS)
PIC............... Pacific Insurance Conference
PIC............... Pacific Intelligence Center (MCD)
PIC............... Pacific Islanders in Communications (SAUS)
PIC............... Paid-In Capital [Finance] (MHDW)
PIC............... Paired-Ion Chromatography
PIC............... Para-iodoclonidine [Biochemistry]
PIC............... Parent Indicator Code (DNAB)

PIC.............. Partially Incinerated Compound [Furnace technology]
PIC.............. Particle in Cell [Gas solid]
PIC.............. Particulate Inorganic Carbon (CARB)
PIC.............. Partners in Change Program [Department of Labor]
PIC.............. Payload Integration Center [NASA] (MCD)
PIC.............. Payload Integration Committee [NASA] (NASA)
PIC.............. Payload Integration Contractor (MCD)
PIC.............. PC Paint image format (SAUS)
PIC.............. Peak Identification Computer
PIC.............. People's Involvement Corp. (EA)
PIC.............. Performance Incentive Contracting (AAGC)
PIC.............. Periodic Inspection Control [Military] (IAA)
PIC.............. Peripheral Interface Controller [Computer science]
PIC.............. Peripherie Controller [Computer science] (IAA)
PIC.............. Pershing Instant Comment [Donaldson, Lufkin & Jenrette] [Database]
PIC.............. Personal Identification Code [Banking]
PIC.............. Personal Information Carrier (SAUS)
PIC.............. Personal Information Communicator (SAUS)
PIC.............. Personal Intelligent Communicator [Computer science] (PCM)
PIC.............. Personal Internet Connection [Fee-based accounts]
PIC.............. Personality Inventory for Children [Psychology]
PIC.............. Personnel Investigations Center
PIC.............. Pesticides Information Center [National Agricultural Library]
                  [Terminated, 1969]
PIC.............. Petrochemical Investing Corp.
PIC.............. Phosphoinositidase C [An enzyme]
PIC.............. Photographic Industries Council (SAUS)
PIC.............. Photographic Industry Council [Defunct] (EA)
PIC.............. Photographic Interpretation Center (MCD)
PIC.............. Photo Interpretation Center (SAUS)
PIC.............. Photo Interpretation Console (IAA)
PIC.............. Physics Information Center (SAUS)
PIC.............. Physics International Co. (SAUS)
PIC.............. Piccadilly Cafeterias [NYSE symbol] (TTSB)
PIC.............. Piccadilly Cafeterias, Inc. [NYSE symbol] (SPSG)
PIC.............. Piccadilly Saloon [London] (DSUE)
pic............... Piccolo (WDAA)
PIC.............. [The] Pickens Railroad Co. [Later, PICK] [AAR code]
PIC.............. Picos [Brazil] [Airport symbol] (AD)
PIC.............. Picrotoxin [Biochemistry]
Pic.............. Pictor [Constellation]
PIC.............. Pictorial (WDAA)
PIC.............. Picture (AABC)
PIC.............. Picture File Format [Computer science] (BTTJ)
PIC.............. Picture Image Compatibility (VLIE)
PIC.............. Picture Interactive Computer System (IAA)
pic............... Pictures [Slang] (WDMC)
PIC.............. Piedmont Interfaith Council (SAUS)
PIC.............. Pig Improvement Co. [British] (ECON)
PIC.............. Pilot in Command [Navy] (DOMA)
PIC.............. Pilot-Integrated Cockpit (AAG)
PIC.............. Pine Cay [British West Indies] [Airport symbol] [Obsolete] (OAG)
PIC.............. Pitch Impregnation Carbonization (MCD)
PIC.............. Planar Integrated Circuit (SAUS)
PIC.............. Planned Insurance Coverage
PIC.............. Plasma Insulin Concentration [Clinical chemistry]
PIC.............. Plastic Igniter Cord (IAA)
PIC.............. Plastic Insulated Cable (IAA)
PIC.............. Plastic-Insulated Cable (SAUS)
PIC.............. Plastic Insulated Conductor
PIC.............. Platform for Internet Content (SAUS)
PIC.............. Plug-In Card (VLIE)
PIC.............. Pocket Ionization Chamber (SAUS)
PIC.............. Point in Call (SAUS)
PIC.............. Poison Information Center (SAUS)
PIC.............. Policy Information Center [Department of Health and Human
                  Services] [Information service or system] (IID)
PIC.............. Polyethylene Insulated Cable (SAUS)
PIC.............. Polyethylene Insulated Conductor [Telecommunications]
PIC.............. Polymer-Impregnated Concrete (KSC)
PIC.............. Polymorphism Information Content [Medicine] (DMAA)
PIC.............. Polyolefin Insulated Cable (SAUS)
PIC.............. Portable Imaging Computer
PIC.............. Position Independent Code [Telecommunications] (TEL)
PIC.............. Positive Immittance Converter (PDAA)
PIC.............. Positive Impedance Converter (IAA)
PIC.............. Positive Ion Chamber
PIC.............. Postinflammatory Corticoid [Medicine]
PIC.............. Potential Icing Category [Meteorology] (DA)
PIC.............. Power Information Center [Interagency Advanced Power Group]
                  [DoD] [Washington, DC]
PIC.............. Power Input Connection (SAUS)
PIC.............. Power Integrated Circuit [Computer science]
PIC.............. Predicted Intercept Contour
PIC.............. Preferred Inter exchange Carrier (SAUS)
PIC.............. Preimpregnated Cable (SAUS)
PIC.............. Preinitiation Complex [Genetics]
PIC.............. Preinstallation Calibration (KSC)
PIC.............. Preinstallation Checkout (NASA)
PIC.............. Presbyterian Interracial Council (EA)
PIC.............. Pressure-Impregnation Carbonization (SAUS)
PIC.............. Pressure Indicated Controlled (SAUS)
PIC.............. Pressure Indicator Controller
PIC.............. Pressurized Ion Chamber (SAUS)
PIC.............. Prices and Income Commission (SAUS)

PIC	Primary Independent Carrier (VLIE)
PIC	Primary Interexchange Carrier [*Telecommunications*] (OTD)
PIC	Primate Information Center [*University of Washington*] [*Seattle, WA*]
pic	Prince Edward Island [*Canada*] [*MARC country of publication code*] [*Library of Congress*] (LCCP)
PIC	Printer Interface Cartridge [*Epson America, Inc.*]
PIC	Prior Informed Consent [*For use of pesticides*]
PIC	Priority Intercept Controller [*Computer science*] (ELAL)
PIC	Private Industry Council [*Generic term for group that helps provide job training*]
PIC	Procedures for Instrument Calibration
PIC	Process Interface Control
PIC	Processor Input Channel (NVT)
PIC	Processor Interconnection Channel (NITA)
PIC	Procurement Information Center
PIC	Procurement Information Circular (AAGC)
PIC	Procurement Information for Contracts [*AFSC*]
PIC	Product Information Catalog (SAUS)
PIC	Product Information Center [*AgriData Resources, Inc.*] [*Information service or system*]
PIC	Production Information and Control (SAUS)
PIC	Production Inventory Control (MHDI)
PIC	Product of Incomplete Combustion [*Environmental Protection Agency*] (ERG)
PIC	Products of Incomplete Combustion (SAUS)
PIC	Professional Image Computer (NITA)
PIC	Professional Instrument Course [*Aeronautics*]
PIC	Professional Interfraternity Conference [*Later, PFA*] (EA)
PIC	Program for Improved Contract Management [*Military*] (AFIT)
PIC	Program Identification Code (MUGU)
PIC	Program Indicator Code (SAUS)
PIC	Program Information Center
PIC	Program Information Code [*Computer science*] (ELAL)
PIC	Program Initiations and Commitments (AAG)
PIC	Program Instruction, Calibration [*Marine Corps*]
PIC	Program Interrupt Control [*Computer science*]
PIC	Programmable Industrial Controller (NITA)
PIC	Programmable Integrated Circuit (SAUS)
PIC	Programmable Interrupt Controller [*Computer science*]
PIC	Programmable Interval Clock (NASA)
PIC	Programmed Information Center
PIC	Programmed Instruction Centre (SAUS)
PIC	Programmed Instruction Counter (VLIE)
PIC	Project for Interface Compatibility
PIC	Project Information Center
PIC	Project Initiation Conference (SAUS)
PIC	Prolonged Illness Coverage [*Insurance*] (PAZ)
PIC	Promotion Industry Club (EA)
PIC	Promotion Industry Council (NTPA)
PIC	Proton Induced Cascade [*Physics*]
PIC	Prudential Insurance Co. of America (EFIS)
PIC	Pseudoisocyanine [*Organic chemistry*]
PIC	Pseudo-Isocytidine [*Antineoplastic compound*]
PIC	Public Information Center [*Nuclear energy*] (NRCH)
PIC	Public Information Committee [*of the NATO Military Committee*] (NATG)
PIC	Public Instruction Course (SAUS)
PIC	Public Interest Campaign (SAUS)
PIC	Publishers' Information Card [*Later, IBIS*] [*British*]
PIC	Pulsed Ionization Chamber
PIC	Pulse-Indicating Cartridge (SAUS)
PIC	Pulse-Induced Collapse (SAUS)
PIC	Pulse Ionisation Chamber (SAUS)
PIC	Purpose Identification Code
PIC	Pursuant to Instructions Contained In (MUGU)
PIC	Pyro Ignition Control (SAUS)
PIC	Pyro Initiator Capacitors (SAUS)
PIC	Pyro Initiator Controller [*NASA*] (NAKS)
PIC	Pyrotechnic Ignition Control (NASA)
PIC	Pyrotechnic Initiator Capacitor (NASA)
PIC	Pyrotechnic Initiator Controller (NASA)
PICA	Palestine Israel Colonization Association (SAUS)
PICA	Palestine Israelite Colonisation Association
PICA	Participating Interest Contingency Agreement
PICA	Picture-Coding Algorithm (VLIE)
PICA	Police Insignia Collectors Association [*British*] (DBA)
PICA	Porch Index of Communicative Ability [*Psychology*]
PICA	Portable Image Computation Architectures (SAUS)
PICA	Posterior Inferior Cerebellar Artery [*Anatomy*]
PICA	Posterior Inferior Communicating Artery [*Cardiology*] (DAVI)
PICA	Posterior Internal Cerebral Artery [*Cardiology*] (DAVI)
PICA	Power Industry Computer Applications (MCD)
PICA	Preliminary Inventory Control Afloat (SAUS)
PICA	Press Independence and Critical Ability (NTCM)
PICA	Pressure Indicated Controlled Alarmed (SAUS)
PICA	Primary Inventory Control Activity (MCD)
PICA	Printing Industry Computer Associates, Inc.
PICA	Private Investment Co. for Asia SA
PICA	Procedures for Inventory Control Afloat [*Navy*]
PICA	Procedures Inventory Control Afloat (SAUS)
PICA	Professional Insurance Communicators of America (EA)
PICA	Programming Interpersonal Curricula for Adolescents [*Learning model*] [*Education*]
PICA	Project for Integrated Catalogue Automation [*Royal Netherlands Library*] [*Cataloging cooperative*] (IID)
PICA	Project Integrated Cataloguing Automation (SAUS)
PICA	Property Services Agency Information on Construction and Architecture [*Property Service Agency Library Service*] [*British*] [*Information service or system*]
PICA	Public Interest Computer Association (EA)
PICA	Pyrotechnic Initiator Control Assembly (SAUS)
PICAA	Permanent International Committee of Agricultural Associations (SAUS)
PICAC	Porch Index of Communicative Ability in Children [*Psychology*]
PICAC	Power Industry Computer Applications Conference (MCD)
PICADAD	Place Identification/Characteristics and Area/Distance and Direction [*Bureau of the Census*]
PICADAD	Place Identification, Characteristics, Area, Distance, and Direction (SAUS)
PICAm	Proceedings of the International Congress of Americanists (SAUS)
PICAO	Provisional International Civil Aviation Organization [*Later, ICAO*]
PICAO Journal	Provisional International Civil Aviation Organization Journal (SAUS)
PICASO	Picture Algorithms-Subroutine Orientated (NITA)
PICASSO	Pen Input to Computer and Scanned Screen Output [*Computer science*] (PDAA)
PICASSO-CENA	Pathfinder Instruments for Cloud and Aerosol Spacebourne Observations-Climatologie Etneduedes des Nuages et des Aerosols [*NASA's proposed launch date is March 2003*]
PICB	Peabody Institute of the City of Baltimore [*Maryland*]
PICB	Peripheral Interface Control Bus (SAUS)
PICC	Partial Inventory Consumption Claim (SAUS)
PICC	Parts for Import Cars Coalition [*Defunct*] (EA)
PICC	Peoples Insurance Company of China (SAUS)
PICC	Peripherally-Inserted Central Catheter [*Medicine*]
PICC	Philadelphia International Convention Center [*Pennsylvania*]
PICC	Philippine International Convention Center [*Pennsylvania*]
PICC	Piccolo
PICC	Plastics in Construction Council [*Later, CCS*] (EA)
PICC	Processor Interface Controller and Communications [*Computer science*] (TIMI)
PICC	Professional Institutions Council for Conservation [*British*]
PICC	Provisional International Computation Center
PICCA	Positive Ion Cluster Composition Analyzer [*Instrumentation*]
PicCafe	Piccadilly Cafeterias, Inc. [*Associated Press*] (SAG)
PICCAP	Pacific Island Climate Change Assistance Programme (SAUS)
PICCED	Pratt Institute Center for Community and Environmental Development [*Research center*] (RCD)
PICCO	Pennsylvania Industrial Chemical Corp. [*Trademark*]
PICD	Preliminary Interface Control Drawing
PICD	Primary Inventory Cutoff Data [*Supply*]
PICD	Primary Irritant Contact Dermatitis [*Medicine*] (DMAA)
PIC Device	Personnel Identity Card Device (SAUS)
PICDG	Polar Icebreaker Canadian Design Group
PICDMS	Picture Database Management System (SAUS)
PICE	Palaeoenvironments from Ice Cores (SAUS)
PICE	Product Improved Compatibility Electronics (MCD)
PICE	Programmable Integrated Control Equipment
PICEA	Private Information Center on Eastern Arabia (SAUS)
PICEE	President's Interagency Committee on Export Expansion [*Absorbed by President's Export Council in 1979*] (EGAO)
PICEL	Picture Element (SAUS)
PICEL	Picture Elements per Line (SAUS)
PICE/PIA	Printing Industry Credit Exchange/PIA [*of the Printing Industries of America*] [*Defunct*] (EA)
PICES	Programmed Interactive Cost Estimating System (ACAE)
PICESP	Put It in Corporate Executives' Swimming Pools [*Waste management slang*]
PICF	Principal Investigator Computing Facilities (ACAE)
PICFS	Postinfective Chronic Fatigue Syndrome [*Medicine*] (DMAA)
PICG	PCTE Interface Control Group (SAUS)
PICG	Pig Industry Consultative Group [*Queensland, Australia*]
PICG	Programme International de Correlation Geologique [*International Geological Correlation Programme - IGCP*] (EAIO)
PICGC	Permanent International Committee for Genetic Congresses
PicGPA	Picrylated Guinea Pig Albumin [*Immunochemistry*]
PICI	Programmed Instruction Center for Industry
PICIC	Pakistan Industrial Credit and Investment Corp. (SAUS)
PICIM	Positive Ion Chemical Ionization Mass Spectroscopy (ACAE)
PICIP	Personal Computer Instrument Product (SAUS)
PICK	Part Information Correlation Key
Pick	Pickens Railroad (SAUS)
PICK	[*The*] Pickens Railroad Co. [*Formerly, PIC*] [*AAR code*]
Pick	Pickering's Massachusetts Supreme Judicial Court Reports [*1822-39*] [*A publication*] (DLA)
PICK	Pickwick [*Refers to an inferior quality cigar*] (DSUE)
Pickle	Pickle's Reports [*85-108 Tennessee*] [*A publication*] (DLA)
PICKLE	Preserving Individual Cultures and Knowledge in Lands Everywhere [*An association*]
PICKLE	President's Intelligence Checklist [*Daily report prepared by CIA*]
Pick (Mass)	Pickering's Massachusetts Reports [*18-41 Massachusetts*] [*A publication*] (DLA)
Pick Stat	Pickering's English Statutes [*A publication*] (DLA)
PICKUP	Professional, Industrial and Commercial Updating [*Vocational training*] [*British*]
PICL	Pest Infestation Control Laboratory (SAUS)
PICL	Presidents Intelligence Checklist (SAUS)
PICL	Proceedings of the International Congress of Linguists (SAUS)
PICLS	Purdue International and Computational Learning System (SAUS)

PICLS............ Purdue University Instructional and Computational Learning System (SAUS)
PICM............ Master Chief Precision Instrumentman [*Navy rating*]
PICM............ Permanent International Committee of Mothers
PICM............ Picom Insurance [*NASDAQ symbol*] (TTSB)
PICM............ PICOM Insurance Co. [*NASDAQ symbol*] (SAG)
PICM............ Production and Inventory Cost Minimizer (SAUS)
PICM............ Professional Group [*NASDAQ symbol*] [*Formerly, Professionals Insurance Co. Management Group*]
PICM............ Professionals Insurance Co. Management Group [*NASDAQ symbol*] (SAG)
PICM Gp...... Professionals Insurance Co. Management Group [*Associated Press*] (SAG)
PIC-MOD...... Purpose Identification Code - Month and Calendar Year of Detachment (DNAB)
PIC-NF......... Picroindigocarmine-Nuclear Fast Red [*A biological stain*]
PICO .... Pacific Islands Contact Office (COE)
PICO .... Partido Independiente de la Clase Obrera [*Panama*] [*Political party*] (EY)
PICO .... Person in Column One [*1980 census*]
PICO .... Physicians Insurance Co. of Ohio [*NASDAQ symbol*] (NQ)
PICO .... PICO Holdings, Inc. [*NASDAQ symbol*] (SAG)
PICO .... Picosecond (GOBB)
PICO .... Polar Ice Core Drilling Office [*National Science Foundation*] (MSC)
PICO .... Polar Ice Coring Office (SAUS)
PICO .... Polio Information Center Online (SAUS)
PiCO .... Portable Interactive Computing Object
PICO .... Preinstallation, Installation, and Checkout (ACAE)
PICO .... Product Improvement Control Office (AFM)
Pico .... Progressive Tools and Industries Co.
PICO .... Purchasing Internal Change Order (MCD)
PICOA .... Physicians Insur Ohio [*NASDAQ symbol*] (TTSB)
PICODE....... Program Indicator-Code [*Computer science*] (ECII)
PICOE .... Programed Initiations, Commitments, Obligations and Expenditures (SAUS)
PICOE .... Programmed Initiations, Commitments, Obligations, and Expenditures [*AFSC*]
PICO Hld..... PICO Holdings, Inc. [*Associated Press*] (SAG)
PICOM .... PICOM Insurance Co. [*Associated Press*] (SAG)
PICOMM ..... Potter Instrument Coordinated Measuring Machine
PICON.......... Process Intelligent Control [*A data processing system from LISP Machine, Inc.*]
PI Controller... Proportional-plus-Integral Controller (SAUS)
PICOP .... Paper Industries Corporation of the Philipines (SAUS)
PicoPd .... Pico Products, Inc. [*Associated Press*] (SAG)
PICOR.......... Pilot Controlled Overtone Reproduction (SAUS)
PICORNAVIRUS... Pico Ribonucleic Acid Virus
PICOS .... Purchased Input Concept Optimization with Suppliers [*Auto industry quality and cost management program*]
PICOST .... Probability of Incurring Estimated Costs [*Military*] (MCD)
PICP............. Prime Inventory Control Point (DNAB)
PICP............. Proceedings of the International Congress of Philosophy (SAUS)
PICP............. Program Interface Control Plan (NASA)
PICPAB .... Phenomena Induced by Charged Particle Beams
PICPS .... Proceedings of the International Congress of Phonetic Sciences (SAUS)
PICPSA .... Permanent International Commission for the Proof of Small Arms (SAUS)
PICPSA .... Permanent International Commission for the Proof of Small-Arms (EAIO)
PICRC .... Pesticide and Industrial Chemicals Research Center [*Public Health Service*] (GRD)
PICRS .... Program Information Control and Retrieval System (NASA)
PICRS .... Program Information Coordination and Review Service [*NASA*] (NASA)
PICS............ Pacific Islands Central School (SAUS)
PICS............ Part Inventory Control System (SAUS)
PICS............ Partnership in Computational Science (SAUS)
PICS............ Payload Integration Control Schedule (SAUS)
PICS............ Permit Imprint Collectors Society (EA)
PICS............ Perpetual Inventory Control System
PICS............ Personnel Information Commission System (SAUS)
PICS............ Personnel Information Communication [*or Control*] System [*Computer science*]
PICS............ Pharmaceutical Information Control System (DIT)
PICS............ Photogrammetric Integrated Control System (SAUS)
PICS............ Photographic Information Condensing System (DNAB)
PICS............ Photographic Integrated Control System (SAUS)
PICS............ Photography in Community Self-Development [*Program of Master Photo Dealers and Finishers Association*]
PICS............ Photo Index and Cataloging System (NASA)
PICS............ Physical Inventory Control System (SAUS)
PICS............ Pioneer Image Converter System [*NASA*]
PICS............ Plastid Isolation Column System [*Analytical chemistry*]
PICS............ Platform for Internet Content Selection [*Computer science*]
PICS............ Platformfor Internet Content Selection (SAUS)
PICS............ Platform for Internet Content Specification [*Computer science*]
PICS............ Plug-in Control System (SAUS)
PICS............ Plug-In Inventory Control System [*Bell System*]
PICS............ Positive Ion Composition Spectrometer (SAUS)
PICS............ Predefined Input Control Sequence (MCD)
PICS............ Procurement Information Control System [*NASA*]
PICS............ Production Information and Control Subsystem (SAUS)
PICS............ Production Information and Control System [*IBM Corp.*] [*Software package*]

PICS............ Productivity Improvement and Control System (BUR)
PICS............ Program Information and Control System (MCD)
PICS............ Programmable Industrial Control Simulation (SAUS)
PICS............ Protocol Implementation Conformance Statement [*Computer science*] (TNIG)
PICS............ Protocol Interoperability Conformance Statment (SAUS)
PICS............ Pulsed Image Converter System (ACAE)
PICS/DCPR... Plug-In Inventory Control System/Detailed Continuing Property Record [*Telecommunications*] (TEL)
PICSO.......... Pressure-Controlled Intermittent Coronary Sinus Occlusion [*Medicine*] (DMAA)
PIC System... Picture Interactive Computer System (SAUS)
PICT............. Format for images used by Apple Macintosh (SAUS)
PICT............. Perceived Instrumentality of the College Test
PICT............. Philips Inventory Control Technique [*Computer science*] (IAA)
Pict .... Pictor [*Constellation*]
PICT............. Pictorial (ROG)
pict .... Pictorial (WDAA)
Pict .... Picture (AL)
PICT............. Picture File Format [*Computer science*] (BTTJ)
PICT............. Project on the Improvement of College Teaching
Pict Dict Rome... Pictorial Dictionary of Ancient Rome [*A publication*] (OCD)
PicTel.......... PictureTel Corp. [*Associated Press*] (SAG)
PICTEL........ Picture Telephone [*Telecommunications*] (EECA)
pictg .... Pictograph (VRA)
PICTOMAP ... Photographic Image Conversion by Tonal Masking Procedures (MCD)
PICTS.......... Photo-Induced Current Transient Spectroscopy (AAEL)
PICU............ Parallel Instruction Control Unit
PICU............ Pediatric Intensive Care Unit [*Medicine*]
PICU............ Priority Interrupt Control Unit [*Computer science*] (MDG)
PICU .... Pulmonary Intensive Care Unit [*Medicine*]
PICUTP .... Permanent and International Committee of Underground Town Planning (SAUS)
PICUTP .... Permanent International Committee of Underground Town Planning (SAUS)
PICUTPC...... Permanent and International Committee of Underground Town Planning and Construction
PICV............ Protected Infantry Combat Vehicle (SAUS)
PIC(WA)...... Potato Industry Council (Western Australia)
PID.............. D. T. Watson Home for Crippled Children, Leetsdale, PA [*OCLC symbol*] (OCLC)
PID............. Pain Intensity Differences [*Medicine*]
PID............. Parallel Interface Device (SAUS)
PID............. Parameter Identification [*Communications*]
PID............. Partial Initial Decision [*Nuclear energy*] (NRCH)
PID............. Particle-Induced Desorption (SAUS)
PID............. Partido de Integracion Democrata [*Democratic Integration Party*] [*Argentina*] [*Political party*] (PPW)
PID............. Partido Izquierda Democratica [*Democratic Left Party*] [*Political party*] (EAIO)
PID............. Passenger Information Display
PID............. Passive Identification Device (SAUS)
PID............. Patrol Input Device (MCD)
PID............. Payload Insertion Device (NASA)
PID............. Pelvic Inflammatory Disease [*Medicine*]
PID............. Perfect-Gas Isentropic Decompression [*Engineering*]
PID............. Peripheral Interface Device [*Computer science*] (EECA)
PID............. Persistent Identifier (SAUS)
PID............. Personal Identification Device (MHDI)
PID............. Personal Identifier (SAUS)
PID............. Personality and Individual Differences [*A publication*]
PID............. Personnel Identification Device [*Navy*] (IAA)
PID............. Personnel Inquiry/Death/Occupational Illness [*Report*] (DNAB)
PID............. Phenindione [*or Phenylindandione*] [*Anticoagulant*]
PID............. Photo-Imageable Dielectric (SAUS)
PID............. Photo-Induced Desorption (SAUS)
PID............. Photointerpretation Department [*Military*]
PID............. Photo Ionisation (or Ionization) Detector (SAUS)
PID............. Photoionization Detector
PID............. Photon-Induced Dissociation [*For spectral studies*]
PID............. Photon Ionization Detector (EEVL)
PID............. Pictorial Information Digitizer [*Computer science*] (DIT)
PID............. Picture Input Device (SAUS)
PID............. Pilot-Induced Deceleration
PID............. Pilot-Induced Decillation (SAUS)
PID............. Plan Identification Number (DOMA)
PID............. Planned Industrial Development (PA)
PID............. Planning and Integration Division (SAUS)
PID............. Plasma-Iron Disappearance [*Hematology*] (MAE)
PID............. Poisons Information Database (SAUS)
PID............. Polarization Image Detector (SAUS)
PID............. Police Intelligence Detail (SAUS)
PID............. Political Intelligence Department [*British*] [*World War II*]
PID............. Port Identification [*Telecommunications*] (TEL)
PID............. Position Identifier (SAUS)
PID............. Primary Immunodeficiency Disease [*Medicine*]
PID............. Prime Input Development
PID............. Prime Item Development (MCD)
PID............. Primitive Interface Definition (SAUS)
PID............. Process & Instrument Design (ACII)
PID............. Process Identification (SAUS)
PID............. Process Identifier [*Computer science*] (PCM)
PID............. Process-Induced Defect
PID............. Procurement Information Digest (AFM)

PID	Procurement Item/Identification Description [DoD]
PID	Product ID (SAUS)
PID	Product Identifier (SAUS)
PID	Product Innovation and Design
PID	Program Identifier (ACAE)
PID	Program Information Department (SAUS)
PID	Program Information Document [NASA] (MCD)
PID	Program Introduction Document (NASA)
PID	Programming Information Distribution (SAUS)
PID	Project Identification Code
PID	Project Implementation Directive [Air Force]
PID	Prolapsed Intervertebral Disc [Medicine]
PID	Proportional, Integral, and Differential Gain (SAUS)
PID	Proportional Integral Derivation
PID	Proportional-Integral Derivative [Engineering]
PID	Proportional Integral Differential [Digital control-algorithm] (IAA)
PID	Proportional Integration Derivation
PID	Proportional Integro-Differential (SAUS)
PID	Proportional plus Integral plus Derivative (SAUS)
PID	Proportional-Plus Integral-Plus Derivative [Digital control algorithm]
PID	Protocol Identification Number (SAUS)
PID	Protocol Identifier (SAUS)
PID	Protruded Intervertebral Disc [Medicine]
PID	Pseudo Interrupt Device
PID	Public Information Division [Army]
PIDA	Payload Installation and Deployment Aid [NASA] (NASA)
PIDA	Pet Industry Distributors Association (EA)
PIDA	Pharmaceutical Industry Development Assistance (SAUS)
PIDA	Phenylindane Dicarboxylic Acid (EDCT)
PIDA	Pig Industry Development Authority [British] (BI)
PIDA Bulletin	Pig Industry Development Authority Bulletin (SAUS)
PIDAS	Perimeter Intrusions Detection Analysis System (SAUS)
PIDAS	Portable Instantaneous Display and Analysis Spectrometer (SAUS)
PIDAS	Portable Instant Intelligent Display and Analysis Spectrometer (SAUS)
PIDAS	Portable Intelligent Display and Analysis Spectrometer (SAUS)
PIDB	Peripheral Interface Data Bus (SAUS)
PIDC	Pakistan Industrial Development Corp. (SAUS)
PIDC	Philadelphia Industrial Development Corp.
PIDC	Photo-Induced Discharge Characteristic (SAUS)
PIDC	Precision Instrument Development Center (SAUS)
PIDC	Procurement Intern Development Center (DNAB)
PIDC	Projects International Development Corp. (SAUS)
PIDC	Prototype International Data Centre [For evaluating seismic signals]
PIDCOM	Process Instruments Digital Communication System [Beckman Industries]
PIDD	Passive Identification/Detection and Direction (MCD)
PIDD	Planned Inactivation or Discontinued Date [Environmental science] (COE)
PIDDP	Planetary Instrument Definition and Development Program (ACAE)
PI/DE	Passive Identification/Direction Finding Equipment (MCD)
PI/DE	Positive Identification and Direction Equipment
PI/DE	Positive Indentification and Direction Finding Equipment
Pid Eng	Pidgin English (SAUS)
PIDEP	Preinterservice Data Exchange Program
PID-Filter	Proportional-Integral-Differential-Filter (SAUS)
PIDG	Proportional, Integral, and Differential Gain (SPST)
PIDI	Philippines Invention Development Institute (SAUS)
Pidico	Project Industrial Development and Investment Corp. (SAUS)
PIDO	Primitive Indian Development Organization (SAUS)
PIDP	Pacific Islands Development Program [East-West Center] [Research center] (RCD)
PIDP	Pilot Information Display Panel
PIDP	Programmable Indicator Data Processor [Military] (CAAL)
PIDR	Product Inspection Discrepancy Report (MCD)
PIDRA	Portable Insulin Dosage-Regulating Apparatus [Medicine]
PIDRS	Photographic Instrumentation Data Recording System (MCD)
PIDS	Parameter Inventory Display System (DNAB)
PIDS	Personal Inspirable Dust Spectrometer (SAUS)
PIDS	Physical Intrusion Detection System (DWSG)
PIDS	Portable Image Display System (NASA)
PIDS	Primary Image Disemination System (SAUS)
PIDS	Primary Immunodeficiency Syndrome [Medicine] (DMAA)
PIDS	Prime Item Development Specification
PIDS	Process Integration, Devices and Structures (SAUS)
PIDS	Public Investment Data System (MHDW)
PIDS	Pylon Integrated Dispenser Station (SEWL)
PIDSA	Population Information Documentation System for Africa
PIDT	Plasma-Iron Disappearance Time [Hematology] (MAE)
PIDX	Petroleum Industry Data Exchange (SAUS)
PIE	Air South West [British] [FAA designator] (FAAC)
PIE	Clearwater-St. Petersburg [Florida] [Airport symbol] (AD)
PIE	Elwyn Institute, Elwyn, PA [OCLC symbol] (OCLC)
PIE	Pacific Information Exchange [Information service or system] (IID)
PIE	Pacific Intercultural Exchange (SAUS)
PIE	Pacific Intermountain Express (SAUS)
PIE	Pacific Islands Ecosystems [Springfield, VA] [Department of the Interior] [No longer available online] [Information service or system]
PIE	Pacing Item Evaluation (MCD)
PIE	Paedophile Information Exchange [British] (ILCA)
PIE	Parallel Instruction Execution [Computer science] (BUR)
PIE	Parallel Interface Element
PIE	Partners in Education (SAUS)
PIE	Patent Information Exploitation [Canadian Patent Office]
PIE	Payload Integration Equipment [NASA] (MCD)
PIE	Payroll Audit, Indexing, and Expiration
PIE	Period of Interruption of Employment (WDAA)
PIE	Peripheral Interface Element [Computer science] (IAA)
PIE	Personal Intelligent Electronics [Computer science] (AGLO)
PIE	Personal Interactive Electronics [Apple Computer Inc.]
PIE	Photo Image Enhancement (ACAE)
PIE	Photo-Induced Electrochromism
PIE	Pietermaritzburg [South Africa] [Seismograph station code, US Geological Survey] [Closed] (SEIS)
PIE	Pipestone Petroleums, Inc. [Toronto Stock Exchange symbol] [Vancouver Stock Exchange symbol]
PIE	P/L Integration Equipment (SAUS)
PIE	Plug-In Electronics
PIE	Plug-In Extension
PIE	Plume Interaction Experiment [Army] (RDA)
PIE	Pocket Internet Explorer [Microsoft Corp.] [Computer science]
PIE	Polar Ice Extent (SAUS)
PIE	Poly(iminoethylene) [Organic chemistry]
PIE	Portable Information Evaluation
PIE	Position Indicating Equipment (SAUS)
PIE	Post-Irradiation Examination [Nuclear energy] (NRCH)
PIE	Post-Irradiation Experiment [Nuclear energy] (NRCH)
PIE	Pre-Impact Event [Automotive safety]
PIE	Preimplantation Embryo
PIE	Price in Effect [Military]
PIE	Primary Industry and Energy
PIE	Program for Increased Education [Military]
PIE	Program Interrupt Element [Computer science] (IAA)
PIE	Program Interrupt Entry [Computer science]
PIE	Programmable Interface Electronics (SAUS)
PIE	Programming and Instrumentation Environment [Computer science]
PIE	Prolog Inference Engine [Computer science]
PIE	Proposal Information Exchange [Military]
PIE	Proto-Indo-European [Language] (BARN)
PIE	Publications Indexed for Engineering [A publication]
PIE	Public Interest Economics Foundation [Defunct] (EA)
PIE	Pulmonary Infiltration with Eosinophilia [Medicine]
PIE	Pulmonary Interstitial Edema [Medicine] (DAVI)
PIE	Pulmonary Interstitial Emphysema [Medicine]
PIE	Pulse Interference Elimination
PIE	Pulse Interference Eliminator [RADAR]
PIE	Pulse Interference Emitting (MCD)
PIE	Pyrotechnically Initiated Explosive (SAUS)
PIE	St. Petersburg [Florida] [Airport symbol] (OAG)
PIEA	Pencil Industry Export Association [Defunct] (EA)
PIEA	Petroleum Industry Electrical Association [Later, ENTELEC] (EA)
PIEA	Petroleum Industry Electrotechnical Association (IAA)
PIEA	Pre-Arrangement Interment Exchange of America [Later, PIAA]
PIE-C	Public Interest Economics Center (EA)
PIECE	Petroleum Industry Environmental Preservation Executive (SAUS)
PIE COST	Probability of Incurring Estimated Cost
PIECOST	Probability of Incurring Estimated Costs [Military]
PIECP	Preliminary Impact Engineering Change Proposal (MCD)
PIED	Piedmont Mining Co., Inc. [NASDAQ symbol] (NQ)
PiedBcp	Piedmont Bancorp, Inc. [Associated Press] (SAG)
PiedBGp	Piedmont Bancgroup [Associated Press] (SAG)
PiedmBc	Piedmont Bancorp, Inc. [Associated Press] (SAG)
PiedMg	Piedmont Managment Co., Inc. [Associated Press] (SAG)
PiedMn	Piedmont Mining Co., Inc. [Associated Press] (SAG)
PiedNG	Piedmont Natural Gas Co., Inc. [Associated Press] (SAG)
PIE-F	Public Interest Economics Foundation [Defunct] (EA)
Piemnt	Piemonte Foods, Inc. [Associated Press] (SAG)
PI Engine	Post Inner Engine (SAUS)
PIEP	Peripheral Infarct Epicardium [Medicine] (DB)
PIEP	Petroleum Industry Environmental Performance
PIEP	Primary Irritation Evaluation (SAUS)
PIEP	Primary Irritation Evaluation Program
PIER	Procedures for Internet/Enterprise Renumbering (SAUS)
PIER	Product Inventory Electronically Recorded (PDAA)
Pier 1	Pier 1 Imports, Inc. [Associated Press] (SAG)
PIERC	Pacific Island Ecosystems Research Center (SAUS)
Pierce RR	Pierce on Railroad Law [A publication] (DLA)
PiercPag	Piercing Pagoda, Inc. [Associated Press] (SAG)
PIERS	Port Import/Export Reporting Service [Journal of Commerce, Inc.] [Information service or system]
PIERS-4	Pressure-Induced Extra Resonance in Four-wave mixing (SAUS)
PIES	Packaged Interchangeable Electronic System
PIES	Penning Ionization Electron Spectroscopy
PIES	Photographic Image Editing System (SAUS)
PIES	Pollution Prevention Information Exchange System [Environmental science]
PIES	Procurement and Inventory of Equipment System (DNAB)
PIES	Procurement Information Exchange System (SAUS)
PIES	Program Information and Evaluation System (SAUS)
PIES	Project Independence Evaluation System [Energy policy]
PIES	Purchasing Information Exchange System (SAUS)
PIESA	Parasite-Induced Erythrocyte Surface Antigen [Immunology]
Piezonator	Piezo-Resonator (SAUS)
PIF	Insured Muni Income Fd [NYSE symbol] (TTSB)
PIF	Package Information Form (IAA)
PIF	Page Image Format (SAUS)
PIF	Paid In Full (SAUS)
PIF	PaineWebber Premium Insured Municipal Income [NYSE symbol] (SPSG)

PIF .... Pakistan Islamic Front [*Pakistan*] [*Political party*] (ECON)
PIF .... Paper Industry Federation (NADA)
PIF .... Partners in Friendship (EA)
PIF .... Payload Integration Facility [*NASA*] (KSC)
PIF .... Peak Inspiratory Flow [*Medicine*] (AAMN)
PIF .... Perpetual Inventory File (DNAB)
PIF .... Personnel Identification Feature [*Navy*] (NVT)
PIF .... Phase Interface Fading (VLIE)
PIF .... Phase Inversion Formulation [*Chemistry*]
PIF .... Photo Interpretation Facility (SAUS)
PIF .... Picture Interchange Format File (SAUS)
PIF .... Pilot Information File [*Army*]
PIF .... Place in Inactive File [*Army*]
PIF .... Point Initiating Fuze
PIF .... Polyisocyanurate Foam (IGSL)
PIF .... Porportional-Integral Filter (SAUS)
PIF .... Positive Identification Feature (MCD)
PIF .... Positive Identification Friend/Foe (SAUS)
PIF .... Postscript Interchange Format (SAUS)
PIF .... Predictive Influence Function [*Statistics*]
PIF .... Preparer Inventory File [*IRS*]
PIF .... Privatization Investment Fund Trust Units [*Toronto Stock Exchange symbol*]
PIF .... Problem Identification Form (ARMP)
PIF .... Process Interchange Format [*Computer science*] (VLIE)
PIF .... Productivity Investment Fund [*Program*] [*Air Force*]
PIF .... Program Information File
PIF .... Programmable Interface [*Computer science*] (VLIE)
PIF .... Proinsulin-Free [*Medicine*] (DB)
PIF .... Project in Foreign Language Pedagogy (AIE)
PIF .... Prolactin Inhibiting Factor [*Endocrinology*] (DAVI)
PIF .... Prolactin-Release Inhibiting Factor [*Also, PRIH*] [*Endocrinology*]
PIF .... Proliferation Inhibitory Factor [*Immunochemistry*]
PIF .... Proportional-Integral Filter (SAUS)
PIF .... Prostatic Interstitial Fluid [*Medicine*] (MELL)
PIF .... Provision of Industrial Facilities [*Army*] (AABC)
PIF .... Pseudo-Identification Feature (MCD)
PIF .... Punjab Irregular Force [*British military*] (DMA)
PIFA .... Packaging and Industrial Films Association [*British*] (DBA)
PIFA .... Pain-Inhibition Fear Avoidance [*Medicine*] (MELL)
PIFA .... Power Input Filter Assembly
PIFAL .... Program Instruction Frequency Analyzer [*Telecommunications*] (IAA)
PIFC .... Pakistan Industrial Finance Corp. (SAUS)
PIFCM .... Pitch Integrated Flight Control Module (MCD)
PI-FET .... Piezoelectric Field-Effect Transistor (PDAA)
PIFEX .... Programmable Image Feature Extractor [*to provide real-time machine vision for the Martian Rover robot*] [*Jet Propulsion Laboratory*] (BYTE)
PIFF .... Punjab Irregular Frontier Force [*British military*] (DMA)
PIFG .... Poor Intrauterine Fetal Growth [*Medicine*] (MELL)
PIFI .... Piedmonte Foods [*NASDAQ symbol*] (TTSB)
PIFI .... Piemonte Foods, Inc. [*NASDAQ symbol*] (NQ)
PIFI .... Pressure-Induced Intracranial Focal Ischemia [*Medicine*]
PIFL .... Pipe Flow (PDAA)
PIFMIL .... Proceedings of the International Federation for Modern Languages and Literatures (SAUS)
PIFOV .... Planet in Field of View [*NASA*]
PIFR .... Peak Inspiratory Flow Rate [*Medicine*]
PIFR .... Program Interrupt Flag Register [*Computer science*] (IAA)
PIFRS .... Prototype Increase Frequency Reporting System (SAUS)
PIFS .... Plume-Induced Flow Separation
PIFS .... Point Coordination Inter Frame Space (SAUS)
PIFS .... Point Inter-Frame Space (SAUS)
PIFS .... Post Infection Fatigue Syndrome [*Medicine*]
PIFS .... Prime Item Fabrication Specification
PIFT .... Platelet Immunofluorescence Test [*Analytical biochemistry*]
PIFT .... Protocol Interbank File Transfer [*Computer science*] (VLIE)
PIFUA .... Powerplant and Industrial Fuel Use Act of 1978
Pig .... drill-pipe internal rust scraper (SAUS)
PIG .... Glenn Mills School, Glenn Mills, PA [*OCLC symbol*] (OCLC)
PIG .... Pacific Institute of Geography
PIG .... Passive-Income Generator [*Investment term*]
PIG .... Pendulous Integrating Gyro
PIG .... Pendulous Integrating Gyroscope
PIG .... Penning Ionization Gauge (IAA)
PIG .... Pertussis Immune Gobulin [*Medicine*] (STED)
PIG .... Phillips Ionization Gauge
PIG .... Phosphatidylinositol Glycan [*Biochemistry*]
PIG .... Photo-Island Grid
pig .... Pigment (BARN)
Pig .... Pigmentation (STED)
Pig .... Pigott's Common Recoveries [*3 eds.*] [*1739-92*] [*A publication*] (DLA)
PIG .... Pipeline Industries Guild (SAUS)
PIG .... Plasma Inert Gas (SAUS)
PIG .... Plasmatron Inert Gas (SAA)
PIG .... Polymeric Immunoglobulin [*Medicine*] (DMAA)
PIG .... Pride, Integrity, Guts [*Police alternative for the appellation applied to police by radical groups*]
PIG .... Process Ink Gamut [*Printing technology*]
PIG .... Product Information Guide (SAUS)
PIG .... Production Image Generator (MCD)
PIG .... Production Installation Group [*Military*] (CAAL)
PIG .... Program Implementation Guideline (EG)
PIG .... Pulse Inert Gas
PIGA .... Pendulous Integrating Gyro Accelerometer

PIGA .... Pendulous Integrating Gyroscope Accelerometers
PIGA .... Pulsed Integrated Gyroscopic Accelerometer (SAUS)
PIGADD .... Permanent Intergovernmental Authority on Drought and Development (SAUS)
Pig & R ...... Pigott and Rodwell's English Registration Appeal Cases [*1843-45*] [*A publication*] (DLA)
PIGDX .... Pioneer Gold Shares Cl.A [*Mutual fund ticker symbol*] (SG)
PIGFET .... P-channel Insulated-Gate Field-Effect Transistor (SAUS)
PIGI .... Pregnancy-Induced Glucose Intolerance (STED)
PIGI .... Pregnancy-Induced Glucose Intolerance [*Medicine*] (MELL)
PIGIT .... Putnam Intermediate Government Income Trust [*Associated Press*] (SAG)
Pig Judg ..... Pigott's Foreign Judgments [*3rd ed.*] [*1908-09*] [*A publication*] (DLA)
PIGLET .... Personalized Intelligently Generated Explanatory Text (SAUS)
PIGLET .... Purchase Information, Gifts, Loans, Exchanges Tracking [*Suggested name for the Library of Congress computer system*]
pigm .... Pigment (STED)
PIGM .... Pigmentum [*Paint*] [*Pharmacy*]
PIGM .... Putnam Investment Grade Municipal Trust [*Associated Press*] (SAG)
PIGMA .... Pressurized Inert Gas Metal Arc (KSC)
PIGME .... Particle-Induced Gamma-ion Emission (SAUS)
PIGME .... Particle-Induced Gamma-Ray Emission (SAUS)
PIGME .... Programmed Inert Gas Multi-Electrode (PDAA)
PIGMI .... Pion Generator for Medical Irradiation [*Radiology*]
PIGMI .... Position Indicating General Measuring Instrument
PIGMI .... Positron-Indicating General Measuring Instrument (SAUS)
Pigm Resin Technol... Pigment and Resin Technology (SAUS)
PIGMT2 .... Putnam Investment Grade Municipal Trust II [*Associated Press*] (SAG)
PIGMT3 .... Putnam Investment Grade Multiple Sectors III [*Associated Press*] (SAG)
PIGPA .... Pyruvate, Inosine, Glucose Phosphate, Adenine (AAMN)
PIGR .... Polymeric Immunoglobulin Receptor [*Biochemistry*]
Pig Rec ...... Pigott's Recoveries [*England*] [*A publication*] (DLA)
PIGS .... PAFEC Interactive Graphics System [*PAFEC Ltd.*] [*Software package*] (NCC)
PIGS .... Passive Infrared Guidance System [*DoD*]
PIGS .... Pesticides in Groundwater Strategy [*Environmental Protection Agency*] (GFGA)
PIGS .... Poles, Italians, Greeks, and Slavs
PIGS .... Portable Inertial Guidance System
PIGS .... Procedures, Information, Guidance & Standards (WDAA)
PIGU .... Pendulous Integrating Gyroscope Unit (SAUS)
PIGU .... Pendulous Integrating Gyro Unit
PIH .... Paper in Hand (SAUS)
PIH .... Passive Immune Hemolysis (PDAA)
PIH .... Permanent Income Hypothesis [*Economics*]
PIH .... Pheniprazine (LDT)
PIH .... Phenylisopropylhydrazine [*Pharmacology*]
PIH .... Pin in Hole (AAEL)
PIH .... Pipeline Induction Heat [*Industrial firm*] [*British*]
PIH .... Pocatello [*Idaho*] [*Airport symbol*] (OAG)
PIH .... Poison Inhalation Hazard (SARE)
PIH .... Population and International Health (SAUS)
PIH .... Pork Industry Handbook [*A publication*]
PIH .... Post-Inflammatory Hyperpigmentation [*Medicine*] (MELL)
PIH .... Pregnancy-Induced Hypertension [*Gynecology*]
PIH .... Primary Intracerebral Hemorrhage (CPH)
PIH .... Prolactin-Inhibiting Hormone (STED)
PIH .... Prolactin-Release Inhibiting Hormone [*Endocrinology*]
PIH .... Public and Indian Housing [*HUD*]
PIH .... St. Gabriel's Hall, Phoenixville, PA [*OCLC symbol*] (OCLC)
PIHC .... PHC, Inc. [*NASDAQ symbol*] (SAG)
PIHC .... PHC Inc.'A' [*NASDAQ symbol*] (TTSB)
PIHCA .... Polyisohexylcyanoacrylate [*Antibacterial*]
PIHCW .... PHC Inc. Wrrt [*NASDAQ symbol*] (TTSB)
PIHF .... Periodic Inhomogeneous Film (SAUS)
PIHH .... Postinfluenza-Like Hyposmia and Hypogeusia (STED)
PIHM .... Polish Institute of Hydrology and Meteorology
PIHM .... Protective Integrated Hood Mask (SAUS)
PIHSMP .... Protocol Relating to Intervention on the High Seas in Cases of Marine Pollution by Substances other than Oil [*Environmental science*] (COE)
PII .... Fairbanks, AK [*Location identifier*] [*FAA*] (FAAL)
PII .... Pershing II [*Army*]
PII .... Petroleum Information International (SAUS)
PII .... Phantom II [*Model of automobile*]
PII .... Plasma Inorganic Iodine [*Clinical chemistry*] (MAE)
PII .... Plasma Ion Implantation (SAUS)
PII .... Polaris Industries [*NYSE symbol*] (TTSB)
PII .... Polaris Industries, Inc. [*NYSE symbol*] (SAG)
PII .... Positive Immittance Inverter (IEEE)
PII .... Predominant Interest Installation (AAGC)
PII .... Primary Irritation Index [*Medicine*] (STED)
PII .... Primary Irritation Indices [*for skin*]
PII .... Printing Industry Institute [*A graphic arts training school*]
PII .... Procurement Instrument Identification (NG)
PII .... Profit in Inventory (TIMI)
PII .... Program Integrated Information (VLIE)
PII .... Publisher Item Identifier
PII .... Sleighton School, Darling, PA [*OCLC symbol*] (OCLC)
PIIC .... Pergamon International Information Corp. [*Information service or system*] (IID)
PIIC .... Public Interest Immunity Certificate [*British*] (ECON)
PIID .... Prediction Interval Initiation Date (DNAB)

PIIF............. Pakistan International Industrial Fair (SAUS)
PIIF............. Proteinase Inhibitor Inducing Factor [Biochemistry]
PIII............. plasma Immersion Ion Implantation (AAEL)
PIIM........... Planned Interdependency Incentive Method
PIIN........... Procurement Instruction Identification Number [Army] (AABC)
PIIN........... Procurement Instrument Identification Number [Military]
PI/INT'L...... Packaging Institute International [Later, IoPP] (EA)
PIIO........... Poultry Industry Investigation Officer [Australia]
PIIP........... Potable Insulin Infusion Pump [Medicine] (STED)
PIIS........... Posterior Inferior Iliac Spine [Medicine] (STED)
PIIX........... PCI IDE/ISA Xcelerator (SAUS)
PIJ............. Palestinian Islamic Jihad (SAUS)
PIJ............. Pickled-in-Jar [Food technology]
PIJAC......... Pet Industry Joint Advisory Council (EA)
PIJR........... Product Improvement Joint Review [Military]
PIK............. Glasgow-Prestwick [Scotland] [Airport symbol] (OAG)
PIK............. Pay in Kind Preferred Stock (TDOB)
PIK............. Payment in Kind
PIK............. Pic Prospectors [Vancouver Stock Exchange symbol]
PIK............. Portable Injection Kit
PIK............. Potsdam Institute for Climate Impact Research
PIK............. Prestwick [Scotland] [Airport symbol] (AD)
PIK............. Programmer's Imaging Kernel [Computer science] (BTTJ)
PIKE........... Pike [Postal Service standard] (OPSA)
Pike........... Pike's Reports [1-5 Arkansas] [A publication] (DLA)
Pike & F Adm Law... Pike and Fischer's Administrative Law [A publication] (DLA)
Pike & F Fed Rules Service... Pike and Fischer's Federal Rules Service [A publication] (DLA)
Pike & Fischer Admin Law... Pike and Fischer's Administrative Law [A publication] (DLA)
Pike H of L... Pike's History of the House of Lords [A publication] (DLA)
PIKES......... Phot-Interpretation Keys Expert System (SAUS)
PIKES......... Pike [Commonly used] (OPSA)
Pikeville...... Pikeville National Corp. [Associated Press] (SAG)
PIK Securities... Payment-in-Kind Securities [Investment term] (DFIT)
PIKT........... Problem Informant/Killer Tool
PIL............. Brazos Santiago, TX [Location identifier] [FAA] (FAAL)
PIL............. Pacific International Lines (SAUS)
PIL............. Page Interchange Language (SAUS)
PIL............. Pair Inter Langues [Bourg La Reine, France] (EAIO)
PIL............. Pakistan International Airlines (SAUS)
PIL............. Parti de l'Independance et de la Liberte [Party for Independence and Liberty] [Congo] [Political party]
PIL............. Parts Identification List (ACAE)
PIL............. Patient Information Leaflet [Pharmacy]
PIL............. Payment in Lieu
PIL............. Percentage Increase in Loss [Statistics]
PIL............. Pest Infestation Laboratory [Agricultural Research Council] (PDAA)
PIL............. Pilar [Argentina] [Seismograph station code, US Geological Survey] (SEIS)
pil............. Pilaster (VRA)
PIL............. Pilot (WGA)
Pil............. Pilula [Pill] [Pharmacology] (DAVI)
Pil............. Pilula [Pill] [Pharmacy]
PIL............. Pistol Petroleum [Vancouver Stock Exchange symbol]
PIL............. Pitt Interpretive Language [Computer science] (DIT)
PIL............. Pittsburgh Interpretive [or Interactive] Language [Computer science] (IAA)
PIL............. Plastic Impregnated Laminate
PIL............. Practice Instrument Landing (ADA)
PIL............. Precision In Line [Electronics] (EECA)
PIL............. Preferred Item List (RDA)
PIL............. Priority Interrupt Level (VLIE)
PIL............. Procedure Implementation Language (SAUS)
PIL............. Processing Information List [Computer science]
PIL............. Procurement Information Letter (MCD)
PIL............. Product Identifier Label (SAUS)
PIL............. Publications International Ltd.
PIL............. Publishing Interchange Language [Computer science] (CDE)
PIL............. Purple Indicating Light (MSA)
PIL............. Purpose in Life [Personality development test] [Psychology]
PILA........... Point Ion Lattice Approximation (SAUS)
PILA........... Power Industry Laboratory Association [Defunct] (EA)
PILAC......... Pulsed Ion Linear Accelerator
PiLam......... Pi Lambda Phi (EA)
PILANS....... Problem-oriented Industrial Languages (SAUS)
PILAR........ Petroleum Industry Local Authority Reporting (PDAA)
PILB.......... Passenger and Immigration Lists Bibliography [A publication]
PILC.......... Paper-Insulated, Lead-Covered Cable [Telecommunications]
PILC.......... Pillared Interlayered Clays [Catalysis technology]
PILC.......... Pregnancy and Infant Loss Center (EA)
PILC Cable... Paper-Insulated, Lead-Covered Cable (SAUS)
PILCX......... PIMCO: International CI.C [Mutual fund ticker symbol] (SG)
PILE.......... Product Inventory Level Estimator (PDAA)
PilgAmer..... Pilgrim American Bank & Thrift Fund, Inc. [Associated Press] (SAG)
PilgAPr...... Pilgrim America Prime Rate Trust [Associated Press] (SAG)
PilgPr....... Pilgrims Pride Corp. [Associated Press] (SAG)
PilgPrm...... Pilgrim Prime Rate Trust [Associated Press] (SAG)
Pilgr......... [The] Passionate Pilgrim [Poetry] (BARN)
Pilgr......... [The] Pilgrim's Progress [Bunyan] (BARN)
PilgRg....... Pilgrim Regional Banc Shares, Inc. [Associated Press] (SAG)
PILI.......... Passenger and Immigration Lists Index [A publication]
PILL.......... Newport Dock [British depot code]
PILL.......... Pilgrim League (PSS)
PILL.......... Programmed Instruction Language Learning [Computer science]

PILL.......... ProxyMed, Inc. [NASDAQ symbol] (SAG)
PILL.......... Proxymed Pharmacy [NASDAQ symbol] (SAG)
PILLS......... Particulate Instrumentation by LASER Light Scattering (PDAA)
PILM.......... Pillared Interlayered Montmorillonite [Catalysis technology]
PILMS........ Precision Insertion Loss Measurement Set (IAA)
PILNAV...... Piloting Navigation (SAUS)
PILO.......... Phased Integrated Laser Optics Technology (ACAE)
pilo.......... pilocarpine (SAUS)
PILO.......... Public Information Liaison Officer [Military]
PILOH........ Pay in Lieu of Holiday (WDAA)
PILOT........ Panel on Instrumentation for Large Optical Telescopes (SAUS)
PILOT........ Paton Lyall Tosh [Rock music group]
PILOT........ Payment in Lieu of Taxes
PILOT........ Permutation Indexed Literature of Technology (IEEE)
PILOT........ Phased Integrated LASER Optics Technology (SEWL)
PILOT........ Piloted Low-Speed Test [Aerospace]
PILOT........ Pod Integrated Localisation, Observation, Transmission (SAUS)
PILOT........ Printing Industry Language for Operations of Typesetting
PILOT........ Programmed Inquiry, Learning or Teaching [Computer science]
PILOT........ Programmed Inquiry, Learning or Technology (SAUS)
PILOT........ Programmed Instruction Learning on Teaching [A simplified programming language for computer-assisted instruction] (EDAC)
PilotACE..... Pilot Automatic Computing Engine (VLIE)
Pilowtex...... Pillowtex Corp. [Associated Press] (SAG)
PILP.......... Parametric Integer Linear Program [Computer science]
PILP.......... Program for Industrial Laboratory Projects (SAUS)
PILP.......... Program of Industry/Laboratory Projects [National Research Council of Canada]
PILP.......... Pseudoinfinite, Logarithmically Periodic
PILP Antenna... Pseudo-Infinite, Logarithmically Periodic Antenna (SAUS)
PILPS......... Program for Intercomparison of Land Surface Parameterization Schemes (SAUS)
PILPS......... Project for Intercomparison of Landsurface Parameterization Schemes (SAUS)
PILS.......... Payload Integration Library System [NASA] (SSD)
PILS.......... Pilsener Lager (DSUE)
PILS.......... Precision Instrument Landing System
PIL STA...... Pilot Station [Nautical charts]
PILT.......... Payment in Lieu of Taxes Program [Department of the Interior]
PILTA......... Payment in Lieu of Taxes Act
PIM........... Grey Nuns - Partners in Ministry (EA)
PIm........... Immaculata College, Immaculata, PA [Library symbol] [Library of Congress] (LCLS)
PIM........... Pacem in Maribus [Secondary name for the International Ocean Institute] (MSC)
PIM........... Pacific Rim Energy [Vancouver Stock Exchange symbol]
PIM........... Parallel Inference Machine [Computer science]
PIM........... Parameter Identification Mechanism
PIM........... Partners-in-Mission [Church of England]
PIM........... Passive Intermodulation (ACAE)
PIM........... Patient Interface Module (SAUS)
PIM........... Payload Integration Manager (SAUS)
PIM........... Peak Integration Method (SAUS)
PIM........... Penalties in Minutes [Hockey]
PIM........... Penicillamine-Induced Myasthenia (STED)
PIM........... Peripheral Interface Module
PIM........... Permanent Information Memory (SAUS)
PIM........... Personal Illumination Marker [Military] (INF)
PIM........... Personal Information Management (or Manager) (SAUS)
PIM........... Personal Information Manager [Computer science]
PIM........... Phosphatidylinositol Mannoside [Biochemistry]
Pi M.......... Pillius Medicinensis [Flourished, 1165-1207] [Authority cited in pre-1607 legal work] (DSA)
PIM........... Pilot Machine (NITA)
PIM........... Pine Mountain, GA [Location identifier] [FAA] (FAAL)
PIM........... Planned Incremental Modernization (DOMA)
PIM........... Planning Interchange Meeting (ACAE)
PIM........... Plan of Intended Movement (MUGU)
PIM........... Plastic Intake Manifold
PIM........... Plated Interconnecting Matrix
PIM........... Plug-In Module (MCD)
PIM........... Point Indicating Machine (IAA)
PIM........... Point of Intended Movement [Military]
PIM........... Polyphase Induction Motor
PIM........... Port Interface Module (SAUS)
PIM........... Position and Intended Movement [or Maneuver] (NATG)
PIM........... Position in Miles (MCD)
PIM........... Position of Intended Movement
PIM........... Powder Injection Molding [Metallurgy]
PIM........... Precision Indicator of the Meridian
PIM........... Precision Instrument Mount
PIM........... Presa Del Infiernillo [Mexico] [Seismograph station code, US Geological Survey] [Closed] (SEIS)
PIM........... Presbyterian Inland Mission
PIM........... Pretrained Individual Manpower (ACAE)
PIM........... Previously Intended Movement (SAUS)
PIM........... Pricing Instructions Memorandum (MCD)
PIM........... Primary Interface Module (SAUS)
PIM........... Priority Interrupt Module (SAUS)
PIM........... Process Interface Module (SAUS)
PIM........... Processor in Memory [Computer science]
PIM........... Processor Interface Module
PIM........... Processor Interrupt Module (SAUS)
PIM........... Product Information Management (SEWL)
PIM........... Product Information Memoranda

PIM..............	Program Initialization Module [*Computer science*] (ECII)
PIM..............	Program Integration Manual
PIM..............	Program Interface Module
PIM..............	Programmatic Interchange Meetings (SAUS)
PIM..............	Pro Independence Movement [*Puerto Rico*]
PIM..............	Provincial Institute of Mining
PIM..............	Public Information Meeting (COE)
PIM..............	Pulse Intensity Modulation
PIM..............	Pulse Interval Modulation
PIM..............	Putnam Master Intermediate Income Trust [*NYSE symbol*] (SPSG)
PIM..,........	Putnam Master Interm Income [*NYSE symbol*] (TTSB)
PIM..............	South Mountain Restoration Center, South Mountain, PA [*OCLC symbol*] (OCLC)
PiMA...........	Ateneo de Manila University, Manila, Philippines [*Library symbol*] [*Library of Congress*] (LCLS)
PIMA...........	Paper Industry Management Association (EA)
PIMA...........	Photographic Industry Marketing Association [*Australia*]
PIMA...........	Plug-In Module Assembly (MCD)
PIMA...........	Polyisocyanurate Insulation Manufacturers Association (EA)
PIMA...........	Portable Intelligence Maintenance Aid [*Army*] (DOMA)
PIMA...........	Prairie Implement Manufacturers Association (SAUS)
PIMA...........	Prime Intermediate Maintenance Activity
PIMA...........	Printing Industry Management Association (DGA)
PIMA...........	Professional Insurance Mass-Marketing Association [*Bethesda, MD*] (EA)
PIMB...........	PCTE Interface Management Board (SAUS)
PIMCC	Packards International Motor Car Club (EA)
PIMCO	Pacific Investment Management Co.
PIMCO	Physicians Insurance Medical Co. (DAVI)
PIMCO	Poultry Industry Manufacturers Council [*Defunct*] (EA)
PimcoAd	Pimco Advisors Ltd. [*Associated Press*] (SAG)
PimCom.......	Pimco Commercial Mortgage [*Associated Press*] (SAG)
PIME	Pontifical Institute for Foreign Missions (TOCD)
pime	Pontifical Institute for Foreign Missions (TOCD)
PIME	Pontifical Institute for Mission Extension [*Roman Catholic men's religious order*]
PIMEG	Program to Increase Minority Engineering Graduates (SAUS)
PIMI	Preinactivation Material Inspection [*Military*] (NVT)
PIMIA..........	Potentiometric Ionophore Modulated Immunoassay [*Electrochemistry*]
PIMIS..........	Portable Integrated Maintenance Information System
PIMISS	Pennsylvania Interagency Management Information Support System (SAUS)
PIMK...........	Portable Injection Molding Kit
PIML...........	Polynomial Propogation Time Immediate Language [*Computer science*] (MHDI)
PIMMA........	Professional Insurance Mass-Marketing Association [*Bethesda, MD*] (EA)
PIMNY	Printing Industries of Metropolitan New York
PIMO	Presentation of Information for Maintenance and Operation [*DoD*]
PIMOS	Parallel Inference Multiprocessor Operating System [*Computer science*]
PIMOS	Pittler Memory Operations System (SAUS)
PIMP	Permissible Individual Maximum Pressure (SAA)
PIMP...........	Peroxisomal Integral Membrane Protein [*Biochemistry*]
PIMP...........	Pimperne [*England*]
PIMP...........	Program for Interactive Multiple Process Simulation (PDAA)
PIMR	Polar Ice Mapping Radiometer (SAUS)
PIMR	Pushbroom Imaging Microwave Radiometer (SAUS)
PIMRA	Pirmasens Missile Repair Activity [*Germany*] [*Army*]
PIMRIS	Pacific Islands Marine Resources Information System [*Marine science*] (OSRA)
PIMS...........	Parts Inventory Management System (SAUS)
PIMS...........	Peacekeeper in Minuteman Silos (DWSG)
PIMS...........	Personnel Inventory Management System [*AT & T*]
PIMS...........	Pesticide Incident Monitoring System [*Environmental Protection Agency*] (EPAT)
PIMS...........	Phase Interference Modulation System (ACAE)
PIMS...........	Photoionization Mass Spectrometry
PIMS...........	Pontifical Institute of Mediaeval Studies [*Canada*] (IRC)
PIMS...........	Preform In-Mold Surfacing [*Plastics technology*]
PIMS...........	Principal Investigator Microgravity Services (SAUS)
PIMS...........	Printers Integrated Management System (DGA)
PIMS...........	Procurement Information Management Services (SAUS)
PIMS...........	Profit Impact of Marketing Strategy
PIMS...........	Program Interface for Multiplex System (ACAE)
PIMS...........	Programmable Implantable Medication System
PIMS...........	Project Information Management System (SAUS)
PIMS...........	Property Information Management System (SAUS)
PIMSA	Prensa Independiente Mexicana Sociedad Anonima [*Press agency*] [*Mexico*]
PIMT...........	Protein Isoaspartyl Methyltransferase [*An enzyme*]
Pim Ten......	Pim on Feudal Tenures [*A publication*] (DLA)
PIMV...........	Plantago Mottle Virus [*Plant pathology*]
PIN..............	AMF Bowling [*NYSE symbol*] (SG)
PIN..............	Jasper, TX [*Location identifier*] [*FAA*] (FAAL)
PIN..............	Pacific Island Nations
PIN..............	Pacific Island Network [*Marine science*] (OSRA)
PIN..............	Page and Item Number
PIN..............	Parallel Input
PIN..............	Parintins [*Brazil*] [*Airport symbol*] (AD)
PIN..............	Particle Inclusion Noise (ACAE)
PIN..............	Particle Induced Noise (SAUS)
PIN..............	Patent Information Network (SAUS)
PIN..............	Patriots Information Network [*Defunct*] (EA)
PIN..............	P-doped, Intrinsic, N-doped (SAUS)
PIN..............	Pennsylvania School for the Deaf, Philadelphia, PA [*OCLC symbol*] (OCLC)
PIN..............	People in Need [*Food program sponsored by family of kidnapped heiress, Patricia Hearst, 1974*]
PIN..............	Personal Identification Name (NITA)
PIN..............	Personal [*or Private*] Identification Number [*Banking*]
PIN..............	Personal Information Network [*Indesys, Inc.*] [*Telecommunications service*] (TSSD)
PIN..............	Personal Injury Notice (AAG)
PIN..............	Personnel Increment Number (DOMA)
PIN..............	Pesticide Information Network [*Environmental Protection Agency*] (AEPA)
PIN..............	Phase Inversion nanoencapsulation [*Materials science*]
PIN..............	Piece Identification Number
PIN..............	Pinedale [*Wyoming*] [*Seismograph station code, US Geological Survey*] [*Closed*] (SEIS)
PIN..............	Pinion (MSA)
Pin..............	Pinney's Wisconsin Supreme Court Reports [*1839-52*] [*A publication*] (DLA)
PIN..............	Plan Identification Number (AFM)
PIN..............	Plant Information Network [*Fish and Wildlife Service*] [*Ceased operation*] (IID)
PIN..............	Plastics Industry Notes [*Later, CIN*]
PIN..............	Police Information Network [*San Francisco Bay area, California*]
PIN..............	Position Indicator
PIN..............	Positive-Intrinsic-Negative [*or P-Type Intrinsic N-Type*]
PIN..............	Power Information Network [*Computer science*]
Pin..............	Power input (SAUS)
PIN..............	Precision Inertial Navigation (SAUS)
PIN..............	Pre-Invitation Notice
PIN..............	Preliminary Imagery Nomination File (MCD)
PIN..............	Private Intelligent Networker (NITA)
PIN..............	Procedural Interrupt Negative (SAUS)
PIN..............	Process Identification Number (SAUS)
PIN..............	Processor Independent NetWare [*Computer science*]
PIN..............	Procurement Information Notice [*Environmental Protection Agency*] (ERG)
PIN..............	Product Identification Number
PIN..............	Product Information Network [*McGraw-Hill Information Systems Co.*] [*Information service or system*] (IID)
PIN..............	Program Identification Number (MUGU)
PIN..............	Program Integrated Network
PIN..............	Programme of International Nature management (SAUS)
PIN..............	Programming Information (SAUS)
PIN..............	Property Inheritance Network Computer
PIN..............	Proposal Identification Number (AAG)
PIN..............	Prostatic Intraepithelial Neoplasia [*Medicine*] (MELL)
PIN..............	Prosthetic Intradithelial Neodlasia [*Medicine*]
PIN..............	Protein Inhibitor of nNOS [*Neuronal Nitric Oxide Synthase*] [*Neuroscience*]
PIN..............	PSI Energy, Inc. [*NYSE symbol*] (SPSG)
PIN..............	P-Type/Insulator/N-Type [*Electronics*] (AAEL)
PIN..............	P-Type Intrinsic N-Type [*or Positive-Intrinsic-Negative*]
PIN..............	P-type Intrinsic-N-type (SAUS)
PIN..............	Publication Identification Number [*Military*] (INF)
P IN²	Parts per Square Inch (WDAA)
P/In3	Parts per Cubic Inch (SAUS)
P IN³	Parts per Cubic Inch (WDAA)
PINA	Pacific Islands News Association [*Australia*]
P in A	Parallax in Altitude [*Navigation*]
PINA	Parallax in Altitude [*Navigation*]
PINA	Parenting in a Nuclear Age (EA)
PINA	Permaculture Institute of North America (SAUS)
PINA	Potash Institute of North America [*Later, PPI*] (EA)
PinBG	Pinnacle Bank Group, Inc. [*Associated Press*] (SAG)
P in C	Paymaster in Chief (SAUS)
P-in-C	Priest-in-Charge [*Church of England*]
PINC	Property Income Certificate [*Investment term*] [*British*]
Pinc C.........	Pincushion Correction (SAUS)
PINCCA.......	Price Index Numbers for Current Cost Accounting [*Service in Information and Analysis*] [*British*] [*Information service or system*] (IID)
PincIF	Pinnacle Financial Services, Inc. [*Associated Press*] (SAG)
PincIFn	Pinnacle Financial Services [*Associated Press*] (SAG)
PincIM........	Pinnacle Micro, Inc. [*Associated Press*] (SAG)
PincIMic	Pinnacle Micro, Inc. [*Associated Press*] (SAG)
PIND	Particle Impact Noise Detection (or Detector) (SAUS)
PIND	Particle Inclusion Noise Detection (ACAE)
PIND	Payload Integration Plan (SAUS)
Pind...........	Pindar [*518-438BC*] [*Classical studies*] (OCD)
PINDEX......	Pollution Index (SAUS)
PIN Diode....	Positive-Intrinsic-Negative Diode (SAUS)
PINE...........	Passive Infrared Equipment (SAUS)
PINE...........	Passive Infrared Night Equipment (MCD)
PINE...........	Pine [*Commonly used*] (OPSA)
PINE...........	Pine is not Elm (SAUS)
PINE...........	Program for Internet News and Email (SAUS)
PINELLAS	Pinellas Plant [*Department of Energy*] [*Largo, FL*] (GAAI)
PINES	Pines [*Commonly used*] (OPSA)
PINES	Public Information Network for Electronic Services
PINES	Public Information on Nuclear Energy Service [*American Nuclear Society*]
PINET.........	Physicians Information Network (SAUS)
PINET.........	Physics Information Network (SAUS)
PINFET........	Positive-Intrinsic-Negative Field-Effect Transistor (SAUS)

ping............ Packet Internet Groper [*Computer science*] (IGQR)
PING............ Packet Internet Groper [*Computer program*] (PCM)
ping............ Pinguis [*Fat, Grease*] [*Latin*] (DAVI)
PING............ Pulsed Inertial Navigation and Guidance (SAUS)
Ping Chat Mortg... Pingrey's Treatise of Chattel Mortgages [*A publication*] (DLA)
PINGO.......... Public Interest Nongovernmental Organization
PINGP.......... Prairie Island Nuclear Generating Plant (NRCH)
PINH............ Pyridoxal Isonicotinoylhydrazone [*Biochemistry*]
PINI............ Plug-in Neutral Injector (SAUS)
PINI............ Positive Ion Neutral Injector [*Nuclear energy*] (NUCP)
Pinktn.......... Pinkerton's, Inc. [*Associated Press*] (SAG)
PINN............ Pinnacle Banc Group [*NASDAQ symbol*] (TTSB)
PINN............ Pinnacle Banc Group, Inc. [*NASDAQ symbol*] (SAG)
PINN............ Pinnacles National Monument
Pinn............ Pinney's Wisconsin Reports [*A publication*] (DLA)
PINN............ Proposed International Nonproprietary Name [*Drug research*]
PinnclBk...... Pinnacle Bank [*Associated Press*] (SAG)
Pinney.......... Pinney's Wisconsin Reports [*A publication*] (DLA)
Pinney (sv)... Pinney's Wisconsin Reports [*A publication*] (DLA)
PinnSyst...... Pinnacle Systems, Inc. [*Associated Press*] (SAG)
PINO............ Positive Input - Negative Output [*Computer science*]
PINPD.......... Positive-Intrinsic-Negative Photodiode (SAUS)
PINPOINT.... Phase Integrating Position Indicator for Transmitters (SAUS)
PINPrB......... PSI Energy, 4.16%cmPfd vtg [*NYSE symbol*] (TTSB)
PINPrC......... PSI Energy, 4.32% Pfd [*NYSE symbol*] (TTSB)
PINPrD......... PSI Energy, 7.15% Pfd [*NYSE symbol*] (TTSB)
PINPrJ......... PSI Energy, 6.875% Pfd [*NYSE symbol*] (TTSB)
PINPrK......... PSI Energy, 7.44% Pfd [*NYSE symbol*] (TTSB)
PinptRtl....... Pinpoint Retail Solutions [*Associated Press*] (SAG)
PINRO.......... Polar Institute of Marine Fishery and Oceanography (SAUS)
PINRO.......... Polar Scientific Research Institute for Marine Fisheries and Oceanography [*Russian*]
PINS............ Palletized Inertial Navigation System [*Military*] (LAIN)
PINS............ Patient in Need of Supervision (MELL)
PINS............ Personnel Information System [*Army*] (AABC)
PINS............ Persons in Need of Supervision [*Classification for delinquent children*]
PINS............ Pipeline Inspection Notification System (PIAV)
PINS............ Point-in-Space (MCD)
PINS............ Political Information System [*Databank of political strategist Richard Wirthlin*]
PINS............ Portable Inertial Navigation System
PINS............ Precise Integrated Navigation System [*Navy*] (DOMA)
PINS............ Precisions Improved Nesting System (SAUS)
PINS............ Professional International Network Society (NTPA)
PINSAC........ PINS [*Portable Inertial Navigation System*] Alignment Console
PINSCH........ Periodic-Index Separate-Confinement Heterostructure (SAUS)
PINSCH QW... Periodic-Index Separate-Confinement Heterostructure Quantum-Well (SAUS)
PINSTD........ Preinserted
PINSTECH.... Pakistan Institute of Nuclear Science and Technology
PINT............ Power Integrated Transistor (SAUS)
PINT............ Power Intelligence (DNAB)
PINT............ Processor Interrupt (SAUS)
PINT............ PSTN and Internet Internetworking (SAUS)
PINT............ Purdue Interpretive Program (SAUS)
PINT............ Purdue Interpretive Programming and Operating System (MCD)
PIN/TAN....... Personal Identification Number/Transaction Number (SAUS)
PINTE.......... Processor Interrupts Enabled [*Computer science*] (MHDI)
PINTEC........ Plastics Institute National Technical Conference (SAUS)
PINTS.......... Ported-Coax Intrusion Sensor [*Military*] (INF)
PInU............ Indiana University of Pennsylvania, Indiana, PA [*Library symbol*] [*Library of Congress*] (LCLS)
PINV............ Post-Imperative Negative Variation [*Medicine*] (DMAA)
Pin (Wis)...... Pinney's Wisconsin Reports [*A publication*] (DLA)
Pin Wis R..... Pinney's Wisconsin Reports [*A publication*] (DLA)
PINWOR........ Pinworm [*Gastroenterology*] (DAVI)
PinWst......... Pinnacle West Capital Corp. [*Associated Press*] (SAG)
pinx............ Pinxit (WDAA)
PINX............ Pinxit [*He, or She, Painted It*] [*Latin*]
PINX............ Private Integrated Services Network Exchange (SAUS)
PINXT.......... Pinxit [*He, or She, Painted It*] [*Latin*] (ROG)
P/Iny............ Parts per Square Inch (SAUS)
PINY............ Polytechnic Institute of New York
PIO.............. Palestine Information Office (EA)
PIO.............. Parallel Input/Output
PIO.............. Parallel Interface Output (SAUS)
PIO.............. Parallel I/O (SAUS)
PIO.............. Parallel/Programmable I/O (SAUS)
PIO.............. Peripheral Input/Output (NITA)
PIO.............. Peripheral Input-Output Controller [*Computer science*] (CIST)
PIO.............. Pheniminooxazolidinone [*Pharmacology*]
PIO.............. Photocomposition Input Option (NITA)
PIO.............. Photographic Interpretation Officer (SAUS)
PIO.............. Photo Interpretation Officer [*Air Force*]
PIO.............. Physical Input-Output [*Computer science*] (IAA)
PIO.............. Pielago [*Ship's rigging*] (ROG)
PIO.............. Pilot-Induced Oscillation
PIO.............. Pilot Information Office
PIO.............. Pilot Information Officer (SAUS)
PIO.............. Pinon, NM [*Location identifier*] [*FAA*] (FAAL)
PIO.............. Pi Omicron National Sorority (EA)
PIO.............. Pioneer [*A publication*]
PIO.............. Pioneer Airlines, Inc. [*ICAO designator*] (FAAC)
PIO.............. Pioneer Corp ADR [*NYSE symbol*] (SG)
PIO.............. Pioneer Electron ADR [*NYSE symbol*] (TTSB)
PIO.............. Pioneer Electronic Corp. [*NYSE symbol*] (SPSG)
PIO.............. Plate Iron Oxide [*Automotive paint*]
PIO.............. Poets International Organisation [*Bangalore, India*] (EAIO)
PIO.............. Port Information Office (SAUS)
PIO.............. Position Iterative Operation
PIO.............. Precision Interactive Operation [*Computer science*]
PIO.............. Precision-Interpret Operation (SAUS)
PIO.............. Precision Iterative Operation (IAA)
PIO.............. Preliminary Inquiry Officer (DNAB)
PIO.............. Private Input/Output [*Telecommunications*] (TEL)
PIO.............. Process Input-Output [*Computer science*] (ECII)
PIO.............. Processor Input-Output [*Computer science*] (MDG)
PIO.............. Programmable Input/Output (SAUS)
PIO.............. Programmed Input/Output
PIO.............. Project Implementation Order (SAUS)
PIO.............. Provisioned Item Order (MCD)
PIO.............. Public Information Office [*or Officer*]
PIO.............. Western Pennsylvania School for the Deaf, Pittsburgh, PA [*OCLC symbol*] (OCLC)
PIOB............ President's Intelligence Oversight Board (DOMA)
PIOBX.......... Pioneer Bond Fund [*Mutual fund ticker symbol*] (SG)
PIO/C........... PIO for Commodities (SAUS)
PIOC............ Program Input-Output Cassette [*Computer science*] (IAA)
PIO/C........... Project Implementation Order/Commodity [*Agency for International Development*]
PIOCA.......... Peruvian Inca Orchid Dog Club of America (EA)
PIOCC.......... Province Intelligence and Operations Coordination Center [*Vietnam*] (VNW)
PIOCS.......... Parallel Input/Output Control System (NITA)
PIOCS.......... Physical Input-Output Control System [*Computer science*] (BUR)
PIODCA........ Peruvian Inca Orchid Dog Club of America (EA)
PIODX.......... Pioneer Fund Cl.A [*Mutual fund ticker symbol*] (SG)
PIOFA.......... Petroleum Ether Insoluble Oxidized Fatty Acid [*Food science*]
PIOFS.......... Parallel I/O File System (SAUS)
PIOG............ Pioneer Group [*NASDAQ symbol*] (TTSB)
PIOG............ [*The*] Pioneer Group, Inc. [*NASDAQ symbol*] (NQ)
PIOM............ Physical Input/Output Manager (SAUS)
pion............. Pi-Meson (BARN)
PION............ Pioneer (AABC)
pion............. Pioneer (GEAB)
PIONA.......... Pioneer Companies, Inc. [*NASDAQ symbol*] (SAG)
PIONA.......... Pioneer Cos. 'A' [*NASDAQ symbol*] (TTSB)
PionCos........ Pioneer Companies, Inc. [*Associated Press*] (SAG)
PioneerC...... Pioneer Commercial Funding Corp. [*Associated Press*] (SAG)
PionF........... Pioneer Financial Services, Inc. [*Associated Press*] (SAG)
PionFS......... Pioneer Financial Services, Inc. [*Associated Press*] (SAG)
PionGp......... [*The*] Pioneer Group, Inc. [*Associated Press*] (SAG)
PionHiB........ Pioneer Hi-Bred International [*Associated Press*] (SAG)
PionInt......... Pioneer Interest Shares [*Associated Press*] (SAG)
PionrC.......... Pioneer Commercial Funding Corp. [*Associated Press*] (SAG)
PionrEl......... Pioneer Electronic Corp. [*Associated Press*] (SAG)
PionStd........ Pioneer Standard Electronics [*Associated Press*] (SAG)
PionStd........ Pioneer-Standard Electronics, Inc. [*Associated Press*] (SAG)
PIOP............ Pharmacists in Ophthalmic Practice (EA)
PIO/P........... PIO for Participant Training (SAUS)
PIOPED........ Prospective Investigation of Pulmonary Embolism Diagnosis [*Medicine*]
PIOPIC......... Protection and Indemnity of Oil Pollution Indemnity Clause [*Insurance*] (DS)
PIOR............ Panstwowa Inspekcja Ochrony Roslin (SAUS)
PioRail......... Pioner Railcorp [*Associated Press*] (SAG)
PIOS............ Pioneer-Standard Electronics, Inc. [*NASDAQ symbol*] (NQ)
PIOS............ Pioneer Std Electr [*NASDAQ symbol*] (TTSB)
PIOS............ Planning Information Overlay System (SAUS)
PIOS............ State Inspectorate for Environmental Protection (SAUS)
PIOSA.......... Pan-Indian Ocean Science Association (NOAA)
PIOSP.......... Process Input-Output Subroutine Package [*Computer science*] (MHDI)
PIO/T........... PIO for Contract Technicians or Contract Services (SAUS)
PIO/T........... Project Implementation Order/Technical [*Agency for International Development*]
PIOTA.......... Post-Irradiation Open Test Assembly [*Nuclear energy*] (NRCH)
PIOTA.......... Proximity Instrumented Open Test Assembly [*Nuclear energy*] (NRCH)
PIOTX.......... Pioneer II Cl.A [*Mutual fund ticker symbol*] (SG)
PIOU............ Parallel Input-Output Unit [*Computer science*] (IEEE)
PIOUS.......... Peripheral Integrated Off-Line Utility System (SAA)
PIP.............. 6-Mercaptopurin, Vincristine, Methotrexate, Citrovorum Factor [*Chemotherapy*] (DAVI)
PIP.............. IGOSS Plan and Implementation Programme (SAUS)
PIP.............. Package Irradiation Plant [*Nuclear energy*] (NUCP)
PIP.............. Packaging and Industrial Polymers [*E.T. DuPont*]
PIP.............. Packet Interface Port (SAUS)
PIP.............. Page Image Processor [*Computer science*] (VLIE)
PIP.............. Pan-Iranist Party [*Political party*] (PPW)
PIP.............. Paper Impact Printing (HGAA)
PIP.............. Para-Isothiocyanatephenethylamine [*Biochemistry*]
PIP.............. Parallel Image Processing (ACAE)
PIP.............. Parallel I/O Port (SAUS)
PIP.............. Paralytic Infantile Paralysis [*Medicine*] (DB)
PIP.............. Parental Involvement Project (AIE)
PIP.............. Participant Instrumentation Package
PIP.............. Participating Irredeemable Preference [*Shares*]
PIP.............. Participation Interest Purchase [*FNMA*] (EMRF)

PIP..............	Partido Independentista Puertorriqueno [*Puerto Rican Independence Party*] [*Political party*] (PPW)
PIP..............	Partner Interface Process [*Computer science*] (VLIE)
PIP..............	Partners in Progress [*Government*] [*Civil rights*]
PIP..............	Parts Improvement Program (ACAE)
PIP..............	Pasuquin [*Philippines*] [*Seismograph station code, US Geological Survey*] (SEIS)
PIP..............	Path Independent Protocol
PIP..............	Pattern and Information Processing (SAUS)
PIP..............	Payload Integration Plan [*NASA*] (NASA)
PIP..............	Payload Interface Plan [*NASA*] (NASA)
PIP..............	Payment in Part [*Business term*]
PIP..............	Peak Inspiratory Pressure [*Medicine*] (DAVI)
PIP..............	Performance Improvement and Productivity Programme (SAUS)
PIP..............	Performance Improvement Program (ACAE)
PIP..............	Performance Improvement Proposal (ACAE)
PIP..............	Periodical Informational Posting (SAUS)
PIP..............	Periodic Interim Payment Program [*Medicare*] (GFGA)
PIP..............	Peripheral Interchange Package (SAUS)
PIP..............	Peripheral Interchange Program [*Computer science*]
PIP..............	Peripheral Interface Programmer [*Circuit*] [*Computer science*]
PIP..............	Permatite Instant Plastic (SAUS)
PIP..............	Persistent Internal Polarization
PIP..............	Personal Identification Program (SAUS)
PIP..............	Personal Identification Project [*Computer science*]
PIP..............	Personal Information Processor (SAUS)
PIP..............	Personal Information Processors (AGLO)
PIP..............	Personal Injury Protection [*Insurance*] (TVEL)
PIP..............	Personal Innovation Program
PIP..............	Personal Interaction Panel (VLIE)
PIP..............	Personnel Identification Project (SAUS)
PIP..............	Personnel Interface Processor (MCD)
PIP..............	Pesticide Information Profiles (GNE)
PIP..............	Petroleum Incentives Program [*Canada*]
PIP..............	Philips-Imperial Petroleum Ltd. (SAUS)
PIP..............	Phosphatidylinositol-4-phosphate (SAUS)
PIP..............	Phosphatidylinositol Phosphate [*Biochemistry*]
PIP..............	Photo Image Processor (MCD)
PIP..............	Photo Interpretive Program (BUR)
PIP..............	Picture-in-a-Picture [*Multi-Vision Products*] [*Video technology*]
PIP..............	Pilot Indoctrination Programme (SAUS)
PIP..............	Pilot Point [*Alaska*] [*Airport symbol*] (OAG)
PIP..............	P-Internet-Protocol (SAUS)
PIP..............	Pipe Inspection Program (SAUS)
PIP..............	Pipeline Image Processor (SAUS)
PIP..............	Piperacillin [*An antibiotic*]
PIP..............	Planning Integration Process (SAUS)
PIP..............	Plant-in-Place
PIP..............	Plant Instrumentation Program
PIP..............	Plot Inconsistencies Project (SAUS)
PIP..............	Plug-in Programmer (SAUS)
PIP..............	Plug-In Protocol (SAUS)
PIP..............	Polar Information Program (SAUS)
PIP..............	Polaris Improvement Program (SAUS)
PIP..............	Policy Improvement Program
PIP..............	Policy Integration Program
PIP..............	Pollution Information Project (NITA)
PIP..............	Population Information Program [*Later, CCP*] (EA)
PIP..............	Portable Instrumentation Package [*Military*] (CAAL)
PIP..............	Position Indicating Probe (IEEE)
PIP..............	Positive Incentive Program (SAUS)
PIP..............	Positive Inspiratory Pressure [*Medicine*] (MELL)
PIP..............	Postal Instant Press (EFIS)
PIP..............	Postinfusion Phlebitis [*Medicine*] (MELL)
PIP..............	Postinspiratory Pressure [*Medicine*] (DAVI)
PIP..............	Poured-in-Place (SAUS)
PIP..............	Power Input Panel
PIP..............	Prearrival Inspection Procedure
PIPD..............	Precise Installation Position
PIP..............	Precision Instrumentation Package (SEWL)
PIP..............	Predicted Impact Point [*Aerospace*] (AAG)
PIP..............	Predicted Intercept Point
PIP..............	Preliminary Information Pamphlet
PIP..............	Preparatory Investment Protection [*For the consortia which invested in deep sea mining*]
PIP..............	Preparedness and Industrial Planning
PIP..............	Pretty Important Person
PIP..............	Primary Indicating Position (IAA)
PIP..............	Primary Indicating Position Data Logger (IEEE)
PIP..............	Prior Immobilization and Positioning [*Roentgenology*]
PIP..............	Probabilistic Information Processing (or Processor) (SAUS)
PIP..............	Problem Identification Program (MCD)
PIP..............	Problem Input Preparation [*Computer science*] (BUR)
PIP..............	Problem Isolation Procedure (VLIE)
PIP..............	Procedural Information Pamphlet
PIP..............	Procedural Interrupt Positive (SAUS)
PIP..............	Proceedings in Print [*A bibliographic publication*]
PIP..............	Process Improvement Proposal (SAUS)
PIP..............	Process-Induced Particles (AAEL)
PIP..............	Process Interface Processor [*Computer science*] (VLIE)
PIP..............	Product Improvement (MCD)
PIP..............	Product Improvement Phase (SAUS)
PIP..............	Product Improvement Plan
PIP..............	Product Improvement Program [*Military*]
PIP..............	Product Improvement Proposal (MCD)
PIP..............	Product Information Package (SAUS)
PIP..............	Product Integration Program (SAUS)
PIP..............	Product Introductory Presentation
PIP..............	Production Implementation Program (AAG)
PIP..............	Production Improvement Program [*Navy*] (NG)
PIP..............	Production Instrumentation Package (NASA)
PIP..............	Productivity Improvement Program [*Office of Management and Budget*] (GFGA)
PIP..............	Productivity Improvement Program [*Department of Labor*]
PIP..............	Professional Information Processor (SAUS)
PIP..............	Professional Intern Program (SAUS)
PIP..............	Profile Ignition Pick-Up [*Automotive engineering*]
PIP..............	Profit Improvement Program
PIP..............	Program Implementation Plan (MCD)
PIP..............	Program Information Package (AAGC)
PIP..............	Program in Process [*Computer science*] (BUR)
PIP..............	Program in Progress [*Computer science*] (IAA)
PIP..............	Program Integrating Plan [*Computer science*] (IAA)
PIP..............	Program Integration Plan
PIP..............	Programmable Interconnect Point [*Computer science*]
PIP..............	Programmable Interface Processor (ACAE)
PIP..............	Programmed Individual Presentation (IAA)
PIP..............	Programmed Interconnection Pattern (VLIE)
PIP..............	Programmed Interconnection Process (SAUS)
PIP..............	Programmer Incentive Plan (SAUS)
PIP..............	Programs for the Improvement of Practice [*Washington, DC*] [*Department of Education*] (GRD)
PIP..............	Progressive Independent Party [*South Africa*] [*Political party*] (EY)
PIP..............	Progressive Inspection Plan [*Navy*] (NG)
PIP..............	Projected Impact Point [*Aviation*]
PIP..............	Project Implementation Plan
PIP..............	Project Implementation Profile [*Test*] (TMMY)
PIP..............	Project Initiation Period
PIP..............	Project Instrumentation Plan [*NASA*] (GFGA)
PIP..............	Project on Information Processing (IEEE)
PIP..............	Proof in Print
PIP..............	Proposal Instruction Package (MCD)
PIP..............	Proprietary Information Protection
PIP..............	Prototype Inlet Piping (SAUS)
PIP..............	Prototypic Inlet Piping [*Nuclear energy*] (NRCH)
PIP..............	Provabilistic Information Processing [*Computer science*] (IAA)
PIP..............	Prove in Plan (MCD)
PIP..............	Proximal Interphalangeal [*Joint*]
PIP..............	Psychotic Inpatient Profile [*Psychology*]
PIP..............	Public and Institutional Property [*Insurance*]
PIP..............	Public Investment Program (SAUS)
PIP..............	Public Involvement Plan (SAUS)
PIP..............	Public Involvement Program (GNE)
PIP..............	Puerto Rican Independence Party [*Political party*] (PD)
PIP..............	Pulsed Integrated (or Integrating) Pendulum (SAUS)
PIP..............	Pulsed Integrating Pendulum
PIP..............	Pulse Input Proportional [*Electro-optical system*]
PIP..............	Pulse Integrating Pendulum
PIP..............	Pulse Interval Processor (SAUS)
PIP..............	Western Psychiatric Institute and Clinic, University of Pittsburgh, Pittsburgh, PA [*OCLC symbol*] (OCLC)
PIPA..............	Pacific Industrial Property Association (EA)
PIPA..............	Pacific Islands Producers Association (SAUS)
PIPA..............	Pulse Integrating Pendulous Accelerometer (SAUS)
PIPA..............	Pulse Integrating Pendulum Accelerometer
PIPA	Pulse Integrating Pendulum Assembly (NASA)
PIPACE	Peacetime Intelligence Plan, Allied Central Europe [*NATO*]
Pip & C Mil L...	Pipon and Collier's Military Law [*3rd ed.*] [*1865*] [*A publication*] (DLA)
PI-PB	Performance Versus Intensity Function for Phonetically Balanced Words (MEDA)
PIPC..............	Percent Indices Process Capable
PIPCST	Piping Cost and Weight Analysis Program (DNAB)
PIPD..............	Planning Input for Program Development (ACAE)
PIPE..............	Consolidated Stainless [*NASDAQ symbol*] (TTSB)
PIPE..............	Consolidated Stainless, Inc. [*NASDAQ symbol*] (SAG)
PIPE..............	Persistent Interstitial Pulmonary Emphysema [*Medicine*] (DMAA)
PIPE..............	Pipestone National Monument
PIPE..............	Plug-In Processing Element (VLIE)
PIPE..............	Plumbing Industry Progress and Education Fund
PIPE..............	Points, Income, Personnel Expense (SAUS)
PIPECO	Photoion-Photoelectron Coincidence [*Spectroscopy*]
PIPEF..........	Pacific Islands Polynesian Education Foundation (SAUS)
PIPEFLEX....	Pipe Flexibility [*Stress Analysis Program*]
PIPEL..........	Pipeline (SAUS)
Pipeline Gas J...	Pipeline and Gas Journal (SAUS)
Pipe Line Ind...	Pipe Line Industry (SAUS)
PIPELN	Pipeline company [*Transportation company classification code*]
PIPEMAID	Piping Program
PIPER	Pulsed Intense Plasma for Experimental Research
PIPER	Pulsed Intense Plasma for Exploratory Research
PiperJaf.......	Piper Jaffray, Inc. [*Associated Press*] (SAG)
PIPES..........	Piperazinediethanesulfonic Acid [*A buffer*]
PIPES..........	Program on International Politics, Economics, and Security [*University of Chicago*]
Pipes Pipelines Int...	Pipes and Pipelines International (SAUS)
PIPEX..........	Pipeline Engineering Exhibition (SAUS)
PIPI..............	Pipelines Inspectorate (HEAS)
PIPICO	Panel on International Programs and International Cooperation in Oceans Affairs [*Department of State*] (NOAA)

PIPICO	Panel on International Programs and International Organizations [*US State Department*] (USDC)
PIPIDA	N-Para-Isopropylacetanilide-Iminodiacetic Acid [*Scan*] [*Radiology*] (DAVI)
PIPIDA	Para-Isopropylphenyl(iminodiacetic Acid)
PIPIT	Peripheral Interface and Program Interrupt Translator (PDAA)
PIPJ	Proximal Interphalangeal Joint [*Anatomy*]
PIP Joint	Proximal Interphalangeal Joint (SAUS)
PIPLC	Phosphatidylinositol-Specific Phospholipase C [*Biochemistry*]
PIPO	Parallel-In Parallel-Out [*Telecommunications*] (TEL)
PIPO	Partition Input-Partition Output (SAUS)
PIPO	Phase-In, Phase-Out (MCD)
PIPPAP	Pile for Producing Power and Plutonium [*Nuclear energy*] (NRCH)
PIPPS	Publication Information Processing and Printing System
Pippy	Person Inheriting Parents' Property [*Lifestyle classification*] [*British*]
PIPQUIC	Program Integration Project Queries Use in Interactive Command (COE)
PIPR	Plant-in-Place Records
PIPR	Polytechnic Institute of Puerto Rico
PIPR	Public Interest Public Relations (EA)
PIPRS	Ping Intercept Passive Ranging SONAR [*Military*]
PIPS	Pan Information Processing System (SAUS)
PIPS	Paperless Item Processing System [*Banking*]
PIPS	Parallel Information Processing System (SAUS)
PIPS	Passivated Implanted Planar Silicon (SAUS)
PIPS	Passive Infrared Personnel Sensor (ACAE)
PIPS	Patient-Identified Physicians Survey [*Department of Health and Human Services*] (GFGA)
PIPS	Pattern Information Processing System
PIPS	PCAC Information Processing System (SAUS)
PIPS	Peabody Intellectual Performance Scale [*Education*]
PIPS	Personal Image Processing System (SAUS)
PIPS	Plans Integration Partitioning System (COE)
PIPS	Polar Ice Prediction System (SAUS)
PIPS	Polymerization-Induced Phase Separation (SAUS)
PIPS	Portable Interactive Planning System (SAUS)
PIPS	Postinjection Propulsion Subsystem [*NASA*]
PIPS	Precision Ion Polishing System (SAUS)
PIPS	Preschool Interpersonal Problem Solving Test
PIPS	Product Information Pipeline System (VLIE)
PIPS	Production Information Processing System (IAA)
PIPS	Professional Improvement Points Program [*Louisiana*] (EDAC)
PIPS	Professional Institute of the Public Service of Canada [*See also IPFP*]
PIPS	Properties of Irregular Parts System (MCD)
PIPS	Pulsed Integrating Pendulums [*NASA*] (QAA)
PIPS	Science and Technology Policies Information Exchange Programme [*SPINES*] [*UNESCO*] [*Superseded by*] [*Information service or system*] (IID)
PIPSAR	Pipe Sizing Program - Air (DNAB)
PIPSCR	Philippine Islands Public Service Commission Reports [*A publication*] (DLA)
PIPSPK	Pipe Sizing Program - Sprinkling (DNAB)
PIPSST	Pipe Sizing Program - Steam (DNAB)
PIPTA	Panel on International Procurement in the Technology Age (AAGC)
PIPUCR	Philippine Islands Public Utility Commission Reports [*A publication*] (DLA)
PIQ	Parallel Instruction Queue
PIQ	Performance Intelligence Quotient [*Psychology*] (DMAA)
PIQ	Performance IQ (SAUS)
PIQ	Program Idea Quotient [*Home testing measurement*] (NTCM)
PIQ	Property in Question
PIQ	State Regional Correctional Facility at Mercer, Mercer, PA [*OCLC symbol*] (OCLC)
PIQA	Procurement Integration Quality Assurance (AAGC)
PIQA	Proofing, Inspection, and Quality Assurance [*Military*]
PIQSY	Probes for the International Quiet Solar Year [*OSS*]
PIR	Packaging Information Record (MCD)
PIR	Parachute Infantry Regiment [*Military*]
PIR	Paragnostic Information Retrieval [*Parapsychology*]
PIR	Parallel Injection Readout (IAA)
PIR	Partido de la Izquierda Revolucionaria [*Party of the Revolutionary Left*] [*Bolivia*] [*Political party*] (PPW)
PIR	Party of Independent Republicans (SAUS)
PIR	Passive Infrared
PIR	Past in Review (EA)
PIR	Payload Integration Review (ACAE)
PIR	Peak Intensity Ratio [*Spectroscopy*]
PIR	Pennsylvania International Raceway [*Auto racing*]
PIR	Pennsylvania Rehabilitation Center, Johnstown, PA [*OCLC symbol*] (OCLC)
PIR	Periodic Incremental Release [*Physiology*]
PIR	Periodic Intelligence Report
PIR	Periodic Intelligence Review [*Supreme Allied Commander, Atlantic*] (NATG)
PIR	Personal Interview Record
PIR	Personnel Information Report (SAUS)
PIR	Personnel Information Roster [*Military*]
PIR	Pesticide Ingredient Review Program [*Chemical Specialties Manufacturers Association*]
PIR	Petrolite Irradiation Reactor
PIR	Philippine Independence Ribbon [*Military decoration*]
PIR	Phoenix International Raceway
PIR	Photographic Intelligence Report [*Military*]
PIR	Photographic Interpretation Report
PIR	Photo Interpretation Report [*Air Force*] (AFM)
PIR	Photon-Induced x-Ray (SAUS)
PIR	Pier 1 Imports [*NYSE symbol*] (SPSG)
PIR	Pierre [*South Dakota*] [*Airport symbol*] (OAG)
PIR	Pilot Request (SAA)
PIR	Piriform (DB)
PIR	Pirmasens [*Federal Republic of Germany*] [*Seismograph station code, US Geological Survey*] (SEIS)
PIR	Plug-In Relay
PIR	Polling Interrupt Routine (SAUS)
PIR	Polyisocyanurate (SAUS)
PIR	Post Implementation Review
PIR	Postinhibitory Rebound [*Physiology*]
PIR	Precision Infrared Radiometer (ARMP)
PIR	Precision Inspection Request (IAA)
PIR	Precision Instrumentation RADAR
PIR	Predicted Intercept Range [*Military*] (CAAL)
PIR	Preliminary Information Report (SAUS)
PIR	Prematriculation Immunization Requirement
PIR	Pressure Ignition Rocket (NATG)
PIR	Pressure Indicated Registered (SAUS)
PIR	Pressure Indicator Recorder (ECII)
PIR	Prim-Air Aps [*Denmark*] [*ICAO designator*] (FAAC)
PIR	Primary Intelligence Requirement [*Military*] (INF)
PIR	Principal Ideal Ring (SAUS)
PIR	Priority Information Requirement [*Military intelligence*] (INF)
PIR	Priority Intelligence Requirement [*Military*] (INF)
PIR	Prisoner-Initiated Review
PIR	Process and Indoctrinate Recruits
PIR	Procurement Information Reporting (ACAE)
PIR	Procurement Initiation Request (MCD)
PIR	Product Improvement Review
PIR	Product Information Release
PIR	Production Inspection Record
PIR	Product of Incomplete Reaction (EEVL)
PIR	Professional Investor Report [*A publication*] (IT)
PIR	Program Incident Report
PIR	Program Information Report [*Head Start Program*] [*Department of Health and Human Services*] (GFGA)
PIR	Program Instruction Register (SAUS)
PIR	Program Interrupt Register [*Computer science*] (IAA)
PIR	Project Independence Report
PIR	Project Internal Result (SAUS)
PIR	Protein Identification Resource [*National Biomedical Research Foundation*] [*Georgetown University Medical Center*] [*Information service or system*] (IID)
PIR	Protein Information Resource (HGEN)
PIR	Protocol-Independent Routing [*Computer science*]
PIR	Publication Illustration Request
PIR	Publication Information Register (IAA)
PIR	Pulse Input Register (SAUS)
PIR	Pure India Rubber [*Cables*]
PIRA	Paper Industries Research Association (NADA)
PIRA	Photographic Instrument Repairing Associates [*British*] (DBA)
PIRA	Positive Identification and Radar Advisory (SAUS)
PIRA	Printing and Packaging Industries Research Association (SAUS)
PIRA	Printing and Packaging Research Association
PIRA	Printing Industry Research Association (NADA)
PIRA	Prison Industries Reorganization Administration [*Terminated, 1940*]
PIRA	Provisional Irish Republican Army
PIRA	Research Association for the Paper and Board, Printing and Packaging Industries [*Research center*] (IRC)
PIRAD	Passive Infrared Detector (ACAE)
PIRAD	Proximity Information, Range, and Disposition
PIRAI	PIRA International [*British*] (EAIO)
PIRAMID	Project: Individualized Reading and Mathematics Inter-District (EDAC)
PIRAS	Polarized Infrared Absorption Spectroscopy
PIRATA	Pilot Research Array in the Tropical Atlantic (SAUS)
PIRATA	Pilot Research Moored Array in the Tropical Atlantic [*Proposed project*] [*Marine science*] (OSRA)
PIRATE	Passive Infra-Red Airborne Track Equipment (SAUS)
PIRATE	Public Information in Rural Areas Technical Experiment (NITA)
PIRATE	Public Information in Rural Areas Technology Experiment [*British Library*] (PDAA)
PIRAZ	Positive Identification RADAR Advisory Zone (NVT)
PIRB	Position Indicating Radio Beacon
PIRC	Portable Inflatable Recompression Chamber (MCD)
PIRC	Pressure Indicator Recorder Controller (ECII)
PIRC	Preventive Intervention Research Center for Child Health [*Yeshiva University*] [*Research center*] (RCD)
PIRC	Protocol Implementation Review Committee [*National Institutes of Health*]
PIR Cable	Pure India Rubber Cable (SAUS)
PIRCS	Passive Infrared Confirming Sensor (MCD)
PIRD	Program Instrumentation Requirements Document [*NASA*]
PIR databases	Protein Information Resource Databases (DOG)
PIRE	Pacific Institute for Research and Evaluation [*Research center*] (RCD)
PI Rep	Philippine Island Reports [*A publication*] (DLA)
PIREP	Pilot Report [*Pertaining to meteorological conditions*] [*FAA*]
PIREP	Pilot Weather Report (PIPO)
PIREPS	Pilot Reports [*Marine science*] (OSRA)
PIRETS	Pittsburgh Information Retrieval System (SAUS)
PIRETS	Pittsburgh Retrieval System (NITA)
PIRF	Perimeter-Insulated Raised Floor [*Residential construction*]

PIRF	Petroleum Industry Research Foundation (NADA)
PIRFC	Pilot Requests Forecast [Aviation] (FAAC)
PIRG	Public Interest Research Group [Formed by consumer-advocate Ralph Nader]
PIRI	Paint Industries Research Institute (SAUS)
P-IRI	Plasma Immunoreactive Insulin [Hematology] (MAE)
PIRI	Psychologists Interested in Religious Issues (EA)
PIRID	Passive Infrared Intrusion Detector (NVT)
PIRINC	Petroleum Industry Research Foundation (EA)
PIRL	Pattern Information Retrieval Language (SAUS)
PIRL	PRISM [Personnel Record Information System for Management] Information RetrievalLanguage [Computer science] (PDAA)
PIRLA	Paleoecological Reconstruction of Recent Lake Acidification (SAUS)
PIRLS	Probe Infrared Laser Spectrometer (ACAE)
PI RM	Pilot Reamer (SAUS)
PIRN	Preliminary Interface Revision Notice [NASA] (KSC)
PIRO	People, Ideas, Resources, Objectives [Management strategy] (DHSM)
PIRO	Pictured Rocks National Lakeshore [National Park Service designation]
PIROGAS	Plasma Injection of Reducing Overheated Gas System (SAUS)
PIROS	Passive Infrared Remote Observation System (SAUS)
PIRP	Prison Information Reform Project (SAUS)
PIRP	Proposed International Reference Preparation (SAUS)
PIRP	Provisional International Reference Preparation
PIRR	Parts Installation and Removal Record [NASA] (KSC)
PIRR	Prepositioned War Reserve Interrogation and Readiness Reporting (MCD)
PIRR	Problem Investigation and Repair Record [NASA] (KSC)
PIRR	PWRS [Prepositioned War Reserve Stock] Interrogation and Readiness Reporting System [Navy]
PIRR	Pyrogen Identifier Rapid Response (SAUS)
PIRRB	Photo Intelligence Requirements Review Board [Military]
PIRRCOM	Project for the Intensification of Regional Research on Cotton, Oilseeds and Minerals (SAUS)
PIRS	Partial Input Record Storage (SAUS)
PIRS	Passive Infrared Seeker
PIRS	Passive Infrared Sensor (ACAE)
PIRS	Personal Information Retrieval System
PIRS	Personnel Information Retrieval System
PIRS	Philosopher's Index Retrieval System (NITA)
PIRS	Philosopher's Information Retrieval System [Bowling Green State University]
PIRS	Plasma Immunoreactive Secretion [Medicine] (DMAA)
PIRS	Pollution Incident Reporting System [Coast Guard]
PIRS	Poseidon Information Retrieval System [Missiles]
PIRS	Project Information Retrieval System [HEW]
PIRS	Pulsed Infrared System (ACAE)
PIRSA	Passive Infrared Situation Awareness (ACAE)
PIRS Method	Partial Input Record Storage Method (SAUS)
PIRT	Placement by an Interchange and Rate Technique (SAUS)
PIRT	Precision Infrared Tracking
PIRT	Precision Infrared Triangulation
PIRT	Pretreatment Implementation Review Task Force [Environmental Protection Agency] (EPA)
PIRT	Programmed Instruction in Real Time (SAUS)
PIRT	Public Information Retrieval Terminal (SAUS)
PIRT System	Preliminary Infrared Triangulation System (SAUS)
PIRU	Public Information Reference Unit [Environmental Protection Agency] (GFGA)
PIRV	Programmed Interrupt Request Vector [Computer science] (ELAL)
Pis	In Pisonem [of Cicero] [Classical studies] (OCD)
PIS	Parts Identification Service
PIS	Passenger Information System
PIS	Passive Infrared System
PIS	Patent Inventor Service (NITA)
PIS	Pathology Information System (SAUS)
PIS	Penning Ionization Spectroscopy (PDAA)
PIS	Photographic Interpretation Section
PIS	Pisa [Italy] [Seismograph station code, US Geological Survey] [Closed] (SEIS)
PIS	Piscivorous
Pis	Pistol (SAUS)
PIS	Pointable Imaging Spectrometer (SAUS)
PIS	Poitiers [France] [Airport symbol] (OAG)
PIS	Polling Interrupt Sequence (SAUS)
PIS	Polyisobutylene (EDCT)
PIS	Portfolio-Management Information System (SAUS)
PIS	Position Indicator System
PIS	Positive Ion Source
PIS	Postal Inspection Service
PIS	Preinfarction Syndrome [Cardiology]
PIS	Preinsert Sequencing
PIS	Pressure-Indicating Switch [Nuclear energy] (NRCH)
PIS	Prime Implicant Solution (IAA)
PIS	Procedure Interrupt Signal (SAUS)
PIS	Process Instrumentation System [Nuclear energy] (NRCH)
PIS	Process Instrument Sheet
PIS	Product Information Specialist
PIS	Provisional International Standard
PIS	Public Information Specialist (COE)
PIS	Public Insurance Service (SAUS)
PIS	Pulsed Illumination Source
PIS	Pulse Integration System
PIS	Stevens Trade School, Lancaster, PA [OCLC symbol] (OCLC)

PISA	Persistent Information Space Architecture [Computer science]
PISA	Phase Invariant Signature Algorithm [Chemistry] (DAVI)
PISA	Polish Independent Student Association (EA)
PISA	Prototype Image Spectrum Analyzer (SAUS)
PISA	Public Interest Satellite Association [Defunct] (EA)
PISAB	Pulse Interference Separation and Blanking [RADAR]
PISAB	Pulse Interference Suppression and Blanking (SAUS)
PISABG	PISA/Business Graphics (SAUS)
PISADB	PISA/Data Base (SAUS)
PISADD	PISA/Data Dictionary (SAUS)
PISAL	Periodicals in South African Libraries (NITA)
PISAMP	PISA/Menue Processor (SAUS)
PISAQL	PISA/Query Language (SAUS)
PISARG	PISA/Report Generator (SAUS)
PISB	People's Institute for Survival and Beyond (EA)
PISC	Pacific International Services Corp. [NASDAQ symbol] (NQ)
PISC	Parris Island, South Carolina [Marine Corps]
PISC	Petroleum Industry Security Council (EA)
PISC	Phoenix International Science Center (SAUS)
Pisc	Pisces [Constellation]
PISC	Programme for the Inspection of Steel Components (HEAS)
PISCES	Paleolimnological Investigations of Salinity, Climatic and Environmental Shifts (SAUS)
PISCES	Percutaneously Inserted Spinal Cord Electrical Stimulation [Medicine] (DMAA)
PISCES	Plessey Integrated Shipborne Combat Electronic Systems (SAUS)
PISCES	Poisson and Continuity Equations Solver (SAUS)
PISCES	Production Information Stocks and Cost Enquiry System (MHDB)
PISD	Pacific Information Systems Division (SAUS)
PISE	No Pilot Balloon Observation Due to Unfavorable Sea Conditions [NWS] (FAAC)
PISE	Pneumatically Installed Stabilized Earth
PISE	Pnuematically-Impacted Stabilized Earth
PISG	Pitcairn Islands Study Group (EA)
PISGA	Palestinian Interim Self-Government Authority [Proposed] (ECON)
PISH	Program Instrumentation Summary Handbook [NASA] (KSC)
PISI	Palmar Intercalated Segmental Instability [Medicine] (MELL)
PISMV	Plantago Severe Mottle Virus [Plant pathology]
PISO	No Pilot Balloon Observation Due to Snow [Meteorology] (FAAC)
PISO	Parallel-In Serial-Out [Telecommunications] (TEL)
PISO	Philippines Investment Systems Organization (SAUS)
PISO	Polyimidesulfone (SAUS)
PISP	PCG-insensitive Streptococcus pneumoniae (SAUS)
PISP	Pipe Springs National Monument
PISP	Polar Ice Sheet Program (SAUS)
PISSC	Programme International sur la Securite des Substances Chimiques [International Programme on Chemical Safety] (EAIO)
PIST	Percent Inspection-Points to Satisfy Tolerances [Manufacturing]
PIST	Piston [Automotive engineering]
Pist	Piston's Mauritius Reports [A publication] (DLA)
Piston	Piston's Mauritius Reports [A publication] (DLA)
PISU	Polyimidesulfone [Organic chemistry]
PISUKI	Pacific Islands Society of the United Kingdom and Ireland (EAIO)
PISYS	Photographic Interpretation Data System (SAUS)
PIT	Pacific Investment Trust [Finance] [British]
PIT	Panair International SRL [Italy] [ICAO designator] (FAAC)
PI/T	Parallel Interface/Timer [Motorola, Inc.]
PIT	Parameter Input Tape (IAA)
PIT	Participate in Archeology
PIT	Parti de l'Independance et du Travail [Party of Independence and Labor] [Senegal] [Political party] (PPW)
PIT	Parti Ivoirien des Travailleurs [Ivorian Workers' Party] [The Ivory Coast] [Political party] (EY)
PIT	Partners in Transition [Poland, Czechoslovakia, and Hungary] (ECON)
PIT	Part-Time, Intermittent, Temporary [Nuclear energy]
PIT	Pasadena Institute of Technology (SAUS)
PIT	Passive Immunotherapy [Medicine] (TAD)
PIT	Passive Integrated Transponder
PIT	Patellar Inhibition Test [Neurology] (DAVI)
Pit	Pateller Inhibition Test (STED)
PIT	Performance Improvement Test (SAUS)
PIT	Performance Improvement Tests
PIT	Peripheral Input Tape [Computer science]
PIT	Peripheral Interface Tests (MCD)
PIT	Permanent Income Theory [Econometrics]
PIT	Permit Improvement Team [Environmental science] (EPAT)
PIT	Personal Income Tax
PIT	Phase Inversion Temperature [Physical Chemistry]
PIT	Photographic Interpretation Technique
PIT	Physical Inventory Taking (MHDB)
PIT	Picture Identification Test [Psychology]
PIT	Picture Impressions Test [Psychology]
PIT	Pilot Instructor Training [Aviation] (FAAC)
PIT	Pirates Gold Corp. [Vancouver Stock Exchange symbol]
Pit	Pitocin [Trademark of Parke, Davis & Co. for Oxytocin, a labor-inducing drug]
Pit	Pitressin [Trademark of Parke, Davis & Co. for Vasopressin, an antidiuretic hormone]
PIT	Pittsburgh [Pennsylvania] [Seismograph station code, US Geological Survey] [Closed] (SEIS)
PIT	Pittsburgh [Pennsylvania] [Airport symbol]
Pit	Pittsburgh Steelers [National Football League] [1941-42, 1945-present] (NFLA)
PIT	Pituitary [Endocrinology] (AAMN)

pit..............	Pituitary (STED)
PIT..............	Plasma Iron Transport [Hematology]
PIT..............	Plasma Iron Turnover [Hematology] (DAVI)
PIT..............	Polar Ionospheric Trough
PIT..............	Polaris Industrial Team [Missiles]
PIT..............	Pole Interpolation Technique (SAUS)
PIT..............	Powder-in-Tube (SAUS)
PIT..............	Pre-Induction Training
PIT..............	Preinstallation Test [NASA] (KSC)
PIT..............	Prevailing-In Torque [Automotive engineering]
PIT..............	Principal, Interest and Taxes (SAUS)
PIT..............	Print Illegal and Trace
PIT..............	Printing and Information Technology (SAUS)
PIT..............	Printing and Information Technology Division (NITA)
PIT..............	Prioritized Image Transmission (SAUS)
PIT..............	Processing Index Terms
PIT..............	Processing of Indexing Terms
PIT..............	Product Improvement Test
PIT..............	Program Instruction Tape [Computer science] (IEEE)
PIT..............	Programmable Interface/Timer [Computer science] (AGLO)
PIT..............	Programmable Interval Timer
PIT..............	Programmed Instruction Text
PIT..............	Progressive Inspection Tag (SAUS)
PIT..............	Projected Inactive Time [Computer science]
PIT..............	Project in Trouble (CCCA)
PIT..............	Property Income Trust [Investment term]
PIT..............	Protection Identification Key (SAUS)
PIT..............	Provincial Institute of Textiles
PIT..............	Psychological Insight Test [Psychometrics]
PIT..............	University of Pittsburgh, Pittsburgh, PA [OCLC symbol] (OCLC)
PITA..........	Pacific International Trapshooting Association (EA)
PITA..........	Pain in the Acronym (SAUS)
PITA..........	Pain in the Anatomy (SAUS)
PITA..........	Paper Industry Technical Association [British] (EAIO)
PITA..........	Parison Inflation Thinning Analysis (SAUS)
PITA..........	Petroleum Industry Training Association (SAUS)
PITA..........	Provincial Institute of Technology and Art
PITA..........	Provincial Intermediate Teachers Association (SAUS)
PITAC........	Pakistan Industrial Technical Assistance Center (or Centre) (SAUS)
PITAS........	Petroleum Industry Training Association Scotland (SAUS)
PITB..........	Pacific Inland Tariff Bureau
PITB..........	Pacific Island Teachers Board (SAUS)
PITB..........	Petroleum Industry Training Board (SAUS)
PITB..........	Poetry in the Branches [Program]
PITB..........	Push Commercial Division [An association] (EA)
PITB..........	PUSH [People United to Save Humanity] International Trade Bureau (EA)
Pitblado Lect...	Isaac Pitblado's Lectures on Continuing Legal Education [A publication] (DLA)
PITC..........	Pacific International Trust Co. (SAUS)
PITC..........	Phenylisothiocyanate [Organic chemistry]
PITC..........	Photoinduced Tunnel Current
Pitc	Pitcairn's Criminal Trials [1488-1624] [Scotland] [A publication] (DLA)
PITC..........	Pittencrieff Communications [NASDAQ symbol] (SAG)
Pitc Crim Tr...	Pitcairn's Ancient Criminal Trials [Scotland] [A publication] (DLA)
PITCOM.......	Parliamentary Information Technology Committee [Political communications] [British]
Pitc Tr	Pitcairn's Criminal Trials [3 Scotland] [A publication] (DLA)
PITDIC	Pacific Islands Tourism Development Council (SAUS)
PitDsm........	Pittsburgh-Des Moines Corp. [Associated Press] (SAG)
PITE..........	Project on Information Technology and Education [Defunct] (EA)
Pitencr........	Pittencrieff Communications [Commercial firm] [Associated Press] (SAG)
PITF..........	Poultry Industry Trust Fund [Australia]
PITFA.........	Product Improvement Through Feature Analysis (SAUS)
PITFC........	Potato Industry Trust Fund Committee [Western Australia]
PIT FE........	Personal Income Tax Filing Enforcement (SAUS)
PITG..........	Payload Integration Task Group [NASA] (NASA)
PITHX	Pioneer Mid Cap Cl.A [Mutual fund ticker symbol] (SG)
PITI..........	Principal, Interest, Taxes, Insurance [Real estate]
Pitisc Lex	Pitisci's Lexicon [A publication] (DLA)
PITL..........	Pacific Islands Transport Line (SAUS)
PITMOS	Post Mode Optimizing System (SAUS)
Pitm Prin & Sur...	Pitman on Principal and Surety [A publication] (DLA)
PITN..........	Polyisothianaphthene [Organic chemistry]
PitnB..........	Pitney-Bowes, Inc. [Associated Press] (SAG)
PitnyBw	Pitney-Bowes, Inc. [Associated Press] (SAG)
PITO..........	Portuguese Information and Tourist Office (SAUS)
PITP..........	Phosphatidylinositol Transfer Protein [Biochemistry]
PITP...........	Pseudoidiopathic Thrombocytopenic Purpura (STED)
PITR..........	Plasma Iron Transport [or Turnover] Rate [Hematology]
PITR..........	Plasma Iron Turnover Rate (SAUS)
PITRI	Petroleum Industry Technology and Research Institute, Inc. (SAUS)
PITS..........	Pacific Islands Training School (SAUS)
PITS..........	Parent-Infant Traumatic Stress (DAVI)
PITS..........	Partners In Transition [Poland, Czech, Hungary - called the Visegrad Trio]
PITS..........	Passive Identification & Targeting System (SAUS)
PITS..........	Passive Intercept Tracking System
PITS..........	Patriot Integration and Test System [Army]
PITS..........	Payload Integration Test Set [NASA] (MCD)
PITS..........	Peak Instantaneous Transients and Subtleties (SEWL)
PITS..........	Petroleum Industry Training Service (SAUS)
PITS..........	Photoinduced Transient Spectroscopy
PITS..........	Position Interrogation and Transmission System (SAUS)

PITS..........	Primary Influent Treatment System
PITS..........	Projected Intensity Triplet Space (SAUS)
PITS..........	Project Information Tracking System [Environmental Protection Agency] (GFGA)
PITS..........	Propellant Injector Tube Simulator (MCD)
PITS..........	Propulsion Integration Test Stand
PitstnMn......	[The] Pittston Co. [Associated Press] (SAG)
PitstnSvc......	[The] Pittston Co. [Associated Press] (SAG)
Pit Sur	Pitman on Principal and Surety [1840] [A publication] (DLA)
Pitt.............	Pittsburgh, PA (DLA)
PITT...........	Polaris Integrated Test Team [Missiles]
PITT...........	Punch-through Injection Transit-Time (SAUS)
Pitt Bank......	Pitt's Bankruptcy Acts [A publication] (DLA)
PITTC.........	Philips International Telecommunications Training Center (IAA)
Pitt CC Pr	Pitt's County Court Practice [A publication] (DLA)
PITTCON......	Pittsburgh Conference (SAUS)
Pitt LJ.........	Pittsburgh Legal Journal [A publication] (DLA)
Pitts	Pittsburgh, PA (DLA)
Pitts	Pittsburgh Reports [A publication] (DLA)
Pittsb	Pittsburgh, PA (DLA)
Pittsb	Pittsburgh Reports [A publication] (DLA)
Pittsb Leg J...	Pittsburgh Legal Journal [Pennsylvania] [A publication] (DLA)
Pittsb Leg J NS...	Pittsburgh Legal Journal, New Series [Pennsylvania] [A publication] (DLA)
Pittsb Leg J (OS)...	Pittsburgh Legal Journal, Old Series [A publication] (DLA)
Pittsb Leg J (PA)...	Pittsburgh Legal Journal [Pennsylvania] [A publication] (DLA)
Pittsb LJ......	Pittsburgh Legal Journal [Pennsylvania] [A publication] (DLA)
Pittsb L Rev...	Pittsburgh Law Review [A publication] (DLA)
Pittsb R (PA)...	Pittsburgh Reporter [A publication] (DLA)
Pittsburgh Leg J...	Pittsburgh Legal Journal [Pennsylvania] [A publication] (DLA)
Pittsburgh Leg Journal...	Pittsburgh Legal Journal [Pennsylvania] [A publication] (DLA)
Pittsburg St U...	Pittsburg State University (GAGS)
Pitts Leg J...	Pittsburgh Legal Journal [Pennsylvania] [A publication] (DLA)
Pitts Leg J (NS)...	Pittsburgh Legal Journal, New Series [Pennsylvania] [A publication] (DLA)
Pitts Leg Jour...	Pittsburgh Legal Journal [Pennsylvania] [A publication] (DLA)
Pitts LJ.......	Pittsburgh Legal Journal [A publication] (DLA)
Pitts LJ (NS)...	Pittsburgh Legal Journal, New Series [A publication] (DLA)
Pitts R	Pittsburgh Reports [Pennsylvania] [A publication] (DLA)
Pitts Rep	Pittsburgh Reports [A publication] (DLA)
Pitts Rep (PA)...	Pittsburgh Reports [Pennsylvania] [A publication] (DLA)
Pittway	Pittway Corp. [Associated Press] (SAG)
Pittwy	Pittway Corp. [Associated Press] (SAG)
PittwyA........	Pittway Corp. [Associated Press] (SAG)
PITU...........	Pipe or Tubing [Freight]
PitWVa........	Pittsburgh & West Virginia Railroad [Associated Press] (SAG)
PITY-EM......	Principal, Interest, Taxes, Energy, and Maintenance [Real estate]
PITYP..........	Pinatype (VRA)
PIU...........	East Pennsylvania Psychiatric Institute, Philadelphia, PA [OCLC symbol] (OCLC)
PIU.............	Path Information Unit [Computer science]
PIU.............	Pathological Internet Use
PIU.............	Performance and Innovation Unit
PIU.............	Peripheral Interface Unit (ELAL)
PIU.............	Photographic Interpretation Unit [Marine Corps]
PIU.............	Pilot Indicator Unit [Aviation] (IAA)
PIU.............	Pilot Information Utilization
PIU.............	Piura [Peru] [Airport symbol] (OAG)
PIU.............	Plug-In Unit
PIU.............	Polymerase-Inducing Unit
PIU.............	Power Integration Unit (SSD)
PIU.............	Power Intercept Unit [Military] (CAAL)
PIU.............	Power Interface Unit (MCD)
PIU.............	Private Lines Unlimited (EA)
PIU.............	Process Input Unit [Computer science] (BUR)
PIU.............	Process Interface Unit
PIU.............	Processor Interface Unit (SAUS)
PIU.............	Programmable Interface Unit (SAUS)
PIU.............	Programmer Interface Unit (MCD)
PIU.............	Public Inspection Unit (SAUS)
PIU.............	Pyrotechnic Initiator Unit (MCD)
PiU.............	University of the Philippines, Quezon City, Philippines [Library symbol] [Library of Congress] (LCLS)
PIUC	Parametric Image Up-Conversion (SAUS)
PIUG	Parti Independantiste de l'Unite Guyanaise [Pro-Independence Party of Guyanese Unity] [Political party] (PPW)
PIUMP	Plug-In Unit Mounting Panel
PIUS	Process Inherent Ultimately Safe [Nuclear reactor]
PI/USA........	Packaging Institute, United States of America [Later, PI/INT'L] (EA)
PIV.............	Parainfluenza Virus
PIV.............	Particle Image Velocimeter (ABAC)
PIV.............	Particle Image Velocimetry [Fluid dynamics]
PIV.............	Peak Inverse Voltage [RADAR]
PIV.............	Peripheral Intravenous [Line] [Pharmacology] (DAVI)
PIV.............	Personal Indentification Verification
PIV.............	Pick Inverse Voltage [Electronics] (ECII)
PIV.............	Piva [Solomon Islands] [Seismograph station code, US Geological Survey] [Closed] (SEIS)
PIV.............	Pivot [Automotive engineering]
PIV.............	Planet in View [NASA]
PIV.............	Plug-In Valve
PIV.............	Positive Infinitely Variable
PIV.............	Post Indicator Valve
PIV.............	Primate Immunodeficiency Virus [Medicine] (MELL)

PIV	Product Inspection Verification
PIV	Propellant Isolation Valve
PIV	Scotland School for Veterans' Children, Scotland, PA [OCLC symbol] (OCLC)
PIV4	Plantago Virus 4 [Plant pathology]
PIVAD	Product Improvement Vulcan Air Defense (MCD)
PIVADS	Product Improved Vulcan Air Defense System (MCD)
PIVD	Protruded Intervertebral Disc [Medicine]
PIVED	Plasma-Injection Vacuum Energy Diverter
PIV Gear	Positive Infinitely Variable Gear (SAUS)
PIVH	Peripheral Intravenous Hyperalimentation [Medicine] (MELL)
PIVI	Parainfluenza Virus Infection [Medicine] (MELL)
PIVKA	Protein-Induced by Vitamin K Antagonist (DB)
PIVKA	Protein in Vitamin K Absence (AAMN)
PIVN	Public Interest Video Network/New Voices Radio (EA)
PIVOT	Planning and Implementing Vocational Readiness in Occupational Therapy
PIVOT	Programmers Interactive Verification and Organizational Tool (SAUS)
PIVR	Pacemaker-Induced Ventricular Rate [Cardiology] (CPH)
PIVS	Particle-Induced Visual Sensations
PIVT	Product Improvement Verification Test
PIVT	Production Improvement Verification Test
PIVX	Plantain Virus X [Plant pathology]
PIW	Period of Incapacity for Work (DI)
PIW	Photo Imaging Workstation (SAUS)
PIW	Plastic Insulated Wire
PIW	Ports and Inland Waterways
PIW	Program Interrupt Word
PIW	Woodhaven Center, Philadelphia, PA [OCLC symbol] (OCLC)
PIWC	Petroleum Industry War Council
PIWG	Permanent Interoperability Working Group (SAUS)
PIWG	Product Improvement Working Group [Military] (AFIT)
PIWI	No Pilot Balloon Observation Due to High, or Gusty, Surface Wind [NWS] (FAAC)
PIWT	Partially Impacted Wisdom Tooth (MELL)
PIWWC	Planetary Initiative for the World We Choose (EA)
PIX	Avenue Entertainment Grp [AMEX symbol] (SG)
PIX	Parallel Interface Extender [Computer science] (IAA)
PIX	Pico Island [Azores] [Airport symbol] (OAG)
PIX	Picture
PIX	Picture Rocks, PA [Location identifier] [FAA] (FAAL)
PIX	Pinxit [He, or She, Painted It] [Latin] (ROG)
PIX	Proton-Induced X-Ray Analysis
PIX	Youth Development Center, Loysville, Loysville, PA [OCLC symbol] (OCLC)
PIX Analysis	Proton Induced X-ray Analysis (SAUS)
Pix Aud	Pixley on Auditors [8th ed.] [1901] [A publication] (DLA)
PIXE	Particle [or Proton]-Induced X-Ray Emission
PIXE	Particle-Induced X-Ray Excitation (SAUS)
PIXE	Photon-Induced X-Ray Emission (SAUS)
pixel	Picture Element (AEBE)
Pixel	Picture Element [Computer science] (ITCA)
pixel	Picture Element (SHCU)
PIXEL	Picture Element [Single element of resolution in image processing]
pixelsat	Picture Element Satellite (ADWA)
PIXES	Particle-Induced X-Ray Emission Spectroscopy (EDCT)
PIXI	Professional Industrial X-Ray Imaging (SAUS)
PIXIE	Particle-Induced X-ray Emission (SAUS)
PIXNET	Parallel Interface Extender Network (SAUS)
PIXR	Pixar [NASDAQ symbol] (TTSB)
PIXSYS	Pictorial Information Extraction System (SAUS)
PIXT	PixTech, Inc. [NASDAQ symbol] (SAG)
PixTech	PixTech, Inc. [Associated Press] (SAG)
PIY	Pembroke Imperial Yeomanry [British military] (DMA)
PIY	Personality Inventory for Youth [Test] (TMMY)
PIY	Youth Development Center, New Castle, New Castle, PA [OCLC symbol] (OCLC)
PIZ	Pizaz European [British] [FAA designator] (FAAC)
PIZ	Point Lay [Alaska] [Airport symbol] (OAG)
PIZ	Point Lay, AK [Location identifier] [FAA] (FAAL)
PIZ	Public Information Zone (HEAS)
PIZ	Youth Development Center, Waynesburg, Waynesburg, PA [OCLC symbol] (OCLC)
pizz	Pizzicato [Plucking] [Italian] [Music] (WDAA)
PIZZ	Pizzicato [Plucked] [Music]
PizzaInn	Pizza Inn, Inc. [Associated Press] (SAG)
PJ	Air St. Pierre [ICAO designator] (AD)
PJ	Bombay High Court Printed Judgments [1869-1900] [India] [A publication] (DLA)
PJ	Netherlands Antilles [International civil aircraft marking] (ODBW)
PJ	Pajamas
PJ	Pancreatic Juice [Medicine] (MELL)
PJ	Panel Jack
PJ	Parnelli Jones [Race car driver]
PJ	Parteijargon [Party Language] [German]
PJ	Participating Jurisdiction
PJ	Peripheral Jet (AAG)
PJ	Petajoule (ADA)
PJ	Peutz-Jeghers [Syndrome] [Medicine] (DB)
PJ	Picojoule [Logic gate efficiency measure] (MDG)
PJ	Plasma Jet (AAG)
PJ	Plastic Jacket
PJ	Police Judge (SAUS)
PJ	Police Justice
PJ	Porcelain Jacket [Dentistry] (MELL)

PJ	Possible Jobs [Test] [Psychology]
PJ	Presiding Judge
PJ	Presiding Probate Judge [British] (ROG)
PJ	Prince of Jerusalem [Freemasonry]
PJ	Probate Judge
PJ	Procurement Justification [Navy]
PJ	Project Jonah [Defunct] (EA)
PJ	Puisne Judge [Australia]
PJ	Pulsejet
PJ	Purchases Journal [Accounting]
PJA	Abington Library Society, Jenkintown, PA [Library symbol] [Library of Congress] [Obsolete] (LCLS)
PJA	Pakistan Jute Association (SAUS)
PJA	Pipe Jacking Association [British] (DBA)
PJA	Proper Job Analysis (COE)
PJAFC	P. J. Allman Fan Club (EA)
PJAL	Progressive Jewish Activism List [An association]
PJAIG	Alverthorpe Gallery, Rosenwald Collection, Jenkintown, PA [Library symbol] [Library of Congress] (LCLS)
PJAM	PJ America, Inc. [NASDAQ symbol] (SAG)
PJ Amer	PJ America, Inc. [Associated Press] (SAG)
PJAS	Project Associates (SAUS)
PJB	Pad Journal Bearing
PJB	Premature Junctional Beat [Cardiology]
PJBD	Permanent Joint Board on Defense [US, Canada]
PJC	Jean Coutu Group (PJC), Inc. [Toronto Stock Exchange symbol]
PJC	Paducah Junior College [Kentucky]
PJC	Paris Junior College [Texas]
PJC	Pensacola Junior College [Florida]
PJC	Perkinston Junior College [Mississippi]
PJC	Piper Jaffray Companies [NYSE symbol] (SPSG)
PJC	Polydox Jewish Federation (SAUS)
PJC	Post Junior College [Connecticut]
PJC	Poteau Junior College [Oklahoma]
PJC	Pratt Junior College [Kansas]
PJC	Premature Junctional Contractions [Cardiology] (DMAA)
PJC	Premature Junctional Tachycardia (SAUS)
PJC	University of Pittsburgh, Johnstown, Johnstown, PA [OCLC symbol] (OCLC)
PJCTL	Projectile (MSA)
Pjctvs	Projectavision, Inc. [Associated Press] (SAG)
Pjctvsn	Projectavision, Inc. [Associated Press] (SAG)
PJD	Pedro Dome [Alaska] [Seismograph station code, US Geological Survey] [Closed] (SEIS)
PJE	Parachute Jumping Exercise
PJE	Private Jet Expeditions, Inc. [ICAO designator] (FAAC)
PJE	Project Engineer
PJE	Pulse Jet Engine
PJES	Photojet Edge Sensor
PJF	Peripheral Jet (Flat-Bottom)
PJF	Pharmaceutical Journal Formulary (ROG)
PJF	Pin Jointed Framework
PJF	Pin Jounted Framework (SAUS)
PJFS	Philip Jose Farmer Society (EA)
PJG	Panjgur [Pakistan] [Airport symbol] (OAG)
PJG	Potts Junction [Guam] [Seismograph station code, US Geological Survey] (SEIS)
PJH	Piper, Jr., H. E., Philadelphia PA [STAC]
PJH	PLRS/JTIDS [Position Location Reporting System/Joint Tactical Information Distribution System] Hybrid (MCD)
PJH	PLRS/JTIDS Hybrid System (SAUS)
PJHI	PLRS/JTIDS [Position Location Reporting System/Joint Tactical Information Distribution System] Hybrid Interface
PJI	Parachute Jump Instructor [Military] [British] (INF)
PJI	Pattern Jury Instructions [A publication]
PJI	Personnel Journal Index [Personnel Journal] [Information service or system] (CRD)
PJI	Point Judith, RI [Location identifier] [FAA] (FAAL)
PJI	Proper Job Instruction (COE)
PJILMCC	Philip C. Jessup International Law Moot Court Competition (EA)
PJIT	Parts Just in Time
PJL	Passive Jammer Location (SAUS)
P JI	Pharmaceutical Journal [A publication] (ROG)
PJL	Power Jets, Limited
PJL	Printer Job Language [Computer science]
PJLB	Lower Burma Printed Judgments [A publication] (DLA)
PJM	Pennsylvania-Jersey-Maryland [Electric power pool]
PJM	Pennsylvania-New Jersey-Maryland (SAUS)
PJM	Polymer Jell Material
PJM	Positive Joint Mobilization [Medicine] (DMAA)
PJM	Postjunctional Membrane
PJM	Power Jets Memorandum
PJM	Project Manager [Military]
PJMA	Pakistan Jute Mills Association (SAUS)
PJM Interconnection	Pennsylvania-New Jersey-Maryland Interconnection (SAUS)
PJM Power Pool	Pennsylvania-New Jersey-Maryland Power Pool (SAUS)
PJN	Fort Lauderdale, FL [Location identifier] [FAA] (FAAL)
PJN	Posteriojugalis Nerve (SAUS)
PJNF	Project Join Normal Form (SAUS)
PJo	Cambria County Library System, Johnstown, PA [Library symbol] [Library of Congress] (LCLS)
PJO	Pioneer Jupiter Orbit [NASA]
PJON	Johnston Island/Johnston Atoll [Johnston Island] [ICAO location identifier] (ICLI)
PJOP	Preliminary Joint Operation Procedure (KSC)

PJoU	University of Pittsburgh at Johnstown, Johnstown, PA [*Library symbol*] [*Library of Congress*] (LCLS)
PJP	Pancreatic Juice Protein [*Medicine*] (DMAA)
PJP	Probate Judge of the Peace (GEAB)
PJPC	Plug/Jack Patch Cord
PJPEG	Progressive JPEG (SAUS)
PJR	Peoria, IL [*Location identifier*] [*FAA*] (FAAL)
PJR	Peterson, J. Robert, New York NY [*STAC*]
PJR	Philadelphia Journalism Review [*A publication*]
PJR	Pipe Joint Record (DNAB)
PJR	Port Jersey [*AAR code*]
PJR	Power Jets Report
P Jr & H	Patton, Jr., and Heath's Reports [*Virginia Special Court of Appeals*] [*A publication*] (DLA)
PJS	Jet Aviation, Business Jets AG [*Switzerland*] [*ICAO designator*] (FAAC)
PJS	Newport News, VA [*Location identifier*] [*FAA*] (FAAL)
PJ's	Pajamas [*Slang*]
PJ's	Paramedic Jumpers
PJS	Peripheral Jet (Skegs)
PJS	Peritoneojugular Shunt [*Medicine*] (DB)
PJS	Peutz-Jeghers Syndrome [*Oncology*]
PJ's	Physical Jerks [*Exercise*] [*Slang*] [*British*] (DSUE)
PJS	Piezojunction Sensor
PJS	Plug and Jack Set
PJS	Production Job Sheet
PJSOR	Proposed Joint Services Operational Requirement (SAUS)
PJSS	PACAF [*Pacific Air Forces*] Jungle Survival School (AFM)
PJST	Peace & Justice Studies (SAUS)
PJT	Paroxysmal Junctional Tachycardia [*Cardiology*]
PJT	Practical Job Training (MCD)
PJT	Pulse Jitter Tester
PJTN	Projection (MSA)
PJTP	Portable Job Ticket Processor (RALS)
PJTR	Projector (MSA)
PJTV	Projectavision, Inc. [*NASDAQ symbol*] (SAG)
PJTVP	Projectavision $0.40 Cv'B'Pfd [*NASDAQ symbol*] (TTSB)
PJTVW	Projectavision Inc. Wrrt [*NASDAQ symbol*] (TTSB)
PJU	Juniata College, Huntingdon, PA [*OCLC symbol*] (OCLC)
PJU	Physician's Journal Update [*Television program*]
PJV	Pump Jet Vehicle
PJVT	Paroxysmal Junctional-Ventricular Tachycardia [*Medicine*] (MEDA)
PJYLARC	Penn Jersey Young Ladies Amateur Radio Certificate (SAUS)
PK	Central Parking [*NYSE symbol*] (TTSB)
PK	Central Parking Corp. [*NYSE symbol*] (SAG)
pK	Dissociation Constant [*Chemistry*] (DAVI)
PK	Kill Probability (SAUS)
pK'	Negative Log of the Dissociation Constant [*Medicine*]
PK	Pack (AAG)
PK	Package [*Shipping*] (MCD)
PK	Pakistan [*ANSI two-letter standard code*] (CNC)
pk	Pakistan [*IYRU nationality code*] [*MARC country of publication code*] [*Library of Congress*] (LCCP)
Pk	Park (DD)
pk	Park (VRA)
PK	Park [*or Parking*]
PK	Parrot-Kaufmann (DB)
PK	Paterson-Kelly [*Syndrome*] [*Medicine*] (DB)
Pk	Peak [*Valve*] (NAKS)
Pk	Peak (NTIO)
PK	Peak [*Maps and charts*]
pK	Peak Value [*Computer science*]
PK	Peck (AAG)
pk	Peck (DMAA)
PK	Penetrating Keratoplasty [*Ophthalmology*] (DAVI)
PK	Pericardial Knock [*Medicine*] (DB)
PK	Peter King [*Afro-jazz band*]
PK	Pharmacokinetic
PK	Phileleftheron Komma [*Liberal Party*] [*Greek*] [*Political party*] (PPE)
PK	Pig Kidney [*Medicine*] (DMAA)
PK	Pike
Pk	Pink (SAUS)
PK	Piringer-Kuschinka [*Syndrome*] [*Medicine*] (DB)
PK	Place Kicker [*Football*] (GOBB)
P$_K$	Plasma Potassium [*Biochemistry*] (DAVI)
PK	Pokhvala Knige [*A publication*]
PK	Pole Cat [*Slang*]
PK	Polyketone (EDCT)
PK	Polymerization Kinetics (SAUS)
PK	Position Keeper
PK	Posta Kutusu [*Postbox*] [*Turkish*] (EY)
PK	Prausnitz-Kuestner [*Reaction*] [*Immunology*]
PK	Prausnitz-Kunstner [*Reaction or Transfer Test*] [*Medicine*] (DAVI)
PK	Preacher's Kid [*Slang*]
PK	Preknock (SAUS)
PK	Pridie Kalendas [*The Day before the Calends*] [*Latin*]
PK	Primary Key [*Computer science*] (PCM)
PK	Principal Keeper [*Slang for a warden*]
PK	Printing Key (SAUS)
PK	Probability of Kill (MCD)
PK	Probable Kill (SAUS)
PK	Programmed Keyboard (SAUS)
PK	Prophets and Kings (BJA)
PK	Protection Key (VLIE)
PK	Protein Kinase [*Also, PKase*] [*An enzyme*]
Pk	Psychokinesis (DIPS)
PK	Psychokinesis
PK	Psychokinetic (DB)
PK	Public Key (VLIE)
PK	Pyruvate Kinase [*An enzyme*]
PK	Soviet Light Machine Gun
PK	West Irian [*Aircraft nationality and registration mark*] (FAAC)
P-K4	Pawn to King Four [*Standard opening to a game of chess. Pawn is moved to the fourth square in front of the king*]
PKA	Equator Airlines Ltd. [*Kenya*] [*ICAO designator*] (FAAC)
PKA	Napaskiak [*Alaska*] [*Airport symbol*] (OAG)
PKA	Napaskiak, AK [*Location identifier*] [*FAA*] (FAAL)
pKa	Negative Log of Dissociation Constant [*Medicine*] (DAVI)
PKA	Paul Kagan Associates, Inc. [*Information service or system*] [*Telecommunications*] (IID)
PKA	Pi Kappa Alpha [*Fraternity*]
PKA	Polk Audio [*AMEX symbol*] (SAG)
PKA	Prekallikrein Activator [*Medicine*] (MELL)
PKA	Primary Knock-on-Atom (MCD)
PKA	Professional Karate Association [*Defunct*] (EA)
PKA	Prokininogenase [*An enzyme*] (MAE)
PKA	Protein Kinase A [*An enzyme*]
PKA	Public Key Algorithm [*Computer science*]
PKAD	Accumulated Dose Special Process (SAUS)
PkAF	Pakistani Air Force
PKAFA	PKA [*Professional Karate Association*] Fighters Association [*Defunct*] (EA)
PKAR	Protein Kinase Activation Ratio [*Medicine*] (DMAA)
PKAS	Parti Kadazan Asli Sabah [*Malaysia*] [*Political party*] (FEA)
PKase	Protein Kinase [*Also, PK*] [*An enzyme*]
PKAWA	Pocket Knife Ancillary Workers' Association [*A union*] [*British*]
PKB	Parkersburg [*West Virginia*] [*Airport symbol*] (OAG)
PKB	Parkersburg, WV [*Location identifier*] [*FAA*] (FAAL)
PKB	Photoelectric Keyboard
PKB	Portable Keyboard
PKB	Protein Kinase B [*An enzyme*]
PKB	Public Key Block (VLIE)
PKBS	Preschool and Kindergarten Behavior Scales [*Test*] (TMMY)
PKC	Cocoa, FL [*Location identifier*] [*FAA*] (FAAL)
PKC	Peckham Road [*California*] [*Seismograph station code, US Geological Survey*] (SEIS)
PKC	Phuket [*Thailand*] [*Airport symbol*] (AD)
PKC	Position Keeping Computer
PKC	Problem-Knowledge Coupler (DMAA)
PKC	Protein Kinase C [*An enzyme*]
PKC	Public Key Cryptography
PKCS	Public Key Cryptographic System (VLIE)
PKCS	Public Key Cryptography Standards [*Telecommunications service*]
PKD	Pac Ed Systems Corp. [*Vancouver Stock Exchange symbol*]
PKD	Packed (IAA)
pkd	Packed
PKD	Parker Drilling [*NYSE symbol*] (TTSB)
PKD	Parker Drilling Co. [*NYSE symbol*] (SPSG)
PKD	Park Rapids, MN [*Location identifier*] [*FAA*] (FAAL)
PKD	Partially Knocked Down [*Consignment*] [*Shipping*] (DS)
PKD	Partly Knocked Down (SAUS)
PKD	Philip K. Dick [*Science fiction writer*]
PKD	Pi Kappa Delta [*Society*]
PKD	Polycystic Kidney Disease [*Medicine*]
PKD	Programmable Keyboard and Display [*Computer science*] (NASA)
PKD	Programmable Keyboard Display (SAUS)
PKD	Proliferative Kidney Disease [*Medicine*] (DMAA)
PKD	Pyruvate Kinase Deficiency [*Medicine*] (MELL)
PKDB	Partai Kebang-Saan Demokratik Brunei [*Brunei National Democratic Party*] [*Political party*] (EY)
PKDG	Professional Knitwear Designers Guild
PKDOM	Pack for Domestic Use
PKD PDR	Packed Powder (WGA)
PKDS	Philip K. Dick Society [*Defunct*] (EA)
PKE	Pacific Kenridge [*Vancouver Stock Exchange symbol*]
PKE	Park Electrochemical [*NYSE symbol*] (TTSB)
PKE	Park Electrochemical Corp. [*NYSE symbol*] (SPSG)
PKE	Parker, CA [*Location identifier*] [*FAA*] (FAAL)
PKE	Parkes [*Australia*] [*Airport symbol*] (OAG)
Pke	Pike (PROS)
PKE	Positive Kinetic Energy [*Automotive emissions*]
PKE	Public-Key Encryption [*Microcomputer technology*]
PKF	Pakistan Investment Fd [*NYSE symbol*] (TTSB)
PKF	Pakistan Investment Fund [*NYSE symbol*] (SPSG)
PKF	Park Falls, WI [*Location identifier*] [*FAA*] (FAAL)
PKF	Parkfield Array [*California*] [*Seismograph station code, US Geological Survey*] (SEIS)
PKF	Permanent Kidney Failure (MELL)
PKF	Phagocytosis and Killing Function [*Immunology*] (AAMN)
PKF	Phosphofructokinase (DB)
PKF	Polarity Correlation Function (IAA)
PKF	Primary Kidney Fold
PKFC	Princess Kitty Fan Club (EA)
pkg	Package (WDMC)
PKG	Package
PKG	Packaging (SAUS)
PKG	Packaging Corp. America [*NYSE symbol*] (SG)
Pkg	Packing (DS)
PKG	Parking (KSC)
PKG	Phonocardiogram [*Cardiology*]

PKG B/M...... Package Bill of Material (SAUS)
PKGD........... Packaged (IAA)
pkge............. Package (WDMC)
PKGE............ Package
Pkg instr...... Packing Instruction (DS)
PKGNG......... Packaging
PKG-POL...... Packaged POL [*Petroleum, Oils and Lubricants*] (DOMA)
Pkgs............ Packages (EBF)
PKG SPEC.... Packaging Specifications (SAUS)
Pkg Technol Sci... Packaging Technology and Science (SAUS)
PKH.......... Park Hill [*California*] [*Seismograph station code, US Geological Survey*] (SEIS)
PKH........... Probability of a Kill Given a Hit [*Military*] (DNAB)
PKHOW....... Pack Howitzer [*Marine Corps*]
PKI............. Parkland Industries Ltd. [*Toronto Stock Exchange symbol*]
PKI............. Partai Katolik Indonesia [*Catholic Party of Indonesia*] [*Political party*]
PKI............. Partai Komunis Indonesia [*Communist Party of Indonesia*] [*Political party*]
PKI............. Partai Kristen Indonesia [*Christian Party of Indonesia*] [*Political party*]
PKI............. Potato Kallikrein Inhibitor [*Medicine*] (DMAA)
PKI............. Protein Kinase Inhibitor [*Biochemistry*]
PKI............. Public Key Infrastructure (AGLO)
PKI............. Public Key Infrastructure (SEWL)
PKI............. Public Key Infrastructure (VLIE)
PKI............. Pyruvate Kinase, Liver Type [*Medicine*] (DMAA)
PKK............. Kurdish Workers' Party [*Turkey*] [*Political party*] (PD)
PKK............. Kurdistan Workers' Party
PKK............. Pakokku [*Myanmar*] [*Airport symbol*] (OAG)
PKK............. Porkkala [*Finland*] [*Seismograph station code, US Geological Survey*] (SEIS)
PKK............. Protein Kinase K [*An enzyme*]
PkKP............ Pakistan National Scientific and Documentation Center, Karachi, Pakistan [*Library symbol*] [*Library of Congress*] (LCLS)
PKL............. Parklane Technologies, Inc. [*Vancouver Stock Exchange symbol*]
PKL............. Pi Kappa Lambda [*Society*]
PKL............. Possum Kingdom Lake (SAUS)
PK-LT........... Psychokinesis on Living Targets
PKM............. Packmaster [*Army*] (WGA)
PKM............. Perigee Kick Motor (MCD)
PKMA........... Eniwetok [*Marshall Islands*] [*ICAO location identifier*] (ICLI)
PK-MB........... Psychokinetic Metal-Bending [*Parapsychology*]
PKMJ............ Majuro [*Marshall Islands*] [*ICAO location identifier*] (ICLI)
PKMKCMD... Perhaps...Kids Meeting Kids Can Make a Difference (EA)
Pkmr............. Packmaster [*Army*]
PKMS........... Pertubohan Kebangsaan Melayu Singapura [*Singapore Malays' National Organization*] [*Political party*] (FEA)
PKN............. Aspen, CO [*Location identifier*] [*FAA*] (FAAL)
PKN............. Pangkalanbuun [*Indonesia*] [*Airport symbol*] (OAG)
PKN............. Parkinsonism [*Medicine*] (DMAA)
PKN............. Pauken [*Kettledrums*]
PKN............. Perkin-Elmer [*NYSE symbol*] (TTSB)
PKN............. Perkin-Elmer Corp. [*NYSE symbol*] (SPSG)
PKNG HSE... Packing House [*Freight*]
PKO............. Parakou [*Benin*] [*Airport symbol*] (OAG)
PKO............. Peace-Keeping Operation (MCD)
PKO............. Perdant par Knockout [*Losing by a Knockout*] [*French*]
PKOH........... Park-Ohio Indus [*NASDAQ symbol*] (TTSB)
PKOH........... Park Ohio Industries [*NASDAQ symbol*] (SAG)
PKOH........... Park-Ohio Industries, Inc. [*NASDAQ symbol*] (NQ)
PKP............. Palestiner Komunistische Partei [*Palestine Communist Party*] [*Political party*] (BJA)
PKP............. Partido Komunista ng Pilipinas [*Communist Party of the Philippines*] [*Political party*] (PPW)
PKP............. Penetrating Keratoplasty [*Ophthalmology*]
PKP............. Perustuslaillinen Kansanpuolue [*Constitutional People's Party*] [*Finland*] [*Political party*] (PPE)
PKP............. Phi Kappa Phi [*Honor society*] (AEE)
PKP............. Polskie Koleje Panstwowe [*Polish State Railways*]
PKP............. Praktische Krankenpflege (SAUS)
PKP............. Predicted Kill Point (SAUS)
PKP............. Preknock Pulse
PKP............. Public Key Partners (VLIE)
PKP............. Pukapuka [*French Polynesia*] [*Airport symbol*] (OAG)
PKP............. Purple-K-Powder
pKp............. purple K powder (SAUS)
PKPA........... Parental Kidnapping Prevention Act (BARN)
PK/PK........... Peak-to-Peak (MCD)
PKpP............ Pennwalt Corp., King Of Prussia, PA [*Library symbol*] [*Library of Congress*] (LCLS)
PKPS........... [*The*] Poughkeepsie Savings Bank FSB [*Poughkeepsie, NY*] [*NASDAQ symbol*] (NQ)
PKPS........... Poughkeepsie Svgs Bank [*NASDAQ symbol*] (TTSB)
PKQ............. Dallas-Fort Worth, TX [*Location identifier*] [*FAA*] (FAAL)
PKR............. Packer (WGA)
PKR............. Phased Knee Rehabilitation (DMAA)
PKR............. Picker
PKR............. P. K. Le Roux Dam [*South Africa*] [*Seismograph station code, US Geological Survey*] (SEIS)
PKR............. Pokhara [*Nepal*] [*Airport symbol*] (OAG)
PKR............. Polycystic Kidney Research Foundation (PAZ)
PKRDD......... Pravitel'stvennaya Komissiya po Raketam Dalnego Deistviya [*State Commission for the Study of the Problems of Long-Range Rockets*] [*Former USSR*]
PKs............. Bayard Taylor Memorial Library, Kennett Square, PA [*Library symbol*] [*Library of Congress*] (LCLS)

PKS.............. Packs of Cigarettes Smoked
PKS.............. Parti Kongres Sarawak [*Malaysia*] [*Political party*] (EY)
PKS.............. Perigee Kick Stage (ACAE)
PKS.............. Phi Kappa Sigma [*Fraternity*]
PKS.............. Photo-Kit System (SAUS)
PKS.............. Polyketide Synthase [*An enzyme*]
PKSAP........ Psychiatric Knowledge and Skills Self-Assessment Program (SAUS)
PKSEA......... Packed for Overseas Use (SAUS)
PKSEA......... Pack for Overseas
PKSh........... Partia Komuniste e Shqiperise [*Communist Party of Albania*] [*Later, PPSh*] [*Political party*] (PPE)
PKSI............ Primus Knowledge Solutions [*NASDAQ symbol*] (SG)
PKsL........... Longwood Gardens Library, Kennett Square, PA [*Library symbol*] [*Library of Congress*] (LCLS)
PKSRP......... Possum Kingdom State Recreation Park (SAUS)
PKSS........... Probability of Kill Single Shot (MCD)
pkt............. Packet (SHCU)
PKT............. Packet
PKT............. Phase Keying Technique
PKT............. Phi Kappa Tau [*Fraternity*]
PKT............. Pittsburgh Theological Seminary, Pittsburgh, PA [*OCLC symbol*] (OCLC)
PKT............. Pocket (MSA)
PKTF............ Printing and Kindred Trades Federation (SAUS)
PKTN............ Pinkerton's, Inc. [*NASDAQ symbol*] (SAG)
PKTR............ Packeteer, Inc. [*NASDAQ symbol*] (SG)
PKU............. Pekanbaru [*Indonesia*] [*Airport symbol*] (OAG)
PKU............. Phenylketonuria [*Congenital metabolism disorder*] [*Medicine*]
PKU............. Pianoforte Keymakers' Union [*British*]
PKU-P........... PKU [*Phenylketonuria*] Parents (EA)
PKuS........... Kutztown State College, Kutztown, PA [*Library symbol*] [*Library of Congress*] (LCLS)
PKV............. Killed Poliomyelitis Vaccine [*Immunology*] (MAE)
PKV............. Peak Kilovolt (SAUS)
PkV............. Peak Kilovolts
PKV............. Port Lavaka, TX [*Location identifier*] [*FAA*] (FAAL)
PK/VAL......... Peak-to-Valley (SAUS)
PKVL............ Pikeville National [*NASDAQ symbol*] (TTSB)
PKVL............ Pikeville National Corp. [*NASDAQ symbol*] (NQ)
PKW............. Kenosha, WI [*Location identifier*] [*FAA*] (FAAL)
PKW............. Personenkraftwagen [*Automobile*] [*German*]
PKW............. Selebi-Phikwe [*Botswana*] [*Airport symbol*] (OAG)
PKWA........... Kwajalein [*Marshall Islands*] [*ICAO location identifier*] (ICLI)
PKWAY......... Parkway (MSA)
P/kWh.......... Pennies per Kilowatt Hour (SAUS)
Pkwy............ Parkway (ASC)
PKWY........... Parkway (KSC)
PKWY........... [*The*] Parkway Co. [*NASDAQ symbol*] (NQ)
PKWYS........ Parkways [*Commonly used*] (OPSA)
PKX............. Pohang Iron & Steel ADS [*NYSE symbol*] (TTSB)
PKX............. Pohang Iron & Steel Co., Ltd. [*NYSE symbol*] (SAG)
PKY............. Pak Lay [*Laos*] [*Airport symbol*] (AD)
PKY............. Palangkaraya [*Indonesia*] [*Airport symbol*] (OAG)
Pky............. Parkway (DD)
PKY............. Parkway (MCD)
PKY............. Pecky (WGA)
Pky............. Pecky (WPI)
PKZ............. Pakse [*Laos*] [*Airport symbol*] (AD)
PKZ............. Pensacola, FL [*Location identifier*] [*FAA*] (FAAL)
PKZIP.......... Phil Katz's Zip (VLIE)
PL............. Aero Peru [*ICAO designator*] (AD)
PL............. Front Line [*Revolutionary group*] [*Italy*]
PL............. Lancaster County Library, Lancaster, PA [*Library symbol*] [*Library of Congress*] (LCLS)
PL............. Packaging List (SAUS)
PL............. Packing List
PL............. Padlock (AAG)
PL............. Pail
PL............. Palm Leaf [*Reaction*] [*Medicine*]
PL............. Pamphlet Law (SAUS)
PL............. Pamphlet Laws [*A publication*] (DLA)
PL............. Panel Left [*Nuclear energy*] (NRCH)
p/l............. panial loss (SAUS)
PL............. Panoramic Lens (SAUS)
PL............. Paperleg [*A favored student*] [*Teen slang*]
PL............. Paper Life Ltd. [*British*]
PL............. Paper Loss (MHDW)
PL............. Paradise Lost (SAUS)
PL............. Parameter List (SAUS)
PL............. Parish Line R. R. [*AAR code*]
PL............. Parity Low Bit (VLIE)
PL............. Partial Loss [*Insurance*]
PL............. Partido Liberal [*Liberal Party*] [*Peru*] [*Political party*] (EY)
PL............. Partido Liberal [*Liberal Party*] [*Panama*] [*Political party*] (PPW)
PL............. Partido Liberal [*Liberal Party*] [*Honduras*] [*Political party*]
PL............. Partido Liberal [*Liberal Party*] [*Paraguay*] [*Political party*] (PPW)
PL............. Partido Liberal [*Liberal Party*] [*Portugal*] [*Political party*] (PPE)
PL............. Partido Liberal [*Liberal Party*] [*Colombia*] [*Political party*] (EY)
PL............. Partido Liberal [*Liberal Party*] [*Spain*] [*Political party*] (PPE)
PL............. Partido Libertador [*Liberating Party*] [*Brazil*] [*Political party*]
PL............. Parti Liberal [*Liberal Party (1974-1979)*] [*Belgium*] [*Political party*] (PPE)
PL............. Parting Line [*Castings*] (AAG)
PL............. Parts List
PL............. Party Line (SAUS)

PL	Passenger Liability [*Insurance*] (BARN)
PL	Pastoral Lease (SAUS)
PL	Patch Loader (SAUS)
PL	Patent Licence (SAUS)
PL	Patent Location (NITA)
PL	Patent Log (SAUS)
PL	Path Length (SAUS)
PL	Path Link (SAUS)
PL	Path Loss [*Communications*]
PL	Patriot League (PSS)
PL	Patrol Land [*Aviation*]
PL	Patrologiae Cursus. Series Latina [*A publication*] (OCD)
Pl	Paul (BJA)
PL	Paulist League (EA)
P/L	Pay Load (ACAE)
PL	Payload [*NASA*] (KSC)
PL	Payload Length (SAUS)
PL	Paymaster-Lieutenant [*Navy*] [*British*]
PL	Peak Loss (IAA)
PL	Peanut Leafspot [*Plant pathology*]
PL	Pearl Language (SAUS)
PL	Pectate Lyase [*An enzyme*]
Pl	Pelagius [*Deceased, 1232*] [*Authority cited in pre-1607 legal work*] (DSA)
PL	Pelusium Line [*Nile delta*] [*Geology*]
pl	Pencil (VRA)
PL	People for Life (EA)
PL	People's Lobby (EA)
PL	Perceived Level [*Noise*]
PL	Perception of Light
PL	Periodic Line (ELAL)
PL	Peroneus Longus [*Muscle*] [*Orthopedics*] (DAVI)
P/L	Personal Lines
PL	Personnel Laboratory [*Air Research and Development Command*] [*Air Force*] (AAG)
PL	Personnel Letters (SAUS)
PL	Petro-Lewis Corp. (EFIS)
PL	Petty Larceny
PL	Pharmacopoeia of London (SAUS)
PL	Phase Line
PL	Phase Locking (SAUS)
PL	Philosophical Library [*A publication*]
PL	Phlogopite (SAUS)
PL	Phone Line
PL	Phospholipid [*Biochemistry*]
PL	Photoconductor Lamp (IAA)
PL	Photolettering (DGA)
PL	Photolithography (SAUS)
PL	Photolocator (MCD)
PL	Photoluminescence
PL	Physical Layer (VLIE)
PL	Physical Limnology (SAUS)
pl	Piazza (VRA)
pl	Picoliter [*One trillionth of a liter*] (MAE)
PL	Pilatus Flugzeugwerke AG [*Switzerland*] [*ICAO aircraft manufacturer identifier*] (ICAO)
PL	Pile
PL	Pilot Lamp (ELAL)
PL	Pilot Lamp (TIMI)
PL	Pilot Line (SAUS)
PL	Pipeline
PL	Pipe Lines Act [*Town planning*] [*British*]
PL	Piping Load [*Nuclear energy*] (NRCH)
PL	Piping Loads (SAUS)
PL	Pitch Line (MSA)
Pl	Place (TBD)
pl	Place (VRA)
PL	Place
PL	Placebo [*Medicine*]
PL	Placental Lactogen [*Endocrinology*]
Pl	Plagioclase [*Lunar geology*]
PL	Plain (MSA)
PL	Plain Language [*As opposed to coded message*] [*Military*]
PL	Plans
PL	Plantagenet [*Genealogy*] (ROG)
PL	Plantar [*Related to the sole of the foot*] (DAVI)
pl	Plasma
Pl	Plasmodium [*The malarial parasite*] [*Infectious diseases*] (DAVI)
PL	Plaster (WGA)
PL	Plastic Laboratory [*Princeton University*] (MCD)
PL	Plastic Limit (IEEE)
PL	Plastic Surgery [*Medicine*]
pl	Plastid [*Botany*]
pl	Plate (DIAR)
PL	Plate (KSC)
PL	Plateau Length
PL	Plated (IAA)
pl	Platelet [*Hematology*] (MAE)
pl	Platelet Lactogen [*Hematology*] (DMAA)
PL	Platinum [*Chemistry*] (ROG)
Pl	Plato [*Fourth century BC*] [*Classical studies*] (OCD)
pl	Platoon (MILB)
PL	Platoon (NATG)
PL	Platoon Leader [*Military*] (INF)
PL	Platz [*Square*] [*German*] (EY)
pl	Platz (VRA)
PL	Players League [*Major league in baseball, 1890*]
pl	Plaza (VRA)
PL	PLC Capital LLC, Inc. [*NYSE symbol*] (SAG)
PL	Pleadings [*Legal shorthand*] (LWAP)
PL	Pleasure (ROG)
PL	[*The*] Plessey Co. Ltd. (MCD)
pl	Pleural [*Medicine*] (MAE)
Pl	Plexus (SAUS)
PL	Plimsoll Line [*Shipping*] (DAS)
PL	Ploshchad [*Square*] [*Russian*] (EY)
PL	Plotter
Pl	Plowden's English King's Bench Commentaries [*or Reports*] [*1550-80*] [*A publication*] (DLA)
PL	Plug (AAG)
PL	Plugged (SAUS)
PL	Plume [*Numismatics*]
pl	Plural (ODBW)
PL	Plural
pl	Plus (ELAL)
PL	Pluto (SAUS)
PL	Plymouth [*Postcode*] (ODBW)
PL	Poet Laureate
PL	Poetry London [*A publication*] [*British*]
Pl	Poiseuille [*Unit of dynamic viscosity*]
PL	Poland [*ANSI two-letter standard code*] (CNC)
pl	Poland [*MARC country of publication code*] [*Library of Congress*] (LCCP)
Pl	Poland (MILB)
PL	Polarized Light
PL	Policy Loan
PL	Poly-L-lysine [*Also, PLL*] [*Biochemical analysis*]
PL	Poor Law [*A publication*] (DLA)
PL	Portable Low-Power [*Reactor*] (NRCH)
PL	Port Line [*Steamship*] (MHDW)
PL	Position Line [*Navigation*]
PL	Position Location [*DoD*]
PL	Post Landing [*NASA*] (KSC)
PL	Post Laundry [*Army*]
PL	Powered Lift (SAUS)
PL	Power Line (IAA)
PL	Power Loading (IAA)
PL	Power Locks (BARN)
PL	Prayers for Life (EA)
PL	Prelaunch (NASA)
PL	Preliminary Leaf [*Bibliography*]
P/L	Presentation Label [*Publishing*]
PL	Presentation Layer (SAUS)
PL	Presley Labs [*Vancouver Stock Exchange symbol*]
PL	Pressurizer Level (IEEE)
PL	Price Level [*Economics*]
PL	Price List
PL	Primary Leading [*Photography*] (DGA)
PL	Primrose League [*British*] (DI)
PL	Prince Line [*Steamship*] (MHDW)
PL	Princess Louise's Sutherland and Argyll Highlanders [*Military*] [*British*] (ROG)
PL	Private Label [*Business term*]
PL	Private Line
PL	Probabilistic Logic (SAUS)
PL	Probability of Leakage (ACAE)
PL	Procedural Language (PCM)
PL	Procedure Library [*Computer science*]
PL	Production Language
PL	Production List (AAG)
PL	Product Liability [*Insurance*]
PL	Product License
PL	Products Liability (SAUS)
PL	Professional Librarian (SAUS)
P/L	Profit and Loss [*Accounting*]
PL	Program Level (IAA)
PL	Program Library [*Computer science*]
PL	Program Logic [*Computer science*] (TEL)
PL	Programmed Learning (SAUS)
PL	Programming Language [*Computer science*]
PL	Programming Logics (SAUS)
PL	Progressive Labor [*A faction of Students for a Democratic Society*]
PL	Projection Lens [*Microscopy*]
PL	Project Leader
PL	Project Lighthawk [*Later, LH*] (EA)
PL	Project Local [*Defunct*] (EA)
PL	Proliferative Layer (SAUS)
PL	Prolymphocytic Leukemia [*Also, PLL*] [*Oncology*]
PL	Promotion List (DICI)
PL	Propagation Loss
PL	Propellant Loading [*NASA*] (KSC)
PL	Property Line [*Real estate*] (MSA)
PL	Proportionality Limit (SAUS)
PL	Proportional Limit
P/L	Proprietary Limited (ADA)
PL	Propulsion Laboratory [*Army*] (GRD)
PL	Prospective Loss
PL	Protected Location [*Shipping*] (DS)
PL	Protective Life Corp. [*NYSE symbol*] (SPSG)
PL	Protectively Located [*Plant layout*]

PL	Provisioning List (MCD)
PL	Proximity Log (SAUS)
PL	Pseudolumina [Anatomy]
PL	Psychological Laboratory (MCD)
PL	Public Law [An act of Congress]
PL	Public Liability [Business term]
PL	Public Library
Pl	Pulmonary Venous Pressure [Medicine] (MAE)
PL	Pulpolingual [Dentistry]
PL	Pulsatility Index [Medicine]
PL	Pulsed Laser (SAUS)
PL	Pulse Length (NVT)
P/L	Purchased Labor (NASA)
PL	Purple-glow Lamp (SAUS)
PL	Pyridoxal [Also, Pxl] [Biochemistry]
PL	Radio Positioning Land Station [ITU designation] (CET)
P_L	Transpulmonary Pressure [Cardiology] (DAVI)
PL/1	Programming Language, Version One [Computer science] (MCD)
PLA	Pakistan Liberation Army (PD)
PLA	Pakistan Librarians Association (SAUS)
PLA	Palau [Palau Islands] [Seismograph station code, US Geological Survey] [Closed] (SEIS)
PLA	Palestine Liberation Army
PLA	Panchromatic Linear Array (SAUS)
PLA	Parachute Location Aid (MCD)
PLA	Para Legal Association [British] (DBA)
PLA	Parlamento Latinoamericano [Latin American Parliament - LAP] [Bogota, Colombia] (EAIO)
PLA	Parlar Resources Ltd. [Vancouver Stock Exchange symbol]
PLA	Partial Look Ahead (SAUS)
PLA	Partido Laborista Agrario [Panama] [Political party] (EY)
PLA	Partido Liberal Autentico [Panama] [Political party] (EY)
PLA	Party of Labor of Albania [Political party] (PPW)
PLA	Passengers' Luggage in Advance [Railway] (ROG)
PLA	Patent Licensing Agreement (SEWL)
PLA	Patriotic Liberation Army [Myanmar] (PD)
PLA	Pedestrian League of America [Later, APA] (EA)
Pla	Pelagius [Deceased, 1232] [Authority cited in pre-1607 legal work] (DSA)
PLA	Pennilane Development [Vancouver Stock Exchange symbol]
PLA	People's Liberation Army [India] (PD)
PLA	People's Liberation Army [National Liberation Front] [North Vietnam] (VNW)
PLA	People's Liberation Army [China]
PLA	Pet Lovers Association (EA)
PLA	Phase Locked Arrays [Physics]
PLA	Philadelphia Library Association (SAUS)
PLA	Philatelic Literature Association [Later, APRL] (EA)
PLA	Phospholipase A [An enzyme] (DAVI)
PLA	Physiological Learning Aptitude (KSC)
PLA	Pitch Lock Actuator (MCD)
PLA	Place (ADA)
PLA	Placebo [Medicine]
Pla	Placentinus [Deceased, 1192] [Authority cited in pre-1607 legal work] (DSA)
PLA	Placita
PLA	Placitum [or Placita] [Agreeable, Agreed Upon] [Latin] [Legal term] (DLA)
PLA	Plain Language Address [Telecommunications] (TEL)
PLA	Plain Language Addressee (SAUS)
PLA	Planned Labor Application [Military] (AFIT)
PLA	Planned Landing Area [NASA]
PLA	Plan of Launch Azimuth [Aerospace] (AAG)
PLA	Plasma Resin Activity (SAUS)
pla	Plaster (VRA)
PLA	Platelet Antigen (DB)
PLA	Playboy Enterprises Cl'B' [NYSE symbol] (TTSB)
PLA	Playboy Enterprises, Inc. [NYSE symbol] (SPSG)
PLA	Plaza (ADA)
PLA	Poetry League of America (EA)
PLA	Polyactide [Chemistry term]
PLA	Polylactic Acid [Organic chemistry] (RDA)
PLA	Poly-L-arginine [Biochemistry]
PLA	Polynesian Air-Ways [ICAO designator] (FAAC)
PLA	Popular Library of Art [A publication]
PLA	Port of London Authority [British]
PLA	Posterior Left Atrial Wall [Cardiology]
PLA	Potential Leaf Area [Botany]
PLA	Potentially Lethal Arrhythmia [Medicine] (DMAA)
PLA	Power Lever Angle
PLA	Practice Landing Approach [Aviation]
PLA	Practise Low Approach (SAUS)
PLA	Prescribed Load Allowance (SAUS)
PLA	Price-Level-Adjusted Accounting (ADA)
PLA	Print Load Analyzer
PLA	Private Libraries Association [British]
PLA	Product Liability Act (SAUS)
PLA	Product License Application [FDA]
PLA	Professional Legal Assistants (EA)
PLA	Program-Length Advertising [Broadcasting] (WDMC)
PLA	Programmable Line Adapter
PLA	Programmable Link Adapter
PLA	Programmable Logic Array [Computer science]
PLA	Project Labor Agreement (AAGC)
PLA	Proton Linear Acceleration (or Accelerator) (SAUS)
PLA	Psycholinguistic Age [Education]
PLA	Psychological Learning Aptitude (MCD)
PLA	Public Library Association (EA)
PLa	Pulpolabial [Dentistry]
PLA	Pulpolinguoaxial [Dentistry]
PLA	Pulsed LASER Annealing [Semiconductor technology]
PLA	Pulverized Limestone Association (EA)
PLA	University of Pittsburgh, Law School, Pittsburgh, PA [OCLC symbol] (OCLC)
PLA$_2$	Phospholipase A$_2$ [An enzyme]
PLAA	Playboy Enterprises'A'(vtg) [NYSE symbol] (TTSB)
PLAA	Positive Low Angle of Attack
PLA AEPS	PLA [Public Library Association] Alternative Education Programs Section
PLAAF	People's Liberation Army Air Force
PLA AFLS	PLA [Public Library Association] Armed Forces Library Section
PLAALLS	Public Library Association Adult Life Long Learning Services
PLAAR	Packaged Liquid Air-Augmented Rocket (MCD)
PLAAS	Plasma Atomic Absorption System [Spectrometry]
PLA AV	PLA [Public Library Association] Audiovisual
PLA AVC	PLA [Public Library Association] Audiovisual Committee
PLAB	Party-Line Adapter Board [Telecommunications] (MHDI)
PLAB	Philadelphia Library Association Bulletin (SAUS)
PLAB	Photronics, Inc. [NASDAQ symbol] (NQ)
PLAB	Professional and Linguistic Assessment Board (AIE)
PLA Bull	Pennsylvania Library Association Bulletin (SAUS)
PLAC	Placebo [Medicine]
Plac	Placentinus [Deceased, 1192] [Authority cited in pre-1607 legal work] (DSA)
PLAC	Post-Launch Analysis of Compliance [NASA]
Plac Abbrev	Placitorum Abbreviatio [Latin] [A publication] (DLA)
Plac Ang Nor	Bigelow's Placita Anglo-Normanica [A publication] (DLA)
PLACE	Place [Commonly used] (OPSA)
PLACE	Positioner Layout and Cell Evaluator [Robotics]
PLACE	Position Location and Aircraft Communication Equipment
PLACE	Position Location and Aircraft Equipment (SAUS)
PLACE	Position Location and Communications Experiment [NASA]
PLACE	Post-LANDSAT Advanced Concept Evaluation (MCD)
PLACE	Programa Latinoamericano de Cooperacion Energetica [Latin American Energy Cooperation Program] (EAIO)
PLACE	Programming Language for Automatic Checkout Equipment
PlacerD	Placer Dome, Inc. [Associated Press] (SAG)
Plac Gen	Placita Generalia [Latin] [A publication] (DLA)
PLACID	Payload Aboard, Caution in Descent [NASA]
PLA CIS	PLA [Public Library Association] Community Information Section
PLACO	Planning Committee [International Organization for Standardization] (IEEE)
PLAD	Paperless LANTIRN Automated Depot (SAUS)
PLAD	Parachute Low-Altitude Delivery [Air Force]
PLAD	Plain Language Address Directory
PLAD	Plasma Diode (SAUS)
PLAD	Price-Level-Adjusted Deposit
PLAD	Public Lands Appreciation Day [A joint effort of Times Mirror Magazines and the Bureau of Land Management] (PS)
PLADS	Parachute Low-Altitude Delivery System [Military]
PLADS	Plain Language Address System (SAUS)
PLADs	Price Level Adjusted Deposits (SAUS)
PLADS	Pulsed LASER Airborne Depth Sounding System [Naval Oceanographic Office]
PLADS	Pulsed Light Airborne Depth Sounder (SAUS)
PLADS System	Pulsed Laser Airborne Depth Sounding System (SAUS)
PLAF	People's Liberation Armed Forces [National Liberation Front] [North Vietnam] (VNW)
PLAFB	Plattsburgh Air Force Base [New York] (AAG)
PLAFSEP	Processing Libraries - Anecdotes, Facetia, Satire, Etc., Periodicals [A publication]
Plag	Plagioclase [Lunar geology]
PLAGM	Placid, Louisiana Land and Exploration, Amerada Hess, Getty, and Marathon [Oil-and gas-holding bloc in Alaska]
PLAI	Potsdam Land-Atmosphere Interaction Model (SAUS)
PLAI	Preschool Language Assessment Instrument [Child development test]
PLAIC	Purdue Laboratory for Applied Industrial Control [Purdue University] [Research center] (RCD)
PLAID	Precision Location and Identification (SEWL)
PLAID	Professional Library Access and Information Delivery [Information service or system] (IID)
PLAID	Programmed Learning Aid
PLAIL	Public Libraries and Independent Learners (TELE)
PLAIN	Plain [Commonly used] (OPSA)
PLAINES	Plains [Commonly used] (OPSA)
PLAINS	Plains [Commonly used] (OPSA)
Plaintr	Plaintree Systems, Inc. [Associated Press] (SAG)
PLAL	Pro-Life Action League (EA)
PLA LC	PLA [Public Library Association] Legislative Committee
PLAM	Peoples Liberation Army of Malawi (SAUS)
PLAM	Plastic Laminate [Technical drawings]
PLAM	Practice Limpet Assembly Modular [Navy] (CAAL)
PLAM	Price-Level-Adjusted Mortgage
plam	price-level adjusted mortgage (SAUS)
PLAME	Propulsive Left Landing with Aerodynamic Maneuvering Entry (PDAA)
PLAME	Propulsive Lift Aerodynamic Maneuvering Entry (SAUS)
PLAMED	Plantas Medicinales [Ministerio de Sanidad y Consumo] [Spain] [Information service or system] (CRD)
PLA MLS	PLA [Public Library Association] Metropolitan Libraries Section

PLA Monthly... Port of London Authority Monthly (SAUS)
PL/AMOS..... Philips Laboratory Air Force Maui Optical Station (SAUS)
PLA MPLSS... PLA [*Public Library Association*] Marketing of Public Library Services Section
PLAN .... Open Plan Systems [*NASDAQ symbol*] (TTSB)
PLAN .... Open Plan Systems, Inc. [*NASDAQ symbol*] (SAG)
PLAN .... Parts Logistics Analysis Network
PLAN .... Paterson Looks Ahead Now (SAUS)
PLAN .... Payload Local Area Network [*NASA*] (SSD)
PLAN .... People's Liberation Army Navy
PLAN .... People's Liberation Army of Namibia [*Political party*] (PPW)
PLAN .... Personal LAN (NITA)
PLAN .... Personal Local Area Network [*Telecommunications*] (OSI)
Plan............ Planet (SAUS)
Plan............ Planetarium (SAUS)
PLAN .... Planned Lifetime Advocacy Network
Plan............ Planning (DLA)
PLAN .... Planning
PLAN .... Positive Locator Aid to Navigation
PLAN .... Prevent Los Angeles Now
PLAN .... Prevent Los Angelization Now (SAUS)
PLAN .... Problem Language Analyzer [*Computer science*]
PLAN .... Professional Local Area Network (NITA)
PLAN .... Program for Learning in Accordance with Needs [*Westinghouse Learning Corp.*]
PLAN .... Program Language Analyzer [*Computer science*] (IEEE)
PLAN .... Programming Language Nineteen-Hundred [*Computer science*]
PLAN .... Protect Life in All Nations (EA)
PLAN .... Public Lands Action Network (SAUS)
PLAN .... Public Libraries Automation Network [*California State Library*] [*Sacramento, CA*]
Plan & Comp... Planning and Compensation Reports [*British*] [*A publication*] (DLA)
PlanarSy...... Planar Systems [*Commercial firm*] [*Associated Press*] (SAG)
PLANAT .... North Atlantic Treaty Regional Planning Group
Planc .... Pro Plancio [*of Cicero*] [*Classical studies*] (OCD)
PLANCODE... Planning, Control, and Decision Evaluation System [*IBM Corp.*]
PLANCODE System... Planning, Control and Decision Evaluation System (SAUS)
PLand .... Professional Landman [*Canada*] (DD)
PL&PD......... Personal Loss and Personal Damage (SAUS)
PL & PD ...... Public Liability and Property Damage [*Insurance*]
Pl & Pr Cas... Pleading and Practice Cases [*1837-38*] [*England*] [*A publication*] (DLA)
PL & R .... Postal Laws and Regulations [*Later, Postal Manual*]
PLANES .... Programmed Language Enquiry System (NITA)
Planet.......... Planetarium (DIAR)
Planet.......... Planetary (SAUS)
PLANET....... Planned Logistics Analysis and Evaluation Technique [*Air Force*]
PLANET....... Planning Evaluation Technique (MCD)
PLANET....... Plant Layout Analysis and Evaluation Technique (SAUS)
PLANET....... Private Line Analysis and Network Engineering Tools (SAUS)
PLANET....... Private Local Area Network [*Racal LAN Systems, Inc.*] [*Boca Raton, FL*] (TSSD)
PLANET....... Probing Lensing Anomalies Network [*Astronomy*]
Planet Rep... Planetary Report (SAUS)
PLANEX .... [*The*] Planning Exchange Database [*Pergamon InfoLine*] [*Database*] [*Information service or system*] (IID)
PLANEX .... Planning Exercise [*Military*] (NVT)
Pl Ang-Norm... Placita Anglo-Normannica Cases (Bigelow) [*A publication*] (DLA)
Plan Higher Ed... Planning for Higher Education [*A publication*]
PlanHlly...... Planet Hollywood International, Inc. [*Associated Press*] (SAG)
Planistor...... Planar Resistor
PLANIT .... Programming Language for Interaction and Teaching [*1966*] [*Computer science*]
PLANIT .... Programming Language for Interactive Teaching
PLANITRON... Planar Integration Electron Tube (SAUS)
Plank .... Plankton (SAUS)
PLANMAN.... Planned Maintenance [*Contract Data Research*] [*Software package*] (NCC)
PLANN......... Plant Location Assistance Nationwide Network
PLANNET ..... Planning Network
PLANOX....... Planar Oxide
PLANOX....... Plane Oxide (SAUS)
PLANS .... Plastic Analysis of Nonlinear Structures (SAUS)
PLANS .... Position Location and Navigation Symposium (SAUS)
PLANS .... Position Location and Navigation System
PLANS .... Position Locator and Navigation System (SAUS)
PLANS .... Program Logistics and Network Scheduling System (IEEE)
PLANS .... Programming Language for Allocation and Network Scheduling [*1975*] [*Computer science*] (CSR)
PlanSci........ Planning Sciences International [*Associated Press*] (SAG)
Plan Soc...... Planetry Society (SAUS)
Plant........... De Plantatione [*Philo*] (BJA)
PLANT .... Program for Linguistic Analysis of Natural Plants (IEEE)
PLANT .... Programming Language for Interaction and Teaching (SAUS)
PLANT .... Programming Language for Interactive Teaching [*Computer science*] (IAA)
Plant Cell Environ... Plant, Cell and Environment (SAUS)
Plant Cell Rep... Plant Cell Reports (SAUS)
Plant Cell Tissue Organ Culture... Plant Cell, Tissue and Organ Culture (SAUS)
Plant Dis ..... Plant Disease (SAUS)
Plant Dis Rep... Plant Disease Reporter (SAUS)
Plant Ecol.... Plant Ecology (SAUS)
Plant Eng.... Plant Engineering (SAUS)
Planters Bull... Planters Bulletin (SAUS)

PLANTFACTS... Steel Plants Information System [*German Iron and Steel Engineers Association*] [*Dusseldorf*] [*Information service or system*] (IID)
plant-flex.... Plantar Flexion [*Orthopedics*] (DAVI)
Plant Growth Regul... Plant Growth Regulation (SAUS)
Plant Mol Biol Rep... Plant Molecular Biology Reporter (SAUS)
Plant Mol Biol Report... Plant Molecular Biology Reporter (SAUS)
Plant Oper Prog... Plant Operation and Progress (SAUS)
Plant Physiol Biochem... Plant Physiology and Biochemistry (SAUS)
Plantron....... Plantronics, Inc. [*Associated Press*] (SAG)
Plant Sci...... Plant Science (SAUS)
Plant Sci Bull... Plant Science Bulletin (SAUS)
Plants Mach... Plants and Machinery (SAUS)
PLANY .... Protestant Lawyers Association of New York (EA)
PLAO .... Parts List Assembly Order (MCD)
PLAP.......... Placental Alkaline Phosphatase [*An enzyme*]
PLAP.......... Port of London Authority Police (SAUS)
PLAP.......... Power Lever Angle Position (MCD)
PLAP.......... Prelaunch, Launch, and Ascent Procedures [*NASA*] (IAA)
PLAP.......... Pulsed-Laser Atom Probe (SAUS)
Pla Par .... Placita Parliamentaria [*Latin*] [*A publication*] (DLA)
PLA/PGA..... Polylactic Acid/Polyglycolic Acid (SAUS)
PLapK......... Keystone Junior College, La Plume, PA [*Library symbol*] [*Library of Congress*] (LCLS)
PLA PLSS ... PLA [*Public Library Association*] Public Library Systems Section
PLAQ .... Planned Quantity (SAUS)
PLA Quarterly... Private Libraries Association Quarterly (SAUS)
PLAR .... Postal Laws and Regulations (IAA)
PLARA .... Packaged Liquid Air-Augmented (IAA)
Plarbage..... Plane-floor garbage (SAUS)
PLARS .... Position Location and Reporting System [*Military*] (INF)
PLAS.......... Plaster (AAG)
plas .... Plastic (VRA)
PLAS.......... Plastic
PLas .... Premier Laser Systems, Inc. [*Associated Press*] (SAG)
PLAS.......... Private Line Assured Service [*Telecommunications*] (TEL)
PLAS.......... Professional Library Automation System (TELE)
PLAS.......... Program Logical Address Space
PLAS.......... Programmable Link Adaptation System (MCD)
PLASA .... Professional Lighting & Sound Association (SAUS)
PLASCAMS... Plastics: Computer Aided Materials Selector [*Rapra Technology Ltd.*] [*Information service or system*] (CRD)
PLASDOC.... Plastic and Polymer Patents (SAUS)
PLASDOC.... Plastics Documentation (SAUS)
PLASI......... Pulsating Visual Approach Slope Indicator [*Aviation*] (FAAC)
PLASI......... Pulse Light Approach Indicator System (SAUS)
PLASI......... Pulse Light Approach Slope Indicator (PDAA)
PLASMA ..... Parents League of American Students of Medicine Abroad [*Defunct*] (EA)
PLASMA ..... Plant Services Maintenance (PDAA)
Plasma .... Plasma & Materials Technologies, Inc. [*Associated Press*] (SAG)
Plasma Chem Plasma Process... Plasma Chemistry and Plasma Processing (SAUS)
Plasma Phys... Plamsa Physics (SAUS)
Plasma Phys Control Fusion... Plasma Physics and Controlled Fusion (SAUS)
PLASMEX .... International Plastics Exhibition
PLASMEX .... International Plastics Machinery, Equipment and Materials Exhibition (SAUS)
PLA SMLS ... PLA [*Public Library Association*] Small and Medium-Sized Libraries Section
Plast .... Plastic (DIAR)
Plast .... Plasticity (SAUS)
Plast .... Plastics (SAUS)
PLAST......... Pre-Engineered Logistical and Administrative Structures (SAUS)
PLAST......... Propellant Loading and All Systems Test [*NASA*] (KSC)
Plast Age..... Plastics Age (SAUS)
Plast Bldg Contr... Plastics in Building Construction (SAUS)
Plast Bubber Int... Plastics and Rubber International (SAUS)
Plast Bubber Process Appl... Plastics and Rubber Processing and Applications (SAUS)
Plast Bus..... Plastics Business (SAUS)
Plast Compounding... Plastics Compounding (SAUS)
Plast Des Forum... Plastics Design Forum (SAUS)
PLASTEC...... Plastics Evaluation Center (SAUS)
PLASTEC...... Plastics Technical Evaluation Center [*Dover, NJ*] [*Army*]
PLASTEC...... Plastics Technology Information Analysis Center (SAUS)
Plast Eng..... Plastics in Engineering (SAUS)
PLASTEUROTEC... European Group of Fabricators of Technical Plastics Parts (SAUS)
PLASTEUROTEC... Groupement Europeen des Fabricants de Pieces Techniques Plastiques [*European Group of Fabricators of Technical Plastics Parts*] (EAIO)
PlasThrm..... Plasma-Therm, Inc. [*Associated Press*] (SAG)
Plast Ind News... Plastics Industry News (SAUS)
PlasTIPS ..... Plastics Training and Information to Promote Safety (SAUS)
PlastLn .... Plasti-Line, Inc. [*Associated Press*] (SAG)
Plast News... Plastics News (SAUS)
Plast News Briefs... Plastics News Briefs (SAUS)
Plast Retail Packag Bull... Plastics in Retail Packaging Bulletin (SAUS)
Plast Rubber Wkly... Plastics and Rubber Weekly (SAUS)
Plast S Africa... Plastics Southern Africa (SAUS)
Plast Technol... Plastics Technology (SAUS)
Plast Today... Plastics Today (SAUS)
Plast World... Plastics World (SAUS)
PLAT.......... Pilot Landing Aid Television (SAUS)
PLAT.......... Pilot Landing Air Television

PLAT............	Pilot Landing Assistance Television
PLAT............	Pilot-LOS [*Line of Sight*] Landing Aid Television (NG)
plat.............	Plate (VRA)
Plat.............	Plateau (NTIO)
Plat.............	Plateau (SAUS)
PLAT............	Plateau [*Board on Geographic Names*]
PLAT............	Platelet [*Hematology*]
PLAT............	Platform (KSC)
PLAT............	Platinum [*Chemical symbol is Pt*] (AAG)
PLAT............	Platinum Technology [*NASDAQ symbol*] (SPSG)
PLAT............	Platonic
plat.............	Platoon (WDAA)
PLAT............	Platoon
PLATF...........	Platt National Park
PLATF...........	Platform (AAG)
Platinum Met Rev...	Platinum Metals Review (SAUS)
PLATL..........	Platelets [*Hematology*] (DAVI)
PLATLDR.....	Platoon Leader [*Military*]
PLATN........	Platinum [*Chemistry*] (ROG)
platn.........	Platinum [*Metal*] (VRA)
PLATO........	Pennzoil Louisiana and Texas Offshore [*Oil industry group*]
PLATO........	Platform Observables (SAUS)
PLATO........	Platform Observables Subassembly
PLATO........	Pollution Liability Agreement Among Tanker Owners [*Insurance*] (DS)
PLATO........	Port Lincoln Advancement Trust Organization (SAUS)
PLATO........	Programmed Learning Automatic Teaching Organization (SAUS)
PLATO........	Programmed Logic for Automated Learning Operation [*Computer science*] (IAA)
PLATO........	Programmed Logic for Automatic Teaching [*or Training*] Operations [*University of Illinois*] [*Programming language*]
PLATON......	Programming Language for Tree Operation (SAUS)
PLATR	Pawling Lattice Test Rig [*United Nuclear Co.*]
PLATS.........	Pilot Landing and Takeoff System (IIA)
PLATS.........	Precision Location and Tracking System (PDAA)
PLatS..........	Saint Vincent College, Latrobe, PA [*Library symbol*] [*Library of Congress*] (LCLS)
PlatSoft.......	Platinum Software Corp. [*Associated Press*] (SAG)
Plat Surf Fin...	Plating and Surface Finishing (SAUS)
PLAT System...	Pilot Landing Aid Television System (SAUS)
PLATT..........	Page Level Availability Time Test [*Computer science*]
Platt...........	Platt on Leases [*A publication*] (DLA)
Platt...........	Platt on the Law of Covenants [*1829*] [*A publication*] (DLA)
PlatTc.........	Platinum Technology, Inc. [*Associated Press*] (SAG)
Platt Cov......	Platt on the Law of Covenants [*A publication*] (DLA)
Platt Leas....	Platt on Leases [*1847*] [*A publication*] (DLA)
PLAT/VLA ...	Pilot Landing Aid Television / Visual Landing Aid [*System*] (DNAB)
Platy...........	Platyhelminthes (SAUS)
Platy...........	Platypoecilus (SAUS)
Platy...........	Platysma (SAUS)
Plaut..........	Plautus [*Third century BC*] [*Classical studies*] (OCD)
PLAV...........	Polish Legion of American Veterans (NADA)
PLAV...........	Polish Legion of American Veterans, USA (EA)
PLAVA	Polish Legion of American Veterans, USA , Ladies Auxiliary (EA)
PLAVLA.......	Polish Legion of American Veterans, USA , Ladies Auxiliary (EA)
PLAW.........	Programming Language for Arc Welding (SAUS)
PLAWM Trough...	Pockels Langmuir Adam Wilson McBain Trough [*Surface film balance*]
Plaxton........	Plaxton's Canadian Constitutional Decisions [*A publication*] (DLA)
PLAY...........	Participate in the Lives of America's Youth
PLAY...........	Players International [*NASDAQ symbol*] (TTSB)
PLAY...........	Players International, Inc. [*NASDAQ symbol*] (NQ)
PLAY...........	Providing Lifetime Activity for Youth
Playby	Playboy Enterprises, Inc. [*Associated Press*] (SAG)
PlayBy	Play By Play Toys & Novelties, Inc. [*Associated Press*] (SAG)
PlaybyA	Playboys Enterprises [*Associated Press*] (SAG)
PlaybyB	Playboys Enterprises [*Associated Press*] (SAG)
PlayCo.........	Play Co. Toys [*Associated Press*] (SAG)
Play Co	Play Co. Toys & Entertainment Corp. [*Associated Press*] (SAG)
Players	Players International Corp. [*Associated Press*] (SAG)
PlaytxPd	Playtex Products, Inc. [*Associated Press*] (SAG)
PLAZA.........	Plaza [*Commonly used*] (OPSA)
PLB.............	Amer Italian Pasta'A' [*NYSE symbol*] (SG)
PLB.............	Packet Length in Bits (SAUS)
PLB.............	Payload Bay [*NASA*] (NAKS)
PLB.............	Per Pound [*Freight*]
PLB.............	Personal Locator Beacon [*Military*] (AFM)
PLB.............	Phopholipase B [*An enzyme*] (DAVI)
PLB.............	Phospholamban [*Biochemistry*]
PLB.............	Picture Level Benchmark [*Computer science*] (CDE)
PLB.............	Plattsburgh, NY [*Location identifier*] [*FAA*] (FAAL)
PLB.............	Plumbing Mart [*Vancouver Stock Exchange symbol*]
PLB.............	Poor Law Board
PLB.............	Porous Layer Bead [*Chromatography*] (DB)
PLB.............	Print Line Buffer [*Computer science*] (VLIE)
PLB.............	Prior-Lien Bond [*Business*] (MHDB)
PLB.............	Proctolin-Like Bioactivity [*Neurobiology*]
PLB.............	Public Light Bus [*British*]
PLB.............	Publisher's Library Binding
PLB.............	Pullbutton (AAG)
PLBB...........	Patent Licensing Bulletin Board [*U.S. Department of Commerce*] (BARN)
PLBD	Payload Bay Door [*NASA*] (MCD)
PLBD	Plugboard (MSA)
PLBG	Plumbing (WGA)
PLBK...........	Playback (NASA)
PLBKAC	Problem Lies Between Keyboard and Chair (SAUS)
PL-BL..........	Plate Block [*Philately*]
PLBLK.........	Pillow Block
PLBOL	Position Launch/Bearing Only Launch
PLBR	Plumber (WGA)
PLBR	Prototype Large Breeder Reactor [*Also, NCBR*] [*Nuclear energy*]
PLC.............	Pacific Lighting Corp. (SAUS)
PLC.............	Pacific Logging Congress (EA)
PLC.............	Packaged Laboratory Chemicals (COE)
PLC.............	Palomares Road [*California*] [*Seismograph station code, US Geological Survey*] (SEIS)
PLC.............	Parti de la Liberte du Citoyen [*Belgium*] [*Political party*] (EY)
PLC.............	Partido Liberal Constitucionalista [*Constitutionalist Liberal Party*] [*Nicaragua*] [*Political party*] (PPW)
PLC.............	Patrice Lumumba Coalition (EA)
PLC.............	Pattern Length Coding (SAUS)
PLC.............	Paymaster-Lieutenant-Commander [*Navy*] [*British*]
PLC.............	Peritoneal Lymphoid Cell (SAUS)
PLC.............	Periventricular Leukomalacia Complex [*Medicine*]
PLC.............	Perry-Link Cubmarine [*A submersible vehicle*]
PLC.............	Personal Line of Credit (SAUS)
PLC.............	Phospholipase C [*An enzyme*]
PLC.............	Phospholysine C [*Biochemistry*]
PLC.............	Pilot Laboratories Corp. [*Vancouver Stock Exchange symbol*]
PLC.............	Placer Development Ltd. [*AMEX symbol*] (SPSG)
PI C.............	Placita Coronae [*Pleas of the Crown*] [*Latin*] [*Legal term*] (DLA)
PLC.............	Plague Locust Commission (SAUS)
PLC.............	Planar Chromatography
PLC.............	Planeta Rica [*Colombia*] [*Airport symbol*] (AD)
PLC.............	Platform Control
PLC.............	Platoon Leader's Class [*Army*]
PLC.............	PLC Capital LLC, Inc. [*Associated Press*] (SAG)
PLC.............	PLC Systems [*AMEX symbol*] (SPSG)
PLC.............	Pneumatic Lead Cutter
PLC.............	Pneumatic Logic Circuit (SAUS)
PLC.............	Poet Laureatus Caesareus [*Imperial Poet Laureate*] [*Latin*] (ROG)
PLC.............	Point Loma College [*California*]
PLC.............	Police
PLC.............	Police Aviation Services [*British*] [*ICAO designator*] (FAAC)
PLC.............	Polymer Liquid Crystal (SAUS)
PLC.............	Poor Law Commissioners [*British*]
PLC.............	Power Lever Control (MCD)
PLC.............	Power Line Carrier
PLC.............	Power Line Communications
PLC.............	Power Line Conditioner (VLIE)
PLC.............	Power Line Converter (SAUS)
PLC.............	Power Line Cycle (SAUS)
PLC.............	Power Loading Control (IAA)
PLC.............	Predictive Linguistic Constraint
PLC.............	Preferred Line of Credit (SAUS)
PLC.............	Prelaunch Computer (SAUS)
PLC.............	Preliminary Loads Cycle (SAUS)
PLC.............	Preparative Layer Chromatography
PLC.............	Presbyterian Lay Committee (EA)
PLC.............	Pressurized Logistics Carrier (SAUS)
PLC.............	Primary Leadership Course [*Army*]
PLC.............	Primary Location Code [*Computer science*]
PLC.............	Prime Level Code
PLC.............	Print Line Complete [*Computer science*] (VLIE)
PLC.............	Private Line Carrier [*Telecommunications*] (IAA)
PLC.............	Probe Launch Complex (SAUS)
PLC.............	Process Limit Count (TIMI)
PLC.............	Process Line Control [*Computer science*] (VLIE)
PLC.............	Process Liquid Chromatography
PLC.............	Production Line Configured [*Military*] (CAAL)
PLC.............	Product Level Control (SAUS)
PLC.............	Product Life Cycle (ODBW)
PLC.............	Products List Circular [*Patents*]
PLC.............	Program-Length Commercial [*Television*]
PLC.............	Program Level Change (VLIE)
PLC.............	Program Level Change Tape [*Computer science*] (IBMDP)
PLC.............	Programmable Line Controller (NITA)
PLC.............	Programmable Logic Control [*Computer science*]
PLC.............	Programming Language Committee [*CODASYL*]
PLC.............	Proinsulin-Like Compound [*Endocrinology*]
PLC.............	Propellant Loading Console (SAUS)
PLC.............	Provisional Legislative Council [*Hong Kong*]
PLC.............	Pseudolymphocytic Choriomeningitis [*Medicine*] (DMAA)
PLC.............	Pseudophase Liquid Chromatography
PLC.............	Public Lands Council (EA)
PLC.............	Public Liability Company (DFIT)
PLC.............	Public Lighting Commission
PLC.............	Public Limited Co. [*British*]
Plc.............	Public Limited Company
PLC.............	Public Utility Company (EBF)
PLCA..........	Parallel Line Communication Adaptor (NITA)
PLCA..........	Pipe Line Contractors Association (EA)
PLCA..........	Pipeline Contractors Association (SAUS)
PLCAA	Professional Lawn Care Association of America (EA)
PLCAC	Pipeline Contractors Association of Canada (SAUS)
PLCAI.........	Pipe Line Contractors Association, International (EA)
PLCB..........	Planetary Liquid-Cooled Brake [*Off-highway equipment*]
PLCB..........	Program List Control Block [*Computer science*] (ELAL)
PLCB..........	Pseudoline Control Block [*Computer science*]

PLC Bulletin... Progressive Librarians Council Bulletin (SAUS)
PLCC........... Paulson Cap [NASDAQ symbol] (TTSB)
PLCC........... Paulson Capital Corp. [NASDAQ symbol] (SAG)
PLCC........... Plastic Chip Carrier (NITA)
PLCC........... Plastic Leaded Chip Carrier [Computer science]
PLCC........... Plastic Leadless Chip Carrier [Computer technology] (PCM)
PLCC........... Power Line Carrier Communication (PDAA)
PLCC........... Primary Liver Cell Cancer [Oncology]
PLCC........... Propulsion Local Control Console (DNAB)
PLCCE......... Preliminary Life-Cycle Cost Estimate
PLCCE......... Program Life-Cycle Cost Estimate [Army]
PLCD .... Product Liability Common Defense [Later, PLPD] [An association]
               (EA)
PLCDR........ Private Line Carrier Divided Ringing [Telecommunications] (IAA)
PLCE........... Children's Place Retail Stores [NASDAQ symbol] (SG)
PLCE........... Peripheral and Loading Control Element (SAUS)
PLCE........... Personal Load Carrying Equipment (SAUS)
PLCEA......... Part-Length Control Element Assembly [Nuclear energy] (NRCH)
PLCEDM ...... Part-Length Control Element Drive Mechanism [Nuclear energy]
               (NRCH)
PLCH .... Kiritimati Island [Christmas Islands] [Kiribati] [ICAO location
               identifier] (ICLI)
PLCHC .... Polymer Life Cycle Hydrocarbons
PLC I/O....... Programmable Logic Controller Input/Output (SAUS)
PLCL........... Phase-Locked Control Loop [NASA] (IAA)
PLCL........... Polyclonal Gammopathy Identified [Immunology] (DAVI)
PLCLAS....... Propagation Loss Classification System [Navy] (NVT)
PL-CLP .... Plantelet Clumps [Hematology] (DAVI)
PLCM.......... Polycom, Inc. [NASDAQ symbol] (SAG)
PLCM.......... Propellant Loading Control Monitor [NASA] (KSC)
PLCM&ND ... Proceedings of the Linguistic Circle of Manitoba and North Dakota
               (SAUS)
PLCMC........ Public Library of Charlotte and Mecklenburg County [North Carolina]
PLCN .... Parts List Change Notice (MCD)
PLCNY .... Publications of the Linguistic Circle of New York (SAUS)
PLCO .... Play Company Toys [NASDAQ symbol] (SAG)
PLCO .... Play Co. Toys & Entertainment Corp. [NASDAQ symbol] (SAG)
PLCO .... Play Co. Toys & Entmt [NASDAQ symbol] (TTSB)
PLCO .... Postoperative Low Cardiac Output [Medicine] (DMAA)
PLCO .... Prostate, Lung, Colorectal, and Ovarian [Cancers]
Pl Com .... Plowden's English King's Bench Commentaries [or Reports]
               [1550-80] [England] [A publication] (DLA)
PL Com .... Poor Law Commissioner [A publication] (DLA)
PLCOP .... Prelaunch Checkout Plan [NASA] (KSC)
PLCOW .... Play Co. Toys & Entmt Wrrt [NASDAQ symbol] (TTSB)
PLCP........... Photochromic Liquid Crystal Polymer [Organic chemistry]
PLCP........... Physical Layer Convergence Procedure (CIST)
PLCP........... Physical Layer Convergence Protocol (MLOA)
PLCR .... Post Launch Checkout Report (ACAE)
Pl Cr Con Tr... Plowden's Criminal Conversation Trials [A publication] (DLA)
PlcrD .... Placer Dome [Associated Press] (SAG)
PLCS........... Proceedings of the London Classical Society (SAUS)
PLCS........... Propellant Loading Control System [NASA] (AAG)
PLC Sys....... PLC Systems [Associated Press] (SAG)
PLCT........... Power Line Carrier Telephony (SAUS)
PLCT........... Prelaunch Certification Test
Pl Cu .... Plain Copper (SAUS)
PLCU .... Programmable Logic Control Unit (SAUS)
PLCU .... Propellant Level Control Unit [NASA] (KSC)
PLCU .... Propellant-Loading Control Unit [NASA] (IAA)
PLCURR....... Plate Current [Electronics] (IAA)
PLCV........... Pelargonium Leaf Curl Virus [Plant pathology]
PLCWTWU... Power Loom Carpet Weavers' and Textile Workers' Union [British]
plcy............ Policy (ELAL)
Plcy .... Policy (TBD)
PLCY.......... Policy
PlcyMg .... Policy Management Systems [Associated Press] (SAG)
PLD............ All Pakistan Legal Decisions [A publication] (ILCA)
PLD............ Package Level Detail (VLIE)
PLD............ Paid Land Diversion Program [Department of Agriculture] (GFGA)
PLD............ Partial Line Down (NITA)
PLD............ Partial Lipodystrophy [Medicine]
PLD............ Partido de la Liberacion Dominicana [Dominican Liberation Party]
               [Dominican Republic] [Political party] (PPW)
PLD............ Parti Liberal-Democrate [Cameroon] [Political party] (EY)
PLd............ Path Loss, Downlink [Communications]
PLD............ Payload [NASA]
PLD............ Periodic Lattice Distortion (SAUS)
PLD............ Peripheral Light Detection (DMAA)
PLD............ Periscope-Like Display (SAUS)
PLD............ Permanently Lubricated Drivetrain
PLD............ Personal Laser Detector (SAUS)
PLD............ Personnel Letdown Device
PLD............ Phase Linked Demodulator (SAUS)
PLD............ Phase Lock Demodulator
PLD............ Phase-Locked Detector (IAA)
PLD............ Phase-Locked Discriminator (IAA)
PLD............ Phospholipase D [An enzyme]
PLD............ Physical Logical Description (MHDI)
PLD............ Plaid (ADA)
PLD............ Plated (MSA)
PLD............ Platelet Defect [Hematology] (MAE)
PlD............ Platform Deck (SAUS)
PLD............ Played Matches [Cricket] (ROG)
PLD............ Policy Liaison Division (AAGC)

PLD............ Polycystic Liver Disease [Medicine] (DMAA)
PLD............ Polymer-Linked Ligand Dimer [Biochemistry]
PLD............ Portland, IN [Location identifier] [FAA] (FAAL)
PLD............ Posterior Latissimus Dorsi [Anatomy]
PLD............ Posterolateral Dendrite [Neurology]
PLD............ Potentially Lethal Damage [Medicine]
PLD............ Precision LASER Designator (RDA)
PLD............ Pregnancy, Labor and Delivery (DAVI)
PLD............ Presentation Logic Domain (SAUS)
PLD............ Primary Layer Depth [Military] (CAAL)
PLD............ Principle of Limit Design
PLD............ Probable Line of Deployment [Army] (AABC)
PLD............ Procurement Legal Division [Later, Office of General Counsel] [Navy]
PLD............ Product Line Development
PLD............ Program Listing Document (MCD)
PLD............ Program Load Disc (SAUS)
PLD............ Programmable Logic Device
PLD............ ProLogis Trust [NYSE symbol] [Formerly, Security Capital Industries
               Trust]
PLD............ Protective LASER Devices (MCD)
PLD............ Pulsed LASER Deposition [Coating technology]
PLD............ Pulse-Length Discriminator (IEEE)
PLD............ Pulse Level Detector (MCD)
PLDA .... Power Line Disturbance Analyser (SAUS)
PLdaC......... Calvary Baptist School of Theology, Lansdale, PA [Library symbol]
               [Library of Congress] (LCLS)
PLDAL .... Pro-Life Direct Action League (EA)
PLDC .... Preliminary List of Design Changes
PLDC .... Primary Leadership Development Course [Army] (INF)
PLDC .... Primary Long-Distance Carrier [Telephone service]
PLDD .... Percutaneous Laser Disc Decompression
PLDD .... Poorly Differentiated Lymphoma, Diffuse [Oncology and pathology]
               (DAVI)
PLDD .... Profiled Lightly Doped Drains (NITA)
PLD Digest... Pakistan Legal Decisions Digest (SAUS)
PLDF.......... Piecewise Linear Discriminant Function (SAUS)
PLDF.......... Pseudo Load Factor (IAA)
PLDG .... Portuguese Language Development Group [Modern Language
               Association of America] (AEBS)
PLDH .... Plasma Lactic Dehydrogenase [An enzyme] (AAMN)
PLDI.......... Payload Data Interleaver [NASA] (MCD)
PLDI.......... Petersburg Long Distance [NASDAQ symbol] (SAG)
PLDI.......... Plastic Die [Tool] (AAG)
PLDI.......... PLD Telekom, Inc. [NASDAQ symbol] (SAG)
PLDI.......... Programming Language Design and Implementation [Computer
               science] (VLIE)
PLDIF........ Petersburg Long Distance [NASDAQ symbol] (TTSB)
PLDIF........ PLD Telekom [NASDAQ symbol] [Formerly, Petersburg Long
               Distance] (SG)
PLDIS .... Public Libraries Development Incentive Scheme (SAUS)
PLDIS .... Public Library Development Incentive Scheme [British]
PLDISS ...... Plate Dissipation [Electronics] (IAA)
PLDK .... Peabody Language Development Kits [Education]
PLDK-P ...... Peabody Language Development Kit: Preschool (EDAC)
PLDM......... Payload Management [NASA] (MCD)
PLDM......... Power Line Disturbance Monitor (SAUS)
PLDMI .... Precise LASER Distance Measuring Instrument
PLDP.......... Parti Liberal Democrate et Pluraliste [Belgium] [Political party] (PPW)
PLDP.......... Public Library Development Plan [American Library Association,
               Public Library Association]
PLD-PACOM... Petroleum Logistical Data - Pacific Command (CINC)
PLDR.......... Potentially Lethal Damage Repair [Medicine]
PLDS .... Payload Support [NASA] (MCD)
PLDS .... Pilot Land Data System (ACAE)
PLDS .... Planetary Land Data System (SAUS)
PLDS .... Public Library Data Service
PLDT.......... Philippine Long Distance Telephone Co.
PLDT C .... Philippine Long Distance Telephone Company (SAUS)
PLD Tele ..... PLD Telekom, Inc. [Associated Press] (SAG)
PLDTS .... Propellant Loading Data Transmission System [NASA] (KSC)
PLDX.......... Polydox (SAUS)
PL DYL .... Placidyl [Ethchlorvynol] [A hypnotic and sedative] (DAVI)
PLE............ Encyclopedia of Pennsylvania Law [A publication] (DLA)
PLE............ Painfully Long Extension (MUSM)
PLE............ Panlobular Emphysema [Medicine] (STED)
PLE............ Personal Level Encryption [Computer science]
PLE............ Phased Loading Entry [Computer science]
PLE............ Phase Loading Entry (SAUS)
PLE............ Photoluminescence Excitation [Physics]
PLE............ Piecewise-Linear Expression (SAUS)
PLE............ Pinnacle Bank [AMEX symbol] (TTSB)
PLE............ Pipeline Element (NITA)
PLE............ [The] Pittsburgh & Lake Erie Railroad Co. [AAR code]
PLE............ Planned Life Extension [Pershing] (MCD)
Ple............ Pleiade [Record label] [France]
PLE............ Plesetsk [Satellite launch complex] [Former USSR]
PLE............ Pleura (SAUS)
PLE............ Porcine Liver Esterase
PLE............ Preliminary Logistics Evaluation
PLE............ Primary Loss Expectancy [Insurance]
PLE............ Product Limit Estimator (MHDB)
PLE............ Professional Land Economist [Canada] (DD)
PLE............ Programmable Logic Element (SAUS)
PL/E.......... Programming Language / Edit [Computer science] (MHDI)
PLE............ Programming Language Evaluation (SAUS)

PLE............	Protein-Losing Enteropathy [*Gastroenterology*] (DAVI)
PLE............	Prudent Limit of Endurance (NVT)
PLE............	Pseudolupus Erythematosus [*Syndrome*] (STED)
PLE............	Public Local Exchange (SAUS)
PLE............	Puerile Light Entertainment (SAUS)
PLE............	Pulsed LASER Experiment
PLE............	Pulse Length Error (MCD)
PLEA..........	Pacific Lumber Exporters Association (EA)
PLEA..........	Poverty Lawyers for Effective Advocacy
PLEA..........	Prototype Language for Economic Analysis [*Computer science*] (IID)
PLEAD........	Place of Last Entered Active Duty [*Military*]
PLEADGS.....	Pleadings [*Legal term*] (ROG)
PLEASE.......	Parolees, Law-Enforcement Assist Student Education [*Project to reduce drug abuse among junior and senior high school students in California*]
PLEASM......	Programmable Logic Elements Assembler (SAUS)
PLeB..........	Bucknell University, Lewisburg, PA [*Library symbol*] [*Library of Congress*] (LCLS)
PLEB..........	Plebeian (WGA)
PLEB..........	Plebiscitum [*A Decree of the People*] [*Latin*] (DLA)
plebe.........	plebeian (SAUS)
PLebHi........	Lebanon County Historical Society, Lebanon, PA [*Library symbol*] [*Library of Congress*] (LCLS)
plebs..........	plebeians (SAUS)
PLebV.........	United States Veterans Administration Hospital, Lebanon, PA [*Library symbol*] [*Library of Congress*] (LCLS)
PLED..........	Periodic Lateralized Epileptiform Discharge [*Medicine*] (MAE)
pled...........	pleaded (SAUS)
pLED..........	Polymeric Light Emitting Diode
PLED..........	Polymer Light Emitting Diode (SAUS)
PLEDM.......	Phase-State Low Electron-Hole-Number Drive Memory
P Leg J.......	Pittsburgh Legal Journal [*Pennsylvania*] [*A publication*] (DLA)
P Leg Jour....	Pittsburgh Legal Journal [*Pennsylvania*] [*A publication*] (DLA)
PLEI..........	Public Law Education Institute (EA)
PLEM.........	Pipeline End Manifold (PDAA)
Plen..........	Plenary (SAUS)
PLEN..........	Plenipotentiary
PLEN..........	Plenum Publishing [*NASDAQ symbol*] (TTSB)
PLEN..........	Plenum Publishing Corp. [*NASDAQ symbol*] (NQ)
PLEN..........	Public Leadership Education Network (EA)
PLENAPS.....	Plans for the Employment of Naval and Air Forces of the Associated Powers in theEastern Theatre in the Event of War with Japan
PLENCH......	Pliers and Wrench [*Combination tool*]
PLENG........	Physical Record Length [*Computer science*] (MHDI)
Plenum.......	Plenum Publishing Corp (SAUS)
PLER..........	Primrose Lake Evaluation Range (SAUS)
PLES..........	Parallel-Line Equal Space [*Medicine*] (DMAA)
PLES..........	Parallel-Line Equal Spacing (STED)
PLES..........	Photoluminescence Excitation Spectroscopy (SAUS)
PLESA........	Programs for Persons with Limited English-Speaking Ability [*Department of Labor*]
PLEU..........	Pleural Fluid [*Medicine*] (DAVI)
Pleur Fl.......	Pleural Fluid [*Medicine*] (MAE)
PLEURO......	Pleuropneumonia [*Veterinary medicine*] (DSUE)
PLEVA........	Pityriasis Lichenoides et Varioliformis Acuta [*Dermatology*] (MAE)
P/L-EX........	Payload Executive (SAUS)
PLEX..........	Plant Experimentation (PDAA)
PLEX..........	Programming Language Extension [*Computer science*] (CIST)
plexg.........	Plexiglass (VRA)
Plexus.......	Plexus Corp. [*Associated Press*] (SAG)
PLEYA........	Public Library Entrepreneur of the Year Award [*Sponsored by Geac Computers Ltd.*]
PLF...........	Franklin and Marshall College, Lancaster, PA [*Library symbol*] [*Library of Congress*] (LCLS)
PLF...........	Free Library of Philadelphia, Philadelphia, PA [*OCLC symbol*] (OCLC)
PLF...........	Pacific Legal Foundation (EA)
PLF...........	Page Length Field
PLF...........	Pala [*Chad*] [*Airport symbol*] (AD)
PLF...........	Palestine Liberation Front [*Political party*] (PD)
PLF...........	Parachute Landing Fall [*Military*]
PLF...........	Pastel Food [*Vancouver Stock Exchange symbol*]
PLF...........	Patient Load Factor (AFM)
PLF...........	Payload Fairing (IGSL)
PLF...........	People's Liberation Forces [*Ethiopia*] [*Political party*] (AF)
PLF...........	Perilymphatic Fistula [*Medicine*] (DMAA)
PLF...........	Perilymph Fistula [*Medicine*]
PLF...........	Phase Lock Frequency
PLF...........	Phone Line Formatter
PLF...........	Plaintiff
PLF...........	Plant Load Factor (SAUS)
PLF...........	Pohjanmaan Lento OY [*Finland*] [*ICAO designator*] (FAAC)
PLF...........	Polar Lipid Fraction [*Biochemistry*]
PLF...........	Polyforming (SAUS)
PLF...........	Positive Lock Fastener
PLF...........	Posterior Lung Fiber [*Medicine*] (DMAA)
plf............	Pounds per Foot (WPI)
PLF...........	Powered-Lift Facility (SAUS)
PLF...........	Power for Level Flight [*Aeronautics*]
PLF...........	Private Line Telephone
P-L F.........	Pro-Life Federation (SAUS)
PLF...........	Proliferin [*Biochemistry*]
PLF...........	Proposition Letter Formula
PLF...........	Public Lands Foundation (EA)
PLFA..........	Phospholipid ester-linked Fatty Acid (SAUS)

PLFA..........	Phospholipid Fatty Acids (COE)
PLFA..........	Polar Lipid Fatty Acid [*Biochemistry*]
PLFA..........	Primary Level Field Activity [*Defense Supply Agency*]
PLFA..........	Tabueran Island [*Fanning Islands*] [*Kiribati*] [*ICAO location identifier*] (ICLI)
PLFC..........	Premature Living Female Child [*Neonatology*] (DAVI)
PLFC..........	Pulaski Furniture [*NASDAQ symbol*] (TTSB)
PLFC..........	Pulaski Furniture Corp. [*NASDAQ symbol*] (NQ)
PLFC & A....	Peggy Lee Fan Club and Archives [*Later, OOPLFC & A*] (EA)
PLFE..........	Presidential Life [*NASDAQ symbol*] (TTSB)
PLFE..........	Presidential Life Corp. [*NASDAQ symbol*] (NQ)
PLFF..........	Plaintiff
PLFP..........	Pity Large Family Present-Buyers
PLFPF.........	Payload Fairing Processing Facility (IGSL)
PLFS..........	Perilymphatic Fistula Syndrome [*Medicine*] (DMAA)
PLFTR........	Please Furnish Transportation Requests (NOAA)
PLFUR........	Please Furnish (NOAA)
PLG...........	Parametric Light Generator (SAUS)
PLG...........	Permanent Liaison Group (SAUS)
PLG...........	Piling (MSA)
PLG...........	Place Resources Corp. [*Toronto Stock Exchange symbol*]
PLG...........	Plane Guard (NVT)
PLG...........	Planning Liaison Group (SAUS)
PLG...........	Plasminogen [*An enzyme*] (DAVI)
PLG...........	Pleural Ganglion [*Medicine*]
PLG...........	Plug (AAG)
PLG...........	Poetae Lyrici Graeci [*A publication*] (OCD)
PLG...........	PolyGram NV [*NYSE symbol*] (SPSG)
PLG...........	Polygyros [*Greece*] [*Seismograph station code, US Geological Survey*] (SEIS)
PLG...........	Poor Law Guardian [*British*]
PLG...........	Private-Label and Generic Brands
PLG...........	Process Line Generator (SAUS)
PLG...........	Progressive Librarians Guild [*American Library Association*]
PLG...........	Prolyl(leucyl)glycinamide [*Biochemistry*]
PLG...........	Pulsed Light Generator
PLGA..........	Polylacticco-Glycolic Acid [*Organic chemistry*]
PLGC..........	Pension Loan Guarantee Corp. (SAUS)
PLGC..........	Presbyterians for Lesbian/Gay Concerns (EA)
PLGL..........	Plasminogen-Like [*Medicine*] (DMAA)
PLGL..........	Plate Glass
PLGL..........	Plateglass (SAUS)
PLGM.........	NYC Parents of Lesbians and Gay Men (EA)
PL/GP........	Philips Laboratory, Geophysics Directorate (SAUS)
PLGR.........	Plunger (MSA)
PLGR.........	Portable Lightweight Global Receiver (SAUS)
PLGR.........	Portable Lightweight GPS Receiver (SAUS)
PLGR.........	Position Location Ground Receiver (SAUS)
PLGR.........	Precision Lightweight Global-Positioning-Satellite Receiver
PLGR.........	Precision Lightweight GPS [*Global Positioning System*] Receiver [*Navigation systems*]
PLGS	Partita Liberale Giovani Somali [*Somali Liberal Youth Party*] [*Political party*]
PLGS	Proceedings of the Liverpool Geological Society (SAUS)
PLGSS	Payload Ground Support Systems [*NASA*] (NASA)
PLGT.........	Prototype Lunar Geologist Tool
P-LGV........	Psittacosis-Lymphogranuloma Venereum [*Medicine*]
PLH...........	Hamilton Watch Co., Lancaster, PA [*Library symbol*] [*Library of Congress*] [*Obsolete*] (LCLS)
PLH...........	Palaemontes-Lightening Hormone
PLH...........	Paroxysmal Localized Hyperhidrosis [*Dermatology*] (DAVI)
PLH...........	Partido Liberal de Honduras [*Liberal Party of Honduras*] [*Political party*] (PPW)
PLH...........	Payload Handling [*NASA*] (NASA)
PLH...........	Pharyngeal Lymphoid Hyperplasia (SAUS)
PLH...........	Pituitaries Luteinizing Hormone (SAUS)
PLH...........	Placental Lactogenic Hormone (DB)
PLH...........	Plaser Light [*Vancouver Stock Exchange symbol*]
PLH...........	Plymouth [*England*] [*Airport symbol*] (OAG)
PLH...........	Posterior Lobe of Hypophysis [*Medicine*] (MELL)
PLH...........	Pulmonary Left Heart (SAUS)
PLH...........	Punjab Light Horse [*British military*] (DMA)
PL-HGH.......	Plasma-treated Human Growth Hormone (SAUS)
PLHi..........	Lancaster County Historical Society, Lancaster, PA [*Library symbol*] [*Library of Congress*] (LCLS)
PLHIC	Programmable Linear Hall Integrated Circuit [*Electronics*]
PLHR	Power Line Harmonic Radiation
PLhS..........	Lock Haven State College, Lock Haven, PA [*Library symbol*] [*Library of Congress*] (LCLS)
PLI...........	Empresa de Transporte Aereo del Peru [*ICAO designator*] (FAAC)
PLI...........	Ltd. Systems [*Vancouver Stock Exchange symbol*]
PLI...........	Pacific Law Institute (SAUS)
pli............	Pali [*MARC language code*] [*Library of Congress*] (LCCP)
PLI...........	Panarea [*Lipari Islands*] [*Seismograph station code, US Geological Survey*] (SEIS)
PLI...........	Partido Liberal Independiente [*Independent Liberal Party*] [*Nicaragua*] [*Political party*] (PPW)
PLI...........	Partito Liberale Italiano [*Italian Liberal Party*] [*Political party*] (PPW)
PLI...........	Passenger and Immigration Lists Index [*A publication*]
PLI...........	Paternal Leukocyte Immunization (ADWA)
PLI...........	Payload Interrogator (MCD)
PLI...........	Phone Line Interface [*IBM Corp.*] (PCM)
PLI...........	Photo-Laboratory-Index (SAUS)
PLI...........	Photo Library Inc (SAUS)
PLI...........	Pilot Location Indicator

PLI .... Plant Location International (SAUS)
PLI .... Polyvision Corp. [*AMEX symbol*] (SAG)
PLI .... Power Level Indicator
PLI .... Power Loss Indicator (SAUS)
PLI .... Practising Law Institute (EA)
PLI .... Preload Indicating
PLI .... Private Line Interface
PLI .... Procedural Language Interface (SAUS)
PLI .... Proctolin-Like Immunoactivity [*Neurobiology*]
PLI .... Product Licensing Index (SAUS)
PLI .... Professional Liability Insurance (DMAA)
PLI .... Programming Language Interface [*Computer science*] (AGLO)
PLI .... Public Lands Institute (EA)
PLI .... Pulsed LASER Interferometry
PLIA .... Pollution Liability Insurance Association [*Defunct*] (EA)
PLIANT .... Procedural Language Implementing Analog Techniques [*Computer science*] (IEEE)
PLIB .... Pacific Lumber Inspection Bureau (EA)
PLIB .... Program Library [*Computer science*]
PLIC .... Procedural Language for Integrity Constraints [*Computer science*] (MHDI)
PLIC .... Programmable Logic Integrated Circuit (SAUS)
PLICE .... Programmable Low Impedance Circuit Element (TIMI)
PLICE .... Programmable Low-Impedance Circuit Element (SAUS)
PLICK .... Pride, Loyalty, Integrity, Capability, Knowledge (DNAB)
PLIDCO .... Pipe Line Development Co. (SAUS)
PLIDCO .... Pipe Line Development Company, Cleveland, Ohio (SAUS)
PLIE .... Phase Linear Interferometer Experiment (MCD)
PLIF .... Planar Laser Induced Fluorescence
PLI F .... Polo Laico Liberali-Repubblicani Federalisti [*Italy*] [*Political party*] (ECED)
PLIF .... Postlumbar Interbody Fusion [*Neurology*] (DAVI)
PLIM .... Post Launch and Instrumentation Message [*NASA*] (IAA)
PLIM .... Post Launch Information Message [*NASA*] (KSC)
PLIM .... Propellant Lining Installation Metal (ACAE)
PLim 1 .... Plimsoll line (SAUS)
PLIMC .... Pipe Line Insurance Managers Conference [*Defunct*] (EA)
PLIMS .... Programming Language for Information Management System [*Computer science*] (MHDI)
PLimT .... Tyler Arboretum, Lima, PA [*Library symbol*] [*Library of Congress*] (LCLS)
PLIN .... Power Line Impedance Network
PLIN .... Private Line Intercity Network (SAUS)
PLINK .... American People/Link [*American Design and Communication*] [*Information service or system*] (IID)
PLIP .... Parallel Line Internet Protocol [*Computer science*] (AGLO)
PLIP .... Preamplifier Limited Infrared (IAA)
PLIP .... Preamplifier Limited Infrared Photoconductor (SAUS)
PLIRRA .... Pollution Liability Insurance and Risk Retention Act (GFGA)
PLIS .... Preclinical Literature Information System [*Computer science*]
PLIS .... Propellant-Level Indicating System (SAUS)
PLIS .... Public Libraries in the Information Society (TELE)
PLISN .... Parts List Item Sequence Number (MCD)
PLISN .... Provisioning List Item Sequence Number (NASA)
PLISS .... Portable Life Support System (SAUS)
PLISSIT .... Permission, Limited Information, Specific Suggestions, and Intensive Therapy [*Occupational therapy*]
PLIST .... Parameters List (SAUS)
PLIT .... Petrolite Corp. [*NASDAQ symbol*] (NQ)
PLITTY .... Private Line Teletypewriter Service [*Telecommunications*] (TEL)
PLIUN .... Partido Liberal Independiente de Unidad Nacional [*Nicaragua*] [*Political party*] (EY)
PLIW .... Preload Indicating Washer
PLJ .... Pacific Law Journal [*A publication*] (ILCA)
PLJ .... Parliamentary Lobby Journalists [*British*]
PLJ .... Pass Lake Resources Ltd. [*Vancouver Stock Exchange symbol*]
PLJ .... Patna Law Journal [*India*] [*A publication*] (ILCA)
PLJ .... Pennsylvania Law Journal [*A publication*] (DLA)
PLJ .... Permanent Loop Junctor (NITA)
PLJ .... Philippine Law Journal [*A publication*] (ILCA)
PLJ .... Pittsburgh Legal Journal [*Pennsylvania*] [*A publication*] (DLA)
PLJ .... Punjab Law Reporter [*India*] [*A publication*] (DLA)
PLJ .... Pure Lemon Juice
PLJ NS .... Pittsburgh Legal Journal, New Series [*Pennsylvania*] [*A publication*] (DLA)
PLK .... Branson, MO [*Location identifier*] [*FAA*] (FAAL)
PLK .... Phi Lambda Kappa [*Fraternity*]
PLK .... Plank (AAG)
PLK .... Ploecker-Lee-Kesler [*Equation of state*]
PLK .... Plucky Little King [*Used by Western diplomats in Amman in reference to King Hussein of Jordan*]
PLK .... Poincare-Lighthill-Kuo [*Method*]
PLK .... Salomon, Inc. [*AMEX symbol*] (SAG)
PLK .... Salomon Inc. 6.125% PRI 'ELKS' [*AMEX symbol*] (TTSB)
PLKR .... Peacoat Locker
PLL .... Pall Corp. [*NYSE symbol*] (SAG)
PLL .... Pallet [*Building construction*]
PLL .... Papers on Language and Literature: A Journal for Scholars and Critics of Language and Literature [*A publication*] (ANEX)
PLL .... Parts Load List (MCD)
PLL .... Passenger Legal Liability [*Insurance*] (AIA)
PLL .... Peripheral Light Loss
PLL .... Permanent Logical Link [*Telecommunications*]
PLL .... Phase-Locked Loop [*NASA*]
PLL .... Pilgrim Lacrosse League (PSS)

PLL .... Plasma Lockload (AAEL)
PI L .... Platt on Leases [*1841*] [*A publication*] (DLA)
PLL .... Polo, IL [*Location identifier*] [*FAA*] (FAAL)
PLL .... Poly-L-lysine [*Also, PL*] [*Biochemistry*]
PLL .... Positive Logic Level
PLL .... Posterior Longitudinal Ligament [*Medicine*] (MELL)
PLL .... Prelinked Library (SAUS)
PLL .... Prescribed Load List [*Vehicle maintenance operation*] [*Army*]
PLL .... Pressure Length Loop (DB)
PLL .... Prince Line Ltd. [*Steamship*] (MHDW)
PLL .... Program Load Limit (SAUS)
PLL .... Prolymphocytic Leukemia [*Also, PL*] [*Oncology*]
PLL .... Pseudoalcoholic Liver Lesions [*Medicine*]
PLLA .... Printer Long Line Adapter (SAUS)
PLLDF .... Phase-Locked Loop with Decision Feedback [*NASA*] (IAA)
PLLE .... Prueba de Lectura y Lenguaje Escrito [*Standardized test of reading and writing in Spanish for students in grades 3 through 10*]
PLLI .... National Institute on Postsecondary Education, Libraries, and Lifelong Learning
PLL-IC .... Phase-Locked Loop-Integrated Circuit (SAUS)
PLLL .... Parallel Petroleum [*NASDAQ symbol*] (TTSB)
PLLL .... Parallel Petroleum Corp. [*NASDAQ symbol*] (NQ)
PLLL .... Posterior Lateral Line Lobe [*Of electric fishes*]
PLLO .... Phase-Locked Loop Oscillators (ADWA)
PLLRC .... Public Land Law Review Commission [*Terminated, 1970*]
PLLS .... Portable Landing Light System (PDAA)
PLLT .... Pallet (NATG)
PLLTN .... Pollution
PLLVM .... Pennsylvania Farm Museum of Landis Valley, Lancaster, PA [*Library symbol*] [*Library of Congress*] (LCLS)
PLM .... Pacific Law Magazine [*A publication*] (DLA)
PLM .... Packaged Liquid Missile
PLM .... Pakistan Liberation Movement [*Political party*] (PD)
PLM .... Palembang [*Indonesia*] [*Airport symbol*] (OAG)
PLM .... Palomar [*California*] [*Seismograph station code, US Geological Survey*] (SEIS)
PLM .... Passive Line Monitor [*Datapoint*]
PLM .... Passive Lunar Marker
PLM .... Payload Management [*NASA*] (NASA)
PLM .... Payload Mangement (SAUS)
PLM .... Payload Monitoring [*NASA*] (NASA)
PLM .... People's Liberation Movement [*Montserrat*] [*Political party*] (PPW)
PLM .... Percent Labeled Mitosis [*Cytology*]
PLM .... Periodic Leg Movement (DMAA)
PLM .... Permanent Longitudinal Magnetism (SAUS)
PLM .... Phleomycin [*Biochemistry*]
PLM .... Phospholemman [*Biochemistry*]
PLM .... Planetary Rotation Machine (IAA)
PLM .... Planned Lighting Maintenance (SAUS)
PLM .... Planned Maintenance (SAUS)
PLM .... Plasma Level Monitoring [*Medicine*] (DMAA)
PLM .... Plastic Laminating Mold (MCD)
PLM .... PLM International [*AMEX symbol*] (TTSB)
PLM .... PLM International, Inc. [*AMEX symbol*] (SPSG)
PLM .... Plymouth Financial [*Vancouver Stock Exchange symbol*]
PLM .... Poetae Latini Minores [*A publication*] (OCD)
PLM .... Polarized Light Microscopy
PLM .... Polymer-Linked Ligand Monomer [*Biochemistry*]
PLM .... Poor Law Magazine [*A publication*] (DLA)
PLM .... Power Line Modulation (AABC)
PLM .... Prelaunch Monitor [*NASA*] (KSC)
PLM .... Preliminary (KSC)
PLM .... Private Label Merchandiser [*USCG*] (TAG)
PLM .... Production Line Maintenance [*Air Force*]
PLM .... Production-Line Maintenance (SAUS)
PLM .... Production Line Manufacturing
PLM .... Product Life-Cycle Management [*Automotive industry*]
PLM .... Product Line Manager
PLM .... Program Library Management (TIMI)
PLM .... Programmable Logic Matrix (SAUS)
PLM .... Programming Language for Microcomputers (SAUS)
PL/M .... Programming Language for Microprocessors (NITA)
PL/M .... Programming Language/Microcomputers [*Intel Corp.*] [*1973*] [*Computer science*] (CSR)
PLM .... Programming Logic Manual
PLM .... Progressive Labor Movement (BARN)
PLM .... Pulse-Length Modulation
PLMA .... Private Label Manufacturers Association (EA)
PLMA .... Producers Livestock Marketing Association [*Later, IPLA*] (EA)
PL Mag .... Poor Law Magazine [*1858-1930*] [*Scotland*] [*A publication*] (DLA)
PLMATH ...... Procedure Library Mathematics [*Computer science*] (IAA)
PLMB .... Plumbing (AAG)
PLMBR .... Plumber
PLMC .... Premature Living Male Child [*Neonatology*] (DAVI)
PLMD .... Payload Mating Dolly [*NASA*]
PLMD .... Periodic Limb Movements Disorder (ADWA)
PLME .... Peak Local Mean Error (MCD)
PLMES .... Planning, Measurement, and Evaluation Section [*PLA*] (AL)
PLMES .... Planning, Measurements & Evaluation Section [*Public Library Association*] [*American Library Association*]
PLMG .... Plumbing (WGA)
PLMG .... Publishers' Library Marketing Group [*Defunct*] (EA)
PLMHi .... Lancaster Mennonite Conference Historical Society, Lancaster, PA [*Library symbol*] [*Library of Congress*] (LCLS)

PLMN.......... Partido Marxista Leninista de Nicaragua [*Political party*] (EY)
PLMN.......... Public Land Mobile Network (CGWS)
PL MO .... Plastic Mould (SAUS)
PLMP.......... Program Logistic Management Plan (MCD)
PLMPA......... Permanent Labourers' Mutual Protective Association [*A union*] [*British*]
PLMR.......... Paris, Lyons, and Mediterranean Railway (ROG)
PLMR.......... Post Launch Memorandum Report
PlmrW .... Palmer Wireless [*Associated Press*] (SAG)
PLMS.......... Palms
PLMS.......... Partitioned Libraries Management System (MHDI)
PLMS.......... Periodic Leg Movements in Sleep (DIPS)
PLMS.......... Periodic Limb Movement when Sleeping (MELL)
PLMS.......... Plastic Master [*Tool*] (AAG)
PLMS.......... Preservation of Library Materials Section [*Resources and Technical Services Division*] [*American Library Association*]
PLMS.......... Program Logistics Master Schedule [*NASA*] (NASA)
PLMS.......... Public Land Mobile Service Data Base [*Comp Comm, Inc.*] [*Information service or system*] (CRD)
PlmSSB .... Palm Springs Savings Bank [*Associated Press*] (SAG)
PLMT .... Pastoral Lands Management Team (SAUS)
PLMT .... Plasmacytoid Lymphocyte [*Hematology*] (DAVI)
PLMV .... Posterior Leaf Mitral Valve [*Cardiology*] (DMAA)
PLMX .... PL/M Extended [*Programming language*] (CSR)
PLN............. Flight Plan [*Aviation code*]
PLN............. Pancreatic Lymph Nodes [*Medicine*] (MELL)
PLN............. Partido de Liberacion Nacional [*National Liberation Party*] [*El Salvador*] [*Political party*] (EY)
PLN............. Partido Liberacion Nacional [*National Liberation Party*] [*Costa Rica*] [*Political party*] (PPW)
PLN............. Partido Liberal Nacionalista [*Nationalist Liberal Party*] [*Nicaragua*]
PLN............. Pellston [*Michigan*] [*Airport symbol*] (OAG)
PLN............. Pellston, MI [*Location identifier*] [*FAA*] (FAAL)
PLN............. Pelvic Lymph Node [*Gynecology*] (DAVI)
PLN............. Peripheral Lymph Node [*Medicine*] (DB)
PLN............. Phospholamban [*Biochemistry*]
Pl-N............ Place-Name (SAUS)
PLN............. Plain
PLN............. Plan (NASA)
PLN............. Plane (MSA)
Pln............. Platen (SAUS)
Pln............. Platoon [*British military*] (DMA)
PLN............. Plauen [*German Democratic Republic*] [*Seismograph station code, US Geological Survey*] (SEIS)
PLN............. Polnippon [*Poland*] [*ICAO designator*] (FAAC)
PLN............. Popliteal Lymph Node [*Anatomy*]
PLN............. Posterior Lip Nerve (DAVI)
PLN............. Posterior Lymph Node (SAUS)
PLN............. Potassium Lithium Niobate (PDAA)
PLN............. Primary Learning Net (SAUS)
PLN............. Primary Learning Network [*Computer science*] (IAA)
PLN............. Private Line Network (CCCA)
PLN............. Program Line Number [*DoD*]
PLN............. Program Logic Network (NASA)
PLN............. Proteoliaisin [*Biochemistry*]
PLN............. Pudendal Lymph Nodes [*Medicine*] (MELL)
PLN............. Pump-Line-Nozzle
PLN............. Purposely Limited Network (SAUS)
PLNAG .... Public Libraries Networking Advisory Group [*British*] (TELE)
PLNAP .... Pro-Life Nonviolent Action Project (EA)
PLNASG ...... Public Libraries Network Awareness Steering Group [*British*] (TELE)
PLNASG ...... Public Library Network Awareness Steering Group (SAUS)
PLNC .... Point Loma Nazarene College (SAUS)
PLNCIAWPRC... Polish National Committee of the International Association on Water Pollution Research and Control (SAUS)
PLND .... Pelvic Lymph Node Dissection [*Medicine*] (MELL)
plnd .... Planned (DA)
Plng .... Planning (TBD)
PLNG .... Planning
PlnMsg .... Plain Message (SAUS)
PLNN .... Planning (MCD)
PLNP .... Port Lincoln National Park (SAUS)
PLNR .... Planar (MSA)
PLNR .... Planar Systems [*NASDAQ symbol*] (SAG)
PLNR .... Planner
PLNRCODE... Planner Code (SAUS)
PlnRsc .... Plains Resources, Inc. [*Associated Press*] (SAG)
PLNS .... Plains
PLNS .... Planning Sciences International [*NASDAQ symbol*] (SAG)
PLNSTD ...... Planned Standard Equipment [*Navy*] (AFIT)
PLNSY .... Planning Sciences ADS [*NASDAQ symbol*] (TTSB)
PLNT .... Planet (MSA)
PLNT .... Plant
PLNTY .... Planetary (MSA)
PLO............. Pacific Launch Operations [*NASA*]
PLO............. Palestina Liberty Organisation (SAUS)
PLO............. Palestine Liberation Organisation (SAUS)
PLO............. Palestine Liberation Organization [*Political party*] (PD)
PLO............. Palestinian Liberation Organization (SAUS)
PLO............. Parliamentary Liaison Officer (ADA)
PLO............. Partial Lunar Orbit [*Planetary science*]
PLO............. Parts List Only (MCD)
PLO............. Payload Officer [*NASA*] (MCD)
PLO............. Pentagon Liaison Office (MCD)
PLO............. Peoples Liberation Organization (NADA)

PLO............. Phase-Locked Oscillator
PLO............. Pipeline Oil (SAUS)
PLO............. Plans Officer
PLO............. Please Leave On (SAUS)
PLO............. Polycystic Lipomembranous Osteodysplasia [*Medicine*] (DMAA)
PLO............. Poly-L-ornithine
PLO............. Poor Law Office (ROG)
PLO............. Port Liaison Officer
PLO............. Port Lincoln [*Australia*] [*Airport symbol*] (OAG)
PLO............. Presidential Libraries Office (NADA)
PLO............. Price-Lifting Operation [*Business term*] (ECON)
PLO............. Probability of Leakage through Overlay
PLO............. Process Limit Option (SAUS)
PLO............. Product Line Organization
PLO............. Program Line Organization
PLO............. Programmed Local Oscillator
PLO............. Project Line Organization
PLO............. Public Land Order [*Interior*]
PLO............. Public Limit Order [*British*] (NUMA)
PLO............. Pulsed LASER Oscillator
PLO............. Pulsed Locked Oscillator
PLOA .... Proposed Letter of Agreement (MCD)
PLOB .... Patrol Log Observations [*Aviation*] (DSUE)
PLOB .... Place of Birth
PLOB .... Public Limit Order Board [*British*] (NUMA)
PLOC .... Payload Operations Contractor [*NASA*] (SSD)
PLOCAP ...... Post Loss-of-Coolant Accident Protection [*Nuclear energy*] (NRCH)
PLOCSA ...... Personal Liaison Officer, Chief of Staff, Army (SAUS)
PLOCSA ...... Personnel Liaison Officer, Chief of Staff, Army (AABC)
PLOD .... Periodic List of Data [*Computer science*]
PLOD .... Planetary Orbit Determination (IEEE)
PLOKTA ...... Press Lots of Keys to Abort [*Computer term*]
P Lom .... Petrus Lombardi [*Flourished, 1154-59*] [*Authority cited in pre-1607 legal work*] (DSA)
PLOM.......... Prescribed Loan Optimization Model [*Army*] (AABC)
PLOME........ Poor Little Old Me Syndrome [*British*]
PLOMS........ Professional Legal Office Management System (SAUS)
PLondon ...... Greek Papyri in the British Museum [*A publication*] (OCD)
PLONEF ...... Plates on Elastic Foundations [*Structures & Computers Ltd.*] [*Software package*] (NCC)
PLONG .... Present Longititude [*Aviation*] (FAAC)
PLOO .... Pacific Launch Operations Office [*NASA*]
PLOP .... Pilot Line Operating Procedure (SAUS)
PLOP .... Planetary Landing Observation Package [*Aerospace*]
PLOP .... Plant Layout Optimization Procedure (SAUS)
PLOP .... Pressure Line of Position [*Air Force*]
PLor........... Saint Francis College, Loretto, PA [*Library symbol*] [*Library of Congress*] (LCLS)
PLOS .... Primary Line of Sight [*Sextants*]
PLOT .... People's Liberation Organization of Tamil Eelam [*Sri Lanka*] [*Political party*]
PLOT .... Piagetian Logical Operations Test (EDAC)
PLOT .... Plotter
PLOT .... Plotting
PLOT .... Porous Layer Open Tubular (SAUS)
PLOT .... Porous Layer, Open Tubular Column [*Gas chromatography*]
PLOT .... Possibility of Launch-on-Time (SAUS)
PLOT .... Probability of Launch on Time (MCD)
Plot........... Vita Plotini [*of Porphyry*] [*Classical studies*] (OCD)
PLOTE .... People's Liberation Organization of Tamil Eelam [*Sri Lanka*] [*Political party*]
PLOW .... Petunia Lovers of the World
Plow .... Plowden's English King's Bench Commentaries [*or Reports*] [*A publication*] (DLA)
Plowd .... Plowden's English King's Bench Commentaries [*or Reports*] [*A publication*] (DLA)
PLOYREP..... Unit Deployment Report (CINC)
PLP............. La Palma [*Panama*] [*Airport symbol*] (OAG)
PLP............. Packet Layer Protocol [*Computer science*] (TNIG)
PLP............. Packet Level Procedure [*or Protocol*] [*Computer programming*] (PCM)
PLP............. Packet Level Protocol (SAUS)
PLP............. Palo [*Philippines*] [*Seismograph station code, US Geological Survey*] (SEIS)
PLP............. Palpus [*Arthropod anatomy*]
PLP............. Parathyroidlike Protein [*Medicine*] (MELL)
PLP............. Parliamentary Labour Party [*British*]
PLP............. Parti de la Liberte et du Progres [*Party of Liberty and Progress*] [*See also PVV*] [*Belgium*] (PPE)
PLP............. Partido de los Pobres [*Poor People's Party*] [*Mexico*] [*Political party*] (PD)
PLP............. Parti Liberal Progressiste [*Liberal Progressive Party*] [*Morocco*] [*Political party*] (PPW)
PLP............. Parti pour la Liberation du Peuple [*People's Liberation Party*] [*Senegal*] [*Political party*] (PPW)
PLP............. Partners for Livable Places (EA)
PLP............. Parts List Page (KSC)
PLP............. Party Line Protocol (SAUS)
PLP............. Passive Low Pass (IAA)
PLP............. Patrol Landplane (SAUS)
PLP............. Pattern Learning Parser
PLP............. People's Liberation Party [*Pakistan*]
PLP............. Periodate Lysine-Paraformaldehyde
PLP............. Periodate-Lysine-Paraformalin (SAUS)
PLP............. Personal LASER Printer [*Computer science*]

PLP............. Phantom Limb Pain (MELL)
PLP............. Phillips Petroleum Co. [Toronto Stock Exchange symbol]
PLP............. Phoenix Aviation [British] [ICAO designator] (FAAC)
PLP............. Photolithographic Process (IAA)
PLP............. Physical Layer Protocol (SAUS)
PLP............. Plastic Lined Pipe (SAUS)
PLP............. Plastic-Lined Pipe
PLP............. Polyoma-Like Particle [Genetics]
PLP............. Polystyrene Latex Particles (DB)
PLP............. Post Launch Phase
PLP............. Power Law Process
PLP............. Preferred Lenders Program [Small Business Administration]
PLP............. Preformed Line Product (IAA)
PLP............. Preformed Line Products (SAUS)
PLP............. Presentation Level Protocol [AT & T Videotex System]
PLP............. Principal Locating Point [Automotive engineering]
PLP............. Prison Link Project (WDAA)
PLP............. Procedural Language Processor
PLP............. Process Layup Procedure
PLP............. Product Liability Prevention [Conference]
PLP............. Product Line Planning (SAUS)
PLP............. Programming Language Processing (or Processor) (SAUS)
PLP............. Progressive Labor Party (EA)
PLP............. Progressive Labour Party [Saint Lucia] [Political party] (EAIO)
PLP............. Progressive Liberal Party [Bahamas] [Political party] (PPW)
PLP............. Prolactin-Like Protein [Biochemistry]
PLP............. Proteolipid [Biochemistry]
PLP............. Proteolipid Protein [Biochemistry]
PLP............. Pyridoxal Phosphate [Also, PALP] [Biochemistry]
PLPA........... Pageable Link Pack Area (SAUS)
PLPA........... Pageable Link-Pack Area
PLPA........... Palmyra, Palymra Island [Line Islands] [ICAO location identifier] (ICLI)
PLPA........... Permissible Low-Pressure Alarm (SAUS)
PLPA........... Permissive Low-Pressure Alarm (IEEE)
Pl Par.......... Placita Parliamentaria [Latin] [A publication] (DLA)
PL PATH..... Plant Pathology (SAUS)
PLPB.......... Petroleum Labor Policy Board [Abolished, 1936]
PLPBD........ Pulpboard
PLPD.......... Product Liability Prevention and Defense [An association] (EA)
PLP FOR..... Foramen of Labial Palpus [Arthropod anatomy]
PLPG.......... Publishers' Library Promotion Group [Later, PLMG] (EA)
PLP GRNDG... Pulp Grinding [Freight]
PLPH.......... Post-Lumbar Puncture Headache [Medicine] (DMAA)
PLPI........... Product Licence Parallel Importation (DB)
PLPLS........ Proceedings of the Leeds Philosophical and Literary Society (SAUS)
PLPO......... Phase-Locked Pulsed Oscillator (SAUS)
PlPolyT....... Planet Polymer Technologies, Inc. [Associated Press] (SAG)
PLPP......... Pennsylvania League for Planned Parenthood (SAUS)
PLPP......... Position Location Post Processor (MCD)
PLPrM........ PLC Capital LLC 'A' 'MIPS' [NYSE symbol] (TTSB)
PLPS.......... Packaged Liquid Propellant System
PLPS.......... Propellant Loading and Pressurization System [NASA]
PLPS.......... Pulse-Locked Power Supply (SAUS)
PLPT.......... Presentation Level Protocol [Computer science]
PLPT.......... Pretreatment Local Program Tracking System (SAUS)
PLPV.......... Pelargonium Line Pattern Virus [Plant pathology]
PLQ........... Photoluminescence Quenching Spectroscopy (SAUS)
PLQ........... Plaque (MSA)
PLQ........... Public Library Quarterly (SAUS)
PLQ........... Tallahassee, FL [Location identifier] [FAA] (FAAL)
PLR........... LaRoche College, Pittsburgh, PA [OCLC symbol] (OCLC)
PLR........... Northwestern Air Lease Ltd. [Canada] [ICAO designator] (FAAC)
PLR........... Pacific Law Reporter [A publication] (DLA)
PLR........... Packet Lost Ratio (SAUS)
PLR........... Pakistan Law Reports [A publication] (DLA)
PLR........... Pakistan Law Review [A publication] (DLA)
PLR........... Parlake Resources Ltd. [Toronto Stock Exchange symbol]
PLR........... Partido Liberal Radical [Radical Liberal Party] [Ecuador] [Political party] (PPW)
PLR........... Partido Liberal Radical [Radical Liberal Party] [Paraguay] [Political party] (PPW)
PLR........... Patent Law Review [A publication] (DLA)
PLR........... Patent Log Reading [Navigation]
PLR........... Patna Law Reporter [India] [A publication] (DLA)
PLR........... Pell City, AL [Location identifier] [FAA] (FAAL)
PLR........... Pennsylvania Law Record [Philadelphia] [A publication] (DLA)
P-LR.......... Pennsylvania Legislative Reference Bureau, Harrisburg, PA [Library symbol] [Library of Congress] (LCLS)
PLR........... Periodic Logistical Report
PLR........... Philippine Liberation Ribbon [Military decoration]
PLR........... Pillar (MSA)
PLR........... Pliers (MSA)
PLR........... Plymouth Rubber Co., Inc. [AMEX symbol] (SPSG)
plr............. Poplar (VRA)
PLR........... Portable LASER Range-Finder
PLR........... Power Line Radiation [Radioscience]
PLR........... Presentation Loss Rate (MCD)
PLR........... Pressure Level Recorder
PLR........... Primary Language Record [Education] (AIE)
PLR........... Primary Loss Retention [Insurance]
PLR........... Private Legislation Reports [Scotland] [A publication] (DLA)
PLR........... Production Limitation Record (SAUS)
PLR........... Product Licence of Right (DB)
PLR........... Program Length Register [Computer science] (VLIE)

PLR........... Program Library Release (VLIE)
PLR........... Program Life Requirement (NG)
PLR........... Program Lock-in Register (NITA)
PLR........... Programming Language for Robots (VLIE)
PLR........... Prolactin Receptor [Biochemistry]
PLR........... Pronation/Lateral Rotation [Fracture] [Orthopedics] (DAVI)
PLR........... Psychological Laboratories [Harvard University] (KSC)
PLR........... Public Law Review [A publication]
PLR........... Public Lending Right [Royalty for books borrowed from public libraries] [British]
PLR........... Puller (MSA)
PLR........... Pulse Link Relay [Telecommunications] (TEL)
PLR........... Pulse Link Repeater [Telecommunications] (TEL)
PLR........... Punjab Law Reporter [India] [A publication] (DLA)
PLR........... Pupillary Light Reflex (SAUS)
PLR. A....... Plymouth Rubber'A'vtg [AMEX symbol] (TTSB)
PLR.B......... Plymouth Rubber Cl'B' [AMEX symbol] (TTSB)
PLRA......... Partido Liberal Radical Autentico [Authentic Liberal Radical Party] [Paraguay] [Political party] (PD)
PLRA......... Pennsylvania Learning Resources Association (EDAC)
PLRA......... Photo Litho Reproducers Association (SAUS)
PLRA......... Photo-Litho Reproducers' Association [British] (BI)
PLRACTA.... Position Location, Reporting, and Control of Tactical Aircraft [Military]
PLRB......... Property Loss Research Bureau (EA)
PLRC......... Pulsed LASER Remote Crosswind Sensor (MCD)
PLRCAE...... Radio Corp. of America, Electron Tube Division, Engineering Section, Lancaster, PA [Library symbol] [Library of Congress] [Obsolete] (LCLS)
PLRD......... Payload Requirements Document (NASA)
PLRD......... Polaroid (VRA)
PLRD......... Procurement, Logistics, and Readiness Division (AAGC)
PLRD......... Pull Rod
PLR Dacca... Pakistan Law Reports, Dacca Series [A publication] (DLA)
PLRE......... Program on Long-Range Forecasting Research [Marine science] (OSRA)
PL Reaction... Palm Leaf Reaction (SAUS)
PLRF......... Pediatric Liver Research Foundation [Defunct] (EA)
pLRF......... Placental Luteinizing Hormone-Releasing Factor [Endocrinology]
PLRF......... Planer Fixture
PLRF......... Program on Long-Range Forecasting Research (SAUS)
PLRG......... Public Libraries Research Group [British] (TELE)
PLRI.......... Posterolateral Rotation Instability [Sports medicine]
PLRJ & K.... Punjab Law Reporter, Jammu and Kashmir Section [India] [A publication] (DLA)
PLR Kar...... Pakistan Law Reports, Karachi Series [1947-53] [A publication] (DLA)
PLR Lah..... Pakistan Law Reports, Lahore Series [1947-55] [A publication] (DLA)
PLRPF........ Personnel Loss Rate Planning Factors (MCD)
PLRS......... Pelorus
PLRS......... Phase Lock Receiving System
PLRS......... Phase-Lock Receiving System (SAUS)
PLRS......... Position Location Reporting System [Military]
PLRS/TIDS... Position Location Reporting System/Tactical Information Distribution Systems [Military] (RDA)
PLRSTN...... Pelorus Stand
PLRT......... Polarity (MSA)
PLRV......... Payload Launch Readiness Verification [NASA] (MCD)
PLRV......... Potato Leafroll Virus
PLRV......... Pseudo Leaf Roll Virus (SAUS)
PLRWP....... Pakistan Law Reports, West Pakistan Series [A publication] (DLA)
pls............. Isoelectric Point (STED)
PLS........... Page Layout System [Graphic arts] (DGA)
PLS........... Palio Air Service [Italy] [ICAO designator] (FAAC)
PLS........... Palletized Loading System
PLS........... Palletized Load System [Army] (RDA)
PLS........... Palomar-Leiden Survey
PLS........... Papillon-Lefevre Syndrome [Medicine] (DMAA)
PLS........... Paracelsus Healthcare Corp. [NYSE symbol] (SAG)
PLS........... Parcels (MSA)
PLS........... Parent Locator Service [A service of the Office of Child Support Enforcement (OCSE)] (PAZ)
PLS........... Parsons Language Sample
PLS........... Partial Least Squares
PLS........... Parti Liberal Suisse [Liberal Party of Switzerland] [Political party] (PPE)
PLS........... Patrol Locator System [Army]
PLS........... Payload Systems [NASA] (MCD)
PLS........... Peerless Tube Co. [AMEX symbol] (SPSG)
PLS........... Peninsula Library System [Belmont, CA] [Library network]
PLS........... People's Law School [Defunct] (EA)
PLS........... Peralto Resources Corp. [Vancouver Stock Exchange symbol]
PLS........... Periodic Log System
PLS........... Personal Learning System (VLIE)
PLS........... Personal Library Software [Commercial firm]
PLS........... Personal Library Systems (SAUS)
PLS........... Personal Locator System (ACAE)
PLS........... Physical Layer Signaling (SAUS)
PLS........... Physical Layer Signalling (VLIE)
PLS........... Physical Signalling (NITA)
PLS........... Picture Line Standard (ELAL)
PLS........... Pitch Limit Switch
PLS........... Plaisance [Mauritius] [Geomagnetic observatory code]
PLS........... Plasma Light Source
PLS........... Plasma Spectrometer (ACAE)
PLS........... Plasma Subsystem (ACAE)

PLS	Plastic Surgery (MELL)
pls	Plates (DIAR)
PLS	Plates [*Classical studies*] (OCD)
PLS	Please (AFM)
PLS	Plugging Switch (IEEE)
PLS	Pneumatic Limit Switch
PLS	Polson, MT [*Location identifier*] [*FAA*] (FAAL)
PLS	Polynomial Solution (IAA)
PLS	Polystyrene Latex Sphere
PLS	Popular Low-Power Schottky [*Electronics*] (MCD)
PLS	Portable Laboratory Salinometer
PLS	Position Location System [*Army*]
PLS	Positive Locking System (SAUS)
PLS	Positive Lubrication System (SAUS)
PLS	Positron Lifetime Spectroscopy (SAUS)
PLS	Post Landing and Safing [*NASA*] (NASA)
PLS	Postsecondary Longitudinal Studies Program [*Department of Education*] (GFGA)
PLS	Precautions, Limitations, and Setpoints [*Nuclear energy*] (NRCH)
PLS	Pre Launch Survivability (ACAE)
PLS	Pre-Launch Survivability (SAUS)
PLS	Preliminary Landing Site (NASA)
PLS	Preliminary Location Summary (VLIE)
PLS	Preschool Language Scale [*Child development test*]
PLS	President of the Linnaean Society [*British*]
PLS	Primary Landing Site (MCD)
PLS	Primary Lateral Sclerosis [*Medicine*] (DMAA)
PLS	Primary Link Station (VLIE)
PLS	Principles and Practice of Land Surveying (SAUS)
PLS	Private Line Service
PLS	Product Line Simulator
PLS	Professional Land Surveyor (SAUS)
PLS	Professional Legal Secretary [*National Association of Legal Secretaries*] [*Designation awarded by*]
PLS	Profit-and-Loss-Sharing Account [*Banking*] (IMH)
PLS	Program Liaison Staff (COE)
PLS	Programmable Limit Switch (SAUS)
PLS	Programmable Logic Sequence (SAUS)
PLS	Programmable Logic Sequencer [*Computer science*]
PLS	Programming Language for System [*Computer science*] (IAA)
PLS	Progressive Learning Systems [*Potomac, MD*] (TSSD)
PLS	Projectile Location System (SAUS)
PLS	Projection of Latent Structures (AAEL)
PLS	Propellant Loading Sequencer (AAG)
PLS	Propellant Loading System
PLS	Prostaglandin-Like Substance [*Biochemistry*] (MAE)
PLS	Providenciales [*British West Indies*] [*Airport symbol*] (OAG)
PLS	Provincial Land Surveyor (SAUS)
PLS	Public Library of Science
PLS	Publishers Licensing Society (DGA)
PLS	Pulse (MSA)
PLS	Pulsed LASER System
PLS	Pulsed Light Source
PLS	Pulser (SAUS)
PLS	Pure Live Seed (SAUS)
PLS	Purnell Library Service [*Commercial firm*]
PLSA	Partner Launch Site Agreement (SAUS)
PLSA	Pulsed Laser Spectrum Analyzer (SAUS)
PLSAP	Physical Layer Service Access Point [*Computer science*] (VLIE)
PLSC	Pacific Logistics Support Command (SAUS)
PLSC	Political Science (SAUS)
PLSC	Project Level Steering Committee (HGAA)
PLSD	Post Hoc Least Significant Difference [*Statistics*]
PLSD	Promotion List Service Date [*Air Force*]
PLSD	Protected Least Significant Difference (DMAA)
PLSFC	Part Load Specific Fuel Consumption [*Gas turbine*]
PLSGT	Platoon Sergeant [*Marine Corps*]
PLSHD	Polished [*Freight*]
Plshr	Polisher (SAUS)
PLSI	Planar Least Squares Inverse (SAUS)
PLSI	Premier Laser Systems, Inc. [*NASDAQ symbol*] (SAG)
PLSI	Programmable Large Scale Integration (SAUS)
PLSIA	Premier Laser Systems 'A' [*NASDAQ symbol*] (TTSB)
PLSIW	Premier Laser Systems Wrrt 'A' [*NASDAQ symbol*] (TTSB)
PLSIZ	Premier Laser Systems Wrrt 'B' [*NASDAQ symbol*] (TTSB)
PLSL	Propellants and Life Support Laboratory [*NASA*] (NASA)
PLSN	Pulsation (MSA)
PL/SNSR	Payload Sensor [*NASA*] (GFGA)
PLSNT	Pleasant
PLSO	Phonetic Letter Spell Out (CCCA)
PLSO	Phonetic Letters Spelled Out (SAUS)
PLSO	Propellant Life Support and Ordnance [*NASA*] (KSC)
PLSP	Payload Signal Processor [*NASA*] (NAKS)
PLSP	Prelaunch Survival Probability (CINC)
PLSPC	Programme on Land-Surface Processes and Climate (SAUS)
PLSPC	Research Programme on Land-Surface Processes and Climate (SAUS)
PL SPKR	Plug for Speaker (SAUS)
PLSPS	Performance Levels of a School Program Survey [*Teacher evaluation test*]
PLSR	Pulsator (MSA)
PLSS	Payload Support Structure [*NASA*] (SSD)
PLSS	Personal Life Support System (SAUS)
PLSS	Portable Life Support Subsystem (SAUS)
PLSS	Portable Life Support System [*or Subsystem*] [*NASA*]

PLSS	Post-Landing Survival System [*NASA*]
PLSS	Pottable Life-Support System (SAUS)
PLSS	Precision Location Strike System [*Air Force*]
PLSS	Prelaunch Status Simulator
PLSS	Primary Life Support Subsystem (SAUS)
PLSS	Primary Life Support System [*or Subsystem*] (NASA)
PLSS	Public Land Survey System (ADWA)
PLSS	Public Library Systems Section [*Public Library Association*]
PLSSRS	Plant and Soil Science Research Station [*Southern Illinois University at Carbondale*] [*Research center*] (RCD)
PLSSU	Portable Life Support Stretcher Unit [*Military*] (CAAL)
PLST	Palletized Loading System Trailer (SAUS)
PLST	Palletized Load System Truck [*Military*]
PLST	Plastering
PLSTC	Plastic (AAG)
PLSTG	Plastering (SAUS)
PLSTR	Plasterer (ADA)
PLSTRER	Plasterer (WGA)
PLSV	Propellant Latching Solenoid Valve
PL Sw	Plub with Switch (SAUS)
PLT	Columbus, NE [*Location identifier*] [*FAA*] (FAAL)
PLT	Lancaster Theological Seminary of the United Church of Christ, Lancaster, PA [*Library symbol*] [*Library of Congress*] (LCLS)
PLT	Lutheran Theological Seminary, Philadelphia, PA [*OCLC symbol*] (OCLC)
PLT	Pacific Lighting (SAUS)
PLT	Page Layout Terminal [*Graphic arts*] (DGA)
PLT	Pallet (AABC)
PLT	Panduit Locking Tie (SAUS)
Plt	Parliament
PLT	Partido Liberal Teete [*Teete Liberal Party*] [*Paraguay*] [*Political party*] (PPW)
PLT	Patna Law Times [*India*] [*A publication*] (DLA)
Plt	Peltier's Orleans Appeals Decisions [*Louisiana*] [*A publication*] (DLA)
PLT	Personal Leave Time (SAUS)
PLT	Phase-Locked Time (SAUS)
PLT	Photoluminescent Thermometer
PLT	Pi Lambda Theta [*An association*] (NTPA)
PLTP	Pilot (AFM)
PLT	Pilot Knob [*California*] [*Seismograph station code, US Geological Survey*] (SEIS)
PLT	Pipeline Time [*Army*]
PLT	Plaint [*Legal term*] (ROG)
PLT	Planar Tube
PLT	Plant
PLT	Plantronics, Inc. [*NYSE symbol*] (SPSG)
PLT	Plate
PLT	Platelet [*Hematology*]
PLT	Platen (SAUS)
PLT	Platoon [*Military*] (AABC)
Plt	Plot (SAUS)
PLT	Plotting (SAUS)
PLT	Port Light
PLT	Post Loading Test (NG)
PLT	Power Line Transient (IEEE)
PLT	Primed Lymphocyte Typing [*Hematology*]
PLT	Princeton Large Torus [*Nuclear reactor*]
PLT	Private Line Telephone
PLT	Private Line Teletypewriter
PLT	Procurement Lead Time [*Army*]
PLT	Production Lead Time
PLT	Program Library Tape [*Computer science*] (IEEE)
PLT	Program List Table [*Computer science*] (VLIE)
PLT	Programmed Learning Textbook
PLT	Programmed Light Table (SAUS)
PLT	Programming-Language Theory (SAUS)
PLT	Progressive Lowering of Temperature
PLT	Project Lead Time
PLT	Project Learning Tree (WPI)
PLT	Psittacosis-Lymphogranuloma Trachoma (SAUS)
PLT	Psittacosis-Lymphogranuloma Venereum Trachoma [*Microbiology*]
PLT	Pulsed Light Theodolite
PLT	Pulse Light Theodolite (SAUS)
PLT	Punjab Law Times [*India*] [*A publication*] (DLA)
PLT	South Carolina Aeronautics Commission [*FAA designator*] (FAAC)
PLTC	Partnership for Long Term Care
PLTC	Political (SAUS)
PLTC	Port Liner Terms Charges [*Shipping*] (DS)
PLTC	Power-Limited Tray Cable (SAUS)
PLTC	Propellant Loading Terminal Cabinet (AAG)
PLTD	Plated
PLTF	Par Leadership Training Foundation [*Defunct*] (EA)
PLTF	Plaintiff [*Legal term*] (ROG)
PLTF	Purple Loosestrife Task Force [*Defunct*] (EA)
PLTFF	Plaintiff
PLTFM	Platform
PLT-G	Giant Platelet [*Hematology*] (DAVI)
PLTG	Plating
PLT GL	Plate Glass [*Freight*]
PLTHS	Pilothouse
PL-TLM	Payload Telemetry (SAUS)
PLT LT	Pilot Light (MSA)
PLTN	Platoon
Plt Off	Pilot Officer [*British military*] (DMA)
PLTP	Phospholipid Transfer Protein [*Biochemistry*]

PLT Press....	Platen Press (SAUS)
PLTR..........	Plan for Long-Range Technical Requirements
PLTR..........	Plotter (MSA)
PLTR..........	Procurement Lead Time Requirement
Pltrsq.........	Plateresque (VRA)
PLTRY........	Poultry [Freight]
PLTS..........	Pacific Lutheran Theological Seminary (SAUS)
PLTS..........	Point Loma Test Site (SAUS)
PLTS..........	Precision LASER Tracking System (NASA)
PltsTrg........	Pilots Training (SAUS)
PLTTNG......	Pilot Training [Air Force]
PLTTNGSq ..	Pilot Training Squadron [Air Force]
PLTTY........	Private Line Teletypewriter [Telecommunications] (IAA)
PLTTY........	Private Line Teletypewriter Service (NITA)
PLTV..........	Percentage Local Thickness Variation (AAEL)
PLTXAU......	Public Telex Access Unit [Telecommunications] (OSI)
PLTY..........	Poultry
PLTYP.........	Plumbeotype (VRA)
PLTZC.........	Pulitzer Publishing Co. (MHDW)
PLU...........	Pacific Lutheran University (SAUS)
PLU...........	Partial Line Up (NITA)
PLU...........	Partido Liberal Unificado [Unified Liberal Party] [Paraguay] [Political party] (PPW)
PLu...........	Path Loss, Uplink [Communications]
PLU...........	Patrice Lumumba University (SAUS)
PLU...........	People Like Us (IIA)
PLU...........	PERT [Program Evaluation and Review Technique] Life Cycle Unified System (IAA)
PLU...........	Phi Lambda Upsilon [Fraternity]
PLU...........	Platoon Leaders Unit [Marine Corps]
PI U..........	Plowden on Usury [A publication] (DLA)
PLU...........	Pluggable Unit (SAA)
plu...........	Plural (WDMC)
PLU...........	Plural
PLU...........	Plurality (SAUS)
PLU...........	Plutonium [Chemical symbol is Pu] (AAG)
PLU...........	Poor Law Union [British]
PLU...........	Position Location Uncertainty (ACAE)
PLU...........	Pratt & Lambert United, Inc. [NYSE symbol] (SAG)
PLU...........	Preservation of Location Uncertainty [Strategy for protecting missiles] [Military]
PLU...........	Pressure Lubrication Unit
PLU...........	Price Look-Up (IAA)
PLU...........	Primary Logical Unit [Computer science] (CIST)
PLU...........	Probability of Leakage through Underlay
PLU...........	Program Library Unit (SAUS)
PLU...........	Program Load Unit
PLU...........	Propellant Loading and Utilization (AAG)
PLUARG......	Pollution from Land Use Activity Reference Group (SAUS)
PLUCON......	Plutonium Decontamination Emergency Team [Army]
PLUG.........	Propellant Loading and Utilization Group (AAG)
PLUG.........	Public Law Utilities Group (SAUS)
PLUGE.......	Picture Line-Up Generating Equipment (SAUS)
PLUGE.......	Picture Line-Up Generator [Television]
PLuL........	Lincoln University, Lincoln University, PA [Library symbol] [Library of Congress] (LCLS)
PLUM........	Payload Launch Module
PLUM........	Payload Umbilical Mast (NASA)
PLUM........	Planning Land Use Model (SAUS)
PLUM........	Priority Low-Use Minimal
PLUM........	Programmes Library Update and Maintenance (PDAA)
PLUM........	Programming Language for Users of MAVIS [Microprocessor-Based Audio Visual Information System] (PDAA)
PLUM........	Programs Library Update and Maintenance (SAUS)
PLUMB.......	Plumber (SAUS)
PLUMB.......	Plumbing (SAUS)
PLUMB.......	Plumbum [Lead] [Pharmacy]
Plum Contr...	Plumptre on Contracts [2nd ed.] [1897] [A publication] (DLA)
PlumCrk......	Plum Creek Timber Co., Inc. [Associated Press] (SAG)
PLUME.......	Pipeline Under Mother Earth (SAUS)
PLUME2D	Two-Dimensional Plumes in Uniform Ground Water Flow (SAUS)
PLUME3D	Three-Dimensional Plumes in Uniform Ground Water Flow (SAUS)
PLUMG.......	Plumbing (SAUS)
PLUMR.......	Plumber (SAUS)
PLUNA........	Primeras Lineas Uruguayas de Navegacion Aerea [Uruguayan National Airlines]
PLund.........	Papyri Lundenses [A publication] (OCD)
PLUNGER	Protocol Link Undoing Network Great Error Rates (SAUS)
PLUOT........	Parts Listing and Used On Technique (SAUS)
PLUOT........	Parts Listing Used On-Line Technique [Computer science] (IAA)
PLUP.........	Pluperfect [Grammar]
PLUPF........	Pluperfect [Grammar]
PLUR.........	Jarvis Island [Line Islands] [ICAO location identifier] (ICLI)
PLUR.........	Photographics Laboratory Usage Reporting
PLUR.........	Photo Lab Usage Reporting (MCD)
plur...........	Plural (NTIO)
PLUR.........	Plural
PLUS.........	Parent Loans for/to Undergraduate Students (SAUS)
PLUS.........	Parent Loans to Undergraduate Students [Later, ALAS] [Department of Education]
PLUS.........	PERT [Program Evaluation and Review Technique] Lifecycle Unified System
PLUS.........	Physically-Limited United Students (SAUS)
PLUS.........	Portable Lightweight Upper Air Sounding System (MCD)
PLUS.........	Potential Long Supply Utilization Screening (NATG)
PLUS	Precision Loading and Utilization System (AAG)
PLUS	Prima Leben und Sparen [Quality Living and Saving] [Brand name and discount store chain in West Germany and US]
PLUS	Procedures for Long Supply Assets Utilization Screening [DoD]
PLUS	Professional Learning Unit System (SAUS)
PLUS	Professional Liability Underwriting Society (NTPA)
PLUS	Program Language for User's System (NITA)
PLUS	Program Language for User Systems (SAUS)
PLUS	Program Library Update System
PLUS	Programmed Learning under Supervision
PLUS	Programming Language for UNIVAC [Universal Automatic Computer] Systems [Computer science] (CSR)
PLUS	Project Literacy United States (SAUS)
PLUS	Project Literacy US [Joint project of American Broadcasting Co. and Public Broadcasting Service]
PLUS	Prudent Laboratory Use System [Health insurance] (GHCT)
PLUS	Room Plus, Inc. [NASDAQ symbol] (SAG)
PLUSS	Point Loma Unmanned Search System (SAUS)
PLUSS	USS Point Loma Unmanned Search System (SAUS)
Plut............	Plutarch [First century AD] [Classical studies] (OCD)
PLUT..........	Plutchnik [Geriatric rating scale] (DMAA)
Plut............	Plutus [of Aristophanes] [Classical studies] (OCD)
PLUTHARCO...	Plutonium, Uranium, Thorium Assembly Reactivity Code
PLUTO	Pipe Line Under the Ocean (SAUS)
PLUTO	Pipeline under the Ocean [British project] [World War II]
PLUTO	Planning Urban Transportation Options [Traffic management]
PLUTO	Plutonium Loop Testing Reactor (SAUS)
PLUTO	Plutonium [Loop-Testing] Reactor [British] (DEN)
PLUTO	Programmed Logic for Automatic Teaching Operation
PLUTO Technique...	Parts Listing Used-on Technique (SAUS)
PLUVUE	Plume Visibility Model [Environmental Protection Agency] (GFGA)
PLUZ..........	Policy Land Use Zone [Australian Capital Territory]
PLV...........	Live Poliomyelitis Vaccine [Immunology] (MAE)
PLV...........	Panleukopenia Virus [Medicine] (MAE)
PLV...........	Peak Left Ventricular [Pressure] [Cardiology]
PLV...........	Personnel Launch Vehicle (ACAE)
PLV...........	Phenylalanine-Lysine-Vasopressin (MAE)
PLV...........	Phu-Lien [Kien-An] [Vietnam] [Seismograph station code, US Geological Survey] (SEIS)
PLV...........	Pitch Line Velocity (SAUS)
PLV...........	Polaravia OY [Finland] [ICAO designator] (FAAC)
PLV...........	Posterior Left Ventricle [Anatomy] (DAVI)
PLV...........	Posterior Left Ventricular Wall [Cardiology]
PLV...........	Postlanding Vent [or Ventilation] [Apollo] [NASA]
PLV...........	Power Limiting Valve
PLV...........	Presentation Level Video (PCM)
PLV...........	Presentation Level Video (SAUS)
PLV...........	Production Level Video (SAUS)
PLV...........	Production Level Video
PLVC..........	Post-Landing Vent Control [NASA] (KSC)
PLVL..........	Present Level [Aviation] (FAAC)
PLVRZD	Pulverized (MSA)
PLVS..........	Pelvis (SAUS)
PLVW..........	Pool View (TRID)
PLW...........	Palau [ANSI three-letter standard code] (CNC)
PLW...........	Palu [Indonesia] [Airport symbol] (OAG)
PLW...........	Patna Law Weekly [India] [A publication] (DLA)
PLW...........	Plastic Engine Technology Corp. [Toronto Stock Exchange symbol]
PLW...........	Plow Snow [NWS] (FAAC)
PLW...........	Preload Washer
PLWA..........	People Living with AIDS [Acquired Immunodeficiency Syndrome] [Medicine] (TAD)
PL/WA........	Plain Washer [Automotive engineering]
PLWA..........	Primary Light Water Addition (COE)
plwd..........	Plywood (BARN)
PLWG	Photographic Laboratories Working Group [Range Commanders Council] [White Sands Missile Range, NM]
PLWHA	People Living With HIV/AIDS [Human Immunodeficiency Virus / Acquired Immune Deficiency Syndrome] [Australia]
PLWP	Programmed Labor Work Performed (SAUS)
PLWR	Pressurized Light Water Reactor (SAUS)
PLWS	Prader-Labhart-Willi Syndrome [Medicine] (DMAA)
PLWS	Pulsed Laser Weapon System (ACAE)
PLX...........	Parallax Developments [Vancouver Stock Exchange symbol]
PLX...........	Plains Resources [AMEX symbol] (TTSB)
PLX...........	Plains Resources, Inc. [AMEX symbol] (SPSG)
PLX...........	Plexus [Medicine]
PLX...........	Position Launch [Search mode wherein X signifies the launch mode number] (MCD)
PLX...........	Propellant Loading Exercise (MCD)
PLX...........	Propellant-Loading Transfer (SAUS)
PLX...........	Robinson, IL [Location identifier] [FAA] (FAAL)
PI x Fe.......	Plastic to Female (SAUS)
PI x PI	Plastic to Plastic (SAUS)
PLXS..........	Plexus Corp. [NASDAQ symbol] (NQ)
PLY...........	Photolimited Yield
PLY...........	Photoluminescence Yield [Spectroscopy]
Ply...........	Plymouth [Record label]
ply...........	Plywood (VRA)
PLY...........	Plywood
PLY...........	Polaris Energy [Vancouver Stock Exchange symbol]
PLY...........	Polyphase Corp. [AMEX symbol] (SPSG)
PLY...........	Prune Extract Lactose Yeast Medium [Microbiology]
plyc..........	Polychrome (VRA)
plyes..........	Polyester (VRA)

PlyGem	Ply-Gem, Inc. [*Associated Press*] (SAG)
PLYINST	Command Comply Current Instructions
PLYM	Plymouth [*England*]
plym	Polymer (VRA)
P-LYM	Prolymphocyte [*Hematology*] (DAVI)
PLYMCHAN	Plymouth Subarea Channel [*NATO*] (NATG)
PLYMCHAN	Plymouth Sub-Area Command Headquarters (SAUS)
Plymouth St C	Plymouth State College (GAGS)
PLYMP	Plympton [*England*]
PLYMT	Plymtree [*England*]
PLYPASSPORT	Application for Passport for Self and/or Dependents Accordance BUPERS Manual [*Navy*]
plypt	Polyptic (VRA)
Plyr	Player (SAUS)
PlyR	Plymouth Rubber Co., Inc. [*Associated Press*] (SAG)
plyst	Polystyrene (VRA)
plyur	Polyurethane (VRA)
plyvn	Polyvinyl (VRA)
PLYWD	Plywood
PLZ	Phenelzine (DMAA)
Plz	Plaza (AD)
plz	Plaza (BEE)
PLZ	Plaza (MCD)
PLZ	Please
PLZ	Polarize (MSA)
PLZ	Port Elizabeth [*South Africa*] [*Airport symbol*] (OAG)
PLZ	Programming Languages for the Zilog [*Computer science*] (CSR)
PLZ	Programming Language Zilog (SAUS)
PLZ	Punch Leading Zeros (TIMI)
PLZA	Plaza [*Commonly used*] (OPSA)
PLZF	Promyelocytic Leukaemia Zinc-Finger [*Protein*]
PLZN	Polarization (MSA)
PLZT	Leading Lanthanum Zirconate Titanate
PLZT	Pb-based Lanthanum-doped Zirconate Titanates
PLZT	Polycrystalline Lead-Zirconate-Titanate (SAUS)
PM	[*The*] Chesapeake & Ohio Railway Co. (Pere Marquette District) [*AAR code*]
PM	Cold Press Molding
PM	Ha-Po'el ha-Mizrahi (BJA)
PM	Pacemaker [*Medicine*] (DMAA)
PM	Pacific Mail (ROG)
P/M	Pacific Molasses (AD)
PM	Pacific Mutual Life Insurance Co. (EFIS)
PM	Package Monitor (SAUS)
PM	Pad Mechanic [*Aerospace*]
PM	Pagemaker (SAUS)
PM	Painting Machine
PM	Pak [*or Phak*] Mai [*New Party*] [*Political party*]
PM	Paleomagnetism (SAUS)
PM	Palmgren-Miner (SAUS)
PM	Pamphlet
PM	Panel Maintenance (IAA)
PM	Panel Meter (IEEE)
pm	Papier Mache (VRA)
PM	Papillary Muscle [*Medicine*] (DB)
PM	Papular Mucinosis (DB)
PM	Parachute Mine [*British military*] (DMA)
PM	Parallel Memory (SAUS)
PM	Paramagnet (SAUS)
PM	Paramagnetic (SAUS)
PM	Parameter [*Computer science*]
pm	Paramilitary (AD)
Pm	Paratid Midle [*Band protein*] (DMAA)
PM	Paraxial Magnification (SAA)
P/M	Parent-Metabolite Ratio [*Medicine*] (MEDA)
PM	Parlor Maid
PM	Partial Mastectomy (MELL)
PM	Partial Remission [*Medicine*] (CDI)
PM	Particulate Matter
PM	Partito Monarchico [*Monarchist Party*] [*Italy*] [*Political party*] (PPE)
P/M	Parts per Million (IEEE)
PM	Passed Midshipman
pm	Passed Motion
PM	Past Master [*Freemasonry*]
PM	Patriotic Majority [*An association*] (EA)
PM	Patriotikon Metopon [*Patriotic Front*] [*Greek Cyprus*] [*Political party*] (PPE)
PM	Patrol Missile Boat (SAUS)
PM	Patternmaker [*Navy rating*]
PM	Pavement Material (SAUS)
PM	Payload Management [*NASA*] (NASA)
PM	Payload Midbody [*NASA*] (MCD)
PM	Pay Master (SAUS)
PM	Paymaster
PM	Peabody Museum (AD)
PM	Peace Museum (EA)
PM	Pectoralis Major [*Anatomy*]
PM	Peculiar Matter (SAUS)
PM	Peculiar Meter
PM	Pelizaeus-Merbacher [*Disease*] [*Medicine*] (DB)
PM	Penalty Minutes [*Hockey*]
PM	Pension Mortgage [*British*]
PM	People Meter [*TV ratings measuring device*] [*Advertising*]
PM	Pere Marquette Railroad
PM	Perfect Master [*Freemasonry*]

PM	Performance Management (SAUS)
PM	Performance Measure (SAUS)
PM	Performance Measurement
PM	Performance Monitor [*NASA*] (NASA)
PM	Performance Monitoring (SAUS)
PM	Periodic Maintenance (AFM)
PM	Peripheral Memory (SAUS)
PM	Peritoneal Macrophage [*Immunology*] (AAMN)
p-m	Permanent Magnet (AD)
PM	Permanent Magnet [*Loudspeaker*]
PM	Permanent Memory (SAUS)
PM	Permanent Mold (SAUS)
PM	Per Metre (SAUS)
PM	Per Million
PM	Per Minute (IAA)
p/m	Per Month (WDAA)
PM	Per Month
PM	Per Thousand (SAUS)
Pm	Petameter (IDOE)
PM	Petit Mal [*Epilepsy*]
PM	Petroleos Mexicanos [*Spanish*] (AD)
PM	Petroleum Marketers, Inc. (EFIS)
PM	Pharmacy (SAUS)
PM	Phased Maintenance (MCD)
PM	Phase Match (IAA)
PM	Phase Modulated (SAUS)
p-m	Phase Modulation (AD)
PM	Phase Modulation [*Radio data transmission*]
PM	PHIGS Monitor (SAUS)
PM	Philip Morris, Inc.
PM	Philosophical Magazine (SAUS)
PM	Phorbol Monomyristate [*Organic chemistry*]
PM	Phosphoramide Mustard [*Antineoplastic drug*]
PM	Photographic Master
PM	Photographic Material (SAUS)
PM	Photomagnetic (SAUS)
PM	Photo Marketing Magazine [*A publication*] (EAAP)
PM	Photo Master (MCD)
PM	Photomechanical (SAUS)
PM	Photomultiplier
PM	Photosynthetic Measurements (SAUS)
PM	Phyllosticta maydis [*A toxin-producing fungus*]
P/M	Physical Medicine [*Medical officer designation*] [*British*]
PM	Physical Medium (MLOA)
PM	Physical Metallurgist (SAUS)
PM	Physical Metallurgy (SAUS)
PM	Physical Modeling (SAUS)
PM	Piae Memoriae [*Of Pious Memory*] [*Latin*]
pm	Picometer [*One trillionth of a meter*]
PM	Picometer (or -metre) (SAUS)
pM	Picomoler [*One trillionth of a mole*] (AAMN)
PM	Pilgrim Airlines [*ICAO designator*] (AD)
PM	Pilot Motor (MSA)
PM	Pioneer Ministries (EA)
PM	Pitching Moment [*Physics*]
PM	Pitch Mark [*Shipfitting*]
PM	Pit Membrane [*Paleobotany*]
PM	Plane Matching Interface (SAUS)
PM	Planetary Mission [*NASA*] (NASA)
PM	Planned Maintenance
PM	Plant Management (SAUS)
PM	Plasmalemma [*Cytology*]
PM	Plasma Membrane [*Cytology*]
PM	Plaster Master (MSA)
PM	Plastic Manoeuvre (SAUS)
PM	Plastic Mold (MCD)
PM	Platelet Microsome [*Medicine*] (DMAA)
PM	Plate Modulated (or Modulation) (SAUS)
P/M	Player/Missile [*Atari computers*]
PM	Plessey Memories (SAUS)
PM	Plus Minus [*More or less*]
PM	Pneumomediastinum [*Medicine*] (AAMN)
pm	Poids Moliculaire [*Molecular Weight*] [*French*] (AD)
PM	Point-to-Multipoint (SAUS)
PM	Polarization-Maintaining [*Optical Film*]
PM	Polarization Microscope (SAUS)
PM	Polarization Modulation (MCD)
PM	Police Magistrate
PM	Police Mutual Assurance Society [*British*]
PM	Policy Memorandum [*Military*]
PM	Poliomyelitis [*Medicine*]
PM	Pollen Mass [*Botany*]
PM	Polling Method (SAUS)
PM	Polling Mode (SAUS)
PM	Pollution Minimum
PM	PolyMedica Industries [*AMEX symbol*] (TTSB)
PM	PolyMedica Industries, Inc. [*AMEX symbol*] (SAG)
PM	Polymeric Material (SAUS)
PM	Polymeric Membrane
PM	Polymer Morphology (SAUS)
PM	Polymethacrylic [*Organic chemistry*]
PM	Polymethylene (SAUS)
PM	Polymorph [*Hematology*]
PM	Polymorphonuclear [*Leukocyte*] [*Hematology*] (DAVI)
PM	Polymyositis [*Medicine*]

pm	Pondmeter (SAUS)
PM	Pondus Medicinale [*Medicinal Weight*] [*Pharmacy*] (ROG)
PM	Pontifex Maximus [*Supreme Pontiff*] [*Latin*]
PM	Poor Metabolism [*Medicine*]
PM	Pope and Martyr [*Church calendars*]
PM	Popular Movement Against the European Community (ECON)
PM	Portable Magnetometer [*NASA*]
PM	Portable Medium-power (SAUS)
PM	Portable Medium Power Plant [*Nuclear energy*] (NRCH)
PM	Postal Manual
PM	Posterior Mitral Leaflet [*Cardiology*]
PM	Postmark [*Deltiology*]
PM	Postmaster
PM	Postmenopausal [*Gynecology*] (DAVI)
PM	Post Meridian
pm	Post Meridiem [*Afternoon*] [*Latin*] (WDMC)
PM	Post Meridiem [*After Noon*] [*Latin*]
PM	Postmodernist [*Architecture*]
pm	Post Mortem (AD)
PM	Post Mortem [*After Death*] [*Latin*]
PM	Postmortem (SAUS)
PM	Potentiometer (DEN)
PM	Potting Mold (MCD)
PM	Pounds per Minute
PM	Powdered Medium (SAUS)
PM	Powder Magnet (SAUS)
PM	Powder Metallurgy
PM	Power Management (NAKS)
PM	Power Mirrors
PM	Power Module (MCD)
PM	Powlesland & Mason [*Railway*] [*Wales*]
PM	Precious Metal
PM	Preincubation Mixture
pm	Premium (AD)
PM	Premium
PM	Premium Memory (SAUS)
PM	Premixer (SAUS)
pm	Premolar [*Dentistry*] (AD)
PM	Premolar [*Dentistry*]
PM	Prenegotiation Memorandum (AAGC)
PM	Preparation Meetings [*Quakers*]
PM	Prepared Message
PM	Presbyterian Men (EA)
PM	Presentation Manager [*Computer science*]
PM	Presidential Memo
PM	Pressure, Manifold
PM	Pressure Multiplier [*Nuclear energy*] (NRCH)
PM	Pressurized Module (SSD)
pm	Presystolic Murmur [*Medicine*] (AD)
PM	Presystolic Murmur [*Cardiology*]
PM	Pretibial Myxedema [*Medicine*] (DMAA)
PM	Preventative Maintenance (SAUS)
pm	Preventive Maintenance (AD)
PM	Preventive Maintenance
PM	Preventive Material
PM	Preventive Medicine [*Also, PVNTMED*] (AFM)
PM	Preventive Medicine, Preventive Maintenance (SAUS)
PM	Priest and Martyr [*Church calendars*]
PM	Primary Marker (SAUS)
PM	Primary Market [*Investment term*]
PM	Primary Memory (DIPS)
PM	Primary Mirror (SAUS)
PM	Primary Motivation [*Psychology*] (DAVI)
PM	Primary Munition
PM	Prime Meridian (SAUS)
PM	Prime Minister
PM	Prime Mover (MCD)
PM	Primitive Methodists (ROG)
PM	Principal Matron [*Navy*] [*British*]
PM	Principle of Multiplying [*New math*]
PM	Printing Mechanism (IAA)
PM	Print Matrix (IAA)
PM	Priority Message (SAUS)
PM	Private Mail (SAUS)
PM	Prize Money
PM	Probability of a Single Failure Causing Other Failures within a Three-Pack [*Department of Defense*]
PM	Procedure Memory (SAUS)
PM	Procedures Manual (IEEE)
PM	Processable Mode (SAUS)
PM	Processing Modflow [*Computer program*] [*Scientific Software Group*]
PM	Processing Module [*Computer science*]
PM	Process Manager (USDC)
PM	Process Manual
PM	Process Module (SAUS)
PM	Processor Module (NITA)
PM	Procurement and Material
PM	Procurement Manual [*US Postal Service*] [*A publication*] (AAGC)
PM	Producers Monthly (SAUS)
PM	Producibility Manual (ACAE)
PM	Production [*or Product*] Manager
PM	Production Mode
PM	Production Monitor (IAA)
PM	Production Monitoring (SAUS)
PM	Product Management (SAUS)

PM	Product Manager
PM	Product Marketing (SAUS)
p/m	Professional/Managerial (WDMC)
PM	Profit Margin (TDOB)
PM	Profit Motivated [*Housing*]
PM	Program (NG)
pm	Program Manager (AD)
PM	Program Manager [*or Management*] (MCD)
PM	Programmed Machine (SAUS)
PM	Program Memorandum (MCD)
PM	Program Method [*Computer science*] (IAA)
PM	Program Milestone [*NASA*] (NASA)
PM	Programming Manual (SAUS)
PM	Programming Matrix (SAUS)
PM	Programming Method
PM	Programming Mode (SAUS)
PM	Programming Module (SAUS)
PM	Program Mode [*Computer science*] (ELAL)
PM	Program Module (SAUS)
PM	Program Monitoring (MUGU)
PM	Project Magic (EA)
pm	Project Management (ABAC)
PM	Project Manager [*Military*]
PM	Pro Memoria [*In Remembrance*] [*Latin*]
PM	Pro Mense [*Per Month*] [*Latin*]
PM	Promethium
Pm	Promethium [*Chemical symbol*]
PM	Pro Mille [*Per Thousand*] [*Latin*]
PM	Propellant Management (KSC)
PM	Proper Motion [*Astronomy*] (BARN)
PM	Property Management (OICC)
PM	Propulsion Memorandum
PM	Propulsion Module [*NASA*] (KSC)
PM	Prostatic Massage [*Medicine*]
PM	Protected Memory (SAUS)
PM	Protected Mode (SAUS)
PM	Protein Methylesterase (DB)
PM	Protocol Machine [*Computer science*] (TNIG)
PM	Provost Marshal [*Army*]
PM	Pseudo Memory (SAUS)
PM	Puberal Macromastia [*Medicine*] (DMAA)
pm	Publicity Man (AD)
PM	Publicity Man [*Slang*]
PM	Pulmonary Macrophages [*Medicine*]
PM	Pulpomesial [*Dentistry*]
PM	Pulsating Mixing (SAUS)
PM	Pulse Code Modulation [*Telecommunications*] (IAA)
pm	Pulse Modulation (AD)
PM	Pulse Modulation
PM	Pulse Modulator (IDOE)
pm	Pumice (AD)
Pm	Pumice [*Quality of the bottom*] [*Nautical charts*]
PM	Punctum Maximum (SAUS)
PM	Punjabi Muslim [*Pakistan*]
PM	Purchase Memo (MCD)
PM	Purchase Memorandum
PM	Purchase Money (SAUS)
pm	Purchase Money Morgage, Premium (EBF)
PM	Purchase-Money Mortgage [*Real estate*]
PM	Purchase Money Mortgage, Premium (EBF)
PM	Purchasing Manager
PM	Purity Meter (SAUS)
PM	Purple Membrane [*Protein*] (DB)
PM	Purpose-Made [*Construction*]
PM	Push Money [*Sales incentive*]
P/M	Put More (VLIE)
P/M	Put of More [*Stock exchange term*]
PM	Pyridoxamine [*Also, Pxm*] [*Biochemistry*]
PM	Pyrometallurgist (SAUS)
PM	Pyrometallurgy (SAUS)
PM	Sisters of the Presentation of Mary [*Roman Catholic religious order*]
PM	St. Pierre and Miquelon [*ANSI two-letter standard code*] (CNC)
PM1	Patternmaker, First Class [*Navy rating*]
PM2	Patternmaker, Second Class [*Navy rating*]
PM3	Patternmaker, Third Class [*Navy rating*]
PM10	Particulate Matter [*Less than 10 microns*]
PM10	Particulate Matter, 10 Millimeters and Less (COE)
PM-10	Particulate Matter of 10 Microns in Diameter or Smaller [*BTS*] (TAG)
PM15	Particulate Matter, 15 Millimeters and Less (COE)
PMA	Allegheny College, Meadville, PA [*Library symbol*] [*Library of Congress*] (LCLS)
PMA	Pacific Maritime Association (EA)
PMA	Pacific Missionary Aviation (SAUS)
PMA	Pan-Macedonian Association (EA)
PMA	Pan Malaysian Air Transport [*ICAO designator*] (FAAC)
PMA	Panorama Resources Ltd. [*Vancouver Stock Exchange symbol*]
PMA	Papillary, Marginal, Attached [*With reference to gingivae*] [*Dentistry*]
pma	Paramethoxyamphetamine (AD)
PMA	Paramethoxyamphetamine
PMA	Parts Manufacturer Approval [*FAA*] (MCD)
PMA	Parts Manufacturing Associates (AD)
PMA	Parts Manufacturing Authority (SAUS)
PMA	Peat Moss Association (EA)
PMA	Pemba Island [*Tanzania*] [*Airport symbol*] (OAG)
PMA	Pencil Makers Association (EA)

PMA.............. Performance Management and Accounting (SAUS)
PMA.............. Performance Management Association (EAIO)
PMA.............. Performance Measurement Analysis (VLIE)
PMA.............. Performance Monitor Annunciator [*NASA*] (MCD)
PMA.............. Permanent Magnet Association (IAA)
PMA.............. Permanent Mailing Address
PMA.............. Permanent Management Arrangements (SAUS)
PMA.............. Personal Managers Association [*British*] (DBA)
PMA.............. Personal Money Allowance
PMA.............. Personnel Management Advisor (NOAA)
PMA.............. Personnel Management Assistance
PMA.............. Perth Market Authority [*Australia*]
PMA.............. Perth Muslim Association [*Australia*]
PMA.............. Petroleum and Minerals Authority (SAUS)
PMA.............. Petroleum Monitoring Agency [*Ministry of Energy, Mines, and
                  Resources*] [*Canada*]
PMA.............. Pharmaceutical Manufacturers Association (EA)
PMA.............. Phased Maintenance Availability [*Navy*] (DOMA)
PMA.............. Phenylmercuric Acetate [*Also, PMAC*] [*Herbicide and fungicide*]
PMA.............. Philadelphia Museum of Art (AD)
PMA.............. Philadelphia Musical Academy
PMA.............. Philippine Mahogany Association [*Defunct*] (EA)
PMA.............. Philippine Military Academy (SAUS)
PMA.............. Phonograph Manufacturers Association (EA)
PMA.............. Phorbol-12-Myristate-13-Acetate (SAUS)
PMA.............. Phorbol Myristate Acetate [*Also, PTA, TPA*] [*Organic chemistry*]
PMA.............. Phosphomolybdic Acid [*Organic chemistry*]
PMA.............. Photo Marketing Association (AD)
PMA.............. Photo Marketing Association International (EA)
PMA.............. Photonic Multichannel Analyzer
PMA.............. Physical Medium Attachment [*Telecommunications*] (OSI)
PMA.............. Physical Memory Address
PMA.............. Pianoforte Manufacturers' Association Ltd. [*British*] (BI)
PMA.............. Pine Manor College, Chestnut Hill, MA [*OCLC symbol*] (OCLC)
PMA.............. Planetary Microbiological Assay [*Aerospace*]
PMA.............. Plasma Membrane Adenosinetriphosphatase (DB)
PMA.............. Plastic Mock-Up Assembly
PMA.............. Plumbers' Merchants Association [*British*] (BI)
PMA.............. PMI Group [*NYSE symbol*] (TTSB)
PMA.............. PMI Group, Inc. [*NYSE symbol*] (SAG)
PMA.............. Pole Mounted Amplifier (SAUS)
PMA.............. Pole-Mounted Amplifier
PMA.............. Police Management Association [*Defunct*] (EA)
PMA.............. Police Marksman Association (EA)
PMA.............. Policy Management Architecture (SAUS)
PM-A .... Polishing Medium-Abrasive (SAUS)
PMA.............. Polish Museum of America (EA)
PMA.............. Political Military Affairs (SAUS)
PMA.............. Politico-Military Affairs [*U.S. Department of State*] (BARN)
PMA.............. Polymethacrylate (SAUS)
PMA.............. Polymethacrylic Acid (SAUS)
PMA.............. Poly(methyl Acrylate) [*Organic chemistry*]
PMA.............. Polymetylacrylate (SAUS)
PMA.............. Polyurethane Manufacturers Association (EA)
PMA.............. Portable Maintenance Aid [*Army*]
PMA.............. Port Moller [*Alaska*] [*Seismograph station code, US Geological
                  Survey*] (SEIS)
pma.............. Positive Mental Attitude (AD)
PMA.............. Positive Mental Attitude
PMA.............. Potato Marketing Authority [*Australia*]
PMA.............. Potato Merchants' Association [*Australia*]
PMA.............. Powder Metallurgy Association (SAUS)
PMA.............. Power Marketing Administration [*Department of Energy*]
PMA.............. Power-Marketing Administration (SAUS)
PMA.............. Preamplifier Module Assembly
PMA.............. Precious Metal Adder (Cost) (MCD)
PMA.............. Precious Metal Anode
PMA.............. Precision Measurement Association (SAUS)
PMA.............. Precision Measurements Association (EA)
PMA.............. Precision Metalforming Association (EA)
PMA.............. Preferred Machine Assist [*Computer science*] (ITCA)
PMA.............. Premarket Approval (SAUS)
PMA.............. Premarket Approval Application [*Food and Drug Administration*]
PMA.............. Pressurized Mating Adapter (SAUS)
PMA.............. Prevalence of Gingivitis [*Dentistry*] (DAVI)
PMA.............. Preventive Maintenance Agreement
PMA.............. Primary Market Area
PMA.............. Primary Mental Abilities [*Test*] [*Education*]
PMA.............. Prime Macro-Assembler (NITA)
PMA.............. Prime Medical Aid
PMA.............. Prinzmetal's Angina [*Cardiology*] (DAVI)
PMA.............. Priority Memory Access
PMA.............. Priority Memory Address (NITA)
PMA.............. Prison Mission Association (EA)
PMA.............. Probability of Mission Abort [*Navy*] (ANA)
PMA.............. Probationary Medical Assistant [*British military*] (DMA)
PMA.............. Procurement and Management Assistance [*Small Business
                  Administration*]
PMA.............. Procurement Methods Analyst (AFM)
PMA.............. Produce Marketing Association [*Newark, DE*] (EA)
PMA.............. Production and Marketing Administration [*Department of Agriculture*]
                  [*Functions dispersed, 1953*]
PMA.............. Production Monitoring Analysis (SAUS)
PMA.............. Professional Managers Association (EA)
PMA.............. Professional Manufacturers' Agents (EA)

PMA.............. Professional Mariners Alliance [*Defunct*] (EA)
PMA.............. Programa Mundial de Alimentos [*World Food Program*] [*Spanish*]
                  (AD)
PMA.............. Program Memory Area [*Computer science*] (DCDG)
PMA.............. Progressive Muscular Atrophy [*Medicine*]
PMA.............. Projected Map Assembly (SAUS)
PMA.............. Project Manager, Air
PMA.............. Project Manager, Air Systems Command [*Navy*]
PMA.............. Project Military Adviser (NATG)
PMA.............. Prompt Maintenance Alarm (SAUS)
PMA.............. Propagation Management Assessment (SEWL)
PMA.............. Property Management Association (SAUS)
PMA.............. Property Management Association of America (EA)
PMA.............. Property Market Analysis [*Consulting firm*] [*British*]
PMA.............. Property Movement Authorization (ACAE)
PMA.............. Prorated Mental Age [*Psychology*]
PMA.............. Protected Memory Address
PMA.............. Provincial Museum of Alberta (SAUS)
PMA.............. Publications of the Mediaeval Academy (SAUS)
PMA.............. Publishers Marketing Association (EA)
PMA.............. Pulpomesioaxial [*Dentistry*]
PMA.............. Pump-Motor Assembly
PMA.............. Purchase Methods Analyst
PMA.............. Pyridylmercuric Acetate [*Fungicide*] [*Organic chemistry*]
PMA.............. Pyromellitic Acid [*Organic chemistry*]
PMAA........... Paper Makers Advertising Association (EA)
PMAA........... Petroleum Marketers Association of America (EA)
PMAA........... Politico-Military Administrative Affairs [*Committee*]
PMAA........... Promotion Marketing Association of America [*New York, NY*] (EA)
PMAA........... Property Management Association of America (EA)
PMAA........... Proprietary Medicines Association of Australia
PMAA........... Propulsion Module Attach Assembly [*NASA*] (SPST)
PM-AAH....... Project Manager, Advanced Attack Helicopter [*Military*]
PMAAH........ Project Manager, Advanced Attack Helicopter
PMA/ARR.... Probable Missed Approach per Arrival [*Aviation*] (PDAA)
PMAC.......... Packet Media Access Control (SAUS)
PMAC.......... Packet Media Access Controller [*Computer science*] (VLIE)
PMAC.......... Parallel Memory Address Counter [*Computer science*]
P-MAC .... Perceptual-Motor Assessment for Children (TES)
PMAC.......... Peripheral Module Access Controller [*Computer science*] (VLIE)
PMAC.......... Personnel Management Advisory Committee (SAUS)
PMAC.......... Pharmaceutical Manufacturers Association of Canada
PMAC.......... Phenyl Mercuric Acetate (SAUS)
PMAC.......... Phenylmercuric Acetate [*Also, PMA*] [*Herbicide and fungicide*]
PMAC.......... PMA Communications, Inc. [*Boston, MA*] (TSSD)
PMAC.......... Polymethacrolein (SAUS)
PMAC.......... Polymethoxy Acetal (EDCT)
PMAC.......... Preliminary Maintenance Allocation Chart (MCD)
PMAC.......... Preliminary Maintenance Allocation Charts (SAUS)
PMAC.......... Project Manager Allocation Chart
PMAC.......... Proprietary Medicines Advisory Committee [*Australia*]
PMAC.......... Provisional Military Administrative Council [*Ethiopia*] [*Political party*]
                  (PD)
PMAC.......... Purchasing Management Association of Canada
PMACODS.... Project Manager, Army Container Oriented Distribution System
                  (MCD)
PM ACS .... Product Manager, Army Communications System
PMACS .... Project Management and Control System (CIST)
PMAD .... Performance Monitor Annunciation Driver [*NASA*] (MCD)
PMAD .... Personnel Management Authorization Document [*Army*]
PMAD .... Polymer Modifiers and Additives Division (SAUS)
PMAD .... Portable Maintenance Aid Device (SAUS)
PMAD .... Power Management and Distribution (NASA)
PMAD .... Public Morals Administrative Division (SAUS)
PMadW........ Westinghouse Electric Corp., Waltz Mill Site Library, Madison, PA
                  [*Library symbol*] [*Library of Congress*] (LCLS)
PMAE.......... Peabody Museum of Archeology and Ethnology (AD)
PMAESA ...... Port Management Association of Eastern and Southern Africa (EA)
PMAF.......... Pharmaceutical Manufacturers Association Foundation (IAA)
PMAF.......... Polaris Missile Assembly Facility
PMAFS........ Public Members Association of the Foreign Service (EA)
PMAG .... Program Management Advisory Group (SAUS)
PMAG .... Program Manager Assistance Group [*Military*] (MCD)
PMAG .... Provisional Military Advisory Group
PMAHPVDC... Permanent Mold Alloy High-Pressure Vacuum Die Casting
PMA-I .... Photo Marketing Association-International (NTPA)
PMAI.......... Piano Manufacturers Association International (EA)
PMAI.......... Powder Metallurgy Association of India (SAUS)
P-MAIL .... Paper Mail (SAUS)
P/Maj.......... Pipe-Major [*British military*] (DMA)
PMALS........ Prototype Miniature Air Launched Segment (SAUS)
PMALS........ Prototype Miniature Air-Launched System
PM Amb ..... Paramedic Ambulance (AMHC)
PMAN .... Piedmont Management Co., Inc. [*NASDAQ symbol*] (NQ)
PMAN .... Polymethacrylonitrile (EDCT)
PM & ACS ... Procurement Management and Acquisition Control System [*Social
                  Security Administration*]
PM&C .... Department of Prime Minister and Cabinet (SAUS)
PM & C........ Plant Monitoring and Control [*IBM Corp.*]
PM&C .... Prime Minister and Cabinet (SAUS)
PM & C-HI ... Plant Monitoring and Control - Host Interface [*IBM Corp.*]
PM&E .... Performance Measurement and Evaluation (SAUS)
PM & OA ..... Printers' Managers and Overseers Association (AD)
pm & r........ Physical Medicine and Rehabilitation (AD)
PM&R .... Physical Medicine and Rehabilitation

PManM........	Mansfield State College, Mansfield, PA [*Library symbol*] [*Library of Congress*] (LCLS)
PMANY........	Pattern Makers Association of New York (EA)
PMAP.........	Performance Monitor Annunciation Panel [*NASA*] (MCD)
PMAP.........	Photomap
PMAP.........	Port Mapper (SAUS)
PMAP.........	Procedure Map (VLIE)
pMAP.........	Professional Map Analysis Package (SAUS)
PMAPS........	Predirected Munitions Automated Planning System (ACAE)
PMAR.........	Page Map Address Register
PMAR.........	Precious Metals Area Representative [*DoD*] (AFIT)
PMAR.........	Preliminary Maintenance Analysis Report [*Aerospace*] (AAG)
PMAR.........	Program Memory Address Register (SAUS)
PMarhSO.....	Sun Oil Co., Marcus Hook, PA [*Library symbol*] [*Library of Congress*] (LCLS)
PMARP.......	Peacetime Manpower Allocation Requirements Plan (CINC)
PMARS.......	Performance Management and Recognition System (MCD)
PMAS.........	Performance Measurement Analysis System (SAUS)
PMAS.........	Photochemical Assessment Monitoring Stations (EPAT)
PMAS.........	Police Mutual Assurance Society [*British*]
PMAS.........	Propulsion Module Attach Structure [*NASA*] (SPST)
PMAS.........	Purdue Master Attitude Scales [*Psychology*]
PMASA.......	Printers' Medical Aid and Sanatoria Association [*British*] (BI)
PMASAL......	Papers of the Michigan Academy of Science, Arts and Letters (SAUS)
PM-ASE......	Project Manager, Aircraft Survivability Equipment [*Military*]
PMASE.......	Project Manager, Aircraft Survivability Equipment
PM-ASH......	Project Manager, Advanced Scout Helicopter [*Military*]
PMASH.......	Project Manager, Advanced Scout Helicopter
PM-ASI.......	Program Management Office for Armored Systems Integration [*Army*] (RDA)
PMAT.........	Page Map Address Table [*NASA*] (NASA)
PMAT.........	Plasma & Materials Technologies [*NASDAQ symbol*] (TTSB)
PMAT.........	Plasma & Materials Technologies, Inc. [*NASDAQ symbol*] (SAG)
PMAT.........	Portable Maintenance Access Terminal [*Computer science*]
PMAT.........	Primary Mental Abilities Test [*Education*]
PMAT.........	Purdue Mechanical Adaptability Test
PMATA........	Paint Manufacture and Allied Trades' Association [*British*] (BI)
PMATA........	Paint Manufacturers and Allied Trades Association (SAUS)
PMATA........	Paper Makers' Allied Trades Association [*British*] (DBA)
PMAWS.......	Passive Missile Approach Warning System [*Military*] (SEWL)
PMax.........	Peak Inspiratory Pressure [*Medicine*] (DAVI)
PMB.........	Canadian Print Measurement Bureau (NITA)
PMB.........	Cis-Platinum, Methotrexate, Bleomycin [*Antineoplastic drug regimen*] (DAVI)
PMB.........	Pacific Motor Tariff Bureau, Inc., Oakland CA [*STAC*]
PMB.........	Palm Beach [*Diocesan abbreviation*] [*Florida*] (TOCD)
PMB.........	Papillomacular Bundle [*Medicine*] (MELL)
PMB.........	Para-Hydroxymercuribenzoate [*Biochemistry*] (MAE)
PMB.........	Paranormal Metal Bending
PMB.........	Pembina, ND [*Location identifier*] [*FAA*] (FAAL)
PMB.........	Pentamethylbenzene (SAUS)
PMB.........	Performance Management Baseline (SAUS)
PMB.........	Performance Measurement Baseline (MCD)
PMB.........	Phenylmercuric Borate (SAUS)
PMB.........	P-Hydroxymercuribenzoate (SAUS)
PMB.........	Physical Metallurgy Branch
PMB.........	Pilot Make Busy (IEEE)
PMB.........	Plant Molecular Biology (SAUS)
PMB.........	Plastic Media Blasting [*Coating technology*]
PMB.........	P-Mercuribenzoate (SAUS)
PMB.........	Polychrome Methylene Blue
PMB.........	Polymethylbenzene [*Organic chemistry*]
PMB.........	Polymorphonuclear Basophilic [*Leucocytes*] [*Hematology*]
PMB.........	Polymyxin B (DB)
pmb.........	Post-Menopausal Bleeding [*Medicine*] (AD)
PMB.........	Postmenopausal Bleeding [*Medicine*]
PMB.........	Potato Marketing Board [*British*]
PMB.........	Practice Multiple Bomb (MCD)
PMB.........	Precision Manned Bomber
PMB.........	Premier Bancshares [*NYSE symbol*]
PMB.........	Print Measurement Bureau [*Founded in 1971*] [*Also the name of a database*] [*Canada*]
PMB.........	Print Measures Bureau (SAUS)
PMB.........	Private Mail Bag
PMB.........	Program Management Board (AFM)
PMB.........	Project Management and Budgeting
PMB.........	PROM [*Programmable Read-Only Memory*] Memory Board
PMBA........	Plant Molecular Biology Association (SAUS)
PMBA........	Professional Master of Business Administration (PGP)
PMB Bulletin...	Pigs Marketing Board Bulletin (SAUS)
PMBC........	Pacific Motor Boat Club (AD)
PMBC........	Phuket Marine Biological Center [*Marine science*] (MSC)
PMBC........	Pilot Make Busy Call
PMBC........	Plywood Manufacturers of British Columbia (SAUS)
PMBC........	Portland Motor Boat Club [*Oregon*] (AD)
PMBC........	Process-Model Based Controller (ACII)
PMB Circuit...	Pilot Make Busy Circuit (AD)
PMBIAS......	Percentage Median Bias [*Statistics*]
PMB Leucocytes...	Polymorphonuclear Basophilic Leucocytes (SAUS)
pmbo.........	Participative Management by Objectives (AD)
PMBOK.......	Project Management Body of Knowledge
PMBR........	Practice Multiple Bomb Rack (NG)
PMBR........	Preliminary Multistate Bar Review (SAUS)
PMBS........	Pelican Man's Bird Sanctuary (EA)
PMBT.........	Propellant Mean Bulk Temperature (SAUS)
PMBU	Personal Member of the Baptist Union [*British*]
pmbx	Private Manual Branch Exchange (AD)
PMBX.........	Private Manual Branch Exchange [*Communications*]
PMC.........	Carnegie-Mellon University, Pittsburgh, PA [*OCLC symbol*] (OCLC)
PMC.........	Chief Patternmaker [*Navy rating*]
PMC.........	Little Missionary Sisters of Charity [*Roman Catholic religious order*]
PMC.........	Pacific Marine Center [*National Oceanic and Atmospheric Administration*]
PMC.........	Pacific Medical Center (BABM)
PMC.........	Pacific Missile Center [*Marine science*] (MSC)
PMC.........	Pan Metal [*formerly, Patton Morgan*] Corp. [*Ammunition manufacturer*]
PMC.........	Parents of Missing Children [*Australia*]
PMC.........	Parents of Murdered Children [*Later, POMC*] (EA)
PMC.........	Partially Mission Capable [*Maintenance and supply*] (MCD)
PMC.........	Partially Mission-Capable (SAUS)
PMC.........	Partial Mission Capability [*Time*]
PMC.........	Partial Mission Capable (SAUS)
PMC.........	Patient Management Categories [*Medicine*] (MEDA)
PMC.........	Patrol/Mine Countermeasure Craft [*British*]
PMC.........	Payload Monitoring and Control [*NASA*] (NASA)
PMC.........	Penguin Modern Classics [*Book publishing*]
PMC.........	Pennsylvania Military Academy (AD)
PMC.........	Pennsylvania Military College
PMC.........	Pentamethyl(hydroxy)chromane [*Organic chemistry*]
PMC.........	People's Mandate Committee (EA)
PMC.........	Percent Modern Carbon [*In atmosphere*]
PMC.........	Performance Management Computer (PDAA)
PMC.........	Performance Measurement Criteria (SAUS)
PMC.........	Peripheral Mononuclear Cell [*Cytology*]
PMC.........	Peritoneal Mast Cell
PMC.........	Permanently Manned Capability (SSD)
PMC.........	Personal Mobile Communicator (SAUS)
PMC.........	Personnel Management Centre [*British*] (ODBW)
PMC.........	Personnel Mobilization Center [*Military*]
PMC.........	Phased Maintenance Checklist (MCD)
PMC.........	Phenolic Molding Compound
PMC.........	Phenylacetamidocoumarin (SAUS)
PMC.........	Phenylmercuric Chloride [*Antiseptic*]
PMC.........	Philatelic Music Circle (EA)
PMC.........	Physical Media Components Sublayer (SAUS)
PMC.........	Physical Medicine Centre (SAUS)
PMC.........	Piperidinomethylcyclohexane [*Organic chemistry*]
PMC.........	Planning Ministers' Conference [*Australia*]
PMC.........	Planning Ministers Council (SAUS)
PMC.........	Plaster-Molded Cornice [*Construction*]
PMC.........	Plutona-Molybdenum CERMET [*Ceramic Metal Element*] (NASA)
PMC.........	PMC Capital [*AMEX symbol*] (TTSB)
PMC.........	PMC Capital, Inc. [*AMEX symbol*] (SPSG)
PMC.........	Polar Mesospheric Cloud (SAUS)
PMC.........	Pollen Mother Cell [*Botany*]
PMC.........	Polymer Matrix Composite [*Materials science*]
PMC.........	Polymer-Matrix Composite (SAUS)
PMC.........	Polymer-Metal Composite (SAUS)
PMC.........	Polymer-Reinforced (SAUS)
PMC.........	Port Management Center (SAUS)
PMC.........	Posterior Medial Corner of Knee [*Sports medicine*]
PMC.........	Post Maintenance Check (MCD)
PMC.........	Post Manufacture Checkout
PMC.........	Post Manufacturing Checkout (KSC)
PMC.........	Post Master's Certificate (PGP)
PMC.........	Post Ministerial Conference (SAUS)
PMC.........	Post-Ministerial Conference [*ASEAN*]
PMC.........	Postmodern Culture (SAUS)
PMC.........	Powdered Metal Cathode
PMC.........	Power-Mate Corp. (IAA)
PMC.........	Powertrain Management Controller [*Automotive engineering*]
PMC.........	Precision Machinery Commercialization
PMC.........	Precision Machining Commercialization (MCD)
PMC.........	Precision Measurement Work Cell (ACAE)
pmc	Precision Mirror Calorimeter (AD)
PMC.........	Predictive Multisensor Correlation
PMC.........	Pre-Mission Calibration (PDAA)
PMC.........	Premium Merchandising Club of New York (EA)
PMC.........	Premotor Cortex [*Neuroanatomy*]
PMC.........	President of the Mess Committee [*Military*] [*British*]
PMC.........	President's Management Council (AAGC)
PMC.........	Pressure-Modulator Cell (EOSA)
PMC.........	Pressurized Membrane Container
pmc	Preventive Maintenance Contract (AD)
PMC.........	Primary Mesenchyme Cell [*Cytology*]
PMC.........	Prime Mover Control [*Valve*]
PMC.........	Princeton Microfilm Corp.
PmC.........	Princeton Microfilm Corporation, Princeton, NJ [*Library symbol*] [*Library of Congress*] (LCLS)
PMC.........	Printing Memory Computer (SAUS)
PMC.........	Private Mailing Card [*Deltiology*]
PMC.........	Private Medical Communication
PMC.........	Private Meter Check [*Telecommunications*] (TEL)
PMC.........	Processed Meats Committee [*Later, DPMC*] (EA)
PMC.........	Process Module Controller (AAEL)
PMC.........	Procurement Committee (MCD)
PMC.........	Procurement Management Code [*Military*] (AFIT)
PMC.........	Procurement, Marine Corps [*An appropriation*]

PMC............ Procurement Method Code (SAUS)
PMC............ Procurement Method Coding [DoD]
PMC............ Professional and Managerial Class [British] (DI)
PMC............ Professional Musicians' Club [Australia]
PMC............ Programmable Machine Control (SAUS)
PMC............ Programmable Machine Controller (NRCH)
PMC............ Programmable Machine Tool Controller (IAA)
PMC............ Programmable Matrix Controller (IAA)
PMC............ Program Management Charter (SAUS)
PMC............ Program Management Control
PMC............ Program Management Course [Army] (RDA)
PMC............ Program Manager Charter (SAUS)
PMC............ Program Marginal Checking
PMC............ Project Management Committee (AD)
PMC............ Project Management Corp. (SAUS)
PMC............ Project Management Course [Army]
PMC............ Project Manufacturing Controller (MCD)
PMC............ Pro Maria Committee (EA)
PMC............ Propellant Monitor and Control (AFM)
PMC............ Pseudo Machine Code [Computer science] (BUR)
PMC............ Pseudomembranous Colitis [Medicine]
PMC............ Public Media Center (EA)
PMC............ Puerto Montt [Chile] [Airport symbol] (OAG)
PMC............ Pumice (MSA)
pMc............ Pure Mexican Cocaine (AD)
PMCA.......... Pennsylvania Manufacturing Confectioners Association (SAUS)
PMCA.......... Purple Martin Conservation Association (EA)
PM-CAWS.... Project Manager for Cannon Artillery Weapon Systems (RDA)
PMCB.......... Partially Mission Capable Both [Maintenance and supply] (MCD)
PMCB.......... Pentamethyl Chlorobenzene (SAUS)
PMCB.......... Project Manager Control Board
P/MCB .... Project/Miscellaneous Change Board (MCD)
PMCC.......... Paper Machine Clothing Council (NTPA)
PMCC.......... Peerless Motor Car Club (EA)
PMCC.......... Pensky-Martens Closed Cup [Flash point test]
PMCC.......... Platform Mission Control Center [NASA]
PMCC.......... Platforms Mission Control Center (SAUS)
PMCC.......... Platoon Mistral Command Centre (SAUS)
PMCC.......... Port Management Control Center (SAUS)
PMCC.......... Post Mark Collectors Club (EA)
PMCCN .... Product-Moment Correlation Co-Efficient (DMAA)
PMCCN .... Performance and Management of Complex Communication Networks (SAUS)
PMC CT ...... PMC Commercial Trust [Associated Press] (SAG)
PMCD .... Post Mortem Core Dump [Computer science]
PMCD .... Process Measurement & Control Division (ACII)
PMCD .... Program Module Connection Diagram (MHDI)
PMCF.......... Partial Mission Capability Factor
PMCF.......... Post Maintenance Check Flight (MCD)
PMCG.......... Pyrrolidylmethyl Cyclopentylphenylglycolate (SAUS)
PMCH.......... Pro-Melanin-Concentrating Hormone (DMAA)
PMCHi .... Crawford County Historical Society, Meadville, PA [Library symbol] [Library of Congress] (LCLS)
PMCHL .... Pro-Melanin-Concentrating Hormone-Like (DMAA)
PM CHS...... Program Manager, Common Hardware Systems (SAUS)
PMCI........... Phosphate Mining Corp. of Christmas Island (EY)
PMCI........... Postmyocardial Infarct [Medicine] (MELL)
PMC INC...... Precision Management of Concordville, Inc. [Media, PA] (TSSD)
PMCIS .... Post-Myocardial Infarction Syndrome [Medicine] (MELL)
PMck .... Carnegie Free Library of McKeesport, McKeesport, PA [Library symbol] [Library of Congress] (LCLS)
PMCL.......... Posterior Medial Collateral Ligament [Anatomy]
PMCL.......... Proposed MAPAD Change Letter (AAGC)
PMCL.......... Proposed Maximum Contaminant Level (SAUS)
PMCL.......... Proposed MILSTRIP Change Letters
PMCLG........ Proposed Maximum Contaminant Level Goal (SAUS)
PMCM......... Master Chief Patternmaker [Navy rating]
PMCM......... Partially Mission Capable Maintenance [Maintenance and supply] (MCD)
PMCM......... Partial Mission Capable, Maintenance (SAUS)
PMCM......... Permanent Mold Casting Mold (MCD)
PMCM......... Pulse Morse Code Modulation (OA)
PMC Model... Preparata, Metze and Chien Model (SAUS)
PMCP.......... Prime Capital Corp. [NASDAQ symbol] (SAG)
PMCPE........ Prime Capital [NASDAQ symbol] (SG)
PMCQ .... Paper Marketing Council of Queensland [Australia]
PMCS.......... Partially Mission Capable Supply [Maintenance and supply] (MCD)
PMCS.......... Partial Mission Capable, Supply (SAUS)
PMCS.......... Partial Mission Capable-Supply
PMCS.......... Patient Management Computer Stimulation (DMAA)
PMCS.......... PMC-Sierra, Inc. [NASDAQ symbol] [Formerly, Sierra Semiconductor] (SG)
PMCS.......... Power Monitoring and Control Systems
PMCS.......... Preventive Maintenance Checks and Services [for Army vehicles] (INF)
PMCS.......... Process Monitoring and Control System
pmcs.......... Process Monitoring and Control Systems (AD)
PMCS.......... Production Management Control System (SAUS)
PMCS.......... Professional Military Comptroller School
PMCS.......... Programmable Modular Communication System (SEWL)
PMCS.......... Program [or Project] Management Control System [Army]
PMCS.......... Project Management Control System
PMCS.......... Pulse-Modulated Communications System
PMCS.......... Senior Chief Patternmaker [Navy rating]

PMCT........... PAL [Permissive Action Link] Management Control Team [Army] (AABC)
PMCT........... Program Management Control Table [Computer science] (ELAL)
PMCTF........ Prime Minister's Country Task Force [Australia]
PMCU......... Personal Member of the Congregational Union [British]
PMCU......... Predominately Minority Colleges and Universities
PMCV......... Politically Motivated Crimes of Violence (SAUS)
PMCV......... Programmed Multichannel Valve [Chromatography]
PMCVG...... Photometric Modelling for Computer Vision and Graphics (VLIE)
PMD........... Packet Mode Data [Computer science] (VLIE)
PMD........... Palmdale, CA [Location identifier] [FAA] (FAAL)
PMD........... Palmdale/Lancaster [California] [Airport symbol] (OAG)
PMD........... Palmer Industries Ltd. [Vancouver Stock Exchange symbol]
PMD........... Panel-Mounted Display (MCD)
PMD........... Part Manufacturing Design
PMD........... Parts Manufacturing Division (SAUS)
PMD........... Payload Mating Dolly [NASA]
PMD........... Payload Module Decoder [NASA]
PMD........... Pelizaeus-Merzbacher Disease [Medicine]
PMD........... Permanent Magnetic Dynamic (SAUS)
PMD........... Personnel Management Division [Environmental Protection Agency] (GFGA)
PMD........... Petroleum and Mines Department (SAUS)
PMD........... Pharmaco-Medical Documentation, Inc. [Information service or system] (IID)
PMD........... Physical Layer, Medium Dependent (SAUS)
PMD........... Physical Layer Medium Dependent Layer (SAUS)
PMD........... Physical Media Dependent (SAUS)
PMD........... Physical Medium Dependent [Computer science]
PMD........... Physical Medium Dependent Layer [Telecommunications] (OSI)
PMD........... Planning and Management Division [Environmental Protection Agency] (GFGA)
PMD........... Point of Maximum Definition (SAUS)
PMD........... Pollution Measurement Division (SAUS)
PMD........... Pollution Monitoring Directory (SAUS)
PMD........... Pontiac Motor Division [General Motors Corp.]
Pmd........... Portmadoc (AD)
PMD........... Positional Macro-Definition (SAUS)
PMD........... Postmortem and Diagnostic Processor (SAUS)
PMD........... Post-Mortem Debugger [Computer science] (PCM)
PMD........... Post Mortem Dump [Computer science]
pmd........... Post-Mortem Dumps (AD)
PMD........... Power Management and Distribution Palmdale [California]
PMD........... Pre-Metal Dielectric (SAUS)
PMD........... Preventive Maintenance, Daily (MCD)
PMD........... Preventive Maintenance Division [Air Force]
PMD........... Primary Myeloproliferative Disease [Medicine]
PMD........... Primary Myocardial Disease [Medicine]
PMD........... Private Management Domain [Computer science] (TNIG)
PMD........... Private Medical Doctor (DAVI)
PMd........... Private Physician
PMD........... Processing, Marketing, and Distribution
PMD........... Product Marketing Division (SAUS)
PMD........... Profile Measurement Device (SAUS)
PMD........... Program for Management Development [Harvard Business School] (DD)
PMD........... Program Management Directive [Air Force]
PMD........... Program Management Document (SAUS)
PMD........... Program Management Documentation [Army]
PMD........... Program Management Documents
PMD........... Programmed Multiple Development [Analytical chemistry]
PMD........... Program Module Dictionary
PMD........... Program Monitoring and Diagnosis
PMD........... Progressive Muscular Dystrophy [Medicine]
PMD........... Project-based Management Development (SAUS)
pmd........... Projected Map Display (AD)
PMD........... Projected Map Display
PMD........... Project Management Division (SAUS)
PMD........... Project Manager Development (MCD)
PMD........... Propellant Management Device (ACAE)
PMD........... Protein Mutant Database (SAUS)
PMD........... Psychemedics Corp. [AMEX symbol] (SAG)
PMD........... Psychiatric Military Duty
PMDA......... Photographic Manufacturers and Distributors Association (EA)
PMDA......... Pianoforte Manufacturers and Distributors Association [British] (DBA)
PMDA......... Plastics Machinery Distributors Association [British] (EAIO)
PMDA......... Pyromellitic Dianhydride [Organic chemistry]
PMDAMT .... Pacific Mobile Depot Activity Maintenance Team (CINC)
PMDA/ODA.. Pyromellitic Dianhydride/Oxydianiline (SAUS)
PMDB......... Program Management Decision Brief [Defense Systems Management College] (DOMA)
PMD/BMI.... Project Management Division/Batelle Memorial Institute (AD)
PMDC .... Pakistan Minerals Development Corp. (AD)
PMDC .... Permanent Magnet Direct Current (SAUS)
PMDC .... Project for Mathematical Development of Children [National Science Foundation]
PMDC .... Project Manager Development Course [Military] (RDA)
PMDD .... Personnel Management Development Directorate [Military Personnel Center] (AABC)
PMDD .... Premenstrual Dysphoric Disorder [Gynecology] (DMAA)
PMDF......... Pascal Memo Distribution Facility [Computer science]
PMDF......... Project Master Data File [For spacecraft]
PMDG .... Pentamethylene Diguanidine [Organic chemistry]
PMDI .... Palmer Drought Severity Index
PMDI .... Polydiphenylmethanediisocyanate (SAUS)

PMDI .... Polymeric MDI (SAUS)
PMDI .... Polymeric Methylene Diphenylene Isocyanate (EDCT)
PMDI .... Polymethylene Diisocyanate (SAUS)
PMDI .... Polymethylene Diphenylene Isocyanate (SAUS)
PMDL......... Palmdale, CA (NASA)
PMDL......... Post M-Day Deployment List [Military] (AABC)
PMDL......... Post Mobilization Deployment List [Department of Defense]
PMDL......... Provisional Military Demarcation Line (CINC)
PMDL Unit.. Post Mobilization Deployment List Unit (SAUS)
PMDM .... Polyhedra Molecular Demonstration Model
PMDM .... Poly(mellitic Dianhydride Methacrylate) [Organic chemistry]
PM/DM .... Polymyositis/Dermatomyositis [Rheumatology] (DAVI)
PMDO .... Phased Maintenance During Overhaul
PMDP .... Pavement Marking Demonstration Program [Federal Highway Administration]
PMDP .... Project Manager Development Program [Army] (RDA)
PMDP .... Prototype Model Design Plan (SAUS)
PMDR .... Parametric Monotone Decreasing Ratio [Statistics]
PMDR .... Phosphorescence-Microwave Double Resonance
PMDR .... Provisioning Master Data Record
PMDRAM.... Page Mode Dynamic Random Access Memory (SAUS)
PM-DRG ..... Pediatric-Modified Diagnosis-Related Group (HCT)
PMDRMU.... Paper Mould and Dandy Roll Makers' Union (DGA)
PMDS .... Peristent Muellerian Duct Syndrome [Medicine] (DMAA)
PMDS .... (Phenylmercury)dodecenyl Succinate [Antimicrobial agent]
PMDS .... Pilot Map Display System
PMDS .... Plant Management, Maintenance/Design Engineering Show (SAUS)
PMDS .... Point Missile Defense System (DNAB)
PMDS .... Portable Diver Monitoring System
PMDS .... Power Management and Distribution System (SAUS)
PMDS .... Primary Myelodysplastic Syndrome [Medicine] (DMAA)
PMDS .... Process Monitoring and Display Software [Computer science] (ECII)
pmds .... Projected Map Display Set (AD)
PMDS .... Projected Map Display System
PMDS .... Property Management and Disposal Service [Abolished, 1973] [General Services Administration]
PMDT......... Park Meditech, Inc. [NASDAQ symbol] (SAG)
PMDT......... Pentamethyldiethylenetriamine [Organic chemistry]
PMDTF........ Park Meditech [NASDAQ symbol] (TTSB)
PMDU .... Projected Map Display Unit (DNAB)
PMDY .... Midway Naval Station [Henderson Field], Sand Island [Midway Islands] [ICAO location identifier] (ICLI)
PME............ Allstate Corp. [NYSE symbol] (SAG)
PME............ Allstate Cp 6.76% Exch Nts '98 [NYSE symbol] (TTSB)
PME............ Caltech Political Military Exercise [International relations simulation game]
PME............ Paramagnetic Meissner Effect [Physics]
PME............ Passive Microelectronic Element
PME............ Pattern Matching Engine (SAUS)
PME............ Peace Movement of Ethiopia (EA)
PME............ Pectin Methylesterase [Also, PE] [An enzyme]
PME............ Pedal Mode Ergometer
PME............ Performance Management and Evaluation
pme .... Performance-Measuring Equipment (AD)
PME............ Performance Monitoring Equipment (NVT)
PME............ Personnel Management Evaluation [Marine science] (OSRA)
PME............ Personnel Management for Executives [Military] (RDA)
PME............ Phosphatidylmonomethylethanolamine [Biochemistry]
PME............ Phosphomonoester [Biochemistry]
PME............ Phosphorylated Monester [Organic chemistry]
PME............ Photomagnet Electric
PME............ Photomagnetoelectric
PME............ Photomagnetoelectric Effect (IAA)
PME............ Photomechanical Effect (SAUS)
PME............ Pinosylvin Methyl Ether [Organic chemistry]
pme .... Planning, Management, Evaluation (AD)
PME............ Planning Market Estimate (SAUS)
PME............ Political Military Exercise (SAUS)
PME............ Polymorphonuclear Eosinophile [Hematology]
P Me........... Portland, Maine (AD)
PME............ Portsmouth [England] [Airport symbol] (AD)
PME............ Postmenopausal Estrogen Therapy [Gynecology] (CPH)
PME............ Precision Measurement Equipment
PME............ Precision Measuring Equipment (AFM)
PME............ Pre-Manufacturing Engineering (SAUS)
PME............ Premature Ejaculation [Medicine] (MELL)
PME............ Preventive Maintenance Effectiveness (SAUS)
PME............ Primary Mission Equipment
PME............ Prime Ministers of England [A publication]
PME............ Prime Mission Equipment
PME............ Process and Manufacturing Engineering (NRCH)
PME............ Processor Memory Enhancement
PME............ Product Market Estimate (SAUS)
PME............ Product Marketing Engineer (TIMI)
PME............ Professional Management for Executives [Army]
PME............ Professional Military Education (AFM)
PME............ Professional Military Ethic (MCD)
PME............ Profession Military Education [Department of Defense]
PME............ Progressive Myoclonus Epilepsy [Medicine] (MELL)
PME............ Project Management Engineering, Inc. (EFIS)
PME............ Project Manager, Electronics System Command [Navy]
pme .... Protective Multiple Earthing (AD)
PME............ Protective Multiple Earthing [Electricity]
PMEA.......... (Phenyl)(methyl)ethanolamine [Organic chemistry]
PMEA.......... Phosphonylmethoxyethyladenine [Antiviral]

PMEA.......... Powder Metallurgy Equipment Association (EA)
P/MEA........ Probationary Marine Engineering Artificer [British military] (DMA)
PMEA.......... Production and Maintenance Engineering Agent (MCD)
PMEA.......... Publishing Manufacturers Executive Association (EA)
PMEAR....... Preliminary Maintenance Engineering Analysis Requirement (MCD)
PMEC......... Postgraduate Medical Education Committee [University of Queensland, Australia]
PMEC......... Professional Military Education Centre (SAUS)
PMEC......... Pseudomembranous Enterocolitis [Medicine] (STED)
PMED......... Paradigm Medical Industries, Inc. [NASDAQ symbol] (SAG)
PMedS........ Delaware County Institute of Science, Media, PA [Library symbol] [Library of Congress] (LCLS)
PMEE......... Prime Mission Electronic Equipment [NASA] (KSC)
PME-Effect... Photomagnetoelectric-Effect (SAUS)
PMEF......... Petroleum Marketing Education Foundation (EA)
PMEG......... Page Map Entry Group (SAUS)
PMEG......... Perforated Metal Export Groups [British] (DBA)
PMEL......... Pacific Marine Environmental Laboratory [Seattle, WA] [National Oceanic and Atmospheric Administration] (GRD)
PMEL......... Precision Measurements Equipment Laboratory [NASA]
PMEL......... Precision Measuring Equipment Laboratory (AD)
PMEL......... Precision Mechanics and Electronics Laboratory (COE)
PME Leucocytes... Polymorphonuclear Eosinophilic Leucocytes (SAUS)
PMEM......... Piezoelectric MEM (SAUS)
PMEM......... Piezoelectric Micro Electro Mechanical (AAEL)
PMEM......... Practical Methods in Electron Microscopy (SAUS)
PMEM......... Processor Memory [Computer science] (CIST)
PM-ENDOR... Polarization Modulated Electron Nuclear Double Resonance [Spectroscopy]
PMEP......... Pumping Mean Effective Pressure [Automotive engine testing]
PMer........... Mercer Free Library, Mercer, PA [Library symbol] [Library of Congress] (LCLS)
PMES......... Personnel Management Evaluation System [Department of Labor]
PMES......... Productivity Measurement and Evaluation System (MCD)
PMES......... Proposed Material Erection Schedule (MCD)
PME School... Professional Military Education School (SAUS)
pmest .... Personality, Matter, Energy, Space, Time (AD)
PMEST........ Personality, Matter, Energy, Space, Time [Colon classification, S. R. Ranganathan] [Library science]
pmet .... Painted Metal (AD)
PMET......... Painter Metal (AAG)
PMEV......... Panel-Mounted Electronic Voltmeter
PMEV......... Panel Mounted (or Mounting) Electronic Voltmeter (SAUS)
PMEXPO...... Property Management Exposition [Bachner Communications] (TSPED)
PMF............ L-Phenylalanine Mustard, 5-Fluorouracil, Methotrexate [Antineoplastic drug regimen] (DAVI)
PMF............ Parts Master File (MCD)
PMF............ Patriot Maintenance Facility [Army]
PMF............ Pennsylvania Mutual Fund (SAUS)
PMF............ Performance Measurement Facility (IAA)
PMF............ Performance Monitor Function [NASA] (NASA)
PMF............ Performance Monitoring Function
PMF............ Perigee Motor Firing [Aerospace] (MCD)
PMF............ Permanent Magnetic Field
PMF............ Permanent Military Force (ADA)
PMF............ Personnel Master File [Army] (AABC)
PMF............ Pilot Mortar Fire
PMF............ Polaris Missile Facility [Military] (IAA)
PMF............ Presidential Medal of Freedom (AD)
PMF............ Price Master File (MCD)
PMF............ Principle Management Facility (MCD)
PMF............ Probability Mass Function (IAA)
PMF............ Probable Maximum Flood [Nuclear energy] (NRCH)
pmf............ Probable Maximum Flooding (AD)
PMF............ Processed Message File (MCD)
PMF............ Processeur Militaire Francais [French]
PMF............ Product Master File (ADWA)
PMF............ Product Measurement Facility (IAA)
PMF............ Professional Medical Film (AABC)
PMF............ Programmable Matched Filter (IAA)
PMF............ Program Management Facility [NASA] (MCD)
pmf............ Progressive Massive Fibrosis [Medicine] (AD)
PMF............ Progressive Massive Fibrosis
PMF............ Project Management File (MCD)
PMF............ Pro Male Fingers [International Bowhunting Organization] [Class equipment]
PMF............ Pro Media Foundation (EA)
PMF............ Protein Motive Force (SAUS)
PMF............ Proton Motive Force [Physics]
PMF............ Pterygomaxillary Fossa (STED)
PMF............ Pulsed Magnetic Field (SAUS)
PMFA.......... Fireman Apprentice, Patternmaker, Striker [Navy rating]
PM-FAC ..... Prednisone, Methotrexate, Fluorouracil, Adriamycin, Cyclophosphamide [Antineoplastic drug regimen]
PM FATDS... Program Manager, Field Artillery Tactical Data Systems (SAUS)
PMFC......... Pacific Marine Fisheries Commission [Later, PSMFC] (EA)
PMFC......... Pacific Marine Fisheries Compact (COE)
PMFC......... Patsy Montana Fan Club (EA)
PMFG......... Peerless Manufacturing Co. [NASDAQ symbol] (NQ)
PMFG......... Peerless Mfg [NASDAQ symbol] (TTSB)
PMFI.......... Perpetual Midwest Financial [NASDAQ symbol] (TTSB)
PMFI.......... Perpetual Midwest Financial, Inc. [NASDAQ symbol] (SAG)
PMFJI......... Pardon Me for Jumping In (ADWA)
PM/FL........ Performance Monitor/Fault Locator [Military] (CAAL)

PMFLT......... Pamphlet (MSA)
PMFN........... Fireman, Patternmaker, Striker [Navy rating]
PMF-PAC ..... Polaris Missile Facility, Pacific (SAUS)
PMFPAC ...... Polaris Missile Facility, Pacific Fleet
PMFS........... Pulsed Magnetic Field System
PM-FTIR ...... Polarization Modulation Fourier Transform InfraRed (SAUS)
PMFWCMA... Paper Mill Fourdrinier Wire Cloth Manufacturers Association [Later, FWC] (EA)
PMG........... Page Map Group (SAUS)
PMG........... Pall Mall Gazette [A publication]
PMG........... Paymaster General [Navy]
PMG........... Permanent Magnet Generator
PMG........... Phase Modulation Generator
PMG........... Photographic Materials Specialty Group (NTPA)
PMG........... Physiological Measurement Group
PMG........... Phytophthora Megasperma F. Sp. Glycinea [A fungus]
PMG........... Pinto Malartic [Vancouver Stock Exchange symbol]
PMG........... Plasma Motor Generator (SAUS)
PMG........... Polymethylgalacturonase [An enzyme]
PMG........... Ponta Pora [Brazil] [Airport symbol] (OAG)
PMG........... Portfolio Marine Group (SAUS)
PMG........... Port Moresby [Papua New Guinea] [Seismograph station code, US Geological Survey] (SEIS)
PmG........... Postmaster General (AD)
PMG........... Postmaster General
PMG........... Poultry Marketing Guide
PMG........... Power Metal Grid (PDAA)
PMG........... Prediction Marker Generator
PMG........... Primary Medical Group [Insurance] (DMAA)
PMG........... Prison-Made Goods Statute (GOBB)
PMG........... Procurement Management Group (SAUS)
PMG........... Program Maintenance Group (SAUS)
PMG........... Propodial Mucus Gland [Zoology]
PMG........... Provisional Military Government [Ethiopia]
PMG........... Provost Marshal General [Army]
PMG........... Putnam Investment Grade Municipal Trade II [NYSE symbol] (SPSG)
PMG........... Putnam Inv Grade Muni Tr II [NYSE symbol] (TTSB)
PMGCT .... Primary Mediastinal Germ-Cell Tumor [Medicine] (DMAA)
PMGDINYC... Production Men's Guild of the Dress Industry of New York City (EA)
PMGFEL....... Preliminary Master Government-Furnished Equipment List (MCD)
PMGI .... Prime Management Group, Inc. [NASDAQ symbol] (SAG)
PMGI .... Princeton Media Group, Inc. [NASDAQ symbol] (SAG)
PMGM .... Program Manager Guidance Memorandum (SAUS)
PMGM .... Program Manager's Guidance Memorandum
PMGO .... Office of the Provost Marshal General [Army]
PM-GPV ...... Project Manager, General Purpose Vehicle (SAA)
PMgr........... Professional Manager (DD)
PMGS .... Predictable Model Guidance Scheme (OA)
PMGS .... Provost Marshal General's School, United States Army
PMGSE .... Provisional Military Government of Socialist Ethiopia (SAUS)
PMGV .... Postmeal Glucose Value [Medicine] (MELL)
PMGW .... Primary Mission Gross Weight
pmh .... Past Medical History (AD)
PMH........... Past Medical History
PMH........... Patrol Missile Hydrofoil (SAUS)
PMH........... Per Man Hour (WDAA)
PMH........... Petroleum Movement History (SAUS)
PMH........... Phenylmercuric Hydroxide [Organic chemistry]
PMH........... Porcine Malignant Hyperthermia (SAUS)
PMH........... Portsmouth, OH [Location identifier] [FAA] (FAAL)
PMH........... Postermedial Hypothalamus (DB)
PMH........... Posteromedial Hypothalamus [Medicine] (DMAA)
PMH........... Previous Medical History (MELL)
PMH........... Prime Mission Hardware (ACAE)
pmh .... Probable Maximum Hurricane (AD)
PMH........... Probable Maximum Hurricane [Nuclear energy] (NRCH)
PMH........... Production per Man-Hour
PMH........... Productive Man Hour (SAUS)
PMH........... Programmed Medical History (STED)
PMH........... Pseudomyocardial Hypertrophy [Medicine] (MELL)
PMH........... Putnam Tax-Free Health Care Fund [NYSE symbol] (SPSG)
PMH........... Putnam Tax-Free Hlth Care Fd [NYSE symbol] (TTSB)
PMHC .... Pyridinylmethylethylene(hydrazinecarbothioamide) [Organic chemistry]
PMHL........... Preferred Measurement Hardware List [NASA] (NASA)
PMH/M .... Productive Man-Hours per Month [Navy] (NG)
PMHP .... Para-Menthane Hydroperoxide [Organic chemistry]
PMHP .... Para-Methane Hydroperoxide
PMHP .... P-Methane Hydroperoxide (SAUS)
PMHP .... Primary Mental Health Project (AD)
PMHR .... Predicted Maximum Heart Rate [Medicine] (DMAA)
PMHRON ..... Patrol Combatant Missile Hydrofoil Squadron (DNAB)
PMHRON MLSG... Patrol Combatant Missile Hydrofoil Squadron Mobile Logistics Support Group (DNAB)
PMHS .... Polymethylhydrosiloxane [Organic chemistry]
PMHS .... Poly(methyl-Hydrostyrene) [Organic chemistry]
PMHSA .... Polish Military History Society of America (EA)
PM-HTV ...... Program Manager for Heavy Tactical Vehicles [Military]
PMHx .... Past Medical History (DAVI)
PMHYT .... Putnam Managed High Yield Trust [Associated Press] (SAG)
PMi............. Milton Public Library, Milton, PA [Library symbol] [Library of Congress] (LCLS)
PMI............. Palma [Mallorca Island] [Airport symbol] (OAG)
PMI............. Palma de Mallorca Balearic Islands, Spain (AD)
PMI............. Paper Money Identifier (ACAE)

PMI............. Parmac Mines [Vancouver Stock Exchange symbol]
PMI............. Partai Muslimin Indonesia [Indonesian Muslim Party] [Political party] (AD)
PMI............. Past [or Previous] Medical Illness
PMI............. Patient Medication Information (MELL)
PMI............. Patient Medication Instruction
PMI............. Pearlitic Malleable Iron (MCD)
PMI............. Pennsylvania Muscle Institute [University of Pennsylvania] [Research center] (RCD)
PMI............. Pensions Management Institute [British] (EAIO)
PMI............. Perioperative Myocardial Infarction [Medicine] (DMAA)
PMI............. Permanent Manufacturing Information (MSA)
PMI............. Personnel Management Information (IAA)
PMI............. Pesticide Monitoring Inventory [Environmental Protection Agency] (AEPA)
PMI............. Petroleum Monitoring, Inc. (EFIS)
PMI............. Phase Measuring Interferometer (AAEL)
PMI............. Phenylmethylisoxazole [Organic chemistry]
PMI............. Phosphomannose Isomerase [An enzyme] (MAE)
PMI............. Phosphomannoseisomerase (SAUS)
pmi............. Photographic Micro-Image (AD)
PMI............. Photographic Microimage Master [Reprography]
PMI............. Place of Maximal Impulse [Medicine] (MELL)
PMI............. Plant Manager Instruction [Nuclear energy] (NRCH)
PMI............. Plasma-Materials Interactions (MCD)
PMI............. Plumbing Manufacturers Institute (EA)
PMI............. Point of Maximal Impulse [Medicine]
PMI............. Point of Maximum Impact (SAUS)
pmi............. Point of Maximum Impulse (AD)
PMI............. Point of Maximum Intensity
PMI............. Polymethacrylimid (SAUS)
PMI............. Polymethacrylimide (EDCT)
PMI............. Positional Macro Instruction (SAUS)
PMI............. Posterior Myocardial Infarction [Medicine] (DMAA)
PMI............. Postmaintenance Inspection (SAUS)
PMI............. Post Mortem Interval [Forensics] [Medicine]
PMI............. Postmortem Intervals (SAUS)
PMI............. Postmyocardial Infarction [Syndrome] [Medicine]
PMI............. Powder Metallurgy International (SAUS)
PMI............. Power Management Inventory [Test]
PMI............. Precious Metals Institute
PMI............. Precision Monolithics Inc (NITA)
PMI............. Preliminary Maintenance Inspection [Department of Defense]
PMI............. Preliminary Marksmanship Instruction [Army]
PMI............. Pre-Marital Inventory (AD)
PMI............. Premark International, Inc. [NYSE symbol] (SPSG)
PMI............. Premark Intl [NYSE symbol] (TTSB)
PMI............. Premarksmanship Instruction [Army]
PMI............. Prescriptive Math Inventory
PMI............. Present Medical Illness
PMI............. Presidential Management Incentives [Office of Management and Budget]
PMI............. Presidential Management Intern (SAUS)
PMI............. Pressed Metal Institute [Later, AMSA]
PMI............. Preventive Maintenance Inspection (AFM)
PMI............. Preventive Maintenance Instruction [Department of Defense]
PMI............. Previous Medical Illness (CPH)
PMI............. Primary Measurement Instrument
PMI............. Principal Maintenance Inspector (NASA)
PMI............. Printed Motors, Inc. (SAUS)
PMI............. Private Memory Interconnect (SAUS)
PMI............. Private Memory Interface (SAUS)
pmi............. Private Mortgage Insurance (AD)
PMI............. Private Mortgage Insurance [Insurance of mortgages by private insurers]
PMI............. Probe Ministries International (EA)
PMI............. Processor Monitoring Instrument [Computer science] (ADA)
PMI............. Programmable Machine Interface (MCD)
PMI............. Programmable Memory Interface [Computer science]
PMI............. Programmable MODEM Interface [Computer science] (MCD)
PMI............. Programmable Multispectral Imager (SAUS)
PMI............. Program Management Instruction [Department of Defense]
PMI............. Project Management Institute (EA)
PMI............. Proposed Military Improvement (CAAL)
PMI............. Protection Mode Indicator (SAUS)
PMI............. Pseudo Matrix Isolation (SAUS)
PMI............. Pseudomatrix Isolation
PMI............. Purchased Materials Inspection
PMIA.......... Parallel Multiplexer Interface Adapter (MCD)
PMIA.......... Powder Metal Industries Association [Australia]
P/MIA......... Powder Metallurgy Industries Association (SAUS)
PMIA.......... Precioas Metals Industry Association (SAUS)
PMIA.......... Presidential Management Improvement Award
PMIC.......... Parallel Multiple Incremental Computer
PMIC.......... Payload Mission Integration Contract [NASA]
PMIC.......... Periodic Maintenance Information Cards
PMIC.......... Personnel Management Information Center [Air Force] (AFM)
PMIC.......... Poultry Meat Industry Committee [New South Wales, Australia]
PMIC.......... Precious Metal Indicator Code
PMIC.......... Precious Metals Institute Conference (SAUS)
PMIC.......... President's Management Improvement Council (AD)
PMIF.......... Powder Metal Industries Federation
PMIG .... Political-Military Interdepartmental Group (AD)
PMIG .... Programmers Minimal Interface to Graphics (MCD)
PMI Gp .... PMI Group, Inc. [Associated Press] (SAG)

PMIIT.......... Putnam Master Intermediate Income Trust [*Associated Press*] (SAG)
PMIJ.......... Pulse Modulated Infrared Jammer (SAUS)
PMIJ.......... Pulse-Modulated Infrared Jammer
PMilan........ Papiri Milanesi [*A publication*] (OCD)
PMilS......... Millersville State College, Millersville, PA [*Library symbol*] [*Library of Congress*] (LCLS)
PMIM.......... Powder Metal Injection Molding (SAUS)
PMI/MO....... Precedence Manual In / Manual Out (DNAB)
PMIN.......... Processor Memory Interconnection Network (SAUS)
PMIP.......... Palaeoclimate Model Inter-comparison Project (SAUS)
PMIP.......... Paleoclimate Modeling Intercomparison Project [*Marine science*] (OSRA)
PMIP.......... Paleoclimatic (or Paleoclimatological) Model Intercomparison Project (SAUS)
PMIP.......... Pan Malayan Islamic Party
PMIP.......... Postmaintenance Inspection Pilot
PMIP.......... Presidential Management Intern Program [*Executive Office of the President*] (GFGA)
PMIPK........ Poly Methyl Isopropenyl Ketone (SAUS)
PMIPK........ Poly(methyl Isopropenyl Ketone) [*Organic chemistry*]
PMI Powder Metall Int... PMI Powder Metallurgy International (SAUS)
PMIR.......... Pressure Modulator Infrared Radiometer (EOSA)
PMIR.......... Program Manager's Integration Review [*NASA*] (NASA)
PMIR.......... Psi-Mediated Instrumental Response [*Parapsychology*]
PMIRD........ Passive Microwave Intercept Receiver Display
PMIRR........ Pressure Modulator Infra-Red Radiometer (VLIE)
PMIRR........ Pressure Modulator Infrared Radiometer (ACAE)
PMIS.......... Passive Microwave Imaging System [*NASA*]
PMIS.......... Patient Medical Information System (OA)
PMIS.......... Personal Management Information System [*Computer science*] (IAA)
PMIS.......... Personnel Management Information System
PMIS.......... Personnel Management Information Systems (SAUS)
PMIS.......... Personnel Marking and Identification System (SAUS)
PMIS.......... Planning Management Information System (AD)
PMIS.......... Plant Management Information System
PMIS.......... Plant Monitoring and Information System [*Nuclear energy*] (NRCH)
PMIS.......... Postmyocardial Infarction Syndrome [*Medicine*] (DMAA)
PMIS.......... Precision Mechanisms in Sodium [*Nuclear energy*] (NRCH)
PMIS.......... Premis Corp. [*NASDAQ symbol*] (SAG)
PMIS.......... Printing Management Information System (SAUS)
PMIS.......... Printing Management Information Systems
PMIS.......... Process Management Information System (ACII)
PMIS.......... Production Management Information System (SAUS)
PMIS.......... Product Management Information System (AD)
PMIS.......... Program Management Information System [*Army*]
PMIS.......... Program Measurement Information System [*Computer science*] (IAA)
PMIS.......... Projects Management Information System [*UNESCO*] (DUND)
PMIS.......... PSRO [*Professional Standards Review Organization*] Management Information System (DHSM)
PMIS.......... Publications Management Information System (SAUS)
PMIS.......... Purchase Management Information System (SAUS)
PMISP........ Personnel Management Information System Plan (SAUS)
PMI Syndrome... Postmyocardial Infarction Syndrome (SAUS)
PMIT.......... Putnam Master Income Trust [*Associated Press*] (SAG)
PMITS........ Post Mobilization Individual Training and Support (MCD)
PM ITTS...... Program Manager, Instrumentation, Targets, and Threat Simulators (SAUS)
PM ITTS...... Project Manager, Instrumentation, Targets, and Threat Simulators (SAUS)
PMJ.......... Porto Murtinho [*Brazil*] [*Airport symbol*] (AD)
PMJ.......... Pulse Modulated Jammer (SAUS)
PMJ.......... Pulse-Modulated Jammer
PMJC......... Pine Manor Junior College (AD)
PMJEG........ Performance Measurement Joint Executive Group (DOMA)
PMJI......... Pardon My Jumping In [*E-Mail discussion*]
PMK.......... Palair Macedonian [*Yugoslavia*] [*ICAO designator*] (FAAC)
PMK.......... Panel Marking Kit
PMK.......... Pitch Mark [*Shipfitting*] (AAG)
pmk.......... Pitch Mark (AD)
PMK.......... Pointe Molloy [*Kerguelen Islands*] [*Seismograph station code, US Geological Survey*] (SEIS)
PMK.......... Portable Molding Kit
pmk.......... Postmark (AD)
PMK.......... Postmark
PMK.......... Primark Corp. [*NYSE symbol*] (SPSG)
PMK.......... Primary Monkey Kidney [*Physiology*]
PMK.......... Primary Rhesus Monkey Kidney (AAMN)
PMKD......... Postmarked (SAUS)
PMKM......... Past Master, Knights of Malta [*Freemasonry*] (ROG)
PMKY......... Pittsburgh, McKeesport & Youghiogheny [*AAR code*]
PML.......... Pacific Micronesian Line (AD)
PML.......... Pakistan Muslim League [*Political party*]
PML.......... Parts Material List
PML.......... Pattern Makers' League of North America (EA)
PML.......... Payload Management Lamp
PML.......... Perfectly Matched Layer (ARMP)
PML.......... Perfect Matched Layer (SAUS)
PML.......... Permitted Maximum Level (SAUS)
P M L........ Phoenix Memorial Laboratory (SAUS)
PML.......... Phoenix Mutual Life Insurance Co. (EFIS)
PML.......... Physical Memory Level
PML.......... Physical Memory Loss [*Computer science*] (CIST)
PML.......... PI Edit's Macro Language [*Iliad Group*] [*Computer science*]
PML.......... [*The*] Pierpont Morgan Library (BJA)

PML.......... Plymouth Marine Laboratory [*Natural Environment Research Council*] [*British*] [*Information service or system*] (IID)
PML.......... Polymer Microdevice Laboratory [*Case Western Reserve University*] [*Research center*] (RCD)
PML.......... Polymorphonuclear Leukocyte [*Hematology*]
PML.......... Port Moller [*Alaska*] [*Airport symbol*] (OAG)
PML.......... Port Moller, AK [*Location identifier*] [*FAA*] (FAAL)
PML.......... Possible Maximum Loss (MARI)
PML.......... Posterior Mitral Leaflet [*Cardiology*]
PML.......... Powder Metallurgy Laboratory (SAUS)
PML.......... Power Minimized Logic (SAUS)
PML.......... Preliminary Materials List [*NASA*]
pml.......... Probable Maximum Loss (AD)
PML.......... Probable Maximum Loss [*Insurance*]
PML.......... Process Modelling Language (VLIE)
PML.......... Production Measurement Log (SAUS)
PML.......... Programmable Macro Logic (NITA)
PML.......... Progressive Multifocal Leucoencephalopathy (SAUS)
PML.......... Progressive Multifocal Leukoencephalopathy [*Oncology*]
PML.......... Promotion Management List [*Pronounced "pemell"*] [*Air Force*]
PML.......... Promyelocytic Leukaemia Protein [*Biochemistry*]
PML.......... Promyelocytic Leukemia [*Medicine*]
PML.......... Putnam Investment Grade Multiple Sectors III [*AMEX symbol*] (SPSG)
PML.......... Putnam Inv Grade Muni Tr III [*AMEX symbol*] (TTSB)
PML.......... University of Windsor, Paul Martin Law Library [*UTLAS symbol*]
pmla......... Parmelia (AD)
PMLA......... Production Music Libraries Association (EA)
PMLA......... Publication of the Modern Language Association of America (AD)
PMLC......... Pooled Mixed Lymphocyte Culture [*Clinical chemistry*]
PMLC......... Previous Micro-Location Counter (VLIE)
PMLC......... Programmed Multiline Controller
PMLD......... Profound and Multiple Learning Difficulties (AIE)
PMLE......... Polymorphous Light Eruption [*Medicine*]
PMLF......... Project Marketing Loan Facility [*Australia*]
PMLG......... Poly(methyl L-Glutamate) [*Organic chemistry*]
PMLM......... Photosensitive Membrane Light Modulation (or Modulator) (SAUS)
PMLM......... Photosensitive Membrane Light Modulator
PMLO......... Partially Maleated Linseed Oil (SAUS)
PMLO......... Philippine Military Liaison Officer (DNAB)
PMLO......... Principal Military Landing Officer (AD)
PMLO......... Principal Military Landing Offices [*British*]
PM Loudspeaker... Permanent Magnetic Loudspeaker (SAUS)
PMLPC........ Permanent Mass Layoffs and Plant Closings Program [*Bureau of Labor Statistics*]
PM-LSM...... Polarization-Modulation Laser-Scanning Microscopy
PML-TNO..... TNO Prins Maurits Laboratory (SAUS)
PMLV......... Permanent Magnet Latch Valve
PMM.......... Military Morale Division [*Coast Guard*]
PMM.......... Paramagnetic Material (SAUS)
PMM.......... Parametric Modelling (SAUS)
PMM.......... Partial Matrix Multiply (IAA)
PMM.......... Peace Mission Movement (EA)
PMM.......... Peat Marwick McLintock [*Accounting firm*] [*British*]
PMM.......... Pedestal-Mounted Manipulator [*Nuclear energy*] (NRCH)
PMM.......... Penobscot Marine Museum (EA)
PMM.......... Permanent Magnet Magnetizer (SAUS)
PMM.......... Permanent Magnet Motor (IAA)
PMM.......... Personnel Management Manual [*A publication*] (ADA)
PMM.......... Petroleum Marketing Management [*Petroleum Marketers Association of America*] [*A publication*]
PMM.......... Petroleum Marketing Monthly [*Department of Energy*] [*Information service or system*] (CRD)
PMM.......... Physical Memory Manager [*Computer science*] (PCM)
PMM.......... Phytophthora Megasperma F.Sp Medicaginia [*A fungus*]
PMM.......... Planar Motion Mechanism (SAUS)
PMM.......... Poly Methyl Methacrylate (SAUS)
PMM.......... Poly(methyl Methacrylate) [*Also, PMMA*] [*Organic chemistry*]
PMM.......... Pool Maintenance Module [*Telecommunications*] (TEL)
PMM.......... Portavideo [*Vancouver Stock Exchange symbol*]
PMM.......... Post Mast Message (IAA)
PMM.......... Post-Merger Management
PMM.......... Presa Malpaso [*Mexico*] [*Seismograph station code, US Geological Survey*] (SEIS)
pmm.......... Preventive Medicine Measures
PMM.......... Primitive Martian Mantle [*Planetary science*]
PMM.......... Probability of Missed Message (CCCA)
PMM.......... Process Monitoring Modules (ACII)
PMM.......... Procom Emerald [*Vancouver Stock Exchange symbol*]
PMM.......... Procurement Material Management (TIMI)
PMM.......... Professional Media Magazine (SAUS)
PMM.......... Professional Music Men, Inc. (EA)
PMM.......... Profile Milling Machine
PMM.......... Programmable Microcomputer Module
PMM.......... Property Management Manual [*NASA*] (MCD)
PMM.......... Protoplast Maintenance Medium (DB)
PMM.......... Pullman, MI [*Location identifier*] [*FAA*] (FAAL)
pmm.......... Pulse Mode Multiplex (AD)
PMM.......... Pulse Mode Multiplex
PMM.......... Purchase-Money Mortgage [*Real estate*]
PMM.......... Putnam Managed Municipal Income [*NYSE symbol*] (SPSG)
PMM.......... Putnam Managed Muni Income [*NYSE symbol*] (TTSB)
PMMA........ Paper Machinery Makers Association (SAUS)
PMMA........ Pere Marquette Memorial Association (EA)
PMMA........ Poly(methyl Methacrylate) [*Also, PMM*] [*Organic chemistry*]

pmma	Polymethylmethacrylate (AD)
PMMA	Poly Methyl Methacrylate Association [*European Council of Chemical Manufacturers Federations*] [*Brussels, Belgium*] (EAIO)
PMMA	Polymethyl Methacrylate Association (SAUS)
PMMAP	Poly(methyl Methacrylate Peroxide) [*Organic chemistry*]
PMMAPA	Poly Methyl Methacrylate Producers Association [*Belgium*] (EAIO)
PMMB	Parallel Memory to Memory Bus (SAUS)
PMMB	Parallel Memory-to-Memory Bus
PMMC	Permanent Magnetic Movable Coil
PMMC	Permanent Magnetic Movable (or Moving) Coil (SAUS)
PMMC	Permanent Magnet Moving Coil (SAUS)
PMMC	Precious Metals Marketing Co.
PM-MCD	Project Manager for Mines, Countermine, and Demolitions [*Army*] (RDA)
PM-MEP	Project Manager - Mobile Electric Power [*DoD*]
PMMEP	Project Manager, Mobile Electric Power (SAUS)
PMMF	Precious Metals Master File [*DoD*] (AFIT)
PMMI	Packaging Machinery Manufacturers Institute (EA)
PMMI	Packaging Machinery Manufacturers (or Manufacturing) Institute (SAUS)
PMMI	Permanent Magnet Movable (or Moving) Iron (SAUS)
PMMI	Polypyromellitimide (EDCT)
PMMI	Putnam Managed Municipal Income Trust [*Associated Press*] (SAG)
PMML	Predictive Model Markup Language (IDAI)
PMMM	Pall Mall Money Management [*Investment group*] [*British*]
PMMO	Particulate Methane Monooxygenase [*Biochemistry*]
PMMO	Projects and Missions Management Office (SAUS)
PMMP	Post Mortem Memory Print (SAUS)
PMMP	Project Managers Master Plan (SAUS)
PMMR	Panel-Mounted Microfilm Reader
PMMR	Passive Multichannel Microwave Radiometer [*NASA*]
PMMRS	Passive Microwave Mapping and Retrieval Simulator (SAUS)
PMMS	Phrenicon Metabolic Monitoring System
PMMS	Plainsong and Mediaeval Music Society (EA)
PMMS	Process Material Management System (SAUS)
PMMS	Program Master Milestone Schedule (MCD)
PMMU	Paged Memory Management Unit [*Computer chip*] (BYTE)
pmmu	Paged Memory-Management Unit (AD)
PMMU	Page Memory Management Unit (SAUS)
PMMV	Pea Mild Mosaic Virus [*Plant pathology*]
PMMW	Passive Millimeter Wave (ADWA)
PMN	Pacific Mountain Network [*Television*]
PMN	Pahute Mesa [*Nevada*] [*Seismograph station code, US Geological Survey*] [*Closed*] (SEIS)
PMN	Pasteurized Milk Network (SAUS)
PMN	Performance Monitoring (VLIE)
PMN	Permian Resources Ltd. [*Vancouver Stock Exchange symbol*]
PMN	Phenyl Mercuric Nitrate (SAUS)
PMN	Phenylmercuric Nitrate [*Antiseptic*]
PMN	Polymorphonuclear [*Hematology*]
pmn	Polymorphonuclear Neutrophil (AD)
PMN	Polymorphonuclear Neutrophilic [*Hematology*]
PMN	Polymorphonucleocyte [*Hematology*] (CPH)
PMN	Postman (DCTA)
PMN	Premanufacture Notification [*Environmental Protection Agency*]
PMN	Pre-Manufacturing Notice [*Government regulations*]
PMN	Premarket Notification [*Requirement for introducing new chemicals into the EEC*]
pmn	Producto Material Neto [*Net Material Product*] [*Spain*] (AD)
PMN	Program Management Network (MCD)
PMN	Program Model Number (SAUS)
PMN	Project Management Network [*Computer science*] (VLIE)
PMN	Proposed Material Need (MCD)
PMN	Pumani [*Papua New Guinea*] [*Airport symbol*] (OAG)
PMN	Putnam New York Investment Grade Municipal [*AMEX symbol*] (SPSG)
PMN	Putnam NY Inv Grade Muni [*AMEX symbol*] (TTSB)
PMNA	Pacific Mountain Network Association (AD)
PMNA	Parkers Marsh Natural Area [*Virginia*]
PM-NAVCON	Project Manager, Navigation and Control [*Military*]
PMNAVCON	Project Manager, Navigation and Control
PMNC	Peripheral Blood Mononuclear Cell [*Medicine*] (DMAA)
PMNC	Pharmaceutical Multinational Company (DB)
PMNF	Premanufacture Notification Form [*Environmental Protection Agency*] (GFGA)
PMNG	Polymorphonuclear Granulocyte [*Hematology*] (DAVI)
PMNH	Peabody Museum of Natural History (NADA)
PMNL	Polymorphonuclear Leucocyte (SAUS)
pmnl	Polymorphonuclear Leukocyte (AD)
PMNL	Polymorphonuclear Leukocyte [*Hematology*]
PMNN	Polymorphonuclear Neutrophil (DB)
PMNP	Platform-Mounted Nuclear Plant (NRCH)
PMNP	Platform Mounted Nuclear Platform (SAUS)
PMNPP	Platform Mounted Nuclear Power Plant (SAUS)
pmnr	Periadenitis Mucosa Necrotica Recurrens (AD)
PMNR	Periadenitis Mucosa Necrotica Recurrens [*Medicine*]
PMNR	Porter McLeod National Retail [*NASDAQ symbol*] (SAG)
PMNR	Porter McLeod Natl Retail [*NASDAQ symbol*] (TTSB)
PMN/SFS	People's Music Network for Songs of Freedom and Struggle (EA)
PMNT	Permanent (IAA)
PMNUC	Project Manager for Nuclear [*Munitions*]
PM-NUC	Project Manager for Nuclear Munitions [*Army*] (RDA)
PMNV	Project Manager, Night Vision (RDA)
PM NV/RSTA	Project Manager for Night Vision/Reconnaissance Surveillance and Target Acquisition [*Military*] (RDA)
PMo	Monessen Public Library, Monessen, PA [*Library symbol*] [*Library of Congress*] (LCLS)
PMO	Palermo [*Italy*] [*Airport symbol*] (OAG)
PMO	Palermo Resources, Inc. [*Vancouver Stock Exchange symbol*]
pmo	Palomar Mountain Observatory (AD)
PMO	Perroni, Martin, O'Reilly [*Commercial firm*]
PMO	Personnel Management Officer [*Army*] (INF)
PMO	Perturbation Molecular Orbital [*Theory*]
PMO	Phenylmercuric Oleate (SAUS)
PMO	Phenyl Mercury Oleate (SAUS)
PMO	Phenylmethyloxadiazole (SAUS)
PMO	Pianissimo [*Very Softly*] [*Music*] (ROG)
pmo	Pianissimo [*Very Softly*] [*Italian*] [*Music*] (AD)
PMO	Pine Mountain Observatory
PMO	Polaris Material Office [*Missiles*]
PMO	Polaris Missile Office
PMO	Pomariorio [*Tuamotu Archipelago*] [*Seismograph station code, US Geological Survey*] (SEIS)
PMO	Port Medical Officer
PMO	Port Meteorological Office [*National Weather Service*]
PMO	Port Meteorological Officer (SAUS)
PMO	Postal Money Order [*Military*]
PMO	Postmenopausal Osteoporosis [*Medicine*]
PMO	Prime Minister's Office
PMO	Principal Medical Officer
pmo	Printed Matter Only (AD)
PMO	Product Management Office [*Army*]
PMO	Product Manager's Office (RDA)
PMO	Product Manufacturing Organization
PMO	Profit Making Organization
PMO	Program Maintenance Office
PMO	Program Management Office [*Environmental Protection Agency*] (GFGA)
PMO	Program Management Office [*NASA*] (KSC)
PMO	Program Management Office [*Army*]
PMO	Program Management Organization (HLLA)
PMO	Program Manager's Office
PMO	Project Management Office [*Army*] (AABC)
PMO	Project Manager's Office
PMO	Property Movement Order
PMO	Provisional [*Program Management*] Office [*Army*]
PMO	Provost Marshal's Office
PMO	Psychiatric Military Officer
PMO	Purple Mountain Observatory, Academia Sinica, Nanjing (SAUS)
PMO	Putnam Municipal Opportunities Trust [*NYSE symbol*] (SPSG)
PMO	Putnam Muni Opport Tr [*NYSE symbol*] (TTSB)
PMOA	Programmatic Memorandum of Agreement (COE)
PMOA	Prospectors and Mine Owners Association (EA)
PMOC	Pioneer Mission Operations Center [*NASA*]
PMOC	Prototype Mission Operations Center (ACAE)
PMODA	Phenyl(mercapto)oxadiazole [*Reagent*]
PMOF	Presidential Medal of Freedom [*Military decoration*] (GFGA)
PM of F	Presidential Medal of Freedom [*Military decoration*] (AABC)
PMOG	Plutonium Maintenance and Operating Gallery [*Nuclear energy*] (NRCH)
PMOG	Proposed Material Ordering Guide (MCD)
pmol	Picomole [*One trillionth of a mole*] (WGA)
PMOLANT	Polaris Material Office, Atlantic Fleet [*Missiles*]
pmole	Picomole [*One trillionth of a mole*] (DAVI)
PMOM	Performance Management Operations Manager
PMOM	Performance Management Operations Manual [*NASA*] (NASA)
PMO-MTV	Project Manager's Office, Medium Tactical Vehicles [*Army*]
PMON	Performance Management Operations Network [*NASA*] (NASA)
P-MONO	Promonocytes [*hematology*] (DAVI)
PMOPAC	Polaris Material Office, Pacific Fleet [*Missiles*]
PMOR	Phar-Mor, Inc. [*NASDAQ symbol*] (SAG)
P Mor	Port Moresby (AD)
PMOR	Probabilistic Methods in Operations Research (SAUS)
PMORW	Phar-Mor Wrrt [*NASDAQ symbol*] (TTSB)
P-MOS	P-Channel Metal-Oxide Semiconductor
PMOS	Permanent Manned Orbital Station (AAG)
PMOS	Physical Movement of Spacecraft (SAA)
PMOS	Positive Channel Metal Oxide Semiconductor (SAUS)
PMOS	Positive-Channel Metal-Oxide Semiconductor [*Telecommunications*] (TEL)
PMOS	Positive Metal-Oxide Semiconductor (SAUS)
PMOS	Primary Military Occupational Specialty [*Army*]
PMOS	Program Management and Operations Staff [*Environmental Protection Agency*] (GFGA)
PMOS	Program Management and Operation Staff (SAUS)
PMOS	P-Type Metal-Oxide Semiconductor (SAUS)
PMOSC	Primary Military Occupational Code (AD)
PMOSC	Primary Military Occupational Specialty Code [*Army*] (AABC)
PMOT	Putnam Municipal Opportunities Trust [*Associated Press*] (SAG)
PMov	Personnel Movements (SAUS)
PMP	Pacific Magazines and Printing Ltd. [*Commercial firm*] [*Australia*]
PMP	Packed Main Parachute
PMP	Pain Management Program [*Neurology*] (DAVI)
PMP	Parallel Microprogrammed Processor [*Computer science*]
PMP	Parent Mass Peak
PMP	Parents' Magazine Press
PMP	Partial Manifold Preheater [*Automotive engineering*]
PMP	Partido ng Masang Pilipino [*Political party*] (EY)
PMP	Parti du Mouvement Populaire de la Cote Francaise des Somalis [*Popular Movement Party of French Somaliland*] [*Political party*]

PMP............	Partito Monarchico Popolare [*Popular Monarchist Party*] [*Italy*] [*Political party*] (PPE)
PMP............	Parts Material Packaging (SAUS)
PMP............	Parts, Materials, and Packaging (MCD)
PMP............	Parts, Materials, and Processes (MCD)
PMP............	Parts, Materials, Processes (SAUS)
PMP............	Passive Measurement Program
PMP............	Past Menstrual Period [*Medicine*]
PMP............	Patient Management Path (SAUS)
PMP............	Patient Management Problem [*Gerontology*]
PMP............	Patient-Management Problem (SAUS)
PMP............	Patient Medication Profile (STED)
PMP............	Patient of the Month Program (SAUS)
PMP............	Payload Mounting Panels (SAUS)
PMP............	Performance Management Package [*NASA*] (NASA)
PMP............	Performance Management Process (SAUS)
PMP............	Performance Monitoring Program (CCCA)
PmP............	Pergamon Press, Inc., Fairview Park, Elmsford, NY [*Library symbol*] [*Library of Congress*] (LCLS)
PMP............	Permanent Manned Presence (SSD)
pmp............	Per-Member Payment (AD)
PMP............	Persistent Mentoposterior [*A fetal position*] [*Obstetrics*]
PMP............	Peter Miller Apparel Group, Inc. [*Toronto Stock Exchange symbol*]
PMP............	Phased Maintenance Program (SAUS)
PMP............	Phased Manufacturing Program (SAUS)
PMP............	Phenyl(methyl)pyrazolone [*An organic pigment*]
PMP............	Photomechanical Process (SAUS)
PMP............	Physical Media Parameter (VLIE)
PMP............	Piecewise Markov Process (PDAA)
PMP............	Pimaga [*Papua New Guinea*] [*Airport symbol*] (OAG)
PMP............	Planar Metallization with Polymer (IAA)
PMP............	Planned Maintenance Plan (MCD)
PMP............	Plan of Actions and Milestones (SAUS)
PMP............	Plantar Metatarsal Padding [*Medicine*] (MELL)
PMP............	Poly(metal Phosphinate) [*Organic chemistry*]
PMP............	Poly(methylpentene) [*Organic chemistry*]
PMP............	Pompano Beach, FL [*Location identifier*] [*FAA*] (FAAL)
PMP............	Pompeii [*Italy*] [*Seismograph station code, US Geological Survey*] [*Closed*] (SEIS)
PMP............	Pontifical Mission for Palestine (EA)
PMP............	Pontryagins Maximum Principle (SAUS)
PMP............	Population Management Plan (SAUS)
PMP............	Portable Medium-Powder Plant (SAUS)
PMP............	Position Management Program
PMP............	Postmastectomy Pain (MELL)
PMP............	Post-Metal Programming (SAUS)
PMP............	Powdered Metal Part
PMP............	Powder Melting Process [*Physics*]
PMP............	Power Management Profile [*Test*]
pmp............	Precious Metal Plating (AD)
PMP............	Precision Mounting Platform (ACAE)
PMP............	Preliminary Management Plan (AD)
PMP............	Preliminary Mission Profile (MCD)
PMP............	Premodulation Processor
PMP............	Preoperational Maintenance Plan
PMP............	Preoperational Monitoring Program [*Nuclear energy*] (NRCH)
PMP............	Pressure Measurement Package
PMP............	Prevention, Mitigation and Preparedness [*Office of U.S. Foreign Disaster Assistance*]
PMP............	Preventive Maintenance Package (SAUS)
PMP............	Preventive Maintenance Periodic [*Inspection*]
PMP............	Preventive Maintenance Plan (KSC)
PMP............	Preventive Maintenance Procedure [*Nuclear energy*] (NRCH)
PMP............	Preventive Maintenance Program (SAUS)
pmp............	Previous Menstrual Period [*Medicine*] (AD)
PMP............	Previous Menstrual Period [*Medicine*]
PMP............	Prime Mission Product (SAUS)
PMP............	Prime Mission Project [*Military*]
PMP............	Prime Motor Inns L.P. [*NYSE symbol*] (TTSB)
PMP............	Prime Motor Inns Ltd. [*NYSE symbol*] (SPSG)
PMP............	Prior Menstrual Period [*Gynecology*] (DAVI)
PMP............	Prism-Mirror-Prism [*For electron microscopy*]
PMP............	Probable Maximum Precipitation [*Nuclear energy*] (NRCH)
PMP............	Procurement Methods and Practices (AD)
PMP............	Product and Marketing Planning (IAA)
PMP............	Product & Market Planning (SAUS)
PMP............	Professor of Moral Philosophy
PMP............	Profit-Maximizing Price (MHDW)
PMP............	Program Management Plan [*NASA*]
PMP............	Program Master Plan [*Department of Defense*]
PMP............	Program Monitor Panel
PMP............	Progressive Merger Procedure [*Econometrics*]
PMP............	Project Management Plan (ABAC)
PMP............	Project Management Plan/System (SAUS)
PMP............	Project Management Professional
PMP............	Project Master Plan [*Army*]
PMP............	Project on Military Procurement [*Later, PGP*] (EA)
PMP............	Property Management Plan [*Australia*]
PMP............	Property Management Planning (SAUS)
PMP............	Protective Mobilization Plan
PMP............	Psychotropic Medication Plan (STED)
PMP............	Pulmonary Mean Pressure [*Medicine*]
PMP............	Pulsed Microwave Power
PMP............	Pump (KSC)
PMP............	Pyridoxamine Phosphate [*Biochemistry*]
PMPA.........	Permanent Magnet Producers Association [*Later, MMPA*] (EA)
PMPA.........	Petroleum Marketing Practices Act
PMPA.........	(Phosphonylmethoxypropyl)adenine [*Antiviral*]
PMPA.........	Powder Metallurgy Parts Association (SAUS)
PMPA.........	Precision Machined Products Association (NTPA)
PMPA.........	Proximal Main Pulmonary Artery [*Anatomy*]
P/M Part.....	Powder Metal Part (SAUS)
PMPCB.......	Part, Material and Processes Control Board (ACAE)
PMPE.........	Punch Memory Parity Error [*Computer science*] (IAA)
PMPEA.......	Professional Motion Picture Equipment Association [*Later, PFVEA*] (EA)
PMPFR.......	Program Manager's Preflight Review [*NASA*] (KSC)
PMPG	Pumping
PMPH	Pamphlet (DLA)
PMPIN.......	Pre-Manufacturing and Pre-Importation Notification (SAUS)
PMPIT.......	Program Management Process Improvement Team (TIMI)
PMPL........	Preferred Mechanical Parts List [*NASA*] (NASA)
PM Plant....	Portable Medium-power Plant (SAUS)
PMPM........	Per Member per Month
PMPM........	Perpetual Motion Poetry Machine
PMPM........	Phase Margin Performance Measure [*Manual control system*]
PMPM........	Programmable Multiple Position Machine (MCD)
PMPM........	Pulse Mode Performance Model (KSC)
PMPMA.......	Plastic and Metal Products Manufacturers Association (EA)
PMPMD.......	Pest Management and Pesticide Monitoring Division (SAUS)
PMPO	Peak Music Power Output (SAUS)
PMPO	Postmenopausal Palpable Ovary [*Gynecology*]
PMPO	Pulse-Modulated Power Oscillator (SAUS)
PMPP........	Program Management Phase-Out Plan [*Military*] (AFIT)
PMPPI.......	Polymethylenepolyphenyl Polyisocyanate [*Organic chemistry*]
PMPPIC......	Polymethylene-Polyphenyl Isocyanate (SAUS)
PMPQ	Professional and Managerial Position Questionnaire [*Test*]
PMPR	Program Management and Performance Review
PMPRB.......	Program to Manage Pesticide Residues in Beef (SAUS)
PM Press....	Powder Metal Press (SAUS)
PMPS.........	Postmastectomy Pain Syndrome [*Medicine*] (DMAA)
PMPS.........	Program Management Planning and Scheduling [*Military*] (DNAB)
PMPSL.......	Part, Material and Processes Selection List (ACAE)
PMPY.........	Per Member per Year
PMQ	Perito Moreno [*Argentina*] [*Airport symbol*] (OAG)
PMQ	Permanent Married Quarters [*Canadian Forces*]
PMQ	Phytylmenaquinone [*Vitamin K*] [*Also, K*] [*Biochemistry*]
PMQ	Prime Minister's Question [*British*] (BARN)
PMQ	Primitive Methodist Quarterly Review [*A publication*] (ROG)
PMR..........	Pacemaker Rhythm [*Medicine*] (MELL)
PMR..........	Pacific Missile Range [*Later, WTR*]
PMR..........	Palmer [*Alaska*] [*Seismograph station code, US Geological Survey*] (SEIS)
PMR..........	Palmerston North [*New Zealand*] [*Airport symbol*] (OAG)
PMR..........	Parabolic Microwave Reflector
PMR..........	Paramagnetic Resonance (IAA)
PMR..........	Partido Mariateguista Revolucionario [*Peru*] [*Political party*] (EY)
PMR..........	Partidul Muncitoresc Roman [*Romanian Workers' Party*] [*Political party*]
PMR..........	Parts Material Requirements File
PMR..........	Passive Microwave Radiometer (SAUS)
PMR..........	Patellar Medial Retinaculum [*Medicine*] (MELL)
PMR..........	Patient Master Record (SAUS)
PMR..........	Patient Medical Record (DB)
PMR..........	Payload Mass Ratio
Pmr..........	Paymaster (AD)
PMR..........	Paymaster
PMR..........	Performance Measurement Report [*NASA*] (NASA)
PMR..........	Performance Monitoring Receiver
PMR..........	Perinatal Mortality Rate [*Medicine*]
PMR..........	Periodic Medical Review (STED)
PMR..........	Phase Modulation Recording (VLIE)
PMR..........	Physical Medicine and Rehabilitation (STED)
PMR..........	Planned Maintenance Requirements
PMR..........	Point of Minimum Radius (IAA)
PMR..........	Polise-Air [*Russian Federation*] [*ICAO designator*] (FAAC)
PMR..........	Pollutant Mass Rate [*Environmental science*] (GFGA)
PMR..........	Polyester Mold Release [*Plastics*]
PMR..........	Polymerizable Monomer Reactant (SAUS)
PMR..........	Polymerization of Monomeric Reactants (SAUS)
PMR..........	Polymerization of Monomer Reactants [*Organic chemistry*]
PMR..........	Polymerized Monomeric Reactant (SAUS)
PMR..........	Polymorphic Reticulosis [*Ophthalmology*] (DAVI)
PMR..........	Polymyalgia Rheumatica [*Medicine*]
PMR..........	Portable Microfiche Reader [*DASA Corp.*]
PMR..........	Portable Microwave Repeater (SAUS)
PMR..........	Portable Multiparameter Radar (SAUS)
PMR..........	Posteromedial Release [*Orthopedics*] (DAVI)
PMR..........	Postmaster (DCTA)
PMR..........	Postmaster Return (SAUS)
PMR..........	Post Mortem Routine (SAUS)
PMR..........	Potential Military Relationship (SAUS)
PMR..........	Potential Military Relevance
PMR..........	Power Master Reset (SAUS)
PMR..........	Power Monitor Relay
PMR..........	Precision Microwave Radiometer (SAUS)
PMR..........	Preliminary Materials Review
P/M/R	Premakeready [*Graphic arts*] (DGA)
PMR..........	Prependicular Mode Recording (SAUS)
pmr............	Pressure-Modulated Radiometer (AD)

PMR............	Pressure Modulation Radiometer
PMR............	Pressure Modulator Radiometer (SAUS)
PMR............	Preventive Maintenance and Repair [*Aviation*] (MCD)
PMR............	Primary Mission Readiness
PMR............	Prime Resources Corp. [*Vancouver Stock Exchange symbol*]
PMR............	Priority Monitor Report
PMR............	Prior Medical Record (DB)
PMR............	Private Milk Records (SAUS)
PMR............	Private Mobile Radio (CGWS)
PMR............	Problem Management Report (SAUS)
PMR............	Procurement Management Review [*DoD*]
PMR............	Profoundly Mentally Retarded
PMR............	Programmable Multiloop Regulator (SAUS)
PMR............	Program Management Responsibilities (SAUS)
PMR............	Program Management Responsibility (MCD)
PMR............	Program Management Review
PMR............	Program Manager's Review [*NASA*] (NASA)
PMR............	Programmed Mixture Ratio (KSC)
PMR............	Program Modification Request (SAUS)
PMR............	Progressive Muscle Relaxation (MELL)
PMR............	Projection Microradiography (IAA)
PMR............	Project Management Report
PMR............	Project Management Review
PMR............	Pro Male Release [*International Bowhunting Organization*] [*Class equipment*]
PMR............	Propellant Mass Ratio (SAA)
PMR............	Property Management Regulation (AAGC)
PMR............	Property Movement Request (MCD)
PMR............	Proportionate Morbidity Ratio [*Statistics*] (DAVI)
PMR............	Proportionate Mortality Rate [*or Ratio*]
PMR............	Proportionate Mortality Ratio (SAUS)
PMR............	Protein Magnetic Resonance [*Medicine*] (MAE)
PMR............	Proton Magnetic Resonance
PMR............	Provisioning Master Record (MCD)
PMR............	Psychomotor Retardation (STED)
PMR............	Public Mobile Radio (WDMC)
PMR............	Pulsational Magnetic Radiation [*Astronomy*]
PMR............	Purchased Material Return (TIMI)
PMRA	Percent of Males Reproductively Active [*Ecology*]
PMRA	Projected Manpower Requirements Account [*Navy*]
PMRAFNS....	Princess Mary's Royal Air Force Nursing Service [*British*]
PMRB	Preliminary Materials Review Board
PMRC	Pakistan Medical Research Council
PMRC	Parents' Music Resource Center (EA)
PMRC	Prepositioned Material Receipt Card [*DoD*]
PMRC	Proctor Maple Research Center [*University of Vermont*] [*Research center*] (RCD)
PMR Cp	PMR Corp. [*Associated Press*] (SAG)
PMRD	Prepositioned Material Receipt Documents (MCD)
PMRDET	Pacific Missile Range Detachment [*Obsolete*] (MUGU)
PM Reactor...	Portable Medium-power Reactor (SAUS)
PMRF	Pacific Missile Range Facility [*Military*] (MUSM)
PMRFAC	Pacific Missile Range Facility [*Obsolete*] (MUGU)
PMRG	Preliminary Materials Review Group [*NASA*] (KSC)
PMRH	Panda Marine River Horizontal (SAUS)
PMRI	Porous Media Research Institute [*University of Waterloo*] [*Research center*] (RCD)
PMRI	Posteromedial Rotation Instability [*Sports medicine*]
PMRI	Prairie Masonry Research Institute (SAUS)
Pmr in C	Paymaster-in-Chief (SAUS)
PMRL	Physical Metallurgy Research Laboratories (SAUS)
PMRL	Pulp Manufacturers' Research League
PMRM	Periodic Maintenance Requirements Manual [*Navy*]
PMRMO	Protectable Mobilization Reserve Materiel Objective [*Army*] (AABC)
PMRMR	Protectable Mobilization Reserve Materiel Requirements [*Army*]
PMRN	Parents' Music Resource Network (EA)
PMR/NMC....	Pacific Missile Range / Naval Missile Center (SAA)
PMRO	Popular Magazine Review Online [*EBSCO Subscription Services*] [*Information service or system*]
PMRP	Petroleum Material Requirements Plan (MCD)
PMRP	PMR Corp. [*NASDAQ symbol*] (SAG)
PMRP	Precious Metals Recovery Program [*DoD*] (AFIT)
PMRP	Program Manager's Recommended Program
PM-RPV	Project Manager, Remotely Piloted Vehicle [*Military*]
PMRPV	Project Manager, Remotely Piloted Vehicles [*Department of Defense*]
PMRR	Pacific Missile Range Representative [*Obsolete*] (MUGU)
PMRR	Pre-Mate Readiness Review [*NASA*] (KSC)
PMRR	Prepositioned Materiel Receipt Record (ACAE)
PMRS	Parachute Medical Rescue Service (EA)
PMRS	Performance Management and Recognition System
PMRS	Performance Management Reporting System (SAUS)
PMRS	Performance Monitoring and Reporting System (SAUS)
PMRS	Physical Medicine and Rehabilitation Service
PMRS	Plasma-Melted Rapidly Solidified (SAUS)
PMRS	Private Mobile Radio Service (CGWS)
PMRS	Production Management and Reporting System
PMRS	Project Management Reporting System (SAUS)
PMRSG	Pacific Missile Range Study Group [*Obsolete*]
PMRT..........	Peabody Mathematics Readiness Test [*Educational test*]
PMRT..........	Program Management Responsibility Transfer (MCD)
PMRT..........	Progressive Muscle Relaxation Training [*Psychology*]
PMRTD	Program Management Responsibility Date (SAUS)
PMRTD	Program Management Responsibility Transfer Date (AFIT)
PMRTD	Project Management Responsibility Date (SAUS)
PMRTF.........	Pacific Missile Range Tracking Facility [*Obsolete*] (MUGU)

PMRTP	Program Management Responsibility Transfer Plan (AFIT)
PMRV-N......	Panda Marine River Vertical (SAUS)
PMRX	Pharmaceutical Marketing Services [*NASDAQ symbol*] (SPSG)
PMRX	Pharmaceutical Mktg Svcs [*NASDAQ symbol*] (TTSB)
PMRY	Pomeroy Computer Resources [*NASDAQ symbol*] (TTSB)
PMRY	Pomeroy Computer Resources, Inc. [*NASDAQ symbol*] (SAG)
PMRY	Presidio of Monterey [*Military*] (AABC)
PMS............	Chorionic Gonadotropin in Pregnant Mare's Serum [*Veterinary medicine*] (DAVI)
PMS............	Packet Memory System (SAUS)
PMS............	Palmer - Arctic Valley [*Alaska*] [*Seismograph station code, US Geological Survey*] (SEIS)
PMS............	Panda Marine Standard (SAUS)
PMS............	Pantone Matching System [*Printing*]
PMS............	Paper Manifesting System
PMS............	Parallel Mass Spectrometer
PMS............	Para-Methylstyrene [*Organic chemistry*]
PMS............	Partial Metric System (MCD)
PMS............	Particle Measurement System
PMS............	Particle Measuring Systems [*Aerosol measurement device*]
PMS............	Partido Mexicano Socialista [*Political party*] (EY)
PMS............	Passive Maternal Smoking (MELL)
PMS............	Pavement Management System [*Australia*]
PMS............	Peabody Museum of Salem (AD)
PMS............	Pedestal Mounted Stinger (SAUS)
PMS............	Pedestal-Mounted Stinger [*Army*]
PMS............	People's Medical Society (EA)
PMS............	People's Message System [*For Apple II computers*] [*Electronic bulletin board*]
PMS............	Performance Management Software (IAA)
PMS............	Performance Management System (HLLA)
PMS............	Performance Measurement System [*Nuclear Regulatory Commission*] (MCD)
PMS............	Performance Monitoring System [*Fort Belvoir, VA*] [*Army*] (NASA)
PMS............	Periodical Management System [*Library science*] (TELE)
PMS............	Peripheral Monitor System (SAUS)
PMS............	Permanent Magnet Speaker
PMS............	Permanent Manual System (AD)
PMS............	Permitted Maximum Signal (SAUS)
PMS............	Personal Mailing System (HGAA)
PMS............	Personnel Management Series [*Civil Service Commission*]
PMS............	Personnel Management Services
PMS............	Personnel Management Specialist (GFGA)
PMS............	Personnel Management Squadron (SAUS)
PMS............	Personnel Management System [*Air Force*] (AFM)
PMS............	Phenazine Methosulfate [*Biochemistry*]
pms............	Phenazine Methosulphate (AD)
PMS............	Phoenix Missile System
PMS............	Physical and Mathematical Sciences (SAUS)
PMS............	Physiological Monitoring System (SAA)
PMS............	Phytophthora Megasperma Var. Sojae [*A fungus*]
PMS............	Piccola Missione per il Sordomuti [*Little Mission for the Deaf-Mute - LMDM*] [*Rome, Italy*] (EAIO)
PMS............	Picturephone Meeting Service [*AT & T*]
PMS............	Pipeline Management System (SAUS)
PMS............	Pitch Microwave System
PMS............	Planemasters Services, Inc. [*ICAO designator*] (FAAC)
PMS............	Planned Maintenance Subsystem
PMS............	Planned Maintenance Support (SAUS)
PMS............	Planned Maintenance System [*SNMMS*]
PMS............	Planned Missile System
PMS............	Planning and Management Staff (SAUS)
PMS............	Plant Monitoring System [*Nuclear energy*] (NRCH)
PMS............	Plasmid Maintenance Sequence [*Genetics*]
PMS............	Plastic Media Stripping (SAUS)
PMS............	Plastic to Metal Seal
PMS............	Platform Management System (SAUS)
PMS............	P-Methylstyrene [*Plastics*]
PMS............	PM Industries, Inc. [*Vancouver Stock Exchange symbol*]
PMS............	Polaris Missile System
PMS............	Polar Meteorological Satellite (SSD)
PMS............	Policy Management System (SAUS)
PMS............	Policy Management Systems [*NYSE symbol*] (SPSG)
PMS............	Policy Mgmt Systems [*NYSE symbol*] (TTSB)
PMS............	Pollution Monitoring Satellite
pms............	Pollution-Monitoring Satellite (AD)
PMS............	Polymethylsorbate (SAUS)
PMS............	Polymethylstyrene [*Organic chemistry*]
PMS............	Poor Miserable Soul (AD)
PMS............	Poor Miserable Soul [*Medical slang*]
PMS............	Popular Music and Society [*A publication*] (BRI)
PMS............	Portable Monitoring Set (MCD)
PMS............	Post-Marketing Surveillance
PMS............	Postmeiotic Segregation [*Genetics*]
pms............	Post-Menopausal Syndrome [*Medicine*] (AD)
PMS............	Postmenopausal Syndrome [*Medicine*]
PMS............	Post-Menstrual Syndrome (SAUS)
PMS............	Post-Merger Syndrome [*Business term*]
PMS............	Postmitochondrial Supernatant [*Medicine*] (MAE)
PMS............	Post-Modern Slut (SAUS)
PMS............	Post-Mortem Survival [*Parapsychology*]
PMS............	Power Management System
PMS............	Power-Management System (SAUS)
PMS............	Prang-Mark Society (EA)
PMS............	Predicted Manning System [*Military*]

pms	Pregnant Mare's Serum (AD)
PMS	Pregnant Mare's Serum [*Endocrinology*]
PMS	Pre-Main-Sequence (SAUS)
PMS	Premature Start [*Yacht racing*] (IYR)
pms	Pre-Menstrual Syndrome [*Medicine*] (AD)
PMS	Premenstrual [*Stress*] Syndrome [*Medicine*]
PMS	Premenstrual Syndrome (SAUS)
PMS	Pre-Midshipmen School
PMS	Pre-Millennial Syndrome (SAUS)
PMS	President of the Meteorological Society [*British*]
PMS	President of the Miniature Society [*British*] (DI)
PmS	Preston Microfilming Services Ltd., Toronto, ON, Canada [*Library symbol*] [*Library of Congress*] (LCLS)
PMS	Preventive Maintenance Services
PMS	Preventive Maintenance System
PMS	Printer Management Software (SAUS)
PMS	Probability of Mission Success [*Aerospace*] (AAG)
PMS	Probable Maximum Surge [*Nuclear energy*] (NRCH)
PMS	Process Measurement Systems Ltd. (NITA)
PMS	Processor, Memories and Switches
PMS	Processor Memory Switch [*Computer science*] (ECII)
PMS	Processors, Memories, and Switches [*Programming language*] (CSR)
p-m-s	Processors-Memories-Switches (AD)
PMS	Production Management Support (SAUS)
PMS	Production Management System [*Safe Computing Ltd.*] [*Software package*] (NCC)
PMS	Product Management System
PMS	Product Monitoring System (SAUS)
PMS	Professor of Military Science
PMS	Program Management Staff (COE)
PMS	Program Management Support [*Army*]
PMS	Program Management System [*Computer science*]
PMS	Program Master Schedule (MCD)
PMS	Programmed Mode Switch (IAA)
PMS	Projected Map System (OA)
PMS	Project Management System [*IBM Corp.*] [*Computer science*]
PMS	Project Manager, Ships
PMS	Project Manager System
PMS	Project Map System (SAUS)
PMS	Project Master Schedule
PMS	Property Management System (TRID)
PMS	Proposal Management System
PMS	Propulsion Module Subsystem (ACAE)
PMS	Prothazin Methosulfate
PMS	Public Management Sources [*A publication*]
PMS	Public Message Service [*Western Union Corp.*]
PMS	Public Message System (SAUS)
PMS	Publisher Management System (NITA)
PMS	Pureed, Mechanical, Soft [*Diet*] (DAVI)
PMS	Region 4 Position Management System (SAUS)
PMSA	Office of the Project Manager Selected Ammunition [*DoD*]
PMSA	Pacific Merchant Shipping Association (AD)
PMSA	Paddy's Market Stallholders' Association [*Australia*]
PMSA	PM [*Product Management*] Materiel Systems Assessment (RDA)
PMSA	Posterior Middle Suprasylvian Area [*Anatomy*]
PMSA	Primary Metropolitan Statistical Area [*Census Bureau*]
PMSA	Professional Master of Science in Accounting (PGP)
P/MSA	Project/Major Subcontractor Affected (MCD)
PMSA	Project Management System Assessment
PMSA	Project Manager for Selected Ammunition
PMSA	Project Manager's System Assessment
PMS & T	Professor of Military Science and Tactics
PMSAT	Pre-Medical Student Assessment Test (EDAC)
PMSC	Pediatric Medical Special Care (DMAA)
PMSC	Pluripotent Myeloid Stem Cell [*Cytology*] (MAE)
PMSC	Prime Minister's Science Council [*Australia*]
PMSD	Parti Mauricien Social-Democrate [*Mauritian Social Democratic Party*] [*Political party*] (PPW)
PMSD	Program Management and Support Division [*Environmental Protection Agency*] (GFGA)
PMS/DOD	Performance Measurement System/Department of Defense
PM-SDR	Project Manager-Soldier (SAUS)
PMSE	Percentage Mean Squared Error [*Statistics*]
PMSE	Permanent Memory with Semi-Elastic Range (MCD)
PMSE	Polar Mesopause Summer Echo (SAUS)
PMSE	Polar Mesosphere Summer Echo (SAUS)
PMSE	Program Management Simulation Exercise [*Aerospace*]
PMSEIC	Prime Minister's Science, Engineering and Innovation Council [*Australia*]
PMSF	Phenylmethanesulfonyl Fluoride (SAUS)
PMSF	Phenylmethylsulfonyl Fluoride [*Analytical chemistry*]
PMSF	Phenylmethylsulfonylfluoride (SAUS)
PMSFN	Planetary Manned Space Flight Network [*Aerospace*] (MCD)
PMSG	Peace Movement Study Group [*Colgate University*] (EA)
pmsg	Pregnant Mare's Serum Gonadotrophin (AD)
PMSG	Pregnant Mare's Serum Gonadotrophin [*Endocrinology*]
PMSGT	Paymaster Sergeant [*Marine Corps*]
PM/SH	Preventive Maintenance and Self-Help [*Program*]
PMS-HD	Panda Marine Standard Heavy Duty (SAUS)
PMSI	Prime Medical Services [*NASDAQ symbol*] (TTSB)
PMSI	Prime Medical Services, Inc. [*NASDAQ symbol*] (NQ)
PMSI	Prime Medics [*NASDAQ symbol*] (SAG)
PMSM	Product Marketing Strategy Model (SAUS)
PMSN	Permission (FAAC)
PMSO	Port Mine Sweeping Officer (SAUS)

PMSO	Program Management and Support Office (SAUS)
PMSO	Project Management Staff Officer [*Military*] (AFIT)
PMSO	Project Management Support Office [*Army*] (RDA)
PMSP	Parallel Modular Signal Processor
PMSP	Photon-Counting Microspectrophotometer
PMSP	Plant Modelling System Program (PDAA)
PMSP	Preliminary Maintainability and Spare Parts
PMSP	Preliminary Message Security Protocol (SAUS)
pm specialists	Paramilitary Specialists (AD)
PMSPS	Project Management Staffing Practices Study [*Navy*] (NG)
PMSR	Patternmaker, Ship Repair [*Navy rating*]
PMSR	Physical, Mental, Social, Religious [*"Fourfold Life" symbol of American Youth Foundation*]
PMSRC	Pittsburgh Mining and Safety Research Center [*Bureau of Mines*]
PMSRP	Physical and Mathematical Sciences Research Paper (IEEE)
PMSS	Personnel Mobility Support System [*Military*]
PMSS	Policy and Management Support Staff (COE)
PMSS	Precision Measuring Subsystem (KSC)
PMSS	Preventive Maintenance Scheduling System (CIST)
PMSS	Program Management Support Staff [*Environmental Protection Agency*] (GFGA)
PMSS	Program Management Support System (SAUS)
PMSS	Program Manager's Support System [*Defense Systems Management College*] [*Fort Belvoir, VA*] (RDA)
PMSSMS	Planned Maintenance System for Surface Missile Ships (AD)
PMST	Professor of Military Science and Tactics (MUGU)
PMSU	Peripheral Motor-Sensory Unit (MELL)
PMSV	Pilot-to-Metro Service
PMSV	Pilot to Metro Services (SAUS)
PMSW	Polymer Microstructure Waveguide (SAUS)
PMSX	Processor Memory Switch Matrix
PMT	Medical Photography Technician [*Navy*]
PMT	Page Map Table [*NASA*] (HGAA)
PMT	Para-Methoxytoluene [*Organic chemistry*]
PMT	Partido Mexicano de los Trabajadores [*Mexican Workers' Party*] [*Political party*] (PPW)
PMT	Passenger-Miles Traveled [*DOE*] (TAG)
pmt	Payment (AD)
PMT	Payment (AFM)
PMT	Pennsylvania Motor Truck Association, Inc., Harrisburg PA [*STAC*]
PMT	Perceptual Maze Test [*Psychology*]
PMT	Perceptual Memory Task (TES)
PMT	Performance Measuring Tool (MCD)
PMT	Periodic Maintenance Team
PMT	Permanent Magnet Tester [*Memory*] [*Bell Laboratories*] (IAA)
PMT	Permanent Magnet Twistor [*Memory*] [*Bell Laboratories*]
PMT	Per Metric Ton (SAUS)
PMT	Permit (FAAC)
PMT	Person-Miles of Travel [*FHWA*] (TAG)
PMT	Personnel Management Team
PMT	Phase Modulated Transmission (SAUS)
PMT	Phase-Modulated Transmission
PMT	Philip Michael Thomas [*Co-star in TV series "Miami Vice"*]
PMT	Photomechanical Transfer [*Negative paper*] [*Eastman Kodak*]
PMT	Photomultiplier Transit (SAUS)
PMT	Photomultiplier Tube [*Electronics*]
pmt	Photomultiplier Tubes (AD)
PMT	Physical Master Tape (IAA)
PMT	Physical Message Type [*Communications*]
PMT	Pine Mountain [*Oregon*] [*Seismograph station code, US Geological Survey*] (SEIS)
PMT	Planning/Management Team [*NASA*] (MCD)
PMT	PMC Technologies Ltd. [*Vancouver Stock Exchange symbol*]
PMT	P-Methoxytoluene (SAUS)
PMT	Polaromicrotribrometry [*Analytical chemistry*]
PMT	Pore Microtubule (SAUS)
PMT	Portable Magnetic Tape
PMT	Porteus Maze Test [*Medicine*] (MAE)
PMT	Portsmouth Marine Terminal
pmt	Positive Matte Technique (AD)
PMT	Post-Maastricht Tension [*European community*] (ECON)
PMT	Post-Market Trading
PMT	Potteries Motor Traction Co. [*British*]
PMT	Power Microwave Tube
PMT	Precious Metal Tip (IAA)
PMT	Pre-Determined Motion-Time [*Management*] (PDAA)
PMT	Predetermined Motion Time (SAUS)
pmt	Premenstrual Tension [*Medicine*] (AD)
PMT	Premenstrual Tension [*Medicine*]
PMT	Premilleniial Tension
PMT	Preparatory Marksmanship Training [*Military*] (INF)
PMT	Prepare Master Tape
PMT	Preventive Maintenance Time (MCD)
PMT	Printed Mechanical Transfer (VLIE)
PMT	Production Monitoring Test (NG)
PMT	Products, Marketing, and Technology [*Bank Administration Institute*] [*A publication*]
PMT	Program Management Team (SAUS)
PMT	Program Master Tape
PMT	Programmed Math Tutorial [*National Science Foundation*]
pmt	Programs, Materials, Techniques (AD)
PMT	Project Management Team (ODBW)
PMT	Pulse Modulator Tube (SAUS)
PMT	Pulse-Modulator Tube
PMT	Pure Milk Tablet (IIA)

PMT	Putnam Master Income Tr [*NYSE symbol*] (TTSB)
PMT	Putnam Master Income Trust [*NYSE symbol*] (SPSG)
PMTA	Page Map Table Address Register [*NASA*] (HGAA)
PMTA	Phosphomolybdic and Phosphotungstic Acid Mixture (SAUS)
PMTA	Phosphomolybdic-Phosphotungstic Acid Mixture (EDCT)
PMTB	Pacific Motor Tariff Bureau (AD)
PMTC	Pacific Missile Test Center [*Point Mugu, CA*] [*Navy*]
PMTC	Parametric Technical [*NASDAQ symbol*] (TTSB)
PMTC	Parametric Technology Corp. [*NASDAQ symbol*] (NQ)
PMTC	Pittsburgh Mining Technology Center [*Department of Energy*] (GRD)
PMTC	Point Mugu Test Center (SAUS)
PMTC	Private Motor Truck Council (SAUS)
PMTCC	Private Motor Truck Council of Canada (SAUS)
PMT Contact	Precious Metal Tip Contact (SAUS)
PMTD	Post Mortem Tape Dump [*Computer science*]
PMTD	Promoted (SAUS)
PMTE	Page Map Table Entry [*NASA*] (IAA)
P/M Technol Newsl	P/M Technology Newsletter (SAUS)
PMT-EM	Project Manager, Training Devices Engineering Management [*Orlando, FL*] [*Army*]
PMTF	Product Management Task Force (AAEL)
PMTHP	Project Mercury Technical History Program [*NASA*]
PMTI	Palomar Medical Technologies [*NASDAQ symbol*] (SAG)
PMTI	Palomar Med Tech [*NASDAQ symbol*] (TTSB)
PM/TMDE	Project Manager for Test, Measurement and Diagnostic Equipment (SAUS)
PM TMDS	Program Manager - Test, Measurement, and Diagnostic Systems [*Army*]
PMTO	Post Mortem Test Object
PMTO	Project Manager Test Offices [*Military*]
PMTP	Production Missile Test Program
PMTP	Program Management Transfer Point (SAUS)
PMTPD	Program Management Transfer Point Date (SAUS)
PMTPM	Program Management Transfer Point Milestone (SAUS)
PMTPP	Program Management Transfer Point Plan (SAUS)
P/MTR	Potentiometer [*Automotive engineering*]
PM TRADE	Office of the Project Manager for Training Devices [*Military*] (RDA)
PM-TRADE	Program Manager for Training Devices (SAUS)
PM-TRADE	Project Manager, Training Devices
PMTR System	Partially Mechanized Traffic Recording System (SAUS)
PMTS	Passive Multi-Target Tracking System (SEWL)
PMTS	PMT Services [*NASDAQ symbol*] (SAG)
PMTS	Precision Missile Tracking System [*Military*] (IAA)
PMTS	Predetermined Motion Time Standards [*Management*] (IAA)
PMTS	Predetermined Motion Time System (SAUS)
PMTS	Predetermined Motion Time Systems [*Management*]
PMTS	Premenstrual Tension Syndrome [*Medicine*]
PMTS Chart	Predetermined Motion Time System Chart (SAUS)
PMTS Codes	Predetermined Motion Time System Codes (SAUS)
PMT Svc	PMT Services [*Associated Press*] (SAG)
PMTT	Phase-Modulated Telemetry Transmission
PMTT	Pulmonary Mean Transit Time [*Medicine*] (MAE)
PMTV	Potato Mop-Top Virus [*Plant pathology*]
PMU	Paimiut, AK [*Location identifier*] [*FAA*] (FAAL)
PMU	Parametric Measurement Unit (VLIE)
PMU	Pattern Makers Union (AD)
PMU	PCM Master Unit (SAUS)
pmu	Performance Monitor Unit (AD)
PMU	Performance Monitor Unit [*Communications*]
PMU	Permanently Medically Unfit
PMU	Personal Messaging Unit (CGWS)
PMU	Physical Mock-Up
pmu	Physical Mockup (AD)
PMU	Pierce Mountain [*Vancouver Stock Exchange symbol*]
PMU	Plant Makeup [*Nuclear energy*] (NRCH)
PMU	Pontifical Missionary Union [*Later, PMUPR*] [*See also OPM*] (EA)
PMU	Population Management Unit (WDAA)
PMU	Portable Memory Unit [*Computer science*]
PMU	Power Management Unit [*Computer science*] (CIST)
PMU	Power Meter Unit (SAUS)
PMU	Precision Measurement Unit (SAUS)
PMU	Precision Mockup (ACAE)
PMU	Pregnant Mare's Urine [*Veterinary medicine*] (BARN)
PMU	Pressure Measuring Unit (KSC)
PMU	Preventive Medicine Unit [*Navy*] (NVT)
pmu	Productive Man Work Unit (AD)
PMU	Program Management Unit [*Computer science*] (IAA)
PMUB	Pulse Modulation Unit (NASA)
PMUB	Presbyterian, Methodist, and United Board [*British military*] (DMA)
PMUPR	Pontifical Missionary Union of Priests and Religious (EA)
PMUS	Permanently Mounted User Set [*Computer science*] (ADA)
PMUSAOAS	Permanent Mission of the United States of America to the Organization of American States (AD)
PM-UTTAS	Project Manager, Utility Tactical Transport Aircraft System [*Military*]
PMUTTAS	Project Manager, Utility Tactical Transport Aircraft System
PMUX	Programmable Multiplex [*Computer science*] (TEL)
PMUX	Propulsion Multiplexer
PMv	Monroeville Public Library, Monroeville, PA [*Library symbol*] [*Library of Congress*] (LCLS)
PMV	Panicum Mosaic Virus
PMV	Papaya Mosaic Virus
PMV	Paramyxovirus
PMV	Parcel Mail Vans [*British railroad term*]
PMV	Passenger Motor Vehicle
PMV	Peach Mosaic Virus (SAUS)
PMV	Peanut Mottle Virus
PMV	Pedal Modulating Valve [*Hydraulics*]
PMV	Plasma Membrane Vesicle [*Cytology*]
PMV	Plate-Motion Vector [*Geology*]
PMV	Plattsmouth, NE [*Location identifier*] [*FAA*] (FAAL)
PMV	Politically Motivated Violence (ADA)
PMV	Porlamar [*Venezuela*] [*Airport symbol*] (OAG)
PMV	Prime Mission Vehicle (MCD)
PMV	Private Market Value [*Investment term*] (DFIT)
PMV	Private Motor Vehicle (DNAB)
PMV	Prolapsing Mitral Valve [*Cardiology*]
PMV	Pro Mundi Vita [*Brussels, Belgium*] [*Defunct*] (EAIO)
PMvAC	Community College of Allegheny County, Boyce Campus, Monroeville, PA [*Library symbol*] [*Library of Congress*] (LCLS)
PMVB	Pocono Mountain Vacation Bureau (AD)
PMVE	Primary Mirror Vortex Fixture (SAUS)
pmvi	Periodic Motor Vehicle Inspection (AD)
PMVI	Periodic Motor Vehicle Inspection (PDAA)
PMvK	Koppers Co., Inc., Research Department, Monroeville, PA [*Library symbol*] [*Library of Congress*] (LCLS)
PMVL	Posterior Mitral Valve Leaflet [*Anatomy*] (AAMN)
PMV-LATA	Passenger Motor Vehicle Labour Adjustment Training Arrangements [*Australia*]
PMVMP	Passenger Motor Vehicle Manufacturing Plan [*Australia*]
pmvp	Precio Maximo de Venta al Publico [*Maximum Price Charged the Public*] [*Spanish*] (AD)
p mvr	Prime Mover (AD)
PMVR	Prime Mover [*Technical drawings*]
PMvS	United States Steel Corp., Research Center Library, Monroeville, PA [*Library symbol*] [*Library of Congress*] (LCLS)
PMW	Pacemaker Wire [*Cardiology*] (DAVI)
PMW	Parts Manufacturing Workmanship
PMW	Passive Microwave (SAUS)
PMW	Pole Mountain [*Wyoming*] [*Seismograph station code, US Geological Survey*] [*Closed*] (SEIS)
PMW	Position Mode Wavelength (ADWA)
PMW	Post-Menopausal Women (MELL)
PMW	Premenopausal Women (MELL)
PMW	Preventive Maintenance Welding (PDAA)
PMW	Private Microwave [*System*]
PMW	Probable Maximum Wind (GOBB)
PMW	Progressive Mine Workers of America
PMW	Project Magic Wand [*Military*] (MCD)
PMW	Project Management Work-Bench (NITA)
PMW	Project Manager Workbench (SAUS)
PMW	Prompt Mobilization Designation Withdrawn
PMW	Pulse-Modulated Wave [*Telecommunications*] (IAA)
PMWCMA	Paper Mill Wire Cloth Manufacturers' Association (DGA)
PMWG	Program Management Working Group (SAUS)
PMWI	PageMart Wireless 'A' [*NASDAQ symbol*] (SG)
PMWIN	Processing MODFLOW for Windows
PMWP	Probable Maximum Winter Precipitation [*Nuclear energy*] (NRCH)
PMWS	Pedestal-Mounted Weapons System (SAUS)
PMWS	Program Management Work Station (TIMI)
PMW System	Private Microwave System (SAUS)
PMX	Packet Multiplexer
PMX	Palmer, MA [*Location identifier*] [*FAA*] (FAAL)
PMX	Pamorex Minerals, Inc. [*Toronto Stock Exchange symbol*]
PMX	Partially Matched Crossover (VLIE)
PMX	Petroleos Mexicanos [*Mexico*] [*ICAO designator*] (FAAC)
PMX	Physical Modeling Extension (SAUS)
PMX	Physical Modelling Extension (NITA)
pmx	Private Manual Exchange (AD)
PMX	Private Manual Exchange
PMX	Protected Message Exchange
PMY	Productive Man Year (SAUS)
PMY	Professional Man-Year (GOBB)
PMyE	Evangelical Congregational School of Theology, Myerstown, PA [*Library symbol*] [*Library of Congress*] (LCLS)
pmyob	Please Mind Your Own Business (AD)
PMYOB	Please Mind Your Own Business
PMZ	Palmar [*Costa Rica*] [*Airport symbol*] (AD)
PMZ	Plymouth, NC [*Location identifier*] [*FAA*] (FAAL)
PMZF	Programmable Multi-Zone Furnace (SAUS)
PN	Coastal Airways [*ICAO designator*] (AD)
PN	Nacionalista [*Nationalist Party*] [*Spain*] [*Political party*] (AD)
Pn	North Celestial Pole (AD)
pn---	North Pacific [*MARC geographic area code*] [*Library of Congress*] (LCCP)
PN	North Pole [*Also, NP*]
PN	Pacific Communications Net [*Air Force*]
PN	Pacific Northern [*Airline*] (AD)
PN	Packet Network (SAUS)
PN	Packet Number (SAUS)
PN	Page Number (SAUS)
PN	Paging Network (SAUS)
PN	Pain (SAUS)
PN	Pakistan Navy
PN	Palus Nebularum [*Lunar area*]
pn	Panama [*MARC country of publication code*] [*Library of Congress*] (LCCP)
PN	Pan American World Airways (SAUS)
PN	Pan-American World Airways [*Stock exchange symbol*] (AD)
PN	Papillary or Nodular Hyperplasia [*Medicine*]

PN	Paranode (SAUS)
PN	Parenteral Nutrition [Medicine]
PN	Parish Nurse (NUJO)
PN	Partenavia Construzioni Aeronautiche SpA [Italy] [ICAO aircraft manufacturer identifier] (ICAO)
PN	Particulate Nitrogen [Chemistry]
PN	Partido Nacional [National Party] [Uruguay] [Political party] (PPW)
PN	Partido Nacional [National Party] [Honduras] [Political party] (PPW)
PN	Partido Nacional [National Party] [Spain] [Political party] (AD)
PN	Partido Nacional [National Party] [Dominican Republic] [Political party]
PN	Parti Nationaliste [Canada]
pn	Partition (AD)
Pn	Partition (WGA)
PN	Partition Number (SAUS)
PN	Partit Nazzjonalista [Nationalist Party] [Malta] [Political party] (EAIO)
pn	Part Number (AD)
P/N	Part Number
PN	Part Number
PN	Party Notified (IAA)
PN	Passive Network (SAUS)
PN	Past Number (SAUS)
PN	Patent Number (NITA)
PN	Path Number (SAUS)
PN	P-Doped N-Doped (SAUS)
PN	Pennaco Energy [AMEX symbol]
PN	Perceived Noise
pn	Percussion Note (AD)
PN	Percussion Note [Physiology]
PN	Percussive Note (SAUS)
PN	Perforation Number (SAUS)
PN	Performance Number
PN	Periarteritis [or Polyarteritis] Nodosa [Also, PAN] [Medicine]
Pn	Perigean Range (AD)
PN	Perigean Range
PN	Peripheral Nerve [Anatomy]
PN	Peripheral Neuropathy [Medicine]
PN	Peroxide Number [Hydrocarbon fuel specifications]
PN	Personal Name (NITA)
PN	Personal Names from Cuneiform Inscriptions of the Cassite Period [A publication] (BJA)
PN	Personnelman [Navy rating]
PN	Personnel Navigant
PN	Petri Net (VLIE)
PN	Phase Name (NITA)
PN	Phenolic Nylon
PN	Philippine Navy
PN	Phon [Unit of loudness level] (IAA)
P/N	Phonogram [British military] (DMA)
PN	Photonegative (SAUS)
PN	Photonic Network (SAUS)
PN	Photonuclear (SAUS)
Pn	Photosynthesis (SAUS)
pN	Piconewton [Unit of force]
PN	Piedmont & Northern Railway Co. [AAR code]
PN	Pilot Navigator (IAA)
P/N	Pilots Name (SAUS)
pn	Pine (VRA)
P/N	Pin Number (AAG)
PN	Pitcairn Islands [ANSI two-letter standard code] (CNC)
PN	Place-Name
PN	Place of Publication Class Number (NITA)
PN	Plain
PN	Planetary Nebula (SAUS)
PN	Planetary Nebulae [Astrophysics]
PN	Planners Network (EA)
PN	Plant Normal [Nuclear energy] (NRCH)
PN	Plaque Neutralization [Dentistry] (DMAA)
PN	Plasticity Number (AAG)
pn	Please Note (AD)
P/N	Please Note [Copyediting] (WDMC)
PN	Please Note
PN	Pneumatic
PN	Pneumonia [Medicine]
PN	Point of No Return (AD)
PN	Pole, North (SAUS)
PN	Polish Notation [Mathematics]
PN	Polnische Notation (SAUS)
PN	Polyarteritis Nodosa [Rheumatology] (DAVI)
PN	Polyneuritis (DB)
PN	Pontine Nuclei [Neuroanatomy]
P/N	Porter/Novelli [A public relations firm] [New York, NY] (WDMC)
pn	Position (AD)
Pn	Position (WGA)
PN	Positional Nystagmus [Physiology] (MAE)
PN	Position Number (ADA)
PN	Position Pennant [Navy] [British]
PN	Positive Negative
P/N	Positive/Negative
PN	Positive Notification (VLIE)
PN	Postal Note (ADA)
PN	Postnasal [Otorhinolaryngology] (DAVI)
PN	Postnatal [Medicine]
PN	Practical Nurse
PN	Preliminary Notification (NRCH)
PN	Press Night
PN	Pressure, Nominal (SAUS)
PN	Pressure, Normal (SAUS)
PN	Primary Node (SAUS)
PN	Princeton Aviation [ICAO designator] (AD)
PN	Printing News (SAUS)
P/N	Print plus Negative (SAUS)
PN	Prior Notice (SAUS)
PN	Procedure Name (SAUS)
PN	Processing Negativity [Computer science]
PN	Processing Node (VLIE)
PN	Processor Number (VLIE)
PN	Proctor Normal (SAUS)
PN	Procurement Notice [NASA] (AAGC)
Pn	Production [Economics]
PN	Production Notice (KSC)
PN	Product Name (NITA)
PN	Programmable Network
PN	Program Notice (KSC)
PN	Program Number [Horse racing]
PN	Progress note [Medical records] (DAVI)
PN	Project de Norme
PN	Projection Neurons [Neuroanatomy]
PN	Project Note
PN	Project Number [Online database field identifier] [Computer science]
pn	Promissory Note (AD)
p/n	Promissory Note (NTIO)
PN	Promissory Note [Business term]
PN	Prompt Neutron (SAUS)
PN	Pronuclei [Embryology]
PN	Proportional Navigation (IAA)
PN	Pseudo Noise (SAUS)
PN	Pseudonoise
PN	Pseudo-Random Noise (NAKS)
PN	Pseudorandom Number
PN	Psychiatric Nurse
pn	Psychiatry-Neurology (AD)
PN	Psychoneurologist
PN	Psychoneurotic [Cases, patients, etc.]
PN	Public Network [Telecommunications]
PN	Publisher's Name [Online database field identifier]
PN	Pulse Network (KSC)
PN	Punch On
pn	Punch-On [Computer science] (AD)
PN	Punch Only (SAUS)
PN	Pupil Nurse [British] (DI)
PN	Putative Neurotransmitter [Biochemistry]
PN	Pyelonephritis [Medicine] (MAE)
PN	Pyridine Nucleotide [Medicine] (DMAA)
PN	Pyridoxine [or Pyridoxol] [Also, Pxn] [Biochemistry]
PN	Pyrrolnitrin [Antifungal antibiotic]
PN	Regular Pending Transaction [IRS]
PN1	Personnelman, First Class [Navy rating]
P_{N2}	Partial Pressure of Nitrogen [Medicine] (DAVI)
PN2	Personnelman, Second Class [Navy rating]
PN20	Partial Pressure of Nitrous Oxide (SAUS)
PN3	Personnelman, Third Class [Navy rating]
Pn6	Partenavia [Airplane code]
PNA	Nomina Anatomica (Paris) [Anatomical Nomenclature] (DAVI)
PNA	Pacific North America (SAUS)
PNA	Pacific/North American [Sector] [Marine science] (OSRA)
PNA	Pacific North Atlantic [Marine science] (OSRA)
PNA	Pacific Northern Airlines (AD)
PNA	Packet Network Adapter (SAUS)
PNA	Packet Network Adaptor (NITA)
PNA	Pakistan National Alliance (PD)
PNA	Palestinian National Authority [Political party] (ECON)
PNA	Pamplona [Spain] [Airport symbol] (OAG)
Pna	Panama (SAUS)
PNA	Panna [India] [Airport symbol] (AD)
PNA	Pa-O National Army [Myanmar] [Political party] (EY)
PNA	Paper Napkin Association
PNA	Parallel and Novel Architectures [British]
PNA	Parallel Network Architecture (SAUS)
PNA	Para-Nitroaniline [Organic chemistry]
PNA	Parenting in a Nuclear Age (EA)
PNA	Parisiensis Nomina Anatomica [Paris Anatomical Nomenclature] [Medicine]
PNA	Partacoona [Australia] [Seismograph station code, US Geological Survey] (SEIS)
PNA	Parti Nationale Africain [African National Party] [Chad] [Political party]
PNA	Passed, but Not Advanced
PNA	Passive Network Array (SAUS)
PNA	Peanut Agglutinin [Immunology]
PNA	Pennsylvania Nurses Association (SAUS)
PNA	Pentose Nucleic Acid (SAUS)
PNA	Pentosenucleic Acid [Biochemistry]
PNA	People's News Agency [An association] (EA)
PNA	Peptide Nucleic Acid [Biochemistry]
PNA	Peripheral Node Adapter (TIMI)
PNA	Philippines News Agency (AD)
PNA	Pinedale, WY [Location identifier] [FAA] (FAAL)
PNa	Plasma Sodium [Organic chemistry] (DAVI)
PNA	Point of No Alternative (SAUS)

PNA .... Polish National Alliance of the United States of North America (EA)
PNA .... Polish Nobility Association (EA)
PNA .... Polyamide Nucleic Acid [*Biochemistry*]
PNA .... Polynuclear Aromatic [*Organic chemistry*]
PNA .... Polynuclear Aromatic Hydrocarbon (ABAC)
PNA .... Price Not Available (DNAB)
PNA .... Probablistic Noise Audibility (EEVL)
PNA .... Processing Terminal Network Architecture [*Computer science*] (BUR)
PNA .... Professional Numismatists' Association [*British*] (BI)
PNA .... Programmable Network Access (SAUS)
PNA .... Project Network Analysis
PNA .... Protein equivalent of Nitrogen Appearance (SAUS)
PNA .... Universal Airlines, Inc. [*ICAO designator*] (FAAC)
PNAB .... Percutaneous Needle Aspiration Biopsy [*Medicine*]
PNAC .... Pacific Northwest Athletic Conference (PSS)
PNAC .... President's National Advisory Committee (NADA)
PNAC .... Psychiatric Nurses' Association of Canada
PNACO .... Past National Commodore (SAUS)
PNA Compounds... Polynuclear Aromatic Compounds (SAUS)
PNAD .... Personnel Nuclear Accident Dosimeter (SAUS)
PNAF .... Plan Name and Address File [*IRS*]
PNAF .... Potential Network Access Facility
PNAF .... Primary Nuclear Airlift Force
PNAH .... Polynuclear Aromatic Hydrocarbon [*Environmental chemistry*]
PNAI .... Provincial Newspapers Association of Ireland (AD)
PNAMBIC.... Pay No Attention to the Man Behind the Curtain [*Computer hacker terminology*] (NHD)
PNAME .... Public Model Name [*Automotive emissions*]
PNAP .... Pro-Life Nonviolent Action Project (EA)
PNAP .... Protected Natural Area Programme (SAUS)
PNAS .... Palletized Night Attack System
PNAS .... Proceedings of the National Academy of Sciences [*A publication*]
PNAS .... Prudent No Added Salt [*Diet*] (DAVI)
PNASA .... Para-Nitroaniline-o-sulfonic Acid [*Organic chemistry*]
PnASat....... PanAmSat Corp. [*Associated Press*] (SAG)
P-NAV .... Personal Navigation
PNAV .... Precise Navigation
PNAV .... Precision Navigation Ambiguity Resolution
PNAV .... Proportional Navigation
pnavq......... Positive-Negative Ambivalent Quotient (AD)
PNAvQ .... Positive-Negative Ambivalent Quotient [*Psychology*]
PNazMHi...... Moravian Historical Society, Nazareth, PA [*Library symbol*] [*Library of Congress*] (LCLS)
PNB .... North Platte, NE [*Location identifier*] [*FAA*] (FAAL)
PNB .... Pacific Northwest Ballet
PNB .... Pacific Northwest Bell (SAUS)
PNB .... Particle/Neutral Beam (MCD)
PNB .... Partido ng Bayan [*Party of the Nation*] [*Philippines*] [*Political party*]
PNB .... Permodalan Nasional Bank [*Malaysia*]
PNB .... Personal Needs Break (WDAA)
PNB .... Philadelphia National Bank (SAUS)
PNB .... Philippine National Bank (AD)
PNB .... Pomio [*New Britain*] [*Seismograph station code, US Geological Survey*] [*Closed*] (SEIS)
PNB .... Porto Nacional [*Brazil*] [*Airport symbol*] (AD)
PNB .... Premature Nodal Beat [*Cardiology*] (DAVI)
PNB .... Premier National Bancorp [*AMEX symbol*] [*Formerly, Hudson Chartered Bancorp*]
pnb .... Producto Nacional Bruto [*Gross National Product*] [*Spanish*] (AD)
PNB .... Produto National Bruto [*Gross National Product*] [*Portugal*] (AD)
PNB .... Prostatic Needle Biopsy [*Oncology*] (DAVI)
PNB .... Punjab National Bank (SAUS)
PNBA.......... Pacific Northwest Booksellers Association (AD)
PNBAS........ ((Para-Nitrophenyl)azo)salicylic Acid [*A dye*] [*Organic chemistry*]
PNBB........ Parc National de la Boucle du Baoule [*Baoule River Bend National Park*] [*French*] [*Mali*]
PNBC .... Pacific Northwest Bibliographic Center [*Library network*]
PNBC .... Princeton National Bancorp [*NASDAQ symbol*] (SAG)
PNBC .... Princeton Natl Bancorp [*NASDAQ symbol*] (TTSB)
PNBF .... Peak Nucleate Boiling Flux
PNBH.......... Petri-Net-Based Hypertext (SAUS)
PNBH.......... P-Nitrobenzaldehyde Hydrazone (SAUS)
PNBK .... Patriot National Bank CT [*NASDAQ symbol*] (SAG)
PNBK .... Patriot Natl Bk [*NASDAQ symbol*] (TTSB)
PNBMS........ Pacific Northwest Bird and Mammal Society [*Later, SNUB*] (EA)
PNBOUNDARY... Positive Negative Boundary (SAUS)
PNBP .... Parc National de la Boucle de la Pendjari [*Penjari River Bend National Park*] [*French*] [*Dahamey*] (AD)
PNBS .... Pyridinium(nitro)benzenesulfonate [*Organic chemistry*]
PNBT .... Paranitroblue Tetrazoleum (SAUS)
PNBT .... Para-Nitroblue Tetrazolium
PNC .... Chief Personnelman [*Navy rating*]
PNc .... New Castle Free Public Library, New Castle, PA [*Library symbol*] [*Library of Congress*] (LCLS)
PNC .... Northampton County Area Community College, Bethlehem, PA [*OCLC symbol*] (OCLC)
PNC .... Paging Network Controller (SAUS)
PNC .... Pakistan National Congress [*Political party*]
PNC .... Palestine National Council (PD)
PNC .... Parity Nonconservation [*Physics*]
PNC .... Parque Nacional Canaima [*Canaima National Park*] [*Venezuela*] (AD)
PNC .... Particulate Nitrocellulose (SAUS)
PNC .... Partido Nacional Ceuti [*Ceuta National Party*] [*Political party*] (PPW)
PNC .... Partido Nacional Conservador [*Nicaragua*] [*Political party*] (EY)

PNC .... Partido Nacional Cristiano [*National Christian Party*] [*Colombia*] [*Political party*] (EY)
PNC .... Partido Nacionalista Ceuti [*Political party*] (EY)
PNC .... Partidual Nationale Crestine [*National Christian Party*] [*Romania*] [*Political party*] (PPE)
PNC .... Parti National Caledonien [*Caledonian National Party*] [*Political party*] (PPW)
PNC .... Passenger Name Check-In (MCD)
pnc............. Pencillin (AD)
PNC .... Pencrude Resources, Inc. [*Vancouver Stock Exchange symbol*]
PNC .... Penicillin
PNC .... People, Networks & Communication (SAUS)
PNC .... People's National Congress [*Guyana*] (PD)
PNC .... Peoples National Convention (SAUS)
PNC .... Peripheral Nerve Conduction [*Neurology*] (DAVI)
PNC .... Peripheral Nucleated Cell (AAMN)
PNC .... Personal Number Calling [*Telecommunications*]
PNACO .... Philatelic-Numismatic Combination [*or Commemorative*]
PNC .... Phosphonitrilic Chloride [*Inorganic chemistry*]
PNC .... Photo-Nitrosation of Cyclohexane (SAUS)
PNC .... Physitest Normalise Canadien [*Canadian Standardized Test of Fitness - CSTF*]
PNC .... Pine Canyon [*California*] [*Seismograph station code, US Geological Survey*] (SEIS)
PNC .... Place Names Committee [*Victoria, Australia*]
pnc............. Plate Number Coil (AD)
PNC .... Plate Number Coil [*Philately*]
PNC .... PNC Bank Corp. [*NYSE symbol*] (TTSB)
PNC .... Pneumotaxic Center [*Medicine*] (DAVI)
PNC .... Police National Computer [*British*]
PNC .... Ponca City [*Oklahoma*] [*Airport symbol*] (OAG)
PNC .... Ponca City, OK [*Location identifier*] [*FAA*] (FAAL)
PNC .... Postnatal Clinic
PNC .... Power Reactor and Nuclear Fuel Development Corp. [*Japan*] (PDAA)
PNC .... Preferred Noise Criteria (SAUS)
PNC .... Preferred Noise Criterion [*L. L. Beranek*] (DIPS)
pnc............. Premature Nodal Contraction (AD)
PNC .... Premature Nodal Contraction [*Cardiology*]
PNC .... Prenatal Care [*Obstetrics*] (DAVI)
PNC .... Prenatal Clinic [*Obstetrics*] (DAVI)
PNC .... Prenodal Contraction [*Cardiology*] (DAVI)
PNC .... Programmed Numerical Control
PNC .... Prohibition National Committee (EA)
PNC .... Provident National Financial Corp. (EFIS)
PNC .... Pseudonurse Cells [*Cytology*]
PN Case ...... Psychoneurotic Case (SAUS)
PNCB .... Pakistan Narcotics Control Board
PNCB .... Para-Nitrochlorobenzene [*Organic chemistry*]
PNCC .... Pacific Northwest College Conference (PSS)
PNCC .... Partial Network Control Center
PNCC .... President's National Crime Commission (AD)
PNCE .... Private New Capital Expenditure
PNCEA .... Paulist National Catholic Evangelization Association (EA)
PNCFN........ Permanent Nordic Committee on Food and Nutrition [*Copenhagen, Denmark*] (EAIO)
PNCH .... Partido Nacional Conservador de Honduras [*National Conservative Party of Honduras*] [*Political party*]
pnch........... Punch (AD)
PNCH.......... Punch
PNCIAWPRC... Philippine National Committee of the International Association on Water Pollution Research and Control (SAUS)
PNCK .... Pancake
PNCL .... Percent Non-Conforming Lots (SAUS)
PNCL .... Pinnacle Micro [*NASDAQ symbol*] (TTSB)
PNCL .... Pinnacle Micro, Inc. [*NASDAQ symbol*] (NQ)
Pncla .... Pensacola, Florida
PNCM .... Master Chief Personnelman [*Navy rating*]
PNC MLA..... Pacific Northwest Chapter of the Medical Library Association (SAUS)
PNCO .... Personnel Noncommissioned Officer
PNCOC........ Primary Noncommissioned Officer Course [*Army*] (INF)
PNCP .... Periphal Mode Control Point (SAUS)
PNCP .... Peripheral Network Control Point (SAUS)
PNCPrC...... PNC Bank Cp $1.60 Cv C Pfd [*NYSE symbol*] (TTSB)
PNCPrD....... PNC Bank Cp $1.80 Cv D Pfd [*NYSE symbol*] (TTSB)
PNC Project... Police National Computer Project (SAUS)
PNCS .... Pakistani National Conservation Strategy (SAUS)
PNCS .... Performance & Navigation Computer System (SAUS)
PNCS .... Private Network Communication Systems (MCD)
PNCS .... Senior Chief Personnelman [*Navy rating*]
PNCTR........ Passive Non-Cooperative Target Recognition (ACAE)
PNCU .... Police National Computer Unit [*British*]
Pnd .... Pandjang (AD)
pnd .... Paroxysmal Nocturnal Dyspnoea (AD)
PND .... Paroxysmal Nocturnal Dyspnea [*Medicine*]
PND .... Parti des Nationalistes du Dahomey [*Dahomean Nationalists Party*] [*Political party*]
PND .... Partido Nacional Democratico [*National Democratic Party*] [*Costa Rica*] [*Political party*] (PPW)
PND .... Partido Nacional Democratico [*National Democratic Party*] [*Dominican Republic*] [*Political party*]
PND .... Partidul National-Democratic [*National Democratic Party*] [*Romania*] [*Political party*] (PPE)
PND .... Parti National Democrate [*Morocco*] [*Political party*] (EY)
PND .... Passive Navigation Device
PND .... Pending

PND	Pictorial Navigation Display (OA)
PND	Position-Navigation Device (SAUS)
PND	Positive-Negative Diode (SAUS)
PND	Postnasal Drainage [or Drip] [Medicine]
pnd	Postnasal Drip [Medicine] (AD)
PND	Postnatal Days
PND	Postnatal Depression [Medicine] (ECON)
pnd	Pound (MAE)
PND	Preliminary Number Deflator [Empirical mathematics] (ECON)
PND	Premodulation Processor - Near Earth Data (KSC)
PND	Prenatal Diagnosis [Medicine]
PND	Present Next Digit
PND	Pressed Notch Depth (PDAA)
PND	Primary Navigation Display (GAVI)
PND	Principal Neutralizing Determinant [Immunology]
PND	Principal Neutralizing Domain [Medicine]
PND	Program Network Diagram [Telecommunications] (TEL)
PND	Pronatriodilatin (DB)
PND	Pseudonyms and Nicknames Dictionary [A publication]
PND	Punta Gorda [Belize] [Airport symbol] (OAG)
PNDA	Panda Project [NASDAQ symbol] (TTSB)
PNDA	[The] Panda Project, Inc. [NASDAQ symbol] (SAG)
PNDA	People for Nuclear Disarmament Australia [An association]
PNDB	Pelerinage a Notre Dame de Beauraing [An association] (EAIO)
pndb	Perceived Noise Decibels (AD)
PNDB	Perceived Noise Decibels
PNdB	Perceived Noise Decibels
PNDC	Parallel Network Digital Computer (IEEE)
PNDC	Partido Nacional de Democracia Centrista [Chile] [Political party] (EY)
PNDC	Progressive Neuronal Degeneration of Childhood [Medicine]
PNDC	Provisional National Defence Council [Ghana] (PD)
PNDC	Provisional National Defense Council (SAUS)
PNDD	Parti National pour la Democratie et le Developpement [Benin] [Political party] (EY)
PNDES	Pulse Doppler Non-Elevation Scan (SAUS)
pndg	Pending (AD)
PNDG	Pending (AFM)
PNDI	Pennsylvania Natural Diversity Inventory [Bureau of Forestry] [Harrisburg] [Information service or system] (IID)
PNDL	Pentland Group plc [LO Symbol] (TTSB)
PNDLR	Parking, Neutral, Driving, Lowgear, Reverse (SAUS)
P-N-D-L-R	Park-Neutral-Drive-Low-Reverse (AD)
PNDLR	Pendular
PNDM	Project Nondesign Memo
PNDMA	Paranitroso-Dimethylalanin (SAUS)
pndnt	Pendentive (VRA)
PNDO	Partial Neglect of Differential Overlap [Physics]
Pndo	Pinedo (AD)
PNDP	Para-Nitrophenyl Diphenyl Phosphate [Organic chemistry]
PNDR	Ponder Industries [NASDAQ symbol] (TTSB)
PNDR	Ponder Industries, Inc. [NASDAQ symbol] (SAG)
PNDT	Parti Nationale pour la Developpement du Tchad [National Party for the Development of Chad]
PNE	Copene-Petroquimica ADS [NYSE symbol] (SG)
PNE	Pacific National Exchange (SAUS)
PNE	Pacific National Exchange Vancouver [Vancouver] (AD)
PNE	Pacific National Exhibition [Vancouver] (AD)
PNE	Pacific National Exhibition Home Show [Southex Exhibitions] (TSPED)
PNE	Paine College, Warren A. Candler Library, Augusta, GA [OCLC symbol] (OCLC)
PNE	Panhandle Eastern Corp. [Toronto Stock Exchange symbol]
pne	Peaceful Nuclear Explosion (AD)
PNE	Peaceful Nuclear Explosion
PNE	Peaceful Nuclear Explosive
PNE	Peaceful Nuclear Explosives (SAUS)
PNE	Philadelphia [Pennsylvania] North Philadelphia [Airport symbol] (OAG)
PNE	Philadelphia, PA [Location identifier] [FAA] (FAAL)
PNE	PINE [Postal Service standard] (OPSA)
PNE	Plasma Norepinephrine [Medicine] (DMAA)
PNE	Pneumoencephalography [Medicine] (CPH)
PNe	Pointe Noire (AD)
pne	Practical Nurse's Education (AD)
PNE	Practical Nurse's Education
PNEA	Parque Nacional El Avila [El Avila National Park] [Spanish] (AD)
PNEAC	Printer's National Environment Assistance Center (AGLO)
PNEC	Part Number Engineering Change
PNEC	Predicted No Effect Concentration [Environmental technology]
PNEC	Primary Navy Enlisted Classification [Code]
PNEC	Proceedings of the National Electronics Conference [A publication]
PNED	Peaceful Nuclear Explosive Device
PNed	Pharmacopeia Nederlandsche [Netherlands Pharmacopoeia]
PNEDC	Programme National D'etude de la Dynamique du Climat [France] [Marine science] (OSRA)
PNEDC	Programme National d'Etudes de la Dynamique du Climat (USDC)
PNEM	Paraneoplastic Encephalomyelitis [Medicine] (DMAA)
PNEM-APROME	Partido Nacionalista Espanol de Melilla - Asociacion pro Melilla [Spanish North Africa] [Political party] (MENA)
PNERL	Pacific Northwest Environmental Research Laboratory [Environmental Protection Agency] (MSC)
Pnes	Pines (AD)
PNES	Pines
PNET	Peaceful Nuclear Explosions Treaty [Officially, Treaty on Underground Nuclear Explosions for Peaceful Purposes]
PNET	Peaceful Nuclear Explosion Treaty (SAUS)
PNET	Peripheral Neuroepithelioma [Medicine] (DMAA)
PNET	Primitive Neuroectodermal Tumor [Oncology]
PNET	ProNet, Inc. [NASDAQ symbol] (NQ)
PNEU	Parents' National Educational Union [British]
PNEU	Parents National Education Union (SAUS)
PNEU	Pneumatic (AAG)
pneu	Pneumatic (AD)
pneu	Pneumonia [Medicine] (MAE)
PNEUC	Physical Non-Elementary Unit Control (SAUS)
PNEUC	Physical Non-Eliminated Unit Check (SAUS)
PNEUD	Pneudraulic
PNEUG	Pneumatic Pressure Generator (MCD)
PNEUM	Pneumatic
PNEUM	Pneumonia (WDAA)
PNEUMO	Pneumothorax [Medicine]
pneumoccon	Pneumocconiosis [Medicine] (AD)
pneumog	Pneumograph (AD)
PNEUMOG	Pneumography (SAUS)
Pneumol	Pneumology (SAUS)
pneumonoultra	Pneumonoultra-Microscopicsilicovolcanoconiosis [Medicine] (AD)
PNEUROP	European Committee of Manufacturers of Compressors, Vacuum Pumps, and Pneumatic Tools (EA)
PNF	Pacific National Financial Corp. [Toronto Stock Exchange symbol] [Vancouver Stock Exchange symbol]
PNF	Palestine National Front [Political party] (PD)
PNF	Partial Neutralization Feed (ABAC)
PNF	Partito Nazionale Fascista [National Fascist Party] [Italy] [Political party] (PPE)
PNF	Peierls-Nabarro Force [Physics]
PNF	Penn Traffic [NYSE symbol] (TTSB)
PNF	Penn Traffic Co. [NYSE symbol] (SAG)
PNF	Phosphonitrilic Fluoroelastomer [Synthetic rubber]
PNF	Pilot Not Flying (GAVI)
PNF	Positive Neutral Finder [Automotive engineering]
PNF	Postnuclear Fraction [Biochemical tissue analysis]
PNF	Prenex Normal Form [Logic]
pnf	Proprioceptive Neuromuscular Facilitation (AD)
PNF	Proprioceptive Neuromuscular Facilitation [Neurology]
pnfd	Present Not for Duty (AD)
PNFD	Present Not for Duty [Military]
PNFE	Prototype Network Front End (SAUS)
PN-FET	Positive-Negative-Field-Effect Transistor (SAUS)
PNFI	Petawawa National Forestry Institute [Canadian Forestry Service] [Research center] (RCD)
PNFI	Pinnacle Financial Services, Inc. [NASDAQ symbol] (NQ)
PNFI	Pinnacle Financial Svcs [NASDAQ symbol] (TTSB)
PNFPP	Philippines National Family Planning Program (SAUS)
PNFS	Peak and Northern Footpaths Society [British] (DBA)
PNFSO	Primary Nonferrous Smelter Order [Environmental Protection Agency]
PNG	Pacific Northern Gas Ltd. [Toronto Stock Exchange symbol] [Vancouver Stock Exchange symbol]
PNG	Papua New Guinea [ANSI three-letter standard code] (CNC)
PNG	Papua New Guinea Banking Corp.
PNG	Papua Nueva Guinea [Papua New Guinea] [Spanish] (AD)
PNG	Paranagua [Brazil] [Airport symbol] (OAG)
PNG	Parque Nacional Guatopo [Guatopo National Park] [Venezuela] [Spanish] (AD)
PNG	Partido Nacional Guevarista [Ecuador] [Political party] (PPW)
PNG	Passive Night Goggles [Military] (WDAA)
PNG	Passive Night-vision Goggles (SAUS)
PNG	Paua New Guinea (SAUS)
Png	Penang (AD)
PNG	Penghu [Hokoto] [Republic of China] [Seismograph station code, US Geological Survey] (SEIS)
PNG	Penicillin G [Medicine] (DMAA)
PNG	Penn-America Group [NYSE symbol] (SG)
PNG	Percent Normalized Gradient (SAUS)
PNG	Persona Non Grata [Unacceptable Person] [Latin]
png	Persona Non Grata [An Unacceptable Person] [Latin] (AD)
PNG	Philippine Natural Gum
PNG	Plant Nitrogen in Grain [Harvest nitrogen index]
PNG	Popondetta [New Guinea] [Airport symbol] (AD)
PNG	Portable Network Graphic [Computer science] (PCM)
PNG	Portable Network Graphics [Computer science] (PCM)
PNG	Professional Numismatists Guild (EA)
PNG	Proportional Navigation Guidance
PNG	Pseudo Noise Generator (SAUS)
PNG	Pseudonoise Generator
PNG	Puerto Rico Air NAtional Guard [FAA designator] (FAAC)
PNGCS	Primary Navigation, Guidance and Control System (KSC)
PNGFA	Pacific Northwest Grain and Feed Association (EA)
PNGI	Papua New Guinea Institute of Chemistry
PNGL	Papua New Guinea Line (AD)
P N G Med J	Papua New Guinea Medical Journal (SAUS)
PNGS	Primary Navigation and Guidance System (SAUS)
PNGS	Primary Navigation System
PNGV	Partnership for a New Generation of Vehicles [Collaboration of government and industry]
PNH	North Hills School District Instructional Materials Center, Pittsburgh, PA [OCLC symbol] (OCLC)
PNH	Pan Head [Design engineering]
pnh	Paroxysmal Nocturnal Hemoglobinuria (AD)

PNH .... Paroxysmal Nocturnal Hemoglobinuria [*Medicine*]
PNH .... Partido Nacional Hondureno [*Honduran National Party*] [*Political party*]
PNH .... Parti National d'Haiti [*National Party of Haiti*] [*Political party*]
PNH .... Phnom Penh [*Cambodia*] [*Airport symbol*] (OAG)
PNH .... Pitcher Mountain [*New Hampshire*] [*Seismograph station code, US Geological Survey*] (SEIS)
PNH .... Polynuclear Hydrocarbon (DMAA)
PNHA .... Physicians National Housestaff Association [*Defunct*]
PNHDL........ Panhandle
PNHP .... Parque Nacional Henri Pittier [*Henri Pittier National Park*] [*Venezuela*] [*Spanish*] (AD)
PNHP .... Phsicians for a National Health Program (EA)
PNHS .... Pacific Northwest Heather Society [*Later, NAHS*] (EA)
PNI .... Aerovias de Poniente SA de CV [*Mexico*] [*ICAO designator*] (FAAC)
PNI .... Pacific Neurosciences Institute (SAUS)
PNI .... Paninternational
PNI .... Parque Nacional Iguazu [*Iguazu National Park*] [*Spanish*] (AD)
PNI .... Partai Nasionalis Indonesia [*Nationalist Party of Indonesia*] [*Political party*]
PNI .... Participate but Do Not Initiate [*Investment term*]
PNI .... Partido Nacional Independiente [*National Independent Party*] [*Costa Rica*] [*Political party*] (PPW)
PNI .... Part Number Index (MCD)
PNI .... Pascoe Nally International [*British*]
PNI .... Peer Nomination Inventory [*Psychology*]
PNI .... Peripheral Nerve Injury [*Medicine*]
PNI .... Pharmaceutical News Index [*UMI/Data Courier*] [*Information service or system*] [*A publication*]
PNI .... Pictorial Navigation Indicator [*Aviation*] (DA)
PNI .... Picture Netwok International, Ltd.
PNI .... Picture Network International [*Commercial firm*] [*Information service or system*]
PNI .... Pinerola [*Italy*] [*Seismograph station code, US Geological Survey*] (SEIS)
PNI .... Ponape [*Caroline Islands*] [*Airport symbol*] (OAG)
pni .... Positive Noninterfering (AD)
PNI .... Positive Noninterfering [*Alarm system*]
PNI .... Postnatal Infection [*Medicine*]
PNI .... Principal Neo-Tech, Inc. [*Toronto Stock Exchange symbol*]
PNI .... Processor Network Interface (SAUS)
PNI .... Prognostic Nutrition Index [*Dietetics*] (DAVI)
PNI .... Protease Nexin I [*Biochemistry*]
pni .... Psychoneuroimmunology (AD)
PNI .... Psychoneuroimmunology
pni .... Pulsed Neutron Interrogation (AD)
PNI .... Pulsed Neutron Interrogation (PDAA)
PNIC .... Pleasure Navigation International Joint Committee [*See also CINP*] [*The Hague, Netherlands*] (EAIO)
P Nic .... Port Nicholson (AD)
PNIC .... Private-data Network Identification Code (SAUS)
PNID .... Peer Nomination Inventory of Depression [*Child development test*] [*Psychology*]
P-NID.......... Precedence Network In-Dialing [*Telecommunications*] (TEL)
PNID/NOD... Priority Network In-Dial / Network Out-Dial (DNAB)
PNIE.......... Priority National Intelligence Estimate [*CIA*] (LAIN)
PNII .... Prentiss Normal and Industrial Institute [*Mississippi*]
PNII .... Protease Nexin II [*Biochemistry*]
PNIMIC .... Pilot NATO Insensitive Munitions Information Center (SAUS)
PNIN .... P-Doped, N-Doped, Intrinsic, N-Doped (SAUS)
PNIN .... Positive-Negative-Intrinsic-Negative (SAUS)
PNIO .... Priority National Intelligence Objectives (MCD)
PNIP .... P-Doped, N-Doped, Intrinsic, P-Doped (SAUS)
PNIP .... Positive-Negative-Intrinsic-Positive [*Electron device*] (MSA)
PNIPAAM...... Poly-N-isopropylacrylamide [*Organic chemistry*]
PNIPAM....... Poly-N-Isopropylacrylamide [*Organic chemistry*]
PNITC .... Pacific Northwest International Trade Council (AD)
PNIU .... Pneumatic Scale Corp. (SAUS)
PNJ .... Paterson [*New Jersey*] [*Airport symbol*] (AD)
PNJ .... Paterson, NJ [*Location identifier*] [*FAA*] (FAAL)
PNJ .... Polar Night Jet Stream (ADA)
PNJ .... Pulsed Noise Jamming (SAUS)
PNJALBB .... Peter Noone Just a Little Bit Better Promotion Club (EA)
PN-Junction... Positive Negative Junction (SAUS)
PNK .... Pink [*Electrical wiring*]
PNK .... Pinkham Creek [*Montana*] [*Seismograph station code, US Geological Survey*] [*Closed*] (SEIS)
PNK .... Pink Pages Publication [*Vancouver Stock Exchange symbol*]
pnk............. Pinl
PNK .... Polynucleotide Kinase [*An enzyme*]
PNK .... Pontianak [*Indonesia*] [*Airport symbol*] (OAG)
PNK .... Pyridoxine Kinase (DMAA)
PNkA........... Aluminum Co. of America, ALCOA Research Laboratories Library, New Kensington, PA [*Library symbol*] [*Library of Congress*] (LCLS)
PNKA .... Protein Induced by Vitamin K Absence and Antagonists (PDAA)
pnksh.......... Pinkish [*Philately*]
PNL .... Aero Personal SA de CV [*Mexico*] [*ICAO designator*] (FAAC)
PNL .... Instrument Panel [*Automotive engineering*]
PNL .... Pacific Naval Laboratories (AD)
PNL .... Pacific Northwest Laboratory [*Department of Energy*] [*Richland, WA*]
PNL .... Pakistan National League [*Political party*]
pnl .... Panel (AD)
PNL .... Panel (KSC)
PNL .... Pantelleria [*Italy*] [*Airport symbol*] (OAG)

PNL............ Partidul National Liberal [*National Liberal Party*] [*Romania*] [*Political party*] (PPE)
PNL............ Parti National Liberal [*National Liberal Party*] [*Lebanon*] [*Political party*] (PPW)
PNL............ Passenger Name List [*Travel industry*]
PNL............ Peanut Lectin [*Immunochemistry*]
PNL............ Peninsula [*Alaska*] [*Seismograph station code, US Geological Survey*] (SEIS)
PNL............ Perceived Noise Level
PNL............ Philippine National Line (AD)
PNL............ Pine Bell Mines [*Vancouver Stock Exchange symbol*]
PNL............ Polytechnic of North London, School of Librarianship, London, England [*OCLC symbol*] (OCLC)
PNL............ Prescribed Nuclear Load [*Military*] (AABC)
PNL............ Pressure Noise Level (MCD)
PNL............ Pulsed Neodymium LASER
PNL............ Pulsed Neutron Logging (SAUS)
PNLA .... Pacific Northwest Library Association
PNLA .... Pacific Northwest Loggers Association (EA)
PNLA .... Percutaneous Needle Lung Aspiration [*Medicine*] (DMAA)
PNLAADA.... Programme National de Lutte Contre l'Abus de l'Alcool et des Drogues chez les Autochtones [*Canada*]
PNLA/BCLA... Pacific Northwest/British Columbia Library Associations
PNL BD .... Panel Board (SAUS)
pnlbd .... Panelboard [*National Electrical Code*] (IEEE)
PNLBRG...... Panel Bridge (MUGU)
PNLF .... Planetary-Nebula Luminosity Function (SAUS)
PNLF .... Probability of no Loss of Function (SAUS)
PNLG .... Phase Nulling LASER Gyroscope
PNL/I .... Provisioning Numerical Listing/Index
PNLM .... Palestine National Liberation Movement [*Political party*] (BJA)
PNLO .... Principal Naval Liaison Officer [*British*]
PNLRM .... Preferred National Land Rights Model [*Australia*]
PNLT.......... Perceived Noise Level, Tone Corrected
PNM.......... Pan-Somali Nationalist Movement [*Political party*]
PNM.......... Partido Nacionalista de Mexicano [*Nationalist Party of Mexico*] [*Political party*]
PNM.......... Partito Nazionale Monarchico [*National Monarchist Party*] [*Italy*] [*Political party*] (PPE)
PNM.......... Path Number Matrix (SAUS)
PNM.......... People's National Movement [*Trinidad and Tobago*] [*Political party*] (PD)
PNM.......... Perinatal Mortality [*Medicine*]
PNM.......... Periodicals/News/Microfilm unit (SAUS)
PNM.......... Peripheral Nerve Myelin [*Medicine*] (MELL)
PNM.......... Phenolic Nylon with Microballoon
PNM.......... Pinnacles National Monument [*California*] (AD)
PNM.......... Portable Anymap (SAUS)
PNM.......... Postneonatal Mortality (STED)
PNM.......... Price Negotiation Memorandum (MCD)
PNM.......... Public Service Co. of New Mexico [*NYSE symbol*] (SPSG)
PNM.A....... Public Svc New Mexico [*NYSE symbol*] (TTSB)
PNM.......... Pulse Number Modulation
PNM.......... Pyranometer (SAUS)
PNM-Aprome... Partido Nacionalista de Melilla - Asociacion Pro Melilla [*Political party*] (EY)
PNMC .... Phenyl Methylcarbamate [*Organic chemistry*]
PNMF .... Pseudo Noise Matched Filter (IAA)
PNMG .... Persistent Neonatal Myasthenia Gravis [*Medicine*] (DAVI)
PNMO .... Provided No Military Objection Exists [*Army*]
PNMP .... Preliminary NMCS Master Plan (SAUS)
PNMR .... Proton Nuclear Magnetic Resonance (SAUS)
PNMT........ Phenylethanolalnine N-Methyltransferase (SAUS)
PNMT........ Phenylethanolamine N-Methyltransferase [*An enzyme*]
PNMT........ Positive Negative Metal Transistor (SAUS)
PNMT........ Positive-Negative Metal Transistor [*Electronics*] (IAA)
PNN .... Penn Engineering & Manufacturing Corp. [*AMEX symbol*] (SPSG)
PNN .... Penn Engr & Mfg [*AMEX symbol*] (TTSB)
PNN .... Pinnacle Mountain [*Alaska*] [*Seismograph station code, US Geological Survey*] (SEIS)
PNN .... Princeton, ME [*Location identifier*] [*FAA*] (FAAL)
PNN.A....... Probabilistic Neural Network (IDAI)
PNN.A....... Penn Engr & Mfg'A' [*AMEX symbol*] (TTSB)
PN-NAIPC ... Patriot Network - National Association of Independent Patriot Clubs (EA)
pn nb.......... Piano Nobile (VRA)
PNNCF........ Pacific Northern Naval Coastal Frontier
PNNI .... Private Node to Network Interface (SAUS)
PNNI .... Public Network Node Interface (SAUS)
PNNL .... Pacific Northwest National Laboratory
PNNT .... Pennant (MSA)
PNNW........ Pennichuck Corp. [*NASDAQ symbol*] (SAG)
PNo............ Montgomery County-Norristown Public Library, Norristown, PA [*Library symbol*] [*Library of Congress*] (LCLS)
PNO .... Nashville, TN [*Location identifier*] [*FAA*] (FAAL)
PNO .... Panaco, Inc. [*AMEX symbol*]
PNO .... Pancontinental Oil Ltd. [*Toronto Stock Exchange symbol*]
PNO .... Pa-O National Organization [*Myanmar*] [*Political party*] (EY)
PNO .... Parque Nacional Ordesa [*Ordesa National Park*] [*Spanish*] (AD)
PNO .... Parti Nationaliste Occitan [*Occitanian Nationalist Party*] [*France*] [*Political party*] (PPE)
PNO .... Party for National Order [*Turkey*] [*Political party*] [*Defunct*] (MENA)
PNO .... Pendleton [*Oregon*] [*Seismograph station code, US Geological Survey*] (SEIS)
pno .... Pergamino [*Parchment*] [*Spanish*] (AD)

pno .... Piano (AD)
PNO .... Piano
pno .... Pianoforte (WDAA)
PNO .... Port of New Orleans (AD)
PNO .... Preliminary Notification [*Nuclear energy*] (NRCH)
PNO .... Premium Notice Ordinary [*Insurance*]
PNO .... Principal Naval Overseer [*British*]
PNO .... Principal Nursing Officer
PNO .... Public Network Operator (SAUS)
PNOA .... Para-Nitro-ortho-anisidine [*Organic chemistry*]
pnob .... Pencil Note on Back [*Philately*]
PNOC .... Philippine National Oil Co. (AD)
PNOC .... Philippines National Oil Co. (SAUS)
PNOC .... Proposed Notice of Change
PNO-CI .... Pair Natural Orbital Configuration Interaction [*Atomic physics*]
PNoH .... Norristown State Hospital, Norristown, PA [*Library symbol*] [*Library of Congress*] (LCLS)
PNohM......... Mary Immaculate Seminary, Northampton, PA [*Library symbol*] [*Library of Congress*] (LCLS)
PNOK .... Primary Next of Kin [*Army*] (AABC)
PNOM .... Procedural Nomenclature (MCD)
PNOPO........ Parliament National Organisations and Public Offices [*British*]
PNortHi....... Historical Society of Montgomery County, Norristown, PA [*Library symbol*] [*Library of Congress*] [*Obsolete*] (LCLS)
PNOT .... Para-Nitro-ortho-toluidine [*Organic chemistry*]
PNOT .... Para-Nitro-o-toluidine [*Organic chemistry*]
PNOT .... Penta-Nitro-O-Toluidine (SAUS)
PNP .... Pakistan National Party [*Political party*] (PD)
PNP .... Panache Resources, Inc. [*Vancouver Stock Exchange symbol*]
PNP .... Pan Pacific Retail Prop. [*NYSE symbol*] (SG)
PNP .... Paranitrophenol
PNP .... Para-Nitrophenol [*or Nitrophenyl*] [*Organic chemistry*]
PNP .... Para-Nitrophenyl (SAUS)
PNP .... Para-Nitrophenyl-Beta-Galactosidase [*An enzyme*] (DAVI)
PNP .... Partido Nacionalista del Pueblo [*Bolivia*] [*Political party*] (PPW)
PNP .... Partido Nacionalista ng Pilipinas [*Philippine Nationalist Party*] [*Political party*] (EY)
PNP .... Partido Nacionalista Popular [*Popular Nationalist Party*] [*Panama*] [*Political party*] (PPW)
PNP .... Partido Nashonal di Pueblo [*National People's Party*] [*Netherlands Antilles*] [*Political party*] (EY)
PNP .... Partido Nuevo Progresista [*New Progressive Party*] [*Puerto Rico*] [*Political party*] (PPW)
PNP .... Partidul National Poporului [*National People's Party*] [*Romania*] [*Political party*] (PPE)
PNP .... Parti National du Progres [*National Progress Party*] [*Congo*] [*Political party*]
PNP .... Parti National Populaire [*National Popular Party*] [*Canada*] [*Political party*] (PPW)
PNP .... Parti National Progressiste [*Haiti*] [*Political party*] (EY)
PNP .... Passive Neighbourhood Pattern (SAUS)
PNP .... Peake's English Nisi Prius Cases [*1790-1812*] [*A publication*] (DLA)
PNP .... Peak Negative Pressure [*Medicine*] (DAVI)
PNP .... Pearl Necklace Polymer [*Organic chemistry*]
PNP .... Pediatric Nephrology [*Medical specialty*] (DHSM)
PNP .... Pediatric Nurse Practitioner
PNP .... Penuelas [*Puerto Rico*] [*Seismograph station code, US Geological Survey*] (SEIS)
PNP .... People's National Party [*Jamaica*] [*Political party*] (PPW)
PNP .... People's National Party [*Ghana*] [*Political party*] (PPW)
PNP .... Peripheral Neuropathy [*Medicine*]
PNP .... Philippine National Police (SAUS)
PNP .... Pick-and-Place Robot (SAUS)
PNP .... Platelet Neutralization Procedure [*Medicine*] (MEDA)
PNP .... Platt National Park [*Oklahoma*] (AD)
PNP .... Plug and Play [*Microsoft Corp.*] [*Computer auto-configuration system*] (PCM)
PnP.............. Plug and Play (PCM)
PnP.............. Plug and Pray (SAUS)
PNP .... Plug N Play (SAUS)
PNP .... Polyneuropathy [*Medicine*] (STED)
PNP .... Popondetta [*Papua New Guinea*] [*Airport symbol*] (OAG)
PNP .... Popular Nationalist Party [*Panama*] [*Political party*] (PD)
pnp.............. Positive Negative Positive (AD)
PNP .... Positive-Negative-Positive [*Transistor*]
PNP .... Post-Nodal Piece (SAUS)
PNP .... Precision Navigation Processor (SAUS)
PNP .... Precision Navigation Project
PNP .... Preliminary Network Plan (SSD)
PNP .... Prenegotiation Position (MCD)
PNP .... Private Non-Profit
PNP .... Probability of No Penetration [*NASA*] (SPST)
PNP .... Programmed Numerical Pathcontroller (SAUS)
PNP .... Progressive National Party [*Turks and Caicos Islands*] [*Political party*] (PPW)
PNP .... Progressive Nuclear Palsy [*Neurology*] (DAVI)
PNP .... Prototype Nuclear Process
PNP .... Psychiatric Nurse Practitioner (NUJO)
PNP .... Psychogenic Nocturnal Polydipsia [*Medicine*]
PNP .... P-Type, N-Type, P-Type Transistor (NITA)
PNP .... Purine-Nucleoside Phosphorylase [*An enzyme*]
PNP .... Purine Nucleotide Phosphorylase [*An enzyme*] (DAVI)
PNP .... Pyridoxine Phosphate [*Biochemistry*]
PNPA .... Para-Nitrophenyl Acetate [*Organic chemistry*]
PNPA .... P-Nitrophenyl Acetate (SAUS)

PN Patient... Psychoneurotic Patient (SAUS)
PNPB .... Positive-Negative Pressure Breathing [*Medicine*] (STED)
PNPBIOS...... Plug and Play Basic Input Output System (SAUS)
PNPDPP....... Para-Nitrophenyl Diphenyl Phosphate [*Organic chemistry*]
PNPF .... Piqua Nuclear Power Facility
PNPG .... Para-Nitrophenylglycerin (SAUS)
PNPG .... Para-Nitrophenylglycerine [*Biochemistry*]
PNPG .... Parti National Populaire Guyanais [*French Guiana*] [*Political party*] (EY)
PNPG .... P-Nitrophenyl-a-Glucopyranoside (SAUS)
PNPG .... P-Nitrophenyl-B-Galactoside [*Chemistry*] (MAE)
PNP-Glu....... Para-Nitrophenyl-a-Glucoside (SAUS)
PNPH .... Parti National Progressiste d'Haiti [*National Progressive Party of Haiti*] [*Political party*]
PNPL .... Para-Nitrophenyl Laurate [*Organic chemistry*]
PNPLS .... Progress at NPL [*National Priorities List*] Sites [*A publication*] [*EPA*]
PNPN .... Positive, Negative, Positive, Negative (SAUS)
pnpn .... Positive-Negative Positive-Negative (AD)
PNPN .... Positive-Negative-Positive-Negative [*Transistor*] (MUGU)
P-NPNN ...... Para-Nitrophenyl Nitronyl Nitroxide
PNPP .... Para-Nitrophenyl Phosphate [*Organic chemistry*]
PNPP .... Perry Nuclear Power Plant (NRCH)
PNPP .... P-Nitrophenyl Phosphate (SAUS)
pnpr........... Positive-Negative Pressure Respiration (AD)
PNPR .... Positive-Negative Pressure Respiration
PN-PRBS ..... Pseudo-Noise, Pseudo-Random Binary String/Stream (CGWS)
PNPS .... Palisades Nuclear Power Station (NRCH)
P-NPS......... Para-Nitrophenylsulfate [*Pharmacology*] (DAVI)
PNPS .... Plant Nitrogen Purge System (IEEE)
PNPS .... Plant Nuclear Protection System (IAA)
PNPSF .... Passive Neighbourhood Pattern Sensitive Fault (SAUS)
PNQ .... Pine Crest Resources [*Vancouver Stock Exchange symbol*]
PNQ .... Poona [*India*] [*Airport symbol*] (OAG)
PNR .... Page Number Register (SAUS)
PNR .... Panair [*Spain*] [*ICAO designator*] (FAAC)
PNR .... Partido Nacionalista Renovador [*Nationalist Renewal Party*] [*Guatemala*] [*Political party*] (PPW)
PNR .... Partido Nacionalista Revolucionario [*Revolutionary Nationalist Party*] [*Ecuador*] [*Political party*] (PPW)
PNR .... Partido Nacional Republicano [*National Republican Party*] [*Portugal*] [*Political party*] (PPE)
PNR .... Partido Nacional Republicano [*National Republican Party*] [*Paraguay*] [*Political party*]
PNR .... Partido Nacional Revolucionario [*National Revolutionary Party*] [*Venezuela*] [*Political party*]
PNR .... Partij Nationalistische Republiek [*Nationalist Republic Party*] [*Surinam*] [*Political party*] (PPW)
PNR .... Passenger Name Record [*Travel industry*] (TRID)
PNR .... Passenger Name Record [*Airlines*]
PNR .... Passenger Now Recorded [*Travel industry*] (TRID)
PNR .... Pennant Resources Ltd. [*Toronto Stock Exchange symbol*]
PNR .... Penrod [*Nevada*] [*Seismograph station code, US Geological Survey*] [*Closed*] (SEIS)
PNR .... Pentair, Inc. [*NYSE symbol*] (TTSB)
PNR .... Philippine National Railways (DS)
PNR .... Photonuclear Reaction (SAUS)
Pnr.............. Pioneer (AD)
PNR .... Pioneer
PNR .... Pittsburgh Naval Reactor (AD)
PNR .... Pittsburgh Naval Reactors Office [*Energy Research and Development Administration*]
PNR .... Pointe Noire [*Congo*] [*Airport symbol*] (OAG)
pnr.............. Point of No Return (AD)
PNR .... Point of No Return [*Aviation*]
PNR .... Polish National Railways (SAUS)
PNR .... Popular News and Review [*A publication*]
PNR .... Preliminary Negotiation Reports
PNR .... Primary Navigation Reference (AAG)
pnr.............. Prior Notice Required (AD)
PNR .... Prior Notice Required (AFM)
PNR .... Prisoner
PNR .... Proved Name Registraton [*Advertising*] (DOAD)
PNR .... Proximal Negative Response
PNR .... Pulletop Nature Reserve [*New South Wales*] (AD)
PNR .... Pulse Nuclear Radiation (AAG)
PNR .... Purchase Notice and Release (SAUS)
PNRBC........ Pacific Northwest River Basin Commission
PNRC.......... Pacific Northwest Regional Commission [*Department of Commerce*]
PNRC.......... Potomac Naval River Command (MCD)
PNRC.......... Projet National de Coordination des Ressources dans le Domaine de la Statistiques et de l'Information Judiciaires [*Canada*]
PNRE .... Pan Atlantic Re, Inc. (MHDW)
PNRG .... Prime Energy [*NASDAQ symbol*] (SAG)
PNRG .... PrimeEnergy Corp. [*NASDAQ symbol*] (SPSG)
PNRHSL...... Pacific Northwest Regional Health Science Library [*Library network*]
PNRI .... Philippines Nuclear Research Institute (SAUS)
PNRL .... Penril DataComm Ntwks [*NASDAQ symbol*] (TTSB)
PNRL .... Penril Data Communication Networks [*NASDAQ symbol*] (SPSG)
PNRO .... Pittsburgh Naval Reactors Office [*Department of Energy*] [*West Mifflin, PA*] (GAAI)
PNRP .... Philadelphia Pulmonary Neoplasm Research Project (AD)
PNRP .... Pollution and Natural Resources Program (SAUS)
PNRS .... Preliminary Natural Resources Survey (GNE)
PNRS .... Project Notification and Review System [*Department of Labor*]
PNRSV........ Prunus Necrotic Ringspot Virus

PNR System...   Passenger Name Record System (SAUS)
PNS ....   Pacific Navigation Systems (AD)
PNS ....   Pakistan Naval Ship (AD)
PNS ....   Parabolized Navier-Stokes Modeling (MCD)
PNS ....   Paraneoplastic Neurodegenarative Syndrome [Medicine]
pns.............   Parasympathetic Nervous System (AD)
PNS ....   Parasympathetic Nervous System
PNS ....   Park-Neutral Switch [Automotive engineering]
PNS ....   Partial Niche Separation
PNS ....   Partial Nonprogressing Stroke (CPH)
PNS ....   Part Number Specification (MCD)
PNS ....   Peacenet Sweden (SAUS)
PNS ....   Peculiar and Non-Standard (SAUS)
PNS ....   Peculiar and Nonstandard Items (AAG)
PNS ....   Penas [Bolivia] [Seismograph station code, US Geological Survey] (SEIS)
PNS ....   Pennington's Stores Ltd. [Toronto Stock Exchange symbol]
PNS ....   Pensacola [Florida] [Airport symbol] (OAG)
Pns ....   Pension (TBD)
PNS ....   People's News Service [British]
PNS ....   Peripheral Nerve Stimulator [Medicine] (MAE)
pns.............   Peripheral Nervous System (AD)
PNS ....   Peripheral Nervous System [Medicine]
PNS ....   Perkins Nuclear Station (NRCH)
PNS ....   Philadelphia & Norfolk Steamship [AAR code]
PNS ....   Philadelphia Naval Shipyard (AD)
PNS ....   Philippine News Service (SAUS)
PNS ....   Philippines News Service
PNS ....   Pic'N'Save Corp. (EFIS)
PNS ....   Pinnacle Data Systems [AMEX symbol]
PNS ....   Plate Number Society [Defunct] (EA)
PNS ....   Polynucleotide Sequence (DB)
PNS ....   Pooled Normal Serum (PDAA)
PNS ....   Portable Navigation System
PNS ....   Portsmouth Naval Shipyard [New Hampshire]
PNS ....   Positive-Negative Selection [Genetic engineering technique]
PNS ....   Posterior Nasal Spine [Medicine] (DMAA)
PNS ....   Post Nickel Strike (PDAA)
PNS ....   Postnuclear Supernatant
PNS ....   PPTP Network Server (SAUS)
PNS ....   Practical Nursing Student (DAVI)
PNS ....   Prescribed Nuclear Stockage [Military] (AABC)
PNS ....   Primary North-South Stationkeeping (ACAE)
PNS ....   Principal Nursing Sister (WDAA)
PNS ....   Probability of Not Having a Space
PNS ....   Professionals for National Security [Defunct] (EA)
PNS ....   Professor of Naval Science
PNS ....   Program on Non-violent Sanctions in conflict & defense (SAUS)
PNS ....   Project of National Significance
PNS ....   Publishers Newspaper Syndicate
PNS ....   Pulsed Neutron Source (SAUS)
PNS ....   Survey Udara (Penas) PT [Indonesia] [ICAO designator] (FAAC)
PNSA ....   Pacific Northwest Ski Association (EA)
PNSA ....   Peanut and Nut Salters Association [Later, PBNPA] (EA)
PNSA ....   Seaman Apprentice, Personnelman, Striker [Navy rating]
PNS & T ......   Professor of Naval Science and Tactics [Naval ROTC]
PNSC ....   Packet Network Service Center (SAUS)
PNSC ....   Packet Network Service Centre (NITA)
PNSC ....   Passenger Network Services Corporation (TRID)
PNSC ....   Philippine National Science Society (SAUS)
PNSCP ....   Plan for Navy Satellite Communications Plan
PNSD ....   Parti National pour la Solidarite et le Developpement [Algeria] [Political party] (EY)
PNSI ....   Polhemus Navigational Sciences, Inc. (MCD)
PNSL ....   Papulonodular Skin Lesion [Medicine] (MELL)
PNSN ....   Pacific Northwest Seismic Network (SAUS)
PNSN ....   Parque Nacional Sierra Nevada [Sierra Nevada National Park] [Venezuela] [Spanish] (AD)
PNSN ....   Pension
PNSN ....   Seaman, Personnelman, Striker [Navy rating]
PNSO ....   Pull Next Stitch Over [Knitting] (BARN)
PNSP ....   Penicillin-Nonsusceptible S. Pneumoniae [Clinical chemistry]
PNSQ ....   Porter Need Satisfaction Questionnaire (EDAC)
PNSRC ....   Plant Nuclear Safety Review Committee (SAUS)
PNSS ....   Pediatric Nutrition Surveillance System [Centers for Disease Control] (DAVI)
PNSS ....   Pregnancy Nutrition Surveillance System (SAUS)
PNSS ....   Pseudonoise Spread Spectrum (SAUS)
PNST ....   Pilot Network System Test (SAUS)
PNSTDC......   Pakistan National Scientific and Technical Documentation Center (AD)
PNSUS........   Place Name Survey of the U.S. (SAUS)
PNSUS........   Placename Survey of the US (EA)
PNSY ....   Portsmouth Naval Shipyard [New Hampshire]
PNt...............   Newtown Library Co., Newtown, PA [Library symbol] [Library of Congress] [Obsolete] (LCLS)
pnt ....   Paint (AD)
PNT.............   Paint (MSA)
PNT.............   Paint Template
Pnt.............   Panart [Record label] [Cuba, USA]
PNT.............   Para-Nitrotoluene [Organic chemistry]
PNT.............   Paroxysmal Nodal Tachycardia [Cardiology]
PNT.............   Parque Nacional Tijuca [Tijuca National Park] [Brazil] [Portuguese] (AD)
PNT.............   Partial Nodular Transformation (DMAA)

PNT.............   Partido Nacionalista de los Trabajadores [Argentina] [Political party] (EY)
PNT.............   Parti National du Travail [Benin] [Political party] (EY)
PNT.............   Parti National du Travail [Haiti] [Political party] (EY)
PNT.............   Patient (AABC)
PNT.............   Penna Enterprises [NYSE symbol] (TTSB)
PNT.............   Penn Enterprises, Inc. [NYSE symbol] (SAG)
Pnt.............   Pentagon (AD)
PNT.............   Pentagon
PNT.............   Penticton [British Columbia] [Seismograph station code, US Geological Survey] (SEIS)
PNT.............   Percutaneous Nephrostomy Tube [Nephrology] (DAVI)
PNT.............   Petromet Resources Ltd. [Toronto Stock Exchange symbol]
PNT.............   Plasma Nitriding (SAUS)
PNT.............   Point
PNT.............   Pontiac, IL [Location identifier] [FAA] (FAAL)
PNT.............   Position-Navigation-Time
PNT.............   Print (SAUS)
PNTA ....   Pacific Northwest Trade Association
PNTA ....   Pentair, Inc. [NASDAQ symbol] (NQ)
Pnt Anx........   Pentagon Annex (AD)
PNtB ....   Bucks County Community College, Newtown, PA [Library symbol] [Library of Congress] (LCLS)
PNTB ....   Peninsula Trust Bank [NASDAQ symbol] (TTSB)
PNTB ....   Peninsula Trust Bank, Inc. [NASDAQ symbol] (SAG)
PNTBT ....   Partial Nuclear Test Ban Treaty (AD)
PNtC ....   Council Rock High School, Newtown, PA [Library symbol] [Library of Congress] (LCLS)
PNTC ....   Panatech Res & Dev [NASDAQ symbol] (TTSB)
PNTC ....   Panatech Research & Development Corp. [NASDAQ symbol] (NQ)
PNTCENS.....   Patient Census Report
PNTCENS Report...   Patient Census Report (SAUS)
pntd ....   Painted (AD)
PNTD ....   Painted
PNTD ....   Personnel Neutron Threshold Detector (IEEE)
PN/TDMA....   Pseudo Noise/Time Division Multiple Access (MCD)
PN-TDMA....   Pseudo-Noise-Time Division Multiple Access (SAUS)
PNtE ....   Ellis College, Newtown, PA [Library symbol] [Library of Congress] [Obsolete] (LCLS)
PNTG ....   Petromet Resources Ltd. [NASDAQ symbol] (NQ)
PNTG ....   Printing (ROG)
PNTGF ....   Petromet Resources [NASDAQ symbol] (TTSB)
PNTGN........   Pentagon (MSA)
PNTK ....   Pentech International [NASDAQ symbol] (TTSB)
PNTK ....   Pentech International, Inc. [NASDAQ symbol] (NQ)
PNTL ....   Phonetel Technologies [NASDAQ symbol] (TTSB)
PNTL ....   Phonetel Technologies, Inc. [NASDAQ symbol] (NQ)
PNTO ....   Portuguese National Tourist Office (EA)
PNTO ....   Principal Naval Transport Officer [British military] (DMA)
PNTOS ....   Para-Nitrotoluene-ortho-sulfonic Acid [Organic chemistry]
pntr ....   Painter (AD)
PNTR ....   Painter
PNTR ....   Permanent Normal Trade Relations
PNTR ....   Pointer (MCD)
PNTRY ....   Pantry
PNts ....   Newtown Public Library, Newtown Square, PA [Library symbol] [Library of Congress] (LCLS)
PNTY ....   Pantry (ADWA)
PNTYP ....   Panno Type (VRA)
PNU ....   Panguitch [Utah] [Airport symbol] (OAG)
PNU ....   Peasants' National Unity [Afghanistan] [Political party] (EY)
PNU ....   Personennamen der Texte aus Ugarit [A publication] (BJA)
PNU ....   Pharmacia & Upjohn [NYSE symbol] (TTSB)
PNU ....   Pharmacia & Upjohn, Inc. [NYSE symbol] (SAG)
PNU ....   Platinum Communication System [Vancouver Stock Exchange symbol]
PNU ....   Pneumatic Scale Corp. [Stock exchange symbol] (AD)
PNU ....   Position Navigation Unit (SEWL)
PNU ....   Protein Nitrogen Units [Clinical chemistry]
PNU ....   Puma Navigation Update programme (SAUS)
PNUA ....   Partito Nazionale Unito Africa [National Party of United Africans] [Somalia] [Political party]
PNUA ....   Polish National Union of America (EA)
PNUD ....   Programa de las Naciones Unidas para el Desarrollo [United Nations Development Program - UNDP] [Spanish] (MSC)
PNUMA........   Chilean National Union for the Enviornment (SAUS)
PNUMA........   Programa de las Naciones Unidas para el Medio Ambiente [United Nations Environmental Programme Regional Office for Latin America] (EAIO)
PNUT ....   Portable Nursing Unit Terminal
PNUT ....   Possible Nuclear Underground Test
pnutbutsan...   Peanut-Butter Sandwich (AD)
p-nut butter...   Peanut-Butter Sandwich (AD)
pnutbutwich...   Peanut-Butter Sandwich (AD)
PNUTS ....   Possible Nuclear Test Site [Pronounced "peanuts"] [Air Force intelligence]
PNUTS ....   Possible Nuclear Underground Test Site
PNV ....   National Velasquista Party [Ecuador] [Political party] (PPW)
PNV ....   Panavia SA [ICAO designator] (FAAC)
PNV ....   Partido Nacionalista Vasco [Basque Nationalist Party] [Spain] [Political party] (PPE)
PNV ....   Partido Nacional Velasquista [National Velasquista Party] [Ecuador] [Political party] (PPW)
PNV ....   Parti National Voltaique [Voltaic National Party] [Political party]
PNV ....   Patino N. V. [Toronto Stock Exchange symbol]

PNV	Pilot Night Vision (SEWL)
PNV	Potential Natural Vegetation (GNE)
PNV	Prenatal Vitamins (DAVI)
PNV	Present Net Value (WPI)
PNVAL	Previously Not Available [Army] (AABC)
PNVD	Passive Night Vision Devices [Army] (AABC)
PNVS	Pilot Night Vision Sensor
PNVS	Pilot Night Vision System [Army] (MCD)
PNVS	Pilot's Night Vision Sensor
PNVS	Pilots Night Vision System (SAUS)
PNVTS	Pyrotechnics No-Voltage Test Set
PNW	Pacific Northwest
PNW	Pacific Northwest Outport [MTMC] (TAG)
PNW	Personal Netware (SAUS)
PNW	Pinnacle West Capital [NYSE symbol] (TTSB)
PNW	Pinnacle West Capital Corp. [NYSE symbol] (SPSG)
PNW	[The] Prescott & Northwestern Railroad Co. [AAR code]
PNW	Project Night Watch (SAUS)
PNW	Protracted Nuclear Warfighting (ACAE)
PNWA	Pacific Northwest Waterways Association (SAUS)
PNW Bulletin...	Pacific Northwest Bulletin (SAUS)
PNWC	Pacific Northwest Writers' Conference
PNwC	Westminster College, New Wilmington, PA [Library symbol] [Library of Congress] (LCLS)
PNWCSC......	Pacific Northwest Canadian Studies Consortium [University of Oregon]
PNWD/BMI...	Pacific Northwest Division/Battelle Memorial Institute (AD)
PNWIS-APCA...	Pacific Northwest International Section-Air Pollution Control Association (SAUS)
PNWL	Pacific Northwest Laboratory [AEC]
PNWR	Piedmont National Wildlife Refuge [Georgia] (AD)
PNWR	Presquile National Wildlife Refuge [Virginia] (AD)
PNWR	Pungo National Wildlife Refuge [North Carolina] (AD)
PNWRBC......	Pacific Northwest River Basins Commission [Water Resources Council] [Terminated, 1981] (NOAA)
PNX	Imperial Airways, Inc. [ICAO designator] (FAAC)
pnx.............	Pneumothorax [Medicine] (AD)
PNX	Pneumothorax [Medicine]
PNX	Private Network Exchange [Computer science] (VLIE)
PNXT	Pinxit [He, or She, Painted It] [Latin]
pnxt	Pinxit [He or She Painted It] [Latin] (AD)
PNY	Camp Parks, CA [Location identifier] [FAA] (FAAL)
PNY	Penny
PNY	Piedmont Natl Gas [NYSE symbol] (TTSB)
PNY	Piedmont Natural Gas Co., Inc. [NYSE symbol] (SPSG)
PNY	Plattsburgh [New York] [Seismograph station code, US Geological Survey] (SEIS)
PNY	Portuguese Navy
PNYA	Port of New York Authority [Later, PANYNJ]
PNYCTC	Pennsylvania New York Central Transportation Co. (AD)
PNZ...........	Pennzoil Co., Exploration Library, Houston, TX [OCLC symbol] (OCLC)
Pnz............	Penzance (AD)
PNZ...........	Petrolina [Brazil] [Airport symbol] (OAG)
PO..............	Aeropelican Intercity Commuter Air Services [ICAO designator] (AD)
po---...........	Oceanica [MARC geographic area code] [Library of Congress] (LCCP)
PO..............	Office of Policy, Planning and Program Evaluation (SAUS)
PO..............	Officer Personnel Division [Coast Guard]
PO..............	Oil City Library, Oil City, PA [Library symbol] [Library of Congress] (LCLS)
PO..............	Oscillopolarograph
PO..............	Paarieto-Occipital [Medicine] (DMAA)
PO..............	Pacific Ocean
PO..............	Page Overflow (SAUS)
PO..............	Palomar Capital [Vancouver Stock Exchange symbol]
PO..............	Paper Out (SAUS)
PO..............	Parallel Output [Computer science] (BUR)
P:O.............	Parent Offspring [Genetics]
PO..............	Parieto-Occipital [Anatomy] (AAMN)
PO..............	Parity Odd
PO..............	Parking Orbit [NASA]
PO..............	Parliamentary Officer [Australia]
PO..............	Parole Officer
PO..............	Partial Pressure of Oxygen (DAVI)
P/O.............	Part Of (KSC)
p/o	Part of (AD)
PO..............	Passport Office [Department of State]
PO..............	Patent Office [Later, PTO] [Department of Commerce]
PO..............	Patents Office (SAUS)
PO..............	Path Operator (SAUS)
PO..............	Patrologia Orientalis [A publication] (ODCC)
PO..............	Performance Objectives (OICC)
PO..............	Performing Organization (NITA)
PO..............	Period of Onset [Medicine]
PO..............	Perioperative [Medicine] (DMAA)
PO..............	Permit Office [British] (ROG)
PO..............	Peroral (SAUS)
PO..............	Per Orally (SAUS)
PO..............	Per Order (WDMC)
PO..............	Per Os [By Mouth] [Pharmacy]
po..............	Per Os [By Mouth] [Latin] (AD)
PO..............	Peroxidase [Also, POD] [An enzyme]
PO..............	Persistent Object (SAUS)
PO..............	Personnel Office [Kennedy Space Center Directorate] (NASA)
PO.............	Personnel Officer
PO.............	Pesticides Office [Environmental Protection Agency]
PO.............	Petroleum Officer (SAUS)
PO.............	Petty Officer [Navy]
PO.............	Phase Optimization (SAUS)
PO.............	Phase Oscillation (SAUS)
PO.............	Phase-Out
PO.............	Phenoxy (EDCT)
PO.............	Philadelphia Orchestra (SAUS)
PO.............	Philharmonic Orchestra [Music]
P/O............	Phone Order [Medicine]
P/O............	Phosphate to Oxygen (BARN)
PO.............	Phymatotrichum omnivorum [A fungus]
PO.............	Physical Oceanography (SAUS)
PO.............	Physical Optics (SAUS)
PO.............	Pilot Officer
P/O............	Pitch Over
PO.............	Planetary Office (IAA)
PO.............	Planetary Orbit
PO.............	Planned Obsolescence (MHDB)
PO.............	Planning Objectives (VLIE)
PO.............	Planted on (SAUS)
PO.............	Plotter-Output (SAUS)
PO.............	Plotting Officer (SAUS)
PO.............	Poco [Somewhat] [Music]
po.............	Poetry (AD)
PO.............	Point (WGA)
PO.............	Polarity (AAG)
po.............	Polarity (AD)
PO.............	Polar-Optical (SAUS)
PO.............	Pole [Unit of measurement]
PO.............	Pole Operator (SAUS)
P/O............	Police Officer (ADWA)
PO.............	Police Officer
PO.............	Political Officer [NATO]
P/O............	Pollen/Ovule Ratio [Botany]
Po.............	Polonium [Chemical element]
PO.............	Polskie Zaklady Lotnicze [Poland] [ICAO aircraft manufacturer identifier] (ICAO)
PO.............	Polymerizable Oligomer (OA)
PO.............	Polymerizable Oligomers (SAUS)
PO.............	Polyolefin [Organic chemistry]
PO.............	Polyot (SAUS)
PO.............	Poly Propylene Oxide (EDCT)
Po.............	Polyzoa [Quality of the bottom] [Nautical charts]
PO.............	Por Orden [By Order] [Spanish]
PO.............	Portal (DB)
PO.............	Port Flag [Navy] [British]
PO.............	Portland Oregonian [A publication] (AD)
PO.............	Port Officer
po.............	Portugal [MARC country of publication code] [Library of Congress] (LCCP)
PO.............	Portugal [NATO]
Po.............	Portuguese [Language, etc.] (DLA)
PO.............	Position Offered
PO.............	Positive Output (SAUS)
Po.............	Possible
PO.............	Postal Officer (DCTA)
PO.............	Postal Order
PO.............	Posterior (MAE)
PO.............	Post Flight Inspection [Air Force]
po.............	Post Office (WDMC)
PO.............	Post Office
PO.............	Post Office Department [Canada]
p-o............	Postoperative (AD)
PO.............	Postoperative [Medicine]
PO.............	Post Orbit [NASA]
PO.............	Postpay Coin Telephone [Telecommunications] (TEL)
PO.............	Potential Officer [British military] (DMA)
PO.............	Power On (VLIE)
po.............	Power-Operated (AD)
PO.............	Power-Operated
po.............	Power Oscillator (AD)
PO.............	Power Oscillator [Electronics]
PO.............	Power Output
PO.............	Pre-Authorization Order
PO.............	Precipitator Outlet (SAUS)
PO.............	Predominating Organism (AAMN)
PO.............	Preoperational (MCD)
PO.............	Preoptic [Area of the brain]
PO.............	Preparation Order (SAUS)
PO.............	Presbyteri Oratorii [Oratorians] [Roman Catholic religious order]
PO.............	Presbyterorum Ordinis [Decree on the Ministry and Life of Priests] [Vatican II document]
P/O............	Preservation by Operation (SAUS)
PO.............	Pressure Oscillation (IAA)
PO.............	Pressure Oxidation (SAUS)
PO.............	Preventive Officer [British] (ROG)
po.............	Previous Orders (AD)
PO.............	Previous Orders [Military]
PO.............	Previous Owner
PO.............	Primary Outlet (SAUS)
PO.............	Primary Output (IAA)
PO.............	Primitive data holding Object (SAUS)
PO.............	Principal Officer [Foreign Service]

PO............	Principal Only (EBF)
PO............	Principal Only Strip [*Mortgage security*]
PO............	Principals Only (SAUS)
PO............	Printout
PO............	Print Output (SAUS)
PO............	Privately Owned (AFM)
PO............	Private Office [*Documents issued by the Secretary General, NATO*] (NATG)
PO............	Privileged Operation (VLIE)
PO............	Probation Officer
PO............	Processing Office [*Bureau of the Census*] (GFGA)
PO............	Procurement Objective (NVT)
PO............	Production Offset (AABC)
PO............	Production Order (KSC)
PO............	Professional Officer
PO............	Professor Ordinarius [*Ordinary Professor*] [*Latin*] (ROG)
PO............	Programmed Operation (SAUS)
PO............	Programmed Oscillator
PO............	Program Objective
PO............	Program Office [*Air Force*] (CET)
PO............	Program Operations (COE)
PO............	Program Originator (AFM)
PO............	Project Office [*or Officer*] [*Military*]
PO............	Project Officer (COE)
PO............	Project ORBIS (EA)
PO............	Project Order [*DoD*]
PO............	Project Overcome (EA)
PO............	Proposals Outstanding
PO............	Proposition One [*Defunct*] (EA)
PO............	Propylene Oxide [*Organic chemistry*]
PO............	Propylene Oxide Homopolymer (SAUS)
PO............	Province of Ontario [*Canada*]
PO............	Provisioning Order (AFM)
PO............	Pseudoadiabatic Operation [*Chemical engineering*]
PO............	Psychological Operation [*Military*] (CINC)
PO............	Public Offering [*Investment term*]
PO............	Public Office [*British*] (ROG)
PO............	Public Officer (SAUS)
PO............	Public Official
PO............	Pull Out (IAA)
PO............	Pulmonary Valve Opening [*Cardiology*]
PO............	Pulsed Carrier without Any Modulation Intended to Carry Information (IEEE)
PO............	Pulse Oscillator (IAA)
PO............	Pulse Output
PO............	Punching Operation (SAUS)
PO............	Punch Off (SAUS)
PO............	Punch On (VLIE)
PO............	Punch Operator (SAUS)
PO............	Punch Out [*Computer science*] (IAA)
PO............	Punted Over [*Boating*] [*British*] (ROG)
PO............	Purchase Option (SAUS)
PO............	Purchase Order
PO............	Purchasing Office [*DoD*] (AFIT)
PO............	Pushout (SAUS)
po............	Putout (ADWA)
PO............	Putout [*Baseball*]
P-O............	Pyrenees-Orientales (AD)
PO............	Radio Positioning Mobile Station [*ITU designation*] [*Telecommunications*] (CET)
PO1............	Petty Officer, First Class [*Navy*]
PO 1/C............	Petty Office First Class [*Military*] (AD)
pO₂............	Oxygen Pressure (DAVI)
PO₂............	Partial Pressure of Oxygen (AAMN)
PO2............	Petty Officer, Second Class [*Navy*]
PO2............	Pressure of Oxygen (SAUS)
PO 2/C............	Petty Office Second Class [*Military*] (AD)
PO3............	Petty Officer, Third Class [*Navy*]
PO 3/C............	Petty Office Third Class [*Military*] (AD)
Po5............	Party of Five [*Television program title*]
PO1/2............	Petty Officer 1st/2nd Class (SAUS)
POA............	Le Point Air [*France*] [*ICAO designator*] (FAAC)
POA............	Pacific Ocean Area [*World War II*]
POA............	Pahoa, HI [*Location identifier*] [*FAA*] (FAAL)
POA............	Palaeovegetation of the Americas (SAUS)
POA₂............	Pancreatic Oncofetal Antigen [*Immunochemistry*]
POA............	Panel of Americans [*Defunct*] (EA)
POA............	Parallel Overlap Assembly [*Computer science*]
POA............	Pay-on-Answer [*Telecommunications*] [*British*]
POA............	Pay on Arrival (SAUS)
POA............	Peacetime Operating Assets [*DoD*] (AFIT)
POA............	Petroleum Operating Agreement (CINC)
POA............	Petty Officer Airman [*British military*] (DMA)
POA............	Phalangeal Osteoarthritis [*Medicine*]
POA............	Phenoxyacetic Acid [*Organic chemistry*]
POA............	Pilot-Operated Absolute System (SAUS)
poa............	Place of Acceptance (AD)
POA............	Place of Acceptance [*Business term*] (DCTA)
POA............	Plan of Action (NASA)
POA............	Plotting Officers Assistant (SAUS)
POA............	Point Of Action (EECA)
POA............	Point of Aim (SAUS)
POA............	Point of Application [*Medicine*] (MAE)
POA............	Polarized Orbital Approximation (PDAA)
POA............	Police Officers' Association [*British*] (BI)

POA............	Pontifica Opera di Assistenza [*Pontifical Relief Organization*]
POA............	Pony of the Americas
PoA............	Pony of the Americas Club (NTPA)
POA............	Portable Object Adapter (VLIE)
POA............	Portland Opera Association [*Oregon*] (AD)
POA............	Porto Alegre [*Brazil*] [*Airport symbol*] (OAG)
POA............	Port of Arrival
POA............	Position of Advantage (SAUS)
PoA............	Power of Attorney (AD)
POA............	Power of Attorney
POA............	Power Open Association [*Computer science*] (CDE)
POA............	Preoptic Area [*of the brain*]
POA............	Price on Application [*Business term*] (ADA)
POA............	Primary Optic Afferents
poa............	Primary Optical Area (AD)
POA............	Primary Optic Atrophy
POA............	Prison Officers' Association [*A union*] [*British*] (DCTA)
POA............	Privately Owned Automobile
POA............	Privately-Owned Open Air-Braked [*Railway wagons*] (PDAA)
POA............	Probability of Acceptance (IAA)
POA............	Problem Oriented Assembler [*Computer science*] (VLIE)
POA............	Problem-Oriented Assembler (SAUS)
POA............	Program Office Approvals (COE)
POA............	Program Operations Assistant (SAUS)
POA............	Proof of Accounts
POA............	Property Owners Association (NTPA)
POA............	Provisional Operating Authorization [*for nuclear power plant*]
POA............	Public Order Act
POA............	Purchased on Assembly (KSC)
POA............	Purchase Option Agreement (TIMI)
POA............	Purchase Order Authorization (SAA)
POA............	Purgeable Organic Analyzer
POAA............	Planetary Operations Analysis Area [*NASA*]
POAA............	Post Office Agents' Association [*Australia*]
POAA............	Property Owners Association of America [*Defunct*] (EA)
POA & M............	Plan of Action and Milestones (NVT)
POAC............	Peace Officers Association of California (AD)
POAC............	Pony of the Americas Club (EA)
POAC............	Port and Ocean Engineering Under Arctic Conditions International Committee (EAIO)
POAC............	Post Office Advisory Committee [*British*]
POAC............	Post Office Advisory Council (AD)
POAC............	Post Office Ambulance Centre [*British*] (DI)
POAC............	Probe Origin Authentication Check (VLIE)
PoACCS Ph II...	Portuguese Air Command & Control System Phase II (SAUS)
POACH............	PC-On-A-Chip
POACH............	Prednisone, Oncovin [*Vincristine*] Cytosine Arabinoside, Cyclophospham ide, and Adriamycin [*Antineoplastic drug regimen*] (DAVI)
POACMN............	Petty Officer Aircrewman [*British military*] (DMA)
POACS............	Prior Other Active Commissioned Service [*Military*]
POAD............	Position Administration Display (SAUS)
POADS............	Portland Air Defense Sector (SAA)
POAE............	Port of Aerial Embarkation [*Air Force*]
POAE............	Principal Officer of Aircraft Equipment [*Ministry of Aircraft Production*] [*British*] [*World War II*]
POAES............	Prior Other Active Enlisted Service [*Military*]
POAF............	Petty Officer Air Fitter [*British military*] (DMA)
POAG............	Peace Officers Association of Georgia (AD)
POAG............	Primary Open Angle Glaucoma (SAUS)
POAG............	Primary Open-Angle Glaucoma [*Ophthalmology*]
POA-HA............	Preoptic Anterior Hypothalamic Area [*Medicine*] (DMAA)
PO/AH Areas...	Preoptic and Anterior Hypothalamic Areas (SAUS)
POAHEDPEARL...	Pacific Ocean Areas Headquarters Pearl Harbor
POALS............	Petty Officers Advanced Leadership School [*Navy*] (MUGU)
POAM............	Polar Ozone Aerosol Measurement
POAM............	Polar Ozone Aerosol Monitor (SAUS)
POAM............	Polar Ozone and Aerosol Measurements (SAUS)
POAN............	Procurement of Ordnance and Ammunition - Navy
PO & CS............	Post Office and Civil Service Committee [*US Senate*] [*Obsolete*]
POANSW............	Property Owners' Association of New South Wales [*Australia*]
POAQ............	Property Owners' Association of Queensland [*Australia*]
POAR............	Postal Laws and Regulations [*Later, Postal Manual*] (IAA)
POAR............	Problem Objective Approach Response (SAUS)
POAR............	Problem-Objective-Approach-Response [*System of planning patient care*] [*Medicine*]
POAR............	Project Order Action Request [*Navy*] (NG)
POAR............	Project Order Action Required
poas-............	American Samoa [*MARC geographic area code*] [*Library of Congress*] (LCCP)
POAS............	Pankypria Omospondia Anexartiton Syntechnion [*Pancyprian Federation of Independent Trade Unions*] [*Cyprus*]
POAS............	Psychological Operations Automated System (COE)
POASP............	Plans and Operations Automated Storage Program [*Military*]
POAT............	Psychological Operations Assessment Team (COE)
POATSC............	Pacific Overseas Air Technical Service Command
POAU............	Protestants and Other Americans for Separation of Church and State (NADA)
POAU............	Protestants and Other Americans United [*for Separation of Church and State*]
POAU............	Protestants and Other Americans United for Separation of Church and State (SAUS)
POB............	Fayetteville, NC [*Location identifier*] [*FAA*] (FAAL)
POB............	Paris Opera Ballet

POB	Parti Ouvrier Belge [*Belgian Workers' Party*] [*Later, Belgian Socialist Party*] [*Political party*] (PPE)
POB	Parts on Change (SAUS)
POB	Peanut Oil and Beeswax (SAUS)
POB	Penicillin, Oil, Beeswax [*Medicine*]
POB	Perfluorooctyl Bromide [*Organic chemistry*]
POB	Periphal Order Buffer (SAUS)
POB	Peripheral Order Buffer [*Computer science*] (VLIE)
pob	Persons on Board (AD)
POB	Persons on Board [*Aviation*]
POB	Phenoxybenzamine [*Later, PBZ*] [*Adrenergic blocking agent*]
pob	Pilot on Board (AD)
POB	Place of Birth
pob	Poblacion [*Population*] [*Spanish*] (AD)
POB	Point of Banking (SAUS)
pob	Point of Beginning (AD)
POB	Point of Beginning
POB	Point of Business
POB	Polyoxybutylene Glycol (SAUS)
PoB	Port of Baltimore (AD)
POB	Postal Bulletin [*A publication*]
POB	Post Office Book (SAUS)
POB	Post Office Box
POB	Power Outlet Box
pob	Prevention of Blindness (AD)
POB	Prevention of Blindness [*Medicine*] (MAE)
POB	Principles of Operation Bulletin (SAUS)
POB	Procurement Opportunities Board (SAUS)
POB	Public Oversight Board
POB	Push-Out Base (IAA)
POB	Servicios Aereos Poblanos, SA de CV [*Mexico*] [*FAA designator*] (FAAC)
POB²	Prepped Out Beyond Belief [*Book title*]
POBA	Patent Office Board of Appeals (IAA)
POBA	Persons Overwhelmed By Acronyms (SAUS)
POBA	Plain Old Balloon Angioplasty [*Cardiology*] [*Facetious*]
PO Bag	Post Office Bag (ASC)
POBAL	Powered Balloon [*System*]
POBAL System	Powered Balloon System (SAUS)
POBAS	Project Oriented Budgeting and Accounting System (SAUS)
POBATO	Propellant on Board at Takeoff
POBCOST	Probabilistic Budgeting and Forward Costing (MCD)
POBE	Profile of Out-of-Body Experiences (STED)
POB-N	Polyoxybutylene Glycol Nylon-12
POBN	(Pyridyloxide)butylnitrone [*Organic chemistry*]
POBN	Pyridyl Oxide-N-tert-butylnitrone [*Organic chemistry*]
POBO	Project Office Business Operations
POBOC	Payment on Behalf of Crown (SAUS)
pobp-	British Solomon Islands [*MARC geographic area code*] [*Library of Congress*] (LCCP)
POBP	Preoperative Bowel Preparation [*Medicine*] (MELL)
POBR	Poe & Brown [*NASDAQ symbol*] (SAG)
POBR	Problem-Oriented Basic Research [*National Science Foundation*]
pobra	Pony and Zebra (AD)
POBS	Portsmouth Bank Shares [*NASDAQ symbol*] (TTSB)
POBS	Portsmouth Bank Shares, Inc. [*NASDAQ symbol*] (NQ)
POBSP	Pacific Ocean Biological Survey Program [*Smithsonian Institution*] (GFGA)
POBT	Postoperative Bleeding Time [*Medicine*] (MELL)
POB Technique	Push-out Base Technique (SAUS)
POB Transistor	Push out Base Transistor (SAUS)
POBY	Prior Operating Budget Year [*Military*] (AFIT)
POC	Clarion State College, Oil City, PA [*Library symbol*] [*Library of Congress*] (LCLS)
POC	La Pocatiere [*Quebec*] [*Seismograph station code, US Geological Survey*] (SEIS)
POC	La Verne, CA [*Location identifier*] [*FAA*] (FAAL)
Po/C	Ocular Pressure (STED)
POC	Packaged Optimization Control [*Engineering*]
POC	Panel of Counselors (SAUS)
POC	Parallel Optical Computer
POC	Paralympic Organizing Committee (SAUS)
POC	Para-Ovarian Cyst [*Medicine*] (MELL)
POC	Parent-Offspring Conflict
POC	Particulate Organic Carbon
POC	Particulate Organic Concentration [*Environmental science*]
POC	Particulate Organic Matter
POC	Parti d'Opposition Congolais [*Congolese Opposition Party*] [*Political party*]
POC	Patch Output Converter (IAA)
Poc	Payload Operations Center [*NASA*] (NAKS)
POc	Payload Operations Center [*NASA*] (NASA)
POC	Peeping Other Chatters (SAUS)
POC	Performance Operating Characteristic (DIPS)
POC	Performance Optimization Code
POC	Personnel Operations Center
POC	Peugeot Owners' Club (EA)
POC	Physical Oceanography Committee (SAUS)
POC	Physical Organic Chemistry (SAUS)
POC	Physics of Control (IAA)
POC	Pick Off, Circuit
POC	Pick-off Circuit (SAUS)
POC	Picosecond Optical Calorimetry (SAUS)
POC	Pittsburgh Opera Co. (AD)
POC	Planning Objective Coordinator

POC	Platoon Operations Center [*Army*]
POC	Plymouth Owners Club (EA)
POC	Pocono Airlines, Inc. [*ICAO designator*] (FAAC)
POC	Poco Petroleums Ltd. [*Toronto Stock Exchange symbol*]
POC	Poculum [*Cup*] [*Pharmacy*]
POC	Point of Care [*Medicine*]
POC	Point of Compliance (FFDE)
POC	Point of Contact (AABC)
poc	Point of Contact (AD)
POC	Policy Oversight Committee [*Library Science*] (TELE)
POC	Porsche Owners Club (EA)
POc	Porte-Oceane [*Record label*] [*France*]
POC	Port of Call
POC	Post Office Corps [*British military*] (DMA)
POC	Post Office Counters Ltd. [*British*]
POC	Post of the Corps
POC	Postoperative Care [*Medicine*]
POC	Postoperative Complication [*Medicine*] (MELL)
POC	Post Oral Ciliary (SAUS)
POC	Postoral Ciliary [*Gland*]
POC	Potential Officer Cadet (WDAA)
POC	Potential Operated Channel (DB)
POC	Power and Clear (SAUS)
POC	Power Control
POC	Power on Clear (MHDI)
POC	Power Oscillator (VLIE)
POC	Precision Oscillator Crystal
POC	Preliminary Operational Capability [*Military*] (AFIT)
POC	Preservation of Capital [*Investment term*]
poc	Principal Operating Component (AD)
POC	Principal Operating Component
POC	Prisoner of Chat (SAUS)
POC	Prisoners of Conscience [*File of persons imprisoned for political or religious beliefs kept by Amnesty International*]
POC	Prison Officer's Club (AD)
poc	Privately Owned Conveyance (AD)
POC	Privately Owned Conveyance [*Army*]
POC	Probability of Chance (MELL)
POC	Procarbazine, Oncovin [*Vincristine*], CCNU [*Lomustine*] [*Antineoplastic drug regimen*]
POC	Proceeding on Course [*Aviation*] (FAAC)
POC	Proceed on Course (SAUS)
POC	Process Operator Console
POC	Processor Outage Control (SAUS)
POC	Procurement Outlook Conference (SAUS)
POC	Productional Operational Capability
POC	Production Office Coordinator (WDMC)
POC	Production Operational Capability
POC	Production Operations Control (TIMI)
POC	Production Order Change (KSC)
POC	Product of Combustion (SAUS)
POC	Products of Combustion (DICI)
POC	Products of Conception [*Medicine*] (MEDA)
POC	Professional Officer Course [*AFROTC*] (AFM)
POC	Program of Cooperation (SAUS)
POC	Program Office Contacts (COE)
POC	Program-Operator Communication [*Computer science*] (DCDG)
POC	Programs of Cooperation (MCD)
POC	Proof of Concept [*Army*]
POC	Proopiocortin [*Biochemistry*]
POC	Public Oil Co. (AD)
Poc	Purchase Order Closeout (NAKS)
POC	Purchase Order Closeout (NASA)
POC	Purchase Order Contract
POC	Purgeable Organic Carbon [*Chemistry*]
POCA	Association of Psychiatric Outpatient Centers of America [*Psychiatric Out patient Centers of America*] [*Acronym is based on former name,*] (EA)
POCA	Pediatric Perioperative Cardiac Arrest (SAUS)
POCA	Petty Officer Caterer [*British military*] (DMA)
POCA	Point of Closet Approach (ACAE)
POCA	Post Office Clerks' Association [*A union*] [*Northern Ireland*]
POCA	Prednisone, Oncovin [*Vincristine*], Cytarabine, Adriamycin [*Antineoplastic drug regimen*]
POCA	Progress Observation and Corrective Action (SAUS)
POCA	Public Offender Counselors Association [*Later, IAAOC*] (EA)
POCAL	Pre-Operational Common Age List
PO Cas	Perry's Oriental Cases [*Bombay*] [*A publication*] (DLA)
POCASEA	Protection of Children Against Sexual Exploitation Act of 1977
POCB	Plain Ol' Country Boy
POCC	Payload Operations Control Center [*NASA*] (NASA)
POCC	Penn Octane [*NASDAQ symbol*] (TTSB)
POCC	Penn Octane Corp. [*NASDAQ symbol*] (SAG)
POCC	Platform Operations Control Center
POCC	Procarbazine, Oncovin [*Vincristine*], Cyclophosphamide, CCNU [*Lomustine*] [*Antineoplastic drug regimen*]
POCC	Program Operation Control Center [*Space science*]
POC Cost	Percentage of Construction Cost (SAUS)
Poc Costs	Pocock on Costs [*1881*] [*A publication*] (DLA)
POCE	Pantone Open Color Environment [*Joint venture between Pantone, Inc. and LightSource Computer Images*] [*Computer science*] (PCM)
POCE	Proof-of-Concept Experiment [*Solar thermal conversion*]
POCEL	Petty Officer Control Electrician [*British military*] (DMA)
POC-ET	Proof of Concept Experimental Testbed (SAUS)

POCET	Proof-of-Concept Experiment Testbed [*Solar thermal conversion*] (MCD)
POC Gland...	Post Oral Ciliary Gland (SAUS)
POCH	Progressiven Organisationen der Schweiz [*Progressive Organizations of Switzerland*] [*Political party*] (PPE)
PochFdl	Pocahontas Federal Savings & Loan Association [*Associated Press*] (SAG)
poci-	Caroline Islands [*MARC geographic area code*] [*Library of Congress*] (LCCP)
POCI	Pontiac-Oakland Club International (EA)
POCI	Precision Optics Corp. [*NASDAQ symbol*] (SAG)
POCI	Precision Optics Mass [*NASDAQ symbol*] (TTSB)
POCIBO.......	Polar Circling Balloon Observatory
POCIL	Pocillum [*Little Cup*] [*Pharmacy*] (ROG)
Pocill	Pocillum [*Little Cup*] [*Pharmacy*]
POCK	Petty Officer Cook [*British military*] (DMA)
pock............	Pocket (AD)
Pocket Bks...	Pocket Books (AD)
POCL	Power on Clear [*Navy Navigation Satellite System*] (DNAB)
POCL	Project Office Change Letter
POCM	Parallel Ocean-Climate Model (SAUS)
POCM	Partido Obrero y Campesino de Mexico [*Mexico*] [*Political party*]
POCM	Postal Contracting Manual [*Postal Service*]
POCN	Purchase Order Change Notice
POCN	Purchase Order Change Number
POCO	European Political Cooperation [*EC*] (ECED)
POCO	Physiology of Chimpanzees in Orbit [*NASA*]
Poco	Politically Correct
POCO	Position Computer (IAA)
POCO	Power On - Clock On [*Aerospace*]
POCO	Power on, Clock on (SAUS)
POCO	Proposed Operational Capability Objective (SAUS)
POCO	Purchase Order Change Order (AAG)
POCO	Purchase Order Close out (SAUS)
POCO	Purchase Order Closeout (AAG)
POCOA........	Post Office Controlling Officers' Association [*A union*] [*British*]
pocp-	Canton and Enderbury Islands [*MARC geographic area code*] [*Library of Congress*] (LCCP)
POC/POT......	Proof of Concept/Proof of Technology (ACAE)
POCR	Processor Oriented Character Recognition (SAUS)
POCR	Program Objectives Change Request [*DoD*]
POCR	Purchase Order Change Request (TIMI)
POCS	Passive Ocean Colour Subsystem (SAUS)
POCS	Patent Office [*later, PTO*] Classification System
POCS	Process Operator Console Support (SAUS)
POCS	Proper Oriented Cut-Set (SAUS)
POCSAG......	Post Office Code Standard Advisory Group (SAUS)
POCSAG.....	Post Office Code Standardization Advisory Group (SAUS)
POCSAG......	Post Office Standardisation Advisory Group (SAUS)
POCSC........	Penn-Ohio Collegiate Swimming Conference (PSS)
POCT	Periodically Oscillating Crystal Temperature (SAUS)
Po Ct	Police Court (DLA)
POCTA	Prevention of Cruelty to Animals Society Member (DSUE)
POCUL	Poculum [*Cup*] [*Pharmacy*] (ROG)
POCV	Proof of Concept Vehicle [*Automotive engineering*]
pocw-..........	Cook Island [*MARC geographic area code*] [*Library of Congress*] (LCCP)
POCW	Park Operations and Capital Works (SAUS)
POCY	Postoperative Chronologic Year (STED)
POD	Pacific Ocean Division [*Army Corps of Engineers*]
pod	Paid on Delivery (AD)
POD	Paper on Demand (SAUS)
POD	Parent Organization Designator (MCD)
POD	Parents of Diabetics
pod	Payable on Death (AD)
POD	Payable on Death [*Insurance*]
POD	Payload Operations Director (SAUS)
POD	Payload Operations Division [*NASA*] (MCD)
POD	Payment on Death (SAUS)
POD	Payment on Delivery (SAUS)
POD	Pay on Delivery [*Shipping*]
POD	Pentoxydase (SAUS)
POD	Period of Disability [*Social Security Administration*] (DHP)
POD	Permissible Operating Distance [*Army*] (AFIT)
POD	Peroxidase [*Also, PO*] [*An enzyme*]
POD	Personal Orientation Dimensions [*Personality development test*] [*Psychology*]
POD	Piece of Data [*Computer science*] (NHD)
POD	Pin-on-Disk (SAUS)
POD	Place of Death (MAE)
POD	Place of Debarkation (SAUS)
POD	Place of Delivery [*Shipping*] (DS)
POD	Place of Discharge
POD	Place of Disembarkation (SAUS)
POD	Plain Old Document (SAUS)
POD	Plain Old Documentation (SAUS)
POD	Plain Old Dos (SAUS)
POD	Planet of Death (SAUS)
POD	Planning and Organization Development (SAUS)
POD	Plan of the Day
POD	Pneumatically Operated Disconnect (KSC)
POD	Pocket Oxford Dictionary [*A publication*]
POD	Podbielniak Analysis (SAUS)
POD Gland...	Podiatry (DAVI)
POD	Podkamennaya [*Former USSR*] [*Geomagnetic observatory code*]

POD	Podor [*Senegal*] [*Airport symbol*] (OAG)
POD	Point of Departure
POD	Point of Discharge (GFGA)
POD	Point of Distribution (SAUS)
POD	Point of Origin Device (SAUS)
pod	Point-of-Origin Device (AD)
POD	Point-of-Origin Device (IEEE)
POD	Points of Domination [*Military*]
POD	Polycystic Ovarian Disease [*Medicine*]
pod	Port of Debarkation (AD)
POD	Port of Debarkation [*Military*]
POD	Port of Delivery [*Shipping*]
pod	Port of Departure (AD)
POD	Port of Destination [*MARAD*] (TAG)
POD	Port of Discharge [*Navy*]
POD	Port of Disembarkation (SAUS)
POD	Postobstructive Diuresis [*Medicine*] (MELL)
POD	Post of Duty
POD	Post Office Department [*Later, United States Postal Service*]
POD	Post Office Directory
POD	Postoperative Day [*Medicine*]
POD	Potential Ozone Depleter
POD	Pounds-Out-the-Door [*Measure of industrial production*]
POD	Power of Deduction (SAUS)
POD	Power on Diagnostics (SAUS)
POD	Precise Orbit Determination (SAUS)
POD	Precision Orbit Determination (MCD)
POD	Precision Orbit Determination Experiment (SAUS)
POD	Preflight Operation Division [*NASA*]
POD	Preflight Operations Division
POD	Preliminary Orbit Determination (IGSL)
POD	Price on Delivery (EBF)
POD	Printing on Demand (SAUS)
POD	Print on Demand (SAUS)
POD	Private Orientation Device (ACAE)
POD	Probability of Damage (ACAE)
POD	Probability of Detect (SAUS)
pod	Probability of Detection (AD)
POD	Probability of Detection (USDC)
POD	Probability of Detention (SAUS)
pod	Process-Oriented Design (AD)
POD	Products Operations Division (ACAE)
POD	Professional and Organizational Development [*In association name Professional and Organizational Development Network in Higher Education*] (EA)
POD	Programmable Option Devices (SAUS)
POD	Programmed Operational Date (AFIT)
POD	Program Objectives Document (AAGC)
POD	Program Office Directive
POD	Program Operation Description
POD	Project Operations Director (BARN)
POD	Project Organization Demographic (SAUS)
POD	Proof of Debt [*Business term*] (DCTA)
POD	Proof of Delivery [*Shipping*] (DS)
POD	Proof of Deposit [*Banking*]
POD	Proof of Design (MCD)
POD	Proposed Operational Dates (SAUS)
POD	Prosthetics and Orthotics Database [*University of Strathclyde*] [*Glasgow, Scotland*] [*Information service or system*] (IID)
POD	Protective Oceanic Device
POD	Proton Omnidirectional Detector (USDC)
POD	Proximity Optical Device (NASA)
POD	Publishing On Demand (SAUS)
POD	Pulse Omission Detector (MCD)
POD	Purchase Order Deviation (KSC)
PO'd............	Put Out [*i.e., angry*] [*Bowdlerized version*]
PODA..........	Piloting of Office Documentation Architecture (NITA)
PODA..........	Piloting of Orientated Demand Assignment (SAUS)
PODA..........	Priority Oriented Demand Assignment [*Computer science*] [*Telecommunications*]
PODA..........	Priority-Oriented Demand Assignment (SAUS)
PODAF........	Post Operation Data Analysis Facility
PODAF........	Power Density, Assigned Frequency Band (SAUS)
PODAF........	Power Density Exceeding a Specified Level over an Area with an Assigned Frequency Band (IEEE)
PoDAG........	Polar DAAC [*Distributed Active Archive Center*] Advisory Group [*Marine science*] (OSRA)
PODAPS......	Portable Data Processing System
PODAS.......	Portable Data Acquisition System
PODBCA......	Post Office Department Board of Contract Appeals (AFIT)
PODCC........	Plan, Organize, Direct, Coordinate, Control [*Principles of management*]
POD/CL.......	Probability of Detection/Confidence Level (SAUS)
Pod D	Doctor of Podiatry
PODE	Pacific Ocean Division Engineers (CINC)
PODEM........	Path Oriented Decision Making (SAUS)
podex..........	Photographic Exercise (AD)
PODF...........	Post of Duty File
PODI	Print On Demand Initiative (SAUS)
podia	Podiatrist (AD)
PODIA	Podiatry (SAUS)
PODIM.........	Poseidon Design Information Memo [*Missiles*]
PODM..........	Preliminary Orbit Determination Method [*Computer*] [*NASA*]
PODM Computer...	Preliminary Orbit Determination Method Computer (SAUS)
POD Mods ...	Power on Demand Modules (SAUS)

POD Network... Professional and Organizational Development Network in Higher Education (NTPA)
PODO Profit on Day One [*Classification for new newspaper*]
PODR Pixel Order (SAUS)
PODRS Patent Office [*later, PTO*] Data Retrieval System [*Department of Commerce*]
PODS Parents of Children with Down Syndrome [*An association*] (EA)
PODS Parents of Down's Syndrome (EA)
PODS Perceptions of Developmental Skills Profile [*Education*] (EDAC)
PODS Pilot Ocean Data System (MCD)
PODS Portable Data Store [*Computer science*] (PDAA)
PODS Portable Digitiser Subsystem (SAUS)
PODS Post Operative Destruct System (SAUS)
PODS Postoperative Destruct System (MCD)
PODS Precise Orbit Determination System (SAUS)
PODSC Parents of Down's Syndrome Children (EA)
PODUC Provided [*Following Named*] Officers Have Not Departed Your Command [*Amend Assignment Instructions as Indicated*] [*Army*] (AABC)
PODx Postoperative Diagnosis [*Medicine*]
PODx Preoperative Diagnosis [*Medicine*]
POE Fort Polk [*Louisiana*] [*Airport symbol*] (OAG)
POE Fort Polk, LA [*Location identifier*] [*FAA*] (FAAL)
POE Pacific Orient Express (WDAA)
POE Panel on the Environment [*of President's Science Advisory Committee*]
POE Payment Option Election (MCD)
POE Peace on Earth [*Australia*] [*Political party*]
POE Pediatric Orthopedic Examination (MELL)
POE People of the Earth [*Also, RAN*] (EA)
POE Petroleum Operations Engineer (SAUS)
POE Pilot Operational Equipment (MCD)
POE Place of Embarkation (SAUS)
POE Plank-on-Edge
POE Pneumatically Operated Equipment (AAG)
POE Point of Entry [*Accounts*]
POE Point of Exposure [*Environmental Protection Agency*] (ERG)
POE Points of Entry (SAUS)
POE Polyexethylene (SAUS)
POE Polyolefin Elastomers [*Plastics*]
poe Polyoxyethylene (AD)
POE Polyoxyethylene [*Organic chemistry*]
POE Port of Embarkation (DFIT)
POE Port of Entry [*Shipping*]
POE Post-Occupancy Evaluation
POE Post-Operations Evaluation (MCD)
POE Postoperative Endophthalmitis [*Ophthalmology*]
POE Postoperative Exercise [*Medicine*] (DAVI)
POE Power Open Environment [*Computer science*]
POE Predicted Operational Environment [*Military*] (CAAL)
POE Pretesting Orientation Exercises [*US Employment Service*] [*Department of Labor*]
POE Primary Organization Element (NOAA)
POE Print Out Effect
POE Program Office Estimate (SAUS)
POE Projected Operational Environment (NVT)
POE Proof of Eligibility [*Medicine*] (DMAA)
POE Property Owning Expenses (SAUS)
POE Pull-Over Enrichment [*Automotive engineering*]
POE Pulsar Energy/Resources [*Vancouver Stock Exchange symbol*]
POE Pulse Oriented Electrophoresis [*Analytical biochemistry*]
poea- Easter Island [*MARC geographic area code*] [*Library of Congress*] (LCCP)
POEA Philippines Overseas Employment Administration (PDAA)
POEA Protection of Offshore Energy Assets [*Navy*] (NVT)
P/OEA3 Probationary Ordnance Electrical Artificer 3rd Class [*British military*] (DMA)
POEAS Planetary Orbiter Error Analysis Study Program
POE Buoy Plank on Edge Buoy (SAUS)
poe buoy Plank-on-Edge Buoy (AD)
PoeBwn Poe & Brown [*Commercial firm*] [*Associated Press*] (SAG)
poecrit Poetry Criticism (AD)
POED Post Office Engineering Department (IAA)
POED Program Organization for Evaluation and Decision
POED Provincial Officer of Establishment Division (SAUS)
PO'ed Put Out [*i.e., angry*] [*Bowdlerized version*]
POEE Post Office Electrical Engineer (IAA)
POEEJ Post Office Electrical Engineers Journal (SAUS)
POEER Pacific Oceanographic Equipment Evaluation Range (NOAA)
POEF Post Office Engineering Federation [*A union*] [*British*]
POEIT Provisional Organization for European Inland Transportation [*World War II*]
POEL(A) Petty Officer Electrician (Air) [*British military*] (DMA)
POEL(AW) Petty Officer Electrician (Air Weapon) [*British military*] (DMA)
POEM Physical Oceanography of the Eastern Mediterranean (SAUS)
POEM Polar-Orbit Earth Observation Mission (SAUS)
POEM Polar Orbiting Earth Mission (SAUS)
POEM Polar-Orbiting Earth Mission [*European Space Agency*] (EOSA)
POEM Polar Orbiting Earth Monitoring (SAUS)
POEM Polar Orbiting Earth-Observation Mission (SAUS)
POEM Portable Object-oriented Entity Manager (SAUS)
POEM Procedure for Optimizing Elastomeric Mountings (SAUS)
POEMs Patient Oriented Evidence that Matters (SAUS)

POEMS Plasma Cell Dyscracia with Polyneuropathy, Organomegaly, Endocrinopathy, Monoclonal Protein [*M-protein*], Skin changes [*Medicine*] (DAVI)
POEMS Platinum Open Enterprise Management System (SAUS)
POEMS Polyneuropathy Associated with Organomegaly Endocrine Disorders, Myeloma, and Skin Modifications
POEMS Polyoxyethylene Monostearate [*Organic chemistry*]
POEMS Positron Electron Magnetic Spectrometer (EOSA)
POEMS Postoperative Expert Medical System (IDAI)
PO Engine Port Outer Engine (SAUS)
POENIT Poenitentia [*Penance*] [*Latin*] (ADA)
POEOP Polyoxyethylene Oxypropylene (SAUS)
POEOP Polyoxyethyleneoxypropylene [*Organic chemistry*]
POEP Primary Operand Execution Pipeline (SAUS)
Poe PI Poe on Pleading and Practice [*A publication*] (DLA)
POERS Post Office Engineering Research Station (SAUS)
POES Polar Operational Environmental Satellite (USDC)
POES Polar Orbiting Environmental Satellite
POES Polar-Orbiting Operational Environmental Satellite (USDC)
POESID Position of Earth Satellite in Digital Display (MCD)
POE STEARATE... Polyoxyethylene Stearate (SAUS)
Poet De Poetis [*of Suetonius*] [*Classical studies*] (OCD)
POET Partially Overlapped Echo Cancelled Transmission (SAUS)
POET Persistent Objects and Extended Database Technology (SAUS)
POET Petty Officer Enroute Training [*Navy*] (NVT)
Poet Poetica [*of Aristotle*] [*Classical studies*] (OCD)
poet Poetical (AD)
Poet Poetry [*A publication*] (BRI)
POET Portable Optic-Electronic Tracker (PDAA)
POET Portable Orders Entry Terminal (IAA)
POET Primed Oscillator Expendable Transponder [*Military*] (CAAL)
POET Psychological Operations Exploitation Team [*Vietnam*]
POET Pulse Oximeter/End Tidal [*Carbon Dioxide*] [*Medicine*] (DAVI)
Poetics T Poetics Today [*A publication*] (BRI)
Poet Mel Gr... Poetae Melici Graeci [*A publication*] (OCD)
POETRI Programme on Exchange and Transfer of Information on Community Water Supply and Sanitation [*International Reference Center for Community Water Supply and Sanitation*] [*Information service or system*] (IID)
POETRI Program on Exchange and Transfer of Information (SAUS)
Poet Rom Vet... Poetarum Romanorum Veterum Reliquiae [*A publication*] (OCD)
POETS Phooey on Everything, Tomorrow's Saturday [*Bowdlerized version*]
POETS Product Operations Estimating Techniques System (ACAE)
POETS Push Off Early, Tomorrow's Saturday [*Bowdlerized version*]
POEU Post Office Engineering Union [*British*]
POEU Post Office Engineers Union (SAUS)
POEW Protracted Offensive Electronic Warfare [*Military*] (SEWL)
POF American Jurisprudence Proof of Facts [*A publication*]
POF Pakistan Ordnance Factories (SAUS)
POF Parts Order Form
POF Philharmonic Orchestra of Florida (AD)
POF Physician's Order Form (MELL)
PoF Physics of Failure [*Program*]
POF Pillar of Fire Church (IIA)
POF Pinhole Occulter Facility (SSD)
POF Planned Outage Factor [*Electronics*] (IEEE)
POF Plastic Optical Fiber [*Automotive electronics*]
pof Please Omit Flowers (AD)
POF Point of Failure (SAUS)
POF Point-of-Failure [*Computer science*] (IBMDP)
POF Police Officer, Female
POF Polymer Optical Fiber [*Telecommunications*]
POF Poplar Bluff [*Missouri*] [*Airport symbol*] (OAG)
POF Poplar Bluff, MO [*Location identifier*] [*FAA*] (FAAL)
POF Positive Opening Fin (MCD)
POF Postovulatory Follicle [*Endocrinology*]
POF Powder on Foil (SAUS)
POF Premature Ovarian Failure [*Medicine*]
POF Primary Ovarian Failure [*Gynecology*] (DMAA)
POF Priority of Fire [*Military*] (INF)
POF Privately Owned Firearm (MCD)
POF Programmed Operator Facility [*Computer science*] (ELAL)
POF Prolific Resources [*Vancouver Stock Exchange symbol*]
POF Pulsed Optical Feedback (SAUS)
POF Pyruvate Oxidation Factor [*Biochemistry*]
P of A Point of Assembly (SAUS)
P of A Pott of Anchorage (SAUS)
POFA Programmed Operational and Functional Appraisals (SAUS)
POFA Programmed Operational Functional Appraisal [*Navy*]
POFA/IPOFA... Programmed Operational Functional Appraisal/Integrated Programmed Operational Functional Appraisal (SAUS)
PofB Ponies of Britain [*An association*] (DBA)
P of D Point of Debarkation (SAUS)
P of E Portal of Entry [*Bacteriology*]
P of E Port of Embarkation [*Military*]
PofE Port of Entry [*Immigration*] (DAVI)
POFF Peripheral Online Oriented Function (SAUS)
POFF Computer... Peripheral Online Oriented Function Computer (SAUS)
P of GP Pearl of Great Price (SAUS)
P of H Patron of Husbandry
POFI Pacific Ocean Fisheries Investigations (SAUS)
POFI Pacific Oceanic Fisheries Investigations (NOAA)
POFI Pacific Oceanographic Fisheries Investigation (SAUS)
pofj- Fiji [*MARC geographic area code*] [*Library of Congress*] (LCCP)
P of L Port of London (ROG)

P of O......... Point of Origin (SAUS)
POFOOGUSA... Protection of Foreign Officials and Official Guests of the United States Act
pofp............. French Polynesia [MARC geographic area code] [Library of Congress] (LCCP)
PO-FY......... Program Objectives for Fiscal Year (DNAB)
POG............ Pacific Oceanographic Group [British Columbia] (AD)
POG............ Parents of Gays (EA)
POG............ Patina Oil & Gas [NYSE symbol] (TTSB)
POG............ Pediatric Oncology Group
POG............ Petty Officer's Guide [A publication] [Navy]
POG............ Piping Instrumentation and Operating Gallery [Nuclear energy] (NRCH)
POG............ Plant Operating Guide (DNAB)
Pog............. Pogonion (DMAA)
POG............ Polyexethylene Glycol (SAUS)
POG............ Polymyositis Ossificans Generalisata (DB)
POG............ Polyoxethylene Glycol (SAUS)
POG............ Port Gentil [Gabon] [Airport symbol] (OAG)
POG............ Position of Germany [British] [World War II]
POG............ Post Office Guide [Book of regulations] [British]
POG............ Project Officer's Group
POG............ Propulsion Operating Guide (DNAB)
POG............ Provisional Ordnance Group [Military]
POG............ Psychological Operations Group (DOMA)
POG.WS....... Patina Oil & Gas Wrrt [NYSE symbol] (TTSB)
POGASIS...... Planetary Observation Geometry and Science Instrument Sequence Program [Aerospace]
POGaz......... Post Office Gazette [British] [A publication] (DCTA)
POGE........... Planning Operational Gaming Experiment [Game]
pogg-.......... Galapagos Islands [MARC geographic area code] [Library of Congress] (LCCP)
pogn-.......... Gilbert and Ellice Islands [Tuvalu] [MARC geographic area code] [Library of Congress] (LCCP)
POGO.......... Pennzoil Offshore Gas Operators (AD)
POGO.......... Personal Objectives and Goals (SAUS)
Pogo........... Pogonomyrinex Occidentalis [A genus of ants]
POGO.......... Pogo Suppression System [NASA]
POGO.......... Polar Orbit Geophysical Observatory (SAUS)
POGO.......... Polar Orbiting Geophysical Observatories [Marine science] (OSRA)
POGO.......... Polar Orbiting Geophysical Observatory [NASA]
POGO.......... Polar Orbiting Geophysical Obsevvatories (or Observatory) (SAUS)
POGO.......... Pop Your Seat Belt, Open the Window, Get Out [Automobile safety]
POGO.......... Pre-Oxidation Gettering of the Other Side (PDAA)
POGO.......... Prime's Online Graduate Opportunities (NITA)
POGO.......... Privately Owned/Government Operated (GFGA)
POGO.......... Privately-Owned/Government-Operated (SAUS)
POGO.......... Problem-Oriented Graphics Operation (SAUS)
POGO.......... Programmer-Oriented Graphics Operation (IEEE)
POGO.......... Program Optimizer (IAA)
POGO.......... Project on Government Oversight (EA)
PogoPd........ Pogo Producing Co. [Associated Press] (SAG)
POGPr.......... Patina Oil & Gas 7.125% Pfd [NYSE symbol] (TTSB)
POGR.......... Poplar Grove National Cemetery
POGS.......... National Association of Post Office and General Service Maintenance Employees [Later, APWU] [AFL-CIO]
POGS........... Polar Orbiting Geomagnetic Satellite (SAUS)
POGSI......... Policy Group on Scientific Information [Marine science] (MSC)
POGT.......... Power-Operated Gun Turret
pogu-.......... Guam [MARC geographic area code] [Library of Congress] (LCCP)
pOH............ Alkalinity Factor (SAUS)
pOH............ Hydroxyl Concentration [Organic chemistry] (MAE)
POH............ Path Overhead [Telecommunications] (ITD)
POH............ Path Section Overhead (SAUS)
POH............ Personal Oral Hygiene (MELL)
POH............ Pilot's Operating Handbook [Aviation] (DA)
POH............ Placed off Hire
POH............ Planned Outage Hours [Electronics] (IEEE)
POH............ Pocahontas, IA [Location identifier] [FAA] (FAAL)
Poh............ Pohang (AD)
POH............ Power-On Hours (ELAL)
POH............ Pull-Out Harness
poh............ Pull Out of Hole (AD)
POHA.......... Preoperative Holding Area [Medicine] (MELL)
Pohang........ Pohang Iron & Steel Co., Ltd. [Associated Press] (SAG)
POHC.......... Principal Organic Hazardous Constituent [Environmental chemistry]
POHI........... Physically or Otherwise Health Impaired
POHM.......... Page-Oriented Holograph Memory [Computer science]
POHMA........ Project for the Oral History of Music in America
POHS.......... Presumed Ocular Histoplasmosis Syndrome [Ophthalmology]
POHWARO... Pulsated, Overheated, Water Rocket [Swiss space rocket]
POI............. Parking Orbit Injection [NASA]
POI............. Parking Orbit Inspection [NASA]
POI............. Parti Oubanguien de l'Independance [Ubangi Independence Party] [Political party]
POI............. Path Overhead Identifier (SAUS)
POI............. Path Overhead Indicator (MLOA)
POI............. Period of Interest (MCD)
POI............. Personal Orientation Inventory [Psychology]
POI............. Personal Outlook Inventory [Employment test]
POI............. Pilkington Optronics Inc. (SAUS)
POI............. Plan of Instruction
POI............. Point of Impact
POI............. Point of Information (SAUS)
POI............. Point of Interaction (SAUS)

POI............. Point of Interception (GNE)
POI............. Point of Interface [Telecommunications]
POI............. Poison
POI............. Post-Ignition
POI............. Postoperative Instructions [Medicine] (MELL)
POI............. Potosi [Bolivia] [Airport symbol] (AD)
POI............. Pre-Overhaul Inspection (MCD)
POI............. Pressure-Operated Initiator (MCD)
POI............. Probability Of Intercept (LAIN)
POI............. Product of Inertia (MCD)
POI............. Program Operator Interface [Computer science] (ELAL)
POI............. Proof of Illness (MELL)
POI............. Public Office of Information (MCD)
POI............. Purchase Order Item (KSC)
POIC........... Payload Operations Integration Centre (SAUS)
POIC........... Petty Officer in Charge [Navy] (NVT)
POIC........... Poly(octyl Isocyanate) [Organic chemistry]
POID........... Post Office Investigation/Intelligence Department [British] (DI)
POIDRT....... Poison Dart (SAUS)
POIF.......... Plan Organization Index File [IRS]
POIG.......... Pairwise Implication Path (SAUS)
poik........... Poikilocyte [or Poikilocytosis] [Medicine] (MAE)
POIL.......... Power Density Imbalance Limit (IAA)
POINT......... Paraplegics on Independent Nature Trails, Dallas (SAUS)
POINT......... Pasadena Online Information Network [Pasadena Public Library] (OLDSS)
POINT......... Performance Oriented Integrated Technology (SAUS)
POINT......... Point [Commonly used] (OPSA)
Point.......... Point of Air (SAUS)
Point.......... Point of Arena (SAUS)
Point.......... Point of Conception (SAUS)
Point.......... Point of Fortin (SAUS)
Point.......... Point of Harbor (SAUS)
Point.......... Point of Lookout (SAUS)
Point.......... Point of Pleasant (SAUS)
POINT......... Pursuing Our Italian Names Together (EA)
POINTER...... Particle Orientation Interferometer [ASD]
POINTER...... Pre-University Orbital Information Tracker Equipment and Recorder (PDAA)
POINTERM... Appointment Will Be Regarded as Having Terminated upon This Date
PoinTIS........ Point of Care, Team Information System (SAUS)
Point Loma C... Point Loma Nazarene College (GAGS)
POINTMAIL... Letter Appointment in Mail
POINTS........ Points [Commonly used] (OPSA)
POINTS........ Precision Optical Interferometer in Space (SAUS)
POIP .... Potential Offender Identification Program
POIPCD........ Patent Office and Industrial Property and Copyright Department [British]
POIQT .... Performance-Oriented Infantry Qualification Test (INF)
POIR .... Project Officers Interim Report [Air Force] (MCD)
POIS .... Parkland On-Line Information Systems [Computer science] (DMAA)
POIS .... Poison (AAMN)
pois .... Poison (AD)
POIS .... Poisoning [FBI standardized term]
POIS .... Polish Osteogenesis Imperfecta Society (SAUS)
POIS .... Post Office Insurance Society [British] (DI)
POIS .... Procurement Operations and Information System (SAUS)
POIS .... Procurement Operations Information System (MCD)
POIS .... Prototype On-Line Instrument System [Computer science] (NRCH)
POIS .... Purchase Order Information System (MCD)
POISE......... Panel on Inflight Scientific Experiments [NASA]
POISE......... Photosynthetic Oxygenation Illuminated by Solar Energy
POISE......... Pointing & Stabilisation platform Experiment (SAUS)
POISE......... Pointing and Stabilization Platform Element [Army] (MCD)
POISE......... Practice-Oriented Information System Experiment (SAUS)
POISE......... Preoperational Inspection Services Engineering (IAA)
POIT........... Power of Influence Test [Psychology]
POIT........... Power-of-Influence Test (SAUS)
POJ............ Patent Office Journal [India] [A publication] (DLA)
POJ............ Selma, AL [Location identifier] [FAA] (FAAL)
poji-........... Johnston Atoll [MARC geographic area code] [Library of Congress] (LCCP)
PoK............ Pakistan-occupied Kashmir (SAUS)
POK............ Power on Okey Signal (SAUS)
POK............ Sacramento, CA [Location identifier] [FAA] (FAAL)
Pokeman ..... Pocket Monsters [Nintendo Co., Ltd.]
poki-........... Kermadec Islands [MARC geographic area code] [Library of Congress] (LCCP)
POKMV .... Pokeweed Mosaic Virus [Plant pathology]
POL............ Pacific Oceanographic Laboratories [Later, Pacific Marine Environmental Laboratory]
POL............ Pacific Oceanographic Laboratory (SAUS)
POL............ Pacific Oceanography Laboratories (SAUS)
POL............ Pair Orthogonalized Lowdin [Physics]
POL............ Parents of Large Families
POL............ Pastoral Occupation Licence (SAUS)
POL............ Patent Office Library (AD)
POL............ Paul Otchakovsky-Laurens [Publishing imprint, named for imprint editor]
POL............ Pemba [Mozambique] [Airport symbol] (OAG)
POL............ Petroleum, Oil, and Lubricants [Military]
pol............ Petroleum-Oil-and-Lubricants (AD)
POL............ Petroleum, Oil and Lubrication (or Lubricants) (SAUS)
POL............ Philips Optical Language (IAA)
POL............ Physician-Owned Laboratory (HCT)

POL............	Physician's Office laboratory
POL............	Physicians Online (SAUS)
POL............	Point of Learning (SAUS)
POL............	Pola [*Yugoslavia*] [*Seismograph station code, US Geological Survey*] [*Closed*] (SEIS)
POL............	Polacca [*Ship's rigging*] (ROG)
POL............	Poland [*ANSI three-letter standard code*] (CNC)
Pol............	Poland (VRA)
pol............	Polar (AD)
POL............	Polar International Airlines, Inc. [*ICAO designator*] (FAAC)
POL............	Polarity [*or Polarize*] (KSC)
POL............	Polarization (SEWL)
Pol............	Polen [*Poland*] [*Norwegian*] (AD)
Pol............	Police (WDAA)
POL............	Police
POL............	Policy
POL............	Policy Division (SAUS)
POL............	Policy Office (SAUS)
POL............	Polish (AAG)
Pol............	Polish (BEE)
pol............	Polish [*MARC language code*] [*Library of Congress*] (LCCP)
pol............	Polished (VRA)
POL............	Polish Ocean Lines (AD)
pol............	Polite (SHCU)
POL............	Polite
Pol............	Politica [*of Aristotle*] [*Classical studies*] (OCD)
POL............	Political
POL............	Political Prisoner (SAUS)
POL............	Political Section [*Foreign service*]
pol............	Politician (NTIO)
POL............	Politician
POL............	Politics On-Line (SAUS)
Pol............	Pollexfen's English King's Bench Reports [*1669-85*] [*A publication*] (DLA)
POL............	Polling (IAA)
POL............	Pollution
POL............	Polonium [*Chemical symbol is Po*] (AAG)
Pol............	Polydor & Deutsche Grammophon [*Record label*] [*Germany, Europe, etc.*]
POL............	Polygram [*Publisher*]
POL............	Polymerase [*An enzyme*]
Pol............	Polyphon [*Record label*] [*Denmark, etc.*]
POL............	Polytranslation Analysis and Programming (SAUS)
POL............	Porto Amelia [*Mozambique*] [*Airport symbol*] (AD)
POL............	Port of Loading [*Shipping*]
POL............	Possession-Only License (GOBB)
POL............	Posterior Oblique Ligaments [*Medicine*]
POL............	Power Optimized Logic (SAUS)
POL............	Practical Quantification Limit [*Metallurgy*]
POL............	Premature Onset of Labor [*Obstetrics*] (DAVI)
pol............	Problem-Oriented Language (AD)
POL............	Problem-Oriented Language [*Computer science*]
POL............	Procedure Oriented Language (SAUS)
POL............	Procedure-Oriented Language [*Computer science*]
POL............	Process Oriented Language (SAUS)
POL............	Process-Oriented Language [*Computer science*] (IEEE)
POL............	Program Oriented Language [*Computer science*] (ECII)
POL............	Proudman Oceanographic Laboratory [*UK*] [*Marine science*] (OSRA)
POL............	Provisional Operating License [*for nuclear power plant*]
POL............	Public Opinion Laboratory [*Northern Illinois University*] [*Research center*] (RCD)
p-ola..........	Payola (AD)
POLA..........	Pointable Optical Linear Array (SAUS)
POLA..........	Polymerase Alpha (DMAA)
POLA..........	Port of London Authority [*England*] (WDAA)
POLA..........	Project on Linguistic Analysis
POLA..........	Prostitutes of Los Angeles [*An association*] (AD)
PolAb..........	Pollution Abstracts
POLAC.........	Problem-Oriented Language for Analytical Chemistry [*Computer science*] (PDAA)
POLACAP.....	Port of London Authority Combined Accident Procedure (SAUS)
Pol Ad	Political Adviser (AD)
polad..........	Political Adviser (AD)
POLAD........	Political Adviser
Polam LJ......	Polamerican Law Journal [*A publication*] (DLA)
polang........	Polarization Angle (AD)
POLANG.......	Polarization Angle [*Telecommunications*]
Polar..........	Global Geospace Science Polar Spacecraft (SAUS)
POLAR	International Solar Terrestrial Physics Program (SAUS)
polar..........	Polarity (AD)
POLAR	Polarity [*or Polarize*] (IAA)
POLAR	Polarize (SAUS)
POLAR	Polar Plasma Laboratory (ADWA)
POLAR	Production Order Locating and Reports (SAUS)
POLAR	Production Order Location and Reporting [*NASA*] (NASA)
POLAR	Projected Operational Logistics Analysis Requirements
Polar BEAR...	Polar Beacon Experiments and Auroral Research (AD)
PolarE........	Polar Express Corp. [*Associated Press*] (SAG)
POLARIS......	Fleet Ballistic Missile Weapons System (SAUS)
POLARIS......	Photochemistry of Ozone Loss in Arctic Region in Summer (SAUS)
Polaris........	Polaris Industries, Inc. [*Associated Press*] (SAG)
POLARIS......	Polar-Motion Analysis by Radio Interferometric Surveying [*Geodetic measuring facilities*]
POLARIS......	Princeton On-Line Accelerator Isotope Separator (SAUS)
Polaroid.......	Polaroid Corp. [*Associated Press*] (SAG)

PolarPAC	Polar Public Access Catalog (SAUS)
Polar Res	Polar Research (SAUS)
POLARS.......	Pathology On-Line Logging and Reporting System [*Computer science*] (PDAA)
POLARSCAT...	Polarimetric Scatterometer (SAUS)
POLAT	Polar Atlantic (SAUS)
POL BKM	Polished Buckram (DGA)
POLC	Petty Officers Leadership Course (SAUS)
Pol C	Political Code [*A publication*] (DLA)
POLCAP......	Petroleum Capability (SAUS)
POLCAP......	Petroleum, Oils, and Lubricants Capabilities (MCD)
POLCATS	Pollution Characterization by Absorption on Spectroscopy (SSD)
POLCO......	Polar Continental (SAUS)
POLCOD......	Police Code [*INTERPOL*]
Pol Code.....	Political Code [*A publication*] (DLA)
Pol Col	Police College (AD)
Pol Com	Police Commissaire [*Interpol*] [*British*] (AD)
Pol Com	Police Commissioner (AD)
pol com	Political Committee (AD)
Pol Cont	Pollock on Contracts [*A publication*] (DLA)
polcrit.........	Political Critic (AD)
POLD	Professional and Occupational Licensing Directory [*A publication*]
POLDAM......	POL [*Petroleum, Oil, and Lubricants*] Installations Damage Report (NATG)
poldamr.......	Petroleum, Oil, and Lubrication Installation Damage Report (AD)
POLDAMR.....	Petroleum, Oil and Lubrication Installations Damage Report (SAUS)
POLDER......	Polarization and Directionality of Earth Reflectances (SAUS)
POLDER......	Polarization and Directionality of the Earth's Reflectances [*Instrumentation*]
Pol Dig Part...	Pollock's Digest of the Laws of Partnership [*A publication*] (DLA)
POLDPS.......	Pioneer Off-Line Data-Processing System [*NASA*]
POLE..........	Point-of-Last-Environment [*Computer science*] (IBMDP)
POLE..........	Polar Ozone Lidar Experiment (SAUS)
POLE..........	Prednisolone, Oncovin [*Vicristine*], L-Asparaginase [*Antineoplastic drug regimen*] (DAVI)
POLE..........	Public Opinion Logical Expectation (SAUS)
POL/ECO......	Political/Economic Section [*Foreign service*]
pol econ	Political Economy (AD)
polem.........	Polemic (AD)
polem.........	polemicist (SAUS)
polem.........	polemicize (SAUS)
Pol Endocrinol...	Polish Endocrinology (SAUS)
Pol Eng.......	Polish Engineering (SAUS)
POLES	Polar Exchange at the Sea Surface (EOSA)
POLEX	Polar Experiment
POLEX	Political Exercise [*International relations game*]
POLEX-NORTH...	Polar Experiment in the Northern Hemisphere (MSC)
POLEX-SOUTH...	Polar Experiment in the Southern Hemisphere (MSC)
polf............	Parents of Large Families (AD)
POLF..........	Parents of Large Families
Pol Fed........	Police Federation [*London*] (AD)
Pol Fedn Newsl...	Police Federation Newsletter [*A publication*] (DLA)
POLFER.......	Polizia Ferroviaria [*Railroad Police*] [*Italian*] (AD)
Pol Found....	Police Foundation [*Washington, D.C.*] (AD)
POLGEN.......	Problem-Oriented Language Generator [*Computer science*] (BUR)
poli...........	Politician (AD)
POLIC	Petroleum Intersectional Command [*Army*] (AABC)
Police Fedn Newsl...	Police Federation Newsletter [*A publication*] (ILCA)
Police J Ct...	Police Justice's Court [*A publication*] (ILCA)
Police LQ....	Police Law Quarterly [*A publication*] (ILCA)
pol ind........	Pollen Index (AD)
POL IND	Pollen Index (WDAA)
pol in the pen...	Politician in the Penitentiary (AD)
Pol in the Pen...	Politician in the Penitentiaty (SAUS)
polio..........	Poliomyelitis [*Medicine*] (AD)
POLIO	Poliomyelitis [*Medicine*]
POLIS	Parliamentary On-Line Information System [*House of Commons Library*] [*Bibliographic database*] [*Information service or system*] [*British*] (IID)
POLIS	Parliamentary Online Library Study (SAUS)
POLIS.........	Petroleum Intersectional Service [*Army*]
POLIS	Political Institutions Simulation [*Game*]
POLIS	Polynomial Interpreting System (SAUS)
POLISARIO...	Popular Front for the Liberation of Saguiet el Hamra and Rio de Oro [*Morocco*]
poli sci	Political Science
PolishTel	Polish Telephones & Microwave Corp. [*Associated Press*] (SAG)
polit...........	Political (AD)
POLIT.........	Political (EY)
Polit...........	Political (TBD)
polit...........	Politics (WDAA)
Polit...........	Politics [*A publication*]
POLITBUREAU...	Political Bureau [*of USSR*]
POLITBURO...	Politicheskoe Byuro [*Political Bureau of USSR*]
Politburo......	Politicheskoe Byuro [*Political Bureau of the Central Committee*] [*Russian*] (AD)
Pol J..........	Police Journal [*A publication*] (ILCA)
POLK	Polk Audio [*NASDAQ symbol*] (TTSB)
POLK	Polk Audio, Inc. [*Baltimore, MD*] [*NASDAQ symbol*] (NQ)
POLKA	Periodical On-Line Keyword Access [*Computer science*] (PDAA)
POLKA	Petroleum, Oil and Lubricants out-of-Kilter Algorithm (SAUS)
PolkAu	Polk Audio, Inc. [*Associated Press*] (SAG)
PolkAud	Polk Audio [*Associated Press*] (SAG)
POLK of A....	Polka Lovers Klub of America (EA)

Poll............. Pollack's Ohio Unreported Judicial Decisions Prior to 1823 [*A publication*] (ILCA)
POLL............ Pollex [*An Inch*] [*Pharmacy*]
Poll............. Pollexfen's English King's Bench Reports [*1669-85*] [*A publication*] (ILCA)
poll............. Pollution (AD)
POLL............ Public Opinion Location Library [*The Roper Center for Public Opinion Research*] [*Information service or system*] (CRD)
POL/LAB...... Political and Labor Section [*Foreign service*]
Pol Law of Nat... Polson's Law of Nations [*1848*] [*A publication*] (DLA)
Poll CC Pr ... Pollock's Practice of the County Courts [*A publication*] (ILCA)
Poll Contr Guide... Pollution Control Guide [*A publication*] (DLA)
Pollex.......... Pollexfen's English King's Bench Reports [*1669-85*] [*A publication*] (ILCA)
Pollexf......... Pollexfen's English King's Bench Reports [*1669-85*] [*A publication*] (ILCA)
Pollexfen..... Pollexfen's English King's Bench Reports [*1669-85*] [*A publication*] (ILCA)
Pollock & Maitl... Pollock and Maitland's History of English Common Law [*A publication*] (DLA)
PolloTrp...... Pollo Tropical [*Commercial firm*] [*Associated Press*] (SAG)
Poll Prod ..... Pollock on the Production of Documents [*A publication*] (DLA)
Pol LQ .... Police Law Quarterly [*A publication*] (DLA)
POLLS .... Parliamentary On-Line Library Study [*Atomic Energy Authority*] [*British*]
POLLUT .... Pollution
Pollut Atmos... Pollution Atmospherique (SAUS)
Pollut Eng.... Pollution Engineering (SAUS)
Pollution Cont Guide (CCH)... Pollution Control Guide (Commerce Clearing House) [*A publication*] (DLA)
POLMI .... Problem-Oriented Machine Independent Language (SAUS)
POL/MIL ...... Political/Military (SAUS)
Pol Mil Dig... Poland's Digest of the Military Laws of the United States [*A publication*] (DLA)
poln-........... Central and Southern Line Islands [*MARC geographic area code*] [*Library of Congress*] (LCCP)
POLN .... Pollution Normal (SAUS)
poln .... polnisch [*Polish*] [*German*] (AD)
POLO .... Pacific Command Operations Liaison Office [*Army*] (AABC)
POLO .... Plant and Office Layout (AD)
POLO .... Polar Orbiting Lunar Observatory [*Satellite*]
POLO .... Problem-Oriented Language Organizer [*Computer science*] (PDAA)
POLO .... Procurement Online Ordering System (MCD)
Polon .... Polonais [*Polish*] [*French*] (AD)
POLOPS...... Polynomial Operations [*Air Force*]
POLOS........ Polar Oceans and the Law of the Sea Project (SAUS)
POLPA .... Polar Pacific (AD)
Pol Part....... Pollock's Digest of the Laws of Partnership [*A publication*] (DLA)
Pol Pharm Trans... Polish Pharmaceutical Transactions (SAUS)
Pol Prod Doc... Pollock on the Power of Courts to Compel the Production of Documents [*A publication*] (DLA)
POLPS........ Polymorphonuclear Leukocytes [*Hematology*] (DAVI)
POLR .... Polar Express Corp. [*NASDAQ symbol*] (SAG)
POLREG...... Polynomial Regression (IAA)
POLREP...... Pollution Report (GNE)
Pol Res Q ... Political Research Quarterly [*A publication*] (BRI)
Pol Rev Radiol Nucl Med... Polish Review of Radiology and Nuclear Medicine (SAUS)
PolrEx......... Polar Express Corp. [*Associated Press*] (SAG)
PolRs.......... Pollution Research and Control Corp. [*Associated Press*] (SAG)
POLRW....... Polar Express Wrrt'B' [*NASDAQ symbol*] (TTSB)
Pol Rze Lud... Polaska Rzeczpospolita Ludowa [*Polish People's Republic*] (AD)
POLS .... Planned Ocean Logistic System (SAUS)
pols .... Political Prisoners (AD)
pols .... Politicians (AD)
POLS .... Politics (SAUS)
PolSc.......... Political Science (DD)
POLSC .... Political Science
pol sci .... Political Science (AD)
PolSciQ........ Political Science Quarterly (SAUS)
Pol Sci Quar... Political Science Quarterly [*A publication*] (ILCA)
POLSG .... Polishing
Pols Nat ...... Polson's Law of Nations [*1848*] [*A publication*] (DLA)
PolSt........... Political Studies (SAUS)
POLSTAR..... Plant for On-Load Short-circuit Testing and Research (SAUS)
POLSTRADA... Polizia Stradale [*Highway Police*] [*Italian*] (AD)
Pol Stud J ... Policy Studies Journal [*A publication*] (BRI)
POLT........... Program Optimizing Low-Thrust Trajectory (ACAE)
Pol Technol News... Polish Technological News (SAUS)
Pol Tech Rev... Polish Technical Review (SAUS)
PolTel......... Polish Telephones & Microwave Corp. [*Associated Press*] (SAG)
POLTHN....... Polyethylene [*Organic chemistry*]
POLTL.......... Political (AFM)
POLTN......... Pollution
Pol Tr Mar... Poland's Law of Trade Marks [*A publication*] (DLA)
POLUT .... Pollution
PolutRs........ Pollution Research and Control Corp. [*Associated Press*] (SAG)
polwar .... Political Warfare (AD)
POLWAR...... Political Warfare
POLWARADDIR... Political Warfare Advisory Directorate
POLX .... Polydex Pharmaceuticals Ltd. [*NASDAQ symbol*] (NQ)
POLXF .... Polydex Pharmaceuticals [*NASDAQ symbol*] (TTSB)
POLY .... Planet Polymer Technologies [*NASDAQ symbol*] (TTSB)
POLY .... Planet Polymer Technologies, Inc. [*NASDAQ symbol*] (SAG)
Pol'y .... Policy (DLA)

poly .... Polydipsia [*Medicine*] (DAVI)
POLY .... Polyester
poly .... Polyethylene (AD)
POLY .... Polyethylene (DEN)
POLY .... Polygamy [*FBI standardized term*]
poly .... Polymer (AD)
POLY .... Polymorphonuclear Leukocyte [*Hematology*]
poly .... Polymorphonuclear Neutrophil Granulocyte [*Hematology*] (DAVI)
Poly .... Polynesia (AD)
poly .... Polyphagia [*Medicine*] (DAVI)
poly .... Polytechnic (AD)
POLY .... Polytechnic
poly .... Polyuria [*Medicine*] (DAVI)
poly .... Polyvinyl (AD)
PolyA .... Polyadenylated
poly(A)........ Polyadenylic Acid [*Biochemistry*] (MAE)
Polyb .... Polybius [*Second century BC*] [*Classical studies*] (OCD)
Pol YB Int'l L... Polish Yearbook of International Law [*Warsaw*] [*A publication*] (DLA)
Pol Yb of Internat L... Polish Yearbook of International Law [*Warsaw*] [*A publication*] (DLA)
poly bot ...... Polyethylene Bottle (AD)
POLYC .... Polychromasia [*Hematology*] (DAVI)
poly-C......... Polycytidylic Acid [*Biochemistry*] (DMAA)
Poly-C........ Polyester Capacitor (SAUS)
PolyCenter... Digitalis new name for DECmcc. (SAUS)
Polycom ..... Polycom, Inc. [*Associated Press*] (SAG)
Polycryst...... Polycrystalline (SAUS)
POLYDAT..... Polymetallic Nodule Deposits Database (SAUS)
Polydex....... Polydex Pharmaceuticals Ltd. [*Associated Press*] (SAG)
POLYDOC .... Polytechnical Documentation (NITA)
POLYDOP .... Polystation Doppler Tracking System (MCD)
POLYED ...... Polymer Education
POLYEST ..... Polyester
polyg .... Polygraph (AD)
POLYG .... Polygraphy (SAUS)
poly-G........ Polyguanylic Acid [*Biochemistry*] (DMAA)
Polyg .... Polygynie (SAUS)
POLYGON .... Oceanographic Experiment in the North-East Atlantic [*Former USSR*] [*Marine science*] (OSRA)
PolyGp........ Polymer Group, Inc. [*Associated Press*] (SAG)
Polygr.......... PolyGram NV [*Associated Press*] (SAG)
poly-I.......... Polyinosinic Acid [*Biochemistry*] (DMAA)
poly I:C........ Polyinosinic Polycytidylic Acid (BARN)
Pol Yid .... Polish Yiddish (SAUS)
Polym .... Polymerized (SAUS)
Polym ....: Polymusic [*Record label*]
POLYMAT..... Polymer Materials [*Deutsches Kunststoff-Institut*] [*Germany*] [*Information service or system*] (CRD)
Polym Bull... Polymer Bulletin (SAUS)
Polym Commun... Polymer Communications (SAUS)
Polym Compos... Polymer Composites (SAUS)
Polym Degrad Stabil... Polymer Degradation and Stability (SAUS)
Polym Dig ... Polymer Digest (SAUS)
Polymed ..... PolyMedica Industries, Inc. [*Associated Press*] (SAG)
POLYMEG .... Polytetramethylene Ether Glycol (SAUS)
Polym Eng Sci... Polymer Engineering and Science (SAUS)
Polym J ...... Polymer Journal (SAUS)
Polym Lett Ed... Polymer Letters Edition of the Journal of Polymer Science (MEC)
Polym Mech... Polymer Mechanics (SAUS)
Polym News... Polymer News (SAUS)
POLYMODE... Polygon Midocean Dynamic Experiment (SAUS)
POLYMODE... Polygon-MODE [*Mid-Ocean Dynamics Experiment*] [*Soviet-US cooperative undersea weather exploration*]
polymorph ... Polymorphonuclear [*Leukocyte*] [*Hematology*] (DAVI)
polymorph ... Polymorphous (AD)
Polym Plast Technol Eng... Polymer-Plastics Technology and Engineering (SAUS)
Polym Prepr Am Chem Soc... Polymer Preprints of the American Chemical Society (SAUS)
Polym Proc Eng... Polymer Process Engineering (SAUS)
Polym Rubb Asia... Polymers and Rubber Asia (SAUS)
Polym Sci... Polymer Science (SAUS)
Polym Sci USSR... Polymer Science USSR (SAUS)
Polym Test... Polymer Testing (SAUS)
POLYMYX.... Polymyxin B Sulfate (SAUS)
Polyn .... Polynesia (VRA)
POLYN .... Polynesia
Polynes........ Polynesian (DIAR)
POLYOX...... Poly(ethylene Oxide) [*Trademark*]
POLYP .... Polyprocessor
Polyph .... Polyphase Instrument Corp. [*Associated Press*] (SAG)
PolyRs........ Polymer Research Corp. of America [*Associated Press*] (SAG)
polys........... polymorphonuclear cells (SAUS)
POLYSAC IRON... Polysaccharide Iron complex (SAUS)
Polysar Prog... Polysar Progress (SAUS)
poly sci........ Political Science (AD)
polysex........ Polysexual (AD)
polys (segs)... Polymorphonuclear Segmented Neutrophils [*Hematology*] (DAVI)
poly-T......... Polythymidylic Acid [*Biochemistry*] (DMAA)
Polytech...... Polytechnic (PROS)
polytech...... Polytechnical (BARN)
POLYTRAN... Polytranslation Analysis (SAUS)
POLYTRAN... Polytranslation Analysis and Programming (IEEE)
Poly U .... Polytechnic University (GÁGS)
poly(U) .... Polyuridylic Acid [*Biochemistry*] (MAE)

Polyvisn.......	Polyvision Corp. [*Associated Press*] (SAG)
Polyvsn....	Polyvision Corp. [*Associated Press*] (SAG)
polywater	Polymerized Water (AD)
POLY-WRI ...	Polytechnic Institute of New York Weber Research Institute [*Farmingdale, NY*]
POM.............	Aurelio y Gustavo Pompa Estrella [*Mexico*] [*FAA designator*] (FAAC)
POM.............	Operation: Peace of Mind [*Later, Runaway Hotline*] [*An association*] (EA)
POM.............	Pain on Motion (STED)
POM.............	Pallet-Only Mode [*NASA*] (NASA)
POM.............	Particulate Organic Matter [*Environmental chemistry*]
POM.............	Pay-off Matrix (SAUS)
POM.............	Pennsylvania-Ohio-Maryland League [*Old baseball league*]
POM.............	Peritronics Med [*Vancouver Stock Exchange symbol*]
POM.............	Persistent Object Manager (SAUS)
POM.............	Personal Opinion Matrix [*Test*] (TES)
POM.............	Personal Opinion Message [*Western Union*] (IIA)
POM.............	Personnel, Operations, Maintenance (MCD)
POM.............	Phase of Moon (SAUS)
POM.............	Phase of the Moon [*Astronomy*] (NHD)
POM.............	Phenomenon of Man [*Project*] (EA)
POM.............	Photo-Optical Memory (SAUS)
POM.............	Pivaloyloxymethyl Chloride (SAUS)
POM.............	Plan Objectives Memorandum (CCCA)
PoM.............	Plan of Management (SAUS)
POM.............	Plate Orifice Meter (SAUS)
POM.............	Polarizing Optical Microscopy
POM.............	Police Officer, Male
POM.............	Polyacetal (SAUS)
POM.............	Polycyclic Organic Material (SAUS)
pom.............	Polycyclic Organic Matter (AD)
POM.............	Polycyclic Organic Matter
POM.............	Polyformaldehyde (EDCT)
POM.............	Polymerized and Oxidized Material [*Food science*]
POM.............	Polymethylene Oxide (SAUS)
POM.............	Polynuclear Organic Matter (FFDE)
POM.............	Polyoxometalate [*Organic chemistry*]
POM.............	Poly(oxymethylene) [*Organic chemistry*]
pom.............	Polyoxymethylene (AD)
POM.............	Polyphenylene Oxide, Modified (SAUS)
pom.............	Pomeranian (AD)
POM.............	Pomeranian Dog (DSUE)
pom.............	Pomeridiano [*Afternoon*] [*Italian*] (AD)
Pom.............	Pommy [*British*] (ODBW)
pom.............	Pomological (AD)
POM.............	Pomona [*California*] [*Seismograph station code, US Geological Survey*] [*Closed*] (SEIS)
POM.............	Pomona, CA [*Location identifier*] [*FAA*] (FAAL)
pom.............	Pom-Pom (AD)
Pom.............	Pompon [*Horticulture*]
POM.............	Pool Operational Module [*Telecommunications*] (TEL)
POM.............	Port Moresby [*Papua New Guinea*] [*Airport symbol*] (OAG)
PoM.............	Port of Miami (AD)
POM.............	Position Modulator (NRCH)
POM.............	Potential Officer Material [*British military*] (DMA)
POM.............	Potomac Electric Power Co. [*NYSE symbol*] (SPSG)
POM.............	Potomac Electric Pwr [*NYSE symbol*] (TTSB)
POM.............	Preobservational Mean [*Statistics*]
pom.............	Preparation for Overseas Movement (AD)
POM.............	Preparation for Overseas Movement [*Military*]
POM.............	Prescription Only Medicine [*British*]
POM.............	Princeton Ocean Model (SAUS)
POM.............	Printer Output Microfilm
POM.............	Print on Metal (DGA)
POM.............	Printout Microfilm (NITA)
POM.............	Priority of Movement (SAUS)
POM.............	Priority of Movements [*Military*] [*British*]
POM.............	Prior to Overseas Movement [*DoD*]
POM.............	Production/Operations Management (SAUS)
POM.............	Production Order Master (SAUS)
POM.............	Professional or Managerial (WDMC)
POM.............	Professionals, Owners, and Managers [*A. C. Nielsen Co.*] [*Demographic category*] (NTCM)
POM.............	Program Objectives Memorandum [*Military*]
POM.............	Program Operating Memorandum (SAUS)
POM.............	Program Operation Mode
POM.............	Project Office Memo
POM.............	Project Officers Meeting
POM.............	Project Operations and Milestones (SAUS)
POM.............	Proof of Manufacturing (ACAE)
POM.............	Public Order Member (NUMA)
POMA.............	Petty Officer Medical Assistant [*British military*] (DMA)
POMA.............	Petty Officer's Military Academy [*Navy*]
POMA.............	Pointable Optical Mosaic Array (SAUS)
POMA.............	Polyoctyl Methacrylate [*Organic chemistry*]
POMALS	Pedestal Operated Multi-Ammunition Launching System (SAUS)
POMAR	Position Operational, Meteorological Aircraft Report
POMAR	Preventive Operational Maintenance and Repair [*Military*] (NVT)
POMAS	Procurement Office for Military Automotive Supplies
pomato	Potato-Tomato (AD)
POMBA	Parents of Multiple Births Associations of Canada
POM/BES	Program Objective Memorandum/Budget Estimate Submission (MCD)
POMC	Parents of Murdered Children (EA)
POMC	Period of Minimum Change (SAUS)
POMC	Pro-Opiomelanocortin [*Endocrinology*]

Pom Code Rem...	Pomeroy on Code Remedies [*A publication*] (DLA)
Pom Const Law...	Pomeroy's Constitutional Law of the United States [*A publication*] (DLA)
Pom Contr ...	Pomeroy on Contracts [*A publication*] (DLA)
pomcus.......	Prepositioned Material Configured in Unit Sets (AD)
POMCUS......	Prepositioned Overseas Material (or Materiel) Configured in/to Unit Sets (AD)
POMCUS......	Pre-positioned Overseas Materiel Configured to Unit Sets (SAUS)
POMCUS......	Prepositioning of Material Configured to Unit Sets (SAUS)
POMCUS......	Prepositioning of Materiel Configured to Unit Sets [*Army*] (AABC)
POMCUS......	Prepositioning of Organisational Material Configured in Unit Sets (SAUS)
POMD	Program Operation Mode (IAA)
POME..........	early convict immigrants (SAUS)
pome-..........	Melanesia [*MARC geographic area code*] [*Library of Congress*] (LCCP)
POME..........	Principal Ordnance Mechanical Engineer [*British military*] (DMA)
POME..........	Prisoner of Mother England [*Nineteenth-century convict in penal colony of Australia, now a nickname for any Australian*]
POME..........	Problems-Objectives-Methods-Evaluation [*Planning method*]
POME..........	Protect Our Mountain Environment [*Colorado*]
POMEM........	Petty Officer Marine Engineering Mechanic [*British military*] (DMA)
Pom Eq Jur...	Pomeroy's Equity Jurisprudence [*A publication*] (DLA)
Pom Eq Juris...	Pomeroy's Equity Jurisprudence [*A publication*] (DLA)
POMERID......	Pomeridianus [*In the Afternoon*] [*Pharmacy*]
Pomeroy.......	Pomeroy Computer Resources, Inc. [*Associated Press*] (SAG)
Pomeroy.......	Pomeroy's Reports [*73-128 California*] [*A publication*] (DLA)
POMF..........	Polaris Missile Facility
POMFLANT...	Polaris Missile Facility, Atlantic (AD)
POMFLANT...	Polaris Missile Facility, Atlantic Fleet
POMFPAC.....	Polaris Missile Facility, Pacific Fleet
POMGEN......	Program Objective Memorandum Generator [*Military*]
POMH	National Association of Post Office Mail Handlers, Watchmen, Messengers, and Group Leaders [*Later, NPOMHWMGL*]
POMI	Photochromic Microimage (IAA)
POMI	Preliminary Operating and Maintenance Instructions [*Aerospace*] (AAG)
POMINS......	Portable Mine Neutralization System (MCD)
POMM	Preliminary Operating and Maintenance Manual [*Military*] (AABC)
Pom Mun Law...	Pomeroy on Municipal Law [*A publication*] (DLA)
POMO	Partially Occupied Molecular Orbitals [*Physical chemistry*]
POMO	Personnel Objectives Monitoring Operation
POMO	Postmodern
POMO	Production Oriented Maintenance Organization (SAUS)
POMO	Production-Oriented Maintenance Organization (MCD)
POMO	Program Operations and Management Office [*Environmental Protection Agency*] (GFGA)
POMOL	POMCUS [*Prepositioning of Materiel Configured to Unit Sets*] Objective Levels [*Military*]
pomol	Pomologic (AD)
POMOL	Pomologist (SAUS)
POMOL	Pomology
POMOLA......	Poor Man's Optical Landing System
Pomp..........	Epistula ad Pompeium [*of Dionysius Halicarnassensis*] [*Classical studies*] (OCD)
Pomp..........	Pompeius [*of Plutarch*] [*Classical studies*] (OCD)
Pomp..........	Pompey (AD)
POMP	Pomposo [*Grandly*] [*Music*] (ROG)
POMP	Pre Coded Originating Mail Processor (PDAA)
POMP	Prednisone, Oncovin [*Vincristine*], Methotrexate, Purinethol [*Mercaptopurine*] [*Antineoplastic drug regimen*]
POMP	Principal Outer Membrane Protein
POMP	Problem-Oriented Management of Patients (SAUS)
POMP	Purinethol, Oncovin, Methotrexate, Prednisone [*Medicine*] (MEDA)
POMPAC.....	Polaris Missile Facility, Pacific (AD)
POMPr........	Potomac Elec Pwr $2.44 Cv Pfd [*NYSE symbol*] (TTSB)
POMPrA......	Potomac El Pwr$3.89'91 Pfd [*NYSE symbol*] (TTSB)
POMPrH......	Potomac Elec Pwr $3.37cm'87 Pfd [*NYSE symbol*] (TTSB)
POM Project...	Phenomenon of Man Project (SAUS)
Pom Rem	Pomeroy on Civil Remedies [*A publication*] (DLA)
Pom Rem & Rem Rights...	Pomeroy on Civil Remedies and Remedial Rights [*A publication*] (DLA)
POMR/PST...	Partido Obrero Marxista Revolucionario/Partido Socialista de los Trabajadores [*Marxist Revolutionary Workers' Party/Socialist Workers' Party*] [*Peru*] [*Political party*] (PPW)
POMS	Panel on Operational Meteorological Satellites
POMS	Persistent Object Management System (NITA)
POMS	Pilot Ocean Monitoring Study (SAUS)
POMS	Plain Old Mail Service (CIST)
POMS	Polar Operational Meteorological Satellite (USDC)
POMS	Polar Orbiting Meteorological Satellite (SAUS)
POMS	Poly-Ortho-methylstyrene [*Organic chemistry*]
POMS	Process Operating Management System [*Manufacturing*]
POMS	Production and Operations Management Society (EA)
POMS	Professional Office Management System (CIST)
POMS	Profile of Mood States [*A questionnaire*]
POMS	Program Operations Manual System [*Social Security Administration*]
POMS	Psychiatric Outpatient Mood Scale (SAUS)
POMSA	Post Office Management Staff Association (SAUS)
POMSA	Post Office Management Staffs Association [*A union*] [*British*] (DCTA)
POMS-BI.....	Profile of Mood States-Bipolar Form
POMSEE......	Performance, Operating (or Operational) and Maintenance Standards for Electronic Equipment (SAUS)

POMSEE ...... Preparation, Operation and Maintenance of Shipboard Electronics Equipment (SAUS)
pomsee........ Preparation, Operation, Maintenance, Shipboard Electronics Equipment (AD)
POMSIP ...... Post Office Management and Service Improvement Program [Obsolete]
Pom Spec Perf... Pomeroy on Specific Performance of Contracts [A publication] (DLA)
POMSS .... Pre-positioned Operational Material Storage Site (SAUS)
POMT.......... Patriot Organizational Maintenance Trainer [Army]
POMT.......... Planning and Operations Management Team (MCD)
POMT.......... Planning Operations Management Team (SAUS)
POMV .... National Federation Post Office Motor Vehicle Employees [Later, APWU] (EA)
POMV .... Privately Owned Motor Vehicle (NATG)
POMWG...... Program Objective Memorandum Working Group (SAUS)
PON .... Paraoxonase [An enzyme]
PON .... Particulate Organic Nitrogen
PON .... Passive Optical Network
P-on .... Phoshorylation (SAUS)
PON .... Phosphorotioate Oligonucleotide [Biochemistry]
PON .... Ponce [Puerto Rico] [Seismograph station code, US Geological Survey] (SEIS)
PON .... Ponder Oils Ltd. [Toronto Stock Exchange symbol]
Pon .... Pontius [Authority cited in pre-1607 legal work] (DSA)
PON .... Pontoon (AAG)
pon .... Pontoon (AD)
PON .... Portuguese Navy [ICAO designator] (FAAC)
PON .... Position (IAA)
PON .... Pride of Newark [Feigenspan beer]
PON .... Primary Olfactory Nerve (SAUS)
PON .... Production Order Notification (SAUS)
PON .... Program Opportunity Notice [Energy Research and Development Administration]
PON .... Program Opportunity Notice (or Notification) (SAUS)
PON .... Program Opportunity Notification (AD)
PON .... Project Originator Number (SAUS)
PON .... Pump Octane Number (SAUS)
PON .... Purchase Order Notice (SAUS)
pona .... Paraffin, Olefin, Naphthene, Aromatic (AD)
PONA.......... Paraffins, Olefins, Naphthenes, Aromatics
PONA.......... Provisions for Ozone Nonattainment Areas [Environmental science] (COE)
PONAM...... Polar North Atlantic Margins (SAUS)
PONAM...... Polar North Atlantic Margins Programme (SAUS)
Pon Ble........ Poncius Blegerii [Flourished, 14th century] [Authority cited in pre-1607 legal work] (DSA)
PonBrg........ Ponton Bridge (SAUS)
PonBrg........ Pontoon Bridge (AD)
PONBRG ...... Pontoon Bridge (MUGU)
PONC .... Price of Non-Conformance (SAUS)
Poncebk...... Poncebank [Associated Press] (SAG)
Ponce Sch Med... Ponce School of Medicine (GAGS)
PONCHO ..... Patrons of Northwest Civic Cultural and Charitable Organizations
POND.......... Parents of Near Drownings [An association] (EA)
POND.......... Pondere [By Weight] [Latin]
pond .... Pondere [By Weigh] [Latin] (AD)
POND.......... Ponderosus [Heavy] [Pharmacy]
Ponder........ Ponder Industries, Inc. [Associated Press] (SAG)
Pondo .... Pondoland (AD)
PONF .... Paediatric Oncology Nurses Forum [British]
PONG.......... Poet of the New Generation [Term used to describe poets writing for entertainment value] (ECON)
PONI .... Positive Output, Negative Input (SAUS)
PONI .... Postoperative Narcotic Infusion (STED)
ponl-........... New Caledonia [MARC geographic area code] [Library of Congress] (LCCP)
ponn-.......... New Hebrides [MARC geographic area code] [Library of Congress] (LCCP)
p-on-n......... Positive on Negative (AD)
PONN.......... Positive-on-Negative (IAA)
PONS .... Platt's Oilgram News Service
PONS .... Portuguese Naval Ship (SAUS)
pons........... Profile of Nonverbal Sensitivity (AD)
PONS.......... Profile of Nonverbal Sensitivity [Psychology]
PONSE .... Personnel of the Naval Shore Establishment [Report] (NG)
PONSE Report... Personnel of the Naval Shore Establishment Report (SAUS)
PONSI......... Program of Noncollegiate Sponsored Instruction (OICC)
Pont .... Epistulae ex Ponto [of Ovid] [Classical studies] (OCD)
Pont .... Pontevedra (AD)
PONT.......... Pontiac [Automotive engineering]
PONT .... Pontifex [Bishop] [Latin] (WGA)
Pont .... Ponton (SAUS)
Pont .... Pontoon (WGA)
PONTA........ Popular New Titles from Abroad [Book acquisition program for libraries]
pont b .... Pontoon Bridge (AD)
Ponti .... Pontiac (AD)
Pont Max .... Pontifex Maximus [Supreme Pontiff] [Latin] (AD)
PonTn .... Ponton Train (SAUS)
ponu-.......... Nauru [MARC geographic area code] [Library of Congress] (LCCP)
PONUC....... Post Office National Users' Council [British]
PONVER...... Project on National Vocational Education Resources (EDAC)
PONY .... Pennsylvania, Ohio, New York Baseball League (IIA)
PONY .... Pennsylvania-Ontario-New York League [Old baseball league]

PONY .... Pride of the Navy Yard (DNAB)
PONY .... Prostitutes of New York
PONY .... Protect Our Nation's Youth [Baseball league] [Name usually written Pony]
PONY .... Purpose of Neighborhood Youth [Foundation]
PONYA........ Port of New York Authority [Later, PANYNJ]
POO .... Pallet of Opportunity (SAUS)
POO .... Panel on Oceanography
POO .... Parents Opposed to Opting Out [An association] (AIE)
POO .... Payload Operations Office [NASA]
POO .... Platform of Opportunity Program [National Oceanic and Atmospheric Administration] (MSC)
POO .... Pocos De Caldas [Brazil] [Airport symbol] (OAG)
Poo .... Poole (AD)
POO .... Poona [India] [Seismograph station code, US Geological Survey] (SEIS)
POO .... Port Operations Officer (DS)
POO .... Port Ordnance Officer (SAUS)
POO .... Post Office Order
POO .... Post Officer Order (SAUS)
POO .... Principal Ordnance Officer (SAUS)
POO .... Priority Operational Objective [Military]
POO .... Program Operations Officer [Social Security Administration]
POOC .... Payload of Opportunity Carrier (SAUS)
POOD.......... Permanent Officer of the Day [or Deck] [Navy]
POOD.......... Permanent Officer of the Deck (SAUS)
pood .... Poodle Dog (AD)
POOD.......... Provisioning Order Obligating (or Obligation) Document (SAUS)
POOEL........ Petty Officer Ordnance Electrician [British military] (DMA)
poof .... Peripheral On-Line-Oriented Function [Computer science] (AD)
POOFF .... Preservation of Our Femininity and Finances [Women's group opposing below-the-knee fashions introduced in 1970]
POOFF .... Professional Oglers of Female Figures [Men's group opposing below-the-knee fashions introduced in 1970]
POOH.......... Postoperative Open-Heart [Surgery] (STED)
POOL .... Parallel Object Orientated Language (SAUS)
POOL .... Pollution of Oceans Originating on Land (SAUS)
POOL .... SCP Pool [NASDAQ symbol] (TTSB)
POOL .... SCP Pool Corp. [NASDAQ symbol] (SAG)
PoolEn........ Pool Energy Services Co. [Associated Press] (SAG)
poop .... Nincompoop (AD)
POOP .... Principles of Operation (SAUS)
POOP .... Process Oriented Observation Program [NORPAX] (MSC)
POOP .... Proper Object Oriented Programming (SAUS)
POOR.......... Poor Clot [Medicine] (STED)
POOR.......... Prevention of Over-Radiation [Military]
Poore Const... Poore's Federal and State Constitution [A publication] (DLA)
Poor L & Local Gov't... Poor Law and Local Government Magazine [A publication] (DLA)
POOS .... Priority Order Output System [Japan] (DIT)
poosslq........ Person of Opposite Sex Sharing Living Quarters (AD)
POOW .... Petty Officer of the Watch [Navy] (NVT)
POoW .... Petty Officer on Watch [Military] (AD)
POOZ .... Permanently Open Ocean Zone (SAUS)
Pop .... Carbonated Beverage (SAUS)
POP .... International Polar Orbiting Platform (SAUS)
POP .... Pacific Ocean Perch
POP .... Package for Online Programming [Computer science] (CDE)
POP .... Palletizing Optimization Potential (AD)
POP .... Palletizing Optimization Program (SAUS)
POP .... Panoramic Office Planning
POP .... Paperless Ordering Placement [System] (DOMA)
POP .... Parallel Ocean Program (SAUS)
POP .... Parallel Output Platform
POP .... Parents of Punkers (EA)
POP .... Paroxypropione [or Paraoxypropiophenone] [Endocrinology]
POP .... Particle-Oriented Paper (IAA)
POP .... Particulate Organic Phosphorus
POP .... Partido de Orientacion Popular [Popular Orientation Party] [El Salvador] [Political party] (PPW)
POP .... Parti Ouvrier et Paysan du Congo [Congolese Workers' and Peasants' Party] [Zaire] [Political party]
POP .... Parti Ouvrier-Progressiste [Canada]
POP .... Patrexes of the Panopticon (EA)
POP .... Payload Optimized Program [NASA] (KSC)
POP .... Pay One Price
POP .... Peak Overpressure [Nuclear energy] (NRCH)
POP .... Perceived Outcome Potential (MHDI)
POP .... Percentage of Precipitation (SAUS)
POP .... Performance-Oriented Packaging [for hazardous materials]
POP .... Period of Performance (MCD)
POP .... Permanently Out of Print (SAUS)
pop .... Perpendicular Ocean Platform (AD)
POP .... Perpendicular Ocean Platform [Oceanography]
POP .... Perpendicular to Orbital Plane
POP .... Perpendicular-to-Orbit Plan
POP .... Perpendicular-to-Orbit Plane [Aerospace] (KSC)
pop .... Persistent Occipito-Posterior (AD)
POP .... Persistent Occipit Posterior [A fetal position] [Obstetrics]
POP .... Persistent Organic Pollutant [Environmental science]
POP- .... Personal Ozone Protection
POP .... Pharmacists in Ophthalmic Practice [Later, PIOP] (EA)
POP .... Picture-outside-Picture [Television technology] (PS)
POP .... Pipeline Outfit, Petroleum (MCD)
POP .... Pituitary Opioid Peptide [Medicine] (DMAA)

POP	Placing Older People (SAUS)
POP	Plasma Oncotic Pressure [*Medicine*] (MAE)
pop	Plasma Osmotic Pressure (AD)
POP	Plasma Osmotic Pressure [*Medicine*]
pop	Plaster of Paris (AD)
POP	Plaster of Paris
POP	Pneumatic Operated Piston (ECII)
POP	Point of Presence [*Telecommunications*] (DOM)
PoP	Point of Presence [*Telecommunications*] (PCM)
POP	Point of Production (SAUS)
POP	Point of Purchase [*Advertising*]
POP	Polar Orbiting Platform (SSD)
POP	Pollution and Overpopulation
POP	Polymyositis Ossificans Progressiva [*Medicine*] (DMAA)
POP	Polyolefin Plastomer [*Organic chemistry*]
POP	Poly Phenylene Oxide (EDCT)
POP	Pope & Talbot [*NYSE symbol*] (TTSB)
POP	Pope & Talbot, Inc. [*NYSE symbol*] (SPSG)
POP	POP from Stack (SAUS)
Pop	Popham's English King's Bench Reports [*1592-1627*] [*A publication*] (DLA)
POP	Popliteal [*Artery*] [*Anatomy*] (AAMN)
POP	Popondetta [*Papua New Guinea*] [*Seismograph station code, US Geological Survey*] [*Closed*] (SEIS)
Pop	Poppa (AD)
pop	Poppet (AD)
POP	Popping [*Mining engineering*]
pop	Popular (AD)
POP	Popular
Pop	Populare [*Record label*] [*Romania*]
POP	Population (AAG)
pop	Population (AD)
Pop	Population (TBD)
POP	Population Division [*Bureau of the Census*] (OICC)
POP	Portugese Overseas Province (AD)
POP	Posterior Odds Processing [*Weather forecasting*] [*National Science Foundation*]
POP	Post Office Preferred (DCTA)
POP	Post Office Protocol [*Telecommunications*]
p-op	Post-Operative (AD)
POP	Postoperative [*Medicine*]
POP	Postoperative Pain [*Medicine*] (MELL)
POP	Power On/Off Protection
POP	Practical Ordered Program (OA)
POP	Preburner Oxidizer Pump (MCD)
POP	Preflight Operations Procedure (MCD)
POP	Prefocused Objective Pinhole (SAUS)
POP	Prelaunch Operations Plan [*NASA*] (NASA)
POP	Premanagement Orientation Program [*LIMRA*]
POP	Pressurizer Overpressure (SAUS)
POP	Pressurizer Overpressure Protection System [*Nuclear energy*] (IEEE)
POP	Primary Operation
pop	Printer of Plates [*MARC relator code*] [*Library of Congress*] (LCCP)
POP	Printing-Out Paper
POP	Probability of Precipitation (SAUS)
POP	Process Optimization Program (SAUS)
POP	Processor on Plug in (SAUS)
POP	Profiler Online Program (SAUS)
POP	Profit Option Plan [*Retailing*]
POP	Programmed Operators and Primitives [*Computer science*]
POP	Program Obligation Plan (KSC)
POP	Program Operating Plan
POP	Progressive Overload Program [*Weight training*]
POP	Project Objective Plan (NG)
POP	Project Operation (SAUS)
POP	Project Optimization Procedure (IAA)
POP	Prompt Ordering Plan
POP	Proof of Principle (SAUS)
POP	Proof-Of Principle [*Test*]
POP	Proof of Purchase
POP	Protection System (SAUS)
POP	Public Offering Price (AD)
POP	Puerto Plata [*Dominican Republic*] [*Airport symbol*] (OAG)
POP	Pump Optimizing Program
POP	Purchase Outside Production (SAA)
POP	SCI-FI Society of Long Island [*Formerly, Patrexes of the Panopticon*] (EA)
POP3	Post Office Protocol 3 [*Computer science*]
POPA	Patent Office Professional Association (EA)
POPA	Payload Ordnance Processing Area (NASA)
POPA	Pet Owners' Protective Association
POPA	POP All registers (SAUS)
Popa	Popayan, Colombia (AD)
POPA	Prevention of Oil Pollution Act [*1971*]
POPA	Property Owners' Protection Association
pop advertising ...	Point-of-Purchase Advertising (AD)
POPAE	Protons on Protons and Electrons [*Physics*]
POPAI	Point-of-Purchase Advertising Institute [*Fort Lee, NJ*] (EA)
POPAL	Pre-Operational Peculiar Age List
POP & B	Proposed Operating Program and Budget [*Army*]
pop art	Popular Art (AD)
popb	Proposed Operating Plan and Budget (AD)
POPC	Pamitoyl-Oleoylphosphatidylcholine [*Biochemistry*]
popc-	Pitcairn [*MARC geographic area code*] [*Library of Congress*] (LCCP)
POP-CON	Populist Conservative [*Wing of the Republican Party represented by Congressmen Gingrich, Kemp, and Lott*]
POPCRU	Police and Prison Civil Rights Union [*Founded in 1989*] [*South Africa*] (ECON)
POPCRU	Police and Prison Service Civil Rights Union (SAUS)
POPCX	PIMCO: Opportunity Cl.C [*Mutual fund ticker symbol*] (SG)
POPD	Power-Operated
POPDA	Polyoxypropylenediamine [*Organic chemistry*]
POPE	Parents for Orthodoxy in Parochial Education [*Group opposing sex education in schools*]
POPE	Polar Orbiting Platform Element (SAUS)
POPE	Product Oriented Procedures Evaluation (AD)
Pope Cust	Pope on Customs and Excise [*11th ed.*] [*1828*] [*A publication*] (DLA)
POP ED	Popular Edition [*Publishing*]
Pope Lun ...	Pope on Lunacy [*A publication*] (DLA)
PopeRes	Pope Resources Ltd. [*Associated Press*] (SAG)
PopeTal	Pope & Talbot, Inc. [*Associated Press*] (SAG)
popex	Population Explosion (AD)
POPEZ	Pope Resources L.P. [*NASDAQ symbol*] (TTSB)
POPEZ	Pope Resources Ltd. [*NASDAQ symbol*] (SPSG)
POPF	POP Flags (SAUS)
popf	Prepared-on-Premises Flavor (AD)
POPGUN	Policy and Procedure Governing the Use of Nicknames [*Army*] (AABC)
Poph	Popham's English King's Bench Reports [*1592-1627*] [*A publication*] (DLA)
Poph (2)	Cases at the End of Popham's Reports [*A publication*] (DLA)
Popham	Popham's English King's Bench Reports [*79 English Reprint*] [*1592-1626*] [*A publication*] (DLA)
Poph Insol ...	Popham's Insolvency Act of Canada [*A publication*] (DLA)
popi	Post Office Position Indicator [*British*] (AD)
POPI	Post Office Position Indicator [*A form of long-range position indicator*] [*British*]
POPIM	Product Operations Planning Instruction Manual (ACAE)
POPIN	Population Information Network [*United Nations*] [*Internet resource*]
POPIN-Africa ...	Population Information Network for Africa (SAUS)
POPINFORM...	Population Information (SAUS)
POPINFORM...	Population Information Network [*UNESCO*]
POPINS	Population Information System [*UNESCO*]
POPL	Principles of Programming Language (SAUS)
POPL	Problem-Oriented Programming Language (SAUS)
POPLAB	International Program of Laboratories for Population Statistics
POPLAB	Program of Laboratories for Population Statistics (SAUS)
POPLINE	Population Information On-Line [*Bibliographic database*] (IID)
POPLINE	Population Online (NITA)
poplit	Popliteal (AD)
POPLIT	Popliteal [*Anatomy*]
POPMail	Post Office Protocol Mail
POPMIP	Portable Ocean Platform Motion Instrumentation Package [*Marine science*] (MSC)
Pop Mo L Tr...	Popular Monthly Law Tracts [*1877-78*] [*A publication*] (DLA)
pop music ...	Popular Music (AD)
POPMV	Poplar Mosaic Virus [*Plant pathology*]
Popn	Population
POPO	Phase One Program Office (ACAE)
POPO	Poured-On, Passed-Over [*Bowdlerized version*]
POPO	Push-On, Pull-Off [*Computer science*]
POPOP	Phenyl Oxazolyl Phenyl Oxazolyl Phenyl (SAUS)
POPP	Prison Officer in a Private Prison (WDAA)
Pop Plast	Popular Plastics (SAUS)
Pop Plast Packag...	Popular Plastics and Packaging (SAUS)
pop psych....	Popular Psychiatry (AD)
popr	Pilot Overhaul Provisioning Review (AD)
POPR	Pilot Overhaul Provisioning Review
POPR	Prototype Organic Power Reactor [*Nuclear energy*]
POPS	Free-Fall Pop-Up Ocean Bottom Seismometer [*Marine science*] (MSC)
POPS	National Beverage Corp. [*NASDAQ symbol*] (SAG)
POPS	Pantograph Optical Projection System (IEEE)
POPS	Paperless Order Processing System (SAUS)
POPS	Parachute Opening Proximity Sensor (MCD)
POPS	Partners of Prisoners & Families Support Group (WDAA)
POPS	People Opposed to Pornography in Schools [*Group opposing sex education in schools*]
POPS	Performance Optimized Page Size (SAUS)
POPS	Performance-Oriented Packing Standard
POPs	Persistent Organic Pollutants (SAUS)
POPS	Platt's Oilgram Price Service
POPs	Points of Presence (SAUS)
pops-	Polynesia [*MARC geographic area code*] [*Library of Congress*] (LCCP)
pops	Popular Concerts (AD)
POPS	Positioning Orbital Propulsion System (MCD)
POPS	Preserve Our Presidential Sites (EA)
POPS	Pressurizer Overpressure Protection System [*Nuclear energy*] (NRCH)
POPS	Primary Oceanographic Prediction System (SAUS)
POPS	Principal Oscillation Patterns Analysis
POPS	Process Operating System [*Toshiba Corp.*] [*Japan*]
POPS	Procurers of Painted-Label Sodas [*Defunct*] (EA)
POPS	Profiles of Problem Solving [*Test*] (TMMY)
POPS	Program for Operator Scheduling [*Bell System computer program*]
POPS	Project Operations [*Navy*] (NVT)
POPS	Protect Our Pelican Society [*Later, PMBS*] (EA)
POPS	Pyrotechnical Optical Plume Simulator (SAUS)

POPS	Pyrotechnic Optical Plume Simulation
POPS	Pyrotechnic Optical Plume Simulator (MCD)
POPSAT	Precise Orbit Positioning Satellite (SAUS)
POPSAT	Precise Orbit Positioning Spacecraft (ACAE)
Pop Sci	Popular Science [*A publication*] (AD)
POP SCI MO...	Popular Science Monthly [*A publication*] (ROG)
POPSE	Project Office for Physical Security Equipment [*Army*] (RDA)
POPSER	Polaris Operational Performance Surveillance Engineering Report [*Missiles*]
POP-Server...	Post Office Protocol-Server (SAUS)
POPSI	Postulate-Based Permuted Subject Indexing (PDAA)
POPSI	Precipitation and Off-Path Scattered Interference [*Report*] [*FCC*]
POPSIPT	Project Operations in Port [*Navy*] (NVT)
POPT	Petty Officer Physical Trainer [*British military*] (DMA)
POPT	Pretesting Orientation on the Purpose of Testing [*US Employment Service*] [*Department of Labor*]
POPU	Push Over Pull Up (NASA)
Popul Rep A...	Population Reports. Series A, Oral Contraceptives (SAUS)
Popul Rep B...	Population Reports. Series B, Intrauterine Devices (SAUS)
Popul Rep C...	Population Reports. Series C, Female Sterilization (SAUS)
Popul Rep D...	Population Reports. Series D, Male Sterilization (SAUS)
Popul Rep E...	Population Reports. Series E, Law and Policy (SAUS)
Popul Rep H...	Population Reports. Series H, Barrier Methods (SAUS)
Popul Rep J...	Population Reports. Series J, Family Planning Programs (SAUS)
Popul Rep L...	Population Reports. Series L, Issues in World Health (SAUS)
Popul Rep M...	Population Reports. Series M, Special Topics (SAUS)
Populuxe	Popular Luxury [*Coined by Thomas Hine, design critic for the Philadelphia Inquirer, to describe the period from the mid-1950's to the mid-1960's*]
POPUS	Post Office Processing Utility Subsystem [*Telecommunications*] (TEL)
POQ	Passing Over Quay (SAUS)
poq	Periodic Order Quantity (AD)
POQ	Period Order Quantity (PDAA)
POQ	Production Offset Quantity [*Military*]
POQ	Provided Otherwise Qualified [*Military*] (AABC)
POQ	Public Opinion Quarterly [*A publication*] (AD)
POQ	Push Off Quickly [*i.e., Be quick about it*] [*British*]
POQL	Probability Outgoing Quality Limit (PDAA)
POQU	Procedure of Questionable Usefulness [*Medicine*] (CPH)
POR	Pacific Ocean Region
POR	Parking Orbit Rendezvous [*NASA*] (MCD)
POR	Partido Obrero Revolucionario [*Revolutionary Workers Party*] [*Bolivia*] [*Political party*] (PPW)
POR	Partido Obrero Revolucionario [*Revolutionary Workers Party*] [*Argentina*] [*Political party*]
POR	Partido Obrero Revolucionario [*Revolutionary Workers Party*] [*Peru*] [*Political party*]
POR	Patent Office Reports [*A publication*] (DLA)
POR	Patrol Operations Report
POR	Payable on Receipt [*Business term*]
p-o-r	Pay-on-Receipt (AD)
POR	Pay on Return [*Business term*]
POR	Peak Overshoot Ratio (IAA)
POR	Periodic Operation Report
POR	Periphal Output Register (SAUS)
POR	Peripheral Order Register (SAUS)
POR	Personnel Occurrence Report [*RAF*] [*British*]
POR	Physician of Record (DAVI)
POR	Pilot Opinion Rating
POR	Place of Receipt (MARI)
POR	Plutonium Organic Recycle [*Nuclear energy*] (NRCH)
POR	Point of No Return (GOBB)
POR	Point of Receive (SAUS)
POR	Point of Resolution (NAKS)
POR	Point of Return (SAUS)
POR	Pola Resources Ltd. [*Vancouver Stock Exchange symbol*]
POR	Policy, Organisation (or Organization) and Rules (SAUS)
POR	Pori [*Finland*] [*Airport symbol*] (OAG)
Por	Porifera (AD)
Por	Porogi [*Waterfall*] [*Russian*] (AD)
por	Porosity (AD)
por	Porous (SAUS)
por	Portage (BARN)
POR	Portec, Inc. [*NYSE symbol*] (SPSG)
POR	Portion
Por	Portland (AD)
POR	Portland [*Maine*] [*Seismograph station code, US Geological Survey*] [*Closed*] (SEIS)
POR	Port of Refuge [*Shipping*]
por	Portrait (RION)
POR	Portrait
Por	Portsmouth Spartans [*National Football League*] [*1930-33*] (NFLA)
Por	Portugal (AD)
Por	Portuguese (AD)
por	Portuguese [*MARC language code*] [*Library of Congress*] (LCCP)
POR	Portuguese
POR	Position of Responsibility (ADA)
POR	Postocclusive Oscillatory Response (DB)
POR	Post Office Return
POR	Post Office Rifles [*Military*] [*British*] (ROG)
POR	Power on Request (ACAE)
POR	Power on Reset (ACAE)
POR	Power-On Reset (AEBE)
POR	Preparation of Overseas Replacement [*Military*] (RDA)
POR	Preparation of Replacements for Oversea Movement [*MTMC*] (TAG)
POR	Press on Regardless [*Automotive marathon*]
POR	Price on Request
POR	Prime contractor Organization (SAUS)
POR	Problem-Oriented Record (SAUS)
POR	Problem-Oriented Records [*Medicine*]
POR	Problem-Oriented Routine (IEEE)
POR	Processing Overseas Replacement Training [*Military*] (VNW)
POR	Process-of-Record (AAEL)
POR	Production Order Records (SAA)
POR	Production Order Request (SAUS)
POR	Program of Requirements (EEVL)
POR	Project Officers Report (MCD)
POR	Propylene Oxide Rubber (SAUS)
POR	Psychotherapy Outcome Research
por	Public Opinion Research (AD)
POR	Purchase Order Request
PORA	Police Officers Research Association (AD)
PORAC	Peace Officers Research Association of California
PORACC	Principles of Radiation and Contamination Control [*Nuclear energy*]
PORAG	Presiding Officers' Review and Advisory Group [*Commonwealth Parliament*] [*Australia*]
PORB	Production Operations Review Board [*NASA*] (NASA)
PORC	Partido Obrero Revolucionario-Combate [*Revolutionary Struggle Workers' Party*] [*Bolivia*] [*Political party*] (PPW)
PORC	Peralta Oaks Research Center (AD)
PORC	Plant Operations Review Committee [*Nuclear energy*] (NRCH)
PORC	Plant Overnight Review Committee [*Environmental science*] (COE)
PORC	Porcelain (AAG)
porc	Porcelain (AD)
PORC	Porphyria, Chester Type (DMAA)
PORC	Purchase Order Release and Control (SAUS)
PORC	Purchase Order Requisition Control (SAUS)
PORCN	Production Order Records Change Notice (KSC)
PORCO	Port Control Office
PORD	Performance and Operations Requirements Document [*NASA*] (NASA)
PORDA	Personnel Officers of Research and Development Agencies
PORDIR	Port Director
PORE	Point Reyes National Seashore [*National Park Service designation*]
POREA	Post Office Regional Employees' Association [*Defunct*] (EA)
POREL(A)	Petty Officer Radio Electrician (Air) [*British military*] (DMA)
POREP	Position Report [*Air Force*]
PORES	Purchase Order Receiving System (MCD)
PORF	Pacific Ocean Research Foundation (EA)
Porg	Person of Restricted Growth [*Slang term used to describe a person of limited cultural awareness*] [*Lifestyle classification*]
PORGIE	Paperback Original [*Award for best original paperback books of the year*]
PORI	Polaris Operational Readiness Instrumentation [*Missiles*]
PORI	Portal Operational Readiness Instrumentation (SAUS)
PORI	Preoperational Readiness Inspection (MCD)
PO-RIP	Purchase Order Receipt in Process (SAUS)
PORIS	Post Office Radio Interference Service [*British*] (DI)
PORIS	Post Office Radio Interference Station (AD)
PORK	Partnership for Over-Regulated Kar [*Humorous description of government-auto industry technology research program*]
porksan	Pork Sandwich (AD)
porkwich	Pork Sandwich (AD)
PORL	Pacific Oceanographic Research Laboratories (SAUS)
PORL	Peninsular/Oriental Steam Nav [*LO Symbol*] (TTSB)
porm	Plus or Minus (AD)
P or M	Plus or Minus (MSA)
PORM	Plus or Minus
PORM-PST...	Partido Obrero Revolucionario Marxista-Partido Socialista de los Trabajadores [*Peru*] [*Political party*] (EY)
porn	Pornographic (AD)
PORN	Pornography (DSUE)
PORN	Protect Our Responsibilities Now [*Book title*]
pornette	Pornographic Cassette (AD)
pornfilm	Pornographic Motion Picture Film (AD)
porno	Pornofilm (AD)
porno	Pornographer (AD)
PORNO	Pornography (DSUE)
PORNO	Purchase Order Number (SAUS)
pornobio	Pornographic Biography (AD)
pornofilm	Pornographic Motion Picture (AD)
porno mag...	Pornographic Magazine (AD)
pornovel	Pornographic Novel (AD)
pornovelist...	Pornographic Novelist (AD)
Porn Squad...	Pornographic Squad (AD)
pornzines	Pornographic Magazines (AD)
PORP	Partial Ossicular Replacement Prosthesis
PORP	Printed on Recycled Paoer (AD)
PORP	Printed on Rice-Paper (SAUS)
P or P	Publish or Perish [*Said of scholars, scientists, etc.*]
porph	Porphyry (VRA)
Porph	Porphyry [*Third century AD*] [*Classical studies*] (OCD)
PORR	Preliminary Operations Requirements Review [*NASA*] (NASA)
PORR	Purchase Order Revision Request
PORS	Portable Oil Reclamation System (SAUS)
PORS	Post Office Research Station (AD)
PORS	Power-On Reset [*Electronics*]
PORS	Product Output Reporting System
PORS	Project Officer Record System (SAUS)

PORSE......... Post Overhaul Reaction Safeguard Examination [Navy] (NVT)
PORSEC....... Pacific Ocean Remote Sensing Conference (SAUS)
PORSHE....... Project of Ocean Rafts System for Hydrogen Economy
PORT.......... Bayport Restaurant Group [NASDAQ symbol] (TTSB)
PORT.......... Bayport Restaurant Group, Inc. [NASDAQ symbol] (SAG)
PORT.......... Partnership Order Retrieval Tool (VLIE)
PORT.......... Patient Outcome Research Team (PCM)
PORT........... Photo-Optical Recorder (or Recording) Tracker (SAUS)
port........... Photo-Optical Recorder Tracker (AD)
PORT.......... Port [Commonly used] (OPSA)
port........... Portable (AD)
PORT......... Portable (KSC)
Port........... Portal (SAUS)
PORT .... Porter (DSUE)
Port............ Porter's Alabama Supreme Court Reports [1834-39] [A publication]
                  (DLA)
Port............ Porter's Indiana Reports [3-7 Indiana] [A publication] (DLA)
PORT.......... Port Financial [NASDAQ symbol] (SG)
Port........... Portfolio (DIAR)
Port........... Portfolio (WGA)
PORT.......... Portland Railroad
PORT.......... Portmanteau (DSUE)
port........... Portrait (AD)
PORT .... Portrait
port........... portraiture (SAUS)
Port............. Portugal (VRA)
PORT.......... Portugal
port........... Portugiesisch [Portuguese] [German] (AD)
Port........... Portuguese (ODBW)
PORT .... Postoperative Respiratory Therapy (DAVI)
PORT .... Prescriptive Objective Reference Testing [Vocational guidance]
PORT .... Presentation Portfolio (VRA)
Port Ade ...... Port Adelaide [South Australia] (AD)
Portage........ Portage Industries Corp. [Associated Press] (SAG)
Portainer ..... Port Container (SAUS)
PORTAL....... Polar Orbiter Remapping and Transformation Application Library
                  (SAUS)
PORTAL....... Process-Oriented Real-Time Algorithmic Language [1978] [Computer
                  science] (CSR)
Port (Ala).... Porter's Alabama Reports [A publication] (DLA)
Port Ala R .. Porter's Alabama Reports [A publication] (DLA)
Port Ald .... Port Alberni [Vancouver Island, British Columbia] (AD)
portalet........ Portable Toilet (AD)
Port Alex ..... Port Alexander [Alaska] (AD)
Port Ant .... Port Antonio [Jamaica] (AD)
PORTAPAK... Portable, Self-Contained, Instrument Package
Port Art........ Port Arthur (AD)
PORTAS....... Penetration of Radiation Through Aperture Simulation (PDAA)
PortBk......... Portsmouth Bank Shares, Inc. [Associated Press] (SAG)
PORT CEM... Portland Cement [Technical drawings] (DAC)
Port Chi .... Port Chicago (AD)
Port Chi .... Portuguese China (AD)
Port Dal .... Port Dalhousie [Ontario, Canada] (AD)
Portec......... Portec, Inc. [Associated Press] (SAG)
PORTER....... Performance Oriented Tracking of Equipment Repair (ACAE)
Porter .... Porter's Alabama Reports [A publication] (DLA)
Porter .... Porter's Indiana Reports [3-7 Indiana] [A publication] (DLA)
Porter (Ala)... Porter's Alabama Reports [A publication] (DLA)
Porter R .... Porter's Alabama Reports [A publication] (DLA)
Porter's Ala R... Porter's Alabama Reports [A publication] (DLA)
Porter's R.... Porter's Alabama Reports [A publication] (DLA)
Porter's Repts... Porter's Alabama Reports [A publication] (DLA)
PortG35....... Portland General Electric Co. [Associated Press] (SAG)
PortGC........ Portland General Corp. [Associated Press] (SAG)
PortgIT........ Portugal Telecom SA [Associated Press] (SAG)
PORTIA....... Port Operations, Transport and Integrated Accountancy (MHDB)
Port Ind .... Portuguese India (AD)
Port Ins........ Porter's Laws of Insurance [A publication] (DLA)
Port Jack ..... Port Jackson Sydney [Sydney, New South Wales, Australia] (AD)
Portland St U... Portland State University (GAGS)
Portland UL Rev... Portland University. Law Review [A publication] (DLA)
Port Liz........ Port Elizabeth [New Jersey] (AD)
Port Liz........ Port Elizabeth [South Africa] (AD)
PORTN........ Portion (ROG)
Port Nick ..... Port Nicholson [Wellington, New Zealand] (AD)
Port of Emb... Port of Embarkation
PORTP......... Partido Obrero Revolucionaria Trotskista Posadista [Bolivia] [Political
                  party] (PPW)
Port P .... Portuguese Pharmacopoeia [A publication]
Port Phil ...... Port Phillip [Melbourne, Victoria, Australia] (AD)
PORTREP..... Port [or Anchorage] Capacity Report [Navy] (NVT)
Port Rich ..... Port Richmond [Staten Island, New York] (AD)
PORTs .... Patient Outcome Research Teams (SAUS)
PORTS........ Physical Oceanographic Real-Time System [Marine science] (OSRA)
PORTS........ Portable Imagery Telecommunications System (ACAE)
PORTS........ Portable Remote Telecommunications System (DOMA)
PORTS........ Port Objective for Real-Time Systems [Marine science] (OSRA)
PORTS........ Ports [Commonly used] (OPSA)
PORTS........ Ports Characteristics File (SAUS)
PORTS........ Portsmouth [City in England]
PORTS......... Portsmouth Gaseous Diffusion Plant [Department of Energy]
                  [Portsmouth, OH] (GAAI)
PORTS........ Preliminary Operations Requirements Test System (ACAE)
PortsBk........ Portsmouth Bank Shares [Associated Press] (SAG)
PORTSM....... Portsmouth [County borough in England]

Ports NSW JI... Ports of New South Wales Journal [A publication]
PORTSREP... Ports Report File (MCD)
Port Sud ..... Port Sudan (AD)
PORTSUM... Port [or Anchorage] Summary Report [Navy] (NVT)
Port Swett .... Port Swettenham [Malaysia] (AD)
PortSys........ Porta Systems Corp. [Associated Press] (SAG)
Port Talb .... Port Talbot [Wales] (AD)
Port Tew .... Port Tewfik [Egypt] (AD)
Port Tim ...... Portuguese Timor (AD)
Portug......... Portugais [Portuguese] [French] (AD)
PortugI....... Portugal Fund [Associated Press] (SAG)
Port UL Rev... Portland University. Law Review [A publication] (DLA)
Port Wash ... Port Washington [Long Island, New York] (AD)
Port Wel .... Port Wellen [Ontario, CAN] (AD)
Port Yid ..... Portuguese Yiddish (SAUS)
PORV .... Pilot-Operated Relief Valve [Nuclear energy] (NRCH)
PORV .... Power-Operated Relief Valve [Nuclear energy] (NRCH)
POS .... Aeroposta SA [Argentina] [ICAO designator] (FAAC)
POS .... Catalina Marketing [NYSE symbol] (TTSB)
POS .... Catalina Marketing Corp. [NYSE symbol] (SPSG)
POS .... Pacific Ocean Ship (NASA)
POS .... Pacific Orchid Society of Hawaii (EA)
POS .... Parent Operating Service (MCD)
POS .... Parosteal Osteosarcoma [Oncology] (DAVI)
POS .... Partially Ordered Set (OA)
POS .... Partial Output Signal (SAUS)
POS .... Part-of-Speech (IDAI)
POS .... Pascal Operating System (ELAL)
POS .... Patella Overload Syndrome [Medicine] (MELL)
POS .... Patent Office Society (EA)
POS .... Peacetime Operating Stock [Military] (CINC)
POS .... Peacetime Operating Stocks (SAUS)
POS .... Pennsylvania Orthopaedic Society (SAUS)
POS .... Period of Service [Military]
POS .... Permanently Out of Stock (SAUS)
POS .... Permanent Orbital Station [NASA] (IAA)
POS .... Persistant Object Service (SAUS)
POS .... Persistent Object Service (SAUS)
POS .... Photo Optic System
POS .... Pico Resources [Vancouver Stock Exchange symbol]
POS .... Piper Owner Society (EA)
POS .... Pivoting Optical Servo (SAUS)
POS .... Planar Oxygen Sensor
POS .... Plan of Service (OICC)
POS .... Plant Operating System [Nuclear energy] (NRCH)
POS .... Play Observation Scale [Test] (TMMY)
pos............. Point of Sale (AD)
POS .... Point of Sale (ODBW)
PoS .... Point of Sale
POS .... Point of Scale (SAUS)
POS .... Point of Service [Health plan option]
POS .... Point of Service Option
POS .... Point-of-Service Plan [Insurance] (PAZ)
POS .... Polar Orbiting Satellite [Marine science] (OSRA)
POs .... Police Officers (AD)
POS .... Policy Statements [Australian Broadcasting Tribunal] [A publication]
POS .... Polycystic Ovarian Syndrome [Also, PCOS] [Gynecology]
POS .... Portable Oxygen System (MCD)
PoS .... Port of Service (AD)
POS .... Port Of Spain [Trinidad and Tobago] [Airport symbol] (OAG)
PoS .... Port of Spain (AD)
POS .... Port(s) of Support (DOMA)
POS .... Position (KSC)
pos............. Position (WDMC)
Pos .... Positioning (SAUS)
pos............. Positive (AD)
POS .... Positive (AFM)
Pos .... Positive Ground
POS .... Possession [or Possessive] (WGA)
pos............. Possibility (AD)
Pos .... Possible
POs .... Postal Orders (AD)
POS .... Post Office Scheme [Regulations] [British]
POS .... Preferred Overseas Shore Duty
POS .... Pressure on Space [Publishing] (DGA)
POS .... Pressure Operated Switch (SAUS)
POS .... Pressure-Operated Switch (IAA)
POS .... Primary Operating Stock [DoD]
POS .... Primary Operating Stocks (SAUS)
POS .... Primary Operating System (IEEE)
POS .... Primary Oxygen System
POS .... Probability of Success (COE)
POS .... Probability of Survival [Automotive componant analysis]
POS .... Problem-Oriented Software (SAUS)
POS .... Problem Oriented System
POS .... Problem-Oriented System (SAUS)
POS .... Processor Operating System (SAUS)
POS .... Production-Oriented Survey (MCD)
pos............. Product of Sums (AD)
POS .... Products of Sums (IAA)
POS .... Professional Operating System (NITA)
POS .... Professions and Occupations Sourcebook [A publication]
POS .... Programmable Object Select [Computer science] (VLIE)
POS .... Programmable Option Select [Computer science]
PoS .... Programme of Study [British] (DET)

POS	Programming Optimizing System (IAA)
POS	Program of Study (AEE)
POS	Program Operations Staff [*Environmental Protection Agency*] (GFGA)
POS	Program Order Sequence
POS	Protection of Shipping (SEWL)
POS	Protein, Oil, and Starch [*Pilot manufacturing plant established by the Canadian government*]
POS	Pupil Observation Survey [*Education*]
POS	Purchase Order Status (SAUS)
POS	Purchase Order Supplement
POSA	Passive Optical Sample Assembly (SAUS)
POSA	Patriotic Order Sons of America (EA)
posa	Payment Outstanding Suspense Accounts (AD)
POSA	Payment Outstanding Suspense Accounts (NATG)
POSA	Petty Officer Stores Accountant [*British military*] (DMA)
POSA	Preliminary Operating Safety Analysis [*Nuclear energy*] (NRCH)
POSA MOS	Polysilicon Oxidation Self-Aligned Metal-Oxide Semiconductor (SAUS)
POSARS	Plan of Service Automated Reporting System [*Employment and Training Administration*] [*Department of Labor*]
posb	Possibly (VRA)
POSB	Post Office Savings Bank
POSC	Little Workers of the Sacred Heart (TOCD)
POSC	Petrotechnical Open Software Corp. (SAUS)
POSC	Primary Operations System Control (SAUS)
POSC	Problem-Oriented System of Charting (AAMN)
posc-	Santa Cruz Islands [*MARC geographic area code*] [*Library of Congress*] (LCCP)
POSCH	Program of Surgical Control of Hyperlipidemia
POSCO	Pohang Iron & Steel Co. (ECON)
POSCOR	Position Correct (CAAL)
POSCORB	Planning, Organizing, Staffing, Coordinating, Reporting, and Budgeting [*Management*]
POSD	Personnel on Station Date [*Army*] (AABC)
POSD	Post Office Savings Department (AD)
POSD	Program for Optical System Design
POSD	Program of Optical System Design (SAUS)
POSD	Project Operation Support Division [*NASA*]
POSDCORB	Planning, Organizing, Staffing, Directing, Coordinating, Reporting, and Budgeting [*Principles of management*]
posdsplt	Port Side Out, Starboard Side Home [*British slang*] (AD)
posdsplt	Positive Displacement (AD)
POSDSPLT	Positive Displacement
POSE	Parents Opposed to Sex Education
POSE	Photogrammetric Ocean Survey Equipment
POSE	Picture-Oriented Software Engineering [*Computer science*] (CIST)
POSE	Portable Operating System Environment
POSE	Portable Operating System Extension [*Computer science*] (VLIE)
POSE	Power Operational Support Equipment
POSE	Promotion of Social Education [*British*] (DI)
PO SEC	Principal Officer's Secretary [*Foreign service*]
POSEIDON	French component of TOPEX POSEIDON (SAUS)
POSEIDON	Positioning Ocean Sea Earth and Ice Dynamics and Orbiting Navigator (SAUS)
POSER	Process Organization to Simplify Error Recovery (PDAA)
POSET	Partially Ordered Set (HGAA)
Posey	Posey's Unreported Cases [*Texas*] [*A publication*] (ILCA)
Posey UC	Texas Unreported Cases [*A publication*] (DLA)
Posey Unrep Cas	Posey's Unreported Cases [*Texas*] [*A publication*] (DLA)
POSF	Port of Support File (DOMA)
POSF	Ports of Support File (SAUS)
POSG	After Glucose Infusion Started [*Biochemistry*] (DAVI)
posh	Permuted on Subject Headings (AD)
POSH	Permuted on Subject Headings [*Indexing technique*]
POSH	Personal & Organizational Security Handbook [*A publication*]
POSH	Port Outwardbound, Starboard Homewardbound [*Refers to shaded cabins of British naval officers in the Far East*]
POSH	Probability of Severe Hail (USDC)
posh	Samoa Islands [*MARC geographic area code*] [*Library of Congress*] (LCCP)
POSI	Parallel-Out, Serial-In (SAUS)
POSI	Personnel On-Site Integration (SAA)
POSI	Portable Operating System Interface (SAUS)
POSI	Positron Corp. [*NASDAQ symbol*] (SAG)
POSI	Promotion Conference for OSI (SAUS)
POS INIT	Position Initialization (GAVI)
POSIP	Portable Ship Instrumentation Package
posistor	Positive Resistor (AD)
posit	Position (AD)
POSIT	Position (NVT)
posit	Positive (AD)
POSIT	Positive
POSIT	Positivism (ROG)
posit	Positron (AD)
POSIT	Profile for Open Systems Internetworking Technologies [*Computer science*] (CDE)
POSIT	Profiles for Open Systems Interconnection Technologies (SAUS)
POSIT	Profiles for Open Systems Interworking Technologies (SAUS)
POSITIVE	Parents of Surrogate-Borne Infants and Toddlers in Verbal Exchange (EA)
Positr	Positron Corp. [*Associated Press*] (SAG)
POSITREPS	Position Reports
positron	Positive Electron (AD)
POSITRON	Positive Electron
Positron	Positron Corp. [*Associated Press*] (SAG)
POSIW	Positron Corp. Wrrt [*NASDAQ symbol*] (TTSB)
POSIX	Portable Operating System based on Unix (SAUS)
POSIX	Portable Operating System Interface Exchange
POSIX	Portable Operating System Interface for Computer Environments (AAGC)
POSIX	Portable Operating System Interface for Computer Systems (SAUS)
POSIX	Portable Operating System Interface for Unix [*Computer science*] (PCM)
POSIX	Portable Operating System Interface for X (SAUS)
POSIX	Portable Operating Systems for Computer Environments (AD)
POSIX	Portable Operating System Specification [*IEEE*]
POSK	Polski Osrodek Spoleczno-Kulturalny [*Polish Social and Cultural Association - PSCA*] (EAIO)
POSKP	Polski Osrodek Spoleczno-Kulturalny Posk [*Polish Social and Cultural Association - PSCA*] (EAIO)
POsl	Papyri Osloenses [*A publication*] (OCD)
POSL	Parti Ouvrier Socialiste Luxembourgeois [*Luxembourg Socialist Workers' Party*] (EAIO)
POSM	National Association of Post Office and General Service Maintenance Employees [*Later, APWU*] [*AFL-CIO*]
posm	Patient-Operated Selected Mechanisms (AD)
POSM	Patient Operated Selected (or Selector) Mechanism (SAUS)
POSM	Patient-Operated Selector Mechanism [*Pronounced "possum"*]
POSMA	Postal Service Manual [*A publication*]
Posmo	Osmotic Permeability [*Biochemistry*] (DAVI)
posn	Position (AD)
POSN	Position (AFM)
posn-	Solomon Islands [*MARC geographic area code*] [*Library of Congress*] (LCCP)
POSNA	Pediatric Orthopaedic Society of North America (EA)
POS/NAV	Positioning/Navigation
POS/NAV	Position/Navigation [*System*] [*Military*] (INF)
POSNO	Position Number [*Military*] (ADDR)
POSN SW	Position Switch (SAUS)
POSNY	People of the State of New York (AD)
POSO	Prosoft I-Net Solutions, Inc. [*NASDAQ symbol*] (SAG)
POSP	Pacific Ocean Stations Program (SAA)
POSPI	Post Office Standards Parts Interface (SAUS)
pos pr	Positive Pressure (MAE)
Pos Press	Positive Pressure (CPH)
pos pron	Possessive Pronoun (AD)
POSR	Peacetime Operating Stock Requirement [*Military*] (AFIT)
POS R	Positive Review [*A publication*] (ROG)
POS REF	Position Reference (GAVI)
PosResp	Positive Response Television [*Associated Press*] (SAG)
POSRIP	People Organized to Stop Rape of Imprisoned Persons (EA)
POSS	Palomar Observatory Sky Survey [*NASA*]
POSS	Passive Optical Satellite Surveillance [*System*] (NATG)
POSS	Passive Optical Surveillance System (SAUS)
POSS	Photo-Optical Surveillance Subsystem
POSS	Photooptical Surveillance System (SAUS)
POSS	Plant Occurrence and Status System (SAUS)
P-O-S S	Point-of-Sale System (AD)
P-O-S S	Point-of-Service System (AD)
POSS	Polar Orbiting Satellite System (SAUS)
POSS	Polyimide on Silicon-mask Substrate (SAUS)
POSS	Portable Oceanographic Survey System (MCD)
poss	Possession (AD)
POSS	Possession [*or Possessive*] (AFM)
Poss	Possession (BEE)
poss	Possessive (WDMC)
poss	Possible (WDMC)
POSS	Possible
poss	Possibly (WDMC)
POSS	Possis Medical [*NASDAQ symbol*] (TTSB)
POSS	Possis Medical, Inc. [*NASDAQ symbol*] (NQ)
POSS	Program Operations Support Staff [*Environmental Protection Agency*] (GFGA)
POSS	Prototype Optical Surveillance Subsystem (SAUS)
POSS	Prototype Optical Surveillance System
POSS	Proximal Over-Shoulder Strap [*Medicine*]
POSSE	Parents of Students in Special Education (SAUS)
POSSE	Parents Opposed to Sex and Sensitivity Education [*An association*]
POSSE	Police Operations Systems Support System Elementary
POSSE	Progressive Onslaught to Stamp out Stock Errors [*Navy*] (NG)
POSSED	Possessed (ROG)
posses	Possessive (AD)
POSSF	Post Office Staff Superannuation Fund [*British*] (DI)
Possis	Possis Medical, Inc. [*Associated Press*] (SAG)
posslq	Person of the Opposite Sex in Same Living Quarters (AD)
POSSLQ	Persons of Opposite Sex Sharing Living Quarters [*Bureau of the Census*]
POSSN	Possession (WGA)
POSSNC	Post Office Senior Staff Negotiating Council [*British*]
POSSON	Possession
POSS System	Passive Optical Satellite Surveillance System (SAUS)
POSSUB	Possible Submarine [*Navy*] (NVT)
POSSUM	Pictures of Specific Syndromes and Unknown Malformations [*Database*]
POSSUM	Polar Orbiting Satellite System - University of Michigan [*Designed by engineering students*]
Post	De Posteritate Caini [*of Philo*] (BJA)
POST	Frederick Post Drafting Equipment (AD)
POST	International Post Ltd. [*NASDAQ symbol*] (SAG)
POST	Intl Post Ltd [*NASDAQ symbol*] (TTSB)

POST	Parliamentary Office of Science and Technology [*British*]
POST	Passive Optical Scan Tracker (MCD)
POST	Passive Optical Seeker Technique
POST	Passive Optical Seeker Technology (SAUS)
POST	Payload Operations Support Team [*NASA*] (MCD)
POST	Peace Officers Standards and Training (SAUS)
POST	Peace Officer Standards and Training
POST	Periodically Oscillating Source Temperature (SAUS)
POST	Peritoneal Ovum Sperm Transfer [*Medicine*]
POST	Piezoelectric-Oscillator Self-Tuned [*Electric system*]
POST	Point-of-Sale Terminal [*Business term*]
POST	Point of Sale Transaction (SAUS)
POST	Point-of-Sale Transaction
POST	Polaris Operation Support Task Group [*Missiles*]
POST	Polar Stratospheric Telescope
POST	Police Officer Student Training (AD)
POST	Portable Optical Sensor Tester (ACAE)
PoST	Portable Satellite Terminal (SAUS)
POST	Positive (AAG)
post	Postage (AD)
POST	Postal (SAUS)
POST	Postemergence [*Weed control*]
POST	[*The*] Poster [*A publication*] (ROG)
post	Poster (VRA)
Post	Posterior (AMHC)
post	Posterior
POST	Posting (SAUS)
post	Post Mortem (AD)
POST	Postmortem (AAMN)
Post	Post's Reports [*23-26 Michigan*] [*A publication*] (DLA)
Post	Post's Reports [*42-64 Missouri*] [*A publication*] (DLA)
POST	Postulate (SAUS)
POST	Power on Self Test (SAUS)
POST	Power-On Self Test [*IBM-PC feature*]
POST	Processes of Science Test (AD)
POST	Production-Oriented Scheduling Technique (SAUS)
POST	Production-Oriented Scheduling Techniques (MCD)
POST	Programmer Operating Standards Technique
POST	Program to Operate Simulated Trajectories
POST	Program to Optimize Shuttle [*or Simulated*] Trajectories [*NASA*] (KSC)
POST	Program to Optimize Simulated Trajectories (SAUS)
POST	Proposed Optical Stinger
POST	Prototype Ocean Surveillance Terminal [*Navy*] (ANA)
POST	Prototype Ocean Surveillance Tracker (SEWL)
Post & Ins ...	Postage and Insurance (ILCA)
Post & Reg...	Postage and Registration (DLA)
post-Aug......	Post-Augustan (AD)
POST AUR ...	Post Aurem [*Behind the Ear*] [*Pharmacy*]
post aur......	Post Aurem [*Behind the Ear*] [*Latin*] (AD)
POSTD	Petty Officer Steward [*British military*] (DMA)
post d	Posterior Diameter (AD)
POSTE	Postage (ROG)
POSTEC	Powder Science and Technology Research Association [*Norway*] (EAIO)
POSTEC	Program of Research in Powder Science and Technology (SAUS)
POSTECH	Pohang Institute of Science and Technology (SAUS)
poster	Posterior (AD)
Poster	Posterity (SAUS)
POSTER	Post Strike Emergency Reporting
pos terminal...	Point-of-Sale Terminal (AD)
Poste's Gai ...	Poste's Translation of Gaius [*A publication*] (ILCA)
Poste's Gaius Inst...	Poste's Translation of Gaius [*A publication*] (DLA)
POSTFAT	Postfinal Acceptance Trials [*Navy*] (NVT)
Postfax	Post Facsimile (SAUS)
POSTFAX	Post Office Facsimile [*British*]
postgangl	Postganglionic [*Medicine*] (MEDA)
PostGradDipAgr...	Postgraduate Diploma in Agriculture
PostGradDipEdStud(IndArts)...	Postgraduate Diploma in Educational Studies (Industrial Arts)
PostGradDipl...	Post-Graduate Diploma (SAUS)
Postgrad Med Inst...	Postgraduate Medical Institute (AD)
Postgraduate D...	Postgraduate Diploma (PGP)
POSTGRES...	POSTGRES Object-Relational Database Mangement System (SAUS)
Posth	Posthumous (DIAR)
POSTH	Posthumous
POST-J	Polymer Science and Technology-Journals (SAUS)
postl	Postlude (AD)
Postl Dict.....	Postlethwaite's Dictionary of Trade and Commerce [*A publication*] (DLA)
post-mort....	Post Mortem (AD)
POSTNET.....	Postal Numeric Encoding Technique (SAUS)
POSTNET.....	Postnumeric Encoding Technique [*US Postal Service*]
post-obit.....	Post Obitum [*After Death*] [*Latin*]
post ofc	Post Office (VRA)
post-op	Post-Operative (AD)
POSTOP	Postoperative [*Medicine*]
POSTOR.......	Photo-Optical Storage [*Computer science*] (VLIE)
POST-P	Polymer Science and Technology Patents (SAUS)
POSTP	Posterior Probability [*Computations*]
POSTP	Postprocessor [*Computer science*]
post part......	Post Partum [*Afterbirth*] [*Latin*] (AD)
PostPr..........	Post Properties, Inc. [*Associated Press*] (SAG)
POSTPRO......	Postprocessor [*Computer science*]
PostPrp........	Post Properties, Inc. [*Associated Press*] (SAG)

POSTS	Positive Occipital Sharp Transients of Sleep [*On electroencephalogram*] [*Neurology*] (DAVI)
Post Sag D...	Posterior Sagittal Diameter [*Anatomy*] (MAE)
Post Script...	Post Script: Essays in Film and the Humanities [*A publication*] (BRI)
POST SING SED LIQ...	Post Singulas Sedes Liquidas [*After Every Loose Stool*] [*Pharmacy*] (ROG)
post-sync....	Post-Synchronization (AD)
POSV	Pilot Operated Solenoid Valve (SAUS)
POSV	Pilot-Operated Solenoid Valve [*Nuclear energy*] (IAA)
POSW	Privately Owned Stored Water (ADWA)
POSWG........	Poseidon Software Working Group [*Missiles*]
pot	Dashpot (IDOE)
POT.............	Paint on Tangent (IAA)
POT.............	Parallel Output
POT.............	Partial Operating Time (SAUS)
POT.............	Part of Title [*Computer science*] (DCDG)
POT.............	Pennsylvania-Ontario Transportation Co. [*AAR code*]
POT.............	Periodic Orbital Theory (SAUS)
POT.............	Periostitis Ossificans Toxica [*Medicine*] (DMAA)
POT.............	Physical Organization Table (HGAA)
POT.............	Picture Object Table (MHDI)
POT.............	Piston Operated Transducer
POT.............	Pitch-Orthogonal Thrust
POT.............	Plain Old Telephone [*Bell System's basic model*]
pot	Point of tangency (AD)
POT.............	Point of Turnaround [*Travel industry*] (TRID)
POT.............	Polet [*Former USSR*] [*FAA designator*] (FAAC)
pot	Portable Outdoor Toilet (AD)
POT.............	Portable Outside Toilet [*A unit of mobility equipment*] [*Military*]
POT.............	Port Antonio [*Jamaica*] [*Airport symbol*] (OAG)
POT.............	Post Office Telecommunications [*British*]
POT.............	Post-Operative Treatment [*Medicine*] (DMAA)
POT.............	Potable
pot	Potash (AD)
POT.............	Potash Corp. of Saskatchewan [*NYSE symbol*] (SPSG)
POT.............	Potash Corp. Saskatchewan [*NYSE symbol*] (TTSB)
pot	Potassa [*Chemistry*] (MAE)
POT.............	Potassium [*Chemical symbol is K*]
POT.............	Potato (ROG)
POT.............	Potentate
pot	Potential (AD)
POT.............	Potential (AFM)
POT.............	Potential Temperature (SAUS)
pot	Potentiometer (IDOE)
POT.............	Potentiometer [*or Potentiometric*]
Pot.............	Potion
POT.............	Potsdam [*Germany*] [*Later, NGK*] [*Seismograph station code, US Geological Survey*] (SEIS)
Pot.............	Potter (SAUS)
POT.............	Pottery
POT.............	Pottle [*Unit of measure*] (ROG)
POT.............	Pottsville Free Public Library, Pottsville, PA [*OCLC symbol*] (OCLC)
POT.............	Potus [*A Drink*] [*Pharmacy*]
POT.............	Prevailing-Out Torque [*Automotive engineering*]
POT.............	Program for Operational Trajectories [*Marine science*] (OSRA)
POT.............	Proof of Technology (ACAE)
POT.............	Propeller Order Transmitter (OA)
POT.............	Pulmonary Oxygen Transfer [*Medicine*] (MELL)
POTA	Planet of the Apes [*Movie title*]
POT ACE......	Potassium Acetate (SAUS)
POT ACID PHOS...	Potassium Acid Phosphate (SAUS)
POTAD	Program for Operational Transport and Dispersion (USDC)
PotAGT	Potential Abnormality of Glucose Tolerance [*Medicine*]
POT&I	Pre-Overhaul Test and Inspection Plan (SAUS)
POT & I	Preoverhaul Tests and Inspections [*Navy*] (NVT)
POTANN.......	Potomac Annex [*Navy*]
Potash	Potash Corp. of Saskatchewan, Inc. [*Associated Press*] (SAG)
Potash	Potassium Carbonate (SAUS)
potash alum...	Potassium Aluminum Sulfate (AD)
potass.........	Potassium [*An element*] (DAVI)
POTASWG.....	Poseidon Test Analysis Software Working Group [*Missiles*]
potats	Potatoes (AD)
POTBI	Places, Organizations, Things, Biographics, Intangibles
POT BICARB...	Potassium Bicarbonate (SAUS)
POT BIT	Potassium Bitartrate (SAUS)
POT CITR	Potassium Citrate (SAUS)
POT CL	Potassium Chloride (SAUS)
POTCP	Partially Oxidized Tetracyanoplatinate Compound [*Inorganic, one-dimensional conductor*]
POTD	Player of the Decade [*Sports*]
P o TD	Port of The Dalles (AD)
POTDIF	Potential Difference [*Electronics*] (IAA)
POTDR.........	Polarization Optical Time-Domain Reflectometry (SAUS)
Pot Dwar	Potter's Edition of Dwarris on Statutes [*A publication*] (DLA)
PotEd25.......	Potomac Edison [*Associated Press*] (SAG)
PotEl..........	Potomac Electric Power Co. [*Associated Press*] (SAG)
POTELECTROMET...	Potentiometric Electrometer (IAA)
POTEN	Potential (AAMN)
POTF...........	Polychromatic Optical Thickness Fringe (OA)
POTF...........	Polychromatic Optical Thickness Fringes (SAUS)
POTF...........	Psychological Operations Task Force [*Army*] (INF)
POTG	Phenylorthotolyl Guanidine (SAUS)
POT GLUC ...	Potassium Gluconate (SAUS)
Poth Cont...	Pothier's Contracts [*A publication*] (DLA)
Poth Contr Sale...	Pothier's Treatise on the Contract of Sale [*A publication*] (DLA)

Poth Cont Sale... Pothier's Treatise on the Contract of Sale [*A publication*] (DLA)
Pothier Pand... Pothier's Pandectae Justinianeae, Etc. [*A publication*] (DLA)
Poth Mar Cont... Pothier's Treatise on Maritime Contracts [*A publication*] (DLA)
Poth Ob ...... Pothier on the Law of Obligations [*A publication*] (DLA)
Poth Obl ...... Pothier on the Law of Obligations [*A publication*] (DLA)
Poth Oblig ... Pothier on the Law of Obligations [*A publication*] (DLA)
Poth Oeuv.... Oeuvres de Pothier [*A publication*] (DLA)
Poth Pand.... Pothier's Pandects [*A publication*] (DLA)
Poth Part.... Pothier on Partnership [*A publication*] (DLA)
Poth Proc Civ... Pothier. Procedure Civile [*A publication*] (DLA)
POTIB .... Polaris Technical Information Bulletin [*Missiles*]
POTIB .... Poseidon Technical Information Bulletin [*A publication*] (AD)
potl- .... Tokelau Islands [*MARC geographic area code*] [*Library of Congress*] (LCCP)
Pot LD .... Pott's Law Dictionary [*3rd ed.*] [*1815*] [*A publication*] (DLA)
Potltch........ Potlatch Corp. [*Associated Press*] (SAG)
POTMC........ Protective Outfit Toxicological Microclimate Controlled (RDA)
PotmEl........ Potomac Electric Power Co. [*Associated Press*] (SAG)
POTMLD....... Potential Mixed Layer Depth
POT NIT ...... Potassium Nitrate (SAUS)
POTO .... Potomac River Basin (SAUS)
poto- .... Tonga [*MARC geographic area code*] [*Library of Congress*] (LCCP)
POTOMAC..... Patent Office Techniques of Mechanized Access and Classification [*Automation project, shut down in 1972*]
potosslq...... Persons of the Opposite Sex Sharing Living Quarters (AD)
POTP .... Paralysis of the Pen (SAUS)
POTP .... Physical Operation Time Projection (SAUS)
POT PHOS ... Potassium Phosphate (SAUS)
potr............. Potrero [*Cattle Ranch*] [*Spanish*] (AD)
POTRK........ Purchase Order Tracking System (SAUS)
POTRK........ Region 3 Purchase Order Tracking System (SAUS)
PotrSvg....... Potters Savings & Loan Co. [*Associated Press*] (SAG)
POTS .... Perials of the Sea (MHDB)
POTS .... Petty Officer Telegraphist Special (DSUE)
POTS .... Photo-Optical Terrain Simulator (MUGU)
pots .... Plain Old Telephone Service (AD)
POTS .... Plain Old Telephone Service [*or System*] [*Humorous term for Long Lines Department of AT & T*] [*See also PANS*]
POTS .... Plain Old Telephone System (SAUS)
POTS .... Plain Old Time-Sharing (SAUS)
POTS .... Plain Ordinary Telephone Service (SAUS)
POTS .... Plain Ordinary Telephone System (SAUS)
POTS .... Plug-on Terminator System (SAUS)
POTS .... PORI [*Polaris Operational Readiness Instrumentation*] Operational Test System [*Missiles*]
POTS .... Post Office Training School (SAUS)
pots .... Potentiometers (AD)
POTS .... Potentiometers (COE)
POTS .... Precision Optical Tracking System (KSC)
POTS .... Preoverhaul Tests [*Navy*] (NVT)
POTS .... Purchase of Telephones and Services Program (AAGC)
POTS .... Purchase of Telephones and Systems (SAUS)
POTS .... Purchase of Telephone Services Contracts
POTSB .... Post Office and Trustee Savings Bank (SAUS)
POT SW....... Potentiometer with Switch (SAUS)
POTT........... Patriot Operator Tactics Trainer (ACAE)
pott............. Pottery (AD)
pott-........... Trust Territory of the Pacific Islands [*MARC geographic area code*] [*Library of Congress*] (LCCP)
Pott Corp ..... Potter on Corporations [*A publication*] (DLA)
Pott Dwarris... Potter's Edition of Dwarris on Statutes [*A publication*] (DLA)
Potter.......... Potter's Reports [*4-7 Wyoming*] [*A publication*] (DLA)
PottrFinl ...... Potters Financial Corp. [*Associated Press*] (SAG)
POTTS .... Post Office Technicians Training School (SAUS)
Potts LD ...... Potts' Law Dictionary [*3rd ed.*] [*1815*] [*A publication*] (DLA)
POTUS........ President of the United States
POTV .... Personnel Orbit Transfer Vehicle (MCD)
pot w .... Portable Water (AD)
POTW .... Potable Water (KSC)
POTW .... Publically-Owned Treatment Works (DNAB)
POTW .... Publicly Owned Treatment Works (EG)
POTWA .... Post and Telecommunications Workers Association (SAUS)
POU .... Paramount Resources Ltd. [*Toronto Stock Exchange symbol*]
POU .... Placenta, Ovary, Uterus [*Medicine*]
POU .... Point of Use
POU .... Poughkeepsie [*New York*] [*Airport symbol*] (OAG)
POU .... Poughkeepsie, NY [*Location identifier*] [*FAA*] (FAAL)
POU .... Pouilloux [*France*] [*Seismograph station code, US Geological Survey*] (SEIS)
POUCC........ Post Office Users Coordination Committee [*British*]
POUCG........ Point of Use Chemical Generation (SAUS)
POUCG........ Point-of-Use Chemical Generation (AAEL)
POUF .... Projects of Optimum Urgency and Feasibility
PoughSv ...... [*The*] Poughkeepsie Savings Bank FSB [*Associated Press*] (SAG)
poul .... Poultry (AD)
POUL .... Poultry
POUM .... Partido Obrero de Unificacion Marxista [*Workers' Party of Marxist Unification*] [*Former USSR*] (LAIN)
POUNC........ Post Office Users' National Council [*British*] (ILCA)
POUP .... Post Overhaul Upkeep Period
poup-......... United States Miscellaneous Pacific Islands [*MARC geographic area code*] [*Library of Congress*] (LCCP)
POU/POE...... Point-of-Use/Point-of-Entry [*Water standards*] (FFDE)
POUR.......... President's Organization for Unemployment Relief (AD)

POUS .... Partido Operario de Unidade Socialista [*Workers' Party for Socialist Unity*] [*Portugal*] [*Political party*] (PPW)
POUT .... Prison Officer under Training (WDAA)
POV Ob .... Peak Operated Valve (MCD)
POV .... Peak Operating Valve
POV .... Peak Operating Voltage
POV .... Pend Oreille Valley Railroad (AD)
POV .... Peroxide Value (SAUS)
POV .... Persistence of Vision - Ray [*Computer program*]
POV .... Personally Owned Vehicle
POV .... Pinch-Off Voltage
POV .... Pittsburgh & Ohio Valley Railway Co. [*AAR code*]
POV .... Plane of Vibration
POV .... Pneumatically Operated Valve
POV .... Pneumatic Operated Valve (SAUS)
POV .... Point of View
p-o-v .... Point-of-View (AD)
POV .... Povidone (SAUS)
POV .... Presov [*Czechoslovakia*] [*Airport symbol*] (AD)
POV .... Pressure-Operated Valve (MCD)
pov .... Privately Owned Vehicle (AD)
POV .... Privately Owned Vehicle (NVT)
POV .... Proximity Operations Vehicle (SSD)
POV .... Purchase, Outside Vendors
POV .... Putting-On Voltage [*Doppler navigation*] (DEN)
POVC.......... Probation Officers and Volunteers in Corrections [*Victoria, Australia*]
POVEU .... Program Operations Vocational Education Unit (OICC)
Pov L Rep ... Poverty Law Reporter [*Commerce Clearing House*] [*A publication*] (DLA)
POVMR........ Problem-Oriented Veterinary Medical Record (SAUS)
POVORTAD... Positive Vorticity Advection (SAUS)
POVT .... Puerperal Ovarian-Vein Thrombophlebitis [*Medicine*]
POW .... Country Potash, Oil and Wheat Country (SAUS)
POW .... Paying Their Own Way
POW .... Pay Order of Withdrawal
POW .... Peoples of the World [*A publication*]
POW .... Perception of Ward [*Scales*] [*Psychology*]
POW .... Peripheral Output Writer (SAUS)
POW .... Petty Officer of the Watch [*Navy*]
POW .... Place of Work (SAUS)
PoW........... Plan of Work (HEAS)
POW........... Powassan Encephalitis [*Medicine*]
POW .... Powder [*Navy*]
pow........... Power (AD)
POW .... Power
POW .... Power Corp. of Canada [*Toronto Stock Exchange symbol*] [*Vancouver Stock Exchange symbol*]
POW .... Powhatan [*Arkansas*] [*Seismograph station code, US Geological Survey*] (SEIS)
P o W .... Prince of Wales (AD)
POW .... Prince of Wales
pow............ Prisoner of War (AD)
PoW........... Prisoner of War (WDAA)
POW .... Prisoner of War [*Also, PW*]
P o W .... Prisoner of Watergate (AD)
POW .... Prisoner Outreach Work (WDAA)
POW .... Progressive Order of the West [*Defunct*] (EA)
POWACO...... Portable Water Coolant Circulator
Pow App Proc... Powell's Law of Appellate Proceedings [*A publication*] (DLA)
PoWBN........ Biblioteka Narodowa [*National Library*], Warsaw, Poland [*Library symbol*] [*Library of Congress*] (LCLS)
PoWC.......... Instytut Informacji Naukowej, Technicznej, i Ekonomicznej, Warsaw, Poland [*Library symbol*] [*Library of Congress*] (LCLS)
POWC .... Program Out-of-Window Collision (SAUS)
Pow Car...... Powell's Inland Carriers [*2nd ed.*] [*1861*] [*A publication*] (DLA)
Pow Cont ..... Powell on Contracts [*A publication*] (DLA)
Pow Conv ..... Powell. Conveyancing [*1810*] [*A publication*] (ILCA)
POW Country... Potash, Oil, and Wheat Country [*Saskatoon, Saskatchewan*] (AD)
powd........... Powder (AD)
POWD .... Powder [*England*]
POWD .... Powdered
Powder Bulk Eng... Powder and Bulk Engineering (SAUS)
Powder Diffr... Powder Diffraction (SAUS)
Powder Handl Process... Powder Handling and Processing (SAUS)
Powder Metall... Powder Metallurgy (SAUS)
Powder Metall Def Technol... Powder Metallurgy in Defense Technology (SAUS)
Powder Metall Int... Powder Metallurgy International (SAUS)
Powder Metall Sci Technol... Powder Metallurgy Science and Technology (SAUS)
Powder Metall Technol... Powder Metallurgy Technology (SAUS)
Powder Sci Eng... Powder Science and Engineering (SAUS)
Powder Technol... Powder Technology (SAUS)
Pow Dev...... Powell's Essay upon the Learning of Devises, Etc. [*A publication*] (DLA)
POWDR........ Protect Our Wetlands and Duck Resources [*Department of the Interior*] [*Washington, DC*]
Powell .... Powell Industries, Inc. [*Associated Press*] (SAG)
POWEP........ Priority Output Writes Execution Process (SAUS)
POWER........ Pennsylvania's Online World of Electronic Resources
POWER........ Pension Opportunities for Workers' Expanded Retirement [*Plan proposed in 1991 by the Department of Labor*]
POWER........ People Organized and Working for Economic Rebirth [*Program for black economic development*] [*Later, Nationway Ventures International Ltd.*]
POWER........ Performance Optimization with Enhanced RISC [*Reduced Instruction Set Computer*] (PCM)

POWER........ Planning Operation With Enabling Resources
POWER........ Power Optimization With Enhanced RISC (SAUS)
POWER........ Priority Output Writers Execution Processor [*Computer science*] (IAA)
POWER........ Priority Output Writers, Execution Processors, and Input Readers (MHDI)
POWER........ Priority Output Writers, Executionprocessors and input Readers (SAUS)
POWER........ Priority Output Writes Execution Process [*Computer science*] (IAA)
POWER........ Producing Organized Writing and Effective Reviewing
POWER........ Professionals Organized for Women's Equal Rights [*Feminist group*]
POWER........ PROFS [*Program for Regional Observing and Forecasting Services*] Operational Weather Education and Research [*Marine science*] (OSRA)
POWER........ Programmed Offline Waste Reduction (SAUS)
power.......... Programmed Operational Warshot Evaluation and Review (AD)
POWER........ Programmed Operational Warshot Evaluation and Review
POWER........ Promote Our Wonderful Energy Resources (EA)
Power Convers Intell Motion... Power Conversion and Intelligent Motion (SAUS)
POWER CTR... Power Center (SAUS)
Power Eng J... Power Engineering Journal (SAUS)
Power Int..... Power International (SAUS)
Power Int Ed... Power International Edition (SAUS)
POWERPC... Performance Optimization with Enhanced RISC-Performance Computing (SAUS)
Powers .... Powers' Reports, New York Surrogate Court [*A publication*] (DLA)
Power's Sur... Powers' Reports, New York Surrogate Court [*A publication*] (DLA)
POWER System... Priority Output Writers, Executionprocessors and input Readers System (SAUS)
Power Transm Des... Power Transmission Design (SAUS)
Power Works Eng... Power and Works Engineering (SAUS)
Pow Ev .... Powell on Evidence [*10th ed.*] [*1921*] [*A publication*] (DLA)
powf-.......... Wallis and Futuna [*MARC geographic area code*] [*Library of Congress*] (LCCP)
POWG.......... Payload Operations Working Group (SAUS)
POWG.......... Procurement Officers Work Group (AAGC)
Pow Inl Car... Powell on the Law of Inland Carriers [*A publication*] (DLA)
POW(J)........ Prisoner of War of Japan
powk-.......... Wake Island [*MARC geographic area code*] [*Library of Congress*] (LCCP)
POWL .... Powell Indus [*NASDAQ symbol*] (TTSB)
POWL .... Powell Industries, Inc. [*NASDAQ symbol*] (NQ)
POW/MIA..... Prisoner of War/Missing in Action (SAUS)
POW/MIG..... Place of Work and Migration Sample [*Bureau of the Census*] (GFGA)
Pow Mort..... Powell on Mortgages [*6th ed.*] [*1826*] [*A publication*] (DLA)
Pow Mortg... Powell on Mortgages [*A publication*] (DLA)
POW/MP...... Prisoner of War/Missing Personnel
POWO.......... Prince [*or Princess*] of Wales' Own [*Military unit*] [*British*] (DMA)
PoWP.......... Biblioteka Golowna Politechniki Warszawsjiej (Warsaw Technical University Central Library), Warsaw, Poland [*Library symbol*] [*Library of Congress*] (LCLS)
POWP.......... Preliminary Overhaul Work Package (DNAB)
POWR.......... Environmental Power [*NASDAQ symbol*] (SAG)
Pow R & D... Power, Rodwell, and Drew's English Election Cases [*1847-56*] [*A publication*] (DLA)
PowrCrv...... PowerCerv Corp. [*Associated Press*] (SAG)
POWREN...... Petty Officer Wren (SAUS)
POWRENAF... Petty Officer WREN [*Women's Royal Naval Service*] Air Fitter [*British military*] (DMA)
POWRENCINE... Petty Officer WREN [*Women's Royal Naval Service*] Cinema Operator [*British military*] (DMA)
POWRENCK... Petty Officer WREN [*Women's Royal Naval Service*] Cook [*British military*] (DMA)
POWRENDHYG... Petty Officer WREN [*Women's Royal Naval Service*] Dental Hygienist [*British military*] (DMA)
POWRENDSA... Petty Officer WREN [*Women's Royal Naval Service*] Dental Surgery Assistant [*British military*] (DMA)
POWRENMET... Petty Officer WREN [*Women's Royal Naval Service*] Meteorological Observer [*British military*] (DMA)
POWRENMT... Petty Officer WREN [*Women's Royal Naval Service*] Motor Transport Driver [*British military*] (DMA)
POWRENPHOT... Petty Officer WREN [*Women's Royal Naval Service*] Photographer [*British military*] (DMA)
POWRENQA... Petty Officer WREN [*Women's Royal Naval Service*] Quarters Assistant [*British military*] (DMA)
POWREN(R)... Petty Officer WREN [*Women's Royal Naval Service*] (RADAR) [*British military*] (DMA)
POWRENREL... Petty Officer WREN [*Women's Royal Naval Service*] Radio Electrician [*British military*] (DMA)
POWRENRS(M)... Petty Officer WREN [*Women's Royal Naval Service*] Radio Supervisor (Morse) [*British military*] (DMA)
POWRENSA... Petty Officer WREN [*Women's Royal Naval Service*] Stores Accountant [*British military*] (DMA)
POWRENS(C)... Petty Officer WREN [*Women's Royal Naval Service*] Stores Assistant (Clothes) [*British military*] (DMA)
POWRENS(S)... Petty Officer WREN [*Women's Royal Naval Service*] Stores Assistant (Stores) [*British military*] (DMA)
POWRENSTD... Petty Officer WREN [*Women's Royal Naval Service*] Steward [*British military*] (DMA)
POWRENS(V)... Petty Officer WREN [*Acromens Royal Naval Service*] Stores Assistant (Victualling) [*British military*] (DMA)
POWRENTEL... Petty Officer WREN [*Women's Royal Naval Service*] Telephonist [*British military*] (DMA)
POWRENTSA... Petty Officer WREN [*Women's Royal Naval Service*] Training Support Assistant [*British military*] (DMA)

POWRENWA... Petty Officer WREN [*Women's Royal Naval Service*] Weapon Analyst [*British military*] (DMA)
POWRENWTR(G)... Petty Officer WREN [*Women's Royal Naval Service*] Writer (General) [*British military*] (DMA)
POWRENWTR(P)... Petty Officer WREN [*Women's Royal Naval Service*] Writer (Pay) [*British military*] (DMA)
POWRENWW... Petty Officer WREN [*Women's Royal Naval Service*] Welfare Worker [*British military*] (DMA)
Powrwv........ Powerwave Technologies, Inc. [*Associated Press*] (SAG)
POWS .... PROFS [*Program for Regional Observing and Forecasting Services*] Operational Work Station [*Marine science*] (OSRA)
POWS .... Project Operating Work Statement [*NASA*] (NASA)
POWS .... Pyrotechnic Outside Warning System (IEEE)
pows-.......... Western Samoa [*MARC geographic area code*] [*Library of Congress*] (LCCP)
POW Scales... Perception of Ward Scales (SAUS)
POW-SIG ..... Pagan/Occult/Witchcraft Special Interest Group (EA)
Pow Str....... Power Steering (SAUS)
Pow Surr ..... Powers' Reports, New York Surrogate Court [*A publication*] (DLA)
POWTECH... International Powder and Bulk Solids Technology Exhibition and Conference
POWTR........ Petty Officer Writer [*British military*] (DMA)
POWU......... Post Office Workers Union (SAUS)
POWU......... Post Office Work Unit [*Computer performance measure*] [*British Telecom*]
PoWU......... Uniwersytet Warszawski [*University of Warsaw*], Warsaw, Poland [*Library symbol*] [*Library of Congress*] (LCLS)
POW:WE...... Peoples of the World: Western Europeans [*A publication*]
POWWER.... Power of World Wide Energy Resources [*In organization name "Natural POWWER"*] (EA)
Pow Wind.... Power Windows (SAUS)
POX .... Partial Oxidation [*Organic chemistry*]
POX .... Point of Exit
POX .... Port Alexander [*Alaska*] [*Airport symbol*] (AD)
P-OX .... Pressure Oxidation
POX .... Purgeable Organic Halogen [*Chemistry*] (FFDE)
POX-AC....... Pox Battery, Acute [*Biochemistry*] (DAVI)
poxd-.......... Mariana Islands [*MARC geographic area code*] [*Library of Congress*] (LCCP)
poxe-.......... Marshall Islands [*MARC geographic area code*] [*Library of Congress*] (LCCP)
poxf-.......... Midway Islands [*MARC geographic area code*] [*Library of Congress*] (LCCP)
poxh-.......... Niue [*MARC geographic area code*] [*Library of Congress*] (LCCP)
POY .... Lovell-Powell [*Wyoming*] [*Airport symbol*] (AD)
POY .... Partially Oriented Yarn (SAUS)
POY .... Partially Oriented Yarns
POY .... Polyester Oriented Yarn (DICI)
POY .... Powell, WY [*Location identifier*] [*FAA*] (FAAL)
POY .... Prairie Oil Royalties Co. Ltd. [*AMEX symbol*] [*Toronto Stock Exchange symbol*] (SPSG)
POY .... Preoriented Polyester Yarn (SAUS)
poy.............. Pre-Oriented Yarn (AD)
Poynt M & D... Poynter on Marriage and Divorce [*2nd ed.*] [*1824*] [*A publication*] (DLA)
POYO.......... Pollo Tropical [*NASDAQ symbol*] (SAG)
Poz.............. Poznan (AD)
POZ.............. Poznan [*Poland*] [*Airport symbol*] (OAG)
POZN .... Pozen, Inc. [*NASDAQ symbol*]
PP................ Brazil [*International civil aircraft marking*] (ODBW)
pp................ by proxy (SAUS)
PP................ Descent through Cloud (SAUS)
PP................ Eisai Co. Ltd. [*Japan*] [*Research code symbol*]
PP................ Free Library of Philadelphia, Philadelphia, PA [*Library symbol*] [*Library of Congress*] (LCLS)
PP................ Head Injury Hotline [*Formerly, Phoenix Project*] (EA)
PP................ Pacific Petroleum (AD)
PP................ Packet Processor (SAUS)
PP................ Page Printer (NVT)
Pp................ Pages (WDMC)
PP................ Pages
pp................ Pages (WDMC)
PP................ Pages from the Past [*Later, PIR*] [*An association*] (EA)
PP................ Painting Processor (SAUS)
PP................ Palisades Plant [*Nuclear energy*] (NRCH)
PP................ Palus Putretudinis [*Lunar area*]
PP................ Pancreatic Polypeptide [*Biochemistry*]
PP................ Pandectes Periodiques [*A publication*] (ILCA)
pp................ Panel Point (AD)
PP................ Panel Point [*Technical drawings*]
PP................ Pangu Pati [*Papua New Guinea*] [*Political party*] (PPW)
PP................ Papa [*Pope*]
Pp................ Papa [*Father*] [*Latin*] (AD)
PP................ Paper Profit
pp................ Papua New Guinea [*MARC country of publication code*] [*Library of Congress*] (LCCP)
PP................ Paradigm Publishing Ltd. [*British*]
PP................ Paradoxical Pulse [*Medicine*] (DMAA)
PP................ Parallel Plate (SAUS)
PP................ Parallel Poll (SAUS)
PP................ Parallel Port (SAUS)
PP................ Parallel Printer (SAUS)
PP................ Parallel Processing (SAUS)
PP................ Parallel Processor
PP................ Parallel Programming (SAUS)

PP	Parametric Programming (SAUS)
pp	Parcel Post (AD)
PP	Parcel Post
PP	Parish Priest
PP	Paris Publications, Inc.
PP	Parity Price (MHDW)
PP	Parliamentary Papers [A publication] [British]
PP	Pars Planitis (SAUS)
PP	Partially Paid (SAUS)
P/P	Partial Pay [Air Force]
pp	Partial Pressure (NAKS)
PP	Partial Pressure
PP	Partial Product (IAA)
PP	Partia Popullore [Popular Party] [Albania] [Political party] (PPE)
PP	Participatory Program (SAUS)
PP	Particular [Named] Port [British] (ROG)
PP	Particulate Phosphorus (SAUS)
PP	Partido Panamenista [Panamanian Party] [Political party] (PPW)
PP	Partido Popular [Popular Party] [Spain] [Political party] (PPE)
PP	Partido Populista [Populist Party] [Argentina] [Political party]
PP	Parti du Peuple [People's Party] [Burundi] [Political party]
pp	Partly Paid (ADWA)
PP	Partners in Politics (EA)
pp	Part Paid (AD)
PP	Part Paid [Business and trade]
PP	Parts Per
PP	Passage Point (SAUS)
PP	[The] Passionate Pilgrim [Shakespearean work]
pp	Passive Participle (AD)
PP	Passive Participle
PP	Password Protection (SAUS)
PP	Pastor Pastorum [Shepherd of the Shepherds] [Latin] (ROG)
pp	Past Participle (WDMC)
PP	Past Participle
PP	Past Patriarch [Freemasonry] (ROG)
PP	Past President
PP	Patchboard Programming (SAUS)
P/P	Patch Panel (NASA)
PP	Patent Bending (SAUS)
PP	Patent Pending (IAA)
PP	Pater Patriae [The Father of His Country] [Latin]
PP	Pathfinder Pilot (SAUS)
PP	Path Provisioning (SAUS)
PP	Patres [Fathers] [Latin]
P/P	Patriotic Party [British]
PP	Patrol Vessels [Navy symbol] (MUGU)
PP	Pattern Processing (SAUS)
PP	Payload Pointer (SAUS)
PP	Pay Period (EEVL)
PP	Payphone (SAUS)
PP	Peace PAC (EA)
PP	Peak Power (IAA)
PP	Peak Pressure
p-p	Peak-to-Peak (AEBE)
PP	Peak-to-Peak
P-P	Peak-to-Peak [Value]
PP	Peanut Pals (EA)
PP	Pedal Power
PP	Pedal Pulse
PP	Peering Point (SAUS)
PP	Pelagra Preventive (SAUS)
PP	Pellagra Preventing (SAUS)
pp	Pellagra Preventive (AD)
PP	Pellagra Preventive [Factor] [See also PPF] [Biochemistry]
P-P	Pellagra-Preventive Factor (AD)
PP	Pellet Plant (SAUS)
PP	Pension Plan
PP	People's Party [Spain] [Political party] (ECON)
PP	People's Party [Halkci Partisi] [Turkey] [Political party] (PPW)
PP	Pep Pill [Slang]
pp	Perceptual Performance (AD)
PP	Percussion Primer (SAUS)
PP	Perfect Prog (SAUS)
PP	Perfect Program (SAUS)
PP	Perforation Pitch (SAUS)
PP	Perfusion Pressure [Cardiology] (DAVI)
PP	Pericardial Pressure (SAUS)
PP	Periodical Publications [British Library shelf designation]
PP	Peripheral Processor [Computer science]
PP	Periportal [Anatomy]
PP	Periproct [Invertebrate anatomy]
PP	Permanent Partial [Dentistry] (MAE)
pp	Permanent Party (AD)
PP	Permanent Party [Military]
PP	Permanent Pasture [Agriculture]
PP	Permanent Press (ADA)
PP	Permanent Professor
PP	Peroxisome Proliferator [Biochemistry]
pp	per paragraph (SAUS)
p/p	per passenger (SAUS)
pp	Per Person (AD)
pp	per pro (SAUS)
PP	Per Procurationem [By Proxy, By the Action Of] [Legal term] [Latin]
PP	Personal Prelatures [Diocesan abbreviation] (TOCD)
PP	Personal Property

P-P	Person to Person [Word processing]
PP	Pet Pride (EA)
PP	Petroleum Point
PP	Petrol Point (SAUS)
PP	Petrus Piccoli de Monteforte [Flourished, 14th century] [Authority cited in pre-1607 legal work] (DSA)
PP	Petticoat Peeping [From one girl to another, in reference to dress disarrangement]
PP	Peyer's Patch [Immunology]
PP	Phase Partitioning (SAUS)
PP	Phillips Airlines [ICAO designator] (AD)
PP	Philo-Phobe [Psychological testing]
PP	Phoenix Project [An association] (EA)
PP	Phony Peach Bacteria [Plant pathology]
PP	Phosphoprotein (SAUS)
PP	Photosynthetic Panel [i.e., leaf] [Slang]
PP	Physical Partition (SAUS)
PP	Physical Plane (SAUS)
pp	Physical Profile (AD)
PP	Physical Profile
pp	Physical Properties (AD)
PP	Physical Properties
PP	Phytophthora Parasitica [A fungus]
pp	Pianissimo [Very Softly] [Italian] [Music] (WDAA)
PP	Pianissimo [Very Softly] [Music]
PP	Picked Ports
pp	Pickpocket (AD)
PP	Pickpocket
PP	Picric Powder (SAUS)
PP	Picture Peace [Defunct] (EA)
pp	Piena Pelle [Full Leather] [Italian] (AD)
P/P	Pier/Pier (SAUS)
PP	Piers Plowman [Middle English poem]
P/P	Pier-to-House Service (SAUS)
P/P	Pier to Pier (ADA)
P/P	Pier-to-Pier Service (SAUS)
PP	Piissimus [Most Holy] [Latin]
PP	Pilotless Plane
PP	Pilot Parents (EA)
PP	Pilot Pulse
PP	Pilot Punch
PP	Pine Bark Mixed with Peat
PP	Pink Puffer [Emphysema] (MAE)
PP	Pinpoint [Pupils] [Ophthalmology] (DAVI)
PP	Pinprick [Medicine] (DMAA)
PP	Pipelined Processor (SAUS)
PP	Pipeline Processor (IAA)
PP	Piping
PP	Piscataqua Pioneers (EA)
PP	Piu Piano [More Softly] [Music]
PP	PIXEL-Processing [Computer science]
PP	Placental Protein [Gynecology]
PP	Place of Publisher (NITA)
PP	Plane Parallel
PP	Plane Polarized [Telecommunications] (TEL)
PP	Planetary Programs [NASA]
PP	Planned Parenthood
pp	Planning Package (NAKS)
PP	Planning Package [NASA] (NASA)
pp	Planning Permission (AD)
PP	Planning Permit (SAUS)
PP	Planning Purpose
PP	Plan Profile
PP	Plant Protection
PP	Plasmapheresis [Hematology]
PP	Plasma Processing (SAUS)
PP	Plasma Protein
PP	Plaster of Paris
PP	Plate Power (IAA)
PP	Plate Pulse (IAA)
PP	Play or Pay (ROG)
PP	Please Pay (ROG)
pp	Plenum Pressure (COE)
PP	Plethysmograph Pressure [Measurement] [Medicine] (DAVI)
PP	Pleural Pressure [Medicine]
PP	Plot Points [Computer science]
PP	Pluripara (SAUS)
PP	Pluvius Policy [Insurance against rain]
PP	Pocketpiece [A. C. Nielsen Co.] [Rating report] (NTCM)
PP	Poetry Project (EA)
P/P	Point/Point (SAUS)
P/P	Point-to-Point [Air Force]
PP	Polar Pacific [American air mass]
PP	Pole Piece (DEN)
PP	Pole Position [Automobile racing]
PP	Polizei Pistole [Police Pistol] [Walther Waffenfabrik, German arms manufacturer]
PP	Pollution Prevention (EEVL)
PP	Polynomial Programming (SAUS)
PP	Polynominal Programming (SAUS)
PP	Polypeptide [Biochemistry]
PP	Polyphosphate [Inorganic chemistry] (AAMN)
PP	Polypropylen (SAUS)
PP	Polypropylene [Organic chemistry]
PP	Polypyrrole [Photovoltaic energy systems]

PP	Polystyrene Agglutination Plate (DB)
PP	Pom-Pom [*Gun*]
PP	Pontificum [*Of the Popes*] [*Latin*]
PP	Popular Party [*European political movement*] (ECON)
PP	Population Planning (DAVI)
PP	Populist Party of America [*Political party*] (EA)
PP	Porcelain Pavers (DICI)
PP	Portability Package (SAUS)
PP	Portable Part (SAUS)
PP	Port Pipe (ADA)
P/P	Port/Port (SAUS)
P/P	Port-to-Port Transport (SAUS)
PP	Posa Piano [*Handle with Care*] [*Shipping*] [*Italian*]
PP	Position Paper (MCD)
PP	Positive Pressure (SAUS)
pp	Postage Paid (AD)
PP	Postage Paid [*Shipping*]
pp	Posted Price (MENA)
PP	Posterior Parietal Cortex [*Neuroanatomy*]
PP	Posterior Pituitary [*Medicine*]
PP	Postglenoid Process (SAUS)
PP	Post Pagado [*Postage Paid*] [*Shipping*] [*Spanish*]
PP	Post Paid (SAUS)
pp	Postpaid
PP	Post Partum [*After Birth*] [*Latin*] (ADA)
pp	postpartum (SAUS)
pp	Post Partum [*Afterbirth*] [*Latin*] (AD)
PP	Postpass
PP	Post Pay (SAUS)
PP	Postponed
PP	Post Position [*Racing*]
PP	Postprandial [*After Meals*] [*Pharmacy*]
PP	Post Processing
PP	Postprocessor [*Computer science*] (IAA)
PP	Pounds Pressure
PP	Pour Point [*Petroleum characteristic*]
PP	Power Package
PP	Power Panel (SAUS)
PP	Power People
PP	Power Plan (IAA)
PP	Power Plant
PP	Power Play [*Hockey*]
pp	Power Pole (NAKS)
PP	Power Pole (NASA)
PP	Power Supplies [*JETDS nomenclature*] [*Military*] (CET)
PP	Practice and Procedure (SAUS)
PP	Practice Projectile (SAUS)
PP	Praemissis Praemittendis [*Omitting Preliminaries, To Whom It May Concern*] [*Latin*]
PP	Praepter Propter [*Approximately*] [*Pharmacy*]
Pp	Pratylenchus penetrans [*A nematode*]
PP	Precautionary Principle (SAUS)
PP	Precision Platform (ACAE)
PP	Predictive Pipelining (SAUS)
PP	Preferred Provider [*Medicine*] (DMAA)
PP	Prentiss Properties Trust [*NYSE symbol*] (SAG)
PP	Prepaid
PP	Preparative Flag [*Navy*] [*British*]
PP	Preparing, Providing [*Pharmacy*] (ROG)
P/P	Pre/Planned (SAUS)
PP	Preposition [*Industrial engineering*]
PP	Prepositional Phrase (BYTE)
PP	Prepregnancy [*Medicine*]
PP	Preprinted
PP	Preprocessor
PP	Preproduction (KSC)
P/P	Pre-Prototype (SAUS)
PP	Prescribed Period [*Social Security Administration*] (OICC)
PP	Presentation Position [*Computer science*] (DCDG)
PP	Presenting Problem (SAUS)
PP	Present Participle [*Grammar*]
pp	Present Position (AD)
PP	Present Position [*Military*]
PP	Present Pupil (AIE)
PP	Press Packed
PP	Press Pressure (SSD)
PP	Pressure Pattern (MCD)
PP	Pressure Plate (SAUS)
PP	Pressure Proof (SAUS)
pp	Pressure-Proof (AD)
PP	Pressure-Proof [*Technical drawings*]
PP	Pretty Poor [*Slang*] [*Bowdlerized version*]
PP	Previous Page (SAUS)
PP	Primarily Primates [*An association*] (EA)
PP	Primary Point (VLIE)
PP	Primary Power (SAUS)
PP	Primary Pressure [*Nuclear energy*] (NRCH)
PP	Primary Processor (SAUS)
PP	Primary Producers (ADA)
PP	Princess Pat's [*Princess Patricia of Connaught's Light Infantry*] [*Military unit*] [*Canada*]
PP	Principal
PP	Principal Point
PP	Principles and Practice (SAUS)
pp	Printed Pages [*Publishing*] (WDAA)
PP	Printer Page [*Computer science*]
PP	Printer Perforator (SAUS)
P/P	Printer/Plotter (NASA)
PP	Print Position (SAUS)
PP	Print Positions
PP	Print Program (SAUS)
P/P	Print Punch
PP	Print-Punch [*Computer science*] (BUR)
PP	Priority Message Precedence [*Telecommunications*] (ADDR)
PP	Priority Pollutant (EEVL)
PP	Priority Processing (SAUS)
PP	Priority Processor
PP	Prior Permission
PP	Private Jet Services AG [*Sweden*] [*ICAO designator*] (ICDA)
pp	Privately Printed (AD)
PP	Privately Printed
P/P	Private Passenger
PP	Private Patient [*Medicine*]
PP	Private Physician (SAUS)
PP	Private Pilot (SAUS)
PP	Private Practice [*Chiropody*] [*British*]
pp	Private Property (AD)
PP	Private Property [*Military*]
PP	Problem Program (VLIE)
PP	Procurement Package (AAGC)
PP	Procurement Plan (MCD)
PP	Producer Price
PP	Production Phase (SAUS)
PP	Production Pool (SAUS)
PP	Production Processes
PP	Product Publication (IAA)
pp	Professional Paper (AD)
PP	Professional Paper
PP	Professor Publicus [*Public Professor*] [*Latin*] (ROG)
PP	Programming Plan (AFM)
PP	Programming Problem (SAUS)
PP	Program Package (MCD)
PP	Program Paper
PP	Program Part (SAUS)
pp	Program Performance (NAKS)
PP	Program Performance (NASA)
PP	Program Performed
PP	Program Planning (COE)
PP	Program Position (SAUS)
PP	Program Processing (SAUS)
PP	Program Product [*Computer science*]
PP	Program Pulse (SAUS)
PP	Progress Payments [*Military procurement*]
PP	Projection Plane (SAUS)
PP	Project Priesthood (EA)
PP	Project Proposal (KSC)
PP	Proletarian Party
PP	Promotion Pamphlet (SAUS)
PP	Proodeftiki Parataxis [*Progressive Front*] [*Greek Cyprus*] [*Political party*] (PPE)
pp	Pro Parte [*In Part*] [*Latin*]
PP	Propeller Pitch
PP	Proportional Part
PP	Proposals Paper
PP	Proposed Plan (BCP)
PP	Propria Persona [*In His or Her Own Person*] [*Latin*] (WGA)
PP	Propulsion Power (KSC)
PP	Protein Phosphatase [*An enzyme*]
PP	Prothrombin-Proconvertin [*Hematology*]
PP	Proton-Proton [*Nuclear physics*]
PP	Protoporphyria [*Medicine*]
PP	Protoporphyrin [*Biochemistry*]
PP	Provisioning Procedures [*Corps of Engineers*]
PP	Proximal Phalanx [*Anatomy*]
PP	Pseudomyxoma Peritonei [*Medicine*] (DMAA)
PP	Pseudoprogram (IAA)
PP	Psychic Phenomena
PP	Psychological Profile
PP	Psychologists and Psychiatrists [*in service*] [*British*]
P/P	Pterocephaliid-Ptychaspid [*Paleogeologic boundary*]
PP	Public Property
PP	Published Price [*of a book*]
PP	Pulmonary Pressure (SAUS)
PP	Pulse Pair (IAA)
PP	Pulse Polarography [*Analytical chemistry*]
PP	Pulse Pressure [*Medicine*]
PP	Pulse Pumped (SAUS)
P-P	Pulse to Pulse
PP	Puls-Polarography (SAUS)
PP	Pulvis Patrum [*The Fathers' Powder (or Jesuits' Powder)*] [*Pharmacy*] (ROG)
PP	Pump-Priming (MHDB)
PP	Punctum Proximum [*Near Point*] [*Latin*]
pp	Purchased Part (AD)
PP	Purchased Part
PP	Purchased Parts
PP	Purchase Power [*Commercial firm*] (EA)
PP	Purchase Price
PP	Purified Protein (SAUS)
PP	Pusher Plane

p-p	Push-Pull (AD)
pp	Push-Pull (NAKS)
PP	Push-Pull [*Technical drawings*]
PP	Pyrophosphate [*Chemistry*]
PP1	Protein Phosphatase 1 [*An enzyme*]
PP1P	Patrol Plane 1st Pilot (SAUS)
PPA	Athenaeum of Philadelphia, Philadelphia, PA [*Library symbol*] [*Library of Congress*] (LCLS)
PPA	National Plant Protection Association
PPA	Pakistan Press Association (AD)
PPA	Paleopathology Association (EA)
PPA	Palpation, Percussion, and Auscultation [*Medicine*]
ppa	Palpitation, Percussion, Auscultation (AD)
PPA	Pampa, TX [*Location identifier*] [*FAA*] (FAAL)
PPA	Panamerican/Panafrican Association (EA)
PPA	Paper Pail Association [*Defunct*] (EA)
PPA	Paper Plate Association [*Later, SSI*] (EA)
PPA	Parallel Port Adapter [*Computer science*] (CIST)
PPA	Parallel Processing Automata (PDAA)
PPA	Parcel Post Association [*Later, PSA*] (EA)
PPA	Parenting Publications of America (NTPA)
PPA	Parent of a Person with Autism (SAUS)
PPA	Parents for Private Adoption [*Defunct*] (EA)
PPA	Partial Peak Area (SAUS)
PPA	Partial Product Array (SAUS)
PPA	Partido Panamenista Autentico [*Panama*] [*Political party*] (EY)
PPA	Partido Patriotico Arubano [*Aruban Patriotic Party*] [*Netherlands Antilles*] [*Political party*] (PPW)
PPA	Partido Peronista Autentico [*Authentic Peronist Party*] [*Argentina*] [*Political party*] (EY)
PPA	Parts Performance Analysis (VLIE)
PPA	Pathology Practice Association (EA)
PPA	Peat Producers Association [*British*] (EAIO)
PPA	Pediatric Pain Assessment (MELL)
PPA	Pensioner Party of Australia [*Political party*]
PPA	Pension Portability Act of 1992 (WYGK)
PPA	Pension Protection Act (GFGA)
PPA	People for Prison Alternatives [*An association*] (AD)
PPA	Peoples Progressive Alliance (SAUS)
PPA	Peppa Resources [*Vancouver Stock Exchange symbol*]
PPA	Perennial Plant Association (EA)
PPA	Performance Partnership Agreement (SARE)
PPA	Periodical Publishers Association [*Later, MCA*] (EA)
PPA	Permian Partnership (SAUS)
PPA	Per Power of Attorney [*Business term*]
ppa	Per Procura [*By Proxy*] [*Latin*]
PPA	Personnel Pool of America [*An association*] (AD)
PPA	Pesticide Producers Association [*Defunct*] (EA)
PPA	Pet Producers of America (EA)
ppa	Phenylpropanolamine (AD)
PPA	Phenylpropanolamine [*Organic chemistry*]
PPA	Phenylpropanolamine(hydrochloride) [*Also, PPH, PPM*] [*Decongestant*]
PPA	Phenyl Pyruvic Acid (SAUS)
PPA	Phenylpyruvic Acid [*Organic chemistry*]
PPA	Phiala Prius Agitata [*Having First Shaken the Bottle*] [*Pharmacy*]
ppa	Phiala Prius Agitate [*Bottle Having First Been Shaken*] [*Latin*] (AD)
PPA	Phosphoric Acid Anodized (PDAA)
PPA	Photographic Peak Analysis
PPA	Photo Peak Analysis (IEEE)
ppa	Photo-Peak Analysis (AD)
PPA	Physical Page Address [*Computer science*] (CIST)
PPA	Pianoforte Publicity Association [*British*] (BI)
PPA	Piano Publicity Association (SAUS)
PPA	Pictorial Photographers of America (EAIO)
PPA	Pie De Palo [*Argentina*] [*Seismograph station code, US Geological Survey*] (SEIS)
PPA	Pilot Pulse Amplitude
PPA	Pilots and Passengers Association [*Defunct*] (EA)
PPA	Pipe Products Association (SAUS)
PPA	Piraeus Ports Authority (SAUS)
PPA	Pitch Precession Amplifier
PPA	Pittsburgh Pneumonia Agent [*Microbiology*]
PPA	Pixel Processing Accelerator [*Computer science*] (VLIE)
PPA	Plane Parallel Approximation (ARMP)
PPA	Planned Program Accomplishment (GNE)
PPA	Plant Patent Act [*1930*]
PPA	Plaque-Producing Agent (SAUS)
PPA	Plasminogen Proactivator [*Hematology*]
PPA	Platform Pointing Angle (ACAE)
PPA	Plutonium Preparation Area [*Nuclear energy*] (GFGA)
PPA	Policyholders Protective Association of America (EA)
PPA	Pollution Prevention Act [*1990*]
PPA	Polycrystalline Products Association (NTPA)
PPA	Polymer Permeation Analyzer
PPA	Polymer Processing Additive (SAUS)
PPA	Polyphenylacetylene (SAUS)
PPA	Poly(phosphoric Acid) [*Inorganic chemistry*]
PPA	Polyphthalamide (SAUS)
PPA	Pool Promoters Association [*British*] (BI)
PPA	Popcorn Processors Association [*Later, PI*]
PPA	Popski's Private Army [*Commando force led by Vladimir Peniakoff*] [*World War II*]
PPA	Population Planning Associates (BABM)
PPA	Portland Port Authority [*Australia*]
PPA	Post Pack Audit (VLIE)
PPA	Postpartum Amenorrhea [*Medicine*]
PPA	Post-Pill Amenorrhea [*Medicine*] (MEDA)
PPA	Potato Processors' Association [*Australia*]
PPA	Poultry Publishers Association (EA)
PPA	Power Plant Automation
PPA	Powerplant Performance Analysis
PPA	Preferred Provider Arrangement [*Information service or system*] (HCT)
PPA	Preliminary Pile Assembly (IAA)
PPA	Prephenic Acid (SAUS)
PPA	Pre-Planned Application (SAUS)
PPA	Pre-Planned Applications (VLIE)
PPA	Pre-Planned Attack (SAUS)
PPA	Preschool Playgrounds Association [*British*]
PPA	Pre-school Playgroups Association (SAUS)
PPA	Prescription Pricing Authority (PDAA)
PPA	Presidents' Professional Association [*Later, Presidents Association*] (EA)
PPA	Press and Publications Administration [*China*]
PPA	Princeton Particle Accelerator (IAA)
PPA	Princeton-Pennsylvania Accelerator [*Closed, 1972*] [*AEC*]
PPA	Princeton-Pennsylvania Proton Accelerator [*Closed, 1972*] [*AEC*] (IAA)
PPA	Principal Port Authority [*British*] (ROG)
PPA	Principle Policy Analyst (SAUS)
PPA	Printers' Provident Association (DGA)
PPA	Printing Platemakers Association [*Later, GPA*]
PPA	Priority Problem Areas (MCD)
PPA	Prison Parole Assessment (WDAA)
PPA	Process Plan Association [*British*] (DS)
PPA	Process Plant Association [*British*] (DBA)
PPA	Produce Packaging Association [*Later, PMA*] (EA)
PPA	Product Performance Analysis (VLIE)
PPA	Professional Paddlesports Association (NTPA)
PPA	Professional Panhellenic Association [*Later, PFA*] (EA)
PPA	Professional Photographers of America (AD)
PPA	Professional Programmers Association (EA)
PPA	Professional Putters Association (EA)
PPA	Program Problem Area
PPA	Program Product Announcement (VLIE)
PPA	Program, Project and Activity (SAUS)
PPA	Progressive Party of America [*Third party in 1948 Presidential race*]
PPA	Progressive Peoples Alliance (SAUS)
PPA	Progress Presse Agentur GmbH [*Press agency*] [*Germany*]
PPA	Proletarian Party of America [*Political party*] (AD)
PPA	Promotional Products Association International (NTPA)
PPA	Prompt Payment Act (AAGC)
PPA	Propane Phosphonic Acid Anhydride [*Organic chemistry*]
PPA	Propane-Precipitated Asphalt [*Petroleum technology*]
PPA	Property Protection Area
PPA	Propheter Construction Co., Inc. [*ICAO designator*] (FAAC)
PPA	Protected Partition Area [*Telecommunications*] (IAA)
PPA	Protestant Press Agency [*British*]
PPA	Prudent Purchaser Arrangement [*Medical insurance*]
PPA	Pseudo Passive Array (SAUS)
PPA	Pseudopassive Array
PPA	Public Personnel Association [*Later, IPMA*] (EA)
PPA	Publishers' Publicity Association (EA)
Ppa	Pulmonary Artery Pressure [*Medicine*] (DMAA)
PPA	Pulmonary Artery Pressure [*Cardiology*]
PPA	Pulsed Plasma Accelerator (SAUS)
PPA	Pulsed Power Amplifier
PPA	Pulse Plasma Accelerator
PPA	Purchase Power Agreement (SAUS)
PPA	Pure Pulmonary Atresia [*Medicine*] (DMAA)
PPA	Purple Plum Association [*Defunct*] (EA)
PPA	Push-Pull Amplifier (IAA)
PPAA	Palynological and Palaeobotanical Association of Australia (QUAC)
PPAA	Patres Amplissimi [*Cardinals*] [*Latin*]
PPAA	Personal Protective Armor Association (EA)
PPAAR	Princeton University, Pennsylvania University, Army Avionics Research (PDAA)
PPAB	Program and Policy Advisory Board [*UN Food and Agriculture Organization*]
PPABP	American Baptist Publication Society, Philadelphia, PA [*Library symbol*] [*Library of Congress*] [*Obsolete*] (LCLS)
PP-AC	Air-Conditioning Power Panel (DAC)
PPAC	Penn-Pacific Corp. (SAUS)
PPAC	Pesticide Policy Advisory Committee [*Environmental Protection Agency*]
PPAC	Primary Progress Assessment Chart [*Psychology*]
PPAC	Private Planning Association of Canada
PPAC	Product Performance Agreement Center [*Military*]
PPAC	Progressive Political Action Committee [*Defunct*]
PPAC	Public Parks Advisory Committee [*South Australia*]
PPACE	United States Army, Corps of Engineers, Philadelphia District Library, Custom House, Philadelphia, PA [*Library symbol*] [*Library of Congress*] (LCLS)
PPACHi	American Catholic Historical Society, Philadelphia, PA [*Library symbol*] [*Library of Congress*] (LCLS)
PPAD	Practical Periodontics & Aesthetic Dentistry (SAUS)
PPADS	Parawing Precision Aerial Delivery System (MCD)
PPAEM	Albert Einstein Medical Center, Northern Division, Philadelphia, PA [*Library symbol*] [*Library of Congress*] (LCLS)

PPAFA	Pennsylvania Academy of the Fine Arts, Philadelphia, PA [*Library symbol*] [*Library of Congress*] [*Obsolete*] (LCLS)
PPAG	Pediatric Pharmacy Advocacy Group (SAUS)
PPAG	Personnel Profile - Age by Grade [*Army*]
PPAG	Proposed Public Affairs Guidance (COE)
PPAI	Pinpoint Assignment Instructions [*Army*] (INF)
PPAK	Atwater Kent Museum, Philadelphia, PA [*Library symbol*] [*Library of Congress*] (LCLS)
PPAL	Pacific Power and Light (SAUS)
PPAL	Pennsylvania Power & Light Co. (IAA)
PPAL	Principal (ROG)
PPalZ	New Jersey Zinc Co., Technical Library, Palmerton (SAUS)
PPalZ	New Jersey Zinc Co. [*of Pennsylvania*], Technical Library, Palmerton, PA [*Library symbol*] [*Library of Congress*] (LCLS)
PPAM	Privileged Primary Access Method (SAUS)
PPAM	Program Product Assurance Manager (ACAE)
PPAmP	American Philosophical Society, Philadelphia, PA [*Library symbol*] [*Library of Congress*] (LCLS)
PPAmS	American Sunday School Union, Philadelphia, PA [*Library symbol*] [*Library of Congress*] [*Obsolete*] (LCLS)
PPAmSR	American Sugar Refining Co., Philadelphia, PA [*Library symbol*] [*Library of Congress*] [*Obsolete*] (LCLS)
PPAmSwM	American Swedish Historical Foundation, Philadelphia, PA [*Library symbol*] [*Library of Congress*] (LCLS)
PPAN	Academy of Natural Sciences of Philadelphia, Philadelphia, PA [*Library symbol*] [*Library of Congress*] (LCLS)
PPAN	Pyrolyzed Polyacrylonitrile [*Organic chemistry*]
PP & A	Palpation, Percussion, and Auscultation [*Medicine*]
pp & a	Palpitation, Percussion, and Auscultation (AD)
PP & A	Percussion, Palpation, and Auscultation [*Medicine*] (DAVI)
pp&b	Paper, Printing, and Binding (AD)
PP & B	Paper, Printing, and Binding [*Publishing*]
PP&C	Payload Planning and Control (SAUS)
PP & C	Pickpocket and Confidence [*Police term*]
PP & C	Production Planning and Control [*Military*] (AABC)
PP&C	Program Planning and Control (SPST)
PP & C	Project Planning and Control (NG)
PP&E	Production Process and Equipment (SAUS)
PP & E	Program Planning and Evaluation (AD)
PP&L	Pacific Power and Light (AD)
PP&L	Pennsylvania Power and Light (AD)
PP&L Res	PP & L Resources, Inc. [*Associated Press*] (SAG)
PP & NA	Private Plants and Naval Activities
PP&O	Plans, Policy and Operations (SAUS)
PP&S	Papers on Poetics and Semiotics (SAUS)
PP & T	Packaging, Preservation, and Transportation
PPAnR	Annenberg Research Institute for Judaic and Middle Eastern Studies, Philadelphia, PA [*Library symbol*] [*Library of Congress*] (LCLS)
PPAp	Apprentices Free Library, Philadelphia (SAUS)
PPAp	Apprentices' Free Library, Philadelphia, PA [*Library symbol*] [*Library of Congress*] [*Obsolete*] (LCLS)
PPAP	Peak Pulmonary Artery Pressure (SAUS)
PPAP	People's Party of Arunachal Pradesh [*India*] [*Political party*] (PPW)
PPAP	Precedents of Private Acts of Parliament [*A publication*] (DLA)
PPAP	Product Part Approval Process
PPA pos	Phenylpyruvic Acid Positive [*Biochemistry*] (DAVI)
PPAR	Paging Partners [*NASDAQ symbol*] (TTSB)
PPAR	Paging Partners Corp. [*NASDAQ symbol*] (SAG)
PPAR	Paterson Parchment Paper Co. (SAUS)
PPAR	Peroxisome Proliferator-Activated Receptor [*Genetics*]
PPAR	Priority Problem Analysis Report [*Military*] (DNAB)
PPAR	Program Page Address Register (ACAE)
PPAR	Project Performance Audit Report
PPARA	ARA Historical Foundation, ARA Industries, Philadelphia, PA [*Closed*] [*Library symbol*] [*Library of Congress*] (LCLS)
PPARC	Particle Physics and Astronomy Research Council [*British*]
PPArmA	Armstrong Association of Philadelphia, Philadelphia, PA [*Library symbol*] [*Library of Congress*] [*Obsolete*] (LCLS)
PPARW	Paging Partners Wrrt [*NASDAQ symbol*] (TTSB)
PPAS	Patti Page Appreciation Society (EA)
PPAS	Peripheral Pulmonary Artery Stenosis [*Medicine*] (DMAA)
PPAS	Personal Property Accountability System (SAUS)
PPAS	Portable Public Address System (MCD)
PPAS	Postpolio Atrophy Syndrome [*Medicine*] (MELL)
PPAS	Potassium Picrate Active Substances [*Measure of detergent content of water*]
PPAS	Precision Pulse Analysis System (SAUS)
PPAS	Probability Proportional to Aggregate Size [*Statistics*]
PPAtR	Atlantic Refining Co., Philadelphia, PA [*Library symbol*] [*Library of Congress*] (LCLS)
PPATRA	Printing, Packaging, and Allied Trades Research Association (AD)
PPATY	Preparatory (ROG)
PPAuC	Automobile Club of Philadelphia, Philadelphia, PA [*Library symbol*] [*Library of Congress*] [*Obsolete*] (LCLS)
PPAUS	Peat Producers Association of the United States (EA)
PPAW	Public Policy Affecting Women Task Force (EA)
PPAWA	Poultry Producers' Association of Western Australia
PPB	Botanical Research Centre (SAUS)
PPB	Paper, Printing, and Binding (ADWA)
Ppb	Pappaband [*Hard Cover*] [*German*] (AD)
PPB	Parachute Paraglider Building [*NASA*] (KSC)
PPB	Part Per Billion (SAUS)
ppb	Parts per Billion (AD)
PPB	Parts per Billion
ppb	Parts per Billion 10 (IDOE)
PPB	Perliminary Parts Breakdown (SAUS)
PPB	Petro-Canada Products, Inc. [*Toronto Stock Exchange symbol*] [*Vancouver Stock Exchange symbol*]
PPB	Philadelphia Bar Association, Philadelphia, PA [*Library symbol*] [*Library of Congress*] (LCLS)
PPB	Planning, Programming, Budgeting (SAUS)
P-P-B	Planning-Programming-Budgeting [*System*] [*Army*]
PPB	Platelet-Poor Blood [*Hematology*] (MAE)
PPB	Platoon Patrol Base [*Military*] (VNW)
PPB	Polar Patrol Balloons (SAUS)
PPB	Political Party Broadcast [*Television*] [*British*]
PPB	Polybrominated-Biphenyl (AD)
PPB	Poly(para-benzamide) [*Organic chemistry*]
PPB	Positive Pressure Breathing [*Aerospace*]
PPb	Postparotid Basic Protein (DMAA)
PPB	Power Plant Bulletin (MCD)
PPB	Precision Pressure Balance
PPB	Preliminary Parts Breakdown (SAUS)
PPB	Preparing, Planning and Budegting (SAUS)
PPB	Prepatellar Bursitis [*Medicine*] (MELL)
PPB	Preprophase Band [*Cytology*]
PPB	Presidente Prudente [*Brazil*] [*Airport symbol*] (AD)
PPB	Pres Prudente [*Brazil*] [*Airport symbol*] (OAG)
PPB	Primary Parts Breakdown (SAUS)
PPB	Primary Propulsion Branch [*Manned Spacecraft Center*]
PPB	Printing, Paper, and Binding [*Publishing*] (WDMC)
PPB	Private Posting Box
PPB	Procurement Policy Board [*ABA Public Contract Law Section*] (AAGC)
PPB	Production Parts Breakdown (MCD)
PPB	Program Performance Baseline (NASA)
PPB	Program Planning Budget (NOAA)
PPB	Program-Planning-Budgeting
PPB	PROM [*Programmable Read-Only Memory*] Programmer Board
PPB	Provisional Parts Breakdown (SAUS)
PPB	Provisioning Parts Breakdown
PPB	Purchasing Power Benefit (ADA)
PPB	Push-Pull Bearing
PPB	Push Pull Button (SAUS)
PPB&G	Positive Pressure Breathing & G System (SAUS)
PPBANSW	Pasture Protection Boards' Association of New South Wales [*Australia*]
PPBAS	Planning, Programming, Budgeting, Accounting System (SAUS)
PPBAS	Planning-Programming-Budgeting-Accounting System (AD)
PPBB	Partai Pesaka Bumiputra Bersatu [*United Traditional Bumiputra Party*] [*Malaysia*] [*Political party*] (PPW)
PPBB	PCI-toPCI Bridge Board (ACII)
PPBB	Prime Power Brass Board (MCD)
PPBC	Pittsburgh Penguins Booster Club (EA)
PPBC	Plant Pathogenic Bacteria Committee (EA)
PPBC	Portland Problem Behavior Checklist (EDAC)
PPBC-R	Portland Problem Behavior Checklist - Revised [*Educational test*]
P PBD	Paper or Paperboard [*Freight*]
PPBD	Port of Palm Beach District [*AAR code*]
PPBE	Passenger Protective Breathing Equipment [*Aviation*] (DA)
PPBE	Postpartum Breast Engorgement [*Medicine*] (MELL)
PPBERS	Program Performance and Budget Execution Review System [*Army*]
PPBES	Planning, Programming, Budgeting, and Execution System [*Army*] (RDA)
PPBES	Planning-Programming-Budgeting-Evaluation System (SAUS)
PPBES	Program Planning and Budget Execution System [*Army*]
PPBES	Program Planning-Budgeting-Evaluation System (SAUS)
PPBESP	Program Planning-Budgeting-Evaluation System Project (EA)
PPBESP	Program Planning-Budgeting-Evaluation System Project (EA)
PPBF	Pan-American Pharmaceutical and Biochemical Federation (SAUS)
PPBF	Pan-American Pharmaceutical and Biochemical Federation
PPBFSPS	Pen and Pocket Blade Forgers' and Smithers' Protective Society [*A union*] [*British*]
PPBH	Pharmaceutical Partners for Better Healthcare (ECON)
PPBI	Balch Institute, Philadelphia, PA [*Library symbol*] [*Library of Congress*] (LCLS)
PPBM	Pulse Polarization (or Polarized) Binary Modulation (SAUS)
PPBMIS	Planning, Programming, and Budgeting Management Information System [*Army*]
PPBP	Pro-Platelet Basic Protein (DMAA)
PPBR	Program Plan and Budget Request (OICC)
PPBS	Planning, Programming, and Budgeting Structure
PPBS	Planning, Programming, and Budgeting System [*Army*]
PPBS	Planning-Programming-Budgeting-System (SAUS)
PPBS	Plant Population Biology Section (SAUS)
PPBS	Positive Pressure Breathing System [*Aerospace*]
PPBS	Postprandial Blood Sugar [*Clinical chemistry*]
PPBS	Professional Programmer Based System (SAUS)
PPBS	Program Performance Budgetary Systems (SAUS)
PPBS	Program Planning and Budgeting Staff [*Environmental Protection Agency*] (GFGA)
PPBS	Program, Planning, and Budgeting System [*Johnson Administration*] [*Executive Office of the President*] (GFGA)
PPBSO	Piping and Pipe Band Society of Ontario [*Canada*]
PPBV	Parts Per Billion by Volume (SAUS)
PPC	Chlorinated Polypropylene (SAUS)
PPC	College of Physicians of Philadelphia, Philadelphia, PA [*Library symbol*] [*Library of Congress*] [*OCLC symbol*] (LCLS)
PP-C	Free Library of Philadelphia, Carson Collection, Philadelphia, PA [*Library symbol*] [*Library of Congress*] (LCLS)

PPC............	Journal of Pension Planning and Compliance (journ.) (SAUS)
PPC............	Palm Personal Computer
PPC............	Pan Pacific Centers [Defunct] (EA)
PPC............	Paperboard Packaging Council (EA)
PPC............	Parallel Path Counter [Electronics] (IAA)
PPC............	Parallel Plate Chambers (SAUS)
PPC............	Parallel Poll Configuration (SAUS)
PPC............	Partial Pay Card
PPC............	Partido Popular Cristiano [Christian Popular Party] [Peru] [Political party] (PPW)
PPC............	Parting Post Calls (MCD)
PPC............	Partitu Populare Corsu [Corsica] [Political party] (PD)
PPC............	Parts Preference Code [Military] (AFIT)
PPC............	Patres Conscripti [Senators] [Latin] (ROG)
PPC............	Patrick Petroleum Co. (EFIS)
PPC............	Patrol Plane Commander
PPC............	Pay Per Channel (SAUS)
PPC............	Peace Promotion Code (SAUS)
PPC............	Peak Power Control [Telecommunications] (TEL)
PPC............	Permission to Photocopy (MCD)
PPC............	Per Pupil Cost (AFM)
PPC............	Persistent Photoconductivity [Physics]
PPC............	Personal Portable Computer
PPC............	Personal Productivity Center
PPC............	Personal Programmable Calculator (MHDI)
PPC............	Personal Programmers Club (SAUS)
PPC............	Personal Protective Clothing (GNE)
PPC............	Pertec Peripherals Corp. (SAUS)
PPC............	Pet Population Control (AD)
PPC............	Petroleum Packaging Council (NTPA)
PPC............	Petroleum Pipeline Company, Cairo (SAUS)
PPC............	Petroleum Planning Committee [Obsolete] [NATO] (NATG)
PPC............	Phased Program Construction (IAA)
PPC............	Phased Provisioning Code (NASA)
PPC............	Philatelic Press Club [Later, IPPC]
PPC............	Philips Petroleum Co. (SAUS)
PPC............	Photographic Processing Cells (AFM)
PPC............	Photo Persistent Conductivity (AAEL)
PpC............	Pick Publishing Corporation, New York, NY [Library symbol] [Library of Congress] (LCLS)
ppc............	Picture Postcard (AD)
PPC............	Picture Postcard
PPC............	Pierce's Perpetual Code [1943] [A publication] (DLA)
PPC............	Pine Pass [British Columbia] [Seismograph station code, US Geological Survey] [Closed] (SEIS)
PPC............	Pin-to-Pin Compatible (SAUS)
PPC............	Plain Paper Copier [Electrophotography]
PPC............	Plain Plaster Cornice [Construction]
PPC............	Planar Positive Column (SAUS)
PPC............	Planar Postive Column (IAA)
PPC............	Plane Paper Copier (IAA)
ppc............	Plan-Paper Copier (AD)
PPC............	Plant Pest Control Division [of ARS, Department of Agriculture]
PPC............	Plant Process Computer
PPC............	Plasma Prothrombin Conversion (DB)
PPC............	Platform Position Computer
PPC............	Platinum-Palladium Colloid (DB)
PPC............	Plug Patch Cord
PPC............	Plutonium Process Cell [Nuclear energy] (NRCH)
PPC............	Plutonium Product Cell [Nuclear energy] (NRCH)
PPC............	Point of Possible Collision [Navigation]
PPC............	Point-to-Point Correlation [Graphing]
PPC............	Polarizable Point Charge [Model for the water molecule]
PPC............	Polar Path Compass (ACAE)
PPC............	Policy and Planning Committee (SAUS)
PPC............	Policy Planning Council [U.S. Department of State] (BARN)
PPC............	Polyphthalate Carbonate (SAUS)
PPC............	Polyphthalate-Polycarbonate
PPC............	Pooled Platelet Concentrate [Medicine] (MEDA)
PPC............	Portable Personal Computer (DGA)
PPC............	Positive Peer Control
PPC............	Positive Peer Culture (AD)
PPC............	Postal code for the Prime Contractor (SAUS)
PPC............	Posterior Parietal Cortex [Brain anatomy]
PPC............	Postoperative Pulmonary Complications (SAUS)
PPC............	Postpulmonary Complications
PPC............	Potential Performance Capability (SAUS)
PPC............	Potential Points of Collision [Navigation]
PPC............	Potentional Performance Capability (IAA)
PPC............	Pour Prendre Conge [To Take Leave] [French]
p p c............	Pour Prendre Conge [To Take Leave] [French] (AD)
PPC............	Power Pack Charger
PPC............	Power PC (SAUS)
PPC............	Power Physics Corp. (SAUS)
PPC............	Power Plant Change (NVT)
PPC............	PPC Oil & Gas Corp. [Toronto Stock Exchange symbol]
PPC............	Practitioners Publishing Company
PPC............	Precipitating Particle Counter (ACAE)
PPC............	Precision Photomechanical Corp.
PPC............	Predicted Point of Collision (SAUS)
PPC............	Predicted Propagation Correction (PDAA)
PPC............	Preliminary Phase Correction (IAA)
PPC............	Preprocessing Center [NASA] (NASA)
PPC............	Pre-Proposal Conference (MCD)
PPC............	Preservation and Packaging Committee
PPC............	President of the Privy Council [Canada]
PPC............	Pressure Pulse Contour [Cardiac computer] (PDAA)
PPC............	Primary Power Control (MCD)
PPC............	Printers' Pension Corp. (DGA)
PPC............	Print Position Counter
PPC............	Priority Placement Certificate [Military] (AFM)
PPC............	Process Problem Chart (SAUS)
PPC............	Process Proximity Correction (SAUS)
PPC............	Production and Planning Control (SAUS)
PPC............	Production Planning and Control
PPC............	Product Planning Committee
PPC............	Professional Personal Computer
PPC............	Professional Personnel Consultant (WDAA)
PPC............	Program Planning and Control (AAG)
PPC............	Program Planning Coordination Office [United Nations]
PPC............	Program Product Center (SAUS)
ppc............	Progressive Patient Care (AD)
PPC............	Progressive Patient Care
PPC............	Projection Printing Camera (SAUS)
PPC............	Project Parts Coordinator
PPC............	Project Physics Course [National Science Foundation]
PPC............	Project Planning and Control (COE)
PPC............	Project Planning Centre for Developing Countries [Research center] [British] (IRC)
PPC............	Project Preparation Committee (SAUS)
PPC............	Proof-of-Passing Certificate (OTD)
PPC............	Pro-Personal Computer (NITA)
PPC............	Prospect Creek, AK [Location identifier] [FAA] (FAAL)
PPC............	Prospective Parliamentary Candidate [British]
PPC............	Protected Personnel Carrier (SAUS)
PPC............	Proximal Palmar Crease [Anatomy]
PPC............	Psychiatric Patient Classes
PPC............	Psychorotrophic Plate Count [Bacteriology]
PPC............	Publishers Publicity Circle
PPC............	Pulsed Power Circuit (IEEE)
PPC............	Pulse Position Code (SAUS)
PPC............	Pulse-to-Pulse Correlation (ACAE)
PPC............	Purchase Price Control (AD)
pPc............	Pure Peruvian Cocaine (AD)
PPCA	Plasma [or Proserum] Prothrombin Conversion Accelerator [Factor VII] [Also, SPCA] [Hematology]
ppca............	Plasma Prothrombin Conversion Accelerator (AD)
PPCA	Plasma Rothrombin Conversion Accelerator (SAUS)
PPCA	Power Plant Contractors Association (SAUS)
PPCA	Preliminary Physical Configuration Audit (SAUS)
PPCA	Proserum Prothrombin Conversion Accelerator (ADWA)
PPCAA	Parole and Probation Compact Administrators Association (EA)
PPCAP	People to People Citizen Ambassador Program (EA)
PPCB	Page Printer Control Block [Computer science]
PPCB	Patrick Petroleum Co. [NASDAQ symbol] (SAG)
PPCC	Carpenters' Co., Philadelphia, PA [Library symbol] [Library of Congress] (LCLS)
PPCC	Particles per Cubic Centimeter
PPCC	Parts per Cubic Centimeter (IAA)
ppcc............	parts per cubic centimetre (SAUS)
PPCC	Port Phillip Conservation Council [Australia]
PPCC	Postmolded Plastic Chip Carrier [Computer science]
PPCCD	Profiled Peristaltic Charge Coupled-Device [Computer science] (IAA)
PPCCD	Profiled Peristaltic Charge-Coupled Device (SAUS)
PPCCH	Chestnut Hill College, Philadelphia, PA [Library symbol] [Library of Congress] (LCLS)
PPC-CPE	Practitioners Publishing Company-CPE (SAUS)
PPCD	Plant Pest Control Division (AD)
PPCD	Polymorphous Posterior Corneal Dystropy [Medicine] (DMAA)
PPCE	Portable Pneumatic Checkout Equipment (KSC)
PPCE	Post-Proline Cleaving Enzyme [Biochemistry]
PPCE	Print Position Control Exit (SAUS)
PPCE&E	Print Position Counter Entry and Exit (SAUS)
ppcf............	Plasma Prothrombin Conversion Factor (AD)
PPCF	Plasmin Prothrombin Conversion Factor [Factor V] [Hematology]
PPCH	People-to-People Committee for the Handicapped (EA)
PPCH	Pilot Pouch (SAUS)
PPCI............	Curtis Institute of Music, Philadelphia, PA [Library symbol] [Library of Congress] (LCLS)
PPCI............	Presentation Protocol Control Information [Telecommunications]
PPCI............	Pressure Piping Components, Inc. (SAUS)
PPCiC	Civic Club of Philadelphia, Philadelphia, PA [Library symbol] [Library of Congress] [Obsolete] (LCLS)
PPCIG	Personal Property Consignment Instruction Guide (MCD)
PPCLI..........	Princess Patricia of Connaught's Light Infantry [Military unit] [Canada]
PPCLI..........	Princess Patricia's Canadian Light Infantry (AD)
PPCM	Perimeter-Portal Continuous Monitoring (SAUS)
PPCM	Philadelphia County Medical Society, Philadelphia, PA [Library symbol] [Library of Congress] [Obsolete] (LCLS)
PPCM	Postpartum Cardiomyopathy [Medicine] (MELL)
PPC-M	Precision Pressure Controller-Monitor (SAUS)
PPCM	Predictive Pulse Code Modulation (SAUS)
PPCO	Periodically Phase-Controlled Oscillator (SAUS)
PPCO	Philadelphia College of Osteopathic Medicine, Philadelphia, PA [Library symbol] [Library of Congress] (LCLS)
PPCO2	Partial Pressure Carbon Dioxide
PPCoC	Community College of Philadelphia, Philadelphia, PA [Library symbol] [Library of Congress] (LCLS)
PPCOD	People-to-People Committee on Disability (EA)

PPCoIP .... Colonial Penn Group, Inc., Marketing Research Library, Philadelphia, PA [*Library symbol*] [*Library of Congress*] (LCLS)

PPComm...... Commercial Museum, Philadelphia, PA [*Library symbol*] [*Library of Congress*] [*Obsolete*] (LCLS)

PPCP .... College of Physicians of Philadelphia, Philadelphia, PA [*Library symbol*] [*Library of Congress*] (LCLS)

PPCP .... People to People Contact for Peace (SAUS)

PPCP .... Power PC Plattform (SAUS)

PPCP .... Propellant Pneumatic Control Panel (KSC)

PPCPC .... Philadelphia City Planning Commission, Philadelphia, PA [*Library symbol*] [*Library of Congress*] (LCLS)

PPCPSG....... Polish POW Camps Philatelic Study Group (EA)

PPCR .... Preliminary Program Change Request (SAUS)

PPCR .... Production Planning Change Request (SAA)

PP Crepe .... Partially Purified Crepe (SAUS)

PPCRGD ...... Pelican (SAUS)

PPCRGD ...... Pelican Pedestrian Crossing Regulations and General Directions (SAUS)

PPCS .... National Carl Schurz Memorial Foundation, Philadelphia, PA [*Library symbol*] [*Library of Congress*] [*Obsolete*] (LCLS)

PPCS .... Page Printer Control System [*Computer science*]

PPCS .... Personnel Protection and Communication Services [*British*] (AD)

PPCS .... Person to Person: Collect and Special Instruction [*Telecommunications*] (TEL)

PPCS .... Person to Person, Collect, Special (SAUS)

PPCS .... Postpericardiotomy Syndrome [*Medicine*] (MELL)

PPCS .... Precision Pointing Control System [*Engineering*]

PPCS .... Primary Producers' Cooperative Society (AD)

PPCS .... Production Planning and Control System

PPCS .... Project Planning and Control System [*Social Security Administration*]

PPCSEAPR... Plant Protection Committee for the South East Asia and Pacific Region (SAUS)

PPCT........... Project Planning and Control Techniques (SAUS)

PPCU .... Parallel Processor Control Unit (SAUS)

PPCuP .... Curtis Publishing Co., Research Library, Philadelphia, PA [*Library symbol*] [*Library of Congress*] [*Obsolete*] (LCLS)

PPCV .... Pulmonary Capillary Venous Pressure (SAUS)

PPD .... A Posteriori Probability Distribution [*Mathematics*]

PPD .... Drexel University, Philadelphia, PA [*Library symbol*] [*Library of Congress*] (LCLS)

PPD .... Humacao-Palmas [*Puerto Rico*] [*Airport symbol*] (OAG)

PPD .... I-GOOS Panel on Products and Distribution (SAUS)

PPD .... Packs per Day [*Cigarettes*] [*Medicine*]

PPD .... Panel Power Distribution (MCD)

PPD .... Panoramic Passive Detection (SAUS)

PPD .... Papered (ROG)

PPD .... Paranoid Personality Disorder (AD)

PPD .... Para-Phenylenediamine [*Organic chemistry*]

PPD ,........... Partial Packet Discard (MLOA)

PPD .... Partido Popular Democratico [*Popular Democratic Party of Puerto Rico*] [*Spanish*] (BARN)

PPD .... Partido por la Democracia [*Democratic Party*] [*Chile*] [*Political party*] (EY)

PPD .... Parti Populaire Djiboutien [*Djibouti People's Party*] [*Political party*] (PPW)

PPD .... Parti Progressiste Dahomeen [*Dahomey Progressive Party*] [*Political party*]

PPD .... Parts Provisioning Document

PPD .... Party for Peace and Democracy [*South Korea*] [*Political party*]

PPD .... Payload Position Data

PPD .... Pay Packets Deficiency (SAUS)

PPD .... Pay Packets Deficiency [*British*]

PPD .... Pepsin Pancreatin Digest [*Food protein digestibility assay*]

PPD .... Peripheral Pulse Distributor (SAUS)

PPD .... Permanent Partial Disability [*Dentistry*] (MAE)

PPD .... Personal Protective Device [*Toxicology*]

PPD .... Personnel Planning Data [*Navy*]

PPD .... Personnel Priority Designator [*Military*] (AFM)

PPD .... Petroleum Production Division (AD)

PPD .... Phenyldiphenyloxadiazole [*Organic chemistry*] (MAE)

PPD .... Piperidine Pentamethylene Dithiocarbonate (SAUS)

PPD .... Pitch Phase Detector

PPD .... Plains Petroleum Co. [*Vancouver Stock Exchange symbol*]

PPD .... Planning Production Data (SAUS)

PPD .... Plot Plan Drawing (SAA)

PPD .... Point Position Data

PPD .... Politieke Partij Democraten 66 [*Political Party Democrats 66*] [*Netherlands*] (EAIO)

PPD .... Portland Public Docks (AD)

PPD .... Port Protection Device [*Computer science*] (ITCA)

PPD .... Portuguese Popular Democrats

PPD .... Posterior Polymorphous Dystrophy [*Neurology*] (DAVI)

ppd .... Postpaid (WDMC)

PPD .... Postpaid

PPD .... Postpartum Day [*Obstetrics*] (DAVI)

PPD .... Postpartum Depression (PAZ)

PPD .... PostScript Printer Description [*Computer science*] (PCM)

PPD .... Preferred Policyholders' Discount [*British*] (BARN)

ppd .... Prepaid (WDMC)

PPD .... Prepaid

PPD .... Prepaid Dental Plan [*Insurance*] (MCD)

PPD .... Pre-Paid Legal Services, Inc. [*AMEX symbol*] (SPSG)

PPD .... Pre-Paid Legal Svcs [*AMEX symbol*] (TTSB)

ppd .... Prepared (MAE)

PPD .... Preprototype Demonstration

PPD .... Presidential Protective Division [*US Secret Service*]

PPD .... Prime Power Distribution

PPD .... Principal Project Designer [*Engineering project management*]

PPD .... Printer Page Description [*Computer science*]

PPD .... Processed Payment Document (GFGA)

PPD .... Product and Process Description (SAUS)

PPD .... Production Program, Douglas

PPD .... Proficiency Pay Designator [*Military*] (AABC)

PPD .... Prognostic Prediction Devices

PPD .... Program Package Document

PPD .... Program Planning Directives [*NASA*] (KSC)

PPD .... Program Planning Document (NG)

PPD .... Progressive Perceptive Deafness [*Medicine*]

PPD .... Projectile Pull and Drain [*Machine*] (MCD)

PPD .... Project Planning Directive (NG)

PPD .... Project Planning Document (ABAC)

PPD .... Prompt Payment Discount (AAGC)

PPD .... Propria Pecunia Dedicavit [*With His Own Money He Offered It*] [*Latin*] (ROG)

PPD .... Propulsion and Power Division [*Manned Spacecraft Center*] [*NASA*]

PPD .... Provisioning Procurement Data

PPD .... Proximity, Point Detonating (SAUS)

PPD .... Pulse-Type Phase Detector

PPD .... Purchasing Power of the Dollar (MHDW)

ppd .... Purified Protein Derivative (AD)

PPD .... Purified Protein Derivative [*Tuberculin*]

PPDA .... Para-Phenylenediamine [*Organic chemistry*]

PPDA .... Phenyl Phosphorodiamidate [*Fertilizer technology*]

PPDA .... Poor Prisoners Defence Act (SAUS)

PPDA .... Produce Packaging Development Association (AD)

PPDB .... Personnel Planning Data Book [*Navy*]

PPDB .... Point Positioning Data Base (SAUS)

PPDB .... Point-Positioning Data Base [*Cartography*] (RDA)

PPD-B .... Purified Protein Derivative - Battey [*Tuberculin*] (AAMN)

PPD-B .... Purified Protein Derivative-Battey (SAUS)

PPDC .... Dental Cosmos Library, Philadelphia, PA [*Library symbol*] [*Library of Congress*] [*Obsolete*] (LCLS)

PPDC .... Paraguayan People's Documentation Center [*Mestre, Italy*] (EAIO)

PPDC .... Partido Popular Democratica Cristiana [*Popular Christian Democratic Party*] [*Spain*] [*Political party*] (PPE)

PPDC .... Perfusion Program Directors Council [*Cardiology*] (DAVI)

PPDC .... Pig Production Development Committee (SAUS)

PPDC .... Polymer Products Development Center (or Centre) (SAUS)

PPDC .... Programming Panels and Decoding Circuits

PPDD .... Peoples Party for Democracy and Development (SAUS)

PPDD .... Pershing Physical Deception Device [*Army*]

PPDD .... Plan Position Data Display

PPDD .... Preliminary Project Design Description (NRCH)

PPDDS .... Private Practice Dental Delivery System

PPDef-M ..... Defense Personnel Support Center, Directorate of Medical Material Library, Philadelphia, PA [*Library symbol*] [*Library of Congress*] (LCLS)

PPDF .... Poisson Probability Distribution Function [*Mathematics*]

PPDF .... Portable Postscript-Document Format [*Computer science*] (ELAL)

PPDG .... Parti Progressiste Democratique Guadeloupeen [*Political party*] (EY)

PPDGF .... Porcine Platelet-Derived Growth Factor [*Biochemistry*]

PPDI .... Paraphenylene Diisocyanate [*Organic chemistry*]

PPDI .... Pharmaceutical Product Development, Inc. [*NASDAQ symbol*] (SAG)

PPDI .... Pharmaceutical Product Devlpmt [*NASDAQ symbol*] (TTSB)

ppdi .... Pilot's Projected-Display Indicator (AD)

PPDI .... Pilots Projected Display Indicator (SAUS)

PPDI .... Pre-Pre-Delivery Inspection [*Automotive project management*]

PPDIL .... Pre-Power-Dependent Insertion Limit [*Nuclear energy*] (NRCH)

PPDio .... Diocesan Library, Philadelphia, PA [*Library symbol*] [*Library of Congress*] [*Obsolete*] (LCLS)

PPDL .... Postscript Page Description Language [*Computer science*] (CIST)

PPDM .... E. I. Du Pont de Nemours & Co., Marshall Laboratory, Philadelphia, PA [*Library symbol*] [*Library of Congress*] (LCLS)

PPDM .... Pseudo-Pinch Design Method [*Heat exchange design*]

PPDMG .... Popular Priced Dress Manufacturers Group [*Later, AMA*] (EA)

ppdo .... Per Person, Double Occupancy (AD)

PPDO .... Per Person, Double Occupancy [*Travel industry*] (TRID)

PPDO .... Personal Paid Days Off

PPDO .... Program and Policy Development Office (SAUS)

PPDO .... Provincial Planning and Development Office (SAUS)

PPDP .... Preliminary Project Development Plan [*NASA*]

PPDP .... Preprogram Definition Phase

PP-DPH....... Free Library of Philadelphia, Library for the Blind and Physically Handicapped, Philadelphia, PA [*Library symbol*] [*Library of Congress*] (LCLS)

PPDR .... Philadelphia Department of Records, Philadelphia, PA [*Library symbol*] [*Library of Congress*] (LCLS)

PPDR .... Pilot Performance Description Record

PP/DR......... Preliminary Performance Design Requirements

PPDR .... Preproliferative Diabetic Retinopathy [*Medicine*] (MELL)

PPDR .... Production Packing Depth Range (NG)

PPDrop .... Dropsie University, Philadelphia, PA [*Library symbol*] [*Library of Congress*] (LCLS)

PPDS .... Personal Printer Data Stream [*IBM Corp.*] (PCM)

PPDS .... Phonologic Programming Deficit Syndrome (DMAA)

PPDS .... Physical Property Data Service [*Institution of Chemical Engineers*] [*Databank*] [*Information service or system*] (IID)

PPDS .... Planning Production Data Sheet

PPDS .... Preservation and Packaging Data Sheet [*DoD*]

PPDS .... Primary Processor and Data Storage (SAUS)

PPDS	Publishers' Parcels Delivery Service (AD)
PPDS	Purchase Parts Data Sheet
PPD-S	Purified Protein Derivative-Standard [*Tuberculin*]
PPDSE	International Plate Printers, Die Stampers, and Engravers' Union of North America
PPDSE	Plate Printers, Die Stampers, and Engravers [*Union*] (AD)
PPDT	(Phenylpyridyl)diphenyltriazine [*Analytical chemistry*]
PPDT	Poly(phenyleneterephthalamide) [*Organic chemistry*]
PPDU	Presentation Protocol Data Unit [*Computer science*] (TNIG)
PPDU	Propulsion Power Distribution Unit (ACAE)
PPDVWG	Population Dynamics and Physical Variability Working Group (SAUS)
PPE	Independent Union of Plant Protection Employees in the Electrical and Machine Industry
PPE	Packet Processing Engine (SAUS)
PP/E	Parallel Print/Exact (VLIE)
PP/E	Parallel Print/Extract (SAUS)
PPE	Park Place Entertainment [*NYSE symbol*] (SG)
PPE	Partial Plasma Exchange (STED)
PPE	Particle Physics Experiments Division (SAUS)
PPE	Parti Populaire Europeen [*European Peoples' Party - EPP*] (EAIO)
PPE	Party for the Protection of the Environment (SAUS)
PPE	PATRIOT Peculiar Equipment (SAUS)
PPE	Pave Paws East (SAUS)
PPE	People, Places and Events (SAUS)
PPE	Peripheral Processor Element [*Computer science*] (VLIE)
PPE	Permeability Pulmonary Edema (STED)
PPE	Personal Protective Equipment [*General Motors Corp.*]
PPE	Personnel Protection Equipment (SAUS)
PPE	Phase Partitioning Experiment (SAUS)
ppe	Philosophy, Politics, and Economics (AD)
PPE	Philosophy, Politics, Economics [*Oxford University*]
PPE	Pholbe Phillips Editions [*Publisher*] [*British*]
PPE	Pipette [*Chemistry*]
PPE	Platform Position Equipment
PPE	Polypentene [*Organic chemistry*]
PPE	Polyphenylene Ether (SAUS)
PPE	Polyphenylene Ether Plastic [*Materials science*]
PPE	Polyphenylether (IEEE)
PPE	Polyphosphate Ester [*Inorganic chemistry*]
PPE	Polyphosphate Ester (SAUS)
PPE	Polyphosphoric Ester (STED)
PPE	Porcine Pancreatic Elastase [*An enzyme*]
PPE	Potomac Pacific Engineering, Inc.
PPE	Predicted Period of Effect (SAUS)
PPE	Predicted Period-of-Effect [*Meteorology*]
PPE	Premodulation Processing Equipment
PPE	Premodulation Processor Equipment (SAUS)
PPE	Preparticipation Physical Exam
PPE	Preparticipation Physical Examination
PPE	Preproduction Engineering
PPE	Preproduction Evaluation (NG)
PPE	Preproduction Proposal Evaluation
PPE	Preproenkephalin [*Biochemistry*]
PPE	Print-Punch Editor [*Computer science*] (SAA)
PPE	Problem Program Efficiency (IEEE)
PPE	Problem Program Evaluator
PPE	Programmed Physical Examination (STED)
PPE	Program Performance Evaluator (NITA)
PPE	Program Planning and Evaluation
PPE	Prototype Production Evaluation (NG)
PPE	Purchasing Power Equivalent
PPE	Pyridoxal Phosphate Effect [*Medicine*]
PPE	Shuman, Psychiatric and Psychological Evidence (SAUS)
PPEA	Plant Performance Evaluation Activity [*Military*] (DNAB)
PPEB	Eastern Baptist Theological Seminary, Philadelphia, PA [*Library symbol*] [*Library of Congress*] (LCLS)
PPEB	[*The*] Pottery of Palestine from the Earliest Times to the End of the EarlyBronze Age [*A publication*] (BJA)
PPEC	Panchayat Polity and Evaluation Committee (SAUS)
PPECC	Philippine Pacific Economic Cooperation Committee
PPECP	Pollution Prevention and Emissions Control Program (COE)
PPEF	Public Policy Education Fund (EA)
PPEFH	E. F. Hutton & Co., Philadelphia, PA [*Library symbol*] [*Library of Congress*] [*Obsolete*] (LCLS)
PPELE	Practical Papers in English Language Education (SAUS)
PPEM	Packed Pixel Expansion Mode
PPEMA	Portable Power Equipment Manufacturers Association (EA)
PPEN	Purchased Parts Equipment Notice (SAA)
PPEng	Engineers' Club, Philadelphia, PA [*Library symbol*] [*Library of Congress*] [*Obsolete*] (LCLS)
PPEP	Eastern Pennsylvania Psychiatric Institute, Philadelphia, PA [*Library symbol*] [*Library of Congress*] (LCLS)
PPEP	Pen Plotter Emulation Plotsoftware (SAUS)
PPEP	Pen Plotter Emulation Program [*Computer science*] (MHDI)
PPEP	Plasma Physics and Environmental Perturbation (NASA)
P/PEP	Progress Performance Evaluation Panel [*Job Corps*]
PPER	Procurement Package Engineering Release (MCD)
PPES	Physical Performance Evaluation System [*Army*]
PPES	Pilot Performance Evaluation System [*Air Force*]
PPES	Planning, Programming, and Execution System [*Army*] (AAGC)
PPeSchw	Schwenkfelder Historical Library, Pennsburg, PA [*Library symbol*] [*Library of Congress*] (LCLS)
PPET	Pangea Petroleum Co. (SAUS)
PPETS	Pretreatment Permitting and Enforcement Tracking System [*Environmental Protection Agency*] (ERG)

PPEWARN	Pave Paws Early Warning phased-Array Radar Network (SAUS)
PPF	Columbus Polar Platform (SAUS)
PPF	Franklin Institute, Philadelphia, PA [*Library symbol*] [*Library of Congress*] [*OCLC symbol*] (LCLS)
PPF	Hancock [*John*] Patriot Preferred Dividend Fund [*NYSE symbol*] (SPSG)
PPF	John Hancock Patr Pfd Div Fd [*NYSE symbol*] (TTSB)
PPF	Pacific Peace Fund (EA)
PPF	Paired-Pulse Facilitation [*Neurophysiology*]
PPF	Panamanian Public Force (AD)
PPF	Panels Per Facing [*Outdoor advertising*] (WDMC)
PPF	Parsons [*Kansas*] [*Airport symbol*] (OAG)
PPF	Parsons, KS [*Location identifier*] [*FAA*] (FAAL)
PPF	Parti Populaire Francais [*French Popular Party*] [*Political party*] (PPE)
PPF	Patriotic People's Front [*Hungary*] [*Political party*]
PPF	Payload Processing Facility [*Air Force*] (NASA)
PPF	Peacetime Planning Factors
PPF	Peak Power Frequency
PPF	Pellagra Preventive Factor [*See also PP*] [*Biochemistry*]
PPF	People's Police Force
PPF	Permanent Power Fuse (SAUS)
ppf	Personal Property Floater [*Insurance*] (AD)
PPF	Personal Property Floater [*Insurance*]
PPF	Phagocytosis Promoting Factor [*Immunology*] (DAVI)
PPF	Phase Pushing Factor
PPF	Photophoretic Force [*Pressure exerted by light*]
PPF	Plain Paper Fax (SAUS)
PPF	Plasma Protein Fraction [*Hematology*]
PPF	Platform Proto-Federation (SAUS)
PPF	Plumbers and Pipefitters [*Union*] (AD)
PPF	Poetarum Philosophorum Graecorum Fragmenta [*A publication*] (OCD)
PPF	Polarization-Preserving Fiber
PPF	Polar Platform (SAUS)
PPF	Poly(phenolformaldehyde) [*Organic chemistry*]
PPF	Porous Polyurethane Foam [*Also, PUF*] [*Plastics technology*]
PPF	Positive Position Feedback
PPF	Post Parturitive Fever (SAUS)
PPF	Power Plant Frame [*Mazda Miata*] [*Connecting engine and transmission to final drive*]
PPF	Presbyterian Peace Fellowship (EA)
PPF	Primary Part Failure (DNAB)
PPF	Principal Profile Forms [*Soil classification*]
PPF	Print Production Format (SAUS)
PPF	Privatefoeretagarnas Partioganisation i Finland [*Finnish Private Entrepreneurs' Party*] [*Political party*] (PPE)
PPF	Production Possibility Frontier [*Economics*]
PPF	Program Preparation Facilities (VLIE)
PPF	Program Production Fee (VLIE)
PPF	Program Protects Flags (VLIE)
PPF	Provision of Production Facilities [*Military*] (AABC)
PPF	United Association of Journeymen and Apprentices of the Plumbing and Pipe Fitting Industry of the United States and Canada
PPFA	Page Printer Formatting Aid [*Computer science*] (CIST)
PPFA	Planned Parenthood Federation of America (EA)
PPFA	Plastic Pipe and Fittings Association (EA)
PPFA	Professional Picture Framers Association (EA)
PPFA	United States Army, Frankford Arsenal Library, Philadelphia, PA [*Library symbol*] [*Library of Congress*] (LCLS)
p-p factor	Pellagra-Preventive Factor (AD)
PPFAR	Federal Archives and Records Center, General Services Administration, Philadelphia, PA [*Library symbol*] [*Library of Congress*] (LCLS)
PPFAS	Past President of the Faculty of Architects and Surveyors [*British*] (DBQ)
PPFAS	Post President of the Faculty of Architects and Surveyors (SAUS)
PPF-B	Biochemical Research Foundation, Franklin Institute, Newark, DE [*Closed*] [*Library symbol*] [*Library of Congress*] (LCLS)
PPFC	Peoples Pearl and Fishery Corp. (SAUS)
PPFC	Philadelphia Fellowship Commission, Philadelphia, PA [*Library symbol*] [*Library of Congress*] [*Obsolete*] (LCLS)
PPFC	Priscilla Presley Fan Club [*Defunct*] (EA)
PPFCA	Philadelphia College of Art Library (SAUS)
PPFD	Photosynthetically Active Photon Flux Density [*Botany*]
PPFD	Photosynthetic Photon Flux Density (SAUS)
PPFF	Poisson Probability Frequency Function [*Mathematics*]
PPF-G	Germantown Laboratories, Inc., Philadelphia, PA [*Library symbol*] [*Library of Congress*] (LCLS)
PPFHi	Historical Society of Frankford, Philadelphia, PA [*Library symbol*] [*Library of Congress*] [*Obsolete*] (LCLS)
PP Film	Polypropylene Film (SAUS)
PPFJC	Federation of Jewish Charities, Philadelphia, PA [*Library symbol*] [*Library of Congress*] [*Obsolete*] (LCLS)
PPFML	Fidelity Mutual Life Insurance Co., Philadelphia, PA [*Library symbol*] [*Library of Congress*] (LCLS)
PPFO	Paris Procurement Field Office
PPFP	Plane Parallel Fabry-Perot (SAUS)
PPFPR	F. P. Ristine & Co., Philadelphia, PA [*Library symbol*] [*Library of Congress*] [*Obsolete*] (LCLS)
PPFr	Friends' Free Library of Germantown, Philadelphia, PA [*Library symbol*] [*Library of Congress*] (LCLS)
PPFR	Plutonium Product Filter Room [*Nuclear energy*] (NRCH)
PPFRB	Federal Reserve Bank of Philadelphia, Philadelphia, PA [*Library symbol*] [*Library of Congress*] (LCLS)

PPFRT	Prototype Preliminary Flight Rating Test
PPFS	Pergamon Professional and Financial Services [*Commercial firm*] [*British*]
PPFS	Pre-Printed Forms System (SAUS)
PPFS	Product Performance Feedback System (SAUS)
PPFS	Purchased Parts Forecasting System (TIMI)
PPFU	Post Program Follow-Up (AGLO)
PPFUN	Post-Processor Function (SAUS)
PPG	German Society of Pennsylvania, Philadelphia, PA [*Library symbol*] [*Library of Congress*] (LCLS)
PPG	Pacific Proving Ground [*AEC*]
PPG	Pago Pago [*Samoa*] [*Airport symbol*] (OAG)
PPG	Pago Pago, AQ [*Location identifier*] [*FAA*] (FAAL)
PPG	Pediatric Pneumogram [*Radiology*] (DAVI)
PPG	Performance Partnership Grant (SAUS)
PPG	Periodical Press Gallery [*US Senate*]
PPG	Permanent Planning Group [*Military*] [*British*]
PPG	Personnel Processing Group [*Army*]
PPG	Photoplethysmography [*Medicine*]
PPG	Picopicogram [*One trillionth of one trillionth of a gram*]
PPG	Piezoelectric Power Generation
PPG	Pipe Plug
PPG	Pittsburgh Paint and Glass [*Company*]
PPG	Pittsburgh Plate Glass [*Commercial firm*]
PPG	Planned Procurement Guide
PPG	Planning and Policy Guidance (MCD)
PPG	Planning and Programming Guidance [*Army*] (AABC)
ppg	Planning and Programming Guidance (AD)
PPG	Plasma Power Generator
PPG	Player Piano Group (EAIO)
PPG	Points per Game (WGA)
PPG	Policies and Procedures Guide (SAA)
PPG	Polymorphonuclear Cells per Glomerulus (STED)
PPG	Poly(propylene Glycol) [*Organic chemistry*]
PPG	Polyurethane-Polyvinyl Graphite (STED)
PPG	Portal Pressure Gradient [*Medicine*] (DMAA)
PPG	Postprandial Glucose (STED)
ppg	Pounds per Gallon
PPGL	Power-Play Goal [*Hockey*]
PPG	PPG Indus [*NYSE symbol*] (TTSB)
PPG	PPG Industries, Inc. [*Formerly, Pittsburgh Plate Glass Co.*] [*Associated Press*] (SAG)
PPG	PPG Industries, Inc., Coatings and Resins Division, Allison Park, PA [*OCLC symbol*] (OCLC)
PPG	Predictive Proportional Guidance
PPG	Pre-School Playgroup [*British*] (DET)
PPG	Pretragal Parotid Gland (STED)
PPG	Primary Pattern Generator [*Bell Laboratories*]
PPG	Prime Power Group
PPG	Print Pattern Generator (IAA)
PPG	Priority Planning Grid (ABAC)
PPG	Program for Population Genetics [*Collaboration of US and China Groups*]
PPG	Programmable Pattern Generator (SAUS)
PPG	Programmable Pulse Generator (IGSL)
PPG	Program Planning Guide (OICC)
PPG	Program Policy Guidelines
PPG	Program Pulse Generator (IEEE)
PPG	Propulsion and Power Generation
PPG	Propylene Gylcol (ACAE)
PPG	Pulses Per Group (SAUS)
PPGA	British Pot Plant Growers Association (SAUS)
PPGA	Pennsylvania Personnel and Guidance Association (AD)
PPGA	Personal Producing General Agent [*Insurance*]
PPGA	Plastic Pin Grid Array (PCM)
PPGA	Post Pill Galactorrhea-Amenorrhea [*Medicine*]
ppga	Post-Pill Galactorrheamenorrhea [*Medicine*] (AD)
PPGA	Pot Plant Growers Association (SAUS)
PPGA	Potplant Growers Association [*British*] (DBA)
PPGA	Preschool Play-Group Association [*British*] (DI)
PPGA	Professional Plant Growers Association (NTPA)
PPGBL	Personal Property Government Bill of Lading (DNAB)
PPGD	Pelvic Plane of Greatest Dimension [*Medicine*] (MELL)
PPGE	General Electric Co., Philadelphia, PA [*Library symbol*] [*Library of Congress*] (LCLS)
PPGE	Partido del Progreso de Guinea Ecuatorial [*Progressive Party of Equatorial Guinea*] [*Political party*] (EY)
PPGE-M	General Electric Co., Missile and Space Vehicle Department, Aerosciences Laboratory, Philadelphia (SAUS)
PPGE-M	General Electric Co., Missile and Space Vehicle Department, Aerosciences Laboratory, Philadelphia, PA [*Library symbol*] [*Library of Congress*] (LCLS)
PPGen	Genealogical Society of Pennsylvania, Philadelphia, PA [*Library symbol*] [*Library of Congress*] (LCLS)
PPGenH	Philadelphia General Hospital Laboratories, Philadelphia, PA [*Library symbol*] [*Library of Congress*] [*Obsolete*] (LCLS)
PPGeo	Geographical Society of Philadelphia, Philadelphia, PA [*Library symbol*] [*Library of Congress*] [*Obsolete*] (LCLS)
PPGF	Polypeptide Growth Factor [*Endocrinology*] (DAVI)
PPGH	Philadelphia General Hospital, Philadelphia, PA [*Library symbol*] [*Library of Congress*] (LCLS)
PPGi	Girard College, Philadelphia, PA [*Library symbol*] [*Library of Congress*] [*Obsolete*] (LCLS)
PPGJW	Past Pro-Grand Junior Warden [*Freemasonry*] (ROG)
PPGL	Polished Plate Glass [*Technical drawings*] (DAC)
PPGM	Past Provincial Grand Master [*Freemasonry*]
PPGM	Planning, Programming and Guidance Memorandum (SAUS)
PPGM	Planning-Programming Guidance Memo [*Navy*]
PPGO	Past Pro-Grand Organist [*Freemasonry*] (ROG)
PPGO	Past Pro-Grand Orient [*Freemasonry*] (ROG)
PPGP	Past Pro-Grand Pursuivant [*Freemasonry*] (ROG)
PPGP	Prepaid Group Practice [*Insurance*] (DHSM)
PPGraph	Graphic Sketch Club, Philadelphia, PA [*Library symbol*] [*Library of Congress*] [*Obsolete*] (LCLS)
PPGratz	Gratz College, Philadelphia, PA [*Library symbol*] [*Library of Congress*] [*Obsolete*] (LCLS)
PPGRC	Public Policy and Government Relations Council
PPGS	Postpartum Glomerulosclerosis [*Medicine*] (MELL)
PPGS	Publications of the Pennsylvana German Society (SAUS)
PPGSB	Past Pro-Grand Sword Bearer [*Freemasonry*] (ROG)
PPGSN	Past Provincial Grand Senior [*Freemasonry*] (ROG)
PPGSW	Past Provincial Grand Senior Warden [*Freemasonry*]
PPGW	Past Pro-Grand Warden [*Freemasonry*] (ROG)
PPH	Pages per Hour
PPH	Paid Personal Holiday
pph	Pamphlet (AD)
PPH	Pamphlet
pph	Papers Per Hour [*News*] (WDMC)
PPH	Parts per Hour (TIMI)
PPH	Parts per Hundred
PPH	Past Pertinent History (SAUS)
PPH	Peak-to-Peak Heights [*Spectrometry*]
PPH	Persistent Pulmonary Hypertension [*Medicine*]
PPH	Petroleum Pipehead
PPH	Phenylpropanolamine(hydrochloride) [*Also, PPA, PPM*] [*Decongestant*]
PPH	Phosphopyruvate Hydratase [*An enzyme*]
PPH	PHP Healthcare [*NYSE symbol*] (TTSB)
PPH	PHP Healthcare Corp. [*NYSE symbol*] (SPSG)
PPH	Plasmapherese (SAUS)
PPH	Postlumbar Puncture Headache [*Medicine*] (MELL)
pph	Post-Partum Hemorrhage [*Medicine*] (AD)
PPH	Postpartum Hemorrhage [*Medicine*]
pph	Pounds Per Hour (AD)
PPH	Pounds per Hour (NG)
PPH	Primary Pulmonary Hypertension [*Medicine*]
PPH	Prophet Resources Ltd. [*Vancouver Stock Exchange symbol*]
PPH	Protocollagen Proline Hydroxylase [*An enzyme*] (MAE)
pph	Pulses Per Hour (AD)
PPH	Pulses per Hour
PPHa	Hahnemann Medical College and Hospital, Philadelphia, PA [*Library symbol*] [*Library of Congress*] (LCLS)
PPHA	Peak Pulse Height Analysis
PPHA	Private Proprietary Homes for Adults
PPHBA	Peruvian Paso Half-Blood Association [*Later, PPPBR*] (EA)
PPHFC	Holy Family College, Philadelphia, PA [*Library symbol*] [*Library of Congress*] (LCLS)
PPH/LB	Pounds per Hour per Pound (SAA)
PPHM	Parts per Hundred Million
P-PH-M	Pulse Phase Modulation (DEN)
PPHN	Persistent Pulmonary Hypertension of the Newborn [*Medicine*]
PPHN	Primary Pulmonary Hypertension of the Newborn [*Medicine*] (NRGU)
PPHOPT	Pseudo-Pseudohypoparathyroidism [*Also, PPHP*] [*Endocrinology*]
PPHor	Pennsylvania Horticultural Society, Philadelphia, PA [*Library symbol*] [*Library of Congress*] (LCLS)
P Php	Port Phillip (AD)
PPHP	Pseudo-Pseudohypoparathyroidism [*Also, PPHOPT*] [*Endocrinology*]
PPHPI	Henry Phipps Institute, Philadelphia, PA [*Library symbol*] [*Library of Congress*] [*Obsolete*] (LCLS)
PPHPI	Henry Phipps Institute, Philadelphia (SAUS)
pphpm	Parts Per Hundred Parts of Mix (AD)
pphpm	Pints Per Hundred Parts of Mix (AD)
pphr	Parts Per Hundred Parts of Rubber (AD)
PPHRII	Parents of Premature and High Risk Infants International (EA)
PPHRNA	Peruvian Paso Horse Registry of North America (EA)
PPHS	Partisan Prohibition Historical Society (EA)
PPHSL	Periodical Publication in Harvard Science Libraries
PPHT	(Phenylethyl-propylamino)hydroxytetralin [*Biochemistry*]
PPHx	Previous Psychiatric History (MEDA)
PPHYS	Plant Physiology (SAUS)
PPi	Carnegie Library of Pittsburgh, Pittsburgh, PA [*Library symbol*] [*Library of Congress*] (LCLS)
PPI	Institute for Psychosomatic and Psychiatric Research and Training [*Research center*] (RCD)
PPI	Pacific Propeller Inc. (SAUS)
PPI	Packing, Postage, and Insurance [*Shipping*]
PPI	Padangpandjang [*Sumatra*] [*Seismograph station code, US Geological Survey*] (SEIS)
ppi	Pages Per Inch (AD)
PPI	Pages per Inch [*Publishing*]
PPI	Pakistan Press International
PPI	Pan Pacific Institute [*Flinders University, Australia*]
PPI	Parallel Peripheral Interface [*Computer science*]
PPI	Parallel Plate Interceptor (SAUS)
PPI	Parallel Port Interface (SAUS)
ppi	Parcel Post Insured (AD)
PPI	Parcel Post, Insured [*Shipping*]
PPI	Particles per Inch
PPI	Partito Popolare Italiano [*Italian Popular Party*] [*Political party*] (WDAA)

PPI.............	Parts Parameter Information (SAUS)
PPI.............	Passe Partout International
PPI.............	Pass Point Instrument (SAUS)
PPI.............	Patient Package Insert [Pharmacy] (DAVI)
PPI.............	Pensioners for Peace International (EAIO)
PPI.............	Pergamon Press, Inc.
PPI.............	Permanent Pacemaker Implantation [Medicine] (MELL)
PPI.............	Personality and Personal Illness Questionnaires [Psychology]
PPI.............	Personalpolitische Information (SAUS)
PPI.............	Personnel Planning Information
PPI.............	Pharate Pupal Integument (SAUS)
PPI.............	Phoenix Precision Instrument Co.
PPI.............	Pickle Packers International (EA)
ppi.............	Picks Per Inch [Weaving] (DICI)
PPI.............	Pico Products [AMEX symbol] (TTSB)
PPI.............	Pico Products, Inc. [AMEX symbol] (SPSG)
PPI.............	Pictorial Position Indicator
PPI.............	Pilgrim Holdings Ltd. [Vancouver Stock Exchange symbol]
PPI.............	PIPA [Pulsed Integrating Pendulous Accelerometer] Pulse Integrator
PPI.............	Piston Position Indicator
PPI.............	PIXEL [Picture Element] per Inch [Computer science] (PCM)
ppi.............	Pixels Per Inch [Computer graphics] (WDMC)
PPI.............	Plane Position Indicator [RADAR]
PPI.............	Plan Position Indication (or Indicator) (SAUS)
ppi.............	Plan Position Indicator (AD)
PPI.............	Plan Position Indicator Mode [Computer science] (ADA)
PPI.............	Plasma Protein Isolate [Food technology]
PPI.............	Plastic Pipe Institute (SAUS)
PPI.............	Plastics Pipe Institute (EA)
PPI.............	Plate Power Input (ELAL)
PPI.............	Plot Position Indicator
PPI.............	Point per Inch (IAA)
ppi.............	Points Per Inch (WDMC)
ppi.............	Policy Proof of Interest (AD)
PPI.............	Policy Proof of Interest
PPI.............	Polymeric Polyisocyanate (EDCT)
PPI.............	Polyphosphonositides
PPI.............	Polyphthalimide [Organic chemistry]
PPI.............	POM [Program Objective Memorandum] Preparation Instructions [Military]
ppi.............	Pores per Inch
PPI.............	Port Pirie [Australia] [Airport symbol] (OAG)
PPI.............	Ports [Harbors] Performance Indicator [Australia]
PPI.............	Postage Paid Impression [Freight] (DCTA)
PPI.............	Potash and Phosphate Institute (EA)
PPI.............	Potato Protease Inhibitor (DB)
PPI.............	Pounds per Inch [Lubrication load]
PPI.............	Power Prime Implicant (VLIE)
PPI.............	Preceding Preparatory Interval [Psychometrics]
PPI.............	Precise Pixel Interpolation (SAUS)
PPI.............	Precise-Pixel Interpolation [Computer science]
PPI.............	Precision Products, Incorporated
PPI.............	Preferred Parts Index
PPI.............	Pre Phase-In
PPI.............	Pre-Planned Product Improvements (ACAE)
PPI.............	Preplant Inc. [Herbicides] [Agriculture]
PPI.............	Prepleading Investigation [Law]
PPI.............	Pre-production Part Index
PPI.............	Preproinsulin [Medicine] (DB)
PPI.............	Present Pain Intensity
PPI.............	Present Position Indication (or Indicator) (SAUS)
PPI.............	Present Position Indicator [Aviation]
PPI.............	Prices Paid Index [Economics]
PPI.............	Primarily Primates, Inc. [An association] (EA)
PPI.............	Primary Personal Interest [Personnel study]
PPI.............	Prime Permissible Implicant (SAUS)
PPI.............	Prince Patrick Island [Canada]
PPI.............	Print Position Indicator (SAUS)
PPI.............	Process Planning Interface [Computer science] (VLIE)
PPI.............	Producer Price Index [Bureau of Labor Statistics] [Information service or system]
PPI.............	Professional Photographers of Israel (PDAA)
PPI.............	Professional Photographers of Israel Organization (SAUS)
PPI.............	Professional Press Inc. (SAUS)
PPI.............	Programmable Parallel Interface (SAUS)
PPI.............	Programmable Peripheral Interface (MCD)
PPI.............	Program Position Indicator
PPI.............	Progressive Policy Institute [Research center] (RCD)
PPI.............	Project Procurement Instruction (SAUS)
PPI.............	Project Procurement Instructions [Jet Propulsion Laboratory, NASA]
PPI.............	Project Public Information [Department of Education] (AEBS)
PPI.............	Property Protection Insurance
PPI.............	Proportional Plus Integral
PPI.............	Protective Packaging, Inc. (AD)
PPI.............	Public-Private Interface
PPI.............	Publishing Partners International (SAUS)
PPI.............	Pulse Position Indicator (MCD)
ppi.............	Pulses Per Inch (WDMC)
PPI.............	Pulses per Inch (CMD)
PPI.............	Pyrophosphate Index [Agronomy]
PPi.............	Pyrophosphate, Inorganic [Chemistry]
PPIA.............	American-Indonesian Friendship Association (SAUS)
PPi-A.............	Carnegie Library of Pittsburgh, Allegheny Regional Branch, Monroeville, PA [Library symbol] [Library of Congress] (LCLS)
PPIA.............	Poultry Products Inspection Act (GFGA)
PPIA.............	Programme du Pipeline des Iles de l'Arctique [Canada]
PPiAC.............	Community College of Allegheny County, Pittsburgh, PA [Library symbol] [Library of Congress] (LCLS)
PPiAL.............	Allegheny County Law Library, Pittsburgh, PA [Library symbol] [Library of Congress] (LCLS)
PPiAM.............	Pittsburgh Academy of Medicine, Pittsburgh, PA [Library symbol] [Library of Congress] (LCLS)
PPIAS.............	Parent-to-Parent Information on Adoption Services [British] (DI)
PPIB.............	Programmable Protocol Interface Board
PPiC.............	Carnegie-Mellon University, Pittsburgh, PA [Library symbol] [Library of Congress] (LCLS)
PPIC.............	Pesticide Programs Information Center (EPAT)
PPIC.............	Plumbing and Piping Industry Council (AD)
PPIC.............	Pollution Prevention Information Clearinghouse [Environmental Protection Agency]
PPiCa.............	Carlow College, Pittsburgh, PA [Library symbol] [Library of Congress] (LCLS)
PPiCa-O.............	Carlow College, Our Lady of Mercy Academy, Pittsburgh, PA [Library symbol] [Library of Congress] (LCLS)
PPiCC.............	Chatham College, Pittsburgh, PA [Library symbol] [Library of Congress] (LCLS)
PPICC.............	Plasma Proinflammatory Cytokine Concentration [Medicine] (MELL)
PPICR.............	Institute for Cancer Research, Philadelphia, PA [Library symbol] [Library of Congress] (LCLS)
PPICS.............	Production Planning Inventory Control System (PDAA)
PPiD.............	Duquesne University, Pittsburgh, PA [Library symbol] [Library of Congress] (LCLS)
PPID.............	Peak Pain Intensity Difference Score [Medicine] (DMAA)
PPID.............	Polaris-Poseidon Intelligence Digest (MCD)
PPID.............	Process Program Identification (AAEL)
PPID.............	Product IBM Program Information Department (SAUS)
PPI Display...	Plan Position Indicator Display (SAUS)
PPiD-L.............	Duquesne University, School of Law, Pittsburgh, PA [Library symbol] [Library of Congress] (LCLS)
PPIDP.............	Pulp and Paper Industries Development Programme (SAUS)
PPiE.............	E. D'Appolonia Consulting Engineers, Pittsburgh, PA [Library symbol] [Library of Congress] (LCLS)
PPIE.............	Prolonged Postictal Encephalopathy [Medicine] (DMAA)
PPIE.............	Pseudophase Ion Exchange [Chemistry]
PPIF.............	Photographic Processing and Interpretation Facilities (SAUS)
PPIF.............	Photographic Processing and Interpretation Facility
PPIF.............	Photo Processing Interpretation Facility
ppif.............	Photo-Processing Interpretation Facility (AD)
PPIFC.............	Pauline Pinkney International Fan Club (EA)
PPIFIA.............	Policy Proof of Interest, Full Interest Admitted (EBF)
PPIG.............	Psychology of Programming Interest Group (SAUS)
PPIGB.............	Plant Pathology Internet Guide Book
PPiGulf.............	Gulf Research & Development Co., Pittsburgh, PA [Library symbol] [Library of Congress] (LCLS)
PPiHB.............	Carnegie-Mellon University, Hunt Institute for Botanical Documentation, Pittsburgh, PA [Library symbol] [Library of Congress] (LCLS)
PPiHi.............	Historical Society of Western Pennsylvania, Pittsburgh, PA [Library symbol] [Library of Congress] (LCLS)
PPiI.............	International Poetry Forum, Pittsburgh, PA [Library symbol] [Library of Congress] (LCLS)
PPiK.............	Ketchum, McLeod & Grove, Inc., Pittsburgh, PA [Library symbol] [Library of Congress] (LCLS)
PPiL.............	LaRoche College, Pittsburgh, PA [Library symbol] [Library of Congress] (LCLS)
PPIL.............	Priced Provisioned Item List (MCD)
p-pille.............	Praeventivpille [Dano-Norwegian] [Contraceptive pill] (AD)
PPiM.............	Carnegie-Mellon University, Mellon Institute, Pittsburgh, PA [Library symbol] [Library of Congress] (LCLS)
PPIM.............	Programmable Peripheral Interface Microcomputer (IAA)
PPiMS.............	Mine Safety Appliances Co., Pittsburgh, PA [Library symbol] [Library of Congress] (LCLS)
PPIMS.............	Past Performance Information Management System [Army]
PPIn.............	Independence National Historical Park, Philadelphia, PA [Library symbol] [Library of Congress] (LCLS)
pp/in.............	Pages Per Inch (AD)
PPINA.............	Insurance Co., of North America, Corporate Archives, Philadelphia, PA [Library symbol] [Library of Congress] (LCLS)
PPINA.............	RADAR Weather Report Not Available [NWS] (FAAC)
PPINE.............	RADAR Weather Report Equipment No Echoes Observed [NWS] (FAAC)
PPINICI.............	Pulsed Positive Ion-Negative Ion Chemical Ionization [Instrumentation]
PPINO.............	RADAR Weather Report Equipment Inoperative Due to Breakdown [NWS] (FAAC)
P/P INS.............	Parts per Installment (SAUS)
PPInstHE.............	Past President of the Institution of Highway Engineers [British] (DI)
PPInstRA.............	Past President of the Institute of Registered Architects (SAUS)
PPIOK.............	RADAR Weather Report Equipment Operation REsumed [NWS] (FAAC)
PPIOM.............	RADAR Weather Report Equipment Inoperative Due to Maintenance [NWS] (FAAC)
PPIP.............	Philippine Poultry Improvement Plant (SAUS)
PPIP.............	Physics Post-Doctoral Information Pool [American Institute of Physics] (PDAA)
PPiPP.............	Point Park College, Pittsburgh, PA [Library symbol] [Library of Congress] (LCLS)
PPiPPG.............	PPG Industries, Inc., Glass Research Center, Information Services Library, Pittsburgh, PA [Library symbol] [Library of Congress] (LCLS)

PPiPT............	Pittsburgh Theological Seminary, Pittsburgh, PA [*Library symbol*] [*Library of Congress*] (LCLS)
PPIR	Personal Property Inventory Report
PPIR	Personnel Planning Information Report (MCD)
PPIR	Personnel Planning Integration Report
PpiR	Rockwell International Corp., Pittsburgh (SAUS)
PPiR	Rockwell International Corp., Pittsburgh, PA [*Library symbol*] [*Library of Congress*] (LCLS)
PPIRG.........	Pave Paws Interface Requirements Group (SAUS)
PPIRO.........	Planned Position Indicator Readout (NVT)
PPiRP	Reformed Presbyterian Theological Seminary, Pittsburgh, PA [*Library symbol*] [*Library of Congress*] (LCLS)
PPIS............	Pesticide Product Information System [*Environmental Protection Agency*] (GFGA)
PPIS............	Pollution Prevention Inventives for States (EPAT)
PPIS............	Product Profile Information System [*Shell Oil Co.*]
PPI Screen...	Plan Position Indicator Screen (SAUS)
PPIStructE ...	Past President of the Institution of Structural Engineers [*British*] (DI)
PPITB..........	Plastics Processing Industry Training Board (SAUS)
PPIU	Policy, Planning and Implementation Unit
PPIU	Probe Power Interface Unit (ACAE)
PPIU	Programmable Peripheral Interface Unit
PPiU	University of Pittsburgh, Pittsburgh, PA [*Library symbol*] [*Library of Congress*] (LCLS)
PPiU-A.........	University of Pittsburgh, Henry Clay Frick Fine Arts Center, Pittsburgh, PA [*Library symbol*] [*Library of Congress*] (LCLS)
PPiU-BL......	University of Pittsburgh, Blair-Lippincott Library, Eye and Ear Hospital of Pittsburgh, Pittsburgh, PA [*Library symbol*] [*Library of Congress*] (LCLS)
PPiU-H.........	University of Pittsburgh, Maurice and Laura Falk Library of the Health Professions, Pittsburgh, PA [*Library symbol*] [*Library of Congress*] (LCLS)
PPiU-IS........	University of Pittsburgh, Archives of Industrial Society, Pittsburgh, PA [*Library symbol*] [*Library of Congress*] (LCLS)
PPiU-L.........	University of Pittsburgh, Law School, Pittsburgh, PA [*Library symbol*] [*Library of Congress*] (LCLS)
PPiU-LS.......	University of Pittsburgh, Graduate School of Library and Information Sciences, Pittsburgh, PA [*Library symbol*] [*Library of Congress*] (LCLS)
PPiU-NS	University of Pittsburgh, Natural Sciences Library, Pittsburgh, PA [*Library symbol*] [*Library of Congress*] (LCLS)
PPiU-PH	University of Pittsburgh, Graduate School of Public Health, Pittsburgh, PA [*Library symbol*] [*Library of Congress*] (LCLS)
PPiU-PIA......	University of Pittsburgh, Graduate School of Public and International Affairs, Pittsburgh, PA [*Library symbol*] [*Library of Congress*] (LCLS)
PPiUS	United States Steel Corp., Pittsburgh, PA [*Library symbol*] [*Library of Congress*] (LCLS)
PPiU-SF......	University of Pittsburgh, Stephen Collins Foster Memorial [*Music*] Library, Pittsburgh, PA [*Library symbol*] [*Library of Congress*] (LCLS)
PPiUSM	United States Department of the Interior, Bureau of Mines, Pittsburgh Research Center, Pittsburgh, PA [*Library symbol*] [*Library of Congress*] (LCLS)
PPIV............	Per Person Interview Value [*Marketing*] (WDMC)
PPIV............	Positive Personnel Identity Verification (PDAA)
PPIVM	Passive Physiological Intervertebral Movement (SAUS)
PPiW	Westinghouse Electric Corp., Research and Development Center, Pittsburgh, PA [*Library symbol*] [*Library of Congress*] (LCLS)
PPiW-N........	Westinghouse Electric Corp., Nuclear Center Library, Pittsburgh, PA [*Library symbol*] [*Library of Congress*] (LCLS)
PPiWP	Western Psychiatric Institute and Clinic, University of Pittsburgh, Pittsburgh, PA [*Library symbol*] [*Library of Congress*] (LCLS)
PPJ	Pressure Plane Joint
PPJ	Pure Pancreatic Juice
PPJ	Thomas Jefferson University, Philadelphia, PA [*Library symbol*] [*Library of Congress*] (LCLS)
PPJea	Jeanes Hospital, Philadelphia, PA [*Library symbol*] [*Library of Congress*] [*Obsolete*] (LCLS)
PPJO............	Pli Premier Jour Officiel [*Official First Day Cover - OFDC*] [*Canada Post Corp.*]
PPJ-S...........	Thomas Jefferson University, Scott Memorial Library, Philadelphia, PA [*Library symbol*] [*Library of Congress*] (LCLS)
PPJW..........	Past Pro-Junior Warden [*Freemasonry*] (ROG)
PPK.............	Paired Perpendicular Keratotomy [*Procedure to correct astigmatism*]
PPK.............	Palmoplantar Keratoderma [*Dermatology*]
PPK.............	Palmoplantar Keratosis [*Medicine*] (DMAA)
PPK.............	Parametrized Post-Keplerian [*Physics*]
PPK.............	Paramp Pump Klystron
PPK.............	Parti Progressiste Katangais [*Political party*]
PPK.............	Personal Preference Kit [*Small bag in which astronauts are allowed to take personal mementos*]
PPK.............	Polizei Pistole Kriminal [*Pistol suitable for undercover police or detective use*] [*Walther Waffenfabrik, German arms manufacturer*]
PPK.............	Programmable Power Key [*Computer science*]
PPK.............	Punt, Pass, and Kick [*Youth competition sponsored by professional football*]
pPk	Purplish Pink (AD)
PPK.............	Ramp 66, Inc. [*ICAO designator*] (FAAC)
PPKB	Partai Perpaduan Kebang-Saan Brunei [*Brunei National United Party*] [*Political party*] (EY)
PPKCA	Pen and Pocket Knife Cutters' Association [*A union*] [*British*]
PPKG	Power Package (MSA)
Ppl...............	Intrapleural Pressure [*Medicine*] (DAVI)
PPL.............	Library Co. of Philadelphia, Philadelphia, PA [*Library symbol*] [*Library of Congress*] (LCLS)
PPL.............	Package Programs of London (NITA)
PPL.............	Palach Press Ltd. [*British*] (EAIO)
PPL.............	Palmer Physical Laboratory [*Princeton University*] (MCD)
PPL.............	Pars Plana Lensectomy (SAUS)
PPL.............	Pars Planus Lensectomy [*Ophthalmology*] (DAVI)
PP/L............	Partial Payload (SAUS)
PPL.............	Participle [*Grammar*] (WGA)
PPL.............	Passed Parameter List (SAUS)
PPL.............	PCBoard Programming Language [*Clark Development Co.*] (PCM)
PPL.............	Pembina Resources Ltd. [*Toronto Stock Exchange symbol*]
PPL.............	Penicilloyl-Polylysin (SAUS)
PPL.............	Penicilloyl Polylysine [*Pharmacology*]
PPL.............	Pennsylvania Power & Light Co. [*NYSE symbol*] (SPSG)
PPL.............	People
PPL.............	Peripheral Blood Leukocyte [*Medicine*] (PDAA)
PPL.............	Per Pupil Limitation (AFM)
PPL.............	Peter Peregrinus Ltd. [*Publisher*]
PPL.............	Phenylpropanolamine [*Organic chemistry*]
PPL.............	Philadelphia Public Library (AD)
PPL.............	Phoenix Public Library (AD)
PPL.............	Phonographic Performance Ltd. [*British*]
PPL.............	Photogrammetric Programming Language [*Computer science*] (PDAA)
PPI.............	Photoplate (SAUS)
PPL.............	Physical Properties Laboratory [*Oklahoma State University*] [*Research center*] (RCD)
ppl..............	Pipeline (AD)
PPL.............	Pittsburgh Public Library (AD)
PPL.............	Pixel per Line [*Computer science*] (IAA)
PPL.............	Planned Parenthood League (AD)
PPL.............	Planning Parts List
PPL.............	Plan Position Landing (DEN)
PPL.............	Plant Physiology Laboratory (SSD)
PPL.............	Plasma Physics Laboratory [*Also known as PPPL*]
PPL.............	Plasma Propulsion Laboratory (MCD)
PPL.............	Plus Programming Language [*Computer science*]
PPL.............	Plutonium Product Loadout [*Nuclear energy*] (NRCH)
PPL.............	Pneumatic Projectile Launcher (SAUS)
PPL.............	Point-to-Point Link (SAUS)
PPL.............	Police Protective League (AD)
PPL.............	Polymorphic Programming Language [*1971*] [*Computer science*] (CSR)
PPL.............	Polypivalolactone (SAUS)
PPL.............	Populated Place [*Board on Geographic Names*]
PPL.............	Population Paper Listing [*US Census Bureau*] [*A publication*]
PPL.............	Porcine Pancreatic Lipase [*An enzyme*]
PPL.............	Portland Public Library (SAUS)
PPL.............	Posterior Pole Plasm [*Insect embryology*]
PPL.............	Posterior Pulmonary (or Pulmonic) Leaflet (SAUS)
PPL.............	Power Plant Laboratory (MUGU)
PPL.............	Power Plate Loading (SAUS)
PPL.............	PP&L Resources [*NYSE symbol*] (TTSB)
PPL.............	PP & L Resources, Inc. [*NYSE symbol*] (SAG)
PPL.............	Precise Participant Location
PPL.............	Predictive Period LASER (KSC)
PPL.............	Preferential Planning List
PPL.............	Prefer Product List (SAUS)
PPL.............	Preferred Parts List
PPL.............	Preferred Products List (ACAE)
PPL.............	Preliminary Parts List
PPL.............	Preliminary Power Laboratory (IAA)
PPL.............	Presbyterians Pro-Life [*An association*] (EA)
PPL.............	Priced Parts List (NASA)
P/PL............	Primary Payload [*NASA*] (NASA)
PPL.............	Princeton Polymer Laboratories
PPL.............	Print Positions per Line [*Computer science*] (MHDI)
PPL.............	Private Pilot's Licence [*British*]
PPL.............	Process Peripherals Ltd. (SAUS)
PPL.............	Process-to-Process Link (SAUS)
PPL.............	Production Practice Level (SAUS)
PPL.............	Production Process Level (SAUS)
PPL.............	Program Production Library [*Computer science*]
PPL.............	Project Priority List [*Environmental Protection Agency*]
PPL.............	Protected Private Land (AD)
PPL.............	Protein-Polysaccharide [*Biochemistry*] (DAVI)
PPL.............	Protein Preprolactin [*Biochemistry*]
PPL.............	Providence Public Library (AD)
PPL.............	Provisioning Parts List (AAG)
PPL.............	Purchased Parts List
PPL.............	Pure Prairie League [*Musical group*]
PPL.............	Purple
PPL.............	Puu Pili [*Hawaii*] [*Seismograph station code, US Geological Survey*] (SEIS)
PpL.............	W. & F. Pascoe Proprietory Ltd., Milsons Point, Australia [*Library symbol*] [*Library of Congress*] (LCLS)
PPLA...........	Practice Precautionary Landing Approach [*Aviation*]
PPLA...........	Professional Photographic Laboratories Association [*British*] (DBA)
P-plane........	Pilotless Airplane (AD)
PPLas	La Salle College, Philadelphia, PA [*Library symbol*] [*Library of Congress*] (LCLS)
PPlase	Peptidylprolyl Cis-Trans Isomerase [*An enzyme*]
PPLB...........	Postprocessor Call Library [*Computer science*] (IAA)
PPLC...........	Patients Protection Law Commission (AD)

PPLCA .... Propellant and Pressurant Loading and Control Assembly (SAUS)

PPLD .... Pikes Peak Library District [*Internationally recognized computerized library system*]

PPLDF .... Professional Protector and Legal Defense Fund

PPLE .... Partial Preliminary Logistic Evaluation

PPLE .... Participle [*Grammar*]

pple .... Past Participle (AD)

PPLE .... Principle (ROG)

PPL/H .... Private Pilot's Licence/Helicopters [*British*] (AIA)

PPLI .... Precise Participant Location-Identification [*Navigation*]

PPLI .... Precise Position Location Information

PPLI .... Provisioning Parts List Index (MCD)

PPLIF .... Pulsed Photolysis LASER-Induced Fluorescence [*Environmental science*]

PPLL .... Military Order of the Loyal Legion of the United States, [*Civil*] War Library and Museum, Philadelphia, PA [*Library symbol*] [*Library of Congress*] (LCLS)

PPLLT .... Provisional Program Load Library Tape [*Computer science*] (MHDI)

PPIn .... Independence National Historical Park, Philadelphia (SAUS)

PPLN .... Periodically Poled Lithium Niobate (SEWL)

PPLN .... Pipeline

PPINIC .... Pulsed Positive Ion-Negative Ion Chemical Ionization (SAUS)

pplo .... Pleuropneumonia-Like Organism (AD)

PPLO .... Pleuropneumonia-Like Organisms [*Bacteriology*]

PPLO .... Pleuropneumonia-Link Oganism [*Medicine*] (WDAA)

PPLOT .... Postprocessor Plot (SPLAT)

PPLOV .... Painless Progressive Loss of Vision (MELL)

PPLP .... Peak Pleural Pressure (SAUS)

PPLP .... Photo Polymers Lithograph Plate (SAUS)

PPLP .... Photopolymers Lithograph Plate

P PLPBD ..... Paper or Pulpboard [*Freight*]

PPLPrA .... Penn Pwr & Lt 4.40% Pfd [*NYSE symbol*] (TTSB)

PPLPrB .... Penn Pwr & Lt 4.50% Pfd [*NYSE symbol*] (TTSB)

ppls .... Peoples [*Internet language*] [*Computer science*]

PPLS .... Peoples Bank Corp. (Indianapolis, IN) [*NASDAQ symbol*] (SAG)

PPLS .... Peoples Bank Indianapolis [*NASDAQ symbol*] (TTSB)

PPLS .... Precision Position Location (or Locator) System (SAUS)

PPLS .... Precision Position Locator System [*Army*]

PPLS .... Preferred Parts List System (MCD)

PPLS .... Propellant and Pressurant Loading System [*NASA*] (KSC)

PPIStructE ... Past President of the Institution of Structural Engineers (SAUS)

PPLT .... Lutheran Theological Seminary, Philadelphia, PA [*Library symbol*] [*Library of Congress*] (LCLS)

PPL-Test ..... Penicilloyl-Polylsin-Test (SAUS)

P-PLUS .... Polar Platform Utilisation Study (SAUS)

PPLV .... Pars Plana Lensectomy-Vitrectomy [*Medicine*] (MELL)

PPLV .... Preliminary Pollutant Limit Value (MCD)

PPLX .... Section of Populated Place [*Board on Geographic Names*]

PPM .... Aberdeen, MD [*Location identifier*] [*FAA*] (FAAL)

PPM .... Frevious processor mode (SAUS)

PPM .... Investment Grade Municipal Income Fund [*NYSE symbol*] (SAG)

PPM .... Investment Grade Muni Inc. [*NYSE symbol*] (TTSB)

PPM .... Mercantile Library, Philadelphia, PA [*Library symbol*] [*Library of Congress*] [*Obsolete*] (LCLS)

PPM .... Page Per Minute (SAUS)

PPM .... Page-per-Minute [*Computer science*] (PCM)

PPM .... Pages per Minute [*Printer technology*]

ppm .... Pages per Minute

ppm .... Papermaker [*MARC relator code*] [*Library of Congress*] (LCCP)

PPM .... Parallel Performance Monitor (SAUS)

PPM .... Parallel Processing Machine [*Computer science*] (IAA)

PPM .... Particuliere Participatiemaatschappy [*Private Joint Stock Company*] [*Dutch*]

PPM .... Partido del Pueblo Mexicano [*Mexican People's Party*] [*Political party*] (PPW)

PPM .... Partido Proletario de Mexico [*Proletarian Party of Mexico*] [*Political party*] (AD)

PPM .... Parti Pekerja-Pekerja Malaysia [*Workers' Party of Malaysia*] [*Political party*] (PPW)

PPM .... Parti Progressiste Martiniquais [*Progressive Party of Martinique*] [*Political party*] (PPW)

PPM .... Partitioned-Pipe Mixer [*Engineering*]

PPM .... Part Per Million (SAUS)

PPM .... Part Program Manager

PPM .... Parts per Mille (SAUS)

ppm .... Parts Per Million (AD)

PPM .... Parts per Million

Ppm .... Parts per Million

PPM .... Parts per Minute (MCD)

PPM .... Pattani People's Movement [*Thailand*] [*Political party*]

PPM .... Peak Power Meter

ppm .... Peak Program Meter (AD)

PPM .... Peak Program Meter [*Television*]

PPM .... Peoples Pharmacy of Mali (SAUS)

PPM .... Perfect Prognosis Method (SAUS)

PPM .... Periodic Permanent Magnet

PPM .... Periodic Permanent Magnet Focusing (IAA)

PPM .... Periodic Pulsed Magnet (SAUS)

PPM .... Periodic Pulse Metering [*Telecommunications*] (TEL)

PPM .... Period Permanent Magnet (SAUS)

PPM .... Permanent Pacemaker [*Cardiology*] (MAE)

PPM .... Perodic Permanent Magnet (SAUS)

PPM .... Pershing Project Manager

PPM .... Personnel Priority Model (MCD)

PPM .... Personnel Program Manager [*Navy*]

PPM .... Persutuan Perpustakaan Malaysia [*Library Association of the Federation of Malaysia*] (AD)

PPM .... Phased Project Management (SAUS)

PPM .... Phase Pulse Modulation (SAUS)

PPM .... Phenylpropanolamine(hydrochloride) [*Also, PPA, PPH*] [*Decongestant*]

PPM .... Phosphopentomutase [*An enzyme*]

PPM .... Physician Practice Management

PPM .... Picks per Minute (SAUS)

PPM .... Picture Processing Machine (SAUS)

PPM .... Pictures per Minute (NTCM)

PPM .... Piecewise Parabolic Method [*Mathematical model of fluid flow*]

PPM .... Pigmented Pupillary Membrane [*Medicine*] (STED)

PPM .... Pileable Pallet Module (SAUS)

PPM .... Pilot Performance Measurement (ACAE)

PPM .... Pilot Production Model [*Military*] (CAAL)

PPM .... Pilot Pulse Missile

PPM .... Pistol Prize Money [*British military*] (DMA)

PPM .... Planned Preventive Maintenance (IEEE)

PPM .... Platform Pointing Mode (ACAE)

PPM .... Policy and Procedures Manual (SAUS)

PPM .... Popocatepetl [*Mexico*] [*Seismograph station code, US Geological Survey*] (SEIS)

PPM .... Portable Pix Map [*Computer science*]

PPM .... Position and Pay Management [*Army*] (AABC)

PPM .... Position and Proper Motion [*Catalog of star positions*]

PPM .... Positions and Proper Motions (SAUS)

PPM .... Postage Prepaid in Money

PPM .... Posterior Papillary Muscle [*Image on transesophageal echocardiography*] [*Cardiology*] (DAVI)

PPM .... Postpass Message

PPM .... Post-Program Monitoring

ppm .... Pounds Per Minute (AD)

PPM .... Pounds per Minute

PPM .... Prairie Print Makers [*Defunct*] (EA)

PPM .... Prediction by Partial Mapping (RALS)

PPM .... Prediction by Partial Matching

PPM .... Prenegotiation Position Memorandum (AAGC)

PPM .... Presentation Protocol Machine [*Telecommunications*] (OSI)

PPM .... Presidential Review Memorandum (SAUS)

PPM .... Previous Processor Mode

PPM .... Prime Period of Maintenance (SAUS)

PPM .... Principal Period of Maintenance (AAGC)

PPM .... Problem Program Monitor (IAA)

PPM .... Process and Production Methods (SAUS)

PPM .... Production Planning Memorandum

PPM .... Product Portfolio Management (SAUS)

PPM .... Program, Project Management [*Army*]

P/PM .... Program/project manager (SAUS)

PPM .... Project Profile Manual

PPM .... Prudential Portfolio Managers Ltd. [*British*]

PPM .... Pulmonary Pressure Method (SAUS)

PPM .... Pulse per Minute (SAUS)

PPM .... Pulse Phase Modulation [*Telecommunications*] (IAA)

ppm .... Pulse Position Modulation (AD)

PPM .... Pulse Position Modulation [*Radio data transmission*]

PPM .... Pulse-Position Modulation (SAUS)

PPM .... Pulse Power Module (RDA)

ppm .... Pulses per Minute (IDOE)

PPM .... Pulses per Minute

PPM .... Pyrite-Pyrrhotite-Magnetite [*Mineralogy*]

PPMA .... Pakistan Paint Manufacturers Association (SAUS)

PPMA .... Petroleum Marketers Association of America

PPMA .... Petrol Pump Manufacturers Association [*British*] (DBA)

PPMA .... Plastic Pipe Manufacturers Association (SAUS)

PPMA .... Plastic Products Manufacturers Association [*Later, Plastic and Metal Products Manufacturers Association*] (EA)

PPMA .... Political Products Manufacturers Association (EA)

PPMA .... Polypropyl Methacrylate [*Organic chemistry*]

ppma .... Post-Polio Muscular Atrophy [*Medicine*] (AD)

PPMA .... Post-Poliomyelitis Muscular Atrophy [*Medicine*]

PPMA .... Precision Potentiometer Manufacturers Association [*Later, Variable Resistive Components Institute*] (EA)

PPMA .... Produce Packaging and Marketing Association [*British*] (DBA)

PPMA .... Progressive Postmyelitis Muscular Atrophy [*Medicine*] (DMAA)

PPMA .... Pulp and Paper Manufacturers Association [*Later, PPMMA*] (EA)

PPMAP .... Power Planning Modeling Application Procedure [*Environmental Protection Agency*] (GFGA)

PPMB .... Palynology and Plant Micropalaeontology of Belgium (SAUS)

PPMC .... Parts per Million Carbon [*Automotive engineering*]

PPMC .... People to People Music Committee (EA)

PPMC .... Petroleum Products Marketing Co. (SAUS)

PPMC .... Physician Practice Management Companies (SAUS)

PPMC .... Physician Practice Management Company (ADWA)

PPMC .... Produce Prepackaging Machinery Co. (SAUS)

PPMCX .... PIMCO: Precious Metals Cl.C [*Mutual fund ticker symbol*] (SG)

PPMD .... Posterior Polymorphous Dystrophy

PPMD .... Posterior Polymorphous Dystrophy of the Cornea [*Ophthalmology*] (DAVI)

PPME .... Pacific Plate Motion Experiment (NASA)

PPME .... Protection and Preservation of the Marine Environment (SAUS)

PPMFA .... Pulp and Paper Manufacturers' Federation of Australia

PPMFC .... Preprints on Precision Measurement and Fundamental Constants [*National Institute of Standards and Technology*]

PPMG .... Professional Publishers Marketing Group (EA)

PPMHD.......	Pulsed Plasma Magnetohydrodynamic (SAUS)
PPMI..........	Pilot Plant Meat Irradiator
PPMI..........	Printed Paper Mat Institute (EA)
PPMI..........	Progressive Pacemaker Inhibition (SAUS)
PPMIN........	Pulses per Minute (MSA)
PPMis.........	Misericordia Hospital, Philadelphia, PA [*Library symbol*] [*Library of Congress*] [*Obsolete*] (LCLS)
PPMIS	Personal Property Management Information System (SAUS)
PPML.........	Preferred Parts and Materials List [*NASA*]
PPMM.........	Postpolycythemia Myeloid Metaplasia [*Medicine*] (AAMN)
PPMMA.......	Pulp and Paper Machinery Manufacturers Association [*Later, APMA*] (EA)
PPMMB.......	Periodical Polytechnical. Mechanical Engineering (SAUS)
PPMMHD....	Pulse Power Magnetohydrodynamic (SAUS)
PPMMS......	Polaris/Poseidon Material Management System (SAUS)
PPMN........	Preliminary Program Management Network [*Military*]
PPMNA	Provisions for Particulate Matter Nonattainment Areas [*Environmental science*] (COE)
PPMO........	Pershing Project Manager's Office (RDA)
PPMO........	Provisional Program Management Office [*Army*]
PPMoi.........	Moore College of Art, Philadelphia, PA [*Library symbol*] [*Library of Congress*] (LCLS)
PPMP.........	Preliminary Program Management Plan
PPMPC	Pilot Parachute Mortar Pyrotechnic Cartridge (SAA)
PPM/PPB	Parts per Million/Parts per Billion (SAUS)
PPMR	Purchased Parts Material Requirements
PPMR	Purchase Parts Material Request
PPMRC	Pre-Positioned Materiel Receipt Card
PPMRD	Pre-Positioned Material Receipt Document
PPMS.........	Pad-Pad Minimum Spacing (SAUS)
PPMS.........	Performax's Personal Matrix System (DMAA)
PPMS.........	Personal Property Management System (SAUS)
PPMS.........	Personal Property Movement and Storage System (SAUS)
PPMS.........	Physical Properties Measurement System (AAEL)
PPMS.........	Pitt Press Mathematical Series [*A publication*]
PPMS.........	Plastic Pipe Manufacturers Society [*British*] (DBA)
PPMS.........	Poly(para-Methylstyrene) [*Organic chemistry*]
PPMS.........	Polyphenylmethylsiloxane [*Organic chemistry*]
PPMS.........	Primary Progressive Multiple Sclerosis (SAUS)
PPMS.........	Product Procedure Maintenance System (SAUS)
PPMS.........	Professional Productivity Management System (HGAA)
PPMS.........	Programme and Project Management System [*United Nations Development Programme*] (DUND)
PPMS.........	Program Planning Management System (ACAE)
PPMS.........	Psychophysiologic Musculoskeletal [*Reaction*] [*Medicine*] (STED)
PPMS.........	Purdue Perceptual-Motor Survey [*Kephart Scale*]
ppmv..........	Parts per Million by Volume [*Marine science*] (OSRA)
PPMV.........	Parts per Million by Volume
PPMV.........	Peach Purple Mosaic Virus (SAUS)
PPMW	Parts per Million by Weight (MCD)
PPMW	Primary Plant Mineralized Water (IAA)
PPN	Numismatic and Antiquarian Society, Philadelphia, PA [*Library symbol*] [*Library of Congress*] [*Obsolete*] (LCLS)
PPN	Papenoo [*Society Islands*] [*Seismograph station code, US Geological Survey*] (SEIS)
PPN	Parameterized Post-Newtonian [*Gravity*]
PPN	Parametrized Post-Newtonian [*Physics*]
PPN	Partial Parenteral Nutrition [*Medicine*] (DMAA)
PPN	Partido Patriotico Nobo [*New Patriotic Party*] [*Aruba*] [*Political party*] (EY)
PPN	Partido Progreso Nacional [*National Progress Party*] [*Costa Rica*] [*Political party*] (PPW)
PPN	Parti Progressiste Nigerien [*Nigerian Progressive Party*] [*Political party*]
PPN	Patient Progress Note (SAUS)
PPN	Patrol Plane Navigator (DNAB)
PPN	Peak-to-Peak Noise [*Instrumentation*]
PPN	Pedunculopontine Nucleus (DMAA)
PPN	Peer-To-Peer Network [*Computer science*] (AGLO)
PPN	Peripendicular Nucleus (SAUS)
PPN	Peripheral Parenteral Nutrition [*Medicine*] (DAVI)
PPN	Peroxypropionyl Nitrate (SAUS)
PPN	Peroxypropionyl Nitride (SAUS)
PPN	Peroxyproprionyl Nitrate [*Organic chemistry*]
PPN	Polyphosphonate [*Organic chemistry*]
PPN	Popayan [*Colombia*] [*Airport symbol*] (OAG)
PPN	Portland Public Library, Portland, ME [*OCLC symbol*] (OCLC)
PPN	Precipitation (WGA)
PPN	Predictive Proportional Navigation
PPN	Preferred Provider Network
PPN	Programmer Project Number (SAUS)
PPN	Project, Programmer Number
ppn..........	Proportion (AD)
PPN	Proportion (ROG)
ppn..........	proportional (SAUS)
PPN	Protoplanetary Nebulae [*Astrophysics*]
PPN	Public Packet Network [*Computer science*] (ODBW)
PPN	Pyramidopallidonigral (DB)
PPNA	Peak Phrenic Nerve Activity [*Medicine*]
PPNA	Pupil-Perceived Needs Assessment [*Education*] (EDAC)
PPNA	Pupil-Perceived-Needs Assessment
PPNAD........	Primary Pigmented Nodular Adrenocortical Disease [*Medicine*] (STED)
PPNB	Pre-Pottery Neolithic B Period [*Paleontology*]
PPNC	Patrol Plane Navigator/Communicator (DNAB)

PPNC	Pre-Pottery Neolithic C Phase [*Paleontology*]
PPNC	Proceedings. Pacific Northwest Conference on Foreign Languages (SAUS)
PPNCFL	Proceedings of the Pacific Northwest Conference on Foreign Languages (SAUS)
PPNDG........	Petition Pending
PPNF	Price-Pottenger Nutrition Foundation (EA)
PPNG	Penicillinase-Producing Neisseria Gonorrheas (SAUS)
PPNG	Penicillinase-Producing Neisseria gonorrhoeae
PPNICI	Pulsed Positive/Negative Ion Chemical Ionization
P/PNL	Pocket Panel [*Automotive engineering*]
PPNICI	Pulsed Positive/Negative Ion Chemical Ionization (SAUS)
PPNMC	United States Navy, Naval Regional Medical Center, Philadelphia, PA [*Library symbol*] [*Library of Congress*] (LCLS)
PPNP	Point Pelee National Park [*Ontario, Canada*] (AD)
PPNR	Photosynthetic Pyridine Nucleotide Reductase (SAUS)
PPNSC	Preferred Procurement Number Selector Code [*Military*] (AFIT)
PPNSCA......	Policy Plans and National Security Council Affairs
PPNS-IE	Preschool and Primary Nowicki-Strickland Internal-External Control Scale (EDAC)
PPNT	Proponent
PPNV	Plum Phloem Necrosis Virus (SAUS)
PPNW	Physicians for the Prevention of Nuclear War (AD)
PPNWA	N. W. Ayer & Son, Philadelphia, PA [*Library symbol*] [*Library of Congress*] [*Obsolete*] (LCLS)
PPO	Diphenyloxazole [*Chemistry*] (DAVI)
PPO	Parking Patrol Officer
PPO	Patriot Project Office [*Army*]
PPO	Peak Pepsin Output (SAUS)
PPO	Pepsi Cola Puerto Rico Bottling [*NYSE symbol*] (SAG)
PPO	Pepsi-Cola Puerto Rico Bott'B' [*NYSE symbol*] (TTSB)
PPO	Performance Prediction Overview (SAUS)
PPO	Permanent Paranormal Object
PPO	Photographic Program Office [*NASA*] (KSC)
PPO	Planning Purposes Only (SAUS)
PPO	Platelet Peroxidase [*An enzyme*]
PPO	Pleuropneumonia Organisms [*Bacteriology*]
PPO	Police Petty Officer (DNAB)
PPO	Pollution Prevention Office [*Environmental Protection Agency*]
PPO	Polyphenelene Oxide (SAUS)
PPO	Polyphenol Oxidase [*An enzyme*]
ppo	Polyphenylene Oxide (AD)
PPO	Polyphenylene Oxide [*Organic chemistry*]
PPO	Polyphenylenoxid (SAUS)
PPO	Polyphenylodine Oxide (SAUS)
PPO	Poly(propylene Oxide) [*Organic chemistry*]
PPO	Port Postal Office (AFM)
PPO	Positive Pole Operation (SAUS)
PPo	Pottsville Free Public Library, Pottsville, PA [*Library symbol*] [*Library of Congress*] (LCLS)
PPO	Power Plant Operating
PPO	Preferred-Provided Organization [*Insurance*] (AD)
PPO	Preferred-Provider Option [*Insurance*]
PPO	Preferred-Provider Organization [*Insurance*]
PPO	Prepaid Purchase Order (SAUS)
PPO	Pre Phase-Out
PPO	Pressed Plutonium Oxide
PPO	Primary Party Organization [*Politics*]
PPO	Principal Period of Operations (ACAE)
PPO	Principal Priority Officer
ppo	Prior Permission Only (AD)
PPO	Prior Permission Only (AFM)
PPO	Procurement Planning Officer
PPO	Program Printout (MCD)
PPO	Projected Program Objective (NG)
PPO	Prototype Program Office
PPO	Publications and Printing Office [*Army*]
PPO	Public Pension Offset [*Federal Employees Retirement System*] (GFGA)
PPO	Pure Plutonium Oxide
PPO	Push-Pull Output (DEN)
PPO$_2$	Partial Pressure of Oxygen (CAAL)
PPOA	Pollution Prevention Opportunity Assessment (SAUS)
PPoAr	Schuylkill County Archives, Pottsville, PA [*Library symbol*] [*Library of Congress*] (LCLS)
PPOC	Per Pupil Operating Cost (ADA)
PPO Cable ...	Polyphenylene Oxide Cable (SAUS)
PP of A........	Professional Photographers of America [*Atlanta, GA*] (WDMC)
PPOG	Polytechnic Personnel Officers Group (AIE)
PPOKE	Pre-Processor Oriented Key Entry (SAUS)
p-p-ola........	Political Plugola (AD)
PPOLL	Parallel Poll (CIST)
ppom	Particulate Polycyclic Organic Matter (AD)
P-POP	Plain Paper Optimized Printing [*Canon*] [*Computer science*]
PPORT	Prostate Patient Outcomes Research Team
PPOS	Present Position (GAVI)
PPOS	Saint George United Methodist Church, Philadelphia, PA [*Library symbol*] [*Library of Congress*] (LCLS)
PPOSN........	Proposition (ROG)
PPOX	Polypropylene Oxide (EDCT)
PPOX	Polypropylene Oxide Plastic
PPP............	Forest Research Centre (SAUS)
PPP............	Glycerintripalmitat (SAUS)
PPP............	Pacific Peacemaker Project [*Defunct*] (EA)
PPP............	Packaged Power Plant (SAUS)

PPP	Package Processing Point
PPP	Pakistan People's Party [*Political party*] (PD)
PPP	Palmar-Plantar Pustulosis
PPP	Palmoplantar Pustulosis [*Medicine*] (DMAA)
PPP	Pan Pacific Petroleum [*Vancouver Stock Exchange symbol*]
PPP	Paper, Printing, Publishing [*Department of Employment*] [*British*]
PPP	Parallel Pattern Processor
PPP	Parallel Push Pull (IAA)
PPP	Parallel Push-Pull (SAUS)
PPP	Pariser-Parr-Pople [*Physical chemistry*]
PPP	Partai Persatuan Pembangunan [*United Development Party*] [*Indonesia*] [*Political party*] (PPW)
PPP	Partido del Pueblo de Panama [*Panamanian People's Party*] [*Political party*] (PPW)
PPP	Passage, Power, and Passenger [*Evaluation of labor progress*] [*Obstetrics*] (DAVI)
PPP	Payload Patch Panel [*NASA*] (NAKS)
ppp	Peak Pulse Power (NAKS)
PPP	Peak Pulse Power
PPP	Pentose Phosphate Pathway (SAUS)
PPP	Pentose-Phosphate Pathway [*Metabolism*]
PPP	Penultimate Profit [*Investment term*] (DFIT)
PPP	Peoples Party of Pakistan [*Political party*] (AD)
PPP	People's Patriotic Party [*Myanmar*] [*Political party*] (PD)
PPP	People's Political Party [*St. Vincent*] [*Political party*] (PPW)
PPP	People's Progressive Party [*Mauritania*] [*Political party*] (EY)
PPP	People's Progressive Party [*Solomon Islands*] [*Political party*] (PPW)
PPP	People's Progressive Party [*Gambia*] [*Political party*] (PPW)
PPP	People's Progressive Party [*Anguilla*] [*Political party*] (PPW)
PPP	People's Progressive Party [*Guyana*] [*Political party*] (PD)
PPP	People's Progress Party [*Papua New Guinea*] [*Political party*] (PPW)
PPP	Permanent Party Personnel (MCD)
PPP	Perpex Peristaltic Pump
PPP	Personal Productivity Products (TIMI)
PPP	Personal Property Policy [*Insurance*]
PPP	Personnel Performance Profile
PPP	Personnel Policies and Practices (SAUS)
PPP	Petroleum Production Pioneers (AD)
PPP	Petty Pet Peeve (SAUS)
PPP	Petty Political Pismire (SAUS)
PPP	Phased Program Planning
PPP	Phased Project Planning [*NASA*] (KSC)
PPP	Pianississimo [*As Softly As Possible*] [*Music*]
PPP	Pickford Projective Pictures [*Psychology*]
PPP	Pipelines, Politics and People. Capital Communications Ltd. (SAUS)
ppp	Piu Pianissimo [*Very Very Softly*] [*Italian*] [*Music*] (AD)
PPP	Planning Purpose Proposal
PPP	Plan Position Presentation
PPP	Plans, Progress, and Problems (ACAE)
PPP	Platelet-Poor Plasma [*Hematology*]
PPP	Platoon Package Program
PPP	Pluripotent Progenitor [*Cytology*]
PPP	Pogo Producing [*NYSE symbol*] (TTSB)
PPP	Pogo Producing Co. [*NYSE symbol*] (SPSG)
PPP	Point-to-Point Protocol [*Computer science*] (PCM)
PPP	Policy, Procedures, and Practice (ACAE)
PPP	Polluter Pays Principle
PPP	Polluter-Pays-Principle (SAUS)
PPP	Pollution Prevention Plan [*Environmental science*] (COE)
PPP	Poly(para-phenylene) [*Organic chemistry*]
PPP	Polyphoretic Phosphate [*Organic chemistry*] (DAVI)
PPP	Polypropylene-Paper-Polypropylene [*Biochemistry*]
PPP	Popular Power Package (IAA)
PPP	Population Policy Panel (SAUS)
PPP	Portable Plotting Package [*Nuclear energy*] (NRCH)
PPP	Positive Pressure Paradox
PPP	Positive Pressur Paradox (SAUS)
PPP	Post-Painted Parts
PPP	Postpartum Psychosis [*Obstetrics*] [*Psychiatry*] (DAVI)
PPP	Powerful Permutation Procedure [*Meteorology*]
PPP	Preferred Pharmacy Program
PPP	Pre-Planned Product Improvement (ACAE)
PPP	Prepositional Procurement Package (DOMA)
PPP	Prepositioning Procurement Package (SAUS)
PPP	Preposition Procurement Package (SAUS)
PPP	Prescriptive Parent Programming [*Education*]
PPP	Prescriptive Program Plan [*Education*]
PPP	Pretty Poor Planning
PPP	Primary Products Promotion [*Australia*]
PPP	Priority Placement Program (DOMA)
PPP	Prior-Participating Preferred [*Stock*] (MHDW)
PPP	Prison Pen Pals (EA)
PPP	Private Patients' Plan [*British*]
PPP	Production Part Pattern (MCD)
PPP	Profit and Performance Planning (DCTA)
PPP	Programmable Power Processor (ACAE)
PPP	Programmed Production Planning (SAUS)
PPP	Program Protection Plan [*DoD*] (RDA)
PPP	Progressive People's Party [*Sudan*] [*Political party*] (EY)
PPP	Progressive People's Party [*Sierra Leone*] [*Political party*] (EY)
PPP	Progressive People's Party [*Liberia*] [*Political party*] (PPW)
PPP	Propria Pecunia Posuit [*Erected at His Own Expense*] [*Latin*]
PPP	Proserpine [*Australia*] [*Airport symbol*] (OAG)
PPP	Protons per Pulse (SAUS)
PPP	Province Pacification Plan (CINC)
PPP	Provisioning Program Plan (MCD)
PPP-I	Public Policy Program [*Australian National University*]
PPP	Public-Private-Partnership (VLIE)
PPP	Purchasing Power Parities (or Parity) (SAUS)
PPP	Purchasing Power Parity [*Economics*]
PPP	Purified Placental Protein (SAUS)
PPP	Push-Pull Power (IAA)
PPPA	Parallel Push-Pull Amplifier (SAUS)
PPPA	Poison Prevention Packaging Act
PPPA	Professional Pool Players Association [*Defunct*] (EA)
PPPA	Protein Phosphatase Alpha (DMAA)
PPPA	Pulp and Paper Prepackaging Association [*Later, SSI*]
PPPA	Push-Pull Power Amplifier (IAA)
PPP&B	Paper, Plates, Print and Bind [*Book publishing*] (GOBB)
PPP & M	Preservation, Packaging, Packing, and Marking
PPPBDD	Iran. Plant Pests and Diseases Research Institute. Department of Botany. Publication (journ.) (SAUS)
PPPBL	Peripheral Pulses Palpable Both Legs [*Medicine*] (DMAA)
PPPBR	Peruvian Paso Part-Blood Registry (EA)
PPPC	Petroleum Pool Pacific Coast
PPPC	Pipe Plug Producers Council (EA)
PPPCA	Philadelphia College of Art Library, Philadelphia, PA [*Library symbol*] [*Library of Congress*] (LCLS)
PPP Circuit	Parallel Push-Pull Circuit (SAUS)
PPPCity	Philadelphia City Institute Branch Free Library, Philadelphia, PA [*Library symbol*] [*Library of Congress*] [*Obsolete*] (LCLS)
PPPCO	Pennsylvania College of Optometry, Philadelphia, PA [*Library symbol*] [*Library of Congress*] (LCLS)
PPPCPh	Philadelphia College of Pharmacy and Science, Philadelphia, PA [*Library symbol*] [*Library of Congress*] (LCLS)
PPPD	Point to Point Protocol Daemon [*Computer science*] (VLIE)
PPPE	Pennsylvania Economy League, Inc., Eastern Division, Philadelphia, PA [*Library symbol*] [*Library of Congress*] (LCLS)
PPPE	People, Plans and the Peace. Peace River Planning Commission (SAUS)
PPPEA	Pulp, Paper, and Paperboard Export Association of the United States (EA)
PPPEC	Philadelphia Electric Co., Philadelphia, PA [*Library symbol*] [*Library of Congress*] (LCLS)
PPPEE	Pulsed Pinch Plasma Electromagnetic Engine (AAG)
PPPF	Positive Pregnancy and Parenting Fitness (EA)
PPPFM	Free and Accepted Masons of Pennsylvania, Grand Lodge Library, Philadelphia, PA [*Library symbol*] [*Library of Congress*] (LCLS)
PPPG	People's Progressive Party of Guyana [*Political party*]
PPPG	Postprandial Plasma Glucose [*Endocrinology*] (DAVI)
PPPH	Forest Research and Development Centre (SAUS)
PPPH	Pennsylvania Hospital, Philadelphia, PA [*Library symbol*] [*Library of Congress*] (LCLS)
PPPHA	Philadelphia Housing Association, Philadelphia, PA [*Library symbol*] [*Library of Congress*] [*Obsolete*] (LCLS)
PPPHC	Philadelphia Tuberculosis and Health Association, Philadelphia, PA [*Library symbol*] [*Library of Congress*] [*Obsolete*] (LCLS)
PPPH-I	Institute of the Pennsylvania Hospital, Philadelphia, PA [*Library symbol*] [*Library of Congress*] (LCLS)
PPPH-I	Institute of the Pennsylvania Hospital, Philadelphia (SAUS)
PPPI	Insurance Society of Philadelphia, Philadelphia, PA [*Library symbol*] [*Library of Congress*] [*Obsolete*] (LCLS)
PPPI	Personnel Performance Problems Inventory [*Test*]
PPPI	Photo Processing and Photo Interpretation (SAUS)
PPPI	Plan Positional Plot Indicator
PPPI	Potential Preplanned Product Improvement (ACAE)
PPPI	Precision Plan Position Indicator
PPPI	Preliminary Process Potential Index
PPPI	Preplanned Product Improvement [*DoD*] (MCD)
PPPI	Primary Private Practice Income [*Medicine*] (MAE)
PPPI	Primary Private Practice Insurance [*Medicine*] (DMAA)
PPPI	Private Pay Phones, Inc. (SAUS)
PPPI	Projection Plan Position Indicator
PPPI	Pulp, Paper & Paperband Institute (SAUS)
PPPI	Pulp, Paper and Paperboard Institute (SAUS)
PPPI	Pulp, Paper, and Paperboard Institute USA [*Later, API*]
PPPIP	Dhak Patiwat Phaochen Islam Pattani (SAUS)
PPPL	Philadelphia Board of Public Education, Pedagogical Library, Philadelphia, PA [*Library symbol*] [*Library of Congress*] (LCLS)
PPPL	Planetary Physical Processes Laboratory (SSD)
PPPL	Princeton Plasma Physics Laboratory [*Also known as PPL - Plasma Physics Laboratory*] [*Princeton, NJ*] [*Department of Energy*]
PPPL	Printed Planning Parts List
PPPL	Program Preferred Parts List
PPPlanP	Planned Parenthood of Southeast Pennsylvania, Philadelphia, PA [*Library symbol*] [*Library of Congress*] (LCLS)
PPPlay	Plays and Players Club, Philadelphia, PA [*Library symbol*] [*Library of Congress*] [*Obsolete*] (LCLS)
P-P plot	Probability-Probability Plot [*Statistics*]
PPPlPh	Philadelphia College of Pharmacy and Science (SAUS)
PPPLS	Public Policy for Public Libraries Section [*Public Library Association*] [*American Library Association*]
PPPM	Philadelphia Museum of Art, Philadelphia, PA [*Library symbol*] [*Library of Congress*] (LCLS)
PPP Method	Pariser, Parr and Pople Method (SAUS)
PPPM-I	Philadelphia Museum of Art, College of Art, Philadelphia, PA [*Library symbol*] [*Library of Congress*] [*Obsolete*] (LCLS)
PPPM-I	Philadelphia Museum of Art, College of Art (SAUS)
PPPO	Personal Property Processing Office (SAUS)
PPPOE	Point-to-Point Protocol over Ethernet [*Computer science*] (VLIE)

PPPoE.........	Point-to-Point Protocol over Ethernet
PPPP	Past Performance and Present Posture (AAG)
PPPP	People's Peace and Prosperity Party [*Defunct*] (EA)
pppp	Piu Piu Piu Pianissimo [*Very, Very, Very Softly*] [*Italian*] [*Music*] (AD)
PPPP	Porokeratosis Punctata Palmaris et Plantaris [*Medicine*] (DMAA)
PPPP	Previous Paragraph was Polemical Position (SAUS)
PPPP	Programmable Powdered Preform Process [*Plastics*]
PPPPI	Photographic Projection Plan Position Indicator (DEN)
PPPPP	Pain, Pallor, Pulse Loss, Paresthesia, Paralysis [*Medicine*] (MEDA)
PPPR	Philadelphia Transportation Co., Philadelphia, PA [*Library symbol*] [*Library of Congress*] [*Obsolete*] (LCLS)
PPPRC........	Poor Richard Club, Philadelphia, PA [*Library symbol*] [*Library of Congress*] [*Obsolete*] (LCLS)
PPPres........	Presbyterian University of Pennsylvania, Scheie Eye Institute Library, Philadelphia, PA [*Library symbol*] [*Library of Congress*] (LCLS)
PPPRF........	Pan Pacific Public Relations Federation [*Thailand*] [*Defunct*]
PPPrHi........	Presbyterian Historical Society, Philadelphia, PA [*Library symbol*] [*Library of Congress*] (LCLS)
PPPrI	Printing Institute, Philadelphia, PA [*Library symbol*] [*Library of Congress*] [*Obsolete*] (LCLS)
PPPrl	Printing Institute, Philadelphia (SAUS)
PPProM	Provident Mutual Life Insurance Co., Philadelphia, PA [*Library symbol*] [*Library of Congress*] [*Obsolete*] (LCLS)
PPPS	People's Press Printing Society [*British*]
PPPs	Public-Private Partnerships
PPPS	Pulse Pairs per Second (SAUS)
PPPSB	Philadelphia College of the Bible, Philadelphia, PA [*Library symbol*] [*Library of Congress*] (LCLS)
PPPTe..........	Philadelphia College of Textiles and Science, Philadelphia, PA [*Library symbol*] [*Library of Congress*] (LCLS)
PPPTP	Central Research Institute for Food Crops (SAUS)
PPQ	Abandoned Police Post [*Board on Geographic Names*]
PPQ	Parts per Quadrillion
PPQ	Person Perception Questionnaire [*Psychology*] (EDAC)
PPQ	Pittsfield, IL [*Location identifier*] [*FAA*] (FAAL)
PPQ	Planning Purpose Quote
PPQ	Plant Protection and Quarantine Programs [*Department of Agriculture*] (IMH)
ppq	Polyphenylquinoxaline (AD)
PPQ	Polyphenylquinoxaline [*Resin*]
PPQ	Possible Parliamentary Question [*Australia*]
PPQ	Pre-Production Qualification (SAUS)
PPQ	Primary Parts Package (SAUS)
PPQ	Pulses Per Quarternote (SAUS)
PPQA	Pageable Partition Queue Area [*Computer science*]
PPQC	Piece Part Quality Control (TIMI)
PPQN	Parts per Quarter Note [*Computer science*] (PCM)
PP/Q Program...	Plant Protection and Quarantine Program (SAUS)
PPQR	Priority Parts Quality Review
PPQT	Parts per Quintillion (SAUS)
PPQT	Preproduction Qualification Test [*Army*]
PPQT & E	Pre-Production Qualification Test and Evaluation [*Army*]
PPR	Page Printing Receiver (SAUS)
PPR	Paid Pensioner Recruiter [*British military*] (DMA)
PPR	Palomino Pony Registry
PPR	Paper
PPr..............	Paraprosthetic (DB)
PPR	Partial Product Read (SAUS)
PPR	Partido Panamenista Republicano [*Panama*] [*Political party*] (EY)
PPR	Partido Patriotico Revolucionario [*Mexico*] [*Political party*] (EY)
PPR	Partido Proletariano Revolucionario [*Proletarian Revolutionary Party*] [*Portugal*] [*Political party*] (PPW)
PPR	Parts Planning Record (SAUS)
PPR	Passenger Profile Record [*Travel industry*] (TRID)
PPR	Payload Preparation Room [*VAFB*] [*NASA*] (MCD)
PPR	Peak Production Rate
PPR	Performance Planning and Revenue (SAUS)
PPR	Periodicals Publishing Record [*Alberta Public Affairs Bureau*] [*Canada*] [*Information service or system*] (CRD)
PPR	Periodic Performance Report (SAUS)
PPR	Periodic Personnel Report
PPR	Permanent Pay Record [*Military*]
PPR	Permanent Personal Registration [*Voting*] (BARN)
PPR	Peste des Petits Ruminants [*Rinderpest-like disease*] [*Veterinary medicine*]
PPR	Photographic Press Review [*A publication*] [*British*]
PPR	Photo-Plastic-Recording
PPR	Photoplastic Recording (SAUS)
PPR	Photopolarimeter Radiometer [*Instrumentation*]
PPR	Photopolarimeter-Radiometer (SAUS)
PPR	Physician-Patient Relation (MELL)
PPR	Physician Payment Reform
PPR	Pilgrim America Prime Rate Trust [*NYSE symbol*] (SAG)
PPR	Pilgrim America Prime Rt [*NYSE symbol*] (TTSB)
PPR	Pilgrim Prime Rate Trust [*NYSE symbol*] (SPSG)
PPR	Pilot, Pressure Regulator (MCD)
PPR	Pinault Printemps-Redoute [*A non-food retail group*] [*France*]
PPR	Pirapora [*Brazil*] [*Airport symbol*] (AD)
PPr..............	Pittsburgh Pirates [*National Football League*] [*1933-40*] (NFLA)
PPR	Planar Plate Reactor (SAUS)
PPR	Polish People's Republic
PPR	Politieke Partij Radikalen [*Radical Political Party*] [*Netherlands*] [*Political party*] (PPE)
PPR	Polska Partia Robotnicza [*Polish Workers' Party*] [*Political party*]
PPR	Portable Propagation Recorder [*Bell System*]
PPr..............	Port Pirie (AD)
PPR	Post-Punch Read (SAUS)
PPR	Potential Problem Report [*Navy*] (CAAL)
PPR	Prepublication Review (SAUS)
ppr..............	Present Participle (AD)
PPR	Present Participle [*Grammar*]
PPR	Press and Public Relations Ltd. (SAUS)
PPR	Price. Procedural Regulation [*United States*] [*A publication*] (DLA)
PPR	Price's Precipitation Reaction [*Medicine*]
PPR	Principal Private Residence [*Income tax*] [*British*]
PPR	Principal Probate Registry (DLA)
ppr..............	Printed Paper Rate (AD)
PPR	Printed Paper Rate [*British*] (ILCA)
ppr..............	Prior Permission Required (AD)
PPR	Prior Permission Required (FAAC)
PPR	Probate Practice Reporter (SAUS)
PPR	Procurement Problem Report (AD)
PPR	Production Parts Record (SAUS)
PPR	Production Parts Release (KSC)
PPR	Production Performance Report (SAUS)
PPR	Production Progress Report (MCD)
PPR	Product Performance Report (SAUS)
PPR	Program Planning Report (IAA)
PPR	Program Progress Report (SAUS)
PPR	Program Progress Review
PPR	Program Proposal Request
PPR	Progress Payment Report (AAGC)
PPR	Project Progress Report (OICC)
PPR	Proper [*Heraldry*]
PPR	Proprietary Procurement Request (NG)
PPR	Protective Partial Reflector (SAUS)
PPR	Provisioning Preparedness Review [*Navy*] (CAAL)
PPR	Purchase Parts Request (KSC)
PPRA	Past President of the Royal Academy [*British*] (EY)
PPRA	Preliminary Personnel Requirements Analysis [*Navy*]
PPRA	Protection of Pupil Rights Amendment
PPRAM	Parallel Processing Random Access Memory (AAEL)
pprbd..........	Paperboard (AD)
PPRBD	Paperboard
PPRC	Peer-to-Peer Remote Copy (SAUS)
PPRC	Personnel Program Review Committee [*Military*]
PPRC	Physician Payment Review Commission
PPRC	Pollution Prevention Research Center [*North Carolina State University*] [*Research center*] (RCD)
PPRCI..........	Rittenhouse Club, Philadelphia, PA [*Library symbol*] [*Library of Congress*] [*Obsolete*] (LCLS)
PPRD	Pontypool Road [*Welsh depot code*]
PPRDS........	Products and Process Research and Development Support (DCTA)
PPRE	Peroxisome Proliferator Response Element [*Biochemistry*]
PPREC	Pulp and Paper Research and Education Center [*Auburn University*] [*Research center*] (RCD)
PPREF	Process Program Reference (AAEL)
PPREP	Periodic Personnel Reports
PPREPT	Periodic Personnel Report [*Military*] (AABC)
PPRETS	Reformed Episcopal Seminary, Philadelphia, PA [*Library symbol*] [*Library of Congress*] [*Obsolete*]
PPRF	Paramedian Pontine Reticular Formation [*Neuroanatomy*]
PPRF	Pontine Paramedian Reticular Formation (SAUS)
PPRF	Postpartum Renal Failure [*Medicine*] (DMAA)
PPRF	Pulse Pair Repetition Frequency (MCD)
PPRF	Rosenbach Foundation, Philadelphia, PA [*Library symbol*] [*Library of Congress*] (LCLS)
PPRG	Precambrian Paleobiology Research Group
PPRGF........	Richard Gimbel Foundation for Literary Research, Philadelphia, PA [*Library symbol*] [*Library of Congress*] [*Obsolete*] (LCLS)
PPRI	PACOM [*Pacific Command*] Priority Number (CINC)
PPRI	Pan-Pacific Research Institution (SAUS)
PPRI	Poloron Products, Inc. (SAUS)
PPRI	Pulp and Paper Research Institute (SAUS)
PPRIBA........	Past President of the Royal Institute of British Architects (EY)
PPRibP........	Phosphoribose Diphosphate [*Biochemistry*]
PPRIC	Pulp and Paper Research Institute of Canada
PPRICA........	Pulp and Paper Research Institute of Canada (AD)
PPRINT	Post-Processor Print (SAUS)
PPrIT	Putnam Premier Income Trust [*Associated Press*] (SAG)
PPRI	Plant Protection Research Institute (SAUS)
PPRL	Poisonous Plant Research Laboratory [*Agricultural Research Service*] [*Research center*] (RCD)
PPRM	Population Protection and Resources Management [*Military*] [*British*]
pprm..........	Preprimer
PPRM	Pure Premium Rating Method [*Insurance*]
PPRN	Preliminary Publication Revision Notice
PPRN	Purchased Parts Requirement Notice (KSC)
PPRNCM......	Professional Performance of the Royal Northern College of Music [*British*] (DBQ)
PPRNS........	Pulse-Phased Radio Navigation System
PPRO	Pattern Processing Technologies, Inc. (SAUS)
PPRO	Per Procuration [*Business term*]
P Proc Hampshire Field Club...	Papers and Proceedings. Hampshire Field Club and Archaeological Society (SAUS)
PPROM........	Prolonged Premature Rupture of Membranes [*Obstetrics*] (DAVI)
PPROP........	Personal Property [*Legal shorthand*] (LWAP)
PProt	Postprotest (SAUS)
PPRP	Polydenosine Diphosphate-Ribose Polymerase (DMAA)

PPRPF .... Regional Planning Federation, Philadelphia, PA [*Library symbol*] [*Library of Congress*] [*Obsolete*] (LCLS)
PPRR .... Performance Planning & Review Record (WDAA)
PPRR .... Program Pre-Release Reviews (SAUS)
PPRS .... Perceptions of Parental Role Scales
PPRS .... Preferred Planning Reporting System (WDAA)
PPRS .... Program Planning and Review Staff [*Environmental Protection Agency*] (GFGA)
PPRS .... Promotion and Placement Referral Subsystem (SAUS)
PPRS .... Promotions and Placements Referral System (MCD)
PPRSA .... Past President of the Royal Society of Arts [*British*] (DI)
PPRV .... Peste des Petits Ruminants Virus [*Rinderpest-like disease*] [*Veterinary medicine*]
PPRWP .... Poor Precordial R-Wave Progression [*Cardiology*]
PPS .... Butte Aviation, Inc. [*FAA designator*] (FAAC)
PPS .... Pacific Passenger Services (AD)
PPS .... Packets per Second [*Computer science*] (PCM)
PPS .... Paco Pharmaceutical Services, Inc (SAUS)
PPS .... Pad-Pad Spacing (SAUS)
PPS .... Paediatric Pathology Society of Europe (SAUS)
PPS .... Page Printing System [*Honeywell, Inc.*] [*Computer science*]
PPS .... Page Processing System (NITA)
PPS .... Pain Producing Substance (SAUS)
PPS .... Paint, Pesticide Chemicals, and Solvents
PPS .... Panoramic Passive Sonar (SAUS)
PPS .... Paper Publications Society [*Amsterdam, Netherlands*] (EA)
PPS .... Parallel Processing System [*Computer science*] (MDG)
PPS .... Parameter Processing System (CAAL)
PPS .... Parliamentary Private Secretary [*British*]
PPS .... Partia e Punes e Shqiperise [*Party of Labor of Albania - PLA*] [*Political party*] (PPW)
PPS .... Partial Pressure Sensor
PPS .... Participating Preferred Stock (MHDW)
PPS .... Partido Popular Salvadoreno [*Salvadoran Popular Party*] [*Political party*] (PPW)
PPS .... Partido Popular Socialista [*Popular Socialist Party*] [*Argentina*] [*Political party*] (PPW)
PPS .... Partido Popular Socialista [*Popular Socialist Party*] [*Mexico*] [*Political party*]
PPS .... Parti du Progres et du Socialisme [*Party of Progress and Socialism*] [*Morocco*] [*Political party*] (PPW)
PPS .... Parti du Progres Social [*Burkina Faso*] [*Political party*] (EY)
PPS .... Parti Populaire Senegalais [*Senegalese People's Party*] [*Political party*] (PPW)
PPS .... Parti Populaire Syrien [*Syrian People's Party*] [*Political party*] (BJA)
PPS .... Parti Progressiste Soudanais [*Sudanese Progressive Party*] [*Political party*]
PPS .... Partitioned Priority System (SAUS)
PPS .... Partito Populare Somalo [*Somali People's Party*]
PPS .... Parts Provisioning System (KSC)
PPS .... Party for Progress and Socialism (SAUS)
PPS .... Party for Progress and Solidarity (SAUS)
PPS .... Passenger Presence Sensor [*Automotive safety systems*]
PPS .... Patchboard Programming System
PPS .... Payload Pointing System (SSD)
PPS .... Payload Power Switch
PPS .... Payphone Power Supply (SAUS)
PPS .... Pennsylvania Prison Society (AD)
PPS .... Peoples Oil Ltd. [*Vancouver Stock Exchange symbol*]
PPS .... Pepsin A [*Medicine*] (MAE)
PPS .... Performance Program Statement [*Australia*]
PPS .... Period per Second (IAA)
PPS .... Periods per Second (SAUS)
PPS .... Peripheral Processing System (SAUS)
PPS .... Peripheral Processor System [*Computer science*] (IAA)
PPS .... Personal Plane Service [*Aircraft restoration firm*] [*British*]
PPS .... Personal Portable Shopper [*Computer science*]
PPS .... Personal Preference Scale [*Psychology*]
PPS .... Personal Printer Series [*IBM Corp.*]
PPS .... Personal Printing System [*Computer science*]
PPS .... Personal Process Service (LAIN)
PPS .... Personal Protection Squad [*of the London Metropolitan Police*]
PPS .... Personnel/Payroll System
PPS .·........... Personnel Preference Scale (SAUS)
PPS .... Personnel Processing Squadron
PPS .... Persutuan Perpustakaan Singapura [*Library Association of Singapore*] (AD)
PPS .... Petroleum Press Service
PPS .... Petroleum Production Survey [*Bureau of Mines*]
PPS .... Phantom Phanatics Society (EA)
PPS .... Philadelphia Programming Society (SAUS)
PPS .... Phlogopite-Peridotite Solidus [*Geology*]
PPS .... Phosphoribosyl-1-pyrophosphatsynthetase (SAUS)
PPS .... Phosphorous Propellant System (KSC)
PPS .... Photophoretic Spectroscopy
PPS .... Photopolarimeter Spectrometer
PPS .... Photovoltaic Power Supply
PPS .... Photovoltaic Power System (SAUS)
pps .... Pictures Per Second (AD)
PPS .... Pictures per Second (WDAA)
PPS .... Piece Part Specification (MCD)
PPSPF .... Pierpont [*South Carolina*] [*Seismograph station code, US Geological Survey*] (SEIS)
PPS .... Pitt Press Series [*A publication*]
PPS .... Plant Parasitic Systems

PPS .... Plant Protection System [*Nuclear energy*] (NRCH)
PPS .... Plasma Power Supply
PPS .... Plasma Protein Solution (SAUS)
PPS .... Plate Power Supply (ELAL)
PPS .... Plutonium Product Storage [*Nuclear energy*] (NRCH)
PPS .... Pneumatic Power Subsystem (NASA)
PPS .... Point-to-Point System (IAA)
PPS .... Policies and Procedures (SAUS)
PPS .... Policy Processing Sheet [*Insurance*]
PPS .... Polonus Philatelic Society (EA)
PPSA .... Polska Partia Socjalistyczna [*Polish Socialist Party*]
PPS .... Poly(para-phenylene Sulfide) [*Organic chemistry*]
PPS .... Polyphensulfid (SAUS)
PPS .... Polyphenylene Sulfide (SAUS)
PPS .... Polyphenylene Sulfide Plastic
PPS .... Polyphenylenesulphone (SAUS)
PPS .... Polyvalance Pneumococcal Polysaccharides [*A vaccine for patients with splenectomies*] [*Medicine*] (DAVI)
PPS .... Portable Personal Shopper
PPS .... Ported Pressure Switch [*Automotive engineering*]
PPS .... Port Presentation Module (SAUS)
PPS .... Postpartum Sterilization [*Gynecology*] (DAVI)
PPS .... Postperfusion Syndrome [*Medicine*]
PPS .... Postpericardiotomy Syndrome [*Medicine*] (DMAA)
PPS .... Post-Polio Sequelae [*Medicine*]
PPS .... Post-Polio Syndrome [*Medicine*] (AD)
p-ps .... Post-Postscriptum [*Further Postscript*] [*Latin*]
PPS .... Post Production Service (AAG)
PPS .... Post Production Support (MCD)
PPS .... Postproduction Support (SAUS)
PPS .... Post Properties [*NYSE symbol*] (TTSB)
PPS .... Post Properties, Inc. [*NYSE symbol*] (SPSG)
PPS .... Postpump Syndrome [*Medicine*] (MAE)
pps .... Pounds Per Second (AD)
PPS .... Pounds per Second (AAG)
PPS .... Power Personal Systems (SAUS)
PPs .... Prairie Provinces (SAUS)
PPS .... Precise Positioning Service [*Military*]
PPS .... Precision Pointing System (SAUS)
PPS .... Precision Positioning Service
PPS .... Precision Power Supply
PPS .... Precision Processing System (SAUS)
PPS .... Pre-Planned Support (SAUS)
PPS .... Prepositioned Stock (NG)
PPS .... Pre-Processeur de Signal [*Computer*] [*French*]
PPS .... Prescribed Payments System (ADA)
PPS .... Preselection Primary Section
PPS .... Primary Paraffin Sulfonate [*Organic chemistry*]
PPS .... Primary Power Standard
PPS .... Primary Power System [*Nuclear energy*] (NRCH)
PPS .... Primary Propulsion System [*Spacecraft*]
PPS .... Primary Protection System [*Computer science*]
PPS .... Prime Power System (SAUS)
PPS .... Principal Private Secretary [*British*]
PPS .... Printer/Plotter System (MCD)
PPS .... Priority Processing System (SAUS)
PPS .... Prior Preferred Stock
pps .... Private Parliamentary Secretary [*British*] (AD)
PPS .... Private Practice Section [*American Physical Therapy Association*] (EA)
PPS .... Probability Proportional to Size [*Statistics*]
PPS .... Proceedings of the Prehistoric Society (SAUS)
PPS .... Procurement Planning Schedule [*DoD*]
PPS .... Production Planning System [*TDS Business Systems Ltd.*] [*Software package*] (NCC)
PPS .... Product Performance Specification (SAUS)
PPS .... Product Performance Surveys (SAUS)
PPS .... Programmable Patch System
PPS .... Programmable Power Supply
PPS .... Programmable Pressure Source (SAUS)
PPS .... Programmed Processor System
PPS .... Programming Program Strela [*Computer science*]
PPS .... Program Performance Specification (CAAL)
PPS .... Program Peripheral Subsystems (CCCA)
PPS .... Program Planning Summary (OICC)
PPS .... Program Planning System [*DoD*]
PPS .... Program Policy Staff [*UN Food and Agriculture Organization*]
PPS .... Program Preparation Subsystem (SAUS)
PPS .... Program Production Supervisor (SAUS)
PPS .... Program Product Specification (SAUS)
PPS .... Progressive Pneumonia of Sheep
PPS .... Project for Public Spaces (EA)
PPS .... Project Planning System (SAUS)
PPS .... Project Profile System (SAUS)
PPS .... Project Proposal Summary (SAUS)
PPS .... Proposal Pricing System (SAUS)
PPS .... Propose (FAAC)
PPS .... Propulsion and Propellant Section [*Picatinny Arsenal*] [*Dover, NJ*]
PPS .... Propulsion Pressurization Subsystem
PPS .... Prospective Payment System [*For hospital care*]
PPS .... Prospective Pricing System [*Information service or system*] (HCT)
PPS .... Protecte Payments System (SAUS)
PPS .... Provincial Peace Structure (SAUS)
PPS .... Provisioning Parts Schedule (MCD)
PPS .... Provisioning Performance Schedule (AFM)

PPS............. Provisioning Policy Statement (MCD)

PPS............. Prudential Property Services [Prudential Group] [British]

PPS............. Public and Private [Nongovernment] Schools [Public-performance tariff class] [British]

PPS............. Public Packet Switching (SAUS)

PPS............. Puerto Princesa [Philippines] [Airport symbol] (OAG)

PPS............. Pulse per Second (SAUS)

pps............. Pulses Per Second (AD)

PPS............. Pulses per Second [Data transmission]

PPS............. Pupil Personnel Services

PPSA .... Pan-Pacific Surgical Association (EA)

PPSA .... Prospect Park Savings & Loan Association (SAUS)

PPSAS .... Program Planning and Status Assessment System [Nuclear energy] (NRCH)

PPSAT .... Peripheral Processor Saturation (MHDI)

PPSAWA .... Pan Pacific and Southeast Asia Women's Association (AD)

PPSB .... Periodical Publishers' Service Bureau (NADA)

PPSB .... Prothrombin, Proconvertin, Stuart Factor, Antihemophilic B Factor [Blood coagulation factors] [Hematology]

PPSC .... Parallel Processing System Compiler (SAUS)

PPSC .... Petroleum Products Supply Corp. (SAUS)

PPSC .... Physical Profile Serial Code [Military]

PPSC .... Privacy Protection Study Commission [Government commission]

PPSC .... Processor Program State Control (NITA)

PPSCA .... Partido Popular Social Cristiano Autentico [Political party] (EY)

PPSCI .... Seamens Church Institute, Philadelphia (SAUS)

PPSCI .... Seamen's Church Institute, Philadelphia, PA [Library symbol] [Library of Congress] [Obsolete] (LCLS)

PPSD .... Personnel and Pay Services Division

PPSD .... Polska Partia Socialno-Demokratyczna [Polish Social-Democrat Party] [Political party]

PPSD .... Proposed

PPSE.......... Programmer Support Environment [Computer science] (LAIN)

PPSE.......... Purpose

PPSEA .... Proceedings of the Prehistoric Society of East Anglia (SAUS)

PPSEAWA .... Pan-Pacific and South-East Asia Women's Association [Tokyo, Japan] (EAIO)

PPSEAWA-USA... Pan Pacific and Southeast Asia Women's Association of the USA (EA)

PPSED3 .... Annual Research Reviews. Physiological and Pathological Aspects of Prolactin Secretion (journ.) (SAUS)

PPSER .... Postgraduate Paediatrics Series (SAUS)

PPSF.......... Palestinian Popular Struggle Front [Political party] (BJA)

PPSF.......... Prefocused-objective Pinhole Spatial Filter (SAUS)

PPSFP .... Parallel-Pattern Single-Fault Propagation [Computer science] (CIST)

PPS-FR .... Polska Partia Socjalistyczna - Frakcja Rewolucyjna [Polish Socialist Party - Revolutionary Faction] [Political party] (PPE)

PPSG .... Piston and Pin Standardization Group [Later, NEPMA] (EA)

PPSG .... Spring Garden College, Philadelphia, PA [Library symbol] [Library of Congress] (LCLS)

PPSh........... Partia e Punes e Shqiperise [Labor Party of Albania] [Formerly, PKSh] [Political party] (PPE)

PPSH .... Pseudovaginal Perineoscrotal Hypospadias [Medicine]

PPSI........... Pacific Physician Services (SPSG)

PPSI........... Pacific Physician Services, Inc. [NASDAQ symbol] (SAG)

PPSI........... Parent Problem-Solving Instrument (EDAC)

PPSI........... Pound-Weight per Square Inch (SAUS)

PPSIA .... "Personal Property Shipping Information" [Pamphlet] Is Applicable [Military] (AABC)

PPSIAD .... Past President of the Society of Industrial Artists and Designers [British] (DI)

PPS II .... Payroll Personnel System

PPSJ........... Pressure Plane Swivel Joint

PPSJ........... Saint Josephs College, Philadelphia (SAUS)

PPSJ........... Saint Joseph's College, Philadelphia, PA [Library symbol] [Library of Congress] (LCLS)

PPSJ-AF ...... Saint Joseph's College, Academy of Food Marketing, Philadelphia, PA [Library symbol] [Library of Congress] (LCLS)

PPSJ-AF ...... Saint Josephs College, Academy of Food Marketing, Philadelpia (SAUS)

PPSKED .... Provisioning Performance Schedule (MCD)

PPSKF .... SmithKline Corp., Philadelphia, PA [Library symbol] [Library of Congress] (LCLS)

PPSL.......... Program Parts Selection List

PPSL.......... Proposed Parts Selection List (SAUS)

PPSL.......... Provisioning Parts Selection List (MCD)

PPSMEC ...... Procurement, Precedence of Supplies, Material and Equipment Committee [Joint Communications Board]

ppsn........... Present Position (AD)

PPSN .... Present Position [Aviation] (FAAC)

PPSN .... Public Packet Switched [or Switching] Network [Telecommunications]

PPSN .... Purchased Part Shortage Notice

ppso........... Per Person, Single Occupancy (AD)

PPSO .... Personal Property Shipping Office [Military]

PPSOPR....... Sun Oil Co., General Office Library, Philadelphia, PA [Library symbol] [Library of Congress] [Obsolete] (LCLS)

PPSP .... Page Printer Spooling System [Computer science]

PPSP .... Pollution Prevention and Safety Panel (SAUS)

PPSP .... Ponderosa Pine or Sugar Pine [Lumber]

PPSP .... Postproduction Support Plan (SAUS)

PPSP .... Power Plant Siting Program [Environmental Protection Agency] (GFGA)

PPS-PODS ... Precise Position System-Precise Orbit Determination System (SAUS)

PPSPS .... Plutonium Product Shipping Preparation Station [Nuclear energy] (NRCH)

PPSQ .... Principal Problem Strategy Questionnaire (EDAC)

PPSR .... Periodic Personnel Strength Report [Army] (AABC)

PPSS .... Foundation for the President's Private Sector Survey on Cost Control (EA)

PPSS .... Polyphenylene Sulfide Sulfone [Organic chemistry]

PPSS .... President's Private Sector Survey

PPSS .... Product and Process Status System (SAUS)

PPSS .... Project Planning and Scheduling System (SAUS)

PPSS .... Public Packet Switching Service (NITA)

PPSSCC .... Foundation for the President's Private Sector Survey on Cost Control (EA)

PPS-SM .... Precise Positioning Service-Security Module (SAUS)

P-PST .... Pre-Professional Skill Test (EDAC)

PPStarr........ Starr Center Association, Philadelphia, PA [Library symbol] [Library of Congress] [Obsolete] (LCLS)

PPStCh .... Saint Charles Borromeo Seminary, Philadelphia, PA [Library symbol] [Library of Congress] (LCLS)

PPSteph...... William B. Stephens Memorial Library, Philadelphia, PA [Library symbol] [Library of Congress] (LCLS)

PPSTH .... Population Post-stimulus Time Histogram [Statistics]

PPSU .... Personal Printer Spooling Utility (SAUS)

PPSU .... Poly Phenylene Sulfone (EDCT)

PPSU .... Polyphenylene Sulfone (SAUS)

PPSU .... Polyphenylene Sulfone Plastic

PPSU .... Programmable Power Supply Unit (EECA)

PPSV .... Plutonium Product Storage Vault [Nuclear energy] (NRCH)

PPSV .... Printing and Publishing Services, Victoria [Australia]

PPSWA .... Plant Protection Society of Western Australia [Australia]

PPS-WRN ... Polska Partia Socjalistyczna - Wolnosc, Rownosc, Niepodleglosc [Polish Socialist Party - Freedom, Equality, Independence] [Political party] (PPE)

PPT............. Palmitoyl-Protein Thioesterase [An enzyme]

PPT............. Pamatai [French Polynesia] [Geomagnetic observatory code]

PPT............. Papeete [French Polynesia] [Airport symbol] (OAG)

PPT............. Papeete [French Polynesia] [Seismograph station code, US Geological Survey] (SEIS)

PPT............. Papeete, Society Islands [Airport] (AD)

PPT............. Parietal Pleural Tissue (DB)

PPT............. Partial Parse Trees (SAUS)

PPT............. Partial Prothrombin Time [Hematology]

PPT............. Parti Progressiste Tchadien [Progressive Party of Chad] [Political party]

PPT............. Part Per Trillion (SAUS)

PPT............. Parts for Printer Terminal (SAUS)

PPT............. Parts per Thousand (DNAB)

ppt............. Parts per Thousand (IDOE)

ppt............. Parts per Trillion [Marine science] (OSRA)

PPT............. Parts per Trillion

PPT............. Parts Procurement Time (SAUS)

p-p-t........... Pay-per-Transaction [Agreement between video cassette rental stores and owners of film rights]

PPT............. Peak-to-Peak Threshold (DB)

PPT............. Pedunculopontine Tegmentum [Neurology]

PPT............. Pericles, Prince of Tyre [A publication] (AD)

PPT............. Periodic Programs Termination [Computer science]

PPT............. Period Pulse Train

PPT............. Peripheral Performance Test (CAAL)

PPT............. Permanent Part-Time (ADA)

PPT............. Personal Portable Telephone (SAUS)

PPT............. Personal Property Tax (MHDW)

PPT............. Perspective-Pole Track (SAUS)

PPT............. Phosphinothricin [Organic chemistry]

PPT............. Pilot's Power Tool

PPT............. Pine Point Mines Ltd. [Toronto Stock Exchange symbol] [Vancouver Stock Exchange symbol]

PPT............. Pitch Precession Torquer

PPT............. Plant Protease Test (MAE)

PPT............. Poly Propylene Terephthalate (EDCT)

PPT............. Polypropylene Terephthalate (SAUS)

PPT............. Polypurine Tract [Genetics]

PPT............. Polypurinetract (SAUS)

PPT............. Polypyrimidine Tract [Genetics]

PPT............. Polysilicon Pressure Transducer (SAUS)

PPT............. Pooh Property Trust [A.A. Milne estate] [British]

PPT............. Poppet [Engineering]

PPT............. Port Processing Time (SAUS)

PPT............. Post Production Test

PPT............. PowerPoint [Computer science] (PCM)

PPT............. Powerpoint Presentation Format (SAUS)

PPT............. Practical Policy Test [Psychology]

PPT............. Praecipitatus [Precipitated] [Pharmacy]

PPT............. Praeparata [Prepared] [Pharmacy] (ROG)

ppt............. Precipitate (AD)

PPT............. Precipitate (MSA)

ppt............. precipitation (SAUS)

ppt............. Precipitat Prepared [Laboratory science] (DAVI)

PPT............. Precision Pressure Transducer

PPT............. Preproduction Test [Army]

PPT............. Preprotachykinin [Biochemistry]

PPT............. Preprototype (SAA)

PPT............. Primary Program operator interface Task (SAUS)

PPT............. Printer Pass-Through (SAUS)

PPT............. Private Purchasing Tariff [British]

PPT............. Probabilistic Potential Theory (PDAA)

PPT............. Process Page Table [Telecommunications] (TEL)

PPT............	Production Prototype
PPT............	Production Prototype Test
PPT............	Production Prove-out Test (SAUS)
PPT............	Product Positioning Time (AFM)
PPT............	Profit per Transaction [*Travel industry*] (TVEL)
PPT............	Programmer Productivity Technique (IAA)
PPT............	Program Processing Table (SAUS)
PPT............	Program Proofing Team (SAUS)
PPT............	Program Punched Tape (SAUS)
PPT............	Project Planning Technique (MCD)
PPT............	Prompt (ROG)
PPT............	Propyl(thio)uracil [*Biochemistry*]
PPT............	Public and Private Transport
PPT............	Pulse Pair Timing (SAUS)
PPT............	Pulse Plasma Thruster
PPT............	Punched Paper Tape [*Computer science*]
PPT............	Punched Plated Thru (SAUS)
PPT............	Putnam Premier Income Tr [*NYSE symbol*] (TTSB)
PPT............	Putnam Premier Income Trust [*NYSE symbol*] (SPSG)
PPT............	Temple University, Philadelphia, PA [*Library symbol*] [*Library of Congress*] (LCLS)
PPT............	Temple University, Physics Library (SAUS)
PPT............	Theosophical Society, Philadelphia, PA [*Library symbol*] [*Library of Congress*] [*Obsolete*] (LCLS)
PPTA............	Post-Primary Teachers Association [*New Zealand*] (WDAA)
PPTA............	Precipitation (SAUS)
PPTB............	Pin-Pack Test Board
PPTBA.........	Pattern and Plastic Tool Builders Association [*Defunct*] (EA)
PPTC............	People-to-People Tennis Committee (EA)
PPTC............	Purchased Part Tab Card
PPTC............	Purchase Part Tab Card
pptd	Precipitated (AD)
PPTD	Precipitated
PPT-D	Temple University, Dental-Pharmacy School, Philadelphia, PA [*Library symbol*] [*Library of Congress*] (LCLS)
PPTE.......	Permanent Part-Time Employment
PPT ERIN......	Priorities and Protection Team (SAUS)
PPTF............	Public Policy Task Force [*Defunct*] (EA)
PPTF............	Public-Private Task Force
ppth............	Parts Per Thousand
pPTH............	Porcine Parathyroid Hormone [*Endocrinology*]
PPT Hole Process...	Punched Plated Thru Hole Process (SAUS)
PPTI............	Passport Travel, Inc. (SAUS)
PPTI............	Protein Polymer Technologies [*NASDAQ symbol*] (TTSB)
PPTI............	Protein Polymer Technologies, Inc. [*NASDAQ symbol*] (SAG)
PPT-ISA......	Picture Personality Test for Indian South Africans
PPTIW	Protein Polymer Technol Wrrt [*NASDAQ symbol*] (TTSB)
PPTJ............	Theodore F. Jenkins Memorial Law Library, Philadelphia, PA [*Library symbol*] [*Library of Congress*] (LCLS)
PPTL............	Postpartum Tubal Ligation [*Medicine*]
PPTL............	Pulp and Paper Traffic League [*Defunct*] (EA)
PPT-L............	Temple University, Law School, Philadelphia, PA [*Library symbol*] [*Library of Congress*] (LCLS)
ppt/lat..........	prompt or later (SAUS)
PPT-M	Temple University, Medical School, Philadelphia, PA [*Library symbol*] [*Library of Congress*] (LCLS)
PPTMR	Personal Property Traffic Management Regulation
pptn	Precipitation (AD)
PPTN	Precipitation
PPTO	Personal Property Transportation Officer
PPTO	Principal Professional and Technology Officer [*British*]
PPTP............	Personnel Performance and Training Program
PPTP............	Point-to-Point Tunneling Protocol [*Microsoft Corp.*]
PPTP............	Power Proportioning Temperature Programmer (SAUS)
PPTPI............	Power-Proportioning Temperature Programmer (IAA)
PPTPI............	Past President of the Town Planning Institute (SAUS)
PPTPP	Promulgators of Public Toilets in Public Parks (AD)
PPTR	Pulsed Photothermal Radiometry (SAUS)
PPTR	Punched Paper Tape Reader [*Computer science*]
PPTri	Tri-Institutional Library, Philadelphia, PA [*Library symbol*] [*Library of Congress*] (LCLS)
PPTS............	Pianoforte Polishers' Trade Society [*A union*] [*British*]
PPTS............	Portable Perishable Tool System (MCD)
PPTS............	Pre-Planned Training System (PDAA)
PPTS............	Pre-Problem Training Situation (SAA)
PPTS............	Punched Paper Tape Speed (SAUS)
PPTS............	Pyridinium Para-Toluenesulfonate [*Organic chemistry*]
PPTS............	Pyridinium-para-Tosylate [*Organic chemistry*]
PP/TSD	Post Placement and Training Support Program for People with Disabilities [*Australia*]
PPT SH	Prompt Ship (SAUS)
PPT-T...........	Temple University, School of Theology, Philadelphia, PA [*Library symbol*] [*Library of Congress*] (LCLS)
PPTTG	Personal Property Transit Time Guide [*MTMC*] (TAG)
pptv	Parts per Trillion by Volume (CARB)
PPTV............	Parts per Trillion by Volume
PPTV............	PPT Vision [*NASDAQ symbol*] (TTSB)
PPTV............	PPT Vision, Inc. [*NASDAQ symbol*] (SAG)
PPT Vis.........	PPT Vision, Inc. [*Associated Press*] (SAG)
PPTW...........	Permanent Part-Time Work
ppty	Property (AD)
PPTY	Property (AFM)
PPU	Cocoa, FL [*Location identifier*] [*FAA*] (FAAL)
PPU	Packaged Power Unit (SAUS)
PPU	Papun [*Myanmar*] [*Airport symbol*] (OAG)
PPU	Parti Populaire des Ueles [*Ueles People's Party*] [*Political party*]
PPU	Payment for Public Use [*Canada*]
PPU	Peace Pledge Union [*British*]
PPU	Peninsula Petroleum Corp. [*Vancouver Stock Exchange symbol*]
PPU	Peoria & Pekin Union Railway Co. [*AAR code*]
PPU	Peripheral Processing Unit [*Computer science*]
PPU	Peripheral Processor Unit (SAUS)
PPU	Picture Processing Unit [*Computer science*]
ppu	Platform Position Unit (AD)
PPU	Platform Position Unit
PPU	Pool Planned Unit (SAUS)
PPU	Power Processing Unit (MCD)
PPU	Pre-Processing Unit (SAUS)
PPU	Pre-Processor Utility (NITA)
PPU	Preproduction Unit (MCD)
PPU	Primary Power Unit
PPU	Primary Producers Union (AD)
PPU	Prime Power Unit
PPU	Professional Psychics Unit (SAUS)
PPU	Professional Psychics United (EA)
PPU	Programmable Processing Unit (SAUS)
PPU	Program Providing Unit (SAUS)
PPU	Projectile Programming Unit (SAUS)
PPU	Promontory Point [*Utah*] [*Seismograph station code, US Geological Survey*] [*Closed*] (SEIS)
PPUAES	Publications. Princeton University Archaeological Expeditions to Syria (SAUS)
PPUC	Probably Permanently Under Construction (SAUS)
PPUG	United Gas Improvement Corp., Philadelphia, PA [*Library symbol*] [*Library of Congress*] [*Obsolete*] (LCLS)
PPUI	Pitch and Putt Union of Ireland (EAIO)
PPUK	Picked Ports United Kingdom (SAUS)
PPULC	Union Library Catalogue of Pennsylvania, Philadelphia, PA [*Library symbol*] [*Library of Congress*] (LCLS)
PPUNA.........	United States Naval Aircraft Factory, Philadelphia, PA [*Library symbol*] [*Library of Congress*] [*Obsolete*] (LCLS)
PPUnC	University Club, Philadelphia, PA [*Library symbol*] [*Library of Congress*] [*Obsolete*] (LCLS)
PPUNH.........	United States Naval Home, Philadelphia, PA [*Library symbol*] [*Library of Congress*] [*Obsolete*] (LCLS)
PPUSDA......	United States Department of Agriculture, Agricultural Research Service, Eastern Utilization Research and Development Division, Philadelphia, PA [*Library symbol*] [*Library of Congress*] (LCLS)
PPV............	Paraphenylene Vinylene [*Organic chemistry*]
PPV............	Pars Plana Vitrectomy
PPV............	Pay per View (SAUS)
ppv............	Pay-Per-View (AD)
PPV............	Pay-per-View [*Pay-television service*]
ppv............	People-Powered Vehicle (AD)
PPV............	People-Powered Vehicle [*Recreational vehicle powered by pedaling*]
PPV............	Pitch Power Valve (IAA)
PPV............	Plum Pox Virus [*Plant pathology*]
PPV............	Polarized Platen Viewer (OA)
PPV............	Poly (Phenylenevinylene) [*Organic chemistry*]
PPV............	Porcine Parvovirus [*Veterinary science*] (DMAA)
PPV............	Positive Predictive Value [*Experimentation*]
PPV............	Positive Pressure Ventilation [*Medicine*]
PPV............	Pre-Production Verification (SAUS)
PPV............	Preprogrammed Vehicles (MCD)
PPV............	Pressure Protection Valve (SAUS)
PPV............	Primary Pressure Vessel (MCD)
PPV............	Progressive Pneumonia Virus [*Medicine*] (DB)
PPV............	Propulsive Propellant Venting (SAUS)
P/PV............	Public/Private Ventures [*Philadelphia, PA*] [*Research center*] (RCD)
PPV............	Purchase Price Variance (TIMI)
PPV............	United States Veterans Administration Hospital, Philadelphia, PA [*Library symbol*] [*Library of Congress*] (LCLS)
PPVL...........	Posterior Pulmonary Valve Leaflet (SAUS)
PPVO...........	Premature Pulmonary Valve Opening (SAUS)
PPVP...........	Posterior Precortical Vitreous Pocket (SAUS)
PPVS...........	Propulsion Propellant Venting System (SAUS)
PPVT...........	Peabody Picture Vocabulary Test [*Education*]
PPVT-R........	Peabody Picture Vocabulary Test - Revised [*Education*]
PP-W...........	Free Library of Philadelphia, H. Josephine Widener Memorial Branch, Philadelphia, PA [*Library symbol*] [*Library of Congress*] [*Obsolete*] (LCLS)
PPW...........	PacifiCorp [*NYSE symbol*] (SPSG)
PPW...........	Pacificorp Capital [*NYSE symbol*] (SAG)
PPW...........	Papa Westray [*Scotland*] [*Airport symbol*] (OAG)
PPW...........	Partial Product Write (SAUS)
PPW...........	Parts per Weight
PPW...........	Patient Protective Wrap
PPW...........	Pave Paws West (SAUS)
PPW...........	Personal Protection Weapon (SAUS)
PPW...........	Petitions for Patent Waiver
PPW...........	Plane-Polarized Wave
PPW...........	Ponderosa Pine Woodwork (SAUS)
PPW...........	Ponderosa Pine Woodwork Association [*NWWDA*] [*Absorbed by*] (EA)
PPW...........	Potato Processing Waste
PPWA...........	Ponderosa Pine Woodwork Association [*NWWDA*] [*Absorbed by*]
PPWa...........	Wagner Free Institute of Science, Philadelphia, PA [*Library symbol*] [*Library of Congress*] (LCLS)
PPWC	Pines to Palms Wildlife Committee (SAUS)
PPWC	Pulp, Paper, and Woodworkers of Canada

PPWD	S. S. White Co., Philadelphia, PA [*Library symbol*] [*Library of Congress*] [*Obsolete*] (LCLS)
PPWe	Westminster Theological Seminary, Philadelphia, PA [*Library symbol*] [*Library of Congress*] (LCLS)
PPWF	Pakistan Petroleum Workers Federation (SAUS)
PPWG	Production Planning Working Group (SAUS)
PPWI	Wistar Institute of Anatomy and Biology, Philadelphia, PA [*Library symbol*] [*Library of Congress*] (LCLS)
PPWiH	Wills Eye Hospital, Philadelphia, PA [*Library symbol*] [*Library of Congress*] (LCLS)
PPWL	Present Practice Waste Load (DICI)
PPWM	Medical College of Pennsylvania, Philadelphia, PA [*Library symbol*] [*Library of Congress*] (LCLS)
PPWP	Planned Parenthood - World Population [*Later, PPFA*] (EA)
PPWPr	PacifiCorp 5% Pfd [*AMEX symbol*] (TTSB)
PPWPrE	PacifiCorp $1.98 cm Pfd [*NYSE symbol*] (TTSB)
PPWR	Pre-Positioned War Reserve (SAUS)
PPWR	Prepositioned War Reserves [*Army*]
PPWRS	Prepositioned War Reserve Stocks [*Army*]
PPWSM	Post Production Weapon System Management (SAUS)
PPWW	Painless, Progressive, Weakening, Wasting painless (SAUS)
PPX	Packet Protocol Extension
PPX	Pipecolylxylidine (SAUS)
PPX	Port Moller, AK [*Location identifier*] [*FAA*] (FAAL)
PPY	Pages per Year [*Facetious criterion for determining insignificance of Supreme Court Justices*] [*Proposed by University of Chicago professor David P. Currie*]
PPY	Pancreatic Polypeptide [*Medicine*] (DMAA)
PPY	Polyacrylonitride Precursor Yarn (SAUS)
PPY	Prophesy Development [*Vancouver Stock Exchange symbol*]
PPYH	Young Men's and Young Women's Hebrew Association, Philadelphia, PA [*Library symbol*] [*Library of Congress*] [*Obsolete*] (LCLS)
PPYU	Party of Popular Yemenite Unity [*Political party*] (PD)
PPZ	Proton Polar Zone
PPZ	Puerto Paez [*Venezuela*] [*Airport symbol*] (AD)
PPZ	Zoological Society of Philadelphia, PA [*Library symbol*] [*Library of Congress*] [*Obsolete*] (LCLS)
PQ	Pack Quickly [*Humorous interpretation for Parti Quebecois*] [*Canada*]
PQ	Panic in Quebec [*Humorous interpretation for Parti Quebecois*] [*Canada*]
PQ	Parametric Quantron [*Physics*]
PQ	Parliamentary Question [*British*]
PQ	Parti Quebecois [*Quebec separatist political party*]
pq	Peculiar (AD)
PQ	Performance Qualification (ACII)
PQ	Performer Quotient [*TV-performer rating*]
pq	Permeability Quotient (AD)
PQ	Permeability Quotient
pq	Personality Quotient (AD)
PQ	Personality Quotient [*Psychology*]
p-q	Phenol-Hydroquinone [*Photography*] (AD)
PQ	Philological Quarterly [*A publication*] (BRI)
PQ	Photo Quality (PCM)
PQ	Physically Qualified
PQ	Physician's Questionnaire (AAMN)
PQ	Planetary Quarantine [*NASA*]
PQ	Plant Quarantine Division [*of ARS, Department of Agriculture*]
PQ	Plasma Quad [*Instrumentation*]
PQ	Plastoquinone [*Biochemistry*]
PQ	Pollution Quotient
PQ	Polyquinoxaline [*Organic chemistry*]
P-Q	Porphyrin-Quinone [*Photochemistry*]
PQ	PQ Corp. [*Formerly, Philadelphia Quartz Co.*]
PQ	Premium Quality (MUGU)
PQ	Preparative Quencher [*Spectroscopy*]
PQ	Presentation Quotient [*Business Term*]
pq	Previous Question (AD)
PQ	Previous Question [*Parliamentary law*]
Pq	Primaquine [*Antimalarial*]
PQ	Pronator Quadratus [*Muscle*] [*Anatomy*] (DAVI)
pq	Pro Querente [*For the Plaintiff*] [*Latin*] [*Legal term*] (DLA)
PQ	Province Quebec [*Quebec*] [*Canadian province*] [*Postal code*]
PQ	Psi Quotient [*Parapsychology*]
PQ	Public Quarters
PQ	Puerto Rico International Airlines, Inc. [*Prinair*] [*ICAO designator*] (OAG)
pq	Punishment Quarters (AD)
PQ	Pyrimethamine-Quinine [*Organic chemistry*] (MAE)
PQ	Quebec [*Postal code*] (CDAI)
PQ	South Pacific Airlines of New Zealand (AD)
PQ	United States Patent Quarterly [*A publication*] (DLA)
PQA	Pacific Coast Airlines [*ICAO designator*] (FAAC)
PQA	Palm Query Applications
PQA	Parts Quality Assurance
PQA	Petroleum Quality Assurance
PQA	Plant Quality Assurance
PQA	Preliminary Qualification Analysis
PQA	Preliminary Quantitative Analysis
pqa	Procurement Quality Assurance (AD)
PQA	Procurement Quality Assurance [*Program*] [*DoD*]
PQA	Production Quality Assurance
PQA	Program Quality Acceptance (SPST)
PQA	Project Quality Assurance
PQA	Protected Queue Area [*Computer science*] (BUR)
PQAA	Province of Quebec Association of Architects [*1890, OAQ from 1974*] [*Canada*] (NGC)
PQAD	Plant Quality Assurance Director [*Nuclear energy*] (NRCH)
PQAE	Program Quality Assurance Engineer (ACAE)
PQAI	Procurement Quality Assurance Instruction
PQAM	Project Quality Assurance Manager [*Nuclear energy*] (NRCH)
PQAM	Purchaser Quality Assurance Manager (ACAE)
PQANSW	Paraplegic and Quadriplegic Association of New South Wales [*Australia*]
PQAP	Planned Quality Assurance Program [*Navy*]
PQAP	Procurement Quality Assurance Program [*DoD*]
PQAQ	Paraplegic and Quadriplegic Association of Queensland [*Australia*]
PQAR	Petroleum Quality Assurance Representative
PQAR	Purchasers Quality Assurance Representative (SAUS)
PQAS	Program Quality Assurance System (SAUS)
PQASA	Paraplegic and Quadriplegic Association of South Australia
PQAV	Paraplegic and Quadriplegic Association of Victoria [*Australia*]
PQAWA	Paraplegic and Quadriplegic Association of Western Australia
PQB	Quebecor CI'A' [*AMEX symbol*] (TTSB)
PQB	Quebecor, Inc. [*AMEX symbol*] (SPSG)
PQC	Chieftain Airways PLC [*British*] [*ICAO designator*] (FAAC)
PQC	Paul Quinn College, Waco, TX [*OCLC symbol*] (OCLC)
PQC	Phuquoc [*South Vietnam*] [*Airport symbol*] (AD)
PQC	Poor-Quality Cost (SAUS)
PQC	Precision Quartz Crystal
PQC	Premium Quality Control (SAUS)
PQC	Procurement Quality Control (IAA)
PQC	Production Quality Compiler (SAUS)
PQC	Production Quality Control
PQCC	Production Quality Compiler Compiler (SAUS)
PQCS	Process Quality Control System
PQD	Partido Quisqueyano Democrata [*Quisqueyan Democratic Party*] [*Dominican Republic*] [*Political party*] (PPW)
PQD	Percentage Quartile Deviation [*Statistics*]
PQD	Plant Quarantine Division (AD)
PQD	Predicted Quarterly Demand
PQD	Pyroelectric Quad Detector
PQDMB	Percentage Quartile Deviation Median Bias [*Statistics*]
PQE	Parents for Quality Education [*Defunct*] (EA)
PQE	Path Quality Evaluation (SAUS)
pqe	Post-Qualification Education (AD)
PQE	Post-Qualification Education (PDAA)
PQE	Precision-Quality-Experience (SAUS)
PQE	Principal Quality Engineers [*British*] (RDA)
PQE	Professional Qualification Examination [*National Security Agency*] (EDAC)
PQE	Project Quality Engineer
PQE	Project Quality Engineering
PQEP	Product Quality Evaluation Plan [*Military*] (AABC)
PQET	Print Quality Enhancement Technology [*IBM*] (PCM)
PQFP	Plastic Quad Flat Package [*Computer science*] (PCM)
PQGS	Propellant Quantity Gauge [*or Gauging*] System [*Apollo*] [*NASA*]
PQI	Personal Quality Improvement (ADWA)
PQI	Presque Isle [*Maine*] [*Airport symbol*] (OAG)
PQI	Presque Isle, ME [*Location identifier*] [*FAA*] (FAAL)
PQI	Print Quality Improvement [*Advanced photo system*]
PQI	Process Quality Indicator (ACAE)
PQI	Product Quality Improvement [*Program*] [*Chrysler Corp.*]
pqi	Professional Qualification Index (AD)
PQI	Professional Qualification Index (AFM)
PQI	Propellant Quantity Indicator (NASA)
PQIH	Plant Quarantine Inspection House (AD)
PQL	Practical Quantitation Level [*Environmental chemistry*] (ERG)
PQL	Practical Quantitation Limit [*Environmental chemistry*]
PQL	Prior Quarter Liability [*IRS*]
PQLI	Physical Quality of Life Index [*Overseas Development Council*]
PQM	Pilotless Drone Missile [*Department of Defense*]
PQM	Pilot Qualified in Model (NVT)
PQM	Post Quartermaster [*Marine Corps*]
PQM	Print Quality Monitor [*Computer science*] (IAA)
PQM	Pulse Quaternary Modulation
PQMC	Philadelphia Quartermaster Center [*Merged with Defense Clothing and Textile Supply Center*] [*Military*]
PQMD	Philadelphia Quartermaster Depot [*Military*]
PQMD	Propellant Quantity Measuring Device
PQMDO	Proposed Quality Material Development Objective (NATG)
PQMF	Parallel Quadrature Mirror Filter (PDAA)
PQMR	Preliminary Quantitative Material Requirements (MCD)
PQMS	Process Quality Measurement System [*Chemical process engineering*]
PQN	Consolidated Petroquin [*Vancouver Stock Exchange symbol*]
PQN	Pahaquarry [*New Jersey*] [*Seismograph station code, US Geological Survey*] (SEIS)
PQN	Pipestone, MN [*Location identifier*] [*FAA*] (FAAL)
PQN	Principal Quantum Number [*Atomic physics*]
PQNCX	PIMCO: Renaissance CI.C [*Mutual fund ticker symbol*] (SG)
PQNS	Protein, Quantity Not Sufficient [*Laboratory science*] (DAVI)
PQO	Phoenix, AZ [*Location identifier*] [*FAA*] (FAAL)
PQO	Principal Quality Officer (SAUS)
PQOL	Perceived Quality of Life [*Medicine*] (DMAA)
PQOS	Pre-Qualified Offsets Supplier
PQOSS	Pre-Qualified Offsets Supplier Status
PQP	Planetary Quarantine Plan [*NASA*]
PQP	Precision Quartz Products (TIMI)
PQP	Preliminary Qualification Procedures (SAUS)

PQP	Prequalification Prototype (KSC)
PQP	Priorities, Quality, Productivity (SAUS)
PQQ	Port Macquarie [Australia] [Airport symbol] (OAG)
PQQ	Pyrroloquinoline Quinone [Biochemistry]
PQQPRI	Preliminary Qualitative and Quantitative Personnel Requirements Information
PQQPRI	Provisional Qualitative and Quantitative Personnel Requirements Information [Army] (AABC)
PQR	Pantan Resources [Vancouver Stock Exchange symbol]
PQR	Performance Qualification Requirement
PQR	Personnel Qualification Record [Military] (INF)
PQR	Personnel Qualification Roster [Military] (AABC)
PQR	Prequalification Review (ACAE)
PQR	Procedure Qualification Record [Nuclear energy] (NRCH)
PQR	Productivity, Quality and Reliability (SAUS)
PQR	Program Quality Review (AD)
PQRI	Product Quality Research Initiative [Drug evalution]
PQRN	Project Quality Requirements Notice (TIMI)
pqrs	Productivity Increases, Quality Control, Robotization, and Savings [Japanese formula for economic success] (AD)
PQRST	Personal Questionnaire Rapid Scaling Technique [Personality development test] [Psychology]
PQRST	Product-Quality-Routing-Service-Timing [Industrial engineering]
PQS	Percentage Quota System (AD)
PQS	Personnel Qualification Standard (AD)
PQS	Personnel Qualification Standards [Military] (NVT)
PQS	Pilot Station [Alaska] [Airport symbol] (OAG)
PQS	Production Quotation Support
PQS	Product Quality System (TIMI)
PQS	Product Quotient Storage (SAUS)
PQS	Progressive Qualification Scheme [British]
PQS	Promotion Qualification Score [Military]
PQSF	Preparative Quencher Stopped Flow [Spectroscopy]
PQSI	Product Quality System for Inspection (TIMI)
PQST	Product Quality System for Test (TIMI)
PQT	Parquet Resources, Inc. [Toronto Stock Exchange symbol]
PQT	PC Quote [AMEX symbol] (TTSB)
PQT	PC Quote, Inc. [AMEX symbol] (SAG)
PQT	Performance Qualification Test (MCD)
PQT	Polyquinazolotriazole [Organic chemistry]
PQT	Preliminary Qualification Test (MCD)
PQT	Production Qualification and Testing
PQT	Production Qualification Test (SAUS)
PQT	Production Qualification Testing
PQT	Production Quality Test (SAUS)
PQT	Professional Qualification Test [of the National Security Agency]
PQT	Prototype Qualification Test
PQT	Prototype Qualification Testing (RDA)
PQT & E	Production Qualification Test and Evaluation
PQT-C	Prototype Qualification Test - Contractor (MCD)
PQT-G	Prototype Qualification Test - Government (MCD)
PQT/LOT	Production Qualification Test / Limited Operational Test
PQTP	Prototype Qualification Test Plan (SAUS)
PQT-SE	Prototype Qualification Test - Service Evaluation (MCD)
PQu	Polycyclic Quinone (SAUS)
PQU	Salisbury, MD [Location identifier] [FAA] (FAAL)
PQUA	Preliminary Quantitative Usage Analysis [Environmental science] (EPAT)
PQUE	Petroquest Energy [Formerly, Optima Petroleum] [NASDAQ symbol]
PQUE	Print Queue Processor [Computer science]
PQV	Procurement Quality Verification (SAUS)
PQV	Program Quality Verification (SAUS)
PQW	Placita de Quo Warranto, Record Commission [England] [A publication] (DLA)
PQX	Physically Qualified Except
PQZ	Premium Quality Zinc
PR	Abbott Laboratories [Research code symbol]
PR	Aircrew Survival Equipmentman [Navy rating]
PR	Deputy Chief of Staff, Requirements and Programs (SAUS)
PR	Directorate of Programs and Resources (SAUS)
PR	Pacific Reporter [A publication] (DLA)
PR	Pacing Response (SAUS)
PR	Packet Radio (SAUS)
PR	Packet Rate (SAUS)
P(R)	Packet (Receive)
PR	Page Reader (SAUS)
PRST	Painter (ADA)
pr	Pair (AD)
PR	Pair (KSC)
PR	Pakistan Railways (DCTA)
PR	Panama Red [Variety of marijuana]
Pr	Panama-Red Marijuana (AD)
PR	Panel Receptacle
PR	Pangenesis Related [Protein chemistry]
PR	Panthere Rose [France] [An association] [Defunct] (EAIO)
pr	Paper (WDAA)
PR	Paper Tape Reader
PR	Papertape Reader (SAUS)
PR	Parachute Rigger [Navy] (KSC)
PR	Paradise Regained [A publication] (AD)
PR	Parallax and Refraction
Pr	Parana (AD)
pr	Parcel Receipt (AD)
PR	Parcel Receipt [Shipping]
PR	Parental Recommendation [Movie rating] (CDAI)

PR	Parents Rights (EA)
PR	Parish Register
P+R	Park and Ride (SAUS)
PR	Park Ranger (AD)
PR	Parliamentary Report [British]
PR	Parliamentary Returns (SAUS)
PR	Parrott Rifle
PR	Partial (WEAT)
PR	Partial Reflector (SAUS)
PR	Partial Reinforcement (DIPS)
PR	Partial Remission [Medicine]
PR	Partial Responder (SAUS)
PR	Partial Response [Medicine] (DAVI)
PR	Partial Reward (DIPS)
PR	Partido Radical [Radical Party] [Spain] [Political party] (PPE)
PR	Partido Radical [Radical Party] [Chile] [Political party]
PR	Partido Reformista [Reformist Party] [Dominican Republic] [Political party] (PPW)
PR	Partido Republicano [Republican Party] [Ecuador] [Political party] (EY)
PR	Partido Republicano [Republican Party] [Panama] [Political party] (EY)
PR	Partido Revolucionario [Revolutionary Party] [Guatemala] [Political party] (PPW)
PR	Partido Riojano [Spain] [Political party] (EY)
PR	Parti Republicain [Republican Party] [Reunion] [Political party] (EY)
PR	Parti Republicain [Republican Party] [New Caledonia] [Political party] (FEA)
PR	Parti Republicain [Republican Party] [Martinique] [Political party] (PPW)
PR	Parti Republicain [Republican Party] [France] [Political party] (PPW)
PR	Partisan Review [A publication] (BRI)
PR	Partito Radicale [Radical Party] [Founded, 1955] [Italy] [Political party] (PPE)
PR	Party of Reunification (SAUS)
PR	Party Raayat [Leftist organization in Singapore]
PR	Passengers' Risk (ROG)
PR	Passive Ranging [Military] (LAIN)
PR	Past in Review [Later, PIR] (EA)
PR	Pastor
PR	Pathogenesis Related [Biology]
PR	Path Replacement (SAUS)
PR	Patient Relations (DAVI)
PR	Patria Roja [Red Fatherland] [Peru] (PD)
PR	Patrol Report (SAUS)
PR	Patrol Vessel, River Gunboat [Navy symbol]
PR	Pattern Recognition (BUR)
PR	Pattern Recognizer (SAUS)
PR	Payload Recorder (SAUS)
PR	Payment Received (SAUS)
pr	Payroll (AD)
PR	Payroll
PR	Peer Review
PR	Peking Review [A publication] (AD)
PR	Pelvic Rock [Orthopedics] (DAVI)
PR	Peng-Robinson [Equation of state]
PR	Penicillium roqueforti [Toxin] [Medicine]
P-R	Pennsylvania-Reading [Seashore Lines] (AD)
PR	Pennsylvania Reports (Penrose and Watts) [A publication] (DLA)
PR	Penny Resistance (EA)
PR	Pen Record (SAA)
PR	Pentium Rating (SAUS)
PR	Per
PR	Percentage Rates
pr	Percentile Rank (AD)
PR	Percentile Rank
PR	Percent Recovery [Plant pathology]
PR	Perforation Rate (SAUS)
PR	Performance Rating (OICC)
PR	Performance Ratio (AAG)
PR	Performance Report (AFM)
PR	Performance Requirement
PR	Perfusion Rate [Cardiology] (DAVI)
PR	Periodic Report (IAA)
PR	Periodic Reversal (IAA)
PR	Periodic Review [Social Security Administration] (DHP)
pr	Peripheral Resistance (AD)
PR	Peripheral Resistance [Medicine]
PR	Peripheral rheumatism [Medicine] (DB)
PR	Perirenal [Nephrology]
PR	Permanens Rector [Permanent Rector]
PR	Permanent Reactor (SAUS)
PR	Permanent Rector (SAUS)
PR	Permeance (IAA)
PR	Permissive Reassignment [Air Force] (AFM)
PR	Per Price [Business term]
PR	Per Recipient (SAUS)
PR	Per Rectum [Medicine]
pr	Per Rectum [By the Rectum] [Latin] (AD)
PR	Pershing Rifles [Honorary military organization]
PR	Persistency Rater [LIMRA]
PR	Personality Record [Psychological testing]
PR	Personnel Request (TIMI)
PR	Personnel Resources (EA)
PR	Person Reporting (GOBB)

PR	Pesikta Rabbati (BJA)
PR	Pesticide Registration [Environmental Protection Agency]
PR	Pesticide Regulation Notice (SAUS)
PR	Pharmaceutical Representative (SAUS)
PR	Phase Resolved (SAUS)
PR	Phenol Red
PR	Philadelphia Reports [Pennsylvania] [A publication] (DLA)
PR	Philanthropic Roundtable (EA)
PR	Philippine Airlines [ICAO designator] (AD)
PR	Philippine Airlines, Inc. (SAUS)
PR	Philippine Island Reports [A publication] (DLA)
P-R	Philips Roxane [Commercial firm] (DAVI)
PR	Phosphate Rock [Petrology]
PR	Phosphorylase-Rupturing [Biochemistry]
PR	Photographic Reconnaissance [Military] (MCD)
PR	Photographic Recorder
PR	Photoreacting [or Photoreactivation] [Biochemistry]
PR	Photo Reconnaissance [ICAO designator] (FAAC)
PR	Photorecorder
PR	Photo Reflectance (SAUS)
PR	Photorefractive [Optics]
PR	Photoresist
P/R	Photosynthesis/Respiration [Biochemistry]
PR	Phrasal Representation (SAUS)
PR	Physical Record [Computer science]
PR	Physican Reviewer (MEDA)
Pr	Piaster (SAUS)
PR	Picture Ratio (IAA)
PR	Piezo Resistive [Automotive electronics]
PR	Piezoresistive (SAUS)
PR	Pilot Rating
PR	Pinar del Rio (AD)
PR	Pinch Runner [Baseball]
PR	Pineal Recess [Neuroanatomy]
PR	Pipe Rail (AAG)
PR	Pipe Rolls (SAUS)
PR	Pitch Ratio
P/R	Pitch/Roll (MCD)
PR	Pitting Rate (SAUS)
PR	Pittsburgh Reports [1853-73] [Pennsylvania] [A publication] (DLA)
PR	Pityriasis [Dermatology]
PR	Pityriasis Rosea [Dermatology] (MAE)
PR	Planetary RADAR [Equipment box]
P/R	Planned Requirements (DNAB)
PR	Planning Reference
PR	Plant Recovery [Nuclear energy] (NRCH)
PR	Plant Report
PR	Please Return
PR	Plotting and RADAR
PR	Ply Rating [Tires] (NATG)
PR	Plyrating-prismary Radar (SAUS)
PR	Pneumatic Retinopathy [Ophthalmology]
PR	Pocket Radio (SAUS)
PR	Point Resistance (SAUS)
PR	Polarization Ratio (SAUS)
PR	Polarized Relay (IAA)
PR	Policy Review (MCD)
PR	Polish Register [Polish ship classification society] (DS)
PR	Polish Register Classification Society (SAUS)
PR	Polskie Radio [Polish Radio] (AD)
PR	Polyarthrite Rheumatisme (SAUS)
PR	Ponceau Red [Biological stain]
PR	Poor Rate [British] (ROG)
PR	Populus Romanus [The Roman People] [Latin]
PR	Port Risks (MARI)
PR	Position Record (NASA)
PR	Position Register (IAA)
PR	Position Report [Air Force]
PR	Positive Real (SAUS)
PR	Postal Regulations (DLA)
PR	Poste Recommandee [Registered Post]
PR	Posterior Repair [Gynecology] (DAVI)
PR	Posterior Ridge
PR	Posterior Right (SAUS)
PR	Posterior Root [Medicine] (DMAA)
PR	Post Request
PR	Post-Resuscitation
PR	Potency Ratio [Medicine] (DMAA)
PR	Pounder [Gun]
PR	Pour Remercier [To Express Thanks] [French]
PR	Power Range [Nuclear energy] (NRCH)
PR	Power Rating
PR	Power Ratio
PR	Power Return
Pr	Praca [Plaza] [Portuguese] (AD)
Pr	Practice Reports [Various jurisdictions] [A publication] (DLA)
Pr	Prairie (AD)
PR	Prairie (MCD)
Pr	Prandtl Number [IUPAC]
PR	Praseodymium
Pr	Praseodymium [Chemical element]
PR	Prayer
PR	Preacher
Pr	Preamble (ILCA)
Pr	Precancelled [Philately]

PR	Precedence Rating [Military] (AFIT)
PR	Precipitation Radar (EOSA)
PR	Preconstruction Requirement [Environmental Protection Agency]
PR	Predicted Rate [Medicine] (DAVI)
Pr	Prednisone [Also, P, PDN, Pred, Pro] [Endocrinology] [Antineoplastic drug]
Pr	Preemphasis (SAUS)
PR	Preferred [Stock exchange term] (SPSG)
pr	Preferred (WDAA)
PR	Prefix [Indicating a private radiotelegram] (BUR)
PR	Prefix Resolution (SAUS)
PR	Preflight
PR	Pregnancy Rate [Medicine]
PR	Preliminary Report
PR	Preliminary Review [Army]
PR	Premature Release [Telecommunications] (TEL)
PR	Prepare (VLIE)
PR	Prepare Reply
PR	Preposition
PR	Pre-Raphaelite
Pr	Presbyopia (AD)
PR	Presbyopia [Ophthalmology]
Pr	Presbyter [Elder] [Latin] (AD)
PR	Presbyterian (ROG)
pr	Present (SHCU)
PR	Present
Pr	Presentation [Gynecology]
PR	Presidency (ROG)
Pr	Press (AD)
pr	Press (RION)
PR	Pressoreceptor [Laboratory science] (DAVI)
PR	Press Release
PR	Press Revise (DGA)
PR	Pressure
PR	Pressure Ratio
PR	Pressure Recorder (NRCH)
PR	Pressure Regulation
PR	Pressure Regulator (KSC)
PR	Preston [Postcode] (ODBW)
PR	Prevention (DAVI)
pr	Price (ODBW)
PR	Price [Online database field identifier]
PR	Price Communications [AMEX symbol] (TTSB)
PR	Price Communications Corp. [AMEX symbol] (SAG)
PR	Price Received
PR	Price Redetermination [Economics]
PR	Price Reduced [of a book]
Pr	Price's English Exchequer Reports [1814-24] [A publication] (DLA)
Pr	Priest (WDAA)
PR	Priest
PR	Primary (NASA)
PR	Primary RADAR (DA)
PR	Primary Rate (SAUS)
PR	Primary Reference [Automobile fuel] (DICI)
PR	Primary Runout (SAUS)
PR	Primary Zone [Environmental science] (COE)
PR	Primitive
Pr	Prince (WDAA)
PR	Prince
PR	Prince Regent (ROG)
PR	Princess Royal's [Military unit] [British]
Pr	Principal
PR	Principal Register [Computer science]
PR	Print [or Printed] (NTCM)
pr	Print (VRA)
PR	Printed [or Printer]
PR	Printer [Computer science] (IAA)
PR	Printing Reperforator (SAUS)
PR	Printing Request (MCD)
PR	Print Register (IAA)
PR	Print Restore [Computer science] (MHDB)
Pr	Prior (SG)
PR	Prior
PR	Priority Country (SAUS)
PR	Priority Regulation
PR	Priority Resolver
PR	Priority Routine (SAUS)
PR	Priory
PR	Prism
pr	Prismatic Tank [Liquid gas carriers]
PR	Prison Riot (WDAA)
Pr	Pristane [Organic chemistry]
pr	Private (DLA)
PR	Private Road [Maps and charts] [British] (ROG)
PR	Prize Ring [Boxing]
PR	Probabilistic Risk Assessment [Computer-based technique for accident prediction]
PR	Probability
Pr	Probable
pr	Probated (GEAB)
PR	Probate Record (SAUS)
PR	Probate Reports [A publication] (DLA)
Pr	Problemata [of Aristotle] [Classical studies] (OCD)
PR	Problem Report (MCD)
Pr	Procarbazine [Also, P, PC, PCB] [Antineoplastic drug]

PR................	Procedural Regulations [*Civil Aeronautics Board*]	
PR................	Procedures Review [*DoD*]	
PR................	Proceedings (IAA)	
PR................	Processor [*Computer science*] (IAA)	
PR................	Process-Reactive [*Scale*] [*Psychometrics*]	
PR................	Proctologist	
Pr................	Proctoscopy (AD)	
PR................	Proctosigmoidoscopy [*Medicine*] (AD)	
PR................	Procurement Regulation [*Military*]	
PR................	Procurement Request [*or Requisition*]	
PR................	Procurement Requisition (SAUS)	
PR................	Producing Region [*Agriculture*]	
PR................	Production Rate	
PR................	Production Requirements [*Military*] (AFIT)	
PR................	Production Review [*Automotive project management*]	
P/R...............	Productivity/Respiration [*Physiology*]	
PR................	Product Register (SAUS)	
PR................	Product-Remainder (SAUS)	
PR................	Product Removal (ABAC)	
PR................	Profile (DAVI)	
PR................	Profile Reliability (MCD)	
PR................	Profit Rate (WGA)	
P-R...............	Progesterone Receptor [*Endocrinology*]	
PR................	Programmed Requirement	
PR................	Programming [*Computer science*] (IAA)	
PR................	Programming Requirement (SAUS)	
PR................	Program Register [*Computer science*] (BUR)	
PR................	Program Repeat (SAUS)	
PR................	Program Requirements (KSC)	
PR................	Program Routine (SAUS)	
PR................	Progressive Resistance	
PR................	Progress Record (SAUS)	
PR................	Progress Report	
PR................	Project Release (EA)	
PR................	Project Report	
PR................	Project Rover (SAA)	
PR................	Prolactin [*Also, LTH, PRL*] [*Endocrinology*]	
PR................	Prolonged-Release [*Pharmacy*]	
Pr................	Promenade (DD)	
Pr................	Promille (SAUS)	
PR................	Promotion Request (SAUS)	
PR................	Pronominal [*Grammar*] (ROG)	
PR................	Pronoun	
PR................	Pronounced	
Pr................	Proof [*Numismatic term*]	
PR................	Propagating Rift [*Geology*]	
PR................	Proper	
PR................	Property	
PR................	Proportional Representation [*in legislatures, etc.*]	
PR................	Proposed Regulation	
PR................	Proposed Request	
PR................	Proposed Rule [*Federal government*] (GFGA)	
PR................	Propulsion Range	
Pr................	Propyl [*Organic chemistry*]	
PR................	Pro Rata	
pr................	Prose	
PR................	Prosthetic-Group Removing [*Enzyme*] [*Biochemistry*] (DAVI)	
PR................	Prosthion [*Medicine*] (MAE)	
PR................	Protease [*Chemistry*]	
PR................	Protective Reaction [*Bombing raid*] [*Vietnam*]	
PR................	Protectorate Regiment [*British military*] (DMA)	
PR................	Protein (MAE)	
PR................	Protestant (ADA)	
PR................	Prothrombinratio (SAUS)	
PR................	Prototype	
PR................	Proved	
PR................	Provencal [*Language, etc.*]	
PR................	Proverb	
Pr................	Proverbs [*Old Testament book*] (BJA)	
PR................	Provisional Release (SAUS)	
PR................	Provost (WDAA)	
Pr................	Proximal	
PR................	Pseudo Random (SAUS)	
PR................	Pseudorandom	
PR................	Pseudoresidual	
PR................	Psychedelic Review [*A publication*]	
PR................	Psychiatric Record (AD)	
PR................	Publicity Release (NTCM)	
pr................	Public Relations (AD)	
PR................	Public Relations	
PR................	Public Responsibility	
PR................	Puerto Rican [*Derogatory term*]	
PR................	Puerto Rico [*ANSI two-letter standard code*] (CNC)	
PR................	Puerto Rico [*Postal code*]	
pr................	Puerto Rico [*IYRU nationality code*] [*MARC country of publication code*] [*Library of Congress*] (LCCP)	
PR................	Puerto Rico Supreme Court Reports [*A publication*] (DLA)	
PR................	Pulmonic Regurgitation [*Cardiology*] (DAVI)	
PR................	Pulsed Reactor (SAUS)	
PR................	Pulse Rate	
PR................	Pulse Ratio (IEEE)	
PR................	Pulse Regeneration (or Regenerator) (SAUS)	
PR................	Pulse Regenerator	
PR................	Punching Rate (SAUS)	
PR................	Punch Routine (SAUS)	
PR................	Punctum Remotum [*Far Point*] [*Latin*]	
pr................	Punctum Remotum [*Remote Point*] [*Latin*] (AD)	
PR................	Punjab Record [*India*] [*A publication*] (DLA)	
PR................	Purchase Request	
PR................	Purchase Requirement (SAUS)	
PR................	Purchase Requisition	
PR................	Pure Rubber (SAUS)	
PR................	Purple (AAG)	
pR................	Purplish Red (AD)	
PR................	Purplish Red	
PR................	Pyke's Reports [*Canada*] [*A publication*] (DLA)	
PR................	Pyramidal Response (DB)	
pr................	Pyrite [*CIPW classification*] [*Geology*]	
PR................	Pyrogallol Red [*Also, PGR*] [*An indicator*] [*Chemistry*]	
PR................	Pyrolytic Release	
PR+..............	Reactor Pressure Plus (NRCH)	
PR................	Reading Public Library, Reading, PA [*Library symbol*] [*Library of Congress*] (LCLS)	
PR................	River Gunboat [*Navy symbol*]	
PR................	Software-Parameter Specification (SAUS)	
PR................	Upper Canada Practice Reports [*1850-1900*] [*Ontario*] [*A publication*] (DLA)	
PR1..............	Parachute Rigger, First Class [*Navy*]	
PR2..............	Parachute Rigger, Second Class [*Navy*]	
PR3..............	Parachute Rigger, Third Class [*Navy*]	
PRA	Albright College, Reading, PA [*Library symbol*] [*Library of Congress*] (LCLS)	
PRA	Division of Policy Research and Analysis [*National Science Foundation*]	
PRA	Page Replacement Algorithm [*Computer science*] (MHDI)	
PRA	Paint Research Association [*British*]	
PRA	Paperwork Reduction Act (GFGA)	
PRA	Parabolic Reflector Aerial (or Antenna) (SAUS)	
PRA	Parabolic Reflector Antenna	
PRA	Parana [*Argentina*] [*Airport symbol*] (OAG)	
PRA	Parool (SAUS)	
PRA	Participant Record Advice	
PRA	Partido Revolucionario Autentico [*Authentic Revolutionary Party*] [*Bolivia*] [*Political party*] (PPW)	
PRA	Parti du Regroupement Africain [*African Regroupment Party*] [*Niger*] [*Political party*] (PD)	
PRA	Parti du Regroupement Africain [*African Regroupment Party*] [*Banned, 1974*] [*Burkina Faso*] [*Political party*]	
PRA	Patent-Rights-Acquisition (SAUS)	
PRA	Paymaster Rear Admiral (SAUS)	
PRA	Paymaster-Rear-Admiral [*Navy*] [*British*]	
PRA	Pay Readjustment Act [*1942*]	
PRA	Pay Record Access	
pra	Payroll Audit (AD)	
PRA	Payroll Auditor [*Insurance*]	
PRA	Peace Research Abstracts (NITA)	
PRA	Peak Recording Accelerograph [*Accelerometer*] (IEEE)	
PRA	Pendulous Reference Axis [*Accelerometer*] (IEEE)	
PRA	Peoples Republic of Albania (SAUS)	
PRA	Peoples Republic of Angola (SAUS)	
PRA	People's Revolutionary Army [*Grenada*]	
PRA	Permanent Restricted Area [*Former USSR*] (NATG)	
PRA	Personal Rights Association [*British*] (BI)	
PRA	Personnel Research Activity [*Later, NPTRL*] [*Navy*]	
PRA	Personnel Research Association (SAUS)	
PRA	Petrol Retailers' Association [*British*]	
PRA	Pharmacy Restructuring Authority [*Australia*]	
PRA	Phosphoribosylamin (SAUS)	
PRA	Phosphoribosylamine	
PRA	Photon Research Associates (ACAE)	
PRA	Pilots Rights Association (EA)	
PRA	Pitch and Roll Attitude (IAA)	
PRA	Planetary Radio Astronomy	
PRA	Planned Regulatory Action [*Federal government*] (GFGA)	
PRA	Planned Restricted Availability [*Military*] (NVT)	
pra	Plasma Renin Activity [*Medicine*] (AD)	
PRA	Plasma Renin Activity [*Hematology*]	
PRA	Plutonium Recycle Acid [*Nuclear energy*] (NRCH)	
PRA	Polar Regions Award (IAA)	
PRA	Policy Research and Analysis	
PRA	Popular Resistance Army (SAUS)	
PRA	Popular Rotorcraft Association (EA)	
PRA	Port Rashid Authority (SAUS)	
PRA	Position Resolution Alarm (TIMI)	
PRA	Postal Reorganization Act (AD)	
PRA	Postal Reorganization Act of 1970 (AAGC)	
PRA	Postrenal Azotemia [*Medicine*] (MELL)	
PRA	Potencia Radiada Aparente (SAUS)	
PRA	Praha [*Prague*] [*Czechoslovakia*] [*Seismograph station code, US Geological Survey*] (SEIS)	
PRA	Prairiefire Rural Action (EA)	
PRA	Prairie Rail Authority	
pra	Prakrit [*MARC language code*] [*Library of Congress*] (LCCP)	
PRA	Precession Axis (SAUS)	
PRA	Precision Axis (KSC)	
PRA	Precision Radar Approach (PIPO)	
PRA	Preliminary Reserve Analysis (SAUS)	
PRA	Premium Audit	
PRA	Prerefund Audit [*IRS*]	
PRA	Pre-Retirement Association [*British*] (DI)	

PRA	President of the Royal Academy [*British*]
PRA	President's Re-Employment Agreement [*New Deal*]
PRA	Primary Area (SAUS)
PRA	Primary Rate Access (VLIE)
PRA	Primary Reviewing Authority
PRA	Prime Responsible Authority (IAA)
PRA	Print Alphamerically (SAUS)
pra	Print Alphanumerically (AD)
PRA	Print Alphanumerically [*Computer science*] (MDG)
PRA	Probabilistic Risk Assessment [*Computer-based technique for accident prediction*]
pra	Probation and Rehabilitation of Airmen (AD)
PRA	Probation and Rehabilitation of Airmen [*Air Force*] (AFM)
PRA	Production Reader Assembly (KSC)
PRA	Production Readiness Assessment [*Army*]
PRA	Progesterone Receptor Assay [*Clinical chemistry*]
PRA	Program Reader Assembly [*Computer science*]
pra	Progressive Retinal Atrophy [*Medicine*] (AD)
PRA	Projected Requisition Authority [*Army*] (AABC)
PRA	Prompt Radiation Analysis (MCD)
PRA	Propionic Acid [*Organic chemistry*]
PRA	Prospair Ltd. [*British*] [*ICAO designator*] (FAAC)
PRA	Proust Research Association (EA)
PRA	Psoriasis Research Association (EA)
PRA	Psychiatric Rehabilitation Association [*British*]
PRA	Psychological Research Associates (or Association) (SAUS)
PRA	Public Resources Association [*Defunct*] (EA)
PRA	Public Roads Administration
PRA	Puerto Rico Area Office [*AEC*]
PRA	Puerto Rico Association (AD)
PRA	Purchase and Resale Agreement [*Canada*] (BARN)
PRA	US 1869 Pictorial Research Associates (EA)
PRAA	Airman Apprentice, Parachute Rigger, Striker [*Navy rating*]
PRAAD	Photo-Resist Apply and Dry (SAUS)
PRAB	Prab Robots, Inc. (SAUS)
Prac	Practical (DLA)
PRAC	Practice (AABC)
prac	Practice (AD)
Prac	Practise (SAUS)
PRAC	Pressure Ratio Acceleration Control [*Gas turbine engine*]
PRAC	Productivity Technologies Corp. [*NASDAQ symbol*] (SAG)
PRAC	Program Resource Advisory Committee [*TRADOC*] (MCD)
PRAC	Public Relations Advisory Committee
PRACA	Problem Reporting and Corrective Action (MCD)
PRACA	Puerto Rican Association for Community Affairs (EA)
Prac Act	Practice Act [*A publication*] (DLA)
Prac Appr Pat TM and Copyright	Practical Approach to Patents, Trademarks and Copyrights (SAUS)
Pra Cas	Prater's Cases on Conflict of Laws [*A publication*] (DLA)
PRACDA	Polarimetric Radar Control and Data Aquisition (SAUS)
PRACE	Photo-Resist Align, Contact and Expose (SAUS)
PRaCHS	Archbishop Carroll High School, Radnor, PA [*Library symbol*] [*Library of Congress*] (LCLS)
PRACL	Page Replacement Algorithm and Control Logic (SAUS)
pracl	Page-Replacement Algorithm and Control Logic (AD)
PRACL	Page-Replacement Algorithm and Control Logic [*Computer science*]
PRACL	Practical
Prac Litig	Practical Litigation (SAUS)
PRACOS	Praxis-Computer-System (SAUS)
PRACSA	Public Remote Access Computer Standards Association (SAUS)
PRACSATS	Practical Satellites
Pract	Practical (DIAR)
PRACT	Practical (ROG)
PRACT	Practice [*Legal shorthand*] (LWAP)
PRAC-T	Practice Tracer (SAUS)
pract	Practitioner (AD)
PRACT	Practitioner
PRACT	Practolol (DB)
Pract Eng	Practical Energy (SAUS)
Pract Law	Practical Lawyer [*A publication*] (DLA)
Pract Med	Practice of Medicine (SAUS)
PRACTNR	Practitioner
Pract Pharm	Practical Pharmacy (SAUS)
Pract Reg	Practical Register in the Common Pleas [*England*] [*A publication*] (DLA)
PRAD	Pitch Radio Adjustment Device
PRAD	Pitch Ratio Adjust Device (MCD)
PRADA	Partido Revolucionario Dominicano Autentico [*Dominican Republic*] [*Political party*]
Pr Adm Dig	Pritchard's Admiralty Digest [*3rd ed.*] [*1887*] [*A publication*] (DLA)
PRADO	Public Radio Association of Development Officers (SAUS)
PRADOR	PRF [*Pulse Repetition Frequency*] Ranging Doppler RADAR
PRADOR	Pulse repetition frequency Ranging Doppler Radar (SAUS)
PRADS	Parachute Retrorocket Airdrop System (MCD)
Prad Wireless	Practical Wireless (SAUS)
praed	praedicative (SAUS)
praef	Praefatio [*Latin*] (OCD)
Praeger	Frederick A. Praeger (AD)
Praegtzr	Praegitzer Industries, Inc. [*Associated Press*] (SAG)
Praem	De Praemiis et Poenis [*of Philo*] (BJA)
praen	Praenomen (AD)
Praep Evang	Praeparatio Evangelica [*of Eusebius*] [*Classical studies*] (OCD)
Praepo	Praepositus [*Deceased, 1509*] [*Authority cited in pre-1607 legal work*] (DSA)
praes	Praesens [*Present Tense*] [*Latin*]
praet	Praeteritum [*Past Tense*] [*Latin*]
PRAF	Passenger-Reserved Air Freight
PRAG	Pensions Research Accountants Group (MHDB)
PRAG	Pragma Bio-Tech, Inc. (SAUS)
prag	Pragmatic (AD)
Prag	Pragmatism (SAUS)
pragma	Processing Routines Aided by Graphics for Manipulation of Arrays (AD)
PRAGMA	Processing Routines Aided by Graphics for Manipulation of Arrays (PDAA)
Prag Micro	Pragmatics Microfiche (SAUS)
Pra H & W	Prater on Husband and Wife [*2nd ed.*] [*1836*] [*A publication*] (DLA)
PrA-HPA	Protein A Hemolytic Plaque Assay [*Medicine*] (DMAA)
PRAI	Peer Review Analysis (EFIS)
PRAI	Phosphoribosyl Anthranilate Isomerase
PRAI	Planning Research and Action Institute (SAUS)
PRAI	Pre-Reading Assessment Inventory [*Education*] (EDAC)
PRAI	Project Research Applied in Industry (SAUS)
PRAIC	President of the Royal Architectural Institute of Canada (NGC)
PRAICO	Puerto Rican American Insurance Co. (AD)
PR Aircraft	Photographic Reconnaissance Aircraft (SAUS)
PRAIRE	Polarization Radar Illinois Rainfall Experiments (SAUS)
PRAIREO	Prairie Oil Royalties Co. Ltd. (SAUS)
PRAIRIE	Prairie [*Commonly used*] (OPSA)
Prairie View A&M U	Prairie View Agricultural and Mechanical University (GAGS)
PRAIS	Passive Ranging Interferometer Sensor
prais	Passive-Ranging Interferometer Sensor (AD)
PRAIS	Pesticide Residue Analysis Information Service [*British*]
PRAISE	Pilot Records of Achievement in Schools Evaluation (AIE)
PRAISE	Prospective Randomized Amlodipine Survival Evaluation [*Medicine*] (DMAA)
Prakruti Utkal Unir J Sci	Prakruti Utkal University Journal of Science (SAUS)
pral	Principal [*Principal*] [*Spanish*] (AD)
Pr Alc	Propyl Alcohol (SAUS)
PRAM	Packet Random Access Memory (SAUS)
PRAM	Page Replacement Analysis Models (SAUS)
PRAM	Parallel Random Access Machine [*Computer science*]
PRAM	Parameter Random Access Memory (ADWA)
PRAM	Parameter Random-Access Memory [*Computer science*] (DCDG)
pram	Perambulator (AD)
PRAM	Perambulator [*British*]
PRAM	Permanent Random-Access Memory (SAUS)
PRAM	Poseidon Random Access Memory [*Missiles*]
Pram	Poseidon Random-Access Memory (AD)
Pram	Prambanam (VRA)
PRAM	Preliminary Repair Level Decision Analysis Model (PDAA)
PRAM	Pre-Recorded Announcement and Boarding Music Reproducer
PRAM	Primary Report of Aircraft Mishap [*Army*] (DOMA)
PRAM	Processing Rate Analytic Model (SAUS)
PRAM	Productivitiy, Reliability, Availability and Maintainability (SAUS)
PRAM	Productivity, Reliability and Maintainability (SAUS)
pram	Productivity, Reliability, Availability, and Maintainability (AD)
PRAM	Productivity, Reliability, Availability, and Maintainability Office [*Air Force*]
PRAM	Product Reliability and Maintainability
PRAM	Programmable Amplifier (SAUS)
PRAM	Programmable Random Access Memory [*Computer science*] (IAA)
p/RAM	Programmable Random Analysis Method (SAUS)
PRAM	Programmes and Measures (SAUS)
PRAM	Program Requirements Analysis Method
PRAM	Propelled Ascent Mine
PRAM	Propelled Rapid Ascent Mine (MCD)
PRAM	Pseudorandom Access Memory [*Computer science*] (IAA)
PRAM	Rocket-Propelled Rising Mine (SAUS)
PRAMPO	Productivity, Reliability, Availability, and Maintenance Program Office [*Air Force*] (DOMA)
PRAMS	Paperwork Reduction Act Management System (SAUS)
PRAMS	Passenger Reservation and Manifesting System (SAUS)
PRAMS	Pregnancy Risk Assessment Monitoring System (SAUS)
PRAMS	Processing Asset Management System (WDAA)
PRAMS	Programmatic Risk Assessment Model System (SAUS)
PRAN	Airman, Parachute Rigger, Striker [*Navy*]
PRAN	Pre-Analysis (VLIE)
PRAN	Prefix Analysis (SAUS)
PRAN	Production Analyser (SAUS)
PRAN	Production Analyzer (IAA)
PRAND	Prandium [*Dinner*] [*Pharmacy*]
prand	Prandium [*dinner*] [*Latin*] (AD)
PR&C	Purchase Request and Commitment (SAUS)
PR & D	Personal Rest and Delay [*Air Force*] (AFM)
PR & D	Power, Rodwell, and Drew's English Election Cases [*1847-56*] [*A publication*] (DLA)
PR&D	Process Research and Development (SAUS)
PR&D	Program Research and Development (SAUS)
PR & D	Public Research and Development
PR & D El Cas	Power, Rodwell, and Drew's English Election Cases [*A publication*] (DLA)
Pr & Div	Law Reports, Probate and Divorce [*England*] [*A publication*] (DLA)
PR & R	Professional Rights and Responsibilities
PR&R	Project Review and Reporting (ACAE)
PRANG	Projection Angle
PRANG	Puerto Rico Air National Guard
PRANS	Proportional Range Scheduling (SAUS)
PRAODP	Agricultural Research Organization. Preliminary Report (journ.) (SAUS)

PRAP .... Passive Radar-Augmented Projectile (SAUS)
PRAP .... Patient Resident Assessment Profile [*Geriatrics*]
PRAP .... Provincial/Regional Library Association Presidents [*Canada*]
PRAP .... Provisions of Following Reference Apply [*Army*] (AABC)
PRAP .... Pylos Regional Archaeological Project (SAUS)
PrAPhA .... Proceedings of the American Philological Association (SAUS)
PRAQ .... Playground and Recreation Association of Queensland [*Australia*]
PRAR .... Partido Revolucionario Autentico Rios [*Bolivia*] [*Political party*] (PPW)
PRAR .... Planetary Radio Astronomy Receiver (SAUS)
PRARE .... Precise Range and Range Rate Equipment (SAUS)
PRARE .... Precise Range and Range Rate Experiment (SAUS)
PRARE .... Precise Range and Range-Rate Experiment
PRARE .... Precision Range and Rate Equipment (SAUS)
PRARE .... Precision Range and Rate Experiment (SAUS)
PRAREE ...... Precise Range and Range Rate Equipment, Extended Version (SAUS)
PRAREE ...... Precise Range and Rate Equipment-Extended Version (EOSA)
PRARIE .... Prairie [*Commonly used*] (OPSA)
PRARS .... Pitch, Roll, Azimuth Reference System (NG)
PRAS .... Pacific Regional Advisory Service [*South Pacific Bureau for Economic Co-Operation*] (EY)
PRAS .... Particle Reactor Analysis Services (AAEL)
PRAS .... Pension and Retirement Annuity System
PRAS .... Prereduced, Anaerobically Sterilized [*Microbiology*]
PRAS .... President of the Royal Astronomical Society (SAUS)
PRAS .... Principle Research Areas (SAUS)
PRAS .... Pseudo-Renal Artery Syndrome [*Medicine*] (DMAA)
PRAS .... Pulsed Realistic Age-Structured [*Model for disease persitence*]
PRASD .... Personnel Research Activity, San Diego [*California*] [*Navy*]
PRASD3 .... Alabama. Agricultural Experiment Station. Progress Report Series (journ.) (SAUS)
PRAT .... Parliamentary Retiring Allowances Trust [*Australia*]
PRAT .... Platelet Radioactive Antiglobulin Test [*Hematology*] (DAVI)
PRAT .... Prattsburgh Railroad (AD)
PRAT .... Predicted Range Against Target [*Military*] (NVT)
PRAT .... Pressure-Retaining Amphipod Trap [*Deep-sea biology*]
PRAT .... Production Reliability Acceptance Test
PRAT .... Production Reliability Assurance Test (SAUS)
P RAT AET... Pro Ratione Aetatis [*According to Age*] [*Pharmacy*] (ROG)
p rat aet ..... Pro Ratione Aetatis [*In Proportion to Age*] [*Latin*] (AD)
P RAT AETAT... Pro Rata Aetatis [*According to Age*] [*Pharmacy*]
p rat aetat ... Pro Ratione Aetatis [*In Proportion to Age*] [*Latin*] (MAE)
PrattHtl .... Pratt Hotel Corp. [*Associated Press*] (SAG)
PratLm .... Pratt & Lambert United, Inc. [*Associated Press*] (SAG)
PRATRA ...... Philippines Relief and Trade Rebilitation Administration (AD)
PRATS .... Pesticides Regulatory Action Tracking System (EPAT)
Pratt............ Pratt's Contraband-of-War Cases [*A publication*] (DLA)
Pratt............ Pratt's Supplement to Bott's Poor Laws [*1833*] [*A publication*] (DLA)
Pratt BS .... Pratt's Law of Benefit Building Societies [*A publication*] (DLA)
Pratt Cont .... Pratt's Contraband-of-War Cases [*A publication*] (DLA)
Pratt Cts Req... Pratt's Statutes Establishing Courts of Request [*A publication*] (DLA)
Pratt Fr Soc... Pratt on Friendly Societies [*15th ed.*] [*1931*] [*A publication*] (DLA)
Pratt High.... Pratt and Mackenzie on Highways [*21st ed.*] [*1967*] [*A publication*] (DLA)
Pratt Inst ..... Pratt Institute (GAGS)
Pratt PL .... Pratt's Edition of Bott on the Poor Laws [*A publication*] (DLA)
Pratt Prop T... Pratt on the Property Tax Act [*A publication*] (DLA)
Pratt Sav B... Pratt on Savings Banks [*6th ed.*] [*1845*] [*A publication*] (DLA)
Pratt SL .... Pratt on Sea Lights [*2nd ed.*] [*1858*] [*A publication*] (DLA)
PRAUD9....... Agricultural Research Institute Ukiriguru. Progress Report (journ.) (SAUS)
PRAUS......... Programme de Recherche sur l'Amiante de l'Universite de Sherbrooke [*Asbestos Research Program*] [*University of Sherbrooke*] [*Quebec*] [*Information service or system*] (IID)
PRAV .... Planned Restricted Availability [*Navy*] (ANA)
PRAV .... Playground and Recreation Association of Victoria [*Australia*]
PRAVT .... Preentry-AV-tachycardia (SAUS)
PRAVT .... Pre-entry-AV-Tachykardie (SAUS)
PRAW .... Personnel Research Activity, Washington, DC [*Obsolete*] [*Navy*]
PRaW .... Wyeth Laboratories, Radnor, PA [*Library symbol*] [*Library of Congress*] (LCLS)
PRAWL .... Puerto Rican American Women's League
Prax............ Bowns Practice (or Precedents) in Chancery (journ.) (SAUS)
Prax............ Browns Practice or Precedents in Chance (SAUS)
Prax............ Brown's Practice (Praxis) [*or Precedents*] in Chancery [*A publication*] (DLA)
PRAX .... Praxis Pharmaceuticals, Inc. (SAUS)
Praxair........ Praxair, Inc. [*Associated Press*] (SAG)
Prax Can..... Praxis Almae Curiae Cancellariae (Brown) [*A publication*] (DLA)
PRAY .... Paul Revere Associated Yeoman (AD)
PRAZ .... Prazosin [*A vasodilator*]
PRB .... Basic Proline-Rich Protein (DMAA)
PRB .... Packet Receive Buffer [*Computer science*] (VLIE)
PRB .... Painters' Registration Board [*Western Australia*]
PRB .... Panel Review Board [*NASA*] (KSC)
PRB .... Parabola [*Mathematics*]
PRB .... Parachute Refurbishment Building [*NASA*] (NASA)
PRB .... Partial Roll-Back (SAUS)
PRB .... Partido de la Revolucion Boliviana [*Bolivian Revolutionary Party*] [*Political party*] (AD)
PRB .... Partido Republicano Brasileiro [*Brazil*] [*Political party*] (EY)
PRB .... Paso Robles [*California*] [*Airport symbol*] (AD)
PRB .... Paso Robles, CA [*Location identifier*] [*FAA*] (FAAL)
PRB .... Pay Review Body (SAUS)

PRB .... Pension Review Board [*Canada*]
PRB .... Pension Review Board Reports (SAUS)
PRB .... People's Republic of Benin (AD)
PRB .... Peoples Republic of Bulgaria (SAUS)
PRB .... Performance Review Board (ACAE)
PRB .... Personal Reaction Blank [*Psychology*] (DAVI)
PRB .... Personnel Reaction Blank [*Psychology*]
PRB .... Personnel Records Branch [*Army*] (AABC)
PRB .... Personnel Requirements Branch (MUGU)
PRB .... Personnel Research Branch [*Army*] (MCD)
PRB .... Personnel Review Board (AD)
PRB .... Physical Record Block (TIMI)
PRB .... Physiotherapists' Registration Board [*New South Wales, Australia*]
PRB .... Planned Requirements - Bureau Directed
PRB .... Plant Review Board [*Nuclear energy*] (NRCH)
PRB .... Podiatrists' Registration Board [*New South Wales, Australia*]
PRB .... Polar Research Board [*National Academy of Sciences*]
PRB .... Population Reference Bureau (EA)
PRB .... Post-Retirement Benefits (AAGC)
PRB .... Powder River Basin
PRB .... Pre-Raphaelite Brotherhood (WDAA)
PRB .... Press-Radio Bureau (NTCM)
prb .... Principal Borehole (AD)
PRB .... Private Radio Bureau [*FCC*] (NTCM)
PRB .... Probex Corp. [*AMEX symbol*] (SG)
PRB .... Problem Review Board (ARMP)
PRB .... Procedure Review Board [*Nuclear energy*] (NRCH)
PRB .... Procurement Review Board (MCD)
PRB .... Professional Registration Boards of the Northern Territory [*Australia*]
PRB .... Program Request Block (IAA)
PRB .... Program Request Buffer (SAUS)
PRB .... Program Review Board
PRB .... Project Review Board [*NASA*] (NASA)
PRB .... Prosthetics Research Board
PRB .... Proteus Air Systeme [*France*] [*ICAO designator*] (FAAC)
PRB .... Pseudo Random Binary (SAUS)
PRB .... Pseudo-Random Binary (AAEL)
PRB .... Psychopharmacology Research Branch (SAUS)
PRB .... Psychosurgery Review Board [*Victoria, Australia*]
PRB .... Public Roads Bureau
PRBA .... Portable Rechargeable Battery Association (NTPA)
PRBA .... Puerto Rican Bar Association (EA)
PRBA(AG).... Personnel Research Board of the Army, Adjutant General
PRBAL .... Previous Balance (VLIE)
PrBayA........ American Junior College of Puerto Rico, Bayamon, PR [*Library symbol*] [*Library of Congress*] (LCLS)
PrBayC........ Bayamon Central University, Bayamon, Puerto Rico (SAUS)
PrBayC........ Bayamon Central University (Universidad Central de Bayamon), Bayamon, Puerto Rico [*Library symbol*] [*Library of Congress*] (LCLS)
PRBBB .... Proximal Right Bundle Branch Block (SAUS)
PRBC .... Packed Red Blood Cells [*Medicine*]
PRBC .... Parasitized Red Blood Cell [*Medicine*]
PRBC .... Peoples Revolution Broadcasting Corp. (SAUS)
PRBC .... Placental Residual Blood Volume [*Medicine*] (DMAA)
PRBC .... Premier Bancorp, Inc. [*NASDAQ symbol*] (NQ)
PRBC .... Prestige Bancorp, Inc. [*NASDAQ symbol*] (SAG)
PRBCH........ Process Biochemistry (SAUS)
PRBD .... Paraboloid
PRBE .... Program Robot by Example (SAUS)
PRBG .... Puerto Rican Board of Guardians [*Defunct*] (EA)
PRBK .... Provident Bancorp [*NASDAQ symbol*] (TTSB)
PRBK .... Provident Bancorp, Inc. [*NASDAQ symbol*] (SAG)
PRBLC .... Parabolic
PRBLTY .... Probability [*NWS*] (FAAC)
PRBMD........ Physical Review B, Condensed Matter (SAUS)
PRBMECAB... Permanent Regional Bureau of the Middle East Committee for the Affairs of the Blind [*Riyadh, Saudi Arabia*] (EAIO)
PRBNT .... Prebent
PRBO .... Position Relief Briefing Observed [*Aviation*] (FAAC)
Pr Br .... Propyl Bromide (SAUS)
PRBS .... Printer Barrier Strip (VLIE)
PRBS .... Pseudo Random Binary Sequence (SAUS)
PRBS .... Pseudorandom Binary Sequence [*Computer science*]
PRBS .... Pseudorandom Binary Signal (SAUS)
PRBSG........ Pseudorandom Binary Sequence Generator [*Computer science*] (NRCH)
PRBT .... Precision Remote Bathythermograph
PRBV .... Placental Residual Blood Volume [*Hematology*] (MAE)
PRC .... Chief Aircrew Survival Equipmentman [*Formerly, Chief Parachute Rigger*] [*Navy rating*]
PRC .... Pacific Air Charter, Inc. [*ICAO designator*] (FAAC)
PRC .... Packed Red Cell [*Hematology*] (MAE)
PRC .... Packed Red Cells (SAUS)
PRC .... Pain Rehabilitation Center (AD)
PRC .... Palestine Red Crescent (AD)
PRC .... Park Requirement Card (SAUS)
PRC .... Park Ridge Center (EA)
PRC .... Partial Read Current (SAUS)
PRC .... Partial Response Coding (IEEE)
PRC .... Partido Regionalista de Cantabria [*Spain*] [*Political party*] (EY)
PRC .... Partido Republicano Calderonista [*Calderonista Republican Party*] [*Costa Rica*] [*Political party*] (PPW)
PRC .... Partido Revolucionario Comunista [*Brazil*] [*Political party*] (EY)
PRC .... Parti Republicain Caledonien [*New Caledonia*] [*Political party*] (FEA)

PRC	Part Requirement Card
PRC	Parts Release Card (KSC)
PRC	Parts Release Curve (SAUS)
PRC	Passaic River Coalition (EA)
PRC	Passenger Reservation Center [Army]
PRC	Pay-Raise Commission (AD)
PRC	Peer Review Committee (SAUS)
PRC	Penrose Resources Corp. [Vancouver Stock Exchange symbol]
PRC	Pension Research Council (EA)
PRC	Pension Rights Center [Washington, DC] (EA)
PRC	People's Redemption Council [Liberia] (PD)
PRC	People's Republic of China [Mainland China]
PRC	People's Republic of the Congo
PRC	Periodic Reverse Current (IAA)
PRC	Period Reverse Current (SAUS)
PRC	Permanent Regular Commissions [Army] [British]
PRC	Permanent Representatives Committee of the European Communities (SAUS)
PRC	Personality Research Center [University of Texas at Austin] [Research center] (RCD)
PRC	Personal Radio Communications (SAUS)
PRC	Personnel Readiness Center [Air Force]
PRC	Personnel Reception Centre [British military] (DMA)
PRC	Personnel Recovery Center [Military]
PRC	Personnel Reporting Code [Army] (AABC)
PRC	Phased Rate of Change (SAUS)
PRC	Phase Rate of Change (SEWL)
PRC	Phase-Response Curve
PRC	Philippine Resource Center [An association] (EA)
PRC	Photo Receptor Cell [Medicine] (MELL)
PRC	Physical Review Council [DoD]
PRC	Picatinny Research Center [Picatinny Arsenal] (AD)
PRC	Pierce (MSA)
PRC	Pilot Resource (SAUS)
PRC	Pitch Radio Controller
PRC	Pitch Rate Command (MCD)
PRC	Pitch Ratio Controller (MCD)
PRC	Planar Random Composite (MCD)
PRC	Planned Requirements, Conversion (NG)
PRC	Planning Research Corp. [Telecommunications service] (TSSD)
PRC	Planning Research Corporation [Marine science] (OSRA)
PRC	Plant Records Center [of the American Horticultural Society] (IID)
PRC	Plasma Renin Concentration [Hematology]
PRC	Plastic Roller Conveyor
PRC	Player Relations Committee [Baseball] (NDBD)
PRC	Plutonium Rework Cell [Nuclear energy] (NRCH)
PRC	Point of Reverse Curve (MSA)
PRC	Point Reyes [California] [Seismograph station code, US Geological Survey] [Closed] (SEIS)
PRC	Polar Research Cell (SAUS)
PRC	Policy Review Committee [Terminated, 1981] [National Security Council] (EGAO)
PRC	Polish Resettlement Corps [British military] (DMA)
prc	Polysulphide Rubber Compound (AD)
prc	Polysulphide Rubber Compound (PDAA)
PRC	Populace and Resources Control (COE)
PRC	Population Research Center [University of Chicago] [Research center] (RCD)
PRC	Population Resource Center (EA)
PRC	Portable Radio Communication (SAUS)
PRC	Portuguese Civilization (SAUS)
PRC	Postal Rate Commission [Federal government]
PRC	Postconsumer Recycled Content [Plastics technology]
PRC	Post Roman Conditam [After the Founding of Rome] [Latin]
PRC	Poultry Research Centre [of the Agricultural Research Council] [British] (ARC)
PRC	Power Reflection Coefficient [of RADAR signals]
PRC	Prattsburgh Railway Corp. [AAR code]
PRC	Precipitation (CARB)
PRC	Preoral Ciliary [Gland]
PRC	Pre-Ranger Course [Army] (INF)
PRC	Prescott [Arizona] [Airport symbol] (OAG)
PRC	Prescott, AZ [Location identifier] [FAA] (FAAL)
PRC	Prescription Rate Carryover [Health insurance] (GHCT)
PRC	Pressure Recorder Controller [Nuclear energy] (NRCH)
PRC	Pressure Response Cell [For chemical kinetic studies]
PRC	Pressure Riser-Less Casting
PRC	Prevention Research Center [Pacific Institute for Research and Evaluation] [Research center] (RCD)
PRC	Price
PRC	Price Redetermination Contract (SAA)
PRC	Primary Reference Clock (SAUS)
PRC	Primary Return Code [Computer science] (ELAL)
PRC	Primary Return Code (SAUS)
PRC	Primary Routing Center [Telecommunications] (TEL)
PRC	Primate Research Center
PRC	Prime Responder Cell (DB)
PRC	Principal Reducing Credit
PRC	Printer Control
PRC	Priory Cell
Pr C	Prize Cases [A publication] (DLA)
PRC	Problem Resolution Coordinator [IRS]
PRC	Procaterol [Pharmacology]
PRC	Procedure Review Committee (AAG)
PRC	Process Communication (SAUS)
PRC	Procession Register Clock
PRC	Proconsul
PRC	Procurement Request Code [Military] (AFIT)
PRC	Production Control (IAA)
PRC	Production Readjustments Committee [WPB]
PRC	Product Regional Center [Department of Supply and Service] [Canada] (IMH)
PRC	Products Research & Chemical Corp. (SAUS)
PRC	Professional Reference Center [Los Angeles County Office of Education] [Downey, CA] [Library network]
PRC	Professional Relations Council [American Chemical Society]
PRC	Programmable Radar Controller (SAUS)
PRC	Programmed Rate Control (NITA)
PRC	Programmed Route Control [Computer science] (VLIE)
PRC	Program Range Change (VLIE)
PRC	Program Request Control (SAUS)
PRC	Program Required Credentials [Computer science] (ELAL)
PRC	Program Required Credentials (SAUS)
PRC	Program Resources Catalog
PRC	Program Rest Code (MCD)
PRC	Program Review Committee (AFM)
PRC	Projects Review Committee (SAUS)
PRC	Prologic Management Systems, Inc. [AMEX symbol] (SAG)
PRC	Promotion Research Committee
PRC	Propeller Change (MCD)
PRC	Propulsion Research Corporation
PRC	Providence College, Phillips Memorial Library, Providence, RI [OCLC symbol] (OCLC)
PRC	Proximal Row Carpectomy [Medicine] (MELL)
PRC	Pseudo-Range Correction
PRC	Public Radio Conference (SAUS)
PRC	Public Relations Club (AD)
PRC	Pyrotechnic Rocket Container
PRC	Revolutionary Socialist Party [Peru] [Political party] (PD)
Pr Ca	Great War Prize Cases, by Evans [England] [A publication] (DLA)
Pr Ca	Great War Prize Cases, by Evans (journ.) (SAUS)
PRCA	Packaging Research [NASDAQ symbol] (TTSB)
PRCA	Packaging Research Corp. [NASDAQ symbol] (SAG)
PRCA	Palomino Rabbit Co-Breeders Association (EA)
PRCA	Parks, Recreation and Cultural Affairs Administration [New York City]
PRCA	People's Republic of China Army (MCD)
PRCA	Pitch and Roll Channel Assembly (MCD)
PRCA	Presbyterian Reformed Church of Australia
PRCA	President of the Royal Cambrian Academy (SAUS)
PRCA	President of the Royal Canadian Academy
PRCA	President of the Royal Canadian Academy of Arts (NGC)
PRCA	Problem Reporting and Corrective Action (NASA)
PRCA	Professional Rodeo Cowboys Association (EA)
PRCA	Public Relations Consultants Association (EAIO)
PRCA	Puerto Rico Communications Authority
PRCA	Pure Red Cell Agenesis [Hematology] (MAE)
PRCA	Pure Red Cell Aplasia [Hematology]
PR Cable	Pure Rubber Cable (SAUS)
PrCaC	Colegio Universitario de Cayey, Cayey, PR [Library symbol] [Library of Congress] (LCLS)
PRCAF	Peoples Republic of China Air Force (SAUS)
PRCAFL	Publications of the Research Center in Anthropology, Folklore and Linguistics (SAUS)
PRCAFL	Publications. Research Center in Anthropology, Folklore and Linguistics (SAUS)
PRC & NW...	Pierre, Rapid City & Northwestern Railroad [Nickname: Plenty Rough Country and No Women]
PR Card	Parts Requisition Card (SAUS)
PRCAW	Packaging Research Wrrt [NASDAQ symbol] (TTSB)
PRCB	Program Requirement Control Board (SAUS)
PRCB	Program Requirements Change Board [NASA] (NASA)
PRCB	Program Requirements Control Board [NASA]
PRCB	Program Review Change Board
PRCB	Program Review Control Board [NASA] (NASA)
PRCBD	Program Requirements Control Board Directive [NASA] (NASA)
PRCBD	Program Review Control Board Directive [NASA] (NASA)
PRCBXSS....	Priority Coinbox with Special Services (SAUS)
PRCC	Partial Rank Correlation Coefficient [Nuclear energy] (NUCP)
PRCC	Parts Request Card Code (SAUS)
PRCC ..../.....	Peoria Record Club [Record label]
PRCC	Pollution Research and Control Corp. [NASDAQ symbol] (SAG)
PRCC	Pollution Resh & Ctl CA [NASDAQ symbol] (TTSB)
PRCC	Procurement Research Coordinating Counsel (AAGC)
PRCC	Puerto Rico Cancer Center [University of Puerto Rico] [Research center] (RCD)
PRC-CAS.....	Polar Research Committee-Chinese Academy of Sciences (SAUS)
PRCCh	Principal Roman Catholic Chaplain [Navy] [British]
PRCCM	Partial Reference Count Contour Machine (SAUS)
PrcCm	Price Communications Corp. [Associated Press] (SAG)
PRCCS	Parts Return Control Card System (SAUS)
PRCCT	Printed Circuit [Computer science] (IAA)
prcd	Priced (AD)
PRCD	Proceed (VLIE)
PRCEC	Pearce Sys Intl [NASDAQ symbol] (TTSB)
PR Cem	Puerto Rican Cement Co., Inc. [Associated Press] (SAG)
PRCESSN....	Processing
PRCF	Petroleum Resources Communications Foundation [Canada]
PRCF	Plutonium Recycle Critical Facility [Nuclear energy]
PRCGT	Confederacion Generale Trabajadores de Puerto Rico
Pr Ch	Parish Church (AD)

PR Ch .... Practical Register in Chancery [*England*] [*A publication*] (DLA)
Pr Ch .... Precedents in Chancery, Edited by Finch [*1689-1722*] [*England*] [*A publication*] (DLA)
PRCH .... Precharge
PRCH .... Proprietary Chapel [*Church of England*]
PRCHNG ...... Purchasing
prchst .... Parachutist (AD)
prcht .... Parachute (AD)
PRCHT .... Parachute (AFM)
Prcht Bad..... Parachutist Badge [*Military decoration*]
PRCI .... Parti Republicain de la Cote d'Ivoire [*Republicaqn Party of the Ivory Coast*] [*Political party*] (EY)
PRCI .... Policy Review Committee Intelligence [*Military*]
PRCI .... Productability Reliability Cost Improvement (SAUS)
PRCI .... Production Reliability Cost Improvement (DWSG)
PRCIX .... Price T. Rowe: New Income [*Mutual fund ticker symbol*] (SG)
Pr CKB .... Practice Cases, in the King's Bench [*England*] [*A publication*] (DLA)
PRCL .... Confederacion Laborista de Puerto Rico
Pr Cl .... Propyl Chlorite (SAUS)
PRCL .... Protocol Common Logic (SAUS)
PRCM .... Master Chief Aircrew Survival Equipmentman [*Formerly, Master Chief Parachute R igger*] [*Navy rating*]
PRCM .... Paleoclimate Reconstructions for Climate Modeling (SAUS)
PRCM .... Passive Radiation Countermeasure [*Military*]
PRCM .... Pericom Semiconductor Corp. [*NASDAQ symbol*] (SAG)
PRCM .... Procom Technology Inc. [*NASDAQ symbol*] (SAG)
PRCM .... Protocom Devices, Inc. (SAUS)
PRCMNT ...... Procurement
PRCMO .... Paleoclimate Reconstructions of Climate Modeling Observatory (SAUS)
PRCMT .... Procurement (MSA)
PRCN .... Peoples Republic of China Navy (SAUS)
PRCN .... Percon, Inc. [*NASDAQ symbol*] (SAG)
PRCN .... Porcine Respiratory Coronavirus (DB)
PRCN .... Precision (MSA)
PR-CNTL...... Product Control Register
PRCO .... Pacific Requisition Control Office [*Navy*]
Pr Co .... Prerogative Court (DLA)
PR Code...... Print Restore Code
PR/COM...... Vessel Delivered in Partially-Completed Status [*Navy*] (DNAB)
Pr Compt..... Pour Compte (SAUS)
Pr Cont........ Pratt's Contraband-of-War Cases [*1861*] [*A publication*] (DLA)
ProOptCp .... Precision Optics Corp. [*Associated Press*] (SAG)
PRCP .... Perceptron, Inc. [*NASDAQ symbol*] (SAG)
PRCP .... Percutaneous Renal Cyst Puncture [*Medicine*] (MELL)
PRCP .... Personnel Readiness Capability Program [*Navy*] (DNAB)
PRCP .... Power Remote Control Panel (AAG)
PRCP .... Practical Register in the Common Pleas [*A publication*] (DLA)
PRCP .... President of the Royal College of Physicians [*British*]
PRCP .... President of the Royal College of Preceptors [*British*] (ROG)
PRCP .... Programmed Communication Electronic Support Program (SAUS)
PRCP .... Puerto Rican Communist Party [*Political party*]
PRC Plating... Periodic Reverse Current Plating (SAUS)
PRCPM .... Partial Response Continuous-Phase-Modulation (SAUS)
PRCPM .... Print Complement (VLIE)
PRCPTN ...... Precipitin [*Test*] [*Immunology*]
PRCR .... Professional Health Care of America, Inc. (SAUS)
PRCR .... Protective Cover (AAG)
PrcREI .... Price REIT, Inc. [*Associated Press*] (SAG)
PRCS .... Passive and Remote Crosswind Sensor (MCD)
PRCS .... People's Republic of China Satellite
PRCS .... Personal Radio Communications System [*General Electric Co.*]
PRCS .... Personal Report of Confidence as a Speaker [*Psychology*]
PRCS .... Polish Red Cross Society
PRCS .... President of the Royal College of Surgeons [*British*]
PRCS .... Prevention and Removal of Corrosion and Scale [*Engineering*]
PRCS .... Primary Reaction Control System (SAUS)
prcs .... Process (AD)
PRCS .... Process (AFM)
PRCS .... Processing (IAA)
PRCS .... Project Revision Control System (SAUS)
P/RCS .... Propulsion and Reaction Control Subsystem [*NASA*] (KSC)
PRCS .... Psychological Response Classification System
PRCS .... Purchase Requisition Change Supplement
PRCS .... Senior Chief Aircrew Survival Equipmentman [*Formerly, Senior Chief Parachute R igger*] [*Navy rating*]
PRCSG........ Processing (MSA)
PRCSR........ Processor
PRCS SPEC... Process Specification (SAUS)
PRCST .... Precast (AAG)
prcst .... Precast (AD)
PRCT .... Pool Repair Cycle Time (MCD)
PRCT .... Procept, Inc. [*NASDAQ symbol*] (SAG)
PRCTN .... Precaution [*ICAO designator*] (FAAC)
PRCU .... Power Regulating and Control Unit (CET)
prcu .... Power Regulation and Control Unit (AD)
PRCUA .... Polish Roman Catholic Union of America (EA)
PRCUI .... Congreso Uniones Industriales de Puerto Rico
PRCV .... Processor Recovery (SAUS)
PRCVS........ Pre-Canvass (SAUS)
PRCY .... ProCyte Corp. [*NASDAQ symbol*] (NQ)
prd .... Partial Reaction of Degeneration (AD)
PRD .... Partial Reaction of Degeneration
PRD .... Parti Democratique Dahomeen [*Dahomey Democratic Party*] [*Political party*]

PRD .... Partido de la Revolucion Democratica [*Mexico*] [*Political party*] (EY)
PRD .... Partido de Renovacion Democratica [*Democratic Renewal Party*] [*Costa Rica*] [*Political party*] (PPW)
PRD .... Partido Reformista Democratico [*Democratic Reformist Party*] [*Spain*] [*Political party*] (PPW)
PRD .... Partido Revolucionario Democratico [*Democratic Revolutionary Party*] [*Panama*] [*Political party*] (PPW)
PRD .... Partido Revolucionario Dominicano [*Dominican Revolutionary Party*] [*Dominican Republic*] [*Political party*] (PPW)
PRD .... Parti du Renouveau Democratique [*Benin*] [*Political party*] (EY)
PRD .... Parti Radical-Democratique Suisse [*Radical Democratic Party of Switzerland*] [*Political party*] (PPE)
PRD .... Part Reference Designator
PRD .... Party for Renovation and Development (SAUS)
PRD .... Party for Reviving Democracy (SAUS)
PRD .... Party of the Democratic Revolution [*Mexico*] [*Political party*]
PRD .... Payload Retention Device (SAUS)
PRD .... Payroll Deduction
PRD .... Performance-Related Pay [*Business term*] (ECON)
PRD .... Period
PRD .... Periodontics and Restorative Dentistry
PRD .... Personal Radiation Dosimeter (KSC)
PRD .... Personnel Readiness Date [*Army*] (AABC)
PRD .... Personnel Records Division [*Army*] (AABC)
PRD .... Personnel Requirements Data (AAG)
PRD .... Personnel Research Division [*Navy*] (MCD)
PRD .... Personnel Resources Data
PRD .... Pesticides Regulation Division (AD)
PRD .... Physician Relations Department (DMAA)
PRD .... Piezoelectric Resonating Device
PRD .... Planned Residential Development
PRD .... Polaroid Corp. [*NYSE symbol*] (SPSG)
PRD .... Political Resource Directory [*A publication*]
PRD .... Polytechnic Research & Development Co. (AAG)
PRD .... Positive Regulatory Domain [*Genetics*]
PRD .... Postal Regulating Detachment [*Military*]
PRD .... Postradiation Dysplasia [*Medicine*]
PRD .... Potentially Reportable Deficiency [*Nuclear energy*] (NRCH)
PRD .... Power Range Detector (IEEE)
PRD .... Power Requirement Data
PRD .... Precompetitive Research and Development
PRD .... Predicted Range of the Day [*Military*] (NVT)
PRD .... Preretro Update Display
PRD .... Presidential Review Directive (USDC)
PRD .... Pressing Direction
PRD .... Previous Device Register (SAUS)
PRD .... Pride
PRD .... Primary Radar Data (SAUS)
PRD .... Prime RADAR Digitizer (IAA)
PRD .... Princeton Reference Design (MCD)
PRD .... Printer Driver
prd .... Printer Dump (AD)
PRD .... Process Requirements Drawing (MCD)
PRD .... Procurement Regulation Directive [*NASA*] (NASA)
PRD .... Procurement Requirements Document [*NASA*] (NASA)
PRD .... Production Responsibilities Document (MCD)
PRD .... Productive (SAUS)
PRD .... Productivity Research Division [*Office of Personnel Management*] (GRD)
PRD .... Product Requirements Document (SAUS)
PRD .... Product Research and Development [*Advertising*] (DOAD)
PRD .... Proficiency Rating Designator [*Military*]
PRD .... Program [*or Project*] Requirement Data [*NASA*] (KSC)
PRD .... Program Requirement Document (SAUS)
PRD .... Program Requirements Document
PRD .... Projected Rotation Date (NG)
PRD .... Project Requirement Document (SAUS)
PRD .... Proline-Rich Domain [*Genetics*]
prd .... Pro-Rata Distribution (AD)
PRD .... Pro Rate Distribution [*Clause*] [*Insurance*]
PRD .... Proton Recoil Detector (SAUS)
PRD .... Puerto Rico, Decisiones [*A publication*] (DLA)
PRD .... Pulse Rate Discriminator (SAUS)
PRD .... Purdue Aeronautics Corporation
PRD .... Push Road (SAUS)
PRD .... Push Rod [*Mechanical engineering*]
PRDA .... Pony Riding for the Disabled Association [*Australia*]
PRDA .... Program Research and Development Agreement (SAUS)
PRDA .... Program Research and Development Announcement [*Energy Research and Development Administration*]
PRDA .... Propfan Research and Development Announcement (SAUS)
PRDC .... Personnel Research and Development Center [*Office of Personnel Management*] (GRD)
PRDC .... Pig Research and Development Corp. [*Australia*]
PRDC .... Polar Research and Development Center [*Army*]
PRDC .... Power Reactor Development Corp. (SAUS)
PRDCTVTY... Productivity
PRDDO .... Partial Retention of Diatomic Differential Overlap [*Physics*]
PRDE .... Pride International [*NASDAQ symbol*] [*Formerly, Pride Petroleum*] (SG)
PRDE .... Pride Petroleum Services, Inc. [*NASDAQ symbol*] (CTT)
PRDE .... Pride Petroleum Svcs [*NASDAQ symbol*] (TTSB)
PrdEn.......... Producers Entertainment Group Ltd. [*Associated Press*] (SAG)
PrdEnt.......... Producers Entertainment Group Ltd. [*Associated Press*] (SAG)
PrdePt .... Pride Petroleum Services, Inc. [*Associated Press*] (SAG)

PRDF	Page Reference Distribution Function [*Computer science*] (IAA)
PRDF	Political Rights Defense Fund [*Defunct*] (EA)
PRDG	Princess Royal's Dragoon Guards [*Military unit*] [*British*] (ROG)
PRDIAG	Primary Diagnosis [*Medicine*]
PRDIALTO	Pre Dial Time-Out (SAUS)
PRDL	Personnel Research and Development Laboratory [*Navy*] (MCD)
prdl	Predella (VRA)
PRDM	Paradigm Technology [*NASDAQ symbol*] (TTSB)
PRDM	Paradigm Technology, Inc. [*NASDAQ symbol*] (SAG)
PRDM	Parti pour le Rassemblement Democratique des Mahorais [*Mayotte*] [*Political party*] (EY)
PRDMD	Private Directory Management Domain (SAUS)
PRDN	Partido de Reconciliacion Democratica Nacional [*Party of National Democratic Reconciliation*] [*Guatemala*] [*Political party*]
PRDNTST	Periodonist
PRDP	Power Reactor Demonstration Program
PRDPC	Pooled Random Donor Platelet Concentrates [*Medicine*] (MELL)
PRDPEC	Power Reactor Development Programme Evaluation Committee [*Canada*] (HGAA)
PRDR	Preproduction Reliability Design Review [*Navy*] (CAAL)
PRDR	Procedure (SAUS)
PRDR	Production Request Design Review
PRDS	Packet Radio Demonstrator System (SAUS)
PRDS	Paradise
PRDS	Post Boost Detection System (ACAE)
PRDS	Processed RADAR Display System (PDAA)
PRDT	Production Reliability Demonstration Test (SAUS)
PRDV	Peak Reading Digital Voltmeter
prdx	paradox (SAUS)
PRDX	Prediction Program [*NASA*]
PRE	Bureau for Private Enterprise
PRE	Federation Europeenne des Fabricants de Produits Refractaires [*Zurich, Switzerland*] (EAIO)
PRE	Partial Reflection Experiment (SAUS)
PRE	Partial Reinforcement Effect (DIPS)
PRE	Partido Republicano Evolucionista [*Republican Evolutionist Party*] [*Portugal*] [*Political party*] (PPE)
PRE	Partido Roldosista Ecuatoriano [*Ecuador*] [*Political party*] (EY)
PRE	Partner-Resisted Exercise [*Army*] (INF)
PRE	Performance Requirements Envelope (ACAE)
PRE	Personal Rescue Enclosure (NASA)
PRE	Personnel Restraint Equipment (SAA)
PRE	Petroleum Refining Engineer
PRE	Photoreactivating
PRE	Physical Reconditioning Exercises [*Orthopedics*] (DAVI)
PRE	Pineridge Capital [*Vancouver Stock Exchange symbol*]
PRE	Planetary Rotation Engine (IAA)
PRE	Portable RADAR Equipment
pre	Pre-Choice [*Advertising*] (WDMC)
PRE	Precinct
PRE	Precision Airlines (SAUS)
PRE	Precision Valley Aviation [*ICAO designator*] (FAAC)
PRE	Predecessor (KSC)
pre	Prefatory (WDMC)
PRE	Prefect
pre	Preferred (WDMC)
pre	Prefix (WDMC)
PRE	Prefix
PRE	Preformatted (SAUS)
Pre	Preliminary (AMHC)
PRE	Preliminary
PRE	Preliminary Amplifier (IAA)
PRE	Premier Industrial Corp. [*NYSE symbol*] (SPSG)
pre	Preoperative [*Surgery*] (WDMC)
PRE	Prepayment Coin Telephone [*Telecommunications*] (TEL)
PRE	Pre-Retirement Education (AIE)
PRE	Presbyterian Historical Society, Philadelphia, PA [*OCLC symbol*] (OCLC)
PRE	Preselection (SAUS)
PRE	President of the Royal Society of Painter-Etchers and Engravers [*British*]
pre	Pretest [*Advertising*] (WDMC)
PRE	Pretoria [*South Africa*] [*Seismograph station code, US Geological Survey*] (SEIS)
PRE	Prime contractors Region (SAUS)
PRE	Problem Reproducer Equipment (SAA)
PRE	Processing Refabrication Experiment [*Nuclear energy*] (NRCH)
PRE	Product-Remainder Extension (SAUS)
PRE	Progesterone [*A hormone*]
PRE	Progesterone Response Element [*Endocrinology*]
PRE	Program Reliability Engineer (ACAE)
PRE	Progressive Resistance (or Resistive) Exercise (SAUS)
PRE	Progressive Resistive Exercise [*Medicine*]
PRE	Proportional Reduction of Error
PRE	Protective Reservation Equipment (SAUS)
PRE	Protein Relaxation Enhancement (OA)
PRE	Protein Retention Efficiency [*Medicine*] (WDAA)
PRE	Proton Relaxation Enhancement [*Physics*]
PRE	Psychophysiological Reeducation (SAUS)
PRE	Public Relations Exchange [*Later, PRXI*] (EA)
PRE	Pulse Radiation Effect
PRE	Realencykopaedie fuer Protestantische Theologie und Kirche [*A publication*] (ODCC)
PRE	Spanish Catalonian Battalion (PD)
PREA	Pension Real Estate Association (EA)

P/REA	Probationary Radio Electrical Artificer [*British military*] (DMA)
PREAG	Parks Residents Environmental Action Group [*Australia*]
PREAG	Photographic Reconnaissance Equipment Advisory Group [*Military*]
PREAMP	Preamplifier (AAG)
preamp	Preamplifier (ADWA)
preamp	Preamplifier (DCDG)
PREAMP	Preliminary Amplifier (SAUS)
PREAP	Prison Research Education Action Project (EA)
PRE-ARM	People's Rights Enforced Against Riots and Murder [*Vigilante group in New Jersey*]
PREB	Prebendary
PREB	Pupil Record of Educational Behavior [*Aptitude test*]
Preb Dig	Preble. Digest, Patent Cases [*A publication*] (DLA)
Preb Pat Cas	Preble. Digest, Patent Cases [*A publication*] (DLA)
PREBS	Pennsylvania Real Estate Brokers and Salesmens (SAUS)
PREC	Palestine Research and Educational Center (EA)
p rec	Per Rectum [*Through the rectum*] [*Pharmacology*] (DAVI)
PREC	Potomac River Enforcement Conference (SAUS)
PREC	Precambrian [*Period, era, or system*] [*Geology*]
PREC	Precedence (AABC)
PREC	Preceding
PREC	Precentor (ROG)
PREC	Precious (ROG)
prec	Precious (VRA)
PREC	Precision (AABC)
Prec	Precite [*Supra, Cited Before*] [*French*] (ILCA)
PREC	Propulsion Research Environmental Chamber
PREC	Public Revenue Education Council (EA)
PrecCst	Precision Castparts Corp. [*Associated Press*] (SAG)
PRECD	Precede (FAAC)
PrecDr	Precision Drilling Corp. [*Associated Press*] (SAG)
PRECEDE	Predisposing, Reinforcing, and Enabling Causes in Educational Diagnosis and Evaluation [*Occupational therapy*]
Preceiver	Preamplifier/Receiver (SAUS)
Pre Ch	Precedents in Chancery, Edited by Finch [*A publication*] (DLA)
Prec in Ch	Precedents in Chancery, Edited by Finch [*24 English Reprint*] [*1689-1722*] [*A publication*] (DLA)
Prec in Ch (Eng)	Precedents in Chancery, Edited by Finch [*24 English Reprint*] [*A publication*] (DLA)
precip	Precipitate [*Laboratory science*] (DAVI)
PRECIP	Precipitated (SAUS)
PRECIP	Precipitation
Precip	Precipitous (AMHC)
PRECIP	Processing of Emissions by Clouds and Precipitation (SAUS)
PRECIS	Pre-Coordinate Indexing System
PRECIS	Preserved Context Index System [*British Library*] [*London, England*] [*Information service or system*]
PRECO	Precision Equipment Co. (SAUS)
PRECO	Preparatory Commission of the United Nations Organization
PRECOM	Precommissioning [*Military*]
PRECOM	Preliminary Communications Search [*Military*] (NVT)
PRECOMDET	Precommissioning Detail [*Navy*] (NVT)
PRECOMG	Precommissioning [*Military*] (NVT)
PRECOMM	Pre-Commissioning (SAUS)
PRECOMM	Preliminary Communications [*Military*] (NVT)
PRECOMMDET	Precommissioning Detail [*Navy*]
PRECOMMSCOL	Precommissioning School [*Navy*]
precomp	Precomputed Loan
PRECOMP	Prediction of Contingency Maintenance and Parts Requirements (MCD)
PRECOMUNIT	Precommissioning Unit [*Navy*] (DNAB)
precon	Previous Conviction (WDAA)
PRECOX	Precision Oxide (SAUS)
PRECP	Processing of Emissions by Clouds and Precipitation (SAUS)
PRECP	Program on Nonlinearity of Acid Precipitation Process (SAUS)
PrecRes	Precision Response Corp. [*Associated Press*] (SAG)
PRECSA	Precision Aerotech, Inc. (SAUS)
PRECSN	Precision
PrecStd	Precision Standard, Inc. [*Associated Press*] (SAG)
PrecSy	Precision Systems, Inc. [*Associated Press*] (SAG)
Pre-D	Predetection (SAUS)
pred	Predicate (SHCU)
PRED	Predicate
PRED	Predictability (SAUS)
PRED-	Predictability, Negative (SAUS)
PRED+	Predictability, Positive (SAUS)
pred	Predicted (STED)
PRED	Predicted
PRED	Prediction (AFM)
Pred	Prednisolone (SAUS)
PRED	Prednisone (DMAA)
Pred	Prednisone [*Also, P, PDN, Pr, Pro*] [*Endocrinology*] [*Antineoplastic drug*]
PreD₃	Previtamin D3 [*A precursor to vitamin D3*] (DAVI)
PREDA	Puerto Rico Economic Development Administration (NADA)
PREDECE	Predecease (ROG)
Pre-Design	Preliminary Design (SAUS)
PREDICT	Pollution Reduction by Information and Control Technology
PREDICT	Prediction of Radiation Effects by Digital Computer Techniques
PREDICT	Process Reliability, Evaluation and Determination of Integrated Circuit Techniques (SAUS)
PREDNIS	Prednisolone (SAUS)
PREDNIS ACE	Prednisolone Acetate (SAUS)
Pr Edw I	Prince Edward Island (DLA)
Pr Edw I	Prince Edward Island Reports [*Canada*] [*A publication*] (DLA)

Pr Edw Isl.... Prince Edward Island (DLA)
Pr Edw Isl.... Prince Edward Island Reports [Canada] [A publication] (DLA)
PREE.......... Partial Reinforcement Extinction Effect (STED)
PRE-EM ...... Preeminence (SAUS)
PRE-EM ...... Preeminent (SAUS)
PRE-EM ...... Preemptible (SAUS)
PRE-EM ...... Preemption (SAUS)
PREEMIE...... Premature Baby [Medical slang] (WDAA)
PRE-EMPTN... Pre-Emption (ROG)
PreES.......... Pre-Enumeration Survey (SAUS)
pref.......... Preface (WDAA)
PREF.......... Preface
pref.......... prefatory (SAUS)
PREF.......... Prefecture
PREF.......... Prefer (SAUS)
PREF.......... Preference [or Preferred] (AFM)
pref.......... Preference (NTIO)
Pref.......... Preference (SG)
pref.......... Preference (SHCU)
PREF.......... Preferred (KSC)
PREF.......... Prefix (AAG)
PREF.......... Prefocused
PREF.......... Propulsion Research Environmental Facility
PREFAB........ Prefabricated (KSC)
PREFACE ...... Pre-Freshman and Cooperative Education for Minorities in Engineering (SAUS)
PRE FA FIRE ORDER... Prepare FA Fire Order (SAUS)
PREF-AP....... Prefect Apostolic (SAUS)
PREF-AP....... Prefect-Apostolic [Roman Catholic]
PREFAT........ Prepare Final Acceptance Trials [Navy] (NVT)
PREFCE........ Preface (ROG)
prefd.......... Preferred (STED)
PREFD .... Preferred (WDAA)
Prefect........ Prefecture (DIAR)
PREFLT......... Preflight (KSC)
PREFLTSCOL... Preflight School [Military]
PREFMD ...... Preformed
PREFRAM..... Prepare Fleet Rehabilitation and Modernization Overhaul [Navy] (NVT)
PREFRAMO... Prepare Fleet Rehabilitation and Modernization Overhaul (SAUS)
preft.......... Prefecture
PREFUN....... Preparatory Function (SAUS)
Preg.......... Pregnancy (AMHC)
PREG .... Pregnancy [or Pregnant]
PREG .... Pregnelone (STED)
PREG .... Pregnenolone [Endocrinology]
pregang....... Preganglionic [Anatomy]
PREGN........ Pregnancy [or Pregnant] (AAMN)
prehis.......... Prehistory [or Prehistoric] (BARN)
PREHIST....... Prehistory [or Prehistoric] (WDAA)
PREIA .... Professional Radio and Electronics Institute of Australia
PREINACT.... Prepare Inactivation [Navy] (NVT)
PREINSURV... Prepare for Board of Inspection and Survey [Navy] (NVT)
PREINSURV... President of Board for Inspection and Survey
PreissM........ Preiss [Byron] Multimedia Co., Inc. [Associated Press] (SAG)
PREJ.......... Prejudice (AABC)
PREL.......... Pain Relief Level [Medicine]
PREL.......... Power-Refrigeration-Electric (SAUS)
PREL.......... Preliminary
PREL.......... Preliminary Evaluation [Orbit identification]
PREL.......... Prelude [Music] (ROG)
PREL.......... Priority Reconnaissance Exploitation List (CINC)
PREL.......... Programmable Rotary Encoded Logic [Computer science] (MHDB)
PRELA .... Prensa Latina, Angencia Informativa Latinoamericana [Press agency] [Cuba]
PRELIM........ Preliminary (AFM)
Prelim .... Preliminary (AL)
prelim.......... Preliminary (STED)
prelim diag... Preliminary Diagnosis [Medicine] (DAVI)
prelims........ Preliminary Pages [Frontmatter] [Publishing]
PRELIMY ...... Preliminary (ROG)
prelm.......... Preliminary (VRA)
PRELOG........ People's Revolutionary League of Ghana [Political party] (PPW)
PRELOGE.... Preliminary Logistics Evolution (SAUS)
PRELORT...... Precision Long-Range Tracking (SAUS)
PRELORT...... Precision Long-Range Tracking RADAR
PRELORT Radar... Precision Long-Range Tracking Radar (SAUS)
PRELUDE..... Pre-Optimization Linearization of Undulation and Detection of Errors (PDAA)
PREM.......... Preliminary Reference Earth Model [Geology]
PREM.......... Premature [Medicine]
prem.......... Prematurity (STED)
PREM.......... Premier (ROG)
prem.......... Premiere (WDMC)
PREM.......... Premier Financial Services, Inc. [Freeport, IL] [NASDAQ symbol] (NQ)
PREM.......... Premier Financial Svcs [NASDAQ symbol] (TTSB)
Prem.......... Premises (TBD)
PREM.......... Premium (AFM)
Prem.......... Premium (EBF)
prem.......... Premium (WDMC)
PREM.......... Probe-Microphone Real Ear Measurement [Audiology]
PREMA........ Pulp Refining Equipment Manufacturers Association (EA)
PremBksh.... Premier Bankshares [Associated Press] (SAG)
Premdr....... Premdor, Inc. [Associated Press] (SAG)

Premed....... Premedical (SAUS)
PREMED...... Premedical Student (WDAA)
PRE-MED.... Previous to Appearance in MEDLINE [Latham, NY] [Bibliographic database]
PREMEDU... Preventive Medicine Unit
Premerk...... Premark International, Inc. [Associated Press] (SAG)
PREMES ...... Premises (ROG)
PremFin....... Premier Financial Bancorp, Inc. [Associated Press] (SAG)
PremFn....... Premier Financial Services [Associated Press] (SAG)
premie....... Premature [Infant] (DAVI)
Premis........ Premis Corp. [Associated Press] (SAG)
PREMIS ...... Premises Information System (SAUS)
PremLiab.... Premises Liability (SAUS)
PREMO...... Presentation Environment for Multimedia Objects (RALS)
PREMOD..... Premodeling Data Output [Environmental Protection Agency]
PREMOD..... Premodulation (NASA)
PRE-MOD.... Premodulation
PREMODE.... Preliminary Mid-Ocean Dynamics Experiment [Marine science] (MSC)
PREMPT ..... Program For Electromagnetic Pulse Testing (SAUS)
Prem Red ... Premium Reducing (SAUS)
Prem Res ... Premium Reserve (SAUS)
PremIn .... Premier Industrial Corp. [Associated Press] (SAG)
pre-mRNA... Precursor-Messenger Ribonucleic Acid
PREMS ...... Premises (DSUE)
PREMSS ...... Photographic Reconnaissance and Exploitation Management Support System (MCD)
PremT........ Premiere Technologies, Inc. [Associated Press] (SAG)
PREN .... European draft standard (SAUS)
PREN .... Price Enterprises [NASDAQ symbol] (TTSB)
PREN .... Price Enterprises, Inc. [NASDAQ symbol] (SAG)
PREN .... Project Engineering (SAUS)
Pren Act ..... Prentice's Proceedings in an Action [2nd ed.] [1880] [A publication] (DLA)
prenat........ Prenatal
PrEng........ Professional Engineer
PrentPr .... Prentiss Properties Trust [Associated Press] (SAG)
preocc .... Preoccupied [Biology, taxonomy]
PRE-OP....... Pre-Operational
PREOP .... Preoperative [Medicine]
PRE-OPS..... Pre-Operational Support [Military]
PREOS .... Performance and Range of Electro-Optical Systems (SAUS)
PREOS .... Predicted Range for Electrooptical Systems [Military] (CAAL)
PREOVHL.... Prepare for Overhaul (SAUS)
PREOVHL.... Prepare for Shipyard Overhaul [Navy] (NVT)
PREP .... Pacific Range Electromagnetic Platform (AAG)
PREP .... Parent Readiness Evaluation of Preschoolers [Child development test]
PREP .... Pattern Reversal Evoked Potential
PREP .... Peace Research and Education Project
PREP .... Peacetime Requirements and Procedures [Strategic Air Command] (MUGU)
PREP .... Pediatrics Review and Education Program (SAUS)
PREP .... Penaeid Prawns Recruitment Project (SAUS)
PREP .... Personal Radio Equipped Police (SAUS)
PREP .... Personal Responsibility Education Process
PREP .... Persons Responsive to Educational Problems (EA)
PREP .... Plan, Rehearse, Edit, and Psych [Public speaking preparation technique]
PREP .... Plasma Rotating Electrode Process [Metallurgy]
PREP .... Population, Resources, and Environment Program [American Association for the Advancement of Science]
PReP .... Power PC [Personal Computer] Reference Platform [Configuration standard] (PCM)
PREP .... PowerPC Reference Plattform (SAUS)
PREP .... Predischarge Education Program [DoD]
PREP .... Pre-Edit Processor (SAUS)
prep.......... Preparation (WDMC)
PREP .... Preparation [or Preparatory]
PREP .... Preparation Rehabilitation Education Program (SAUS)
Prep.......... Preparations (AL)
Prep.......... Preparatory (AL)
prep.......... Preparatory (NTIO)
PREP .... Preparatory (SAUS)
PREP ...... Prepare (AFM)
prep.......... Prepare (WDMC)
prep.......... Preposition (WDMC)
PREP .... Preposition
PREP .... Preprocessing (SAUS)
PREP .... Productivity Research and Extension Program [North Carolina State University] [Research center] (RCD)
PREP .... Programmable Electronics Performance Corp. (SAUS)
PREP .... Programmed Educational Package
PREP .... Programmed Electronics Pattern (PDAA)
PREP .... Pupil Record of Educational Progress [Education] (AEBS)
PREP .... Purchasing, Receiving, and Payable System
PREP .... Putting Research into Educational Practice [Information service of ERIC]
Prepak........ People's Revolutionary Party of Kungleipak [India] [Political party] (PD)
PREPARE.... Premarital Personal and Relationship Evaluation
PREPAS ...... Precise Personnel Assignment System [Marine Corps] (GFGA)
PREPCOM... Preparatory Commission for the International Seabed Authority and for the International Tribunal for the Law of the Sea (SAUS)

PrepCom...... Preparatory Committee [*United Nations Committee on Environment and Development*]
PREPCOM.... Preparatory Consultations Meeting (SAUS)
PREPD .... Prepared
PREPE .... Prepare (ROG)
PREP FA MVMT REQ... Prepare FA Movement Request (SAUS)
Prep Frt ...... Prepaid Freight (SAUS)
PREPG .... Preparing
PREPN .... Preparation
PREPnet ...... [*The*] Pennsylvania Research & Economic Partnership Network [*Computer science*] (TNIG)
Prepo........... Praepositus [*Deceased, 1509*] [*Authority cited in pre-1607 legal work*] (DSA)
PREPO .... Pre Positioning (ACAE)
Prepos......... Praepositus [*Deceased, 1509*] [*Authority cited in pre-1607 legal work*] (DSA)
PREPOS...... Preposition (AABC)
PREPOSN ... Prepared Position (SAUS)
PREPOSTOR... Prepositioned Storage [*Army*] (AABC)
PREPP .... Process Experimental Pilot Plant (COE)
PREPPSA..... Prepare Postshakedown Availability [*Navy*] (NVT)
Preppy........ Preparatory School Alumnus [*Lifestyle classification*]
Prepr Am Cbem Soc Div Fuel Chem... Preprints. American Chemical Society. Division of Fuel Chemistry (SAUS)
Prepr Amer Wood Pres Ass... Preprint. American Wood Preservers Association (SAUS)
PREP/RAMP... Pre-Edit Processor/Report and Message Processor (SAUS)
PREPREG..... Pre-Impregnated Glass Fibers [*Fiberglass production*]
PREPRO...... Prepositioning [*Ship*] [*Navy*] (DOMA)
PREPRO...... Preprocessor [*Computer*] [*Coast Guard*]
PREPROD .... Pre Production (ACAE)
PREPROD .... Preproduction Model [*Military*] (AFIT)
Prepr Pap Annu Conf Australas Corros Assoc... Australasian Corrosion Association. Preprinted Papers of the Annual Conference (journ.) (SAUS)
Prepr Pap Natl Meet Dir Water Air Waste Chem Am Chem Soc... Preprints of Papers Presented at National Meeting. Division of Water, Air and Waste Chemistry. American Chemical Society (SAUS)
PREPS .... Predischarge Remedial Education Program [*For servicemen*]
PREPS .... Program of Research and Evaluation in Public Schools [*Mississippi State University*] [*Research center*] (RCD)
PREPSCOL.... Preparatory School
PREPSYS..... Preparedness for Operations Status System (SAUS)
PREPTP ...... digit preparation type and application point (SAUS)
Prepub........ Prepublication (SAUS)
prepub......... Prepublication
PREQUAL..... Prequalified [*NASA*] (KSC)
Prer .... Prerogative Court (DLA)
PRER .... Putting Research into Educational Research
PRE-RE........ Prerefunded Municipal Note [*Investment term*] (DFIT)
PRERECPAC... Preplanned Reconnaissance Pacific (CINC)
PREREQ...... Prerequisite (WGA)
Prer Hum Serv... Prevention in Human Services (SAUS)
PRERLA....... Pupils Round, Equal, React to Light and Accommodation [*Medicine*] (MAE)
Prerog Ct ..... Prerogative Court, New Jersey (DLA)
PRES.......... Precision Resources, Inc. (SAUS)
PRES.......... Premises (ROG)
PRES.......... Pre-Release Employment Scheme (WDAA)
PRES.......... Presbyterian
pres............. Prescriptions (SAUS)
PRES.......... Presence
PRES.......... Present (AAG)
pres........... Present (NTIO)
Pres............ Presentation (EBF)
PRES.......... Preserved
PRES.......... Preset (SAUS)
PRE-S .... Preshaving (MSA)
pres .... President (DD)
PRES.......... President (EY)
Pres............ President (ODBW)
PRES.......... President of the Royal Entomological Society [*British*]
PRES.......... Pressure (FAAC)
PRES.......... Preston R. R. [*AAR code*]
PRES.......... Presumptive [*Grammar*]
PRES.......... Prime Residential, Inc. [*NASDAQ symbol*] (SAG)
PRES.......... Program Reporting and Evaluation System (ACAE)
PRES........ Promotion Recommendation Forms (SAUS)
PRES.......... Proton Resonance (IAA)
PRES.......... Puerto Rico Employment Service (SAUS)
PRES100..... Presidential's Hundred Tab [*Military*]
Pres Abs...... Preston's Abstracts of Title [*2nd ed.*] [*1823-24*] [*A publication*] (DLA)
PRESAC....... Photographic Reconnaissance System Analysis by Computer
PRESAGE..... Program to Realistically Evaluate Strategic Anti-Ballistic-Missile Gaming Effect (SAUS)
PRESAILEDREP... Forecast Sailing Report [*Navy*] (NVT)
PRESAIR...... Pressurized Air Compressor (DNAB)
Presb.......... Presbyterian (NTIO)
PRESB .... Presbyterian
PRESB .... Prescribe (AABC)
Presb&Ref R... Presbyterian and Reformed Review (SAUS)
PresBnc ...... Prestige Bancorp, Inc. [*Associated Press*] (SAG)
presby .... presbyopic (SAUS)
PRESBY ...... Presbyterian
presby .... Presbytery (VRA)
PRESBY ...... Presbytery

Presbyt-St Lukes Hosp Med Bull... Presbyterian-St. Lukes Hospital. Medical Bulletin (SAUS)
Presbyt-St Lukes Hosp Res Rep... Presbyterian-St. Lukes Hospital. Research Report (SAUS)
PresCasn .... President Casinos, Inc. [*Associated Press*] (SAG)
Pres C of E Ch... Presbyterian Church of England Chaplain [*Navy*] [*British*]
PRESCOM.... Personnel Command [*Army*] (DOMA)
Pres Conv.... Preston on Conveyancing [*5th ed.*] [*1819-29*] [*A publication*] (DLA)
PRESCORE... Program for the Rapid Estimation of Construction Requirements
PRESCR....... Prescription (MSA)
Presd.......... Presidio Oil Co. [*Associated Press*] (SAG)
PRESDL....... Presidential (WGA)
PresDuSta ... Present Duty Station (SAUS)
presen .... Presentation (VRA)
Preserv........ Preservation (DIAR)
PRESERV..... Preservation
Pres Est...... Preston on Estates [*3rd ed.*] [*1829*] [*A publication*] (DLA)
PRESET........ Preset Spin Echo Technique
Pres Fal....... Falconer's Decisions, Scotch Court of Session [*1744-51*] [*A publication*] (DLA)
Pres Fal....... Gilmour & Falconer Reports, Court of Session (SAUS)
Pres Fal....... Gilmour and Falconer's Reports, Scotch Court of Session [*A publication*] (DLA)
Pres Falc..... President Falconer's Scotch Session Cases (Gilmour and Falconer) [*1681-86*] [*A publication*] (DLA)
PRESFR....... Pressure Falling Rapidly [*NWS*] (FAAC)
PRESIG....... Pressurizing (KSC)
PRESIGN...... Procedure Sign
Presilection... Presidential Election (SAUS)
PRESINSURV... Inspection and Survey Board [*Navy*]
Pres Leg...... Preston on Legacies [*1824*] [*A publication*] (DLA)
PresLf.......... Presidential Life Corp. [*Associated Press*] (SAG)
Presly......... Presley Companies [*Associated Press*] (SAG)
Pres Mer ..... Preston on Merger [*A publication*] (DLA)
PRESNAVWARCOL... Naval War College
PRES PART... Present Participle [*Grammar*] (WDAA)
Pres Proc.... Presidential Proclamation (AAGC)
PRESPROC... Presidential Proclamation
PresR......... Presidential Realty Corp. [*Associated Press*] (SAG)
PRESRR..... Pressure Rising Rapidly [*NWS*] (FAAC)
PRESS .... Pacific Range Electromagnetic Signature Studies [*or System*] [*Military*] (NG)
PRESS .... Pacific Range Electromagnetic Signature System (SAUS)
PRESS .... Parti Republicain Social du Senegal [*Social Republican Party of Senegal*] [*Political party*]
PRESS .... Peace Research and European Security Studies (SAUS)
PRESS .... Predicted Residual Sum of Squares
PRESS .... Prediction Error Sum of Squares (AAEL)
PRESS .... Prereading Expectancy Screening Scale [*Educational test*]
PRESS .... Pressurant (NAKS)
PRESS .... Pressure (MCD)
PRESS .... Product Records Engineering Support System (SAUS)
PRESS .... Project Review, Evaluation and Scheduling System (SAUS)
PRESS .... Prolog Equation Solving System (BYTE)
PRESS .... Property Record for Equipment Servicing and Sharing (MCD)
PRESSAR..... Presentation Equipment for Slow Scan RADAR
PRESSDUCTOR... Pressure Inductor (IAA)
PRESSFR..... Pressure Falling Rapidly [*Meteorology*] (WEAT)
PRESSO....... Program for Elective Surgical Second Opinion [*Blue Cross/Blue Shield*]
Pres SQ ...... Presidential Studies Quarterly [*A publication*] (BRI)
PRESSRA..... Presentation Equipment for Slow Scan Radar (SAUS)
PRESSRR..... Pressure Rising Rapidly [*Meteorology*] (WEAT)
Pressure Eng... Plessure Engineering (SAUS)
PRESSURS... Pre-Strike Surveillance/Reconnaissance System (MCD)
PREST .... Party on Scientific and Technical Research Policy [*European community*] (MHDB)
PREST .... Policy Research in Engineering, Science and Technology (SAUS)
PREST .... Present (ROG)
PRES'T .... President
PRE-ST .... Prestart (AAG)
PREST .... Programme of Policy Research in Engineering Science and Technology [*British*]
Prest Conv... Preston on Conveyancing [*A publication*] (DLA)
Prestek .... Presstek, Inc. [*Associated Press*] (SAG)
Prestel........ Press button on Telephone-Lines (SAUS)
Prest Est..... Preston on Estates [*A publication*] (DLA)
PrestFn....... Prestige Financial Corp. [*Associated Press*] (SAG)
Prest Merg... Preston on Merger [*A publication*] (DLA)
PRESTMO .... Prestissimo [*Very Fast*] [*Music*] (ROG)
PRESTO ...... Personnel Response and Evaluation System for Target Obscuration [*Military*] (RDA)
PRESTO ...... Precursory Research for Embryonic Science and Technology (SAUS)
PRESTO ...... Prediction of Radiological Effects Due to Shallow Trench Operations [*Environmental Protection Agency*] (AEPA)
PRESTO ...... Prestissimo [*Very Fast*] [*Music*] (ROG)
PRESTO ...... Program for Rapid Earth-to-Space Trajectory Optimization [*NASA*]
PRESTO ...... Programmable Etalon Spectrometer for Twilight Observations (SAUS)
PRESTO ...... Program Reporting and Evaluation System for Total Operation (SAUS)
PRESTO ...... Program Reporting and Evaluation System for Total Operations [*AFSC*]
PRESTO ...... Project Release Status Operation (SAUS)
PRE-STORM.. Preliminary Regional Experiment for STORM [*Stormscale Operational and Research Meteorology*] [*Marine science*] (OSRA)

PRE-STORM...   Preliminary Research Experiment-Stormscale Operational and Research Meteorology (SAUS)
Prest Shep T...   Sheppard's Touchstone by Preston [*A publication*] (DLA)
PRESUB.......   Pre-Subscript (SAUS)
Presv ....   Preservation (AL)
presv ....   Preservation (BARN)
Presync.......   Presynchronization
PRET...........   Periodic Reliability Evaluation Test (MCD)
PRET...........   Preterit [*Past tense*] [*Grammar*] (ROG)
Pret.............   Preterite (SAUS)
PRET...........   Pretoria [*South Africa*] (ROG)
PRET...........   Program for the Recovery of the Economy in Transition (SAUS)
PRETACS .....   Prediction of Tax Cases System (SAUS)
PRETCHREP...   Preliminary Technical Report (MCD)
PRETECHREP...   Preliminary Technical Report [*Army*] (AABC)
PRETOS ....   Proofreading Tests of Spelling [*Educational test*]
Pretrial Conf...   Pretrial Conference (SAUS)
PRETTYBLUEBATCH...   Philadelphia Regular Exchange Tea Total Young Belles Lettres Universal Experimental Bibliographical Association To Civilize Humanity [*From Edgar Allan Poe essay "How to Write a Blackwood Article"*]
pretz ....   pretzel (SAUS)
PREV ....   Medical and Psychological Previews [*Database*] [*BRS Information Technologies*] [*Information service or system*] (IID)
PREV ....   Prevent (SAUS)
PREV ....   Prevention
PREV ....   Previous (AFM)
prev ....   Previous (NTIO)
prev ....   Previous (SHCU)
PREV ....   Previously (SAUS)
PREV ....   Previous Program Selection [*In-car entertainment*] [*Electronics*]
PrevAGT ......   Previous Abnormality of Glucose Tolerance
PREVAN.......   Precompiler for Vector Analysis (SAUS)
PREVEN ....   Preventive (SAUS)
PREVENT.....   Pacific Northwest Regional Visibility Experiment using Natural Tracers [*Marine science*] (OSRA)
PREVENT.....   Pacific NW Regional Visibility EXperiment using Natural Tracers (USDC)
PREVENT.....   Precertification to Verify Necessary Treatment
PRevere.......   Paul Revere Corp. [*Associated Press*] (SAG)
PREVLINE....   Prevention Online (SAUS)
PREVLV ....   Prevalve
PrevMed ......   Preventive Medicine (DAVI)
PREVMEDU...   Preventive Medicine Unit
pre-voc........   Prevocational [*Education*] (DAVI)
PREVT ....   Preventative
PREWI ....   Press Wireless [*A radio service for the transmission of news*]
PREWI ....   Press Wireless, Inc. (SAUS)
Pr Exch........   Price's English Exchequer Reports [*1814-24*] [*A publication*] (DLA)
PREXTEND...   Prestel Extended (SAUS)
PREZ...........   President Casinos [*NASDAQ symbol*] (TTSB)
PREZ...........   President Riverboat Casinos [*NASDAQ symbol*] (SAG)
PRF.............   Palestine Rejection Front (BJA)
PRF.............   Parachute Refurbishment Facility [*NASA*] (NASA)
PRF.............   Parliament Reference (SAUS)
PRF.............   Partial Refund [*Travel industry*] (TVEL)
PRF.............   Partial Reinforcement [*Training*]
PRF.............   Partido Revolucionario Febrerista [*Febrerista Revolutionary Party*] [*Paraguay*] [*Political party*] (PPW)
PRF.............   Patient Record Form
PRF.............   Patient Report Form (DB)
PRF.............   Penetration Room Filtration [*Nuclear energy*] (NRCH)
prf.............   Performer [*MARC relator code*] [*Library of Congress*] (LCCP)
PRF.............   Permanent Requirements File [*Computer science*] (CIST)
PRF.............   Personality Research Form [*Psychology*]
PRF.............   Personnel Readiness File [*Army*] (AABC)
PRF.............   Personnel Resources File (SAUS)
PRF.............   Petroleum Research Fund
PRF.............   Phenol/Resorcinol/Formaldehyde [*Plastics technology*]
PRF.............   Plant Response Fertilization [*Agriculture*]
PRF.............   Plasmacytoma Repressor Factor [*Cytology*]
PRF.............   Plastics Recycling Foundation (EA)
PRF.............   Plug Representing Fuze (SAUS)
PRF.............   Plutonium Reclamation Facility [*Nuclear energy*]
PRF.............   Plymouth Rock Foundation (EA)
PRF.............   Plywood Research Foundation (EA)
PRF.............   Porpoise Rescue Foundation (EA)
PRF.............   Point Response Function [*Of a telescope*]
PRF.............   Polyclonal Rheumatoid Factor [*Medicine*] (DMAA)
PRF.............   Pontine Reticular Formation [*Neurophysiology*]
PRF.............   Potential Requirements File (NITA)
PRF.............   Power Radio Frequency [*Telecommunications*] (IAA)
PRF.............   Prefac Enterprises, Inc. [*Toronto Stock Exchange symbol*]
PRF.............   Preferences (SAUS)
PRF.............   Preformed [*Technical drawings*]
PRF.............   Pride Co. $2.60cm Cv L.P. [*NYSE symbol*] (TTSB)
PRF.............   Pride Companies Ltd. [*NYSE symbol*] (SPSG)
PRF.............   Primary Reference Fuel [*Automotive engineering*]
PRF.............   Priority-Reserved Flight (SAUS)
PRF.............   Problem Report Form (SAUS)
PRF.............   Processor Request Flag [*Telecommunications*] (TEL)
PRF.............   Progressive Renal Failure [*Medicine*] (AAMN)
PRF.............   Prolactin Releasing Factor (SAUS)
PRF Shep T...   Prolactin-Releasing Factor [*Endocrinology*]
PRF.............   Proliferation Regulatory Factor [*Biochemistry*]

PRF.............   Proof (KSC)
prf...............   Proof (VRA)
Pr F ....   Propyl Fluoride (SAUS)
PRF.............   Protein Research Foundation (SAUS)
PRF.............   Protein Rich Fraction [*Food analysis*]
PRF.............   Protein Rich Fractions (SAUS)
PRF.............   Psychiatric Research Foundation
PRF.............   Psychical Research Foundation (EA)
PRF.............   Psychosynthesis Research Foundation (EA)
PRF.............   Publications Reference File [*Government Printing Office*] [*Database*] [*Washington, DC*] (MCD)
PRF.............   Public Relations Foundation
PRF.............   Public Residential Facility
PRF.............   Puerto Rico Federal Reports [*A publication*] (DLA)
PRF.............   Pulse Rate Frequency (MUGU)
PRF.............   Pulse Recurrence Frequency
prf.............   Pulse Repetition Frequency (IDOE)
PRF.............   Pulse Repetition Frequency [*Computer science*]
PRF.............   Pulsese Repetition Frequency (SAUS)
PRF.............   Purchase Rate Factor
PRF.............   Purdue Research Foundation [*Purdue University*] [*Research center*] (MCD)
PRFA ....   Plasma Recognition Factor Activity [*Hematology*] (AAMN)
Pr Falc........   President Falconer's Scotch Session Cases [*1744-51*] [*A publication*] (DLA)
PRFAW ....   Personnel Research Field Activity, Washington [*Navy*] (MUGU)
PrfBcp.........   Professional Bancorp [*Associated Press*] (SAG)
PRFC ....   Plymouth Rock Fanciers Club (EA)
PRFC ....   Potomac River Fisheries Commission [*Maryland and Virginia*] (NOAA)
PRFCN ....   Purification
PRFCS ....   Pattern Recognition Feedback Control System [*Computer science*] (IAA)
PRFCS ....   Prefocus
PRFD ....   Pulse Recurrence Frequency Discrimination [*Telecommunications*] (TEL)
PRFD ....   Pulse Repetition Frequency Distribution (SAUS)
PRFDX........   Price T. Rowe: Equity Income [*Mutual fund ticker symbol*] (SG)
PRFE..........   Polar Reflection Faraday Effect
PRFE..........   Polar-Reflection Faraday Effect (SAUS)
PR Fed ....   Puerto Rico Federal Reports [*A publication*] (DLA)
PRFG..........   Proofing [*Freight*]
PRFH..........   Pseudo-Random Frequency-Hopping (SAUS)
PRFI...........   Portable Range-Finder/Illuminator
PRFI...........   Puerto Rican Family Institute (EA)
PRFIA ....   Phase-Resolved Fluoroimmunoassay
PRFIC ....   Plume RADAR Frequency Interference Code (MCD)
PrfIOF ....   Preferred Income Opportunity Fund [*Associated Press*] (SAG)
PRFL..........   Pressure Fed Liquid (KSC)
PRFM..........   Performance (MSA)
PRFM..........   Perfumania, Inc. [*NASDAQ symbol*] (SAG)
PRFM..........   Premature [*or Prolonged*] Rupture of Fetal Membrane [*Gynecology*] (MAE)
PRFM..........   Prolonged Rupture of Fetal Membranes [*Obstetrics*] (DAVI)
PRFM..........   Pseudorandom Frequency Modulated [*Computer science*]
PRFN..........   Prestige Financial [*NASDAQ symbol*] (TTSB)
PRFN..........   Prestige Financial Corp. [*NASDAQ symbol*] (SAG)
PRFNL........   Professional (SAUS)
PRFP..........   Preliminary Request for Proposal (SAUS)
PRFPT ....   Federacion Puertorriqueno de Trabajadores
PRFR ....   Proofer [*Freight*]
PRFR ....   Proof Reader (SAUS)
PRFR ....   Proofreader (SAUS)
PRFRD........   Proofread (MSA)
PRFRT ....   Partially Relaxed Fourier Transform (DB)
PRFS ....   Phase-Resolved Fluorescence Spectroscopy
PRFS ....   Pulse Recurrence Frequency Stagger (OA)
PRFs ....   Pulse Repetition Frequencies (SAUS)
PRFSS ....   Peterborough Royal Foxhound Show Society [*British*] (DBA)
PRFT..........   Partially Relaxed Fourier Transform [*Mathematics*]
PRFT..........   Portable Rod-and-Frame Test (EDAC)
PRFT..........   Presser Foot
PRFT..........   Press Fit
PRFT..........   Proffitt's, Inc. [*NASDAQ symbol*] (NQ)
PRFU..........   Processor Reader for Use (SAUS)
PRFU..........   Processor Ready for Use [*Telecommunications*] (TEL)
PRG ....   Empresa Aero-Servicios Parrague Ltd. [*Chile*] [*ICAO designator*] (FAAC)
PRG ....   Gilbert Associates, Inc., Reading, PA [*Library symbol*] [*Library of Congress*] (LCLS)
PRG ....   PAL Programming Department (SAUS)
PRG ....   Parabolic Radius Gage (MCD)
PRG ....   Paris, IL [*Location identifier*] [*FAA*] (FAAL)
PRG ....   Patient Related Groups (SAUS)
PRG ....   Peacekeeper Rail Garrison [*Cancelled 1991*] [*Air Force*] (DOMA)
PRG ....   Peerless Carpet Corp. [*Toronto Stock Exchange symbol*]
PRG ....   Peer Review Group (MELL)
PRG ....   People's Revolutionary Government [*Grenada*] (PD)
PRG ....   Perennial Rye Grass [*Immunology*]
PRG ....   Performance Related Gift [*Business Management*]
PRG ....   Personnel Requirements Generator
PRG ....   Personnel Resources Group [*Military*]
PRG ....   Perugia [*Italy*] [*Seismograph station code, US Geological Survey*] (SEIS)
PRG ....   Phleborrheogram [*Hematology*] (DAVI)

PRG	Physician Resources Group, Inc. [*NYSE symbol*] (SAG)
PRG	Physicians Resource Group [*NYSE symbol*] (TTSB)
PRG	Pick Resources Guide [*ALLM Books*] [*England*] [*Information service or system*] (IID)
PRG	Plastic Radial Grating
PRG	Policy Research Group [*Australian Labor Party*]
PRG	Powerful Radio Galaxy [*Cosmology*]
PRG	Prague [*Former Czechoslovakia*] [*Airport symbol*] (OAG)
PRG	Procedure Review Group [*Nuclear energy*] (NRCH)
PRG	Program Control Mode (SAUS)
PRG	Program Regulation Guide
PRG	Program Resources Group (SAUS)
PRG	Program Review Group [*Military*]
PRG	Provisional Revolutionary Government [*Political arm of the Vietcong*] (VNW)
PRG	Psychological Readers Guide (SAUS)
PRG	Purge (AAG)
PRGC	Past Royal Grand Cross [*Freemasonry*] (ROG)
Prg Chk	Program Check (SAUS)
Prg E	Program End (SAUS)
Prg Exp	Program Expander (SAUS)
PRGFX	Price T. Rowe: Growth Stock [*Mutual fund ticker symbol*] (SG)
PRG/I	Pick Resources Guide/International [*ALLM Books*] [*Information service or system*] (IID)
PRGIX	Price T. Rowe: Growth & Income [*Mutual fund ticker symbol*] (SG)
PRGM	Program (AFM)
Prgm	Program (PHSD)
PRGMG	Programming (MSA)
PRGMNG	Programming
PRGMR	Programmer (AFM)
Prgmr	Programmer (AL)
PRGM RGTR	Program Register (SAUS)
PRGO	Perrigo Co. [*NASDAQ symbol*] (SPSG)
PRGPrB	Pub Sv E&G 4.18% Pfd [*NYSE symbol*] (TTSB)
PRGR	ProGroup, Inc. [*NASDAQ symbol*] (NQ)
PRGR	Proving Ground (SAUS)
Prg Reg	Program Register (SAUS)
PRGRMR	Programmer
PRGS	President of the Royal Geographical Society [*British*]
PRGS	Proceedings of the Royal Geographical Society (SAUS)
PRGS	Prognosis (AABC)
PRGS	Progress Software [*NASDAQ symbol*] (SPSG)
Prg Sh	Program Shift (SAUS)
PrgSoft	Progress Software Corp. [*Associated Press*] (SAG)
Prg Sup	Program Suppress (SAUS)
PRGVN	Provisional Revolutionary Government of South Vietnam (VNW)
PRGX	Profit Recovery Group International, Inc. (The) [*NASDAQ symbol*] (SAG)
PRGX	Profit Recovery Grp Intl [*NASDAQ symbol*] (TTSB)
PRGY	Prodigy Communications [*NASDAQ symbol*] (SG)
PRH	Partido Revolucionario Hondureno [*Honduras Revolutionary Party*] [*Political party*] (PPW)
PRH	Petrol Railhead
PRH	Phrae [*Thailand*] [*Airport symbol*] (OAG)
PrH	Prepositus Hypoglossi [*Neuroanatomy*]
PRH	Preretinal Hemorrhage [*Medicine*] (MELL)
PRH	Program Requirements Handbook (MUGU)
PRH	Prolactin-Releasing Hormone [*Endocrinology*]
PRH	Promus Hotel [*NYSE symbol*] (TTSB)
PRH	Promus Hotel Corp. [*NYSE symbol*] (SAG)
PRH	Psychiatric Regional Hospital [*Health insurance*] (GHCT)
PRH	Pulmonary Right Heart (SAUS)
PRHA	People Refreshment House Association [*British*] (BI)
PRHA	President of the Royal Hibernian Academy [*British*]
PRHB	Pacific Rehabilitation & Sports Medicine, Inc. [*NASDAQ symbol*] (SAG)
PRHB	Pacific Rehab/Sports Medicine [*NASDAQ symbol*] (TTSB)
PRHBF	Peak Reactive Hyperemia Blood Flow [*Hematology*] (MAE)
Pr HC Ch	Practice of the High Court of Chancery [*A publication*] (DLA)
PRHi	Historical Society of Berks County, Reading, PA [*Library symbol*] [*Library of Congress*] (LCLS)
PRHS	Port Richmond High School
PRHYX	Price T. Rowe: High Yield [*Mutual fund ticker symbol*] (SG)
PRI	Farmington, MO [*Location identifier*] [*FAA*] (FAAL)
PRI	Institutional Revolutionary Party [*Mexico*] [*Political party*]
PRI	Pacific Research Institute for Public Policy (EA)
PRI	Pacific Resources, Inc. (EFIS)
PRI	Pain Rating Index
PRI	Paint Research Institute [*Defunct*] (EA)
PRI	Paleontological Research Institution (EA)
PRI	Partial Response Impuls (SAUS)
PRI	Partido Revolucionario Institucional [*Party of the Institutionalized Revolution*] [*Mexico*] [*Political party*]
PRI	Partito Repubblicano Italiano [*Italian Republican Party*] [*Political party*] (PPW)
PRI	Partner Relationship Inventory [*Marital relations test*] [*Psychology*]
PRI	Partnership for Rural Improvement [*Washington*] (EDAC)
PRI	Peace Research Institute [*Later, Institute for Policy Studies*] (EA)
PRI	Performance Registry International
PRI	Performance Review Institutes
PRI	Periodic Reinvestigation (SAUS)
PRI	Personal Reaction Index [*Interpersonal skills and attitudes test*]
PRI	Personal Resource Inventory (DB)
PRI	Personnel Research, Inc. [*Information service or system*] (IID)
PRI	Personnel Research Institute Test (AEBS)
PRI	Petroleum Recovery Institute [*Research center*] (RCD)
PRI	Phosphate Rock Institute [*Defunct*] (EA)
PRI	Phosphoribose Isomerase [*An enzyme*] (MAE)
PRI	Photographic Radar Intelligence
PRI	Photographic Reconnaissance and Interpretation (NATG)
PRI	Photo RADAR Intelligence
PRI	Pineapple Research Institute (SAUS)
PRI	Pineapple Research Institute of Hawaii (EA)
PRI	Pittsburgh Research Institute (SAUS)
PRI	Plan Repeater Indicator (IAA)
PRI	Plasticity Retention Index [*Rubber test method*]
PRI	Plastics and Rubber Institute [*Institution of the Rubber Industry and Pla stics Institute*] [*Formed by a merger of*] (EAIO)
PRI	Polymer Research Institute [*University of Massachusetts*] [*Research center*] (RCD)
PRI	Polymer Research Institute [*Polytechnic Institute of New York*] [*Research center*] (RCD)
PRI	Population Reference Intake (WDAA)
PRI	Potomac Research, Incorporated
PRI	Practice Training Index
PRI	Praslin Island [*Seychelles Islands*] [*Airport symbol*] (OAG)
PRI	Pre-Ignition
PRI	Preliminary Rifle Instruction [*Military*]
PRI	Prescriptive Reading Inventory
PRI	President of the Royal Institute (SAUS)
PRI	President of the Royal Institute (of Painters in Water Colours) [*British*] (ROG)
PRI	President of the Royal Institution (London) (ROG)
PRI	President Regimental Institutes [*British*]
PRI	Pressure Rate Index (SAUS)
PRI	Pressure Ratio Indicator (SAUS)
PRI	Prevention Routiere Internationale [*International Road Safety Organization*] [*Luxembourg*] (EAIO)
Pri	Price's English Exchequer Reports [*1814-24*] [*A publication*] (DLA)
Pri	Price's English Mining Commissioners' Cases [*A publication*] (DLA)
PRI	Priest [*California*] [*Seismograph station code, US Geological Survey*] (SEIS)
pri	Primary (IDOE)
PRI	Primary (KSC)
PRI	Primary Rate, Inc.
PRI	Primary Rate Interface (PCM)
PRI	Primary Rifle Instruction (SAUS)
PRI	Primary Winding (IAA)
PRI	Primate Research Institute [*New Mexico State University*] [*Hollman, NM*]
PRI	Prime Computer Inc., Corporation Library, Framingham, MA [*OCLC symbol*] (OCLC)
PRI	Primer (IAA)
PRI	Princeville Airways, Inc. [*ICAO designator*] (FAAC)
PRI	Printer Interface [*Computer science*] (CIST)
PRI	Priority (AFM)
PRI	Priority Repair Induction [*Code*]
PRI	Priority Requirement for Information (AFM)
Pri	Priscianus [*Authority cited in pre-1607 legal work*] (DSA)
PRI	Prison
PRI	Private
PRI	Prize [*or Prizeman*] [*British*] (ROG)
PRI	Processing Research Institute [*Carnegie Mellon University*]
PRI	Production Rate Index (OA)
PRI	Production Records, Inc. (EA)
PRI	Program Interrupt [*Computer science*] (IAA)
PRI	Program Revision Intent
PRI	Projection Readout Indicator [*Aviation*] (OA)
PRI	Projector Rectile Image (SAUS)
PRI	Proteus Resources, Inc. [*Vancouver Stock Exchange symbol*]
PRI	Prout Research Institute (EA)
PRI	Psoriasis Research Institute (EA)
PRI	Public Radio International
PRI	Public Relations Institute (SAUS)
PRI	Public Relations Institute of Ireland (BI)
PRI	Puerto Rican Independence [*Later, GPRG*] [*An association*] (EA)
PRI	Puerto Rico [*ANSI three-letter standard code*] (CNC)
PRI	Pulse Rate Increase [*Medicine*]
PRI	Pulse Rate Indicator
PRI	Pulse Recurrence [*or Repetition*] Interval (NATG)
PRI	Pulse Repetition Internal
PRI	Pulse Repetition Interval (CIST)
PRI	Pure Research Institute [*Later, BRINC*] (EA)
PRIA	Peer Review Improvement Act (SAUS)
PRIA	Peer Review Improvement Act of 1982
PRIA	President of the Royal Irish Academy
PRIA	Priam Corp. (SAUS)
PRIA	PRI Automation [*NASDAQ symbol*] (SAG)
PRIA	Proceedings of the Royal Irish Academy (SAUS)
PRIA	Public Rangelands Improvement Act (SAUS)
PRIA	Public Rangelands Improvement Act of 1978
PRIA	Society for Participatory Research in Asia [*India*] (EAIO)
PRIAM	Precision Range Information Analysis for Missiles (MCD)
PRIAM	Pre-Normative Requirements for Intelligent Actuation & Measurements (ACII)
PRIAS	Packard's Radioimmunoassay System [*Medicine*] (DMAA)
PRIAS	Plant Register/Fixed Assets and Inflation Accounting System (SAUS)
PrIAU-SJ	Inter-American University of Puerto Rico, San Juan Campus, San Juan, PR [*Library symbol*] [*Library of Congress*] (LCLS)
PRI Auto	PRI Automation [*Associated Press*] (SAG)

PRIB .... Private Brands, Inc. (SAUS)
PRIBA .... President of the Royal Institute of British Architects
PRIBAG .... Priority Baggage (DNAB)
PRI BIL .... Primary Billet (DNAB)
Pribilovs ...... Pribilov Islands in the Bering Sea off Alaska (SAUS)
PRIC .... Dec. Puerto Rico Industrial Commission Decisions (SAUS)
PRIC .... Peripheral Interface Controller (SAUS)
PRICAI .... Pacific Rim International Conference on Artificial Intelligence (SAUS)
PRICALL ...... Priority Call (SAUS)
PRIC Dec ..... Puerto Rico Industrial Commission Decisions [*A publication*] (DLA)
PRICE .... Peroxy Radicals Inter Comparison Exercise (EA)
PRICE .... Physicians for Research in Cost-Effectiveness (EA)
Price .... Price's English Exchequer Reports [*A publication*] (DLA)
Price .... Price's English Mining Commissioners' Cases [*A publication*] (DLA)
PRICE .... Pricing Review to Intensify Competitive Environment [*Computer science*]
PRICE .... Productivity Improvement and Cost Effectiveness (SAUS)
PRICE .... Programmed Review of Information for Costing and Estimation (or Evaluation) (SAUS)
PRICE .... Programmed Review of Information for Costing and Evaluation (MCD)
PRICE .... Protection, Rest, Ice, Compression, Evaluation [*Medicine*]
Price & St ... Price and Stewart's Trade Mark Cases [*A publication*] (DLA)
PriceCst .... Price Costco, Inc. [*Associated Press*] (SAG)
PriceEnt .... Price Enterprises, Inc. [*Associated Press*] (SAG)
Price Gen Pr ... Price's General Practice [*A publication*] (DLA)
Price Liens ... Price on Maritime Liens [*1940*] [*A publication*] (DLA)
Pricell .... Pricellular Corp. [*Associated Press*] (SAG)
Price Min Cas ... Price's Mining Cases [*A publication*] (DLA)
PRICEMMM ... Protection, Rest, Ice, Compression, and Elevation
Price Notes PC ... Price's Notes of Practice Cases in Exchequer [*1830-31*] [*England*] [*A publication*] (DLA)
Price Notes PP ... Price's Notes of Points of Practice, English Exchequer Cases [*A publication*] (DLA)
Price PC ...... Price's English Practice Cases [*1830-31*] [*A publication*] (DLA)
Price Pr Cas ... Price's English Practice Cases [*A publication*] (DLA)
Price R Est ... Price on Acts Relating to Real Estate [*A publication*] (DLA)
PRICE-S .... Software Costing Model (SAUS)
PriceTR .... Price [*T. Rowe*] Associates, Inc. [*Associated Press*] (SAG)
Prickett .... Prickett's Reports [*1 Idaho*] [*A publication*] (DLA)
PRICOM .... Prison Commission [*British*]
PRI-D .... Peace Research Institute - Dundas [*Canada*] (IRC)
PRID .... Peace Research Institute, Dundas (SAUS)
PRID .... Planning Record Identifier (SAUS)
PRID .... Pridie [*The Day Before*] [*Latin*]
PriD .... Princeton Datafilm, Inc. (SAUS)
PriD .... Princeton Datafilm, Inc., Princeton, NJ [*Library symbol*] [*Library of Congress*] (LCLS)
PRID .... Processor Identity Number (SAUS)
Prid & C ...... Prideaux and Cole's English Reports [*4 New Sessions Cases*] [*1850-51*] [*A publication*] (DLA)
Prid & Co .... Prideaux and Cole's English Reports [*4 New Sessions Cases*] [*1850-51*] [*A publication*] (DLA)
Prid Ch W .... Prideaux's Directions to Churchwardens [*10th ed.*] [*1835*] [*A publication*] (DLA)
PRIDCO .... Puerto Rico Industrial Development Co.
Prid Conv ..... Prideaux's Forms and Precedents in Conveyancing [*24th ed.*] [*1952*] [*A publication*] (DLA)
PRIDE .... National Parents' Resource Institute for Drug Education (EA)
PRIDE .... Parents Resource Institute for Drug Education (SAUS)
PRIDE .... People and Resources Identified for Distributed Environments (TELE)
PRIDE .... People for Rehabilitating and Integrating the Disabled through Education [*New York City*]
PRIDE .... Perfection Requires Individual Defect Elimination
PRIDE .... Performance Readiness Initiatives Decision Evaluation System (SAUS)
PRIDE .... Personalized Recruiting for Immediate and Delayed Entry (SAUS)
PRIDE .... Personal Responsibility in Daily Effort [*Military Airlift Command's acronym for the Zero Defects Program*]
PRIDE .... Personal Responsibility in Defect Elimination (SAUS)
PRIDE .... Policy based Routing, Implementation and Deployment in Europe (SAUS)
PRIDE .... Preschool and Kindergarten Interest Descriptor [*Educational test*]
Pride .... Pride Companies Ltd. [*Associated Press*] (SAG)
PRIDE .... PRIDE Foundation, Inc. (NRGU)
PRIDE .... Priority Receiving with Inter-Departmental Efficiency [*Computer science*]
PRIDE .... Production of Reliable Items Demands Excellence [*Navy*] (NG)
PRIDE .... Production Review Integrated Database (SAUS)
PRIDE .... Productive Rehabilitation Institute of Dallas for Ergonomics [*Research center*] (RCD)
PRIDE .... Productivity Improvements for the Decade of the Eighties
PRIDE .... Productivity-Resourcefulness-Incentives-Dedication-Excellence (SAUS)
PRIDE .... Professional Results in Daily Effort [*Strategic Air Command's acronym for the Zero Defects Program*]
PRIDE .... Profitable Information by Design (MHDI)
PRIDE .... Profitable Information by Design through Phased Planning and Control (MHDB)
PRIDE .... Programmed Reliability in Design (SAUS)
PRIDE .... Programmed Reliability in Design Engineering
PRIDE .... Promote Real Independence for the Disabled and Elderly (EA)
PRIDE .... Prompt Response Insurance Delivery Express
PRIDE .... Protection of Reefs and Islands from Degradation and Exploitation
PRIDE .... Provisioning Review Input Data Evaluation (MCD)

PRIDE .... Puerto Rico Information and Decision Environment (SAUS)
PRIDE .... Pulse RADAR Intelligent Diagnostic Environment [*US Army Missile Command*] (RDA)
PrideA .... Pride Automotive Group, Inc. [*Associated Press*] (SAG)
PrideAto ...... Pride Automotive Group, Inc. [*Associated Press*] (SAG)
Prid Judg ..... Prideaux's Judgments and Crown Debts [*4th ed.*] [*1854*] [*A publication*] (DLA)
PRIEA .... Priority Issues Requiring Experimentation and Analysis (SAUS)
PRI-EOM ..... Procedure Interrupt-End-of-Message (SAUS)
PRI-EOP ..... Procedure Interrupt-End-of-Producedure (SAUS)
PRIF .... Peace Research Institute Frankfurt (SAUS)
PRIF .... Prior Year Refund Information File [*IRS*]
PRI-FLY .... Primary Flight Control [*on an aircraft carrier*] [*Navy*]
PRIG .... Packet Radio Interest Group (SAUS)
PRIH .... Pineapple Research Institute of Hawaii (SAUS)
PRIH .... Prolactin-Release Inhibiting Factor [*Also, PIF*] [*Endocrinology*]
PRIH .... Prolactin Release Inhibiting Hormone (SAUS)
PRIISM .... Pacific Research Institute for Information Systems and Management [*University of Hawaii at Manoa*] [*Research center*] (RCD)
PRIL .... Penarth Research International Ltd. [*British*]
PRIL .... Processor in The Loop (SAUS)
PRIM .... Pac Rim Holding [*NASDAQ symbol*] (SPSG)
PRIM .... Plans and Reports Improvement Memorandum [*Military*] (CAAL)
PRIM .... Plume Radiation Intensity Measurement (MUGU)
PRIM .... Pre-Referral Intervention Manual [*Test*] (TMMY)
PRIM .... Primary (AFM)
prim .... Primary (NTIO)
PRIM .... Primase (DMAA)
PRIM .... Primate
PRIM .... Primitive
prim .... primordial (SAUS)
PRIM .... Program for Information Managers [*Later, AIM*] [*An association*]
PRIM .... Programmed Instruction for Management Education (HGAA)
PRIMA .... Pollutant Response in Marine Animals [*Marine science*] (MSC)
PRIMA .... Primary Care Information Management across Anglia (SAUS)
PRIMA .... Public Radio in Mid-America (NTCM)
PRIMA .... Public Risk and Insurance Management Association [*Washington, DC*] (EA)
PRIMA .... Public Risk Management Association (NTPA)
Primadn .... Primadonna Resorts, Inc. [*Associated Press*] (SAG)
PrimaE .... Prima Energy Corp. [*Associated Press*] (SAG)
PRIM & R .... Public Responsibility in Medicine and Research (EA)
PRIMAR .... Program to Improve Management of Army Resources (AABC)
PrimaryB ...... Primary Bank [*Associated Press*] (SAG)
Primary Ed ... Primary Education [*A publication*]
Primary J .... Primary Journal (SAUS)
PRIMAS .... Precipitation Radar Image Management System (SAUS)
PRIMATE ..... Personal Retrieval of Information by Microcomputer and Terminal Ensemble
PRIM BIB .... Primary Bibliography (DGA)
Prim Care .... Primary Care, Clinics in Office Practice (SAUS)
PRIMCOM .... Pacific Rim Interactive Multimedia Computing [*Australia*]
Prim Comm Cen ... Primary Communication Center (SAUS)
PRIME .... Phantom Run Instrumented MILES Engagement (SAUS)
PRIME .... Philadelphia Regional Introduction for Minorities to Engineering (SAUS)
PRIME .... Plankton Reactivity in the Marine Environment (SAUS)
PRIME .... Planning through Retrieval of Information for Management Extrapolation (SAUS)
PRIME .... Precision Integrator for Meteorological Echoes (IEEE)
PRIME .... Precision Range Integrated Maneuver Exercise [*Army*] (RDA)
PRIME .... Precision Recovery Including Maneuvering Entry [*Air Force*]
PRIME .... Pre-Injection Metering [*Automotive fuel systems*]
PRIME .... Prematriculation Program in Medical Education (DMAA)
PRIME .... Preparedness of Resources in Mission Evaluation (SAA)
PRIME .... Prescribed Right to Income and Maximum Equity
PRIME .... Primary Initiatives in Mathematics Education (AIE)
PRIME .... Primate Information Management Experiment (SAUS)
PRIME .... Prime Computer, Inc. (SAUS)
PRIME .... Priority Improved Management Effort (KSC)
PRIME .... Priority Improvement Effort [*DoD*]
PRIME .... Priority Management Effort [*Army*]
PRIME .... Priority Management Engineering System (SAUS)
PRIME .... Priority Management Evaluation [*Navy*]
PRIME .... Procarbazine, Ifosfamide, Methotrexate [*Antineoplastic drug regimen*]
PRIME .... Processing, Research, Inspection, and Marine Extension Program [*National Oceanic and Atmospheric Administration*] (MSC)
PRIME .... Profession Related Intern-Mentorship Experience
PRIME .... Program for Innovation in Microenterprise (SAUS)
PRIME .... Program Independence, Modularity, Economy
PRIME .... Programmed Instruction for Management Education [*American Management Association*]
PRIME .... Programme for International Managers in Europe [*Business program*]
PRIME .... Program Research in Integrated Multiethnic Education [*Defunct*] (EA)
PRIME .... Purdue Rare Isotope Measurement Laboratory (SAUS)
PRIME BEEF ... Priority Improvement Management Effort Base Engineering Emergency Force [*Air Force*] (DOMA)
PrimeCp .... Prime Capital Corp. [*Associated Press*] (SAG)
Prim Ed-Pop Ed ... Primary Education-Popular Educator (SAUS)
PrimeMg .... Prime Management Group, Inc. [*Associated Press*] (SAG)
PRIMENET .... Prime Network Software Package [*Prime Computer, Inc.*]
PrimEq .... Prime Equities International [*Associated Press*] (SAG)
PRIMER .... Patient Record Information for Education Requirements [*Computer science*]

PRIME RIBS... Priority Improvement Management Effort Readiness in Base Services [*Air Force*] (DOMA)
PrimeRsd .... Prime Residential, Inc. [*Associated Press*] (SAG)
PRIMES .... Pennsylvania Retrieval of Information in Mathematics Education System (SAUS)
PRIMES .... Preflight Integration of Munitions and Electronic Systems (MCD)
PRIMES .... Productivity Integrated Measurement System [*Army*]
PrimeSrc .... PrimeSource Corp. [*Associated Press*] (SAG)
PRIMEX .... Primary Care Extender [*Insurance*] (DMAA)
primex......... Primex Technologies, Inc. [*Associated Press*] (SAG)
PRIMEX .... Private Message Switching [*Telecommunications*] [*British*]
PRIMIP .... Primipara [*Woman bearing first child*] [*Medicine*] (AAMN)
PRIMIR....... Product Improvement Information Report (SAUS)
PRIMIR....... Product Improvement Management Information Report
PRIM LUC.. Prima Luce [*Early in the Morning*] [*Pharmacy*]
PRIM M .... Primo Mane [*Early in the Morning*] [*Pharmacy*]
PRIM METH... Primitive Methodist [*A publication*]
PRIMO .... International Research Programme in the Western Mediterranean (SAUS)
PRIMO .... Programmable, Realtime, Incoherent, Matrix, Optical Processor [*Computer science*]
PRIMORDIAL... Primary Order Dial (NITA)
PRIMOS....... Prime Operating System [*Prime Computer, Inc.*]
PRIMP .... Primipara [*Woman bearing first child*] [*Obstetrics*] (DAVI)
PRI-MPS..... Procedure Interrupt-Multipage Signal (SAUS)
Prim Rel Sta... Primary Relay Station (SAUS)
Primrk .... Primark Corp. [*Associated Press*] (SAG)
PRIMS .... Product Requirement Information Management System (MCD)
PRIMSCO..... Pilot Run Item Master Schedule Committee (IAA)
PRIMTEC .... Pacific Rim Interactive Multi-Media Technology
PRIMTRA..... Air Primary Training
PRIMTRA..... Primary Training (SAUS)
PRIMUS .... Physician Reservists in Medical Universities and Schools [*Military*]
PRIMUS....... Primary Medical Care for the Uniformed Services [*DoD*]
PrimusT....... Primus Telecommunications Group, Inc. [*Associated Press*] (SAG)
PRIN .... Partido Revolucionario de la Izquierda Nacionalista [*National Leftist Revolutionary Party*] [*Bolivia*] [*Political party*] (PPW)
PRIN .... Peace Research Institute of Nigeria (SAUS)
PRIN .... Performance Risk Index Number (NG)
PRIN .... Powerec International
PRIN .... Princeton [*New Jersey*] [*Seismograph station code, US Geological Survey*] (SEIS)
Prin............. Principal (AL)
prin............. Principal (PROS)
PRIN .... Principal
PRIN .... Principality (ROG)
PRIN .... Principally (ROG)
PRIN .... Principia [*Elements*] [*Latin*] (ROG)
PRIN .... Principle (ROG)
prin............. Principle (VRA)
PRIN .... Printer Replaceable Item (SAUS)
PRINAIR ...... Puerto Rico International Airlines (SAUS)
PRINAIR ...... Puerto Rico National Airlines
PrinAm .... Princeton American Corp. [*Associated Press*] (SAG)
PRINC......... Principal
PRINC......... Principle
PRINC-APIC... Princeton Reliability Information Center-Apollo Parts Information Center (SAUS)
PRINCE....... Pans Reliability Information Center (SAUS)
PRINCE....... Parts, Reliability and Information Center (SAUS)
PRINCE....... Parts Reliability Information Center [*NASA*]
PRINCE....... Prediction Integrated with Code for Finite Elements [*Durability testing*]
PRINCE....... Programed International Computer Environment (SAUS)
PRINCE....... Programed Reinforced Instruction Necessary for Continuing Education (SAUS)
PRINCE....... Programmed International Computer Environment [*International relations simulation game*]
PRINCE....... Programmed Reinforced Instruction Necessary to Continuing Education (SAUS)
PRINCE/APIC... Parts Reliability Information Center/Apollo Parts Information Center [*NASA*]
PrinceM....... Princeton Media Group, Inc. [*Associated Press*] (SAG)
Prince NML... Prince's New Mexico Laws [*A publication*] (DLA)
Princeton U... Princeton University (GAGS)
PRINCIR ...... Printed Circuit (IAA)
PrincNtl ...... Princeton National Bancorp [*Associated Press*] (SAG)
Princ Univ Bull... Princeton University Bulletin (SAUS)
PRIND......... Present Indication [*Aviation*] (IAA)
PRIND......... Prolonged Reversible Ischemic Neurologic Deficit [*Medicine*] (DMAA)
PRINDI........ Princeton Diagnostic Laboratories of America, Inc. (SAUS)
PRINDUS ..... Prison Industries [*Industries conducted in English prisons*]
PRINFO....... Printed Information Distribution (SAA)
PRINFOD ..... Printed Information Distribution
PRING......... Partido Revolucionario de Izquierda Nacional Gueiler [*Revolutionary Party of the National Left - Gueiler Wing*] [*Bolivia*] [*Political party*] (PPW)
PRIN-L........ Partido Revolucionario de la Izquierda Nacional Laboral [*Political party*] (PPW)
PRINM........ Partido Revolucionario de la Izquierda Nacional Moller [*Bolivia*] [*Political party*] (PPW)
PRINMUS .... Principal Musician [*Marine Corps*]
PRINOBC/NEC... Primary Navy Officer Billet Classification and Navy Enlisted Classification
Prin PL .... Eden's Principles of Penal Law [*A publication*] (DLA)

Prin PL .... Eden's Principles of the Penal Law (SAUS)
Prin Pts .... Principal Parts (SAUS)
PRINS........... Partially Reversible Ischemic Neurologic Symptoms (SAUS)
Prins & Conderlag... Prins and Conderlag's Reports [*Ceylon*] [*A publication*] (ILCA)
PrinsRec..... Prins Recycling Corp. [*Associated Press*] (SAG)
PRINSYS..... Product Information System (IAA)
PRINSYS..... Production Information System (SAUS)
PRINT .... Preedited Interpreter (or Interpretive) (SAUS)
PRINT .... Pre-Edited Interpretive System [*Computer science*]
print........... Printing (WDMC)
PRINT .... Print Recognition Input Terminal (SAUS)
PRINT .... Public Release of Information and Transcripts [*Student legal action organization*]
Print&Pub... Printing and Publishing (SAUS)
Print Coll Q... Print Collectors Quarterly (SAUS)
PRINTF .... Print with Formatting (SAUS)
PRINTG....... Printing
printout........ Printer Output [*Computer science*] (CDE)
PRINTR....... Printer
PRINT System... Preedited Interpretive System (SAUS)
PRINUL....... Puerto Rico International Undersea Laboratory
PRIO .... International Peace Research Institute (SAUS)
PRIO .... International Peace Research Institution, Oslo [*Norway*]
PRIO .... Peace Research Institute (or Institution), Oslo (SAUS)
prio............. Priority (ELAL)
PRIO .... Priority [*Telecommunications*]
PRION.......... Proteinaceous Infectious Particle
PRIONS....... Proteinaceous Infectious Particles (SAUS)
PRIOR.......... Program for In-Orbital Rendezvous [*Antisatellite system*] [*Air Force*]
PRIORCBX ... Priority Coinbox (SAUS)
PRIOSUB .... Priority Subscriber (SAUS)
PRIOSUBS ... Priority Subscriber with Special Services (SAUS)
PRIP .... Park Restoration and Improvement Program [*National Park Service*]
PRIP .... Pattern Recognition and Image Processing (SAUS)
PRIP .... Planned Retirement Income Program [*Institute of Financial Management*]
PRIP .... Product Reliability Improvement Program
PRIP .... PSP Radar Improvement Program (SAUS)
PRIPACSEVOCAM... Primary Pacific Secure Voice Communications [*Navy*] (CAAL)
PRI-PL .... Primary Payload (SAUS)
PRIPP .... Pacific Research Institute for Public Policy (EA)
PRIP System... Pattern Recognition and Image Processing System (SAUS)
PRIR .... Parts Reliability Improvement Route (or Routing) (SAUS)
PR/IR .... Public Relations/Investor Relations (SAUS)
PRIRA......... Primary RADAR (FAAC)
PRIS .... Pacific Range Instrumentation Satellite (MUGU)
PRIS .... Personnel Resource Impact System (SAUS)
PRIS .... Pest Management Research Information System [*Agriculture Canada*] [*Information service or system*] (IID)
PRIS .... Prison (ROG)
PRIS .... Prisoner (AFM)
PRIS .... Program Resource Information System [*Department of Agriculture*]
PRIS .... Propeller Revolution Indicator System (MSA)
PRIS .... Protective Response Inducing Substance (SAUS)
PRIS .... Publications Reliability Inspection Sheet
PRISA .... Primary Slot Allocation (SAUS)
PRISA .... Public Radio Internet Service Alliance (SAUS)
PR/ISC .... Public Relations/Information Services Control (SAUS)
PRISCO........ Price Stabilisation Corp. (SAUS)
PRISCO........ Price Stabilization Corp.
PrisCoeff..... Prismatic Coefficient (SAUS)
PRISE .... Page Reader Input System with Editing (NVT)
PRISE .... Pennsylvania Resources and Information Center for Special Education [*Montgomery County Intermediate Unit*] [*King of Prussia*] [*Information service or system*] (IID)
PRISE .... Pennsylvania's Regional Instruction System for Education [*Network of colleges and universities*]
PRISE .... Primary Care Sharing the Evidence (SAUS)
PRISE .... Program for Integrated Shipboard Electronics
Pri Seq .... Primary Sequence (SAUS)
PRISIC........ Photographic Reconnaissance Interpretation Section [*Squadron*] IntelligenceCenter [*JICPOA*]
PRISM .... Parallel Instruction Set Multiprocessor (SAUS)
PRISM .... Parallel Reduced Instruction Set Multiprocessing (or -processor) (SAUS)
PRISM .... Parameter Related Internal Standard Method [*Statistical procedure*]
PRISM .... Paraxial-Ray Imaging Spectro Microscope
PRISM .... Partnership for Regulatory Innovation and Sustainable Manufacturing
PRISM .... Passive RADAR Identification System (SEWL)
PRISM .... Pattern Recognition Information Synthesis Modeling [*Market analysis*]
PRISM .... Peace and Reconciliation Inter-Schools Movement (AIE)
PRISM .... Pediatric Risk of Mortality [*Medicine*]
PRISM .... Pediatric Risk of Mortality Score [*Medicine*] (STED)
PRISM .... Personal Records Information System Management (SAUS)
PRISM .... Personnel Record Information System (SAUS)
PRISM .... Personnel Record Information Systems for Management
PRISM .... Personnel Related Information System for Management (NITA)
PRISM .... Personnel Requirements Information System Methodology (NVT)
PRISM .... Photo-Refractive Information Storage Material (SAUS)
PRISM .... Photorefractive Information Storage Materials Consortium (CDE)
PRISM .... Pittsburgh Research-Based Instructional Supervising Model (EDAC)
PRISM .... Plant Risk Status Information Management System [*Environmental science*] (COE)
PRISM .... Pliocene Research, Interpretations and Synoptic Mapping [*Climatology*]

PRISM .... Powerful Resource for Information and System Management [*Computer science*] (IAA)
PRISM .... Power Reactor Inherently Safe Module [*Nuclear energy*]
PRISM .... Power Reactor Innovation Small Module [*Nuclear energy*]
PRISM .... Priorities in School Mathematics Project (EDAC)
PRISM .... Prioritized Requirement, Impacts and Schedule Milestones (ACAE)
PRISM .... Prioritized Requirements, Impacts and Schedule Milestones (SAUS)
PRISM .... Prism Entertainment Corp. (SAUS)
Prism .... Prism Group [*Associated Press*] (SAG)
PRISM .... Production Requirements for Industrial Scheduling Manpower (SAUS)
PRISM .... Programmable Integrated Scripts for MIRROR [*Management Information Reporting and review of Operational Resources Systems*] [*Computer Language*] (PCM)
PRISM .... Programmed Integrated System Maintenance (NG)
PRISM .... Programming Information and Scheduling Management (SAUS)
PRISM .... Program Reliability Information System for Management [*Polaris*]
PRISM .... Program Reporting and Information System for Management (SAUS)
PRISM .... Progressive Refinement of Integrated Supply Management (AFM)
PRISM .... Projection and Integrated Stand alone Monitor (SAUS)
PRISM .... Projection and Integrated Standalone Monitor [*Dolch Computer Systems*] [*Computer science*] (PCM)
PRISM .... Prospective Record of the Impact and Severity of Menstrual symptoms (SAUS)
PRISM .... Pulse Repetition Interval Sorting Matrix (VLIE)
PRISMA .... Primary Imaging System for Multiple Applications (SEWL)
PrismEnt ...... Prism Entertainment Corp. [*Associated Press*] (SAG)
PRISM Internatl... Professional Records and Information Services Management International (NTPA)
PRISMS .... Phoenix Real-time Instrumentation for Surface Meteorological Studies network (SAUS)
PRISMS .... Plan of Research for Integrated Soil Moisture Studies (SAUS)
PrismS.......... Prism Solutions [*Associated Press*] (SAG)
PRISN .... Prime Stock Number
PRISN .... Procurement Instrument Serial Number (SAUS)
PRISNET ...... Private Switching Network Service [*Telecommunications*]
Prison L Reptr... Prison Law Reporter [*A publication*] (ILCA)
Prison L Rptr... Prison Law Reporter [*A publication*] (DLA)
Prison Serv J... Prison Service Journal [*A publication*] (DLA)
PRISS .... Post Deployment Software Support Real-Time Interactive Simulation System
PRISSECIMP... Primary Secondary Impedance (IAA)
PrissSys ...... Peerless Systems Corp. [*Associated Press*] (SAG)
PRIST .... Paper Radioimmunosorbent Test [*Analytical biochemistry*]
PRIT .... Pig Research Institute Taiwan (SAUS)
PRITAC .... Primary Tactical Radio Circuit (IAA)
Pritch Adm Dig... Pritchard's Admiralty Digest [*3rd ed.*] [*1887*] [*A publication*] (DLA)
Pritch M & D... Pritchard's Divorce and Matrimonial Causes [*3rd ed.*] [*1874*] [*A publication*] (DLA)
Pritch Quar Sess... Pritchard's Quarter Sessions [*A publication*] (DLA)
PRITMR .... Primary Timer (VLIE)
PRITX .... Price T. Rowe: Intl. Stock [*Mutual fund ticker symbol*] (SG)
PRIV .... Privacy (SAUS)
priv .... Private (STED)
PRIV .... Private
PRIV .... Privation (SAUS)
PRIV .... Privative
priv .... privet (SAUS)
PRIV .... Privilege
priv .... privily (SAUS)
priv .... privy (SAUS)
PRIVAUTH ... Travel Authorized via Privately-Owned Vehicle with Understanding No Additional Cost to Government Involved
Priv C App... Privy Council Appeals [*England*] [*A publication*] (DLA)
Priv CDI .... Indian Privy Council Decisions [*A publication*] (DLA)
Priv Counc App... Privy Council Appeals [*England*] [*A publication*] (DLA)
Priv Counc DI... Privy Council Decisions [*India*] [*A publication*] (DLA)
PRIVE .... Private (ROG)
Priv Found Rep... Private Foundations Reporter (SAUS)
Priv Fran Cont... Private Franchise Contracts (SAUS)
Priv Hous Fin... Private Housing Finance [*A publication*] (DLA)
Priv Inv Abroad... Private Investments Abroad (SAUS)
Priv Lond..... Privilegia Londini [*A publication*] (DLA)
Priv Maintd... Privately Maintained [*Nautical charts*]
PRIV PR ...... Privately Printed (SAUS)
PRIV PROP... Private Property [*Military*] (DNAB)
PRIV PUB .... Privately Published (SAUS)
Priv St .... Private Statutes (SAUS)
PRIVX .... Private Exchange (IAA)
Pri X .... Primary X (SAUS)
Pri X Pu....... Primary X Pickup (SAUS)
PRIZE.......... Program for Research in Information Systems Engineering [*University of Michigan*] [*Research center*] (RCD)
Prize CR ...... Prize Court Reports [*South Africa*] [*A publication*] (DLA)
PRIZM .... Potential Rating Index by ZIP [*Zone Improvement Plan*] Market [*Advertising*]
PRIZM .... Potential Rating Index for ZIP Markets (SAUS)
PRJ............. Aero Servicios Pro-Bajio, SA de CV [*Mexico*] [*FAA designator*] (FAAC)
PRJ............. American Junior College of Puerto Rico, Bayamon, PR [*OCLC symbol*] (OCLC)
PRJ............. Capri [*Italy*] [*Airport symbol*] (AD)
PRJ............. Payroll Journal [*Accounting*]
PRJ............. Port Royal [*Jamaica*] [*Seismograph station code, US Geological Survey*] (SEIS)

PRJ............. Projected RADAR Jammer (SEWL)
PRJC........... Pearl River Junior College [*Poplarville, MS*]
PRJC........... Puerto Rico Junior College
PRJMP........ Pressure Jump [*NWS*] (FAAC)
PRK .... Democratic People's Republic of Korea [*ANSI three-letter standard code*] (CNC)
PRK ....: Paraskevi [*Lesbos*] [*Greece*] [*Seismograph station code, US Geological Survey*] (SEIS)
PRK .... Park
PRK .... Park National Corp. [*AMEX symbol*] (SAG)
PRK .... Parkside Petroleum, Inc. [*Toronto Stock Exchange symbol*] [*Vancouver Stock Exchange symbol*]
PRK .... People's Republic of Kampuchea [*From 1979 to 1989*] [*Formerly, Cambodia*] [*Later, SOC*] (PD)
PRK .... Phase Reversal Keying [*Computer science*] (IAA)
PRK .... Photorefractive Keratectomy [*Ophthalmology*]
PRK .... Pridie Kalendas [*The Day before the Calends*] [*Latin*]
PRK .... Primary Rabbit Kidney [*Medicine*] (DMAA)
PRK .... Primary Rat Kidney [*Cells*]
PRKB .... Printer Keyboard (VLIE)
PR-KB .... Printer-Keyboard (SAUS)
PRKC .... Protein Kinase C (DMAA)
PRKCA .... Protein Kinase C Alpha (DMAA)
PRK Cells .... Primary Rat Kidney Cells (SAUS)
PRKG .... Parking
PRKNG........ Parking (SAUS)
PRKO .... Progesterone Receptor Knockout [*Mouse strain*]
PRKR .... Parkervision, Inc. [*NASDAQ symbol*] (SAG)
PRL .... Aviaprima [*Russian Federation*] [*ICAO designator*] (FAAC)
PRL .... Pacht, Ross et Al, Los Angeles, CA [*OCLC symbol*] (OCLC)
PRL .... Package Research Laboratory (SAUS)
PRL .... Page Revision Log (NASA)
prl .... Parallel (ELAL)
PRL .... Parallel (MSA)
PRL .... Partido Radical Liberal [*Radical Liberal Party*] [*Ecuador*] [*Political party*]
PRL .... Parti Reformateur Liberal [*Liberal Reform Party*] [*Belgium*] [*Political party*] (PPW)
PRL .... Parti Republicain de la Liberte [*Republican Party for Liberty*] [*France*] [*Political party*] (PPE)
PRL .... Parti Republicain de la Liberte [*Republican Party for Liberty*] [*Burkina Faso*] [*Political party*]
PRL .... Parts Requirement List (KSC)
PRL .... Paul Revere [*NYSE symbol*] (SPSG)
PRL .... Peace Research Laboratory [*Later, LPRL*] [*An association*] (EA)
prl .... Pearl (VRA)
PRL .... Periodical (SAUS)
PRL .... Periodical Requirements (SAUS)
PRL .... Personnel Research Laboratory [*Lackland Air Force Base, TX*]
PRL .... Pesticide Research Laboratory and Graduate Study Center [*Pennsylvania State University*] [*Research center*] (RCD)
PRL .... Petroleum Refining Laboratory [*Pennsylvania State University*] (MCD)
PRL .... Philco Resources [*Vancouver Stock Exchange symbol*]
PRL .... Philips Research Laboratories (NITA)
PRL .... Photoreactivating Light
PRL .... Physical Research Laboratory (CARB)
PRL .... Physical Review Letters [*A publication*]
P R L.......... Physics Research Laboratory (SAUS)
PRL .... Physiological Research Laboratories [*University of California at San Diego*] [*Research center*]
PRL .... Pick-Resistant Lock (SAUS)
PRL .... Pioneering Research Laboratory [*Massachusetts*] [*Army*]
PRL .... Planning Requirements List (MCD)
PRL .... Plastics Research Laboratory [*MIT*] (MCD)
PRL .... Polar Research Laboratory [*USA*] [*Marine science*] (OSRA)
PRL .... Polished-Rod Load (SAUS)
PRL .... Political Risk Letter [*Database*] [*Frost & Sullivan, Inc.*] [*Information service or system*] (CRD)
PRL............ Population Research Laboratory [*University of Alberta*] [*Research center*] (RCD)
PRL .... Postal Reform League (IAA)
PRL .... Prairie Research Laboratory (SAUS)
PRL .... Preamble
PRL .... Precision Reduction Laboratory (AFM)
PRL .... Predicted Repair Level (MCD)
PRL .... Pressure Ratio Limiter (MCD)
PRL .... Price Reduction League (SAUS)
PRL .... Princes Risborough Laboratory (SAUS)
PRL .... Print Lister (VLIE)
PRL .... Priority Rate Limiting (MCD)
Pr L .... Private Laws (SAUS)
PRL .... Private Relocatable Library (SAUS)
PRL .... Processor Level (VLIE)
PRL .... Programming Research Ltd. (SAUS)
PRL .... Program Reference Library (VLIE)
PRL .... Progressive Republican League
PRL .... Project Records List (SAUS)
PRL .... Project Research Laboratory
Prl .... Prolactin (DIPS)
Prl .... Prolactin (STED)
PRL .... Prolactin [*Also, LTH, PR*] [*Endocrinology*]
PRL .... Prolong International [*AMEX symbol*] (SG)
PRL .... Properties Research Laboratory [*Purdue University*] [*Lafayette, IN*]
PRL .... Propulsion Research Laboratory
PRL............ Proton Reference Level [*Chemistry*]

PRL.............. Publication Requirements List (SAUS)
PRL.............. Publications Requirements List (NG)
PRL.............. Pulse Reflection Logic (SAUS)
PRL.............. Pulse-Reflection Logic (IAA)
PRLA .... Prairie Religious Library Association
PRLA .... Pupils React to Light and Accommodation [Medicine] (STED)
PRI&RB .... Puerto Rico Inspection and Rating Bureau (SAUS)
PrLas........... Premier Laser Systems, Inc. [Associated Press] (SAG)
PRLASR........ Population Research Laboratory. University of Alberta. Department of Sociology. Alberta Series Report (SAUS)
PrIAU-SJ..... Inter-American University of Puerto Rico, San Juan Campus (SAUS)
PR Laws Ann... Laws of Puerto Rico, Annotated [A publication] (DLA)
PRLC .... Pittsburgh Regional Library Center [Chatham College] [Pittsburgh, PA] [Library network]
PRLCA .... Power Research Library of Contemporary Art [University of Sydney, Australia]
Prl Cmm...... Parole Commission (SAUS)
PRLD .... Pick-Resistant Locking Device (SAUS)
PRLDEF .... Puerto Rican Legal Defense and Education Fund (EA)
PRLG .... Prologue (SAUS)
PRLI............ Purchase Request Line Item [DoD]
PRLINK....... Public Relations Society of America Online Information Service (IID)
PRLM.......... Preliminary (VLIE)
PRIMORDIAL... Primary Order Dial (SAUS)
PRLN .... Paracelsian, Inc. [NASDAQ symbol] (SAG)
Pr Ln .... Prior Lien [Business term] (MHDW)
PRINOBC/NEC... Primary Navy Officer Billet Classifcation and Navy Enlisted Classification (SAUS)
PRLNW .... Paracelsian Inc. Wrrt [NASDAQ symbol] (TTSB)
PRLO .... Prologic Management Systems, Inc. [NASDAQ symbol] (SAG)
PRLO .... PROLOGIC Mgmt Sys [NASDAQ symbol] (TTSB)
PRLOW........ PROLOGIC Mgmt Sys Wrrt [NASDAQ symbol] (TTSB)
PRLP .... Planetary Rocket Launcher Platform (AAG)
PRLP .... Puerto Rico Legal Project [of the National Lawyers Guild] (EA)
PRIPACSEVOCAM... Primary Pacific Secure Voice Communications (SAUS)
PRLR .... Parlor
PRLS .... Peerless Systems Corp. [NASDAQ symbol] (SAG)
PRLS .... Pima Regional Library Service [Library network]
PRLS Ln ...... Prepaid Rental-Listing Service (SAUS)
PRLS .... Pulsed Ruby LASER System
PRLS .... Pulse Ruby Laser System (SAUS)
PRISM .... Program Integrated System Maintenance (SAUS)
PRISMA....... PRimary Imaging Systems for Multiple Application (SAUS)
PRLST .... Price List
PRLTRL & M... Printer, Lithographer, and Multilith Operator [Navy]
PRLW .... Parti des Reformes et de la Liberte de Wallonie [Belgium] [Political party] (PPW)
PRLWCSR.... Population Research Laboratory. University of Alberta. Department of Sociology. Western Canada Series Report (SAUS)
PRLX .... Parallax (AAG)
PRLX .... Parlex Corp. [NASDAQ symbol] (NQ)
PRM............. Panarim Resources, Inc. [Vancouver Stock Exchange symbol]
PRM............. Parameter (ECII)
PRM............. Parma Byzantine [Diocesan abbreviation] [Ohio] (TOCD)
Prm............. Parmenides [of Plato] [Classical studies] (OCD)
PRM............. Parsons Mountain [South Carolina] [Seismograph station code, US Geological Survey] (SEIS)
PRM............. Partially Reflecting Mirror
PRM............. Partially Regulated Module
PRM............. Partial Refund Message [Travel industry] (TRID)
PRM............. Partial Response Method
PRM............. Partner Relationship Management
PRM............. Payload Retention Mechanism [NASA] (NASA)
PRM............. Period of Reduced Melting [Climatology]
PRM............. Personal Radiation Monitor
PRM............. Petition [or Proposal] for Rule Making (NRCH)
PRM............. Phase Retarder Module (SAUS)
PRM............. Phase Reversal Modulation (SAUS)
PRM............. Phosphoribomutase [An enzyme] (MAE)
PRM............. Photoreceptor Membrane [Of the eye]
PRM............. Pilots Radio Manual
PRM............. Pit Rib Meristem [Botany]
PRM............. Pocket Radiation Monitor (SAUS)
PRM............. Portable Radiation Monitor (SAUS)
PRM............. Posigrade Rocket Motor (NASA)
PRM............. Positron Reemission Microscopy (SAUS)
PRM............. Power Range Monitor (IEEE)
PRM............. Precision Runway Monitor [FAA] (TAG)
PRM............. Preformed Road Markings [Road markings embedded in the pavement rather than painted on street's surface]
PRM............. Preliminary Requirements Model [NASA]
PRM............. Prematurely Ruptured Membrane [Medicine] (STED)
PRM............. Premature [or Prolonged] Rupture of Membranes [Gynecology] (MAE)
PRM............. Premium
PRM............. Presbyterian Renewal Ministries (EA)
PRM............. Presidential Review Memo (SAUS)
PRM............. Presidential Review Memorandum [Jimmy Carter Administration]
PRM............. Pressure Monitoring Module [Mechanical engineering]
PRM............. Pressure Remanent Magnetization
PRM............. Prevention Reference Manuals [Environmental science] (COE)
PRM............. Preventive Medicine (MAE)
PRM............. Primary Reference Material [Library science] (DAVI)
PRM............. Primary Reference Material [Medicine] (MAE)
PRM............. Prime (AAG)

PRM............. Prime Air, Inc. [ICAO designator] (FAAC)
PRM............. Prime Computer, Inc. (SAUS)
PRM............. PRIMEDIA, Inc. [NYSE symbol] [Formerly, K-III Communications] (SG)
prm............. Primer
PRM............. Primidone [Antiepileptic drug]
PRM............. Priming (SAUS)
PRM............. Process Radiation Monitor [Nuclear energy] (NRCH)
PRM............. Process Resource Manager (SAUS)
PRM............. Production Release Meeting (SAUS)
PRM............. Program Memory (SAUS)
PRM............. Programmer Reference Manual [Computer science]
PRM............. Programmers Reference Manual (SAUS)
PRM............. Programming and Resources Management [NASA] (MCD)
PRM............. Program Reference Manual (VLIE)
PRM............. Program Resolution Monitor (SAUS)
PRM............. Project Review Meeting (SAUS)
PRM............. Promote (AABC)
PRM............. Publications Requirements Manager [DoD]
PRM............. Puerto Lopez [Colombia] [Airport symbol] (AD)
PRM............. Pulse Rate Modulation
PRM............. Pulse Ratio Modulator
PRM............. Pulse Repetition Per Minute (SAUS)
PRM............. Pyrradiometer (SAUS)
PRMA .... Permeator Corp. (SAUS)
PRMA .... Primadonna Resorts [NASDAQ symbol] (TTSB)
PRMA .... Primadonna Resorts [NASDAQ symbol] (SAG)
PRMA .... Puerto Rican Maritime Authority (SAUS)
PrMan.......... Prayer of Manasses [Apocrypha] (BJA)
PRMAR .... Primary Mission Area [Military] (CAAL)
PrmBcp........ Prime Bancorp, Inc. [Associated Press] (SAG)
PrmBn .... Premier Bankshares Corp. [Associated Press] (SAG)
PRMC .... Pacific Regional Monitoring Center (SAUS)
PRMC .... Paper and Plastic Representatives Management Council (NTPA)
PRMC .... Periodically Replenished Magma Chambers [Geology]
PRMC .... Puerto Rican Migration Consortium (EA)
PRMD .... Private Management Domain [Telecommunications] (OSI)
PRME .... Prime Capital Corp. (SAUS)
PRME .... Prime Response [NASDAQ symbol] (SG)
PRME .... Prime Retail [NASDAQ symbol] (TTSB)
PRME .... Prime Retail, Inc. [NASDAQ symbol] (SAG)
PrmEgy........ Prime Energy [Associated Press] (SAG)
PrmeMd........ Prime Medics [Associated Press] (SAG)
PRMEP .... Prime Retail 8.5%Ptc Cv'B'Pfd [NASDAQ symbol] (TTSB)
PRMF.......... Preretinal Macular Fibrosis [Medicine] (MELL)
PrmFar .... Premier Farnell PLC [Associated Press] (SAG)
PRMFN .... Prime Partners Ltd (SAUS)
PRMG .... Piston Ring Manufacturers Group [Later, NEPMA] (EA)
PRM GR .... Permanent Grade (DNAB)
PRMGX........ Principal Balanced Fund Cl.A [Mutual fund ticker symbol] (SG)
PRMH .... Parti Republicain Modere Haitien [Political party] (EY)
PRMH .... Profoundly Retarded Multiply Handicapped (AIE)
PrmHsp........ Prime Hospitality Corp. [Associated Press] (SAG)
Prmian......... Permian Basin Royalty Trust [Associated Press] (SAG)
Pr Min .... Printed Minutes of Evidence [A publication] (DLA)
PR/MIPR...... Purchase Request/Military Interdepartmental Purchase Request (AFIT)
PRMIS .... Printing Resources Management Information System (DNAB)
Prmisy......... Premisys Communications [Associated Press] (SAG)
Prmk........... Paramark Enterprises, Inc. [Associated Press] (SAG)
PRML.......... Partial Response Maximum Likelihood [Computer science]
PrmLasr....... Premier Laser Systems, Inc. [Associated Press] (SAG)
PRMLD .... Premolded [Technical drawings] (MSA)
PR/MIPR...... Purchase Request/Military Interdepartmental Purchase Request (SAUS)
PrMLtd........ Prime Motor Inns Ltd. [Associated Press] (SAG)
PRMMI .... Puerto Rico Marine Management (SAUS)
PRMO .... Premenos Technology [NASDAQ symbol] (TTSB)
PRMO .... Premenos Technology Corp. [NASDAQ symbol] (SAG)
PRMOD........ Printer Module (SAUS)
PrmosT........ Premenos Technology Corp. [Associated Press] (SAG)
PRMP .... Plutonium Recovery Modification Project [Department of Energy]
PRMP .... Production Readiness Master Plan
PrmPks........ Premier Parks, Inc. [Associated Press] (SAG)
PRMR .... Pitch Rate/Moment Ratio [Automotive engineering]
PRMR .... Primer (MSA)
PrmRad .... Premier Radio Network [Associated Press] (SAG)
PrmrBc .... Premier Bancorp, Inc. [Associated Press] (SAG)
PrmRetl .... Prime Retail, Inc. [Associated Press] (SAG)
PrmRtl .... Prime Retail, Inc. [Associated Press] (SAG)
PRMS .... Personnel Recovery Mission Software (SEWL)
PRMS .... Plans Review Management System (SAUS)
PRMS .... Premisys Communications [NASDAQ symbol] (SAG)
PRMSA .... Puerto Rico Maritime Shipping Authority (SAUS)
PRM-SDX .... Pyrimethamine-Sulfadoxine [Pharmacology] (DAVI)
PrmsH .... Promus Hotel Corp. [Associated Press] (SAG)
PRMSS .... Patriotic Resistance Movement of South Sudan [Political party]
PRMSS .... Pregnancy-Related Mortality Surveillance System (MELL)
PRMTR .... Parameter (AAG)
PRMV .... Peach Rosette Mosaic Virus [Plant pathology]
PRMX .... Primex Technologies, Inc. [NASDAQ symbol] (SAG)
PRN .... Greenville, AL [Location identifier] [FAA] (FAAL)
PRN .... Packet Radio Network [Telecommunications] (OSI)
PRN .... Pahrock Range [Nevada] [Seismograph station code, US Geological Survey] (SEIS)

PRN	Park Reverse Neutral [*Automotive engineering*]
PRN	Partido de la Resistencia Nicaraguense [*Political party*] (EY)
PRN	Partido de la Revolucion Nacional [*Party of the National Revolution*] [*Bolivia*] [*Political party*] (PPW)
PRN	Partido de Reconstrucao Nacional [*Brazil*] [*Political party*] (EY)
PRN	Partido Republicano Nacional [*National Republican Party*] [*Costa Rica*] [*Political party*]
PRN	Parts Requirement Notice (KSC)
PRN	Peace Research Network [*Later, PSA*] (EA)
PRN	Peace RES Network (EA)
PRN	Periodic-Random Noise (SAUS)
PRN	Pesticide Registration Notice (EEVL)
PRN	Physicians Radio Network
PRN	Polyradiculoneuropathy [*Medicine*] (DB)
PRN	Post-Rotatory Nystagmus
PRN	Practice Notes of the Australian Broadcasting Tribunal (SAUS)
PRN	Preference Rating Number (SAUS)
PRN	Previous Result Negative (IAA)
PRN	Pridie Nonas [*The Day before the Nones*] [*Latin*]
PRN	Princess Air [*British*] [*ICAO designator*] (FAAC)
PRN	Printer [*Computer science*]
PRN	Print Numerically (DEN)
PRN	Pristina [*Former Yugoslavia*] [*Airport symbol*] (OAG)
PRN	PR Newswire [*PR Newswire, Inc.*] [*Information service or system*] (IID)
PRN	Procurement Reallocation Notice
PRN	Program Release Notice [*NASA*] (NASA)
PRN	Program Revision Number (SAUS)
PRN	Prominent Resources Corp. [*Vancouver Stock Exchange symbol*]
PRN	Pronasale [*Anatomy*]
PRN	Pro Re Nata [*Whenever Necessary*] [*Pharmacy*]
PRN	Pseudo Random Noise (SAUS)
PRN	Pseudorandom Noise
PRN	Pseudorandom Number
PRN	Pseudo-Rustler-Noise (SAUS)
PRN	Puerto Rican Cement [*NYSE symbol*] (TTSB)
PRN	Puerto Rican Cement Co., Inc. [*NYSE symbol*] (SPSG)
PRN	Pulse Ranging Navigation
PRN	Pulse Ranging Network (KSC)
PRN	Purchase Request Notice [*Banking*]
PRN	Purchase Request Number
PRNA	Plasmid RNA (SAUS)
pRNA	Ribonucleic Acid, Polysomal [*Biochemistry, genetics*]
PRNAV	Precision RNAV (SAUS)
PRNC	Potomac River Naval Command [*Washington, DC*]
PRNC	Prince
PRNC	Puerto Rico Nuclear Center
PRND	Prophylactic Regional Node Dissection [*Medicine*] (MELL)
PRNDI	Public Radio News Directors (NTPA)
PRNDI	Public Radio News Directors Inc. (SAUS)
PRNDL	Park, Reverse, Neutral, Drive, Low [*Automotive term for automatic gearshift indicator in cars; pronounced "prindle"*]
PrnDn	Princeton Dental Management Corp. [*Associated Press*] (SAG)
PrnDnt	Princeton Dental Management Corp. [*Associated Press*] (SAG)
PRNET	Packed Radio Network (SAUS)
PRNET	Packet Radio Network
PRNET	Pocket Radio Network (CCCA)
PRNEX	Price T. Rowe: New Era [*Mutual fund ticker symbol*] (SG)
PRNG	Paper Negative (VRA)
PRNG	Pseudo Random Number Generator (SAUS)
PRNG	Purging (MSA)
PRNHX	Price T. Rowe: New Horizons [*Mutual fund ticker symbol*] (SG)
PRNI	Premiere Radio Networks [*NASDAQ symbol*] (TTSB)
PRNI	Premier Radio Network [*NASDAQ symbol*] (SAG)
PRNIA	Premiere Radio Networks 'A' [*NASDAQ symbol*] (TTSB)
PRNL	Pictured Rocks National Lakeshore (SAUS)
prnnl	Perennial [*Botany*]
PRNP	Prion Protein (DMAA)
PRNS	Point Reyes National Seashore (SAUS)
PRNS	Prins Recycling [*NASDAQ symbol*] (TTSB)
PRNS	Prins Recycling Corp. [*NASDAQ symbol*] (SAG)
PRNSA	Pseudo-Random Noise Assembly (SAUS)
PRNSA	Pseudo Random Noise Signal Assembly (SAUS)
PRNT	Plaque Reduction Neutralization Test [*Immunochemistry*]
PRNTDEV	Print Device (SAUS)
PRNTG	Printing (MSA)
PRNTMODE	Print Mode (SAUS)
PRNTR	Printer
PRNTV	Preventive
PRNU	Photoresponse Nonuniformity
PRNWR	Parker River National Wildlife Refuge (SAUS)
PRO	Digital Equipment Corporation (SAUS)
PRO	Pacific Research Office (CINC)
PRO	Pacific Research Onice (SAUS)
PRO	Parallel Rod Oscillator
PRO	Parents Reaching Out [*An association*] (EA)
PRO	Parents Rights Organization (EA)
PRO	Particle Reduction Oven
PRO	Parts Release Order
PRO	Patients' Rights Organization (EA)
PRO	Pay and Records Office [*British military*] (DMA)
PRO	Peer Review Organization [*Medicare*]
PRO	Pen Recorder Output (SAA)
PRO	Performing Rights Organization [*Formerly, BMI-Canada Ltd.*] [*Canada*]

PRO	Perry, IA [*Location identifier*] [*FAA*] (FAAL)
PRO	Personnel Relations Officer [*for Shore Stations*] [*Navy*]
PRO	Photographic Reconnaissance Officer (SAUS)
PR/O	Pilot Repair/Overhaul [*Military*]
PRO	Pitch Response Operator
PRO	Planned Requirements, Outfitting [*Navy*] (NG)
PRO	Planning Resident Order (KSC)
PRO	Plant Representative Officer (MCD)
PRO	Plastic Repair Optimized (SAUS)
PRO	Population Renewal Office (EA)
PRO	Precision Risc Organisation (or Organization) (SAUS)
PRO	Precision RISC [*Reduced Instruction Set Computer*] Organization
Pro	Prednisone [*Also, P, PDN, PR, Pred*] [*Antineoplastic drug, Endocrinology*]
PRO	Press Officer (SAUS)
PRO	Principal Public Library [*Library network*]
PRO	Principal Reducing Option
PRO	Print Octal (DEN)
pro	Probate (GEAB)
PRO	Probate
PRO	Probation [*or Probationer*]
PRO	Probation Services for Adults (PHSD)
PRO	Problem Resolution Office [*IRS*]
PRO	Procedure (AABC)
PRO	Proceed (NAKS)
Pro	Proculus [*Flourished, 1st century*] [*Authority cited in pre-1607 legal work*] (DSA)
PRO	Procurement Research Office [*Army*]
PRO	Production Repair Order
pro	Professional (ODBW)
PRO	Professional
PRO	Professional Dental Technologies, Inc. [*AMEX symbol*] (SAG)
PRO	Professionally (SAUS)
PRO	Professional Racing Organization of America [*Later, USCF*] (EA)
PRO	Professional Resellers Organization [*Defunct*] (EA)
PRO	Professional Review Organization [*Medicare*]
PRO	Proficiency
PRO	Proflavine [*An antiseptic*]
PRO	Programmable Remote Operation [*Computer Devices, Inc.*]
PRO	Programming Online (SAUS)
PRO	Program Representative Office (AAGC)
PRO	Progressive
pro	Proline [*An amino acid*] (DOG)
Pro	Proline [*Also, P*] [*An amino acid*]
Pro	Prolyl [*Biochemistry*]
PRO	Pronation [*Medicine*]
PRO	Pronoun [*Grammar*] (WGA)
PRO	Pronto Explorations Ltd. [*Toronto Stock Exchange symbol*]
PRO	Propagation [*Military*]
PRO	Propagation Prediction Report (SAA)
PRO	Propair, Inc. [*Canada*] [*ICAO designator*] (FAAC)
PRO	Propeller Order
PRO	Prophylactic (AABC)
PRO	Prospect Referral Operation (SAUS)
PRO	Prostitute (ADA)
Pro	Protein
Pro	Protest (EBF)
PRO	Protest
Pro	Prothrombin [*Factor II*] [*Hematology*]
PRO	Proved
pro	Provencal [*MARC language code*] [*Library of Congress*] (LCCP)
Pro	Proverbs [*Old Testament book*] (BJA)
PRO	Providence [*Diocesan abbreviation*] [*Rhode Island*] (TOCD)
PRO	Province (ROG)
PRO	Provost
PRO	Public Radio Online (SAUS)
PRO	Public Record Office [*British*]
PRO	Public Relations Office [*or Officer*] [*Usually military*]
PRO	Public Relations Officer (ADWA)
PRO	Puchase Request Order
PRO.EC	Professional Dental Tech [*ECM, Symbol*] (TTSB)
PROA	Polymer Research Corp. of America [*NASDAQ symbol*] (NQ)
PROA	Polymer Research Corporation of America (SAUS)
PROA	Polymer Resh America [*NASDAQ symbol*] (TTSB)
PROA	Public Record Office Archives (SAUS)
PROA	Puerto Rico Operations Area
ProActiv	ProActive Technologies, Inc. [*Associated Press*] (SAG)
PRO-AM	Professional-Amateur (WDAA)
pro-am	Professionals and Amateurs [*Sports*] (WDMC)
PROANTAR	Brazilian Antarcic Program (SAUS)
PROAP	Principal Regional Office for Asia and the Pacific [*UNESCO*]
Prob	English Probate and Admiralty Reports for Year Cited (journ.) (SAUS)
Prob	Law Reports, Probate Division [*England*] [*A publication*] (DLA)
PROB	Probability (KSC)
PROB	Probability Percentage (PIAV)
PROB	Probable (GOBB)
prob	Probable
prob	Probably (VRA)
PROB	Probably
Prob	Probate [*Legal term*] (DLA)
PROB	Probation [*FBI standardized term*]
PROB	Problem
Prob	Quod Omnis Probus Liber Sit [*of Philo*] (BJA)
PROB40	Probability 40 Percent [*ICAO*] (FAAC)

Prob (1891)... Law Reports, Probate Division [*1891*] [*England*] [*A publication*] (DLA)
Prob&Adm... Div. Probate and Admiralty Division Law Reports (SAUS)
Prob & Adm Div... Probate and Admiralty Division Law Reports [*A publication*] (DLA)
Prob & Div... Probate and Divorce, English Law Reports [*A publication*] (DLA)
Prob & Mat... Probate and Matrimonial Cases [*A publication*] (DLA)
PROBAR ...... Programmable Band Radiometer (SAUS)
Probat... Probation [*Legal term*] (DLA)
Probation & Parole L Rep... Probation and Parole Law Reports [*A publication*] (DLA)
Probation & Parole L Summ... Probation and Parole Law Summaries [*A publication*] (DLA)
Probat J....... Probation Journal [*A publication*] (ILCA)
Prob C........ Probate Code [*A publication*] (DLA)
PROBCOST... Probabilistic Budgeting and Forward Costing
PROBCOST... Probable Cost (SAUS)
Prob Ct Rep... Probate Court Reporter [*Ohio*] [*A publication*] (DLA)
PROBDAM... Probably Damaged (SAUS)
PROBDET... Probability of Detection [*Navy*] (NVT)
Prob Div ...... Probate Division, English Law Reports [*A publication*] (DLA)
PROBE........ Performance Review of Base Supply Effectiveness [*Air Force*] (AFM)
PROBE........ Performance Review of Base-supply Effectiveness (SAUS)
PROBE........ Pilot Radiation Observation Experiment [*Marine science*] (OSRA)
PROBE........ Portable Remote Observation of the Environment (SAUS)
PROBE........ Practical Research into Organizational Behavior and Effectiveness (EDAC)
PROBE........ Pre-Recognition of Baleful Error (SAUS)
PROBE...... Profile Resolution Obtained by Excitation (PDAA)
PROBE........ Program for Research on Objectives-Based Evaluation [*UCLA*]
PROBE........ Program Optimization and Budget Evaluation [*Military*]
PROBE........ Pro-Recognition of Baleful Errors (SAUS)
PROBE........ Prototype Radiation Observation Experiment (SAUS)
PROBES....... Processes and Resources of the Bering Sea Shelf [*University of Alaska*]
PROBFOR .... Probability Forecasting [*Computer program*] [*Bell System*]
PRO BIKE... Bicycle Federation of America (EA)
PROBIT....... Probability Unit [*Statistics*]
Prob J.......... Probation Journal [*A publication*] (DLA)
Probl Hetmatol Blood Transfus... Problems of Hematology and Blood Transfusion (SAUS)
Probl Psychol... Problems of Psychology (SAUS)
Probl Radiobiol... Problems of Radiobiology (SAUS)
Prob LT... Probyn on Land Tenure [*4th ed.*] [*1881*] [*A publication*] (DLA)
Probl Virol... Problems of Virology (SAUS)
PROBO......... Product/Ore/Bulk/Oil Carrier [*Shipping*] (DS)
Prob Off....... Probation Officer (SAUS)
PROBOUT .... Proceed On or About (MUGU)
Prob Pr Act... Probate Practice Act [*A publication*] (DLA)
Prob R .... Probate Reports [*A publication*] (DLA)
Prob Rep ...... Probate Reports [*A publication*] (DLA)
Prob Rep Ann... Probate Reports, Annotated [*A publication*] (DLA)
PROBSUB .... Probable Submarine (NVT)
PROBUS ...... Program Budget System [*Military*]
Proby.......... Probationary [*British military*] (DMA)
PROC........... Performing Rights Organization of Canada [*See also SDE*]
PROC........... Performing Rights Organisation of Canada (SAUS)
PROC........... Preliminary Required Operational Capability [*Military*]
PROC........... Procaine hydrochloride (SAUS)
Proc............ Procedere (SAUS)
PROC........... Procedure (AAG)
Proc............ Proceeding (SAUS)
Proc............ Proceedings (DIAR)
proc............ Proceedings (WDMC)
PROC........... Proceedings
PROC........... Pro-Cel International, Inc. (SAUS)
PROC........... Process (AABC)
proc............ Process (VRA)
Proc............ Processes (AL)
Proc............ Processing (AL)
proc............ Processing (ELAL)
PROC........... Processing (SAUS)
PROC........... Procession (ROG)
PROC........... Processor [*or Processing*]
Proc............ Proclamation (DLA)
PROC........... Proctor
PROC........... Procure (AABC)
PROC........... Procurement (MSA)
PROC........... Programming Computer [*Computer science*]
PROC........... Proposed Required Operational Capability [*Military*] (AABC)
PROC........... Protein C (DMAA)
PROCAARE... Program for Collaboration Against AIDS and Related Epidemics (SAUS)
Proc Abstr Soc Biol Chem... Proceedings and Abstracts. Society of Biological Chemists (SAUS)
Proc Acad Sci Georgian SSR... Proceedings. Academy of Sciences. Georgian SSR (SAUS)
Proc Acad Sci USSR... Proceedings. Academy of Sciences of the USSR. Geochemistry Section (SAUS)
Proc A Conv Am Cranberry Growers Ass... Proceedings. Annual Convention. American Cranberry Growers Association (SAUS)
PROCADES... Project for Training in Rural, Economic and Social Development (SAUS)
PROCAL....... Programmable Calculator [*Computer science*] (IAA)
Proc Amer Math Soc... Proceedings of the American Mathematical Society (SAUS)

Proc Amer Power Conf... Proceedings of the American Power Conference (SAUS)
Proc Amer Soc Civ Engrs... Proceedings of the American Society of Civil Engineers (SAUS)
Proc Amer Soc of Internat L... Proceedings. American Society of International Law [*A publication*] (DLA)
Proc Amp..... Processing Amplifier (NTCM)
Proc Am Pet Inst... Proceedings. American Petroleum Institute (SAUS)
Proc Am Pharm Manuf Assoc Annu Meet... Proceedings. American Pharmaceutical Manufacturers Association. Annual Meeting (SAUS)
Proc Am Pharm Manuf Assoc Midyear East Sect Meet... Proceedings. American Pharmaceutical Manufacturers Association. Midyear Eastern Section Meeting (SAUS)
Proc Am Soc Civ Eng Transp Eng J... Proceedings. American Society of Civil Engineers.Transportation Engineering Journal (SAUS)
Proc Annu Allerton Conf Circuit Syst Theory... Proceedings. Annual Allerton Conference on Circuit and System Theory (SAUS)
Proc Annu Allerton Conf Commun Control Comput... Proceedings. Annual Allerton Conference on Communication, Control and Computing (SAUS)
Proc Annu Conf Int Symp N Am Lake Manage Soc... Proceedings. Annual Conference and International Symposium. North American Lake Management Society (SAUS)
Proc Annu Conv Assoc Am Pestic Control Off... Proceedings Annual Convention Association. American Pesticide Control Officials (SAUS)
Proc Annu Conv Flavoring Ext Manuf Assoc US... Proceedings. Annual Convention. Flavoring Extract Manufacturers Association of the United States (SAUS)
Proc Annu Conv Sugar Technol Assoc India... Proceedings. Annual Convention. Sugar Technologists Association of India (SAUS)
Proc Annu Conv West Can Water Sewage Conf... Proceedings. Annual Convention. Western Canada Water and Sewage Conference (SAUS)
Proc Annu Eng Geol Soils Eng Symp... Proceedings. Annual Engineering Geology and Soils Engineering Symposium (SAUS)
Proc Annu Fall Meet Calif Nat Gasoline Assoc... Proceedings. Annual Fall Meeting California Natural Gasoline Association (SAUS)
Proc Annu Meet Am Asso Vet Lab Diagn... Proceedings. Annual Meeting. American Association of Veterinary Laboratory Diagnosticians (SAUS)
Proc Annu Meet Biochem... Proceedings. Annual Meeting of Biochemistry (SAUS)
Proc Annu Meet Hawaii Sugar Plant Ass... Proceedings. Annual Meeting. Hawaiian Sugar Planters Association (SAUS)
Proc Annu Meet Int Magnesium Ass... Proceedings. Annual Meeting. International Magnesium Association (SAUS)
Proc Annu Meet Med Sect Am Counc Life Insur... Proceedings. Annual Meeting Medical Section. American Council of Life Insurance (SAUS)
Proc Annu Meet Med Sect Am Counc Life Insur... Proceedings, Annual Meeting of the Medical Section of the American Council of Life Insurance (SAUS)
Proc Annu Meet Nat Ass Wheat Growers... Proceedings. Annual Meeting National Association of Wheat Growers (SAUS)
Proc Annu Sci Meet Comm Probl Drug Depend US Nat Res Counc... Proceedings. Annual Scientific Meeting. Committee on Problems of Drug Dependence. United States National Research Counci (SAUS)
Proc Annu Symp Comput Appl Med Care... Proceedings of the Annual Symposium on Computer Applications in Medical Care (SAUS)
Proc Annu Tech Meet Tech Assa Graphic Arts... Proceedings. Annual Technical Meeting. Technical Association. Graphic Arts (SAUS)
Proc AOS..... Proceedings of the American Oriental Society (SAUS)
PRO CAPILL... Pro Capillis [*For the Hair*] [*Pharmacy*]
Procarb......... Procarbazine [*Antineoplastic drug*] (DAVI)
PROCAS....... Process Calculation System (SAUS)
PROCAS....... Process-Oriented Contract Administration Services
Proc Asiat Soc... Proceedings. Asiatic Society (SAUS)
Proc Assoc Am Physicians... Proceedings of the Association of American Physicians (SAUS)
Proc Astron Soc Aust... Proceedings of the Astronomical Society of Australia (SAUS)
Proc Aust Biochem Soc... Proceedings of the Australian Biochemical Society (SAUS)
Proc Aust Bldg Res Congr... Australian Building Research Congress. Proceedings (journ.) (SAUS)
Proc Aust Clay Miner Conf... Australian Clay Minerals Conference. Proceedings (journ.) (SAUS)
Proc Aust Conf Nucl Tech Anal... Australian Conference on Nuclear Techniques of Analysis. Proceedings (journ.) (SAUS)
Proc Australal Inst Min Me... Proceedings of the Australasian Institute of Mining and Metallurgy (SAUS)
Proc Aust Soc Anim Prod... Proceedings of the Australian Society of Animal Production (SAUS)
Proc Aust Soc Med Res... Proceedings of the Australian Society for Medical Research (SAUS)
Proc B & B... Proctor's Bench and Bar of New York [*A publication*] (DLA)
Proc Br Ceram Soc... Proceedings of the British Ceramic Society (SAUS)
Proc Br Crop Prot Conf... Proceedings. British Crop Protection Conference. Weeds (SAUS)
Proc Can Nucl Assoc Annu Int Conf... Proceedings Canadian Nuclear Association Annual International Conference (SAUS)
Proc Cen...... Procurement Center (SAUS)
Proc Ch........ Proceedings in Chancery [*A publication*] (DLA)
PROC CHECK... Process Check (SAUS)
Proc Chem Soc... Proceedings of the Chemical Society (SAUS)
Proc Cir........ Procurement Circular (AAGC)
PROCCIR ..... Procurement Circular [*Air Force*] (AFIT)
Proc Coll Nat Sci... Proceedings. College of Natural Sciences (SAUS)
Proc Conf Aust Soc Sugar Cane Technol... Australian Society of Sugar Cane Technologists. Proceedings of the Conference (journ.) (SAUS)

Proc Congr Int Assoc Sci Study Ment Defic... Proceedings Congress of the International Association for the Scientific Study of Mental Deficiency (SAUS)

Proc Congr S Afr Sug Technol Ass... Proceedings. Congress of the South African Sugar Technologists Association (SAUS)

Proc Cotteswold Natur Fld Club... Proceedings. Cotteswold Naturalists Field Club (SAUS)

Proc Counc Econ AIME... Proceedings. Council of Economics. American Institute of Mining, Metallurgical and Petroleum Engineers (SAUS)

Proc Coventry Dist Natur Hist Sci Soc... Proceedings. Coventry District Natural History and Scientifc Society (SAUS)

Proc Cumberland Geol Soc... Proceedings. Cumberland Geological Society (SAUS)

PROCD......... Procedure (AFM)

procd........... Procedure (ELAL)

PROCD......... Proceed (AFM)

Proc Dir Refin Am Pet Inst... Proceedings. Division of Refining. American Petroleum Institute (SAUS)

Proc Dist ..... Procurement District (SAUS)

Proc Dorset Soc... Dorset Natural History and Archaeological Society. Proceedings (journ.) (SAUS)

PROCDRE .... Procedure (ROG)

Proc East Afr Acad... Proceedings. East African Acdemy (SAUS)

PROCED......... Procedure

Proceed of the Canmbridge Philol Soc... Cambridge Philological Society, Cambridge, England, Proceedings (SAUS)

PRO-CELEB... Professional Celebrit (SAUS)

Proc Elec Assoc Aust... Proceedings. Electrical Association of Australia [A publication]

Proc Elec Assoc NSW... Proceedings. Electrical Association of New South Wales [Australia] [A publication]

Proc Eng Assoc NSW... Proceedings. Engineering Association of New South Wales [Australia] [A publication]

Proc Eng Soc West PA... Proceedings. Engineers Society of Western Pennsylvania (SAUS)

Procept........ Procept, Inc. [Associated Press] (SAG)

Process Eecon Int... Process Economis International (SAUS)

Process Eng Plant and Control... Process Engineering. Plant and Control (SAUS)

Proces-Verb Seances Soc Sci Phys Nat Bordeaux... ProcSs-Verbaux des Seances. Societe des Sciences Physiques et Naturelles de Bordeaux (SAUS)

Proc Eur Dial Transplant Assoc Eur Renal Assoc... Proceedings. European Dialysis and Transplant Association-European Renal Association (SAUS)

PROCEVAL... Procurement Evaluation (SAUS)

Proc Fac Eng Tokai Univ... Proceedings. Faculty of Engineering Tokai University (SAUS)

Proc Fla Anti-Mosq... Proceedings. Florida Anti-Mosquito Association (SAUS)

Proc Fla State Hort Soc... Proceedings of the Florida State Horticultural Society (SAUS)

Proc Florida State Hortic Soc... Florida. State Horticultural Society. Proceedings (journ.) (SAUS)

Proc Geol Assoc... Proceedings. Geologists Association (SAUS)

Proc Geol Assoc London... Proceedings. Geologists Association of London (SAUS)

Proc Ger Soc Neurosurg... Proceedings. German Society of Neurosurgery (SAUS)

Proc Hokuriku Br Crop Sci Soc... Proceedings. Hokuriku Branch of Crop Science Society (SAUS)

PROCIEE...... Proceedings of the Institute of Electrical Engineers [A publication] (IAA)

Proc IEE-A ... Institution of Electrical Engineers. Proceedings. A (journ.) (SAUS)

Proc IEE-B ... Institution of Electrical Engineers. Proceedings. B (journ.) (SAUS)

Proc IEE-C ... Institution of Electrical Engineers. Proceedings. C (journ.) (SAUS)

Proc IEE D ... Institution of Electrical Engineers. Proceedings. D (journ.) (SAUS)

Proc IEE F ... Institution of Electrical Engineers. Proceedings. F (journ.) (SAUS)

Proc IEE G ... Institution of Electrical Engineers. Proceedings. G (journ.) (SAUS)

Proc Indiana Aad Sci... Proceedings. Indiana Academy of Science (SAUS)

Proc Indiana Acad Sci... Proceedings of the Indiana Academy of Science (SAUS)

Proc Indian Acad Sci... Proceedings of the Indian Academy of Sciences (SAUS)

Proc Indian Acad Sci Sect A Earth Planetary Sci... Indian Academy of Sciences. Proceedings. Section A. Earth and Planetary Sciences (journ.) (SAUS)

Proc Indian Natl Sci Acad... Proceedings. Indian National Science Academy (SAUS)

Proc Indian Natl Sci Acad... Proceedings of the Indian National Science Academy (SAUS)

Proc Indian Soc of Internat L... Proceedings of the Conference, The Indian Society of International Law (SAUS)

Proc Inst Automob Eng... Proceedings. Institution of Automobile Engineers (SAUS)

Proc Inst Chem... Proceedings. Institution of Chemists (SAUS)

Proc Inst Criminol Univ Sydney... University of Sydney. Institute of Criminology. Proceedings [A publication]

Proc Inst Elect Electron E... Proceeding of the Institute of Electrical and Electronic Engineers (SAUS)

Proc Inst Electr Eng... Proceedings of the Institution of Electrical Engineers (SAUS)

Proc Inst Mech Eng... Proceedings of the Institution of Mechanical Engineers (SAUS)

Proc Inst Med Chicago... Proceedings of the Institute of Medicine of Chicago (SAUS)

Proc Instn Radio Eng Aust... Proceedings. Institution of Radio Engineers of Australia [A publication]

Proc Inst Pomol... Proceedings. Research Institute of Pomology (SAUS)

ProcInstRadEng... Proceedings of Institute of Radio Ingineers (SAUS)

Proc Inst Radio Engrs... Proceedings of the Institute of Radio Engineers (SAUS)

Proc Int Assoc Theor Appl Limnol... Proceedings. International Association of Theoretical and Applied Limnology (SAUS)

Proc Int Ass Test Mater... Proceedings. International Association for Testing Materials (SAUS)

Proc Int Congr Ecol... Proceedings of the International Congress of Ecology (SAUS)

Proc Int Pharmacol Meet... Proceedings. International Pharmalogical Meeting (SAUS)

Proc Int Pl Propag Soc... Proceedings. International Plant Propagators Society (SAUS)

Proc Int Sci Congr Cultiv Edible Fungi... Proceedings. International Scientifc Congress on the Cultivation of Edible Fungi (SAUS)

Proc Int Symp Boreal For... Proceedings of the International Symposium on Boreal Forest (SAUS)

Proc Int Union Biol Sci... Proceedings. International Union of Biological Sciences (SAUS)

Proc Iowa Acad Sci... Proceedings of the Iowa Academy of Science (SAUS)

Proc IRE ...... Proceedings of the IRE (SAUS)

Proc La Acad Sci... Proceedings of the Louisiana Academy of Sciences (SAUS)

PROCLIB...... Procedure Library [Computer science]

Proc Lincoln Coll Farmers Conf... Proceedings. Lincoln College. Farmers Conference (SAUS)

Proc Med-Leg Soc Vic... Medico-Legal Society of Victoria. Proceedings [A publication]

Proc Microscopical Soc Vic... Proceedings. Microscopical Society of Victoria [Australia] [A publication]

ProcmT........ Procom Technology Inc. [Associated Press] (SAG)

Proc Nat Conf AIAS... Proceedings. National Conference. Australian Institute of Agricultural Science (SAUS)

Proc Natl Acad Sci USA... Proceedings of the National Academy of Science of the United States of America (MEC)

Proc Natl Counc Sci Dev... Proceedings. National Council on Science Development (SAUS)

Proc Natl Inst Sci... Proceedings. National Institute of Sciences (SAUS)

Proc Natl Sci Counc... Proceedings of the National Science Council (SAUS)

Proc Natl Telecommon Conf... Proceedings. National Telecommunications Conference (SAUS)

Proc Natn Ent Soc... Proceedings. National Entomological Society (SAUS)

Proc Near E S Afr Irrig Pract Semin... Proceedings. Near East-South Africa Irrigation Practices Seminar (SAUS)

PROCNEC...... Proceeding of the National Electrical Conference (SAUS)

Proc Nutr Soc... Proceedings of the Nutrition Society (SAUS)

PROCO......... Procurement Officer [Military]

PROCO......... Programmed Combustion [Ford Motor Co.]

PROCO......... Projects for Continental Operations [World War II]

Proc of the SJCC... Proceedings of the Summer Joint Computer Conference (SAUS)

Proc of the WJCC... Proceedings of the Winter Joint Computer Conference (SAUS)

PROCOL....... Process Control Language (NITA)

PROCOL....... Process Control Oriented Language [Computer science] (IAA)

ProCom........ IEEE-SA Standards Board Procedures Committee (SAUS)

PROCOM...... Procedures Committee [Institute of Electrical and Electronics Engineers] (IEEE)

PROCOM...... Procurement Committee

PROCOM...... Prognose Compiler [Computer science] (IAA)

PROCOM...... Projection Compositor (SAUS)

PROCOMEXCHI... Mexican-Chicano Cooperative Programs on Mexican-US-Chicano Futures (EA)

PROCOMM... Program Communication (SAUS)

PROCOMP...... Process Compiler [Computer science] (IAA)

PROCOMP ... Process Computer [Computer science]

PROCOMP ... Program Compiler [Computer science] (IEEE)

PROCON ...... Project Control (SAUS)

PROCON ...... Protocol Converter (DA)

PROCON ...... Request Diagnosis, Prognosis, Present Condition, Probable Date and Mode of Disposition of Following Patient Reported in Your Hospital [Military]

Procop......... Procopius [Sixth century AD] [Classical studies] (OCD)

PROCOP ...... Project Control Package (SAUS)

PROCOPT .... Processing Option [Computer science] (MHDB)

Proc Osaka Prefect Inst Public Health... Proceedings. Osaka Prefecture Institute of Public Health (SAUS)

PROCOTIP ... Promotion Cooperative du Transport Individuel Publique [Public cars for private use to reduce traffic congestion] [Also known as TIP] [France]

Proc Phil Educ Soc... Proceedings. Philosophy of Education Society (SAUS)

Proc Phys Soc... Proceedings. Physical Society (SAUS)

Proc Plant Propagators Soc... Proceedings. Plant Propagators. Society (SAUS)

Proc PN Lebedev Phys Inst... Proceedings of the P.N. Lebedev Physics Institute (SAUS)

Proc Pr .... Proctor's Practice [A publication] (DLA)

Proc Prac..... Proctor's Practice [A publication] (DLA)

PROCR....... Processor (VLIE)

Proc Reg Conf Int Potash Inst... Proceedings. Regional Conferene. International Potash Institute (SAUS)

Proc Reliab Maint Conf... Proceedings of Reliability and Maintainability Conference (SAUS)

Proc Rep S Seedmens Ass... Proceedings and Reports. Southern Seedmens Association (SAUS)

Proc Res Inst Oceanogr Fish... Proceedings. Research Institute of Oceanography and Fisheries (SAUS)

Proc Res Soc Jap Sugar Refin Technol... Proceedings. Research Society of Japan Sugar Refineries Technologists (SAUS)

Proc Roy Anthtropol Inst... Proceedings. Royal Anthropological Institute (SAUS)

Proc Roy Aust Chem Inst... Proceedings of the Royal Australian Chemical Institute (SAUS)

Proc Roy Soc... Proceeding of the Royal Society (SAUS)

Proc Roy Soc Med... Proceedings of the Royal Society of Medicine (SAUS)

Proc Roy Soc Qld... Proceedings. Royal Society of Queensland [*Australia*] [*A publication*]

Proc Roy Soc Vic... Proceedings. Royal Society of Victoria [*Australia*] [*A publication*]

Proc R Soc Edin... Proceedings of the Royal Society of Edinburgh (MEC)

Proc R Soc London... Proceedings of the Royal Society of London (MEC)

Proc Ruakura Farmers Conf... Proceedings. Ruakura Farmers Conference (SAUS)

PROCS......... Proceedings

Proc S Afr Soc Anim Proc... Proceedings. South African Society of Animal Production (SAUS)

PROCSCAN... Procedure Library Scanning (SAUS)

Proc Sci Soc Univ Adel... Proceedings. Scientific Society. University of Adelaide [*A publication*]

PROCSD... Processed

Proc Second Malays Soil Conf... Proceedings. Second Malaysian Soil Conference (SAUS)

Proc Semin Biomass Energy City Farm Ind... Proceedings. Seminar on Biomass Energy for City, Farm and Industry (SAUS)

PROCSEQ... Processing Sequence [*Computer science*] (MHDB)

Proc Shikoku Br Crop Sci Soc... Proceedings. Shikoku Branch of Crop Science Society (SAUS)

PROCSIM... Processor Simulation (SAUS)

PROCSIM..... Processor Simulation Language [*Computer science*] (PDAA)

PROCSIM Language... Processor Simulation Language (SAUS)

Proc SJCC... Proceeding of the Spring Joint Computer Conference (SAUS)

Proc Soc Anal Chem... Proceedings of the Society for Analytical Chemistry (SAUS)

Proc Soc Chem Indust Vic... Proceedings. Society of Chemical Industry of Victoria [*Australia*] [*A publication*]

Proc Soc Exp Biol Med... Proceedings of the Society for Experimental Biology and Medicine (SAUS)

PROCSTEP... Procedure Step (SAUS)

PROCSTOR... Program Storage [*Computer science*] (VLIE)

Proc Study Fauna Flora USSR... Proceedings on the Study of the Fauna and Flora of the USSR (SAUS)

PROCSY....... Purdue Remote Online Console System (SAUS)

Proc Symp Effects Ionizing Radiat Seed Signific Crop Impr... Proceedings. Symposium on the Effects of Ionizing Radiation on Seeds and Their Significance for Crop Improvement (SAUS)

Proc Symp Isotop Plant Nutr Physiol... Proceedings. Symposium on Isotopes in Plant Nutrition and Physiology (SAUS)

Proc Symp Use Radioisotop Soil Plant Nutr Stud... Proceedings Symposium on the Use of Radioisotopes in Soil-Plant Nutrition Studies (SAUS)

Proct........... Proctology [*Medicine*] (AMHC)

PROCT........ Proctology

ProctGm ...... Procter & Gamble Co. [*Associated Press*] (SAG)

PROCTO...... Proctocolitis (SAUS)

PROCTO...... Proctocolonoscopy (SAUS)

PROCTO...... Proctology [*Gastroenterology*] (DAVI)

PROCTO...... Proctoplegia (SAUS)

PROCTO...... Proctoscopy [*Medicine*]

PROCTO...... Proctosigmoidectomy (SAUS)

PROCTOR .... Priority Routine Organizer for Computer Transfers and Operations of Registers

Proc Tree Wardens Arborists Util Conf... Proceedings. Tree Wardens, Arborists and Utilities Conference (SAUS)

PROCU......... Processing Unit

PROCUP ...... Partido Revolucionario Obrerista y Clandestino de Union Popular [*Mexico*] [*Political party*] (EY)

PROCURE .... Command Procurement System (SAUS)

Proc Utah Acad Sci... Proceedings. Utah Academy of Sciences, Arts and Letters (SAUS)

PROCVAL..... Validation Procedures Library [*Social Security Administration*]

Proc WA Instn Eng... Proceedings. Western Australian Institution of Engineers [*A publication*]

Proc West For Conserv Ass... Proceedings Western Forestry Conference. Western Forestry and Conservation Association (SAUS)

Proc West Pharmacol Soc... Proceedings of the Western Pharmacology Society (SAUS)

Proc World Congr Anaesthesiol... Anaesthesiology. Proceedings of the World Congress of Anaesthesiologists (journ.) (SAUS)

Procyt......... ProCyte Corp. [*Associated Press*] (SAG)

PROD........... Office of Production [*National Security Agency*]

PROD........... Photographic Retrieval from Optical Disk

prod............ Produce (WDAA)

PROD........... Produce

PROD........... Producer (GOBB)

PROD........... Product [*or Production*] (AABC)

prod............ Product (WDMC)

Prod............ Production (AAGC)

PROD........... Production (DOMA)

prod............ Production (WDMC)

Prod............ Produzent (SAUS)

PROD........... Professional Drivers Council for Safety and Health

PROD........... Professional Over-the-Road Drivers [*Part of Teamsters Union*]

PROD........... Program for Orbit Development (SAUS)

PRODAC ..... Production Advisers Consortium (NADA)

PRODAC ..... Programmed Digital Automatic Control [*Computer science*]

PRODAM..... Production Orientated Draughting and Manufacturing (PDAA)

PRODAN ...... Propionyl(dimethylamino)naphthalene [*Organic chemistry*]

PRODASE .... Protein Database

Prod Aust ... Productivity Australia [*A publication*]

PRODC........ Production Command [*Army*]

PROD Code... Product Code (SAUS)

PROD/DEPL... Production and Deployment [*Phase*] (DOMA)

PRODEM...... Project on Demilitarisation (SAUS)

Proden......... Proyecto de Desarrollo Nacional [*Project for National Development*] [*Chile*] (PPW)

ProDex......... ProDex, Inc. [*Associated Press*] (SAG)

PRODISCO... Producers Distributing Corp.

Prod Liab..... Products Liability (SAUS)

Prod Liab Int'l... Product Liability International [*A publication*] (DLA)

Prod Liab Rep... Product Liability Reporter [*Commerce Clearing House*] [*A publication*] (DLA)

Prod Liab Rep... Products Liability Reporter (or Reports) (SAUS)

PRODN .... Production

Prodn......... Production

PRODNG ..... Producing

ProDnt .... Professional Dental Technologies, Inc. [*Associated Press*] (SAG)

PRODOC ...... Procedure Documentation [*Computer science*] (MHDB)

PRODON ...... Production

ProdOp .... Production Operators Corp. [*Associated Press*] (SAG)

PRO DOS .... Pro Dose [*For a Dose*] [*Pharmacy*]

ProDOS....... Professional Disk Operating System [*Computer science*]

Prod Proj Trends Bldg... Products, Projects and Trends in Building (SAUS)

PRODR .... Producer

Prods........... Products (AAGC)

Prod Safety & Liab Rep... Product Safety and Liability Reporter [*A publication*] (DLA)

PRODSEC .... Product Security (ACAE)

PRODT........ Product

Prod Tech... Production and Technique (SAUS)

PRODUCE .... Production Distribution Using Component Evaluation (IAA)

Product....... Productivity Technologies Corp. [*Associated Press*] (SAG)

PRODUCTN... Production

Productv ..... Productivity Technologies Corp. [*Associated Press*] (SAG)

PRODUTAS... Proceed on Duty Assigned [*Military*]

PRODVAL .... Product Validation (MCD)

PROE .... Programme Regional Oceanien de l'Environnement [*South Pacific Regional Environmental Programme - SPREP*] (EAIO)

Proe Divers Gas Purity Symp... Proceedings. Divers Gas Purity Symposium (SAUS)

PRO EL........ Protein Electrophoresis [*Biochemistry*] (DAVI)

Proe NJ Mosq Control Assoc... Proceedings. New Jersey Mosquito Control Association (SAUS)

Pro Ex.......... Protein Exchange [*Dietetics*]

PROF .... Parameter Profile (SAUS)

PROF .... Peace Research Organization Fund

PROF .... Personal Radio Operators Federation [*Defunct*] (EA)

PROF .... Prediction and Optimization of Failure (SAUS)

PROF .... Prediction and Optimization of Failure Rate (MHDB)

PROF .... Premixed One-Dimensional Flame Code (SAUS)

PROF .... Profanity [*FBI standardized term*]

PROF .... Profession [*or Professional*]

Prof............ Professional (AL)

prof............ Professional (NTIO)

prof............ Professional (SHCU)

PROF .... Professional Investors Insurance Group, Inc. (SAUS)

PROF .... Professional Office System

PROF .... Professor (EY)

Prof............ Professor (ODBW)

prof............ Professor (PROS)

PROF .... Profile (GAVI)

prof............ Profile (VRA)

Prof............ Profile

prof............ profundus (SAUS)

PROF .... Pupil Registering and Operational Filing [*Computer science*]

ProFac......... Pro-Fac Cooperative, Inc. [*Associated Press*] (SAG)

PROFAC...... Propulsive Fluid Accumulator

PROFACTS... Product Formulation, Accounting and Cost System (SAUS)

PROFACTS... Production Formulation, Accounting, and Cost System (MHDI)

Prof Admin... Professional Administrator [*A publication*]

PROFAGTRANS... Proceed by First Available Government Transportation [*Military*]

PROFAT .... Projet des Francophones de l'Atlantique [*Canada*]

pro-fax......... Production Facilities (WDMC)

Pro-Fax........ Production Facility (NTCM)

ProfBTM ...... Professional Business and Technical Management [*British*] [*An association*] (DBA)

Prof Burd..... Commemoratio Professorum Burdigalensium [*of Ausonius*] [*Classical studies*] (OCD)

Prof Corp..... Proffatt on Private Corporations in California [*A publication*] (DLA)

Prof Corp Guide... Professional Corporation Guide (SAUS)

Prof Corp Guide (P-H)... Professional Corporation Guide (Prentice-Hall, Inc.) [*A publication*] (DLA)

PROFCRE.... Professional Care, Inc. (SAUS)

PROFCY....... Proficiency

PROF-E........ Programmed Review of Operator Functions - Elementary (DNAB)

Prof Eng ..... Professional Engineer

Prof Engr .... Professional Engineer [*A publication*]

PROFERI...... Programme for Refugee Reintegration and Rehabilitation of Resettlement Areas in Eritrea

PROFESSL.... Professional

PROFFENS... Prototype Flash Flood Estimation and Nowcasting System (SAUS)

PROFFIS ...... Professional Filler System [*Military*]

Proffitt .... Proffitt's, Inc. [*Associated Press*] (SAG)

PROFIBUS ... Process Field Bus (SAUS)

Profile .... Passive Radio Frequency Interference Location Experiment (SAUS)

PROFILE ...... Programmed Functional Indices for Laboratory Evaluation [*RAND Corp.*]

PROFILE ...... Program Overview and File (SAUS)

PROFILES.... Personal Reflection on Family Life and Employment Stressors [*Psychology*]
PROFINE...... Proximity Fuze Intercept and Analysis Equipment (SAUS)
PROFIS........ Professional Officer Filler Information System (SAUS)
PROFIS........ Programminformationssystem Sozialwissenschaften [*Informationszentrum Sozialwissenschaften*] [*Germany*] [*Defunct*] [*Information service or system*] (CRD)
PROFISS..... Professional Filter System (SAUS)
PROFIT....... Planners Remote Offline Form Image Tape (SAUS)
PROFIT........ Program for Financed Insurance Techniques
PROFIT........ Program for Financed (or Financial) Insurance Technic (or Techniques) (SAUS)
PROFIT........ Programmed Receiving, Ordering and Forecasting Inventory Technique (SAUS)
PROFIT........ Programmed Reviewing, Ordering, and Forecasting Inventory Technique
PROFIT........ Propulsion Flight Control Integration Technology (MCD)
PROFIT........ Propulsion/Flight Control Technology (SAUS)
PROFITS System... Personalized Realtime-Oriented Financial Institutions Time Saving System (SAUS)
Prof Jur....... Proffatt on Trial by Jury [*A publication*] (DLA)
PROFL......... Professional
Prof Lib Pr... Professional Library Press (SAUS)
PR of MAN... [*The*] Prayer of Manasses, King of Judah [*Apocrypha*]
PROFNET..... Procurement & Financial Management of Logistics Supplies (SAUS)
Prof Not....... Proffatt on Notaries [*A publication*] (DLA)
Prof Officer... Professional Officer [*A publication*]
PROFP......... Proficiency Pay [*Military*]
PROF PHONO PL... Professional Phonograph Plug (SAUS)
PROF PHONO SKT... Professional Phonograph Socket (SAUS)
PROF Rate... Prediction and Optimization of Failure Rate (SAUS)
ProfRec........ Profit Recovery Group International, Inc. (The) [*Associated Press*] (SAG)
PROFS......... Professional Office System [*IBM Corp.*]
profs........... professors (SAUS)
PROFS........ Program for Regional Observing and Forecasting Services [*Boulder, CO*] [*Department of Commerce*] (GRD)
PROFS........ Prototype for Regional Observing and Forecasting Service (SAUS)
PROFS........ Prototype Regional Observation and Forecasting Service [*National Oceanic and Atmospheric Administration*] (GRD)
PROFS........ Prototype Regional Observation (or Observing) and Forecasting Service (SAUS)
Profsnl........ Professional (TBD)
ProfStaff...... Professional Staff [*Associated Press*] (SAG)
Prof Wills.... Proffatt on Wills [*A publication*] (DLA)
PROG........... Peer Review Oversight Group [*National Institutes of Health*]
PROG........... Progenitor (SAUS)
PROG........... Progeny (SAUS)
prog........... Progesterone [*Endocrinology*] (DAVI)
prog........... Prognathism [*Dentistry*] (DAVI)
Prog........... Prognose (SAUS)
PROG........... Prognosis [*or Prognostication*] (AAG)
prog........... prognostic (SAUS)
PROG........... Prognostication (SAUS)
PROG........... Prognosticator (SAUS)
Prog........... Program (AL)
PROG........... Program (KSC)
PROG........... Programmable (SAUS)
PROG........... Programmed (SAUS)
PROG........... Programmer [*or Programming*]
PROG........... Programmer's Paradise [*NASDAQ symbol*] (TTSB)
PROG........... Programmers Paradise, Inc. [*NASDAQ symbol*] (SAG)
PROG........... Programs Division (SAUS)
PROG........... Progress (AABC)
Prog........... Progress (DIAR)
Prog........... Progressive [*A publication*] (BRI)
PROG........... Progressive (GOBB)
Prog Allergol... Progress of Allergology (SAUS)
Prog Arch .... Progressive Architecture [*A publication*] (BRI)
PROG BK .... Programmed Book [*Publishing*]
ProgBk........ Progressive Bank, Inc. [*Associated Press*] (SAG)
ProgCp........ Progressive Corp. [*Associated Press*] (SAG)
Prog F .... Progressive Fire (SAUS)
Prog Fish-Cult... Progressive Fish Culturist (SAUS)
ProgFn......... Progress Financial Corp. [*Associated Press*] (SAG)
Prog Instr&Ed Tech... Programmed Instruction and Educational Technology (SAUS)
PROGLIB...... Production Program Library [*Social Security Administration*]
PRO GM ...... Pro Grand Master [*Freemasonry*]
PROGMAN ... Program Manager (VLIE)
Prog Med..... Progress in Medicine (SAUS)
Prog Med Parasitol... Progress in Medical Parasitology (SAUS)
PROGMG ..... Programming
PROGN .... Prognosis (AAMN)
Prog Neurol Psyciatry... Progress in Neurology and Psychiatry (journ.) (SAUS)
Prog Neuro-Psychopharmacol&Biol Psychiatry... Progress in Neuro-Psychopharmacology and Biological Psychiatry (SAUS)
PROGNO........ Prognosen-Trends-Entwicklungen [*Forecasts-Trends-Developments*] [*Society for Business Information*] [*Information service or system*] (IID)
PROG-NOSAG... European Centre for Applied Economic Research (SAUS)
PROGO........ Program Guidance and Objectives (SAUS)
Prog Odontostomatol... ProgrSs Odonto-Stomatologique (SAUS)
PROGOFOP... Program of Operation [*Computer science*]
Prog Oto-Rhino-Laryngol... ProgrSs en Oto-Rhino-Laryngologie (SAUS)
ProgPar....... Programmers Paradise, Inc. [*Associated Press*] (SAG)

Prog Physiol Sci... Progress in Physiological Sciences (SAUS)
Prog Protozool... Progress in Protozoology (SAUS)
PROGR .... Programmer (ECII)
progr.......... Progress (DAVI)
PROGRAM... Programming (SAUS)
Program Abstr Am Soc Parasitol Annu Meet... Program and Abstracts. American Society of Parasitologists. Annual Meeting (SAUS)
Program/Proc Natl Horsemens Semin... Program/Proceedings. National Horsemens Seminar (SAUS)
Progr Bull...... Progress Bulletin (SAUS)
Prog Rep Exp Stn Colorado State Univ... Colorado State University. Experiment Station. Progress Report (journ.) (SAUS)
Prog Rep Minist Agric Fish Fd Exp Husb Fms Exp Hort Stns... Progress Report. Ministry of Agriculture, Fisheries and Food. Experimental Husbandry Farms and Experimental Horticultur (SAUS)
Progr Math... Progress of Mathematics (SAUS)
Progrp .... ProGroup, Inc. [*Associated Press*] (SAG)
Progr Polym Sci... Progress in Polymer Science (MEC)
Progr Rev For Prod Lab... Program Review. Forest Products Laboratory (SAUS)
PROGS......... Prognosis (SAUS)
PROGS......... Progressive
PROGS......... Progressive Proofs [*Graphic arts*] (DGA)
PROGSYS...... Programming System (SAUS)
PROGTOT .... Progressive Total (VLIE)
PROGVAL .... Validation Program Library [*Social Security Administration*]
PROH.......... Prohibit
PROH.......... Prohibition [*FBI standardized term*]
Prohib......... Prohibited
PROI.......... CFI ProServices [*NASDAQ symbol*] (TTSB)
PROI.......... CFI Proservices, Inc. [*NASDAQ symbol*] (SAG)
PROI.......... President of the Royal Institute of Oil Painters [*British*]
PROI.......... Project Return on Investment (MHDW)
PRO-IF....... Personal Radio Operators International Federation [*Formerly, ARC*] (EA)
PROIMREP... Proceed Immediately - Report for Purpose Indicated [*Military*]
PROIMREP... Proceed Immediately-Report for Purpose Indicated (SAUS)
Pro Indian Soc of Internat L... Proceedings of the Conference. Indian Society of International Law [*New Delhi, India*] [*A publication*] (DLA)
Proj............ Project (TBD)
proj........... Project (VRA)
PROJ.......... Project
PROJ.......... Projectile (AFM)
PROJ.......... Projection (SAUS)
PROJ.......... Projector [*or Projection*]
PROJACS..... Project Analysis and Control System (MHDI)
PROJD........ Projected (SAUS)
PROJECT...... Project Engineering Control
PROJENGR... Project Engineer
PROJID........ Project Identification [*Computer science*]
PROJMGR.... Project Manager [*Military*]
PROJMGRASWS... Project Manager, Antisubmarine Warfare Systems
PROJMGRFBM... Project Manager, Fleet Ballistic Missile [*Navy*]
PROJMGRSMS... Project Manager, Surface Missile Systems [*Navy*]
ProjSft .... Project Software & Development, Inc. [*Associated Press*] (SAG)
projt........... Projector (VRA)
PROJTRNS... Project Transition [*DoD*]
PROL.......... Priority Requirement Objective List (AFM)
Prol............ Prologic Management Systems, Inc. [*Associated Press*] (SAG)
prol........... Prologue (WDAA)
PROL.......... Prologue
PRO L .... Province Laws (DLA)
PROLAC....... Prolactin [*Biochemistry*] (DAVI)
PROLAMAT... International Conference on Programming Languages for Numerically Controlled Machines (SAUS)
PROLAMAT... Programming Language for Numerically Controlled Machine Tools (SAUS)
PROLAMAT... Programming Languages for Machine Tools [*Conference*]
PROLAMAT... Programming Languages for Numerically Controlled Machine Tools [*Conference*] [*Computer science*] (IAA)
PROLAN....... Processed Language [*Computer science*]
PROLAN....... Processing Language (SAUS)
PROLDI........ Annual Research Reviews. Prolactin (journ.) (SAUS)
prole.......... Proletarian (ADWA)
PROLE .... Proletarian (WDAA)
Proler .... Proler International Corp. [*Associated Press*] (SAG)
PROLETCULT... Proletarian Culture
PROLIB........ Project Library (SAUS)
Prolif .... Proliferative [*or Proliferation*]
PROLLAP...... Professional Library Literature Acquisition Program
PRO LOC et TEM... Pro Loco et Tempore [*For the Place and Time*] [*Latin*] (ROG)
PROLOG ...... Production of Onshore Lower 48 Oil and Gas Model [*Department of Energy*] (GFGA)
PROLOG ...... Program Logistics (NG)
PROLOG ...... Programming in Logic [*Programing language*] [*1970*]
PROLOG ...... Programming Logic (SAUS)
PROLOG ...... Project Logic Planning (SAUS)
Prolog......... Prologic Management Systems, Inc. [*Associated Press*] (SAG)
Prologc........ Prologic Management Systems, Inc. [*Associated Press*] (SAG)
Prologic....... Prologic Management Systems, Inc. [*Associated Press*] (SAG)
PROLOG Planning... Project Logic Planning (SAUS)
prolong........ Prolongatus [*Prolonged*] [*Latin*] (DAVI)
prolong........ prolonged (SAUS)
PROLOPLA... Program Logical Plan (SAUS)
PROLT .... Procurement Lead Time
PROM .... Partial Read Only Memory (SAUS)

PROM	Passive Range of Motion [Medicine]
PROM	Pockel's Readout Optical Memory
PROM	Pockels Readout Optical Modulator
PROM	Pockels-Readout-Optical Modulator (SAUS)
PROM	Pockets Readout Optical Modulator (SAUS)
PROM	Premature [or Prolonged] Rupture of Membranes [Gynecology]
PROM	Programable Read Only Memory (SAUS)
PROM	Programmable Read-Only Memory [Computer science]
PROM	Program, Resources, Objectives, Management [Air Force Systems Command technique]
PROM	Progressive Range of Motion [Medicine]
PROM	Prolonged Rupture of Membranes [Gynecology] (DAVI)
prom	Promenade (DD)
PROM	Promenade [Maps and charts]
PROM	Prominent
PROM	Promise [Legal shorthand] (LWAP)
Prom.	Promissory [A publication] (DLA)
PROM	Promontory
PROM	Promote [or Promotion] (AFM)
PROM	Promoter (SAUS)
PROM	Promotion
PROM	Promotor (SAUS)
PROM	Prompter (SAUS)
PROM	Promulgate (AABC)
PROM	Promulgation (SAUS)
Pro-MACE	Prednisone, Methotrexate with Leucovorin, Adriamycin, Cyclophosphamide, Epipodophyllin [Etoposide, VP-16] [Antineoplastic drug regimen]
PROMACE-MOPP...	Procarbazine, Methotrexate, Adriamycin, Cyclophosphamide, Etoposide, Mustargen [Nitrogen mustard], Oncovin , Procarbazine, Prednisone [Vincristine] [Antineoplastic drug regimen]
PROMACE-MOPP...	Procarbazine, Methotrexate, Adriamycin, Cyclophosphamide, Etoposide, Mustargen, Oncovin, Procarbazine, Prednisone (SAUS)
PROMACX...	Production Management and Control System (SAUS)
PROMAG...	Production Management Action Group [British]
PROMAP	Program for the Refinement of the Materiel Acquisition Process [Army] (AABC)
PROMAST...	Production Master Scheduling System (PDAA)
PROMATS...	Probabilistic Materials System (PDAA)
PROMATS...	Programmable Magnetic Tape System [Computer science] (VLIE)
PROMCOM...	Project Monitoring and Control Method (SAUS)
Prom dk...	Promenade Deck [of a ship] (DS)
ProMED	Program for Monitoring Emerging Diseases (SAUS)
ProMED	Program to Monitor Emerging Diseases
PROMED	Pro-Med Capital Corp.
PROMEE	Promisee [Legal shorthand] (LWAP)
PROMESS...	Penmarch Radar Oceanographic Microwave Experiment on Signature Studies (SAUS)
PROMETH	Promethazine Hydrochloride (SAUS)
PROMETHEUS...	Program for European Traffic with Highest Efficiency and Unprecedented Safety (ECON)
PROMEX	Productivity Measurement Experiment [National Institute of Standards and Technology]
PROMIM	Programmable Multiple Ion Monitor
PROMIS	Polar Regions and Outer Magnetosphere (ACAE)
PROMIS	Problem Oriented Medical Guidance System
PROMIS	Problem-Oriented Medical Information System [Computerized patient-management system]
PROMIS	Process Management and Information System [I. P. Sharp Associates Ltd.] [Software package] (NCC)
PROMIS	Procurement Management Information System (SAUS)
PROMIS	Production Management Information System (TIMI)
PROMIS	Project Management Integrated System (NITA)
PROMIS	Project-Oriented Management Information System
PROMIS	Prosecution Management Information System (SAUS)
PROMIS	Prosecutor's Management Information System [Law Enforcement Assistance Administration]
PROMISE	Programming Managers Information System (MHDI)
PROMISE	Prospective Randomized Milrinone Survival Evaluation [Medicine]
PROMISS	Packaging Requirements for Optimum Malfunction Isolation by Systematic Substitution (IAA)
PROML	Promulgate
PROMMIS...	Programmed Restructuring of Maintenance Management Information System (SAUS)
PROMO	Promotion [Slang] (DSUE)
promo	Promotional (TVEL)
PROMO	Promotional Advertising (GOBB)
Promo	Promotional Announcement (NTCM)
PROMOCM...	Project Monitor and Control Method (SAUS)
PROMOR	Promisor [Legal shorthand] (LWAP)
Promot.	Promotion (DIAR)
PROMPT	Production, Reviewing, Organizing, and Monitoring of Performance Techniques (BUR)
PROMPT	Program Monitoring and Planning Techniques (IEEE)
PROMPT	Program Reporting, Organization, and Management Planning Technique (IAA)
PROMPT	Program to Record Official Mail Point-to-Point Times [Postal Service program]
PROMPT	Project Management and Production Team Technique [Computer science]
PROMPT	Project Reporting Organization and Management Planning Technique
PROMS	Procurement Management System (MCD)
PROMS	Programmable Read Only Memory System [Computer science]

PROMS	Program Modelling and Simulation (SAUS)
PROMS	Program Modelling System (SAUS)
PROMS	Program Monitoring System (MCD)
PROMS	Projectile Measurement System [Computer science] [Army]
PROMSS	Procedures and Relationships for the Operation of Manual Stations and Spaces (DNAB)
PROM STAT...	Promotion Status (DNAB)
PROMT	Precision Optimized Measurement Time [Spectroscopy]
PROMT	Predicasts Overview of Markets and Terminology (NITA)
PROMT	Predicasts Overviews of Marketing and Technology [Business database]
PROMT	Programmable Miniature Message Terminal (MCD)
PROMUS	Provincial-Municipal Simulator [Computer-based urban management system]
Pro Mus Orc...	Pro Musica Orchestra (SAUS)
PROMY	Promissory (ROG)
PRON	Patriotyczny Ruch Odrodzenia Narodowego [Patriotic Movement for National Rebirth] [Poland] (EY)
PRON	Procurement Request and Order Number (SAUS)
PRON	Procurement Request Order Number [Army] (AABC)
ProN	Progressive Number (SAUS)
PRON	Pronation
PRON	Pronominal (ADA)
pron	Pronoun (NTIO)
PRON	Pronoun
PRON	Pronounced
PRON	Pronouncement (SAUS)
PRON	Pronunciation (ROG)
pron	Pronunciation (WDMC)
Pron A	Prenominal Adjective (SAUS)
PRONED	Promotion of Non-Executive Directors (ODBW)
Pronet	ProNet, Inc. [Associated Press] (SAG)
PRO-NICA	Professionals - Nicaragua [An association] (EA)
Pro-Nica	Professionals - Nicaragua (EA)
Pro Note	Promissory Note (SAUS)
PRONTO	Program for Numeric Tool Operation [Computer science]
PRONTO	Programmable Network Telecommunications Operating System
pronun	pronunciate (SAUS)
prooem	Prooemium (BJA)
PROOF	Parole Resource Office and Orientation Facility (SAUS)
PROOF	Precision Recording (Optical) of Fingerprints
PROOF	Projected Return on Open Office Facilities [Computer program]
proOLMC	Pro-Opiolipomelanocortin [Endocrinology]
PRO-OP	Project Optimization [Industrial engineering]
PROP	Panel Review of Products (SAUS)
PROP	Performance Review for Operating Programs (BUR)
PROP	Pilot Repair Overhaul and Provisioning (MUGU)
PROP	Planetary Rocket Ocean Platform
PROP	Portland Regional Opportunities Program (SAUS)
PROP	Prerelease Orientation Program [Reformatory program]
PROP	Preservation of the Rights of Prisoners [An association] [British]
PROP	Primary Operand (SAUS)
PROP	Primary Operand Pipeline (SAUS)
PROP	Primary Operand Unit (IAA)
PROP	Prisoners' Right of Privacy [British] (DI)
PROP	Production Operators [NASDAQ symbol] (TTSB)
PROP	Production Operators Corp. [NASDAQ symbol] (NQ)
PROP	Production Planning (IAA)
PROP	Profit Rating of Projects
PROP	Program for the Refinement of Orbital Parameters (SAUS)
PROP	Proof of Purchase (WDMC)
PROP	Propaganda (AFM)
Prop	Propagate [Botany]
PROP	Propellant (KSC)
PROP	Propelled (SAUS)
PROP	Propeller
prop	Proper (NTIO)
PROP	Proper
prop	properly (SAUS)
PROP	Propertius [Roman poet, c. 29BC] [Classical studies] (ROG)
Prop	Property (TBD)
prop	Property (WDAA)
PROP	Property
PROP	Property Release Option Program [HUD]
PROP	Proportional (KSC)
PROP	Proportioning (NAKS)
PROP	Proposal (AAG)
PROP	Proposed (AFM)
PROP	Proposition
PROP	Propranolol (DB)
prop	propriertary (SAUS)
prop	Proprietor (WDAA)
PROP	Proprietor
PROP	Propulsion (AAG)
PROP	Propulsion Engineer (NAKS)
PROP	Propulsor (SAUS)
PROP	Propylthiouracil [Also, PT, PTU] [Thyroid inhibitor]
PROP	Protected Areas Programme (SAUS)
PROPAC	Progressive Political Action Committee [Defunct] (EA)
PROPAC	Prospective Payment Assessment Commission [Washington, DC] (EGAO)
ProPAC	Prospective Payment Assessment Commission
propaed	propaedutics (SAUS)
PROPAKASIA...	International Food Processing and Packaging Technology Exhibition and Conferencefor South East Asia

PROPAL....... Programmed PAL (SAUS)
PROPAL....... Proportional
Prop & Comp... Property and Compensation Reports [*A publication*] (DLA)
Prop & Comp R... Property and Compensation Reports [*A publication*] (DLA)
PRO-PAY ..... Proficiency Pay [*Military*]
Propcon .... Conferences Prop and Pulpwood Charter (SAUS)
PropCT......... Property Capital Trust [*Associated Press*] (SAG)
pro per .... Propria Persona [*In His or Her Own Person*] [*Latin*] (WGA)
PROPER COUNT... Property Accountability (MCD)
PROPH......... Porphyrins [*Chemistry*] (DAVI)
PROPH......... Profile of Phonology (AIE)
proph .... prophetic (SAUS)
PROPH......... Prophylactic
Proph........... Prophylaxis (SAUS)
Proph21....... Prophet 21, Inc. [*Associated Press*] (SAG)
PROPHET..... Proactive Rehabilitation of Outside Plant Using Heuristic Expert Techniques [*GTE computer software*]
prophy .... Prophylactic (DAVI)
PROPIN........ Proprietary Information
PROPL......... Proportional
Prop Law..... Property Lawyer [*1826-30*] [*A publication*] (DLA)
Prop Law Bull... Property Law Bulletin [*A publication*] (DLA)
Prop Law NS... Property Lawyer, New Series [*England*] [*A publication*] (DLA)
PROPLING.... Propelling
PROPLOSS... Propagation Loss (NVT)
PROPLT....... Propellant (NASA)
PROPN......... Propane
PROPN......... Proportion (MSA)
proPO .... Prophenoloxidase
PROPON...... Proportion (ROG)
PROPORICH... Proceed to Port in Which Unit is Located [*Navy*] (DNAB)
PROPR......... Proprietary (ROG)
PROPR......... Proprietor (EY)
propr........... Proprietor (WDAA)
PROPRCS.... Propulsion Reaction Control System (SAUS)
PROPRE....... Property Press (DLA)
PROPRSS.... Proprietress (ROG)
PROPSIM..... Propagation Simulator (SAUS)
ProPTH .... Proparathyroid Hormone (SAUS)
PROPTRY .... Proprietary [*Freight*]
PROPUL....... Propulsion
Prop Wash... Propeller Wash (SAUS)
PROPY......... Proprietary
Pro Quer...... Pro Querente [*For the Plaintiff*] [*Latin*] (ILCA)
PROR.......... Predicted Orbit
PROR........... Proposal Online Reparation (SAUS)
PRORA........ Program for Research on Romance Authors (SAUS)
PRORA........ Programs for Research on Romance Authors
PRORAT....... Projected Rating
PRO RAT AET... Pro Ratione Aetatis [*According to Age*] [*Pharmacy*]
PRO RECT ... Pro Recto [*Rectal*] [*Pharmacy*]
pro rect....... pro recto [*By rectum*] [*Latin*] [*Pharmacy*] (DAVI)
PROREP....... Proceed Ship, Command Station Reporting Duty or Purpose Indicated [*Military*]
PRORM........ Pay and Records Office-Royal Marines (SAUS)
PROS.......... Preventive Maintenance, Repair, and Operational Services (ODBW)
PROS.......... Procurement Squadron
PROS.......... Professional Reactor Operator Society (EA)
PROS.......... Proscenium [*Theater term*] (DSUE)
PROS.......... Prosecution (ROG)
PROS.......... Prosody
PROS.......... Prospect Group [*NASDAQ symbol*] (TTSB)
PROS.......... [*The*] Prospect Group, Inc. [*New York, NY*] [*NASDAQ symbol*] (NQ)
pros .... Prostate [*Anatomy*] (DAVI)
PROS.......... Prosthetic (AABC)
PROS.......... Prostitute (DSUE)
PROS.......... Prostrate
PROSA......... Programming System with Symbolic Addresses [*Computer science*] (IAA)
PROSAM...... Programmed Single-Axis Mount [*Military camera*]
PROSAMO ... Planned Release of Selected and Modified Organisms [*British*]
Pros Atty...... Prosecuting Attorney (DLA)
pros atty...... Prosecuting Attorney (NTIO)
PROSC......... Proscenium [*Theater term*] (WDAA)
PRosC.......... Rosemont College, Rosemont, PA [*Library symbol*] [*Library of Congress*] (LCLS)
PROSD........ Performance Records for Optimizing System Design (IAA)
PROSE........ Partnership to Reduce Operation and Support Costs, Engine
PROSE........ Personal Record of School Experiences (EDAC)
PROSE........ Problem Solution Engineering [*Programming language*] [*Computer science*] (CSR)
PROSE........ Production Scheduler (SAUS)
PROSE........ Program System Example (SAA)
PROSEA...... Plant Resources of South-East Asia [*A publication*]
PROSECON... Prosecution (ROG)
PROSEL....... Process Control and Sequencing Language [*Computer science*] (IAA)
PROSEL....... Process-control and Sequencing Language (SAUS)
PROSEL....... Process Sequencing Language (SAUS)
ProsGp........ [*The*] Prospect Group, Inc. [*Associated Press*] (SAG)
PROSI......... Public Relations Office of the Sugar Industry
PROSIG........ Procedure Signal [*Navy*]
PROSIGN..... Procedure Sign [*Military*] (AABC)
PROSIM...... Production System Simulator [*Computer science*]
PROSIN....... Procedure Sign [*Military*] (IAA)

PROSINE...... Procedure Sign [*Military*]
Pros J Natl Dist Atty A... Prosecutor. Journal of the National District Attorneys Association (SAUS)
PROSMATEC... Progressive Shift Schedule Management Technology [*Automotive engineering*]
PROSO......... Protamine Sulfate [*Biochemistry*] (DAVI)
ProSoc........ Prometheus Society (EA)
Prosoft........ Prosoft I-Net Solutions, Inc. [*Associated Press*] (SAG)
Prosop Att ... Prosopographia Attica [*A publication*] (OCD)
PROSP......... Prospecting (SAUS)
prosp........... Prospectively (DLA)
PROSPEC.... PRO Specification (NITA)
PROSPECT... Proponent Sponsored Engineer Corps Training [*Army Corps of Engineers*]
PROSPECTRA... Program by development by Specification and Transformation (SAUS)
PROSPER .... Procedure for Personalizing an envelope program (SAUS)
PROSPER .... Profit Simulating (or Simulation) Planning and Evaluation of Risk (SAUS)
PROSPER .... Profit Simulation, Planning and Evaluation of Risk (MHDB)
PROSPIN ..... Project Profile Screening and Pre-appraisal Information System (SAUS)
ProSport ...... Professional Sports Care Management, Inc. [*Associated Press*] (SAG)
ProsSt......... Prospect Street High Income Portfolio, Inc. [*Associated Press*] (SAG)
PROST........ Pronuclear Oocyte and Sperm Transfer [*Embryology*]
PROST........ Pronuclear Stage Tubal Transfer (SAUS)
prost........... Prostate (CPH)
PROST........ Prostitute [*or Prostitution*] [*FBI standardized term*]
Prostaglandins Leukotrienes Med... Prostaglandins, Leukotrienes and Medicine (SAUS)
PROSTAT..... Prostatic (AAMN)
Prostate Suppl... Prostate. Supplement (SAUS)
PROSTH...... Prosthesis
PROSY........ People's Republic of South Yemen (BJA)
prot............ Protect (ELAL)
PROT .... Protect [*or Protection*] (MSA)
PROT .... Protected (SAUS)
PROT .... Protected Reservation [*Travel industry*] (TVEL)
PROT .... Protective Life Corp. (SAUS)
Prot............ Protectorate (WDAA)
PROT .... Protein
PROT .... Protest (ROG)
Prot............ Protestant (WDAA)
PROT .... Protestant
PROT .... Proteus [*Bacterium*]
PROT .... Protinus [*Speedily*] [*Pharmacy*]
Prot............ Protocol (DLA)
PROT .... Prototype
Prot... Protozoa (SAUS)
PROT .... Protractor (AAG)
PROTA........ Protection Actual [*Probability for avoidance of ship*]
ProTACA ...... Procurement Technical Assistance Cooperative Agreement Program [*DoD*]
PROTAG...... Protagonist (SAUS)
PROTAP...... Professional Opportunities through Academic Partnership [*National War College*]
PROTAP...... Protonotary Apostolic [*Roman Catholic*]
Prot CJ .... Protocol on the Statute of the European Communities Court of Justice [*A publication*] (DLA)
PROTCT ...... Protective (AAG)
PROT DEV ... Protective Device (SAUS)
ProtDg .... Protein Design Labs [*Associated Press*] (SAG)
PROTEC ...... Protection
ProTech ...... Prospective Technology Communication System (SAUS)
PROTECON... Process and Test Control [*Pendar Technical Association Ltd.*] [*Software package*] (NCC)
PROTECT ..... Probabilities Recall Optimizing the Employment of Calibration Time (KSC)
PROTECT ..... Protection
Protect......... Protection
ProtectO ...... Protection One, Inc. [*Associated Press*] (SAG)
PROTEL ...... Procedure Oriented Type Enforcing Language (SAUS)
PRO TEM ..... Pro Tempore [*For the Time Being*] [*Latin*]
Pro tem ...... Pro Tempore-for the time being (SAUS)
PRO TEM et LOC... Pro Tempore et Loco [*For the Time and Place*] [*Latin*] (ROG)
Proteon........ Proteon, Inc. [*Associated Press*] (SAG)
PRO/TEST..... Profitable approach to Testing (SAUS)
PROTEUS.... Profile Telemetry of Upper Ocean Currents [*Marine science*] (OSRA)
PROTEUS.... Project to Research Objects Theories, Extraterrrestrials, and Unusual Sightings (EA)
PROTEUS..... Propulsion Research and Openwater Testing of Experimental Underwater System (SAUS)
PROTEUS..... Propulsion Research and Open Water Testing of Experimental Underwater Systems (MCD)
PROTEUS..... Prototype Real-Time Operational Test, Evaluation and User Simulation (SAUS)
Proth........... Prothetics (SAUS)
PROTHROM... Prothrombin [*Hematology*]
Proth Time... Prothrombin Time (SAUS)
Pro Time ..... Prothrombin Time (SAUS)
PROTIMEREP... Proceed in Time Report Not Later Than [*Hour and/or date indicated*] [*Military*]
ProtLf......... Protective Life Corp. [*Associated Press*] (SAG)
PROTN........ Procedure Turn (SAUS)

PROTO	Protoporphyrin [*Hematology*]
Proto	ProtoSource Corp. [*Associated Press*] (SAG)
PROTO	Prototype (KSC)
Protoch	Protochorda (SAUS)
PROTO-E Language	Programming Tool Extensible Language (SAUS)
ProtoS	ProtoSource Corp. [*Associated Press*] (SAG)
protozool	protozoologist (SAUS)
protozool	protozoology (SAUS)
ProtP	Protein Polymer Technologies, Inc. [*Associated Press*] (SAG)
Prot P I	Protocol on Privileges and Immunities (SAUS)
Prot PI	Protocol on Privileges and Immunities of the European Economic Community [*A publication*] (DLA)
ProtPoly	Protein Polymer Technologies, Inc. [*Associated Press*] (SAG)
PROTR	Protractor (MSA)
Protr	Protrepticus [*of Clemens Alexandrinus*] [*Classical studies*] (OCD)
ProtSy	Protocol Systems, Inc. [*Associated Press*] (SAG)
PROT TP	Prototyp (SAUS)
PROTYP	Processor Type code (SAUS)
Proud Dom Pub	Proudhon's Domaine Public [*A publication*] (DLA)
Proudf Land Dec	United States Land Decisions (Proudfit) [*A publication*] (DLA)
PROUS	Proceed to a Pon in Continental United States (SAUS)
PROUS	Proceed to a Port in Continental United States [*Military*]
PRO US EXT	Pro Usu Externo [*For External Use*] [*Pharmacy*]
Prouty	Prouty's Reports [*61-68 Vermont*] [*A publication*] (DLA)
Prov	De Providentia [*of Seneca the Younger*] [*Classical studies*] (OCD)
PROV	Provedor (SAUS)
prov	Provenance (VRA)
prov	Provencal (BEE)
PROV	Provencal [*Language, etc.*]
PROV	Provence [*France*] (ROG)
PROV	Proverb
Prov	Proverbs [*Old Testament book*]
PROV	Provide (KSC)
Prov	Providence (SAUS)
PROV	Provident Financial Holdings, Inc. [*NASDAQ symbol*] (SAG)
prov	Province (ELAL)
PROV	Province
Prov	Provincial (AL)
PROV	Provincial
PROV	Provinciale [*Provincial*] [*Netherlands*] (EY)
PROV	Proving Ground [*Navy*]
PROV	Provision [*or Provisional*] (AFM)
Prov	Provisional (TBD)
Prov	Provisional Light [*Navigation signal*]
PROV	Provisioning
PROV	Provost
ProvBcp	Provident Bancorp, Inc. [*Associated Press*] (SAG)
Prov Can Stat	Statutes of the Province of Canada [*A publication*] (DLA)
ProvCo	Provident Companies, Inc. [*Associated Press*] (SAG)
Prov Cons	De Provinciis Consularibus [*of Cicero*] [*Classical studies*] (OCD)
PROVCORPV	Provisional Corps, Vietnam
PROVD	Provided
Prov Eng	Provincial English (SAUS)
PROVER	Procurement for Minimum Total Cost through Value Engineering and Reliability
PROVER	Procurement, Value, Economy, Reliability
ProvFinl	Provident Financial Holdings, Inc. [*Associated Press*] (SAG)
ProvGM	Provincial Grand Master [*Freemasonry*]
PROVGR	Proving Grounds
PROVIB	Propulsion System Decision and Vibration Analysis (DNAB)
Provid	De Providentia [*of Philo*] (BJA)
Providence C	Providence College (GAGS)
Providn	Providian Corp. [*Formerly, Capital Holding*] [*Associated Press*] (SAG)
PROVIMI	Proteins, Vitamins, and Minerals [*Pharmacology*] (DAVI)
PROVIS	Provision
provl	provisional (SAUS)
PROVMAAG	Provisional Military Assistance Advisory Group (CINC)
PROVMAAG-K	Provisional Military Assistance Advisory Group, Korea (CINC)
PROVMAIN	Other Provisions Basic Orders Remain in Effect
PROVMAINTCO	Provisional Maintenance Company [*Navy*] (DNAB)
PROVMUSTCO	Provisional Medical Unit Self-Contained Company [*Navy*] (DNAB)
PROVN	Provision (SAUS)
PROVNC	Province
provns	Provisions (DLA)
PROVNS	Provision Store (SAUS)
PROVO	Proviso [*Contract clause*] (ROG)
PROVO	Provocateur (DSUE)
PROVONS	Provisions
Provor	Provisor (SAUS)
PROVORG	Providing Organization (DOMA)
PROVSN	Provision
Prov St	Statutes, Laws, of the Province of Massachusetts [*A publication*] (DLA)
PROVSUPDEP	Provision Supply Depot (SAUS)
PROWDELREP	Proceed Without Delay Report Duty or Purpose Indicated [*Military*]
PROWL	Procedure Work Log System (IAA)
PROWLER	Programmable Robot Observer with Logical Enemy Response [*Developed by Robot Defense Systems of Thornton, CO*]
PROWL System	Procedure Work Log System (SAUS)
PROWORD	Procedure Word
PROWS	Projected Warhead System (SAUS)
PROX	Preferential Oxidation [*Vehicle power systems*]
PRO-X	Prothrombin Time [*Hematology*] (CPH)
prox	Proximal (CPH)

PROX	Proxim, Inc. [*NASDAQ symbol*] (SAG)
PROX	Proximity (AABC)
Prox	Proximo (EBF)
PROX	Proximo [*In Next Month*] [*Latin*]
prox	Proximo [*In Next Month*] [*Latin*] (ODBW)
PROX ACC	Proxime Accessit [*Next in Order of Merit*] [*Latin*]
PRO-XAN	Protein-Xanthophyll [*Alfalfa protein concentrate process*]
PRO-XAN	Protein-Xantophyll (SAUS)
PROXI	Projection by Reflection Optics of Xerographic Images (IEEE)
Proxim	Proxim, Inc. [*Associated Press*] (SAG)
Proxima	Proxima Corp. [*Associated Press*] (SAG)
prox luc	Proxima Luce [*Day Before*] [*Latin*] (MAE)
Proxymd	ProxyMed, Inc. [*Associated Press*] (SAG)
PRP	Panretinal Photocoagulation [*Ophthalmology*]
PRP	Paper, Rubber and Plastics (SAUS)
PRP	Parent Rule Point (MCD)
PRP	Partial Read Pulse (SAUS)
PRP	Parti de la Revolution Populaire [*People's Revolutionary Party*] [*Zaire*] [*Political party*] (PD)
PRP	Partido de Renovacion Puertorriqueno [*Puerto Rican Renewal Party*] [*Political party*] (EY)
PRP	Partido de Representacao Popular [*Brazil*] [*Political party*]
PRP	Partido Renovacion Patriotica [*Honduras*] [*Political party*] (EY)
PRP	Partido Republicano Portugues [*Portuguese Republican Party*] [*Political party*] (PPE)
PRP	Partido Revolucionario Popular [*Popular Revolutionary Party*] [*Portugal*] [*Political party*] (PPE)
PRP	Parti Republicain du Progres [*Republican Progress Party*] [*Central Africa*] [*Political party*] (PD)
PRP	Parti Republicain Progressif [*Algeria*] [*Political party*] (EY)
PRP	Peace Resource Project (EA)
PRP	Peak Radiated Power (CET)
PRP	Peer Review Panel (ABAC)
PRP	Penicillinase-Resistant Penicillin [*Medicine*] (MELL)
PRP	People's Redemption Party [*Nigeria*] [*Political party*] (PPW)
PRP	People's Reform Party [*Philippines*] [*Political party*] (EY)
PRP	People's Revolutionary Party [*North Vietnam*] [*Political party*]
PRP	People's Revolutionary Party [*Benin*] [*Political party*]
PRP	Peptide Recognition Protein [*Biochemistry*]
PRP	Perfect Reading Prosthesis (SAUS)
PRP	Performance Recovery Program (SAUS)
PRP	Performance-Related Pay (ECON)
PRP	Performance, Requirements, Practices [*Military*]
PRP	Personnel Reliability Program [*Air Force*]
PRP	Petrol Refilling Point (SAUS)
PRP	Phantom Range Pod (MCD)
PRP	Phase Review Package (MCD)
PRP	Physical Readiness Program [*Navy*] (DNAB)
PRP	Physiologic Rest Position [*Medicine*] (DMAA)
PRP	Pick-up Release Point (SAUS)
PRP	Pickup-Zone Release Point
PRP	Pipelined Resampling Processor (ACAE)
PRP	Pityriasis Rubra Pilaris [*Dermatology*] (MAE)
PRP	Placement Route and Patch [*Computer science*] (IAA)
PRP	Placement-Route-and-Patch (SAUS)
PRP	Platelet-Rich Plasma [*Hematology*]
PRP	Pneumatically-Released Pilot (DNAB)
PRP	Polymer of Ribose Phosphate [*Organic chemistry*] (MAE)
PRP	Polyribitol Phosphate [*Organic chemistry*]
PRP	Polyribophosphate (SAUS)
PRP	Position Report Printout
PRP	Postbuckled Rectangular Plate
PRP	Potentially Responsible Party [*Environmental Protection Agency*]
PRP	Power-Deployed Reserve Parachute (MCD)
PRP	Precision Registration Processor (SAUS)
PRP	Premature-Removal Period (MCD)
PRP	Prepare (FAAC)
PRP	Prerigor Pressurization [*Meat processing*]
PR P	Present Participle (WGA)
PRP	Presidential Reorganizational Project
PRP	President's Reorganization Project [*Carter Administration*] [*Executive Office of the President*] (GFGA)
PRP	Pressure Rate Product [*In treadmill test*]
PRP	Preventral Protractor (SAUS)
PRP	Previous Record Pointer (SAUS)
PRP	Primary Raynaud's Phenomenon [*Medicine*]
PRP	Principality (SAUS)
PRP	Principal Responsible Party
PRP	Print Out [*Computer science*] (IAA)
PrP	Prion Protein [*Biochemistry*]
PRP	Problem Resolution Program [*IRS*]
PRP	Procedure-Related Pain (MELL)
PRP	Procurement Requirements Package (MCD)
PRP	Production Readiness Plan
PRP	Production Requirements Plan
PRP	Production Reserve Policy
PRP	Product Requirements Plan
PRP	Profit-Related Pay [*Economics*]
PRP	Programmed Random Process (SAUS)
PRP	Program Random Process (PDAA)
PRP	Program Requirements Package [*Computer science*]
PRP	Program Review Panel [*Army*] (AABC)
PRP	Progressive Rework Plan
PRP	Progressive Rubella Panencephalitis [*Medicine*]
PRP	Proliferative Retinopathy Photocoagulation

PRP	Proliferin Related Protein [Biochemistry]
PRP	Proline-Rich Protein [Biochemistry]
PRP	Proper Return Port [Shipping]
PRP	Prospective Reimbursement Plan [Medicaid]
PRP	Protease-Resistant Prion [Medicine]
PrP	Protease-Resistant Protein [Microbiology]
PrP	Protein Phosphatase [An enzyme]
PRP	Pseudorandom Pulse
PRP	Psychotic Reaction Profile [Psychology]
PRP	Public Relations Personnel [Navy]
PRP	Pulse Recurrence [or Repetition] Period (CET)
PRP	Pulse Repetition Frequency [Medicine] (DAVI)
PRP	Pulse Repetition Period [Computer science] (IAA)
PRP	Purchase Request Package [Shipping] (MCD)
PRP	Purple (MSA)
PRP	Purpose (MSA)
PRP	Reformed Presbyterian Theological Seminary, Pittsburgh, PA [OCLC symbol] (OCLC)
PRPA	Professional Race Pilots Association [Later, USARA] (EA)
PRPA	Projectile Raye a Propulsion Additionelle (SAUS)
PRPA	Puerto Rico Ports Authority (SAUS)
PRPB	Parti de la Revolution Populaire du Benin [Benin People's Revolutionary Party] [Political party] (PD)
PRPB	Peoples Revolution Party of Benin (SAUS)
PRPC	Parti Republicain du Peuple Camerounais [Political party] (EY)
PRPC	Public Relations Policy Committee [NATO] (NATG)
PrPCU-L	Catholic University of Puerto Rico, Law Library, Ponce, Puerto Rico [Library symbol] [Library of Congress] (LCLS)
PRP-D	Polyribosylribitol Phosphate-Diptheria Toxoid [Medicine]
PRPD	Public Radio Program Directors
PRPDA	Public Radio Program Directors Association (NTPA)
PrpdLg	Pre-Paid Legal Services, Inc. [Associated Press] (SAG)
PRPE	Prairie Pacific Energy Corp. (SAUS)
PRPF	Parameter Profile (SAUS)
PRPF	Planar Radial Peaking Factor [Network analysis] (IEEE)
PRPG	Political Resident Persian Gulf (SAUS)
PRPG	Proportioning
PRPGA	Puerto Rico Personne and Guidance Association (SAUS)
PRPH	Peripherin (DMAA)
Pr/Ph	Pristane/Phytane Ratio [Environmental science]
PRPHL	Peripheral
PRPIT	Process Management for Process Identifier Table (SAUS)
PRPL	PACOM [Pacific Command] Reconnaissance Priority List (CINC)
PRPL	People's Democratic Republic of Laos
PRPL	Procurement Repair Parts List (AAG)
prpl	Purple
PRPLN	Propulsion (MSA)
PRPLNT	Propellant (KSC)
PRPLT	Propellant (MSA)
PRPNE	Propane [Organic chemistry]
PRPOOS	Plankton Rate Processes in Oligotrophic Oceans [Cooperative research project]
Pr Pos Ctl Ex...	Print Position Control Exit (SAUS)
Pr Pos Ctr E&E...	Print Position Counter Entry and Exit (SAUS)
Pr Pos Ctr Ent&Ex...	Print Position Counter Entry and Exit (SAUS)
Pr Pos Ent ...	Print Position Entry (SAUS)
Pr Pos Ex....	Print Position Exit (SAUS)
PRPP	Phosphoribosyl Pyrophosphate (SAUS)
PRPP	Phosphoribosylpyrophosphate [Biochemistry]
PRPP	Phosphorylribose Pyrophosphate [Biochemistry]
PRPP	Pseudoresidual Plot Program
PRPQ	Programming Request for Price Quotation [Computer science]
PRPQ	Program Request for Price Quotation (SAUS)
PR PR...........	Praeter Propter [About, Nearly] [Latin] (ROG)
PRPR	Puerto Rico Pool-type Reactor (SAUS)
PRPRR	Preparer
PRPS	Pressure Rise per Stage (MCD)
PRPS	Programming Requirements Process Specification (SAUS)
PRPS	Programming Requirements Process Specifications
PRPS	Program Requirement Process Specification [NASA] (KSC)
PRPS	Prostatic Secretory Protein (DMAA)
PRPSA	Personal Report of Public Speaking Apprehension (EDAC)
PRPSD	Proposed (MSA)
PRPSL	Proposal (MSA)
PRPT	Parti Revolutionnaire du Peuple Tunisien [Revolutionary Party of the Tunisian People] [Political party] (PD)
PRP-T	Polyribosylribitol Phosphate Conjugated to Tetanus Toxoid [Medicine]
PRPT	Prescriptive Reading Performance Test [Educational test]
prpt.............	proportional (SAUS)
PRPUC.........	Philippine Republic Presidential Unit Citation [Military decoration]
PRPUCE.......	Philippine Republic Presidential Unit Citation Emblem [Military decoration]
prpylm.........	Propylaeum (VRA)
PRQ	Houston, TX [Location identifier] [FAA] (FAAL)
PRQ	Partition Request Queue (SAUS)
PRQ	Personal Resources Questionnaire (DMAA)
PRQ	Presidente Roque Saenz Pena [Argentina] [Airport symbol] (AD)
PRQA	Passenger Ride Quality Apparatus [Public transportation]
PRR	Partner Airlines [Former USSR] [FAA designator] (FAAC)
PRR	Parts Replacement Request (KSC)
PRR	Passenger Reservation Request (NVT)
PRR	Passive Ranging RADAR
PRR	Pawling Research Reactor
PRR	Pennsylvania Railroad Co. [AAR code] [Obsolete]
PRR	Performance-Related Remuneration (ADA)

PRR	Perrine, FL [Location identifier] [FAA] (FAAL)
PRR	Perris [California] [Seismograph station code, US Geological Survey] [Closed] (SEIS)
PRR	Personnel Requirements Report [Army]
PRR	Philippine Research Reactor (SAA)
PRR	Placement Revision Request
PRR	Planning & Requirements Review (SAUS)
PRR	Planning Release Record (AAG)
PRR	Plans and Requirements Review
PRR	Political Risk Review [A publication] (EAAP)
PRR	Post-Recall Release (WDAA)
Pr R	Practice Reports [Quebec] [A publication] (DLA)
Pr R	Practice Reports [Ontario] [A publication] (DLA)
PRR	Practise Rocket (SAUS)
PRR	Prairie [Commonly used] (OPSA)
PRR	Prelaunch Readiness Review (ACAE)
PRR	Preliminary Requirements Review [NASA] (KSC)
PRR	Premature Removal Rate
PRR	Pre-Readiness Review (SAUS)
PRR	Presbyterian and Reformed Renewal Ministries International [Formerly, PCC] (EA)
PRR	Pressure Rise Rate [Nuclear energy] (NRCH)
PRR	Primary Production Required [Resource management]
PRR	Prioritized Round-Robin (SAUS)
PRR	Prism Resources Ltd. [Vancouver Stock Exchange symbol]
PRR	Problem Reporting and Resolution
PRR	Producer's Reliability Risk
PRR	Production Readiness Review
PRR	Production Release Request (SAUS)
PRR	Production Research Reports
PRR	Professional Rights and Responsibilities
PRR	Program Request Register (SAUS)
PRR	Program Requirements Review [NASA] (NASA)
PRR	Program Revision Report (KSC)
PRR	Project Requirements Review (SAUS)
PRR	Proline-Rich Protein [Biochemistry]
PRR	Pro Racing Regulation [Automobile racing]
PRR	Proton Relaxation Rate
PRR	Pseudoresident Reader (MHDB)
PRR	Publication Revision Request (AAG)
PRR	Puerto Rico Reactor (NRCH)
PRR	Puerto Rico Supreme Court Reports [A publication] (DLA)
PRR	Pulse Radar Repair (SAUS)
PRR	Pulse Recurrence [or Repetition] Rate (MUGU)
PrRA	Academia Maria Reina, Rio Piedras, PR [Library symbol] [Library of Congress] (LCLS)
PRRA	Puerto Rico Reconstruction Administration [Terminated, 1955]
PrRadA	Premiere Radio Networks, Inc. [Associated Press] (SAG)
PRR & Regs...	Commonwealth of Puerto Rico Rules and Regulations [A publication] (DLA)
PRR&Regs...	Commonwealth of Puerto Rico Rules and Regulations (journ.) (SAUS)
PRRB	Provider Reimbursement Review Board [Medicare]
PRRC	New Mexico Petroleum Recovery Research Center [New Mexico Institute of Mining and Technology] [Research center] (RCD)
PRRC	Pitch/Roll Rate Changer Assembly (MCD)
PRRC	Precision Response Corp. [NASDAQ symbol] (SAG)
PRRD	Proprietary Rights to Registration Data
PrRe	Evangelical Seminary, Rio Piedras, PR [Library symbol] [Library of Congress] (LCLS)
PRRE	Pupils Round, Regular, and Equal [Medicine] (MAE)
Pr Reg BC ...	Practical Register in the Bail Court [A publication] (DLA)
Pr Reg Ch...	Practical Register in Chancery [1 vol.] [A publication] (DLA)
Pr Reg CP ...	Practical Register in the Common Pleas [1705-42] [A publication] (DLA)
Pr Rep	Practice Reports [Ontario] [A publication] (DLA)
Pr Rep	Practice Reports [England] [A publication] (DLA)
Pr Rep BC ...	Lowndes, Maxwell, and Pollock's English Bail Court Practice Reports [1850-51] [A publication] (DLA)
PRRFC.........	Planar Randomly Reinforced Fiber Composite
PRRI	Puerto Rico Rum Institute [Later, PRRPA]
PRRM	Presbyterian and Reformed Renewal Ministries International (EA)
PRRM	Program Review and Resources Management [NASA]
PRRM	Pulse Repetition Rate Modulation [Data transmission] [Computer science] (TEL)
PRRMI.........	Presbyterian and Reformed Renewal Ministries International (EA)
PRRPA.........	Puerto Rico Rum Producers Association [Defunct] (EA)
PRRR	Pioneer Railcorp [NASDAQ symbol] (SAG)
PRRS	Porcine Reproductive and Respiratory Syndrome (SAUS)
PRRS	Positioning Reporting Recording System (RDA)
PRRS	Problem Reporting and Resolution System [Military] (CAAL)
PR-RSV.......	Rous Sarcoma Virus, Prague Strain
PRRWO.......	Puerto Rican Revolutionary Workers Organization (NADA)
PRS	Pacific Railroad Society (EA)
PRS	Pacific Rocket Society (EA)
PRS	Packaged Reefer Space unit (SAUS)
PRS	Padre Resources [Vancouver Stock Exchange symbol]
PRS	Paint Research Station [British] (BI)
PRS	Pairs
PRS	Pakistan Railway Standard (SAUS)
PRS	Parachute Rocket System (SAUS)
PRS	Paraiso [California] [Seismograph station code, US Geological Survey] (SEIS)
PRS	Parametric Ruled Surface (MCD)
PRS	Parasi [Solomon Islands] [Airport symbol] (OAG)

PRS	Park and Ride Scheme	(SAUS)
PRS	Parliamentary Research Services	[British]
PRS	Pars Systems (CRS) [ICAO designator]	(FAAC)
PRS	Partei fuer Renten-, Steuer-, und Soziale Gerechtigkeit [Party for Equitable Pensions, Taxation, and Social Services] [Germany] [Political party]	(PPW)
PR's	Partial Responders [to medication]	
PRS	Partial Response Signalling	(NITA)
PRS	Partial Response System	(SAUS)
PRS	Parti de la Revolution Socialiste [Party of Socialist Revolution] [Senegal] [Political party]	
PRS	Parti de la Revolution Socialiste [Party of Socialist Revolution] [Benin] [Political party]	
PRS	Partido de la Revolucion Socialista [Party of the Socialist Revolution] [Cuba] [Political party]	
PRS	Partido para a Renovacao Social [Party for Social Renovation] [Guinea-Bissau] [Political party]	(EY)
PRS	Partido Revolucionario Socialista [Mexico] [Political party]	(EY)
PRS	Partito Republicano Sammarinese [Republican Party] [San Marino] [Political party]	(EY)
PRS	Passive RADAR Surveillance [Military]	(CAAL)
PRS	Passive Ranging Sonar	(SAUS)
PRS	Pattern Recognition Society	(EA)
PRS	Pattern Recognition System	
PRS	Payload Retention Subsystem [NASA]	(NASA)
PRS	Peer Review Systems, Inc.	
PRS	Pennsylvania Radiological Society	(SAUS)
PRS	Pennsylvania-Reading Seashore Lines [Absorbed into Consolidated Rail Corp.]	
PRS	Perceptual Respresentation System [Memory]	
PRS	Performance Rating System	(OICC)
PRS	Performing Right Society	[British]
PRS	Performing Rights Society	(SAUS)
PRS	Periphal Reset	(SAUS)
PRS	Personality Rating Scale [Psychology]	
PRS	Personal Radio Services	(SAUS)
PRS	Personal Recording System	
PRS	Personal Relations Survey [Managerial skills test]	
PRS	Personal Response System	(SAUS)
PRS	Personnel Readiness System [Air Force]	
PRS	Personnel Rescue Service [NASA]	(NASA)
PRS	Personnel Rescue System [NASA]	(MCD)
PRS	Personnel Research Section [Army]	
PRS	Personnel Research Staff [Department of Agriculture]	
PRS	Pesticides Registration Section	(HEAS)
PRS	Philatelic Research Society	
PRS	Philosophical Research Society	(EA)
PRS	Photographic Reconnaissance System	
PRS	Photo Resist Spinner	
PRS	Physically Restricted Status [Military]	
PRS	Pierre Robin Syndrome	(MELL)
PRS	Pipe Roll Society	(EA)
PRS	Placement Research Service	
PRS	Planar Rider System	
PRS	Planners Referral Service [Information service or system]	(IID)
PRS	Planning Record Sheet	
PR's	Planning References	(AAG)
PRS	Planning Reference System	(SAUS)
PRS	Planning Research & Systems Ltd. [British]	
PRS	Planning Research & Systems PLC	(SAUS)
PRS	Plasma Renin Substrate [Hematology]	
PRS	Pneumatic Reading System	
PRS	Pointing Reference System	(KSC)
PRS	Polynomial Remainder Sequence	(SAUS)
PRS	Polynominal Remainder Sequence	(SAUS)
PRS	Population Research Service [Information service or system]	(IID)
PRS	Portable Radar Simulator	(ACAE)
PRS	Positive Rolandic Spikes [Neurology]	(DAVI)
PRS	Potential Routes	(SAUS)
PRS	Power Reactant Subsystem [NASA]	(NASA)
PRS	Power Reactant System	
PRS	Power Relay Satellite	
PRS	Prayers	(ROG)
PRS	Precipitate Reduction Sinter [Metal]	(DICI)
PRS	Precision Ranging System	
PRS	Precision Rotary Stripper	
PRS	Precision Roughness Standard	(SAUS)
PRS	Present	(WGA)
PRS	Presidential Airways	(SAUS)
PRS	President of the Royal Society	[British]
PRS	Presidio Oil Co. [AMEX symbol]	(SPSG)
PRS	Presidio, TX [Location identifier] [FAA]	(FAAL)
PRS	Press	(MSA)
PRS	Pressure	(SAUS)
PRS	Pressure Reducing Station	
PRS	Pressure Response Spectrum [Nuclear energy]	(NRCH)
PR/S	Prestrike	(SAA)
PRS	Price Reporting System	(NUMA)
PRS	Primary Recovery Ship [NASA]	
PRS	Primary Recovery Site [NASA]	(KSC)
PRS	Primary Representational System	(EDAC)
PRS	Primary Rescue Site [NASA]	(NASA)
PRS	Printed Record Storage	(SAUS)
PRS	Print Management Service	(SAUS)
PRS	Priority Reservation System	(SAUS)
PRs	Problem Reports	(SAUS)
PRS	Procedure Review Section [Social Security Administration]	
PRS	Process Radiation Sampler [Nuclear energy]	(NRCH)
PRS	Procurement Tracking System	(SAUS)
PRS	Production Recording System	
PRS	Production Release System	(MCD)
PRS	Production Reporting System	(SAUS)
PRS	Product Requirement Schedule	(MCD)
PRS	Product Requirement Specification	(SAUS)
PRS	Programmed RADAR Simulator	(IAA)
PRS	Program Rating Summary Report [Television ratings]	(NTCM)
PRS	Program Request System	(SAUS)
PRS	Program Requirements Summary	(MUGU)
PRS	Prolonged Respiratory Support	(MELL)
PRS	Property Recovery Section	
PRS	Property Recovery Squad	(SAUS)
PRS	Propodial Sinus [Zoology]	
PRS	Proportional Representation Society	
PRS	Prospective Reimbursement System [Health insurance]	(GHCT)
PRS	Prospectors Air [Vancouver Stock Exchange symbol]	
PRS	Protective Research Section	(SAUS)
PRS	Protestant Reformation Society	(EA)
PRS	Provide Repair Service [Navy]	(NVT)
PRS	Provisioning Requirements Statement	
PRS	Pseudorandom Sequence	
PRS	Pseudo-Random Signal	(SAUS)
PRS	Psycholinguistic Rating Scale	
PRS	Public Radio Stations	(SAUS)
PRS	Public Rehabilitation Scheme	(SAUS)
PRS	Public Relations Section [Library Administration and Management Association]	
PRS	Puerto Lempira [Honduras] [Airport symbol]	(AD)
PRS	Pupil Rating Scale	(SAUS)
PRS	Pure Random Search [Optimization method]	
PRS	Pure Resources [NYSE symbol]	
PRSA	Pan-Rhodian Society of America	(EA)
PRSA	Permigewasset River Study Act of 1989	(COE)
PRSA	Polarizer-Retarder-Sample-Analyzer	(SAUS)
PRSA	Power Reactant Storage Assembly [NASA]	(MCD)
PRSA	President of the Royal Scottish Academy	
PRSA	Proportional Representation Society of Australia	
PRSA	Public Relation Society of America	(SAUS)
PRSA	Public Relations Society of America	(EA)
PRSA	Puerto Rico Statehood Commission	(EA)
PrSaC	Colegio Universitario del Sagrado Corazon [College of the Sacred Heart], Santurce, PR [Library symbol] [Library of Congress]	(LCLS)
Prsbytn	Presbytarian	(BEE)
PRSC	Parametric Response Surface Control	(AAEL)
PRSC	Plutonium Rework Sample Cell [Nuclear energy]	(NRCH)
PRSC	Puerto Rico Solidarity Committee	(EA)
Pr Scale	Prejudice Scale [Psychology]	(DHP)
PR Scale	Process-Reactive Scale	(SAUS)
PRSCHL	Preschool	
PRSCR	Puerto Rico Supreme Court Reports [A publication]	(DLA)
PRSD	Portable Rectilinear Scanning Device	
PRSD	Power Reactant Storage [or Supply] and Distribution [NASA]	(NASA)
PRSD	Power Reactant Supply and Distribution	
PRSD	Pressed	(AAG)
PRSDMET	Pressed Metal	(SAUS)
PRSDS	Power Reactant Storage and Distribution System	(MCD)
PrSE	El Mundo Publishing Co., San Juan, PR [Library symbol] [Library of Congress]	(LCLS)
PRSE	Precise Software Solutions [NASDAQ symbol]	
PRSE	President of the Royal Society of Edinburgh	
PRSEC	Payroll Section	
PRSF	Portal Software [NASDAQ symbol]	(SG)
Prsfdr	Pressfeeder [Printing]	
PRSG	Personal Radio Steering Group [Ann Arbor, MI] [Telecommunications service]	(TSSD)
PRSG	Pressing	
PRSG	Pseudo Random Signal Generator	(SAUS)
PRSG	Pulse-Rebalanced Strapdown Gyro	(MCD)
PRSH	President of the Royal Society for the Promotion of Health [British]	
PRSI	Pay Related Social Insurance	(SAUS)
PRSIG	Pacific Rim SMDS Interest Group	(SAUS)
PRSIS	Prospective Rate Setting Information System [Medicine]	(DMAA)
PRS Journal	Philosophical Research Society Journal	(SAUS)
PRSL	Pennsylvania-Reading Seashore Lines [Absorbed into Consolidated Rail Corp.] [AAR code]	
PRSL	Progressive Savings & Loan Association	(SAUS)
PRSM	Parachute Rocket System Modified	(SAUS)
PRSM	Prism Group [NASDAQ symbol]	(SAG)
PR/SM	Processor Resource/Systems Manager [Computer science]	(CDE)
prsmc	Prismacolor	(VRA)
PRSMC	Prism Group [NASDAQ symbol]	(TTSB)
PRSMN	Pressman	(AABC)
Pr Smp	Print Sample	(SAUS)
PRSN	Phased-Array Responsive Spot Noise	(SEWL)
PRSN	Provisional Relative Sunspot Number [NASA]	
PRSNG	Pressing	
PRSNL	Personal	
PRSNNL	Personnel	
PRSNT	Present [NWS]	(FAAC)
PRSP	Penicillin-Resistant S. Pneumoniae [Clinical chemistry]	

PRSP .... Poverty Reduction Strategy Paper
PRSP .... Prereading Screening Procedures (SAUS)
PRSP .... Puerto Rico Socialist Party (NADA)
PRSPL .... Planning and Role Setting for Public Libraries [*Public Library Association*] [*A publication*]
PRSPT .... Sindicato de Obreros Unidos del Sur de Puerto Rico
PRSPT .... Sindicato Puertorriqueno de Trabajadores
PRSR .... Presser (MSA)
PR/SR .... Price Redetermination/Service Reallocation (AAGC)
PRSRV .... Preservative (AAG)
PRSRZ .... Pressurize (MSA)
PRSS .... Passive Ranging Sub-System (SEWL)
PRSS .... Pennsylvania-Reading Seashore Lines [*Absorbed into Consolidated Rail Corp.*]
PRSS .... Polystatic Radar Satellite System (ACAE)
PRSS .... Problem Report Squawk Sheet [*NASA*] (NASA)
PRSSA .... Public Relations Student Society of America (EA)
PRSSA .... Puerto Rico Mainland US Statehood Students Association (EA)
PRSSD .... Pressed
PRST .... Persist (FAAC)
PrST .... Prairie Standard Time (SAUS)
PRST .... Presstek, Inc. [*NASDAQ symbol*] (NQ)
PRST .... Priest
PRST .... Probability Ration Sequential Test [*Quality management*]
PRST .... Probability Reliability Sequential Tests (MCD)
PRST .... Puerto Rican Standard Time (SAUS)
PRSTAT .... Pressure-Test Status [*Automotive emissions*]
Pr Stat .... Private Statutes [*Legal term*] (DLA)
PRSTC .... Prosthetic
PRSTCOM ..... Pressure Test Comments [*Automotive emissions*]
PRSTG .... Prestige
PRSU .... Police Requirements Support Unit [*Home Office*] [*British*]
Pr Sup .... Print Suppression (SAUS)
PRSV .... Papaya Ringspot Virus [*Plant pathology*]
PRSV .... Peach Red Suture Virus (SAUS)
PRSV .... Preserving
PRSVN .... Preservation (AABC)
PRSW .... President of the Royal Scottish Water Colour Society
PRSW .... Pure Software [*NASDAQ symbol*] (TTSB)
PRSW .... Pure Software, Inc. [*NASDAQ symbol*] (SAG)
PrSW .... World University, San Juan, PR [*Library symbol*] [*Library of Congress*] (LCLS)
PrSW-I .... World University, International Institute of the Americas, Barbosa Esq. Guayama, San Juan, PR [*Library symbol*] [*Library of Congress*] (LCLS)
PRT .... Air Cargo Carriers, Inc. [*ICAO designator*] (FAAC)
PRT .... Pacemaker-Re-entry Tachykardie (SAUS)
PRT .... Parachute Radio Transmitter [*Telecommunications*] (IAA)
PRT .... Pararescue Team (COE)
PRT .... Parliamentary Remuneration Tribunal [*New South Wales, Australia*]
PRT .... Parr Terminal Railroad [*AAR code*]
PRT .... Part (AAG)
PRT .... Participating Research Teams [*Department of Energy*]
PRT .... Partido Revolucionario de los Trabajadores [*Revolutionary Workers' Party*] [*Costa Rica*] [*Political party*] (EY)
PRT .... Partido Revolucionario de los Trabajadores [*Workers' Revolutionary Party*] [*Argentina*] [*Political party*] (PD)
PRT .... Partido Revolucionario de los Trabajadores [*Workers' Revolutionary Party*] [*Peru*] [*Political party*] (PPW)
PRT .... Partido Revolucionario de los Trabajadores [*Workers' Revolutionary Party*] [*Uruguay*] [*Political party*] (PD)
PRT .... Partido Revolucionario de Trabajadores [*Revolutionary Worker's Party*] [*Colorado*] [*Political party*] (EY)
PRT .... Passage Reading Test [*Education*] (EDAC)
PRT .... Patient Refused Test (SAUS)
PRT .... Patient Review Tribunal [*Queensland, Australia*]
PRT .... Patten Recognition Technology (NITA)
PRT .... Pattern Recognition Technique
PRT .... Patter Recognition Technique
PRT .... Payroll Tax (ADA)
PRT .... Penicillium Roqueforti Toxin (DB)
PRT .... Periodic Reevaluation Tests
PRT .... Permanent Recording Traffic [*Telecommunications*] (IAA)
PRT .... Personalized Rapid Transport (SAUS)
PRT .... Personal Rapid Transit [*Computer-guided transit system*]
PRT .... Personnel Research Test [*Military*]
PRT .... Petroleum Revenue Tax [*British*]
PRT .... Pharmaceutical Research and Testing [*Public Health Service*] (GRD)
PRT .... Philadelphia Rapid Transit (SAUS)
PRT .... Philadelphia Reading Test [*Education*]
PRT .... Phosphoribosyltransferase [*Also, PRTase*] [*An enzyme*]
PRT .... Photoradiation Therapy [*Oncology*]
PRT .... Physical Readiness Training [*Army*] (INF)
PRT .... Pictorial Reasoning Test [*Job screening test*]
PRT .... Planar Resistor Technology (AAEL)
PRT .... Platinum Resistance Thermometer
PRT .... Point Retreat, AK [*Location identifier*] [*FAA*] (FAAL)
PRT .... Polysilicon Resonant pressure Transducer (SAUS)
PRT .... Port
PRT .... Portable Radiation Thermometer
PRT .... Portable Radio Telephone
PRT .... Portable Remote Terminal
PRT .... Portable Router Template (MCD)
PRT .... Portable Router Tool
PRT .... Portland [*Diocesan abbreviation*] [*Maine*] (TOCD)

PRT .... Portugal [*ANSI three-letter standard code*] (CNC)
PRT .... Power Recovery Turbine
PRT .... Prato [*Italy*] [*Seismograph station code, US Geological Survey*] (SEIS)
PRT .... Precision Radiation Thermometer
PRT .... Preliminary Reference Trajectory [*NASA*] (KSC)
PRT .... Pressure Ratio Transducer (SAUS)
PRT .... Pressurized Relief Tank (NRCH)
PRT .... Primary Ranging Test (OA)
PRT .... Print
PRT .... Printed Receive Tape (SAUS)
prt .... Printer [*MARC relator code*] [*Library of Congress*] (LCCP)
PRT .... Printer [*Computer science*] (MDG)
PRT .... Prison Reform Trust (WDAA)
Prt. .... Private [*British military*] (DMA)
PRT .... Problem Resolution Tasking System [*Army*] (INF)
PRT .... Processing Response Time (SAUS)
PRT .... Procurement Review Team
PRT .... Procurement Round Table (EA)
PRT .... Production Reliability Test
PRT .... Production Run Tape
PRT .... Product Range Testing [*Business term*]
PRT .... Product Reliability Test (SAUS)
PRT .... Program Reference Table
PRT .... Program Review Team [*Navy*] (DNAB)
PRT .... Project Readiness Test (ACAE)
PRT .... Promotion, Transfer, and Redundancy [*Railway union agreement*] [*British*] (ECON)
PRT .... Prompt Air, Inc. [*FAA designator*] (FAAC)
PRT .... Prompt Relief Trip [*Nuclear energy*] (NRCH)
Prt. .... Protagoras [*of Plato*] [*Classical studies*] (OCD)
PRT .... Prova di Restituzione Termica [*Italy*] [*Medicine*]
PRT .... Provost
PRT .... Prudential Realty Trust (SAUS)
PRT .... Psychiatric Rehabilitation Team (EA)
PRT .... Publications Requirements Tables (AAG)
PRT .... Pulsed RADAR Transmitter
prt .... Pulse Frequency (IDOE)
PRT .... Pulse Recurrence [*or Repetition*] Time (CET)
PRT .... Pulse Repetition Time
PRTA .... Proximal Renal Tubular Acidosis [*Medicine*] (MELL)
PRTA .... Public Road Transport Association (SAUS)
PRTase .... Phosphoribosyltransferase [*Medicine*] (MEDA)
PRTAX .... Price T. Rowe: Tax-Free Income [*Mutual fund ticker symbol*] (SG)
PRTB .... Partido Revolucionario de Trabajadores Bolivianos [*Bolivian Workers' Revolutionary Party*] [*Political party*] (PD)
PRTB .... Pursue Real-Time BASIC (SAUS)
PRTB .... Soviet Mobile Rocket Technical Base
prTBR .... Draft Technical Basis for Regulations (SAUS)
PRTBR .... Partido Revolucionario de los Trabajadores de Bolivia Romero [*Bolivia*] [*Political party*] (PPW)
PRTC .... Partido Revolucionario de los Trabajadores Centroamericanos [*Revolutionary Party of Central American Workers*] [*El Salvador*] [*Political party*] (PD)
PRTC .... Pediatric Research and Training Center [*University of Connecticut*] [*Research center*] (RCD)
PRTC .... Ports Canada
PRTC .... Precision Technologies (SAUS)
PRTC .... Priority Real Time Command (ADWA)
PRTC .... Professional Rate Training Course (DNAB)
PRTC .... Puerto Rico Telephone Co. (SAUS)
PRTCAL .... Priority Testcall (SAUS)
PRTCALSS ... Priority Testcall to Special Services (SAUS)
PRTCD .... Puerto Rico Tax Court Decisions [*A publication*] (DLA)
PRTC-H .... Partido Revolucionario de los Trabajadores Centroamericanos - Seccion de Hondur as [*Revolutionary Party of Central American Workers - Honduras*] [*Political party*]
PRTCM .... Professional Register of Traditional Chinese Medicine (SAUS)
PRTCT .... Protection (SAUS)
PRTCTV ...... Protective
PRTD .... Portland Traction Co. [*AAR code*]
PRTD .... Printed (DGA)
prtd .... Printed (VRA)
PRTE .... Primary Route (SAUS)
PRTE .... Profit Technology, Inc. (SAUS)
PRTEID .... Primary Route Identity (SAUS)
PRTF .... Pheromone and Receptor Transcription Factor [*Genetics*]
PRTF .... Psychiatric Review Technique Form [*Social Security Administration*]
PRTG .... Printing (AFM)
PRTH .... Pituitary Resistance to Thyroid Hormone [*Medicine*] (DMAA)
PRTH .... Prothrombin Time [*Hematology*] (DAVI)
PRTH-C .... Prothrombin Time Control [*Hematology*] (DAVI)
PRTHS .... Pennsylvania Railroad Technical and Historical Society (EA)
PRTI .... Physical and Recreational Training Instructor [*British military*] (DMA)
PRTI .... Professional Realtime Interface (SAUS)
PRTK .... Presto-Tek Corp. (SAUS)
PRTKT .... Parts Kit
PRTL .... Portable (DNAB)
PRTL .... Primus Telecommunications Group, Inc. [*NASDAQ symbol*] (SAG)
PRTIMG ...... Print Image (SAUS)
PRTLS .... Powered Return to Launch Site [*NASA*] (MCD)
PRTLSP .... Printer Line Spacing (SAUS)
PRTLY .... Partially
PRTM .... Printing Response-Time Monitor
PrtMcled ...... Porter McLeod National Retail [*Associated Press*] (SAG)

PRTN	Partition
PRTN	Proteinase (DMAA)
PRTN	Proton Energy Sys. [*NASDAQ symbol*]
PRTNR	Partner
PRTNRSHP	Partnership
PRTO	Preservation Research and Testing Office [*Library of Congress*] (EA)
PRTOT	Prototype Real-Time Optical Tracker [*Computer science*]
PRTOV	Printer Overflow (SAUS)
PRTP	Prototype (IAA)
PRTQ	Peer Role-Taking Questionnaire [*Psychology*] (EDAC)
PRTR	Plutonium Recycle Test Reactor [*Nuclear energy*]
PRTR	Pollutant Release and Transfer Registers (SAUS)
PRTR	Porter
PRTR	Printer
PRTRC	Printer Controller (SAUS)
Prt Rep	Practice Reports [*A publication*] (DLA)
PRTRL	Printer, Lithographer [*Navy*]
PRTRM	Printer, Offset Process [*Navy*]
PRTRNS	Programmable Transformer Converter (MCD)
Prtronx	Printronix, Inc. [*Associated Press*] (SAG)
PRTS	Parallel Run-Time Support library (SAUS)
PRTS	Personal Rapid Transit System [*Computer-guided transit system*]
PRTS	Ports [*Postal Service standard*] (OPSA)
PRTS	Pretoria Theological Series [*A publication*] (BJA)
PRTS	Processor Resident Testing Software (SAUS)
PrtSc	Print Screen [*Computer keyboard*]
PRTSTNT	Protestant
PRT System	Personal Rapid Transport System (SAUS)
PRTV	Positive Response Television [*NASDAQ symbol*] (SAG)
Prtw	Propeller Twist [*Genetics*]
PRTY	Priority
PrtyCty	Party City Corp. [*Associated Press*] (SAG)
PRTYPOLS	Priority Pollutants (SAUS)
PRU	Packed Radio Unit (SAUS)
PRU	Packet Radio Unit
PRU	Paranagua [*Brazil*] [*Airport symbol*] (AD)
PRU	Pararescue Unit (COE)
PRU	Percent Reduction of Urea (SAUS)
PRU	Performance Reference Unit (SAUS)
PRU	Peripheral Resistance Unit [*Medicine*]
PRU	Personnel Readiness Unit (SAUS)
PRU	Photographic Reconnaissance Unit [*Aircraft*] [*Marine Corps*]
PRU	Photo Reconnaissance Unit (SAUS)
PRU	Physical Record Unit (NITA)
PRU	Physical Research Unit (IAA)
PRU	Pneumatic Regulation Unit (AAG)
PRU	Polarity Reversal Unit [*Electrochemistry*]
PRU	Polish-Russian Union (NADA)
PRU	Power Regulator Unit (SAUS)
PRU	Pressure Reduction Unit (SAUS)
PRU	Primary Replacement Unit
PRU	Printer Unit (SAUS)
PRU	Prisoner's Rights Union (EA)
PRU	Program Research Unit (SAUS)
PRU	Programs Research Unit (KSC)
PRU	Prome [*Myanmar*] [*Airport symbol*] (OAG)
PRU	Provincial Reconnaissance Unit [*Military*]
pru	prude (SAUS)
pru	prudent (SAUS)
PRU	Prudential Property & Casualty Insurance Co., Holmdel, NJ [*OCLC symbol*] (OCLC)
PRU	Pruhonice [*Czechoslovakia*] [*Seismograph station code, US Geological Survey*] (SEIS)
PrU	University of Puerto Rico, Rio Piedras, PR [*Library symbol*] [*Library of Congress*] (LCLS)
PRUAA	President of the Royal Ulster Academy of Arts
PRUC	Partido Revolucionario de Union Civico [*Revolutionary Party for Civic Union*] [*Costa Rica*] [*Political party*]
PRUC	Practice Reports [*1848-1900*] [*Upper Canada*] [*A publication*] (DLA)
PRUCIS	Philippine Rural Community Improvement Society (SAUS)
PRUCOL	Permanently Residing Under Color Of Law (SAUS)
PRUD	Partido Revolucionario de Unification Democratica [*Revolutionary Party of Democratic Unification*] [*El Salvador*]
PrudRe	Prudential Reinsurance Holdings, Inc. [*Associated Press*] (SAG)
PrU-H	University of Puerto Rico, Humacao Regional College, Humacao, PR [*Library symbol*] [*Library of Congress*] (LCLS)
PRUL	Programs Unlimited (SAUS)
PrU-L	University of Puerto Rico, Law Library, San Juan, PR [*Library symbol*] [*Library of Congress*] (LCLS)
PrU-M	University of Puerto Rico, School of Medicine, San Juan, PR [*Library symbol*] [*Library of Congress*] (LCLS)
PrU-MA	University of Puerto Rico, Mayaguez Campus, Mayaguez, Puerto Rico [*Library symbol*] [*Library of Congress*] (LCLS)
PrU-MS	University of Puerto Rico, Department of Marine Sciences, Mayaguez (SAUS)
PrU-MS	University of Puerto Rico, Department of Marine Sciences, Mayaguez, PR [*Library symbol*] [*Library of Congress*] (LCLS)
PRUNCATS	Program Relay Universal Card Analysis Test System (SAUS)
PRUNIT	Photo Roentgen Unit (IAA)
PrU-NS	University of Puerto Rico, Natural Science Iibrary, Rio Piedras, PR [*Library symbol*] [*Library of Congress*] (LCLS)
PRURDCO	Puerto Rico Undersea Research and Development Corp. (SAUS)
PRUS	Prussia [*Obsolete*]
Prus	Prussian [*Philately*]
PRUSAF	Puerto Rico, USA Foundation (EA)

PRV	Papaya Ringspot Virus
PRV	Parsley Rhabdovirus [*Plant pathology*]
PRV	Peach Rosette Virus (SAUS)
PRV	Peak Rated Voltage (IAA)
PRV	Peak Reserve Voltage (IAA)
PRV	Peak Reverse Voltage
PRV	Pearl River Valley Railroad Co. [*AAR code*]
PRV	Permanently Resident Volume (VLIE)
PRV	Peugeot Renault Volvo [*Automobile joint project partners*]
PRV	Polycythemia Rubra Vera [*Medicine*]
PRV	Porvoo [*Finland*] [*Seismograph station code, US Geological Survey*] [*Closed*] (SEIS)
PRV	Posterior wall of Right Ventricle (SAUS)
PRV	Pour Rendre Visite [*To Make a Call*] [*French*]
PRV	Pressure Reduce Valve (SAUS)
PRV	Pressure Reducing (or Reduction) Valve (SAUS)
PRV	Pressure Reducing [*or Regulation or Relief*] Valve
PRV	Pressure Reduction Valve
PRV	Pressure Regulation Valve
PRV	Pressure Regulator Valve (COE)
PRV	Pressure Relief Valve
PRV	Princess Ventures [*Vancouver Stock Exchange symbol*]
PRV	Prior Record Variable [*Criminal sentencing*]
prv	Private (VRA)
PRV	Programmed Rate-of-rise of Voltage (SAUS)
PRV	Propeller Revolution
Prv	Proverbs [*Old Testament book*]
PRV	Provincial
PRV	Provincial Express, Inc. [*Canada*] [*ICAO designator*] (FAAC)
PRV	Provisional Reconnaissance Unit
PRV	Pseudorabies Virus
PRV	Pseudo Register Vector (VLIE)
PRV	Pseudorelative Velocity
Prv	Pyruvenol [*Biochemistry*]
PRVA	Programmable Rotary Vane Attenuator (SAUS)
PrvAm	Provident American Corp. [*Associated Press*] (SAG)
PrvBksh	Provident Bankshares Corp. [*Associated Press*] (SAG)
PRVCAR	Private Rail Car Company [*Transportation company classification code*]
prv coll	Private Collection (VRA)
PRVD	Procurement [*or Purchase*] Request for Vendor Data (AAG)
PRVD	Provide (SAUS)
PRVD	Purchase Request for Vendor Data (SAUS)
PRVDNC	Providence
Prvena	Provena Foods, Inc. [*Associated Press*] (SAG)
PrvEng	Providence Energy Corp. [*Associated Press*] (SAG)
PRVEP	Pattern Reversal Visual Evoked Potential
PrvLf	Provident Life & Accident Insurance Co. of America [*Associated Press*] (SAG)
PrvLLC	Providian LLC, Inc. [*Associated Press*] (SAG)
PRVNTN	Prevention
PRVNTV	Preventive
PrVOBl	Preisverordnungsblatt (SAUS)
PRVS	Penetration Room Ventilation System [*Nuclear energy*] (IEEE)
PRVS	Previous (VLIE)
PRVT	Production Readiness Verification Testing (MCD)
PRVT	Production Reliability Verification Test
PRVT	Product Reliability Validation Test (MCD)
PRVW	Preview (MSA)
PrvWor	Providence & Worcester Railroad Co. [*Associated Press*] (SAG)
PrvWor	Providence Worcester Railroad Co. [*Associated Press*] (SAG)
PRW	Paired Wire [*Telecommunications*] (TEL)
PRW	Passive Radar Warning (SAUS)
PRW	Per cent Rated Wattage (SAUS)
PRW	Percent Rated Wattage
PRW	Polymerized Ragweed [*Immunology*]
PRW	Press Relations Wire [*Commercial firm*] (EA)
PRW	Promark Software [*Vancouver Stock Exchange symbol*]
PRW	Prosser [*Washington*] [*Seismograph station code, US Geological Survey*] (SEIS)
PRW	Quebecor Printing [*NYSE symbol*] (TTSB)
PRW	Quebecor Printing, Inc. [*NYSE symbol*] (SAG)
PRW	World University, San Juan, PR [*OCLC symbol*] (OCLC)
PRWAD	Professional Rehabilitation Workers with the Adult Deaf [*Later, ADARA*] (EA)
PRWD	Priority Regular World Day
PRWI	Prince William Forest Park [*National Park Service designation*]
PRWO	Puerto Rican Revolutionary Workers Organization
PRWP	Poor R-Wave Progression [*On electrocardiogram*] [*Cardiology*] (DAVI)
PRWRA	Puerto Rican Water Resources Authority
PRWRA	Puerto Rico Water Resources Authority (SAUS)
PRWS	Plasma and Radio Wave Spectrometer (ACAE)
PRWS	President of the Royal Society of Painters in Water Colours [*British*]
PRWV	Peak Reserve Working Voltage
PRX	Paris [*Texas*] [*Airport symbol*] (OAG)
PRX	Paris, TX [*Location identifier*] [*FAA*] (FAAL)
PRX	Pharmaceutical Resources [*NYSE symbol*] (SPSG)
PRX	Pressure Regulation Exhaust
PRX	Pressure Regulator Exhaust (SAUS)
PRX	Proximity (SAUS)
PRX	Pseudoexfoliation (DMAA)
PRXI	PRX [*Public Relations Exchange*] International (EA)
PRXL	Parexel International Corp. [*NASDAQ symbol*] (SAG)
PRXL	PAREXEL Intl [*NASDAQ symbol*] (TTSB)

PRXM	Proxima Corp. [*NASDAQ symbol*] (SAG)
PRXS	Praxis Biologics, Inc. (SAUS)
PRY	Paraguay [*ANSI three-letter standard code*] (CNC)
PRY	Parys [*South Africa*] [*Seismograph station code, US Geological Survey*] (SEIS)
PRY	Pittsburgh Railways Corp. (SAUS)
PRY	Pittway Corp. [*AMEX symbol*] (SPSG)
PRY	Primary (SAUS)
PRY.A	Pittway Corp.'A' [*AMEX symbol*] (TTSB)
P Ryl	Catalogue of the Greek Papyri in the John Rylands Library at Manchester [*A publication*] (OCD)
P Ryl	Catalogue of the Greek Papyri in the John Rylands Library at Manchester (journ.) (SAUS)
PRZ	Peoples Republic of Zanzibar (SAUS)
PRZ	Polarized Return-to-Zero (VLIE)
PRZ	Portales, NM [*Location identifier*] [*FAA*] (FAAL)
PRZ	Potential Repository Zone [*Nuclear waste storage*]
PRZ	Pressoreceptor Zone [*Medicine*] (MELL)
PRZ	Prism Entertainment [*AMEX symbol*] (TTSB)
PRZ	Prism Entertainment Corp. [*AMEX symbol*] (SPSG)
PRZ	Prize Energy [*AMEX symbol*] (SG)
PRZ	Przhevalsk [*Former USSR*] [*Seismograph station code, US Geological Survey*] (SEIS)
PRZF	Pyrazofurin [*Antineoplastic drug*]
PRZM	Pesticide Root Zone Model [*Environmental Protection Agency*] (AEPA)
PRZM	Prism Solutions [*NASDAQ symbol*] (SAG)
PRZR	Polarized Return-to-Zero Recording (VLIE)
PS	Abbott Laboratories [*Research code symbol*]
PS	American Political Science Association. Quarterly [*A publication*]
PS	Chemical Agent/Tear Gas, Chloropicrin (SAUS)
PS	Chloropicrin [*Poison gas*] [*Army symbol*]
PS	Elementary and Early Childhood Education [*Educational Resources Information Center (ERIC) Clearinghouse*] [*University of Illinois*] (PAZ)
PS	Pacemaker Syndrome [*Medicine*] (MELL)
PS	Pace Setter (MHDI)
PS	Pacifc Southwest Airlines (SAUS)
PS	Pacific Southwest Airlines [*ICAO designator*] (OAG)
PS	Pacific Star Communication [*Vancouver Stock Exchange symbol*]
P(S)	Packet (Send)
PS	Packet Send Sequence Number
PS	Packet Switch (SAUS)
PS	Packet Switcher (or Switching) (SAUS)
PS	Packet Switching [*Telecommunications*]
PS	Packet Switch Stream [*British*] [*Computer science*] (TNIG)
PS	Packing Sheet (MCD)
PS	Packing Standards (SAUS)
PS	Paddle Steamer (ADA)
PS	Paediatric Surgery
PS	Paget-Schroetter [*Syndrome*] [*Medicine*] (DB)
PS	Painting System
PS	Pakistan Standard (IAA)
PS	Paleontological Society (EA)
PS	Palm Society [*Later, IPS*] (EA)
PS	Paltauf-Sternberg [*Disease*] [*Medicine*] (DB)
PS	Pan Salicornia Zone [*Ecology*]
PS	Paper Structure (SAUS)
PS	Parachute Subsystem [*NASA*] (NASA)
PS	Parade State (SAUS)
PS	Paradoxical Sleep
P/S	Parallel/Serial (SAUS)
PS	Parallel Single [*Outdoor advertising*] (NTCM)
PS	Parallel to Serial (NITA)
P/S	Parallel to Serial Converter (MCD)
PS	Paramagnetic Scheromak
PS	Parameter Set for (SAUS)
PS	Paranoid Schizophrenia [*Medicine*] (MELL)
PS	Parapsychological Society (SAUS)
PS	Paraspinous (SAUS)
PS	Parenteral Society (SAUS)
PS	Parents of Suicides (EA)
PS	Parents' Section of the Alexander Graham Bell Association for the Deaf (EA)
PS	Parity Switch
PS	Parliamentary Secretary [*British*]
PS	Parlor Snake [*Slang for "to escort visitors around post"*]
PS	Parochial School
PS	Parrot Society (EA)
ps	PARSEC [*Parallax Second*] [*See PARSEC*]
PS	Par Selling (MHDB)
PS	Partially Sighted (AIE)
PS	Partially Smutted [*Plant pathology*]
PS	Partially Synergistic [*Pharmacology*]
PS	Partial Seizure (MELL)
PS	Participating Scientist (ACAE)
PS	Particle Simulation (SAUS)
PS	Partido Socialista [*Socialist Party*] [*Uruguay*] [*Political party*]
PS	Partido Socialista [*Socialist Party*] [*Chile*] [*Political party*]
PS	Partido Socialista Portuguesa [*Portuguese Socialist Party*] [*Political party*] (PPE)
PS	Partido Socialista - Uno [*Socialist Party - One*] [*Also, PS-1*] [*Bolivia*] [*Political party*] (PPW)
PS	Parti Socialiste [*Socialist Party*] [*Belgium*] [*Political party*] (PPW)

PS	Parti Socialiste - Federation de la Reunion [*Reunion Federation of the Socialist Party*] [*Political party*] (PPW)
PS	Parts Shipped (or Shipper) (SAUS)
PS	Parts Shipper
PS	Part Surface (IAA)
PS	Passed School of Instruction [*of Officers*] [*British*]
PS	Passenger Service
PS	Passenger Steamer
PS	Passing Scuttle
PS	Passive Smoke (MELL)
ps	Pastel (VRA)
PS	Pastel Society [*British*]
PS	Pathological Staging (SAUS)
PS	Pathological (Surgical) Staging [*For Hodgkin's Disease*]
PS	Pathologic Stage
PS	Patient's Serum [*Medicine*]
PS	Patrologia Syriaca (BJA)
PS	Patrol Service [*British military*] (DMA)
PS	Patrol Ship (CINC)
PS	Patton Society (EA)
PS	Pause Statement (SAUS)
P/S	Pause/Still [*Video technology*]
PS	Payload Shroud (MCD)
PS	Payload Specialist [*NASA*] (MCD)
PS	Payload Station [*NASA*] (MCD)
PS	Payload Support [*NASA*] (NASA)
PS	Paymaster Sergeant
PS	Pedal Sinus
PS	Pediatric Surgery (DAVI)
PS	Pellegrini-Stieda [*Disease*] [*Medicine*] (DB)
PS	Pellet Size
PS	Penal Servitude
PS	Penny Stock [*Investment term*]
PS	Pension Trust, Profit-Sharing, Stock Bonus or Annuity Plan (SAUS)
PS	Pentagrid Switch (SAUS)
PS	Peperomia Society [*Later, PEPS*] (EA)
PS	Perception Schedule
PS	Perceptual Speed (Test) [*Psychology*]
PS	Percussion Shrapnel (SAUS)
PS	Perfect Shuffle (MHDI)
PS	Performance Score
PS	Performance Specification
PS	Performance Standard
PS	Performance Status [*Rehabilitation*] (DAVI)
PS	Performing Scale [*Medicine*] (MAE)
PS	Perform Statement (SAUS)
PS	Perimeter Surveillance (LAIN)
PS	Periodic Syndrome [*Medicine*]
P/S	Periods per Second (SAUS)
PS	Peripheral Shock [*Psychology*]
PS	Permanent Secretary
PS	Permanent Signal [*Telecommunications*] (TEL)
PS	Permutation Sequence (SAUS)
PS	Per Second (AAMN)
PS	Per Ship
PS	Personal Secretary (DCTA)
PS	Personal Skills
PS	Personal Survival
PS	Personal System [*IBM computer introduced in 1987*]
PS	Personnel Strength (SAUS)
PS	Personnel Subsystem [*Army*]
PS	Per Speculum [*Medicine*]
PS	Peru Solidarity [*An association*] (EA)
Ps	Peseta [*Monetary unit*] [*Andorra and Spain*] (BARN)
PS	Petrol Station (SAUS)
PS	Pet Switchboard [*Defunct*] (EA)
PS	Petty Sessions (DLA)
PS	Pharmaceutical Society (NADA)
P/S	Phaser/Subarray
PS	Phase Separation
P/S	Phase Shift (ACAE)
PS	Phase-Shift
PS	Phasing System [*Telecommunications*] (OA)
PS	Phenix Society (EA)
PS	Phenolsteroid (SAUS)
PS	Phenol Steroids (SAUS)
PS	Phenomenally Speedy Ordinary [*Photographic plates*] (ROG)
PS	Philalethes Society (EA)
PS	Phillnathean Society (EA)
PS	Philolexian Society (EA)
PS	Philological Society (EAIO)
PS	Philomathean Society (EA)
PS	Phosphate-Saline [*A buffer*] [*Cell culture*]
PS	Phosphatidylserine [*Biochemistry*]
PS	Photochemical System
PS	Photoemission Scintillation (MCD)
PS	Photoemmission Scintillation (SAUS)
PS	Photographic Service
PS	Photographic Squadron
PS	Photometer System (KSC)
PS	Photosystems
PS	Phototelegraph Station (SAUS)
PS	Phrase Structure (WGA)
PS	Phrenic Stimulation [*Medicine*] (MELL)
PS	Phylaxis Society (EA)

P S	Physical Science (SAUS)
PS	Physical Sciences
PS	Physical Security
PS	Physical Sequential (HGAA)
PS	Physical Status [Medicine]
PS	Physics Specification (SAUS)
PS	Physiological Society (BUAC)
PS	Physiologic Saline [Medicine] (MELL)
PS	Picket Ships [Navy]
PS	Pico Second (SAUS)
ps	Picosecond [One trillionth of a second]
PS	Picosecond
PS	Picture Storage (SAUS)
PS	Picture System (ELAL)
PS	Pilgrim Power Station (NRCH)
PS	Pilgrim Society (EA)
PS	Pineal Stalk [Neuroanatomy]
PS	Pine Bark Mixed with Clay Loam Soil
PS	Pine Siskin [Ornithology]
PS	Pink Sheet [Investment term]
PS	Pioneer School (SAUS)
PS	Piper Syndrome (SAUS)
PS	Pipe Size (BARN)
PS	Pirandello Society (EA)
PS	Pisosecond (IAA)
PS	Pistol Sharpshooter [Army]
PS	Pitot/Static Tube (MCD)
PS	[The] Pittsburg & Shawmut Railroad Co. [AAR code]
PS	Pituitary Stalk [Neuroanatomy]
PS	Planetary Society (EA)
PS	Planetary Surface (IAA)
PS	Planning and Scheduling
PS	Planning Staff (SAUS)
PS	Planning Study (AAG)
PS	Plant Stress [Horticulture]
PS	Plastic Surgery [Medicine]
PS	Plate Sunk [Printing] (DGA)
PS	Platform (Sided) (DCTA)
P/S	Platoon/Section [Army]
PS	Plea Side (ROG)
PS	Pleural Sclerite [Entomology]
PS	Plotter System (SAUS)
PS	Plotting System
PS	Plus
PS	Pneumatic Suspension [Automotive engineering]
PS	Pneumatic System
PS	Poetry Society [British]
P/S	Point of Shipment
PS	Point of Switch
PS	Point of Symmetry
PS	Point Setting (SAUS)
PS	Point Shifting (SAUS)
PS	Point Source (COE)
PS	Point Sparger [Engineering]
PS	Point Spread [In visual cortex]
PS	Polanyi Society (EA)
PS	Polaris Standard [Missiles]
PS	Polarity Scale [Psychology]
PS	Polarity Selector (IAA)
PS	Polar Stereographic (SAUS)
PS	Police Sergeant [Scotland Yard]
PS	Policy Statement
PS	Polio Society (EA)
PS	Polite Society (BUAC)
PS	Political Science (SAUS)
PS	Polling Signal (SAUS)
Ps	Polyporus sulphureus [A fungus]
PS	Polysaccharide (DB)
PS	Polystyrene [Organic chemistry]
PS	Polysulfone [Also, PSO] [Organic chemistry]
P/S	Polyunsaturated/Saturated [Fatty acid ratio]
PS	Population Sample (MAE)
PS	Porlock Society (EA)
PS	Porous Silicon [Physics]
PS	Portable Station (SAUS)
P/S	Port and Starboard (SAUS)
PS	Porter-Silber Chromogen [Medicine] (MAE)
PS	Port Security
PS	Port Store [Telecommunications] (TEL)
PS	Port Strobe [Telecommunications] (TEL)
PS	Pos-Escrito [Postscript] [Portuguese]
PS	Position-Specific Antigen
PS	Positive Value (DA)
Ps	Positronium (SAUS)
PS	Postal Satsang [An association] (EA)
PS	Postal Service [US]
PS	Posterior Synechia (SAUS)
PS	Poster Society (EA)
PS	Post Script (SAUS)
ps	PostScript [Computer science]
PS	PostScript [Adobe printer language]
P S	Post Scriptum [Written Afterwards, Postscript] [Latin]
PS	Post Status (SAUS)
PS	Potassium Sorbate [Food additive]
PS	Potentiometer Synchro
PS	Potentiometer Synchronometer
P/S	Power Section (NG)
PS	Power Series (IAA)
PS	Power Shift (SAUS)
PS	Power Shutdown (SAUS)
PS	Power Source
PS	Power-Specific (MCD)
PS	Power Spectra [Neurophysiology]
PS	Power Spectrum (SAUS)
PS	Power Station (MCD)
PS	Power Steering [Automobile ads]
PS	Powerstroke (SAUS)
PS	Power Supply
PS	Powys Society (EA)
PS	Prairie Schooner [A publication] (BRI)
PS	Prairies Service [Record series prefix] [Canada]
PS	Predictive Saccades [Ophthalmology]
PS	Preduzece Soko [Former Yugoslavia] [ICAO aircraft manufacturer identifier] (ICAO)
PS	Preferred Stock [Investment term]
PS	Pregnant Serum (SAUS)
PS	Prehistoric Society (EA)
PS	Preliminary Study
PS	Preparedness Staff [Environmental Protection Agency] (GFGA)
Ps	Prescription (AAMN)
PS	Presenilin [Biochemistry]
PS	Presentation Services [Computer science] (IBMDP)
PS	Present State (SAUS)
PS	Present Symptoms (SAUS)
PS	Press Secretary (ILCA)
PS	Press to Start (KSC)
Ps	Pressure (HLLA)
PS	Pressure [or Propellant] Seal
P-S	Pressure-Sensitive
PS	Pressure Sensor
PS	Pressure Sore (MELL)
PS	Pressure Steam (SAUS)
PS	Pressure Support (SAUS)
PS	Pressure Switch
Ps	Pressure, Systolic [Cardiology]
PS	Price Spreading [Business term]
PS	Primary School (ADA)
PS	Primary Section (SAUS)
PS	Primary Sequence (SAUS)
PS	Primary Storage (SAUS)
PS	Primary Syphilis (MELL)
PS	Prime Select (MCD)
PS	Prime Sponsor
PS	Principal Sojourner [Freemasonry] (ROG)
PS	Principal Subject [In a sonata or rondo] [Music] (ROG)
PS	Printer Start (SAUS)
PS	Printing Speed (SAUS)
PS	Print Scan [Computer science] (IAA)
PS	Print Storage (SAUS)
PS	Priority Service (SAUS)
PS	Prior Service [Military]
PS	Private Screenings [Cable TV programming service]
PS	Private Secretary
PS	Private Security Program [Association of Independent Colleges and Schools specialization code]
PS	Private Siding [Rail] [Shipping] (DS)
PS	Privilege Service (SAUS)
PS	Privy Seal [British]
PS	Probability of mission Success (SAUS)
PS	Probability of Survival (MCD)
PS	Problem Space
PS	Problem Specification
PS	Problem Statement [Computer science] (IAA)
PS	Procambial Strand [Botany]
PS	Procedure Signal (SAUS)
PS	Procedure Statement (SAUS)
PS	Processing State (SAUS)
PS	Processing Station (SAUS)
PS	Processor Status
PS	Processor Storage (SAUS)
PS	Process Sheet
PS	Process Solution (MCD)
PS	Process Solvent (SAUS)
PS	Process Specification
PS	Process Status (SAUS)
PS	Process Stop Ship (SAUS)
PS	Process Storage [Computer science] (IAA)
PS	Process Subsystem [Telecommunications] (TEL)
PS	Procurement Specification (MCD)
PS	Production Set (SAUS)
PS	Production Sharing (SAUS)
PS	Production Support (SAUS)
PS	Production System (SAUS)
PS	Product Service (IAA)
PS	Product Sharing (SAUS)
PS	Product Software (MCD)
PS	Product Specification (SAUS)
P/S	Product Standards (MCD)
PS	Product Support
PS	Profit Sharing [Business term]

PS	Programmable Switch [*Computer science*] (IAA)
PS	Programmed Symbols (MEDA)
PS	Programming System
PS	Program Scheduling (SAUS)
PS	Program Section [*Computer science*] (IAA)
PS	Program Segment (SAUS)
PS	Program Selector (SAUS)
PS	Program Service (SAUS)
PS	Program Shift (SAUS)
PS	Program Simulation (OICC)
PS	Program Sound (SAUS)
PS	Program Source [*Computer science*] (IAA)
PS	Program Specification (MCD)
PS	Program Start (KSC)
PS	Program Stateword [*Computer science*] (IAA)
PS	Program Status [*Computer science*] (IAA)
PS	Program Store [*Computer science*] (IEEE)
PS	Program Structure (SAUS)
PS	Program Summary (NG)
PS	Program System
PS	Progressive Stroke (SAUS)
PS	Project Scientist (SAUS)
PS	Project Slip
PS	Project Start [*Milestone chart*]
PS	Project Stock [*Military*] (AABC)
PS	Project Study [*British military*] (DMA)
PS	Proler International Corp. [*NYSE symbol*] (SPSG)
PS	Proler Intl [*NYSE symbol*] (TTSB)
PS	Prolifers for Survival [*Defunct*] (EA)
PS	Prometheus Society (EA)
PS	Prompt Side [*of a stage*] [*i.e., the right side*] [*A stage direction*]
PS	Proof Shot [*Ammunition*]
PS	Proof Stress
PS	Propellant Seal
PS	Propellant Supply (KSC)
PS	Propellant System
PS	Proportional Spacing [*Typography*] (WDMC)
PS	Propulsion Section
Ps	Proseminar (SAUS)
PS	Prostaglandin Synthetase [*An enzyme*]
PS	Prostatic Secretion [*Medicine*] (MELL)
PS	Protected Ship (SAUS)
PS	Protection Strategy (COE)
PS	Protective Security (SAUS)
PS	Protective Service
PS	Protective Shelter
PS	Protective Silver (SAUS)
PS	Protective Structure
PS	Protective Subsystem [*Military*] (INF)
PS	Protect Status (MHDB)
PS	Protein Society (BUAC)
PS	Protein Synthesis
PS	Proton Synchrotron [*Nuclear energy*]
PS	Proton Synchrotron Division (SAUS)
PS	Protoplasmic Surface [*Freeze etching in microscopy*]
PS	Proto-Semitic (BJA)
PS	Provision Supply (SAUS)
PS	Provost-Sergeant
ps	Psalm (GROV)
PS	Psalm
Ps	Psalms [*Biblical*] (RION)
PS	Pseudo [*Classical studies*] (OCD)
Ps	Pseudomonas [*Bacterium*] (MAE)
PS	Pseudomonas Stutzeri [*Bacterium*]
PS	Pseudonym (WGA)
PS	Psychiatric (MAE)
PS	Psychology Society (EA)
PS	Psychometric Society (EA)
PS	Psychonomic Society (EA)
PS	Psychotic
PS	Publication Standard
PS	Public Safety (SAUS)
PS	Public Sale
PS	Public School
PS	Public Service
PS	Public Statutes [*Legal term*] (DLA)
PS	Public Stenographer
PS	Public Storage (EFIS)
PS	Publishing Services [*American Library Association*]
PS	Puget Sound [*Also, Puget Sound Naval Shipyard*] [*Washington*]
P-S	Pullman-Standard (SAUS)
PS	Pull Switch
PS	Pulmonary Sequestration
PS	Pulmonary Stenosis [*Medicine*]
PS	Pulse per Second (IAA)
PS	Pulse Sensor (KSC)
PS	Pulse Shaper
PS	Pulses per Second [*Data transmission*] (DEN)
PS	Pulse Stretcher
PS	Pumping Station (NATG)
PS	Purdon's Pennsylvania Statutes [*A publication*] (DLA)
PS	Purity-Supreme [*Supermarkets*]
PS	Pyloric Stenosis [*Medicine*]
PS	Serum From a Pregnant Woman (DAVI)
Ps	South Celestial Pole (SAUS)
ps---	South Pacific [*MARC geographic area code*] [*Library of Congress*] (LCCP)
PS	South Pole [*Also, SP*]
PS	Static Pressure
PS	Swarthmore Public Library, Swarthmore, PA [*Library symbol*] [*Library of Congress*] (LCLS)
PS	Transport [*Russian aircraft symbol*]
PS	US Postal Service (AAGC)
PS-1	Partido Socialista - Uno [*Socialist Party - One*] [*Also, PS*] [*Bolivia*] [*Political party*] (PD)
PS/2	Personal System/2 [*IBM Corp.*]
PS2	Picture System 2 [*Evans & Sutherland Computer Corp.*] (MCD)
PS2	PlayStation 2 [*Video game console*]
PS2	Power Station Two
PS^2	Profound Sensitivity Syndrome [*Psychology*]
PS3	PROBE [*Program Optimization and Budget Evaluation*] Staff Support System [*Military*]
PS2000	Public Service 2000 Program [*Canada*]
PSA	Pacific Island Aviation, Inc. [*Mariana Islands*] [*ICAO designator*] (FAAC)
PSA	Pacific Science Association [*Hawaii*] (BUAC)
PSA	Pacific Sciences Association (SAUS)
PSA	Pacific Seedsmens Association (BUAC)
PSA	Pacific South American (SAUS)
PSA	Pacific Southwest Airlines
PSA	Packers and Stockyards Administration (SAUS)
PSA	Pakistan Sociological Association (BUAC)
PSA	Panda Standard Asynchron (SAUS)
PSA	Parallel Signature Analyzer (TIMI)
PSA	Parametric Semiconductor Amplifier
PSA	Parametric Sound Amplifier [*Blaupunkt*]
PSA	Parcel Shippers Association (EA)
PSA	Partial Starting Address (SAUS)
PSA	Particle Size Analyzer
PSA	Particularly Sensitive Sea Area (SAUS)
PSA	Partido Socialista Aponte [*Bolivia*] [*Political party*] (PPW)
PSA	Partido Socialista Argentino [*Socialist Party of Argentina*] [*Political party*]
PSA	Parti Socialiste Autonome [*Autonomous Socialist Party*] [*France*] [*Political party*] (PPE)
PSA	Parti Solidaire Africain [*African Solidarity Party*] [*Congo*] [*Political party*]
PSA	Partito Socialista Autonomo [*Autonomous Socialist Party*] [*Switzerland*] [*Political party*] (PPW)
PSA	Part Stress Analysis (MCD)
PSA	Passenger Service Agent [*Travel industry*] (TVEL)
PSA	Passenger Shipping Association [*British*] (DBA)
PSA	Passive Situation Awareness (ACAE)
PSA	Pastel Society of America (EA)
PSA	Past Shakedown Availability [*Military*]
PSA	Path of Steepest Ascent [*Statistical design of experiments*]
PSA	Path Selection Algorithm [*Telecommunications*] (TEL)
PSA	Patient Care Associate [*Medicine*]
PSA	Payload Service Area [*NASA*] (NASA)
PSA	Payload Support Avionics [*NASA*] (NASA)
PSA	Peace and Solidarity Alliance (EA)
PSA	Peace Studies Association (EA)
PSA	People's Supreme Assembly [*Yemen*] [*Political party*] (PPW)
PSA	Peripherals Suppliers Association (ELAL)
PSA	Permanent Storage Area (SAUS)
PSA	Personal Service Agreements (MCD)
PSA	Personal Statement Analyzer (HGAA)
PSA	Personnel and Service Area [*Nuclear energy*] (NRCH)
PSA	Personnel Support Activity (DOMA)
PSA	Personnel Support Agency
PSA	Petersburg [*Alaska*] [*Seismograph station code, US Geological Survey*] (SEIS)
PSA	Petites Soeurs de l'Assumption [*Little Sisters of the Assumption - LSA*] [*Paris, France*] (EAIO)
PSA	Peugot Societe Anonyme [*Peugeot Co. Ltd.*] [*French*]
PSA	Philippine Standards Association (IAA)
PSA	Philippine Sugar Association [*Later, PSC*] (EA)
PSA	Philosophy of Science Association (EA)
PSA	Phlebology Society of America (NTPA)
PSA	Phobia Society of America [*Later, ADAA*] (EA)
PSA	Photographic Society of America (EA)
PSA	Phycological Society of America (EA)
PSA	Physical Sector Address (SAUS)
PSA	Pickles and Sauces Association [*British*] (DBA)
PSA	Pipe Stress Analysis (PDAA)
PSA	Pirandello Society of America (EA)
PSA	Pisa [*Italy*] [*Airport symbol*] (OAG)
PsA	Pisces Austrinus [*Constellation*]
PSA	Pisces Society of America
PSA	Pitch Servo Assembly (SAUS)
PSA	Planning Simulation Accounting (SAUS)
PSA	Play Schools Association (EA)
PSA	Pleasant Sunday Afternoons
PSA	Plumeria Society of America (EA)
PSA	Pneumatic Sensor Assembly
PSA	Poe Studies Association (EA)
PSA	Poetry Society of America (EA)
PSA	Police Superintendents' Association [*New Zealand*] (WDAA)
PSA	Political Studies Association [*British*]
PSA	Political Studies Association of the United Kingdom (BUAC)

PSA............. Polycrystalline Silicon Self-Aligned [*Photovoltaic energy systems*] (MHDI)
PSA............. Polyethylene Sulfonic Acid [*Organic chemistry*] (MAE)
PSA............. Polysialic Acid [*Organic chemistry*]
PSA............. Polysilicic Acid [*Organic chemistry*]
PSA............. Polysilicon Self-Aligned (SAUS)
PSA............. Poly-Substance Abuse [*Medicine*] (MELL)
PSA............. Portable Sanitation Association (EA)
PSA............. Portable Sound Analyzer
PSA............. Port Storage Area [*Telecommunications*] (TEL)
PSA............. Port Support Activity (DOMA)
PSA............. Post Shakedown Availability
PSA............. Post Sleep Activity (SAUS)
PSA............. Post-Sleep Activity
PSA............. Post Strike Assessment (SAUS)
PSA............. Potential Surface Analysis (ADA)
PSA............. Potentiometric Stripping Analysis (ABAC)
PSA............. Potters' Society of Australia
PSA............. Poultry Science Association (EA)
PSA............. Power and Servo Assembly
PSA............. Power Saw Association [*British*] (BI)
PSA............. Power Servo Amplifier (KSC)
PSA............. Power Servo Assembly (MCD)
PSA............. Power Supply Assembly
PSA............. Power Switching Amplifier
PSA............. Power Switching Assembly
PSA............. Precipitation Series Algorithm [*Marine science*] (OSRA)
PSA............. Prefabricated Surfacing Aluminum
PSA............. Preferred Storage Area (MCD)
PSA............. Preferred Supplier Agreement (SAUS)
PSA............. Prefix Save Area (SAUS)
PSA............. Prefix Storage Area [*Computer science*] (OA)
PSA............. Preliminary Safety Analysis [*NASA*] (SSD)
PSA............. Preliminary Site Assessment (SARE)
PSA............. Pre/Post Sleep Activity (NASA)
PSA............. Prepseudoarthrosis [*Medicine*] (MELL)
PSA............. President of the Society of Antiquaries [*British*]
PSA............. Pre Sleep Activity (SAUS)
PSA............. Pressure Sensitive Adhesive [*Trademark*]
PSA............. Pressure Suit Assembly
PSA............. Pressure Swing Absorption (SAUS)
PSA............. Pressure-Swing Adsorption [*Chemical engineering*]
PSA............. Pressure Switch Assembly (NASA)
PSA............. Pressure Switching Alarm [*Engineering*]
PSA............. Presunrise Authority
PSA............. Presunrise Service Authority (NTCM)
PSA............. Pretrial Service Agency (SAUS)
PSA............. Prices Surveillance Authority (BUAC)
PSA............. Primary Store Address (SAUS)
PSA............. Principal Staff Assistants
PSA............. Principal Supervisory Agent (EBF)
PSA............. Private Schools Association [*British*]
PSA............. Probabilistic Safety Analysis (NRCH)
PSA............. Problem Specification Analyzer (RALS)
PSA............. Problem Statement Analyser (or Analyzer) (SAUS)
PSA............. Problem Statement Analyzer [*Computer science*] (IAA)
PSA............. Proceedings of the Society of Antiquaries (SAUS)
PSA............. Process Service Area (IAA)
PSA............. Procurement Seminar for Auditors [*Army*]
PSA............. Product Safety Association [*Defunct*] (EA)
PSA............. Product Support Administration (MCD)
PSA............. Product Support Analysis (SAUS)
PSA............. Professional Sales Association (NTPA)
PSA............. Professional Salespersons of America [*Defunct*] (EA)
PSA............. Professional Service Association (EA)
PSA............. Professional Services Agreement (COE)
PSA............. Professional Skaters Association (NTPA)
PSA............. Professional Skills Alliance (EA)
PSA............. Professional Squash Association (NTPA)
PSA............. Professional Stringers Association [*Defunct*] (EA)
PSA............. Programmed Shutter and Aperture [*Photography*] (DICI)
PSA............. Program Study Authorization (KSC)
PSA............. Progressive Spinal Ataxia [*Medicine*] (DMAA)
PSA............. Project-Specific Analysis (SAUS)
PSA............. Project Support Agreement (SAUS)
PSA............. Prolonged Sleep Apnea
PSA............. Promoting Stress & Anxiety (WDAA)
PSA............. Promotional Sourcing Association (BUAC)
PSA............. Property Services Agency [*Department of the Environment*] [*British*]
PSA............. Prostate-Specific Antigen [*Immunochemistry*]
PSA............. Protected Storage Address [*Computer science*] (VLIE)
PSA............. Protective Security Attendant [*Australia*]
PSA............. Protocol-Specific Annex (SAUS)
PSA............. Province Senior Advisor [*Army*] (VNW)
PSA............. Provisional Site Acceptance (NATG)
PSA............. Provisional System Acceptance (SAUS)
PSA............. Provisional System Approval (SAUS)
PSA............. Provisions Stowage Assembly (NASA)
PSA............. Psalm
Psa............. Psalms [*Old Testament book*]
PSA............. Pseudomonic Acid [*Biochemistry*]
PsA............. Psoriatic Arthritis (DAVI)
Psa............. Psychoanalysis (DIPS)
PSA............. Psychological Operations Support Activity [*Military*] (MCD)
PSA............. Psychological Semantic Analysis (NITA)

PSA............. Psychological Society of America (SAUS)
PSA............. Psychological Stress Analyzer (SAUS)
PSA............. Psychologists for Social Action [*Defunct*] (EA)
PSA............. Publication Systems Associates, Inc. [*Information service or system*] (IID)
PSA............. Public Securities Association [*Database producer*] (EA)
PSA............. Public Servants Association (SAUS)
PSA............. Public Service Act
PSA............. Public Service Administration (SAUS)
PSA............. Public Service Advertising (SAUS)
PSA............. Public Service Alliance (BUAC)
PSA............. Public Service Announcement
PSA............. Public Service Association [*New Zealand*] (WDAA)
PSA............. Public Storage [*NYSE symbol*] (TTSB)
PSA............. Public Storage, Inc. [*NYSE symbol*] (SAG)
PSA............. Push Down Stack Automaton [*Computer science*]
PSA............. Storage Properties, Inc. [*AMEX symbol*] (SPSG)
PSAA............ Pacific Special Activities Area [*Military*]
PSAA............ Pakistan Students' Association of America
PSAA............ Plasma Sciences and Applications (IAA)
PSAA............ Polish Singers Alliance of America (EA)
PSAA............ Polwarth Sheepbreeders' Association of Australia
PSAA............ Poststimulatory Auditory Adaptation
PSAAV .... Provincial Sewerage Authorities Association of Victoria [*Australia*]
PSAB .... Pathology Services Accreditation Board [*Victoria, Australia*]
PSAB .... Prime Bancorp [*NASDAQ symbol*] (TTSB)
PSAB .... Prime Bancorp, Inc. [*NASDAQ symbol*] (CTT)
PSAB .... Production Systems Acceptance Branch [*Social Security Administration*]
PSAB .... Public Schools Appointments Bureau (SAUS)
PSAC .... Passive Satellite Attitude Control
PSAC .... Pated-System Auxiliary Control element (SAUS)
PSAC .... Peak Sound Absorption Concentration (SAUS)
PSAC .... Pennsylvania State Athletic Conference (PSS)
P sac .... Pericardial Cavity (SAUS)
PSAC .... Personnel Service Company [*Army*] (AABC)
PSAC .... Policy Signing and Accounting Centre [*Insurance firm*] [*British*]
PSAC .... Preferred Stock Advisory Committee [*New Deal*]
PSAC .... Presidential Scientific Advisory Committee (SAUS)
PSAC .... President's Science Advisory Committee [*Terminated, 1973*] [*Executive Office of the President*]
PSAC .... Presidents Science Advisory Committee (or Council) (SAUS)
PSAC .... Private Security Advisory Council [*Terminated, 1977*] [*Department of Justice*] (EGAO)
PSAC .... Production Statistics Advisory Committee (BUAC)
PSAC .... Product Safety Advisory Council [*Consumer Product Safety Commission*]
PSAC .... Professional Services Advisary Committee (SAUS)
PSAC .... Professional Skating Association of Canada
PSAC .... Public Service Alliance of Canada [*Labor union of federal government employees*]
PSACEI ...... Propulsion Subsystem for Attitude Control and Engine Ignition (IGSL)
PSACH .... Pseudoachondrodysplasia [*Medicine*] (DMAA)
PSACN .... Process Specification Advance Change Notice (SAA)
PSACO .... Papillary Serous Adenocarcinoma of Ovary [*Medicine*] (MELL)
PSAcPh....... Prostate-Specific Acid Phosphatase [*An enzyme*]
PSACPOO .... President's Scientific Advisory Committee Panel on Oceanography [*Marine science*] (MSC)
PSACS .... Pilot Selection and Classification System (SAUS)
PSAD .... Passive Sensor for Aircraft Detection [*Military*] (SEWL)
PSAD .... Political/Statistical Area Description (SAUS)
PSAD .... Predicted Site Acquisition Data [*NASA*]
PSAD .... Prediction, Simulation, Adaptation, Decision [*Computer science*]
PSAD .... Prediction, Simulation, Adaption and Decision (SAUS)
PSAD .... Procurement and Systems Acquisition Division (AAGC)
PSAD .... Prostate-Specific Antigen Density [*Medicine*] (MELL)
PSAE .... Philippine Society of Agricultural Engineers (BUAC)
PSAF .... Print Services Access Facility [*Computer science*] (VLIE)
PSAF .... Private Sector Adjustment Factor [*Banking*]
PSAG .... Pelvic Sonoangiography [*Medicine*] (DMAA)
PSAG .... Probabilistic Systems Assessment Group (SAUS)
PSAG .... Program System Analysis Guide (VLIE)
PSAG-CD ..... Public Service Advisory Group/Collection Development (SAUS)
PSAGN........ Poststreptococcal Acute Glomerulonephritis [*Medicine*]
PSAG-PS..... Public Service Advisory Group/Public Services (SAUS)
PSAG-TS..... Public Service Advisory Group/Technical Services (SAUS)
PSAI........... Pediatric Services of Amer [*NASDAQ symbol*] (TTSB)
PSAI........... Pediatric Services of America, Inc. [*NASDAQ symbol*] (SAG)
PSAI........... Political Studies Association of Ireland (BUAC)
PSAI........... Portable Sanitation Association International (NTPA)
PSAI........... Proceedings of the Suffolk Archaeological Institute (SAUS)
PSAIR .... Priority Specific Air Information Request [*Defense Mapping Agency*] (MCD)
PSAJ........... Peace Studies Association of Japan (BUAC)
PSA Journal... Photographic Society of America Journal (SAUS)
PSAL.......... Permanent Supplementary Artificial Lighting (IAA)
PSAL.......... Programming System Activity Log [*Computer science*]
PSAL.......... Programming Systems Activity Log (SAUS)
PSAL.......... Public Schools Athletic League
PSALI.......... Permanent Supplementary Artificial Lighting Interiors (SAUS)
PSALI.......... Permanent Supplementary Artificial Lighting of Interiors (IEEE)
P Salin .... Petrus de Salinis [*Flourished, 13th century*] [*Authority cited in pre-1607 legal work*] (DSA)
PSALM........ Project Structured Analysis of LOGEX [*Logistical Exercise*] Methodology (MCD)

PSAM.......... Partitioned Sequence (or Sequential) Access Method (SAUS)
PSAM.......... Point Source Ambient Monitoring [*Environmental Protection Agency*] (GFGA)
PSAM.......... Probabilistic Structural Analysis Methodology (ACAE)
PSAM.......... Proceedings of Symposia in Applied Mathematics (SAUS)
PSAMPP...... Philadelphia Society for Alleviating the Miseries of Public Prisons (SAUS)
PSAMS........ Plessey Scientific-Atlanta Multistar System (NITA)
PSAN.......... Phase Stabilized Ammonium Nitrate (MCD)
PSAN.......... Polystyrolakrylnitril (SAUS)
PSAn.......... Psychoanalysis [*or Psychoanalyst*] (DAVI)
psan............ psychoanalyze (SAUS)
PS & A........ Pharmacy, Supply, and Administration (DOMA)
PS & B........ Power Steering and Brakes [*Automotive engineering*] (IIA)
PS & C........ Private Siding and Collected One End
PS&C.......... Private Siding and Collected (or Collection) (SAUS)
PS&C.......... Production Scheduling and Control (AAGC)
PS&C.......... Program Scheduling and Control (SAUS)
PS & CC...... Packaging, Storage, and Containerization Center [*DARCOM*] (MCD)
PS & D........ Private Siding and Delivered One End
PS & DS...... Program Statistics and Data Systems
PS & E........ Plans, Specifications, and Estimates [*Construction*]
PS & ER...... Production Support and Equipment Replacement [*Military*] (AABC)
PS & L........ Power Switching and Logic
PS & M........ Personnel Supervision and Management Division of ASTSECNAV's Office [*Absorbed into SECP, 1944*]
PS&SC........ Public Service and Safety Committee (SAUS)
PS&SSU...... Power Supply & System Selector Unit (SAUS)
PS & T........ Pay, Subsistence, and Transportation [*Military*]
PSANDT...... Pay, Subsistence, and Transportation [*Military*]
PS & TC...... Population Studies and Training Center [*Brown University*] [*Research center*] (RCD)
PS & TN...... Pay, Subsistence, and Transportation, Navy
PS & W........ Pacific, Southern & Western Railroad [*Nickname: Play Safe and Walk*]
PS&W.......... Philadelphia Steel and Wire (SAUS)
PSANP........ Phenol-Soluble Acidic Nuclear Protein [*s*] [*Biochemistry*]
PSANZ........ Perinatal Society of Australia & New Zealand (SAUS)
PSAO.......... Pharmacy Services Administrative Organization
PSAO.......... Primary Staff Action Officer [*Military*]
PSAODAP.... Presidential Special Action Office for Drug Abuse Prevention (SAUS)
PSAP.......... Particle/Soot Absorption Photometer (SAUS)
PSAP.......... Pennsylvania Student Assistance Program (SAUS)
PSAP.......... Pharmacotherapy Self-Assessment Program (SAUS)
PSAP.......... Phenylsulfonylacetophenone
PSAP.......... Plane Stress Analysis and Plot [*Computer science*]
PSAP.......... Power Supply for Asynchron Peripheral replaceable item (SAUS)
PSAP.......... Presentation Service Access Point [*Telecommunications*] (OSI)
PSAP.......... Primary Public Safety Answering Point (DMAA)
PSAP.......... Program Status Area Pointer (SAUS)
PSAP.......... Public Safety Answering Point [*Telecommunications*] (TEL)
PSAP.......... Public Service Answering Point
PSAP.......... Pulmonary Surfactant Apoprotein [*Biochemistry*]
PSAPI.......... Presentation Space Application Programming Interface (SAUS)
PSAPR........ Pathology Society of Asia and Pacific Region (BUAC)
PSAPrA........ Public Storage 10% cm'A'Pfd [*NYSE symbol*] (TTSB)
PSAPrB........ Public Storage 9.20% cm'B'Pfd [*NYSE symbol*] (TTSB)
PSAPrC........ Public Storage Adj Rt'C'Pfd [*NYSE symbol*] (TTSB)
PSAPrD........ Public Storage 9.50%'D'Pfd [*NYSE symbol*] (TTSB)
PSAPrE........ Public Storage 10%'E'Pfd [*NYSE symbol*] (TTSB)
PSAPrF........ Public Storage 9.75% 'F' Pfd [*NYSE symbol*] (TTSB)
PSAPrG........ Public Storage 8.875% Dep Pfd [*NYSE symbol*] (TTSB)
PSAPrH........ Public Storage 8.45%'H'Dep Pfd [*NYSE symbol*] (TTSB)
PSA-Process... Poly-silicon Self-Aligned Process (SAUS)
PSAPrX........ Public Storage 8.25%Cv Pfd [*NYSE symbol*] (TTSB)
PSAR.......... Parts and Supplies Adjustment Request (SAUS)
PSAR.......... Platform Shock Attenuation and Realignment System (MCD)
PSAR.......... Pneumatic [*or Pressure*] System Automatic Regulator (AAG)
PSAR.......... Preliminary Safety Analysis Report
PSAR.......... Pressure System Automatic Regulator (IAA)
PSAR.......... Process Storage Address Register [*Computer science*] (IAA)
PSAR.......... Programmable Synchronous/Asynchronous Receiver (IEEE)
PSAR.......... Propulsion Systems Analysis Report (SAA)
PS Area....... Posterior Speech Area (SAUS)
PSarg.......... Pre-Sargonic (BJA)
PSARP........ Programmable Signal and Response Processor (SAUS)
PSaS.......... Personally Safe and Sound (SAUS)
PSAS.......... Prespeech Assessment Scale [*Occupational therapy*]
PSAS.......... Production Systems Acceptance Section [*Social Security Administration*]
PSAS.......... Programming System Announcement Summary (VLIE)
PSAS.......... Program Support and Advanced Systems (SAA)
PSASA........ Public Service Association of South Australia
PSASS........ Perishable Subsistence Automated Supply System [*DoD*]
PSASV........ Phase-Sensitive Anodic Stripping Voltammetry
PSAT.......... Palm Springs Aerial Tramway (SAUS)
PSAT.......... Percent Saturation of Transferrin (SAUS)
PSAT.......... Pluribus Satellite Interface Message Processor (ACAE)
PSAT.......... Predicted Site Acquisition Table [*NASA*]
PSAT.......... Programmable Synchronous/Asynchronous Transmitter (IEEE)
PSAT.......... Prostate-Specific Antigen Test [*Medicine*] (MELL)
PSAT/NMSQT... Preliminary Scholastic Aptitude/National Merit Scholarship Qualifying Test (PAZ)
PSAUK........ Political Studies Association of the United Kingdom
PSAUSA...... Polish Socialist Alliance of the United States of America (EA)
PSAX.......... Pacific Southwest Airlines [*Air carrier designation symbol*]
PSB............ Bellefonte-Clearfield-Philipsburg [*Pennsylvania*] [*Airport symbol*] (AD)
PSB............ Harbor Patrol Boat [*Navy*]
PSB............ Pacific Science Board [*National Academy of Sciences*]
PSB............ Paradox Salt Basin (SAUS)
PSB............ Paratytic Shellfish Poisoning (SAUS)
PSB............ Passive-Sonobuoy (SAUS)
PSB............ Path State Block (SAUS)
PSB............ Phase Shifting Blank (AAEL)
PSB............ Philatelic Sales Branch [*Later, PSD*] [*US Postal Service*]
PSB............ Philipsburg, PA [*Location identifier*] [*FAA*] (FAAL)
PSB............ Phosphorus-Solubilizing Bacteria [*Microbiology*]
PSB............ Plant Safety Bureau
PSB............ Plant Service Building [*Nuclear energy*] (NRCH)
PSB............ Plough, Sweeper, and Blower (DA)
PSB............ Police Superannuation Board [*Australia*]
PSB............ Polished Silica Block (SAUS)
PSB............ Polytechnic of the South Bank [*London, England*]
PSB............ Post-Strike-Base (SAUS)
PSB............ Power Supply Bar (SAUS)
PSB............ Premium Savings Bond [*British*] (DCTA)
PSB............ Procedure Status Block (TIMI)
PSB............ Process Specification Block (SAUS)
PSB............ Product Symbology Block (SAUS)
PSB............ Professional and Statutory Board (AIE)
PSB............ Professional Staffs Branch (HEAS)
PSB............ Programmspezifikationsblock (SAUS)
PSB............ Program Specification Block [*IBM Corp.*]
PSB............ Program Station Basis [*Rating system*] (WDMC)
PSB............ Program Status Book (SAUS)
PSB............ Protected Specimen Brush [*Medicine*]
PSB............ Protein S Beta (DMAA)
PSB............ PS Booster (SAUS)
PSB............ PS Business Parks, Inc. [*AMEX symbol*] (SPSG)
PSB............ Psychological Services Bureau (AEBS)
PSB............ Psychological Strategy Board [*Military*] (LAIN)
PSB............ Public Safety Building (SARE)
PSB............ Public Security Bureau (SAUS)
PSB............ Public Service Board (NADA)
PSBA.......... Pennsylvania School Boards Association (SAUS)
PSBA.......... Power-Specific Biological Activity [*Engine emissions testing*]
PSBA.......... Proceedings of the Society of Biblical Archaeology (SAUS)
PSBA.......... Public School Bursars' Association [*British*] (BI)
PSBBF........ Pearl S. Buck Birthplace Foundation (EA)
PSBBrc........ Peoples Savings Bank of Brockton [*Associated Press*] (SAG)
PSBCA........ Painted Soda Bottles Collectors Association (EA)
PSBCA........ Postal Service Board of Contract Appeals (AAGC)
PSBDIR........ Program Specification Block Directory (SAUS)
PSbetaG...... Pregnancy-Specific Beta-1-Glycoprotein [*Medicine*] (DMAA)
PSBF.......... Pearl S. Buck Foundation (EA)
PSBG.......... Pregnancy-Specific beta-Glycoprotein [*Gynecology*]
PSBGEN...... Program Specification Block Generator (VLIE)
PSBGEN...... PSG Generation (SAUS)
PSBH.......... Pad Safety in Blockhouse
PSBH.......... Phonon Side-Band Hole [*Spectroscopy*]
PSBI.......... Performance Standardization Branch Instruction (SAA)
PSBK.......... Progressive Bank [*NASDAQ symbol*] (TTSB)
PSBK.......... Progressive Bank, Inc. [*Pawling, NY*] [*NASDAQ symbol*] (NQ)
PSBL.......... Possible (FAAC)
PSBLS........ Permanent Space Based Logistics System
PSBLS........ Permanent Space-Based Logistics System (SAUS)
PSBMA........ Professional Services Business Management Association [*Later, PSMA*] (EA)
PsbMV........ Pea Seed-Borne Mosaic Virus
PSBNAME.... Program Specification Block Name [*Computer science*] (MHDB)
PSBO.......... Partial Small Bowel Obstruction [*Medicine*] (MEDA)
PSBO.......... Public Savings Bond Office (SAUS)
PSBP.......... PS Business Parks, Inc. [*Associated Press*] (SAG)
PSBPrB........ Pub Sv Colo, 8.40% Pfd [*NYSE symbol*] (TTSB)
PSBR.......... Pennsylvania State University Breazeale Nuclear Reactor [*Research center*] (RCD)
PSBR.......... Public Sector Borrowing Requirement
PSBR.......... Pyridine Styrene Butadiene Rubber (SAUS)
PSBR.......... Vinylpyridine-Styrene-Butadiene Rubber (SAUS)
PSBS.......... Phoenix Society for Burn Survivors (EA)
PSBT.......... Pilot Self-Briefing Terminal [*Aviation*] (FAAC)
PSBU.......... Propeller Shaft Bearing Unit [*Truck engineering*]
PSBU.......... Public Sector and Broadcasting Union [*Australia*]
PSBUS........ Path Selection Bus (SAUS)
PSBV.......... Public Service Board Victoria [*Australia*]
PSC............ Congolese Socialist Party [*Zaire*] [*Political party*] (PD)
psc............ geomagnetic pulsation (SAUS)
PSC............ Isla De Pascua [*Easter Island*] [*Seismograph station code, US Geological Survey*] [*Closed*] (SEIS)
PSC............ Pacifc Sea Council (SAUS)
PSC............ Pacific Salmon Commission (EA)
PSC............ Pacific Science Center
PSC............ Pacific Science Council
PSC............ Pacific South Coast Freight Bureau, San Francisco CA [*STAC*]
PSC............ Pacific Studies Center (EA)
PSC............ Packet Switching Center (VLIE)
PSC............ Pakistan Shipping Corp. (SAUS)
PSC............ Palaeontological Society of China (BUAC)
PSC............ Palestine Solidarity Campaign (BUAC)
PSC............ Palestine Solidarity Committee [*Defunct*] (EA)

PSC	Palmer Skin Conductance
PSC	Palynological Society of China (QUAC)
PSC	Paper Skip Character [Computer science] (VLIE)
PSC	Papillary Serous Cyst [Medicine] (MELL)
PSC	Parallel Switch Control (MCD)
PSC	Parallel to Serial Converter
PSC	Parallel to Series Converter
PSC	Parents Sharing Custody (EA)
PSC	Partido Social Conservador Colombiano [Colombian Social Conservative Party] [Political party] (EY)
PSC	Partido Social Cristiano [Social Christian Party] [Ecuador] [Political party] (PPW)
PSC	Partido Social Cristiano [Social Christian Party] [Bolivia] [Political party]
PSC	Partido Social Cristiano [Social Christian Party] [Guatemala] [Political party] (PPW)
PSC	Partido Socialcristiano Nicaraguense [Nicaraguan Social Christian Party] [Political party] (PPW)
PSC	Partido Socialista de Catalunya [Catalan Socialist Party] [Spain] [Political party] (PPE)
PSC	Parti Socialiste Caledonien [New Caledonia] [Political party] (FEA)
PSC	Parti Socialiste Camerounais [Cameroon Socialist Party] [Political party]
PSC	Parti Socialiste Centrafricain [Central African Socialist Party] [Political party] (PD)
PSC	Pasco [Washington] [Airport symbol] (OAG)
PSC	Pasco, WA [Location identifier] [FAA] (FAAL)
PSC	Passaic Byzantine [Diocesan abbreviation] [New Jersey] (TOCD)
PSC	Passed Staff College [British]
PSC	Passenger Services Conference [IATA] (DS)
psc	Passes Staff College [British] (WA)
PSC	Patriot Steering Committee
PSC	Paul Smiths College [New York]
PSC	Payphone Speech Circuit (SAUS)
PSC	Peacetime Subcontract
PSC	Peachtree Support Center (SAUS)
PSC	Pembroke State College [North Carolina]
PSC	Peralta Shipping Corp. (SAUS)
PSC	Percentage of Successful Collisions [Obstetrics]
PSC	Performance Seeking Control (SAUS)
PSC	Performing Support Center (SAUS)
PSC	Periodic Surveillance Committees (SAUS)
PSC	Permanent Split Capacitor (IAA)
PSC	Personal Service Contract (SAUS)
PSC	Personal Service Corporation (EBF)
PSC	Personal Services Contractor
PSC	Personal Super Computer (SAUS)
PSC	Personal Supercomputer [Culler Scientific Systems Corp.]
PSC	Personnel Service Center [or Company] [Military] (INF)
PSC	Personnel Status Change (KSC)
PSC	Personnel Subsystem Cost
PSC	Personnel Support Company [Army]
PSC	Per Standard Compass [Navigation]
PSC	Petroleum Supply Command (SAUS)
PSC	Petty Sessional Court [British] (ROG)
PSC	Phase-Sensitive Converter
PSC	Philadelphia Service Center [IRS]
PSC	Philadelphia Suburban Corp. [NYSE symbol] (SPSG)
PSC	Philander Smith College [Little Rock, AR]
PSC	Phila Suburban [NYSE symbol] (TTSB)
PSC	Philippine Sugar Commission (EA)
PSC	Phonemic Spelling Council [Defunct] (EA)
PSC	Photographic Sciences Corp. (EFIS)
PSC	Photosensitive Cell (IEEE)
PSC	Phylogenetic Species Concept [Biology]
PSC	Physical Sciences Center
PSC	Physical Sciences Committee [Terminated, 1977] [NASA] (EGAO)
PSC	Physical Security/Pilferage Code (MCD)
PSC	Physical Signaling Components Sublayer (SAUS)
PSC	Pipe Smokers' Council (BUAC)
Psc	Pisces [Constellation]
PSC	Pittsburgh Scientific Center (SAUS)
PSC	Pittsburgh Steel Co. (SAUS)
PSC	Pittsburgh Supercomputer (or Supercomputing) Center (SAUS)
PSC	Pittsburgh Supercomputing Center [National Science Foundation] [Research center] (RCD)
PSC	Pittsburgh Superconducting Center [Pennsylvania] (GRD)
PSC	Plant Simulation Code (ABAC)
pSC	Plasmid Stanley Cohen [Molecular biology]
PSC	Platform Support Center [NASA] (SSD)
PSC	Pluripotent Stem Cell [Cytology]
PSC	Plutonium Stripping Concentrate [Nuclear energy] (NRCH)
PSC	Point Shipping Co. [Steamship] (MHDW)
PSC	Point Stress Criterion (SAUS)
PSC	Polaroid Stereoscopic Chroncyclegraph
PSC	Polar Science Center [University of Washington] [Research center] (RCD)
PSC	Polar Stratospheric Cloud [Meteorology]
PSC	Police Staff College (SAUS)
PSC	Polish Steamship Co. (SAUS)
PSC	Population Studies Center [University of Michigan] [Research center] (RCD)
PSC	Porcelain on Steel Council [Defunct] (EA)
PSC	Porcelain-on-Steel Council (SAUS)
PSC	Porous Silicon Capacitor (AAEL)

PSC	Porter-Silber Chromogen [Medicine] (MAE)
PSC	Portland Society for Calligraphy (EA)
PSC	Port Service Charge (SAUS)
PSC	Postal Service Center (AFM)
PSC	Posterior Subcapsular Cataracts [Ophthalmology]
PSC	Post-Storage Checkout [NASA] (KSC)
PSC	Postsynaptic Current [Neurophysiology]
PSC	Potentiometer Strip Chart
PSC	Potomac State College [of West Virginia University]
PSC	Power Supply Calibrator
PSC	Power System Communications (IAA)
PSC	Power System Control (VLIE)
PSC	Prairie Swine Centre [University of Saskatchewan] [Canada] (IRC)
PSC	Prairie Swine Centre, Inc. [Canada] (BUAC)
PSC	Preferred Semiconductor Circuit [Electronics] (IAA)
PSC	Pressure Suit Circuit (KSC)
PSC	Pressure System Control (AAG)
PSC	Prestressed Cement (EDCT)
PSC	Prestressed Concrete (ADA)
PSC	Presumptive Hematopoietic Stem Cell
PSC	Price Signal Code [Military] (AABC)
PSC	Primary Sclerosing Cholangitis [Medicine]
PSC	Primary Store Capacity (SAUS)
PSC	Primary Subordinate Commands (SAUS)
PSC	Prime Service Contractor (SAUS)
PSC	Prime Systems Contractor
PSC	Principal Surface Combatant (MILB)
PSC	Principle Surface Combatants (SAUS)
PSC	Print Scan Counter [Computer science] (VLIE)
PSC	Print Server Command (SAUS)
PSC	Private Secretary's Certificate [British] (DI)
PSC	Private Sector Council (EA)
PSC	Probability Saturation Counter (SAUS)
PSC	PROBE [Program Optimization and Budget Evaluation] Steering Committee [Military]
PSC	Problem Specification Card (SAUS)
PSC	Processing and Spectral Control
PSC	Processing Service Centers [Social Security Administration]
PSC	Process Schedule Control (SAUS)
PSC	Procurement Source Code (AFM)
PSC	Procurement Strategy Corp. (SAUS)
PSC	Product and Service Code (AAGC)
PSC	Production Schedule Confirmation (SAUS)
PSC	Production Scheduling and Control (IAA)
PSC	Product Safety Committee [New South Wales, Australia]
PSC	Product Service Center (SAUS)
PSC	Product Support Confidential (AAG)
PSC	Professional Service Corporation [Medicine] (HCT)
PSC	Professional Services Corp. (SAUS)
PSC	Professional Services Council [Washington, DC] (EA)
PSC	Programmable Sample Changer [Spectroscopy]
PSC	Programmable System Component (TIMI)
PSC	Programming Sciences Corp. (SAUS)
PSC	Program Schedule Chart (NASA)
PSC	Program Sequence Control (NITA)
PSC	Program Service Center [Social Security Administration] (OICC)
PSC	Program Site Coordinator [Environmental science] (EPAT)
PSC	Program Standards Checker [Computer science]
PSC	Program Status Chart [Computer science]
PSC	Program Structure Code (AFM)
PSC	Program Support Center
PSC	Program Support Contract (SSD)
PSC	Program Support Contractor (SAUS)
PSC	Program Support Coordinator (SAUS)
PSC	Program Switching Center [Computer science] (IAA)
PSC	Prohibited Species Catch (SAUS)
PSC	Project Systems Control (MCD)
PSC	Propagating Space Charge (PDAA)
PSC	Protosolar Cloud [Astronomy]
PSC	Prototype System Characteristics
PSC	PSC, Inc. [Associated Press] (SAG)
PSC	Pseudo-Store Cell (SAUS)
PSC	Public Safety Calling system (SAUS)
PSC	Public Service Careers [Program] [Department of Labor]
PSC	Public Service Co.
PSC	Public Service Commission [Canada] (BUAC)
PSC	Public Service Commission [Usually, of a specific state]
PSC	Pulse Shape Control (SAUS)
PSC	Pulse Shape Control Circuit (IAA)
PSC	Pulse Synchronized Contraction [In the vascular system] [Medicine]
PSC	Sandoz AG [Switzerland] [Research code symbol]
PSc	Scranton Public Library, Scranton, PA [Library symbol] [Library of Congress] (LCLS)
PSC	Swarthmore College, Swarthmore, PA [Library symbol] [Library of Congress] [OCLC symbol] (LCLS)
PSCA	Parliamentary Select Committee on Agriculture [British]
PscA	Pisces Austrinus [Constellation]
PSCA	Polish Social and Cultural Association [British] (EAIO)
PSCA	Pressure Suit Conditioning Assembly (MCD)
PSCA	Profit Sharing Council of America (EA)
PSCACM	Permanent Secretariat of the Central American Common Market
PSCAGNT	Podhale Social-Cultural Association of Gypsies in Nowy Targ [Poland] (BUAC)
PSCAN	P-Scanner (SAUS)
PSCAN	Purchase Order Scan

PS Cap	Polystyrene Capacitor (SAUS)
PSCAV	Professional Squash Coaches' Association of Victoria [*Australia*]
PSCB	Padded Sample Collection Bag [*NASA*]
PSCB	Parliamentary Standing Committee on Broadcasting [*Australia*]
PSCB	Presentation Services Command Processor (SAUS)
PSCBG	Paper Shipping-Containers Buyers Group
PSCC	Packaging, Storage, and Containerization Center
PSCC	Photo Systems Controller Console (KSC)
PSCC	Polymer Supply and Characterization Center (SAUS)
PSCC	Posterior Subcapsular Cataract [*Medicine*] (STED)
PSCC	Power System Communications (IAA)
PSCC	Power System Computation Conference
PSCC	Projets de Services Communautaires du Canada
PSC Circuit	Pulse Shape Control Circuit (SAUS)
PSCD	Patrol Service Central Depot (SAUS)
PSCD	Plutonium Stripping Concentration Distillate [*Nuclear energy*] (NRCH)
PSCD	Postcard (VRA)
PSCD	Program for the Study of Crime and Delinquency [*Ohio State University*] [*Research center*] (RCD)
PSCE	Presurgical Coagulation Evaluation [*Medicine*] (DAVI)
PSCEC	Planning Status of Committed Engineering Changes (SAA)
PSCF	Personal Security Clearance File
PSCF	Primary System Control Facility [*Computer science*] (ELAL)
PSCF	Processor Storage Control Function
PSCFB	Pacific South Coast Freight Bureau
PSCFB	Pacific Southcoast Freight Bureau (SAUS)
PSCG	PATRIOT Security Classification Guide (SAUS)
PSCG	Power Supply and Control Gear
PSCG	Power Supply Control Group [*Military*] (CAAL)
PSCH	Periodic Scheduler (SAUS)
PSCH	Postoperative Suprachoroidal Hemorrhage [*Medicine*]
PSChE	Pseudocholinesterase (STED)
PSC-Hi	Friends Historical Library of Swarthmore College, Swarthmore, PA [*Library symbol*] [*Library of Congress*] (LCLS)
PSCI	Perez Self-Concept Inventory [*Psychology*] (EDAC)
PSCI	Plastic Shipping Container Institute (EA)
Psci	Pressure at Slow Component Intercept [*Medicine*] (STED)
PSCI	Primary Self-Concept Inventory [*Psychology*] (EDAC)
PSCJ	Perseverance Society of Carpenters and Joiners [*A union*] [*British*]
PSCJ	Progressive Society of Carpenters and Joiners [*A union*] [*British*]
PSCL	Programmed Sequential Control Language
PSCL	Programmed Sequential Control Logic (SAUS)
PSCL	Propellants System Components Laboratory [*Kennedy Space Center*] [*NASA*]
PSCL	Propellant Systems Cleaning Laboratory [*NASA*] (NASA)
PScL	Scranton Public Library, Scranton, PA [*Library symbol*] [*Library of Congress*] (LCLS)
PScLL	Lackawanna Bar Association Law Library, Scranton, PA [*Library symbol*] [*Library of Congress*] (LCLS)
PSCLS	Potentiostatic Stress Corrosion Life Curve (SAUS)
PScM	Marywood College, Scranton, PA [*Library symbol*] [*Library of Congress*] (LCLS)
PSCM	Pilot Scale Ceramic Melter (ABAC)
PSCM	Pokeweed Activated Spleen Conditioned Medium [*Medicine*] (STED)
PSCM	Process Steering and Control Module [*Telecommunications*] (TEL)
PSCM	Professinal Sports Care Management, Inc. [*NASDAQ symbol*] (SAG)
PSCM	Professional Sports Care Mgmt [*NASDAQ symbol*] (TTSB)
PSC Motor	Permanent Split Capacitor Motor
PSCN	Partido Socialcristiano Nicaraguense [*Nicaraguan Social Christian Party*] [*Political party*] (PPW)
PSCN	Permanent System Control Number (MCD)
PSCN	Preliminary Specification Change Notice [*NASA*] (NASA)
PSCN	Program Support Communication Network (SAUS)
PSCN	Program Support Communications Network (SSD)
PSCN	Program Support Computer Network (SAUS)
PSCN	Proposed Specification Change Notice
PSCNet	Pittsburgh Supercomputing Center Network [*Pennsylvania*]
PSCNET	Pittsburgh Superconducting Center Network
PSCO	Pennsylvania State College of Optometry
PSCO	Personnel Survey Control Officer [*Military*] (AABC)
PSCO	ProtoSource Corp. [*NASDAQ symbol*] (SAG)
PSCOE	Power Sources Center of Excellence
PSCol	Public Service Co. of Colorado [*Associated Press*] (SAG)
P/score	Pressure Score [*Medicine*] (STED)
PSCOU	ProtoSource Corp. Unit [*NASDAQ symbol*] (TTSB)
PSCOW	ProtoSource Corp. Wrrt [*NASDAQ symbol*] (TTSB)
PSCP	Palestine Symphonic Choir Project (EA)
P/S CP	Platoon/Section Command Post
PSCP	Polar Continental Shelf Project [*Canada*]
PSCP	Posterior Subcapsular Cataractous Plaque [*Ophthalmology*] (DAVI)
PSCP	Public School Construction Program (SAUS)
PSCP	Public Service Careers Program [*Department of Labor*]
PSC-P	Swarthmore College Peace Collection, Swarthmore, PA [*Library symbol*] [*Library of Congress*] (LCLS)
PSCPD	Philadelphia Signal Corps Procurement District [*Army*]
PSC-PSOE	Partit dels Socialistes de Catalunya [*Party of Socialists of Catalonia*] [*Political party*] (PPW)
PSCPT	Preschool Self-Concept Picture Test [*Psychology*]
PSCR	Permanent Scratch File [*Computer science*]
PSCR	Photo-Selective Copper Reduction [*For circuit board manufacture*]
PSCR	Priority System Change Request
PSCR	Production Schedule Completion Report [*DoD*]
PSCR	Programmable Scanning Receiver (DWSG)
PSCR	Public Service Commission Reports [*A publication*] (DLA)
PSCRC	Portable Small Computer Requirements Contract (SAUS)

PSCRD	Program Support Communications Requirements Document (SSD)
PSCRL	Patent Security Category Review List (AAGC)
PSCRT	Passive Satellite Communications Research Terminal (SAA)
PSCS	Pacific Scatter Communications System [*Air Force*] (CET)
PSCS	Packet-Switched Communication System (CIST)
PSCS	Photographic Sensor Control System (SAUS)
PSCS	Program Support Control System
PSCS	Pulse Signature Classification System (SAUS)
Pscs calculator	Pascals calculator (SAUS)
PSCT	Peripheral Stem Cell Transplant [*Medicine*] (MELL)
PSCT	Permanent Service on Crustal Thickness (SAUS)
PSCT	Politte Sentence Completion Test (TES)
PSCT	Polymer Stabilized Cholesteric Texture (SAUS)
PSCU	Power Supply Control Unit (CET)
PSCU	Power-Supply Control Unit
PSCU	Private Sector Casemix Unit (ADWA)
PScU	University of Scranton, Scranton, PA [*Library symbol*] [*Library of Congress*] (LCLS)
PSCUS	Peters' United States Surpeme Court Reports [*26-41 United States*] [*A publication*] (DLA)
PSCX	PSC, Inc. [*Formerly, Photographic Sciences Corp.*] [*NASDAQ symbol*] (NQ)
PSD	Destour Socialist Party [*Tunisia*] [*Political party*] (PD)
PSD	Doctor of Political Science
Ps D	Doctor of Psychology
Ps D	Doctor of Psychology in Metaphysics
PSD	Doctor of Public Service
PSD	Packed Switched Data
PSD	Packet Switched Data (SAUS)
PSD	Parallel Shift and Dwell (SAUS)
PSD	Partial Sleep Deprivation (MELL)
PSD	Particle Size Distribution
PSD	Partido Socialdemocracia [*Social Democratic Party*] [*Chile*] [*Political party*] (EY)
PSD	Partido Social Democrata [*Social Democratic Party*] [*Spain*] [*Political party*] (PPE)
PSD	Partido Social Democrata [*Social Democratic Party*] [*Mexico*] [*Political party*] (PPW)
PSD	Partido Social Democrata [*Social Democratic Party*] [*Bolivia*] [*Political party*] (PPW)
PSD	Partido Social Democratico [*Social Democratic Party*] [*Nicaragua*] [*Political party*] (PPW)
PSD	Partido Social Democratico [*Social Democratic Party*] [*El Salvador*] [*Political party*]
PSD	Partido Social Democratico [*Social Democratic Party*] [*Brazil*] [*Political party*]
PSD	Partido Socialista Democratico [*Social Democratic Party*] [*Guatemala*] [*Political party*] (PD)
PSD	Partido Socialista Democratico [*Social Democratic Party*] [*Argentina*] [*Political party*] (EY)
PSD	Parti Social-Democrate [*Algeria*] [*Political party*] (EY)
PSD	Parti Social-Democrate [*Social Democratic Party*] [*France*] [*Political party*] (PPW)
PSD	Parti Social Democrate de Madagascar et des Comores [*Social Democratic Party of Madagascar and Comores*]
PSD	Parti Social-Democratie [*Benin*] [*Political party*] (EY)
PSD	Parti Socialiste Democratique [*Cameroon*] [*Political party*] (EY)
PSD	Passed (ROG)
PSD	Passing Scene Display
PSD	Past Start Date
PSD	Patent Search Documentation (NITA)
PSD	Paternal Sister Dam (OA)
PSD	Patient Symptom Diary
PSD	Pay Supply Depot (WDAA)
PSD	Peptone-Starch-Dextrose [*Microbiology*] (MAE)
PSD	Performance and Security Document (SAUS)
PSD	Perform Security block Defence (SAUS)
PSD	Permanent Signal Detection [*Telecommunications*] (TEL)
PSD	Personal Services Department [*Navy*] [*British*]
PSD	Personal Smoke Device
PSD	Personnel Services Division [*Army*]
PSD	Personnel Support Detachment (DOMA)
PSD	Personnel System [*or Subsystem*] Development (AAG)
PSD	Pescadero [*California*] [*Seismograph station code, US Geological Survey*] (SEIS)
PSD	Pesticides Safety Directorate (BUAC)
PSD	Petroleum Safety Data [*American Petroleum Institute*]
PSD	Petroleum Storage Depot (SAUS)
PSD	Petty Session Division [*Legal term*] (DLA)
PSD	Phase-Sensitive Demodulator [*or Detector*]
PSD	Phase-Sensitive Detection (SAUS)
PSD	Phase-Sensitive Detector (SAUS)
PSD	Phase Shifter Driver
PSD	Philadelphia Signal Depot (SAUS)
PSD	Philatelic Sales Division [*Formerly, PSB*] [*US Postal Service*]
PSD	Photoconductive, Semiconductive Device
PSD	Photon Stimulated Desorption [*For analysis of surfaces*]
PSD	Photo-Sensitive Detection (or Detector) (SAUS)
PSD	Photoshop image format (SAUS)
PSD	Photo-Stimulated Desorption (SAUS)
PSD	Pictorialized Scatter Diagram [*Botany*]
PSD	Pitch Servo Drive
PSD	Pittsburgh Steamship Division (SAUS)
PSD	Planning Systems Division (COE)
PSD	Platform Specific Driver [*Computer science*]

PSD .... Polysilicon Diode (IAA)
PSD .... Polystyrene, Deuterated [*Organic chemistry*]
PSD .... Pore Size Distribution
PSD .... Port Said [*Egypt*] [*Airport symbol*] (AD)
PSD .... Port Security Detachment [*Military*] (GFGA)
PSD .... Port Sharing Device (ACAE)
PSD .... Port Status Display (AAEL)
PSD .... Position-Sensitive Detection (or Detector) (SAUS)
PSD .... Position Sensitive Light Detector (IAA)
PSD .... Postal Security Device [*Computer science*]
PSD .... Post Sending Delay
PSD .... Poststenotic Dilatation [*Medicine*] (MELL)
PSD .... Postsurgical Distress [*Medicine*] (MELL)
PSD .... Postsynaptic Density [*Neurophysiology*]
PSD .... Power Sliding Door [*Automotive engineering*]
PSD .... Power Spectral [*or Spectrum*] Density
PSD .... Power Spectrum Distribution [*Electronics*]
PSD .... Power Supply & Distribution (SAUS)
PSD .... Power System Demonstrator (SAUS)
PSD .... Preferred Sea Duty
PSD .... Prepare Simulation Data (ACAE)
PSD .... Pre-Shipment Document (SAUS)
PSD .... Pressure-Sensitive Devices (MCD)
PSD .... Prevention of Significant Deterioration [*Environmental Protection Agency*]
PSD .... Prevent Significant Deterioration
PSD .... Primary Standard Data (SAUS)
PSD .... Printed Side Down [*Graphic arts*] (DGA)
PSD .... Printer Sharing Device (SAUS)
PSD .... Printing Systems Division (NITA)
PSD .... Private-Sector Development (ECON)
PSD .... Procedural Support Data
PSD .... Processing Status Display [*NASA*]
PSD .... Process Specification Departure (SAA)
PSD .... Procurement Surveys Division [*NASA*] (MCD)
PSD .... Professional Service Dates [*Formerly, ADBD*]
PSD .... Professional Systems Division [*American Institute of Architects Service Corp.*] [*Information service or system*] (IID)
PSD .... Programmable System Design [*Computer science*] (AGLO)
PSD .... Programmed Slip Differential [*Automotive engineering*]
PSD .... Programmers Supplementary Documents (SAUS)
PSD .... Programme Support and Development [*British*]
PSD .... Program Status Documents [*Computer science*]
PSD .... Program Status Double Word (SAUS)
PSD .... Program Status Doubleword
PSD .... Program Support Document (MUGU)
PSD .... Program System Description (SAA)
PSD .... Program Systems Division [*Environmental Protection Agency*] (GFGA)
PSD .... Promotion Service Date
PSD .... Propellant Slosh Dynamics
PSD .... Propellant Storage Depot [*NASA*]
PSD .... Proportional Stock Density [*Pisciculture*]
PSD .... Propulsion System Demonstrator [*Marine Corps*] (DOMA)
PSD .... Protective Serum Dilution
PSD .... Protective Structures Division [*Office of Civil Defense*]
PSD .... Pseudosingle Domain [*Behavior of grains in rocks*] [*Geophysics*]
PSD .... Pseudo Stow Document (DNAB)
PSD .... Public Safety Division (SAUS)
PSD .... Puget Sound P&L [*NYSE symbol*] (TTSB)
PSD .... Puget Sound Power & Light Co. [*NYSE symbol*] (SPSG)
PSD .... Pulse Shape Discrimination (or Discriminator) (SAUS)
PSD .... Pulse Shape Discriminator
PSD .... Pure Screw Dislocation
PSDA .... Paper Sack Development Association [*British*] (BI)
PSDA .... Partial Source Data Automation (NVT)
PSDA .... Particle Size Distribution Analysis [*Statistics*]
PSDA .... Patient Self-Determination Act
PSDA .... Post-Storm Data Acquisition (SAUS)
P/SDA .... Power/Signal Distribution Assembly
PSDA .... Psychoactive Substance Dependence and Abuse (MELL)
PSDB .... Partido da Social Democracia Brasiliera [*Brazilian Social Democratic Party*] [*Political party*] (EY)
PSDB .... Physical Segment Descriptor Block (SAUS)
PSDB .... Police Scientific Development Branch [*British*] (WDAA)
PSDC .... Pennsylvania State Data Center [*Middletown*] [*Information service or system*] (IID)
PSDC .... Plant Sciences Data Center [*Formerly, Plant Records Center*] [*American Horticultural Society*] [*Mt. Vernon, VA*]
PSDC .... Power Sprayer and Duster Council (EA)
PSDC .... Protective Structures Development Center [*Military*]
PSDC .... Public Switched (or Switching) Digital Capability (SAUS)
PSD Circuit... Permanent Signal Detection Circuit (SAUS)
PSDD .... Planetary Science Data Dictionary (SAUS)
PSDD .... Preliminary System Design Description [*Nuclear energy*] (NRCH)
PSDDS .... Pilot [*or Public*] Switched Digital Data Service [*Telecommunications*] (TEL)
PS de G .... Partido dos Socialistas de Galicia [*Spain*] [*Political party*] (EY)
Psdepgr .... Pseudepigrapha (BJA)
PSDF .... People's Self-Defense Force [*South Vietnamese militia force*] (VNW)
PSDF .... Popular Self-Defense Force [*Local armed units protecting Vietnamese hamlets*]
PSDF .... Propulsion Systems Development Facility (KSC)
PSDI .... Partido Social Democratico Independente [*Independent Social Democratic Party*] [*Portugal*] [*Political party*] (PPE)

PSDI .... Partito Socialista Democratico Italiano [*Italian Social Democratic Party*] [*Political party*]
PSDI .... Presence Sensing Device Initiation (SARE)
PSDI .... Project Software & Development, Inc. [*NASDAQ symbol*] (SAG)
PSDI .... Project Software & Dvlp [*NASDAQ symbol*] (TTSB)
PSDIAD .... Photostimulated Desorption Ion Angular Distribution [*Surface analysis*]
PSDIS .... Partito Socialista Democratico Indipendente Sammarinese [*Independent Social Democratic Party of San Marino*] [*Political party*] (PPE)
PSDL .... Product Support Data List (SAUS)
PSDL .... Region 4 PSD Log System (SAUS)
PSdM .... Mennonite Publishing House, Scottsdale, PA [*Library symbol*] [*Library of Congress*] (LCLS)
PSDM .... Presentation Services for Data Management (MHDB)
PSD(MS)..... Photon Stimulated Desorption (Mass Spectroscopy) (MCD)
PSDN .... Packed Switched Data Network (SAUS)
PSDN .... Packet Swiched Data Network (SAUS)
PSDN .... Packet Switched Data Network [*Telecommunications*]
PSDN .... Packet Switched Digital Network (SAUS)
PSDN .... Packet Switching Data System (SAUS)
PSDN .... Packet-Switching Data Network [*Computer science*] (DOM)
PSDN .... Packet Switching Digital Network (SAUS)
PSDN .... Public Switched Data Network (NITA)
PSDN .... Public Switched (or Switching) Digital Network (SAUS)
PSDNA .... Power System Dynamic Network Analyzer (SAUS)
Psdo .... Pseudonym (SAUS)
PSDOS .... Public Switched Digital Data Service (SAUS)
PSDP .... Payload Station Distribution Panel [*NASA*] (MCD)
PSDP .... Personnel Subsystem Development Plan
PSDP .... Phase Structure and Dependency Parser (SAUS)
PSDP .... Phrase Structure and Dependency Parser (DIT)
PSDP .... Professional Skills Development Program [*Bureau of the Census*] (GFGA)
PSDP .... Programmable Signal Data Processor (SAUS)
PSDPC .... Polar Satellite Data Processing Centre (CARB)
PSDPr .... Puget Sound P&L 7.875% Pfd [*NYSE symbol*] (TTSB)
PSDPrB .... Puget Sound P&L Adj Rt'B'Pfd [*NYSE symbol*] (TTSB)
PSDR .... Planning and Scheduling Document Record [*NASA*] (NASA)
PSDR .... Process Storage Data Register (IAA)
PSDR .... Program Status Doubleword Register [*Computer science*] (MHDB)
PSDR .... Public Sector Debt Repayment [*British*] (ECON)
PSDS .... Packet Switch Data System [*Information retrieval*] (IID)
PSDS .... Packet Switched Data Service [*Telecommunications*] (TEL)
PSDS .... Partito Socialista Democratico Sammarinese [*Social Democratic Party of San Marino*] [*Political party*] (PPE)
PSDS .... Passing Scene Display System
PSDS .... Permanently Separated from Duty Station [*Military*]
PSDS .... Postal Source Data System [*U.S. Postal Service*] (CIST)
PSDS .... Prison Service Drug Strategy (WDAA)
PSDS .... Public Switched Data Service [*Telecommunications*]
PSDS .... Public Switched Digital Service [*Computer science*] (TNIG)
PSDS Matrix... Positive Semi-Definite Symmetric Matrix (SAUS)
PSDSP .... Pious Society of the Daughters of Saint Paul [*See also FSP*] [*Rome, Italy*] (EAIO)
PSDT .... President (ROG)
PSDTC .... Pacific Securities Depository Trust Co.
PSDTN .... Packet Switched Data Transmission Network (SAUS)
PSDU .... Personnel Services Delivery Unit (HEAS)
PSDU .... Polish Social Democratic Union [*Political party*]
PSDU .... Power Switching Distribution Unit
PSDU .... Presentation Service Data Unit [*Telecommunications*] (OSI)
PSDUPD ...... Port of San Diego Unified Port District (SAUS)
PSDVB .... Poly(styrene-Divinylbenzene) [*Organic chemistry*]
PSE .... Aeroservicio Sipse SA de CV [*Mexico*] [*ICAO designator*] (FAAC)
PSE .... Pacific School of English [*Australia*]
PSE .... Pacific Stock Exchange (EA)
PSE .... Packet Switched Exchange (SAUS)
PSE .... Packet Switch Exchange (SAUS)
PSE .... Packet Switching Exchange [*Telecommunications*]
PSE .... Pale Soft Exudative [*Pork*]
PSE .... Paper Surface Efficiency (DGA)
PSE .... Partido Socialista de Euskadi [*Basque Socialist Party*] [*Spain*] [*Political party*] (EY)
PSE .... Partido Socialista Ecuatoriano [*Ecuadorean Socialist Party*] [*Political party*] (PPW)
PSE .... Passage
PSE .... Passive Seismic Experiment [*NASA*]
PSE .... Passive Smoke Exposure (MELL)
PSE .... Path Switching Element (SAUS)
PSE .... Payload Service Equipment [*NASA*] (MCD)
PSE .... Payload Service (or Servicing) Equipment (SAUS)
PSE .... Payload Servicing Equipment [*NASA*] (NAKS)
PSE .... Payload Support Equipment [*NASA*] (MCD)
PSE .... Peculiar Support Equipment [*NASA*] (NASA)
PSE .... Penicillin-Sensitive Enzymes [*Biochemistry*]
PSE .... Personal and Social Education (DET)
PSE .... Personal Security Environment (SAUS)
PSE .... Personnel Subsystem Elements [*Army*] (AABC)
PSE .... Perth Stock Exchange [*Australia*]
PSE .... Phase Shifter, Electronic (SAUS)
PSE .... Phase-Shifter, Electronic
PSE .... Philadelphia Stock Exchange
PSE .... Philippine Stock Exchange
PSE .... Photosensitive Epilepsy

PSE............ Physical Security Equipment [*Army*] (RDA)
PSE............ Physiological Systems Experiment (SAUS)
PSE............ Phytochemical Society of Europe (EA)
PSE............ Pigin Signed English
PSE............ Pi Sigma Epsilon (EA)
PSE............ Pitch Steering Error
pse............ Planed and Square-Edge (DAC)
PSE............ Planed and Square Edged (SAUS)
PSE............ Pleasant Saturday Evenings
PSE............ Pleasant Sunday Evenings (ROG)
PSE............ Please (MDG)
PSE............ Pneumatic System Equipment [*Automotive engineering*]
PSE............ Point of Subjective Equality [*Psychology*]
PSE............ Polestar Exploration, Inc. [*Vancouver Stock Exchange symbol*]
PSE............ Ponce [*Puerto Rico*] [*Airport symbol*] (OAG)
PSE............ Portal Systemic Encephalopathy [*Medicine*]
PSE............ Post-Separation Employment
PSE............ Postshunt Encephalopathy [*Medicine*]
PSE............ Power Spectrum Equalization [*Electronics*]
PSE............ Power Switching Electronics (ACAE)
PSE............ Power System Engineering (MCD)
PSE............ Present State Examination [*Medicine*] (DMAA)
PSE............ Pressurized Subcritical Experiment [*Nuclear energy*]
PSE............ Pre-Stamped Envelope
PSE............ Prevention of Stripping Equipment (NATG)
PSE............ Principal Staff Element [*Defense Supply Agency*]
PSE............ Print Scan Emitter [*Computer science*] (VLIE)
PSE............ Priority Standardization Effort [*Army*] (AABC)
PSE............ Prison Service Establishment (AIE)
PSE............ Probability of Successful Engagement [*Military*] (CAAL)
PSE............ Processor Speed Enhancement (SAUS)
PSE............ Process Systems Engineering
PSE............ Producer Subsidy Equivalent [*OECD model for the study of farm-support policies in the EC, Japan, America, Canada, Australia, and New Zealand*]
PSE............ Product Support Engineering (MCD)
PSE............ Programmed System Evolution (MCD)
PSE............ Programming Support Environment
PSE............ Program Sub-Element (SAUS)
PSE............ Program Supplement (COE)
PSE............ Protein Separation Efficiency [*Food technology*]
PSE............ Proximal Sequence Element [*Genetics*]
PSE............ Proximal Stimulating Electrode (DB)
PSE............ Psychological Stress Evaluation
PSE............ Psychological Stress Evaluator [*Lie detector*]
PSE............ Public Sector [*or Service*] Employment
PSE............ Public Service Electric & Gas Co., Newark, NJ [*OCLC symbol*] (OCLC)
PSE............ Public Service Employment (EBF)
PSE............ Pulse Sense
PSE............ Purified Spleen Extract [*Medicine*] (DMAA)
PSEA............ Pacific and Southeast Asia (DNAB)
PSEA............ Pennsylvania State Education Association (SAUS)
PSEA............ Physical Security Equipment Agency [*Army*]
PSEA............ Pleaters, Stitchers, and Embroiderers Association (EA)
PSEAG .... Physical Security Equipment Action Group [*Department of Defense*] (SEWL)
PSE & C ..... Power Supply Engineering and Construction [*Nuclear energy*] (NRCH)
PSE & G ...... Public Service Electric & Gas Co.
PSEB............ Poisoning Surveillance and Epidemiology Branch [*Defunct*] (EA)
PSEB............ Punjab State Electricity Board [*India*] (BUAC)
PSEBM......... Proceedings of the Society for Experimental Biology and Medicine [*A publication*]
P/SEC........... Personal Secretary (DCTA)
psec............ Picosecond [*Alternative of preferred ps*] (IDOE)
PSEC............ Picosecond [*One trillionth of a second*]
PSECT......... Program Section (VLIE)
PSECU .... Pennsylvania State Employees Credit Union (SAUS)
PSED........... Preliminary Systems Engineering Design
PSEDGP...... Perth South East Division Division of General Practice (SAUS)
PSEF........... Pennsylvania Science and Engineering Foundation
PSEF........... Plastic Surgery Educational Foundation (EA)
PSEFA......... Production Standard Evolution Form-Airframe (SAUS)
PSEFC......... Production Standard Evolution Form-Engines (SAUS)
PSEG .... PSE & G Capital Trust [*Associated Press*]
PSEG .... Public Service Electric & Gas Co. [*Associated Press*] (SAG)
PSEG .... Public Service Enterprise Group, Inc. (EFIS)
PSEK........... Probability of Single Shot Engagement Kill [*Military*]
PSEK........... Progressive Symmetrical Erythrokeratoderma [*Medicine*] (DMAA)
PSEL........... Plant Specific Emission Limit (SARE)
PSEL........... Presentation Selector (VLIE)
PSeIS........... Susquehanna University, Selinsgrove, PA [*Library symbol*] [*Library of Congress*] (LCLS)
PSEM........... Philips Scanning Electron Microscope (SAUS)
PSEMA........ Parti Social d'Education des Masses Africaines [*African Party for Social Education of the Masses*] [*Burkina Faso*]
PSE Muscle... Pale, Soft Exudative Muscle (SAUS)
PSEN .... Pupils with Special Educational Needs (SAUS)
PseOG .... Pease Oil & Gas Co. [*Associated Press*]
PSEP........... Passive Seismic Experiments Package [*NASA*]
PSEP........... Physical Security Evaluation Procedure [*US Army Construction Engineering Research Laboratory*] (RDA)
PSEQ .... Pupil Services Expectation Questionnaire
PSER .... Peak Systolic Ejection Rate (SAUS)

PSER .... Production Support and Equipment Replacement (SAUS)
PSERC .... Public Sector Economics Research Centre [*University of Leicester*] [*British*] (CB)
PSERVER.... Print Server [*Computer science*] (VLIE)
PSES........... P-bit Severely Errored Seconds (SAUS)
PSES........... Pretreatment Standards for Existing Sources [*Environmental Protection Agency*]
PSET........... Permanent Service on Earth Tides (SAUS)
PSET........... Pre-Selection English Test [*Australia*]
P Sett .... Previous Settlement (SAUS)
PSEU........... Production Support Equipment Unit (MCD)
PSEU........... Public Service Executive Union [*Ireland*] (BUAC)
PSEU........... Public Services Employees' Union [*Afghanistan*] (BUAC)
PSEU........... Pylon Servo Electronic Unit (SAUS)
pseud........... pseudandry (SAUS)
Pseud........... Pseudepigrapha (BJA)
pseud........... pseudepigraphy (SAUS)
pseud........... pseudograph (SAUS)
pseud........... pseudojyn (SAUS)
pseud........... Pseudonym (BEE)
PSEUD........ Pseudonym
pseud........... pseudonyma (SAUS)
Pseudep....... Pseudepigrapha (BJA)
PSEUDO...... Pseudonym [*Legal shorthand*] (LWAP)
PSEUDOEPH... Pseudoephedrine Hydrochloride (SAUS)
PSEUDOEPH SULF... Pseudoephedrine Sulfate (SAUS)
PSEUDOEPH TAN... Pseudoephedrine Tannate (SAUS)
PSEW........... Project on the Status and Education of Women (EA)
PSewD......... Dixmont State Hospital, Sewickley, PA [*Library symbol*] [*Library of Congress*] (LCLS)
PSF............ Pakistan Science Foundation
PSF............ Panama Sea Frontier
PSF............ Panhandle & Santa Fe Railway Co. [*AAR code*]
PSF............ Parents for Safe Food [*An association*] (BUAC)
PSF............ Parti Social Francais [*French Social Party*] [*Political party*] (PPE)
PSF............ Passive Solar Foundation [*Defunct*] (EA)
PSF............ Pattern Sensitive Fault (SAUS)
PSF............ Payload Servicing Fixture (SAUS)
PSF............ Payload Structure Fuel [*Ratio*]
PSF............ Peptide Supply Factor [*Biochemistry*]
PSF............ Performance Shaping Factor [*Engineering*]
PSF............ Performance Shaping Factors (SAUS)
PSF............ Permanent Signal Finder
PSF............ Permanent Swap File (SAUS)
PSF............ Personal Silicon Foundry (IAA)
PSF............ Per Square Foot (ADA)
PSF............ Phelps-Stokes Fund (SAUS)
PSF............ Philippine Sea Frontier
PSF............ Pittsfield [*Massachusetts*] [*Airport symbol*] (AD)
PSF............ Pittsfield, MA [*Location identifier*] [*FAA*] (FAAL)
PSF............ Plutonium Stripper Feed [*Nuclear energy*] (NRCH)
PSF............ Point Spread Function
PSF............ Polystyrene Foam (SAUS)
PSF............ Polysulfon (SAUS)
PSF............ Polysulfone [*Organic chemistry*]
PSF............ Popular Struggle Front [*Palestine*] [*Political party*] (PD)
PSF............ Port Stanley [*Falkland Islands*] [*Seismograph station code, US Geological Survey*] [*Closed*] (SEIS)
PSF............ Posterior Spinal Fusion [*Medicine*] (DAVI)
PSF............ Post Stimulus Flow (SAUS)
PSF............ Pound-Force per Square Foot (IAA)
PSF............ Pound-force/Square Foot (SAUS)
psf............ Pounds per Square Foot (IDOE)
PSF............ Pounds per Square Foot
PSF............ Power Separation Filter (IAA)
PSF............ Preservation Services Fund
PSF............ Presidio of San Francisco [*Military*] (AABC)
PSF............ Prime Subframe (MCD)
PSF............ Print Services Facility (SAUS)
PSF............ Private Sector Financing (SAUS)
PSF............ Private Source Funds (DNAB)
PSF............ Probability of Spurious Fire [*Military*] (CAAL)
PSF............ Probability Sample File [*Human Relations Area Files*] [*Information retrieval*]
PSF............ Processing and Staging Facility [*Solid rocket booster*] (NASA)
PSF............ Processing and Storage Facility [*NASA*] (NASA)
PSF............ Process Signal Former (IAA)
PSF............ Production Sharin Formula (SAUS)
PSF............ Product Sharing Formula (SAUS)
PSF............ Program for the Study of the Future (EA)
PSF............ Program Support Facility (USDC)
PSF............ Progressive Space Forum [*Defunct*] (EA)
PSF............ Progres Social Francais [*French Social Progress*] [*Political party*] (PPE)
PSF............ Provisional Sinn Fein [*Northern Ireland*]
PSF............ Provisional System Feature [*Telecommunications*] (TEL)
PSF............ Pseudosarcomatous Fasciitis [*Medicine*]
PSF............ Saint Francis College, Loretto, PA [*OCLC symbol*] (OCLC)
PSFAM........ Parameter Sensitive Frequency Assignment Method (MCD)
PSFC........... Pacific Salmon Fisheries Commission (BUAC)
PS/FC......... Power Supply / Frequency Converter (DWSG)
PSFC........... Power Supply/Fuel Cell (NAKS)
PS/FC......... Power Supply/Fuel Cell
PSFC........... Process Supercritical Fluid Chromatography
PSFC........... Provisional Special Forces Co. (CINC)

PSFC/HIMH... Buzzcocks Fan Club/Harmony in My Head (EA)
PSFC/HIMH... Pete Shelley Fan Club/Harmony in My Head (EA)
PSFD .... Public Sector Financial Deficit
PSFG .... Permanent Service for the Fluctuation of Glaciers (SAUS)
PSFHQ........ Philippine Sea Frontier Headquarters (SAUS)
PSFI .... PS Financial, Inc. [NASDAQ symbol] (SAG)
PS Fincl...... PS Financial, Inc. [Associated Press] (SAG)
PSFL .... Puget Sound Freight Lines [AAR code]
PSFQ .... Pupil Services Fulfillment Questionnaire
PSF Ratio .... Payload, Structure, Fuel Ratio (SAUS)
PSFS.......... Philadelphia Savings Fund Society (SAUS)
PSFT.......... Peoplesoft, Inc. [NASDAQ symbol] (SAG)
PSG .... Pacific Seabird Group (EA)
PSG .... Palestine Study Group (EA)
PSG .... Parachute Study Group (EA)
PSG .... Parti Socialiste Guyanais [Guiana Socialist Party] [Political party] (PPW)
PSG .... Passage [NWS] (FAAC)
psg........... passing (SAUS)
PSG .... Passiv Sonar Geraet (SAUS)
PSG .... Peak Systolic Gradient [Medicine] (MAE)
PSG .... Permanent Steering Group
PSG .... Pershing [Missile] (GFGA)
PSG .... Personnel Subsystem Group (SAA)
PSG .... Peru Support Group (BUAC)
PSG .... Petersburg [Alaska] [Airport symbol] (OAG)
PSG .... Petersburg, AK [Location identifier] [FAA] (FAAL)
PSG .... Phenol Sector Group [European Council of Chemical Manufacturers Federations] [Belgium] (EAIO)
PSG .... Phosphate-Saline-Glucose [A buffer] [Cell culture]
PSG .... Phosphor-Silicate Glass (SAUS)
PSG .... Phosphosilicate Glass (IEEE)
PSG .... Phrase Structure Grammar (SAUS)
PSG .... Phrase-Structure Grammar [Computer science]
PSG .... Planning Systems Generator
PSG .... Platoon Sergeant [Army] (AABC)
PSG .... Polysomnogram [Medicine] (MAE)
PSG .... Polysomnography (DIPS)
PSG .... Post Stall Gyration (MCD)
PSG .... Power Subsystem Group [NASA] (MCD)
PSG .... Prask-Structive Grammar (SAUS)
PSG .... Pregnancy-Specific Glycoprotein [Biochemistry]
PSG .... Presystolic Gallop [Cardiology]
PSG .... Production Support Group (NITA)
PSG .... Production System Generator
PSG .... Production Systems Group (SAUS)
PSG .... Product Support Group (SAUS)
PSG .... Professional Service Group (SAUS)
PSG .... Professional Specialty Group
PSG .... Programmable Sequence Generator [Computer science] (CIST)
PSG .... Programmable Signal Generator (SAUS)
PSG .... Programmable Sound Generator [Chip] [Atari, Inc.]
PSG .... Programmable Symbol Generator
PSG .... Program Systems Guide (SAUS)
PSG .... Project Science Group (ACAE)
PSG .... Pseudomonas Syringae PV Glycinea [Plant pathology]
PSG .... PS Group Holdings [NYSE symbol] [Formerly, PS Group, Inc.] (SG)
PSG .... PS Group, Inc. [NYSE symbol] (SPSG)
PSG .... Psychogalvanometer
PSG .... Psychogalvanometric (SAUS)
PSG .... Psychological Studies Group [Military] (VNW)
PSG .... Public Strategies Group, Inc. [Consulting firm hired in 1993 to improve Minneapolis school district] (ECON)
PSG .... Publishing Systems Group [Later, CPSUG] (EA)
PSG .... Pulsed Strain Gauge (IAA)
PSG .... Pulse Sequence Generation [Instrumentation]
PSG .... Pulse Signal Generator (IAA)
PSG .... Pulse Sweep Generator (SAUS)
PSGA .... Parkinson Support Groups of America (EA)
PSGA .... Pedal Steel Guitar Association (EA)
PSGA .... Professional Skaters Guild of America (EA)
PSGAG........ Polysulfated glycosaminoglycan (SAUS)
PSGB .... Pharmaceutical Society of Great Britain
PSGB .... Primate Society of Great Britain (DBA)
PSGBI........ Pathological Society of Great Britain and Ireland (SAUS)
PSGCU........ Palm Springs Golf 'Unit' [NASDAQ symbol] (TTSB)
PSGD .... Past Senior Grand Deacon [Freemasonry]
PSGE .... Partido Socialdemocrata de Guinea Ecuatorial [Social Democratic Party of Equatorial Guinea] [Political party] (EY)
PSGE .... Passage [Postal Service standard] (OPSA)
PSGE .... Photosynthetic Gas Exchanger (SAA)
PSGE .... Project Specification Group Engineer
PSG-EG........ Partido Socialista Galego - Esquerda Galega [Spain] [Political party] (EY)
PSGI .... Permanent Service for Geomagnetic Indices (SAUS)
PSGI .... Permanent Service on Geomagnetic Indices (SAUS)
PSGL .... P-Selectin Glycoprotein Ligand [Biochemistry]
PSGM .... Past Supreme Grand Master [Freemasonry]
PSG Mask... Phosphosilicate Glass Mask (SAUS)
PSGN .... Post-Streptococcal Glomerulonephritis [Medicine]
PSGR.......... Passenger (AFM)
psgr........... Passenger (TVEL)
PSGR LNG.. Passenger Lounge (SAUS)
PS Grp......... PS Group, Inc. [Associated Press] (SAG)
P-SGT .... P-channel Silicon Gate (SAUS)

PSGT .... Platoon Sergeant [Military]
PSGTCAEI... Permanent Secretariat of the General Treaty on Central American Economic Integration (EAIO)
PSGV .... Pacific Sentinel Gold Corp. [NASDAQ symbol] (SAG)
PSGVF .... Pacific Sentinel Gold [NASDAQ symbol] (TTSB)
PSGW .... Past Senior Grand Warden [Freemasonry]
PSH .... Friends Historical Library of Swarthmore College, Swarthmore, PA [OCLC symbol] (OCLC)
PSH .... Parshall, ND [Location identifier] [FAA] (FAAL)
PSH .... Past Social History (CPH)
PSH .... Past Surgical History [Medicine] (DMAA)
PSH .... Permanent Shift of Hearing
PSH .... Peshawar [Pakistan] [Seismograph station code, US Geological Survey] (SEIS)
PSH .... Phase Shift (MSA)
PSH .... Physical Services Header (SAUS)
PSH .... Polystyrene, Hydrogenous [Organic chemistry]
PSH .... Postspinal Headache (AAMN)
PSH .... Post-Stimulus Histogram [Psychometrics]
PSH .... Preselect Heading (NG)
PSH .... Pressure Switch, High [Nuclear energy] (NRCH)
PSH .... Productive Standard Hour (PDAA)
PSH .... Program Support Handbook
PSH .... Provisional Site Handover (SAUS)
PSH .... Proximity Sensing Head
PSH .... Publications Statistiques Hongroises [Hungary]
PSH .... Public Storage Canadian Properties IIIa Ltd. [Toronto Stock Exchange symbol]
P-Shaw....... George Bernard Shaw (SAUS)
P Shaw....... Patrick Shaw's Justiciary Cases [1819-31] [Scotland] [A publication] (DLA)
PSHB .... Persistent Spectral Hole-Burning [Spectroscopy]
PSHC .... Permanent Secretariat of the Hemispheric Congress (EA)
PSHC .... Public Speaking and Humor Club (EA)
PSHCJ .... Philanthropic Society of House Carpenters and Joiners [A union] [British]
PSHD .... Phase-Shift Driver (MSA)
PSHD .... Port Security Harbor Defense (DOMA)
PSHF .... Polysulfone Hollow Fiber [Filtration membrane]
PSHFA .... Public Servants' Housing and Finance Association [British] (BI)
PSHR .... Project Safety & Health Review (SAUS)
PSHR .... Pusher [Freight]
PSHRPQ ...... Program Support for Hardware RPQ (SAUS)
PSHS .... Propulsion Systems Hazards Subcommittee [Military]
PShS........... Shippensburg State College, Shippensburg, PA [Library symbol] [Library of Congress] (LCLS)
PSHSGB....... Polar System History Society of Great Britain (BUAC)
PSHT .... Powys Self-Help Trust [British]
PSHTM .... Pilot Scale High Temperature Melter (ABAC)
PSI........... Pacific Semiconductors, Inc. (MCD)
PSI........... Pacific Stratus Investigation [Marine science] (OSRA)
PSI........... Pacific Sulfur Investigation [Marine science] (OSRA)
PSI........... Pacific Sulfur/Stratus Investigation (USDC)
PSI........... Packet Switching Interface (SAUS)
PSI........... Packet Switch Interface (SAUS)
PSI........... Page Survival Index (PDAA)
PSI........... Paid Service Indication [Telecommunications] (TEL)
PSI........... Pakistan Standards Institution (IAA)
PSI........... Palmar Sweat Index (EDAC)
PSI........... Parameter Setting Instruction (SAUS)
PSI........... Parameter Signature Identification (SAUS)
PSI........... Parapat [Sumatra] [Seismograph station code, US Geological Survey] (SEIS)
PSI........... Parapsychological Services Institute (EA)
PSI........... Parapsychology (SAUS)
PSI........... Parenting Stress Index [Psychology]
PSI........... Partai Socialis Indonesia [Socialist Party of Indonesia]
PSI........... Participation Systems, Inc. [Electronics Communications Co.] [Winchester, MA] [Telecommunications] (TSSD)
PSI........... Particle-Sizing Interferometer (MCD)
PSI........... Parti Socialiste Ivoirien [Ivorian Socialist Party] [The Ivory Coast] [Political party] (EY)
PSI........... Partito Socialista Italiano [Italian Socialist Party] [Political party] (PPE)
PSI........... Pasni [Pakistan] [Airport symbol] (OAG)
PSI........... Passive Solar Institute [Defunct] (EA)
PSI........... Pathfinder Systems Inc. (SAUS)
PSI........... Paul Scherrer Institute [Switzerland] (BUAC)
PSI........... Percent Similarity Index
PSI........... Performance Systems International (SAUS)
PSI........... Performance Systems International, Inc.
PSI........... Peripherally Synapsing Interneuron [Neurology]
PSI........... Peripheral Subsystem Interface [Computer science] (IAA)
PSI........... Permanent Staff Instructor [Military] [British]
PSI........... Permuterm Subject Index [Institute for Scientific Information] [A publication] (IID)
PsI........... Perpetual Storage, Inc., Salt Lake City, UT [Library symbol] [Library of Congress] (LCLS)
PSI........... Personalised System of Induction (AIE)
PSI........... Personalized System of Instruction
PSI........... Personal Security Identifier [Computer science] (ELAL)
PSI........... Personal Sequential-Inference Machine [Computer science]
PSI........... Personal Sequential Interface (SAUS)
PSI........... Personal Service Income
PSI........... Personal Style Indicator [Test] (TMMY)

PSI...............	Personnel Security Investigation [*Military*]
PSI...............	Personnel Selection Inventory [*Test*]
PSI...............	Person of Special Importance [*British military*] (DMA)
PSI...............	Per Square Inch (ADA)
PSI...............	Petit SystSme Informatique (SAUS)
PSI...............	Pet Sitters International (NTPA)
PSI...............	Pharmaceutical Society of Ireland (BI)
PSI...............	Phenomenological Systems, Inc.
PSI...............	Photographic Society International (EA)
PSI...............	Photographic Society of Ireland (BI)
PSI...............	Photometric Sunspot Index
PSI...............	Photon Science Instruments (SAUS)
PSI...............	Photo Services Industrial Ltd. [*British*]
PSI...............	Physical, Sensitivity, Intellectual [*Biorhythmics*]
PSI...............	Physicians Services Inc. (SAUS)
PSI...............	Pilot Steering Indicator (SAUS)
PSI...............	Planned Speed Indicator
PSI...............	Planned Start Installation [*Telecommunications*] (TEL)
PSI...............	Plan Shear Indicator (SAUS)
PSI...............	Plan Speed Indicator [*Military*]
PSI...............	Plas Speed Indicator (IAA)
PSI...............	Platoon Sector Indicator [*Army*]
PSI...............	Play Skills Inventory
PSI...............	Policy Studies Institute [*Research center*] [*British*] (IRC)
PSI...............	Pollutant Standards Index [*Environmental Protection Agency*]
PSI...............	Pollution Standards Index (SARE)
p-Si	Polycrystalline Silicon [*Photovoltaic energy systems*]
PSI...............	Population Services Inc. (SAUS)
PSI...............	Population Services International (BUAC)
PSI...............	Porta Systems [*AMEX symbol*] (TTSB)
PSI...............	Porta Systems Corp. [*AMEX symbol*] (SPSG)
PSI...............	Positive Self-Image [*Psychology*]
PSI...............	Posterior Sagittal Index [*Anatomy*] (AAMN)
PSI...............	Posterior Superior Iliac Spine [*Posterosuperior iliac spine*] [*Anatomy*] (DAVI)
PSI...............	Postpartum Support, International (EA)
PSI...............	Postscript Interpreter (SAUS)
PSI...............	Post-Tensioning Institute (WPI)
PSI...............	Potential Savings Index (SAUS)
PSI...............	Pound-Force per Square Inch (IAA)
psi	Pounds per Square Inch (IDOE)
PSI...............	Pounds per Square Inch
PSI...............	Pounds per Square Inch Absolute (IAA)
PSI...............	Power per Square Inch
PSI...............	Power Semiconductors, Inc. (SAUS)
PSI...............	Power Static Inverter (NASA)
PSI...............	Praed Street Irregulars (EA)
PSI...............	Preprogrammed Self-Instruction [*Computer science*] (IEEE)
PSI...............	Preschool Inventory (EDAC)
PSI...............	Pre-Sentence Investigation (OICC)
PSI...............	Present Serviceability Index (IEEE)
PSI...............	Preservice Inspection [*Nuclear energy*] (NRCH)
PSI...............	Pre-Shipment and Inspection (SAUS)
PSI...............	Preshipment Inspection [*International trade*]
PSI...............	President of the Service Institute (SAUS)
PSI...............	Pressure per Square Inch (EEVL)
PSI...............	Pressure Sensitive Identification
PSI...............	Pressurized Sphere Injection (DNAB)
PSI...............	Pressurized Sphere Injector (SAUS)
PSI...............	Presynaptic Inhibition (SAUS)
PSI...............	Prime System Indicator
PSI...............	Private Sector Initiatives (SAUS)
PSI...............	Probe Systems, Inc.
PSI...............	Problem-Solving and Inference Machine (IAA)
PSI...............	Problem Solving Information (SAUS)
PSI...............	Problem-Solving Information [*Apparatus*]
PSI...............	Problem-Solving Interpreter [*Computer language*]
PSI...............	Processor Simulator (SAUS)
PSI...............	Process Safety Information (SAUS)
PSI...............	Process System Index
PSI...............	Process Systems, Inc.
PSI...............	Process to Support Interoperability (SAUS)
PSI...............	Proctorial System of Instruction (IEEE)
PSI...............	Production Stock Item (MCD)
PSI...............	Product Support Instructions (AAG)
PSI...............	Professional Secretaries International [*Kansas City, MO*] (EA)
PSI...............	Professional Services Income (WDAA)
PSI...............	Programmable Series Interface (SAUS)
PSI...............	Programmed School Input (NVT)
PSI...............	Program Status Information [*Computer science*] (MCD)
PSI...............	Program Supply Interest (MCD)
PSI...............	Project Security Instruction (SAUS)
PSI...............	Project Starlight International (EA)
PSI...............	Protosynthetic Indexing (NITA)
PSI...............	Protosynthex Index
PSI...............	Pseudomonas Sp. Lipase
PSI...............	PSI Energy [*Associated Press*] (SAG)
PSI...............	Psychiatric Society for Informatics (SAUS)
PSI...............	Psychological Screening Inventory [*Personality development test*]
PSI...............	Psychological Society of Ireland (BUAC)
PSI...............	Psychosomatic Inventory [*Psychology*]
PSI...............	Publications Standing Instruction (AAG)
PSI...............	Public Services International [*See also ISP*] [*Ferney Voltaire, France*] (EAIO)
PSI...............	Pulsepower Systems Incorporated
PSI...............	Pulse Sciences, Inc.
PSIA............	Paper Stock Institute of America (EA)
PSIA............	Pound-Force per Square Inch, Absolute (SAUS)
psia	Pounds per Square Inch Absolute (IDOE)
PSIA............	Pounds per Square Inch Absolute
PSIA............	President of the Society of Industrial Artists [*British*]
PSIA............	Pressure Absolute [*AGA*] (TAG)
PSIA............	Production System Integration Area
PSIA............	Professional Ski Instructors of America (EA)
PSIA............	Public Security Investigation Agency [*Japan*] (CINC)
PSI Apparatus...	Problem Solving Information Apparatus
PSI-B	Personnel Selection Inventory for Banking [*Test*] (TES)
PSIC............	Pacific Scientific Information Center (SAUS)
PSIC............	Passenger Service Improvement Corp.
PSIC............	Passive Solar Industries Council (EA)
PSIC............	Planning and Systems Integration Center (SAUS)
PSIC............	Process Signal Interface Controller
PSIC............	Production Scheduling and Inventory Control
P-SiC	P-type Silicon-Carbide (SAUS)
PSICOMP....	Predicted Speech Intelligibility Computer (IAA)
Psicor	PSICOR, Inc. [*Associated Press*] (SAG)
PSID	Panel Study of Income Dynamics
PSID	Partial Seismic Intrusion Device (MCD)
PSID	Patrol Seismic Intrusion Detector [*or Device*] [*DoD*]
PSID	Postscript Image Data
PSID	Pounds per Square Inch Differential (MCD)
psid	Pounds per Square Inch, Differential [*Marine science*] (OSRA)
PSID	Preliminary Safety Information Document [*Nuclear energy*] (NRCH)
PSID	Presentation Space Identifier (SAUS)
PSIDC	Punjab State Industrial Development Corp. [*India*] (BUAC)
PS/IDS	Physical Security/Intrusion Detection System (MCD)
PSIEP.........	Project on Scientific Information Exchange in Psychology [*Superseded by Office of Communication*]
PSIF............	Prison Service Industries & Farming (WDAA)
PSIF............	Prison Service Industries and Farms (BUAC)
PSIFC.........	Pat Shea International Fan Club (EA)
PSIFET.......	Power Silicon Field-Effect Transistor (SAUS)
PSIFT.........	Platelet Suspension Immunofluorescence Test [*Medicine*] (DMAA)
PSIG	Partial Signalling (SAUS)
PSIG	Per-Square-Inch Gauge (AAGC)
PSIG	Per Square Inch on the Gauge (SAUS)
PSIG	Pound-Force per Square Inch, Gauge (SAUS)
psig	Pounds per Square Inch Gauge (IDOE)
psig	Pressure per Square Inch Gauge (COE)
PSIG	Pressure per Square Inch Gauge (EPAT)
PSIG	Propulsion Systems Integration Group [*NASA*] (NASA)
PSII............	Plasma Source Ion Implantation (AAEL)
PSII............	Process Safety Incident Investigation [*Engineering*]
PSII............	Psychiatric Severity of Illness Index (SAUS)
PSIL............	Philippine Society of International Law (BUAC)
PSIL............	Potential Selected Item List (MCD)
PSIL............	Preferred Speech Interference Level
PSI-LOGO	Listing of Oil and Gas Opportunities [*Online Resource Exchange, Inc.*] [*Database*]
PSIM..........	Power System Instrumentation and Measurement (MCD)
PSIM..........	Problem-Solving Instructional Material [*National Science Foundation project*]
PSI-Machine...	Personal Sequential Inference Machine (SAUS)
PSIMPLE.....	Problem-Solving In Medical Physiology, Logically Explained (SAUS)
PSINet	PSINet, Inc. [*Associated Press*] (SAG)
PSIO	Performance Scales Intelligence Quotient (EDAC)
PSIP..........	Periodic Smoke Inspection Program [*Diesel engine emissions*]
PSIP..........	Poultry Stock Improvement Plan (SAUS)
PSIP..........	Private Sector Initiative Program [*Department of Labor*]
PSIP..........	Project on Scientific Information in Psychology (SAUS)
PSIPU........	Postscript-Intelligent Processing Unit (SAUS)
PSIR..........	Passenger-Side Inflatable Restraint [*Automotive safety systems*]
PSIR	Phase-Sampled Impulse-Response (SAUS)
PSIR Filter...	Phase-Sampled Impulse-Response Filter (SAUS)
PSIS..........	Permanent Secretaries Committee on the Intelligence Services (SAUS)
PSIS..........	Plastic Surgery Information Service (SAUS)
PSIS..........	Posterior Sacroiliac Spine [*Anatomy*] (DAVI)
PSIS..........	Posterior Superior Iliac Spine [*Medicine*] (STED)
PSIS..........	Pounds per Square Inch per Second
psis...........	Pounds per Square Inch Sealed (NAKS)
PSIS..........	Pounds per Square Inch Sealed (NASA)
PSIS..........	Programme for Strategic and International Security Studies [*Switzerland*] (PDAA)
PSIS..........	Programming Systems Information System (SAUS)
PSISIG.......	Psychic Science International Special Interest Group (EA)
PSIT..........	Property Security Investment Trust [*British*]
PSIT..........	PSi Technologies Hldg. ADS [*NASDAQ symbol*] (SG)
PSIU	Packet Switch Interface Unit (SAUS)
PSIU	Power/Sequence Interface Unit (MCD)
PSIUP........	Partito Socialista Italiano di Unita Proletaria [*Italian Socialist Party of Proletarian Unity (1945-1947)*] [*Political party*] (PPE)
PSIV...........	Passive
PSIX...........	Performance Systems International, Inc. [*NASDAQ symbol*] (SAG)
PSIX...........	PSINet, Inc. [*NASDAQ symbol*] [*Formerly, Performance Systems International*] (SG)
PSJ	Palynological Society of Japan (QUAC)
PSJ	Parallel Swivel Joint
PSJ	Petites Soeurs de Jesus [*Little Sisters of Jesus*] [*Italy*] (EAIO)
PSJ	Petsec Energy ADS [*NYSE symbol*] (SG)

PSJ	Pharmaceutical Society of Japan (BUAC)
psj	Planed and Square-Jointed (DAC)
PSJ	Plane Swivel Joint
PSJ	Point Spread Junction (IAA)
PSJ	Policy Studies Journal
PSJ	Poso [Indonesia] [Airport symbol] (OAG)
PSJ	Pressure Switch Joint
PSJ	Public Service Job (OICC)
PSJF	Preemptive Shortest Job First (SAUS)
PSJS	Pier and Span Junction Set (MCD)
PSK	Dublin, VA [Location identifier] [FAA] (FAAL)
PSK	Personal Survival Kit (SAUS)
PSK	Phase Shift Keyed (SAUS)
PSK	Phase Shift Keying [Computer science]
PSK	PostSparKasse [Post Office Savings Bank] [Austria]
PSK	Power Supply Kit
PSK	Private Secretary to the King [British]
PSK	Program Selection Key [Computer science] (BUR)
PSK	Protection Survey Kit
PSK	Protein Serine Kinase (DMAA)
PSK	Public Storage Properties IX, Inc. [AMEX symbol] (SAG)
PSK	Pulse Shift Keying (CAAL)
PSKL	Program Skelton Language (SAUS)
PSKM	Phase Shift Keyed Modulation (NITA)
PSKM	Phase-Shift Keying MODEM
PSK-PCM	Phase-Shift Keying - Pulse Code Modulation
PSL	Environmental Study Center (SAUS)
PSL	Pacific Star Line (SAUS)
PSL	Pakistan Shipping Line (SAUS)
PSL	Paleobotanical Society of Lucknow (SAUS)
PSL	Palouse Silt Loam [Agronomy]
PSL	Parallel Strand Lumber
PSL	Parasternal Line [Anatomy] (MAE)
PSL	Parti Social-Liberal [Algeria] [Political party] (EY)
PSL	Parts Selection List (SPST)
PSL	Patterson Strategy Letter (SAUS)
PSL	Paymaster-Sub-Lieutenant [Navy] [British]
PSL	PD Service Lage (SAUS)
PSL	Peabody Short Line R. R. [Army]
PSL	Percent Stroke Length [Medicine] (STED)
PSL	Permanent Seat License (SAUS)
PSL	Perpendicular to the Sun Line (SAUS)
PSL	Personnel Skill Levels (AAG)
PSL	Perth [Scotland] [Airport symbol] (AD)
PSL	Peruvian State Line (SAUS)
PSL	Petroleum Ether-Soluble Lipid
PSL	Phase Sequence Logic (IAA)
PSL	Phase Sequency Logic (SAUS)
PSL	Philharmonic Society of London (SAUS)
PSL	Photographic Science Laboratory [Navy]
PSL	Photostimulated Luminescence [Physics]
PSL	Physical Science Libraries (SAUS)
PSL	Physical Sciences Laboratory [Bethesda, MD] [National Institutes of Health] (GRD)
PSL	Physical Sciences Laboratory [University of Wisconsin - Madison, New Mexico State University] [Research center]
PSL	Pipe Sleeve
PSL	Pocket Select Language [Burroughs Corp.]
PSL	Polskie Stronnictwo Ludowe [Polish Peasant Party] [Political party] (PPE)
PSL	Poly-crystalline Silicon Layer (SAUS)
PSL	Polystyrene Latex (PDAA)
PSL	Portable Standard List Processing [Computer science]
PSL	Port Service Ltd. (SAUS)
PSLF	Potassium, Sodium Chloride, Sodium Lactate [Solution] (AAMN)
PSL	Potential Source List (MCD)
PSL	Power and Signal List [Telecommunications] (TEL)
PSL	Power Source Logic
PSL	Power Systems Laboratories (ACAE)
PSL	Practical Storage Life
PSL	Pressure Seal (NASA)
PSL	Pressure Sensitive Label (SAUS)
PSL	Pressure-Sensitive Label
PSL	Pretoria State Library (SAUS)
PSL	Primary Standards Laboratory
PSL	Private Sector Liquidity
PSL	Problem-Solving Language
PSL	Problem Specification Language
PSL	Problem Statement Language [Computer science] (IAA)
PSL	Processor Status Longword (SAUS)
PSL	Process Simulation Language [Computer science] (TEL)
PSL	Process Status Longword [Number] [Computer science] (BYTE)
PSL	Professionnel Air Systems [France] [ICAO designator] (FAAC)
PSL	Programming Script Language (PCM)
PSL	Programming Support Library
PSL	Program Structuring Language (SAUS)
PSL	Program Supply Logic Unit (SAUS)
PSL	Program Support Letter (SAUS)
PSL	Program Support Library (MCD)
PSL	Project Support Laboratory [Military] (CAAL)
PSL	Propellant Seal
PSL	Propulsion Systems Laboratory [USATACOM] (RDA)
PSL	Public School League [Sports]
PSL	Public Software Library (SAUS)
PSL	Public Storage Properties X, Inc. [AMEX symbol] (SAG)

PSL	Public Storage Prop'A' X [AMEX symbol] (TTSB)
PSL	Pycnocline Scattering Layer (DNAB)
PSL	South Hills Library Association, Pittsburgh, PA [OCLC symbol] (OCLC)
PSLA	Palaung State Liberation Army [Myanmar] [Political party] (EY)
PSLA	Pennsylvania School Librarians Association
PSLA	Polish Sea League of America (EA)
PSLA	Pre-School Learning Alliance (WDAA)
PSLC	Post-Schistosomal Liver Cirrhosis [Medicine]
PSLC	Private Security Liaison Council (EA)
PSLD	Parasympatholytic Drug [Medicine] (MELL)
PSLI	Packet Switch Level Interface
PSLI	Partito Socialista dei Lavoratori Italiani [Socialist Party of Italian Workers] [Political party] (PPE)
PSLI	Physalaemin-Like Immunoreactivity [Medicine]
P-slip	Process Slip
PSL-Lewica	Polskie Stronnictwo-Lewica [Polish Peasant Party-Left (1947-1949)] [Political party] (PPE)
PSL-Lewica	Polskie Stronnictwo Ludowe-Lewica [Polish Peasant Party-Left (1913-1920)] [Political party] (PPE)
PSLLS	Pulsed Solid-State LASER Light Source
PSLM	Priority Search-Lock Monitor (SAUS)
PSL-NW	Polskie Stronnictwo Ludowe-Nowe Wyzwolenie [Polish Peasant Party-New Liberation] [Political party] (PPE)
PSLO	Palaung State Liberation Organization [Myanmar] [Political party] (EY)
PSLO	Provost & Security Liaison Officer (SAUS)
PSLP	Private Sector Linkages Program (SAUS)
PSL-Piast	Polskie Stronnictwo Ludowe-Piast [Polish Peasant Party-Piast] [Political party] (PPE)
PSL/PSA	Problem Statement Language/Problem Specification Analyzer [Computer science]
PSL/PSA	Problem Statement Language/Problem Statement Analysis (SAUS)
PSLR	Peak Side Lobe Ratio (SAUS)
PSLR	Product Safety and Liability Reporter [A publication]
PSLS	Pan Stock Line Station (MCD)
PSLS	Polystyrene Latex Sphere (AAEL)
PSL SOL	Potassium, Sodium Chloride, Sodium Lactate Solution (BABM)
PSL sol	Potassium, Sodium Chloride, Sodium Lactate Solution [Pharmacology] (DAVI)
PSLT	Picture Story Language Test
PSLT	Port Side Light (IAA)
PSLT	Pressurized Sonobuoy Launch Tube [Navy] (CAAL)
pslt	Psalter (VRA)
PSLU	Power Supply Logic Unit (SAUS)
PSLV	Poa Semilatent Virus
PSLV	Polar Satellite Launch Vehicle
PSLV	Polar Space Launch Vehicle [Indian Space Research]
PSL-Wyzwolenie	Polskie Stronnictwo Ludowe-Wyzwolenie [Polish Peasant Party-Liberation] [Political party] (PPE)
PSM	Packet Service Module (SAUS)
PSM	Packet Switched Signaling Message (CIST)
PSM	Packet-switched Signalling Message (SAUS)
PSM	Packet Switching Module (SAUS)
PSM	Panasystolic Murmur [Cardiology] (DAVI)
PSM	Parallel Slit Map (OA)
PSM	Parcel Sorting Machine [Freight] (DCTA)
PSM	Parc Saint-Maur [France] [Later, CLF] [Geomagnetic observatory code]
PSM	Particle Size Monitor [Instrumentation]
PSM	Parti Socialiste Mauricien [Mauritian Socialist Party] [Political party] (EY)
PSM	Parti Socialiste Monegasque [Monaco Socialist Party] [Political party] (PPW)
psm	Passed School of Music [Certificate of the Royal Military School of Music] (WDAA)
PSM	Passenger Service Manager [Travel industry]
PSM	Paste Striping Machine (SAUS)
PSM	Past Savio Movement [Defunct] (EA)
PSM	Peak Selector Memory [Computer science]
PSM	People for Self Management [An association] (NADA)
PSM	Persistent Stored Modules (SAUS)
PSM	Personal Skills Map [Career effectiveness test]
PSM	Personal Software Marketing (SAUS)
PSM	Personal Storage Module (SAUS)
PSM	Personnel Subsystem Manager [Army] (AABC)
PSM	Personnel Systems Management [Air Force] (AFM)
PSM	Personnel Systems Manager (SAUS)
PSM	Petroleum Supply Monthly [Database] [Department of Energy] [Information service or system] (CRD)
PSM	Phase-Sensitive Modulator (SAUS)
PSM	Phase-Sensitive Modulator (MCD)
PSM	Phase Shifter Module (SAUS)
PSM	Phase-Shifter Module
PSM	Phase Shifting Mask (AAEL)
PSM	Phase-Shift Mask (SAUS)
PSM	Phase Shift Modification (SAUS)
PSM	Photo Sensing Mark (SAUS)
PSM	Physical Society of Moldova (BUAC)
PSM	Physician and Sports Medicine [A publication]
PSM	Pia Societas Missionum [Fathers of the Pious Society of Missions, Pallottini] [Roman Catholic religious order]
PSM	Pioneer Metals Corp. [Toronto Stock Exchange symbol] [Vancouver Stock Exchange symbol]
PSM	Platyschisma Shale Member [Geology]

PSM............	Please See Me
PSM........	Plymouth State College of the University of New Hampshere, Plymouth, NH [*OCLC symbol*] (OCLC)
PSM..........	Point Scattering Model (SAUS)
PSM..........	Point Source Modeling (SAUS)
PSM..........	Point Source Monitoring [*Environmental Protection Agency*] (GFGA)
PSM..........	Portal-Systemic Myelopathy [*Medicine*] (MELL)
PSM..........	Portsmouth [*New Hampshire*] [*Airport symbol*] (AD)
PSM..........	Portsmouth, NH [*Location identifier*] [*FAA*] (FAAL)
PSM..........	Position Switching Module (SAUS)
PSM..........	Positive Sample Mode (SAUS)
PSM..........	Postal Service Manual [*A publication*] (AFM)
PSM..........	Postmitochondrial Supernatant [*Medicine*] (DMAA)
PSM..........	Postsynaptic Membrane [*Neurology*]
PSM..........	Power Strapping Machine
PSM..........	Power Supply Module (MHDI)
PSM..........	Power System Module
PSM..........	Preservation Security Manager
PSM..........	Pressure-Sensitive Mat
PSM..........	Pressure Switch Manifold [*Automotive transmissions*]
PSM..........	Presystolic Murmur [*Cardiology*]
PSM..........	Printing Systems Manager (SAUS)
PSM..........	Print Management System (SAUS)
PSM..........	Prism (MSA)
PSM..........	Probabilistic Sequential Machine (RALS)
PSM..........	Process Safety Management [*Chemical engineering*]
PSM..........	Producibility Study Memorandum (SAUS)
PSM..........	Production Systems Management (IAA)
PSM..........	Productive Standard Minute (MHDI)
PSM..........	Product Sales Manager (SAUS)
PSM..........	Product Support Manual (AAG)
PSM..........	Professional Service Manager (SAUS)
PSM..........	Professional Staff Member [*Congress*] (DOMA)
PSM..........	Programming Support Monitor [*Texas Instruments, Inc.*]
PSM..........	Programming System Memorandum (SAUS)
PSM..........	Programming Systems Manual (SAUS)
PSM..........	Program Security Manager (SAUS)
PSM..........	Program Sensitive Malfunction (SAUS)
PSM..........	Program-Sensitive Malfunction
PSM..........	Program Support Management [*NASA*] (KSC)
PSM..........	Program Support Material (SAUS)
PSM..........	Program Support Monitor [*Computer science*] (ELAL)
PSM..........	Progressive Series Modulator (IAA)
PSM..........	Project Safety Management
PSM..........	Project Security Manager (ADWA)
PSM..........	Propellant Storage Module [*NASA*]
PSM..........	Proportional Spacing Machine [*Computer science*] (ELAL)
PSM..........	Pro Sanctity Movement (EA)
PSM..........	Public Service Medal
PSM..........	Public Storage Properties XI, Inc. [*AMEX symbol*] (SAG)
PSM..........	Public Storage Prop'A' XI [*AMEX symbol*] (TTSB)
PSM..........	Pulse Slope Modulation (IAA)
PSM..........	Pulse-Spacing Modulation (ECII)
PSM..........	Pulse Step Modulation (SAUS)
PSM..........	Purse-String Mouth (MELL)
PSM..........	Pyro Substitute Monitor [*NASA*] (NASA)
PSM..........	Pyrotechnic Substitute Monitor
PSm............	Thesaurus Syriacus [*R. Paine Smith*] [*A publication*] (BJA)
PSMA........	Power Saw Manufacturers Association [*Later, CSMA*] (EA)
PSMA........	Power Sources Manufacturers Association (NTPA)
PSMA........	Power Supply Manufacturers Association [*British*] (DBA)
PSMA........	President of the Society of Marine Artists [*British*]
PSMA........	Pressure Sensitive Manufacturers Association [*British*] (DBA)
PSMA........	Professional Services Management Association [*Alexandria, VA*] (EA)
PSMA........	Progressive Spinal Muscular Atrophy [*Medicine*]
PSMA........	Progressive Streptococcal Muscular Atrophy [*Medicine*] (MELL)
PSMA........	Prostate-Specific Membrane Antigen [*Medicine*]
PSMA........	Proximal Spinal Muscular [*Medicine*] (DMAA)
PSMA........	Proximal Spinal Muscular Atrophy [*Medicine*] (DMAA)
PSMA........	Pyrotechnic Signal Manufacturers Association (EA)
PSMC........	Pre-Selected Manual Control (SAUS)
PSMD........	Photo Selective Metal Deposition
PSMD........	Photo-Selective Metal Deposition (SAUS)
PSME........	Partido Socialista de Melilla [*See also PSOE*] [*Spanish North Africa*] [*Political party*] (MENA)
PSME........	Personal Social and Moral Education (AIE)
PSMed........	Psychosomatic Medicine (DAVI)
PSME-PSOE...	Partido Socialista de Melilla - Partido Socialista Obrero Espanol [*Political party*] (EY)
PSMF........	Protein Sparing Modified Fast
PSMFC........	Pacific States Marine Fisheries Commission
PSMI........	Phase-Shift Modal Interference
PSMI........	Precise Ship Motion Instrument
PS/Min........	Private Secretary to the Minister (SAUS)
PSMIT........	Programming Services for Multimedia Industry Terminals [*IBM Corp.*]
PSML........	Processor System Modeling Language [*1976*] [*Computer science*] (CSR)
PSML........	Processor System Modelling Language (SAUS)
PSMM........	Multimission Patrol Ship [*Symbol*]
PSMM........	Patrol Ship Multi-Mission (SAUS)
PSMMA........	Plastic Soft Materials Manufacturers Association (EA)
P/S Mode.....	Parallel/Serial Mode (SAUS)
PSMP........	Program on Short- and Medium-Range Weather Prediction Research [*Marine science*] (OSRA)

PSMP..........	Project Software Management Plan (SSD)
PSMP..........	Public Sector Management Programme (SAUS)
PSMPA........	Per Square Meter per Annum
PSMR..........	Part Specification for Reliability (SAUS)
PSMR..........	Parts Specification Management for Reliability
PSMR..........	Pneumatic [*or Pressure*] System Manifold Regulator [*or Manual*] (AAG)
PSMR........	Pneumatic System Manual Regulator (SAUS)
PSMR........	Pressure System Manifold Regulator (SAUS)
PSMR........	Pressure System Manual Regulator (SAUS)
PSMRD........	Postsurgical Minimum Residual Disease [*Medicine*] (DB)
PSMS..........	Permanent Section of Microbiological Standardization (MCD)
PSMS..........	Physical Self Maintenance Scale
PSMSL........	Permanent Service for Mean Sea Level [*of the Federation of Astronomical and Geophysical Data Analysis Services*] [*Birkenhead, Merseyside, England*] (EAIO)
PSMT..........	Paced Sequential Memory Task (PDAA)
PSMT..........	Pedestal Sight Manipulation Test (IAA)
PSMT..........	Perishable Sheet Metal Tool (MCD)
PSMT..........	Psychiatric Services Management Team (STED)
PSMTA........	Power Supply Modulator Test Adapter (ACAE)
PSMU..........	Power Supply and Multiplexer Unit [*Telecommunications*] (TSSD)
PSMV..........	Paspalum Striate Mosaic Virus [*Plant pathology*]
PSMV..........	Pea Seed-Borne Mosaic Virus [*Plant pathology*]
PSN............	Package Sequence Number
PSN............	Packet Switched Network
PSN............	Packet Switching Network (SAUS)
PSN............	Packet Switching Node
PSN............	Packet Switch Node
PSN............	Palestine, TX [*Location identifier*] [*FAA*] (FAAL)
PSN............	Parent Support Network [*Australia*]
PSN............	Partial Shipment Number [*DoD*]
PSN............	Parti de la Solidarite Nationale [*Party of National Solidarity*] [*Luxembourg*] [*Political party*] (PPE)
PSN	Partido Socialista Nicaraguense [*Nicaraguan Socialist Party*] [*Political party*] (PPW)
PSN	Payment Systems Network, Inc. (TBD)
PSN	Penicillin, Streptomycin and Neomycin (SAUS)
PSN	Pentium Serial Number [*Computer science*]
PSN	Perfect Shuffle Network (SAUS)
PSN	Permanent Sort Number [*Computer science*]
PSN	Polish Surname Network (EA)
PSN	Poor Sisters of Nazareth (TOCD)
PSN	Position
Psn	Positioning (SAUS)
PSN	Position Sequence Number (SAUS)
PSN	Potassium Sodium Niobate (SAUS)
PSN	Potosina del Aire SA de CV [*Mexico*] [*ICAO designator*] (FAAC)
PSN	Print Sequence Number [*Computer science*] (ELAL)
PSN	Private Satellite Network (SAUS)
PSN	Private Satellite Network, Inc. [*New York, NY*] [*Telecommunications*] (TSSD)
PSN	Private Switching Networks (SAUS)
PSN	Processing Serial Number (MCD)
PSN	Processor Serial Number
PSN	Professional Speakers Network (NTPA)
PSN	Program Summary Network (MCD)
PSN	Progressive Student Network (EA)
PSN	Provisioning Sequence Number (MCD)
PSN	Public Storage Properties XII, Inc. [*AMEX symbol*] (SAG)
PSN	Public Storage Prop'A' XII [*AMEX symbol*] (TTSB)
PSN	Public Switched Network (BUR)
PSN	Purge Sequence Number (SAUS)
PSNA	Phytochemical Society of North America (EA)
PSNA	Powys Society of North America (EA)
PSNAL	Personal (FAAC)
PSNAP	Programmable Steerable Nulling Antenna Processor (SAUS)
PSNB	Public-Sector Net Borrowing
PSNB	Puget Sound Bancorp (EFIS)
PSNC	Pacific Steam Navigation Co. (MHDW)
PSNC	Parti Socialiste de la Nouvelle Caledonie [*Socialist Party of New Caledonia*] [*Political party*] (PPW)
PSNC	Pharmaceutical Services Negotiating Committee (BUAC)
PSNCF	Pacific Southern Naval Coastal Frontier
PSNCO	Personnel Staff Noncommissioned Officer [*Military*]
PSNI	Pharmaceutical Society of Northern Ireland (BUAC)
PSNL	Personnel (FAAC)
PSNP	Partial Sequence Number Packet (SAUS)
PSNP	Pebble Springs Nuclear Plant (NRCH)
PSNR	Pasifik Satelit Nusantara (PT) [*NASDAQ symbol*] (SAG)
PSNR	Peak Signal to Noise Ratio (SAUS)
PSNR	Positioner
PSNR	Power Signal-to-Noise Ratio
PSNRL	Peak Signal-to-Noise Ratio Loss (SAUS)
PSNRP	Position Report [*Aviation*] (FAAC)
PSNS	Parasympathetic Nervous System (STED)
PSNS	Physical Science for Nonscience Students
PS NS	Picket Ship, Navy Service (SAUS)
PSNS	Pretreatment Standards for New Indirect Sources [*Environmental Protection Agency*]
PSNS	Pretreatment Standards for New Sources (SAUS)
PSNS	Programmable Sampling Network Switch
PSNS	Puget Sound Naval Shipyard [*Bremerton, WA*] (MCD)
PSNS-MATLABS...	Puget Sound Naval Shipyard Material Laboratories [*Bremerton, WA*]

PSNSR........	Position Sensor (MCD)
P SNSR.......	Position Sensor
PSNSW........	Philatelic Society of New South Wales [Australia]
PSNSY........	Puget Sound Naval Shipyard [Bremerton, WA]
PSNT..........	Present [Legal term] (ROG)
PSNZ..........	Perinatal Society of New Zealand (BUAC)
PSNZ..........	Pharmaceutical Society of New Zealand (SAUS)
PSO............	Pad Safety Officer [Aerospace] (MCD)
PSO............	Paint Spray Outfit
PSO............	Pasadena Symphony Orchestra (SAUS)
PSO............	Paseo
PSO............	Pasto [Colombia] [Airport symbol] (OAG)
PSO............	Pasto [Colombia] [Seismograph station code, US Geological Survey] (SEIS)
PSO............	Pauli Spin Operator [Physics]
PSO............	Peacetime Stockage Objective [DoD] (AFIT)
PSO............	Pearson plc ADR [NYSE symbol]
PSO............	Pending Service Order (SAUS)
PSO............	Penobscot Shoe [AMEX symbol] (TTSB)
PSO............	Penobscot Shoe Co. [AMEX symbol] (SPSG)
PSO............	Personal Staff Officer [Australia]
PSO............	Personnel Security Officer [Military]
PSO............	Personnel Selection Officer [British military] (DMA)
PSO............	Personnel Services Organisation [Australia]
PSO............	Phoenix Symphony Orchestra (SAUS)
PSO............	Phorate Sulfoxide (SAUS)
PSO............	Piano-Shaped Object
PSO............	Pilot Systems Officer (SAUS)
PSO............	Pilot Systems Operator
PSO............	Pittsburgh Symphony Orchestra (SAUS)
PSO............	Planet Sensor Output
PSO............	Point Surface Origin
PSO............	Polaris Systems Officer [British military] (DMA)
PSO............	Policy Studies Organization (EA)
PSO............	Political Survey Officer (SAUS)
PSO............	Political Survey Officers [Navy]
PSO............	Polysulfon (SAUS)
PSO............	Polysulfone [Also, PS] [Organic chemistry]
PSO............	Portland Symphony Orchestra (SAUS)
PSO............	Port Services Office [or Officer] (DNAB)
PSO............	Prague Symphony Orchestra (SAUS)
PSO............	Primary Standardization Office [Military] (AABC)
PSO............	Principal Scientific Officer [British]
PSO............	Principal Staff Officer [British military] (DMA)
PSO............	Procurement Services Office
PSO............	Product Support Organization
PSO............	Profco Resources Ltd. [Vancouver Stock Exchange symbol]
PSO............	Programmable Storage Oscilloscope (CIST)
PSO............	Program Secretarial Officer (COE)
PSO............	Program Senior Official (COE)
PSO............	Program Staff Officer
PSO............	Progressive Supranuclear Ophthalmoplegia (CPH)
PSO............	Project Science Office (EOSA)
PSO............	Prospective Supply Officer (DNAB)
PSO............	Protective Security Officer
PSO............	Protective Service Operations (SAUS)
PSO............	Protocol Supporting Organization (SAUS)
PSO............	Provider Sponsored Organization
PSO............	Provisions Supply Office [Military]
PSO............	Proximal Subungual Onychomycosis
PSO............	Psychiatric Services Officer [Australia]
PSO............	Publications Supply Officer [Military]
PSO............	Publicity Security Officer [Navy]
PSO............	Public Safety Officer
PSO............	Public Service Obligation [Australia]
PSO............	Public Service Organisation [Government grant] [British]
PSOA..........	Postal Supervisory Officers' Association [Australia]
PSOA..........	Pro Stock Owners Association (EA)
PSOB..........	Paper Society for the Overseas Blind [Defunct] (EA)
PSOC..........	Preliminary System Operational Concept (MCD)
PSOE..........	Partido Socialista Obrero Espanol [Spanish Socialist Workers' Party] [See also PSME] [Political party] (PPE)
PSOJ..........	Private Sector Organisation of Jamaica (BUAC)
P SOL.........	Partially Soluble (SAUS)
P sol..........	Partly Soluble [Chemistry] (DAVI)
P Sol..........	Partly Soluble (WGA)
PSOLMHT....	Pious Society of Our Lady of the Most Holy Trinity (EA)
PSom..........	Mary S. Biesecker Public Library, Somerset, PA [Library symbol] [Library of Congress] (LCLS)
PSOM..........	Persistency framework in Somobjects (SAUS)
PSomHi.......	Somerset County Historical and Genealogical Society, Somerset, PA [Library symbol] [Library of Congress] (LCLS)
PSOMT........	Public Sector Organisation for Maritime Transport (SAUS)
PSON..........	Paul-Son Gaming [NASDAQ symbol] (TTSB)
PSON..........	Paul-Son Gaming Corp. [NASDAQ symbol] (SAG)
PSON..........	Person (ROG)
PSONAL.......	Personal (ROG)
PSOP..........	Parti Socialiste des Ouvriers et Paysans [Socialist Party of Workers and Peasants] [France] [Political party]
PSOP..........	Payload Systems Operating Procedures [NASA] (NASA)
PSOP..........	Power System Optimization Program [Computer science]
PSOR..........	Passenger-Seat Occupant Recognition [Automotive safety systems]
PSOR..........	Preliminary System of Requirements
PSOS..........	Personal Services Operating System (SAUS)
PSOS..........	Probably Secure Operating System (MHDB)
PSOT..........	Patch Start of Transaction (SAUS)
PSP............	Pace-Setting Potential [Physiology]
PSP............	Pacific Security Pact (SAUS)
PSP............	Pacifistische Socialistische Partij [Pacific Socialist Party] [Political party] [Netherlands]
PSP............	Package Size Proneness [Marketing]
PSP............	Packaging Shipping Procedures
PSP............	Packet Satellite Program terminal (SAUS)
PSP............	Packet Switching Processor
PSP............	Pad Safety Plan
PSP............	Paint Shop Pro (SAUS)
PSP............	Palm Springs [California] [Airport symbol] (OAG)
PSP............	Palm Springs, CA [Location identifier] [FAA] (FAAL)
PSP............	Palynological Society of Poland (QUAC)
PSP............	Pancreatic Spasmolytic Peptide [Biochemistry]
PSP............	Paralytic Seafood Poisoning (SAUS)
PSP............	Paralytic Shellfish Poisoning [Marine biology]
PSP............	Parathyroid Secretory Protein [Biochemistry]
PSP............	Parti de la Solidarite du Peuple [Cameroon] [Political party] (EY)
PSP............	Partido Socialista del Peru [Socialist Party of Peru] [Political party] (PPW)
PSP............	Partido Socialista Popular [Popular Socialist Party] [Spain] [Political party] (PPE)
PSP............	Partido Socialista Popular [Popular Socialist Party] [Peru] [Political party] (PPW)
PSP............	Partido Socialista Portuguesa [Portuguese Socialist Party] [Political party] (PPW)
PSP............	Partido Social Progresista [Social Progressive Party] [Brazil] [Political party]
PSP............	Parti Socialiste Polynesien [Polynesian Socialist Party] [Political party] (PPW)
PSP............	Parti Social pour le Progres [Tunisia] [Political party] (EY)
PSP............	Parti Soudanais Progressiste [Sudanese Progressive Party] [Political party]
PSP............	Parts Screening Program
PSP............	Patrol Seaplane
PSP............	Pauli Sound Pressure (SAUS)
PSP............	Pauli Speech Power (SAUS)
PSP............	Payload Signal Processor [NASA] (NASA)
PSP............	Payload Specialist Panel [NASA] (NASA)
PSP............	Payload Support Plan [NASA] (MCD)
PSP............	Payroll Savings Plan (GFGA)
PSP............	Peace Shield Program (SAUS)
PSP............	Peak Sideband Power (DEN)
PSP............	Peak Systolic Pressure (SAUS)
PSP............	Peoples Solidarity Party (SAUS)
PSP............	Perforated Steel Planking (SAA)
PSP............	Perforated Steel Plate (VNW)
PSP............	Perforated Steel Plating (DNAB)
PSP............	Performance Shaping Parameter (SAUS)
PSP............	Performance Shaping Parameters (IEEE)
PSP............	Performance Share Plan [Human resources] (WYGK)
PSP............	Performance Standards Program
PSP............	Periodic Short Pulse (MAE)
PSP............	Permanent Sample Plot [For ecological studies]
PSP............	Personal Security Preview [Psychology] (DAVI)
PSP............	Personal Software Process (SAUS)
PSP............	Personal Software Products (SAUS)
PSP............	Personal Success Program
PSP............	Personal Survival Pack (SAUS)
PSP............	Personnel Subsystem Process [Army] (AABC)
PSP............	Pharmaceutical Society of Pakistan (BUAC)
PSP............	Pharmacological Sciences Program [Bethesda, MD] [National Institute of General Medical Sciences] (GRD)
PSP............	Phased Support Plan (SAUS)
PSP............	Phenolsulfonephthalein [Chemical indicator]
PSP............	Pierced Steel Planking [Military]
PSP............	Pierce Steel Plating (SAUS)
PSP............	Plane Strain Plastometer
PSP............	Planet Scan Platform [NASA] (KSC)
PSP............	Planned Standard Programming [Computer science]
PSP............	Plasma Separations Process (SAUS)
PSP............	Plasma Spraying [Welding]
PSP............	Plasmon Surface Polariton [Physics]
PSP............	Platform Sensor Package
PSP............	Pocahontas State Park (SAUS)
PSP............	Pointed Soft Point [Ammunition]
PSP............	Pointed Soft Point Bullet
PSP............	Police Service Pistol
PSP............	Policies, Systems, and Procedures
PSP............	Polyfactorial Study of Personality [Psychology]
PSP............	Poly(styrene peroxide) [Organic chemistry]
PSP............	Popular Socialist Party [Political party] (BUAC)
PSP............	Portable Service Processor (IEEE)
PSP............	Positive Screened Print (SAUS)
PSP............	Positive Spike Pattern (MAE)
PSP............	Posterior Spinous Process (SAUS)
psp............	Posterior Subcapsular Plaque [Ophthalmology] (DAVI)
PSP............	Postipankki [National savings bank] [Finland]
PSP............	Post-Shoring-Polyethylene [Method of constructing underground homes]
PSP............	Post-Surgical Pain [Medicine]
PSP............	Postsynaptic Potential [Neurophysiology]
PSP............	Potential for Successful Performance [Test]
PSP............	Power System Planning

PSP............ Praja Socialist Party [*India*] [*Political party*] (PPW)
PSP............ Precision Spectral Pyranometer (SAUS)
PSP............ Precision Spot Positioning
PSP............ Predictable System Performance (SAA)
PSP............ Predictive Smooth Pursuit [*Ophthalmology*]
PSP............ Pre-Season Predictor Model [*Television ratings*] (NTCM)
PSP............ Presending Pause (NITA)
PSP............ Presensitized Photoplate
PSP............ Pre-Series Phase (SAUS)
PSP............ Prestart Panel [*Aerospace*] (AAG)
PSP............ Pre-Stock Point
PSP............ Priced Spare Parts [*Military*] (AFIT)
PSP............ Price-Subsidy Program (SAUS)
PSP............ Price-Support Program (SAUS)
PSP............ Primary and Secondary Power system (SAUS)
PSP............ Primary Smog Product (PDAA)
PSP............ Primary Sodium Pump [*Nuclear energy*] (NRCH)
PSP............ Primary Supply Point [*Military*] (AFM)
PSP............ Primary Support Point [*Military*] (AFM)
PSP............ Printing Summary Punch (SAUS)
PSP............ Priority Strike Plan (SAUS)
PSP............ Priority Strike Program
PSP............ Probability-of-Single-Pulse (SAUS)
PSP............ Problem Solving Process
PSP............ Product Service Publication [*General Motors Corp.*]
PSP............ Product Structure Plan (SAUS)
PSP............ Product Support Plan (SAUS)
PSP............ Product Support Program (NG)
PSP............ Professional and Scholarly Publishing Division [*Association of American Publishers*] (EDAC)
PSP............ Professional Scholarly Publishing
PSP............ Profit Sharing Plan [*Business term*] (MHDW)
PSP............ Programmable Signal Processor (MCD)
PSP............ Program Segment Prefix [*Computer science*]
PSP............ Programs Support Plan (SAUS)
PSP............ Program Support Plan [*NASA*]
PSP............ Program Support Plans (SAUS)
PSP............ Progressive Socialist Party [*Lebanon*] [*Political party*] (BJA)
psp............ Progressive Supernuclear Palsy (SAUS)
PSP............ Progressive Supranuclear Palsy [*Neurology*]
PSP............ Project Schedule Plan (NASA)
PSP............ Project Standard Practice (DNAB)
PSP............ Project Structure Plan (SAUS)
PSP............ Prone Sleeping Position (MELL)
PSP............ Protective Shielding Program
PSP............ Protocol for Specific Purpose
PSP............ Pseudopregnancy [*Gynecology*]
PSP............ Pseudostatic Spontaneous Potential (IAA)
PSP............ Public School Pronunciation (SAUS)
PSP............ Public Security Police (SAUS)
PSP............ Public Storage Canadian Properties [*Limited Partnership Units*] [*Toronto Stock Exchange symbol*]
PSP............ Public Storage Properties XIV, Inc. [*AMEX symbol*] (SAG)
PSP............ Public Storage Prop'A' XIV [*AMEX symbol*] (TTSB)
PSP............ Puerto Rican Socialist Party [*Political party*] (PD)
PSP............ Swarthmore College Peace Collection, Swarthmore, PA [*OCLC symbol*] (OCLC)
PSPA .... Pacific Seafood Processors Association (EA)
PSPA .... Passive Solar Products Association (EA)
PSPA .... Physician Services Practice Analysis (ADWA)
PSPA .... Plant Site Property Administrator (ACAE)
PSPA .... Pre-School Play Apparatus (WDAA)
PSPA .... Pressure Static Probe Assembly (MCD)
PSPA .... Professional School Photographers of America (EA)
PSPA .... Professional Sports Photographers Association [*British*] (EAIO)
PSPA .... Systolic Pulmonary Artery Pressure (SAUS)
PSP & E ...... Product Support Planning and Estimating (AAG)
PSPB .... Pulse Code Modulation Speech Bus (SAUS)
PSPC .... Partido Socialista del Pueblo de Ceuta [*Political party*] (EY)
PSPC .... Permanent South Pacific Commission (BUAC)
PSPC .... Physical Security / Pilferage Code
PSPC .... Polystyrene Packaging Council (EA)
PSPC .... Position-Sensitive Proportional Counter [*Instrumentation*]
PSPC .... Position Sensitive Proportional Counters (SAUS)
PSPCA .... President's Soviet Protocol Committee [*World War II*]
PSPCA .... Pennsylvania Society for the Prevention of Cruelty to Animals
PSPCD .... Puget Sound Pollution-Control District (SAUS)
PSPD .... Permits and State Programs Division [*Environmental Protection Agency*] (GFGA)
PSPD .... Position-Sensitive Proportional Detector [*For X-ray diffraction*]
PSPDC .... Polar Satellite Precipitation Data Centre (SAUS)
PSPDN .... Packet Switched Public Data Network [*Computer science*] (TNIG)
PSPDN .... Packet-Switched Public Data Network (SAUS)
PSPDN .... Packet Switching Public Data Network (SAUS)
PSPEN .... Primary/Secondary Peace Education Network [*Later, PEN*] (EA)
PSPF........... Potential Single Point Failures [*NASA*] (KSC)
PSPF........... Prostacyclin Stimulating Plasma Factor [*Endocrinology*]
PSPFLI........ Pulsed Single Photon Fluorescence Lifetime Instrumentation
PSPG .... Phase-Shifting Pulse Gate (WDAA)
PSPGV .... Primary Sodium Pump Guard Vessel [*Nuclear energy*] (NRCH)
PSphR .... Rohm & Haas Co., Research Library Services, Spring House, PA [*Library symbol*] [*Library of Congress*] (LCLS)
PSPI........... Psychosocial Pain Inventory [*Psychology*]
PSPL........... Priced Spare Parts List
PSPL........... Progressive Socialist Party of Lebanon

PSPL............ Prototype Spare Parts List (SAUS)
PSPL Pre-Op... Prices Square Parts List-Pre-Operational
PSPLR .... Priced Spare Parts List Revision
PSPM .... Procurement Seminar for Project Management [*Army*]
PSPMW .... International Brotherhood of Pulp, Sulphite, and Paper Mill Workers [*Later, UPIU*]
PSPMW .... Pulp, Sulphite and Paper Mill Workers (SAUS)
P-Spot .... Preceding Spot (SAUS)
PSPP .... Preliminary System Package Plan
PSPP .... Preliminary System Package Program
PSPP .... Proposed System Package Plan [*Military*]
PSPR .... Personnel Subsystem Products [*Army*] (AABC)
PSPR .... Programmable Signal Processor RADAR
PSPRT .... Partial Sequential Probability Ratio Test (PDAA)
PSPS .... Paddle Steamer Preservation Society [*British*] (BI)
PSPS .... Passive Surface Pressure Sounder (SAUS)
PSPS .... Pesticides Safety Precautions Scheme [*British*]
PSPS .... Planar Silicon Photoswitch (IEEE)
PSPS .... Postsurgical Pain Syndrome (MELL)
PSPs .... Post-Synaptic Potentials (SAUS)
PSPS .... Power-Steering Pressure Sensor [*Automotive engineering*]
PSPS .... Power Steering Pressure Switch [*Automotive engineering*]
PSPS .... Primary Solar Piping System (SAUS)
PSPS .... Product Support Procurement Summary (MCD)
PSPSK .... Previous Signaling Element Phase Shift Keying [*Computer science*] (IAA)
PS-PSK....... Previous Signalling-element Phase Shift Keying (SAUS)
PSPSV........ Pre-School Playgroup Support Visitor (WDAA)
PSPT.......... Parisi Spanish Proficiency Test (EDAC)
PSPT.......... Passport (AABC)
PSPT.......... Planar Silicon Power Transistor
PSptv......... PerSeptive Biosystems, Inc. [*Associated Press*] (SAG)
PSPV .... Partido Socialista del Pais Valenciano [*Spain*] [*Political party*] (EY)
PSQ .... Parent Symptom Questionnaire [*Medicine*] (DMAA)
PSQ .... Patient Satisfaction Questionnaire [*Medicine*] (DMAA)
PSQ .... Personal Security Questionnaire (SAUS)
PSQ .... Personnel Security Questionnaire
PSQ .... Personnel Squadron
PSQ .... Political Science Quarterly [*A publication*] (BRI)
PSQ .... Protein Sequence Query
PSQ .... Public Storage Properties XV [*AMEX symbol*] (SPSG)
PSQ .... Public Storage Prop'A' XV [*AMEX symbol*] (TTSB)
PSQA .... Pageable System Queue Area [*Computer science*] (MCD)
PSQC .... Philippine Society for Quality Control (BUAC)
PSQI .... Pittsburgh Sleep Quality Index
PSQL .... Platinum Software [*NASDAQ symbol*] (TTSB)
PSQL .... Platinum Software Corp. [*NASDAQ symbol*] (SAG)
PSQL .... Process Screening Quality Level (SAUS)
PSR .... Pacific School of Religion (SAUS)
PSR .... Pacific Security Region
PSR .... Pacific-Sierra Research Corp.
PSR .... Packed Snow on Runway [*NWS*] (FAAC)
PSR .... Pad Safety Report [*NASA*]
PSR .... Page Send-Receive [*Teletypewriter*]
PSR .... Pain Sensitivity Range [*Biometrics*]
PSR .... Panoramic Stereo Rectification
PSR .... Paper Stock Record (DGA)
PSR .... Parachute Status Report [*Army*] (AABC)
PSR .... Partido Socialista Revolucionario [*Revolutionary Socialist Party*] [*Portugal*] [*Political party*] (PPE)
PSR .... Partido Socialista Revolucionario [*Revolutionary Socialist Party*] [*Mexico*] [*Political party*] (PPW)
PSR .... Partido Socialista Revolucionario [*Revolutionary Socialist Party*] [*Peru*] [*Political party*] (PPW)
PSR .... Parts and Supplies (or Supply) Requisition (SAUS)
PSR .... Parts and Supply Requisition (IAA)
PSR & E...... Party Socialiste Revolutionnaire [*Socialist Revolutionary Party*] [*Lebanon*] [*Political party*] (PPW)
PSR .... Passenger Service Representative [*Travel industry*] (TRID)
PSR .... Passenger Space Ratio (SAUS)
PSR .... Passive Ranging Sonar (SAUS)
psr .... Paternal Sex Ratio Gene [*Genetics*]
PSR .... Paul's Scarlet Rose [*Plant cell line*]
PSR .... Pelvispondylite Rheumatismale (SAUS)
PSR .... Pennsylvania State Reports [*A publication*] (DLA)
PSR .... Pennsylvania State University Reactor (NRCH)
PSR .... Perfectly Stirred Reactor
PSR .... Performance Summary Report (NG)
PSR .... Peripheral Shim Rod [*Nuclear energy*] (NRCH)
PSR .... Personal Service Radio
PSR .... Personnel Status Report [*Military*]
PSR .... Pescara [*Italy*] [*Airport symbol*] (OAG)
PSR .... Petaluma & Santa Rosa Railroad Co. [*AAR code*]
PSR .... Petrostates Resource Corp. [*Vancouver Stock Exchange symbol*]
PSR .... Pharmaceutical Sales Representative
PSR .... Phase Sensitive Rectifier (NITA)
PSR .... Phase Sequence Relay
PSR .... Phase Shift Register (SAUS)
PSR .... Philatelic Societies' Record [*A publication*] [*British*]
PSR .... Photo Scale Reciprocal (DNAB)
PSR .... Physical Sciences Research Program [*North Carolina State University*] [*Research center*] (RCD)
PSR .... Physicians for Social Responsibility (EA)
PSR .... Plow-Steel Rope
PSR .... Point of Safe Return (MCD)

PSR	Point Source Range (IAA)
PSR	Policy Status Report [*Insurance*]
PSR	Political and Social Reform Movement [*British*]
PSR	Political Science Reviewer [*A publication*] (BRI)
PSR	Poly Static Radar (ACAE)
PSR	Portable Seismic Recorder
PSR	Portal Systemic Resistance [*Medicine*] (MELL)
PSR	Port State Register (SAUS)
PSR	Positive Support Review (SAUS)
PSR	Positive Support Review, Inc. [*Telecommunications service*] (TSSD)
PSR	Postal Service Representative [*British*] (DCTA)
PSR	Post-Sinusoidal Resistance
PSR	Post-Strike Reconnaissance (SAUS)
PSR	Power Supply Regulation (SAUS)
PSR	Power Supply Rejection (SAUS)
PSR	Power System Relaying (MCD)
PSR	Predicted SONAR Range [*Military*] (NVT)
PSR	Pre-Sentence Report (WDAA)
PSR	Present Serviceability Rating [*FHWA*] (TAG)
PSR	Pre Shipment Review (ACAE)
PSR	Presidential Special Representative (BARN)
PSR	Pressure (SAUS)
PSR	Price-Sales Ratio [*Economics*]
PSR	Primary Surveillance RADAR
PSR	Primary System Relief (COE)
PSR	Priority Status Register (SAUS)
PSR	Problem Status Report (MCD)
PSR	Processor State Register
PSR	Procurement Status Report (IEEE)
PSR	Productivity Savings Reward (AAGC)
PSR	Product Specific Realizations (SAUS)
PSR	Product Specific Release (SAUS)
PSR	Professional Sportscar Racing
PSR	Programming Status Report [*Computer science*]
PSR	Programming Support Representative [*IBM Corp.*]
PSR	Program Status Register
PSR	Program Status Report [*or Review*]
PSR	Program Status Review [*NASA*] (NASA)
PSR	Program Study Request (AAG)
PSR	Program Summary Record [*Military*] (AFIT)
PSR	Program Support Representative (NITA)
PSR	Program Support Requirements (KSC)
PSR	Progress Summary Report
PSR	Project Safe Run (EA)
PSR	Project Scan Record
PSR	Project Summary Report (MCD)
PSR	Proliferative Sickle Retinopathy (DB)
PSR	Propeller Shaft Rate [*Navy*] (CAAL)
PSR	Pro Seniors [*International Bowhunting Organization*] [*Class Equipment*]
PSR	Protected Service Routine (SAUS)
PSR	Proton Storage Ring [*Nuclear physics*]
PSR	Prototype Systems Review
PSR	Provisioning Support Request [*Military*] (CAAL)
PSR	Public Service Company of Colorado [*AMEX symbol*] (SAG)
PSR	Public Service Co. of Colorado [*NYSE symbol*] (SPSG)
PSR	Public Social Responsibility [*Unit of the Anglican Church of Canada General Synod*]
PSR	Public SvcColorado [*NYSE symbol*] (TTSB)
PSR	Pulmonary Stretch Receptors [*Medicine*]
PSR	Pulsar (SAUS)
PSRA	Persil Stain Release Agent (WDAA)
PSRA	Presunrise Service Authorization [*Telecommunications*] (OTD)
PSRA	Problem Status Report Analysis (SAA)
PSRA	Professional Soccer Reporter's Association (EA)
PSRAAALAA	President's Special Representative and Adviser on African, Asian, and Latin American Affairs [*Department of State*]
PSRAM	Physical Security Requirements Assessment Methodology [*Civil Engineering Research Laboratory*] [*Navy*] (RDA)
PSRAM	Pseudostatic Random Access Memory [*Apple Computer Inc.*]
PSRBOW	Premature Spontaneous Rupture of Bag of Waters [*Medicine*] (MEDA)
PSRC	Plastic Surgery Research Council (EA)
PSRC	Pretrial Services Resource Center (EA)
PSRC	PrimeSource Corp. [*NASDAQ symbol*] (SAG)
PSRC	Public Service Research Council (EA)
PSRCA	Professional Standards Review Council of America (EA)
PSRD	Personnel Shipment Ready Date [*Army*] (AABC)
PSRD	Program Support Requirements Document [*NASA*] (KSC)
PSRE	Partido Socialista Revolucionario Ecuatoriano [*Socialist Revolutionary Party of Ecuador*] [*Political party*] (PPW)
PSRE	Propulsion System Rocket Engine (MCD)
PSRF	Point Source Response Function
PSRF	Product Support Reports and Functions
PSRF	Profit Sharing Research Foundation (EA)
PSRG	Privacy and Security Research Group (SAUS)
PSRGN	Pacific Southwest Regional Genetics Network (SAUS)
PSRI	Particulate Solid Research Institute
PSRI	Personnel Specialities and Record Inventory (SAA)
PSRI	Position Subject to Return of Incumbent (SAUS)
PSRI	Position Subject to Return of Incumbent [*Aviation*] (FAAC)
PSRI	Psycho-Social Rehabilitation International (EAIO)
PSRI	Public Systems Research Institute (SAUS)
PSRL	Post Strike Reconnaissance List [*Military*] (CINC)
PSRM	Pacific Southwest Railway Museum (SAUS)

PSRM	Parti Sosialis Rakyat Malaya [*People's Socialist Party of Malaya*]
PSRM	Post-Scram Reactivity Monitor [*Nuclear energy*] (NRCH)
PSRM	Pressurization Systems Regulator Manifold (AAG)
PSRM	Processor State Register Main [*Computer science*]
PSRMA	Pacific Southwest Railway Museum Association [*Later, SDRM*] (EA)
PSR-ML/MIR	Partido Socialista Revolucionario (Marxista-Leninista)/Movimiento de Izquierda Revolucionaria [*Revolutionary Socialist Party (Marxist-Leninist)/Mi litant Movement of the Revolutionary Left*] [*Peru*] [*Political party*] (PPW)
PSRMLS	Pacific Southwest Regional Medical Library [*Library network*]
PSRMT	Piecewise-Sinusoidal Reaction Matching Technique [*Antenna*] [*Navy*]
PSRO	Passenger Standing Route Order [*Army*] (AABC)
PSRO	Professional Services Review Organization (SAUS)
PSRO	Professional Standards Review Organization (NADA)
PSR-P	Packed Snow on Runway - Patchy [*Aviation*] (DNAB)
PSRP	Physical Sciences Research Papers [*Air Force*] (MCD)
PSRP	Production Support Repair Plan (SAA)
PSRPP	Public Safety and Resource Protection Program (SAUS)
PSRPr	Pub Sv of Colo.,4 1/4% Pfd [*AMEX symbol*] (TTSB)
PSRPrA	Pub Sv Colo.,7.15% Pfd [*NYSE symbol*] (TTSB)
PSRR	Parachute Supported Radio Relay
PSRR	Power Supply Rejection Ratio (IAA)
PSRR	Product and Support Requirements Request [*Computer science*] (IBMDP)
PSRS	Patient Service Records System
PSRS	Pictographic Self-Rating Scale [*Psychology*] (AEBS)
PSRS	Portable Seismic Recording System
PSRS	Position Subject to Rotating Shifts [*Aviation*] (FAAC)
PSRS	Psychiatric Self-Rating Scale (SAUS)
PSrS	Slippery Rock State College, Slippery Rock, PA [*Library symbol*] [*Library of Congress*] (LCLS)
PSRT	Passive Satellite Research Terminal
PSRT	Postscript Round Table (SAUS)
PS-RTP	Paper-Substrate Room-Temperature Phosphorescence [*Analytical chemistry*]
PSRU	Processor State Register Utility [*Computer science*]
PSRU	Production Support Repair Unit (SAA)
PSS	Hastings, NE [*Location identifier*] [*FAA*] (FAAL)
PSS	International Production, Service, and Sales Union
PSS	Packet Switched System (NITA)
PSS	Packet Switching Service [*Telecommunications*] [*Information service or system*] [*British*] (IID)
PSS	Packet Switching Stream (SAUS)
PSS	Packet Switching System (SAUS)
PSS	Packet Switch Stream (SAUS)
PSS	Packet SwitchStream [*British Telecommunications Plc*] [*London*] [*Information service or system*] (IID)
PSS	Packet Switchstream Service (SAUS)
PSS	Pad Safety Supervision [*Aerospace*] (AAG)
PSS	Pad Safety Supervision (or Supervisor) (SAUS)
PSS	Pad Safety Supervisor [*NASA*] (NAKS)
PSS	Painful Shoulder Syndrome (MELL)
PSS	Palomar Sky Survey [*NASA*]
PSS	Parallel Search Storage (SAUS)
PSS	Parents for Student Safety (SAUS)
PSS	Partially Sighted Society [*British*]
PSS	Partia Socialiste e Shqiperise [*Socialist Party of Albania*] [*Political party*] (EAIO)
PSS	Parti de Solidarite Senegalaise [*Senegalese Solidarity Party*] [*Political party*]
PSS	Parti Socialiste Suisse [*Social Democratic Party of Switzerland*] [*Political party*] (PPE)
PSS	Partito Socialista Sammarinese [*Socialist Party of San Marino*] [*Political party*] (PPE)
PSS	Partito Socialista Somalo [*Somali Socialist Party*] [*Political party*] (PPE)
PSS	Passenger Sensing System [*Automotive safety*]
PSS	Passenger Service Supervisor [*Travel industry*]
PSS	Passenger Service Systems [*Airlines*]
PSS	Patent Searching System (SAUS)
PSS	Patent Search System [*Pergamon*] [*Database*] [*Computer science*] [*British*]
PSS	Pauli Spin Susceptibility [*Physics*]
PSS	Payless ShoeSource [*NYSE symbol*] (TTSB)
PSS	Payless ShoeSource, Inc. [*NYSE symbol*] (SAG)
PSS	Payload Specialist Station [*NASA*] (NASA)
PSS	Payload Support System [*NASA*] (MCD)
PSS	Perceived Stress Scale [*Psychology*] (DHP)
PSS	Performance Standard Sheet
PSS	Performance Summary Sheet
PSS	Performance Support System [*Human resources*] (WYGK)
PSS	Periodic Steady State (SAUS)
PSS	Periscope Simulation System [*Navy*]
PSS	Persian Shipping Services, Teheran (SAUS)
PSS	Personal Security System (SAUS)
PSS	Personnel Security Staff (SAUS)
PSS	Personnel Security System (ACAE)
PSS	Personnel Service Support [*Army*] (DOMA)
PSS	Personnel Staffing Specialist (GFGA)
PSS	Personnel Subsystem [*Air Force*] (AFM)
PSS	Personnel Support System [*Army*] (AABC)
PSS	Perturbed Stationary State (SAUS)
PSS	Phase-System Switching [*Physical chemistry*]
PSS	Physical Security Specialist (SAUS)
PSS	Physical Security Subsystem
PSS	Physical Security System (SAUS)

PSS............. Physiological Saline Solution [*Physiology*]
PSS............. Physiological Stability Score (SAUS)
PSS............. Physiologic Saline Solution (SAUS)
PSS............. Planetary Scan System [*or Subsystem*]
PSS............. Planned Systems Schedule (AAG)
PSS............. Planning Summary Sheets (AAG)
PSS............. Plant Science Seminar [*Later, ASP*]
PS/S............ Plumbing Supervisor/Specialist (AAG)
PSS............. Plume Suppression System [*Combustion technology*]
PSS............. Plunger Snap Switch
PSS............. Pneumatic Supply Subsystem (AAG)
PSS............. Polar Subsurface Sounder (SSD)
PSS............. Poly(styrenesulfonate) [*Organic chemistry*]
PSS............. Polystyrene Sulfonate (SAUS)
PSS............. Porcine Stress Syndrome [*Veterinary medicine*]
PSS............. Portable Simulation System (MCD)
PSS............. Port Safety and Security [*USCG*] (TAG)
PSS............. Portsmouth Signal School
PSS............. Posadas [*Argentina*] [*Airport symbol*] (OAG)
PSS............. Possible Signal Sample (SAUS)
PSS............. Postal Savings System [*Terminated, 1966*]
PSS............. Postal Separation System
PSS............. Postscripta [*Postscripts*] [*Latin*]
PSS............. Power Subsystem (SAUS)
PSS............. Power Supply Section
PSS............. Power Supply Subsystem (IAA)
PSS............. Power Supply System (SAUS)
PSS............. Power Switching System (SAUS)
PSS............. Power System Synthesizer
PSS............. Precancel Stamp Society (EA)
PSS............. Precision Sun Sensor (ACAE)
PSS............. Premature Separation Switch (SAA)
PSS............. Premature Separation System (ACAE)
PSS............. Presbyteri Sancti Sulpicii [*Sulpicians*] [*Roman Catholic men's religious order*]
PSS............. Pre-School Screening (SAUS)
PSS............. Preselection Secondary Section (SAUS)
PSS............. Pressure Sensitive Schottky (SAUS)
P/S/S.......... Price/Stern/Sloan Publishers, Inc.
PSS............. Primary Sampling System [*Nuclear energy*] (NRCH)
PSS............. Princess (ROG)
PSS............. Printer Storage System [*Computer science*] (MHDI)
PSS............. Printing and Stationery Service (SAUS)
PSS............. Priority Scheduling System (SAUS)
PSS............. Private Schools Survey (SAUS)
PSS............. Private Signalling System (SAUS)
PSS............. Probabilistic Safety Study [*Nuclear energy*] (NRCH)
PSS............. Probe Support Subsystem (ACAE)
PSS............. Problem Solving State (SAUS)
PSS............. Process Sampling System [*Nuclear energy*] (NRCH)
PSS............. Process Standard Specification
PSS............. Process Switching Service (IAA)
PSS............. Production System Support (SAUS)
PSS............. Product Support System (SAUS)
PSS............. Professional Services Section (BARN)
PSS............. Professor of Sacred Scripture
PSS............. Programmable Store System (SAUS)
PSS............. Programming Support System (SAA)
PSS............. Programming Systems Support (SAUS)
PSS............. Program Support Staff [*Environmental Protection Agency*] (GFGA)
PSS............. Progressive Science Series [*A publication*]
PSS............. Progressive Systemic Sclerosis [*Medicine*]
PSS............. Projected Smoke System (SEWL)
PSS............. Project Summary Sheet (SAUS)
PSS............. Propellant Supply Subsystem (SAUS)
PSS............. Propellant Supply System [*or Subsystem*]
PSS............. Proposed Sale of Securities (GFGA)
PSS............. Proprietary Software Systems [*Computer science*] (IEEE)
PSS............. Proprietary System [*Computer science*] (IAA)
PSS............. Propulsion Subsystem Structure
PSS............. Propulsion Support System (KSC)
PSS............. Protection Security Service
PSS............. Protective Security Service
PSS............. Protective Signature Service (MCD)
PSS............. Psalms [*Old Testament book*]
Pss............. Pseudomonas Syringae Syringae [*Plant pathology*]
PSS............. Pseudo-Sense Switch
PSS............. Pseudo Spread Spectrum (MCD)
PSS............. Pseudo Steady State (SAUS)
PSS............. Psychiatric Services Section [*of the American Hospital Association*] [*Later, SCSMHPS*] (EA)
PSS............. Psychiatric Status Schedules [*Psychology*]
PSS............. Psychological Saline Solution (BARN)
PSS............. Public Services Satellite
PSS............. Public Service System (SAUS)
PSS............. Public Storage Canadian Properties II [*Limited Partnership Units*] [*Toronto Stock Exchange symbol*]
PSS............. PUREX Sludge Supernatant liquid (SAUS)
PSS............. Push-Button Selection Station
PSSA.......... Payload Support Structural Assembly (SAUS)
PSSA.......... Photogrammetric Society of South Africa (SAUS)
PS(SA)........ Photographic Society of Southern Africa (BUAC)
PSSA.......... Pilot Signal Selector Adaptor (SAA)
PSSA.......... Pilots Stick Sensor Assembly (SAUS)
PSSA.......... Pitch Starting Synchro Assembly

PSSA.......... Pitch Static Stability Angle [*Automotive safety*]
PSSA.......... Polycristalline Silicon Selfaligned (SAUS)
PSSA.......... Postsunset Service Authorization [*Telecommunications*] (OTD)
PSSA.......... Pseudo-Steady-State Approximation [*Chemical engineering*]
PSSA.......... Pyroelectric Solid State Array (ACAE)
PSSAA........ Pacific Stars and Stripes Alumni Association (EA)
PSSAANDPS... Permanent Secretariat of the South American Agreement on Narcotic Drugs and Psychotropic Substances (EAIO)
PSSB.......... Palm Springs Savings Bank [*Palm Springs, CA*] [*NASDAQ symbol*] (NQ)
PSSB.......... Palm Springs Svgs Bk [*NASDAQ symbol*] (TTSB)
PSSB.......... Passing Stopped School Bus [*Traffic offense charge*]
PSSBB........ Public School System Blanket Bond [*Insurance*]
PSSC.......... Packaging, Shipping and Safety Committee (SAUS)
PSSC.......... Parachute Subsystem Sequence Controller [*NASA*] (SAA)
PSSC.......... Personal Social Services Council [*British*] (DI)
PSSC.......... Petroleum Security Subcommittee [*of Foreign Petroleum Supply Committee*] [*Terminated, 1976*] (EGAO)
PSSC.......... Philippine Social Science Council
PSSC.......... Physical Science Study Committee [*National Science Foundation*]
PSSC.......... Pious Society of Missionaries of St. Charles [*Later, CS*] [*Roman Catholic men's religious order*]
PSSC.......... Pressure-Sensitive Safety Controller [*Electronics*]
PSSC.......... Professional Staff Selection Committe (SAUS)
PSSC.......... Programmer and Star-tracker Signal Controller (SAUS)
PSSC.......... Public Service Satellite Consortium (EA)
PSSCC........ Peter Symonds School Cadet Corps [*British military*] (DMA)
PSSCP........ Partially Submerged Supercaviating Propeller (SAUS)
PSSD.......... Parallel-Serial Scan Design [*Electronics*]
PSSD.......... Personnel Service Support Directorate (DOMA)
PSSDC........ Production Service and Sales District Council (NTPA)
PSSDS........ Portable Surface Supported Diving System (PDAA)
PSSEK........ Probability of Single Shot Engagement Kill (SAUS)
PSSEK........ Probability of Single Shot Engagement Kill [*Military*]
PSSEP........ Preliminary System Safety Engineering Plan
PSSES........ Public Service Senior Executive Service [*Australia*]
PSSF.......... Petites Soeurs de la Sainte-Famille [*Little Sisters of the Holy Family*] [*Sherbrooke, PQ*] (EAIO)
PSSG.......... Payload Specialist Support Group (SAUS)
PSSG.......... Physical Science Study Group
PSSG.......... Protocol Standards Steering Group (SAUS)
PSSGNR..... Passenger
PSSHAK..... Primary Support Structures and Housing Assembly Kit (SAUS)
PSSI.......... Pacific/Sulfur/Stratus Investigation (SAUS)
PSS-I......... Peace Science Society (International) (EA)
PSSI.......... Physician Sales & Service [*NASDAQ symbol*] (TTSB)
PSSI.......... Physician Sales & Service, Inc. [*NASDAQ symbol*] (SAG)
PSSI.......... Plasma Source Ion Implantation
PSSI.......... Primary Specialty Skill Identifier [*Military*] (AABC)
PSSI.......... PSS World Medical [*NASDAQ symbol*] (SG)
PSSIIS....... Partito Socialista: Sezione Italiana del Internazionale Socialista [*Socialist Party: Italian Section of International Socialism*] [*Political party*] (PPE)
PSS(Int)...... Peace Science Society (International)
PSSJ.......... Poor Sisters of St. Joseph (TOCD)
PSSK.......... Probability of Single Shot Kill [*Of a guided missile*]
PSSK.......... Probability of Single-Shot Kill (SAUS)
PSSL.......... Princeton University Solid State and Materials Laboratory [*New Jersey*]
PSSL.......... Private Source Statement Library (SAUS)
PSSL.......... Program Source Status List (SAUS)
PSSM.......... Parking Systems Simulation Model (SAUS)
PSSM.......... Photographic Systems Simulation Model (SAUS)
PSSM.......... Planar Supercell Stack Method (SAUS)
PSSM.......... Polish Society of Social Medicine (SAUS)
PSSM.......... Preliminary Science Meeting [*NASA*]
PSSMA........ Paper Shipping Sack Manufacturers Association (EA)
PSSMLF...... Provincial Society of Spanish and Moroccan Leather Finishers [*A union*] [*British*]
PSSNY........ Philharmonic Symphony Society of New York (SAUS)
PSSO.......... Passed Slip Stitch Over (SAUS)
PSSO.......... Pass Slip Stitch Over [*Knitting*]
PsSol......... Psalms of Solomon [*Pseudepigrapha*] (BJA)
PSSP.......... Partition with Self Substitution Property (IAA)
PSSP.......... Partition with Self-Substitution Property (SAUS)
PSSP.......... Payload Specialist Station Panel [*NASA*] (MCD)
PSSP.......... Personnel Security and Surety Program [*Military*] (ADDR)
PSSP.......... Personnel Surety and Security Program
PSSP.......... Phone Center Staffing and Sizing Program [*Telecommunications*] (TEL)
PSSP.......... Pilot Stick Sensor Assembly (SAUS)
PSSR.......... Parallel-Shaft Speed Reducer
PSSR.......... Pre-Startup Safety Review [*Chemical engineering*]
PSSR.......... Primary School Staff Relations [*Project*] (AIE)
PSSR.......... Problem Status and Summary Report [*NASA*] (KSC)
PSSR.......... Provisioning Supply Support Requests [*DoD*]
PSSRA........ Public Service Staff Relations Act [*Canada*]
PSSRB........ Public Service Staff Relations Board [*Canada*]
PSSS.......... Polish Society of Soil Science (SAUS)
PSSS.......... Presidential Survivability Support System
PSSS.......... Psychiatric Status Schedule (SAUS)
Pss Sol....... Psalms of Solomon [*Biblical*] (RION)
PSST.......... Periodic Significant Scheduled Tasks [*NASA*] (NASA)
PSST.......... Prairie State Standard Time (SAUS)
PSS(T)........ Pregnancy Support Service (Tasmania) [*Australia*]

PSST	Public Sector Standardization Team (SAUS)	
PSSTA	Port Security Station [*Coast Guard*]	
PSS Transistor	Pressure Sensitive Schottky Transistor (SAUS)	
PSSU	Patch Survey and Switching Unit (MCD)	
PSSU	Pilots Stick Sensor Unit	
PSSW	Parliamentary Secretary of State for War (SAUS)	
PST	Airwork (New Zealand) Ltd. [*ICAO designator*] (FAAC)	
PST	Pacific Standard Time	
PST	Pacific Summer Time	
PST	Pad Service Tower (IGSL)	
PST	Paired Selected Ternary (IAA)	
PST	Pair Selected Ternary [*Computer science*]	
PST	Pakistan Standard Time (SAUS)	
PST	Pancreastatin [*Biochemistry*]	
PST	Pancreatic Suppression Test [*Medicine*] (AAMN)	
PST	Paroxysmal Superaventricular Tachycardia [*Medicine*] (MEDA)	
PST	Paroxysmal Supraventricular Tachycardia [*Cardiology*] (DAVI)	
PST	Partido Socialista de los Trabajadores [*Socialist Workers Party*] [*Panama*] [*Political party*] (EY)	
PST	Partido Socialista de los Trabajadores [*Socialist Workers' Party*] [*Colombia*] [*Political party*] (PPW)	
PST	Partido Socialista de los Trabajadores [*Socialist Workers' Party*] [*Mexico*] [*Political party*] (PPW)	
PST	Partition Specification Table (MHDI)	
PST	Pascal-Suttle Test [*Psychology*] (DAVI)	
PST	Pass Time [*Military*]	
pst	Paste (VRA)	
PST	Paste	
PST	Pastry (MSA)	
PST	Pasture Canyon [*Utah*] [*Seismograph station code, US Geological Survey*] [*Closed*] (SEIS)	
PST	Penicillin, Streptomycin, and Tetracycline [*Antibiotics*] (MAE)	
PST	Penicillin, Streptomycin,Tetracyclin (SAUS)	
PSt	Pennsylvania State University, University Park, PA [*Library symbol*] [*Library of Congress*] (LCLS)	
PST	Pentobarbital Sleeping Time (SAUS)	
PST	Performance Specification Tree	
PST	Periodic Self-Test [*Computer science*]	
PST	Peristimulus Time [*Neurophysiology*]	
PST	Personnel Subsystem Team [*Military*] (AFIT)	
PST	Peseta [*Monetary unit*] [*Spain and Latin America*]	
PST	Pesticide	
PST	Petrie Stores (EFIS)	
PST	Petrie Stores Corp. [*NYSE symbol*] (SPSG)	
PST	Phase Space Theory [*Physical chemistry*]	
PST	Phenol Sulfotransferase [*An enzyme*]	
PST	Philadelphia Suburban Transportation [*AAR code*]	
PST	Picture Story Test (SAUS)	
PST	Piston Shock Tunnel	
PST	Planetary Spectroscopy Telescope (SSD)	
PST	Plan Specification Tools (SAUS)	
PST	Platelet Survival Time [*Medicine*] (MELL)	
PST	Point of Spiral Tangent (KSC)	
PST	Polaris Star Tracker [*Missiles*]	
PST	Polished Surface Technique (IEEE)	
PST	Pooled Superannuation Trust	
PST	Porcine Somatotropin [*Gene-spliced animal hormone*] [*Monsanto Co.*]	
PST	Portuguese Speaking Test [*Center for Applied Linguistics*] (TES)	
PST	Positive Sign Trigger (SAUS)	
PST	Post-Stall (SAUS)	
PST	Poststenotic [*Medicine*] (DMAA)	
PST	Post Stimulus Time (SAUS)	
PST	Post-Stimulus Time	
PST	Pound Static Thrust (SAUS)	
PST	Precision Static Toroid (SAUS)	
PST	Prefrontal Sonic Treatment (SAUS)	
PST	Preliminary Safety Training (SAUS)	
PST	Preparing for Settlement and Trial (SAUS)	
PST	Pressure Sensitive Tape (SAUS)	
PST	Pressure-Sensitive Tape	
PST	Preston [*Cuba*] [*Airport symbol*] (AD)	
PST	Pre-Stretched Tubing (SAUS)	
PST	Pre-Structured Technology (SAUS)	
PST	Primary Surge Tank [*Nuclear energy*] (NRCH)	
PST	Priority Selection Table [*Computer science*] (IBMDP)	
PST	Prior Service Training [*US Army Reserve*] (INF)	
PST	Production Sampling Test (IAA)	
PST	Production Special Tooling (MCD)	
PST	Production Surveillance Test (MCD)	
PST	Product Support Technician	
PST	Professional, Scientific, and Technical	
PST	Profit Sharing Trustee (DLA)	
PST	Profit-Sharing Trustee (SAUS)	
PST	Program Status Table [*Computer science*] (IAA)	
PST	Program Synchronization Table (CMD)	
PST	Project ST [*Later, NSTA*] (EA)	
PST	Project Support Team (SAUS)	
PST	Propeller STOL [*Short Takeoff and Landing*] Transport	
PST	Propulsion Systems Trainer (SAUS)	
PST	Pro Sight Technology	
PST	Pro-Stock Truck [*Automobile racing*]	
PST	Provincial Standard Time (TRID)	
PST	Shepard's Preparing for Settlement and Trial [*A publication*]	
Pst	Static Transpulmonary Pressure at a Specific Lung Volume [*Medicine*] (DAVI)	
PSTA	Monterey Pasta [*NASDAQ symbol*] (SAG)	
PSTA	Packaging Science and Technology Abstracts [*International Food Information Service*] [*Germany*] [*Information service or system*]	
PSTA	Partido Socialista Tito Atahuichi [*Bolivia*] [*Political party*] (PPW)	
PSt-A	Pennsylvania State University, Agricultural Library, University Park, PA [*Library symbol*] [*Library of Congress*] (LCLS)	
PSTA	Pre-Sea Trial Audit (MCD)	
PSTA	Public Safety and Training Association (NADA)	
PSt-All	Pennsylvania State University, Allentown Campus, Allentown, PA [*Library symbol*] [*Library of Congress*] (LCLS)	
PSt-Alt	Pennsylvania State University, Altoona Campus, Altoona, PA [*Library symbol*] [*Library of Congress*] (LCLS)	
PSTAR	Portable Search and Target-Acquisition RADAR (SEWL)	
PSTART	Page Start register (SAUS)	
P-STATIC	Precipitation Static	
PSt-B	Pennsylvania State University, Berks Campus, Wyomissing, PA [*Library symbol*] [*Library of Congress*] (LCLS)	
PSTB	Perpetual State Bank (North Carolina) [*NASDAQ symbol*] (SAG)	
PSTB	Picture Story Test Blank [*Psychology*]	
PSTB	Propulsion System Test Bed [*for ABC helicopters*] (RDA)	
PSTB	Puget Sound Tug & Barge [*AAR code*]	
pstbd	Pasteboard (VRA)	
PSt-Be	Pennsylvania State University, Beaver Campus, Monaca, PA [*Library symbol*] [*Library of Congress*] (LCLS)	
PSTC	Pressure Sensitive Tape Council (EA)	
PSTC	Product Support Task Control (AAG)	
PSTC	Public Switched Telephone Circuits [*Telecommunications*] (TEL)	
PStcA	American Philatelic Research Library, State College, PA [*Library symbol*] [*Library of Congress*] (LCLS)	
PSt-Ca	Pennsylvania State University, Capitol Campus, Middletown, PA [*Library symbol*] [*Library of Congress*] (LCLS)	
PSTCA	Public Services Temporary Clerks' Association [*A union*] [*British*]	
PStcH	HRB-Singer, Inc., Science Park, State College, PA [*Library symbol*] [*Library of Congress*] (LCLS)	
PSTCO	Per Steering Compass [*Navigation*] (DNAB)	
PST Code	Paired Selected Ternary Code	
PSt-D	Pennsylvania State University, DuBois Campus, DuBois, PA [*Library symbol*] [*Library of Congress*] (LCLS)	
PSTD	Potato Spindle Tuber Disease	
PSTD	Prison Service Training Depot (SAUS)	
PSTD	Promotable Second-Tier Debt [*Economics*]	
PstdE	Eastern College, St. Davids, PA [*Library symbol*] [*Library of Congress*] (LCLS)	
PSt-De	Pennsylvania State University, Delaware Campus, Chester, PA [*Library symbol*] [*Library of Congress*] (LCLS)	
PST Deflection Yoke	Precision Static Toroid Deflection Yoke (SAUS)	
PSt-E	Pennsylvania State University, Behrend Campus, Erie, PA [*Library symbol*] [*Library of Congress*] (LCLS)	
PSTE	Personnel Subsystem Test and Evaluation [*Military*]	
PST-E	Priority Selection Table Extension [*Computer science*] (IBMDP)	
PSTE	Production Special Testing Equipment (MCD)	
PSTEP	Pre-Service Teacher Education Program [*National Science Foundation*]	
PSTE Program	Personnel Subsystem Test and Evaluation Program (SAUS)	
PSTF	Payload Spin Test Facility (MCD)	
PSt-F	Pennsylvania State University, Fayette Campus, Uniontown, PA [*Library symbol*] [*Library of Congress*] (LCLS)	
PSTF	Pioneer Station Training Facility [*NASA*]	
PSTF	Pressure Suppression Test Facility [*Nuclear energy*] (IEEE)	
PSTF	Privately-Owned Sewage Treatment Facility	
PSTF	Professional Staff [*NASDAQ symbol*] (SAG)	
PSTF	Profit Sharing Trust Fund	
PSTF	Proximity Sensor Test Facility [*Nuclear energy*] (NRCH)	
PSTF	Pump Seal Test Facility [*Nuclear energy*] (NRCH)	
PSTG	Postage (WGA)	
PSTGC	Per Steering Compass [*Navigation*]	
PSt-H	Pennsylvania State University, Hazelton Campus, Hazelton, PA [*Library symbol*] [*Library of Congress*] (LCLS)	
PSTH	Peristimulus Time Histogram	
PSTH	Posthumously	
PSTH	Poststimulus Time Histigram [*Medical statistics*]	
PSTH	Poststimulus Time-Histogramm (SAUS)	
PSTH	Poststimulus Time Histograph (STED)	
PSTH	Professional Sports Teams Histories [*A publication*]	
PSTI	Pancreatic Secretory Trypsin Inhibitor [*Biochemistry*]	
PSTIAC	Pavements and Soil Trafficability Information Analysis Center [*Army Corps of Engineers*] (IID)	
PSt-KP	Pennsylvania State University, King of Prussia Graduate Center, King of Prussia, PA [*Library symbol*] [*Library of Congress*] (LCLS)	
PSTL	Pastoral	
PSTL	Pistol (MSA)	
PSTL	Postal (AFM)	
PSTL	Pressure Model Static and Transient Launch Configuration (SAA)	
PSTM	Persistent Standoff Target Marker (MCD)	
PSTM	Photon Scanning Tunnelling Microscope	
PSTMA	Paper Stationery and Tablet Manufacturers Association [*Later, PCA*] (EA)	
PSt-MA	Pennsylvania State University, Mont Alto Campus, Mont Alto, PA [*Library symbol*] [*Library of Congress*] (LCLS)	
PSt-McK	Pennsylvania State University, McKeesport Campus, McKeesport, PA [*Library symbol*] [*Library of Congress*] (LCLS)	
PSTN	Pesticide Safety Team Network (GNE)	
PSTN	Piston (MSA)	

PSTN .... Position
PSTN .... Public Service Telephone Network (WDAA)
PSTN .... Public Switched (or Switching) Telephone Network (SAUS)
PSt-NK........ Pennsylvania State University, New Kensington Campus, New Kensington, PA [Library symbol] [Library of Congress] (LCLS)
PSt-O .... Pennsylvania State University, Ogontz Campus, Abington, PA [Library symbol] [Library of Congress] (LCLS)
PSTO .... Principal Sea Transport Officer
PSTO .... Purdue Student-Teacher Opinionaire [Test]
PSTOL .... Spacecraft Test Operations Language (SAUS)
PSTOP .... Page Stop register (SAUS)
PS to PS ...... Private Siding to Private Siding
PS to S .... Private Siding to Station
PSTP .... Pentasodium Triphosphate (STED)
PSTP .... Programmable Strategy Theorem Prover (SAUS)
PSTP .... Protocol Standards Technical Panel (SAUS)
PSt-PiN........ Pennsylvania State University, School of Nursing, Allegheny General Hospital, Pittsburgh, PA [Library symbol] [Library of Congress] (LCLS)
PSTR .... Pastor
PSTR .... Penn State TRIGA [Training Reactor, Isotopes General Atomic] Reactor
PSTR .... Pennsylvania State University Triga Reactor (SAUS)
PSTR .... Propulsion System Training Rig (SAUS)
P/STRG .... Power Steering [Automotive engineering]
P-Strip .... P-shaped Strip (SAUS)
PSTS .... Passive SONAR Tracking System
PSt-S .... Pennsylvania State University, Scranton Campus, Scranton, PA [Library symbol] [Library of Congress] (LCLS)
PSTS .... Personnel Selection Training School (SAUS)
PSTS .... Primary School Teachers and Science [Project] (AIE)
PSt-Sk .... Pennsylvania State University, Schuylkill Campus, Schuylkill Haven, PA [Library symbol] [Library of Congress] (LCLS)
PSt-SV .... Pennsylvania State University, Shenango Valley Campus, Sharon, PA [Library symbol] [Library of Congress] (LCLS)
PSTTX........ Pioneer Short Term Income [Mutual fund ticker symbol] (SG)
PSTV .... Potato Spindle Tuber Viroid (STED)
PSTV .... Potato Spindle Tuber Virus
PSTV .... Protocol Specification, Testing and Verification (SAUS)
PSTV .... PST Vans [NASDAQ symbol] (TTSB)
PSTV .... PST Vans, Inc. [NASDAQ symbol] (SAG)
PSTVd .... Potato Spindle Tuber Viroid [Plant pathology]
PST Vn .... PST Vans, Inc. [Associated Press] (SAG)
PSt-WB........ Pennsylvania State University, Wilkes-Barre Campus, Wilkes-Barre, PA [Library symbol] [Library of Congress] (LCLS)
PSt-WS .... Pennsylvania State University, Worthington Scranton Campus, Dunmore, PA [Library symbol] [Library of Congress] (LCLS)
PSt-X .... Pennsylvania State University, Off-Campus Libraries [Library symbol] [Library of Congress] (LCLS)
PSt-Y .... Pennsylvania State University, York Campus, York, PA [Library symbol] [Library of Congress] (LCLS)
pstyl .... Peristyle (VRA)
P'STYL........ Pronestyl [Procainamide] [Bristol-Myers Squibb Co.] [Pharmacology] (DAVI)
PSTZ .... Pasteurize (SAUS)
PSTZD .... Pasteurized (SAUS)
PSTZG .... Pasteurizing [Freight]
PSU .... Aeropeninsular, SA de CV [Mexico] [FAA designator] (FAAC)
PSu .... John R. Kaufman, Jr., [Sunbury] Public Library, Sunbury, PA [Library symbol] [Library of Congress] (LCLS)
PSU .... Package Size Unspecified
PSU-O .... Packet Switching Unit
PSU .... Page Storage Unit (SAUS)
PSU .... Partido Socialista Unificado [Socialist Unification Party] [Argentina] [Political party] (PPW)
PSU .... Partido Socialista Uruguayo [Uruguayan Socialist Party] [Political party] (PD)
PSU .... Partidul Socialist Unitar [Unitary Socialist Party] [Romania] [Political party] (PPE)
PSU .... Parti Socialiste Unifie [Unified Socialist Party] [France] [Political party] (PPW)
PSU .... Partito Socialista Unificato [Unified Socialist Party] [Italy] [Political party] (PPE)
PSU .... Partito Socialista Unitario [Socialist Unity Party] [Italy] [Political party] (PPE)
PSU .... Path Setup [Telecommunications] (TEL)
PSU .... Penn State University (SAUS)
PSU .... Pennsylvania State University
PSU .... Pennsylvania State University, University Park (USDC)
PSU .... Peripheral Switching Unit (CIST)
PSU .... Pet Services, Unlimited [Commercial firm] (EA)
PSU .... Philatelic Sales Unit
PSU .... Photosynthetic Unit
PSU .... Plasma Spray Unit
PSU .... Polyphenylene Sulfone [Organic chemistry]
PSU .... Portable Storage Unit (SAUS)
PSU .... Portland State University
PSU .... Port Security Unit [Coast Guard] (DOMA)
PSU .... Port Sharing Unit (IAA)
PSU .... Port Storage Utility [Telecommunications] (TEL)
PSU .... Postsurgical Unit (DAVI)
PSU .... Power Sensor Unit
PSU .... Power Supply Unit (MSA)
PSU .... Power Switching Unit (MCD)
PSU .... Practical Salinity Unit

PSU .... Pressure Speed-Up (SAUS)
PSU .... Pressure Status Unit (AAG)
PSU .... Primary Sampling Unit [Statistics]
PSU .... Primary Switching Unit (SAUS)
PSU .... Printed Side Up [Graphic arts] (DGA)
PSU .... Probability Sampling Unit (WDMC)
PSU .... Problem Statement Unit (SAUS)
PSU .... Processor Service Unit (ECII)
PSU .... Processor Speed Up [Computer memory core]
PSU .... Processor Storage Unit [Computer science] (CIST)
PSU .... Program Storage Unit [Computer science] (MDG)
PSU .... Pseudo (ACAE)
PSU .... Publications Services Unit (SAUS)
PSU .... Public Sector Unit (SAUS)
PSU .... Public Security Unit (SAUS)
PSU .... Public Services Unit (EERA)
PSU .... Public Storage Properties XVI [AMEX symbol] (SPSG)
PSU .... Public Storage Prop'A'XVI [AMEX symbol] (TTSB)
PSU .... Pyrotechnic Switching Unit (ACAE)
PSU .... Tatoo-a-Pet [Commercial firm] (EA)
PSUB .... Piston Supported Upper Bearing (SAUS)
PSUB .... Piston-Supported Upper Bearing
P-Substance... Protein Substance (SAUS)
PSUC .... Partit Socialista Unificat de Catalunya [Unified Socialist Party of Catalonia] [Spain] [Political party] (PPE)
PSUD .... Psychoactive Substance Use Disorder
PSU/IRL....... Pennsylvania State University Ionosphere Research Laboratory
PSU-IRL....... Pennsylvania State University-Ionosphere Research Laboratory (SAUS)
PSUL .... Power Supply Unit Launching (SAUS)
PSULI .... Partito Socialista Unitario de Lavoratori Italiani [Unitary Socialist Party of Italian Workers] [Political party] (PPE)
PSU-MRL..... Pennsylvania State University-Materials Research Laboratory (SAUS)
PSUN .... Pacific Sunwear of Calif [NASDAQ symbol] (TTSB)
PSUN .... Pacific Sunwear of California, Inc. [NASDAQ symbol] (SAG)
PSUP .... Pennsylvania State University Press (DGA)
PSUR .... Pennsylvania State University Reactor
PSURAO ..... Pennsylvania State University Radio Astronomy Observatory
PSurg.......... Plastic Surgeon (SAUS)
PSurg.......... Plastic Surgery [Medicine]
P-SURG ...... Presurgery Coagulation Profile [Hematology and surgery] (DAVI)
PSUSAM..... Philippine Statehood USA Movement [An association] (EA)
PSUT .... Phase Shifter Under Test (SAUS)
PSV .... Pair Shield Video (NITA)
PSV .... Paleosecular Variation [Geology]
PSV .... Papillitis Stenosans Vateri (DB)
PSV .... Peanut Stunt Virus
PSV .... Photographic-Spatial Volume (SAA)
PSV .... Pictorial Study of Values [Psychology]
PSV .... Pilot Secure Voice (SAUS)
PSV .... Planetary Space Vehicle [NASA] (NASA)
PSV .... Platform Supply Vessel (SAUS)
PSV .... Polished Stone Value (SAUS)
PSV .... Polished-Stone Value (PDAA)
PSV .... Portable Sensor Verifier (AAG)
PSV .... Positive Start Voltage
PSV .... Preliminary Site Visit (SAUS)
PSV .... Present State Variable (SAUS)
PSV .... Preserve (MSA)
PSV .... Pressure Safety Valve
PSV .... Pressure Support Ventilation [Medicine] (DAVI)
PSV .... Probability State Variable [Statistics]
PSV .... Program Status Vector (SAUS)
PSV .... Progressieve Surinaamse Volkspartij [Progressive Suriname People's Party] [Political party] (PPW)
PSV .... Project Salt Vault (SAUS)
PSV .... Pseudo-Synthetic Video (DOMA)
PSV .... Psychological, Social, and Vocational [Adjustment factors]
PSV .... Public Service Vehicle
PSV .... Public Storage Properties XVII, Inc. [AMEX symbol] (SAG)
PSV .... Public Storage Prop'A'XVII [AMEX symbol] (TTSB)
PSV .... Saint Vincent College, Latrobe, PA [OCLC symbol] (OCLC)
PSVC .... Power alarm on Service Cluster (SAUS)
PSvcBad...... Presidential Service Badge [Military decoration] (AABC)
PSvCol........ Public Service Co. of Colorado [Associated Press] (SAG)
PSVD .... Polystyrene-Divinylbenzene Copolymer [Organic chemistry]
PSV Device... Probabilistic State Variable Device (SAUS)
PSVER .... Pattern-Shift Visual Evoked Response [Medicine] (MEDA)
PSVL .... Peak Signal Voltage Loss (SAUS)
PSVM.......... Phase Sensitive Voltmeter (SAUS)
PSVM.......... Phase-Sensitive Voltmeter
psvm.......... Phase-Sensitive Voltmeter (IDOE)
PSVM.......... Phase Shift Voltmeter (SAUS)
PSVN .... Pilot Secure Voice Network (SAUS)
PSvNM........ Public Service Co. of New Mexico [Associated Press] (SAG)
PSVOA........ Purse Seine Vessel Owners Association (EA)
PSVOMA..... Purse Seine Vessel Owners Marketing Association [Later, PSVOA] (EA)
PSVP .... Pilot Secure Voice Project [NATO Integrated Communications System] (NATG)
PSVT.......... Paroxysmal Supraventricular Tachycardia [Cardiology]
PSVT.......... Passivate [Metallurgy]
PSVT.......... Pilot Secure Voice Terminal (SAUS)
PSVTN .... Preservation (MSA)
PSVTV .... Preservative (MSA)

PSVX	Pilot Secure Voice Exchange (SAUS)	
PSW............	Japan/Korea/Pacific South West Service (SAUS)	
PSW............	Pacific South West (SAUS)	
PSW............	Pacific Southwest Forest and Range Experiment Station [*Berkeley, CA*] [*Department of Agriculture*] (GRD)	
PSW............	Past Sleepwalker (STED)	
PSW............	Peripheral Switching Unit (NITA)	
PSW............	Pinetree Software Canada Ltd. [*Vancouver Stock Exchange symbol*]	
PSW............	Planar Stich Wire	
PSW............	Plasma Spray Welder	
PSW............	Politically Simulated World [*Computer-assisted political science game*]	
PSW............	Potential Switch	
PSW............	Potentiometer Slide Wire (SAUS)	
PSW............	Potentiometer Slidewire	
PSW............	Powerplant Specific Weight	
PSW............	Primary Shield Water (DNAB)	
PSW............	Processor Status Word	
PSW............	Process Status Word	
PSW............	Programming Status Word (SAUS)	
PSW............	Program Status Word [*Computer science*]	
PSW............	Program Support Workstation (ACAE)	
PSW............	Pskov State Aviation Enterprise [*Former USSR*] [*FAA designator*] (FAAC)	
PSW............	Psychiatric Social Worker [*British*]	
PSW............	Public Storage Properties XVIII [*AMEX symbol*] (SPSG)	
PSW............	Public Storage Prop'A'XVIII [*AMEX symbol*] (TTSB)	
PSW............	PUREX Sludge Waste (SAUS)	
PSWA	Partially Smooth Water Area (DS)	
PSWAD	Perspective Study of World Agricultural Development [*FAO*] [*United Nations*] (MSC)	
PSWB	Patented Steel Wire Bureau [*British*] (BI)	
PSWB	Plateau State Water Board (SAUS)	
PSWB	Public School Word-Book [*A publication*]	
PSWBD	Power Switchboard	
PSWBS	Project Summary Work Breakdown Structure	
PSWC	Pacifc Tsunami Warning Center (SAUS)	
PSWC	Payload Systems Weight Capability (IGSL)	
PSWF..........	Prolate Spheroidal Wave Function (PDAA)	
PSWFA	Prestige Saltwater Fly Anglers	
PSWFRES	Pacific Southwest Forest and Range Experiment Station [*Berkeley, CA*] (SAA)	
PSWG	Pressure Sine Wave Generator	
PSWG	Product Support Working Group (SAUS)	
PSWHQ........	Primary Static War Headquarters (SAUS)	
PSWHQ........	Primary Subordinate War Headquarters (SAUS)	
PSWIE	Proceedings of the South Wales Institute of Engineers (SAUS)	
PSWM	Postscript Window Manager (SAUS)	
PSWMOW	Psychiatric Social Work in Mental Observation Wards [*British*]	
PSWMRL	Pasture Systems and Watershed Management Research Lab	
PSWO	Picture and Sound World Organization	
PSWO	Princess of Wales' Own [*Military unit*] [*British*] (ROG)	
PSWO	Product Support Work Order	
PSWOPC	Psychiatric Social Work in Out-Patient Clinics [*British*]	
PSWP	Plant Service Water Pump (IEEE)	
PSWR	Powell Sport Wagon Registry (EA)	
PSWR	Power Standing Wave Ratio	
PSWR	Program Status Word Register [*Computer science*] (MHDB)	
PSWS	Peak Systolic Wall Stress (SAUS)	
PSWS	Potable and Sanitary Water System [*Nuclear energy*] (NRCH)	
PSwS	Smith, Kline & French Co. [*Later, SmithKline Corp.*], Swedeland, PA [*Library symbol*] [*Library of Congress*] (LCLS)	
PSWT..........	Polysonic Wind Tunnel (MCD)	
PSWT..........	Psychiatric Social Work Training [*British*]	
PSWTE........	Proceedings of the Society for Water Treatment and Examinations (SAUS)	
PSWTUF	Public Service Workers' Trade Union Federation [*Ceylon*]	
PSWU	Public Services Workers Union (SAUS)	
PSW Unit.....	Processor Status Word Unit	
PSX............	Pacific Scientific [*NYSE symbol*] (TTSB)	
PSX............	Pacific Scientific Co. [*NYSE symbol*] (SPSG)	
PSX............	Pacific South West Express (SAUS)	
PSX............	Palacios, TX [*Location identifier*] [*FAA*] (FAAL)	
PSX............	Pseudoexfoliation (DMAA)	
PSY............	Port Stanley [*Falkland Islands*] [*Airport symbol*]	
PSY............	PSM Technologies, Inc. [*Vancouver Stock Exchange symbol*]	
PSY............	Psychiatry	
PSY............	Psychological (CINC)	
PSY............	Public Storage Properties XIX, Inc. [*AMEX symbol*] (SAG)	
PSY............	Public Storage Prop'A' XIX [*AMEX symbol*] (TTSB)	
PSYC	Psychologist	
PSYC	Psychology	
PsyCp..........	Psychemedics Corp. [*Associated Press*] (SAG)	
PSYCH	Psychiatrist (DSUE)	
PSYCH	Psychiatry	
PSYCH	Psychic (ROG)	
Psych	Psychical (SAUS)	
PSYCH	Psychology (AFM)	
Psych	Psychology (DD)	
psych	Psychology (NTIO)	
PSYCHABS...	Psychological Abstracts	
Psych & MLJ..	Psychological and Medico-Legal Journal [*A publication*] (DLA)	
PSYCHC.......	Psychiatric	
PSYCH/D......	Psychological Death (SAUS)	
PSYCHE	Programming Systems Yearly Cost Headcount Estimate (SAUS)	

PSYCHEM....	Psychiatric Chemistry	
PSyCHES	Psychiatric Case History Event System (PDAA)	
PSYCHIAT....	Psychiatric (SAUS)	
psychiat.......	Psychiatry [*or Psychiatric*] (DAVI)	
PSYCHL	Psychological (AFM)	
PSYCHO.......	Psychoanalysis (DSUE)	
psycho	Psychopath [*Psychiatry*] (DAVI)	
Psychoan.....	Psychoanalist (SAUS)	
psychoan	Psychoanalysis [*Medicine*] (DMAA)	
Psychoanal...	Psychoanalysis (BEE)	
psychobio.....	psychobiological (SAUS)	
PSYCHOBIO...	Psychobiologist (SAUS)	
PSYCHOBIO...	Psychobiology (SAUS)	
PSYCHOBIOG...	Psychiographer (SAUS)	
PSYCHOBIOG...	Psychobiographer (SAUS)	
PSYCHOBIOG...	Psychobiographic (SAUS)	
PSYCHOBIOG...	Psychobiography (SAUS)	
PSYCHOCHRON...	Psychochronicle (SAUS)	
PSYCHOCHRON...	Psychochronologer (SAUS)	
PSYCHOCHRON...	Psychochronologic (SAUS)	
PSYCHOCHRON...	Psychochronology (SAUS)	
PSYCHOCHRONICLE...	Psychiatric Chronicle (SAUS)	
PSYCHOCHRONICLE...	Psychological Chronicle (SAUS)	
PSYCHODELS...	Psychodelics (SAUS)	
PSYCHOGEOG...	Psychogeographer (SAUS)	
PSYCHOGEOG...	Psychogeography (SAUS)	
PSYCHOHIST...	Psychohistorian (SAUS)	
PSYCHOHIST...	Psychohistorical (SAUS)	
PSYCHOHIST...	Psychohistory (SAUS)	
PSYCHOL.....	Psychology	
PSYCHOMET...	Psychometric (SAUS)	
Psychonomic Sci...	Psychonomic Science (SAUS)	
PSYCHOPATHOL...	Psychopathological (SAUS)	
PSYCHOPATHOL...	Psychopathologist (SAUS)	
psychopathol...	Psychopathology (DAVI)	
PSYCHOPHYS...	Psychophysical (SAUS)	
PSYCHOPHYS...	Psychophysicist (SAUS)	
psychophys...	Psychophysics [*Psychiatry*] (DAVI)	
psychophysiol...	psychophysiological (SAUS)	
PSYCHOPHYSIOL...	Psychophysiologist (SAUS)	
psychophysiol...	Psychophysiology [*Psychiatry*] (DAVI)	
PSYCHOPRISON...	Psychiatric Hospital Prison (SAUS)	
PSychosMed...	Psychosomatic Medicine [*Psychiatry*] (DAVI)	
PSYCHOSURG...	Psychosurgeon (SAUS)	
PSYCHOSURG...	Psychosurgery (SAUS)	
psychot........	psychotic (SAUS)	
PSYCHOTHER...	Psychotherapist (SAUS)	
psychother...	Psychotherapy [*Psychiatry*] (DAVI)	
PSYCHO WARD...	Psychopathic Ward (SAUS)	
Psych Qtly ...	Psychoanalytic Quarterly (SAUS)	
Psych Test...	Psychological Testing (SAUS)	
PSYCHY.......	Psychiatry	
PsycINFO.....	Psychological Abstracts Information Services [*American Psychological Association*] (IID)	
PSYCINFO....	Psychological Information (NITA)	
PSYCINFO....	Psychological Information (SAUS)	
PSYCO........	Peripheral System Checkout (SAUS)	
PSYCTRC	Psychiatric	
PSYCTRY	Psychiatry	
PSYCY	Psychology	
PsyD	Doctor of Psychology	
PsyD, LCP ...	Doctor of Psychology, Licensed Clinical Psychologist	
PSYDOC.......	Psychiatrist Doctor (SAUS)	
PSYETA........	Psychologists for the Ethical Treatment of Animals [*An association*] (EA)	
PsyETA	Psychologists for the Ethical Treatment of Animals (EA)	
Psy M	Master of Psychology (PGP)	
PSYNC........	Processor Synchronous (SAUS)	
PSYOP........	Psychological Operation [*Military*]	
PSYOPS.......	Psychological Operations [*Military*]	
PSY-OPS......	Psychological Warfare Operations (DNAB)	
psy-path......	Psychopath [*Psychiatry*] (DAVI)	
Psy-ped......	Psychologie-Pedagogie [*French*] (CPGU)	
PSYRES	Psychotherapeutische Forschungsstelle in Stuttgart (SAUS)	
PSYS	Precision Systems [*NASDAQ symbol*] (TTSB)	
PSYS	Precision Systems, Inc. [*NASDAQ symbol*] (SAG)	
Psy S	Specialist in Psychology (PGP)	
PSY-SDIV	Psychological Sciences Division [*Office of Naval Research*] (DNAB)	
psy-som.......	Psychosomatic (DAVI)	
PsySR	Psychologists for Social Responsibility (EA)	
PSYU	Public Sustained Yield Unit [*Forestry*]	
PSYWAR......	Psychological Warfare	
PSYWPN......	Psychological Weapon [*Military*] (AFM)	
PSZ............	Partially Stabilized Zirconia (SAUS)	
PSZ............	Partially-Stabilized Zirconia [*Ceramics*]	
PSZ............	Partly Stabilized Zirconia (SAUS)	
PSZ............	Piszkesteto [*Hungary*] [*Seismograph station code, US Geological Survey*] (SEIS)	
PSZ............	Pressure Sealing Zipper	
PSZ............	Pro Air Service [*ICAO designator*] (FAAC)	
PSZ............	Public Storage Properties XX [*AMEX symbol*] (SPSG)	
PSZ............	Public Storage Prop'A' XX [*AMEX symbol*] (TTSB)	
PSZ............	Puerto Suarez [*Bolivia*] [*Airport symbol*] (OAG)	
PSZN	Pubblicazioni. Stazione Zoologica di Napoli [*A publication*]	

PT	Advanced Planning and Technology Office [*Kennedy Space Center Directorate*] (NASA)
PT	Brazil [*International civil aircraft marking*] (ODBW)
PT	Duffryn Yard [*Welsh depot code*]
PT	Motor Torpedo Boat [*Navy symbol*] [*Obsolete*]
PT	Pacific Time
PT	Packaged Terminal (SAUS)
PT	Packed Tower (EEVL)
PT	Packet Terminal (NITA)
PT	Packet Trunk (SAUS)
PT	Packet Type (SAUS)
PT	Page Table [*Computer science*] (IAA)
PT	Page Teleprinter (SAUS)
PT	Page Terminator (SAUS)
pt	Paint (VRA)
PT	Pain Threshold
PT	Pallet Truck (DCTA)
P-T	Palomero Toluqueno [*Race of maize*]
PT	Paper Tape
PT	Paper Title [*Business term*]
PT	Paper Trooper [*One who salvaged paper for war effort*] [*World War II*]
PT	Para-Terphenyl [*Organic chemistry*]
PT	Parathormone (DB)
PT	Parathyroid [*Medicine*]
PT	Parcel Ticket [*Freight*]
PT	Paroxysmal Tachycardia [*Cardiology*]
pt	Part (DAVI)
Pt.	Part
PT	Part [*Online database field identifier*]
PT	Partially Tested (IAA)
PT	Participative Teams (MCD)
PT	Partido de los Trabajadores [*Paraguay*] [*Political party*] (EY)
PT	Partido Trabajador [*Mexico*] [*Political party*] (EY)
PT	Partition Table [*Computer science*] (IAA)
PT	Part Throttle [*Engines*]
PT	Part Time (EEVL)
P-T	Part-Time [*Employment*]
PT	Part-Timers (SAUS)
PT	Part Total [*Earnings less than weekly benefit amount*] [*Unemployment insurance*] (OICC)
PT	Paschale Tempore [*Easter Time*] [*Latin*]
PT	Passage Time (SAUS)
PT	Passenger Traffic [*MTMC*] (TAG)
PT	Passenger Train (SAUS)
PT	Passenger Transport
PT	Passing Title [*Real estate*]
PT	Passive Track [*Military*] (CAAL)
PT	Past Tense
PT	Pataca [*Monetary unit*] [*Macau*]
PT	Patch Test [*Medicine*] (MELL)
PT	Patellar Tendon [*Anatomy*]
PT	Patentee (NITA)
PT	Path & Thread (SAUS)
Pt.	Patient (WDAA)
PT	Patient
PT	Patrol Torpedo (ADWA)
PT	Patrol Torpedo Boat [*Later, PTF*] [*Navy symbol*]
PT	Pattern Transfer (SAUS)
PT	Paying Teller [*Banking*]
PT	Payload Type (SAUS)
pt	Payment (WDMC)
PT	Payment
PT	Payout Time [*Business term*]
PT	Pay Tone [*Telecommunications*] (TEL)
PT	Peacetime (SEWL)
PT	Peak Time (SAUS)
PT	Pencil Tube
PT	Penetrant Test [*Nuclear energy*] (NRCH)
PT	Penetration Test (NATG)
PT	Peninsula Terminal (SAUS)
PT	Peninsula Terminal Co. [*AAR code*]
PT	Pennant [*British naval signaling*]
P-T	Pensacola-Tallahassee [*Diocesan abbreviation*] [*Florida*] (TOCD)
PT	Pension Trustee (DLA)
PT	Perfect Title [*Business term*]
PT	Perforated Tape [*Computer science*] (IAA)
PT	Perforated Type (SAUS)
PT	Performance Technology [*Human resources*] (WYGK)
PT	Performance Test
PT	Performance Testing
PT	Pericardial Tamponade [*Medicine*] (DMAA)
PT	Periodic Test [*Nuclear energy*] (NRCH)
PT	Period Tapering (IAA)
PT	Peripheral Transfer (SAUS)
PT	Permanent and Total (SAUS)
PT	Permeability Transition [*Biochemistry*]
PT	Peroneal Tendonitis [*Medicine*] (MELL)
PT	Perpetual Traveller (ECON)
PT	Persepolis Texts (BJA)
PT	Persistent Tease [*Slang*] [*Bowdlerized version*]
P/T	Personal Time [*Employment*]
PT	Personal Trade [*Marketing and retail terminology referring to customers*]
PT	Personal Transporter
PT	Personnel & Training (SAUS)
PT	Personnel Training
PT	Perstetur [*Let It Be Continued*] [*Pharmacy*]
PT	Per Ton (SAUS)
PT	Per Truck
PT	Perturbation Theory [*Physical chemistry*]
PT	Pertussis Toxin [*Pharmacology*]
PT	Peseta [*Monetary unit*] [*Spain and Latin America*]
Pt.	Peter [*New Testament book*]
PT	Petrol Tractor [*British*]
PT	Petty Theft
PT	Phase Transfer [*Physical chemistry*]
PT	Phase Transition (SAUS)
PT	Phase Type (NITA)
PT	Pheasant Trust (EA)
PT	Phenolthiazine (SAUS)
PT	Phenytoin [*Pharmacology*] (DAVI)
PT	Philadelphia Transportation (SAUS)
PT	Phoenix Theatre [*Defunct*] (EA)
PT	Photoconductive Thermoplastic [*Materials science*]
PT	Photographic Intelligenceman [*Navy rating*]
PT	Photo Technician (SAUS)
PT	Phototherapy [*Medicine*]
PT	Phototoxity [*Medicine*]
PT	Phototransistor (NRCH)
PT	Physical Teardown (MCD)
PT	Physical Therapy [*or Therapist*]
PT	Physical Training [*Military*]
PT	Physiotherapy [*Medicine*]
PT	Piaster [*Monetary unit*] [*Spain, Republic of Vietnam, and some Middle Eastern countries*] (IMH)
PT	Picture Telegraphy [*Telecommunications*] (IAA)
PT	Picture Transmission (SAUS)
PT	Pigeon-Toed (MELL)
PT	Pilot Tape (SAUS)
PT	Pilot Test (SAUS)
PT	Pine Tar [*Medicine*]
pt	Pint (ODBW)
PT	Pint
PT	Pipe Tap (MSA)
PT	Pipe Thread (SAUS)
Pt.	Pitch (SAUS)
PT	Pitch Trim (MCD)
PT	Placebo Treated [*Medicine*]
PT	Plain Talk (EA)
PT	Plain Test (MCD)
PT	Plain Text (SAUS)
PT	Plane Table (SAUS)
PT	Planning and Timing [*of Investments*]
Pt.	Plantinum (SAUS)
PT	Planum Temporale [*Brain anatomy*]
P-T	Plasma Thermocouple Reactor [*Nuclear energy*] (NRCH)
PT	Plasma Triode (SAUS)
PT	Plasticized Transparent [*Flexography*] (DGA)
PT	Plastics Technology [*A publication*]
PT	Plastic Training (SAUS)
PT	Plastic Tube
PT	Platinum
Pt.	Platinum [*Chemical element*]
PT	Platoon Truck [*British*]
PT	Pleno Titulo [*With Full Title*] [*Latin*]
PT	Plenty Tough [*Slang*]
PT	Plenty Trouble [*Slang*]
PT	Plonia Technica
PT	Plotting Equipment [*JETDS nomenclature*] [*Military*] (CET)
PT	Plot Titles [*Test*] [*Psychology*]
PT	Pneumatic Tube [*Technical drawings*]
PT	Pneumothorax [*Medicine*]
PT	Pocket Telephone
PT	Poetry Treasury [*An association*] [*Defunct*] (EA)
pt	Point (ODBW)
PT	Point [*Maps and charts*]
Pt.	Point (SHCU)
P/T	Pointer/Tracker (MCD)
PT	Point location (SAUS)
PT	Point of Tangency
PT	Point of Turn [*Navigation*]
Pt.	Points, typographische (SAUS)
PT	Pollen Tube [*Botany*]
PT	Poll-Tax Rolls [*British*]
PT	Polymeric Triglyceride [*Food science*]
PT	Polythiophene [*Organic chemistry*]
PT	Polyvalent Tolerance (BABM)
PT	Pool Temperature [*Nuclear energy*] (NRCH)
PT	Pope and Talbot [*Steamship*] (MHDW)
PT	Popliteal Tendon [*Anatomy*]
pt	Port (ODBW)
PT	Port
PT	Portal Tract [*Anatomy*]
PT	Port Number [*Telecommunications*] (TEL)
Pt.	Porto (SAUS)
PT	Port Talbot Railway [*Wales*]
PT	Port Taxes (TRID)
PT	Port Tower (SAUS)
PT	Portugal [*ANSI two-letter standard code*] (CNC)

PT	Portugal Telecom ADS [*NYSE symbol*] (TTSB)
PT	Portugal Telecom SA [*NYSE symbol*] (SAG)
pt	Portuguese Timor [*io (Indonesia) used in records cataloged after January 1978*] [*MARC country of publication code*] [*Library of Congress*] (LCCP)
PT	Positional Tolerance (AAEL)
PT	Positional Tolerancing
PT	Position Location Reporting System Terminal
PT	Postal Telegraph (SAUS)
PT	Postal Telegraph Co. [*Terminated*]
PT	Post and Telegraph (SAUS)
PT	Post and Telegraphy [*Telecommunications*] (IAA)
PT	Poste e Telegrafi [*Post and Telegraph Service*] [*Italy*]
PT	Posterior Tibial [*Anatomy*]
PT	Posterior Tibial pulse (SAUS)
PT	Posts and Telecommunications (SAUS)
PT	Post Town
PT	Potential Transformer
PT	Power Train (SAUS)
PT	Power Transfer (KSC)
PT	Power Turbine (SAUS)
PT	Prachakorn Thai [*Thai Citizens Party*] [*Political party*]
PT	Practice Tracer (SAUS)
PT	Precision Teaching
PT	Precision Time (SAUS)
PT	Precision Time Fuze
P/T	Precision-to-Tolerance ratio (SAUS)
PT	Precision Tracker (SAUS)
PT	Precision Transform [*Eastman Kodak Co.*] [*Computer science*] (PCM)
PT	Preferential Treatment (OICC)
PT	Premium Transfer (SAUS)
PT	Preoperational Test [*Nuclear energy*] (NRCH)
PT	Prepunched Tape (SAUS)
PT	Press Test [*Psychology*]
P/T	Pressure/Temperature (KSC)
PT	Pressure Test (AAG)
PT	Pressure Time Fuel System [*Cummins Engine Co., Inc.*]
PT	Pressure Transducer (KSC)
PT	Pressure Transmitter (NRCH)
PT	Pressure Tubing
PT	Pretectal [*Neuroanatomy*]
pt	Preterit [*Past tense*] [*Grammar*]
PT	Previous Operating Time (AFIT)
PT	Primal Therapy
PT	Primary Target [*Army*]
PT	Primary Timer (SAUS)
PT	Primary Trainer [*Aircraft*]
PT	Print (MSA)
PT	Printed Text
PT	Printer Terminal
PT	Printing Tape (SAUS)
PT	Print Text (SAUS)
PT	Priority Telegram
PT	Prior Treatment [*Medicine*]
PT	Prismatic Tank (SAUS)
PT	Private Terms
PT	Procedure Trainer (SAUS)
PT	Procedure Turn [*FAA*] (TAG)
PT	Processing Tax Division [*United States Internal Revenue Bureau*] (DLA)
PT	Processing Time
PT	Processor Terminal (SAUS)
PT	Process Time (SAUS)
PT	Process Type (SAUS)
PT	Production Techniques (MCD)
PT	Production Test [*Military*]
PT	Productive Time [*Computer order entry*]
PT	Product Team (AAGC)
PT	Product Test (IAA)
PT	Proficiency Testing
PT	Profile Template
PT	Profit Taking [*Investment term*]
PT	Program (Exercise) on Treadmill
PT	Programmable Terminal [*Computer science*]
PT	Programmed Testing (SAUS)
PT	Programmed Timing (SAUS)
PT	Programmer and Timer
PT	Programmer Training (SAUS)
PT	Programming Theory (SAUS)
PT	Programming Time (SAUS)
PT	Program Tab (SAUS)
PT	Program Table (SAUS)
PT	Program Tape (SAUS)
PT	Program Termination (SAUS)
PT	Program Test (SAUS)
PT	Program Text (SAUS)
PT	Program Time (SAUS)
PT	Program Timer (SAUS)
PT	Program Track (SAUS)
PT	Program Transfer (SAUS)
PT	Program Translation (SAUS)
PT	Program Transmitter (SAUS)
pt	Progress in Technology [*Automotive industry*]
PT	Progressive Tax (MHDW)
PT	Prohibited Telegrams
PT	Project Team (SAUS)
PT	Project Technology (ACAE)
PT	Project Tibet (EA)
PT	Project Transition [*DoD*] (OICC)
PT	Project Trust (EAIO)
PT	Prolong Tablets [*Pharmacy*]
PT	Pronator Teres [*Musle*] [*Orthopedics*] (DAVI)
PT	Proof Test (AAG)
PT	Propanethiol [*Organic chemistry*]
PT	Propanthiol
PT	Propellant Injection Pressure
PT	Propellant Temperature (SAUS)
PT	Propellant Transfer
PT	Propeller Torpedo [*Boat*]
PT	Property Tax (MHDW)
PT	Property Transfer [*Real estate*] (KSC)
PT	Property Type
PT	Prophet
PT	Propylthiouracil [*Also, PROP, PTU*] [*Thyroid inhibitor*]
PT	Pro Tempore [*For the Time Being*] [*Latin*]
PT	Prothrombin Time [*Hematology*]
PT	Prototype (IAA)
PT	Provascular Tissue [*Botany*]
PT	Provincetown-Boston Airline [*ICAO designator*] (AD)
PT	Provisioning Team (AAG)
PT	Pseudoternary (SAUS)
PT	Pseudotetrade (SAUS)
Pt	Pseudoword Target [*Psychology*]
PT	Psychology Today [*A publication*] (BRI)
Pt	Pteropods [*Quality of the bottom*] [*Nautical charts*]
PT	PTP Resource Corp. [*Formerly, Petrologic Petroleum Ltd.*] [*Vancouver Stock Exchange symbol*]
PT	Publication Type [*Online database field identifier*]
PT	Public Transport (DA)
PT	Public Trustee
PT	Pull-Through [*Gun cleaning*]
PT	Pulmonary Trunk (SAUS)
PT	Pulmonary Tuberculosis [*Medicine*]
PT	Pulp Testing [*Dentistry*]
PT	Pulse Time (SAUS)
PT	Pulse Timer
PT	Pulse Train
PT	Pulse Transformator (SAUS)
PT	Pulse Transformer (IAA)
PT	Punched Tape [*Computer science*]
PT	Punch Through [*Computer science*] (IAA)
PT	Punch Transfer (SAUS)
PT	Pupil Teacher
PT	Purchase Tax [*British*]
PT	Pure Telepathy [*Psychical research*]
PT	Pyramidal Tract [*Anatomy*]
PT	Pyramid Texts (BJA)
PT	Pyrotechnic Material (SAUS)
PT	[*Serum Glutamic*] Pyruvic Transaminase [*Also, SGPT*] [*An enzyme*] (DAVI)
PT	Test Plan (SAUS)
PT	Total Pressure
PT1	Photographic Intelligenceman, First Class [*Navy rating*]
PT2	Photographic Intelligenceman, Second Class [*Navy rating*]
PT3	Photographic Intelligenceman, Third Class [*Navy rating*]
PTA	African Preferential Trade Area (SAUS)
PTA	Eastern and Southern African Preferential Trade-Area (SAUS)
PTA	National Postal Transport Association [*Later, APWU*]
PTA	Packed Tower Aeration (MEC)
PTA	Page Table Address [*Computer science*] (IAA)
PTA	Palatines to America (EA)
PTA	Pantorama Industries, Inc. [*Toronto Stock Exchange symbol*]
PTA	Paper and Twine Association (EA)
PTA	Paper Tape Accessory (MHDI)
PTA	Paper Towel Association [*British*] (BI)
PTA	Parallel Tubular Array [*Cytology*]
PTA	Parathyroid Adenoma [*Medicine*] (STED)
PTA	Parent-Teacher Association
PTA	Part Throttle Acceleration [*Engines*] (EG)
PTA	Part Time Alcoholic (SAUS)
PTA	Passenger Transport Authorities [*British*]
PTA	Passenger Transport Authority (SAUS)
PTA	Passive Towed Array (SAUS)
PTA	Patient-Triggered Analgesia (SAUS)
PTA	Penn Treaty American [*NYSE symbol*] (SG)
PTA	People Taking Action
PTA	Percent Time Active (CAAL)
PTA	Percutaneous Transluminal Angiography (SAUS)
PTA	Percutaneous Transluminal Angioplasty [*Medicine*]
PTA	Periodical Title Abbreviations [*A publication*]
PTA	Peritonsillar Abscess [*Medicine*]
PTA	Persistent Truncus Arteriosus [*Medicine*] (MAE)
PTA	Peseta [*Monetary unit*] [*Spain and Latin America*]
PTA	Pet Traders Association
PTA	Phenyltrimethylammonium [*Also, PTM, PTMA*] [*Organic chemistry*]
PTA	Philippine Tobacco Administration (SAUS)
PTA	Philippine Travel Authority (SAUS)
PTA	Phorbol Tetradecanoyl Acetate [*Also, PMA, TPA*] [*Organic chemistry*]
PTA	Phosphoryl Triamide [*Organic chemistry*]

PTA............. Phosphotransacetylase [*An enzyme*]
PTA............. Phosphotungstic Acid [*Inorganic chemistry*]
PTA............. Photographers' Telegraph Association
PTA............. Photo Transistor Amplifier (SAUS)
PTA............. Phototransistor Amplifier
PTA............. Physical Therapy Assistant
PTA............. Pianoforte Tuners' Association [*British*] (DBA)
PTA............. Piano Tuners Association (SAUS)
PTA............. Picatinny Arsenal [*New Jersey*] [*Later, Armament Development Center*] [*Army*]
PTA............. Pilotless Target Aircraft [*Military*]
PTA............. Pitch Trim Adjustment
PTA............. Pitch Trim Angle
PTA............. Planar Turbulence Amplifier (IEEE)
PTA............. Plasma Thrombin Antecedent (SAUS)
PTA............. Plasma Thromboplastin Antecedent [*Factor XI*] [*Hematology*]
PTA............. Plasma Transferred Arc [*Metallurgy*]
PTA............. Platelet Thromboplastin Antecendent [*Medicine*] (STED)
PTA............. Platinized Titanium Anode
PTA............. Point of Total Assumption (MCD)
PTA............. Polish Telegraphic Agency (SAUS)
PTA............. Pope and Talbot (SAUS)
PTA............. Port Alsworth [*Alaska*] [*Airport symbol*] (OAG)
PTA............. Postal Transportation Association (SAUS)
PTA............. Postcard Traders' Association [*British*] (DBA)
PTA............. Posterior Tibial [*Pulse*] [*Medicine*] (DAVI)
PTA............. Post-Tensioning Association (SAUS)
PTA............. Post-Test Analysis [*NASA*] (NASA)
PTA............. Post-Timeline Assessment (SEWL)
PTA............. Post-Traumatic Amnesia [*Medicine*]
PTA............. Potential Toxic Area (NASA)
PTA............. Power Transfer Assembly (IAA)
PTA............. Preferential Trade Arrangements [*ASEAN*] (IMH)
PTA............. Premium Transportation Authorization (AAG)
PTA............. Prepaid Ticket Advice [*Travel industry*] (TRID)
PTA............. Preparation through Acceptance
PTA............. Pressure Transducer Assembly
PTA............. Pre-Treatment Anxiety [*Medicine*] (DMAA)
PTA............. Prevention of Terrorism Act [*British*] (ECON)
PTA............. Price-Tag Awareness [*See also PTS*]
PTA............. Primary Target Area [*Military*]
PTA............. Primary Tungsten Association [*British*] (EAIO)
PTA............. Principle Technical Advisor (SAUS)
PTA............. Printing Trades Alliance [*British*] (DBA)
PTA............. Prior to Administration (AMHC)
PTA............. Prior to Admission [*Medicine*]
PTA............. Prior to Arrival [*Medicine*] (MAE)
PTA............. Procrustes Target Analysis [*Marine science*] (OSRA)
PTA............. Procurement Technical Assistance
PTA............. Profan Test Assessment [*NASA*]
PTA............. Profiler Triangle Analysis package (SAUS)
PTA............. Programmable Translation Array
PTA............. Programmed Time of Arrival (ACAE)
PTA............. Programmed Translation Array (SAUS)
PTA............. Program Time Analyzer
PTA............. Propfan Technology Assessment (SAUS)
PTA............. Propfan Test Assessment (ACAE)
PTA............. Proposed Technical Approach
PTA............. Propulsion Test Article [*NASA*] (NASA)
PTA............. Protestant Teachers Association (NADA)
PTA............. Prothrombin Activity [*Hematology*]
PTA............. Protionamid (SAUS)
PTA............. Proton Target Area
PTA............. Ptarmigan Airways Ltd. [*Canada*] [*ICAO designator*] (FAAC)
PTA............. Pulse Torquing Assembly (KSC)
PTA............. Punta Arenas [*Chile*] [*Seismograph station code, US Geological Survey*] [*Closed*] (SEIS)
PTA............. Purchase Transaction Analysis
PTA............. Pure Terephthalic Acid (DICI)
PTA............. Pure Tone Acuity (STED)
PTA............. Pure Tone Audiometry (MELL)
PTA............. Pure Tone Average [*Otorhinolaryngology*] (DAVI)
PTA............. Purified Terephthalic Acid [*Organic chemistry*]
PTAA............. Airman Apprentice, Photographic Intelligenceman, Striker [*Navy rating*]
PTA-A........ Periodical Title Abbreviations: by Abbreviation [*A publication*]
PTAA............. Professional Tattooists Association of Australia
PTAB............. Photographic Technical Advisory Board [*American National Standards Institute*]
PTAB............. Program Status Table [*Computer science*] (IAA)
PTAB............. Project Technical Advisory Board (AAEL)
PTAC............. Penn Treaty American [*NASDAQ symbol*] (TTSB)
PTAC............. Penn Treaty American Corp. [*NASDAQ symbol*] (NQ)
PTAC............. Plant Transportation Advisory Committee
PTAC............. Procurement Technical Assistance Centers (SAUS)
PTAC............. Professional and Technical Advisory Committee [*JCAH*]
P'TACH........ Parents for Torah for All Children [*Program for learning disabled children*]
PTACV........ Prototype Aircushioned Vehicle (SAUS)
PTACV........ Prototype Tracked Air-Cushion Vehicle
PTACX........ PIMCO: Target Cl.C [*Mutual fund ticker symbol*] (SG)
PTAD........... (Phenyl)triazolinedione [*Organic chemistry*]
PTAD........... Productivity and Technical Assistance Division [*Mutual Security Agency, Abolished, 1953*]
PTADB......... Planning Terrain Analysis Data Base (SAUS)

PTADSIM..... Program Tactical Air (SAUS)
PT AEQ........ Partes Aequales [*Equal Parts*] [*Pharmacy*]
PTAF............ Platelet Activating Factor (DMAA)
PTAF............ Policy Target Adjustment Factor (MEDA)
PTAFR........ Platelet Activating Factor Receptor (DMAA)
PTAG........... Portable Tactical Aircraft Guidance (SAUS)
PTAG........... Portable Tactical Approach Guidance (SAUS)
PTAG........... Professional Tattoo Artists Guild (EA)
P-TAG......... Target-Attaching Globulin Precursor [*Medicine*] (STED)
PTAH........... Phosphotungstic Acid-Hematoxylin [*A stain*]
PTAL........... Para-Tolualdehyde [*Organic chemistry*]
PTAL........... Payment Transaction Application Layer [*Computer science*] (ITCA)
PTA Modulation... Phase-to-Amplitude Modulation (SAUS)
PTAN........... Airman, Photographic Intelligenceman, Striker [*Navy rating*]
PT & E........ Physical Teardown and Evaluation (MCD)
PT & E........ Progress Tests and Examinations
PT & ER...... Physical Teardown and Evaluation Review (MCD)
PT & ME...... Physical Teardown and Maintenance Evaluation [*Army*]
PT&Rec Sch... Physical Training and Recreational School (SAUS)
PT & W........ Physical Training and Welfare [*British military*] (DMA)
PTANYC...... Protestant Teachers Association of New York City (EA)
PTAP........... Phenyltrimethylammonium Perbromide [*Organic chemistry*]
PTAP........... Porsche Technology Apprenticeship Program [*Automotive industry*]
PTAP........... Profiler Triangle Analysis Package [*Marine science*] (OSRA)
PTAP........... Purified Diphtheria Toxoid Precipitated by Aluminum Phosphate (AAMN)
PTAP........... Purified Toxoid precipitated by Aluminum Phosphate (SAUS)
PTAR........... Prime Time Access Rule [*Television*]
PTAS........... Pilotless Target Aircraft Squadron (SAUS)
PTAS........... Productivity and Technical Assistance Secretariat (SAUS)
PTASE......... Phosphatase [*An enzyme*] (DHSM)
PTA-T......... Periodical Title Abbreviations: by Title [*A publication*]
PTAT........... Pesticides, Toxics, and Air Team (COE)
PTAT........... Private Trans Atlantic Telecommunications (SAUS)
PTAT........... Proportional to Absolute Temperature (IAA)
PTAT........... Pure Tone Average Threshold (DMAA)
PTAT Cable... Private Transatlantic Telephone Cable (SAUS)
PTAV........... Percutaneous Transluminal Aortic Valvuloplasty [*Cardiology*] (CPH)
PTAVE......... Parents and Teachers Against Violence in Education (EA)
PTAWT........ Atlantic Wind Test Site, Tignish, Prince Edward Island [*Library symbol*] [*National Library of Canada*] (NLC)
PTB............. Page Table Base [*Computer science*] (IAA)
PTB............. Paragon Trade Brands [*NYSE symbol*] (SPSG)
ptB............. Part Bunkers [*Shipping*] (DS)
PTB............. Partial Test Ban (SAUS)
PTB............. Partido Trabalhista Brasileiro [*Brazilian Labor Party*] [*Political party*] (PPW)
PTB............. Parti du Travail de Belgique [*Belgian Labour Party*] [*Political party*] (EY)
PTB............. Parti du Travail du Burkina [*Burkina Faso*] [*Political party*] (EY)
PTB............. Patellar Tendon Bearing [*Medicine*]
PTB............. Patrol Torpedo Boat (WDAA)
PTB............. Payload Timing Buffer [*NASA*] (NASA)
PTB............. Perishables Tariff Bureau, Atlanta GA [*STAC*]
PTB............. Permian-Triassic Boundary [*Geology*]
PTB............. Persistent, Toxic and Bioaccumulative substances (SAUS)
PTB............. Personnel Test Battery
PTB............. Petersburg, VA [*Location identifier*] [*FAA*] (FAAL)
PTB............. Phenacylthiazolium Bromide [*Organic chemistry*]
PTB............. Phosphotyrosine-Binding [*Biochemistry*]
PTB............. Physical Transaction Block
PTB............. Physikalisch Technische Bundesanstalt (ACII)
PTB............. Point Barrow [*Alaska*] [*Later, BRW*] [*Seismograph station code, US Geological Survey*] [*Closed*] (SEIS)
PTB............. Pounds per Thousand Barrels [*Petroleum technology*]
PTB............. Pressure Test Barrel
PTB............. Prior to Birth [*Medicine*]
PTB............. Processor Test Bus (SAUS)
PTB............. Process Technical Bulletin (MCD)
PTB............. Production and Test Branch (IAA)
PTB............. Program Time Base [*Military*] (AFIT)
PTB............. Protected Terminal Block (SAUS)
PTB............. Prothrombin (SAUS)
PTB............. PT Boats, Inc. (EA)
PTBA........... Percutaneous Transluminal Balloon Angioplasty [*Cardiology*] (DMAA)
PTBA........... Privat Termination Basic Access (SAUS)
PTBA........... Proud to be Australian [*Political party*]
PTBB........... Para-tertiary-butylbenzaldehyde [*Organic chemistry*]
PTBBA .... Para-tertiary-butylbenzoic Acid [*Organic chemistry*]
PTBD .... Percutaneous Transhepatic Biliary Drainage [*Medicine*]
PTBD .... Percutaneous Transluminal Balloon Dilatation [*Medicine*] (MELL)
PTBD-EF..... Percutaneous Transhepatic Biliary Drainage - Enteric Feeding [*Medicine*] (DAVI)
PTBE .... Pyretic Tick-Borne Encephalitis [*Medicine*] (DMAA)
PTBF .... Portal Tributary Blood Flow [*Physiology*]
PTBI .... PT Boats, Inc. (EAIO)
PTBIPK .... Poly(t-Butyl Isopropenyl Ketone) [*Organic chemistry*]
PTBK .... Partbook [*Music*]
PTBL .... Portable (AABC)
PTBL .... Potable (SAUS)
PT boat........ Patrol Boat (SAUS)
PTBPD .... Posttraumatic Borderline Personality Disorder [*Medicine*] (DMAA)
PTBR .... Processing Tax Board of Review Decisions [*United States Internal Revenue Bureau*] [*A publication*] (DLA)
PTBR .... Punched Tape Block Reader [*Computer science*]

PtBS	Poly(tertiary-butylstyrene) [*Organic chemistry*]
PTBS	Posttraumatic Brain Syndrome [*Medicine*] (DMAA)
PTBT	Para-tertiary-butyltoluene [*Organic chemistry*]
PTBT	Partial Test Ban Treaty (SAUS)
PTBT	Partial Test-Ban Treaty
PTBT	Pretransplant Blood Transfusion [*Medicine*]
PTBVK	Poly(t-Butyl Vinyl Ketone) [*Organic chemistry*]
ptbx	Partbook (GROV)
PTC	Chief Photographic Intelligenceman [*Navy rating*]
PTC	Motor Boat Subchaser [*Navy symbol*] [*Obsolete*]
PTC	Pacific Telecommunications Conference (or Council) (SAUS)
PTC	Pacific Telecommunications Council (EA)
PTC	Pacific Theological College (SAUS)
PTC	Pacific Tin Consolidated (SAUS)
PTC	Pacific Tuna Conference
PTC	Paisley Technical College (SAUS)
PTC	Paket-Test-Center (SAUS)
PTC	Pakistan Television Corporation Ltd. (SAUS)
PTC	Paper Tape Code (SAUS)
PTC	Paper Tape Control (SAUS)
PTC	Parallel Test Component (SAUS)
PTC	PAR Technology [*NYSE symbol*] (TTSB)
PTC	PAR Technology Corp. [*NYSE symbol*] (SPSG)
Ptc	Participating [*Business term*]
PTC	Parti Travailliste Congolais [*Congolese Labor Party*] [*Political party*]
PTC	Part Through Crack [*Alloy tension*]
PTC	Passive Thermal Control
PTC	Patent, Trademark, and Copyright Institute [*Franklin Pierce College*] (IID)
PTC	Patrol Vessel, Motor Torpedo Boat, Submarine Chaser [*Navy symbol*]
PTC	Payload Training Complex (SAUS)
PTC	Peace Tax Campaign [*Australia*]
PTC	Peace Through Confrontation (SAUS)
PTC	Pentagon Telecommunications Center (MCD)
PTC	Peoples Telephone Co., Inc. (EFIS)
PTC	Peoria Terminal (SAUS)
PTC	Peoria Terminal Co. [*AAR code*]
PTC	Percutaneous Cholangiography [*Medicine*]
PTC	Percutaneous Transhepatic Cholangiogram [*Medicine*]
PTC	Percutaneous Transhepatic Cholangiography (SAUS)
PTC	Performance Test Chamber (MCD)
PTC	Performance Test Code
PTC	Performance Test Codes (SAUS)
PTC	Periscope Television Camera [*Telecommunications*] (IAA)
PTC	Permission to Take Classes [*Education*]
PTC	Personal Transfer Capsule
PTC	Personal Typing Centre (NITA)
PTC	Personnel Transfer Capsule [*Undersea technology*]
PTC	Personnel Transfer Chamber (SAUS)
PTC	Personnel Transit Center (SAUS)
PTC	Personnel Transport Carrier
PTC	Phase Transfer Catalysis [*Physical chemistry*]
PTC	Phenylisothiocyanate [*Organic chemistry*]
PTC	Phenylthiocarbamide [*or Phenylthiocarbamyl*] [*Organic chemistry*]
PTC	Pheochromocytoma, Thyroid Carcinoma Syndrome [*Oncology*] (MAE)
PTC	Philadelphia Transportation Co. (SAUS)
PTC	Photographic Training Centre [*British*] (CB)
PTC	Photographic Type Composition (ADA)
PTC	Physical Training Centre (SAUS)
PTC	Physical Training Course (SAUS)
PTC	Pine Tree Camp (SAUS)
PTC	Pipe and Tobacco Council (SAUS)
PTC	Pipe and Tobacco Council of America [*Defunct*] (EA)
PTC	Pipe Tobacco Council (EA)
PTC	Pitch Trim Compensator
PTC	Pitch Trim Controller (MCD)
PTC	Plan to Clear [*Aviation*] (FAAC)
PTC	Plasma Thromboplastin Component [*Factor IX*] [*Also, CF*] [*Hematology*]
PTC	Plastics Technology Centre (SAUS)
PTC	Plastic Training Cartridge [*Army*] (INF)
PTC	Platelet Count (SAUS)
PTC	Plugged Telescoping Catheter [*Clinical chemistry*]
PTC	Pneumatic Temperature Control
PTC	Pneumatic Test Console
PTC	Points to Consider
PTC	Police Training Centre [*British*]
PTC	Portable Tele-Transaction Computer [*Telxon*]
PTC	Portable Temperature Control (KSC)
PTC	Portable Temperature Controller [*NASA*] (NAKS)
PTC	Porto Cannone [*Italy*] [*Seismograph station code, US Geological Survey*] (SEIS)
PTC	Portuguese Trade Commission (EA)
PTC	Positive Target Control [*Aviation*] (FAAC)
PTC	Positive Temperature Coefficient
PTC	Positive Transmitter Control
PTC	Postal and Telegraphic Censorship [*Telecommunications*] (IAA)
PTC	Postal Telegraph Cable
PTC	Post and Telecommunications Corp. (SAUS)
PTC	Posterior Trabeculae Carneae [*Heart anatomy*]
PTC	Posts and Telecommunications Corp. (SAUS)
PTC	Post-Tensioned Concrete [*Technical drawings*]
PTC	Post-Turnover Change [*Nuclear energy*] (NRCH)
PTC	Power Testing Code (MCD)
PTC	Power Transfer Coefficient
PTC	Power Transmission Council
PTC	Practical Tonnage Capacity (SAUS)
PTC	Pre- and Post-Process Treatment Chambers (AAEL)
PTC	Prehead Triple Coil (SAUS)
PTC	Premature Tricuspid Closure [*Medicine*] (DMAA)
PTC	Preoperative Testing Center
PTC	Preparatory Technical Committee (SAUS)
PTC	Press Trust of Ceylon (SAUS)
PTC	Pressure and Temperature Control (KSC)
PTC	Pressure Transducer Calibrator
PTC	Pre-Temperature Control (SAUS)
PTC	Primary Teaching Certificate [*Australia*]
PTC	Primary Technical Control (SAUS)
PTC	Primary Technical Course [*Military*]
PTC	Primary Training Center (SAUS)
PTC	Primary Training Centre [*British military*] (DMA)
PTC	Princeton Resources Corp. [*Vancouver Stock Exchange symbol*]
PTC	Printer Terminal Control
PTC	Private Truck Council (SAUS)
PTC	Process and Test Control (SAUS)
PTC	Programmable Telecommunication Interface (SAUS)
PTC	Programmable Temperature Controls
PTC	Programmable Test Console
PTC	Programmed Transmission Control (BUR)
PTC	Programmer Training Center
PTC	Programming and Training Center (SAUS)
PTC	Programming through the Connector [*Electronics*]
PTC	Program of Technical Cooperation [*Organization of American States*]
PTC	Program Test Controller
PTC	Promotional Telephone Call [*Marketing*] (OICC)
PTC	Proof Test Capsule [*NASA*]
PTC	Propellant Tanking Console (AAG)
PTC	Propeller Technical Committee
PTC	Propensity to Consume (MHDW)
PTC	Propulsion Test Complex (KSC)
PTC	Prothrombin Complex [*Hematology*]
PTC	Pseudotumor Cerebri [*Medicine*] (AAMN)
PTC	Psychophysical Timing Curve
PTC	Public Services, Tax & Commerce Union (WDAA)
PTC	Publishing Technology Corp. [*Information service or system*] (IID)
PTC	Pulse Time Code
PTC	Punched Tape Card (SAUS)
PTC	Punched Tape Check (SAUS)
PTC	Punched.Tape Code (SAUS)
PTC	Push-to-Connect [*Pneumatic systems*]
PTCA	Patience T'ai Chi Association (EA)
PTCA	Percutaneous Transhepatic Cholangiogram (SAUS)
PTCA	Percutaneous Transluminal Catheter Angioplasty (SAUS)
PTCA	Percutaneous Transluminal Coronary Angioplasty [*Medicine*]
PTCA	Plains Tribal Council of Assam [*India*] [*Political party*] (PPW)
PTCA	Postal Telegraph Clerks' Association [*A union*] [*British*]
PTCA	Pressure Technology Corp. of America
PTCA	Private Truck Council of America (EA)
PTCA	Professional Tennis Coaches' Association [*Australia*]
PTCAA	Professional Turkey Calling Association of America (EA)
PTCAD	Provisional Troop Carrier Airborne Division
PTCC	Pacific Division Transport Control Center
PTCC	Pacific-Division Transport Control Center (SAUS)
PTCC	PerSeptive Tech II Corp. [*NASDAQ symbol*] (SAG)
PT/CC	Problem Tracking and Change Control [*Computer science*]
PTCCS	Polaris Target Card Computing System [*Missiles*]
PtcD	Phosphatidylcholine [*Biochemistry*]
PTCD	Private Training College for the Disabled (AIE)
PTCE	Patient Treatment Clinical Exercise (SAUS)
PTCE	Peripheral Terminal Control Element (SAUS)
PTCE	Permanent Test Facility Control Element (SAUS)
PT-Cephalgia	Posttraumatic Cephalgia (SAUS)
PTCF	Primary Technical Control Facility (SAUS)
PTCH	Pacer Technology [*NASDAQ symbol*] (NQ)
PTCHY	Patchy [*Meteorology*] (DA)
PTCI	Programmable Telecommunications Interface (MCD)
PTCI	Programmable Terminal Communications Interface (MCD)
PTCL	Pakistan Telecommunication Company Limited
PT CL	Part Called [*Stock exchange term*] (MHDB)
PTCL	Peripheral T-Cell Lymphoma [*Oncology*]
PTCLD	Part Called [*Stock exchange term*] (SPSG)
PTCLD	Port Called (SAUS)
PTCLDY	Partly Cloudy (SAUS)
PTCM	Master Chief Photographic Intelligenceman [*Navy rating*]
PTCMA	Plastic Tanks and Cisterns Manufacturers Association (SAUS)
Pt Copyright & TM Cas	Patent, Copyright, and Trade Mark Cases [*United States*] [*A publication*] (DLA)
PTCP	Parameter Test Control Program [*Computer science*] (IAA)
PTCP	Participate (FAAC)
PTCP	Positive Turnaround Control Point (MCD)
PTCPY	Paper Tape Copy (SAUS)
PTCR	Pad Terminal Connection Room [*NASA*]
PTCR	Patent, Trademark and Copyright Research Institute (SAUS)
PTCR	Payload Terminal Connector Room [*NASA*] (MCD)
PTCR	Percutaneous Transluminal Coronary Recanalization [*Cardiology*] (DMAA)
PTCR	Positive Temperature Coefficient of Resistance (SAUS)
PTCR	Positive Temperature Coefficient Resistance [*Materials science and technology*]

PTCRA .... Percutaneous Transluminal Coronary Rotational Ablation [*Cardiology*] (DMAA)
PTCRM .... Partial Thermochemical Remanent Magnetization
Pt/CrNe .... Plantinum Cromium Neon-onboard spectral calibration (SAUS)
PTCS .... Passive Thermal Control Section [*NASA*] (NASA)
PTCS .... Passive Thermal Control System (NASA)
PTCS .... Pax Tibi cum Sanctis [*Peace to Thee with the Saints*] [*Latin*]
PTCS .... Pentagon Telecommunication Center System (SAUS)
PTCS .... Percutaneous Transhepatic Cholangioscopy [*Medicine*]
PTCS .... Phenyltrichlorosilane [*Organic chemistry*]
PTCS .... Planning, Training, and Checkout System [*NASA*] (MCD)
PTCS .... Portable Tracking & Control Station (SAUS)
PTCS .... Powertrain Control Signal [*Automotive engineering*]
PTCS .... Pressure Transducer Calibration System
PTCS .... Propellant Tanking Computer System (KSC)
PTCS .... Senior Chief Photographic Intelligenceman [*Navy rating*]
PTCT .... Path Count (SAUS)
PtCT .... Patient Care Technologies (ADWA)
PTCT .... Protect (MSA)
PT-CT .... Prothrombin Time Control [*Hematology*] (DAVI)
PTC Thermistor... Positive Temperature Coefficient Thermistor (SAUS)
PTCU .... Punched Tape Control Unit (SAUS)
PTCU .... Pilot-Operated Temperature Control Valve
PTCV .... Plowright Tissue Culture Vaccine [*Against rinderpest*]
PTD .... Package Travel Directive (WDAA)
PTD .... Painted (AAG)
ptd .... Painted (VRA)
PTD .... Paper Tape Date (SAUS)
PTD .... Paper Towel Dispenser [*Technical drawings*]
PTD .... Parallel Transfer Disk [*Computer science*]
PTD .... Parallel Transfer Drive
PTD .... Particle Transfer Device
PTD .... Part Throttle Deceleration [*Engines*] (EG)
PTD .... Patented (IAA)
PTD .... Percutaneous Transluminal Dilatation [*Medicine*] (DMAA)
PTD .... Period to Discharge [*Medicine*] (DAVI)
PTD .... Permament Total Diabilitty (SAUS)
PTD .... Permanent Total Disability [*Medicine*]
PTD .... Personality Trait Disorder (MELL)
PTD .... Phenyltriazolinedione [*Organic chemistry*]
Ptd .... Phosphatidic (SAUS)
Ptd .... Phosphatidyl
PTD .... Photodiode Detector [*Instrumentation*]
PTD .... Photothermal Deflection
PTD .... Physical Teardown (MCD)
PTD .... Physical Theory of Diffraction (SAUS)
PTD .... Pilot to Dispatcher
PTD .... Plant Test Date [*Telecommunications*] (TEL)
PTD .... Pointed (WGA)
PTD .... Portland [*Oregon*] [*Seismograph station code, US Geological Survey*] (SEIS)
PTD .... Posttuning Drift
PTD .... Potsdam, NY [*Location identifier*] [*FAA*] (FAAL)
PTD .... Potter Distilleries Ltd. [*Toronto Stock Exchange symbol*] [*Vancouver Stock Exchange symbol*]
PTD .... Printed
PTD .... Prior to Delivery (MELL)
PTD .... Prior to Discharge [*Medicine*] (MAE)
PTD .... Professional Training and Development (SAUS)
PTD .... Programmable Thermal Desorber (SAUS)
PTD .... Programmable Threshold Detector (MCD)
PTD .... Programmed Thermal Desorber
PTD .... Program Test Director (CCCA)
PTD .... Provisional Technical Documentation (SAUS)
PTD .... Provisioning Technical Data
PTD .... Provisioning Technical Documentation
PTD .... Provisioning Transcript Documentation (MCD)
PTDA .... Passive Target Data Analysis (SAUS)
PTDA .... Per Task Data Area [*Computer science*] (BYTE)
Ptd A .... Pointed Arch (SAUS)
PTDA .... Power Transmission Distributors Association (EA)
PTDA .... Professional Tournament Directors Association (SAUS)
PTDB .... Point Target Data Base (SAA)
PTDC .... Pacific Trade and Development Conference [*OPTAD*] (FEA)
PTDC .... Pakistan Tourism Development Corp. (SAUS)
PtdCho .... Phosphatidylcholine (STED)
PTD Drive .... Parallel Transfer Disk Drive (SAUS)
PTDDSS ...... Provisioning Technical Documentation Data Selection Sheet [*NASA*] (NASA)
PTDDSS ...... PTD Data Selection Sheet (SAUS)
PTD/E .... Physical Teardown Evaluation
Pt Dest .... Port of Destination (SAUS)
PtdEtn .... Phosphatidylethanolamine (STED)
PTDF .... Pacific Tuna Development Foundation (EA)
PTDF .... Procurement Technical Data File [*DoD*]
PtdGro .... Phosphatidylglycerol (SAUS)
Pt Dhgtr ..... Patient's Daughter [*Also, Pt DTR*] (DAVI)
PTDI .... Punched Tape Data Input (SAUS)
PTDIA .... Professional Truck Driver Institute of America (EA)
PtdIns .... Phosphatidylinositol [*Also, PI*] [*Biochemistry*]
Pt Disch ...... Port of Discharge
Pt Disch Decl... Port of Discharge Declared (SAUS)
PTDL .... Programmable Tapped Delay Line (PDAA)
PTDOS .... Processor Technology Disk Operating System
PTDP .... Permanent Transvenous Demand Pacemaker (STED)

PTDP .... Preliminary Technical Data Package (SAUS)
PTDP .... Preliminary Technical Development Plan (AFM)
PTDP .... Production Technical Data Package (SAUS)
PTDP .... Proposed Technical Development Plan
PTDQ .... Polymerized Trimethyl Dihydro Quinoline (SAUS)
PTDQ .... Polymerized Trimethyldihydroquinoline [*Organic chemistry*]
PTDR .... Post-Test Disassembly Report (SAUS)
PtdS .... Phosphatidylserine [*Biochemistry*]
PTDS .... Photo Target Detection System
PtdSer .... Phosphatidylserine (STED)
PTDTL .... Pumped Tunnel Diode Transistor Logic
PTDTL Circuit... Pumped Tunnel Diode Transistor Logic Circuit (SAUS)
PT DTR....... Patient's Daughter [*Also, Pt Dhgtr*] (DAVI)
PTDU .... Pointing and Tracking Demonstration Unit (MCD)
PTe .... Indian Valley Public Library, Telford, PA [*Library symbol*] [*Library of Congress*] (LCLS)
PTE .... International Federation of Professional and Technical Engineers
PTE .... Nouadhibou [*Mauritania*] [*Airport symbol*] (AD)
PTE .... Packet Transfer Engine [*Newbridge Networks Corp.*]
PTE .... Packet Transport Equipment [*Computer science*] (PCM)
PTE .... Page Table Entry
PTE .... Parathyroid Extract (SAUS)
PTE .... Parathyroid Extract [*Medicine*]
PTE .... Partido de Trabajadores Espanoles [*Spanish Workers' Party*] [*Political party*] (PPE)
PTE .... Part-Time Education (WDAA)
PTE .... Party to Exemption [*RSPA*] (TAG)
PTE .... Passenger Transport Executive [*British*]
PTE .... Path Terminating Equipment
PTE .... Peace through Education Project [*An association*]
PTE .... Pectin transeliminase [*or Pectate Lyase*] [*An enzyme*]
PTE .... Peculiar Test Equipment
PTE .... Perforated Tape Exchange (SAUS)
PTE .... Permanent Total Enclosure (EEVL)
PTE .... Personal Terminal Environment (SAUS)
PTE .... Photographic Tasks and Equipment [*NASA*]
PTE .... Plant Transaction Entry (SAUS)
PTE .... Plasma Thromboplastin Enzyme (SAUS)
PTE .... Plate (ROG)
PTE .... Portable Test Equipment (AAG)
PTE .... Portage [*Alaska*] [*Seismograph station code, US Geological Survey*] (SEIS)
PTE .... Port Stephens [*Australia*] [*Airport symbol*] (OAG)
PTE .... Posttraumatic Endophthalmitis (STED)
PTE .... Post-Traumatic Epilepsy (MELL)
PTE .... Potentially Toxic Element
PTE .... Potential to Emit (GNE)
PTE .... Power Transport Equipment
PTE .... Pressure Test Equipment (MCD)
PTE .... Pressure-Tolerant Electronics (IEEE)
PTE .... Pretax Earnings [*Employment*]
PTE .... Pretibial Edema [*Medicine*] (DAVI)
PTE .... Primrose Technology Corp. [*Vancouver Stock Exchange symbol*]
Pte .... Private (WDAA)
PTE .... Private [*British*]
PTE .... Private Trade Entity
PTE .... ProActive Technologies, Inc. [*AMEX symbol*] (SAG)
PTE .... Problem Trend Evaluation (MCD)
PTE .... Process and Test Equipment (SAUS)
PTE .... Production Test Equipment (MCD)
PTE .... Protect Error (SAUS)
PTE .... Proximal Tibial Epiphysis [*Orthopedics*] (DAVI)
PTE .... Proxylem Tracheary Element [*Botany*]
Pte .... Pteroyl [*Biochemistry*]
PTE .... Pulmonary Thromboembolism [*Medicine*]
PTE .... Punched Tape Equipment (SAUS)
PTEA .... Preliminary Training Effectiveness Analysis
PTEA .... Pulmonary Thromboendarterectomy [*Medicine*] (ADWA)
PTEAR .... Physical Teardown
PTEAR .... Physical Teardown and Maintenance Allocation Review (MCD)
PTeb .... Tebtunis Papyri [*A publication*] (OCD)
PTEC .... Phoenix Technologies [*NASDAQ symbol*] (TTSB)
PTEC .... Phoenix Technologies Ltd. [*NASDAQ symbol*] (NQ)
PTEC .... Plastics Technical Evaluation Center [*Military*]
pt ed .... Patient Education (DAVI)
PTED .... Pulmonary Thromboembolic Disease [*Medicine*]
PteGlu .... Pteroylmonoglutamic Acid [*Folic acid*] [*Also, FA, PGA*] [*Biochemistry*]
PTEK .... Premiere Technologies [*NASDAQ symbol*] (TTSB)
PTEK .... Premiere Technologies, Inc. [*NASDAQ symbol*] (SAG)
PTEL .... Peoples Telephone Co. [*NASDAQ symbol*] (TTSB)
PTEL .... People's Telephone Co., Inc. [*NASDAQ symbol*] (NQ)
PT Employment... Part-Time Employment (SAUS)
PTEN .... Patterson Energy [*NASDAQ symbol*] (TTSB)
PTEN .... Patterson Energy, Inc. [*NASDAQ symbol*] (SAG)
PTEN .... Pentaerythritol Tetranitrate [*An explosive and a vasodilator*] [*Cardiology*] (DAVI)
PTEN .... Prime Time Entertainment Network [*Television broadcasting*]
pter .... End of Short Arm of Chromosome [*Medicine*] (STED)
PTER .... Physical Teardown and Evaluation Review (MCD)
PTERM .... Physical Terminal (SAUS)
PTES .... Productivity Trend Evaluation System (MCD)
PTES .... Purdue Teacher Evaluation Scale
PTET .... Platinum Entertainment [*NASDAQ symbol*] (TTSB)
PTETD .... Production Test Engineering Task Description (MCD)
PTE Technology... Pressure Tolerant Electronic Technology (SAUS)

PTETPC	Party to Expose the Petrov Conspiracy [*Australia*] [*Political party*]
PTETS	Pioneer Television and Electronic Technicians Society [*Defunct*] (EA)
PT EX	Part Exchange (WDAA)
PTF	fast patrol boat (SAUS)
PTF	Fast Patrol Craft (SAUS)
PTF	Malololailai [*Fiji*] [*Airport symbol*] (OAG)
PTF	Paralemniscal Tegmental Field [*Neuroanatomy*]
PTF	Parathyroid Fever [*Medicine*] (CPH)
PTF	Particulars to Follow (SAUS)
PTF	Parts Transfer Form (SAA)
PTF	Part-Time Force (SAUS)
PTF	Patch and Test Facility
PTF	Patient Treatment File [*Medicine*] (DMAA)
PTF	Patrol Torpedo Boat, Fast [*Formerly, PT*] [*Navy symbol*]
PTF	Payload Test Facility [*VAFB*] [*NASA*] (MCD)
PTF	Payload Training Facility (SAUS)
PTF	Permanent Test Facility (SAUS)
PTF	Permit to Fly [*Aviation*] (AIA)
PTF	Petersfield Oil & Minerals [*Vancouver Stock Exchange symbol*]
PTF	Phase Transfer Function (MCD)
ptf	Plaintiff (GEAB)
PTF	Plaintiff [*Legal term*] (ROG)
PTF	Plasma Thromboplastin Factor [*Factor VIII*] [*Also, AHF, AHG, TPC*] [*Hematology*]
PTF	Police Training Foundation
PTF	Polymer Thick Film
PTF	Polytetrafluoroethylene (EDCT)
PTF	Pool Transmission Facility (SAUS)
PTF	Port Task Force
PTF	Power Test Fail
PTF	Problem Temporary/Trouble Fix (SAUS)
PTF	Production Tabulating Form (AAG)
PTF	Programming Temporary Fixed (SAUS)
PTF	Program Temporary Fix [*Computer science*]
PTF	Program Trouble Fix (SAUS)
PTF	Proof Test Facility [*Nuclear energy*]
PTF	Propellant Tank Flow
PTF	Propulsion Test Facilities (or Facility) (SAUS)
PTF	Proximal Tubule Fluid [*Laboratory science*] (DAVI)
PTF	Pthread Framework (SAUS)
PTF	Pulse Transfer Function
PTF	Punched Tape Feed (SAUS)
PTF	Punch-Through Factor (SAUS)
PTF	Reengineering Task Force
PTFA	Preliminary Tool and Facility Analysis (MCD)
PTFA	Prothrombin Time Fixing Agent (DMAA)
PTFACE	Permanent Test Facility Auxiliary Control Element (SAUS)
PTFC	Pretty Things Fan Club (EA)
PTFCE	Polytrifluorochloroethene (BARN)
PTFD	Personnel, Training and Force Development [*Army*]
PTFD	Punched Tape Feed Device (SAUS)
PTFDA	Professional Travel Film Directors Association [*Later, Professional Travelogue Sponsors - PTS*] (EA)
PTFE	Polyterafluoroethylene (SAUS)
PTFE	Polytetrafluorethylen (SAUS)
PTFE	Polytetrafluoroethene (SAUS)
PTFE	Polytetrafluoroethylene [*Organic chemistry*]
PTFG	Large Guided Missile Motorboat [*Navy symbol*] (DNAB)
PTFHA	Physician Task Force on Hunger in America [*Defunct*] (EA)
PTFHC	Putnam Tax Free Health Care Fund [*Associated Press*] (SAG)
PTFM	Passive Target Flow Management
PTFM	Platform (AAG)
PTFMA	Peacetime Force Material Assets [*Navy*] (AFIT)
PTFMA	Public Telecommunications Financial Management Association (EA)
PTFMO	Peacetime Force Materiel Objective [*Army*]
PTFMPO	Peacetime Force Materiel Procurement Objective [*Army*]
PTFMR	Peacetime Force Material Request
PTFMR	Peacetime Force Materiel Requirements [*Army*]
PTFMR-A	Peacetime Force Materiel Requirements - Acquisition [*Army*] (AABC)
PTFMR-R	Peacetime Force Materiel Requirements - Retention [*Army*] (AABC)
PTFP	Prime-Time Family Programming (SAUS)
PTFP	Public Telecommunications Facilities Program [*Department of Commerce*]
PTFS	Pilot-to-Forecaster Service (NOAA)
PTFS	Posttraumatic Fibromyalgia Syndrome [*Medicine*] (DMAA)
PTFT	Production Temporary Facility Tool (SAA)
PTFUR	President's Task Force on Urban Renewal (EA)
PTFX	Plating Fixture (AAG)
ptg	Painting (VRA)
PTG	Parathyroid Gland [*Medicine*] (DMAA)
PTG	Parent-Teacher Group
PTG	Pennington Gap, VA [*Location identifier*] [*FAA*] (FAAL)
PTG	Personal Training Guide (SAUS)
PTG	Piano Technicians Guild (EA)
PTG	Pietersburg [*South Africa*] [*Airport symbol*] (OAG)
PTG	Place to Go (IAA)
PTG	Place-to-Go (SAUS)
PTG	Planed, Tongued, and Grooved (DAC)
PTG	Planning and Tracking Group
PTG	Pointing (SAUS)
PTG	Polaris Task Group [*Missiles*]
PTG	Portage Industries Corp. [*AMEX symbol*] (SPSG)
PTG	Portageville [*Missouri*] [*Seismograph station code, US Geological Survey*] [*Closed*] (SEIS)
PTG	Port Task Group (SAUS)
PTG	Portuguese (ROG)
PTG	Precise Tone Generator [*Telecommunications*] (TEL)
PTG	Pressure Test Gauge
PTG	Pressure Transfer Gauge
ptg	Printing (WDMC)
PTG	Printing
PTG	Professional Technical Group
PTG	Prothoracic Gland [*Insect anatomy*]
PTG	Pulse Target Generator
PTG	Small Guided Missile Motorboat [*Navy symbol*] (DNAB)
PTG	Teniposide [*Antineoplastic drug regimen*] (DAVI)
PTGA	Pteroyltriglutamic Acid [*Pharmacology*]
PTGANE	Professional Technical Group on Aerospace and Navigational Electronics (SAUS)
PTGAP	Professional Technical Group on Antennas and Propagation [*of the IEEE*]
PTGBD	Percutaneous Transhepatic Gallbladder Drainage [*Medicine*]
PTGC	Programmed Temperature Gas Chromatography
PTG CYL	Printing Cylinder (DGA)
PTGEC	Professional Technical Group on Electronic Computers [*Later, IEEE Computer Society*]
PT GEO	Posted to Geographics
PTGEWS	Professional Technical Group on Engineering Writing and Speech [*of the IEEE*]
pTGF	Porcine Transforming Growth Factor
PTGL	Pyrolysis to Gases and Liquids [*Chemical processing*]
PTGRFI	Professional Technical Group on Radio Frequency Interference (SAUS)
PTGS	Paper Trade Golfing Society [*British*]
PTGS	Picosecond Transient Grating Spectroscopy
PTGS	Portable Telemetry Ground Station
Ptg Std	Petrograd Standard (SAUS)
PTGT	Primary Target [*Military*]
PTGWO	Philippine Transport and General Workers Organisations (SAUS)
PTH	Hydrofoil Motor Torpedo Boat [*Ship symbol*] (NATG)
PTH	Pacer Technology (EFIS)
PTH	Pallet Torque Hook
PTH	Panther Mines Ltd. [*Vancouver Stock Exchange symbol*]
PTH	Paper Tape Half-Duplex
PTH	Parathormon (SAUS)
PTH	Parathormone [*Medicine*] (MAE)
PTH	Parathyroid Hormone [*Endocrinology*]
PTH	Path (GAVI)
PTH	Pathology [*Medical specialty*] (DHSM)
PTH	Peak Tanning Hours [*Supposedly occurring between 10am and 2pm*] [*See also BROTS, SROTS*]
PTH	Phenylthiohydantoin [*Organic chemistry*]
PTH	Pin-Through-Hole (SAUS)
PTH	Plasma Thromboplastin Component [*Medicine*] (DMAA)
PTH	Plated through Hole
Pth	Polythiophene [*Organic chemistry*]
PTH	Port Heiden [*Alaska*] [*Airport symbol*] (OAG)
PTH	Port Heiden, AK [*Location identifier*] [*FAA*] (FAAL)
PTH	Post-Transfusion Hepatitis [*Medicine*]
PTH	Processor Test Handler (SAUS)
PTH	Project Team Head (MHDI)
PTH	Project Top Hat [*Defunct*] (EA)
PTH	Psychotherapeutische Medizin (SAUS)
PtHA	Pinto Horse Association of America (EA)
P Th B	Bachelor of Practical Theology
PTH Circuit	Plated Through Hole Circuit (SAUS)
PThD	Punch-Through Device (PDAA)
PtHeat	Petroleum Heat & Power Corp. [*Associated Press*] (SAG)
PtHel	Petroleum Helicopter, Inc. [*Associated Press*] (SAG)
PTHF	Polytetrahydrofuran [*Organic chemistry*]
PtHg	Partially Hearing (AIE)
PTHLGST	Pathologist
PTH-LP	Parathyroid Hormone-Like Peptide [*Endocrinology*]
PT/HR	Pints per Hour (SAUS)
PTHrP	Parathormon related Peptides (SAUS)
PTHrP	Parathyroid Hormone-Related Protein [*Biochemistry*]
PTHrP	PTH-related Proteins (SAUS)
PTHS	Parathyroid Hormone Secretion Rate [*Endocrinology*] (MAE)
PTHS	Profile Total Hip System (MELL)
PTHSE	Penthouse (TVEL)
PTI	First USA Paymentech [*NYSE symbol*] (TTSB)
PTI	First USA Paymentech, Inc. [*NYSE symbol*] (SAG)
PTI	I-GOOS Panel on Technical Implementation (SAUS)
PTI	Pacific Telecom, Incorporated
PTI	Package Turn In (MCD)
PTI	Packet Type Identifier (SAUS)
PTI	Pancreatic Trypsin Inhibitor [*Biochemistry*]
PTI	Parent Training and Information [*Centers*] [*Established under the Individuals with Disabilities Education Act (IDEA)*] (PAZ)
PTI	Parkes-Tidbinbilla Interferometer [*Astronomy*]
PTI	Party Identity [*Telecommunications*] (TEL)
PTI	Pathways to Independence [*An association*] (EA)
PTI	Payload Type Identifier
PTI	Payload Type Indicator (SAUS)
PTI	Paymentech, Inc. [*NYSE symbol*] [*Formerly, First USA Paymentech*]
PTI	Pennsylvania Transportation Institute [*Pennsylvania State University*] [*Research center*] (RCD)
PTI	Penn Telecom, Inc. [*Gibsonia, PA*] (TSSD)
PTI	Persistent Tolerant Infection

PTI.............	Personnel Tests for Industry
PTI.............	Personnel Transaction Identifier [*Air Force*] (AFM)
PTI.............	Philadelphia Textile Institute
PTI.............	Physical-Technical Institute [*Former USSR*]
PTI.............	Physical Therapy Intervention (AMHC)
PTI.............	Physical Training Instructor [*British*]
PTI.............	Physico-Technical Institute (SAUS)
PTI.............	Pictorial Test of Intelligence [*Education*]
PTI.............	Pipe Test Insert [*Liquid Metal Engineering Center*] [*Energy Research and Development Administration*] (IEEE)
PTI.............	Plant Transfer In (SAUS)
PTI.............	Plugging Temperature Indicator [*Nuclear energy*] (NRCH)
PTI.............	Poetry Therapy Institute (EA)
PTI.............	Porous Tungsten Ionizer
PTI.............	Portable Test Instrument (SAUS)
PTI.............	Post-Tensioning Institute [*Defunct*] (EA)
PTI.............	Power Tool Institute (EA)
PTI.............	Power Tool Institute, Inc. (SAUS)
PTI.............	Practice Training Index
PTI.............	Precision Technology, Inc. (AAG)
PTI.............	Preliminary Test Information (KSC)
PTI.............	Pre-programmed Test Input (SAUS)
PTI.............	Presentation of Technical Information (SAUS)
PTI.............	Presistent Tolerant Infection (SAUS)
PTI.............	[*The*] Press Trust of India
PTI.............	Pretrial Intervention (BARN)
PTI.............	Pre-Trial Investigation (DNAB)
PTI.............	Pre-Trip Inspection [*Shipping*]
PTI.............	Previously-Taxed Income
PTI.............	Prinicipal-Teacher Interaction Study (EDAC)
PTI.............	Production Training Indicator [*Computer science*]
PTI.............	Product Test Interface (SAUS)
PTI.............	Programmed Test Input (MCD)
PTI.............	Programming Tools and Information [*IBM Corp.*] [*Computer science*]
PTI.............	Program Transfer Interface
PTI.............	Promethean Technologies, Inc. [*Vancouver Stock Exchange symbol*]
PTI.............	Protein Technologies International
PTI.............	Publicacoes Tecnicas Internacionais Ltda. [*International Technical Publications Ltd.*] [*Information service or system*] (IID)
PTI.............	Public Technology, Inc. [*Research center*] (RCD)
PTI.............	Public Tool Interface [*Computer science*] (ODBW)
PTI.............	Punched Tape Information (SAUS)
PTI.............	Puntilla Lake, AK [*Location identifier*] [*FAA*] (FAAL)
PTIA...........	Pet Trade and Industry Association (EAIO)
PTIC...........	Patent and Trade Mark Institute of Canada
PTIC...........	Patent and Trademark Institute of Canada (SAUS)
PTIDG	Presentation of Technical Information Discussion Group (SAUS)
PTIDG	Presentatson of Technical Information Discussion Group (SAUS)
PTIE	Pet Trade and Industry Exhibition [*British*] (ITD)
PTIG...........	Presentation of Technical Information Group (SAA)
PTIHd........	PTI Holding, Inc. [*Associated Press*] (SAG)
PTI Hold	PTI Holding, Inc. [*Associated Press*] (SAG)
PTII...........	PTI Holding [*NASDAQ symbol*] (TTSB)
PTII...........	PTI Holding, Inc. [*NASDAQ symbol*] (SAG)
PTIIW.........	PTI Hldg Wrrt [*NASDAQ symbol*] (TTSB)
PTIL...........	Parts Test Information List (KSC)
PTIM..........	Punched Tape Invoicing Machine (SAUS)
PTIME........	Periodic Timer (SAUS)
PTIO...........	Pesticides Technical Information Office (SAUS)
PTI-ODT.....	Personnel Tests for Industry - Oral Directions Test
PTIOS........	Paper Tape Input/Output System (SAUS)
PTIOS........	Plant Transfer In Operating System (SAUS)
PTIP..........	Physical Therapist in Independent Practice (GFGA)
PTIP..........	Pluribus Terminal Interface Processor [*Computer science*] (CIST)
PTIR..........	Precision Track Illuminator RADAR (SEWL)
PTIRFM.......	Polarized Total Internal Reflection Fluorescence Microscopy
PTIS...........	Pacific Triangle Information Services [*Information service or system*] (IID)
PTIS...........	Photothermal Infrared Spectroscopy (SAUS)
PTIS...........	Photo Thermal Ionization Spectroscopy (AAEL)
PTIS...........	Photothermal Ionization Spectroscopy (SAUS)
PTIS...........	Photo Thermical Ionization Spectroscopy (SAUS)
PTIS...........	Piano Teachers Information Service (SAUS)
PTIS...........	Plasma Therm [*NASDAQ symbol*] (TTSB)
PTIS...........	Plasma-Therm, Inc. [*NASDAQ symbol*] (NQ)
PTIS...........	Powertrain Input Signal [*Automotive engineering*]
PTIS...........	Programmed Test Input System (MCD)
PTIS...........	Program Test Input System (SAUS)
PTIS...........	Propulsion Test Instrumentation System (KSC)
PTIWU	Posts and Telegraphs Industrial Workers' Union [*India*]
PTIX...........	Performance Technologies [*NASDAQ symbol*] (TTSB)
PTIX...........	Performance Technologies, Inc. [*NASDAQ symbol*] (SAG)
PTJ	Part-Time Job
PTJ	Portland [*Australia*] [*Airport symbol*] (OAG)
PTJ	Pulse Train Jitter [*Computer science*] (IAA)
PTJ	Pulse-Train Jitter (SAUS)
PTJA..........	Plan to Join Airways (SAUS)
PTK	Passport to Knowledge [*Program*]
PTK	Phototherapeutic Keratectomy [*Ophthalmology*]
PTK	Polishing Tool Kit
PTK	Pontiac, MI [*Location identifier*] [*FAA*] (FAAL)
PTK	Potentiometer Tapping Kit
PTK	Probability of Track [*Military*]
PTK	Protein-Tyrosine Kinase [*An enzyme*]
PTKK..........	Truk [*Caroline Islands*] [*ICAO location identifier*] (ICLI)

PTL.............	Pain Tolerance Level (MELL)
PTL.............	Parameter Table Load (SAUS)
PTL.............	Partial Total Loss [*Insurance*] (DS)
PTL.............	Part Time Legislature
PTL.............	Part Truck Load (SAUS)
PTL.............	Pass the Loot (SAUS)
PTL.............	Patrol [*or Patrolman*] (AABC)
PTL.............	Patrol Boat
PTL.............	Peacetime Losses [*Military*]
PTL.............	Penteli [*Greece*] [*Seismograph station code, US Geological Survey*] (SEIS)
PTL.............	[*Sodium*] Pentothal [*An anesthetic*] (DAVI)
PTL.............	People That Live (SAUS)
PTL.............	People That Love [*Of television's "PTL Club"*] [*Facetious translations: "Pass the Loot" and "Pay the Lady"*]
PTL.............	Perinatal Telencephalic Leukoencephalopathy [*Medicine*]
PTL.............	Peripheral T-Cell Lymphoma [*Oncology*]
PTL.............	Petroleum Testing Laboratory
PTL.............	Phase Tracking Loop (MCD)
PTI.............	Philips Telecommunicatie Industrie (SAUS)
PTL.............	Photographic Technology Laboratory (KSC)
PTL.............	Physikalisch-Technisches Labor (SAUS)
PTI.............	Pictorial Test of Intelligence (SAUS)
PTL.............	Pietermaritzburg [*South Africa*] [*Airport symbol*] (AD)
PTL.............	Pintle [*Design engineering*]
PTL.............	Pittsburgh Testing Laboratory (EFIS)
PTL.............	Planning Test List
PTL.............	Pocket Testament League (EA)
ptl.............	Portal (VRA)
PTL.............	Posterior Tricuspid Leaflet (SAUS)
PTL.............	Power Transmission Line (OA)
PTL.............	Praga Tools (SAUS)
PTL.............	Praise the Lord [*Of television's "PTL Club"*] [*Facetious translations: "Pass the Loot" and "Pay the Lady"*]
PTL.............	Pressure, Torque, and Load
PTL.............	Preterm Labor [*Obstetrics*] (DAVI)
PTL.............	Pre-Test Laboratory (DNAB)
PTL.............	Pretty Tough Lawyer [*Refers to Melvin Belli, attorney for Tammy and Jim Bakker of the PTL Club*]
PTL.............	Primary Target Line [*Military*]
PTL.............	Process and Test Language
PTL.............	Project Title (SAUS)
PTI.............	Protect the Innocent (SAUS)
PTL.............	Providence Air Charter [*ICAO designator*] (FAAC)
PTL.............	Public Television Library
PTL.............	Pulse Transmission Logic (IAA)
PTLA...........	Praise the Lord Anyway
PTLA...........	Publishers' Trade List Annual
PTLAP.........	Petroleum Test Laboratory Accreditation Program
PTLBD	Particleboard
PTLC...........	Piedmont Triad Library Council [*Library network*]
PTLC...........	Precipitation Thin-Layer Chromatography [*Medicine*] (DMAA)
PTLC...........	Preparative Thin-Layer Chromatography (DB)
PT-LD	Physical Teardown - Logistics Demonstration (MCD)
PTLD...........	Post-Transfusion Liver Disease [*Medicine*]
PTLD...........	Prescribed Tumor Lethal Dose [*Oncology*]
PTLEF.........	Peace through Law Education Fund (EA)
PTLEN........	Petal Length [*Botany*]
PTLF..........	Pressure, Temperature, Level, and Flow [*Chemical engineering*]
PTLL..........	Pittsburgh Toy Lending Library (SAUS)
PTL Network...	Praise the Lord Television Network (SAUS)
PTLP..........	Pre-Timeline Planning (SEWL)
PTLRS	Publications and Technical Literature Research Section [*Environmental Protection Agency*] (IID)
PTLS..........	Program-controlled Train Leading System (SAUS)
PTLV..........	Peach Twisted Leaf Virus (SAUS)
PTLV..........	Primate T-Lymphotropic Viruses
PTLX..........	Patlex Corp. [*NASDAQ symbol*] (SAG)
PTLY..........	Partly [*NWS*] (FAAC)
Ptly Pd.......	Partly Paid (SAUS)
PTM...........	Packet Transfer Mode (SAUS)
PTM...........	Packet Transport Mode (SAUS)
PTM...........	Packet Trunk Module (SAUS)
PTM...........	Palmarito [*Venezuela*] [*Airport symbol*] (OAG)
PTM...........	Pancake Torque Motor (SAUS)
PTM...........	Pancake Torquer Motor (SAA)
PTM...........	Parasite Tubing Method (PDAA)
PTM...........	Passenger Ton Miles (SAUS)
PTM...........	Passenger Traffic Manager
PTM...........	Pass Through Mode (SAUS)
PTM...........	Patient Monitored (MELL)
PTM...........	Pattern Test Mount (SAUS)
PTM...........	Pattern Transformation Memory
PTM...........	Performance Test Model (OA)
PTM...........	Petromac Energy, Inc. [*Vancouver Stock Exchange symbol*]
PTM...........	Phase Time Modulation
PTM...........	Phase-Time Modulation (SAUS)
PTM...........	Phenyltrimethylammonium [*Also, PTA, PTMA*] [*Organic chemistry*]
PTM...........	Photomultiplier (IAA)
PTM...........	Photon Tunneling Microscope
PTM...........	Photo Tracing Machine (SAUS)
PTM...........	Physical Teardown and Maintenance (MCD)
PTM...........	Pietermaritzburg [*South Africa*] [*Seismograph station code, US Geological Survey*] (SEIS)
PTM...........	Pilot Training Missile (ACAE)

PTM............	Please Tell Me (SAUS)
PTM............	Pneumatic Telescope Mast
PTM............	Polaris Tactical Missile
PTM............	Portable Traffic Monitor [Telecommunications] (TEL)
PTM............	Portland Terminal Co. [AAR code]
PTM............	Posttransfusion Mononucleosis [Medicine]
PTM............	Post-Traumatic Meningitis [Medicine] (MELL)
PTM............	Pressure Time per Minute (SAUS)
PTM............	Pressure-Transmitting Medium [Engineering]
Ptm............	Pressure Transmural [Pretaining to an airway or blood vessel] [Medicine] (DAVI)
PTM............	Preterm Milk [Medicine]
PTM............	Pretuned Module [Telecommunications] (IAA)
PTM............	Primary Thickening Meristem [Botany]
PTM............	Priority Timing Module
PTM............	Product Test Monitor (SAUS)
PTM............	Professional, Technical and Management (SAUS)
PTM............	Programmable Terminal Multiplexer [Texas Instruments, Inc.]
PTM............	Programmable Timer Module
PTM............	Program Time Multiplex (SAUS)
PTM............	Program Timing and Maintenance [Electronics] (IAA)
PTM............	Program Timing and Miscellaneous [Electronics]
PTM............	Program Trouble Memoranda (or Memorandum) (SAUS)
PTM............	Program Trouble Memorandum [NASA] (IAA)
PTM............	Proof Test Model [NASA]
PTM............	Propellant-Pressurant Tank Module (ACAE)
PTM............	Prototype Model (SAUS)
PTM............	Pulse Tie Modulation (SAUS)
PTM............	Pulse Time Modulation [Radio]
PTM............	Pulse Time (or Modulation) (SAUS)
PTM............	Pulse Transmission Mode (MCD)
PTM............	Punched Tape Memory (SAUS)
PTM............	Punch-Through Modulation (SAUS)
PTM............	Putnam Managed High Yield Trust [NYSE symbol] (SPSG)
PTM............	Putnam Managed Hi Yield Tr [NYSE symbol] (TTSB)
PTM............	Southeastern Airways Corp. [ICAO designator] (FAAC)
PTMA............	Phenyltrimethylammonium [Also, PTA, PTM] [Organic chemistry]
PTMA............	Phosphotungstomolybdic Acid [Inorganic chemistry]
PTMA............	Prednisolone Trimethylacetate (SAUS)
PTMA............	Prothymosin Alpha (DMAA)
PTMAS........	Professional, Technical, Managerial, and Administrative Staff
PTMC............	Photomechanical (VRA)
PTMC............	Polaris Tender Management Computer [Missiles]
PTMC............	Polish Telephones & Microwave Corp. [NASDAQ symbol] (SAG)
PTMC............	Polish Tels & Microwave Corp. [NASDAQ symbol] (TTSB)
PTMCA............	Pit Tub and Mine Car Manufacturers' Association [British] (BI)
PTMCW........	Polish Tels & Microwave Wrrt [NASDAQ symbol] (TTSB)
PTMD............	Propellant Toxicity Monitoring Device (SAUS)
PTMD............	Propellant Toxicity Monitoring Devices (KSC)
PTMDF........	Pupils, Tension, Media, Disc, Fundus [Medicine]
PTME............	Physical Teardown/Maintenance Evaluation
PTMEG........	Polytetramethylene Ether Glycol [Organic chemistry]
PTMG............	Polytetramethylene Glycol (SAUS)
PTML............	PNP [Positive-Negative-Positive] Transistor Magnetic Logic (IEEE)
PTML............	Positive Negative, Positive Negative Transistor Magnetic Logic
PTML............	Proxicom Template Markup Language [Computer science]
PTMOD........	Paper Tape Module (SAUS)
PTM/OS........	Programmable Terminal Monitor/Operating System (NITA)
PTMPY........	Per Thousand Members per Year (DMAA)
PTMR............	Percutaneous Transmyocardial Revascularization [Medicine]
PTMS............	Parathymosin (DMAA)
PTMS............	Para-Toluidine-meta-sulfonic Acid [Also, PTMSA] [Organic chemistry]
PTMS............	Pattern Transformation Memory System
PTMS............	Precision Torque Measuring System (NASA)
PTMS............	Publication Text Management System (MCD)
PTMS............	Public Transportation Facilities and Equipment Management System [FHWA] (TAG)
PTMSA........	Para-Toluidine-meta-sulfonic Acid [Also, PTMS] [Organic chemistry]
PTMSP........	Poly(trimethylsilyl-propyne) [Organic chemistry]
PTMT............	Poly(tetramethylene Terephthalate) [Organic chemistry]
PTMTCS......	Power-Tape-to-Magnetic-Tape Conversion System (SAUS)
PTMTLG........	Pitometer-Log [Engineering]
PTMU............	Power and Temperature Monitor Unit (KSC)
PTMU............	Pressure & Temperature Measurement Unit (SAUS)
PTMUX........	Pulse Time Multiplex (MSA)
PTMV............	Percutaneous Transvenous Mitral Valvotomy [Cardiology]
PTM x ESV...	Pressure Timer per Minute x Endsystolic Volume (SAUS)
PTN............	Morgan City/Patterson [Louisiana] [Airport symbol] (OAG)
PTN............	Pantanal Linhas Aereas Sul-Matogrossenses SA [Brazil] [ICAO designator] (FAAC)
PTN............	Particulate Total Nitrogen [Analytical chemistry]
PTN............	Partido Trabalhista Nacional [National Workers' Party] [Brazil]
PTN............	Partition (KSC)
PTN............	Patterson, LA [Location identifier] [FAA] (FAAL)
PTN............	Peace Through NATO (SAUS)
PTN............	Personal Telecommunications Number (SAUS)
PTN............	Personal Telephone Number (SAUS)
PTN............	Phenotemperature Normogram [Phenology]
PTN............	Phenytoin [Anticonvulsant]
PTN............	Photographic Trade News (SAUS)
PTN............	Plant Test Number [Telecommunications] (TEL)
PTN............	Pluton Industries Ltd. [Vancouver Stock Exchange symbol]
Ptn............	Portion (SAUS)
PTN............	Potsdam [New York] [Seismograph station code, US Geological Survey] (SEIS)
PTN............	Private Telecommunication Network [Telecommunications] (OSI)
PTN............	Procedure Turn [ICAO] (FAAC)
Ptn............	Pterin [Biochemistry]
PTN............	Public Telephone Network (DA)
PTN............	Pull-Thru Network (EA)
PTN............	Pyramidal Tract Neuron (SAUS)
PTNA............	Pituitary Tumor Network Association (EA)
PTNA............	Professional Travel Nurses Association (SAUS)
PTNB............	Preterm Newborn (MELL)
pTNM............	Postsurgical, Tumor, Nodes, and Metastases [Classifications for postsurgical resection pathological staging of cancer] [Oncology] (DAVI)
PTNR............	Partner (ROG)
Ptnr............	Partner (TBD)
PTNRSHIP ...	Partnership (ROG)
PTNX............	Printronix, Inc. [NASDAQ symbol] (NQ)
PTNX............	Private Telecommunication Network Exchange [Telecommunications] (OSI)
PTO............	Desiderio & Taylor,Planning Tax-Exempt Organizations (SAUS)
PTO............	North West Geomatics Ltd. [Canada] [ICAO designator] (FAAC)
PTO............	Pacific Theater of Operations [World War II]
PTO............	Packard Truck Organization [Defunct] (EA)
PTO............	Paid Time Off (NFD)
PTO............	Parent-Teacher Organization (SAUS)
PTO............	Participating Test Organization [Air Force]
PTO............	Partners Oil & Mining [Vancouver Stock Exchange symbol]
PTO............	Part Time Operation (DA)
PTO............	Patent and Trademark Office [Formerly, PO] [Department of Commerce]
PTO............	Pato Branco [Brazil] [Airport symbol] (OAG)
PTO............	People, Topics, Opinions [A publication] [British]
PTO............	Percutaneous Transhepatic Obliteration (STED)
PTO............	Perlsucht Tuberculin Original [Medicine] (MAE)
PTO............	Perlsucht-Tuberculin Original
PTO............	Permeability Tuned Oscillator (SAUS)
PTO............	Permeability-Tuned Oscillator (IAA)
PTO............	Personal Time Off (DAVI)
PTO............	Personal Trust Officer [Banking] (TBD)
PTO............	Physical Training Officer (SAUS)
PTO............	Plant Transfer Out (SAUS)
pto............	Please Turn Over (WDMC)
PTO............	Please Turn Over [the page]
PTO............	Porto [Serro Do Pilar] [Portugal] [Seismograph station code, US Geological Survey] (SEIS)
PTO............	Port Transportation Officer
PTO............	Power Takeoff [Automotive engineering]
PTO............	Power Test Operations (MCD)
PTO............	Powertrain Operations [Auto manufacturer corporate structure]
PTO............	Preliminary Technical Order (ACAE)
PTO............	Prevent Take-Off (SAUS)
PTO............	Primary Test Organization (ACAE)
PTO............	Principal Technical Officer (SAUS)
PTO............	Professional and Technology Officer [British]
PTO............	Project Technical Office [Military] (DNAB)
PTO............	Project Type Organization (AAG)
PTO............	Proof Test Orbiter [NASA]
PTO............	Propellant Transfer Operation (AFM)
PTO............	Provisional Topographic Overprint (SAUS)
PTO............	Public Telecommunication Network Operator (SAUS)
PTO............	Public Telecommunications Operator (NITA)
PTO............	Public Trust Office [Australia]
PTO............	Punched Tape Output (SAUS)
PTO............	Purdue Teacher Opinionaire [Test]
PTO............	Pyridinethiol Oxide [Pharmacology]
PTOA............	Projective Tests of Attitudes
PTOA............	Public Television Outreach Alliance (SAUS)
PTobA............	United States Army, Tobyhanna Army Depot Library, Tobyhanna, PA [Library symbol] [Library of Congress] (LCLS)
PTO Board ...	Patent and Trademark Office Board of Patent Appeals and Interferences (AAGC)
PTOC	Platoon Tactical Operations Center (ACAE)
PTOCA............	Presentation Text Object Content Architecture (SAUS)
PTOE............	Planned Table of Organization and Equipment (SAUS)
P to F	Poor to Fair (SAUS)
PToG............	General Telephone & Electronics, GTE Sylvania, Inc., Towanda, PA [Library symbol] [Library of Congress] (LCLS)
PTOJ............	Passive Track-On-Jam
PTOJ............	Passsive Track On Jam (SAUS)
PTOL............	Peacetime Operating Level (AFM)
Ptol............	Ptolemaeus Mathematicus [Second century AD] [Classical studies] (OCD)
Ptol............	Ptolemaic (BJA)
PTOMAIN.....	Project to Optimize Many Individual Numbers (SAA)
PTON............	Proteon, Inc. [NASDAQ symbol] (SPSG)
P to P	Peak-to-Peak (SAUS)
P to P	Plate to Plate (DEN)
P-to-P	Plate-to-Plate (SAUS)
P-to-P	Point-to-Point (SAUS)
P to P	Port to Port [Shipping] (DS)
PTOPC............	Program to Program Communications (MHDI)
PTOS	Paper Tape Oriented Operating System
PTOS	Paper Tape-oriented Operating System (SAUS)
PTOS	Patent and Trademark Office Society (EA)
PTOS	Patriot Tactical Operations Simulator [Army]
PTOS	Peacetime Operating Stock [Military]

PTOS	Punched Tape Oriented System (SAUS)
PTOUT	Printout (MSA)
PTP	Association of Professional Team Physicians (SAUS)
PTP	Paper Tape Perforator [or Punch]
PTP	Paper Tape Printer (SAUS)
PTP	Parameter Test Program (SAA)
PTP	Parent to Parent, Inc. [Australia]
PTP	Parti Togolais du Progres [Party for Togolese Progress]
PTP	Part-Time Pimp (SAUS)
PTP	Patch and Test Panel (SAUS)
PTP	Peak-to-Peak [Nuclear energy]
PTP	Pensions for Technical Professionals [An association]
PTP	People-to-People
PTP	People to People International (EA)
PTP	percutaneous Transhepatic Portography (STED)
PTP	Percutaneous Transhepatic Selective Portography [Roentgenography]
PTP	Periodic Tasker Process (SAUS)
PTP	Peripheral Target Position (ABAC)
PTP	Petrologic Petroleum [Vancouver Stock Exchange symbol]
PTP	Phenyltetrahydropyridine [Biochemistry]
PTP	Physical Training Phase
PTP	Platinum Temperature Probe
PTP	Pointe-A-Pitre [Guadeloupe] [Airport symbol] (OAG)
PTP	Point Park College, Pittsburgh, PA [Inactive] [OCLC symbol] (OCLC)
PTP	Point-to-Point [Robotics] [Telecommunications]
PTP	Point-to-Point Phone (NAKS)
PTP	Pollution Transfer Program [Marine science] (MSC)
PTP	Porous Tungsten Plug
PTP	Posterior Tibial Pulse [Cardiology] (DAVI)
PTP	Posto Telefonico Pubblico [Public Telephone] [Italy]
PTP	Post-Tetanic Potentiation [Neurology]
PTP	Post-Transfusion Purpura [Medicine]
PTP	Potato Tuber Peroxidase [An enzyme]
PTP	Preferred Target Point (KSC)
PTP	Preliminary Task Plan (MCD)
PTP	Preoperational Test Procedure (SAUS)
PTP	Pretransmission Precautionary Answer to Nature's Call [Especially before a long program] [Television]
PTP	Pre-Turbo Pressure
PTP	Primary Target Point [NASA]
PTP	Printing Tape Puncher (SAUS)
PTP	Print-to-Point [Telecommunications] (IAA)
PTP	Prior to Program [Medicine] (MAE)
PTP	Probability to Penetrate (SAUS)
PTP	Processor to Processor (SAUS)
PTP	Production Test Plan (MCD)
PTP	Production Test Procedure (NATG)
PTP	Productive Thinking Program (SAUS)
PTP	Professional Tax Planner
PTP	Programmable Telemetry Processor (SAUS)
PTP	Programmable Text Processor [Programming language] (CSR)
PTP	Programmable Touch Panel [Electronics]
PTP	Programmed Text Processing (SAUS)
PTP	Programmed Turn Phase
PTP	Program Tape Punch (SAUS)
PTP	Program Task Planning (MCD)
PTP	Project Test Plan (SAUS)
PTP	Promise to Pay (MHDW)
PTP	Protect the Planet [Manual]
PTP	Protein Tyrosine Phosphatase [An enzyme]
PTP	Prothrombin-Proconvertin (STED)
PTP	Prothrombin-Procovertin (STED)
PTP	Proximal Tubular Pressure (STED)
PTP	Proximity Test Plug [Nuclear energy] (NRCH)
PTP	Publicly Traded Partnership (SAUS)
PTP	Pueblo to People (EA)
PTP	Pumped Two-Phase Mounting Plate (SAUS)
PTP	Punched Tape Perforator (SAUS)
PTP	Punched Tape Programming (SAUS)
Ptp	Transpulmonary Pressure (MAE)
PTPA	Portal-to-Portal Act of 1947 (WYGK)
PTPA	Public Television Programmers Association (SAUS)
PT-PAC	Physical Therapy Political Action Committee
PTPase	Protein Tyrosine Phosphatase [An enzyme]
PTPC	Permeability Transition Pore Complex [Biochemistry]
PTPC	Professional Teaching Practices Commission (OICC)
PTPC	Protein-Tyrosine Phosphatase C (DMAA)
PTPD	Part Paid [Business term]
Pt Pd	Part paid (EBF)
PTPD	Post-Traumatic Personality Defect (MELL)
PTPE	Powertrain Product Engineering [Automotive]
PTP'er	Prime Time Performer [In book title, "Vitale: Just Your Average Bald, One-Eyed Basketball Wacko Who Beat the Ziggy and Became a PTP'er"]
PTPF	Payee TIN [Taxpayer Identification Number] Perfection File [IRS]
PTPG	Participating (SAUS)
PTPG	Protein-Tyrosine Phosphatase Gamma (DMAA)
PTPI	People to People International (EAIO)
PTPI	Post-Traumatic Pulmonary Insufficiency [Medicine] (MELL)
PTPI	Professional and Technical Programs, Inc.
PT Plane	Patrol Torpedo Plane (SAUS)
PTPLU	Point Source Gaussian Diffusion Model (SAUS)
PTPM	Posttraumatic Progressive Myelopathy [Neurology] (DAVI)
PTPN	Peripheral [Vein] Total Parenteral Nutrition [Gastroenterology] (DAVI)
PTPN	Ponape Island [Caroline Islands] [ICAO location identifier] (ICLI)
PTPN	Protein-Tyrosine Phosphatase, Non-Receptor (DMAA)
PTPO	Painted Thermoplastic Olefin [Plastics]
PTP Programming	Point-to-Point Programming (SAUS)
PTPR	Production Test Program Report
PTPS	Package Test Power Supply
PTPS	Parallel Funed Parallel Stabilized (SAUS)
PTPS	Parallel Tuned Parallel-Stabilized (SAUS)
PTPS	Parallel-Tuned Parallel-Stabilized (IAA)
PTPS	Parker Team Player Survey [Test] (TMMY)
PTPS	Photothermal Phase-shift Spectroscopy (SAUS)
PTPS	Propellant Transfer Pressurization System (KSC)
PTPS	Pumped Two-Phase System (SSD)
PTPSC	People-to-People Sports Committee (EA)
PTPSH	Provide this Passenger Special Handling (SAUS)
PT-PSK	Pilot-Tone Phase Shift Keyed (or Keying) (SAUS)
PTPSK	Pilot Tone Phase Shift Keying [Computer science] (IAA)
PTPT	Platinum Print (VRA)
PT/PT	Point-to-Point (SAUS)
P-TPT	Portable Tactual Performance Test [Child development test] [Psychology]
PTQ	Ludlow Aviation, Inc. [FAA designator] (FAAC)
PTQ	Parent-Teacher Questionnaire (DMAA)
PTQ	Poly(tolyquinoxaline) [Organic chemistry]
PTQ	Pulse-Taking Questionnaire
PTR	Nova Scotia Department of Lands and Forests [Canada] [FAA designator] (FAAC)
PTR	Pacific Test Range (MUGU)
ptr	Painter (VRA)
PTR	Painter
PTR	Paper Tape Reader
PTR	Paper Tape Reading (SAUS)
PTR	Paper Towel Receptor [Technical drawings]
PTR	Parr Terminal Railroad (MHDW)
PTR	Partido Tercera Republica [Chile] [Political party] (EY)
PTR	Partner
PTR	Parts Tool Requirements File
PTR	Parts Transfer Record (SAA)
PTr	Part Throttle Reheat [Aviation] (OA)
PTR	Patellar Tendon Reflex (SAUS)
PTR	Patient Termination Record [Medicine] (DB)
PTR	Patient to Return (MELL)
PTR	Patuxent River [Navy] (MCD)
PTR	Perforated Tape Reader
PTR	Peripheral Total Resistance [Medicine] (MAE)
PTR	Perlsucht Tuberculin Rest [Medicine] (MAE)
PTR	Perlsucht-Tuberculin Rest (SAUS)
PTR	Permanent Traffic Recording (SAUS)
P/Tr	Permian/Triassic [A geological period boundary]
PTR	Personal Technology Research [Commercial firm]
PTR	Peterson [Alabama] [Seismograph station code, US Geological Survey] (SEIS)
Ptr	Petrine [Of, or relating to, Peter the Apostle or Peter the Great] (BJA)
PTR	Photoelectric Tape Reader
PTR	Physical Technical Reactor (SAUS)
PTR	Physikalisch-Technische Reichsanstalt
PTR	Pilot Training Rate [Navy]
PTR	Platinum Resistance (SAUS)
PTR	Pleasant Harbor [Alaska] [Airport symbol] (OAG)
PTR	Plug-Type Receptacle
PTR	Pointer [Computer science]
PTR	Pointer Record (SAUS)
PTR	Point in Time Repair [Computer science]
PTR	Polar to Rectangular (SAA)
PTR	Polar-to-Rectangular (SAUS)
PTR	Pool Test Reactor [Nuclear energy]
PTR	Pool Thermal Reactor (SAUS)
PTR	Pool Training Reactor [Nuclear energy]
PTR	Poor Transmission [Telecommunications] (TEL)
PTr	Porcine Trypsin (DB)
PTR	Portable Tape Recorder
PTR	Port Macquarie [New South Wales] [Airport symbol] (AD)
PTR	Port Thermal Radiator (SPST)
PTR	Position Track RADAR
PTR	Positive Termination Rate [Job Training and Partnership Act] (OICC)
PTR	Postetanic Repetition (SAUS)
PTR	Post-Tenure Review (SAUS)
PTR	Post-Tetanic Repetition (SAUS)
PTR	Post-Trip Review
PTR	Power Transformers (MCD)
PTR	Precision Transmitter Receiver
PTR	Preliminary Technical Report
PTR	Preliminary Test Report [NASA] (KSC)
PTR	Pressure Test Record
PTR	Pressure Transmitter Recorder (ECII)
PTR	Pressure Tube Reactor (SAUS)
PTR	Pressure-Tube Reactor [Nuclear energy]
PTR	Pressurized Tube Reactor (SAUS)
PTR	Pretransmit Receiving
PTR	Pre-Trial Release (OICC)
PTR	Primary Tactical Reconnaissance (SAUS)
PTR	Printer (MSA)
P Tr	Private Trust [Includes testamentary, investment, life insurance, holding title, etc.] [Legal term] (DLA)

PTR............	Problem Trouble Report (CTAS)
PTR............	Processor Tape Read
PTR............	Processor Tape Reader
PTR............	Production Test Record
PTR............	Production Test Requirements (KSC)
PTR............	Professional Tennis Registry, USA (EA)
PTR............	Proficiency Testing Research (EA)
PTR............	Programmer Trouble Report [Nuclear energy] (GFGA)
PTR............	Program Technical Report (CTAS)
PTR............	Program Technical Review (MCD)
PTR............	Program Test Routine (SAUS)
PTR............	Program Trouble Report [NASA] (KSC)
PTR............	Proof Test Reactor [Nuclear energy]
PTR............	Prothrombin Time Ratio [Medicine] (MELL)
PTR............	Pulmonary Total Resistance (SAUS)
PTR............	Pulse Transient Recorder
PTR............	Punched Tape Reader [Computer science]
PTR............	Punched Tape Reading (SAUS)
PTR............	Punched Tape Recorder (SAUS)
PTR............	Pupil-Teacher Ratio
PTR............	Security Capital Pacific Trust [NYSE symbol] (SAG)
PTR............	Security Cap Pacific Tr [NYSE symbol] (TTSB)
PTRA	Paper Tape Reader Adapter (SAUS)
PTRA	Percutaneous Transluminal Renal Angioplasty [Medicine] (DMAA)
PTRA	Port Terminal Railroad Association
PTRA	Power-Motion Technology Representatives Association (NTPA)
PTRA	Power Transmission Representatives Association (EA)
PTRAC	Planning and Transport Research Advisory Council (SAUS)
P/TRAC	Positraction [Automotive engineering]
PTR Algorithm...	Polygon-to-Rectangle Algorithm (SAUS)
PTrB............	Betz Laboratories, Inc., Trevose, PA [Library symbol] [Library of Congress] (LCLS)
PTRC	Paper Tape Reader Control (SAUS)
PTRC	Personnel and Training Research Center [Air Force]
PTRD	Part Redeemed [Stock exchange term] (SPSG)
PTRD	Percutaneous Transluminal Renal Dilatation (SAUS)
PTRE...........	PartnerRe Ltd. [NASDAQ symbol] (SAG)
PTRE...........	Pressure Tube Reactor Experiment [Nuclear energy] (NUCP)
PTREF..........	PartnerRe Ltd [NASDAQ symbol] (TTSB)
PTRF...........	Peacetime Rate Factor [Military] (AABC)
PTRF...........	Peacetime Replacement Factor [Military]
PTR File	Parts Tool Requirements File (SAUS)
PTRH	Punched Tape Reading Head (SAUS)
PTRI...........	Pharmaceutical and Toxicological Research Institute [Ohio State University] [Research center] (RCD)
PTRIA	Polystyrene-Tube Radioimmunoassay [Medicine] (DMAA)
PtrixMd.......	Pediatrix Medical Group, Inc. [Associated Press] (SAG)
PTRJ...........	Powered Thermocouple Reference Junction
PTRM	Partial Thermoremanent Magnetization [Geophysics]
PTRN	Photran Corp. [NASDAQ symbol] (TTSB)
PTRNMKR...	Patternmaker (WGA)
PTRO	Koror [Caroline Islands] [ICAO location identifier] (ICLI)
PTRO	Personnel Transaction Register by Originator [Military] (AABC)
PTRO	Petrominerals Corp. [NASDAQ symbol] (NQ)
PTRO	Preoverhaul Test Requirement Outline
PTRP	Paper Tape Reader Punch [Computer science] (IAA)
PTRP	Post-Treatment Resource Program [Medicine]
PTRPrA.......	Security Cap Pac Cv'A'Pfd [NYSE symbol] (TTSB)
PTRPrB.......	Security Cap Pac Tr Sr'B'Pfd [NYSE symbol] (TTSB)
PTRR	Port Townsend Railroad, Inc. [Formerly, PTS] [AAR code]
PTRRS	Pipeline Time Recording and Reporting Systems (SAUS)
PTRS	Philosophical Transactions. Royal Society of London [A publication]
PTRS	Potters Financial [NASDAQ symbol] (TTSB)
PTRS	Potters Financial Corp. [NASDAQ symbol] (SAG)
PTRS	Potters Savings & Loan Co. [NASDAQ symbol] (SAG)
PTRT...........	Part Task Radar Trainer (SAUS)
ptrt...........	Portrait (VRA)
PTR-t	Punch Tape Reader (SAUS)
PTRU	Petro Union, Inc. [NASDAQ symbol] (SAG)
PT Rulings...	Pay-Roll Tax Rulings [Australia] [A publication]
PTRUQ	Petro Union [NASDAQ symbol] (TTSB)
PTRV	Peak Transient Reverse Voltage [Electronics] (IAA)
Ptry...........	Pantry (SAUS)
PTRY	Pantry, Inc. [NASDAQ symbol]
Ptry...,.......	Poetry (SAUS)
ptry.............	Pottery (VRA)
PTRY	Pottery [Freight]
PTS.............	Painful Tonic Seizure (AAMN)
PTS.............	Pali Text Society (EA)
PTS.............	Panoramic Thermic Sight (SAUS)
PTS.............	Paper Tape Sender
PTS.............	Paper Tape System [Computer science] (IAA)
PTS.............	Paper Tape-to-Magnetic Tape Conversion System (DIT)
PTS.............	Papiertechnische Stiftung [Database producer]
PTS.............	Parachute Training School [British military] (DMA)
PTS.............	Parameter Test Setup
PTS.............	Para-Toluenesulfonic Acid
PTS.............	Park-Tronic System [Automotive engineering]
Pts.............	Participating (EBF)
PTS.............	Parts
Pts.............	Parts
PTS.............	Parts Tracking System (SAUS)
PTS.............	Part-Task Simulator (SAUS)
PTS.............	Patellar-Tendon Supracondylar [Anatomy]
PTS.............	Payload Test Set [NASA] (NASA)
PTS.............	Payload Transportation System [NASA] (MCD)
PTS.............	People's Translation Service (EA)
PTS.............	Perforated Tape Subsystem [Computer science] (IAA)
PTS.............	Performance Tracking System
PTS.............	Permanent Threshold Shift [Hearing evaluation]
PTS.............	Personal Telecommunications System (SAUS)
PTS.............	Personal Typography System (DGA)
PTS.............	Personnel Transfer Submersible (SAUS)
PTS.............	Petro-Sun International, Inc. [Toronto Stock Exchange symbol]
PTS.............	Philatelic Traders' Society Ltd. [British] (BI)
PTS.............	Philips Theological Seminary (SAUS)
PTS.............	Phosphotransferase System [Organic chemistry]
PTS.............	Photogrammetric Target System [Air Force]
PTS.............	Photogrammetric Triangulation System [Air Force] (IAA)
PTS.............	Photothermal Spectroscopy
PTS.............	Phototransmission System [Telecommunications] (IAA)
PTS.............	Phototypesetting (DGA)
PTS.............	Pilot Training Squadron [Air Force]
PTS.............	Pilot Training System (SAUS)
PTS.............	Pinchless Tracing Simulator (SAUS)
PTS.............	Pi Tau Sigma [Society]
PTS.............	Pittsburg, KS [Location identifier] [FAA] (FAAL)
PTS.............	Plane Transport System (DA)
PTS.............	Planning Tracking System (MCD)
PTS.............	Plasma Technology Section (SAUS)
PTS.............	Player Trade Society [A union] [British]
PTS.............	Pneumatic Target System (SAUS)
PTS.............	Pneumatic Test Sequencer (AFM)
PTS.............	Pneumatic Test Set (KSC)
PTS.............	Pneumatic Tube System
PTS.............	Pod Tail Section
PTS.............	Pointing and Tracking Scope
PTS.............	Points [Postal Service standard] (OPSA)
PTS.............	Points of Call Airlines Ltd. [Canada] [ICAO designator] (FAAC)
PTS.............	Polar Track Structure [Aviation] (FAAC)
PTS.............	Pollution Technical Services Ltd., Abingdon (SAUS)
PTS.............	Polymer Thick Film (SAUS)
PTS.............	Portsmouth Torpedo School (SAUS)
PTS.............	Port Townsend Railroad, Inc. [Later, PTRR] [AAR code]
PTS.............	Postal Transportation Service (SAUS)
PTS.............	Post and Telecommunications Service (IAA)
PTS.............	Post-Traumatic Stress [Medicine]
PTS.............	Potential Tax Savings (SAUS)
PTS.............	Power Transfer Switch
PTS.............	Power Transient Suppressor (IEEE)
PTS.............	Practical Test Standards [FAA] (TAG)
PTS.............	Precision Timing System
PTS.............	Predicasts Terminal System (SAUS)
PTS.............	Predicasts Terminal Systems [Predicasts, Inc.] [Cleveland, OH] [Database]
PTS.............	Predicasts Time Series [Series of databases] [Predicasts, Inc.] [Cleveland, OH]
PTS.............	Preflight Test Set (DNAB)
PTS.............	Preliminary Training School (SAUS)
PTS.............	Pressure Test Station (DNAB)
PTS.............	Pressure Tuning Spectroscopy (SAUS)
PTS.............	Pressurized Thermal Shock [Nuclear energy]
PTS.............	Price-Tag Shock [See also PTA]
PTS.............	Primary Trait System (EDAC)
PTS.............	Prime Time Sunday [TV program]
PTS.............	Princeton Theological Seminary (SAUS)
PTS.............	Princeton Theological Seminary, Princeton, NJ [OCLC symbol] (OCLC)
PTS.............	Printing Technical School (DGA)
PTS.............	Prior to Surgery (DAVI)
PTS.............	Private Telecommunications Systems [Radio-Suisse Ltd.] [Switzerland] [Telecommunications]
PTS.............	Proactive TMDE Support (RDA)
PTS.............	Proceed to Select [Telecommunications] (TEL)
PTS.............	Proceed-to-Select (SAUS)
PTS.............	Proceed to Send [Telecommunications] (TEL)
PTS.............	Proceed-to-Send (SAUS)
PTS.............	Processor Transaction Server [Computer science] (CIST)
PTS.............	Production Test Specification
PTS.............	Professional Tank Services, Ltd. (EFIS)
PTS.............	Professional Travelogue Sponsors (EA)
PTS.............	Programmable Terminal System [Computer science] (IAA)
PTS.............	Programmer Test Station
PTS.............	Program of Technology and Society [Later, DTS] (EA)
PTS.............	Program Test System [Computer science] (IEEE)
PTS.............	Program Triple Store
PTS.............	Projectile Tracking System (SAUS)
PTS.............	Project Tracking System [Environmental Protection Agency] (ERG)
PTS.............	Propellant Transfer System
PTS.............	Protestant Truth Society [British] (DBA)
PTS.............	Protoflight Telescope Subassembly (SAUS)
PTS.............	Provisional Technical Secretariat [United Nations]
PTS.............	Public Telephone Service [or System] [Telecommunications] (TEL)
PTS.............	Public Telephone System (SAUS)
PTS.............	Punched Tape Speed (SAUS)
PTS.............	Pure Time Sharing [Computer science] (IEEE)
PTS.............	Put to Sleep [ASPCA terminology]
PTSA...........	Kusaie [Caroline Islands] [ICAO location identifier] (ICLI)
PTSA...........	Para-Toluenesulfonamide (SAUS)
PTSA...........	Para-Toluenesulfonic Acid [Organic chemistry]

PTSA............	Para-Toluene Sulphonic Acid (SAUS)
PTSA............	Parent-Teacher Student Association (SAUS)
PTSA............	Parent-Teacher-Student Association [Nickname: "Pizza"]
PTSA............	Piano Trade Suppliers' Association [British] (BI)
PTSA............	Professional Trucking Services Association (EA)
PTSC...........	Paper Tape Selectric Composer (DGA)
PT-S/C.........	Proof Test Spacecraft [NASA]
PTSD...........	Pesticides and Toxic Substances Division [Environmental Protection Agency] (GFGA)
PTSD...........	Post Traumatic Stress Disorder (SAUS)
PTSD...........	Post-Traumatic Stress Disorder [Psychiatry]
PTSDT.........	Proceed to Send Data Tone (SAUS)
PTSE...........	Paper Tape Splicing Equipment
PTSE...........	PNNI Topology State Element (SAUS)
PTSED.........	Pesticides and Toxic Substances Enforcement Division (COE)
PTSH...........	Poststimulus Time Histogram [Medicine] (DMAA)
pts/hr..........	parts per hour (SAUS)
pts/hr..........	pieces per hour (SAUS)
PTSI............	PAM Transportation Services, Inc. [NASDAQ symbol] (NQ)
PTSI............	P.A.M. Transportation Svcs [NASDAQ symbol] (TTSB)
PTSI............	Para-Toluene Sulfonylisocyanate [Organic chemistry]
PtSi............	Platinum Silicide (SAUS)
PTSM...........	Plant, Technology, and Safety Management (HCT)
PTSO...........	Personnel Transaction Summary by Originator [Military] (AABC)
PTSP...........	Paper Tape Software Package (NITA)
PTSP...........	Peacetime Support Period [DoD]
PT/SP..........	Pressure Tube to Spool Piece [Nuclear energy] (NRCH)
PTSP...........	Proceed-to-Select Protocol (SAUS)
PTS PROMT...	Predicasts Overview of Markets and Technology [Predicasts, Inc.] [Cleveland, OH] [Bibliographic database]
PTSR...........	Performance Technical Survey Report
PTSR...........	Preliminary Technical Survey Report [Military] (AFIT)
PTSR...........	Pressure Tube Superheat Reactor (SAUS)
PTSR...........	Pressure-Tube Superheat Reactor [Nuclear energy]
PTSS...........	Parallel Tuned Series Stabilized (IAA)
PTSS...........	Personnel Target Subsystem (SAUS)
PTSS...........	Photon Target Scoring System (AAG)
PTSS...........	Posttraumatic Stress Syndrome [Medicine] (DMAA)
PTSS...........	Post-Traumatic Stress System [Medicine]
PTSS...........	Princeton Time Sharing Services, Inc.
PTSS...........	Princeton Time-Sharing System (SAUS)
ptst............	Paintstick (VRA)
PTST...........	Personnel Transaction Summary by Type Transaction [Military] (AABC)
PTST...........	Pretransfusion Serologic Testing
PTST...........	Prime Time School Television [Defunct] (EA)
PTSTV.........	Prime Time School Television (SAUS)
PTT.............	Paper Tape Transmission (SAUS)
PTT.............	Paper Tape Typewriter (SAUS)
PTT.............	Parity Test Track (SAUS)
PTT.............	Partial Thromboplastin Time [Hematology]
PTT.............	Particle Transport Time (MAE)
PTT.............	Part Task Trainer (MCD)
PTT.............	Party Test [Telecommunications] (TEL)
PTT.............	Patellar Tendon Transfer [Medicine] (MELL)
PTT.............	Peak Twitch Tension [Physiology]
PTT.............	Perforated Tape Transmitter (SAUS)
PTT.............	Perth Theatre Trust [Australia]
PTT.............	Petrotex Resources [Vancouver Stock Exchange symbol]
PTT.............	Physical Therapist Technician
PTT.............	Platform Terminal Transmitter (SAUS)
PTT.............	Platform Transmitter Terminal [Satellite-based tracking system]
PTT.............	Postal, Telegraph, and Telephone Administration (NATG)
PTT.............	Postal, Telephone, and Telegraph
PTT.............	Postes, Telegraphes, et Telediffusion [Post, Telegraph, and Telephone] [General Post Office] [Facetious translation: Prostitution Telematique et Telephonique] [France]
PTT.............	Post-Target Turn (SAUS)
PTT.............	Post, Telegraph and Telephone Authority (NITA)
PTT.............	Post, Telephone, and Telegraph [Telecommunications] (IAA)
PTT.............	Post Telephone & Telegraph Administration (WDAA)
PTT.............	Post Telephone or Telex (NITA)
PTT.............	Post, Telephone, Telegraph (SAUS)
PTT.............	Post, Telephon und Telegraphenbetriebe [Switzerland] [Telecommunications]
PTT.............	Post Ten Tumblers [Pseudonym used by William Maginn]
PTT.............	Post und Telegraphenverwaltung [Postal and Telegraph Administration] [Austria] [Telecommunications]
PTT.............	Pratt, KS [Location identifier] [FAA] (FAAL)
PTT.............	Prenegotiated Target Time (SAUS)
PTT.............	Press-to-Talk (IDOE)
PTT.............	Press-to-Test (SAUS)
PTT.............	Press to Transmit
PTT.............	Press-to-Transmit (SAUS)
PTT.............	Pressure Temperature Time (SAUS)
PTT.............	Private Tombs at Thebes [Oxford] [A publication] (BJA)
PTT.............	Processing Telecom Technologies (PCM)
PTT.............	Production Type Test
PTT.............	Program Technical Training (AFM)
PTT.............	Program Test Tape [Computer science] (IEEE)
PTT.............	Protein Truncation Test [Analytical biochemistry]
PTT.............	Prothrombin Time [Hematology] (AAMN)
PTT.............	Public Telecommunications Trust [Proposed replacement for Corporation for Public Broadcasting]
PTT.............	Pulmonary Transit Time [Physiology]

PTT.............	Pulse Transmission Time [Medicine] (DMAA)
PTT.............	Punched Tape Technique (SAUS)
PTT.............	Push to Talk
PTT.............	Push-to-Talk (SAUS)
PTT/8..........	Paper Tape Code on Eight Levels (NITA)
PTTA...........	Postal Telegraph and Telephone Authority (SAUS)
PTT Administration...	Postal, Telegraph and Telephone Administration (SAUS)
PTT Bulletin...	Post-, Telephon- and Telegraphen-Bulletin (SAUS)
PTTC...........	Pacific Transportation Terminal Command [Army]
PTTC...........	Paper Tape and Transmission Code
PTTC...........	Paper Tape Transmission Code (SAUS)
PTTC...........	Perforated Tape and Transmission Code [Telecommunications] (IAA)
PTTC...........	Perforated Tape and Transmission Control (SAUS)
PTTC...........	Petroleum Technology Transfer Council (NTPA)
PTTC...........	Public Telephone and Telegraph Codes (SAUS)
PTT-CT........	Activated Partial Thromboplastin Time, Control [Hematology] (DAVI)
PTTDAR......	Personnel Training and Training Devices Analysis Report (MCD)
PTTH...........	Prothoracicotropic Hormone
PTTI............	Postal, Telegraph, and Telephone International [See also IPTT] [Geneva, Switzerland] (EAIO)
PTTI............	Post, Telegraph and Telephone International (SAUS)
PTTI............	Precise Time and Time Interval (SAUS)
PTTK...........	Kosrae Island [Caroline Islands] [ICAO location identifier] (ICLI)
PTTK...........	Partial Thromboplastin Time with Kaolin [Hematology]
PTTL...........	Photo-Transferred Thermoluminescence (PDAA)
PTTL...........	Press-to-Test Light
Pt-Tm..........	Part-Time (SAUS)
PTTM..........	Power alarm on Trunk Testing Module (SAUS)
PTTMC........	PACOM [Pacific Command] Tactical Target Materials Catalog (CINC)
PTTNMKR ...	Patternmaker (SAUS)
Pt to Pt.......	Point-to-Point (SAUS)
PTTRN........	Pattern
PTTS...........	Pressure Temperature Test Set (DWSG)
PTTS...........	Private Telegraph and Telephone Service [Telecommunications] (IAA)
PTTY...........	Petty
PTU............	Package Transfer Unit
PTU............	Pallet Transporter Unit [Military] (CAAL)
PTU............	Paper Tape Unit (SAUS)
PTU............	Parallel Transmission Unit (AAG)
PTU............	Part-Throttle Unlock [Automotive engineering]
PTU............	Pathology Transcription Unit
PTU............	Phenylthiourea [Organic chemistry]
PTU............	Pilot Test Unit [Air Force]
PTU............	Planning Tracking Unit (MCD)
PTU............	Platinum [Alaska] [Airport symbol] (OAG)
PTU............	Platinum, AK [Location identifier] [FAA] (FAAL)
PTU............	Plumbers Trade Union (SAUS)
PTU............	Plumbing Trades Union [British]
PTU............	Plumbing Trade Union (NADA)
PTU............	Portable Test Unit
PTU............	Power Transfer Unit
PTU............	Power Transmission Unit (SAUS)
PTU............	Pressure, Temperature, Humidity (SAUS)
PTU............	Probe Transducer Unit (SAUS)
PTU............	Processor Transfer Unit (SAUS)
PTU............	Programmable Test Unit (SAUS)
PTU............	Program Track Unit [Telecommunications] (LAIN)
PTU............	Propylthiouracil [Also, PROP, PT] [Thyroid inhibitor]
PTU............	Protection Training Unit (SAUS)
PTU............	Psychiatric Treatment Unit (SAUS)
PTU............	Punched Tape Unit (SAUS)
P-TUBE.......	Pneumatic Tube (NAKS)
P-Tube........	Pneumatic Tube
PTUC..........	Pacific Trade Union Community [Australia] (EAIO)
PTUC..........	Philippines Trade Union Council (SAUS)
PTUC..........	Philippine Trade Unions Council (SAUS)
PTUF...........	Palestine Trade Union Federation (SAUS)
PTUF...........	Professional Tennis Umpires Federation (SAUS)
PTUSR........	Processor Transfer Unit Status Register (SAUS)
PTUV..........	Public Tenants' Union of Victoria [Australia]
PTV............	Pakistan Television Corp. (SAUS)
PTV............	Parachute Test Vehicle
PTV............	Paratransit Vehicle
PTV............	Passenger Transfer Vehicle [Airport transportation]
PTV............	Passenger Transport Vehicle
PTV............	Pathfinder Test Vehicle [NASA] (MCD)
PTV............	Pay Television
PTV............	Peach Tree Valley [California] [Seismograph station code, US Geological Survey] (SEIS)
PTV............	Peak-to-Valley
PTV............	Penetration Test Vehicle [Aerospace]
PTV............	Personal Transportation Vehicle (SAUS)
PTV............	Pietas Tutissima Virtus [Piety Is the Safest Virtue] [Motto of Ernst, Margrave of Brandenburg (1583-1613)] [Latin]
PTV............	Pitch Thrust Vector (KSC)
PTV............	Poly(thienylenevinylene) [Organic chemistry]
PTV............	Porous Tungsten Vaporizer
PTV............	Porterville, CA [Location identifier] [FAA] (FAAL)
PTV............	Posterior Tibial Vein (SAUS)
PTV............	Predetermined Time Value (IEEE)
PTV............	Programmable Temperature Vaporizer
PTV............	Programmed-Temperature Vaporizing [Analytical chemistry]
PTV............	Projection Television (SAUS)
PTV............	Propulsion Technology Validation (MCD)

PTV	Propulsion Test Vehicle
PTV	Prototype Test Vehicle (MCD)
PTV	Public Television
PTV	Punched Tape Verifier [Computer science]
PTV	Purich through Varactor [Computer science] (IAA)
PTV	Punch-Through Varactor (SAUS)
PTV	Puntavia Air Services [Djibouti] [FAA designator] (FAAC)
PTVA	Propulsion Test Vehicle Assembly [NASA]
PTVAA	Portland Television Appliance Association (SAUS)
PTVC	Pitch Thrust Vector Control (KSC)
PTVD	Portable Toxic Vapor Detector
PTVE	Propulsion and Terrain Vehicle Engineering [NASA]
PTVE	Propulsion Test Vehicle Engineering [NASA] (MCD)
PTVL	Preview Travel [NASDAQ symbol] (SG)
PTVST	Port Visit [Navy] (NVT)
PTVV	Peak-to-Valley Variation (MCD)
PTW	Page Table Word [Computer science] (IAA)
PTW	Permit to Work (HEAS)
PTW	Personal Typesetting Workstation (DGA)
PTW	Per Thousand Words (SAUS)
PTW	Per Ton Weight (SAUS)
PTW	Physikalisch-Technische-Werkstatten [Roentgenology]
PTW	Pilot Training Wing [Air Force]
PTW	Playing to Win (EA)
PTW	Point Target Weapon
PTW	Pork Tapeworm [Medicine] (MELL)
PTW	Pottstown, PA [Location identifier] [FAA] (FAAL)
PTW	Pressure-Treated Wood
PTW	Pressure-Type Window
PTW	Primary Translation Word (SAUS)
PTW	Programmable Typewriter (SAUS)
PTWAM	Page Table Word Associative Memory [Computer science] (IAA)
PTWC	Pacific Tsunami Warning Center [National Weather Service] (MSC)
PTWC	Project on Technology, Work, and Character (EA)
PT-WEX	Part-Time Work Experience Program [Texas] (EDAC)
PTWF	Pakistan Transport Workers' Federation
PTWG	Planning Tracking Working Group
PTWG	Provisioning Technical Working Group
PTWI	Provisional Tolerable Weekly Intake [Toxicology]
PTWM	Power Transformation Weighting Method [Mathematics]
PTWMASA	Private Treaty Wool Merchants' Association of South Australia
PTWMAV	Private Treaty Wool Merchants' Association of Victoria [Australia]
PTWMAWA	Private Treaty Wool Merchants' Association of Western Australia
P-TWP	Post-Township
PTWT	Photo-Type Traveling Wave Tube (NG)
PTWT	Photo-type Travelling Wave Tube (SAUS)
PTWU	Postal and Telecommunications Workers Union (SAUS)
PTX	Aereo Postal de Mexico SA de CV [ICAO designator] (FAAC)
PTX	Pacific Trans-Ocean Resources Ltd. [Toronto Stock Exchange symbol]
PTX	Packet transmitted bit in TCR (SAUS)
PTX	Palytoxin [Organic chemistry]
PTx	Parathyroidectomy [Medicine]
PTX	Pertussis Toxin [Pharmacology]
PTX	Picrotoxin [Biochemistry]
PTX	Pillowtex Corp. [NYSE symbol] (SPSG)
PTX	Pneumothorax [Medicine] (AAMN)
PTX	Polythermalex (IAA)
PTX	Polythiazide [Organic chemistry]
PTX	Pressure Temperature Composition (SAUS)
PTX	Pressure-Temperature Composition
PTX	Proprietary Format [Computer science]
PTX	Pullman Taconite Express (SAUS)
PTXA	Parathyroidectomy and Autotransplantation [Endocrinology] (DAVI)
PTXB	Pumiliotoxin B [Organic chemistry]
PTXes	Pneumothoraces (SAUS)
PTXT	Pressure Temperature Composition Time (SAUS)
PTY	Panama City [Panama] [Airport symbol] (OAG)
PTY	Parity (IAA)
PTY	Party (AAG)
PTY	Program Type (SAUS)
PTY	Proplythiouracil (SAUS)
Pty	Proprietary (DD)
pty	Proprietary (NTIO)
PTY	Proprietary
PTY	Pseudo-Terminal driver (SAUS)
PTYA	Yap [Caroline Islands] [ICAO location identifier] (ICLI)
P-type	Jungian perceptive type (SAUS)
P-Type SC	P-Type Semicondctor (SAUS)
PTZ	Pan Tilt Zoom (SAUS)
PTZ	Pentylenetetrazol (SAUS)
PTZ	Pentylenetetrazole [CNS stimulant]
PTZ	Phenothiazine (EDCT)
PTZ	Pulitzer Publishing [NYSE symbol] (TTSB)
PTZ	Pulitzer Publishing Co. [NYSE symbol] (SPSG)
PU	Pacifc University (SAUS)
PU	Pack Unit [Single title, multiple orders] [Publishing] [British]
PU	Paid Up [Insurance] (SAUS)
pu	Paid Up [Insurance] (ODBW)
PU	Parents United (EA)
PU	Participating Unit (NVT)
PU	Parts Used [Medicine]
PU	Passed Urine [Medicine]
PU	Pass Urine (SAUS)
PU	Paste Up (ADA)

PU	Peptic Ulcer [Medicine]
PU	Perbonate Unit [Analytical biochemistry]
PU	Percent Utilization [Anesthesiology]
PU	Peripheral Unit [Computers] (MSA)
PU	Personnel, Utility [British military] (DMA)
PU	Persons Using [Television] (WDMC)
PU	Peru [IYRU nationality code] (IYR)
PU	Per Unit (EECA)
PU	Per-Unit
PU	Per Urethra [Medicine]
PU	Philips University (SAUS)
PU	Physical Unit [Computer science] (IBMDP)
PU	Pickup
PU	Planning Unit (HEAS)
PU	Plant Unit
PU	Players' Union [Football] [British]
PU	Pluggable Unit (SAA)
PU	Pluna [Airline flight code] (ODBW)
PU	Plutonium
Pu	Plutonium [Chemical element]
PU	Polysulfide Urethane (SAUS)
PU	Polyurethane [Also, PUR] [Organic chemistry]
PU	Port-Unit (SAUS)
PU	Power Equipment [JETDS nomenclature] [Military] (CET)
PU	Power Unit
PU	Prefix Update (SAUS)
PU	Pregnancy Urine [Medicine]
PU	Prilled Urea [A fertilizer]
PU	Primary User (SAUS)
PU	Princeton University
PU	Printing Unit (SAUS)
PU	Print Unit (SAUS)
PU	Prisoner's Union [Later, PRU] (EA)
PU	Processing Unit [Computer science]
PU	Processor Unit (SAUS)
PU	Processor Utility [Telecommunications] (TEL)
PU	Production Unit (CAAL)
PU	Program Unit (SAUS)
PU	Propellant Unit (NASA)
PU	Propellant Utilization [Aerospace]
PU	Propulsion Unit (SAUS)
PU	Propyleneurea [Organic chemistry]
PU	Prostatic Urethra [Anatomy] [Urology] (DAVI)
PU	Protection Unearthed (SAUS)
PU	Proteolytic Unit (SAUS)
PU	Proutist Universal (EA)
PU	Publications (MCD)
PU	Publisher [Online database field identifier]
PU	Puetzer [Germany] [ICAO aircraft manufacturer identifier] (ICAO)
PU	Pumps (RIMS)
PU	Pump Unit (AAG)
Pu	Punic (BJA)
Pu	Punjab Regiment [India] [Army]
PU	Purdue University
Pu	Purine [Biochemistry]
PU	Purple (ROG)
PU	University of Pennsylvania, Philadelphia, PA [Library symbol] [Library of Congress] (LCLS)
PU3S	Power-Up 3-State (SAUS)
PUA	Pacific Union Association (SAUS)
PUA	Partido de Unificacion Anticomunista [Anti-Communist Unification Party] [Guatemala] [Political party] (PPW)
PUA	Patient Unit Assistant [Medicine] (DMAA)
PUA	Physical Unit Address (SAUS)
PUA	Plant-Unique Analysis [Nuclear energy] (NRCH)
PUA	Polish Union of America (EA)
PUA	Pride Users' Association [Defunct] (EA)
PUA	Primeras Lineas Uruguayas de Navegacion Aerea [Uruguay] [ICAO designator] (FAAC)
PUA	Profiling User Agent (SAUS)
PU-A	University of Pennsylvania, Morris Arboretum, Philadelphia, PA [Library symbol] [Library of Congress] (LCLS)
PUAA	Public Utilities Advertising Association [Later, PUCA] (EA)
PUAC	Propellant Utilization Acoustical (or Acoustics) Checkout (SAUS)
PUAC	Public Athletic Conference (PSS)
PU-AC	University of Pennsylvania, Annenberg School of Communications, Philadelphia, PA [Library symbol] [Library of Congress] (LCLS)
PUAD	Pueblo Army Depot [Colorado] (AABC)
PUADA	Pueblo Army Depot Activity (AABC)
PUAE	Agreement on Peaceful Uses of Atomic Energy (SAUS)
PUAG	Purpose Use Arrestor Gear (SAUS)
PUAID	Parti d'Unite Arabe Islamique-Democratique [Algeria] [Political party] (EY)
PU & D	Pick Up and Delivery [Business term]
PUAR	Pulse Acquisition RADAR [Military] (MSA)
PU-Ar	University of Pennsylvania Archives, Philadelphia, PA [Library symbol] [Library of Congress] (LCLS)
PUAS	Postal Union for America and Spain (SAUS)
PUAS	Postal Union of the Americas and Spain [See also UPAE] [Montevideo, Uruguay] (EAIO)
PUASP	Postal Union of the Americas, Spain, and Portugal [Uruguay] (EAIO)
PUB	Partido Union Boliviana [Bolivian Unity Party] [Political party] (PPW)
PUB	Percutaneous Umbilical Blood [Pediatrics] (CPH)
PUB	Phycourobilin [Biochemistry]
PUB	Physical Unit Block [Computer science]

PUB .... Puale Bay [*Alaska*] [*Seismograph station code, US Geological Survey*] (SEIS)
Pub .... Public (TBD)
pub .... Public (WDMC)
PUB .... Public
pub .... publican (SAUS)
PUB .... Publication (AFM)
pub .... Publication (WDMC)
pub .... Public House (ODBW)
PUB .... Public House [*A drinking establishment*] [*British*]
PUB .... Publicis Groupe S.A. ADS [*NYSE symbol*]
PUB .... Publicity
PUB .... Public Utilities Board (NADA)
pub .... publish (SAUS)
PUB .... Published (AABC)
pub .... Published (WDMC)
PUB .... Publisher
Pub .... Publishers Announcement (SAUS)
PUB .... Pueblo [*Colorado*] [*Airport symbol*] (OAG)
PUB .... Pueblo, CO [*Location identifier*] [*FAA*] (FAAL)
PUBAFF .... Public Affairs (DNAB)
PUBAFFRRU... Public Affairs Ready Reserve Unit (DNAB)
Pub Aide...... Publication Aide (SAUS)
Pub&Loc Laws... Public and Local Laws (SAUS)
Pub Auth...... Public Authorities (SAUS)
Pub Bargaining Cas... Public Bargaining Cases (SAUS)
Pub Bargaining Cas (CCH)... Public Bargaining Cases (Commerce Clearing House) [*A publication*] (DLA)
PUB BDG ...... Publisher's Binding (DGA)
Pub Bldgs ..... Public Buildings (SAUS)
PUBC .... Presbyterians United for Biblical Concerns [*Later, PBC*] (EA)
Pubcaster .... Public Broadcaster [*Radio or TV station affiliated with NPR or PBS*]
Pub Cit .... Public Citizen (SAUS)
PubcoC .... Pubco Corp [*Associated Press*] (SAG)
PUBD .... Published (ROG)
pubd .... Published (WDAA)
PUBDIS........ Publishing Distribution System (SAUS)
Pub Doc .... Public Document (SAUS)
PUB DOC ..... Public Documents (ROG)
PUB ED........ Publication Editor (SAUS)
Pub Employee Bargaining Rep (CCH)... Public Employee Bargaining Reports (Commerce Clearing House) [*A publication*] (DLA)
Pub Employee Rel Rep... Public Employee Relations Reports [*A publication*] (DLA)
Pub Ent Advert & Allied Fields LQ... Publishing, Entertainment, Advertising, and Allied Fields Law Quarterly [*A publication*] (DLA)
Pub Gen Laws... Public General Laws [*A publication*] (DLA)
PUB HA........ Public Hall [*Freemasonry*] (ROG)
Pub Health... United States Public Health Service, Court Decisions [*A publication*] (DLA)
Pub Hist ...... [*The*] Public Historian [*A publication*]
Pub Hous ..... Public Housing (SAUS)
PUBINFO...... Office of Public Information [*Formerly, OPR*] [*Navy*]
PUBINFO...... Public Information (SAUS)
Pub Int......... Public Interest [*A publication*]
Pub Intl L .... Public International Law (SAUS)
publ .... Public (MILB)
PUBL .... Public (WGA)
PUBL .... Publication [*or Published or Publisher*] (EY)
PUBL .... Public Health Library (SAUS)
Publ .... Publicity (DIAR)
PUBL .... Publish (FAAC)
publ .... Published (PROS)
Publ .... Publisher (AL)
Publ .... Publishing (AL)
Publ Admin... Public Administration [*A publication*]
Publ Amer Assoc Adv Sci... Publication of the American Association for the Advancement of Science (SAUS)
Pub Land L Rev... Public Land Law Review [*A publication*] (DLA)
Pub Lands... Public Lands (SAUS)
Pub Lands Dec... Department of the Interior, Decisions Relating to Public Lands [*A publication*] (DLA)
Pub Lands Dec... Department of the Interior, Decisions Relating to Public Lands (SAUS)
Publ Ashon Soc Pac... Publications of the Astronomical Society of the Pacific (SAUS)
Pub Law ...... Public Law (AAGC)
Pub Laws ..... Public Laws (SAUS)
PUBLCTN..... Publication
PUBLD .... Published (ROG)
Pub LF......... Public Law Forum [*A publication*] (DLA)
Publ Finance Q... Public Finance Quarterly (SAUS)
public .... Publicist
PUBLICA..... Public Libraries Concerted Action (TELE)
Public Adm... Public Administration (SAUS)
Publick .... Publicker Industries, Inc. [*Associated Press*] (SAG)
Public Works Local Gov Eng... Public Works and Local Government Engineering (SAUS)
Publ Interest... Public Interest (SAUS)
PUBLINX...... Public Links [*Amateur golf*]
Pub Loc Laws... Public Local Laws (SAUS)
Publ Pers Rev... Public Personnel Review (SAUS)
PUBLR .... Publisher
Publ Serv Rev... Public Service Review [*A publication*]
PUBLSHG .... Publishing (DCTA)
Publ Stud..... Public Studies (SAUS)

Pub Manag... Public Management (SAUS)
Pubn .... Publication (AL)
PUBN .... Publication (MSA)
pubn .... Publication (WDAA)
PUBNET ...... American Association of Publishers' electronic ordering system
PUBO .... Pubco Corp. [*NASDAQ symbol*] (NQ)
Pub Op Q..... Public Opinion Quarterly [*A publication*] (BRI)
Pub Papers... Public Papers of the President [*A publication*] (DLA)
Pub Rel .... Public Relations
Pub Rel Bull... Public Relations Bulletin [*American Bar Association*] [*A publication*] (DLA)
Pub Rel J..... Public Relations Journal [*A publication*] (BRI)
Pub Res....... Public Resolution (AAGC)
Pub Res....... Public Resources (SAUS)
Pub Res C ... Public Resources Code [*California*] [*A publication*] (ILCA)
Pub Res No... Public Resolution Number [*Congress*] (ILCA)
PUB RM...... Publisher's Ream (DGA)
PUBS .... Elephant & Castle Group, Inc. [*NASDAQ symbol*] (SAG)
PUBS .... Percutaneous Umbilical Blood Sampling [*Medicine*]
PUBS .... Percutaneous Umbilical Cord Sampling [*Also, Cordocentesus*] [*Medical test*] (PAZ)
PUBS .... Pop-Up Bottom Seismograph [*Marine science*] (MSC)
PUBS .... Prairie University Biological Seminars (SAUS)
PUBS .... Publications (CDAI)
PUBS .... Publication Series
PUBS .... Purple Urine Bag Syndrome [*Medicine*] (DMAA)
Pub Safety... Public Safety
PUBSAT ...... Publications Ships Assistance Team [*Navy*]
PUBSAT ...... Publications Special Assistance Team [*Military*]
Pub Sec...... Public Securities and Obligations (SAUS)
Pub Sect Lab Rel... Public Sector Labor Relations Conference Board (SAUS)
Pub Ser Comm... Public Service Commission [*Usually, of a specific state*] (DLA)
Pub Serv...... Public Service (SAUS)
PUBSF .... Elephant & Castle Group [*NASDAQ symbol*] (TTSB)
PubSNC ...... Public Service Co. North Carolina [*Associated Press*] (SAG)
PUBS Recorder... Pop-Up Bottom Seismic Recorder (SAUS)
Pub St .... Public Statutes [*A publication*] (DLA)
PubSt .... Public Storage, Inc. [*Associated Press*] (SAG)
PubStrg........ Public Storage, Inc. [*Associated Press*] (SAG)
Pub U Rep... Public Utilities Reports [*A publication*] (DLA)
Pub Util .... Public Utilities (SAUS)
Pub Util C.... Public Utilities Code [*A publication*] (DLA)
Pub Util Comm... Public Utilities Commission (SAUS)
Pub Util L Anthol... Public Utilities Law Anthology [*A publication*] (DLA)
Pub Util Rep... Public Utilities Reports [*A publication*] (DLA)
Pub Wks...... Public Works (SAUS)
PubWorkCen... Public Works Center (SAUS)
PU-BZ .... University of Pennsylvania, Biology Library, Philadelphia, PA [*Library symbol*] [*Library of Congress*] (LCLS)
PUC .... Pacific Unicorn [*Vancouver Stock Exchange symbol*]
PUC .... Pacific Union College [*Angwin, CA*]
PUC .... Papers under Consideration
PUC .... Parti de l'Unite Congolaise [*Congolese Unity Party*] [*Political party*]
PUC .... Pediatric Urine Collector [*Medicine*]
PUC .... Peoples University of China (SAUS)
PUC .... Peripheral Unit Controller [*Computer science*] (CIST)
PUC .... Permanent Unit Code (NG)
PUC .... Pick-Up Car
PUC .... Planification d'Urgence Canada [*Emergency Planning Canada - EPC*]
PUC .... Plant of Unit Control (SAUS)
PUC .... Player Unit Component (MCD)
PUC .... Pontificia Universidade Catolica [*Rio de Janeiro*]
PUC .... Popular Unity of Chile [*Political party*]
PUC .... Portee Utile de Combat (SAUS)
PUC .... Port Utilization Committee
PUC .... Post Urbem Conditam [*After the Building of the City of Rome*] [*Latin*]
PUC .... Premature Uterine Contractions (SAUS)
PUC .... Presidential Unit Citation [*Military decoration*]
PUC .... Price [*Utah*] [*Airport symbol*] (OAG)
PUC .... Price, UT [*Location identifier*] [*FAA*] (FAAL)
PUC .... Processing Unit Cabinet [*Computer science*]
PUC .... Production Urgency Committee [*WPB*]
PUC .... Program Under Control (NITA)
PUC .... Program Unit Code [*Military*] (AFIT)
PUC .... Provided You Concur [*Army*]
PUC .... Public Utilities and Corporations (SAUS)
PUC .... Public Utilities Code (SAUS)
PUC .... Public Utilities Commission
PUC .... Public Utility Co.
PUC .... Public Utility Commissioner (SAUS)
PUC .... Punctured Uniform Code [*Computer science*] (IAA)
PU-C .... University of Pennsylvania, Chemistry Library, Philadelphia, PA [*Library symbol*] [*Library of Congress*] (LCLS)
PUCA .... Partido Unionista Centro Americana [*Nicaragua*] [*Political party*] (EY)
PUCA .... Public Utilities Communicators Association [*Later, UCI*] [*New Castle, PA*] (EA)
PUCaILL ...... Publications of the University of California in Languages and Literature (SAUS)
PUCC .... Port Users Consultative Committee (SAUS)
PUCC .... Port Utilities [*AAR code*]
PUCC .... Purdue University Computing Center (SAUS)
PUCF .... Polyurethane Coated Fabrics (SAUS)
PUCF .... Polyurethane-Coated Fibers (SAUS)
PUCK .... Florida Panthers Holdings, Inc. [*NASDAQ symbol*] (SAG)
PUCK .... Propellant Utilization Checkout Kit (KSC)

PUCK	Pucklechurch [England]
PuCl	Plutonium Chloride
PUCM	Progressive Union of Cabinet Makers [British]
PUCP	Physical Unit Control Point (SAUS)
PUCP	Process Unit Control Panel [Computer science] (IAA)
PU:CPI	Processing Unit for Coordination Processor Interface (SAUS)
PUCR	Plant Unit Cost Report (SAUS)
PUCS	Propellant Utilization Control System (KSC)
PUCU	Propellant Utilization Control Unit
PUD	Parallel Undocumented Development (PDAA)
PUD	Partido Union Democratica [Guatemala] [Political party]
PUD	Party of Union and Development (SAUS)
PUD	Peptic Ulcer Disease
PUD	Peri-Urethral Diathermy [Medicine]
PUD	Physical Unit Directory [Computer science] (MHDI)
PUD	Pick Up and Delivery [Business term]
PUD	Pick-up and Delivery (SAUS)
PUD	Planned Unit Development [Housing]
PUD	Planned Urban Development
PUD	Preretro Update Display
PUD	Prisoner under Detention (ADA)
PUD	Public Utility District [Bonds]
pud	Pudding (BARN)
pud	puddle (SAUS)
PUD	Pudendal (DMAA)
PUD	Puerto Deseado [Argentina] [Airport symbol] (OAG)
PuD	Pulmonary Disease [Medicine] (STED)
PUD	Pulmonary Disease [Medicine]
PuD	Pulmonary Disorder [Medicine] (MELL)
PU-D	University of Pennsylvania, Evans Dental Library, Philadelphia, PA [Library symbol] [Library of Congress] (LCLS)
PUDA	Pueblo Depot Activity [Colorado] [Army]
PUDD	Programmable Universal Direct Drive
PUDEMO	Peoples United Democratic Movement (SAUS)
PUDG	Pudgie's Chicken [NASDAQ symbol] (TTSB)
PUDG	Pudgies Chicken, Inc. [NASDAQ symbol] (SAG)
Pudgie	Pudgies Chicken, Inc. [Associated Press] (SAG)
Pudgies	Pudgies Chicken, Inc. [Associated Press] (SAG)
PUDGW	Pudgies Chicken Wrrt [NASDAQ symbol] (TTSB)
PUDL	Push Down List [Computer science] (IAA)
PUDL Memory	Push Down List Memory (SAUS)
PUDN	Perpetuation of Unit Documentation Number (MCD)
PUDN	Perpetuation of Unit Document Number (SAUS)
PUDOC	Centrum voor Landbouwpublikaties en Landbouwdocumentatie [Center for Agricultural Publishing and Documentation] [Ministry of Agriculture and Fisheries] [Information service or system] (IID)
PU-DPL	Princeton University Device Physics Laboratory [New Jersey]
PUDS	Propulsion Unit Data Sheet (SAUS)
PUDT	Personal User Data Terminal (SAUS)
PUDT	Propellant Utilization Data Translator (AAG)
PUDVM	Pulsed Ultrasound Doppler Velocity Meter
PUE	Phosphorus Utilization Efficiency [Ecology]
PUE	Physiotherapists' Union of Employees [Australia]
PUE	Pick-up Electrode (SAUS)
PUE	Polyurethanen (SAUS)
PUE	Presidential Unit Emblem [Military decoration] (AABC)
PUE	Prestocked Unit Equipment (SAUS)
PUE	Pre-Stock Unit Equipment [Military] [British]
PUE	Processing Unit, Extension (SAUS)
PUE	Propellant Utilization Exerciser
PUE	Puebla [Mexico] [Seismograph station code, US Geological Survey] [Closed] (SEIS)
PUE	Puerto Obaldia [Panama] [Airport symbol] (OAG)
PUE	Pyrexia of Unknown Etiology [Medicine]
PUEC	Portsmouth Uranium Enrichment Complex (COE)
PUE:CPI	Processing Unit, Extension for Coordination Processor Interface (SAUS)
PU-EI	University of Pennsylvania, Moore School of Electrical Engineering, Philadelphia, PA [Library symbol] [Library of Congress] (LCLS)
Puerto Rico	Puerto Rico Reports [A publication] (DLA)
Puerto Rico F	Puerto Rico Federal Reports [A publication] (DLA)
Puerto Rico Fed	Puerto Rico Federal Reports [A publication] (DLA)
Puerto Rico Rep	Puerto Rico Supreme Court Reports [A publication] (DLA)
PUETO	Panhellenic Union of Exporters of Table Olives (SAUS)
PUF	Partially Unfolded Form [Biochemistry]
PUF	Partido Union Federal [Federal Union Party] [Argentina] [Political party]
PUF	Pau [France] [Airport symbol] (OAG)
PUF	People's United Front [Papua New Guinea] [Political party] (PPW)
PUF	People's United Front [Bangladesh] [Political party]
PUF	Percent Unaccounted For
PUF	Physical Update File (SAUS)
PUF	Planning Units File (SAUS)
PUF	Polyurethane Film [Plastics technology]
PUF	Polyurethane Foam
PUF	Polyurethanfaser (SAUS)
PUF	Porous Polyurethane Foam [Also, PPF] [Plastics technology]
PUF	Prime Underwriting Facility [Banking]
PUF	Proper Use Factor (SAUS)
PUF	Public Use Form (SAUS)
Puf	Puffendorf's Law of Nature and Nations [A publication] (DLA)
PUF	Pure Ultrafiltration (DMAA)
PU-F	University of Pennsylvania, H. H. Furness Memorial Library, Philadelphia, PA [Library symbol] [Library of Congress] (LCLS)
PUFA	Polyunsaturated Fatty Acid [Nutrition]

PU-FA	University of Pennsylvania, School of Fine Arts, Philadelphia, PA [Library symbol] [Library of Congress] (LCLS)
PUFF	People United to Fight Frustrations (EA)
PUFF	Picofarad (MDG)
PUFF	Proposed Uses of Federal Funds [Health Planning and Resource Development Act of 1974]
PUFFIN	Pedestrian User-Friendly Intelligent Crossing (WDAA)
PUFFS	Passive Underwater Fire Control Feasibility Study
PUFFS	Passive Underwater Fire-control Feasibility Study (SAUS)
PUFFS	Passive Underwater Fire Control Feasibility System
PUFFS	Passive Underwater Fire-control Feasibility System (SAUS)
PUFFT	Purdue University Fast FORTRAN [Formula Translation] Translator [Computer science]
PUFI	Packed under Federal Inspection
PUFI	Pair-Usage-Frequency Indicator (SAUS)
PUFL	Pump Fed Liquid (KSC)
PUFM	Pull Up Field Mast (SAUS)
PUFO	Pack Up and Fade Out [End of military exercise] [British] (DSUE)
PUFS	Programmer's Utility Filing System (DIT)
PUFS	Proposed Underwater Fire Control Feasibility Study (SAA)
PUG	Partially Underground [Military]
PUG	PASCAL Users Glroup (SAUS)
PUG	PASCAL Users' Group [Defunct] (EA)
PUG	Penta Users Group (EA)
PUG	Port Augusta [Australia] [Airport symbol] (OAG)
PUG	Prestel Users Group (NITA)
PUG	PRIME Users Group (EA)
PUG	Print under Glaze [Ceramics]
PUG	Propellant Utilization and Gauging [Apollo] [NASA]
pug	pugilism (SAUS)
PUG	Pugilist
PUG	Pugillus [A Handful] [Pharmacy] (ROG)
Pug	Pugsley's New Brunswick Reports [14-16 New Brunswick] [A publication] (DLA)
PUG	Pulsed Universal Grid
PUG	Pure Gold Resources, Inc. [Toronto Stock Exchange symbol]
PugetP	Puget Sound Power & Light Co. [Associated Press] (SAG)
PUGLIG	PUG Library Information Group (NITA)
PUGS	Propellant Utilization and Gaging System (NAKS)
PUGS	Propellant Utilization and Gauging System [Apollo] [NASA] (KSC)
Pugs	Pugsley's New Brunswick Reports [14-16 New Brunswick] [A publication] (DLA)
Pugs & Bur	Pugsley and Burbridge's New Brunswick Reports [17-20 New Brunswick] [A publication] (DLA)
Pugs & Burg	Pugsley and Burbridge's New Brunswick Reports [17-20 New Brunswick] [A publication] (DLA)
Pugs & T	Pugsley and Trueman's New Brunswick Reports [A publication] (DLA)
Pugs & Tru	Pugsley and Trueman's New Brunswick Reports [1882-83] [A publication] (DLA)
PUGT	Puget Sound Basin (SAUS)
PugtP	Puget Sound Power & Light Co. [Associated Press] (SAG)
PUH	Pauahi [Hawaii] [Seismograph station code, US Geological Survey] (SEIS)
PUH	Pregnancy Urine Hormone [Endocrinology]
PUHCA	Public Utility Holding Co. Act of 1935
PUHCA	Public Utility Holding Company Act (SAUS)
PUHS	Phoenix Union High School (SAUS)
PUHS	Propulsion Unit History Sheet (SAUS)
PUI	Pen User Interface [Computer science]
PUI	Physical Unit of Information [Computer science] (IAA)
PUI	Picoscopic User Interface (SAUS)
PUI	Pilot-under-Instruction [Navy]
PUI	Platelet Uptake Index [Clinical chemistry]
PUIC	Project Unique Identification Code (AAGC)
PUID	Physical Unit Identifier (SAUS)
PU Imp	Pickup Impulse (SAUS)
PU-Ind	University of Pennsylvania, Industrial Research Department, Philadelphia, PA [Library symbol] [Library of Congress] [Obsolete] (LCLS)
PUIWP	People for a United India and World Peace (EA)
PUJ	Punta Cana [Dominican Republic] [Airport symbol] (OAG)
PUJC	Priority, Urgency, Justification and Category (SAUS)
PUJO	Peoples Union of Justice and New Order (SAUS)
PUJT	Programmable Unijunction Transistor (IAA)
PUK	Pack-Up Kit (MCD)
PUK	Paducah [Kentucky] [Airport symbol] (AD)
PUK	Parti d'Unite Katangaise [Katanga Unity Party] [Political party]
PUK	Patriotic Union of Kurdistan [Iraq] [Political party] (PD)
PUK	Pechiney-Ugine-Kuhlmann [France] [Commercial firm]
PUK	Prourokinase [Thrombolytic] [An enzyme]
PUK	Prudential plc ADS [NYSE symbol]
PUK	Pukarua [French Polynesia] [Airport symbol] (OAG)
PUKO	Pan American Union of Karatedo Organisations (SAUS)
PUKO	Pan-American Union of Karatedo Organizations (EA)
PUKS	Pivotal Unknowables
PUL	Packet Underway Limit (SAUS)
PUL	Percutaneous Ultrasonic Lithotripsy [Medicine]
PUL,	Per-Unit-Length (SAUS)
PUL	Preconfiguration Unit Load
PUL	Press Union of Liberia
PUL	Princeton University Library (SAUS)
PUL	Princeton University, Princeton, NJ [Inactive] [OCLC symbol] (OCLC)
PUL	Program Update Library
PUL	Propellant Utilization and Loading

PUL............ Publicker Indus [*NYSE symbol*] (TTSB)
PUL............. Publicker Industries, Inc. [*NYSE symbol*] (SPSG)
PUL............ Pubourethral Ligament (STED)
PUL............ Pulkovo [*Former USSR*] [*Seismograph station code, US Geological Survey*] (SEIS)
PUL............ Pulley (AAG)
pul............ Pulmonary (STED)
PUL............ Pulmonary
PUL............ Pul. Przedsiebiorstwo Uslug Lotniczych [*Poland*] [*ICAO designator*] (FAAC)
Pul............ Pulse (SAUS)
PUL............ Pulse Resources [*Vancouver Stock Exchange symbol*]
PUL............ Punjab University Library (SAUS)
PU-L .... University of Pennsylvania, Biddle Law Library, Philadelphia, PA [*Library symbol*] [*Library of Congress*] (LCLS)
PULA .... Patani United Liberation Organisation (SAUS)
PULA .... Public Laws
PulaskF....... Pulaski Furniture Corp. [*Associated Press*] (SAG)
PulaskiB ..... Pulaski Bank, A Savings Bank [*Associated Press*] (SAG)
PULB .... Pulaski Bank, A Savings Bank [*NASDAQ symbol*] (SAG)
PULB .... Pulaski Bank A Svgs Bk MO [*NASDAQ symbol*] (TTSB)
PULHEEMS... Physical Capacity, Upper and Lower Limbs, Hearing, Eyesight, Emotional Capacity, Mental Stability (SAUS)
PULHES .... Physical Capacity, Upper Extremities, Lower Extremities, Hearing, Eyes, and Psychiatric System (DNAB)
PULHHEEMS... Physical Capacity, Upper Limbs, Left Hearing, Right Hearing, Left Eye, Right Eye, Mental Capacity, Stability [*Military medical assessment*] (WDAA)
PUL INS...... Pulmonary Insufficiency (SAUS)
PULL............ Power for Underwater Logistics and Living
Pull Acc..... Pulling on Mercantile Accounts [*1846*] [*A publication*] (DLA)
Pull Accts ... Pulling's Law of Mercantile Accounts [*A publication*] (DLA)
Pull Att .... Pulling on Attorneys and Solicitors [*3rd ed.*] [*1862*] [*A publication*] (DLA)
Pull Laws & Cust Lond... Pulling's Treatise on the Laws, Customs, and Regulations of the City and Port o f London [*A publication*] (DLA)
Pull Port of London... Pulling's Treatise on the Laws, Customs, and Regulations of the City and Port ofLondon [*A publication*] (DLA)
PULM........... Programmable Universal Logic Module (SAUS)
pulm .... Pulmentum [*Gruel Pulmonary*] [*Latin*] (MAE)
pulm............ Pulmonary (MELL)
PULM........... Pulmonary
PULM EMB... Pulmonary Embolism (SAUS)
PULMO .... Pulmoaortic (SAUS)
PULMO .... Pulmology (SAUS)
PULMO .... Pulmometer (SAUS)
PULMO .... Pulmometric (SAUS)
PULMO .... Pulmometry (SAUS)
PULMO .... Pulmonectomy (SAUS)
PULMO .... Pulmonitis (SAUS)
PULMO .... Pulmonologist (SAUS)
pulmo .... pulmotor (SAUS)
Pulmotor...... Pulmonary Motor (SAUS)
PULO .... Patani United Liberation Organisation (SAUS)
PULO .... Pattani United Liberation Organization [*Thailand*] [*Political party*] (PD)
PULO .... Pattini United Liberation Organisation (SAUS)
PULP .... Premium Unleaded Petrol
pulpbd .... Pulpboard (VRA)
PULPP .... Peripheral Ultra-Low Power Processor (PDAA)
pulpwd........ Pulpwood (VRA)
PULS .... Performance Utility Luxury Society [*Electric vehicles*]
PULS .... Poseidon Undersea Launching System (NOAA)
PULS .... Propellant Utilization Loading System (AAG)
PULS .... Pulse Bancorp [*NASDAQ symbol*] (TTSB)
PULS .... Pulse Bancorp, Inc. [*NASDAQ symbol*] (SAG)
PULSAR....... Pulsated Uniform Laser-Stimulated Artificial Radiation (SAUS)
PULSAR...... Pulsating Star
PULSAR...... Pulsed Sequential Access Relay [*Electronics*] (ECII)
PULSAR....... Pulsed Uniform LASER-Stimulated Artificial Radiation [*Proposed acronymic designation for pulsars, in the event they are found to be artificially caused by intelligent life from outer space*]
PULSAR....... Pulsed Uniform Laser Stimulated Artificial Radiation (SAUS)
PULSAR....... Pulse Star (SAUS)
PULSE .... Patented Uniform Lateral Stability Element
PULSE .... Program of Universal Logic Simulation for Electronics (SAUS)
PULSE .... Public and Local Services Efficiency Campaign (SAUS)
PULSE .... Public Urban Locator Service
PulseBcp .... Pulse Bancorp, Inc. [*Associated Press*] (SAG)
PULSES .... Physical Condition, Upper Extremity Function, Lower Extremity Function, Sensory and Communication Abilities, Excretory Control, Social Support [*A neurological disability profile*]
Pulsifer (ME)... Pulsifer's Reports [*35-68 Maine*] [*A publication*] (DLA)
PULSTAR..... Pulse Training Assembled Reactor [*Nuclear energy*] (NRCH)
Pul Sten ...... Pulmonary Stenosis (SAUS)
Pult............. Pulton. De Pace Regis [*A publication*] (DLA)
Pulte............ Pulte Corp. [*Associated Press*] (SAG)
PultzPb ...... Pulitzer Publishing Co. [*Associated Press*] (SAG)
PULV .... Pulverization (SAUS)
PULV .... Pulverized
PULV .... Pulvis [*Powder*] [*Pharmacy*]
PULV CONSPER... Pulvis Conspersus [*Dusting Powder*] [*Pharmacy*]
pulv gros .... Pulvis Grossus [*Coarse Powder*] [*Pharmacy*] [*Latin*] (MAE)
pulv subtil ... Pulvis Subtilis [*Smooth Powder*] [*Pharmacy*] [*Latin*] (MAE)
pulv tenu ..... Pulvis Tenuis [*Very fine powder*] [*Latin*] (DMAA)

PUM............ Packet User Module (SAUS)
PUM............ Partido Unificado Mariateguista [*Peru*] [*Political party*] (EY)
PUM............ Peanut Urinary Mucins (DB)
PUM............ Pennsylvania University Museum
PUM............ Per Unit Monthly (DNAB)
PUM............ Pomalaa [*Indonesia*] [*Airport symbol*] (OAG)
PUM............ Pop-Up Mechanism (SAUS)
PUM............ Postal Union Mail (SAUS)
PUM............ President of the United Mineworkers
PUM............ Processor Utility Monitor [*Telecommunications*] (TEL)
PUMA.......... Frogrammable universal manipulator.
PUMA.......... Passive Underbody Main Absorber [*Automotive emissions*]
PUMA.......... Powered Ultralight Manufacturers Association [*Defunct*] (EA)
PUMA.......... Processor-Upgradable Microcomputer Architecture [*DFI, Inc.*] (PCM)
PUMA.......... Processor Upgradable Modular Architecture (SAUS)
PUMA.......... Programmable Universal Machine for Assembly [*Robot*]
PUMA.......... Programmable Universal Manipulator (NITA)
PUMA.......... Programmable Universal Manipulator for Assembly [*General Motors Corp. assembly robot*]
PUMA.......... Programmable Universal Mechanical Assembly (SAUS)
PUMA.......... Programmable Universal Micro Accelerator [*Computer science*] (CDE)
PUMA.......... Prostitutes' Union of Massachusetts
PUMA.......... Public Use Microdata Area (SAUS)
PUMA.......... Puma Technology, Inc. [*NASDAQ symbol*] (SAG)
PumaT......... Puma Technology, Inc. [*Associated Press*] (SAG)
PU-Math ..... University of Pennsylvania, Mathematics-Physics Library, Philadelphia, PA [*Library symbol*] [*Library of Congress*] (LCLS)
PUMC .... Public Utilities Management Co. (SAUS)
PUMCODOXPURSACOMLOPAR... Pulse-Modulated Coherent Doppler-Effect X-Band Pulse-Repetition Synthetic-Array Pulse Compression Side Lobe Planar Array
PU-Med .... University of Pennsylvania, Medical School, Philadelphia, PA [*Library symbol*] [*Library of Congress*] (LCLS)
PU-Med-TS... University of Pennsylvania, Medical School, Hospital Nurses Library, Philadelphia, PA [*Library symbol*] [*Library of Congress*] (LCLS)
PUMF........... Peaceful Uses of Military Forces
PUMGC........ Pious Union of Our Mother of Good Counsel [*See also SMBC*] [*Genazzano, Italy*] (EAIO)
PUMICE .... Precision Unmanned Integrated Control Equipment (SAUS)
PUMP .... Parts Usage Maintenance Program [*Computer science*] (IAA)
PUMP .... Plant Uncoupling Mitochondrial Protein [*Biochemistry*]
PUMP .... Production Upgrade Management Program (DNAB)
PUMP .... Protesting Unfair Marketing Practices [*Student legal action organization*]
PUMP .... Pumping (SAUS)
PUMPA........ Purine Metabolic Patients' Association (NRGU)
Pump Ct ..... Pump Court (SAUS)
PUMS .... Permanently Unfit for Military Service [*British*]
PUMS .... Physical Unit Management Services [*Computer science*] (CIST)
PUMS .... Public Use Microdata Sample [*Bureau of the Census*] (GFGA)
PUMS .... Public Use Microdata Samples
PUMS .... Public Use Micro Sample
PUM:SIMP... Processing Unit Memory for Signaling Management Processor (SAUS)
PUMST .... Polish Underground Movement (1939-1945) Study Trust (EA)
PUMT.......... Programmable Universal Module Tester (SAUS)
PU-Mu .... University of Pennsylvania, University Museum, Philadelphia, PA [*Library symbol*] [*Library of Congress*] (LCLS)
PU-Music..... University of Pennsylvania, School of Music, Philadelphia, PA [*Library symbol*] [*Library of Congress*] (LCLS)
Pun .... All India Reporter, Punjab [*A publication*] (DLA)
Pun .... All India Reporter, Punjab (journ.)
Pun .... Indian Law Reports Punjab (journ.) (SAUS)
Pun .... Indian Law Reports, Punjab Series [*A publication*] (DLA)
PUN .... Parti de l'Unite Nationale [*Party of National Unity*] [*Haiti*] [*Political party*] (PPW)
PUN .... Partido Union Nacional [*National Union Party*] [*Costa Rica*] [*Political party*]
PUN .... Physical Unit Number (SAUS)
PUN .... Plasma Urea Nitrogen (AAMN)
PUN .... Plutonyl Nitrate [*Inorganic chemistry*]
PUN .... Precision Underwater Navigation
PUN .... Punch
PUN .... Puncheon [*Unit of measurement*]
PUN .... Punia [*Zaire*] [*Airport symbol*] (AD)
Pun .... Punica [*of Silius Italicus*] [*Classical studies*] (OCD)
PUN .... Punishment (DSUE)
PUN .... Puno [*Peru*] [*Seismograph station code, US Geological Survey*] (SEIS)
PUN .... Punta [*Flamenco dance term*]
PU-N .... University of Pennsylvania, Center for the Study of the History of Nursing, Philadelphia, PA [*Library symbol*] [*Library of Congress*] (LCLS)
PUNA .... Parti de l'Unite Nationale [*National Unity Party*] [*Congo*]
PUNC .... Partido de Unidad Nacional Conservadora [*Nicaragua*] [*Political party*] (EY)
PUNC .... Possibly Uncommitted (SAUS)
PUNC .... Practical, Unpretentious, Nomographic Computer
PUNC .... Probable Ultimate Net Cost [*Accounting*]
PUNC .... Punctuation
PUNC .... Puncture (DAVI)
punceq........ Punctuated Equilibrium [*Bacteriology*]
PUNCT .... Punctuation (ROG)

PUNGA......... Parti de l'Unite Nationale Gabonaise [*Party for Gabonese National Unity*] [*Political party*]
P-UNI........... Private User Network Interface (SAUS)
Punj Rec...... Punjab Record [*India*] [*A publication*] (DLA)
PUNL........... Percutaneous Ultrasonic Nephrolithotripsy [*Nephrology*] [*Radiology*] (DAVI)
PUN Press... Punching Press (SAUS)
PUNS........... Partido de Union Nacional del Sahara [*Western Sahara*] [*Political party*]
PUNS.......... Permanently Unfit for Naval Service [*British*]
PUNSW....... Poets' Union of New South Wales [*Australia*]
PUO............. Placed under Observation [*Medicine*]
PUO............. Pneumonia (SAUS)
PUO............. Princeton University Observatory [*New Jersey*]
PUO............. Prudhoe Bay [*Arkansas*] [*Airport symbol*] (OAG)
PUO............. Prudhoe Bay, AK [*Location identifier*] [*FAA*] (FAAL)
Puo............. [*A*] Purine Nucleoside [*Also, R*]
PUO............. Put Under Observation (SAUS)
PUO............. Pyrexia [*fever*] of Unknown Origin [*Commonly called Trench Fever*]
PuO2........... Plutonium Dioxide
PUOS.......... Public Understanding of Science Program (EDAC)
PU-OSC...... Pulsed Oscillator (SAUS)
PUOW......... Proposed Units of Work
PUP............. Paid-Up Policy [*Insurance*] (DSUE)
PUP............. PARC Universal Packet protocol (SAUS)
PUP............. Parti de l'Unite du Peuple Gabonais [*Political party*] (EY)
PUP............. Parti de l'Unite Populaire [*Tunisia*] [*Political party*] (EY)
PUP............. Partido Union Patriotica [*Patriotic Union Party*] [*Dominican Republic*] [*Political party*] (PPW)
PUP............. Patch Utility Program (SAUS)
PUP............. Peacetime Utilization Program
PUP............. Peak Underpressure [*Nuclear energy*] (NRCH)
PUP............. People's United Party [*Belize*] [*Political party*] (PPW)
PUP............. Peoples Unity Party (SAUS)
PUP............. Performance Units Plan (MHDB)
PUP............. Performance Update Program [*Air Force*] (DOMA)
PUP............. Performance Upgrade Program (ACAE)
PUP............. Peripheral Unit Processor [*Computer science*]
PUP............. Peripheral Universal Processor (NITA)
PUP............. Pick-Up (TVEL)
PUP............. Pick-up-Point (SAUS)
PUP............. Pious Union of Prayer (EA)
PUP............. Plutonium Utilization Program [*Nuclear Regulatory Commission*] (NRCH)
PUP............. Po [*Upper Volta*] [*Airport symbol*] (AD)
PUP............. Polytechnic University of the Philippines (SAUS)
PUP............. Popular Unity Party [*Bangladesh*] [*Political party*] (PPW)
PUP............. Pop Up Point (ACAE)
PUP............. Power Upgrade Program
PUP............. Power Utility Pak [*Computer software*] [*Jwalk and Associates*] (PCM)
PUP............. Pregnant Urban Professional (SAUS)
Pup............. Pre-Urban Professional [*Acronym coined by TeenAge magazine to describe it s typical reader*] [*Lifestyle classification*]
PUP............. Prime Unit Processor (SAUS)
PUP............. Princeton University Press (DGA)
PUP............. Principal User Processing (SAUS)
PUP............. Principal User Processor (SAUS)
PUP............. Principle User Processor (SAUS)
PUP............. Principle User Product (SAUS)
PUP............. Product Update Program (SAUS)
PUP............. Product Upgrade Program (MUSM)
PUP............. Progressive Unionist Party [*Northern Ireland*] [*Political party*] (PPW)
PUP............. Public Utilities Panel [*EECE*]
PUP............. Pull Up Point
PUP............. Pupakea [*Hawaii*] [*Seismograph station code, US Geological Survey*] [*Closed*] (SEIS)
PUP............. Pupil (DSUE)
Pup............. Puppis [*Constellation*]
PUPA.......... Polish Union Printers Association [*Chicago*]
PUPE.......... Production Unit Price Estimate (SAUS)
PU-Penn...... University of Pennsylvania, Penniman Library of Education, Philadelphia, PA [*Library symbol*] [*Library of Congress*] [*Obsolete*] (LCLS)
PUPG.......... Production Unit Price Goals (MCD)
PUPID......... Pulp and Paper Industry Division [*Instrument Society of America*]
PUPM.......... Party for Unity and Progress in Mali (SAUS)
PUPO.......... Pull-Up, Push-Out
PUPO.......... Pull Up Push Over (NASA)
PUPP.......... Pruritic Urticarial Papules and Plaques [*Dermatology*] (BARN)
Pupp.......... Puppis [*Constellation*]
PUPPI........ Pop-Up Pore Pressure Instrument [*Oceanography*]
Puppie........ Pregnant Urban Professional [*Terminology used in "The Yuppie Handbook"*] [*Lifestyle classification*]
PUPPP........ Pruritic Urticarial Papules and Plaques of Pregnancy [*Medicine*]
PUPS.......... Portable Universal Programming System (SEWL)
PU-PSW...... University of Pennsylvania, Pennsylvania School of Social Work, Philadelphia, PA [*Library symbol*] [*Library of Congress*] (LCLS)
PUQ............. Punta Arenas [*Chile*] [*Airport symbol*] (OAG)
PUR............. Partido de Unificacion Revolucionaria [*Party of Revolutionary Unification*] [*Guatemala*] [*Political party*]
PUR............. Partido Union Revolucionaria [*Cuba*]
PUR............. Patch Unit Radio [*Bell System*]
PUR............. Persons Using Radio [*Radio ratings*] (WDMC)
PUR............. Polyurethane [*Also, PU*] [*Organic chemistry*]
PUR............. Procurement Request [*Army*] (IAA)

PUR............. Program of University Research
PUR............. Program Utility Routines [*Computer science*]
PUR............. Public Utilities Reports [*A publication*] [*Information service or system*] (IID)
PUR............. Purari [*Papua New Guinea*] [*Seismograph station code, US Geological Survey*] (SEIS)
PUR............. Purchase (AFM)
PUR............. Purchasing Receipt [*Business term*]
PUR............. Purdue University Reactor
PUR............. Purdue University Research (MCD)
PUR............. Purgative [*Medicine*] (ROG)
PUR............. Purge (SAUS)
PUR............. Purichlor Technology Ltd. [*Vancouver Stock Exchange symbol*]
pur............. purified (SAUS)
PUR............. Purifier (AAG)
pur............. purify (SAUS)
Pur............. [*A*] Purine [*Biochemistry*]
PUR............. Purity [*of the Drug*] [*Pharmacy*] (ROG)
PUR............. Puromycin [*Trypanocide*] [*Antineoplastic drug*]
pur............. Purple [*Philately*]
pur............. purplish (SAUS)
PUR............. Purpure [*Purple*] [*Heraldry*]
PUR............. Pursuant (AABC)
PUR............. Pursuit (AABC)
pur............. Purus [*Pure*] [*Latin*]
PUR............. Spurwing Airlines (Pty) Ltd. [*South Africa*] [*ICAO designator*] (FAAC)
PUR 3d........ Public Utilities Reports, Third Series [*A publication*] (DLA)
PURA.......... PACOM [*Pacific Command*] Utilization and Redistribution Agency
PURA.......... Public Utilities Review Act [*1934*]
PURAC........ Personal Use Radio Advisory Committee [*FCC*] [*Defunct*] (TSSD)
PURAVAL.... Purchase Availability (SAUS)
PURB.......... Purbeck [*District in England*]
PURC.......... Pacific Utilization Research Center [*Marine science*] (MSC)
PURC.......... Princeton University Research Center [*Marine science*] (MSC)
PURC.......... Public Utility Research Center [*University of Florida*] [*Research center*] (RCD)
PURC.......... Purchasing
Purch......... Purchase (TBD)
PURCH........ Purchase
purch......... Purchasing (DD)
PURCHG...... Purchasing (ROG)
PURDAX..... Public Utility Revenue Data Acquisition (SAUS)
Purd Dig...... Purdon's Digest of Laws [*Pennsylvania*] [*A publication*] (DLA)
Purd Dig Laws... Purdon's Digest of Laws [*Pennsylvania*] [*A publication*] (DLA)
Purdue........ Purdue University Press (SAUS)
Purdue U .... Purdue University (GAGS)
Purdue U (Calumet)... Purdue University-Calumet (GAGS)
PURE.......... Innovative Medical Services [*NASDAQ symbol*] (SAG)
PURE.......... People United for Rural Education (EA)
PURE.......... POMCUS Unit Residual Equipment (SAUS)
PURE.......... Present University Research Efforts [*Database*] [*Harperson Data Services*]
PURE.......... Purepac, Inc [*NASDAQ symbol*] (SAG)
Pure Appl Chem... Pure and Applied Chemistry (MEC)
PureAtria.... Pure Atria Corp. [*Associated Press*] (SAG)
PURE MAT... Pure Machine-Aided Translation (SAUS)
PURE MT.... Pure Machine Translation (SAUS)
Purepac....... Purepac, Inc. [*Associated Press*] (SAG)
PUREQ........ Purchase Requisition (NOAA)
PureSf........ Pure Software, Inc. [*Associated Press*] (SAG)
PureTc......... Pure Tech International, Inc. [*Associated Press*] (SAG)
PureWld ..... Pure World, Inc. [*Associated Press*] (SAG)
PUREX........ Plutonium Uranium Extraction [*Nuclear energy*]
PUREX........ Plutonium-Uranium Extraction (SAUS)
PUREX-Verfahren... Plutonium and Uranium Recovery by Extraction (SAUS)
purg........... Purgativus [*Cathartic, purgative*] [*Latin*] (MAE)
PURGE........ Pearson Universal Random Generator
PURIF......... Purification
PURL.......... Permanent Uniform Resource Locator (SAUS)
PURL.......... Permanent Universal Resource Locator (SAUS)
PURL.......... Persistent Uniform Resource Locator [*Computer science*] (IGQR)
PURL.......... Persistent Universal Resource Locator [*Computer science*]
PURL.......... Persistent URL (SAUS)
PURM.......... Project for Utilization and Redistribution of Materiel [*Air Force*]
PUR (NS).... Public Utilities Reports, New Series [*A publication*] (DLA)
PURO.......... Puromycin (SAUS)
PURP.......... Purple (SAUS)
PURP.......... Purpose (AFM)
PURP.......... Purpure [*Purple*] [*Heraldry*] (ROG)
PURPA........ Public Utilities Regulatory Policies Act (SAUS)
PURPA........ Public Utilities Regulatory Policy Act [*1978*]
Purple's St... Purple's Statutes, Scates' Compilation [*A publication*] (DLA)
PurR.......... Purine Repressor [*Biochemistry*]
PURRC........ Polyurethane Recycle and Recovery Council [*Plastics recycling research*]
PURRE........ Plutonium Recycle Reactor Experiment (SAUS)
PURS.......... Partido de la Union Republicana Socialista [*Socialist Republican Union Party*] [*Bolivia*]
PURS.......... Pursuit
PURS.......... Purus, Inc. [*NASDAQ symbol*] (SAG)
PURSC........ Partido Unido de la Revolucion Socialista Cubana [*Cuba*] [*Political party*] (EY)
PURSCE...... Pursuance (ROG)
PURSIS........ Peking University Real-World Spatial Information System (SAUS)
PURSIS........ Peking University Remote Sensing Information System (SAUS)

PURST .... Pursuant
PURT .... PureTec Corp. [*NASDAQ symbol*] [*Formerly, Pure Tech International*] (SG)
PURT .... Pure Tech International, Inc. [*NASDAQ symbol*] (NQ)
Purus .... Purus, Inc. [*Associated Press*] (SAG)
PURV .... Powered Underwater Research Vehicle [*Navy*]
Purv Coll ..... Purvis' Collection of the Laws of Virginia [*A publication*] (DLA)
PURW .... Pure World, Inc. [*NASDAQ symbol*] (SAG)
PUS .... Parliamentary Under Secretary [*British*]
PUS .... Passive Ultrasonic Sensor (PDAA)
PUS .... Permanently Unfit for Service [*Military*] (ADA)
PUS .... Permanent Under Secretary [*British*]
PUS .... Permanent Under-Secretary (SAUS)
PUS .... Personnel Utilization Sheet
PUS .... Pharmacopeia of the United States
PUS .... President of the United States
PUS .... Processor Upgrade Socket (SAUS)
PUS .... Processor Utility Subsystem [*Telecommunications*] (TEL)
PUS .... Propellant Utilization System
PUS .... Propulsion Utilization System (SAUS)
PUS .... Public Understanding of Science (SAUS)
PUS .... Public Use Samples
PUS .... Pusan [*South Korea*] [*Airport symbol*] (OAG)
PUS .... Pusan [*South Korea*] [*Seismograph station code, US Geological Survey*] [*Closed*] (SEIS)
pus .... Pushto [*MARC language code*] [*Library of Congress*] (LCCP)
PUS .... Section for Staff Development at Lund University (SAUS)
PU-S .... University of Pennsylvania, Edgar Fah Smith Memorial Library, Philadelphia, PA [*Library symbol*] [*Library of Congress*] (LCLS)
PUSAS .... Proposed United States of America Standard
PUSC .... Partido Unidad Social Cristiana [*Costa Rica*] [*Political party*] (EY)
PU-Sc .... University of Pennsylvania, Towne Scientific School, Philadelphia, PA [*Library symbol*] [*Library of Congress*] (LCLS)
PUSCC .... Portugal-United States Chamber of Commerce (NTPA)
PUSD .... Partido Unido Social Democratico [*United Social-Democratic Party*] [*Guinea-Bissau*] [*Political party*] (EY)
PUSD .... Polska Unia Socjaldemokratyczna [*Polish Social Democratic Union*] [*Political party*]
PUSE .... Propellant Utilization System Exerciser
PUSEC .... Polish-US Economic Council (EA)
PUSGX .... Pioneer Amer. Income Cl.A [*Mutual fund ticker symbol*] (SG)
PUSH .... People United to Save Humanity [*In organization name "Operation PUSH"*]
PUSH .... Play Units for Severely Handicapped (EDAC)
PUSH .... Public Use Sample Helper (PDAA)
PUSHA .... Push All Registers (SAUS)
PUSHF .... Push Flags (SAUS)
PUSI .... Peripheral Unit Selection Instruction (SAUS)
PUSJD .... Pious Union of St. Joseph for the Dying [*Defunct*] (EA)
PUSJDS .... Pious Union of St. Joseph for Dying Sinners [*Later, PUSJD*] (EA)
PU/SIB .... Processing Unit and Signal Buffer (SAUS)
PUSLITBANGNAK... Central Research Institute for Animal Science (SAUS)
PU:SIMP .... Processing Unit for Signaling Management Processor (SAUS)
PUSMM .... Parti d'Union Socialiste des Musulmans Mauritaniens [*Party for Socialist Unity of Moslems of Mauritania*] [*Political party*]
PUSO .... Principal Unit Security Officer (AAG)
PU-Sp .... University of Pennsylvania, Van Pelt Library, Special Collections, Philadelphia, PA [*Library symbol*] [*Library of Congress*] (LCLS)
PUSR .... Peripheral Unit Selection Register (SAUS)
PU-SRS .... University of Pennsylvania, South Asia Regional Studies Library, Philadelphia, PA [*Library symbol*] [*Library of Congress*] (LCLS)
PUSS .... Pallet Utility Support Structure [*NASA*] (MCD)
PUSS .... Pilots Universal Sighting System
PUSSI .... Prostitutes United for Social and Sexual Integration [*British*] (DI)
PUSSW .... Parliamentary Under-Secretary of State for War (SAUS)
PUST .... Panafrican Union of Science and Technology
PUSTAT .... Purge Status [*Automotive emissions*]
PUSTCOM.... Purge Status Comments [*Automotive emissions*]
PUSU .... Policy Unit Support Unit (HEAS)
PUSVC Manager... Physical Unit Services Manager (SAUS)
PUSWA .... Public Utilities Street Works Act (SAUS)
PUT .... Aeroput [*Yugoslavia*] [*ICAO designator*] (FAAC)
PUT .... Passenger-Unit-Transport-System (SAUS)
PUT .... Persons Using Television [*Television ratings*]
pU/T .... Pilot Under Training [*Aviation*] (DA)
PUT .... Pop-Up Test of missiles (SAUS)
PUT .... Programmable Unijunction Transistor
PUT .... Program Update Tape
PUT .... Property Unit Trust [*Finance*] [*British*]
PUT .... Provocative Use Test [*Medicine*] (DMAA)
PUT .... Punta De Talca [*Chile*] [*Seismograph station code, US Geological Survey*] (SEIS)
PUT .... Putao [*Burma*] [*Airport symbol*] (AD)
PUT .... Putnam, CT [*Location identifier*] [*FAA*] (FAAL)
PUT .... Putrescine [*Organic chemistry*]
PUTB .... Put-Back (SAUS)
PUTC .... Pittsburgh Urban Transit Council (SAUS)
PUTC .... Put Character (SAUS)
PUTCO .... Pittsburgh Urban Transit Council (SAUS)
PUTCO .... Public Utility Transport Corp.
Puter Ch .... Puterbaugh's Illinois Chancery Pleading [*A publication*] (DLA)
Puter Pl .... Puterbaugh's Illinois Common Law Pleading [*A publication*] (DLA)
PUTF .... Put Formatted (SAUS)
PUTI .... Peripheral Unit Test Instruction (SAUS)

Putnam .... Putnam's Proceedings before the Justice of the Peace [*A publication*] (DLA)
PutnCA .... Putnam California Investment Grade [*Associated Press*] (SAG)
PutNY .... Putnam New York Investment Grade [*Associated Press*] (SAG)
PUTP .... Put Packed (SAUS)
PUTR .... Pacific Underwater Test Range (SAA)
PUTT .... Brassie Golf Corp. [*NASDAQ symbol*] (SAG)
PUTT .... Portable Underwater Tracking Transducer
PUTT .... Propellant Utilization Time Trace
PUTWS .... Put Word in String (SAA)
PUU .... Piute Reservoir [*Utah*] [*Seismograph station code, US Geological Survey*] (SEIS)
PUU .... Puerto Asis [*Colombia*] [*Airport symbol*] (OAG)
PU-UH .... University of Pennsylvania, University Hospital, Philadelphia, PA [*Library symbol*] [*Library of Congress*] (LCLS)
PU-UH-DeS... University of Pennsylvania, University Hospital, De Schweinitz Collection of Ophthalmology, Philadelphia, PA [*Library symbol*] [*Library of Congress*] (LCLS)
PUUSNA ...... Polish Union of the United States of North America (EA)
PUV .... Positive contrast Ultra Violet (SAUS)
PUV .... Posterior Urethral Valve [*Medicine*] (DMAA)
PUV .... Propellant Utilization Valve [*NASA*] (NASA)
PUV .... Pulaski [*Virginia*] [*Seismograph station code, US Geological Survey*] [*Closed*] (SEIS)
PUV .... Puumala Virus
PU-V .... University of Pennsylvania, School of Veterinary Medicine, Philadelphia, PA [*Library symbol*] [*Library of Congress*] (LCLS)
PUVA .... Photochemotherapy with Ultraviolet A [*Oncology*]
PUVA .... Psoralens and Ultraviolet A [*Therapy*] [*Medicine*]
PUVD .... Pulsed Ultrasonic Blood Velocity Detector (AAMN)
PUVEP .... Propellant Utilization Vehicleborne Electronic Package (SAUS)
PUVEP .... Propellant Utilization Vehicle Electronic Package (MCD)
PUVLV .... Propellant Utilization Valve [*NASA*] (AAG)
PUW .... Pick-Up Walker (MEDA)
PUW .... Pullman [*Washington*] [*Airport symbol*] (OAG)
PUW .... Pullman, WA [*Location identifier*] [*FAA*] (FAAL)
PU-W .... University of Pennsylvania, Wharton School of Finance and Commerce, Philadelphia, PA [*Library symbol*] [*Library of Congress*] (LCLS)
PUWP .... Polish United Workers' Party [*See also PZPR*] [*Political party*] (PD)
PUY .... Pula [*Former Yugoslavia*] [*Airport symbol*] (OAG)
PUZ .... Puerto Cabezas [*Nicaragua*] [*Airport symbol*] (AD)
PV .... Association Quebecoise Plaidoyer-Victimes (AC)
PV .... Eastern Provincial Airways [*Labrador*] [*ICAO designator*] (OAG)
P-V .... Panton-Valentine [*Leukocidin*] [*Bacteriology*] (DAVI)
PV .... Papillomavirus
PV .... Parameter Value (SAUS)
PV .... Paravane [*Anti-moored-mine device*] [*Obsolete*]
PV .... Paraventricular [*Neuroanatomy*] (MAE)
PV .... Paravertebral [*Medicine*] (MELL)
P/V .... Parity/overflow (SAUS)
PV .... Parole Violator
PV .... Paromomycin-Vancomycin [*Blood agar*] [*Microbiology*]
PV .... Par Value [*Finance*]
pv .... Pathovar [*Microbiology*]
PV .... Path Verification
PV .... Patrol Vessel
PV .... Paving [*Technical drawings*]
PV .... Peach Virus (SAUS)
P/V .... Peak-to-Valley
PV .... Pemphigus Vulgaris [*Dermatology*]
PV .... [*The*] People's Voice [*Pre-World War II publication of Adam Clayton Powell, Jr., and Charlie Buchanan*]
PV .... Peripheral Vascular [*Medicine*]
PV .... Peripheral Vein [*Anatomy*]
PV .... Peripheral Vessel [*Cardiology*] (MAE)
PV .... Peritoneo-Venous (WDAA)
PV .... Permanganate Value (SAUS)
PV .... Peroxide Value [*Food analysis*]
PV .... Personal Visit (SAUS)
P/V .... Per Vagina (SAUS)
P/V .... Per Vaginam [*Medicine*]
PV .... Petite Vitesse [*Goods train*] [*French*]
PV .... Pfeiffer Vacuum Technology AG [*NYSE symbol*] (SAG)
PV .... Photographic Vision [*Filter*]
PV .... Photovoltaic
Pv .... Photovoltaics (COE)
PV .... Physical Volume (SAUS)
PV .... Physical Vulnerability [*Number*] (NATG)
PV .... Piccola Velocity (SAUS)
pV .... Picovolt (IDOE)
PV .... Pigment Volume
PV .... Pilot Vessel
PV .... Pioneer Venus [*Spacecraft*]
PV .... Pipe Ventilated
PV .... Piston Valve [*Automotive engineering*]
PV .... Pisum Virus [*Plant pathology*]
PV .... Planetary Vehicle [*NASA*]
PV .... Planuebergang [*Grade Crossing*] [*German military - World War II*]
PV .... Plan View (MSA)
PV .... Plasma Value (SAUS)
PV .... Plasma Volume [*Medicine*]
PV .... Plastic Viscosity
PV .... Playback Verifier (MCD)
PV .... Plummer-Vinson [*Syndrome*] [*Medicine*] (DB)

P/V .... Pneumatic-to-Voltage (SAUS)
PV .... Pole Vault
PV .... Polio Vaccine
PV .... Poliovirus
PV .... Polycythemia Vera [*Also, PCV*] [*Hematology*]
PV .... Polydor/Deutsche-Grammophon Variable Microgroove [*Record label*] [*Germany*]
PV .... Polyoma Virus
PV .... Polyoma-Virus (SAUS)
PV .... Polyvinyl (WGA)
p/v .... Pool View
PV .... Pore Volume [*Geology*]
PV .... Pornovision [*Television*]
PV .... Portal Vein [*Anatomy*]
PV .... Position Vacant (ADA)
PV .... Position Value
PV .... Positively Vet [*British*] (BARN)
PV .... Positive Vetting (SAUS)
PV .... Positive Volume (IEEE)
PV .... Postvaccination
PV .... Post Village
PV .... Post-Virgil
PV .... Postvoiding [*Medicine*] (MAE)
PV .... Potential Viewer [*Television ratings*] (NTCM)
PV .... Potential Vorticity [*Meteorology*] [*Fluid mechanics*]
PV .... Precision Visuals (SAUS)
PV .... Present Value [*Finance*]
PV .... Pressure [*or Pressurized*] Control Valve (IAA)
P/V .... Pressure/Vacuum
P/V .... Pressure Valve (SAUS)
PV .... Pressure Velocity
PV .... Pressure Vessel (MSA)
P-V .... Pressure-Volume
PV .... Pressurization Valve
PV .... Prevailing Visibility
PV .... Prevalve (NASA)
PV .... Prevention of Violence (DICI)
P/V .... Preview
PV .... Preview Monitor [*A TV monitor*] [*Filmmaking*] (WDMC)
PV .... Price Variation (SAUS)
PV .... Priest Vicar
PV .... Primary Valve
PV .... Prime Vertical
PV .... Princess Victoria's Royal Irish Fusiliers [*Military*] [*British*] (ROG)
PV .... Principal Value (SAUS)
PV .... Private Varnish [*Privately owned railroad cars*]
PV .... Private Venture (SAUS)
PV .... Privileged Information (SAUS)
PV .... Process Variable (IAA)
PV .... Production Validation [*Military*] (AABC)
PV .... Production Verification (SAUS)
PV .... Product Verification (SAUS)
PV .... Professional Virgin (DSUE)
PV .... Professional Volunteer
P/V .... Profit Volume (SAUS)
P/V .... Profit/Volume Ratio
PV .... Project Verification (COE)
PV .... Project Volunteer (EA)
PV .... Prometheus Vinctus [*of Aeschylus*] [*Classical studies*] (OCD)
PV .... Propellant Valve (SAUS)
PV .... Proteus Vulgaris [*Bacterium*]
PV .... Protoverin (SAUS)
PV .... Public Volunteer
PV .... Public Voucher
PV .... Pull and Void (MCD)
PV .... Pulmonary Valve (SAUS)
PV .... Pulmonary Valvotomy [*Cardiology*]
PV .... Pulmonary Vascularity [*Medicine*]
PV .... Pulmonary Vein [*Medicine*]
PV .... Pulmonic Valve [*Cardiology*] (DAVI)
PV .... Pulse Voltammetry [*Analytical chemistry*]
PV .... Pyrocatechol Violet [*Also, PCV*] [*An indicator*] [*Chemistry*]
Pv .... Ventral Pressure Neurons [*of a leech*]
PV .... Villanova University, Villanova, PA [*Library symbol*] [*Library of Congress*] (LCLS)
PV1 .... Private E-1 [*Army*]
PV-1(M) .... Poliovirus Type 1, Maloney
PV2 .... Private E-2 [*Army*]
PV-2(L) .... Poliovirus Type 2, Lansing
PV 4 .... Pickup Trucks, Vans, and Four-Wheel-Drive Vehicles [*Initialism used as title of a publication*]
PVA .... Aerotransportes Privados SA de CV [*Mexico*] [*ICAO designator*] (FAAC)
PVA .... Paralyzed Veterans of America (EA)
PVA .... Parameter Variation Analysis (SAUS)
PVA .... Passenger Vessel Association (NTPA)
PVA .... Perigee Velocity Augmentation (SAUS)
PVA .... Personal Values Abstract [*Scale*]
PVA .... Personal Virtual Assistant
PVA .... Platinova Resources Ltd. [*Toronto Stock Exchange symbol*]
PVA .... Poly Vinyl Acetate (SAUS)
PVA .... Polyvinyl Acetate [*Organic chemistry*] (IAA)
PVA .... Poly(vinyl Alcohol) [*Also, PVAL*] [*Organic chemistry*]
PVA .... Population Viability Analysis [*Biology*]
PVA .... Portable Vehicle Analyzer [*Auto repair*] [*Electronics*]

PVA .... Positive Vorticity Advection [*NWS*] (FAAC)
PVA .... Potato Virus A [*Plant pathology*]
PVA .... Preburner Valve Actuator [*NASA*] (NASA)
PVA .... Present Value Analysis (MCD)
PVA .... Prison Visitors' Association (NADA)
PVA .... Privacy Act (MCD)
PVA .... Procedure Value Analysis (PDAA)
PVA .... Propellant Valve Actuator (MCD)
PVA .... Providencia [*Colombia*] [*Airport symbol*] (OAG)
PVA .... Provident Life Accident Insurance Co. of America [*NYSE symbol*] (SPSG)
PVA .... Pulmonary Valve Atresia (SAUS)
PVAA .... Polyvinylacetat (SAUS)
PVAC .... Peak Volts Alternating Current (KSC)
PVAC .... Polyvinil Acetate
PVAC .... Poly(vinyl Acetate) [*Organic chemistry*]
PVAC .... Present Value of Annual Charges
PVAD .... Position Velocity and Attitude Display (SAUS)
PVAE .... Poly(vinyl Acetate) [*Organic chemistry*]
PVAHI .... Augustinian Historical Institute, Villanova University, Villanova, PA [*Library symbol*] [*Library of Congress*] (LCLS)
PVAL .... Poly(vinyl Alcohol) [*Also, PVA*] [*Organic chemistry*]
PVAL .... Polyvinylalkohol (SAUS)
P-Value .... Probability Value (SAUS)
PV & D .... Purge, Vent, and Drain (NASA)
PVAR .... Percentage Variance [*Statistics*]
PVAS .... Postvasectomy Specimen [*Urology*] (DAVI)
PVAS .... Primary Voice Alerting System (SAUS)
PVAS .... Primary Voice Alert System [*NORAD*] (MCD)
PVASI .... Pulsating/Steady Visual Approach Slope Indicator [*Aviation*] (FAAC)
PVAT .... Paravant Computer Systems, Inc. [*NASDAQ symbol*] (SAG)
PVat II .... II Papiro Vaticano Greco II [*A publication*] (OCD)
PVAX .... Personal Virtual Address Extension [*Computer science*] (CIST)
PVB .... Platinol [*Cisplatin*], Vinblastine, Bleomycin [*Antineoplastic drug regimen*]
PVB .... Platteville, WI [*Location identifier*] [*FAA*] (FAAL)
PVB .... Polyvinyl Benzene (SAUS)
PVB .... Poly Vinyl Butyral (SAUS)
PVB .... Poly(vinyl Butyral) [*Safety glass laminating material*] [*Organic chemistry*]
PVB .... Polyvinylbutyrat (SAUS)
PVB .... Polyvinyl Butyryl (SAUS)
PVB .... Portametric Voltmeter Bridge
PVB .... Post-Vacation Blues
PVB .... Potentiometer Voltmeter Bridge (SAUS)
PVB .... Potentiometric Voltmeter Bridge (SAUS)
PVB .... Potentionmetric Voltmeter Bridge (IAA)
PVB .... Premature Ventricular Beat [*Cardiology*]
PVB .... Provident Life & Accident Insurance Co. of America [*NYSE symbol*] (SPSG)
PV-B .... Villanova University, Business and Finance Library, Villanova, PA [*Library symbol*] [*Library of Congress*] (LCLS)
PVBE .... Polyvinyl Butyl Ether [*Organic chemistry*]
PVBr .... Polyvinyl Bromide (PDAA)
PVBr .... Polyvinyl Butyral (SAUS)
PVBS .... Possible Vertebral-Basilar System [*Medicine*] (BABM)
PVC .... Pacvest Capital, Inc. [*Toronto Stock Exchange symbol*]
PVC .... Particle Vibration Coupling (SAUS)
PVC .... Partido de Veteranos Civiles [*Civilian Veterans' Party*] [*Dominican Republic*] [*Political party*] (PPW)
PVC .... Peripheral Vasoconstriction [*Medicine*]
PVC .... Periscope Viewer/Controller (MCD)
PVC .... Permanent Virtual Channel
PVC .... Philippine Volconology Commission (SAUS)
PVC .... Photovoltaic Cell (IAA)
PVC .... Pigment Volume Concentration
PVC .... Point of Vertical Curve
PVC .... Poly n-Vinyl Carbazole (SAUS)
PVC .... Polyvinyl Carbazol (IAA)
PVC .... Polyvinylchlorid (SAUS)
PVC .... Poly(vinyl Chloride) [*Organic chemistry*]
PVC .... Port Vila [*New Hebrides*] [*Seismograph station code, US Geological Survey*] (SEIS)
PVC .... Position and Velocity Computer
PVC .... Postvoiding Cystogram [*Medicine*] (MAE)
PVC .... Potential Volume Change
PVC .... Precision Valve Corp. (SAUS)
PVC .... Premature Ventricular Contraction [*Cardiology*]
PVC .... Pressure Vacuum Chamber
PVC .... Pressure Velocity Correction (AAEL)
PVC .... Pressure Volume Compensator (KSC)
PVC .... Pressure Volume Control (SAUS)
pvc .... Price Variation Clause (DS)
PVC .... Primary Visual Cortex [*Anatomy*]
PVC .... Private Virtual Circuit [*Telecommunications*]
PVC .... Prosthetic Valve (Disk) Closing [*Cardiology*]
PVC .... Pro-Vice-Chancellor (SAUS)
PVC .... Provincetown [*Massachusetts*] [*Airport symbol*] (OAG)
PVC .... Provincetown, MA [*Location identifier*] [*FAA*] (FAAL)
PVC .... Provisioned Virtual Connection (SAUS)
PVC .... Pulmonary Venous Congestion [*Medicine*]
PVC .... Pulse Voltage Converter (OA)
PVC .... Punch Validity Check (SAUS)
PVC .... PVC Container Corp. [*Associated Press*] (SAG)
PVCA .... Polyvinyl Chloride Acetate (SAUS)

PVCA	Polyvinylchloride Acetate [*Organic chemistry*]
PVCBMA	PVC [*Polyvinylchloride*] Belting Manufacturers Association [*Defunct*] (EA)
PVCC	Permanent Virtual Channel Connection (DDC)
PVCC	Piedmont Virginia Community College (SAUS)
PVCC	PVC Container [*NASDAQ symbol*] (TTSB)
PVCC	PVC Container Corp. [*Eatontown, NJ*] [*NASDAQ symbol*] (NQ)
PVCCF	Polyvinyl-Chloride-Coated Fibers (SAUS)
PVCF	Phase Variable Canonical Form (PDAA)
PVCF	Present Value Cash Flow [*Finance*]
PVCH	Polyvinylcyclohexane (SAUS)
PV CHART	Profit-Volume Chart (SAUS)
PVCI	Peripheral Vision Command Indicator
PVCN	Poly(vinyl Cinnamate) [*Organic chemistry*]
PVCN	Priced Vocabulary of Clothing and Necessaries (SAUS)
PVCO	Pulmonary Venous Channel Obstruction (SAUS)
PVco2	Venous Carbon Dioxide Pressure [*Medicine*] (MAE)
PVCP	Pulmonary Venous Capillary Pressure (SAUS)
PVCS	Portable Voice Communications System
PVCT	Posterior Vena Caval Thrombosis (SAUS)
PVCV	Pelargonium Vein Clearing Virus [*Plant pathology*]
PVCz	Poly-N-Vinylcarbazole (SAUS)
PVD	Administradora de Fondos ADS [*NYSE symbol*] (TTSB)
PVD	Administradora de Fondos de Pensiones Provida SA [*NYSE symbol*] (SAG)
PVD	Pancreatic Ventral Duct [*Anatomy*]
PVD	Paravisual Director [*British*]
PVD	Parent Very Disturbed [*Pediatrics*] (DAVI)
PVD	Percussion, Vibration, and Drainage [*Medicine*] (DAVI)
PVD	Peripheral Vascular Disease [*Medicine*]
PVD	Periphered Vision Display (SAUS)
PVD	Persistent Virus Disease [*Medicine*] (WDAA)
PVD	Photovoltaic Detection
PVD	Physical Vapor Deposition [*Coating technology*]
PVD	Physical Vulnerability Division [*Air Force*]
PVD	Planned Variations Demonstration [*HUD*]
PVD	Planned View Display (SAUS)
PVD	Plan Video Display (NITA)
PVD	Plan View Display (GAVI)
PVD	Polyvinyl Dichloride (EDCT)
PVD	Polyvinylidenchlorid (SAUS)
PVD	Polyvinylidene Chloride (SAUS)
PVD	Posterior Vitreous Detachment [*Ophthalmology*]
PVD	Primary Volume Descriptor (SAUS)
PVD	Product Verification Demonstration (MCD)
PVD	Protective Vehicle Division [*US Secret Service*]
PVD	Providence [*Rhode Island*] [*Airport symbol*] (OAG)
PVD	Pulmonary Vascular Disease [*Medicine*]
PVD	Purge, Vent, Drain System (MCD)
PVD	Theodore Francis Green State Airport [*FAA*] (TAG)
PvdA	Partij van de Arbeid [*Labor Party*] [*Netherlands*] [*Political party*] (PPE)
PVDA	Polyvinylidene Acetate (SAUS)
PvdA/PTA	Partij van de Arbeid van Belgiee/Parti du Travail de Belgique [*Belgian Labor Party*] [*Political party*] (PPW)
PVDC	Polyvinyldichlorid (SAUS)
PVDC	Polyvinyl Dichloride (EDCT)
PVDC	Poly(vinylidene Chloride) [*Organic chemistry*]
PVDF	Polyvinyldene Fluoride (SAUS)
PVDF	Polyvinyl Difluoride (SAUS)
PVDF	Poly(vinylidene Difluoride) [*Organic chemistry*]
PVDF	Poly(vinylidene Fluoride) [*Organic chemistry*]
PVDF	Polyvinylidenfluorid (SAUS)
PVDL	Precision Variable Delay Line
PVDS	Physical Vulnerability Data Sheets (MCD)
PVDS	Propelled Variable-Depth SONAR (SEWL)
PVDSTOW	Plan View Display STOW (SAUS)
PvdV	Partij van de Vrijheid [*Party of Freedom*] [*Netherlands*] [*Political party*] (PPE)
PVE	Perivenous Encephalomyelitis [*Neurology*] (DAVI)
PVE	Pine Valley Explorers [*Vancouver Stock Exchange symbol*]
PVE	Polyvinyl Ether [*Organic chemistry*]
PVE	Porvenir [*Panama*] [*Airport symbol*] (OAG)
PVE	Premature Ventricular Extrasystole [*Cardiology*] (AAMN)
PVE	Process Validation Enterprise [*Army*] (RDA)
PVE	Prolonged Vacuum Exposure
PVE	Prosthetic Valve Echogram [*Cardiology*]
PVE	Prosthetic Valve Endocarditis [*Medicine*]
PVE	Provisioning Engineer
PVE	Pulmonary Vascular Effect [*Physiology*]
PVED	Parity Violating Energy Difference [*Physical chemistry*]
PVED	Parity Violation Energy Difference [*Physics*]
PVED	Periventricular Echo Density (DB)
PVEE	Polyvinyl Ethyl Ether [*Organic chemistry*]
PVEM	Pulse-Vector Emittance Meter (SAUS)
PVEN	Primate Vaccine Evaluation Network
PVEP	Pattern Visual Evoked Potential [*neurology*] (DAVI)
PVEPP	Preliminary Value Engineering Program Plan (MCD)
PVF	Peak Visibility Factor
PVF	Pension Valuation Factor
PVF	Peripheral Visual Field [*Optics*]
PVF	Placerville, CA [*Location identifier*] [*FAA*] (FAAL)
PVF	Political Victory Fund [*National Rifle Association*]
PVF	Polyvinylfluorid (SAUS)
PVF	Poly(vinyl Fluoride) [*Organic chemistry*]

PVF	Polyvinyl Formal [*Organic chemistry*]
PVF	Portal Venous Flow [*Physiology*]
PVF	Posterior Vitreous Face [*Ophthalmology*] (DAVI)
PVF	Primary Ventricular Fibrillation (CPH)
PVF2	Fluorinated polymer used in tactile sensing in robots etc. (SAUS)
PVF2	Poly(vinylidene Fluoride) [*Organic chemistry*]
PVFC	PVF Capital [*NASDAQ symbol*] (TTSB)
PVFC	PVF Capital Corp. [*NASDAQ symbol*] (SAG)
PVFCap	PVF Capital Corp. [*Associated Press*] (SAG)
PVFD	Pipe Ventilated, Forced Draught
PVfHi	Valley Forge Historical Society, Valley Forge, PA [*Library symbol*] [*Library of Congress*] (LCLS)
PVFHP	Public Voice for Food and Health Policy (EA)
PV Filter	Panchromatic Vision Filter (SAUS)
PVFM	Polyvinyl Formal [*Organic chemistry*]
PVFM	Polyvinylformal (SAUS)
PVFO	Polyvinyl Formal (EDCT)
PVfP	Philadelphia Quartz Co., Valley Forge, PA [*Library symbol*] [*Library of Congress*] (LCLS)
PVFS	Physicians for a Violence-Free Society
PVFS	Pinnacle Virtual File System [*Pinnacle Micro, Inc.*] [*Computer science*] (PCM)
PVFS	Postviral Fatigue Syndrome [*Medicine*] (DMAA)
PVG	Periventricular Gray [*Neurobiology*]
PVG	Polyvinylene Glycol (SAUS)
PVG	Portsmouth, VA [*Location identifier*] [*FAA*] (FAAL)
PVG	Programmable Variations Generator [*Computer science*]
PVG	Project on the Vietnam Generation [*Later, II*] (EA)
PVG	Proportional Valve Group [*Hydraulics*]
PVG	Pulmonary Valve Gradient [*Medicine*] (DMAA)
PVGA	Processed Vegetable Growers Association [*British*] (DBA)
PVGC	Pioneer Venus Gas Chromatograph [*NASA*]
PVG GND	Proving Ground (SAUS)
PVH	Papilloma Virus Hominis (DB)
PVH	Paraventricular Hypothalmic Nucleus [*Neuroanatomy*]
PVH	Periventricular Hemorrhage [*Medicine*]
PVH	Phillips-Van Heusen [*NYSE symbol*] (TTSB)
PVH	Phillips-Van Heusen Corp. [*NYSE symbol*] (SPSG)
PVH	Pope Valley Holding [*Vancouver Stock Exchange symbol*]
PVH	Porto Velho [*Brazil*] [*Airport symbol*] (OAG)
PVH	Propane-Vacuum-Hydrogen (SAUS)
PVH	Pulmonary Venous Hypertension [*Medicine*]
PVHE	Polyvinyl Hexyl Ether [*Organic chemistry*]
PVHO	Pressure Vessel for Human Occupancy [*Deep-sea diving*]
PVHS	Photorefractive Volume Holographic Storage
PVI	Pacific Vocational Institute Library [*UTLAS symbol*]
PVI	Paranavai [*Brazil*] [*Airport symbol*] (AD)
PVI	Peripheral Vascular Insufficiency [*Medicine*]
PVI	Perpendicular Vegetation Index [*Botany*]
PVI	Personal Values Inventory [*Psychology*]
PVI	Picture Vocational Interest Questionnaire for Adults [*Vocational guidance test*]
PVI	Pilot Vehicle Interface (SAUS)
PVI	Pilot-Vehicle Interface [*Search technology*]
PVI	Placental Villus Inflammation [*Medicine*] (MELL)
PVI	Point of Vertical Intersection
PVI	Poly(vinyl Isobutyl Ether) [*Organic chemistry*]
PVI	Portal Vein Inflow [*Physiology*]
PVI	Postage Validation Imprinter
PVI	Post-Vaccination Immunity [*Medicine*] (MELL)
PVI	Precision Visuals International (SAUS)
PVI	Premature Vulcanization Inhibitor (MCD)
PVI	Present Value Index (EBF)
PVI	Pre-Vulcanisation (or Vulcanization) Inhibitor (SAUS)
PVI	Prevulcanization Inhibitor
PVI	Primary Vocational Interest [*Personnel study*]
PVI	Product Verification Inspection [*DoD*]
PVI	Programmable Video Interface
PVID	Pipe Ventilated, Induced Draught
PVIF	Present Value Interest Factor [*Finance*]
PVIFA	Present Value Interest Factor of an Annuity [*Real estate*]
PVIIX	Putnam Voyager II Cl.A [*Mutual fund ticker symbol*] (SG)
PVIM	Pulse Vector Immittance Meter (SAUS)
PVIR	Penn Virginia [*NASDAQ symbol*] (TTSB)
PVIR	Penn Virginia Corp. [*NASDAQ symbol*] (NQ)
PVIS	Pneumatic Vertical-Indicating Scale (SAUS)
PVIS	Program Verification Information System (SAUS)
PVITL	Program-Variation-in-the-Large (SAUS)
PVITS	Program-Variation-in-the-Small (SAUS)
PVIZT	Phenyl(vinyl)imidazolidinethione [*Organic chemistry*]
PVJ	Pauls Valley, OK [*Location identifier*] [*FAA*] (FAAL)
PVJC	Palo Verde Junior College [*California*]
PVK	Packaged Ventilation Kit [*Civil Defense*]
PVK	Penicillin V Potassium [*Medicine*] (DMAA)
PVK	Photoconductive Polyvinyl Carbazole (SAUS)
PVK	Polyvinylcarbazol [*Organic chemistry*] (IEEE)
PVK	Polyvinyl Carbazole (SAUS)
PVK	Preveza/Lefkas [*Greece*] [*Airport symbol*] (OAG)
P-VL	Panton-Valentine Leukocidin
PVL	Parameter Value Language (ADWA)
PVL	Pavlikeny [*Bulgaria*] [*Seismograph station code, US Geological Survey*] (SEIS)
PVL	Perivalvular Leakage [*Medicine*] (DMAA)
PVL	Periventricular Leukomalacia [*Medicine*]
PVL	Periventricular Lucencies (SAUS)

PVL............	Permanent Vision Loss [*Medicine*] (DMAA)
PVL............	Polyporus Versicolor Laccase (SAUS)
PVL............	Pressure to Vertical Locks
PVL............	Prevail (FAAC)
PV-L...........	Villanova University, Law School, Villanova, PA [*Library symbol*] [*Library of Congress*] (LCLS)
PVLR	Publisher/Vendor/Library Relations [*Committee of Association for Library Collections and Technical Services*]
PVLR	Publisher/Vendor-Library Relations Committee [*ALCTS*] (AL)
PVLT...........	Prevalent (FAAC)
PVM............	Parallel Virtual Machine [*Software package*]
PVM............	Parasitophorous Vacuole Membrane [*Malaria*]
PVM............	Pass-through Virtual Machine (SAUS)
PVM............	Passthru Virtual Machine (SAUS)
PVM............	Performance Verification Matrix (SAUS)
PVM............	Pneumonia Virus of Mice
PVM............	Point Visibility Meter (SAUS)
PVM............	Polyvinyl Methyl (SAUS)
PVM............	Poly(vinyl Methyl Ether) [*Organic chemistry*]
PVM............	Posterior Ventral Microtubule [*Anatomy*]
PVM............	Potato Virus M [*Plant pathology*]
PVM............	Potentiometric Voltmeter
PVM............	Power Vacuum Module [*Automotive engineering*]
PVM............	Pressure Vessel Material
PVM............	Preventive Medicine (MELL)
PVM............	Prisons Video Magazine (WDAA)
PVM............	Process Evaluation Module (SAUS)
PVM............	Progressive Minerals [*Vancouver Stock Exchange symbol*]
PVM............	Projection Video Monitor
PVM............	Protein-Vitamin-Mineral (SAUS)
PVM............	Protein, Vitamins, Minerals [*J. B. Williams Co. brand of liquid protein*]
PVM............	Proton Vector Magnetometer (NOAA)
PVMA..........	Pressure Vessel Manufacturers Association (EA)
PVMA..........	Protoverin-6-Monoacetat (SAUS)
PVMB..........	Potential Variation Mixed Basis [*Photovoltaic energy systems*]
PVMD..........	Parallel Virtual Machine Daemon (CTAS)
PVME..........	Poly(vinyl Methyl Ether) [*Organic chemistry*]
PVMed........	Preventative Medicine (DAVI)
PVMI..........	Parish Visitors of Mary Immaculate [*Roman Catholic women's religious order*]
PVMK..........	Polyvinyl Methyl Ketone [*Organic chemistry*] (DICI)
PVMNM	Perrys Victory Memorial National Monument (SAUS)
PVMNT	Pavement (SAUS)
PVMS..........	Paged Virtual Memory System (SAUS)
PVMT..........	Pavement [*Technical drawings*]
pvmt	Pavement
PVMTD	Preservation Method
PVMV..........	Panda Vehicle Module Vertical (SAUS)
PVMV..........	Pepper Veinal Mottle Virus [*Plant pathology*]
PVMVH	Panda Vehicle Module Horizontal (SAUS)
PVMV-N	Panda Vehicle Module Vertical (SAUS)
PVN	Paraventricular Nuclei (SAUS)
PVN	Paraventricular Nucleus [*Brain anatomy*]
PVN	Patient Very Nervous [*Medicine*] (WDAA)
PVN	Peters Valley [*New Jersey*] [*Seismograph station code, US Geological Survey*] [*Closed*] (SEIS)
PVN	Poly(vinyl Nitrate) [*Organic chemistry*]
PVN	Private Virtual Network (SAUS)
PVN	Programmable Virtual Network (SAUS)
PVN	Proven Resources Ltd. [*Vancouver Stock Exchange symbol*]
PVN	Providian Corp. [*Formerly, Capital Holding*] [*NYSE symbol*] (SAG)
PVN	Providian LLC [*NYSE symbol*] (SAG)
PVNGS........	Palo Verde Nuclear Generating Station (NRCH)
PVNO..........	Polyvinylpyridine-N-Oxide [*Organic chemistry*]
PVNO..........	Polyvinylpyridin-N-oxid (SAUS)
PVNO..........	Polyvinylpyridinoxid (SAUS)
PVNPrM......	Providian LLC'MIPS' [*NYSE symbol*] (TTSB)
PVNPS........	Post-Vietnam Psychiatric Syndrome
PVNS..........	Pigmented Villonodular Synovitis [*Also, PVS*] [*Medicine*]
PVNT..........	Prevent (AAG)
PVNT..........	Preventile (SAUS)
PVNT..........	Preventive (SAUS)
PVNTMED	Preventive Medicine [*Also, PM*]
PVO	Atlantic City, NJ [*Location identifier*] [*FAA*] (FAAL)
PVO	Bearing Supplies Ltd. [*British*] [*ICAO designator*] (FAAC)
PVO	Peripheral Vascular Occlusion [*Medicine*] (DAVI)
PVO	Phosphorus Vanadium Oxide [*Inorganic chemistry*]
PVO	Pioneer Venus Orbiter [*NASA*]
PVO	Portoviejo [*Ecuador*] [*Airport symbol*] (OAG)
PVO	Principal Veterinary Officer (ROG)
PVO	Principal Visiting Officer [*Australia*]
PVO	Private Voluntary Organization
PVO	Privileged Visiting Order (WDAA)
PVO	Project Vietnam Orphans [*British*] (DI)
PVO	Prosthetic Valve (Disk) Opening [*Cardiology*]
PVO	Protivo-Voxdushnaia Oborona [*Antiaircraft Defense*] [*Former USSR*]
PVO	Pulmonary Venous Obstruction [*Medicine*] (DMAA)
PVO	Pulmonary Venous Occlusion [*Cardiology*] (DAVI)
PVO	Soviet designation for Air Defence (SAUS)
PvO₂	Partial Pressure of Venous Oxygen [*Hematology*] (CPH)
PVOA..........	Passenger Vehicle Operators Association Ltd. [*British*] (BI)
PVOA..........	Passenger Vehicle Operators Association (SAUS)
PVOA..........	Public Vehicle Operators' Association [*Later, CBRPT*] [*British*] (DI)
PVOD..........	Peripheral Vascular Occlusive Disease [*Medicine*]
PVOD..........	Pulmonary Vascular Obstructive Disease [*Medicine*] (MELL)
PVOD..........	Pulmonary Veno-Occlusive Disease [*Medicine*] (STED)
PVOD..........	Pulmonary Venous Obstructive Disease [*Cardiology*] (DAVI)
PVOH..........	Polyvinyl Alcohol (EDCT)
PVOR..........	Precision VHF [*Very High-Frequency*] Omnidirectional Range (IAA)
PVOR..........	Precision VHF Omnirange
PVOR..........	Precision Vision Omnirange (SAUS)
PVOUVS......	Pioneer Venus Orbiter Ultraviolet Spectrometer [*NASA*]
PVOYX........	Putnam Voyager Cl.A [*Mutual fund ticker symbol*] (SG)
PVP............	Packet Video Processor (SAUS)
PVP............	Packet Video Protocol (SAUS)
PVP............	Parallel Vector Processing (SAUS)
PV-P	Past Vice-President
PVP............	Penicillin V Potassium [*Biochemistry*] (MAE)
PVP............	Performance Verification Plan (SAUS)
PVP............	Peripheral Vein Plasma [*Cardiology*] (MAE)
PVP............	Peripheral Venous Pressure [*Cardiology*]
PVP............	Permanent Virtual Path (SEWL)
PVP............	Photovoltaic Power (SAUS)
PVP............	Pipelined Vector Processor (NITA)
PVP............	Plant Variety Protection
PVP............	Plasma Vaporization Process
PVP............	Polyvinyl Propionate (SAUS)
PVP............	Polyvinylpyridine
PVP............	Polyvinylpyrrolidon (SAUS)
PVP............	Poly(vinylpyrrolidone) [*Organic chemistry*]
PVP............	Polyvinyl Pyrrolidone (SAUS)
PVP............	Portal Venous Pressure [*Physiology*]
PVP............	Preferred Vision Provider
PVP............	President's Veterans Program [*Employment*]
PVP............	Pre-Volume Production [*Automotive term*] (GOBB)
PVP............	Professional Video Productions, Inc. [*Telecommunications service*] (TSSD)
PVP............	Prototype-Validation Phase (SAUS)
PVP............	Pueblo Viejo [*Peru*] [*Seismograph station code, US Geological Survey*] [*Closed*] (SEIS)
PVP............	Pulmonary Venous Pressure [*Medicine*] (STED)
PVPA	Plant Variety Protection Act [*1970*]
PVPC	Permanent Virtual Path Connection (DDC)
PVPC	Principal Vertical Polar Curve (SAUS)
PVPDC	Poly(vinylpyridinium) Dichromate [*Organic chemistry*]
PVP-I	Poly(vinylpyrrolidone) Iodine Complex
PVP-I	Polyvinylpyrrolidone Povidone-Iodine (STED)
PVPMPC	Perpetual Vice-President-Member Pickwick Club [*From "The Pickwick Papers" by Charles Dickens*]
PVPO	Plant Variety Protection Office [*Department of Agriculture*]
PVPP	Polyvinyl Polypyrrolidone (SAUS)
PVPS	Plasma Varactor Phase Shifter
PVQ	Deadhorse, AK [*Location identifier*] [*FAA*] (FAAL)
PVQ	Personal Value Questionnaire [*Navy*]
PVR	Palos Verdes [*California*] [*Seismograph station code, US Geological Survey*] [*Closed*] (SEIS)
PVR	Paraventricular Nuclear Stratum (STED)
PVR	Peripheral Vascular Resistance [*Cardiology*]
PVR	Permanent Virtual Route (SAUS)
PVR	Personnel Vehicle Radar (LAIN)
PVR	Phase Volume Ratio [*Physical chemistry*]
PVR	Photo Voltaic Relay (NITA)
PVR	Police Volunteer Reserves (SAUS)
PVR	Poltable Volume-controlled Respirator (SAUS)
PVR	Pontefract Volunteer Rifles [*British military*] (DMA)
PVR	Portable Vehicular Ramp [*MTMC*] (TAG)
PVR	Portable Volume-controlled Respirator (SAUS)
PVR	Portal Venous Pressure [*Medicine*] (MELL)
PVR	Postvoiding Residual [*Medicine*]
PVR	Precision Voltage Reference (MDG)
PVR	Prefix Value Register (SAUS)
PVR	Premature Voluntary Release [*British military*] (DMA)
PVR	Premature Voluntary Requirement (SAUS)
PVR	Premature Voluntary Retirement (SAUS)
PVR	Procedure Validation Report (AAG)
PVR	Process Variable Record
PVR	Product Verification Review (ACAE)
PVR	Profit/Volume Ratio
PVR	Proliferative Vitreoretinopathy [*Ophthalmology*]
PVR	Puerto Vallarta [*Mexico*] [*Airport symbol*] (OAG)
PVR	Pulmonary Vascular Resistance [*Physiology*]
PVR	Pulmonary Venous Redistribution (STED)
PVR	Pulse Volume Rate [*Physiology*]
PVR	Pulse Volume Recording [*Medicine*]
PVR	Pure and Vulcanized Rubber (IAA)
P/V Ratio	Peak to Valley Ratio (SAUS)
PVRC	Pressure Vessel Research Committee [*National Institute of Standards and Technology*]
PVRD	Purge, Vent, Repressurize, and Drain (NASA)
PVRI	Pulmonary Vascular Resistance Index [*Medicine*] (DMAA)
PVRO	Plant Variety Rights Office [*Ministry of Agriculture, Fisheries, and Food*] [*British*]
PVRO	Pyrotechnics (NAKS)
PVRS	Personal Video Recorders
PVRV	Purified Vero-Cell Rabies Vaccine [*Medicine*] (DB)
PVS............	Panoramic Vision System (SAUS)
PVS............	Parallel Visualization Server (SAUS)
PVS............	Partner Violence Screen [*Health*]
PVS............	Passive Night Vision (SAUS)
PVS............	[*The*] Pecos Valley Southern Railway Co. [*AAR code*]

PVS.............	Percussion, Vibration and Suction [*Medicine*] (DAVI)
PVS.............	Performance Verification System
PVS.............	Peripheral Vascular Surgery [*Cardiology*] (DAVI)
PVS.............	Peritoneovenous Shunt [*Medicine*]
PVS.............	Periventricular Nuclear Stratum (DB)
PVS.............	Periventricular System (SAUS)
PVS.............	Permanent Vendor Support (SAUS)
PVS.............	Persistent Vegetative State [*Medicine*]
PVS.............	Personal Value System (SAUS)
PVS.............	Personal Videoconferencing Station [*Widcom, Inc.*] [*Los Gatos, CA*] [*Telecommunications service*] (TSSD)
PVS.............	Personal Videoconferencing System (NITA)
PVS.............	Photovoltage Spectroscopy (SAUS)
PVS.............	Photovoltaic System
PVS.............	Pigmented Villonodular Synovitis [*Also, PVNS*] [*Medicine*]
PVS.............	Pilot Vision System (SAUS)
PVS.............	Plant Vent Stack [*Nuclear energy*] (NRCH)
PVS.............	Plexus Visibility Score [*Medicine*]
PVS.............	Polyvinylsulfonate [*Organic chemistry*]
PVS.............	Ported Vacuum Switch [*Automotive engineering*]
PVS.............	Postal Vehicle Service
PVS.............	Post-Vietnam Syndrome
PVS.............	Postviral Syndrome [*Medicine*] (WDAA)
PVS.............	Potato Virus S [*Plant pathology*]
PVS.............	Potentially Visible Set (SAUS)
PVS.............	Premature Ventricular Systole [*Cardiology*] (MAE)
PVS.............	Present Value Service [*LIMRA*]
PVS.............	Pressure Vacuum System
PVS.............	Prime Vendor Support [*Army*]
PVS.............	Principal Veterinary Surgeon [*British*]
PVS.............	Priority Ventures [*Vancouver Stock Exchange symbol*]
PVS.............	Private Viewdata System [*Computer science*]
PVS.............	Private Vocational Schools
PVS.............	Proceedings of the Virgil Society (SAUS)
PVS.............	Product Verification Specification
PVS.............	Professional Video Services Corp. [*Telecommunications service*] (TSSD)
PVS.............	Professional Vision Services (SAUS)
PVS.............	Programmed Ventricular Stimulation (DB)
PVS.............	Program Validation Services [*Computer science*]
PVS.............	Propellant Venting System
PVS.............	Prototype Verification System (RALS)
PVS.............	Pulmonary Valve Stenosis [*Cardiology*]
PVS.............	Purified for Volumetric Standardization (SAUS)
PVSA	Parkvale Financial [*NASDAQ symbol*] (TTSB)
PVSA	Parkvale Financial Corp. [*NASDAQ symbol*] (NQ)
PVSA	Peripheral Vascular Society of America (SAUS)
PVSC	Professional Video Services Corp. [*Telecommunications service*] (TSSD)
PVSE...........	Primary Vehicle System Engineer (SAUS)
PVSG	Paravertebral Sympathetic Ganglion [*Neuroanatomy*]
PVSG	Periscope Visual Scene Generation
PVSG	Polycythemia Vera Study Group (MEDA)
PV Slg	Polyvalent Surface Immunoglobulin [*Immunology*]
PVST...........	Premate Verification System Test [*NASA*]
PV/ST..........	Premate Verification/System Test [*NASA*] (KSC)
PVT.............	Pacific Vending Technology Ltd. [*Vancouver Stock Exchange symbol*]
PVT.............	Packet Voice Terminal (SAUS)
PVT.............	Page View Terminal [*Typography*] [*Videotex terminal*]
PVT.............	Parameter Variable Table (CIST)
PVT.............	Parameter/Variable Table (SAUS)
PVT.............	Paroxysmal Ventricular Tachycardia [*Medicine*]
PVT.............	Par Voie Telegraphique [*By Telegraph*] [*French*]
PVT.............	Performance Validation Test (CIST)
PVT.............	Performance Verification Test
PVT.............	Permanent Virtual Terminal (SAUS)
PVT.............	Personal Verifier Terminal (DA)
PVT.............	Persons Viewing Television [*Television ratings*] (NTCM)
PV/T...........	Photovoltaic/Thermal
PVT.............	Physical Vapor Transport [*Materials processing*]
PVT.............	Pivot (MSA)
PVT.............	Point of Vertical Tangent
PVT.............	Polyvalent Tolerance [*Immunology*]
PVT.............	Poly(vinyltoluene) [*Organic chemistry*]
PVT.............	Polyvinyl Toluene
PVT.............	Portal Vein Thrombosis [*Physiology*]
PVT.............	Position Velocity-Time
PVT.............	Potato Virus T [*Plant pathology*]
PVT.............	Precision Verification Team
PVT.............	Precision Verification Test (MCD)
PVT.............	Preflight Verification Test (NASA)
PVT.............	Pressure, Volume, Temperature
Pvt.............	Private (DD)
pvt..............	Private (GEAB)
PVT.............	Private
PVT.............	Private Patient [*Medicine*] (DMAA)
PVT.............	Probe Velocity Transducer (KSC)
PVT.............	Process, Voltage, Temperature (SAUS)
PVT.............	Production Validation Testing
PVT.............	Product Verification Test (MCD)
PVT.............	Protected Tube-Launched Optically Tracked Wire-Guided Anti-Tank Missile Vehicle
PVT.............	Prototype Validation Test (MCD)
PVT.............	Provident Companies [*NYSE symbol*] (TTSB)

PVT.............	Provident Companies, Inc. [*NYSE symbol*] (SAG)
PVT.............	Provisioning Technician
PVT.............	Pulse Video Thermography [*Nondestructive testing technique*]
PVT.............	Pyrotechnic Verification Test [*NASA*] (NASA)
PVTA	Philippine Virginia Tobacco Administration (SAUS)
PVTA	Protoverin-3,6,16-Triacetat (SAUS)
PVTAP	Photovoltaic Transient Analysis Computer Program
PVTB	Private Bancorp, Inc. [*NASDAQ symbol*]
PVT-C	Production Validation Test - Contractor (MCD)
PVT-C	Product Verification Test - Contractor (MCD)
PVT-C	Prototype Validation Test - Contractor (MCD)
PVTCA	Polyvinyl Trichloracetate (SAUS)
PVTD	PNNL Vitrification Technology Department (SAUS)
PVTE	Private
PVT-G	Production Validation Test - Government
PVT-G	Product Verification Test-Government
PVT-G	Prototype Validation Test - Government
PVTI	Piping and Valve Test Insert [*Nuclear energy*] (NRCH)
PVTM	Physical Vulnerability Technical Memorandum (MCD)
PVTOS	Physical Vapor Transport of Organic Solids (SAUS)
PVTOS	Physical Vapor Transport of Organic Solutions [*Materials processing*]
PVTPr	Provident Companies Dep Pfd [*NYSE symbol*] (TTSB)
PVTR	Portable Video Tape Recorder
PVTS	Pressure Vessel Thermal Shock (PDAA)
PVU	Perimeter Ventures Ltd. [*Vancouver Stock Exchange symbol*]
PVU	Prairie View University (SAUS)
PVU	Precision Velocity Update (MCD)
PVU	Production Verification Unit (ACAE)
PVU	Provo [*Utah*] [*Airport symbol*] (OAG)
PVU	Provo, UT [*Location identifier*] [*FAA*] (FAAL)
PVU	Villanova University, Villanova, PA [*OCLC symbol*] (OCLC)
PVV	Fondation Europeenne "Pro Venetia Viva" [*European Foundation "Pro Venetia Viva"*] (EAIO)
PVV	Partij voor Vrijheid en Vooruitgang [*Freedom and Progress Party*] [*See also PLP*] [*Belgium*] [*Political party*] (PPW)
PVV	Path Variability Value (SAUS)
PVV	Portal Venous Velocity [*Physiology*]
PVV	Pressure, Vent, and Vacuum
PVW	Plainview, TX [*Location identifier*] [*FAA*] (FAAL)
PVW	Posterior Vaginal Wall [*Medicine*] (DMAA)
PVW	Program Control Word (SAUS)
PVW	Pure Virgin Wool (SAUS)
PVW	Wilson College, Chambersburg, PA [*OCLC symbol*] (OCLC)
PVWA	Planned Value of Work Accomplished
PVWA	Plan Value Work Accounting (MCD)
PVWS	Planned Value of Work Scheduled (MCD)
PVX	Phosphorous-Doped Vapor-Deposited Oxide (IAA)
PVX	Potato Virus X [*Plant pathology*]
PVY	Pope Vanoy [*Alaska*] [*Airport symbol*] (OAG)
PVY	Potato Virus Y
PVY	Providence Energy [*AMEX symbol*] (TTSB)
PVY	Providence Energy Corp. [*AMEX symbol*] (SPSG)
PVYV	Pittosporum Vein Yellowing Virus [*Plant pathology*]
PVZ	Painesville, OH [*Location identifier*] [*FAA*] (FAAL)
PW.............	Citizens Library, Washington, PA [*Library symbol*] [*Library of Congress*] (LCLS)
PW.............	Pacific Western Airlines Ltd. [*Canada*] [*ICAO designator*] (OAG)
PW.............	Packed Weight
PW.............	Paine Webber, Inc. (EFIS)
PW.............	Palau [*ANSI two-letter standard code*] (CNC)
PW.............	Paper Wrapper (ADA)
PW.............	Paraguay Watch (EA)
PW.............	Parallel With (IAA)
PW.............	Parameter Word (SAUS)
PW.............	Parkes-Weber [*Syndrome*] [*Medicine*] (DB)
PW-C	Passing Window (MSA)
PW.............	Pass Word (SAUS)
PW.............	Password [*Computer science*]
PW.............	Pathetic Wanker (SAUS)
PW.............	Peak Watt (SAUS)
PW.............	Peere-Williams' English Chancery Reports [*1695-1736*] [*A publication*] (DLA)
PW.............	Penetrating Wound (MELL)
PW.............	Pension for Wounds [*Navy*] [*British*] (ROG)
PW.............	Peptone Water (SAUS)
PW.............	Pericardium Wall [*Medicine*]
PW.............	Permanent Way (SAUS)
PW.............	Personal Workstation (SAUS)
pw.............	Per Week (ODBW)
PW.............	Per Week
PW.............	Petroleum Week [*A publication*]
PW.............	Philadelphia & Western Railroad [*AAR code*] [*Terminated*]
pW.............	Picowatt
PW.............	Picowatts
PW.............	Pilot Wire (MSA)
PW.............	Pine Bark Mixed with Weblite and Peat
PW.............	Pitts & W Va RR SBI [*AMEX symbol*] (TTSB)
PW.............	Pittsburgh & West Virginia (SAUS)
PW.............	Pittsburgh & West Virginia Railroad [*AMEX symbol*] (SPSG)
PW.............	Pivoted Window (AAG)
PW.............	Plain Washer (MSA)
PW.............	Plantar Wart [*Orthopedics*] (DAVI)
PW.............	Plated Wire (SAUS)
PW.............	Platoon Weapons [*British military*] (DMA)
PW.............	Poets and Writers (EA)

PW	Policewoman (WDAA)
PW	Ports and Waterways
PW	Port-Wine Stain
PW	Port Wing (SAUS)
PW	Position Wanted [Employment]
PW	Positive Women [An association] [Australia]
PW	Postal Wire [Telecommunications] (IAA)
PW	Posterior Wall [Medicine]
PW	Postwar
PW	Potable Water [Nuclear energy] (NRCH)
PW	Powder Weight (SAUS)
PW	Power
PW	Power Wagon [Military vehicle]
PW	Power Windows [Automobile ads]
P-W	Prader-Willi [Syndrome] [Medicine] (AAMN)
PW	Pratt and Whitney
PW	Precipitable Water (CARB)
PW	Precise Word (SAUS)
PW	PRECIS Word (NITA)
PW	Presbyterian Women [An association] (EA)
PW	Present Worth [Economics]
PW	Pressurized Water
PW	Prevailing Wage (MHDW)
PW	Price Waterhouse (SAUS)
PW	Prime Western [Zinc]
PW	Prince of Wales [Military unit] [British]
PW	Printed Wiring (MSA)
PW	Printing World [A publication] (DGA)
PW	Prisoner of War [Also, POW]
PW	Private Wire (NATG)
PW	Procedure Word (SAUS)
PW	Process Water [Environmental science] (COE)
PW	Progesterone Withdrawal [Endocrinology]
PW	Program Word [Computer science] (IAA)
PW	Projected Window (MSA)
PW	Projection Welding
PW	Proven Winners
PW	Providence & Worcester Co. [AAR code]
PW	Psychological Warfare
PW	Public Welfare
PW	Public Works
PW	Publishers Weekly [A publication] (BRI)
PW	Pulmonary Wedge [Pressure] (DB)
PW	Pulpwash [Byproduct of citrus processing]
PW	Pulse Wave (SAUS)
PW	Pulse Width [RADAR]
pW	Pulse Width
PW	Puncture Wound (MELL)
PW	Purlwise [Knitting]
PW	Royal Warrant for Pay and Promotion [British military] (DMA)
PW	State Department of Public Welfare (SAUS)
Pw	Transthoracic Pressure [Medicine] (DAVI)
pW0p	Picowatts, Psophometrically Weighted at a Point of Zero Reference Level
PW2	Personal Workstation 2 [Computer hardware] [Unisys Corp.] (PCM)
PWA	Challeng'Air [France] [FAA designator] (FAAC)
PWA	Oklahoma City, OK [Location identifier] [FAA] (FAAL)
PWA	Pacific Western Airlines (SAUS)
PWA	Pacific Western Airlines Ltd. [Toronto Stock Exchange symbol] [Vancouver Stock Exchange symbol]
PWA	Palmer-Houston [Alaska] [Seismograph station code, US Geological Survey] (SEIS)
PWA	Patient [or Person] with [AIDS] Acquired Immunodeficiency Syndrome [Immunology] (DAVI)
PWA	People with AIDS Coalition (EA)
PWA	Performance Warehouse Association (EA)
PWA	Person with AIDS [Acquired Immune Deficiency Syndrome] [Medicine]
PWA	Pharmaceutical Wholesalers Association [Later, DWA]
PWA	Please Wait Awhile [Humorous interpretation for Pacific Western Airlines Corp.]
PWA	Polish Women's Association [Australia]
PWA	Portuguese West Africa [Angola]
PWA	Power and Water Authority [Northern Territory, Australia]
PWA	Pratt & Whitney Aircraft (MCD)
PWA	Pray while Aloft [Humorous interpretation for Pacific Western Airlines Corp.]
PWA	Premiumwear, Inc. [NYSE symbol] (SG)
PWA	Printed Wire Assembly [Computer science]
PWA	Printed Wiring Assemblies (or Assembly) (SAUS)
PWA	Prison Wardens Association (NADA)
PWA	Private Eye Writers of America [An association]
PWA	Private Write Area [NASA] (NASA)
PWA	Probably Won't Arrive [Humorous interpretation for Pacific Western Airlines Corp.]
PWA	Process Waste Assessment [Environmental science] (COE)
PWA	Product Work Authorization (NASA)
PWA	Professional Women's Association
PWA	Professional Writers of America (NADA)
PWA	Project Work Authorization
PWA	Psychic Workers Association (NADA)
PWA	Public Works Act (SAUS)
PWA	Public Works Administration [All functions transferred to office of Federal Works Agency, 1943]

PWA	Publishers' Weekly Announcements [Title changed to Forthcoming Books] [A publication]
PWA	PWA Corp. [Toronto Stock Exchange symbol] [Vancouver Stock Exchange symbol]
PWa	Warren Library Association and County Division, Warren, PA [Library symbol] [Library of Congress] (LCLS)
PWA	Waynesburg College, Waynesburg, PA [OCLC symbol] (OCLC)
PWAA	Paint and Wallpaper Association of America [Later, NDPA] (EA)
PWAA	Polish Western Association of America (EA)
PWAA	Polish Women's Alliance of America (EA)
PWAA	Professional Women's Appraisal Association (EA)
PWAAS	Passive Wide Area Alerting System (SAUS)
PWAC	Periodical Writers Association of Canada
PWAC	Pratt & Whitney Aircraft (AAG)
PWAC	Present Worth of Annual Charges [Pronounced "p-wack"] [Bell System]
PWAcD	Present Worth of Annual Cost (SAUS)
PWAcD	David Library of the American Revolution, Washington Crossing, PA [Library symbol] [Library of Congress] (LCLS)
PWAF	Polish Workers' Aid Fund [Defunct] (EA)
PWAFRR	Present Worth of All Future Revenue Requirements [Finance]
PW AIDS	Persons With AIDS (SAUS)
PWAIT Acknowledge	Processor Wait Acknowledge (SAUS)
PWAK	Wake Island Air Force Base [Wake Island] [ICAO location identifier] (ICLI)
PWal	Helen Kate Furness Free Library, Wallingford, PA [Library symbol] [Library of Congress] (LCLS)
PWalPH	Pendle Hill Library, Wallingford, PA [Library symbol] [Library of Congress] (LCLS)
PW & B	Philadelphia, Wilmington & Baltimore Railroad
PWAP	Public Works of Art Projects [New Deal]
PWAR	Posterior Wall of Aortic Root (SAUS)
PWARC	Person With AIDS-Related Complex (CPH)
PWarN	United States Naval Air Development Center, Technical Information Library, Warminster, PA [Library symbol] [Library of Congress] (LCLS)
PWASA	Poliomyelitis Welfare Association of South Australia
PWASS	Precision Wide Area Surveillance System (ACAE)
PWAV	Powerwave Technologies, Inc. [NASDAQ symbol] (SAG)
P-Wave	Pressure Wave (SAUS)
P-Wave	Primary compressional Wave (SAUS)
P-Wave	Primary seismic Wave (SAUS)
PWayC	Waynesburg College, Waynesburg, PA [Library symbol] [Library of Congress] (LCLS)
PWB	Directorate of Post War Building [British] (DAS)
PWb	Osterhout Free Library, Wilkes-Barre, PA [Library symbol] [Library of Congress] (LCLS)
PWB	Partial Weight Bearing [Medicine]
PWB	Pencil Writing on Back [Deltiology]
PWB	Permanent Water Ballast (DS)
PWB	Pilot Weather Briefing [Aviation] (FAAC)
PWB	Printed Wire Board (NAKS)
PWB	Printed Wiring Board (DOMA)
PWB	Printer Wire (or Wiring) Board (SAUS)
PWB	Printing Wiring Board (SAUS)
PWB	Private Wine Buyers' Society [British] (BI)
PWB	Programmer's Workbench [Microsoft, Inc.] (PCM)
PWB	Programmers Work Bench (SAUS)
PWB	Psychological Warfare Branch [Allied Forces] [World War II]
PWB	Public Web Browser
PWB	Pulling Whaleboat
PWBA	Pension and Welfare Benefits Administration [Department of Labor]
PWBA	Plane-Wave Born Approximation
PWBA	Printed Wiring Board Assembly (MCD)
PWBA	Printing Wiring Board Assembly (SAUS)
PWBA	Professional Women Bowlers Association [Later, LPBT] (EA)
PWBC	PennFirst Bancorp [NASDAQ symbol] (SAG)
PWBC	Peripheral White Blood Cells [Medicine]
PWbH	Wyoming Historical and Geological Society, Wilkes-Barre, PA [Library symbol] [Library of Congress] (LCLS)
PWBI	Posterior Wall of Bronchus Intermedius [Anatomy]
PWbK	King's College, Wilkes-Barre, PA [Library symbol] [Library of Congress] (LCLS)
PWBK	Pennwood Savings Bank [NASDAQ symbol] (SAG)
PWB/MM	Programmer's Workbench Memorandum Macros [Computer science] (MHDI)
PWB/MM	Programmers Work Bench/Memorandum Macros (SAUS)
PWBP	Pension and Welfare Benefit Programs [Labor-Management Services Administration]
PWBRT	Prophylactic Whole Brain Radiation Therapy [Medicine] (DMAA)
PWBS	Program Work Breakdown Structure (NASA)
PWBS	Project Work Breakdown (SAUS)
PWbW	Wilkes College, Wilkes-Barre, PA [Library symbol] [Library of Congress] (LCLS)
PWC	Chester County District Library Center, Exton, PA [OCLC symbol] (OCLC)
PWC	Pacific War Council [World War II]
PWC	Pacific Weather Centre (SAUS)
PWC	Pacific Westbound Conference (SAUS)
PWC	Pairwise Comparison (SAUS)
PWC	Parents Who Care [An association] (NADA)
PWC	Paws with a Cause [An association] (EA)
PWC	Peak Work Capacity
PWC	Peasants Work Cooperatives (SAUS)
PWC	Pentecostal World Conference [Emmetten, Switzerland] (EA)

PWC............	Peoples World Convention (SAUS)
PWC............	Personal Watercraft
PWC............	Pfeifer-Weber-Christian [Syndrome] [Medicine] (DB)
PWC............	Physical Work Capacity
PWC............	Physical Working Capacity (SAUS)
PWC............	Physicians Who Care (EA)
PWC............	Piecewise Constant (SAUS)
PWC............	Pilgrim Wrestling Conference (PSS)
PWC............	Poland Watch Center [Defunct] (EA)
PWC............	Portable Windows Change [Computer science]
PWC............	Port Workers' Committee [British]
PWC............	Pratt & Whitney Aircraft of Canada (SAUS)
PWC............	Pratt & Whitney Canada, Inc. [ICAO designator] (FAAC)
PWC............	Precipitation Water Content (SAUS)
PWC............	PricewaterhouseCoopers
PWC............	Primary Work Code (SSD)
PWC............	Printed Wiring Card (SAUS)
PWC............	Printed Wiring Cards [Telecommunications]
PWC............	Prisoner of War Cage
PWC............	Prisoner of War Camp
PWC............	Prisoner of War Command
PWC............	Prisoner of War Compound
PWC............	Prisoner of War Convention (SAUS)
PWC............	Process Water Cooler (MSA)
PWC............	Professional Women in Construction (EA)
PWC............	Professional Women's Caucus (EA)
PWC............	Provincial Warning Center [NATO] (NATG)
PWC............	Public Work Center (SAUS)
PWC............	Public Works Canada [See also TPC]
PWC............	Public Works Center [Navy]
PWC............	Pulse-Width Coded (or Coder, or Coding) (SAUS)
PWC............	Pulse Width Controlled (SAUS)
PWCA..........	Peoples World Constituent Assembly (SAUS)
PWCA..........	Pure White Cell Aplasia [Medicine] (DMAA)
PWCACE......	Public Works Center Activity Civil Engineer [Navy] (DNAB)
PWCB..........	Provincial Water Conservancy Bureau (SAUS)
PWcC..........	Chester County District Library Center, West Chester, PA [Library symbol] [Library of Congress] (LCLS)
PWCC..........	Political Warfare Coordination Committee [London] [World War II]
PWCCA........	Pembroke Welsh Corgi Club of America (EA)
PWCDET......	Public Works Center Detachment [Navy] (DNAB)
PWCEN........	Public Works Center [Navy]
PWCF..........	Person with Cystic Fibrosis
PWCFC........	Proceedings of the West Cornwall Field Club (SAUS)
PWcHi.........	Chester County Historical Society, West Chester, PA [Library symbol] [Library of Congress] (LCLS)
PWCI...........	Price Warehouse Coopers & Lybrand
PW/CI/DET...	Prisoner of War/Civilian Internees/Detainees (MCD)
PW Circuit...	Pilot Wire Circuit (SAUS)
PWCLANT....	Public Works Center, Atlantic [Navy]
PWCM.........	Pulse Width with Carrier Modulation (SAUS)
PWCMIS......	Public Works Center Management Information System [Navy] (DNAB)
PWCMS.......	Public Works Center Management System [Navy]
PW Coll Pt...	Prisoners of War Collecting Point (SAUS)
PWCOU.......	Public Workers and Constructional Operatives' Union [British]
PWCPAC......	Public Works Center, Pacific [Navy]
PWCR.........	Prader-Willi Chromosome Region [Medicine] (DMAA)
PWcS..........	West Chester State College, West Chester, PA [Library symbol] [Library of Congress] (LCLS)
PWCT..........	Passenger Will Contact [Travel industry] (TVEL)
PwCtIT........	Power Control Technologies, Inc. [Associated Press] (SAG)
PWD	Pan World Ventures, Inc. [Vancouver Stock Exchange symbol]
PWD	Participative Work Design
PWD	Participatory Work Design (SAUS)
PWD	People with Disabilities
PWD	Permanent Wants Directory [A publication]
PWD	Permissible Weekly Dose (SAUS)
PWD	Petroleum Warfare Department [Ministry of Fuel and Power] [British] [World War II]
PWD	Philadelphia Water Department (SAUS)
PWD	Plentywood, MT [Location identifier] [FAA] (FAAL)
PWD	Plywood [Technical drawings]
PWD	Post-Write Disturb (IAA)
PWD	Powder (KSC)
PWD	Powder Distributor (SAUS)
PWD	Power Distributor (KSC)
PWD	Powered (IAA)
PWD	Practice Weapon Dispenser (SAUS)
PWD	Present Working Directory (SAUS)
PWD	Print Working Directory (SAUS)
PWD	Processor Word (SAUS)
PWD	Process Word (IAA)
PWD	Procurement Work Directive [Army] (AABC)
PWD	Programmed Warhead Detonation (SAUS)
PWD	Proximity Warning Device (MCD)
PWD	Psychological Warfare Division [SHAEF] [World War II]
PWD	Public Works Department (NADA)
PWD	Pulse-Width Detection (or Detector) (SAUS)
PWD	Pulse-Width Detector [or Discriminator] [RADAR]
PWD	Pulse-Width Discriminating (or Discrimination, or Discriminator) (SAUS)
PWD	Pulse Width Distortion (SAUS)
PWDC.........	Philippine War Damage Commission [Post-World War II]
PWDCA........	Portuguese Water Dog Club of America (EA)
PWDEPT	Public Works Department [Navy]
PWDG.........	Prince of Wales' Dragoon Guards [Military] [British] (ROG)
PWDI..........	Program with Developing Institutions (EA)
PWDMS......	Public Works Developmental Management System [Navy]
PWDP.........	Powder Passing
PWDR.........	Partial Wave Dispersing (or Dispersion) Relation (SAUS)
PWDR.........	Partial Wave Dispersing Relation
pwdr	Powder [Pharmacy] (DAVI)
PWDRD.......	Powdered [Freight]
PWDS	Postweaning Diarrhea Syndrome [Medicine] (DMAA)
PWDS	Protected Wireline Distribution System (CET)
PWDTS........	Peacekeeper Warranty Data Tracking System (SAUS)
PWDY	PaineWebber Group [Associated Press] (SAG)
PWDY496	PaineWebber Group [Associated Press] (SAG)
PWE............	Pauli-Weiakopf Equation (SAUS)
PWE............	Pauli-Weisskopf Equation [Physics]
PWE............	Pawnee City, NE [Location identifier] [FAA] (FAAL)
PWE............	Political Warfare Executive [World War II]
PWE............	Posterior Wall Excursion [Anatomy] (DMAA)
PWE............	Present Working Estimate (ABAC)
PWE............	Present Worth Expenditures [Telecommunications] (TEL)
PWE............	Pre-Warfare Executive (WDAA)
PWE............	Primary Weapons and Equipment
PWE............	Prisoner of War Enclosure
PWE............	Pulse-Width Encoder (or Encoding) (SAUS)
PWEA.........	Printed Wiring and Electronic Assemblies [NASA]
PWEA.........	Public Works Employment Act (AAGC)
P-WEAR......	Preliminary Work Breakdown Structure Element Audit Review (SAUS)
PW/ED........	Pratt & Whitney Engineering Division
PWEDA.......	Public Works and Economic Development Act
PWEDA.......	Public Works and Economic Development Association (EA)
PWEHC.......	Public Works Emergency Housing Corp. [New Deal]
PWES.........	Price Waterhouse Energy Solutions
PWesAC.......	Community College of Allegheny County, South Campus, West Mifflin, PA [Library symbol] [Library of Congress] (LCLS)
PWesD.......	Dresser Industries, Inc., Harbison-Walker Refractories Co., West Mifflin, PA [Library symbol] [Library of Congress] (LCLS)
PWF............	Pacific Whale Foundation (EA)
PWF............	Package Will Follow [Birthday-card notation]
PWF............	Pax World Foundation (EA)
PWF............	Permanent Wood Foundation [Building term]
PWF............	Personnel Working File (DOMA)
PWF............	Photoelectric Work Function
PWF............	Pop Warner Football (EA)
PWF............	Portable Windows Format [Computer science]
PWF............	Power Financial Corp. [Toronto Stock Exchange symbol]
PWF............	Power Warning Feature (SAUS)
PWF............	Pregnancy Without Fear (SAUS)
PWF............	Present Worth Factor [Real estate]
PWF............	Private Wagon Federation [British] (DBA)
PWF............	Propellant Weight Fraction (NATG)
PWF............	Pulse Wave Form
PWF............	Pure Water Flux [Engineering]
PWFA.........	Papermakers' Woven Felt Association (DGA)
PWFA.........	Petroleum Workers Federation of Aruba (SAUS)
PWFG.........	Primary Waveform Generator [Telecommunications] (TEL)
PWFN.........	Projection Weld Flange Nut
PWFR.........	Plantwide Failure Reporting (MCD)
PWFS.........	Price Waterhouse Financial Solutions
PWG	Panzerwagen [Tank] [German military - World War II]
PWG	Parliamentary Working Group (SAUS)
PWG	Pathology Work Group (GNE)
PWG	Permanent Working Group (NATG)
PWG	Permanent Working Group of European Junior Hospital Doctors (SAUS)
PWG	Photoelectric Web Guide
PWG	Plastic Wire Guide
PWG	Powergem Resources Corp. [Vancouver Stock Exchange symbol]
PWG	Powergen PLC [NYSE symbol] (SAG)
PWG	PowerGen PLC ADS [NYSE symbol] (TTSB)
PWG	Printer Working Group (SAUS)
PWG	Province Working Group (SAUS)
PWG.PP.......	PowerGen PLC Interim ADS [NYSE symbol] (TTSB)
PWG C........	PWG Capital Trust I [Associated Press] (SAG)
PWGCA.......	Permanent Working Group on Cooperation in Antarctica (SAUS)
PWGM........	Process Water Gamma Monitor [Environmental science] (COE)
PwgnADS....	Powergan PLC [Associated Press] (SAG)
PwgnIntr.....	Powergan PLC [Associated Press] (SAG)
PWGS.........	Pacific Weather Graphics System (SAUS)
PWGSC.......	Public Works and Government Services Canada (ACII)
PWH	Pellet Warhead
PWH	Person infected With HIV (SAUS)
PWH	Per Workable Hatch (RIMS)
PWH	Poliokeawe [Pali] [Hawaii] [Seismograph station code, US Geological Survey] (SEIS)
PWH	Precision Welding-Head
PWH	Proprietor of Copyright on a Work Made for Hire
PWH	Prototype Wave Height
PWHA.........	Peace/War Headquarters (SAUS)
PWHA.........	Plutonium Waste Handling Area [Nuclear energy] (NRCH)
PWHD.........	Per Workable Hatch per Day (SAUS)
Pwhe..........	Person Who Has Everything [Lifestyle classification]
PWhi...........	Whitehall Township Public Library, Whitehall, PA [Library symbol] [Library of Congress] (LCLS)
PWHK.........	PaineWebber Group, Inc. [Associated Press] (SAG)

PWHQ	Peace War Headquarters (NATG)
PWHQ	Primary War Headquarters (SAUS)
PWHS	Public Works Historical Society (EA)
PWHT	Post-Weld Heat Treatment [Nuclear energy] (NRCH)
PWHWwd	Per Workable Hatch per Weather Working Day (SAUS)
PWI	Alas Panamenas SA [Panama] [ICAO designator] (FAAC)
PWI	PACOM [Pacific Command] Warning Intelligence [Army]
PWI	Participation with Industry (ACAE)
PWI	Permanent Ware Institute [Defunct] (EA)
PWI	Permanent Way Institution [Fleet, Hampshire, England] (EAIO)
PWI	Perry Williams, Inc. (EFIS)
PWI	Physiological Workload Index [Aviation]
PWI	Piecewise-Linear (IAA)
PWI	Pilot Warning Indicator [or Instrument] [Aviation]
PWI	Pilot Warning Instrument (SAUS)
PWI	Plasma Wave Instrument [Physics]
PWI	Platoon Weapons Instructor [British military] (DMA)
PWI	Portable Water Intake (SAUS)
PWI	Posterior Wall Infarct [Anatomy] (MAE)
PWI	Posterior Wall Infarction (SAUS)
PWI	Potable Water Intake
PWI	Precedence Work Item
PWI	Prince of Wales' Island (ROG)
PWI	Prisoner of War Interrogation
PWI	Projects with Industry Program [Department of Education]
PWI	Proximity Warning Indication (or Indicator) (SAUS)
PWI	Proximity Warning Indicator [or Instrument] [Aviation]
PWI	Proximity Warning Instrument
PWI	Public Windows Initiative (SAUS)
PWI	Public Windows Interface [Computer science] (PCM)
PWIA	Personal Watercraft Industry Association (EA)
PWIB	Prisoner of War Information Bureau [Post-World War II]
PWIC	Prisoner of War Information Center (DOMA)
PWIF	Plantation Workers' International Federation [Later, IFPAAW]
PWIFC	Porter Wagoner International Fan Club [Defunct] (EA)
PWIN	Prototype WWMCCS Intercomputer Network (MCD)
PWINO	Precipitation Identifier Information Not Available [NWS] (FAAC)
PWIP	Participative Work Improvement Program (SAUS)
PWIP	Physical Work in Process (SAUS)
PWIR	Palmar Wireless [NASDAQ symbol] (SAG)
PWIR	Palmer Wireless 'A' [NASDAQ symbol] (TTSB)
PWIS	Prisoner of War Information System (DOMA)
PWIS	Prisoners of War Information System (SAUS)
PWI System	Pilot Warning Indicator System (SAUS)
PWJ	Paine Webber Group [NYSE symbol] (TTSB)
PWJ	PaineWebber Group, Inc. [NYSE symbol] (SPSG)
PWJ	Pulsating Water-Jet Lavager [Medicine] (RDA)
PWJ	PWG Capital Trust I [NYSE symbol] (SAG)
PWJC	Paine, Webber, Jackson & Curtis [Later, Paine Webber, Inc.]
PWJC	Piney Woods Junior College (SAUS)
PWK	Chicago/Wheeling, IL [Location identifier] [FAA] (FAAL)
PWK	Prestwick BAE [British] [ICAO designator] (FAAC)
PWL	Password List (SAUS)
PWL	Petroleum and Water Logistics [Army] (RDA)
PWL	Piecewire-Linear (SAUS)
PWL	Piecewise-Linear
PWL	Piecework Linear
PWL	Port Wells [Alaska] [Seismograph station code, US Geological Survey] (SEIS)
PWL	Poughkeepsie, NY [Location identifier] [FAA] (FAAL)
PWL	Powell Air Ltd. [Canada] [ICAO designator] (FAAC)
PWL	Power Level
PWL	Printed Wiring Laboratory (MCD)
PWLA	Posterior Wall of Left Atrium (SAUS)
PWL-AROM	P-Wave Logger (SAUS)
PWLB	Public Works Loan Board [British]
PWIF	Plantation Workers International Federation (SAUS)
PWLV	Posterior Wall of Left Ventricle [Anatomy] (AAMN)
PWM	Parentship for World Mission (NADA)
PWM	Partnership for World Mission (SAUS)
PWM	Planar Wing Module (MCD)
PWM	Plated Wire Memory
PWM	Pokeweed Mitogen [Genetics]
PWM	Portable Welding Machine
PWM	Portland [Maine] [Airport symbol] (OAG)
PWM	Portland, ME [Location identifier] [FAA] (FAAL)
PWM	Printed Wiring Master
PWM	Probability of Wrong Message (CCCA)
PWM	Pulse-Width Modulated (or Modulating, or Modulation, or Modulator) (SAUS)
PWM	Pulse Width Modulation [Electronic instrumentation]
PWM	Pulse-Width Multiplier (IEEE)
PWM	Puls Width Modulation
PWMA	Portable Wear Metal Analyzer [Air Force]
PWMA	Primary Warfare Mission Area [Military] (SEWL)
PWMAF	Pulse-Width Modulated Audio Frequency (IAA)
PWM-AF	Pulse-Width-Modulated Audio-Frequency (SAUS)
PWM-AM	Pulse-Width Modulation-Amplitude Modulation (SAUS)
PWMD	Printed Wiring Master Drawing (NASA)
PWM-FM	Pulse-Width Modulation - Frequency Modulation [RADAR]
PWMI	Plastic Waste Management Institute
PWMI	Pulse-Width-Modulated Inverter (SAUS)
PWmL	Lycoming College, Williamsport, PA [Library symbol] [Library of Congress] (LCLS)
PWML	Patchy White Matter Lesion [Medicine]
PWMM	Polly Woodside Maritime Museum [Australia]
PWmP	James V. Brown Library of Williamsport and Lycoming County, Williamsport, PA [Library symbol] [Library of Congress] (LCLS)
PWMR	Periventricular White-Matter Radiolucency [Medicine]
P Wms	Peere-Williams' English Chancery Reports [1695-1736] [A publication] (DLA)
PWMS	Public Works Management System [Navy]
PWMSCM	Pokeweed Mitogen-Stimulated Spleen-Cell-Conditioned Medium [For growing cells]
P Wms (Eng)	Peere-Williams' English Chancery Reports [1695-1736] [A publication] (DLA)
PW/MSF	Prairie Warrior/Mobile Strike Force (SAUS)
PWMSP	People with Multiple Social Problems (SAUS)
PWMSP	Persons With Multiple Social Problems (SAUS)
PWN	Cash America International, Inc. [NYSE symbol] (SPSG)
PWN	Cash Amer Intl [NYSE symbol] (TTSB)
PWN	Patna Weekly Notes [India] [A publication] (ILCA)
PWN	Peacenet World News (SAUS)
PWN	Pinewood Nematode
PWN	Pulsar Wind Nebula [Astronomy]
PWN	West Plains, MO [Location identifier] [FAA] (FAAL)
PWNA	Power Washers of North America (NTPA)
PWNBKR	Pawnbroker
PWNDA	Provincial Wholesale Newspaper Distributors' Association [British] (BI)
PWNP	Parra Wirra National Park (SAUS)
PW-NWLZOA	Pioneer Women/Na'amat, the Women's Labor Zionist Organization of America [Later, MWWV] (EA)
PWO	Parliamentarians for World Order (EA)
PWO	Performance Work Standard (AAGC)
PWO	Plane-Wave Orbital [Physics]
PWO	Prince of Wales' Own [Military unit] [British]
PWO	Principal Weapons Officer
PWO	Principal Welfare Officer [Navy] [British]
PWO	Principle Warfare Officer [British]
PWO	Production Work Order (MCD)
PWO	Public Works Officer [Navy]
PWOC	Protestant Women of the Chapel
PWOP	Pregnant Without Official Permission (SAUS)
PWOP	Pregnant without Permission [Military] [World War II]
PWOR	Prince of Wales' Own Royal [Military unit] [British]
PWORC-E	P&W Overhaul and Repair Center-Europe (SAUS)
PWP	Barrio Florida [Puerto Rico] [Seismograph station code, US Geological Survey] (SEIS)
PWP	Chemical Agent/Plastized (SAUS)
PWP	PaineWebber Group [NYSE symbol] (SAG)
PWP	Parents without Partners (EA)
PWP	Partial Write Pulse (SAUS)
PWP	Particles per Wafer Pass (AAEL)
PWP	Past Worthy Patriarch
PWP	Peasants' and Workers' Party [India] [Political party] (PPW)
PWP	Personal Water Purifier (SAUS)
PWP	Personal Word Processor (WDMC)
PWP	Personnel Work Plan (HEAS)
PWP	Picowatt Power (CET)
PWP	Picowatt Psophometric (IAA)
PWP	Picowatt Psophometrically Weighted (SAUS)
pWp	Picowatts, Psophometrically Weighted
PWP	Plain Writing Printer (SAUS)
PWP	Planning Work Package (MCD)
PWP	Plasticized White Phosphorus
PWP	Plastic Waste Processor (DWSG)
PWP	Polish Workers' Party
PWP	Portable Word Processor
PWP	Postwar Planning [World War II]
PWP	Prelaunch Wind Profile (SAA)
PWP	Preliminary Working Paper (AAGC)
PWP	Presidents Working Party (SAUS)
P-W-P	Product-with-Purchase (WDMC)
p-w-p	Product-with-Purchase (WDMC)
PWP	Professional Women Photographers (EA)
PWP	Programmable Weld Positioner (SAUS)
PWP	Public Watering Place (ADA)
PWP	Public Works Planning (GFGA)
PWP	Pulmonary Wedge Pressure [Medicine]
PWP	Purchase-with-Purchase [Sales promotion]
PWPHIT	PaineWebber Premier High Income Trust [Associated Press] (SAG)
PWPIM	PaineWebber Premier Insured Municipal Income Fund [Associated Press] (SAG)
PWpM	Merck, Sharp & Dohme [Later, Merck & Co., Inc.] Research Laboratories, Library Services, West Point, PA [Library symbol] [Library of Congress] (LCLS)
PWPO	PWP Measured at a Point of Zero Reference Level (SAUS)
PWPP	Professionwide Pension Plan [American Chemical Society]
PWPS	Pure Water Preservation Society [British]
PWQ	Petersburg, WV [Location identifier] [FAA] (FAAL)
PWQ	Preferred and Well Qualified [Candidate designation]
PWQM	Protection Water Quality Management
PWR	Partially Whitened Representation (SAUS)
PWR	Passive Warning Radar (SAUS)
PWR	Passive Warning Receiver (SAUS)
PWR	Peak Watt Rating [Electrical engineering]
PWR	Pilot Wire Regulator
PWR	Placement and Wire Routing (SAUS)
PWR	Point of Weapon Release [Military]

PWR .... Police War Reserve [*British*] (DAS)
PWR .... Port Walter, AK [*Location identifier*] [*FAA*] (FAAL)
PWR .... Post-War Reconstruction (SAUS)
pwr .... Power (IDOE)
PWR .... Power (KSC)
PWR .... Power Explorations, Inc. [*Toronto Stock Exchange symbol*]
PWR .... Power On [*Modem status information light*] [*Computer science*] (IGQR)
PWR .... Power Reactor (SAUS)
PWR .... Power Wirewound Resistor
PWR .... Pressurised Water Reactor (SAUS)
PWR .... Pressurized Water Reactor (SAUS)
PWR .... Pressurized Water Reactor [*Nuclear energy*]
PWR .... Prevailing Wage Rate [*US Employment Service*] [*Department of Labor*]
PWR .... Prince of Wales' Royal [*Military unit*] [*British*]
PWR .... Processor Write (SAUS)
PWR .... Program Work Request
PWR .... Project Work Review [*Army*] (AFIT)
PWR .... Publication Work Request (MCD)
PWR .... Public Worship Regulation Act [*1874*] [*British*] (ROG)
PWR .... Punjab Weekly Reporter [*India*] [*A publication*] (ILCA)
PWRA .... Professional Women's Rodeo Association
PWRC .... FMS Patuxent Wildlife Research Center Financial Management System (SAUS)
PWRC .... Patuxent Wildlife Research Center (SAUS)
PWRCB .... President's War Relief Control Board [*World War II*]
PWRDEVELENGR... Power Development Engineer (IAA)
PWRE .... Prepositioned War Reserve Equipment [*Army*]
PWREMR .... Prepositioned War Reserve Material Requirements [*Navy*] (MCD)
PWREMS .... Prepositioned War Reserve Material Stocks [*Navy*] (MCD)
PWR-FA .... Pressurized Water Reactor-Flexible Assembly (SAUS)
PWR-FLECHT... Pressurized Water Ractor - Full Length Emergency Cooling Heat Transfer [*Nuclear energy*] (PDAA)
PWRH .... Powerhouse (MSA)
PwrhsRs ...... Powerhouse Resources, Inc. [*Associated Press*] (SAG)
PWRIMC .... Prince of Wales Royal Indian Military College [*British military*] (DMA)
PWRM .... Prepositioned War Reserve Materiel (MCD)
PWRMON .... Power Monitor (IAA)
PWRMR .... Prepositioned War Reserve Materiel Requirement (NVT)
PWRMRB .... Prepositioned War Reserve Materiel Requirement Balance (AFIT)
PWRMS .... Prepositioned War Reserve Materiel Stock (NVT)
PWRNO .... Power Failure (FAAC)
PWRO .... Pending Work Release Order (MCD)
PWROK .... Power Restored (FAAC)
PWRPLT .... Power Plant (IAA)
PWRPNL ...... Power Panel (IAA)
PWRR .... Passive Warning Radar Receiver (SAUS)
PWRR .... Prepositioned War Reserve Requirements [*Army*] (NG)
PWRR .... Providence and Worcester Railroad Co. [*NASDAQ symbol*] (NQ)
PWRR .... Providence & Worcester RR [*NASDAQ symbol*] (TTSB)
PWRR .... Providence Worcester Railroad Co. [*NASDAQ symbol*] (SAG)
PWRR-MF .... Prepositioned War Reserve Requirements for Medical Facilities [*Army*] (AABC)
PWRS .... Pacific War Research Society (SAUS)
PWRS .... Prepositioned War Reserve Stocks [*Army*]
PWRS .... Preposition War Reserve Stock (SAUS)
PWRS .... Programmable Weapons Release System (IEEE)
PWRSEMICOND... Power Semiconductor (IAA)
PWRS-MF .... Prepositioned War Reserve Stocks for Medical Facilities [*Army*] (AABC)
PWR SPLY... Power Supply (SAUS)
PWRSUP...... Power Supply (IAA)
Pwr Sw ..... Power Switch (SAUS)
PWRU .... Power Unit (IAA)
PWS............ Paddle-Wheel Steamer [*Shipping*] (ROG)
PWS............ Parallel Working System
PWS............ Pattern Weavers' Society [*A union*] [*British*] (DCTA)
PWS............ Pax World Service (EA)
PWS............ Peer Web Services (SAUS)
PWS............ Performance Work Standard
PWS............ Performance Work Statement [*DoD*]
PWS............ Periyar Wildlife Sanctuary (SAUS)
PWS............ Peter Warlock Society (EA)
PWS............ Petrified Wood Society (EA)
PWS............ Petroleum and Water Systems [*Army*] (RDA)
PWS............ Phoenix Weapons System
PWS............ Plane Wave Spectrum (SAUS)
PWS............ Plane-Wave Spectrum
PWS............ Plasma Wave Guide Switch (IAA)
PWS............ Plasma Waveguide Switch (SAUS)
PWS............ Plasma Wave Science (SAUS)
PWS............ Plasma Wave Source [*Physics*]
PWS............ Plasma Wave System [*Instrumentation*]
PWS............ Pore-Water Sampler (SAUS)
PWS............ Portable Work Station (SPST)
PWS............ Port-Wine Stain
PWS............ Potable Water System (KSC)
PWS............ Power Web Suite (SAUS)
PWS............ Powys (SAUS)
PWS............ Prader-Willi Syndrome (SAUS)
PWS............ Prader-Willi Syndrome Association (EA)
PWS............ Predicted Wave Signaling
PWS............ Predicted Wave Signalling (SAUS)
PWS............ Preliminary Work Statement (MCD)

PWS............ Present Weather Sensor (ARMP)
PWS............ Pressure Wave Supercharger [*Automotive engineering*]
PWS............ Pricing Work Statement (MCD)
PWS............ Prisoners' Wives' Service (WDAA)
PWS............ Private Web Server (SAUS)
PWS............ Private Wire Service
PWS............ Private Wire System (AAG)
PWS............ Professional Work Station (SAUS)
PWS............ Programmable Work Station (SAUS)
PWS............ Programmers Work Station (SAUS)
PWS............ Programmer Work Station
PWS............ Program Work Statement (MCD)
PWS............ Project Work Schedule [*Computer science*]
PWS............ Proximity Warning System (IAA)
PWS............ Psychological Warfare Service [*Allied Forces*] [*World War II*]
PWS............ Psychological Warfare Society [*Birmingham, England*] (EA)
PWS............ Public Water Supply (PA)
PWS............ Public Water System (GFGA)
PWS............ Pulau-Weh [*Sumatra*] [*Seismograph station code, US Geological Survey*] [*Closed*] (SEIS)
PWSA .... Pheasant and Waterfowl Society of Australia
PWSA .... Ports and Waterways Safety Act (GFGA)
PWSA .... Prader-Willi Syndrome Association (SAUS)
PWSA .... Professional Women Singers Association (EA)
PWSC .... Post-War Scientific Collaboration [*British*]
PWSC .... Preferred Weapon System Concept [*Military*] (SEWL)
PWSCC .... Prince William Sound Community College [*Alaska*]
PWSCS .... Programmable Workstation Communication Services (SAUS)
PWSN .... Public Safety Wireless Network (SEWL)
PWSO .... Pilot Weapons System Officer
PWSP .... Project Workpackage Structure Plan (SAUS)
PWSP .... Public Weather Services Programme (SAUS)
PWSPMid ... PaineWebber Group, Inc. [*Associated Press*] (SAG)
PWSPP .... Payne Whitney Suicide Prevention Program [*New York Hospital*] (EA)
PWSS .... Port War Signal Station [*British military*] (DMA)
PWSS .... Public Water Supply System (GFGA)
PWST .... Protected Water Storage Tank [*Nuclear energy*] (NRCH)
PWSWA ...... Processed Woodchip, Sawdust and Woodfloor Association (SAUS)
PW System... Pilot Warning System (SAUS)
PWT............ Bremerton, WA [*Location identifier*] [*FAA*] (FAAL)
PWT............ Pacific War Time (IAA)
PWT............ Pacific Winter Time (IAA)
PWT............ Penn West Petroleum Ltd. [*Toronto Stock Exchange symbol*]
PWT............ Pennyweight
PWT............ Pennyweight Troy (SAUS)
PWT............ Picture World Test [*Psychology*]
PWT............ Posterior Wall Thickness (SAUS)
PWT............ Professional Walleye Trail
PWT............ Progressive Wave Tube
PWT............ Propulsion Wind Tunnel (SAUS)
PWT............ Propulsion Wind Tunnel Facility [*Arnold Air Force Base, TN*] [*Air Force*]
PWT............ Pulse Wave Time (SAUS)
PWTAG ...... Pool Water Treatment Advisory Group (SAUS)
PWTC .... Public Works Training Center [*Navy*]
PWTC .... Public Works Transportation Center (MCD)
PWTCVA ..... Procurement of Weapons and Tracked Combat Vehicles, Army (AABC)
PWTF .... Polish Workers Task Force (EA)
PWTN .... Power Train (AABC)
PWTO .... Principal Wireless Telegraphy Officer (IAA)
PWTP......... Process Waste Treatment Plant [*Engineering*]
PWTR......... Pewter (MSA)
PWTR......... Philadelphia War Tax Resistance (EA)
PWTVA ...... Procurement of Weapons and Tracked Vehicles, Army (AABC)
PWU .... Pacific Western University [*Hawaii*]
PWU .... Political World Union (EA)
PWU .... Power Up (SAUS)
PWU .... Pressure Work up (SAUS)
PWU .... Provision Wholesalers Union (SAUS)
P W/U......... Public Works & Utilities (SAUS)
PWUSA ...... Project Wolf USA (EA)
PWUSD...... PaineWebber Group, Inc. [*Associated Press*] (SAG)
PWUSJ ...... PaineWebber Group [*Associated Press*] (SAG)
PWV .... Passionfruit Woodiness Virus [*Plant pathology*]
PWV .... Peach Wart Virus (SAUS)
PWV .... Pittsburgh & West Virginia Railroad [*AAR code*]
PWV .... Polistes Wasp Venom [*Laboratory science*] (DAVI)
PWV .... Precipitable Water Vapor
PWV .... Pressure Wave Velocity [*Cardiology*]
PWV .... Pretoria-Witwatersrand [*South Africa*]
PWV .... Prince of Wales' Volunteers [*Military unit*] [*British*]
PWV .... Pulse Wave Velocity
PWV .... Pulse-Width Valve (SAUS)
PWVA .... Pacific War Veterans of America [*Defunct*]
PWVS .... Prince of Wales' Volunteer Service [*British*]
PW/VSE ..... Programmers Work Station/Virtual Storage Extended (SAUS)
PWW .... Planar Wing Weapon, a canceled alternative for CWW (SAUS)
PWW .... Plannar Wing Weapon (MCD)
PWW .... Point Weather Warning
PWW .... Project West Wing (MCD)
PWW .... Washington and Jefferson College, Washington, PA [*Library symbol*] [*Library of Congress*] (LCLS)
PWWC .... Post War World Council [*Defunct*] (EA)

PWWD	Per Weather Working Day (RIMS)
PWWH	Per Weather Working Hour (SAUS)
PW-WLZOA	Pioneer Women, the Women's Labor Zionist Organization of America [Later, PW-MWLZOA] (EA)
PWWR	Power Wirewound Resistor
PWWT	Pacific Winter War Time (SAUS)
PWX	Permanent Working Staff [NATO] (NATG)
PWX	Prisoners of War Executive [Branch of SHAEF] [World War II]
PWY	PaineWebber Group [AMEX symbol] (SAG)
PX	Air Niugini [Air New Guinea] [ICAO designator] (AD)
PX	Aspen Airways (SAUS)
PX	Heavenly Bodies Polar Distance (SAUS)
PX	Pancreatectomized [Medicine]
PX	Part Exchange [Automobile classified advertising]
Px	Past History (DAVI)
PX	Pedro Ximenez [A blending sherry]
PX	Peroxidase [Also, PO, POD] [An enzyme]
PX	Phantom Coil (SAUS)
PX	Physical Examination
Px	Physican examination (SAUS)
PX	Piroxicam [Anti-inflammatory]
Px	Plantwax [A fungicide]
PX	Please Exchange
PX	Pneumothorax [Medicine]
PX	Post Exchange [Military]
PX	Praxair, Inc. [NYSE symbol] (SPSG)
PX	Pressure Transmitter (SAUS)
PX	Primary Index (SAUS)
PX	Private Examination (WDAA)
PX	Private Exchange
PX	Production Executive of the War Cabinet [World War II]
Px	Prognosis [Medicine] (WGA)
PX	Pulse Stretcher (SAUS)
PX	Pulse Transformer (SAUS)
PX	Pyroxene [Also, PYX] [A mineral]
PXA	Parana [Brazil] [Airport symbol] (AD)
PXA	Place Index in Address (SAA)
PXA	primary X-ray Analysis (SAUS)
PXA	Pulsed Xenon Arc
PXA-Lamp	Pulsed Xenon Arc Lamp (SAUS)
PXC	Proximity Computer (MCD)
PXCMD	Phoenix Contract Management District (SAA)
PXD	Pioneer Natural Resources [NYSE symbol] [Formerly, Parker & Parsley Petrol] (SG)
PXD	Place Index in Decrement
PXD	Post-Exercise Discussion [NATO] (NATG)
PXD	Price Ex-Dividend [Stock market]
PXDV	Peach X-Disease Virus (SAUS)
PXE	Pacific Exchange, Inc.
PXE	Pacific Research & Engineering Corp. [AMEX symbol] (SAG)
PXE	Phenylxylylethane [Organic chemistry]
PXE	Piezo-Oxide (SAUS)
PXE	Piezoxide (SAUS)
PXE	Poly(xylenyl ether) [Organic chemistry]
PXE	Preboot Execution Environment (SAUS)
PXE	Provinces X Explorations [Vancouver Stock Exchange symbol]
PXE	Pseudoxanthoma Elasticum [Medicine]
PXE.U	Pacific Res & Engineering Unit [AMEX symbol] (TTSB)
PXF	Primex Forest Industries Ltd. [Toronto Stock Exchange symbol] [Vancouver Stock Exchange symbol]
PXG	Phoenix Gold Mines Ltd. [Toronto Stock Exchange symbol]
PXH	Pacific Express Holdings Ltd. [New Zealand] [ICAO designator] (FAAC)
PXI	Pax Christi International (EA)
PXI	PCI Extension for Instrumentation (SAUS)
PXI	Pulsed Xenon Illuminator
PXI	Pulse Xenon Illuminator (SAUS)
PxIMP	Peroxisomal Integral Membrane Protein [Biochemistry]
PX In	Arrival Time [Aviation]
PXISA	PXI Systems Alliance (SAUS)
PXL	Poney Explorations Ltd. [Vancouver Stock Exchange symbol]
PXL	Pulsed Xenon Lamp (SAUS)
PXL	Pulsed Xenon LASER
Pxl	Pyridoxal [Also, PL] [Biochemistry]
PXL Aircraft	Patrol, Experimental Landbased Aircraft (SAUS)
PXLS	Pulsed Xenon Light Source
PXLSS	Pulsed Xenon Light Source System
PXM	Projection X-Ray Microscope
Pxm	Pyridoxamine [Also, PM] [Biochemistry]
PX Me	Report My Arrival or Departure [Aviation slang]
PXML	Private Exchange Master List (SAUS)
PXN	Panoche, CA [Location identifier] [FAA] (FAAL)
PXN	Paxson Communications Corp. [AMEX symbol] (SAG)
PXN	Paxson Communications 'A' [AMEX symbol] (TTSB)
Pxn	Pyridoxine [Also, PN] [Biochemistry]
PXO	Porto Santo [Portugal] [Airport symbol] (OAG)
PXO	Preservation by Operation
PXO	Prospective Executive Officer
PX Out	Takeoff Time [Aviation]
PXP	Packet Exchange Protocol [Computer science] (TNIG)
PXP	Phoenix Investment Partners [NYSE symbol] [Formerly, Phoenix Duff & Phelps]
PXPPL	Pull and Push Plate
PXR	Paxar Corp. [NYSE symbol] (SAG)

PXR	Plus-X-Reversal
PXR	Post-Exercise Report (SAUS)
PXR	Praxis Resources Ltd. [Vancouver Stock Exchange symbol]
PXRD	Powder X-Ray Diffraction
PXRE	Phoenix Re Corp. [NASDAQ symbol] (NQ)
PXRE	PXRE Corp. [NASDAQ symbol] (TTSB)
PXRE Cp	PXRE Corp. [Associated Press] (SAG)
PXS	Plexus Resources Corp. [Toronto Stock Exchange symbol]
PXS	Port Exchange
PXS	primary X-ray Spectroscopy (SAUS)
PXS	Pulsed Xenon System
PXS	Pulsed X-ray System (SAUS)
PXSC	Proximity Sensing Computer (MCD)
PXSS	Pulsed Xenon Solar Simulator
PXSTR	Phototransistor (IEEE)
PXT	Patuxent River, MD [Location identifier] [FAA] (FAAL)
PXT	Pinxit [He, or She, Painted It] [Latin]
PXT	Praxis Technologies Corp. [Toronto Stock Exchange symbol]
PXU	Pleiku [South Vietnam] [Airport symbol] (AD)
PXU	Portable X-Ray Unit
PXV	Evansville, IN [Location identifier] [FAA] (FAAL)
PXV	Pedro Ximenez Viejo [A blending sherry]
PXX	Aroostook Aviation, Inc. [FAA designator] (FAAC)
PXX	Porto Alfonso [Brazil] [Airport symbol] (AD)
PXXI	Prophet 21, Inc. [NASDAQ symbol] (SAG)
PXY	Milwaukee, WI [Location identifier] [FAA] (FAAL)
Pxy	Pyridoxyl [Biochemistry]
PY	Martin Memorial [York City and County] Library, York, PA [Library symbol] [Library of Congress] (LCLS)
PY	Pack Year [Cigarettes] (MEDA)
PY	Pack Years [of cigarette consumption] (DAVI)
PY	Paraguay [ANSI two-letter standard code] (CNC)
Py	Paraguay (MILB)
py	Paraguay [IYRU nationality code] [MARC country of publication code] [Library of Congress] (LCCP)
PY	Patrol Vessel, Yacht [Navy symbol]
PY	Patrol Yacht (SAUS)
PY	Pechiney ADS [NYSE symbol] (TTSB)
PY	Pembroke Yeomanry [British military] (DMA)
PY	Person Years [After radiation exposure]
p/y	Per Year (WDAA)
Py	Phosphopyridoxal [Medicine] (DMAA)
PY	Physical Year
P/Y	Pitch or Yaw
PY	Polygon
Py	Polyoma Virus [Medicine] (DMAA)
PY	Polysar Ltd. [Toronto Stock Exchange symbol] [Vancouver Stock Exchange symbol]
PY	Prior Year (AABC)
py	Program Year (NAKS)
PY	Project Yedid [Defunct] (EA)
PY	Proto Yiddish (BJA)
PY	Publication Year [Online database field identifier]
Py	Pyrene [Organic chemistry] (AAMN)
Py	Pyridine [Organic chemistry]
Py	Pyrimidine (DOG)
Py	Pyrogen [Medicine]
PY	Pyrometer (IEEE)
PY	Pyronin Y [A biological dye]
PY	Pyrrolidine (SAUS)
PY	Pythium [A fungus]
PY	Spray [ICAO] (FAAC)
PY	Surinam Airways [ICAO designator] (AD)
PYA	Partners Preferred Yield [AMEX symbol] (SAG)
PYA	Partners Preferred Yld'A' [AMEX symbol] (TTSB)
PYA	Penn Yan, NY [Location identifier] [FAA] (FAAL)
PYA	Pioneer Youth of America (EA)
PYA	Pittsburgh, Youngstown & Ashland Railway Co. (IIA)
PYA	Plan, Year, and Age [Insurance designations]
PYA	Psychoanalysis [Medicine]
PYA	Pyatigorsk [Former USSR] [Seismograph station code, US Geological Survey] (SEIS)
PYA	Pyroair Tech [Vancouver Stock Exchange symbol]
PYAC	Penn-York Athletic Conference (PSS)
PYAR	Person-Years-at-Risk [After radiation exposure] (FFDE)
PYarE	Electric Storage Battery Co., Yardley, PA [Library symbol] [Library of Congress] (LCLS)
Py B	Bachelor of Pedagogy
PYB	Borg-Warner Corp., York Division, York, PA [Library symbol] [Library of Congress] (LCLS)
PYB	[The] Palestine Year Book [New York] [A publication] (BJA)
PYB	Partners Preferred Yield II [AMEX symbol] (SAG)
PYB	Partners Preferred Yld'A' II [AMEX symbol] (TTSB)
PYB	Pittsburgh Youth Ballet
PYBT	[The] Prince's Youth Business Trust [British]
PYBURO	Pyrethrum Bureau (SAUS)
PYBV	Peach Yellow Blotch Virus (SAUS)
PYC	Aeropycsa SA de CV [Mexico] [ICAO designator] (FAAC)
PYC	Kuparuk, AK [Location identifier] [FAA] (FAAL)
PYC	Pale Yellow Candle [Baltic coffee-house] [London] (DSUE)
PYC	Partners Preferred Yield III [AMEX symbol] (SAG)
PYC	Partners Preferred Yld'A' III [AMEX symbol] (TTSB)
PYC	Patrol Vessel, Yacht, Coastal [Navy symbol] [Obsolete]
PYC	Patrol Yacht, Coastal (SAUS)
PYC	Pembroke Yeomanry Cavalry [British military] (DMA)

PYC............	Perishability Code [Military] (AFIT)
PYC............	Playon Chico [Panama] [Airport symbol] (OAG)
PYC............	Pope and Young Club (EA)
PYC............	Proteose-Yeast Castione (SAUS)
PYC............	Proteose-Yeast Castione Medium [Microbiology] (MAE)
PyC............	Pyogenic Culture [Medicine] (MAE)
PyC............	Pyrocarbon (SAUS)
PYC............	York College of Pennsylvania, York, PA [Library symbol] [Library of Congress] (LCLS)
PyCCD	Profiled Peristaltic Charge-Coupled Device (SAUS)
PYCG	Pyrochromatogram [Analytical chemistry]
PyCIL	Powered Programmable Current-Injection Logic (SAUS)
PYCR	Pyrroline-5-Carboxylate Reductase (DMAA)
Pyd	[A] Pyrimidine Nucleoside [Also, Y]
PYDV	Potato Yellow Dwarf Virus [Plant pathology]
PYE	Peptone Yeast Extract [Medium] [Microbiology] (DAVI)
PYE	Point Reyes, CA [Location identifier] [FAA] (FAAL)
PYE	Protect Your Environment [Groups]
PYE	Pryme Energy Resources [Vancouver Stock Exchange symbol]
PYF	French Polynesia [ANSI three-letter standard code] (CNC)
PYF	Pyrenees [France] [Seismograph station code, US Geological Survey] (SEIS)
Py-FD-MS ...	Pyrolysis Field Desorption Mass Spectrometry
PYFV	Parsnip Yellow Fleck Virus [Plant pathology]
PYG	Peptone Yeast Glucose (SAUS)
PYG	Peptone-Yeast-Glucose [Medium] [Microbiology]
PYG Broth...	Proteose-Yeast-Glucose Broth (SAUS)
PYGC	Pyrolysis Gas Chromatography
PYGM	Peptone-Yeast-Glucose-Maltose (SAUS)
PYGM	Peptone-Yeast Glucose Maltose Agar [Microbiology] (MAE)
PYGN	Pyrogen Unit [Biochemistry]
PYGS	Church of Jesus Christ of Latter-Day Saints, Genealogical Society Library, Gettysburg Branch, York, PA [Library symbol] [Library of Congress] (LCLS)
PYGS	Proceedings of the Yorkshire Geological Society (SAUS)
PYH	Puerto Ayacucho [Venezuela] [Airport symbol] (OAG)
PYH	York Hospital, York, PA [Library symbol] [Library of Congress] (LCLS)
PYHi	Historical Society of York County, York, PA [Library symbol] [Library of Congress] (LCLS)
Py-HRMS.....	Pyrolysis High-Resolution Mass Spectrometry
PYI	Presidential Young Investigator (SAUS)
PYI	Presidential Young Investigator Program [National Science Foundation]
PYJ	Louisville, KY [Location identifier] [FAA] (FAAL)
Pyke...........	Pyke's Lower Canada King's Bench Reports [1809-10] [A publication] (ILCA)
Pyke LC	Pyke's Lower Canada King's Bench Reports [1809-10] [A publication] (ILCA)
Pyke's R	Pyke's Lower Canada King's Bench Reports [1809-10] [A publication] (ILCA)
PYL	Perry Island, AK [Location identifier] [FAA] (FAAL)
PYLL	Potential Years of Life Lost [Medicine] (DMAA)
PYLR	Peach Yellow Leaf Roll [Plant pathology]
PYLV...........	Peach Yellow Leafroll Virus (SAUS)
PYM	Martin Memorial [York City and County] Library, York, PA [OCLC symbol] (OCLC)
PYM	Pan-African Youth Movement (EA)
PYM	Plymouth, MA [Location identifier] [FAA] (FAAL)
PYM	Psychosomatic [Medicine] (DMAA)
PYM	Psychosomatic Medicine
PYM	Putnam High Yield Municipal [NYSE symbol] (SPSG)
PYM	Putnam Hi Yield Muni [NYSE symbol] (TTSB)
Py-MS	Pyrolysis Mass Spectrometry
pymt	Payment (GEAB)
PYMT	Payment
Pymt	Payment
PYMV	Peanut Yellow Mottle Virus [Plant pathology]
PYN	Chicago, IL [Location identifier] [FAA] (FAAL)
PYN	Poneloya [Nicaragua] [Seismograph station code, US Geological Survey] (SEIS)
PYN	Pyloric Nerve (SAUS)
PYNC	Prior Year Notice [IRS]
PYO	Person-Years of Observation [Medicine]
PYO	Pick Your Own [Fruits and vegetables] (DSUE)
PYO	Prior Year Overhead (AAGC)
PYO	Pyongyang [Heizo] [North Korea] [Seismograph station code, US Geological Survey] [Closed] (SEIS)
PYOL	Pyramid Oil (EFIS)
PYoW..........	Westmoreland County Community College, Youngwood, PA [Library symbol] [Library of Congress] (LCLS)
PYP	Photoactive Yellow Protein [Biochemistry]
PYP	Pyrophosphate [Scintiscanning]
PYPER	Promote Yard Performance Efficiency and Reliability (DNAB)
PYPH	Polyphase
PYR	Pitch, Yaw, Roll (SAUS)
P-Y-R..........	Pitch-Yaw-Roll (AAG)
PYR	Player Resources, Inc. [Vancouver Stock Exchange symbol]
PYR	Prior Year Report
PYR	Prior Year's Return [IRS]
Py R............	Pyke's Lower Canada King's Bench Reports [1809-10] [A publication] (ILCA)
Pyr	Pyralidae [Entomology]
PYR	Pyramid [California] [Seismograph station code, US Geological Survey] (SEIS)
pyr	Pyramid
PYR	Pyramid Air Lines [Egypt] [ICAO designator] (FAAC)
Pyr	Pyramidal Tract [Neuroanatomy]
PYR	Pyrgos [Greece] [Airport symbol] (AD)
PYR	Pyridine [Organic chemistry]
Pyr	[A] Pyrimidine [Biochemistry]
PYR	Pyrocap International Corp. [AMEX symbol] (SAG)
Pyr	Pyrocap International Corp. [Associated Press] (SAG)
PYR	Pyrometer (AAG)
PYR	Pyruvate [Biochemistry]
PYR.EC........	Pyrocap International [ECM Symbol] (TTSB)
PYRA	Pyramidal (SAUS)
pyrcrts........	Pyramid Cartons
PYRETH	Pyrethrum [Pellitory] [Pharmacology] (ROG)
PYRIL	Pyrilamine maleate (SAUS)
PYRIL TAN...	Pyrilamine Tannate (SAUS)
PYRKAL.......	Greek Powder & Cartridge Company S.A. (SAUS)
PYRKIN........	Pyruvate Kinase [An enzyme] (DAVI)
pyrm	Pyramid (VRA)
PYRMD	Pyramid [Freight]
PYRMD	Pyramided (SAUS)
PYRO	Pyrogallic Acid (ROG)
PYRO	Pyromaniac (WDAA)
PYRO	Pyrotechnic
Pyro	Pyroxylin (SAUS)
Pyrocp........	Pyrocap International Corp. [Associated Press] (SAG)
PYROELEC...	Pyroelectricity (SAUS)
PYROM	Pyrometer [Engineering]
PYROM	Pyrometry (SAUS)
PYROTECH..	Pyrotechnical (ROG)
pyrox	Pyroxiline (VRA)
PYROX GN ...	Pyroxene Gneisses [Agronomy]
PyrP............	Pyridoxamine Phosphate [or Pyridoxyl Phosphate] [Organic chemistry] (DAVI)
PyrP............	Pyridoxyl (Pyridoxamine) Phosphate (BABM)
Pyrr............	Pyrrhotite (SAUS)
PYRR	Pyrrolidine [Organic chemistry]
PYRREC.......	Pyrrolidinoethyl Chloride [Organic chemistry]
Pyrrh..........	Pyrrhus [of Plutarch] [Classical studies] (OCD)
PYRS	Pyramids [Board on Geographic Names]
PYRUV	Pyruvate [Organic chemistry] (DAVI)
PYS	Parietal Yolk Sac [Cells] (DB)
PYS	Partial Yield Spectroscopy (MCD)
PYS	Photoelectron Yield Spectroscopy
PYS	Photo-emission Yield Spectroscopy (SAUS)
PYS	Photo Yield Spectroscopy (AAEL)
PYS	Primitive Yolk Sac [Embryology]
PYSZ	Partially Yttria-Stabilized Zirconia [Industrial ceramics]
PYT	Payment (DCTA)
PYT	Playitas [Nicaragua] [Seismograph station code, US Geological Survey] (SEIS)
PYT	Prentiss, MS [Location identifier] [FAA] (FAAL)
PYT	Pretty Young Thing [In song title from the Michael Jackson album "Thriller"]
PYT	Pyng Tech [Vancouver Stock Exchange symbol]
Pyth	Pythian [of Pindar] [Classical studies] (OCD)
Py-TRMS	Pyrolysis Time-Resolved Mass Spectrometry
PYTV...........	TV Filme, Inc. [NASDAQ symbol] (SAG)
PYV	Payton Ventures [Vancouver Stock Exchange symbol]
PYV	Peach Yellow Virus (SAUS)
PyV	Polyoma Virus
PYV	Yaviza [Panama] [Airport symbol] (OAG)
PYX	Perryton, TX [Location identifier] [FAA] (FAAL)
PYX	Playtex Products [NYSE symbol] (SPSG)
PYX	Pyroxene [Also, PX] [A mineral]
Pyx	Pyxis [Constellation]
Pyxi	Pyxis [Constellation]
Pyxis	Pyxis Corp. [Associated Press] (SAG)
PYXS	Pyxis Corp. [NASDAQ symbol] (SAG)
PZ	Canal Zone [ANSI two-letter standard code] [Obsolete] (CNC)
PZ	Pancreozymin [Also, CCK] [Endocrinology]
PZ	Panzerbrechend [Armor-Piercing] [German military - World War II]
PZ	Pastural Zone [Agriculture]
PZ	Past Z
PZ	Paterson Zochonis [Commercial firm] [British]
PZ	Peak-to-Zero (IAA)
PZ	Pelletizing (SAUS)
PZ	Penzance [British depot code]
PZ	Performing organization Zip code (SAUS)
PZ	Peripheral Zone [Botany] [Anatomy]
PZ	Phase Zero
Pz	Phenylazobenzyloxycarbonyl [Biochemistry]
PZ	Pick Up Zone [Shipping]
PZ	Pickup Zone [Military] (INF)
pz................	Pieze [Unit of pressure]
PZ	Pie Zeses [May You Live Piously] [Italian]
PZ	Pizza
PZ	Plus Zero (SAUS)
PZ	Poland [IYRU nationality code] (IYR)
PZ	Police Zone (SAUS)
PZ	Potez [Etablissements Henri Potez] [France] [ICAO aircraft manufacturer identifier] (ICAO)
PZ	Prazosin [A vasodilator]
PZ	Pregnancy Zone Protein (AAMN)
PZ	Primary Zone [Military]

PZ	Prisoner of Zion (BJA)
PZ	Proliferative Zone (MELL)
PZ	Promethazine (SAUS)
PZ	Protective Zone
PZ	Prozone Phenomenon [Immunology]
PZ	Psychic Zodiac
PZ	Pulse Zero (SAUS)
PZ	Puls Zero (SAUS)
PZ	Pyrazine [Organic chemistry]
PZ	Surinam [Aircraft nationality and registration mark] (FAAC)
PZA	Patrol Zone Area (MCD)
PZA	Paz De Ariporo [Colombia] [Airport symbol] (OAG)
PZA	Pizzeria
PZA	Provena Foods [AMEX symbol] (TTSB)
PZA	Provena Foods, Inc. [AMEX symbol] (SPSG)
PZA	Pyrazinamide [Antibacterial compound]
PZA	Pyrazinoic Acid (MELL)
PZAA	Polarized Zeeman Atomic Absorption
PZB	Parenzyme Buccal (SAUS)
PZB	Pietermaritzburg [South Africa] [Airport symbol] (OAG)
PZB	Pittston Brinks Group [NYSE symbol] [Formerly, Pittston Services Group] (SG)
PZB	Pittston Brinks Grp [NYSE symbol] (TTSB)
PZC	Pezamerica Resources Corp. [Vancouver Stock Exchange symbol]
PZC	Point of Zero Change (SAUS)
PZC	Point of Zero Charge [Electrochemistry]
PZC	Progressive Zionist Caucus (EA)
PZ-CCK	Pancreozymin-Cholecystokinin [Endocrinology] (MAE)
PZCO	Pickup-Zone Control Officer [Military] (INF)
PZD	Partial Zona Dissection [In-vitro fertilization] (PAZ)
PZD	Partial Zonal Drilling [In vitro fertilization] [Medicine] (BARN)
PZD	Phase Zero Defense
PZDF	Phil Zimmermann Defense Fund (SAUS)
PZDV	Panzer-Division [Armored Division] [German military]
PZE	PennzEnergy Co. [NYSE symbol] (SG)
PZE	Penzance [England] [Airport symbol] (OAG)
PZE	Piezoelectric
PZEV	Partial-Zero-Emission-Vehicle
PZFC	Pia Zadora Fan Club (EA)
PZH	Zhob [Pakistan] [Airport symbol] (OAG)
PZI	Indiana University of Pennsylvania, Indiana, PA [OCLC symbol] (OCLC)
PZI	Protamine Zinc Insulin
PZKPFW	Panzerkampfwagen [German tank] [World War II]
PZKW	Panzerkampfwagen [German tank] [World War II]
PZL	Panstwowe Zaklady Lotnicze [Poland] [ICAO designator] (FAAC)
PZL	Pennzoil Co. [NYSE symbol] [Toronto Stock Exchange symbol] (SPSG)
PZL	Pennzoil-Quaker State [NYSE symbol] (SG)
PZL	Progressive Zionist League-Hashomer Hatzair (EA)
PZM	Piezoelectric Mount (IAA)
PZM	Pittston Minerals Group [NYSE symbol] (SPSG)
PZM	Pressure-Zone Microphone (SAUS)
PZM	Pressurized Zone Microphone
PZN	Prison Realty Trust [NYSE symbol] (SG)
PZO	Peebles, OH [Location identifier] [FAA] (FAAL)
PZO	Puerto Ordaz [Venezuela] [Airport symbol] (OAG)
PZP	Phase Zero Program
PZP	Porcine Zona Pellucida [Experimental animal contraceptive]
PZP	Pregnancy Zone Protein
PZPR	Polska Zjednoczona Partia Robotnicza [Polish United Workers' Party - PUWP] [Political party] (PPW)
PZ-Protein	Pregnancy Zone Protein (SAUS)
PZQ	Rogers City, MI [Location identifier] [FAA] (FAAL)
PZ(R)	Penetration Zone (Radius) (MCD)
PZR	Pressurizer (NRCH)
PZR LCS	Pressurizer Level Control System [Nuclear energy] (GFGA)
PZR PCS	Pressurizer Pressure Control System [Nuclear energy] (GFGA)
PZS	Pittston Services Group [Formerly, The Pittston Co.] [NYSE symbol] (SPSG)
PZS	President of the Zoological Society [British]
PZSV	Pelargonium Zonate Spot Virus [Plant pathology]
PZT	Lead [Plumbum] Zirconate-Titanate [Piezoelectric transducer]
PZT	Photographic Zenith Telescope (SAUS)
PZT	Photographic Zenith Tube
PZT	Piezoelectric (SAUS)
PZT	Piezoelectric Transducer [or Translator]
PZT	Piezoelectric Zirconate Titanate
PZT	Plumbum-Zirconate-Titanate (SAUS)
PZT	Polycrystalline Lead Zirconate Titanate [Piezoelectricity]
PZU	Port Sudan [Sudan] [Airport symbol] (OAG)
PZV	New York, NY [Location identifier] [FAA] (FAAL)
PZX	Heavenly Bodys Azimuth (SAUS)
PZX	Paragould, AR [Location identifier] [FAA] (FAAL)
PZX	Pittston BAX Group [NYSE symbol] [Formerly, Pittston Burlington Group]
PZX	Pittston Burlington Group [NYSE symbol] (TTSB)
PZY	Performance Executive Airlines Ltd. [British] [ICAO designator] (FAAC)
PZY	Piestany [Former Czechoslovakia] [Airport symbol] (OAG)
PZZ	Pizza Patio Ltd. [Vancouver Stock Exchange symbol]
PZZA	Papa Johns International, Inc. [NASDAQ symbol] (SAG)
PZZA	Papa John's Intl [NASDAQ symbol] (TTSB)
PZZI	Pizza Inn [NASDAQ symbol] (TTSB)
PZZI	Pizza Inn, Inc. [NASDAQ symbol] (SAG)

3 1001 00011758 1